2024
Harris
Ohio
Industrial Directory

Published July 2024 next update July 2025

WARNING: Purchasers and users of this directory may not use this directory to compile mailing lists, other marketing aids and other types of data, which are sold or otherwise provided to third parties. Such use is wrongful, illegal and a violation of the federal copyright laws.

CAUTION: Because of the many thousands of establishment listings contained in this directory and the possibilities of both human and mechanical error in processing this information, Mergent Inc. cannot assume liability for the correctness of the listings or information on which they are based. Hence, no information contained in this work should be relied upon in any instance where there is a possibility of any loss or damage as a consequence of any error or omission in this volume.

Publisher

Mergent Inc.
444 Madison Ave
New York, NY 10022

©Mergent Inc All Rights Reserved
2024 Mergent Business Press
ISSN 1080-2614
ISBN 979-8-89251-119-3

TABLE OF CONTENTS

Summary of Contents & Explanatory Notes 4
User's Guide to Listings 6

Geographic Section
County/City Cross-Reference Index 9
Firms Listed by Location City 13

Standard Industrial Classification (SIC) Section
SIC Alphabetical Index 725
SIC Numerical Index 729
Firms Listed by SIC 735

Alphabetic Section
Firms Listed by Firm Name 1007

Product Section
Industrial Product Index 1277
Firms Listed by Product Category 1291

SUMMARY OF CONTENTS

Number of Companies 16,575
Number of Decision Makers 25,050
Minimum Number of Employees 6

EXPLANATORY NOTES

How to Cross-Reference in This Directory

Sequential Entry Numbers. Each establishment in the Geographic Section is numbered sequentially (G-0000). The number assigned to each establishment is referred to as its "entry number." To make cross-referencing easier, each listing in the Geographic, SIC, Alphabetic and Product Sections includes the establishment's entry number. To facilitate locating an entry in the Geographic Section, the entry numbers for the first listing on the left page and the last listing on the right page are printed at the top of the page next to the city name.

Source Suggestions Welcome

Although all known sources were used to compile this directory, it is possible that companies were inadvertently omitted. Your assistance in calling attention to such omissions would be greatly appreciated. A special form on the facing page will help you in the reporting process.

Analysis

Every effort has been made to contact all firms to verify their information. The one exception to this rule is the annual sales figure, which is considered by many companies to be confidential information. Therefore, estimated sales have been calculated by multiplying the nationwide average sales per employee for the firm's major SIC/NAICS code by the firm's number of employees. Nationwide averages for sales per employee by SIC/NAICS codes are provided by the U.S. Department of Commerce and are updated annually. All sales—sales (est)—have been estimated by this method. The exceptions are parent companies (PA), division headquarters (DH) and headquarter locations (HQ) which may include an actual corporate sales figure—sales (corporate-wide) if available.

Types of Companies

Descriptive and statistical data are included for companies in the entire state. These comprise manufacturers, machine shops, fabricators, assemblers and printers. Also identified are corporate offices in the state.

Employment Data

This directory contains companies with 6 or more employees. The employment figure shown in the Geographic Section includes male and female employees and embraces all levels of the company: administrative, clerical, sales and maintenance. This figure is for the facility listed and does not include other plants or offices. It should be recognized that these figures represent an approximate year-round average. These employment figures are broken into codes A through G and used in the Product and SIC Sections to further help you in qualifying a company. Be sure to check the footnotes on the bottom of pages for the code breakdowns.

Standard Industrial Classification (SIC)

The Standard Industrial Classification (SIC) system used in this directory was developed by the federal government for use in classifying establishments by the type of activity they are engaged in. The SIC classifications used in this directory are from the 1987 edition published by the U.S. Government's Office of Management and Budget. The SIC system separates all activities into broad industrial divisions (e.g., manufacturing, mining, retail trade). It further subdivides each division. The range of manufacturing industry classes extends from two-digit codes (major industry group) to four-digit codes (product).

For example:

Industry Breakdown	Code	Industry, Product, etc.
*Major industry group	20	Food and kindred products
Industry group	203	Canned and frozen foods
*Industry	2033	Fruits and vegetables, etc.

*Classifications used in this directory

Only two-digit and four-digit codes are used in this directory.

Arrangement

1. The **Geographic Section** contains complete in-depth corporate data. This section is sorted by cities listed in alphabetical order and companies listed alphabetically within each city. A County/City Index for referencing cities within counties precedes this section.

> IMPORTANT NOTICE: It is a violation of both federal and state law to transmit an unsolicited advertisement to a facsimile machine. Any user of this product that violates such laws may be subject to civil and criminal penalties, which may exceed $500 for each transmission of an unsolicited facsimile. Mergent Inc. provides fax numbers for lawful purposes only and expressly forbids the use of these numbers in any unlawful manner.

2. The **Standard Industrial Classification (SIC) Section** lists companies under approximately 500 four-digit SIC codes. An alphabetical and a numerical index precedes this section. A company can be listed under several codes. The codes are in numerical order with companies listed alphabetically under each code.

3. The **Alphabetic Section** lists all companies with their full physical or mailing addresses and telephone number.

4. The **Product Section** lists companies under unique Harris categories. An index preceding this section lists all product categories in alphabetical order. Companies can be listed under several categories.

USER'S GUIDE TO LISTINGS

GEOGRAPHIC SECTION

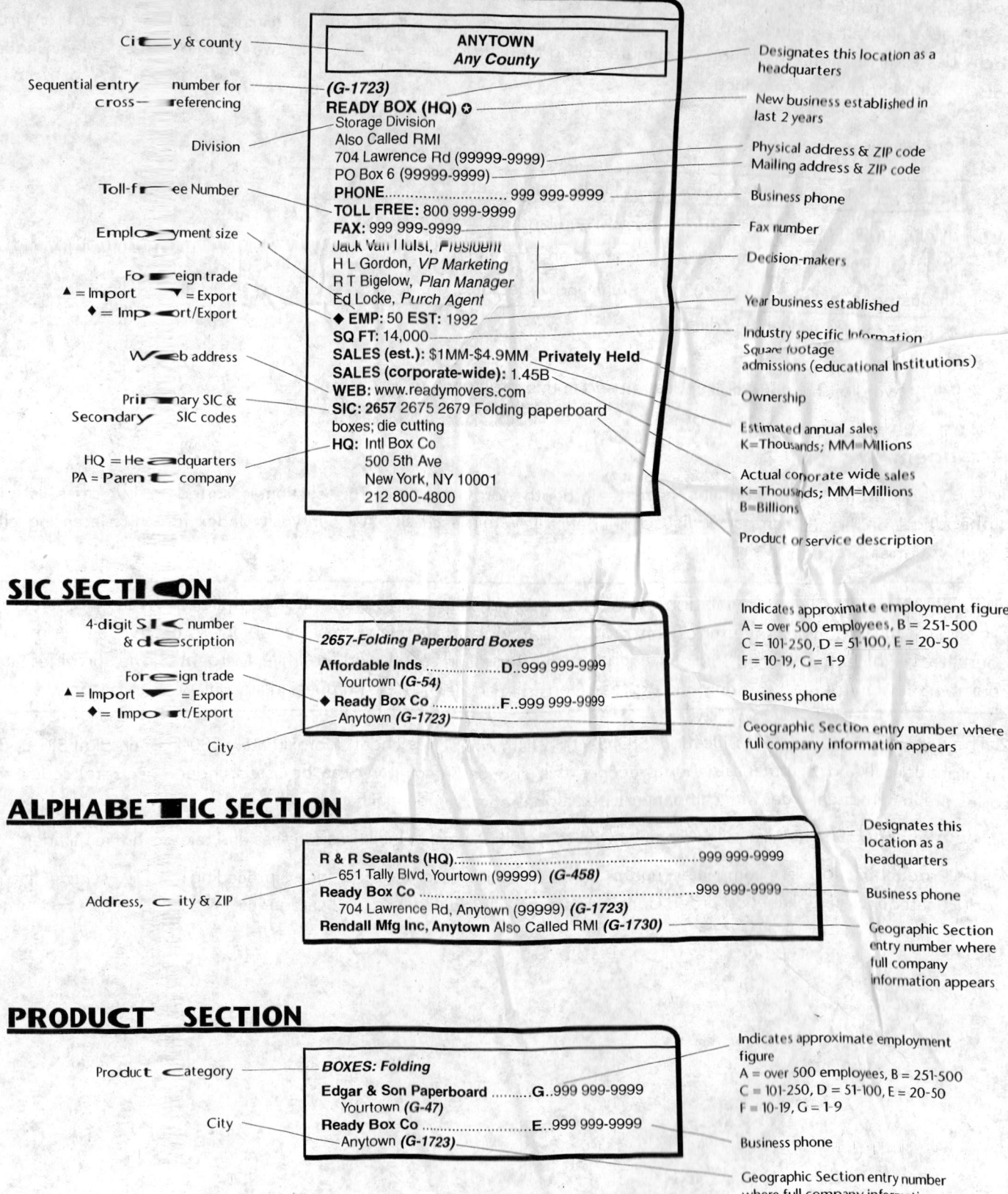

SIC SECTION

ALPHABETIC SECTION

PRODUCT SECTION

GEOGRAPHIC SECTION

Companies sorted by city in alphabetical order
In-depth company data listed

STANDARD INDUSTRIAL CLASSIFICATIONS

Alphabetical index of classification descriptions
Numerical index of classification descriptions
Companies sorted by SIC product groupings

ALPHABETIC SECTION

Company listings in alphabetical order

PRODUCT INDEX

Product categories listed in alphabetical order

PRODUCT SECTION

Companies sorted by product and manufacturing service classifications

COUNTY/CITY CROSS-REFERENCE INDEX

Adams
City	Entry #
Manchester	(G-9617)
Peebles	(G-12325)
Seaman	(G-13114)
Winchester	(G-16072)

Allen
City	Entry #
Beaverdam	(G-1096)
Bluffton	(G-1498)
Cairo	(G-1905)
Delphos	(G-6759)
Elida	(G-7093)
Lima	(G-9217)
Spencerville	(G-13485)

Ashland
City	Entry #
Ashland	(G-549)
Hayesville	(G-8315)
Loudonville	(G-9448)
Nova	(G-12002)
Perrysville	(G-12447)

Ashtabula
City	Entry #
Andover	(G-483)
Ashtabula	(G-625)
Austinburg	(G-741)
Conneaut	(G-5916)
Geneva	(G-7929)
Jefferson	(G-8744)
Kingsville	(G-8932)
North Kingsville	(G-11796)
Orwell	(G-12164)
Pierpont	(G-12473)
Roaming Shores	(G-12830)
Rock Creek	(G-12831)
Rome	(G-12848)
Williamsfield	(G-15868)
Windsor	(G-16075)

Athens
City	Entry #
Albany	(G-382)
Amesville	(G-472)
Athens	(G-672)
Coolville	(G-5941)
Glouster	(G-7983)
Nelsonville	(G-11356)
The Plains	(G-14059)

Auglaize
City	Entry #
Cridersville	(G-6041)
Lima	(G-9303)
Minster	(G-11047)
New Bremen	(G-11398)
New Hampshire	(G-11445)
New Knoxville	(G-11447)
Saint Marys	(G-12944)
Wapakoneta	(G-15105)
Waynesfield	(G-15295)

Belmont
City	Entry #
Barnesville	(G-902)
Bellaire	(G-1183)
Belmont	(G-1249)
Bridgeport	(G-1647)
Flushing	(G-7586)
Lansing	(G-9050)
Martins Ferry	(G-9895)
Morristown	(G-11222)
Powhatan Point	(G-12684)
Saint Clairsville	(G-12894)
Shadyside	(G-13146)
Somerton	(G-13451)

Brown
City	Entry #
Aberdeen	(G-1)
Fayetteville	(G-7464)
Georgetown	(G-7950)
Mount Orab	(G-11239)
Ripley	(G-12819)
Sardinia	(G-13106)

Butler
City	Entry #
Fairfield	(G-7328)
Fairfield Township	(G-7430)
Hamilton	(G-8174)
Liberty Township	(G-9206)
Liberty Twp	(G-9212)
Middletown	(G-10800)
Monroe	(G-11093)
Okeana	(G-12066)
Overpeck	(G-12208)
Oxford	(G-12210)
Seven Mile	(G-13132)
Shandon	(G-13159)
Somerville	(G-13452)
Trenton	(G-14539)
West Chester	(G-15359)

Carroll
City	Entry #
Carrollton	(G-2303)
Dellroy	(G-6758)
Malvern	(G-9608)
Mechanicstown	(G-10287)

Champaign
City	Entry #
Mechanicsburg	(G-10285)
Saint Paris	(G-12970)
Urbana	(G-14825)

Clark
City	Entry #
Donnelsville	(G-6806)
Enon	(G-7250)
Medway	(G-10397)
New Carlisle	(G-11411)
South Charleston	(G-13454)
Springfield	(G-13526)
Tremont City	(G-14538)

Clermont
City	Entry #
Amelia	(G-447)
Batavia	(G-906)
Bethel	(G-1318)
Cincinnati	(G-2544)
Felicity	(G-7467)
Goshen	(G-7992)
Loveland	(G-9474)
Miamiville	(G-10710)
Milford	(G-10889)
Williamsburg	(G-15864)

Clinton
City	Entry #
Blanchester	(G-1347)
Martinsville	(G-9902)
New Vienna	(G-11543)
Sabina	(G-12887)
Wilmington	(G-16037)

Columbiana
City	Entry #
Columbiana	(G-5025)
East Liverpool	(G-6988)
East Palestine	(G-7003)
Homeworth	(G-8554)
Kensington	(G-8790)
Leetonia	(G-9127)
Lisbon	(G-9307)
Negley	(G-11354)
New Waterford	(G-11553)
Rogers	(G-12847)
Salem	(G-12975)
Salineville	(G-13037)
Summitville	(G-13950)
Wellsville	(G-15334)

Coshocton
City	Entry #
Coshocton	(G-5968)
Fresno	(G-7821)
Walhonding	(G-15091)
West Lafayette	(G-15616)

Crawford
City	Entry #
Bucyrus	(G-1849)
Crestline	(G-6033)
Galion	(G-7857)
New Washington	(G-11545)

Cuyahoga
City	Entry #
Bay Village	(G-963)
Beachwood	(G-972)
Bedford	(G-1097)
Bedford Heights	(G-1163)
Berea	(G-1263)
Brecksville	(G-1604)
Broadview Heights	(G-1654)
Brooklyn	(G-1675)
Brooklyn Heights	(G-1682)
Brookpark	(G-1703)
Chagrin Falls	(G-2365)
Cleveland	(G-3569)
Cleveland Heights	(G-4937)
East Cleveland	(G-6983)
Euclid	(G-7258)
Garfield Heights	(G-7911)
Gates Mills	(G-7927)
Glenwillow	(G-7982)
Highland Heights	(G-8383)
Independence	(G-8650)
Lakewood	(G-8965)
Maple Heights	(G-9746)
Mayfield Heights	(G-10247)
Mayfield Hts	(G-10257)
Mayfield Village	(G-10258)
Middleburg Heights	(G-10715)
Moreland Hills	(G-11218)
Newburgh Heights	(G-11613)
North Olmsted	(G-11816)
North Royalton	(G-11865)
Oakwood Village	(G-12035)
Olmsted Falls	(G-12074)
Olmsted Twp	(G-12085)
Parma	(G-12286)
Richmond Heights	(G-12805)
Rocky River	(G-12836)
Seven Hills	(G-13131)
Shaker Heights	(G-13149)
Solon	(G-13304)
South Euclid	(G-13457)
Strongsville	(G-13800)
University Heights	(G-14798)
Walton Hills	(G-15097)
Warrensville Heights	(G-15226)
Westlake	(G-15727)

Darke
City	Entry #
Arcanum	(G-518)
Greenville	(G-8035)
New Madison	(G-11473)
Osgood	(G-12173)
Rossburg	(G-12861)
Union City	(G-14776)
Versailles	(G-14976)
Yorkshire	(G-16293)

Defiance
City	Entry #
Defiance	(G-6667)
Hicksville	(G-8370)
Sherwood	(G-13202)

Delaware
City	Entry #
Ashley	(G-622)
Columbus	(G-5059)
Delaware	(G-6699)
Galena	(G-7853)
Lewis Center	(G-9143)
Ostrander	(G-12174)
Powell	(G-12662)
Radnor	(G-12696)
Sunbury	(G-13951)
Westerville	(G-15646)

Erie
City	Entry #
Berlin Heights	(G-1312)
Castalia	(G-2318)
Huron	(G-8625)
Kelleys Island	(G-8788)
Milan	(G-10882)
Sandusky	(G-13040)
Vermilion	(G-14971)

Fairfield
City	Entry #
Amanda	(G-445)
Baltimore	(G-843)
Bremen	(G-1638)
Carroll	(G-2294)
Lancaster	(G-8985)
Lithopolis	(G-9331)
Millersport	(G-11010)
Pickerington	(G-12454)
Sugar Grove	(G-13915)

Fayette
City	Entry #
Bloomingburg	(G-1353)
Jeffersonville	(G-8764)
Washington Court Hou	(G-15232)
Wshngtn Ct Hs	(G-16225)

Franklin
City	Entry #
Blacklick	(G-1330)
Canal Winchester	(G-1977)
Columbus	(G-5074)
Dublin	(G-6856)
Etna	(G-7253)
Gahanna	(G-7828)
Galloway	(G-7904)
Grove City	(G-8071)
Groveport	(G-8129)
Hilliard	(G-8392)
Lockbourne	(G-9334)
New Albany	(G-11363)
Obetz	(G-12057)
Reynoldsburg	(G-12748)
Upper Arlington	(G-14799)
Urbancrest	(G-14852)
Westerville	(G-15691)
Worthington	(G-16189)

Fulton
City	Entry #
Archbold	(G-520)
Delta	(G-6779)
Fayette	(G-7461)
Lyons	(G-9531)
Metamora	(G-10603)
Pettisville	(G-12451)
Swanton	(G-13967)
Wauseon	(G-15256)

Gallia
City	Entry #
Bidwell	(G-1324)
Cheshire	(G-2477)
Crown City	(G-6053)
Gallipolis	(G-7888)
Rio Grande	(G-12818)
Thurman	(G-14073)
Vinton	(G-15011)

Geauga
City	Entry #
Burton	(G-1880)
Chagrin Falls	(G-2386)
Chardon	(G-2440)
Chesterland	(G-2478)
Huntsburg	(G-8620)
Middlefield	(G-10729)
Montville	(G-11148)
Newbury	(G-11621)
Novelty	(G-12006)
Parkman	(G-12283)
Thompson	(G-14061)

Greene
City	Entry #
Alpha	(G-439)
Beavercreek	(G-1037)
Beavercreek Township	(G-1084)
Bellbrook	(G-1191)
Cedarville	(G-2322)
Dayton	(G-6151)
Fairborn	(G-7307)
Jamestown	(G-8740)
Spring Valley	(G-13490)
Xenia	(G-16247)
Yellow Springs	(G-16282)

Guernsey
City	Entry #
Byesville	(G-1893)

COUNTY/CITY CROSS-REFERENCE

	ENTRY #
Cambridge	(G-1918)
Cumberland	(G-6054)
Derwent	(G-6798)
Kimbolton	(G-8927)
Lore City	(G-9446)
Quaker City	(G-12691)
Senecaville	(G-13130)

Hamilton

	ENTRY #
Addyston	(G-8)
Blue Ash	(G-1356)
Cincinnati	(G-2578)
Cleves	(G-4945)
Harrison	(G-8263)
Miamitown	(G-10705)
Montgomery	(G-11129)
Newtown	(G-11661)
North Bend	(G-11703)
Norwood	(G-11994)
Reading	(G-12747)
Sharonville	(G-13170)
Springdale	(G-13525)
West Chester	(G-15530)

Hancock

Arcadia	(G-516)
Arlington	(G-548)
Findlay	(G-7469)
Mc Comb	(G-10268)
Mount Cory	(G-11228)
Rawson	(G-12743)
Van Buren	(G-14903)
Vanlue	(G-14969)

Hardin

Ada	(G-2)
Alger	(G-384)
Dunkirk	(G-6976)
Forest	(G-7589)
Kenton	(G-8880)
Mount Victory	(G-11301)

Harrison

Bowerston	(G-1544)
Cadiz	(G-1903)
Freeport	(G-7761)
Hopedale	(G-8557)
Jewett	(G-8767)
Scio	(G-13111)
Tippecanoe	(G-14169)

Henry

Deshler	(G-6799)
Hamler	(G-8260)
Holgate	(G-8489)
Liberty Center	(G-9204)
Malinta	(G-9604)
Mc Clure	(G-10265)
Napoleon	(G-11308)
Okolona	(G-12071)
Ridgeville Corners	(G-12815)

Highland

Greenfield	(G-8026)
Hillsboro	(G-8455)
Leesburg	(G-9122)

Hocking

Laurelville	(G-9054)
Logan	(G-9358)

Holmes

	ENTRY #
Berlin	(G-1302)
Big Prairie	(G-1328)
Charm	(G-2471)
Glenmont	(G-7980)
Holmesville	(G-8541)
Killbuck	(G-8916)
Lakeville	(G-8962)
Millersburg	(G-10937)
Mount Hope	(G-11237)
Walnut Creek	(G-15094)
Winesburg	(G-16077)

Huron

Bellevue	(G-1221)
Collins	(G-5004)
Greenwich	(G-8066)
Monroeville	(G-11122)
New London	(G-11460)
North Fairfield	(G-11776)
Norwalk	(G-11952)
Plymouth	(G-12608)
Wakeman	(G-15073)
Willard	(G-15859)

Jackson

Jackson	(G-8707)
Oak Hill	(G-12016)
Wellston	(G-15326)

Jefferson

Bergholz	(G-1300)
Brilliant	(G-1651)
Irondale	(G-8693)
Mingo Junction	(G-11044)
Rayland	(G-12745)
Richmond	(G-12802)
Steubenville	(G-13660)
Tiltonsville	(G-14116)
Toronto	(G-14534)
Wintersville	(G-16084)
Yorkville	(G-16294)

Knox

Bladensburg	(G-1346)
Centerburg	(G-2357)
Danville	(G-6148)
Fredericktown	(G-7738)
Gambier	(G-7906)
Howard	(G-8558)
Mount Vernon	(G-11260)

Lake

Concord Township	(G-5900)
Eastlake	(G-7016)
Fairport Harbor	(G-7454)
Grand River	(G-8011)
Kirtland	(G-8939)
Madison	(G-9587)
Mentor	(G-10401)
Mentor On The Lake	(G-10600)
Painesville	(G-12215)
Perry	(G-12349)
Wickliffe	(G-15823)
Willoughby	(G-15871)
Willoughby Hills	(G-16021)
Willowick	(G-16030)

Lawrence

Chesapeake	(G-2472)
Ironton	(G-8694)

	ENTRY #
Kitts Hill	(G-8943)
Proctorville	(G-12686)
South Point	(G-13463)

Licking

Alexandria	(G-383)
Croton	(G-6051)
Etna	(G-7254)
Granville	(G-8014)
Heath	(G-8316)
Hebron	(G-8334)
Homer	(G-8552)
Johnstown	(G-8768)
Newark	(G-11560)
Pataskala	(G-12296)
Saint Louisville	(G-12942)
Utica	(G-14856)

Logan

Belle Center	(G-1195)
Bellefontaine	(G-1199)
De Graff	(G-6664)
East Liberty	(G-6984)
Huntsville	(G-8622)
Lakeview	(G-8961)
Lewistown	(G-9194)
Rushsylvania	(G-12874)
Russells Point	(G-12876)
West Liberty	(G-15622)
West Mansfield	(G-15625)

Lorain

Amherst	(G-473)
Avon	(G-758)
Avon Lake	(G-796)
Columbia Station	(G-5005)
Elyria	(G-7104)
Grafton	(G-7996)
Lagrange	(G-8946)
Lorain	(G-9399)
North Ridgeville	(G-11826)
Oberlin	(G-12048)
Sheffield Lake	(G-13178)
Sheffield Village	(G-13179)
Wellington	(G-15303)

Lucas

Holland	(G-8492)
Maumee	(G-10159)
Monclova	(G-11092)
Oregon	(G-12098)
Sylvania	(G-13969)
Toledo	(G-14172)
Waterville	(G-15239)
Whitehouse	(G-15815)

Madison

London	(G-9379)
Mount Sterling	(G-11253)
Plain City	(G-12558)
West Jefferson	(G-15608)

Mahoning

Austintown	(G-751)
Beloit	(G-1250)
Berlin Center	(G-1309)
Boardman	(G-1510)
Campbell	(G-1966)
Canfield	(G-1995)
Damascus	(G-6147)
Lowellville	(G-9510)

	ENTRY #
New Middletown	(G-11478)
New Springfield	(G-11539)
North Jackson	(G-11777)
North Lima	(G-11801)
Petersburg	(G-12450)
Poland	(G-12610)
Sebring	(G-13116)
Struthers	(G-13898)
Youngstown	(G-16295)

Marion

Caledonia	(G-1915)
La Rue	(G-8945)
Marion	(G-9847)
Morral	(G-11221)
Prospect	(G-12689)
Waldo	(G-15089)

Medina

Brunswick	(G-1745)
Chippewa Lake	(G-2543)
Hinckley	(G-8471)
Homerville	(G-8553)
Litchfield	(G-9328)
Lodi	(G-9344)
Medina	(G-10288)
Seville	(G-13133)
Sharon Center	(G-13162)
Spencer	(G-13479)
Valley City	(G-14860)
Wadsworth	(G-15014)

Meigs

Pomeroy	(G-12613)
Portland	(G-12638)
Racine	(G-12693)
Tuppers Plains	(G-14618)

Mercer

Burkettsville	(G-1879)
Celina	(G-2324)
Chickasaw	(G-2490)
Coldwater	(G-4981)
Fort Recovery	(G-7613)
Maria Stein	(G-9771)
Rockford	(G-12833)
Saint Henry	(G-12934)

Miami

Bradford	(G-1599)
Casstown	(G-2317)
Conover	(G-5935)
Covington	(G-6016)
Ludlow Falls	(G-9528)
Piqua	(G-12501)
Pleasant Hill	(G-12606)
Tipp City	(G-14118)
Troy	(G-14548)
West Milton	(G-15629)

Monroe

Beallsville	(G-1034)
Clarington	(G-3562)
Hannibal	(G-8261)
Sardis	(G-13110)
Woodsfield	(G-16086)

Montgomery

Beavercreek	(G-1068)
Brookville	(G-1728)
Centerville	(G-2359)

	ENTRY #
Clayton	(G-3563)
Dayton	(G-6177)
Englewood	(G-7221)
Farmersville	(G-7460)
Germantown	(G-7951)
Huber Heights	(G-8575)
Kettering	(G-8902)
Miamisburg	(G-10604)
Moraine	(G-11150)
New Lebanon	(G-11448)
Oakwood	(G-12026)
Trotwood	(G-14543)
Union	(G-14773)
Vandalia	(G-14931)
W Carrollton	(G-15013)
West Carrollton	(G-15349)

Morgan

Malta	(G-9606)
Mcconnelsville	(G-10281)
Pennsville	(G-12348)

Morrow

Cardington	(G-2274)
Edison	(G-7084)
Iberia	(G-8647)
Marengo	(G-9766)
Mount Gilead	(G-11232)

Muskingum

Adamsville	(G-7)
Chandlersville	(G-2439)
Dresden	(G-6855)
Frazeysburg	(G-7714)
Nashport	(G-11335)
New Concord	(G-11430)
Norwich	(G-11992)
Roseville	(G-12859)
South Zanesville	(G-13477)
Zanesville	(G-16493)

Noble

Caldwell	(G-1906)
Dexter City	(G-6801)
Sarahsville	(G-13105)

Ottawa

Curtice	(G-6056)
Elmore	(G-7099)
Genoa	(G-7947)
Gypsum	(G-8171)
Lakeside	(G-8959)
Lakeside Marblehead	(G-8960)
Marblehead	(G-9764)
Oak Harbor	(G-12009)
Port Clinton	(G-12615)
Williston	(G-15870)

Paulding

Antwerp	(G-491)
Grover Hill	(G-8169)
Haviland	(G-8309)
Latty	(G-9053)
Oakwood	(G-12030)
Paulding	(G-12311)
Payne	(G-12321)

Perry

Corning	(G-5957)
Crooksville	(G-6043)
Glenford	(G-7979)

2024 Harris Ohio Industrial Directory

COUNTY/CITY CROSS-REFERENCE

	ENTRY #		ENTRY #		ENTRY #		ENTRY #		ENTRY #
Junction City	(G-8783)	Bellville	(G-1241)	Brewster	(G-1642)	North Bloomfield	(G-11712)	Little Hocking	(G-9332)
Mount Perry	(G-11249)	Butler	(G-1891)	Canal Fulton	(G-1967)	Southington	(G-13478)	Lower Salem	(G-9519)
New Lexington	(G-11451)	Lexington	(G-9195)	Canton	(G-2023)	Vienna	(G-14994)	Marietta	(G-9774)
Shawnee	(G-13177)	Lucas	(G-9520)	East Canton	(G-6977)	Warren	(G-15134)	New Matamoras	(G-11476)
Somerset	(G-13449)	Mansfield	(G-9620)	East Sparta	(G-7013)	West Farmington	(G-15605)	Vincent	(G-15006)
Thornville	(G-14065)	Ontario	(G-12090)	Greentown	(G-8034)			Waterford	(G-15235)
		Shelby	(G-13190)	Hartville	(G-8299)	**Tuscarawas**		Whipple	(G-15813)
Pickaway		Shiloh	(G-13203)	Louisville	(G-9455)	Baltic	(G-833)		
Ashville	(G-667)			Magnolia	(G-9596)	Bolivar	(G-1522)	**Wayne**	
Circleville	(G-3540)	**Ross**		Massillon	(G-10072)	Dennison	(G-6793)	Apple Creek	(G-495)
New Holland	(G-11446)	Bainbridge	(G-830)	Middlebranch	(G-10714)	Dover	(G-6807)	Burbank	(G-1877)
Orient	(G-12113)	Chillicothe	(G-2491)	Minerva	(G-11025)	Dundee	(G-6962)	Creston	(G-6038)
Williamsport	(G-15869)	Frankfort	(G-7657)	Navarre	(G-11340)	Gnadenhutten	(G-7984)	Dalton	(G-6130)
		Kingston	(G-8931)	North Canton	(G-11713)	Midvale	(G-10874)	Doylestown	(G-6852)
Pike		Londonderry	(G-9398)	North Lawrence	(G-11798)	Mineral City	(G-11017)	Fredericksburg	(G-7717)
Beaver	(G-1035)	Richmond Dale	(G-12804)	Paris	(G-12282)	New Philadelphia	(G-11484)	Kidron	(G-8913)
Latham	(G-9051)	South Salem	(G-13475)	Uniontown	(G-14780)	Newcomerstown	(G-11640)	Marshallville	(G-9893)
Piketon	(G-12475)			Waynesburg	(G-15292)	Port Washington	(G-12631)	Mount Eaton	(G-11229)
Waverly	(G-15278)	**Sandusky**		Wilmot	(G-16065)	Strasburg	(G-13742)	Orrville	(G-12116)
		Clyde	(G-4971)			Sugarcreek	(G-13918)	Rittman	(G-12821)
Portage		Fremont	(G-7762)	**Summit**		Uhrichsville	(G-14761)	Shreve	(G-13208)
Atwater	(G-702)	Gibsonburg	(G-7955)	Akron	(G-9)	Zoarville	(G-16575)	Smithville	(G-13298)
Aurora	(G-703)	Millersville	(G-11016)	Barberton	(G-850)			Sterling	(G-13659)
Deerfield	(G-6666)	Woodville	(G-16091)	Bath	(G-962)	**Union**		West Salem	(G-15632)
Diamond	(G-6804)			Clinton	(G-4968)	Marysville	(G-9904)	Wooster	(G-16093)
Garrettsville	(G-7912)	**Scioto**		Copley	(G-5942)	Milford Center	(G-10927)		
Hiram	(G-8481)	Franklin Furnace	(G-7712)	Coventry Township	(G-6003)	Raymond	(G-12746)	**Williams**	
Kent	(G-8792)	Haverhill	(G-8308)	Cuyahoga Falls	(G-6060)	Richwood	(G-12813)	Alvordton	(G-444)
Mantua	(G-9734)	Lucasville	(G-9521)	Fairlawn	(G-7433)			Bryan	(G-1803)
Mogadore	(G-11065)	Mc Dermott	(G-10273)	Green	(G-8025)	**Van Wert**		Edgerton	(G-7071)
North Benton	(G-11709)	Minford	(G-11043)	Hudson	(G-8581)	Convoy	(G-5940)	Edon	(G-7085)
Randolph	(G-12697)	New Boston	(G-11396)	Lakemore	(G-8958)	Middle Point	(G-10713)	Montpelier	(G-11133)
Ravenna	(G-12699)	Otway	(G-12205)	Macedonia	(G-9534)	Van Wert	(G-14904)	Pioneer	(G-12488)
Rootstown	(G-12850)	Portsmouth	(G-12640)	Munroe Falls	(G-11303)	Venedocia	(G-14970)	Stryker	(G-13907)
Streetsboro	(G-13752)	South Webster	(G-13476)	New Franklin	(G-11435)			West Unity	(G-15636)
		Wheelersburg	(G-15808)	Northfield	(G-11904)	**Vinton**			
Preble				Norton	(G-11936)	Hamden	(G-8172)	**Wood**	
Camden	(G-1962)	**Seneca**		Peninsula	(G-12337)	Mc Arthur	(G-10262)	Bowling Green	(G-1547)
Eaton	(G-7054)	Alvada	(G-440)	Richfield	(G-12781)	New Plymouth	(G-11533)	Bradner	(G-1603)
Eldorado	(G-7092)	Attica	(G-700)	Sagamore Hills	(G-12893)	Ray	(G-12744)	Dunbridge	(G-6961)
Gratis	(G-8023)	Bettsville	(G-1319)	Silver Lake	(G-13297)	Zaleski	(G-16492)	Grand Rapids	(G-8008)
Lewisburg	(G-9185)	Bloomville	(G-1354)	Stow	(G-13680)			Luckey	(G-9527)
New Paris	(G-11480)	Fostoria	(G-7627)	Tallmadge	(G-14021)	**Warren**		Millbury	(G-10930)
Verona	(G-14975)	New Riegel	(G-11534)	Twinsburg	(G-14620)	Carlisle	(G-2287)	North Baltimore	(G-11694)
West Alexandria	(G-15339)	Old Fort	(G-12072)			Franklin	(G-7659)	Northwood	(G-11916)
West Manchester	(G-15624)	Tiffin	(G-14074)	**Trumbull**		Kings Mills	(G-8929)	Pemberville	(G-12334)
				Bristolville	(G-1652)	Lebanon	(G-9059)	Perrysburg	(G-12358)
Putnam		**Shelby**		Brookfield	(G-1668)	Maineville	(G-9598)	Portage	(G-12633)
Cloverdale	(G-4970)	Anna	(G-488)	Burghill	(G-1878)	Mason	(G-9945)	Risingsun	(G-12820)
Columbus Grove	(G-5896)	Botkins	(G-1541)	Cortland	(G-5960)	Morrow	(G-11223)	Rossford	(G-12863)
Continental	(G-5937)	Fort Loramie	(G-7596)	Girard	(G-7958)	Pleasant Plain	(G-12607)	Walbridge	(G-15078)
Fort Jennings	(G-7595)	Jackson Center	(G-8729)	Hartford	(G-8298)	South Lebanon	(G-13461)	Weston	(G-15804)
Gilboa	(G-7957)	Kettlersville	(G-8912)	Hubbard	(G-8561)	Springboro	(G-13493)		
Glandorf	(G-7978)	Port Jefferson	(G-12630)	Kinsman	(G-8935)	Waynesville	(G-15297)	**Wyandot**	
Kalida	(G-8784)	Russia	(G-12881)	Leavittsburg	(G-9057)			Carey	(G-2277)
Leipsic	(G-9132)	Sidney	(G-13216)	Masury	(G-10155)	**Washington**		Mc Cutchenville	(G-10272)
Ottawa	(G-12177)			Mc Donald	(G-10276)	Belpre	(G-1252)	Nevada	(G-11361)
Ottoville	(G-12197)	**Stark**		Mineral Ridge	(G-11019)	Beverly	(G-1320)	Sycamore	(G-13988)
		Alliance	(G-386)	Newton Falls	(G-11652)	Fleming	(G-7585)	Upper Sandusky	(G-14803)
Richland		Beach City	(G-968)	Niles	(G-11662)	Graysville	(G-8024)		

GEOGRAPHIC SECTION

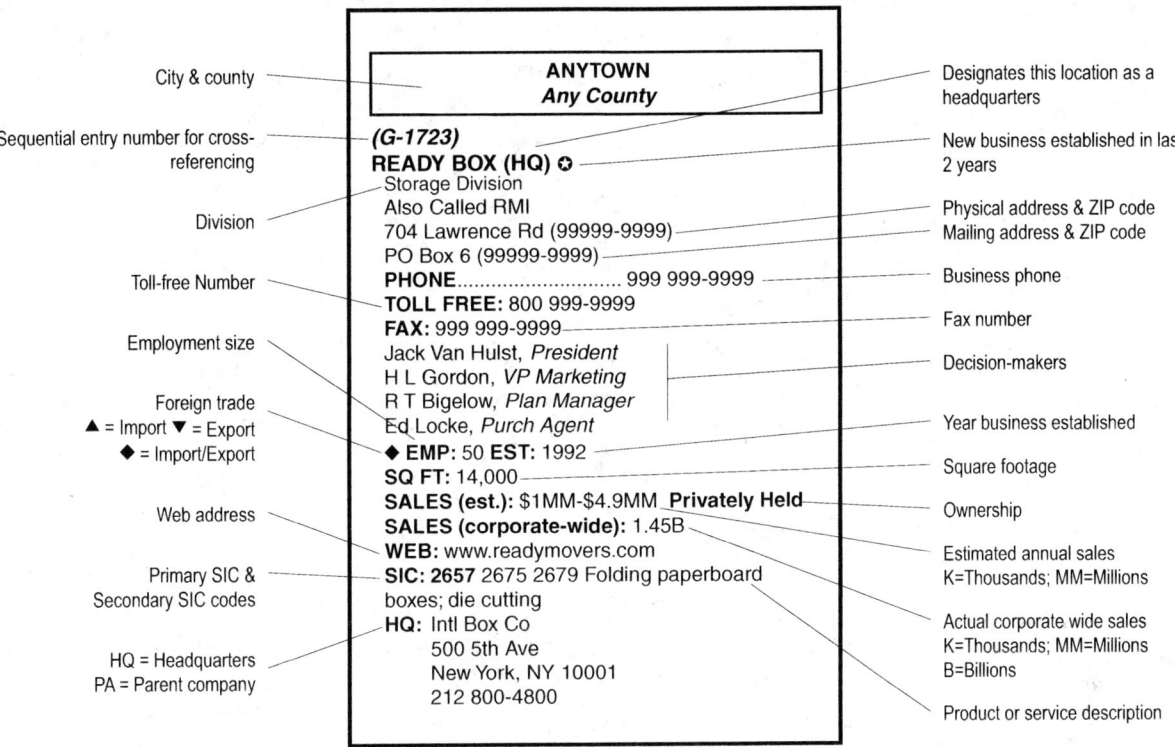

See footnotes for symbols and codes identification.
- This section is in alphabetical order by city.
- Companies are sorted alphabetically under their respective cities.
- To locate cities within a county refer to the County/City Cross Reference Index.

IMPORTANT NOTICE: It is a violation of both federal and state law to transmit an unsolicited advertisement to a facsimile machine. Any user of this product that violates such laws may be subject to civil and criminal penalties which may exceed $500 for each transmission of an unsolicited facsimile. Harris InfoSource provides fax numbers for lawful purposes only and expressly forbids the use of these numbers in any unlawful manner.

Aberdeen
Brown County

(G-1)
HILLTOP BASIC RESOURCES INC
Also Called: Maysville Ready Mix Con Co
8030 Rte 52 Us (45101)
PHONE..................937 795-2020
John F Steele Junior, *CEO*
EMP: 10
SALES (corp-wide): 59.62MM **Privately Held**
Web: www.hilltopcompanies.com
SIC: 3273 Ready-mixed concrete
PA: Hilltop Basic Resources, Inc.
50 E Rvrcnter Blvd Ste 10
Covington KY 41011
513 651-5000

Ada
Hardin County

(G-2)
ADA TECHNOLOGIES INC (HQ)
805 E North Ave (45810-1809)
PHONE..................419 634-7000
▲ **EMP:** 240 **EST:** 1995
SQ FT: 156,000
SALES (est): 45.65MM **Privately Held**
Web: www.adatechinc.com
SIC: 3714 Motor vehicle transmissions, drive assemblies, and parts
PA: Atsumitec Co.,Ltd.
4-6-1, Takaokanishi, Chuo-Ku
Hamamatsu SZO 433-8

(G-3)
ASSOCIATED PLASTICS CORP
502 Eric Wolber Dr (45810-1100)
PHONE..................419 634-3910
Fred Wolber, *Pr*
George Wolber, *
Samuel W Diller, *
▲ **EMP:** 70 **EST:** 1976
SQ FT: 63,000
SALES (est): 8.41MM **Privately Held**
Web: www.associatedplasticscorp.com
SIC: 3089 Injection molding of plastics

(G-4)
NASG OHIO LLC
Also Called: North American Stamping Group
605 E Montford Ave (45810-1804)
P.O. Box 265 (45810-0265)
PHONE..................419 634-3125
EMP: 11 **EST:** 2002
SALES (est): 5.2MM
SALES (corp-wide): 250.69MM **Privately Held**
Web: www.nasg.net
SIC: 3469 Stamping metal for the trade
PA: North American Stamping Group, Llc
119 Kirby Dr
Portland TN 37148
615 323-0500

(G-5)
SAY SECURITY GROUP USA LLC (PA)
520 E Montford Ave (45810-1821)
PHONE..................419 634-0004
Jason Szuch, *Managing Member*
▲ **EMP:** 18 **EST:** 2003
SQ FT: 10,000
SALES (est): 913.18K
SALES (corp-wide): 913.18K **Privately Held**
Web: www.saysecurity.com
SIC: 7382 3699 Security systems services; Security devices

(G-6)
WILSON SPORTING GOODS CO
217 Liberty St (45810-1135)
P.O. Box 116 (45810-0116)
PHONE..................419 634-9901
Dan Riegle, *Mgr*
EMP: 170
SQ FT: 30,000
Web: www.wilson.com
SIC: 3949 Sporting and athletic goods, nec
HQ: Wilson Sporting Goods Co.
1 Prudntial Pl 130 E Rndl
Chicago IL 60601
773 714-6400

Adamsville
Muskingum County

(G-7)
EXCO RESOURCES (PA) LLC
4100 Valley Rd (43802)
PHONE..................740 796-5231
EMP: 16
SALES (corp-wide): 394.03MM **Privately Held**

Addyston - Hamilton County (G-8)

SIC: 1311 Crude petroleum production
HQ: Exco Resources, Llc
12377 Merit Dr Ste 1700
Montoursville PA 17754

Addyston
Hamilton County

(G-8)
INEOS ABS (USA) LLC
Also Called: Ineos
356 Three Rivers Pkwy (45001)
P.O. Box 39 (45001)
PHONE...............513 467-2400
Clint Herring, *VP*
Rebecca Libourel, *
◆ **EMP: 185 EST: 2007**
SQ FT: 372,600
SALES (est): 48.67MM
SALES (corp-wide): 917.38K Privately Held
Web: www.ineos-abs.com
SIC: 2821 7389 Plastics materials and resins; Business Activities at Non-Commercial Site
HQ: Ineos Industries Limited
Hawkslease
Lyndhurst HANTS SO43
238 028-7000

Akron
Summit County

(G-9)
1ST IMPRESSIONS PLUS LLC
1868 Akron Peninsula Rd (44313-4808)
PHONE...............330 696-7605
EMP: 6 EST: 2016
SALES (est): 80.61K Privately Held
SIC: 2732 2759 Book printing; Card printing and engraving, except greeting

(G-10)
A BEST TRMT & PEST CTRL SUPS
Also Called: A-Best Termite and Pest Ctrl
891 Gorge Blvd (44310-3462)
PHONE...............330 434-5555
EMP: 6 EST: 1995
SALES (est): 441.31K Privately Held
Web: www.abestpest.com
SIC: 7342 2879 5191 Pest control in structures; Insecticides and pesticides; Pesticides

(G-11)
A-A BLUEPRINT CO INC
2757 Gilchrist Rd (44305-4400)
PHONE...............330 794-8803
Daisy Scalia, *Prin*
John Scalia, *
EMP: 32 EST: 1968
SQ FT: 30,000
SALES (est): 4.85MM Privately Held
Web: www.aablueprint.com
SIC: 2791 2759 7334 2789 Typesetting; Letterpress printing; Photocopying and duplicating services; Bookbinding and related work

(G-12)
A/C LASER TECHNOLOGIES INC
471 Rutland Ave (44305-3161)
PHONE...............330 784-3355
Jo Ann Wilson, *Pr*
Frank Wilson, *Treas*
EMP: 10 EST: 1988
SALES (est): 490.43K Privately Held
Web: www.businesssupply.com

SIC: 3555 7699 5999 Printing trades machinery; Printing trades machinery and equipment repair; Business machines and equipment

(G-13)
ABATEMENT LEAD TSTG RISK ASSSS
404 Abbyshire Rd (44319-3806)
PHONE...............330 785-6420
EMP: 6
SALES (est): 143.71K Privately Held
SIC: 1031 Lead and zinc ores

(G-14)
ACC AUTOMATION CO INC
475 Wolf Ledges Pkwy (44311-1199)
PHONE...............330 928-3821
Frank Rzicznek, *VP*
EMP: 25 EST: 1962
SQ FT: 7,500
SALES (est): 2.38MM Privately Held
SIC: 8711 3536 Consulting engineer; Cranes, overhead traveling

(G-15)
ACCENT MANUFACTURING INC
80 Cole Ave (44301-1605)
PHONE...............330 724-7704
Gregory Todd, *Mgr*
EMP: 12
SALES (corp-wide): 1.38MM Privately Held
Web: www.accentcustommarble.com
SIC: 3281 Marble, building: cut and shaped
PA: Accent Manufacturing, Inc.
1026 Gardner Blvd
Norton OH 44203
330 724-7704

(G-16)
ACE PRECISION INDUSTRIES INC
925 Moe Dr (44310-2518)
PHONE...............330 633-8523
Sandy A Di Fiore, *Prin*
James S Wolf, *
Jerry S Wolf, *
Beverly Wolf, *
▲ **EMP: 25 EST: 1974**
SQ FT: 15,000
SALES (est): 4.86MM Privately Held
Web: www.aceprecisionind.com
SIC: 3599 Machine shop, jobbing and repair

(G-17)
ACRO TOOL & DIE COMPANY
Also Called: Metalcraft Solutions
325 Morgan Ave (44311-2494)
PHONE...............330 773-5173
Pamela Thielo, *Pr*
T T Thompson, *
Pamela Perrin, *
▲ **EMP: 37 EST: 1951**
SQ FT: 27,000
SALES (est): 4.69MM Privately Held
Web: www.acrotool.com
SIC: 0781 0811 3541 3444 Landscape services; Christmas tree farm; Machine tools, metal cutting type; Sheet metalwork

(G-18)
ACU-SERVE CORP (PA)
121 S Main St Ste 102 (44308-1436)
PHONE...............330 923-5258
Angie Barone, *Pr*
Timothy Barone, *VP*
EMP: 140 EST: 1993
SALES (est): 13.52MM Privately Held
Web: www.acuservecorp.com

SIC: 7372 6411 Prepackaged software; Medical insurance claim processing, contract or fee basis

(G-19)
AD COMPANY HOLDINGS INC
Also Called: Auto Data
3245 Pickle Rd (44312-5333)
PHONE...............404 256-3544
Craig Harris, *Pr*
Jason Clift, *Sec*
David Andersen, *VP*
EMP: 24 EST: 1985
SALES (est): 480.53K Privately Held
Web: www.driverse.com
SIC: 7372 Prepackaged software

(G-20)
ADA EXTRUSIONS INC
505 W Wilheth Rd (44314-3717)
PHONE...............440 285-7653
EMP: 6 EST: 2014
SALES (est): 244.43K Privately Held
SIC: 3089 Injection molding of plastics

(G-21)
ADH INDUSTRIES INC
2854 Morrison St (44312-1727)
PHONE...............330 283-5822
Anthony Hornbeck, *Pr*
EMP: 6 EST: 2016
SALES (est): 85.18K Privately Held
SIC: 3469 Machine parts, stamped or pressed metal

(G-22)
ADVANCED CRYOGENIC ENTPS LLC
1034 Home Ave (44310-3502)
PHONE...............330 922-0750
David Norton, *Managing Member*
EMP: 8 EST: 2006
SQ FT: 52,000
SALES (est): 484.62K Privately Held
SIC: 7389 3679 Grinding, precision: commercial or industrial; Cryogenic cooling devices for infrared detectors, masers

(G-23)
ADVANCED POLY-PACKAGING INC (PA)
1331 Emmitt Rd (44306-3807)
P.O. Box 7040 (44306-0040)
PHONE...............330 785-4000
▲ **EMP: 116 EST: 1978**
SALES (est): 20.59MM
SALES (corp-wide): 20.59MM Privately Held
Web: ecom.advancedpoly.com
SIC: 3565 5199 Packaging machinery; Packaging materials

(G-24)
AIR ENTERPRISES INC
735 Glaser Pkwy (44306-4160)
PHONE...............330 794-9770
Dorothy Gaffney, *Ch Bd*
Ed Gaffney Junior, *CEO*
James Dowey, *Pr*
EMP: 516 EST: 1964
SQ FT: 100,000
SALES (est): 8.81MM
SALES (corp-wide): 315.22MM Privately Held
Web: www.airenterprises.com
SIC: 3822 3585 3564 Air conditioning and refrigeration controls; Air conditioning units, complete: domestic or industrial; Blowers and fans
PA: Resilience Capital Partners Llc
25101 Chgrin Blvd Ste 350
Cleveland OH 44122

216 292-0200

(G-25)
AJINOMOTO HLTH NTRTN N AMER IN
Also Called: More Than Gourmet
929 Home Ave (44310-4107)
PHONE...............330 762-6652
EMP: 73
Web: www.ajihealthandnutrition.com
SIC: 2032 Soups and broths, canned, jarred, etc.
HQ: Ajinomoto Health & Nutrition North America, Inc.
250 E Devon Ave
Itasca IL 60143
630 931-6800

(G-26)
AKROCHEM CORPORATION (PA)
3770 Embassy Pkwy (44333-8367)
PHONE...............330 535-2100
◆ **EMP: 60 EST: 1929**
SALES (est): 139.59MM
SALES (corp-wide): 139.59MM Privately Held
Web: www.akrochem.com
SIC: 5169 2851 Synthetic resins, rubber, and plastic materials; Paints and paint additives

(G-27)
AKRON BELTING & SUPPLY COMPANY
1244 Home Ave (44310-2511)
PHONE...............330 633-8212
Joe Mentzer, *Pr*
Joe Clark, *Pr*
Mark Brotherton, *VP*
EMP: 8 EST: 1989
SQ FT: 2,500
SALES (est): 2.46MM Privately Held
Web: www.akronbelting.com
SIC: 5085 3496 Hose, belting, and packing; Conveyor belts

(G-28)
AKRON CENTL ENGRV MOLD MCH INC
2680 Cory Ave (44314-1329)
PHONE...............330 475-1388
Frank Muhl, *Prin*
EMP: 9 EST: 1969
SALES (est): 110K Privately Held
Web: www.acemm.com
SIC: 2499 Trophy bases, wood

(G-29)
AKRON CENTL ENGRV MOLD MCH INC
1625 Massillon Rd (44312-4204)
PHONE...............330 794-8704
Frank James Muhl, *Pr*
John Kaeberlein, *Pr*
Frank R Muhl, *Stockholder*
EMP: 20 EST: 1969
SQ FT: 15,000
SALES (est): 2.55MM Privately Held
Web: www.acemm.com
SIC: 3544 8742 4213 Industrial molds; New products and services consultants; Automobiles, transport and delivery

(G-30)
AKRON COATING ADHESIVES CO INC
365 Stanton Ave (44301-1468)
PHONE...............330 724-4716
John Questel, *Pr*
John C Questel, *Stockholder*
Clifford C Questel, *Stockholder*

Lynn Questel, *Stockholder*
EMP: 10 **EST:** 1977
SQ FT: 17,000
SALES (est): 2.42MM **Privately Held**
Web: www.akroncoating.com
SIC: 2891 Adhesives

(G-31)
AKRON COCA-COLA BOTTLING CO
Also Called: Coca-Cola
1560 Triplett Blvd (44306-3306)
PHONE.................................330 784-2653
Matt Cartaglia, *Genl Mgr*
▲ **EMP:** 1300 **EST:** 1985
SALES (est): 86.56MM
SALES (corp-wide): 45.75B **Publicly Held**
Web: www.coca-cola.com
SIC: 2086 Bottled and canned soft drinks
HQ: Coca-Cola Refreshments Usa, Inc.
1 Coca Cola Plz Nw
Atlanta GA 30313
770 989-3000

(G-32)
AKRON COTTON PRODUCTS INC
437 W Cedar St (44307-2321)
PHONE.................................330 434-7171
Michael Zwick, *Pr*
EMP: 9 **EST:** 1929
SQ FT: 26,000
SALES (est): 981.24K **Privately Held**
Web: www.akroncotton.com
SIC: 2211 5999 Scrub cloths; Cleaning equipment and supplies

(G-33)
AKRON FOUNDRY CO (PA)
2728 Wingate Ave (44314-1300)
P.O. Box 27028 (44319-7028)
PHONE.................................330 745-3101
George Ostich, *Pr*
Geraldine Ostich, *
Michael Ostich, *
Ronald C Allan, *
EMP: 175 **EST:** 1969
SQ FT: 100,000
SALES (est): 49.84MM
SALES (corp-wide): 49.84MM **Privately Held**
Web: www.akronfoundry.com
SIC: 3369 5063 3365 3363 Castings, except die-castings, precision; Boxes and fittings, electrical; Aluminum foundries; Aluminum die-castings

(G-34)
AKRON GEAR & ENGINEERING INC
501 Morgan Ave (44311-2431)
P.O. Box 269 (44309-0269)
PHONE.................................330 773-6608
W Thomas James Iii, *Pr*
Carl G James, *VP*
John A Neuman, *VP Fin*
Gary Davis, *Asst Tr*
William Moore, *CUST SVCS*
EMP: 21 **EST:** 1911
SQ FT: 25,000
SALES (est): 5.08MM
SALES (corp-wide): 1.51B **Privately Held**
Web: www.akrongear.com
SIC: 3568 3566 3545 3462 Sprockets (power transmission equipment); Gears, power transmission, except auto; Machine tool accessories; Iron and steel forgings
PA: Forge Industries, Inc.
4450 Market St
Youngstown OH 44512
330 960-2468

(G-35)
AKRON LEGAL NEWS INC
60 S Summit St (44308)
PHONE.................................330 296-7578
John L Burleson, *Pr*
EMP: 12 **EST:** 1922
SQ FT: 4,000
SALES (est): 424.82K **Privately Held**
Web: www.akronlegalnews.com
SIC: 2711 8111 Newspapers: publishing only, not printed on site; Legal services

(G-36)
AKRON LITHO-PRINT COMPANY INC
1026 S Main St (44311-2346)
PHONE.................................330 434-3145
Pete P Ripplinger, *Pr*
Sharon Ripplinger, *Sec*
EMP: 12 **EST:** 1935
SQ FT: 5,500
SALES (est): 2.26MM **Privately Held**
Web: www.lithoprintco.com
SIC: 2752 2759 Lithographing on metal; Letterpress printing

(G-37)
AKRON ORTHOTIC SOLUTIONS INC
582 W Market St (44303-1839)
PHONE.................................330 253-3002
EMP: 8 **EST:** 1995
SALES (est): 540.02K **Privately Held**
SIC: 3842 5999 Braces, orthopedic; Orthopedic and prosthesis applications

(G-38)
AKRON PAINT & VARNISH INC
Also Called: APV Engineered Coatings
1390 Firestone Pkwy (44301-1695)
PHONE.................................330 773-8911
Dave Venarge, *Pr*
Ed Apsega, *General Vice President*
Mike Summers, *Purchasing*
◆ **EMP:** 90 **EST:** 1878
SQ FT: 160,000
SALES (est): 22.49MM **Privately Held**
Web: www.apvcoatings.com
SIC: 2851 2891 3953 Paints and paint additives; Adhesives and sealants; Marking devices

(G-39)
AKRON PLATING CO INC
1774 Hackberry St (44301-2493)
PHONE.................................330 773-6878
Robert Ormsby Junior, *Pr*
Fred Beidle, *VP*
Jennifer Ormsby, *Sec*
EMP: 10 **EST:** 1948
SQ FT: 7,500
SALES (est): 1.01MM **Privately Held**
Web: www.akronplating.com
SIC: 3471 Electroplating of metals or formed products

(G-40)
AKRON POLYMER PRODUCTS INC (PA)
1471 Exeter Rd (44306-3856)
PHONE.................................330 628-5551
Greg C Anderson, *Pr*
Kevin Gandee, *
▲ **EMP:** 68 **EST:** 1986
SALES (est): 9.77MM
SALES (corp-wide): 9.77MM **Privately Held**
Web: www.akronpolymer.com
SIC: 3089 3082 Extruded finished plastics products, nec; Tubes, unsupported plastics

(G-41)
AKRON PORCELAIN & PLASTICS CO (PA)
Also Called: Akron Porcelain & Plastic Co
2739 Cory Ave (44314-1308)
P.O. Box 15157 (44314-5157)
PHONE.................................330 745-2159
George H Lewis Junior, *Ch Bd*
Michael B Dunphy, *
Robert Briggs, *
▲ **EMP:** 140 **EST:** 1890
SQ FT: 120,000
SALES (est): 18.26MM
SALES (corp-wide): 18.26MM **Privately Held**
Web: www.akronporcelain.com
SIC: 3089 3264 Injection molded finished plastics products, nec; Porcelain electrical supplies

(G-42)
AKRON REBAR CO (PA)
Also Called: Cleveland Rebar
809 W Waterloo Rd (44314-1527)
P.O. Box 3710 (44314-0710)
Michael B Humphrey, *Prin*
Michael Humphrey Ii, *CEO*
▲ **EMP:** 32 **EST:** 1978
SQ FT: 32,600
SALES (est): 7.02MM
SALES (corp-wide): 7.02MM **Privately Held**
Web: www.akronrebar.com
SIC: 3441 3449 Fabricated structural metal; Bars, concrete reinforcing: fabricated steel

(G-43)
AKRON SPECIAL MACHINERY INC (PA)
Also Called: Poling Group, The
2740 Cory Ave (44314-1396)
PHONE.................................330 753-1077
David Poling Senior, *Pr*
Marlene Poling, *
David Poling Junior, *CFO*
▼ **EMP:** 49 **EST:** 1978
SQ FT: 60,000
SALES (est): 10.6MM
SALES (corp-wide): 10.6MM **Privately Held**
Web: www.polinggroup.com
SIC: 3599 Machine shop, jobbing and repair

(G-44)
AKRON STEEL FABRICATORS CO
Also Called: Poling Group
3291 Manchester Rd (44319)
PHONE.................................330 644-0616
David Poling Senior, *Pr*
Keith Kline, *
Marlene M Poling, *
David Poling Junior, *CFO*
Carolyn Clay, *
▼ **EMP:** 30 **EST:** 1947
SQ FT: 28,000
SALES (est): 5.11MM **Privately Held**
Web: www.polinggroup.com
SIC: 3491 Process control regulator valves

(G-45)
AKRON STEEL TREATING CO
336 Morgan Ave (44311-2424)
P.O. Box 2290 (44309-2290)
PHONE.................................330 773-8211
Christopher Powell, *CEO*
Joseph A Powell, *
Jim Stewart, *
Rick Miller, *
EMP: 45 **EST:** 1943
SQ FT: 46,000
SALES (est): 9.58MM **Privately Held**
Web: www.akronsteeltreating.com
SIC: 3398 3479 Metal heat treating; Painting, coating, and hot dipping

(G-46)
AKRON THERMOGRAPHY INC
Also Called: B C T
3506 Fortuna Dr (44312-5284)
PHONE.................................330 896-9712
Randal S Teague, *Prin*
EMP: 11 **EST:** 1995
SALES (est): 371.45K **Privately Held**
Web: www.evoprint.com
SIC: 2752 Commercial printing, lithographic

(G-47)
AKRON THERMOGRAPHY INC
Also Called: B C T
3406 Fortuna Dr (44312)
PHONE.................................330 896-9712
EMP: 17 **EST:** 1995
SALES (est): 736.32K **Privately Held**
Web: www.evoprint.com
SIC: 2752 Commercial printing, lithographic

(G-48)
AKRON VAULT COMPANY INC
Also Called: Akron Crematory
2399 Gilchrist Rd (44305-4496)
PHONE.................................330 784-5475
Marty Ebie, *Pr*
Phil Kauffman, *Sec*
EMP: 24 **EST:** 1944
SQ FT: 11,000
SALES (est): 1MM **Privately Held**
SIC: 3272 Burial vaults, concrete or precast terrazzo

(G-49)
ALCO-CHEM INC (PA)
Also Called: Alco
45 N Summit St (44308-1933)
PHONE.................................330 253-3535
Anthony Mandala Junior, *Pr*
Bart Mandala, *
Robert Mandala, *
▲ **EMP:** 34 **EST:** 1966
SQ FT: 22,000
SALES (est): 21.28MM
SALES (corp-wide): 21.28MM **Privately Held**
Web: www.alco-chem.com
SIC: 5087 2869 2842 Janitors' supplies; Industrial organic chemicals, nec; Polishes and sanitation goods

(G-50)
ALCON TOOL CO LTD
561 Lafollette St (44311-1824)
PHONE.................................330 773-9171
EMP: 6 **EST:** 2015
SALES (est): 104.54K **Privately Held**
Web: www.alcontool.com
SIC: 3541 Machine tools, metal cutting type

(G-51)
ALCON TOOL COMPANY
Also Called: Alcon
565 Lafollette St (44311-1824)
PHONE.................................330 773-9171
Charles E Conner, *CEO*
▼ **EMP:** 50 **EST:** 1946
SQ FT: 100,000
SALES (est): 9.37MM **Privately Held**
Web: www.alcontool.com
SIC: 3541 Machine tools, metal cutting type

(G-52)
ALEXANDER PIERCE CORP
1874 Englewood Ave (44312-1002)

Akron - Summit County (G-53)

GEOGRAPHIC SECTION

PHONE.............................330 798-9840
Kim Hocevar-claxon, *Prin*
EMP: 14 **EST:** 2019
SALES (est): 992.29K **Privately Held**
Web:
www.alexanderpiercerestaurant.com
SIC: 3479 Coating of metals and formed products

(G-53)
ALL-TECH MANUFACTURING LTD
1477 Industrial Pkwy (44310-2601)
PHONE.............................330 633-1095
Joseph Manijak, *Managing Member*
Frank Manijak, *Managing Member*
EMP: 21 **EST:** 1992
SQ FT: 9,000
SALES (est): 2.02MM **Privately Held**
SIC: 3599 Machine shop, jobbing and repair

(G-54)
ALLEN RANDALL ENTERPRISES INC
70 E Miller Ave (44301-1324)
P.O. Box 1117 (44309-1117)
PHONE.............................330 374-9850
Jim Bradshaw, *Pr*
EMP: 10 **EST:** 1988
SQ FT: 12,500
SALES (est): 953.79K **Privately Held**
Web: www.allen-randall.com
SIC: 3599 Machine shop, jobbing and repair

(G-55)
ALLIANCE FORGING GROUP LLC
847 Pier Dr # 1000 (44307-2267)
PHONE.............................330 680-4861
David Risher, *Managing Member*
EMP: 6 **EST:** 2013
SQ FT: 100,000
SALES (est): 383.34K **Privately Held**
SIC: 3462 Ornamental metal forgings, ferrous

(G-56)
ALTERRA ENERGY LLC
1200 E Waterloo Rd (44306-3806)
PHONE.............................800 569-6061
EMP: 7 **EST:** 2019
SALES (est): 1.03MM
SALES (corp-wide): 24.92B **Privately Held**
Web: www.alterraenergy.com
SIC: 2899 Chemical preparations, nec
PA: Neste Oyj
Keilaranta 21
Espoo 02150
1045811

(G-57)
AMERI-KART CORP
1293 S Main St (44301-1302)
PHONE.............................800 232-0847
Michael Mcgaugh, *Pr*
EMP: 88
SALES (corp-wide): 813.07MM **Publicly Held**
Web:
www.myersengineeredsolutions.com
SIC: 3089 Injection molding of plastics
HQ: Ameri-Kart Corp.
17196 State Road 120
Bristol IN 46507

(G-58)
AMERICAN BOTTLING COMPANY
1259 George Washington Blvd (44312-3007)
PHONE.............................330 733-3830
Joe Laduto, *Mgr*
EMP: 27
Web: www.keurigdrpepper.com
SIC: 2086 Soft drinks: packaged in cans, bottles, etc.

HQ: The American Bottling Company
6425 Hall Of Fame Ln
Frisco TX 75034

(G-59)
AMERICAN MADE BAGS LLC
999 Sweitzer (44311-2359)
PHONE.............................330 475-1385
Thomas Armour, *Pr*
EMP: 19 **EST:** 2010
SALES (est): 1.18MM **Privately Held**
SIC: 2393 Canvas bags

(G-60)
AMERICAN ORGINAL BLDG PDTS LLC
1000 Arlington Cir (44306-3973)
PHONE.............................330 786-3000
Dale V Wilson, *Managing Member*
Gordon F Keeler Junior, *Managing Member*
EMP: 7 **EST:** 2007
SALES (est): 693.86K **Privately Held**
Web: www.americanoriginalsiding.com
SIC: 2952 Siding materials

(G-61)
AMERICAN POLYMERS CORPORATION (PA)
231 Springside Dr Ste 145 (44333-2455)
PHONE.............................330 666-6048
Kevin Copeland, *Prin*
Phil Farensworth, *Sr VP*
EMP: 6 **EST:** 1999
SQ FT: 2,000
SALES (est): 1.44MM
SALES (corp-wide): 1.44MM **Privately Held**
SIC: 2821 Plastics materials and resins

(G-62)
AMERICAN PRINTING INC
1121 Tower Dr (44305-1089)
PHONE.............................330 630-1121
David Hall, *Pr*
Kim Krietz, *Sec*
EMP: 10 **EST:** 1928
SQ FT: 15,000
SALES (est): 999.6K **Privately Held**
Web: www.americanprintinginc.com
SIC: 2752 Offset printing

(G-63)
ANANDA ANANI LLC ✪
1769 E Waterford Ct Apt 912 (44313-8375)
PHONE.............................440 406-6086
Cara Mitthell, *Managing Member*
EMP: 7 **EST:** 2022
SALES (est): 78.58K **Privately Held**
SIC: 2371 Apparel, fur

(G-64)
ARIEL CORPORATION
3360 Miller Park Rd (44312-5342)
PHONE.............................330 896-2660
Karen Buchwald Wright, *Pr*
EMP: 69
SALES (corp-wide): 105.04MM **Privately Held**
Web: www.arielcorp.com
SIC: 3563 Air and gas compressors including vacuum pumps
PA: Ariel Corporation
35 Blackjack Road Ext
Mount Vernon OH 43050
740 397-0311

(G-65)
ASH SEWER & DRAIN SERVICE
451 E North St (44304-1217)
PHONE.............................330 376-9714

Greg Ash, *Prin*
EMP: 6 **EST:** 1987
SALES (est): 577.51K **Privately Held**
SIC: 3272 4959 Sewer pipe, concrete; Sanitary services, nec

(G-66)
ASTER INDUSTRIES INC
275 N Arlington St Ste B (44305-1600)
PHONE.............................330 762-7965
Kimberly Oplinger, *Pr*
Michael J Oplinger, *
EMP: 26 **EST:** 1990
SQ FT: 14,500
SALES (est): 5.21MM **Privately Held**
Web: www.asterind.com
SIC: 3999 2599 Advertising display products; Bar, restaurant and cafeteria furniture

(G-67)
ATCPC OF OHIO LLC
Also Called: Klutch Cannabis
1055 Home Ave (44310-3501)
PHONE.............................330 670-9900
Adam Thomarios, *Pr*
EMP: 51 **EST:** 2009
SALES (est): 2.24MM **Privately Held**
SIC: 3999

(G-68)
AURIS NOBLE LLC (PA)
160 E Voris St (44311-1514)
P.O. Box 522 (44309-0522)
PHONE.............................330 321-6649
Patrick Deeringer, *COO*
Lou Britton, *Manager*
EMP: 22 **EST:** 2011
SQ FT: 2,000
SALES (est): 4.78MM
SALES (corp-wide): 4.78MM **Privately Held**
Web: www.aurisnoble.com
SIC: 3341 4953 5093 Secondary precious metals; Recycling, waste materials; Nonferrous metals scrap

(G-69)
AUSTIN PARTS & SERVICE
56 N Union St (44304-1347)
PHONE.............................330 253-7791
Joe Hickin, *Owner*
EMP: 6 **EST:** 2015
SALES (est): 189.66K **Privately Held**
Web: www.austinpartsandservice.com
SIC: 3714 Motor vehicle parts and accessories

(G-70)
AUTO DEALER DESIGNS INC
303 W Bartges St (44307-2205)
P.O. Box 2379 (44224-1200)
PHONE.............................330 374-7666
John Volpe, *CEO*
David Volpe, *Pr*
Paul Volpe, *VP*
Paula Volpe, *Sec*
Marilyn Volpe, *Treas*
EMP: 22 **EST:** 1971
SQ FT: 16,152
SALES (est): 2.32MM **Privately Held**
Web: www.autodealerdesigns.com
SIC: 3993 5199 Signs and advertising specialties; Advertising specialties

(G-71)
AXIOM INTERNATIONAL INC
3517 Embassy Pkwy Ste 150 (44333-8407)
PHONE.............................330 396-5942
Wayne Stair, *Pr*
Cinda Klatil, *Contrlr*
Mike Leidhty, *CFO*

EMP: 8 **EST:** 2011
SQ FT: 7,500
SALES (est): 183.09K **Privately Held**
Web: www.americasinternational.com
SIC: 2821 Plastics materials and resins

(G-72)
B RICHARDSON INC
Also Called: Talk of Town Silkscreen & EMB
25 Elinor Ave (44305-4005)
PHONE.............................330 724-2122
Becky Waidmann, *Pr*
Herb Waidmann, *Sec*
EMP: 9 **EST:** 1985
SQ FT: 5,000
SALES (est): 432.92K **Privately Held**
Web: www.talkofthetownsilkscreen.com
SIC: 2262 7299 Screen printing: manmade fiber and silk broadwoven fabrics; Stitching, custom

(G-73)
BABCOCK & WILCOX COMPANY (HQ)
1200 E Market St Ste 650 (44305)
P.O. Box 351 (44203)
PHONE.............................330 753-4511
Mark Low, *Sr VP*
Jimmy Morgan, *
Louis Salamone, *
◆ **EMP:** 1000 **EST:** 1867
SQ FT: 16,000
SALES (est): 896.25MM
SALES (corp-wide): 999.35MM **Publicly Held**
Web: www.babcock.com
SIC: 1629 1711 3443 7699 Industrial plant construction; Plumbing, heating, air-conditioning; Fabricated plate work (boiler shop); Boiler and heating repair services
PA: Babcock & Wilcox Enterprises, Inc.
1200 E Market St Ste 650
Akron OH 44305
330 753-4511

(G-74)
BABCOCK & WILCOX ENTPS INC (PA)
1200 E Market St Ste 650 (44305)
PHONE.............................330 753-4511
Kenneth M Young, *Ch Bd*
Louis Salamone, *CAO*
Henry E Bartoli, *CSO*
Robert M Caruso, *CIO*
John J Dziewisz, *CCO*
EMP: 106 **EST:** 1867
SALES (est): 999.35MM
SALES (corp-wide): 999.35MM **Publicly Held**
Web: www.babcock.com
SIC: 3621 3829 Power generators; Nuclear instrument modules

(G-75)
BABCOCK & WILCOX HOLDINGS INC
1200 E Market St Ste 650 (44305-4067)
PHONE.............................704 625-4900
EMP: 2400 **EST:** 2017
SALES (est): 48.92MM **Privately Held**
Web: www.babcock.com
SIC: 3511 8711 Turbines and turbine generator sets; Engineering services

(G-76)
BABCOX MEDIA INC
3550 Embassy Pkwy (44333-8318)
PHONE.............................330 670-1234
William E Babcox, *Pr*
Greg Cira, *
Lance Goeddel, *CAO*
EMP: 75 **EST:** 1913

GEOGRAPHIC SECTION

Akron - Summit County (G-101)

SQ FT: 40,000
SALES (est): 23.2MM **Privately Held**
Web: www.babcox.com
SIC: **2721** Magazines: publishing only, not printed on site

(G-77)
BAKER MEDIA GROUP LLC
Also Called: Akron Life
1653 Merriman Rd Ste 116 (44313-5293)
PHONE..................................330 253-0056
Don Baker Junior, *Managing Member*
Colin Baker Publ, *Prin*
EMP: 11 EST: 2004
SQ FT: 3,000
SALES (est): 965.83K **Privately Held**
Web: www.akronlife.com
SIC: **2721** Magazines: publishing only, not printed on site

(G-78)
BAUMGARDNER PRODUCTS CO
295 Silver St (44303-2229)
PHONE..................................330 376-2466
Robert Donatelli, *Prin*
EMP: 7 EST: 2016
SALES (est): 183.31K **Privately Held**
Web: www.baumgardnerproducts.com
SIC: **3272** Burial vaults, concrete or precast terrazzo

(G-79)
BAXTERS LLC
1259 Ashford Ln (44313-6870)
PHONE..................................234 678-5484
Jerry Mallo, *Prin*
EMP: 6 EST: 2012
SALES (est): 138.32K **Privately Held**
SIC: **2834** Pharmaceutical preparations

(G-80)
BDU HOLDINGS INC
467 Dan St (44310-3906)
PHONE..................................330 374-1810
Tim Lowe, *Pr*
EMP: 10 EST: 1983
SQ FT: 20,000
SALES (est): 760K **Privately Held**
SIC: **3069** Custom compounding of rubber materials

(G-81)
BEAVER PRODUCTIONS
2251 Cooledge Ave (44305-2162)
PHONE..................................330 352-4603
Joshua Beaver, *Prin*
EMP: 6 EST: 2008
SALES (est): 413.29K **Privately Held**
Web: www.beaverproductions.com
SIC: **2741** Guides: publishing and printing

(G-82)
BERINGER PLATING INC
1211 Devalera St (44310-2488)
PHONE..................................330 633-8409
James Beringer Junior, *Pr*
Laura Beringer, *Sec*
EMP: 8 EST: 1953
SQ FT: 21,000
SALES (est): 1.18MM **Privately Held**
Web: www.beringerplating.com
SIC: **3471** 8471 Electroplating of metals or formed products; Engineering services

(G-83)
BERRAN INDUSTRIAL GROUP INC
570 Wolf Ledges Pkwy (44311-1022)
PHONE..................................330 253-5800
Randy P Adair, *Pr*
Don Schultz, *

EMP: 26 EST: 1980
SQ FT: 18,000
SALES (est): 4.37MM **Privately Held**
Web: www.berranindustrialgroup.com
SIC: **3599** 3441 3549 3444 Custom machinery; Fabricated structural metal; Metalworking machinery, nec; Sheet metalwork

(G-84)
BEST MOLD & MANUFACTURING INC
1546 E Turkeyfoot Lake Rd (44312)
P.O. Box 544 (44685)
PHONE..................................330 896-9988
EMP: 45 EST: 2000
SQ FT: 26,000
SALES (est): 8.49MM **Privately Held**
Web: www.bestmmi.com
SIC: **3599** Machine shop, jobbing and repair

(G-85)
BESTEN EQUIPMENT INC
388 S Main St Ste 700 (44311-1060)
PHONE..................................216 581-1166
Lynn Bisantz, *Prin*
EMP: 35 EST: 2005
SALES (est): 3.22MM **Publicly Held**
Web: www.bestenequipment.com
SIC: **2891** Sealants
PA: Quanex Building Products Corporation
945 Bunker Hl Rd Ste 900
Houston TX 77024

(G-86)
BIF CO LLC
Also Called: Bif, LLC
1405 Home Ave (44310-2514)
PHONE..................................330 564-0941
Mark Schoenbaechler, *Pr*
EMP: 10 EST: 2001
SQ FT: 150,000
SALES (est): 2.51MM
SALES (corp-wide): 16.2MM **Privately Held**
Web: www.bifwater.com
SIC: **3824** Impeller and counter driven flow meters
PA: Logan Machine Company
1405 Home Ave
Akron OH 44310
330 633-6163

(G-87)
BLINGED & BRONZED
2303 Manchester Rd (44314-3602)
PHONE..................................330 631-1255
Danielle Stoll, *Pr*
EMP: 10 EST: 2020
SALES (est): 581.61K **Privately Held**
SIC: **2869** Tanning agents, synthetic organic

(G-88)
BNOAT ONCOLOGY
411 Wolf Ledges Pkwy Ste 105 (44311-1028)
PHONE..................................330 285-2537
EMP: 6 EST: 2010
SALES (est): 459.88K **Privately Held**
Web: www.nitricoxidelab.com
SIC: **2834** Pharmaceutical preparations

(G-89)
BOGIE INDUSTRIES INC LTD
Also Called: Weaver Fab & Finishing
1100 Home Ave (44310-3504)
PHONE..................................330 745-3105
Jim Lauer, *Pr*
Fuzzy Helton, *
Marian Lauer, *
EMP: 38 EST: 1998

SQ FT: 40,000
SALES (est): 8.99MM **Privately Held**
Web: www.weaverfab.com
SIC: **3444** 1799 3399 Sheet metalwork; Coating of metal structures at construction site; Powder, metal

(G-90)
BOIVIN MACHINE
400 Lombard St (44310-2322)
PHONE..................................330 928-3942
Harry Boivin, *Prin*
EMP: 7 EST: 2002
SALES (est): 68.95K **Privately Held**
Web: www.hhmachine.com
SIC: **3599** Machine shop, jobbing and repair

(G-91)
BONNOT COMPANY
1301 Home Ave (44310-2654)
PHONE..................................330 896-6544
George W Bain, *Pr*
John Negrelli, *
▼ EMP: 25 EST: 1891
SQ FT: 40,000
SALES (est): 5.79MM **Privately Held**
Web: www.thebonnotco.com
SIC: **3599** Custom machinery

(G-92)
BRIDGESTONE AMRCAS TIRE OPRTONS
1670 Firestone Pkwy (44301-1659)
PHONE..................................330 379-3714
EMP: 76
Web: www.bridgestoneamericas.com
SIC: **3011** Tires and inner tubes
HQ: Bridgestone Americas Tire Operations, Llc
200 4th Ave S Ste 100
Nashville TN 37201
615 937-1000

(G-93)
BRIGHT STAR BOOKS INC
1357 Home Ave (44310-2549)
PHONE..................................330 888-2156
Keith Seher, *Dir*
Nancy Baxter, *Dir*
Iriel Hopkins, *Dir*
Dave Plahuta, *Dir*
Christin Seher, *Dir*
EMP: 7 EST: 2017
SALES (est): 162.14K **Privately Held**
Web: www.brightstarbooks.org
SIC: **2731** Book publishing

(G-94)
BUCKEYE READY MIX CONCRETE
1562 Massillon Rd (44312-4203)
PHONE..................................330 798-5511
John Chafe, *Pr*
EMP: 7 EST: 1996
SALES (est): 178.39K **Privately Held**
SIC: **3273** Ready-mixed concrete

(G-95)
BURGHARDT MANUFACTURING INC
1524 Massillon Rd (44306-4162)
PHONE..................................330 253-7590
Adam Burghardt, *Pr*
EMP: 9 EST: 1987
SQ FT: 8,000
SALES (est): 1.84MM **Privately Held**
SIC: **3441** Fabricated structural metal for bridges

(G-96)
BURGHARDT METAL FABG INC
1638 Mcchesney Rd (44306-4396)

PHONE..................................330 794-1830
Craig Shuster, *Pr*
Cindy Archer, *Sec*
EMP: 18 EST: 1958
SQ FT: 22,000
SALES (est): 2.21MM **Privately Held**
Web: www.burgmetalfab.com
SIC: **3449** 3441 Miscellaneous metalwork; Fabricated structural metal

(G-97)
BURT MANUFACTURING COMPANY INC
Also Called: Thycurb
44 E South St (44311-2031)
PHONE..................................330 762-0061
Marvin Ricklefs, *CEO*
EMP: 37 EST: 1890
SQ FT: 120,000
SALES (est): 2.25MM
SALES (corp-wide): 49.99MM **Privately Held**
SIC: **3564** 3442 3444 Blowers and fans; Metal doors, sash, and trim; Ventilators, sheet metal
PA: Thybar Corporation
913 S Kay Ave
Addison IL 60101
630 543-5300

(G-98)
CALIBER MOLD AND MACHINE INC
2200 Massillon Rd (44312-4234)
P.O. Box 847 (45701-0847)
PHONE..................................330 633-8171
Jack Thornton, *Pr*
Thomas Thornton, *
EMP: 40 EST: 1986
SALES (est): 5.14MM **Privately Held**
Web: jax.tiremolds.com
SIC: **3544** Industrial molds

(G-99)
CARDINAL PRINTING INC
112 W Wilbeth Rd (44301-2415)
P.O. Box 678 (44232-0678)
PHONE..................................330 773-7300
Vince Rosnack, *Pr*
Pam Rosnack, *Sec*
EMP: 8 EST: 1980
SQ FT: 6,700
SALES (est): 507.48K **Privately Held**
Web: www.cardinalprinting.net
SIC: **2752** Offset printing

(G-100)
CARGILL INCORPORATED
Also Called: Cargill
2065 Manchester Rd (44314-1770)
PHONE..................................330 745-0031
Wayne A Brown, *Mgr*
EMP: 105
SALES (corp-wide): 176.74B **Privately Held**
Web: www.cargill.com
SIC: **2048** Prepared feeds, nec
PA: Cargill, Incorporated
15407 Mcginty Rd W
Wayzata MN 55391
800 227-4455

(G-101)
CCSI INC
1868 Akron Peninsula Rd (44313-4808)
PHONE..................................800 742-8535
Frank Orlando, *VP*
EMP: 10 EST: 2013
SALES (est): 886.9K **Privately Held**
Web: www.ccsi-inc.com
SIC: **3829** Measuring and controlling devices, nec

Akron - Summit County (G-102)

GEOGRAPHIC SECTION

(G-102)
CEC ELECTRONICS CORP
1739 Akron Peninsula Rd (44313-5157)
P.O. Box 3870 (44223-7870)
PHONE..................................330 916-8100
Dan Lujan, *Pr*
EMP: 7 **EST:** 1981
SQ FT: 3,000
SALES (est): 2.95MM **Privately Held**
Web: www.cecelectronics.info
SIC: 3679 Electronic circuits

(G-103)
CECIL C PECK CO
1029 Arlington Cir (44306-3959)
PHONE..................................330 785-0781
Paul Stewart, *Pr*
▲ **EMP:** 10 **EST:** 1945
SQ FT: 8,350
SALES (est): 874.51K **Privately Held**
Web: www.summitmachinesolutions.com
SIC: 3699 8/11 Welding machines and equipment, ultrasonic; Designing: ship, boat, machine, and product

(G-104)
CED PROCESS MINERALS INC (PA)
863 N Cleveland Massillon Rd
(44333-2167)
PHONE..................................330 666-5500
Leland D Cole, *VP*
William M Douglas, *Sec*
Nolan E Douglas, *Treas*
▼ **EMP:** 18 **EST:** 1981
SQ FT: 2,368
SALES (est): 3.95MM
SALES (corp-wide): 3.95MM **Privately Held**
Web: www.cedprocessminerals.com
SIC: 1446 Foundry sand mining

(G-105)
CENTRAL COCA-COLA BTLG CO INC
Also Called: Coca-Cola
1560 Triplett Blvd (44306-3306)
PHONE..................................330 875-1487
EMP: 34
SALES (corp-wide): 45.75B **Publicly Held**
Web: www.coca-cola.com
SIC: 2086 8741 Bottled and canned soft drinks; Management services
HQ: Central Coca-Cola Bottling Company, Inc.
555 Taxter Rd Ste 550
Elmsford NY 10523
914 789-1100

(G-106)
CHARLES AUTO ELECTRIC CO INC
600 Grant St (44311-1502)
P.O. Box 2872 (44720-0872)
PHONE..................................330 535-6269
Daniel Ardelean, *Pr*
Erik S Ardelean, *VP*
Mary Ardelean, *Treas*
EMP: 8 **EST:** 1972
SQ FT: 8,000
SALES (est): 673.91K **Privately Held**
Web: www.charlesautoelectric.com
SIC: 3694 3621 Generators, automotive and aircraft; Starters, for motors

(G-107)
CHARLES COSTA INC
Also Called: Costa Machine
924 Home Ave (44310-4108)
PHONE..................................330 376-3636
George Marino, *Pr*
Carl Prentiss, *VP*
EMP: 18 **EST:** 1972
SQ FT: 10,000
SALES (est): 218.75K **Privately Held**
Web: www.costamachine.com
SIC: 3599 Machine shop, jobbing and repair

(G-108)
CHOCOLATE ECSTASY INC
879 Home Ave (44310-4120)
PHONE..................................330 434-4199
Cindy Mason, *Prin*
EMP: 7 **EST:** 1997
SALES (est): 160K **Privately Held**
SIC: 2066 Chocolate and cocoa products

(G-109)
CHROME DEPOSIT CORPORATION
1566 Firestone Pkwy (44301-1626)
PHONE..................................330 773-7800
Philip Court, *Pr*
EMP: 29
SALES (corp-wide): 21.07B **Publicly Held**
Web: www.chromedeposit.com
SIC: 3471 Chromium plating of metals or formed products
HQ: Chrome Deposit Corporation
6640 Melton Rd
Portage IN 46368
219 763-1571

(G-110)
CIMS INCORPORATED
2701 Gilchrist Rd (44305-4434)
P.O. Box 1610 (44309-1610)
PHONE..................................330 794-8102
Susan L Kruder, *Pr*
EMP: 20 **EST:** 1973
SQ FT: 7,200
SALES (est): 385.04K **Privately Held**
Web: www.cimstireregistration.com
SIC: 7534 Tire retreading and repair shops

(G-111)
CIOFFI HOLDINGS LLC
1001 Eastwood Ave (44305-1127)
P.O. Box 412 (44278-0412)
PHONE..................................330 794-9448
Jamie Stone, *Prin*
EMP: 16 **EST:** 2019
SALES (est): 2.37MM **Privately Held**
Web: www.libertyredimix.com
SIC: 3273 Ready-mixed concrete

(G-112)
CLASSIC COUNTERTOPS LLC
1519 Kenmore Blvd (44314-1661)
PHONE..................................330 882-4220
EMP: 6 **EST:** 2008
SQ FT: 4,700
SALES (est): 312.23K **Privately Held**
Web: www.classiccountertops.net
SIC: 3131 1799 Counters; Counter top installation

(G-113)
CLEARSONIC MANUFACTURING INC
1025 Evans Ave (44305-1020)
PHONE..................................828 772-9809
▲ **EMP:** 8 **EST:** 1995
SALES (est): 749.02K **Privately Held**
Web: www.clearsonic.com
SIC: 3999 Barber and beauty shop equipment

(G-114)
COMBS MANUFACTURING INC
380 Kennedy Rd (44305-4422)
PHONE..................................330 784-3151
▲ **EMP:** 70
SIC: 3599 7692 2421 Machine shop, jobbing and repair; Welding repair; Sawmills and planing mills, general

(G-115)
COS BLUEPRINT INC
590 N Main St (44310-3145)
P.O. Box 4931 (44310-0931)
PHONE..................................330 376-0022
Jim Scalia, *Pr*
Martin Hyatt, *
Linda Scalia, *
EMP: 24 **EST:** 1985
SQ FT: 12,000
SALES (est): 2.08MM **Privately Held**
Web: www.reprosinc.com
SIC: 2752 5999 5712 5943 Offset printing; Typewriters and business machines; Office furniture; Office forms and supplies

(G-116)
COUNTRY PURE FOODS INC (PA)
222 S Main St Ste 401 (44308-1525)
PHONE..................................330 753-2293
◆ **EMP:** 120 **EST:** 1995
SALES (est): 273.99MM **Privately Held**
Web: www.countrypure.com
SIC: 2033 2037 2086 Fruit juices: fresh; Fruit juice concentrates, frozen; Fruit drinks (less than 100% juice): packaged in cans, etc.

(G-117)
CRAWFORD AE LLC
Also Called: Hickok Ae LLC
735 Glaser Pkwy (44306-4166)
PHONE..................................330 794-9770
Brian Powers, *
◆ **EMP:** 95 **EST:** 2017
SALES (est): 22.12MM
SALES (corp-wide): 143.89MM **Publicly Held**
SIC: 3585 Heating and air conditioning combination units
PA: Crawford United Corporation
10514 Dupont Ave
Cleveland OH 44108
216 541-8060

(G-118)
CREATIVE IP LLC
1653 Merriman Rd Ste L1 (44313-5293)
PHONE..................................234 571-2466
Kim Mitzo Thompson, *Pr*
▲ **EMP:** 7 **EST:** 2014
SALES (est): 396.19K **Privately Held**
SIC: 2789 2721 Bronzing books, cards, or paper; Comic books: publishing only, not printed on site

(G-119)
CURTIS STEEL & SUPPLY INC
1210 Curtis St (44301-1428)
PHONE..................................330 376-7141
Tom Poinar, *Pr*
Michael S Poinar, *VP*
EMP: 14 **EST:** 1947
SQ FT: 22,000
SALES (est): 1.06MM **Privately Held**
SIC: 3599 5051 Machine shop, jobbing and repair; Ferrous metals

(G-120)
CUSTOM CRAFT CONTROLS INC
Also Called: Custom Craft
1620 Triplett Blvd (44306-3308)
P.O. Box 7363 (44306-0363)
PHONE..................................330 630-9599
Kenneth Mike Dunaway, *Pr*
Debbie Dunaway, *Pr*
EMP: 18 **EST:** 1986
SQ FT: 10,000
SALES (est): 3MM **Privately Held**
Web: www.customcraftcontrols.com
SIC: 3613 8711 Control panels, electric; Engineering services

(G-121)
D & L MACHINE CO INC
1029 Arlington Cir (44306-3959)
PHONE..................................330 785-0781
Charles Bell, *Pr*
Naaman Elliott, *
EMP: 25 **EST:** 1943
SQ FT: 18,100
SALES (est): 2.71MM **Privately Held**
Web: www.summitmachinesolutions.com
SIC: 3599 Machine shop, jobbing and repair

(G-122)
D AND D PLASTICS INC
581 E Tallmadge Ave (44310-2402)
P.O. Box 285 (44278-0285)
PHONE..................................330 376-0668
Charles Hay, *Pr*
Terri Hay, *Treas*
EMP: 10 **EST:** 1982
SQ FT: 8,000
SALES (est): 730.52K **Privately Held**
Web: www.d-dplastics.com
SIC: 3089 Extruded finished plastics products, nec

(G-123)
DATAQ INSTRUMENTS INC
241 Springside Dr (44333-2432)
PHONE..................................330 668-1444
John J Bowers, *Pr*
Roger Lockhart, *VP*
Karen Bowers, *Sec*
EMP: 24 **EST:** 1984
SQ FT: 4,000
SALES (est): 5.04MM **Privately Held**
Web: www.dataq.com
SIC: 3577 Computer peripheral equipment, nec

(G-124)
DAUPHIN HOLDINGS INC
Also Called: Arnold's Candies
931 High Grove Blvd (44312-3405)
PHONE..................................330 733-4022
Laurel Dauphin, *Pr*
EMP: 11 **EST:** 2011
SALES (est): 486.62K **Privately Held**
SIC: 2064 Candy and other confectionery products

(G-125)
DC LEGACY CORP
3300 Massillon Rd (44312)
PHONE..................................330 896-4220
Michael Hochschwender, *CEO*
Albert Kungl, *
▲ **EMP:** 40 **EST:** 1971
SQ FT: 26,000
SALES (est): 4.67MM **Privately Held**
Web: www.delcollc.com
SIC: 3544 Special dies and tools

(G-126)
DIAMOND AMERICA CORPORATION
Also Called: Akron Tool and Die
96 E Miller Ave (44301-1325)
PHONE..................................330 762-9269
▲ **EMP:** 22 **EST:** 1943
SALES (est): 4.83MM **Privately Held**
Web: www.daextrusion.com
SIC: 3544 3469 Extrusion dies; Machine parts, stamped or pressed metal

(G-127)
DIAMOND DESIGNS INC
231 Springside Dr Ste 145 (44333-2455)
PHONE..................................330 434-6776
Philip H Gross, *Pr*
Bradley Gross, *VP*

GEOGRAPHIC SECTION

Akron - Summit County (G-151)

EMP: 8 EST: 1980
SALES (est): 723.9K **Privately Held**
SIC: **3911** Jewelry, precious metal

(G-128)
DIAMOND POLYMERS INCORPORATED
1353 Exeter Rd (44306-3853)
PHONE..............................330 773-2700
◆ EMP: 66
SIC: **2821** 2295 Plastics materials and resins; Resin or plastic coated fabrics

(G-129)
DIE-GEM CO INC
Also Called: Kel-Eez
394 Greenwood Ave (44320-1245)
PHONE..............................330 784-7400
James Adams, *Pr*
James Adams, *Pr*
Diane Adams, *VP*
EMP: 15 EST: 1971
SQ FT: 17,000
SALES (est): 1.14MM **Privately Held**
Web: www.die-gem.com
SIC: **3089** Injection molding of plastics

(G-130)
DIGITAL COLOR INTL LLC
Also Called: D C I
1653 Merriman Rd Ste 211 (44313-5276)
EMP: 18 EST: 2011
SQ FT: 38,000
SALES (est): 1.28MM **Privately Held**
Web: www.digitalcolorinternational.com
SIC: **7336** 2752 2653 7331 Creative services to advertisers, except writers; Commercial printing, lithographic; Display items, solid fiber: made from purchased materials; Direct mail advertising services

(G-131)
DJ SIGNS MD LLC
224 W Exchange St Ste 290 (44302-1722)
PHONE..............................330 344-6643
EMP: 15
SALES (corp-wide): 86.89K **Privately Held**
SIC: **3993** Signs and advertising specialties
PA: D.J. Signs, M.D., Llc
8 Brandywine Dr
Hudson OH

(G-132)
DLH ENTERPRISES LLC
Also Called: Hotcards of Akron
2086 Romig Rd Ste 2 (44320-3874)
PHONE..............................330 253-6960
EMP: 6 EST: 2010
SALES (est): 260.63K **Privately Held**
SIC: **2759** Commercial printing, nec

(G-133)
DOWCO LLC
Also Called: Finite Fibers
1374 Markle St (44306-1801)
PHONE..............................330 773-6654
▲ EMP: 22 EST: 2005
SQ FT: 1,500
SALES (est): 4.76MM **Privately Held**
Web: www.finitefiber.com
SIC: **2824** Nylon fibers

(G-134)
DRB HOLDINGS LLC
3245 Pickle Rd (44312-5333)
PHONE..............................330 645-3299
Bill Morgenstern, *CEO*
EMP: 285 EST: 2003
SALES (est): 10.71MM **Privately Held**
Web: www.drb.com

SIC: **7373** 7371 7372 Systems software development services; Custom computer programming services; Prepackaged software

(G-135)
DRB SYSTEMS LLC (HQ)
Also Called: Drb Tunnel Solutions
3245 Pickle Rd (44312-5333)
P.O. Box 550 (44685-0550)
PHONE..............................330 645-3299
Dale Brott, *Pr*
Donald A Brott, *
Kenneth Brott, *
EMP: 259 EST: 1984
SALES (est): 86.19MM
SALES (corp-wide): 3.1B **Publicly Held**
Web: www.drb.com
SIC: **7373** 7371 7372 Systems software development services; Custom computer programming services; Prepackaged software
PA: Vontier Corporation
5438 Wade Park Blvd # 601
Raleigh NC 27607
984 275-6000

(G-136)
EARTHQUAKER DEVICES LLC
Also Called: Earthquaker Devices
350 W Bowery St (44307-2538)
PHONE..............................330 252-9220
Jamie Stillman, *Pt*
Jamie Stillman, *Managing Member*
▲ EMP: 41 EST: 2007
SALES (est): 3.01MM **Privately Held**
Web: www.earthquakerdevices.com
SIC: **3931** Guitars and parts, electric and nonelectric

(G-137)
ELLET NEON SALES & SERVICE INC
Also Called: E S C
3041 E Waterloo Rd (44312-4058)
P.O. Box 6063 (44312-0063)
PHONE..............................330 628-9907
Gregory Peters, *Pr*
Claudia Peters, *
Mike Croston, *
Johnathan Webb, *
Amy Yelling, *
EMP: 50 EST: 1956
SQ FT: 7,000
SALES (est): 8.89MM **Privately Held**
Web: www.elletneon.com
SIC: **3993** Electric signs

(G-138)
ELLORAS CAVE PUBLISHING INC
1056 Home Ave (44310-3502)
P.O. Box 937 (44223-0937)
PHONE..............................330 253-3521
Patty L Marks, *CEO*
Tina M Engler, *
Christina M Brashear, *
EMP: 25 EST: 2002
SQ FT: 12,960
SALES (est): 502.76K **Privately Held**
SIC: **2741** 2731 Miscellaneous publishing; Book publishing

(G-139)
ENDURANCE MANUFACTURING INC
1615 E Market St (44305-4210)
PHONE..............................330 628-2600
Thomas J Turkalj, *Prin*
EMP: 12 EST: 2011
SALES (est): 1.3MM **Privately Held**
SIC: **2813** Industrial gases

(G-140)
ENERGY HBR NCLEAR GNRATION LLC
168 E Market St (44308-2014)
PHONE..............................888 254-6359
John Judge, *Pr*
EMP: 6 EST: 2007
SALES (est): 4.6MM
SALES (corp-wide): 14.78B **Publicly Held**
SIC: **3443** Nuclear reactors, military or industrial
HQ: Energy Harbor Corp.
168 E Market St
Akron OH 44308
888 254-6359

(G-141)
ENGINEERED PLASTICS CORP
420 Kenmore Blvd (44301-1038)
PHONE..............................330 376-7700
Jim Rauh, *Pr*
Joe Raugh, *
▲ EMP: 24 EST: 1994
SQ FT: 1,000,000
SALES (est): 525.81K **Privately Held**
SIC: **3052** Plastic belting

(G-142)
ENLARGING ARTS INC
161 Tarbell St (44303-2233)
PHONE..............................330 434-3433
EMP: 8 EST: 1994
SALES (est): 548.38K **Privately Held**
SIC: **2752** 7384 3993 7336 Commercial printing, lithographic; Photofinish laboratories; Signs and advertising specialties; Commercial art and graphic design

(G-143)
ESI-EXTRUSION SERVICES INC
305 W North St (44303-2350)
PHONE..............................330 374-3388
EMP: 35 EST: 1981
SALES (est): 5.38MM **Privately Held**
Web: www.esi-extrusion.com
SIC: **3544** 3559 3549 3541 Special dies, tools, jigs, and fixtures; Plastics working machinery; Metalworking machinery, nec; Machine tools, metal cutting type

(G-144)
ESP AKRON SUB LLC
240 W Emerling Ave (44301-1620)
PHONE..............................330 374-2242
Thomas Holleran, *CEO*
EMP: 72 EST: 2020
SALES (est): 3.86MM **Privately Held**
SIC: **2899** Chemical preparations, nec

(G-145)
EVONIK CORPORATION
Also Called: Degussa
3500 Embassy Pkwy Ste 100 (44333-8327)
PHONE..............................330 668-2235
Salena Wilson, *Prin*
EMP: 24
SALES (corp-wide): 2.27B **Privately Held**
Web: corporate.evonik.com
SIC: **2869** Industrial organic chemicals, nec
HQ: Evonik Corporation
2 Turner Pl
Piscataway NJ 08854
732 982-5000

(G-146)
EZURIO LLC (PA)
50 S Main St Ste 1100 (44308-1831)
PHONE..............................330 434-7929
Bill Steinike, *CEO*

Bob Sallmann, *
EMP: 75 EST: 2019
SALES (est): 98.1MM
SALES (corp-wide): 98.1MM **Privately Held**
Web: www.ezurio.com
SIC: **3674** Computer logic modules

(G-147)
F M MACHINE CO
1114 Triplett Blvd (44306-3098)
PHONE..............................330 773-8237
Robert R Christian, *Pr*
Joel Christian, *
Shannon Adolph, *
Courtney Wagner, *
EMP: 45 EST: 1963
SQ FT: 36,000
SALES (est): 7.14MM **Privately Held**
Web: www.fmmachine.com
SIC: **3599** 3441 Machine shop, jobbing and repair; Fabricated structural metal

(G-148)
FALLS MTAL FBRCTORS INDUS SVCS
380 Kennedy Rd (44305)
PHONE..............................330 253-7181
Daniel Pugh, *Pr*
Daniel R Pugh, *Pr*
Stephanie Pugh, *Treas*
EMP: 13 EST: 2014
SALES (est): 2.27MM **Privately Held**
Web: www.fmfis.com
SIC: **1542** 1541 3542 Nonresidential construction, nec; Factory construction; Punching, shearing, and bending machines

(G-149)
FALLS TOOL AND DIE INC
1416 Piedmont Ave (44310-2614)
PHONE..............................330 633-4884
Marvin Hardy, *Pr*
David Cunningham, *Contrlr*
EMP: 8 EST: 1964
SQ FT: 18,500
SALES (est): 815.24K **Privately Held**
SIC: **3469** 3544 3465 Stamping metal for the trade; Special dies and tools; Automotive stampings

(G-150)
FAMOUS INDUSTRIES INC (DH)
Also Called: Johnson Contrls Authorized Dlr
2620 Ridgewood Rd Ste 200 (44313-3507)
PHONE..............................330 535-1811
Pat Mccaffrey, *Pr*
EMP: 50 EST: 1948
SALES (est): 51.14MM
SALES (corp-wide): 3.83B **Privately Held**
Web: www.johnsoncontrols.com
SIC: **3444** 5065 5074 Metal ventilating equipment; Telephone equipment; Plumbing and heating valves
HQ: Flex-Tek Group Llc
1473 Gould Dr
Cookeville TN 38506
931 432-7212

(G-151)
FENIX FABRICATION INC
2689 Wingate Ave (44314-1301)
PHONE..............................330 745-8731
Christopher J Forgan, *Pr*
EMP: 24 EST: 2007
SALES (est): 2.35MM **Privately Held**
Web: www.fenixfab.com
SIC: **3441** Fabricated structural metal

Akron - Summit County (G-152)

(G-152)
FERRIOT INC
1000 Arlington Cir (44306-3973)
P.O. Box 7670 (44306-0670)
PHONE....................................330 786-3000
Gordon Keeler, *CEO*
George D Grosso, *
David Ferriot, *
▲ **EMP:** 170 **EST:** 1929
SQ FT: 220,000
SALES (est): 47.45MM **Privately Held**
Web: www.ferriot.com
SIC: 3089 3544 Injection molding of plastics; Industrial molds

(G-153)
FIRESTONE POLYMERS LLC (PA)
381 W Wilbeth Rd (44301-2465)
P.O. Box 26611 (44319-6611)
PHONE....................................330 379-7000
◆ **EMP:** 73 **EST:** 2001
SALES (est): 117.67MM
SALES (corp-wide): 117.67MM **Privately Held**
Web: www.firestonepolymers.com
SIC: 3069 Latex, foamed

(G-154)
FIVE STAR HEALTHY VENDING LLC
388 S Main St Ste 440 (44311-1064)
PHONE....................................330 549-6011
EMP: 11
SALES (est): 452.49K **Privately Held**
SIC: 3581 Automatic vending machines

(G-155)
FLEXSYS AMERICA LP (HQ)
Also Called: Flexsys America
260 Springside Dr (44333-4554)
PHONE....................................330 666-4111
◆ **EMP:** 65 **EST:** 1995
SQ FT: 85,000
SALES (est): 52.96MM
SALES (corp-wide): 105.28MM **Privately Held**
SIC: 3069 8731 2899 2823 Reclaimed rubber and specialty rubber compounds; Commercial physical research; Chemical preparations, nec; Cellulosic manmade fibers
PA: Flexsys Holdings, Inc.
    260 Springside Dr
    Akron OH 44333
    330 666-4111

(G-156)
FLEXSYS INC (PA)
260 Springside Dr (44333-4554)
PHONE....................................212 605-6000
Sandip Tyagi, *CEO*
Tony Lee, *Treas*
EMP: 500 **EST:** 2021
SALES (est): 360MM
SALES (corp-wide): 360MM **Privately Held**
Web: www.flexsys.com
SIC: 2819 7389 Industrial inorganic chemicals, nec; Business Activities at Non-Commercial Site

(G-157)
FOUNDATION INDUSTRIES INC (PA)
Also Called: F I C
880 W Waterloo Rd Ste B (44314-1519)
PHONE....................................330 564-1250
Richard Huscroft, *Pr*
◆ **EMP:** 40 **EST:** 1991
SQ FT: 109,000
SALES (est): 22.36MM **Privately Held**
Web: www.foundationind.com

SIC: 3999 Barber and beauty shop equipment

(G-158)
FREEDOM FORKLIFT SALES LLC
1114 Garman Rd (44313-6614)
PHONE....................................330 289-0879
David Dye, *Prin*
EMP: 7 **EST:** 2017
SALES (est): 271.73K **Privately Held**
Web: www.freedomforkliftsales.com
SIC: 3537 Forklift trucks

(G-159)
G&O RESOURCES LTD
96 E Crosier St (44311-2342)
PHONE....................................330 253-2525
Robert Nelson, *CEO*
EMP: 12 **EST:** 1997
SALES (est): 953.02K **Privately Held**
SIC: 1382 Oil and gas exploration services

(G-160)
GABRIEL PHENOXIES INC (PA)
240 W Emerling Ave (44301)
PHONE....................................704 499-9801
Seth Tomasch, *CEO*
◆ **EMP:** 24 **EST:** 1993
SALES (est): 11.01MM
SALES (corp-wide): 11.01MM **Privately Held**
SIC: 2821 Plastics materials and resins

(G-161)
GALENAS LLC
1956 S Main St (44301-2877)
PHONE....................................330 208-9423
Geoffrey Korff, *Managing Member*
EMP: 11 **EST:** 2016
SALES (est): 3.03MM **Privately Held**
Web: www.galenas.com
SIC: 2834 Pharmaceutical preparations

(G-162)
GARRO TREAD CORPORATION (PA)
Also Called: Ace Rubber Products Division
100 Beech St (44308-1916)
P.O. Box 4567 (44310-0567)
PHONE....................................330 376-3125
Charles Garro, *Pr*
Greg Garro, *VP*
EMP: 9 **EST:** 1980
SQ FT: 100,000
SALES (est): 2.42MM
SALES (corp-wide): 2.42MM **Privately Held**
Web: www.acerubber.net
SIC: 3069 5531 Mats or matting, rubber, nec ; Automotive tires

(G-163)
GEAR STAR AMERICAN PERFORMANCE
132 N Howard St (44308-1937)
PHONE....................................330 434-5216
Zack Farah, *Pr*
Derek Kriebel, *Prin*
◆ **EMP:** 6 **EST:** 2001
SALES (est): 791K **Privately Held**
Web: www.gearstar.com
SIC: 3714 5571 5013 Motor vehicle transmissions, drive assemblies, and parts; Motorcycle parts and accessories; Motor vehicle supplies and new parts

(G-164)
GEHM & SONS LIMITED
825 S Arlington St (44306-2498)
PHONE....................................330 724-8423
Juanita Gehm, *Pr*

EMP: 6 **EST:** 1929
SQ FT: 5,780
SALES (est): 2.18MM **Privately Held**
Web: www.4dryice.com
SIC: 5145 2086 5169 Syrups, fountain; Carbonated beverages, nonalcoholic: pkgd. in cans, bottles; Dry ice

(G-165)
GEN DIGITAL INC
Also Called: Symantec
159 S Main St (44308-1317)
PHONE....................................330 252-1171
Joe Cassner, *Brnch Mgr*
EMP: 8
SALES (corp-wide): 3.34B **Publicly Held**
Web: www.nortonlifelock.com
SIC: 3674 Semiconductors and related devices
PA: Gen Digital Inc.
    60 E Rio Salado Pkwy # 1
    Tempe AZ 85281
    650 527-8000

(G-166)
GENERAL METALS POWDER CO LLC (PA)
Also Called: Gempco
1195 Home Ave (44310-2576)
PHONE....................................330 633-1226
Jerry Lynch, *Pr*
Louis L Cseko Junior, *VP*
Barry P Alvord, *
EMP: 43 **EST:** 1929
SQ FT: 30,000
SALES (est): 9.19MM
SALES (corp-wide): 9.19MM **Privately Held**
Web: www.gmpfriction.com
SIC: 3499 3714 3568 Friction material, made from powdered metal; Motor vehicle parts and accessories; Power transmission equipment, nec

(G-167)
GENERAL POLYMERS
567 E Turkeyfoot Lake Rd (44319-4107)
PHONE....................................330 896-7126
Sherwin Williams, *Pr*
EMP: 11 **EST:** 2002
SALES (est): 469.77K **Privately Held**
Web: www.sherwin-williams.com
SIC: 2821 Epoxy resins

(G-168)
GENTZLER TOOL & DIE CORP (PA)
3903 Massillon Rd (44312)
P.O. Box 158 (44232-0158)
PHONE....................................330 896-1941
David W Gentzler, *Pr*
Geraldine Gentzler, *Pr*
David Gentzler, *VP*
EMP: 20 **EST:** 1953
SQ FT: 20,000
SALES (est): 2.79MM
SALES (corp-wide): 2.79MM **Privately Held**
Web: www.gentzlertoolanddie.com
SIC: 3469 3544 Stamping metal for the trade ; Special dies and tools

(G-169)
GOJO CANADA INC
1 Gojo Plz Ste 500 (44311-1085)
PHONE....................................330 255-6000
EMP: 12 **EST:** 2011
SALES (est): 399.74K **Privately Held**
Web: www.gojo.com
SIC: 2842 Polishes and sanitation goods

(G-170)
GOJO INDUSTRIES INC (PA)
Also Called: Gojo
1 Gojo Plz Ste 500 (44311)
P.O. Box 991 (44311)
PHONE....................................330 255-6000
Joseph Kanfer, *Ch Bd*
Mark Lerner, *
◆ **EMP:** 200 **EST:** 1946
SQ FT: 500,000
SALES (est): 425.22MM
SALES (corp-wide): 425.22MM **Privately Held**
Web: www.gojo.com
SIC: 2842 3586 2844 Polishes and sanitation goods; Measuring and dispensing pumps; Perfumes, cosmetics and other toilet preparations

(G-171)
GOODYEAR TIRE & RUBBER COMPANY (PA)
Also Called: Goodyear
200 E Innovation Way (44316)
PHONE....................................330 796-2121
Mark Stewart, *Pr*
Laurette T Koellner, *
Christina L Zamarro, *Chief Financial Officer USA*
Darren R Wells, *CAO*
David E Phillips, *CLO*
◆ **EMP:** 2602 **EST:** 1898
SALES (est): 20.07B
SALES (corp-wide): 20.07B **Publicly Held**
Web: www.goodyear.com
SIC: 3011 5531 7534 7538 Inner tubes, all types; Automotive tires; Tire retreading and repair shops; General automotive repair shops

(G-172)
GRADY MCCAULEY INC
Also Called: LSI Graphic Solutions Plus
5127 Boyer Pkwy (44312-4272)
PHONE....................................330 494-9444
David Mccauley, *Pr*
EMP: 100 **EST:** 1963
SALES (est): 32.27MM
SALES (corp-wide): 496.98MM **Publicly Held**
SIC: 3993 2759 Electric signs; Screen printing
PA: Lsi Industries Inc.
    10000 Alliance Rd
    Cincinnati OH 45242
    513 793-3200

(G-173)
GREAT LAKES POLYMER PROC INC (PA)
1210 Massillon Rd (44306-3327)
PHONE....................................313 655-4024
Alan Mitchell, *CEO*
EMP: 19 **EST:** 2020
SALES (est): 500K
SALES (corp-wide): 500K **Privately Held**
SIC: 2822 Ethylene-propylene rubbers, EPDM polymers

(G-174)
GROUP ENDEAVOR LLC
1750 Canton Rd (44312-4006)
PHONE....................................234 571-5096
EMP: 86
SALES (corp-wide): 340.51K **Privately Held**
SIC: 2531 Seats, automobile
PA: Group Endeavor, Llc
    3732 Fishcreek Rd 950
    Stow OH 44224
    234 571-5096

GEOGRAPHIC SECTION

(G-175)
H & H MACHINE SHOP AKRON INC
955 Grant St (44311-2490)
PHONE..................330 773-3327
Henry R Haas, *Pr*
Anna Haas, *Sec*
EMP: 21 EST: 1959
SQ FT: 24,000
SALES (est): 3.85MM **Privately Held**
Web: www.hhmachine.com
SIC: 3599 7692 Machine shop, jobbing and repair; Welding repair

(G-176)
H & M METAL PROCESSING CO (HQ)
1414 Kenmore Blvd (44314-1600)
PHONE..................330 745-3075
Robert Mcmillen, *Pr*
Robert Mcmillen Iv, *Stockholder*
Ben Mcmillen, *Stockholder*
Alexandra Evanko, *Stockholder**
EMP: 42 **EST:** 1942
SQ FT: 7,000
SALES (est): 13.07MM **Privately Held**
Web: www.blacknitride.com
SIC: 3398 Metal heat treating
PA: Moore, Mc Millen Holdings, Inc
1850 Front St
Cuyahoga Falls OH 44221

(G-177)
HALLER ENTERPRISES INC
1621 E Market St (44305-4210)
PHONE..................330 733-9693
TOLL FREE: 800
David Haller, *Pr*
Harriet Haller, *VP*
Daid Haller Junior, *VP*
EMP: 10 **EST:** 1966
SQ FT: 6,000
SALES (est): 930.76K **Privately Held**
SIC: 2097 5999 Manufactured ice; Ice

(G-178)
HAMLIN NEWCO LLC
2741 Wingate Ave (44314-1301)
PHONE..................330 753-7791
Charles N Biehara, *
▲ **EMP:** 52 **EST:** 2007
SQ FT: 110
SALES (est): 9.82MM **Privately Held**
Web: www.hnmetalstamping.com
SIC: 3469 Stamping metal for the trade

(G-179)
HAMLIN STEEL PRODUCTS LLC
2741 Wingate Ave (44314-1301)
PHONE..................330 753-7791
EMP: 45 **EST:** 1978
SQ FT: 110,000
SALES (est): 4.89MM **Privately Held**
Web: www.hnmetalstamping.com
SIC: 3469 Stamping metal for the trade

(G-180)
HARRY C LOBALZO & SONS INC
Also Called: Hobart Sales & Service
61 N Cleveland Massillon Rd Unit A (44333)
PHONE..................330 666-6758
Mike Lobalzo, *Ch*
Joe Saporito, *
Rick Lobalzo, *Vice Chairman**
▲ **EMP:** 45 **EST:** 1956
SQ FT: 20,000
SALES (est): 10.79MM **Privately Held**
Web: www.retailfoodequip.com
SIC: 5046 7699 3556 Restaurant equipment and supplies, nec; Restaurant equipment repair; Food products machinery

(G-181)
HERBERT USA INC
1480 Industrial Pkwy (44310-2602)
PHONE..................330 929-4297
Mathias Walter, *Pr*
Todd Jarvis, *
▲ **EMP:** 55 **EST:** 1974
SQ FT: 25,000
SALES (est): 4.78MM **Privately Held**
Web: www.herbert.eu
SIC: 3544 Industrial molds

(G-182)
HERITAGE INDUSTRIAL FINSHG INC
1874 Englewood Ave (44312-1002)
PHONE..................330 798-9840
Agathonico Pamboukis, *Ch*
Nicholas Pamboukis, *
Russell Kemppel, *
Frank J Witschey, *
Marla Kay, *
▲ **EMP:** 58 **EST:** 1965
SQ FT: 35,000
SALES (est): 8.26MM **Privately Held**
Web: www.heritageindustrialfinishing.com
SIC: 3479 Painting of metal products

(G-183)
HEXPOL COMPOUNDING LLC
Also Called: Hexpol Silicone
1497 Exeter Rd (44306-3856)
PHONE..................440 682-4038
EMP: 121
SALES (corp-wide): 2.12B **Privately Held**
Web: www.hexpol.com
SIC: 3069 Medical and laboratory rubber sundries and related products
HQ: Hexpol Compounding Llc
14330 Kinsman Rd
Burton OH 44021
440 834-4644

(G-184)
HIGH LOW WINERY
3867 Medina Rd (44333-4506)
PHONE..................844 466-4456
EMP: 8 **EST:** 2017
SALES (est): 378.79K **Privately Held**
Web: www.searchhighandlow.com
SIC: 2084 Wines

(G-185)
HUNTSMAN ADVNCED MTLS AMRCAS L
240 W Emerling Ave (44301-1620)
PHONE..................330 374-2424
EMP: 30
SALES (corp-wide): 6.11B **Publicly Held**
Web: www.huntsman.com
SIC: 2821 Plastics materials and resins
HQ: Huntsman Advanced Materials Americas Llc
10003 Woodloch Forest Dr # 260
The Woodlands TX 77380
281 719-6000

(G-186)
HUNTSMAN ADVNCED MTLS AMRCAS L
Also Called: Gabriel Performance Products
240 W Emerling Ave (44301-1620)
PHONE..................866 800-2436
EMP: 33
SALES (corp-wide): 6.11B **Publicly Held**
Web: www.huntsman.com
SIC: 2821 Plastics materials and resins
HQ: Huntsman Advanced Materials Americas Llc
10003 Woodloch Forest Dr # 260
The Woodlands TX 77380
281 719-6000

(G-187)
HUNTSMAN CORPORATION
Also Called: Cvc Thermoset Specialties
240 W Emerling Ave (44301-1620)
PHONE..................330 374-2418
Jeffrey Michaels, *Prin*
EMP: 100
SALES (corp-wide): 6.11B **Publicly Held**
Web: www.huntsman.com
SIC: 2899 2821 Chemical preparations, nec; Plastics materials and resins
PA: Huntsman Corporation
10003 Woodloch Forest Dr
The Woodlands TX 77380
281 719-6000

(G-188)
HYGENIC COMPANY LLC
Also Called: Performance Health
1245 Home Ave (44310-2510)
PHONE..................330 633-8460
Marshall Dahneke, *Pr*
Niels Lichti, *
Ralph Buster, *Corporate Vice President**
◆ **EMP:** 324 **EST:** 1925
SQ FT: 135,000
SALES (est): 97.23MM
SALES (corp-wide): 182.7MM **Privately Held**
Web: www.hygenic.com
SIC: 3069 3061 Medical and laboratory rubber sundries and related products; Mechanical rubber goods
PA: Cogr, Inc.
140 E 45th St Fl 43
New York NY 10017
212 370-5600

(G-189)
IMPORTERS DIRECT LLC
1559 S Main St (44301-1632)
PHONE..................330 436-3260
Timothy Adkins, *Pr*
EMP: 10 **EST:** 2008
SQ FT: 15,400
SALES (est): 446.92K **Privately Held**
Web: www.cheapdjgear.us
SIC: 1731 3648 7359 3646 Sound equipment specialization; Stage lighting equipment; Sound and lighting equipment rental; Commercial lighting fixtures

(G-190)
INDUSTRIAL TECHNOLOGIES INC
1643 Massillon Rd (44312-4273)
PHONE..................330 434-2033
Gregg Caprez, *Pr*
Michelle H Caprez, *VP*
EMP: 7 **EST:** 1997
SQ FT: 3,000
SALES (est): 907.83K **Privately Held**
Web: www.industrialtech.info
SIC: 3543 Industrial patterns

(G-191)
INSTANT GRAPHICATIONS INC
1025 Bloomfield Ave (44302-1147)
PHONE..................330 819-5267
John Hunyadi, *Prin*
EMP: 6 **EST:** 2010
SALES (est): 130.83K **Privately Held**
Web: www.instantgraphications.com
SIC: 2752 Commercial printing, lithographic

(G-192)
INTEL INTERPEACE
1342 Easton Dr (44310-1557)
PHONE..................330 922-4450
EMP: 7 **EST:** 2016
SALES (est): 102.97K **Privately Held**

SIC: 3674 Semiconductors and related devices

(G-193)
IROK INC
753 N Main St (44310-3044)
PHONE..................330 819-3612
Michael Thomas, *Prin*
EMP: 6 **EST:** 2015
SALES (est): 105.9K **Privately Held**
Web: www.beaconjournal.com
SIC: 2711 Newspapers

(G-194)
ITEM NA
925 Glaser Pkwy (44306-4161)
PHONE..................216 271-7241
EMP: 7 **EST:** 2018
SALES (est): 169.52K **Privately Held**
Web: www.itemnorthamerica.com
SIC: 3999 Manufacturing industries, nec

(G-195)
JDA SOFTWARE GROUP INC
Also Called: JDA SOFTWARE GROUP, INC.
308 N Cleveland Massillon Rd (44333-9302)
PHONE..................480 308-3000
Kurt Thomiet, *Brnch Mgr*
EMP: 13
Web: www.blueyonder.com
SIC: 7372 Prepackaged software
HQ: Blue Yonder Group, Inc.
15059 N Scttsdale Rd Ste
Scottsdale AZ 85254

(G-196)
JILCO PRECISION MOLD MCH INC
Also Called: Jilco
1245 Devalera St (44310-2457)
PHONE..................330 633-9645
John Shepherd, *Pr*
EMP: 6 **EST:** 1983
SQ FT: 3,300
SALES (est): 515.47K **Privately Held**
Web: www.jilco.us
SIC: 3599 Machine shop, jobbing and repair

(G-197)
JORDANKELLY LLC
165 Ira Ave (44301-1117)
PHONE..................216 855-8550
EMP: 11 **EST:** 2018
SALES (est): 989.38K **Privately Held**
SIC: 3531 4231 Construction machinery; Trucking terminal facilities

(G-198)
JRB ATTACHMENTS LLC (DH)
820 Glaser Pkwy (44306-4133)
PHONE..................330 734-3000
Steve Andrews, *CEO*
Steve Klyn, *CFO*
Jeremy Wild, *Contrlr*
Michael Flannery, *VP*
Robert Hunt, *Contrlr*
▲ **EMP:** 7 **EST:** 1983
SALES (est): 43.51MM
SALES (corp-wide): 15.78B **Publicly Held**
Web: www.paladinattachments.com
SIC: 3531 Construction machinery attachments
HQ: Paladin Brands Group, Inc.
2800 Zeeb Rd
Dexter MI 48130
319 378-3696

(G-199)
JSC EMPLOYEE LEASING CORP (PA)
1560 Firestone Pkwy (44301-1626)

Akron - Summit County (G-200)

GEOGRAPHIC SECTION

PHONE..............................330 773-8971
Jack Jeter, *Pr*
Nicholas George, *Sec*
Pam Love, *Ex VP*
EMP: 92 **EST:** 1971
SQ FT: 150,000
SALES (est): 19.37MM
SALES (corp-wide): 19.37MM **Privately Held**
SIC: 2522 5021 Office cabinets and filing drawers, except wood; Filing units

(G-200)
JSH INTERNATIONAL LLC
124 Darrow Rd Ste 5 (44305-3835)
PHONE..............................330 734-0251
Kevin Mulvihill, *Managing Member*
EMP: 6 **EST:** 2008
SALES (est): 541.92K **Privately Held**
Web: www.jshinternational.net
SIC: 5084 2836 Industrial machinery and equipment; Biological products, except diagnostic

(G-201)
KARMAN RUBBER COMPANY
2331 Copley Rd (44320-1499)
PHONE..............................330 864-2161
David W Mann, *Pr*
G Jay Hearty, *
EMP: 90 **EST:** 1945
SQ FT: 55,000
SALES (est): 9.96MM **Privately Held**
Web: www.karman.com
SIC: 3069 3829 3822 3061 Molded rubber products; Measuring and controlling devices, nec; Environmental controls; Mechanical rubber goods

(G-202)
KAYLO ENTERPRISES LLC
540 S Main St Ste 115 (44311-1023)
PHONE..............................330 535-1860
Thomas A Lovick, *Pr*
EMP: 8 **EST:** 2015
SALES (est): 294.27K **Privately Held**
SIC: 2621 7389 3579 2262 Book, bond and printing papers; Advertising, promotional, and trade show services; Mailing, letter handling, and addressing machines; Screen printing: manmade fiber and silk broadwoven fabrics

(G-203)
KENMORE DEVELOPMENT & MCH CO
1395 Kenmore Blvd (44314-1658)
PHONE..............................330 753-2274
Richard Roten, *Pr*
EMP: 10 **EST:** 1939
SQ FT: 20,000
SALES (est): 757.02K **Privately Held**
Web: www.bdwlegal.com
SIC: 3599 Machine shop, jobbing and repair

(G-204)
KENMORE GEAR & MACHINE CO INC
2129 Jennifer St (44313-4763)
PHONE..............................330 753-6671
David Ingham, *Pr*
Pamela S Ballinger, *VP*
Gary Ballinger, *Treas*
David Ingham Junior, *Sec*
EMP: 7 **EST:** 1926
SQ FT: 9,352
SALES (est): 570.87K **Privately Held**
SIC: 3566 Speed changers, drives, and gears

(G-205)
KENT STOW SCREEN PRINTING INC
Also Called: Mascot Shop, The
1340 Home Ave Ste F (44310-2570)
PHONE..............................330 923-5118
William C Sauders, *Pr*
EMP: 6 **EST:** 1978
SQ FT: 3,000
SALES (est): 244.1K **Privately Held**
SIC: 7336 2396 Silk screen design; Automotive and apparel trimmings

(G-206)
KILLBUCK OIL AND GAS LLC
52 Marvin Ave (44302-1048)
PHONE..............................330 447-8423
Nathan Mcintyre, *Prin*
EMP: 6 **EST:** 2016
SALES (est): 154.54K **Privately Held**
SIC: 1389 Oil and gas field services, nec

(G-207)
KILLIAN LATEX INC
2064 Killian Rd (44312-4897)
PHONE..............................330 644-6746
Timothy J Killian, *Pr*
Joan Killian Fisk, *Sec*
EMP: 15 **EST:** 1975
SQ FT: 65,000
SALES (est): 2.69MM **Privately Held**
Web: www.killianlatex.com
SIC: 3069 3087 Custom compounding of rubber materials; Custom compound purchased resins

(G-208)
KILTEX CORPORATION
2064 Killian Rd (44312-4830)
PHONE..............................330 644-6746
Timothy J Killian, *Pr*
Joan Killian-fisk, *Sec*
EMP: 15 **EST:** 1983
SALES (est): 853.92K **Privately Held**
Web: www.killianlatex.com
SIC: 3069 Custom compounding of rubber materials

(G-209)
KING INDUSTRIES LLC
1324 Newton St (44305-3327)
PHONE..............................330 733-9106
EMP: 7 **EST:** 2018
SALES (est): 48.34K **Privately Held**
Web: www.kingindustries.com
SIC: 3999 Manufacturing industries, nec

(G-210)
KING MODEL COMPANY
Also Called: King Castings
365 Kenmore Blvd (44301-1053)
PHONE..............................330 633-0491
Michael Wells, *Pr*
Gifford Wells, *
John Horrell, *
EMP: 31 **EST:** 1975
SQ FT: 15,000
SALES (est): 2.46MM **Privately Held**
Web: www.kingmachinemolds.com
SIC: 3999 Models, general, except toy

(G-211)
KIRTLEY MOLD INC
Also Called: Signature Mold and Fabrication
1986 Manchester Rd (44314-2479)
PHONE..............................330 472-2427
EMP: 7 **EST:** 2015
SALES (est): 503.07K **Privately Held**
Web: www.signaturemoldfab.com
SIC: 2821 Molding compounds, plastics

(G-212)
KRUPP RUBBER MACHINERY
103 Western Ave (44313-6300)
PHONE..............................330 864-0800
William Bradshaw, *Prin*
EMP: 9 **EST:** 2007
SALES (est): 398.5K **Privately Held**
SIC: 3069 5084 Fabricated rubber products, nec; Plastic products machinery

(G-213)
KURTZ BROS COMPOST SERVICES
2677 Riverview Rd (44313-4719)
PHONE..............................330 864-2621
Thomas Kurtz, *Pr*
▲ **EMP:** 12 **EST:** 1990
SALES (est): 486.44K **Privately Held**
SIC: 2875 8741 Compost; Management services

(G-214)
LABABIDI ENTERPRISES INC
2167 Forest Oak Dr (44312-2234)
PHONE..............................330 733-2907
Wallid Lababidi, *Owner*
EMP: 7 **EST:** 1998
SALES (est): 213.67K **Privately Held**
SIC: 3841 8011 Anesthesia apparatus; Offices and clinics of medical doctors

(G-215)
LAIRD TECHNOLOGIES INC
50 S Main St Ste 1100 (44308-1831)
PHONE..............................330 434-7929
EMP: 12
SALES (corp-wide): 2.93B **Publicly Held**
Web: www.lairdtech.com
SIC: 3679 Electronic circuits
HQ: Laird Technologies, Inc.
16401 Swingley Ridge Rd
Chesterfield MO 63017
636 898-6000

(G-216)
LANCER DISPERSIONS INC
1680 E Market St (44305-4246)
EMP: 65
Web: www.akrondispersions.com
SIC: 3089 3087 2816 Coloring and finishing of plastics products; Custom compound purchased resins; Inorganic pigments

(G-217)
LANDMARK PLASTIC CORPORATION (PA)
1331 Kelly Ave (44306-3773)
PHONE..............................330 785-2200
Robert G Merzweiler, *CEO*
◆ **EMP:** 190 **EST:** 1984
SQ FT: 200,000
SALES (est): 23.73MM
SALES (corp-wide): 23.73MM **Privately Held**
Web: www.landmarkplastic.com
SIC: 3089 Plastics containers, except foam

(G-218)
LEHNER SCREW MACHINE LLC
1169 Brittain Rd (44305-1004)
PHONE..............................330 688-6616
Thomas Bader, *Pr*
John Bader, *VP*
EMP: 21 **EST:** 1950
SQ FT: 10,524
SALES (est): 1.46MM **Privately Held**
Web: www.lehnerscrewmachine.com
SIC: 3451 3599 Screw machine products; Machine shop, jobbing and repair

(G-219)
LELAND-GIFFORD INC
1029 Arlington Cir (44306-3959)
PHONE..............................330 785-9730
Robert Hartford, *Pr*
EMP: 9 **EST:** 1984
SQ FT: 20,000
SALES (est): 982.12K **Privately Held**
Web: www.summitmachinesolutions.com
SIC: 3541 Drilling and boring machines

(G-220)
LIPPINCOTT AND PETO INC
Also Called: Rubber World Magazine
1741 Akron Peninsula Rd (44313-5157)
P.O. Box 5451 (44334-0451)
PHONE..............................330 864-2122
Joe Lippincott, *Pr*
EMP: 17
SQ FT: 2,500
SALES (est): 26.60K **Privately Held**
Web: www.rubberworld.com
SIC: 2721 Trade journals: publishing only, not printed on site

(G-221)
LOCK 15 BREWING COMPANY LLC
21 W North St (44304-1035)
PHONE..............................234 900-8277
EMP: 42 **EST:** 2015
SALES (est): 1.13MM **Privately Held**
Web: www.lock15brewing.com
SIC: 5813 2082 Bars and lounges; Malt beverages

(G-222)
LOCKHEED MRTIN INTGRTED SYSTEM
Also Called: Aerospace Simulations
1210 Massillon Rd (44315-0001)
PHONE..............................330 796-2800
Dan Fiest, *Mgr*
EMP: 176
SIC: 3812 Search and navigation equipment
HQ: Lockheed Martin Integrated Systems, Llc
6801 Rockledge Dr
Bethesda MD 20817

(G-223)
LOGAN MACHINE COMPANY (PA)
Also Called: LMC
1405 Home Ave (44310-2586)
PHONE..............................330 633-6163
Mark Schoenbaechler, *Pr*
Kenneth Schoenbaechler, *
▲ **EMP:** 64 **EST:** 1943
SQ FT: 96,000
SALES (est): 16.2MM
SALES (corp-wide): 16.2MM **Privately Held**
Web: www.loganmachine.com
SIC: 3599 3728 3544 3469 Custom machinery; Aircraft parts and equipment, nec; Special dies, tools, jigs, and fixtures; Metal stampings, nec

(G-224)
LOWRY FURNACE CO INC
Also Called: Hvac
663 Flora Ave (44314-1754)
PHONE..............................330 745-4822
Gregory Shiflett, *Pr*
EMP: 6 **EST:** 1945
SQ FT: 3,000
SALES (est): 603.24K **Privately Held**
Web: www.lowryfurnace.com
SIC: 1711 3444 Warm air heating and air conditioning contractor; Sheet metalwork

GEOGRAPHIC SECTION

(G-225)
LUND EQUIPMENT COMPANY
2400 N Cleveland Massillon Rd
(44333-1251)
P.O. Box 213 (44210-0213)
PHONE..................................330 659-4800
John Skeel, *Pr*
Raymond Smiley, *VP*
EMP: 20 **EST:** 1932
SQ FT: 5,000
SALES (est): 2.29MM **Privately Held**
Web: www.lundkey.com
SIC: 3444 Sheet metalwork

(G-226)
LYONDLLBSELL ADVNCED PLYMERS I
1353 Exeter Rd (44306-3853)
PHONE..................................330 773-2700
EMP: 124
Web: www.lyondellbasell.com
SIC: 2821 Molding compounds, plastics
HQ: Lyondellbasell Advanced Polymers Inc.
1221 Mckinney St Ste 300
Houston TX 77010
713 309-7200

(G-227)
LYONDLLBSELL ADVNCED PLYMERS I
790 E Tallmadge Ave (44310-3564)
PHONE..................................330 630-0308
Derold Hines, *Brnch Mgr*
EMP: 202
SQ FT: 104,823
Web: www.lyondellbasell.com
SIC: 2821 Molding compounds, plastics
HQ: Lyondellbasell Advanced Polymers Inc.
1221 Mckinney St Ste 300
Houston TX 77010
713 309-7200

(G-228)
LYONDLLBSELL ADVNCED PLYMERS I
1183 Home Ave (44310-2508)
PHONE..................................330 630-3315
Joe Ocampo, *Brnch Mgr*
EMP: 93
SQ FT: 52,766
Web: www.lyondellbasell.com
SIC: 2821 Molding compounds, plastics
HQ: Lyondellbasell Advanced Polymers Inc.
1221 Mckinney St Ste 300
Houston TX 77010
713 309-7200

(G-229)
LYONDLLBSELL ADVNCED PLYMERS I
1353 Exeter Rd (44306-3853)
PHONE..................................330 498-4840
A Maghes, *Brnch Mgr*
EMP: 50
Web: www.lyondellbasell.com
SIC: 2821 Plastics materials and resins
HQ: Lyondellbasell Advanced Polymers Inc.
1221 Mckinney St Ste 300
Houston TX 77010
713 309-7200

(G-230)
M & J MACHINE COMPANY
2420 Pickle Rd (44312-4227)
PHONE..................................330 645-0042
James Kuts, *Pr*
Charlene Kuts, *VP*
Jonathan Kuts, *Sec*
EMP: 10 **EST:** 1977
SQ FT: 15,000
SALES (est): 1.01MM **Privately Held**
Web: www.mjmachine.net
SIC: 3599 Machine shop, jobbing and repair

(G-231)
M&MS AUTOSALES LLC
2203 Manchester Rd (44314-3723)
PHONE..................................234 334-7022
EMP: 10 **EST:** 2020
SALES (est): 486.42K **Privately Held**
SIC: 2396 Automotive and apparel trimmings

(G-232)
M7 HRP LLC
Also Called: Harwood Rubber Products
75 E Market St (44308)
PHONE..................................330 923-3256
Ryan Smith, *Managing Member*
EMP: 17 **EST:** 1965
SALES (est): 1.15MM **Privately Held**
SIC: 3069 Fabricated rubber products, nec

(G-233)
MA WORKWEAR LLC
2048 Akron Peninsula Rd (44313-4802)
PHONE..................................800 459-4405
Michael Allio, *VP*
Rick Kenny Allio, *COO*
Mark Allio, *CFO*
EMP: 7 **EST:** 2012
SQ FT: 3,500
SALES (est): 461.96K **Privately Held**
Web: www.maworkwear.com
SIC: 2389 Men's miscellaneous accessories

(G-234)
MACK CONCRETE INDUSTRIES INC
Also Called: Mack Ready-Mix
124 Darrow Rd Ste 7 (44305-3835)
PHONE..................................330 784-7008
EMP: 35
SALES (corp-wide): 134.58MM **Privately Held**
Web: www.mackconcrete.com
SIC: 3273 Ready-mixed concrete
HQ: Mack Concrete Industries, Inc.
201 Columbia Rd
Valley City OH 44280
330 483-3111

(G-235)
MARK-ALL ENTERPRISES LLC
Also Called: Excelsior Marking
888 W Waterloo Rd (44314-1528)
PHONE..................................800 433-3615
▲ **EMP:** 22 **EST:** 1905
SQ FT: 32,000
SALES (est): 4.18MM **Privately Held**
Web: www.excelsiormarking.com
SIC: 3953 2796 3999 Figures (marking devices), metal; Platemaking services; Badges, metal: policemen, firemen, etc.

(G-236)
MARKETHTCH INC D/B/A MH EYE CA
Also Called: J G Pads
91 E Voris St (44311)
P.O. Box 1151 (44309)
PHONE..................................330 376-6363
EMP: 10 **EST:** 1993
SQ FT: 9,400
SALES (est): 1.51MM **Privately Held**
Web: www.mheyecare.us
SIC: 3841 5047 Surgical and medical instruments; Medical equipment and supplies

(G-237)
MARKHAM MACHINE COMPANY INC
160 N Union St (44304-1355)
PHONE..................................330 762-7676
James M Markham, *Pr*
EMP: 18 **EST:** 1965
SQ FT: 13,000
SALES (est): 2.38MM **Privately Held**
SIC: 3599 Machine shop, jobbing and repair

(G-238)
MARTIN ALLEN TRAILER LLC
Also Called: AMG Trailer and Equipment
837 N Cleveland Massillon Rd (44333-2167)
PHONE..................................330 942-0217
Dean Martin, *Pr*
EMP: 10 **EST:** 2014
SALES (est): 220.55K **Privately Held**
Web: www.peterbilt.com
SIC: 3715 5084 Truck trailers; Trailers, industrial

(G-239)
MAXION WHEELS SEDALIA LLC
428 Seiberling St (44306-3205)
PHONE..................................330 794-2300
Randy Arnst, *Brnch Mgr*
EMP: 834
Web: www.maxionwheels.com
SIC: 3714 Motor vehicle parts and accessories
HQ: Hayes Lemmerz International-- Sedalia, Llc
3610 W Main St
Sedalia MO 65301
660 827-3640

(G-240)
MCNEIL & NRM INC (HQ)
96 E Crosier St (44311-2342)
PHONE..................................330 761-1855
Paul Yared, *CEO*
F H Yared, *
A Melek, *
A P Singh, *
◆ **EMP:** 65 **EST:** 1979
SQ FT: 35,000
SALES (est): 23.42MM
SALES (corp-wide): 23.42MM **Privately Held**
Web: www.mcneilnrm.com
SIC: 3559 3599 3542 Rubber working machinery, including tires; Custom machinery; Machine tools, metal forming type
PA: Mcneil & Nrm Intl., Inc.
96 E Crosier St
Akron OH 44311
330 253-2525

(G-241)
MCNEIL & NRM INTL INC (PA)
96 E Crosier St (44311-2342)
PHONE..................................330 253-2525
F H Yared, *Ch Bd*
Al M Melek, *
R A Nelson, *
Joel Siegfried, *
EMP: 75 **EST:** 1979
SQ FT: 35,000
SALES (est): 23.42MM
SALES (corp-wide): 23.42MM **Privately Held**
Web: www.mcneilnrm.com
SIC: 3559 3599 Rubber working machinery, including tires; Custom machinery

(G-242)
MEASUREMENT SPECIALTIES INC
2236 N Cleveland Massillon Rd Ste A (44333-1288)
PHONE..................................330 659-3312
Robert Visger, *Brnch Mgr*
EMP: 28
Web: www.te.com
SIC: 3829 Measuring and controlling devices, nec
HQ: Measurement Specialties, Inc.
1000 Lucas Way
Hampton VA 23666
757 766-1500

(G-243)
MEGGITT ARCFT BRKING SYSTEMS C (DH)
Also Called: Mabsc
1204 Massillon Rd (44306-4188)
P.O. Box 7670 (44306-0670)
PHONE..................................330 796-4400
Luke Duardogan, *Pr*
◆ **EMP:** 769 **EST:** 1989
SQ FT: 733,000
SALES (est): 286.11MM
SALES (corp-wide): 19.07B **Publicly Held**
Web: www.kfabsc.com
SIC: 3728 Brakes, aircraft
HQ: Meggitt Limited
Pilot Way
Coventry W MIDLANDS CV7 9
247 682-6900

(G-244)
MEGGITT ROCKMART INC
1204 Massillon Rd (44306-4188)
PHONE..................................770 684-7855
EMP: 28 **EST:** 2019
SALES (est): 5.33MM **Privately Held**
Web: www.meggitt-mabs.com
SIC: 3728 Aircraft parts and equipment, nec

(G-245)
METALCTTING SPCLISTS GROUP LTD
468 Molane Ave (44313-6620)
PHONE..................................330 962-4980
EMP: 9 **EST:** 2009
SALES (est): 110K **Privately Held**
Web: www.metalcutting.us
SIC: 3599 Air intake filters, internal combustion engine, except auto

(G-246)
METALICO AKRON INC (HQ)
Also Called: Metalico Annaco
943 Hazel St (44305)
P.O. Box 1148 (44309)
PHONE..................................330 376-1400
TOLL FREE: 800
Jeffery Bauer, *Genl Mgr*
EMP: 14 **EST:** 1930
SQ FT: 30,000
SALES (est): 17.7MM
SALES (corp-wide): 156.94MM **Privately Held**
Web: www.metalico.com
SIC: 5093 4953 3341 Ferrous metal scrap and waste; Refuse systems; Secondary nonferrous metals
PA: Metalico, Inc.
135 Dermody St
Cranford NJ 07016
908 497-9610

(G-247)
MEYER DESIGN INC
100 N High St (44308-1918)
PHONE..................................330 434-9176
TOLL FREE: 800
Christopher Meyer, *Pr*
EMP: 22 **EST:** 1974
SQ FT: 18,000
SALES (est): 490.55K **Privately Held**
Web: www.meyerdesign.com

Akron - Summit County (G-248)

SIC: 3949 Playground equipment

(G-248)
MIKRON INDUSTRIES INC (HQ)
388 S Main St Ste 700 (44311-1060)
PHONE..................................713 961-4600
Scott Zuehlke, *CFO*
Paul Cornett, *Sec*
George Wilson, *CEO*
EMP: 55 **EST:** 1969
SALES (est): 27.72MM **Publicly Held**
Web: www.quanex.com
SIC: 3081 3089 Vinyl film and sheet; Extruded finished plastics products, nec
PA: Quanex Building Products Corporation
945 Bunker Hl Rd Ste 900
Houston TX 77024

(G-249)
MILESTONE SERVICES CORP
551 Beacon St (44311-1805)
PHONE..................................330 374-9500
EMP: 6 **EST:** 1997
SQ FT: 200
SALES (est): 590K **Privately Held**
Web: www.milestoneservicescorp.com
SIC: 3471 Plating and polishing

(G-250)
MILLERS APLUS CMPT SVCS LLC
Also Called: Mapcs
1067 Mercer Ave (44320-3613)
P.O. Box 1901 (44309-1901)
PHONE..................................330 620-5288
Alisa Miller, *Prin*
EMP: 10 **EST:** 2020
SALES (est): 547.26K **Privately Held**
Web: www.millers.com
SIC: 8748 8243 8742 7373 Systems engineering consultant, ex. computer or professional; Operator training, computer; Management information systems consultant; Office computer automation systems integration

(G-251)
MOHICAN INDUSTRIES INC
1225 W Market St (44313-7107)
PHONE..................................330 869-0500
Judy Dipaola, *Pr*
EMP: 8 **EST:** 1980
SQ FT: 20,000
SALES (est): 836.66K
SALES (corp-wide): 6.03MM **Privately Held**
SIC: 2822 Synthetic rubber
PA: Sovereign Chemical Company
4040 Embassy Pkwy Ste 190
Akron OH 44333
330 869-0500

(G-252)
MONTGOMERY & MONTGOMERY LLC
80 N Pershing Ave (44313-6258)
PHONE..................................330 858-9533
EMP: 7 **EST:** 2014
SALES (est): 117.35K **Privately Held**
SIC: 7692 Welding repair

(G-253)
MORE THAN GOURMET HOLDINGS INC
929 Home Ave (44310-4107)
PHONE..................................330 762-6652
Brad Sacks, *CEO*
▲ **EMP:** 50 **EST:** 1993
SALES (est): 21.29MM **Privately Held**
Web: www.morethangourmet.com

SIC: 5149 2032 Seasonings, sauces, and extracts; Soups and broths, canned, jarred, etc.
HQ: Ajinomoto Health & Nutrition North America, Inc.
250 E Devon Ave
Itasca IL 60143
630 931-6800

(G-254)
MOTOROLA SOLUTIONS INC
3875 Embassy Pkwy Ste 280 (44333-8345)
PHONE..................................330 664-1610
EMP: 6 **EST:** 2013
SALES (est): 88.38K **Privately Held**
Web: www.motorolasolutions.com
SIC: 3663 Radio and t.v. communications equipment

(G-255)
MT VERNON MOLD WORKS INC
2200 Massillon Rd (44312-4234)
PHONE..................................618 242-6040
EMP: 21 **EST:** 1991
SALES (est): 5.55MM
SALES (corp-wide): 24.79MM **Privately Held**
SIC: 3544 7692 Special dies and tools; Welding repair
PA: Saehwa Imc Na, Inc.
2200 Massillon Rd
Akron OH 44312
330 645-6653

(G-256)
MUELLER ELECTRIC COMPANY INC (HQ)
2850 Gilchrist Rd Ste 5 (44305-4445)
P.O. Box 92922 (44194-2922)
PHONE..................................216 771-5225
Arnold Siemer, *Pr*
▲ **EMP:** 50 **EST:** 2011
SALES (est): 16.54MM
SALES (corp-wide): 180.13MM **Privately Held**
Web: www.muellerelectric.com
SIC: 3644 3643 3694 3496 Insulators and insulation materials, electrical; Current-carrying wiring services; Harness wiring sets, internal combustion engines; Miscellaneous fabricated wire products
PA: Desco Corporation
7795 Walton Pkwy Ste 175
New Albany OH 43054
614 888-8855

(G-257)
MULTI-VALVE TECHNOLOGY INC
1100 Triplett Blvd (44306-3029)
PHONE..................................330 608-4096
Christopher Wright, *Pr*
EMP: 6 **EST:** 2018
SALES (est): 136.54K **Privately Held**
SIC: 3999 Manufacturing industries, nec

(G-258)
MYE AUTOMOTIVE INC
1293 S Main St (44301-1302)
PHONE..................................330 253-5592
John C Orr, *Pr*
EMP: 59 **EST:** 1999
SALES (est): 2.47MM
SALES (corp-wide): 813.07MM **Publicly Held**
Web: www.myersindustries.com
SIC: 3089 Pallets, plastics
PA: Myers Industries, Inc.
1293 S Main St
Akron OH 44301
330 253-5592

(G-259)
MYERS INDUSTRIES INC
Akro-Mils Division
1293 S Main St (44301-1339)
P.O. Box 989 (44309-0989)
PHONE..................................330 253-5592
David Grider, *Genl Mgr*
EMP: 57
SALES (corp-wide): 813.07MM **Publicly Held**
Web: www.myersindustries.com
SIC: 3089 3443 Molding primary plastics; Fabricated plate work (boiler shop)
PA: Myers Industries, Inc.
1293 S Main St
Akron OH 44301
330 253-5592

(G-260)
MYERS INDUSTRIES INC (PA)
Also Called: Myers Industries
1293 S Main St (44301-1339)
PHONE..................................330 253-5592
Michael Mcgaugh, *Pr*
F Jack Liebau Junior, *Ch Bd*
Sonal P Robinson, *Ex VP*
Daniel W Hoehn, *Corporate Controller*
Lorelei Evans, *Pers/VP*
EMP: 50 **EST:** 1933
SQ FT: 129,000
SALES (est): 813.07MM
SALES (corp-wide): 813.07MM **Publicly Held**
Web: www.myersindustries.com
SIC: 3089 3086 3069 3052 Pallets, plastics; Plastics foam products; Rubber automotive products; Automobile hose, rubber

(G-261)
NETWORK POLYMERS INC
1353 Exeter Rd (44306-3853)
PHONE..................................330 773-2700
◆ **EMP:** 29
Web: www.networkpolymers.com
SIC: 2821 5162 Plastics materials and resins; Plastics resins

(G-262)
NEW CASTINGS INC
Also Called: Quality Molded
2200 Massillon Rd (44312-4234)
PHONE..................................330 645-6653
Mike Cingel, *Pr*
EMP: 108 **EST:** 1994
SQ FT: 15,000
SALES (est): 1.98MM
SALES (corp-wide): 24.79MM **Privately Held**
SIC: 3544 Industrial molds
PA: Saehwa Imc Na, Inc.
2200 Massillon Rd
Akron OH 44312
330 645-6653

(G-263)
NEWSOME & WORK METALIZING CO
258 Kenmore Blvd (44301)
P.O. Box 27091 (44319-7091)
PHONE..................................330 376-7144
Michael Newsome, *Pr*
EMP: 7 **EST:** 1958
SQ FT: 10,000
SALES (est): 945.23K **Privately Held**
SIC: 3471 Sand blasting of metal parts

(G-264)
NIDEC MOTOR CORPORATION
Imperial Electric
3030 Gilchrist Rd (44305-4420)
PHONE..................................575 434-0633
EMP: 125

Web: acim.nidec.com
SIC: 3621 Motors, electric
HQ: Nidec Motor Corporation
8050 W Florissant Ave
Saint Louis MO 63136

(G-265)
NORKAAM INDUSTRIES LLC
Also Called: Maple Valley Cleaners
1477 Copley Rd (44320-2656)
PHONE..................................330 873-9793
Eugene Norris, *Mgr*
EMP: 9 **EST:** 2016
SALES (est): 459.52K **Privately Held**
SIC: 3999 Manufacturing industries, nec

(G-266)
NORTH COAST THEATRICAL INC
2181 Killian Rd (44312-4887)
PHONE..................................330 762-1768
Richard Arconti, *Pr*
John Kramanak, *VP*
EMP: 9 **EST:** 1991
SALES (est): 995.32K **Privately Held**
Web: www.northcoasttheatrical.com
SIC: 3993 7922 Signs and advertising specialties; Theatrical production services

(G-267)
NORTH HILL MARBLE & GRANITE CO
448 N Howard St (44310-3185)
PHONE..................................330 253-2179
TOLL FREE: 800
Miles V Buzzi, *Pr*
Miles V Buzzi Ii, *VP*
Paul Buzzi, *Sec*
EMP: 10 **EST:** 1919
SQ FT: 4,000
SALES (est): 890K **Privately Held**
Web: www.northhillmarbleandgranite.com
SIC: 5999 1741 3993 3281 Monuments, finished to custom order; Masonry and other stonework; Signs, not made in custom sign painting shops; Cut stone and stone products

(G-268)
NORTHHILL T-SHIRT PRINT DSIGN
509 E Glenwood Ave (44310-3470)
PHONE..................................330 208-0338
EMP: 7 **EST:** 2021
SALES (est): 308.68K **Privately Held**
SIC: 3161 Clothing and apparel carrying cases

(G-269)
NSA TECHNOLOGIES LLC
3867 Medina Rd Ste 256 (44333-4525)
PHONE..................................330 576-4600
EMP: 7 **EST:** 2007
SALES (est): 183.75K **Privately Held**
Web: www.nsatechnology.com
SIC: 7372 8742 8731 Publisher's computer software; Marketing consulting services; Commercial physical research

(G-270)
OHIO GASKET AND SHIM CO INC (PA)
Also Called: Ogs Industries
976 Evans Ave (44305-1019)
PHONE..................................330 630-0626
John S Bader, *Pr*
Thomas Bader, *
◆ **EMP:** 45 **EST:** 1959
SQ FT: 84,000
SALES (est): 21.3MM
SALES (corp-wide): 21.3MM **Privately Held**

Web: www.ogsindustries.com
SIC: **3469** 3053 3599 3499 Stamping metal for the trade; Gaskets, all materials; Machine shop, jobbing and repair; Shims, metal

(G-271)
OHIO PURE FOODS INC (HQ)
681 W Waterloo Rd (44314-1547)
PHONE..................................330 753-2293
Kenny Sadai, *Ch Bd*
Thomas Kolb, *
▲ **EMP:** 89 **EST:** 1949
SQ FT: 100,000
SALES (est): 10.72MM **Privately Held**
SIC: **2033** 2086 Fruit juices: fresh; Fruit drinks (less than 100% juice): packaged in cans, etc.
PA: Country Pure Foods, Inc.
222 S Main St Ste 401
Akron OH 44308

(G-272)
ONQ SOLUTIONS INC
2213 Romig Rd (44320-3823)
PHONE..................................234 542-0289
EMP: 6
Web: www.onqsolutions.com
SIC: **2542** Stands, merchandise display: except wood
PA: Onq Solutions, Inc.
24540 Clawiter Rd
Hayward CA 94545

(G-273)
PALMER PRODUCTS INC
Also Called: Palmer Products
920 Moe Dr (44310-2519)
PHONE..................................330 630-9397
Leonard Palmer, *Pr*
Leonard Palmer Junior, *Pr*
Len Senior, *Pr*
EMP: 7 **EST:** 1973
SQ FT: 8,000
SALES (est): 914.78K **Privately Held**
Web: www.palmerbearings.com
SIC: **3599** Machine shop, jobbing and repair

(G-274)
PERFECT PRCISION MACHINING LTD
920 Clay St (44311-2214)
PHONE..................................330 475-0324
Margaret Habib, *Prin*
EMP: 9 **EST:** 2004
SALES (est): 970.7K **Privately Held**
Web: www.ppm-ohio.com
SIC: **3599** Machine shop, jobbing and repair

(G-275)
PIN OAK ENERGY PARTNERS LLC (PA)
388 S Main St Ste 401b (44311-4407)
PHONE..................................888 748-0763
Christopher Halvorson, *CEO*
Mark Van Tyne, *Chief Business Development Officer*
Christine Shepard-dessai, *VP*
Heidi Ewing, *Accounting*
EMP: 15 **EST:** 2015
SALES (est): 10.44MM
SALES (corp-wide): 10.44MM **Privately Held**
Web: www.pinoakep.com
SIC: **1311** Crude petroleum and natural gas production

(G-276)
PIONEER PLASTICS CORPORATION
3330 Massillon Rd (44312-5397)
PHONE..................................330 896-2356
Ralph J Danesi Junior, *Pr*

Jakob Denzinger, *
EMP: 125 **EST:** 1975
SQ FT: 45,000
SALES (est): 24.06MM **Privately Held**
Web: www.pioneerplasticscorp.com
SIC: **3089** Injection molding of plastics

(G-277)
PLATE-ALL METAL COMPANY INC
1210 Devalera St (44310-2483)
PHONE..................................330 633-6166
John L Burg, *Pr*
Irene Burg, *Contrlr*
Charles Killinger, *Manager*
EMP: 8 **EST:** 1945
SQ FT: 6,660
SALES (est): 786.59K **Privately Held**
Web: www.plateallmetal.com
SIC: **3471** 8711 Chromium plating of metals or formed products; Engineering services

(G-278)
PMBP LEGACY CO INC (PA)
Also Called: Ruscoe
485 Kenmore Blvd (44301-1013)
P.O. Box 3858 (44314-0858)
PHONE..................................330 253-8148
Angel Esplin, *CEO*
Betty Pfaff, *
EMP: 49 **EST:** 1949
SQ FT: 24,000
SALES (est): 10.51MM
SALES (corp-wide): 10.51MM **Privately Held**
Web: www.ruscoe.com
SIC: **2891** 3297 2851 Adhesives and sealants; Nonclay refractories; Paints and allied products

(G-279)
PMBP LEGACY CO INC
219 E Miller Ave (44301-1326)
P.O. Box 3858 (44314-0858)
PHONE..................................330 253-8148
Paul Michalec, *Dir*
EMP: 15
SALES (corp-wide): 10.51MM **Privately Held**
Web: www.ruscoe.com
SIC: **2865** Color pigments, organic
PA: Pmbp Legacy Co., Inc.
485 Kenmore Blvd
Akron OH 44301
330 253-8148

(G-280)
POLY-MET INC
1997 Nolt Dr (44312-4862)
P.O. Box 10024 (44310-0024)
PHONE..................................330 630-9006
Frank Moore, *Pr*
Laura Moore, *VP*
EMP: 15 **EST:** 1971
SQ FT: 10,000
SALES (est): 404.68K **Privately Held**
SIC: **3479** Hot dip coating of metals or formed products

(G-281)
POLYMET RECOVERY LLC
1280 Devalera St (44310-2418)
PHONE..................................330 630-9006
Frank Moore, *Pr*
EMP: 7 **EST:** 2015
SALES (est): 546.85K **Privately Held**
Web: www.polymetrecovery.com
SIC: **3471** Plating and polishing

(G-282)
PORTAGE MACHINE CONCEPTS INC
Also Called: Portage Knife Company
75 Skelton Rd (44312-1821)
P.O. Box 248 (44260-0248)
PHONE..................................330 628-2343
Jeannine Lizak, *Pr*
Christopher Michalec, *Treas*
W Duane Huff, *Sec*
▲ **EMP:** 16 **EST:** 1981
SQ FT: 6,500
SALES (est): 2.61MM **Privately Held**
Web: www.portageknife.com
SIC: **3541** Machine tools, metal cutting type

(G-283)
PRESSLERS MEATS INC
2553 Pressler Rd (44312-5500)
PHONE..................................330 644-5636
Roger H Pressler, *Pr*
Richard Pressler, *VP*
EMP: 15 **EST:** 1944
SQ FT: 1,800
SALES (est): 1.75MM **Privately Held**
SIC: **2011** Meat packing plants

(G-284)
PRO-FAB INC
2570 Pressler Rd (44312-5554)
PHONE..................................330 644-0044
Anna Myers, *CEO*
Monroe W Townsend, *VP*
EMP: 24 **EST:** 1978
SQ FT: 15,000
SALES (est): 1.15MM **Privately Held**
Web: www.profabincorporated.net
SIC: **3441** 1791 Fabricated structural metal; Structural steel erection

(G-285)
PRO-GRAM ENGINEERING CORP
1680 Hampton Rd (44305-3575)
PHONE..................................330 745-1004
Kenneth Anderson, *Pr*
Dadan Anderson, *VP*
EMP: 9 **EST:** 1984
SALES (est): 780.58K **Privately Held**
Web: www.billetspeedworks.com
SIC: **3599** Machine shop, jobbing and repair

(G-286)
PROGRESSIVE MFG CO INC
Also Called: Progrssive Mtllizing Machining
300 Massillon Rd (44312-1914)
PHONE..................................330 784-4717
Doris Datsko, *Pr*
David Datsko, *VP*
George Datsko Junior, *Sec*
EMP: 8 **EST:** 1972
SQ FT: 18,000
SALES (est): 978.93K **Privately Held**
Web: www.prorebuild.com
SIC: **3599** 3479 5084 Machine shop, jobbing and repair; Painting, coating, and hot dipping; Industrial machinery and equipment

(G-287)
PUR HAIR EXTENSIONS LLC
1088 E Tallmadge Ave (44310-3516)
PHONE..................................330 786-5772
EMP: 6 **EST:** 2018
SALES (est): 86.29K **Privately Held**
Web: www.purhairextensions.com
SIC: **7389** 7231 3999 Business Activities at Non-Commercial Site; Cosmetology and personal hygiene salons; Hair and hair-based products

(G-288)
Q MODEL INC
3414 E Waterloo Rd (44312-4011)
P.O. Box 25 (44260-0025)
PHONE..................................330 733-6545
Todd Strohfus, *Pr*
Laverne Strohfus, *CFO*
EMP: 15 **EST:** 1989
SQ FT: 35,000
SALES (est): 4.83MM **Privately Held**
Web: www.qmodelinc.net
SIC: **3469** 3069 Patterns on metal; Molded rubber products

(G-289)
QT EQUIPMENT COMPANY (PA)
151 W Dartmore Ave (44301-2462)
PHONE..................................330 724-3055
Daniel Root, *Pr*
Dave Root, *
▼ **EMP:** 35 **EST:** 1992
SQ FT: 20,000
SALES (est): 10.3MM **Privately Held**
Web: www.qtequipment.com
SIC: **7532** 5531 3713 Body shop, trucks; Automotive tires; Utility truck bodies

(G-290)
QUANEX BUILDING PRODUCTS CORP
388 S Main St Ste 700 (44311-1060)
PHONE..................................360 345-1241
EMP: 13
Web: www.quanex.com
SIC: **3272** Building materials, except block or brick: concrete
PA: Quanex Building Products Corporation
945 Bunker Hl Rd Ste 900
Houston TX 77024

(G-291)
QUANEX IG SYSTEMS INC (HQ)
Also Called: Quanex Building Products
388 S Main St Ste 700 (44311-1060)
PHONE..................................216 910-1500
◆ **EMP:** 99 **EST:** 1994
SQ FT: 400,000
SALES (est): 71.79MM **Publicly Held**
Web: www.quanex.com
SIC: **3061** 3053 Mechanical rubber goods; Gaskets; packing and sealing devices
PA: Quanex Building Products Corporation
945 Bunker Hl Rd Ste 900
Houston TX 77024

(G-292)
QUARRYMASTERS INC
1644 Berna Rd (44312-5434)
PHONE..................................330 612-0474
Joseph A Della, *Pr*
Jacalyn Tutthill, *VP*
▲ **EMP:** 9 **EST:** 2006
SALES (est): 417.56K **Privately Held**
SIC: **3281** 8742 Granite, cut and shaped; General management consultant

(G-293)
QUIKEY MANUFACTURING CO INC (PA)
1500 Industrial Pkwy (44310-2600)
PHONE..................................330 633-8106
Michael W Burns, *Pr*
Thomas Stiller, *
Patrick P Burns, *
William B Stiller, *
Mary Lou Burns, *Stockholder**
▲ **EMP:** 125 **EST:** 1959
SQ FT: 50,000
SALES (est): 22.67MM
SALES (corp-wide): 22.67MM **Privately Held**

Akron - Summit County (G-294)

Web: www.quikey.com
SIC: 3993 Advertising novelties

(G-294)
R C MUSSON RUBBER CO
1320 E Archwood Ave (44306-2825)
P.O. Box 7038 (44306-0038)
PHONE.................................330 773-7651
Bennie D Segers, *Ch Bd*
Frank W Rockhold, *VP*
Robert S Segers, *VP*
William J Segers, *VP*
Billie H Dreyer, *Sec*
EMP: 20 **EST:** 1945
SQ FT: 40,000
SALES (est): 3.92MM **Privately Held**
Web: www.mussonrubber.com
SIC: 3069 5085 Mats or matting, rubber, nec ; Rubber goods, mechanical

(G-295)
RAINBOW MASTER MIXING INC
467 Dan St (44310-3900)
PHONE.................................330 374-1810
Tim Lowe, *Managing Member*
EMP: 11 **EST:** 2007
SALES (est): 2.57MM **Privately Held**
Web: www.rainbowmastermixing.com
SIC: 3069 Medical and laboratory rubber sundries and related products

(G-296)
RANDY LEWIS INC
Also Called: Acme Fence & Lumber
1053 Bank St (44305-2507)
PHONE.................................330 784-0456
Randy Lewis, *Pr*
EMP: 16 **EST:** 1939
SQ FT: 10,000
SALES (est): 2.14MM **Privately Held**
Web: www.acmefence.com
SIC: 3446 2499 3315 3089 Fences or posts, ornamental iron or steel; Fencing, wood; Chain link fencing; Fences, gates, and accessories: plastics

(G-297)
RANSOME AC LLC ✪
1235 Tioga Ave (44305-1153)
PHONE.................................234 205-6907
Jada Ransome, *Managing Member*
EMP: 6 **EST:** 2023
SALES (est): 78.58K **Privately Held**
SIC: 3231 7231 3999 7389 Products of purchased glass; Beauty shops; Manufacturing industries, nec; Business services, nec

(G-298)
RAUH POLYMERS INC
420 Kenmore Blvd (44301-1038)
PHONE.................................330 376-1120
Joseph M Rauh, *Pr*
James T Rauh, *VP*
▲ **EMP:** 15 **EST:** 2004
SALES (est): 4.86MM **Privately Held**
Web: www.rauhpolymers.com
SIC: 2821 Plastics materials and resins

(G-299)
RCM ENGINEERING COMPANY
2089 N Cleveland Massillon Rd (44333-1258)
P.O. Box 517 (44210-0517)
PHONE.................................330 666-0575
Robert C Mc Dowell, *Owner*
EMP: 9 **EST:** 1903
SQ FT: 2,200
SALES (est): 725.79K **Privately Held**
SIC: 1311 1321 Natural gas production; Natural gasoline production

(G-300)
REGENCY SEATING INC
Also Called: Regency Office Furniture
2375 Romig Rd (44320-3824)
PHONE.................................330 848-3700
John Summerville, *Pr*
Aaron Summerville, *
◆ **EMP:** 35 **EST:** 1941
SQ FT: 100,000
SALES (est): 4.99MM **Privately Held**
Web: www.regencyof.com
SIC: 2426 Furniture stock and parts, hardwood

(G-301)
REPORTER NEWSPAPER INC
1088 S Main St (44301-1206)
P.O. Box 2042 (44309-2042)
PHONE.................................330 535-7061
William Ellis Junior, *Pr*
EMP: 10 **EST:** 1951
SALES (est): 590.52K **Privately Held**
Web: www.thereporternewspaperonline.com
SIC: 2711 Newspapers: publishing only, not printed on site

(G-302)
REVLIS CORPORATION (PA)
255 Fountain St (44304-1920)
PHONE.................................330 535-2100
▲ **EMP:** 38 **EST:** 1971
SALES (est): 10.05MM
SALES (corp-wide): 10.05MM **Privately Held**
SIC: 2865 2869 Dyes and pigments; Industrial organic chemicals, nec

(G-303)
REVVITY HEALTH SCIENCES INC
520 S Main St Ste 2423 (44311-1086)
PHONE.................................330 825-4525
Chritine Gradisher, *Mgr*
EMP: 44
SALES (corp-wide): 2.75B **Publicly Held**
Web: www.perkinelmer.com
SIC: 2835 2836 5049 Diagnostic substances ; Biological products, except diagnostic; Laboratory equipment, except medical or dental
HQ: Revvity Health Sciences, Inc.
940 Winter St
Waltham MA 02451
781 663-6900

(G-304)
RICHARDS WHL FENCE CO INC
Also Called: Richard's Fence Company
1600 Firestone Pkwy (44301-1659)
PHONE.................................330 773-0423
Richard Peterson, *Pr*
Bill Peterson, *
▲ **EMP:** 30 **EST:** 1968
SQ FT: 235,000
SALES (est): 12.28MM **Privately Held**
Web: www.richardsfence.com
SIC: 3315 5039 Chain link fencing; Wire fence, gates, and accessories

(G-305)
RIVER VALLEY PAPER COMPANY LLC
Also Called: River Valley Paper
131 N Summit St (44304-1277)
P.O. Box 1191 (44309-1191)
PHONE.................................330 535-1001
Rick Torbeck, *Managing Member*
EMP: 29 **EST:** 2016
SALES (est): 2.73MM **Privately Held**
Web: www.intfiber.com

SIC: 2611 Pulp manufactured from waste or recycled paper

(G-306)
RJS CORPORATION
Also Called: Rjs
3400 Massillon Rd (44312-5392)
PHONE.................................330 896-2387
◆ **EMP:** 45 **EST:** 1948
SALES (est): 7.5MM **Privately Held**
Web: www.rjscorp.com
SIC: 3559 3546 3496 Rubber working machinery, including tires; Power-driven handtools; Miscellaneous fabricated wire products

(G-307)
ROCHLING AUTOMOTIVE USA LLP
2275 Picton Pkwy (44312-4270)
PHONE.................................330 400-5785
EMP: 75
SALES (corp-wide): 2.7B **Privately Held**
Web: www.roechling.com
SIC: 3714 Motor vehicle engines and parts
HQ: Rochling Automotive Usa Llp
245 Parkway E 29334
Duncan SC 29334
864 486-0888

(G-308)
ROETMANS WELDING LLC
155 Beaver St (44304-1907)
PHONE.................................216 385-5938
Robert Roetman, *Pr*
EMP: 9 **EST:** 2013
SALES (est): 464.4K **Privately Held**
Web: www.roetmansweldingllc.com
SIC: 7692 Welding repair

(G-309)
ROGERS INDUSTRIAL PRODUCTS INC
532 S Main St (44311-1018)
PHONE.................................330 535-3331
John Cole, *Pr*
◆ **EMP:** 35 **EST:** 1951
SQ FT: 239,000
SALES (est): 5.01MM **Privately Held**
Web: www.rogersusa.com
SIC: 3542 3625 3491 3643 Presses: hydraulic and pneumatic, mechanical and manual; Industrial electrical relays and switches; Pressure valves and regulators, industrial; Current-carrying wiring services

(G-310)
ROTOCAST TECHNOLOGIES INC
1900 Englewood Ave (44312-1004)
PHONE.................................330 798-9091
EMP: 30 **EST:** 1996
SQ FT: 25,000
SALES (est): 3.86MM **Privately Held**
Web: www.rotocastmold.com
SIC: 3365 3544 Aluminum and aluminum-based alloy castings; Special dies, tools, jigs, and fixtures

(G-311)
ROYALTON MANUFACTURING INC
1169 Brittain Rd (44305)
P.O. Box 33190 (44133)
PHONE.................................440 237-2233
Kenneth Wesner, *Pr*
William Calfee, *VP*
Judith Wesner, *Treas*
EMP: 34 **EST:** 1978
SQ FT: 12,000
SALES (est): 471.98K **Privately Held**
SIC: 3599 Machine shop, jobbing and repair

(G-312)
RUBBER CITY MACHINERY CORP
Also Called: R C M
One Thousand Sweitzer Avenue (44311)
P.O. Box 2043 (44309-2043)
PHONE.................................330 434-3500
George B Sobieraj, *Pr*
Robert J Westfall, *
Bernie Sobieraj, *
Robert F Longano, *Prin*
▲ **EMP:** 32 **EST:** 1980
SQ FT: 100,000
SALES (est): 5.7MM **Privately Held**
Web: www.rcmc.com
SIC: 3559 5084 7629 Rubber working machinery, including tires; Industrial machinery and equipment; Electrical repair shops

(G-313)
RUBBER WORLD MAGAZINE INC
1741 Akron Peninsula Rd (44313-5157)
PHONE.................................330 864-2122
EMP: 8 **EST:** 1984
SALES (est): 177.37K **Privately Held**
Web: www.rubberworld.com
SIC: 2721 Periodicals

(G-314)
RUSCOE COMPANY
485 Kenmore Blvd (44301-1013)
PHONE.................................330 253-8148
Angel Esplin, *CFO*
EMP: 33 **EST:** 2020
SALES (est): 2.87MM **Privately Held**
SIC: 2891 Adhesives and sealants

(G-315)
RUSSELL PRODUCTS CO INC
Also Called: Akron Anodizing & Coating Div
1066 Home Ave (44310-3502)
PHONE.................................330 535-3391
Daniel Dzurovcin, *VP*
EMP: 9
SALES (corp-wide): 4.28MM **Privately Held**
Web: www.russprodco.com
SIC: 3471 Finishing, metals or formed products
PA: Russell Products Co., Inc.
275 N Forge St
Akron OH 44304
330 535-9246

(G-316)
RUSSELL PRODUCTS CO INC
De Valera Division
275 N Forge St Ste 1 (44304-1440)
PHONE.................................330 535-9246
Robert Evans, *Prin*
EMP: 10
SQ FT: 14,000
SALES (corp-wide): 4.28MM **Privately Held**
Web: www.russprodco.com
SIC: 3479 3471 Painting of metal products; Anodizing (plating) of metals or formed products
PA: Russell Products Co., Inc.
275 N Forge St
Akron OH 44304
330 535-9246

(G-317)
RUSSELL PRODUCTS CO INC (PA)
Also Called: Falholt Division
275 N Forge St (44304-1440)
PHONE.................................330 535-9246
◆ **EMP:** 10 **EST:** 1959
SALES (est): 4.28MM
SALES (corp-wide): 4.28MM **Privately Held**

GEOGRAPHIC SECTION

Akron - Summit County (G-339)

Web: www.russprodco.com
SIC: 3479 3471 Painting of metal products; Anodizing (plating) of metals or formed products

(G-318)
RUSSELL STANDARD CORPORATION
Also Called: Jasa Asphalt Russell Standard
990 Hazel St (44305-1610)
PHONE..................................330 733-9400
Robert Gunther, Mgr
EMP: 6
SALES (corp-wide): 121.53MM Privately Held
Web: www.russellstandard.com
SIC: 5032 2951 Asphalt mixture; Concrete, bituminous
PA: Russell Standard Corporation
    285 Kappa Dr Ste 300
    Pittsburgh PA 15238
    412 449-0700

(G-319)
S & A INDUSTRIES CORPORATION
1500 Exeter Rd (44306)
PHONE..................................330 733-6040
EMP: 22
Web: www.s-aindustries.com
SIC: 3086 Plastics foam products
HQ: S & A Industries Corporation
    1471 Exeter Rd
    Akron OH 44306

(G-320)
S & A INDUSTRIES CORPORATION (DH)
1471 Exeter Rd (44306-3856)
PHONE..................................330 733-6040
▲ EMP: 66 EST: 2010
SQ FT: 42,000
SALES (est): 33.02MM Privately Held
Web: www.s-aindustries.com
SIC: 3086 Plastics foam products
HQ: Sekiso Corporation
    1-3, Hinakitamachi
    Okazaki AIC 444-0

(G-321)
S I T STRINGS CO INC
2493 Romig Rd (44320-4109)
PHONE..................................330 434-8010
Virgil Lay, Pr
Robert C Hird, VP
Edwin Speedy, Ex VP
EMP: 20 EST: 1980
SQ FT: 16,000
SALES (est): 2.45MM Privately Held
Web: www.sitstrings.com
SIC: 3931 5736 Guitars and parts, electric and nonelectric; Musical instrument stores

(G-322)
SACO LOWELL PARTS LLC
1395 Triplett Blvd (44306-3124)
PHONE..................................330 794-1535
Bruce Weick, VP
John Daenes, Pr
Russell Dunlap, VP
EMP: 26 EST: 2001
SALES (est): 518.39K Privately Held
Web: www.wwwilliams.com
SIC: 3469 Machine parts, stamped or pressed metal

(G-323)
SAEHWA IMC NA INC (PA)
Also Called: Versitech Mold Div
2200 Massillon Rd (44312-4234)
PHONE..................................330 645-6653

Mike Cingel, Pr
Stanley B Migdal, *
Mike Politis, *
Jerry Candiliotis, *
Jim Finfield, *
▲ EMP: 100 EST: 1978
SQ FT: 83,821
SALES (est): 24.79MM
SALES (corp-wide): 24.79MM Privately Held
SIC: 3544 Industrial molds

(G-324)
SAINT-GOBAIN PRFMCE PLAS CORP
2664 Gilchrist Rd (44305-4412)
PHONE..................................330 798-6981
Chris Mattern, Manager
EMP: 200
SQ FT: 100,000
SALES (corp-wide): 397.78MM Privately Held
Web: plastics.saint-gobain.com
SIC: 3061 3083 Medical and surgical rubber tubing (extruded and lathe-cut); Laminated plastics plate and sheet
HQ: Saint-Gobain Performance Plastics Corporation
    20 Moores Rd
    Malvern PA 19355
    440 836-6900

(G-325)
SCANDINAVIAN TOB GROUP LN LTD
Also Called: Stg Lane
1424 Diagonal Rd (44320-4016)
PHONE..................................770 934-4594
J Kelly Michols, CEO
W David Parrish, Finance Treasurer
Phil Gee, Managing Director US Operations
Daniel Mcgee, Sec
Elliot Fledz, Asst Tr
◆ EMP: 130 EST: 1975
SALES (est): 22.36MM Privately Held
Web: www.st-group.com
SIC: 2131 5194 Smoking tobacco; Tobacco and tobacco products

(G-326)
SCHOTT METAL PRODUCTS COMPANY
Also Called: Design Wheel and Hub
2225 Lee Dr (44306-4399)
PHONE..................................330 773-7873
Samuel Schott, Pr
F W Schott, *
Paul Graham, *
EMP: 20 EST: 1945
SQ FT: 90,000
SALES (est): 1.16MM Privately Held
SIC: 3469 3714 Stamping metal for the trade; Motor vehicle parts and accessories

(G-327)
SHIN-ETSU SILICONES AMER INC
963 Evans Ave (44305-1041)
PHONE..................................330 630-9860
EMP: 11 EST: 2010
SALES (est): 1.45MM Privately Held
Web: www.shinetsusilicones.com
SIC: 2869 Industrial organic chemicals, nec

(G-328)
SHIN-ETSU SILICONES OF AMERICA INC (HQ)
1150 Damar Dr (44305-1066)
PHONE..................................330 630-9460
◆ EMP: 150 EST: 1985
SALES (est): 102.95MM Privately Held
Web: www.shinetsusilicones.com

SIC: 5169 2822 2869 Silicon lubricants; Silicone rubbers; Industrial organic chemicals, nec
PA: Shin-Etsu Chemical Co., Ltd.
    1-4-1, Marunouchi
    Chiyoda-Ku TKY 100-0

(G-329)
SHINCOR SILICONES INC
1030 Evans Ave (44305-1021)
PHONE..................................330 630-9460
▲ EMP: 50
Web: www.shinetsusilicones.com
SIC: 2822 2891 2869 Silicone rubbers; Adhesives and sealants; Industrial organic chemicals, nec

(G-330)
SHOOK MANUFACTURED PDTS INC (PA)
1017 Kenmore Blvd (44314-2153)
P.O. Box 15058 (44314-5058)
PHONE..................................330 848-9780
Roy Knittle, Pr
Thomas Johns, VP
▲ EMP: 9 EST: 1968
SQ FT: 10,000
SALES (est): 1.06MM
SALES (corp-wide): 1.06MM Privately Held
Web: www.shookmfg.com
SIC: 3545 5072 Chucks: drill, lathe, or magnetic (machine tool accessories); Hardware

(G-331)
SIGNET ENTERPRISES LLC (PA)
19 N High St (44308-1912)
PHONE..................................330 762-9102
Anthony S Manna, Managing Member
EMP: 24 EST: 2011
SQ FT: 26,000
SALES (est): 12.07MM
SALES (corp-wide): 12.07MM Privately Held
Web: www.signetllc.com
SIC: 2899 Chemical preparations, nec

(G-332)
SK SCREEN PRINTING INC
89 Monroe Ave (44301)
PHONE..................................330 475-0286
EMP: 23
SIC: 2759 Screen printing
PA: Sk Screen Printing Inc
    1340 Home Ave Ste F
    Akron OH 44310

(G-333)
SOUTH AKRON AWNING CO (PA)
763 Kenmore Blvd (44314-2196)
PHONE..................................330 848-7611
Ranell Minear, Pr
Kathleen Mueller, Sec
Michelle Halafa, VP
EMP: 14 EST: 1913
SQ FT: 19,000
SALES (est): 2.22MM
SALES (corp-wide): 2.22MM Privately Held
Web: www.southakronawning.com
SIC: 2394 1799 7359 Awnings, fabric: made from purchased materials; Awning installation; Tent and tarpaulin rental

(G-334)
STANDARD JIG BORING SVC LLC (HQ)
Also Called: Sjbs
3360 Miller Park Rd (44312-5388)

PHONE..................................330 896-9530
Ginger Townsend, Managing Member
Jeffrey R Wahl, *
▲ EMP: 20 EST: 2007
SQ FT: 30,000
SALES (est): 10.62MM
SALES (corp-wide): 105.04MM Privately Held
SIC: 3599 Machine shop, jobbing and repair
PA: Ariel Corporation
    35 Blackjack Road Ext
    Mount Vernon OH 43050
    740 397-0311

(G-335)
STANDARD JIG BORING SVC LLC
3194 Massillon Rd (44312-5363)
PHONE..................................330 644-5405
George Koberlein, Brnch Mgr
EMP: 79
SALES (corp-wide): 105.04MM Privately Held
SIC: 3599 Machine shop, jobbing and repair
HQ: Standard Jig Boring Service, Llc
    3360 Miller Park Rd
    Akron OH 44312
    330 896-9530

(G-336)
STAR PRINTING COMPANY INC
125 N Union St (44304-1390)
PHONE..................................330 376-0514
Vicki Lauck, Pr
Robert D Lauck Junior, VP
Paul M Lauck, VP
Lynda Moore, Sec
EMP: 22 EST: 1932
SQ FT: 20,000
SALES (est): 2.33MM Privately Held
Web: www.starptg.com
SIC: 2752 2759 2789 Offset printing; Letterpress printing; Bookbinding and related work

(G-337)
STEEL STRUCTURES OF OHIO LLC
1324 Firestone Pkwy Unit A (44301-1624)
PHONE..................................330 374-9900
James L Rench, Managing Member
EMP: 11 EST: 2003
SQ FT: 5,000
SALES (est): 544.91K Privately Held
SIC: 3449 Bars, concrete reinforcing: fabricated steel

(G-338)
STERLING ASSOCIATES INC
Also Called: Fastsigns
1783 Brittain Rd (44310-1801)
PHONE..................................330 630-3500
Milton L Liming, Pr
Brent B Liming, VP
Elaine Liming, Sec
EMP: 8 EST: 1962
SQ FT: 2,000
SALES (est): 810.59K Privately Held
Web: www.fastsigns.com
SIC: 3993 2721 Signs, not made in custom sign painting shops; Periodicals

(G-339)
SUMMIT DESIGN AND TECH INC ✪
Also Called: West Reserve Controls
1147 Sweitzer Ave (44301-1337)
PHONE..................................330 733-6662
Jay Mendpara, CEO
EMP: 18 EST: 2022
SALES (est): 1.15MM Privately Held
Web: www.anzer-usa.com
SIC: 3559 Electronic component making machinery

Akron - Summit County (G-340) GEOGRAPHIC SECTION

(G-340)
SUMMIT MACHINE SOLUTIONS LLC
Also Called: Cecil Peck Co
1029 Arlington Cir (44306-3959)
PHONE..................................330 785-0781
Jay Hofner, *Managing Member*
EMP: 9 **EST:** 2010
SALES (est): 936.11K **Privately Held**
Web: www.summitmachinesolutions.com
SIC: 3548 Welding apparatus

(G-341)
SUMMIT TOOL COMPANY (HQ)
Also Called: Ken-Tools
768 E North St (44305-1164)
P.O. Box 9320 (44305-0320)
PHONE..................................330 535-7177
Larry Sorles, *Dir*
Douglas Romstadt, *
▲ **EMP:** 65 **EST:** 1932
SQ FT: 70,000
SALES (est): 18.82MM **Privately Held**
Web: www.kentool.com
SIC: 3544 Special dies and tools
PA: North Coast Holdings Incorporated
768 E North St
Akron OH 44305

(G-342)
SYNTHOMER INC
1380 Tech Way (44306-2572)
PHONE..................................330 734-1237
EMP: 10
SALES (corp-wide): 2.46B **Privately Held**
Web: www.omnova.com
SIC: 2819 Industrial inorganic chemicals, nec
HQ: Synthomer Inc.
25435 Harvard Rd
Beachwood OH 44122
216 682-7000

(G-343)
SYSTEMS KIT LLC MB
Also Called: Industrial Profile Systems
925 Glaser Pkwy (44306-4161)
PHONE..................................330 945-4500
Rick Sabo, *VP*
EMP: 25 **EST:** 2019
SALES (est): 9.34MM
SALES (corp-wide): 77.71K **Privately Held**
Web: www.industrialprofile.com /
SIC: 3354 8711 Shapes, extruded aluminum, nec; Mechanical engineering
HQ: Weiss North America, Inc.
3860 Ben Hur Ave Unit 2
Willoughby OH 44094
440 269-8031

(G-344)
T & CS REPAIRS & RETAIL LLC
1153 Marcy St (44301-1305)
PHONE..................................704 964-7325
EMP: 20 **EST:** 2020
SALES (est): 703.97K **Privately Held**
SIC: 3161 Clothing and apparel carrying cases

(G-345)
T L SQUIRE AND COMPANY INC
4040 Embassy Pkwy Ste 300 (44333-8341)
PHONE..................................330 668-2604
Joseph Wozny, *Pr*
David Schierenbeck, *VP*
Ed Brodbeck, *VP*
EMP: 6 **EST:** 1982
SQ FT: 1,800
SALES (est): 43.9MM **Privately Held**
Web: www.tlsquire.com
SIC: 2822 Synthetic rubber

(G-346)
T W CORPORATION
99 South Seiberling Street (44305-4216)
PHONE..................................440 461-3234
Thomas T Whims, *Pr*
Thomas T Whims, *Pr*
Thomas M Seger, *Sec*
EMP: 22 **EST:** 1994
SQ FT: 28,000
SALES (est): 249.97K **Privately Held**
Web: www.twdesignbuild.com
SIC: 3365 Aerospace castings, aluminum

(G-347)
TALLMADGE FINISHING CO INC
879 Moe Dr Ste C20 (44310-2558)
PHONE..................................330 633-7466
David Mann, *Pr*
Paul Cooper, *
EMP: 10 **EST:** 1981
SALES (est): 173K **Privately Held**
SIC: 3069 Hard rubber and molded rubber products

(G-348)
TALLMADGE SPINNING & METAL CO
2783 Gilchrist Rd Unit A (44305-4406)
P.O. Box 58 (44278-0058)
PHONE..................................330 794-2277
John Sasanecki, *Pr*
Jacob Sasanecki, *VP*
Linda Sasanecki, *Treas*
EMP: 15 **EST:** 1947
SQ FT: 15,000
SALES (est): 4MM **Privately Held**
Web: www.tsm1947.com
SIC: 3444 Sheet metalwork

(G-349)
TB BACKSTOP INC
4478 Regal Dr (44321)
PHONE..................................330 434-4442
Thomas Brennan, *Pr*
EMP: 14 **EST:** 1985
SALES (est): 2.36MM **Privately Held**
Web: www.valleyrubber.com
SIC: 3069 Reclaimed rubber and specialty rubber compounds

(G-350)
TECH PRO INC
3030 Gilchrist Rd (44305-4420)
PHONE..................................330 923-3546
John Putman, *Pr*
Kay Putman, *
▲ **EMP:** 9 **EST:** 1982
SQ FT: 30,000
SALES (est): 177.92K **Privately Held**
SIC: 7699 3821 3829 3825 Laboratory instrument repair; Laboratory apparatus and furniture; Measuring and controlling devices, nec; Instruments to measure electricity

(G-351)
TEMPLE ISRAEL
Also Called: Jewish Synagogue
91 Springside Dr (44333-2428)
PHONE..................................330 762-8617
Pastor David Lipper, *Prin*
Milton I Wiskind, *Pr*
Doctor Davis Meckler, *VP*
Henry Nagel, *VP*
Fabian Velia, *Sec*
EMP: 9 **EST:** 1866
SALES (est): 424.95K **Privately Held**
Web: www.templeisraelakron.org
SIC: 8661 3625 Synagogue; Switches, electric power

(G-352)
THE R C A RUBBER COMPANY
1833 E Market St (44305-4214)
P.O. Box 9240 (44305-0240)
PHONE..................................330 784-1291
◆ **EMP:** 80
Web: www.rcarubber.com
SIC: 3069 Molded rubber products

(G-353)
THEKEN COMPANIES LLC
1800 Triplett Blvd (44306-3311)
PHONE..................................330 733-7600
EMP: 15 **EST:** 2013
SQ FT: 30,000
SALES (est): 860.67K **Privately Held**
Web: www.nextsteparthropedix.com
SIC: 3841 Surgical and medical instruments

(G-354)
THEKEN PORT PARK LLC
1800 Triplett Blvd (44306-3311)
PHONE..................................330 733-7600
EMP: 57 **EST:** 2015
SALES (est): 5.71MM **Privately Held**
Web: www.nextsteparthropedix.com
SIC: 3313 Alloys, additive, except copper: not made in blast furnaces

(G-355)
THERMELECTRICITY LLC
411 Wolf Ledges Pkwy Ste 100 (44311-1028)
PHONE..................................330 972-8054
EMP: 8 **EST:** 2012
SALES (est): 248.12K **Privately Held**
SIC: 3621 Power generators

(G-356)
THERMO-RITE MFG COMPANY
Also Called: Star Fire Distributing
1355 Evans Ave (44305-1038)
PHONE..................................330 633-8680
Roy Allen, *CEO*
EMP: 36 **EST:** 1946
SQ FT: 120,000
SALES (est): 9.05MM **Privately Held**
Web: www.star-fire.com
SIC: 3429 Fireplace equipment, hardware: andirons, grates, screens

(G-357)
THYME INC
3245 Pickle Rd (44312-5333)
PHONE..................................484 872-8430
Robert N Sampson, *Pr*
EMP: 19 **EST:** 1987
SALES (est): 513.7K **Privately Held**
SIC: 7371 7373 5734 3578 Computer software development; Computer integrated systems design; Software, computer games; Calculating and accounting equipment

(G-358)
TINYCIRCUITS
540 S Main St (44311-1079)
PHONE..................................330 329-5753
EMP: 8 **EST:** 2013
SALES (est): 3.99MM **Privately Held**
Web: www.tinycircuits.com
SIC: 3679 Electronic circuits

(G-359)
TLT-BABCOCK INC
260 Springside Dr (44333-2433)
PHONE..................................330 867-8540
▲ **EMP:** 92
SIC: 3564 3822 Blowers and fans; Damper operators: pneumatic, thermostatic, electric

(G-360)
TLT-TURBO INC
2693 Wingate Ave (44314)
P.O. Box 3830 (44314)
PHONE..................................330 776-5115
John A Landis, *Dir*
▲ **EMP:** 6 **EST:** 2014
SALES (est): 3.79MM
SALES (corp-wide): 92.38B **Privately Held**
Web: www.tlt-turbo.com
SIC: 3564 Ventilating fans: industrial or commercial
HQ: Tlt-Turbo Gmbh
Gleiwitzstr. 7
Zweibrucken RP 66482
63328080

(G-361)
TOTAL CALL CENTER SOLUTIONS
1014 Margate Dr Ste 200 (44313-5808)
PHONE..................................330 869-9844
Mark Thorne, *Pr*
Gary Cooper, *VP*
Rhonda Thorne, *Stockholder*
EMP: 10 **EST:** 1990
SALES (est): 601K **Privately Held**
SIC: 3661 7389 Telephone dialing devices, automatic; Telephone services

(G-362)
TRI CAST LIMITED PARTNERSHIP
2128 Killian Rd (44312-4898)
PHONE..................................330 733-8718
John Voight, *CEO*
EMP: 24 **EST:** 2000
SQ FT: 18,712
SALES (est): 2.4MM **Privately Held**
Web: www.tri-cast.com
SIC: 3321 Gray iron castings, nec

(G-363)
TRI-CAST INC (PA)
2128 Killian Rd (44312-4898)
PHONE..................................330 733-8718
John Voight, *CEO*
EMP: 30 **EST:** 1967
SQ FT: 28,000
SALES (est): 4.42MM
SALES (corp-wide): 4.42MM **Privately Held**
Web: www.tri-cast.com
SIC: 3321 Gray iron castings, nec

(G-364)
TRUSEAL TECHNOLOGIES INC (HQ)
388 S Main St Ste 700 (44311)
PHONE..................................216 910-1500
August J Coppola, *CEO*
Lee Burroughs, *
David Marlar, *
Joseph Stevenot, *
Joel Falck, *
◆ **EMP:** 35 **EST:** 1997
SQ FT: 80,000
SALES (est): 27.31MM **Publicly Held**
Web: www.truseal.com
SIC: 2891 Sealants
PA: Quanex Building Products Corporation
945 Bunker Hl Rd Ste 900
Houston TX 77024

(G-365)
TS SALES LLC
Also Called: Top Shot Ammunition
847 Pier Dr (44307-2267)
PHONE..................................727 804-8060
Mark Schneider, *Managing Member*
EMP: 15 **EST:** 2014

▲ = Import ▼ = Export
◆ = Import/Export

GEOGRAPHIC SECTION

Alliance - Stark County (G-389)

SALES (est): 2MM **Privately Held**
SIC: **5941** 3484 Firearms; Guns (firearms) or gun parts, 30 mm. and below

(G-366)
UNINTERRUPTED LLC
3800 Embassy Pkwy Ste 360 (44333-8389)
PHONE..............................216 771-2323
Maverick Carter, *CEO*
EMP: 15 **EST:** 2014
SALES (est): 963.4K **Privately Held**
SIC: **7372** Application computer software

(G-367)
UNITED FEED SCREWS LTD
487 Wellington Ave (44305-2680)
PHONE..............................330 798-5532
Paul Norton, *Pr*
Joe Norton Senior, *TechI Dir*
▲ **EMP:** 10 **EST:** 1998
SQ FT: 14,500
SALES (est): 1.9MM **Privately Held**
Web: www.unitedfeedscrews.com
SIC: **3061** Oil and gas field machinery rubber goods (mechanical)

(G-368)
V-I-S-C-E-R-O-T-O-N-I-C INC
118 W Market St (44303-2359)
PHONE..............................330 690-3355
Christopher Cook, *Pr*
Rich Cook, *VP*
EMP: 100 **EST:** 2021
SALES (est): 3.66MM **Privately Held**
SIC: **2515** Mattresses and bedsprings

(G-369)
VERTICAL DATA LLC
Also Called: Medtrace
2169 Chuckery Ln (44333-4742)
P.O. Box 38 (44210-0038)
PHONE..............................330 289-0313
EMP: 15 **EST:** 2015
SALES (est): 561.41K **Privately Held**
Web: www.vertical-data.com
SIC: **7372** Application computer software

(G-370)
VIRTUAL HOLD TECH SLUTIONS LLC (DH)
Also Called: Mindful
3875 Embassy Pkwy Ste 350 (44333)
PHONE..............................330 670-2200
EMP: 29 **EST:** 1995
SQ FT: 18,000
SALES (est): 23.35MM
SALES (corp-wide): 534MM **Privately Held**
Web: www.getmindful.com
SIC: **7371** 7372 Computer software development; Prepackaged software
HQ: Medallia, Inc.
6220 Stnrdge Mall Rd Fl 2
Pleasanton CA 94588
650 321-3000

(G-371)
VULCAN MACHINERY CORPORATION
20 N Case Ave (44305-2598)
PHONE..............................330 376-6025
David Jacobs, *Pr*
Bradley J Jacobs, *
EMP: 21 **EST:** 1966
SALES (est): 2.42MM **Privately Held**
Web: www.vulcanmachinery.com
SIC: **3559** 7299 Plastics working machinery; Banquet hall facilities

(G-372)
W G LOCKHART CONSTRUCTION CO
800 W Waterloo Rd (44314-1528)
PHONE..............................330 745-6520
Alexander R Lockhart, *Pr*
Richard Stanley, *
EMP: 23 **EST:** 1918
SQ FT: 5,000
SALES (est): 676.6K **Privately Held**
SIC: **1611** 3273 Highway and street construction; Ready-mixed concrete

(G-373)
WEAVER INDUSTRIES PROPAK
480 Baltimore Ave (44306-2506)
PHONE..............................330 475-8160
EMP: 7 **EST:** 2017
SALES (est): 56.44K **Privately Held**
Web: www.weaverindustries.org
SIC: **3999** Manufacturing industries, nec

(G-374)
WHITE INDUSTRIAL TOOL INC
Also Called: White Tool
102 W Wilbeth Rd (44301-2415)
PHONE..............................330 773-6889
Ronald White Junior, *Pr*
Richard White, *VP*
Christopher White, *Treas*
Robert White, *Sec*
Ronald White Senior, *Stockholder*
EMP: 12 **EST:** 1965
SQ FT: 18,000
SALES (est): 472.95K **Privately Held**
Web: www.whiteindtool.com
SIC: **3423** Hand and edge tools, nec

(G-375)
WI INC
Also Called: Wek Industries, Inc.
1293 S Main St (44301-1302)
PHONE..............................440 576-6940
EMP: 125
SIC: **3089** Injection molding of plastics

(G-376)
WISE EDGE LLC
Also Called: Ovs Knife Co.
981 Home Ave (44310-4107)
PHONE..............................330 208-0889
Jeffery Wise, *Pr*
Ashley Combs, *Mgr*
EMP: 7 **EST:** 2010
SALES (est): 925.15K **Privately Held**
SIC: **3599** 3423 3555 3541 Grinding castings for the trade; Hand and edge tools, nec; Printing trades machinery; Machine tools, metal cutting type

(G-377)
WRC HOLDINGS INC
Also Called: Wrc
1485 Exeter Rd (44306-3856)
PHONE..............................330 733-6662
◆ **EMP:** 18 **EST:** 1990
SALES (est): 4.17MM **Privately Held**
Web: www.wrcakron.com
SIC: **3625** 8711 Relays and industrial controls; Designing: ship, boat, machine, and product

(G-378)
YANKE BIONICS INC (PA)
303 W Exchange St (44302-1702)
PHONE..............................330 762-6411
Mark Yanke, *Pr*
Gary Charton, *
Jim Kraus, *
EMP: 44 **EST:** 1993
SQ FT: 15,000
SALES (est): 9.61MM
SALES (corp-wide): 9.61MM **Privately Held**
Web: www.yankebionics.com
SIC: **3842** Limbs, artificial

(G-379)
YOKOHAMA TWS NORTH AMERICA INC (DH)
Also Called: Trellborg Whl Systems Amrcas I
1501 Exeter Rd (44306-3889)
PHONE..............................866 633-8473
Alberto Crema, *Dir Fin*
◆ **EMP:** 40 **EST:** 1991
SQ FT: 600,000
SALES (est): 63.32MM
SALES (corp-wide): 4.26B **Privately Held**
SIC: **3011** 3061 Industrial tires, pneumatic; Mechanical rubber goods
HQ: Trelleborg Corporation
200 Veterans Blvd Ste 3
South Haven MI 49090
269 639-9891

(G-380)
YUGO MOLD INC
1733 Wadsworth Rd (44320-3141)
PHONE..............................330 606-0710
Zack Milkovich, *Pr*
Milo Milkovich, *VP*
Sam Milkovich, *Ch Bd*
EMP: 12 **EST:** 1985
SQ FT: 6,050
SALES (est): 302.05K **Privately Held**
SIC: **3544** Industrial molds

(G-381)
ZIEGLER TIRE AND SUPPLY CO
Also Called: Ziegler Tire Oil
547 Wolf Ledges Pkwy (44311-1091)
PHONE..............................330 434-7126
EMP: 9
SALES (corp-wide): 111.76MM **Privately Held**
Web: www.zieglertire.com
SIC: **5014** 5531 7534 Automobile tires and tubes; Automotive tires; Tire repair shop
PA: The Ziegler Tire And Supply Company
4150 Millennium Blvd Se
Massillon OH 44646
330 834-3332

Albany
Athens County

(G-382)
WEDGEWOOD CONNECT OHIO LLC ✪
2364 Blizzard Ln (45710-9287)
PHONE..............................800 331-8272
Marcy Bliss, *CEO*
Joseph Costa, *Pr*
Maria Kraus, *CFO*
EMP: 6 **EST:** 2023
SALES (est): 96.79K **Privately Held**
SIC: **2834** Pharmaceutical preparations

Alexandria
Licking County

(G-383)
COUNTRY OUTDOOR WD STOVES COWS
6040 Castle Rd (43001-9762)
PHONE..............................740 967-0315
Duane Larason, *Admn*
EMP: 6 **EST:** 2015
SALES (est): 85.87K **Privately Held**
SIC: **2499** Wood products, nec

Alger
Hardin County

(G-384)
WIWA LLC
107 N Main St (45812-8506)
P.O. Box 398 (45812-0398)
PHONE..............................419 757-0141
Jeffrey Wold, *Genl Mgr*
▲ **EMP:** 10 **EST:** 2001
SQ FT: 12,000
SALES (est): 3.25MM
SALES (corp-wide): 13.75MM **Privately Held**
Web: www.wiwausa.com
SIC: **3563** Spraying and dusting equipment
PA: Wiwa Wilhelm Wagner Gmbh & Co. Kg
Gewerbestr. 1-3
Lahnau HE 35633
64416090

(G-385)
WIWA LP
107 N Main St (45812-8506)
P.O. Box 398 (45812-0398)
PHONE..............................419 757-0141
EMP: 8 **EST:** 2011
SALES (est): 1.19MM **Privately Held**
Web: www.wiwausa.com
SIC: **3563** Robots for industrial spraying, painting, etc.

Alliance
Stark County

(G-386)
A R SCHOPPS SONS INC
14536 Oyster Rd (44601-9243)
P.O. Box 2513 (44601-0513)
PHONE..............................330 821-8406
Robert Schopp, *Pr*
David Schopp, *
Mary Schopp, *
▲ **EMP:** 50 **EST:** 1898
SQ FT: 3,084
SALES (est): 2.55MM **Privately Held**
Web: www.arschopp.com
SIC: **3931** Organ parts and materials

(G-387)
ACME INDUSTRIAL GROUP INC
540 N Freedom Ave (44601-1816)
P.O. Box 2388 (44601-0388)
PHONE..............................330 821-3900
Richard Burton Junior, *Pr*
Deborah Burton, *VP*
EMP: 23 **EST:** 1952
SALES (est): 418.56K **Privately Held**
SIC: **3471** Electroplating of metals or formed products

(G-388)
ACME SURFACE DYNAMICS INC
555 N Freedom Ave (44601-1873)
P.O. Box 2388 (44601-0388)
PHONE..............................330 821-3900
EMP: 10 **EST:** 2012
SALES (est): 1.19MM **Privately Held**
Web: www.acmesdi.com
SIC: **3312** Stainless steel

(G-389)
ALL COATINGS CO INC
510 W Ely St (44601-1610)
PHONE..............................330 821-3806

Alliance - Stark County (G-390)

Scott Brothers, *Pr*
Wanda Lou Brothers, *Sec*
EMP: 7 **EST:** 1998
SQ FT: 70,000
SALES (est): 910K **Privately Held**
Web: www.allcoatings.com
SIC: 2951 2851 Asphalt paving mixtures and blocks; Paints and paint additives

(G-390)
ALLIANCE ABRASIVES LLC
23649 State Route 62 (44601-9027)
P.O. Box 3447 (44601-7447)
PHONE.................................330 823-7957
▲ **EMP:** 15
Web: www.allianceabrasives.com
SIC: 3291 Abrasive products

(G-391)
ALLIANCE CASTINGS COMPANY LLC
1001 E Broadway St (44601-2602)
PHONE.................................330 829-5600
▲ **EMP:** 20 **EST:** 2003
SALES (est): 9.35MM
SALES (corp-wide): 3.96B **Privately Held**
SIC: 3743 Railroad equipment
HQ: Amsted Rail Company, Inc.
311 S Wacker Dr Ste 5300
Chicago IL 60606

(G-392)
ALLIANCE EQUIPMENT COMPANY INC
1000 N Union Ave (44601-1392)
PHONE.................................330 821-2291
Patricia Antonosanti, *Pr*
Matthew Antonosanti, *VP*
▲ **EMP:** 11 **EST:** 1982
SQ FT: 49,000
SALES (est): 2.41MM **Privately Held**
Web: www.alliance-equipment.com
SIC: 3089 Plastics and fiberglass tanks

(G-393)
ALLIANCE PUBLISHING CO INC (HQ)
Also Called: Review, The
40 S Linden Ave (44601-2447)
P.O. Box 9901 (44711-0901)
PHONE.................................330 453-1304
Chuck Dix, *Pr*
R Victor Dix, *
Robert C Dix, *
David E Dix, *
Timothy Dix, *
EMP: 125 **EST:** 1888
SQ FT: 25,000
SALES (est): 46.01MM
SALES (corp-wide): 467.21MM **Privately Held**
SIC: 2711 2752 Newspapers, publishing and printing; Commercial printing, lithographic
PA: Dix 1898, Inc.
212 E Liberty St
Wooster OH
330 264-3511

(G-394)
ALLIANCE REDI-MIX INC
22138 Hartley Rd (44601-9013)
PHONE.................................330 821-9244
Jeff Schrader, *null S*
EMP: 11 **EST:** 1999
SALES (est): 292.02K **Privately Held**
SIC: 3273 Ready-mixed concrete

(G-395)
BANCO DIE INC
11322 Union Ave Ne (44601-1398)
PHONE.................................330 821-8511
Michael Bresnahan, *Pr*
Joseph E Bender, *VP*
Patti Bresnahan, *Treas*
Martha Bender, *Sec*
Chris Carmen, *Mgr*
EMP: 17 **EST:** 1948
SQ FT: 7,500
SALES (est): 423.19K **Privately Held**
SIC: 3544 Special dies and tools

(G-396)
BUCKEYE PACKAGING CO INC
12223 Marlboro Ave Ne (44601-9772)
PHONE.................................330 935-0301
EMP: 80 **EST:** 1952
SALES (est): 9.56MM **Privately Held**
Web: www.buckeyepackaging.com
SIC: 2673 2759 3081 Bags: plastic, laminated, and coated; Commercial printing, nec; Packing materials, plastics sheet

(G-397)
C JS SIGNS
1670 Charl Ann Dr (44601-3688)
PHONE.................................330 821-7446
Christopher Liebhart, *Owner*
EMP: 6 **EST:** 1998
SALES (est): 257.58K **Privately Held**
Web: www.cjsigns.net
SIC: 3993 Signs and advertising specialties

(G-398)
CENTRAL COATED PRODUCTS INC
2025 Mccrea St (44601-2794)
P.O. Box 3348 (44601-7348)
PHONE.................................330 821-9830
Thomas A Tormey, *Pr*
Steven T Porter, *
Pamela Porter, *Stockholder**
Anne Tormey, *Stockholder**
▲ **EMP:** 60 **EST:** 1976
SQ FT: 77,500
SALES (est): 429.41K **Privately Held**
Web: www.centralcoated.com
SIC: 2672 2671 Paper; coated and laminated, nec; Paper, coated or laminated for packaging

(G-399)
CUSTOM POLY BAG LLC
9465 Edison St Ne (44601-9799)
PHONE.................................330 935-2408
EMP: 57 **EST:** 1969
SALES (est): 10.07MM
SALES (corp-wide): 433.54MM **Privately Held**
Web: www.ppcflex.com
SIC: 2673 3089 2759 Plastic bags: made from purchased materials; Extruded finished plastics products, nec; Flexographic printing
PA: Ppc Flexible Packaging, Llc
1111 Busch Pkwy
Buffalo Grove IL 60089
847 541-0000

(G-400)
DAMON INDUSTRIES INC (PA)
12435 Rockhill Ave Ne (44601-1065)
P.O. Box 2120 (44601-0120)
PHONE.................................330 821-5310
TOLL FREE: 800
◆ **EMP:** 90 **EST:** 1938
SALES (est): 8.37MM
SALES (corp-wide): 8.37MM **Privately Held**
Web: www.damonq.com
SIC: 2842 2899 3541 2879 Cleaning or polishing preparations, nec; Water treating compounds; Buffing and polishing machines; Agricultural chemicals, nec

(G-401)
DAVIS TECHNOLOGIES INC
Also Called: Dti
837 W Main St (44601-2208)
P.O. Box 2475 (44601-0475)
PHONE.................................330 823-2544
EMP: 12 **EST:** 1987
SQ FT: 7,500
SALES (est): 781.56K **Privately Held**
Web: www.moretraction.com
SIC: 8711 3625 Electrical or electronic engineering; Control equipment, electric

(G-402)
DOM TUBE CORP
640 Keystone St (44601-1886)
P.O. Box 2298 (44601-0298)
PHONE.................................412 299-2616
◆ **EMP:** 657
SIC: 3317 Seamless pipes and tubes

(G-403)
FILNOR INC (PA)
227 N Freedom Ave (44601-1897)
P.O. Box 2328 (44601-0328)
PHONE.................................330 821-8731
Ronald L Neely, *CEO*
James C Neely, *Pr*
Craig Clarke, *VP*
Daren Szekely, *VP*
Renee Shahaden, *Treas*
◆ **EMP:** 12 **EST:** 1970
SQ FT: 72,000
SALES (est): 8.63MM
SALES (corp-wide): 8.63MM **Privately Held**
Web: www.filnor.com
SIC: 3625 5063 Electric controls and control accessories, industrial; Electrical apparatus and equipment

(G-404)
FOREPLEASURE
14461 Gaskill Dr Ne (44601-1142)
PHONE.................................330 821-1293
EMP: 6 **EST:** 2001
SALES (est): 212.37K **Privately Held**
SIC: 2252 Hosiery, nec

(G-405)
GNW ALUMINUM INC
1356 Beeson St Ne (44601-6201)
P.O. Box 2418 (44601-0418)
PHONE.................................330 821-7955
Nathan Hoopes, *Pr*
Adam Hoopes, *
Beatrice K Hoopes, *
EMP: 40 **EST:** 2002
SALES (est): 6.56MM **Privately Held**
SIC: 3341 Aluminum smelting and refining (secondary)

(G-406)
HOLOPHANE CORPORATION
12720 Beech St Ne (44601-8778)
PHONE.................................330 823-5535
Steve Oyster, *Brnch Mgr*
EMP: 956
SALES (corp-wide): 3.95B **Publicly Held**
Web: holophane.acuitybrands.com
SIC: 3646 Commercial lighting fixtures
HQ: Holophane Corporation
3825 Columbus Rd Bldg A
Granville OH 43023

(G-407)
KEENER RUBBER COMPANY
14700 Commerce St Ne (44601-1035)
P.O. Box 2717 (44601-0717)
PHONE.................................330 821-1880
Richard A Michelson, *CEO*
EMP: 18 **EST:** 1956
SQ FT: 30,000
SALES (est): 1.96MM **Privately Held**
Web: www.keenerrubber.com
SIC: 3069 Rubber bands

(G-408)
MAC MANUFACTURING INC (HQ)
Also Called: Mac
14599 Commerce St Ne (44601)
PHONE.................................330 823-9900
Michael Conny, *Prin*
Dan Tubbs, *
Jenny Conny, *
Steve Hallas, *Prin*
Bill Ogden, *Prin*
▲ **EMP:** 700 **EST:** 1995
SALES (est): 108.7MM **Privately Held**
Web: www.mactrailer.com
SIC: 3715 5012 Truck trailers; Trailers for trucks, new and used
PA: Mac Trailer Manufacturing, Inc.
14599 Commerce St Ne
Alliance OH 44601

(G-409)
MAC STEEL TRAILER LTD
14599 Commerce St Ne (44601-1003)
PHONE.................................330 823-9900
Michael A Conny, *Managing Member*
EMP: 24 **EST:** 1999
SALES (est): 666.55K **Privately Held**
Web: www.mactrailer.com
SIC: 3715 Truck trailers

(G-410)
MAC STRAIGHT TRUCK BODIES INC
14599 Commerce St Ne (44601-1003)
PHONE.................................800 647-9424
EMP: 13 **EST:** 2019
SALES (est): 1.4MM **Privately Held**
Web: www.mactrailer.com
SIC: 3715 Truck trailers

(G-411)
MAC TRAILER MANUFACTURING INC (PA)
14599 Commerce St Ne (44601-1003)
PHONE.................................800 795-8454
Michael A Conny, *Pr*
Bill Ogden, *CFO*
◆ **EMP:** 1300 **EST:** 1992
SQ FT: 220,000
SALES (est): 182.08MM **Privately Held**
Web: www.mactrailer.com
SIC: 3715 5012 5013 5015 Truck trailers; Trailers for trucks, new and used; Motor vehicle supplies and new parts; Motor vehicle parts, used

(G-412)
MAC TRAILER SERVICE INC
14504 Commerce St Ne (44601-1000)
PHONE.................................330 823-9190
Michael Conny, *Pr*
EMP: 40 **EST:** 1997
SALES (est): 9.61MM **Privately Held**
Web: www.mactrailer.com
SIC: 3715 Truck trailers

(G-413)
MARLBORO MANUFACTURING INC
11750 Marlboro Ave Ne (44601-9798)
PHONE.................................330 935-2221

GEOGRAPHIC SECTION

Alliance - Stark County (G-437)

Thomas Naughton, *Pr*
Renee Milliken, *
Daniel Lough, *
Patrick Whitaker, *
▲ **EMP:** 50 **EST:** 1960
SQ FT: 54,000
SALES (est): 9.01MM **Privately Held**
Web: www.marlborohinge.com
SIC: 3429 Piano hardware

(G-414)
MORGAN ENGINEERING SYSTEMS INC
1182 E Summit St (44601-3224)
PHONE................330 821-4721
James Broch, *Brnch Mgr*
EMP: 38
SALES (corp-wide): 33.18MM **Privately Held**
Web: www.morganengineering.com
SIC: 3536 Cranes, overhead traveling
PA: Morgan Engineering Systems, Inc.
1049 S Mahoning Ave
Alliance OH 44601
330 823-6130

(G-415)
MORGAN ENGINEERING SYSTEMS INC (PA)
1049 S Mahoning Ave (44601-3212)
PHONE................330 823-6130
▼ **EMP:** 50 **EST:** 1868
SALES (est): 33.18MM
SALES (corp-wide): 33.18MM **Privately Held**
Web: www.morganengineering.com
SIC: 3536 Cranes, overhead traveling

(G-416)
MORGAN SITE SERVICES INC
1049 S Mahoning Ave (44601-3212)
PHONE................330 823-6120
Brian Mertes, *CEO*
EMP: 25
SALES (est): 1.25MM **Privately Held**
SIC: 3999 Manufacturing industries, nec

(G-417)
MYERS INDUSTRIES INC
Also Called: Trilogy Plastics
2290 W Main St (44601-2272)
PHONE................330 821-4700
Andrean Horton, *Pr*
EMP: 154
SALES (corp-wide): 813.07MM **Publicly Held**
Web: www.myersindustries.com
SIC: 3089 Injection molding of plastics
PA: Myers Industries, Inc.
1293 S Main St
Akron OH 44301
330 253-5592

(G-418)
PHILLIPS MFG & MCH CORP
118 1/2 E Ely St (44601-1809)
P.O. Box 2627 (44601-0627)
PHONE................330 823-9178
Deborah L Williamson, *Pr*
EMP: 9 **EST:** 1914
SQ FT: 20,000
SALES (est): 687.28K **Privately Held**
SIC: 3599 Machine shop, jobbing and repair

(G-419)
PITTMAN ENGINEERING INC
15835 Armour St Ne (44601-9349)
P.O. Box 3734 (44601-7734)
PHONE................330 821-4365
Michael Anstine, *Pr*
EMP: 18 **EST:** 1997
SQ FT: 23,000
SALES (est): 2.16MM **Privately Held**
Web: www.anstine.net
SIC: 3599 3441 Machine shop, jobbing and repair; Fabricated structural metal

(G-420)
PREMIER BANDAG 8 INC
1469 W Main St (44601-2153)
PHONE................330 823-3822
Will Tollerton, *Pr*
EMP: 13 **EST:** 1998
SALES (est): 835.18K **Privately Held**
SIC: 7534 Tire retreading and repair shops

(G-421)
PTC ALLIANCE LLC
640 Keystone St (44601-1886)
PHONE................330 821-5700
Peter Whiting, *Brnch Mgr*
EMP: 50
SALES (corp-wide): 54.57MM **Privately Held**
Web: www.ptcalliance.com
SIC: 3317 Steel pipe and tubes
HQ: Ptc Alliance Llc
6051 Wallace Road Ext # 200
Wexford PA 15090
412 299-7900

(G-422)
SAMS GRAPHIC INDUSTRIES
Also Called: Graphic Industries
611 Homeworth Rd (44601-9072)
PHONE................330 821-4710
Sam Schuette, *Owner*
EMP: 10 **EST:** 1966
SQ FT: 6,000
SALES (est): 468.9K **Privately Held**
SIC: 2796 2759 Engraving platemaking services; Engraving, nec

(G-423)
SANCAP LINER TECHNOLOGY INC
16125 Armour St Ne (44601-9301)
PHONE................330 821-1166
EMP: 90
SIC: 3081 Unsupported plastics film and sheet

(G-424)
SILMARILLION PARTNERS INC (PA)
2290 W Main St (44601-2272)
P.O. Box 2600 (44601-0600)
PHONE................330 821-4700
Stephen Osborn, *Pr*
Rex Roseberry, *
Bruce Frank, *
EMP: 152 **EST:** 1896
SQ FT: 90,000
SALES (est): 21.97MM
SALES (corp-wide): 21.97MM **Privately Held**
Web: www.myersengineeredsolutions.com
SIC: 3089 Injection molding of plastics

(G-425)
SMITH MACHINE INC
20651 Lake Park Blvd (44601-3319)
PHONE................330 821-9898
David F Smith, *Pr*
Eileen R Smith, *VP*
Tim Smith, *Genl Mgr*
EMP: 7 **EST:** 1976
SALES (est): 782.5K **Privately Held**
SIC: 3599 Machine shop, jobbing and repair

(G-426)
SPECIALTY MFG & SERVICE
12280 Rockhill Ave Ne (44601-1064)
P.O. Box 2928 (44601-0928)
PHONE................330 821-4675
EMP: 6 **EST:** 2018
SALES (est): 95.57K **Privately Held**
SIC: 3999 Manufacturing industries, nec

(G-427)
STEEL EQP SPECIALISTS INC (PA)
Also Called: S.E.S. Engineering
1507 Beeson St Ne (44601-2142)
PHONE................330 823-8260
James R Boughton, *CEO*
T Virgil Huggett, *Ch Bd*
Donald Watkins, *Ex VP*
Wayne W Weisenburger, *VP*
Allan Wolfgang, *VP*
▲ **EMP:** 72 **EST:** 1976
SQ FT: 32,000
SALES (est): 27.78MM
SALES (corp-wide): 27.78MM **Privately Held**
Web: www.seseng.com
SIC: 7699 3599 7629 3593 Industrial machinery and equipment repair; Custom machinery; Electrical repair shops; Fluid power cylinders and actuators

(G-428)
STUCHELL PRODUCTS LLC
Also Called: Sare Plastics
12240 Rockhill Ave Ne (44601-1064)
PHONE................330 821-4299
EMP: 45 **EST:** 2005
SALES (est): 9.8MM **Privately Held**
Web: www.sareplastics.com
SIC: 3089 Injection molded finished plastics products, nec

(G-429)
SUN AMERICA LLC
46 N Rockhill Ave (44601-2211)
PHONE................330 821-6300
Dwayne Robinson, *CFO*
EMP: 26 **EST:** 2018
SALES (est): 9.68MM **Privately Held**
Web: www.sun-america.com
SIC: 2671 Paper; coated and laminated packaging

(G-430)
SUNAMERICACONVERTING LLC
46 N Rockhill Ave (44601-2211)
PHONE................330 821-6300
▲ **EMP:** 55 **EST:** 2004
SQ FT: 72,000
SALES (est): 8.47MM **Privately Held**
Web: www.sun-america.com
SIC: 2656 Paper cups, plates, dishes, and utensils

(G-431)
T & W FORGE INC
Also Called: T & W Forge
562 W Ely St (44601-6409)
EMP: 60
Web: www.pair.com
SIC: 3462 Iron and steel forgings

(G-432)
T AND W STAMPING ACQUISITION (PA)
930 W Ely St (44601-1500)
PHONE................330 821-5777
EMP: 6 **EST:** 2017
SALES (est): 211.98K
SALES (corp-wide): 211.98K **Privately Held**
SIC: 3469 Stamping metal for the trade

(G-433)
TRAILSTAR INTERNATIONAL INC (PA)
Also Called: Trailstar
20700 Harrisburg Westville Rd (44601)
P.O. Box 2086 (44601-0086)
PHONE................330 821-9900
Michael Conny, *CEO*
Tom Hahn, *Pr*
EMP: 76 **EST:** 2012
SALES (est): 10.7MM
SALES (corp-wide): 10.7MM **Privately Held**
Web: www.trailstarintl.com
SIC: 3715 Truck trailers

(G-434)
TRILOGY PLASTICS ALLIANCE INC
Also Called: Trilogy Plastics
2290 W Main St (44601-2272)
P.O. Box 2600 (44601-0600)
PHONE................330 821-4700
EMP: 21 **EST:** 2005
SALES (est): 2.18MM
SALES (corp-wide): 813.07MM **Publicly Held**
Web: www.myersengineeredsolutions.com
SIC: 3089 Injection molding of plastics
PA: Myers Industries, Inc.
1293 S Main St
Akron OH 44301
330 253-5592

(G-435)
W J EGLI COMPANY INC (PA)
205 E Columbia St (44601-2563)
P.O. Box 2605 (44601-0605)
PHONE................330 823-3666
William J Egli, *Pr*
Garth Egli, *VP*
Cheryl A Stuffel, *Sec*
▼ **EMP:** 15 **EST:** 1968
SQ FT: 100,000
SALES (est): 2.41MM
SALES (corp-wide): 2.41MM **Privately Held**
Web: www.wjegli.com
SIC: 2541 3496 3498 3444 Display fixtures, wood; Miscellaneous fabricated wire products; Fabricated pipe and fittings; Sheet metalwork

(G-436)
WHITACRE GREER COMPANY (PA)
1400 S Mahoning Ave (44601-3433)
P.O. Box 2960 (44601-0960)
PHONE................330 823-1610
J B Whitacre Junior, *Ch Bd*
Janet Kaboth, *Vice Chairman*
L A Morrison, *
EMP: 38 **EST:** 1916
SALES (est): 12.96MM
SALES (corp-wide): 12.96MM **Privately Held**
Web: www.wgpaver.com
SIC: 3251 3255 Paving brick, clay; Clay refractories

(G-437)
WIELAND METAL SVCS FOILS LLC
2081 Mccrea St (44601-2704)
PHONE................330 823-1700
Kevin Bense, *Pr*
Robert M James, *VP*
Marc R Bacon, *CFO*
Greg Keown, *Genl Mgr*
▲ **EMP:** 53 **EST:** 1986
SQ FT: 80,000

Alliance - Stark County (G-438)

SALES (est): 28.04MM **Privately Held**
SIC: 3341 3353 3471 3497 Secondary nonferrous metals; Aluminum sheet, plate, and foil; Plating and polishing; Metal foil and leaf
HQ: Wieland Metal Services, Llc
301 Metro Center Blvd # 204
Warwick RI 02886
401 736-2600

(G-438)
WINKLE INDUSTRIES INC
2080 W Main St (44601-2187)
PHONE..................................330 823-9730
Joe Schatz, *CEO*
Beth A Felger, *
Christina M Schatz, *
▲ **EMP:** 55 **EST:** 1949
SQ FT: 85,000
SALES (est): 11.57MM **Privately Held**
Web: www.winkleindustries.com
SIC: 7699 3499 5063 Industrial machinery and equipment repair; Magnets, permanent: metallic; Control and signal wire and cable, including coaxial

Alpha
Greene County

(G-439)
UNISON INDUSTRIES LLC
2070 Heller Rd (45301)
PHONE..................................937 426-0621
EMP: 11 **EST:** 1998
SALES (est): 309.4K **Privately Held**
Web: www.unisonindustries.com
SIC: 7699 3315 Typewriter repair, including electric; Steel wire and related products

Alvada
Seneca County

(G-440)
B M MACHINE (PA)
11722 W County Road 6 (44802-9721)
PHONE..................................419 595-2898
Robert Mathias, *Owner*
EMP: 6 **EST:** 1998
SALES (est): 904.52K
SALES (corp-wide): 904.52K **Privately Held**
Web: www.bmmachine.com
SIC: 3599 Machine shop, jobbing and repair

(G-441)
BR PALLET INC
21395 County Road 7 (44802-9620)
P.O. Box 68 (44802-0068)
PHONE..................................419 427-2200
Carl Ruehle, *Ch*
Dwayne Hoschar, *
Bryan Ruhle, *
EMP: 36 **EST:** 1990
SQ FT: 1,500
SALES (est): 2.2MM **Privately Held**
SIC: 2448 Pallets, wood

(G-442)
CIRCUIT BOARD MINING LLC
23546 Us Highway 224 (44802-9641)
PHONE..................................419 348-1057
EMP: 6 **EST:** 2021
SALES (est): 446.95K **Privately Held**
SIC: 3341 Secondary nonferrous metals

(G-443)
MIDWEST LASER SYSTEMS INC
Also Called: MLS Systems
4777 S Us Highway 23 (44802-9702)
PHONE..................................419 424-0062
Chad Bouillon, *Pr*
William J Hunter, *
EMP: 25 **EST:** 1980
SALES (est): 2.93MM **Privately Held**
Web: www.mlssystems.com
SIC: 3599 3549 Custom machinery; Metalworking machinery, nec

Alvordton
Williams County

(G-444)
PIONEER INDUSTRIAL SYSTEMS LLC (PA)
16442 Us Highway 20 (43501-9707)
PHONE..................................419 737-9506
Todd Hendricks Senior, *Pr*
▲ **EMP:** 7 **EST:** 2003
SQ FT: 7,500
SALES (est): 4.99MM
SALES (corp-wide): 4.99MM **Privately Held**
Web: www.pioneerindsys.com
SIC: 3599 Machine shop, jobbing and repair

Amanda
Fairfield County

(G-445)
CLEAR CREEK SCREW MACHINE CO
4900 Julian Rd Sw (43102-9514)
PHONE..................................740 969-2113
George Bartrom, *Pr*
EMP: 8 **EST:** 1959
SQ FT: 15,000
SALES (est): 986.88K **Privately Held**
SIC: 3599 3451 Machine shop, jobbing and repair; Screw machine products

(G-446)
MID-WEST FABRICATING CO (PA)
Also Called: Mid West Fabricating Co
313 N Johns St (43102-9002)
PHONE..................................740 969-4411
Jennifer Johns Friel, *Pr*
Julia Johns, *
Ann Custer, *
♦ **EMP:** 125 **EST:** 1945
SQ FT: 280,000
SALES (est): 28.07MM
SALES (corp-wide): 28.07MM **Privately Held**
Web: www.midwestfab.com
SIC: 3496 Miscellaneous fabricated wire products

Amelia
Clermont County

(G-447)
A & A SAFETY INC (PA)
1126 Ferris Rd (45102-1892)
PHONE..................................513 943-6100
William N Luttmer, *Pr*
Francis Luttmer, *
EMP: 50 **EST:** 1979
SQ FT: 12,300
SALES (est): 22.88MM
SALES (corp-wide): 22.88MM **Privately Held**
Web: www.aasafetyinc.com
SIC: 7359 3993 5084 1721 Work zone traffic equipment (flags, cones, barrels, etc.); Signs and advertising specialties; Safety equipment; Painting and paper hanging

(G-448)
ACREO INC
3209 Marshall Dr (45102-9213)
P.O. Box 361 (45157-0361)
PHONE..................................513 734-3327
Roger Williams, *Pr*
EMP: 7 **EST:** 1994
SQ FT: 10,000
SALES (est): 415.49K **Privately Held**
SIC: 7389 3556 Design, commercial and industrial; Food products machinery

(G-449)
ALCON INC (HQ)
1132 Ferris Rd (45102-1020)
PHONE..................................513 722-1037
Michael Ball, *Ch*
EMP: 40 **EST:** 1967
SQ FT: 15,000
SALES (est): 1.36B **Privately Held**
Web: www.alcon-inc.net
SIC: 3643 Connectors and terminals for electrical devices
PA: Alcon Ag
0
Freiburg FR 1701

(G-450)
ALL WRITE RIBBON INC
3916 Bach Buxton Rd (45102-1014)
P.O. Box 67 (45102-0067)
PHONE..................................513 753-8300
William E Lyon, *Pr*
Harold Wolfe, *
▲ **EMP:** 16 **EST:** 1981
SQ FT: 20,000
SALES (est): 946.47K **Privately Held**
Web: www.allwriteribbon.com
SIC: 3955 Print cartridges for laser and other computer printers

(G-451)
AMELIA PLASTICS
3202 Marshall Dr Bldg 8 (45102-9212)
PHONE..................................513 386-4926
EMP: 6 **EST:** 2016
SALES (est): 228.22K **Privately Held**
SIC: 3089 Injection molding of plastics

(G-452)
AMON INC
3214 Marshall Dr (45102-9212)
PHONE..................................513 734-1700
EMP: 39 **EST:** 1994
SALES (est): 478.14K **Privately Held**
SIC: 3599 Machine shop, jobbing and repair

(G-453)
ASAP READY MIX INC
250 Mount Holly Rd (45102-9740)
PHONE..................................513 797-1774
Dan Dunham, *Prin*
EMP: 8 **EST:** 2009
SALES (est): 197.55K **Privately Held**
SIC: 3273 Ready-mixed concrete

(G-454)
DEIMLING/JELIHO PLASTICS INC
4010 Bach Buxton Rd (45102-1048)
PHONE..................................513 752-6653
William Deimling, *Pr*
Mary Ann Deimling, *
▼ **EMP:** 83 **EST:** 1975
SQ FT: 60,000
SALES (est): 18.54MM **Privately Held**
Web: www.deimling-jeliho.com
SIC: 3089 3599 Injection molding of plastics; Machine shop, jobbing and repair

(G-455)
GREENS PURE COATINGS LLC
1186 Sycamore Ln (45102-1232)
PHONE..................................513 907-2765
Nicholas Green, *Prin*
EMP: 6 **EST:** 2018
SALES (est): 179.65K **Privately Held**
SIC: 3479 Metal coating and allied services

(G-456)
HARRISON WELDING SERVICES LLC
3462 Winter Holly Dr (45102-8006)
PHONE..................................513 405-6581
Zachary Harrison, *Prin*
EMP: 6 **EST:** 2018
SALES (est): 26.00K **Privately Held**
Web: www.hwscincy.com
SIC: 7692 Welding repair

(G-457)
JLC INDUSTRIAL LLC
3048 Bachelier Rd (45102-2302)
PHONE..................................513 236-0462
Jamie Callihan, *Admn*
EMP: 6 **EST:** 2009
SALES (est): 392.04K **Privately Held**
Web: www.jlcindustrial.com
SIC: 3599 Machine shop, jobbing and repair

(G-458)
KOEBBE PRODUCTS INC (PA)
1132 Ferris Rd (45102-1020)
PHONE..................................513 753-4200
Dick Koebbe, *Pr*
EMP: 60 **EST:** 1969
SQ FT: 38,400
SALES (est): 19.74MM
SALES (corp-wide): 19.74MM **Privately Held**
Web: www.egerproducts.com
SIC: 3644 3544 5039 Insulators and insulation materials, electrical; Forms (molds), for foundry and plastics working machinery; Ceiling systems and products

(G-459)
LT MOSES WILLARD INC
3972 Bach Buxton Rd (45102-1099)
PHONE..................................513 248-5500
Christopher L Nordloh, *Pr*
EMP: 32 **EST:** 1965
SQ FT: 18,000
SALES (est): 2.92MM **Privately Held**
SIC: 3645 Residential lighting fixtures

(G-460)
MOBILE CONVERSIONS INC
3354 State Route 132 (45102-2249)
PHONE..................................513 797-1991
EMP: 14 **EST:** 1994
SQ FT: 2,176
SALES (est): 2.44MM **Privately Held**
Web: www.mobileconversions.com
SIC: 7532 2451 Van conversion; Mobile homes

(G-461)
PRINTINK INC
3976 Bach Buxton Rd (45102-1014)
PHONE..................................513 943-0599
Glenn Pearson, *Pr*
EMP: 9 **EST:** 2000
SQ FT: 25,000
SALES (est): 889.53K **Privately Held**
SIC: 2893 Printing ink

(G-462)
ROMANS MOBILE WELDING LLC
1238 Nottingham Rd (45102-9207)
PHONE.................................513 603-0961
Roman Calderon, *Managing Member*
EMP: 6
SALES (est): 78.58K **Privately Held**
SIC: 3548 7389 Welding apparatus; Business services, nec

(G-463)
S DH FLOW CONTRO LS LLC
1118 Ferris Rd (45102-1002)
PHONE.................................513 834-8432
EMP: 7 **EST:** 2012
SALES (est): 353.47K **Privately Held**
Web: www.sdhflowcontrols.com
SIC: 3491 Industrial valves

(G-464)
SANREED MANAGEMENT GROUP LLC
Also Called: Alcon Connectors
1132 Ferris Rd (45102-1020)
PHONE.................................513 722-1037
EMP: 4585 **EST:** 2019
SALES (est): 71.45MM **Privately Held**
SIC: 3643 Connectors and terminals for electrical devices

(G-465)
SOUTHERN OHIO MFG INC
3214 Marshall Dr (45102-9212)
PHONE.................................513 943-2555
Dave Rechtin, *Pr*
EMP: 27 **EST:** 1984
SALES (est): 379.87K **Privately Held**
Web: www.southernohiomfg.com
SIC: 3599 Machine shop, jobbing and repair

(G-466)
STEWART FILMSCREEN CORP
3919 Bach Buxton Rd (45102-1013)
PHONE.................................513 753-0800
Grant Stewart, *Pr*
EMP: 40
SALES (corp-wide): 26.51MM **Privately Held**
Web: www.stewartfilmscreen.com
SIC: 3861 Screens, projection
PA: Stewart Filmscreen Corp.
   1161 Sepulveda Blvd
   Torrance CA 90502
   310 784-5300

(G-467)
SUN CHEMICAL CORPORATION
Colors Dispersion Division
3922 Bach Buxton Rd (45102-1098)
PHONE.................................513 753-9550
Edward Polaski, *Mgr*
EMP: 67
SQ FT: 7,200
Web: www.sunchemical.com
SIC: 2893 2865 Printing ink; Cyclic crudes and intermediates
HQ: Sun Chemical Corporation
   35 Waterview Blvd Ste 104
   Parsippany NJ 07054
   973 404-6000

(G-468)
TRI STATE COREBUYERS LLC
1427 Glenwood Ct (45102-2553)
PHONE.................................513 288-8063
Joshua Mckinney, *Brnch Mgr*
EMP: 10
SALES (corp-wide): 55.56K **Privately Held**
SIC: 3714 Motor vehicle parts and accessories
PA: Tri State Corebuyers Llc
   906 Staghorn Dr
   Cincinnati OH

(G-469)
TRI-STATE FABRICATORS INC
1146 Ferris Rd (45102-1020)
PHONE.................................513 752-5005
Richard Mark Vogt, *Pr*
Jeffrey G Vogt, *
Joanne Vogt, *
Jay Richard Vogt, *
EMP: 50 **EST:** 1983
SQ FT: 120,000
SALES (est): 10.84MM **Privately Held**
Web: www.tristatefabricators.com
SIC: 3441 3444 3471 3479 Fabricated structural metal; Sheet metalwork; Plating and polishing; Painting of metal products

(G-470)
WELLEX AMG
3214 Marshall Dr (45102-9212)
PHONE.................................513 734-1700
EMP: 6 **EST:** 2012
SALES (est): 126.33K **Privately Held**
Web: www.wellexmfg.com
SIC: 3599 Machine shop, jobbing and repair

(G-471)
WELLEX MANUFACTURING INC
3214 Marshall Dr (45102-9212)
PHONE.................................513 734-1700
John Born, *Pr*
David Uible, *Pr*
John Born, *Pr*
Marliese Born, *Prin*
EMP: 7 **EST:** 1963
SQ FT: 3,400
SALES (est): 895.47K **Privately Held**
Web: www.wellexmfg.com
SIC: 3599 Machine shop, jobbing and repair

Amesville
Athens County

(G-472)
THIRD SALVO COMPANY
16355 Tick Ridge Rd (45711-9522)
PHONE.................................740 818-9669
Joseph Gillespie, *Prin*
EMP: 9 **EST:** 2017
SALES (est): 498.59K **Privately Held**
SIC: 1741 1521 1389 1542 Foundation and retaining wall construction; Single-family housing construction; Construction, repair, and dismantling services; Garage construction

Amherst
Lorain County

(G-473)
CLOVERVALE FARMS LLC (DH)
Also Called: Clovervale Foods
8133 Cooper Foster Park Rd (44001)
PHONE.................................440 960-0146
Richard Cawrse Junior, *Pr*
Suzanne Graham, *
Richard Cecil, *
EMP: 100 **EST:** 1920
SQ FT: 38,000
SALES (est): 28.27MM
SALES (corp-wide): 52.88B **Publicly Held**
Web: clovervalefarms.openfos.com
SIC: 2032 2033 2038 0191 Puddings, except meat: packaged in cans, jars, etc.; Fruits: packaged in cans, jars, etc.; Frozen specialties, nec; General farms, primarily crop
HQ: Advancepierre Foods, Inc.
   9990 Prnceton Glendale Rd
   West Chester OH 45246
   513 874-8741

(G-474)
CURRIER RICHARD & JAMES
Also Called: Amherst Party Shop
540 Mcintosh Ln (44001-3108)
P.O. Box 500 (44001-0500)
PHONE.................................440 988-4132
Richard Currier, *Pt*
James Currier, *Pt*
EMP: 6 **EST:** 1954
SALES (est): 491.32K **Privately Held**
Web: www.amherstpartyshop.com
SIC: 5921 2086 Beer (packaged); Bottled and canned soft drinks

(G-475)
DURAY MACHINE COMPANY INC
400 Ravenglass Blvd (44001-2383)
PHONE.................................440 277-4119
Wayne Duray, *Pr*
Janet Dadas, *Sec*
EMP: 10 **EST:** 1961
SQ FT: 18,000
SALES (est): 650.81K **Privately Held**
SIC: 3599 7692 Machine shop, jobbing and repair; Welding repair

(G-476)
ECO FUEL SOLUTION LLC
779 Sunrise Dr (44001-1660)
PHONE.................................440 282-8592
James Bodnar, *Prin*
EMP: 6 **EST:** 2011
SALES (est): 110.92K **Privately Held**
SIC: 2869 Fuels

(G-477)
KTM NORTH AMERICA INC (PA)
Also Called: Gasgas North America
1119 Milan Ave (44001-1319)
PHONE.................................855 215-6360
Di Stefan Pierer, *CEO*
Rod Bush, *
Selvaraj Narayana, *
John S Harden, *
Jon-erik Burleson, *Treas*
▲ **EMP:** 87 **EST:** 1992
SQ FT: 5,000
SALES (est): 53.86M **Privately Held**
Web: www.ktm.com
SIC: 5012 3751 Motorcycles; Motorcycles, bicycles and parts

(G-478)
NORDSON CORPORATION
300 Nordson Dr (44001-2422)
PHONE.................................440 985-4496
Wendy Jordan, *Brnch Mgr*
EMP: 432
SALES (corp-wide): 2.63B **Publicly Held**
Web: www.nordson.com
SIC: 3563 Air and gas compressors
PA: Nordson Corporation
   28601 Clemens Rd
   Westlake OH 44145
   440 892-1580

(G-479)
NORDSON CORPORATION
444 Gordon Ave Dock C1-C3 (44001)
PHONE.................................440 985-4458
EMP: 32
SALES (corp-wide): 2.63B **Publicly Held**
Web: www.nordson.com
SIC: 3563 Spraying outfits: metals, paints, and chemicals (compressor)
PA: Nordson Corporation
   28601 Clemens Rd
   Westlake OH 44145
   440 892-1580

(G-480)
NORDSON CORPORATION
100 Nordson Dr M 81 (44001-2454)
PHONE.................................440 985-4000
Michael Hilton, *Pr*
EMP: 500
SALES (corp-wide): 2.63B **Publicly Held**
Web: www.nordson.com
SIC: 3563 Spraying outfits: metals, paints, and chemicals (compressor)
PA: Nordson Corporation
   28601 Clemens Rd
   Westlake OH 44145
   440 892-1580

(G-481)
PAPA JOES PIES INC (PA)
Also Called: Mama Jo Homestyle Pies
1969 Cooper Foster Park Rd (44001-1207)
PHONE.................................440 960-7437
Johanna Mann, *Pr*
EMP: 11 **EST:** 1993
SALES (est): 1.22MM
SALES (corp-wide): 1.22MM **Privately Held**
Web: www.mamajopies.com
SIC: 2051 Pies, bakery: except frozen

(G-482)
PRO IMAGE SIGN & DESIGN INC
8087 Leavitt Rd (44001-2711)
PHONE.................................440 986-8888
EMP: 22
SALES (corp-wide): 67.16K **Privately Held**
Web: www.proimagesign.com
SIC: 3993 Signs and advertising specialties
PA: Pro Image Sign & Design, Inc.
   5349 Oakwood Dr
   Sheffield Village OH 44054
   216 403-7727

Andover
Ashtabula County

(G-483)
ADVANCED TECHNOLOGY CORP
101 Parker Dr (44003-9456)
PHONE.................................440 293-4064
Seymour S Stein, *Ch Bd*
Anthony Stavole, *
Sherry Epstein, *
◆ **EMP:** 17 **EST:** 1951
SQ FT: 220,000
SALES (est): 7.61MM
SALES (corp-wide): 43.51MM **Privately Held**
Web: www.atc-lighting-plastics.com
SIC: 3647 3469 Vehicular lighting equipment; Metal stampings, nec
HQ: Atc Lighting & Plastics, Inc.
   101 Parker Dr
   Andover OH 44003

(G-484)
ATC GROUP INC (PA)
Also Called: Atc Lighting & Plastics
101 Parker Dr (44003-9456)
P.O. Box 1120 (44003-1120)
PHONE.................................440 293-4064
Seymour S Stein Ph.d., *Pr*

Andover - Ashtabula County (G-485)

Sherry Epstein, *
▲ EMP: 100 EST: 1984
SQ FT: 50,000
SALES (est): 43.51MM
SALES (corp-wide): 43.51MM Privately Held
Web: www.oneatlas.com
SIC: 3647 3089 3841 Vehicular lighting equipment; Injection molded finished plastics products, nec; Surgical and medical instruments

(G-485)
ATC LIGHTING & PLASTICS INC (HQ)
Also Called: Kdlamp Company
101 Parker Dr (44003-9456)
P.O. Box 1120 (44003-1120)
PHONE..................440 466-7670
Seymour S Stein Ph.d., Ch Bd
▲ EMP: 155 EST: 1991
SALES (est): 24.23MM
SALES (corp-wide): 43.51MM Privately Held
Web: www.atc-lighting-plastics.com
SIC: 3647 3714 3713 3648 Motor vehicle lighting equipment; Motor vehicle parts and accessories; Truck and bus bodies; Lighting equipment, nec
PA: Atc Group, Inc.
    101 Parker Dr
    Andover OH 44003
    440 293-4064

(G-486)
K-D LAMP COMPANY
Also Called: Etc Lighthing and Plastic
101 Parker Dr (44003-9456)
PHONE..................440 293-4064
Seymour Stein, Treas
Doctor Seymour Stein, Pr
Sherry Epstein, *
▲ EMP: 49 EST: 2005
SALES (est): 16.33MM
SALES (corp-wide): 43.51MM Privately Held
SIC: 3647 Headlights (fixtures), vehicular
PA: Atc Group, Inc.
    101 Parker Dr
    Andover OH 44003
    440 293-4064

(G-487)
LIGHTING PRODUCTS INC
101 Parker Dr (44003-9456)
P.O. Box 1120 (44003-1120)
PHONE..................440 293-4064
▲ EMP: 6 EST: 1994
SALES (est): 6.36MM
SALES (corp-wide): 43.51MM Privately Held
Web: www.atc-lighting-plastics.com
SIC: 3647 Motor vehicle lighting equipment
HQ: Atc Lighting & Plastics, Inc.
    101 Parker Dr
    Andover OH 44003

Anna
Shelby County

(G-488)
AGRANA FRUIT US INC
16197 County Road 25a (45302-9498)
PHONE..................937 693-3821
Jeff Elliot, Mgr
EMP: 150
SALES (corp-wide): 68.66MM Privately Held
Web: us.agrana.com
SIC: 8734 2099 2087 Food testing service; Food preparations, nec; Flavoring extracts and syrups, nec
HQ: Agrana Fruit Us, Inc.
    6850 Southpointe Pkwy
    Brecksville OH 44141
    440 546-1199

(G-489)
CHILLTEX LLC
Also Called: Honeywell Authorized Dealer
7440 Hoying Rd (45302-9616)
PHONE..................937 710-3308
Matt Eilerman, Prin
EMP: 9 EST: 2005
SALES (est): 1.79MM Privately Held
Web: www.chilltexllc.com
SIC: 3585 Heating equipment, complete

(G-490)
L & O TIRE SERVICE INC
14555 State Route 119 E (45302-9416)
PHONE..................937 394-8462
Paul Opperman, Pr
Shirley Opperman, Sec
EMP: 8 EST: 1981
SQ FT: 4,000
SALES (est): 496.39K Privately Held
Web: www.lotireservice.com
SIC: 5531 5014 7534 7538 Automotive tires; Automobile tires and tubes; Tire repair shop; General truck repair

Antwerp
Paulding County

(G-491)
ANTWERP TOOL & DIE INC
3167 County Road 424 (45813-9416)
P.O. Box 712 (45813-0712)
PHONE..................419 258-5271
Gerald A Snyder, Pr
EMP: 15 EST: 1985
SQ FT: 10,500
SALES (est): 1.69MM Privately Held
Web: www.antwerptool.com
SIC: 3544 3545 Special dies and tools; Machine tool accessories

(G-492)
ATWOOD MOBILE PRODUCTS LLC
5406 County Road 424 (45813)
PHONE..................419 258-5531
EMP: 81
SALES (corp-wide): 2.84B Privately Held
Web: www.dometic.com
SIC: 3714 Motor vehicle parts and accessories
HQ: Atwood Mobile Products Llc
    1120 N Main St
    Elkhart IN 46514

(G-493)
K & L TOOL INC
5141 County Road 424 (45813)
P.O. Box 1086 (45813-1086)
PHONE..................419 258-2086
Kirk L Hopkins, Pr
Laurel Hopkins, VP
EMP: 20 EST: 1977
SQ FT: 4,500
SALES (est): 516.37K Privately Held
SIC: 3542 3544 Bending machines; Special dies and tools

(G-494)
WEST BEND PRINTING & PUBG INC
101 N Main St (45813-8406)
P.O. Box 1008 (45813-1008)
PHONE..................419 258-2000
Bryce Steiner, Pr
EMP: 6 EST: 2005
SQ FT: 3,000
SALES (est): 402.28K Privately Held
Web: www.westbendprinting.com
SIC: 2752 Offset printing

Apple Creek
Wayne County

(G-495)
BUCKEYE WOODWORKING
5556 Mount Hope Rd (44606-9340)
PHONE..................330 698-1070
Wayne Hershberger, Prin
EMP: 6 EST: 2008
SALES (est): 270.46K Privately Held
SIC: 2431 Millwork

(G-496)
COBLENTZ BROTHERS INC
7101 S Kohler Rd (44606-9613)
PHONE..................330 857-7211
Wayne Liechty, Pr
Jonas Coblentz, *
Ray Coblentz, *
EMP: 28 EST: 1961
SQ FT: 20,100
SALES (est): 6.64MM Privately Held
Web: www.coblentzpallet.com
SIC: 2448 2421 Pallets, wood; Sawmills and planing mills, general

(G-497)
CROWNPLACE BRANDS LTD
Also Called: Crown Place Brands
13110 Emerson Rd (44606-9813)
PHONE..................888 332-5534
Clint M Leibolt, Managing Member
▲ EMP: 7 EST: 2012
SALES (est): 218.18K Privately Held
Web: www.efel-usa.com
SIC: 5932 5947 5399 3949 Antiques; Gift shop; Country general stores; Fishing equipment

(G-498)
ELDORADO STONE LLC
Stone Craft
167 Maple St (44606-9599)
PHONE..................330 698-3931
Melanie Garcia, Mgr
EMP: 30
Web: www.eldoradostone.com
SIC: 3272 1771 Concrete products, precast, nec; Concrete work
HQ: Eldorado Stone Llc
    3817 Ocean Ranch Blvd # 114
    Oceanside CA 92056
    800 925-1491

(G-499)
ELY ROAD REEL COMPANY LTD
9081 Ely Rd (44606-9320)
PHONE..................330 683-1818
Marvin Weaver, Pt
Robert Weaver, *
EMP: 25 EST: 1987
SQ FT: 16,000
SALES (est): 2.19MM Privately Held
Web: www.elyroadreel.com
SIC: 2499 Spools, reels, and pulleys: wood

(G-500)
FOUNTAIN NOOK WOODCRAFT
5528 Fountain Nook Rd (44606-9748)
PHONE..................330 473-2162
EMP: 6 EST: 2008
SALES (est): 92.22K Privately Held
SIC: 2511 Wood household furniture

(G-501)
GROSS LUMBER INC
8848 Ely Rd (44606-9799)
PHONE..................330 683-2055
Rick Grossniklaus, Pr
Don Grossniklaus, *
Rick Grossniklaus, VP
EMP: 15 EST: 1957
SQ FT: 30,000
SALES (est): 426.69K Privately Held
Web: www.jlgrosslumber.com
SIC: 2448 5031 5099 2426 Pallets, wood; Lumber: rough, dressed, and finished; Wood and wood by-products; Hardwood dimension and flooring mills

(G-502)
JAE TECH INC
32 Hunter St (44606-9600)
PHONE..................330 698-2000
Ian Cameron, Prin
EMP: 55 EST: 2000
SQ FT: 37,500
SALES (est): 9.89MM Privately Held
Web: www.jaetechinc.com
SIC: 3714 Axle housings and shafts, motor vehicle

(G-503)
L E SOMMER KIDRON INC
6856 Kidron Rd (44606-9326)
P.O. Box 230 (44636-0230)
PHONE..................330 857-2031
Glenford Steiner, Pr
EMP: 8 EST: 1997
SALES (est): 198.21K Privately Held
Web: www.lesommerkidron.com
SIC: 2048 Livestock feeds

(G-504)
MCKAY-GROSS DIVISION
8848 Ely Rd (44606-9319)
PHONE..................330 683-2055
EMP: 12 EST: 2016
SALES (est): 721.99K Privately Held
SIC: 2426 Lumber, hardwood dimension

(G-505)
MILLWOOD INC
Also Called: Litco Wood Products
8208 S Kohler Rd (44606-9420)
PHONE..................330 857-3075
Ely Miller, Brnch Mgr
EMP: 69
Web: www.millwoodinc.com
SIC: 2448 Pallets, wood
PA: Millwood, Inc.
    3708 International Blvd
    Vienna OH 44473

(G-506)
MILLWOOD INCORPORATED
13407 Dover Rd (44606-9387)
PHONE..................330 704-6707
Lionel Trebilcock, Pr
EMP: 10 EST: 1998
SALES (est): 546.3K Privately Held
Web: www.millwoodinc.com
SIC: 2448 Pallets, wood

(G-507)
MOWHAWK LUMBER LTD
2931 S Carr Rd (44606-9306)
PHONE..................330 698-5333
EMP: 20 EST: 2008
SALES (est): 1.25MM Privately Held
Web: www.mohawklumber.com

SIC: 2421 Sawmills and planing mills, general

(G-508)
OMEGA CEMENTING CO
3776 S Millborne Rd (44606-9757)
P.O. Box 357 (44606-0357)
PHONE.................................330 695-7147
Donald Gaddis, *CEO*
EMP: 7 **EST:** 1986
SQ FT: 3,000
SALES (est): 926.95K **Privately Held**
SIC: 1389 1081 7349 Well plugging and abandoning, oil and gas; Metal mining exploration and development services; Cleaning service, industrial or commercial

(G-509)
RAY H MILLER LOGGING LUMB
8848 Ely Rd (44606-9319)
PHONE.................................330 683-2055
EMP: 6 **EST:** 2019
SALES (est): 470.35K **Privately Held**
SIC: 2411 Logging

(G-510)
ROCK DECOR COMPANY
Also Called: Casa Di Sassi
167 Maple Street (44606-9599)
P.O. Box 148 (44606-0148)
PHONE.................................330 830-9760
Gary Miller, *Prin*
EMP: 35 **EST:** 2010
SALES (est): 3.51MM **Privately Held**
Web: www.rock-decor.com
SIC: 3272 Stone, cast concrete

(G-511)
STEIN-WAY EQUIPMENT
12335 Emerson Rd (44606-9798)
PHONE.................................330 857-8700
Oris Steiner, *Pt*
Oris Steiner, *Genl Pt*
EMP: 8 **EST:** 1976
SQ FT: 20,000
SALES (est): 695.39K **Privately Held**
Web: www.steinwayequipment.com
SIC: 3523 Barn, silo, poultry, dairy, and livestock machinery

(G-512)
VERSI-TECH INCORPORATED
Also Called: Versa Tech Technologies
32 Hunter St (44606-9600)
PHONE.................................586 944-2230
Ron Schroeder, *Prin*
EMP: 10 **EST:** 1973
SALES (est): 2.12MM
SALES (corp-wide): 46.21MM **Privately Held**
Web: www.versatechmi.com
SIC: 3599 Machine shop, jobbing and repair
PA: Mid-West Forge Corporation
2778 S M Ctr Rd Ste 200
Willoughby OH 44094
216 481-3030

(G-513)
WAYNEDALE TRUSS AND PANEL CO
8971 Dover Rd (44606-9407)
PHONE.................................330 698-7373
James Fry, *Pr*
Diane Fry, *
EMP: 34 **EST:** 1978
SQ FT: 2,000
SALES (est): 2.09MM **Privately Held**
Web: www.waynedaletruss.com
SIC: 2439 Trusses, wooden roof

(G-514)
WEAVER WOODCRAFT L L C
9652 Harrison Rd (44606-9623)
PHONE.................................330 695-2150
Dave Weaver, *Prin*
EMP: 9 **EST:** 2008
SALES (est): 497.48K **Privately Held**
SIC: 2511 Wood household furniture

(G-515)
Y & T WOODCRAFT INC
10861 Lautenschlager Rd (44606-9353)
PHONE.................................330 464-3432
Nelson Troyer, *Prin*
EMP: 8 **EST:** 2004
SALES (est): 271.59K **Privately Held**
Web: www.ytwoodcraft.com
SIC: 2512 Upholstered household furniture

Arcadia
Hancock County

(G-516)
MAASS MIDWEST MFG INC
Also Called: Dickens Foundry
19710 State Route 12 (44804-9503)
PHONE.................................419 894-6424
Mike Wedge, *Ltd Pt*
EMP: 9
SALES (corp-wide): 9.36MM **Privately Held**
Web: www.maassmidwest.com
SIC: 3366 3491 3432 Brass foundry, nec; Industrial valves; Plumbing fixture fittings and trim
PA: Maass - Midwest Mfg. Inc.
11283 Dundee Rd
Huntley IL 60142
847 669-5135

(G-517)
RPM CARBIDE DIE INC
Also Called: RPM
202 E South St (44804-9773)
P.O. Box 278 (44804-0278)
PHONE.................................419 894-6426
Eric E Metcalfe, *CEO*
Joseph E Phillips, *
EMP: 38 **EST:** 1967
SQ FT: 18,500
SALES (est): 5.03MM **Privately Held**
Web: www.rpmcarbidedie.com
SIC: 3544 Special dies and tools

Arcanum
Darke County

(G-518)
HOFMANNS LURES INC
3937 Kilbourn Rd (45304-9732)
PHONE.................................937 684-0338
Denis Short, *Pr*
EMP: 8 **EST:** 1987
SALES (est): 392.76K **Privately Held**
Web: www.hofmannslures.com
SIC: 3949 Masks: hockey, baseball, football, etc.

(G-519)
RED BARN CABINET CO
8046 State Route 722 (45304-9409)
PHONE.................................937 884-9800
Mark Angle, *Pr*
EMP: 7 **EST:** 2005
SALES (est): 259.06K **Privately Held**
Web: www.redbarncabinetco.net

SIC: 2434 Wood kitchen cabinets

Archbold
Fulton County

(G-520)
AMERICAN POWER PULL CORP
2022 S Defiance St (43502)
P.O. Box 96 (43502-0096)
PHONE.................................419 335-7050
Edward S Kraemer, *Pr*
◆ **EMP:** 8 **EST:** 1919
SQ FT: 36,600
SALES (est): 1.01MM **Privately Held**
Web: www.americanpowerpull.com
SIC: 3423 3531 3536 Jacks: lifting, screw, or ratchet (hand tools); Winches; Hoists, cranes, and monorails

(G-521)
ARCHBOLD BUCKEYE INC
207 N Defiance St (43502-1187)
PHONE.................................419 445-4466
Ross William Taylor, *Pr*
Brent C Taylor, *VP*
Sharon S Taylor, *Sec*
EMP: 10 **EST:** 1905
SQ FT: 2,800
SALES (est): 658.44K **Privately Held**
Web: www.archboldbuckeye.com
SIC: 2711 Newspapers: publishing only, not printed on site

(G-522)
ARCHBOLD CONTAINER CORP
800 W Barre Rd (43502-9595)
P.O. Box 10 (43502-0010)
PHONE.................................800 446-2520
Lynn Aschliman, *Pr*
Lynn Aschliman, *Pr*
Elvin D Yoder, *
EMP: 150 **EST:** 1970
SQ FT: 230,000
SALES (est): 25.13MM
SALES (corp-wide): 1.87B **Privately Held**
Web: www.gbp.com
SIC: 2653 3086 Boxes, corrugated: made from purchased materials; Packaging and shipping materials, foamed plastics
PA: Green Bay Packaging Inc.
1700 N Webster Ave
Green Bay WI 54302
920 433-5111

(G-523)
ARCHBOLD FURNITURE CO
733 W Barre Rd (43502-9304)
PHONE.................................567 444-4666
Pat Mcnamara, *Pr*
Pete Gstaldar, *
◆ **EMP:** 32 **EST:** 1978
SALES (est): 11.09MM **Privately Held**
Web: www.archboldfurniture.com
SIC: 5712 2511 Furniture stores; Unassembled or unfinished furniture, household: wood

(G-524)
ARROW TRU-LINE INC (PA)
2211 S Defiance St (43502-9151)
PHONE.................................419 446-2785
Marvin Miller, *Pr*
Stacy Sauber, *
◆ **EMP:** 150 **EST:** 1959
SQ FT: 63,000
SALES (est): 72.73MM
SALES (corp-wide): 72.73MM **Privately Held**
Web: www.arrowtruline.com

SIC: 3469 Metal stampings, nec

(G-525)
BIL-JAX INC (DH)
Also Called: Biljax Scaffolding
125 Taylor Pkwy (43502)
PHONE.................................419 445-8915
◆ **EMP:** 13 **EST:** 1947
SALES (est): 23.37MM
SALES (corp-wide): 920.13K **Privately Held**
Web: www.biljax.com
SIC: 3446 Scaffolds, mobile or stationary: metal
HQ: Haulotte Group
Rue Emile Zola
Lorette 42420
477292424

(G-526)
CLANCYS CABINETS LLC
3751 County Road 26 (43502-9434)
PHONE.................................419 445-4455
EMP: 9 **EST:** 1990
SQ FT: 4,000
SALES (est): 474.3K **Privately Held**
Web: www.clancyscabinets.com
SIC: 2434 Wood kitchen cabinets

(G-527)
CONAGRA BRANDS INC
La Choy Food Products Division
901 Stryker St (43502-1053)
PHONE.................................419 445-8015
Ron Corkins, *Brnch Mgr*
EMP: 78
SALES (corp-wide): 12.28B **Publicly Held**
Web: www.conagrabrands.com
SIC: 2032 2099 Chinese foods, nec: packaged in cans, jars, etc.; Food preparations, nec
PA: Conagra Brands, Inc.
222 W Mdse Mart Plz Ste 1
Chicago IL 60654
312 549-5000

(G-528)
FROZEN SPECIALTIES INC
Also Called: FSI
720 W Barre Rd (43502-9304)
P.O. Box 410 (43502-0410)
PHONE.................................419 445-9015
Khun Anat Julintron, *CEO*
▼ **EMP:** 140 **EST:** 1969
SALES (est): 47.55MM **Privately Held**
Web: www.frozenspecialties.com
SIC: 2038 Pizza, frozen
HQ: Bellisio Foods, Inc
701 Washington Ave N # 400
Minneapolis MN 55401

(G-529)
GERALD GRAIN CENTER INC
3265 County Road 24 (43502-9415)
PHONE.................................419 445-2451
Chet Phillips, *Brnch Mgr*
EMP: 30
SALES (corp-wide): 20.13MM **Privately Held**
Web: www.geraldgrain.com
SIC: 3523 5191 Elevators, farm; Animal feeds
PA: Gerald Grain Center, Inc.
14540 County Road U
Napoleon OH 43545
419 598-8015

(G-530)
HAULOTTE NORTH AMERICA MFG INC
125 Taylor Pkwy (43502-9122)

Archbold - Fulton County (G-531)

PHONE..................................567 444-4159
EMP: 9 **EST:** 2021
SALES (est): 617.09K **Privately Held**
Web: www.haulotte-usa.com
SIC: 3446 Scaffolds, mobile or stationary: metal

(G-531)
HAULOTTE US INC (DH)
Also Called: Bil-Jax
125 Taylor Pkwy (43502-9122)
PHONE..................................419 445-8915
Mike Garvaglia, *CEO*
Lynn Yarnell, *CFO*
◆ **EMP:** 17 **EST:** 2001
SQ FT: 14,700
SALES (est): 11.11MM
SALES (corp-wide): 920.13K **Privately Held**
Web: www.haulotte-usa.com
SIC: 3531 Aerial work platforms: hydraulic/ elec. truck/carrier mounted
HQ: Haulotte Group
Rue Emile Zola
Lorette 42420
477292424

(G-532)
HIT TROPHY INC
4989 State Route 66 (43502-9362)
PHONE..................................419 445-5356
Tom Wyse, *Pr*
Abe Wyse, *Mktg Dir*
EMP: 6 **EST:** 1949
SALES (est): 860.52K **Privately Held**
Web: www.hittrophy.com
SIC: 3499 5999 2499 Trophies, metal, except silver; Trophies and plaques; Trophy bases, wood

(G-533)
LAUBER MANUFACTURING CO
3751 County Road 26 (43502-9434)
P.O. Box 175 (43502-0175)
PHONE..................................419 446-2450
Bruce Lauber, *Pr*
Elizabeth Grime, *Sec*
Graeme O Lauber Junior, *Treas*
EMP: 7 **EST:** 1929
SQ FT: 43,000
SALES (est): 456.18K **Privately Held**
Web: www.lauberinsurance.org
SIC: 2511 Wood household furniture

(G-534)
LIECHTY SPECIALTIES INC
Also Called: Industrial WD Prts Fabrication
1901 S Defiance St (43502-9438)
P.O. Box 6 (43502-0006)
PHONE..................................419 445-6696
Allen K Liechty, *Pr*
Virgina Liechty, *Sec*
EMP: 8 **EST:** 1965
SQ FT: 25,000
SALES (est): 611.76K **Privately Held**
Web: www.nefltd.com
SIC: 2431 Millwork

(G-535)
LOGO THIS
301 Ditto St Ste E (43502-1111)
PHONE..................................419 445-1355
Dan Rychener, *Pr*
EMP: 6 **EST:** 2000
SALES (est): 614.17K **Privately Held**
Web: www.logothisohio.com
SIC: 2395 Embroidery products, except Schiffli machine

(G-536)
MILLER BROS PAVING INC (HQ)
1613 S Defiance St (43502-9488)
P.O. Box 30 (43502-0030)
PHONE..................................419 445-1015
Dean Miller, *Pr*
Robert Miller, *VP*
Steven A Everhart, *Sec*
Bradley Dmiller Pe, *Pr*
EMP: 10 **EST:** 1972
SQ FT: 48,000
SALES (est): 6.56MM **Privately Held**
Web: www.mbcholdings.com
SIC: 2951 Asphalt paving mixtures and blocks
PA: Mbc Holdings, Inc.
1613 S Defiance St
Archbold OH 43502

(G-537)
NAPOLEON SPRING WORKS INC (HQ)
111 Weires Dr (43502-9153)
P.O. Box 160 (43502-0160)
PHONE..................................419 445-1010
Robert Shram Senior, *Pr*
◆ **EMP:** 143 **EST:** 1960
SALES (est): 49.6MM
SALES (corp-wide): 15.37MM **Privately Held**
Web: www.lynx-nsw.com
SIC: 3493 3429 Torsion bar springs; Builders' hardware
PA: Industries Lynx Inc
175 Rue Upper Edison
Saint-Lambert QC J4R 2
514 866-1068

(G-538)
NEF LTD
Also Called: Liechty Specialties
1901 S Defiance St (43502-9438)
P.O. Box 6 (43502-0006)
PHONE..................................419 445-6696
Nisha E Francis, *Pr*
EMP: 6 **EST:** 2017
SALES (est): 920.31K **Privately Held**
Web: www.nefltd.com
SIC: 2452 Prefabricated buildings, wood

(G-539)
NOFZIGER DOOR SALES INC
111 Taylor Pkwy (43502-9309)
PHONE..................................419 445-2961
Tom Rufenacht, *Mgr*
EMP: 13
SALES (corp-wide): 39.6MM **Privately Held**
Web: www.dublinohiogaragedoors.com
SIC: 3442 5211 Metal doors; Garage doors, sale and installation
PA: Nofziger Door Sales, Inc.
320 Sycamore St
Wauseon OH 43567
419 337-9900

(G-540)
P T I INC
100 Taylor Pkwy (43502-9309)
P.O. Box 53256 (43553-0256)
PHONE..................................419 445-2800
▲ **EMP:** 27 **EST:** 1998
SALES (est): 1.03MM **Privately Held**
SIC: 3089 Plastics processing

(G-541)
POWDER COATING PLUS LLC
2010 S Defiance St (43502-9112)
PHONE..................................419 446-0089
EMP: 10 **EST:** 2006
SALES (est): 565.12K **Privately Held**
Web: www.powdercoatingplus.net
SIC: 3479 Painting, coating, and hot dipping

(G-542)
PROGRESSIVE FURNITURE INC (HQ)
Also Called: Progressive International
502 Middle St (43502-1559)
P.O. Box 308 (43502-0308)
PHONE..................................419 446-4500
Kevin Sauder, *Pr*
Dan Kendrick, *Ex VP*
John Boring, *VP Fin*
◆ **EMP:** 25 **EST:** 1985
SQ FT: 8,000
SALES (est): 26.16MM
SALES (corp-wide): 543.69MM **Privately Held**
Web: www.progressivefurniture.com
SIC: 2511 2517 5021 Bed frames, except water bed frames: wood; Home entertainment unit cabinets, wood; Tables, occasional
PA: Sauder Woodworking Co.
502 Middle St
Archbold OH 43502
419 446-2711

(G-543)
QUADCO REHABILITATION CTR INC
Also Called: Northwest Products Div
600 Oak St (43502-1579)
P.O. Box 336 (43502-0336)
PHONE..................................419 445-1950
Phillip Zuver, *Brnch Mgr*
EMP: 35
SALES (corp-wide): 1.38MM **Privately Held**
Web: www.quadcorehab.org
SIC: 8331 2448 Vocational rehabilitation agency; Wood pallets and skids
PA: Quadco Rehabilitation Center, Inc.
427 N Defiance St
Stryker OH 43557
419 682-1011

(G-544)
SAUDER MANUFACTURING CO (HQ)
Also Called: Wieland
930 W Barre Rd (43502-9320)
P.O. Box 230 (43502-0230)
PHONE..................................419 445-7670
Virgil L Miller, *Pr*
William Ogden, *
Phil Bontrager, *
◆ **EMP:** 220 **EST:** 1945
SQ FT: 300,000
SALES (est): 160.81MM
SALES (corp-wide): 543.69MM **Privately Held**
Web: www.saudermfg.com
SIC: 2531 Church furniture
PA: Sauder Woodworking Co.
502 Middle St
Archbold OH 43502
419 446-2711

(G-545)
SAUDER WOODWORKING CO
330 N Clydes Way (43502-9170)
PHONE..................................419 446-2711
EMP: 10
SALES (corp-wide): 543.69MM **Privately Held**
Web: www.sauder.com
SIC: 2519 5021 Fiberglass and plastic furniture; Furniture
PA: Sauder Woodworking Co.
502 Middle St
Archbold OH 43502
419 446-2711

(G-546)
SAUDER WOODWORKING CO (PA)
Also Called: Sauder
502 Middle St (43502-1500)
P.O. Box 156 (43502-0156)
PHONE..................................419 446-2711
Kevin Sauder, *CEO*
Patrick Sauder, *Ex VP*
◆ **EMP:** 2100 **EST:** 1934
SQ FT: 5,000,000
SALES (est): 543.69MM
SALES (corp-wide): 543.69MM **Privately Held**
Web: www.sauder.com
SIC: 5021 2512 Household furniture; Upholstered household furniture

(G-547)
SYSTECH HANDLING INC
120 Taylor Pkwy (43502-9309)
PHONE..................................419 445-8226
Wendell Lantz, *Pr*
Mike Waidelich, *VP*
EMP: 12 **EST:** 1999
SQ FT: 12,500
SALES (est): 2.51MM **Privately Held**
Web: www.systechhandling.com
SIC: 3599 8711 7692 3444 Custom machinery; Engineering services; Welding repair; Sheet metalwork

Arlington
Hancock County

(G-548)
BASF
522 Crawford Rd (45814-9670)
PHONE..................................419 408-5398
EMP: 40 **EST:** 2015
SALES (est): 1.48MM **Privately Held**
Web: www.basf.com
SIC: 2869 Industrial organic chemicals, nec

Ashland
Ashland County

(G-549)
ACTIVE METAL AND MOLDS INC
2219 Cottage St (44805-1296)
PHONE..................................419 281-9623
▲ **EMP:** 12
Web: www.activemetalinc.com
SIC: 3444 3449 3599 7692 Sheet metalwork; Miscellaneous metalwork; Machine shop, jobbing and repair; Welding repair

(G-550)
ALTEC INDUSTRIES
1236 Township Road 1175 (44805-1979)
PHONE..................................419 289-6066
Bob Donaldson, *Prin*
EMP: 8 **EST:** 2005
SALES (est): 931.72K **Privately Held**
Web: www.altec.com
SIC: 3531 Construction machinery

(G-551)
ASHLAND PRECISION TOOLING LLC
1750 S Baney Rd (44805-3522)
P.O. Box 129 (44691-0129)
PHONE..................................419 289-1736
EMP: 21 **EST:** 2002
SQ FT: 56,000
SALES (est): 1.01MM **Privately Held**
Web: www.ashlandprecisiontooling.com
SIC: 3599 Machine shop, jobbing and repair

GEOGRAPHIC SECTION

Ashland - Ashland County (G-572)

(G-552)
ASHLAND PUBLISHING CO
Also Called: Ashland Times Gazette
40 E 2nd St (44805-2304)
P.O. Box 693 (44805-0693)
PHONE..............................419 281-0581
Timothy Dix, *Sec*
G Charles Dix Ii, *Treas*
Troy Dix, *
▲ **EMP:** 451 **EST:** 1850
SQ FT: 12,400
SALES (est): 2.48MM
SALES (corp-wide): 467.21MM **Privately Held**
Web: www.times-gazette.com
SIC: 2711 Newspapers, publishing and printing
PA: Dix 1898, Inc.
  212 E Liberty St
  Wooster OH
  330 264-3511

(G-553)
ASHLAND WATER GROUP INC (PA)
1899 Cottage St (44805)
PHONE..............................877 326-3561
Larry Donelson, *Pr*
Jody Bartter, *Treas*
▲ **EMP:** 7 **EST:** 2008
SQ FT: 3,000
SALES (est): 6.16MM
SALES (corp-wide): 6.16MM **Privately Held**
Web: www.ashlandpump.com
SIC: 3561 Pumps and pumping equipment

(G-554)
ATLAS BOLT & SCREW COMPANY LLC (DH)
Also Called: Atlas Fasteners For Cnstr
1628 Troy Rd (44805-1398)
PHONE..............................419 289-6171
Robert W Moore, *Pr*
Robert C Gluth, *Ex VP*
Robert Webb, *Sec*
▲ **EMP:** 175 **EST:** 1986
SQ FT: 75,000
SALES (est): 47.18MM
SALES (corp-wide): 364.48B **Publicly Held**
Web: www.atlasfasteners.com
SIC: 3452 5085 5051 5072 Washers, metal; Fasteners, industrial: nuts, bolts, screws, etc.; Metals service centers and offices; Hardware
HQ: Marmon Group Llc
  181 W Madison St Ste 3900
  Chicago IL 60602
  312 372-9500

(G-555)
BARBASOL LLC
2011 Ford Dr (44805-1277)
PHONE..............................419 903-0738
▲ **EMP:** 36 **EST:** 2009
SQ FT: 80,000
SALES (est): 5.2MM
SALES (corp-wide): 18.91MM **Privately Held**
Web: www.barbasol.com
SIC: 2844 Toilet preparations
PA: Perio, Inc.
  6156 Wilcox Rd
  Dublin OH 43016
  614 791-1207

(G-556)
BENDON INC (PA)
Also Called: Bendon Publishing Intl
1840 S Baney Rd (44805-3524)
PHONE..............................419 207-3600
Benjamin Ferguson, *CEO*
Benjamin Ferguson, *Pr*
Terry Gerwig, *
Jenny Hastings, *
David Swank, *
▲ **EMP:** 54 **EST:** 2001
SQ FT: 220,000
SALES (est): 28.5MM
SALES (corp-wide): 28.5MM **Privately Held**
Web: www.bendonpub.com
SIC: 5999 5961 5092 2731 Educational aids and electronic training materials; Educational supplies and equipment, mail order; Educational toys; Books, publishing only

(G-557)
BOOKMASTERS INC (HQ)
Also Called: Baker & Taylor Publisher Svcs
30 Amberwood Pkwy (44805-9765)
PHONE..............................419 281-1802
Raymond Sevin, *Pr*
Thomas Wurster, *
◆ **EMP:** 157 **EST:** 1972
SQ FT: 180,000
SALES (est): 49.92MM **Privately Held**
Web: www.btpubservices.com
SIC: 7389 2752 2731 2791 Printers' services: folding, collating, etc.; Commercial printing, lithographic; Book publishing; Typesetting
PA: Baker & Taylor, Llc
  2810 Clseum Cntre Dr Ste
  Charlotte NC 28217

(G-558)
BOR-IT MFG CO INC
1687 Cleveland Rd (44805-1929)
P.O. Box 789 (44805-0789)
PHONE..............................419 289-6639
Michael W Albers, *Pr*
Michelle Albers, *Sec*
▼ **EMP:** 20 **EST:** 1987
SQ FT: 12,500
SALES (est): 2.33MM **Privately Held**
Web: www.bor-it.com
SIC: 3541 Drilling and boring machines

(G-559)
BOSTIK INC
1745 Cottage St (44805-1237)
PHONE..............................419 289-9588
Barry Sheets, *Brnch Mgr*
EMP: 23
SALES (corp-wide): 125.67MM **Privately Held**
Web: www.bostik.com
SIC: 2891 Adhesives and sealants
HQ: Bostik, Inc.
  11320 W Watertwn Plnk Rd
  Wauwatosa WI 53226
  414 774-2250

(G-560)
BYLER TRUSS
1271 State Route 96 (44805-9357)
PHONE..............................330 465-5412
Harvey Byler, *Ofcr*
EMP: 6 **EST:** 2014
SALES (est): 74.3K **Privately Held**
SIC: 2439 Trusses, wooden roof

(G-561)
CABINET RESTYLERS INC
Also Called: Cabinet Restylers
419 E 8th St (44805-1953)
PHONE..............................419 281-8449
Eric Thiel, *Pr*
Denise Appleby, *VP*
EMP: 56 **EST:** 1968
SQ FT: 50,000
SALES (est): 9.23MM **Privately Held**
Web: www.thiels.com
SIC: 1751 2541 5211 1799 Window and door (prefabricated) installation; Cabinets, lockers, and shelving; Cabinets, kitchen; Bathtub refinishing

(G-562)
CENTERRA CO-OP (PA)
813 Clark Ave (44805-1967)
PHONE..............................419 281-2153
Jean Bratton, *CEO*
William Bullock, *
▲ **EMP:** 30 **EST:** 2003
SALES (est): 174.64MM
SALES (corp-wide): 174.64MM **Privately Held**
Web: www.centerracoop.com
SIC: 5983 5261 5999 2048 Fuel oil dealers; Fertilizer; Feed and farm supply; Bird food, prepared

(G-563)
CERTIFIED LABS & SERVICE INC
535 E 7th St (44805-2553)
PHONE..............................419 289-7462
Gary E Funkhouser, *Pr*
Michael C Huber, *VP*
Harret Funkhouser, *Treas*
Pam Huber, *Sec*
▲ **EMP:** 6 **EST:** 1984
SQ FT: 5,000
SALES (est): 461.8K **Privately Held**
Web: www.certifiedlabsservice.com
SIC: 7699 3822 3561 Pumps and pumping equipment repair; Hydronic controls; Pumps, domestic: water or sump

(G-564)
CHANDLER SYSTEMS INCORPORATED
Also Called: Best Controls Company
710 Orange St (44805-1725)
PHONE..............................888 363-9434
William Chandler III, *Pr*
Polly Chandler, *
Bill Chandler, *
▲ **EMP:** 65 **EST:** 1993
SQ FT: 52,000
SALES (est): 20.61MM **Privately Held**
Web: www.chandlersystemsinc.com
SIC: 5074 3625 Water purification equipment ; Relays and industrial controls

(G-565)
CITY OF ASHLAND
City Services
310 W 12th St (44805-1756)
P.O. Box Remont Ave (44805)
PHONE..............................419 289-8728
EMP: 9
SALES (corp-wide): 29.24MM **Privately Held**
Web: www.ashland-ohio.com
SIC: 3589 Garbage disposers and compactors, commercial
PA: City Of Ashland
  206 Claremont Ave Ste 1
  Ashland OH 44805
  419 289-8170

(G-566)
COLORING BOOK SOLUTIONS LLC
426 E 8th St (44805-1909)
PHONE..............................419 281-9641
Don Myers Iii, *Managing Member*
▲ **EMP:** 9 **EST:** 2003
SQ FT: 15,000
SALES (est): 966.71K **Privately Held**
Web: www.coloringbooksolutions.com
SIC: 2759 Commercial printing, nec

(G-567)
CONERY MANUFACTURING INC
1380 Township Road 743 (44805-8926)
PHONE..............................419 289-1444
Scott Conery, *Pr*
Chris Shafer, *VP*
▲ **EMP:** 16 **EST:** 1979
SQ FT: 24,000
SALES (est): 2.36MM **Privately Held**
Web: www.conerymfg.com
SIC: 3822 Liquid level controls, residential or commercial heating

(G-568)
CONVERGE GROUP INC
1850 S Baney Rd (44805-3524)
PHONE..............................419 281-0000
Mike Sloan, *Genl Mgr*
EMP: 6 **EST:** 2013
SQ FT: 25,000
SALES (est): 230.57K **Privately Held**
Web: www.convergegroup.org
SIC: 3089 Injection molding of plastics

(G-569)
CRAZY MONKEY BAKING INC
1191 Commerce Pkwy (44805-8955)
PHONE..............................419 903-0403
▲ **EMP:** 8 **EST:** 2007
SALES (est): 6.16MM
SALES (corp-wide): 6.16MM **Privately Held**
Web: www.crazymonkeybaking.com
SIC: 2064 Candy and other confectionery products
PA: Ashland Water Group, Inc.
  1899 Cottage St
  Ashland OH 44805
  877 326-3561

(G-570)
CUSTOM HOISTS INC (HQ)
771 County Road 30a (44805-9227)
PHONE..............................419 368-4721
Rick Hiltunen, *Pr*
▲ **EMP:** 165 **EST:** 1973
SQ FT: 110,000
SALES (est): 46.95MM
SALES (corp-wide): 741.05MM **Publicly Held**
Web: www.customhoists.com
SIC: 3593 Fluid power cylinders and actuators
PA: Standex International Corporation
  23 Keewaydin Dr
  Salem NH 03079
  603 893-9701

(G-571)
FARR AUTOMATION INC
58 Sugarbush Ct (44805-9737)
PHONE..............................419 289-1883
Ross Farr, *Pr*
Karen Farr, *Sec*
EMP: 15 **EST:** 1999
SQ FT: 26,000
SALES (est): 1.17MM **Privately Held**
Web: www.farrautomation.com
SIC: 3599 Custom machinery

(G-572)
FLOW CONTROL US HOLDING CORP
Also Called: Pentair Water Ashland Oper
1101 Myers Pkwy (44805-1969)
PHONE..............................419 289-1144
EMP: 145
SALES (corp-wide): 15.16B **Publicly Held**
SIC: 3561 Pumps and pumping equipment
HQ: Flow Control Us Holding Corporation

Ashland - Ashland County (G-573)

5500 Wayzata Blvd Ste 800
Minneapolis MN 55416
763 545-1730

(G-573)
FOLDING CARTON SERVICE INC
608 Westlake Dr (44805-1378)
PHONE.................................419 281-4099
Mina Risha, *Pr*
EMP: 12 **EST:** 1988
SQ FT: 24,000
SALES (est): 950.17K **Privately Held**
Web: www.fcsohio.com
SIC: 2653 Boxes, corrugated: made from purchased materials

(G-574)
FOLLETT HGHER EDCATN GROUP INC
Also Called: Baker & Taylor Publisher Svcs
30 Amberwood Pkwy (44805-9765)
PHONE.................................419 281-5100
Bob Gospodarek, *Sr VP*
EMP: 180
SALES (corp-wide): 906.01MM **Privately Held**
Web: www.btpubservices.com
SIC: 2731 Book publishing
PA: Follett Higher Education Group, Llc
3 Westbrook Corp Ctr Ste
Westchester IL 60154
800 365-5388

(G-575)
FUTURE MOLDING INC
Also Called: Hedstrom Injection
1850 S Baney Rd (44805-3524)
PHONE.................................419 281-0000
Chris Shafer, *Pr*
EMP: 10 **EST:** 2012
SALES (est): 757.13K **Privately Held**
SIC: 3089 Injection molding of plastics

(G-576)
GENCO
1250 George Rd (44805-8916)
PHONE.................................419 207-7648
EMP: 9 **EST:** 2014
SALES (est): 85.84K **Privately Held**
Web: www.genco.us
SIC: 1389 Oil field services, nec

(G-577)
HARRIS WELDING AND MACHINE CO
2219 Cottage St (44805-1296)
P.O. Box 317 (44805-0317)
PHONE.................................419 281-8351
John Kochenderfer, *Pr*
Tracy Kochenderfer, *Sec*
EMP: 10 **EST:** 1964
SQ FT: 7,500
SALES (est): 898.94K **Privately Held**
Web: www.machlev.com.br
SIC: 7692 3599 Welding repair; Machine shop, jobbing and repair

(G-578)
HEDSTROM PLASTICS LLC
100 Hedstrom Dr (44805)
PHONE.................................419 289-9310
Rod Mitchell, *
Scott Conery, *
EMP: 75 **EST:** 2020
SALES (est): 7.07MM **Privately Held**
Web: www.hedstromplastics.com
SIC: 3086 Plastics foam products

(G-579)
HILLMAN PRECISION INC
462 E 9th St Ste 1 (44805-1923)
PHONE.................................419 289-1557
Geoff Hillman Senior, *CEO*
Geoff Hillman Junior, *Pr*
EMP: 16 **EST:** 1991
SQ FT: 37,000
SALES (est): 1.76MM **Privately Held**
Web: www.hillmanprecision.com
SIC: 3599 Machine shop, jobbing and repair

(G-580)
HYDROMATIC PUMPS INC
1101 Myers Pkwy (44805-1969)
PHONE.................................419 289-1144
Keith Lang, *Pr*
▼ **EMP:** 67 **EST:** 1959
SALES (est): 1.53MM **Privately Held**
Web: www.hydromatic.com
SIC: 3561 Pumps and pumping equipment

(G-581)
JRS MBL WLDG FABRICATION LLC
992 County Road 601 (44805-8918)
PHONE.................................567 307-5460
Josh Hahn, *Prin*
EMP: 6 **EST:** 2016
SALES (est): 74.38K **Privately Held**
SIC: 7692 Welding repair

(G-582)
JUST NAME IT INC
110 Hedstrom Dr (44805-3586)
PHONE.................................614 626-8662
Joe Grubbs, *Pr*
EMP: 7 **EST:** 2010
SALES (est): 412.73K **Privately Held**
Web: just-name-it.square.site
SIC: 2759 Screen printing

(G-583)
KAR-DEL PLASTICS INC
1177 Faultless Dr (44805-1250)
PHONE.................................419 289-9739
Scott Pay, *Pr*
Shari L Regan, *VP*
Teresa Pay, *Sec*
EMP: 8 **EST:** 1984
SQ FT: 14,000
SALES (est): 915.14K **Privately Held**
Web: www.kar-delplastics.com
SIC: 3089 Plastics and fiberglass tanks

(G-584)
KEEN PUMP COMPANY INC
Also Called: Keen Pump
471 E State Rte 250 E (44805)
PHONE.................................419 207-9400
Gregory W Keener, *Pr*
Frank Yuhafz, *
Suzzanne Keener, *
Jacob Studer, *
▲ **EMP:** 35 **EST:** 2007
SQ FT: 100,000
SALES (est): 5.48MM **Privately Held**
Web: www.keenpump.com
SIC: 3561 Pumps and pumping equipment

(G-585)
KEHL-KOLOR INC
824 Us Highway 42 (44805-9516)
P.O. Box 770 (44805-0770)
PHONE.................................419 281-3107
Jon B Kehl, *Pr*
Mark Kehl, *
▲ **EMP:** 32 **EST:** 1971
SQ FT: 60,000
SALES (est): 2.42MM **Privately Held**
Web: www.kehlkolor.com

SIC: 2752 2796 2791 2789 Offset printing; Lithographic plates, positives or negatives; Typesetting; Bookbinding and related work

(G-586)
KENAG INC
101 E 7th St (44805-1702)
P.O. Box 326 (44805-0326)
PHONE.................................419 281-1204
Doug Patton, *Pr*
▲ **EMP:** 21 **EST:** 1997
SQ FT: 35,000
SALES (est): 2.24MM **Privately Held**
Web: www.kenag.com
SIC: 2621 5085 Milk filter disks; Filters, industrial

(G-587)
KNOWLTON MACHINE INC
726 Virginia Ave (44805-1944)
P.O. Box 656 (44805-0656)
PHONE.................................419 281-6802
James Knowlton, *Pr*
EMP: 6 **EST:** 1988
SQ FT: 6,000
SALES (est): 688.29K **Privately Held**
Web: www.knowltonmachine.com
SIC: 3599 1799 Machine shop, jobbing and repair; Welding on site

(G-588)
LAKE ERIE FROZEN FOODS MFG CO
1830 Orange Rd (44805-1335)
PHONE.................................419 289-9204
Mike Buckingham, *CEO*
William Buckingham, *
Mike Buckingham, *VP*
▲ **EMP:** 80 **EST:** 1962
SQ FT: 30,000
SALES (est): 9.12MM **Privately Held**
Web: www.leffco.net
SIC: 2038 2037 2022 Snacks, incl. onion rings, cheese sticks, etc.; Vegetables, quick frozen & cold pack, excl. potato products; Cheese; natural and processed

(G-589)
LIQUI-BOX CORPORATION
Also Called: Bag & Bottle Manufacturing
1817 Masters Ave (44805-1291)
PHONE.................................419 289-9696
Sheff Sweet, *Brnch Mgr*
EMP: 44
SALES (corp-wide): 5.49B **Publicly Held**
Web: www.liquibox.com
SIC: 2673 3089 3081 2671 Plastic bags: made from purchased materials; Plastics processing; Unsupported plastics film and sheet; Paper; coated and laminated packaging
HQ: Liqui-Box Corporation
2415 Cascade Pointe Blvd
Charlotte NC 28208
804 325-1400

(G-590)
MAVERICK INNVTIVE SLUTIONS LLC
Also Called: Mis
532 County Road 1600 (44805)
PHONE.................................419 281-7944
James Dygert, *Rep*
Todd Meldrum, *Rep*
◆ **EMP:** 75 **EST:** 1937
SQ FT: 50,000
SALES (est): 9.83MM **Privately Held**
SIC: 3556 3585 Food products machinery; Refrigeration and heating equipment

(G-591)
MCGRAW-HILL SCHL EDCATN HLDNGS
Also Called: Mc Graw-Hill Educational Pubg
1250 George Rd (44805-8916)
PHONE.................................419 207-7400
Maryellen Valaitis, *Prin*
EMP: 750
Web: www.mheducation.com
SIC: 2731 5192 Books, publishing and printing; Books, periodicals, and newspapers
HQ: Mcgraw-Hill School Education Holdings, Llc
2 Penn Plz Fl 20
New York NY 10121
646 766-2000

(G-592)
MIDWEST CONVEYOR PRODUCTS INC
Also Called: Ashland Conveyor Products
1919 Cellar Dr (44805-1275)
PHONE.................................419 281-1235
William Waltz, *Pr*
Tim Swineford, *VP*
EMP: 23 **EST:** 1998
SQ FT: 50,000
SALES (est): 10.43MM **Privately Held**
Web: www.ashlandconveyor.com
SIC: 5084 3535 Conveyor systems; Belt conveyor systems, general industrial use

(G-593)
MORITZ MATERIALS INC (PA)
859 Faultless Dr (44805-1274)
P.O. Box 392 (44805-0392)
PHONE.................................419 281-0575
James Moritz, *Pr*
Joseph Moritz, *VP*
EMP: 22 **EST:** 1985
SQ FT: 2,000
SALES (est): 2.36MM
SALES (corp-wide): 2.36MM **Privately Held**
Web: www.moritzmaterials.com
SIC: 3273 5032 Ready-mixed concrete; Concrete building products

(G-594)
MP TECHNOLOGIES INC
Also Called: Manufacturing Process Tech
532 County Road 1600 (44805-9207)
PHONE.................................440 838-4466
Paul Takacs, *Pr*
Laraine Takacs, *VP*
EMP: 17 **EST:** 1985
SALES (est): 2.21MM **Privately Held**
Web: www.mptechnologiesltd.com
SIC: 3463 Machinery forgings, nonferrous

(G-595)
NOVATEX NORTH AMERICA INC
1070 Faultless Dr (44805-1247)
PHONE.................................419 282-4264
Michael Donofrio, *Pr*
▲ **EMP:** 55 **EST:** 2006
SALES (est): 10.26MM
SALES (corp-wide): 924.96K **Privately Held**
Web: www.novatex.us
SIC: 3069 3085 3089 Nipples, rubber; Plastics bottles; Injection molded finished plastics products, nec
HQ: Novatex Gmbh
Werner-Von-Siemens-Str. 14
Pattensen NI 30982
510191950

▲ = Import ▼ = Export
◆ = Import/Export

GEOGRAPHIC SECTION

Ashland - Ashland County (G-621)

(G-596)
OHIO TOOL WORKS LLC
1374 Township Road 743 (44805-8926)
PHONE..................................419 281-3700
John C Hovsepian, *Pr*
Sharon Parrish, *
EMP: 59 **EST:** 2004
SQ FT: 45,000
SALES (est): 10.07MM
SALES (corp-wide): 474.81MM **Privately Held**
Web: www.ohiotoolworks.com
SIC: 3599 Machine shop, jobbing and repair
HQ: Hardinge Inc.
79 W Paces Ferry Rd Nw # 2
Atlanta GA 30305
607 734-2281

(G-597)
PACKAGING CORPORATION AMERICA
Also Called: Pca/Ashland 307
929 Faultless Dr (44805-1246)
P.O. Box 367 (44805-0367)
PHONE..................................419 282-5809
Jeff Kaser, *Brnch Mgr*
EMP: 110
SALES (corp-wide): 8.48B **Publicly Held**
Web: www.packagingcorp.com
SIC: 2653 Boxes, corrugated: made from purchased materials
PA: Packaging Corporation Of America
1 N Field Ct
Lake Forest IL 60045
847 482-3000

(G-598)
PENTAIR PUMP GROUP INC
740 E 9th St (44805-1954)
PHONE..................................419 281-9918
EMP: 12 **EST:** 2017
SALES (est): 562.94K **Privately Held**
Web: www.femyers.com
SIC: 3561 Pumps and pumping equipment

(G-599)
PERFOMANCE FEED & SEEDS INC
1379 Township Road 1353 (44805-9364)
PHONE..................................419 496-0531
Jason Bryant, *Prin*
EMP: 8 **EST:** 2020
SALES (est): 403.52K **Privately Held**
Web: www.performancefeedandseeds.com
SIC: 3999 Seeds, coated or treated, from purchased seeds

(G-600)
PHILWAY PRODUCTS INC
521 E 7th St (44805-2553)
PHONE..................................419 281-7777
EMP: 195
Web: www.philway.com
SIC: 3672 Printed circuit boards

(G-601)
PIONEER NATIONAL LATEX INC
114 E 7th St (44805-1701)
PHONE..................................419 289-3300
Daniel Derick, *Brnch Mgr*
EMP: 70
SALES (corp-wide): 228.74MM **Privately Held**
Web: www.pioneernational.com
SIC: 3069 Toys, rubber
HQ: Pioneer National Latex, Inc.
246 E Fourth St
Wichita KS 67220
419 289-3300

(G-602)
PIONEER NATIONAL LATEX INC
Also Called: Packaging Department
244 Commercial Ave (44805)
PHONE..................................419 289-3300
EMP: 20
SALES (corp-wide): 228.74MM **Privately Held**
Web: www.pioneernational.com
SIC: 3069 3944 Toys, rubber; Games, toys, and children's vehicles
HQ: Pioneer National Latex, Inc.
246 E Fourth St
Wichita KS 67220
419 289-3300

(G-603)
PLAID HAT GAMES
1172 State Route 96 (44805-1071)
PHONE..................................419 552-5490
Colby Dauch, *CEO*
EMP: 8 **EST:** 2020
SALES (est): 472.44K **Privately Held**
Web: www.plaidhatgames.com
SIC: 3944 Board games, puzzles, and models, except electronic

(G-604)
PLAID HAT GAMES LLC
1172 State Route 96 (44805)
PHONE..................................419 552-5490
Colby Dauch, *CEO*
EMP: 8 **EST:** 2020
SALES (est): 519.25K **Privately Held**
Web: www.plaidhatgames.com
SIC: 3944 Board games, puzzles, and models, except electronic

(G-605)
PRECISION DESIGN INC
Also Called: Ohio Electric Control
2221 Ford Dr (44805-1280)
PHONE..................................419 289-1553
Robert Mcmullen, *Pr*
EMP: 6 **EST:** 1995
SALES (est): 520K **Privately Held**
Web: www.ohioelectriccontrol.com
SIC: 3621 Control equipment for electric buses and locomotives

(G-606)
PURVI OIL INC
654 Us Highway 250 E (44805-9755)
PHONE..................................419 207-8234
EMP: 6 **EST:** 2014
SALES (est): 235.59K **Privately Held**
SIC: 1311 Crude petroleum and natural gas

(G-607)
PWP INC
532 County Road 1600 (44805-9207)
PHONE..................................216 251-2181
Micheal Hooper, *CEO*
▲ **EMP:** 45 **EST:** 1953
SALES (est): 8.56MM
SALES (corp-wide): 26.25MM **Privately Held**
Web: www.progresswire.com
SIC: 3496 Miscellaneous fabricated wire products
PA: Tahoma Enterprises, Inc.
255 Wooster Rd N
Barberton OH 44203
330 745-9016

(G-608)
R & J AG MANUFACTURING INC
Also Called: All-Plant Liquid Plant Food
821 State Route 511 (44805-9562)
PHONE..................................419 962-4707
Roger D Shopbell, *Pr*
James Shopbell, *Treas*
Joan Shopbell, *VP*
Pam Tobias, *Sec*
EMP: 10 **EST:** 1982
SQ FT: 5,000
SALES (est): 1.9MM **Privately Held**
SIC: 2873 5999 Nitrogenous fertilizers; Farm equipment and supplies

(G-609)
RAIN DROP PRODUCTS LLC
2121 Cottage St (44805-1245)
PHONE..................................419 207-1229
Mark Williams, *Pr*
Michael Hooper, *
James Cox, *
◆ **EMP:** 30 **EST:** 1999
SQ FT: 30,000
SALES (est): 5.05MM **Privately Held**
Web: www.rain-drop.com
SIC: 3949 Water sports equipment

(G-610)
RETURN POLYMERS INC
400 Westlake Dr (44805-1397)
PHONE..................................419 289-1998
David Foell, *Pr*
EMP: 65 **EST:** 1992
SQ FT: 26,000
SALES (est): 19.31MM
SALES (corp-wide): 1.37B **Publicly Held**
Web: www.returnpolymers.com
SIC: 2821 Plastics materials and resins
PA: The Azek Company Inc
1330 W Fulton St Ste 350
Chicago IL 60607
877 275-2935

(G-611)
ROTOSOLUTIONS INC
1401 Jacobson Ave (44805-1846)
PHONE..................................419 903-0800
Ralph Kirkpatrick, *CEO*
EMP: 15 **EST:** 2013
SALES (est): 2.44MM **Privately Held**
Web: www.rotosolutions.com
SIC: 3089 Injection molding of plastics

(G-612)
SCHOONOVER INDUSTRIES INC
1440 Simonton Rd (44805-1906)
P.O. Box 69 (44805-0069)
PHONE..................................419 289-8332
Robert P Schoonover, *Pr*
EMP: 26 **EST:** 1983
SQ FT: 12,000
SALES (est): 5.18MM **Privately Held**
Web: www.schoonoveronline.com
SIC: 3441 3444 Fabricated structural metal; Sheet metalwork

(G-613)
SEPTIC PRODUCTS INC
1378 Township Road 743 (44805-8926)
PHONE..................................419 282-5933
Rod Mitchell, *Pr*
EMP: 8 **EST:** 2005
SALES (est): 966.92K **Privately Held**
Web: www.septicproducts.com
SIC: 3272 Septic tanks, concrete

(G-614)
SJE RHOMBUS CONTROLS
2221 Ford Dr (44805-1280)
PHONE..................................419 281-5767
Vic Olivieri, *Prin*
EMP: 8 **EST:** 2018
SALES (est): 1.61MM **Privately Held**
Web: www.sjeinc.com
SIC: 3822 Environmental controls

(G-615)
STEEL CITY CORPORATION (PA)
1000 Hedstrom Dr (44805-3587)
P.O. Box 1227 (44501-1227)
PHONE..................................330 792-7663
Chris Shafer, *Pr*
Rod Mitchell, *Prin*
Scott Conery, *Prin*
◆ **EMP:** 20 **EST:** 1939
SQ FT: 161,000
SALES (est): 2.11MM
SALES (corp-wide): 2.11MM **Privately Held**
Web: www.scity.com
SIC: 2678 Newsprint tablets and pads: made from purchased materials

(G-616)
STRAIGHTAWAY FABRICATIONS LTD
481us Highway 250 E (44805-9771)
PHONE..................................419 281-9440
David Bowles, *Pr*
EMP: 14 **EST:** 2004
SQ FT: 1,500
SALES (est): 1.75MM **Privately Held**
Web: www.straightawayfab.com
SIC: 3441 Fabricated structural metal

(G-617)
TAHOMA ENGINEERED SOLUTIONS INC
Also Called: Tahoma Engineered Solutions
532 County Road 1600 (44805)
PHONE..................................330 345-6169
EMP: 29 **EST:** 1966
SALES (est): 4.36MM **Privately Held**
Web: www.tahomaengineeredsolutions.com
SIC: 3599 Machine shop, jobbing and repair

(G-618)
TREMCO CPG INC
1451 Jacobson Ave (44805-1865)
PHONE..................................419 289-2050
James Mongiardo, *Brnch Mgr*
EMP: 50
SALES (corp-wide): 7.26B **Publicly Held**
Web: www.tremcosealants.com
SIC: 2891 Adhesives and sealants
HQ: Tremco Cpg Inc.
3735 Green Rd
Beachwood OH 44122
216 292-5000

(G-619)
UPS STORE
Also Called: UPS
1130 E Main St (44805-2832)
PHONE..................................419 289-6688
Albert Welsch, *Prin*
EMP: 6 **EST:** 2008
SALES (est): 146.44K **Privately Held**
Web: locations.theupsstore.com
SIC: 2752 Business form and card printing, lithographic

(G-620)
WAUGS INC
956 State Route 302 (44805-9578)
PHONE..................................440 315-4851
EMP: 8 **EST:** 2006
SALES (est): 540.57K **Privately Held**
Web: www.waugs.com
SIC: 3089 Injection molding of plastics

(G-621)
ZEPHYR INDUSTRIES INC
600 Township Road 1500 (44805-9759)

(PA)=Parent Co (HQ)=Headquarters
✪ = New Business established in last 2 years

PHONE..............................419 281-4485
Vincent Richilano, *Pr*
David E Richilano, *Sec*
EMP: 8 **EST:** 1958
SQ FT: 20,000
SALES (est): 883.94K **Privately Held**
Web: www.zephyrindustries.com
SIC: 3365 3569 3599 Machinery castings, aluminum; Firefighting and related equipment; Machine shop, jobbing and repair

Ashley
Delaware County

(G-622)
IMPERIAL ON-PECE FIBRGLS POOLS
255 S Franklin St (43003-9749)
PHONE..............................740 747-2971
TOLL FREE: 800
Charles Levings Junior, *Pr*
Carol Mash, *VP*
Glen Mash, *Prin*
John Mash, *Prin*
EMP: 10 **EST:** 1969
SQ FT: 10,000
SALES (est): 607.1K **Privately Held**
SIC: 3949 1799 Swimming pools, except plastic; Swimming pool construction

(G-623)
ROTARY PRODUCTS INC
202 W High St (43003-9703)
P.O. Box 370 (43003-0370)
PHONE..............................740 747-2623
Chris Buechel, *Pr*
EMP: 15
SALES (corp-wide): 2.98MM **Privately Held**
Web: www.rotaryproductsinc.com
SIC: 3081 Unsupported plastics film and sheet
PA: Rotary Products, Inc.
    117 E High St
    Ashley OH 43003
    740 747-2623

(G-624)
ROTARY PRODUCTS INC (PA)
117 E High St (43003)
P.O. Box 370 (43003-0370)
PHONE..............................740 747-2623
Christopher Buechel, *Pr*
EMP: 14 **EST:** 1958
SQ FT: 9,000
SALES (est): 2.98MM
SALES (corp-wide): 2.98MM **Privately Held**
Web: www.rotaryproductsinc.com
SIC: 3081 Vinyl film and sheet

Ashtabula
Ashtabula County

(G-625)
AAM MOLD AND MACHINE INC
1015 Westwood Dr (44004-2369)
PHONE..............................440 998-2040
Anthony Martino, *Pr*
EMP: 16 **EST:** 2010
SALES (est): 1.87MM **Privately Held**
Web: www.aammold.com
SIC: 3599 Machine shop, jobbing and repair

(G-626)
AKALINA ASSOCIATES INC
2751 West Ave (44004-3117)
P.O. Box 398 (44005-0398)
PHONE..............................440 992-2195
Nicholas J Jammal, *Pr*
▲ **EMP:** 200 **EST:** 1945
SQ FT: 72,000
SALES (est): 21.98MM **Privately Held**
Web: www.ashtabularubber.com
SIC: 3061 3069 3053 Mechanical rubber goods; Hard rubber and molded rubber products; Gaskets, all materials

(G-627)
CICOGNA ELECTRIC AND SIGN CO (PA)
Also Called: Cicogna
4330 N Bend Rd (44004-9797)
P.O. Box 234 (44005-0234)
PHONE..............................440 998-2637
Frank Cicogna, *Pr*
James M Timonere, *
EMP: 75 **EST:** 1975
SQ FT: 55,000
SALES (est): 9.83MM
SALES (corp-wide): 9.83MM **Privately Held**
Web: www.cicognasign.com
SIC: 3993 Neon signs

(G-628)
CREATIVE MILLWORK OHIO INC
1801 W 47th St (44004)
P.O. Box 1157 (44005)
PHONE..............................440 992-3566
Joseph J Lalli, *COO*
Brian A Estock, *
Cynthia Estock, *
Joann Andersen, *
EMP: 80 **EST:** 1987
SQ FT: 67,000
SALES (est): 14MM **Privately Held**
Web: www.creativemillwork.com
SIC: 3089 3442 Window frames and sash, plastics; Window and door frames

(G-629)
CRUISIN TIMES HOLDINGS LLC
5239 Lake Rd W (44004-8520)
PHONE..............................234 646-2095
Chris Paczak, *Managing Member*
EMP: 6
SALES (est): 78.58K **Privately Held**
SIC: 2721 Magazines: publishing and printing

(G-630)
CUSTOM CRAFT COLLECTION INC
Also Called: Russel Upholstery
5422 Main Ave (44004-7058)
PHONE..............................440 998-3000
TOLL FREE: 888
EMP: 10 **EST:** 1994
SQ FT: 10,000
SALES (est): 608.03K **Privately Held**
Web: www.russellupholstery.com
SIC: 2512 7641 2522 Upholstered household furniture; Reupholstery and furniture repair; Office furniture, except wood

(G-631)
ELCO CORPORATION
1100 State Rd (44004-3943)
PHONE..............................440 997-6131
Tom Steiv, *Mgr*
EMP: 28
Web: www.lubeperformanceadditives.com
SIC: 2869 2819 2899 Industrial organic chemicals, nec; Industrial inorganic chemicals, nec; Chemical preparations, nec
HQ: Elco Corporation
    1000 Belt Line Ave
    Cleveland OH 44109
    800 321-0467

(G-632)
ESAB GROUP INCORPORATED
3325 Middle Rd (44004-3974)
P.O. Box 943 (44005-0943)
PHONE..............................440 813-2506
Cheri Houser, *Prin*
EMP: 7 **EST:** 2016
SALES (est): 236.87K **Privately Held**
SIC: 3356 Nonferrous rolling and drawing, nec

(G-633)
FREZERVE INC
1218 Lake Ave (44004-2932)
P.O. Box 890 (44005-0890)
PHONE..............................440 661-4037
David Hellmer, *Pr*
EMP: 8 **EST:** 2021
SALES (est): 500K **Privately Held**
SIC: 2034 2095 Fruits, freeze-dried; Freeze-dried coffee

(G-634)
G M R TECHNOLOGY INC
2131 Aetna Rd (44004-6291)
PHONE..............................440 992-6003
Connie J Speakman, *Prin*
Peter P Zawaly Junior, *Prin*
◆ **EMP:** 30 **EST:** 1984
SQ FT: 45,000
SALES (est): 4.67MM **Privately Held**
SIC: 3089 Injection molding of plastics

(G-635)
GRAND RIVER RUBBER & PLASTICS COMPANY
2029 Aetna Rd (44004-6298)
P.O. Box 477 (44005-0477)
PHONE..............................440 998-2900
◆ **EMP:** 200 **EST:** 1976
SALES (est): 31.45MM **Privately Held**
Web: www.grandriverrubber.com
SIC: 3069 3053 Washers, rubber; Gaskets, all materials

(G-636)
GREAT LAKES PRINTING INC
2926 Lake Ave (44004-4964)
P.O. Box 245 (44047-0245)
PHONE..............................440 993-8781
Jeff Lampson, *Pr*
Jeff Lampson, *VP*
EMP: 18 **EST:** 1976
SQ FT: 2,460
SALES (est): 461.8K **Privately Held**
Web: www.millerbuildersinc.com
SIC: 2752 2759 Offset printing; Letterpress printing

(G-637)
HALMAN INC
3901 N Bend Rd (44004-9778)
P.O. Box 3108 (44005-3108)
EMP: 14 **EST:** 1986
SALES (est): 2.19MM **Privately Held**
Web: www.halmaninc.com
SIC: 3441 1541 Fabricated structural metal; Renovation, remodeling and repairs: industrial buildings

(G-638)
HONES HARBOR HOUSE GIFTS
720 E 6th St (44004-3520)
PHONE..............................216 334-9836
Lynn Homes, *Prin*
EMP: 6 **EST:** 2012
SALES (est): 71.95K **Privately Held**
SIC: 3291 Hones

(G-639)
INEOS KOH INC
3509 Middle Rd (44004-3915)
P.O. Box 858 (44005-0858)
PHONE..............................440 997-5221
Ashley Reed, *CEO*
Lucie David, *
▲ **EMP:** 117 **EST:** 1989
SALES (est): 45.77MM
SALES (corp-wide): 917.38K **Privately Held**
Web: www.ashtachemicals.com
SIC: 2812 Caustic potash, potassium hydroxide
HQ: Ineos Enterprises Us Holdco Llc
    23425 W Amoco Rd
    Channahon IL 60410
    614 787-2058

(G-640)
INEOS PIGMENTS ASU LLC
2501 Middle Rd (44004-3917)
PHONE..............................440 994-1999
James Koutras, *Managing Member*
EMP: 26 **EST:** 2013
SQ FT: 30,000
SALES (est): 1.23MM
SALES (corp-wide): 917.38K **Privately Held**
SIC: 2819 Industrial inorganic chemicals, nec
HQ: Ineos Enterprises Holdings Limited
    15-19 Britten Street
    London SW3 3
    192 851-6948

(G-641)
INEOS PIGMENTS USA INC
Also Called: Millennium
2900 Middle Rd (44004-3925)
P.O. Box 160 (44005-0160)
PHONE..............................440 994-1400
Joseph Dezman, *Mgr*
EMP: 200
SALES (corp-wide): 917.38K **Privately Held**
SIC: 2819 Industrial inorganic chemicals, nec
HQ: Ineos Pigments Usa Inc.
    6752 Baymeadow Dr
    Glen Burnie MD 21060
    410 762-1000

(G-642)
ITEN INDUSTRIES INC (PA)
Also Called: Plant 2
4602 Benefit Ave (44004-5455)
P.O. Box 2150 (44005-2150)
PHONE..............................440 997-6134
Peter D Huggins, *CEO*
Peter D Huggins, *Pr*
Bill Kane, *
Terry Warren, *
◆ **EMP:** 172 **EST:** 1922
SQ FT: 175,000
SALES (est): 46.58MM
SALES (corp-wide): 46.58MM **Privately Held**
Web: www.itenindustries.com
SIC: 3089 Laminating of plastics

Ashtabula - Ashtabula County (G-663)

(G-643)
ITEN INDUSTRIES INC
3500 N Ridge Rd W (44004-6370)
PHONE..................440 997-6134
EMP: 10
SALES (corp-wide): 46.58MM **Privately Held**
Web: www.itenindustries.com
SIC: 3089 Laminating of plastics
PA: Iten Industries, Inc.
4602 Benefit Ave
Ashtabula OH 44004
440 997-6134

(G-644)
KOSKI CONSTRUCTION CO (PA)
5841 Woodman Ave (44004-7919)
P.O. Box 1038 (44005-1038)
PHONE..................440 997-5337
Donald R Koski, *Pr*
Thomas Pope, *VP*
David C Sheldon, *Treas*
EMP: 6 **EST:** 1921
SQ FT: 3,500
SALES (est): 4.14MM
SALES (corp-wide): 4.14MM **Privately Held**
Web: www.koski-construction.com
SIC: 1611 1794 1771 2951 Surfacing and paving; Excavation work; Concrete work; Asphalt and asphaltic paving mixtures (not from refineries)

(G-645)
LAKE CITY PLATING LLC (PA)
Also Called: Lake City Plating
1701 Lake Ave (44004-3099)
PHONE..................440 964-3555
Todd Bendis, *CEO*
Ryan Carroll, *
EMP: 107 **EST:** 1949
SQ FT: 60,000
SALES (est): 22.53MM
SALES (corp-wide): 22.53MM **Privately Held**
Web: www.lakecityplating.com
SIC: 3471 Electroplating of metals or formed products

(G-646)
LINDE INC
Praxair
3102 Lake Rd E (44004-3829)
PHONE..................440 994-1000
J J Redmond, *Brnch Mgr*
EMP: 12
Web: www.lindeus.com
SIC: 2813 Oxygen, compressed or liquefied
HQ: Linde Inc
10 Riverview Dr
Danbury CT 06810
203 837-2000

(G-647)
MEESE INC
Meese Orbitron Dunne
4920 State Rd (44004-6237)
P.O. Box 607 (44005-0607)
PHONE..................440 998-1202
Robert W Dunne Junior, *Pr*
EMP: 13
Web: www.meese-inc.com
SIC: 3429 3089 3544 3444 Hardware, nec; Injection molded finished plastics products, nec; Special dies, tools, jigs, and fixtures; Sheet metalwork
HQ: Meese, Inc.
1745 Cragmont St
Madison IN 47250
800 829-4535

(G-648)
MFG COMPOSITE SYSTEMS COMPANY
Also Called: Mfg CSC
2925 Mfg Pl (44004-9701)
P.O. Box 675 (44005-0675)
PHONE..................440 997-5851
Richard Morrison, *Pr*
Andy Juhola, *
Alec Raffa, *
Keith Bihary, *
Dan Plona, *
◆ **EMP:** 350 **EST:** 1948
SALES (est): 87.55MM
SALES (corp-wide): 360.86MM **Privately Held**
Web: www.mfgcsc.com
SIC: 3229 2823 Glass fiber products; Cellulosic manmade fibers
PA: Molded Fiber Glass Companies
2925 Mfg Pl
Ashtabula OH 44004
440 997-5851

(G-649)
MODROTO
4920 State Rd (44004-6237)
PHONE..................440 998-1202
Bob Dunne, *Pr*
EMP: 9 **EST:** 2015
SALES (est): 242.24K **Privately Held**
SIC: 2655 2599 5085 Fiber cans, drums, and containers; Carts, restaurant equipment; Bins and containers, storage

(G-650)
MOLDED FIBER GLASS COMPANIES (PA)
2925 Mfg Pl (44004-9445)
P.O. Box 675 (44005-0675)
PHONE..................440 997-5851
Richard Morrison, *CEO*
Dave Denny, *
Darren Schwede, *
Greg Tilton, *
Carl Lafrance, *CIO*
◆ **EMP:** 685 **EST:** 1946
SQ FT: 265,000
SALES (est): 360.86MM
SALES (corp-wide): 360.86MM **Privately Held**
Web: www.moldedfiberglass.com
SIC: 3089 Molding primary plastics

(G-651)
MOLDED FIBER GLASS COMPANIES
Also Called: Msg Premier Molded Fiber
4401 Benefit Ave (44004-5458)
P.O. Box 675 (44005-0675)
PHONE..................440 997-5851
Richard Morrison, *CEO*
EMP: 55
SQ FT: 168,000
SALES (corp-wide): 360.86MM **Privately Held**
Web: www.moldedfiberglass.com
SIC: 3089 Molding primary plastics
PA: Molded Fiber Glass Companies
2925 Mfg Pl
Ashtabula OH 44004
440 997-5851

(G-652)
MOLDED FIBER GLASS COMPANIES
1315 W 47th St (44004-5403)
PHONE..................440 994-5100
Pete Emrich, *Brnch Mgr*
EMP: 50
SALES (corp-wide): 360.86MM **Privately Held**
Web: www.moldedfiberglass.com
SIC: 3089 Plastics containers, except foam
PA: Molded Fiber Glass Companies
2925 Mfg Pl
Ashtabula OH 44004
440 997-5851

(G-653)
NORTHEAST BOX COMPANY
1726 Griswold Ave (44004-9213)
P.O. Box 370 (44005-0370)
PHONE..................440 992-5500
Ronald Marchewka, *Pr*
Craig Parker, *Stockholder*
Richard Selip, *Stockholder*
Robert Jessup, *Stockholder*
Joseph Misinic, *Stockholder*
EMP: 55 **EST:** 1978
SQ FT: 110,000
SALES (est): 6.28MM **Privately Held**
Web: www.northeastbox.com
SIC: 2653 Boxes, corrugated: made from purchased materials

(G-654)
PESKA INC (PA)
Also Called: Sports & Sports
3600 N Ridge Rd E (44004-4316)
PHONE..................440 998-4664
Steve Reichert, *Pr*
Edith M Reichert, *Prin*
Paul A Reichert, *Prin*
EMP: 10 **EST:** 1983
SQ FT: 6,000
SALES (est): 919.58K
SALES (corp-wide): 919.58K **Privately Held**
Web: www.sportsnsports.com
SIC: 5941 2396 Sporting goods and bicycle shops; Screen printing on fabric articles

(G-655)
PINNEY DOCK & TRANSPORT LLC
1149 E 5th St (44004-3513)
P.O. Box 41 (44004-0041)
PHONE..................440 964-7186
◆ **EMP:** 57 **EST:** 1953
SQ FT: 20,000
SALES (est): 1.65MM **Publicly Held**
SIC: 3731 4491 5032 Drydocks, floating; Docks, piers and terminals; Limestone
PA: Kinder Morgan Inc
1001 La St Ste 1000
Houston TX 77002

(G-656)
PROFESSIONAL MARINE REPAIR LLC
1453 Dover Cntr Rd (44004)
PHONE..................440 409-9957
EMP: 8 **EST:** 2018
SALES (est): 400K **Privately Held**
SIC: 3731 Lighters, marine: building and repairing

(G-657)
REESE MACHINE COMPANY INC
2501 State Rd (44004-5235)
P.O. Box 1396 (44005-1396)
PHONE..................440 992-3942
Dale Reese, *Pr*
EMP: 10 **EST:** 1965
SALES (est): 1.01MM **Privately Held**
Web: www.reesemc.com
SIC: 3599 Machine shop, jobbing and repair

(G-658)
RELOADING SUPPLIES CORP
Also Called: Ohio Guns
3916 Edgewater Dr (44004-2132)
PHONE..................440 228-0367
Daryl G Upole Iii, *Admn*
Daryl Upole, *Pr*
EMP: 8 **EST:** 2009
SALES (est): 996.58K **Privately Held**
Web: www.ohioguns.us
SIC: 3484 5941 Machine guns and grenade launchers; Ammunition

(G-659)
REX INTERNATIONAL USA INC
Also Called: Wheeler Manufacturing
3744 Jefferson Rd (44004-9601)
P.O. Box 688 (44005-0688)
PHONE..................800 321-7950
John Miyagawa, *CEO*
◆ **EMP:** 20 **EST:** 1988
SQ FT: 22,000
SALES (est): 6.23MM **Privately Held**
Web: www.wheelerrex.com
SIC: 3423 3546 3545 3541 Hand and edge tools, nec; Power-driven handtools; Machine tool accessories; Pipe cutting and threading machines
HQ: Rex Industries Co., Ltd.
1-9-3, Hishiyahigashi
Higashi-Osaka OSK 578-0

(G-660)
SHORT RUN MACHINE PRODUCTS INC
4744 Kister Ct (44004-8974)
PHONE..................440 969-1313
Scott Ray, *Pr*
EMP: 12 **EST:** 1989
SALES (est): 1.02MM **Privately Held**
Web: www.shortrunmachine.com
SIC: 3599 3544 Machine shop, jobbing and repair; Special dies, tools, jigs, and fixtures

(G-661)
STAN-KELL LLC
2621 West Ave (44004-3115)
P.O. Box 429 (44005-0429)
PHONE..................440 998-1116
Brian Lewis, *Pr*
Steve Berndt, *VP*
EMP: 30 **EST:** 1963
SQ FT: 18,450
SALES (est): 1.96MM **Privately Held**
Web: www.pencotool.com
SIC: 3544 3599 7692 Industrial molds; Machine shop, jobbing and repair; Welding repair

(G-662)
ULTIMATE CHEM SOLUTIONS INC
1800 E 21st St (44004-4012)
P.O. Box 1768 (44005-1768)
PHONE..................440 998-6751
Yogi V Chokshi, *Pr*
EMP: 16 **EST:** 2010
SALES (est): 2.21MM **Privately Held**
SIC: 2869 Industrial organic chemicals, nec

(G-663)
VEITSCH-RADEX AMERICA LLC
4741 Kister Ct (44004-8975)
PHONE..................717 793-7122
David Lawrie, *Pr*
Carlo A D'amicis, *COO*
Craig Powell, *STEEL*
Giovanni Tancredo, *INDUSTRIAL*
Kelly L Myers, *Sec*
EMP: 65 **EST:** 2002
SALES (est): 8.46MM **Privately Held**
SIC: 3255 Brick, clay refractory
HQ: Veitsch-Radex Gmbh & Co Og
Kranichberggasse 6
Wien 1120
502130

Ashtabula — Ashtabula County (G-664)

(G-664)
VIBRANTZ COLOR SOLUTIONS INC (DH)
Also Called: Chromaflo
2600 Michigan Ave (44004-3140)
P.O. Box 816 (44005-0816)
PHONE.................................440 997-5137
Scott Becker, *CEO*
Jim Hill, *
◆ **EMP:** 137 **EST:** 1970
SQ FT: 175,000
SALES (est): 257.16MM
SALES (corp-wide): 1.88B **Privately Held**
Web: www.vibrantz.com
SIC: 2816 3087 2865 Inorganic pigments; Custom compound purchased resins; Color pigments, organic
HQ: Vibrantz Technologies Inc.
16945 Northchase Dr # 2000
Houston TX 77060
646 747-4222

(G-665)
WITT ENTERPRISES INC
2024 Aetna Rd (44004-6260)
PHONE.................................440 992-8333
Ron Kister Junior, *Pr*
EMP: 26 **EST:** 1986
SQ FT: 600
SALES (est): 966.51K **Privately Held**
Web: www.cw2.com
SIC: 3471 Sand blasting of metal parts

(G-666)
ZEHRCO-GIANCOLA COMPOSITES INC (PA)
1501 W 47th St (44004-5419)
PHONE.................................440 994-6317
Anthony Giancola, *Pr*
▼ **EMP:** 105 **EST:** 2003
SQ FT: 150,000
SALES (est): 26.65MM
SALES (corp-wide): 26.65MM **Privately Held**
Web: www.zehrco-giancola.com
SIC: 3089 Injection molding of plastics

Ashville
Pickaway County

(G-667)
COLUMBUS INDUSTRIES INC (HQ)
2938 State Route 752 (43103)
P.O. Box 257 (43103)
PHONE.................................740 983-2552
Harold T Pontius, *Ch Bd*
Jeffrey Pontius, *Pr*
Eric Pontius, *VP*
Wayne Vickers, *Ex VP*
Debbie Vickers, *VP*
◆ **EMP:** 100 **EST:** 1965
SQ FT: 78,000
SALES (est): 103.8MM
SALES (corp-wide): 1.05B **Privately Held**
Web: www.columbusindustries.com
SIC: 3569 Filters
PA: Filtration Group Corporation
1 Tower Ln
Oakbrook Terrace IL 60181
630 968-1730

(G-668)
COLUMBUS INDUSTRIES ONE LLC
2938 State Route 752 (43103-9543)
P.O. Box 257 (43103-0257)
PHONE.................................740 983-2552
Wayne Vickers, *Managing Member*
EMP: 10 **EST:** 2000
SALES (est): 956.12K **Privately Held**
SIC: 3569 Filters

(G-669)
NOVELIS ALR ROLLED PDTS LLC
1 Reynolds Rd (43103-9204)
PHONE.................................740 983-2571
EMP: 829
Web: www.novelis.com
SIC: 3355 Aluminum rolling and drawing, nec
HQ: Novelis Alr Rolled Products, Llc
25825 Science Park Dr # 400
Beachwood OH 44122
216 910-3400

(G-670)
NOVELIS CORPORATION
1 Reynolds Rd (43103-9204)
P.O. Box 197 (43103-0197)
PHONE.................................740 983-2571
EMP: 156
Web: www.novelis.com
SIC: 3341 3444 Secondary nonferrous metals; Sheet metalwork
HQ: Novelis Corporation
One Phpps Plz 3550 Pchtre
Atlanta GA 30326
404 760-4000

(G-671)
OWENS CORNING SALES LLC
Also Called: Owens Corning
1 Reynolds Rd (43103-9204)
P.O. Box 197 (43103-0197)
PHONE.................................740 983-1300
Rodney Sawall, *Mgr*
EMP: 13
SIC: 3444 3354 Siding, sheet metal; Aluminum extruded products
HQ: Owens Corning Sales, Llc
1 Owens Corning Pkwy
Toledo OH 43659
419 248-8000

Athens
Athens County

(G-672)
AC GREEN LLC
6648 Hudnell Rd (45701)
PHONE.................................740 292-2604
Claire Green, *Pr*
EMP: 12 **EST:** 2021
SALES (est): 1.12MM **Privately Held**
SIC: 3441 Fabricated structural metal

(G-673)
ADAMS PUBLISHING GROUP LLC (HQ)
Also Called: Apg Media of Ohio
9300 Johnson Hollow Rd (45701-9028)
PHONE.................................740 592-6612
Mark Adams, *CEO*
Robert Wallace, *CFO*
EMP: 47 **EST:** 2013
SALES (est): 17.7MM
SALES (corp-wide): 333.51MM **Privately Held**
Web: www.adamspg.com
SIC: 2711 Newspapers, publishing and printing
PA: Adams Publishing Group, Llc
4095 Coon Rapids Blvd Nw
Minneapolis MN 55433
218 348-3391

(G-674)
ALL POWER EQUIPMENT LLC (PA)
Also Called: Kubota Authorized Dealer
8880 United Ln (45701-3667)
PHONE.................................740 593-3279
EMP: 19 **EST:** 1997
SQ FT: 6,000
SALES (est): 2.39MM **Privately Held**
Web: www.allpowerequipment.com
SIC: 5261 5561 3799 5083 Lawnmowers and tractors; Camper and travel trailer dealers; All terrain vehicles (ATV); Farm and garden machinery

(G-675)
ATHENS MOLD AND MACHINE INC
180 Mill St (45701-2627)
P.O. Box 847 (45701-0847)
PHONE.................................740 593-6613
Jack D Thornton, *Pr*
Mark Thornton, *
EMP: 81 **EST:** 1985
SQ FT: 70,000
SALES (est): 7.81MM **Privately Held**
Web: www.tiremolds.com
SIC: 3544 3599 7692 Special dies and tools; Machine shop, jobbing and repair; Welding repair

(G-676)
ATHENS TECHNICAL SPECIALISTS
Also Called: Atsi
8157 Us Highway 50 (45701-9303)
PHONE.................................740 592-2874
Ted Gilfert, *VP*
James Gilfert, *Pr*
Una Gilfert, *Sec*
▲ **EMP:** 14 **EST:** 1982
SQ FT: 6,000
SALES (est): 2.24MM **Privately Held**
Web: www.bectactical.com
SIC: 3669 8748 Traffic signals, electric; Traffic consultant

(G-677)
BRIDGESTONE RET OPERATIONS LLC
Also Called: Firestone
820 E State St (45701-2112)
PHONE.................................740 592-3075
Greg Myers, *Mgr*
EMP: 6
Web: www.bridgestoneamericas.com
SIC: 5531 7534 Automotive tires; Rebuilding and retreading tires
HQ: Bridgestone Retail Operations, Llc
333 E Lake St Ste 300
Bloomingdale IL 60108
630 259-9000

(G-678)
BUCKEYE SMOOTHIES LLC
145 Columbus Rd (45701-1356)
PHONE.................................740 589-2900
Thomas Kostohryz, *Prin*
EMP: 7 **EST:** 2007
SALES (est): 114.82K **Privately Held**
SIC: 2037 Frozen fruits and vegetables

(G-679)
CITY OF ATHENS
395 W State St (45701-1527)
PHONE.................................740 592-3344
EMP: 22
SALES (corp-wide): 25.51MM **Privately Held**
Web: ci.athens.oh.us
SIC: 3589 4941 Water treatment equipment, industrial; Water supply
PA: City Of Athens
8 E Washington St Ste 101
Athens OH 45701
740 592-3338

(G-680)
CRUMBS INC
Also Called: Crumbs Bakery
94 Columbus Rd (45701-1312)
P.O. Box 315 (45701-0315)
PHONE.................................740 592-3803
Jeremy Bowman, *Pr*
EMP: 10 **EST:** 1986
SALES (est): 714.43K **Privately Held**
Web: crumbsbakery.a-zcompanies.com
SIC: 2051 5461 Bakery: wholesale or wholesale/retail combined; Retail bakeries

(G-681)
DIAGNOSTIC HYBRIDS INC
2005 E State St Ste 100 (45701-2125)
PHONE.................................740 593-1784
David R Scholl Ph.d., *Pr*
James L Brown, *
Geoff Morgan, *
Gail Pres-regulatory Goodrum V, *Quality Affairs*
Paul D Olivo Ph.d., *Research Vice President*
EMP: 220 **EST:** 1982
SQ FT: 25,000
SALES (est): 46.99MM
SALES (corp-wide): 3B **Publicly Held**
Web: www.quidelortho.com
SIC: 2835 3841 Diagnostic substances; Diagnostic apparatus, medical
HQ: Quidel Corporation
9975 Summers Ridge Rd
San Diego CA 92121
858 552-1100

(G-682)
FUSION NOODLE COMPANY INC
30 E Union St (45701-2911)
PHONE.................................740 589-5511
EMP: 8 **EST:** 2013
SALES (est): 414.57K **Privately Held**
Web: www.fusionnoodleathens.com
SIC: 2098 Noodles (e.g. egg, plain, and water), dry

(G-683)
G & J PEPSI-COLA BOTTLERS INC
Also Called: Pepsi-Cola
2001 E State St (45701-2125)
PHONE.................................740 593-3366
Curt Allison, *Brnch Mgr*
EMP: 44
SALES (corp-wide): 404.54MM **Privately Held**
Web: www.gjpepsi.com
SIC: 2086 5149 Carbonated soft drinks, bottled and canned; Beverages, except coffee and tea
PA: G & J Pepsi-Cola Bottlers Inc
9435 Waterstone Blvd # 390
Cincinnati OH 45249
513 785-6060

(G-684)
GEM COATINGS LTD
5840 Industrial Park Rd (45701-8736)
PHONE.................................740 589-2998
Karry Gemmell, *Pt*
EMP: 19 **EST:** 2001
SQ FT: 55,000
SALES (est): 680.89K **Privately Held**
Web: www.coatingsllc.com
SIC: 3479 Coating of metals with plastic or resins

(G-685)
GLOBAL COOLING INC
Also Called: Stirling Ultracold
6000 Poston Rd (45701)
PHONE.................................740 274-7900

◆ EMP: 121 EST: 1993
SQ FT: 15,000
SALES (est): 42.14MM Publicly Held
Web: www.biolifesolutions.com
SIC: 3821 Freezers, laboratory
PA: Biolife Solutions, Inc.
3303 Mnte Vlla Pkwy Ste 3
Bothell WA 98021

(G-686)
HOCKING VALLEY CONCRETE INC
748 W Union St (45701-9408)
PHONE..................740 592-5335
EMP: 8 EST: 2008
SALES (est): 512.39K Privately Held
Web: www.hockingvalleyconcrete.com
SIC: 3273 Ready-mixed concrete

(G-687)
MCHAPPYS DONUTS OF PARKERSBURG
Also Called: Mc Happys Donuts
384 Richland Ave (45701-3204)
PHONE..................740 593-8744
Bonnie Boring, Mgr
EMP: 75
SALES (corp-wide): 22.71MM Privately Held
Web: www.mchappys.com
SIC: 5461 2051 Doughnuts; Doughnuts, except frozen
HQ: Mchappy's Donuts Of Parkersburg, Inc.
2515 Washington Blvd
Belpre OH 45714
740 423-6351

(G-688)
MESSENGER PUBLISHING COMPANY
Also Called: Athens Messenger, The
9300 Johnson Hollow Rd (45701-9028)
P.O. Box 4210 (45701-4210)
PHONE..................740 592-6612
Mark Policinski, Pr
Clarence Brown Junior, Ch Bd
Joyce Brown, *
John Aston, *
EMP: 125 EST: 1825
SQ FT: 25,000
SALES (est): 10.91MM
SALES (corp-wide): 333.51MM Privately Held
Web: www.athensmessenger.com
SIC: 2711 2752 Newspapers, publishing and printing; Offset printing
HQ: Adams Publishing Group, Llc
9300 Johnson Hollow Rd
Athens OH 45701
740 592-6612

(G-689)
OHIO GUITAR SHOWS INC
23 Curtis St (45701-3724)
P.O. Box 66 (45780-0066)
PHONE..................740 592-4614
EMP: 6 EST: 1985
SALES (est): 152.04K Privately Held
Web: www.ohioguitarshow.com
SIC: 2721 Magazines: publishing only, not printed on site

(G-690)
PETRO QUEST INC (PA)
3 W Stimson Ave (45701-2679)
P.O. Box 268 (45701-0268)
PHONE..................740 593-3800
Paul J Gerig, Pr
Christian Gerig, VP
Debora Jarvis, Sec
EMP: 6 EST: 1983
SQ FT: 2,200
SALES (est): 874.3K
SALES (corp-wide): 874.3K Privately Held
SIC: 1381 8111 Drilling oil and gas wells; General practice attorney, lawyer

(G-691)
PLEASANT HILL VINEYARDS LLC
5015 Pleasant Hill Rd (45701-8752)
PHONE..................740 502-3567
Sandra Corder, Prin
EMP: 6 EST: 2013
SALES (est): 241.23K Privately Held
Web: www.pleasanthillvineyardsllc.com
SIC: 2084 Wines

(G-692)
PRECISION IMPRINT
26 E State St (45701-2540)
PHONE..................740 592-5916
Randy Shoup, Owner
EMP: 8 EST: 1988
SQ FT: 5,000
SALES (est): 653.13K Privately Held
Web: www.precisionimprint.com
SIC: 2261 5136 5137 2759 Screen printing of cotton broadwoven fabrics; Sportswear, men's and boys'; Sportswear, women's and children's; Screen printing

(G-693)
QUICK LOADZ CONTAINER SYS LLC
Also Called: Quickloadz
5850 Industrial Park Rd (45701)
P.O. Box 272 (45780-0272)
PHONE..................888 304-3946
▲ EMP: 30 EST: 2013
SALES (est): 3.22MM Privately Held
Web: www.quickloadz.com
SIC: 3715 Trailer bodies

(G-694)
QUIDEL CORPORATION
2005 E State St # 100 (45701-2125)
PHONE..................858 552-1100
Scott Mccloud, Brnch Mgr
EMP: 53
SALES (corp-wide): 3B Publicly Held
Web: www.quidelortho.com
SIC: 2835 Diagnostic substances
HQ: Quidel Corporation
9975 Summers Ridge Rd
San Diego CA 92121
858 552-1100

(G-695)
QUIDEL CORPORATION
1055 E State St Ste 100 (45701-7911)
PHONE..................740 589-3300
EMP: 22
SALES (corp-wide): 3B Publicly Held
Web: www.quidelortho.com
SIC: 2835 Diagnostic substances
HQ: Quidel Corporation
9975 Summers Ridge Rd
San Diego CA 92121
858 552-1100

(G-696)
QUIDEL DHI
2005 E State St (45701-2125)
PHONE..................740 589-3300
Chris Ridgway, Mgr
EMP: 11 EST: 2013
SALES (est): 1.79MM
SALES (corp-wide): 3B Publicly Held
Web: www.quidelortho.com
SIC: 3829 Medical diagnostic systems, nuclear
HQ: Quidel Corporation
9975 Summers Ridge Rd
San Diego CA 92121
858 552-1100

(G-697)
SMITH CONCRETE CO
5240 Hebbardsville Rd (45701-9359)
PHONE..................740 593-5633
Phil Parsons, Mgr
EMP: 8
SALES (corp-wide): 5.07MM Privately Held
Web: www.shellyco.com
SIC: 3273 Ready-mixed concrete
PA: Smith Concrete Co
2301 Progress St
Dover OH 44622
740 373-7441

(G-698)
STEWART-MACDONALD MFG CO (PA)
Also Called: Stewart McDnalds Guitar Sp Sup
21 N Shafer St (45701-2304)
PHONE..................740 592-3021
Kay Tousley, CEO
Jay Hostetler, VP
John A Woodrow, CFO
▲ EMP: 40 EST: 1969
SQ FT: 12,000
SALES (est): 16.72MM
SALES (corp-wide): 16.72MM Privately Held
Web: www.stewmac.com
SIC: 3931 5736 Banjos and parts; Musical instrument stores

(G-699)
SUNPOWER INC
2005 E State St Ste 104 (45701-2125)
PHONE..................740 594-2221
Jeffrey Hatfield, VP
EMP: 95 EST: 1974
SQ FT: 16,000
SALES (est): 20.87MM
SALES (corp-wide): 6.6B Publicly Held
Web: www.sunpowerinc.com
SIC: 8731 8711 8733 3769 Commercial physical research; Engineering services; Physical research, noncommercial; Space vehicle equipment, nec
HQ: Advanced Measurement Technology, Inc.
801 S Illinois Ave
Oak Ridge TN 37830
865 482-4411

Attica
Seneca County

(G-700)
EITLE MACHINE TOOL INC
6036 Coder Rd (44807-9638)
PHONE..................419 935-8753
Jerrold Eitle, Pr
EMP: 7 EST: 1972
SALES (est): 542.51K Privately Held
SIC: 3599 Machine shop, jobbing and repair

(G-701)
KS TECHNOLOGIES & CSTM MFG LLC
12178 E County Road 6 (44807-9793)
P.O. Box 122 (44807-0122)
PHONE..................419 426-0172
Ron Waldock, Owner
EMP: 8 EST: 2015
SALES (est): 305.55K Privately Held
Web: www.kstech-custom.com
SIC: 8731 3999 Commercial physical research; Manufacturing industries, nec

Atwater
Portage County

(G-702)
CURTIS HILBRUNER
Also Called: Acorn Rubber
1315 Bank St (44201-9302)
P.O. Box 126 (44201-0126)
PHONE..................330 947-3527
Curtis Hilbruner, Owner
EMP: 9 EST: 1977
SALES (est): 500.86K Privately Held
Web: www.acornrubber.co.uk
SIC: 3069 Hard rubber and molded rubber products

Aurora
Portage County

(G-703)
ACCURATE FAB LLC
760 Deep Woods Dr (44202-9762)
PHONE..................330 562-3140
EMP: 10
SALES (est): 312.38K Privately Held
SIC: 3441 Fabricated structural metal

(G-704)
ADIDAS NORTH AMERICA INC
Also Called: Adidas Outlet Store Aurora
549 S Chillicothe Rd (44202-7848)
PHONE..................330 562-4689
EMP: 15
SALES (corp-wide): 23.29B Privately Held
SIC: 2329 Athletic clothing, except uniforms: men's, youths' and boys'
HQ: Adidas North America, Inc.
3449 N Anchor St Ste 500
Portland OR 97217
971 234-2300

(G-705)
ADVANCED INNOVATIVE MFG INC
Also Called: A.I.M.
116 Lena Dr (44202-9202)
PHONE..................330 562-2468
Joseph A Hawald, Pr
Mark J Hawald, *
EMP: 58 EST: 2014
SQ FT: 68,000
SALES (est): 5.02MM Privately Held
Web: www.a-i-mfg.com
SIC: 3541 Machine tools, metal cutting type

(G-706)
ATRIUM AT ANNA MARIA INC
849 N Aurora Rd (44202-9537)
PHONE..................330 562-7777
Aaron Baker, Admn
EMP: 14 EST: 2014
SALES (est): 902.77K Privately Held
Web: www.annamariaofaurora.com
SIC: 2711 Newspapers, publishing and printing

(G-707)
AUTOMATION PLASTICS CORP
150 Lena Dr (44202-9202)
PHONE..................330 562-5148
Harry Smith, Pr
EMP: 60 EST: 1978
SQ FT: 43,000
SALES (est): 14.6MM Privately Held
Web: www.automationplastics.com
SIC: 3089 3544 Injection molding of plastics; Special dies, tools, jigs, and fixtures

Aurora - Portage County (G-708)

(G-708)
BARRACUDA TECHNOLOGIES INC
2900 State Route 82 (44202-9395)
PHONE..................................216 469-1566
EMP: 7 **EST:** 2011
SALES (est): 91.6K **Privately Held**
SIC: 3644 Noncurrent-carrying wiring devices

(G-709)
BERRY PLASTICS FILMCO INC
1450 S Chillicothe Rd (44202-9282)
PHONE..................................330 562-6111
David Meldren, *Pr*
Judy Ciocca, *Prin*
▲ **EMP:** 81 **EST:** 1997
SQ FT: 85,000
SALES (est): 14.1MM **Publicly Held**
SIC: 3081 Plastics film and sheet
HQ: Berry Global, Inc.
101 Oakley St
Evansville IN 47710

(G-710)
CANTEX INC
11444 Chamberlain Rd # 1 (44202-9306)
PHONE..................................330 995-3665
Mike Schafer, *Brnch Mgr*
EMP: 86
Web: www.cantexinc.com
SIC: 3084 3089 Plastics pipe; Fittings for pipe, plastics
HQ: Cantex Inc.
301 Commerce St Ste 2700
Fort Worth TX 76102

(G-711)
CUSTOM PULTRUSIONS INC (HQ)
1331 S Chillicothe Rd (44202-8066)
PHONE..................................330 562-5201
Jay Lund, *CEO*
EMP: 62 **EST:** 2009
SALES (est): 12.57MM
SALES (corp-wide): 1.78B **Privately Held**
Web: www.custompultrusions.com
SIC: 3089 Injection molding of plastics
PA: Andersen Corporation
100 4th Ave N
Bayport MN 55003
651 264-5150

(G-712)
EATON CORPORATION
Synflex Division
115 Lena Dr (44202-9202)
PHONE..................................330 274-0743
Phil Corvo, *Mgr*
EMP: 35
SQ FT: 7,568
Web: www.dix-eaton.com
SIC: 3089 3494 3429 3052 Plastics containers, except foam; Valves and pipe fittings, nec; Hardware, nec; Rubber and plastics hose and beltings
HQ: Eaton Corporation
1000 Eaton Blvd
Cleveland OH 44122
440 523-5000

(G-713)
ELECTRIC SPEED INDICATOR CO
650 Cedar Bark Dr (44202-7750)
PHONE..................................216 251-2540
Robert P Riley, *Pr*
EMP: 10 **EST:** 1934
SALES (est): 566.74K **Privately Held**
Web: www.electricspeedindicator.com
SIC: 3829 7699 Geophysical and meteorological testing equipment; Meteorological instrument repair

(G-714)
EPG INC
500 Lena Dr (44202-9245)
PHONE..................................330 995-5125
Michael Orazen, *Mgr*
EMP: 64
SALES (corp-wide): 4.26B **Privately Held**
SIC: 3053 3061 Gaskets, all materials; Mechanical rubber goods
HQ: Epg, Inc.
1780 Miller Pkwy
Streetsboro OH 44241
330 995-9725

(G-715)
FREEDOM HEALTH LLC
65 Aurora Industrial Pkwy (44202-8088)
PHONE..................................330 562-0888
Mark Yoho, *VP*
Patrick Warczak Junior, *VP*
Vincenzo Franco, *VP*
▲ **EMP:** 20 **EST:** 2004
SQ FT: 50,000
SALES (est): 6.76MM **Privately Held**
Web: www.succeed-equine.com
SIC: 2023 Dietary supplements, dairy and non-dairy based

(G-716)
GODFREY & WING INC (PA)
220 Campus Dr (44202-6663)
PHONE..................................330 562-1440
Alexander Alford, *CEO*
Christopher Gilmore, *
Karen Gilmore, *
Brad Welch, *
▲ **EMP:** 41 **EST:** 1947
SQ FT: 68,000
SALES (est): 19.38MM
SALES (corp-wide): 19.38MM **Privately Held**
Web: www.godfreywing.com
SIC: 3479 8734 Coating of metals with plastic or resins; Testing laboratories

(G-717)
GUNNISON ASSOCIATES LLC
114 Barrington Town Square Dr # 11 (44202-7792)
PHONE..................................330 562-5230
EMP: 6 **EST:** 1998
SALES (est): 327.27K **Privately Held**
SIC: 3565 Packaging machinery

(G-718)
HEINENS INC
Also Called: Heinen's 8
115 N Chillicothe Rd (44202-7797)
PHONE..................................330 562-5297
Paul Otoole, *Mgr*
EMP: 150
SALES (corp-wide): 337.91MM **Privately Held**
Web: www.heinens.com
SIC: 5411 2051 Supermarkets, chain; Bread, cake, and related products
PA: Heinen's, Inc.
4540 Richmond Rd
Warrensville Heights OH 44128
216 475-2300

(G-719)
HF GROUP LLC (PA)
400 Aurora Commons Cir Unit 74 (44202)
P.O. Box 74 (44202-0074)
PHONE..................................440 729-2445
Jay B Fairfield, *Managing Member*
EMP: 10 **EST:** 2006
SQ FT: 6,000
SALES (est): 111.11MM **Privately Held**
Web: www.hfgroup.com

SIC: 2732 Book printing

(G-720)
INTEGRITY PARKING LLC ✪
Also Called: Consulting
400 Aurora Commons Cir Unit 438 (44202)
PHONE..................................440 543-4123
Lee Shorts, *CEO*
Lee Shorts, *Managing Member*
EMP: 16 **EST:** 2023
SALES (est): 723.35K **Privately Held**
Web: www.integrityparking.com
SIC: 3559 8742 7521 Parking facility equipment and supplies; Transportation consultant; Parking structure

(G-721)
LAYERZERO POWER SYSTEMS INC
1500 Danner Dr (44202-9298)
PHONE..................................440 399-9000
Milind Bhanoo, *Pr*
James M Oalm, *
EMP: 25 **EST:** 2001
SALES (est): 8.96MM **Privately Held**
Web: www.layerzero.com
SIC: 3613 Power switching equipment

(G-722)
LERNER ASSOC
665 E Homestead Dr (44202-8790)
P.O. Box 651 (44202-0651)
PHONE..................................330 348-0360
EMP: 8 **EST:** 2019
SALES (est): 243.28K **Privately Held**
Web: www.lernerandassoc.com
SIC: 3089 Injection molding of plastics

(G-723)
LYNK PACKAGING INC (PA)
Also Called: Jit Milrob
1250 Page Rd (44202-6666)
PHONE..................................330 562-8080
David R Jones, *Ch*
Elaine Jones, *VP*
EMP: 22 **EST:** 1985
SQ FT: 60,000
SALES (est): 10.61MM
SALES (corp-wide): 10.61MM **Privately Held**
Web: www.lynkpkg.com
SIC: 2448 5113 5085 2653 Pallets, wood; Corrugated and solid fiber boxes; Industrial supplies; Corrugated and solid fiber boxes

(G-724)
MERIDIAN LLC
Also Called: Meridian
325 Harris Dr (44202-7539)
PHONE..................................330 995-0371
EMP: 9 **EST:** 2010
SALES (est): 161.13K **Privately Held**
Web: www.meridianmed.net
SIC: 3841 Surgical and medical instruments

(G-725)
MERIDIENNE INTERNATIONAL INC
Also Called: Atlantic Water Gardens
125 Lena Dr (44202-9202)
PHONE..................................330 274-8317
William Lynne, *Pr*
▲ **EMP:** 7 **EST:** 1983
SALES (est): 2.41MM
SALES (corp-wide): 189.01MM **Privately Held**
Web: www.atlantic-oase.com
SIC: 3083 1799 3271 0781 Laminated plastics plate and sheet; Fountain installation; Blocks, concrete: landscape or retaining wall; Landscape services
PA: Oase Living Water Gmbh
Tecklenburger Str. 161

Horstel NW 48477
5454800

(G-726)
NATURAL ESSENTIALS INC
115 Lena Dr (44202-9202)
PHONE..................................330 562-8022
EMP: 10
Web: www.naturalessentialsinc.com
SIC: 2844 Perfumes, cosmetics and other toilet preparations
PA: Natural Essentials Incorporated
1830 Miller Pkwy
Streetsboro OH 44241

(G-727)
NETWORK TECHNOLOGIES INC
1275 Danner Dr (44202-8054)
PHONE..................................330 562-7070
◆ **EMP:** 96 **EST:** 1984
SALES (est): 9.11MM **Privately Held**
Web: www.networktechinc.com
SIC: 3678 Electronic connectors

(G-728)
OASE NORTH AMERICA INC
125 Lena Dr (44202-9202)
PHONE..................................800 365-3880
Andreas Szabados, *CEO*
Birgit Kempe-heeger, *Sec*
Ansgar Paul, *Sec*
◆ **EMP:** 6 **EST:** 1994
SALES (est): 6.28MM
SALES (corp-wide): 189.01MM **Privately Held**
Web: us.oase-livingwater.com
SIC: 3594 3524 5251 Fluid power pumps; Lawn and garden equipment; Pumps and pumping equipment
HQ: Oase International Holding Gmbh
Tecklenburger Str. 161
Horstel NW
5454800

(G-729)
OHIO FIRE SUPPRESSION LLC
10481 Maryland St (44202-8506)
PHONE..................................216 269-6032
EMP: 8 **EST:** 2018
SALES (est): 403.36K **Privately Held**
Web: www.ohiofiresuppression.com
SIC: 3672 Printed circuit boards

(G-730)
OMEGA POLYMER TECHNOLOGIES INC (PA)
Also Called: Opti
1331 S Chillicothe Rd (44202-8066)
PHONE..................................330 562-5201
Ronald Baker, *Pr*
Bob Jackson, *Sec*
EMP: 6 **EST:** 1994
SALES (est): 32.58MM **Privately Held**
SIC: 3089 Injection molding of plastics

(G-731)
OMEGA PULTRUSIONS INCORPORATED
1331 S Chillicothe Rd (44202-8066)
PHONE..................................330 562-5201
Donald F Borraccini, *Pr*
EMP: 169 **EST:** 1970
SQ FT: 95,000
SALES (est): 1.99MM **Privately Held**
SIC: 3089 Injection molding of plastics
PA: Omega Polymer Technologies, Inc.
1331 S Chillicothe Rd
Aurora OH 44202

▲ = Import ▼ = Export
◆ = Import/Export

GEOGRAPHIC SECTION

Austintown - Mahoning County (G-753)

(G-732)
PHILPOTT RUBBER LLC
Also Called: Philpott Rubber and Plastics
375 Gentry Dr (44202-7540)
　PHONE..................................330 225-3344
　EMP: 8
　SALES (corp-wide): 28.02MM **Privately Held**
　Web: www.philpottsolutions.com
　SIC: 3069 Medical sundries, rubber
　HQ: Philpott Rubber Llc
　　1010 Industrial Pkwy N
　　Brunswick OH 44212
　　330 225-3344

(G-733)
RADIX WIRE CO
350 Harris Dr (44202-7536)
　PHONE..................................330 995-3677
　EMP: 18
　SQ FT: 10,000
　SALES (corp-wide): 20.56MM **Privately Held**
　Web: www.radix-wire.com
　SIC: 3357 Nonferrous wiredrawing and insulating
　PA: Radix Wire Co
　　30333 Emerald Valley Pkwy
　　Solon OH 44139
　　216 731-9191

(G-734)
ROBECK FLUID POWER CO
Also Called: Robeck
350 Lena Dr (44202-8098)
　PHONE..................................330 562-1140
　Peter Becker, *Pr*
　Ken Traeger, *
　Ida Becker, *
　▲ **EMP:** 65 **EST:** 1983
　SQ FT: 6,000
　SALES (est): 26.14MM **Privately Held**
　Web: www.robeckfluidpower.com
　SIC: 5084 3593 3594 3494 Hydraulic systems equipment and supplies; Fluid power cylinders and actuators; Fluid power pumps and motors; Valves and pipe fittings, nec

(G-735)
SACO AEI POLYMERS INC
Also Called: Macro Meric
1395 Danner Dr (44202-9273)
　PHONE..................................330 995-1600
　Matt Mclaughlin, *Brnch Mgr*
　EMP: 16
　SQ FT: 28,829
　SALES (corp-wide): 96.26MM **Privately Held**
　Web: www.sacoaei.com
　SIC: 2821 Plastics materials and resins
　PA: Saco Aei Polymers, Inc.
　　3220 Crocker Ave
　　Sheboygan WI 53081
　　920 803-0778

(G-736)
THYSSNKRUPP ROTHE ERDE USA INC (DH)
Also Called: Rotek
1400 S Chillicothe Rd (44202-9282)
P.O. Box 312 (44202-0312)
　PHONE..................................330 562-4000
　Mark Girman, *Pr*
　Jose Muzzi, *
　Frank Kuepper, *SLS & ENGINEERING*
　▲ **EMP:** 160 **EST:** 1855
　SQ FT: 132,000
　SALES (est): 53.13MM
　SALES (corp-wide): 40.78B **Privately Held**
　Web: www.rotek-inc.com
　SIC: 3562 3462 3463 3321 Ball bearings and parts; Iron and steel forgings; Nonferrous forgings; Gray and ductile iron foundries
　HQ: Thyssenkrupp North America, Llc
　　111 W Jckson Blvd Ste 240
　　Chicago IL 60604
　　312 525-2800

(G-737)
TRELLBORG SLING PRFILES US INC
Also Called: Trelleborg
285 Lena Dr (44202-9247)
P.O. Box 639 (46507-0639)
　PHONE..................................330 995-9725
　Smitty Mckee, *Pr*
　Gabe Orazen, *
　Michael Scanlon, *
　EMP: 130 **EST:** 2006
　SALES (est): 45.19MM
　SALES (corp-wide): 4.26B **Privately Held**
　SIC: 3089 3465 Extruded finished plastics products, nec; Body parts, automobile: stamped metal
　HQ: Trelleborg Corporation
　　200 Veterans Blvd Ste 3
　　South Haven MI 49090
　　269 639-9891

(G-738)
UNIVERSAL HEAT TREATING INC
Also Called: Universal Black Oxiding
60 Samantha Dr (44202-9801)
　PHONE..................................216 641-2000
　Ernie D'amato, *CEO*
　Michael D Amato, *
　Kevin D'amato, *VP*
　EMP: 32 **EST:** 1965
　SALES (est): 4.82MM **Privately Held**
　Web: www.uhtcle.com
　SIC: 3398 Metal heat treating

(G-739)
USA INSTRUMENTS INC
Also Called: GE
1515 Danner Dr (44202-9273)
　PHONE..................................330 562-1000
　Eric Stahre, *Pr*
　▲ **EMP:** 250 **EST:** 1993
　SQ FT: 58,000
　SALES (est): 53.51MM
　SALES (corp-wide): 19.55B **Publicly Held**
　SIC: 3677 Electronic coils and transformers
　HQ: Ge Healthcare Inc.
　　251 Locke Dr
　　Marlborough MA 01752
　　732 457-8667

(G-740)
VIDEO PRODUCTS INC
Also Called: VPI
1275 Danner Dr (44202-8054)
　PHONE..................................330 562-2622
　Carl Jagatich, *Pr*
　EMP: 60 **EST:** 1977
　SQ FT: 8,000
　SALES (est): 4.56MM **Privately Held**
　Web: www.vpi.us
　SIC: 3577 Computer peripheral equipment, nec

Austinburg
Ashtabula County

(G-741)
AUSTINBURG MACHINE INC
2899 Industrial Park Dr (44010-9764)
　PHONE..................................440 275-2001
　Richard Pildner, *Pr*
　John Pildner, *VP*
　Lynetta Pildner, *Sec*
　EMP: 8 **EST:** 1970
　SQ FT: 8,200
　SALES (est): 890.32K **Privately Held**
　SIC: 3599 Machine shop, jobbing and repair

(G-742)
BISMARK LAWNCARE LLC
4057 State Route 307 (44010-9705)
　PHONE..................................440 361-5561
　Robert W Bismark, *Pt*
　EMP: 12 **EST:** 2013
　SALES (est): 979.94K **Privately Held**
　SIC: 0782 1389 Lawn care services; Construction, repair, and dismantling services

(G-743)
COLORAMIC PROCESS INC
2883 Industrial Park Dr (44010-9764)
P.O. Box 12 (44010-0012)
　PHONE..................................440 275-1199
　Donald Pikounik, *Pr*
　Robert Pikounik, *Pr*
　Fred Zust, *VP*
　Marilyn Pikounik, *Sec*
　EMP: 11 **EST:** 1959
　SALES (est): 444.55K **Privately Held**
　Web: www.coloramic.com
　SIC: 2752 Offset printing

(G-744)
ENCAPSULATION TECHNOLOGIES LLC
2937 Industrial Park Dr (44010-9763)
　PHONE..................................419 819-6319
　Canaima Technologies, *Prin*
　EMP: 9 **EST:** 2017
　SALES (est): 52.58K **Privately Held**
　Web: www.salvona.com
　SIC: 2834 Pharmaceutical preparations

(G-745)
EUCLID REFINISHING COMPNAY INC
Also Called: Surftech
2937 Industrial Park Dr (44010-9763)
　PHONE..................................440 275-3356
　Nicholas Cottone, *CEO*
　EMP: 10 **EST:** 1988
　SQ FT: 15,000
　SALES (est): 1.46MM **Privately Held**
　Web: www.euclidrefinishing.com
　SIC: 3479 Coating of metals and formed products

(G-746)
FARIN INDUSTRIES INC
2844 Industrial Park Dr (44010-9764)
P.O. Box 185 (44010-0185)
　PHONE..................................440 275-2755
　Michael F Farinacci, *Pr*
　EMP: 18 **EST:** 1984
　SQ FT: 10,000
　SALES (est): 521.59K **Privately Held**
　Web: www.farin.us
　SIC: 3714 Motor vehicle parts and accessories

(G-747)
FUTURE CONTROLS CORPORATION
1419 State Route 45 (44010-9749)
P.O. Box 130 (44010-0130)
　PHONE..................................440 275-3191
　John Williams, *Pr*
　Jeremy Sutch, *
　Philip Bunnell, *
　EMP: 41 **EST:** 1985
　SQ FT: 33,000
　SALES (est): 5.3MM **Privately Held**
　Web: www.futurecontrols.com
　SIC: 3823 3625 3822 Temperature instruments: industrial process type; Relays and industrial controls; Environmental controls

(G-748)
PAINESVILLE PUBLISHING INC
2883 Industrial Park Dr (44010-9764)
P.O. Box 12 (44010-0012)
　PHONE..................................440 354-4142
　Don Tiknovnik, *Pr*
　Marie Baker, *VP*
　EMP: 7 **EST:** 1941
　SQ FT: 3,000
　SALES (est): 524.39K **Privately Held**
　Web: www.painesvillepublishing.com
　SIC: 2752 2791 2789 Offset printing; Typesetting; Bookbinding and related work

(G-749)
RTS COMPANIES (US) INC
2900 Industrial Park Dr (44010-9763)
　PHONE..................................440 275-3077
　Graham Lobban, *Pr*
　◆ **EMP:** 40 **EST:** 2008
　SALES (est): 8.31MM **Privately Held**
　Web: www.rtscompaniesinc.com
　SIC: 3089 Injection molding of plastics

(G-750)
SPRING TEAM INC
2851 Industrial Park Dr (44010)
P.O. Box 215 (44010)
　PHONE..................................440 275-5981
　Russ Bryer, *Pr*
　Richard Kovach, *
　Gary Van Buren, *
　Nancy Sidley, *
　Ed Hall, *
　▼ **EMP:** 67 **EST:** 1968
　SQ FT: 42,000
　SALES (est): 9.81MM **Privately Held**
　Web: www.springteam.com
　SIC: 3496 3495 Miscellaneous fabricated wire products; Wire springs

Austintown
Mahoning County

(G-751)
COWLES INDUSTRIAL TOOL CO LLC
Also Called: Cowles Industrial Tool
185 N Four Mile Run Rd (44515-3006)
　PHONE..................................330 799-9100
　David Smith, *Pr*
　EMP: 35 **EST:** 2012
　SQ FT: 30,000
　SALES (est): 5.31MM **Privately Held**
　Web: www.cowles-tool.com
　SIC: 3545 Tools and accessories for machine tools

(G-752)
L M ENGINEERING INC
Also Called: Lm Cases
3760 Oakwood Ave (44515)
　PHONE..................................330 270-2400
　Joann Laguardia, *Pr*
　William Laguardia, *
　EMP: 25 **EST:** 1982
　SQ FT: 40,000
　SALES (est): 4.45MM **Privately Held**
　Web: www.lmcases.com
　SIC: 3161 Musical instrument cases

(G-753)
OHIO LUXURY BULDERS LLC
Also Called: Ohio Luxury Builders
4958 Mahoning Ave (44515-1704)

Austintown - Mahoning County (G-754)

PHONE.....................330 881-0073
Corey Kemp, *Managing Member*
EMP: 8 **EST:** 2017
SALES (est): 493.51K **Privately Held**
SIC: 1521 1389 1799 1761 Single-family home remodeling, additions, and repairs; Construction, repair, and dismantling services; Building site preparation; Roofing, siding, and sheetmetal work

(G-754)
PRECISION FOAM FABRICATION INC
3760 Oakwood Ave Ste B (44515-3041)
PHONE.....................330 270-2440
Joann Laguargia, *Pr*
EMP: 13 **EST:** 1998
SALES (est): 809.98K **Privately Held**
Web: www.precisionfoam.com
SIC: 3089 Injection molding of plastics

(G-755)
T&W STAMPING INC ◎
207 N Four Mile Run Rd (44515-3008)
PHONE.....................330 270-0891
EMP: 7 **EST:** 2022
SALES (est): 755.15K **Privately Held**
Web: www.twstamping.com
SIC: 3469 Stamping metal for the trade

(G-756)
TRANSUE & WILLIAMS STAMPG CORP
207 N Four Mile Run Rd (44515-3008)
PHONE.....................330 821-5777
John Staudt, *VP*
John Beringer, *Treas*
▲ **EMP:** 32 **EST:** 1986
SALES (est): 7.26MM **Privately Held**
Web: www.twstamping.com
SIC: 3469 Stamping metal for the trade

(G-757)
XALOY LLC (PA)
375 Victoria Rd Ste 1 (44515-2053)
PHONE.....................330 726-4000
Kamal K Tiwari, *CEO*
Keith Young, *
◆ **EMP:** 190 **EST:** 2021
SALES (est): 106.67MM
SALES (corp-wide): 106.67MM **Privately Held**
Web: www.xaloy.com
SIC: 3089 8711 Automotive parts, plastic; Engineering services

Avon
Lorain County

(G-758)
A J ROSE MFG CO (PA)
38000 Chester Rd (44011-4022)
PHONE.....................216 631-4645
Daniel T Pritchard, *Pr*
Douglas E Krzywicki, *
Dale A Pritchard, *
Terry J Sweeney, *
◆ **EMP:** 235 **EST:** 1922
SQ FT: 270,000
SALES (est): 74.13MM
SALES (corp-wide): 74.13MM **Privately Held**
Web: www.ajrose.com
SIC: 3469 Perforated metal, stamped

(G-759)
ACCEL CORPORATION (DH)
Also Called: Accel Color
38620 Chester Rd (44011-1074)
PHONE.....................440 934-7711
▲ **EMP:** 60 **EST:** 1998
SALES (est): 10.29MM **Privately Held**
SIC: 3087 Custom compound purchased resins
HQ: Techmer Pm, Llc
1 Quality Cir
Clinton TN 37716
865 457-6700

(G-760)
ACCEL CORPORATION
Also Called: Accel Color
38620 Chester Rd (44011-1074)
PHONE.....................440 327-7418
Dwight Morgan, *Mgr*
EMP: 7
SIC: 2865 Dyes and pigments
HQ: Accel Corporation
38620 Chester Rd
Avon OH 44011

(G-761)
ADVANCED POLYMER COATINGS LTD
951 Jaycox Rd (44011-1351)
P.O. Box 269 (44011-0269)
PHONE.....................440 937-6218
Donald Keehan, *Ch*
Denise Keehan, *
▲ **EMP:** 26 **EST:** 1987
SQ FT: 35,000
SALES (est): 9.48MM **Privately Held**
Web: www.adv-polymer.com
SIC: 3081 Plastics film and sheet

(G-762)
AIRCRAFT WHEEL & BRAKE LLC ◎
1160 Center Rd (44011-1208)
PHONE.....................440 937-6211
Ian Walsh, *CEO*
EMP: 99 **EST:** 2022
SALES (est): 25.34MM
SALES (corp-wide): 775.85MM **Privately Held**
Web: www.kaman.com
SIC: 3728 Wheels, aircraft
PA: Kaman Corporation
1332 Blue Hills Ave
Bloomfield CT 06002
860 243-7100

(G-763)
BENDIX COML VHCL SYSTEMS LLC (DH)
Also Called: Bendix
35500 Chester Rd (44011)
P.O. Box 4016 (44035)
PHONE.....................440 329-9000
Piotr Sroka, *Pr*
Piotr Sroka, *
Carlos Hungria, *
Dave Kralic, *
◆ **EMP:** 350 **EST:** 2001
SALES (est): 997.21MM
SALES (corp-wide): 2.67MM **Privately Held**
Web: www.bendix.com
SIC: 3714 5013 5088 Motor vehicle brake systems and parts; Automotive supplies and parts; Combat vehicles
HQ: Knorr-Bremse Ag
Moosacher Str. 80
Munchen BY 80809
8935470

(G-764)
BRIMAR PACKAGING INC
37520 Colorado Ave (44011-1534)
PHONE.....................440 934-3080
EMP: 40 **EST:** 1992
SALES (est): 2.57MM **Privately Held**

Web: www.brimarpackaging.com
SIC: 2449 2653 5085 2657 Wood containers, nec; Boxes, corrugated: made from purchased materials; Commercial containers; Folding paperboard boxes

(G-765)
CHALFANT MANUFACTURING COMPANY (DH)
1050 Jaycox Rd (44011-1312)
PHONE.....................330 273-3510
Gloria Slaga, *CEO*
John Slaga, *Pr*
▼ **EMP:** 7 **EST:** 1945
SALES (est): 8.3MM **Privately Held**
Web: www.chalfant-obo.com
SIC: 3643 Current-carrying wiring services
HQ: Obo Bettermann Holding Gmbh & Co. Kg
Huingser Ring 52
Menden (Sauerland) NW
2373890

(G-766)
CLEAN REMEDIES LLC
1431 Lear Industrial Pkwy Ste A (44011-1359)
PHONE.....................440 670-2112
Meredith Farrow, *CEO*
EMP: 13 **EST:** 2018
SALES (est): 2.14MM **Privately Held**
Web: www.cleanremedies.com
SIC: 2833 Drugs and herbs: grading, grinding, and milling

(G-767)
CLEVELAND WHEELS
Also Called: Aircraft Wheels and Breaks
1160 Center Rd (44011-1208)
PHONE.....................440 937-6211
Manny Nnay Bajakfoujian, *CEO*
EMP: 9 **EST:** 1936
SALES (est): 2.35MM **Privately Held**
SIC: 5088 3799 Aircraft equipment and supplies, nec; Transportation equipment, nec

(G-768)
COMPREHENSIVE LOGISTICS CO INC
1200 A Chester Industrial Pkwy (44011-1081)
PHONE.....................440 934-3517
Daryl Legg, *Brnch Mgr*
EMP: 20
Web: www.complog.com
SIC: 3714 Motor vehicle transmissions, drive assemblies, and parts
PA: Comprehensive Logistics, Co., Inc.
8200 Hlth Ctr Blvd Ste 10
Bonita Springs FL 34135

(G-769)
CORE TECHNOLOGY INC
1260 Moore Rd Ste E (44011-4021)
PHONE.....................440 934-9935
▲ **EMP:** 10 **EST:** 1995
SQ FT: 5,500
SALES (est): 1.51MM **Privately Held**
Web: www.core-techs.com
SIC: 3629 Power conversion units, a.c. to d.c.: static-electric

(G-770)
CUTTING DYNAMICS INC
35050 Avon Commerce Pkwy (44011-1374)
PHONE.....................440 249-4666
William V Carson Junior, *Brnch Mgr*
EMP: 61
SALES (corp-wide): 63.28MM **Privately Held**

Web: www.cuttingdynamics.com
SIC: 3599 Amusement park equipment
HQ: Cutting Dynamics, Inc.
980 Jaycox Rd
Avon OH 44011
440 249-4150

(G-771)
ECP CORPORATION
Also Called: Polycase Division
1305 Chester Industrial Pkwy (44011-1083)
PHONE.....................440 934-0444
Steven Began, *Pr*
▲ **EMP:** 48 **EST:** 1951
SQ FT: 40,000
SALES (est): 9.36MM **Privately Held**
Web: www.polycase.com
SIC: 3469 Electronic enclosures, stamped or pressed metal

(G-772)
EIDP INC
Also Called: Dupont
38620 Chester Rd (44011-1074)
PHONE.....................440 934-6444
Bob Langenderfer, *Mgr*
EMP: 10
SALES (corp-wide): 17.23B **Publicly Held**
Web: www.dupont.com
SIC: 2911 Petroleum refining
HQ: Eidp, Inc.
9330 Zionsville Rd
Indianapolis IN 46268
833 267-8382

(G-773)
ELITE MANUFACTURING INDS LLC
2395 Muirwood Rd (44011-4734)
PHONE.....................440 934-0920
EMP: 7 **EST:** 2005
SALES (est): 142.68K **Privately Held**
Web: www.elitemfgind.com
SIC: 3999 Barber and beauty shop equipment

(G-774)
FLAVORSEAL LLC
35179 Avon Commerce Pkwy (44011-1374)
PHONE.....................440 937-3900
◆ **EMP:** 99 **EST:** 2010
SQ FT: 40,000
SALES (est): 23.46MM
SALES (corp-wide): 23.46MM **Privately Held**
Web: www.flavorseal.com
SIC: 2673 Bags: plastic, laminated, and coated
PA: M&Q Acquisition Llc
3 Earl Ave
Schuylkill Haven PA

(G-775)
FREEMAN MANUFACTURING & SUP CO (PA)
1101 Moore Rd (44011-4043)
PHONE.....................440 934-1902
Lou Turco, *Pr*
Gerald W Rusk, *Ch Bd*
EMP: 50 **EST:** 1942
SQ FT: 110,000
SALES (est): 50.71MM
SALES (corp-wide): 50.71MM **Privately Held**
Web: www.freemansupply.com
SIC: 5084 3087 3543 2821 Industrial machinery and equipment; Custom compound purchased resins; Industrial patterns; Plastics materials and resins

GEOGRAPHIC SECTION

Avon Lake - Lorain County (G-799)

(G-776)
GREEN ACQUISITION LLC
Also Called: Green Bearing Co
1141 Jaycox Rd (44011-1366)
PHONE.................................440 930-7600
EMP: 15 **EST:** 1940
SALES (est): 2.21MM
SALES (corp-wide): 23.91MM **Privately Held**
SIC: 3714 Bearings, motor vehicle
PA: Bearing Technologies, Ltd.
33554 Pin Oak Pkwy
Avon Lake OH 44012
800 597-3486

(G-777)
KAYDON CORPORATION
1500 Nagel Rd (44011-1337)
PHONE.................................231 755-3741
◆ **EMP:** 71 **EST:** 1962
SALES (est): 18.93MM
SALES (corp-wide): 9.24B **Privately Held**
SIC: 3562 Ball bearings and parts
HQ: Kaydon Corporation
2723 S State St Ste 300
Ann Arbor MI 48104
734 747-7025

(G-778)
L & W INC
Also Called: L&W Cleveland
1190 Jaycox Rd (44011-1313)
PHONE.................................734 397-6300
Steve Schafer, Mgr
EMP: 33
SALES (corp-wide): 3.1B **Privately Held**
Web: www.autokiniton.com
SIC: 3469 3465 3441 3429 Stamping metal for the trade; Automotive stampings; Fabricated structural metal; Hardware, nec
HQ: L & W, Inc.
17757 Woodland Dr
New Boston MI 48164
734 397-6300

(G-779)
LEISURE TIME PDTS DESIGN CORP
1284 Miller Rd (44011-1004)
P.O. Box 276 (44011-0276)
PHONE.................................440 934-1032
EMP: 6 **EST:** 1992
SALES (est): 501.72K **Privately Held**
Web: www.leisuretimecorp.com
SIC: 2326 3069 3844 3949 Aprons, work, except rubberized and plastic: men's; Aprons, vulcanized rubbed or rubberized fabric; X-ray apparatus and tubes; Camping equipment and supplies

(G-780)
LOGISYNC CORPORATION
Also Called: Logisync
1313 Lear Industrial Pkwy (44011-1360)
P.O. Box 368 (44011-0368)
PHONE.................................440 937-0388
▲ **EMP:** 13 **EST:** 1992
SALES (est): 378.86K **Privately Held**
Web: www.logisync.com
SIC: 7373 3672 3822 3625 Computer integrated systems design; Printed circuit boards; Environmental controls; Relays and industrial controls

(G-781)
MAROON INTRMDIATE HOLDINGS LLC
1390 Jaycox Rd (44011-1372)
PHONE.................................440 937-1000
Jean-luc Joye, Prin
EMP: 9 **EST:** 2014
SALES (est): 779.41K **Privately Held**

Web: www.barentz-na.com
SIC: 2869 5169 Industrial organic chemicals, nec; Chemicals and allied products, nec

(G-782)
PARKER-HANNIFIN CORPORATION
Parker Hannifin Corp
1160 Center Rd (44011-1297)
P.O. Box 158 (44011-0158)
PHONE.................................440 937-6211
EMP: 110
SALES (corp-wide): 14.35B **Publicly Held**
Web: www.parker.com
SIC: 3728 Wheels, aircraft
PA: Parker-Hannifin Corporation
6035 Parkland Blvd
Cleveland OH 44124
216 896-3000

(G-783)
PRO-TEC INDUSTRIES INC
Also Called: Protech Industries
1384 Lear Industrial Pkwy (44011-1368)
PHONE.................................440 937-4142
Kurt F Van Luit, Pr
Jeff Leonard, VP
EMP: 6 **EST:** 1992
SQ FT: 6,000
SALES (est): 785.77K **Privately Held**
SIC: 3089 Plastics hardware and building products

(G-784)
QUAL-FAB INC
34250 Mills Rd (44011-2471)
PHONE.................................440 327-5000
Gary Vanek, Pr
Craig Hartzell, *
Jeffrey Ogle, *
Kathy Bennett, *
David Peter, *
▼ **EMP:** 48 **EST:** 2000
SQ FT: 80,000
SALES (est): 9.71MM **Privately Held**
Web: www.qual-fab.net
SIC: 3312 3498 3433 Stainless steel; Fabricated pipe and fittings; Heating equipment, except electric

(G-785)
RAILROAD BREWING COMPANY
1010 Center Rd (44011-1206)
PHONE.................................440 723-8234
Thomas R Wagner, Pr
Thomas Wager, Pr
Jerome Moore, VP
Tom Culler, Treas
EMP: 9 **EST:** 2015
SQ FT: 4,000
SALES (est): 338.8K **Privately Held**
Web: test.railroad.beer
SIC: 5813 3556 Tavern (drinking places); Brewers' and maltsters' machinery

(G-786)
RDA GROUP LLC
2131 Clifton Way (44011-2809)
PHONE.................................440 724-4347
Robert Desmarais, Prin
EMP: 6 **EST:** 2008
SALES (est): 79.46K **Privately Held**
SIC: 3559 Sewing machines and attachments, industrial, nec

(G-787)
RICHTECH INDUSTRIES INC
34000 Lear Industrial Pkwy (44011-1375)
PHONE.................................440 937-4401
Kurt Van Luit, CEO
EMP: 9 **EST:** 1990
SALES (est): 1.02MM **Privately Held**

Web: www.richtechindustries.com
SIC: 3299 1799 Moldings, architectural: plaster of paris; Waterproofing

(G-788)
SOLAS LTD
Also Called: Solas Global Solutions
33587 Streamview Dr (44011-2598)
PHONE.................................650 501-0889
William Sammon, Managing Member
EMP: 21 **EST:** 2010
SALES (est): 1.13MM **Privately Held**
SIC: 5113 2656 2653 2499 Disposable plates, cups, napkins, and eating utensils; Straws, drinking: made from purchased material; Pallets, solid fiber: made from purchased materials; Trays: wood, wicker, and bagasse

(G-789)
TECHNIFAB INC (PA)
Also Called: Technifab Engineered Products
1355 Chester Industrial Pkwy (44011-1083)
PHONE.................................440 934-8324
Jeffrey L Petras, Pr
◆ **EMP:** 21 **EST:** 1994
SQ FT: 40,000
SALES (est): 8.2MM **Privately Held**
Web: www.technifabinc.com
SIC: 3086 Insulation or cushioning material, foamed plastics

(G-790)
VALENSIL TECHNOLOGIES LLC
34910 Commerce Way (44011)
P.O. Box 388 (44011-0388)
PHONE.................................440 937-8181
Richard A West, Prin
EMP: 26 **EST:** 2014
SALES (est): 1.24MM **Privately Held**
Web: www.valensil.com
SIC: 3841 8733 Surgical and medical instruments; Medical research

(G-791)
WESTLAKE TOOL & DIE MFG CO
1280 Moore Rd (44011-1014)
PHONE.................................440 934-5305
Seamus Walsh, CEO
EMP: 100 **EST:** 2017
SALES (est): 8.66MM **Privately Held**
Web: www.westlaketool.com
SIC: 3469 Stamping metal for the trade

(G-792)
WONDER MACHINE SERVICES INC
35340 Avon Commerce Pkwy (44011-1374)
PHONE.................................440 937-7500
George Woyansky, Pr
Jeanine Woyansky, *
Diane Woyansky, *
EMP: 30 **EST:** 1976
SQ FT: 22,500
SALES (est): 4.64MM **Privately Held**
Web: www.wondermachine.com
SIC: 3599 3541 Machine shop, jobbing and repair; Machine tools, metal cutting type

(G-793)
WOODMAN AGITATOR INC
1404 Lear Industrial Pkwy (44011)
PHONE.................................440 937-9865
James Bielozer, Pr
Mary Bielozer, VP
Keith M Bielozer, VP
◆ **EMP:** 17 **EST:** 1947
SALES (est): 2.68MM **Privately Held**
Web: www.woodmanagitator.com
SIC: 3559 Paint making machinery

(G-794)
WTD REAL ESTATE INC
1280 Moore Rd (44011-1014)
P.O. Box 240 (44011-0240)
PHONE.................................440 934-5305
Seamus E Walsh, Pr
Theresa Walsh, VP
EMP: 60 **EST:** 1968
SQ FT: 65,100
SALES (est): 6.29MM **Privately Held**
Web: www.westlaketool.com
SIC: 3469 Stamping metal for the trade

(G-795)
ZEPHYR SOLUTIONS LLC
1050 Lear Industrial Pkwy Bldg 1 (44011-1388)
PHONE.................................440 937-9993
Scott Mccullough, CEO
Brian Bastock, Pr
Ryan Keating, CFO
EMP: 19 **EST:** 2016
SQ FT: 12,000
SALES (est): 4.44MM **Privately Held**
Web: www.zephyrsolutions.com
SIC: 2813 Industrial gases

Avon Lake
Lorain County

(G-796)
APPLIED SPECIALTIES INC
Also Called: Asi Chemical Company
33555 Pin Oak Pkwy (44012-2319)
P.O. Box 307 (44012-0307)
PHONE.................................440 933-9442
◆ **EMP:** 30 **EST:** 1981
SALES (est): 8.46MM **Privately Held**
Web: www.appliedspecialties.com
SIC: 2899 8742 Water treating compounds; Industry specialist consultants

(G-797)
AVIENT CORPORATION (PA)
Also Called: Avient
33587 Walker Rd (44012)
PHONE.................................440 930-1000
Robert M Patterson, Ch Bd
Jamie A Beggs, Sr VP
Lisa K Kunkle, Sr VP
Joao Jose San Martin Neto, Chief Human Resource Officer
Joel R Rathbun, Sr VP
◆ **EMP:** 73 **EST:** 1885
SALES (est): 3.14B **Publicly Held**
Web: www.avient.com
SIC: 2821 3087 5162 3081 Thermoplastic materials; Custom compound purchased resins; Resins; Unsupported plastics film and sheet

(G-798)
AVIENT CORPORATION
33587 Walker Rd # Rdb-418 (44012-1145)
P.O. Box 31480 (44131-0480)
PHONE.................................440 930-3727
EMP: 13
Web: www.avient.com
SIC: 2821 Plastics materials and resins
PA: Avient Corporation
33587 Walker Rd
Avon Lake OH 44012

(G-799)
AVON LAKE PRINTING
227 Miller Rd (44012-1004)
PHONE.................................440 933-2078
Thomas Brock, Owner
EMP: 9 **EST:** 1985

Avon Lake - Lorain County (G-800)

SQ FT: 8,000
SALES (est): 859.86K **Privately Held**
Web: www.minuteman.com
SIC: **2752** 5943 Offset printing; Office forms and supplies

(G-800)
AVON LAKE SHEET METAL CO
33574 Pin Oak Pkwy (44012-2320)
P.O. Box 64 (44012-0064)
PHONE..................440 933-3505
Carl Wetzig Junior, *Pr*
Gary Wightman, *
EMP: 38 EST: 1953
SQ FT: 32,000
SALES (est): 8.06MM **Privately Held**
Web: www.avonlakesheetmetal.com
SIC: **3444** 1761 Sheet metalwork; Sheet metal work, nec

(G-801)
CATANIA MEDALLIC SPECIALTY INC
Also Called: Catania Medallic Specialities
668 Moore Rd (44012-2315)
PHONE..................440 933-9595
Vince Frank, *Pr*
Trisha Frank, *
▲ EMP: 27 EST: 1971
SQ FT: 12,000
SALES (est): 1.91MM **Privately Held**
Web: www.cataniainc.com
SIC: **3469** 3965 3369 2395 Ornamental metal stampings; Fasteners, buttons, needles, and pins; Nonferrous foundries, nec; Pleating and stitching

(G-802)
CUTTING DYNAMICS INC
33597 Pin Oak Pkwy (44012-2319)
PHONE..................440 930-2862
William V Carson Junior, *Pr*
EMP: 61
SALES (corp-wide): 63.28MM **Privately Held**
Web: www.cuttingdynamics.com
SIC: **3599** Machine shop, jobbing and repair
HQ: Cutting Dynamics, Inc.
980 Jaycox Rd
Avon OH 44011
440 249-4150

(G-803)
DANCO METAL PRODUCTS LLC
760 Moore Rd (44012-2317)
PHONE..................440 871-2300
EMP: 95
Web: www.dancometal.com
SIC: **3444** 3644 3469 3443 Metal housings, enclosures, casings, and other containers; Noncurrent-carrying wiring devices; Metal stampings, nec; Fabricated plate work (boiler shop)

(G-804)
ECHOPRESS LTD
Also Called: Proforma Echopress
444 Avon Point Ave (44012-2810)
PHONE..................216 373-7560
EMP: 8 EST: 2009
SALES (est): 391.22K **Privately Held**
Web: www.echopress.com
SIC: **2741** Miscellaneous publishing

(G-805)
ELECTRA SOUND INC (PA)
Also Called: Electrasound TV & Appl Svc
32483 English Turn (44012-3321)
PHONE..................216 433-9600
TOLL FREE: 800
Robert C Masa Junior, *CEO*
Patricia Masa, *
Charles C Masa, *
EMP: 70 EST: 1968
SALES (est): 12.2MM
SALES (corp-wide): 12.2MM **Privately Held**
Web: www.techni-car.com
SIC: **3694** 7622 5065 5731 Automotive electrical equipment, nec; Television repair shop; Sound equipment, electronic; Automotive sound equipment

(G-806)
EMPIRE SYSTEMS INC
33683 Walker Rd (44012)
PHONE..................440 653-9300
Jeffery Eagens, *CEO*
Cheryle Hayley, *CFO*
◆ EMP: 10 EST: 2003
SQ FT: 41,000
SALES (est): 1.8MM **Privately Held**
Web: www.empiresystemsinc.com
SIC: **8711** 3559 Consulting engineer; Foundry machinery and equipment

(G-807)
FORD MOTOR COMPANY
Also Called: Ford
650 Miller Rd (44012-2398)
PHONE..................440 933-1215
Deborah S Kent, *Engr*
EMP: 247
SALES (corp-wide): 176.19MM **Publicly Held**
Web: www.ford.com
SIC: **5511** 3711 Automobiles, new and used; Motor vehicles and car bodies
PA: Ford Motor Company
1 American Rd
Dearborn MI 48126
313 322-3000

(G-808)
GAYSON SILICON DISPERSIONS INC
33587 Walker Rd (44012-1145)
PHONE..................330 848-8422
EMP: 6 EST: 2016
SALES (est): 433.32K **Privately Held**
SIC: **2821** Plastics materials and resins

(G-809)
GEON PERFORMANCE SOLUTIONS LLC
556 Moore Rd (44012-2313)
PHONE..................440 930-1000
EMP: 32
SALES (corp-wide): 2.67MM **Privately Held**
Web: www.geon.com
SIC: **2821** Thermoplastic materials
HQ: Geon Performance Solutions, Llc
25777 Detroit Rd Ste 202
Westlake OH 44145
800 438-4366

(G-810)
HASHIER & HASHIER MFG
644 Moore Rd (44012-2315)
PHONE..................440 933-4883
Frank Hashier, *Pr*
EMP: 6 EST: 1976
SQ FT: 6,000
SALES (est): 400K **Privately Held**
Web: www.hashiermfg.com
SIC: **3469** Stamping metal for the trade

(G-811)
HELICAL LINE PRODUCTS CO
659 Miller Rd (44012-2306)
P.O. Box 217 (44012-0217)
PHONE..................440 933-9263
Albert C Bonds, *Pr*
William T Bonds, *
Robert S Bonds, *
▼ EMP: 23 EST: 1964
SQ FT: 33,000
SALES (est): 2.38MM **Privately Held**
Web: www.helical-line.com
SIC: **3496** Miscellaneous fabricated wire products

(G-812)
HINKLEY LIGHTING INC (PA)
Also Called: Fredrick Ramond
33000 Pin Oak Pkwy (44012-2641)
PHONE..................440 653-5500
Jess Wiedemer, *Pr*
Eric Wiedemer, *
◆ EMP: 45 EST: 1922
SQ FT: 100,000
SALES (est): 23.2MM
SALES (corp-wide): 23.2MM **Privately Held**
Web: www.hinkley.com
SIC: **3645** 3646 3634 Residential lighting fixtures; Commercial lighting fixtures; Ceiling fans

(G-813)
JOHN CHRIST WINERY INC
32421 Walker Rd (44012-2226)
PHONE..................440 933-9672
Dean Gunter, *Genl Mgr*
EMP: 8 EST: 2001
SALES (est): 456.9K **Privately Held**
Web: johnchristwine.homestead.com
SIC: **2084** Wines

(G-814)
KLINGSHIRN WINERY INC
33050 Webber Rd (44012-2330)
PHONE..................440 933-6666
Lee Klingshirn, *Pr*
Lee Klingshirn, *Pr*
Nancy Klingshirn, *VP*
EMP: 8 EST: 1935
SQ FT: 3,850
SALES (est): 623.55K **Privately Held**
Web: www.klingshirnwine.com
SIC: **2084** Wines

(G-815)
LUBRIZOL GLOBAL MANAGEMENT INC
550 Moore Rd (44012-2313)
P.O. Box 134 (44012-0134)
PHONE..................440 933-0400
Joseph Lazeunick, *Brnch Mgr*
EMP: 50
SALES (corp-wide): 364.48B **Publicly Held**
Web: www.lubrizol.com
SIC: **2899** 2821 Chemical preparations, nec; Plastics materials and resins
HQ: Lubrizol Global Management, Inc.
9911 Brecksville Rd
Cleveland OH 44141
216 447-5000

(G-816)
MARKERS INC
33490 Pin Oak Pkwy (44012-2318)
PHONE..................440 933-5927
Dale Hlavin, *Stockholder*
EMP: 6 EST: 1987
SALES (est): 465.18K **Privately Held**
Web: www.markersinc.com
SIC: **2399** 5261 Banners, pennants, and flags; Lawn and garden supplies

(G-817)
MEXICHEM SPECIALTY RESINS INC (HQ)
33653 Walker Rd (44012)
P.O. Box 277 (44012)
PHONE..................440 930-1435
Nicholas Peter Ballas, *CEO*
Jorge Alberto Barron Garcia, *
◆ EMP: 27 EST: 2013
SALES (est): 82.66MM **Privately Held**
SIC: **2822** 2821 Ethylene-propylene rubbers, EPDM polymers; Polymethyl methacrylate resins, plexiglass
PA: Orbia Advance Corporation, S.A.B. De C.V.
Av. Paseo De La Reforma No. 483
Piso 47
Mexico CMX 06500

(G-818)
NATIONAL FLEET SVCS OHIO LLC
607 Miller Rd (44012-2306)
PHONE..................440 930-5177
Tim Lariviere, *Pr*
EMP: 12 EST: 2008
SALES (est): 2.46MM **Privately Held**
Web: www.nationalfleetservices.com
SIC: **3089** 7532 Automotive parts, plastic; Van conversion

(G-819)
NORTH AMERICAN COMPOSITES
33660 Pin Oak Pkwy (44012-2322)
PHONE..................440 930-0602
EMP: 7 EST: 2019
SALES (est): 551.84K **Privately Held**
Web: www.ip-corporation.com
SIC: **2821** Plastics materials and resins

(G-820)
PIN OAK DEVELOPMENT LLC
32329 Orchard Park Dr (44012-2167)
PHONE..................440 933-9862
David Rickey, *Owner*
EMP: 7 EST: 2011
SALES (est): 358.38K **Privately Held**
SIC: **3452** Pins

(G-821)
POLYMER DIAGNOSTICS INC
33587 Walker Rd (44012-1145)
PHONE..................440 930-1361
Tom Waltermire, *CEO*
EMP: 20 EST: 1998
SALES (est): 6.86MM **Publicly Held**
Web: www.polymerdiagnostics.com
SIC: **2869** Laboratory chemicals, organic
PA: Avient Corporation
33587 Walker Rd
Avon Lake OH 44012

(G-822)
POLYONE FUNDING CORPORATION
33587 Walker Rd (44012-1145)
PHONE..................440 930-1000
EMP: 31 EST: 2002
SALES (est): 4.52MM **Publicly Held**
Web: www.avient.com
SIC: **2821** Thermoplastic materials
PA: Avient Corporation
33587 Walker Rd
Avon Lake OH 44012

(G-823)
POLYONE LLC
33587 Walker Rd (44012-1145)
PHONE..................440 930-1000
Robert M Patterson, *Pr*
EMP: 30 EST: 2013
SALES (est): 4.78MM **Publicly Held**

Web: www.avient.com
SIC: 2821 Thermoplastic materials
PA: Avient Corporation
33587 Walker Rd
Avon Lake OH 44012

(G-824)
SPARTECH MEXICO HOLDING CO TWO
33587 Walker Rd (44012-1145)
PHONE..................................440 930-3619
Richard N Altice, *Pr*
EMP: 27 **EST:** 2015
SALES (est): 853.21K **Privately Held**
SIC: 2821 Plastics materials and resins

(G-825)
THOGUS PRODUCTS COMPANY
33490 Pin Oak Pkwy (44012-2318)
PHONE..................................440 933-8850
Helen Thompson, *CEO*
Matthew Grantson, *
◆ **EMP:** 96 **EST:** 1958
SQ FT: 50,000
SALES (est): 20.27MM **Privately Held**
Web: www.thogus.com
SIC: 3089 3494 3492 Injection molding of plastics; Valves and pipe fittings, nec; Fluid power valves and hose fittings

(G-826)
VOO DOO INDUSTRIES LLC
33640 Pin Oak Pkwy Ste 4 (44012-3510)
PHONE..................................440 653-5333
Robert Ueker, *Prin*
▲ **EMP:** 6 **EST:** 2004
SALES (est): 262.01K **Privately Held**
Web: www.voodoomoto.com
SIC: 3999 Manufacturing industries, nec

(G-827)
W R G INC
Also Called: Buckeye Metals
631 Parkside Dr (44012-4006)
PHONE..................................216 351-8494
EMP: 25
SIC: 5093 3341 Nonferrous metals scrap; Secondary nonferrous metals

(G-828)
WATTEREDGE LLC (DH)
Also Called: Watteredge
567 Miller Rd (44012-2304)
PHONE..................................440 933-6110
Joseph P Langhenry, *Pr*
◆ **EMP:** 64 **EST:** 1970
SQ FT: 65,000
SALES (est): 25.11MM
SALES (corp-wide): 1.7B **Privately Held**
Web: www.watteredge.com
SIC: 5085 3643 5051 3052 Industrial supplies; Current-carrying wiring services; Metals service centers and offices; Rubber and plastics hose and beltings
HQ: Coleman Cable, Llc
1 Overlook Pt
Lincolnshire IL 60069
847 672-2300

(G-829)
WOLFF TOOL & MFG COMPANY INC
Also Called: O G Bell
139 Lear Rd (44012-1904)
PHONE..................................440 933-7797
Alan Wolff, *Pr*
Barbara Wolff, *VP*
EMP: 10 **EST:** 1946
SQ FT: 1,610
SALES (est): 749.62K **Privately Held**
Web: www.ogbell.com
SIC: 3599 Machine shop, jobbing and repair

Bainbridge
Ross County

(G-830)
COUNTRY CRUST BAKERY
4918 State Route 41 S (45612-9613)
PHONE..................................888 860-2940
EMP: 6 **EST:** 2008
SALES (est): 189.68K **Privately Held**
SIC: 2051 Bakery: wholesale or wholesale/retail combined

(G-831)
KNISLEY LUMBER
160 Potts Hill Rd (45612-9768)
P.O. Box 488 (45612-0488)
PHONE..................................740 634-2935
Mark A Knisley, *Owner*
EMP: 11 **EST:** 1980
SQ FT: 4,000
SALES (est): 423.26K **Privately Held**
SIC: 2421 2435 2426 Sawmills and planing mills, general; Hardwood veneer and plywood; Hardwood dimension and flooring mills

(G-832)
RANDY CARTER LOGGING INC
1100 Schmidt Rd (45612-3700)
PHONE..................................740 634-2604
Randy L Carter, *Prin*
EMP: 6 **EST:** 2004
SALES (est): 106.59K **Privately Held**
SIC: 2411 Logging camps and contractors

Baltic
Tuscarawas County

(G-833)
ANDAL WOODWORKING
1411 Township Road 151 (43804-9627)
PHONE..................................330 897-8059
Andrew Yoder, *Prin*
Andrew Yoder, *Owner*
EMP: 10 **EST:** 2008
SALES (est): 582.1K **Privately Held**
SIC: 2511 Wood bedroom furniture

(G-834)
BALTIC COUNTRY MEATS
Also Called: Baltic Meats
3320 State Route 557 (43804-9609)
PHONE..................................330 897-7025
Susie Raber, *Owner*
Dan Miller, *Owner*
EMP: 6 **EST:** 1987
SALES (est): 457.21K **Privately Held**
SIC: 2011 5411 Meat packing plants; Delicatessen stores

(G-835)
COUNTY LINE WOOD WORKING LLC
1482 County Road 600 (43804-9642)
PHONE..................................330 316-3057
Marvin Miller, *Prin*
EMP: 7 **EST:** 2015
SALES (est): 326.89K **Privately Held**
SIC: 2499 Wood products, nec

(G-836)
FLEX TECHNOLOGIES INC
Also Called: Poly Flex
3430 State Route 93 (43804-9705)
P.O. Box 300 (43804-0300)
PHONE..................................330 897-6311
Brian Harrison, *Mgr*
EMP: 53
SQ FT: 20,000
SALES (corp-wide): 6MM **Privately Held**
Web: www.flextechnologies.com
SIC: 2821 5169 3087 Molding compounds, plastics; Synthetic resins, rubber, and plastic materials; Custom compound purchased resins
PA: Flex Technologies, Inc.
5479 Gundy Dr
Midvale OH 44653
740 922-5992

(G-837)
GERBER & SONS INC (PA)
Also Called: Gerber & Sons
201 E Main St (43804-3516)
P.O. Box 248 (43804-0248)
PHONE..................................330 897-6201
Thomas Gerber, *Pr*
Michael Gerber, *
Douglas A Davis, *
Steven Gerber, *
EMP: 33 **EST:** 1905
SQ FT: 7,200
SALES (est): 6.06MM
SALES (corp-wide): 6.06MM **Privately Held**
Web: www.gerberandsons.com
SIC: 2048 5999 Livestock feeds; Farm equipment and supplies

(G-838)
HOLMES PANEL LLC
3052 State Route 557 (43804-7504)
PHONE..................................330 897-5040
Junior Keim, *Pt*
Dan Hershberger, *Pt*
Wayne Hershberger, *Pt*
EMP: 9 **EST:** 2000
SQ FT: 600
SALES (est): 714.4K **Privately Held**
SIC: 5211 2511 Lumber and other building materials; Wood household furniture

(G-839)
LIL TURTLES
504 N Ray St (43804-7500)
PHONE..................................330 897-6400
Matthew Miller, *Prin*
EMP: 6 **EST:** 2021
SALES (est): 496.01K **Privately Held**
Web: www.lilturtles.com
SIC: 2066 Chocolate and cocoa products

(G-840)
POLYNEW INC
3557 State Rte 93 (43804)
P.O. Box 318 (43804)
PHONE..................................330 897-3202
Robert Burket, *Pr*
Gail Burket, *Sec*
EMP: 6 **EST:** 1988
SQ FT: 12,000
SALES (est): 475.56K **Privately Held**
Web: www.polynew.com
SIC: 2821 Plastics materials and resins

(G-841)
TBONE SALES LLC
Also Called: Tbone Sales
410 N Ray St (43804-8901)
P.O. Box 75 (43804-0075)
PHONE..................................330 897-6131
EMP: 12 **EST:** 1954
SQ FT: 7,500
SALES (est): 1.1MM **Privately Held**
Web: www.tbonesales.com
SIC: 5411 7549 5531 5511 Convenience stores; Automotive maintenance services; Auto and truck equipment and parts; Trucks, tractors, and trailers: new and used

(G-842)
TRI STATE DAIRY LLC (PA)
Also Called: Es Steiner Dairy
9946 Fiat Rd Sw (43804-9049)
PHONE..................................330 897-5555
EMP: 6 **EST:** 2011
SALES (est): 1.19MM
SALES (corp-wide): 1.19MM **Privately Held**
SIC: 2022 Cheese; natural and processed

Baltimore
Fairfield County

(G-843)
CARAUSTAR INDUSTRIES INC
Ohio Paperboard
310 W Water St (43105-1276)
PHONE..................................740 862-4167
EMP: 56
SALES (corp-wide): 5.22B **Publicly Held**
Web: www.greif.com
SIC: 2631 2611 Paperboard mills; Pulp mills
HQ: Caraustar Industries, Inc.
5000 Astell Pwdr Sprng Rd
Austell GA 30106
770 948-3101

(G-844)
FILTER TECHNOLOGY INC
11885 Paddock View Ct Nw (43105-9556)
PHONE..................................614 921-9801
Ray Reisiger, *Prin*
EMP: 6 **EST:** 2011
SALES (est): 99.67K **Privately Held**
SIC: 3569 Filters

(G-845)
GREEN GOURMET FOODS LLC
515 N Main St (43105-1214)
PHONE..................................740 400-4212
EMP: 10 **EST:** 2011
SQ FT: 150,000
SALES (est): 241.03K **Privately Held**
Web: www.greengourmetfoods.net
SIC: 2034 Potato products, dried and dehydrated

(G-846)
RAYMOND W REISIGER
11885 Paddock View Ct Nw (43105-9556)
PHONE..................................740 400-4090
Ray Reisiger, *Prin*
EMP: 6 **EST:** 2010
SALES (est): 99.74K **Privately Held**
SIC: 3569 Filters

(G-847)
SAW DUST LTD
4799 Refugee Rd Nw (43105-9424)
PHONE..................................740 862-0612
James Wagenbrenner, *Owner*
EMP: 8 **EST:** 1995
SALES (est): 374.13K **Privately Held**
Web: www.edrichlumber.com
SIC: 2431 Woodwork, interior and ornamental, nec

(G-848)
TRI-TECH LED SYSTEMS LLC
Also Called: Tri-Tech
600 W Market St (43105-1176)
PHONE..................................614 593-2868
Scott Graham, *CEO*

David Hanson, *CFO*
Timothy Bosick, *VP*
Terry Nicopolis, *VP*
Bill Mcguire, *Acctnt*
EMP: 7 **EST:** 2012
SQ FT: 2,000
SALES (est): 483.42K **Privately Held**
SIC: 3674 Light emitting diodes

(G-849)
WOODEN HORSE
204 N Main St (43105-1212)
PHONE.................................740 503-5243
Wade Messmer, *Owner*
Barbara Messmer, *Pt*
EMP: 6 **EST:** 1979
SQ FT: 2,400
SALES (est): 241.82K **Privately Held**
SIC: 5947 5092 2426 8299 Gift, novelty, and souvenir shop; Toys and hobby goods and supplies; Hardwood dimension and flooring mills; Arts and crafts schools

Barberton
Summit County

(G-850)
A&D MACHINING LLC
1464 Waterloo Rd (44203-1204)
PHONE.................................330 786-0964
Ashley Anderson, *Mgr*
EMP: 8 **EST:** 2014
SALES (est): 516.85K **Privately Held**
Web: www.admachiningllc.com
SIC: 3599 Machine shop, jobbing and repair

(G-851)
ACE BOILER & WELDING CO INC
2891 Newpark Dr (44203-1047)
PHONE.................................330 745-4443
Robert Kille, *Pr*
Cynthia Kille, *Stockholder*
EMP: 8 **EST:** 1962
SQ FT: 15,000
SALES (est): 623.67K **Privately Held**
Web: www.aceboilerandwelding.com
SIC: 3599 3441 Machine shop, jobbing and repair; Fabricated structural metal

(G-852)
AKAY HOLDINGS INC
1031 Lambert St (44203-1611)
PHONE.................................330 753-8458
Albert Kay, *Pr*
Charles Kay, *Marketing**
John Lindeman, *
EMP: 23 **EST:** 1946
SQ FT: 90,000
SALES (est): 5.1MM **Privately Held**
Web: www.asbindustries.com
SIC: 1799 3599 3542 4215 Coating, caulking, and weather, water, and fireproofing; Machine shop, jobbing and repair; Presses: hydraulic and pneumatic, mechanical and manual; Courier services, except by air

(G-853)
AKRON BLDG CLOSEOUT MTLS LLC
Also Called: ABC Materials
425 Fairview Ave (44203-2774)
PHONE.................................234 738-0867
EMP: 6 **EST:** 2013
SALES (est): 317.9K **Privately Held**
Web: www.akronmaterials.com
SIC: 1799 1389 5051 Kitchen and bathroom remodeling; Construction, repair, and dismantling services; Steel decking

(G-854)
AMERICAN MOLDING COMPANY INC
711 Wooster Rd W (44203-2444)
PHONE.................................330 620-6799
Laverne J Strohfus, *Prin*
EMP: 8 **EST:** 2014
SALES (est): 167.04K **Privately Held**
Web: www.americanmolding.us
SIC: 3089 Injection molding of plastics

(G-855)
ANDERSON GRAPHICS INC
711 Wooster Rd W (44203-2444)
PHONE.................................330 745-2165
John Anderson, *Pr*
Larry Okolish, *
EMP: 30 **EST:** 1979
SALES (est): 2.08MM **Privately Held**
Web: www.anderson-graphics.com
SIC: 2752 2759 2789 2791 Offset printing; Commercial printing, nec; Bookbinding and related work; Typesetting

(G-856)
AXXESS LLC
61 E State St (44203-2730)
PHONE.................................330 861-0911
Tom Gerstenslager, *Prin*
EMP: 8 **EST:** 2006
SALES (est): 125.21K **Privately Held**
SIC: 3541 Vertical turning and boring machines (metalworking)

(G-857)
B & C RESEARCH INC
Also Called: B & C Research
842 Norton Ave (44203-1750)
P.O. Box 70 (44203-0070)
PHONE.................................330 848-4000
Bob Clements, *Ch Bd*
Louis Bilinovich, *
▲ **EMP:** 500 **EST:** 1985
SQ FT: 100,000
SALES (est): 116MM
SALES (corp-wide): 6.64B **Publicly Held**
SIC: 3599 Machine shop, jobbing and repair
HQ: Howmet Securities Llc
101 Cherry St Ste 400
Burlington VT 05401
802 658-2561

(G-858)
B & P POLISHING INC
123 9th St Nw (44203-2455)
P.O. Box 408 (44203-0408)
PHONE.................................330 753-4202
Louie Vilinovach, *Pr*
▲ **EMP:** 11 **EST:** 2001
SALES (est): 1.3MM **Privately Held**
SIC: 3291 Buffing or polishing wheels, abrasive or nonabrasive

(G-859)
B&C MACHINE CO LLC
401 Newell St (44203-2018)
P.O. Box 345 (44203-0345)
PHONE.................................330 745-4013
EMP: 23 **EST:** 2002
SQ FT: 300,000
SALES (est): 766.1K **Privately Held**
SIC: 3599 3714 3743 3398 Machine shop, jobbing and repair; Motor vehicle parts and accessories; Locomotives and parts; Metal heat treating

(G-860)
BABCOCK & WILCOX COMPANY
Also Called: Barberton Facility
91 Stirling Ave (44203-2600)
PHONE.................................330 753-4511

Doug Garlock, *Brnch Mgr*
EMP: 20
SALES (corp-wide): 999.35MM **Publicly Held**
Web: www.babcock.com
SIC: 3443 Fabricated plate work (boiler shop)
HQ: The Babcock & Wilcox Company
1200 E Market St Ste 650
Akron OH 44305
330 753-4511

(G-861)
BARBERTON STEEL INDUSTRIES INC
240 E Huston St (44203-3044)
P.O. Box 350 (44203-0350)
PHONE.................................330 745-6837
EMP: 48 **EST:** 2004
SALES (est): 5.35MM **Privately Held**
Web: www.barbertonsteel.net
SIC: 3321 Gray iron castings, nec

(G-862)
BUCKEYE ABRASIVE INC
1020 Eagon St (44203-1604)
PHONE.................................330 753-1041
Robert J Armour, *Pr*
EMP: 10 **EST:** 1954
SQ FT: 14,400
SALES (est): 978.29K **Privately Held**
Web: www.buckeyeabrasive.com
SIC: 3291 Wheels, abrasive

(G-863)
BWX TECHNOLOGIES INC
91 Stirling Ave (44203-2615)
PHONE.................................330 860-1692
EMP: 50
SIC: 3823 Process control instruments
PA: Bwx Technologies, Inc.
800 Main St Fl 4
Lynchburg VA 24504

(G-864)
CARDINAL RUBBER COMPANY
939 Wooster Rd N (44203-1698)
PHONE.................................330 745-2191
Diane Mcconnell, *Pr*
Thomas R Schnee, *
Robert F Schnee Junior, *Stockholder*
▲ **EMP:** 30 **EST:** 1944
SQ FT: 80,000
SALES (est): 2.59MM **Privately Held**
Web: www.cardinalrubbercompany.com
SIC: 3069 3061 3479 2891 Molded rubber products; Automotive rubber goods (mechanical); Bonderizing of metal or metal products; Adhesives and sealants

(G-865)
CUSTOM KERF WOODWORKING LLC
927 Raymond Ave (44203-6656)
PHONE.................................330 745-7651
Paul Ratay, *Prin*
EMP: 6 **EST:** 2017
SALES (est): 65.49K **Privately Held**
Web: www.customkerf.com
SIC: 2431 Millwork

(G-866)
DAVIS PRINTING COMPANY
Also Called: Davis Graphic Comm Solutions
101 Robinson Ave (44203-3502)
PHONE.................................330 745-3113
◆ **EMP:** 38 **EST:** 1906
SALES (est): 5.24MM **Privately Held**
Web: www.davisgcs.com

SIC: 2752 3993 2791 2789 Commercial printing, lithographic; Signs and advertising specialties; Typesetting; Bookbinding and related work

(G-867)
FLOHR MACHINE COMPANY INC
Also Called: Flohrmachine.com
1028 Coventry Rd (44203-1636)
PHONE.................................330 745-3030
Gerard Flohr, *Pr*
Ivan W Flohr, *
William Flohr, *
Joseph Flohr, *
Jude Flohr, *
EMP: 24 **EST:** 1966
SQ FT: 6,000
SALES (est): 3.47MM **Privately Held**
Web: www.flohrmachine.com
SIC: 3599 Machine shop, jobbing and repair

(G-868)
FREDS WOODWORKING & REMODELIN
665 Fairview Ave (44203-3870)
PHONE.................................330 802-8646
Fred Lambert, *Prin*
EMP: 6 **EST:** 2008
SALES (est): 198.6K **Privately Held**
Web: www.fredswoodworking.com
SIC: 2431 Millwork

(G-869)
GLAS ORNAMENTAL METALS INC
1559 Waterloo Rd (44203-1335)
PHONE.................................330 753-0215
John Glas, *Pr*
Rita Glas, *Ch Bd*
Karol Glas, *Sec*
EMP: 9 **EST:** 1961
SQ FT: 6,300
SALES (est): 972.58K **Privately Held**
Web: www.glasornamental.com
SIC: 3446 Railings, prefabricated metal

(G-870)
GLASS SURFACE SYSTEMS INC
Also Called: G S S
24 Brown St (44203-2315)
P.O. Box 311 (44203-0311)
PHONE.................................330 745-8500
Barry Jacobs, *Pr*
EMP: 75 **EST:** 1970
SQ FT: 17,000
SALES (est): 4.69MM **Privately Held**
Web: www.glasscoat.com
SIC: 3231 Strengthened or reinforced glass

(G-871)
HANNECARD ROLLER COATINGS INC
1031 Lambert St (44203-1611)
PHONE.................................330 753-8458
Dirk Vidts, *CEO*
Charles Kay, *
Peter De Marre, *
EMP: 33 **EST:** 2020
SALES (est): 2.82MM **Privately Held**
Web: www.asbindustries.com
SIC: 3069 Top roll covering, for textile mill machinery: rubber

(G-872)
HOWMET AEROSPACE INC
Also Called: HOWMET AEROSPACE INC
842 Norton Ave (44203-1715)
PHONE.................................330 848-4000
Tim Doyle, *Brnch Mgr*
EMP: 135
SALES (corp-wide): 6.64B **Publicly Held**

Barberton - Summit County (G-896)

Web: www.howmet.com
SIC: 3353 Aluminum sheet and strip
PA: Howmet Aerospace Inc.
201 Isabella St Ste 200
Pittsburgh PA 15212
412 553-1950

(G-873)
HYCOM INC
374 5th St Nw (44203-2127)
PHONE.................................330 753-2330
EMP: 45 EST: 1993
SQ FT: 126,684
SALES (est): 8.3MM Privately Held
Web: www.hycominc.com
SIC: 3498 Tube fabricating (contract bending and shaping)

(G-874)
IDEAL DRAPERY COMPANY INC
1024 Wooster Rd N (44203-1626)
PHONE.................................330 745-9873
FAX: 330 745-1504
EMP: 17
SQ FT: 4,000
SALES (est): 993.92K Privately Held
SIC: 2395 7389 Decorative and novelty stitching: for the trade; Sewing contractor

(G-875)
JOHNDOW INDUSTRIES INC
151 Snyder Ave (44203-4007)
PHONE.................................330 753-6895
Drew Dawson, *Pr*
Robert Christy, *
◆ EMP: 24 EST: 1981
SQ FT: 120,000
SALES (est): 4.99MM Privately Held
Web: www.johndow.com
SIC: 3559 Automotive maintenance equipment

(G-876)
KEM ADVERTISING AND PRTG LLC
564 W Tuscarawas Ave Ste 104 (44203-8213)
PHONE.................................330 818-5061
Kimberly Okolish, *Prin*
EMP: 7 EST: 2014
SALES (est): 224.43K Privately Held
SIC: 2752 Commercial printing, lithographic

(G-877)
LINDE INC
Also Called: Praxair
4805 Fairland Rd (44203-3913)
P.O. Box 509 (44203-0509)
PHONE.................................330 825-4449
EMP: 6
Web: www.lindeus.com
SIC: 2813 Industrial gases
HQ: Linde Inc.
10 Riverview Dr
Danbury CT 06810
203 837-2000

(G-878)
MAG RESOURCES LLC
711 Wooster Rd W (44203-2444)
P.O. Box 590 (44203-0590)
PHONE.................................330 294-0494
▲ EMP: 16 EST: 2007
SQ FT: 3,300
SALES (est): 2.83MM Privately Held
Web: www.magresources.net
SIC: 5023 2431 2591 8742 Venetian blinds; Blinds (shutters), wood; Window blinds; Business planning and organizing services

(G-879)
MALCO PRODUCTS INC (PA)
Also Called: Malco Products
361 Fairview Ave (44203-2700)
P.O. Box 892 (44203-0892)
PHONE.................................330 753-0361
◆ EMP: 175 EST: 1953
SALES (est): 63.82MM
SALES (corp-wide): 63.82MM Privately Held
Web: www.malcopro.com
SIC: 2842 8742 2899 2841 Polishes and sanitation goods; Marketing consulting services; Chemical preparations, nec; Soap and other detergents

(G-880)
MAY LIN SILICONE PRODUCTS INC
955 Wooster Rd W (44203-7149)
P.O. Box 335 (44203-0335)
PHONE.................................330 825-9019
Linda Weaver, *Pr*
Dave Weaver, *VP*
EMP: 6 EST: 1958
SQ FT: 1,800
SALES (est): 539.01K Privately Held
Web: www.may-lin.com
SIC: 3069 3053 Molded rubber products; Gaskets, all materials

(G-881)
MCCOY GROUP INC
1020 Eagon St (44203-1604)
PHONE.................................330 753-1041
Penni Cooper, *Prin*
EMP: 6 EST: 2019
SALES (est): 203.91K Privately Held
Web: www.buckeyeabrasive.com
SIC: 2431 Millwork

(G-882)
MERRYWEATHER FOAM INC (PA)
Also Called: Merryweather
11 Brown St (44203-2300)
PHONE.................................330 753-0353
▲ EMP: 35 EST: 1944
SALES (est): 16.67MM
SALES (corp-wide): 16.67MM Privately Held
Web: www.merryweather.com
SIC: 3086 3069 3089 2891 Plastics foam products; Sponge rubber and sponge rubber products; Extruded finished plastics products, nec; Adhesives and sealants

(G-883)
MITCHELL PLASTICS INC
130 31st St Nw (44203-7238)
PHONE.................................330 825-2461
Mitchell E Volk, *Pr*
EMP: 22 EST: 1976
SQ FT: 15,000
SALES (est): 2.37MM Privately Held
Web: www.mpicase.com
SIC: 3069 3993 Laboratory sundries: cases, covers, funnels, cups, etc.; Signs and advertising specialties

(G-884)
NOVATION SOLUTIONS LLC
25 Foundation Pl (44203-3520)
PHONE.................................330 620-6721
Thomas J Tupa, *Prin*
EMP: 11 EST: 2012
SALES (est): 5.12MM Privately Held
Web: www.novationsi.com
SIC: 2869 Industrial organic chemicals, nec

(G-885)
OGONEK CUSTOM HARDWOOD INC (PA)
61 E State St (44203-2730)
PHONE.................................833 718-2531
Daniel Ogonek, *Pr*
EMP: 7 EST: 1985
SALES (est): 798.97K
SALES (corp-wide): 798.97K Privately Held
Web: www.ogonekhardwoods.com
SIC: 2431 2426 7389 Millwork; Furniture stock and parts, hardwood; Interior designer

(G-886)
OHIO PRECISION MOLDING INC
Also Called: Opm
122 E Tuscarawas Ave (44203-2628)
PHONE.................................330 745-9393
Bruce Vereecken, *Pr*
Joe Vereecken, *
David Vereecken, *
Karen Vereecken, *Stockholder*
▲ EMP: 30 EST: 1994
SQ FT: 30,000
SALES (est): 6.94MM Privately Held
Web: www.ohioprecisionmolding.com
SIC: 3089 Injection molding of plastics

(G-887)
OLSON SHEET METAL CNSTR CO
465 Glenn St (44203-1499)
PHONE.................................330 745-8225
John Sveda, *Pr*
Joanne Sveda, *Sec*
EMP: 6 EST: 1938
SALES (est): 509.91K Privately Held
SIC: 3441 Fabricated structural metal

(G-888)
PARATUS SUPPLY INC
30 2nd St Sw (44203-2620)
PHONE.................................330 745-3600
Craig Cutcher, *VP*
John Sesic, *Genl Mgr*
EMP: 10 EST: 2010
SALES (est): 973.22K Privately Held
Web: www.paratussupply.com
SIC: 3563 3086 Spraying and dusting equipment; Insulation or cushioning material, foamed plastics

(G-889)
PATHFINDER CMPT SYSTEMS INC
345 5th St Ne (44203-2863)
PHONE.................................330 928-1961
EMP: 7 EST: 1990
SALES (est): 863.23K Privately Held
Web: www.pathfindercs.com
SIC: 7372 7371 Prepackaged software; Custom computer programming services

(G-890)
PLASTIC MOLD TECHNOLOGY INC
40 Stuver Pl (44203-2416)
PHONE.................................330 848-4921
Damir Petkovic, *Pr*
Robin Petkovic, *Sec*
EMP: 8 EST: 1994
SQ FT: 6,500
SALES (est): 875.25K Privately Held
SIC: 3544 Industrial molds

(G-891)
PPG INDUSTRIES INC
Also Called: South Plant
4829 Fairland Rd (44203-3905)
PHONE.................................330 825-0831
Carl E Johnson, *Brnch Mgr*
EMP: 24
SALES (corp-wide): 17.65B Publicly Held
Web: www.ppg.com
SIC: 2851 Paints and paint additives
PA: Ppg Industries, Inc.
1 Ppg Pl
Pittsburgh PA 15272
412 434-3131

(G-892)
PREFERRED COMPOUNDING CORP (HQ)
Also Called: Preferred Compounding
1020 Lambert St (44203-1612)
PHONE.................................330 798-4790
Mikael Fryklund, *Pr*
Joe Hudson, *
Scott Lieberman, *
Andrew Chan, *
Randy Niedermier, *
▲ EMP: 109 EST: 2002
SQ FT: 70,000
SALES (est): 98.21MM
SALES (corp-wide): 2.12B Privately Held
Web: www.preferredperforms.com
SIC: 3069 Custom compounding of rubber materials
PA: Hexpol Ab
Skeppsbron 3
MalmO 211 2
40254660

(G-893)
REVLIS CORPORATION
Also Called: Revlon
2845 Newpark Dr (44203-1047)
PHONE.................................330 535-2108
Brad Wehman, *Mgr*
EMP: 18
SQ FT: 10,000
SALES (corp-wide): 10.05MM Privately Held
Web: www.akrochem.com
SIC: 2816 Inorganic pigments
PA: Revlis Corporation
255 Fountain St
Akron OH 44304
330 535-2100

(G-894)
RICHARDSON PUBLISHING COMPANY
Also Called: Barberton Herald
70 4th St Nw Ste 1 (44203-8283)
P.O. Box 830 (44203-0830)
PHONE.................................330 753-1068
Dave Richardson, *Pr*
Cathy Robertson, *VP*
EMP: 11 EST: 1923
SALES (est): 467.39K Privately Held
Web: www.barbertonherald.com
SIC: 2711 Newspapers: publishing only, not printed on site

(G-895)
ROTARY SMER SPCALIST GROUP LLC
Also Called: Rss Maclin
635 Wooster Rd W (44203-2440)
PHONE.................................330 299-8210
Anthony Ganni, *Managing Member*
Christopher Ganni, *Managing Member*
EMP: 6 EST: 2019
SALES (est): 240.01K Privately Held
SIC: 3599 Machine and other job shop work

(G-896)
SPARTON ENTERPRISES LLC
3717 Clark Mill Rd (44203)
PHONE.................................877 772-7866
James E Little Junior, *Pr*
Andy Little, *

Barberton - Summit County (G-897)   GEOGRAPHIC SECTION

▲ EMP: 25 EST: 1969
SQ FT: 110,000
SALES (est): 6.09MM Privately Held
Web: www.spartonenterprises.com
SIC: 3069 Reclaimed rubber (reworked by manufacturing processes)

(G-897)
TAHOMA ENTERPRISES INC (PA)
255 Wooster Rd N (44203-2560)
PHONE..................330 745-9016
William P Herrington, CEO
EMP: 100 EST: 2007
SALES (est): 26.25MM
SALES (corp-wide): 26.25MM Privately Held
SIC: 3069 3089 5199 5162 Reclaimed rubber (reworked by manufacturing processes); Plastics processing; Foams and rubber; Plastics products, nec

(G-898)
TAHOMA RUBBER & PLASTICS INC (HQ)
Also Called: Rondy & Co.
255 Wooster Rd N (44203-2560)
PHONE..................330 745-9016
William P Herrington, CEO
▼ EMP: 100 EST: 1965
SQ FT: 750,000
SALES (est): 17.69MM
SALES (corp-wide): 26.25MM Privately Held
Web: www.tahomarubberplastics.com
SIC: 3069 3089 5199 5162 Reclaimed rubber (reworked by manufacturing processes); Plastics processing; Foams and rubber; Plastics products, nec
PA: Tahoma Enterprises, Inc.
  255 Wooster Rd N
  Barberton OH 44203
  330 745-9016

(G-899)
TENNEY TOOL & SUPPLY CO
973 Wooster Rd N (44203-1625)
PHONE..................330 666-2807
David Masa, Pr
Daniel Braun, VP
Donald Kepple, Sec
EMP: 9 EST: 1947
SQ FT: 11,000
SALES (est): 658.87K Privately Held
SIC: 5085 3599 Industrial tools; Machine shop, jobbing and repair

(G-900)
WINERY AT WOLF CREEK
2637 S Cleveland Massillon Rd (44203-6417)
PHONE..................330 666-9285
Andrew Troutman, Owner
EMP: 10 EST: 1981
SALES (est): 909.09K Privately Held
Web: www.wineryatwolfcreek.com
SIC: 2084 Wines

(G-901)
WRIGHT TOOL COMPANY
1 Wright Pl (44203-2798)
P.O. Box 512 (44203-0512)
PHONE..................330 848-0600
Richard Wright, Ch Bd
Terry G Taylor, *
Tom Futey, *
▲ EMP: 160 EST: 1927
SQ FT: 124,000
SALES (est): 43.31MM Privately Held
Web: www.wrighttool.com
SIC: 3462 3423 Iron and steel forgings; Wrenches, hand tools

Barnesville
Belmont County

(G-902)
BUCKEYE STEEL INC
607 Watt Ave (43713-1272)
P.O. Box 458 (43713-0458)
PHONE..................740 425-2306
EMP: 10 EST: 1994
SQ FT: 34,000
SALES (est): 958.21K Privately Held
SIC: 3441 Fabricated structural metal

(G-903)
K & J MACHINE INC
326 Fairmont Ave (43713-9669)
PHONE..................740 425-3282
Homer Luyster, Pr
Martha L Luyster, VP
Sharon Lucas, Sec
EMP: 10 EST: 1971
SQ FT: 3,300
SALES (est): 383.48K Privately Held
SIC: 7699 3599 7692 Aircraft and heavy equipment repair services; Machine shop, jobbing and repair; Welding repair

(G-904)
RODNEY WELLS
Also Called: Rods Welding and Rebuilding
34225 Holland Rd (43713-9602)
PHONE..................740 425-2266
EMP: 7 EST: 1991
SALES (est): 607.31K Privately Held
Web: www.rodsweld.com
SIC: 7692 Welding repair

(G-905)
SUN SHINE AWARDS
36099 Bethesda Street Ext (43713-9619)
PHONE..................740 425-2504
Danny Kimble, Owner
EMP: 10 EST: 1987
SALES (est): 453.39K Privately Held
SIC: 5999 2395 Trophies and plaques; Embroidery and art needlework

Batavia
Clermont County

(G-906)
A-1 FABRICATORS FINISHERS LLC
4220 Curliss Ln (45103-3276)
PHONE..................513 724-0383
Dennis Doane, Managing Member
Joe Strack, *
Jamie Doane, *
EMP: 78 EST: 2003
SQ FT: 80,000
SALES (est): 10.69MM Privately Held
Web: www.a1fabricators.com
SIC: 3441 Fabricated structural metal

(G-907)
AAG GLASS LLC
760 Kent Rd (45103-1704)
PHONE..................513 286-8268
Frank Lauch, Managing Member
EMP: 20 EST: 2018
SALES (est): 2.48MM Privately Held
Web: www.aagglass.com
SIC: 3231 Windshields, glass: made from purchased glass

(G-908)
AMERICAN MICRO PRODUCTS INC (PA)
4288 Armstrong Blvd (45103)
PHONE..................513 732-2674
◆ EMP: 199 EST: 1957
SALES (est): 23.14MM
SALES (corp-wide): 23.14MM Privately Held
Web: www.american-micro.com
SIC: 3451 3452 3678 Screw machine products; Bolts, nuts, rivets, and washers; Electronic connectors

(G-909)
AUTO TEMP INC
Also Called: ATI
950 Kent Rd (45103-1738)
P.O. Box 631690 (45263-1690)
PHONE..................513 732-6969
Frank Lauch, CEO
Matt Fassler, *
Doug Fassler, *
◆ EMP: 155 EST: 1991
SQ FT: 210,000
SALES (est): 24.96MM Privately Held
Web: www.autotempinc.com
SIC: 3231 Tempered glass: made from purchased glass

(G-910)
AVENUE FABRICATING INC
1281 Clough Pike (45103-2501)
PHONE..................513 752-1911
Gretchen Nichols, Pr
Robert Nichols, *
EMP: 41 EST: 1989
SQ FT: 17,800
SALES (est): 8.27MM Privately Held
Web: www.avenuefabricating.com
SIC: 3441 Fabricated structural metal

(G-911)
BEAUMONT MACHINE LLC
4001 Borman Dr (45103-1684)
P.O. Box 624 (45103-0624)
PHONE..................513 383-5061
EMP: 10 EST: 1998
SALES (est): 173.94K Privately Held
Web: www.beaumontmachine.com
SIC: 3599 Machine shop, jobbing and repair

(G-912)
BECKMAN ENVIRONMENTAL SVCS INC
Also Called: Besco
4259 Armstrong Blvd (45103-1697)
PHONE..................513 732-3570
Joan Beckman, Pr
John Beckman, General Vice President
EMP: 12 EST: 1973
SQ FT: 6,700
SALES (est): 2.13MM Privately Held
Web: www.bescosales.com
SIC: 3589 7699 Sewage treatment equipment; Sewer cleaning and rodding

(G-913)
BLACK MACHINING & TECH INC
4020 Bach Buxton Rd (45103-2525)
PHONE..................513 752-8625
EMP: 10 EST: 1983
SALES (est): 943.77K Privately Held
SIC: 3599 Machine shop, jobbing and repair

(G-914)
CINCHEMPRO INC
Also Called: Cincinnati Chemical Processing
458 W Main St (45103-1712)
PHONE..................513 724-6111
John Glass, CEO
EMP: 105 EST: 1970
SQ FT: 22,000
SALES (est): 7.37MM Privately Held
Web: www.cinchempro.com
SIC: 2899 Chemical preparations, nec

(G-915)
CINCINNATI MACHINES INC
4165 Half Acre Rd (45103-3247)
PHONE..................513 536-2432
Rose Acree, Supervisor
▲ EMP: 21 EST: 1998
SALES (est): 511.67K Privately Held
Web: www.cinmac.com
SIC: 3088 Plastics plumbing fixtures

(G-916)
CLERMONT STEEL FABRICATORS LLC
2565 Old State Route 32 (45103-3205)
PHONE..................513 732-6033
Robert Mampe, CEO
Ken Miller, *
◆ EMP: 70 EST: 2004
SQ FT: 144,000
SALES (est): 9.94MM Privately Held
Web: www.clermontsteel.com
SIC: 3441 Fabricated structural metal

(G-917)
COLLOTYPE LABELS USA INC
4053 Clough Woods Dr (45103-2587)
PHONE..................513 381-1480
David Buse, Pr
EMP: 100 EST: 1903
SALES (est): 24.26MM
SALES (corp-wide): 14.52B Privately Held
SIC: 2759 Labels and seals: printing, nsk
HQ: Multi-Color Corporation
  4053 Clough Woods Dr
  Batavia OH 45103
  513 381-1480

(G-918)
CORE COMPOSITES CINCINNATI LLC
4174 Half Acre Rd (45103-3250)
PHONE..................513 724-6111
John Glass, Prin
EMP: 60 EST: 2004
SALES (est): 24.99MM Publicly Held
Web: www.coremt.com
SIC: 3089 Injection molding of plastics
PA: Core Molding Technologies, Inc.
  800 Manor Park Dr
  Columbus OH 43228

(G-919)
D&D DESIGN CONCEPTS INC
Also Called: W.T.nickell Co.
4360 Winding Creek Blvd (45103-1729)
PHONE..................513 752-2191
Rick Meyer, Pr
EMP: 10 EST: 1960
SQ FT: 8,000
SALES (est): 977.52K Privately Held
Web: www.wtnickell.com
SIC: 2759 Labels and seals: printing, nsk

(G-920)
DELTEC INCORPORATED
4230 Grissom Dr (45103-1669)
PHONE..................513 732-0800
Chris Dugle, Ch
Jason Dugle, *
EMP: 46 EST: 1970
SQ FT: 42,000
SALES (est): 8.96MM Privately Held
Web: www.deltec-inc.com
SIC: 3599 Machine shop, jobbing and repair

GEOGRAPHIC SECTION
Batavia - Clermont County (G-943)

(G-921)
ELECTRODYNE COMPANY INC
4188 Taylor Rd (45103-9736)
P.O. Box 321 (45103-0321)
PHONE.................513 732-2822
Scott Blume, *Pr*
Cathy Brinkman, *VP*
▲ **EMP:** 14 **EST:** 1972
SQ FT: 22,000
SALES (est): 1.11MM **Privately Held**
Web: www.edyne.com
SIC: 3264 Porcelain electrical supplies

(G-922)
ELLIS & WATTS GLOBAL INDS INC
4400 Glen Willow Lake Ln (45103-2379)
PHONE.................513 752-9000
Gina Cottrell, *Pr*
EMP: 21 **EST:** 2014
SALES (est): 18.71MM
SALES (corp-wide): 364.48B **Publicly Held**
Web: www.elliswatts.com
SIC: 3585 Refrigeration and heating equipment
HQ: Marmon Holdings, Inc.
   181 W Madison St Ste 3900
   Chicago IL 60602
   312 372-9500

(G-923)
ENGINEERED MBL SOLUTIONS INC
Also Called: E M S
4155 Taylor Rd (45103-9792)
PHONE.................513 724-0247
Bryce Johnson, *VP*
EMP: 15 **EST:** 2007
SALES (est): 2.82MM **Privately Held**
Web: www.engmobilesolutions.com
SIC: 3715 Truck trailers

(G-924)
FREEMAN ENCLOSURE SYSTEMS LLC
4160 Half Acre Rd (45103-3250)
PHONE.................877 441-8555
Dale Freeman, *Pr*
EMP: 210 **EST:** 2010
SQ FT: 120,000
SALES (est): 61.08MM **Publicly Held**
Web: www.freemanenclosures.com
SIC: 3444 Sheet metalwork
HQ: Ies Infrastructure Solutions, Llc
   800 Nave Rd Se
   Massillon OH 44646
   330 830-3500

(G-925)
HUHTAMAKI INC
1985 James E Sauls Sr Dr (45103-3246)
PHONE.................513 201-1525
EMP: 112
SALES (corp-wide): 4.53B **Privately Held**
Web: www.huhtamaki.com
SIC: 3565 2656 Labeling machines, industrial ; Ice cream containers: made from purchased material
HQ: Huhtamaki, Inc.
   9201 Packaging Dr
   De Soto KS 66018
   913 583-3025

(G-926)
INGREDIENT MASTERS INC
Also Called: Manufacturing Animal Food Phrm
377 E Main St (45103-3001)
PHONE.................513 231-7432
Scott Culshaw, *Pr*
Cheryl Culshaw, *Sec*
▼ **EMP:** 7 **EST:** 1980
SALES (est): 812.68K **Privately Held**
Web: www.ingredientmasters.com
SIC: 3556 3559 Bakery machinery; Refinery, chemical processing, and similar machinery

(G-927)
KEY RESIN COMPANY (DH)
4050 Clough Woods Dr (45103-2586)
PHONE.................513 943-4225
Eric Borglum, *Pr*
◆ **EMP:** 16 **EST:** 1993
SQ FT: 18,000
SALES (est): 8.77MM
SALES (corp-wide): 7.26B **Publicly Held**
Web: www.keyresin.com
SIC: 2821 2822 Epoxy resins; Ethylene-propylene rubbers, EPDM polymers
HQ: The Euclid Chemical Company
   19215 Redwood Rd
   Cleveland OH 44110
   800 321-7628

(G-928)
KOEBBE PRODUCTS INC
4226 Grissom Dr (45103-1669)
PHONE.................513 735-1400
Scott Mclarin, *Brnch Mgr*
EMP: 90
SQ FT: 2,128
SALES (corp-wide): 19.74MM **Privately Held**
Web: www.egerproducts.com
SIC: 3089 Injection molding of plastics
PA: Koebbe Products, Inc.
   1132 Ferris Rd
   Amelia OH 45102
   513 753-4200

(G-929)
LOUIS G FREEMAN CO
4064 Clough Woods Dr (45103-2586)
PHONE.................513 263-1720
Louis Freeman, *Prin*
EMP: 7 **EST:** 2010
SALES (est): 123.6K **Privately Held**
Web: www.freemanschwabe.com
SIC: 3089 Plastics products, nec

(G-930)
MAGNET ENGINEERING INC
2690 Riggs Ln (45103-8487)
PHONE.................513 248-4578
Debbie Schafer, *Owner*
EMP: 8 **EST:** 2000
SALES (est): 246.09K **Privately Held**
Web: www.magnetengineering.com
SIC: 3499 Magnets, permanent: metallic

(G-931)
MAVERICK NAIL & STAPLE LTD
1680 Autumn Oak Dr Ste 100 (45103-8416)
PHONE.................513 843-5270
Roger Brofft, *Managing Member*
EMP: 6 **EST:** 2015
SALES (est): 90.89K **Privately Held**
SIC: 3315 Staples, steel: wire or cut

(G-932)
MCC-NORWAY LLC
4053 Clough Woods Dr (45103-2587)
PHONE.................513 381-1480
EMP: 12 **EST:** 2010
SALES (est): 2.4MM
SALES (corp-wide): 14.52B **Privately Held**
SIC: 2759 Labels and seals: printing, nsk
HQ: Multi-Color Corporation
   4053 Clough Woods Dr
   Batavia OH 45103
   513 381-1480

(G-933)
MET FAB FABRICATION AND MCH
2974 Waitensburg Pike (45103)
P.O. Box 363 (45103-0363)
PHONE.................513 724-3715
Rod Stouder, *Pr*
Debbie Stouder, *Treas*
EMP: 6 **EST:** 1984
SQ FT: 14,000
SALES (est): 652.47K **Privately Held**
Web: www.met-fabinc.com
SIC: 3535 3599 Conveyors and conveying equipment; Machine and other job shop work

(G-934)
MIDWEST MOLD & TEXTURE CORP
4270 Armstrong Blvd (45103-1670)
PHONE.................513 732-1300
Yoji Tatematsu, *Ch*
Katsumi Kawaguchi, *
Marico Cummings, *
▲ **EMP:** 38 **EST:** 1987
SQ FT: 20,000
SALES (est): 9.98MM **Privately Held**
Web: www.mmtcorp.com
SIC: 3544 Industrial molds
HQ: Tmw Co., Ltd.
   27-1, Okudasawacho
   Inazawa AIC 492-8

(G-935)
MILACRON HOLDINGS CORP (HQ)
Also Called: Milacron
4165 Half Acre Rd (45103-3247)
PHONE.................513 487-5000
Thomas Goeke, *Pr*
Bruce Chalmers, *
Mark Miller, *Chief Human Resources Officer**
Hugh O'donnell, *VP*
EMP: 245 **EST:** 1860
SALES (est): 1.24B **Publicly Held**
Web: www.milacron.com
SIC: 3544 Industrial molds
PA: Hillenbrand, Inc.
   1 Batesville Blvd
   Batesville IN 47006

(G-936)
MILACRON MARKETING COMPANY LLC (DH)
Also Called: Wear Technology
4165 Half Acre Rd (45103-3247)
PHONE.................513 536-2000
◆ **EMP:** 51 **EST:** 2009
SQ FT: 275,000
SALES (est): 411.38MM **Publicly Held**
Web: www.milacron.com
SIC: 3541 Machine tools, metal cutting type
HQ: Milacron Llc
   10200 Alliance Rd Ste 200
   Blue Ash OH 45242

(G-937)
MILACRON PLAS TECH GROUP LLC (DH)
4165 Half Acre Rd (45103-3247)
PHONE.................513 536-2000
Tom Goeke, *CEO*
Ron Krisanda, *COO*
Richard A Oleary, *VP*
▲ **EMP:** 156 **EST:** 2009
SALES (est): 117.83MM **Publicly Held**
Web: www.milacron.com
SIC: 3544 Forms (molds), for foundry and plastics working machinery
HQ: Milacron Llc
   10200 Alliance Rd Ste 200
   Blue Ash OH 45242

(G-938)
MULTI-COLOR AUSTRALIA LLC (DH)
4053 Clough Woods Dr (45103-2587)
PHONE.................513 381-1480
EMP: 58 **EST:** 2010
SALES (est): 7.29MM
SALES (corp-wide): 14.52B **Privately Held**
SIC: 2754 2752 2759 Commercial printing, gravure; Commercial printing, lithographic; Advertising literature: printing, nsk
HQ: Multi-Color Corporation
   4053 Clough Woods Dr
   Batavia OH 45103
   513 381-1480

(G-939)
MULTI-COLOR CORPORATION (HQ)
Also Called: McC Label
4053 Clough Woods Dr (45103)
PHONE.................513 381-1480
Hassan H Rmaile, *Pr*
▲ **EMP:** 16 **EST:** 1985
SQ FT: 392,527
SALES (est): 1.59B
SALES (corp-wide): 14.52B **Privately Held**
Web: www.mcclabel.com
SIC: 2759 2679 2672 Labels and seals: printing, nsk; Labels, paper: made from purchased material; Labels (unprinted), gummed: made from purchased materials
PA: Clayton, Dubilier & Rice, Inc.
   375 Park Ave Fl 18
   New York NY 10152
   212 407-5200

(G-940)
NEWACT INC
2084 James E Sauls Sr Dr (45103-3259)
PHONE.................513 321-5177
Rodney J Newman, *Pr*
Tom Vale, *VP Mktg*
Ennes Ireton Iii, *VP Engg*
EMP: 17 **EST:** 1987
SQ FT: 16,000
SALES (est): 5.8MM **Privately Held**
Web: www.newactinc.com
SIC: 5085 3643 3069 Industrial supplies; Electric connectors; Molded rubber products

(G-941)
ON DISPLAY LTD
1250 Clough Pike (45103-2502)
PHONE.................513 841-1600
EMP: 20 **EST:** 1996
SQ FT: 35,000
SALES (est): 5.17MM **Privately Held**
Web: www.ondisplay.net
SIC: 3999 Advertising display products

(G-942)
ORBIT MANUFACTURING INC
4291 Armstrong Blvd (45103-1697)
P.O. Box 144 (45103-0144)
PHONE.................513 732-6097
James S Paul, *Pr*
Kathy Paul, *Sec*
EMP: 13 **EST:** 1984
SQ FT: 10,000
SALES (est): 446.73K **Privately Held**
Web: www.orbitman.com
SIC: 3089 Injection molding of plastics

(G-943)
PLASTIKOS CORPORATION
Also Called: Multi-Form Plastics
700 Kent Rd (45103-1704)
P.O. Box 138 (45103-0138)
PHONE.................513 732-0961
Richard Bates, *Ch*
EMP: 22 **EST:** 1979
SQ FT: 48,000

Batavia - Clermont County (G-944)

SALES (est): 2.61MM **Privately Held**
Web: www.multiformplasticsinc.com
SIC: 3089 Thermoformed finished plastics products, nec

(G-944)
PRINTERS BINDERY SERVICES INC
Also Called: Printers Bindery
4564 Winners Cir (45103-9256)
PHONE..................513 821-8039
Joyce Bowman, *Pr*
▲ **EMP:** 68 **EST:** 1985
SALES (est): 4.89MM **Privately Held**
Web: www.printersbinderyohio.com
SIC: 2789 2675 Binding only: books, pamphlets, magazines, etc.; Die-cut paper and board

(G-945)
PROCOAT PAINTING INC
601 W Main St (45103-1715)
PHONE..................513 735-2300
Steve Hickey, *Prin*
EMP: 6 **EST:** 2014
SALES (est): 503.55K **Privately Held**
Web: www.procoatptg.com
SIC: 1721 3479 Painting and paper hanging; Painting of metal products

(G-946)
S & K METAL POLSG & BUFFING
4194 Taylor Rd (45103-9736)
PHONE..................513 732-6662
Aldena Sons, *Pr*
Everett J Sons, *VP*
EMP: 7 **EST:** 1971
SQ FT: 17,500
SALES (est): 739.91K **Privately Held**
SIC: 3471 Electroplating of metals or formed products

(G-947)
SAVOR SEASONINGS LLC
4292 Armstrong Blvd (45103-1600)
PHONE..................513 732-2333
Jeff Higgins, *Managing Member*
Shelly Higgins, *Pr*
EMP: 19 **EST:** 2002
SQ FT: 10,000
SALES (est): 4.39MM **Privately Held**
Web: www.savorseasonings.com
SIC: 2099 Seasonings and spices

(G-948)
SENECA ENTERPRISES INC
4053 Clough Woods Dr (45103-2587)
PHONE..................814 432-7890
Randy L Hicks, *Pr*
Edward Mc Mullen, *Sec*
Joseph Schwabenbauer, *VP*
Dennis Pascarella, *CEO*
Robert Puleo, *VP Opers*
EMP: 13 **EST:** 1995
SALES (est): 509.63K **Privately Held**
SIC: 2752 Tickets, lithographed

(G-949)
SPECTRA-TECH MANUFACTURING INC
4013 Borman Dr (45103-1684)
PHONE..................513 735-9300
Scott Reilman, *Pr*
Shirley Reilman, *
Jason Jasper, *
Craig Wilson, *
◆ **EMP:** 47 **EST:** 1998
SQ FT: 18,000
SALES (est): 18.81MM **Privately Held**
Web: www.4spectra.com

SIC: 3613 Panelboards and distribution boards, electric

(G-950)
STRAIGHT CREEK BUSHMAN LLC
202 E Main St (45103-2905)
PHONE..................513 732-1698
Robert Stearns, *Prin*
EMP: 6 **EST:** 2013
SALES (est): 161.31K **Privately Held**
SIC: 1221 Bituminous coal and lignite-surface mining

(G-951)
SUPERIOR STEEL SERVICE LLC
2760 Old State Route 32 (45103-3210)
PHONE..................513 724-7888
Jeffrey A Brewsaugh, *Managing Member*
EMP: 15 **EST:** 2004
SQ FT: 12,000
SALES (est): 2.72MM **Privately Held**
Web: www.superiorsteelservice.com
SIC: 3441 Fabricated structural metal

(G-952)
TEN DOGS GLOBAL INDUSTRIES LLC
4400 Glen Willow Lake Ln (45103-2320)
PHONE..................513 752-9000
EMP: 9 **EST:** 2009
SALES (est): 460.41K **Privately Held**
Web: www.elliswatts.com
SIC: 3585 Refrigeration and heating equipment

(G-953)
TIPTON ENVIRONMENTAL INTL INC
4446 State Route 132 (45103-1229)
PHONE..................513 735-2777
EMP: 10 **EST:** 1995
SQ FT: 3,600
SALES (est): 826.25K **Privately Held**
Web: www.fluencecorp.com
SIC: 3589 Water treatment equipment, industrial

(G-954)
TREEFROGG SPECIALTIES INC
1786 Craver Rd (45103-9615)
PHONE..................513 212-3581
Gene Conroy, *Prin*
▲ **EMP:** 6 **EST:** 2012
SALES (est): 143K **Privately Held**
Web: www.treefroggapparel.com
SIC: 2759 Screen printing

(G-955)
TSP INC
2009 Glenn Pkwy (45103-1676)
PHONE..................513 732-8900
J Stuart Newman, *Pr*
EMP: 20 **EST:** 1986
SQ FT: 30,000
SALES (est): 1.68MM **Privately Held**
Web: www.tspinc.com
SIC: 3479 3089 3081 Painting, coating, and hot dipping; Windows, plastics; Plastics film and sheet

(G-956)
UNILOY MILACRON INC
4165 Half Acre Rd (45103)
PHONE..................513 487-5000
John C Francy, *Pr*
◆ **EMP:** 78 **EST:** 1998
SALES (est): 62.73MM **Publicly Held**
Web: www.milacron.com
SIC: 2821 Plastics materials and resins
HQ: Milacron Llc
 10200 Alliance Rd Ste 200

Blue Ash OH 45242

(G-957)
UNIVERSAL PACKG SYSTEMS INC
Also Called: Paklab
5055 State Route 276 (45103-1211)
PHONE..................513 732-2000
Richard Burton, *Brnch Mgr*
EMP: 158
SALES (corp-wide): 379.38MM **Privately Held**
Web: www.paklab.com
SIC: 2844 7389 3565 2671 Cosmetic preparations; Packaging and labeling services; Bottling machinery: filling, capping, labeling; Plastic film, coated or laminated for packaging
PA: Universal Packaging Systems, Inc.
 14570 Monte Vista Ave
 Chino CA 91710
 909 517-2442

(G-958)
UNIVERSAL PACKG SYSTEMS INC
5069 State Route 276 (45103-1211)
PHONE..................513 735-4777
EMP: 158
SALES (corp-wide): 379.38MM **Privately Held**
Web: www.paklab.com
SIC: 2844 7389 3565 2671 Cosmetic preparations; Packaging and labeling services; Bottling machinery: filling, capping, labeling; Plastic film, coated or laminated for packaging
PA: Universal Packaging Systems, Inc.
 14570 Monte Vista Ave
 Chino CA 91710
 909 517-2442

(G-959)
VERSTRETE IN MOLD LBELS USA IN
Also Called: Multi-Color
4101 Founders Blvd (45103-3616)
PHONE..................513 943-0080
Mike Henry, *Pr*
Sharon Birkett, *CFO*
EMP: 15 **EST:** 2017
SQ FT: 115,000
SALES (est): 7.03MM
SALES (corp-wide): 14.52B **Privately Held**
SIC: 2759 2679 Labels and seals: printing, nsk; Labels, paper: made from purchased material
HQ: Multi-Color Corporation
 4053 Clough Woods Dr
 Batavia OH 45103
 513 381-1480

(G-960)
WHITEWATER FOREST PRODUCTS LLC
Also Called: White Water Forest
1970 Clark Ln (45103-1752)
P.O. Box 429 (45103-0429)
PHONE..................513 724-0157
Dan Shiels, *Managing Member*
EMP: 15 **EST:** 2013
SQ FT: 60,000
SALES (est): 2.5MM **Privately Held**
Web: www.whitewaterforest.com
SIC: 2421 Sawmills and planing mills, general

(G-961)
WILSON SEAT COMPANY
199 Foundry Ave (45103-2606)
P.O. Box 323 (45103-0323)
PHONE..................513 732-2460
Michael A Wilson, *Pr*
Mark Wilson, *VP*

EMP: 10 **EST:** 1961
SQ FT: 33,000
SALES (est): 451.07K **Privately Held**
SIC: 3713 3993 Truck bodies and parts; Signs, not made in custom sign painting shops

Bath
Summit County

(G-962)
WARMUS AND ASSOCIATES INC
Also Called: Smith Carl E Cnslting Engneers
2324 N Cleveland Massillon Rd (44210)
P.O. Box 807 (44210-0807)
PHONE..................330 659-4440
Alfred T Warmus, *Pr*
Roy P Stype Iii, *VP*
Brain Warmus, *Sec*
EMP: 12 **EST:** 1935
SQ FT: 7,000
SALES (est): 479.13K **Privately Held**
SIC: 8711 3441 5063 Consulting engineer; Tower sections, radio and television transmission; Electrical apparatus and equipment

Bay Village
Cuyahoga County

(G-963)
ARCHER PUBLISHING LLC
27101 E Oviatt Rd (44140-3307)
PHONE..................440 338-5233
Janelle Regotti, *Prin*
EMP: 7 **EST:** 2019
SALES (est): 310K **Privately Held**
SIC: 2741 Miscellaneous publishing

(G-964)
CLEARVUE PRODUCTS LLC
24620 Wolf Rd (44140-2767)
PHONE..................440 871-4209
Thomas Hortel, *Prin*
EMP: 10 **EST:** 2016
SALES (est): 50.22K **Privately Held**
SIC: 3441 Fabricated structural metal

(G-965)
GENERATIONS ACE INC
Also Called: Super Suppers
29121 Inverness Dr (44140-1836)
PHONE..................440 835-4872
James Bracken, *Pr*
Jody Bracken, *VP*
EMP: 8 **EST:** 2006
SALES (est): 389.94K **Privately Held**
SIC: 2099 Emulsifiers, food

(G-966)
RESERVE INDUSTRIES INC
Also Called: Reserve Industries
386 Lake Park Dr (44140-2963)
PHONE..................440 871-2796
John Megyimori, *Pr*
John Ruminsky, *VP*
EMP: 9 **EST:** 1958
SQ FT: 26,000
SALES (est): 372.7K **Privately Held**
SIC: 3089 3544 Injection molding of plastics; Special dies and tools

(G-967)
SOLO DYNA SYSTEMS LTD
24220 Bruce Rd (44140-2936)
PHONE..................440 871-7112
Arthur W Zimmerman, *Prin*
EMP: 6 **EST:** 2006

SALES (est): 89.94K **Privately Held**
Web: www.solodynasystems.biz
SIC: 3714 Motor vehicle parts and accessories

Beach City
Stark County

(G-968)
MERIDIAN INDUSTRIES INC
Also Called: Kleen Test Products
9901 Chestnut Ridge Rd Nw (44608-9417)
PHONE.................................330 359-5809
Peter Morton, Mgr
EMP: 24
SQ FT: 15,000
SALES (corp-wide): 331.16MM **Privately Held**
Web: www.meridiancompanies.com
SIC: 2299 2844 Pads, fiber: henequen, sisal, istle; Perfumes, cosmetics and other toilet preparations
PA: Meridian Industries, Inc.
 735 N Water St Ste 630
 Milwaukee WI 53202
 414 220-0610

(G-969)
MILLER CORE II INC
9823 Chestnut Ridge Rd Nw (44608-9480)
PHONE.................................330 359-0500
Joseph Miller, Pr
Reuben Miller, VP
Linda Miller, Sec
EMP: 8 EST: 2005
SALES (est): 927.71K **Privately Held**
Web: www.millercore2.com
SIC: 3567 Core baking and mold drying ovens

(G-970)
PROGRESSIVE FOAM TECH INC
6753 Chestnut Ridge Rd Nw (44608-9464)
PHONE.................................330 756-3200
Patrick Culpepper, Pr
Richard Wilson, *
▲ EMP: 120 EST: 1990
SQ FT: 100,000
SALES (est): 23.83MM **Privately Held**
Web: www.progressivefoam.com
SIC: 2821 Polystyrene resins

(G-971)
STARK TRUSS COMPANY INC
Also Called: Stark Truss Beach City Lumber
6855 Chestnut Ridge Rd Nw (44608-9462)
PHONE.................................330 756-3050
EMP: 63
SALES (corp-wide): 99.05MM **Privately Held**
Web: www.starktruss.com
SIC: 2439 2421 Trusses, wooden roof; Sawmills and planing mills, general
PA: Stark Truss Companies, Inc.
 109 Miles Ave Sw
 Canton OH 44710
 330 478-2100

Beachwood
Cuyahoga County

(G-972)
ALCHEM ALUMINUM EUROPE INC
25825 Science Park Dr Ste 400 (44122-7323)
PHONE.................................216 910-3400
Sean Stack, Pr
EMP: 9 EST: 2009
SALES (est): 183.29K **Privately Held**
SIC: 3555 Printing trades machinery

(G-973)
ALERIS RM INC
25825 Science Park Dr Ste 400 (44122-7323)
PHONE.................................216 910-3400
EMP: 580 EST: 2015
SALES (est): 9.65MM **Privately Held**
SIC: 3355 Aluminum rolling and drawing, nec
HQ: Novelis Alr Aluminum Holdings Corporation
 3550 Peachtree Rd Ne
 Atlanta GA 30326

(G-974)
BIP PRINTING SOLUTIONS LLC
24755 Highpoint Rd (44122-6050)
PHONE.................................216 832-5673
Nancy Mcgraw, Pr
EMP: 10 EST: 2014
SQ FT: 13,000
SALES (est): 402.32K **Privately Held**
Web: www.simplesolutions.org
SIC: 2732 2789 Books, printing and binding; Trade binding services

(G-975)
BOAT DECOR LLC
3700 Park East Dr (44122-4305)
PHONE.................................216 831-1889
Frank Dottore, Prin
EMP: 7 EST: 2010
SALES (est): 204.71K **Privately Held**
Web: www.gulfcoastmariner.com
SIC: 3089 Plastics boats and other marine equipment

(G-976)
CFO NTIC
23205 Mercantile Rd (44122-5911)
PHONE.................................216 450-5700
EMP: 6 EST: 2011
SALES (est): 125.11K **Privately Held**
Web: www.ntic.com
SIC: 2899 Chemical preparations, nec

(G-977)
CLEVELAND JEWISH PUBL CO FDN
23800 Commerce Park (44122-5828)
PHONE.................................216 454-8300
EMP: 11 EST: 1964
SALES (est): 210.66K **Privately Held**
Web: www.clevelandjewishnews.com
SIC: 2711 Newspapers, publishing and printing

(G-978)
COHESANT INC (PA)
3601 Green Rd Ste 308 (44122-5719)
PHONE.................................216 910-1700
EMP: 45
SALES (est): 20.9MM **Privately Held**
Web: www.cohesant.com
SIC: 3563 3559 3586 Spraying outfits: metals, paints, and chemicals (compressor); Paint making machinery; Measuring and dispensing pumps

(G-979)
COLUMBUS JEWISH NEWS
23880 Commerce Park Ste 1 (44122-5830)
PHONE.................................216 342-5184
EMP: 7 EST: 2019
SALES (est): 161.03K **Privately Held**
Web: www.clevelandjewishnews.com
SIC: 2711 Newspapers, publishing and printing

(G-980)
COMMONWEALTH ALUMINUM MTLS LLC
25825 Science Park Dr Ste 400 (44122-7323)
PHONE.................................216 910-3400
EMP: 11 EST: 2009
SALES (est): 721.43K **Privately Held**
SIC: 3555 Printing trades machinery

(G-981)
CONCEPT XXI INC
23600 Mercantile Rd Ste 101 (44122)
PHONE.................................216 831-2121
Irving Kaplan, Pr
EMP: 9 EST: 1979
SQ FT: 2,000
SALES (est): 332.02K **Privately Held**
Web: www.concept21.com
SIC: 7379 7372 Computer related consulting services; Prepackaged software

(G-982)
CURRENT LIGHTING SOLUTIONS LLC (HQ)
Also Called: GE Current, A Daintree Company
25825 Science Park Dr Ste 400 (44122)
PHONE.................................216 462-4700
Steve Harris, CEO
Barry Webb, CFO
◆ EMP: 430 EST: 1998
SQ FT: 20,890
SALES (est): 669.52MM
SALES (corp-wide): 1.6B **Privately Held**
Web: www.gecurrent.com
SIC: 3646 3641 2819 Commercial lighting fixtures; Electric lamps; Industrial inorganic chemicals, nec
PA: Current Lighting Holdco, Inc.
 25825 Science Park Dr # 400
 Beachwood OH 44122
 216 462-4700

(G-983)
DATATRAK INTERNATIONAL INC
3690 Orange Pl Ste 375 (44122-4466)
PHONE.................................440 443-0082
James R Ward, Pr
Julia Henderson, *
Alex Tabatabai, *
EMP: 47 EST: 1991
SQ FT: 4,300
SALES (est): 7.16MM **Privately Held**
Web: www.fountayn.com
SIC: 7374 7372 Data processing and preparation; Prepackaged software

(G-984)
DEEP BRAIN INNOVATIONS LLC
22901 Millcreek Blvd Ste 10 (44122)
PHONE.................................216 378-9106
EMP: 10 EST: 2012
SALES (est): 60.4K **Privately Held**
Web: www.deepbraininnovations.com
SIC: 3845 Electromedical equipment

(G-985)
EATON CORPORATION
Also Called: Fluid Power Plant
1000 Eaton Blvd (44122-6058)
PHONE.................................440 523-5000
Joy Davis, Brnch Mgr
EMP: 500
Web: www.dix-eaton.com
SIC: 3714 3824 Motor vehicle electrical equipment; Mechanical and electromechanical counters and devices
HQ: Eaton Corporation
 1000 Eaton Blvd
 Cleveland OH 44122
 440 523-5000

(G-986)
EATON LEASING CORPORATION
1000 Eaton Blvd (44122)
PHONE.................................216 382-2292
Richard Fearon, Pr
Billie Rawot, VP
EMP: 500 EST: 1981
SQ FT: 1,200
SALES (est): 60.88MM **Privately Held**
SIC: 7359 3612 3594 3593 Equipment rental and leasing, nec; Transformers, except electric; Fluid power pumps and motors; Fluid power cylinders and actuators
HQ: Eaton Corporation
 1000 Eaton Blvd
 Cleveland OH 44122
 440 523-5000

(G-987)
ETS SCHAEFER LLC (DH)
3700 Park East Dr Ste 300 (44122-4399)
PHONE.................................330 468-6600
Terrance Hogan, CEO
Michael Hobey, CFO
EMP: 27 EST: 2018
SALES (est): 10.36MM
SALES (corp-wide): 372.45MM **Privately Held**
Web: www.etsschaefer.com
SIC: 3297 3433 Nonclay refractories; Heating equipment, except electric
HQ: Real Alloy Recycling, Llc
 3700 Park East Dr Ste 300
 Beachwood OH 44122
 216 755-8900

(G-988)
GENERAL ENVMTL SCIENCE CORP
3659 Green Rd Ste 306 (44122-5715)
PHONE.................................216 464-0680
Barton Gilbert, Pr
Elaine Gilbert, VP
EMP: 8 EST: 1974
SALES (est): 902.27K **Privately Held**
Web: www.generalenvironmentalscience.com
SIC: 2836 Bacteriological media

(G-989)
HELIX LINEAR TECHNOLOGIES INC
23200 Commerce Park (44122-5802)
PHONE.................................216 485-2263
Jaseph Nook, Prin
EMP: 43 EST: 2013
SALES (est): 10.54MM **Privately Held**
Web: www.helixlinear.com
SIC: 3549 Screw driving machines

(G-990)
HELIX OPERATING COMPANY LLC
23200 Commerce Park (44122-5802)
PHONE.................................855 435-4958
Jaseph Nook, Managing Member
EMP: 8 EST: 2016
SALES (est): 699.99K **Privately Held**
SIC: 3451 3549 Screw machine products; Screw driving machines

(G-991)
IMCO RECYCLING OF INDIANA INC
25825 Science Park Dr Ste 400 (44122-7323)
PHONE.................................216 910-3400
Michael D Friday, Pr
EMP: 8 EST: 2009
SALES (est): 209.1K **Privately Held**
SIC: 3555 Printing trades machinery

Beachwood - Cuyahoga County (G-992) **GEOGRAPHIC SECTION**

(G-992)
ITL LLC
Also Called: Industrial Timber and Lumber
23925 Commerce Park Rd (44122-5821)
PHONE..................................216 831-3140
EMP: 23 EST: 2015
SALES (est): 1.1MM Privately Held
SIC: 2426 Lumber, hardwood dimension
PA: Northwest Hardwoods, Inc.
2600 Network Blvd Ste 600
Frisco TX 75034

(G-993)
KIRTLAND CAPITAL PARTNERS LP (PA)
Also Called: K C P
3201 Enterprise Pkwy Ste 200 (44122)
PHONE..................................216 593-0100
◆ EMP: 46 EST: 1992
SQ FT: 4,031
SALES (est): 44.69MM Privately Held
Web: www.kirtlandcapital.com
SIC: 5051 3312 3498 3494 Metals service centers and offices; Tubes, steel and iron; Fabricated pipe and fittings; Valves and pipe fittings, nec

(G-994)
LEWIS UNLIMITED INC
3690 Orange Pl Ste 340 (44122-4438)
PHONE..................................216 514-8282
Joseph Lewis, Pr
Nina Lewis, VP
EMP: 7 EST: 1993
SQ FT: 3,000
SALES (est): 879.53K Privately Held
Web: www.lewisunlimited.com
SIC: 3599 Machine shop, jobbing and repair

(G-995)
LIDSEN PUBLISHING INC
2000 Auburn Dr Ste 200 (44122-4314)
PHONE..................................216 378-7542
Bingke Lv, Prin
EMP: 6 EST: 2016
SALES (est): 72K Privately Held
Web: www.lidsen.com
SIC: 2741 Miscellaneous publishing

(G-996)
MAKERGEAR LLC
23632 Mercantile Rd Ste I (44122-5916)
PHONE..................................216 765-0030
▲ EMP: 6 EST: 2009
SALES (est): 712.55K Privately Held
Web: www.makergear.com
SIC: 3999 Education aids, devices and supplies

(G-997)
MASTER BLDRS SLTONS ADMXTRES U (HQ)
Also Called: Mbcc Group
23700 Chagrin Blvd (44122-5506)
PHONE..................................216 839-7500
Boris Gorella, CEO
Bruce J Christensen, Pr
Christian Hammel, CFO
Karsten Eller, COO
EMP: 49 EST: 2019
SALES (est): 146.86MM Privately Held
Web: www.master-builders-solutions.com
SIC: 2899 Concrete curing and hardening compounds
PA: Sika Ag
Zugerstrasse 50
Baar ZG 6341

(G-998)
MASTER BUILDERS LLC (HQ)
Also Called: Degussa Construction
23700 Chagrin Blvd (44122-5506)
PHONE..................................800 228-3318
Anthony Price, CEO
◆ EMP: 50 EST: 1911
SALES (est): 467.64MM Privately Held
Web: master-builders-solutions.basf.us
SIC: 2899 2851 1799 Concrete curing and hardening compounds; Epoxy coatings; Caulking (construction)
PA: Sika Ag
Zugerstrasse 50
Baar ZG 6341

(G-999)
MASTERBRAND CABINETS LLC (HQ)
Also Called: Decora
3300 Enterprise Pkwy Ste 300 (44122)
P.O. Box 420 (47547-0420)
PHONE..................................812 482-2527
Dave Banyard, Pr
Angela M Pla, *
Matthew C Lenz, *
Andi Simon, *
▲ EMP: 300 EST: 1986
SALES (est): 1.3B
SALES (corp-wide): 2.73B Publicly Held
Web: www.masterbrand.com
SIC: 2434 7371 Wood kitchen cabinets; Computer software development
PA: Masterbrand, Inc.
1 Masterbrand Cabinets Dr
Jasper IN 47546
812 482-2527

(G-1000)
MIM SOFTWARE INC (PA)
25800 Science Park Dr Ste 180 (44122-7311)
PHONE..................................216 455-0600
Andrew Nelson, CEO
Jonathan Piper, *
Peter Simmelink, *
Jerimy Brockway, *
Mark Cain, *
EMP: 160 EST: 2003
SALES (est): 35.87MM
SALES (corp-wide): 35.87MM Privately Held
Web: www.mimsoftware.com
SIC: 7372 Application computer software

(G-1001)
NATIONAL BIOLOGICAL CORP
23700 Mercantile Rd (44122-5900)
PHONE..................................216 831-0600
Kenneth Oif, Pr
Michael Kaufman, *
▲ EMP: 50 EST: 1965
SQ FT: 36,000
SALES (est): 10.96MM Privately Held
Web: www.natbiocorp.com
SIC: 3841 3648 Surgical and medical instruments; Ultraviolet lamp fixtures

(G-1002)
NEUROWAVE SYSTEMS INC
25825 Science Park Dr Ste 250 (44122-7300)
PHONE..................................216 361-1591
Robert N Schmidt, CEO
Mo Modarres, Pr
Andrew Balint, Contrlr
EMP: 7 EST: 2003
SQ FT: 10,000
SALES (est): 2.26MM Privately Held
Web: www.neurowavesystems.com
SIC: 5047 3845 Patient monitoring equipment; Ultrasonic scanning devices, medical

(G-1003)
NOVELIS ALR ALMNUM-ALABAMA LLC
25825 Science Park Dr Ste 400 (44122-7323)
PHONE..................................256 353-1550
EMP: 48 EST: 1993
SALES (est): 7.35MM Privately Held
SIC: 3353 Aluminum sheet, plate, and foil

(G-1004)
NOVELIS ALR ALUMINUM LLC
Also Called: Davenport Rolling Mill
25825 Science Park Dr Ste 400 (44122-7323)
PHONE..................................216 910-3400
EMP: 542 EST: 2007
SALES (est): 105.62MM Privately Held
Web: www.novelis.com
SIC: 3355 3354 Aluminum rolling and drawing, nec; Shapes, extruded aluminum, nec
HQ: Novelis Alr Rolled Products, Inc.
3550 Peachtree Rd Ne # 11
Atlanta GA 30326
216 910-3400

(G-1005)
NOVELIS ALR ROLLED PDTS LLC (DH)
25825 Science Park Dr Ste 400 (44122-7323)
PHONE..................................216 910-3400
Sean Stack, Managing Member
▲ EMP: 21 EST: 2000
SALES (est): 191.65MM Privately Held
Web: www.novelis.com
SIC: 3355 Aluminum rolling and drawing, nec
HQ: Novelis Alr Aluminum Holdings Corporation
3550 Peachtree Rd Ne
Atlanta GA 30326

(G-1006)
OHIO NITROGEN LLC
25800 Science Park Dr (44122-7339)
PHONE..................................216 839-5485
EMP: 7 EST: 2019
SALES (est): 242.51K Privately Held
SIC: 2813 Nitrogen

(G-1007)
OLD RAR INC
3700 Park East Dr Ste 300 (44122-4399)
PHONE..................................216 545-7249
EMP: 1000 EST: 2009
SQ FT: 7,000
SALES (est): 136.73MM Privately Held
SIC: 3341 Secondary nonferrous metals

(G-1008)
OMNOVA WALLCOVERING USA INC
25435 Harvard Rd (44122-6201)
PHONE..................................216 682-7000
Kevin Mc Mullin, CEO
EMP: 100 EST: 1998
SALES (est): 47.43MM
SALES (corp-wide): 2.46B Privately Held
Web: www.omnova.com
SIC: 2819 Industrial inorganic chemicals, nec
HQ: Synthomer Inc.
25435 Harvard Rd
Beachwood OH 44122
216 682-7000

(G-1009)
PCC AIRFOILS LLC
25201 Chagrin Blvd Ste 290 (44122-5600)
PHONE..................................216 766-6206
EMP: 10 EST: 2017
SALES (est): 1MM Privately Held
Web: www.pccairfoils.com
SIC: 3369 Nonferrous foundries, nec

(G-1010)
PHILIPS MED SYSTEMS CLVLAND IN
100 Park Ave Ste 300 (44122-8203)
PHONE..................................617 245-5510
EMP: 75
SALES (corp-wide): 18.51B Privately Held
Web: www.emergin.com
SIC: 3844 X-ray apparatus and tubes
HQ: Philips Medical Systems (Cleveland), Inc.
595 Miner Rd
Cleveland OH 44143
440 483-3000

(G-1011)
POWERTECH INC
25805 Fairmount Blvd Apt 203 (44122)
PHONE..................................901 850-9393
Danny Holmes, Pr
Barbara Gross, Ex VP
◆ EMP: 9 EST: 1999
SQ FT: 10,000
SALES (est): 514.73K Privately Held
Web: www.powertechcontrols.com
SIC: 3674 Semiconductors and related devices

(G-1012)
PRIME CONDUIT INC (PA)
23240 Chagrin Blvd Ste 405 (44122-5468)
P.O. Box 22897 (44122-0897)
PHONE..................................216 464-3400
Jim Abel, Pr
Kay Condon, Sec
◆ EMP: 18 EST: 2008
SALES (est): 19.78MM Privately Held
Web: www.primeconduit.com
SIC: 2821 3312 Polyvinyl chloride resins, PVC; Pipes and tubes

(G-1013)
REAL ALLOY RECYCLING LLC (HQ)
3700 Park East Dr Ste 300 (44122-4399)
PHONE..................................216 755-8900
▲ EMP: 100 EST: 2018
SQ FT: 7,000
SALES (est): 345.81MM
SALES (corp-wide): 372.45MM Privately Held
Web: www.realalloy.com
SIC: 3341 Secondary nonferrous metals
PA: Real Alloy Holding, Llc
3700 Park East Dr Ste 300
Beachwood OH 44122
216 755-8900

(G-1014)
REAL ALLOY SPECIALTY PDTS LLC (DH)
3700 Park East Dr Ste 300 (44122-4399)
PHONE..................................216 755-8836
Terry Hogan, Pr
EMP: 1000 EST: 2018
SALES (est): 222.46MM
SALES (corp-wide): 372.45MM Privately Held
SIC: 3341 3313 3334 Secondary nonferrous metals; Ferromanganese, not made in blast furnaces; Pigs, aluminum
HQ: Real Alloy Recycling, Llc
3700 Park East Dr Ste 300
Beachwood OH 44122
216 755-8900

▲ = Import ▼ = Export
◆ = Import/Export

GEOGRAPHIC SECTION
Beaver - Pike County (G-1036)

(G-1015)
REAL ALLOY SPECIALTY PDTS LLC (DH)
3700 Park East Dr Ste 300 (44122-4399)
PHONE...................216 755-8836
Terry Hogan, *Pr*
Michael Hobey, *
EMP: 159 **EST:** 1992
SQ FT: 36,500
SALES (est): 111.66MM
SALES (corp-wide): 112.7MM **Publicly Held**
Web: www.realalloy.com
SIC: 3355 Aluminum rolling and drawing, nec
HQ: Real Alloy Intermediate Holdings, Llc
3700 Park East Dr Ste 300
Beachwood OH

(G-1016)
REAL ALLOY SPECIFICATION LLC (DH)
3700 Park East Dr Ste 300 (44122-4399)
PHONE...................216 755-8900
Terrance J Hogan, *Pr*
EMP: 83 **EST:** 2018
SALES (est): 57.64MM
SALES (corp-wide): 372.45MM **Privately Held**
Web: www.realalloy.com
SIC: 3334 3341 3313 Pigs, aluminum; Secondary nonferrous metals; Ferromanganese, not made in blast furnaces
HQ: Real Alloy Recycling, Llc
3700 Park East Dr Ste 300
Beachwood OH 44122
216 755-8900

(G-1017)
RELIABLE WHEELCHAIR TRANS
28899 Harvard Rd (44122-4741)
PHONE...................216 390-3999
Lapetha Ruffin, *Prin*
EMP: 6 **EST:** 2010
SALES (est): 81.88K **Privately Held**
SIC: 3842 Wheelchairs

(G-1018)
REXON COMPONENTS INC
24500 Highpoint Rd (44122-6002)
PHONE...................216 292-7373
M R Farukhi, *Pr*
Zaid H Farukhi, *VP*
Steve Fink, *Sec*
◆ **EMP:** 20 **EST:** 1983
SQ FT: 10,000
SALES (est): 2.39MM **Privately Held**
Web: www.rexon.com
SIC: 3674 Semiconductors and related devices

(G-1019)
ROCKHEAD GROUP USA LLC
25370 Letchworth Rd (44122-4159)
PHONE...................216 310-1569
Jonathan Kaplin, *Managing Member*
EMP: 6 **EST:** 2017
SALES (est): 180.48K **Privately Held**
Web: www.rockheadsusa.com
SIC: 2399 7371 Fabricated textile products, nec; Computer software development and applications

(G-1020)
RSI COMPANY (PA)
Also Called: Worthington
24050 Commerce Park Ste 200 (44122-5833)
PHONE...................216 360-9800
Steve Sords, *Pr*
Robert Sords, *CFO*
▼ **EMP:** 19 **EST:** 1990
SQ FT: 60,000
SALES (est): 3.24MM **Privately Held**
Web: www.rsi.com
SIC: 3559 3585 Recycling machinery; Refrigeration and heating equipment

(G-1021)
SAMEGOAL INC
3401 Enterprise Pkwy Ste 340 (44122)
PHONE...................216 766-5713
Andrew Hochhaus, *Mgr*
EMP: 9 **EST:** 2016
SALES (est): 266.83K **Privately Held**
Web: www.samegoal.com
SIC: 7372 Prepackaged software

(G-1022)
SEAFORTH MINERAL & ORE CO INC (PA)
3690 Orange Pl Ste 495 (44122)
PHONE...................216 292-5820
Gary Mcclurg, *Ch Bd*
James Mcclurg, *Pr*
▲ **EMP:** 15 **EST:** 1957
SQ FT: 3,500
SALES (est): 15.15MM
SALES (corp-wide): 15.15MM **Privately Held**
Web: www.seaforthinc.com
SIC: 5052 3295 Nonmetallic minerals and concentrate; Minerals, ground or treated

(G-1023)
SHAQ INC
Also Called: Shaw Stainless
22901 Millcreek Blvd Ste 650 (44122)
PHONE...................770 427-0402
EMP: 70 **EST:** 2021
SALES (est): 12.11MM
SALES (corp-wide): 2.16B **Publicly Held**
SIC: 5085 5051 3312 Valves and fittings; Pipe and tubing, steel; Stainless steel
PA: Olympic Steel, Inc.
22901 Mllcreek Blvd Ste 6
Cleveland OH 44122
216 292-3800

(G-1024)
SIKA MBCC US LLC
Also Called: Master Bldrs Sltons Cnstr Syst
23700 Chagrin Blvd (44122-5506)
PHONE...................216 839-7500
Boris Gorella, *CEO*
Christian Hammel, *CFO*
Karsten Eller, *COO*
Bruce Christensen, *Pr*
EMP: 512 **EST:** 2020
SALES (est): 134.1MM **Privately Held**
Web: www.master-builders-solutions.com
SIC: 1771 2891 1799 Flooring contractor; Sealants; Coating, caulking, and weather, water, and fireproofing
HQ: Master Builders Solutions Admixtures Us, Llc
23700 Chagrin Blvd
Beachwood OH 44122
216 839-7500

(G-1025)
SYNTHOMER INC (HQ)
25435 Harvard Rd (44122-6201)
PHONE...................216 682-7000
Calum G Maclean, *Pr*
Stephen G Bennett, *
Richard Atkinson, *
◆ **EMP:** 140 **EST:** 1952
SALES (est): 736.2MM
SALES (corp-wide): 2.46B **Privately Held**
Web: www.omnova.com
SIC: 2819 2211 3069 3081 Industrial inorganic chemicals, nec; Decorative trim and specialty fabrics, including twist weave; Roofing, membrane rubber; Unsupported plastics film and sheet
PA: Synthomer Plc
Temple Mead
Harlow CM20
127 943-6211

(G-1026)
SYNTHOMER USA LLC (HQ)
25435 Harvard Rd (44122-6201)
PHONE...................678 400-6655
Calum Maclean, *CEO*
Julia Harp, *Development PROD*
Richard Cochran, *CFO*
◆ **EMP:** 24 **EST:** 2016
SALES (est): 24.7MM
SALES (corp-wide): 2.46B **Privately Held**
SIC: 2891 3479 Adhesives; Painting, coating, and hot dipping
PA: Synthomer Plc
Temple Mead
Harlow CM20
127 943-6211

(G-1027)
THE CLEVELAND JEWISH PUBL CO
23880 Commerce Park Ste 1 (44122-5830)
PHONE...................216 454-8300
Rob Certner, *Prin*
EMP: 26 **EST:** 2012
SALES (est): 32.9K **Privately Held**
Web: www.clevelandjewishnews.com
SIC: 2711 Newspapers, publishing and printing

(G-1028)
TOA TECHNOLOGIES INC (PA)
3333 Richmond Rd Ste 420 (44122-4194)
PHONE...................216 925-5950
Yuval Brisker, *Pr*
Irad Carmi, *
Brian Cook, *
Bruce Grainger, *
Michael Mcdonnell, *VP*
EMP: 216 **EST:** 2003
SALES (est): 25.39MM
SALES (corp-wide): 25.39MM **Privately Held**
Web: www.oracle.com
SIC: 7372 Prepackaged software

(G-1029)
TRAPEZE SOFTWARE GROUP INC
23215 Commerce Park Ste 200 (44122-5803)
PHONE...................905 629-8727
EMP: 17
SALES (corp-wide): 6.62B **Privately Held**
Web: www.trapezegroup.com
SIC: 7372 Prepackaged software
HQ: Trapeze Software Group, Inc.
1110 Continental Pl Ne
Cedar Rapids IA 52402
480 991-2427

(G-1030)
TREMCO CPG INC
23150 Commerce Park (44122-5807)
PHONE...................216 514-7783
EMP: 14
SALES (corp-wide): 7.26B **Publicly Held**
Web: www.tremcocpg.com
SIC: 2891 Sealants
HQ: Tremco Cpg Inc.
3735 Green Rd
Beachwood OH 44122
216 292-5000

(G-1031)
TREMCO INCORPORATED (HQ)
3735 Green Rd (44122-5730)
◆ **EMP:** 265 **EST:** 1980
SALES (est): 740.14MM
SALES (corp-wide): 7.26B **Publicly Held**
Web: www.tremcocpg.com
SIC: 2891 2952 1761 1752 Sealants; Roofing materials; Roofing contractor; Floor laying and floor work, nec
PA: Rpm International Inc.
2628 Pearl Rd
Medina OH 44256
330 273-5090

(G-1032)
WALTER H DRANE CO INC
23811 Chagrin Blvd Ste 344 (44122-5525)
PHONE...................216 514-1022
William Kenneweg, *Pr*
EMP: 8 **EST:** 1955
SALES (est): 549.88K **Privately Held**
SIC: 2741 Technical manual and paper publishing

(G-1033)
ZEKELMAN INDUSTRIES INC
3201 Entp Pkwy Ste 150 (44122)
PHONE...................216 910-3700
Frank A Riddick Iii, *Brnch Mgr*
EMP: 31
Web: www.zekelman.com
SIC: 3317 Steel pipe and tubes
PA: Zekelman Industries, Inc.
227 W Monroe St Ste 2600
Chicago IL 60606

Beallsville
Monroe County

(G-1034)
DONALD E DORNON
44592 Game Ridge Rd (43716-9318)
PHONE...................740 926-9144
Donald E Dornon, *Prin*
EMP: 7 **EST:** 2006
SALES (est): 232.99K **Privately Held**
SIC: 3531 Backhoes

Beaver
Pike County

(G-1035)
BEAVER WOOD PRODUCTS
190 Buck Hollow Rd (45613-9498)
P.O. Box 404 (45613-0404)
PHONE...................740 226-6211
Walter Thornsberry, *Pt*
Rick Thornsberry, *Pt*
EMP: 17 **EST:** 1988
SALES (est): 774.44K **Privately Held**
SIC: 2421 2436 2435 2426 Sawmills and planing mills, general; Softwood veneer and plywood; Hardwood veneer and plywood; Hardwood dimension and flooring mills

(G-1036)
WISEMAN BROS FABG & STL LTD
2598 Glade Rd (45613-9613)
P.O. Box 307 (45613-0307)
PHONE...................740 988-5121
EMP: 10 **EST:** 1995
SQ FT: 8,000
SALES (est): 2.28MM **Privately Held**
Web: www.wisemanbrothers.com
SIC: 3441 Fabricated structural metal

Beavercreek
Greene County

(G-1037)
A C HADLEY - PRINTING INC
Also Called: Hadley Printing
1530 Marsetta Dr (45432-2733)
PHONE..................937 426-0952
Nancy Hadley, *Pr*
Scott Hadley, *VP*
Michael Hadley, *Sec*
EMP: 6 **EST:** 1959
SQ FT: 4,800
SALES (est): 330.25K **Privately Held**
SIC: 2396 2759 Automotive and apparel trimmings; Thermography

(G-1038)
A SERVICE GLASS INC
1363 N Fairfield Rd (45432-2693)
PHONE..................937 426-4920
Donald T Sullivan, *Pr*
Donald J Sullivan, *Pr*
William C Sullivan, *VP*
Glenn Sullivan, *Sec*
EMP: 24 **EST:** 1959
SQ FT: 8,000
SALES (est): 1.96MM **Privately Held**
Web: www.aserviceglass.com
SIC: 5231 3231 1793 5039 Glass; Doors, glass: made from purchased glass; Glass and glazing work; Glass construction materials

(G-1039)
ADVANT-E CORPORATION (PA)
2434 Esquire Dr (45431-2573)
PHONE..................937 429-4288
Jason K Wadzinski, *Ch Bd*
James E Lesch, *CFO*
EMP: 10 **EST:** 1994
SQ FT: 19,000
SALES (est): 12.55MM
SALES (corp-wide): 12.55MM **Privately Held**
Web: www.advant-e.com
SIC: 7372 7375 Application computer software; Information retrieval services

(G-1040)
ARCTOS MISSION SOLUTIONS LLC
2601 Mission Point Blvd (45431-6600)
PHONE..................813 609-5591
James Fugit, *CEO*
Steven Shugart, *
Todd J Schweitzer, *
Brian Overstreet, *
David Joseph, *
EMP: 40 **EST:** 2008
SALES (est): 4.65MM
SALES (corp-wide): 67.58MM **Privately Held**
Web: www.arctos-us.com
SIC: 7379 5045 3728 Computer related consulting services; Computers, peripherals, and software; Aircraft parts and equipment, nec
HQ: Arctos, Llc
2601 Mssion Pt Blvd Ste 3
Beavercreek OH 45431
478 923-9995

(G-1041)
ASTRO INDUSTRIES INC
4403 Dayton Xenia Rd (45432-1805)
PHONE..................937 429-5900
Kailash Mehta, *Pr*
EMP: 24 **EST:** 1967
SQ FT: 24,000
SALES (est): 4.87MM **Privately Held**
Web: www.astro-ind.com
SIC: 3678 3679 5063 3357 Electronic connectors; Electronic circuits; Wiring devices; Communication wire

(G-1042)
CARBIDE PROBES INC
1328 Research Park Dr (45432-2897)
PHONE..................937 429-9123
Greg Shellabarger, *Pr*
Dan Shellabarger, *Prin*
Roberta Lee Shellabarger, *VP*
Cheryl Terry, *Treas*
Jessica Ross, *Admn*
EMP: 22 **EST:** 1955
SQ FT: 10,000
SALES (est): 2.57MM **Privately Held**
Web: www.carbideprobes.com
SIC: 3545 Machine tool attachments and accessories

(G-1043)
COMMUNICATION CONCEPTS INC
508 Mill Stone Dr (45434-5840)
PHONE..................937 426-8600
Rodger L Southworth, *Pr*
Marlis Southworth, *Sec*
EMP: 6 **EST:** 1978
SALES (est): 500K **Privately Held**
Web: www.communication-concepts.com
SIC: 5961 3674 Mail order house, nec; Semiconductors and related devices

(G-1044)
CREEK SMOOTHIES LLC
3195 Dayton Xenia Rd (45434-6390)
PHONE..................937 429-1519
EMP: 6 **EST:** 2011
SALES (est): 488.67K **Privately Held**
SIC: 2037 Frozen fruits and vegetables

(G-1045)
DECIBEL RESEARCH INC
Also Called: DECIBEL RESEARCH, INC
2661 Commons Blvd Ste 136 (45431-3704)
PHONE..................256 705-3341
Bassem Mahafza, *Brnch Mgr*
EMP: 49
SALES (corp-wide): 13.17MM **Privately Held**
Web: www.decibelresearch.com
SIC: 3812 Radar systems and equipment
PA: Decibel Research, Inc.
325 Bob Heath
Huntsville AL 35806
256 716-0787

(G-1046)
DRS ADVANCED ISR LLC (DH)
2601 Mission Point Blvd Ste 250 (45431)
PHONE..................937 429-7408
Angella Cowan, *
Sandra L Hodgkinson, *
Terence J Murphy, *
EMP: 150 **EST:** 2009
SQ FT: 25,000
SALES (est): 86.78MM
SALES (corp-wide): 15.28B **Publicly Held**
Web: www.leonardodrs.com
SIC: 3812 Navigational systems and instruments
HQ: Drs Defense Solutions, Llc
4910 Executive Ct S
Frederick MD 21703

(G-1047)
DRS LEONARDO INC
Also Called: Leonardo Drs Arbr Intllgnce Sy
2601 Mission Point Blvd Ste 250 (45431)
PHONE..................937 429-7408
EMP: 46
SALES (corp-wide): 15.28B **Publicly Held**
Web: www.leonardodrs.com
SIC: 3812 Search and navigation equipment
HQ: Leonardo Drs, Inc.
2345 Crystal Dr Ste 1000
Arlington VA 22202
703 416-8000

(G-1048)
DRS SIGNAL TECHNOLOGIES INC
4393 Dayton Xenia Rd (45432-1803)
PHONE..................937 429-7470
Leo Torresani, *Pr*
EMP: 47 **EST:** 1990
SALES (est): 2.73MM
SALES (corp-wide): 15.28B **Publicly Held**
Web: www.leonardodrs.com
SIC: 3825 7371 Electrical energy measuring equipment; Custom computer programming services
HQ: Leonardo Drs, Inc.
2345 Crystal Dr Ste 1000
Arlington VA 22202
703 416-8000

(G-1049)
EDICT SYSTEMS INC
2434 Esquire Dr (45431-2573)
PHONE..................937 429-4288
Ason K Wadzinski, *Ch Bd*
EMP: 45 **EST:** 1989
SQ FT: 12,000
SALES (est): 11.71MM
SALES (corp-wide): 12.55MM **Privately Held**
Web: www.edictsystems.com
SIC: 7372 Prepackaged software
PA: Advant-E Corporation
2434 Esquire Dr
Beavercreek OH 45431
937 429-4288

(G-1050)
EDL DISPLAYS INC
1304 Research Park Dr (45432-2818)
PHONE..................937 429-7423
Charles W Mc Intire, *Pr*
Michael J Mc Ardle, *General Vice President*
EMP: 20 **EST:** 1993
SQ FT: 10,000
SALES (est): 1.86MM **Privately Held**
SIC: 3663 Television monitors

(G-1051)
GENERAL DYNMICS MSSION SYSTEMS
2673 Commons Blvd Ste 200 (45431-3505)
PHONE..................513 253-4770
Bob Kiley, *Mgr*
EMP: 11
SALES (corp-wide): 42.27B **Publicly Held**
Web: www.gdmissionsystems.com
SIC: 3669 3812 Transportation signaling devices; Search and navigation equipment
HQ: General Dynamics Mission Systems, Inc.
12450 Fair Lakes Cir
Fairfax VA 22033
877 449-0600

(G-1052)
GRID SENTRY LLC
3915 Germany Ln (45431-1688)
PHONE..................937 490-2101
EMP: 6 **EST:** 2008
SALES (est): 224.93K **Privately Held**
Web: www.gridsentry.us
SIC: 3822 Thermostats and other environmental sensors

(G-1053)
KETCO INC
1348 Research Park Dr (45432-2818)
PHONE..................937 426-9331
Richard D Harding, *Pr*
Steven Gerbic, *VP*
EMP: 20 **EST:** 1973
SQ FT: 15,000
SALES (est): 1.95MM **Privately Held**
Web: www.ketco.com
SIC: 3543 Industrial patterns

(G-1054)
LEAR ENGINEERING CORP
2942 Stauffer Dr (45434-6247)
PHONE..................937 429-0534
Dennis M Swing, *Pr*
EMP: 6 **EST:** 1975
SQ FT: 2,400
SALES (est): 242.65K **Privately Held**
Web: www.learengineering.com
SIC: 3827 Optical test and inspection equipment

(G-1055)
LEIDOS INC
3745 Pentagon Blvd (45431-2369)
PHONE..................937 656-8433
Dennis Anders, *Brnch Mgr*
EMP: 77
Web: www.leidos.com
SIC: 8731 7371 7373 8742 Commercial physical research; Computer software development; Systems engineering, computer related; Training and development consultant
HQ: Leidos, Inc.
1750 Presidents St
Reston VA 20190
571 526-6000

(G-1056)
MONARCH WATER SYSTEMS INC
689 Greystone Dr (45434-4202)
PHONE..................937 426-5773
TOLL FREE: 888
John Glaser, *VP*
Patricia A Glaser, *Pr*
EMP: 10 **EST:** 1918
SQ FT: 7,500
SALES (est): 701.73K **Privately Held**
SIC: 3589 Water filters and softeners, household type

(G-1057)
NUCOR CORPORATION
Also Called: Vulcraft
3000 Presidential Dr Ste 110 (45324-6208)
PHONE..................937 390-2300
Sean Murphy, *Mgr*
EMP: 8
SALES (corp-wide): 34.71B **Publicly Held**
Web: www.nucor.com
SIC: 3312 Blast furnaces and steel mills
PA: Nucor Corporation
1915 Rexford Rd
Charlotte NC 28211
704 366-7000

(G-1058)
PRIORITY CUSTOM MOLDING INC
2628 Colonial Pkwy (45434-6288)
PHONE..................937 431-8770
Carol S Williams, *Pr*
Dennie Williams, *VP*
Bob Abbitt, *Treas*
Angela Abbit, *Sec*
▲ **EMP:** 10 **EST:** 1997
SALES (est): 488.52K **Privately Held**

SIC: 3089 3081 Molding primary plastics;
Unsupported plastics film and sheet

(G-1059)
RAYTHEON COMPANY
Also Called: Raytheon
2970 Presidential Dr Ste 300 (45324-6752)
PHONE..................................937 429-5429
Mike Evans, *Brnch Mgr*
EMP: 10
SALES (corp-wide): 68.92B **Publicly Held**
Web: www.rtx.com
SIC: 3812 Sonar systems and equipment
HQ: Raytheon Company
 870 Winter St
 Waltham MA 02451
 781 522-3000

(G-1060)
RELIABLE HERMETIC SEALS LLC
Also Called: Rh Seals
4156 Dayton Xenia Rd (45432-1904)
PHONE..................................888 747-3250
EMP: 12 **EST:** 2012
SALES (est): 1MM **Privately Held**
Web: www.rhseals.com
SIC: 3643 3679 Bus bars (electrical conductors); Hermetic seals, for electronic equipment

(G-1061)
SHOPS BY TODD INC (PA)
Also Called: Occassionally Yours
2727 Fairfield Commons Blvd Spc W273 (45431-5748)
PHONE..................................937 458-3192
Todd Bettman, *Pr*
EMP: 9 **EST:** 1985
SQ FT: 1,750
SALES (est): 951.97K **Privately Held**
Web: www.occasionallyyoursgifts.com
SIC: 5947 2759 Gift shop; Invitation and stationery printing and engraving

(G-1062)
SIERRA NEVADA CORPORATION
2611 Commons Blvd (45431-3704)
PHONE..................................937 431-2800
William Sullivan, *Prin*
EMP: 111
SALES (corp-wide): 2.38B **Privately Held**
Web: www.sncorp.com
SIC: 8731 3577 Electronic research; Computer peripheral equipment, nec
PA: Sierra Nevada Corporation
 444 Salomon Cir
 Sparks NV 89434
 775 331-0222

(G-1063)
SIGN WRITE
3348 Dayton Xenia Rd (45432-2747)
PHONE..................................937 559-4388
Kristine Sturr, *Prin*
EMP: 6 **EST:** 2010
SALES (est): 99.34K **Privately Held**
SIC: 3993 Signs and advertising specialties

(G-1064)
SONALYSTS INC
2940 Presidential Dr Ste 160 (45324-6564)
PHONE..................................937 429-9711
EMP: 21
SALES (corp-wide): 69.66MM **Privately Held**
Web: www.sonalysts.com
SIC: 3211 Window glass, clear and colored
PA: Sonalysts, Inc.
 215 Parkway N
 Waterford CT 06385
 860 442-4355

(G-1065)
TERADYNE INC
Avionics Interface Tech
2689 Commons Blvd Ste 201 (45431-3822)
PHONE..................................937 427-1280
Andy Kragick, *Mgr*
EMP: 15
SALES (corp-wide): 2.68B **Publicly Held**
Web: www.teradyne.com
SIC: 3829 Measuring and controlling devices, nec
PA: Teradyne, Inc.
 600 Riverpark Dr
 North Reading MA 01864
 978 370-2700

(G-1066)
THREAD WORKS CUSTOM EMBROIDERY
Also Called: Thread Wrks EMB Screenprinting
2630 Colonel Glenn Hwy (45324-6559)
PHONE..................................937 478-5231
▲ **EMP:** 6 **EST:** 1993
SQ FT: 1,700
SALES (est): 354.44K **Privately Held**
Web: www.twlogo.com
SIC: 2395 Embroidery and art needlework

(G-1067)
WOOD DUCK ENTERPRISES LTD
2225 La Grange Rd (45431-3159)
PHONE..................................937 776-0606
Teresa Chromey, *Prin*
EMP: 6 **EST:** 2010
SALES (est): 208.54K **Privately Held**
SIC: 2491 Wood products, creosoted

Beavercreek
Montgomery County

(G-1068)
A & A SAFETY INC
4080 Industrial Ln (45430-1017)
PHONE..................................937 567-9781
Tim Weeks, *Mgr*
EMP: 10
SALES (corp-wide): 22.88MM **Privately Held**
Web: www.aasafetyinc.com
SIC: 7359 1721 5084 1611 Work zone traffic equipment (flags, cones, barrels, etc.); Painting and paper hanging; Safety equipment; Highway and street sign installation
PA: A & A Safety, Inc.
 1126 Ferris Rd
 Amelia OH 45102
 513 943-6100

(G-1069)
ALEKTRONICS INC
4095 Executive Dr (45430-1062)
PHONE..................................937 429-2118
Alan Eakle, *CEO*
EMP: 16 **EST:** 1988
SQ FT: 4,800
SALES (est): 3.71MM **Privately Held**
Web: www.alekcompanies.com
SIC: 3672 Printed circuit boards

(G-1070)
ATK SPACE SYSTEMS LLC
1365 Technology Ct (45430-2212)
PHONE..................................937 490-4121
Todd Henrich, *VP*
EMP: 135
Web: www.northropgrumman.com
SIC: 3812 Search and navigation equipment
HQ: Atk Space Systems Llc
 6033 Bandini Blvd
 Commerce CA 90040
 323 722-0222

(G-1071)
ATK SYSTEMS
1365 Technology Ct (45430-2212)
PHONE..................................937 429-8632
EMP: 9
SALES (est): 263.04K **Privately Held**
SIC: 3812 Search and navigation equipment

(G-1072)
CERTIFIED COMPARATOR PRODUCTS
1174 Grange Hall Rd (45430-1094)
PHONE..................................937 426-9677
Rod Murch, *Pr*
EMP: 6 **EST:** 2012
SALES (est): 517.09K **Privately Held**
Web: www.qvii.com
SIC: 5065 3545 Electronic parts and equipment, nec; Comparators (machinists' precision tools)

(G-1073)
EXITO MANUFACTURING LLC
4120 Industrial Ln Ste B (45430-1004)
PHONE..................................937 291-9871
EMP: 7 **EST:** 2000
SALES (est): 816.82K **Privately Held**
Web: www.exitomfg.com
SIC: 3544 3542 3728 3714 Special dies, tools, jigs, and fixtures; Machine tools, metal forming type; Aircraft parts and equipment, nec; Motor vehicle parts and accessories

(G-1074)
HII MISSION TECHNOLOGIES CORP
1430 Oak Ct (45430-1069)
PHONE..................................937 426-3421
Charlie Schwegman, *Brnch Mgr*
EMP: 8
Web: www.hii.com
SIC: 8711 3721 Engineering services; Aircraft
HQ: Hii Mission Technologies Corp.
 8350 Broad St Ste 1400
 Mc Lean VA 22102
 703 918-4480

(G-1075)
MATRIX RESEARCH INC
3844 Research Blvd (45430-2104)
PHONE..................................937 427-8433
Robert Hawley, *Pr*
Robert W Hawley, *
James Lutz, *
William Pierson, *
EMP: 80 **EST:** 2005
SQ FT: 4,000
SALES (est): 16.31MM **Privately Held**
Web: www.matrixresearch.com
SIC: 3829 8711 Measuring and controlling devices, nec; Engineering services

(G-1076)
NORTHROP GRMMAN INNVTION SYSTE
1365 Technology Ct (45430-2212)
PHONE..................................937 429-9261
Don Hairston, *Prin*
EMP: 150
Web: www.northropgrumman.com
SIC: 3812 Search and navigation equipment
HQ: Northrop Grumman Innovation Systems, Inc.
 2980 Fairview Park Dr
 Falls Church VA 22042

(G-1077)
NORTHROP GRUMMAN SYSTEMS CORP
Also Called: Aerontics Systems Arspc Strctr
1365 Technology Ct (45430-2212)
PHONE..................................937 490-4111
Richard Passmore, *Brnch Mgr*
EMP: 174
Web: www.northropgrumman.com
SIC: 3812 Search and navigation equipment
HQ: Northrop Grumman Systems Corporation
 2980 Fairview Park Dr
 Falls Church VA 22042
 703 280-2900

(G-1078)
PROGRAM MANAGERS INC
Also Called: World Digital Imaging
1138 Richfield Ctr (45430-1121)
PHONE..................................937 431-1982
Craig Howick, *Prin*
Jerry Warner, *Prin*
EMP: 7 **EST:** 1998
SALES (est): 813.55K **Privately Held**
Web: www.worlddigitalimaging.com
SIC: 2752 Offset printing

(G-1079)
RCF KITCHENS INDIANA LLC
Also Called: Really Cool Foods
87 Shelford Way (45440-3657)
PHONE..................................765 478-6600
Don Gillun, *Managing Member*
EMP: 9 **EST:** 2007
SQ FT: 1,500
SALES (est): 1.66MM **Privately Held**
SIC: 2015 Chicken, processed: fresh

(G-1080)
RESONANT SCIENCES LLC
3975 Research Blvd (45430-2107)
PHONE..................................937 431-8180
Jeremy North, *Pr*
EMP: 49 **EST:** 2014
SALES (est): 10.47MM **Privately Held**
Web: www.resonantsciences.com
SIC: 8711 3825 Aviation and/or aeronautical engineering; Radio frequency measuring equipment

(G-1081)
SUPERIOR SODA SERVICE LLC
3626 Napanee Dr (45430-1322)
P.O. Box 341450 (45434-1450)
PHONE..................................937 657-9700
EMP: 6 **EST:** 2010
SALES (est): 443.9K **Privately Held**
Web: www.superiorsodaservice.com
SIC: 7699 3441 Vending machine repair; Fabricated structural metal

(G-1082)
THE SCHAEFER GROUP INC (PA)
1300 Grange Hall Rd (45430-1013)
PHONE..................................937 253-3342
▲ **EMP:** 50 **EST:** 1956
SALES (est): 20.24MM
SALES (corp-wide): 20.22MM **Privately Held**
Web: www.theschaefergroup.com
SIC: 3567 1741 Metal melting furnaces, industrial: electric; Refractory or acid brick masonry

(G-1083)
WERNLI REALTY CORPORATION
1300 Grange Hall Rd (45430-1013)
PHONE..................................937 258-7878
Richard L Schaefer, *Pr*

Beavercreek Township - Greene County (G-1084)

John Miltenberger, *
EMP: 11 **EST:** 1956
SQ FT: 20,000
SALES (est): 249.68K **Privately Held**
Web: www.theschaefergroup.com
SIC: 3441 6512 Building components, structural steel; Nonresidential building operators

Beavercreek Township
Greene County

(G-1084)
FLUID APPLIED ROOFING LLC
Also Called: Manufacturing
830 Space Dr (45434-7163)
PHONE..................855 860-2300
Sonny Arwood, *CEO*
EMP: 17 **EST:** 2012
SALES (est): 2.56MM **Privately Held**
Web: www.fluidappliedroofing.com
SIC: 2952 Roofing materials

(G-1085)
MOSHER MACHINE & TOOL CO INC
2201 Valley Springs Rd (45434-6100)
PHONE..................937 258-8070
Kevin Mosher, *Pr*
Michael Mosher, *VP*
EMP: 29 **EST:** 1973
SALES (est): 2.41MM **Privately Held**
Web: www.moshermachine.com
SIC: 3451 3599 Screw machine products; Machine shop, jobbing and repair

(G-1086)
NORTHROP GRMMAN TCHNCAL SVCS I
Also Called: Ngts
4065 Colonel Glenn Hwy (45431-1601)
PHONE..................937 320-3100
Saju Kuruvilla, *Brnch Mgr*
EMP: 66
SIC: 3812 8711 7373 Search and navigation equipment; Engineering services; Computer integrated systems design
HQ: Northrop Grumman Technical Services, Inc.
7575 Colshire Dr
Mc Lean VA 22102
703 556-1144

(G-1087)
NORTHROP GRUMMAN SYSTEMS CORP
4065 Colonel Glenn Hwy (45431-1601)
PHONE..................937 429-6450
Mel Meadows, *Brnch Mgr*
EMP: 79
Web: www.northropgrumman.com
SIC: 3812 Search and navigation equipment
HQ: Northrop Grumman Systems Corporation
2980 Fairview Park Dr
Falls Church VA 22042
703 280-2900

(G-1088)
OCULII CORP
829 Space Dr (45434-7162)
PHONE..................937 912-9261
Feng-ming Wang, *CEO*
EMP: 25 **EST:** 2012
SALES (est): 2.89MM
SALES (corp-wide): 226.47MM **Publicly Held**
Web: www.oculii.com
SIC: 3812 Radar systems and equipment
PA: Ambarella, Inc.

3101 Jay St
Santa Clara CA 95054
408 734-8888

(G-1089)
PHILLIPS COMPANIES (PA)
620 Phillips Dr (45434-7230)
P.O. Box 187 (45301-0187)
PHONE..................937 426-5461
George E Phillips, *Ch*
Richard L Phillips Ii, *Pr*
Dennis Phillips, *Sec*
Bradley Phillips, *VP*
Jason Phillips, *Treas*
EMP: 20 **EST:** 1942
SQ FT: 2,000
SALES (est): 12.47MM
SALES (corp-wide): 12.47MM **Privately Held**
Web: www.phillipscompanies.com
SIC: 1442 6552 1794 Sand mining; Subdividers and developers, nec; Excavation work

(G-1090)
PHILLIPS READY MIX CO
620 Phillips Dr (45434-7230)
P.O. Box 187 (45301-0187)
PHONE..................937 426-5151
EMP: 23 **EST:** 1960
SALES (est): 442K **Privately Held**
Web: www.phillipscompanies.com
SIC: 1771 3273 7353 5191 Concrete pumping; Ready-mixed concrete; Heavy construction equipment rental; Farm supplies

(G-1091)
QQE SUMMIT LLC
802 Orchard Ln (45434-7217)
PHONE..................937 236-3250
Ryan Kelly, *Prin*
EMP: 10 **EST:** 2020
SALES (est): 978.97K **Privately Held**
Web: www.qqe.com
SIC: 3599 Machine shop, jobbing and repair

(G-1092)
QUALITY QUARTZ ENGINEERING INC
802 Orchard Ln (45434-7217)
PHONE..................937 236-3250
◆ **EMP:** 52 **EST:** 2007
SALES (est): 11.21MM **Privately Held**
Web: www.qqe.com
SIC: 3679 Quartz crystals, for electronic application
PA: Quality Quartz Engineering, Incorporated
802 Orchard Ln
Beavercreek Township OH 45434

(G-1093)
QUALITY QUARTZ ENGINEERING INC (PA)
802 Orchard Ln (45434-7217)
PHONE..................510 791-1013
▲ **EMP:** 24 **EST:** 1995
SALES (est): 11.52MM **Privately Held**
Web: www.qqe.com
SIC: 3679 Quartz crystals, for electronic application

(G-1094)
SONOCO PRODUCTS COMPANY
Sonoco Consumer Products
761 Space Dr (45434-7171)
PHONE..................937 429-0040
Norwood Bizzell, *Mgr*
EMP: 62

SALES (corp-wide): 6.78B **Publicly Held**
Web: www.sonoco.com
SIC: 2655 5113 2891 Cans, fiber: made from purchased material; Paper tubes and cores; Adhesives and sealants
PA: Sonoco Products Company
1 N 2nd St
Hartsville SC 29550
843 383-7000

(G-1095)
W&W AUTOMOTIVE & TOWING INC
Also Called: W & W Automotive
680 Orchard Ln (45434-7205)
PHONE..................937 429-1699
Regina White, *Pr*
EMP: 10 **EST:** 1981
SQ FT: 16,000
SALES (est): 999.12K **Privately Held**
Web: www.wandwautomotive.com
SIC: 3711 7532 Chassis, motor vehicle; Body shop, automotive

Beaverdam
Allen County

(G-1096)
GOODYEAR TIRE & RUBBER COMPANY
Also Called: Goodyear
415 E Main St (45808-9728)
PHONE..................419 643-8273
Paul Morton, *Brnch Mgr*
EMP: 10
SALES (corp-wide): 20.07B **Publicly Held**
Web: www.goodyear.com
SIC: 7534 5531 Tire retreading and repair shops; Automotive tires
PA: The Goodyear Tire & Rubber Company
200 Innovation Way
Akron OH 44316
330 796-2121

Bedford
Cuyahoga County

(G-1097)
277 NORTHFIELD INC
277 Northfield Rd (44146-4648)
PHONE..................440 439-1029
Guriqbal Multani, *Admn*
EMP: 12 **EST:** 2013
SALES (est): 500.85K **Privately Held**
SIC: 3441 Fabricated structural metal

(G-1098)
ADEMCO INC
Also Called: ADI Global Distribution
7710 First Pl Ste A (44146-6718)
PHONE..................440 439-7002
Mark Blackburn, *Mgr*
EMP: 6
SALES (corp-wide): 6.24B **Publicly Held**
Web: www.adiglobaldistribution.us
SIC: 5063 3669 3822 Electrical apparatus and equipment; Emergency alarms; Environmental controls
HQ: Ademco Inc.
275 Bradhollow Rd Ste 400
Melville NY 11747
631 692-1000

(G-1099)
ALS HIGH TECH INC (PA)
Also Called: Al's Electric Motor Service
135 Northfield Rd (44146-4606)
PHONE..................440 232-7090
Dale Ochwat, *Pr*

Elaine Ochwat, *CEO*
Lynn O Meffen, *Sec*
EMP: 11 **EST:** 1955
SQ FT: 45,000
SALES (est): 975.29K
SALES (corp-wide): 975.29K **Privately Held**
Web: www.alselectricmotorservice.com
SIC: 7694 5063 Electric motor repair; Electrical apparatus and equipment

(G-1100)
AM CASTLE & CO
Also Called: Oliver Steel Plate
26800 Miles Rd (44146-1405)
PHONE..................330 425-7000
Scott J Dolan, *Brnch Mgr*
EMP: 19
SALES (corp-wide): 1.3B **Privately Held**
Web: www.oliversteel.com
SIC: 5051 3444 3443 3398 Steel; Sheet metalwork; Fabricated plate work (boiler shop); Metal heat treating
HQ: A.M. Castle & Co.
1420 Kensington Rd # 220
Oak Brook IL 60523
847 455-7111

(G-1101)
APEX WELDING INCORPORATED
Also Called: Apex Bulk Handlers
1 Industry Dr (44146-4413)
P.O. Box 46199 (44146-0199)
PHONE..................440 232-6770
D J Warner, *Pr*
B A Danna, *VP*
EMP: 15 **EST:** 1947
SQ FT: 15,200
SALES (est): 2.38MM **Privately Held**
Web: www.apexbulkhandlers.com
SIC: 3444 3443 Hoppers, sheet metal; Fabricated plate work (boiler shop)

(G-1102)
ARTISTIC PHOTOGRAPHY PRTG INC
1119 Broadway Ave (44146-4557)
PHONE..................813 310-6965
Glenda S Madaris, *Prin*
EMP: 6 **EST:** 2011
SALES (est): 80.42K **Privately Held**
SIC: 2752 Commercial printing, lithographic

(G-1103)
AUTOMATED PACKG SYSTEMS INC
Sidepouch
25900 Solon Rd (44146-4788)
PHONE..................330 342-2000
Bob Stinger, *Mgr*
EMP: 30
SQ FT: 59,780
SALES (corp-wide): 5.49B **Publicly Held**
Web: www.autobag.com
SIC: 3565 2673 Packaging machinery; Bags: plastic, laminated, and coated
HQ: Automated Packaging Systems, Llc
10175 Philipp Pkwy
Streetsboro OH 44241
330 528-2000

(G-1104)
BEAUTY CFT MET FABRICATORS INC
5439 Perkins Rd (44146-1856)
PHONE..................440 439-0710
Ronald Walnsch, *Pr*
Brian Walnsch, *VP*
Mary Walnsch, *Sec*
EMP: 10 **EST:** 1976
SQ FT: 7,000
SALES (est): 936.87K **Privately Held**

GEOGRAPHIC SECTION
Bedford - Cuyahoga County (G-1127)

Web: www.beautycraftmetalfabricators.com
SIC: **3441** Fabricated structural metal

(G-1105)
BEN VENUE LABORATORIES INC
Also Called: Bedford Laboratories
300 Northfield Rd (44146-4650)
P.O. Box 46568 (44146-0568)
PHONE..................................800 989-3320
▲ **EMP:** 1336
Web: www.boehringer-ingelheim.com
SIC: **2834** Pharmaceutical preparations

(G-1106)
BEST RESULT MARKETING INC
Also Called: Cashman Kiosk
7730 First Pl Ste E (44146-6720)
PHONE..................................234 212-1194
Nilu Patel, *CEO*
Janie Horsburgh, *Prin*
EMP: 6 **EST:** 2020
SALES (est): 281.55K **Privately Held**
SIC: **3581** Automatic vending machines

(G-1107)
BRAINMASTER TECHNOLOGIES INC
195 Willis St # 3 (44146-3508)
P.O. Box 46725 (44146-0725)
PHONE..................................440 232-6000
Thomas F Collura, *Pr*
Terri Collura, *Ex VP*
William Mrklas, *VP Opers*
EMP: 9 **EST:** 1999
SALES (est): 1.51MM **Privately Held**
Web: www.brainmaster.com
SIC: **3845** 7371 Electromedical equipment; Computer software development

(G-1108)
CANNON SALT & SUPPLY INC
26041 Cannon Rd (44146-1835)
PHONE..................................440 232-1700
Robert Foster, *Pr*
EMP: 6 **EST:** 2010
SALES (est): 928.57K **Privately Held**
Web: www.cannonsaltandsupply.com
SIC: **3524** 3423 Lawn and garden equipment ; Garden and farm tools, including shovels

(G-1109)
CAR BROS INC
7177 Northfield Rd (44146-5403)
PHONE..................................440 232-1840
Duane A Carr Junior, *Admn*
EMP: 10 **EST:** 2010
SALES (est): 712.77K **Privately Held**
Web: www.carrbros.net
SIC: **3273** Ready-mixed concrete

(G-1110)
CARR BROS INC
7177 Northfield Rd (44146-5403)
P.O. Box 46387 (44146-0387)
PHONE..................................440 232-3700
Mike Carr, *Owner*
EMP: 15 **EST:** 2015
SALES (est): 6.39MM **Privately Held**
Web: www.carrbros.net
SIC: **3273** Ready-mixed concrete

(G-1111)
CERTON TECHNOLOGIES INC (PA)
Also Called: Har Adhesive Technologies
60 S Park St (44146-3635)
PHONE..................................440 786-7185
Joe Cerino, *Prin*
Joseph Cerino, *Pr*
Diane Cerino, *VP*
EMP: 11 **EST:** 1996

SQ FT: 30,000
SALES (est): 4.52MM
SALES (corp-wide): 4.52MM **Privately Held**
Web: www.haradhesive.com
SIC: **2891** 2851 7699 7359 Adhesives; Paints and paint additives; Professional instrument repair services; Home cleaning and maintenance equipment rental services

(G-1112)
COMMAND PLASTIC CORPORATION
22475 Aurora Rd (44146)
PHONE..................................800 321-8001
Richard S Ames, *Pr*
Ann Ames, *Dir*
Ron Brengartner, *Pr*
▲ **EMP:** 19 **EST:** 1971
SALES (est): 2MM **Privately Held**
Web: www.commandplastic.com
SIC: **2671** 3081 2673 Plastic film, coated or laminated for packaging; Unsupported plastics film and sheet; Bags: plastic, laminated, and coated

(G-1113)
CONTINENTAL BUSINESS ENTPS INC (PA)
Also Called: Ace Metal Stamping Company
7311 Northfield Rd (44146)
PHONE..................................440 439-4400
Louis P Trolli, *Pr*
Richard L Laribee, *Sec*
Lynn Di Geronimo House, *Sec*
EMP: 16 **EST:** 1966
SQ FT: 33,000
SALES (est): 2.47MM
SALES (corp-wide): 2.47MM **Privately Held**
Web: www.acemetalstamping.com
SIC: **3469** 3544 Stamping metal for the trade ; Special dies, tools, jigs, and fixtures

(G-1114)
CUSTOM SURFACES INC
26185 Broadway Ave (44146-6512)
PHONE..................................440 439-2310
Tim Mcconnell, *Pr*
EMP: 9 **EST:** 1975
SQ FT: 9,000
SALES (est): 620.86K **Privately Held**
SIC: **2511** Wood household furniture

(G-1115)
DENGENSHA AMERICA CORPORATION
Also Called: Dengensha America
7647 First Pl (44146-6701)
PHONE..................................440 439-8081
Donald Grisez, *Pr*
▲ **EMP:** 13 **EST:** 1985
SALES (est): 7.17MM **Privately Held**
Web: www.dengensha.com
SIC: **3559** 5084 Automotive related machinery; Industrial machinery and equipment
PA: Dengensha Toa Co., Ltd.
   1-23-1, Masugata, Tama-Ku
   Kawasaki KNG 214-0

(G-1116)
DEUFOL WORLDWIDE PACKAGING LLC
19800 Alexander Rd (44146-5346)
PHONE..................................440 232-1100
Rich Stillman, *Brnch Mgr*
EMP: 22
SIC: **5113** 3412 3086 Boxes and containers; Metal barrels, drums, and pails; Plastics foam products
HQ: Deufol Worldwide Packaging Llc

924 S Meridian St
Sunman IN 47041
888 845-2843

(G-1117)
DIVERSIFIED BRANDS
26300 Fargo Ave (44146-1310)
PHONE..................................216 595-8777
Gayle Dlougon, *Prin*
EMP: 6 **EST:** 2010
SALES (est): 309.45K **Privately Held**
Web: www.krylon.com
SIC: **2819** Industrial inorganic chemicals, nec

(G-1118)
DONE-RITE BOWLING SERVICE CO (PA)
Also Called: Paragon Machine Company
20434 Krick Rd (44146-4422)
PHONE..................................440 232-3280
Robert W Gable, *CEO*
Glenn Gable, *Pr*
Dave Patz, *VP*
Gale Burns, *VP*
Ann Gable, *Stockholder*
▲ **EMP:** 22 **EST:** 1950
SQ FT: 20,000
SALES (est): 2.22MM
SALES (corp-wide): 2.22MM **Privately Held**
Web: www.donerite.com
SIC: **3949** 1752 5091 Bowling equipment and supplies; Floor laying and floor work, nec; Bowling equipment

(G-1119)
E J SKOK INDUSTRIES (PA)
Also Called: Skok Industries
26901 Richmond Rd (44146-1416)
PHONE..................................216 292-7533
Edward J Skok, *Pr*
Richard Skok, *Sec*
EMP: 20 **EST:** 1974
SQ FT: 18,000
SALES (est): 1.92MM
SALES (corp-wide): 1.92MM **Privately Held**
Web: www.skokind.com
SIC: **2541** 2434 Table or counter tops, plastic laminated; Wood kitchen cabinets

(G-1120)
FEDERAL METAL COMPANY (HQ)
Also Called: FM
7250 Division St (44146-5495)
PHONE..................................440 232-8700
David R Nagusky, *CEO*
Peter Nagusky, *Pr*
Chris Greenfield, *VP*
Robert I Kohn, *VP*
Mike Buyarski, *COO*
EMP: 16 **EST:** 1913
SQ FT: 65,000
SALES (est): 23.65MM **Privately Held**
Web: www.federalmetal.com
SIC: **3351** 3364 Copper and copper alloy sheet, strip, plate, and products; Copper and copper alloy die-castings
PA: Oakwood Industries Inc.
   7250 Division St
   Bedford OH 44146

(G-1121)
FERRO CORPORATION
FERRO CORPORATION
7050 Krick Rd (44146-4416)
PHONE..................................216 577-7144
Kent Lee, *Brnch Mgr*
EMP: 72
SALES (corp-wide): 1.88B **Privately Held**
Web: www.vibrantz.com

SIC: **2851** 2869 2842 2836 Paint driers; Industrial organic chemicals, nec; Polishes and sanitation goods; Biological products, except diagnostic
HQ: Vibrantz Corporation
   6060 Parkland Blvd # 250
   Mayfield Heights OH 44124
   216 875-5600

(G-1122)
GROUNDHOGS 2000 LLC
33 Industry Dr (44146-4413)
PHONE..................................440 653-1647
EMP: 6 **EST:** 2006
SALES (est): 616.96K **Privately Held**
Web: www.groundhogs2000.com
SIC: **1381** 1623 7389 Directional drilling oil and gas wells; Water, sewer, and utility lines ; Business Activities at Non-Commercial Site

(G-1123)
HAR EQUIPMENT SALES INC
60 S Park St (44146-3635)
PHONE..................................440 786-7189
Dennis Grosel, *Prin*
EMP: 10 **EST:** 2005
SALES (est): 910.5K **Privately Held**
Web: www.haradhesive.com
SIC: **2891** Adhesives

(G-1124)
HIKMA PHARMACEUTICALS USA INC
Also Called: Research & Development Div
300 Northfield Rd (44146-4650)
PHONE..................................732 542-1191
EMP: 14
SALES (corp-wide): 2.88B **Privately Held**
Web: www.hikma.com
SIC: **2834** Pharmaceutical preparations
HQ: Hikma Pharmaceuticals Usa Inc.
   200 Connell Dr Ste 4100
   Berkeley Heights NJ 07922
   908 673-1030

(G-1125)
HY-TECH CONTROLS INC
7411 First Pl (44146-6712)
PHONE..................................440 232-4040
EMP: 30 **EST:** 1983
SALES (est): 9.17MM **Privately Held**
Web: www.hy-techcontrols.com
SIC: **3613** Control panels, electric

(G-1126)
I SCHUMANN & CO LLC
Also Called: I Schumann & Co
22500 Alexander Rd (44146-5576)
PHONE..................................440 439-2300
Scott Schumann, *Managing Member*
David Schumann, *
Michael Schumann, *Managing Member**
Anthony Schumann, *
Don Robertson, *
◆ **EMP:** 104 **EST:** 1917
SQ FT: 150,000
SALES (est): 23.31MM **Privately Held**
Web: www.ischumann.com
SIC: **3341** Brass smelting and refining (secondary)

(G-1127)
ILLINOIS TOOL WORKS INC
Anchor Fasteners
26101 Fargo Ave (44146-1305)
PHONE..................................216 292-7161
Ray Belcher, *Brnch Mgr*
EMP: 35
SALES (corp-wide): 16.11B **Publicly Held**
Web: www.itw.com

Bedford - Cuyahoga County (G-1128)   GEOGRAPHIC SECTION

SIC: 3496 Miscellaneous fabricated wire products
PA: Illinois Tool Works Inc.
155 Harlem Ave
Glenview IL 60025
847 724-7500

(G-1128)
INTERARMS MANUFACTURING LTD
7400 Northfield Rd (44146-6108)
PHONE.................................440 201-9850
EMP: 6 EST: 2012
SALES (est): 39.69K **Privately Held**
Web: www.interarmstx.com
SIC: 3999 Manufacturing industries, nec

(G-1129)
INTERNATIONAL SOURCES INC
380 Golden Oak Pkwy (44146-6525)
PHONE.................................440 735-9890
Gregory Neal, Pr
▲ EMP: 6 EST: 2015
SALES (est): 389.38K **Privately Held**
SIC: 3069 Fabricated rubber products, nec

(G-1130)
IOPPOLO CONCRETE CORPORATION
10 Industry Dr (44146-4414)
PHONE.................................440 439-6606
Anthony Ioppolo Junior, Pr
EMP: 26 EST: 1958
SQ FT: 6,000
SALES (est): 1MM **Privately Held**
Web: www.ioppoloconcrete.com
SIC: 3273 1711 7353 4959 Ready-mixed concrete; Plumbing, heating, air-conditioning; Heavy construction equipment rental; Snowplowing

(G-1131)
KCN TECHNOLOGIES LLC
Also Called: Ace Hydraulics
1 W Interstate St # 13 (44146-4215)
PHONE.................................440 439-4219
EMP: 8 EST: 1996
SALES (est): 678.19K **Privately Held**
SIC: 1799 7694 7629 Hydraulic equipment, installation and service; Armature rewinding shops; Electrical repair shops

(G-1132)
KOLTCZ CONCRETE BLOCK CO
7660 Oak Leaf Rd (44146-5554)
PHONE.................................440 232-3630
Stanley M Koltcz, Pr
EMP: 26 EST: 1938
SQ FT: 55,000
SALES (est): 4.59MM **Privately Held**
Web: www.koltczblock.com
SIC: 3271 5032 5211 Blocks, concrete or cinder: standard; Masons' materials; Masonry materials and supplies

(G-1133)
LEGENDS AUTO SPA LLC
600 Turney Rd Apt 219 (44146-3369)
PHONE.................................216 333-8030
EMP: 6 EST: 2020
SALES (est): 487K **Privately Held**
SIC: 3589 Car washing machinery

(G-1134)
LOMBARDO GELATO COMPANY
552 Turney Rd Apt A (44146-7340)
PHONE.................................480 274-1018
Jean R Lombardo, Pr
Beatrice A Lombardo, *
EMP: 6 EST: 2004
SALES (est): 242.81K **Privately Held**

Web: www.lombardogelato.com
SIC: 2024 Ice cream and frozen deserts

(G-1135)
LOVEMAN STEEL CORPORATION
5455 Perkins Rd (44146-1856)
PHONE.................................440 232-6200
Anthony Murru, CEO
Robin Davis Ray, Prin
David Loveman, *
Rob Loveman, *
James Loveman, *
◆ EMP: 75 EST: 1928
SQ FT: 80,000
SALES (est): 14.18MM **Privately Held**
Web: www.lovemansteel.com
SIC: 5051 3443 Plates, metal; Weldments

(G-1136)
MAJESTIC FIREPLACE DISTR
7500 Northfield Rd (44146-6110)
PHONE.................................440 400-1040
EMP: 7 EST: 2018
SALES (est): 166.93K **Privately Held**
Web: www.masonsteel.com
SIC: 3462 Iron and steel forgings

(G-1137)
MARLEN MANUFACTURING & DEV CO (PA)
Also Called: Marlen
5150 Richmond Rd (44146-1331)
PHONE.................................216 292-7060
Gary Fenton, Pr
Michael Magar, Treas
▲ EMP: 6 EST: 1952
SQ FT: 45,000
SALES (est): 8.85MM
SALES (corp-wide): 8.85MM **Privately Held**
Web: www.marlenmfg.com
SIC: 3842 Surgical appliances and supplies

(G-1138)
MOLDING DYNAMICS INC
7009 Krick Rd (44146-4415)
PHONE.................................440 786-8100
Charles F Connors Iii, Pr
EMP: 15 EST: 1979
SQ FT: 14,000
SALES (est): 4.24MM **Privately Held**
Web: www.moldingdynamics.net
SIC: 3089 Injection molding of plastics

(G-1139)
MOONLIGHT WOODWORKS LLC
17607 Egbert Rd (44146-4222)
PHONE.................................440 836-3738
Eric Seme, Prin
EMP: 6 EST: 2010
SALES (est): 76K **Privately Held**
SIC: 2431 Millwork

(G-1140)
MORGAN MATROC (ES)
232 Forbes Rd (44146-5418)
PHONE.................................440 232-8600
Peter Morten, Prin
EMP: 7 EST: 2005
SALES (est): 233.88K **Privately Held**
SIC: 3825 Semiconductor test equipment

(G-1141)
MT PLEASANT PHARMACY LLC
631 Lee Rd Apt 1228 (44146-6605)
PHONE.................................216 672-4377
Michael Asiedu-gyekye, Prin
EMP: 6 EST: 2011
SALES (est): 96.86K **Privately Held**

SIC: 3842 Adhesive tape and plasters, medicated or non-medicated

(G-1142)
MTC ELECTROCERAMICS
232 Forbes Rd (44146-5418)
PHONE.................................440 232-8600
Peter Martin, Prin
EMP: 7 EST: 2011
SALES (est): 188.03K **Privately Held**
SIC: 3299 Nonmetallic mineral products,

(G-1143)
NEON WORKSHOP
21417 Aurora Rd (44146-1017)
PHONE.................................216 832-5236
Richard Holzer, Owner
EMP: 6 EST: 2001
SALES (est): 114.37K **Privately Held**
Web: www.xactosigns.com
SIC: 3993 Signs and advertising specialties

(G-1144)
NEW YORK FROZEN FOODS INC (DH)
25900 Fargo Ave (44146-1302)
PHONE.................................216 292-5655
Bruce Rosa, Pr
Donald Penn, *
Larry R Linhart, Prin
EMP: 260 EST: 1978
SQ FT: 55,000
SALES (est): 64.52MM
SALES (corp-wide): 1.82B **Publicly Held**
SIC: 2051 Bread, all types (white, wheat, rye, etc); fresh or frozen
HQ: T.Marzetti Company
380 Polaris Pkwy Ste 400
Westerville OH 43082
614 846-2232

(G-1145)
NPK CONSTRUCTION EQUIPMENT INC (HQ)
7550 Independence Dr (44146-5541)
PHONE.................................440 232-7900
Dan Tyrell, Pr
Nick Shah, *
◆ EMP: 60 EST: 1985
SQ FT: 150,000
SALES (est): 57.56MM **Privately Held**
Web: www.npkce.com
SIC: 5082 3599 3546 3532 General construction machinery and equipment; Machine shop, jobbing and repair; Power-driven handtools; Mining machinery
PA: Nippon Pneumatic Manufacturing Co.,Ltd.
4-11-5, Kamiji, Higashinari-Ku
Osaka OSK 537-0

(G-1146)
OAKWOOD INDUSTRIES INC (PA)
Also Called: Federal Metal Co
7250 Division St (44146-5406)
PHONE.................................440 232-8700
David R Nagusky, Pr
Malvin E Bank, *
◆ EMP: 60 EST: 1986
SQ FT: 65,000
SALES (est): 50.14MM **Privately Held**
Web: www.federalmetal.com
SIC: 3341 3364 Brass smelting and refining (secondary); Nonferrous die-castings except aluminum

(G-1147)
ONE WISH LLC
Also Called: Audimute Sndprfing Mdic Bttrie
23700 Aurora Rd (44146-1796)

PHONE.................................800 505-6883
EMP: 18 EST: 2003
SALES (est): 3.19MM **Privately Held**
Web: www.audimute.com
SIC: 5063 5999 8742 1742 Batteries; Batteries, non-automotive; Marketing consulting services; Acoustical and insulation work

(G-1148)
OVERSEAS PACKING LLC
Also Called: United Packaging Supply Co Div
19800 Alexander Rd (44146-5346)
PHONE.................................440 232-2917
EMP: 21 EST: 1940
SQ FT: 52,000
SALES (est): 471.92K **Privately Held**
SIC: 2449 3412 4783 Wood containers, nec; Metal barrels, drums, and pails; Packing goods for shipping

(G-1149)
PALEOMD LLC
26245 Broadway Ave Ste B (44146-6524)
PHONE.................................248 854-0031
Patricia Urcuyo, Managing Member
EMP: 7 EST: 2015
SALES (est): 476.03K **Privately Held**
Web: www.paleomdpizza.com
SIC: 2038 Pizza, frozen

(G-1150)
PRECISION MCHNING SRFACING INC
20637 Krick Rd (44146-5412)
PHONE.................................440 439-9850
David Slifka, Pr
EMP: 6 EST: 2000
SALES (est): 746.9K **Privately Held**
Web: www.pre-machining.com
SIC: 3599 Machine shop, jobbing and repair

(G-1151)
REA ELEKTRONIK INC
7307 Young Dr Ste B (44146-5385)
PHONE.................................440 232-0555
Ray Turchi, Pr
▲ EMP: 11 EST: 2005
SQ FT: 5,400
SALES (est): 2.9MM **Privately Held**
Web: www.rea-jet.com
SIC: 3953 5112 Marking devices; Marking devices

(G-1152)
RELIANT WORTH CORP
20638 Krick Rd (44146-5409)
PHONE.................................440 232-1422
Don Shumay, Pr
EMP: 7 EST: 1967
SQ FT: 2,500
SALES (est): 704.03K **Privately Held**
Web: www.arconequipment.com
SIC: 3691 Storage batteries

(G-1153)
RESERVE MILLWORK LLC
26881 Cannon Rd (44146)
PHONE.................................216 531-6982
Tony Azzolina, Pr
Virginia Azzolina, VP
EMP: 32 EST: 1980
SQ FT: 18,000
SALES (est): 9.41MM **Privately Held**
Web: www.reservemillwork.com
SIC: 2431 2434 2541 Ornamental woodwork: cornices, mantels, etc.; Wood kitchen cabinets; Wood partitions and fixtures

GEOGRAPHIC SECTION

Bedford Heights - Cuyahoga County (G-1177)

(G-1154)
S & H INDUSTRIES INC (PA)
5200 Richmond Rd (44146-1387)
PHONE..................................216 831-0550
Eric Turk, *CEO*
Steve Perney, *Treas*
EMP: 16 **EST:** 1978
SALES (est): 2.72MM
SALES (corp-wide): 2.72MM **Privately Held**
Web: www.shindustries.com
SIC: 3423 Mechanics' hand tools

(G-1155)
SMITH-LUSTIG PAPER BOX MFG CO
22475 Aurora Rd (44146-1270)
PHONE..................................216 621-0453
Richard Ames, *Pr*
Graham Klintworth, *
Ann Ames, *
▲ **EMP:** 14 **EST:** 1932
SQ FT: 75,000
SALES (est): 273.18K **Privately Held**
Web: www.smithlustigbox.com
SIC: 2631 2653 Folding boxboard; Boxes, corrugated: made from purchased materials

(G-1156)
TAVENS CONTAINER INC
Also Called: Tavens Packg Display Solutions
22475 Aurora Rd (44146-1270)
PHONE..................................216 883-3333
Richard Ames, *
Graham Klintworth, *
EMP: 60 **EST:** 1957
SQ FT: 87,000
SALES (est): 10.45MM **Privately Held**
Web: www.tavens.com
SIC: 2653 3412 Boxes, corrugated: made from purchased materials; Metal barrels, drums, and pails

(G-1157)
THERMO GAMMA-METRICS LLC (HQ)
1 Thermo Fisher Way (44146-6536)
PHONE..................................858 450-9811
Ken Berger, *Pr*
Sandra Lambert, *Sec*
▲ **EMP:** 20 **EST:** 1980
SALES (est): 12MM
SALES (corp-wide): 44.91B **Publicly Held**
SIC: 3824 3826 3812 3823 Controls, revolution and timing instruments; Environmental testing equipment; Search and detection systems and instruments; Process control instruments
PA: Thermo Fisher Scientific Inc.
168 3rd Ave
Waltham MA 02451
781 622-1000

(G-1158)
TOTH MOLD & DIE INC
380 Solon Rd Ste 6 (44146-3809)
PHONE..................................440 232-8530
Timothy Toth, *Pr*
Thomas Toth, *Sec*
EMP: 10 **EST:** 1982
SALES (est): 956.61K **Privately Held**
Web: www.tothmold.net
SIC: 3089 Injection molded finished plastics products, nec

(G-1159)
VITEC INC
26901 Cannon Rd (44146-1809)
PHONE..................................216 464-4670
Richard A Wynveen, *CEO*
Franz H Schubert, *Stockholder*
EMP: 17 **EST:** 1974
SQ FT: 15,000
SALES (est): 1.08MM **Privately Held**
Web: www.vitec-inc.com
SIC: 3823 Process control instruments

(G-1160)
WALTON PLASTICS INC
Also Called: Wal Plax
20493 Hannan Pkwy (44146-5356)
PHONE..................................440 786-7711
Steven Wake, *CEO*
Marvin Bollinger, *Stockholder*
Tim Bollinger, *Stockholder*
Marinko Milos, *CFO*
Larry Crystal, *Prin*
▲ **EMP:** 21 **EST:** 1992
SQ FT: 44,000
SALES (est): 6.27MM **Privately Held**
Web: www.waltonplastics.com
SIC: 3081 Vinyl film and sheet

(G-1161)
YOUNG REGULATOR COMPANY INC
7100 Krick Rd Ste A (44146-4443)
PHONE..................................440 232-9452
Michael E Mcguigan, *Pr*
EMP: 20 **EST:** 1930
SQ FT: 40,000
SALES (est): 4.5MM **Privately Held**
Web: www.youngregulator.com
SIC: 3822 1711 Air conditioning and refrigeration controls; Plumbing, heating, air-conditioning

(G-1162)
ZENEX INTERNATIONAL
7777 First Pl (44146-6733)
PHONE..................................440 232-4155
George Kniere, *Owner*
▲ **EMP:** 16 **EST:** 2006
SALES (est): 8.43MM **Privately Held**
Web: www.zenexint.com
SIC: 2813 Aerosols

Bedford Heights
Cuyahoga County

(G-1163)
AMERICAN SPRING WIRE CORP (PA)
Also Called: Asw
26300 Miles Rd (44146-1072)
PHONE..................................216 292-4620
Timothy W Selhorst, *CEO*
Timothy W Selhorst, *Pr*
Greg Bokar, *
◆ **EMP:** 200 **EST:** 1968
SQ FT: 360,500
SALES (est): 23.38MM
SALES (corp-wide): 23.38MM **Privately Held**
Web: www.americanspringwire.com
SIC: 3272 3315 3316 3339 Concrete products, nec; Wire products, ferrous/iron: made in wiredrawing plants; Wire, flat, cold-rolled strip: not made in hot-rolled mills; Primary nonferrous metals, nec

(G-1164)
ASWPENGG LLC
Also Called: Amrican Spring Wire
26300 Miles Rd (44146-1410)
PHONE..................................216 292-4620
Manish Ishwar, *CEO*
EMP: 21 **EST:** 2016
SALES (est): 2.4MM **Privately Held**
SIC: 3592 3495 Valves; Wire springs

(G-1165)
BRIDGE ANALYZERS INC
5198 Richmond Rd (44146-1331)
PHONE..................................216 332-0592
David Anderson, *Prin*
EMP: 11 **EST:** 2017
SALES (est): 2.26MM **Privately Held**
Web: www.bridgeanalyzers.com
SIC: 3826 Analytical instruments

(G-1166)
CARDINAL FSTENER SPECIALTY INC
Also Called: Cardinal Fastener
5185 Richmond Rd (44146-1330)
PHONE..................................216 831-3800
Bill Boak, *Pr*
Denise R Muha, *
Bill Walczak, *
Wendy L Brugmann, *
▲ **EMP:** 50 **EST:** 1983
SQ FT: 100,000
SALES (est): 4.39MM **Privately Held**
SIC: 3965 Fasteners

(G-1167)
CLEVELAND COCA-COLA BTLG INC
Also Called: Coca-Cola
25000 Miles Rd (44146-1319)
PHONE..................................216 690-2653
George M Gernhardt, *
H C Gram, *Prin*
William L Arnett, *Prin*
Peter E Benzino, *
Charles R Hanlon, *
EMP: 220 **EST:** 1911
SQ FT: 220,000
SALES (est): 24.95MM **Privately Held**
Web: www.abartacocacola.com
SIC: 2086 Bottled and canned soft drinks

(G-1168)
CLEVELAND STEEL SPECIALTY CO
26001 Richmond Rd (44146-1435)
P.O. Box 1687 (44224-0687)
PHONE..................................216 464-9400
Robert W Ehrhardt Senior, *Pr*
Robert W Ehrhardt Senior, *CEO*
Robert W Ehrhardt Junior, *Pr*
EMP: 30 **EST:** 1924
SQ FT: 24,000
SALES (est): 4.69MM **Privately Held**
Web: www.clevelandsteel.com
SIC: 3443 3429 3444 Metal parts; Builders' hardware; Sheet metalwork

(G-1169)
CWH GRAPHICS LLC
Also Called: Ink Well
23196 Miles Rd Ste A (44128-5490)
P.O. Box 22651 (44122-0651)
PHONE..................................866 241-8515
EMP: 7 **EST:** 2005
SQ FT: 4,000
SALES (est): 666.15K **Privately Held**
Web: www.shortstackprinting.com
SIC: 2752 Offset printing

(G-1170)
ELECTRODATA INC
23400 Aurora Rd Ste 5 (44146-1738)
P.O. Box 31780 (44131-0780)
PHONE..................................216 663-3333
Eddy Wright, *Pr*
Jim Spoth, *Sec*
EMP: 11 **EST:** 1972
SQ FT: 11,000
SALES (est): 488.26K **Privately Held**
Web: www.ncs-netcommsolutions.com
SIC: 3661 Telephone and telegraph apparatus

(G-1171)
FLOUR MANAGEMENT LLC
Also Called: Flour Pasta Company
26800 Fargo Ave Ste E (44146-1341)
PHONE..................................216 910-9019
EMP: 19
SALES (corp-wide): 406.59K **Privately Held**
SIC: 2098 Macaroni and spaghetti
PA: Flour Management Llc
34205 Chagrin Blvd
Moreland Hills OH 44022
216 910-9019

(G-1172)
FOOD EQUIPMENT MFG CORP
Also Called: Femc
22201 Aurora Rd (44146-1273)
PHONE..................................216 672-5859
Robert Sauer, *Pr*
EMP: 20 **EST:** 1977
SQ FT: 65,000
SALES (est): 3.87MM **Privately Held**
Web: www.femc.com
SIC: 3565 Packaging machinery

(G-1173)
FROHN NORTH AMERICA INC
23800 Corbin Dr Ste B (44128-5402)
PHONE..................................770 819-0089
◆ **EMP:** 8 **EST:** 1994
SQ FT: 24,000
SALES (est): 2.25MM **Privately Held**
Web: www.frohn.com
SIC: 3369 Nonferrous foundries, nec

(G-1174)
HOIST EQUIPMENT CO INC (PA)
26161 Cannon Rd (44146-1896)
PHONE..................................440 232-0300
Nicholas Gambatesa, *CEO*
Jeffrey Sadar, *
EMP: 25 **EST:** 1953
SQ FT: 40,000
SALES (est): 5.17MM
SALES (corp-wide): 5.17MM **Privately Held**
Web: www.hoistequipment.com
SIC: 3537 3535 3536 Cranes, industrial truck; Overhead conveyor systems; Hoists

(G-1175)
LAKE ERIE STEEL & FABRICATION
5455 Perkins Rd (44146-1856)
PHONE..................................440 232-6200
EMP: 8 **EST:** 2017
SALES (est): 103.91K **Privately Held**
Web: www.lovemansteel.com
SIC: 3441 Fabricated structural metal

(G-1176)
METRON INSTRUMENTS INC
5198 Richmond Rd (44146-1331)
P.O. Box 39325 (44139-0325)
PHONE..................................216 332-0592
David Anderson, *Pr*
EMP: 8 **EST:** 2003
SALES (est): 896.03K **Privately Held**
Web: www.bridgeanalyzers.com
SIC: 3826 Analytical instruments

(G-1177)
MOLDED EXTRUDED
23940 Miles Rd (44128-5425)
PHONE..................................216 475-5491
Frank Novak, *Prin*
EMP: 7 **EST:** 2012
SALES (est): 97.69K **Privately Held**
Web: www.mespecialties.com

Bedford Heights - Cuyahoga County (G-1178)

GEOGRAPHIC SECTION

SIC: 3089 Injection molding of plastics

(G-1178)
NATIONAL PEENING
23800 Corbin Dr Unit B (44128-5402)
PHONE.....................216 342-9155
Don Kvorka, *Pr*
EMP: 14 **EST:** 2013
SALES (est): 765.07K **Privately Held**
Web: www.sintoamerica.com
SIC: 3398 Shot peening (treating steel to reduce fatigue)

(G-1179)
THE PERFECT SCORE COMPANY
Also Called: Perfect Score, The
25801 Solon Rd (44146-4759)
PHONE.....................440 439-9320
Ed Fraschetti, *Pr*
Megan Gross, *Sec*
FMP: 15 **EST:** 1996
SQ FT: 2,000
SALES (est): 1.59MM **Privately Held**
SIC: 3556 Bakery machinery

(G-1180)
UNITREX LTD
Also Called: Sparoom
5060 Taylor Dr Ste D (44128)
PHONE.....................216 831-1900
Anthony Padrazo, *CEO*
▲ **EMP:** 68 **EST:** 2012
SALES (est): 60MM **Privately Held**
Web: www.sparoom.com
SIC: 2899 Oils and essential oils

(G-1181)
WAXMAN INDUSTRIES INC (PA)
24460 Aurora Rd (44146-1794)
PHONE.....................440 439-1830
Larry Waxman, *Pr*
Melvin Waxman, *Ch Bd*
Laurence Waxman, *Pr*
Mark Wester, *Sr VP*
◆ **EMP:** 110 **EST:** 1962
SQ FT: 21,000
SALES (est): 99.88MM
SALES (corp-wide): 99.88MM **Privately Held**
Web: www.waxmanind.com
SIC: 5072 5074 3494 3491 Hardware; Plumbing and hydronic heating supplies; Valves and pipe fittings, nec; Industrial valves

(G-1182)
ZENA BABY SOAP COMPANY
6651 Hedgeline Dr (44146-4870)
PHONE.....................216 317-6433
Dawn Schwark, *CEO*
Dawn Schwark, *Pr*
Donnita Diggs-owens, *Pr*
Latonya Moore, *Pr*
Karen Teague, *Pr*
EMP: 6 **EST:** 2018
SALES (est): 269.7K **Privately Held**
SIC: 2844 Perfumes, cosmetics and other toilet preparations

Bellaire
Belmont County

(G-1183)
BELMONT COMMUNITY HOSPITAL
Also Called: Belmont Community Health Ctr
4697 Harrison Rd (43906-1303)
PHONE.....................740 671-1216
Garry Gould, *CEO*
EMP: 22
SALES (corp-wide): 4.66B **Privately Held**
SIC: 2599 Hospital beds
HQ: Belmont Community Hospital
 4697 Harrison St
 Bellaire OH 43906
 740 671-1200

(G-1184)
CHARLES WISVARI
Also Called: Vivid Graphix
3266 Guernsey St (43906-1545)
PHONE.....................740 671-9960
Charles Wisvari, *Owner*
EMP: 6 **EST:** 1988
SQ FT: 10,500
SALES (est): 309.47K **Privately Held**
Web: www.vividgraphix.com
SIC: 2396 2395 5699 Screen printing on fabric articles; Embroidery products, except Schiffli machine; Customized clothing and apparel

(G-1185)
COUNTRY CLB RTRMENT CTR IV LLC
55801 Conno Mara Dr (43906-9698)
PHONE.....................740 676-2300
EMP: 9 **EST:** 2015
SALES (est): 4.52MM **Privately Held**
Web: www.countryclubretirementcampus.com
SIC: 3949 Indian clubs

(G-1186)
GERDAU AMERISTEEL US INC
5310 Guernsey St (43906-9516)
PHONE.....................740 671-9410
EMP: 8
SALES (corp-wide): 1.56B **Privately Held**
Web: www.gerdau.com
SIC: 3499 3312 1771 Bank chests, metal; Blast furnaces and steel mills; Concrete work
HQ: Gerdau Ameristeel Us Inc.
 4221 W Boy Scout Blvd # 600
 Tampa FL 33607
 813 286-8383

(G-1187)
GUMBYS LLC
2300 Belmont St (43906-1733)
PHONE.....................740 671-0818
Beau Lamotte, *Brnch Mgr*
EMP: 12
Web: www.gumbys.com
SIC: 3999 Cigarette and cigar products and accessories
PA: Gumby's, L.L.C.
 98 E Cove Ave Ste 1
 Wheeling WV 26003

(G-1188)
LION INDUSTRIES LLC
423 53rd St (43906-9514)
P.O. Box 455 (43950-0455)
PHONE.....................740 676-1100
David A Humphreys Junior, *Managing Member*
EMP: 20 **EST:** 2008
SALES (est): 2.75MM **Privately Held**
Web: www.lionind.com
SIC: 3443 3449 Fabricated plate work (boiler shop); Custom roll formed products

(G-1189)
MOUNTAINEER INDUSTRIES LLC
5310 Guernsey St (43906-9516)
PHONE.....................740 676-1100
EMP: 10 **EST:** 2019
SALES (est): 358.41K **Privately Held**

SIC: 3599 Machine shop, jobbing and repair

(G-1190)
XTO ENERGY INC
Also Called: Xto Energy
2358 W 23rd St (43906-9614)
PHONE.....................740 671-9901
EMP: 8
SALES (corp-wide): 344.58B **Publicly Held**
Web: www.xtoenergy.com
SIC: 1311 Crude petroleum production
HQ: Xto Energy Inc.
 22777 Sprngwoods Vlg Pkwy
 Spring TX 77389

Bellbrook
Greene County

(G-1191)
DAIRY SHED
55 Bellbrook Plz (45305-1954)
PHONE.....................937 848-3504
Roger Mcconnell, *Prin*
EMP: 6 **EST:** 1990
SALES (est): 211.07K **Privately Held**
Web: www.bellbrookdairyshed.com
SIC: 2024 Ice cream, bulk

(G-1192)
ERNST ENTERPRISES INC
Also Called: Sugarcreek Ready Mix
2181 Ferry Rd (45305-9728)
PHONE.....................937 848-6811
John Ernst Junior, *Pr*
EMP: 27
SQ FT: 5,000
SALES (corp-wide): 240.08MM **Privately Held**
Web: www.ernstconcrete.com
SIC: 3273 Ready-mixed concrete
PA: Ernst Enterprises, Inc.
 3361 Successful Way
 Dayton OH 45414
 937 233-5555

(G-1193)
GOLDEN SPRING COMPANY INC
2143 Ferry Rd (45305-9728)
P.O. Box 244 (45305-0244)
PHONE.....................937 848-2513
Paul Smith, *Pr*
Rita Treser, *VP*
EMP: 10 **EST:** 1953
SQ FT: 5,100
SALES (est): 779.95K **Privately Held**
Web: www.golden-spring.com
SIC: 3493 Coiled flat springs

(G-1194)
SUPPLY ONE CORPORATION
4146 Woodedge Dr (45305-1617)
PHONE.....................937 297-1111
Allen Pippenger, *Pr*
▲ **EMP:** 14 **EST:** 1940
SQ FT: 128,000
SALES (est): 1.48MM **Privately Held**
SIC: 2434 Wood kitchen cabinets

Belle Center
Logan County

(G-1195)
BELLE CENTER AIR TOOL CO INC
202 N Elizabeth St (43310-9684)
P.O. Box 37 (43310-0037)
PHONE.....................937 464-7474
Carroll Doty, *Pr*

Ruth Doty, *Sec*
▲ **EMP:** 9 **EST:** 1985
SQ FT: 9,500
SALES (est): 2.23MM **Privately Held**
Web: belle-corner.edan.io
SIC: 5084 3532 Pneumatic tools and equipment; Drills, bits, and similar equipment

(G-1196)
HEINTZ FARMS ENTERPRISE PARTNR
4367 State Route 273 W (43310-9710)
PHONE.....................937 464-2535
William Heintz, *Pt*
EMP: 9 **EST:** 2017
SALES (est): 499.44K **Privately Held**
SIC: 3523 Driers (farm): grain, hay, and seed

(G-1197)
HIGHS WELDING INC
3065 County Road 150 (43310-1107)
PHONE.....................937 464-3029
Nick S High, *Pr*
EMP: 6 **EST:** 1972
SALES (est): 508.75K **Privately Held**
SIC: 7692 Welding repair

(G-1198)
TROYERS CABINET SHOP LTD
9442 County Road 101 (43310-9589)
PHONE.....................937 464-7702
Leon H Troyer, *Pt*
Marcus Troyer, *Pt*
Nathan Troyer, *Pt*
EMP: 10 **EST:** 1979
SALES (est): 617.56K **Privately Held**
SIC: 2434 Wood kitchen cabinets

Bellefontaine
Logan County

(G-1199)
5 CORE INC
1221 W Sandusky Ave (43311-1046)
PHONE.....................951 386-6372
Amarjit Singh Kalra, *Pr*
Amarjit Singh Kalra, *Pr*
Surinder Kalra Ctrl, *Prin*
Kaneer Karla, *Finance*
EMP: 17 **EST:** 2020
SALES (est): 3.7MM **Privately Held**
Web: www.5core.com
SIC: 5722 3651 Electric household appliances; Audio electronic systems

(G-1200)
ARDEN J NEER SR
Also Called: Neer's Engineering Labs
4859 Township Road 45 (43311-9624)
PHONE.....................937 585-6733
Arden J Neer Senior, *Owner*
EMP: 15 **EST:** 1927
SQ FT: 7,500
SALES (est): 820.53K **Privately Held**
Web: www.neerssandandgravel.com
SIC: 1442 Construction sand mining

(G-1201)
AXIS CORPORATION
314 Water Ave (43311-1734)
P.O. Box 668 (43311-0668)
PHONE.....................937 592-1958
Matt Oldiges, *Pr*
Linda Luebke, *Sec*
Thomas Oldiges, *Stockholder*
EMP: 10 **EST:** 1969
SQ FT: 20,000
SALES (est): 2.01MM **Privately Held**

Web: www.axiscorporation.com
SIC: 3441 Fabricated structural metal

(G-1202)
CLAYTON HOMES
2720 Us Highway 68 S (43311-8900)
PHONE.................................937 592-3039
EMP: 10 EST: 2019
SALES (est): 144.08K **Privately Held**
Web: www.claytonhomes.com
SIC: 2451 Mobile homes

(G-1203)
COUNTY CLASSIFIEDS
Also Called: The County Classified's
117 E Patterson Ave (43311-1912)
P.O. Box 596 (43311-0596)
PHONE.................................937 592-8847
Leah Frank, *Pr*
EMP: 8 EST: 1987
SALES (est): 498.17K **Privately Held**
Web: www.thecountyclassifiedsonline.com
SIC: 2711 2752 2741 Job printing and newspaper publishing combined; Commercial printing, lithographic; Miscellaneous publishing

(G-1204)
D H S LLC
220 Reynolds Ave (43311-3003)
P.O. Box 3083 (43016-0040)
PHONE.................................937 599-2485
EMP: 15 EST: 1993
SQ FT: 3,500
SALES (est): 500K **Privately Held**
SIC: 3679 Harness assemblies, for electronic use: wire or cable

(G-1205)
DAIDO METAL BELLEFONTAINE LLC
1215 S Greenwood St (43311-1628)
PHONE.................................937 592-5010
▲ EMP: 62 EST: 1997
SQ FT: 224,000
SALES (est): 7.33MM **Privately Held**
Web: www.daidometal.com
SIC: 3714 Motor vehicle parts and accessories
PA: Daido Metal Co., Ltd.
   2-3-1, Sakae, Naka-Ku
   Nagoya AIC 460-0

(G-1206)
DESIGNED HARNESS SYSTEMS INC
Also Called: Dhs Innovations
227 Water Ave (43311-1731)
P.O. Box 37 (43311-0037)
PHONE.................................937 599-2485
Craig Lingon, *Pr*
EMP: 10 EST: 2010
SALES (est): 911.58K **Privately Held**
SIC: 3714 Automotive wiring harness sets

(G-1207)
DMG TOOL & DIE LLC
1215 S Greenwood St (43311-1628)
PHONE.................................937 407-0810
EMP: 6 EST: 2009
SQ FT: 10,000
SALES (est): 938.55K **Privately Held**
Web: www.dmgtool.com
SIC: 3544 Special dies and tools

(G-1208)
EWH SPECTRUM LLC
221 W Chillicothe Ave (43311-1467)
PHONE.................................937 593-8010
Robert L Robinson, *Pr*
Jean Robinson, *

EMP: 74 EST: 1992
SQ FT: 27,500
SALES (est): 9.17MM **Privately Held**
Web: www.ewhspectrum.com
SIC: 3679 3694 Harness assemblies, for electronic use: wire or cable; Engine electrical equipment

(G-1209)
FAST TRACK SIGNS LLC
813 N Main St (43311-2308)
PHONE.................................937 593-9990
Dennis Chaub, *Prin*
EMP: 6 EST: 2005
SALES (est): 278.77K **Privately Held**
Web: www.fasttracksigns.net
SIC: 3993 Signs, not made in custom sign painting shops

(G-1210)
HBD/THERMOID INC
1301 W Sandusky Ave (43311-1082)
PHONE.................................937 593-5010
R Greely, *Brnch Mgr*
EMP: 194
SALES (corp-wide): 241.4MM **Privately Held**
Web: www.thermoid.com
SIC: 3429 3052 Hardware, nec; Rubber and plastics hose and beltings
HQ: Hbd/Thermoid, Inc.
   5200 Upper Metro Pl # 110
   Dublin OH 43017

(G-1211)
HI-POINT GRAPHICS LLC
127 E Chillicothe Ave (43311-1957)
PHONE.................................937 407-6524
Andrea Wrocklage, *Prin*
Rodney Wrocklage, *Prin*
EMP: 8 EST: 2013
SALES (est): 559.12K **Privately Held**
Web: www.hi-pointgraphics.com
SIC: 2752 Offset printing

(G-1212)
HUBBARD PUBLISHING CO
127 E Chillicothe Ave (43311-1957)
P.O. Box 40 (43311-0040)
PHONE.................................937 592-3060
Janet Hubbard, *Pr*
Jon B Hubbard, *
EMP: 24 EST: 1891
SQ FT: 13,000
SALES (est): 838.68K **Privately Held**
Web: www.examiner.org
SIC: 2711 2752 2791 Commercial printing and newspaper publishing combined; Offset printing; Typesetting

(G-1213)
IEG PLASTICS LLC
223 Lock And Load Rd (43311-2500)
PHONE.................................937 565-4211
Jim Moore, *Prin*
EMP: 16 EST: 2014
SALES (est): 4.88MM **Privately Held**
Web: www.ieg-llc.com
SIC: 3089 Injection molding of plastics

(G-1214)
INSTANT REPLAY LTD
334 E Columbus Ave (43311-2002)
PHONE.................................937 592-0534
Lisa Russell, *Off Mgr*
EMP: 9 EST: 2014
SALES (est): 247.51K **Privately Held**
Web: www.rtcservices.org
SIC: 2752 Commercial printing, lithographic

(G-1215)
MAJESTIC PLASTICS INC
811 N Main St (43311-2376)
P.O. Box 47 (43311-0047)
PHONE.................................937 593-9500
Sean Ammons, *Pr*
EMP: 61 EST: 2000
SQ FT: 7,800
SALES (est): 5.82MM **Privately Held**
SIC: 3089 Injection molding of plastics

(G-1216)
MCKNIGHT INDUSTRIES INC
Also Called: National Extrusion & Mfg Co
Orchard & Elm Street (43311)
P.O. Box 460 (43311-0460)
PHONE.................................937 592-9010
Christopher A Kerns, *Pr*
Craig Johnson, *
Carsten Lemkau, *
John D Bishop, *
▲ EMP: 32 EST: 1949
SQ FT: 41,942
SALES (est): 1.93MM **Privately Held**
SIC: 3354 Aluminum extruded products

(G-1217)
OHIO WIRE HARNESS LLC
225 Lincoln Ave (43311-1717)
P.O. Box 27 (43311-0027)
PHONE.................................937 292-7355
EMP: 10 EST: 2011
SALES (est): 1.01MM **Privately Held**
Web: www.theohiowireharness.com
SIC: 3679 Harness assemblies, for electronic use: wire or cable

(G-1218)
SCREAMING EAGLE BOATS
227 Water Ave (43311-1731)
PHONE.................................937 292-7674
Todd Lamb, *Prin*
EMP: 6 EST: 2015
SALES (est): 169.2K **Privately Held**
Web: www.spectrepowerboats.com
SIC: 3732 Boatbuilding and repairing

(G-1219)
SIEMENS INDUSTRY INC
811 N Main St (43311-2300)
PHONE.................................937 593-6010
Larry Falk, *Mgr*
EMP: 45
SALES (corp-wide): 84.48B **Privately Held**
Web: new.siemens.com
SIC: 3612 3613 3643 Transformers, except electric; Switchgear and switchboard apparatus; Current-carrying wiring services
HQ: Siemens Industry, Inc.
   100 Technology Dr
   Alpharetta GA 30005
   847 215-1000

(G-1220)
SPECTRE POWERBOATS LLC
227 Water Ave (43311-1731)
P.O. Box 78 (43035-0078)
PHONE.................................937 292-7674
EMP: 7 EST: 2019
SALES (est): 515.36K **Privately Held**
Web: www.spectrepowerboats.com
SIC: 3732 Boatbuilding and repairing

Bellevue
Huron County

(G-1221)
AMCOR RIGID PACKAGING USA LLC

975 W Main St (44811-9011)
PHONE.................................419 483-4343
Dave Hoover, *BD*
EMP: 6
SALES (corp-wide): 14.69B **Privately Held**
SIC: 3089 Plastics containers, except foam
HQ: Amcor Rigid Packaging Usa, Llc
   10521 S M 52
   Manchester MI 48158

(G-1222)
AMERICAN BALER CO
800 E Center St (44811-1748)
P.O. Box 29 (44811-0029)
PHONE.................................419 483-5790
Dave Kowaleski, *Pr*
E E Moulton, *
Frank B Cameron, *
Richard R Hollington, *
Roger Williams, *
EMP: 65 EST: 1945
SQ FT: 80,133
SALES (est): 18.11MM
SALES (corp-wide): 474.53MM **Privately Held**
Web: www.americanbaler.com
SIC: 3569 3523 Baling machines, for scrap metal, paper, or similar material; Farm machinery and equipment
PA: Avis Industrial Corporation
   1909 S Main St
   Upland IN 46989
   765 998-8100

(G-1223)
BELLEVUE MANUFACTURING COMPANY (PA)
520 Goodrich Rd (44811-1139)
PHONE.................................419 483-3190
EMP: 95 EST: 1915
SQ FT: 150,000
SALES (est): 23.33MM
SALES (corp-wide): 23.33MM **Privately Held**
Web: www.tbmc.net
SIC: 3714 Filters: oil, fuel, and air, motor vehicle

(G-1224)
BUNGE NORTH AMERICA EAST LLC
605 Goodrich Rd (44811-1142)
P.O. Box 369 (44811-0369)
PHONE.................................419 483-5340
Ray Bowns, *Brnch Mgr*
EMP: 8
SALES (corp-wide): 687.86MM **Privately Held**
Web: www.bunge.com
SIC: 2075 2041 Soybean oil, cake or meal; Flour and other grain mill products
PA: Bunge North America (East), L.L.C.
   1391 Tmbrlake Mnor Pkwy S
   Chesterfield MO 63017
   314 292-2000

(G-1225)
CAPITOL ALUMINUM & GLASS CORP
1276 W Main St (44811-9424)
PHONE.................................800 331-8268
Robert C Wagner, *Ch Bd*
Gail P Coe, *
Tory J Woodard, *
Dean Kemp, *
EMP: 55 EST: 1955
SQ FT: 75,000
SALES (est): 11.07MM **Privately Held**
Web: www.capitol-windows.com
SIC: 3442 Metal doors

(G-1226)
DONALD E DIDION II
Also Called: Didion's Mechanical
1027b County Road 308 (44811-9497)
PHONE.............................419 483-2226
Donald E Didion Ii, *Owner*
EMP: 25 **EST:** 1977
SQ FT: 20,000
SALES (est): 3.56MM **Privately Held**
Web: www.didionvessel.com
SIC: 3499 8711 Fire- or burglary-resistive products; Engineering services

(G-1227)
HB FULLER COMPANY
400 N Buckeye St (44811-1210)
PHONE.............................833 672-1482
EMP: 6
SALES (corp-wide): 3.51B **Publicly Held**
Web: www.hbfuller.com
SIC: 2891 Adhesives and sealants
PA: H.B. Fuller Company
1200 Willow Lake Blvd
Saint Paul MN 55110
651 236-5900

(G-1228)
INTERNATIONAL METAL HOSE CO
520 Goodrich Rd (44811-1160)
PHONE.............................419 483-7690
◆ **EMP:** 75 **EST:** 1956
SALES (est): 10.5MM **Privately Held**
Web: www.metalhose.com
SIC: 3599 Flexible metal hose, tubing, and bellows

(G-1229)
MITSUBISHI CHEMICAL AMER INC
Also Called: McPp-Detroit
350 N Buckeye St (44811-1208)
PHONE.............................586 755-1660
Keith Thomas, *Manager*
EMP: 220
Web: www.mcpp-global.com
SIC: 2821 2822 Plastics materials and resins; Synthetic rubber
HQ: Mitsubishi Chemical America, Inc.
9115 Harris Corners Pkwy # 300
Charlotte NC 28269
980 580-2839

(G-1230)
MITSUBISHI CHEMICAL AMER INC
Also Called: McPp
350 N Buckeye St (44811-1208)
PHONE.............................419 483-2931
Lee Wilson, *Brnch Mgr*
EMP: 95
Web: www.mitsubishi-motors.com
SIC: 5511 2891 Automobiles, new and used; Adhesives
HQ: Mitsubishi Chemical America, Inc.
9115 Harris Corners Pkwy # 300
Charlotte NC 28269
980 580-2839

(G-1231)
QUALITY WELDING INC
104 Ronald Ln (44811)
P.O. Box 273 (44811-0273)
PHONE.............................419 483-6067
Charles Tinnel, *Pr*
EMP: 25 **EST:** 1976
SQ FT: 2,800
SALES (est): 1.18MM **Privately Held**
Web: www.qwi-inc.com
SIC: 7692 Welding repair

(G-1232)
R AND S TECHNOLOGIES INC
2474 State Route 4 (44811-9742)
PHONE.............................419 483-3691
Paul Ritz, *Pr*
Gary Shingledecker, *VP*
EMP: 11 **EST:** 1985
SQ FT: 2,400
SALES (est): 1.88MM **Privately Held**
Web: www.r-s-t-inc.com
SIC: 3089 3599 Molding primary plastics; Machine and other job shop work

(G-1233)
SCS GEARBOX INC
739 W Main St (44811-9312)
PHONE.............................419 483-7278
Craig Sage, *Pr*
EMP: 11 **EST:** 1979
SQ FT: 10,000
SALES (est): 1.57MM **Privately Held**
Web: www.scsgearbox.com
SIC: 3714 Gears, motor vehicle

(G-1234)
SENECA RAILROAD & MINING CO
Also Called: Seneca
1075 W Main St (44811-9012)
PHONE.............................419 483-7764
Raymond Wasson, *Pr*
Pat Mira, *Sec*
EMP: 18 **EST:** 1981
SQ FT: 16,300
SALES (est): 573.76K **Privately Held**
Web: www.senecarail.com
SIC: 3312 Rail joints or fastenings

(G-1235)
SOLAE LLC
Also Called: Solae Central Soya
300 Great Lakes Pkwy (44811)
P.O. Box 369 (44811-0369)
PHONE.............................419 483-0400
Dale Perman, *Mgr*
EMP: 122
SALES (corp-wide): 11.48B **Publicly Held**
SIC: 2075 Soybean oil, cake or meal
HQ: Solae, Llc
4300 Duncan Ave
Saint Louis MO 63110
314 659-3000

(G-1236)
SOLAE LLC
605 Goodrich Rd (44811-1142)
PHONE.............................419 483-5340
Dale Hoffman, *Mgr*
EMP: 16 **EST:** 2013
SALES (est): 2.52MM
SALES (corp-wide): 11.48B **Publicly Held**
SIC: 2099 Food preparations, nec
PA: International Flavors & Fragrances Inc.
521 W 57th St
New York NY 10019
212 765-5500

(G-1237)
SPIRALCOOL COMPANY
186 Sheffield St Ste 188 (44811-1528)
P.O. Box 128 (44811-0128)
PHONE.............................419 483-2510
Thomas Artino, *Pr*
Richard A Hopkins, *Pr*
EMP: 9
SQ FT: 5,000
SALES (est): 999.73K **Privately Held**
Web: www.bestbackingpad.com
SIC: 3069 Hard rubber and molded rubber products

(G-1238)
THOMAS STEEL INC
305 Elm St (44811-1564)
PHONE.............................419 483-7540
Jake Thomas, *CEO*
Steve Roth, *
Carl Koselke, *
Lynn E Thomas, *
Chuck Gerber, *
EMP: 38 **EST:** 1959
SQ FT: 50,000
SALES (est): 5.4MM **Privately Held**
Web: www.tsifab.com
SIC: 3441 Building components, structural steel

(G-1239)
TOWER ATMTIVE OPRTONS USA I LL
630 Southwest St (44811-9314)
PHONE.............................419 483-1500
Mike Jenkins, *Brnch Mgr*
EMP: 192
SALES (corp-wide): 3.1B **Privately Held**
Web: www.autokiniton.com
SIC: 3714 Motor vehicle parts and accessories
HQ: Tower Automotive Operations Usa I, Llc
17757 Woodland Dr
New Boston MI 48164

(G-1240)
WINDSOR MOLD USA INC (DH)
Also Called: Autoplas Division
560 Goodrich Rd (44811-1139)
PHONE.............................419 483-0653
Brian K Moll, *Pr*
▲ **EMP:** 19 **EST:** 1992
SALES (est): 38.57MM
SALES (corp-wide): 32.64B **Publicly Held**
Web: www.windsormoldgroup.com
SIC: 3089 Injection molding of plastics
HQ: Windsor Mold Inc
4035 Malden Rd
Windsor ON N9C 2
519 972-9032

Bellville
Richland County

(G-1241)
D H BOWMAN & SONS INC
1201 Mill Rd (44813-1282)
PHONE.............................419 886-2711
John Ellis, *Pr*
EMP: 7 **EST:** 1946
SQ FT: 1,200
SALES (est): 800K **Privately Held**
SIC: 1771 1794 1442 Blacktop (asphalt) work; Excavation work; Sand mining

(G-1242)
GATTON PACKAGING INC
99 East St (44813-1003)
PHONE.............................419 886-2577
John R Gatton, *Pr*
Larry Gatton, *Sec*
EMP: 6 **EST:** 1987
SQ FT: 10,000
SALES (est): 740.12K **Privately Held**
SIC: 2653 Boxes, corrugated: made from purchased materials

(G-1243)
JACKSON WELLS SERVICES
1201 Mill Rd (44813-1282)
PHONE.............................419 886-2017
Cory Jackson, *Owner*
EMP: 10 **EST:** 2011
SALES (est): 650.51K **Privately Held**
Web: www.jacksonwellservices.com
SIC: 1381 Service well drilling

(G-1244)
LUCYS BARKERY LLC
5527 Etzwiler Rd (44813-9105)
PHONE.............................419 886-3779
Nancy K Leach, *Prin*
EMP: 6 **EST:** 2010
SALES (est): 130.53K **Privately Held**
Web: www.pettreatsbylucy.com
SIC: 3999 Manufacturing industries, nec

(G-1245)
NATURAL OPTONS ARMATHERAPY LLC
Also Called: Holistic Botanicals
610 State Route 97 W (44813-8813)
PHONE.............................419 886-3736
George Cox, *Prin*
EMP: 13 **EST:** 2010
SALES (est): 3.6MM **Privately Held**
Web: www.bestaromatherapyproducts.com
SIC: 2833 Medicinals and botanicals

(G-1246)
NORTH CENTRAL INSULATION INC (PA)
7539 State Route 13 (44813)
P.O. Box 368 (44813)
PHONE.............................419 886-2030
TOLL FREE: 800
D Brent Dudgeon, *Pr*
Andrew Dungeon, *VP*
Linda Dudgeon, *Sec*
John Dudgeon, *Sls Mgr*
▲ **EMP:** 18 **EST:** 1980
SQ FT: 10,000
SALES (est): 24.79MM
SALES (corp-wide): 24.79MM **Privately Held**
Web: www.nci-ins.com
SIC: 1741 1742 3231 Foundation building; Insulation, buildings; Products of purchased glass

(G-1247)
PROTEUS ELECTRONICS INC
161 Spayde Rd (44813-9011)
P.O. Box 725 (44813-0725)
PHONE.............................419 886-2296
Thomas Clabaugh, *Pr*
Mark Molnar, *VP*
EMP: 8 **EST:** 1980
SQ FT: 3,500
SALES (est): 882.17K **Privately Held**
Web: www.proteuselectronics.com
SIC: 3629 Electronic generation equipment

(G-1248)
TIMOTHY WHATMAN
6617 Stoffer Rd (44813-9362)
PHONE.............................419 883-2443
Tim Whatman, *Brnch Mgr*
EMP: 23
Web: www.whatmanhardwoods.com
SIC: 2426 Flooring, hardwood
PA: Timothy Whatman
847 Wagner Rd
Bellville OH 44813

Belmont
Belmont County

(G-1249)
STINGRAY PRESSURE PUMPING LLC (PA)
42739 National Rd (43718-9669)

GEOGRAPHIC SECTION   Berea - Cuyahoga County (G-1270)

PHONE..........................405 648-4177
Bob Maughmer, *Managing Member*
▲ **EMP:** 69 **EST:** 2012
SALES (est): 125.79MM
SALES (corp-wide): 125.79MM **Privately Held**
Web: www.mammothenergy.com
SIC: **1389** Gas field services, nec

Beloit
Mahoning County

(G-1250)
BENDER ENGINEERING COMPANY
17934 Mill St (44609-9512)
P.O. Box 238 (44609-0238)
PHONE..........................330 938-2355
Dennis Patterson, *Pr*
Lois Patterson, *VP*
EMP: 7 **EST:** 1983
SQ FT: 2,000
SALES (est): 653.1K **Privately Held**
SIC: **8711** 3545 Engineering services; Machine tool accessories

(G-1251)
MAHONING VALLEY MANUFACTURING
17796 Rte 62 (44609)
P.O. Box 247 (44619-0247)
PHONE..........................330 537-4492
Tony Sampedro, *CEO*
Susan Sampedro, *VP*
EMP: 20 **EST:** 1973
SQ FT: 35,000
SALES (est): 2.06MM **Privately Held**
Web: www.mvmi.com
SIC: **3944** 3469 Strollers, baby (vehicle); Stamping metal for the trade

Belpre
Washington County

(G-1252)
ELECTRNIC DSIGN FOR INDUST INC
Also Called: E D I
100 Ayers Blvd (45714-9303)
PHONE..........................740 401-4000
Richard Wynn, *Pr*
Nancy Wynn, *VP*
Jay Pottmeyer, *VP*
Sam Wynn, *Sec*
EMP: 21 **EST:** 1981
SQ FT: 2,700
SALES (est): 5.12MM
SALES (corp-wide): 5.12MM **Privately Held**
Web: www.cimarron.com
SIC: **3533** 5084 Oil and gas field machinery; Oil refining machinery, equipment, and supplies
PA: Edi Holding Company, Llc
   100 Ayers Blvd
   Belpre OH 45714
   740 401-4000

(G-1253)
GHOSTBLIND INDUSTRIES INC
801 Ashberry Dr (45714-1148)
PHONE..........................740 374-6766
Kevin Pottmeyer, *CEO*
▲ **EMP:** 6 **EST:** 2008
SALES (est): 939.56K **Privately Held**
Web: www.shadowhunterblinds.com
SIC: **5091** 3949 Hunting equipment and supplies; Hunting equipment

(G-1254)
HENDERSHOT PERFORMANCE LLC
3015 State Route 339 (45714-8051)
PHONE..........................740 315-0090
Larry Hendershot, *Managing Member*
EMP: 7 **EST:** 2015
SALES (est): 306.9K **Privately Held**
Web: www.hendershotperformance.com
SIC: **7699** 3949 Motorcycle repair service; Archery equipment, general

(G-1255)
KRATON CORPORATION
2419 State Route 618 (45714-2086)
PHONE..........................740 423-7571
EMP: 64
Web: www.kraton.com
SIC: **2821** Plastics materials and resins
PA: Kraton Corporation
   9950 Woodloch Forest Dr
   Spring TX 77380

(G-1256)
KRATON EMPLYEES RECREATION CLB
2419 State Route 618 (45714-2086)
P.O. Box 235 (45714-0235)
PHONE..........................740 423-7571
EMP: 11 **EST:** 2011
SALES (est): 386.34K **Privately Held**
Web: www.kraton.com
SIC: **2822** Synthetic rubber

(G-1257)
KRATON POLYMERS US LLC
Also Called: Kraton Polymers
2419 State Route 618 (45714)
P.O. Box 235 (45714-0235)
PHONE..........................740 423-7571
Bob Rose, *Brnch Mgr*
EMP: 400
Web: www.kraton.com
SIC: **2822** 5169 2821 Synthetic rubber; Synthetic resins, rubber, and plastic materials; Plastics materials and resins
HQ: Kraton Polymers U.S. Llc
   9950 Woodloch Forest Dr
   Spring TX 77380
   281 504-4700

(G-1258)
ORION ENGINEERED CARBONS LLC
11135 State Route 7 (45714-9496)
PHONE..........................740 423-9571
Donnie Loubiere, *Manager*
EMP: 48
SALES (corp-wide): 2.67MM **Privately Held**
Web: www.orioncarbons.com
SIC: **2869** Industrial organic chemicals, nec
HQ: Orion Engineered Carbons Llc
   1700 City Plaza Dr # 300
   Spring TX 77389
   832 445-3300

(G-1259)
OVP INC
Also Called: Ohio Dalley Press
305 Washington Blvd (45714-2458)
PHONE..........................740 423-5171
John E Baker, *Pr*
EMP: 8 **EST:** 1967
SQ FT: 4,000
SALES (est): 494.76K **Privately Held**
SIC: **2752** Commercial printing, lithographic

(G-1260)
PIONEER CITY CASTING COMPANY
904 Campus Dr (45714-2342)
P.O. Box 425 (45714-0425)
PHONE..........................740 423-7533
Don W Simmons, *Pr*
EMP: 30 **EST:** 1946
SQ FT: 55,000
SALES (est): 2.57MM **Privately Held**
Web: www.pioneercitycasting.com
SIC: **3321** 3322 Gray iron castings, nec; Malleable iron foundries

(G-1261)
WAL-BON OF OHIO INC (PA)
Also Called: Napoli's Pizza
210 Main St (45714-1612)
P.O. Box 508 (45714-0508)
PHONE..........................740 423-6351
Wayne D Waldeck, *Ch Bd*
William D Waldeck, *Pr*
Charles A Bonnist, *Prin*
Doris C Celli, *Prin*
Guy J Celli Senior, *Prin*
EMP: 15 **EST:** 1966
SQ FT: 6,000
SALES (est): 22.71MM
SALES (corp-wide): 22.71MM **Privately Held**
Web: www.napolis.com
SIC: **2051** 5812 Bakery: wholesale or wholesale/retail combined; Pizzeria, independent

(G-1262)
WAL-BON OF OHIO INC
Also Called: Mc Happy's Bake Shoppe
708 Main St (45714-1622)
P.O. Box 508 (45714-0508)
PHONE..........................740 423-8178
William Waldeck, *Mgr*
EMP: 17
SQ FT: 8,000
SALES (corp-wide): 22.71MM **Privately Held**
Web: www.mchappys.com
SIC: **5461** 2051 2099 Doughnuts; Doughnuts, except frozen; Food preparations, nec
PA: Wal-Bon Of Ohio, Inc.
   210 Main St
   Belpre OH 45714
   740 423-6351

Berea
Cuyahoga County

(G-1263)
A & F MACHINE PRODUCTS CO
454 Geiger St (44017-1392)
PHONE..........................440 826-0959
Fred J Helwig Senior, *Pr*
Fred J Helwig Junior, *VP*
EMP: 24 **EST:** 1960
SQ FT: 12,000
SALES (est): 9.05MM **Privately Held**
Web: www.helwigpumps.com
SIC: **3561** Industrial pumps and parts

(G-1264)
ALLOY ENGINEERING COMPANY (PA)
844 Thacker St (44017-1698)
PHONE..........................440 243-6800
Lou Petonovich, *Pr*
Jeffrey Hood, *
▼ **EMP:** 65 **EST:** 1943
SQ FT: 45,000
SALES (est): 25.17MM
SALES (corp-wide): 25.17MM **Privately Held**
Web: www.alloyengineering.com
SIC: **3443** Plate work for the metalworking trade

(G-1265)
AUDION AUTOMATION LTD
Clamco
775 Berea Industrial Pkwy (44017-2948)
PHONE..........................216 267-1911
Mark E Goldman, *Brnch Mgr*
EMP: 25
SALES (corp-wide): 4.98MM **Privately Held**
Web: www.pacmachinery.com
SIC: **3565** Packaging machinery
PA: Audion Automation, Ltd.
   775 Berea Industrial Pkwy
   Berea OH 44017
   216 267-1911

(G-1266)
AUDION AUTOMATION LTD (PA)
775 Berea Industrial Pkwy (44017-2948)
PHONE..........................216 267-1911
Mark Goldman, *CEO*
▲ **EMP:** 10 **EST:** 2001
SQ FT: 64,000
SALES (est): 4.98MM
SALES (corp-wide): 4.98MM **Privately Held**
Web: www.pacmachinery.com
SIC: **3565** Packing and wrapping machinery

(G-1267)
BEREA MANUFACTURING INC
480 Geiger St (44017-1319)
PHONE..........................440 260-0590
Ed Casper, *Pr*
Earl Sunkel, *Sec*
Mike Pandoli, *VP*
▲ **EMP:** 10 **EST:** 2002
SALES (est): 255.03K **Privately Held**
SIC: **3599** Machine and other job shop work

(G-1268)
BEREA PRINTING COMPANY
95 Pelret Industrial Pkwy (44017-2940)
P.O. Box 38251 (44138-0251)
PHONE..........................440 243-1080
James Dettmer, *Pr*
Linda Dettmer, *Sec*
EMP: 9 **EST:** 1967
SALES (est): 1.07MM **Privately Held**
Web: www.bereaprinting.com
SIC: **2752** 2759 Offset printing; Letterpress printing

(G-1269)
CLEVELAND HOYA CORP
Also Called: Advance Lens Labs
94 Pelret Industrial Pkwy (44017-2940)
PHONE..........................440 234-5703
William Bennedict, *CEO*
▲ **EMP:** 24 **EST:** 1995
SALES (est): 2.14MM **Privately Held**
Web: www.hoya.com
SIC: **3827** 3851 Optical instruments and lenses; Ophthalmic goods
PA: Hoya Corporation
   6-10-1, Nishishinjuku
   Shinjuku-Ku TKY 160-0

(G-1270)
CLEVELAND METAL STAMPING CO
1231 W Bagley Rd Ste 1 (44017-2911)
PHONE..........................440 234-0010
Frank Ghinga, *VP*
Florian Ghinga, *Manager*
EMP: 15 **EST:** 1974
SQ FT: 23,000
SALES (est): 1.41MM **Privately Held**
Web: www.cmstamping.com
SIC: **3469** Stamping metal for the trade

Berea - Cuyahoga County (G-1271)　　　GEOGRAPHIC SECTION

(G-1271)
CLEVELAND SHUTTERS INC
204 Depot St (44017-1810)
PHONE...................................440 234-7600
Shannon Harris, *Asst Sec*
EMP: 8 **EST:** 2018
SALES (est): 499.97K **Privately Held**
Web: www.clevelandshutters.com
SIC: 3442 Shutters, door or window: metal

(G-1272)
COLORMATRIX CORPORATION (HQ)
680 N Rocky River Dr (44017-1628)
PHONE...................................216 622-0100
◆ **EMP:** 120 **EST:** 1978
SALES (est): 44.96MM **Publicly Held**
Web: www.avient.com
SIC: 2865 2816 Dyes and pigments; Inorganic pigments
PA: Avient Corporation
　33587 Walker Rd
　Avon Lake OH 44012

(G-1273)
DEARBORN INC
678 Front St (44017-1607)
PHONE...................................440 234-1353
Kenneth Dearborn, *Pr*
EMP: 50 **EST:** 1944
SQ FT: 30,000
SALES (est): 9.69MM **Privately Held**
Web: www.dearborninc.com
SIC: 3599 Machine shop, jobbing and repair

(G-1274)
DENTAL PURE WATER INC
336 Daisy Ave Ste 102b (44017-1729)
PHONE...................................440 234-0890
Frank Falat, *Prin*
EMP: 10 **EST:** 2001
SALES (est): 389.21K **Privately Held**
Web: www.dentalpurewaterinc.com
SIC: 5499 3843 Water: distilled mineral or spring; Dental chairs

(G-1275)
EFG HOLDINGS INC
Also Called: EFG HOLDINGS, INC.
777 W Bagley Rd (44017-2901)
PHONE...................................440 325-4337
EMP: 613
SALES (corp-wide): 70MM **Privately Held**
Web: www.mwcomponents.com
SIC: 3965 Fasteners
PA: Efg Holdings, Llc
　288 Holbrook Dr
　Wheeling IL 60090
　812 689-8990

(G-1276)
EMPIRE PLOW COMPANY INC (DH)
343 W Bagley Rd Ste 214 (44017-1357)
P.O. Box 39 (50220-0039)
PHONE...................................216 641-2290
David Pitt, *Pr*
EMP: 25 **EST:** 1840
SALES (est): 31.63MM
SALES (corp-wide): 838.71K **Privately Held**
Web: www.mckaytillage.com
SIC: 3523 3423 Farm machinery and equipment; Hand and edge tools, nec
HQ: Ralph Mckay Industries Inc
　130 Hodsman Rd
　Regina SK S4N 5
　306 721-9292

(G-1277)
ES THERMAL INC
Also Called: Brown Fired Heater Div
388 Cranston Dr (44017-2205)
PHONE...................................440 323-3291
David Hoecke, *Pr*
John Somodi, *
Keith J Phillips, *
EMP: 25 **EST:** 1974
SALES (est): 2.58MM **Privately Held**
Web: www.es-thermal.com
SIC: 3433 Oil burners, domestic or industrial

(G-1278)
ESTABROOK ASSEMBLY SVCS INC
Also Called: Easi
700 W Bagley Rd (44017-2900)
P.O. Box 804 (44017-0804)
PHONE...................................440 243-3350
Jeffrey W Tarr, *Pr*
Rich Zsigray, *VP*
▼ **EMP:** 15 **EST:** 1991
SQ FT: 14,000
SALES (est): 2.39MM **Privately Held**
Web: www.easiassembly.com
SIC: 3822 Energy cutoff controls, residential or commercial types

(G-1279)
FASTENER INDUSTRIES INC
Also Called: Ohio Nut & Bolt Company Div
33 Lou Groza Blvd (44017-1237)
PHONE...................................440 891-2031
Tim Morgan, *Mgr*
EMP: 50
SALES (corp-wide): 46.16MM **Privately Held**
Web: www.fastenerind.com
SIC: 3452 5084 Bolts, nuts, rivets, and washers; Lift trucks and parts
PA: Fastener Industries, Inc.
　1 Berea Cmns Ste 209
　Berea OH 44017
　440 243-0034

(G-1280)
FASTENER INDUSTRIES INC (PA)
Also Called: Buckeye Fasteners Company
1 Berea Cmns Ste 209 (44017-2577)
PHONE...................................440 243-0034
◆ **EMP:** 7 **EST:** 1905
SALES (est): 46.16MM
SALES (corp-wide): 46.16MM **Privately Held**
Web: www.fastenerind.com
SIC: 3452 5084 Bolts, nuts, rivets, and washers; Lift trucks and parts

(G-1281)
FLAMING RIVER INDUSTRIES INC
800 Poertner Dr (44017-2936)
PHONE...................................440 826-4488
Jeanette Ladina, *Pr*
Ralph A Deluca, *Treas*
▲ **EMP:** 18 **EST:** 1987
SQ FT: 25,000
SALES (est): 4.03MM **Privately Held**
Web: www.flamingriver.com
SIC: 3714 Motor vehicle engines and parts

(G-1282)
HORIZON METALS INC
8059 Lewis Rd Ste 102 (44017-2943)
P.O. Box 38310 (44138-0310)
PHONE...................................440 235-3338
Paul Froehlich, *Pr*
James Batcha, *VP*
▲ **EMP:** 20 **EST:** 1997
SQ FT: 38,000
SALES (est): 2.34MM **Privately Held**
Web: www.horizonmetals.net
SIC: 3441 Fabricated structural metal

(G-1283)
HUNT IMAGING LLC (PA)
210 Sheldon Rd (44017-1234)
PHONE...................................440 826-0433
◆ **EMP:** 31 **EST:** 1930
SQ FT: 2,040
SALES (est): 7.29MM **Privately Held**
Web: www.huntimaging.com
SIC: 2869 2899 Industrial organic chemicals, nec; Chemical preparations, nec

(G-1284)
JACO MANUFACTURING COMPANY
90 Karl St (44017-1320)
P.O. Box 619 (44017-0619)
PHONE...................................440 234-4000
Annmarie Brian, *Mgr*
EMP: 20
SQ FT: 12,000
SALES (corp-wide): 22.24MM **Privately Held**
Web: www.jacomfg.com
SIC: 3089 3559 Injection molded finished plastics products, nec; Plastics working machinery
PA: Jaco Manufacturing Company
　468 Geiger St
　Berea OH 44017
　440 234-4000

(G-1285)
JACO MANUFACTURING COMPANY (PA)
468 Geiger St (44017-1319)
P.O. Box 619 (44017-0619)
PHONE...................................440 234-4000
Stephen C Campbell, *Ch*
Thomas Campell, *
Susan Sexton, *SYS**
EMP: 100 **EST:** 1949
SQ FT: 70,000
SALES (est): 22.24MM
SALES (corp-wide): 22.24MM **Privately Held**
Web: www.jacomfg.com
SIC: 3089 Injection molding of plastics

(G-1286)
JOYCE MANUFACTURING CO
Also Called: Joyce Windows
1125 Berea Industrial Pkwy (44017-2928)
PHONE...................................440 239-9100
Russell Schmidt, *Pr*
Gary Winkler, *
John Caputo, *
EMP: 70 **EST:** 1955
SQ FT: 100,000
SALES (est): 17.3MM **Privately Held**
Web: www.joycemfg.com
SIC: 3448 3446 3444 Prefabricated metal buildings; Architectural metalwork; Awnings, sheet metal

(G-1287)
MASTER PRINTING GROUP INC
Also Called: Master Printing & Mailing
95 Pelret Industrial Pkwy (44017)
PHONE...................................216 351-2246
Jeremy Dobos, *Pr*
EMP: 13 **EST:** 1928
SALES (est): 2.4MM **Privately Held**
Web: www.masterprintinggroup.com
SIC: 2752 7331 Commercial printing, lithographic; Mailing service

(G-1288)
MGM CONSTRUCTION INC
Also Called: MGM Roofing
1480 W Bagley Rd Ste 1 (44017-2951)
PHONE...................................440 234-7600
Michael Lyon, *Pr*
EMP: 18 **EST:** 2000
SALES (est): 2.37MM **Privately Held**
SIC: 1389 1542 1761 1799 Construction, repair, and dismantling services; Commercial and office building contractors; Roofing contractor; Athletic and recreation facilities construction

(G-1289)
NORTH COAST MEDICAL EQP INC
96 Lincoln Ave (44017-1662)
PHONE...................................440 243-6189
Edward Gibbs, *CEO*
EMP: 10 **EST:** 1982
SQ FT: 2,694
SALES (est): 829.17K **Privately Held**
SIC: 3844 X-ray apparatus and tubes

(G-1290)
NOSHOK INC (PA)
1010 W Bagley Rd (44017-2906)
PHONE...................................440 243-0888
Jeff N Scott, *Pr*
Christian F L, *Coll Vice President*
Jeffrey S Mendrala, *
Danielle Lusinchi, *
▲ **EMP:** 33 **EST:** 1980
SQ FT: 50,000
SALES (est): 10.02MM
SALES (corp-wide): 10.02MM **Privately Held**
Web: www.noshok.com
SIC: 3823 Process control instruments

(G-1291)
QRP INC
1000 W Bagley Rd Ste 101 (44017-2906)
PHONE...................................910 371-0700
Dave Werner, *Pr*
Jordan Law, *
Gabriel Yuen, *
EMP: 85 **EST:** 1986
SQ FT: 63,000
SALES (est): 10.83MM
SALES (corp-wide): 15.78B **Publicly Held**
SIC: 3452 Bolts, metal
HQ: Consolidated Aerospace
　Manufacturing, Llc
　1425 S Acacia Ave
　Fullerton CA 92831
　714 989-2797

(G-1292)
RADS LLC
Also Called: Radcliffe Steel
135 Blaze Industrial Pkwy (44017-2930)
P.O. Box 13862 (44334-3862)
PHONE...................................330 671-0464
EMP: 19 **EST:** 1992
SQ FT: 16,000
SALES (est): 1.94MM **Privately Held**
Web: www.dcradcliffe.com
SIC: 3441 Fabricated structural metal

(G-1293)
SAVVY MTNGS SPECIAL EVENTS LTD
281 Bonds Pkwy (44017-1271)
PHONE...................................916 774-3838
K M Smith Authorized Represent, *Prin*
EMP: 6 **EST:** 2004
SALES (est): 119.91K **Privately Held**
SIC: 2448 Wood pallets and skids

(G-1294)
STANDBY SCREW MACHINE PDTS CO
1122 W Bagley Rd (44017-2908)
PHONE...................................440 243-8200
Frederick W Marcell, *Ch Bd*

Sal Caroniti, *
Patt Hanna, *
E J Miller, *
J Albert Lowell, *
◆ **EMP:** 375 **EST:** 1939
SALES (est): 44.77MM **Privately Held**
Web: www.standbyscrew.com
SIC: 3599 Machine shop, jobbing and repair

(G-1295)
TALENT TOOL & DIE INC
777 Berea Industrial Pkwy (44017-2948)
PHONE................................440 239-8777
Tam Pham, *Ch Bd*
Thanh Pham, *
Kha Vu, *
▲ **EMP:** 40 **EST:** 1981
SQ FT: 80,000
SALES (est): 9.41MM **Privately Held**
Web: www.talent-tool.com
SIC: 3469 3544 Metal stampings, nec; Special dies, tools, jigs, and fixtures

(G-1296)
TIMCO RUBBER PRODUCTS INC (PA)
125 Blaze Industrial Pkwy (44017-2930)
PHONE................................216 267-6242
John Kuzmick, *CEO*
Joe Hoffman, *
Randy Dahlke, *
EMP: 27 **EST:** 1956
SQ FT: 4,500
SALES (est): 6.9MM
SALES (corp-wide): 6.9MM **Privately Held**
Web: www.timcorubber.com
SIC: 3069 Bags, rubber or rubberized fabric

(G-1297)
TMG PERFORMANCE PRODUCTS LLC
Also Called: Volant Performance
140 Blaze Industrial Pkwy (44017-2930)
PHONE................................440 891-0999
▲ **EMP:** 60 **EST:** 1988
SALES (est): 12.23MM
SALES (corp-wide): 195.05MM **Privately Held**
Web: www.tmgperformance.com
SIC: 3714 Exhaust systems and parts, motor vehicle
PA: Race Winning Brands, Inc.
7201 Industrial Park Blvd
Mentor OH 44060
440 951-6600

(G-1298)
VOSS INDUSTRIES LLC
1000 W Bagley Rd (44017-2906)
PHONE................................216 771-7655
James Callan, *Pr*
EMP: 99
SALES (corp-wide): 15.78B **Publicly Held**
Web: www.camaerospace.com
SIC: 3429 Hardware, nec
HQ: Voss Industries, Llc
2168 W 25th St
Cleveland OH 44113
216 771-7655

(G-1299)
VRC INC
Also Called: Vrc Manufacturers
696 W Bagley Rd (44017)
PHONE................................440 243-6666
Christopher W Lovell, *CEO*
EMP: 54 **EST:** 1967
SQ FT: 42,000
SALES (est): 8.33MM **Privately Held**
Web: www.vrcmfg.com
SIC: 3599 Machine shop, jobbing and repair

Bergholz
Jefferson County

(G-1300)
DENOON LUMBER COMPANY LLC (PA)
571 County Road 52 (43908-7961)
PHONE................................740 768-2220
EMP: 96 **EST:** 1963
SALES (est): 10.43MM
SALES (corp-wide): 10.43MM **Privately Held**
Web: www.denoon.com
SIC: 2421 2449 2431 2426 Lumber: rough, sawed, or planed; Wood containers, nec; Millwork; Hardwood dimension and flooring mills

(G-1301)
ROSEBUD MINING COMPANY
Also Called: Bergholz 7
9076 County Road 53 (43908-7948)
PHONE................................740 768-2275
William Denoon, *Brnch Mgr*
EMP: 90
SALES (corp-wide): 221.86MM **Privately Held**
Web: www.rosebudmining.com
SIC: 1222 1221 Bituminous coal-underground mining; Bituminous coal and lignite-surface mining
PA: Rosebud Mining Company
301 Market St
Kittanning PA 16201
724 545-6222

Berlin
Holmes County

(G-1302)
AMISH COUNTRY SOAP CO
Also Called: Amish Country Soaps & Sundries
4826 E Main St (44610)
PHONE................................866 687-1724
EMP: 25
SALES (corp-wide): 129.42K **Privately Held**
Web: www.amishcountrysoapco.com
SIC: 2841 Soap and other detergents
PA: Amish Country Soap Co.
4663 Us 62
Berlin OH 44610
866 687-1724

(G-1303)
BERLIN GARDENS GAZEBOS LTD
5045 State Rte 39 (44610)
PHONE................................330 893-3411
EMP: 16 **EST:** 1988
SALES (est): 464.66K **Privately Held**
Web: www.berlingardensllc.com
SIC: 2511 Wood household furniture

(G-1304)
BERLIN WOOD PRODUCTS INC
5039 County Rd 120 (44610)
P.O. Box 184 (44610-0184)
PHONE................................330 893-3281
John A Yoder, *Pr*
Arthur Yoder, *
EMP: 9 **EST:** 1965
SQ FT: 50,000
SALES (est): 239.48K **Privately Held**
Web: www.hcmohio.com
SIC: 2499 3944 Dowels, wood; Wagons: coaster, express, and play: children's

(G-1305)
CENTOR INC
5091 County Rd 120 (44610)
PHONE................................800 321-3391
Mitch Stein, *Brnch Mgr*
EMP: 150
SALES (corp-wide): 2.1B **Privately Held**
Web: www.centorrx.com
SIC: 2631 Container, packaging, and boxboard
HQ: Centor Inc.
1899 N Wilkinson Way
Perrysburg OH 43551
567 336-8094

(G-1306)
DUTCH HERITAGE WOODCRAFT
4363 State Route 39 (44610)
P.O. Box 358 (44610-0358)
PHONE................................330 893-2211
John Wengerd, *Pt*
John Schrock, *Pt*
EMP: 10 **EST:** 1988
SQ FT: 20,000
SALES (est): 149.22K **Privately Held**
SIC: 2511 2431 2426 Wood household furniture; Millwork; Hardwood dimension and flooring mills

(G-1307)
HOLMES LIMESTONE CO (PA)
4255 State Rte 39 (44610)
P.O. Box 295 (44610-0295)
PHONE................................330 893-2721
Merle Mullet, *Pr*
Wade Mullet, *Sec*
William Hummel, *Treas*
EMP: 7 **EST:** 1949
SQ FT: 10,000
SALES (est): 1.86MM
SALES (corp-wide): 1.86MM **Privately Held**
Web: www.holmeslimestone.com
SIC: 1221 Strip mining, bituminous

(G-1308)
ROBIN INDUSTRIES INC
5200 County Rd 120 (44610)
P.O. Box 330 (44610-0330)
PHONE................................330 893-3501
David Theiss, *Brnch Mgr*
EMP: 18
SALES (corp-wide): 74.78MM **Privately Held**
Web: www.robin-industries.com
SIC: 3061 3069 1481 Mechanical rubber goods; Molded rubber products; Mine development, nonmetallic minerals
PA: Robin Industries, Inc.
6500 Rockside Rd Ste 230
Independence OH 44131
216 631-7000

Berlin Center
Mahoning County

(G-1309)
MASTROPIETRO WINERY INC
14558 Ellsworth Rd (44401-9742)
PHONE................................330 547-2151
Daniel Mastropietro, *Pr*
Marianne Mastropietro, *VP*
EMP: 8 **EST:** 2004
SQ FT: 1,512
SALES (est): 669.8K **Privately Held**
Web: www.mastropietrowinery.com
SIC: 2084 Wines

(G-1310)
OHIO WINDMILL & PUMP CO INC
8389 S Pricetown Rd (44401-9701)
PHONE................................330 547-6300
Craig Donges, *Pr*
EMP: 9 **EST:** 1997
SALES (est): 417.86K **Privately Held**
SIC: 3523 Windmills for pumping water, agricultural

(G-1311)
PARKER-HANNIFIN CORPORATION
Also Called: Parker Hannifin
14010 Ellsworth Rd (44401-9749)
PHONE................................330 261-1618
EMP: 6
SALES (corp-wide): 19.07B **Publicly Held**
Web: www.parker.com
SIC: 3594 Fluid power pumps and motors
PA: Parker-Hannifin Corporation
6035 Parkland Blvd
Cleveland OH 44124
216 896-3000

Berlin Heights
Erie County

(G-1312)
AUTOGATE INC
7306 Driver Rd (44814-9661)
P.O. Box 50 (44814-0050)
PHONE................................419 588-2796
TOLL FREE: 800
William Rodwancy, *Pr*
Donald Rodwancy, *
Diane Mongiardo, *
EMP: 34 **EST:** 1985
SQ FT: 28,750
SALES (est): 8.63MM **Privately Held**
Web: www.autogate.com
SIC: 3446 Gates, ornamental metal

(G-1313)
E & R WELDING INC
32 South St (44814-9320)
PHONE................................440 329-9387
Edwin E Charles, *Pr*
Roberta Charles, *Pr*
EMP: 7 **EST:** 1977
SQ FT: 28,000
SALES (est): 204.31K **Privately Held**
SIC: 7692 Welding repair

(G-1314)
ELITE INDUSTRIAL CONTROLS INC
7308 Driver Rd (44814-9661)
PHONE................................567 234-1057
EMP: 20 **EST:** 2018
SALES (est): 3.2MM **Privately Held**
Web: www.eliteindustrialcontrols.com
SIC: 3625 Relays and industrial controls

(G-1315)
KERNELLS AUTMTC MACHINING INC
10511 State Rte 61 N (44814)
P.O. Box 41 (44814-0041)
PHONE................................419 588-2164
Claude Kernell, *Pr*
Vicky Seck, *
Jeff Kernell, *
▲ **EMP:** 50 **EST:** 1969
SQ FT: 20,500
SALES (est): 5.7MM **Privately Held**
Web: www.kernellsautomatic.com
SIC: 3451 Screw machine products

Berlin Heights - Erie County (G-1316)

(G-1316)
LASER GRAPHICS
4606 Mason Rd (44814-9652)
PHONE..............................419 433-2509
William Laughlin, *Owner*
EMP: 6 **EST:** 2005
SALES (est): 139.86K **Privately Held**
Web: www.lasergraphicsonline.com
SIC: 2759 Embossing on paper

(G-1317)
WELD TECH LLC
12316 Berlin Rd (44814-9504)
PHONE..............................419 357-3214
Walt Wlodarsky, *Admn*
EMP: 6 **EST:** 2010
SALES (est): 410.13K **Privately Held**
Web: www.weldtech-metalfab.com
SIC: 3444 Sheet metalwork

Bethel
Clermont County

(G-1318)
AFFORDABLE CABINET DOORS
205 S Main St (45106-1327)
PHONE..............................513 734-9663
Jason Johnson, *Owner*
▲ **EMP:** 6 **EST:** 2012
SALES (est): 149.62K **Privately Held**
SIC: 2434 Wood kitchen cabinets

Bettsville
Seneca County

(G-1319)
CARMEUSE LIME INC
Also Called: Carmeuse Natural Chemicals
1967 W County Rd 42 (44815)
P.O. Box 708 (44815-0708)
PHONE..............................419 986-5200
Thomas A Buck, *CEO*
EMP: 47
SALES (corp-wide): 2.67MM **Privately Held**
Web: www.carmeuse.com
SIC: 1422 Crushed and broken limestone
HQ: Carmeuse Lime, Inc.
11 Stanwix St Fl 21
Pittsburgh PA 15222
412 995-5500

Beverly
Washington County

(G-1320)
SCHILLING TRUSS INC
230 Stony Run Rd (45715-5051)
P.O. Box 187 (45715-0187)
PHONE..............................740 984-2396
Charles L Schilling, *Pr*
Jeff Schilling, *Pr*
Charles L Schilling, *VP*
Lori Meek, *Sec*
EMP: 14 **EST:** 1986
SALES (est): 667.95K **Privately Held**
Web: www.schillingtruss.com
SIC: 2439 Trusses, wooden roof

(G-1321)
SKINNER FIRESTONE INC
Also Called: Firestone
226 Fifth St (45715-1165)
P.O. Box 428 (45715-0428)
PHONE..............................740 984-4247
Vernon Skinner, *Pr*
William Leroy Skinner, *Prin*
EMP: 10 **EST:** 1961
SQ FT: 6,600
SALES (est): 543.07K **Privately Held**
Web: www.skinnerfirestone.com
SIC: 5531 7534 Automotive tires; Tire recapping

(G-1322)
UNLIMITED ENERGY SERVICES LLC
19371 State Route 60 (45715-5055)
P.O. Box 474 (26378-0474)
PHONE..............................304 517-7097
Michael Goodwin, *Pr*
EMP: 10 **EST:** 2018
SALES (est): 2.47MM
SALES (corp-wide): 50.58MM **Privately Held**
SIC: 4953 1382 Refuse systems; Oil and gas exploration services
PA: American Energy Partners, Inc.
616 Hamilton St
Allentown PA 18101
610 217-3275

(G-1323)
WATERFORD TANK FABRICATION LTD
203 State Route 83 (45715-8938)
P.O. Box 392 (45744-0392)
PHONE..............................740 984-4100
Matt Brook, *Pr*
Matt Brook, *Pr*
Larry Lang, *
▲ **EMP:** 80 **EST:** 2006
SQ FT: 80,000
SALES (est): 16.92MM **Privately Held**
Web: www.waterfordtanks.com
SIC: 3399 3441 Iron ore recovery from open hearth slag; Building components, structural steel

Bidwell
Gallia County

(G-1324)
BOB EVANS FARMS INC
Also Called: Bob Evans
791 Farmview Rd (45674-9230)
P.O. Box 198 (45674-0198)
PHONE..............................740 245-5305
Rain Mckinniss, *Mgr*
EMP: 1559
Web: www.bobevansgrocery.com
SIC: 2011 Sausages, from meat slaughtered on site
HQ: Bob Evans Farms, Inc.
8200 Walton Pkwy
New Albany OH 43054
614 492-7700

(G-1325)
OHIO VALLEY TRACKWORK INC
39 Fairview Rd (45614-1100)
P.O. Box 153 (45674-0153)
PHONE..............................740 446-0181
Mike Little, *Pr*
Bret Little, *VP*
Adam Little, *Dir*
EMP: 16 **EST:** 2001
SALES (est): 2.29MM **Privately Held**
Web: www.ohiovalleytrackwork.com
SIC: 3743 Railroad equipment

(G-1326)
RUTLAND TOWNSHIP
33325 Jessie Creek Rd (45614-9600)
P.O. Box 203 (45775-0203)
PHONE..............................740 742-2805
EMP: 6 **EST:** 2011
SALES (est): 472.66K **Privately Held**
SIC: 2951 Asphalt paving mixtures and blocks

(G-1327)
SOUTHERN CABINETRY INC
41 International Blvd (45614-8002)
PHONE..............................740 245-5992
Don Strieter, *Pr*
EMP: 35 **EST:** 1994
SALES (est): 4.01MM **Privately Held**
SIC: 3083 Plastics finished products, laminated

Big Prairie
Holmes County

(G-1328)
DOMETIC SANITATION CORPORATION
Also Called: Dometic Sanitation
13128 State Route 226 (44611-9522)
P.O. Box 38 (44611-0038)
PHONE..............................330 439-5550
Doug Whyte, *Pr*
▲ **EMP:** 48 **EST:** 1998
SALES (est): 12.23MM
SALES (corp-wide): 2.84B **Privately Held**
Web: www.dometicsanitation.com
SIC: 3089 Plastics containers, except foam
HQ: Dometic Corporation
5600 N River Rd Ste 250
Rosemont IL 60018

(G-1329)
PRIDE OF THE HILLS MANUFACTURING INC
8275 State Route 514 (44611-9692)
PHONE..............................330 567-3108
EMP: 100
Web: www.lastarrowmfg.com
SIC: 3533 Oil and gas field machinery

Blacklick
Franklin County

(G-1330)
ACTION GROUP INC
411 Reynoldsburg New Albany Rd (43004-9796)
PHONE..............................614 868-8868
Frank De Nutte, *Pr*
Nancy De Nute, *
EMP: 98 **EST:** 1983
SQ FT: 155,000
SALES (est): 22MM **Privately Held**
Web: www.actiongroupinc.com
SIC: 3449 2541 Bars, concrete reinforcing: fabricated steel; Wood partitions and fixtures

(G-1331)
BESA LIGHTING CO INC
6695 Taylor Rd (43004-9614)
PHONE..............................614 475-7046
◆ **EMP:** 47 **EST:** 1993
SQ FT: 48,500
SALES (est): 7.38MM **Privately Held**
Web: www.besalighting.com
SIC: 3646 3645 Commercial lighting fixtures; Residential lighting fixtures

(G-1332)
BLACKLICK MACHINE COMPANY
265 North St (43004-9139)
P.O. Box 105 (43004-0105)
PHONE..............................614 866-9300
John Boggs, *Pr*
Morgan Brooks, *Rgnl Mgr*
EMP: 7 **EST:** 1954
SQ FT: 7,200
SALES (est): 500K **Privately Held**
Web: www.machinedesignohio.com
SIC: 3599 Machine shop, jobbing and repair

(G-1333)
CEDAR CRAFT PRODUCTS INC
776 Reynoldsburg New Albany Rd (43004-0145)
P.O. Box 9 (43004-0009)
PHONE..............................614 759-1600
Rick Van Walsen, *Pr*
Magdlen Maggie Van Walsen, *Sec*
EMP: 11 **EST:** 1986
SQ FT: 4,800
SALES (est): 353.89K **Privately Held**
Web: www.cedar-craft.com
SIC: 2441 Boxes, wood

(G-1334)
DANA OFF HIGHWAY PRODUCTS LLC
6635 Taylor Rd (43004-9600)
PHONE..............................614 864-1116
Terry Casto, *Brnch Mgr*
EMP: 60
Web: www.dana.com
SIC: 3714 3599 Motor vehicle parts and accessories; Machine shop, jobbing and repair
HQ: Dana Off Highway Products, Llc
3939 Technology Dr
Maumee OH 43537

(G-1335)
DIAMOND CHILD CLOTHING CO LLC
7647 Schneider Way (43004-6034)
PHONE..............................614 575-6238
Arthur Norman, *Owner*
EMP: 6 **EST:** 2011
SALES (est): 120K **Privately Held**
SIC: 3496 Diamond cloth

(G-1336)
DRAGONFLY CSTM FABRICATION LLC
179 Malloy Ln (43004-9351)
P.O. Box 118 (43004-0118)
PHONE..............................614 522-9618
Russell Branham, *Brnch Mgr*
EMP: 8
SALES (corp-wide): 56.1M **Privately Held**
SIC: 7692 Welding repair
PA: Dragonfly Custom Fabrication, Llc
4713 Harbinger Cir E
Columbus OH 43213
614 405-2673

(G-1337)
HP LIQUIDATING INC
725 Reynoldsburg New Albany Rd (43004-9638)
P.O. Box 350 (43004-0350)
PHONE..............................614 861-1791
EMP: 90 **EST:** 1971
SQ FT: 72,000
SALES (est): 11.89MM **Privately Held**
Web: www.hubplastics.com
SIC: 3089 Plastics containers, except foam

(G-1338)
INDUSTRIAL CONTAINER SVCS LLC
1385 Blatt Blvd Gahanna Indsutrial Pk (43004)
PHONE..............................614 864-1900
Ron Grannan, *Prin*

▲ = Import ▼ = Export
◆ = Import/Export

GEOGRAPHIC SECTION

Blue Ash - Hamilton County (G-1360)

EMP: 46
Web: www.mauserpackaging.com
SIC: 3443 3412 3411 Fabricated plate work (boiler shop); Metal barrels, drums, and pails; Metal cans
HQ: Industrial Container Services Llc
 375 Northridge Rd Ste 600
 Atlanta GA 30350
 407 930-4182

(G-1339)
MARINE JET POWER INC
6740 Commerce Court Dr (43004-9200)
PHONE.................................614 759-9000
Kevin Kirby, *Pr*
▲ **EMP:** 6 **EST:** 1981
SQ FT: 7,000
SALES (est): 1MM
SALES (corp-wide): 60.24MM **Privately Held**
Web: www.marinejetpower.com
SIC: 3483 Jet propulsion projectiles
HQ: Marine Jet Power Ab
 Hansellisgatan 6
 Uppsala 754 5
 101651000

(G-1340)
MCGRAW-HILL GLOBAL EDUCATN LLC
860 Taylor Station Rd (43004-9540)
P.O. Box 182605 (43218-2605)
PHONE.................................614 755-4151
EMP: 500
Web: www.mheducation.com
SIC: 2731 Book publishing
HQ: Mcgraw-Hill Global Education, Llc
 2 Penn Plz Fl 20
 New York NY 10121
 646 766-2000

(G-1341)
MURPHY DOG LLC
225 Business Center Dr (43004-9452)
PHONE.................................614 755-4278
◆ **EMP:** 45 **EST:** 2006
SQ FT: 27,000
SALES (est): 9.82MM **Privately Held**
Web: www.artbrands.com
SIC: 2759 Screen printing

(G-1342)
REYNOLDS INDUSTRIES GROUP LLC
97 Hallowell Dr (43004-6054)
P.O. Box 563 (43004-0563)
PHONE.................................614 363-9149
David Reynolds, *Pr*
EMP: 45 **EST:** 2010
SALES (est): 1.29MM **Privately Held**
SIC: 2731 Book publishing

(G-1343)
RICHARDSON WOODWORKING
3834 Mann Rd (43004-9741)
PHONE.................................614 893-8850
Craig Richardson, *Pr*
EMP: 6 **EST:** 2000
SALES (est): 331.39K **Privately Held**
SIC: 2431 Interior and ornamental woodwork and trim

(G-1344)
RIGHT RESTORATION LLC
405 N Brice Rd (43004-9453)
PHONE.................................440 614-0480
Denise A Dolly, *Prin*
EMP: 9 **EST:** 2013
SALES (est): 963.24K **Privately Held**
Web: www.rightrestoration.com

SIC: 3069 Plumbers' rubber goods

(G-1345)
WIRELESS RETAIL LLC
Also Called: Cricket
6750 Commerce Court Dr (43004-9200)
PHONE.................................614 657-5182
Matt Starkin, *Managing Member*
EMP: 10 **EST:** 2018
SALES (est): 1MM **Privately Held**
SIC: 3663 Mobile communication equipment

Bladensburg
Knox County

(G-1346)
DERRICK PETROLEUM INC
Market Street (43005)
P.O. Box 145 (43005-0145)
PHONE.................................740 668-5711
Duane Dugan, *Pr*
Duane Dugan, *
Vickie Dugan, *Sec*
EMP: 6 **EST:** 1977
SQ FT: 500
SALES (est): 990K **Privately Held**
SIC: 1311 Crude petroleum production

Blanchester
Clinton County

(G-1347)
BIC PRECISION MACHINE CO INC
3004 Cherry St (45107-7915)
P.O. Box 188 (45107-0188)
PHONE.................................937 783-1406
Sarah Burns, *CEO*
EMP: 42 **EST:** 1997
SQ FT: 4,000
SALES (est): 4.94MM **Privately Held**
Web: www.bicprecisionmachine.com
SIC: 3599 Machine shop, jobbing and repair

(G-1348)
BLANCHESTER FOUNDRY CO INC
2121 S State Route 133 (45107-9364)
P.O. Box 126 (45107-0126)
EMP: 14 **EST:** 1947
SALES (est): 448.42K **Privately Held**
Web: www.blanchesterfoundry.com
SIC: 3321 Gray iron castings, nec

(G-1349)
CCPI INC (PA)
Also Called: Consolidated Ceramic Products
838 Cherry St (45107-1316)
PHONE.................................937 783-2476
◆ **EMP:** 50 **EST:** 1957
SALES (est): 22.69MM
SALES (corp-wide): 22.69MM **Privately Held**
Web: www.ccpi-inc.com
SIC: 3297 3479 Castable refractories, nonclay; Enameling, including porcelain, of metal products

(G-1350)
HITACHI ASTEMO AMERICAS INC
960 Cherry St (45107-7883)
PHONE.................................937 783-4961
EMP: 195
Web: www.hitachi-automotive.us
SIC: 3694 Engine electrical equipment
HQ: Hitachi Astemo Americas, Inc.
 955 Warwick Rd
 Harrodsburg KY 40330
 859 734-9451

(G-1351)
J-C-R TECH INC
936 Cherry St (45107-1318)
P.O. Box 65 (45107-0065)
PHONE.................................937 783-2296
Rick Carmean, *Pr*
▲ **EMP:** 15 **EST:** 1973
SQ FT: 18,000
SALES (est): 703.33K **Privately Held**
Web: www.jcrtech.com
SIC: 3541 7629 3544 Machine tool replacement & repair parts, metal cutting types; Electrical repair shops; Special dies, tools, jigs, and fixtures

(G-1352)
R & R TOOL INC
1449a Middleboro Rd (45107-8765)
PHONE.................................937 783-8665
Bonnie Reed, *Pr*
Dan Reed, *
Daniel Reed, *
▲ **EMP:** 46 **EST:** 1985
SQ FT: 30,000
SALES (est): 9.62MM **Privately Held**
Web: www.rrtoolinc.com
SIC: 3429 Hardware, nec

Bloomingburg
Fayette County

(G-1353)
BLOOMNGBURG SPRING WIRE FORM I
83 Main St (43106-9008)
P.O. Box 158 (43106-0158)
PHONE.................................740 437-7614
▲ **EMP:** 20 **EST:** 1946
SQ FT: 27,000
SALES (est): 2.39MM **Privately Held**
Web: www.bloomingburgspring.com
SIC: 3495 3496 Wire springs; Miscellaneous fabricated wire products

Bloomville
Seneca County

(G-1354)
BUECOMP INC
Also Called: Bucyrus Extruded Composites
7016 S State Route 19 (44818-9203)
PHONE.................................419 284-3840
Nelfred G Kimerline, *Pr*
Charles W Kimerline, *
Norm Tackett, *
EMP: 9 **EST:** 1969
SQ FT: 19,000
SALES (est): 435.51K **Privately Held**
Web: www.buecomp.com
SIC: 3089 Injection molding of plastics

(G-1355)
HEIDELBERG MTLS MDWEST AGG INC
4575 S County Road 49 (44818-8400)
P.O. Box 128 (44818-0128)
PHONE.................................419 983-2211
Dan Lepp, *Mgr*
EMP: 8
SALES (corp-wide): 23.02B **Privately Held**
SIC: 2951 1422 Asphalt paving mixtures and blocks; Limestones, ground
HQ: Heidelberg Materials Midwest Agg, Inc.
 300 E John Carpenter Fwy
 Irving TX

Blue Ash
Hamilton County

(G-1356)
ABSTRACT DISPLAYS INC
6465 Creek Rd (45242-4113)
PHONE.................................513 985-9700
Carla Eng, *Pr*
Michael Eng, *VP*
EMP: 15 **EST:** 2001
SALES (est): 3.87MM **Privately Held**
Web: www.abstractdisplays.com
SIC: 5046 7389 3577 7336 Display equipment, except refrigerated; Exhibit construction by industrial contractors; Graphic displays, except graphic terminals; Graphic arts and related design

(G-1357)
ADDUP INC
5101 Creek Rd (45242-3931)
PHONE.................................513 745-4510
Ken Wright, *CEO*
Clement Mailet, *CFO*
Rodney Teach, *Sec*
EMP: 20 **EST:** 2017
SQ FT: 10,000
SALES (est): 9.19MM
SALES (corp-wide): 409.51MM **Privately Held**
Web: www.addupsolutions.com
SIC: 3499 5084 Friction material, made from powdered metal; Welding machinery and equipment
HQ: Fives
 3 Rue Drouot
 Paris 75009
 145237575

(G-1358)
ADEMCO INC
Also Called: ADI Global Distribution
5601 Creek Rd Ste A (45242-4037)
PHONE.................................513 772-1851
Erin Fletcher, *Brnch Mgr*
EMP: 10
SALES (corp-wide): 6.24B **Publicly Held**
Web: www.adiglobaldistribution.us
SIC: 5063 3669 3822 Alarm systems, nec; Emergency alarms; Environmental controls
HQ: Ademco Inc.
 275 Bradhollow Rd Ste 400
 Melville NY 11747
 631 692-1000

(G-1359)
ADVANTAGE PRODUCTS CORPORATION (PA)
11559 Grooms Rd (45242-1409)
PHONE.................................513 489-2283
Robert Weber, *Pr*
EMP: 9 **EST:** 1990
SALES (est): 1.23MM **Privately Held**
Web: www.treds.com
SIC: 3021 Protective footwear, rubber or plastic

(G-1360)
AERPIO THERAPEUTICS LLC
9987 Carver Rd Ste 420 (45242-5563)
PHONE.................................513 985-1920
Joseph H Gardner, *CEO*
Kevin Peters, *CSO*
Steve Pakola, *CMO*
EMP: 21 **EST:** 2011
SALES (est): 3.34MM
SALES (corp-wide): 24.35MM **Publicly Held**

Blue Ash - Hamilton County (G-1361)

GEOGRAPHIC SECTION

SIC: 2834 Pharmaceutical preparations
PA: Aadi Bioscience, Inc.
  17383 W Sunset Blvd A250
  Pacific Palisades CA 90272
  424 744-8055

(G-1361)
ALIMENTO VENTURES INC
10001 Alliance Rd (45242-4750)
PHONE.............................855 510-2866
Kevin R Feazell, Pr
EMP: 21 EST: 2013
SALES (est): 533.36K Privately Held
Web: www.alimentoventures.com
SIC: 2099 Seasonings and spices

(G-1362)
APRECIA PHARMACEUTICALS LLC (HQ)
10901 Kenwood Rd (45242-2813)
PHONE.............................513 984-5000
Kyle Smith, Pr
Chris Gilmore, CEO
Mike Rohlfs, CFO
Kyle Smith, Pr
EMP: 15 EST: 2003
SQ FT: 14,000
SALES (est): 21.7MM
SALES (corp-wide): 90.46MM Privately Held
Web: www.aprecia.com
SIC: 2834 Pharmaceutical preparations
PA: Prasco, Llc
  6125 Commerce Ct
  Mason OH 45040
  513 204-1100

(G-1363)
APSX LLC
11121 Kenwood Rd (45242-1817)
PHONE.............................513 716-5992
Cevik Burak, Prin
EMP: 10 EST: 2006
SALES (est): 918.07K Privately Held
Web: www.apsx.com
SIC: 3541 3089 Milling machines; Injection molding of plastics

(G-1364)
BAXTERS NORTH AMERICA INC
Also Called: Right Away Division
4700 Creek Rd (45242-2808)
PHONE.............................513 552-7463
Matt Femia, Contrlr
EMP: 26
SALES (corp-wide): 559.89MM Privately Held
Web: www.baxtersna.com
SIC: 2032 Canned specialties
HQ: Baxters North America, Inc.
  4700 Creek Rd
  Cincinnati OH 45242
  513 552-7485

(G-1365)
BAXTERS NORTH AMERICA INC
10825 Kenwood Rd (45242-2808)
PHONE.............................513 552-7400
EMP: 118
SALES (corp-wide): 559.89MM Privately Held
Web: www.baxtersna.com
SIC: 2032 Canned specialties
HQ: Baxters North America, Inc.
  4700 Creek Rd
  Cincinnati OH 45242
  513 552-7485

(G-1366)
BAXTERS NORTH AMERICA INC
Also Called: Wornick Foods
4602 Ilmenau Way (45242-7563)
PHONE.............................513 552-7728
Diana Frazier, Mgr
EMP: 46
SALES (corp-wide): 559.89MM Privately Held
Web: www.baxtersna.com
SIC: 2032 Baby foods, including meats: packaged in cans, jars, etc.
HQ: Baxters North America, Inc.
  4700 Creek Rd
  Cincinnati OH 45242
  513 552-7485

(G-1367)
BEEBE WORLDWIDE GRAPHICS SIGN
Also Called: Worldwide Graphics and Sign
9933 Alliance Rd Ste 2 (45242-5662)
PHONE.............................513 241-2726
Christian Beebe, Pr
EMP: 6 EST: 2006
SQ FT: 6,000
SALES (est): 402.29K Privately Held
Web: www.worldwidegraphics.com
SIC: 3993 Signs, not made in custom sign painting shops

(G-1368)
BEVCORP INDUSTRIES LLC
10885 Millington Ct (45242-4019)
P.O. Box 428701 (45242-8701)
PHONE.............................513 673-8520
Raegan Martin, Prin
▲ EMP: 6 EST: 2010
SALES (est): 152.31K Privately Held
Web: www.bevcorp.com
SIC: 3999 Manufacturing industries, nec

(G-1369)
BEVERAGES HOLDINGS LLC
10300 Alliance Rd Ste 500 (45242-4767)
PHONE.............................513 483-3300
EMP: 860
SIC: 2086 2037 Fruit drinks (less than 100% juice): packaged in cans, etc.; Fruit juice concentrates, frozen

(G-1370)
BINDUSA
6819 Ashfield Dr (45242-4108)
PHONE.............................513 247-3000
EMP: 11
SALES (est): 1.48MM Privately Held
Web: www.bindusa.com
SIC: 2789 Bookbinding and related work

(G-1371)
BLD PHARMATECH CO LIMITED
10999 Reed Hartman Hwy Ste 304b (45242-8331)
PHONE.............................330 333-6550
Long Dai, CEO
EMP: 7 EST: 2019
SALES (est): 251.58K Privately Held
Web: www.bldpharm.com
SIC: 2834 Pharmaceutical preparations

(G-1372)
BLUE ASH TOOL & DIE CO INC
4245 Creek Rd (45241-2999)
PHONE.............................513 793-4530
Ronald Siderits, Pr
Otto Siderits, Stockholder
Anna Siderits, VP
Caroline Siderits, VP
Michael Siderits, Stockholder
EMP: 15 EST: 1965
SQ FT: 20,000
SALES (est): 2.33MM Privately Held
Web: www.batd.com
SIC: 3545 3544 Gauge blocks; Special dies, tools, jigs, and fixtures

(G-1373)
BRAMKAMP PRINTING COMPANY INC
9933 Alliance Rd Ste 2 (45242-5662)
PHONE.............................513 241-1865
Kevin Murray, VP
Larry Kuhlman, *
EMP: 29 EST: 1921
SQ FT: 200,000
SALES (est): 1.17MM Privately Held
Web: www.graphicvillage.com
SIC: 2759 2752 Letterpress printing; Offset printing

(G-1374)
BROWN PUBLISHING INC LLC
4229 Saint Andrews Pl (45236-1057)
PHONE.............................513 794-5040
EMP: 7 EST: 2010
SALES (est): 439.17K Privately Held
SIC: 2711 Newspapers: publishing only, not printed on site

(G-1375)
C M M S - RE LLC
Also Called: Forward Technologies
6130 Interstate Cir (45242-1425)
PHONE.............................513 489-5111
Bradley Meyers, Pr
Brian Collins, VP
Scott Mayson, VP
Andrew Schultz, VP
EMP: 15 EST: 2014
SQ FT: 6,500
SALES (est): 2.38MM Privately Held
SIC: 3365 3541 Aluminum foundries; Machine tools, metal cutting: exotic (explosive, etc.)

(G-1376)
CAUDABE LLC
4480 Lake Forest Dr Ste 304 (45242-3753)
PHONE.............................513 501-9799
EMP: 8 EST: 2012
SALES (est): 248.94K Privately Held
Web: www.caudabe.com
SIC: 3629 5065 Electronic generation equipment; Sound equipment, electronic

(G-1377)
CEQUENCE SECURITY INC
10805 Indeco Dr Ste B (45241-2965)
PHONE.............................650 437-6338
EMP: 110
SALES (corp-wide): 1.17MM Privately Held
SIC: 7372 Prepackaged software
PA: Cequence Security, Inc.
  100 S Murphy Ave Ste 300
  Sunnyvale CA
  844 978-3258

(G-1378)
CERKL INCORPORATED
Also Called: Cerkl
11126 Kenwood Rd (45242-1897)
P.O. Box 42458 (45242-0458)
PHONE.............................513 813-8425
Tarek Kamil, CEO
EMP: 100 EST: 2014
SALES (est): 11.33MM Privately Held
Web: www.cerkl.com
SIC: 2741 7371 7372 Internet publishing and broadcasting; Software programming applications; Prepackaged software

(G-1379)
CINCINNATI FAMILY MAGAZINE
10945 Reed Hartman Hwy Ste 221 (45242-2853)
PHONE.............................513 842-0077
Jeffrey Pyle, Prin
EMP: 7 EST: 2007
SALES (est): 381.04K Privately Held
Web: www.cincinnatifamilymagazine.com
SIC: 2721 Magazines: publishing only, not printed on site

(G-1380)
CINCINNATI THERMAL SPRAY INC
5901 Creek Rd (45242-4011)
PHONE.............................513 793-1037
Scott Paschke, Brnch Mgr
EMP: 50
Web: www.cts-inc.net
SIC: 3479 Coating of metals and formed products
PA: Cincinnati Thermal Spray, Inc.
  10904 Deerfield Rd
  Blue Ash OH 45242

(G-1381)
CINCINNATI THERMAL SPRAY INC (PA)
Also Called: CTS
10904 Deerfield Rd (45242-4110)
PHONE.............................513 793-0670
▲ EMP: 10 EST: 1987
SALES (est): 26.54MM Privately Held
Web: www.cts-inc.net
SIC: 3479 Coating of metals and formed products

(G-1382)
COMPLETE MECHANICAL SVCS LLC
Also Called: Cincinnati Mechanical Svcs LLC
11399 Grooms Rd (45242-1405)
PHONE.............................513 489-3080
Bruce Ducker, *
Daniel G Dulle, *
Robert Sambrookes, *
Wyane Miller, *
EMP: 97 EST: 2000
SQ FT: 20,000
SALES (est): 24.79MM Privately Held
Web: www.completemech.com
SIC: 1711 3443 Mechanical contractor; Tank towers, metal plate

(G-1383)
CREST CRAFT CO
4460 Lake Forest Dr Ste 232 (45242-3741)
PHONE.............................513 271-4858
Bradley Olsen, Pr
EMP: 10 EST: 1946
SQ FT: 44,000
SALES (est): 1.6MM Privately Held
Web: www.crestcraft.com
SIC: 3499 Novelties and giftware, including trophies

(G-1384)
CUMMINS - ALLISON CORP
Also Called: Cummins
11256 Cornell Park Dr (45242-1821)
PHONE.............................513 469-2924
EMP: 7
SALES (corp-wide): 1.39MM Publicly Held
Web: www.cranepi.com

GEOGRAPHIC SECTION

Blue Ash - Hamilton County (G-1408)

SIC: 5046 3519 Commercial equipment, nec; Internal combustion engines, nec
HQ: Cummins-Allison Corp.
852 Feehanville Dr
Mount Prospect IL 60056
800 786-5528

(G-1385)
DORAN MFG LLC
4362 Glendale Milford Rd (45242-3706)
PHONE...............................866 816-7233
Dave Robinson, *CFO*
EMP: 75 **EST:** 2003
SQ FT: 10,000
SALES (est): 3.61MM **Privately Held**
Web: www.doranmfg.com
SIC: 5013 3714 Motor vehicle supplies and new parts; Sanders, motor vehicle safety
PA: Evolving Enterprises, Inc.
8748 Old Indian Hill Rd
Cincinnati OH 45243

(G-1386)
DSK IMAGING LLC
Also Called: Allegra Marketing Print Mail
6839 Ashfield Dr (45242-4108)
PHONE...............................513 554-1797
Steve Kapuscinski, *Prin*
EMP: 10 **EST:** 2005
SQ FT: 4,000
SALES (est): 1.93MM **Privately Held**
Web: www.allegramarketingprint.com
SIC: 2752 Offset printing

(G-1387)
EAJ SERVICES LLC
Also Called: Nextstep Networking
4350 Glendale Milford Rd Ste 170 (45242)
PHONE...............................513 792-3400
Andrew Johnson, *VP*
EMP: 18 **EST:** 1986
SQ FT: 5,500
SALES (est): 4.39MM **Privately Held**
Web: www.nextstepnetworking.com
SIC: 7373 7378 3571 Computer integrated systems design; Computer maintenance and repair; Electronic computers

(G-1388)
EASTERN SHEET METAL INC (DH)
8959 Blue Ash Rd (45242-7800)
PHONE...............................513 793-3440
William K Stout Senior, *Ch Bd*
William K Stout Junior, *Pr*
Robert Fedders, *Sec*
Margaret Geiger, *Treas*
▲ **EMP:** 61 **EST:** 1978
SQ FT: 80,000
SALES (est): 13.22MM **Privately Held**
Web: www.easternsheetmetal.com
SIC: 3444 Ducts, sheet metal
HQ: Johnson Controls, Inc.
5757 N Green Bay Ave
Milwaukee WI 53209
920 245-6409

(G-1389)
ETHICON ENDO-SURGERY INC (HQ)
4545 Creek Rd (45242-2839)
PHONE...............................513 337-7000
Andrew K Ekdahl, *Pr*
▲ **EMP:** 1440 **EST:** 1992
SQ FT: 31,330
SALES (est): 783.51MM
SALES (corp-wide): 85.16B **Publicly Held**
SIC: 3841 5047 Surgical instruments and apparatus; Medical equipment and supplies
PA: Johnson & Johnson
1 Johnson & Johnson Plz
New Brunswick NJ 08933
732 524-0400

(G-1390)
ETHICON INC
Also Called: Ethicon Endo - Surgery
10123 Alliance Rd (45242-4707)
PHONE...............................513 786-7000
Frank J Ryan, *Mgr*
EMP: 225
SALES (corp-wide): 85.16B **Publicly Held**
SIC: 3842 Surgical appliances and supplies
HQ: Ethicon Inc.
1000 Route 202
Raritan NJ 08869
800 384-4266

(G-1391)
ETHICON US LLC (DH)
4545 Creek Rd # 3 (45242-2839)
PHONE...............................513 337-7000
Timothy H Schmid, *Pr*
Thomas N Graney, *Treas*
Marianne R Lopapa, *Asst Tr*
Michael W Calvani, *Asst Tr*
Dirk Brinckman, *Sec*
EMP: 229 **EST:** 2012
SALES (est): 27.22MM
SALES (corp-wide): 85.16B **Publicly Held**
SIC: 3841 Surgical instruments and apparatus
HQ: Ethicon Endo-Surgery, Inc.
4545 Creek Rd
Blue Ash OH 45242
513 337-7000

(G-1392)
EVERYTHINGS IMAGE INC
9933 Alliance Rd Ste 2 (45242-5662)
PHONE...............................513 469-6727
Kirk Morris, *Pr*
Daniel Mcbride, *VP*
EMP: 13 **EST:** 2002
SQ FT: 5,500
SALES (est): 483.65K **Privately Held**
Web: www.everythingsimage.com
SIC: 2759 Promotional printing

(G-1393)
F+W MEDIA INC
Also Called: Novel Writing Workshop
9912 Carver Rd Ste 100 (45242-5541)
P.O. Box 78000 (48278-0001)
PHONE...............................513 531-2690
▲ **EMP:** 650
Web: www.goldenpeakmedia.com
SIC: 2721 2731 4813 Magazines: publishing only, not printed on site; Books, publishing only; Online service providers

(G-1394)
FEINTOOL CINCINNATI INC (DH)
11280 Cornell Park Dr (45242-1888)
PHONE...............................513 247-0110
Christoph Trachsler, *CEO*
Ralph Hardt, *
Karl Frydryk, *
Paul Frauchiger, *
Rolf Haag, *
▲ **EMP:** 240 **EST:** 1978
SALES (est): 100.69MM **Privately Held**
Web: www.feintool.com
SIC: 3465 Automotive stampings
HQ: Feintool U.S. Operations, Inc.
11280 Cornell Park Dr
Cincinnati OH 45242
513 247-0110

(G-1395)
FLEXOPLATE INC
6504 Corporate Dr (45242-2101)
PHONE...............................513 489-0433
Thomas M Bock, *Pr*
EMP: 13 **EST:** 1960
SQ FT: 10,000
SALES (est): 422.4K **Privately Held**
Web: www.flexoplate.com
SIC: 3555 2796 2791 Printing plates; Platemaking services; Typesetting

(G-1396)
FOOD PLANT ENGINEERING LLC
10816 Millington Ct Ste 110 (45242-4026)
PHONE...............................513 618-3165
EMP: 14 **EST:** 2015
SALES (est): 62.38K **Privately Held**
Web: www.foodplantengineering.com
SIC: 2011 5149 5451 Meat packing plants; Bakery products; Cheese

(G-1397)
GATE WEST COAST VENTURES LLC
Also Called: Tsjmedia
4901 Hunt Rd Ste 200 (45242-6990)
PHONE...............................513 891-1000
Josh Guttman, *Genl Mgr*
Brian Wiles, *Mgr*
EMP: 18 **EST:** 2005
SALES (est): 642.07K **Privately Held**
SIC: 2711 Newspapers, publishing and printing

(G-1398)
GLENROCK COMPANY
10852 Millington Ct (45242-4017)
PHONE...............................513 489-6710
Joe Amrein, *Prin*
EMP: 7
SALES (corp-wide): 24.17MM **Privately Held**
Web: www.glenrockcompany.com
SIC: 2891 Adhesives and sealants
PA: Glenrock Company
200 W Wrightwood Ave
Elmhurst IL 60126
630 530-9600

(G-1399)
GRAPHIC VILLAGE LLC
4440 Creek Rd (45242-2802)
PHONE...............................513 241-1865
EMP: 171 **EST:** 2012
SALES (est): 46.95MM **Privately Held**
Web: www.graphicvillage.com
SIC: 2752 Offset printing

(G-1400)
GRIFFIN INDUSTRIES LLC
11315 Reed Hartman Hwy (45241-2429)
PHONE...............................513 549-0041
EMP: 11
SALES (corp-wide): 6.53B **Publicly Held**
Web: www.griffinind.com
SIC: 5159 2077 Furs, raw; Animal and marine fats and oils
HQ: Griffin Industries Llc
4221 Alexandria Pike
Cold Spring KY 41076
859 781-2010

(G-1401)
H & G EQUIPMENT INC (PA)
10837 Millington Ct (45242-4019)
PHONE...............................513 761-2060
Eric Kuehne, *Pr*
Dave Meiners, *VP*
EMP: 11 **EST:** 1978
SQ FT: 4,400
SALES (est): 1.9MM
SALES (corp-wide): 1.9MM **Privately Held**
Web: www.hgequipment.us
SIC: 3565 Packaging machinery

(G-1402)
H MACK CHARLES & ASSOCIATES INC
Also Called: Ch Mack
10101 Alliance Rd Ste 10 (45242-4715)
PHONE...............................513 791-4456
EMP: 22
Web: www.chmack.com
SIC: 7371 7372 Computer software development; Prepackaged software

(G-1403)
HARTMANN INC
4615 Carlynn Dr (45241-2202)
PHONE...............................513 276-7318
Carolyn Hartmann, *Pr*
EMP: 7 **EST:** 2011
SALES (est): 156.12K **Privately Held**
Web: www.hartmann.ruhr
SIC: 2752 Offset printing

(G-1404)
HB FULLER COMPANY
Also Called: Adhesves Sealants Coatings Div
4450 Malsbary Rd (45242-5695)
PHONE...............................513 719-3600
Todd Trushenski, *Mgr*
EMP: 42
SQ FT: 23,000
SALES (corp-wide): 3.51B **Publicly Held**
Web: www.hbfuller.com
SIC: 2891 Adhesives
PA: H.B. Fuller Company
1200 Willow Lake Blvd
Saint Paul MN 55110
651 236-5900

(G-1405)
HB FULLER COMPANY
4440 Malsbary Rd (45242-5623)
PHONE...............................513 719-3600
Todd Trushenski, *Brnch Mgr*
EMP: 10
SALES (corp-wide): 3.51B **Publicly Held**
Web: www.hbfuller.com
SIC: 2891 Adhesives
PA: H.B. Fuller Company
1200 Willow Lake Blvd
Saint Paul MN 55110
651 236-5900

(G-1406)
HELIUM SEO
11311 Cornell Park Dr (45242-1889)
PHONE...............................513 563-3065
EMP: 54 **EST:** 2018
SALES (est): 6.15MM **Privately Held**
Web: www.helium-seo.com
SIC: 2813 Helium

(G-1407)
HERITAGE HILL LLC
11563 Grooms Rd (45242-1409)
PHONE...............................513 237-0240
EMP: 6 **EST:** 2019
SALES (est): 497.86K **Privately Held**
Web: www.hhcoop.org
SIC: 2211 Apparel and outerwear fabrics, cotton

(G-1408)
ILLINOIS TOOL WORKS INC
Also Called: ITW Evercoat
6600 Cornell Rd (45242-2033)
PHONE...............................513 489-7600
Steven Levine, *Genl Mgr*
EMP: 130
SALES (corp-wide): 16.11B **Publicly Held**
Web: www.itw.com

Blue Ash - Hamilton County (G-1409)

GEOGRAPHIC SECTION

SIC: **2821** 3714 2891 Polyesters; Motor vehicle parts and accessories; Adhesives and sealants
PA: Illinois Tool Works Inc.
155 Harlem Ave
Glenview IL 60025
847 724-7500

(G-1409)
INFINIT NUTRITION LLC
11240 Cornell Park Dr Ste 110 (45242-1800)
PHONE..................................513 791-3500
▲ EMP: 10 EST: 2004
SALES (est): 1.43MM **Privately Held**
Web: www.infinitnutrition.us
SIC: **2023** Dietary supplements, dairy and non-dairy based

(G-1410)
INTERWEAVE PRESS LLC
10151 Carver Rd Ste 200 (45242-4760)
PHONE..................................513 531-2690
EMP: 7 EST: 2013
SALES (est): 158.75K **Privately Held**
SIC: **2741** Miscellaneous publishing

(G-1411)
JATIGA INC (PA)
Also Called: Hanser Music Group
9933 Alliance Rd Ste 1 (45242-5662)
PHONE..................................859 817-7100
John Hanser Iii, *Pr*
Gary Hanser, *
Timothy Hanser, *
David Rasfeld, *
▲ EMP: 80 EST: 1924
SALES (est): 4.06MM
SALES (corp-wide): 4.06MM **Privately Held**
SIC: **3931** 5099 Musical instruments; Musical instruments

(G-1412)
JENZABAR INC
10300 Alliance Rd Ste 200 (45242-4764)
PHONE..................................513 563-4542
EMP: 16
SALES (corp-wide): 375.6K **Privately Held**
Web: www.jenzabar.com
SIC: **7372** Educational computer software
PA: Jenzabar, Inc.
111 Huntington Ave # 530
Boston MA 02199
617 492-9099

(G-1413)
JEWISH FEDERATION OF CINTI
4380 Malsbary Road Ste 150 (45242-5648)
PHONE..................................513 487-4900
Jewish Cincinnati, *Mgr*
EMP: 7 EST: 2017
SALES (est): 232.28K **Privately Held**
Web: www.jewishcincinnati.org
SIC: **2741** Miscellaneous publishing

(G-1414)
JPS TECHNOLOGIES INC (PA)
11110 Deerfield Rd (45242-2022)
PHONE..................................513 984-6400
Robert J Brandner, *Pr*
Nancy K Meyer, *VP*
EMP: 10 EST: 1970
SQ FT: 7,500
SALES (est): 9.77MM
SALES (corp-wide): 9.77MM **Privately Held**
Web: www.jpstechnologies.com
SIC: **5084** 3089 Industrial machinery and equipment; Plastics processing

(G-1415)
JPS TECHNOLOGIES INC
11118 Deerfield Rd (45242-2022)
PHONE..................................513 984-6400
Nancy Meyers, *Mgr*
EMP: 12
SALES (corp-wide): 9.77MM **Privately Held**
Web: www.jpstechnologies.com
SIC: **5084** 3089 Industrial machinery and equipment; Plastics processing
PA: Jps Technologies, Inc.
11110 Deerfield Rd
Blue Ash OH 45242
513 984-6400

(G-1416)
KARDOL QUALITY PRODUCTS LLC (PA)
9933 Alliance Rd Ste 2 (45242-5662)
PHONE..................................513 933-8206
Eric Kahn, *CEO*
Mike Darding, *CFO*
Mark Bedwell, *Pr*
◆ EMP: 6 EST: 1984
SQ FT: 5,000
SALES (est): 5.02MM
SALES (corp-wide): 5.02MM **Privately Held**
Web: www.kardol.com
SIC: **2672** 2841 2842 2821 Paper; coated and laminated, nec; Soap and other detergents; Polishes and sanitation goods; Plastics materials and resins

(G-1417)
KOLINAHR SYSTEMS INC
6840 Ashfield Dr (45242-4108)
PHONE..................................513 745-9401
EMP: 15 EST: 1993
SALES (est): 2.55MM **Privately Held**
Web: www.kolinahrsystems.com
SIC: **3535** 5084 3565 Conveyors and conveying equipment; Industrial machinery and equipment; Packaging machinery

(G-1418)
LANDRUM BROWN WRLDWIDE SVCS LL
Also Called: Landrum & Brown
4445 Lake Forest Dr # 700 (45242-3739)
PHONE..................................513 530-5333
Dennis Peters, *Prin*
EMP: 10 EST: 2000
SALES (est): 96.22K **Privately Held**
Web: www.landrumbrown.com
SIC: **3812** Aircraft/aerospace flight instruments and guidance systems

(G-1419)
LARMAX INC
Also Called: Kwik Kopy Printing
10945 Reed Hartman Hwy Ste 210 (45242-2828)
PHONE..................................513 984-0783
Larry Richardson, *Pr*
Maxine Richardson, *VP*
EMP: 6 EST: 1980
SQ FT: 1,500
SALES (est): 526.29K **Privately Held**
Web: www.kwikkopyblueash.com
SIC: **2752** Offset printing

(G-1420)
LEADEC CORP (DH)
Also Called: Leadec Services
9395 Kenwood Rd Ste 200 (45242-6819)
PHONE..................................513 731-3590
William Bell, *CEO*
Donald G Morsch, *
▲ EMP: 34 EST: 1984
SQ FT: 18,000
SALES (est): 341.34MM
SALES (corp-wide): 2.67MM **Privately Held**
Web: www.leadec-services.com
SIC: **7349** 8741 3714 Building cleaning service; Management services; Motor vehicle parts and accessories
HQ: Leadec Holding Bv & Co. Kg
Meitnerstr. 11
Stuttgart BW 70563
71178410

(G-1421)
LEARN21 A FLXBLE LRNG CLLBRTIV
5959 Hagewa Dr (45242-6240)
PHONE..................................513 402-2121
William Fritz, *Ex Dir*
EMP: 15 EST: 2008
SALES (est): 1.19MM **Privately Held**
Web: www.learn21.org
SIC: **8351** 7372 Child day care services; Educational computer software

(G-1422)
LEGRAND AV INC
Polacoat Divison
11500 Williamson Rd (45241-2271)
PHONE..................................574 267-8101
Bob St Martin, *Mgr*
EMP: 25
SQ FT: 41,700
Web: www.legrandav.com
SIC: **3861** 3643 Motion picture apparatus and equipment; Current-carrying wiring services
HQ: Legrand Av Inc.
6436 City West Pkwy
Eden Prairie MN 55344
866 977-3901

(G-1423)
LIGHTING SYSTEMS INC
10000 Alliance Rd (45242-4738)
PHONE..................................513 372-3332
EMP: 9 EST: 2016
SALES (est): 452.6K **Privately Held**
Web: www.lsicorp.com
SIC: **3479** Metal coating and allied services

(G-1424)
LMG HOLDINGS INC (PA)
Also Called: Scram Systems
4290 Glendale Milford Rd (45242-3704)
PHONE..................................905 829-3541
Marc Jourlait, *Ch*
Kyle Macemore, *CFO*
Concetta Rand, *CRO*
EMP: 27 EST: 2010
SALES (est): 98.79MM
SALES (corp-wide): 98.79MM **Privately Held**
Web: www.lifesafer.com
SIC: **3829** Measuring and controlling devices, nec

(G-1425)
LSI INDUSTRIES INC
LSI Midwest Lighting
10000 Alliance Rd (45242-4706)
PHONE..................................913 281-1100
Dennis Oberling, *Mgr*
EMP: 200
SALES (corp-wide): 496.98MM **Publicly Held**
Web: www.lsicorp.com
SIC: **3646** 5063 Commercial lighting fixtures; Lighting fixtures
PA: Lsi Industries Inc.
10000 Alliance Rd
Cincinnati OH 45242
513 793-3200

(G-1426)
LSI LIGHTRON INC
10000 Alliance Rd (45242-4706)
PHONE..................................845 562-5500
Gene Littman, *CEO*
Barry White, *
▲ EMP: 1000 EST: 1946
SALES (est): 322.71MM
SALES (corp-wide): 496.98MM **Publicly Held**
Web: www.lsicorp.com
SIC: **3646** 5063 Commercial lighting fixtures; Electrical apparatus and equipment
PA: Lsi Industries Inc.
10000 Alliance Rd
Cincinnati OH 45242
513 793-3200

(G-1427)
LUMINEX HM DCOR FRGRNCE HLDG C (PA)
Also Called: Luminex HD&f Company
10521 Millington Ct (45242-4022)
PHONE..................................513 563-1113
Calvin Johnston, *CEO*
EMP: 498 EST: 1976
SALES (est): 260.78MM
SALES (corp-wide): 260.78MM **Privately Held**
Web: www.candle-lite.com
SIC: **5023** 2844 Decorative home furnishings and supplies; Perfumes, cosmetics and other toilet preparations

(G-1428)
MAT BASICS INCORPORATED
4546 Cornell Rd (45241-2425)
PHONE..................................513 793-0313
Suzie L Johnson, *Prin*
EMP: 6 EST: 2011
SALES (est): 245.67K **Privately Held**
Web: www.matbasics.com
SIC: **2273** Carpets and rugs

(G-1429)
MATDAN CORPORATION
10855 Millington Ct (45242-4019)
PHONE..................................513 794-0500
David Arand, *Pr*
▲ EMP: 35 EST: 1992
SQ FT: 10,000
SALES (est): 3.72MM **Privately Held**
Web: www.matdanfasteners.com
SIC: **3452** 3429 Bolts, metal; Hardware, nec

(G-1430)
MAVERICK CORPORATION
11285 Grooms Rd (45242-1428)
PHONE..................................513 469-9919
EMP: 14 EST: 1993
SQ FT: 2,300
SALES (est): 2.45MM **Privately Held**
Web: www.maverickcorp.com
SIC: **3089** 3299 Thermoformed finished plastics products, nec; Ceramic fiber

(G-1431)
MAVERICK MOLDING CO
11359 Grooms Rd (45242-1405)
PHONE..................................513 387-6100
Jack Rubino, *Ex VP*
Laurel Mesing, *Prin*
Brad Love, *Prin*
▲ EMP: 17 EST: 2005
SALES (est): 2.57MM **Privately Held**
Web: www.maverickmolding.com

GEOGRAPHIC SECTION

Blue Ash - Hamilton County (G-1456)

SIC: 3728 Aircraft parts and equipment, nec

(G-1432)
MBAS PRINTING INC
11401 Deerfield Rd (45242-2106)
PHONE................513 489-3000
Richard P Vollet, *Pr*
EMP: 8 **EST:** 2009
SALES (est): 474.2K **Privately Held**
SIC: 2752 Offset printing

(G-1433)
MEDALLION
6100 Hagewa Dr (45242-6231)
PHONE................513 936-0597
Kristy Brown, *Mgr*
EMP: 7 **EST:** 2002
SALES (est): 101.74K **Privately Held**
SIC: 3429 Keys, locks, and related hardware

(G-1434)
MEGADYNE MEDICAL PRODUCTS INC
4545 Creek Rd (45242)
PHONE................801 576-9669
Paul Borgmeier, *Admn*
Robert Farnsworth, *
Andrew K Ekdahl, *
Veera Rastogi, *
Michael Facer, *
▼ **EMP:** 140 **EST:** 1985
SALES (est): 21.78MM
SALES (corp-wide): 85.16B **Publicly Held**
SIC: 3841 Surgical instruments and apparatus
HQ: Ethicon Endo-Surgery, Inc.
4545 Creek Rd
Blue Ash OH 45242
513 337-7000

(G-1435)
META MANUFACTURING CORPORATION
8901 Blue Ash Rd Ste 1 (45242-7809)
PHONE................513 793-6382
David Mc Swain, *Pr*
EMP: 50 **EST:** 1988
SQ FT: 54,000
SALES (est): 6.02MM **Privately Held**
Web: www.metamfg.com
SIC: 3599 7692 Machine shop, jobbing and repair; Welding repair

(G-1436)
METAL IMPROVEMENT COMPANY LLC
11131 Luschek Dr (45241-2434)
PHONE................513 489-6384
Dan Richardson, *Mgr*
EMP: 74
SQ FT: 15,031
SALES (corp-wide): 2.85B **Publicly Held**
Web: www.imrtest.com
SIC: 3398 Shot peening (treating steel to reduce fatigue)
HQ: Metal Improvement Company, Llc
80 E Rte 4 Ste 310
Paramus NJ 07652
201 843-7800

(G-1437)
METALEX MANUFACTURING INC (PA)
5750 Cornell Rd (45242-2083)
PHONE................513 489-0507
Kevin Kummerle, *CEO*
Werner Kummerle, *
Sue Kummerle, *
◆ **EMP:** 112 **EST:** 1972
SQ FT: 120,000
SALES (est): 23.72MM
SALES (corp-wide): 23.72MM **Privately Held**
Web: www.metalexmfg.com
SIC: 3599 3511 3544 3769 Custom machinery; Turbines and turbine generator sets; Special dies, tools, jigs, and fixtures; Space vehicle equipment, nec

(G-1438)
MICHELMAN INC (PA)
Also Called: Michelman
9080 Shell Rd (45236-1232)
P.O. Box 538702 (45253-8702)
PHONE................513 793-7766
◆ **EMP:** 160 **EST:** 1949
SALES (est): 123.72MM
SALES (corp-wide): 123.72MM **Privately Held**
Web: www.michelman.com
SIC: 2869 Industrial organic chemicals, nec

(G-1439)
MILACRON LLC (DH)
10200 Alliance Rd Ste 200 (45242-4716)
PHONE................513 487-5000
Tom Goeke, *CEO*
Hugh Odonnell, *
Bruce Chalmers, *
Ron Krisanda, *
John Gallagher, *
◆ **EMP:** 35 **EST:** 2009
SALES (est): 1.22B **Publicly Held**
Web: www.milacron.com
SIC: 3549 2899 Metalworking machinery, nec; Correction fluid
HQ: Milacron Intermediate Holdings Inc.
3010 Disney St
Cincinnati OH 45209
513 536-2000

(G-1440)
MILLENNIUM PRINTING LLC
Also Called: Millprint
11401 Deerfield Rd (45242-2106)
PHONE................513 489-3000
EMP: 6 **EST:** 2003
SALES (est): 510.35K **Privately Held**
Web: www.perfectionprintmedia.com
SIC: 2752 Offset printing

(G-1441)
MOLDERS WORLD INC
11471 Deerfield Rd (45242-2106)
PHONE................513 469-6653
Russell Bowen, *Prin*
EMP: 10 **EST:** 2007
SALES (est): 247.1K **Privately Held**
Web: www.moldersworld.com
SIC: 3089 Molding primary plastics

(G-1442)
MULTI-CRAFT LITHO INC
4440 Creek Rd (45242-2802)
PHONE................859 581-2754
EMP: 48
SIC: 2791 2789 2759 2732 Typesetting; Bookbinding and related work; Commercial printing, nec; Book printing

(G-1443)
NEW PUBLISHING HOLDINGS LLC
10151 Carver Rd Ste 200 (45242-4760)
PHONE................513 531-2690
Gregory J Osberg, *CEO*
David Nussbaum, *
EMP: 651 **EST:** 2005
SALES (est): 33.45MM **Privately Held**
SIC: 2731 2721 Books, publishing only; Magazines: publishing only, not printed on site

(G-1444)
NUTONE INC
9825 Kenwood Rd Ste 301 (45242-6252)
P.O. Box 270140 (53027-7140)
PHONE................888 336-3948
EMP: 625
Web: www.broan-nutone.com
SIC: 3634 Electric housewares and fans

(G-1445)
OLAY LLC
Also Called: Procter Gamble Olay Co - Cayey
11530 Reed Hartman Hwy (45241-2422)
PHONE................787 535-2191
Ag Lafley, *CEO*
EMP: 13 **EST:** 2007
SALES (est): 816.2K
SALES (corp-wide): 82.01B **Publicly Held**
Web: www.olay.com
SIC: 2844 Cosmetic preparations
HQ: Procter & Gamble International Operations Sa
Route De Saint-Georges 47
Petit-Lancy GE 1213

(G-1446)
OMYA INC (DH)
Also Called: Callahan AMS Machine Company
9987 Carver Rd Ste 300 (45242-5563)
PHONE................513 387-4600
◆ **EMP:** 150 **EST:** 1894
SALES (est): 193.19MM **Privately Held**
Web: www.omya.com
SIC: 2819 Calcium compounds and salts, inorganic, nec
HQ: Omya Industries, Inc
4605 Duke Dr Ste 700
Mason OH 45040
513 387-4600

(G-1447)
ORGANIZED LIGHTNING LLC
Also Called: Shelter Studios
5601 Belleview Ave (45242-7427)
PHONE................407 965-2730
Jonathan Weiner, *Managing Member*
EMP: 6 **EST:** 2013
SQ FT: 3,500
SALES (est): 124.29K **Privately Held**
SIC: 2741 Internet publishing and broadcasting

(G-1448)
OSBORNE COINAGE COMPANY LLC (PA)
Also Called: Doran Manufacturing Co.
4362 Glendale Milford Rd (45242-3706)
PHONE................877 480-0456
Thomas E Stegman, *Pr*
Todd R Stegman, *
Jeffrey J Stegman, *
▲ **EMP:** 70 **EST:** 1835
SALES (est): 19.01MM
SALES (corp-wide): 19.01MM **Privately Held**
Web: www.osbornecoin.com
SIC: 3644 3613 5999 Terminal boards; Panelboards and distribution boards, electric; Coins and stamps

(G-1449)
PACIFIC PISTON RING CO INC
11379 Grooms Rd (45242-1405)
PHONE................513 387-6100
Dirkson Charles, *Pr*
Glenn Dalessandro, *
EMP: 50 **EST:** 1959
SALES (est): 14MM **Privately Held**

SIC: 3728 Aircraft body assemblies and parts

(G-1450)
PATHEON PHARMACEUTICALS INC
4750 Lake Forest Dr (45242-3852)
PHONE................513 948-9111
EMP: 1807
SALES (corp-wide): 44.91B **Publicly Held**
SIC: 2834 Pharmaceutical preparations
HQ: Patheon Pharmaceuticals Inc.
3900 Paramount Pkwy
Morrisville NC 27560
919 226-3200

(G-1451)
PLASTIC MOLDINGS COMPANY LLC (PA)
Also Called: P M C
9825 Kenwood Rd Ste 302 (45242-6252)
PHONE................513 921-5040
Thomas R Gerdes, *
Lisa Jennings, *
▲ **EMP:** 75 **EST:** 1929
SQ FT: 63,500
SALES (est): 24.78MM
SALES (corp-wide): 24.78MM **Privately Held**
Web: www.pmcsmartsolutions.com
SIC: 3089 Injection molding of plastics

(G-1452)
PMC SMART SOLUTIONS LLC
9825 Kenwood Rd Ste 300 (45242-6252)
PHONE................513 921-5040
Lisa Jennings, *Pr*
EMP: 74 **EST:** 2013
SALES (est): 5.02MM **Privately Held**
Web: www.pmcsmartsolutions.com
SIC: 3089 Injection molding of plastics

(G-1453)
PMP INDUSTRIES INC
4460 Lake Forest Dr Ste 228 (45242-3755)
PHONE................513 563-3028
Alessandro Borsetti, *Pr*
EMP: 6 **EST:** 2007
SALES (est): 2.21MM **Privately Held**
Web: www.pmp-industries.com
SIC: 3612 Transformers, except electric
HQ: Pmp Pro Mec Spa
Via Dell'industria 2
Coseano UD 33030
043 286-3611

(G-1454)
POSITECH CORP
11310 Williamson Rd (45241-2233)
PHONE................513 942-7411
▲ **EMP:** 18 **EST:** 1996
SQ FT: 12,400
SALES (est): 1.07MM **Privately Held**
Web: www.positechcorp.net
SIC: 3599 Machine shop, jobbing and repair

(G-1455)
PRECISION ANLYTICAL INSTRS INC
Also Called: P A I
10857 Millington Ct (45242-4019)
PHONE................513 984-1600
EMP: 6
SQ FT: 2,100
SALES (est): 966.3K **Privately Held**
Web: www.toolsforanalysis.com
SIC: 3826 Analytical instruments

(G-1456)
PRESTIGE ENTERPRISE INTL INC
11343 Grooms Rd (45242-1405)
PHONE................513 469-6044
Charles Gabbour, *Pr*

Blue Ash - Hamilton County (G-1457) GEOGRAPHIC SECTION

Jeff Gabbour, *
◆ **EMP:** 51 **EST:** 1977
SQ FT: 10,000
SALES (est): 4.91MM **Privately Held**
Web: www.prestigefloor.com
SIC: 2426 Flooring, hardwood

(G-1457)
PROCTER & GAMBLE COMPANY
Also Called: Procter & Gamble
11530 Reed Hartman Hwy (45241-2422)
PHONE..............................513 626-2500
Gale Britton, *Mgr*
EMP: 24
SALES (corp-wide): 82.01B **Publicly Held**
Web: us.pg.com
SIC: 2844 Deodorants, personal
PA: The Procter & Gamble Company
1 Procter & Gamble Plz
Cincinnati OH 45202
513 983-1100

(G-1458)
PURETI GROUP LLC
10931 Reed Hartman Hwy Ste C
(45242-2862)
PHONE..............................513 708-3631
EMP: 11 **EST:** 2013
SALES (est): 961.24K **Privately Held**
Web: www.pureti.com
SIC: 2819 Chemicals, high purity: refined from technical grade

(G-1459)
RA CONSULTANTS LLC
10856 Kenwood Rd (45242-2812)
PHONE..............................513 469-6600
Marijo Flamm, *
EMP: 30 **EST:** 2004
SALES (est): 5.26MM **Privately Held**
Web: www.raconsultantsllc.com
SIC: 8711 3679 Civil engineering; Commutators, electronic

(G-1460)
RENEGADE MATERIALS CORP
11379 Grooms Rd (45242-1405)
PHONE..............................513 469-9919
Laurie Mesing, *Contrlr*
EMP: 7 **EST:** 2019
SALES (est): 79.54K **Privately Held**
Web: www.renegadematerials.com
SIC: 2821 Plastics materials and resins

(G-1461)
ROSS GROUP INC
4555 Lake Forest Dr Ste 650 (45242-3785)
PHONE..............................937 427-3069
Steve Woody, *Brnch Mgr*
EMP: 6
Web: www.rossgroupinc.com
SIC: 7372 Business oriented computer software
PA: The Ross Group Inc
3400 Chapel Hill Rd
Douglasville GA

(G-1462)
RSW DISTRIBUTORS LLC
Also Called: Culinary Standards
4700 Ashwood Dr Ste 200 (45241-2424)
PHONE..............................502 587-8877
Mark A Littman, *
EMP: 21 **EST:** 2008
SQ FT: 27,111
SALES (est): 908.5K **Privately Held**
SIC: 2038 Frozen specialties, nec

(G-1463)
SAMUEL L PETERS LLC
10001 Alliance Rd Ste 1 (45242-4751)
PHONE..............................513 745-1500
EMP: 8 **EST:** 2016
SALES (est): 415.29K **Privately Held**
SIC: 2711 Commercial printing and newspaper publishing combined

(G-1464)
SAMUELS PRODUCTS INC
9851 Redhill Dr (45242-5694)
PHONE..............................513 891-4456
Millard Samuels, *Pr*
Thomas J Samuels, *
William Fitzpatric, *
EMP: 30 **EST:** 1903
SQ FT: 61,000
SALES (est): 5.66MM **Privately Held**
Web: www.samuelsproducts.com
SIC: 2759 5122 Flexographic printing; Druggists' sundries, nec

(G-1465)
SCHAEFFERS INVESTMENT RESEARCH INC
Also Called: Option Advisor, The
5151 Pfeiffer Rd Ste 450 (45242-4865)
PHONE..............................513 589-3800
EMP: 65 **EST:** 1981
SALES (est): 7.01MM **Privately Held**
Web: www.schaeffersresearch.com
SIC: 2741 6282 2721 Newsletter publishing; Investment advice; Periodicals

(G-1466)
SERMATECH INTERNATIONAL
11495 Deerfield Rd (45242-2106)
PHONE..............................513 489-9800
Rick Kellerman, *Prs Mgr*
EMP: 9 **EST:** 2018
SALES (est): 291.84K **Privately Held**
Web: www.linde-amt.com
SIC: 3479 Coating of metals and formed products

(G-1467)
ST MEDIA GROUP INTL INC
Also Called: St Media Group International
11262 Cornell Park Dr (45242-1828)
PHONE..............................513 421-2050
Jerry Swormstedt, *Ch*
Tedd Swormstedt, *
Murray Kasmenn, *
Wade Swormstedt, *
Brian Soos, *
▲ **EMP:** 65 **EST:** 1906
SQ FT: 30,000
SALES (est): 8.85MM **Privately Held**
Web: www.stmediagroupintl.com
SIC: 2721 2731 2791 Magazines: publishing only, not printed on site; Book publishing; Typesetting

(G-1468)
STACK CONSTRUCTION TECH INC (PA)
9999 Carver Rd (45242-5584)
PHONE..............................513 445-5122
Phil Ogilby, *CEO*
Ray Dezenzo, *
EMP: 15 **EST:** 2007
SALES (est): 10.19MM
SALES (corp-wide): 10.19MM **Privately Held**
Web: www.stackct.com
SIC: 7372 Business oriented computer software

(G-1469)
STANDARD BARIATRICS INC
4300 Glendale Milford Rd (45242-3706)
PHONE..............................513 620-7751
Jonathan Thompson, *Pr*
Matt Sokany, *CEO*
Adam Dunki-jacobs, *COO*
Kurt Azarbarzin, *Ch Bd*
EMP: 30 **EST:** 2016
SALES (est): 5.9MM **Privately Held**
Web: www.standardbariatrics.com
SIC: 3841 Surgical and medical instruments

(G-1470)
STITCHING GLUING SOLUTIONS LLC
9848 Redhill Dr (45242-5627)
P.O. Box 429375 (45242-9375)
PHONE..............................513 588-3168
Jeffrey Jensen, *Pr*
EMP: 6 **EST:** 2016
SALES (est): 530.05K **Privately Held**
Web: www.stitchingandgluing.com
SIC: 3545 Cutting tools for machine tools

(G-1471)
STOLLE PROPERTIES INC
6954 Cornell Rd Ste 100 (45242-3001)
P.O. Box 815 (45036-0815)
PHONE..............................513 932-8664
William Faulkner, *Pr*
EMP: 580 **EST:** 1999
SQ FT: 1,876
SALES (est): 409.65K
SALES (corp-wide): 47.88MM **Privately Held**
SIC: 3469 Metal stampings, nec
PA: The Ralph J Stolle Company
6990 Cornell Rd
Blue Ash OH 45242
513 489-7184

(G-1472)
SUGAR CREEK PACKING CO (PA)
Also Called: Sugar Creek
4350 Indeco Ct (45241-3399)
PHONE..............................740 335-3586
John Richardson, *Ch Bd*
Alex Hauck, *
Thomas J Bollinger, *
Michael Richardson, *
Allan Riney, *
◆ **EMP:** 299 **EST:** 1966
SQ FT: 80,000
SALES (est): 700MM
SALES (corp-wide): 700MM **Privately Held**
Web: www.sugarcreek.com
SIC: 2013 Bacon, side and sliced: from purchased meat

(G-1473)
SUPERALLOY MFG SOLUTIONS CORP
11230 Deerfield Rd (45242-2024)
PHONE..............................513 489-9800
John Wilbur, *CEO*
Robert Segal, *
Leonard Levie, *
▲ **EMP:** 200 **EST:** 1945
SQ FT: 175,000
SALES (est): 50MM **Privately Held**
Web: www.superalloymfg.com
SIC: 3724 Aircraft engines and engine parts

(G-1474)
SUPERALLOY MFG SOLUTIONS CORP
11495 Deerfield Rd (45242-2106)
PHONE..............................513 605-8380
EMP: 12 **EST:** 1986
SALES (est): 327.29K **Privately Held**
Web: www.superalloymfg.com
SIC: 3599 Machine shop, jobbing and repair

(G-1475)
SURGRX INC
4545 Creek Rd (45242-2803)
PHONE..............................650 482-2400
David Clapper, *Pr*
Edward Unkard, *CFO*
EMP: 14 **EST:** 2000
SQ FT: 20,000
SALES (est): 4.78MM
SALES (corp-wide): 85.16B **Publicly Held**
SIC: 3841 Surgical and medical instruments
HQ: Ethicon Endo-Surgery, Inc.
4545 Creek Rd
Blue Ash OH 45242
513 337-7000

(G-1476)
SUTTER LLC
Also Called: BBC Technology Solutions
11105 Deerfield Rd (45242-2021)
PHONE..............................513 891-2261
Michael Sutter, *CEO*
Michael Sutter, *Managing Member*
EMP: 10 **EST:** 2006
SALES (est): 505.53K **Privately Held**
Web: www.enlivenedtech.com
SIC: 8748 3577 7373 Business consulting, nec; Computer peripheral equipment, nec; Value-added resellers, computer systems

(G-1477)
TAPPAN CHAIRS LLC
Also Called: Shaker Workshops
9115 Blue Ash Rd (45242-6821)
PHONE..............................800 840-9121
EMP: 8 **EST:** 2013
SALES (est): 234.26K **Privately Held**
Web: www.tappanchairs.com
SIC: 2511 Wood household furniture

(G-1478)
TECHNOSOFT INC
11180 Reed Hartman Hwy Ste 200 (45242-1824)
PHONE..............................513 985-9877
Adel Chemaly, *Pr*
EMP: 10 **EST:** 1992
SALES (est): 959.47K **Privately Held**
Web: www.technosoft.com
SIC: 7372 7371 Prepackaged software; Custom computer programming services

(G-1479)
TEKWORX LLC
4538 Cornell Rd (45241-2425)
PHONE..............................513 533-4777
Larry Tillack, *Research & Development*
EMP: 15 **EST:** 2002
SALES (est): 2.05MM **Privately Held**
Web: www.tekworx.us
SIC: 8748 8711 1731 3625 Systems analysis and engineering consulting services; Energy conservation engineering; Energy management controls; Electric controls and control accessories, industrial

(G-1480)
THE FECHHEIMER BROTHERS CO (HQ)
4545 Malsbary Rd (45242-5624)
PHONE..............................513 793-5400
Dan Dudley, *CEO*
Fred Heldman, *
◆ **EMP:** 200 **EST:** 1842
SQ FT: 108,000
SALES (est): 106.42MM
SALES (corp-wide): 364.48B **Publicly Held**

Web: www.fechheimer.com
SIC: 2311 2337 2339 5699 Men's and boys' uniforms; Women's and misses' suits and coats; Women's and misses' outerwear, nec ; Uniforms
PA: Berkshire Hathaway Inc.
   3555 Farnam St Ste 1440
   Omaha NE 68131
   402 346-1400

(G-1481)
THE SHEFFER CORPORATION (HQ)
6990 Cornell Rd (45242-3025)
PHONE.................................513 489-9770
▲ EMP: 85 EST: 1956
SALES (est): 23.85MM
SALES (corp-wide): 47.88MM **Privately Held**
Web: www.sheffercorp.com
SIC: 3593 3492 3494 Fluid power cylinders, hydraulic or pneumatic; Control valves, fluid power: hydraulic and pneumatic; Valves and pipe fittings, nec
PA: The Ralph J Stolle Company
   6990 Cornell Rd
   Blue Ash OH 45242
   513 489-7184

(G-1482)
TORAX MEDICAL INC
4545 Creek Rd (45242-2803)
PHONE.................................651 361-8900
Tod Berg, *Pr*
Chas Mckhann, *CCO*
EMP: 18 EST: 2002
SALES (est): 5.61MM
SALES (corp-wide): 85.16B **Publicly Held**
SIC: 3845 Electromedical apparatus
HQ: Ethicon Inc.
   1000 Route 202
   Raritan NJ 08869
   800 384-4266

(G-1483)
TOYO SEIKI USA INC
11130 Luschek Dr (45241-2434)
PHONE.................................513 546-9657
Nobukaizu Kaike, *Prin*
EMP: 17 EST: 2008
SALES (est): 467.74K **Privately Held**
SIC: 2822 Ethylene-propylene rubbers, EPDM polymers
PA: Toyo Seiki Seisaku-Sho, Ltd.
   5-15-4, Takinogawa
   Kita-Ku TKY 114-0

(G-1484)
TRANS-ACC INC (PA)
11167 Deerfield Rd (45242-2021)
PHONE.................................513 793-6410
John Weinkam, *Pr*
Mary Weinkam, *
EMP: 24 EST: 1967
SQ FT: 27,000
SALES (est): 3.99MM
SALES (corp-wide): 3.99MM **Privately Held**
Web: www.trans-acc.com
SIC: 3471 3479 Finishing, metals or formed products; Coating of metals and formed products

(G-1485)
TRAXX NORTH AMERICA INC
10810 Kenwood Rd (45242-2812)
PHONE.................................513 554-4700
EMP: 11 EST: 2015
SALES (est): 337.73K **Privately Held**
Web: www.advertisingvehicles.com
SIC: 3993 Signs and advertising specialties

(G-1486)
UNITED AIR SPECIALISTS INC
Also Called: UAS
4440 Creek Rd (45242-2802)
PHONE.................................513 891-0400
TOLL FREE: 800
◆ EMP: 250
Web: www.uasinc.com
SIC: 3563 3564 Spraying and dusting equipment; Air cleaning systems

(G-1487)
VALENTINE RESEARCH INC
10280 Alliance Rd (45242-4710)
PHONE.................................513 984-8900
Michael Valentine, *Pr*
Stephen Scholl, *
Margaret Valentine, *
EMP: 26 EST: 1983
SQ FT: 11,000
SALES (est): 5.19MM **Privately Held**
Web: www.valentine1.com
SIC: 3812 Radar systems and equipment

(G-1488)
VORTEC AND PAXTON PRODUCTS
10125 Carver Rd (45242-4719)
PHONE.................................513 891-7474
David Spears, *CEO*
William Ooh, *Genl Mgr*
EMP: 14 EST: 1957
SQ FT: 25,000
SALES (est): 2.54MM **Privately Held**
Web: www.paxtonproducts.com
SIC: 3564 Blowers and fans

(G-1489)
VORTEC CORPORATION
Also Called: Vortec-An Illinois TI Works Co
10125 Carver Rd (45242-4798)
Lois Lannigan, *Pr*
EMP: 22 EST: 1992
SALES (est): 6.13MM
SALES (corp-wide): 16.11B **Publicly Held**
Web: www.vortec.com
SIC: 3585 3499 3699 3498 Refrigeration and heating equipment; Nozzles, spray: aerosol, paint, or insecticide; Electrical equipment and supplies, nec; Fabricated pipe and fittings
PA: Illinois Tool Works Inc.
   155 Harlem Ave
   Glenview IL 60025
   847 724-7500

(G-1490)
WHATIFSPORTSCOM INC
10200 Alliance Rd Ste 301 (45242-4716)
PHONE.................................513 333-0313
Tarek Kamil, *Pr*
EMP: 8 EST: 2000
SALES (est): 197.9K **Privately Held**
Web: www.whatifsports.com
SIC: 7372 Home entertainment computer software

(G-1491)
WHITEHOUSE BROS INC
4393 Creek Rd (45241-2923)
P.O. Box 2981 (45201-2981)
PHONE.................................513 621-2259
Joseph G Vogelsang, *Pr*
Gary Domsher, *Mgr*
▲ EMP: 9 EST: 1906
SQ FT: 1,200
SALES (est): 704.28K **Privately Held**
Web: www.whitehousebrothers.com
SIC: 3911 Jewelry, precious metal

(G-1492)
WITTROCK WDWKG & MFG CO INC
4201 Malsbary Rd (45242-5509)
PHONE.................................513 891-5800
David Wittrock, *Pr*
Joseph Wittrock, *
Christopher Wittrock, *
▲ EMP: 70 EST: 1963
SQ FT: 11,000
SALES (est): 9.44MM **Privately Held**
Web: www.wittrockinc.com
SIC: 2431 Millwork

(G-1493)
WOLF MACHINE COMPANY (PA)
5570 Creek Rd (45242-4004)
PHONE.................................513 791-5194
Scott E Andre, *Pr*
EMP: 35 EST: 1888
SQ FT: 50,000
SALES (est): 17.69MM
SALES (corp-wide): 17.69MM **Privately Held**
Web: www.wolfmachine.com
SIC: 5084 3552 3556 3546 Machine tools and accessories; Textile machinery; Food products machinery; Power-driven handtools

(G-1494)
WOODLAWN RUBBER CO
11268 Williamson Rd (45241-2281)
PHONE.................................513 489-1718
Kirk Heithaus, *Pr*
Donald Heithaus, *Treas*
EMP: 18 EST: 1964
SQ FT: 21,000
SALES (est): 2.48MM **Privately Held**
Web: www.woodlawnrubber.com
SIC: 3069 3061 Molded rubber products; Mechanical rubber goods

(G-1495)
WORNICK HOLDING COMPANY INC
4700 Creek Rd (45242-2808)
PHONE.................................513 794-9800
Jon P Geisler, *Pr*
Dustin Mcdulin, *CFO*
Michael Hyche, *
John Kowalchik, *
EMP: 42 EST: 2008
SALES (est): 10.27MM
SALES (corp-wide): 66.66MM **Privately Held**
Web: www.baxtersna.com
SIC: 2032 Canned specialties
HQ: Polen Capital Credit, Llc
   1075 Main St Ste 320
   Waltham MA 02451

(G-1496)
WV CHS PHARMACY SERVICES LLC ✪
Also Called: Pharmacy Solutions Group of WV
10123 Alliance Rd Ste 320 (45242-4707)
PHONE.................................844 595-4652
EMP: 6 EST: 2023
SALES (est): 133.41K **Privately Held**
SIC: 2834 Pharmaceutical preparations

(G-1497)
XOMOX CORPORATION
Also Called: Crane Xomox
4477 Malsbary Rd (45242-5622)
PHONE.................................513 745-6000
EMP: 6
SALES (corp-wide): 2.09B **Publicly Held**
Web: www.cranecpe.com
SIC: 3491 Process control regulator valves
HQ: Xomox Corporation
   4526 Res Frest Dr Ste 400
   The Woodlands TX 77381
   936 271-6500

Bluffton
Allen County

(G-1498)
A TO Z PORTION CTRL MEATS INC
201 N Main St (45817-1283)
PHONE.................................419 358-2926
Lee Ann Kagy, *Pr*
Sean Kagy, *
Leslie Barnes, *
EMP: 34 EST: 1945
SQ FT: 20,000
SALES (est): 9.64MM **Privately Held**
Web: www.atozmeats.com
SIC: 5142 2013 Meat, frozen: packaged; Sausages and other prepared meats

(G-1499)
BLUFFTON NEWS PUBG & PRTG CO
Also Called: Hopscotch Magazine
103 N Main St (45817-1209)
P.O. Box 227 (45817-0227)
PHONE.................................419 358-4610
Thomas Edwards, *Pr*
EMP: 7 EST: 1945
SALES (est): 208.44K **Privately Held**
Web: www.blufftonnews.com
SIC: 2741 Miscellaneous publishing

(G-1500)
BLUFFTON PRECAST CONCRETE CO
8950 Dixie Hwy (45817-8566)
P.O. Box 161 (45817-0161)
PHONE.................................419 358-6946
David P Akin, *Pr*
Michael J Akin, *VP Opers*
James D Akin, *Stockholder*
Carlin Porter, *Sec*
EMP: 21 EST: 1963
SQ FT: 3,000
SALES (est): 6.26MM **Privately Held**
Web: www.blufftonprecast.com
SIC: 3272 Septic tanks, concrete

(G-1501)
BLUFFTON STONE CO
310 Quarry Dr (45817)
P.O. Box 26 (45817-0026)
PHONE.................................419 358-6941
Brent Gerken, *Pr*
Mike Gerken, *Sec*
EMP: 39 EST: 1930
SQ FT: 1,800
SALES (est): 1.87MM **Privately Held**
Web: www.bluffton.edu
SIC: 1422 3274 2951 Crushed and broken limestone; Lime; Asphalt paving mixtures and blocks

(G-1502)
CARPE DIEM INDUSTRIES LLC
Also Called: Diamond Machine and Mfg
505 E Jefferson St (45817-1349)
PHONE.................................419 358-0129
Ryan Smith, *Mgr*
EMP: 55
SQ FT: 271,000
SALES (corp-wide): 9.25MM **Privately Held**
Web: www.colonialsurfacesolutions.com
SIC: 3471 3398 3479 1799 Cleaning and descaling metal products; Metal heat treating; Painting of metal products; Coating of metal structures at construction site

Bluffton - Allen County (G-1503)

PA: Carpe Diem Industries, Llc
4599 Campbell Rd
Columbus Grove OH 45830
419 659-5639

(G-1503)
DIAMOND MFG BLUFFTON LTD
505 E Jefferson St (45817-1349)
PHONE..............................419 358-0129
Tom Langhals, *
EMP: 65 EST: 2010
SQ FT: 120,000
SALES (est): 8.54MM Privately Held
Web: www.diamondmb.com
SIC: 3441 Fabricated structural metal

(G-1504)
GROB SYSTEMS INC
Also Called: Machine Tool Division
1070 Navajo Dr (45817-9666)
PHONE..............................419 358-9015
Michael Hutecker, CEO
David Kuenzli, Sec
◆ EMP: 590 EST: 1981
SQ FT: 262,000
SALES (est): 151.63MM
SALES (corp-wide): 355.83K Privately Held
Web: www.grobgroup.com
SIC: 3535 7699 Robotic conveyors; Industrial equipment services
PA: Grob-Werke Burkhart Grob E.K.
Industriestr. 4
Mindelheim BY 87719
82619960

(G-1505)
MASTERPIECE SIGNS & GRAPHICS
902 N Main St (45817-9710)
P.O. Box 124 (45817-0124)
PHONE..............................419 358-0077
Tim Boutwell, Owner
EMP: 11 EST: 2016
SALES (est): 925.36K Privately Held
Web: www.masterpiecesign.com
SIC: 3993 Signs and advertising specialties

(G-1506)
RICHLAND TOWNSHIP BD TRUSTEES
8435 Dixie Hwy (45817-9543)
PHONE..............................419 358-4897
Rod Goldsberry, Pr
Gary Lugibihl, Prin
Donald Brauen, Prin
Neil Reichenbach, Prin
EMP: 15 EST: 2019
SALES (est): 976.88K Privately Held
SIC: 3531 Road construction and maintenance machinery

(G-1507)
SUMIRIKO OHIO INC (HQ)
320 Snider Rd (45817-9573)
PHONE..............................419 358-2121
Akira Kikuta, Pr
M Fujiwara, Ch Bd
Yuichi Ariga, Treas
◆ EMP: 41 EST: 1988
SQ FT: 240,000
SALES (est): 162.06MM Privately Held
Web: us.sumiriko.com
SIC: 3052 3069 3829 3714 Automobile hose, rubber; Molded rubber products; Measuring and controlling devices, nec; Motor vehicle parts and accessories
PA: Sumitomo Riko Company Limited.
3-1, Higashi
Komaki AIC 485-0

(G-1508)
TOWER ATMTIVE OPRTONS USA I LL
Also Called: Tower Automotive
18717 County Road 15 (45817-9693)
PHONE..............................419 358-8966
Mike Jenkins, Mgr
EMP: 283
SALES (corp-wide): 3.1B Privately Held
Web: www.autokiniton.com
SIC: 3465 Automotive stampings
HQ: Tower Automotive Operations Usa I, Llc
17757 Woodland Dr
New Boston MI 48164

(G-1509)
TRIPLETT BLUFFTON CORPORATION
Also Called: Lfe Instruments
1 Triplett Dr (45817-1055)
P.O. Box 13 (45817-0013)
PHONE..............................419 358-8750
Warren J Hess, Pr
Kyle Apkarian, CFO
▲ EMP: 9 EST: 1932
SQ FT: 150,000
SALES (est): 921.9K Privately Held
Web: www.triplett.com
SIC: 3825 3824 Test equipment for electronic and electrical circuits; Fluid meters and counting devices

Boardman
Mahoning County

(G-1510)
BOARDMAN NEWS
8302 Southern Blvd Ste 2 (44512-3390)
PHONE..............................330 758-6397
Jack Darnell, Owner
EMP: 8 EST: 1947
SQ FT: 3,500
SALES (est): 316.44K Privately Held
Web: www.boardmannews.net
SIC: 2711 Newspapers, publishing and printing

(G-1511)
EMPYRACOM INC (PA)
7510 Market St Ste 8 (44512-6021)
PHONE..............................330 744-5570
Shanthi Subramanyam, Pr
Viswanath Subramanya, VP
EMP: 16 EST: 1994
SQ FT: 2,500
SALES (est): 3.92MM
SALES (corp-wide): 3.92MM Privately Held
Web: www.empyra.com
SIC: 7379 7372 7371 Computer related consulting services; Prepackaged software; Computer software systems analysis and design, custom

(G-1512)
EXCALIBUR BARBER LLC
7401 Market St (44512-5621)
PHONE..............................330 729-9006
Kelan Bilal, Pr
EMP: 10 EST: 2010
SALES (est): 388.25K Privately Held
Web: www.excaliburbarber.com
SIC: 7241 3999 5087 Barber shops; Barber and beauty shop equipment; Beauty salon and barber shop equipment and supplies

(G-1513)
GORANT CHOCOLATIER LLC (PA)
Also Called: Gorant's Yum Yum Tree
8301 Market St (44512-6257)
P.O. Box 1014 (44406-5014)
PHONE..............................330 726-8821
Joseph M Miller, Managing Member
Gary Weiss, Pr
EMP: 120 EST: 1946
SQ FT: 60,000
SALES (est): 27.29MM
SALES (corp-wide): 27.29MM Privately Held
Web: www.gorant.com
SIC: 5441 5947 5145 3999 Candy; Greeting cards; Candy; Candles

(G-1514)
GREENHART RSTORATION MLLWK LLC
6001 Southern Blvd Ste 105 (44512)
PHONE..............................330 502-6050
John Angelilli, Prin
EMP: 9 EST: 2017
SALES (est): 404.2K Privately Held
Web: www.greenheartcompanies.com
SIC: 2431 Millwork

(G-1515)
JAMESON INDUSTRIES LLC
7997 Hitchcock Rd (44512-5845)
PHONE..............................330 533-5579
Daniel Zarlenga, Prin
EMP: 6 EST: 2018
SALES (est): 239.84K Privately Held
SIC: 3999 Manufacturing industries, nec

(G-1516)
PITA WRAP LLC
4721 Market St (44512-1526)
PHONE..............................330 886-8091
Marlene A Bassil, Pr
EMP: 7 EST: 2012
SQ FT: 3,700
SALES (est): 501.68K Privately Held
Web: www.sauceeino.com
SIC: 2099 Food preparations, nec

(G-1517)
RL BEST COMPANY
723 Bev Rd (44512-6423)
PHONE..............................330 758-8601
Richard L Best, CEO
Ted Best, Pr
Mark Best, VP
William Kavanaugh, VP
◆ EMP: 32 EST: 1972
SQ FT: 35,000
SALES (est): 4.7MM Privately Held
Web: www.sms-group.com
SIC: 7539 3599 Machine shop, automotive; Machine shop, jobbing and repair

(G-1518)
STRUGGLE GRIND SUCCESS LLC
6414 Market St (44512-3434)
PHONE..............................330 834-6738
EMP: 6 EST: 2019
SALES (est): 120.88K Privately Held
SIC: 7389 2211 Apparel designers, commercial; Apparel and outerwear fabrics, cotton

(G-1519)
TREEMEN INDUSTRIES INC
Also Called: Tii Treeman Industries
691 Mcclurg Rd (44512-6408)
P.O. Box 3777 (44513-3777)
PHONE..............................330 965-3777
George Ogletree, Pr
Daniel Solmen, *
Violet Ogletree, *
EMP: 40 EST: 1998
SQ FT: 35,900
SALES (est): 6.22MM Privately Held
Web: www.treemen.com
SIC: 3479 3089 3646 3647 Aluminum coating of metal products; Injection molding of plastics; Commercial lighting fixtures; Vehicular lighting equipment

(G-1520)
ZIDIAN MANAGEMENT CORP (PA)
574 Mcclurg Rd (44512-6405)
PHONE..............................330 743-6050
Tom Zidian, Pr *
Michelle Gross, *
EMP: 25 EST: 2000
SALES (est): 91.82MM
SALES (corp-wide): 91.82MM Privately Held
Web: www.summergardenfood.com
SIC: 2099 Food preparations, nec

(G-1521)
ZIDIAN MANUFACTURING INC
Also Called: Summer Garden Food Mfg
500 Mcclurg Rd (44512-6405)
PHONE..............................330 965-8455
Tom Zidian, CEO
▲ EMP: 54 EST: 2000
SALES (est): 11.31MM
SALES (corp-wide): 91.82MM Privately Held
Web: www.summergardenfood.com
SIC: 2099 Sauce, gravy, dressing, and dip mixes
PA: Zidian Management Corp.
574 Mcclurg Rd
Boardman OH 44512
330 743-6050

Bolivar
Tuscarawas County

(G-1522)
AMERICAN HIGHWAY PRODUCTS LLC
11723 Strasburg Bolivar Rd Nw (44612-8554)
P.O. Box 640 (44612-0640)
PHONE..............................330 874-3270
Scott Fier, Pr
Eric Fier, VP
EMP: 10 EST: 1978
SQ FT: 10,400
SALES (est): 1.01MM Privately Held
Web: www.ahp1.com
SIC: 3531 Road construction and maintenance machinery

(G-1523)
DIVERSIFIED HONING INC
11036 Industrial Pkwy Nw (44612-8992)
PHONE..............................330 874-4663
William Blackwell, Pr
Bonnie L Blackwell, Treas
EMP: 9 EST: 1995
SALES (est): 386.29K Privately Held
Web: www.diversifiedhoning.com
SIC: 3541 Honing and lapping machines

(G-1524)
ELEET CRYOGENICS INC (PA)
11132 Industrial Pkwy Nw (44612-8993)
PHONE..............................330 874-4009
▲ EMP: 33 EST: 1997
SQ FT: 47,000
SALES (est): 11.58MM Privately Held
Web: www.eleetcryogenics.com
SIC: 3443 7353 2761 5088 Cryogenic tanks, for liquids and gases; Oil field equipment, rental or leasing; Manifold business forms; Tanks and tank components

GEOGRAPHIC SECTION

Bowerston - Harrison County (G-1546)

(G-1525)
FSRC TANKS INC
11029 Industrial Pkwy Nw (44612-8992)
PHONE..................234 221-2015
EMP: 9 **EST:** 2011
SALES (est): 248.4K **Privately Held**
Web: www.fsrctanks.com
SIC: 1791 3443 Storage tanks, metal: erection; Reactor containment vessels, metal plate

(G-1526)
GEMINI FIBER CORPORATION
11145 Industrial Pkwy Nw (44612-8993)
P.O. Box 487 (44612-0487)
PHONE..................330 874-4131
▲ **EMP:** 12 **EST:** 1993
SQ FT: 15,000
SALES (est): 4.28MM **Privately Held**
Web: www.geminifiber.com
SIC: 2679 Paper products, converted, nec

(G-1527)
HOLDSWORTH INDUSTRIAL FABG LLC
10407 Welton Rd Ne (44612-8833)
P.O. Box 643 (44697-0643)
PHONE..................330 874-3945
Randy Holdsworth, *Owner*
EMP: 6 **EST:** 1980
SQ FT: 5,000
SALES (est): 474.18K **Privately Held**
SIC: 1799 7692 Welding on site; Welding repair

(G-1528)
INVENTIVE EXTRUSIONS CORP
Also Called: I E C
10882 Fort Laurens Rd Nw (44612-8942)
PHONE..................330 874-3000
Steven Martin, *Pr*
EMP: 13 **EST:** 1986
SQ FT: 12,000
SALES (est): 448.4K **Privately Held**
Web: www.premereinc.com
SIC: 3089 3082 Extruded finished plastics products, nec; Unsupported plastics profile shapes

(G-1529)
MYERS MACHINING INC
11789 Strasburg Bolivar Rd Nw (44612-8555)
P.O. Box 645 (44612-0645)
PHONE..................330 874-3005
David Myers, *Pr*
Brenda Myers, *VP*
EMP: 19 **EST:** 1981
SQ FT: 16,000
SALES (est): 445.3K **Privately Held**
SIC: 3599 Machine shop, jobbing and repair

(G-1530)
NILODOR INC
10966 Industrial Pkwy Nw (44612-8991)
P.O. Box 660 (44612-0660)
PHONE..................800 443-4321
Les Mitson, *Pr*
Kurt Peterson, *
Jeff Wilkof, *
◆ **EMP:** 43 **EST:** 1956
SQ FT: 43,000
SALES (est): 9.09MM
SALES (corp-wide): 465.45MM **Privately Held**
Web: www.hospecobrands.com
SIC: 2842 Deodorants, nonpersonal
PA: The Tranzonic Companies
26301 Curtiss Wright Pkwy # 340
Cleveland OH 44143
216 535-4300

(G-1531)
OSTER SAND AND GRAVEL INC
3467 Dover Zoar Rd Ne (44612-8922)
PHONE..................330 874-3322
Dan Morrisset, *Mgr*
EMP: 6
SALES (corp-wide): 2.5MM **Privately Held**
Web: www.ostersandandgravelnorthcantonoh.com
SIC: 1442 Construction sand and gravel
PA: Oster Sand And Gravel, Inc.
5947 Whipple Ave Nw
Canton OH 44720
330 494-5472

(G-1532)
PREMERE ENTERPRISES INC
10882 Fort Laurens Rd Nw (44612-8942)
PHONE..................330 874-3000
Garry D Martin, *Pr*
Richard D Dodez, *Prin*
EMP: 6 **EST:** 1996
SALES (est): 955.25K **Privately Held**
Web: www.premereinc.com
SIC: 3544 Special dies, tools, jigs, and fixtures

(G-1533)
PREMIERE MOLD AND MACHINE CO
10882 Fort Laurens Rd Nw (44612-8942)
PHONE..................330 874-3000
Robert L Martin, *Ch Bd*
Garry Martin, *Pr*
Richard Dodez, *Sec*
EMP: 6 **EST:** 1972
SQ FT: 33,000
SALES (est): 656.95K **Privately Held**
Web: www.premereinc.com
SIC: 3089 Injection molding of plastics

(G-1534)
PROGRSSIVE MOLDING BOLIVAR INC
10882 Fort Laurens Rd Nw (44612-8942)
PHONE..................330 874-3000
James C Dukat, *Prin*
Garry Martin, *
Robert L Martin, *
Richard D Dodez, *
Sandra K Scott, *
EMP: 22 **EST:** 1976
SQ FT: 33,000
SALES (est): 685.58K **Privately Held**
Web: www.premereinc.com
SIC: 3544 3089 Dies, plastics forming; Thermoformed finished plastics products, nec

(G-1535)
QUILTING CREATIONS INTL
8778 Towpath Rd Ne (44612-8556)
P.O. Box 512 (44697-0512)
PHONE..................330 874-4741
Aaron Bell, *Pr*
EMP: 7 **EST:** 1996
SALES (est): 446.94K **Privately Held**
Web: www.quiltingcreations.com
SIC: 2631 5949 Stencil board; Quilting materials and supplies

(G-1536)
RHC INC
Also Called: Ragon House Collection
10841 Fisher Rd Nw (44612-8487)
PHONE..................330 874-3750
Mary Ragon, *Pr*
Joshua Ragon, *VP Opers*
Kerrie Thomas, *Sec*
▲ **EMP:** 22 **EST:** 2004
SALES (est): 2.23MM **Privately Held**
Web: www.ragonhouse.com

SIC: 3999 5023 5999 Christmas tree ornaments, except electrical and glass; Decorating supplies; Christmas lights and decorations

(G-1537)
SLM LLC
Also Called: Clp Services
125 Canal St Ne (44612-9730)
P.O. Box 378 (44612-0378)
PHONE..................330 874-7131
EMP: 9 **EST:** 2020
SALES (est): 892.76K **Privately Held**
SIC: 3089 Toilets, portable chemical: plastics

(G-1538)
SUBURBAN PLASTICS CO (PA)
509 Water St Sw (44612-8986)
PHONE..................847 741-4900
Stuart Buzz Baxter, *Pr*
Jeremy Baxter, *
Cheri A Baxter, *
◆ **EMP:** 325 **EST:** 1946
SALES (est): 24.03MM
SALES (corp-wide): 24.03MM **Privately Held**
Web: www.suburbanplastics.com
SIC: 3089 Injection molding of plastics

(G-1539)
TORQUE 2020 CMA ACQISITION LLC (PA)
Also Called: Cablecraft Motion Controls
10896 Industrial Pkwy Nw (44612-8990)
P.O. Box 409 (44612-0409)
PHONE..................330 874-2900
Daniel Pappano, *Pr*
Kimberly Mcbride, *CFO*
▲ **EMP:** 200 **EST:** 1974
SQ FT: 61,000
SALES (est): 114.74MM
SALES (corp-wide): 114.74MM **Privately Held**
Web: www.cablecraft.com
SIC: 3315 3568 3714 Cable, steel: insulated or armored; Ball joints, except aircraft and auto; Ball joints, motor vehicle

(G-1540)
US TECHNOLOGY MEDIA INC
509 Water St Sw (44612-8986)
P.O. Box 526 (44612-0526)
PHONE..................330 874-3094
EMP: 10 **EST:** 2015
SALES (est): 989.37K **Privately Held**
SIC: 3291 Abrasive products

Botkins
Shelby County

(G-1541)
BOOMERANG RUBBER INC
105 Dinsmore St (45306-9632)
P.O. Box 538 (45306-0538)
PHONE..................937 693-4611
Mark Sultman, *Pr*
EMP: 22 **EST:** 2009
SALES (est): 6.74MM **Privately Held**
Web: www.boomerangrubber.com
SIC: 3069 Reclaimed rubber and specialty rubber compounds

(G-1542)
BROWN INDUSTRIAL INC
311 W South St (45306-8019)
P.O. Box 74 (45306-0074)
PHONE..................937 693-3838
Christopher D Brown, *Pr*
Ruth C Brown, *

Craig D Brown, *
EMP: 45 **EST:** 1937
SQ FT: 32,000
SALES (est): 9.14MM **Privately Held**
Web: www.brownindustrial.com
SIC: 3713 5012 5084 7692 Truck bodies (motor vehicles); Truck bodies; Industrial machinery and equipment; Automotive welding

(G-1543)
RIDLEY USA INC
Also Called: Hubbard Feeds
104 Oak St (45306-8031)
P.O. Box 1105 (42241-1105)
PHONE..................800 837-8222
Roger Allen, *Mgr*
EMP: 10
SALES (corp-wide): 1.49B **Privately Held**
Web: www.hubbardfeeds.com
SIC: 2048 5191 Livestock feeds; Animal feeds
HQ: Ridley Usa Inc.
111 W Cherry St Ste 500
Mankato MN 56001
507 388-9400

Bowerston
Harrison County

(G-1544)
BOWERSTON SHALE COMPANY (PA)
515 Main St (44695-9512)
P.O. Box 199 (44695-0199)
PHONE..................740 269-2921
Mark Willard, *Pr*
Edward C Milliken, *
Beth Hillyer, *
EMP: 30 **EST:** 1929
SQ FT: 100,000
SALES (est): 23.2MM
SALES (corp-wide): 23.2MM **Privately Held**
Web: www.bowerstonshale.com
SIC: 3255 3251 2951 Clay refractories; Brick clay: common face, glazed, vitrified, or hollow; Asphalt paving mixtures and blocks

(G-1545)
NOLAN COMPANY
300 Boyce Dr (44695-9760)
PHONE..................740 269-1512
EMP: 7
SALES (corp-wide): 37.01MM **Privately Held**
Web: www.nolancompany.com
SIC: 3743 3532 Railroad equipment; Mining machinery
HQ: The Nolan Company
1016 9th St Sw
Canton OH 44707

(G-1546)
NOVO MANUFACTURING LLC (DH)
Also Called: Woodsmiths Design & Mfg
35280 Scio Bowerston Rd (44695-9731)
PHONE..................740 269-2221
Rob Brown, *CEO*
Craig Kurtz, *
Jordan Stephens, *
Jeff Leys, *
Jeff Broene, *
▲ **EMP:** 53 **EST:** 1991
SQ FT: 180,000
SALES (est): 61.7MM
SALES (corp-wide): 2.58B **Privately Held**
Web: www.ljsmith.com
SIC: 2431 Staircases, stairs and railings
HQ: Novo Building Products Holdings, Llc
8181 Logistics Dr

Zeeland MI 49464
616 772-7272

Bowling Green
Wood County

(G-1547)
A-GAS US HOLDINGS INC (DH)
Also Called: A-Gas Americas
1100 Haskins Rd (43402-9363)
PHONE..............................419 867-8990
Monte Roach, *Pr*
Patricia Burns, *VP*
Jason Zilles, *CFO*
EMP: 14 **EST:** 2012
SALES (est): 158.73MM **Privately Held**
Web: www.agas.com
SIC: 5099 2869 4953 3399 Fire extinguishers; Freon; Chemical detoxification; Reclaiming ferrous metals from clay
HQ: A-Gas International Limited
  Banyard Road
  Bristol BS20
  127 537-6600

(G-1548)
AARDVARK SCREEN PRTG & EMB LLC
123 S Main St (43402-2910)
P.O. Box 128 (43402-0128)
PHONE..............................419 354-6686
TOLL FREE: 888
EMP: 10 **EST:** 2016
SQ FT: 3,000
SALES (est): 809.97K **Privately Held**
Web: www.aardvarkspe.com
SIC: 2759 7311 Screen printing; Advertising agencies

(G-1549)
ABSORBENT PRODUCTS COMPANY INC
455 W Woodland Cir (43402-8834)
PHONE..............................419 352-5353
Paul Rankin, *Pr*
◆ **EMP:** 35 **EST:** 1989
SALES (est): 8.93MM
SALES (corp-wide): 87.38MM **Privately Held**
SIC: 2676 Diapers, paper (disposable): made from purchased paper
PA: Principle Business Enterprises, Inc.
  20189 Pine Lake Rd
  Bowling Green OH 43402
  419 352-1551

(G-1550)
ADVANCED SPECIALTY PRODUCTS
428 Clough St (43402-2914)
P.O. Box 210 (43402-0210)
PHONE..............................419 882-6528
Kenneth T Kujawa, *Pr*
Eugene Kujawa, *
◆ **EMP:** 7 **EST:** 1983
SQ FT: 24,000
SALES (est): 462.75K **Privately Held**
Web: www.aspohio.com
SIC: 5082 7389 2759 Construction and mining machinery; Packaging and labeling services; Commercial printing, nec

(G-1551)
AEROPACT MANUFACTURING LLC
Also Called: Martin Machine
435 W Woodland Cir (43402-8834)
PHONE..............................419 373-1711
Rajkumar Nagarajan, *Pr*
EMP: 11 **EST:** 2019
SALES (est): 1.57MM **Privately Held**

Web: www.aeropact.com
SIC: 3324 Aerospace investment castings, ferrous

(G-1552)
BARNES INTERNATIONAL LLC
Also Called: Henry Filters
555 Van Camp Rd (43402-9011)
PHONE..............................419 352-7501
Steve Volmer, *Brnch Mgr*
EMP: 28
SALES (corp-wide): 110.62MM **Privately Held**
Web: www.barnesintl.com
SIC: 3677 Electronic coils and transformers
HQ: Barnes International, Llc
  814 Chestnut St
  Rockford IL 61102
  815 964-8661

(G-1553)
BASIC COATINGS LLC
400 Van Camp Rd (43402-9062)
PHONE..............................419 241-2156
EMP: 19 **EST:** 2005
SALES (est): 9.66MM
SALES (corp-wide): 140.16MM **Privately Held**
Web: www.basiccoatings.com
SIC: 2851 Paints and allied products
PA: Betco Corporation
  400 Van Camp Rd
  Bowling Green OH 43402
  419 241-2156

(G-1554)
BETCO CORPORATION LTD (HQ)
400 Van Camp Rd (43402-9062)
PHONE..............................419 241-2156
Paul C Betz, *CEO*
Tony Lyons, *VP*
James Betz, *Sec*
◆ **EMP:** 200 **EST:** 1994
SALES (est): 53.51MM
SALES (corp-wide): 140.16MM **Privately Held**
Web: www.betco.com
SIC: 2842 Polishes and sanitation goods
PA: Betco Corporation
  400 Van Camp Rd
  Bowling Green OH 43402
  419 241-2156

(G-1555)
BIO-SYSTEMS CORPORATION
Also Called: BSC Environmental
400 Van Camp Rd (43402-9062)
PHONE..............................608 365-9550
Malcolm Peacock, *Pr*
Marilyn Peacock, *
Lisa Peacock, *
EMP: 23 **EST:** 1986
SALES (est): 2.2MM **Privately Held**
Web: www.envirozyme.com
SIC: 2819 Industrial inorganic chemicals, nec

(G-1556)
BIOFIT ENGINEERED PRODUCTS LIMITED PARTNERSHIP (PA)
15500 Bio Fit Way (43402-9290)
P.O. Box 109 (43566-0109)
PHONE..............................419 823-1089
▲ **EMP:** 45 **EST:** 1992
SALES (est): 9.29MM **Privately Held**
Web: www.biofit.com
SIC: 3444 2531 2599 2522 Sheet metalwork; Public building and related furniture; Stools, factory; Chairs, office: padded or plain: except wood

(G-1557)
CENTAUR TOOL & DIE INC
2019 Wood Bridge Blvd (43402-8913)
PHONE..............................419 352-7704
Paul E Faykosh, *Pr*
Jack Faykosh, *VP*
Jeff Faykosh, *VP*
EMP: 24 **EST:** 1973
SQ FT: 16,400
SALES (est): 2.4MM **Privately Held**
Web: www.centaurtool.com
SIC: 3544 Die sets for metal stamping (presses)

(G-1558)
CENTURY MARKETING CORPORATION
1145 Fairview Ave (43402-1204)
PHONE..............................419 354-2591
EMP: 149
SALES (corp-wide): 52.62MM **Privately Held**
Web: www.centurylabel.com
SIC: 2759 Labels and seals: printing, nsk
HQ: Century Marketing Corporation
  12836 S Dixie Hwy
  Bowling Green OH 43402
  419 354-2591

(G-1559)
CHEMRON CORP
1142 N Main St (43402-1309)
PHONE..............................419 352-5565
Dennis Callan, *Prin*
EMP: 6 **EST:** 2010
SALES (est): 176.91K **Privately Held**
SIC: 2843 Surface active agents

(G-1560)
CLARK FIXTURE TECHNOLOGIES INC
410 N Dunbridge Rd (43402-8963)
PHONE..............................419 354-1541
EMP: 36 **EST:** 1980
SALES (est): 5.9MM **Privately Held**
Web: www.clarkfixtures.com
SIC: 3829 3544 Measuring and controlling devices, nec; Special dies, tools, jigs, and fixtures

(G-1561)
CMC GROUP INC (PA)
12836 S Dixie Hwy (43402-9697)
PHONE..............................419 354-2591
Albert J Caperna, *Ch*
Craig Dixon, *
Jeff Palmer, *
Bob Copple, *
Tammy Corral, *
▲ **EMP:** 66 **EST:** 1999
SQ FT: 2,268
SALES (est): 52.62MM
SALES (corp-wide): 52.62MM **Privately Held**
Web: www.cmcgp.com
SIC: 2759 7389 Labels and seals: printing, nsk; Telemarketing services

(G-1562)
COOPER-STANDARD AUTOMOTIVE INC
Also Called: Cooper
1175 N Main St (43402-1310)
P.O. Box 1108 (43402-1108)
PHONE..............................419 352-3533
Robert Huey, *Brnch Mgr*
EMP: 90
SALES (corp-wide): 2.82B **Publicly Held**
Web: www.cooperstandard.com

SIC: 3052 Automobile hose, rubber
HQ: Cooper-Standard Automotive Inc.
  40300 Traditions Dr
  Northville MI 48168
  248 596-5900

(G-1563)
DOW JONES & COMPANY INC
Also Called: Dow Jones
1100 Brim Rd (43402-9351)
PHONE..............................419 352-4696
Nick Barbosa, *Brnch Mgr*
EMP: 39
SALES (corp-wide): 9.88B **Publicly Held**
Web: www.dowjones.com
SIC: 2711 Newspapers, publishing and printing
HQ: Dow Jones & Company, Inc.
  1211 Ave Of The Americas
  New York NY 10036
  800 369-5663

(G-1564)
DOWA THT AMERICA INC
2130 S Woodland Cir (43402-8832)
PHONE..............................419 354-4144
Masanari Konomi, *Pr*
Sandy Hill, *
▲ **EMP:** 35 **EST:** 1997
SALES (est): 11.23MM **Privately Held**
Web: www.dowa-tht.com
SIC: 3398 Metal heat treating
HQ: Dowa Thermotech Co., Ltd.
  19-1, Ukishimacho, Mizuho-Ku
  Nagoya AIC 467-0

(G-1565)
ENVIROZYME LLC
Also Called: Envirozyme
400 Van Camp Rd (43402-9062)
PHONE..............................800 232-2847
EMP: 34 **EST:** 2010
SALES (est): 5.68MM **Privately Held**
Web: www.envirozyme.com
SIC: 2836 Bacteriological media

(G-1566)
GELOK INTERNATIONAL CORP
20189 Pine Lake Rd (43402-4091)
P.O. Box 69 (43414-0069)
PHONE..............................419 352-1482
Charles Stocking, *Pr*
Micheal Kirby, *CFO*
Carol Stocking, *Sec*
▲ **EMP:** 21 **EST:** 1983
SQ FT: 20,000
SALES (est): 706.88K **Privately Held**
Web: www.gelok.com
SIC: 3842 Surgical appliances and supplies

(G-1567)
GKN DRIVELINE BOWL GREEN INC (DH)
2223 Wood Bridge Blvd (43402-8873)
PHONE..............................419 373-7700
Kevin Cumming, *CEO*
▲ **EMP:** 30 **EST:** 1998
SALES (est): 5.99MM
SALES (corp-wide): 4.18B **Privately Held**
SIC: 3999 Barber and beauty shop equipment
HQ: Gkn Limited
  2nd Floor, One Central Boulevard
  Solihull W MIDLANDS B90 8
  121 210-9800

(G-1568)
GKN DRIVELINE NORTH AMER INC
Also Called: GKN Driveline Bowling Green
2223 Wood Bridge Blvd (43402-8873)
PHONE..............................419 354-3955

▲ = Import ▼ = Export
◆ = Import/Export

GEOGRAPHIC SECTION

Bowling Green - Wood County (G-1591)

Hideo Miyagi, *Brnch Mgr*
EMP: 62
SALES (corp-wide): 4.18MM **Privately Held**
SIC: 3714 Motor vehicle parts and accessories
HQ: Gkn Driveline North America, Inc.
2200 N Opdyke Rd
Auburn Hills MI 48326
248 296-7000

(G-1569)
KEL-MAR INC
436 N Enterprise St (43402)
P.O. Box 424 (43402-0424)
PHONE................................419 806-4600
Burr Sterling, *Pr*
EMP: 25 **EST:** 1981
SALES (est): 2.46MM **Privately Held**
SIC: 3471 Finishing, metals or formed products

(G-1570)
LBZB RESTAURANTS INC
132 E Wooster St (43402-2919)
PHONE................................567 413-4700
Zachariah Baroudi, *CEO*
EMP: 12 **EST:** 2018
SALES (est): 550.41K **Privately Held**
SIC: 2035 5812 2099 Dressings, salad: raw and cooked (except dry mixes); Fast-food restaurant, chain; Dressings, salad: dry mixes

(G-1571)
LIFEFORMATIONS INC
Also Called: Lifeformations
2029 Wood Bridge Blvd (43402-8913)
PHONE................................419 352-2101
Rodney Hailigmann, *Pr*
EMP: 50 **EST:** 1991
SQ FT: 8,000
SALES (est): 5.28MM **Privately Held**
Web: www.lfstudios.com
SIC: 3559 Robots, molding and forming plastics

(G-1572)
MACK INDUSTRIES
507 Derby Ave (43402-3973)
PHONE................................419 353-7081
Betsie Mack, *Pr*
EMP: 26 **EST:** 1910
SALES (est): 10.25MM
SALES (corp-wide): 134.58MM **Privately Held**
Web: www.mackconcrete.com
SIC: 3272 5211 1711 Burial vaults, concrete or precast terrazzo; Masonry materials and supplies; Septic system construction
PA: Mack Industries, Inc.
1321 Industrial Pkwy N # 500
Brunswick OH 44212
330 460-7005

(G-1573)
MARATHON SPECIAL PRODUCTS CORP
427 Van Camp Rd (43402-9020)
P.O. Box 468 (43402-0468)
PHONE................................419 352-8441
Bret Banks, *VP*
EMP: 175 **EST:** 1956
SQ FT: 68,000
SALES (est): 25.65MM
SALES (corp-wide): 6.25B **Publicly Held**
Web: www.marathonsp.com
SIC: 3613 3643 Fuses and fuse equipment; Current-carrying wiring services
HQ: Regal Beloit America, Inc.
111 W Michigan St
Milwaukee WI 53203
608 364-8800

(G-1574)
MARKHAM CONVERTING LIMITED
12830 S Dixie Hwy (43402-9697)
PHONE................................419 353-2458
EMP: 15 **EST:** 2007
SALES (est): 764.32K
SALES (corp-wide): 52.62MM **Privately Held**
Web: www.cmcgp.com
SIC: 2759 2679 Labels and seals: printing, nsk; Tags and labels, paper
PA: Cmc Group, Inc.
12836 S Dixie Hwy
Bowling Green OH 43402
419 354-2591

(G-1575)
MCCORD PRODUCTS INC
Also Called: McCord Monuments
1135 N Main St (43402-1310)
P.O. Box 648 (43402-0648)
PHONE................................419 352-3691
Kraig Hanneman, *Pr*
Kris Hanneman, *VP*
Mercene Hanneman, *Sec*
EMP: 6 **EST:** 1941
SQ FT: 8,200
SALES (est): 290.5K **Privately Held**
Web: www.mccordcasketsandvaults.com
SIC: 3995 Burial vaults, fiberglass

(G-1576)
MESTEK INC
American Warming & Vent Div
219 S Church St # 200 (43402-2816)
PHONE................................419 288-2703
Paul Quinlan, *Mgr*
EMP: 61
SALES (corp-wide): 689.94MM **Privately Held**
Web: www.mestek.com
SIC: 3822 3444 3442 Air flow controllers, air conditioning and refrigeration; Sheet metalwork; Metal doors, sash, and trim
PA: Mestek, Inc.
260 N Elm St
Westfield MA 01085
413 568-9571

(G-1577)
NOVAVISION LLC (PA)
524 E Woodland Cir (43402-8966)
PHONE................................419 354-1427
▲ **EMP:** 58 **EST:** 1994
SQ FT: 39,000
SALES (est): 12.6MM **Privately Held**
Web: www.novavisioninc.com
SIC: 2759 3471 Flexographic printing; Electroplating of metals or formed products

(G-1578)
NRG INDUSTRIAL LIGHTING MFG CO
7458 Linwood Rd (43402-9545)
P.O. Box 12 (43402-0012)
PHONE................................419 354-8207
Kenneth Stinehart, *Pr*
EMP: 8 **EST:** 2005
SALES (est): 690K **Privately Held**
SIC: 3646 Commercial lighting fixtures

(G-1579)
O D L LLC
19260 Dunbridge Rd (43402-9105)
PHONE................................419 833-2533
David Eckel, *Prin*
EMP: 6 **EST:** 2010
SALES (est): 58.02K **Privately Held**
SIC: 3714 Motor vehicle parts and accessories

(G-1580)
P-MAC LTD
14208 Cross Creek Rd (43402-9434)
PHONE................................419 235-2245
Pat Mcclure, *Prin*
EMP: 6 **EST:** 2010
SALES (est): 247.76K **Privately Held**
SIC: 3324 Steel investment foundries

(G-1581)
PALM PLASTICS LTD
843 Miller Dr (43402-8601)
PHONE................................561 776-6700
EMP: 7 **EST:** 2017
SALES (est): 86.67K **Privately Held**
SIC: 3843 Dental equipment and supplies

(G-1582)
PALMER BROS TRANSIT MIX CON (PA)
Also Called: Fostoria Concrete
12205 E Gypsy Lane Rd (43402-9516)
PHONE................................419 352-4681
Randolph G Schmeltz, *Pr*
Jesse Schmeltz, *VP*
EMP: 15 **EST:** 1974
SQ FT: 2,000
SALES (est): 5.86MM
SALES (corp-wide): 5.86MM **Privately Held**
SIC: 3273 Ready-mixed concrete

(G-1583)
PHOENIX TECHNOLOGIES INTL LLC (HQ)
Also Called: Pti
1098 Fairview Ave (43402-1233)
PHONE................................419 353-7738
Thomas E Brady, *Managing Member*
▲ **EMP:** 50 **EST:** 1992
SQ FT: 100,000
SALES (est): 32.1MM **Privately Held**
Web: www.phoenixtechnologies.net
SIC: 3085 5169 Plastics bottles; Synthetic resins, rubber, and plastic materials
PA: Far Eastern New Century Corporation
36f, No. 207, Dunhua S. Rd., Sec. 2
Taipei City TAP 10605

(G-1584)
PINNACLE INDUSTRIAL ENTPS INC
Also Called: Pinnacle Plastic Products
513 Napoleon Rd (43402-4822)
P.O. Box 286 (43402-0286)
PHONE................................419 352-8688
Kevin J Tearney, *Pr*
Gary Gratop, *
Mike Hagen, *
▲ **EMP:** 125 **EST:** 1995
SQ FT: 90,000
SALES (est): 23.12MM **Privately Held**
Web: www.pinnacleplasticproducts.com
SIC: 3089 Injection molding of plastics

(G-1585)
PIONEER PACKING CO
510 Napoleon Rd (43402-4821)
P.O. Box 171 (43402-0171)
PHONE................................419 352-5283
Brian Contris, *Pr*
EMP: 70 **EST:** 1945
SQ FT: 30,000
SALES (est): 5.27MM **Privately Held**
Web: www.pioneerpacking.com
SIC: 2011 Meat packing plants

(G-1586)
PRINCIPLE BUSINESS ENTPS INC (PA)
Also Called: Tranquility
20189 Pine Lake Rd (43402-4091)
P.O. Box 129 (43414-0129)
PHONE................................419 352-1551
Andrew Stocking, *Pr*
Carol Stocking, *Vice Chairman**
Charles A Stocking, *
Michael Kirby, *
Chuck Tull, *
▲ **EMP:** 200 **EST:** 1961
SQ FT: 105,000
SALES (est): 87.38MM
SALES (corp-wide): 87.38MM **Privately Held**
Web: www.principlebusinessenterprises.com
SIC: 2676 3142 Diapers, paper (disposable): made from purchased paper; House slippers

(G-1587)
RECLAMATION TECHNOLOGIES INC
Also Called: Remtec International
1100 Haskins Rd (43402-9363)
PHONE................................800 372-1301
◆ **EMP:** 38
SIC: 2869 Freon

(G-1588)
REGAL BELOIT AMERICA INC
Marathon Special Products
427 Van Camp Rd (43402-9020)
P.O. Box 468 (43402-0468)
PHONE................................419 352-8441
Larry Minnich, *Genl Mgr*
EMP: 200
SALES (corp-wide): 6.25B **Publicly Held**
Web: www.marathonsp.com
SIC: 3613 3644 Fuse mountings, electric power; Noncurrent-carrying wiring devices
HQ: Regal Beloit America, Inc.
111 W Michigan St
Milwaukee WI 53203
608 364-8800

(G-1589)
SOUTHEASTERN CONTAINER INC
307 Industrial Pkwy (43402-1347)
PHONE................................419 352-6300
John Johnson, *Brnch Mgr*
EMP: 61
SALES (corp-wide): 319.93MM **Privately Held**
Web: www.secontainer.com
SIC: 3085 3089 Plastics bottles; Plastics containers, except foam
PA: Southeastern Container, Inc.
1250 Sand Hill Rd
Enka NC 28728
828 350-7200

(G-1590)
TBT HAULING LLC
500 Lehman Ave Ste 103 (43402-3068)
PHONE................................904 635-7631
EMP: 6 **EST:** 2021
SALES (est): 502.96K **Privately Held**
SIC: 3537 Trucks: freight, baggage, etc.: industrial, except mining

(G-1591)
TH PLASTICS INC
843 Miller Dr (43402-8601)
PHONE................................419 352-2770
Patrick Haas, *Owner*
EMP: 78
SALES (corp-wide): 94.97MM **Privately Held**

(PA)=Parent Co (HQ)=Headquarters
✪ = New Business established in last 2 years

Bowling Green - Wood County (G-1592)   **GEOGRAPHIC SECTION**

Web: www.thplastics.com
SIC: 3089 Injection molding of plastics
PA: Th Plastics, Inc.
   106 E Main St
   Mendon MI 49072
   269 496-8495

(G-1592)
TOLEDO MOLDING & DIE LLC
515 E Gypsy Lane Rd (43402-8739)
PHONE.................................419 354-6050
Tom Pasche, *Mgr*
EMP: 127
Web: www.tmdinc.com
SIC: 3089 Injection molding of plastics
HQ: Toledo Molding & Die, Llc
   1429 Coining Dr
   Toledo OH 43612

(G-1593)
TRENCHLESS RSRCES GLOBL HLDNGS
Also Called: Vylon Pipe
420 Industrial Pkwy (43402-1326)
PHONE.................................419 419-6498
George Foos, *CEO*
EMP: 11 EST: 2018
SALES (est): 1.82MM **Privately Held**
Web: www.vylonpipe.com
SIC: 3312 Pipes and tubes

(G-1594)
VEHTEK SYSTEMS INC
2125 Wood Bridge Blvd (43402-9164)
PHONE.................................419 373-8741
Christian Holzer, *Prin*
◆ EMP: 700 EST: 2004
SALES (est): 103.18MM
SALES (corp-wide): 37.84B **Privately Held**
SIC: 3465 Body parts, automobile: stamped metal
PA: Magna International Inc
   337 Magna Dr
   Aurora ON L4G 7
   905 726-2462

(G-1595)
VITAL & FHR NORTH AMERICA LLC
1201 Brim Rd (43402-9393)
PHONE.................................650 405-9975
Feng Xiong, *Managing Member*
EMP: 35
SALES (est): 3.04MM **Privately Held**
SIC: 3399 Primary metal products

(G-1596)
WOOD COUNTY OHIO
Also Called: Laser Cartridge Express
991 S Main St (43402-4708)
PHONE.................................419 353-1227
Gaile Brooker, *Mgr*
EMP: 8
SALES (corp-wide): 130MM **Privately Held**
Web: www.woodcountydd.org
SIC: 3955 Print cartridges for laser and other computer printers
PA: County Of Wood
   1 Courthouse Sq
   Bowling Green OH 43402
   419 354-9100

(G-1597)
XORB CORPORATION
455 W Woodland Cir (43402-8834)
PHONE.................................419 354-6021
Ralph Temple, *Pr*
Paul Dunlavey, *Sec*
EMP: 7 EST: 1992
SQ FT: 10,000
SALES (est): 1.33MM **Privately Held**
Web: www.xorbcorp.com
SIC: 3826 Analytical instruments

(G-1598)
ZERES INC
2018 Clearwater Cir (43402-8778)
P.O. Box 487 (43402-0487)
PHONE.................................419 354-5555
EMP: 26 EST: 1984
SALES (est): 3.91MM **Privately Held**
Web: www.zeresinc.com
SIC: 2893 Printing ink

Bradford
Miami County

(G-1599)
BOSCOTT METALS INC
Also Called: Boscott
138 S Miami Ave (45308-1321)
P.O. Box 23 (45308-0023)
PHONE.................................937 448-2018
Mark Quinner, *Pr*
EMP: 27 EST: 1935
SQ FT: 20,000
SALES (est): 1.31MM **Privately Held**
SIC: 3365 Aluminum and aluminum-based alloy castings

(G-1600)
C F POEPPELMAN INC (PA)
Also Called: Pepcon Concrete
4755 N State Route 721 (45308-9425)
PHONE.................................937 448-2191
James Poeppelman, *Pr*
Fred Poeppelman, *VP*
EMP: 20 EST: 1950
SQ FT: 1,500
SALES (est): 4.42MM
SALES (corp-wide): 4.42MM **Privately Held**
Web: www.poeppelmanmaterials.com
SIC: 3273 1442 Ready-mixed concrete; Construction sand and gravel

(G-1601)
PRODUCTION PAINT FINISHERS INC
Also Called: P P F
140 Center St (45308-1202)
P.O. Box 127 (45308-0127)
PHONE.................................937 448-2627
Kenneth L Robertson, *Prin*
Lawrence F Francis, *
Allen J Francis, *
Russell Francis, *
Barbara Francis, *
EMP: 80 EST: 1970
SQ FT: 67,000
SALES (est): 9.42MM **Privately Held**
Web: www.productionpaint.com
SIC: 3479 Coating of metals and formed products

(G-1602)
TWENTY ONE BARRELS LTD
9717 Horatio Harris Creek Rd (45308-9686)
PHONE.................................937 467-4498
Danielle Pierce, *CEO*
EMP: 8 EST: 2020
SALES (est): 100K **Privately Held**
Web: www.21barrels.com
SIC: 2084 Wines

Bradner
Wood County

(G-1603)
MESTEK INC
America Wariming & Ventraling
120 Plin St (43406-7735)
P.O. Box 677 (43406-0677)
PHONE.................................419 288-2703
Todd Whightman, *Brnch Mgr*
EMP: 10
SALES (corp-wide): 689.94MM **Privately Held**
Web: www.mestek.com
SIC: 3822 3564 3444 3442 Hardware for environmental regulators; Blowers and fans ; Sheet metalwork; Metal doors, sash, and trim
PA: Mestek, Inc.
   260 N Elm St
   Westfield MA 01085
   413 568-9571

Brecksville
Cuyahoga County

(G-1604)
AB RESOURCES LLC
6802 W Snowville Rd Ste E (44141-3296)
PHONE.................................440 922-1098
EMP: 25 EST: 2005
SQ FT: 7,500
SALES (est): 2.17MM **Privately Held**
Web: www.abresourcesllc.com
SIC: 1382 Oil and gas exploration services

(G-1605)
AGRANA FRUIT US INC (DH)
6850 Southpointe Pkwy (44141-3260)
PHONE.................................440 546-1199
◆ EMP: 50 EST: 1977
SALES (est): 65.58MM
SALES (corp-wide): 68.66MM **Privately Held**
Web: us.agrana.com
SIC: 2087 Flavoring extracts and syrups, nec
HQ: Agrana Fruit Austria Gmbh
   MuhlwaldstraBe 1
   Gleisdorf 8200
   311222260

(G-1606)
APPLIED MEDICAL TECHNOLOGY INC
Also Called: Amt
8006 Katherine Blvd (44141-4202)
PHONE.................................440 717-4000
George J Picha, *Pr*
Robert J Crump, *
EMP: 30 EST: 1979
SQ FT: 14,000
SALES (est): 8.21MM **Privately Held**
Web: www.appliedmedical.net
SIC: 3841 3083 8731 Surgical and medical instruments; Laminated plastics plate and sheet; Medical research, commercial

(G-1607)
BARNES GROUP INC
Also Called: Hyson Products
10367 Brecksville Rd (44141-3335)
PHONE.................................440 526-5900
Mike Gaudiani, *Brnch Mgr*
EMP: 8
SQ FT: 53,593
SALES (corp-wide): 1.26B **Publicly Held**
Web: www.onebarnes.com
SIC: 3469 3495 Metal stampings, nec; Wire springs
PA: Barnes Group Inc.
   123 Main St
   Bristol CT 06010
   860 583-7070

(G-1608)
BENJAMIN MEDIA INC
10050 Brecksville Rd (44141-3219)
P.O. Box 190 (44264-0190)
PHONE.................................330 467-7588
Bernard P Krzys, *Pr*
▲ EMP: 28 EST: 1992
SQ FT: 2,744
SALES (est): 5.01MM **Privately Held**
Web: www.benjaminmedia.com
SIC: 2721 Trade journals: publishing and printing

(G-1609)
BLACK BOX CORPORATION
6650 W Snowville Rd Ste R (44141-4301)
PHONE.................................800 676-8850
Randy Reffert, *Brnch Mgr*
EMP: 10
Web: www.blackbox.com
SIC: 3577 Computer peripheral equipment, nec
HQ: Black Box Corporation
   1000 Park Dr
   Lawrence PA 15055
   724 746-5500

(G-1610)
BRECKSVLL-BRDVIEW HTS GZTTE IN
Also Called: Parma Seven Hills Gazette
7014 Mill Rd (44141-1814)
PHONE.................................440 526-7977
Joyce Mcfadden, *Pr*
EMP: 7 EST: 1975
SQ FT: 816
SALES (est): 398.41K **Privately Held**
Web: www.gazette-news.com
SIC: 2711 Newspapers, publishing and printing

(G-1611)
CURTISS-WRIGHT FLOW CONTROL
Also Called: Sprague Products
10195 Brecksville Rd (44141-3205)
PHONE.................................440 838-7690
EMP: 30
SQ FT: 77,847
SALES (corp-wide): 2.85B **Publicly Held**
Web: www.curtisswright.com
SIC: 3491 Industrial valves
HQ: Curtiss-Wright Flow Control Corporation
   1966 Broadhollow Rd Ste E
   Farmingdale NY 11735
   631 293-3800

(G-1612)
DEMATIC CORP
6930 Treeline Dr (44141-3367)
PHONE.................................440 526-2770
John Baysore, *Pr*
EMP: 95
SALES (corp-wide): 12.43B **Privately Held**
Web: www.dematic.com
SIC: 3535 Conveyors and conveying equipment
HQ: Dematic Corp.
   756 W Peachtree St Nw
   Atlanta GA 30308

GEOGRAPHIC SECTION

Bremen - Fairfield County (G-1639)

(G-1613)
DIRECT DISPOSABLES LLC
10605 Snowville Rd (44141-3446)
P.O. Box 470451 (44147-0451)
PHONE.................................440 717-3335
EMP: 7 **EST:** 2000
SALES (est): 485.26K **Privately Held**
Web: www.directdisposables.com
SIC: 2389 Disposable garments and accessories

(G-1614)
DONLON MANUFACTURING LLC
10680 Springhill Dr (44141-3536)
P.O. Box 41034 (44141-0034)
PHONE.................................847 437-7360
Daniel M Ferrara, *Prin*
EMP: 6 **EST:** 2014
SALES (est): 422.31K **Privately Held**
SIC: 3999 Manufacturing industries, nec

(G-1615)
EAGLESTONE PRODUCTS LLC
8057 Amber Ln (44141-1915)
PHONE.................................440 463-8715
Stephen C Hudak, *Managing Member*
EMP: 9 **EST:** 2002
SALES (est): 504.06K **Privately Held**
Web: www.eaglestoneproducts.com
SIC: 3993 Signs and advertising specialties

(G-1616)
EXACT CUTTING SERVICE INC
Also Called: Experimental Machine
6892 W Snowville Rd Ste 108 (44141)
P.O. Box 470535 (44147-0535)
PHONE.................................440 546-1319
Jerry Narduzzi, *Pr*
▲ **EMP:** 25 **EST:** 1974
SQ FT: 20,000
SALES (est): 338.24K **Privately Held**
Web: www.exactcut.com
SIC: 7389 3599 Metal cutting services; Machine shop, jobbing and repair

(G-1617)
FULTON MANUFACTURING INDS LLC
6600 W Snowville Rd # 6500 (44141-3257)
EMP: 34 **EST:** 2004
SQ FT: 55,000
SALES (est): 4.67MM **Privately Held**
SIC: 3469 Metal stampings, nec

(G-1618)
GLOBAL LIGHTING TECH INC
55 Andrews Cir Ste 1 (44141-3269)
PHONE.................................440 922-4584
Jeffery Parker, *Pr*
Michael Mayer, *General Vice President**
▲ **EMP:** 24 **EST:** 2000
SQ FT: 16,500
SALES (est): 8.59MM **Privately Held**
Web: www.glthome.com
SIC: 3648 3993 Lighting equipment, nec; Signs and advertising specialties
PA: Global Lighting Technologies Inc.
  C/O: Maples & Calder Limited
  George Town GR CAYMAN

(G-1619)
GLOBAL PLASTIC TECH INC
7762 Sunstone Dr (44141-2170)
PHONE.................................330 963-6830
Daryl F Wene, *Pr*
EMP: 25 **EST:** 1994
SQ FT: 12,000
SALES (est): 2.3MM **Privately Held**
SIC: 3089 Injection molded finished plastics products, nec

(G-1620)
HOMBRE CAPITAL INC
5945 W Snowville Rd (44141-3266)
PHONE.................................440 838-5335
Jim Urbanski, *Pr*
EMP: 10 **EST:** 1991
SQ FT: 24,000
SALES (est): 2.5MM **Privately Held**
Web: info.triadtechnologies.com
SIC: 3492 5074 Hose and tube fittings and assemblies, hydraulic/pneumatic; Plumbing and heating valves

(G-1621)
INDUSTRIAL MFG CO LLC (HQ)
8223 Brecksville Rd Ste 100 (44141)
PHONE.................................440 838-4700
◆ **EMP:** 10 **EST:** 1979
SQ FT: 4,700
SALES (est): 458.33MM
SALES (corp-wide): 541.5MM **Privately Held**
Web: www.mfgco.com
SIC: 2542 3728 3566 Lockers (not refrigerated): except wood; Aircraft body and wing assemblies and parts; Speed changers, drives, and gears
PA: Summa Holdings, Inc.
  8223 Brecksville Rd # 100
  Cleveland OH 44141
  440 838-4700

(G-1622)
INTEGRATED CHEM CONCEPTS INC
Also Called: ICC
6650 W Snowville Rd Ste F (44141-4301)
PHONE.................................440 838-5666
EMP: 9 **EST:** 1989
SQ FT: 9,300
SALES (est): 809K **Privately Held**
Web: www.integratedchemicalconcepts.com
SIC: 2821 Plastics materials and resins

(G-1623)
JCB ARROWHEAD PRODUCTS INC
8223 Brecksville Rd Ste 100 (44141-1371)
PHONE.................................440 546-4288
EMP: 8 **EST:** 2016
SALES (est): 370.02K **Privately Held**
SIC: 3728 Aircraft parts and equipment, nec

(G-1624)
JOHNSON CONTROLS INC
Also Called: Johnson Controls
6650 W Snowville Rd (44141-4301)
PHONE.................................216 587-0100
Todd Van Denbusche, *Prin*
EMP: 33
Web: www.johnsoncontrols.com
SIC: 2531 Seats, automobile
HQ: Johnson Controls, Inc.
  5757 N Green Bay Ave
  Milwaukee WI 53209
  920 245-6409

(G-1625)
LUBRIZOL ADVANCED MTLS INC (HQ)
9911 Brecksville Rd (44141-3201)
PHONE.................................216 447-5000
Arnau Pano, *Pr*
EMP: 16 **EST:** 2000
SALES (est): 23.45MM
SALES (corp-wide): 364.48B **Publicly Held**
Web: www.lubrizol.com
SIC: 2899 Chemical preparations, nec
PA: Berkshire Hathaway Inc.
  3555 Farnam St Ste 1440
  Omaha NE 68131
  402 346-1400

(G-1626)
LUBRIZOL CORPORATION
9921 Brecksville Rd (44141-3201)
PHONE.................................216 447-5447
EMP: 12 **EST:** 2019
SALES (est): 1.11MM **Privately Held**
Web: www.lubrizol.com
SIC: 2899 Chemical preparations, nec

(G-1627)
MILO FAMILY VINEYARDS LTD
8869 Brecksville Rd Ste A (44141-1945)
PHONE.................................440 922-0190
Loretta Dichiro, *Prin*
EMP: 6 **EST:** 2016
SALES (est): 79.45K **Privately Held**
SIC: 2084 Wines

(G-1628)
NATURES OWN SOURCE LLC
7033 Mill Rd (44141-1813)
PHONE.................................440 838-5135
EMP: 8 **EST:** 2013
SALES (est): 820K **Privately Held**
Web: www.naturesownsource.com
SIC: 2899 Desalter kits, sea water

(G-1629)
NAUTICUS INC
8080 Snowville Rd (44141-3413)
PHONE.................................440 746-1290
John Agro, *Pr*
John Deagro, *Pr*
▲ **EMP:** 6 **EST:** 1998
SALES (est): 500.06K **Privately Held**
Web: www.nauticusinc.com
SIC: 3732 Motorized boat, building and repairing

(G-1630)
RBR ENTERPRISES LLC
Also Called: Hudson Workwear
6910 Miller Rd (44141-3227)
PHONE.................................866 437-9327
Heidi Sweeney, *Managing Member*
EMP: 11 **EST:** 2000
SALES (est): 1.27MM **Privately Held**
Web: www.hudsonworkwear.com
SIC: 5136 5137 5699 3143 Apparel belts, men's and boys'; Apparel belts, women's and children's; Uniforms and work clothing; Work shoes, men's

(G-1631)
SUMMIT AEROSPACE PRODUCT CORP
10250 Brecksville Rd (44141-3342)
PHONE.................................440 652-6829
EMP: 7 **EST:** 2017
SALES (est): 500.43K **Privately Held**
Web: www.summitapc.com
SIC: 3728 Aircraft parts and equipment, nec

(G-1632)
SYSTEM SEALS INC
6600 W Snowville Rd (44141-3257)
PHONE.................................216 220-1800
EMP: 28
SALES (corp-wide): 1.01MM **Privately Held**
Web: www.systemseals.com
SIC: 3953 5084 Embossing seals and hand stamps; Hydraulic systems equipment and supplies
HQ: System Seals, Inc.
  9505 Midwest Ave
  Cleveland OH 44125

(G-1633)
TELEHEALTH CARE SOLUTIONS LLC
2551 Sweetwater Dr (44141-4102)
PHONE.................................440 823-6023
James Cireddu, *Prin*
EMP: 7 **EST:** 2013
SALES (est): 370K **Privately Held**
SIC: 7372 Publisher's computer software

(G-1634)
TEREX SERVICES
6400 W Snowville Rd Ste 1 (44141-3248)
PHONE.................................440 262-3200
EMP: 6 **EST:** 2013
SALES (est): 67.5K **Privately Held**
SIC: 7692 Welding repair

(G-1635)
TEST-FUCHS CORPORATION
10325 Brecksville Rd (44141-3335)
PHONE.................................440 708-3505
Peter Barnhart, *CEO*
EMP: 8 **EST:** 2017
SQ FT: 168
SALES (est): 1.96MM **Privately Held**
Web: www.test-fuchs.com
SIC: 3826 3829 3728 Analytical instruments; Measuring and controlling devices, nec; Military aircraft equipment and armament

(G-1636)
TRACKER MANAGEMENT SYSTEMS
10091 Brecksville Rd (44141-3396)
PHONE.................................800 445-2438
James Weaver, *Pr*
Terri Weaver, *VP*
EMP: 7 **EST:** 1984
SALES (est): 1.14MM **Privately Held**
Web: www.traxero.com
SIC: 7372 Business oriented computer software

(G-1637)
WICKED PREMIUMS LLC
8748 Brecksville Rd Ste 224 (44141-1986)
PHONE.................................216 364-0322
Ken Chelko, *Prin*
EMP: 6 **EST:** 2013
SALES (est): 73.66K **Privately Held**
Web: www.wickedpremiums.com
SIC: 2752 Commercial printing, lithographic

Bremen
Fairfield County

(G-1638)
INLINE UNDGRD HRZNTAL DRCTNAL
Also Called: Inline Underground Hdd
5440 Marietta Rd Sw (43107-9503)
PHONE.................................740 808-0316
Steven Thompson, *Prin*
EMP: 8 **EST:** 2020
SALES (est): 437.62K **Privately Held**
Web: www.inlinehdd.com
SIC: 1389 Construction, repair, and dismantling services

(G-1639)
STUART BURIAL VAULT CO INC
527 Ford St (43107-1111)
P.O. Box 146 (43107-0146)
PHONE.................................740 569-4158
John A Boone, *Pr*
Mary Lyle Boone, *VP*
EMP: 25 **EST:** 1919
SQ FT: 16,500
SALES (est): 1.22MM **Privately Held**
Web: www.stuartburialvaults.com

Bremen - Fairfield County (G-1640)

SIC: 3272 Burial vaults, concrete or precast terrazzo

(G-1640)
WESTERMAN INC (PA)
245 N Broad St (43107-1003)
P.O. Box 125 (43107-0125)
PHONE...................................800 338-8265
John Moorefield, *Ch*
Jacob Garrett, *
Nick Chrzanowski, *
Dave Cline, *
Brian Kariker, *
◆ EMP: 185 EST: 1957
SQ FT: 150,000
SALES (est): 126.49MM
SALES (corp-wide): 126.49MM Privately Held
Web: www.westermaninc.com
SIC: 3825 1389 Electrical energy measuring equipment; Oil field services, nec

(G-1641)
WORTHINGTON CYLINDER CORP
245 N Broad St (43107-1003)
P.O. Box 125 (43107-0125)
PHONE...................................740 569-4143
EMP: 95
SALES (corp-wide): 4.92B Publicly Held
Web: www.worthingtonenterprises.com
SIC: 3443 Cylinders, pressure: metal plate
HQ: Worthington Cylinder Corporation
200 W Old Wilson Bridge Rd
Worthington OH 43085
614 840-3210

Brewster
Stark County

(G-1642)
BREWSTER CHEESE COMPANY (PA)
Also Called: Brewster Cheese
800 Wabash Ave S (44613-1464)
PHONE...................................330 767-3492
Fritz Leeman, *CEO*
Thomas Murphy, *
Emil Alecusan, *
▼ EMP: 200 EST: 1964
SQ FT: 78,914
SALES (est): 136.03MM
SALES (corp-wide): 136.03MM Privately Held
Web: www.brewstercheese.com
SIC: 2022 Natural cheese

(G-1643)
BREWSTER SUGARCREEK TWP HISTO
Also Called: BREWSTER HISTORICAL SOCIETY
45 Wabash Ave S (44613-1210)
PHONE...................................330 767-0045
Robert Lucking, *Owner*
EMP: 10 EST: 1976
SQ FT: 3,196
SALES (est): 515.12K Privately Held
SIC: 3732 8412 Boat kits, not models; Museum

(G-1644)
L & J DRIVE THRU LLC
212 Wabash Ave N (44613-1040)
PHONE...................................330 767-2185
EMP: 6 EST: 2007
SALES (est): 232.14K Privately Held
SIC: 2086 Carbonated beverages, nonalcoholic: pkged. in cans, bottles

(G-1645)
MICRO MACHINE LTD
275 7th St Sw (44613-1457)
PHONE...................................330 438-7078
Ronald Pollock, *Pt*
Harold Byer, *Pt*
EMP: 7 EST: 2001
SALES (est): 466.12K Privately Held
SIC: 3599 Machine shop, jobbing and repair

(G-1646)
SHEARERS FOODS LLC
Also Called: Shearer's Snacks
692 Wabash Ave N (44613-1020)
PHONE...................................330 767-3426
Angie Hostetler, *Brnch Mgr*
EMP: 7
SALES (corp-wide): 14.52B Privately Held
Web: www.shearers.com
SIC: 2096 Potato chips and similar snacks
HQ: Shearer's Foods, Llc
100 Lincoln Way E
Massillon OH 44646
800 428-6843

Bridgeport
Belmont County

(G-1647)
JERRY HAROLDS DOORS UNLIMITED
Also Called: Doors Unlimited
415 Hall St (43912-1343)
PHONE...................................740 635-4949
Jerry Brocht, *Pr*
Harold Games, *VP*
EMP: 7 EST: 1987
SQ FT: 1,600
SALES (est): 967.65K Privately Held
Web: www.doorsunlimited.net
SIC: 5031 3446 5211 Doors, nec; Architectural metalwork; Garage doors, sale and installation

(G-1648)
RECON
54382 National Rd (43912-9804)
PHONE...................................740 609-3050
Ray Hieronymus, *Pr*
EMP: 99 EST: 2017
SALES (est): 8.69MM Privately Held
Web: www.reconoilfieldservices.com
SIC: 1389 Oil field services, nec

(G-1649)
SKYLINER
225 Main St (43912-1345)
PHONE...................................740 738-0874
Donald Rhodes, *Owner*
Robyn Rhodes, *Prin*
Witney Stewski, *Prin*
EMP: 8 EST: 2015
SALES (est): 144.3K Privately Held
SIC: 7299 2051 Party planning service; Bakery: wholesale or wholesale/retail combined

(G-1650)
TRIPLE J OILFIELD SERVICES LLC
54382 National Rd (43912-9804)
PHONE...................................740 609-3050
EMP: 7 EST: 2010
SALES (est): 448.18K Privately Held
Web: www.reconoilfieldservices.com
SIC: 1389 Oil field services, nec

Brilliant
Jefferson County

(G-1651)
STEEL VALLEY TANK & WELDING
24 County Road 7e (43913-1079)
P.O. Box 8 (43913-0008)
PHONE...................................740 598-4994
Gary Kessler, *Owner*
EMP: 10 EST: 1987
SALES (est): 897.94K Privately Held
SIC: 3443 Industrial vessels, tanks, and containers

Bristolville
Trumbull County

(G-1652)
K M B INC
Also Called: King Bros Feed & Supply
1306 State Route 88 (44402-8743)
P.O. Box 240 (44402-0240)
PHONE...................................330 889-3451
Marlene King, *Pr*
Rex King, *
EMP: 26 EST: 1956
SQ FT: 4,200
SALES (est): 778.28K Privately Held
SIC: 3273 5211 5261 5191 Ready-mixed concrete; Lumber and other building materials; Fertilizer; Feed

(G-1653)
MAHAN PACKING CO
6540 State Route 45 (44402-9730)
PHONE...................................330 889-2454
K Ray Mahan, *Pr*
Nancy Mahan, *
EMP: 17 EST: 1958
SQ FT: 15,000
SALES (est): 756.49K Privately Held
Web: mahan-packing.edan.io
SIC: 2011 Meat packing plants

Broadview Heights
Cuyahoga County

(G-1654)
10155 BROADVIEW BUSINESS
10155 Broadview Rd (44147-3296)
PHONE...................................440 546-1901
David M Leneghan, *Prin*
EMP: 7 EST: 2007
SALES (est): 125.12K Privately Held
Web: www.statesharp.com
SIC: 3629 Power conversion units, a.c. to d.c.: static-electric

(G-1655)
BECKERS BAKE SHOP INC
436 Countryside Dr (44147-3413)
PHONE...................................216 752-4161
Joe J Becker, *Pr*
Jaean Becker, *Asst VP*
EMP: 9 EST: 1973
SALES (est): 225.42K Privately Held
Web: www.beckersbakeshop.com
SIC: 2051 2052 Cakes, bakery: except frozen ; Cookies

(G-1656)
BENJAMIN P FORBES COMPANY
Also Called: Forbes Chocolate
800 Ken Mar Industrial Pkwy (44147-2922)
PHONE...................................440 838-4400
Keith Geringer, *Pr*
▲ EMP: 13 EST: 1913
SQ FT: 16,687
SALES (est): 8.7MM Privately Held
Web: www.forbeschocolate.com
SIC: 2066 Powdered cocoa

(G-1657)
CHICAGO PNEUMATIC TOOL CO LLC
9100 Market Pl Rear (44147-2861)
PHONE...................................704 883-3500
EMP: 18
SALES (corp-wide): 13.47B Privately Held
Web: www.cp.com
SIC: 3546 Power-driven handtools
HQ: Chicago Pneumatic Tool Company Llc
1815 Clubhouse Dr
Rock Hill SC 29730
803 817-7100

(G-1658)
CLINICL OTCMS MNGMNT SYST LLC
Also Called: Coms Interactive
9200 S Hills Blvd Ste 200 (44147-3520)
PHONE...................................330 650-9900
EMP: 59 EST: 2009
SQ FT: 1,400
SALES (est): 8.14MM
SALES (corp-wide): 77.37MM Privately Held
SIC: 7372 Business oriented computer software
HQ: Pointclickcare Technologies Inc
5570 Explorer Dr
Mississauga ON L4W 0
905 858-8885

(G-1659)
KEBAN INDUSTRIES INC
Also Called: Stefan Restoration
1263 Royalwood Rd (44147-1728)
PHONE...................................216 446-0159
Ken Stefan, *Prin*
EMP: 7 EST: 1997
SALES (est): 719.06K Privately Held
SIC: 3599 Custom machinery

(G-1660)
KONECRANES INC
Also Called: Crane Pro Services
331 Treeworth Blvd (44147-2985)
PHONE...................................440 461-8400
EMP: 10
Web: www.konecranes.com
SIC: 3536 7389 Hoists, cranes, and monorails; Crane and aerial lift service
HQ: Konecranes, Inc.
4401 Gateway Blvd
Springfield OH 45502

(G-1661)
MANTRA HAIRCARE LLC
305 Ken Mar Industrial Pkwy (44147-2954)
PHONE...................................440 526-3304
EMP: 10 EST: 2007
SQ FT: 10,000
SALES (est): 331.14K Privately Held
SIC: 2844 Hair preparations, including shampoos

(G-1662)
NATIONAL POLISHING SYSTEMS INC
Also Called: NPS
9299 Market Pl (44147-2866)
PHONE...................................330 659-6547
Robert Tetmayer, *Pr*
EMP: 28 EST: 2007
SALES (est): 4.2MM Privately Held
Web: www.nationalpolishing.com
SIC: 3471 Cleaning, polishing, and finishing

GEOGRAPHIC SECTION

Brooklyn Heights - Cuyahoga County (G-1687)

(G-1663)
NELSON LABS FAIRFIELD INC
9100 S Hills Blvd (44147-3518)
PHONE......................973 227-6882
Daniel L Prince, *Pr*
EMP: 50 **EST:** 1970
SALES (est): 10.56MM
SALES (corp-wide): 1.05B **Publicly Held**
Web: www.nelsonlabs.com
SIC: 3841 8734 Diagnostic apparatus, medical; Testing laboratories
PA: Sotera Health Company
9100 S Hills Blvd Ste 300
Broadview Heights OH 44147
440 262-1410

(G-1664)
NRKA CORP
Also Called: Fastsigns
1100 W Royalton Rd Ste A (44147-3947)
PHONE......................440 817-0700
Bob Bottomley, *Prin*
EMP: 10 **EST:** 2017
SALES (est): 189.1K **Privately Held**
Web: www.fastsigns.com
SIC: 3993 Signs and advertising specialties

(G-1665)
OHIO MACHINERY CO (PA)
Also Called: Caterpillar Authorized Dealer
3993 E Royalton Rd (44147-2898)
PHONE......................440 526-6200
Ken Taylor, *Pr*
Paul Liesem, *
Kelly Love, *
Eric W Emch, *
David J Blocksom, *
◆ **EMP:** 160 **EST:** 1946
SQ FT: 92,000
SALES (est): 185.86MM
SALES (corp-wide): 185.86MM **Privately Held**
Web: www.ohiocat.com
SIC: 7513 6159 7699 5082 Truck rental, without drivers; Machinery and equipment finance leasing; Aircraft and heavy equipment repair services; General construction machinery and equipment

(G-1666)
SALTED DOUGH
9174 Broadview Rd (44147-2515)
PHONE......................216 288-2124
EMP: 6 **EST:** 2019
SALES (est): 837.33K **Privately Held**
Web: www.salteddough.com
SIC: 2024 Ice cream and frozen deserts

(G-1667)
SQUARE D SERVICES
2525 E Royalton Rd Ste 6 (44147-2842)
PHONE......................440 526-9070
Bill Mchenry, *Prin*
EMP: 6 **EST:** 2010
SALES (est): 149.84K **Privately Held**
SIC: 3699 Electrical equipment and supplies, nec

Brookfield
Trumbull County

(G-1668)
E-Z STOP SERVICE CENTER
Also Called: E-Z Label Co
354 Bedford Rd Se (44403-9727)
PHONE......................330 448-2236
Frank Zurawsky, *Pt*
Dave Zurawsky, *Pt*
EMP: 9 **EST:** 1979
SQ FT: 3,000
SALES (est): 381.95K **Privately Held**
SIC: 2754 2671 Labels: gravure printing; Paper; coated and laminated packaging

(G-1669)
ENREVO PYRO LLC
6874 Strimbu Dr (44403-9526)
PHONE......................203 517-5002
Philip Smith, *CEO*
EMP: 6 **EST:** 2012
SQ FT: 15,000
SALES (est): 341.19K **Privately Held**
SIC: 1311 2911 Coal pyrolysis; Fractionation products of crude petroleum, hydrocarbons, nec

(G-1670)
INDUSTRIAL TANK & CONTAINMENT
411 State Route 7 Se Ste 3 (44403-9555)
P.O. Box 267 (44403-0267)
PHONE......................330 448-4876
Raymond Graff, *Pr*
EMP: 10 **EST:** 2001
SQ FT: 10,000
SALES (est): 1.04MM **Privately Held**
Web: www.apitankrepair.com
SIC: 3443 Fabricated plate work (boiler shop)

(G-1671)
IPSCO TUBULARS INC
Also Called: IPSCO TUBULARS, INC.
6880 Parkway Dr (44403-9797)
PHONE......................330 448-6772
EMP: 51
Web: www.tenaris.com
SIC: 3498 Fabricated pipe and fittings
HQ: Ipsco Tubulars Inc.
2200 West Loop S Ste 800
Houston TX 77027

(G-1672)
PANELMATIC BLDG SOLUTIONS INC
6882 Parkway Dr (44403-9797)
PHONE......................330 619-5235
Richard Leach, *Prin*
Sean Fightmaster, *
Dan Vodhanel, *
EMP: 30 **EST:** 2019
SALES (est): 4.19MM
SALES (corp-wide): 56.9MM **Privately Held**
Web: www.panelmatic.com
SIC: 3613 Control panels, electric
PA: Panelmatic, Inc.
6806 Willow Brook Park
Houston TX 77066
888 757-1957

(G-1673)
SADAF OIL & GAS INC
7257 Warren Sharon Rd (44403-9628)
PHONE......................330 448-6631
Jean Wojton, *Mgr*
EMP: 6 **EST:** 2009
SALES (est): 257.22K **Privately Held**
SIC: 1382 Oil and gas exploration services

(G-1674)
SILCOR OILFIELD SERVICES INC
6874 Strimbu Dr (44403-9526)
PHONE......................330 448-8500
Terri D Presco, *Prin*
EMP: 15 **EST:** 1992
SALES (est): 935.72K **Privately Held**
SIC: 1382 Oil and gas exploration services

Brooklyn
Cuyahoga County

(G-1675)
AREWAY ACQUISITION INC
8525 Clinton Rd (44144-1014)
PHONE......................216 651-9022
John S Hadgis, *Pr*
John Hadgis, *
EMP: 99 **EST:** 2010
SQ FT: 100,000
SALES (est): 9.41MM **Privately Held**
SIC: 3471 Polishing, metals or formed products

(G-1676)
AREWAY LLC
8525 Clinton Rd (44144-1014)
PHONE......................216 651-9022
▲ **EMP:** 99 **EST:** 1967
SALES (est): 9.31MM **Privately Held**
SIC: 3714 3541 Motor vehicle engines and parts; Buffing and polishing machines

(G-1677)
ENESPRO PPE ✪
10601 Memphis Ave (44144-2053)
PHONE......................800 553-0672
EMP: 6 **EST:** 2023
SALES (est): 78.58K **Privately Held**
SIC: 3699 Electrical equipment and supplies, nec

(G-1678)
HMI INDUSTRIES INC (PA)
Also Called: Health-Mor
1 American Rd Ste 1250 (44144-2355)
PHONE......................440 846-7800
Daniel Duggan, *CEO*
Timothy Duggan, *VP*
Sorin Fulea, *Treas*
Ken Skoczen, *VP*
◆ **EMP:** 50 **EST:** 1928
SQ FT: 73,000
SALES (est): 22.67MM
SALES (corp-wide): 22.67MM **Privately Held**
Web: www.filterqueen.com
SIC: 3634 Air purifiers, portable

(G-1679)
MMI TEXTILES INC (PA)
Also Called: Ndw Textiles
1 American Rd Ste 950 (44144-2356)
PHONE......................440 899-8050
Amy Hammond, *Pr*
Kathleen Stevens, *CFO*
Nick Rivera, *COO*
▲ **EMP:** 7 **EST:** 2000
SQ FT: 5,000
SALES (est): 4.82MM **Privately Held**
Web: www.mmitextiles.com
SIC: 2211 2221 2262 5131 Duck, cotton; Manmade and synthetic broadwoven fabrics ; Chemical coating or treating of manmade broadwoven fabrics; Broadwoven fabrics

(G-1680)
MPC PLATING INC ✪
9921 Clinton Rd (44144-1035)
PHONE......................216 881-7220
EMP: 7 **EST:** 2022
SALES (est): 453.27K **Privately Held**
Web: www.mpcplating.com
SIC: 3471 Electroplating of metals or formed products

(G-1681)
RHINOSYSTEMS INC
Also Called: Navage
One American Way Ste 1100 (44144-2357)
PHONE......................216 351-6262
Martin Hoke, *Pr*
EMP: 10 **EST:** 2007
SQ FT: 9,000
SALES (est): 2.57MM **Privately Held**
Web: www.navage.com
SIC: 3841 Inhalation therapy equipment

Brooklyn Heights
Cuyahoga County

(G-1682)
APPLIED MATERIALS FINSHG LTD
1040 Valley Belt Rd (44131-1433)
PHONE......................330 336-5645
Faith Ortiz, *Prin*
EMP: 25 **EST:** 2012
SALES (est): 4.63MM **Privately Held**
SIC: 3341 Secondary nonferrous metals

(G-1683)
APPLIED METALS TECH LTD
1040 Valley Belt Rd (44131-1433)
PHONE......................216 741-3236
Lisa Virost, *Pr*
EMP: 47 **EST:** 2001
SQ FT: 30,000
SALES (est): 6.34MM **Privately Held**
Web: www.amtcleveland.com
SIC: 3471 Finishing, metals or formed products

(G-1684)
BEVERAGE ENGINEERING INC
4705 Van Epps Rd (44131-1013)
PHONE......................216 641-6678
Paul L Csank, *Managing Member*
EMP: 12 **EST:** 1987
SALES (est): 250.14K **Privately Held**
SIC: 3585 Beer dispensing equipment

(G-1685)
BRILLIANT ELECTRIC SIGN CO LTD
4811 Van Epps Rd (44131-1082)
PHONE......................216 741-3800
James R Groh, *Managing Member*
EMP: 55 **EST:** 1929
SQ FT: 55,000
SALES (est): 5.05MM **Privately Held**
Web: www.brilliantsign.com
SIC: 3993 1799 Electric signs; Sign installation and maintenance

(G-1686)
C T I AUDIO INC
220 Eastview Dr Ste 1 (44131-1039)
PHONE......................440 593-1111
William Ross, *Ch Bd*
EMP: 9 **EST:** 1987
SQ FT: 70,000
SALES (est): 204.03K **Privately Held**
SIC: 3651 Microphones

(G-1687)
CI DISPOSITION CO
1000 Valley Belt Rd (44131-1433)
PHONE......................216 587-5200
Gary Tarnowski, *VP*
EMP: 89 **EST:** 1952
SQ FT: 56,000
SALES (est): 2.07MM **Privately Held**
SIC: 3699 5085 Linear accelerators; Industrial supplies

Brooklyn Heights - Cuyahoga County (G-1688)

(G-1688)
COVENTYA INC
Also Called: COVENTYA, INC.
4639 Van Epps Rd Frnt (44131-1050)
PHONE..................315 768-6635
EMP: 17
SALES (corp-wide): 2.33B **Publicly Held**
Web: www.coventya.com
SIC: 2899 Plating compounds
HQ: Coventya Inc.
   132 Clear Rd
   Oriskany NY 13424
   216 351-1500

(G-1689)
DIE-MATIC CORPORATION
201 Eastview Dr (44131-1074)
PHONE..................216 749-4656
Louie J Zeitler, *CEO*
Jerry Zeitler, *
John A Gorman, *
Cynthia Graor, *Stockholder*
▲ EMP: 55 EST: 1958
SQ FT: 120,000
SALES (est): 15.47MM **Privately Held**
Web: www.die-matic.com
SIC: 3469 3544 Stamping metal for the trade; Special dies, tools, jigs, and fixtures

(G-1690)
DIGICOM INC
5405 Valley Belt Rd Ste A (44131-1470)
PHONE..................216 642-3838
EMP: 10 EST: 1985
SALES (est): 223.36K **Privately Held**
SIC: 2711 2732 Commercial printing and newspaper publishing combined; Pamphlets: printing only, not published on site

(G-1691)
GRAFTECH INTERNATIONAL LTD (PA)
Also Called: Graftech International
982 Keynote Cir Ste 6 (44131)
PHONE..................216 676-2000
EMP: 91 EST: 1886
SALES (est): 620.5MM **Publicly Held**
Web: graftech2022cr.q4web.com
SIC: 3624 Carbon and graphite products

(G-1692)
GRAFTECH INTL HOLDINGS INC (HQ)
Also Called: UCAR Carbon
982 Keynote Cir Ste 6 (44131-1872)
PHONE..................216 676-2000
David Rintaul, *CEO*
◆ EMP: 197 EST: 1988
SQ FT: 10,000
SALES (est): 135.5MM **Publicly Held**
Web: graftech2022cr.q4web.com
SIC: 3624 Electrodes, thermal and electrolytic uses: carbon, graphite
PA: Graftech International Ltd.
   982 Keynote Cir
   Brooklyn Heights OH 44131

(G-1693)
J & L BODY INC
4848 Van Epps Rd (44131-1016)
PHONE..................216 661-2323
Mike Litteria, *Pr*
Rosemary Nelson, *Sec*
Robert Daley, *VP*
EMP: 10 EST: 1963
SQ FT: 16,000
SALES (est): 785.03K **Privately Held**
Web: www.jlbody.com
SIC: 3715 7549 7539 Truck trailers; Trailer maintenance; Trailer repair

(G-1694)
KWEEN AND CO
994 Valley Belt Rd (44131-1446)
PHONE..................440 724-4342
Alexandra Bonar, *CEO*
Alexandra Kathryn Bonar, *CEO*
EMP: 15 EST: 2019
SALES (est): 803.34K **Privately Held**
Web: www.oat.haus
SIC: 2045 2043 Bread and bread type roll mixes: from purchased flour; Cereal breakfast foods

(G-1695)
MIDWEST PRECISION
1000 Valley Belt Rd (44131-1433)
PHONE..................216 658-0058
EMP: 7 EST: 2014
SALES (est): 73.41K **Privately Held**
Web: www.midwestllc.com
SIC: 3599 Machine shop, jobbing and repair

(G-1696)
NORTH SHORE STRAPPING COMPANY (PA)
1400 Valley Belt Rd (44131-1441)
PHONE..................216 661-5200
Bridget A Leneghan, *Pr*
Kevin Leneghan, *
David M Leneghan, *
▲ EMP: 50 EST: 1982
SQ FT: 225,000
SALES (est): 8.04MM
SALES (corp-wide): 8.04MM **Privately Held**
Web: www.northshorestrapping.com
SIC: 3081 3499 3312 2992 Unsupported plastics film and sheet; Strapping, metal; Wire products, steel or iron; Lubricating oils and greases

(G-1697)
R&D MARKETING GROUP INC
Also Called: Proforma Signature Solutions
4597 Van Epps Rd (44131-1009)
PHONE..................216 398-9100
Dave Mader, *Pr*
Tony Zayas, *Dir*
EMP: 8 EST: 2011
SALES (est): 2.28MM **Privately Held**
Web: www.proforma-solutions.com
SIC: 6794 2759 2752 Franchises, selling or licensing; Commercial printing, nec; Commercial printing, lithographic

(G-1698)
REL ENTERPRISES INC (DH)
Also Called: Diversified Air Systems
4760 Van Epps Rd (44131-1014)
PHONE..................216 741-1700
Bob Lisi, *Pr*
Vincent Lisi, *Sec*
EMP: 20 EST: 1995
SQ FT: 20,000
SALES (est): 2.01MM **Privately Held**
Web: www.diversifiedair.com
SIC: 5084 5075 7694 Compressors, except air conditioning; Compressors, air conditioning; Armature rewinding shops
HQ: Motion & Control Enterprises Llc
   100 Williams Dr
   Zelienople PA 16063
   724 452-6000

(G-1699)
RS INDUSTRIES INC
1455 E Schaaf Rd (44131-1321)
PHONE..................216 351-8200
Nicholas J Russo Senior, *Pr*
Nick Russo Junior, *CFO*
EMP: 9 EST: 1987
SALES (est): 2.3MM **Privately Held**
Web: www.rsind.com
SIC: 5046 3556 Commercial cooking and food service equipment; Food products machinery

(G-1700)
SHIELDS WRIGHT RUBBER CO
4800 Van Epps Rd Ste 104 (44131-1059)
PHONE..................216 741-8200
Bill Wagner, *Prin*
EMP: 7 EST: 2010
SALES (est): 192.61K **Privately Held**
SIC: 3069 Fabricated rubber products, nec

(G-1701)
SIMS-LOHMAN INC
1500 Valley Belt Rd (44131-1450)
PHONE..................440 799-8285
EMP: 78
SALES (corp-wide): 96.65MM **Privately Held**
Web: www.sims-lohman.com
SIC: 3281 Cut stone and stone products
PA: Sims-Lohman, Inc.
   6325 Este Ave
   Cincinnati OH 45232
   513 651-3510

(G-1702)
TREK DIAGNOSTICS INC
982 Keynote Cir (44131-1872)
PHONE..................440 808-0000
EMP: 12 EST: 2017
SALES (est): 276.83K **Privately Held**
SIC: 3826 Analytical instruments

Brookpark
Cuyahoga County

(G-1703)
AMERICAN SOLVING INC
6519 Eastland Rd Ste 5 (44142-1347)
PHONE..................440 234-7373
Orley Aten, *Pr*
Julia Aten, *Treas*
▲ EMP: 6 EST: 1991
SQ FT: 5,000
SALES (est): 500.02K **Privately Held**
Web: www.solvinginc.com
SIC: 3535 5084 Pneumatic tube conveyor systems; Materials handling machinery

(G-1704)
AMPEX METAL PRODUCTS COMPANY (PA)
5581 W 164th St (44142-1513)
PHONE..................216 267-9242
Andrew S Pastor, *Pr*
Robert Pastor, *Product Vice President*
EMP: 55 EST: 1960
SQ FT: 24,000
SALES (est): 6.02MM
SALES (corp-wide): 6.02MM **Privately Held**
Web: www.ampexmetal.com
SIC: 3469 3544 3452 3429 Stamping metal for the trade; Special dies, tools, jigs, and fixtures; Bolts, nuts, rivets, and washers; Hardware, nec

(G-1705)
AZSR TECHNOLOGIES DISTR LLC
14380 Gallatin Blvd (44142-2511)
PHONE..................216 315-8285
EMP: 7
SALES (est): 78.58K **Privately Held**
SIC: 3559 7389 Electronic component making machinery; Business services, nec

(G-1706)
BACKATTACK SNACKS
5121 W 161st St (44142-1604)
PHONE..................216 236-4580
EMP: 6 EST: 2018
SALES (est): 186.4K **Privately Held**
Web: www.backattacksnacks.com
SIC: 2096 Potato chips and similar snacks

(G-1707)
CERAMIC HOLDINGS INC (DH)
Also Called: Cetek
20600 Sheldon Rd (44142-1312)
PHONE..................216 362-3900
Derek Scott, *Pr*
Kathlene Stevens, *
◆ EMP: 120 EST: 1981
SALES (est): 27.04MM **Privately Held**
Web: www.integratedglobal.com
SIC: 7629 7692 Electrical repair shops; Welding repair
HQ: Fosbel Holding, Inc.
   20600 Sheldon Rd
   Cleveland OH 44142

(G-1708)
CRITERION TOOL & DIE INC
Also Called: Criterion Instrument
5349 W 161st St (44142-1609)
PHONE..................216 267-1733
Tanya Disalvo, *Pr*
Dennis M Ondercin, *
Theodore D Ward, *
EMP: 40 EST: 1953
SQ FT: 20,000
SALES (est): 4.93MM **Privately Held**
Web: www.criteriontool.com
SIC: 3599 3544 3541 Machine shop, jobbing and repair; Special dies, tools, jigs, and fixtures; Machine tools, metal cutting type

(G-1709)
CUSTOM FLOATERS LLC
5161 W 161st St (44142-1604)
PHONE..................216 337-9118
Dianne Malone, *Admn*
EMP: 6 EST: 2012
SALES (est): 141.02K **Privately Held**
Web: www.customfloaters.com
SIC: 3465 Body parts, automobile: stamped metal

(G-1710)
CUSTOM FLOATERS LLC
6519 Eastland Rd Ste 101 (44142-1347)
PHONE..................216 536-8979
EMP: 10 EST: 2017
SALES (est): 954.3K **Privately Held**
Web: www.customfloaters.com
SIC: 3714 Motor vehicle parts and accessories

(G-1711)
CUYAHOGA MACHINE COMPANY LLC
5250 W 137th St (44142-1828)
PHONE..................216 267-3560
Irene Bogdan, *Managing Member*
Nona Betz, *Sec*
EMP: 19 EST: 2013
SALES (est): 956.59K **Privately Held**
Web: www.cuyahogamachine.com
SIC: 7699 3599 Industrial machinery and equipment repair; Machine shop, jobbing and repair

GEOGRAPHIC SECTION

Brookville - Montgomery County (G-1734)

(G-1712)
DD FOUNDRY INC (PA)
15583 Brookpark Rd (44142-1518)
PHONE..................216 362-4100
David Dolata, *CEO*
Jerry Kovatch, *
Mary Miller, *Stockholder*
Sandra Catlett, *
David Zanto, *
▲ **EMP:** 12 **EST:** 1946
SQ FT: 80,000
SALES (est): 23.75MM
SALES (corp-wide): 23.75MM **Privately Held**
SIC: 3364 3324 3369 3365 Nonferrous die-castings except aluminum; Commercial investment castings, ferrous; Nonferrous foundries, nec; Aluminum foundries

(G-1713)
E L MUSTEE & SONS INC (PA)
5431 W 164th St (44142-1586)
PHONE..................216 267-3100
Kevin Mustee, *Pr*
◆ **EMP:** 98 **EST:** 1932
SQ FT: 140,000
SALES (est): 15.87MM
SALES (corp-wide): 15.87MM **Privately Held**
Web: www.mustee.com
SIC: 3088 Tubs (bath, shower, and laundry), plastics

(G-1714)
ELGIN FASTENER GROUP
6519 Eastland Rd (44142-1347)
PHONE..................440 239-1165
EMP: 7
SALES (est): 152.51K **Privately Held**
Web: www.mwcomponents.com
SIC: 3452 Bolts, nuts, rivets, and washers

(G-1715)
FORD MOTOR COMPANY
Also Called: Ford
17601 Brookpark Rd (44142-1518)
P.O. Box 9900 (44142)
PHONE..................216 676-7918
Timothy M Duperron, *Brnch Mgr*
EMP: 98
SQ FT: 2,320,000
SALES (corp-wide): 176.19MM **Publicly Held**
Web: www.ford.com
SIC: 3714 3321 Motor vehicle parts and accessories; Gray and ductile iron foundries
PA: Ford Motor Company
1 American Rd
Dearborn MI 48126
313 322-3000

(G-1716)
GREENKOTE USA INC
6435 Eastland Rd (44142-1305)
PHONE..................440 243-2865
Mark Gore, *Dir*
James Thomson, *Sec*
▲ **EMP:** 8 **EST:** 2008
SALES (est): 1.34MM **Privately Held**
Web: www.greenkote.com
SIC: 3479 Coating of metals and formed products

(G-1717)
H&M MTAL STAMPING ASSEMBLY INC
5325 W 140th St (44142-1759)
PHONE..................216 898-9030
Kathryn Mabin, *Pr*
EMP: 19 **EST:** 2008
SALES (est): 1.02MM **Privately Held**
Web: www.hm-metalstamping.com
SIC: 3469 Stamping metal for the trade

(G-1718)
HONEYWELL INTERNATIONAL INC
Also Called: Honeywell
2100 Apollo Dr (44142-4103)
PHONE..................216 459-6048
Dan Stankey, *CFO*
EMP: 18
SALES (corp-wide): 36.66B **Publicly Held**
Web: www.honeywell.com
SIC: 3724 Turbines, aircraft type
PA: Honeywell International Inc.
855 S Mint St
Charlotte NC 28202
704 627-6200

(G-1719)
IVOSTUD LLC
6430 Eastland Rd Ste C (44142-1340)
PHONE..................440 925-4227
Mike Quinn, *CEO*
EMP: 7 **EST:** 2018
SALES (est): 2.69MM
SALES (corp-wide): 374.78K **Privately Held**
Web: www.ivostud.com
SIC: 3452 3548 Bolts, nuts, rivets, and washers; Electric welding equipment
HQ: Avistud Gmbh
Schutzenstr. 6-8
Breckerfeld
233 887-0990

(G-1720)
K-M-S INDUSTRIES INC
Also Called: K.M.S.
6519 Eastland Rd Ste 1 (44142-1347)
PHONE..................440 243-6680
Gerald Korman, *Pr*
Richard Malone Junior, *VP*
Diane Malone, *Treas*
EMP: 17 **EST:** 1980
SQ FT: 25,000
SALES (est): 484.97K **Privately Held**
Web: www.kmsindustries.com
SIC: 3599 5531 7692 Machine shop, jobbing and repair; Automotive parts; Welding repair

(G-1721)
LAKE ERIE GRAPHICS INC
5372 W 130th St (44142-1801)
PHONE..................216 575-1333
James K Dietz, *Pr*
EMP: 30 **EST:** 1990
SQ FT: 25,000
SALES (est): 4.76MM **Privately Held**
Web: www.lakeeriegraphics.com
SIC: 3993 Signs and advertising specialties

(G-1722)
NORTH COAST SEAL INCORPORATED
Also Called: Ncs
5163 W 137th St (44142-1809)
PHONE..................216 898-5000
Thomas Sasura, *Pr*
Edward D Montgomery, *Pr*
▲ **EMP:** 10 **EST:** 1985
SQ FT: 14,000
SALES (est): 1.85MM **Privately Held**
Web: www.northcoastseal.com
SIC: 5085 3069 3053 3089 Gaskets and seals; Sponge rubber and sponge rubber products; Gaskets; packing and sealing devices; Extruded finished plastics products, nec

(G-1723)
PRINTING CONNECTION INC
5205 W 161st St (44142-1606)
PHONE..................216 898-4878
Frank Metro, *Prin*
EMP: 8 **EST:** 2009
SALES (est): 453.27K **Privately Held**
Web: www.printwithpci.com
SIC: 2752 Offset printing

(G-1724)
RELIACHECK MANUFACTURING INC
Also Called: Ecil Met TEC
6550 Eastland Rd (44142-1307)
P.O. Box 303 (44012-0303)
PHONE..................440 933-6162
Luis Antonio Srerie, *Pr*
David Updegraff, *
▲ **EMP:** 26 **EST:** 2002
SALES (est): 5.39MM
SALES (corp-wide): 2.47B **Privately Held**
SIC: 3317 Seamless pipes and tubes
PA: Vesuvius Plc
165 Fleet Street
London EC4A
207 822-0000

(G-1725)
ROLL-IN SAW INC
15851 Commerce Park Dr (44142-2020)
PHONE..................216 459-9001
Donald Borman, *Pr*
Marcus Borman, *VP*
▼ **EMP:** 10 **EST:** 1940
SQ FT: 15,000
SALES (est): 1.5MM **Privately Held**
Web: www.rollinsaw.com
SIC: 3541 Sawing and cutoff machines (metalworking machinery)

(G-1726)
THERMAL SOLUTIONS MFG INC
15600 Commerce Park Dr (44142-2015)
PHONE..................800 776-4225
EMP: 10 **EST:** 2013
SALES (est): 528.53K **Privately Held**
Web: www.thermalsolutionsmfg.com
SIC: 3714 Radiators and radiator shells and cores, motor vehicle

(G-1727)
WELDERS SUPPLY INC
5575 Engle Rd (44142-1533)
PHONE..................216 267-4470
EMP: 45
SALES (corp-wide): 12.38MM **Privately Held**
SIC: 7692 5999 5984 Welding repair; Welding supplies; Propane gas, bottled
HQ: Welders Supply Inc
2020 Train Ave
Cleveland OH 44113
216 241-1696

Brookville
Montgomery County

(G-1728)
ADMARK PRINTING INC
310 Sycamore St (45309-1731)
PHONE..................937 833-5111
Patrick J Bruchs, *Pr*
EMP: 6 **EST:** 1980
SQ FT: 15,000
SALES (est): 498.3K **Privately Held**
SIC: 2752 Offset printing

(G-1729)
ANTIQUE AUTO SHEET METAL INC
718 Albert Rd (45309-9202)
PHONE..................937 833-4422
Raymond Gollahon, *Pr*
Donna Gollahon, *
EMP: 15 **EST:** 1972
SQ FT: 21,000
SALES (est): 2.72MM **Privately Held**
Web: www.brookvilleroadster.com
SIC: 3711 3444 3465 Motor vehicles and car bodies; Sheet metalwork; Body parts, automobile: stamped metal

(G-1730)
BROOKVILLE ROADSTER INC
718 Albert Rd (45309-9202)
PHONE..................937 833-4605
Ray Gollahon, *Pr*
EMP: 10 **EST:** 1986
SALES (est): 723.8K **Privately Held**
Web: www.brookvilleroadster.com
SIC: 3711 5013 Automobile assembly, including specialty automobiles; Automotive supplies and parts

(G-1731)
CSA NUTRITION SERVICES INC
10 Nutrition Way (45309-8884)
PHONE..................800 257-3788
Richard J Chernesky, *Prin*
EMP: 26 **EST:** 1974
SALES (est): 29.65K
SALES (corp-wide): 176.74B **Privately Held**
SIC: 2048 Prepared feeds, nec
PA: Cargill, Incorporated
15407 Mcginty Rd W
Wayzata MN 55391
800 227-4455

(G-1732)
CYCLE ELECTRIC INC
8734 Dayton Greenville Pike (45309-9232)
P.O. Box 81 (45322-0081)
PHONE..................937 884-7300
Karl Fahringer, *Pr*
Roxanne Fahringer, *VP*
EMP: 25 **EST:** 1982
SQ FT: 8,000
SALES (est): 831.52K **Privately Held**
Web: www.cycleelectricinc.com
SIC: 3694 Generators, automotive and aircraft

(G-1733)
D M TOOL & PLASTICS INC
11150 Baltimore Phillipsburg Rd (45309-8687)
PHONE..................937 962-4140
Pat Meyer, *Mgr*
EMP: 11
SALES (corp-wide): 4.78MM **Privately Held**
SIC: 3089 3599 Injection molding of plastics; Machine shop, jobbing and repair
PA: D M Tool & Plastics, Inc.
4140 Us Route 40 E
Lewisburg OH 45338
937 962-4140

(G-1734)
DIGISOFT SYSTEMS CORPORATION
4520 Clayton Rd (45309-9332)
PHONE..................937 833-5016
Gary E Brazier, *Pr*
Betty L Brazier, *
Christopher F Cowan, *Sec*
EMP: 7 **EST:** 1986
SQ FT: 600
SALES (est): 572.38K **Privately Held**

Brookville - Montgomery County (G-1735)

SIC: 7372   Business oriented computer software

(G-1735)
FIBRE GLAST DVLPMENTS CORP LLC
385 Carr Dr (45309-1921)
PHONE................................937 833-5200
Mark Knight, *Prin*
EMP: 15 EST: 2021
SALES (est): 1.04MM **Privately Held**
Web: www.fibreglast.com
SIC: 2821   Plastics materials and resins

(G-1736)
FLOW DRY TECHNOLOGY INC (HQ)
379 Albert Rd (45309)
P.O. Box 190 (45309)
PHONE................................937 833-2161
Douglas Leconey, *Pr*
▲ EMP: 111 EST: 1946
SQ FT: 65,000
SALES (est): 22.56MM
SALES (corp-wide): 1.05B **Privately Held**
Web: www.flowdry.com
SIC: 3053 2834   Gasket materials; Druggists' preparations (pharmaceuticals)
PA: Filtration Group Corporation
    1 Tower Ln
    Oakbrook Terrace IL 60181
    630 968-1730

(G-1737)
FTD INVESTMENTS LLC
379 Albert Rd (45309-9247)
PHONE................................937 833-2161
Doug Le, *Prin*
EMP: 1120 EST: 2006
SQ FT: 65,000
SALES (est): 756.05K **Privately Held**
Web: www.flowdry.com
SIC: 3714 2834   Air conditioner parts, motor vehicle; Druggists' preparations (pharmaceuticals)
PA: Blackstreet Capital Management, Llc
    7250 Woodmont Ave Ste 210
    Bethesda MD 20814

(G-1738)
GREEN TOKAI CO LTD (DH)
Also Called: GTC
55 Robert Wright Dr (45309-1931)
PHONE................................937 833-5444
Daniel Bowers, *Pr*
◆ EMP: 525 EST: 1987
SQ FT: 246,000
SALES (est): 103.87MM **Privately Held**
Web: www.greentokai.com
SIC: 3714 3069   Motor vehicle body components and frame; Rubber automotive products
HQ: Tokai Kogyo Co.,Ltd.
    4-1, Naganecho
    Obu AIC 474-0

(G-1739)
IMAGE PAVEMENT MAINTENANCE
425 Carr Dr (45309-1935)
P.O. Box 157 (45309-0157)
PHONE................................937 833-9200
Michael Gartrell, *Pr*
EMP: 12 EST: 1992
SALES (est): 2.33MM **Privately Held**
Web: www.imagepavement.com
SIC: 1611 2951 1799 1771   Surfacing and paving; Asphalt paving mixtures and blocks ; Parking lot maintenance; Driveway contractor

(G-1740)
KUHNS MOLD & TOOL CO INC
Also Called: K & B Molded Products
9360 National Rd (45309-9675)
PHONE................................937 833-2178
EMP: 75 EST: 1964
SALES (est): 9.47MM **Privately Held**
Web: www.kandbmoldedproducts.com
SIC: 3089 3544   Injection molded finished plastics products, nec; Industrial molds

(G-1741)
MCGREGOR & ASSOCIATES INC
365 Carr Dr (45309-1921)
PHONE................................937 833-6768
Larry Mcgregor, *Pr*
Beverly Mcgregor, *Sec*
Don Wurst, *
▲ EMP: 120 EST: 1971
SQ FT: 16,000
SALES (est): 15.97MM **Privately Held**
Web: www.mcgregor-surmount.com
SIC: 3672   Printed circuit boards

(G-1742)
NORGREN INC
Also Called: IMI Precision
325 Carr Dr (45309-1929)
PHONE................................937 833-4033
Michael Vinski, *Brnch Mgr*
EMP: 147
SALES (corp-wide): 2.74B **Privately Held**
Web: www.norgren.com
SIC: 3625   Actuators, industrial
HQ: Norgren Llc
    5400 S Delaware St
    Littleton CO 80120
    303 794-5000

(G-1743)
R & J TOOL INC
10550 Upper Lewisburg Salem Rd (45309)
P.O. Box 118 (45309-0118)
PHONE................................937 833-3200
Richard Rohrer, *Pr*
Marilyn K Rohrer, *VP*
EMP: 10 EST: 1974
SQ FT: 5,000
SALES (est): 901.25K **Privately Held**
Web: www.rjtoolinc.com
SIC: 3599   Machine shop, jobbing and repair

(G-1744)
SOELTER CORPORATION
385 Carr Dr (45309-1921)
PHONE................................800 838-8984
Marilyn Soelter, *Pr*
▼ EMP: 17 EST: 1955
SALES (est): 4.79MM **Privately Held**
Web: www.fibreglast.com
SIC: 2821   Plastics materials and resins

Brunswick
Medina County

(G-1745)
696 LEDGEROCK CIR
2950 Westway Dr (44212-5665)
PHONE................................330 289-0996
Allen Higgins, *Prin*
EMP: 9 EST: 2010
SALES (est): 244.07K **Privately Held**
SIC: 3571   Minicomputers

(G-1746)
A G INDUSTRIES INC
2963 Interstate Pkwy (44212-4327)
PHONE................................330 220-0050
EMP: 27 EST: 1991
SQ FT: 4,000
SALES (est): 1.99MM **Privately Held**
Web: www.agind.co
SIC: 3544   Special dies, tools, jigs, and fixtures

(G-1747)
ALTERNATIVE SURFACE GRINDING
Also Called: Ring Masters
1093 Industrial Pkwy N (44212-4319)
PHONE................................330 273-3443
EMP: 8 EST: 2010
SALES (est): 226.12K **Privately Held**
Web: www.alternativesurfacegrind.com
SIC: 3599   Machine shop, jobbing and repair

(G-1748)
AMERICAN CUBE MOLD INC
Also Called: Acm
1636 W 130th St (44212-2322)
PHONE................................330 558-0044
Frank J Kichurchak, *Pr*
EMP: 6 EST: 1986
SQ FT: 3,800
SALES (est): 792.01K **Privately Held**
Web: www.americancubemold.com
SIC: 3544 3829   Industrial molds; Testing equipment: abrasion, shearing strength, etc.

(G-1749)
AUTOMATION TOOL & DIE INC
3005 Interstate Pkwy (44212-4328)
PHONE................................330 558-8128
Beth Welding, *Mgr*
EMP: 7 EST: 2014
SALES (est): 290.74K **Privately Held**
Web: www.automationtd.com
SIC: 3544   Special dies and tools

(G-1750)
AXESS INTERNATIONAL LLC
4641 Stag Thicket Ln (44212-5800)
PHONE................................330 460-4840
EMP: 7 EST: 2010
SALES (est): 498.26K **Privately Held**
Web: www.axess-int.com
SIC: 2522   Office furniture, except wood

(G-1751)
CHEMICAL METHODS INCORPORATED
2853 Westway Dr # A (44212-5657)
PHONE................................216 476-8400
Daniel E Richards, *Pr*
EMP: 30 EST: 1971
SALES (est): 2.83MM **Privately Held**
Web: www.chemicalmethods.com
SIC: 2842 3471 2992 2899   Cleaning or polishing preparations, nec; Plating and polishing; Lubricating oils and greases; Chemical preparations, nec

(G-1752)
COLONY MACHINE & TOOL INC
1300 Industrial Pkwy N (44212-2346)
P.O. Box 126 (44212-0126)
PHONE................................330 225-3410
Roger Reich, *Pr*
Mark Borcoman, *VP*
EMP: 8 EST: 1967
SQ FT: 20,000
SALES (est): 841.5K **Privately Held**
Web: www.colonymachine.com
SIC: 3751   Motorcycle accessories

(G-1753)
COLUMBIA CHEMICAL CORPORATION
1000 Western Dr (44212-4330)
PHONE................................330 225-3200
Brett Larick, *Pr*
D J Hudak, *Prin*
William E Rosenberg, *Prin*
Herbert H Geduld, *Prin*
◆ EMP: 22 EST: 1975
SALES (est): 5.53MM **Privately Held**
Web: www.columbiachemical.com
SIC: 2819   Zinc chloride

(G-1754)
COMPONENT MFG & DESIGN
3121 Interstate Pkwy (44212-4329)
P.O. Box 845 (44212-0845)
PHONE................................330 225-8080
Edward C Crist, *Pr*
EMP: 10 EST: 1976
SQ FT: 12,000
SALES (est): 492.46K **Privately Held**
Web: www.cmd-tip.com
SIC: 3599   Machine shop, jobbing and repair

(G-1755)
CONTROLLED ACCESS INC
Also Called: Sentronic
1535 Industrial Pkwy (44212-2359)
P.O. Box 430 (44233-0430)
PHONE................................330 273-6185
Michelle Sherba, *Pr*
Mike Sherba, *Stockholder*
Sylvia Hayes, *Treas*
▲ EMP: 16 EST: 1984
SALES (est): 2.25MM **Privately Held**
Web: www.controlledaccess.com
SIC: 3829   Turnstiles, equipped with counting mechanisms

(G-1756)
D C SYSTEMS INC
1251 Industrial Pkwy N (44212-2341)
PHONE................................330 273-3030
Thomas E Schira, *Pr*
Katherine Schira, *Sec*
EMP: 10 EST: 1967
SQ FT: 22,600
SALES (est): 994.83K **Privately Held**
Web: www.associatedequip.com
SIC: 5063 3692 7699 3629   Batteries; Dry cell batteries, single or multiple cell; Battery service and repair; Battery chargers, rectifying or nonrotating

(G-1757)
DESTINY MANUFACTURING INC
2974 Interstate Pkwy (44212-4323)
PHONE................................330 273-9000
Josef Schuessler, *Pr*
Reinhold Rock, *
Michael Schuessler, *
Bernard Karthan, *
◆ EMP: 44 EST: 1998
SQ FT: 100,000
SALES (est): 8.75MM **Privately Held**
Web: www.destinymfg.com
SIC: 3469 3399   Appliance parts, porcelain enameled; Metal powders, pastes, and flakes

(G-1758)
DIE-MENSION CORPORATION
3020 Nationwide Pkwy (44212-2360)
PHONE................................330 273-5872
Karen Thompson, *Pr*
Rick Thompson, *VP*
▼ EMP: 12 EST: 1985
SQ FT: 14,250
SALES (est): 1.61MM **Privately Held**
Web: www.diemension.com
SIC: 3544 3469   Special dies and tools; Metal stampings, nec

GEOGRAPHIC SECTION
Brunswick - Medina County (G-1785)

(G-1759)
FM SYSTEMS
4295 Center Rd (44212-2917)
PHONE.................................330 273-3000
Ben Halack, *Prin*
EMP: 12 **EST:** 2004
SALES (est): 599.17K **Privately Held**
Web: www.fmsystems.com
SIC: 3699 Security control equipment and systems

(G-1760)
FORMATECH INC
3024 Interstate Pkwy (44212-4324)
PHONE.................................330 273-2800
Craig F Wahl, *Pr*
Carol Wahl, *Sec*
▲ **EMP:** 20 **EST:** 1985
SALES (est): 2.81MM **Privately Held**
Web: www.formatechexhibits.com
SIC: 2542 2541 Counters or counter display cases, except wood; Counters or counter display cases, wood

(G-1761)
FREMAR INDUSTRIES INC
2808 Westway Dr (44212-5656)
PHONE.................................330 220-3700
Marcus Bauman, *CEO*
Donald Brandt, *
▼ **EMP:** 40 **EST:** 1982
SQ FT: 26,000
SALES (est): 1.93MM **Privately Held**
Web: www.fre-mar.com
SIC: 3544 Special dies and tools

(G-1762)
FUNKY INK PRINTS LLC
1736 W 130th St Ste 110 (44212-6333)
PHONE.................................330 241-7291
Tabitha Birce, *Prin*
EMP: 6 **EST:** 2018
SALES (est): 240.2K **Privately Held**
Web: www.funkyinkprints.com
SIC: 2759 Screen printing

(G-1763)
GALLEY PRINTING INC
Also Called: Galley Printing Company
2892 Westway Dr (44212-5656)
PHONE.................................330 220-5577
Richard Stitch, *CEO*
Barbara Stitch, *
EMP: 25 **EST:** 1959
SALES (est): 2.84MM **Privately Held**
Web: www.galleyprinting.com
SIC: 2752 Offset printing

(G-1764)
GEM INSTRUMENT COMPANY INC
2832 Nationwide Pkwy (44212-2362)
P.O. Box 830 (44212-0830)
PHONE.................................330 273-6117
Spiras Arfaras, *Pr*
Joan Arfaras, *VP*
EMP: 11 **EST:** 1937
SQ FT: 10,000
SALES (est): 766K **Privately Held**
Web: www.gem-instrument.com
SIC: 3823 3829 Digital displays of process variables; Measuring and controlling devices, nec

(G-1765)
GLOBAL SPECIALTIES INC
2950 Westway Dr Ste 110 (44212-5666)
PHONE.................................800 338-0814
Clyde Kanz, *Prin*
EMP: 8 **EST:** 2004
SALES (est): 428.42K **Privately Held**
SIC: 3965 Fasteners

(G-1766)
GRAPHTECH COMMUNICATIONS INC
2892 Westway Dr (44212-5656)
PHONE.................................216 676-1020
Stephen L Adamson, *Pr*
William Kall, *VP*
EMP: 10 **EST:** 1977
SALES (est): 943.25K **Privately Held**
Web: www.graphtechcommunications.com
SIC: 2752 Offset printing

(G-1767)
GRIND-ALL CORPORATION
1113 Industrial Pkwy N (44212-2371)
PHONE.................................330 220-1600
Henry Matousek Senior, *Pr*
Mary Matousek, *
EMP: 38 **EST:** 1974
SALES (est): 2.88MM **Privately Held**
Web: www.grindall.com
SIC: 3541 Grinding machines, metalworking

(G-1768)
GROENEVELD ATLANTIC SOUTH
1130 Industrial Pkwy N Ste 7 (44212-5605)
PHONE.................................330 225-4949
Yan Isscs, *Pr*
Glenn Isscs, *Pr*
▲ **EMP:** 9 **EST:** 1999
SALES (est): 457.76K **Privately Held**
SIC: 3569 Lubricating equipment

(G-1769)
ID IMAGES INC
1120 W 130th St (44212-2317)
PHONE.................................330 220-7300
EMP: 21
SALES (est): 5.37MM **Privately Held**
Web: www.idimages.com
SIC: 3577 Bar code (magnetic ink) printers

(G-1770)
ID IMAGES LLC (PA)
1120 W 130th St (44212-2317)
PHONE.................................330 220-7300
▲ **EMP:** 65 **EST:** 1995 .
SQ FT: 24,200
SALES (est): 59.34MM **Privately Held**
Web: www.idimages.com
SIC: 2672 Chemically treated papers, made from purchased materials

(G-1771)
INTERNATIONAL MACHINING INC
2885 Nationwide Pkwy (44212-4314)
PHONE.................................330 225-1963
John Strobel, *Pr*
Bruce Sherman, *
EMP: 40 **EST:** 1981
SQ FT: 26,000
SALES (est): 4.05MM **Privately Held**
Web: www.imimachining.com
SIC: 3599 Machine shop, jobbing and repair

(G-1772)
JET DI INC
1736 W 130th St Ste 200 (44212-6338)
PHONE.................................330 607-7913
David Dempsey, *Pr*
EMP: 7 **EST:** 2013
SALES (est): 683.38K **Privately Held**
Web: www.jet-di.com
SIC: 3544 8711 Special dies, tools, jigs, and fixtures; Machine tool design

(G-1773)
L & R RACING INC
Also Called: Drr USA
1261 Industrial Pkwy N Ste 1a (44212-4310)
P.O. Box 875 (44212-0875)
PHONE.................................330 220-3102
Louis Allan, *CEO*
◆ **EMP:** 20 **EST:** 2000
SALES (est): 3.38MM **Privately Held**
Web: www.drrusa.com
SIC: 5012 5013 3799 Motorcycles; Motorcycle parts; Recreational vehicles

(G-1774)
MURPHY TRACTOR & EQP CO INC
Also Called: John Deere Authorized Dealer
1550 Industrial Pkwy N (44212-2349)
PHONE.................................330 220-4999
EMP: 8
Web: www.murphytractor.com
SIC: 3531 5082 Construction machinery; Construction and mining machinery
HQ: Murphy Tractor & Equipment Co., Inc.
    5375 N Deere Rd
    Park City KS 67219
    855 246-9124

(G-1775)
NABORS & NABORS LTD
627 Redstone Cir (44212-4355)
PHONE.................................440 846-0000
James Nabors, *Prin*
EMP: 6 **EST:** 2017
SALES (est): 174.32K **Privately Held**
Web: www.nabors.com
SIC: 1389 Oil field services, nec

(G-1776)
NUFACTURING INC ✪
2845 Center Rd (44212-2331)
PHONE.................................330 814-5259
Jordan Adair, *Pr*
Jordan Adair, *Managing Member*
EMP: 24 **EST:** 2022
SALES (est): 2.3MM **Privately Held**
Web: www.nufacturing.com
SIC: 2833 Vitamins, natural or synthetic: bulk, uncompounded

(G-1777)
OPTICS INCORPORATED
2936 Westway Dr (44212-5658)
PHONE.................................800 362-1337
Dale Springer Senior, *Pr*
Cheryl Springer, *Sec*
EMP: 22 **EST:** 1960
SQ FT: 10,000
SALES (est): 4.9MM **Privately Held**
Web: www.opticsinc.com
SIC: 3827 Optical instruments and lenses

(G-1778)
PACIFIC TOOL & DIE CO
1035 Western Dr (44212-4331)
PHONE.................................330 273-7363
Charles W Smith, *Pr*
Jeffrey Smith, *VP*
EMP: 26 **EST:** 1959
SQ FT: 20,000
SALES (est): 488.12K **Privately Held**
SIC: 3544 Dies and die holders for metal cutting, forming, die casting

(G-1779)
PAVLETICH MANUFACTURING
2774 Nationwide Pkwy (44212-2357)
PHONE.................................440 382-0997
Jason Tichy, *Prin*
EMP: 6 **EST:** 2017
SALES (est): 249.83K **Privately Held**
Web: www.pavletich-mfg.com
SIC: 3999 Manufacturing industries, nec

(G-1780)
PHILPOTT RUBBER LLC (HQ)
Also Called: Philpott Rubber Company
1010 Industrial Pkwy N (44212-4318)
PHONE.................................330 225-3344
David Ferrell, *CEO*
Mike Baach, *
Russell E Schabel, *
Gregory C Stafford, *
Jeffrey Rog, *
▲ **EMP:** 28 **EST:** 1889
SQ FT: 30,000
SALES (est): 10.94MM
SALES (corp-wide): 28.02MM **Privately Held**
Web: www.philpottsolutions.com
SIC: 3069 Medical sundries, rubber
PA: Philpott Solutions Group Inc.
    1010 Industrial Pkwy N
    Brunswick OH 44212
    330 225-3344

(G-1781)
POMACON INC
2996 Interstate Pkwy (44212-4323)
PHONE.................................330 273-1576
Rodger Post, *Pr*
EMP: 15 **EST:** 1985
SQ FT: 14,000
SALES (est): 2MM **Privately Held**
Web: www.pomacon.com
SIC: 3535 5084 5999 Conveyors and conveying equipment; Conveyor systems; Alcoholic beverage making equipment and supplies

(G-1782)
PRAGMATIC MFG LLC
2774 Nationwide Pkwy Unit 18 (44212-2357)
PHONE.................................330 222-6051
EMP: 10 **EST:** 2019
SALES (est): 505.98K **Privately Held**
Web: www.pragmaticmanufacturing.com
SIC: 3999 Manufacturing industries, nec

(G-1783)
PROKLEAN SERVICES LLC (PA)
3041 Nationwide Pkwy (44212-2361)
P.O. Box 729 (44212-0729)
PHONE.................................330 273-0122
EMP: 24 **EST:** 2016
SALES (est): 2.21MM
SALES (corp-wide): 2.21MM **Privately Held**
Web: www.prokleanservices.com
SIC: 2899 Chemical preparations, nec

(G-1784)
PT SOLUTIONS LLC
2985 Nationwide Pkwy (44212-2365)
PHONE.................................844 786-6300
EMP: 6
SALES (est): 165.07K **Privately Held**
SIC: 3841 Surgical and medical instruments

(G-1785)
QUAD FLUID DYNAMICS INC
2826 Westway Dr (44212-5656)
P.O. Box 429 (44212-0429)
PHONE.................................330 220-3005
Kenneth H Oleksiak, *Pr*
Barbara Oleksiak, *VP*
David E Williams, *VP*
EMP: 10 **EST:** 1978
SQ FT: 10,000
SALES (est): 1.66MM **Privately Held**

Brunswick - Medina County (G-1786)

(G-1786)
Web: www.quadfluiddynamics.com
SIC: **5085** 3594 7699 Valves and fittings; Fluid power pumps and motors; Hydraulic equipment repair

(G-1786)
RAINBOW CULTURED MARBLE
1442 W 130th St (44212-2320)
PHONE................................330 225-3400
Carrie Fuller, *Prin*
Dale Boss, *Prin*
EMP: 11 **EST:** 1975
SQ FT: 6,000
SALES (est): 474.46K **Privately Held**
Web: www.rainbowmarbleinc.com
SIC: **3281** Bathroom fixtures, cut stone

(G-1787)
REALEFLOW LLC
150 Pearl Rd (44212-1116)
PHONE................................855 545-2095
EMP: 7 **EST:** 2007
SALES (est): 1.19MM **Privately Held**
Web: www.realeflow.com
SIC: **7372** Business oriented computer software

(G-1788)
ROCKSTEDT TOOL & DIE INC
2974 Interstate Pkwy (44212-4323)
PHONE................................330 273-9000
Josef Schuessler, *Pr*
EMP: 16 **EST:** 1965
SQ FT: 100,000
SALES (est): 924.35K **Privately Held**
Web: www.rockstedtwireedm.com
SIC: **3544** Special dies and tools

(G-1789)
RONLEN INDUSTRIES INC
2809 Nationwide Pkwy (44212-2363)
PHONE................................330 273-6468
Leonard Lutch, *Pr*
Ron Bryant, *
Greg Lutch, *
EMP: 26 **EST:** 1978
SQ FT: 25,000
SALES (est): 5.71MM **Privately Held**
Web: www.ronlen.com
SIC: **3469** 3544 Stamping metal for the trade ; Special dies and tools

(G-1790)
SCHERBA INDUSTRIES INC
Also Called: Inflatable Images
2880 Interstate Pkwy (44212-4322)
PHONE................................330 273-3200
Robert J Scherba, *Pr*
David M Scherba, *
▲ **EMP:** 100 **EST:** 1982
SQ FT: 63,000
SALES (est): 22.3MM **Privately Held**
Web: www.inflatableimages.com
SIC: **3081** 3069 2394 Vinyl film and sheet; Balloons, advertising and toy: rubber; Canvas and related products

(G-1791)
SENECA LABEL INC
1120 W 130th St (44212-2317)
PHONE................................440 237-1600
Michael Hoopingarner, *Pr*
John Hoopingarner, *
EMP: 35 **EST:** 1968
SALES (est): 5.05MM **Privately Held**
Web: www.senecalabel.com
SIC: **2759** Labels and seals: printing, nsk

(G-1792)
STANDOUT STICKERS INC
2991 Interstate Pkwy (44212-4327)
PHONE................................877 449-7703
Jeffrey Nemecek, *CEO*
EMP: 6 **EST:** 2010
SALES (est): 565.5K **Privately Held**
Web: www.standoutstickers.com
SIC: **2759** Screen printing

(G-1793)
TECHNICAL TOOL & GAUGE INC
2914 Westway Dr (44212-5658)
PHONE................................330 273-1778
Jeff Butcher, *Owner*
EMP: 25 **EST:** 1989
SALES (est): 731.03K **Privately Held**
SIC: **3544** Special dies and tools

(G-1794)
TIGER CAT FURNITURE
294 Marks Rd (44212-1042)
PHONE................................330 220-7232
Audrey F Bledsoe, *Owner*
EMP: 8 **EST:** 1999
SALES (est): 349.71K **Privately Held**
Web: www.tigercatsfurniture.com
SIC: **3999** Novelties, bric-a-brac, and hobby kits

(G-1795)
TINNERMAN PALNUT ENGINEERED PR
1060 W 130th St (44212-2316)
PHONE................................330 220-5100
◆ **EMP:** 23 **EST:** 2011
SALES (est): 1.38MM **Privately Held**
SIC: **3452** Screws, metal

(G-1796)
TURF CARE SUPPLY LLC (PA)
Also Called: Allied Nutrients
50 Pearl Rd Ste 200 (44212-5703)
PHONE................................877 220-1014
Mark Mangan, *Pr*
Michael Randall, *CFO*
▼ **EMP:** 64 **EST:** 1974
SQ FT: 5,000
SALES (est): 80.8MM **Privately Held**
Web: www.turfcaresupply.com
SIC: **2873** Nitrogenous fertilizers

(G-1797)
UNITED MEDICAL SUPPLY COMPANY
2948 Nationwide Pkwy (44212-2364)
P.O. Box 862 (44212-0862)
PHONE................................866 678-8633
Ted Walsh, *CEO*
Anthony Fidram, *Pr*
EMP: 13 **EST:** 2016
SALES (est): 2.54MM **Privately Held**
Web: www.unitedmedsupply.com
SIC: **3841** 5047 Surgical and medical instruments; Hospital equipment and supplies, nec

(G-1798)
VERSATILE AUTOMATION TECH CORP
2853 Westway Dr (44212-5657)
PHONE................................330 220-2600
James Byrne, *Pr*
EMP: 6 **EST:** 2018
SALES (est): 455.33K **Privately Held**
SIC: **3569** 5084 Robots, assembly line: industrial and commercial; Robots, industrial

(G-1799)
VNL MOLDING LTD
669 Marguerite Way (44212-4366)
PHONE................................330 220-5951
Darrell C Christian, *Prin*
EMP: 7 **EST:** 2001
SALES (est): 111.51K **Privately Held**
SIC: **3089** Molding primary plastics

(G-1800)
WALEST INCORPORATED
Also Called: Kol-Cap Manufacturing Co
306 Aynesly Way (44212-4610)
PHONE................................216 362-8110
Mike Gorbulja, *Pr*
EMP: 8 **EST:** 1958
SALES (est): 932.21K **Privately Held**
SIC: **3544** 3599 Special dies and tools; Machine shop, jobbing and repair

(G-1801)
WARD INDUSTRIAL SERVICES INC
1040 Industrial Pkwy N (44212-4318)
PHONE................................877 459-9272
Carol Braunschweig, *Prin*
EMP: 8 **EST:** 2004
SALES (est): 39.69K **Privately Held**
Web: www.wis-co.biz
SIC: **3999** Dock equipment and supplies, industrial

(G-1802)
X-PRESS TOOL INC
2845 Interstate Pkwy (44212-4326)
PHONE................................330 225-8748
Bob Koch, *Pr*
EMP: 13 **EST:** 1999
SALES (est): 206.24K **Privately Held**
SIC: **7999** 3546 3545 Golf services and professionals; Power-driven handtools; Machine tool accessories
PA: Blackhawk Industrial Distribution, Inc.
    10810 E 45th St Ste 100
    Tulsa OK 74146

Bryan
Williams County

(G-1803)
AIRMATE CO INC
16280 County Road D (43506-9552)
PHONE................................419 636-3184
Carol Schreder Czech, *Pr*
Carol Schreder, *
Neil Oberlin, *
▲ **EMP:** 57 **EST:** 1946
SQ FT: 24,000
SALES (est): 7.55MM **Privately Held**
Web: www.airmateplasticfabrication.com
SIC: **3823** 7311 Process control instruments; Advertising consultant

(G-1804)
ALLIED MOULDED PRODUCTS INC (PA)
222 N Union St (43506-1450)
PHONE................................419 636-4217
Aaron T Herman, *Pr*
◆ **EMP:** 239 **EST:** 1958
SQ FT: 110,000
SALES (est): 78.31MM
SALES (corp-wide): 78.31MM **Privately Held**
Web: www.alliedmoulded.com
SIC: **3089** 3699 Injection molded finished plastics products, nec; Electrical equipment and supplies, nec

(G-1805)
ALTENLOH BRINCK & CO INC
2105 County Road 12c (43506-8301)
PHONE................................419 636-6715
Brian Roth, *Pr*
D Kip Winzeler, *
▲ **EMP:** 135 **EST:** 1981
SQ FT: 200,000
SALES (est): 47.11MM
SALES (corp-wide): 380.76MM **Privately Held**
Web: www.spax.us
SIC: **3452** Pins
HQ: Altenloh, Brinck & Co. Us, Inc.
    2105 Williams Co Rd 12 C
    Bryan OH 43506

(G-1806)
ALTENLOH BRINCK & CO US INC (DH)
Also Called: Trufast
2105 County Road 12c (43506-8301)
PHONE................................419 636-6715
Brian Roth, *Pr*
Kip Winzeler, *VP*
▲ **EMP:** 18 **EST:** 2005
SALES (est): 71.49MM
SALES (corp-wide): 380.76MM **Privately Held**
Web: www.spax.us
SIC: **3452** Screws, metal
HQ: Abc Finanzierungs- Und Beteiligungs Gmbh
    Kolner Str. 71-77
    Ennepetal NW
    23337990

(G-1807)
ANDERSON & VREELAND INC
Also Called: Anderson Vreeland Midwest
15348 Us Highway 127 Ew (43506)
P.O. Box 527 (43506-0527)
PHONE................................419 636-5002
EMP: 80
SQ FT: 3,000
SALES (corp-wide): 49.53MM **Privately Held**
Web: www.andersonvreeland.com
SIC: **5084** 3555 3542 2796 Printing trades machinery, equipment, and supplies; Printing trades machinery; Machine tools, metal forming type; Platemaking services
PA: Anderson & Vreeland, Inc.
    8 Evans St
    Fairfield NJ 07004
    973 227-2270

(G-1808)
ARROW TRU-LINE INC
720 E Perry St (43506-2223)
P.O. Box 704 (43506-0704)
PHONE................................419 636-7013
Curtis Anderson, *Ch Bd*
EMP: 8
SALES (corp-wide): 72.73MM **Privately Held**
Web: www.arrowtruline.com
SIC: **3429** 3469 3449 Builders' hardware; Metal stampings, nec; Miscellaneous metalwork
PA: Arrow Tru-Line, Inc.
    2211 S Defiance St
    Archbold OH 43502
    419 446-2785

(G-1809)
BARD MANUFACTURING COMPANY INC (PA)
1914 Randolph Dr (43506-2253)
P.O. Box 607 (43506-0607)
PHONE................................419 636-1194

GEOGRAPHIC SECTION
Bryan - Williams County (G-1833)

William Steel, *Pr*
Paul Matz, *
▼ **EMP:** 82 **EST:** 2006
SALES (est): 246.93K **Privately Held**
Web: www.bardhvac.com
SIC: 3585 Refrigeration and heating equipment

(G-1810)
BRICKER PLATING INC
612 E Edgerton St (43506-1408)
PHONE..................419 636-1990
Tim Bricker, *Pr*
EMP: 6 **EST:** 1950
SQ FT: 4,800
SALES (est): 569.48K **Privately Held**
SIC: 3471 Electroplating of metals or formed products

(G-1811)
BRYAN PUBLISHING COMPANY (PA)
Also Called: County Line
211 W High St Ste A (43506-1604)
PHONE..................419 636-1111
Christopher Cullis, *Pr*
Tom Voight, *
Elizabeth Cullis, *
EMP: 80 **EST:** 1863
SALES (est): 5.12MM
SALES (corp-wide): 5.12MM **Privately Held**
Web: www.bryantimes.com
SIC: 2711 Newspapers, publishing and printing

(G-1812)
BRYAN WEST MAIN STOP
Also Called: Marathon Oil
1310 W High St (43506-1544)
PHONE..................419 636-1616
EMP: 6 **EST:** 2016
SALES (est): 138.25K **Privately Held**
Web: www.marathonoil.com
SIC: 2711 Newspapers, publishing and printing

(G-1813)
C E ELECTRONICS INC
2107 Industrial Dr (43506-8773)
PHONE..................419 636-6705
Garry L Courtney, *Pr*
EMP: 85 **EST:** 1980
SALES (est): 23.04MM **Privately Held**
Web: www.ceelectronics.com
SIC: 3679 3672 Electronic circuits; Printed circuit boards

(G-1814)
CLARIOS LLC
Also Called: Johnson Controls
918 S Union St (43506-2246)
PHONE..................419 636-4211
Kevin Cagala, *Mgr*
EMP: 54
Web: www.clarios.com
SIC: 2531 Seats, automobile
HQ: Clarios, Llc
5757 N Green Bay Ave
Milwaukee WI 53209

(G-1815)
DAAVLIN DISTRIBUTING CO
Also Called: Daavlin
205 W Bement St (43506-1264)
P.O. Box 626 (43506-0626)
PHONE..................419 636-6304
David W Swanson, *Pr*
Tracey Mckelvey, *VP*
Traci Hartman, *
Sandrine Woolace, *
▼ **EMP:** 48 **EST:** 1981
SQ FT: 24,000
SALES (est): 8.87MM **Privately Held**
Web: www.daavlin.com
SIC: 3841 Diagnostic apparatus, medical

(G-1816)
DURACOAT POWDER FINISHING INC (PA)
1012 E Wilson St (43506-9358)
P.O. Box 715 (43517-0715)
PHONE..................419 636-3111
Frank Monosmith, *Pr*
Dock Pigmon, *CFO*
EMP: 13 **EST:** 1992
SQ FT: 45,000
SALES (est): 1.02MM **Privately Held**
Web: www.duracoatpowderfinishing.com
SIC: 3479 Coating of metals and formed products

(G-1817)
ENVASES MEDIA INC
1 Toy St (43506-1853)
P.O. Box 524 (43506-0524)
PHONE..................419 636-5461
Thomas P Dillon, *Pr*
▲ **EMP:** 31 **EST:** 2007
SALES (est): 6.7MM **Privately Held**
Web: www.envases.mx
SIC: 3411 3221 Food and beverage containers; Bottles for packing, bottling, and canning: glass
HQ: Envases Europe A/S
Hedenstedvej 14
Losning 8723
63124200

(G-1818)
FLUID HANDLING DYNAMICS LTD
815 Navarre Ave (43506-1528)
PHONE..................419 633-0560
Nick Kozumplik Junior, *Prin*
EMP: 10 **EST:** 2019
SALES (est): 491.63K **Privately Held**
SIC: 3652 Prerecorded records and tapes

(G-1819)
GENDRON INC
520 W Mulberry St Ste 100 (43506-1159)
PHONE..................419 636-0848
EMP: 22
Web: www.gendroninc.com
SIC: 3842 Surgical appliances and supplies

(G-1820)
H MACHINING INC
720 Commerce Dr (43506-9198)
PHONE..................419 636-6890
Denny Herman, *Pr*
Sherrie Herman, *Sec*
EMP: 11 **EST:** 1988
SQ FT: 18,000
SALES (est): 879.67K **Privately Held**
Web: www.hmachining.net
SIC: 3545 3544 Drills (machine tool accessories); Special dies and tools

(G-1821)
ILLINOIS TOOL WORKS INC
Also Called: ITW Filtration Products
730 E South St (43506-2433)
PHONE..................262 248-8277
EMP: 22
SALES (corp-wide): 16.11B **Publicly Held**
Web: www.itw.com
SIC: 3677 3714 3564 Filtration devices, electronic; Motor vehicle parts and accessories; Blowers and fans
PA: Illinois Tool Works Inc.
155 Harlem Ave
Glenview IL 60025

(G-1822)
ILLINOIS TOOL WORKS INC
Also Called: ITW Powertrain Components
730 E South St (43506-2433)
PHONE..................419 633-3236
Martin Collins, *Brnch Mgr*
EMP: 100
SALES (corp-wide): 16.11B **Publicly Held**
Web: www.itw.com
SIC: 3089 Injection molding of plastics
PA: Illinois Tool Works Inc.
155 Harlem Ave
Glenview IL 60025
847 724-7500

(G-1823)
ILLINOIS TOOL WORKS INC
ITW Tomco
730 E South St (43506-2433)
PHONE..................419 636-3161
Tom Mack, *VP*
EMP: 9
SQ FT: 75,000
SALES (corp-wide): 16.11B **Publicly Held**
Web: www.itw.com
SIC: 3089 Injection molding of plastics
PA: Illinois Tool Works Inc.
155 Harlem Ave
Glenview IL 60025
847 724-7500

(G-1824)
KENLEY ENTERPRISES LLC
418 N Lynn St (43506-1218)
P.O. Box 7036 (43506-7036)
PHONE..................419 630-0921
EMP: 11 **EST:** 2004
SALES (est): 1.37MM **Privately Held**
Web: www.kenleyenterprises.com
SIC: 3549 3498 3714 Wiredrawing and fabricating machinery and equipment, ex. die; Tube fabricating (contract bending and shaping); Motor vehicle parts and accessories

(G-1825)
L E SMITH COMPANY (PA)
1030 E Wilson St (43506)
P.O. Box 766 (43506)
PHONE..................419 636-4555
Laura Juarez, *Pr*
Craig Francisco, *
Mindy Hess, *
Steve Smith, *
Mari Ivan, *
▲ **EMP:** 100 **EST:** 1950
SQ FT: 90,000
SALES (est): 12.22MM
SALES (corp-wide): 12.22MM **Privately Held**
Web: www.lesmith.com
SIC: 2431 5072 2541 Interior and ornamental woodwork and trim; Builders' hardware, nec; Wood partitions and fixtures

(G-1826)
LEADER ENGNRNG-FABRICATION INC
County Rd D-50 (43506)
PHONE..................419 636-1731
EMP: 6
SALES (corp-wide): 8.29MM **Privately Held**
Web: www.axisengineering.com
SIC: 3599 Machine shop, jobbing and repair
PA: Leader Engineering-Fabrication, Inc.
695 Independence Dr
Napoleon OH 43545
419 592-0008

(G-1827)
MANUFACTURED HOUSING ENTPS INC
Also Called: Mansion Homes
9302 Us Highway 6 (43506-9516)
PHONE..................419 636-4511
Mary Jane Fitzcharles, *CEO*
Nathan Kimpel, *
Janet Rice, *
EMP: 25 **EST:** 1966
SQ FT: 250,000
SALES (est): 2.11MM **Privately Held**
Web: www.mheinc.com
SIC: 2451 1521 Mobile homes, except recreational; Single-family housing construction

(G-1828)
MINTEQ INTERNATIONAL INC
719 E High St (43506-1824)
PHONE..................419 636-4561
Tim Connors, *Mgr*
EMP: 12
Web: www.mineralstech.com
SIC: 3297 High temperature mortar, nonclay
HQ: Minteq International Inc.
35 Highland Ave
Bethlehem PA 18017

(G-1829)
NASG SEATING BRYAN LLC
633 Commerce Dr (43506-9197)
PHONE..................419 633-0662
David Vondeylen, *Managing Member*
▲ **EMP:** 92 **EST:** 2001
SQ FT: 80,000
SALES (est): 10.72MM **Privately Held**
Web: www.nasg.net
SIC: 3469 Stamping metal for the trade

(G-1830)
NORTH AMRCN STAMPING GROUP LLC
633 Commerce Dr (43506-9197)
PHONE..................419 633-0662
EMP: 7
SALES (est): 466.88K **Privately Held**
Web: www.nasg.net
SIC: 3599 Machine shop, jobbing and repair

(G-1831)
NOSTRUM LABORATORIES INC
705 E Mulberry St (43506-1734)
PHONE..................419 636-1168
EMP: 46
SQ FT: 91,100
Web: www.nostrumlabs.com
SIC: 2834 Syrups, pharmaceutical
PA: Nostrum Laboratories Inc.
1800 N Topping Ave
Kansas City MO 64120

(G-1832)
OBIC LLC
525 Winzeler Dr # 1 (43506-8303)
PHONE..................419 633-3147
EMP: 8 **EST:** 2018
SALES (est): 1.06MM **Privately Held**
Web: www.obicproducts.com
SIC: 3589 Water filters and softeners, household type

(G-1833)
OHIO ART COMPANY (PA)
1 Toy St (43506-1853)
P.O. Box 111 (43506-0111)
PHONE..................419 636-3141
William C Killgallon, *Ch Bd*
Martin L Killgallon Ii, *Pr*
Martin L Killgallon Iii, *Sr VP*

Bryan - Williams County (G-1834)

Larry Killgallon, *
▲ **EMP:** 77 **EST:** 1908
SQ FT: 661,000
SALES (est): 13.58MM
SALES (corp-wide): 13.58MM **Privately Held**
Web: www.ohioart.com
SIC: 2752 5945 Commercial printing, lithographic; Toys and games

(G-1834)
OTTOKEE GROUP INC
17768 County Road H 50 (43506-9429)
PHONE.................................419 636-1932
Keith Krovath, Mgr
EMP: 6
SALES (corp-wide): 2MM **Privately Held**
SIC: 2875 Fertilizers, mixing only
PA: Ottokee Group, Inc.
  21450 County Rd J
  Archbold OH 43502
  419 445-0440

(G-1835)
PAHL READY MIX CONCRETE INC (PA)
Also Called: Pahl Ready Mix Concrete
14586 Us Highway 127 Ew (43506-9754)
PHONE.................................419 636-4238
TOLL FREE: 800
Thomas G Weber, Pr
Judy Weber, VP
EMP: 17 **EST:** 1968
SQ FT: 500
SALES (est): 4.76MM
SALES (corp-wide): 4.76MM **Privately Held**
Web: www.pahlreadymix.com
SIC: 3273 Ready-mixed concrete

(G-1836)
PRECISE METAL FORM INC
810 Commerce Dr (43506-8861)
P.O. Box 764 (43506-0764)
PHONE.................................419 636-5221
James Bloir, Pr
Linda Bloir, Sec
EMP: 10 **EST:** 1969
SALES (est): 890.65K **Privately Held**
SIC: 3441 Fabricated structural metal

(G-1837)
REECE BROTHERS INC
1 Toy St (43506-1853)
PHONE.................................419 212-9226
EMP: 7 **EST:** 2016
SALES (est): 232.38K **Privately Held**
SIC: 2759 Commercial printing, nec

(G-1838)
SPANGLER CANDY COMPANY (PA)
400 N Portland St (43506-1257)
P.O. Box 71 (43506-0071)
PHONE.................................419 636-4221
▲ **EMP:** 175 **EST:** 1906
SALES (est): 94.36MM
SALES (corp-wide): 94.36MM **Privately Held**
Web: www.spanglercandy.com
SIC: 2064 Candy and other confectionery products

(G-1839)
TGM LLC
401 N Union St (43506-1455)
PHONE.................................419 636-8567
EMP: 15 **EST:** 2011
SQ FT: 17,000
SALES (est): 300K **Privately Held**
Web: www.tgminc.com

SIC: 3599 Machine shop, jobbing and repair

(G-1840)
TITAN TIRE CORPORATION
Also Called: Titan Tire Corporation Bryan
927 S Union St (43506-2252)
PHONE.................................419 633-4221
Tom Jagielski, Mgr
EMP: 400
SQ FT: 750,000
SALES (corp-wide): 1.82B **Publicly Held**
Web: www.titan-intl.com
SIC: 3011 Tires and inner tubes
HQ: Titan Tire Corporation
  2345 E Market St
  Des Moines IA 50317

(G-1841)
TITAN TIRE CORPORATION BRYAN
927 S Union St (43506-2252)
PHONE.................................419 633-4224
Paul Reitz, CEO
EMP: 36 **EST:** 2006
SALES (est): 1.81MM
SALES (corp-wide): 1.82B **Publicly Held**
Web: www.titan-intl.com
SIC: 3011 Tires and inner tubes
PA: Titan International, Inc.
  1525 Kautz Rd Ste 600
  West Chicago IL 60185
  630 377-0486

(G-1842)
TRANE TECHNOLOGIES COMPANY LLC
Also Called: Ingersoll-Rand
209 N Main St (43506-1319)
P.O. Box 151 (43506-0151)
PHONE.................................419 633-6800
EMP: 49
Web: www.tranetechnologies.com
SIC: 3546 4225 3823 3594 Power-driven handtools; General warehousing and storage; Process control instruments; Fluid power pumps and motors
HQ: Ingersoll-Rand Industrial U.S., Inc.
  800 Beaty St Ste E
  Davidson NC 28036
  704 655-4000

(G-1843)
TRANE TECHNOLOGIES COMPANY LLC
Ingersoll-Rand
1 Aro Ctr (43506)
PHONE.................................419 636-4242
EMP: 8
Web: www.tranetechnologies.com
SIC: 3561 Pumps and pumping equipment
HQ: Ingersoll-Rand Industrial U.S., Inc.
  800 Beaty St Ste E
  Davidson NC 28036
  704 655-4000

(G-1844)
WEBER SAND & GRAVEL INC
14586 Us Highway 127 Ew (43506-9754)
PHONE.................................419 636-7920
Tom Weber, Pr
EMP: 8 **EST:** 1968
SALES (est): 531.44K **Privately Held**
SIC: 1442 Gravel mining

(G-1845)
WESTAR PLASTICS LLC
Also Called: Westar Plastics
4271 County Road 15d (43506-9442)
PHONE.................................419 636-1333
Steve Goltare, Managing Member
EMP: 7 **EST:** 1996

SQ FT: 12,000
SALES (est): 927.67K **Privately Held**
Web: www.westarplastics.com
SIC: 3089 Injection molding of plastics

(G-1846)
YANFENG US AUTO INTR SYSTEMS I
Also Called: YANFENG US AUTOMOTIVE INTERIOR SYSTEMS II LLC
918 S Union St (43506-2246)
PHONE.................................419 636-4211
Kevin Cagala, Mgr
EMP: 7
SIC: 3089 Injection molding of plastics
HQ: Yanfeng International Automotive Technology Us Ii Llc
  41935 W 12 Mile Rd
  Novi MI 48377
  248 319-7333

(G-1847)
YANFENG US AUTO INTR SYSTEMS I
Also Called: YANFENG US AUTOMOTIVE INTERIOR SYSTEMS I LLC
918 S Union St (43506-2246)
PHONE.................................419 633-1873
EMP: 51
Web: www.yanfeng.com
SIC: 3089 3465 3479 3714 Injection molding of plastics; Automotive stampings; Painting, coating, and hot dipping; Motor vehicle parts and accessories
HQ: Yanfeng International Automotive Technology Us I Llc
  41935 W 12 Mile Rd
  Novi MI 48377
  248 319-7333

(G-1848)
YANFENG US AUTO INTR SYSTEMS I
Also Called: YANFENG US AUTOMOTIVE INTERIOR SYSTEMS I LLC
715 E South St (43506-2434)
PHONE.................................616 834-9422
Joseph Magdy, Brnch Mgr
EMP: 100
Web: www.yanfeng.com
SIC: 3714 Motor vehicle parts and accessories
HQ: Yanfeng International Automotive Technology Us I Llc
  41935 W 12 Mile Rd
  Novi MI 48377
  248 319-7333

Bucyrus
Crawford County

(G-1849)
ADVANCED FIBER LLC
100 Crossroads Blvd (44820-1361)
PHONE.................................419 562-1337
Doug Leuthold, Pr
EMP: 20 **EST:** 2018
SALES (est): 5.28MM
SALES (corp-wide): 2.78B **Publicly Held**
Web: www.advanced-fiber.com
SIC: 2821 2951 2823 Cellulose derivative materials; Asphalt paving mixtures and blocks; Cellulosic manmade fibers
PA: Installed Building Products, Inc.
  495 S High St Ste 50
  Columbus OH 43215
  614 221-3399

(G-1850)
BUCYRUS BLADES INC (DH)
260 E Beal Ave (44820-3492)
PHONE.................................419 562-6015

Alvin Collins, Ch
Jon Owens, *
Kevin Thomas, *
Eric Blackburn, *
◆ **EMP:** 154 **EST:** 1951
SQ FT: 130,000
SALES (est): 60MM
SALES (corp-wide): 3.29B **Privately Held**
Web: www.escocorp.com
SIC: 3531 Blades for graders, scrapers, dozers, and snow plows
HQ: Esco Group Llc
  2141 Nw 25th Ave
  Portland OR 97210
  503 228-2141

(G-1851)
BUCYRUS GRAPHICS INC
Also Called: Quality Printing Co
214 W Liberty St (44820-2639)
P.O. Box 454 (44820-0454)
PHONE.................................419 562-2906
W Gary Mc Kee, Pr
Judy Mc Kee, Sec
EMP: 10 **EST:** 1968
SQ FT: 5,000
SALES (est): 687.24K **Privately Held**
Web: www.1officesolution.com
SIC: 2752 Offset printing

(G-1852)
BUCYRUS PRECISION TECH INC
Also Called: B P T
200 Crossroads Blvd (44820-1363)
P.O. Box 2748 (44906-0748)
PHONE.................................419 563-9950
▲ **EMP:** 189 **EST:** 1995
SQ FT: 107,000
SALES (est): 48.17MM **Privately Held**
Web: www.bucyrusprecisiontech.com
SIC: 3714 3568 5531 Motor vehicle engines and parts; Power transmission equipment, nec; Automotive accessories
PA: Kaneta Kogyo Co.,Ltd.
  3-18-5, Takaokahigashi, Chuo-Ku
  Hamamatsu SZO 433-8

(G-1853)
CHECKMATE MARINE INC
3691 State Route 4 (44820-9466)
P.O. Box 351 (44820-0351)
PHONE.................................419 562-3881
EMP: 10 **EST:** 2006
SALES (est): 386.19K **Privately Held**
SIC: 3732 Boatbuilding and repairing

(G-1854)
COOPERS MILL INC
1414 N Sandusky Ave (44820-1330)
P.O. Box 149 (44820-0149)
PHONE.................................419 562-4215
Jason Mcmullan, Pr
Justin Mcmullan, VP
EMP: 12 **EST:** 1969
SQ FT: 17,300
SALES (est): 961.35K **Privately Held**
Web: www.crossroadscandles.com
SIC: 2033 5431 5149 Jams, jellies, and preserves, packaged in cans, jars, etc.; Fruit stands or markets; Pickles, preserves, jellies, and jams

(G-1855)
COOPERS MILL INCORPORATED
115 Crossroads Blvd (44820-1362)
PHONE.................................419 562-2878
Justin Mcmullen, Prin
EMP: 7 **EST:** 2019
SALES (est): 144.36K **Privately Held**
Web: www.crossroadscandles.com
SIC: 3999 Candles

GEOGRAPHIC SECTION

Burghill - Trumbull County (G-1878)

(G-1856)
D PICKING & CO
119 S Walnut St (44820-2325)
PHONE..................................419 562-6891
Helen Picking Neff, *Owner*
EMP: 6 **EST:** 1874
SQ FT: 5,000
SALES (est): 450.08K **Privately Held**
Web: www.bucyruscopperkettle.com
SIC: 3364 3931 3366 3321 Copper and copper alloy die-castings; Musical instruments; Copper foundries; Gray and ductile iron foundries

(G-1857)
DIAMOND WIPES INTL INC
1375 Isaac Beal Rd (44820-9604)
PHONE..................................419 562-3575
Diane Belcher, *Prin*
EMP: 8
SALES (corp-wide): 51.1MM **Privately Held**
Web: www.diamondwipes.com
SIC: 3441 Fabricated structural metal
PA: Diamond Wipes International, Inc.
4651 Schaefer Ave
Chino CA 91710
909 230-9888

(G-1858)
EAGLE CRUSHER CO INC
521 E Southern Ave (44820-3258)
P.O. Box 537 (44833-0537)
PHONE..................................419 562-1183
EMP: 95
SQ FT: 200,000
SALES (corp-wide): 39.86MM **Privately Held**
Web: www.eaglecrusher.com
SIC: 3531 Construction machinery
PA: Eagle Crusher Co Inc
525 S Market St
Galion OH 44833
419 468-2288

(G-1859)
EAST SIDE FUEL PLUS OPERATIONS
1505 N Sandusky Ave (44820-1333)
PHONE..................................419 563-0777
Bridgette J Liedorff, *Prin*
EMP: 8 **EST:** 2011
SALES (est): 168.31K **Privately Held**
SIC: 2869 Fuels

(G-1860)
GANYMEDE TECHNOLOGIES CORP
Also Called: J3 Point-Of-Sale
1685 Marion Rd (44820-3116)
P.O. Box 1138 (44820-1138)
PHONE..................................419 562-5522
EMP: 6 **EST:** 2005
SALES (est): 1.09MM **Privately Held**
Web: www.j3pos.biz
SIC: 7371 3578 Computer software development; Calculators and adding machines

(G-1861)
GENERAL ELECTRIC COMPANY
Also Called: GE
1250 S Walnut St (44820-3266)
PHONE..................................419 563-1200
Peter Gabriel, *Brnch Mgr*
EMP: 276
SALES (corp-wide): 67.95B **Publicly Held**
Web: www.ge.com
SIC: 3641 Lamps, fluorescent, electric
PA: General Electric Company
1 Aviation Way
Cincinnati OH 45215
617 443-3000

(G-1862)
IMASEN BUCYRUS TECHNOLOGY INC
Also Called: I B-Tech
260 Crossroads Blvd (44820-1363)
PHONE..................................419 563-9590
Katsumi Ito, *Pr*
Joe Downing, *
Koichi Fukui, *
◆ **EMP:** 220 **EST:** 1997
SALES (est): 49.08MM **Privately Held**
Web: www.bucyrusohio.com
SIC: 3714 Motor vehicle parts and accessories
PA: Imasen Electric Industrial Co., Ltd.
1, Kakibata
Inuyama AIC 484-0

(G-1863)
NATIONAL LIME AND STONE CO
4580 Bethel Rd (44820-9754)
P.O. Box 69 (44820-0069)
PHONE..................................419 562-0771
Eric Johnson, *Prin*
EMP: 28
SALES (corp-wide): 167.89MM **Privately Held**
Web: www.natlime.com
SIC: 1411 3281 1422 Limestone, dimension-quarrying; Cut stone and stone products; Crushed and broken limestone
PA: The National Lime And Stone Company
551 Lake Cascade Pkwy
Findlay OH 45840
419 422-4341

(G-1864)
OAK VIEW ENTERPRISES INC
100 Crossroads Blvd (44820-1361)
PHONE..................................513 860-4446
Doug Leuthold, *Pr*
Jeff Miller, *Prin*
Phil Taylor, *Prin*
Sandi Leuthold, *Prin*
EMP: 26 **EST:** 1988
SALES (est): 8.29MM **Privately Held**
Web: www.advanced-fiber.com
SIC: 2821 5084 Cellulose derivative materials; Paper manufacturing machinery

(G-1865)
QUALITOR SUBSIDIARY H INC
1232 Whetstone St (44820-3539)
PHONE..................................419 562-7987
Andrew Ason, *Pr*
Ralph Reins, *
EMP: 127 **EST:** 1984
SALES (est): 5.08MM
SALES (corp-wide): 8.03B **Privately Held**
SIC: 3714 3451 3429 5013 Motor vehicle brake systems and parts; Screw machine products; Hardware, nec; Automotive supplies and parts
HQ: Transportation Aftermarket Enterprise Inc
1840 Mccullough St
Lima OH

(G-1866)
R L RUSH TOOL & PATTERN INC
Also Called: Rush, R L Tool & Pattern
1620 Whetstone St (44820-3557)
P.O. Box 763 (44820-0763)
PHONE..................................419 562-9849
Roger Rush, *Pr*
Phyllis Rush, *Sec*
EMP: 7 **EST:** 1974
SQ FT: 7,000
SALES (est): 557.37K **Privately Held**

Web: www.rushtool.com
SIC: 3543 3469 Industrial patterns; Stamping metal for the trade

(G-1867)
REGO MANUFACTURING CO INC
1870 E Mansfield St (44820-2018)
P.O. Box 838 (44820-0838)
PHONE..................................419 562-0466
Raymond L Kincaid, *Ch Bd*
Timothy Stenson, *
Ken Kincaid, *
Claudia Kincaid, *
EMP: 63 **EST:** 1973
SQ FT: 15,000
SALES (est): 2.54MM **Privately Held**
Web: www.regoonline.com
SIC: 3911 Jewelry apparel

(G-1868)
RYDER-HEIL BRONZE INC
126 E Irving St (44820-1409)
P.O. Box 647 (44820-0647)
PHONE..................................419 562-2841
Herbert D Kleine, *Pr*
EMP: 35 **EST:** 1910
SQ FT: 39,750
SALES (est): 4.47MM **Privately Held**
Web: www.ryderheil.com
SIC: 3366 Copper foundries

(G-1869)
TRANSCO RAILWAY PRODUCTS
820 Hopley Ave (44820-2855)
PHONE..................................419 562-1031
Randy Stinnett, *Mgr*
EMP: 8 **EST:** 2018
SALES (est): 144.36K **Privately Held**
Web: www.transcorailway.com
SIC: 3537 Industrial trucks and tractors

(G-1870)
TWM LLC
314 N Sandusky Ave (44820-1805)
PHONE..................................419 562-9622
Wendy Magette, *Prin*
EMP: 6 **EST:** 2008
SALES (est): 212.63K **Privately Held**
SIC: 3999 Cigarette and cigar products and accessories

(G-1871)
VAL CASTING INC
108 E Rensselaer St (44820-2320)
P.O. Box 374 (44820-0374)
PHONE..................................419 562-2499
Val Fawley, *Pr*
Michael Romanoff, *
EMP: 10 **EST:** 1983
SQ FT: 4,500
SALES (est): 491.11K **Privately Held**
Web: www.valjewelry.com
SIC: 3911 Jewelry, precious metal

(G-1872)
VELVET ICE CREAM COMPANY
Also Called: Bucyrus Ice Company
1233 Whetstone St (44820-3540)
PHONE..................................419 562-2009
TOLL FREE: 800
Jack Rogers, *Mgr*
EMP: 30
SALES (corp-wide): 21.87MM **Privately Held**
Web: www.velveticecream.com
SIC: 5143 2097 Ice cream and ices; Manufactured ice
PA: Velvet Ice Cream Company
11324 Mount Vernon Rd
Utica OH 43080
740 892-3921

(G-1873)
W E LOTT COMPANY
1432 Isaac Beal Rd (44820-9604)
P.O. Box 628 (44820-0628)
PHONE..................................419 563-9400
Richard Olt, *Pr*
W E Lott, *Sec*
▲ **EMP:** 11 **EST:** 1958
SQ FT: 20,000
SALES (est): 2.36MM **Privately Held**
Web: www.welott.com
SIC: 3462 3321 3322 3324 Iron and steel forgings; Gray and ductile iron foundries; Malleable iron foundries; Steel investment foundries

(G-1874)
W M DAUCH CONCRETE INC
900 Nevada Rd (44820-1744)
PHONE..................................419 562-6917
William Dauch, *Pr*
EMP: 7 **EST:** 1968
SALES (est): 510.31K **Privately Held**
Web: www.dauchconcrete.com
SIC: 3273 1771 Ready-mixed concrete; Concrete work

(G-1875)
WILLIAM DAUCH CONCRETE COMPANY
900 Nevada Wynford Rd (44820-9440)
PHONE..................................419 562-6917
Tim Corrigan, *Mgr*
EMP: 10
SALES (corp-wide): 9.78MM **Privately Held**
Web: www.dauchconcrete.com
SIC: 3273 Ready-mixed concrete
PA: William Dauch Concrete Company Inc
84 Cleveland Rd
Norwalk OH 44857
419 668-4458

(G-1876)
XT INNOVATIONS LTD
4799 Stetzer Rd (44820-9391)
PHONE..................................419 562-1989
EMP: 6 **EST:** 2008
SALES (est): 194.16K **Privately Held**
Web: www.xt-innovations.com
SIC: 2273 Carpets and rugs

Burbank
Wayne County

(G-1877)
PISCIONE WELDING
10147 Franchester Rd (44214-9603)
PHONE..................................440 653-3985
Chad Piscione, *Prin*
EMP: 8 **EST:** 2008
SALES (est): 202.01K **Privately Held**
SIC: 7692 Welding repair

Burghill
Trumbull County

(G-1878)
DESIGNER DOORS INC
4810 State Route 7 (44404-9701)
PHONE..................................330 772-6391
Ron Seidle Junior, *Pr*
Robert Seidle, *
◆ **EMP:** 17 **EST:** 1972
SQ FT: 23,500
SALES (est): 233.45K **Privately Held**
Web: www.cambek.com

SIC: 2431 Doors, wood

Burkettsville
Mercer County

(G-1879)
WERLING AND SONS INC
Also Called: Burkettsville Stockyard
100 Plum St (45310-5017)
P.O. Box 148 (45310-0148)
PHONE.................................937 338-3281
Edward J Werling, Pr
James R Werling, Sec
EMP: 10 **EST:** 1886
SALES (est): 1.92MM **Privately Held**
Web: www.werlingandsons.com
SIC: 5154 2011 Livestock; Meat packing plants

Burton
Geauga County

(G-1880)
HEXPOL COMPOUNDING LLC
Also Called: Burton Rubber Processing
14330 Kinsman Rd (44021-9648)
PHONE.................................440 834-4644
John Gorrell, Mgr
EMP: 200
SALES (corp-wide): 2.12B **Privately Held**
Web: www.hexpol.com
SIC: 3087 2865 5162 2899 Custom compound purchased resins; Dyes and pigments; Resins; Chemical preparations, nec
HQ: Hexpol Compounding Llc
14330 Kinsman Rd
Burton OH 44021
440 834-4644

(G-1881)
HEXPOL COMPOUNDING LLC (DH)
Also Called: Hexpol Polymers
14330 Kinsman Rd (44021-9648)
P.O. Box 415000 (37241-5000)
PHONE.................................440 834-4644
Gary Moore, Pr
Tracy Garrison, Pr
Ernie Ulmer, CFO
▲ **EMP:** 50 **EST:** 2004
SALES (est): 491.43MM
SALES (corp-wide): 2.12B **Privately Held**
Web: www.hexpol.com
SIC: 3087 2821 Custom compound purchased resins; Thermoplastic materials
HQ: Hexpol Holding Inc.
14330 Kinsman Rd
Burton OH 44021
440 834-4644

(G-1882)
HEXPOL HOLDING INC (HQ)
14330 Kinsman Rd (44021-9648)
PHONE.................................440 834-4644
Georg Brunstam, Pr
EMP: 10 **EST:** 2012
SALES: 1.07B
SALES (corp-wide): 2.12B **Privately Held**
Web: www.hexpol.com
SIC: 2821 3087 6719 Plastics materials and resins; Custom compound purchased resins; Investment holding companies, except banks
PA: Hexpol Ab
Skeppsbron 3
MalmO 211 2
40254660

(G-1883)
KEN EMERICK MACHINE PRODUCTS
14504 Main Market Rd (44021-9615)
PHONE.................................440 834-4501
Ken Emerick, Pr
Pam Emerick, VP
EMP: 8 **EST:** 1965
SQ FT: 12,500
SALES (est): 943.59K **Privately Held**
Web: www.emerickmachine.com
SIC: 3541 Machine tools, metal cutting type

(G-1884)
MAINE RUBBER PREFORMS LLC
14481 Butternut Rd (44021-9528)
PHONE.................................216 387-1268
EMP: 6 **EST:** 2012
SALES (est): 119.66K **Privately Held**
Web: www.mainerubberpreforms.com
SIC: 3069 Molded rubber products

(G-1885)
OHIO BOX & CRATE INC
Also Called: Ohio Box and Crate Co
16751 Tavern Rd (44021-9605)
PHONE.................................440 526-3133
Sarmite S Grava, Pr
EMP: 15 **EST:** 1975
SQ FT: 15,000
SALES (est): 441.89K **Privately Held**
SIC: 2441 2448 Boxes, wood; Skids, wood and wood with metal

(G-1886)
STEPHEN M TRUDICK
Also Called: Hardwood Lumber Co
13813 Station Road (44021)
P.O. Box 15 (44021)
PHONE.................................440 834-1891
Stephen M Trudick, Owner
▲ **EMP:** 41 **EST:** 1958
SQ FT: 80,000
SALES (est): 2.29MM **Privately Held**
Web: www.hardwood-lumber.com
SIC: 3991 2426 5031 3442 Brooms and brushes; Dimension, hardwood; Lumber: rough, dressed, and finished; Metal doors, sash, and trim

(G-1887)
TROY CHEMICAL INDUSTRIES INC (PA)
Also Called: Troy Chemical
17040 Rapids Rd (44021-9754)
P.O. Box 430 (44021-0430)
PHONE.................................440 834-4408
Lee Imhof, Pr
Richard B Keyse, VP
Joyce Pope, Sec
▲ **EMP:** 19 **EST:** 1971
SQ FT: 25,000
SALES (est): 4.6MM
SALES (corp-wide): 4.6MM **Privately Held**
Web: www.troychemical.com
SIC: 2842 Polishes and sanitation goods

(G-1888)
TROY MANUFACTURING CO
Also Called: Troy
17090 Rapids Rd (44021-9754)
P.O. Box 448 (44021-0448)
PHONE.................................440 834-8262
David Cseplo, Pr
Charles Fath, *
Wynne Bogert, *
Richard Taylor, *
EMP: 32 **EST:** 1952
SQ FT: 40,000
SALES (est): 8.08MM **Privately Held**
Web: www.troy-mfg.com

SIC: 3599 Machine shop, jobbing and repair

(G-1889)
TROY PRECISION CARBIDE DIE INC
Also Called: Troy Precision Carbide
17720 Claridon Troy Rd (44021-9658)
PHONE.................................440 834-4477
James Dewalt, Pr
Kelly Amon, VP
Jeff Amon, Sec
EMP: 17 **EST:** 1952
SQ FT: 10,000
SALES (est): 512.2K **Privately Held**
Web: www.troyprecisioncarbidedie.com
SIC: 3544 Special dies and tools

(G-1890)
WB INDUSTRIES INC
16461 Messenger Rd. (44021)
PHONE.................................440 708-0309
William Bertman, Owner
EMP: 9 **EST:** 2002
SQ FT: 1,550
SALES (est): 81.86K **Privately Held**
SIC: 3589 Car washing machinery

Butler
Richland County

(G-1891)
WENGERDS WELDING & REPAIR LLC
21701 Pealer Mill Rd (44822-9241)
PHONE.................................740 599-9071
EMP: 7 **EST:** 2000
SALES (est): 293.92K **Privately Held**
SIC: 7692 Welding repair

(G-1892)
YODER WOODWORKING
21198 Swendal Rd (44822-9214)
PHONE.................................740 399-9400
Mervin Yoder, Prin
EMP: 7 **EST:** 2008
SALES (est): 438.37K **Privately Held**
SIC: 2431 Millwork

Byesville
Guernsey County

(G-1893)
DAVID R HILL INC
132 S 2nd St (43723-1304)
P.O. Box 247 (43723-0247)
PHONE.................................740 685-5168
David R Hill, CEO
EMP: 6 **EST:** 1982
SALES (est): 802.5K **Privately Held**
SIC: 1382 Geological exploration, oil and gas field

(G-1894)
DETROIT DESL RMNFCTRNG-AST INC
60703 Country Club Rd (43723-9730)
PHONE.................................740 439-7701
Roger S Penske, Ch Bd
James Morrow, *
Mike Chuich, General Vice President*
◆ **EMP:** 500 **EST:** 1989
SQ FT: 128,000
SALES (est): 75.56MM
SALES (corp-wide): 60.75B **Privately Held**
Web: northamerica.daimlertruck.com
SIC: 3519 Diesel engine rebuilding
HQ: Detroit Diesel Remanufacturing Llc
100 Lodestone Way
Tooele UT 84074

(G-1895)
DETROIT DIESL SPECIALTY TL INC
60703 Country Club Rd (43723-9730)
PHONE.................................740 435-4452
Wayne Prouty, Pr
▲ **EMP:** 110 **EST:** 2001
SALES (est): 2.04MM
SALES (corp-wide): 60.75B **Privately Held**
SIC: 3599 Electrical discharge machining (EDM)
HQ: Detroit Diesel Corporation
13400 W Outer Dr
Detroit MI 48239
313 592-5000

(G-1896)
FAMOUS INDUSTRIES INC
Also Called: L B Manufacturing
356 Main St (43723-1123)
PHONE.................................740 685-2592
EMP: 17
SALES (corp-wide): 3.83B **Privately Held**
Web: www.johnsoncontrols.com
SIC: 3469 3585 3564 3498 Stamping metal for the trade; Refrigeration and heating equipment; Blowers and fans; Fabricated pipe and fittings
HQ: Famous Industries, Inc.
2620 Ridgewood Rd Ste 200
Akron OH 44313
330 535-1811

(G-1897)
FAMOUS REALTY CLEVELAND INC
Also Called: Famous Supply
354 Main St (43723-1123)
PHONE.................................740 685-2533
Eric St Claire, Mgr
EMP: 10
SALES (corp-wide): 1.08MM **Privately Held**
SIC: 3585 5074 Heating and air conditioning combination units; Plumbing fittings and supplies
PA: Famous Realty Of Cleveland, Inc.
109 N Union St
Akron OH 44304
330 762-9621

(G-1898)
ISLAND ASEPTICS LLC
100 Hope Ave (43723-9460)
P.O. Box 280 (43723-0280)
PHONE.................................740 685-2548
▲ **EMP:** 150
SIC: 2656 Food containers (liquid tight), including milk cartons

(G-1899)
KERRY INC
Also Called: Kerry Ingredients
100 Hope Ave (43723-9460)
PHONE.................................760 685-2548
EMP: 45
Web: www.kerry.com
SIC: 2656 5149 Food containers (liquid tight), including milk cartons; Condiments
HQ: Kerry Inc.
3400 Millington Rd
Beloit WI 53511
608 363-1200

(G-1900)
TIMCO INC
57051 Marietta Rd (43723-9709)
PHONE.................................740 685-2594
Tim Brown, Pr
EMP: 12 **EST:** 1982
SQ FT: 2,000

GEOGRAPHIC SECTION

Cambridge - Guernsey County (G-1921)

SALES (est): 923.17K **Privately Held**
Web: www.timcoinc.net
SIC: **1381** 3533 Drilling oil and gas wells; Oil and gas field machinery

(G-1901)
VELOCITY CONCEPT DEV GROUP LLC
8824 Clay Pike (43723-9712)
PHONE.................................740 685-2637
Eric Fehrman, *Brnch Mgr*
EMP: 8
SALES (corp-wide): 6.17MM **Privately Held**
Web: www.velocityfast.com
SIC: **3544** Industrial molds
PA: Velocity Concept Development Group, Llc
    4393 Digital Way
    Mason OH 45040
    513 204-2100

(G-1902)
W P BROWN ENTERPRISES INC
57051 Marietta Rd (43723-9709)
PHONE.................................740 685-2594
William P Brown, *Pr*
EMP: 6 EST: 1978
SALES (est): 600.58K **Privately Held**
Web: www.brownrentalsinc.com
SIC: **1311** Crude petroleum production

Cadiz
Harrison County

(G-1903)
HARRISON NEWS HERALD INC
Also Called: Schloss Media
144 S Main St Lowr (43907-1167)
P.O. Box 127 (43907-0127)
PHONE.................................740 942-2118
David Schloss, *Pr*
EMP: 8 EST: 1882
SALES (est): 220.01K **Privately Held**
Web: www.harrisonnewsherald.com
SIC: **2711** Newspapers, publishing and printing

(G-1904)
STANLEY BITTINGER
Also Called: Bittinger Carbide
81331 Hines Rd (43907-9535)
PHONE.................................740 942-4302
Stanley Bittinger, *Owner*
Sheila Bittinger, *Off Mgr*
EMP: 7 EST: 1981
SQ FT: 1,800
SALES (est): 505.69K **Privately Held**
Web: www.bittingercarbide.com
SIC: **3546** 5084 3545 Power-driven handtools; Industrial machinery and equipment; Machine tool accessories

Cairo
Allen County

(G-1905)
CHEMTRADE REFINERY SVCS INC
7680 Ottawa Rd (45820)
PHONE.................................419 641-4151
Tim Handiford, *Brnch Mgr*
EMP: 10
SALES (corp-wide): 1.34B **Privately Held**
Web: www.chemtradelogistics.com
SIC: **2819** Industrial inorganic chemicals, nec
HQ: Chemtrade Refinery Services Inc.
    440 N 9th St
    Lawrence KS 66044
    785 843-2290

Caldwell
Noble County

(G-1906)
ANTERO RESOURCES CORPORATION
44510 Marietta Rd (43724-9209)
PHONE.................................303 357-7310
Austin Beeler, *Mgr*
EMP: 33
Web: www.anteroresources.com
SIC: **1382** Oil and gas exploration services
PA: Antero Resources Corporation
    1615 Wynkoop St
    Denver CO 80202

(G-1907)
BEAR WELDING SERVICES LLC
18210 Myrtle Ake Rd (43724-9136)
PHONE.................................740 630-7538
Jeremy Leonard, *Managing Member*
EMP: 10 EST: 2014
SALES (est): 231.89K **Privately Held**
SIC: **7692** Welding repair

(G-1908)
CALDWELL LUMBER & SUPPLY CO
Also Called: Do It Best
17990 Woodsfield Rd (43724-9435)
PHONE.................................740 732-2306
Edward Crock, *Pr*
Brandon Crock, *
EMP: 26 EST: 1948
SQ FT: 25,000
SALES (est): 4.39MM **Privately Held**
Web: caldwell.doitbest.com
SIC: **5251** 3273 Hardware stores; Ready-mixed concrete

(G-1909)
INTERNTNAL CNVRTER CLDWELL INC
Also Called: I-Convert
17153 Industrial Hwy (43724-9779)
PHONE.................................740 732-5665
Phil Harris, *Pr*
Mohammed Nadeem, *Care Vice President**
Gerry Medlin, *
Jerry Lawrence, *
Craig Lemieux, *
◆ EMP: 241 EST: 1993
SQ FT: 75,000
SALES (est): 57.45MM
SALES (corp-wide): 32.64B **Publicly Held**
Web: www.novolex.com
SIC: **3089** 3353 3083 Laminating of plastics; Aluminum sheet, plate, and foil; Laminated plastics plate and sheet
HQ: Packaging Dynamics Corporation
    3900 W 43rd St
    Chicago IL 60632

(G-1910)
MAGNUM MAGNETICS CORPORATION
17289 Industrial Hwy (43724-9779)
PHONE.................................740 516-6237
EMP: 39
Web: www.magnummagnetics.com
SIC: **2893** Printing ink
PA: Magnum Magnetics Corporation
    801 Masonic Park Rd
    Marietta OH 45750

(G-1911)
MAGNUM TAPES FILMS
17289 Industrial Hwy (43724-9779)
PHONE.................................877 460-8402
EMP: 7 EST: 2018
SALES (est): 262.82K **Privately Held**
Web: www.magnumtapes.com
SIC: **2672** 3069 3081 Adhesive papers, labels, or tapes: from purchased material; Film, rubber; Polyethylene film

(G-1912)
R C MOORE LUMBER CO
Also Called: MOORE, R C LUMBER CO (INC)
820 Miller St (43724-1044)
P.O. Box 139 (43724-0139)
PHONE.................................740 732-4950
Chad Moore, *Pr*
EMP: 12
SALES (corp-wide): 2.02MM **Privately Held**
SIC: **2431** 5211 Doors, combination screen-storm, wood; Lumber products
PA: R. C. Moore Lumber Co.
    46000 County Road 56
    Caldwell OH
    740 732-2326

(G-1913)
SHARON STONE INC
44895 Sharon Stone Rd (43724-9534)
P.O. Box 100 (45727-0100)
PHONE.................................740 732-7100
John Mccort, *Pr*
Carl Baker Junior, *VP*
Robert Cunningham, *Sec*
EMP: 6 EST: 1985
SQ FT: 980
SALES (est): 482.54K **Privately Held**
SIC: **1422** Limestones, ground

(G-1914)
TRINITY WATER SOLUTIONS LLC
17226 Industrial Hwy (43724-9779)
P.O. Box 4074 (45750-7074)
PHONE.................................740 318-0585
EMP: 25 EST: 2021
SALES (est): 1.74MM **Privately Held**
SIC: **3589** Water treatment equipment, industrial

Caledonia
Marion County

(G-1915)
GLEN-GERY CORPORATION
Also Called: Glen-Gery Caledonia Plant
5692 Rinker Rd (43314-9791)
P.O. Box 207 (43325-0207)
PHONE.................................419 845-3321
Ken Hagberg, *Mgr*
EMP: 66
Web: www.glengery.com
SIC: **3251** 5211 3255 Brick clay: common face, glazed, vitrified, or hollow; Brick; Clay refractories
HQ: Glen-Gery Corporation
    1166 Spring St
    Reading PA 19610
    610 374-4011

(G-1916)
INSTA-GRO MANUFACTURING INC
8217 Linn Hipsher Rd (43314-9736)
PHONE.................................419 845-3046
Allan Farrow, *Pr*
EMP: 6 EST: 1978
SALES (est): 951.41K **Privately Held**
Web: www.instagro.com
SIC: **2875** 5261 Fertilizers, mixing only; Fertilizer

(G-1917)
PILLSBURY COMPANY LLC
Also Called: Pillsbury
4136 Martel Rd (43314-9634)
PHONE.................................419 845-3751
Craig Olinger, *Brnch Mgr*
EMP: 39
SALES (corp-wide): 20.09B **Publicly Held**
Web: www.pillsbury.com
SIC: **2041** 2033 Flour and other grain mill products; Canned fruits and specialties
HQ: The Pillsbury Company Llc
    1 General Mills Blvd
    Minneapolis MN 55426

Cambridge
Guernsey County

(G-1918)
ACI SERVICES INC (PA)
Also Called: Gas Products
125 Steubenville Ave (43725-2243)
PHONE.................................740 435-0240
Chad Brahler, *Pr*
Norm Shade, *
Dwayne Hickman, *
EMP: 40 EST: 1960
SQ FT: 25,000
SALES (est): 10.47MM
SALES (corp-wide): 10.47MM **Privately Held**
Web: www.aciservices.com
SIC: **3563** Air and gas compressors including vacuum pumps

(G-1919)
AMERICAN CULVERT & FABG CO
Also Called: American Culvert
201 Wheeling Ave (43725-2256)
P.O. Box 757 (43725-0757)
PHONE.................................740 432-6334
Herman Rogovin, *Pr*
EMP: 12 EST: 1936
SQ FT: 5,000
SALES (est): 182.9K **Privately Held**
SIC: **3444** 3312 Pipe, sheet metal; Blast furnaces and steel mills

(G-1920)
AMG ALUMINUM NORTH AMERICA LLC (HQ)
Also Called: AMG Aluminum
60790 Southgate Rd (43725)
PHONE.................................659 348-3620
Tom Centa, *Managing Member*
◆ EMP: 15 EST: 1986
SALES (est): 28.44MM
SALES (corp-wide): 937.12MM **Privately Held**
Web: www.amg-al.com
SIC: **3355** 3354 3365 3339 Aluminum rod and bar; Aluminum extruded products; Aluminum foundries; Primary nonferrous metals, nec
PA: Amg Critical Materials N.V.
    Strawinskylaan 1343
    Amsterdam NH 1077
    207147140

(G-1921)
APPALACHIAN SOLVENTS LLC
5041 Skyline Dr (43725-9729)
P.O. Box 1286 (43725-6286)
PHONE.................................740 680-3649
Jonathan Hudson, *Owner*
EMP: 8 EST: 2013
SALES (est): 296.82K **Privately Held**
SIC: **2911** Solvents

Cambridge - Guernsey County (G-1922)

(G-1922)
APPALACHIAN WELL SURVEYS INC
10291 Ohio Ave (43725-3201)
P.O. Box 1058 (43725-6058)
PHONE..................................740 255-7652
Jonathan W Hudson, *Pr*
Mary Ann Hudson, *VP*
EMP: 8 **EST:** 1987
SALES (est): 983.98K **Privately Held**
Web: www.appalachianwellsurveysinc.com
SIC: 1389 Oil field services, nec

(G-1923)
BLUE RACER MIDSTREAM LLC
11388 E Pike Rd Unit B (43725-9669)
PHONE..................................740 630-7556
EMP: 66 **EST:** 2013
SALES (est): 3.31MM **Privately Held**
Web: www.blueracermidstream.com
SIC: 1382 Oil and gas exploration services

(G-1924)
CAMBRDGE OHIO PROD ASSMBLY COR
Also Called: Copac
1521 Morton Ave (43725-2750)
PHONE..................................740 432-6383
Mike Arent, *Pr*
Andrew E Yandora, *VP*
Andrew Balik, *VP Sls*
EMP: 8 **EST:** 1992
SQ FT: 39,500
SALES (est): 510.81K **Privately Held**
Web: www.spinemedspecialists.com
SIC: 3578 3643 Accounting machines and cash registers; Current-carrying wiring services

(G-1925)
CAMBRIDGE PACKAGING INC
Also Called: Cambridge Box & Gift Shop
60794 Southgate Rd (43725-9414)
PHONE..................................740 432-3351
Larry Knellinger, *Pr*
Margaret F Knellinger, *
Bill Knellinger, *
Rick Knellinger, *
EMP: 31 **EST:** 1982
SQ FT: 26,000
SALES (est): 5.48MM **Privately Held**
Web: www.cambridgepackaging.com
SIC: 2653 5199 Boxes, corrugated: made from purchased materials; Packaging materials

(G-1926)
CASTLE PRINTING INC
139 N 7th St (43725-2320)
PHONE..................................740 439-2208
Brenda Taylor, *Prin*
EMP: 6 **EST:** 2017
SALES (est): 83.91K **Privately Held**
SIC: 2752 Offset printing

(G-1927)
CENTRIA INC
Also Called: Hh Robertsons Flooring
530 N 2nd St (43725-1214)
P.O. Box 198 (15003-0198)
PHONE..................................740 432-7351
EMP: 6
SALES (corp-wide): 34.71B **Publicly Held**
Web: www.centria.com
SIC: 3479 3471 Etching and engraving; Finishing, metals or formed products
HQ: Centria, Inc.
1550 Corpls Hts Rd # 500
Moon Township PA 15108
412 299-8000

(G-1928)
CHAMPION SPARK PLUG CMBRDGE PL
6420 Glenn Hwy (43725-9805)
PHONE..................................740 432-2393
Steve Trilliot, *Mgr*
EMP: 6 **EST:** 2018
SALES (est): 242.38K **Privately Held**
SIC: 3714 Motor vehicle parts and accessories

(G-1929)
COLGATE-PALMOLIVE COMPANY
Also Called: Colgate-Palmolive
8800 Guernsey Industrial Blvd (43725-8913)
PHONE..................................212 310-2000
Rick Spann, *Mgr*
EMP: 250
SALES (corp-wide): 19.46B **Publicly Held**
Web: www.colgatepalmolive.com
SIC: 2844 Perfumes, cosmetics and other toilet preparations
PA: Colgate-Palmolive Company
300 Park Ave
New York NY 10022
212 310-2000

(G-1930)
CRESCENT SERVICES LLC
11137 E Pike Rd (43725-8949)
PHONE..................................405 603-1200
Susan Leonard, *Prin*
EMP: 6 **EST:** 2012
SALES (est): 179.1K **Privately Held**
SIC: 1389 Oil field services, nec

(G-1931)
DETROIT DESL RMNUFACTURING LLC
8475 Reitler Rd (43725-8660)
PHONE..................................740 439-7701
Cheryl Meyer, *Brnch Mgr*
EMP: 121
SALES (corp-wide): 60.75B **Privately Held**
SIC: 3519 Diesel engine rebuilding
HQ: Detroit Diesel Remanufacturing Llc
100 Lodestone Way
Tooele UT 84074

(G-1932)
DEVCO OIL INC
Also Called: Devco Trucking
2522 Glenn Hwy (43725-9028)
PHONE..................................740 439-3833
Phillip Dever, *Pr*
Roger Frantz, *VP*
Linda Dever, *Treas*
EMP: 12 **EST:** 1975
SALES (est): 517.38K **Privately Held**
SIC: 1311 Crude petroleum production

(G-1933)
DONOHUES HILLTOP ICE CO LTD
Also Called: Donahue's Hilltop Supply
1112 Highland Ave (43725-8809)
PHONE..................................740 432-3348
John Brent Hoffman, *Owner*
John B Hoffman, *Owner*
EMP: 22 **EST:** 1914
SQ FT: 8,000
SALES (est): 672.99K **Privately Held**
SIC: 2097 Block ice

(G-1934)
EMERSON PROFESSIONAL TOOLS LLC
9877 Brick Church Rd (43725-9420)
PHONE..................................740 432-8782
EMP: 51 **EST:** 2019
SALES (est): 11.9MM
SALES (corp-wide): 15.16B **Publicly Held**
SIC: 3823 Process control instruments
PA: Emerson Electric Co.
8000 W Florissant Ave
Saint Louis MO 63136
314 553-2000

(G-1935)
ENCORE INDUSTRIES INC (DH)
Also Called: Encore Plastics
725 Water St (43725-1241)
PHONE..................................419 626-8000
Timothy J Rathbun, *CEO*
Craig Rathbun, *
▲ **EMP:** 223 **EST:** 2000
SQ FT: 250,000
SALES (est): 49.56MM
SALES (corp-wide): 816.52K **Privately Held**
SIC: 3089 Thermoformed finished plastics products, nec
HQ: Plastiques Ipl Inc
1155 Boul Rene-Levesque O Bureau 4100
Montreal QC H3B 3
418 789-2880

(G-1936)
GEORGETOWN VINEYARDS INC
Also Called: Georgetown Vineyards
62920 Georgetown Rd (43725-9749)
PHONE..................................740 435-3222
John Nicolozakes, *Pr*
Kay Nicolozakes, *VP*
Emma Mcvicker, *Sec*
Sam Nicolozakes, *Treas*
EMP: 25 **EST:** 2004
SQ FT: 600
SALES (est): 1.28MM **Privately Held**
Web: www.georgetowntavern.com
SIC: 2084 5812 2082 Wine cellars, bonded: engaged in blending wines; Pizza restaurants; Near beer

(G-1937)
J E NICOLOZAKES CO
62920 Georgetown Rd (43725-9749)
PHONE..................................740 310-1606
John Nicolozakes, *Prin*
EMP: 6 **EST:** 1992
SALES (est): 95.06K **Privately Held**
SIC: 2084 Wines

(G-1938)
KENNEDYS BAKERY INC
1025 Wheeling Ave (43725-2441)
P.O. Box 396 (43725-0396)
PHONE..................................740 432-2301
T Noralee Kennedy, *Pr*
Bob Kennedy, *VP*
EMP: 14 **EST:** 1925
SQ FT: 8,000
SALES (est): 454.1K **Privately Held**
Web: www.kennedysbakery.com
SIC: 5461 2052 2051 Doughnuts; Cookies and crackers; Bread, cake, and related products

(G-1939)
KINGSLY COMPRESSION INC
Also Called: Kingsly Compression
3956 Glenn Hwy (43725-8575)
PHONE..................................740 439-0772
EMP: 8
Web: www.kingslycompression.com
SIC: 3563 5084 Air and gas compressors; Processing and packaging equipment
PA: Kingsly Compression, Inc.
3750 S Noah Dr
Saxonburg PA 16056

(G-1940)
LILIENTHAL/SOUTHEASTERN INC
1609 N 11th St (43725-1009)
P.O. Box 580 (43725-0580)
PHONE..................................740 439-1640
Richard W Lilienthal, *Pr*
EMP: 8 **EST:** 1875
SQ FT: 6,000
SALES (est): 234.92K **Privately Held**
Web: www.lilseinc.com
SIC: 2752 2782 2759 2789 Offset printing; Blankbooks; Letterpress printing; Bookbinding and related work

(G-1941)
MATTMARK PARTNERS INC
Also Called: Mattmark Drilling Company
61234 Southgate Rd (43725-8945)
PHONE..................................740 439-3109
Gerald J Benson, *Pr*
Georgia Benson, *VP*
EMP: 14 **EST:** 1985
SQ FT: 5,400
SALES (est): 671.97K **Privately Held**
SIC: 1381 Drilling oil and gas wells

(G-1942)
METAL COATERS
Also Called: Centria Coil Coating Services
530 N 2nd St (43725-1214)
PHONE..................................740 432-7351
Charlie Hamilton, *Mgr*
EMP: 100
SALES (corp-wide): 34.71B **Publicly Held**
Web: centrial-nucortransitioncs.msappproxy.net
SIC: 3444 Sheet metalwork
HQ: Centria, Inc.
1550 Corpls Hts Rd # 500
Moon Township PA 15108
412 299-8000

(G-1943)
MO-TRIM INC
240 Steubenville Ave (43725-2215)
P.O. Box 850 (43725-0850)
PHONE..................................740 439-2725
Jack O Cartner, *Pr*
EMP: 9 **EST:** 1962
SQ FT: 10,000
SALES (est): 934.79K **Privately Held**
Web: www.motrim.net
SIC: 3524 Lawn and garden tractors and equipment

(G-1944)
MOSSER GLASS INC
9279 Cadiz Rd (43725-9564)
PHONE..................................740 439-1827
Timmy J Mosser, *Pr*
Thomas R Mosser, *
Timmy J Mosser, *VP*
Mindy Hartly, *
▲ **EMP:** 30 **EST:** 1961
SALES (est): 2.36MM **Privately Held**
Web: www.mosserglass.com
SIC: 3229 5199 5719 Novelty glassware; Glassware, novelty; Glassware

(G-1945)
OHIO BRIDGE CORPORATION
Also Called: U.S. Bridge
201 Wheeling Ave (43725-2256)
P.O. Box 757 (43725-0757)
PHONE..................................740 432-6334
Daniel Rogovin, *CEO*
Richard Rogovin, *
▼ **EMP:** 140 **EST:** 1952
SQ FT: 250,000
SALES (est): 22.38MM **Privately Held**
Web: www.usbridge.com

GEOGRAPHIC SECTION

Canal Fulton - Stark County (G-1967)

SIC: **1622** 3449 Bridge construction; Bars, concrete reinforcing: fabricated steel

(G-1946)
PACKAGING MATERIALS INC
62805 Bennett Ave (43725-9490)
P.O. Box 731 (43725-0731)
PHONE...............................740 432-6337
Marc Radasky, *Pr*
▼ **EMP:** 38 **EST:** 1970
SQ FT: 48,000
SALES (est): 3.5MM
SALES (corp-wide): 25.17MM **Privately Held**
Web: www.packagingmaterialsinc.com
SIC: **3081** 2759 2673 Unsupported plastics film and sheet; Commercial printing, nec; Bags: plastic, laminated, and coated
PA: Columbia Burlap And Bag Company, Inc.
1475 Walnut St
Kansas City MO 64106
816 421-4121

(G-1947)
PANHANDLE OLFLD SVC CMPNIES IN
62787 Philips Rd (43725-8684)
PHONE...............................330 340-9525
EMP: 20
Web: www.posci.net
SIC: **1389** Oil field services, nec
PA: Panhandle Oilfield Service Companies, Inc.
14000 Quail Springs Pkwy # 300
Oklahoma City OK 73134

(G-1948)
PLASTIC COMPOUNDERS INC
1125 Utica Dr (43725-2578)
P.O. Box 664 (43725-0664)
PHONE...............................740 432-7371
Dick Eubanks, *Pr*
Scott Eubanks, *
EMP: 40 **EST:** 1965
SQ FT: 50,000
SALES (est): 5.2MM **Privately Held**
Web: www.plasticcompounders.net
SIC: **2821** Plastics materials and resins

(G-1949)
QUANEX IG SYSTEMS INC
Also Called: Quanex Custom Mixing
804 Byesville Rd (43725-9327)
PHONE...............................740 435-0444
Jim Nixon, *Brnch Mgr*
EMP: 74
Web: www.quanex.com
SIC: **2891** Rubber cement
HQ: Quanex Ig Systems, Inc.
388 S Main St Ste 700
Akron OH 44311

(G-1950)
QUANEX IG SYSTEMS INC
Also Called: Quanex Building Products
800 Cochran Ave (43725-9317)
PHONE...............................740 439-2338
Michael Hovan, *Brnch Mgr*
EMP: 43
Web: www.quanex.com
SIC: **3061** 3053 Mechanical rubber goods; Gaskets; packing and sealing devices
HQ: Quanex Ig Systems, Inc.
388 S Main St Ste 700
Akron OH 44311

(G-1951)
RIDGE TOOL COMPANY
Also Called: North American Dist Ctr
9877 Brick Church Rd (43725-9420)

PHONE...............................740 432-8782
Brian Shanahann, *Mgr*
EMP: 81
SALES (corp-wide): 15.16B **Publicly Held**
Web: www.ridgid.com
SIC: **3541** Machine tools, metal cutting type
HQ: Ridge Tool Company
400 Clark St
Elyria OH 44035
440 323-5581

(G-1952)
SMITH CONCRETE
61539 Southgate Rd (43725-9456)
PHONE...............................740 439-7714
EMP: 11 **EST:** 2019
SALES (est): 144.3K **Privately Held**
Web: www.shellyco.com
SIC: **3273** Ready-mixed concrete

(G-1953)
SNIDER TIRE INC
Also Called: Snider General Tire
9501 Sunrise Rd (43725-9116)
PHONE...............................740 439-2741
Jerry Vandyne, *Mgr*
EMP: 23
SALES (corp-wide): 436.36MM **Privately Held**
Web: www.sniderfleet.com
SIC: **5531** 7534 Automotive tires; Tire retreading and repair shops
PA: Snider Tire, Inc.
1081 Red Ventures Dr
Fort Mill SC 29707
336 691-5480

(G-1954)
SPECTRUM PUBLICATIONS
831 Wheeling Ave (43725-2316)
PHONE...............................740 439-3531
Peggy Murgatroyd, *Genl Mgr*
EMP: 6 **EST:** 2017
SALES (est): 39.41K **Privately Held**
Web: www.daily-jeff.com
SIC: **2711** Newspapers, publishing and printing

(G-1955)
SPORTSMANS HAVEN INC
14695 E Pike Rd (43725-9166)
P.O. Box 403 (43773-0403)
PHONE...............................740 432-7243
Brent Umberger, *Pr*
EMP: 6 **EST:** 1961
SQ FT: 600
SALES (est): 496.54K **Privately Held**
SIC: **2426** 7699 5941 Gun stocks, wood; Gunsmith shop; Firearms

(G-1956)
SUPERIOR HARDWOODS OHIO INC
Also Called: Superior Hardwoods Cambridge
9911 Ohio Ave (43725-9307)
P.O. Box 1358 (43725-6358)
PHONE...............................740 439-2727
Fred Lander, *Mgr*
EMP: 20
SALES (corp-wide): 8.88MM **Privately Held**
Web: www.superiorhardwoodsofohio.com
SIC: **2421** 2426 Sawmills and planing mills, general; Hardwood dimension and flooring mills
PA: Superior Hardwoods Of Ohio, Inc.
134 Wellston Indus Pk Rd
Wellston OH 45692
740 384-5677

(G-1957)
TAYLOR QUICK PRINT
Also Called: Quick Print
1008 Woodlawn Ave # A (43725-2951)
PHONE...............................740 439-2208
Brenda Taylor, *Prin*
EMP: 6 **EST:** 2007
SALES (est): 338.19K **Privately Held**
SIC: **2752** Offset printing

(G-1958)
TELLING INDUSTRIES LLC
2105 Larrick Rd (43725-3064)
PHONE...............................740 435-8900
Steve Linch, *Mgr*
EMP: 37
SALES (corp-wide): 31.59MM **Privately Held**
Web: www.tellingindustries.com
SIC: **3316** Bars, steel, cold-finished, from purchased hot-rolled
PA: Telling Industries, Llc
4420 Sherwin Rd Ste 4
Willoughby OH 44094
440 974-3370

(G-1959)
VARIETY GLASS INC
201 Foster Ave (43725-1219)
PHONE...............................740 432-3643
Thomas R Mosser, *Pr*
Timothy J Mosser, *VP*
EMP: 10 **EST:** 1959
SQ FT: 16,000
SALES (est): 958K **Privately Held**
Web: www.mosserglass.com
SIC: **3229** Scientific glassware

(G-1960)
W A S P INC
59100 Claysville Rd (43725-8943)
PHONE...............................740 439-2398
Jeffrey L Carpenter, *Prin*
EMP: 6 **EST:** 2010
SALES (est): 148.04K **Privately Held**
SIC: **5074** 3432 Plumbing and hydronic heating supplies; Plumbing fixture fittings and trim

(G-1961)
ZEKELMAN INDUSTRIES INC
Also Called: Wheatland Tube Company
9208 Jeffrey Dr (43725-9417)
PHONE...............................740 432-2146
Ned Feeney, *Pr*
EMP: 186
SQ FT: 58,000
Web: www.zekelman.com
SIC: **3317** 3498 5074 3644 Pipes, seamless steel; Fabricated pipe and fittings; Plumbing fittings and supplies; Noncurrent-carrying wiring devices
PA: Zekelman Industries, Inc.
227 W Monroe St Ste 2600
Chicago IL 60606

Camden
Preble County

(G-1962)
CAMDEN READY MIX CO (PA)
478 Camden College Corner Rd (45311-9520)
P.O. Box 5 (45381-0005)
PHONE...............................937 456-4539
John D Wysong, *Pr*
Carroll Wysong, *VP*
EMP: 6 **EST:** 1947
SALES (est): 820.22K

SALES (corp-wide): 820.22K **Privately Held**
Web: www.preblecountystorage.com
SIC: **3273** Ready-mixed concrete

(G-1963)
PRECISION WOOD PRODUCTS INC (PA)
2456 Aukerman Creek Rd (45311-9706)
P.O. Box 10 (45311-0010)
PHONE...............................937 787-3523
Anthony Metzger, *Pr*
Lloyd W Kinzie, *Pr*
Glen D Knaus, *VP*
H Ronald Knaus, *VP*
Barbara Knaus, *Sec*
EMP: 10 **EST:** 1977
SQ FT: 32,000
SALES (est): 3.23MM
SALES (corp-wide): 3.23MM **Privately Held**
Web: www.precisionwoodproducts.com
SIC: **2431** Doors, wood

(G-1964)
TWIN CREEK MFG LLC
8111 Lantis Geeting Rd (45311-8971)
PHONE...............................937 634-3470
Ben Stevic, *Prin*
EMP: 6 **EST:** 2018
SALES (est): 246.52K **Privately Held**
Web: www.twincreekmfg.com
SIC: **3599** Machine shop, jobbing and repair

(G-1965)
WYSONG GRAVEL CO INC
120 Camden College Corner Rd (45311-9520)
P.O. Box 5 (45381-0005)
PHONE...............................937 452-1523
Tom Caden, *Genl Mgr*
EMP: 7
SQ FT: 3,452
SALES (corp-wide): 2.59MM **Privately Held**
Web: www.preblecountystorage.com
SIC: **1442** Gravel mining
PA: Wysong Gravel Co Inc
2332 State Route 503 N
West Alexandria OH 45381
937 456-4539

Campbell
Mahoning County

(G-1966)
SEACOR PAINTING CORPORATION
98 Creed Cir (44405-1277)
P.O. Box 588 (44405-0588)
PHONE...............................330 755-6361
Nicholas Frangos, *Pr*
EMP: 8 **EST:** 1997
SALES (est): 984.82K **Privately Held**
Web: www.seacorpainting.com
SIC: **3479** Painting of metal products

Canal Fulton
Stark County

(G-1967)
ASTRO-TEC MFG INC
550 Elm Ridge Ave (44614-9369)
P.O. Box 608 (44614-0608)
PHONE...............................330 854-2209
Stephanie Hopper, *Pr*
◆ **EMP:** 22 **EST:** 1963
SQ FT: 15,328
SALES (est): 1.94MM **Privately Held**

Canal Fulton - Stark County (G-1968)

Web: www.astro-tec.com
SIC: 3441 Fabricated structural metal

(G-1968)
BIRDS EYE FOODS INC
611 Elm Ridge Ave (44614-8476)
PHONE..................330 854-0818
Bill Gaster, *Brnch Mgr*
EMP: 59
SALES (corp-wide): 312.2MM **Privately Held**
SIC: 2096 3523 Potato chips and similar snacks; Peanut combines, diggers, packers, and threshers
PA: Birds Eye Foods, Inc.
121 Woodcrest Rd
Cherry Hill NJ 08003

(G-1969)
C MASSOUH PRINTING CO INC
Also Called: C Massouh Printing
590 Elm Ridge Ave (44614-9369)
PHONE..................330 408-7330
Carl Massouh, *Pr*
Chris Massouh, *VP*
EMP: 10 EST: 1989
SALES (est): 986.65K **Privately Held**
Web: www.cmassouhprinting.com
SIC: 2752 Offset printing

(G-1970)
COMMUNICATION EXHIBITS INC
1119 Milan St N (44614-9737)
PHONE..................330 854-4040
EMP: 60 EST: 1977
SALES (est): 9.13MM **Privately Held**
Web: www.ceilink.com
SIC: 3993 2542 Signs and advertising specialties; Partitions and fixtures, except wood

(G-1971)
JONMAR GEAR AND MACHINE INC
13786 Warwick Dr Nw (44614-9738)
PHONE..................330 854-6500
Larry Murgatroyd, *Pr*
Brent A Murgatroyd, *VP*
EMP: 6 EST: 2000
SQ FT: 18,000
SALES (est): 694.28K **Privately Held**
Web: www.jonmargear.com
SIC: 3566 7699 Gears, power transmission, except auto; Industrial machinery and equipment repair

(G-1972)
LINDSAY PRECAST LLC (PA)
6845 Erie Ave Nw (44614-8509)
PHONE..................800 837-7788
TOLL FREE: 800
Roland Lindsay Senior, *Pr*
Timothy Gesaman, *
Linda Lindsay, *
▼ EMP: 49 EST: 1968
SALES (est): 98.36MM
SALES (corp-wide): 98.36MM **Privately Held**
Web: www.lindsayprecast.com
SIC: 3272 3699 Septic tanks, concrete; Security devices

(G-1973)
MIDWEST KNIFE GRINDING INC
492 Elm Ridge Ave Ste 4 (44614-9369)
PHONE..................330 854-1030
James M Richmond Ii, *Pr*
EMP: 10 EST: 1986
SQ FT: 12,000
SALES (est): 967.85K **Privately Held**
Web: www.midwestknife.com

SIC: 7699 3541 3423 Knife, saw and tool sharpening and repair; Machine tools, metal cutting type; Hand and edge tools, nec

(G-1974)
RACK COATING SERVICE INC
5760 Erie Ave Nw (44614-9726)
P.O. Box 486 (44614-0486)
PHONE..................330 854-2869
John L Hexamer, *Pr*
EMP: 18 EST: 1963
SQ FT: 2,500
SALES (est): 533.86K **Privately Held**
Web: www.rackpowdercoating.com
SIC: 3479 Coating of metals and formed products

(G-1975)
SUMMIT ENGINEERED PRODUCTS INC
516 Elm Ridge Ave (44614-9309)
PHONE..................330 854-5388
Dick Lutz, *Pr*
EMP: 10 EST: 2006
SALES (est): 1.88MM **Privately Held**
SIC: 3315 Steel wire and related products

(G-1976)
TEK GROUP INTERNATIONAL
Also Called: Tek Manufacturing
567 Elm Ridge Ave (44614-9369)
PHONE..................330 706-0000
Chris Willison, *Pr*
Cliff Willison, *
EMP: 35 EST: 2003
SQ FT: 12,000
SALES (est): 7.2MM **Privately Held**
Web: www.tekusa.com
SIC: 3599 Machine shop, jobbing and repair

Canal Winchester
Franklin County

(G-1977)
A K ATHLETIC EQUIPMENT INC
8015 Howe Industrial Pkwy (43110-7890)
PHONE..................614 920-3069
Angela Katz, *Pr*
EMP: 34 EST: 1993
SQ FT: 32,000
SALES (est): 7.5MM **Privately Held**
Web: www.akathletics.com
SIC: 3496 5091 Mats and matting; Gymnasium equipment

(G-1978)
ALBANESE CONCESSIONS LLC
6983 Greensview Village Dr (43110-8454)
PHONE..................614 402-4937
EMP: 8 EST: 2007
SALES (est): 489.22K **Privately Held**
SIC: 2064 Candy and other confectionery products

(G-1979)
ATWOOD ROPE MANUFACTURING INC
121 N Trine St (43110-1154)
PHONE..................614 920-0534
Curtis Atwood, *Pr*
Curtis Atwood, *Owner*
▲ EMP: 40 EST: 2000
SALES (est): 3.87MM **Privately Held**
Web: www.atwoodrope.com
SIC: 5091 5085 2298 Boat accessories and parts; Rope, cord, and thread; Ropes and fiber cables

(G-1980)
BABBERT REAL ESTATE INV CO LTD (PA)
7415 Diley Rd (43110-8813)
P.O. Box 203 (43110-0203)
PHONE..................614 837-8444
Ervin C Babbert, *CEO*
Chuck Babbert, *
Ronald Babbert, *
Bonnie Babbert, *
EMP: 100 EST: 1998
SQ FT: 20,000
SALES (est): 8.11MM
SALES (corp-wide): 8.11MM **Privately Held**
Web: www.ecbabbert.com
SIC: 3272 Liquid catch basins, tanks, and covers: concrete

(G-1981)
BREWDOG BREWING COMPANY LLC (PA)
Also Called: Brewdog
96 Gender Rd (43110-7539)
PHONE..................614 908-3051
Martin Macdonald, *Genl Mgr*
EMP: 18 EST: 2016
SALES (est): 11.61MM
SALES (corp-wide): 11.61MM **Privately Held**
Web: www.brewdog.com
SIC: 2082 5813 Beer (alcoholic beverage); Bars and lounges

(G-1982)
BRIDGESTONE RET OPERATIONS LLC
Also Called: Firestone
6574 Winchester Blvd (43110-2056)
PHONE..................614 834-3672
EMP: 6
Web: www.bridgestoneamericas.com
SIC: 5531 7534 Automotive tires; Tire retreading and repair shops
HQ: Bridgestone Retail Operations, Llc
333 E Lake St Ste 300
Bloomingdale IL 60108
630 259-9000

(G-1983)
CAPSA SOLUTIONS LLC
8170 Dove Pkwy (43110-9674)
PHONE..................800 437-6633
David Burns, *CEO*
EMP: 90
SALES (corp-wide): 111.12MM **Privately Held**
Web: www.capsahealthcare.com
SIC: 3572 Computer storage devices
PA: Capsa Solutions Llc
8170 Dove Pkwy
Canal Winchester OH 43110
800 437-6633

(G-1984)
DAWSDUKE LTD
9655 Salem Church Rd (43110-9247)
PHONE..................614 270-6278
Charles C Linn, *Prin*
EMP: 6 EST: 2008
SALES (est): 105.02K **Privately Held**
SIC: 3599 Industrial machinery, nec

(G-1985)
E C BABBERT INC
7415 Diley Rd (43110-8813)
P.O. Box 203 (43110-0203)
PHONE..................614 837-8444
Ervin C Babbert, *CEO*
Charles Babbert, *

Rick Gibbs Cntllr, *Prin*
EMP: 72 EST: 2009
SALES (est): 8.63MM **Privately Held**
Web: www.ecbabbert.com
SIC: 3272 Liquid catch basins, tanks, and covers: concrete

(G-1986)
FIFTH AVENUE LUMBER CO
Lumbercraft
5200 Winchester Pike (43110-9723)
PHONE..................614 833-6655
Chris Kealey, *Mgr*
EMP: 39
SALES (corp-wide): 27.1MM **Privately Held**
Web: www.straitandlamp.com
SIC: 2431 2439 2452 2435 Millwork; Trusses, wooden roof; Prefabricated wood buildings; Hardwood veneer and plywood
HQ: Fifth Avenue Lumber Co (Inc)
479 E 5th Ave
Columbus OH 43201
614 294-0068

(G-1987)
HFI LLC (PA)
59 Gender Rd (43110-9733)
PHONE..................614 491-0700
Mark Lecher, *CEO*
Kevin Geiger, *
Neil Fillman, *
Kurt Stuckenbrock, *
◆ EMP: 350 EST: 1969
SQ FT: 140,000
SALES (est): 521.26MM
SALES (corp-wide): 521.26MM **Privately Held**
Web: www.hfi-inc.com
SIC: 2396 2821 3714 3429 Automotive trimmings, fabric; Polyurethane resins; Motor vehicle parts and accessories; Hardware, nec

(G-1988)
KELLOGG CABINETS INC
Also Called: Kci Works
7711 Diley Rd (43110-9616)
PHONE..................614 833-9596
Judy A Kellogg, *CEO*
Douglas E Kellogg, *VP*
Judy Kellogg, *CEO*
◆ EMP: 9 EST: 1975
SQ FT: 28,850
SALES (est): 967.15K **Privately Held**
Web: www.kciworks.com
SIC: 2541 2542 2434 Cabinets, except refrigerated: show, display, etc.: wood; Partitions and fixtures, except wood; Wood kitchen cabinets

(G-1989)
NIFCO AMERICA CORPORATION (HQ)
8015 Dove Pkwy (43110-9697)
PHONE..................614 920-6800
Toshiyuki Yamamoto, *Ch*
Michael Rodenberg, *CEO*
Tom Day, *VP*
John Kosik, *CFO*
▲ EMP: 312 EST: 1996
SQ FT: 50,000
SALES (est): 223.73MM **Privately Held**
Web: www.nifcousa.com
SIC: 3089 Automotive parts, plastic
PA: Nifco Inc.
5-3, Hikarinooka
Yokosuka KNG 239-0

GEOGRAPHIC SECTION

Canfield - Mahoning County (G-2011)

(G-1990)
NIFCO AMERICA CORPORATION
Also Called: Canal Winchester Facility
7877 Robinett Way (43110-8165)
PHONE.....................614 836-3808
Tom Day, *Genl Mgr*
EMP: 155
Web: www.nifcousa.com
SIC: 3089 Automotive parts, plastic
HQ: Nifco America Corporation
  8015 Dove Pkwy
  Canal Winchester OH 43110
  614 920-6800

(G-1991)
NORDIC LIGHT AMERICA INC
6320 Winchester Blvd (43110-6536)
PHONE.....................614 981-9497
Kenneth Johansson, *Pr*
▲ **EMP:** 10 **EST:** 2011
SALES (est): 3.87MM
SALES (corp-wide): 4.03MM **Privately Held**
Web: www.itab.com
SIC: 7389 3646 Interior design services; Ceiling systems, luminous
PA: Nordic Light Ab
  Svedjevagen 12
  SkellefteA 931 3
  910733790

(G-1992)
TARMAN MACHINE COMPANY INC
8215 Dove Pkwy (43110-7717)
P.O. Box 192 (43147-0192)
PHONE.....................614 834-4010
Randy Tarman, *Pr*
EMP: 17 **EST:** 1966
SQ FT: 13,000
SALES (est): 1.94MM **Privately Held**
Web: www.tarmanmachine.com
SIC: 3599 Machine shop, jobbing and repair

(G-1993)
TS TRIM INDUSTRIES INC (DH)
6380 Canal St (43110-9640)
PHONE.....................614 837-4114
▲ **EMP:** 400 **EST:** 1986
SALES (est): 84.46MM **Privately Held**
Web: www.tstech.com
SIC: 5013 3465 3714 3083 Automotive supplies and parts; Moldings or trim, automobile: stamped metal; Motor vehicle parts and accessories; Laminated plastics plate and sheet
HQ: Ts Tech Americas, Inc.
  8458 E Broad St
  Reynoldsburg OH 43068
  614 575-4100

(G-1994)
WORLD HARVEST CHURCH INC (PA)
Also Called: Breakthrough Media Ministries
4595 Gender Rd (43110-9149)
P.O. Box 428 (43110-0428)
PHONE.....................614 837-1990
Pastor Rodney Parsley, *Prin*
EMP: 200 **EST:** 1976
SQ FT: 200,000
SALES (est): 23.49MM
SALES (corp-wide): 23.49MM **Privately Held**
Web: www.whc.life
SIC: 7812 2731 Video tape production; Books, publishing and printing

Canfield
Mahoning County

(G-1995)
ADVETECH INC (PA)
Also Called: Perfection In Carbide
445 W Main St (44406-1436)
PHONE.....................330 533-2227
David Scott Owens, *CEO*
David Smith, *
EMP: 30 **EST:** 1917
SQ FT: 30,000
SALES (est): 4.82MM
SALES (corp-wide): 4.82MM **Privately Held**
Web: www.advetech.com
SIC: 3421 3599 3423 3541 Knife blades and blanks; Machine shop, jobbing and repair; Knives, agricultural or industrial; Machine tools, metal cutting type

(G-1996)
ADVETECH INC
451 W Main St (44406-1425)
P.O. Box 163216 (43216-3216)
PHONE.....................330 533-2227
EMP: 34
SALES (corp-wide): 4.82MM **Privately Held**
Web: www.advetech.com
SIC: 3423 Knives, agricultural or industrial
PA: Advetech, Inc.
  445 W Main St
  Canfield OH 44406
  330 533-2227

(G-1997)
AFC COMPANY
Also Called: Canfield Industrial Park
5183 W Western Reserve Rd (44406-8112)
PHONE.....................330 533-5581
Judith Raber, *Pr*
EMP: 14 **EST:** 1915
SQ FT: 2,500
SALES (est): 488.08K **Privately Held**
Web: www.afcind.com
SIC: 6512 7389 3255 3251 Commercial and industrial building operation; Grinding, precision: commercial or industrial; Clay refractories; Ceramic glazed brick, clay

(G-1998)
ALSTART ENTERPRISES LLC
Also Called: USA Rolls
451 W Main St (44406-1425)
P.O. Box 1076 (44406-5076)
PHONE.....................330 533-3222
Kevin M Sheldon, *Pr*
EMP: 18 **EST:** 2009
SQ FT: 55,000
SALES (est): 4.69MM **Privately Held**
Web: www.usarolls.com
SIC: 3559 Plastics working machinery

(G-1999)
ALUMINUM EXTRUSION TECH LLC
Also Called: Aluminum Extrusion Tech
6155 State Route 446 (44406-9428)
PHONE.....................330 533-3994
Andrew Ruhl, *Managing Member*
EMP: 8 **EST:** 2010
SALES (est): 1.41MM **Privately Held**
Web: www.aluextech.com
SIC: 3355 Extrusion ingot, aluminum: made in rolling mills

(G-2000)
BAIRD BROTHERS SAWMILL INC
7060 Crory Rd (44406-9720)
PHONE.....................330 533-3122
TOLL FREE: 800
Paul Baird, *Pr*
Helen Perrine, *
EMP: 115 **EST:** 1960
SQ FT: 350,000
SALES (est): 16.89MM **Privately Held**
Web: www.bairdbrothers.com
SIC: 2431 Doors and door parts and trim, wood

(G-2001)
BETTS CO DBA BETTS HD
430 W Main St (44406-1434)
P.O. Box 707 (44406-0707)
PHONE.....................330 533-0111
EMP: 7 **EST:** 2014
SALES (est): 720.49K **Privately Held**
SIC: 3493 Steel springs, except wire

(G-2002)
CANFIELD COATING LLC
460 W Main St (44406-1434)
PHONE.....................330 533-3311
EMP: 24 **EST:** 2013
SALES (est): 4.7MM
SALES (corp-wide): 120.84MM **Privately Held**
Web: www.materialsciencescorp.com
SIC: 3479 5051 Galvanizing of iron, steel, or end-formed products; Metals service centers and offices
PA: Material Sciences Corporation
  6855 Commerce Blvd
  Canton MI 48187
  734 207-4444

(G-2003)
CANFIELD METAL COATING CORP
460 W Main St (44406-1434)
PHONE.....................330 702-3876
Ronald W Jandrokovic, *Pr*
George S Bokros, *
Paul Pirko, *
EMP: 52 **EST:** 2001
SALES (est): 12.41MM
SALES (corp-wide): 1.91B **Publicly Held**
Web: www.materialsciencescorp.com
SIC: 3479 5051 Galvanizing of iron, steel, or end-formed products; Metals service centers and offices
HQ: Handy & Harman Ltd.
  590 Madison Ave Fl 32
  New York NY 10022

(G-2004)
DLAC INDUSTRIES INC
3755 Sugarbush Dr (44406-9107)
PHONE.....................330 519-4789
D L Cicoretti, *Prin*
EMP: 6 **EST:** 2011
SALES (est): 74K **Privately Held**
SIC: 3999 Manufacturing industries, nec

(G-2005)
ERIC ALLSHOUSE LLC
9666 Lisbon Rd (44406-8425)
PHONE.....................330 533-4258
Eric Allshouse, *Pt*
EMP: 8 **EST:** 2007
SALES (est): 220.64K **Privately Held**
Web: www.ericallshousellc.com
SIC: 3561 8741 Cylinders, pump; Construction management

(G-2006)
EVERFLOW EASTERN PARTNERS LP (PA)
585 W Main St (44406)
P.O. Box 629 (44406)
PHONE.....................330 533-2692

Brian A Staebler, *Pr*
Michael W Rathburn, *CAO*
EMP: 6 **EST:** 1990
SQ FT: 6,400
SALES (est): 5.95MM **Privately Held**
SIC: 1382 1311 Oil and gas exploration services; Crude petroleum and natural gas

(G-2007)
HORSESHOE EXPRESS INC
8045 Camden Way (44406-8165)
PHONE.....................330 692-1209
Margaret Garwood, *Prin*
EMP: 8 **EST:** 2012
SALES (est): 184.65K **Privately Held**
SIC: 3462 Horseshoes

(G-2008)
IES SYSTEMS INC
464 Lisbon St (44406-1423)
P.O. Box 89 (44406-0089)
PHONE.....................330 533-6683
Mark Brucoli, *Pr*
Rob Mcandrew, *Ex VP*
David Wigal, *
Bill Yobi, *
Kelly Weiss, *
EMP: 45 **EST:** 2000
SQ FT: 27,000
SALES (est): 8.67MM **Privately Held**
Web: www.ies-us.com
SIC: 7389 3821 Design, commercial and industrial; Laboratory apparatus and furniture

(G-2009)
LINDE HYDRAULICS CORPORATION (DH)
5089 W Western Reserve Rd (44406-9564)
PHONE.....................330 533-6801
Doctor Ferdinand Megerlin, *Ch Bd*
Frank Cobb, *
Lewis P Kasper, *
John Kumler, *
▲ **EMP:** 38 **EST:** 1970
SQ FT: 80,000
SALES (est): 10.75MM **Privately Held**
Web: www.lhy.com
SIC: 3594 3566 3714 3621 Pumps, hydraulic power transfer; Gears, power transmission, except auto; Motor vehicle parts and accessories; Motors and generators
HQ: Linde Hydraulics Gmbh & Co. Kg
  Wailandtstr. 13
  Aschaffenburg BY 63741
  602115000

(G-2010)
LTF ACQUISITION LLC
Also Called: Lifetime Fenders
430 W Main St (44406-1434)
PHONE.....................330 533-0111
EMP: 27 **EST:** 2007
SQ FT: 25,000
SALES (est): 2.79MM
SALES (corp-wide): 81.77MM **Privately Held**
SIC: 3714 Motor vehicle parts and accessories
PA: Betts Company
  2843 S Maple Ave
  Fresno CA 93725
  559 498-3304

(G-2011)
MATERIAL SCIENCES CORPORATION
460 W Main St (44406-1434)
PHONE.....................330 702-3882
EMP: 105
SALES (corp-wide): 120.84MM **Privately Held**

(PA)=Parent Co (HQ)=Headquarters
✪ = New Business established in last 2 years

Canfield - Mahoning County (G-2012)

Web: www.materialsciencescorp.com
SIC: 3479 Painting of metal products
PA: Material Sciences Corporation
6855 Commerce Blvd
Canton MI 48187
734 207-4444

(G-2012)
MOLOROKALIN INC (DH)
Also Called: Carepoint Partners
4137 Boardman Canfield Rd Ste Ll04 (44406)
PHONE......................330 629-1332
Ralph Dimuccio, *Ch Bd*
Leonard Holman, *Pr*
Greg Krieger, *VP*
John Appel, *Treas*
Harold Cullar, *Sec*
EMP: 30 EST: 1986
SQ FT: 5,000
SALES (est): 3.48MM Publicly Held
SIC: 2834 Intravenous solutions
HQ: Carepoint Partners, Llc
4623 Wesley Ave Ste H
Cincinnati OH 45212

(G-2013)
MRT LLC
5670 Mission Hills Dr (44406-8218)
PHONE......................330 533-0721
Daniel J Santon, *Prin*
EMP: 6 EST: 2010
SALES (est): 54.74K Privately Held
SIC: 3599 Machine shop, jobbing and repair

(G-2014)
PIERSANTE AND ASSOCIATES INC
230 Russo Dr (44406-9679)
PHONE......................330 533-9904
Thomas S Piersante, *Prin*
EMP: 6 EST: 2010
SALES (est): 206.9K Privately Held
SIC: 3494 Valves and pipe fittings, nec

(G-2015)
R J MANRAY INC
Also Called: Simply Bags
7320 Akron Canfield Rd Ste B (44406)
PHONE......................330 559-6716
Joanne Shirilla, *Pr*
Robert Shirilla, *Mktg Dir*
EMP: 8 EST: 1982
SALES (est): 443.36K Privately Held
Web: www.simply-bags.com
SIC: 5947 7389 2393 2211 Gift shop; Advertising, promotional, and trade show services; Duffle bags, canvas: made from purchased materials; Blankets and blanketings, cotton

(G-2016)
RELATED METALS INC
6011 Deer Spring Run (44406-7609)
PHONE......................330 799-4866
Lori Dripps, *Pr*
Mary Dripps, *VP*
Lawson Dripps, *Sec*
Thomas Dripps, *Treas*
EMP: 7 EST: 1986
SQ FT: 2,000
SALES (est): 750.41K Privately Held
SIC: 1761 3444 Roofing contractor; Sheet metalwork

(G-2017)
RUST BELT BRONCOS LLC
6145 State Route 446 (44406-9428)
PHONE......................330 533-0048
Nathan Miller, *Managing Member*
EMP: 20 EST: 2014
SALES (est): 1.01MM Privately Held

Web: www.rustbeltbroncos.com
SIC: 3052 5531 Transmission belting, rubber; Automotive parts

(G-2018)
STAR EXTRUDED SHAPES INC
7055 Herbert Rd (44406-8660)
P.O. Box 553 (44406-0553)
PHONE......................330 533-9863
EMP: 300 EST: 1983
SALES (est): 27.99MM Privately Held
Web: www.starext.com
SIC: 3354 Aluminum extruded products

(G-2019)
STAR FAB INC (PA)
7055 Herbert Rd (44406-8660)
P.O. Box 553 (44406-0553)
PHONE......................330 533-9863
Kenneth W George Junior, *Pr*
Nick Mistovich, *
▲ EMP: 120 EST: 2001
SQ FT: 100,000
SALES (est): 15.54MM
SALES (corp-wide): 15.54MM Privately Held
Web: www.starext.com
SIC: 3354 3479 Aluminum extruded products; Painting of metal products

(G-2020)
TEXTRON AVIATION INC
449 Greenmont Dr (44406-9658)
PHONE......................330 286-3043
EMP: 6
SALES (corp-wide): 12.87B Publicly Held
Web: www.txtav.com
SIC: 3721 Aircraft
HQ: Textron Aviation Inc.
1 Cessna Blvd
Wichita KS 67215
316 517-6000

(G-2021)
TIGER INDS OIL & GAS LSG LLC
8050 Camden Way (44406-8164)
PHONE......................330 533-1776
EMP: 8 EST: 2012
SALES (est): 328.47K Privately Held
SIC: 3999 Manufacturing industries, nec

(G-2022)
UNITED EXTRUSION DIES INC
5171 W Western Reserve Rd (44406-8112)
P.O. Box 117 (44406-0117)
PHONE......................330 533-2915
John Fritz, *Pr*
James Rektor, *VP*
Sharon Crawford, *Sec*
EMP: 10 EST: 1984
SQ FT: 8,000
SALES (est): 825.27K Privately Held
Web: www.extrusionsupplies.com
SIC: 3544 Special dies and tools

Canton
Stark County

(G-2023)
3D PARTNERS LLC
1817 20th St Ne (44714-2123)
PHONE......................330 323-6453
EMP: 8 EST: 2019
SALES (est): 508.9K Privately Held
SIC: 3441 Fabricated structural metal

(G-2024)
A GATEHOUSE MEDIA COMPANY
500 Market Ave S (44702-2112)
PHONE......................330 580-8579
Kirk Davis, *CEO*
EMP: 14 EST: 2011
SALES (est): 489.66K Privately Held
Web: www.cantonrep.com
SIC: 2711 Newspapers, publishing and printing

(G-2025)
ABC TECHNOLOGIES DLHB INC
2310 Leo Ave Sw (44706)
PHONE......................330 479-7595
Tom Huskey, *Brnch Mgr*
EMP: 44
SALES (corp-wide): 32.64B Publicly Held
Web: www.dlhbowles.com
SIC: 3089 Injection molding of plastics
HQ: Abc Technologies Dlhb, Inc
2122 Leo Ave Sw
Canton OH 44706
330 478-2503

(G-2026)
ABC TECHNOLOGIES DLHB INC (DH)
Also Called: Dlhbowles, Inc.
2422 Leo Ave Sw (44706-2344)
PHONE......................330 478-2503
Daniel Konrad, *Pr*
◆ EMP: 450 EST: 1977
SQ FT: 107,000
SALES (est): 239.01MM
SALES (corp-wide): 32.64B Publicly Held
Web: www.dlhbowles.com
SIC: 3714 Motor vehicle parts and accessories
HQ: Abc Technologies Inc
2 Norelco Dr
North York ON M9L 2
416 246-1782

(G-2027)
ACCU-RITE TOOL & DIE CO CORP
7295 Sunset Strip Ave Nw (44720)
P.O. Box 2651 (44720)
PHONE......................330 497-9959
John Snyder, *Pr*
Susan Snyder, *Sec*
Tom Snyder, *VP*
EMP: 6 EST: 1979
SQ FT: 5,000
SALES (est): 501.45K Privately Held
SIC: 3544 Special dies and tools

(G-2028)
ADELMANS TRUCK PARTS CORP (PA)
Also Called: Adelman's Truck Sales
2000 Waynesburg Dr Se (44707-2194)
PHONE......................330 456-0206
Carl Adelman, *Pr*
Larry Adelman, *
◆ EMP: 30 EST: 1921
SQ FT: 120,000
SALES (est): 10.01MM
SALES (corp-wide): 10.01MM Privately Held
Web: www.adelmans.com
SIC: 5013 3714 Truck parts and accessories; Power transmission equipment, motor vehicle

(G-2029)
AIRFASCO INC
2655 Harrison Ave Sw (44706-3047)
PHONE......................330 430-6190
Dennis Dent, *CEO*

Jeff Parker, *
Marlene Veobides, *
Tim West, *OF CORP Quality**
EMP: 42 EST: 1984
SQ FT: 25,000
SALES (est): 5.23MM Privately Held
Web: www.airfasco.com
SIC: 3452 Bolts, metal

(G-2030)
AIRFASCO INDS FSTNER GROUP LLC
2655 Harrison Ave Sw (44706-3047)
PHONE......................330 430-6190
EMP: 40 EST: 2009
SALES (est): 4.42MM Privately Held
Web: www.airfasco.com
SIC: 3452 Bolts, nuts, rivets, and washers

(G-2031)
AIRGAS USA LLC
2505 Shepler Ave Sw (44706)
PHONE......................330 454-1330
Rod St John, *Brnch Mgr*
EMP: 26
SALES (corp-wide): 101.26MM Privately Held
Web: www.airgas.com
SIC: 2813 Oxygen, compressed or liquefied
HQ: Airgas Usa, Llc
259 N Radnor Chester Rd
Radnor PA 19087
216 642-6600

(G-2032)
AK FABRICATION INC
1500 Allen Ave Se (44707-3768)
PHONE......................330 458-1037
Chris Kulenics, *Pr*
EMP: 12 EST: 1999
SQ FT: 10,000
SALES (est): 2.47MM Privately Held
SIC: 1751 3548 Carpentry work; Welding apparatus

(G-2033)
ALL POWER BATTERY INC
1387 Clarendon Ave Sw Ste 6 (44710-2190)
PHONE......................330 453-5236
William Ferris, *Pr*
EMP: 6 EST: 1986
SQ FT: 4,000
SALES (est): 292.33K Privately Held
Web: www.allpowerbattery.com
SIC: 7699 5013 3691 Battery service and repair; Automotive batteries; Lead acid batteries (storage batteries)

(G-2034)
AMBAFLEX INC
1530 Raff Rd Sw (44710-2322)
PHONE......................330 478-1858
David Spencer, *Genl Mgr*
◆ EMP: 22 EST: 2010
SALES (est): 4.83MM Privately Held
Web: www.ambaflex.com
SIC: 3535 Conveyors and conveying equipment

(G-2035)
AMERICAN ALUMINUM EXTRUSIONS
Also Called: A A E
4416 Louisville St Ne (44705-4848)
PHONE......................330 458-0300
Samuel Popa, *Pr*
Ken Hendricks, *Managing Member**
Barb Kepner, *
Diane Hendricks, *Managing Member**
▲ EMP: 105 EST: 2001
SQ FT: 240,000

GEOGRAPHIC SECTION
Canton - Stark County (G-2060)

SALES (est): 10.96MM **Privately Held**
Web: www.americanaluminum.com
SIC: 3354 Aluminum extruded products

(G-2036)
AMERICAN MADE FUELS INC
717 Warner Rd Se (44707-3380)
P.O. Box 500 (44608-0500)
PHONE...................330 417-7663
EMP: 6 **EST:** 2007
SALES (est): 85.49K **Privately Held**
SIC: 2869 Fuels

(G-2037)
ANHEUSER-BUSCH LLC
Also Called: Anheuser-Busch
1611 Marietta Ave Se (44707-2573)
PHONE...................330 438-2036
TOLL FREE: 800
EMP: 53
SQ FT: 34,360
SALES (corp-wide): 1.31B **Privately Held**
Web: www.budweisertours.com
SIC: 2082 Beer (alcoholic beverage)
HQ: Anheuser-Busch, Llc
1 Busch Pl
Saint Louis MO 63118
800 342-5283

(G-2038)
ARCHER CORPORATION
Also Called: Archer Sign
1917 Henry Ave Sw (44706-2941)
PHONE...................330 455-9995
Jerry Archer, *CEO*
Michael Minor, *
EMP: 40 **EST:** 1965
SQ FT: 70,000
SALES (est): 7.44MM **Privately Held**
Web: www.archersign.com
SIC: 1799 3993 Sign installation and maintenance; Signs and advertising specialties

(G-2039)
ARCONIC
1935 Warner Rd Se (44707-2273)
PHONE...................330 471-1844
EMP: 29 **EST:** 2019
SALES (est): 2.43MM **Privately Held**
Web: www.arconic.com
SIC: 2816 Inorganic pigments

(G-2040)
ASSOCTED VSUAL CMMNCATIONS INC
Also Called: A V C
7000 Firestone Ave Ne (44721-2594)
PHONE...................330 452-4449
Raymond Gonzalez, *Pr*
Paul Anthony, *
EMP: 25 **EST:** 1983
SALES (est): 2.06MM **Privately Held**
Web: www.avcprint.com
SIC: 2759 Screen printing

(G-2041)
AZZ INC
1723 Cleveland Ave Sw (44707-3646)
PHONE...................330 456-3241
Tim Myers, *Mgr*
EMP: 52
SALES (corp-wide): 1.54B **Publicly Held**
Web: www.azz.com
SIC: 3699 Electrical equipment and supplies, nec
PA: Azz Inc.
3100 W 7th St Ste 500
Fort Worth TX 76107
817 810-0095

(G-2042)
BADBOY BLASTERS INCORPORATED
1720 Wallace Ave Ne (44705-4056)
PHONE...................330 454-2699
Andrea Bandi Cain, *Pr*
Mark Cain, *VP*
▲ **EMP:** 10 **EST:** 2006
SQ FT: 13,000
SALES (est): 949.45K **Privately Held**
Web: www.badboyblasters.com
SIC: 3471 Sand blasting of metal parts

(G-2043)
BALL CORPORATION
2121 Warner Rd Se (44707-2273)
PHONE...................234 360-2141
EMP: 23
SALES (corp-wide): 14.03B **Publicly Held**
Web: www.ball.com
SIC: 2631 Paperboard mills
PA: Ball Corporation
9200 W 108th Cir
Westminster CO 80021
303 469-3131

(G-2044)
BARNHART PRINTING CORP
Also Called: Barnhart Publishing
1107 Melchoir Pl Sw (44707-4220)
PHONE...................330 456-2279
Brent A Barnhart, *Ch*
John F Waechter, *Pr*
EMP: 19 **EST:** 1930
SQ FT: 10,000
SALES (est): 810.28K **Privately Held**
SIC: 2752 2759 2789 Offset printing; Letterpress printing; Bookbinding and related work

(G-2045)
BDI INC
Also Called: Bdi
417 Applegrove St Nw (44720-1617)
PHONE...................330 498-4980
Tom Carlouzzi, *Brnch Mgr*
EMP: 103
SALES (corp-wide): 1.51B **Privately Held**
Web: www.bdiexpress.com
SIC: 3568 Power transmission equipment, nec
HQ: Bdi, Inc.
8000 Hub Pkwy
Cleveland OH 44125
216 642-9100

(G-2046)
BEAD SHOPPE AT HOME
2872 Whipple Ave Nw (44708-1532)
PHONE...................330 479-9598
Shelley Lantz, *Owner*
EMP: 6 **EST:** 2006
SALES (est): 131.99K **Privately Held**
SIC: 3999 Beads, unassembled

(G-2047)
BETTER LIVING CONCEPTS INC
Also Called: Compu-Print
7233 Freedom Ave Nw (44720-7123)
P.O. Box 2340 (44720-0340)
PHONE...................330 494-2213
Jeff Davies, *Pr*
EMP: 10 **EST:** 1984
SQ FT: 5,400
SALES (est): 187.02K **Privately Held**
Web: www.gbscorp.com
SIC: 2759 Imprinting

(G-2048)
BIG KAHUNA GRAPHICS LLC
Also Called: Big Kahuna Graphics
1255 Prospect Ave Sw (44706-1627)
PHONE...................330 455-2625
EMP: 9 **EST:** 1987
SALES (est): 786.21K **Privately Held**
Web: www.bigkahunagraphics.com
SIC: 2396 2395 2759 Stamping fabric articles ; Pleating and stitching; Screen printing

(G-2049)
BOLER COMPANY
Hendrickson Trailer Commercial
2070 Industrial Pl Se (44707-2641)
PHONE...................330 445-6728
Perry Bahr, *Brnch Mgr*
EMP: 250
SALES (corp-wide): 758.84MM **Privately Held**
Web: www.hendrickson-intl.com
SIC: 3714 Motor vehicle parts and accessories
PA: The Boler Company
2021 Parkside Dr
Schaumburg IL 60173
630 773-9111

(G-2050)
BOLONS CUSTOM KITCHENS INC
6287 Promler St Nw (44720-7609)
PHONE...................330 499-0092
Guy Bolon, *CEO*
Terry Bolon, *Pr*
EMP: 9 **EST:** 1976
SQ FT: 1,500
SALES (est): 489.19K **Privately Held**
Web: www.bolonskitchens.com
SIC: 5722 2599 Kitchens, complete (sinks, cabinets, etc.); Cabinets, factory

(G-2051)
BOWDIL COMPANY
2030 Industrial Pl Se (44707-2641)
PHONE...................800 356-8663
Brite Morrow, *Pr*
J Britton Morrow, *Sec.*
EMP: 17 **EST:** 1923
SQ FT: 50,000
SALES (est): 3.27MM **Privately Held**
Web: www.bowdil.com
SIC: 3532 3599 3398 Mining machinery; Custom machinery; Metal heat treating

(G-2052)
BRENDEL PRODUCING COMPANY
8215 Arlington Ave Nw (44720-5111)
PHONE...................330 854-4151
Frank Brendel Junior, *Pr*
Kay Morgan, *Mgr*
EMP: 8 **EST:** 1928
SQ FT: 1,200
SALES (est): 475.41K **Privately Held**
Web: www.doylepc.com
SIC: 1381 1311 Directional drilling oil and gas wells; Crude petroleum and natural gas

(G-2053)
BRIDGESTONE RET OPERATIONS LLC
Also Called: Firestone
3032 Atlantic Blvd Ne (44705-3929)
PHONE...................330 454-9478
David Rapp, *Mgr*
EMP: 8
SQ FT: 2,340
Web: www.bridgestoneamericas.com
SIC: 5531 7534 Automotive tires; Rebuilding and retreading tires
HQ: Bridgestone Retail Operations, Llc
333 E Lake St Ste 300
Bloomingdale IL 60108
630 259-9000

(G-2054)
BUCKEYE PAPER CO INC
5233 Southway St Sw Ste 523 (44706-1943)
P.O. Box 711 (44648-0711)
PHONE...................330 477-5925
Edward N Bast Senior, *Pr*
Edward Bast Junior, *VP*
▼ **EMP:** 32 **EST:** 1981
SQ FT: 54,000
SALES (est): 7.06MM **Privately Held**
Web: www.buckeyepaper.com
SIC: 2679 5113 Paper products, converted, nec; Industrial and personal service paper

(G-2055)
BUCKEYE TERMINALS
807 Hartford Ave Se (44707-3376)
PHONE...................330 453-4170
EMP: 7 **EST:** 2018
SALES (est): 173.18K **Privately Held**
Web: www.buckeye.com
SIC: 2999 Petroleum and coal products, nec

(G-2056)
BUDDY HUNTING INC
3440 Overhill Dr Nw (44718-3245)
PHONE...................330 353-6850
Mitch Ciccarone, *Prin*
EMP: 6 **EST:** 2017
SALES (est): 38.29K **Privately Held**
Web: www.blizzardbuddy.com
SIC: 3949 Sporting and athletic goods, nec

(G-2057)
CAGE GEAR & MACHINE LLC
1776 Gateway Blvd Se (44707-3503)
PHONE...................330 452-1532
EMP: 23 **EST:** 2000
SQ FT: 22,900
SALES (est): 5.42MM **Privately Held**
Web: www.cagegear.com
SIC: 3599 3566 Machine shop, jobbing and repair; Gears, power transmission, except auto

(G-2058)
CAMMEL SAW COMPANY
4898 Hills And Dales Rd Nw (44708-1495)
PHONE...................330 477-3764
Dennis Cammel, *Pr*
EMP: 14 **EST:** 1968
SQ FT: 10,000
SALES (est): 827.53K **Privately Held**
Web: www.cammelsaw.com
SIC: 7699 5072 5251 3425 Knife, saw and tool sharpening and repair; Saw blades; Tools; Saws, hand: metalworking or woodworking

(G-2059)
CANDLE COACH
1501 Perry Dr Sw (44710-1038)
PHONE...................330 455-4444
EMP: 8 **EST:** 2018
SALES (est): 398.68K **Privately Held**
Web: www.ledtransportation.com
SIC: 3999 Candles

(G-2060)
CANTON BANDAG CO
922 Benskin Ave Sw (44710-1438)
PHONE...................330 454-3025
TOLL FREE: 800
Dave Richards Junior, *CEO*
EMP: 15 **EST:** 1962
SALES (est): 1.09MM **Privately Held**

Canton - Stark County (G-2061)

Web: www.cantonbandag.com
SIC: 5531 7534 Automotive tires; Tire retreading and repair shops

(G-2061)
CANTON DROP FORGE INC
Also Called: Canton Drop Forge
4575 Southway St Sw (44706-1995)
PHONE.................................330 477-4511
Brad Ahbe, Pr
◆ EMP: 259 EST: 1903
SQ FT: 245,000
SALES (est): 68.96MM
SALES (corp-wide): 1.66B Publicly Held
Web: www.cantondropforge.com
SIC: 3462 3463 3356 3312 Iron and steel forgings; Nonferrous forgings; Nonferrous rolling and drawing, nec; Blast furnaces and steel mills
PA: Park-Ohio Holdings Corp.
6065 Parkland Blvd Ste 1
Cleveland OH 44124
440 947-2000

(G-2062)
CANTON GALVANIZING
2300 Allen Ave Se (44707-3673)
PHONE.................................330 685-7316
EMP: 7 EST: 2019
SALES (est): 233.73K Privately Held
Web: www.hotdipgalvanizing.com
SIC: 3479 Galvanizing of iron, steel, or end-formed products

(G-2063)
CANTON GALVANIZING LLC
1821 Moore Ave Se (44707-2233)
PHONE.................................330 685-9060
Anthony Codispoti, Managing Member
EMP: 27 EST: 2015
SALES (est): 2.06MM Privately Held
SIC: 3479 Etching and engraving

(G-2064)
CANTON GEAR MFG DESIGNING INC
1600 Tuscarawas St E (44707-3199)
PHONE.................................330 455-2771
Matthew Weida, Pr
Barbara Bettis, VP
EMP: 10 EST: 1960
SALES (est): 1.02MM Privately Held
Web: www.cantongears.com
SIC: 3566 Gears, power transmission, except auto

(G-2065)
CANTON OH RUBBER SPECLTY PRODS
Also Called: Cors Products
1387 Clarendon Ave Sw Bldg 13 (44710-2190)
P.O. Box 20188 (44701-0188)
PHONE.................................330 454-3847
EMP: 8 EST: 2008
SQ FT: 15,000
SALES (est): 1.45MM Privately Held
Web: www.corsproducts.com
SIC: 3061 2869 3069 2822 Appliance rubber goods (mechanical); Silicones; Weather strip, sponge rubber; Ethylene-propylene rubbers, EPDM polymers

(G-2066)
CANTON OIL WELL SERVICE INC
7793 Pittsburg Ave Nw (44720-6947)
PHONE.................................330 494-1221
Robert J Hutcheson, Prin
Thomas R Hutcheson, CEO
James Paumier, VP
Kevin W Hutcheson, Pr
EMP: 21 EST: 1962

SQ FT: 7,500
SALES (est): 1.61MM Privately Held
SIC: 1382 Oil and gas exploration services

(G-2067)
CANTON PLATING CO INC
903 9th St Ne (44704-1400)
PHONE.................................330 452-7808
Mark Kast, Pr
Denise Kast, Sec
EMP: 6 EST: 1955
SQ FT: 3,480
SALES (est): 463.31K Privately Held
SIC: 3471 Electroplating of metals or formed products

(G-2068)
CANTON STERILIZED WIPING CLOTH
Also Called: Sentry Products
1401 Waynesburg Dr Se (44707-2115)
P.O. Box 7227 (44705-0227)
PHONE.................................330 455-5179
Robert Shapiro, Pr
Ronald Shapiro, VP
EMP: 8 EST: 1924
SQ FT: 42,000
SALES (est): 908.21K Privately Held
Web: www.sentryproducts.com
SIC: 2211 5199 5113 Scrub cloths; Chamois leather; Napkins, paper

(G-2069)
CARMEL PUBLISHING INC
4501 Hills And Dales Rd Nw (44708-1572)
PHONE.................................330 478-9200
Ernie Blood, Pr
Melody Blood, *
Karen Hought, *
EMP: 14 EST: 1989
SALES (est): 500.09K Privately Held
SIC: 2721 2731 Magazines: publishing and printing; Book publishing

(G-2070)
CASE FARMS
3436 Lesh St Ne (44705-4350)
PHONE.................................330 452-0230
EMP: 8 EST: 2020
SALES (est): 203.54K Privately Held
Web: www.casefarms.com
SIC: 2015 Poultry slaughtering and processing

(G-2071)
CENTRAL ALLIED ENTERPRISES INC (PA)
1243 Raff Rd Sw (44710-1498)
P.O. Box 80449 (44708-0449)
PHONE.................................330 477-6751
EMP: 47 EST: 1929
SALES (est): 21.96MM
SALES (corp-wide): 21.96MM Privately Held
Web: www.shellyco.com
SIC: 1611 2951 1442 Highway and street construction; Asphalt and asphaltic paving mixtures (not from refineries); Construction sand and gravel

(G-2072)
CHECKPOINT SYSTEMS INC
Alpha Security
1510 4th St Se (44707-3206)
PHONE.................................330 456-7776
Tim Williams, Brnch Mgr
EMP: 87
SALES (corp-wide): 4.75B Privately Held
Web: www.checkpointsystems.com

SIC: 3699 Security control equipment and systems
HQ: Checkpoint Systems, Inc.
101 Wolf Dr
West Deptford NJ 08086
800 257-5540

(G-2073)
CHEMSPEC LTD (DH)
Also Called: Chemspec Polymer Additives
4450 Belden Village St Nw Ste 507 (44718-2552)
PHONE.................................330 896-0355
David Moreland, Pr
Chris Wagner, COO
Aaron Shaffer, CFO
◆ EMP: 20 EST: 2003
SQ FT: 1,500
SALES (est): 13.39MM
SALES (corp-wide): 166.77K Privately Held
Web: www.safic-alcan.com
SIC: 2891 2952 3011 Adhesives and sealants; Mastic roofing composition; Automobile tires, pneumatic
HQ: Safic Alcan
Tour Pacific
Puteaux 92800
146926464

(G-2074)
CINTAS CORPORATION NO 2
Also Called: Cintas
3865 Highland Park Nw (44720-4537)
P.O. Box 3010 (44720-8010)
PHONE.................................330 966-7800
TOLL FREE: 800
EMP: 81
SQ FT: 17,084
SALES (corp-wide): 8.82B Publicly Held
Web: www.cintas.com
SIC: 5084 2326 2337 Safety equipment; Work uniforms; Uniforms, except athletic: women's, misses', and juniors'
HQ: Cintas Corporation No. 2
6800 Cintas Blvd
Mason OH 45040

(G-2075)
CITY OF CANTON
Also Called: Traffic Engineering Department
2436 30th St Ne (44705-2568)
PHONE.................................330 489-3370
Dan Moeglin, Admn
EMP: 51
Web: www.cantonohio.gov
SIC: 3669 9111 Traffic signals, electric; Mayors' office
PA: City Of Canton
218 Cleveland Ave Sw
Canton OH 44702
330 438-4300

(G-2076)
CLARK OPTIMIZATION LLC
1222 Easton St Ne (44721-2455)
PHONE.................................330 417-2164
Steve Clark, Pr
Douglas B Crawford, Financial Chief
EMP: 20 EST: 2011
SALES (est): 689.39K Privately Held
Web: www.clarkoptimization.com
SIC: 2741 Internet publishing and broadcasting

(G-2077)
CLARK SUBSTATIONS LLC
Also Called: Clark Substations
2240 Allen Ave Se (44707-3612)
PHONE.................................330 452-5200
EMP: 12 EST: 1950

SALES (est): 907.43K Privately Held
Web: www.vsschuler.com
SIC: 3612 3699 3625 Distribution transformers, electric; Electrical equipment and supplies, nec; Relays and industrial controls

(G-2078)
COMBI PACKAGING SYSTEMS LLC
6299 Dressler Rd Nw (44720-7607)
P.O. Box 9326 (44711-9326)
PHONE.................................330 456-9333
John F Fisher, CEO
Barbara A Karch, Pr
◆ EMP: 70 EST: 1979
SQ FT: 119,000
SALES (est): 23MM Privately Held
Web: www.combi.com
SIC: 3565 Packaging machinery

(G-2079)
COMMUNICATION RESOURCES INC
4786 Dressler Rd Nw Ste 309 (44718-2555)
PHONE.................................800 992-2144
Robert W Fisher, Ch
Randall S Coy, Pr
Georgia A Fisher, VP
EMP: 9 EST: 1979
SQ FT: 2,000
SALES (est): 140.11K Privately Held
Web: www.comresources.com
SIC: 2731 2721 Pamphlets: publishing and printing; Periodicals

(G-2080)
CONTINNTAL HYDRDYNE SYSTEMS IN
2216 Glenmont Dr Nw (44708-2036)
PHONE.................................330 494-2740
Theodore F Savastano, Prin
EMP: 8 EST: 1980
SALES (est): 237.48K Privately Held
Web: www.hydrodynesystems.com
SIC: 3821 Chemical laboratory apparatus, nec

(G-2081)
COPLEY OHIO NEWSPAPERS INC (HQ)
Also Called: Repository
500 Market Ave S (44702-2112)
PHONE.................................585 598-0030
Garrett J Cummings Attorney, Prin
Kevin Kampman, *
Darryl Hudson, *
James Porter, *
EMP: 53 EST: 2000
SALES (est): 79.91MM
SALES (corp-wide): 2.66B Publicly Held
Web: www.cantonrep.com
SIC: 2711 Commercial printing and newspaper publishing combined
PA: Gannett Co., Inc.
175 Sullys Trl Ste 203
Pittsford NY 14534
585 598-0030

(G-2082)
CORDIER GROUP HOLDINGS INC
4575 Southway St Sw (44706-1933)
PHONE.................................330 477-4511
James J O'sullivan Junior, Ch
EMP: 301 EST: 1985
SALES (est): 25.63MM Privately Held
Web: www.cantondropforge.com
SIC: 3462 Iron and steel forgings

GEOGRAPHIC SECTION
Canton - Stark County (G-2106)

(G-2083)
CRAMERS INC
4944 Southway St Sw (44706-1990)
PHONE..................................330 477-4571
 E Robert Schellhase, *Prin*
 Don Hoover, *
 Lynn Herdlick, *
 Dana Cramer, *
 R C Cramer, *
EMP: 25 **EST:** 1946
SQ FT: 15,000
SALES (est): 4.76MM **Privately Held**
Web: www.cramersinc.com
SIC: 3444 3446 3443 3441 Sheet metal specialties, not stamped; Architectural metalwork; Fabricated plate work (boiler shop); Fabricated structural metal

(G-2084)
CSI AMERICA INC
121 14th St Se (44707-3963)
PHONE..................................330 305-1403
 Paul G Gulling, *Pr*
EMP: 9 **EST:** 2012
SALES (est): 82.45K **Privately Held**
SIC: 3999 Manufacturing industries, nec

(G-2085)
CUSTOM TRUCK ONE SOURCE LP
3522 Middlebranch Ave Ne (44705-5012)
PHONE..................................330 409-7291
 Paul Sackett, *Acctg Mgr*
EMP: 26
SALES (corp-wide): 1.87B **Publicly Held**
Web: www.customtruck.com
SIC: 3713 Utility truck bodies
HQ: Custom Truck One Source, L.P.
 7701 E 24 Hwy
 Kansas City MO 64125
 855 931-1852

(G-2086)
CUSTOM WELD & MACHINE CORP
1500 Henry Ave Sw (44706-2852)
PHONE..................................330 452-3935
 Tom Greening, *CEO*
 Tim Savage, *VP*
EMP: 10 **EST:** 1957
SQ FT: 31,500
SALES (est): 252.22K **Privately Held**
SIC: 7692 Welding repair

(G-2087)
D & L ENERGY INC
3930 Fulton Dr Nw Ste 200 (44718-3040)
PHONE..................................330 270-1201
 Ben W Lupo, *CEO*
 Susan A Faith, *Pr*
EMP: 35 **EST:** 1986
SQ FT: 13,637
SALES (est): 2.33MM **Privately Held**
SIC: 1311 Natural gas production

(G-2088)
DARTING AROUND LLC
3058 Cromer Ave Nw (44709-2908)
PHONE..................................330 639-3990
 Jeff Bowman, *Prin*
EMP: 10 **EST:** 2007
SALES (est): 434.16K **Privately Held**
Web: www.dartingaround.com
SIC: 3949 Darts and table sports equipment and supplies

(G-2089)
DE VORE ENGRAVING CO
1017 Tuscarawas St E (44707-3154)
PHONE..................................330 454-6820
 Alan J De Vore, *Pr*
 Chris De Vore, *VP*
EMP: 6 **EST:** 1963
SQ FT: 400
SALES (est): 476.35K **Privately Held**
Web: www.devoreengraving.com
SIC: 3479 Painting, coating, and hot dipping

(G-2090)
DECISION SYSTEMS INC
Also Called: Midland Engineering
2935 Woodcliff Dr Nw (44718-3331)
PHONE..................................330 456-7600
 Peter E Voss, *Pr*
 E R Frederick, *Ex VP*
 Kay Wieschaus, *Treas*
EMP: 19 **EST:** 1978
SQ FT: 5,000
SALES (est): 2.29MM **Privately Held**
SIC: 3559 8711 3535 Separation equipment, magnetic; Engineering services; Conveyors and conveying equipment

(G-2091)
DIANO CONSTRUCTION AND SUP CO
Also Called: Diano Supply Co
1000 Warner Rd Se (44707-3398)
PHONE..................................330 456-7229
 Anthony Diano Junior, *Pr*
 Darlene Guynup, *VP*
EMP: 14 **EST:** 1929
SQ FT: 1,500
SALES (est): 1.01MM **Privately Held**
Web: www.dianosupplyco.com
SIC: 3273 Ready-mixed concrete

(G-2092)
DIEBOLD NIXDORF INCORPORATED
818 Mulberry Rd Se (44707-3201)
PHONE..................................330 490-4000
 Diane Pellegrene, *Brnch Mgr*
EMP: 59
SALES (corp-wide): 1.63B **Publicly Held**
Web: www.dieboldnixdorf.com
SIC: 3578 Automatic teller machines (ATM)
PA: Diebold Nixdorf, Incorporated
 350 Orchard Ave Ne
 North Canton OH 44720
 330 490-4000

(G-2093)
DIOGUARDIS ITALIAN FOODS INC
3116 Market Ave N (44714-1430)
PHONE..................................330 492-3777
 Jeff Labowitz, *Pr*
EMP: 15 **EST:** 2010
SALES (est): 1.11MM **Privately Held**
Web: www.dioguardis.com
SIC: 2038 5411 Spaghetti and meatballs, frozen; Grocery stores, independent

(G-2094)
EDW C LEVY CO
3715 Whipple Ave Sw (44706-3535)
PHONE..................................330 484-6328
 Jack Sines, *Mgr*
EMP: 9
SQ FT: 5,200
SALES (corp-wide): 513.22MM **Privately Held**
Web: www.edwclevy.com
SIC: 5093 3295 Scrap and waste materials; Minerals, ground or treated
PA: Edw. C. Levy Co.
 9300 Dix
 Dearborn MI 48120
 313 429-2200

(G-2095)
ELECTRA TARP INC
2900 Perry Dr Sw (44706-2268)
PHONE..................................330 477-7168
TOLL FREE: 800
 Susan Paul, *Pr*
 Betsy Paul, *Pr*
EMP: 19 **EST:** 1974
SQ FT: 20,000
SALES (est): 2.21MM **Privately Held**
Web: www.electratarp.com
SIC: 2394 5091 2591 2391 Canvas and related products; Sporting and recreation goods; Shade, curtain, and drapery hardware; Cottage sets (curtains), made from purchased materials

(G-2096)
EMAXX NORTHEAST OHIO LLC
Also Called: Akron Canton Waste Oil
1701 Sherrick Rd Se (44707-2201)
PHONE..................................844 645-6299
EMP: 7 **EST:** 2018
SALES (est): 123.95K **Privately Held**
SIC: 2992 Lubricating oils and greases

(G-2097)
EMBROIDME
3611 Cleveland Ave S (44707-1447)
PHONE..................................330 484-8484
 Scott Leuenberger, *Mgr*
EMP: 6 **EST:** 2010
SALES (est): 487.21K **Privately Held**
Web: www.embroidmeofcanton.com
SIC: 2395 Embroidery and art needlework

(G-2098)
ESMET INC
1406 5th St Sw (44702-2062)
P.O. Box 9238 (44711-9238)
PHONE..................................330 452-9132
◆ **EMP:** 34 **EST:** 1937
SALES (est): 6.12MM **Privately Held**
Web: www.esmet.com
SIC: 3429 2542 Keys, locks, and related hardware; Racks, merchandise display or storage: except wood
PA: Tuscany Inc
 1406 5th St Sw
 Canton OH

(G-2099)
EVANS INDUSTRIES INC
606 Walnut Ave Ne (44702-1029)
PHONE..................................330 453-1122
 Sue Ann Evans, *Pr*
 Bevan Evans, *Sec*
EMP: 20 **EST:** 1977
SQ FT: 15,000
SALES (est): 1.12MM **Privately Held**
Web: www.evansind.net
SIC: 3089 Injection molding of plastics

(G-2100)
EVERHARD PRODUCTS INC (PA)
Also Called: Everhard
1016 9th St Sw (44707-4100)
PHONE..................................330 453-7786
 G R Lucas, *Ch Bd*
 James L Anderson, *
 Scott Anderson, *
 Rick Lucas, *
 J D Anderson, *
◆ **EMP:** 119 **EST:** 1960
SQ FT: 154,000
SALES (est): 24.57MM
SALES (corp-wide): 24.57MM **Privately Held**
Web: www.everhard.com
SIC: 3423 Hand and edge tools, nec

(G-2101)
FLAWLESS LOGISTICS LLC
5010 Quincy St Nw (44708-3476)
P.O. Box 35904 (44735-5904)
PHONE..................................330 201-7070
 Cheyenne Moseley, *Mgr*
EMP: 6 **EST:** 2020
SALES (est): 422.46K **Privately Held**
SIC: 3537 Trucks: freight, baggage, etc.: industrial, except mining

(G-2102)
FOLTZ MACHINE LLC
2030 Allen Ave Se (44707-3691)
PHONE..................................330 453-9235
 David Dicola, *Pr*
 Lee Dicola, *
 Linda R Polsinelli, *
EMP: 30 **EST:** 1970
SQ FT: 37,500
SALES (est): 4.43MM **Privately Held**
Web: www.foltzmachine.com
SIC: 3599 Machine shop, jobbing and repair

(G-2103)
FORMCO INC
5175 Stoneham Rd (44720-1540)
PHONE..................................330 966-2111
 Richard Bourne, *Pr*
 Carol Bourne, *Sec*
 Christopher Bourne, *Treas*
EMP: 7 **EST:** 1976
SQ FT: 9,000
SALES (est): 687.98K **Privately Held**
Web: www.moldeddevices.com
SIC: 3089 Injection molding of plastics

(G-2104)
FOUNDATION SYSTEMS ANCHORS INC (PA)
Also Called: F S A
2300 Allen Ave Se (44707-3673)
PHONE..................................330 454-1700
 Anthony Codispoti, *Pr*
 Dennis Dinarda, *VP*
 Karen Hawk, *Sec*
▲ **EMP:** 15 **EST:** 1985
SQ FT: 2,500
SALES (est): 5.38MM
SALES (corp-wide): 5.38MM **Privately Held**
Web: www.fsabolt.com
SIC: 3449 Fabricated bar joists and concrete reinforcing bars

(G-2105)
FRESH MARK INC
1600 Harmont Ave Ne (44705-3398)
PHONE..................................330 455-5253
EMP: 886
SALES (corp-wide): 1.38B **Privately Held**
Web: www.freshmark.com
SIC: 2011 2013 Meat packing plants; Sausages and other prepared meats
PA: Fresh Mark, Inc.
 1888 Southway St Sw
 Massillon OH 44646
 330 832-7491

(G-2106)
FRITO-LAY NORTH AMERICA INC
Also Called: Frito-Lay
4030 16th St Sw (44710-2354)
PHONE..................................330 477-7009
 Mike Kulbacki, *Brnch Mgr*
EMP: 51
SQ FT: 36,400
SALES (corp-wide): 86.39B **Publicly Held**
Web: www.fritolay.com
SIC: 2096 2099 Potato chips and other potato-based snacks; Food preparations, nec
HQ: Frito-Lay North America, Inc.
 7701 Legacy Dr
 Plano TX 75024

Canton - Stark County (G-2107)

(G-2107)
FULLY PROMOTED OF CANTON
Also Called: Fully Promoted
3611 Cleveland Ave S (44707-1447)
PHONE..................330 484-8484
EMP: 6 EST: 2018
SALES (est): 59.06K **Privately Held**
Web: www.fullypromoted.com
SIC: 2395 Embroidery and art needlework

(G-2108)
GALT ALLOYS ENTERPRISE
1550 Marietta Ave Se (44707-2568)
PHONE..................330 309-8194
Phil Pennington, *Pr*
EMP: 11 EST: 2010
SALES (est): 840.54K **Privately Held**
SIC: 1081 Metal mining exploration and development services

(G-2109)
GALT ALLOYS INC MAIN OFC
122 Central Plz N (44702-1448)
PHONE..................330 453-4678
Stephen R Giangiordano, *Prin*
EMP: 6 EST: 2010
SALES (est): 376.95K **Privately Held**
SIC: 3339 Primary nonferrous metals, nec

(G-2110)
GASPAR INC
Also Called: Gaspar
1545 Whipple Ave Sw (44710-1373)
PHONE..................330 477-2222
Gary W Gaspar, *Pr*
Judy Gaspar, *
EMP: 55 EST: 1967
SQ FT: 36,000
SALES (est): 8.71MM **Privately Held**
Web: www.gasparinc.com
SIC: 3443 7692 3444 Tanks, standard or custom fabricated: metal plate; Welding repair; Sheet metalwork

(G-2111)
GENERAL ELECTRIC COMPANY
Also Called: GE
5555 Massillon Rd Bldg D (44720-1339)
PHONE..................330 458-3200
June Mutter, *Mgr*
EMP: 50
SALES (corp-wide): 67.95B **Publicly Held**
Web: www.ge.com
SIC: 3646 Commercial lighting fixtures
PA: General Electric Company
1 Aviation Way
Cincinnati OH 45215
617 443-3000

(G-2112)
GERDAU MCSTEEL ATMSPHERE ANNLI
Also Called: Advanced Bar Technology
1501 Raff Rd Sw (44710-2356)
PHONE..................330 478-0314
Saminathan Ramaswamy, *Prin*
EMP: 28
SQ FT: 31,316
SALES (corp-wide): 1.56B **Privately Held**
SIC: 7389 3398 Metal cutting services; Metal heat treating
HQ: Gerdau Macsteel Atmosphere Annealing
209 W Mount Hope Ave # 1
Lansing MI 48910
517 782-0415

(G-2113)
GLASSES GUY LLC
5151 Tuscarawas St W (44708-5015)
PHONE..................970 624-9019
Frank Soto, *CEO*
EMP: 20 EST: 2019
SALES (est): 703.97K **Privately Held**
SIC: 3851 Eyeglasses, lenses and frames

(G-2114)
GMELECTRIC INC
4606 Southway St Sw (44706-1935)
PHONE..................330 477-3392
George H Mountcastle, *Prin*
EMP: 6 EST: 2008
SALES (est): 669.81K **Privately Held**
Web: www.gmelectric.biz
SIC: 3694 5013 3679 Engine electrical equipment; Automotive supplies and parts; Harness assemblies, for electronic use: wire or cable

(G-2115)
GONZOIL INC
5200 Fulton Dr Nw (44718-1906)
PHONE..................330 497-5888
Douglas W Gonzalez, *Pr*
Frank W Gonzalez, *Sec*
EMP: 9 EST: 1988
SQ FT: 1,000
SALES (est): 824.63K **Privately Held**
Web: www.gonzoilinc.com
SIC: 1382 Oil and gas exploration services

(G-2116)
GOODYEAR TIRE & RUBBER COMPANY
Also Called: Goodyear
6850 Frank Ave Nw (44720-7010)
PHONE..................330 966-1274
Lenny Mullen, *Mgr*
EMP: 9
SALES (corp-wide): 20.07B **Publicly Held**
Web: www.goodyear.com
SIC: 5531 7534 Automotive tires; Tire repair shop
PA: The Goodyear Tire & Rubber Company
200 Innovation Way
Akron OH 44316
330 796-2121

(G-2117)
GREGORY INDUSTRIES INC (PA)
4100 13th St Sw (44710-1464)
PHONE..................330 477-4800
T Stephen Gregory, *Prin*
T Stephen Gregory, *CEO*
Joseph Weaver, *
◆ EMP: 80 EST: 1957
SQ FT: 145,000
SALES (est): 41.63MM
SALES (corp-wide): 41.63MM **Privately Held**
Web: www.gregorycorp.com
SIC: 3441 Fabricated structural metal

(G-2118)
GREGORY ROLL FORM INC
4100 13th St Sw (44710-1464)
P.O. Box 80508 (44708-0508)
PHONE..................330 477-4800
T Stephen Gregory, *CEO*
T Raymond Gregory, *
Joseph Weaver, *
EMP: 100 EST: 1978
SQ FT: 160,000
SALES (est): 4.66MM
SALES (corp-wide): 41.63MM **Privately Held**
Web: www.gregorycorp.com
SIC: 3312 Galvanized pipes, plates, sheets, etc.: iron and steel
PA: Gregory Industries, Inc.
4100 13th St Sw
Canton OH 44710
330 477-4800

(G-2119)
H W FAIRWAY INTERNATIONAL INC
1016 9th St Sw (44707-4108)
PHONE..................330 678-2540
Lee J Strange Presceo, *Prin*
Alice Kandes, *VP*
Charles Zuehmker, *Sec*
EMP: 18 EST: 1940
SALES (est): 890.21K **Privately Held**
Web: www.hwfairway.com
SIC: 3699 3823 3621 Laser systems and equipment; Process control instruments; Starters, for motors

(G-2120)
HAINES PUBLISHING INC
8050 Freedom Ave Nw (44720-6912)
P.O. Box 900820 (84090-0820)
PHONE..................330 494-9111
William Haines Junior, *Pr*
EMP: 25 EST: 1991
SQ FT: 20,000
SALES (est): 1.29MM **Privately Held**
Web: www.haines.com
SIC: 2741 Directories, nec: publishing and printing

(G-2121)
HANNON COMPANY (PA)
Also Called: Charles Rewinding Div
1605 Waynesburg Dr Se (44707-2137)
PHONE..................330 456-4728
Christopher Meister, *Pr*
Mike Mcallister, *Superintnt*
Gary Gonzalez, *
Gary Griswold, *
Ann Paris, *
EMP: 75 EST: 1926
SQ FT: 65,000
SALES (est): 35.51MM
SALES (corp-wide): 35.51MM **Privately Held**
Web: www.hannonelectric.com
SIC: 3621 3825 5084 3699 Motors, electric; Test equipment for electronic and electrical circuits; Industrial machinery and equipment ; Electrical equipment and supplies, nec

(G-2122)
HARRISON PAINT COMPANY (PA)
Also Called: Harrison Paint
1329 Harrison Ave Sw (44706-1596)
PHONE..................330 455-5120
Patrick Lauber, *Pr*
◆ EMP: 27 EST: 1911
SQ FT: 173,000
SALES (est): 6.88MM
SALES (corp-wide): 6.88MM **Privately Held**
Web: www.harrisonpaint.com
SIC: 2851 Paints and allied products

(G-2123)
HEINEMANN SAW COMPANY
2017 Navarre Rd Sw (44706-5499)
PHONE..................330 456-4721
Thomas Dickey, *Pr*
Arthur Poorman, *
▲ EMP: 45 EST: 1917
SQ FT: 20,000
SALES (est): 4.76MM **Privately Held**
Web: www.heinemannsaw.com
SIC: 3425 3421 Saw blades and handsaws; Knives: butchers', hunting, pocket, etc.

(G-2124)
HENDRICKSON USA LLC
Also Called: Hendrcksn Trlr Coml Vhcl Syst
2070 Industrial Pl Se (44707-2641)
PHONE..................330 456-7288
Perry Bahr, *Genl Mgr*
EMP: 150
SALES (corp-wide): 758.84MM **Privately Held**
Web: www.hendrickson-intl.com
SIC: 3714 Motor vehicle parts and accessories
HQ: Hendrickson Usa, L.L.C.
840 S Frontage Rd
Woodridge IL 60517

(G-2125)
HOLMES LUMBER & BLDG CTR INC
1532 Perry Dr Sw (44710-1039)
PHONE..................330 479-8314
EMP: 46
SALES (corp-wide): 32.18MM **Privately Held**
Web: www.holmeslumber.com
SIC: 5031 5211 2439 2434 Lumber, plywood, and millwork; Lumber and other building materials; Structural wood members, nec; Wood kitchen cabinets
PA: Holmes Lumber & Building Center, Inc.
6139 Hc 39
Millersburg OH 44654
330 674-9060

(G-2126)
HUNTER HYDRAULICS INC
Also Called: Hhi
2512 Columbus Rd Ne (44705-3707)
P.O. Box 7117 (44705-0117)
PHONE..................330 455-3983
Larry R Hunter, *Pr*
Judith Kay Hunter, *VP*
EMP: 6 EST: 1968
SQ FT: 10,000
SALES (est): 999K
SALES (corp-wide): 2.36MM **Privately Held**
SIC: 3542 7699 Presses: hydraulic and pneumatic, mechanical and manual; Hydraulic equipment repair
PA: The H H I Company Inc
2512 Columbus Rd Ne
Canton OH 44705
330 455-3983

(G-2127)
HYDRODEC INC (PA)
2021 Steinway Blvd Se (44707-2644)
PHONE..................330 454-8202
EMP: 9 EST: 2006
SALES (est): 9.54MM **Privately Held**
Web: www.hydrodec.com
SIC: 2911 Oils, partly refined: sold for rerunning

(G-2128)
HYDRODEC OF NORTH AMERICA LLC
2021 Steinway Blvd Se (44707-2644)
PHONE..................330 454-8202
Ian Smale, *CEO*
Colin Moynihan, *Ch*
Chris Ellis, *CFO*
▼ EMP: 29 EST: 2007
SQ FT: 15,000
SALES (est): 9.54MM **Privately Held**
Web: www.hydrodec.com
SIC: 2911 Oils, partly refined: sold for rerunning
PA: Hydrodec Inc.
2021 Steinway Blvd Se
Canton OH 44707

GEOGRAPHIC SECTION

Canton - Stark County (G-2153)

(G-2129)
IML CONTAINERS OHIO INC
5365 E Center Dr Ne (44721-3734)
PHONE..................................330 754-1066
John P Lacroix, *Pr*
EMP: 15 **EST:** 2018
SALES (est): 4.28MM
SALES (corp-wide): 355.83K **Privately Held**
SIC: 3089   Plastics containers, except foam
HQ: Les Contenants I.M.L. D'amerique Du Nord Inc
2625 Rte 344
Saint-Placide QC J0V 2
450 258-3130

(G-2130)
IMPERIAL CONVEYING SYSTEMS LLC
4155 Martindale Rd Ne (44705-2727)
PHONE..................................330 491-3200
Brian Rostedt, *Managing Member*
EMP: 14 **EST:** 2020
SALES (est): 1.28MM **Privately Held**
Web: www.imperialconveyingsystems.com
SIC: 3535   Robotic conveyors

(G-2131)
INDUSTRIAL FABRICATION AND MCH
3216 Kuemerle Ct Ne (44705-5076)
PHONE..................................330 454-7644
Jim Stout, *Pt*
Ray Meyers, *Pt*
EMP: 8 **EST:** 1992
SQ FT: 11,000
SALES (est): 730.58K **Privately Held**
SIC: 3443   Fabricated plate work (boiler shop)

(G-2132)
INTERIOR GRAPHIC SYSTEMS LLC
4550 Aultman Rd (44720-1525)
PHONE..................................330 244-0100
Jim Weisburn, *Managing Member*
EMP: 8 **EST:** 1980
SQ FT: 10,000
SALES (est): 491.85K **Privately Held**
Web: www.interiorgraphicsystems.com
SIC: 3993   Signs, not made in custom sign painting shops

(G-2133)
INVUE SECURITY PRODUCTS INC
1510 4th St Se (44707-3206)
PHONE..................................330 456-7776
Farrokh Abadi, *Pr*
▼ **EMP:** 47 **EST:** 2003
SALES (est): 1.93MM
SALES (corp-wide): 4.75B **Privately Held**
Web: www.invue.com
SIC: 3699   Security devices
HQ: Checkpoint Systems, Inc.
101 Wolf Dr
West Deptford NJ 08086
800 257-5540

(G-2134)
JACODAR FSA LLC
2300 Allen Ave Se (44707-3673)
PHONE..................................330 454-1832
Vincent Codispoti, *Prin*
EMP: 21 **EST:** 2013
SALES (est): 841.68K
SALES (corp-wide): 5.38MM **Privately Held**
SIC: 3452   Bolts, metal
PA: Foundation Systems And Anchors, Inc.
2300 Allen Ave Se
Canton OH 44707
330 454-1700

(G-2135)
JANSON INDUSTRIES
1200 Garfield Ave Sw (44706-1639)
P.O. Box 6090 (44706-0090)
PHONE..................................330 455-7029
Richard Janson, *Pt*
Eric H Janson, *Mng Pt*
EMP: 100 **EST:** 1927
SQ FT: 120,000
SALES (est): 14.9MM **Privately Held**
Web: www.jansonindustries.com
SIC: 1799 2391 3999   Rigging and scaffolding; Curtains and draperies; Stage hardware and equipment, except lighting

(G-2136)
JMW WELDING AND MFG INC
512 45th St Sw (44706-4432)
PHONE..................................330 484-2428
John Slutz, *Pt*
Michael Slutz, *
Neal Slutz, *
EMP: 30 **EST:** 1983
SQ FT: 12,000
SALES (est): 2.71MM **Privately Held**
Web: www.jmwcompanies.net
SIC: 3443 7692   Industrial vessels, tanks, and containers; Welding repair

(G-2137)
KEBCO PRCISION FABRICATORS INC
2006 Allen Ave Se (44707-3608)
P.O. Box 20057 (44701-0057)
PHONE..................................330 456-0808
Eric Keblesh, *Admn*
Eric James Keblesh, *Prin*
Michael Todd Cogan, *Prin*
EMP: 12 **EST:** 2008
SALES (est): 2.04MM **Privately Held**
Web: www.kebcofab.com
SIC: 3441   Fabricated structural metal

(G-2138)
KERR FRICTION PRODUCTS INC
2512 Columbus Rd Ne (44705-3707)
P.O. Box 7117 (44705-0117)
PHONE..................................330 455-3983
Larry R Hunter, *Pr*
Judith K Hunter, *VP*
EMP: 16 **EST:** 1987
SQ FT: 10,000
SALES (est): 372.97K **Privately Held**
SIC: 3714   Motor vehicle brake systems and parts

(G-2139)
KLENK INDUSTRIES INC
Also Called: Klenk
1016 9th St Sw (44707-4108)
PHONE..................................330 453-7857
James Andreson, *Pr*
EMP: 15 **EST:** 1934
SQ FT: 5,000
SALES (est): 224.1K **Privately Held**
SIC: 3421   Shears, hand

(G-2140)
KLINGSTEDT BROTHERS COMPANY
425 Schroyer Ave Sw (44702-2012)
P.O. Box 6088 (44706-0088)
PHONE..................................330 456-8319
James R Cassler, *Pr*
Janet Cassler, *Sec*
EMP: 15 **EST:** 1912
SQ FT: 15,000
SALES (est): 425.91K **Privately Held**
Web: www.klingstedtbrothers.com
SIC: 2752 2754   Offset printing; Rotary photogravure printing

(G-2141)
KMS 2000 INC (PA)
Also Called: P P I Graphics
315 12th St Nw (44703)
P.O. Box 21220 (44701)
PHONE..................................330 454-9444
Kevin Smith, *Pr*
EMP: 14 **EST:** 1932
SALES (est): 1.83MM
SALES (corp-wide): 1.83MM **Privately Held**
Web: www.ppigraphics.com
SIC: 2752 2759   Offset printing; Letterpress printing

(G-2142)
KOHLER COATING INC
Also Called: KOHLER COATING
1205 5th St Sw (44707-4625)
PHONE..................................330 499-1407
Herb Kohler, *Pr*
▲ **EMP:** 29 **EST:** 2001
SALES (est): 3.41MM **Privately Held**
Web: www.kohlercoating.com
SIC: 3554   Paper industries machinery

(G-2143)
LANE FIELD MATERIALS INC
530 Walnut Ave Ne (44702-1273)
PHONE..................................330 526-8082
Jason D Terrell, *Prin*
Krystal Fisher, *Prin*
EMP: 7 **EST:** 2020
SALES (est): 688.79K **Privately Held**
SIC: 3537   Industrial trucks and tractors

(G-2144)
LAZARS ART GLLERY CRTIVE FRMNG
2940 Woodlawn Ave Nw (44708)
PHONE..................................330 477-8351
TOLL FREE: 800
Lazer Tarzan, *Pr*
Elizabeth Tarzan, *VP*
EMP: 8 **EST:** 1969
SALES (est): 478.06K **Privately Held**
Web: www.lazarsartgallery.com
SIC: 2499 5999   Picture and mirror frames, wood; Art dealers

(G-2145)
LEGALCRAFT INC
302 Hallum St Sw (44720-4217)
P.O. Box 8500 (44711-8500)
PHONE..................................330 494-1261
Robert Beck, *Pr*
EMP: 15 **EST:** 1933
SQ FT: 2,000
SALES (est): 862.53K **Privately Held**
SIC: 2752   Offset printing

(G-2146)
LOVING CHOICE ADOPTION-PRNTNG
625 Cleveland Ave Nw (44702-1805)
PHONE..................................330 994-1451
Rose Debevec, *Mgr*
EMP: 8 **EST:** 2017
SALES (est): 89.64K **Privately Held**
Web: www.commquest.org
SIC: 2752   Commercial printing, lithographic

(G-2147)
LUSTROUS METAL COATINGS INC
1541 Raff Rd Sw (44710-2321)
PHONE..................................330 478-4653
Michael Paxos, *Pr*
EMP: 40 **EST:** 1980
SQ FT: 34,000
SALES (est): 4.48MM **Privately Held**
Web: www.lustrousmetal.com
SIC: 3471   Electroplating of metals or formed products

(G-2148)
M A C MACHINE
1111 Faircrest St Se (44707-1229)
PHONE..................................410 944-6171
Allen Craig, *Owner*
EMP: 6 **EST:** 1980
SQ FT: 5,400
SALES (est): 390.31K **Privately Held**
SIC: 3599   Machine shop, jobbing and repair

(G-2149)
M K MORSE COMPANY (PA)
1101 11th St Se (44707-3400)
P.O. Box 8677 (44711-8677)
PHONE..................................330 453-8187
Nancy Sonner, *CEO*
Sally Dale, *
James Batchelder, *
Thomas Herrick Junior, *CFO*
George Briercheck, *
◆ **EMP:** 446 **EST:** 1963
SQ FT: 375,000
SALES (est): 93.36MM
SALES (corp-wide): 93.36MM **Privately Held**
Web: www.mkmorse.com
SIC: 3425   Saw blades, for hand or power saws

(G-2150)
M T SYSTEMS INC
400 Schroyer Ave Sw (44702-2013)
P.O. Box 2086 (61834-2086)
PHONE..................................330 453-4646
Mark E Church, *Pr*
EMP: 8 **EST:** 1985
SQ FT: 12,500
SALES (est): 2.18MM **Privately Held**
Web: www.mt-systems.com
SIC: 7373 3823 3561   Computer integrated systems design; Process control instruments; Pumps and pumping equipment

(G-2151)
M TECHNOLOGIES INC
Also Called: Northern Mobile Electric
1818 Hopple Ave Sw (44706-1909)
PHONE..................................330 477-9009
Rodney Mccauley, *Mng Pt*
Diane Broderick, *Pt*
EMP: 12 **EST:** 1981
SQ FT: 6,000
SALES (est): 2.3MM **Privately Held**
Web: www.northernmobile.com
SIC: 3625 5531   Starter, electric motor; Automotive parts

(G-2152)
MARY ANN DONUT SHOPPE INC (PA)
Also Called: Mary Ann Donuts
5032 Yukon St Nw (44708-5018)
PHONE..................................330 478-1655
Patrick J Welden, *Pr*
Dorothy Schweitzer, *VP*
EMP: 8 **EST:** 1947
SALES (est): 2.5MM
SALES (corp-wide): 2.5MM **Privately Held**
Web: www.maryanndonuts.com
SIC: 5461 2051   Doughnuts; Doughnuts, except frozen

(G-2153)
MATALCO (US) INC (DH)
4420 Louisville St Ne (44705-4848)
PHONE..................................330 452-4760

Canton - Stark County (G-2154)   GEOGRAPHIC SECTION

▲ **EMP:** 76 **EST:** 2010
SALES (est): 98.29MM
SALES (corp-wide): 6.29MM **Privately Held**
Web: www.matalco.com
SIC: 3363 Aluminum die-castings
HQ: Matalco Inc
850 Intermodal Dr
Brampton ON L6T 0
905 790-2511

(G-2154)
MATRIX MANAGEMENT SOLUTIONS
5200 Stoneham Rd (44720-1584)
PHONE................................330 470-3700
Mark Terpylak, *Pr*
EMP: 21 **EST:** 2007
SALES (est): 4.45MM **Privately Held**
Web: www.nextgen.com
SIC: 7372 7373 Prepackaged software; Computer integrated systems design
HQ: Nextgen Healthcare, Inc.
18111 Von Karman Ave # 6
Irvine CA 92612
949 255-2600

(G-2155)
MC CONCEPTS LLC
2459 55th St Ne (44721-3425)
PHONE................................330 933-6402
EMP: 7 **EST:** 2008
SALES (est): 461.8K **Privately Held**
SIC: 2095 Roasted coffee

(G-2156)
MCCANN COLOR INC
Also Called: Team Remington Cadillac
8562 Port Jackson Ave Nw (44720-5467)
PHONE................................330 498-4840
EMP: 24
SIC: 2816 2851 Color pigments; Paints and allied products

(G-2157)
MCCANN PLASTICS LLC
Also Called: McCann
5600 Mayfair Rd (44720-1539)
PHONE................................330 499-1515
Nicole Windemuth, *CFO*
EMP: 85 **EST:** 1989
SQ FT: 157,800
SALES (est): 26.82MM
SALES (corp-wide): 2.12B **Privately Held**
SIC: 3087 Custom compound purchased resins
PA: Hexpol Ab
Skeppsbron 3
Malmo 211 2
40254660

(G-2158)
MDI OF OHIO INC
Also Called: Formco
5175 Stoneham Rd (44720-1540)
PHONE................................937 866-2345
John E Dempsey, *Pr*
EMP: 26 **EST:** 2013
SALES (est): 4.49MM
SALES (corp-wide): 61.99MM **Privately Held**
Web: www.moldeddevices.com
SIC: 3089 Injection molded finished plastics products, nec
PA: Molded Devices, Inc.
740 W Knox Rd
Tempe AZ 85284
480 785-9100

(G-2159)
METALLUS INC (PA)
1835 Dueber Ave Sw (44706)
PHONE................................330 471-7000
Michael S Williams, *Pr*
Ronald A Rice, *Non-Executive Chairman of the Board*
Kristopher R Westbrooks, *Ex VP*
Kristine C Syrvalin, *Chief Human Resources Officer*
Kevin A Raketich, *CCO*
◆ **EMP:** 1158 **EST:** 1899
SALES (est): 1.36B
SALES (corp-wide): 1.36B **Publicly Held**
Web: www.metallus.com
SIC: 3312 Blast furnaces and steel mills

(G-2160)
METALLUS INC
2311 Shepler Church Ave Sw (44706-3073)
PHONE................................216 825-2533
EMP: 9
SALES (corp-wide): 1.36B **Publicly Held**
Web: www.metallus.com
SIC: 3312 Blast furnaces and steel mills
PA: Metallus Inc.
1835 Dueber Ave Sw
Canton OH 44706
330 471-7000

(G-2161)
METALLUS INC
4748 Navarre Rd (44706-2339)
PHONE................................800 967-1218
EMP: 18
SALES (corp-wide): 1.36B **Publicly Held**
Web: www.metallus.com
SIC: 3312 Blast furnaces and steel mills
PA: Metallus Inc.
1835 Dueber Ave Sw
Canton OH 44706
330 471-7000

(G-2162)
METALLUS INC
Also Called: Harrison Plant
1835 Dueber Ave Sw (44706-2728)
PHONE................................330 471-7000
EMP: 38
SALES (corp-wide): 1.36B **Publicly Held**
Web: www.metallus.com
SIC: 3312 Blast furnaces and steel mills
PA: Metallus Inc.
1835 Dueber Ave Sw
Canton OH 44706
330 471-7000

(G-2163)
METALLUS INC
Also Called: Timkensteel Fircrest Stl Plant
4511 Faircrest St Sw (44706-3513)
PHONE................................330 471-7000
Ron Balyint, *Prin*
EMP: 47
SALES (corp-wide): 1.36B **Publicly Held**
Web: www.metallus.com
SIC: 3317 Steel pipe and tubes
PA: Metallus Inc.
1835 Dueber Ave Sw
Canton OH 44706
330 471-7000

(G-2164)
MIDWEST SIGN CTR
Also Called: Midwest Sign Center
4210 Cleveland Ave Nw (44709-2350)
PHONE................................330 493-7330
Melvin R Lloyd, *Pr*
Carolyn P Lloyd, *VP*
EMP: 6 **EST:** 1973
SQ FT: 3,000
SALES (est): 200.59K **Privately Held**
Web: www.midwestsigncenter.com
SIC: 3993 Signs, not made in custom sign painting shops

(G-2165)
MILK HNEY CNDY SODA SHOPPE LLC
3400 Cleveland Ave Nw Ste 1 (44709-2784)
PHONE................................330 492-5884
Dwayne Cornell, *Pt*
EMP: 14 **EST:** 1954
SQ FT: 2,500
SALES (est): 452.53K **Privately Held**
Web: www.milkandhoneychocolates.com
SIC: 5451 5812 2066 2064 Ice cream (packaged); Restaurant, lunch counter; Chocolate and cocoa products; Candy and other confectionery products

(G-2166)
MONIQUE BATH AND BODY LTD
6545 Market Ave N (44721-2430)
PHONE................................513 440-7370
Monique Blue, *Managing Member*
EMP: 8 **EST:** 2020
SALES (est): 381.04K **Privately Held**
SIC: 2844 Shampoos, rinses, conditioners: hair

(G-2167)
MPLX TERMINALS LLC
Also Called: Marathon Canton Refinery
2408 Gambrinus Ave Sw (44706-2365)
PHONE................................330 479-5539
Mike Armbrester, *Brnch Mgr*
EMP: 78
SIC: 5172 2951 Gasoline; Asphalt paving mixtures and blocks
HQ: Mplx Terminals Llc
200 E Hardin St
Findlay OH 45840
419 421-2414

(G-2168)
MULTI GALVANIZING LLC
825 Navarre Rd Sw (44707-4058)
PHONE................................330 453-1441
Charles E Decker Ii, *Managing Member*
EMP: 6 **EST:** 2003
SQ FT: 30,000
SALES (est): 620K **Privately Held**
Web: www.multigalvanizing.com
SIC: 3547 Galvanizing lines (rolling mill equipment)

(G-2169)
MURPHY TRACTOR & EQP CO INC
Also Called: John Deere Authorized Dealer
1509 Raff Rd Sw (44710-2321)
PHONE................................330 477-9304
EMP: 8
Web: www.murphytractor.com
SIC: 3531 5082 Construction machinery; Construction and mining machinery
HQ: Murphy Tractor & Equipment Co., Inc.
5375 N Deere Rd
Park City KS 67219
855 246-9124

(G-2170)
MYERS CONTROLLED POWER LLC
133 Taft Ave Ne (44720-2527)
PHONE................................909 923-1800
EMP: 21
SALES (corp-wide): 172.09MM **Privately Held**
Web: www.myerspower.com
SIC: 3629 Inverters, nonrotating: electrical
HQ: Myers Controlled Power, Llc
219 E Maple St 100-200e
North Canton OH 44720
330 834-3200

(G-2171)
NEW BLTMORE ICE CREAM PDTS INC
2932 Clearview Ave Nw (44718-3428)
PHONE................................330 904-6687
EMP: 31 **EST:** 2009
SALES (est): 2.09MM **Privately Held**
SIC: 2024 Ice cream and frozen deserts

(G-2172)
NEWCO INDUSTRIES
4057 Glenmoor Rd Nw (44718-2253)
PHONE................................717 566-9560
Patricia Newell, *Owner*
EMP: 10 **EST:** 2000
SALES (est): 908.9K **Privately Held**
SIC: 3569 Assembly machines, non-metalworking

(G-2173)
NOLAN COMPANY (HQ)
1016 9th St Sw (44707-4108)
PHONE................................330 453-7922
Dan Epstein, *CEO*
EMP: 27 **EST:** 1909
SQ FT: 52,000
SALES (est): 9.17MM
SALES (corp-wide): 37.01MM **Privately Held**
Web: www.nolancompany.com
SIC: 3743 3532 Railroad equipment; Mining machinery
PA: Resource Pro Llc
60 E 42nd St Ste 1500
New York NY 10165
888 577-7552

(G-2174)
NORCIA BAKERY
624 Belden Ave Ne (44704-2229)
PHONE................................330 454-1077
Donald C Horne, *Pr*
Jim Butler, *
EMP: 13 **EST:** 1920
SQ FT: 3,200
SALES (est): 862.51K **Privately Held**
Web: www.norciabakery.com
SIC: 2051 5461 5149 2052 Bakery: wholesale or wholesale/retail combined; Bread; Groceries and related products, nec; Cookies and crackers

(G-2175)
NORRIS NORTH MANUFACTURING
1500 Henry Ave Sw (44706-2852)
PHONE................................330 691-0449
Tyler Palumbo, *Prin*
EMP: 13 **EST:** 2014
SALES (est): 1.13MM **Privately Held**
SIC: 3999 Manufacturing industries, nec

(G-2176)
NORTH CANTON PLASTICS INC
6658 Promway Ave Nw (44720-7316)
PHONE................................330 497-0071
John Kuebel, *Pr*
Karen Kuebel, *
EMP: 38 **EST:** 1988
SQ FT: 26,000
SALES (est): 3.17MM **Privately Held**
Web: www.ncplasticsco.com
SIC: 3089 Injection molding of plastics

GEOGRAPHIC SECTION

Canton - Stark County (G-2202)

(G-2177)
NORTH CANTON TOOL CO
1156 Marion Ave Sw (44707-4138)
P.O. Box 20169 (44701-0169)
PHONE.................................330 452-0545
David Pool, *Pr*
Rebecca Perez, *VP*
EMP: 9 **EST:** 1950
SQ FT: 10,000
SALES (est): 921.41K **Privately Held**
SIC: 3599 Machine shop, jobbing and repair

(G-2178)
NORTHEASTERN OILFIELD SVCS LLC (PA)
1537 Waynesburg Dr Se (44707-2135)
PHONE.................................330 581-3304
David D Krutilek, *Prin*
EMP: 6 **EST:** 2013
SALES (est): 780K
SALES (corp-wide): 780K **Privately Held**
Web: www.northeasternoilfieldservicesllc.com
SIC: 1389 Oil field services, nec

(G-2179)
NORTHEASTERN PLASTICS INC
112 Navarre Rd Sw (44707-3950)
PHONE.................................330 453-5925
EMP: 6 **EST:** 1993
SQ FT: 4,800
SALES (est): 483.17K **Privately Held**
Web: www.northeasternplastics.com
SIC: 2759 2396 Screen printing; Automotive and apparel trimmings

(G-2180)
OBS INC
Also Called: Obs Specialty Vehicles
1324 Tuscarawas St W (44702-2036)
PHONE.................................330 453-3725
Robert Ferne, *Pr*
▲ **EMP:** 13 **EST:** 1998
SQ FT: 28,000
SALES (est): 2.54MM **Privately Held**
Web: www.obsinc.net
SIC: 3711 7532 Mobile lounges (motor vehicle), assembly of; Body shop, automotive

(G-2181)
OGC INDUSTRIES INC
934 Wells Ave Nw (44703-3500)
PHONE.................................330 456-1500
Orlando Chiarucci, *Pr*
EMP: 10 **EST:** 1984
SQ FT: 80,000
SALES (est): 1.78MM **Privately Held**
Web: www.ogcind.com
SIC: 4731 3679 Brokers, shipping; Harness assemblies, for electronic use: wire or cable

(G-2182)
OHIO AUTO SUPPLY COMPANY
Also Called: Professional Detailing Pdts
1128 Tuscarawas St W (44702-2086)
PHONE.................................330 454-5105
Michael Dickson, *Pr*
Stanley R Rubin, *
EMP: 15 **EST:** 1933
SQ FT: 15,000
SALES (est): 2.16MM **Privately Held**
Web: www.professionaldetailingproducts.com
SIC: 5013 2842 5531 3714 Automotive supplies and parts; Cleaning or polishing preparations, nec; Automotive parts; Motor vehicle parts and accessories

(G-2183)
OHIO EMBROIDERY LLC
1321 Davis St Sw (44706-4503)
PHONE.................................330 479-0029
Sarah Kennedy, *Prin*
EMP: 6 **EST:** 2014
SALES (est): 145.03K **Privately Held**
Web: www.ohioembroidery.com
SIC: 2395 Embroidery and art needlework

(G-2184)
OHIO GRATINGS INC (PA)
5299 Southway St Sw (44706-1992)
PHONE.................................800 321-9800
John Bartley, *Pr*
David Bartley, *
Ronald Lenney, *
Jeff Davis, *
Juanita Finley, *
♦ **EMP:** 300 **EST:** 1970
SQ FT: 150,000
SALES (est): 104.87MM
SALES (corp-wide): 104.87MM **Privately Held**
Web: www.ohiogratings.com
SIC: 3446 3444 3441 3312 Gratings, open steel flooring; Sheet metalwork; Fabricated structural metal; Blast furnaces and steel mills

(G-2185)
OHIO PAPER TUBE CO
3422 Navarre Rd Sw (44706-1856)
PHONE.................................330 478-5171
William Natale Junior, *Pr*
Dennis Natale, *
Timothy Natale, *
EMP: 26 **EST:** 1968
SQ FT: 46,000
SALES (est): 4.31MM **Privately Held**
Web: www.ohiopapertube.com
SIC: 2655 5113 Tubes, fiber or paper: made from purchased material; Paper tubes and cores

(G-2186)
OHIO PRECISION INC
1239 Market Ave S (44707-3968)
PHONE.................................330 453-9710
EMP: 8 **EST:** 1995
SALES (est): 846.23K **Privately Held**
SIC: 3599 Machine shop, jobbing and repair

(G-2187)
OHIO VERTICAL HEAT TREAT INC
2030 Industrial Pl Se (44707-2641)
PHONE.................................330 456-7176
EMP: 7 **EST:** 2015
SALES (est): 254.66K **Privately Held**
Web: www.ov-ht.com
SIC: 3398 Metal heat treating

(G-2188)
OMWP COMPANY
3620 Progress St Ne (44705-4438)
P.O. Box 7069 (44705-0069)
PHONE.................................330 453-8438
EMP: 35 **EST:** 1954
SALES (est): 2.21MM **Privately Held**
SIC: 3545 Machine tool accessories

(G-2189)
OSTER SAND AND GRAVEL INC (PA)
5947 Whipple Ave Nw (44720-7692)
PHONE.................................330 494-5472
Marlene Oster, *Pr*
Valerie Newman, *Treas*
Scott Oster, *VP*
EMP: 7 **EST:** 1967
SQ FT: 3,000
SALES (est): 2.5MM
SALES (corp-wide): 2.5MM **Privately Held**
Web: www.ostersandandgravelnorthcantonoh.com
SIC: 1442 Gravel mining

(G-2190)
P & M ENTERPRISES GROUP INC
1900 Mahoning Rd Ne (44705-1449)
PHONE.................................330 316-0387
EMP: 7 **EST:** 2011
SALES (est): 123.89K **Privately Held**
SIC: 1389 5963 Construction, repair, and dismantling services; Home related products, direct sales

(G-2191)
PARAGRAPHICS INC
2011 29th St Nw (44709-3218)
PHONE.................................330 493-1074
James S Bosworth, *Pr*
Peter A Bosworth, *
Andrew Bosworth, *
▲ **EMP:** 30 **EST:** 1975
SQ FT: 18,000
SALES (est): 4.78MM **Privately Held**
Web: www.para-inc.com
SIC: 2752 Offset printing

(G-2192)
PATRIOT PRECISION PRODUCTS
8817 Pleasantwood Ave Nw (44720-4759)
PHONE.................................330 966-7177
Ronald Dillard, *Pr*
EMP: 9 **EST:** 1992
SQ FT: 41,000
SALES (est): 225.16K **Privately Held**
SIC: 3599 Machine shop, jobbing and repair

(G-2193)
PATRIOT SOFTWARE LLC
4883 Dressler Rd Nw Ste 301 (44718-3665)
PHONE.................................877 968-7147
Michael J Kappel, *Pr*
Todd Schmitt, *
EMP: 100 **EST:** 2002
SQ FT: 1,120
SALES (est): 13.67MM **Privately Held**
Web: www.patriotsoftware.com
SIC: 7372 Business oriented computer software

(G-2194)
PATRIOT SPECIAL METALS INC
2201 Harrison Ave Sw (44706-3076)
P.O. Box 1562 (14092-8562)
PHONE.................................330 580-9600
Frank Carchidi, *CEO*
Paul Olah, *
Ron Brattin, *Managing Member*
EMP: 70 **EST:** 1994
SALES (est): 23.58MM
SALES (corp-wide): 51.08MM **Privately Held**
Web: www.republicspecialmetals.com
SIC: 3356 Nonferrous rolling and drawing, nec
PA: Patriot Forge Co.
280 Henry St
Brantford ON
519 758-8100

(G-2195)
PAXOS PLATING INC
4631 Navarre Rd Sw (44706-2336)
PHONE.................................330 479-0022
Mike Paxos, *Pr*
EMP: 25 **EST:** 1996
SQ FT: 35,000
SALES (est): 2.54MM **Privately Held**
Web: www.paxosplating.com
SIC: 3471 Electroplating of metals or formed products

(G-2196)
PHASE II ENTERPRISES INC
Also Called: Marino Maintenance Co
2154 Bolivar Rd Sw (44706-3055)
PHONE.................................330 484-2113
Richard Marino, *Pr*
EMP: 8 **EST:** 1989
SQ FT: 5,200
SALES (est): 686.89K **Privately Held**
Web: www.cobrarolloff.com
SIC: 7349 3446 Building maintenance services, nec; Stairs, fire escapes, balconies, railings, and ladders

(G-2197)
PINNACLE PRESS INC
2960 Harrisburg Rd Ne (44705-2562)
PHONE.................................330 453-7060
Robert Kettlewell, *Pr*
Shelly Poyser, *Treas*
EMP: 11 **EST:** 1976
SQ FT: 9,700
SALES (est): 453K **Privately Held**
Web: www.pinnaclepressinc.com
SIC: 2752 Offset printing

(G-2198)
PRECISION COMPONENT INDS LLC ✪
5325 Southway St Sw (44706-1943)
PHONE.................................330 477-6287
Karen Bartley, *Managing Member*
EMP: 25 **EST:** 2023
SALES (est): 2.93MM **Privately Held**
SIC: 3599 Machine shop, jobbing and repair

(G-2199)
PRECISION POWDER COATING INC
1530 Raff Rd Sw (44710-2322)
PHONE.................................330 478-0741
EMP: 44 **EST:** 1995
SQ FT: 100,000
SALES (est): 2.39MM **Privately Held**
SIC: 3398 3471 Metal heat treating; Finishing, metals or formed products

(G-2200)
PRIDE 821 LLC
401 Cherry Ave Ne (44702-1154)
PHONE.................................330 754-6320
EMP: 8 **EST:** 2020
SALES (est): 561.64K **Privately Held**
SIC: 2599 Bar, restaurant and cafeteria furniture

(G-2201)
PRIME ENGINEERED PLASTICS CORP
1505 Howington Cir Se (44707-2214)
PHONE.................................330 452-5110
Patrick M Nolan, *Pr*
EMP: 15 **EST:** 1996
SQ FT: 14,400
SALES (est): 2.57MM **Privately Held**
Web: www.prime-plastics.com
SIC: 3089 Injection molding of plastics

(G-2202)
PRINT SHOP OF CANTON INC
6536 Promler St Nw (44720-7630)
PHONE.................................330 497-3212
Jeff Grametbauer, *Pr*
Joyce Grametbauer, *Sec*
EMP: 11 **EST:** 1972
SQ FT: 2,600
SALES (est): 879.01K **Privately Held**

Canton - Stark County (G-2203)

Web: www.printshopinc.com
SIC: 2752 Offset printing

(G-2203)
PRO-DECAL INC
3638 Cleveland Ave S (44707-1448)
PHONE...................................330 484-0089
EMP: 6 EST: 1996
SQ FT: 800
SALES (est): 650K Privately Held
Web: www.prodecalinc.com
SIC: 2752 3993 Decals, lithographed; Signs and advertising specialties

(G-2204)
PROFILE PLASTICS INC
1226 Prospect Ave Sw (44706-1628)
PHONE...................................330 452-7000
Bryan Knowles, Prin
Sandra Knowles, Sec
EMP: 21 EST: 1993
SQ FT: 16,000
SALES (est): 4.56MM Privately Held
Web: www.profileplastics.com
SIC: 3089 Extruded finished plastics products, nec

(G-2205)
QUASS SHEET METAL INC
5018 Yukon St Nw (44708-5018)
PHONE...................................330 477-4841
John Angerer, Pr
Joyce Angerer, VP
EMP: 9 EST: 1936
SQ FT: 9,500
SALES (est): 957.34K Privately Held
Web: www.metalfabricationquass.com
SIC: 3444 Sheet metalwork

(G-2206)
QUICKDRAFT INC
1525 Perry Dr Sw (44710-1098)
PHONE...................................330 477-4574
Matthew C Litler, Pr
Matthew C Litzler, Pr
William J Urban, Treas
EMP: 45 EST: 1953
SQ FT: 45,000
SALES (est): 12.03MM
SALES (corp-wide): 25.92MM Privately Held
Web: www.quickdraft.com
SIC: 3535 3564 Conveyors and conveying equipment; Blowers and fans
PA: C.A. Litzler Holding Company
4800 W 160th St
Cleveland OH 44135
216 267-8020

(G-2207)
R G SMITH COMPANY (PA)
Also Called: Rgs
1249 Dueber Ave Sw (44706-1635)
P.O. Box 9067 (44711-9067)
PHONE...................................330 456-3415
EMP: 95 EST: 1909
SALES (est): 21.47MM
SALES (corp-wide): 21.47MM Privately Held
Web: www.rgscontractors.com
SIC: 3444 1761 1541 3496 Ducts, sheet metal; Roofing contractor; Industrial buildings and warehouses; Miscellaneous fabricated wire products

(G-2208)
R H LITTLE CO
4434 Southway St Sw (44706-1894)
PHONE...................................330 477-3455
David Little, Pr
Robert Brady, VP
Genevieve Little, Sec
EMP: 8 EST: 1940
SQ FT: 22,000
SALES (est): 640.76K Privately Held
SIC: 3743 Railroad equipment

(G-2209)
R W SIDLEY INCORPORATED
7545 Pittsburg Ave Nw (44720-6943)
PHONE...................................330 499-5616
R W Sidley, Pr
EMP: 7
SALES (corp-wide): 83.57MM Privately Held
Web: www.rwsidley.com
SIC: 3273 Ready-mixed concrete
PA: R. W. Sidley Incorporated
436 Casement Ave
Painesville OH 44077
440 352-9343

(G-2210)
RANDALL RICHARD & MOORE LLC
Also Called: Cutter Equipment Company
3710 Progress St Ne (44705-4438)
PHONE...................................330 455-8873
EMP: 29 EST: 1998
SALES (est): 1.71MM Privately Held
Web: www.cutteronline.com
SIC: 3523 Turf and grounds equipment

(G-2211)
RELADYNE RELIABILITY SVCS INC (HQ)
3713 Progress St Ne (44705-4437)
PHONE...................................888 478-6996
Larry Stoddard, CEO
▲ EMP: 27 EST: 2011
SALES (est): 21.33MM Privately Held
SIC: 3569 Lubrication machinery, automatic
PA: Reladyne Inc.
8280 Montgomery Rd # 101
Cincinnati OH 45236

(G-2212)
RELIABLE READY MIX CO
1606 Allen Ave Se (44707-3770)
P.O. Box 6359 (44706-0359)
PHONE...................................330 453-8266
James Lombardi, CEO
EMP: 42 EST: 2003
SALES (est): 5.67MM Privately Held
SIC: 3273 Ready-mixed concrete

(G-2213)
REPUBLIC STEEL
Also Called: Canton Hot Rolled Plant
2633 8th St Ne (44704-2311)
PHONE...................................330 438-5533
John Ridgeway, Mgr
EMP: 10
Web: www.republicsteel.com
SIC: 3312 Blast furnaces and steel mills
HQ: Republic Steel
2633 8th St Ne
Canton OH 44704
330 438-5435

(G-2214)
REPUBLIC STEEL (DH)
2633 8th St Ne (44704-2311)
PHONE...................................330 438-5435
Jaime Vigil, Pr
Noel J Huettich, VP
Ted Thielens, VP
John A Willoughby, VP
Joseph A Kaczka, CFO
◆ EMP: 11 EST: 1993
SQ FT: 800,000
SALES (est): 674.25MM Privately Held
Web: www.republicsteel.com

SIC: 3312 Bars, iron: made in steel mills
HQ: Grupo Simec, S.A.B. De C.V.
Av. Lazaro Cardenas No. 601 Edif. A
Guadalajara JAL 44470

(G-2215)
REPUBLIC STORAGE SYSTEMS LLC
1038 Belden Ave Ne (44705-1454)
PHONE...................................330 438-5800
EMP: 400
SIC: 2542 3441 Lockers (not refrigerated): except wood; Fabricated structural metal

(G-2216)
RMI TITANIUM COMPANY LLC
Also Called: Galt Alloys
208 15th St Sw (44707-4009)
PHONE...................................330 471-1844
Bruce Whatzel, Mgr
EMP: 208
SALES (corp-wide): 6.64B Publicly Held
Web: www.howmet.com
SIC: 3312 3341 Blast furnace and related products; Secondary nonferrous metals
HQ: Rmi Titanium Company, Llc
1000 Warren Ave
Niles OH 44446
330 652-9952

(G-2217)
RMI TITANIUM COMPANY LLC
Also Called: Rti Alloys
1550 Marietta Ave Se (44707-2568)
PHONE...................................330 453-2118
George Hilana, Mgr
EMP: 108
SALES (corp-wide): 6.64B Publicly Held
SIC: 3312 3341 Tool and die steel and alloys; Secondary nonferrous metals
HQ: Rmi Titanium Company, Llc
1000 Warren Ave
Niles OH 44446
330 652-9952

(G-2218)
RMI TITANIUM COMPANY LLC
Also Called: Rti Alloys Tpd
1935 Warner Rd Se (44707-2273)
PHONE...................................330 455-4010
Cheryl Lyons, Prin
EMP: 134
SALES (corp-wide): 6.64B Publicly Held
Web: www.howmet.com
SIC: 3499 Friction material, made from powdered metal
HQ: Rmi Titanium Company, Llc
1000 Warren Ave
Niles OH 44446
330 652-9952

(G-2219)
ROBERT SMART INC
Also Called: Superior Machine Co
1100 High Ave Sw (44707-4116)
PHONE...................................330 454-8881
Robert Scott Smart, Pr
EMP: 16 EST: 1939
SALES (est): 471.72K Privately Held
SIC: 3599 Machine shop, jobbing and repair

(G-2220)
SELF MADE HOLDINGS LLC
5325 Southway St Sw (44706-1943)
PHONE...................................330 477-1052
Patricia Gerak, CEO
Anthony J Gerak, *
EMP: 30 EST: 1957
SQ FT: 56,000
SALES (est): 4.9MM Privately Held
Web: www.precision-component.com

SIC: 3599 3544 3545 Machine shop, jobbing and repair; Special dies and tools; Shear knives

(G-2221)
SEQUA CAN MACHINERY INC
Also Called: C I P
4150 Belden Village St Nw Ste 504 (44718-2595)
PHONE...................................330 493-0444
James Mcclung, Pr
Manuel Rubalcava, *
EMP: 24 EST: 1993
SQ FT: 2,000
SALES (est): 8.28MM
SALES (corp-wide): 1.54B Publicly Held
Web: www.cip.co.za
SIC: 3599 5084 Custom machinery; Industrial machinery and equipment
PA: Azz Inc.
3100 W 7th St Ste 500
Fort Worth TX 76107
817 810-0095

(G-2222)
SHAHEEN ORIENTAL RUG CO INC (PA)
Also Called: Abbey Carpet
4120 Whipple Ave Nw (44718-2970)
PHONE...................................330 493-9000
Nicholas H Shaheen Junior, Pr
Dawn Shaheen, VP
EMP: 10 EST: 1901
SQ FT: 12,800
SALES (est): 2.19MM
SALES (corp-wide): 2.19MM Privately Held
Web: www.shaheenrugs.com
SIC: 5713 7217 2295 Carpets; Carpet and furniture cleaning on location; Tape, varnished: plastic, and other coated (except magnetic)

(G-2223)
SHANAFELT MANUFACTURING CO (PA)
2633 Winfield Way Ne (44705-2069)
P.O. Box 7040 (44705-0040)
PHONE...................................330 455-0315
Leo Kovachic, Pr
Jon Lindseth, *
Joseph Sullivan, *
EMP: 35 EST: 1893
SQ FT: 50,000
SALES (est): 4.59MM
SALES (corp-wide): 4.59MM Privately Held
Web: www.shanafelt.com
SIC: 3537 3451 Containers (metal), air cargo; Screw machine products

(G-2224)
SHEETMETAL CRAFTERS
435 Walnut Ave Se (44702-1348)
PHONE...................................330 452-6700
EMP: 10 EST: 2020
SALES (est): 936.54K Privately Held
Web: www.sheetmetalcrafters.com
SIC: 3444 Sheet metalwork

(G-2225)
SHEETMETAL CRAFTERS INC
325 5th St Se (44702-1314)
P.O. Box 20648 (44701-0648)
PHONE...................................330 452-6700
David Grabowsky, Pr
EMP: 15 EST: 1989
SQ FT: 600
SALES (est): 2.21MM Privately Held
Web: www.sheetmetalcrafters.com
SIC: 3444 Sheet metalwork

GEOGRAPHIC SECTION

Canton - Stark County (G-2247)

(G-2226)
SLIMANS PRINTERY INC
Also Called: SPI Mailing
624 5th St Nw (44703-2625)
PHONE.................................330 454-9141
Samuel Sliman Junior, *Pr*
Judy Sliman Humphries, *VP*
EMP: 14 **EST:** 1947
SQ FT: 9,000
SALES (est): 1.6MM **Privately Held**
Web: www.slimansprintery.com
SIC: 2752 2759 Offset printing; Letterpress printing

(G-2227)
SOLMET DRILLING SOLUTIONS LLC
2025 Dueber Ave Sw (44706-2732)
PHONE.................................330 455-4328
Matthew Halter, *Prin*
Kyle Sheposh, *Prin*
EMP: 10 **EST:** 2020
SALES (est): 482.6K **Privately Held**
Web: www.solmet.net
SIC: 3599 Machine shop, jobbing and repair

(G-2228)
SOLMET TECHNOLOGIES INC
2716 Shepler Church Ave Sw (44706-4114)
PHONE.................................330 915-4160
Joseph R Halter Junior, *Pr*
E Scott Jackson, *
Lee Dicola, *
Matthew Halter, *
EMP: 50 **EST:** 1985
SALES (est): 11.1MM **Privately Held**
Web: www.solmet.net
SIC: 3462 Iron and steel forgings

(G-2229)
SPECIAL PACK INC
5555 Massillon Rd (44720-1339)
PHONE.................................330 458-3204
Greg Brumbaugh, *Genl Mgr*
◆ **EMP:** 20 **EST:** 1997
SALES (est): 939.87K **Privately Held**
SIC: 2621 Packaging paper

(G-2230)
STANDARD PRINTING CO OF CANTON
Also Called: Standard Printing Company
1115 Cherry Ave Ne (44704-1325)
P.O. Box 9276 (44711-9276)
PHONE.................................330 453-8247
EMP: 70 **EST:** 1923
SALES (est): 10.07MM **Privately Held**
Web: www.spcoc.com
SIC: 2752 2791 2789 Offset printing; Typesetting; Bookbinding and related work

(G-2231)
STARK CNTY FDRTION CNSRVTION C
6323 Richville Dr Sw (44706-3131)
PHONE.................................330 268-1652
Michael W Rutledge, *Prin*
Jim Adkins, *
Kathy Griffin, *
Debbie Bonk, *
Bob Hess, *
EMP: 25 **EST:** 2018
SALES (est): 1.01MM **Privately Held**
Web: www.the-review.com
SIC: 2711 Newspapers, publishing and printing

(G-2232)
STARK MATERIALS INC
Also Called: Northstar Asphalt
7345 Sunset Strip Ave Nw (44720-7040)
P.O. Box 2646 (44720-0646)
PHONE.................................330 497-1648
EMP: 15 **EST:** 1985
SQ FT: 1,404
SALES (est): 500.65K **Privately Held**
Web: www.northstarasphalt.com
SIC: 2911 2951 Asphalt or asphaltic materials, made in refineries; Asphalt paving mixtures and blocks

(G-2233)
STARK TRUSS COMPANY INC
4933 Southway St Sw (44706-1979)
PHONE.................................330 478-2100
Rob Blyer, *Brnch Mgr*
EMP: 47
SALES (corp-wide): 99.05MM **Privately Held**
Web: www.starktruss.com
SIC: 2439 2511 Trusses, wooden roof; Wood household furniture
PA: Stark Truss Company, Inc.
109 Miles Ave Sw
Canton OH 44710
330 478-2100

(G-2234)
STARK TRUSS COMPANY INC
Stark Forest Products
1601 Perry Dr Sw (44706-1919)
P.O. Box 80808 (44708-0808)
PHONE.................................330 478-6063
EMP: 7
SALES (corp-wide): 99.05MM **Privately Held**
Web: www.starktruss.com
SIC: 2439 Trusses, wooden roof
PA: Stark Truss Company, Inc.
109 Miles Ave Sw
Canton OH 44710
330 478-2100

(G-2235)
STARK TRUSS COMPANY INC (PA)
Also Called: S T C
109 Miles Ave Sw (44710-1261)
P.O. Box 80469 (44708-0469)
PHONE.................................330 478-2100
Abner Yoder, *CEO*
Stephen Yoder, *Pr*
Javan Yoder, *Ex VP*
Todd Pallotta, *VP*
Wendy Spillman, *Sec*
EMP: 18 **EST:** 1968
SQ FT: 4,300
SALES (est): 99.05MM
SALES (corp-wide): 99.05MM **Privately Held**
Web: www.starktruss.com
SIC: 5031 2439 Lumber, plywood, and millwork; Trusses, wooden roof

(G-2236)
STOLLE MACHINERY COMPANY LLC
Also Called: Canton Tool
1007 High Ave Sw (44707-4131)
PHONE.................................330 244-0555
Mike Felpovich, *Mgr*
EMP: 55
SALES (corp-wide): 492.99MM **Privately Held**
Web: www.stollemachinery.com
SIC: 3411 Tin cans
PA: Stolle Machinery Company, Llc
6949 S Potomac St
Centennial CO 80112
303 708-9044

(G-2237)
STUDIO ARTS AND GLASS INC
7495 Strauss Ave Nw (44720-7103)
PHONE.................................330 494-9779
TOLL FREE: 800
Robert Joliet, *Pr*
Wendy Warren, *VP*
EMP: 10 **EST:** 1983
SQ FT: 7,000
SALES (est): 872.87K **Privately Held**
Web: www.studioartsandglass.com
SIC: 3231 8299 Stained glass: made from purchased glass; Arts and crafts schools

(G-2238)
SUN STATE PLASTICS INC
4045 Kevin St Nw (44720-6981)
PHONE.................................330 494-5220
Rick Dewees, *Pr*
EMP: 40 **EST:** 1949
SQ FT: 37,000
SALES (est): 3.7MM **Privately Held**
Web: www.sunstateplastics.com
SIC: 3089 Injection molding of plastics

(G-2239)
SUPERIOR DAIRY INC
Also Called: Creative Edge Group
4719 Navarre Rd Sw (44706-2300)
PHONE.................................330 477-4515
EMP: 220 **EST:** 1922
SALES (est): 55.15MM **Privately Held**
Web: www.mimilk.com
SIC: 2026 2024 Fluid milk; Ice cream and frozen deserts

(G-2240)
SUSPENSION TECHNOLOGY INC
1424 Scales St Sw (44706-3081)
PHONE.................................330 458-3058
David Croston, *Pr*
Ervin Vandenberg, *Prin*
EMP: 15 **EST:** 2000
SQ FT: 12,000
SALES (est): 455.37K **Privately Held**
Web: www.b-tek.com
SIC: 3537 5084 Lift trucks, industrial: fork, platform, straddle, etc.; Lift trucks and parts

(G-2241)
TECHNIBUS INC
1501 Raff Rd Sw Ste 6 (44710-2356)
PHONE.................................330 479-4202
Mike Rice, *Pr*
Jacob Isaacson, *Dir Fin*
▲ **EMP:** 100 **EST:** 2006
SQ FT: 150,000
SALES (est): 33.61MM **Publicly Held**
Web: www.technibus.com
SIC: 3444 Ducts, sheet metal
HQ: Ies Infrastructure Solutions, Llc
800 Nave Rd Se
Massillon OH 44646
330 830-3500

(G-2242)
TEK GEAR & MACHINE INC
1220 Camden Ave Sw (44706-1618)
PHONE.................................330 455-3331
Kevin Aronhalt, *Pr*
Thomas Mertz, *VP*
Emil Bueno, *Treas*
EMP: 8 **EST:** 1990
SQ FT: 6,000
SALES (est): 900K **Privately Held**
Web: www.tekgearinc.com
SIC: 3599 Machine shop, jobbing and repair

(G-2243)
THE BELDEN BRICK COMPANY LLC (HQ)
700 Tuscarawas St W Uppr (44702-2063)
P.O. Box 20910 (44701-0910)
PHONE.................................330 456-0031
◆ **EMP:** 34 **EST:** 1885
SALES (est): 94.32MM
SALES (corp-wide): 140.04MM **Privately Held**
Web: www.beldenbrick.com
SIC: 3251 Structural brick and blocks
PA: Belden Holding & Acquisition Company, Inc.
700 Tuscarawas St W
Canton OH 44702
330 456-0031

(G-2244)
THE W L JENKINS COMPANY
Also Called: Chaplet & Chill Division
1445 Whipple Ave Sw (44710-1321)
PHONE.................................330 477-3407
Susan E Jenkins, *Pr*
EMP: 16 **EST:** 1997
SQ FT: 65,000
SALES (est): 651.46K **Privately Held**
Web: www.wljenkinsco.com
SIC: 3679 3931 3469 3699 Electronic circuits ; Musical instruments; Metal stampings, nec ; Security devices

(G-2245)
TIM L HUMBERT
Also Called: Humbert Screen Graphix
6535 Promler St Nw (44720-7626)
P.O. Box 2476 (44720-0476)
PHONE.................................330 497-4944
Tim L Humbert, *Owner*
EMP: 8 **EST:** 1983
SQ FT: 6,200
SALES (est): 238.18K **Privately Held**
SIC: 2396 2791 Screen printing on fabric articles; Typesetting

(G-2246)
TIMKENSTEEL MATERIAL SVCS LLC
1835 Dueber Ave Sw (44706-2728)
P.O. Box 90246 (77290-0246)
PHONE.................................281 449-0319
Tim Timken, *Prin*
Barbara Moore, *
Shawn Seanor, *
Phillip R Cox, *Prin*
Randall Edwards, *Prin*
▼ **EMP:** 120 **EST:** 1972
SALES (est): 22.58MM
SALES (corp-wide): 1.36B **Publicly Held**
Web: www.metallus.com
SIC: 3599 Machine shop, jobbing and repair
PA: Metallus Inc.
1835 Dueber Ave Sw
Canton OH 44706
330 471-7000

(G-2247)
TRANSFORMER ASSOCIATES LIMITED
831 Market Ave N (44702-1175)
PHONE.................................330 430-0750
Rodney Herndon, *Pr*
Tonya Cihon, *Mgr*
EMP: 6 **EST:** 2004
SALES (est): 732.81K **Privately Held**
Web: www.transformerassociates.com
SIC: 3612 Voltage regulating transformers, electric power

Canton - Stark County (G-2248)

(G-2248)
TRI-K ENTERPRISES INC
935 Mckinley Ave Sw (44707-4163)
PHONE..................330 832-7380
Robert S Black, *Pr*
Kerry Black, *VP*
Kevin Black, *VP*
Joan Black, *Sec*
EMP: 6 **EST:** 1977
SALES (est): 510.63K **Privately Held**
SIC: 3451 3542 Screw machine products; Presses: hydraulic and pneumatic, mechanical and manual

(G-2249)
UHRDEN INC
Also Called: Tubar Eureka Industrial Group
700 Tuscarawas St W (44702-2048)
P.O. Box 705 (44681-0705)
PHONE..................330 456-0031
Kenneth L Cook, *Ch Bd*
Hemmy Acharya, *
▲ **EMP:** 46 **EST:** 1952
SQ FT: 82,000
SALES (est): 4.09MM **Privately Held**
Web: www.tubareureka.com
SIC: 3535 3561 3537 3536 Conveyors and conveying equipment; Pumps and pumping equipment; Industrial trucks and tractors; Hoists, cranes, and monorails

(G-2250)
UNION METAL CORPORATION
1432 Maple Ave Ne (44705-1700)
PHONE..................330 456-7653
◆ **EMP:** 390
Web: www.unionmetal.com
SIC: 3648 Public lighting fixtures

(G-2251)
UNION METAL INDUSTRIES CORP
1432 Maple Ave Ne (44705-1700)
PHONE..................330 456-7653
Ryan Macvoy, *CEO*
Zach Macvoy, *CEO*
EMP: 36 **EST:** 2018
SALES (est): 11.33MM **Privately Held**
Web: www.unionmetal.com
SIC: 3669 Traffic signals, electric

(G-2252)
UNITED ABRASIVES & WELDING LLC
2751 Wisemill Cir Ne (44721-2160)
PHONE..................304 996-1490
J T Olinger Authorized Represn t, *Prin*
EMP: 6 **EST:** 2007
SALES (est): 25.09K **Privately Held**
SIC: 7692 Welding repair

(G-2253)
UNITED ENGINEERING & FNDRY CO
1400 Grace Ave Ne (44705-2035)
PHONE..................330 456-2761
Ronald A Martin, *Pr*
Edward Bauer, *COO*
EMP: 34 **EST:** 1986
SQ FT: 5,000
SALES (est): 209.48K **Privately Held**
Web: www.whemco.com
SIC: 3325 Rolling mill rolls, cast steel

(G-2254)
UNITED GRINDING AND MACHINE CO
2315 Ellis Ave Ne (44705-4696)
PHONE..................330 453-7402
Allan J Pfabe, *Pr*
Dennis Pfabe, *
Karen Essig, *

▲ **EMP:** 42 **EST:** 1967
SQ FT: 65,000
SALES (est): 4.84MM **Privately Held**
Web: www.unitedgrinding.com
SIC: 3599 Machine shop, jobbing and repair

(G-2255)
UNITED ROLLS INC (DH)
Also Called: Whemco
1400 Grace Ave Ne (44705-2035)
PHONE..................330 456-2761
J Douglas Nesom Junior, *Ch Bd*
Robin Ingols, *
Paula Harbaugh, *
Carl Maskiewicz, *
Edward Bauer, *
◆ **EMP:** 83 **EST:** 2010
SQ FT: 225,000
SALES (est): 32.57MM
SALES (corp-wide): 367.37MM **Privately Held**
Web: www.whemco.com
SIC: 3547 3613 Rolling mill machinery; Control panels, electric
HQ: Whemco Inc.
 5 Hot Metal St Ste 300
 Pittsburgh PA 15203
 412 390-2700

(G-2256)
UNITED SURFACE FINISHING INC
2202 Gilbert Ave Ne (44705-4634)
PHONE..................330 453-2786
Robert R Horger, *Pr*
Beth Horger, *VP*
EMP: 26 **EST:** 1954
SQ FT: 18,000
SALES (est): 3.21MM **Privately Held**
Web: www.unitedsurfacefinishing.com
SIC: 3471 Electroplating of metals or formed products

(G-2257)
UNIVERSAL METALS CUTTING INC
2656 Harrison Ave Sw (44706-3085)
PHONE..................330 580-5192
EMP: 7 **EST:** 1996
SQ FT: 8,140
SALES (est): 723.6K **Privately Held**
SIC: 3312 Tubes, steel and iron

(G-2258)
US TECHNOLOGY CORPORATION
4200 Munson St Nw (44718-2981)
PHONE..................330 455-1181
Raymond F Williams, *Pr*
Robert B Putnam, *
◆ **EMP:** 42 **EST:** 1985
SQ FT: 2,000
SALES (est): 6.71MM **Privately Held**
Web: www.ustechnology.com
SIC: 3291 3728 Abrasive products; Aircraft parts and equipment, nec

(G-2259)
USA QUICKPRINT INC (PA)
Also Called: Quick Print
409 3rd St Sw (44702-1910)
PHONE..................330 455-5119
Gerald Hohler, *Pr*
Jocelyn Hohler, *VP*
EMP: 15 **EST:** 1979
SQ FT: 2,000
SALES (est): 2.39MM
SALES (corp-wide): 2.39MM **Privately Held**
Web: www.usaqp.com
SIC: 2752 Offset printing

(G-2260)
V & S SCHULER ENGINEERING INC (DH)
2240 Allen Ave Se (44707-3612)
PHONE..................330 452-5200
Brian Miller, *Pr*
Paul Balster Ctrl, *Prin*
EMP: 33 **EST:** 1939
SQ FT: 40,000
SALES (est): 27.23MM
SALES (corp-wide): 1.03B **Privately Held**
Web: www.vsschuler.com
SIC: 3441 3444 Fabricated structural metal; Sheet metalwork
HQ: Voigt & Schweitzer Llc
 987 Buckeye Park Rd
 Columbus OH 43207
 614 449-8281

(G-2261)
VER MICH LTD
4310 Cleveland Ave Nw (44709-2350)
PHONE..................330 493-7330
Melvin R Lloyd, *Pr*
EMP: 8 **EST:** 2005
SALES (est): 266.2K **Privately Held**
SIC: 2399 Fabricated textile products, nec

(G-2262)
VERSALIFT EAST INC
Also Called: VERSALIFT EAST, INC.
4884 Corporate St Sw (44706-1907)
PHONE..................610 866-1400
EMP: 352
SALES (corp-wide): 266.43MM **Privately Held**
Web: east.versalift.com
SIC: 3534 Elevators and moving stairways
HQ: Versalift East, L.L.C.
 7601 Imperial Dr
 Waco TX 76712

(G-2263)
W W CROSS INDUSTRIES INC
2510 Allen Ave Se (44707-3614)
PHONE..................330 588-8400
Thomas Trudeau, *Pr*
Phillip Lattavo, *VP*
Christine Trudeau, *Treas*
EMP: 10 **EST:** 2002
SALES (est): 1.14MM **Privately Held**
Web: www.wwcross.com
SIC: 3965 Fasteners

(G-2264)
WACKER CHEMICAL CORPORATION
Also Called: Silmix Division
2215 International Pkwy (44720-1372)
PHONE..................330 899-0847
Jake Miller, *Off Mgr*
EMP: 118
SALES (corp-wide): 8.53B **Privately Held**
Web: www.wacker.com
SIC: 2869 Silicones
HQ: Wacker Chemical Corporation
 4950 S State Rd
 Ann Arbor MI 48108
 517 264-8500

(G-2265)
WALLACE FORGE COMPANY
3700 Georgetown Rd Ne (44704-2697)
PHONE..................330 488-1203
Dean Wallace, *Pr*
Sheila A Ghezzi, *
William A Peterson, *
▲ **EMP:** 65 **EST:** 1966
SQ FT: 55,000
SALES (est): 8.68MM **Privately Held**
Web: www.wallaceforge.com

SIC: 3462 3321 3463 3452 Iron and steel forgings; Gray and ductile iron foundries; Nonferrous forgings; Bolts, nuts, rivets, and washers

(G-2266)
WERNET INC
Also Called: Commercial Press
606 Cherry Ave Ne (44702-1046)
PHONE..................330 452-2200
Greg Wernet, *Pr*
Susan Wernet, *Sec*
EMP: 6 **EST:** 1926
SQ FT: 8,800
SALES (est): 301.46K **Privately Held**
SIC: 2752 Offset printing

(G-2267)
WESTERN BRANCH DIESEL LLC
Also Called: John Deere Authorized Dealer
1616 Metric Ave Sw (44706-3087)
PHONE..................330 454-8800
Mike Mcelwain, *Brnch Mgr*
EMP: 17
SQ FT: 22,400
SALES (corp-wide): 192.64MM **Privately Held**
Web: www.westernbranchdiesel.com
SIC: 5084 5531 5063 3714 Engines and parts, diesel; Truck equipment and parts; Generators; Motor vehicle parts and accessories
HQ: Western Branch Diesel, Llc
 3504 Shipwright St
 Portsmouth VA 23703
 757 673-7000

(G-2268)
WHITACRE ENGINEERING COMPANY (PA)
4645 Rebar Ave Ne (44705-4473)
P.O. Box 8444 (44711-8444)
PHONE..................330 455-8505
▲ **EMP:** 37 **EST:** 1920
SALES (est): 7.71MM
SALES (corp-wide): 7.71MM **Privately Held**
Web: www.whitacrerebar.com
SIC: 3441 Fabricated structural metal

(G-2269)
WHITEBROOK INC
1824 Whipple Ave Nw (44708-2839)
PHONE..................330 575-7405
Ralph Brooks, *Prin*
EMP: 6 **EST:** 2019
SALES (est): 109.99K **Privately Held**
SIC: 3599 Machine shop, jobbing and repair

(G-2270)
WYOMING CASING SERVICE INC
1414 Raff Rd Sw (44710-2320)
PHONE..................330 479-8785
EMP: 70
SALES (corp-wide): 49.6MM **Privately Held**
Web: www.wyomingcasing.com
SIC: 1389 Oil field services, nec
PA: Wyoming Casing Service, Inc.
 198 40th St E
 Dickinson ND 58601
 701 225-8521

(G-2271)
XCEL MOLD AND MACHINE INC
7661 Freedom Ave Nw (44720-6987)
PHONE..................330 499-8450
Bruce Cain, *Pr*
Bob Johnson, *VP*
EMP: 25 **EST:** 1956
SQ FT: 25,000

GEOGRAPHIC SECTION

Carlisle - Warren County (G-2293)

SALES (est): 908.78K **Privately Held**
SIC: **3544** Industrial molds

(G-2272)
ZEIGER INDUSTRIES INC
4704 Wiseland Ave Se (44707-1054)
PHONE..................................330 484-4413
Donald Zeiger, *Pr*
Sandi Zeiger, *VP*
EMP: 22 **EST:** 1981
SQ FT: 2,500
SALES (est): 2.57MM **Privately Held**
Web: www.zeigerindustries.com
SIC: 3599 Machine shop, jobbing and repair

(G-2273)
ZIEGLER TIRE AND SUPPLY CO
Also Called: Affordable Tire
4300 Tuscarawas St W (44708-5427)
PHONE..................................330 477-3463
Rick Hall, *Brnch Mgr*
EMP: 9
SALES (corp-wide): 111.76MM **Privately Held**
Web: www.zieglertire.com
SIC: 5531 7534 Automotive tires; Tire retreading and repair shops
PA: The Ziegler Tire And Supply Company
4150 Millennium Blvd Se
Massillon OH 44646
330 834-3332

Cardington
Morrow County

(G-2274)
CARDINGTON YUTAKA TECH INC (DH)
575 W Main St (43315-9796)
PHONE..................................419 864-8777
▲ **EMP:** 750 **EST:** 1995
SQ FT: 300,000
SALES (est): 147.98MM **Privately Held**
Web: www.yutakatech.com
SIC: 3714 Exhaust systems and parts, motor vehicle
HQ: Yutaka Giken Co.,Ltd.
508-1, Yutakacho, Chuo-Ku
Hamamatsu SZO 431-3

(G-2275)
HOFFMAN MEAT PROCESSING
157 S 4th St (43315-9726)
PHONE..................................419 864-3994
Mike Hoffman, *Owner*
EMP: 7 **EST:** 1969
SALES (est): 488.18K **Privately Held**
SIC: 2013 5421 Sausages and other prepared meats; Meat markets, including freezer provisioners

(G-2276)
MARENGO FABRICATED STEEL LTD (PA)
Also Called: Lincoln Center Manufacturing
2896 State Route 61 (43315)
P.O. Box 8 (43321)
PHONE..................................800 919-2652
EMP: 17 **EST:** 1996
SQ FT: 60,000
SALES (est): 4.02MM **Privately Held**
Web: www.lcmohio.com
SIC: 3713 5084 7692 Dump truck bodies; Food product manufacturing machinery; Welding repair

Carey
Wyandot County

(G-2277)
BOSSERMAN AVIATION EQUIPMENT INC
2327 State Highway 568 (43316-9583)
PHONE..................................419 722-2879
◆ **EMP:** 50
Web: www.bossermanaviationequip.com
SIC: 3728 Fuel tanks, aircraft

(G-2278)
CAREY PRECAST CONCRETE COMPANY
3420 Township Highway 98 (43316-9763)
P.O. Box 129 (43316-0129)
PHONE..................................419 396-7142
TOLL FREE: 800
Kathryn Beck, *Pr*
Dean Beck, *Sec*
EMP: 6 **EST:** 1985
SQ FT: 2,000
SALES (est): 610.52K **Privately Held**
Web: www.careyprecast.com
SIC: 3272 Concrete products, precast, nec

(G-2279)
HANON SYSTEMS USA LLC
581 Arrowhead Dr (43316-7503)
PHONE..................................313 920-0583
Thomas Charnesky, *Manager*
EMP: 140
Web: www.hanonsystems.com
SIC: 3714 3585 3699 Air conditioner parts, motor vehicle; Compressors for refrigeration and air conditioning equipment ; Heat emission operating apparatus
HQ: Hanon Systems Usa, Llc
39600 Lewis Dr
Novi MI 48377
248 907-8000

(G-2280)
MINERAL PROCESSING COMPANY
1855 County Highway 99 (43316-9722)
PHONE..................................419 396-3501
Daniel Allen, *Pr*
John Uliveto, *VP*
Harry Allen, *Sec*
Victoria C Allen, *Treas*
EMP: 6 **EST:** 1988
SQ FT: 15,000
SALES (est): 1.03MM
SALES (corp-wide): 14.75B **Publicly Held**
SIC: 3275 3274 Gypsum products; Lime
PA: The Andersons Inc
1947 Briarfield Blvd
Maumee OH 43537
419 893-5050

(G-2281)
NATIONAL LIME AND STONE CO
370 N Patterson St (43316-1057)
P.O. Box 8 (43316-0008)
PHONE..................................419 396-7671
Ryan Phillips, *Brnch Mgr*
EMP: 40
SALES (corp-wide): 167.89MM **Privately Held**
Web: www.natlime.com
SIC: 1422 3291 3281 3274 Lime rock, ground; Abrasive products; Cut stone and stone products; Lime
PA: The National Lime And Stone Company
551 Lake Cascade Pkwy
Findlay OH 45840
419 422-4341

(G-2282)
OHIO POWER SYSTEMS LLC
Also Called: Ops Wireless
807 E Findlay St (43316-1331)
PHONE..................................419 396-4041
Michael R Brooks, *Managing Member*
Dustin Brooks, *Contrlr*
EMP: 14 **EST:** 2004
SQ FT: 10,500
SALES (est): 2.1MM **Privately Held**
Web: www.opscontrols.com
SIC: 3679 Video triggers, except remote control TV devices

(G-2283)
PROGRESSOR TIMES
1198 E Findlay St (43316-9760)
P.O. Box 37 (43316-0037)
PHONE..................................419 396-7567
EMP: 6 **EST:** 1873
SALES (est): 485.62K **Privately Held**
Web: www.theprogressortimes.com
SIC: 7313 2711 Newspaper advertising representative; Newspapers

(G-2284)
QUALITY PLLETS RECYCLABLES LLC
410 E Findlay St (43316-1209)
PHONE..................................419 396-3244
Edward J Gretzinger, *Prin*
EMP: 7 **EST:** 2007
SALES (est): 270.3K **Privately Held**
SIC: 2448 Pallets, wood and wood with metal

(G-2285)
TEIJIN AUTOMOTIVE TECH INC
Also Called: CSP Carey
2915 County Highway 96 (43316)
PHONE..................................419 396-1980
Mike Bishop, *Brnch Mgr*
EMP: 253
Web: www.teijinautomotive.com
SIC: 3089 3714 Injection molding of plastics; Motor vehicle parts and accessories
HQ: Teijin Automotive Technologies, Inc.
255 Rex Blvd
Auburn Hills MI 48326
248 237-7800

(G-2286)
WYANDOT DOLOMITE INC
Also Called: Stoneco
1794 County Highway 99 (43316-9722)
P.O. Box 99 (43316-0099)
PHONE..................................419 396-7641
Dennis Overacker, *Prin*
EMP: 25 **EST:** 1949
SQ FT: 3,500
SALES (est): 1.87MM **Privately Held**
SIC: 1411 1611 2951 3272 Limestone, dimension-quarrying; Surfacing and paving; Asphalt and asphaltic paving mixtures (not from refineries); Concrete products, nec

Carlisle
Warren County

(G-2287)
CONVERTERS/PREPRESS INC
301 Industry Dr (45005-6330)
PHONE..................................937 743-0935
Mike Zimmer, *Brnch Mgr*
EMP: 17
SALES (corp-wide): 2.2MM **Privately Held**
Web: www.cpinc.net
SIC: 2796 7336 Engraving platemaking services; Commercial art and graphic design

PA: Converters/Prepress, Inc.
1070 Tower Ln
Bensenville IL 60106
630 860-9400

(G-2288)
INDUSTRIAL ELECTRONIC SERVICE
Also Called: Dc- Digital
325 Industry Dr (45005-6309)
PHONE..................................937 746-9750
Jim Staffan, *Prin*
Pete Staffan, *Prin*
EMP: 11 **EST:** 1965
SQ FT: 3,700
SALES (est): 850.13K **Privately Held**
Web: www.ledscoreboard.com
SIC: 3993 3579 7622 1731 Scoreboards, electric; Time clocks and time recording devices; Intercommunication equipment repair; Electronic controls installation

(G-2289)
KITTYHAWK MOLDING COMPANY INC
10 Eagle Ct (45005-6321)
PHONE..................................937 746-3663
Wilbur V Wisecup Junior, *CEO*
Dave Holmes, *
Anita Holmes, *
Sue Little, *
EMP: 29 **EST:** 1989
SQ FT: 20,500
SALES (est): 4.99MM **Privately Held**
Web: www.kittyhawkmolding.com
SIC: 3089 Injection molding of plastics

(G-2290)
NARROW WAY CUSTOM TECH INC
100 Industry Dr (45005-6304)
PHONE..................................937 743-1611
Timothy Williams, *Pr*
EMP: 29 **EST:** 1998
SQ FT: 5,600
SALES (est): 4.18MM **Privately Held**
Web: www.narrowway100.com
SIC: 3599 7629 Custom machinery; Electrical repair shops

(G-2291)
PATRIOT MFG GROUP INC
512 Linden Ave (45005-3345)
PHONE..................................937 746-2117
Phillip Hubbell, *Pr*
EMP: 54 **EST:** 2005
SALES (est): 8.1MM **Privately Held**
Web: www.patriot-mg.com
SIC: 3599 Machine shop, jobbing and repair

(G-2292)
QIBCO BUFFING PADS INC (PA)
Also Called: American Buffing
301 Industry Dr Ste B (45005-6330)
PHONE..................................937 743-0805
Jeff Phipps, *VP*
▲ **EMP:** 6 **EST:** 1996
SALES (est): 1.42MM **Privately Held**
Web: www.americanbuffing.com
SIC: 3291 Abrasive buffs, bricks, cloth, paper, stones, etc.

(G-2293)
REFRESCO US INC
Also Called: Refresco North America
300 Industry Dr (45005-6308)
PHONE..................................937 790-1400
EMP: 110
Web: www.refresco.com
SIC: 2033 Fruit juices: packaged in cans, jars, etc.
HQ: Refresco Us, Inc.
6655 S Lewis Ave

Carroll
Fairfield County

Tulsa OK 74136

(G-2294)
ARTISAN EQUIPMENT INC
5770 Winchester Rd (43112-9204)
P.O. Box 500 (43112-0500)
PHONE.....................740 756-9135
Stuart Brengman, *Pr*
Keith C Brengman, *VP*
Marsha Brengman, *Sec*
EMP: 10 **EST:** 1975
SQ FT: 12,700
SALES (est): 961.25K **Privately Held**
Web: www.artisanequipment.com
SIC: 3599 3469 3544 Custom machinery; Machine parts, stamped or pressed metal; Special dies, tools, jigs, and fixtures

(G-2295)
CW MACHINE WORX LTD
4805 Scooby Ln (43112-9446)
PHONE.....................740 654-5304
Shannon Heston, *Managing Member*
EMP: 12 **EST:** 2009
SQ FT: 15,000
SALES (est): 2.44MM **Privately Held**
Web: www.companywrench.com
SIC: 3531 Construction machinery

(G-2296)
DELTA H TECHNOLOGIES LLC (PA)
62 High St (43112-9018)
PHONE.....................740 756-7676
Richard Conway, *Managing Member*
EMP: 6 **EST:** 2009
SALES (est): 3.63MM
SALES (corp-wide): 3.63MM **Privately Held**
Web: www.delta-h.com
SIC: 3567 Industrial furnaces and ovens

(G-2297)
F C BRENGMAN AND ASSOC LLC
86 High St (43112-9793)
P.O. Box 470 (43112-0470)
PHONE.....................740 756-4308
Bill Mason, *Owner*
Bill Mason, *Managing Member*
Robert Mason, *
EMP: 28 **EST:** 1949
SQ FT: 12,000
SALES (est): 2.34MM **Privately Held**
Web: www.fcbrengman.com
SIC: 3469 Stamping metal for the trade

(G-2298)
FAIRFIELD MACHINED PDTS INC
6215 Columbus Lancaster Rd Nw (43112-9202)
P.O. Box 410 (43112-0410)
PHONE.....................740 756-4409
David Riggenbach, *Pr*
Frederick Marshall, *VP*
Ronnie Wyne, *Sec*
EMP: 18 **EST:** 2002
SALES (est): 484.62K **Privately Held**
Web: www.fairfieldmachinedproducts.com
SIC: 3451 Screw machine products

(G-2299)
LLOYD F HELBER
3820 Columbus Lancaster Rd Nw (43112-9720)
PHONE.....................740 756-9607
Lloyd Helber, *Owner*
EMP: 7 **EST:** 1988
SQ FT: 2,756
SALES (est): 402.6K **Privately Held**
SIC: 6531 5812 2754 7519 Real estate leasing and rentals; Italian restaurant; Commercial printing, gravure; Trailer rental

(G-2300)
MARTIN PAPER PRODUCTS INC
5907 Columbus Lancaster Rd Nw (43112-7700)
P.O. Box 102 (43112-0102)
PHONE.....................740 756-9271
Robert A Martin, *Pr*
Clara R Martin, *Prin*
Ronald Martin, *Sec*
EMP: 15 **EST:** 1975
SQ FT: 8,100
SALES (est): 495.71K **Privately Held**
SIC: 2653 2631 Corrugated boxes, partitions, display items, sheets, and pad; Paperboard mills

(G-2301)
RELIABLE MANUFACTURING LLC
5594 Winchester Rd (43112)
PHONE.....................740 756-9373
Jesse Whittington, *Managing Member*
EMP: 23 **EST:** 2021
SALES (est): 10MM **Privately Held**
SIC: 3824 Fluid meters and counting devices

(G-2302)
RELIABLE MFG CO LLC
4411 Carroll Southern Rd (43112-9794)
PHONE.....................740 756-9373
EMP: 6 **EST:** 2002
SQ FT: 8,500
SALES (est): 1.05MM **Privately Held**
SIC: 2813 Industrial gases

Carrollton
Carroll County

(G-2303)
AERO PALLETS INC
348 Raley Ave Se (44615-1443)
P.O. Box 311 (44663-0311)
PHONE.....................330 260-7107
Paul Collier, *Pr*
EMP: 30 **EST:** 2015
SALES (est): 1.78MM **Privately Held**
SIC: 2448 Wood pallets and skids

(G-2304)
CARROLL HILLS INDUSTRIES
540 High St Nw (44615-1116)
P.O. Box 567 (44615-0567)
PHONE.....................330 627-5524
Matt Champbell, *Superintnt*
EMP: 16 **EST:** 1980
SQ FT: 4,640
SALES (est): 561.83K **Privately Held**
Web: www.carrollcbdd.org
SIC: 8331 3999 Sheltered workshop; Barber and beauty shop equipment

(G-2305)
CARROLLTON PUBLISHING COMPANY
Also Called: Free Press Standard
43 E Main St (44615-1221)
P.O. Box 37 (44615-0037)
PHONE.....................330 627-5591
William Peterson, *Genl Mgr*
Maynard Buck, *Sec*
EMP: 14 **EST:** 1965
SQ FT: 4,800
SALES (est): 252.42K **Privately Held**
Web: www.freepressstandard.com
SIC: 2711 Commercial printing and newspaper publishing combined

(G-2306)
ERNST ENTERPRISES INC
Also Called: Valley Concrete
4710 Soldiers Home Rd (44615)
P.O. Box 638 (44615-0638)
PHONE.....................937 866-9441
John Mcaffee, *Genl Mgr*
EMP: 13
SALES (corp-wide): 240.08MM **Privately Held**
Web: www.ernstconcrete.com
SIC: 3273 Ready-mixed concrete
PA: Ernst Enterprises, Inc.
3361 Successful Way
Dayton OH 45414
937 233-5555

(G-2307)
FUSION CERAMICS INC (PA)
160 Scio Rd Se (44615-9502)
P.O. Box 127 (44615-0127)
PHONE.....................330 627-5821
Richard Hannon Junior, *Pr*
Dave Schneider, *
Joyce J Hannon, *
◆ **EMP:** 40 **EST:** 1971
SQ FT: 20,000
SALES (est): 9.78MM
SALES (corp-wide): 9.78MM **Privately Held**
Web: www.fusionceramics.com
SIC: 2899 Chemical preparations, nec

(G-2308)
HALL ACQUISITION LLC
1209 N Lisbon St (44615-9404)
P.O. Box 24 (44615-0024)
PHONE.....................330 627-2119
Donald Hall, *Pr*
EMP: 24 **EST:** 1965
SQ FT: 11,800
SALES (est): 452.84K **Privately Held**
SIC: 3599 Machine shop, jobbing and repair

(G-2309)
HERITAGE PLASTICS LIQUIDATION INC
Also Called: Heritage Plastics
861 N Lisbon St (44615-9401)
PHONE.....................330 627-8002
▼ **EMP:** 70
Web: www.atkore.com
SIC: 3084 Plastics pipe

(G-2310)
J P INDUSTRIAL PRODUCTS INC
755 N Lisbon St (44615)
PHONE.....................330 627-1377
EMP: 10
SALES (corp-wide): 15.95MM **Privately Held**
Web: www.jpindustrial.com
SIC: 2821 Plastics materials and resins
PA: J. P. Industrial Products, Inc.
11988 State Route 45
Lisbon OH 44432
330 424-1110

(G-2311)
JOMAC LTD
Also Called: Jones Propane Supply
182 Scio Rd Se (44615-8521)
P.O. Box 337 (44615-0337)
PHONE.....................330 627-7727
EMP: 38 **EST:** 1983
SALES (est): 5.39MM **Privately Held**
Web: www.jomacltd.com
SIC: 3441 5984 Fabricated structural metal; Propane gas, bottled

(G-2312)
NOMAC DRILLING LLC
1258 Panda Rd Se (44615-9657)
PHONE.....................330 476-7040
EMP: 139
SALES (corp-wide): 4.15B **Publicly Held**
Web: www.patenergy.com
SIC: 1381 Drilling oil and gas wells
HQ: Nomac Drilling, L.L.C.
3400 S Radio Rd
El Reno OK 73036
405 422-2754

(G-2313)
RCE HEAT EXCHANGERS LLC
3165 Folsam Rd Nw (44615-8201)
PHONE.....................330 627-0300
Mike Earl, *Mng Pt*
Robert Strobel, *VP*
EMP: 20 **EST:** 2005
SALES (est): 1.76MM **Privately Held**
Web: www.rceheatexchangers.com
SIC: 3443 Heat exchangers, condensers, and components

(G-2314)
REINALT-THOMAS CORPORATION
5125 Canton Rd Nw (44615-9015)
PHONE.....................330 863-1936
Gene Dunn, *Brnch Mgr*
EMP: 6
SALES (corp-wide): 3.69B **Privately Held**
SIC: 3089 Automotive parts, plastic
PA: The Reinalt-Thomas Corporation
20225 N Scottsdale Rd
Scottsdale AZ 85255
480 606-6000

(G-2315)
SEVEN RANGES MFG CORP
330 Industrial Dr Sw (44615-8569)
P.O. Box 206 (44615-0206)
PHONE.....................330 627-7155
Fred D Tarr Senior, *Pr*
David Richard Tarr, *
EMP: 26 **EST:** 1982
SQ FT: 29,000
SALES (est): 4.29MM **Privately Held**
Web: www.sevenranges.com
SIC: 3469 Stamping metal for the trade

(G-2316)
TWIN CITIES CONCRETE CO
1031 Kensington Rd Ne (44615-9403)
P.O. Box 400 (44622-0400)
PHONE.....................330 627-2158
Louis Cline, *Mgr*
EMP: 483
SALES (corp-wide): 32.72B **Privately Held**
SIC: 3273 Ready-mixed concrete
HQ: Twin Cities Concrete Co.
141 S Tuscarawas Ave
Dover OH 44622
330 343-4491

Casstown
Miami County

(G-2317)
STEEL AVIATION AIRCRAFT SALES
4433 E State Route 55 (45312-9579)
PHONE.....................937 332-7587
Jaime Steel, *Prin*
EMP: 7 **EST:** 2004
SALES (est): 837.42K **Privately Held**
Web: www.steelaviation.com

GEOGRAPHIC SECTION

Celina - Mercer County (G-2342)

SIC: 3721 Airplanes, fixed or rotary wing

Castalia
Erie County

(G-2318)
ABJ EQUIPFIX LLC
Also Called: Abj
202 Lucas St W (44824-9254)
PHONE.....................419 684-5236
Alan D Strause, *CEO*
EMP: 20 **EST:** 2001
SQ FT: 7,000
SALES (est): 2.1MM **Privately Held**
Web: www.abjequipment.com
SIC: 7699 3556 Industrial machinery and equipment repair; Food products machinery

(G-2319)
CASTALIA TRENCHING & RDYMX LLC
4814 State Route 269 S (44824-9359)
PHONE.....................419 684-5502
Joe Verb, *Prin*
Denise Verb, *Prin*
EMP: 16 **EST:** 2013
SALES (est): 1.46MM **Privately Held**
Web: www.ctrmohio.com
SIC: 3273 Ready-mixed concrete

(G-2320)
CASTALIA TRENCHING & READY MIX
4814 State Route 269 S (44824-9359)
PHONE.....................419 684-5502
TOLL FREE: 800
Francis Winkel, *Pr*
James Winkel, *Sec*
Larry Winkel, *VP*
John Winkel, *VP*
EMP: 10 **EST:** 1954
SQ FT: 8,000
SALES (est): 1MM **Privately Held**
Web: www.ctrmohio.com
SIC: 3273 1794 Ready-mixed concrete; Excavation work

(G-2321)
CRUSHED STONE SANDUSKY
9220 Portland Rd (44824-9260)
PHONE.....................419 483-4390
Roetta Moore, *Prin*
EMP: 7 **EST:** 2007
SALES (est): 175.72K **Privately Held**
SIC: 1422 Crushed and broken limestone

Cedarville
Greene County

(G-2322)
APPLIED SCIENCES INC (PA)
141 W Xenia Ave (45314-9529)
P.O. Box 579 (45314-0579)
PHONE.....................937 766-2020
Max Lake, *Pr*
Inga Lake, *VP*
EMP: 19 **EST:** 1984
SQ FT: 6,600
SALES (est): 4.33MM
SALES (corp-wide): 4.33MM **Privately Held**
Web: www.apsci.com
SIC: 8731 3624 Commercial research laboratory; Carbon and graphite products

(G-2323)
PYROGRAF PRODUCTS INC
154 W Xenia Ave (45314-9529)
P.O. Box 579 (45314-0579)
PHONE.....................937 766-2020
Max Lake, *Pr*
Inga Lake, *Sec*
EMP: 16 **EST:** 1996
SQ FT: 6,600
SALES (est): 936.08K
SALES (corp-wide): 4.33MM **Privately Held**
Web: www.pyrografproducts.com
SIC: 2821 Plastics materials and resins
PA: Applied Sciences, Inc.
141 W Xenia Ave
Cedarville OH 45314
937 766-2020

Celina
Mercer County

(G-2324)
BUCKEYE VALLEY PIZZA HUT LTD
Also Called: Pizza Hut
1152 E Market St (45822-1934)
PHONE.....................419 586-5900
EMP: 31
SALES (corp-wide): 7.97MM **Privately Held**
Web: www.pizzahut.com
SIC: 5812 2099 Pizzeria, chain; Food preparations, nec
PA: Buckeye Valley Pizza Hut, Ltd.
65 S Main St
Springboro OH 45066
937 748-3338

(G-2325)
CELINA ALUM PRECISION TECH INC
Also Called: Capt
7059 Staeger Rd (45822-9395)
PHONE.....................419 586-2278
▲ **EMP:** 500 **EST:** 1994
SQ FT: 160,000
SALES (est): 98.62MM **Privately Held**
Web: www.capt-celina.com
SIC: 3592 Pistons and piston rings
HQ: Honda Foundry Co., Ltd.
1620, Matoba
Kawagoe STM 350-1

(G-2326)
CELINA PERCISION MACHINE
1201 Havemann Rd (45822-1391)
PHONE.....................419 586-9222
EMP: 10 **EST:** 2019
SALES (est): 490.69K **Privately Held**
Web: www.machine-pro.com
SIC: 3599 Machine shop, jobbing and repair

(G-2327)
CELINA TENT INC
5373 State Route 29 (45822-9210)
PHONE.....................419 586-3610
◆ **EMP:** 94 **EST:** 1996
SQ FT: 27,000
SALES (est): 11.54MM **Privately Held**
Web: www.celinatent.com
SIC: 2394 Tents: made from purchased materials

(G-2328)
CROWN EQUIPMENT CORPORATION
Also Called: Crown Lift Trucks
410 Grand Lake Rd (45822-1869)
PHONE.....................419 586-1100
Chuck Post, *Brnch Mgr*
EMP: 49
SALES (corp-wide): 7.12B **Privately Held**
Web: www.crown.com
SIC: 3537 Lift trucks, industrial: fork, platform, straddle, etc.
PA: Crown Equipment Corporation
44 S Washington St
New Bremen OH 45869
419 629-2311

(G-2329)
DOLL INC
Also Called: Doll Printing
1901 Havemann Rd (45822)
P.O. Box 412 (45822-0412)
PHONE.....................419 586-7880
Robert A Doll, *Pr*
Phyllis Doll, *Sec*
EMP: 8 **EST:** 1928
SQ FT: 6,200
SALES (est): 939.44K **Privately Held**
Web: www.dollprinting.com
SIC: 2752 Offset printing

(G-2330)
EIGHTH FLOOR PROMOTIONS LLC
Also Called: Awardcraft
1 Visions Pkwy (45822-7500)
P.O. Box 42501 (45042-0501)
PHONE.....................419 586-6433
Dave Willis, *Pr*
Les Dorfman, *
▲ **EMP:** 190 **EST:** 1977
SQ FT: 83,000
SALES (est): 23.13MM **Privately Held**
Web: www.8thfloorpromotions.com
SIC: 3993 Signs and advertising specialties

(G-2331)
ERGO DESKTOP LLC
457 Grand Lake Rd (45822-1839)
PHONE.....................567 890-3746
▲ **EMP:** 23 **EST:** 2009
SQ FT: 2,500
SALES (est): 2.41MM **Privately Held**
Web: www.ergodesktop.com
SIC: 2522 7389 Office furniture, except wood ; Business services, nec

(G-2332)
FALLEN OAK CANDLES INC
917 Lilac St (45822-1326)
PHONE.....................419 204-8162
Brian Brim, *Pr*
EMP: 7 **EST:** 2009
SALES (est): 275.65K **Privately Held**
SIC: 3999 Candles

(G-2333)
FUEL AMERICA
204 E Market St (45822-1733)
PHONE.....................419 586-5609
Penny Zizelman, *Prin*
EMP: 7 **EST:** 2010
SALES (est): 129.12K **Privately Held**
SIC: 2869 Fuels

(G-2334)
GRYPMAT INC
6886 Nancy Ave (45822-9268)
PHONE.....................419 953-7607
Tom Burden, *CEO*
EMP: 7 **EST:** 2017
SALES (est): 484.92K **Privately Held**
Web: www.grypmat.com
SIC: 3069 Trays, rubber

(G-2335)
H & S COMPANY INC
7219 Harris Rd (45822-9370)
PHONE.....................419 394-4444
Kurtis Hoelscher, *Pr*
Kellie Hoelscher, *Finance*
EMP: 20 **EST:** 1981
SQ FT: 6,480
SALES (est): 954.33K **Privately Held**
Web: www.wheeledtrenchers.com
SIC: 3533 3523 Oil field machinery and equipment; Farm machinery and equipment

(G-2336)
HAULETTE MANUFACTURING INC
8271 Us Route 127 (45822-9416)
PHONE.....................419 586-1717
Fred Kremer, *CEO*
Steven Braun, *
EMP: 53 **EST:** 1958
SQ FT: 50,000
SALES (est): 4.79MM **Privately Held**
Web: www.haulette.com
SIC: 3599 3715 Machine shop, jobbing and repair; Trailer bodies

(G-2337)
HOLES CUSTOM WOODWORKING
6875 Nancy Ave (45822-9268)
PHONE.....................419 586-8171
Jane Hole, *Prin*
EMP: 6 **EST:** 2010
SALES (est): 158.62K **Privately Held**
Web: www.karmaresale.com
SIC: 2431 Millwork

(G-2338)
JAVANATION
108 S Main St (45822-2228)
PHONE.....................419 584-1705
Vance Nation, *Owner*
EMP: 10 **EST:** 2009
SALES (est): 462.63K **Privately Held**
Web: www.webdesignandcompany.com
SIC: 3269 Pottery products, nec

(G-2339)
JES FOODS/CELINA INC
1800 Industrial Dr (45822-1376)
PHONE.....................419 586-7446
EMP: 13 **EST:** 1995
SQ FT: 24,000
SALES (est): 1.19MM **Privately Held**
Web: www.jesfoods.com
SIC: 2033 2035 2032 Canned fruits and specialties; Pickles, sauces, and salad dressings; Canned specialties
PA: J.E.S. Foods, Inc.
865 W Liberty St Ste 200
Medina OH 44256

(G-2340)
MACHINE-PRO TECHNOLOGIES INC
1321 W Market St (45822-9285)
PHONE.....................419 584-0086
▲ **EMP:** 57 **EST:** 1994
SQ FT: 24,000
SALES (est): 8.82MM **Privately Held**
Web: www.machine-pro.com
SIC: 3599 Machine shop, jobbing and repair

(G-2341)
MSK TRENCHER MFG INC
7219 Harris Rd (45822-9370)
PHONE.....................419 394-4444
Kurtis Hoelscher, *Pr*
Kellie Hoelscher, *Sec*
EMP: 10 **EST:** 1990
SALES (est): 912.9K **Privately Held**
SIC: 3531 Construction machinery

(G-2342)
PAX MACHINE WORKS INC
5139 Monroe Rd (45822-9033)
P.O. Box 338 (45822-0338)
PHONE.....................419 586-2337

(PA)=Parent Co (HQ)=Headquarters
✪ = New Business established in last 2 years

Celina - Mercer County (G-2343)

Francis J Pax, *Pr*
Michael Pax, *
Deborah Guingrich, *
▼ **EMP:** 97 **EST:** 1948
SQ FT: 451,000
SALES (est): 18.2MM **Privately Held**
Web: www.paxmachine.com
SIC: 3469 Stamping metal for the trade

(G-2343)
PAX PRODUCTS INC
5097 Monroe Rd (45822-9033)
P.O. Box 257 (45822-0257)
PHONE.................................419 586-2337
Francis J Pax, *Pr*
Steven Pax, *VP*
Michael Pax, *Treas*
Deborah Guingrich, *Sec*
EMP: 11 **EST:** 1980
SQ FT: 36,500
SALES (est): 2.36MM **Privately Held**
Web: www.paxproducts.com
SIC: 3569 Lubricating equipment

(G-2344)
PHI WERKES LLC
1201 Havemann Rd (45822-1391)
PHONE.................................419 586-9222
EMP: 8 **EST:** 2003
SQ FT: 13,800
SALES (est): 582.12K **Privately Held**
SIC: 3599 Machine shop, jobbing and repair

(G-2345)
RENOIR VISIONS LLC
Also Called: Accents By Renoir
1 Visions Pkwy (45822-7500)
PHONE.................................419 586-5679
EMP: 9 **EST:** 1995
SQ FT: 65,000
SALES (est): 176.57K **Privately Held**
Web: www.visionsawards.com
SIC: 3993 5094 Signs and advertising specialties; Jewelry and precious stones

(G-2346)
REYNOLDS AND REYNOLDS COMPANY
Reynolds & Reynolds
824 Murlin Ave (45822-2459)
P.O. Box 999 (45822-0999)
PHONE.................................419 584-7000
Ray Grassman, *Brnch Mgr*
EMP: 10
SALES (corp-wide): 1.54B **Privately Held**
Web: www.reyrey.com
SIC: 2761 2759 2752 Manifold business forms; Commercial printing, nec; Commercial printing, lithographic
HQ: The Reynolds And Reynolds Company
1 Reynolds Way
Kettering OH 45430
937 485-2000

(G-2347)
S & K PRODUCTS COMPANY
Also Called: Plant 1
4540 St Rt 127 (45822)
P.O. Box 166 (45828-0166)
PHONE.................................419 268-2244
EMP: 45 **EST:** 1949
SALES (est): 5.05MM **Privately Held**
Web: www.skproductsco.com
SIC: 3469 3429 Metal stampings, nec; Hardware, nec

(G-2348)
SCHUCK MTAL FBRCTION DSIGN INC
8319 Us 127 N (45822)
P.O. Box 354 (45822-0354)
PHONE.................................419 586-1054
EMP: 15 **EST:** 1985
SQ FT: 15,000
SALES (est): 1.45MM **Privately Held**
Web: www.schuckcushionhitches.com
SIC: 3441 Fabricated structural metal

(G-2349)
SOCIETY OF THE PRECIOUS BLOOD
Also Called: Messinger Press
2860 Us Route 127 (45822-9533)
PHONE.................................419 925-4516
Father James Seibert, *Brnch Mgr*
EMP: 40
SALES (corp-wide): 1.12MM **Privately Held**
Web: www.messenger-press.com
SIC: 2732 8661 8211 Pamphlets: printing only, not published on site; Brethren Church; Private elementary and secondary schools
PA: The Society Of The Precious Blood
431 E 2nd St
Dayton OH 45402
937 228-9263

(G-2350)
STANDARD PRINTING CO INC
Also Called: Daily Standard The
123 E Market St (45822-1730)
P.O. Box 140 (45822-0140)
PHONE.................................419 586-2371
Frank Snyder, *Pr*
EMP: 20 **EST:** 1851
SQ FT: 20,000
SALES (est): 1.01MM **Privately Held**
Web: www.dailystandard.com
SIC: 2711 Commercial printing and newspaper publishing combined

(G-2351)
STEALTH ARMS LLC
4939 Kittle Rd (45822-9191)
PHONE.................................419 925-7005
EMP: 8 **EST:** 2013
SALES (est): 535.46K **Privately Held**
Web: www.stealtharms.net
SIC: 3484 Guns (firearms) or gun parts, 30 mm. and below

(G-2352)
THEES MACHINE & TOOL COMPANY
2007 State Route 703 (45822-2525)
PHONE.................................419 586-4766
John E Thees, *Pr*
Carolann Thees, *VP*
EMP: 6 **EST:** 1973
SQ FT: 7,000
SALES (est): 511.48K **Privately Held**
SIC: 3599 Machine shop, jobbing and repair

(G-2353)
THIEMAN TAILGATES INC
600 E Wayne St (45822-1566)
PHONE.................................419 586-7727
Thomas A Thieman, *Pr*
Sandra Thieman, *Sec*
Todd Thieman, *VP*
EMP: 90 **EST:** 1987
SQ FT: 130,000
SALES (est): 9.95MM **Privately Held**
Web: www.thiemantailgates.com
SIC: 3561 Industrial pumps and parts

(G-2354)
VAN TILBURG FARMS INC
Also Called: Vantilburg Farms
8398 Celina Mendon Rd (45822-9339)
PHONE.................................419 586-3077
James Van Tilburg, *Pr*
Brenda Vantilburg, *Sec*
EMP: 12 **EST:** 1942
SQ FT: 2,000
SALES (est): 5.07MM **Privately Held**
Web: www.vantilburgfarms.com
SIC: 5153 2875 Grains; Compost

(G-2355)
VERSA-PAK LTD
500 Staeger Rd (45822)
P.O. Box 69 (45822)
PHONE.................................419 586-5466
Jeffrey C Bruns, *Rep*
Kenneth Gerlach, *
Mark A Bruns, *
EMP: 45 **EST:** 2000
SQ FT: 23,000
SALES (est): 21.72MM **Privately Held**
Web: www.versa-pak.com
SIC: 5199 2671 Packaging materials; Plastic film, coated or laminated for packaging

(G-2356)
WINGS N WHEELS
1217 Brooke Ave (45822-8713)
PHONE.................................419 586-6531
Matthew Berry, *Prin*
EMP: 6 **EST:** 2010
SALES (est): 97K **Privately Held**
SIC: 3312 Wheels

Centerburg
Knox County

(G-2357)
COLUMBUS MOBILE WELDING LLC
110 S Preston St (43011-9779)
PHONE.................................614 352-6052
David Stewart, *Prin*
EMP: 6 **EST:** 1998
SALES (est): 70.47K **Privately Held**
Web: www.mobileweldingcolumbus.com
SIC: 7692 Welding repair

(G-2358)
TRADYE MACHINE & TOOL INC
3116a Wilson Rd (43011-9467)
PHONE.................................740 625-7550
Tracy Payne, *Pr*
Diana Payne, *Mgr*
EMP: 7 **EST:** 1994
SQ FT: 12,000
SALES (est): 707.04K **Privately Held**
Web: www.tradye.com
SIC: 3544 3599 Special dies and tools; Machine shop, jobbing and repair

Centerville
Montgomery County

(G-2359)
ASSOCIATES TIRE AND SVC INC
Also Called: Grismer Tire
1099 S Main St (45458-3840)
PHONE.................................937 436-4692
Andrew Stewart, *Brnch Mgr*
EMP: 10
SALES (corp-wide): 2.02MM **Privately Held**
SIC: 5014 5531 7534 Automobile tires and tubes; Automotive tires; Tire repair shop
PA: Associates Tire And Service Inc.
3411 Office Park Dr
Dayton OH
937 643-2526

(G-2360)
BAILEY & JENSEN INC
442 Yankee Tr (45458-3980)
PHONE.................................937 272-1784
Sharon Bailey, *CEO*
Jerry Bailey, *Pr*
EMP: 6 **EST:** 2012
SALES (est): 64.49K **Privately Held**
Web: www.baileyjensen.com
SIC: 2514 5021 Metal household furniture; Mattresses

(G-2361)
DIMCOGRAY CORPORATION (PA)
Also Called: Dimco-Gray Company
900 Dimco Way (45458-2709)
PHONE.................................937 433-7600
TOLL FREE: 800
Michael Sieron, *CEO*
Terry Tate, *
▲ **EMP:** 90 **EST:** 1924
SQ FT: 48,000
SALES (est): 16.08MM
SALES (corp-wide): 16.08MM **Privately Held**
Web: www.dimcogray.com
SIC: 3089 3873 3965 3625 Injection molding of plastics; Watches, clocks, watchcases, and parts; Fasteners; Relays and industrial controls

(G-2362)
FIRESTONE COMPLETE AUTO CARE
199 E Alex Bell Rd (45459-2797)
PHONE.................................937 528-2496
EMP: 6 **EST:** 2015
SALES (est): 45.49K **Privately Held**
Web: local.firestonecompleteautocare.com
SIC: 7538 7534 General automotive repair shops; Tire retreading and repair shops

(G-2363)
GRISMER TIRE COMPANY (PA)
1099 S Main St (45458-3840)
P.O. Box 337 (45401-0337)
PHONE.................................937 643-2526
Charles L Marshall Ii, *Pr*
John L Marshall, *
Robert Hupp, *
▲ **EMP:** 28 **EST:** 1932
SQ FT: 40,000
SALES (est): 18.33MM
SALES (corp-wide): 18.33MM **Privately Held**
Web: www.grismertire.com
SIC: 5531 7538 5014 7534 Automotive tires; General automotive repair shops; Automobile tires and tubes; Rebuilding and retreading tires

(G-2364)
ROBERT TURNER
8116 Julian Pl (45458-7315)
P.O. Box 751234 (45475-1234)
PHONE.................................937 434-1346
Robert Turner, *Pt*
EMP: 6 **EST:** 2018
SALES (est): 117.77K **Privately Held**
Web: turner.house.gov
SIC: 2711 Newspapers

Chagrin Falls
Cuyahoga County

(G-2365)
1-2-3 GLUTEN FREE INC
125 Orange Tree Dr (44022-1560)
PHONE.................................216 378-9233

GEOGRAPHIC SECTION

Kim Ullner, *Prin*
EMP: 6 **EST:** 2007
SALES (est): 992.3K **Privately Held**
Web: www.123glutenfree.com
SIC: 2041 Flour mixes

(G-2366)
11 92 HOLDINGS LLC
8 E Washington St Ste 200 (44022-3057)
PHONE.................................216 920-7790
Mike Owens, *Prin*
EMP: 10 **EST:** 2014
SALES (est): 886.07K **Privately Held**
SIC: 2591 Blinds vertical
HQ: Vertical Knowledge Llc
8 E Washington St Ste 200
Chagrin Falls OH 44022
216 920-7790

(G-2367)
ADVERTISING JOE LLC MEAN
33 River St Ste 7 (44022-3020)
PHONE.................................440 247-8200
Todd Berk, *Pr*
EMP: 7 **EST:** 2012
SALES (est): 356.1K **Privately Held**
Web: www.meanjoeadvertising.com
SIC: 7311 2759 Advertising agencies; Commercial printing, nec

(G-2368)
CABINETWORKS GROUP MICH LLC
25 N Franklin St (44022-3009)
PHONE.................................440 247-3091
EMP: 41
SALES (corp-wide): 1.6B **Privately Held**
Web: www.cabinetworksgroup.com
SIC: 2434 Wood kitchen cabinets
PA: Cabinetworks Group Michigan, Llc
20000 Victor Pkwy
Livonia MI 48152
734 205-4600

(G-2369)
CATERPILLAR INDUSTRIAL INC
45 E Washington St Ste 203 (44022-3040)
PHONE.................................440 247-8484
EMP: 27 **EST:** 1965
SALES (est): 654.89K
SALES (corp-wide): 67.06B **Publicly Held**
Web: www.caterpillar.com
SIC: 3531 Construction machinery
PA: Caterpillar Inc.
5205 N Ocnnor Blvd Ste 10
Irving TX 75039
972 891-7700

(G-2370)
CHAGRIN VALLEY PUBLISHING CO
Also Called: Chagrin Valley Times
525 Washington St (44022)
P.O. Box 150 (44022)
PHONE.................................440 247-5335
Harold Douthit, *Pr*
EMP: 24 **EST:** 1971
SQ FT: 4,000
SALES (est): 988.44K **Privately Held**
Web: www.chagrinvalleytoday.com
SIC: 2711 Newspapers, publishing and printing

(G-2371)
CLEVELAND LETTER SERVICE INC
8351 Clover Ln (44022-3810)
PHONE.................................216 781-8300
Charles E Janes, *Pr*
EMP: 9 **EST:** 1945
SQ FT: 12,000
SALES (est): 248.68K **Privately Held**
Web: www.clevelandletterservice.com

SIC: 7331 2752 2789 Addressing service; Offset printing; Bookbinding and related work

(G-2372)
COMPLETE STUD WELDING INC
3700 Chagrin River Rd (44022-1130)
PHONE.................................216 533-8482
EMP: 7 **EST:** 2012
SALES (est): 179.95K **Privately Held**
Web: www.completestudweld.com
SIC: 7692 Welding repair

(G-2373)
DOUGLAS W & B C RICHARDSON
62 Wychwood Dr (44022-6853)
PHONE.................................440 247-5262
Barbara C Richardson, *Prin*
EMP: 7 **EST:** 2010
SALES (est): 190K **Privately Held**
SIC: 2992 Lubricating oils and greases

(G-2374)
E TECHNOLOGIES INC
300 Industrial Pkwy Ste A (44022-4420)
PHONE.................................440 247-7000
John Englhardt, *Pr*
Suellen Englehardt, *VP*
EMP: 6 **EST:** 1998
SQ FT: 2,500
SALES (est): 2.23MM **Privately Held**
Web: www.etechnologies.com
SIC: 3612 Transformers, except electric

(G-2375)
E-Z GRADER COMPANY
300 Industrial Pkwy Ste A (44022-4420)
PHONE.................................440 247-7511
Jill Richards, *Pr*
Bruce Richards, *VP*
EMP: 8 **EST:** 1952
SALES (est): 751.71K **Privately Held**
Web: www.ezgrader.com
SIC: 5961 2679 Educational supplies and equipment, mail order; Paperboard products, converted, nec

(G-2376)
EDMAR CHEMICAL COMPANY
539 Washington St (44022-4400)
P.O. Box 598 (44022-0598)
PHONE.................................440 247-9560
Jack Binder, *Pr*
Dan Berick, *Sec*
Jack Ahern, *Treas*
EMP: 9 **EST:** 1940
SALES (est): 1.02MM **Privately Held**
Web: www.edmarchem.com
SIC: 2841 2842 Soap: granulated, liquid, cake, flaked, or chip; Fabric softeners

(G-2377)
EL OSTENDORF INC
Also Called: Shuler Pewter
3425 Roundwood Rd (44022-6634)
PHONE.................................440 247-7631
Ed L Ostendorf, *Pr*
EMP: 7 **EST:** 1956
SQ FT: 12,000
SALES (est): 340.58K **Privately Held**
SIC: 6531 3645 Real estate agent, commercial; Residential lighting fixtures

(G-2378)
GLX POWER SYSTEMS INC
46 Chagrin Plaza Ste 201 (44022)
PHONE.................................440 338-6526
Kent Kristensen, *Pr*
EMP: 9 **EST:** 2018
SALES (est): 333.62K **Privately Held**

SIC: 3692 3691 Primary batteries, dry and wet; Storage batteries

(G-2379)
HP ACQUISITION II LLC
Also Called: Hotcards
22 N Main St Fl 2 (44022-3006)
PHONE.................................216 241-4040
EMP: 11 **EST:** 2015
SALES (est): 1.87MM **Privately Held**
Web: www.hotcards.com
SIC: 2752 Offset printing

(G-2380)
INTEGRATED DEVELOPMENT & MFG (PA)
Also Called: Environmental Growth Chambers
510 Washington St (44022-4448)
PHONE.................................440 247-5100
Adrian Rule, *Pr*
Adrian Rule Iv, *VP*
Raymond F Pletcher, *Treas*
EMP: 16 **EST:** 1952
SQ FT: 28,000
SALES (est): 16.94MM
SALES (corp-wide): 16.94MM **Privately Held**
Web: integrated-development-manufacturing.sbcontract.com
SIC: 3822 1711 Environmental controls; Refrigeration contractor

(G-2381)
KATIMEX USA INC
15241 Hemlock Point Rd (44022-3832)
P.O. Box 4000 (44065-0299)
PHONE.................................440 338-3500
Mary Ann Ondrus, *Pr*
Tom Ondrus, *VP*
EMP: 9 **EST:** 1984
SALES (est): 360.3K **Privately Held**
SIC: 2298 Cable, fiber

(G-2382)
MEYER COMPANY (PA)
Also Called: Tomlinson Industries
7180 Sugar Bush Ln (44022)
PHONE.................................216 587-3400
H F Meyer, *Pr*
Donald Calkins, *
Michael E Figas, *
H F Meyer Iii, *VP*
Heidi Figas, *
◆ **EMP:** 170 **EST:** 1897
SALES (est): 22.49MM
SALES (corp-wide): 22.49MM **Privately Held**
SIC: 3556 Food products machinery

(G-2383)
MILLENNIUM ADHESIVE PDTS LLC
178 E Washington St Ste 1 (44022-2978)
PHONE.................................440 708-1212
Ronald Janoski, *Pr*
Mark Rundo, *VP Sls*
EMP: 10 **EST:** 1997
SQ FT: 7,000
SALES (est): 2.2MM
SALES (corp-wide): 3.51B **Publicly Held**
SIC: 2891 Adhesives and sealants
PA: H.B. Fuller Company
1200 Willow Lake Blvd
Saint Paul MN 55110
651 236-5900

(G-2384)
RSP INDUSTRIES INC
415 Hazelwood Dr (44022-3926)
PHONE.................................440 823-4502
EMP: 11 **EST:** 2016

SALES (est): 1.01MM **Privately Held**
Web: www.sapproductsllc.com
SIC: 2493 Wall tile, fiberboard

(G-2385)
SHOOK MANUFACTURED PDTS INC
3801 Wiltshire Rd (44022-1151)
PHONE.................................440 247-9130
EMP: 8
SALES (corp-wide): 1.06MM **Privately Held**
Web: www.shookmfg.com
SIC: 3545 Chucks: drill, lathe, or magnetic (machine tool accessories)
PA: Shook Manufactured Products, Inc.
1017 Kenmore Blvd
Akron OH 44314
330 848-9780

Chagrin Falls
Geauga County

(G-2386)
AB TIRE & REPAIR
9685 Washington St (44023-2757)
PHONE.................................440 543-2929
Edward Klempay, *Owner*
EMP: 7 **EST:** 2007
SALES (est): 584.44K **Privately Held**
Web: www.radiatorinfo.com
SIC: 5531 7534 Automotive tires; Tire repair shop

(G-2387)
ABANAKI CORPORATION (PA)
Also Called: Aerodyne
17387 Munn Rd (44023-5400)
PHONE.................................440 543-7400
Mark Thomas Hobson, *Pr*
▲ **EMP:** 14 **EST:** 1968
SQ FT: 7,700
SALES (est): 3.69MM
SALES (corp-wide): 3.69MM **Privately Held**
Web: www.abanaki.com
SIC: 3569 Filters

(G-2388)
ACTIVE CHEMICAL SYSTEMS INC
16755 Park Circle Dr (44023-4562)
PHONE.................................440 543-7755
Bruno Thut, *CEO*
Kristine Thut, *Pr*
EMP: 17 **EST:** 1974
SQ FT: 16,000
SALES (est): 1.79MM **Privately Held**
Web: www.activechemicalsystems.com
SIC: 3443 3624 Heat exchangers, condensers, and components; Carbon and graphite products

(G-2389)
ARCHITCTRAL MLLWK CBINETRY INC
16715 W Park Circle Dr (44023-4549)
PHONE.................................440 708-0086
Gary Spaeth, *Pr*
EMP: 8 **EST:** 2002
SALES (est): 1.21MM **Privately Held**
SIC: 5031 5211 3442 1751 Molding, all materials; Cabinets, kitchen; Molding, trim, and stripping; Cabinet and finish carpentry

(G-2390)
BUMMIN BEAVER BREWERY LLC
11610 Washington St (44023-9214)
PHONE.................................440 543-9900
Tony Solitro, *Managing Member*
EMP: 7 **EST:** 2019

Chagrin Falls - Geauga County (G-2391)

SALES (est): 352.37K **Privately Held**
Web: www.bumminbeaver.com
SIC: 2082 Beer (alcoholic beverage)

(G-2391)
CRAFTED SURFACE AND STONE LLC
16625 Wren Rd (44023-4517)
PHONE...............440 658-3799
Allen Gleine, *Managing Member*
EMP: 25 EST: 2018
SALES (est): 2.28MM **Privately Held**
Web: www.craftedss.com
SIC: 1799 2541 Counter top installation; Counter and sink tops

(G-2392)
DESIGNED IMAGES INC
10121 Stafford Rd Ste C (44023-5128)
PHONE...............440 708-2526
Thomas Hoenigman, *Pr*
Renee Hoenigman, *VP*
EMP: 7 EST: 2001
SALES (est): 592.66K **Privately Held**
Web: www.designedimages.net
SIC: 3083 Plastics finished products, laminated

(G-2393)
DYNAMIC DESIGN & SYSTEMS INC
7639 Washington St (44023-4403)
PHONE...............440 708-1010
Richard E Doerr, *Pr*
Marilyn N Doerr, *VP*
◆ EMP: 6 EST: 1982
SQ FT: 3,000
SALES (est): 902.86K **Privately Held**
Web: www.dynamicdes.com
SIC: 2759 2752 Screen printing; Decals, lithographed

(G-2394)
ESPI ENTERPRISES INC (PA)
Also Called: Essential Sealing Products
10145 Queens Way (44023-5407)
P.O. Box 23699 (44023-0699)
PHONE...............440 543-8108
Joshua Botnick, *CEO*
Joshua Botnick, *Pr*
Bruce Pyle, *VP*
Pat Stipp, *Treas*
EMP: 8 EST: 1981
SQ FT: 30,000
SALES (est): 1.7MM
SALES (corp-wide): 1.7MM **Privately Held**
Web: www.espsealing.com
SIC: 3053 Gaskets, all materials

(G-2395)
ETNA PRODUCTS INCORPORATED
Also Called: Master Draw Lubricants
16824 Park Circle Dr (44023-4516)
P.O. Box 23609 (44023-0609)
PHONE...............440 543-9845
Catharine Tripp Golden, *CEO*
Mike Washington, *
◆ EMP: 30 EST: 1943
SQ FT: 35,000
SALES (est): 7.04MM **Privately Held**
Web: www.etna.com
SIC: 2992 2821 2899 Oils and greases, blending and compounding; Polyethylene resins; Chemical preparations, nec

(G-2396)
FIRELANDS MEDIA GROUP LLC (PA)
16759 W Park Circle Dr (44023-4549)
P.O. Box 221230 (44122-0996)
PHONE...............440 543-8566
EMP: 6 EST: 2005
SALES (est): 348.47K

SALES (corp-wide): 348.47K **Privately Held**
Web: www.firelandsmedia.com
SIC: 2721 Magazines: publishing only, not printed on site

(G-2397)
GEAUGA GROUP LLC
11024 Wingate Dr (44023-6181)
PHONE...............440 543-8797
Henry Milnark, *Pr*
James Mecsko, *VP*
Janet Mecsko, *Treas*
EMP: 9 EST: 2010
SALES (est): 86.86K **Privately Held**
Web: geauga.oh.gov
SIC: 2326 2339 7213 Aprons, work, except rubberized and plastic: men's; Aprons, except rubber or plastic: women's, misses', juniors'; Apron supply

(G-2398)
GLOBAL METAL SERVICES LTD
8401 Chagrin Rd Ste 14a (44023-4702)
P.O. Box 297 (44021-0297)
PHONE...............440 591-1264
Chi Cheung, *Managing Member*
▲ EMP: 6 EST: 2012
SALES (est): 487.96K **Privately Held**
Web: www.gmsamerica.com
SIC: 3312 Plate, steel

(G-2399)
HB FULLER COMPANY
17340 Munn Rd (44023-5476)
PHONE...............440 708-1212
Ron Janoski, *Brnch Mgr*
EMP: 8
SALES (corp-wide): 3.51B **Publicly Held**
Web: www.hbfuller.com
SIC: 2891 Adhesives
PA: H.B. Fuller Company
   1200 Willow Lake Blvd
   Saint Paul MN 55110
   651 236-5900

(G-2400)
HIGH TEMPERATURE SYSTEMS INC
16755 Park Circle Dr (44023-4562)
PHONE...............440 543-8271
Bruno Thut, *CEO*
Bruno Thut, *Ch Bd*
Kristine Thut, *Pr*
▲ EMP: 11 EST: 1971
SQ FT: 16,000
SALES (est): 1.86MM **Privately Held**
Web: www.hitemp.com
SIC: 3559 Smelting and refining machinery and equipment

(G-2401)
HYPER TOOL COMPANY
16829 Park Circle Dr (44023-4515)
PHONE...............440 543-5151
Morton C Mc Clennan, *Pr*
Donald Felton, *VP*
EMP: 24 EST: 1948
SQ FT: 12,000
SALES (est): 415.23K **Privately Held**
Web: www.hypertool.com
SIC: 3541 3545 Machine tools, metal cutting type; Machine tool accessories

(G-2402)
IBI BRAKE PRODUCTS INC
Also Called: Brake Products
16751 Hilltop Park Pl (44023-4500)
P.O. Box 23547 (44023-0547)
PHONE...............440 543-7962
John Hooper, *Pr*
EMP: 6 EST: 1985

SQ FT: 9,000
SALES (est): 775.26K **Privately Held**
Web: www.brakeproducts.com
SIC: 3499 5084 7389 3536 Wheels: wheelbarrow, stroller, etc.: disc, stamped metal; Industrial machinery and equipment; Crane and aerial lift service; Hoists, cranes, and monorails

(G-2403)
INTEGRATED DEVELOPMENT & MFG
8401 Washington St (44023-4511)
PHONE...............440 543-2423
Adrian O Rule Iii, *Mgr*
EMP: 19
SALES (corp-wide): 16.94MM **Privately Held**
Web: integrated-development-manufacturing.sbcontract.com
SIC: 3822 Environmental controls
PA: Integrated Development & Mfg
   510 Washington St
   Chagrin Falls OH 44022
   440 247-5100

(G-2404)
L HABERNY CO INC
10115 Queens Way (44023-5407)
PHONE...............440 543-5999
Dale Haberny, *Pr*
EMP: 12 EST: 1983
SQ FT: 7,000
SALES (est): 1.63MM **Privately Held**
Web: www.lhaberny.com
SIC: 3567 1796 Industrial furnaces and ovens; Pollution control equipment installation

(G-2405)
LASER AUTOMATION INC
16771 Hilltop Park Pl (44023-4500)
PHONE...............440 543-9291
John Herkes, *Pr*
Carol Scerba, *Sec*
EMP: 16 EST: 1977
SQ FT: 12,000
SALES (est): 897.1K **Privately Held**
Web: www.laserautomationinc.com
SIC: 3699 5049 3535 Laser welding, drilling, and cutting equipment; Scientific and engineering equipment and supplies; Conveyors and conveying equipment

(G-2406)
LATTICE COMPOSITES LLC
10095 Queens Way (44023-5406)
PHONE...............440 543-7526
Ruchir Shanbhag, *CEO*
EMP: 321 EST: 2012
SALES (est): 2.51MM
SALES (corp-wide): 109.73MM **Privately Held**
Web: www.latticecomposites.com
SIC: 2821 Epoxy resins
PA: Mar-Bal, Inc.
   10095 Queens Way
   Chagrin Falls OH 44023
   440 543-7526

(G-2407)
MAR-BAL INC (PA)
10095 Queens Way (44023-5406)
PHONE...............440 543-7526
Scott Balogh, *Pr*
Steven Balogh, *Ex VP*
Carolyn E Balogh, *VP*
Kevin Casey, *VP*
Jim Wojtila, *CFO*
◆ EMP: 93 EST: 1970
SALES (est): 109.73MM

SALES (corp-wide): 109.73MM **Privately Held**
Web: www.mar-bal.com
SIC: 3089 2821 3081 Molding primary plastics; Polyesters; Unsupported plastics film and sheet

(G-2408)
NATIONAL POLYMER DEV CO INC
10200 Gottschalk Pkwy Ste 4 (44023-5470)
PHONE...............440 708-1245
Adrian De Krom, *Pr*
EMP: 7 EST: 2009
SALES (est): 520.46K **Privately Held**
Web: www.nationalpolymer.com
SIC: 2821 Plastics materials and resins

(G-2409)
NATIONAL POLYMER INC
10200 Gottschalk Pkwy (44023-5470)
P.O. Box 343 (44065-0343)
PHONE...............440 708-1245
Adrian De Krom, *Pr*
Daniel Bess, *Dir*
EMP: 11 EST: 2004
SQ FT: 6,000
SALES (est): 2.66MM **Privately Held**
Web: www.nationalpolymer.com
SIC: 8734 5169 2891 Testing laboratories; Adhesives and sealants; Adhesives, plastic

(G-2410)
NATURES WAY BIRD PRODUCTS LLC
9054 Washington St (44023-2744)
PHONE...............440 554-6166
Keith Moone, *CEO*
EMP: 20 EST: 2011
SALES (est): 20MM **Privately Held**
Web: www.natureswaybirds.com
SIC: 2048 7389 Bird food, prepared; Business services, nec

(G-2411)
NELSON ALUMINUM FOUNDRY INC
17093 Munn Rd (44023-5412)
PHONE...............440 543-1941
Russell Nelson, *Pr*
EMP: 6 EST: 1951
SALES (est): 519.25K **Privately Held**
SIC: 3365 3369 Machinery castings, aluminum; Nonferrous foundries, nec

(G-2412)
P & T MILLWORK INC
10090 Queens Way (44023-5403)
PHONE...............440 543-2151
Joe Tesauro, *CEO*
Randall Pistone, *VP*
David Koci, *Sec*
EMP: 17 EST: 1987
SQ FT: 21,500
SALES (est): 480.99K **Privately Held**
Web: www.ptmillwork.com
SIC: 2499 5211 2431 Decorative wood and woodwork; Door and window products; Millwork

(G-2413)
PANELTECH LLC
17525 Haskins Rd (44023-5729)
PHONE...............440 516-1300
EMP: 14 EST: 2012
SALES (est): 2.13MM **Privately Held**
Web: www.paneltech.com
SIC: 3825 Test equipment for electronic and electric measurement

GEOGRAPHIC SECTION

Chardon - Geauga County (G-2440)

(G-2414)
PEDIAVASCULAR INC
7181 Chagrin Rd Ste 250 (44023-1130)
PHONE.................................216 236-5533
Timothy Moran, *CEO*
EMP: 6 **EST:** 2011
SALES (est): 246.7K **Privately Held**
Web: www.pediavascular.com
SIC: 3841 Inhalation therapy equipment

(G-2415)
PERSISTENCE OF VISION INC
Also Called: Pov Print Communications
16715 W Park Circle Dr (44023-4549)
PHONE.................................440 591-5443
Chris Yuhasz, *Pr*
EMP: 9 **EST:** 1993
SQ FT: 3,000
SALES (est): 954.56K **Privately Held**
Web: www.povprintingservices.com
SIC: 2752 Offset printing

(G-2416)
PHOENIX ASSOCIATES
16760 W Park Circle Dr (44023-4550)
PHONE.................................440 543-9701
EMP: 25 **EST:** 1972
SQ FT: 12,000
SALES (est): 2.49MM **Privately Held**
Web: www.phoenixassociates.com
SIC: 3053 Gaskets, all materials

(G-2417)
PRINTING SERVICES
16750 Park Circle Dr (44023-4563)
PHONE.................................440 708-1999
Robert Roulan, *Pr*
EMP: 10 **EST:** 2000
SQ FT: 16,000
SALES (est): 221.78K **Privately Held**
Web: www.povprintingservices.com
SIC: 7389 2752 Printers' services: folding, collating, etc.; Commercial printing, lithographic

(G-2418)
QUBE CORPORATION
16744 W Park Circle Dr (44023-4550)
PHONE.................................440 543-2393
William C Mc Coy, *Pr*
Steve L Clark, *VP*
EMP: 13 **EST:** 1992
SQ FT: 13,000
SALES (est): 2.42MM **Privately Held**
Web: www.qubeinc.com
SIC: 3089 Injection molding of plastics

(G-2419)
RESERVE ENERGY EXPLORATION CO
10155 Gottschalk Pkwy Ste 1 (44023-5465)
P.O. Box 23278 (44023-0278)
PHONE.................................440 543-0770
Joseph Haas, *Pr*
EMP: 8 **EST:** 2001
SALES (est): 991.66K **Privately Held**
Web: www.reserve-energy.com
SIC: 1382 Oil and gas exploration services

(G-2420)
ROYAL ADHESIVES
10255 Queens Way (44023-5408)
PHONE.................................440 708-1212
EMP: 6 **EST:** 2020
SALES (est): 267.78K **Privately Held**
Web: www.hbfuller.com
SIC: 2891 Adhesives

(G-2421)
ROYAL ADHESIVES & SEALANTS LLC
17340 Munn Rd (44023-5476)
PHONE.................................440 708-1212
Ron Janoski, *Pr*
EMP: 10
SALES (corp-wide): 3.51B **Publicly Held**
Web: www.hbfuller.com
SIC: 2891 Sealants
HQ: Royal Adhesives And Sealants Llc
2001 W Washington St
South Bend IN 46628
574 246-5000

(G-2422)
SAPPHIRE CREEK WNERY GRDNS LLC
16965 Park Circle Dr (44023-6502)
PHONE.................................440 543-7777
EMP: 10 **EST:** 2018
SALES (est): 1.29MM **Privately Held**
Web: www.sapphire-creek.com
SIC: 2084 Wines

(G-2423)
SPECTRE INDUSTRIES LLC
10185 Gottschalk Pkwy Ste 1 (44023-5461)
P.O. Box 39562 (44139-0562)
PHONE.................................440 665-2600
EMP: 6 **EST:** 2018
SALES (est): 42.85K **Privately Held**
Web: www.spectreind.com
SIC: 3999 Manufacturing industries, nec

(G-2424)
STOCK EQUIPMENT COMPANY INC
Also Called: Stock
16490 Chillicothe Rd (44023-4398)
PHONE.................................440 543-6000
◆ **EMP:** 240
SIC: 3535 Conveyors and conveying equipment

(G-2425)
STOUTHEART CORPORATION
7205 Chagrin Rd Ste 4 (44023-1127)
P.O. Box 39219 (44139-0219)
PHONE.................................800 556-6470
David Martinelli, *Pr*
EMP: 37 **EST:** 2002
SQ FT: 500
SALES (est): 4.16MM **Privately Held**
SIC: 3351 Strip, copper and copper alloy

(G-2426)
SUSAN HILL HAMS
1900 Barton Springs Road Unit 5032 (44023)
PHONE.................................440 543-5967
C Martin Harris, *Prin*
EMP: 7 **EST:** 2000
SALES (est): 116.45K **Privately Held**
SIC: 2013 Prepared pork products, from purchased pork

(G-2427)
TANGENT COMPANY LLC
10175 Queens Way Ste 1 (44023-5435)
P.O. Box 23008 (44023-0008)
PHONE.................................440 543-2775
James Bolton, *Managing Member*
EMP: 9 **EST:** 2008
SALES (est): 908.45K **Privately Held**
Web: www.tangentcompany.com
SIC: 3999 8711 8734 8733 Grinding and pulverizing of materials, nec; Engineering services; Testing laboratories; Noncommercial research organizations

(G-2428)
TARKETT INC
16910 Munn Rd (44023-5411)
PHONE.................................440 543-8916
Bruce Ziegler, *Dir*
EMP: 39
Web: www.tarkettna.com
SIC: 3069 Flooring, rubber: tile or sheet
HQ: Tarkett, Inc.
30000 Aurora Rd
Solon OH 44139
800 899-8916

(G-2429)
TARKETT USA INC
16910 Munn Rd (44023-5411)
PHONE.................................440 543-8916
Jeff Fenwick, *Pr*
EMP: 279
Web: www.tarkett-group.com
SIC: 3253 Ceramic wall and floor tile
HQ: Tarkett Usa Inc.
30000 Aurora Rd
Solon OH 44139
877 827-5388

(G-2430)
TRIAD METAL PRODUCTS COMPANY
12990 Snow Rd (44023)
PHONE.................................216 676-6505
Patricia Basista, *Pr*
Richard Basista, *Pr*
Wally Klubert, *Ex VP*
▲ **EMP:** 47 **EST:** 1945
SQ FT: 150,000
SALES (est): 1.33MM **Privately Held**
Web: www.triadmetal.com
SIC: 3469 Stamping metal for the trade

(G-2431)
UTILITY RELAY CO LTD
Also Called: Urc
10100 Queens Way (44023-5404)
PHONE.................................440 708-1000
EMP: 42 **EST:** 1994
SQ FT: 15,000
SALES (est): 7.53MM **Privately Held**
Web: www.utilityrelay.com
SIC: 3625 Industrial electrical relays and switches

(G-2432)
VENTCO INC
66 Windward Way (44023-6706)
PHONE.................................440 834-8888
Joseph Ventimiglia, *Pr*
Frank Ventimiglia, *VP*
▼ **EMP:** 10 **EST:** 1983
SQ FT: 15,500
SALES (est): 839.89K **Privately Held**
SIC: 2842 2992 Cleaning or polishing preparations, nec; Lubricating oils and greases

(G-2433)
VIRTUS STUNTS LLC
16320 Snyder Rd (44023-4312)
PHONE.................................440 543-0472
Ted Batchelor, *Prin*
EMP: 6 **EST:** 2010
SALES (est): 243.4K **Privately Held**
SIC: 2721 Television schedules: publishing only, not printed on site

(G-2434)
WHIP GUIDE CO
Also Called: Gizmo
16829 Park Circle Dr (44023-4515)
PHONE.................................440 543-5151
Morton C Mc Clennan, *Pt*
Walter C Mc Clennan, *Pt*
EMP: 10 **EST:** 1946
SQ FT: 10,000
SALES (est): 899.52K **Privately Held**
Web: www.gizmowhipguide.com
SIC: 3545 3366 Drilling machine attachments and accessories; Copper foundries

(G-2435)
WIHOLI INC
17050 Munn Rd (44023-5413)
PHONE.................................440 543-8233
George C Wick Junior, *Pr*
George F Howson Junior, *VP*
Craig Liechty, *CFO*
EMP: 15 **EST:** 1945
SQ FT: 31,000
SALES (est): 2.63MM **Privately Held**
Web: www.speedselector.com
SIC: 3568 Power transmission equipment, nec

(G-2436)
XACT SPEC INDUSTRIES LLC (PA)
16959 Munn Rd (44023-5410)
PHONE.................................440 543-8157
Peter Barnhart, *Managing Member*
EMP: 33 **EST:** 2008
SQ FT: 32,000
SALES (est): 5.39MM **Privately Held**
Web: www.xactspec.com
SIC: 3599 Machine shop, jobbing and repair

(G-2437)
XACT SPEC INDUSTRIES LLC
Aerospace Operations
16959 Munn Rd (44023-5410)
PHONE.................................440 543-8157
Peter Barnhart, *Mng Pt*
EMP: 9
Web: www.xactspec.com
SIC: 3599 Machine shop, jobbing and repair
PA: Xact Spec Industries Llc
16959 Munn Rd
Chagrin Falls OH 44023

(G-2438)
ZOOK ENTERPRISES LLC (PA)
16809 Park Circle Dr (44023-4515)
P.O. Box 419 (44022-0419)
PHONE.................................440 543-1010
Gregory D Clark, *CEO*
▲ **EMP:** 20 **EST:** 1971
SQ FT: 8,400
SALES (est): 8.01MM
SALES (corp-wide): 8.01MM **Privately Held**
Web: www.zookdisk.com
SIC: 3559 Petroleum refinery equipment

Chandlersville
Muskingum County

(G-2439)
G-ROD WELDING & FABG LLC
5065 Chandlersville Rd (43727-9754)
PHONE.................................740 588-0609
EMP: 6 **EST:** 2016
SALES (est): 38.7K **Privately Held**
SIC: 7692 Welding repair

Chardon
Geauga County

(G-2440)
BOEHRNGER INGLHEIM PHRMCCTCALS

Chardon - Geauga County (G-2441)

11540 Autumn Ridge Dr (44024-8764)
PHONE..................................440 286-5667
Rick Oprzadek, Prin
EMP: 41 EST: 2010
SALES (est): 541.9K Privately Held
SIC: 2834 Pharmaceutical preparations

(G-2441)
BUCKEYE PIPE INSPECTION LLC
10770 Mayfield Rd (44024-9323)
PHONE..................................440 476-8369
Linda Browne, Prin
EMP: 6 EST: 2013
SALES (est): 863.83K Privately Held
Web: www.buckeyepipe.com
SIC: 1389 Oil field services, nec

(G-2442)
CHARDON CUSTOM POLYMERS LLC
373 Washington St (44024-1129)
PHONE..................................440 285-2161
EMP: 16 EST: 2010
SALES (est): 4.73MM Privately Held
Web: www.chardoncp.com
SIC: 3061 3069 Mechanical rubber goods; Molded rubber products

(G-2443)
CHARDON METAL PRODUCTS CO
206 5th Ave (44024-1007)
PHONE..................................440 285-2147
Anderson Allyn Junior, Ch Bd
Duke Allyn, *
Aric Allyn, *
Anderson Allyn Iii, CFO
EMP: 32 EST: 1945
SQ FT: 31,000
SALES (est): 4.68MM Privately Held
Web: www.chardonmetal.com
SIC: 3498 3451 3599 Tube fabricating (contract bending and shaping); Screw machine products; Machine shop, jobbing and repair

(G-2444)
CHARDON SQUARE AUTO & BODY INC (PA)
Also Called: Chardon Tire and Brake
525 Water St (44024-1146)
PHONE..................................440 286-7600
John Colello, Pr
EMP: 10 EST: 1991
SQ FT: 7,800
SALES (est): 2.2MM Privately Held
Web: www.csautoandtire.com
SIC: 7532 7534 7539 Body shop, automotive; Tire retreading and repair shops; Brake services

(G-2445)
CHARDON TOOL & SUPPLY CO INC
115 Parker Ct (44024-1112)
P.O. Box 291 (44024-0291)
PHONE..................................440 286-6440
Weldon Bennett, Pr
EMP: 40 EST: 1986
SQ FT: 4,800
SALES (est): 4.41MM Privately Held
Web: www.chardontool.com
SIC: 3545 5085 Diamond cutting tools for turning, boring, burnishing, etc.; Diamonds, industrial: natural, crude

(G-2446)
CITY OF CHARDON
Also Called: Water & Sewer
201 N Hambden St (44024-1175)
PHONE..................................440 286-2657
David Lelkl, Mgr
EMP: 27
Web: www.chardon.cc
SIC: 3589 Sewage and water treatment equipment
PA: City Of Chardon
111 Water St 2nd Fl
Chardon OH 44024
440 286-2600

(G-2447)
DAVE KRISSINGER
12335 Old State Rd (44024-9560)
PHONE..................................440 669-9957
Dave Krissinger, Prin
EMP: 6 EST: 2010
SALES (est): 85.88K Privately Held
Web: www.garlicdave.com
SIC: 2035 Spreads, garlic

(G-2448)
DE NORA TECH INC
DE NORA TECH, INC.
464 Center St (44024-1068)
PHONE..................................440 285-0100
Dennis L Baxendale, Brnch Mgr
EMP: 161
SALES (corp-wide): 885.74MM Privately Held
Web: business.painesvilleohchamber.org
SIC: 3643 3823 Current-carrying wiring services; Electrolytic conductivity instruments, industrial process
HQ: De Nora Tech, Llc
7590 Discovery Ln
Concord Township OH 44077
440 710-5334

(G-2449)
EGC OPERATING COMPANY LLC (PA)
Also Called: Egc Enterprises
140 Parker Ct (44024-1112)
PHONE..................................440 285-5835
Hugh Slater, CEO
John Popovich, VP
Paul Clark, COO
Lisa Sutton, Contrlr
EMP: 66 EST: 2014
SALES (est): 5.69MM
SALES (corp-wide): 5.69MM Privately Held
Web: www.egcgraphite.com
SIC: 2891 3053 Sealants; Gaskets; packing and sealing devices

(G-2450)
ELEMENT 41 INC (PA)
141 Main St (44024-1244)
PHONE..................................216 410-5646
EMP: 6 EST: 2017
SALES (est): 932.76K
SALES (corp-wide): 932.76K Privately Held
Web: www.element41chardon.com
SIC: 2819 Elements

(G-2451)
GEAUGA COATINGS LLC
15120 Sisson Rd (44024-8507)
PHONE..................................440 221-7286
Brian Milks, Prin
EMP: 8 EST: 2011
SALES (est): 983.99K Privately Held
Web: www.geaugacoatings.com
SIC: 3312 Chemicals and other products derived from coking

(G-2452)
HOWLING PRINT AND PROMO INC
10974 Leader Rd (44024-8938)
P.O. Box 692 (44024-0692)
PHONE..................................440 363-4999
Edward Hamner, Owner
EMP: 8 EST: 2018
SALES (est): 372.41K Privately Held
Web: www.howlingpromo.com
SIC: 2752 Commercial printing, lithographic

(G-2453)
HUTTER RACING ENGINES LTD
12550 Gar Hwy (44024-8232)
PHONE..................................440 285-2175
Ronald Hutter, Pt
Thalia Hutter, Pt
Trevor Hutter, Pt
EMP: 10 EST: 1970
SQ FT: 6,000
SALES (est): 824.93K Privately Held
Web: www.hutterperformance.com
SIC: 3599 7538 Machine shop, jobbing and repair; General automotive repair shops

(G-2454)
KEY MANEUVERS INC (PA)
Also Called: K.M.I. Printing
10639 Grant St Ste C (44024-1282)
P.O. Box 51 (44024-0051)
PHONE..................................440 285-0774
Randy Bennett, Pr
EMP: 7 EST: 1988
SQ FT: 3,000
SALES (est): 1.02MM Privately Held
Web: www.kmiprinting.com
SIC: 2752 Offset printing

(G-2455)
KONA BLACKBIRD INC
Also Called: Black Lab Custom Products
11730 Ravenna Rd (44024-7005)
PHONE..................................440 285-3189
▲ EMP: 29
SIC: 2899 3241 3251 2842 Fluxes; brazing, soldering, galvanizing, and welding; Masonry cement; Flooring brick, clay; Cleaning or polishing preparations, nec

(G-2456)
KTS CSTM LGS/XCLSVELY YOU INC
602 South St Ste C-2 (44024-1459)
PHONE..................................440 285-9803
Kevin R Temple, Pr
Melissa Temple, VP
EMP: 7 EST: 2002
SQ FT: 2,800
SALES (est): 490.31K Privately Held
Web: www.ktscustomlogos.com
SIC: 2395 7389 Embroidery and art needlework; Advertising, promotional, and trade show services

(G-2457)
KTS CUSTOM LOGOS
602 South St Ste C-2 (44024)
PHONE..................................440 285-9803
Kevin R Temple, Pr
Melissa Temple, VP
Ken Temple, Prin
EMP: 7 EST: 1998
SALES (est): 500.96K Privately Held
Web: www.ktscustomlogos.com
SIC: 2395 Embroidery and art needlework

(G-2458)
MAPLEDALE FARM INC
Also Called: Mapledale Landscaping
12613 Woodin Rd (44024-9177)
PHONE..................................440 286-3389
EMP: 10 EST: 1982
SALES (est): 503.27K Privately Held
Web: www.mapledalelandscaping.com
SIC: 0782 4959 2087 5251 Landscape contractors; Snowplowing; Beverage bases, concentrates, syrups, powders and mixes; Snowblowers

(G-2459)
NOF METAL COATINGS N AMER INC (HQ)
275 Industrial Pkwy (44024-1052)
PHONE..................................440 285-2231
Shin Masuda, Pr
Norman Gertz, *
▲ EMP: 50 EST: 1984
SQ FT: 20,000
SALES (est): 17.72MM Privately Held
Web: www.nofmetalcoatings.com
SIC: 2899 Chemical preparations, nec
PA: Nof Corporation
4-20-3, Ebisu
Shibuya-Ku TKY 150-0

(G-2460)
NORTH AMERICAN CAST STONE INC
11546 Claridon Troy Rd (44024-8437)
PHONE..................................440 286-1999
Richard T Rickelman, Prin
EMP: 17 EST: 2002
SALES (est): 366.07K Privately Held
Web: www.northamericancaststone.com
SIC: 3272 Concrete products, precast, nec

(G-2461)
OHIO ORDNANCE WORKS INC
310 Park Dr (44024-1057)
P.O. Box 687 (44024-0687)
PHONE..................................440 285-3481
Robert I Landies, Pr
Robert E Conroy Junior, VP
◆ EMP: 40 EST: 1992
SALES (est): 8.3MM Privately Held
Web: www.oowinc.com
SIC: 3484 Guns (firearms) or gun parts, 30 mm. and below

(G-2462)
ORWELL PRINTING
10639 Grant St Ste C (44024-1282)
P.O. Box 51 (44024-0051)
PHONE..................................440 285-2233
Randy Bennett, Pr
EMP: 8 EST: 1948
SQ FT: 1,900
SALES (est): 873.31K Privately Held
Web: www.orwellprinting.com
SIC: 2752 Offset printing
PA: Key Maneuvers, Inc.
10639 Grant St Ste C
Chardon OH 44024

(G-2463)
PEDAGOGY FURNITURE
745 South St (44024-2800)
PHONE..................................888 394-8484
EMP: 6 EST: 2021
SALES (est): 46.28K Privately Held
Web: www.pedagogyfurniture.com
SIC: 2511 Wood household furniture

(G-2464)
QUANTUM ENERGY LLC (PA)
10405 Locust Grove Dr (44024-8861)
PHONE..................................440 285-7381
EMP: 15 EST: 1996
SALES (est): 1.71MM
SALES (corp-wide): 1.71MM Privately Held
SIC: 1382 Oil and gas exploration services

GEOGRAPHIC SECTION

(G-2465)
RHEIN CHEMIE CORPORATION
145 Parker Ct (44024-1112)
PHONE..................................440 279-2367
◆ EMP: 250
Web: www.lanxess.com
SIC: 3069 5169 Reclaimed rubber and specialty rubber compounds; Industrial chemicals

(G-2466)
RICHARDS MAPLE PRODUCTS INC
545 Water St (44024-1142)
PHONE..................................440 286-4160
TOLL FREE: 800
Debra Richards, *Pr*
Colin Rennie, *VP*
Annette Polson, *Sec*
EMP: 6 EST: 1910
SALES (est): 878.83K **Privately Held**
Web: www.richardsmapleproducts.com
SIC: 2064 5149 Candy and other confectionery products; Syrups, except for fountain use

(G-2467)
SHIFFLER EQUIPMENT SALES INC (PA)
745 S St (44024-2800)
P.O. Box 232 (44024-0232)
PHONE..................................440 285-9175
John Shiffler, *CEO*
Gloria S Shiffler, *
Mark C Lewis, *
▲ EMP: 41 EST: 1971
SQ FT: 30,000
SALES (est): 20.62MM
SALES (corp-wide): 20.62MM **Privately Held**
Web: www.shifflerequip.com
SIC: 2531 School furniture

(G-2468)
SOLON MANUFACTURING COMPANY
425 Center St (44024-1054)
PHONE..................................440 286-7149
David J Carpenter, *Ch*
J Timothy Dunn, *
George Davet, *
Perry Blossom, *
Jim Young, *
▲ EMP: 38 EST: 1949
SQ FT: 30,000
SALES (est): 9.39MM **Privately Held**
Web: www.solonmfg.com
SIC: 3823 3493 3643 3495 Pressure measurement instruments, industrial; Cold formed springs; Current-carrying wiring services; Wire springs

(G-2469)
SPALDING
12860 Mayfield Rd (44024-8963)
PHONE..................................440 286-5717
Richard Spalding, *Prin*
EMP: 10 EST: 2010
SALES (est): 237.96K **Privately Held**
Web: www.spalding.com
SIC: 2253 Jerseys, knit

(G-2470)
WECALL INC
510 Center St (44024-1004)
P.O. Box 39 (44076-0039)
PHONE..................................440 437-8202
Paul David Doherty, *Pr*
Bernard Doherty, *VP*
EMP: 9 EST: 1969
SALES (est): 1.94MM **Privately Held**
Web: www.wecallinc.com
SIC: 3429 3452 Metal fasteners; Bolts, nuts, rivets, and washers

Charm
Holmes County

(G-2471)
RABER LUMBER CO
4112 State Rte 557 (44617)
P.O. Box 26 (44617-0026)
PHONE..................................330 893-2797
Edward Raber, *Pt*
EMP: 7 EST: 1965
SQ FT: 1,000
SALES (est): 552.43K **Privately Held**
SIC: 2421 2448 Sawmills and planing mills, general; Pallets, wood

Chesapeake
Lawrence County

(G-2472)
AQUA OHIO INC
Also Called: Union Rome Sewer System
32 Private Dr 11100 (45619)
P.O. Box 430 (45619-0430)
PHONE..................................740 867-8700
EMP: 10
SALES (corp-wide): 2.05B **Publicly Held**
Web: www.lawcomunicourt.com
SIC: 3589 Sewage and water treatment equipment
HQ: Aqua Ohio, Inc.
6650 South Ave
Youngstown OH 44512
330 726-8151

(G-2473)
G BIG INC (PA)
Also Called: Pickett Concrete
441 Rockwood Ave (45619-1120)
PHONE..................................740 867-5758
John W Galloway, *Pr*
Todd A Galloway, *VP*
James W Galloway, *VP*
EMP: 20 EST: 1960
SQ FT: 2,000
SALES (est): 2.51MM
SALES (corp-wide): 2.51MM **Privately Held**
Web: www.pickettconcrete.com
SIC: 3273 1771 Ready-mixed concrete; Concrete work

(G-2474)
GERALD D DAMRON
197 Township Road 1156 (45619-8905)
PHONE..................................740 894-3680
Gerald Damron, *Prin*
EMP: 7 EST: 2009
SALES (est): 219.61K **Privately Held**
SIC: 2411 Logging

(G-2475)
INK SLINGERS LLC
1564 County Road 36 (45619-7955)
PHONE..................................740 867-3528
EMP: 6 EST: 2014
SALES (est): 214.79K **Privately Held**
Web: www.inkslingersllc.com
SIC: 2759 Screen printing

(G-2476)
PRECISION COMPONENT & MCH INC
17 Rosslyn Rd (45619)
P.O. Box 580 (45619)
PHONE..................................740 867-6366
EMP: 38 EST: 1996
SQ FT: 24,000
SALES (est): 4.66MM **Privately Held**
Web: www.pcmohio.com
SIC: 3599 Machine shop, jobbing and repair

Cheshire
Gallia County

(G-2477)
ENVIRI CORPORATION
5486 State Rte 7 (45620-9522)
P.O. Box 371 (45620-0371)
PHONE..................................740 367-7322
James D Taylor, *Mgr*
EMP: 9
SQ FT: 300
SALES (corp-wide): 2.07B **Publicly Held**
Web: www.enviri.com
SIC: 3295 Slag, crushed or ground
PA: Enviri Corporation
100-120 N 18th St # 17
Philadelphia PA 19103
267 857-8715

Chesterland
Geauga County

(G-2478)
AEROTECH ENTERPRISE
8511 Mulberry Rd (44026)
P.O. Box 596 (44026)
PHONE..................................440 729-2616
Mike Matic, *Pr*
Andrea Matic, *Sec*
EMP: 15 EST: 1973
SQ FT: 6,000
SALES (est): 2.16MM **Privately Held**
Web: www.aerotechcnc.com
SIC: 3599 Machine shop, jobbing and repair

(G-2479)
AMERICAN FLUID POWER INC
7407 Tattersall Dr (44026-2036)
PHONE..................................440 773-7462
EMP: 6 EST: 2017
SALES (est): 340.24K **Privately Held**
Web: www.amerfluidpower.com
SIC: 3599 Machine shop, jobbing and repair

(G-2480)
CHESTERLAND NEWS INC
Also Called: Chesterland News
8389 Mayfield Rd Ste B-4 (44026-2553)
PHONE..................................440 729-7667
EMP: 7 EST: 1967
SALES (est): 194.49K **Privately Held**
Web: www.geaugamapleleaf.com
SIC: 2711 Newspapers, publishing and printing

(G-2481)
HF GROUP LLC
8844 Mayfield Rd (44026-2632)
PHONE..................................440 729-9411
Terry Hymas, *Brnch Mgr*
EMP: 179
Web: www.hfgroup.com
SIC: 2732 Books, printing and binding
PA: Hf Group, Llc
400 Arora Cmmons Cir Unit
Aurora OH 44202

(G-2482)
HF GROUP LLC
Also Called: General Book Binding
8844 Mayfield Rd (44026-2632)
PHONE..................................440 729-9411
Jim Bratton, *Brnch Mgr*
EMP: 112
Web: www.hfgroup.com
SIC: 2789 Bookbinding and related work
PA: Hf Group, Llc
400 Arora Cmmons Cir Unit
Aurora OH 44202

(G-2483)
INNOVEST ENERGY GROUP LLC
8834 Mayfield Rd Ste A (44026-2696)
P.O. Box 179 (44045-0179)
PHONE..................................440 644-1027
Mike Yukich, *Prin*
EMP: 9 EST: 2019
SALES (est): 525.38K **Privately Held**
Web: www.innovestenergygroup.com
SIC: 3643 Lightning protection equipment

(G-2484)
MEISTERMATIC INC
12446 Bentbrook Dr (44026-2459)
PHONE..................................216 481-7773
Edward Kurnava, *Pr*
Terry Kurnava, *
EMP: 20 EST: 1963
SQ FT: 70,000
SALES (est): 326.81K **Privately Held**
SIC: 3451 Screw machine products

(G-2485)
METZENBAUM SHELTERED INDS INC
Also Called: MSI
8090 Cedar Rd (44026-3465)
P.O. Box 538 (44065-0538)
PHONE..................................440 729-1919
Robert Voss, *Prgrm Mgr*
Robert Preston, *
Diane Buehner, *Head Secretary**
EMP: 73 EST: 1969
SQ FT: 12,000
SALES (est): 1.51MM **Privately Held**
Web: www.geaugadd.org
SIC: 8331 7389 3672 Sheltered workshop; Packaging and labeling services; Printed circuit boards

(G-2486)
NITROJECTION
8430 Mayfield Rd (44026-2580)
PHONE..................................440 729-2711
Ana Leben, *Prin*
EMP: 8 EST: 2011
SALES (est): 526.59K **Privately Held**
Web: www.nitrojection.com
SIC: 3089 Injection molding of plastics

(G-2487)
ORGANON INC
7407 Cedar Rd (44026-3464)
PHONE..................................440 729-2290
EMP: 10 EST: 2009
SALES (est): 196.79K **Privately Held**
Web: www.organon.com
SIC: 2834 Pharmaceutical preparations

(G-2488)
PNEUMATIC SPECIALTIES INC
Also Called: PSI
11677 Chillicothe Rd Unit 1 (44026-1905)
PHONE..................................440 729-4400
Lisa Labanc, *CEO*
Lisa Labanc, *Pr*
EMP: 6 EST: 1987
SALES (est): 945.41K **Privately Held**
Web: www.psiproductspecialists.com
SIC: 2841 2842 5999 7218 Soap and other detergents; Degreasing solvent; Safety supplies and equipment; Safety glove supply

(G-2489)
T A BACON CO
Also Called: Tabco
11655 Chillicothe Rd (44026-1927)
P.O. Box 21150 (44121-0150)
PHONE.................................216 851-1404
Timothy Bacon, *Pr*
▲ **EMP:** 22 **EST:** 1975
SQ FT: 45,000
SALES (est): 2.45MM **Privately Held**
Web: www.tabcoparts.com
SIC: 3465 5013 Automotive stampings; Automotive stampings

Chickasaw
Mercer County

(G-2490)
CHICKASAW MACHINE & TL CO INC
0050 Chickasaw Rd (15826-1522)
P.O. Box 35 (45826-0035)
PHONE.................................419 925-4325
Norbert B Tangeman, *Pr*
Ted Homan, *VP*
Dave Tangeman, *VP*
▼ **EMP:** 26 **EST:** 1960
SQ FT: 18,000
SALES (est): 922.03K **Privately Held**
Web: www.chickasawmachine.com
SIC: 3599 Machine shop, jobbing and repair

Chillicothe
Ross County

(G-2491)
ADVANTAGE TENT FITTINGS INC
11661 Pleasant Valley Rd (45601-8315)
PHONE.................................740 773-3015
Benjamin Hall, *Pr*
Robert Hall, *Ch Bd*
▼ **EMP:** 15 **EST:** 1991
SQ FT: 14,000
SALES (est): 2.09MM **Privately Held**
Web: www.advantagetent.com
SIC: 2431 5091 2394 Millwork; Sporting and recreation goods; Canvas and related products

(G-2492)
ALL SIGNS OF CHILLICOTHE INC
Also Called: All Signs
12035 Pleasant Valley Rd (45601-9785)
PHONE.................................740 773-5016
Kris Oliver, *VP*
EMP: 9 **EST:** 1989
SALES (est): 993.17K **Privately Held**
Web: www.allsignsofohio.com
SIC: 3993 1799 Electric signs; Sign installation and maintenance

(G-2493)
AUTOMATOR MARKING SYSTEMS INC
475 Douglas Ave (45601-3663)
PHONE.................................740 983-0157
Gregory Mcdaniel, *Pr*
EMP: 9 **EST:** 2017
SALES (est): 531.82K **Privately Held**
Web: www.automator.com
SIC: 3599 Machine and other job shop work

(G-2494)
BBB MUSIC LLC
643 Central Ctr (45601-2249)
P.O. Box 903 (45601-0903)
PHONE.................................740 772-2262
EMP: 8 **EST:** 2009

SALES (est): 547.43K **Privately Held**
Web: www.bbbmusiccenter.com
SIC: 3931 5736 Musical instruments; Musical instrument stores

(G-2495)
BELL LOGISTICS CO
27311 Old Route 35 (45601)
P.O. Box 91 (45601)
PHONE.................................740 702-9830
Jon Bell, *Pr*
Deana Bell, *
EMP: 30 **EST:** 2007
SQ FT: 25,000
SALES (est): 4.53MM **Privately Held**
Web: www.jbexpress.com
SIC: 3715 Truck trailers

(G-2496)
BROCK RAD WLDG FABRICATION INC
Also Called: Brocks RAD Wldg Fabrication I
370 Douglas Ave (45601-3662)
PHONE.................................740 773-2540
David J Brock, *Pr*
Nancy Brock, *Sec*
EMP: 8 **EST:** 1945
SQ FT: 12,000
SALES (est): 608.15K **Privately Held**
SIC: 7539 7692 Radiator repair shop, automotive; Automotive welding

(G-2497)
CHILLICOTHE PACKAGING CORP
Also Called: Churmac Industries
4168 State Route 159 (45601-8695)
P.O. Box 466 (45601-0466)
PHONE.................................740 773-5800
Michael Mccarty, *Pr*
EMP: 40 **EST:** 1978
SQ FT: 60,000
SALES (est): 4.48MM **Privately Held**
SIC: 2653 Boxes, corrugated: made from purchased materials

(G-2498)
CHURMAC INDUSTRIES INC
Also Called: Chillicothe Packing
4168 State Route 159 (45601-8695)
P.O. Box 205 (45601-0205)
PHONE.................................740 773-5800
Michael Mccarty, *Pr*
EMP: 16 **EST:** 1983
SQ FT: 60,000
SALES (est): 485.3K **Privately Held**
SIC: 2631 Paperboard mills

(G-2499)
CONSOLIDATED METCO INC
351 Chamber Dr (45601-8257)
PHONE.................................740 772-6758
EMP: 50
SALES (corp-wide): 3.96B **Privately Held**
Web: www.conmet.com
SIC: 3089 Injection molding of plastics
HQ: Consolidated Metco, Inc.
5701 Se Columbia Way
Vancouver WA 98661
360 828-2599

(G-2500)
CRISPIE CREME CHILLICOTHE INC
Also Called: Grandpa Jack's
47 N Bridge St (45601-2615)
PHONE.................................740 774-3770
Richard Renison, *Pr*
James M Renison, *
EMP: 8 **EST:** 1929
SQ FT: 2,500
SALES (est): 429.68K **Privately Held**
Web: www.chillicotheohio.com

SIC: 2051 5461 Doughnuts, except frozen; Doughnuts

(G-2501)
DEES FAMILY RACEWAY LLC
906 Charleston Pike (45601-9312)
PHONE.................................740 772-5431
Carmel G Tackett, *Admn*
EMP: 6 **EST:** 2010
SALES (est): 105.52K **Privately Held**
SIC: 3644 Raceways

(G-2502)
FIFTY WEST BREWING COMPANY LLC
1 N Paint St (45601-3116)
PHONE.................................740 775-2337
EMP: 25
SALES (corp-wide): 4.56MM **Privately Held**
Web: www.fiftywestbrew.com
SIC: 2082 Beer (alcoholic beverage)
PA: Fifty West Brewing Company, Llc
7668 Wooster Pike
Cincinnati OH 45227
513 834-8789

(G-2503)
FLOSSYS SWEET TOOTH LLC
5888 Marietta Rd (45601-9194)
PHONE.................................614 425-7939
Jennifer Szatkowski, *Prin*
EMP: 8
SALES (est): 78.58K **Privately Held**
SIC: 2064 Candy and other confectionery products

(G-2504)
G & J PEPSI-COLA BOTTLERS INC
Also Called: Pepsico
400 E 7th St (45601-3455)
PHONE.................................740 774-2148
Henry Thrapp, *Brnch Mgr*
EMP: 23
SALES (corp-wide): 404.54MM **Privately Held**
Web: www.gjpepsi.com
SIC: 2086 Carbonated soft drinks, bottled and canned
PA: G & J Pepsi-Cola Bottlers Inc
9435 Waterstone Blvd # 390
Cincinnati OH 45249
513 785-6060

(G-2505)
GILLS PETROLEUM LLC
213 S Paint St (45601-3828)
PHONE.................................740 702-2600
Barry Rahe, *Prin*
EMP: 6 **EST:** 2016
SALES (est): 217.62K **Privately Held**
SIC: 1381 Drilling oil and gas wells

(G-2506)
GLATFELTER CORPORATION
353 S Paint St (45601-3814)
P.O. Box 2500 (45601-0997)
PHONE.................................740 772-3893
EMP: 9
SALES (corp-wide): 1.39B **Publicly Held**
Web: www.glatfelter.com
SIC: 2621 Book paper
PA: Glatfelter Corporation
4350 Congress St Ste 600
Charlotte NC 28209
704 885-2555

(G-2507)
GLATFELTER CORPORATION
311 Caldwell St (45601-3332)

PHONE.................................740 775-6119
Dawn Limle, *Brnch Mgr*
EMP: 11
SALES (corp-wide): 1.39B **Publicly Held**
Web: www.glatfelter.com
SIC: 2621 Book paper
PA: Glatfelter Corporation
4350 Congress St Ste 600
Charlotte NC 28209
704 885-2555

(G-2508)
GLATFELTER CORPORATION
Also Called: Chillicothe Facility
232 E 8th St (45601-3364)
P.O. Box 2500 (45601-0997)
PHONE.................................740 772-3111
EMP: 100
SALES (corp-wide): 1.39B **Publicly Held**
Web: www.glatfelter.com
SIC: 2621 Book paper
PA: Glatfelter Corporation
4350 Congress St Ste 600
Charlotte NC 28209
704 885-2555

(G-2509)
HERR FOODS INCORPORATED
476 E 7th St (45601-3455)
PHONE.................................740 773-8282
Scott Carmenan, *Mgr*
EMP: 42
SQ FT: 1,000
SALES (corp-wide): 392.21MM **Privately Held**
Web: www.herrs.com
SIC: 2096 Potato chips and other potato-based snacks
PA: Herr Foods Incorporated
20 Herr Dr
Nottingham PA 19362
610 932-9330

(G-2510)
HERR FOODS INCORPORATED
104 S Mcarthur St (45601-3600)
PHONE.................................800 344-3777
EMP: 16
SALES (corp-wide): 392.21MM **Privately Held**
Web: www.herrs.com
SIC: 2096 Potato chips and other potato-based snacks
PA: Herr Foods Incorporated
20 Herr Dr
Nottingham PA 19362
610 932-9330

(G-2511)
INDUSTRIAL RLBLITY SPCLSTS INC (PA)
Also Called: Irr
370 Douglas Ave (45601-3662)
PHONE.................................800 800-6345
Robert A Rivenbark Senior, *Prin*
EMP: 6 **EST:** 2018
SALES (est): 266.24K
SALES (corp-wide): 266.24K **Privately Held**
SIC: 3542 Arbor presses

(G-2512)
INFOSIGHT CORPORATION
20700 Us Highway 23 (45601-9016)
P.O. Box 5000 (45601-7000)
PHONE.................................740 642-3600
John A Robertson, *CEO*
G D Hudelson, *
Barbara Robertson, *
Rob Underhill, *
▲ **EMP:** 65 **EST:** 1993

GEOGRAPHIC SECTION

Chillicothe - Ross County (G-2536)

SQ FT: 30,000
SALES (est): 15.53MM **Privately Held**
Web: www.infosight.com
SIC: **3953** Figures (marking devices), metal

(G-2513)
INGLE-BARR INC (PA)
Also Called: Ibi
20 Plyleys Ln (45601)
P.O. Box 874 (45601)
PHONE..............................740 702-6117
Jeffrey Poole, *Pr*
Rod Poole, *
EMP: 100 EST: 1967
SQ FT: 6,500
SALES (est): 19.09MM
SALES (corp-wide): 19.09MM **Privately Held**
Web: www.4ibi.com
SIC: **1521** 1541 1542 2541 General remodeling, single-family houses; Renovation, remodeling and repairs: industrial buildings; Commercial and office building, new construction; Bar fixtures, wood

(G-2514)
JASON C GIBSON
414 Bethel Rd (45601-8060)
PHONE..............................740 663-4520
Jason C Gibson, *Owner*
EMP: 10 EST: 2005
SALES (est): 494.9K **Privately Held**
SIC: **2411** Logging

(G-2515)
M & M FABRICATION INC
18828 Us Highway 50 (45601-9268)
PHONE..............................740 779-3071
Gary Timmons, *Pr*
Ardath I Wise Incorp, *Prin*
Jessie B Wise Incorp, *Prin*
Joseph S Wise Incorp, *Prin*
EMP: 10 EST: 2001
SALES (est): 2.04MM **Privately Held**
Web: www.mmfabrication.com
SIC: **3441** Building components, structural steel

(G-2516)
MCNEAL ENTERPRISES LLC
807 E 2nd St (45601-2750)
PHONE..............................740 703-7108
EMP: 8 EST: 2015
SALES (est): 717.05K **Privately Held**
SIC: **3089** Injection molding of plastics

(G-2517)
MCRD ENTERPRISES LLC
Also Called: Art Tech
337 E Main St (45601-3415)
PHONE..............................740 775-2377
EMP: 10 EST: 2007
SALES (est): 693.13K **Privately Held**
SIC: **3993** Signs, not made in custom sign painting shops

(G-2518)
MIDWEST MOTOPLEX LLC
98 Consumer Center Dr (45601-2667)
PHONE..............................740 772-5300
EMP: 7 EST: 2011
SQ FT: 13,000
SALES (est): 503.55K **Privately Held**
SIC: **3799** 5012 All terrain vehicles (ATV); Motorcycles

(G-2519)
MISCELLNOUS MTALS FBRCTION INC
18828 Us Highway 50 (45601-9268)
PHONE..............................740 779-3071
Robert J Onda, *Pr*
EMP: 10 EST: 1999
SALES (est): 244.83K **Privately Held**
SIC: **3499** Friction material, made from powdered metal

(G-2520)
NATIONAL INDUS CONCEPTS INC
Also Called: Nic Global
170 N Park Dr (45601-7823)
PHONE..............................615 989-9101
EMP: 235
SALES (corp-wide): 107.03MM **Privately Held**
Web: www.nicglobalms.com
SIC: **3444** Sheet metal specialties, not stamped
PA: National Industrial Concepts, Inc.
23518 63rd Ave Se
Woodinville WA 98072
425 489-4300

(G-2521)
ON THE MANTLE LLC
Also Called: W.britain Model Figures
20 E Water St (45601-2534)
PHONE..............................740 702-1803
Edward Kunzelman, *Managing Member*
EMP: 6 EST: 2020
SALES (est): 271.06K **Privately Held**
SIC: **3999** Miniatures

(G-2522)
PACCAR INC
Paccar
65 Kenworth Dr (45601-8829)
P.O. Box 2345 (45601-0998)
PHONE..............................740 774-5111
Doug Littick, *Bmch Mgr*
EMP: 76
SALES (corp-wide): 35.13B **Publicly Held**
Web: www.paccar.com
SIC: **3711** 3715 3713 Truck and tractor truck assembly; Truck trailers; Truck and bus bodies
PA: Paccar Inc
777 106th Ave Ne
Bellevue WA 98004
425 468-7400

(G-2523)
PARRY CO
33630 Old Route 35 (45601-9117)
PHONE..............................740 884-4893
Dave Merideth, *Pr*
Cassandra Bolt-merideth, *VP*
EMP: 9 EST: 1936
SQ FT: 30,000
SALES (est): 934.53K **Privately Held**
Web: www.parryco.com
SIC: **1442** Construction sand and gravel

(G-2524)
PELLETIER BROTHERS MFG INC
4000 Sulphur Lick Rd (45601)
PHONE..............................740 774-4704
Chris Pelletier, *Pr*
Mark Pelletier, *VP*
EMP: 16 EST: 1992
SQ FT: 7,000
SALES (est): 1.89MM **Privately Held**
Web: www.pellbro.com
SIC: **3479** Coating of metals and formed products

(G-2525)
PIXELLE SPCIALTY SOLUTIONS LLC
232 E 8th St (45601-3564)
PHONE..............................740 772-3111
EMP: 959
SALES (corp-wide): 760.06MM **Privately Held**
Web: www.pixelle.com
SIC: **2621** Specialty or chemically treated papers
PA: Pixelle Specialty Solutions Llc
228 S Main St
Spring Grove PA 17362
717 225-4711

(G-2526)
PPG INDUSTRIES INC
Also Called: PPG Chillicothe
7012 Chillicoth (45601)
PHONE..............................740 774-8734
Amanda Moore, *Acctnt*
EMP: 34
SALES (corp-wide): 17.65B **Publicly Held**
Web: www.ppg.com
SIC: **2851** Paints and allied products
PA: Ppg Industries, Inc.
1 Ppg Pl
Pittsburgh PA 15272
412 434-3131

(G-2527)
PPG INDUSTRIES INC
Also Called: PPG Regional Support Center
848 Southern Ave (45601-9123)
PHONE..............................740 774-7600
Melissa Wills, *Brnch Mgr*
EMP: 37
SALES (corp-wide): 17.65B **Publicly Held**
Web: www.ppg.com
SIC: **2851** Paints and allied products
PA: Ppg Industries, Inc.
1 Ppg Pl
Pittsburgh PA 15272
412 434-3131

(G-2528)
PPG INDUSTRIES INC
Also Called: PPG Aerospace
848 Southern Ave (45601-9123)
P.O. Box 7011 (45601)
PHONE..............................740 774-7600
EMP: 44
SALES (corp-wide): 17.65B **Publicly Held**
Web: www.ppg.com
SIC: **2851** Paints and allied products
PA: Ppg Industries, Inc.
1 Ppg Pl
Pittsburgh PA 15272
412 434-3131

(G-2529)
PRINTEX INCORPORATED (PA)
Also Called: Printex-Same Day Printing
185 E Main St (45601-2507)
P.O. Box 1626 (45601-5626)
PHONE..............................740 773-0088
TOLL FREE: 800
Jeffrey G Marshall, *Pr*
Gene T Marshall, *VP*
EMP: 10 EST: 1975
SQ FT: 3,000
SALES (est): 944.88K
SALES (corp-wide): 944.88K **Privately Held**
Web: www.visitprintex.com
SIC: **2759** 2752 Letterpress printing; Offset printing

(G-2530)
R L S CORPORATION
Also Called: R L S Recycling
990 Eastern Ave (45601-3658)
P.O. Box 327 (45601-0327)
PHONE..............................740 773-1440
Charles Stevens, *Pr*

EMP: 13 EST: 1923
SQ FT: 14,000
SALES (est): 855.08K **Privately Held**
SIC: **5093** 3341 Ferrous metal scrap and waste; Secondary nonferrous metals

(G-2531)
R L WALLER CONSTRUCTION INC
645 Alum Cliff Rd (45601-8533)
PHONE..............................740 772-6185
R l Waller, *Prin*
EMP: 11 EST: 2002
SALES (est): 883.13K **Privately Held**
SIC: **1521** 3441 General remodeling, single-family houses; Building components, structural steel

(G-2532)
RIFFLE MACHINE WORKS INC (PA)
Also Called: Riffle & Sons
5746 State Route 159 (45601-8956)
PHONE..............................740 775-2838
Bob Riffle, *Pr*
Mike Riffle, *VP*
Tim Riffle, *VP*
Mark Riffle, *VP*
EMP: 8 EST: 1980
SQ FT: 3,500
SALES (est): 2.61MM **Privately Held**
SIC: **3599** Machine shop, jobbing and repair

(G-2533)
ROSS-CO REDI-MIX CO INC (PA)
6430 State Route 159 (45601-8956)
PHONE..............................740 775-4466
Todd Wrightsel, *Pr*
Connie Wrightsel, *Sec*
Thomas Overly, *Prin*
EMP: 15 EST: 1962
SALES (est): 2.96MM
SALES (corp-wide): 2.96MM **Privately Held**
SIC: **3273** Ready-mixed concrete

(G-2534)
SHELLY MATERIALS INC
1177 Hopetown Rd (45601-8224)
PHONE..............................740 775-4567
Rusty Scott, *Mgr*
EMP: 26
SALES (corp-wide): 32.72B **Privately Held**
Web: www.shellyco.com
SIC: **3273** Ready-mixed concrete
HQ: Shelly Materials, Inc.
80 Park Dr
Thornville OH 43076
740 246-6315

(G-2535)
STAR CITY PRESS LLC
931 E Water St (45601-2772)
P.O. Box 6023 (45601-6023)
PHONE..............................740 500-0320
EMP: 6 EST: 2020
SALES (est): 75.6K **Privately Held**
Web: www.metro-ds.com
SIC: **2741** 2732 Miscellaneous publishing; Books, printing and binding

(G-2536)
STAT INDUSTRIES INC (PA)
Also Called: Stat Index Tab
137 Stone Rd (45601-9709)
PHONE..............................740 779-6561
Robert Kellough, *CEO*
Susanna Kellough, *CFO*
Chris Kellough, *Prin*
EMP: 7 EST: 1991
SQ FT: 6,000
SALES (est): 900.68K **Privately Held**
Web: www.statindex.com

Chillicothe - Ross County (G-2537)

SIC: 2675 Index cards, die-cut: made from purchased materials

(G-2537)
STAT INDUSTRIES INC
Also Called: Stat Index Tab Company
137 Stone Rd (45601-9709)
PHONE................................740 779-6561
EMP: 6
Web: www.statindex.com
SIC: 2675 Index cards, die-cut: made from purchased materials
PA: Stat Industries, Inc.
   137 Stone Rd
   Chillicothe OH 45601

(G-2538)
THE KITCHEN COLLECTION LLC
Also Called: Le Gourmet Chef
71 E Water St (45601-2535)
PHONE................................740 773-9150
▲ **EMP:** 1495
SIC: 3634 5719 Toasters, electric: household; Kitchenware

(G-2539)
TRIM SYSTEMS OPERATING CORP
75 Chamber Dr (45601-7612)
PHONE................................740 772-5998
EMP: 373
SALES (corp-wide): 994.68MM **Publicly Held**
Web: www.cvgrp.com
SIC: 2396 Automotive and apparel trimmings
HQ: Trim Systems Operating Corp.
   7800 Walton Pkwy
   New Albany OH 43054
   614 289-5360

(G-2540)
TYKMA INC
Also Called: Tykma Electrox
370 Gateway Dr (45601-3976)
P.O. Box 917 (45601-0917)
PHONE................................877 318-9562
Terry Allison, *CEO*
Karen Cyrus, *CFO*
Gregory Cox, *Genl Mgr*
EMP: 53 **EST:** 1970
SQ FT: 50,000
SALES (est): 10.19MM
SALES (corp-wide): 31.96MM **Privately Held**
Web: www.permanentmarking.com
SIC: 3541 3555 Machine tools, metal cutting type; Engraving machinery and equipment, except plates
PA: 600 Group Public Limited Company(The)
   42 Berkeley Square
   London W1J 5

(G-2541)
VITATOE INDUSTRIES INC (PA)
100 Chamber Dr (45601-7612)
P.O. Box 224 (45601-0224)
PHONE................................740 773-2425
EMP: 44 **EST:** 1981
SALES (est): 9.08MM
SALES (corp-wide): 9.08MM **Privately Held**
Web: www.vitatoe.com
SIC: 3713 Truck and bus bodies

(G-2542)
YSK CORPORATION
1 Colomet Rd (45601-8819)
PHONE................................740 774-7315
Kenzaburo Matsuo, *Pr*
H Naiki, *
Reiichi Hohda, *

▲ **EMP:** 279 **EST:** 1988
SQ FT: 200,000
SALES (est): 50.95MM **Privately Held**
SIC: 3469 Machine parts, stamped or pressed metal
HQ: Yanagawa Seiki Co., Ltd.
   1-3-5, Shinsayama
   Sayama STM 350-1

Chippewa Lake
Medina County

(G-2543)
ULTRABILT PLAY SYSTEMS NOVA LT
437 Northvale Dr (44215-9719)
PHONE................................234 248-4414
Julie J Bennett, *Prin*
EMP: 6 **EST:** 2010
SALES (est): 213.94K **Privately Held**
SIC: 3949 Sporting and athletic goods, nec

Cincinnati
Clermont County

(G-2544)
5ME LLC
4270 Ivy Pointe Blvd Ste 100 (45245-0004)
P.O. Box 541085 (45254-1085)
PHONE................................513 719-1600
William A Horwarth, *Pr*
Jeffery Price, *
Chris Chapman, *
EMP: 45 **EST:** 2013
SALES (est): 9.68MM
SALES (corp-wide): 9.68MM **Privately Held**
Web: www.5me.com
SIC: 3544 8742 Special dies, tools, jigs, and fixtures; Business management consultant
PA: 5me Holdings Llc
   4270 Ivy Pointe Blvd # 240
   Cincinnati OH 45245
   859 534-4872

(G-2545)
A & P TECHNOLOGY INC
4622 E Tech Dr (45245-1000)
PHONE................................513 688-3200
Andrew Head, *Brnch Mgr*
EMP: 50
Web: www.braider.com
SIC: 2241 Narrow fabric mills
PA: A & P Technology, Inc.
   4595 E Tech Dr
   Cincinnati OH 45245

(G-2546)
A & P TECHNOLOGY INC
4578 E Tech Dr (45245-1054)
PHONE................................513 688-3200
Andrew Head, *Brnch Mgr*
EMP: 50
Web: www.braider.com
SIC: 2241 Narrow fabric mills
PA: A & P Technology, Inc.
   4595 E Tech Dr
   Cincinnati OH 45245

(G-2547)
A & P TECHNOLOGY INC
4624 E Tech Dr (45245)
PHONE................................513 688-3200
Rhonda Slominski, *Brnch Mgr*
EMP: 50
SQ FT: 1,880
Web: www.braider.com
SIC: 2241 Narrow fabric mills
PA: A & P Technology, Inc.

4595 E Tech Dr
Cincinnati OH 45245

(G-2548)
A & P TECHNOLOGY INC
4599 E Tech Dr (45245-1055)
PHONE................................513 688-3200
Keith Cnarr, *Mgr*
EMP: 50
Web: www.braider.com
SIC: 2241 Webbing, braids and belting
PA: A & P Technology, Inc.
   4595 E Tech Dr
   Cincinnati OH 45245

(G-2549)
A & P TECHNOLOGY INC (PA)
4595 E Tech Dr (45245-1055)
PHONE................................513 688-3200
◆ **EMP:** 20 **EST:** 1994
SQ FT: 75,000
SALES (est): 43.75MM **Privately Held**
Web: www.braider.com
SIC: 2241 Webbing, braids and belting

(G-2550)
ADGO INCORPORATED
3988 Mcmann Rd (45245-2308)
PHONE................................513 752-6880
Robert C Reynolds, *Pr*
Rick Elliott, *
Mike Cliett, *
Kelly Throckmorton, *
EMP: 23 **EST:** 1957
SQ FT: 30,000
SALES (est): 4.86MM **Privately Held**
Web: www.adgoinc.com
SIC: 3613 Control panels, electric

(G-2551)
ALUFAB INC
Also Called: Alufab
1018 Seabrook Way (45245)
PHONE................................513 528-7281
Doug Nimmo, *Pr*
Fred Mileham, *VP*
▲ **EMP:** 6 **EST:** 2005
SQ FT: 4,000
SALES (est): 938.93K **Privately Held**
Web: www.alufabinc.com
SIC: 3354 Aluminum extruded products

(G-2552)
ANTHE MACHINE WORKS INC
2 Locust Hill Rd (45245-3114)
PHONE................................859 431-1035
Donald H Anthe, *Pr*
Mark F Anthe, *Sec*
Douglas J Anthe, *Sls Mgr*
EMP: 7 **EST:** 1897
SALES (est): 641.35K **Privately Held**
Web: www.vintagemachinery.org
SIC: 5084 3545 Machine tools and accessories; Cutting tools for machine tools

(G-2553)
BEACHS TREES SLCTIVE HRVSTG LL
Also Called: Beachs Trees
915 Wilma Cir (45245-2220)
PHONE................................513 289-5976
Brian Beach, *Prin*
EMP: 9 **EST:** 2013
SQ FT: 2,500
SALES (est): 488.71K **Privately Held**
Web: www.beachstrees.com
SIC: 2411 Logging camps and contractors

(G-2554)
CINCINNATI EYE INST - ESTGATE
601 Ivy Gtwy Ste 301 (45245-1899)
PHONE................................513 984-5133
EMP: 13 **EST:** 1945
SALES (est): 75.74K **Privately Held**
Web: www.cincinnatieye.com
SIC: 8049 3827 Offices of health practitioner; Optical instruments and lenses

(G-2555)
CLIPPER PRODUCTS INC
Also Called: Clipper Products
675 Cincinnati Batavia Pike (45245-1028)
PHONE................................513 688-7300
David J Durham, *Pr*
Gerold J Zobrist, *Ch Bd*
▲ **EMP:** 6 **EST:** 1971
SQ FT: 16,000
SALES (est): 622.74K **Privately Held**
Web: www.clippercorp.com
SIC: 3161 Cases, carrying, nec

(G-2556)
CURTISS-WRIGHT FLOW CTRL CORP
Also Called: Qualtech NP
4600 E Tech Dr (45245-1000)
PHONE................................513 528-7900
EMP: 82
SALES (corp-wide): 2.85B **Publicly Held**
Web: www.curtisswright.com
SIC: 3443 8734 Fabricated plate work (boiler shop); Testing laboratories
HQ: Curtiss-Wright Flow Control Corporation
   1966 Broadhollow Rd Ste E
   Farmingdale NY 11735
   631 293-3800

(G-2557)
DRS LEONARDO INC
4043 Mcmann Rd (45245-1960)
PHONE................................513 943-1111
Rich Reynolds, *Brnch Mgr*
EMP: 29
SALES (corp-wide): 15.28B **Publicly Held**
Web: www.leonardodrs.com
SIC: 3812 Search and navigation equipment
HQ: Leonardo Drs, Inc.
   2345 Crystal Dr Ste 1000
   Arlington VA 22202
   703 416-8000

(G-2558)
ELITE BIOMEDICAL SOLUTIONS LLC
756 Cincinnati Batavia Pike Ste C (45245-1277)
PHONE................................513 207-0602
Jeff Smith, *Managing Member*
EMP: 13 **EST:** 2012
SALES (est): 5.51MM **Privately Held**
Web: www.elitebiomedicalsolutions.com
SIC: 3841 7699 7389 Surgical and medical instruments; Medical equipment repair, non-electric; Business services, nec

(G-2559)
FUNTOWN PLAYGROUNDS INC
839 Cypresspoint Ct (45245-3352)
PHONE................................513 871-8585
Orville Wright, *Pr*
Marty Kremer, *VP*
EMP: 11 **EST:** 1979
SALES (est): 420.44K **Privately Held**
Web: www.thinklocalsouthernindiana.com
SIC: 3949 Playground equipment

Cincinnati - Hamilton County

(G-2560)
GBC INTERNATIONAL LLC
1091 Ohio Pike (45245-2339)
PHONE..................513 943-7283
Michael R Adams, *Prin*
EMP: 9 **EST:** 2015
SALES (est): 413.72K **Privately Held**
SIC: 2653 Corrugated and solid fiber boxes

(G-2561)
GENERAL DATA COMPANY INC (PA)
4354 Ferguson Dr (45245-1667)
P.O. Box 541165 (45254-1165)
PHONE..................513 752-7978
Peter Wenzel, *Pr*
Jim Burns, *
Erin Johnson, *
Michele Marsh, *
◆ **EMP:** 280 **EST:** 1980
SQ FT: 175,000
SALES (est): 91.21MM
SALES (corp-wide): 91.21MM **Privately Held**
Web: www.general-data.com
SIC: 2679 5046 5084 2759 Labels, paper: made from purchased material; Commercial equipment, nec; Printing trades machinery, equipment, and supplies; Commercial printing, nec

(G-2562)
GENERAL DATA HEALTHCARE INC
4043 Mcmann Rd (45245-1960)
PHONE..................513 752-7978
Peter Wenzel, *CEO*
EMP: 9 **EST:** 2015
SALES (est): 1.5MM **Privately Held**
Web: www.general-data.com
SIC: 3565 Labeling machines, industrial

(G-2563)
HAWKS & ASSOCIATES INC
Also Called: Hawks Tag
1029 Seabrook Way (45245-1964)
P.O. Box 541207 (45254-1207)
PHONE..................513 752-4311
James M Hawks, *Pr*
EMP: 28 **EST:** 1973
SQ FT: 15,000
SALES (est): 6.16MM **Privately Held**
Web: www.hawkstag.com
SIC: 2759 2752 Flexographic printing; Commercial printing, lithographic

(G-2564)
HDT EXPEDITIONARY SYSTEMS INC
1032 Seabrook Way (45245-1963)
PHONE..................513 943-1111
EMP: 17
Web: www.hdtglobal.com
SIC: 3429 Hardware, nec
HQ: Hdt Expeditionary Systems, Inc.
30500 Aurora Rd Ste 100
Solon OH 44139
216 438-6111

(G-2565)
HUNTER DEFENSE TECH INC
1032 Seabrook Way (45245-1963)
PHONE..................513 943-7880
Angela Cowan, *Brnch Mgr*
EMP: 12
Web: www.hdtglobal.com
SIC: 3812 Search and navigation equipment
PA: Hunter Defense Technologies, Inc.
30500 Aurora Rd Ste 100
Solon OH 44139

(G-2566)
INSTANT SURFACE SOLUTIONS INC
3572 Calumet Dr (45245-3046)
PHONE..................513 266-1667
Deborah Eccard, *Prin*
EMP: 6 **EST:** 2007
SALES (est): 135.04K **Privately Held**
SIC: 2752 Commercial printing, lithographic

(G-2567)
J BEST INC
Also Called: Fastsigns
4476 Glen Este Withamsville Rd (45245)
PHONE..................513 943-7000
EMP: 6 **EST:** 2020
SALES (est): 262.4K **Privately Held**
Web: www.fastsigns.com
SIC: 3993 Signs and advertising specialties

(G-2568)
L3 TECHNOLOGIES INC
Electro Fab Division
3975 Mcmann Rd (45245-2307)
PHONE..................513 943-2000
Charls King, *Genl Mgr*
EMP: 40
SALES (corp-wide): 19.42B **Publicly Held**
Web: www.l3harris.com
SIC: 3672 Printed circuit boards
HQ: L3 Technologies, Inc.
600 3rd Ave Fl 34
New York NY 10016
321 727-9100

(G-2569)
L3HARRIS ELECTRODYNAMICS INC
Also Called: Electrodynamics, Inc.
3975 Mcmann Rd (45245-2307)
PHONE..................847 259-0740
Donald A Spetter, *Pr*
Stephen Post, *
Steven M Post, *
EMP: 195 **EST:** 1981
SQ FT: 46,000
SALES (est): 77.99MM
SALES (corp-wide): 19.42B **Publicly Held**
Web: www.l3harris.com
SIC: 3577 3812 3824 3823 Data conversion equipment, media-to-media: computer; Flight recorders; Controls, revolution and timing instruments; Process control instruments
HQ: L3 Technologies, Inc.
600 3rd Ave Fl 34
New York NY 10016
321 727-9100

(G-2570)
L3HARRIS FZING ORD SYSTEMS INC
3975 Mc Mann Rd (45245-2307)
PHONE..................513 943-2000
Michael T Strianese, *CEO*
Eric Ellis, *Pr*
Curtis Brunson, *Ex VP*
Ralph G D'ambrosio, *CFO*
Steven M Post, *Sr VP*
EMP: 575 **EST:** 1967
SQ FT: 236,000
SALES (est): 215.82MM
SALES (corp-wide): 19.42B **Publicly Held**
Web: www.l3harris.com
SIC: 3483 Arming and fusing devices for missiles
HQ: L3 Technologies, Inc.
600 3rd Ave Fl 34
New York NY 10016
321 727-9100

(G-2571)
LINTECH ELECTRONICS LLC
4435 Aichoitz Rd Ste 500 (45245-1692)
P.O. Box 54436 (45254-0436)
PHONE..................513 528-6190
EMP: 18 **EST:** 1994
SALES (est): 1.15MM **Privately Held**
Web: www.lintech-electronics.com
SIC: 8711 3679 Electrical or electronic engineering; Electronic circuits

(G-2572)
PRO AUDIO
671 Cincinnati Batavia Pike (45245-1002)
PHONE..................513 752-7500
Frank Marino, *Owner*
EMP: 6 **EST:** 2002
SALES (est): 325.65K **Privately Held**
Web: www.proaudio.com
SIC: 3651 Audio electronic systems

(G-2573)
QUEEN CITY FORGING COMPANY
Also Called: Qcforge.com
1019 Seabrook Way (45245-1964)
PHONE..................513 321-2003
Howard R Mayer, *Ch Bd*
John Mayer, *VP*
Ron Secen, *VP*
George C Allen, *Prin*
▲ **EMP:** 16 **EST:** 1881
SQ FT: 36,000
SALES (est): 4.69MM **Privately Held**
Web: www.qcforge.com
SIC: 3462 Iron and steel forgings

(G-2574)
TAKE IT FOR GRANITE LLC
3898 Mcmann Rd (45245-2347)
PHONE..................513 735-0555
Dustin Wallace, *Managing Member*
Amy Jo Wallace, *Managing Member*
▲ **EMP:** 15 **EST:** 2002
SQ FT: 12,000
SALES (est): 1.11MM **Privately Held**
Web: www.takeitforgranitecincy.com
SIC: 3281 Cut stone and stone products

(G-2575)
TWR SERVICES LLC
871 Meadow Ridge Dr (45245-1805)
PHONE..................513 604-4796
Thomas W Runck, *Prin*
EMP: 6 **EST:** 2012
SALES (est): 329.91K **Privately Held**
SIC: 3471 Electroplating of metals or formed products

(G-2576)
UNITED TOOL SUPPLY INC
Also Called: K M I
851 Ohio Pike Ste 101 (45245-2293)
PHONE..................513 752-6000
Russell F Young, *Pr*
EMP: 6 **EST:** 1973
SQ FT: 8,000
SALES (est): 1.59MM **Privately Held**
Web: www.united-tool.com
SIC: 5085 3823 Industrial supplies; Process control instruments

(G-2577)
XCITE SYSTEMS CORPORATION
675 Cincinnati Batavia Pike (45245-1028)
PHONE..................513 965-0300
EMP: 6 **EST:** 1997
SQ FT: 2,000
SALES (est): 692.56K **Privately Held**
Web: www.xcitesystems.com

SIC: 3829 8711 Stress, strain, and flaw detecting/measuring equipment; Engineering services

Cincinnati
Hamilton County

(G-2578)
1 A LIFESAFER INC (PA)
Also Called: Ignition Interlock
3630 Park 42 Dr Ste 140c (45241-2131)
PHONE..................513 651-9560
Chris Linchwaite, *CEO*
Richard Freund, *
Craig Armstrong, *
Glenn Kermes, *
EMP: 21 **EST:** 1992
SALES (est): 14.21MM **Privately Held**
Web: www.lifesafer.com
SIC: 3829 Measuring and controlling devices, nec

(G-2579)
2C TRANSPORT LLC
2344 Kemper Ln (45206-7500)
PHONE..................513 799-5278
EMP: 6 **EST:** 2021
SALES (est): 150K **Privately Held**
SIC: 3537 Trucks, tractors, loaders, carriers, and similar equipment

(G-2580)
400 SW 7TH STREET PARTNERS LTD
Also Called: Ohio Construction News
3825 Edwards Rd Ste 800 (45209-1289)
PHONE..................440 826-4700
Tim Blaicher, *Brnch Mgr*
EMP: 39
Web: www.constructionjournal.com
SIC: 2721 Periodicals
PA: 400 Sw 7th Street Partners, Ltd.
3825 Edwards Rd Ste 800
Cincinnati OH 45209

(G-2581)
400 SW 7TH STREET PARTNERS LTD (PA)
Also Called: Construction Journal
3825 Edwards Rd Ste 800 (45209-1289)
PHONE..................772 781-2144
EMP: 41 **EST:** 1996
SALES (est): 7.67MM **Privately Held**
Web: www.constructionjournal.com
SIC: 2721 Trade journals: publishing only, not printed on site

(G-2582)
A & B DEBURRING COMPANY
Also Called: A & B
525 Carr St (45203-1815)
PHONE..................513 723-0444
TOLL FREE: 800
Robert Wegman, *Pr*
EMP: 14 **EST:** 1946
SQ FT: 25,000
SALES (est): 4.97MM **Privately Held**
Web: www.abdeburr.com
SIC: 5084 3471 Metal refining machinery and equipment; Polishing, metals or formed products

(G-2583)
A AND V GRINDING INC
Also Called: Midwest Centerless Grinding
1115 Straight St 17 (45214-1735)
PHONE..................937 444-4141
Albert Benedetti, *Pr*
Vera Benedetti, *VP*
EMP: 6 **EST:** 1982

Cincinnati - Hamilton County (G-2584)

GEOGRAPHIC SECTION

SQ FT: 12,500
SALES (est): 497.19K **Privately Held**
Web: www.mpgrinding.com
SIC: 3599 Machine shop, jobbing and repair

(G-2584)
A GOOD MOBILE DETAILING LLC ◆
2464 8 Mile Rd (45244-2614)
PHONE.................513 316-3802
Todd Knight, *Managing Member*
EMP: 6 **EST:** 2022
SALES (est): 273.59K **Privately Held**
Web: www.agoodmobiledetailing.com
SIC: 3714 7389 Cleaners, air, motor vehicle; Business services, nec

(G-2585)
A Z PRINTING INC (PA)
Also Called: A-Z Discount Printing
10122 Reading Rd (45241-3110)
PHONE.................513 733-3900
Bruce Hassel, *Pr*
EMP: 6 **EST:** 1978
SQ FT: 4,000
SALES (est): 725.12K
SALES (corp-wide): 725.12K **Privately Held**
Web: www.printing-cincinnati.com
SIC: 2752 Offset printing

(G-2586)
A&E SIGNS AND LIGHTING LLC
1030 Straight St (45214-1734)
PHONE.................513 541-0024
Elvera Maier, *Prin*
EMP: 15
SALES (est): 625.8K **Privately Held**
SIC: 3993 Signs and advertising specialties

(G-2587)
AA HAND SANITIZER
2230 Park Ave Ste 202 (45206-2782)
PHONE.................513 506-7575
Alex Ebner, *Mgr*
Alex Ebner, *Pt*
David Bade, *COO*
EMP: 9 **EST:** 2020
SALES (est): 500K **Privately Held**
Web: saferhands.zachzeltman.com
SIC: 2844 Cosmetic preparations

(G-2588)
AAA GALVANIZING - JOLIET INC
Also Called: Azz Galvanizing - Cincinnati
4454 Steel Pl (45209-1135)
PHONE.................513 871-5700
Lori Wilp, *Manager*
EMP: 13
SALES (corp-wide): 1.54B **Publicly Held**
SIC: 3479 Hot dip coating of metals or formed products
HQ: Aaa Galvanizing - Joliet, Inc.
625 Mills Rd
Joliet IL 60433

(G-2589)
AB BONDED LOCKSMITHS INC
Also Called: Tri County Locksmith
4344 Montgomery Rd (45212-3104)
PHONE.................513 531-7334
Russell Mcgurrin, *Pr*
Russell Mcgurrin, *CEO*
Cindy Mcgurrin, *CFO*
EMP: 7 **EST:** 1933
SQ FT: 5,000
SALES (est): 702.15K **Privately Held**
Web: www.ablocks.com
SIC: 7699 3429 Locksmith shop; Hardware, nec

(G-2590)
ABC SIGNS INC
38 W Mcmicken Ave (45202-7718)
PHONE.................513 241-8884
Cliff Meyer, *Pr*
Thomas Meyer, *VP*
EMP: 10 **EST:** 1979
SQ FT: 30,500
SALES (est): 844.41K **Privately Held**
Web: www.abcsign.com
SIC: 3993 2394 1799 7359 Electric signs; Awnings, fabric: made from purchased materials; Sign installation and maintenance; Sign rental

(G-2591)
ABEL MANUFACTURING COMPANY
3474 Beekman St (45223-2425)
PHONE.................513 681-5000
Carl Abel Junior, *Pr*
Michael Nagel, *VP*
Ardath Abel, *Sec*
Katherine Nagel, *Treas*
Mark Abel, *VP*
EMP: 15 **EST:** 1966
SQ FT: 14,000
SALES (est): 2.22MM **Privately Held**
Web: www.abelfab.com
SIC: 3451 Screw machine products

(G-2592)
ABRA AUTO BODY & GLASS LP
Also Called: ABRA Autobody & Glass
6947 E Kemper Rd (45249-1085)
PHONE.................513 247-3400
EMP: 8
Web: www.abraauto.com
SIC: 7532 2851 Body shop, automotive; Paint removers
HQ: Abra Auto Body & Glass Lp
7225 Northland Dr N # 110
Brooklyn Park MN 55428
888 872-2272

(G-2593)
ABRASIVE PRODUCTS
1028 Rosetree Ln (45230-4041)
PHONE.................513 502-9150
Brent Cassil, *Prin*
EMP: 8 **EST:** 2016
SALES (est): 67.51K **Privately Held**
Web: www.surfaceprep.com
SIC: 3291 Abrasive products

(G-2594)
ACCRETECH SBS INC (PA)
8790 Governors Hill Dr (45249-1307)
PHONE.................513 373-4844
Shigeru Umenaka, *Pr*
▲ **EMP:** 7 **EST:** 2009
SALES (est): 840.07K
SALES (corp-wide): 840.07K **Privately Held**
Web: toseiengineering.accretech.com
SIC: 5045 3545 Computers, peripherals, and software; Balancing machines (machine tool accessories)

(G-2595)
ACCURATE GEAR MANUFACTURING CO
16 E 73rd St (45216-2038)
PHONE.................513 761-3220
Dennis M Pauly, *Pr*
David Schachere, *VP*
EMP: 9 **EST:** 1974
SQ FT: 10,500
SALES (est): 947.41K **Privately Held**
Web: www.accurategearmfg.com

SIC: 3462 Iron and steel forgings

(G-2596)
ACTIVE DAILY LIVING LLC
3308 Bishop St (45220-1858)
PHONE.................513 607-6769
Daniel E Ansel, *Prin*
EMP: 7 **EST:** 2013
SALES (est): 155.55K **Privately Held**
Web: www.activedailyliving.com
SIC: 2711 Newspapers, publishing and printing

(G-2597)
ADLER & COMPANY INC
Also Called: Camargo Construction
6801 Shawnee Run Rd (45243-2417)
PHONE.................513 248-1500
Harry Adler Senior, *Pr*
Harry Adler Junior, *Sec*
EMP: 7 **EST:** 2003
SALES (est): 128.86K **Privately Held**
SIC: 3272 Paving materials, prefabricated concrete

(G-2598)
ADVANCED GROUND SYSTEMS
Also Called: Agse Tooling
1650 Magnolia Dr (45215-1976)
PHONE.................513 402-7226
Roy Stone, *Mgr*
EMP: 18
SALES (corp-wide): 26.13MM **Privately Held**
Web: www.agsecorp.com
SIC: 3724 Aircraft engines and engine parts
HQ: Advanced Ground Systems Engineering Llc
10805 Painter Ave
Santa Fe Springs CA 90670
562 906-9300

(G-2599)
AFFINITY DISP EXPOSITIONS INC
Also Called: Adex International
1375 Spring Park Walk (45215-0046)
PHONE.................513 771-2339
EMP: 16
SALES (corp-wide): 19.2MM **Privately Held**
Web: www.adex-intl.com
SIC: 3993 Signs and advertising specialties
PA: Affinity Displays & Expositions, Inc.
1301 Glendale Milford Rd
Cincinnati OH 45215
513 771-2339

(G-2600)
AFFINITY DISP EXPOSITIONS INC (PA)
Also Called: Adex International
1301 Glendale Milford Rd (45215-1210)
PHONE.................513 771-2339
Timothy Murphy, *Pr*
Walt Pottschmidt, *Ex VP*
Mike Pierdiluca, *VP*
Joe Rickard, *CFO*
▲ **EMP:** 100 **EST:** 1978
SQ FT: 250,000
SALES (est): 19.2MM
SALES (corp-wide): 19.2MM **Privately Held**
Web: www.adex-intl.com
SIC: 3993 Displays and cutouts, window and lobby

(G-2601)
AG ANTENNA GROUP LLC (PA)
11923 Montgomery Rd (45249-2019)
PHONE.................513 289-6521
EMP: 9 **EST:** 2014

SQ FT: 2,500
SALES (est): 702.19K
SALES (corp-wide): 702.19K **Privately Held**
Web: www.agantennagroup.com
SIC: 3663 Antennas, transmitting and communications

(G-2602)
AGNONE-KELLY ENTERPRISES INC
Also Called: Thermalgraphics
11658 Baen Rd (45242-1600)
P.O. Box 428543 (45242-8543)
PHONE.................800 634-6503
Kevin Kelly, *Pr*
Elizabeth Kelly, *VP*
EMP: 6 **EST:** 1987
SQ FT: 20,000
SALES (est): 512.21K **Privately Held**
SIC: 2759 Commercial printing, nec

(G-2603)
AHALOGY
1140 Main St # 3 (45202-7236)
PHONE.................314 974-5599
Michael Wohlschlaeger, *CEO*
EMP: 32 **EST:** 2014
SALES (est): 915.89K **Privately Held**
Web: www.quotient.com
SIC: 2741 Internet publishing and broadcasting

(G-2604)
AIRECON MANUFACTURING CORP
5271 Brotherton Rd (45227-2103)
PHONE.................513 561-5522
Joseph E Gutierrez, *Pr*
Timothy Kidd, *
David W Miller, *
▲ **EMP:** 50 **EST:** 1979
SQ FT: 30,000
SALES (est): 10.66MM **Privately Held**
Web: www.airecon.com
SIC: 3564 Air purification equipment

(G-2605)
AIRTX INTERNATIONAL LTD
6320 Wiehe Rd (45237-4214)
PHONE.................513 631-0660
Michael Rawlings, *Pt*
Michael Rawlings, *Pr*
EMP: 10 **EST:** 1993
SQ FT: 7,500
SALES (est): 992.82K **Privately Held**
Web: www.airtx.com
SIC: 3563 Air and gas compressors

(G-2606)
ALDERWOODS (OKLAHOMA) INC
Also Called: Cremation Association Shawnee
311 Elm St Ste 1000 (45202-2736)
PHONE.................903 597-6611
EMP: 8 **EST:** 1967
SALES (est): 246.07K **Privately Held**
SIC: 2711 Newspapers, publishing and printing

(G-2607)
ALL AROUND PRIMO LOGISTICS LLC
6027 Magnolia Woods Way (45247-2608)
PHONE.................513 725-7888
EMP: 6 **EST:** 2021
SALES (est): 510.7K **Privately Held**
SIC: 3537 Trucks: freight, baggage, etc.: industrial, except mining

(G-2608)
ALL CRAFT MANUFACTURING CO
Also Called: Talisman Racing

6500 Glenway Ave Side 2 (45211-4451)
P.O. Box 58651 (45258-0651)
PHONE..............................513 661-3383
Robert W Farrell, *Pr*
Paula Farrell, *VP*
EMP: 15 **EST:** 1987
SQ FT: 3,200
SALES (est): 2.19MM **Privately Held**
Web: www.allcraftmfg.com
SIC: 3599 Machine shop, jobbing and repair

(G-2609)
ALLERGAN SALES LLC
Also Called: Allergan
5000 Brotherton Rd (45209-1105)
PHONE..............................513 271-6800
Doug Yelton, *Brnch Mgr*
EMP: 190
SALES (corp-wide): 54.32B **Publicly Held**
Web: www.abbvie.com
SIC: 2834 Pharmaceutical preparations
HQ: Allergan Sales, Llc
　　2525 Dupont Dr
　　Irvine CA 92612

(G-2610)
ALLERGAN SALES LLC
3941 Brotherton Rd (45209)
PHONE..............................513 271-6800
Greg Yurchak, *Brnch Mgr*
EMP: 23
SALES (corp-wide): 54.32B **Publicly Held**
Web: www.abbvie.com
SIC: 2834 Pharmaceutical preparations
HQ: Allergan Sales, Llc
　　2525 Dupont Dr
　　Irvine CA 92612

(G-2611)
ALLGEIER & SON INC (PA)
6386 Bridgetown Rd (45248-2933)
PHONE..............................513 574-3735
Michael Allgeier, *Owner*
Margaret A Steigerwald, *Treas*
EMP: 18 **EST:** 1964
SQ FT: 800
SALES (est): 3.07MM
SALES (corp-wide): 3.07MM **Privately Held**
Web: www.allgeierandson.com
SIC: 1794 1422 1795 Excavation and grading, building construction; Crushed and broken limestone; Wrecking and demolition work

(G-2612)
ALUCHEM INC (PA)
1 Landy Ln Ste 1 (45215-3489)
PHONE..............................513 733-8519
Ronald P Zapletal, *Pr*
Ronald L Bell, *
Edward L Butera, *
William A Kist, *
◆ **EMP:** 47 **EST:** 1978
SQ FT: 200,000
SALES (est): 24.04MM
SALES (corp-wide): 24.04MM **Privately Held**
Web: www.aluchem.com
SIC: 2819 Industrial inorganic chemicals, nec

(G-2613)
ALUMINUM EXTRUDED SHAPES INC
Also Called: AES
10549 Reading Rd (45241-2524)
PHONE..............................513 563-2205
Robert E Hoeweler, *Pr*
Alan Hoeweler, *Prin*
Reuven Katz, *Prin*
EMP: 115 **EST:** 1946
SQ FT: 130,000
SALES (est): 14.64MM **Privately Held**
Web: www.alum-ext.com
SIC: 3354 3471 3444 Aluminum extruded products; Plating and polishing; Sheet metalwork

(G-2614)
AMANTEA NONWOVENS LLC
6715 Steger Dr (45237-3097)
PHONE..............................513 842-6600
Gianni Boscolo, *
Tom Grabo, *
▲ **EMP:** 12 **EST:** 2004
SQ FT: 77,000
SALES (est): 356.35K **Privately Held**
SIC: 2297 Nonwoven fabrics

(G-2615)
AMERICAN BOTTLING COMPANY
125 E Court St Ste 820 (45202-1201)
PHONE..............................513 381-4891
EMP: 70
Web: www.keurigdrpepper.com
SIC: 2086 Soft drinks: packaged in cans, bottles, etc.
HQ: The American Bottling Company
　　6425 Hall Of Fame Ln
　　Frisco TX 75034

(G-2616)
AMERICAN BOTTLING COMPANY
Also Called: 7 Up/ Royal Crown
5151 Fischer Ave (45217-1157)
PHONE..............................513 242-5151
Mark Wendling, *Mgr*
EMP: 87
Web: www.keurigdrpepper.com
SIC: 2086 Soft drinks: packaged in cans, bottles, etc.
HQ: The American Bottling Company
　　6425 Hall Of Fame Ln
　　Frisco TX 75034

(G-2617)
AMERICAN CITY BUS JOURNALS INC
Also Called: Cincinnati Business Courier
120 E 4th St Ste 230 (45202-4099)
PHONE..............................513 337-9450
Douglas Bolton, *Brnch Mgr*
EMP: 212
SALES (corp-wide): 2.88B **Privately Held**
Web: www.acbj.com
SIC: 2711 2741 Newspapers: publishing only, not printed on site; Miscellaneous publishing
HQ: American City Business Journals, Inc.
　　120 W Morehead St Ste 400
　　Charlotte NC 28202
　　704 973-1000

(G-2618)
AMERICAN GILD OF ENGLISH HNDBE
201 E 5th St (45202-4152)
PHONE..............................937 438-0085
Jennifer Cauhorn, *Ex Dir*
EMP: 9 **EST:** 1986
SQ FT: 2,253
SALES (est): 683.86K **Privately Held**
Web: www.handbellmusicians.org
SIC: 8699 7929 2741 7041 Personal interest organization; Entertainers and entertainment groups; Music, sheet: publishing only, not printed on site; Membership-basis organization hotels

(G-2619)
AMERICAN LEGAL PUBLISHING CORP
525 Vine St Ste 300 (45202-3121)
PHONE..............................513 421-4248
Stephen G Wolf, *Pr*
Cynthia Poweleit, *
EMP: 40 **EST:** 1978
SALES (est): 4.21MM **Privately Held**
Web: www.amlegal.com
SIC: 2731 2741 Books, publishing only; Miscellaneous publishing

(G-2620)
AMERICAN QUICKSILVER COMPANY
646 Rushton Rd (45226-1124)
PHONE..............................513 871-4517
Barney Pogue, *Pr*
Mara Pogue, *Sec*
▲ **EMP:** 9 **EST:** 1993
SALES (est): 739.69K **Privately Held**
Web: www.americanquicksilverco.com
SIC: 3421 Knife blades and blanks

(G-2621)
AMERICRAFT MFG CO INC
7937 School Rd (45249-1533)
PHONE..............................513 489-1047
Erin Giblin, *Pr*
EMP: 11 **EST:** 1979
SQ FT: 55,000
SALES (est): 3.91MM **Privately Held**
Web: www.americraftmfg.com
SIC: 3564 Blowers and fans

(G-2622)
AMPAC HOLDINGS LLC (HQ)
Also Called: Proampac
12025 Tricon Rd (45246-1719)
PHONE..............................513 671-1777
Greg Tucker, *Managing Member*
◆ **EMP:** 700 **EST:** 2001
SQ FT: 220,000
SALES (est): 420.05MM
SALES (corp-wide): 1.58B **Privately Held**
Web: www.proampac.com
SIC: 2673 2677 3081 2674 Plastic bags: made from purchased materials; Envelopes; Unsupported plastics film and sheet; Shopping bags: made from purchased materials
PA: Proampac Holdings Inc.
　　12025 Tricon Rd
　　Cincinnati OH 45246
　　513 671-1777

(G-2623)
AMPAC PACKAGING LLC (HQ)
Also Called: Ampac
12025 Tricon Rd (45246-1719)
PHONE..............................513 671-1777
John Baumann, *CEO*
◆ **EMP:** 106 **EST:** 2006
SALES (est): 412.5MM
SALES (corp-wide): 1.58B **Privately Held**
Web: www.proampac.com
SIC: 3086 5084 Packaging and shipping materials, foamed plastics; Processing and packaging equipment
PA: Proampac Holdings Inc.
　　12025 Tricon Rd
　　Cincinnati OH 45246
　　513 671-1777

(G-2624)
AMPAC PLASTICS LLC
Also Called: Ampac
12025 Tricon Rd (45246-1792)
PHONE..............................513 671-1777
Greg Tucker, *CEO*
Eric Bradford, *
Bob Wheeler, *
▲ **EMP:** 300 **EST:** 1965
SQ FT: 210,000
SALES (est): 112.79MM
SALES (corp-wide): 1.58B **Privately Held**
Web: www.proampac.com
SIC: 2621 2671 Packaging paper; Paper, coated or laminated for packaging
HQ: Ampac Holdings, Llc
　　12025 Tricon Rd
　　Cincinnati OH 45246
　　513 671-1777

(G-2625)
AMPACET CORPORATION
4705 Duke Dr # 400 (45249)
PHONE..............................513 247-5400
Vicky Willsey, *Mgr*
EMP: 12
SALES (corp-wide): 455.35MM **Privately Held**
Web: www.ampacet.com
SIC: 3089 5162 Coloring and finishing of plastics products; Plastics materials and basic shapes
PA: Ampacet Corporation
　　660 White Plins Rd Ste 36
　　Tarrytown NY 10591
　　914 631-6600

(G-2626)
ANCHOR FLANGE COMPANY (PA)
Also Called: Anchor Fluid Power
5553 Murray Ave (45227-2707)
PHONE..............................513 527-3512
▲ **EMP:** 79 **EST:** 1983
SALES (est): 17.98MM
SALES (corp-wide): 17.98MM **Privately Held**
Web: www.anchorfluidpower.com
SIC: 3462 5085 3594 3494 Flange, valve, and pipe fitting forgings, ferrous; Industrial supplies; Fluid power pumps and motors; Valves and pipe fittings, nec

(G-2627)
ANDYS MDTERRANEAN FD PDTS LLC
906 Nassau St (45206-2508)
PHONE..............................513 281-9791
▲ **EMP:** 6 **EST:** 2008
SQ FT: 9,000
SALES (est): 236.9K **Privately Held**
Web: www.andyskabob.com
SIC: 2099 Food preparations, nec

(G-2628)
ANTHONY FLOTTEMESCH & SON INC
8201 Camargo Rd Ste 1 (45243-1469)
PHONE..............................513 561-1212
James Flottemesch, *Pr*
James Flottimish Junior, *VP*
EMP: 10 **EST:** 1942
SQ FT: 13,000
SALES (est): 664.99K **Privately Held**
Web: www.aflottemesch.com
SIC: 2511 2434 2431 Wood household furniture; Wood kitchen cabinets; Millwork

(G-2629)
ANZA INC
3265 Colerain Ave Ste 2 (45225-3301)
PHONE..............................513 542-7337
John Busse, *Pr*
David Burbink, *VP*
▲ **EMP:** 8 **EST:** 1985
SQ FT: 6,000
SALES (est): 508.74K **Privately Held**
Web: www.anzadesign.com
SIC: 3999 Models, general, except toy

Cincinnati - Hamilton County (G-2630)

(G-2630)
APPLE OF HIS EYE INC
Also Called: Apple
796 Denier Pl (45224-1310)
PHONE.....................513 521-0655
Rhyanne Mcdade, *Prin*
EMP: 7 **EST:** 2015
SALES (est): 114.5K **Privately Held**
Web: www.aohei.org
SIC: 3571 Electronic computers

(G-2631)
ARCHER COUNTER DESIGN INC
4433 Verne Ave (45209-1223)
PHONE.....................513 396-7526
Robert Lewis, *Pr*
Tony Williams, *VP*
▲ **EMP:** 9 **EST:** 1983
SQ FT: 15,000
SALES (est): 810K **Privately Held**
SIC: 2541 Table or counter tops, plastic laminated

(G-2632)
ARKU INC
7251 E Kemper Rd (45249-1030)
PHONE.....................513 985-0500
Nicholas Miller, *Pr*
Franck Hirschmann, *
▲ **EMP:** 30 **EST:** 2004
SALES (est): 7.07MM
SALES (corp-wide): 65.95MM **Privately Held**
Web: www.arku.com
SIC: 3549 Wiredrawing and fabricating machinery and equipment, ex. die
PA: Arku Maschinenbau Gmbh
Siemensstr. 11
Baden-Baden BW 76532
722150090

(G-2633)
ARSCO CUSTOM METALS LLC
Also Called: Arsco Manufacturing Company
3330 E Kemper Rd (45241-1538)
PHONE.....................513 385-0555
Gregory Hemmert, *Managing Member*
EMP: 69 **EST:** 1926
SQ FT: 3,000
SALES (est): 10.81MM **Privately Held**
Web: www.arscometals.com
SIC: 3444 Sheet metalwork

(G-2634)
ART GUILD BINDERS INC
Also Called: Happy Booker
1068 Meta Dr (45237-5008)
PHONE.....................513 242-3000
TOLL FREE: 800
Timothy Hugenberg, *Pr*
Gregory M Hugenberg, *
Donald F Cooper, *
▲ **EMP:** 23 **EST:** 1948
SQ FT: 28,000
SALES (est): 2.32MM **Privately Held**
Web: www.artguildbinders.com
SIC: 2782 2675 2789 Looseleaf binders and devices; Die-cut paper and board; Bookbinding and repairing: trade, edition, library, etc.

(G-2635)
ART WOODWORKING & MFG CO
4238 Dane Ave (45223-1856)
PHONE.....................513 681-2986
Ralph R Dickman, *Pr*
EMP: 30 **EST:** 1922
SQ FT: 23,000
SALES (est): 4.91MM **Privately Held**
Web: www.artwoodmfg.net
SIC: 2431 Millwork

(G-2636)
ASPEC INC
5810 Carothers St (45227-2350)
PHONE.....................513 561-9922
Kerry L Bollmer, *Pr*
EMP: 9 **EST:** 1978
SQ FT: 11,000
SALES (est): 994.54K **Privately Held**
Web: www.aspecplastics.com
SIC: 3089 3544 Injection molding of plastics; Forms (molds), for foundry and plastics working machinery

(G-2637)
ASSOCIATED PREMIUM CORPORATION
1870 Summit Rd (45237-2804)
PHONE.....................513 679-4444
◆ **EMP:** 40 **EST:** 1975
SALES (est): 9.29MM **Privately Held**
Web: www.apcpromos.com
SIC: 5199 5064 3993 3911 Advertising specialties; Electrical appliances, television and radio; Signs and advertising specialties; Jewelry, precious metal

(G-2638)
ASTRO MET INC (PA)
9974 Springfield Pike (45215-1425)
PHONE.....................513 772-1242
Donald Graham, *Pr*
EMP: 18 **EST:** 1961
SQ FT: 39,000
SALES (est): 2.54MM
SALES (corp-wide): 2.54MM **Privately Held**
Web: www.astromet.com
SIC: 3299 Ceramic fiber

(G-2639)
AT&T CORP
Also Called: AT&T
7875 Montgomery Rd Ofc (45236-4305)
PHONE.....................513 792-9300
EMP: 9
SALES (corp-wide): 122.43B **Publicly Held**
Web: www.att.com
SIC: 4813 3661 3357 3571 Local and long distance telephone communications; Telephone and telegraph apparatus; Communication wire; Electronic computers
HQ: At&t Enterprises, Llc
208 S Akard St
Dallas TX 75202
800 403-3302

(G-2640)
ATLANTIC SIGN COMPANY INC
2328 Florence Ave (45206-2431)
PHONE.....................513 383-1504
William Yusko, *Pr*
Cj Mcdonald, *VP*
Aleisa Yusko, *
EMP: 27 **EST:** 2003
SQ FT: 15,000
SALES (est): 4.82MM **Privately Held**
Web: www.atlanticsigncompany.com
SIC: 3993 Signs and advertising specialties

(G-2641)
ATR DISTRIBUTING COMPANY (PA)
Also Called: Atr Automation
11857 Kemper Springs Dr (45240-1641)
P.O. Box 85 (45002-0085)
PHONE.....................513 353-1800
EMP: 8 **EST:** 1981
SALES (est): 4.74MM
SALES (corp-wide): 4.74MM **Privately Held**
Web: www.atrautomation.com
SIC: 7371 7372 Computer software systems analysis and design, custom; Business oriented computer software

(G-2642)
ATR DISTRIBUTING COMPANY
Wonderware Cincinnati
11857 Kemper Springs Dr (45240)
PHONE.....................513 353-1800
Joe Murray, *Brnch Mgr*
EMP: 19
SALES (corp-wide): 4.74MM **Privately Held**
Web: www.atrautomation.com
SIC: 7372 Prepackaged software
PA: Atr Distributing Company
11857 Kemper Springs Dr
Cincinnati OH 45240
513 353-1800

(G-2643)
ATRIUM CENTERS INC
1400 Mallard Cove Dr (45246-3941)
PHONE.....................513 830-5014
Jason Reese, *Brnch Mgr*
EMP: 28
SALES (corp-wide): 50.09MM **Privately Held**
Web: www.atriumlivingcenters.com
SIC: 3442 Metal doors, sash, and trim
PA: Atrium Centers, Inc.
2550 Corp Exchange Dr # 200
Columbus OH 43231
614 416-0600

(G-2644)
AUBREY ROSE APPAREL LLC
3862 Race Rd (45211-4346)
PHONE.....................513 728-2681
EMP: 6 **EST:** 2009
SALES (est): 436.25K **Privately Held**
Web: www.aubreyrose.org
SIC: 7389 2395 Advertising, promotional, and trade show services; Embroidery and art needlework

(G-2645)
AUTOMTED CMPNENT SPCALISTS LLC
7740 Reinhold Dr (45237-2806)
PHONE.....................513 335-4285
Andy Hillard, *Managing Member*
EMP: 25 **EST:** 2020
SALES (est): 1.2MM **Privately Held**
Web: www.automatedcomponentspecialists.com
SIC: 2298 8711 7389 3442 Ropes and fiber cables; Engineering services; Field warehousing; Molding, trim, and stripping

(G-2646)
AVARI AERO LLC
Also Called: Avari Aerospace
7711 Affinity Pl (45231-3567)
PHONE.....................513 828-0860
EMP: 8
SALES (est): 299.29K **Privately Held**
Web: www.avariaero.com
SIC: 3721 Aircraft

(G-2647)
AVC INC
4625 Red Bank Rd Ste 200 (45227-1552)
PHONE.....................513 458-2600
EMP: 10 **EST:** 2015
SALES (est): 2.44MM **Publicly Held**
SIC: 3569 Gas separators (machinery)
PA: Ceco Environmental Corp.
14651 Dallas Pkwy Ste 500
Dallas TX 75254

(G-2648)
AVERY DENNISON CORPORATION
11101 Mosteller Rd Ste 2 (45241-1882)
PHONE.....................513 682-7500
EMP: 50
SALES (corp-wide): 8.36B **Publicly Held**
Web: www.averydennison.com
SIC: 2672 Adhesive backed films, foams and foils
PA: Avery Dennison Corporation
8080 Norton Pkwy
Mentor OH 44060
440 534-6000

(G-2649)
B & J BAKING COMPANY
4056 Colerain Ave (45223-2561)
PHONE.....................513 541-2386
Steve Toleski, *Pr*
Tatsa Toleski, *Sec*
EMP: 11 **EST:** 1924
SQ FT: 10,000
SALES (est): 809.9K **Privately Held**
SIC: 2051 Buns, bread type: fresh or frozen

(G-2650)
B & R FABRICATORS & MAINT INC
4524 W Mitchell Ave (45232-1912)
P.O. Box 17211 (45217-0211)
PHONE.....................513 641-2222
Randy Allen, *Pr*
Bruce Allen, *VP*
EMP: 12 **EST:** 1993
SQ FT: 5,000
SALES (est): 996.89K **Privately Held**
SIC: 7692 Welding repair

(G-2651)
B P OIL COMPANY
Also Called: BP
1201 Omniplex Dr (45240-1280)
PHONE.....................513 671-4107
Pat Hoelle, *Prin*
EMP: 6 **EST:** 2010
SALES (est): 144.11K **Privately Held**
SIC: 2869 Fuels

(G-2652)
B R PRINTERS INC
Also Called: BR Ohio
3962 Virginia Ave (45227-3412)
PHONE.....................513 271-6035
Adam Damaestri, *Pr*
EMP: 80
Web: www.brprinters.com
SIC: 2752 Offset printing
PA: B R Printers, Inc.
665 Lenfest Rd
San Jose CA 95133

(G-2653)
B&G FOODS INC
5204 Spring Grove Ave (45217-1031)
PHONE.....................513 482-8226
EMP: 50
SALES (corp-wide): 2.06B **Publicly Held**
Web: www.bgfoods.com
SIC: 2013 2032 2033 2035 Canned meats (except baby food), from purchased meat; Beans and bean sprouts, canned, jarred, etc.; Canned fruits and specialties; Pickles, sauces, and salad dressings
PA: B&G Foods, Inc.
4 Gatehall Dr Ste 110
Parsippany NJ 07054
973 401-6500

(G-2654)
BAERLOCHER PRODUCTION USA LLC

GEOGRAPHIC SECTION

Cincinnati - Hamilton County (G-2678)

5890 Highland Ridge Dr (45232-1440)
PHONE...................................513 482-6300
David Kuebel, *
▲ EMP: 50 EST: 1999
SQ FT: 50,000
SALES (est): 56.71MM
SALES (corp-wide): 591.42MM **Privately Held**
Web: www.baerlocherusa.com
SIC: 2819 Nonmetallic compounds
HQ: Baerlocher Gmbh
   Freisinger Str. 1
   UnterschleiBheim BY 85716
   89143730

(G-2655)
BANBURY INVESTMENTS INC
Also Called: AlphaGraphics
9160 Union Cemetery Rd (45249-2006)
PHONE...................................513 677-4500
Doug Banbury, Pr
Malisa Banbury, Treas
EMP: 8 EST: 1991
SQ FT: 4,800
SALES (est): 560.16K **Privately Held**
Web: www.alphagraphics.com
SIC: 2752 Commercial printing, lithographic

(G-2656)
BARDES CORPORATION
Also Called: Ilsco
4730 Madison Rd (45227-1426)
PHONE...................................513 533-6200
David Fitzgibbon, CEO
Merrilyn Q Bardes, *
Andrew Quinn, *
James E Valentine, *
▲ EMP: 500 EST: 1996
SQ FT: 300,000
SALES (est): 83.11MM **Privately Held**
SIC: 3643 Electric connectors

(G-2657)
BARR LABORATORIES INC
5040 Duramed Rd (45213-2520)
PHONE...................................513 731-9900
S Goldstein, Prin
EMP: 934
Web: www.tevausa.com
SIC: 2834 Pharmaceutical preparations
HQ: Barr Laboratories, Inc.
   400 Interpace Pkwy Bldg A
   Parsippany NJ 07054
   215 591-3000

(G-2658)
BASF CORP
3131 Spring Grove Ave (45225-1862)
PHONE...................................513 681-9100
EMP: 6 EST: 2018
SALES (est): 538.92K **Privately Held**
Web: www.basf.com
SIC: 2869 Industrial organic chemicals, nec

(G-2659)
BASF CORPORATION
4900 Este Ave (45232-1491)
PHONE...................................513 482-3000
EMP: 145
SALES (corp-wide): 74.89B **Privately Held**
Web: www.basf.com
SIC: 2869 Industrial organic chemicals, nec
HQ: Basf Corporation
   100 Park Ave
   Florham Park NJ 07932
   800 962-7181

(G-2660)
BAXTER BURIAL VAULT SVC INC
Also Called: Baxter-Wilbert Burial Vault
909 E Ross Ave (45217-1159)
PHONE...................................513 641-1010
R Douglas Baxter, Pr
EMP: 16 EST: 1924
SALES (est): 1.33MM **Privately Held**
Web: www.baxterburialvault.com
SIC: 5087 3272 Concrete burial vaults and boxes; Concrete products, nec

(G-2661)
BAXTERS NORTH AMERICA INC (DH)
Also Called: Wornick Foods
4700 Creek Rd (45242)
P.O. Box 42634 (45242)
PHONE...................................513 552-7485
John Kowalchik, CEO
Jack Fields, *
Doug Herald, *
Randy Newbold, *
Dustin Mcdulin, CFO
▼ EMP: 26 EST: 2003
SQ FT: 600,000
SALES (est): 489.6MM
SALES (corp-wide): 559.89MM **Privately Held**
Web: www.baxtersna.com
SIC: 2032 Baby foods, including meats: packaged in cans, jars, etc.
HQ: Baxters Food Group Limited
   Fochabers IV32
   134 382-0393

(G-2662)
BECKER GLLAGHER LEGAL PUBG INC
8790 Governors Hill Dr Ste 102 (45249-1307)
PHONE...................................513 677-5044
B J Becker, Pr
John Gallagher, VP
EMP: 10 EST: 1984
SQ FT: 3,000
SALES (est): 965.36K **Privately Held**
Web: www.beckergallagher.com
SIC: 2741 Miscellaneous publishing

(G-2663)
BECKMAN MACHINE LLC
4684 Paddock Rd (45229-1002)
P.O. Box 37655 (45222-0655)
PHONE...................................513 242-2700
Mary Kathryn Lynch, Pr
Charles Beckman, VP
EMP: 20 EST: 1989
SALES (est): 1.97MM **Privately Held**
Web: www.beckmanmachine.com
SIC: 3599 Machine shop, jobbing and repair

(G-2664)
BENCH MADE WOODWORKING LLC
5150 Kieley Pl (45217-1120)
PHONE...................................513 702-2698
EMP: 8 EST: 2016
SALES (est): 255.12K **Privately Held**
Web: www.benchmadewoodworking.com
SIC: 2431 Millwork

(G-2665)
BERGHAUSEN CORPORATION
4524 Este Ave (45232-1763)
P.O. Box 43400 (45243-0400)
PHONE...................................513 591-4491
Fritz Berghausen, Pr
August Ritt, Prin
◆ EMP: 20 EST: 1863
SQ FT: 38,000
SALES (est): 2.44MM **Privately Held**
Web: www.berghausen.com
SIC: 2843 2087 2865 Emulsifiers, except food and pharmaceutical; Extracts, flavoring ; Food dyes or colors, synthetic

(G-2666)
BERNARD LABORATORIES INC
1738 Townsend St (45223-2710)
PHONE...................................513 681-7373
Boyd J Piper Junior, Pr
▲ EMP: 22 EST: 1980
SQ FT: 30,000
SALES (est): 3.71MM **Privately Held**
Web: www.bernardlab.com
SIC: 7389 2899 Packaging and labeling services; Chemical preparations, nec

(G-2667)
BERRY COMPANY
312 Plum St Ste 600 (45202-4809)
PHONE...................................513 768-7800
Pete Luongo, Pr
EMP: 6 EST: 1910
SALES (est): 449.46K **Privately Held**
Web: www.bal.com
SIC: 2741 Directories, telephone: publishing and printing

(G-2668)
BEST GRAPHICS & PRINTING INC
11836 Stone Mill Rd (45251-4128)
PHONE...................................513 535-3529
Jeffrey Best, Prin
EMP: 6 EST: 2012
SALES (est): 132.63K **Privately Held**
SIC: 2752 Commercial printing, lithographic

(G-2669)
BIOWISH TECHNOLOGIES INC
Also Called: Biowish
2724 Erie Ave Ste B (45208-2125)
PHONE...................................312 572-6700
▲ EMP: 9 EST: 2009
SALES (est): 3.97MM **Privately Held**
Web: www.biowishtechnologies.com
SIC: 2869 Enzymes

(G-2670)
BIOWISH TECHNOLOGIES INC
2717 Erie Ave (45208-2103)
PHONE...................................312 572-6700
EMP: 38 EST: 2009
SALES (est): 4.16MM **Privately Held**
SIC: 2869 Industrial organic chemicals, nec

(G-2671)
BLACK SQUIRREL HOLDINGS INC
Also Called: Frame Usa, Inc.
225 Northland Blvd (45246)
PHONE...................................513 577-7107
◆ EMP: 20 EST: 1990
SQ FT: 7,000
SALES (est): 6.89MM
SALES (corp-wide): 8.02MM **Privately Held**
Web: www.frameusa.com
SIC: 2499 5999 3499 Picture frame molding, finished; Picture frames, ready made; Picture frames, metal
PA: Posterservice, Incorporated
   225 Northland Blvd
   Cincinnati OH 45246
   513 577-7100

(G-2672)
BLU BIRD LLC
Also Called: Stone Center
4820 Stafford St (45227-2539)
PHONE...................................513 271-5646
Steve Piehl, Mgr
EMP: 11
SQ FT: 7,500
SALES (corp-wide): 2.34MM **Privately Held**
Web: www.stonecenters.com
SIC: 3281 Cut stone and stone products
PA: Blu Bird Llc
   1736 Mckinley Ave
   Columbus OH 43222
   614 276-3585

(G-2673)
BLUE CHIP TOOL INC
11511 Goldcoast Dr (45249-1620)
PHONE...................................513 489-3561
William Riehle, Pr
John Kilgore, VP Mfg
Eileen Riehle, Sec
EMP: 19 EST: 1983
SQ FT: 5,000
SALES (est): 995.92K **Privately Held**
Web: www.bluechiptool.com
SIC: 3599 Machine shop, jobbing and repair

(G-2674)
BODOR VENTS INC
Also Called: Vents US
400 Murray Rd (45217-1013)
PHONE...................................513 348-3853
EMP: 7 EST: 2005
SALES (est): 968.51K **Privately Held**
Web: www.vents-us.com
SIC: 3585 Refrigeration and heating equipment

(G-2675)
BODYCOTE THERMAL PROC INC
710 Burns St (45204-1904)
PHONE...................................513 921-2300
Kevin Mccurdy, Brnch Mgr
EMP: 46
SALES (corp-wide): 1B **Privately Held**
Web: www.bodycote.com
SIC: 3398 Metal heat treating
HQ: Bodycote Thermal Processing, Inc.
   12750 Merit Dr Ste 1400
   Dallas TX 75251
   214 904-2420

(G-2676)
BOHLENDER ENGRAVING COMPANY
Also Called: Bohlender Engravg
1599 Central Pkwy (45214-2863)
PHONE...................................513 621-4095
Randy Brunk, Pr
EMP: 9 EST: 1895
SQ FT: 7,500
SALES (est): 239.31K **Privately Held**
SIC: 2759 2752 Commercial printing, nec; Commercial printing, lithographic

(G-2677)
BONSAL AMERICAN INC
5155 Fischer Ave (45217-1157)
PHONE...................................513 398-7300
Marshal Lewis, Mgr
EMP: 11
SQ FT: 8,100
SALES (corp-wide): 32.72B **Privately Held**
SIC: 1442 Construction sand and gravel
HQ: Bonsal American, Inc.
   625 Griffith Rd Ste 100
   Charlotte NC 28217
   704 525-1621

(G-2678)
BOSTON BEER COMPANY
1625 Central Pkwy (45214-2423)
PHONE...................................267 240-4429
Jeremy Roza, Prin
▲ EMP: 19 EST: 2010
SALES (est): 10.23MM **Privately Held**
Web: www.samueladams.com
SIC: 3585 Beer dispensing equipment

Cincinnati - Hamilton County (G-2679)

GEOGRAPHIC SECTION

(G-2679)
BRACKISH MEDIA LLC
2662 Mckinley Ave (45211-7206)
PHONE..................513 394-2871
Terrell Hill, *CEO*
EMP: 11 **EST:** 2014
SALES (est): 706.75K **Privately Held**
SIC: 4899 3577 7313 Communication services, nec; Data conversion equipment, media-to-media: computer; Radio, television, publisher representatives

(G-2680)
BRENTWOOD PRINTING & STY
8630 Winton Rd (45231-4817)
PHONE..................513 522-2679
Scott Finke, *Owner*
EMP: 8 **EST:** 1979
SQ FT: 1,250
SALES (est): 908.33K **Privately Held**
Web: www.brentwood-printing.com
SIC: 2752 Offset printing

(G-2681)
BREWER COMPANY
7300 Main St (45244-3015)
PHONE..................513 576-6300
Laura Graber, *Plng Mgr*
EMP: 7
SALES (corp-wide): 12.34MM **Privately Held**
Web: www.thebrewerco.com
SIC: 2952 2891 Coating compounds, tar; Adhesives and sealants
PA: The Brewer Company
25 Whitney Dr Ste 104
Milford OH 45150
800 394-0017

(G-2682)
BREWPRO INC
Also Called: Brewer Products Co
9483 Reading Rd (45215-3550)
P.O. Box 62065 (45262-0065)
PHONE..................513 577-7200
David Brewer, *Pr*
EMP: 6 **EST:** 1987
SALES (est): 843.93K **Privately Held**
Web: www.brewerproducts.com
SIC: 5082 3531 7353 5169 Road construction equipment; Airport construction machinery; Heavy construction equipment rental; Adhesives and sealants

(G-2683)
BRIDGESTONE RET OPERATIONS LLC
Also Called: Michel Tires Plus 227565
272 W Mitchell Ave (45232-1908)
PHONE..................513 681-7682
EMP: 8
Web: www.bridgestoneamericas.com
SIC: 7534 5531 Tire retreading and repair shops; Automotive tires
HQ: Bridgestone Retail Operations, Llc
333 E Lake St Ste 300
Bloomingdale IL 60108
630 259-9000

(G-2684)
BRIDGESTONE RET OPERATIONS LLC
Also Called: Firestone
7800 Montgomery Rd Unit 18 (45236-4388)
PHONE..................513 793-4550
Derek Lester, *Mgr*
EMP: 7
SQ FT: 6,000
Web: www.bridgestoneamericas.com
SIC: 5531 7534 Automotive tires; Tire retreading and repair shops
HQ: Bridgestone Retail Operations, Llc
333 E Lake St Ste 300
Bloomingdale IL 60108
630 259-9000

(G-2685)
BRIDGESTONE RET OPERATIONS LLC
Also Called: Firestone
9107 Fields Ertel Rd (45249-8209)
PHONE..................513 677-5200
EMP: 7
SQ FT: 6,600
Web: www.bridgestoneamericas.com
SIC: 5531 7534 Automotive tires; Tire retreading and repair shops
HQ: Bridgestone Retail Operations, Llc
333 E Lake St Ste 300
Bloomingdale IL 60108
630 259-9000

(G-2686)
BRIGHTON SCIENCE ◆
4914 Gray Rd (45232-1513)
PHONE..................513 469-1800
Andy Reeher, *CEO*
Tom Perazzo, *CFO*
Blake Bristow, *VP*
EMP: 7 **EST:** 2022
SALES (est): 143.81K **Privately Held**
Web: www.brighton-science.com
SIC: 3823 Process control instruments

(G-2687)
BROADWAY PRINTING LLC
530 Reading Rd (45202-1407)
PHONE..................513 621-3429
EMP: 6 **EST:** 2000
SALES (est): 357.12K **Privately Held**
SIC: 2759 Commercial printing, nec

(G-2688)
BROCAR PRODUCTS INC
4335 River Rd (45204-1041)
P.O. Box 42295 (45242-0295)
PHONE..................513 922-2888
John Helmsderfer, *Pr*
EMP: 21 **EST:** 1992
SQ FT: 16,000
SALES (est): 2.11MM **Privately Held**
Web: www.ceobrocar.com
SIC: 2531 Chairs, table and arm

(G-2689)
BRODWILL LLC
3900 Rose Hill Ave Ste C (45229-1454)
PHONE..................513 258-2716
Rick Williams, *Pr*
EMP: 8 **EST:** 2005
SALES (est): 485.85K **Privately Held**
Web: www.brodwill.com
SIC: 2599 Hospital furniture, except beds

(G-2690)
BROODLE BRANDS LLC
8361 Broadwell Rd Ste 100 (45244-1609)
P.O. Box 54461 (45254-0461)
PHONE..................855 276-6353
Kent Arnold, *Managing Member*
EMP: 8 **EST:** 2011
SQ FT: 10,000
SALES (est): 226.67K **Privately Held**
Web: www.broodlebrands.com
SIC: 3411 Food and beverage containers

(G-2691)
BROOKWOOD GROUP INC
Also Called: Schauer Battery Chargers
3210 Wasson Rd (45209-2382)
PHONE..................513 791-3030
Jonathan Chaiken, *CEO*
▲ **EMP:** 10 **EST:** 2009
SQ FT: 10,000
SALES (est): 951.74K **Privately Held**
Web: www.battery-chargers.com
SIC: 3629 Battery chargers, rectifying or nonrotating

(G-2692)
BT 4 LLC
Also Called: Third Eye Brewing Company
11276 Chester Rd (45246-4013)
PHONE..................513 771-2739
Tom Schaefer, *Managing Member*
Mark Buchy, *Managing Member*
Tim Collins, *Managing Member*
Terry Krieg, *Managing Member*
Tom Collins, *Managing Member*
EMP: 7 **EST:** 2016
SALES (est): 290.42K **Privately Held**
SIC: 2082 Malt beverage products

(G-2693)
BUCKLEY MANUFACTURING COMPANY
148 Caldwell Dr (45216-1522)
PHONE..................513 821-4444
Michael G Strotman, *Pr*
Mary Reardon, *Sec*
Thomas M Strotman, *Treas*
Kathleen Strotman, *Asst Tr*
C M Pulskamp, *Prin*
EMP: 18 **EST:** 1947
SALES (est): 2.37MM **Privately Held**
SIC: 3469 3714 Stamping metal for the trade; Gas tanks, motor vehicle

(G-2694)
BUILDING CTRL INTEGRATORS LLC
300 E Business Way Ste 200 (45241)
PHONE..................513 247-6154
Dave Milar, *Brnch Mgr*
EMP: 6
SALES (corp-wide): 11.3MM **Privately Held**
Web: www.bcicontrols.com
SIC: 3822 Temperature controls, automatic
PA: Building Control Integrators, Llc
383 N Liberty St
Powell OH 43065
614 334-3300

(G-2695)
BUSKEN BAKERY INC (PA)
2675 Madison Rd (45208-1389)
PHONE..................513 871-2114
D Page Busken, *Pr*
Brian Busken, *
EMP: 90 **EST:** 1928
SQ FT: 21,000
SALES (est): 18.43MM
SALES (corp-wide): 18.43MM **Privately Held**
Web: www.busken.com
SIC: 2045 5461 5149 Blended flour: from purchased flour; Bread; Bakery products

(G-2696)
BWAY CORPORATION
Also Called: Bwaypackaging
8200 Broadwell Rd (45244-1608)
PHONE..................513 388-2200
Melissa Williams, *Bmch Mgr*
EMP: 20
Web: www.bwaycorp.com
SIC: 3411 Metal cans
HQ: Bway Corporation
1515 W 22nd St Ste 1100
Oak Brook IL 60523

(G-2697)
C & W CUSTOM WDWKG CO INC
11949 Tramway Dr (45241-1666)
PHONE..................513 891-6340
Dave Williams, *Prin*
Steven Cornett, *Prin*
EMP: 13 **EST:** 2000
SQ FT: 3,000
SALES (est): 1.17MM **Privately Held**
Web: www.candwcustomwoodworking.com
SIC: 2431 Millwork

(G-2698)
CAMARGO PHRM SVCS LLC (DH)
1 E 4th St Ste 1400 (45202-3708)
PHONE..................513 561-3329
Daniel S Duffy, *CEO*
Ray Dawkins, *CMO*
Jim Beach, *COO*
Carter Gaither, *CFO*
Reeves Mcgee, *CCO*
EMP: 11 **EST:** 2003
SALES (est): 8.12MM
SALES (corp-wide): 25.54MM **Privately Held**
Web: www.premierconsulting.com
SIC: 2834 Proprietary drug products
HQ: Premier Research International Llc
3800 Parmnt Pkwy Ste 400
Morrisville NC 27560

(G-2699)
CANDLE-LITE COMPANY LLC
Also Called: Factory Direct
6252 Glenway Ave (45211-6321)
PHONE..................513 662-8616
Gary Pramtero, *CFO*
EMP: 216
SALES (corp-wide): 260.78MM **Privately Held**
Web: www.candle-lite.com
SIC: 3999 Candles
HQ: Candle-Lite Company, Llc
250 Eastern Ave
Leesburg OH 45135
937 780-2563

(G-2700)
CAPS INC
2170 Struble Rd (45231-1736)
PHONE..................513 377-0800
Jayna Smith, *Dir*
EMP: 7 **EST:** 2018
SALES (est): 88.97K **Privately Held**
SIC: 3089 Plastics products, nec

(G-2701)
CARAUSTAR INDUSTRIES INC
Also Called: Cincinnati Paperboard
5500 Wooster Pike (45226-2227)
PHONE..................513 871-7112
Allen Hall, *Manager*
EMP: 45
SALES (corp-wide): 5.22B **Publicly Held**
Web: www.greif.com
SIC: 2631 Paperboard mills
HQ: Caraustar Industries, Inc.
5000 Astell Pwdr Sprng Rd
Austell GA 30106
770 948-3101

(G-2702)
CARGILL INCORPORATED
Cargill
5204 River Rd (45233-1643)
PHONE..................513 941-7400
Robert Mattock, *Mgr*
EMP: 10
SQ FT: 12,000
SALES (corp-wide): 176.74B **Privately Held**

Web: www.peterschocolate.com
SIC: 2869 2899 Industrial organic chemicals, nec; Chemical preparations, nec
PA: Cargill, Incorporated
15407 Mcginty Rd W
Wayzata MN 55391
800 227-4455

(G-2703)
CARLISLE AND FINCH COMPANY
4562 W Mitchell Ave (45232-1759)
PHONE..............................513 681-6080
Kurtis Finch, *CEO*
Brent R Finch, *
Garth Finch, *
EMP: 30 EST: 1897
SQ FT: 45,000
SALES (est): 6.56MM **Privately Held**
Web: www.carlislefinch.com
SIC: 3648 3471 3641 Searchlights; Plating and polishing; Electric lamps

(G-2704)
CARRILLO PALLETS LLC
1292 Glendale Milford Rd (45215-1209)
PHONE..............................513 942-2210
Francisco Carrillo, *Prin*
EMP: 7 EST: 2010
SALES (est): 141.92K **Privately Held**
SIC: 2448 Pallets, wood

(G-2705)
CARUSO FOODS LLC ✪
3465 Hauck Rd (45241-1601)
PHONE..............................513 860-9200
James S Caruso, *CEO*
Jeff Burt, *Pr*
Steven J Caruso, *Ex VP*
David Brown, *CFO*
EMP: 59 EST: 2023
SALES (est): 4.48MM
SALES (corp-wide): 41.72MM **Privately Held**
SIC: 2099 Sandwiches, assembled and packaged: for wholesale market
PA: Caruso, Inc.
3465 Hauck Rd
Cincinnati OH 45241
513 860-9200

(G-2706)
CASCO MFG SOLUTIONS INC
3107 Spring Grove Ave (45225-1821)
PHONE..............................513 681-0003
Thomas Mangold, *Ch*
Melissa Mangold, *
Terri Mangold, *
▲ EMP: 60 EST: 1959
SQ FT: 72,000
SALES (est): 9.93MM **Privately Held**
Web: www.cascomfg.com
SIC: 2515 7641 3841 2522 Mattresses, containing felt, foam rubber, urethane, etc.; Upholstery work; Surgical and medical instruments; Office furniture, except wood

(G-2707)
CAST-FAB TECHNOLOGIES INC (PA)
3040 Forrer St (45209-1016)
PHONE..............................513 758-1000
EMP: 241 EST: 1940
SALES (est): 23.42MM
SALES (corp-wide): 23.42MM **Privately Held**
Web: www.cast-fab.com
SIC: 3499 3321 3441 3322 Machine bases, metal; Gray iron castings, nec; Fabricated structural metal; Malleable iron foundries

(G-2708)
CATALOG MERCHANDISER INC
Also Called: Portico Merchandising
10525 Chester Rd Ste A (45215-1254)
P.O. Box 196 (52052-0196)
▲ EMP: 11 EST: 1997
SALES (est): 993.07K **Privately Held**
SIC: 3993 Signs, not made in custom sign painting shops

(G-2709)
CATERINGSTONE
6119 Kenwood Rd (45243-2307)
PHONE..............................513 410-1064
Doctor David Pensak, *CEO*
EMP: 6
SALES (est): 224.65K **Privately Held**
SIC: 2599 Carts, restaurant equipment

(G-2710)
CBP CO INC
6545 Wiehe Rd (45237-4217)
PHONE..............................513 860-9053
James Yockey, *Pr*
EMP: 13 EST: 1990
SALES (est): 2.32MM
SALES (corp-wide): 4MM **Privately Held**
Web: www.cpprinters.com
SIC: 2752 Offset printing
PA: Sjs Packaging Group, Inc.
6545 Wiehe Rd
Cincinnati OH 45237
513 841-1351

(G-2711)
CBST ACQUISITION LLC
Also Called: Dynus Technologies
6900 Steger Dr (45237-3096)
PHONE..............................513 361-9600
EMP: 90 EST: 1983
SQ FT: 80,000
SALES (est): 9.95MM **Privately Held**
SIC: 5065 7629 3357 7622 Telephone equipment; Telecommunication equipment repair (except telephones); Fiber optic cable (insulated); Radio and television repair

(G-2712)
CDC PUBLISHING
3825 Edwards Rd Ste 800 (45209-1289)
PHONE..............................772 770-6003
EMP: 8 EST: 2019
SALES (est): 201.62K **Privately Held**
Web: www.cdcnews.com
SIC: 2741 Miscellaneous publishing

(G-2713)
CECO FILTERS INC
4625 Red Bank Rd Ste 200 (45227-1552)
PHONE..............................513 458-2600
Mary Buckius, *Pr*
EMP: 9 EST: 2015
SALES (est): 2.48MM **Publicly Held**
Web: www.cecoenviro.com
SIC: 3564 Filters, air: furnaces, air conditioning equipment, etc.
PA: Ceco Environmental Corp.
14651 Dallas Pkwy Ste 500
Dallas TX 75254

(G-2714)
CECO GROUP GLOBAL HOLDINGS LLC (HQ)
4625 Red Bank Rd Ste 200 (45227)
PHONE..............................513 458-2600
EMP: 6 EST: 2013
SALES (est): 7.64MM **Publicly Held**
SIC: 3564 Purification and dust collection equipment

PA: Ceco Environmental Corp.
14651 Dallas Pkwy Ste 500
Dallas TX 75254

(G-2715)
CENTENNIAL BARN
110 Compton Rd (45215-4141)
PHONE..............................513 761-1697
Mary Ann Montgomery, *Prin*
EMP: 7 EST: 2011
SALES (est): 193.65K **Privately Held**
Web: www.franciscanministriesinc.org
SIC: 2335 Wedding gowns and dresses

(G-2716)
CENTRAL INVESTMENT LLC (PA)
7265 Kenwood Rd Ste 240 (45236-4411)
PHONE..............................513 563-4700
Keven Shell, *Pr*
Carl Myers, *VP*
Manny Zapata, *VP*
William P Martin, *Sec*
EMP: 15 EST: 2004
SALES (est): 47.16MM **Privately Held**
Web: www.pepsico.com
SIC: 2086 Carbonated soft drinks, bottled and canned

(G-2717)
CENTRAL READY MIX LLC (PA)
6310 E Kemper Rd Ste 125 (45241-2370)
P.O. Box 70 (45050-0070)
PHONE..............................513 402-5001
TOLL FREE: 888
EMP: 30 EST: 1934
SQ FT: 8,000
SALES (est): 11.19MM
SALES (corp-wide): 11.19MM **Privately Held**
Web: www.centralrm.com
SIC: 3273 1442 Ready-mixed concrete; Sand mining

(G-2718)
CENTRAL READY-MIX OF OHIO LLC
6310 E Kemper Rd Ste 125 (45241-2370)
PHONE..............................614 252-3452
EMP: 9 EST: 2000
SALES (est): 423.54K **Privately Held**
SIC: 3273 Ready-mixed concrete

(G-2719)
CENTRAL USA WIRELESS LLC
11210 Montgomery Rd (45249-2311)
PHONE..............................513 469-1500
EMP: 15 EST: 2013
SALES (est): 827.43K **Privately Held**
Web: www.centralusawireless.com
SIC: 7622 3663 Antenna repair and installation; Antennas, transmitting and communications

(G-2720)
CFGSC LLC
Also Called: Madisono's Gelato
5927 Belmont Ave (45224-2365)
PHONE..............................513 772-5920
Bryan Madison, *Managing Member*
EMP: 6 EST: 2010
SALES (est): 314.47K **Privately Held**
Web: www.madisonogelato.com
SIC: 2024 Ice cream and ice milk

(G-2721)
CFM INTERNATIONAL INC
111 Merchant St (45246-3730)
PHONE..............................513 563-4180
EMP: 11
SALES (corp-wide): 15.7MM **Privately Held**

SIC: 3724 Aircraft engines and engine parts
PA: Cfm International, Inc.
6440 Aviation Way
West Chester OH 45069
513 552-2787

(G-2722)
CFM INTERNATIONAL INC
1 Neumann Way (45215-1900)
PHONE..............................513 563-4180
Pierre Fabre, *Brnch Mgr*
EMP: 11
SALES (corp-wide): 15.7MM **Privately Held**
Web: www.cfmaeroengines.com
SIC: 3724 Aircraft engines and engine parts
PA: Cfm International, Inc.
6440 Aviation Way
West Chester OH 45069
513 552-2787

(G-2723)
CFM RELIGION PUBG GROUP LLC (PA)
8805 Governors Hill Dr Ste 400 (45249-3314)
PHONE..............................513 931-4050
Matthew Thibeau, *Pr*
EMP: 52 EST: 2007
SALES (est): 43.18MM **Privately Held**
Web: www.cfmpublishing.com
SIC: 2721 8741 Magazines: publishing only, not printed on site; Management services

(G-2724)
CH TRANSITION COMPANY LLC (DH)
Also Called: Campbell Group
225 Pictoria Dri Ste 210 (45246-1616)
PHONE..............................800 543-6400
Terry Atwater, *Pr*
Dave Kohlmayer, *
◆ EMP: 112 EST: 1987
SQ FT: 3,000
SALES (est): 70.54MM
SALES (corp-wide): 364.48B **Publicly Held**
SIC: 3563 3546 3548 Air and gas compressors including vacuum pumps; Power-driven handtools; Welding apparatus
HQ: The Marmon Group Llc
181 W Madison St Ste 3900
Chicago IL 60602

(G-2725)
CHAMPION OPCO LLC (DH)
Also Called: Champion Windows
12121 Champion Way (45241-6419)
PHONE..............................513 327-7338
Jim Mishler, *CEO*
Donald R Jones, *
Joe Faisant, *
▲ EMP: 300 EST: 2007
SQ FT: 500,000
SALES (est): 496.44MM **Privately Held**
Web: www.championwindow.com
SIC: 3089 1761 3442 Window frames and sash, plastics; Siding contractor; Storm doors or windows, metal
HQ: Great Day Improvements, Llc
700 Highland Rd E
Macedonia OH 44056

(G-2726)
CHARLES J MEYERS
Also Called: American Custom Polishing
866 Suncreek Ct (45238-4837)
PHONE..............................513 922-2866
Charles J Meyers, *Owner*
EMP: 7 EST: 2002
SALES (est): 182.91K **Privately Held**

Cincinnati - Hamilton County (G-2727)

SIC: 3471 Polishing, metals or formed products

(G-2727)
CHASE INDUSTRIES INC
11502 Century Blvd (45246-3305)
PHONE..............................513 603-2936
EMP: 21 EST: 2018
SALES (est): 2.47MM Privately Held
Web: www.chasedoors.com
SIC: 3442 Metal doors, sash, and trim

(G-2728)
CHATTANOOGA LASER CUTTING LLC
891 Redna Ter (45215-1110)
PHONE..............................513 779-7200
EMP: 10 EST: 1998
SQ FT: 34,000
SALES (est): 459.64K Privately Held
SIC: 3441 Fabricated structural metal

(G-2729)
CHC FABRICATING CORP (PA)
10270 Wayne Ave (45215-1127)
PHONE..............................513 821-7757
EMP: 58 EST: 1961
SALES (est): 4.25MM
SALES (corp-wide): 4.25MM Privately Held
Web: www.chcfab.com
SIC: 1791 3446 3441 Structural steel erection; Stairs, staircases, stair treads: prefabricated metal; Fabricated structural metal

(G-2730)
CHC MANUFACTURING INC (PA)
10270 Wayne Ave (45215-1127)
PHONE..............................513 821-7757
Patrick Mclaughlin, CEO
Mark Lambert, Pr
Robert J Christen, VP
EMP: 21 EST: 2007
SALES (est): 6.13MM
SALES (corp-wide): 6.13MM Privately Held
Web: www.chcfab.com
SIC: 3446 3441 Stairs, staircases, stair treads: prefabricated metal; Fabricated structural metal

(G-2731)
CHESTER LABS INC
900 Section Rd Ste A (45237)
PHONE..............................513 458-3871
Robert King, Prin
EMP: 17 EST: 1946
SALES (est): 366.78K Privately Held
SIC: 2834 Pharmaceutical preparations

(G-2732)
CHICA BANDS LLC
6216 Madison Rd (45227-1908)
P.O. Box 30537 (45230-0537)
PHONE..............................513 871-4300
Marguerita Perez, Prin
EMP: 7 EST: 2011
SALES (est): 176.57K Privately Held
Web: www.chicabands.com
SIC: 3089 Bands, plastics

(G-2733)
CHOICE BRANDS ADHESIVES LTD
Also Called: Choice Adhesives
666 Redna Ter Ste 500 (45215-1166)
PHONE..............................800 330-5566
Robert Johnson, CEO
EMP: 25 EST: 2010
SALES (est): 4.48MM
SALES (corp-wide): 923.49MM Privately Held
Web: www.choicebrandsadhesives.com
SIC: 2891 Adhesives
PA: Innovative Chemical Products Group, Llc
150 Dascomb Rd
Andover MA 01810
978 623-9980

(G-2734)
CHRIS ERHART FOUNDRY & MCH CO
Also Called: Erhart Foundry
1240 Mehring Way (45203)
PHONE..............................513 421-6550
Daniel J Erhart, Pr
EMP: 24 EST: 1854
SQ FT: 40,000
SALES (est): 1.83MM Privately Held
Web: www.erhart.com
SIC: 3321 Gray iron castings, nec

(G-2735)
CIMX LLC
Also Called: Cimx Software
2368 Victory Pkwy Ste 120 (45206-2810)
PHONE..............................513 248-7700
EMP: 30 EST: 1996
SALES (est): 4.22MM Privately Held
Web: www.cimx.com
SIC: 7372 7371 Prepackaged software; Custom computer programming services

(G-2736)
CINCINNATI - VULCAN COMPANY
5353 Spring Grove Ave (45217-1026)
PHONE..............................513 242-5300
Garry C Ferraris, Pr
EMP: 87 EST: 1912
SQ FT: 6,000
SALES (est): 2.24MM
SALES (corp-wide): 11.67MM Privately Held
SIC: 5983 2992 5171 2899 Fuel oil dealers; Oils and greases, blending and compounding; Petroleum bulk stations; Chemical preparations, nec
HQ: Coolant Control, Inc.
5353 Spring Grove Ave
Cincinnati OH 45217
513 471-8770

(G-2737)
CINCINNATI A FLTER SLS SVC INC
Also Called: Cafco Filter
4815 Para Dr (45237-5009)
PHONE..............................513 242-3400
TOLL FREE: 800
Edward W Flick, CEO
Mark Flick, Pr
EMP: 21 EST: 1945
SQ FT: 12,500
SALES (est): 8.11MM Privately Held
Web: www.cafcoservices.com
SIC: 5075 7349 3564 Air filters; Building component cleaning service; Filters, air: furnaces, air conditioning equipment, etc.

(G-2738)
CINCINNATI ABRASIVE SUPPLY CO
5700 Hillside Ave (45233-1508)
PHONE..............................513 941-8866
Thomas Spinnenweber, Pr
Kathleen Spinnenweber, VP
Larry Kite, Treas
EMP: 6 EST: 1974
SALES (est): 771.67K Privately Held
SIC: 5085 3471 Abrasives; Finishing, metals or formed products

(G-2739)
CINCINNATI AIR CONDITIONING CO
Also Called: Honeywell Authorized Dealer
2080 Northwest Dr (45231-1700)
PHONE..............................513 721-5622
Mark Radtke, Pr
Michael Geiger, *
EMP: 55 EST: 1939
SQ FT: 30,000
SALES (est): 15.51MM Privately Held
Web: www.cincinnatiair.com
SIC: 1711 3822 Warm air heating and air conditioning contractor; Environmental controls

(G-2740)
CINCINNATI ASSN FOR THE BLIND
2045 Gilbert Ave (45202-1403)
PHONE..............................513 221-8558
TOLL FREE: 888
John Mitchell, CEO
Ginny Backscheider, SERVICES*
Jennifer Dubois, *
Amy Scrivner, OF Development
COMMUNITY Relations*
Bill Neyer, OF Business Development*
▲ EMP: 125 EST: 1910
SQ FT: 88,000
SALES (est): 12.08MM Privately Held
Web: www.cincyblind.org
SIC: 8331 8322 2891 Sheltered workshop; Association for the handicapped; Adhesives and sealants

(G-2741)
CINCINNATI BEVERAGE COMPANY
242 W Mcmicken Ave (45214-2314)
PHONE..............................513 904-8910
Jay Woffington, CEO
Stacey Schultz, Prin
EMP: 20 EST: 2020
SALES (est): 1.11MM Privately Held
SIC: 2082 Beer (alcoholic beverage)

(G-2742)
CINCINNATI BINDERY & PACKG INC
2838 Spring Grove Ave (45225-2268)
PHONE..............................859 816-0282
EMP: 7 EST: 2010
SALES (est): 540.73K Privately Held
Web: www.cincybindery.com
SIC: 2789 Bookbinding and related work

(G-2743)
CINCINNATI BIOREFINING CORP (HQ)
470 Este Ave (45232)
PHONE..............................513 482-8800
EMP: 10 EST: 2009
SALES (est): 18.97MM Publicly Held
SIC: 2079 Edible fats and oils
PA: Marathon Petroleum Corporation
539 S Main St
Findlay OH 45840

(G-2744)
CINCINNATI CONVERTORS INC
1730 Cleneay Ave (45212-3506)
PHONE..............................513 731-6600
Kristin Goltra, Pr
EMP: 12 EST: 1973
SQ FT: 15,000
SALES (est): 535.47K Privately Held
Web: www.cincinnaticonvertors.com
SIC: 2752 Commercial printing, lithographic

(G-2745)
CINCINNATI CRT INDEX PRESS INC
119 W Central Pkwy (45202-1075)
PHONE..............................513 241-1450
Gregory Arvanetes, Pr
Joseph W Shea Iii, VP
Mark Beatty, Genl Mgr
EMP: 9 EST: 1892
SALES (est): 305.48K Privately Held
Web: www.courtindex.com
SIC: 2741 Miscellaneous publishing

(G-2746)
CINCINNATI CTRL DYNAMICS INC
4924 Para Dr (45237-5012)
PHONE..............................513 242-7300
Jeffrey Bao, Pr
Jeffrey Bad, Dir
Kweesun Ng, Dir
EMP: 8 EST: 1976
SQ FT: 20,000
SALES (est): 1.61MM Privately Held
Web: www.airflowmachines.com
SIC: 3625 3829 7373 Control equipment, electric; Measuring and controlling devices, nec; Systems software development services

(G-2747)
CINCINNATI CUSTOM SIGNS INC
417 Northland Blvd (45240-3210)
PHONE..............................513 322-2559
EMP: 6 EST: 2015
SALES (est): 147.06K Privately Held
Web: www.cincicustomsigns.com
SIC: 3993 Signs and advertising specialties

(G-2748)
CINCINNATI ENQUIRER
312 Elm St Fl 18 (45202-2721)
PHONE..............................513 721-2700
EMP: 100 EST: 2008
SALES (est): 5.28MM Privately Held
Web: www.cincinnati.com
SIC: 2711 Newspapers, publishing and printing

(G-2749)
CINCINNATI GASKET PKG MFG INC
Also Called: Cincinnati Gasket & Indus GL
40 Illinois Ave (45215-5512)
PHONE..............................513 761-3458
Lawrence Uhlenbrock, Pr
Pete Knecht, *
Frank Duttenhofer, *
Henry D Hopf, *
◆ EMP: 45 EST: 1907
SQ FT: 75,000
SALES (est): 6.35MM Privately Held
Web: www.cgindustrialglass.com
SIC: 3229 3053 Glassware, industrial; Gaskets, all materials

(G-2750)
CINCINNATI GEARING SYSTEMS INC
301 Milford Pkwy (45227)
PHONE..............................513 527-8634
Kenneth Kiehl, VP
EMP: 30
SALES (corp-wide): 22.68MM Privately Held
Web: www.cincinnatigearingsystems.com
SIC: 3462 Gears, forged steel
PA: Cincinnati Gearing Systems Incorporated
5757 Mariemont Ave
Cincinnati OH 45227
513 527-8600

(G-2751)
CINCINNATI GEARING SYSTEMS INC (PA)
5757 Mariemont Ave (45227-4216)
PHONE..............................513 527-8600

Kenneth Kiehl, *Pr*
Walter L Rye, *
EMP: 75 **EST:** 1941
SQ FT: 100,000
SALES (est): 22.68MM
SALES (corp-wide): 22.68MM **Privately Held**
Web: www.cincinnatigearingsystems.com
SIC: 3398 3471 Metal heat treating; Plating and polishing

(G-2752)
CINCINNATI GILBERT MCH TL LLC
3366 Beekman St (45223-2424)
PHONE..................................513 541-4815
▲ **EMP:** 19 **EST:** 1995
SQ FT: 50,000
SALES (est): 1.23MM **Privately Held**
Web: www.cincinnatigilbert.com
SIC: 3541 Drilling machine tools (metal cutting)

(G-2753)
CINCINNATI LASER CUTTING LLC
Also Called: Cincinnati Metal Fabricating
891 Redna Ter (45215-1110)
PHONE..................................513 779-7200
Eric Hill, *Pr*
EMP: 40 **EST:** 1999
SQ FT: 45,000
SALES (est): 9.92MM **Privately Held**
Web: www.cincymetalfab.com
SIC: 3441 Fabricated structural metal

(G-2754)
CINCINNATI MEDIA LLC
Also Called: Cincinnati Magazine
1818 Race St Ste 301 (45202-7740)
PHONE..................................513 562-2755
Stefan Wanczyk, *CEO*
John Balardo, *Pr*
EMP: 43 **EST:** 2017
SALES (est): 163.26K **Privately Held**
Web: www.cincinnatimedia.com
SIC: 2721 Magazines: publishing and printing

(G-2755)
CINCINNATI MINE MACHINERY CO (PA)
2950 Jonrose Ave (45239-5319)
PHONE..................................513 522-7777
Robert J Stenger, *Pr*
William D Stenger, *
Jane Wegman, *
Ron Paolello, *
▲ **EMP:** 51 **EST:** 1924
SQ FT: 75,000
SALES (est): 9.41MM
SALES (corp-wide): 9.41MM **Privately Held**
Web: www.cinmine.com
SIC: 3541 3535 Machine tools, metal cutting type; Conveyors and conveying equipment

(G-2756)
CINCINNATI MTALS FBRCATION INC
6305 Lisbon Ave (45213-1227)
PHONE..................................513 382-2988
Eaon Latimore, *Prin*
EMP: 6 **EST:** 2014
SALES (est): 215.29K **Privately Held**
Web: www.cincymetals.com
SIC: 3499 Fabricated metal products, nec

(G-2757)
CINCINNATI PATTERN COMPANY
2405 Spring Grove Ave (45214-1727)
PHONE..................................513 241-9872
Michael J Ballard, *Pr*
EMP: 20 **EST:** 1972
SQ FT: 8,000
SALES (est): 943.44K **Privately Held**
Web: www.cinpat.com
SIC: 3543 Foundry patternmaking

(G-2758)
CINCINNATI PREMIER CANDY LLC
Also Called: Marpro
5141 Fischer Ave (45217-1157)
PHONE..................................513 253-0079
Bill Clark, *
Fred Runk, *
Sandy Runk, *
EMP: 8 **EST:** 1936
SQ FT: 30,000
SALES (est): 192.71K **Privately Held**
SIC: 2064 2099 Candy and other confectionery products; Food preparations, nec

(G-2759)
CINCINNATI RENEWABLE FUELS LLC
4700 Este Ave (45232-1415)
PHONE..................................513 482-8800
Jeffrie Defraties, *
Rajive Khosla, *
◆ **EMP:** 75 **EST:** 2002
SALES (est): 18.97MM **Publicly Held**
Web: www.twinriverstechnologies.com
SIC: 2079 Edible fats and oils
HQ: Cincinnati Biorefining Corp
 470 Este Ave
 Cincinnati OH 45232

(G-2760)
CINCINNATI SITE SOLUTIONS LLC
36 E 7th St Ste 1650 (45202-4452)
PHONE..................................513 373-5001
Stephen R Ramsey Esq, *Admn*
EMP: 6 **EST:** 2017
SALES (est): 67.98K **Privately Held**
Web: www.cincinnati.com
SIC: 2711 Newspapers, publishing and printing

(G-2761)
CINCINNATI STAIR & HANDRAIL
1220 Hill Smith Dr Ste C (45215-1250)
PHONE..................................513 722-3947
Dustin Kreiger, *Owner*
EMP: 13 **EST:** 1975
SALES (est): 395.01K **Privately Held**
Web: www.cincinnatistair.com
SIC: 2431 Millwork

(G-2762)
CINCINNATI STL TREATING CO LLC
5701 Mariemont Ave (45227-4299)
PHONE..................................513 271-3173
Robert W Rye, *Pr*
Walter L Rye, *Ch Bd*
Michael Reichling, *VP*
EMP: 40 **EST:** 2013
SALES (est): 407.2K **Privately Held**
Web: www.steeltreating.com
SIC: 3398 Metal heat treating

(G-2763)
CINCINNATI WINDOW SHADE INC (PA)
Also Called: Cincinnati Window Decor
3004 Harris Ave (45212-2404)
PHONE..................................513 631-7200
James G Frederick, *Pr*
Janet Frederick, *Treas*
James M Frederick, *Sec*
EMP: 16 **EST:** 1934
SQ FT: 15,000
SALES (est): 4.65MM
SALES (corp-wide): 4.65MM **Privately Held**
Web: www.blindsplusandmore.com
SIC: 5023 5719 2591 Window furnishings; Window shades, nec; Window shades

(G-2764)
CINCY CUPCAKES LLC
7940 Hosbrook Rd, (45243-1720)
PHONE..................................513 985-4440
EMP: 12 **EST:** 2012
SALES (est): 210.03K **Privately Held**
SIC: 2051 Bread, cake, and related products

(G-2765)
CINCY GLASS INC
3249 Fredonia Ave (45229-3309)
P.O. Box 141476 (45250-1476)
PHONE..................................513 241-0455
Michael T Brown, *Pr*
EMP: 8 **EST:** 1994
SALES (est): 891.49K **Privately Held**
Web: www.cincyglassig.com
SIC: 3441 Fabricated structural metal

(G-2766)
CINDUS CORPORATION
Also Called: Ptp of Mississippi
515 Station Ave (45215-6899)
PHONE..................................513 948-9951
▲ **EMP:** 100 **EST:** 1923
SALES (est): 18.7MM **Privately Held**
Web: www.cindus.com
SIC: 2679 Crepe paper or crepe paper products: purchased material

(G-2767)
CINEX INC
2641 Cummins St (45225-2099)
PHONE..................................513 921-2825
Gary R Smith, *Pr*
Judith A Smith, *
EMP: 25 **EST:** 1966
SQ FT: 35,000
SALES (est): 1MM **Privately Held**
Web: www.cinexinc.com
SIC: 3599 Machine shop, jobbing and repair

(G-2768)
CINFAB LLC
Also Called: Cinfab
5240 Lester Rd (45213-2522)
PHONE..................................513 396-6100
EMP: 140 **EST:** 1982
SQ FT: 36,500
SALES (est): 22.41MM **Privately Held**
Web: www.cinfab.com
SIC: 3444 Sheet metalwork

(G-2769)
CINTAS CORPORATION (PA)
Also Called: Cintas
6800 Cintas Blvd (45262)
P.O. Box 625737 (45262-5737)
PHONE..................................513 459-1200
Todd M Schneider, *Pr*
Scott D Farmer, *Ex Ch Bd*
James N Rozakis, *Ex VP*
J Michael Hansen, *Ex VP*
D Brock Denton, *Sr VP*
◆ **EMP:** 1500 **EST:** 1968
SALES (est): 8.82B
SALES (corp-wide): 8.82B **Publicly Held**
Web: www.cintas.com
SIC: 2326 2337 7218 5084 Work uniforms; Uniforms, except athletic: women's, misses', and juniors'; Industrial uniform supply; Safety equipment

(G-2770)
CINTAS CORPORATION
Also Called: Cintas Uniforms AP Fcilty Svcs
5570 Ridge Ave (45213-2516)
PHONE..................................513 631-5750
Marie Seng, *Brnch Mgr*
EMP: 100
SALES (corp-wide): 8.82B **Publicly Held**
Web: www.cintas.com
SIC: 2326 2337 7218 5084 Work uniforms; Uniforms, except athletic: women's, misses', and juniors'; Industrial uniform supply; Safety equipment
PA: Cintas Corporation
 6800 Cintas Blvd
 Cincinnati OH 45262
 513 459-1200

(G-2771)
CINTAS SALES CORPORATION (HQ)
Also Called: Cintas
6800 Cintas Blvd (45262)
PHONE..................................513 459-1200
Richard T Farmer, *Ch Bd*
Robert J Kohlhepp, *
Scott Farmer, *
Bill Gale, *
EMP: 450 **EST:** 1987
SALES (est): 22.08MM
SALES (corp-wide): 8.82B **Publicly Held**
SIC: 7218 2326 5136 5137 Industrial uniform supply; Work uniforms; Uniforms, men's and boys'; Uniforms, women's and children's
PA: Cintas Corporation
 6800 Cintas Blvd
 Cincinnati OH 45262
 513 459-1200

(G-2772)
CITYWIDE MATERIALS INC
Also Called: Citywide Ready Mix
5263 Wooster Pike (45226-2228)
PHONE..................................513 533-1111
Jerry Powell Junior, *Ch Bd*
Mark Cassiere, *Pr*
EMP: 20 **EST:** 1992
SQ FT: 560
SALES (est): 2.46MM **Privately Held**
Web: www.citywidematerials.com
SIC: 3273 Ready-mixed concrete

(G-2773)
CLARKE POWER SERVICES INC
Also Called: Clarke Fire Protection Product
3133 E Kemper Rd (45241-1516)
PHONE..................................513 771-2200
Dane Petrie, *Mgr*
EMP: 19
SALES (corp-wide): 225.9MM **Privately Held**
Web: www.clarkepowerservices.com
SIC: 3463 Pump, compressor, turbine, and engine forgings, except auto
PA: Clarke Power Services, Inc.
 3133 E Kemper Rd
 Cincinnati OH 45241
 513 771-2200

(G-2774)
CLIPSONS METAL WORKING INC
Also Called: Clipson S Metalworking
127 Novner Dr (45215-1300)
PHONE..................................513 772-6393
Stuart Clipson, *Pr*
Patricia Clipson, *VP*
EMP: 7 **EST:** 1982
SQ FT: 7,500
SALES (est): 962.44K **Privately Held**

Cincinnati - Hamilton County (G-2775)   GEOGRAPHIC SECTION

SIC: 3599 7692 3441 Machine shop, jobbing and repair; Welding repair; Fabricated structural metal

(G-2775)
CLOVERNOOK CTR FOR BLIND VSLLY (PA)
7000 Hamilton Ave (45231)
PHONE.................513 522-3860
Robin Usalis, Pr
Christopher Faust, *
Douglas Jacques, *
Betsy Baugh, *
Jacqueline L Conner, *
EMP: 125 EST: 1958
SQ FT: 40,000
SALES (est): 6.34MM
SALES (corp-wide): 6.34MM Privately Held
Web: www.clovernook.org
SIC: 2656 8322 7389 Paper cups, plates, dishes, and utensils; Rehabilitation services; Fund raising organizations

(G-2776)
CLUB 513 LLC
201 E 5th St 19th Fl (45202-4152)
PHONE.................800 530-2574
Aaron R Chiles, Managing Member
EMP: 6 EST: 2004
SQ FT: 3,500
SALES (est): 182.96K Privately Held
Web: www.club513llc.com
SIC: 7929 2759 5099 Entertainment group; Letterpress and screen printing; Novelties, durable

(G-2777)
CMT IMPORTS INC (PA)
2930 Glendale Milford Rd Ste 330 (45241)
PHONE.................513 615-1851
Wendell Hunsucker, Pr
Emily Triantos, VP Sls
Brent Atrick, VP Opers
▲ EMP: 6 EST: 2001
SQ FT: 2,300
SALES (est): 4.19MM
SALES (corp-wide): 4.19MM Privately Held
Web: www.cmtimports.com
SIC: 5051 3363 3321 3324 Castings, rough: iron or steel; Aluminum die-castings; Ductile iron castings; Commercial investment castings, ferrous

(G-2778)
CNC PAINTING INC
3244 Vittmer Ave (45238-2206)
PHONE.................513 662-1018
Becky Clark, Prin
EMP: 11 EST: 2010
SALES (est): 41K Privately Held
Web: www.pridetool.com
SIC: 3599 Machine shop, jobbing and repair

(G-2779)
COCA COLA OFFICES
4343 Cooper Rd (45242-5612)
PHONE.................678 327-8959
EMP: 6 EST: 2017
SALES (est): 103.79K Privately Held
Web: www.coca-cola.com
SIC: 2086 Bottled and canned soft drinks

(G-2780)
COCA-COLA CONSOLIDATED INC
Also Called: Coca-Cola
5100 Duck Creek Rd (45227-1450)
PHONE.................513 527-6600
John Whitaker, Mgr
EMP: 1183

SALES (corp-wide): 6.65B Publicly Held
Web: www.cokeconsolidated.com
SIC: 2086 Bottled and canned soft drinks
PA: Coca-Cola Consolidated, Inc.
    4100 Coca-Cola Plz
    Charlotte NC 28211
    704 557-4400

(G-2781)
COLYER C & SONS TRUCK SERVICE
11536 Reading Rd (45241-2241)
PHONE.................513 563-0663
Kirk Colyer, Pr
Charles Colyer, VP
EMP: 9 EST: 1970
SQ FT: 7,000
SALES (est): 439.52K Privately Held
Web: www.colyertruck.com
SIC: 7538 7534 5531 General truck repair; Tire repair shop; Automotive tires

(G-2782)
COMBINED CONTAINERBOARD INC
7741 School Rd (45249-1513)
PHONE.................513 530-5700
Phil Wenger, Genl Mgr
EMP: 52 EST: 1987
SQ FT: 162,000
SALES (est): 13.5MM
SALES (corp-wide): 5.22B Publicly Held
SIC: 2653 Sheets, corrugated: made from purchased materials
HQ: Greif Packaging Llc
    5800 Cane Run Rd
    Louisville KY 40258

(G-2783)
COMMUNICATIONS AID INC
Also Called: University Hring Aid Assctions
222 Piedmont Ave Ste 5200 (45219-4222)
PHONE.................513 475-8453
Stephanie Lockhart, Pr
Myles Pensak, Dir
EMP: 10 EST: 1978
SALES (est): 538.14K Privately Held
SIC: 5999 3842 Communication equipment; Hearing aids

(G-2784)
COMPLETE CYLINDER SERVICE INC
1240 Glendale Milford Rd (45215-1269)
PHONE.................513 772-1500
David Kleier, Prin
EMP: 8 EST: 2012
SALES (est): 895.79K Privately Held
Web: complete-cylinder-service.business.site
SIC: 3272 Cylinder pipe, prestressed or pretensioned concrete

(G-2785)
COMPOSITE SOLUTIONS LLC
3415 Paxton Ave (45208-2314)
PHONE.................513 321-7337
John Doyle, Prin
EMP: 6 EST: 2017
SALES (est): 94.58K Privately Held
Web: www.phoenix-mi.com
SIC: 3728 Aircraft parts and equipment, nec

(G-2786)
CONCENTRIX CVG LLC (DH)
201 E 4th St (45202-4248)
PHONE.................972 454-8000
James A Milton, Managing Member
David W Branderburg, *
Michael J Willner, *
Craig E Holmes, *
Dean C Howell, *
EMP: 109 EST: 2011
SALES (est): 241.52MM

SALES (corp-wide): 7.11B Publicly Held
SIC: 3661 PBX equipment, manual or automatic
HQ: Concentrix Cvg Corporation
    201 E 4th St
    Cincinnati OH 45202
    800 747-0583

(G-2787)
CONSOLDTED ANLYTCAL SYSTEMS IN
Also Called: Cas
2629 Spring Grove Ave (45214-1731)
PHONE.................513 542-1200
Seth Cloran, Pr
Jim Tish, VP
John Tish, Sec
EMP: 14 EST: 2012
SALES (est): 2.57MM Privately Held
Web: www.cas-en.com
SIC: 8711 2452 3448 3823 Consulting engineer; Prefabricated buildings, wood; Prefabricated metal buildings and components; Chromatographs, industrial process type

(G-2788)
CONSOLIDATED METAL PDTS INC (PA)
1028 Depot St (45204-2073)
PHONE.................513 251-2624
John Bernloehr, Pr
Hugh M Gallagher Junior, Pr
John J Kropp, *
EMP: 77 EST: 1945
SQ FT: 150,000
SALES (est): 23.63MM
SALES (corp-wide): 23.63MM Privately Held
Web: www.cmpubolt.com
SIC: 3452 3316 3356 Bolts, metal; Cold finishing of steel shapes; Nonferrous rolling and drawing, nec

(G-2789)
CONTACT CONTROL INTERFACES LLC
231 W 12th St Ste 201c (45202-8001)
PHONE.................609 333-3264
Thomas Buchanan, Prin
EMP: 20 EST: 2016
SALES (est): 772.78K Privately Held
Web: www.contact.ci
SIC: 3577 Computer peripheral equipment, nec

(G-2790)
CONTINENTAL MINERAL PROCESSING CORPORATION
11817 Mosteller Rd (45241-1524)
P.O. Box 62005 (45262-0005)
PHONE.................513 771-7190
◆ EMP: 20 EST: 1948
SALES (est): 7MM Privately Held
Web: www.continentalmineral.com
SIC: 3295 Minerals, ground or treated

(G-2791)
CONTROL CRAFT LLC
1123 Hickorywood Ct (45233-4845)
PHONE.................513 674-0056
EMP: 10 EST: 2000
SALES (est): 1.01MM Privately Held
Web: www.controlcraftllc.com
SIC: 3613 Control panels, electric

(G-2792)
CONTROLLED RELEASE SOCIETY INC
110 E 69th St (45216-2008)

PHONE.................513 948-8000
Danny Lachman, Ofcr
EMP: 7 EST: 2014
SALES (est): 349.12K Privately Held
Web: www.controlledreleasesociety.org
SIC: 2869 Industrial organic chemicals, nec

(G-2793)
CONTROLS AND SHEET METAL INC (PA)
1051 Sargent St (45203-1858)
PHONE.................513 721-3610
Rick Schaible, Pr
Danny D Bishop, Prin
Anthony S Knuckles, Prin
EMP: 21 EST: 1983
SQ FT: 40,000
SALES (est): 9.33MM
SALES (corp-wide): 9.33MM Privately Held
SIC: 5075 3444 Warm air heating and air conditioning; Ducts, sheet metal

(G-2794)
COOL TIMES
6127 Fairway Dr (45212-1307)
PHONE.................513 608-5201
Calvin Lanier, Prin
EMP: 8 EST: 2010
SALES (est): 440.79K Privately Held
Web: www.cooltimeshvac.com
SIC: 3822 Air flow controllers, air conditioning and refrigeration

(G-2795)
COOLANT CONTROL INC (HQ)
5353 Spring Grove Ave (45217-1095)
PHONE.................513 471-8770
Greg Battle, CEO
Garry C Ferraris, *
Jorge Costa, *
Larry Schirmann, *
▲ EMP: 33 EST: 1975
SQ FT: 30,000
SALES (est): 11.67MM
SALES (corp-wide): 11.67MM Privately Held
Web: www.coolantcontrol.com
SIC: 2899 2819 Chemical preparations, nec; Industrial inorganic chemicals, nec
PA: Kodiak, Llc
    1800 Murray Ave
    Pittsburgh PA 15217
    724 812-6595

(G-2796)
CORE OPTIX INC
821 Melbourne St (45229-3311)
PHONE.................855 267-3678
Joseph Kreidler, Pr
Joseph Kreidler, Pr
John Thomson, VP
◆ EMP: 10 EST: 2011
SQ FT: 8,000
SALES (est): 516.9K Privately Held
Web: www.coreoptix.com
SIC: 2298 3357 3351 Cable, fiber; Fiber optic cable (insulated); Wire, copper and copper alloy

(G-2797)
CORPORATE DCMENT SOLUTIONS INC (PA)
11120 Ashburn Rd (45240-3813)
PHONE.................513 595-8200
Mary C Percy, Pr
Harold B Percy Junior, VP
EMP: 9 EST: 1992
SQ FT: 15,000
SALES (est): 2.7MM Privately Held
Web: www.cdsprint.com

GEOGRAPHIC SECTION   **Cincinnati - Hamilton County (G-2822)**

SIC: **7334** 2752 2759 Photocopying and duplicating services; Offset and photolithographic printing; Commercial printing, nec

(G-2798)
CORRUGATED CHEMICALS INC
Also Called: Corrugated Chemicals
3865 Virginia Ave (45227-3409)
PHONE.................................513 561-7773
Tod Sistrunk, *Mgr*
EMP: 6
SQ FT: 23,940
SALES (corp-wide): 5.1MM **Privately Held**
Web: www.corrugatedchemicals.com
SIC: **2869** 5169 Industrial organic chemicals, nec; Chemicals and allied products, nec
PA: Corrugated Chemicals, Inc.
5410 Homberg Dr Ste 20
Knoxville TN 37919
865 588-2471

(G-2799)
COVIDIEN HOLDING INC
Also Called: Covidien
2111 E Galbraith Rd (45237-1624)
PHONE.................................513 948-7219
EMP: 151
Web: www.covidien.com
SIC: **3841** Surgical and medical instruments
HQ: Covidien Holding Inc.
710 Medtronic Pkwy
Minneapolis MN 55432

(G-2800)
CPG - OHIO LLC (HQ)
470 Northland Blvd (45240-3211)
PHONE.................................513 825-4800
Chaim Kaufman, *
EMP: 51 **EST:** 2016
SALES (est): 10.07MM
SALES (corp-wide): 57.46MM **Privately Held**
Web: www.conpackgroup.com
SIC: **2671** 2673 Plastic film, coated or laminated for packaging; Plastic bags: made from purchased materials
PA: Consolidated Packaging Group, Inc.
30 Bergen Tpke
Ridgefield Park NJ 07660
201 440-4240

(G-2801)
CRACO EMBROIDERY INC
37 Techview Dr (45215-1980)
PHONE.................................513 563-6999
Bob Crable, *Pr*
Rick Crable, *VP*
EMP: 9 **EST:** 1991
SQ FT: 1,200
SALES (est): 369.17K **Privately Held**
SIC: **2395** Emblems, embroidered

(G-2802)
CREE LOGISTICS LLC
Also Called: UPS Store 7395
7439 Wooster Pike (45227-3895)
PHONE.................................513 978-1112
James W Cree, *Mgr*
EMP: 6 **EST:** 2021
SALES (est): 300K **Privately Held**
SIC: **3861** Printing frames, photographic

(G-2803)
CROWN EQUIPMENT CORPORATION
Also Called: Crown Lift Trucks
10685 Medallion Dr (45241-4827)
PHONE.................................513 874-2600
EMP: 85
SALES (corp-wide): 7.12B **Privately Held**
Web: www.crown.com

SIC: **3537** Lift trucks, industrial: fork, platform, straddle, etc.
PA: Crown Equipment Corporation
44 S Washington St
New Bremen OH 45869
419 629-2311

(G-2804)
CSP GROUP INC
7141 E Kemper Rd (45249-1028)
PHONE.................................513 984-9500
EMP: 20
Web: www.lumisigns.com
SIC: **3993** Signs and advertising specialties

(G-2805)
CTEK TOOL & MACHINE COMPANY
11310 Southland Rd (45240-3201)
PHONE.................................513 742-0423
Phyllis Couch, *Pr*
James Couch, *VP*
EMP: 6 **EST:** 1993
SQ FT: 6,500
SALES (est): 508.23K **Privately Held**
Web: www.ctektool.com
SIC: **3599** Machine shop, jobbing and repair

(G-2806)
CTS WATERJET LLC
2865 Compton Rd (45251-2633)
PHONE.................................513 641-0600
Steve Goldschmidt, *Prin*
EMP: 7 **EST:** 2019
SALES (est): 493.25K **Privately Held**
Web: www.cts-waterjet.com
SIC: **3599** Machine shop, jobbing and repair

(G-2807)
CUSTOM CARVING SOURCE LLC
3182 Beekman St (45223-2422)
PHONE.................................513 407-1008
EMP: 8 **EST:** 2008
SALES (est): 194.58K **Privately Held**
SIC: **2431** Moldings, wood: unfinished and prefinished

(G-2808)
CUSTOM MATERIAL HDLG EQP LLC
7868 Gapstow Brg (45231-6058)
PHONE.................................513 235-5336
EMP: 6 **EST:** 2006
SALES (est): 410.87K **Privately Held**
SIC: **2411** Logging camps and contractors

(G-2809)
CUSTOM QUALITY PRODUCTS INC
1645 Blue Rock St (45223-7500)
EMP: 23 **EST:** 1982
SALES (est): 2.2MM **Privately Held**
Web: www.cqpinc.com
SIC: **3442** Metal doors, sash, and trim

(G-2810)
CUSTOM TOOLING COMPANY
603 Wayne Park Dr (45215-2848)
PHONE.................................513 733-5790
Thomas Brune, *Pr*
Charles Brune, *VP*
EMP: 10 **EST:** 1963
SQ FT: 5,000
SALES (est): 1.57MM **Privately Held**
Web: www.custom-tooling.com
SIC: **3599** Machine shop, jobbing and repair

(G-2811)
D & M SAW & TOOL INC
Also Called: Eccles Saw & Tool
2974 P G Graves Ln (45241-3155)
PHONE.................................513 871-5433
Michael Hugenberg, *Pr*

EMP: 9 **EST:** 1954
SQ FT: 6,000
SALES (est): 453.86K **Privately Held**
Web: www.ecclessaw.com
SIC: **7699** 5251 3423 Knife, saw and tool sharpening and repair; Chainsaws; Cutting dies, except metal cutting

(G-2812)
D C MORRISON COMPANY INC
11959 Tramway Dr (45241-1666)
P.O. Box 12586 (41012-0586)
PHONE.................................859 581-7511
Henry E Reder, *Pr*
Roger E Reder, *
Bernice Reder, *
Greg Reder, *
EMP: 30 **EST:** 1963
SALES (est): 2.69MM **Privately Held**
Web: www.dcmorrison.com
SIC: **3545** 3542 Machine tool attachments and accessories; Machine tools, metal forming type

(G-2813)
D F ELECTRONICS INC
200 Novner Dr (45215-6002)
PHONE.................................513 772-7792
Donald Fine, *Pr*
Ann Fine, *
EMP: 75 **EST:** 1975
SQ FT: 27,000
SALES (est): 9.05MM **Privately Held**
Web: www.dfelectronics.com
SIC: **3674** Solid state electronic devices, nec

(G-2814)
D+H USA CORPORATION
Also Called: DH
312 Plum St Ste 500 (45202-4810)
PHONE.................................513 381-9400
EMP: 173
SALES (corp-wide): 1.24B **Privately Held**
SIC: **7372** Application computer software
HQ: D+H Usa Corporation
1320 Sw Broadway Ste 100
Portland OR 97204
407 804-6600

(G-2815)
D-G CUSTOM CHROME LLC
5200 Lester Rd (45213-2522)
PHONE.................................513 531-1881
Alex Wyatt, *Pr*
Don Gorman, *
Victoria Gorman, *
EMP: 9 **EST:** 2002
SQ FT: 10,162
SALES (est): 1.01MM **Privately Held**
Web: www.dgcustomchrome.com
SIC: **5013** 3471 Automotive supplies and parts; Plating and polishing

(G-2816)
DADCO INC
Also Called: Rpp Containers
10111 Evendale Commons Dr (45241-2689)
PHONE.................................513 489-2244
Scott Denoma, *Pr*
Jim West, *VP*
EMP: 17 **EST:** 1998
SALES (est): 8.59MM **Privately Held**
Web: www.rppcontainers.com
SIC: **5085** 3089 Bins and containers, storage ; Plastics containers, except foam

(G-2817)
DALE KESTLER
Also Called: Apollo GL Mirror Win Screen Co
3475 Cardiff Ave (45209-1317)

PHONE.................................513 871-9000
Dale Kestler, *Pr*
EMP: 8 **EST:** 1991
SQ FT: 1,500
SALES (est): 993.53K **Privately Held**
Web: www.apolloglassmirror.com
SIC: **5231** 5719 5211 3442 Glass; Mirrors; Door and window products; Screens, window, metal

(G-2818)
DANGELICO GUITARS ✪
10346 Evendale Dr (45241-2512)
PHONE.................................513 218-3985
EMP: 6 **EST:** 2022
SALES (est): 78.58K **Privately Held**
Web: www.dangelicoguitars.com
SIC: **3931** Guitars and parts, electric and nonelectric

(G-2819)
DARLING INGREDIENTS INC
Also Called: Cincinnati Transfer Station
3105 Spring Grove Ave (45225-1821)
PHONE.................................972 717-0300
Tim Fontaine, *Mgr*
EMP: 9
SALES (corp-wide): 6.53B **Publicly Held**
Web: www.darlingii.com
SIC: **2077** Animal and marine fats and oils
PA: Darling Ingredients Inc.
5601 N Macarthur Blvd
Irving TX 75038
972 717-0300

(G-2820)
DATA PROCESSING SCIENCES CORPORATION
Also Called: Dpsciences
2 Camargo Cyn (45243-2945)
PHONE.................................513 791-7100
▼ **EMP:** 65
SIC: **4813** 5045 3669 3577 Telephone communication, except radio; Computers, peripherals, and software; Intercommunication systems, electric; Computer peripheral equipment, nec

(G-2821)
DB PARENT INC
3630 E Kemper Rd (45241-2011)
PHONE.................................513 475-3265
Tom Heintz, *CFO*
EMP: 7 **EST:** 2013
SALES (est): 195.52K **Privately Held**
SIC: **2819** Industrial inorganic chemicals, nec

(G-2822)
DEBRA-KUEMPEL INC (HQ)
Also Called: De Bra - Kuempel
3976 Southern Ave (45227)
P.O. Box 701620 (45227)
PHONE.................................513 271-6500
Fred B De Bra, *Ch Bd*
Joe D Clark, *
Morris H Reed, *
Debbie Biggs, *
Bill Flaugher, *
EMP: 73 **EST:** 1944
SQ FT: 20,079
SALES (est): 59.73MM
SALES (corp-wide): 12.58B **Publicly Held**
Web: www.dkemcor.com
SIC: **3446** 1711 3443 3441 Architectural metalwork; Mechanical contractor; Fabricated plate work (boiler shop); Fabricated structural metal
PA: Emcor Group, Inc.
301 Merritt 7
Norwalk CT 06851
203 849-7800

(PA)=Parent Co (HQ)=Headquarters
✪ = New Business established in last 2 years

Cincinnati - Hamilton County (G-2823)

GEOGRAPHIC SECTION

(G-2823)
DEGUSSA INCORPORATED
620 Shepherd Dr (45215-2104)
PHONE..................513 733-5111
Probyn Forbes, *Prin*
▲ **EMP:** 8 **EST:** 2008
SALES (est): 249.84K **Privately Held**
SIC: 2816 Inorganic pigments

(G-2824)
DELTA POWER SUPPLY INC
10330 Chester Rd (45215-1225)
PHONE..................513 771-3835
▲ **EMP:** 11 **EST:** 1995
SQ FT: 7,500
SALES (est): 1.1MM **Privately Held**
SIC: 3648 Lighting equipment, nec

(G-2825)
DERRICK COMPANY INC
4560 Kellogg Ave (45226-2499)
PHONE..................513 321-8122
Gary Schmid, *CEO*
Jason Schmid, *
Kathie Schmid, *
EMP: 25 **EST:** 1923
SQ FT: 170,000
SALES (est): 2.79MM **Privately Held**
Web: www.derrickcompany.com
SIC: 3398 3471 Metal heat treating; Sand blasting of metal parts

(G-2826)
DESIGN MASTERS INC
800 Redna Ter (45215-1111)
PHONE..................513 772-7175
Terry Masters, *Pr*
EMP: 6 **EST:** 1994
SALES (est): 452.25K **Privately Held**
Web: www.dmisigns.com
SIC: 3993 7532 7319 Signs, not made in custom sign painting shops; Truck painting and lettering; Display advertising service

(G-2827)
DEVICOR MED PDTS HOLDINGS INC
300 E Business Way Fl 5 (45241-2384)
PHONE..................513 864-9000
EMP: 550 **EST:** 2010
SALES (est): 48.56MM **Privately Held**
Web: www.mammotome.com
SIC: 3841 Surgical and medical instruments

(G-2828)
DIAMANT POLYMERS INC
3495 Mustafa Dr (45241-1668)
PHONE..................513 979-4011
EMP: 6 **EST:** 2020
SALES (est): 140.78K **Privately Held**
Web: www.diamantpolymersinc.com
SIC: 2821 Plastics materials and resins

(G-2829)
DIP COAT CUSTOMS LLC
2303 Beechmont Ave (45230-5317)
PHONE..................513 503-1243
Chad Wiseman, *CEO*
EMP: 21
SALES (est): 1.32MM **Privately Held**
Web: www.dipcoatcustom.com
SIC: 2851 Vinyl coatings, strippable

(G-2830)
DITSCH USA LLC
311 Northland Blvd (45246-3690)
PHONE..................513 782-8888
Gary Gottenbusch, *CEO*
Brian Tooley, *CFO*
EMP: 50 **EST:** 2014
SQ FT: 100,000
SALES (est): 11.26MM **Privately Held**
Web: www.ditsch.com
SIC: 2052 5149 Pretzels; Bakery products
HQ: Valora Holding Ag
Hofackerstrasse 40
Muttenz BL 4132

(G-2831)
DIVERSEYLEVER INC
3630 E Kemper Rd (45241-2011)
PHONE..................513 554-4200
Richard Koch, *Pr*
EMP: 9 **EST:** 2017
SALES (est): 343.2K **Privately Held**
Web: www.duboischemicals.com
SIC: 2819 Industrial inorganic chemicals, nec

(G-2832)
DIVERSIFIED OPHTHALMICS INC
Also Called: Diversified SE Division
250 Mccullough St (45226-2145)
PHONE..................803 783-3434
Sara Baldwin, *Mgr*
EMP: 42
SIC: 5048 3851 5049 Contact lenses; Contact lenses; Optical goods
HQ: Diversified Ophthalmics, Inc.
250 Mccullough St
Cincinnati OH
800 852-8089

(G-2833)
DIVERSIPAK INC
838 Reedy St (45202-2216)
PHONE..................513 321-7884
Dan Kunkemoeller, *CEO*
Jennifer Kunkemoeller, *
Greg Lamping, *
Douglas Hearn, *
Jake Linz, *
EMP: 50 **EST:** 1998
SQ FT: 15,000
SALES (est): 15.5MM **Privately Held**
Web: www.diversipak.com
SIC: 2671 Paper, coated or laminated for packaging

(G-2834)
DIVISION OVERHEAD DOOR INC (PA)
Also Called: Cincinnati Prof Door Sls Div
861 Dellway St (45229-3305)
P.O. Box 12588 (41012-0588)
PHONE..................513 872-0888
Robert H Mc Kibben Junior, *Pr*
Pat Higgins, *VP*
Jim Morrison, *Sec*
EMP: 19 **EST:** 1942
SQ FT: 12,000
SALES (est): 1.76MM
SALES (corp-wide): 1.76MM **Privately Held**
Web: www.divisionoverheaddoor.com
SIC: 3442 2431 7699 1751 Garage doors, overhead: metal; Garage doors, overhead, wood; Garage door repair; Garage door, installation or erection

(G-2835)
DMG MORI
300 E Business Way Ste 200 (45241)
PHONE..................513 808-4842
Roopan Dey, *Prin*
EMP: 6 **EST:** 2017
SALES (est): 218.61K **Privately Held**
Web: en.dmgmori-ag.com
SIC: 3541 Machine tools, metal cutting type

(G-2836)
DOMINION LIQUID TECH LLC
Also Called: D L T
3965 Virginia Ave (45227-3411)
PHONE..................513 272-2824
Charles Cain, *Managing Member*
EMP: 41 **EST:** 2003
SQ FT: 54,000
SALES (est): 7.32MM **Privately Held**
Web: www.dltdelivers.com
SIC: 2087 2033 Syrups, drink; Barbecue sauce: packaged in cans, jars, etc.

(G-2837)
DOSMATIC USA INC (PA)
3798 Round Bottom Rd (45244-2413)
PHONE..................972 245-9765
Jeff Rowe, *Pr*
Steve Vogel, *VP*
▲ **EMP:** 18 **EST:** 1990
SQ FT: 25,000
SALES (est): 4.98MM **Privately Held**
Web: www.hydrosystemsco.com
SIC: 3569 Liquid automation machinery and equipment

(G-2838)
DOVER WIPES COMPANY
1 Procter And Gamble Plz (45202-3315)
PHONE..................513 983-1100
EMP: 88 **EST:** 1999
SALES (est): 5.38MM
SALES (corp-wide): 82.01B **Publicly Held**
SIC: 2844 Deodorants, personal
PA: The Procter & Gamble Company
1 Procter & Gamble Plz
Cincinnati OH 45202
513 983-1100

(G-2839)
DOWNHOME INC
Also Called: Down Decor Ohio Feather
1910 South St (45204-2034)
PHONE..................513 921-3373
EMP: 33
Web: www.downdecor.com
SIC: 2392 Pillows, bed: made from purchased materials
PA: Downhome, Inc.
1 Kovach Dr
Cincinnati OH 45215

(G-2840)
DOWNHOME INC (PA)
Also Called: Down Decor
1 Kovach Dr (45215)
PHONE..................513 921-3373
▲ **EMP:** 44 **EST:** 1994
SALES (est): 10.13MM **Privately Held**
Web: www.downdecor.com
SIC: 2392 Pillows, bed: made from purchased materials

(G-2841)
DRAPERY STTCH - CINCINNATI INC
5601 Wooster Pike (45227-4120)
PHONE..................513 561-2443
EMP: 10 **EST:** 1987
SALES (est): 358.64K **Privately Held**
Web: www.draperystitch.com
SIC: 2391 Draperies, plastic and textile: from purchased materials

(G-2842)
DSS INSTALLATIONS LTD
Also Called: Dss/Drect Tv/Rfs/Ms/rmediation
6721 Montgomery Rd Ste 1 (45236-3890)
P.O. Box 36520 (45236-0520)
PHONE..................513 761-7000
Allen Sheff, *Pt*
Allen Sheff, *Managing Member*
EMP: 17 **EST:** 1990
SALES (est): 429.31K **Privately Held**
Web: www.dssinstallations.com
SIC: 5731 1731 7622 3825 Antennas, satellite dish; Cable television installation; Antenna repair and installation; Radio frequency measuring equipment

(G-2843)
DSWDWK LLC
Also Called: Taft's Brewpourium Cincinnati
4831 Spring Grove Ave (45232-1938)
PHONE..................513 853-5021
EMP: 6 **EST:** 2013
SALES (est): 1.07MM **Privately Held**
Web: www.taftsbeer.com
SIC: 2082 Malt beverages

(G-2844)
DWD2 INC
10200 Wayne Ave (45215-1127)
P.O. Box 15627 (45215-0627)
PHONE..................513 563-0070
David Draginoff, *CEO*
Candra Draginoff, *Sec*
Jack Taylor Contl, *Prin*
Mike Trovillo, *VP*
EMP: 17 **EST:** 1972
SQ FT: 11,500
SALES (est): 3.87MM **Privately Held**
Web: www.pridetool.com
SIC: 3599 Machine shop, jobbing and repair

(G-2845)
DYNAMIC INDUSTRIES INC
3611 Woodburn Ave (45207-1019)
PHONE..................513 861-6767
Phillip J Mitchell, *Pr*
Henry W Ochs, *
EMP: 33 **EST:** 1985
SQ FT: 150,000
SALES (est): 6.47MM **Privately Held**
Web: www.dynamicindustries.com
SIC: 3599 Machine shop, jobbing and repair

(G-2846)
DYNEON LLC
2165 Cablecar Ct (45244-4101)
PHONE..................859 334-4500
Thomasine Miller, *Mgr*
EMP: 271
SALES (corp-wide): 32.68B **Publicly Held**
SIC: 3087 Custom compound purchased resins
HQ: Dyneon Llc
6744 33rd St N
Oakdale MN 55128

(G-2847)
E & J GALLO WINERY
125 E Court St (45202-1212)
PHONE..................513 381-4050
Holly Mcclelland, *Mgr*
EMP: 38
SALES (corp-wide): 2.11B **Privately Held**
Web: www.gallo.com
SIC: 2084 Wines
PA: E. & J. Gallo Winery
600 Yosemite Blvd
Modesto CA 95354
209 341-3111

(G-2848)
E C SHAW COMPANY OF OHIO
1242 Mehring Way (45203-1836)
PHONE..................513 721-6334
Joseph Grome, *Pr*
Robert Grome, *OF Purchasing*
Kenneth Grome, *
EMP: 30 **EST:** 1912
SQ FT: 12,000
SALES (est): 2.79MM **Privately Held**
Web: www.ecshaw.com

GEOGRAPHIC SECTION

Cincinnati - Hamilton County (G-2871)

SIC: 3555 3953 3469 2821 Printing plates; Marking devices; Metal stampings, nec; Plastics materials and resins

(G-2849)
E I CERAMICS LLC
2600 Commerce Blvd (45241-1552)
PHONE.................................513 772-7001
Graham J Roberts, *Managing Member*
▲ **EMP:** 60 **EST:** 2002
SALES (est): 11.8MM **Privately Held**
SIC: 3297 Graphite refractories: carbon bond or ceramic bond
HQ: Ifgl Refractories Limited
3, Netaji Subash Road,
Kolkata WB 70000

(G-2850)
E P S SPECIALISTS LTD INC
7875 School Rd (45249-1531)
PHONE.................................513 489-3676
Ed L Wilkson, *Pr*
Lee Wilkinson, *VP*
EMP: 6 **EST:** 1989
SALES (est): 170.46K **Privately Held**
Web: www.lamlite.com
SIC: 2821 Plastics materials and resins

(G-2851)
E&O FBN INC
2230 Gilbert Ave (45206-2531)
PHONE.................................513 241-5150
Robert J Van Lear, *Pr*
Gayle Sherman, *VP*
EMP: 12 **EST:** 1963
SQ FT: 10,000
SALES (est): 327.23K **Privately Held**
Web: www.dovgraphics.com
SIC: 2791 2752 2759 Photocomposition, for the printing trade; Offset printing; Letterpress printing

(G-2852)
EAGLE CREEK INC
Also Called: EAGLE CREEK, INC.
9799 Prechtel Rd (45252-2117)
PHONE.................................513 385-4442
EMP: 83
SALES (corp-wide): 24.6MM **Privately Held**
Web: www.eaglecreek.com
SIC: 3161 Traveling bags
PA: Eagle Creek Ip, Llc
2620 S Cop Frntge Rd Uni
Steamboat Springs CO 80487
760 431-6400

(G-2853)
EAGLEBURGMANN INDUSTRIES LP
3478 Hauck Rd Ste A (45241-4604)
PHONE.................................513 563-7325
Matt Vaupel, *Mgr*
EMP: 10
SALES (corp-wide): 12.23B **Privately Held**
Web: www.eagleburgmann.us
SIC: 3053 Gaskets; packing and sealing devices
HQ: Eagleburgmann Industries Lp
10035 Brookriver Dr
Houston TX 77040
713 939-9515

(G-2854)
EASTGATE CUSTOM GRAPHICS LTD
Also Called: Loveland Graphics
4459 Mount Carmel Tobasco Rd (45244-2225)
PHONE.................................513 528-7922
Donald R Hall, *Pt*
EMP: 7 **EST:** 1994
SQ FT: 42,000

SALES (est): 814.77K **Privately Held**
Web: www.ecgraphix.com
SIC: 7336 5999 2395 Silk screen design; Banners; Embroidery and art needlework

(G-2855)
EASY WAY LEISURE COMPANY LLC (PA)
Also Called: Easy Way Products
8950 Rossash Rd (45236-1210)
PHONE.................................513 731-5640
Jon Randman, *Pr*
Scott Szymkowicz, *
Steve Coppel, *
Pamela Ruvle, *
◆ **EMP:** 40 **EST:** 1947
SQ FT: 100,000
SALES (est): 48.88MM
SALES (corp-wide): 48.88MM **Privately Held**
Web: www.easywayproducts.com
SIC: 2392 Cushions and pillows

(G-2856)
EBEL-BINDER PRINTING CO INC
Also Called: Ebel Tape & Label
1630 Dalton Ave # 1 (45214-2020)
PHONE.................................513 471-1067
Thomas Heidemann, *Pr*
Marian Dulle, *VP*
James Dulle, *Treas*
EMP: 7 **EST:** 1937
SQ FT: 3,000
SALES (est): 640.63K **Privately Held**
SIC: 2759 Flexographic printing

(G-2857)
ECM INDUSTRIES LLC
Also Called: Ecm Industries, Llc
3898 Duck Creek Rd (45227)
PHONE.................................513 533-6242
EMP: 26
SALES (corp-wide): 135.91MM **Privately Held**
Web: www.ilsco.com
SIC: 3643 3369 3451 3678 Current-carrying wiring services; Nonferrous foundries, nec; Screw machine products; Electronic connectors
HQ: Ilsco, Llc
4730 Madison Rd
Cincinnati OH 45227
513 533-6200

(G-2858)
ECOPAC LLC ✪
Also Called: Distrubutors
8100 Reading Rd (45237-1404)
PHONE.................................732 715-0236
Srinivas Bandinani, *Managing Member*
EMP: 6 **EST:** 2022
SALES (est): 593.95K **Privately Held**
Web: www.ecopackamerica.com
SIC: 2674 Paper bags: made from purchased materials

(G-2859)
ECU CORPORATION (PA)
11500 Goldcoast Dr (45249-1621)
PHONE.................................513 898-9294
Mike Fox, *Pr*
Hank Worsley, *VP*
◆ **EMP:** 18 **EST:** 2006
SQ FT: 25,000
SALES (est): 4.54MM **Privately Held**
Web: www.ecucorp.com
SIC: 3585 Air conditioning units, complete: domestic or industrial

(G-2860)
EKCO CLEANING INC
4055 Executive Park Dr Ste 240 (45241-4029)
PHONE.................................513 733-8882
Peter Campanella, *Pr*
C Robert Kidder, *Ch Bd*
EMP: 220 **EST:** 1926
SALES (est): 33.9MM
SALES (corp-wide): 995.27MM **Privately Held**
SIC: 5199 2392 3991 Broom, mop, and paint handles; Mops, floor and dust; Brushes, household or industrial
HQ: Instant Brands Llc
3025 Highland Pkwy # 700
Downers Grove IL 60515
847 233-8600

(G-2861)
ELECTRIC SERVICE CO INC
5331 Hetzell St (45227-1513)
PHONE.................................513 271-6387
Helen Snyder, *Pr*
EMP: 34 **EST:** 1912
SQ FT: 35,000
SALES (est): 2.41MM **Privately Held**
Web: www.elscotransformers.com
SIC: 7629 3677 3621 Electronic equipment repair; Transformers power supply, electronic type; Phase or rotary converters (electrical equipment)

(G-2862)
ELECTRONAUTS LLC
621 Wilmer Ave (45226-1859)
PHONE.................................859 261-3600
Douglas E Gilb, *Managing Member*
◆ **EMP:** 18 **EST:** 1979
SQ FT: 55,000
SALES (est): 8.39MM **Privately Held**
Web: www.electronauts.com
SIC: 3679 Electronic circuits

(G-2863)
ELEEO BRANDS LLC
Also Called: Boogie Wipes
212 E 3rd St (45202-5500)
▲ **EMP:** 6 **EST:** 2020
SALES (est): 1.1MM **Privately Held**
Web: www.boogiewipes.com
SIC: 2676 Sanitary paper products

(G-2864)
ELEEO BRANDS LLC
2150 Winchell Ave (45214-1853)
PHONE.................................513 572-8100
Richard Palmer Mng, *Mgr*
EMP: 8 **EST:** 2020
SALES (est): 1.01MM **Privately Held**
Web: www.eleeobrands.com
SIC: 4783 2676 Packing goods for shipping; Sanitary paper products

(G-2865)
EMERSON ELECTRIC CO
Also Called: Emerson
6000 Fernview Ave (45212-1312)
PHONE.................................513 731-2020
Brent Schroeder, *Mgr*
EMP: 200
SALES (corp-wide): 15.16B **Publicly Held**
Web: www.emerson.com
SIC: 3823 Process control instruments
PA: Emerson Electric Co.
8000 W Florissant Ave
Saint Louis MO 63136
314 553-2000

(G-2866)
EMERY OLEOCHEMICALS LLC (HQ)
Also Called: Emery
4900 Este Ave (45232-1491)
PHONE.................................513 762-2500
Robert J Squires, *Managing Member*
◆ **EMP:** 32 **EST:** 2005
SQ FT: 4,032
SALES (est): 159.56MM **Privately Held**
Web: www.emeryoleo.com
SIC: 2899 Acids
PA: Edenor Oleochemicals (M) Sdn. Bhd.
Lot 1 Jalan Perak
Telok Panglima Garang SLG 42500

(G-2867)
EMPIRICAL MANUFACTURING CO INC
7616 Reinhold Dr (45237-3312)
PHONE.................................513 948-1616
Gloria Tarver, *Pr*
Gloria Jenkins, *Pr*
EMP: 37 **EST:** 1986
SQ FT: 8,200
SALES (est): 562.77K **Privately Held**
Web: www.empirical-co.com
SIC: 2311 Men's and boys' uniforms

(G-2868)
ENCLOSURE SUPPLIERS LLC
Also Called: Champion
12119 Champion Way (45241-6419)
PHONE.................................513 782-3900
▲ **EMP:** 30 **EST:** 1990
SQ FT: 160,000
SALES (est): 12.14MM **Privately Held**
Web: www.esi-blinds.com
SIC: 3448 5031 3231 Prefabricated metal buildings; Lumber, plywood, and millwork; Products of purchased glass
HQ: Champion Opco, Llc
12121 Champion Way
Cincinnati OH 45241
513 327-7338

(G-2869)
ENCOMPASS WOODWORKING LLC
1303 Monmouth St (45225-1349)
PHONE.................................513 569-2841
Adam Schwoeppe, *Managing Member*
EMP: 9 **EST:** 2014
SALES (est): 653.74K **Privately Held**
Web: www.encompasswoodworking.com
SIC: 2431 Millwork

(G-2870)
ENDURANCE INDUSTRIES LLC
5055 Madison Rd (45227-1431)
PHONE.................................513 285-8503
EMP: 8 **EST:** 2018
SALES (est): 464.31K **Privately Held**
Web: www.endurance.industries
SIC: 3999 Manufacturing industries, nec

(G-2871)
ENERFAB INC
ENERFAB, INC.
11861 Mosteller Rd (45241-1524)
PHONE.................................513 771-2300
Steve Zoller, *Genl Mgr*
EMP: 6
SQ FT: 250,000
SALES (corp-wide): 550.89MM **Privately Held**
Web: www.enerfab.com
SIC: 3559 Pharmaceutical machinery
PA: Enerfab, Llc
4430 Chickering Ave
Cincinnati OH 45232
513 641-0500

(PA)=Parent Co (HQ)=Headquarters
✪ = New Business established in last 2 years

Cincinnati - Hamilton County (G-2872)

(G-2872)
ENERFAB LLC (PA)
4430 Chickering Ave (45232-1931)
PHONE..................513 641-0500
Wendell R Bell, *CEO*
Dave Herche, *
Jeffrey P Hock, *
Daniel J Sillies, *
Mark Schoettmer, *
◆ **EMP:** 330 **EST:** 1912
SQ FT: 180,000
SALES (est): 550.89MM
SALES (corp-wide): 550.89MM **Privately Held**
Web: www.enerfab.com
SIC: 3443 1629 1541 1711 Tanks, standard or custom fabricated: metal plate; Power plant construction; Industrial buildings and warehouses; Mechanical contractor

(G-2873)
ENON SAND AND GRAVEL LLC
11641 Mosteller Rd Ste 2 (45241-1520)
PHONE..................513 771-0820
EMP: 9 **EST:** 2005
SALES (est): 564.93K **Privately Held**
Web: www.jrjnet.com
SIC: 1442 Construction sand and gravel

(G-2874)
ENQUIRER PRINTING CO INC
7188 Main St (45244-3019)
PHONE..................513 241-1956
John G Anderson, *Pr*
Michael W Anderson, *VP*
Steve Anderson, *Treas*
EMP: 10 **EST:** 1894
SQ FT: 19,000
SALES (est): 979.4K **Privately Held**
SIC: 2752 Offset printing

(G-2875)
ENQUIRER PRINTING COMPANY
7188 Main St (45244-3019)
PHONE..................513 241-1956
Steve Anderson, *Prin*
EMP: 8 **EST:** 1928
SALES (est): 411.31K **Privately Held**
SIC: 2752 Commercial printing, lithographic

(G-2876)
ENTERTAINMENT JUNCTION
Also Called: Watson's
2721 E Sharon Rd (45241-1944)
PHONE..................513 326-1100
Eric Mueller, *Owner*
EMP: 9 **EST:** 2006
SALES (est): 221.18K **Privately Held**
Web: www.entertrainmentjunction.com
SIC: 2519 Household furniture, nec

(G-2877)
ENVOI DESIGN INC
1332 Main St Frnt (45202-7849)
PHONE..................513 651-4229
Denise Calmus, *Pr*
Steve Weinstein, *VP*
EMP: 7 **EST:** 1988
SQ FT: 1,200
SALES (est): 479.17K **Privately Held**
Web: www.envoidesign.com
SIC: 2752 7336 Commercial printing, lithographic; Graphic arts and related design

(G-2878)
EP BOLLINGER LLC
Also Called: Myrlen
2664 Saint Georges Ct (45233-4290)
PHONE..................513 941-1101
Ed P Bollinger, *Managing Member*

EMP: 501 **EST:** 2015
SQ FT: 22,000
SALES (est): 29.26MM **Privately Held**
Web: www.controlconceptsusa.com
SIC: 2821 Plastics materials and resins

(G-2879)
EPANEL PLUS LTD
271 Northland Blvd (45246-3603)
P.O. Box 18220 (45218-0220)
PHONE..................513 772-0888
EMP: 9 **EST:** 2000
SQ FT: 10,200
SALES (est): 259.74K **Privately Held**
Web: www.epanelplus.com
SIC: 3613 Control panels, electric

(G-2880)
EPS SPECIALTIES LTD INC
7875 School Rd # 77 (45249-1531)
PHONE..................513 489-3676
Edgar L Wilkinson, *Pr*
Lee Wilkinson, *VP*
▲ **EMP:** 12 **EST:** 1983
SALES (est): 2.24MM **Privately Held**
Web: www.lamlite.com
SIC: 3086 Packaging and shipping materials, foamed plastics

(G-2881)
EQM TECHNOLOGIES & ENERGY INC (PA)
1800 Carillion Blvd (45240)
PHONE..................513 825-7500
Jon Colin, *CEO*
Jack S Greber, *Sr VP*
Robert Galvin, *CFO*
EMP: 34 **EST:** 2008
SQ FT: 1,000
SALES (est): 27.32MM **Privately Held**
Web: www.eqm.com
SIC: 2869 Industrial organic chemicals, nec

(G-2882)
EQUIPPING MINISTRIES INTL INC
3908 Plainville Rd # 200 (45227-3202)
PHONE..................513 742-1100
David Ping, *Interim Director*
EMP: 8 **EST:** 1972
SALES (est): 290.49K **Privately Held**
Web: www.equippingministries.org
SIC: 8299 2731 Religious school; Pamphlets: publishing and printing

(G-2883)
EQUISTAR CHEMICALS LP
11530 Northlake Dr (45249-1642)
PHONE..................513 530-4000
Peter Hanik, *Brnch Mgr*
EMP: 74
Web: www.lyondellbasell.com
SIC: 2869 Industrial organic chemicals, nec
HQ: Equistar Chemicals, Lp
1221 Mckinney St Ste 300
Houston TX 77010

(G-2884)
ESSENTIAL ELEMENTS USA LLC
4775 Paddock Rd (45229-1003)
P.O. Box 29075 (45229-0075)
PHONE..................513 482-5700
Todd Wisener, *Genl Mgr*
EMP: 25
SALES (corp-wide): 10.14MM **Privately Held**
Web: www.solvay.com
SIC: 2819 2899 Catalysts, chemical; Chemical preparations, nec
PA: Essential Elements Usa, Llc
504 Carnegie Ctr
Princeton NJ 08540

609 860-4000

(G-2885)
EUROSTAMPA NORTH AMERICA INC
1440 Seymour Ave (45237-3006)
PHONE..................513 821-2275
Gianmario Cillario, *CEO*
▲ **EMP:** 217 **EST:** 2007
SALES (est): 92.59MM **Privately Held**
Web: www.eurostampa.com
SIC: 2752 Offset printing
HQ: Industria Grafica Eurostampa Spa
Viale Rimembranza 20
Bene Vagienna CN 12041
017 265-1811

(G-2886)
EVERS ENTERPRISES INC
Aurand Manufacturing & Eqp Co
1210 Ellis St (45223-1843)
PHONE..................513 541-7200
Ray Evers, *Pr*
EMP: 6
SALES (corp-wide): 2.24MM **Privately Held**
Web: www.aurand.net
SIC: 3589 Commercial cleaning equipment
PA: Evers Enterprises Inc
4849 Blue Rock Rd
Cincinnati OH

(G-2887)
EVERS WELDING CO INC
4849 Blue Rock Rd (45247-5504)
P.O. Box 53426 (45253-0426)
PHONE..................513 385-7352
Edward G Evers, *Pr*
Jacqueline Evers, *
EMP: 17 **EST:** 1957
SQ FT: 3,000
SALES (est): 494.27K **Privately Held**
Web: www.everssteel.com
SIC: 1791 3441 Structural steel erection; Fabricated structural metal

(G-2888)
EVOLUTION CRTIVE SOLUTIONS INC
7107 Shona Dr (45237-3808)
PHONE..................513 681-4450
Cathy Lindemann, *Pr*
EMP: 45 **EST:** 1994
SQ FT: 22,000
SALES (est): 7.87MM **Privately Held**
Web: www.evo-creative.com
SIC: 2752 Color lithography

(G-2889)
EVONIK CORPORATION
Also Called: Coatings & Colorants
620 Shepherd Dr (45215-2104)
PHONE..................513 554-8969
Joseph Won, *Manager*
EMP: 75
SALES (corp-wide): 2.27B **Privately Held**
Web: corporate.evonik.com
SIC: 2819 Industrial inorganic chemicals, nec
HQ: Evonik Corporation
2 Turner Pl
Piscataway NJ 08854
732 982-5000

(G-2890)
EVP INTERNATIONAL LLC
Also Called: Mn8-Foxfire
2701 Short Vine St # 200 (45219-2018)
PHONE..................513 761-7614
EMP: 6 **EST:** 2010
SALES (est): 1.13MM **Privately Held**
Web: www.mn8foxfire.com
SIC: 3646 Commercial lighting fixtures

(G-2891)
EXAIR CORPORATION
11510 Goldcoast Dr (45249-1621)
P.O. Box 00766 (45264)
PHONE..................513 671-3322
Bryan Peters, *Pr*
Roy O Sweeney, *
Brian Peters, *
Jackie Sweeney, *
Bob West, *
EMP: 50 **EST:** 1983
SQ FT: 42,000
SALES (est): 14.16MM **Privately Held**
Web: www.exair.com
SIC: 3499 Nozzles, spray: aerosol, paint, or insecticide

(G-2892)
EXPRESS GRPHICS PRTG DSIGN INC
9695 Hamilton Ave (45231-2351)
PHONE..................513 728-3344
Craig Keller, *Owner*
EMP: 8 **EST:** 1998
SQ FT: 2,400
SALES (est): 714.09K **Privately Held**
Web: www.xgraph1.com
SIC: 2752 Offset printing

(G-2893)
FABRIC FORMS INC
1320 Bates Ave (45225-1310)
PHONE..................513 281-6300
EMP: 7 **EST:** 1991
SQ FT: 4,000
SALES (est): 465.25K **Privately Held**
Web: www.fabricformsawnings.com
SIC: 2394 Awnings, fabric: made from purchased materials

(G-2894)
FAMILY MOTOR COACH ASSN INC (PA)
8291 Clough Pike (45244-2756)
PHONE..................513 474-3622
Lana Makin, *CEO*
EMP: 46 **EST:** 1963
SQ FT: 22,000
SALES (est): 14.9MM
SALES (corp-wide): 14.9MM **Privately Held**
Web: www.fmca.com
SIC: 8641 2721 Social associations; Magazines: publishing and printing

(G-2895)
FAMILY MOTOR COACHING INC
Also Called: Family Motor Coaching
8291 Clough Pike (45244-2756)
PHONE..................513 474-3622
Don Moore, *Pr*
Don Eversmann, *
EMP: 57 **EST:** 1963
SQ FT: 20,000
SALES (est): 5.66MM
SALES (corp-wide): 14.9MM **Privately Held**
Web: www.fmca.com
SIC: 2721 Magazines: publishing only, not printed on site
PA: Family Motor Coach Association, Inc.
8291 Clough Pike
Cincinnati OH 45244
513 474-3622

(G-2896)
FASTSIGNS
Also Called: Fastsigns
12125 Montgomery Rd (45249-1730)
PHONE..................513 489-8989

GEOGRAPHIC SECTION

Cincinnati - Hamilton County (G-2919)

William Jamison, *Prin*
EMP: 9 **EST**: 2008
SALES (est): 454.97K **Privately Held**
Web: www.fastsigns.com
SIC: 3993 Signs and advertising specialties

(G-2897)
FAWN CONFECTIONERY INC (PA)
4271 Harrison Ave (45211-3340)
PHONE..................513 574-9612
Kathy Guenther, *CEO*
Jane Guenther, *Treas*
Jackie Copenhaver, *Sec*
EMP: 15 **EST**: 1946
SALES (est): 1.56MM
SALES (corp-wide): 1.56MM **Privately Held**
Web: www.fawncandy.com
SIC: 5441 2064 2066 Candy; Candy and other confectionery products; Chocolate and cocoa products

(G-2898)
FBF LIMITED
Also Called: Queen City Steel Treating Co
2980 Spring Grove Ave (45225-2146)
PHONE..................513 541-6300
Judith T Houchens, *Pr*
Michael E Fourney, *
William L Fourney, *
EMP: 35 **EST**: 1922
SALES (est): 2.59MM **Privately Held**
Web: www.qcst.com
SIC: 3398 Brazing (hardening) of metal

(G-2899)
FEDERAL EQUIPMENT COMPANY (DH)
5298 River Rd (45233-1688)
PHONE..................513 621-5260
George Whittier, *CEO*
Doug Ridenour, *
Robert Starr, *
Jay Mcfadyen, *CCO*
Jared Barefield, *CAO**
▲ **EMP**: 70 **EST**: 1982
SALES (est): 45.42MM
SALES (corp-wide): 653.43MM **Privately Held**
Web: www.fairbanksmorsedefense.com
SIC: 3699 3728 3534 3535 Electrical equipment and supplies, nec; Aircraft parts and equipment, nec; Elevators and moving stairways; Conveyors and conveying equipment
HQ: Fairbanks Morse, Llc
701 White Ave
Beloit WI 53511
800 356-6955

(G-2900)
FEINTOOL US OPERATIONS INC (DH)
11280 Cornell Park Dr (45242)
PHONE..................513 247-0110
Richard Surico, *CEO*
Ralph E Hardt, *
Christoph Trachsler, *
▲ **EMP**: 250 **EST**: 1978
SALES (est): 145.59MM **Privately Held**
Web: www.feintool.com
SIC: 3469 3465 Metal stampings, nec; Automotive stampings
HQ: Feintool International Holding Ag
Industriering 8
Lyss BE 3250

(G-2901)
FIEDELDEY STL FABRICATORS INC
8487 E Miami River Rd (45247-2208)
PHONE..................513 353-3300

Bernard A Fiedeldey Junior, *Pr*
EMP: 20 **EST**: 1974
SQ FT: 20,000
SALES (est): 4.94MM **Privately Held**
Web: www.fiedeldeysteel.com
SIC: 3441 Fabricated structural metal

(G-2902)
FIELD APPARATUS SERVICE & TSTG
Also Called: F A S T
4040 Rev Dr (45232-1914)
PHONE..................513 353-9399
EMP: 7 **EST**: 1995
SALES (est): 474.94K **Privately Held**
SIC: 8711 3825 Electrical or electronic engineering; Test equipment for electronic and electric measurement

(G-2903)
FIELD AVIATION INC (PA)
8044 Montgomery Rd Ste 530 (45236)
PHONE..................513 792-2282
EMP: 23 **EST**: 2010
SALES (est): 50.32MM **Privately Held**
Web: www.fieldav.com
SIC: 3728 Aircraft parts and equipment, nec

(G-2904)
FIFTH THIRD PROC SOLUTIONS INC
38 Fountain Square Plz (45202-3102)
PHONE..................800 972-3030
EMP: 17 **EST**: 2011
SALES (est): 837.01K **Privately Held**
SIC: 7372 Prepackaged software

(G-2905)
FINN GRAPHICS INC
220 Stille Dr (45233-1695)
PHONE..................513 941-6161
Dan Finn, *Pr*
Robert Finn, *
Jack Roch, *
EMP: 40 **EST**: 1940
SQ FT: 30,000
SALES (est): 4.52MM **Privately Held**
Web: www.finn-line.com
SIC: 2752 3993 2395 Offset printing; Advertising novelties; Pleating and stitching

(G-2906)
FLAVOR PRODUCERS LLC
2429 E Kemper Rd (45241-1811)
PHONE..................513 771-0777
EMP: 42
SALES (corp-wide): 40.88MM **Privately Held**
Web: www.flavorproducers.com
SIC: 2087 Concentrates, flavoring (except drink)
PA: Flavor Producers, Llc
8521 Fllbrook Ave Ste 380
West Hills CA 91304
661 257-3400

(G-2907)
FLAVOR SYSTEMS INTL INC (HQ)
5404 Duff Dr (45246)
PHONE..................513 870-4900
William W Wasz, *Pr*
John Disebastian, *VP*
William Baker, *VP*
▲ **EMP**: 20 **EST**: 1994
SQ FT: 50,000
SALES (est): 10.67MM **Privately Held**
Web: www.flavorsystems.com
SIC: 2087 Flavoring extracts and syrups, nec
PA: Exponent Private Equity Llp
30 Broadwick Street
London

(G-2908)
FLEXOMATION LLC
11701 Chesterdale Rd (45246-3405)
P.O. Box 40537 (45240-0537)
PHONE..................513 825-0555
EMP: 9 **EST**: 2004
SALES (est): 370.11K **Privately Held**
Web: www.flexomation.com
SIC: 3549 Assembly machines, including robotic

(G-2909)
FLINT CPS INKS NORTH AMER LLC
410 Glendale Milford Rd (45215-1103)
PHONE..................513 619-2089
Mike Ledford, *Brnch Mgr*
EMP: 30
SALES (corp-wide): 1.91B **Privately Held**
Web: www.flintgrp.com
SIC: 2865 2893 Color pigments, organic; Printing ink
HQ: Flint Cps Inks North America Llc
17177 N Laurel Park Dr # 300
Livonia MI 48152
734 781-4600

(G-2910)
FLOW TECHNOLOGY INC
4444 Cooper Rd (45242-0259)
PHONE..................513 745-6000
Bill Hayes, *Pr*
Bill Hays, *Pr*
EMP: 48 **EST**: 1978
SALES (est): 2.12MM
SALES (corp-wide): 2.09B **Publicly Held**
Web: www.ftimeters.com
SIC: 3491 Valves, automatic control
HQ: Xomox Corporation
4526 Res Frest Dr Ste 400
The Woodlands TX 77381
936 271-6500

(G-2911)
FLUFF BOUTIQUE
6539 Harrison Ave (45247-7822)
PHONE..................513 227-6614
EMP: 6 **EST**: 2013
SQ FT: 2,000
SALES (est): 434.53K **Privately Held**
SIC: 7363 5621 5137 5963 Help supply services; Women's clothing stores; Women's and children's clothing; Clothing sales, house-to-house

(G-2912)
FLYPAPER STUDIO INC
311 Elm St Ste 200 (45202-2743)
PHONE..................602 801-2208
Patrick Sullivan, *CEO*
Don Perison, *
Pat Stoner, *
Greg Head, *
Sunil Padiyar, *
EMP: 14 **EST**: 2003
SQ FT: 16,778
SALES (est): 374.02K **Privately Held**
SIC: 7372 Educational computer software

(G-2913)
FOODIES VEGAN LTD
Also Called: Five Star Foodies
4524 Este Ave (45232-1763)
PHONE..................513 487-3037
Valerie Williams, *CEO*
Christian Stroud, *CFO*
EMP: 12 **EST**: 2007
SALES (est): 1.2MM **Privately Held**
Web: www.foodiesvegan.com
SIC: 5142 2099 Packaged frozen goods; Tofu, except frozen desserts

(G-2914)
FORCAM INC
3825 Edwards Rd (45209-1262)
PHONE..................513 878-2780
EMP: 15 **EST**: 2012
SALES (est): 2.03MM **Privately Held**
Web: www.forcam.com
SIC: 7371 7372 Computer software development and applications; Application computer software

(G-2915)
FOREST CONVERTING CO INC
4701 Forest Ave (45212-3399)
P.O. Box 12238 (45212-0238)
PHONE..................513 631-4190
R Douglas Lojinger, *Pr*
EMP: 6 **EST**: 1949
SQ FT: 22,000
SALES (est): 584.05K **Privately Held**
Web: www.forestconverting.com
SIC: 2675 Paper die-cutting

(G-2916)
FORMICA CORPORATION (DH)
10155 Reading Rd (45241-4805)
PHONE..................513 786-3400
Frank Riddick, *Pr*
Michael Fischer V, *President SFCE America*
Catherine Vernon, *VP*
Mitchell P Quint, *Pr*
R Gerard Bollman, *VP*
◆ **EMP**: 20 **EST**: 1913
SQ FT: 14,000
SALES (est): 292.94MM
SALES (corp-wide): 355.83K **Privately Held**
Web: www.formica.com
SIC: 2541 2679 Counter and sink tops; Paperboard products, converted, nec
HQ: Broadview Holding B.V.
Willemsplein 2
's-Hertogenbosch NB 5211

(G-2917)
FORUM III INC
436 Mcgregor Ave (45206-2364)
PHONE..................513 961-5123
Michael Evans, *Pr*
Jeffrey Crosby, *
EMP: 8 **EST**: 1985
SQ FT: 8,800
SALES (est): 398.74K **Privately Held**
Web: www.fremont-umc.com
SIC: 2434 2431 2541 Wood kitchen cabinets ; Millwork; Wood partitions and fixtures

(G-2918)
FORWARD MOVEMENT PUBLICATIONS
Also Called: Forward Day By Day
412 Sycamore St Fl 2 (45202-6202)
PHONE..................513 721-6659
Richard Schmidt, *Dir*
▲ **EMP**: 24 **EST**: 1935
SALES (est): 1.9MM **Privately Held**
Web: www.forwardmovement.org
SIC: 2759 Publication printing

(G-2919)
FOSTER TRANSFORMER COMPANY
3820 Colerain Ave (45223-2586)
PHONE..................513 681-2420
◆ **EMP**: 25 **EST**: 1937
SALES (est): 3.84MM
SALES (corp-wide): 4.91MM **Privately Held**
Web: www.foster-transformer.com
SIC: 3677 3612 Electronic transformers; Transformers, except electric
PA: Harrison Corporation

Cincinnati - Hamilton County (G-2920)

GEOGRAPHIC SECTION

3820 Colerain Ave
Cincinnati OH 45223
513 681-2420

(G-2920)
FRANK L HARTER & SON INC
3778 Frondorf Ave (45211-4421)
PHONE.............................513 574-1330
Michael Harter, *Pr*
Barb Harter, *Sec*
EMP: 6 **EST:** 1928
SQ FT: 800
SALES (est): 931.12K **Privately Held**
SIC: 5143 5144 5148 2099 Butter; Eggs; Fresh fruits and vegetables; Salads, fresh or refrigerated

(G-2921)
FRANKLIN COVEY CO
7875 Montgomery Rd Spc 1202 (45236-4344)
PHONE.............................513 080-0975
Jason Mast, *Mgr*
EMP: 8
SALES (corp-wide): 262.84MM **Publicly Held**
Web: www.franklincovey.com
SIC: 2741 Miscellaneous publishing
PA: Franklin Covey Co.
2200 W Parkway Blvd
Salt Lake City UT 84119
801 817-1776

(G-2922)
FREDERICK STEEL COMPANY LLC
Also Called: Bfs Supply
630 Glendale Milford Rd (45215-1105)
PHONE.............................513 821-6400
Burke Byer, *Prin*
Timothy Nagy, *Sec*
Jay Binder, *Prin*
Jeff Ginter, *Prin*
Jonas Allen, *Prin*
EMP: 60 **EST:** 2013
SALES (est): 9.24MM
SALES (corp-wide): 99.72MM **Privately Held**
Web: www.fredericksteel.com
SIC: 1791 3441 Structural steel erection; Building components, structural steel
PA: Benjamin Steel Company, Inc.
777 Benjamin Dr
Springfield OH 45502
937 322-8600

(G-2923)
FROST ENGINEERING INC
3408 Beekman St (45223-2425)
PHONE.............................513 541-6330
EMP: 42 **EST:** 1995
SQ FT: 15,000
SALES (est): 4.32MM **Privately Held**
Web: www.frosteng.net
SIC: 3556 8711 Smokers, food processing equipment; Engineering services

(G-2924)
G & J PEPSI-COLA BOTTLERS INC (PA)
Also Called: Pepsi-Cola
9435 Waterstone Blvd Ste 390 (45249-8227)
PHONE.............................513 785-6060
Timothy S Trant, *CEO*
Daniel D Sweeney, *COO*
Tim Hardid, *COO*
Stanley Kaplan, *Ch*
Thomas D Heekin, *V Ch Bd*
EMP: 10 **EST:** 1968
SQ FT: 8,052
SALES (est): 404.54MM

SALES (corp-wide): 404.54MM **Privately Held**
Web: www.gjpepsi.com
SIC: 2086 Carbonated soft drinks, bottled and canned

(G-2925)
G A AVRIL COMPANY (PA)
Also Called: Brass & Bronze Ingot Division
4445 Kings Run Dr (45232-1401)
P.O. Box 32066 (45232-0066)
PHONE.............................513 641-0566
Thomas B Avril, *Pr*
John G Avril, *VP*
EMP: 10 **EST:** 1946
SQ FT: 47,000
SALES (est): 31.02K
SALES (corp-wide): 31.02K **Privately Held**
Web: www.gaavril.com
SIC: 3341 3356 Brass smelting and refining (secondary); Nonferrous rolling and drawing, nec

(G-2926)
G A AVRIL COMPANY
White Metal Products Division
2108 Eagle Ct (45237-4754)
P.O. Box 12050 (45212-0050)
PHONE.............................513 731-5133
Philip V Schneider, *Mgr*
EMP: 10
SQ FT: 66,782
SALES (corp-wide): 31.02K **Privately Held**
Web: www.gaavril.com
SIC: 3356 Lead and lead alloy bars, pipe, plates, shapes, etc.
PA: The G A Avril Company
4445 Kings Run Dr
Cincinnati OH 45232
513 641-0566

(G-2927)
G L PIERCE INC
Also Called: Cincinnati GL Blck Dyton GL Bl
12100 Mosteller Rd Ste 500 (45241-6404)
PHONE.............................513 772-7202
Gregory Pierce, *Pr*
Gregory L Pierce, *Pr*
EMP: 7 **EST:** 2018
SALES (est): 493.22K **Privately Held**
Web: www.daytonglassblock.com
SIC: 3229 1741 Blocks and bricks, glass; Concrete block masonry laying

(G-2928)
GARDEN STREET IRON & METAL INC (PA)
2885 Spring Grove Ave (45225-2222)
PHONE.............................513 721-4660
Earl J Weber Junior, *Pr*
Margaret Weber, *
▲ **EMP:** 39 **EST:** 1959
SQ FT: 43,000
SALES (est): 8.17MM
SALES (corp-wide): 8.17MM **Privately Held**
Web: www.gardenst.com
SIC: 4953 3341 3312 Recycling, waste materials; Secondary nonferrous metals; Blast furnaces and steel mills

(G-2929)
GARDNER BUSINESS MEDIA INC
6925 Valley Ln (45244-3029)
PHONE.............................513 527-8800
Margaret Kline, *Mgr*
EMP: 10
SQ FT: 17,600
SALES (corp-wide): 21.03MM **Privately Held**
Web: www.gardnerweb.com

SIC: 2721 2731 Trade journals: publishing only, not printed on site; Books, publishing and printing
PA: Gardner Business Media, Inc.
6915 Valley Ave
Cincinnati OH 45244
513 527-8800

(G-2930)
GARDNER BUSINESS MEDIA INC (PA)
6915 Valley Ln (45244-3029)
PHONE.............................513 527-8800
EMP: 120 **EST:** 1928
SALES (est): 21.03MM
SALES (corp-wide): 21.03MM **Privately Held**
Web: www.gardnerweb.com
SIC: 2721 2731 2741 Trade journals: publishing only, not printed on site; Books, publishing only; Miscellaneous publishing

(G-2931)
GARY DATTILO
1329 E Kemper Rd (45246-5101)
PHONE.............................513 671-2117
Gary Dattilo, *Owner*
EMP: 9 **EST:** 2002
SALES (est): 120.83K **Privately Held**
SIC: 3861 Photographic equipment and supplies

(G-2932)
GARYS CHESECAKES FINE DESSERTS
5285 Crookshank Rd Side (45238-3372)
PHONE.............................513 574-1700
Gary Haas, *Owner*
EMP: 8 **EST:** 2003
SALES (est): 434.23K **Privately Held**
Web: www.garyscheesecakes.com
SIC: 2051 Bread, cake, and related products

(G-2933)
GASLIGHT HOLDINGS LLC
Also Called: Gaslight
5910 Hamilton Ave (45224)
PHONE.............................513 470-3525
Peter Kananen, *CEO*
Doug Alcorn, *
EMP: 50 **EST:** 2017
SALES (est): 4.85MM **Privately Held**
Web: www.teamgaslight.com
SIC: 7372 Prepackaged software

(G-2934)
GE AVIATION SYSTEMS LLC
Also Called: GE Aviation
10270 Saint Rita Ln (45215-1215)
PHONE.............................513 470-2889
EMP: 27
SALES (corp-wide): 67.95B **Publicly Held**
Web: www.geaerospace.com
SIC: 3812 Aircraft control systems, electronic
HQ: Ge Aviation Systems Llc
1 Neumann Way
Cincinnati OH 45215
937 898-9600

(G-2935)
GE AVIATION SYSTEMS LLC (HQ)
Also Called: GE Aviation
1 Neumann Way (45215)
PHONE.............................937 898-9600
R F Ehr, *Pr*
J B Hines, *Pr*
Peter Page, *Ex VP*
Jeff Immelt, *Ch*
▲ **EMP:** 8 **EST:** 1987
SALES (est): 2.46B

SALES (corp-wide): 67.95B **Publicly Held**
Web: www.geaerospace.com
SIC: 3812 Aircraft control systems, electronic
PA: General Electric Company
1 Aviation Way
Cincinnati OH 45215
617 443-3000

(G-2936)
GE ENGINE SERVICES LLC
Also Called: GE
201 W Crescentville Rd (45246-1713)
PHONE.............................513 977-1500
John Ousley, *Brnch Mgr*
EMP: 300
SALES (corp-wide): 67.95B **Publicly Held**
Web: www.geaerospace.com
SIC: 3728 Aircraft parts and equipment, nec
HQ: Ge Engine Services, Llc
1 Aviation Way
Cincinnati OH 45215
513 243-2000

(G-2937)
GE HEALTHCARE INC
346 Gest St (45203-1822)
PHONE.............................513 241-5955
Mark Nybo, *Mgr*
EMP: 15
SALES (corp-wide): 19.55B **Publicly Held**
Web: www.cytivalifesciences.com
SIC: 2835 Diagnostic substances
HQ: Ge Healthcare Inc.
251 Locke Dr
Marlborough MA 01752
732 457-8667

(G-2938)
GE MILITARY SYSTEMS
1 Neumann Way (45215-1900)
PHONE.............................513 243-2000
Russ Sparks, *Of Mil Strat*
EMP: 51 **EST:** 1996
SALES (est): 4.9MM
SALES (corp-wide): 67.95B **Publicly Held**
Web: www.geaerospace.com
SIC: 3724 Aircraft engines and engine parts
PA: General Electric Company
1 Aviation Way
Cincinnati OH 45215
617 443-3000

(G-2939)
GE ROLLS ROYCE FIGHTER
One Neumann Way, Md H318 A (45215-1900)
PHONE.............................513 243-2787
Robert H Griswold, *Pr*
EMP: 12 **EST:** 2004
SALES (est): 569.69K
SALES (corp-wide): 67.95B **Publicly Held**
SIC: 3519 Jet propulsion engines
PA: General Electric Company
1 Aviation Way
Cincinnati OH 45215
617 443-3000

(G-2940)
GENERAL CHAIN & MFG CORP
3274 Beekman St (45223-2423)
PHONE.............................513 541-6005
Eric Schaumloffel, *Pr*
EMP: 40 **EST:** 1919
SALES (est): 6.05MM **Privately Held**
Web: www.generalchain.com
SIC: 3496 Miscellaneous fabricated wire products

GEOGRAPHIC SECTION

Cincinnati - Hamilton County (G-2963)

(G-2941)
GENERAL ELECTRIC COMPANY
Also Called: GE
445 S Cooper Ave (45215-4565)
PHONE.................................513 948-4170
Carol Mase, *Mgr*
EMP: 8
SALES (corp-wide): 67.95B **Publicly Held**
Web: www.ge.com
SIC: 3724 Aircraft engines and engine parts
PA: General Electric Company
1 Aviation Way
Cincinnati OH 45215
617 443-3000

(G-2942)
GENERAL ELECTRIC COMPANY (PA)
Also Called: General Electric
1 Aviation Way (45215)
PHONE.................................617 443-3000
H Lawrence Culp Junior, *Ch Bd*
Rahul Ghai, *Sr VP*
L Kevin Cox, *Chief Human Resources Officer*
Michael J Holston, *Sr VP*
Robert Giglietti, *CAO*
EMP: 44087 **EST:** 1892
SALES (est): 67.95B
SALES (corp-wide): 67.95B **Publicly Held**
Web: www.ge.com
SIC: 3812 3519 4581 5088 Aircraft/ aerospace flight instruments and guidance systems; Jet propulsion engines; Aircraft maintenance and repair services; Aircraft engines and engine parts

(G-2943)
GENERAL ELECTRIC COMPANY
Also Called: GE
201 W Crescentville Rd (45246-1733)
PHONE.................................513 977-1500
Bill Fitzgerald, *Mgr*
EMP: 36
SALES (corp-wide): 67.95B **Publicly Held**
Web: www.ge.com
SIC: 7629 3769 3728 3537 Aircraft electrical equipment repair; Space vehicle equipment, nec; Aircraft parts and equipment, nec; Industrial trucks and tractors
PA: General Electric Company
1 Aviation Way
Cincinnati OH 45215
617 443-3000

(G-2944)
GENERAL MILLS INC
General Mills
11301 Mosteller Rd (45241-1827)
PHONE.................................513 771-8200
Jerry Kelley, *Bmch Mgr*
EMP: 89
SALES (corp-wide): 20.09B **Publicly Held**
Web: www.generalmills.com
SIC: 2043 2099 Cereal breakfast foods; Food preparations, nec
PA: General Mills, Inc.
1 General Mills Blvd
Minneapolis MN 55426
763 764-7600

(G-2945)
GENERAL PLASTICS NORTH CORP
5220 Vine St (45217-1028)
PHONE.................................800 542-2466
Zetta Bouligaraki, *Pr*
EMP: 365 **EST:** 1950
SQ FT: 150,000
SALES (est): 5.27MM
SALES (corp-wide): 1.71B **Privately Held**
Web: www.generalplasticscorp.com
SIC: 3479 Coating of metals and formed products
HQ: Pmc, Inc.
12243 Branford St
Sun Valley CA 91352
818 896-1101

(G-2946)
GENERAL TOOL COMPANY (PA)
101 Landy Ln (45215-3495)
PHONE.................................513 733-5500
William J Kramer Junior, *CEO*
William J Kramer Iii, *CFO*
John Cozad, *
Elliot Adams, *
Paul Kramer, *
▲ **EMP:** 235 **EST:** 1947
SQ FT: 150,000
SALES (est): 39.89MM
SALES (corp-wide): 39.89MM **Privately Held**
Web: www.gentool.com
SIC: 3599 3443 3444 3544 Machine shop, jobbing and repair; Fabricated plate work (boiler shop); Sheet metalwork; Special dies and tools

(G-2947)
GENPACT LLC
100 Tri County Pkwy Ste 200 (45246-3244)
PHONE.................................513 763-7660
EMP: 43
Web: www.genpact.com
SIC: 8711 3812 Mechanical engineering; Electronic field detection apparatus (aeronautical)
HQ: Genpact Llc
521 5th Ave Fl 14
New York NY 10175
212 896-6600

(G-2948)
GENTHERM MEDICAL LLC (HQ)
12011 Mosteller Rd (45241-1528)
PHONE.................................513 772-8810
EMP: 236 **EST:** 1940
SALES (est): 79.8MM **Publicly Held**
Web: www.gentherm.com
SIC: 3823 3841 Controllers, for process variables, all types; Surgical and medical instruments
PA: Gentherm Incorporated
21680 Haggerty Rd Ste 101
Northville MI 48167

(G-2949)
GERALD L HERRMANN COMPANY INC
Also Called: Master Print Center
3325 Harrison Ave (45211-5618)
P.O. Box 11560 (45211-0560)
PHONE.................................513 661-1818
TOLL FREE: 800
Gerald Herrmann, *Pr*
Suzanne Herrmann, *Sec*
EMP: 11 **EST:** 1961
SQ FT: 7,500
SALES (est): 2.12MM **Privately Held**
Web: www.addresserbasedsystems.com
SIC: 7331 2752 Addressing service; Photo-offset printing

(G-2950)
GILLETTE COMPANY LLC
Also Called: Gillette
1 Procter And Gamble Plz (45202-3315)
P.O. Box 5319 (45201-5319)
PHONE.................................513 983-1100
David S Taylor, *Ch Bd*
EMP: 63 **EST:** 2016
SALES (est): 26.7MM
SALES (corp-wide): 82.01B **Publicly Held**
Web: www.gillette.com
SIC: 3421 Razor blades and razors
PA: The Procter & Gamble Company
1 Procter & Gamble Plz
Cincinnati OH 45202
513 983-1100

(G-2951)
GIMINETTI BAKING COMPANY
2900 Gilbert Ave (45206-1207)
P.O. Box 6050 (45206-0050)
PHONE.................................513 751-7655
James Ciuccio, *Pr*
EMP: 10 **EST:** 1985
SALES (est): 221.9K **Privately Held**
Web: www.giminetti.com
SIC: 2051 5461 Bakery: wholesale or wholesale/retail combined; Retail bakeries

(G-2952)
GIRINDUS AMERICA INC
Also Called: Avecia
10608 Deercreek Ln (45249-3506)
PHONE.................................513 679-3000
EMP: 30
SIC: 2834 Pharmaceutical preparations

(G-2953)
GIVAUDAN FLAVORS CORPORATION
100 E 69th St (45216-2008)
PHONE.................................513 948-3428
EMP: 16
Web: www.givaudan.com
SIC: 2869 Flavors or flavoring materials, synthetic
HQ: Givaudan Flavors Corporation
1199 Edison Dr
Cincinnati OH 45216

(G-2954)
GIVAUDAN FLAVORS CORPORATION
110 E 69th St (45216)
PHONE.................................513 786-0124
EMP: 6
SIC: 2869 2087 Flavors or flavoring materials, synthetic; Flavoring extracts and syrups, nec
HQ: Givaudan Flavors Corporation
1199 Edison Dr
Cincinnati OH 45216

(G-2955)
GIVAUDAN FLAVORS CORPORATION (DH)
Also Called: Givaudan
1199 Edison Dr 1-2 (45216-2265)
P.O. Box 17038 (45217-0038)
PHONE.................................513 948-8000
◆ **EMP:** 199 **EST:** 1988
SALES (est): 543.21MM **Privately Held**
SIC: 2869 2087 Flavors or flavoring materials, synthetic; Flavoring extracts and syrups, nec
HQ: Givaudan Flavors And Fragrances, Inc.
1199 Edison Dr
Cincinnati OH 45216

(G-2956)
GIVAUDAN FLAVORS CORPORATION
110 E 70th St (45216-2011)
PHONE.................................513 948-8000
EMP: 9
SIC: 2087 Flavoring extracts and syrups, nec
HQ: Givaudan Flavors Corporation
1199 Edison Dr
Cincinnati OH 45216

(G-2957)
GIVAUDAN FRAGRANCES CORP
100 E 69th St (45216-2008)
PHONE.................................513 948-3428
Gary Schmidt, *Mgr*
EMP: 45
SIC: 2869 2087 Flavors or flavoring materials, synthetic; Flavoring extracts and syrups, nec
HQ: Givaudan Fragrances Corporation
1199 Edison Dr Ste 1-2
Cincinnati OH 45216
513 948-8000

(G-2958)
GIVAUDAN FRAGRANCES CORP (DH)
1199 Edison Dr Ste 1-2 (45216-2265)
P.O. Box 17038 (45217-0038)
PHONE.................................513 948-8000
Gilles Andrier, *CEO*
◆ **EMP:** 386 **EST:** 2000
SQ FT: 78,000
SALES (est): 554.64MM **Privately Held**
SIC: 2869 Perfume materials, synthetic
HQ: Givaudan Flavors And Fragrances, Inc.
1199 Edison Dr
Cincinnati OH 45216

(G-2959)
GLOBAL SRCING SUPPORT SVCS LLC
260 E University Ave (45219-2356)
PHONE.................................800 645-2986
▲ **EMP:** 6 **EST:** 2005
SALES (est): 446.18K **Privately Held**
SIC: 3599 Custom machinery

(G-2960)
GM PALLETS COMPANY
121 Citycentre Dr Unit 2 (45216-1657)
P.O. Box 16116 (45216-0116)
PHONE.................................859 408-1781
EMP: 11 **EST:** 2019
SALES (est): 2.36MM **Privately Held**
Web: www.gmpalletsco.com
SIC: 2448 Pallets, wood

(G-2961)
GMP WELDING & FABRICATION INC
11175 Adwood Dr (45240-3235)
PHONE.................................513 825-7861
Leonard J Mee, *Pr*
Tyler Mee, *VP*
Linda Conrad, *Sec*
EMP: 9 **EST:** 1979
SALES (est): 421.73K **Privately Held**
Web: www.gmpwelding.com
SIC: 7692 Welding repair

(G-2962)
GOLD MEDAL PRODUCTS CO (PA)
Also Called: Gold Medal-Carolina
10700 Medallion Dr (45241-4807)
PHONE.................................513 769-7676
◆ **EMP:** 300 **EST:** 1931
SALES (est): 98.56MM
SALES (corp-wide): 98.56MM **Privately Held**
Web: www.gmpopcorn.com
SIC: 3556 3589 5145 3581 Food products machinery; Cooking equipment, commercial; Confectionery; Automatic vending machines

(G-2963)
GOLD STAR CHILI INC (PA)
Also Called: Gold Star Chili
650 Lunken Park Dr (45226-1800)
PHONE.................................513 231-4541

Cincinnati - Hamilton County (G-2964)

Roger David, *Pr*
Suhaila B David, *Stockholder**
Fahid S Daoud, *Stockholder**
Frank S Daoud, *Stockholder**
Basheer S David, *Stockholder**
EMP: 33 **EST:** 1965
SQ FT: 5,000
SALES (est): 22.38MM
SALES (corp-wide): 22.38MM **Privately Held**
Web: www.goldstarchili.com
SIC: 5812 2099 6794 5499 Chili stand; Food preparations, nec; Franchises, selling or licensing; Spices and herbs

(G-2964)
GOLD STAR CHILI INC
Also Called: Gold Star Chili
5420 Ridge Ave (45213-2514)
PHONE.................................513 631-1990
Rusa Abusway, *Owner*
EMP: 50
SALES (corp-wide): 22.38MM **Privately Held**
Web: www.goldstarchili.com
SIC: 5812 2099 Chili stand; Food preparations, nec
PA: Gold Star Chili, Inc.
650 Lunken Park Dr
Cincinnati OH 45226
513 231-4541

(G-2965)
GOMEZ SALSA LLC
8575 Coolwood Ct (45236-1301)
PHONE.................................513 314-1978
Andrew Gomez, *Prin*
EMP: 24 **EST:** 2012
SALES (est): 393.62K **Privately Held**
Web: www.gomezsalsa.com
SIC: 2099 Dips, except cheese and sour cream based

(G-2966)
GOSUN INC
5151 Fischer Ave (45217-1157)
PHONE.................................888 868-6154
Patrick Sherwin, *CEO*
EMP: 10 **EST:** 2016
SALES (est): 5.87MM **Privately Held**
Web: www.gosun.co
SIC: 3631 Barbecues, grills, and braziers (outdoor cooking)

(G-2967)
GOVERNMENT ACQUISITIONS INC
2060 Reading Rd Fl 4 (45202-1400)
PHONE.................................513 721-8700
Roger Brown, *CEO*
Roger Brown, *Owner*
Stan Jones, *
Bobby Brown, *
EMP: 35 **EST:** 1989
SQ FT: 20,000
SALES (est): 21.95MM **Privately Held**
Web: www.gov-acq.com
SIC: 7378 3577 5045 Computer maintenance and repair; Computer peripheral equipment, nec; Computer software

(G-2968)
GRAETERS ICE CREAM COMPANY (PA)
1175 Regina Graeter Way (45216)
PHONE.................................513 721-3323
Richard Graeter Ii, *Pr*
Tom Kunzelman, *
EMP: 60 **EST:** 1870
SQ FT: 25,000
SALES (est): 53.65MM
SALES (corp-wide): 53.65MM **Privately Held**
Web: www.graeters.com
SIC: 2024 2051 2064 2066 Ice cream, packaged: molded, on sticks, etc.; Bread, cake, and related products; Candy and other confectionery products; Chocolate and cocoa products

(G-2969)
GRAPHIC PRINT SOLUTIONS INC
7633 Production Dr (45237-3208)
P.O. Box 37690 (45222-0690)
PHONE.................................513 948-3344
EMP: 8 **EST:** 2017
SALES (est): 338.99K **Privately Held**
Web: www.graphicps.com
SIC: 2752 Offset printing

(G-2970)
GREATER CINCINNATI BOWL ASSN
611 Mercury Dr (45244-1412)
P.O. Box 54290 (45254-0290)
PHONE.................................513 761-7387
Willie Dean, *Pr*
Tom Taylor, *VP*
Joe Mcfarland, *VP*
EMP: 22 **EST:** 1895
SQ FT: 1,700
SALES (est): 779.22K **Privately Held**
Web: www.pincincinnati.org
SIC: 8699 2721 7933 Bowling club; Periodicals; Bowling centers

(G-2971)
GREENDALE HOME FASHIONS LLC
5500 Muddy Creek Rd (45238-2030)
PHONE.................................859 916-5475
▲ **EMP:** 80 **EST:** 1954
SALES (est): 5.26MM **Privately Held**
Web: www.greendalehomefashions.com
SIC: 3842 2392 Life preservers, except cork and inflatable; Cushions and pillows

(G-2972)
GREG G WRIGHT & SONS LLC
10200 Springfield Pike (45215-1116)
PHONE.................................513 721-3310
Tracey A Chriske, *Prin*
EMP: 30 **EST:** 1860
SQ FT: 34,000
SALES (est): 2.05MM **Privately Held**
Web: www.gregwrightandsons.com
SIC: 3953 3993 Textile marking stamps, hand: rubber or metal; Name plates: except engraved, etched, etc.: metal

(G-2973)
GRIFFIN FISHER CO INC
1126 William Howard Taft Rd (45206-2031)
PHONE.................................513 961-2110
Whitney Fisher, *CEO*
Branden Fisher, *Pr*
EMP: 9 **EST:** 1909
SQ FT: 3,800
SALES (est): 504.9K **Privately Held**
Web: www.fishergriffinco.com
SIC: 2394 2396 2399 Convertible tops, canvas or boat: from purchased materials; Automotive trimmings, fabric; Seat covers, automobile

(G-2974)
GRIPPO FOODS INC (PA)
6750 Colerain Ave (45239-5542)
PHONE.................................513 923-1900
Ralph W Pagel Ii, *Pr*
James Pagel, *
Linda Foster, *
Nancy Schreiber, *
Dorothy Saylor, *
EMP: 79 **EST:** 1919
SQ FT: 27,000
SALES (est): 12.01MM
SALES (corp-wide): 12.01MM **Privately Held**
Web: www.grippos.com
SIC: 2096 Potato chips and similar snacks

(G-2975)
GRIPPO POTATO CHIP CO INC
6750 Colerain Ave (45239-5542)
PHONE.................................513 923-1900
Ralph W Pagel Ii, *Pr*
James Pagel, *
Linda Foster, *
Dorothy Saylor, *
EMP: 24 **EST:** 1919
SQ FT: 27,000
SALES (est): 2.89MM **Privately Held**
Web: www.grippos.com
SIC: 2096 2099 Potato chips and other potato-based snacks; Food preparations, nec

(G-2976)
GT INDUSTRIAL SUPPLY INC
Also Called: Gt Industrial Supply
7775 E Kemper Rd (45249-1611)
PHONE.................................513 771-7000
EMP: 10 **EST:** 2009
SALES (est): 6MM **Privately Held**
Web: www.gtindustrialsupply.com
SIC: 2671 5063 5087 5199 Paper; coated and laminated packaging; Lighting fixtures; Janitors' supplies; Packaging materials

(G-2977)
GTLP HOLDINGS LLC (PA)
Also Called: Premier Southern Ticket
7911 School Rd (45249-1533)
PHONE.................................513 489-6700
EMP: 28 **EST:** 2009
SQ FT: 35,000
SALES (est): 4.37MM **Privately Held**
Web: www.premiersouthern.com
SIC: 2752 Tag, ticket, and schedule printing: lithographic

(G-2978)
GUS HOLTHAUS SIGNS INC
Also Called: Holthaus Lackner Signs
817 Ridgeway Ave (45229-3222)
P.O. Box 29373 (45229-0373)
PHONE.................................513 861-0060
Kevin Holthaus, *Pr*
Scott Holthaus, *
Kerry Holthaus, *
EMP: 40 **EST:** 1929
SQ FT: 38,600
SALES (est): 4.86MM **Privately Held**
Web: www.hlsigns.com
SIC: 3993 1799 Electric signs; Sign installation and maintenance

(G-2979)
H HAFNER & SONS INC
5445 Wooster Pike (45226-2226)
PHONE.................................513 321-1895
Justin Cooper, *Pr*
Linda Hafner, *
Andrew O Haefner, *
Maryellen Maltry, *
Paul J Hengge, *
EMP: 42 **EST:** 1923
SQ FT: 5,500
SALES (est): 9.18MM **Privately Held**
Web: www.hafners.com
SIC: 5191 2499 4212 4953 Soil, potting and planting; Mulch, wood and bark; Dump truck haulage; Recycling, waste materials

(G-2980)
H LEE PHILIPPI CO
3660 Hyde Park Ave (45208-1497)
P.O. Box 9845 (45209-0845)
PHONE.................................513 321-5330
Hiram Lee Philippi, *Pr*
Richard W Scott, *VP*
EMP: 15 **EST:** 1964
SQ FT: 20,000
SALES (est): 2.43MM **Privately Held**
SIC: 2679 Paperboard products, converted, nec

(G-2981)
H NAGEL & SON CO
Also Called: Brighton Mills
2641 Spring Grove Ave (45214-1731)
PHONE.................................513 665-4550
Brian Mitchell, *Genl Mgr*
EMP: 10
SALES (corp-wide): 4.51MM **Privately Held**
Web: www.brightonmills.com
SIC: 2041 Flour: blended, prepared, or self-rising
PA: H. Nagel & Son Co.
707 Harrison Brkvl Rd Uni
West Harrison IN 47060
513 665-4550

(G-2982)
H&G LEGACY CO (PA)
1085 Summer St (45204-2037)
PHONE.................................513 921-1075
Mike Lawry, *CEO*
Ryan Canfield, *Pr*
EMP: 14 **EST:** 1896
SQ FT: 15,000
SALES (est): 8.69MM
SALES (corp-wide): 8.69MM **Privately Held**
Web: www.hillandgriffith.com
SIC: 2899 2869 3565 3542 Chemical preparations, nec; Industrial organic chemicals, nec; Packaging machinery; Machine tools, metal forming type

(G-2983)
HADRONICS INC
4570 Steel Pl (45209-1189)
PHONE.................................513 321-9350
Michael G Green, *Pr*
Kenneth J Green, *
Jeffrey Mccarty, *S&M/VP*
Pat Mcdonough, *
EMP: 56 **EST:** 1970
SALES (est): 8.72MM **Privately Held**
Web: www.hadronics.com
SIC: 3471 3479 3555 3366 Electroplating of metals or formed products; Etching and engraving; Printing trades machinery; Copper foundries

(G-2984)
HANCHETT PAPER COMPANY
Also Called: Shorr Packaging
12121 Best Pl (45241-6402)
PHONE.................................513 782-4440
EMP: 73
SALES (corp-wide): 245.19MM **Privately Held**
Web: www.shorr.com
SIC: 2621 Paper mills
PA: Hanchett Paper Company
4000 Ferry Rd
Aurora IL 60502
888 885-0055

GEOGRAPHIC SECTION
Cincinnati - Hamilton County (G-3006)

(G-2985)
HARLAN GRAPHIC ARTS SVCS INC
4752 River Rd (45233-1633)
P.O. Box 643806 (45264-3806)
PHONE.................................513 251-5700
Larry Ehrman, *Pr*
Jeff Ehrman, *VP*
Kim Springer, *CFO*
EMP: 22 **EST:** 1980
SQ FT: 40,000
SALES (est): 5.81MM **Privately Held**
Web: www.harlangraphics.com
SIC: 2791 Typesetting

(G-2986)
HARRAY LLC
266 W Mitchell Ave (45232-1908)
PHONE.................................888 568-8371
EMP: 6 **EST:** 2005
SALES (est): 797.08K **Privately Held**
Web: www.archlouvers.com
SIC: 3444 Sheet metalwork

(G-2987)
HARVEY BROTHERS INC (PA)
3492 Spring Grove Ave (45223-2417)
PHONE.................................513 541-2622
Stephen Kyle, *Pr*
EMP: 8 **EST:** 1920
SQ FT: 5,600
SALES (est): 1.41MM
SALES (corp-wide): 1.41MM **Privately Held**
Web: www.harveybrothersinc.com
SIC: 3441 Fabricated structural metal

(G-2988)
HASON USA CORP
1080 Nimitzview Dr Ste 402 (45230-4332)
PHONE.................................513 248-0287
Dennis Blain, *Prin*
EMP: 11 **EST:** 2014
SALES (est): 274.99K **Privately Held**
SIC: 3443 Tanks, standard or custom fabricated: metal plate

(G-2989)
HATHAWAY STAMP CO
Also Called: Hathaway Stamp
304 E 8th St (45202-2231)
PHONE.................................513 621-1052
Peter Ruttenberg, *Pr*
Robert C Ruwe, *
EMP: 43 **EST:** 1902
SALES (est): 714.88K
SALES (corp-wide): 23.91MM **Privately Held**
Web: www.hathawaystamps.com
SIC: 3953 3089 5999 5943 Embossing seals and hand stamps; Engraving of plastics; Rubber stamps; Office forms and supplies
PA: Volk Corporation
455 E Cady St
Northville MI 48167
248 477-6700

(G-2990)
HATHAWAY STAMP IDNTFCTION CNCN
Also Called: Hathaway Stamp Identification
304 E 8th St (45202-2231)
PHONE.................................513 621-1052
EMP: 6 **EST:** 2012
SALES (est): 729.89K
SALES (corp-wide): 23.91MM **Privately Held**
Web: www.hathawaystamps.com
SIC: 3953 3479 Marking devices; Name plates: engraved, etched, etc.
PA: Volk Corporation
455 E Cady St
Northville MI 48167
248 477-6700

(G-2991)
HCC/SEALTRON (DH)
9705 Reading Rd (45215-3515)
PHONE.................................513 733-8400
Wes Hausman, *Prin*
EMP: 184 **EST:** 1986
SQ FT: 38,000
SALES (est): 51.7MM
SALES (corp-wide): 6.6B **Publicly Held**
SIC: 3678 Electronic connectors
HQ: Hcc Industries Leasing, Inc.
4232 Temple City Blvd
Rosemead CA 91770
626 443-8933

(G-2992)
HELMART COMPANY INC
Also Called: Countertops Helmart
4960 Hillside Ave (45233-1621)
PHONE.................................513 941-3095
Jeff Wittwer, *Pr*
Marlene Wittwer, *Treas*
Mark Wittwer, *Prin*
EMP: 7 **EST:** 1979
SQ FT: 6,000
SALES (est): 1.04MM **Privately Held**
Web: www.helmartgranitecountertops.com
SIC: 5032 1411 2541 Marble building stone; Granite dimension stone; Table or counter tops, plastic laminated

(G-2993)
HEN OF WOODS LLC
Also Called: Wholesale
2116 Colerain Ave (45214-1838)
P.O. Box 867 (45201-0867)
PHONE.................................513 954-8871
Nick Marckwald, *CEO*
Jason Dranschak, *CFO*
EMP: 7 **EST:** 2012
SQ FT: 9,000
SALES (est): 2.29MM **Privately Held**
Web: www.henofthewoods.com
SIC: 5145 2099 2087 5961 Snack foods; Seasonings and spices; Beverage bases, concentrates, syrups, powders and mixes; Catalog and mail-order houses

(G-2994)
HENKEL US OPERATIONS CORP
9435 Waterstone Blvd (45249-8226)
PHONE.................................513 830-0260
EMP: 28
SALES (corp-wide): 23.39B **Privately Held**
Web: www.henkel.com
SIC: 2891 Adhesives
HQ: Henkel Us Operations Corporation
1 Henkel Way
Rocky Hill CT 06067
860 571-5100

(G-2995)
HENTY USA LLC
7260 Edington Dr (45249-1063)
PHONE.................................513 984-5590
Tyler Scott, *Prin*
Tylor Scott, *CEO*
▲ **EMP:** 10 **EST:** 2013
SALES (est): 425.38K **Privately Held**
Web: www.henty-usa.com
SIC: 2392 Bags, garment storage: except paper or plastic film

(G-2996)
HERMETIC SEAL TECHNOLOGY INC
Also Called: Hst
2150 Schappelle Ln (45240-4602)
PHONE.................................513 851-4899
EMP: 10 **EST:** 1994
SALES (est): 1.68MM **Privately Held**
Web: www.glass-to-metal.com
SIC: 3643 Connectors and terminals for electrical devices

(G-2997)
HESKAMP PRINTING CO INC
5514 Fair Ln (45227-3402)
PHONE.................................513 871-6770
J David Heskamp, *Pr*
Jane Heskamp, *Sec*
EMP: 6 **EST:** 1922
SQ FT: 7,500
SALES (est): 486.11K **Privately Held**
SIC: 2752 2759 Offset printing; Letterpress printing

(G-2998)
HICKMAN WILLIAMS & COMPANY (PA)
250 E 5th St Ste 300 (45202)
P.O. Box 538 (45201)
PHONE.................................513 621-1946
Robert E Davis, *Pr*
Robert J Gray, *VP*
Terry L Meadors, *VP*
Steven W Stark, *VP*
Stuart M Shroyer, *VP*
◆ **EMP:** 11 **EST:** 1890
SQ FT: 5,000
SALES (est): 50.64MM
SALES (corp-wide): 50.64MM **Privately Held**
Web: www.hicwilco.com
SIC: 5051 5052 5169 5085 Steel; Coal and other minerals and ores; Chemicals and allied products, nec; Abrasives

(G-2999)
HILLTOP BASIC RESOURCES INC
Also Called: Hilltop Cmpnies St Brnard Rdym
900 Kieley Pl (45217-1153)
PHONE.................................513 242-8400
Cody Steele, *Brnch Mgr*
EMP: 14
SALES (corp-wide): 59.62MM **Privately Held**
Web: www.hilltopcompanies.com
SIC: 3273 Ready-mixed concrete
PA: Hilltop Basic Resources, Inc.
50 E Rvrcnter Blvd Ste 10
Covington KY 41011
513 651-5000

(G-3000)
HILLTOP BASIC RESOURCES INC
Also Called: Hilltop Concrete
511 W Water St (45202-3400)
PHONE.................................513 621-1500
Mike Marchioni, *Mgr*
EMP: 56
SQ FT: 1,758
SALES (corp-wide): 59.62MM **Privately Held**
Web: www.hilltopcompanies.com
SIC: 3273 3272 1442 Ready-mixed concrete; Concrete products, nec; Construction sand and gravel
PA: Hilltop Basic Resources, Inc.
50 E Rvrcnter Blvd Ste 10
Covington KY 41011
513 651-5000

(G-3001)
HILLTOP BIG BEND QUARRY LLC
1 W 4th St Ste 1100 (45202-3610)
PHONE.................................513 651-5000
John F Steele Junior, *Prin*
EMP: 22 **EST:** 2005
SALES (est): 699.97K **Privately Held**
Web: www.hilltopcompanies.com
SIC: 3273 Ready-mixed concrete

(G-3002)
HILLTOP GLASS & MIRROR LLC
7612 Hamilton Ave (45231-3102)
PHONE.................................513 931-3688
EMP: 6 **EST:** 2020
SALES (est): 277.92K **Privately Held**
Web: www.hilltopglass.co
SIC: 5712 3229 1799 1459 Furniture stores; Pressed and blown glass, nec; Special trade contractors, nec; Clay and related minerals, nec

(G-3003)
HOLLAND ASSOCTS LLC DBA ARCHOU
Also Called: Archoustics Mid-America
316 W 4th St Ste 201 (45202-2675)
PHONE.................................513 891-0006
EMP: 10 **EST:** 2007
SALES (est): 1.01MM **Privately Held**
Web: www.rhcontract.com
SIC: 5065 3699 1742 Sound equipment, electronic; Electric sound equipment; Acoustical and insulation work

(G-3004)
HOMAN METALS LLC
1253 Knowlton St (45223-1844)
PHONE.................................513 721-5010
EMP: 8 **EST:** 1940
SQ FT: 60,000
SALES (est): 963.2K **Privately Held**
Web: www.homanmetals.com
SIC: 5093 3334 4953 3355 Ferrous metal scrap and waste; Aluminum ingots and slabs; Recycling, waste materials; Aluminum ingot

(G-3005)
HOME CITY ICE COMPANY
11920 Kemper Springs Dr (45240-1642)
PHONE.................................513 851-4040
Jason Dugas, *Brnch Mgr*
EMP: 8
SQ FT: 14,040
SALES (corp-wide): 100.42MM **Privately Held**
Web: www.homecityice.com
SIC: 2097 Ice cubes
PA: The Home City Ice Company
6045 Bridgetown Rd Ste 1
Cincinnati OH 45248
513 574-1800

(G-3006)
HONEYBAKED HAM COMPANY (PA)
11935 Mason Montgomery Rd Ste 200 (45249-3702)
PHONE.................................513 583-9700
Craig Kurz, *CEO*
George J Kurz, *
George S Kurz, *
Keith Kurz, *
EMP: 25 **EST:** 1957
SQ FT: 12,000
SALES (est): 26.79MM
SALES (corp-wide): 26.79MM **Privately Held**
Web: www.honeybaked.com
SIC: 5421 2099 2024 2013 Meat markets, including freezer provisioners; Food preparations, nec; Ice cream and frozen deserts; Sausages and other prepared meats

---

(PA)=Parent Co (HQ)=Headquarters
✪ = New Business established in last 2 years

Cincinnati - Hamilton County (G-3007)

(G-3007)
HONEYWELL INTERNATIONAL INC
Also Called: Honeywell
1280 Kemper Meadow Dr (45240-1632)
PHONE.................513 745-7200
EMP: 7
SALES (corp-wide): 36.66B **Publicly Held**
Web: www.honeywell.com
SIC: 3724 7372 Aircraft engines and engine parts; Prepackaged software
PA: Honeywell International Inc.
855 S Mint St
Charlotte NC 28202
704 627-6200

(G-3008)
HORMEL FOODS CORP SVCS LLC
Also Called: Hormel
4055 Executive Park Dr Ste 300 (45241-4020)
PHONE.................513 563-0211
Jim Tupy, Mgr
EMP: 17
SALES (corp-wide): 12.11B **Publicly Held**
Web: www.hormelfoods.com
SIC: 2011 Meat packing plants
HQ: Hormel Foods Corporate Services, Llc
1 Hormel Pl
Austin MN 55912

(G-3009)
HORNELL BREWING CO INC
Also Called: Arizona Beverages
644 Linn St Ste 318 (45203-1734)
PHONE.................516 812-0384
Francie Patton, VP
EMP: 6
SALES (corp-wide): 284.65MM **Privately Held**
SIC: 2086 Bottled and canned soft drinks
PA: Hornell Brewing Co., Inc.
60 Crossways Park Dr W # 400
Woodbury NY 11797
516 812-0300

(G-3010)
HORRORHOUND LTD
1706 Republic St (45202-6421)
P.O. Box 710 (45150-0710)
PHONE.................513 239-7263
Jeremy Sheldon, Pt
EMP: 13 **EST:** 2005
SALES (est): 839.41K **Privately Held**
Web: www.horrorhound.com
SIC: 2731 Book publishing

(G-3011)
HRH DOOR CORP
2136 Stapleton Ct (45240-2780)
PHONE.................513 674-9300
EMP: 31
SALES (corp-wide): 616.75MM **Privately Held**
SIC: 3442 2431 Garage doors, overhead: metal; Garage doors, overhead, wood
PA: Hrh Door Corp.
1 Door Dr
Mount Hope OH 44660
850 208-3400

(G-3012)
HUNKAR TECHNOLOGIES INC (PA)
2368 Victory Pkwy Ste 210 (45206-2810)
PHONE.................513 272-1010
Eric R Thiemann, Pr
C Kevin Whaley, *
Jeannine Martin, *
James K Rice, Corporate Secretary*
EMP: 140 **EST:** 1962
SQ FT: 47,000
SALES (est): 24.81MM
SALES (corp-wide): 24.81MM **Privately Held**
Web: www.hunkar.com
SIC: 3565 3823 3577 3441 Labeling machines, industrial; Controllers, for process variables, all types; Bar code (magnetic ink) printers; Fabricated structural metal

(G-3013)
HYDE PARK LUMBER COMPANY
Also Called: Do It Best
3360 Red Bank Rd (45227-4107)
P.O. Box 8085 (45208-0085)
PHONE.................513 271-1500
Mills C Judy Junior, Pr
Vicki Clephane, *
EMP: 35 **EST:** 1902
SQ FT: 80,000
SALES (est): 7.32MM
SALES (corp-wide): 9.86MM **Privately Held**
Web: www.hydeparklumber.com
SIC: 5251 2431 Hardware stores; Millwork
PA: The Judy Mills Company Inc
3360 Red Bank Rd
Cincinnati OH 45227
513 271-4241

(G-3014)
I AM KING APPAREL LLC
8778 Planet Dr (45231-4162)
PHONE.................513 284-9195
William Daniels Iii, Admn
EMP: 6 **EST:** 2014
SALES (est): 71.2K **Privately Held**
SIC: 3544 Special dies, tools, jigs, and fixtures

(G-3015)
I T VERDIN CO (PA)
Also Called: Verdin Company
444 Reading Rd (45202-1432)
PHONE.................513 241-4010
F B Wersel, CEO
Robert R Verdin Junior, CEO
James R Verdin, *
David E Verdin, *
F B Wersel, Prin
◆ **EMP:** 30 **EST:** 1842
SQ FT: 13,000
SALES (est): 18.87MM
SALES (corp-wide): 18.87MM **Privately Held**
Web: www.verdin.com
SIC: 3931 3699 3873 Carillon bells; Bells, electric; Clocks, except timeclocks

(G-3016)
IGEL TECHNOLOGY AMERICA LLC
2106 Florence Ave (45206-2427)
PHONE.................954 739-9990
Jim Volpenhein, CEO
EMP: 31 **EST:** 2009
SALES (est): 886.96K **Privately Held**
Web: www.igel.com
SIC: 7372 Prepackaged software

(G-3017)
ILSCO LLC (HQ)
Also Called: Utilco Div
4730 Madison Rd (45227)
PHONE.................513 533-6200
▲ **EMP:** 250 **EST:** 1894
SALES (est): 114.78MM
SALES (corp-wide): 135.91MM **Privately Held**
Web: www.ilsco.com
SIC: 3643 3369 3451 3678 Electric connectors; Nonferrous foundries, nec; Screw machine products; Electronic connectors
PA: Ecm Industries, Llc
16250 W Woods Edge Rd
New Berlin WI 53151
800 624-4320

(G-3018)
IMPERIAL POOLS INC
12090 Best Pl (45241-1569)
PHONE.................513 771-1506
Mike Grant, Brnch Mgr
EMP: 19
SALES (corp-wide): 71.38MM **Privately Held**
Web: www.imperialpoolsb2b.com
SIC: 3949 Swimming pools, except plastic
PA: Imperial Pools, Inc.
33 Wade Rd
Latham NY 12110
518 786-1200

(G-3019)
INDUSTRIAL COATING TECH INC
Also Called: Ict Sales
1011 Sunset Ave (45205-1503)
PHONE.................513 376-9945
Michael Hernandez, Prin
EMP: 6 **EST:** 2017
SALES (est): 90.18K **Privately Held**
SIC: 3479 Metal coating and allied services

(G-3020)
INDUSTRIAL CONTAINER SVCS LLC
Also Called: Ics-Cargo Clean
1258 Knowlton St (45223-1845)
PHONE.................513 921-2056
Gary Craig, Brnch Mgr
EMP: 43
Web: www.mauserpackaging.com
SIC: 3443 3089 Fabricated plate work (boiler shop); Plastics and fiberglass tanks
HQ: Industrial Container Services Llc
375 Northridge Rd Ste 600
Atlanta GA 30350
407 930-4182

(G-3021)
INDUSTRIAL CONTAINER SVCS LLC
Also Called: Ics-Cargo Clean
837 Depot St (45204-2005)
PHONE.................513 921-8811
John Stephens, Brnch Mgr
EMP: 44
Web: www.mauserpackaging.com
SIC: 3443 3412 3411 Fabricated plate work (boiler shop); Metal barrels, drums, and pails; Metal cans
HQ: Industrial Container Services Llc
375 Northridge Rd Ste 600
Atlanta GA 30350
407 930-4182

(G-3022)
INDUSTRIAL THERMAL SYSTEMS INC
3914 Virginia Ave (45227-3412)
PHONE.................513 561-2100
Robert Jackson, Pr
Susan Jackson, Treas
◆ **EMP:** 15 **EST:** 1982
SQ FT: 34,000
SALES (est): 2.17MM **Privately Held**
Web: www.industrialthermal.com
SIC: 3559 3613 Kilns; Control panels, electric

(G-3023)
INNOVATIVE WOODWORKING INC
1901 Ross Ave (45212-2019)
PHONE.................513 531-1940
Robert Rodenfels, Pr
Robert W Rodenfels Ii, Pr
Janet A Rodenfels, VP
EMP: 9 **EST:** 1984
SQ FT: 13,000
SALES (est): 963.05K **Privately Held**
SIC: 2522 2521 Office bookcases, wallcases and partitions, except wood; Wood office filing cabinets and bookcases

(G-3024)
INSTRMNTATION CTRL SYSTEMS INC
Also Called: Ics Electrical Services
11355 Sebring Dr (45240-2796)
PHONE.................513 662-2600
John Guenther, Pr
▲ **EMP:** 43 **EST:** 1997
SQ FT: 15,500
SALES (est): 8.53MM **Privately Held**
Web: www.icselectricalservices.com
SIC: 1731 7629 3613 General electrical contractor; Electrical measuring instrument repair and calibration; Control panels, electric

(G-3025)
INTER AMERICAN PRODUCTS INC (HQ)
Also Called: Kenlake Foods
1240 State Ave (45204-1728)
PHONE.................800 645-2233
David B Dillon, Ch
Rodney Mcmullen, Pr
Bill Lucia, Genl Mgr
David Hipenbecker, Dir
EMP: 54 **EST:** 1989
SALES (est): 99.38MM
SALES (corp-wide): 150.04B **Publicly Held**
Web: www.interamericanproducts.com
SIC: 2095 2099 2033 2079 Roasted coffee; Spices, including grinding; Jellies, edible, including imitation: in cans, jars, etc.; Salad oils, except corn: vegetable refined
PA: The Kroger Co
1014 Vine St
Cincinnati OH 45202
513 762-4000

(G-3026)
INTERCONTINENTAL CHEMICAL CORP (PA)
4660 Spring Grove Ave (45232-1995)
PHONE.................513 541-7100
Cameron W Cord, Pr
Paul Shaver, *
EMP: 25 **EST:** 1964
SQ FT: 54,000
SALES (est): 3.09MM
SALES (corp-wide): 3.09MM **Privately Held**
Web: www.icc-chemicals.com
SIC: 2899 Chemical preparations, nec

(G-3027)
INTERLUBE CORPORATION
Also Called: Lube & Chem Products
4646 Baker St (45212-2594)
PHONE.................513 531-1777
Elmer Cleave, Pr
Elmer B Cleves, *
EMP: 10 **EST:** 1969
SQ FT: 4,464
SALES (est): 1.89MM **Privately Held**
Web: www.interlubecorp.com
SIC: 2992 Lubricating oils and greases

(G-3028)
INTERNATIONAL BRAND SERVICES
Also Called: Graeter's Ice Cream
3397 Erie Ave Apt 215 (45208-1638)
PHONE.................513 376-8209
Kellie Manning, Genl Mgr

GEOGRAPHIC SECTION
Cincinnati - Hamilton County (G-3053)

EMP: 9 EST: 2003
SALES (est): 310.9K Privately Held
Web: www.graeters.com
SIC: 2024 5812 Ice cream and ice milk; Ice cream stands or dairy bars

(G-3029)
INTERNATIONAL BUS MCHS CORP
Also Called: IBM
1 Procter And Gamble Plz (45202-3315)
PHONE....................513 826-1001
Michael Flood, Opers Mgr
EMP: 8
SALES (corp-wide): 61.86B Publicly Held
Web: www.ibm.com
SIC: 3613 Distribution cutouts
PA: International Business Machines Corporation
1 New Orchard Rd
Armonk NY 10504
914 499-1900

(G-3030)
IOWA QUALITY MEATS LTD
805 E Kemper Rd (45246-2515)
PHONE....................515 225-6868
Pat Watkins, Genl Mgr
EMP: 160 EST: 1980
SQ FT: 24,000
SALES (est): 41.54MM Privately Held
SIC: 2013 Prepared pork products, from purchased pork
HQ: Smithfield Packaged Meats Corp.
805 E Kemper Rd
Cincinnati OH 45246
513 782-3800

(G-3031)
IREPORTSOURCE
7864 Camargo Rd (45243-2652)
PHONE....................888 294-9578
Nancy Koors, Prin
EMP: 11 EST: 2017
SALES (est): 360.19K Privately Held
Web: www.ireportsource.com
SIC: 7372 Prepackaged software

(G-3032)
IRVING MATERIALS INC
2792 Glendale Milford Rd (45241-3127)
PHONE....................513 769-3666
Jay Snider, Brnch Mgr
EMP: 6
SALES (corp-wide): 814.09MM Privately Held
Web: www.irvmat.com
SIC: 3273 Ready-mixed concrete
PA: Irving Materials, Inc.
8032 N State Road 9
Greenfield IN 46140
317 326-3101

(G-3033)
JACOBS MECHANICAL CO
Also Called: Jacobs
4500 W Mitchell Ave (45232-1912)
PHONE....................513 681-6800
John E Mc Donald, Pr
EMP: 125 EST: 1922
SQ FT: 20,000
SALES (est): 23.6MM Privately Held
Web: www.jacobsmech.com
SIC: 1711 3444 Ventilation and duct work contractor; Sheet metalwork

(G-3034)
JAKMAR INCORPORATED
3280 Hageman Ave (45241-1907)
PHONE....................513 631-4303
William Thaman, Pr
EMP: 10 EST: 2001

SALES (est): 226.8K Privately Held
SIC: 3061 Mechanical rubber goods

(G-3035)
JAMES C FREE INC
Also Called: James Free Jewellers
9555 Main St Ste 1 (45242-7670)
PHONE....................513 793-0133
Zackery Karaman, VP
EMP: 6
SALES (corp-wide): 3.45MM Privately Held
Web: www.jamesfree.com
SIC: 3911 5944 Jewelry, precious metal; Jewelry, precious stones and precious metals
PA: James C. Free, Inc.
3100 Far Hills Ave
Dayton OH 45429
937 298-0171

(G-3036)
JAMES C ROBINSON
Also Called: J C Robinson Products
442 Chestnut St Apt 1 (45203-1454)
PHONE....................513 969-7482
James C Robinson, Owner
EMP: 9 EST: 1981
SALES (est): 576.49K Privately Held
SIC: 5149 7231 2842 Dried or canned foods; Beauty shops; Automobile polish

(G-3037)
JAMES L DECKEBACH LLC
4575 Eastern Ave (45226-1805)
PHONE....................513 321-3733
James Deckebach, Owner
EMP: 9 EST: 2016
SALES (est): 221.64K Privately Held
SIC: 2511 Wood household furniture

(G-3038)
JBNOVEMBER LLC
3950 Virginia Ave (45227-3412)
PHONE....................513 272-7000
EMP: 30
SIC: 2752 Offset printing

(G-3039)
JEFFREY D LAYTON
6788 High Meadows Dr (45230-3805)
PHONE....................513 706-4352
EMP: 6 EST: 2009
SALES (est): 170.54K Privately Held
SIC: 2431 Millwork

(G-3040)
JEN-COAT INC (DH)
Also Called: Prolamina
12025 Tricon Rd (45246-1719)
P.O. Box 274 (01086-0274)
PHONE....................513 671-1777
Gregory Tucker, CEO
Eric Bradford, CFO
◆ EMP: 230 EST: 1972
SQ FT: 375,000
SALES (est): 53.97MM
SALES (corp-wide): 1.58B Privately Held
Web: www.proampac.com
SIC: 3554 Die cutting and stamping machinery, paper converting
HQ: Prolamina Corporation
132 N Elm St
Westfield MA 01086

(G-3041)
JERRY TOOLS INC
6200 Vine St (45216-2199)
PHONE....................513 242-3211
David Inboldt, Pr

David Imholt, Pr
Don Daniels, VP
Debra Imholt, VP
EMP: 16 EST: 1965
SQ FT: 15,625
SALES (est): 2.12MM Privately Held
Web: www.jerrytools.com
SIC: 3545 3452 Chucks: drill, lathe, or magnetic (machine tool accessories); Nuts, metal

(G-3042)
JFDB LTD
Also Called: Hvac Mech Cntrcto Plbg Ppfttin
10036 Springfield Pike (45215-1452)
PHONE....................513 870-0601
Jonathan Feldkamp, Pr
Joel Feldkamp, *
EMP: 150 EST: 2006
SQ FT: 18,000
SALES (est): 21.84MM Privately Held
Web: www.jfeldkampdesignbuild.com
SIC: 1711 3499 Mechanical contractor; Aerosol valves, metal

(G-3043)
JOHN FRIEDA PROF HAIR CARE INC (DH)
2535 Spring Grove Ave (45214-1729)
P.O. Box 145444 (45250-5444)
PHONE....................800 521-3189
William J Gentner, Pr
Joseph B Workman, *
EMP: 40 EST: 1990
SALES (est): 24.98MM Privately Held
Web: www.mykaoshop.com
SIC: 2844 Hair preparations, including shampoos
HQ: Kao Usa Inc.
2535 Spring Grove Ave
Cincinnati OH 45214
513 421-1400

(G-3044)
JOHN R JURGENSEN CO (PA)
11641 Mosteller Rd (45241-1520)
PHONE....................513 771-0820
▲ EMP: 440 EST: 1930
SALES (est): 225.16MM
SALES (corp-wide): 225.16MM Privately Held
Web: www.jrjnet.com
SIC: 1611 1442 General contractor, highway and street construction; Sand mining

(G-3045)
JOHN STEHLIN & SONS CO
Also Called: Stehlin, John & Sons Meats
10134 Colerain Ave (45251-4902)
PHONE....................513 385-6164
John Stehlin, Pr
Ronald Stehlin, VP
Richard Stehlin, Sec
Dennis Stehlin, VP
EMP: 10 EST: 1913
SQ FT: 3,600
SALES (est): 456.01K Privately Held
Web: www.stehlinsmeatmarket.com
SIC: 5421 2013 2011 Meat markets, including freezer provisioners; Sausages and other prepared meats; Beef products, from beef slaughtered on site

(G-3046)
JOHNNY HULSMAN SIGNS
2955 Spring Grove Ave (45225-2117)
PHONE....................513 638-9788
EMP: 6 EST: 2018
SALES (est): 189.72K Privately Held
Web: johnny-hulsman-signs-inc.business.site

SIC: 3993 Signs and advertising specialties

(G-3047)
JOHNSON & JOHNSON SERVICES LLC
273 Mccormick Pl (45219-2811)
PHONE....................513 289-4514
Danny Johnson, Mgr
EMP: 10 EST: 2021
SALES (est): 100K Privately Held
Web: www.jnj.com
SIC: 3524 Lawnmowers, residential: hand or power

(G-3048)
JOHNSON CONTROLS INC
Also Called: Johnson Controls
7863 Palace Dr (45249-1635)
PHONE....................513 489-0950
Brian Ballitch, Brnch Mgr
EMP: 52
Web: www.johnsoncontrols.com
SIC: 2531 Seats, automobile
HQ: Johnson Controls, Inc.
5757 N Green Bay Ave
Milwaukee WI 53209
920 245-6409

(G-3049)
JOHNSON CONTROLS INC
Also Called: Johnson Controls
11648 Springfield Pike (45246-3019)
PHONE....................513 671-6338
EMP: 16
Web: www.johnsoncontrols.com
SIC: 2531 7382 Seats, automobile; Security systems services
HQ: Johnson Controls, Inc.
5757 N Green Bay Ave
Milwaukee WI 53209
920 245-6409

(G-3050)
JORDAN VALVE
3170 Wasson Rd (45209-2329)
PHONE....................513 533-5600
EMP: 7 EST: 2021
SALES (est): 252.92K Privately Held
Web: www.jordanvalve.com
SIC: 3599 Industrial machinery, nec

(G-3051)
JOS BERNING PRINTING CO
1850 Dalton Ave (45214-2056)
PHONE....................513 721-0781
Michael Berning, Pr
EMP: 18 EST: 1883
SQ FT: 11,800
SALES (est): 1MM Privately Held
Web: www.josberningprinting.com
SIC: 2752 Offset printing

(G-3052)
JRM 2 COMPANY
Also Called: Cushman Foundry Div
425 Shepherd Ave (45215-3114)
P.O. Box 15527 (45215-0527)
PHONE....................513 554-1700
▲ EMP: 100
SIC: 3365 3325 3369 3341 Aluminum and aluminum-based alloy castings; Alloy steel castings, except investment; Nonferrous foundries, nec; Secondary nonferrous metals

(G-3053)
JUDY MILLS COMPANY INC (PA)
3360 Red Bank Rd (45227-4107)
PHONE....................513 271-4241
Mike Judy, Pr

Cincinnati - Hamilton County (G-3054)

EMP: 36 EST: 1922
SALES (est): 9.86MM
SALES (corp-wide): 9.86MM **Privately Held**
Web: www.doitbest.com
SIC: **5251** 5211 2431 Hardware stores; Lumber and other building materials; Millwork

(G-3054)
K & H INDUSTRIES LLC
1041 Evans St (45204-2019)
PHONE..................513 921-6770
EMP: 15 EST: 1905
SQ FT: 60,000
SALES (est): 1.18MM **Privately Held**
Web: www.kh-ind.com
SIC: **3469** Stamping metal for the trade

(G-3055)
K F T INC
726 Mehring Way (45203-1809)
PHONE..................513 241-5910
Ronald Eubanks, *Pr*
Richard Eubanks, *Stockholder**
EMP: 60 EST: 1941
SQ FT: 45,000
SALES (est): 4.88MM **Privately Held**
Web: www.tkf.com
SIC: **1796** 3535 Millwright; Overhead conveyor systems

(G-3056)
KAFFENBARGER TRUCK EQP CO
3260 E Kemper Rd (45241-1519)
PHONE..................513 772-6800
Rodney Swigert, *Mgr*
EMP: 25
SQ FT: 18,280
SALES (corp-wide): 22.65MM **Privately Held**
Web: www.knapheide.com
SIC: **7538** 5531 3713 3532 Truck engine repair, except industrial; Truck equipment and parts; Truck bodies and parts; Mining machinery
PA: Kaffenbarger Truck Equipment Co Inc
10100 Ballentine Pike
New Carlisle OH 45344
937 845-3804

(G-3057)
KAHNY PRINTING INC
4766 River Rd (45233-1633)
PHONE..................513 251-2911
John S Kahny, *Pr*
Linda Knierim, *
EMP: 25 EST: 1956
SQ FT: 14,000
SALES (est): 2.3MM **Privately Held**
Web: www.kahny.com
SIC: **2752** Offset printing

(G-3058)
KAISER FOODS INC (PA)
500 York St (45214-2490)
PHONE..................513 621-2053
David Kaiser, *Ch*
Donald J Kaiser, *VP*
Kim Speed, *VP*
Kimberly Speed, *COO*
▲ EMP: 20 EST: 1920
SQ FT: 50,000
SALES (est): 25.65MM
SALES (corp-wide): 25.65MM **Privately Held**
Web: www.kaiserpickles.com
SIC: **5149** 2035 Pickles, preserves, jellies, and jams; Cucumbers, pickles and pickle salting

(G-3059)
KAISER PICKLES LLC (HQ)
500 York St (45214-2416)
PHONE..................513 621-2053
David Kaiser, *CEO*
Kim Speed, *
EMP: 6 EST: 2003
SALES (est): 5.61MM
SALES (corp-wide): 25.65MM **Privately Held**
Web: www.kaiserpickles.com
SIC: **2035** Pickled fruits and vegetables
PA: Kaiser Foods, Inc.
500 York St
Cincinnati OH 45214
513 621-2053

(G-3060)
KAISER PICKLES LLC
422 York St (45214-2414)
PHONE..................513 621-2053
FMP: 16
SALES (corp-wide): 25.65MM **Privately Held**
Web: www.kaiserpickles.com
SIC: **2035** Pickled fruits and vegetables
HQ: Kaiser Pickles, Llc
500 York St
Cincinnati OH 45214
513 621-2053

(G-3061)
KAO BRANDS COMPANY
1231 Draper St (45214-1758)
PHONE..................513 977-2931
EMP: 9 EST: 2019
SALES (est): 174.89K **Privately Held**
Web: www.kao.com
SIC: **2844** Cosmetic preparations

(G-3062)
KAO USA INC (HQ)
2535 Spring Grove Ave (45214-1729)
P.O. Box 145444 (45250-5444)
PHONE..................513 421-1400
Karen B Frank, *Ch Bd*
John Nosek, *VP*
◆ EMP: 400 EST: 1971
SQ FT: 489,000
SALES (est): 569.98MM **Privately Held**
Web: www.kao.com
SIC: **2844** 2841 Cosmetic preparations; Soap: granulated, liquid, cake, flaked, or chip
PA: Kao Corporation
1-14-10, Nihombashikayabacho
Chuo-Ku TKY 103-0

(G-3063)
KAO USA INC
312 Plum St (45202-2697)
PHONE..................513 629-5210
Bill Gentner, *Pr*
EMP: 15
Web: www.kao.com
SIC: **2844** Cosmetic preparations
HQ: Kao Usa Inc.
2535 Spring Grove Ave
Cincinnati OH 45214
513 421-1400

(G-3064)
KARRIKIN SPIRITS COMPANY LLC
3717 Jonlen Dr (45227-4103)
PHONE..................513 561-5000
EMP: 11 EST: 2017
SALES (est): 2.51MM **Privately Held**
Web: www.karrikinspirits.com
SIC: **2085** 5812 Distilled and blended liquors; Eating places

(G-3065)
KATCH KITCHEN LLC
4172 Hamilton Ave (45223-2247)
PHONE..................513 537-8056
EMP: 20 EST: 2020
SALES (est): 540K **Privately Held**
SIC: **2499** Food handling and processing products, wood

(G-3066)
KAWS INC
Also Called: RB Tool & Mfg. Co.
2680 Civic Center Dr (45231-1312)
PHONE..................513 521-8292
Kathy Schaeper, *CEO*
Al Schaeper, *
EMP: 26 EST: 1995
SQ FT: 20,000
SALES (est): 7.17MM **Privately Held**
Web: www.rbtoolandmfg.com
SIC: **3599** Machine shop, jobbing and repair

(G-3067)
KC MARKETING LLC ◎
Also Called: Kodiak Chemical
5353 Spring Grove Ave (45217-1026)
PHONE..................513 471-8770
Kevin Dickey, *Managing Member*
EMP: 28 EST: 2022
SALES (est): 9MM
SALES (corp-wide): 9MM **Privately Held**
SIC: **2992** 2819 2869 Lubricating oils and greases; Calcium metal; Industrial organic chemicals, nec
PA: Kodiak, Llc
5353 Spring Grove Ave
Cincinnati OH 45217
513 471-8770

(G-3068)
KDM SIGNS INC
2996 Exon Ave (45241-2521)
PHONE..................513 554-1393
EMP: 6
SALES (corp-wide): 69.1MM **Privately Held**
Web: www.kdmpop.com
SIC: **2759** Commercial printing, nec
PA: Kdm Signs, Inc.
10450 Medallion Dr
Cincinnati OH 45241
513 769-1932

(G-3069)
KDM SIGNS INC (PA)
Also Called: Kdm Screen Printing
10450 N Medallion Dr (45241-3199)
PHONE..................513 769-1932
Robert J Kissel, *Pr*
Kathy Mcqueen, *Sec*
▲ EMP: 230 EST: 1984
SQ FT: 150,000
SALES (est): 69.1MM
SALES (corp-wide): 69.1MM **Privately Held**
Web: www.kdmpop.com
SIC: **3993** 2759 Signs and advertising specialties; Screen printing

(G-3070)
KDM SIGNS INC
Kdm Retail
3000 Exon Ave (45241-2550)
PHONE..................513 769-3900
Lee Diss, *Brnch Mgr*
EMP: 11
SALES (corp-wide): 69.1MM **Privately Held**
Web: www.kdmpop.com
SIC: **2541** Display fixtures, wood
PA: Kdm Signs, Inc.

10450 Medallion Dr
Cincinnati OH 45241
513 769-1932

(G-3071)
KEEBLER COMPANY
Also Called: Keebler
1 Trade St (45227-4509)
PHONE..................513 271-3500
Sam Bristle, *Mgr*
EMP: 67
SALES (corp-wide): 15.31B **Publicly Held**
Web: www.keebler.com
SIC: **2052** Cookies
HQ: Keebler Company
1 Kellogg Sq
Battle Creek MI 49017
269 961-2000

(G-3072)
KELLANOVA
Also Called: Kellog
1 Trade St (45227-4509)
PHONE..................513 271-3500
Jerry Morgan, *Dir*
EMP: 284
SALES (corp-wide): 15.31B **Publicly Held**
Web: www.kellanova.com
SIC: **2052** 2051 Biscuits, dry; Bread, cake, and related products
PA: Kellanova
412 N Wells St
Chicago IL 60654
269 961-2000

(G-3073)
KENDALL/HUNT PUBLISHING CO
Also Called: Rcl Benziger
8805 Governors Hill Dr Ste 400 (45249-3314)
PHONE..................877 275-4725
Peter Ashpostio, *Brnch Mgr*
EMP: 109
SALES (corp-wide): 85.52MM **Privately Held**
Web: www.rclbenziger.com
SIC: **2731** Books, publishing and printing
PA: Kendall/Hunt Publishing Company
4050 Westmark Dr
Dubuque IA 52002
563 589-1000

(G-3074)
KENNEDY INK COMPANY INC (PA)
5230 Wooster Pike (45226-2229)
PHONE..................513 871-2515
Jim Scott, *Pr*
James H Scott, *Prin*
Ralph W Wagner, *Prin*
Donald M Kennedy, *Prin*
EMP: 10 EST: 1956
SQ FT: 8,000
SALES (est): 2.54MM
SALES (corp-wide): 2.54MM **Privately Held**
Web: www.perfectdomain.com
SIC: **2893** Printing ink

(G-3075)
KETTERING ROOFING & SHTMTL INC
3210 Jefferson Ave Ste 1 (45220-2290)
PHONE..................513 281-6413
Timothy Kettering, *Pr*
Christina Kettering, *Sec*
EMP: 13 EST: 1929
SQ FT: 5,000
SALES (est): 464.91K **Privately Held**
SIC: **1761** 3444 2952 Sheet metal work, nec; Sheet metalwork; Asphalt felts and coatings

GEOGRAPHIC SECTION
Cincinnati - Hamilton County (G-3098)

(G-3076)
KING BAG AND MANUFACTURING CO (PA)
1500 Spring Lawn Ave (45223-1699)
PHONE.................513 541-5440
Connie M Kirsch, *Pr*
Ronald Kirsch Senior, *VP*
Ronald Kirsch Junior, *VP*
◆ **EMP:** 25 **EST:** 1985
SQ FT: 18,000
SALES (est): 13.75MM
SALES (corp-wide): 13.75MM **Privately Held**
Web: www.kingbag.com
SIC: 2393 2221 Textile bags; Polyethylene broadwoven fabrics

(G-3077)
KINSELLA MANUFACTURING CO INC
7880 Camargo Rd (45243-2652)
PHONE.................513 561-5285
George P Kinsella, *Pr*
John Kinsella, *Sec*
Kevin Kinsella, *VP*
EMP: 10 **EST:** 1961
SQ FT: 10,000
SALES (est): 712.08K **Privately Held**
Web: www.kinsellakitchens.com
SIC: 5211 2541 2434 Cabinets, kitchen; Counters or counter display cases, wood; Wood kitchen cabinets

(G-3078)
KIRK & BLUM MANUFACTURING CO (DH)
4625 Red Bank Rd Ste 200 (45227-1552)
PHONE.................513 458-2600
◆ **EMP:** 200 **EST:** 1907
SQ FT: 250,000
SALES (est): 48.76MM **Publicly Held**
Web: www.cecoenviro.com
SIC: 1761 3444 3443 Sheet metal work, nec; Sheet metal specialties, not stamped; Fabricated plate work (boiler shop)
HQ: Ceco Group, Inc.
4625 Red Bank Rd Ste 200
Cincinnati OH 45227
513 458-2600

(G-3079)
KIRWAN INDUSTRIES INC
8390 Ridge Rd (45236-1338)
PHONE.................513 333-0766
Ronan Kirwan, *Pr*
EMP: 8 **EST:** 1994
SALES (est): 987.93K **Privately Held**
Web: www.kirwanindustries.com
SIC: 3441 Building components, structural steel

(G-3080)
KITCHENS BY RUTENSCHROER INC (PA)
Also Called: Kbr
950 Laidlaw Ave (45237-5004)
PHONE.................513 251-8333
Steven Rutenschroer, *Pr*
Missy Rutenschroer, *VP*
G Robert Hines, *Prin*
Kathy Frisby, *Prin*
Steven D Rutenschroer, *Prin*
▲ **EMP:** 9 **EST:** 1978
SQ FT: 8,000
SALES (est): 4.48MM
SALES (corp-wide): 4.48MM **Privately Held**
Web: www.kbrmfg.com

SIC: 5722 2519 2541 2511 Kitchens, complete (sinks, cabinets, etc.); Household furniture, except wood or metal: upholstered ; Wood partitions and fixtures; Wood household furniture

(G-3081)
KLOSTERMAN BAKING CO LLC
1000 E Ross Ave (45217-1132)
PHONE.................513 242-5667
EMP: 62
SALES (corp-wide): 190.57MM **Privately Held**
Web: www.klostermanbakery.com
SIC: 5149 2051 Bakery products; Bread, cake, and related products
PA: Klosterman Baking Co., Llc
4760 Paddock Rd
Cincinnati OH 45229
513 242-1004

(G-3082)
KLOSTERMAN BAKING CO LLC (PA)
Also Called: Klosterman
4760 Paddock Rd (45229-1047)
PHONE.................513 242-1004
Ross Anderson, *Pr*
EMP: 30 **EST:** 1892
SQ FT: 10,000
SALES (est): 190.57MM
SALES (corp-wide): 190.57MM **Privately Held**
Web: www.klostermanbakery.com
SIC: 2051 Bakery: wholesale or wholesale/retail combined

(G-3083)
KN8DESIGNS LLC
4016 Allston St (45209-1743)
PHONE.................859 380-5926
Nathan Ward, *Prin*
EMP: 9 **EST:** 2009
SALES (est): 508.65K **Privately Held**
Web: www.kn8designs.com
SIC: 2621 Printing paper

(G-3084)
KNOBLE GLASS & METAL INC (PA)
Also Called: K G M
8650 Green Rd (45255-5016)
PHONE.................513 753-1246
David Knoble, *Pr*
EMP: 9 **EST:** 1999
SALES (est): 896.42K
SALES (corp-wide): 896.42K **Privately Held**
Web: www.knobelglassandmetal.com
SIC: 3229 3354 Glass fibers, textile; Aluminum extruded products

(G-3085)
KNOWLTON MANUFACTURING CO INC
2524 Leslie Ave (45212-4299)
PHONE.................513 631-7353
Kenneth Jenkins, *Pr*
John Fricker, *VP*
Allan Marcuse, *CFO*
Karen Fanroy, *CFO*
EMP: 15 **EST:** 2009
SQ FT: 44,000
SALES (est): 2.9MM **Privately Held**
Web: www.knowltonmfg.com
SIC: 3469 3544 Stamping metal for the trade ; Special dies and tools

(G-3086)
KOHL & MADDEN INC
5000 Spring Grove Ave (45232-1926)
PHONE.................513 326-6900
Rudi Lenz, *Prin*

EMP: 15 **EST:** 2008
SALES (est): 508.1K **Privately Held**
Web: www.sunchemical.com
SIC: 2893 Printing ink

(G-3087)
KOOP DIAMOND CUTTERS INC
214 E 8th St Fl 4 (45202-2173)
PHONE.................513 621-2838
Clarence E Koop, *Pr*
Richard J Louis, *Sec*
EMP: 10 **EST:** 1965
SQ FT: 4,300
SALES (est): 791.6K **Privately Held**
Web: www.koopdiamondcutters.com
SIC: 3911 7631 3915 Jewelry, precious metal ; Jewelry repair services; Jewel cutting, drilling, polishing, recutting, or setting

(G-3088)
KOST USA INC (DH)
Also Called: Kgi Holdings
1000 Tennessee Ave (45229-1008)
PHONE.................513 583-7070
EMP: 23 **EST:** 1985
SALES (est): 72.38MM **Privately Held**
Web: www.kostusa.com
SIC: 2899 2992 Antifreeze compounds; Lubricating oils
HQ: Recochem Inc.
600 5th Ave Fl 22
New York NY 10020
800 361-6030

(G-3089)
KREHBIEL HOLDINGS INC
3962 Virginia Ave (45227-3412)
PHONE.................
▼ **EMP:** 93 **EST:** 1871
SQ FT: 170,000
SALES (est): 15MM **Privately Held**
Web: www.cjkusa.com
SIC: 2752 Offset printing

(G-3090)
KRIEG REV 2 INC
10600 Chester Rd (45215-1206)
PHONE.................513 542-1522
Terry L Krieg, *Pr*
EMP: 29 **EST:** 1975
SQ FT: 30,000
SALES (est): 2.63MM **Privately Held**
Web: www.printing4thetrade.com
SIC: 2752 2789 Offset printing; Bookbinding and related work

(G-3091)
KUHLS HOT SPORTSPOT
6701 Beechmont Ave (45230-2905)
PHONE.................513 474-2282
Robert Kuhl, *Owner*
EMP: 10 **EST:** 1987
SALES (est): 993.61K **Privately Held**
Web: www.cincysportsshop.com
SIC: 2395 Embroidery products, except Schiffli machine

(G-3092)
KUROME THERAPEUTICS INC
3536 Edwards Rd Ste 100 (45208-1358)
PHONE.................513 445-3852
Jan Rosenbaum, *Pr*
John Rice, *Ofcr*
EMP: 6 **EST:** 2021
SALES (est): 1.04MM **Privately Held**
Web: www.kurometherapeutics.com
SIC: 2834 Pharmaceutical preparations

(G-3093)
KYOCERA SENCO INDUS TLS INC (HQ)

8450 Broadwell Rd (45244-1612)
PHONE.................513 388-2000
Cliff Mentrup, *CEO*
▲ **EMP:** 70 **EST:** 1948
SALES (est): 92.87MM **Privately Held**
Web: www.senco.com
SIC: 3546 7389 Power-driven handtools; Business services, nec
PA: Kyocera Corporation
6, Takedatobadonocho, Fushimi-Ku
Kyoto KYO 612-8

(G-3094)
LA MFG INC
Also Called: Brewer Products
9483 Reading Rd (45215-3550)
P.O. Box 62065 (45262-0065)
PHONE.................513 577-7200
David Brewer, *Pr*
EMP: 6 **EST:** 1989
SALES (est): 493.29K **Privately Held**
Web: www.brewerproducts.com
SIC: 3569 5199 5082 General industrial machinery, nec; Nondurable goods, nec; Construction and mining machinery

(G-3095)
LANGDON INC
9865 Wayne Ave (45215-1403)
P.O. Box 15308 (45215-0308)
PHONE.................513 733-5955
David Sandman, *Pr*
Michael Sandman, *
▲ **EMP:** 40 **EST:** 1966
SQ FT: 42,000
SALES (est): 6.92MM **Privately Held**
Web: www.langdonsheetmetal.com
SIC: 3444 1711 3564 3446 Ducts, sheet metal; Warm air heating and air conditioning contractor; Blowers and fans; Architectural metalwork

(G-3096)
LATE FOR SKY PRODUCTION CO
1292 Glendale Milford Rd (45215-1209)
PHONE.................513 531-4400
Robyn L Wilson, *Prin*
William C Schulte Junior, *VP*
Mark Hunter, *
Chris Niehaus, *
▲ **EMP:** 48 **EST:** 1985
SQ FT: 60,000
SALES (est): 9.29MM **Privately Held**
Web: www.lateforthesky.com
SIC: 3944 Board games, children's and adults'

(G-3097)
LAURENEE LTD
Also Called: Deerfield Digital
3509 Harrison Ave (45211-5544)
PHONE.................513 662-2225
Timothy R Roedersheimer, *Managing Member*
EMP: 8 **EST:** 1975
SQ FT: 8,500
SALES (est): 928.37K **Privately Held**
Web: www.deerfielddigital.com
SIC: 2752 2791 Offset printing; Typesetting

(G-3098)
LECTORA
311 Elm St Ste 200 (45202-2743)
PHONE.................513 929-0188
EMP: 9 **EST:** 2019
SALES (est): 75.07K **Privately Held**
Web: www.elblearning.com
SIC: 7372 Prepackaged software

Cincinnati - Hamilton County (G-3099)

(G-3099)
LEE CORPORATION
Also Called: Lee Printers
12055 Mosteller Rd (45241-1589)
PHONE......................513 771-3602
Thomas Krieg, *Pr*
Carol Krieg, *Sec*
Ronald Krieg, *Treas*
Lee Krieg, *VP*
EMP: 7 **EST:** 1905
SQ FT: 35,000
SALES (est): 864.78K **Privately Held**
Web: www.leeprinters.com
SIC: 2752 2759 2791 2789 Offset printing; Letterpress printing; Typesetting; Bookbinding and related work

(G-3100)
LEHIGH PORTLAND CEMENT
2792 Glendale Milford Rd (45241-3127)
PHONE......................513 769-3666
EMP: 6 **EST:** 2017
SALES (est): 68.89K **Privately Held**
SIC: 3241 Portland cement

(G-3101)
LEICA BIOSYSTEMS - TAS
300 E Business Way Fl 5 (45241-2384)
PHONE......................513 864-9671
EMP: 24 **EST:** 2018
SALES (est): 5.09MM **Privately Held**
SIC: 3841 Surgical and medical instruments

(G-3102)
LEONHARDT PLATING COMPANY
5753 Este Ave (45232-1499)
PHONE......................513 242-1410
Kerry Leonhardt, *Pr*
Daniel Leonhardt, *Stockholder*
EMP: 16 **EST:** 1950
SQ FT: 20,500
SALES (est): 508.6K **Privately Held**
Web: www.leonhardtplating.com
SIC: 3471 2899 2851 2842 Electroplating of metals or formed products; Chemical preparations, nec; Paints and allied products; Polishes and sanitation goods

(G-3103)
LIB THERAPEUTICS INC
5375 Medpace Way (45227-1543)
PHONE......................859 240-7764
David Cory, *CEO*
Dennis Thompson, *CFO*
EMP: 10 **EST:** 2017
SALES (est): 1.07MM **Privately Held**
Web: www.libtherapeutics.com
SIC: 2834 Pharmaceutical preparations

(G-3104)
LIFE IS SWEET LLC (PA)
6926 Main St (45244-3009)
PHONE......................330 342-0172
EMP: 13 **EST:** 2018
SALES (est): 9.87MM
SALES (corp-wide): 9.87MM **Privately Held**
Web: www.lisbrands.com
SIC: 2064 Candy and other confectionery products

(G-3105)
LIFESTYLE NUTRACEUTICALS LTD
Also Called: Pun-U
5911 Turpin Hills Dr Ste 101 (45244-3857)
PHONE......................513 376-7218
Collin Literski, *CEO*
Diane Literski, *Dir*
Graham Clark, *Dir*
Brad Bolton Sales, *Prin*
EMP: 6 **EST:** 2005
SALES (est): 119.12K **Privately Held**
SIC: 2023 5149 8731 Dietary supplements, dairy and non-dairy based; Health foods; Agricultural research

(G-3106)
LIGHT VISION
1776 Mentor Ave (45212-3554)
PHONE......................513 351-9444
EMP: 12 **EST:** 1996
SQ FT: 3,000
SALES (est): 341.71K **Privately Held**
SIC: 2064 Candy and other confectionery products

(G-3107)
LINDE GAS & EQUIPMENT INC
Also Called: Praxair
8376 Reading Rd (45237-1407)
PHONE......................513 821-2192
Joe R Smith, *Mgr*
EMP: 8
Web: www.lindeus.com
SIC: 2813 5084 5999 Carbon dioxide; Welding machinery and equipment; Welding supplies
HQ: Linde Gas & Equipment Inc.
10 Riverview Dr
Danbury CT 06810
844 445-4633

(G-3108)
LISTERMANN MFG CO INC
Also Called: Listermann Brewery Supply
4120 Forest Ave (45212-3340)
PHONE......................513 731-1130
Daniel Listermann, *Pr*
Sue Listermann, *VP*
EMP: 8 **EST:** 1991
SALES (est): 1.47MM **Privately Held**
Web: www.listermannbrewing.com
SIC: 3556 Brewers' and maltsters' machinery

(G-3109)
LIVE OFF LOYALTY INC
12019 Hitchcock Dr (45240-1816)
PHONE......................513 413-2401
Derrick Ferguson, *CEO*
EMP: 7 **EST:** 2015
SALES (est): 226.54K **Privately Held**
SIC: 2782 Record albums

(G-3110)
LONE STAR INDUSTRIES INC
6381 River Rd (45233-1360)
PHONE......................513 467-0430
Mike Mcrae, *Prin*
EMP: 10 **EST:** 2006
SALES (est): 125.61K **Privately Held**
SIC: 3241 Cement, hydraulic

(G-3111)
LONG-LOK LLC (PA)
10630 Chester Rd (45215-1249)
PHONE......................336 343-7319
Bryan Perkins, *Managing Member*
EMP: 30 **EST:** 2019
SALES (est): 9.6MM
SALES (corp-wide): 9.6MM **Privately Held**
Web: www.longlok.com
SIC: 3728 R and D by manuf., aircraft parts and auxiliary equipment

(G-3112)
LONG-LOK FASTENERS CORPORATION
10630 Chester Rd (45215-1249)
PHONE......................513 772-1880
Aaron Dollenmeyer, *Mgr*
EMP: 35
SQ FT: 33,000
SALES (corp-wide): 23.95MM **Privately Held**
Web: www.longlok.com
SIC: 3452 Bolts, nuts, rivets, and washers
HQ: Long-Lok Fasteners Corporation
14755 Preston Rd Ste 520
Dallas TX 75254
888 656-9450

(G-3113)
LOROCO INDUSTRIES INC
Also Called: Royal Pad Products
10600 Evendale Dr (45241-2518)
PHONE......................513 891-9544
James Lallathin, *Pr*
Lee Rozin, *
Jim Myers, *
▼ **EMP:** 75 **EST:** 1898
SALES (est): 11.47MM **Privately Held**
Web: www.lorocoindustries.com
SIC: 2675 2671 3479 3544 Paperboard die-cutting; Paper; coated and laminated packaging; Painting, coating, and hot dipping; Dies, steel rule

(G-3114)
LOSANTIVILLE WINERY LLC
38 W Mcmicken Ave (45202-7718)
PHONE......................513 918-3015
EMP: 9 **EST:** 2014
SALES (est): 237.14K **Privately Held**
Web: www.losantivillecc.com
SIC: 2084 Wines

(G-3115)
LSI INDUSTRIES INC (PA)
Also Called: LSI Industries
10000 Alliance Rd (45242)
P.O. Box 42728 (45242)
PHONE......................513 793-3200
James A Clark, *Pr*
Wilfred T O'gara, *Ch Bd*
James E Galeese, *Ex VP*
Thomas A Caneris, *Ex VP*
Jeffery S Bastian, *CAO*
EMP: 264 **EST:** 1976
SQ FT: 243,000
SALES: 496.98MM
SALES (corp-wide): 496.98MM **Publicly Held**
Web: www.lsicorp.com
SIC: 3648 3993 3663 Lighting equipment, nec; Electric signs; Light communications equipment

(G-3116)
LUXFER MAGTECH INC (HQ)
Also Called: Heatermeals
2940 Highland Ave Ste 210 (45212-2402)
PHONE......................513 772-3066
Brian Purves, *CEO*
Marc Lamensdorf, *
Deborah Simsen, *
Deepak Madan, *
EMP: 37 **EST:** 2014
SALES (est): 7.78MM
SALES (corp-wide): 405MM **Privately Held**
Web: www.heatermeals.com
SIC: 2899 5149 Desalter kits, sea water; Groceries and related products, nec
PA: Luxfer Holdings Plc
Ancorage Gateway
Salford LANCS M50 3
161 300-0611

(G-3117)
LYLE INDUSTRIES INC
6633 Wyndwatch Dr (45230-5270)
PHONE......................513 233-2803
Kelly Lyle, *Prin*
EMP: 6 **EST:** 2010
SALES (est): 125.53K **Privately Held**
SIC: 3999 Manufacturing industries, nec

(G-3118)
LYONDELL CHEMICAL COMPANY
11530 Northlake Dr (45249-1642)
PHONE......................513 530-4000
Norma Maraschin, *Mgr*
EMP: 143
Web: www.lyondellbasell.com
SIC: 2869 2822 8731 Olefins; Polyethylene, chlorosulfonated, hypalon; Commercial physical research
HQ: Lyondell Chemical Company
1221 Mckinney St Ste 300
Houston TX 77010
713 309-7200

(G-3119)
M R I EDUCATION FOUNDATION
5400 Kennedy Ave (45213-2664)
PHONE......................513 281-3400
Steve J Pomeranz Md, *Pr*
James Kereiakes, *Stockholder*
EMP: 24 **EST:** 1988
SQ FT: 5,600
SALES (est): 368.34K **Privately Held**
Web: www.proscan.com
SIC: 8249 2741 Medical training services; Miscellaneous publishing

(G-3120)
M ROSENTHAL COMPANY
3125 Exon Ave (45241-2547)
PHONE......................513 563-0081
Edward L Etter Iii, *Mng Pt*
EMP: 19 **EST:** 1888
SQ FT: 30,000
SALES (est): 4.2MM **Privately Held**
Web: www.mrosenthal.com
SIC: 2759 2752 Letterpress printing; Offset and photolithographic printing

(G-3121)
MACHINE DEVELOPMENT CORP
Also Called: Marine Development
7707 Affinity Dr (45231-3567)
PHONE......................513 825-5885
Gary Fay, *Pr*
EMP: 8 **EST:** 1979
SQ FT: 7,800
SALES (est): 888.58K **Privately Held**
Web: cnc-machinists.cmac.ws
SIC: 3599 Machine shop, jobbing and repair

(G-3122)
MACHINE DRIVE COMPANY
2513 Crescentville Rd (45241-1575)
PHONE......................513 793-7077
EMP: 52
SIC: 5063 3625 Electrical apparatus and equipment; Control equipment, electric

(G-3123)
MACKE BROTHERS INC
10355 Spartan Dr (45215-1220)
PHONE......................513 771-7500
Joseph D Macke Senior, *Pr*
Joseph D Macke Junior, *VP*
Bill Macke, *
Nick Macke, *
EMP: 21 **EST:** 1908
SQ FT: 43,000
SALES (est): 669.85K **Privately Held**
Web: www.mackebrothers.com
SIC: 2789 7331 Pamphlets, binding; Mailing service

GEOGRAPHIC SECTION
Cincinnati - Hamilton County (G-3148)

(G-3124)
MADISON PROPERTY HOLDINGS INC
5055 Madison Rd (45227-1431)
PHONE.................................800 215-3210
EMP: 25 **EST:** 1940
SALES (est): 3.91MM **Privately Held**
Web: www.kett-tool.com
SIC: 3546 3542 3421 Power-driven handtools; Machine tools, metal forming type; Cutlery

(G-3125)
MAGNA MACHINE CO (PA)
11180 Southland Rd (45240-3202)
PHONE.................................513 851-6900
Scott Kramer, *CEO*
Scott Kramer, *Pr*
William Kramer Junior, *Sec*
James Parker, *
Greg Bodenburg, *
▼ **EMP:** 101 **EST:** 1953
SQ FT: 80,000
SALES (est): 21.65MM
SALES (corp-wide): 21.65MM **Privately Held**
Web: www.magna-machine.com
SIC: 3556 3554 3599 Bakery machinery; Paper industries machinery; Machine shop, jobbing and repair

(G-3126)
MAGNA THREE LLC
2668 Cyclorama Dr (45211-8315)
PHONE.................................513 389-0776
John Dorey, *Prin*
EMP: 8 **EST:** 2016
SALES (est): 103.91K **Privately Held**
SIC: 3829 Measuring and controlling devices, nec

(G-3127)
MAIN AWNING & TENT INC
415 W Seymour Ave (45216-1862)
PHONE.................................513 621-6947
Hyman Goldfarb, *Pr*
Leslie Goldfarb, *Pr*
Robert Goldfarb, *VP*
◆ **EMP:** 9 **EST:** 1933
SALES (est): 971.45K **Privately Held**
Web: www.awningscincinnati.com
SIC: 2394 Awnings, fabric: made from purchased materials

(G-3128)
MANE INC
10261 Chester Rd (45215-1581)
PHONE.................................513 248-9876
EMP: 141
SIC: 2087 Flavoring extracts and syrups, nec
HQ: Mane, Inc.
2501 Henkle Dr
Lebanon OH 45036
513 248-9876

(G-3129)
MANITOU CANDLE CO LLC
7 W 7th St Ste 1400 (45202-2451)
PHONE.................................513 429-5254
EMP: 7 **EST:** 2016
SALES (est): 247.85K **Privately Held**
Web: www.manitoucandleco.com
SIC: 3999 Candles

(G-3130)
MARCH FIRST MANUFACTURING LLC (PA)
Also Called: March First Brewing
7885 E Kemper Rd (45249-1622)
PHONE.................................513 266-3076
Mark Stuhlreyer, *Pr*
EMP: 8 **EST:** 2016
SALES (est): 4.82MM
SALES (corp-wide): 4.82MM **Privately Held**
Web: www.marchfirstbrewing.com
SIC: 2085 Distilled and blended liquors

(G-3131)
MARINERS LANDING INC
Also Called: Mariner's Landing Marina
7405 Forbes Rd (45233-1014)
PHONE.................................513 941-3625
Pamela Tonne, *Pr*
EMP: 14 **EST:** 1990
SQ FT: 6,992
SALES (est): 443.09K **Privately Held**
Web: www.mariners-landing.com
SIC: 4493 5551 3732 Boat yards, storage and incidental repair; Boat dealers; Boatbuilding and repairing

(G-3132)
MARKUS JEWELERS LLC
Also Called: Marcus Jewelers
2022 8 Mile Rd (45244-2607)
PHONE.................................513 474-4950
Mark Ogier, *Owner*
EMP: 7 **EST:** 1990
SQ FT: 1,100
SALES (est): 470K **Privately Held**
SIC: 3911 5944 Jewelry, precious metal; Jewelry stores

(G-3133)
MASTER COMMUNICATIONS INC
Also Called: Asia For Kids
2692 Madison Rd Ste N1-307 (45208-1321)
P.O. Box 9096 (45209-0096)
PHONE.................................208 821-3473
▲ **EMP:** 9 **EST:** 1994
SALES (est): 452.61K **Privately Held**
Web: www.master-comm.com
SIC: 7812 2731 Video tape production; Book publishing

(G-3134)
MATLOCK ELECTRIC CO INC
2780 Highland Ave (45212)
PHONE.................................513 731-9600
TOLL FREE: 800
Thomas J Geoppinger, *Ch*
Joseph P Geoppinger, *Pr*
▼ **EMP:** 36 **EST:** 1920
SQ FT: 25,000
SALES (est): 8.3MM **Privately Held**
Web: www.matlockelectric.com
SIC: 7694 5063 3699 3612 Electric motor repair; Motors, electric; Electrical equipment and supplies, nec; Transformers, except electric

(G-3135)
MAX ROUSH
661 Polo Woods Dr (45244-5014)
PHONE.................................937 288-2557
Max Roush, *Owner*
EMP: 6 **EST:** 2001
SALES (est): 72.86K **Privately Held**
SIC: 3523 Tractors, farm

(G-3136)
MCRON FINANCE CORP
3010 Disney St (45209-5028)
PHONE.................................513 487-5000
EMP: 44
SALES (est): 2.1MM **Publicly Held**
SIC: 3544 Forms (molds), for foundry and plastics working machinery
HQ: Milacron Holdings Corp.
4165 Half Acre Rd
Batavia OH 45103
513 487-5000

(G-3137)
MCSWAIN MANUFACTURING LLC
Also Called: Midstate Machine
189 Container Pl (45246-1708)
PHONE.................................513 619-1222
Michael Meshay, *Pr*
◆ **EMP:** 180 **EST:** 1942
SQ FT: 70,000
SALES (est): 24.13MM **Privately Held**
Web: www.midstateusa.com
SIC: 3599 Machine shop, jobbing and repair

(G-3138)
MECHANICAL FINISHERS INC LLC
Also Called: Mfi
6350 Este Ave (45232-1450)
PHONE.................................513 641-5419
Nico Cottone, *CEO*
EMP: 30 **EST:** 2015
SALES (est): 2.51MM **Privately Held**
Web: www.mechfin.com
SIC: 3471 Electroplating of metals or formed products

(G-3139)
MECHANICAL FINISHING INC
6350 Este Ave (45232-1450)
PHONE.................................513 641-5419
Jerry Stenger, *Pr*
EMP: 23 **EST:** 1992
SQ FT: 40,000
SALES (est): 781.48K **Privately Held**
Web: www.mechfin.com
SIC: 3471 Finishing, metals or formed products

(G-3140)
MEDER SPECIAL-TEES LTD
618 Delhi Ave (45204-1222)
PHONE.................................513 921-3800
Jerome A Meder, *Owner*
EMP: 8 **EST:** 1984
SQ FT: 3,000
SALES (est): 855.21K **Privately Held**
Web: www.medertees.com
SIC: 2759 Screen printing

(G-3141)
MEDPACE CORE LABORATORIES LLC
5375 Medpace Way (45227-1543)
PHONE.................................513 579-9911
EMP: 18 **EST:** 2017
SALES (est): 11.88MM
SALES (corp-wide): 1.89B **Publicly Held**
Web: www.medpace.com
SIC: 2834 Pharmaceutical preparations
PA: Medpace Holdings, Inc.
5375 Medpace Way
Cincinnati OH 45227
513 579-9911

(G-3142)
MEDPACE HOLDINGS INC (PA)
Also Called: MEDPACE
5375 Medpace Way (45227)
PHONE.................................513 579-9911
August J Troendle, *Ch Bd*
Jesse J Geiger, *LABORATORY Operations*
Susan E Burwig, *Ofcr*
Stephen P Ewald, *Corporate Secretary*
EMP: 246 **EST:** 1992
SQ FT: 600,000
SALES (est): 1.89B
SALES (corp-wide): 1.89B **Publicly Held**
Web: www.medpace.com
SIC: 2834 8731 Pharmaceutical preparations ; Commercial physical research

(G-3143)
MEGGITT (ERLANGER) LLC
Also Called: Edac Composites
10293 Burlington Rd (45231-1901)
PHONE.................................513 851-5550
Steve Hartke, *Brnch Mgr*
EMP: 70
SALES (corp-wide): 19.07B **Publicly Held**
Web: www.meggitt.com
SIC: 3089 3544 2851 2822 Molding primary plastics; Special dies, tools, jigs, and fixtures; Paints and allied products; Synthetic rubber
HQ: Meggitt (Erlanger), Llc
1400 Jamike Ave
Erlanger KY 41018
859 525-8040

(G-3144)
MEGGITT POLYMERS & COMPOSITES
10293 Burlington Rd (45231-1901)
PHONE.................................513 851-5550
EMP: 10 **EST:** 2016
SALES (est): 197.73K **Privately Held**
SIC: 3728 Aircraft parts and equipment, nec

(G-3145)
MEIERJOHAN-WENGLER INC
10340 Julian Dr (45215-1131)
PHONE.................................513 771-6074
Steve Jones, *Pr*
▲ **EMP:** 52 **EST:** 1941
SQ FT: 34,000
SALES (est): 2.77MM
SALES (corp-wide): 1.88B **Publicly Held**
SIC: 3366 Bronze foundry, nec
HQ: Aurora Casket Company, Llc
10944 Marsh Rd
Aurora IN 47001
800 457-1111

(G-3146)
MEIERS WINE CELLARS INC
Also Called: John C Meier Grape Juice Co
6955 Plainfield Rd (45236-3793)
PHONE.................................513 891-2900
Paul Lux, *Pr*
Barbara Boyd Ctrl, *Prin*
◆ **EMP:** 30 **EST:** 1895
SQ FT: 20,000
SALES (est): 9.95MM
SALES (corp-wide): 283.23MM **Publicly Held**
Web: www.drinkmeiers.com
SIC: 2033 2084 2086 Fruit juices: fresh; Wines; Bottled and canned soft drinks
PA: Vintage Wine Estates, Inc.
937 Tahoe Blvd Ste 210
Incline Village NV 89451
707 346-3640

(G-3147)
MELVIN STONE CO LLC
11641 Mosteller Rd Ste 2 (45241-1520)
PHONE.................................513 771-0820
Susan B Salyer, *Prin*
EMP: 16 **EST:** 2006
SALES (est): 906.08K **Privately Held**
Web: www.jrjnet.com
SIC: 3281 Cut stone and stone products

(G-3148)
MENARD INC
2789 Cunningham Rd (45241-1390)
PHONE.................................513 250-4566
EMP: 12
SALES (corp-wide): 1.7B **Privately Held**

Cincinnati - Hamilton County (G-3149)

Web: www.menards.com
SIC: 2431 Millwork
PA: Menard, Inc.
 5101 Menard Dr
 Eau Claire WI 54703
 715 876-2000

(G-3149)
MERIDIAN BIOSCIENCE INC (PA)
Also Called: Meridian Bioscience
3471 River Hills Dr (45244-3023)
PHONE..................513 271-3700
Jack Kenny, *CEO*
Andrew S Kitzmiller, *
Tony Serafini-Iamanna, *Ex VP*
Lourdes G Weltzien, *Ex VP*
Julie Smith, *CAO*
EMP: 188 **EST:** 1976
SALES (est): 333.02MM
SALES (corp-wide): 333.02MM **Privately Held**
Web: www.meridianbioscience.com
SIC: 2835 2834 Diagnostic substances; Pharmaceutical preparations

(G-3150)
MERIDIAN LIFE SCIENCE INC (HQ)
Also Called: Viral Antigens
3471 River Hills Dr (45244-3023)
PHONE..................513 271-3700
Rick Eberly, *Pr*
EMP: 19 **EST:** 1982
SQ FT: 34,000
SALES (est): 20.69MM
SALES (corp-wide): 333.02MM **Privately Held**
Web: www.meridianbioscience.com
SIC: 2835 Veterinary diagnostic substances
PA: Meridian Bioscience, Inc.
 3471 River Hills Dr
 Cincinnati OH 45244
 513 271-3700

(G-3151)
MESA INDUSTRIES INC (PA)
Also Called: Airplaco Equipment Company
4027 Eastern Ave (45226-1747)
PHONE..................513 321-2950
Terry S Segerberg, *CEO*
Kent Sexton, *
James R Sexton, *
◆ **EMP:** 32 **EST:** 1966
SQ FT: 100,000
SALES (est): 24.71MM
SALES (corp-wide): 24.71MM **Privately Held**
Web: www.mesa-intl.com
SIC: 3531 5085 5082 Bituminous, cement and concrete related products and equip.; Hose, belting, and packing; Construction and mining machinery

(G-3152)
MESA INDUSTRIES INC
4141 Airport Rd (45226-1643)
PHONE..................513 999-9781
EMP: 13
SALES (corp-wide): 24.71MM **Privately Held**
Web: www.mesa-intl.com
SIC: 3531 Bituminous, cement and concrete related products and equip.
PA: Mesa Industries, Inc.
 4027 Eastern Ave
 Cincinnati OH 45226
 513 321-2950

(G-3153)
MET-PRO TECHNOLOGIES LLC (HQ)
4625 Red Bank Rd (45227-1500)
PHONE..................513 458-2600
Dennis Sadlowski, *Pr*
EMP: 15 **EST:** 2013
SALES (est): 21.57MM **Publicly Held**
Web: www.cecoenviro.com
SIC: 3564 Air purification equipment
PA: Ceco Environmental Corp.
 14651 Dallas Pkwy Ste 500
 Dallas TX 75254

(G-3154)
METAL POLISHING SPC L L C
5170 Wooster Pike (45226-2329)
PHONE..................513 321-0363
EMP: 6
SALES (corp-wide): 475.21K **Privately Held**
Web: www.metalpolishingspecialties.com
SIC: 2842 Metal polish
PA: Metal Polishing Specialties L L C
 1002 Valley View Dr
 Milford OH

(G-3155)
METALPHOTO OF CINCINNATI INC
1080 Skillman Dr (45215-1137)
PHONE..................513 772-8281
Herbert Wainer, *Prin*
Patrick Hollis, *
EMP: 26 **EST:** 1959
SQ FT: 21,000
SALES (est): 4.83MM
SALES (corp-wide): 32.87MM **Privately Held**
Web: www.mpofcinci.com
SIC: 3993 Name plates: except engraved, etched, etc.: metal
PA: Horizons Incorporated
 18531 S Miles Rd
 Cleveland OH 44128
 216 475-0555

(G-3156)
METCUT RESEARCH ASSOCIATES INC (PA)
Also Called: Metcut Research, Inc.
3980 Rosslyn Dr (45209-1110)
PHONE..................513 271-5100
John P Kahles, *Pr*
John H Clippinger, *
William P Koster, *
John H More, *
Robert T Keeler, *
EMP: 85 **EST:** 1948
SQ FT: 25,000
SALES (est): 24.93MM
SALES (corp-wide): 24.93MM **Privately Held**
Web: www.metcut.com
SIC: 8734 3599 Metallurgical testing laboratory; Machine and other job shop work

(G-3157)
METLWEB LTD
3330 E Kemper Rd (45241-1538)
PHONE..................513 563-8822
EMP: 16 **EST:** 1996
SALES (est): 212.97K **Privately Held**
Web: www.arscometals.com
SIC: 3444 3441 Sheet metal specialties, not stamped; Fabricated structural metal

(G-3158)
METRO CONTAINERS INC
4927 Beech St (45212-2315)
PHONE..................513 351-6800
EMP: 77
SIC: 2653 Boxes, corrugated: made from purchased materials

(G-3159)
METZGER MACHINE CO
2165 Spring Grove Ave (45214-1790)
PHONE..................513 241-3360
David L Brown, *Pr*
Virginia Brown, *Sec*
EMP: 10 **EST:** 1876
SQ FT: 10,000
SALES (est): 1.07MM **Privately Held**
Web: www.metzgermachine.com
SIC: 3599 5085 Machine shop, jobbing and repair; Industrial supplies

(G-3160)
MEYER TOOL INC (PA)
3055 Colerain Ave (45225-1827)
PHONE..................513 681-7362
Arlyn Easton, *Pr*
Larry Allen, *
Jerry Flyr, *General Vice President*
Christine Steele, *
◆ **EMP:** 650 **EST:** 1951
SQ FT: 365,000
SALES (est): 344.81MM
SALES (corp-wide): 344.81MM **Privately Held**
Web: www.meyertool.com
SIC: 3724 3599 Aircraft engines and engine parts; Machine shop, jobbing and repair

(G-3161)
MICRO METAL FINISHING LLC
3448 Spring Grove Ave (45225-1328)
PHONE..................513 541-3095
John A Rose, *Pr*
Karen Lafkas, *
EMP: 61 **EST:** 1995
SQ FT: 100,000
SALES (est): 4.57MM **Privately Held**
Web: www.micrometalfinishing.com
SIC: 3471 Finishing, metals or formed products

(G-3162)
MICROPYRETICS HEATERS INTL INC
Also Called: Mhi
750 Redna Ter (45215-1109)
PHONE..................513 772-0404
Anu Vissa, *COO*
▲ **EMP:** 20 **EST:** 1991
SALES (est): 2.24MM **Privately Held**
Web: www.mhi-inc.com
SIC: 3567 Industrial furnaces and ovens

(G-3163)
MIDSTATE MACHINE OHIO FACILITY
189 Container Pl (45246-1708)
PHONE..................513 619-1222
EMP: 11 **EST:** 2016
SALES (est): 329.57K **Privately Held**
Web: www.midstateusa.com
SIC: 3599 Machine shop, jobbing and repair

(G-3164)
MIDWEST WOODWORKING CO INC
4019 Montgomery Rd (45212-3694)
PHONE..................513 631-6684
Frank David, *Pr*
EMP: 10 **EST:** 1946
SQ FT: 60,000
SALES (est): 176.22K **Privately Held**
SIC: 2431 2541 2434 Millwork; Display fixtures, wood; Wood kitchen cabinets

(G-3165)
MILLSTONE COFFEE INC (HQ)
1 Procter And Gamble Plz (45202-3315)
PHONE..................513 983-1100
R Kerry Clark, *Pr*
Clayton C Daley Junior, *VP Fin*
S P Donovan Junior, *VP*
Doctor Walker, *VP*
H J Kangis, *
▲ **EMP:** 80 **EST:** 1981
SALES (est): 112.05MM
SALES (corp-wide): 8.53B **Publicly Held**
SIC: 2095 Coffee roasting (except by wholesale grocers)
PA: The J M Smucker Company
 1 Strawberry Ln
 Orrville OH 44667
 330 682-3000

(G-3166)
MINUTEMAN PRESS INC
Also Called: Minuteman Press
9904 Colerain Ave (45251-1431)
PHONE..................513 741-9056
Portia Ash, *Prin*
EMP: 10 **EST:** 2010
SALES (est): 262.1K **Privately Held**
Web: www.mmpcolerain.com
SIC: 2752 Commercial printing, lithographic

(G-3167)
MISWEST AMBRODERY
8060 Reading Rd (45237-1414)
PHONE..................513 661-2770
EMP: 10 **EST:** 2015
SALES (est): 199.97K **Privately Held**
SIC: 2395 Embroidery products, except Schiffli machine

(G-3168)
MMP PRINTING INC
Also Called: Minuteman Press
10570 Chester Rd (45215-1263)
PHONE..................513 381-0990
Melody Tuttle, *Pr*
William Tuttle, *VP*
EMP: 23 **EST:** 1995
SQ FT: 30,000
SALES (est): 1.89MM **Privately Held**
Web: www.mmpcincy.com
SIC: 2752 2791 2789 2759 Commercial printing, lithographic; Typesetting; Bookbinding and related work; Commercial printing, nec

(G-3169)
MODEL PATTERN & FOUNDRY CO
3242 Spring Grove Ave (45225-1373)
PHONE..................513 542-2322
Shirley Kipp, *Pr*
Kenneth Kipp, *
David Kipp, *
EMP: 19 **EST:** 1943
SQ FT: 16,500
SALES (est): 935.31K **Privately Held**
SIC: 3363 3364 3366 3365 Aluminum die-castings; Brass and bronze die-castings; Copper foundries; Aluminum foundries

(G-3170)
MODERN ICE EQUIPMENT & SUP CO (PA)
Also Called: Modern Tour
5709 Harrison Ave (45248-1601)
PHONE..................513 367-2101
Gary E Jerow, *Pr*
John Murphy, *VP*
◆ **EMP:** 20 **EST:** 1990
SQ FT: 12,000
SALES (est): 22.4MM **Privately Held**
Web: www.modernice.com
SIC: 5078 3444 Refrigeration equipment and supplies; Sheet metalwork

GEOGRAPHIC SECTION

Cincinnati - Hamilton County (G-3193)

(G-3171)
MODERN MANUFACTURING INC (PA)
Also Called: M&S Machine and Manufacturing
240 Stille Dr (45233-1647)
PHONE..................................513 251-3600
Patrick Sexton, *Pr*
EMP: 6 **EST:** 2001
SQ FT: 30,000
SALES (est): 3.39MM
SALES (corp-wide): 3.39MM **Privately Held**
Web: www.modmfg.net
SIC: 2531 3444 3544 Public building and related furniture; Sheet metal specialties, not stamped; Special dies, tools, jigs, and fixtures

(G-3172)
MONTI INCORPORATED (PA)
4510 Reading Rd (45229-1230)
PHONE..................................513 761-7775
Gavin J Narburgh, *CEO*
Gavin J Narburgh, *Pr*
Beverly Narburgh, *
John Narburgh, *
Brian Tibbs, *
▲ **EMP:** 72 **EST:** 1971
SQ FT: 137,000
SALES (est): 54.14MM
SALES (corp-wide): 54.14MM **Privately Held**
Web: www.monti-inc.com
SIC: 3644 3599 Insulators and insulation materials, electrical; Machine shop, jobbing and repair

(G-3173)
MORGAN4140 LLC
Also Called: Sixteen Brcks Artsan Bakehouse
4760 Paddock Rd Ste B (45229-1048)
PHONE..................................513 873-1426
Ryan Morgan, *Managing Member*
EMP: 10 **EST:** 2012
SALES (est): 581.05K **Privately Held**
Web: www.sixteenbricks.com
SIC: 2051 Bread, cake, and related products

(G-3174)
MORRIS TECHNOLOGIES INC
11988 Tramway Dr (45241-1664)
PHONE..................................513 733-1611
EMP: 45 **EST:** 1994
SQ FT: 25,000
SALES (est): 4.36MM **Privately Held**
SIC: 8711 3999 3313 3841 Mechanical engineering; Models, except toy; Alloys, additive, except copper: not made in blast furnaces; Surgical and medical instruments

(G-3175)
MORROW GRAVEL COMPANY INC (PA)
11641 Mosteller Rd (45241-1520)
PHONE..................................513 771-0820
James P Jurgensen, *Pr*
Tim St Clair, *VP*
EMP: 20 **EST:** 1958
SQ FT: 15,000
SALES (est): 25.39MM
SALES (corp-wide): 25.39MM **Privately Held**
Web: www.jrjnet.com
SIC: 1442 1771 2951 Construction sand mining; Blacktop (asphalt) work; Asphalt and asphaltic paving mixtures (not from refineries)

(G-3176)
MORTON SALT INC
Also Called: Morton Salt
5336 River Rd (45233-1686)
PHONE..................................513 941-1578
Jim Benton, *Brnch Mgr*
EMP: 9
SALES (corp-wide): 1.22B **Privately Held**
Web: www.mortonsalt.com
SIC: 2899 Salt
HQ: Morton Salt, Inc.
444 W Lake St Ste 3000
Chicago IL 60606

(G-3177)
MR LABEL INC
5018 Gray Rd (45232-1514)
PHONE..................................513 681-2088
Patrick H Meehan Junior, *Pr*
Timothy F Meehan, *
Brigid Hoffman, *
▼ **EMP:** 25 **EST:** 1976
SQ FT: 19,200
SALES (est): 4.51MM **Privately Held**
Web: www.mrlabelco.com
SIC: 2759 2672 Flexographic printing; Paper; coated and laminated, nec

(G-3178)
MWGH LLC
Also Called: Metalworking Group, The
9070 Pippin Rd (45251-3174)
PHONE..................................513 521-4114
Doug J Watts, *Managing Member*
EMP: 135 **EST:** 2019
SALES (est): 42.2MM
SALES (corp-wide): 42.2MM **Privately Held**
SIC: 3444 Sheet metalwork
PA: Mwg Holdings, Inc.
9070 Pippin Rd
Cincinnati OH 45251
513 521-4119

(G-3179)
NATIONAL ACCESS DESIGN LLC
Also Called: N A D
1871 Summit Rd (45237-2803)
PHONE..................................513 351-3400
Cheryl White, *Pr*
EMP: 13 **EST:** 2011
SALES (est): 2.3MM **Privately Held**
Web: www.nationalaccessdesign.com
SIC: 3442 3089 Metal doors, sash, and trim; Doors, folding: plastics or plastics coated fabric

(G-3180)
NATIONAL MACHINE TOOL COMPANY
2013 E Galbraith Rd (45215-5633)
PHONE..................................513 541-6682
Harold J Rembold, *Pr*
Chris K Rembold, *VP*
EMP: 9 **EST:** 1903
SQ FT: 5,998
SALES (est): 809.02K **Privately Held**
Web: www.keyseaters.com
SIC: 3541 Machine tools, metal cutting: exotic (explosive, etc.)

(G-3181)
NATIONAL SCOREBOARDS LLC
Also Called: N S B
8044 Montgomery Rd Ste 700 (45236-2926)
PHONE..................................513 791-5244
Nick Mckenzie, *Managing Member*
Aaron Todd, *Managing Member*
EMP: 7 **EST:** 2003
SQ FT: 1,000
SALES (est): 394.83K **Privately Held**
SIC: 3993 Scoreboards, electric

(G-3182)
NATURES MARK LLC
415 Greenwell Ave (45238-5302)
PHONE..................................513 557-3200
Sean O'conner, *Prin*
EMP: 8 **EST:** 2008
SALES (est): 107.08K **Privately Held**
SIC: 3499 Fabricated metal products, nec

(G-3183)
NAVISTAR INC
Also Called: Navistar
11775 Highway Dr (45241-2005)
PHONE..................................513 733-8500
David Mannin, *Brnch Mgr*
EMP: 6
SALES (corp-wide): 350.31B **Privately Held**
Web: www.navistar.com
SIC: 3711 Truck and tractor truck assembly
HQ: Navistar, Inc.
2701 Navistar Dr
Lisle IL 60532
331 332-5000

(G-3184)
NAVISTONE INC
231 W 12th St Ste 200w (45202-8001)
PHONE..................................844 677-3667
Larry Kavanagh, *CEO*
Allen Abbott, *COO*
Efrain Torres, *CFO*
Lori Paikin, *CRO*
EMP: 38 **EST:** 2016
SALES (est): 3.91MM **Privately Held**
Web: www.navistone.com
SIC: 7371 7372 Computer software development; Application computer software

(G-3185)
NEHEMIAH MANUFACTURING CO LLC
1907 South St (45204-2033)
PHONE..................................513 351-5700
Daniel Meyer, *CEO*
Richard T Palmer, *Pr*
Mike Pachko, *COO*
▲ **EMP:** 100 **EST:** 2009
SQ FT: 33,706
SALES (est): 27.6MM **Privately Held**
Web: www.nehemiahmfg.com
SIC: 2844 5122 Perfumes, cosmetics and other toilet preparations; Toiletries

(G-3186)
NEPTUNE EQUIPMENT COMPANY
11082 Southland Rd (45240-3713)
PHONE..................................513 851-8008
Robert W Becker, *Pr*
Mary Ellen Shouse, *Sec*
EMP: 26 **EST:** 1934
SQ FT: 4,000
SALES (est): 4.15MM **Privately Held**
Web: www.necowater.com
SIC: 3825 1623 Meters: electric, pocket, portable, panelboard, etc.; Aqueduct construction

(G-3187)
NETHERLAND RUBBER COMPANY (PA)
2931 Exon Ave (45241-2593)
P.O. Box 62165 (45262-0165)
PHONE..................................513 733-0883
Timothy Clarke, *Pr*
Robert Pater, *VP*
Sue Clarke, *Treas*
EMP: 17 **EST:** 1931
SQ FT: 69,000
SALES (est): 8.87MM
SALES (corp-wide): 8.87MM **Privately Held**
Web: www.netherlandrubber.com
SIC: 5085 3053 3492 5099 Rubber goods, mechanical; Gaskets, all materials; Hose and tube fittings and assemblies, hydraulic/pneumatic; Safety equipment and supplies

(G-3188)
NEW DAIRY CINCINNATI LLC
415 John St (45215-5481)
PHONE..................................214 258-1200
Gregg Engles, *CEO*
EMP: 83 **EST:** 2020
SALES (est): 472.58K
SALES (corp-wide): 447.94MM **Privately Held**
SIC: 2021 Creamery butter
PA: New Dairy Opco, Llc
12400 Coit Rd Ste 200
Dallas TX 75251
214 258-1200

(G-3189)
NEW DIRY CINCINNATI TRNSPT LLC
415 John St (45215-5481)
PHONE..................................214 258-1200
Gregg Engles, *CEO*
EMP: 55 **EST:** 2020
SALES (est): 546.43K
SALES (corp-wide): 447.94MM **Privately Held**
SIC: 2023 Dry, condensed and evaporated dairy products
PA: New Dairy Opco, Llc
12400 Coit Rd Ste 200
Dallas TX 75251
214 258-1200

(G-3190)
NEW PME INC
Also Called: Plant Maintenance Engineering
518 W Crescentville Rd (45246-1222)
PHONE..................................513 671-1717
Charles Walter, *Pr*
EMP: 21 **EST:** 1980
SALES (est): 620.54K **Privately Held**
Web: www.pmebabbittbearings.com
SIC: 3599 Machine shop, jobbing and repair

(G-3191)
NEWMAN BROTHERS INC
5609 Center Hill Ave (45216-2305)
P.O. Box 43460 (45243-0460)
EMP: 29 **EST:** 1882
SQ FT: 65,000
SALES (est): 2.05MM **Privately Held**
Web: www.newmanbrothers.com
SIC: 3446 Ornamental metalwork

(G-3192)
NEWTON SOFTWARE
4811 Montgomery Rd (45212-2163)
PHONE..................................714 469-5773
EMP: 11 **EST:** 2019
SALES (est): 561.67K **Privately Held**
Web: www.paycor.com
SIC: 7372 Prepackaged software

(G-3193)
NEXT GENERATION HEARING CASE
4223 Harrison Ave (45211-3379)
PHONE..................................513 451-0360
EMP: 6 **EST:** 2014
SALES (est): 163.5K **Privately Held**
Web: www.helpuhear.net
SIC: 2834 Pharmaceutical preparations

Cincinnati - Hamilton County (G-3194) GEOGRAPHIC SECTION

(G-3194)
NEXTGEN FIBER OPTICS LLC (PA)
720 E Pete Rose Way Ste 410
(45202-3579)
PHONE.................513 549-4691
EMP: 7 EST: 2002
SALES (est): 1.58MM
SALES (corp-wide): 1.58MM **Privately Held**
SIC: 3229 Fiber optics strands

(G-3195)
NEXTMED SYSTEMS INC (PA)
16 Triangle Park Dr (45246-3411)
PHONE.................216 674-0511
David Shute, *CEO*
James Bennett, *
EMP: 44 EST: 1999
SQ FT: 3,000
SALES (est): 3.37MM
SALES (corp-wide): 3.37MM **Privately Held**
SIC: 7372 Business oriented computer software

(G-3196)
NEYRA INTERSTATE INC (PA)
10700 Evendale Dr (45241)
PHONE.................513 733-1000
EMP: 25 EST: 1975
SALES (est): 26.99MM
SALES (corp-wide): 26.99MM **Privately Held**
Web: www.neyra.com
SIC: 2952 2891 2865 Coating compounds, tar; Adhesives and sealants; Cyclic crudes and intermediates

(G-3197)
NIGERIAN ASSN PHARMACISTS & PH
483 Northland Blvd (45240-3210)
PHONE.................513 861-2329
Nnodum Iheme, *Prin*
EMP: 7 EST: 2007
SALES (est): 125.12K **Privately Held**
SIC: 2834 Pharmaceutical preparations

(G-3198)
NILPETER USA INC
Also Called: Next
11550 Goldcoast Dr (45249-1640)
PHONE.................513 489-4400
Lenny Degirolmo, *Prin*
Timothy Taggart, *
Eric Vandenburg, *
◆ EMP: 110 EST: 1987
SQ FT: 35,000
SALES (est): 26.76MM
SALES (corp-wide): 90.35K **Privately Held**
Web: www.nilpeter.com
SIC: 3555 3554 3565 2759 Printing trades machinery; Die cutting and stamping machinery, paper converting; Packaging machinery; Commercial printing, nec
PA: Nilpeter-Fonden
Elmedalsvej 20-22
Slagelse
58528311

(G-3199)
NINE GIANT BREWING LLC
6095 Montgomery Rd (45213-1617)
PHONE.................510 220-5104
Brandon Hughes, *Owner*
EMP: 8 EST: 2016
SALES (est): 517.01K **Privately Held**
Web: www.ninegiant.com
SIC: 2082 Malt beverages

(G-3200)
NKH-SAFETY INC
1375 Kemper Meadow Dr Ste 12 (45240-1650)
PHONE.................513 771-3839
William Neal, *Pr*
EMP: 11 EST: 1990
SQ FT: 4,000
SALES (est): 130.24K **Privately Held**
Web: www.nkhsafety.com
SIC: 3845 8748 Electromedical equipment; Safety training service

(G-3201)
NNODUM PHARMACEUTICALS CORP
483 Northland Blvd (45240-3210)
P.O. Box 19725 (45219-0725)
PHONE.................513 861-2329
EMP: 12 EST: 1995
SQ FT: 16,000
SALES (est): 2.16MM **Privately Held**
Web: www.zikspain.com
SIC: 2834 Pharmaceutical preparations

(G-3202)
NOBLE DENIM WORKSHOP
2929 Spring Grove Ave (45225-2157)
PHONE.................513 560-5640
EMP: 6 EST: 2013
SALES (est): 136.7K **Privately Held**
Web: www.nobledenim.com
SIC: 2211 Denims

(G-3203)
NOLTE PRECISE MANUFACTURING INC
6850 Colerain Ave (45239-5544)
PHONE.................513 923-3100
EMP: 54 EST: 1916
SALES (est): 5.6MM **Privately Held**
Web: www.nolteprecise.com
SIC: 3451 Screw machine products

(G-3204)
NORTHFIELD BLOCK CO
5155 Fischer Ave (45217-1157)
PHONE.................513 242-3644
EMP: 6 EST: 2019
SALES (est): 1.01MM **Privately Held**
Web: www.oldcastlelogistics.com
SIC: 3271 Concrete block and brick

(G-3205)
NORTON OUTDOOR ADVERTISING
5280 Kennedy Ave (45213-2620)
PHONE.................513 631-4864
Thomas Norton, *CEO*
Thomas Norton, *Pr*
Daniel Norton, *
Michael Norton, *
EMP: 24 EST: 1949
SQ FT: 7,500
SALES (est): 2.24MM **Privately Held**
Web: www.norton-outdoor.com
SIC: 7312 3993 Poster advertising, outdoor; Signs and advertising specialties

(G-3206)
NOVARTIS CORPORATION
Also Called: Novartis Vaccines & Diagnostic
1880 Waycross Rd (45240-2825)
PHONE.................919 577-5000
EMP: 6
Web: www.novartis.com
SIC: 2834 Pharmaceutical preparations
HQ: Novartis Corporation
1 Health Plz
East Hanover NJ 07936
212 307-1122

(G-3207)
NU-TECH POLYMERS CO INC
3220 E Sharon Rd (45241-1945)
PHONE.................513 942-6003
R Douglas Pendery, *Pr*
EMP: 8 EST: 1985
SALES (est): 2.12MM **Privately Held**
Web: www.nu-techpolymers.com
SIC: 2821 Plastics materials and resins

(G-3208)
NUCOR CORPORATION
P.O. Box 5810 (45201-5810)
PHONE.................407 855-2990
EMP: 28
SALES (corp-wide): 34.71B **Publicly Held**
Web: www.nucor.com
SIC: 3312 Blast furnaces and steel mills
PA: Nucor Corporation
1915 Rexford Rd
Charlotte NC 28211
704 000-7000

(G-3209)
NUCOR CORPORATION
Also Called: Nucor Load Center
300 Pike St Fl 4 (45202-4241)
PHONE.................901 275-3826
Susie Eaddy, *Brnch Mgr*
EMP: 15
SALES (corp-wide): 34.71B **Publicly Held**
Web: www.nucor.com
SIC: 3312 Blast furnaces and steel mills
PA: Nucor Corporation
1915 Rexford Rd
Charlotte NC 28211
704 366-7000

(G-3210)
OAK HILLS CARTON CO
6310 Este Ave (45232-1450)
PHONE.................513 948-4200
Kenneth Kabel, *Pr*
EMP: 25 EST: 1951
SQ FT: 40,000
SALES (est): 4MM **Privately Held**
Web: www.oakhillscarton.com
SIC: 2679 2657 Paperboard products, converted, nec; Folding paperboard boxes

(G-3211)
OCCIDENTAL CHEMICAL CORP
4701 Paddock Rd (45229-1003)
PHONE.................513 242-2900
Eugene Thomas, *Brnch Mgr*
EMP: 31
SALES (corp-wide): 28.92B **Publicly Held**
SIC: 2812 2874 2869 2821 Alkalies and chlorine; Phosphatic fertilizers; Industrial organic chemicals, nec; Plastics materials and resins
HQ: Occidental Chemical Corporation
14555 Dallas Pkwy Ste 400
Dallas TX 75254
972 404-3800

(G-3212)
OHIO CBD GUY LLC
7875 Montgomery Rd (45236-4344)
PHONE.................513 417-9806
Jason Friedman, *Owner*
EMP: 6 EST: 2018
SALES (est): 168.09K **Privately Held**
Web: www.ohiocbdguy.com
SIC: 3999

(G-3213)
OHIO FEATHER COMPANY INC
1 Kovach Dr (45215-1000)
PHONE.................513 921-3373
Gabriel Guigui, *Pr*
Daniel Guigui, *VP*
▲ EMP: 6 EST: 1986
SALES (est): 503.65K **Privately Held**
Web: www.sustainabledown.com
SIC: 3999 Feathers and feather products

(G-3214)
OHIO FLAME HARDENING COMPANY (PA)
3944 Miami Rd Apt 106 (45227-3736)
PHONE.................513 336-6160
Robert Bokon, *Pr*
EMP: 24 EST: 1975
SALES (est): 1.47MM
SALES (corp-wide): 1.47MM **Privately Held**
SIC: 3398 Brazing (hardening) of metal

(G-3215)
OHIO HYDRAULICS INC
2510 E Sharon Rd (45241-1891)
PHONE.................513 771-2590
Kathleen Hilliard, *Pr*
John Davis, *
Robert Farwick, *
Tamera Fair, *
EMP: 25 EST: 1971
SQ FT: 13,500
SALES (est): 4.38MM **Privately Held**
Web: www.ohiohydraulics.com
SIC: 3492 3599 5084 7699 Hose and tube fittings and assemblies, hydraulic/pneumatic; Flexible metal hose, tubing, and bellows; Hydraulic systems equipment and supplies; Tank repair and cleaning services

(G-3216)
OHIO PULP MILLS INC
2100 Losantiville Ave Ste 3 (45237-7100)
PHONE.................513 631-7400
Steve Baker, *Mgr*
EMP: 25
SQ FT: 19,000
SALES (corp-wide): 3.15MM **Privately Held**
Web: www.doncosolutions.com
SIC: 2621 Paper mills
PA: Ohio Pulp Mills Inc
737 N Michigan Ave # 1450
Chicago IL 60611
312 337-7822

(G-3217)
OHIO TILE & MARBLE CO
3809 Spring Grove Ave (45223-2693)
PHONE.................513 541-4211
Sean Dowers, *Pr*
Ruth Dowers, *VP*
Clyde Dowers, *Stockholder*
▲ EMP: 23 EST: 1937
SQ FT: 21,500
SALES (est): 2.58MM **Privately Held**
Web: www.ohiotile.com
SIC: 5032 5211 3281 3253 Tile, clay or other ceramic, excluding refractory; Tile, ceramic; Marble, building: cut and shaped; Ceramic wall and floor tile

(G-3218)
OHIO WOOD CONNECTION LLC
8805 Lancaster Ave (45242-7832)
PHONE.................513 581-0361
EMP: 7 EST: 2019
SALES (est): 491.25K **Privately Held**
Web: www.ohiowoodconnection.com
SIC: 2431 Millwork

▲ = Import ▼ = Export
◆ = Import/Export

GEOGRAPHIC SECTION

Cincinnati - Hamilton County (G-3241)

(G-3219)
OHIO WOODWORKING CO INC
5035 Beech St (45212-2399)
PHONE..................513 631-0870
Thomas R Frank Junior, *Pr*
Peggy Frank, *Sec*
EMP: 8 **EST:** 1931
SQ FT: 17,000
SALES (est): 971.6K **Privately Held**
Web:
www.ohiowoodworkingcompany.com
SIC: 2541 2431 Display fixtures, wood; Millwork

(G-3220)
OKL CAN LINE INC
11235 Sebring Dr (45240-2714)
Anthony Lacey, *CEO*
◆ **EMP:** 47 **EST:** 1983
SQ FT: 50,000
SALES (est): 11.04MM
SALES (corp-wide): 11.04MM **Privately Held**
Web: www.oklcan.com
SIC: 3565 7699 Bottling and canning machinery; Industrial machinery and equipment repair
PA: Allcan Global Services, Inc
  11235 Sebring Dr
  Cincinnati OH 45240
  513 825-1655

(G-3221)
OMI SURGICAL PRODUCTS
4900 Charlemar Dr (45227-1550)
PHONE..................513 561-2241
Teck Awa, *Engr*
EMP: 11 **EST:** 2013
SALES (est): 106.14K **Privately Held**
SIC: 3841 Surgical and medical instruments

(G-3222)
OMNICARE PHRM OF MIDWEST LLC (DH)
201 E 4th St Ste 900 (45202-1513)
PHONE..................513 719-2600
Joel Gemunder, *Prin*
EMP: 100 **EST:** 1964
SALES (est): 36.9MM
SALES (corp-wide): 357.78B **Publicly Held**
Web: www.omnicare.com
SIC: 5122 5912 2834 Drugs and drug proprietaries; Drug stores; Pharmaceutical preparations
HQ: Neighborcare Pharmacy Services, Inc.
  201 E 4th St Ste 900
  Cincinnati OH 45202

(G-3223)
ONE CLOUD SERVICES LLC
Also Called: Zimcom Internet Solutions
1080 Nimitzview Dr Ste 400 (45230-4314)
PHONE..................513 231-9500
Anne Zimmerman, *Pr*
Steve Searles, *VP*
EMP: 6 **EST:** 2016
SALES (est): 1.07MM **Privately Held**
Web: www.zimcom.net
SIC: 7372 Business oriented computer software
PA: Liberty Noc, Llc
  4815 Delemere Ave
  Royal Oak MI 48073

(G-3224)
ONE THREE ENERGY INC
Also Called: Edgeenergy
5460 Muddy Creek Rd (45238-2033)
PHONE..................513 996-6973
Greg York, *CEO*
Ben Morris, *VP*
Jon Holland, *CFO*
EMP: 10 **EST:** 2020
SALES (est): 1.3MM **Privately Held**
Web: www.edgeenergyev.com
SIC: 3621 Storage battery chargers, motor and engine generator type

(G-3225)
ONETOUCHPOINT EAST CORP
Also Called: Touch Print Solution
1441 Western Ave (45214-2041)
PHONE..................513 421-1600
Christopher A Illman, *CEO*
William Pearson, *
Larry Halenkamp, *
EMP: 87 **EST:** 1969
SQ FT: 102,000
SALES (est): 23.24MM
SALES (corp-wide): 412.03MM **Privately Held**
Web: www.1touchpoint.com
SIC: 2789 2752 2759 2791 Bookbinding and related work; Commercial printing, lithographic; Commercial printing, nec; Typesetting
HQ: Onetouchpoint Corp.
  1225 Walnut Ridge Dr
  Hartland WI 53029

(G-3226)
ONX HOLDINGS LLC (DH)
Also Called: Onx Enterprise Solutions
221 E 4th St (45202)
PHONE..................866 587-2287
EMP: 57 **EST:** 2006
SALES (est): 95.76MM
SALES (corp-wide): 3.15B **Privately Held**
Web: www.altafiber.com
SIC: 7379 7372 Computer related consulting services; Business oriented computer software
HQ: Cincinnati Bell Inc.
  221 E 4th St Ste 700
  Cincinnati OH 45202
  513 397-9900

(G-3227)
OPTUM INFUSION SVCS 550 LLC (DH)
Also Called: Diplomat Spclty Infusion Group
7167 E Kemper Rd (45249-1028)
PHONE..................866 442-4679
EMP: 63 **EST:** 2004
SALES (est): 50.08MM
SALES (corp-wide): 371.62B **Publicly Held**
Web: www.biorxhemophilia.com
SIC: 5122 8748 2834 5047 Pharmaceuticals; Business consulting, nec; Pharmaceutical preparations; Medical and hospital equipment
HQ: Optum, Inc.
  11000 Optum Cir
  Eden Prairie MN 55344
  952 936-1300

(G-3228)
ORFLEX INC
470 West Northland Blvd (45240-3211)
EMP: 270
SIC: 2671 Paper; coated and laminated packaging

(G-3229)
ORGANIZED LIVING
12115 Ellington Ct (45249-1000)
PHONE..................513 277-3700
EMP: 6 **EST:** 2019
SALES (est): 245.14K **Privately Held**
Web: www.organizedliving.com

SIC: 3499 Fabricated metal products, nec

(G-3230)
ORGANIZED LIVING INC (PA)
Also Called: Organized Living
3100 E Kemper Rd (45241-1517)
PHONE..................513 489-9300
John D Kokenge, *CEO*
Patrick Taylor, *
Steve Mccamley, *VP Mktg*
Robert J Lamping, *
Kevin Ball, *
◆ **EMP:** 40 **EST:** 1919
SQ FT: 16,000
SALES (est): 46.72MM
SALES (corp-wide): 46.72MM **Privately Held**
Web: www.organizedliving.com
SIC: 3083 3411 2542 1799 Laminated plastics plate and sheet; Metal cans; Partitions and fixtures, except wood; Home/office interiors finishing, furnishing and remodeling

(G-3231)
OWL BE SWEATIN
Also Called: Hoot and Holler,
4914 Ridge Ave (45209-1035)
PHONE..................513 260-2026
K C Debra, *Pt*
Mallory Debra, *Pt*
EMP: 6 **EST:** 2012
SALES (est): 123.86K **Privately Held**
SIC: 2339 5632 Scarves, hoods, headbands, etc.: women's; Women's accessory and specialty stores

(G-3232)
P & C METAL POLISHING INC
9766 Pinto Ct (45242-5413)
PHONE..................513 771-9143
Perry Pullum, *Pr*
Donna Williamson, *VP*
EMP: 11 **EST:** 1967
SALES (est): 324.99K **Privately Held**
Web: www.pcmetalpolishing.com
SIC: 3471 Electroplating of metals or formed products

(G-3233)
P-AMERICAS LLC
Also Called: Pepsico
2121 Sunnybrook Dr (45237-2107)
PHONE..................513 948-5100
Bob Goodman, *Brnch Mgr*
EMP: 400
SQ FT: 150,000
SALES (corp-wide): 86.39B **Publicly Held**
Web: www.pepsico.com
SIC: 2086 Carbonated soft drinks, bottled and canned
HQ: P-Americas Llc
  1 Pepsi Way
  Somers NY 10589
  336 896-5740

(G-3234)
PANEL-FAB INC
10520 Taconic Ter (45215-1125)
PHONE..................513 771-1462
Robert A Harrison, *Pr*
Stephen T Williford, *
Nancy J Shurlow, *
EMP: 90 **EST:** 1979
SQ FT: 25,000
SALES (est): 25.47MM **Privately Held**
Web: www.panel-fab.com
SIC: 3613 Control panels, electric

(G-3235)
PATHEON PHARMACEUTICALS INC
2110 E Galbraith Rd (45237-1625)
PHONE..................513 948-9111
Teresa C Turnbow, *Mgr*
EMP: 1807
SALES (corp-wide): 44.91B **Publicly Held**
SIC: 2834 Pharmaceutical preparations
HQ: Patheon Pharmaceuticals Inc.
  3900 Paramount Pkwy
  Morrisville NC 27560
  919 226-3200

(G-3236)
PATIO ENCLOSURES (PA)
11949 Tramway Dr (45241-1666)
PHONE..................513 733-4646
Ronald J Molnar, *Pr*
Donna Molnar, *Sec*
EMP: 19 **EST:** 1973
SQ FT: 10,000
SALES (est): 2.41MM
SALES (corp-wide): 2.41MM **Privately Held**
Web: www.patioenclosures.com
SIC: 5039 2452 1521 Prefabricated structures; Prefabricated wood buildings; Patio and deck construction and repair

(G-3237)
PATRICK J BURKE & CO
Also Called: Burke & Company
901 Adams Crossing Fl 1 (45202-1693)
PHONE..................513 455-8200
Patrick Burke, *Owner*
EMP: 41 **EST:** 1984
SALES (est): 5.72MM **Privately Held**
Web: www.burkecpa.com
SIC: 8721 7372 Certified public accountant; Prepackaged software

(G-3238)
PATRIGRAPHICA LTD
2249 Townsend Rd (45238-3251)
PHONE..................513 460-5380
Ryan J Thelen, *Prin*
EMP: 6 **EST:** 2012
SALES (est): 105.43K **Privately Held**
Web: www.patrigraphica.com
SIC: 2741 Miscellaneous publishing

(G-3239)
PATRIOT SIGNAGE INC
5725 Dragon Way (45227-4519)
PHONE..................859 655-9009
Kevin L Keefe, *Pr*
Mike Maier, *Prin*
EMP: 9 **EST:** 1991
SALES (est): 924.09K **Privately Held**
Web: www.patriotsigns.com
SIC: 3993 Signs, not made in custom sign painting shops

(G-3240)
PAUL H ROHE COMPANY INC
11641 Mosteller Rd (45241-1520)
PHONE..................513 326-6789
James P Jurgensen Ii, *Pr*
EMP: 9 **EST:** 2009
SALES (est): 558.08K **Privately Held**
Web: www.jrjnet.com
SIC: 3273 Ready-mixed concrete

(G-3241)
PAUL WILKE & SON INC
1965 Grand Ave (45214-1505)
PHONE..................513 921-3163
Charles S Wilke, *Pr*
EMP: 14 **EST:** 1920
SQ FT: 22,000

(PA)=Parent Co (HQ)=Headquarters
✪ = New Business established in last 2 years

2024 Harris Ohio Industrial Directory

Cincinnati - Hamilton County (G-3242)

SALES (est): 1.84MM **Privately Held**
Web: www.paulwilkeandson.com
SIC: **3444** 3599 7692 Sheet metal specialties, not stamped; Machine shop, jobbing and repair; Welding repair

(G-3242)
PAVESTONE LLC
8479 Broadwell Rd (45244-1693)
PHONE.................513 474-3783
EMP: 67
SQ FT: 54,837
Web: www.pavestone.com
SIC: **3272** 3281 Paving materials, prefabricated concrete; Cut stone and stone products
HQ: Pavestone, Llc
    5 Concourse Pkwy Ste 1900
    Atlanta GA 30328
    404 926-3167

(G-3243)
PAYCOR HCM INC (HQ)
Also Called: Paycor
4811 Montgomery Rd (45212)
PHONE.................800 381-0053
Raul Villar Junior, *CEO*
Adam Ante, *CFO*
Alice Geene, *CLO*
Ryan Bergstrom, *CPO*
Charles Mueller, *CRO*
EMP: 14 EST: 1990
SQ FT: 135,577
SALES (est): 552.69MM
SALES (corp-wide): 552.69MM **Publicly Held**
Web: www.paycor.com
SIC: **7372** 8742 Prepackaged software; Human resource consulting services
PA: Pride Aggregator, Lp
    601 Lexington Ave Fl 53
    New York NY 10022
    212 753-6300

(G-3244)
PE USA LLC
Also Called: P.E. Labellers
89 Partnership Way (45241-1580)
P.O. Box 62067 (45262-0067)
PHONE.................513 771-7374
▲ EMP: 16 EST: 1961
SALES (est): 3.88MM **Privately Held**
Web: www.pelabellers.com
SIC: **5084** 3565 3469 Packaging machinery and equipment; Packaging machinery; Machine parts, stamped or pressed metal

(G-3245)
PEERLESS PRINTING COMPANY
2250 Gilbert Ave Ste 1 (45206-2531)
PHONE.................513 721-4657
Ken Schrand, *Pr*
Paul Dimario, *Prin*
Jay Heidemann, *Prin*
Steve Lyons, *Prin*
Ryan Schrand, *Prin*
EMP: 17 EST: 1900
SQ FT: 4,400
SALES (est): 916.19K **Privately Held**
Web: www.peerlessprinting.com
SIC: **2752** Offset printing

(G-3246)
PERFECT PROBATE
2036 8 Mile Rd (45244-2607)
PHONE.................513 791-4100
Shawn Wood, *Owner*
EMP: 6 EST: 1994
SALES (est): 334.12K **Privately Held**
Web: www.perfectprobate.com

SIC: **7372** 8111 Prepackaged software; Legal services

(G-3247)
PERFORMANCE ELECTRONICS LTD
11529 Goldcoast Dr (45249-1620)
PHONE.................513 777-5233
Brian Lewis, *Mng Pt*
EMP: 8 EST: 1999
SALES (est): 1.73MM **Privately Held**
Web: www.pe-ltd.com
SIC: **3679** Electronic circuits

(G-3248)
PERFORMANCE PLASTICS LTD
Also Called: Performance Plastics
4435 Brownway Ave (45209-1264)
PHONE.................513 321-8404
EMP: 75 EST: 1982
SQ FT: 20,000
SALES (est): 20.9MM
SALES (corp-wide): 295.68MM **Privately Held**
Web: www.performanceplastics.com
SIC: **3089** Injection molding of plastics
PA: Pexco Llc
    6470 E Johns Xing Ste 430
    Johns Creek GA 30097
    678 990-1523

(G-3249)
PETE GAIETTO & ASSOCIATES INC
1900 Section Rd (45237-3308)
PHONE.................513 771-0903
Jordan Gaietto, *CEO*
▲ EMP: 75 EST: 2005
SQ FT: 3,880
SALES (est): 7.81MM **Privately Held**
Web: www.petergaietto.com
SIC: **2542** Office and store showcases and display fixtures

(G-3250)
PETER CREMER N AMER ENRGY INC
Also Called: Peter Cremer North America
3131 River Rd (45204-1211)
PHONE.................513 557-3943
EMP: 30 EST: 2009
SALES (est): 11.92MM **Privately Held**
Web: www.petercremerna.com
SIC: **2843** Surface active agents

(G-3251)
PETER CREMER NORTH AMERICA LP (DH)
Also Called: Pcna
3131 River Rd (45204-1211)
PHONE.................513 471-7200
Ian Van Handel, *CEO*
◆ EMP: 60 EST: 1998
SALES (est): 115.36MM
SALES (corp-wide): 188.69K **Privately Held**
Web: www.petercremerna.com
SIC: **2899** Oils and essential oils
HQ: Peter Cremer Gmbh
    GlockengieBerwall 3
    Hamburg HH 20095
    40320110

(G-3252)
PETNET SOLUTIONS INC
2139 Auburn Ave (45219-2906)
PHONE.................865 218-2000
EMP: 6
SALES (corp-wide): 84.48B **Privately Held**
Web: www.siemens.com
SIC: **2835** Radioactive diagnostic substances
HQ: Petnet Solutions, Inc.
    810 Innovation Dr
    Knoxville TN 37932
    865 218-2000

(G-3253)
PFPC ENTERPRISES INC
5750 Hillside Ave (45233-1508)
PHONE.................513 941-6200
Peter F Coffaro, *Ch Bd*
James Coffaro, *
Stephen Stout, *
Jerry Jung, *Prin*
EMP: 19 EST: 1963
SQ FT: 52,000
SALES (est): 718.3K **Privately Held**
SIC: **5023** 5084 3594 3535 Floor coverings; Industrial machinery and equipment; Fluid power pumps and motors; Conveyors and conveying equipment

(G-3254)
PGT HEALTHCARE LLP (HQ)
1 Procter And Gamble Plz (45202-3315)
PHONE.................513 983-1100
David S Taylor, *Pr*
Mark Biegger, *Chief Human Resource Officer*
Linda Clement-holmes, *CIO*
Deborah Majoras, *CLO*
EMP: 21 EST: 2014
SALES (est): 2.37MM
SALES (corp-wide): 82.01B **Publicly Held**
SIC: **2676** Towels, napkins, and tissue paper products
PA: The Procter & Gamble Company
    1 Procter & Gamble Plz
    Cincinnati OH 45202
    513 983-1100

(G-3255)
PICKENS WINDOW SERVICE INC
7824 Hamilton Ave (45231-3106)
PHONE.................513 931-4432
Brian Pickens, *Pr*
Kendall Pickens, *Sec*
EMP: 12 EST: 1952
SQ FT: 10,000
SALES (est): 395.59K **Privately Held**
Web: www.pickenswindowparts.com
SIC: **5211** 7699 2431 Windows, storm: wood or metal; Door and window repair; Window screens, wood frame

(G-3256)
PINNACLE ROLLER CO
2147 Spring Grove Ave (45214-1721)
PHONE.................513 369-4830
Mike Brown, *Prin*
EMP: 13 EST: 2004
SALES (est): 1.14MM **Privately Held**
Web: www.pinnacleroller.com
SIC: **3069** Rubber rolls and roll coverings

(G-3257)
PIP PRINTING
Also Called: PIP Printing
5628 Cheviot Rd (45247-7006)
PHONE.................513 245-0590
EMP: 7 EST: 2018
SALES (est): 101.53K **Privately Held**
Web: www.pip.com
SIC: **2752** Offset printing

(G-3258)
PIQUA MATERIALS INC (PA)
11641 Mosteller Rd Ste 1 (45241-1520)
PHONE.................513 771-0820
James Jurgensen, *Pr*
Tim Saintclair, *Sec*
James Jurgenson Ii, *VP*
EMP: 21 EST: 1989
SALES (est): 8.6MM **Privately Held**
Web: www.jrjnet.com
SIC: **1422** Limestones, ground

(G-3259)
PKI INC
Also Called: Powder Kote Industries
4500 Reading Rd (45229-1230)
PHONE.................513 832-8749
Jeff Cox, *Pr*
EMP: 10 EST: 1973
SQ FT: 10,000
SALES (est): 1.07MM **Privately Held**
Web: www.powdercoatinc.com
SIC: **3479** 3471 Coating of metals and formed products; Sand blasting of metal parts

(G-3260)
PLASTICRAFT USA LLC
3101 Exon Ave (45241-2547)
PHONE.................513 761-2999
EMP: 6 EST: 1996
SQ FT: 2,800
SALES (est): 431.86K **Privately Held**
SIC: **3229** 3089 Industrial-use glassware; Molding primary plastics

(G-3261)
PLASTIGRAPHICS INC
722 Redna Ter (45215-1109)
PHONE.................513 771-8848
Robert Heinold, *Pr*
Sandy Miller, *Sec*
EMP: 12 EST: 1971
SQ FT: 6,500
SALES (est): 1.08MM **Privately Held**
Web: www.plastigraphics.com
SIC: **3993** 3861 Signs, not made in custom sign painting shops; Graphic arts plates, sensitized

(G-3262)
PMC SPECIALTIES GROUP INC (DH)
Also Called: Pmcsg
501 Murray Rd (45217-1014)
PHONE.................513 242-3300
◆ EMP: 21 EST: 1984
SQ FT: 7,500
SALES (est): 15.8MM
SALES (corp-wide): 1.71B **Privately Held**
Web: www.pmcsg.com
SIC: **2819** 2816 Industrial inorganic chemicals, nec; Inorganic pigments
HQ: Pmc, Inc.
    12243 Branford St
    Sun Valley CA 91352
    818 896-1101

(G-3263)
PMC SPECIALTIES GROUP INC
5220 Vine St (45217-1028)
PHONE.................513 242-3300
EMP: 18
SALES (corp-wide): 1.71B **Privately Held**
Web: www.pmcsg.com
SIC: **2819** 2816 Industrial inorganic chemicals, nec; Inorganic pigments
HQ: Pmc Specialties Group, Inc.
    501 Murray Rd
    Cincinnati OH 45217

(G-3264)
PME OF OHIO INC (PA)
Also Called: PME- Babbit Bearings
518 W Crescentville Rd (45246-1222)
PHONE.................513 671-1717
Charles Walter, *Pr*
EMP: 20 EST: 1980
SQ FT: 20,000
SALES (est): 8.47MM
SALES (corp-wide): 8.47MM **Privately Held**
Web: www.pmebabbittbearings.com

GEOGRAPHIC SECTION

Cincinnati - Hamilton County (G-3286)

SIC: 3599 Machine shop, jobbing and repair

(G-3265)
PORTER PRECISION PRODUCTS CO (PA)
Also Called: Porter
2734 Banning Rd (45239-5504)
PHONE.................................513 385-1569
John Cipriani Junior, Pr
Mary M Cipriani, *
Dale Warlaumont, *
EMP: 79 EST: 1947
SQ FT: 33,200
SALES (est): 18.01MM
SALES (corp-wide): 18.01MM Privately Held
Web: www.porterpunch.com
SIC: 3544 Special dies and tools

(G-3266)
PORTER-GUERTIN CO INC
2150 Colerain Ave (45214-1873)
P.O. Box 14177 (45250-0177)
PHONE.................................513 241-7663
James F Gentil, Pr
Kathleen Gentil, Sec
EMP: 15 EST: 1953
SQ FT: 12,000
SALES (est): 780.76K Privately Held
Web: www.porterguertinco.com
SIC: 3471 Electroplating of metals or formed products

(G-3267)
POSITROL INC
Also Called: Positrol Workholding
3890 Virginia Ave (45227-3410)
PHONE.................................513 272-0500
David C Weber, Pr
Jonathan T Weber, *
EMP: 30 EST: 1947
SQ FT: 11,000
SALES (est): 4.99MM Privately Held
Web: www.positrol.com
SIC: 3545 Machine tool attachments and accessories

(G-3268)
POSTERSERVICE INCORPORATED (PA)
225 Northland Blvd (45246-3603)
PHONE.................................513 577-7100
Daniel P Regenold, Ch
Dana W Gore, Pr
Rebecca Regenold, Sec
▲ EMP: 6 EST: 1983
SQ FT: 30,000
SALES (est): 8.02MM
SALES (corp-wide): 8.02MM Privately Held
Web: www.artandcanvas.com
SIC: 5199 2741 Posters; Posters: publishing and printing

(G-3269)
PPG ARCHITECTURAL FINISHES INC
Porter Paints
4600 Reading Rd (45229-1232)
PHONE.................................513 242-3050
Beny Cado, Mgr
EMP: 10
SQ FT: 1,600
SALES (corp-wide): 17.65B Publicly Held
Web: www.ppg.com
SIC: 2851 Paints and allied products
HQ: Ppg Architectural Finishes, Inc.
   1 Ppg Pl
   Pittsburgh PA 15272
   412 434-3131

(G-3270)
PPG ARCHITECTURAL FINISHES INC
Glidden Professional Paint Ctr
2960 Exon Ave (45241-2521)
PHONE.................................513 563-0220
EMP: 10
SALES (corp-wide): 17.65B Publicly Held
Web: www.ppg.com
SIC: 2851 Paints and allied products
HQ: Ppg Architectural Finishes, Inc.
   1 Ppg Pl
   Pittsburgh PA 15272
   412 434-3131

(G-3271)
PRECISION SWISS LLC
9580 Wayne Ave (45215-2252)
PHONE.................................513 716-7000
Ron Hinks, Owner
Tatyana Hinks, CFO
EMP: 9 EST: 2011
SQ FT: 17,000
SALES (est): 994.52K Privately Held
SIC: 3843 Dental equipment and supplies

(G-3272)
PREMIER INDUSTRIES INC
5721 Dragon Way Ste 113 (45227-4518)
PHONE.................................513 271-2550
J Paul Taylor, Pr
Suzanne Gerwin, *
EMP: 39 EST: 1935
SQ FT: 45,000
SALES (est): 382.09K
SALES (corp-wide): 4.51MM Privately Held
SIC: 2656 3556 Plates, paper: made from purchased material; Food products machinery
PA: Taylor Company
   5721 Dragon Way Ste 117
   Cincinnati OH 45227
   513 271-2550

(G-3273)
PREMIER SOUTHERN TICKET CO INC
7911 School Rd (45249-1596)
PHONE.................................513 489-6700
Kirk Schulz, Pr
Jim Raike, *
◆ EMP: 38 EST: 1883
SQ FT: 38,000
SALES (est): 1.07MM Privately Held
Web: www.premiersouthern.com
SIC: 2759 Tickets: printing, nsk
PA: Gtlp Holdings, Llc
   7911 School Rd
   Cincinnati OH 45249

(G-3274)
PRIDE CAST METALS INC
2737 Colerain Ave (45225-2263)
PHONE.................................513 541-1295
Thomas Hamm, Pr
Kenneth Bechtol, *
▲ EMP: 100 EST: 1983
SQ FT: 150,000
SALES (est): 7.5MM Privately Held
Web: www.pridecastmetals.com
SIC: 3365 3366 3599 Aluminum and aluminum-based alloy castings; Castings (except die), nec, bronze; Machine shop, jobbing and repair

(G-3275)
PRIMAX COATING
2101 E Kemper Rd (45241-1805)
PHONE.................................513 455-0629
EMP: 6 EST: 2011
SALES (est): 126.71K Privately Held
SIC: 3479 Coating of metals and formed products

(G-3276)
PRIMO SERVICES LLC
1937 Clarion Ave (45207-1242)
PHONE.................................513 725-7888
Shanel Gentry, CEO
EMP: 15 EST: 2014
SALES (est): 1.17MM Privately Held
SIC: 1389 7349 Construction, repair, and dismantling services; Janitorial service, contract basis

(G-3277)
PRINTERY INC
Also Called: Pink Pages
4460 Bridgetown Rd (45211-4411)
P.O. Box 20206 (45220-0206)
PHONE.................................513 574-1099
Donald B Flick, Pr
EMP: 6 EST: 1970
SQ FT: 1,500
SALES (est): 410K Privately Held
SIC: 2741 2791 Directories, telephone: publishing only, not printed on site; Photocomposition, for the printing trade

(G-3278)
PRO MACH INC
89 Partnership Way (45241-1580)
PHONE.................................513 771-7374
EMP: 64 EST: 2019
SALES (est): 4.11MM Privately Held
SIC: 3535 Conveyors and conveying equipment
HQ: Pro Mach, Inc.
   50 E Rvrcnter Blvd Ste 18
   Covington KY 41011
   513 831-8778

(G-3279)
PROAMPAC ORLANDO INC (PA)
12025 Tricon Rd (45246)
PHONE.................................513 671-1777
EMP: 11 EST: 1990
SALES (est): 17.03MM
SALES (corp-wide): 17.03MM Privately Held
SIC: 3086 5084 Packaging and shipping materials, foamed plastics; Processing and packaging equipment

(G-3280)
PROCTER & GAMBLE COMPANY (PA)
Also Called: P&G
1 Procter And Gamble Plz (45202)
P.O. Box 599 (45201)
PHONE.................................513 983-1100
Jon R Moeller, Ch Bd
Shailesh Jejurikar, COO
Andre Schulten, CFO
M Tracey Grabowski, Chief Human Resources Officer
Susan Street Whaley, CLO
◆ EMP: 2997 EST: 1837
SALES (est): 82.01B
SALES (corp-wide): 82.01B Publicly Held
Web: us.pg.com
SIC: 2844 2842 2676 3634 Hair preparations, including shampoos; Specialty cleaning; Towels, napkins, and tissue paper products; Razors, electric

(G-3281)
PROCTER & GAMBLE COMPANY
Also Called: Procter & Gamble
6210 Center Hill Ave (45224-1708)
PHONE.................................513 983-1100
Matt Wagner, Pr
EMP: 98
SALES (corp-wide): 82.01B Publicly Held
Web: us.pg.com
SIC: 2844 2676 3421 2842 Deodorants, personal; Towels, napkins, and tissue paper products; Razor blades and razors; Specialty cleaning
PA: The Procter & Gamble Company
   1 Procter & Gamble Plz
   Cincinnati OH 45202
   513 983-1100

(G-3282)
PROCTER & GAMBLE COMPANY
Also Called: Procter & Gamble
5280 Vine St (45217-1028)
PHONE.................................513 266-4375
Ed Allie, Mgr
EMP: 12
SALES (corp-wide): 82.01B Publicly Held
Web: us.pg.com
SIC: 2844 2676 3421 2842 Deodorants, personal; Towels, napkins, and tissue paper products; Razor blades and razors; Specialty cleaning
PA: The Procter & Gamble Company
   1 Procter & Gamble Plz
   Cincinnati OH 45202
   513 983-1100

(G-3283)
PROCTER & GAMBLE COMPANY
Also Called: Procter & Gamble
654 Wilmer Ave Hngr 4 (45226-1860)
PHONE.................................513 871-7557
David Tobertge, Mgr
EMP: 8
SALES (corp-wide): 82.01B Publicly Held
Web: us.pg.com
SIC: 2844 2676 3421 2842 Deodorants, personal; Towels, napkins, and tissue paper products; Razor blades and razors; Specialty cleaning
PA: The Procter & Gamble Company
   1 Procter & Gamble Plz
   Cincinnati OH 45202
   513 983-1100

(G-3284)
PROCTER & GAMBLE COMPANY
Also Called: Procter & Gamble
5299 Spring Grove Ave (45217-1025)
PHONE.................................513 983-1100
John E Pepper, Ch Bd
EMP: 24
SALES (corp-wide): 82.01B Publicly Held
Web: us.pg.com
SIC: 2844 Deodorants, personal
PA: The Procter & Gamble Company
   1 Procter & Gamble Plz
   Cincinnati OH 45202
   513 983-1100

(G-3285)
PROCTER & GAMBLE COMPANY
6110 Center Hill Ave (45224-1706)
PHONE.................................513 634-2070
Terry Fabisiak, Mgr
EMP: 11
SALES (corp-wide): 82.01B Publicly Held
Web: us.pg.com
SIC: 2844 Deodorants, personal
PA: The Procter & Gamble Company
   1 Procter & Gamble Plz
   Cincinnati OH 45202
   513 983-1100

(G-3286)
PROCTER & GAMBLE COMPANY
Also Called: Procter & Gamble
4460 Kings Run Rd. (45232)

Cincinnati - Hamilton County (G-3287)

GEOGRAPHIC SECTION

PHONE..................513 482-6789
Joe Kelly, Opers Mgr
EMP: 10
SALES (corp-wide): 82.01B Publicly Held
Web: us.pg.com
SIC: 2844 2676 3421 2842 Deodorants, personal; Towels, napkins, and tissue paper products; Razor blades and razors; Specialty cleaning
PA: The Procter & Gamble Company
1 Procter & Gamble Plz
Cincinnati OH 45202
513 983-1100

(G-3287)
PROCTER & GAMBLE COMPANY
Also Called: Procter & Gamble
6300 Center Hill Ave Fl 2 (45224-1795)
PHONE..................513 634-5069
D L Miller, Mgr
EMP: 19
SALES (corp-wide): 82.01B Publicly Held
Web: us.pg.com
SIC: 2844 Deodorants, personal
PA: The Procter & Gamble Company
1 Procter & Gamble Plz
Cincinnati OH 45202
513 983-1100

(G-3288)
PROCTER & GAMBLE COMPANY
Also Called: Procter & Gamble
1 Plaza (45246)
PHONE..................513 983-3000
EMP: 205
SALES (corp-wide): 82.01B Publicly Held
Web: us.pg.com
SIC: 2844 2676 3421 2842 Deodorants, personal; Towels, napkins, and tissue paper products; Razor blades and razors; Specialty cleaning
PA: The Procter & Gamble Company
1 Procter & Gamble Plz
Cincinnati OH 45202
513 983-1100

(G-3289)
PROCTER & GAMBLE COMPANY
Also Called: Procter & Gamble
5348 Vine St (45217-1030)
PHONE..................513 627-7115
Joe Barbro, Brnch Mgr
EMP: 23
SALES (corp-wide): 82.01B Publicly Held
Web: us.pg.com
SIC: 2844 2676 3421 2842 Deodorants, personal; Towels, napkins, and tissue paper products; Razor blades and razors; Specialty cleaning
PA: The Procter & Gamble Company
1 Procter & Gamble Plz
Cincinnati OH 45202
513 983-1100

(G-3290)
PROCTER & GAMBLE COMPANY
Also Called: Procter & Gamble
1340 Clay St (45202-7608)
PHONE..................513 658-9853
David Kuehler, Brnch Mgr
EMP: 7
SALES (corp-wide): 82.01B Publicly Held
Web: us.pg.com
SIC: 2844 Deodorants, personal
PA: The Procter & Gamble Company
1 Procter & Gamble Plz
Cincinnati OH 45202
513 983-1100

(G-3291)
PROCTER & GAMBLE COMPANY
Also Called: Procter & Gamble
2 Procter And Gamble Plz (45202-3315)
PHONE..................513 983-1100
Sharon Shea, Brnch Mgr
EMP: 500
SALES (corp-wide): 82.01B Publicly Held
Web: us.pg.com
SIC: 2844 Deodorants, personal
PA: The Procter & Gamble Company
1 Procter & Gamble Plz
Cincinnati OH 45202
513 983-1100

(G-3292)
PROCTER & GAMBLE COMPANY
Also Called: Procter & Gamble
6280 Center Hill Ave (45224-1708)
PHONE..................513 945-0340
EMP: 17
SALES (corp-wide): 82.01B Publicly Held
Web: us.pg.com
SIC: 2844 2676 3421 2842 Deodorants, personal; Towels, napkins, and tissue paper products; Razor blades and razors; Specialty cleaning
PA: The Procter & Gamble Company
1 Procter & Gamble Plz
Cincinnati OH 45202
513 983-1100

(G-3293)
PROCTER & GAMBLE COMPANY
Procter & Gamble
5289 Vine St (45217-1027)
PHONE..................513 242-5752
EMP: 25
SALES (corp-wide): 82.01B Publicly Held
Web: us.pg.com
SIC: 2844 Deodorants, personal
PA: The Procter & Gamble Company
1 Procter & Gamble Plz
Cincinnati OH 45202
513 983-1100

(G-3294)
PROCTER & GAMBLE DISTRG CO
1 Procter And Gamble Plz (45202)
PHONE..................513 983-1100
EMP: 6 EST: 1902
SALES (est): 183.27K Privately Held
SIC: 2844 Toilet preparations

(G-3295)
PROCTER & GAMBLE FAR EAST INC (HQ)
One Procter & Gamble Plz (45202-3393)
PHONE..................513 983-1100
C Daley, Prin
A G Lafley, Pr
Rl Antoine, VP
F Benvegnu, VP
Rg Pease, VP
EMP: 110 EST: 1837
SQ FT: 1,600,000
SALES (est): 96.32MM
SALES (corp-wide): 82.01B Publicly Held
SIC: 2842 2844 2676 Laundry cleaning preparations; Toilet preparations; Napkins, sanitary: made from purchased paper
PA: The Procter & Gamble Company
1 Procter & Gamble Plz
Cincinnati OH 45202
513 983-1100

(G-3296)
PROCTER & GAMBLE HAIR CARE LLC
1 Procter And Gamble Plz (45202-3393)
PHONE..................513 983-4502
David S Taylor, Ch Bd
EMP: 106 EST: 2001
SALES (est): 12.99MM
SALES (corp-wide): 82.01B Publicly Held
SIC: 2844 Shampoos, rinses, conditioners: hair
PA: The Procter & Gamble Company
1 Procter & Gamble Plz
Cincinnati OH 45202
513 983-1100

(G-3297)
PROCTER & GAMBLE MEXICO INC
1 Procter And Gamble Plz (45202-3393)
PHONE..................513 983-1100
EMP: 7 EST: 2015
SALES (est): 673.79K
SALES (corp-wide): 82.01B Publicly Held
SIC: 2844 2676 3421 2842 Perfumes, cosmetics and other toilet preparations; Towels, napkins, and tissue paper products; Razor blades and razors; Specialty cleaning
PA: The Procter & Gamble Company
1 Procter & Gamble Plz
Cincinnati OH 45202
513 983-1100

(G-3298)
PROCTER & GAMBLE MFG CO (HQ)
Also Called: Procter & Gamble
1 Procter And Gamble Plz (45202-3393)
P.O. Box 599 (45201-0599)
PHONE..................513 983-1100
Jon R Moeller, Ch Bd
John Jensen, VP
C Daley Junior, Prin
John Goodwin, VP
Chris Walther, Sec
◆ EMP: 15 EST: 1910
SQ FT: 1,600,000
SALES (est): 1.27B
SALES (corp-wide): 82.01B Publicly Held
Web: us.pg.com
SIC: 2841 2079 2099 2844 Soap: granulated, liquid, cake, flaked, or chip; Shortening and other solid edible fats; Peanut butter; Toilet preparations
PA: The Procter & Gamble Company
1 Procter & Gamble Plz
Cincinnati OH 45202
513 983-1100

(G-3299)
PROCTER & GAMBLE PAPER PDTS CO (HQ)
Also Called: Procter & Gamble
1 Procter And Gamble Plz (45202-3393)
P.O. Box 599 (45201-0599)
PHONE..................513 983-1100
David S Taylor, Pr
Doctor Walker, VP
E G Nelson, VP Fin
C C Daley, VP
T L Overbey, Sec
◆ EMP: 15 EST: 1893
SQ FT: 1,600,000
SALES (est): 1.96B
SALES (corp-wide): 82.01B Publicly Held
Web: us.pg.com
SIC: 2676 Towels, napkins, and tissue paper products
PA: The Procter & Gamble Company
1 Procter & Gamble Plz
Cincinnati OH 45202
513 983-1100

(G-3300)
PROCTER & GAMBLE PAPER PDTS CO
Also Called: Procter & Gamble
301 E 6th St (45202-3339)
PHONE..................513 983-2222
EMP: 25
SALES (corp-wide): 82.01B Publicly Held
Web: us.pg.com
SIC: 2676 Towels, paper: made from purchased paper
HQ: The Procter & Gamble Paper Products Company
1 Procter And Gamble Plz
Cincinnati OH 45202
513 983-1100

(G-3301)
PROFESSIONAL AWARD SERVICE
Also Called: ID Plastech Engraving
3901 N Bend Rd (45211-4814)
PHONE..................513 389-3600
Ronald Jeremiah, Pr
EMP: 8 EST: 1982
SQ FT: 3,818
SALES (est): 495.81K Privately Held
Web: www.awardsanddesign.com
SIC: 3914 7389 Silverware and plated ware; Engraving service

(G-3302)
PROFILES IN DESIGN INC
860 Dellway St (45229-3306)
PHONE..................513 751-2212
EMP: 14 EST: 1996
SQ FT: 20,000
SALES (est): 907.92K Privately Held
Web: www.profilesindesign.com
SIC: 2434 Vanities, bathroom: wood

(G-3303)
PROFT & GAMBLE
6280 Center Hill Ave (45224-1708)
PHONE..................513 945-0340
Debbie Schurgast, Prin
▲ EMP: 7 EST: 2005
SALES (est): 505.68K Privately Held
SIC: 2844 Shampoos, rinses, conditioners: hair

(G-3304)
PROMINENCE ENERGY CORPORATION
1325 Spring St (45202-7420)
PHONE..................513 818-8329
Howard M Plevyak Junior, Prin
EMP: 6 EST: 2016
SALES (est): 49.89K Privately Held
Web: www.prominenceenergy.com.au
SIC: 1382 Oil and gas exploration services

(G-3305)
PROSPIANT INC (HQ)
5513 Vine St (45217-1022)
PHONE..................513 242-0310
Mark Dunson, Pr
EMP: 48 EST: 1999
SALES (est): 21.71MM
SALES (corp-wide): 1.38B Publicly Held
Web: www.prospiant.com
SIC: 3448 Greenhouses, prefabricated metal
PA: Gibraltar Industries, Inc.
3556 Lake Shore Rd # 100
Buffalo NY 14219
716 826-6500

(G-3306)
PROTECTIVE PACKG SOLUTIONS LLC
10345 S Medallion Dr (45241-4825)
PHONE..................513 769-5777
EMP: 30 EST: 2011
SALES (est): 4.32MM Privately Held

Web:
www.protectivepackagingsolutions.com
SIC: 2653 5199 Boxes, corrugated: made from purchased materials; Packaging materials

(G-3307)
PROTEIN TECHNOLOGIES LTD
4015 Executive Park Dr (45241-4017)
PHONE...............................513 769-0840
F Harrison Green, *Prin*
EMP: 8 EST: 2010
SALES (est): 169.66K **Privately Held**
SIC: 2836 Biological products, except diagnostic

(G-3308)
QC SOFTWARE LLC
50 E Business Way (45241-2397)
PHONE...............................513 469-1424
Kevin Tedford, *CEO*
EMP: 50 EST: 1996
SQ FT: 2,900
SALES (est): 4.56MM
SALES (corp-wide): 40.69MM **Privately Held**
Web: www.kpisolutions.com
SIC: 7371 7372 Computer software development; Prepackaged software
PA: Kuecker Pulse Integration, L.P.
   801 W Markey Rd
   Belton MO 64012
   844 574-1010

(G-3309)
QCA INC
2832 Spring Grove Ave (45225-2220)
PHONE...............................513 681-8400
James Bosken, *Pr*
Andrea Winterhalter, *VP*
EMP: 19 EST: 1950
SQ FT: 35,000
SALES (est): 202.49K **Privately Held**
Web: www.go-qca.com
SIC: 3652 Master records or tapes, preparation of

(G-3310)
QUALITY CONTROLS INC
3411 Church St (45244-3409)
PHONE...............................513 272-3900
Thomas M Pulskamp, *Pr*
Annette Pulskamp, *Sec*
EMP: 11 EST: 1994
SQ FT: 15,000
SALES (est): 2.4MM **Privately Held**
Web: www.qcipanels.com
SIC: 3625 3829 Motor control accessories, including overload relays; Measuring and controlling devices, nec

(G-3311)
QUALITY MECHANICALS INC
1225 Streng St (45223-2642)
PHONE...............................513 559-0998
Richard Doll, *Pr*
Denise Albright, *
EMP: 35 EST: 1985
SQ FT: 4,000
SALES (est): 5.4MM **Privately Held**
Web: www.qualitymechanicals.com
SIC: 3498 Fabricated pipe and fittings

(G-3312)
QUALITY MFG COMPANY INC
4323 Spring Grove Ave (45223-1834)
PHONE...............................513 921-4500
Edward J Bemerer, *Pr*
Richard Lipps, *VP*
Paul A Kapper, *Sec*
EMP: 8 EST: 1975

SQ FT: 16,000
SALES (est): 1.03MM **Privately Held**
Web: www.qmfgco.com
SIC: 3599 Machine shop, jobbing and repair

(G-3313)
QUANTA INTERNATIONAL LLC
1 Landy Ln (45215-3405)
PHONE...............................513 354-3639
Augusto Quinones, *Pr*
EMP: 11 EST: 2011
SALES (est): 1MM **Privately Held**
SIC: 2819 Industrial inorganic chemicals, nec

(G-3314)
QUEBECOR WORLD JOHNSON HARDIN
3600 Red Bank Rd (45227-4142)
PHONE...............................614 326-0299
Chuck Miotke, *Pr*
James H Bossart, *
Jeffery R Herman, *
EMP: 40 EST: 1902
SQ FT: 200,000
SALES (est): 474.28K **Privately Held**
SIC: 2759 2752 2732 Magazines: printing, nsk; Offset printing; Books, printing only

(G-3315)
QUEEN CITY AWNING & TENT CO
Also Called: Queen City Awning
7225 E Kemper Rd (45249-1030)
PHONE...............................513 530-9660
Peter Weingartner, *Pr*
Robert P Weingartner Senior, *Ch*
James Weingartner, *
EMP: 35 EST: 1877
SQ FT: 27,000
SALES (est): 2.82MM **Privately Held**
Web: www.queencityawning.com
SIC: 2394 5712 Awnings, fabric: made from purchased materials; Outdoor and garden furniture

(G-3316)
QUEEN CITY CARPETS LLC
6539 Harrison Ave 304 (45247-7822)
PHONE...............................513 823-8238
Terry Hensley, *VP*
EMP: 10 EST: 2012
SALES (est): 347.76K **Privately Held**
SIC: 2393 Cushions, except spring and carpet: purchased materials

(G-3317)
QUEEN CITY OFFICE MACHINE
3984 Trevor Ave (45211-3407)
PHONE...............................513 251-7200
Ronald Swing, *Prin*
EMP: 10 EST: 1971
SQ FT: 6,000
SALES (est): 965.63K **Privately Held**
Web: www.queencityoffice.com
SIC: 5112 7629 2759 Office supplies, nec; Business machine repair, electric; Laser printing

(G-3318)
QUEEN CITY PALLETS INC
Also Called: Qcp Pallet Services
7744 Reinhold Dr (45237-2806)
PHONE...............................513 821-2700
Mike Unthank, *CEO*
Garry Unthank, *
EMP: 40 EST: 2006
SQ FT: 30,000
SALES (est): 4.56MM **Privately Held**
Web: www.qcpallets.com
SIC: 2448 Pallets, wood

(G-3319)
QUEEN CITY REPROGRAPHICS
2863 E Sharon Rd (45241-1923)
PHONE...............................513 326-2300
EMP: 105 EST: 1963
SALES (est): 11.43MM
SALES (corp-wide): 281.2MM **Publicly Held**
SIC: 5049 7334 7335 2752 Drafting supplies; Blueprinting service; Commercial photography; Lithographing on metal
PA: Arc Document Solutions, Inc.
   12657 Alcosta Blvd # 200
   San Ramon CA 94583
   925 949-5100

(G-3320)
QUEEN CITY SPIRIT LLC
Also Called: Queen City Mascots and Logos
8211 Blue Ash Rd (45236-1987)
PHONE...............................513 533-2662
Deanna Regruth, *Owner*
EMP: 10 EST: 2011
SALES (est): 737.21K **Privately Held**
SIC: 2395 2759 7389 Embroidery and art needlework; Screen printing; Engraving service

(G-3321)
R A HELLER COMPANY
10530 Chester Rd (45215-1262)
PHONE...............................513 771-6100
Steve Heller, *Pr*
Laura Heller, *Sec*
EMP: 11 EST: 1946
SQ FT: 20,000
SALES (est): 1.46MM **Privately Held**
Web: www.raheller.com
SIC: 3471 3599 3545 Chromium plating of metals or formed products; Machine shop, jobbing and repair; Cutting tools for machine tools

(G-3322)
R VANDEWALLE INC
Also Called: Van Engineering Co
4030 Delhi Ave (45204-1276)
PHONE...............................513 921-2657
Robert Vandewalle, *Pr*
Richard Vandewalle, *VP*
EMP: 8 EST: 1942
SQ FT: 7,000
SALES (est): 665.73K **Privately Held**
SIC: 3599 Machine shop, jobbing and repair

(G-3323)
RAD TECHNOLOGIES INCORPORATED
Also Called: Precision Temp
3428 Hauck Rd Ste G (45241-4603)
PHONE...............................513 641-0523
Robert Muhlhauser, *CEO*
Gerry Wolters, *Prin*
Fred Rothzeid, *CFO*
▲ EMP: 12 EST: 2010
SALES (est): 2.13MM **Privately Held**
Web: www.precisiontemp.com
SIC: 3639 Hot water heaters, household

(G-3324)
RANDY GRAY
Also Called: Brat Printing
4142 Airport Rd Unit 1 (45226-1627)
PHONE...............................513 533-3200
EMP: 6 EST: 1993
SQ FT: 9,000
SALES (est): 501.96K **Privately Held**
Web: www.bratprinting.com

SIC: 3552 2395 2396 Textile machinery; Emblems, embroidered; Automotive and apparel trimmings

(G-3325)
RCL PUBLISHING GROUP LLC
8805 Governors Hill Dr Ste 400 (45249-3314)
PHONE...............................972 390-6400
Rcl Benziger, *Prin*
▼ EMP: 11 EST: 2011
SALES (est): 657.23K **Privately Held**
SIC: 2741 Miscellaneous publishing

(G-3326)
RECARO CHILD SAFETY LLC
Also Called: Recaro
4921 Para Dr (45237-5011)
PHONE...............................248 904-1570
◆ EMP: 8 EST: 2011
SQ FT: 40,000
SALES (est): 242.94K **Privately Held**
SIC: 3944 5099 Child restraint seats, automotive; Child restraint seats, automotive

(G-3327)
RECORD HERALD PUBLISHING CO (DH)
Also Called: Record Herald
5050 Kingsley Dr (45227-1115)
P.O. Box 271 (17268-0271)
PHONE...............................717 762-2151
Denise Igram, *Genl Mgr*
Denise Igram, *Mgr*
EMP: 50 EST: 1847
SALES (est): 8.86MM
SALES (corp-wide): 2.66B **Publicly Held**
Web: www.therecordherald.com
SIC: 2711 2752 Commercial printing and newspaper publishing combined; Commercial printing, lithographic
HQ: Gatehouse Media, Llc
   175 Sullys Trl Ste 203
   Pittsford NY 14534
   585 598-0030

(G-3328)
RECTO MOLDED PRODUCTS INC
4425 Appleton St (45209-1290)
PHONE...............................513 871-5544
Per Flem, *Pr*
EMP: 65 EST: 1913
SQ FT: 65,000
SALES (est): 13.81MM **Privately Held**
Web: www.rectomolded.com
SIC: 3089 3083 Injection molding of plastics; Laminated plastics plate and sheet

(G-3329)
REIKI LADI
9693 Loralinda Dr (45251-2132)
PHONE...............................513 235-7515
EMP: 6 EST: 2001
SALES (est): 96.76K **Privately Held**
Web: www.stillpointtherapy.com
SIC: 2833 Medicinals and botanicals

(G-3330)
REILLY-DUERR TANK CO
698 W Columbia Ave (45215-3169)
P.O. Box 15189 (45215-0189)
PHONE...............................513 554-1022
Kevin Graham, *Prin*
EMP: 7 EST: 2002
SALES (est): 142.96K **Privately Held**
Web: www.valleymetalworks.com
SIC: 3444 Sheet metalwork

Cincinnati - Hamilton County (G-3331)

(G-3331)
RELIABLE CASTINGS CORPORATION (PA)
3530 Spring Grove Ave (45223-2448)
EMP: 100 **EST:** 1922
SALES (est): 34MM
SALES (corp-wide): 34MM **Privately Held**
Web: www.reliablecastings.com
SIC: 3365 3543 Aluminum and aluminum-based alloy castings; Industrial patterns

(G-3332)
RENEE GRACE LLC
Also Called: Renee Grace Bridal
11176 Main St (45241-2672)
PHONE.................513 399-5616
Teresa Eklund, *Prin*
EMP: 8 **EST:** 2018
SALES (est): 205.86K **Privately Held**
Web: www.reneegrace.com
SIC: 2335 Bridal and formal gowns

(G-3333)
REVEL OTR URBAN WINERY
111 E 12th St (45202-7203)
PHONE.................513 929-4263
EMP: 7 **EST:** 2017
SALES (est): 216.02K **Privately Held**
Web: www.revelotr.com
SIC: 2084 Wines

(G-3334)
RHGS COMPANY
1150 W 8th St Ste 111 (45203-1245)
PHONE.................513 721-6299
Gregg Sample, *Pr*
Ronald E Heithaus, *Prin*
EMP: 6 **EST:** 2004
SQ FT: 8,000
SALES (est): 964.33K **Privately Held**
Web: www.thetormaxxcompany.com
SIC: 3545 Machine tool accessories

(G-3335)
RHI US LTD (DH)
3956 Virginia Ave (45227-3412)
PHONE.................513 527-6160
◆ **EMP:** 9 **EST:** 2010
SALES (est): 10.21MM **Privately Held**
Web: www.interstop-usa.com
SIC: 3823 Refractometers, industrial process type
HQ: Dutch Us Holding B.V.
   Hofplein 19
   Rotterdam ZH 3032
   263635763

(G-3336)
RHINEGEIST HOLDING COMPANY INC
1910 Elm St (45202-7751)
PHONE.................513 381-1367
Robert Bonder, *Prin*
EMP: 11 **EST:** 2021
SALES (est): 305.16K **Privately Held**
Web: www.rhinegeist.com
SIC: 2082 Malt beverages

(G-3337)
RIBS KING INC
9406 Main St (45242-7616)
PHONE.................513 791-1942
Evan Andrews, *VP*
Thomas Gregory, *Pr*
Dean Gregory, *VP*
Victoria Siegel, *VP*
EMP: 9 **EST:** 1990
SQ FT: 21,000
SALES (est): 758.43K **Privately Held**
Web: www.montgomeryinnribsking.com
SIC: 2035 Seasonings and sauces, except tomato and dry

(G-3338)
RICHARD BENHASE & ASSOC INC
11741 Chesterdale Rd (45246-3405)
PHONE.................513 772-1896
Richard Benhase, *Pr*
Linda Benhase, *VP*
EMP: 9 **EST:** 1979
SQ FT: 15,000
SALES (est): 490.68K **Privately Held**
Web: www.benhasecarrestorations.com
SIC: 2521 2511 2434 Cabinets, office: wood; Wood household furniture; Wood kitchen cabinets

(G-3339)
RICHARDS INDUSTRIALS INC (PA)
Also Called: Richards Industrials
3170 Wasson Rd (45209-2329)
PHONE.................513 533-5600
Jordan Bast, *Pr*
John Speridakos, *
Bill Metz, *
Jim Gray, *
▲ **EMP:** 75 **EST:** 1961
SQ FT: 150,000
SALES (est): 49.62MM
SALES (corp-wide): 49.62MM **Privately Held**
Web: www.richardsind.com
SIC: 3491 3494 3823 Industrial valves; Pipe fittings; Process control instruments

(G-3340)
RIDGE ENGINEERING INC
Also Called: Delhi Welding Co
1700 Blue Rock St (45223-2505)
PHONE.................513 681-5500
Rob Shean, *Genl Mgr*
EMP: 9 **EST:** 1984
SQ FT: 14,000
SALES (est): 595.99K **Privately Held**
Web: www.ridgeeng.com
SIC: 7692 Welding repair

(G-3341)
RINA SYSTEMS LLC
8180 Corporate Park Dr Ste 140 (45242)
PHONE.................513 469-7462
EMP: 6 **EST:** 1995
SALES (est): 842.09K **Privately Held**
Web: www.rinasystems.com
SIC: 7372 Prepackaged software

(G-3342)
RIPPER WOODWORK INC
6450 Mapleton Ave (45233-4529)
PHONE.................513 922-1944
Gerard Holthaus, *Prin*
EMP: 6 **EST:** 2009
SALES (est): 209.55K **Privately Held**
SIC: 2431 Millwork

(G-3343)
RIVER CITY BODY COMPANY
2660 Commerce Blvd (45241-1552)
PHONE.................513 772-9317
John Mc Henry, *Pr*
EMP: 11 **EST:** 1989
SQ FT: 10,000
SALES (est): 2.49MM **Privately Held**
Web: www.rivercitybody.com
SIC: 3537 5531 Trucks, tractors, loaders, carriers, and similar equipment; Truck equipment and parts

(G-3344)
RIVERSIDE CNSTR SVCS INC
218 W Mcmicken Ave (45214-2314)
PHONE.................513 723-0900
Robert S Krejci, *Pr*
Timothy L Pierce, *
EMP: 32 **EST:** 1993
SQ FT: 21,000
SALES (est): 4.74MM **Privately Held**
Web: www.riversidearchitectural.com
SIC: 2431 1751 2434 Millwork; Carpentry work; Wood kitchen cabinets

(G-3345)
RLM & SQG INDUSTRIES INC
3714 Jonlen Dr (45227-4103)
PHONE.................513 527-4057
Raymond Rytel, *Prin*
EMP: 7 **EST:** 2010
SALES (est): 149K **Privately Held**
Web: www.rlm-sqg.com
SIC: 3999 Manufacturing industries, nec

(G-3346)
RM ADVISORY GROUP INC
5300 Vine St (45217)
PHONE.................513 242-2100
Robert Moskowitz, *Pr*
Ira Moskowitz, *
EMP: 35 **EST:** 1901
SQ FT: 70,000
SALES (est): 4.57MM **Privately Held**
SIC: 5093 3341 Ferrous metal scrap and waste; Secondary nonferrous metals

(G-3347)
RMT ACQUISITION INC
Also Called: Young & Bertke Air Systems Co.
3111 Spring Grove Ave (45225)
PHONE.................513 241-5566
Roger Young, *Pr*
Tim Rohrer, *
Michael Munafo, *
Phillip C Young, *Stockholder**
EMP: 28 **EST:** 1920
SQ FT: 51,000
SALES (est): 4.47MM **Privately Held**
Web: www.youngbertke.com
SIC: 1761 3441 3564 3444 Sheet metal work, nec; Fabricated structural metal; Blowers and fans; Sheet metalwork

(G-3348)
ROBBINS INC (PA)
Also Called: Robbins Sports Surfaces
4777 Eastern Ave (45226-2339)
PHONE.................513 871-8988
James H Stoehr Iii, *Ch*
Dave Fulton, *
Mike Niese, *
John Williams, *
Beth Smith, *
◆ **EMP:** 35 **EST:** 1970
SQ FT: 3,000
SALES (est): 43.54MM
SALES (corp-wide): 43.54MM **Privately Held**
Web: www.robbinsfloor.com
SIC: 2426 Flooring, hardwood

(G-3349)
ROLCON INC
510 Station Ave (45215-5439)
PHONE.................513 821-7259
Don Mileham, *Admn*
EMP: 10
Web: www.rolconrollers.com
SIC: 3535 3561 Conveyors and conveying equipment; Cylinders, pump
PA: Rolcon, Inc
   134 Carthage Ave
   Cincinnati OH 45215

(G-3350)
RON TOELKE
4377 Oakville Dr (45211-2485)
PHONE.................513 598-1881
Ronald G Toelke, *Prin*
EMP: 6 **EST:** 2010
SALES (est): 97.78K **Privately Held**
SIC: 2752 Commercial printing, lithographic

(G-3351)
ROTEX GLOBAL LLC
Also Called: Gundlach
1230 Knowlton St (45223-1800)
P.O. Box 630317 (45263-0317)
PHONE.................513 541-1236
William J Herkamp, *Pr*
Robert W Dieckman, *
Gary Armstrong, *
Mark J Moore, *
Richard B Paulsen, *
◆ **EMP:** 166 **EST:** 1844
SQ FT: 150,000
SALES (est): 48.04MM **Publicly Held**
Web: www.rotex.com
SIC: 3569 3826 Sifting and screening machines; Particle size analyzers
PA: Hillenbrand, Inc.
   1 Batesville Blvd
   Batesville IN 47006

(G-3352)
ROUGH BROTHERS MFG INC
5513 Vine St (45217-1022)
PHONE.................513 242-0310
Richard Reilly, *Pr*
David Roberts, *
◆ **EMP:** 90 **EST:** 1992
SQ FT: 100,000
SALES (est): 86.1MM
SALES (corp-wide): 1.38B **Publicly Held**
Web: www.prospiant.com
SIC: 1542 3448 Greenhouse construction; Greenhouses, prefabricated metal
HQ: Rough Brothers Holding Co., Inc
   3556 Lake Shore Rd # 100
   Buffalo NY 14219
   716 826-6500

(G-3353)
RPI COLOR SERVICE INC
Also Called: RPI Graphic Data Solutions
1950 Radcliff Dr (45204-1823)
PHONE.................513 471-4040
Patricia A Raker, *Pr*
Karen E Rellar, *Communication Secretary**
Denise L Rellar, *
William E Rellar, *
EMP: 70 **EST:** 1980
SQ FT: 65,000
SALES (est): 9.85MM **Privately Held**
Web: www.rpigraphic.com
SIC: 2752 Offset printing

(G-3354)
RUDD EQUIPMENT COMPANY INC
11807 Enterprise Dr (45241-1511)
PHONE.................513 321-7833
Mike Rudd, *Pr*
EMP: 62
Web: www.ruddequipment.com
SIC: 3462 7699 Construction or mining equipment forgings, ferrous; Industrial machinery and equipment repair
HQ: Rudd Equipment Company, Inc.
   4344 Poplar Level Rd
   Louisville KY 40213
   502 456-4050

GEOGRAPHIC SECTION

Cincinnati - Hamilton County (G-3378)

(G-3355)
RUMPKE TRANSPORTATION CO LLC (HQ)
10795 Hughes Rd (45251-4598)
PHONE.................513 851-0122
William J Rumpke, *Pr*
Phil Wehrman, *CFO*
EMP: 10 **EST:** 1999
SQ FT: 10,000
SALES (est): 93.25MM **Privately Held**
Web: www.rumpke.com
SIC: 3561 5084 7537 4953 Pumps and pumping equipment; Hydraulic systems equipment and supplies; Automotiv e transmission repair shops; Refuse systems
PA: Rumpke Consolidated Companies, Inc.
3990 Generation Dr
Cincinnati OH 45251

(G-3356)
RUMPKE TRANSPORTATION CO LLC
Also Called: Rumpke Container Service
553 Vine St (45202-3105)
PHONE.................513 242-4600
EMP: 263
Web: www.rumpke.com
SIC: 4953 3341 3231 2611 Recycling, waste materials; Secondary nonferrous metals; Products of purchased glass; Pulp mills
HQ: Rumpke Transportation Company, Llc
10795 Hughes Rd
Cincinnati OH 45251
513 851-0122

(G-3357)
RUSSOS RAVIOLI LLC
5950 Montgomery Rd (45213-1610)
PHONE.................513 833-7700
Diane Jennings, *Mgr*
EMP: 15
SALES (corp-wide): 129.21K **Privately Held**
Web: www.russosravioli.com
SIC: 2099 Food preparations, nec
PA: Russo's Ravioli Llc
8338 Gwilada Dr
Cincinnati OH 45236
513 833-7700

(G-3358)
S J ROTH ENTERPRISES INC
900 Kieley Pl (45217-1153)
PHONE.................513 543-1140
Steven Roth, *Pr*
Frank J Roth, *
EMP: 70 **EST:** 1980
SQ FT: 1,200
SALES (est): 5.63MM **Privately Held**
SIC: 3273 Ready-mixed concrete

(G-3359)
SAKRETE INC
5155 Fischer Ave (45217-1157)
PHONE.................513 242-3644
John G Avril, *Ch Bd*
J Craig Avril, *
EMP: 35 **EST:** 1936
SQ FT: 35,000
SALES (est): 3.27MM **Privately Held**
SIC: 3273 6794 Ready-mixed concrete; Patent buying, licensing, leasing

(G-3360)
SAMHAIN PUBLISHING LTD (LLC)
11821 Mason Montgomery Rd # 2 (45249-3705)
PHONE.................513 453-4688
EMP: 9
SALES (est): 932.68K **Privately Held**
SIC: 2741 Miscellaneous publishing

(G-3361)
SAMUEL ADAMS BREWERY COMPANY LTD
1625 Central Pkwy (45214-2423)
PHONE.................513 412-3200
◆ **EMP:** 100
Web: www.samadamscincy.com
SIC: 2082 Beer (alcoholic beverage)

(G-3362)
SANGER & EBY DESIGN LLC
501 Chestnut St (45203-1420)
PHONE.................513 784-9046
Donna Eby, *Pt*
Lisa Sanger, *Pt*
EMP: 16 **EST:** 1988
SQ FT: 6,300
SALES (est): 1.9MM **Privately Held**
Web: www.sangereby.com
SIC: 7336 7372 Graphic arts and related design; Application computer software

(G-3363)
SATURDAY KNIGHT LTD (PA)
Also Called: Skl Home
4330 Winton Rd (45232-1827)
PHONE.................513 641-1400
Frank Kling, *Ch Bd*
Jim Lewis, *Pr*
Dianne Weidman, *VP*
Ed Diller, *Dir*
Bryan Kelley, *CFO*
◆ **EMP:** 100 **EST:** 1975
SQ FT: 450,000
SALES (est): 18.17MM
SALES (corp-wide): 18.17MM **Privately Held**
Web: www.sklhome.com
SIC: 2392 Towels, fabric and nonwoven: made from purchased materials

(G-3364)
SAUERWEIN WELDING
605 Wayne Park Dr (45215-2848)
P.O. Box 15033 (45215-0033)
PHONE.................513 563-2979
Donald Sauerwein, *Pr*
EMP: 7 **EST:** 1964
SQ FT: 5,000
SALES (est): 430K **Privately Held**
Web: www.sauerweinwelding.com
SIC: 7692 Welding repair

(G-3365)
SB TRANS LLC
300 E Business Way Ste 200 (45241)
PHONE.................407 477-2545
EMP: 10 **EST:** 2018
SALES (est): 1.02MM **Privately Held**
SIC: 3537 Trucks: freight, baggage, etc.: industrial, except mining

(G-3366)
SCALLYWAG TAG
5055 Glencrossing Way (45238-3362)
PHONE.................513 922-4999
James Leopold, *Owner*
EMP: 6 **EST:** 2008
SALES (est): 170.23K **Privately Held**
Web: www.scallywagtag.com
SIC: 3845 Laser systems and equipment, medical

(G-3367)
SCHAAF CO INC
2440 Spring Grove Ave (45214-1755)
PHONE.................513 241-7044
TOLL FREE: 800

Walter A Smith, *Pr*
Chuck Smith, *VP*
Barb Meeks, *Sec*
EMP: 9 **EST:** 1928
SQ FT: 6,500
SALES (est): 493.04K **Privately Held**
Web: www.schaafcincy.com
SIC: 2394 Awnings, fabric: made from purchased materials

(G-3368)
SCHAERER MEDICAL USA INC
675 Wilmer Ave (45226-1802)
P.O. Box 645110 (45264-0301)
PHONE.................513 561-2241
Michal Palazzola, *CEO*
William Tobler, *Sec*
Mark D Budde, *CEO*
Hans Rudolf Saegesser, *Ch Bd*
Jan Osborne, *Prin*
▲ **EMP:** 11 **EST:** 1965
SQ FT: 100,000
SALES (est): 2.78MM **Privately Held**
Web: www.schaerermayfieldusa.com
SIC: 5999 3842 Medical apparatus and supplies; Surgical appliances and supplies

(G-3369)
SCHENZ THEATRICAL SUPPLY INC
2959 Colerain Ave (45225-2103)
PHONE.................513 542-6100
John J Schenz, *Pr*
EMP: 10 **EST:** 1967
SQ FT: 15,000
SALES (est): 151.67K **Privately Held**
Web: www.schenz.com
SIC: 2389 5999 7922 Theatrical costumes; Theatrical equipment and supplies; Equipment rental, theatrical

(G-3370)
SCOTT MODELS INC
607 Redna Ter Ste 400 (45215-1183)
PHONE.................513 771-8005
Thomas Scott, *Pr*
EMP: 15 **EST:** 1974
SQ FT: 10,000
SALES (est): 1MM **Privately Held**
Web: www.scottmodels.com
SIC: 3999 Models, except toy

(G-3371)
SCS CONSTRUCTION SERVICES INC
2130 Western Ave (45214-1744)
PHONE.................513 929-0260
Jerry Back, *Pr*
Larry Back, *
EMP: 25 **EST:** 2000
SQ FT: 8,000
SALES (est): 10.01MM **Privately Held**
Web: www.scscincinnati.com
SIC: 1542 3231 1761 3449 Commercial and office building, new construction; Doors, glass: made from purchased glass; Skylight installation; Curtain walls for buildings, steel

(G-3372)
SDI INDUSTRIES
8561 New England Ct (45236-2093)
PHONE.................513 561-4032
Edward Boll, *Prin*
EMP: 6 **EST:** 2010
SALES (est): 178.85K **Privately Held**
Web: www.sdi.systems
SIC: 3999 Manufacturing industries, nec

(G-3373)
SEALTRON INC
9705 Reading Rd (45215-3515)
PHONE.................513 733-8400
Andy Goldfarb, *Pr*

Christopher Bateman, *
EMP: 144 **EST:** 1971
SQ FT: 38,000
SALES (est): 13.8MM
SALES (corp-wide): 6.6B **Publicly Held**
SIC: 3823 Process control instruments
PA: Ametek, Inc.
1100 Cassatt Rd
Berwyn PA 19312
610 647-2121

(G-3374)
SECURITY FENCE GROUP INC (PA)
4260 Dane Ave (45223-1855)
PHONE.................513 681-3700
Christine Frankenstein, *CEO*
Christine Frankenstein, *Pr*
George Frankenstein, *
Angela Case, *
EMP: 37 **EST:** 1960
SQ FT: 140,000
SALES (est): 18.5MM **Privately Held**
Web: www.sfence.com
SIC: 1611 1799 5039 1731 Guardrail construction, highways; Fence construction; Wire fence, gates, and accessories; General electrical contractor

(G-3375)
SEEMLESS PRINTING LLC
717 Linn St (45203-1703)
PHONE.................513 871-2366
Alicia Wilhelmy, *Pt*
EMP: 6 **EST:** 2002
SALES (est): 500.95K **Privately Held**
Web: www.seemlessprinting.com
SIC: 2752 Offset printing

(G-3376)
SEILKOP INDUSTRIES INC
Also Called: Hitech Shapes & Designs
7211 Market Pl (45216-2020)
PHONE.................513 679-5680
Ken Seilkop, *Owner*
EMP: 10
SALES (corp-wide): 19.44MM **Privately Held**
Web: www.seilkopindustries.com
SIC: 3543 3369 3365 3363 Foundry patternmaking; Nonferrous foundries, nec; Aluminum foundries; Aluminum die-castings
PA: Seilkop Industries, Inc.
425 W North Bend Rd
Cincinnati OH 45216
513 761-1035

(G-3377)
SEILKOP INDUSTRIES INC (PA)
Also Called: Epcor Foundries
425 W North Bend Rd (45216-1731)
PHONE.................513 761-1035
Dave Seilkop, *Pr*
Ken Seilkop, *
Robin Vogel, *
EMP: 50 **EST:** 1946
SQ FT: 35,000
SALES (est): 19.44MM
SALES (corp-wide): 19.44MM **Privately Held**
Web: www.seilkopindustries.com
SIC: 3363 3544 3553 3469 Aluminum die-castings; Special dies and tools; Pattern makers' machinery, woodworking; Patterns on metal

(G-3378)
SELBY SERVICE/ROXY PRESS INC
2020 Elm St (45202-4911)
PHONE.................513 241-3445
Clarence Stricker, *Ch Bd*
Robert Stricker, *Pr*

Cincinnati - Hamilton County (G-3379)

Loretta Stricker, *Treas*
Jeanne Meinzen, *Sec*
Bob Furnish, *VP*
EMP: 6 **EST:** 1938
SALES (est): 466.43K **Privately Held**
SIC: 2752 7331 2759 Offset printing; Addressographing service; Letterpress printing

(G-3379)
SENIOR IMPACT PUBLICATIONS LLC
5980 Kugler Mill Rd (45236-2075)
PHONE.................513 791-8800
Robert Jutze, *Pr*
EMP: 10 **EST:** 1997
SALES (est): 500.68K **Privately Held**
Web: www.seniorimpact.com
SIC: 2741 Miscellaneous publishing

(G-3380)
SENNECA HOLDINGS INC (HQ)
Also Called: Door Engineering and Mfg
11502 Century Blvd (45246-3305)
PHONE.................800 543-4455
Robert G Isaman, *CEO*
Jeffrey Stark, *
Michael Rubiera, *CCO*
Karl Adrian, *
Pat Mcmullen, *CFO*
EMP: 20 **EST:** 2010
SALES (est): 65.96MM
SALES (corp-wide): 448.01MM **Privately Held**
Web: www.senneca.com
SIC: 3442 Metal doors, sash, and trim
PA: Kohlberg & Co., L.L.C.
111 Radio Circle Dr
Mount Kisco NY 10549
914 241-5190

(G-3381)
SENSE DIAGNOSTICS INC
1776 Mentor Ave Ste 426 (45212-3583)
PHONE.................513 702-0376
Geoff Klass, *CEO*
Dan Kincaid, *COO*
Matt Flaherty, *CCO*
Ope Adeoye, *CMO*
EMP: 9 **EST:** 2013
SALES (est): 147.95K **Privately Held**
Web: www.senseneuro.com
SIC: 3841 Diagnostic apparatus, medical

(G-3382)
SENSORY ROBOTICS INC
9711 Winton Hills Ln (45215-2059)
PHONE.................513 545-9501
Chris Edwards, *CEO*
EMP: 7 **EST:** 2020
SALES (est): 469.55K **Privately Held**
Web: www.sensoryrobotics.com
SIC: 3569 Robots, assembly line: industrial and commercial

(G-3383)
SERVATII INC
3774 Paxton Ave (45209-2306)
PHONE.................513 271-5040
EMP: 9
SALES (corp-wide): 14.87MM **Privately Held**
Web: www.servatii.com
SIC: 2051 Bread, cake, and related products
PA: Servatii, Inc.
3888 Virginia Ave
Cincinnati OH 45227
513 271-5040

(G-3384)
SESH COMMUNICATIONS
Also Called: N J E M A Magazine
3440 Burnet Ave Ste 130 (45229-2857)
PHONE.................513 851-1693
EMP: 15 **EST:** 1998
SALES (est): 863.37K **Privately Held**
Web: www.thecincinnatiherald.com
SIC: 2711 2721 Newspapers, publishing and printing; Periodicals

(G-3385)
SETCO INDUSTRIES INC
5880 Hillside Ave (45233-1524)
PHONE.................513 941-5110
Jeff Clark, *CEO*
EMP: 40 **EST:** 2017
SALES (est): 3.93MM **Privately Held**
Web: www.setco.com
SIC: 3545 Machine tool accessories

(G-3386)
SHARPS VALET PARKING SVC INC
11650 Greenhaven Ct (45251-4211)
PHONE.................574 223-5230
Dennis M Packer, *Prin*
EMP: 7 **EST:** 1999
SALES (est): 164.33K **Privately Held**
SIC: 1442 Construction sand and gravel

(G-3387)
SHAWNEE SYSTEMS INC
4221 Brandonmore Dr (45255-3656)
P.O. Box 1446 (30009-1446)
PHONE.................513 561-9932
▲ **EMP:** 57
Web: www.shawneesystems.com
SIC: 2761 2752 Manifold business forms; Commercial printing, lithographic

(G-3388)
SIDEWAY SIGNS LLC
4842 Hanley Rd (45247-3537)
PHONE.................501 400-4013
Edward Kutz, *Ofcr*
EMP: 7 **EST:** 2021
SALES (est): 46.08K **Privately Held**
Web: www.sidewaysigns.com
SIC: 3993 Signs and advertising specialties

(G-3389)
SIEBTECHNIK TEMA INC
7806 Redsky Dr (45249-1632)
PHONE.................513 489-7811
EMP: 17 **EST:** 2019
SALES (est): 172.85K **Privately Held**
Web: www.siebtechnik-tema.com
SIC: 3089 Plastics products, nec

(G-3390)
SIEBTECHNIK TEMA INC
7806 Redsky Dr (45249-1632)
PHONE.................513 489-7811
Michael Mullins, *Pr*
J Neal Gardner, *
▲ **EMP:** 26 **EST:** 1977
SQ FT: 15,000
SALES (est): 20.16MM
SALES (corp-wide): 466.88MM **Privately Held**
SIC: 3599 3589 3532 3569 Custom machinery; Commercial cooking and foodwarming equipment; Mineral beneficiation equipment; Centrifuges, industrial
HQ: Siebtechnik Gmbh
Platanenallee 46
Mulheim An Der Ruhr NW 45478
208580100

(G-3391)
SIGMATEK SYSTEMS LLC (HQ)
Also Called: Sigma T E K
1445 Kemper Meadow Dr (45240-1637)
PHONE.................513 674-0005
Ben Terreblanche, *CEO*
EMP: 65 **EST:** 1993
SQ FT: 23,000
SALES (est): 26.66MM
SALES (corp-wide): 11.77B **Privately Held**
Web: www.sigmanest.com
SIC: 7372 Prepackaged software
PA: Sandvik Ab
Hogbovagen 45
Sandviken 811 3
26260000

(G-3392)
SIGNALYSIS INC
539 Glenrose Ln (45244-1509)
PHONE.................513 528-6164
Robert Neil Coleman, *Pr*
Kyle Coleman, *VP*
Phil Wilkin, *Stockholder*
EMP: 12 **EST:** 1987
SALES (est): 2.69MM **Privately Held**
Web: www.signalysis.com
SIC: 8711 7371 3695 7389 Consulting engineer; Computer software development and applications; Computer software tape and disks: blank, rigid, and floppy; Business services, nec

(G-3393)
SIMPLEVMS LLC
7373 Beechmont Ave Ste 130 (45230-4100)
PHONE.................888 255-8918
Jason Oswald, *Pr*
EMP: 19 **EST:** 2011
SALES (est): 3.76MM **Privately Held**
Web: www.simplevms.com
SIC: 7372 7371 8742 8748 Business oriented computer software; Computer software development and applications; Human resource consulting services; Business consulting, nec
PA: Avionte, Llc
4300 Marketpointe Dr # 250
Minneapolis MN 55435

(G-3394)
SIMPLY UNIQUE SNACKS LLC
4420 Haight Ave (45223-1705)
PHONE.................513 223-7736
Steve Hofford, *Pr*
EMP: 6 **EST:** 2014
SALES (est): 330K
SALES (corp-wide): 1.1MM **Privately Held**
Web: www.simplyuniquesnacks.com
SIC: 2013 2037 2068 7389 Snack sticks, including jerky: from purchased meat; Fruit juices, frozen; Salted and roasted nuts and seeds; Business Activities at Non-Commercial Site
PA: United Snacks Of America Llc
42 Phipps Ln
Plainview NY 11803
516 319-9448

(G-3395)
SIMS-LOHMAN INC (PA)
Also Called: Sims-Lohman Fine Kitchens Gran
6325 Este Ave (45232)
PHONE.................513 651-3510
Steve Steinman, *CEO*
John Beiersdorfer, *
▲ **EMP:** 50 **EST:** 1974
SQ FT: 153,000
SALES (est): 96.65MM
SALES (corp-wide): 96.65MM **Privately Held**
Web: www.sims-lohman.com
SIC: 2435 5031 Hardwood veneer and plywood; Kitchen cabinets

(G-3396)
SK TEXTILE INC
Also Called: Sk
1 Knollcrest Dr (45237-1608)
PHONE.................800 888-9112
Kim Morris Heiman, *Pr*
▲ **EMP:** 105 **EST:** 1986
SALES (est): 4.66MM **Privately Held**
Web: www.standardtextile.com
SIC: 2391 2211 Curtains and draperies; Bedspreads, cotton

(G-3397)
SMALL BUSINESS PRODUCTS
8603 Winton Rd (45231-4816)
P.O. Box 297257 (33029-7257)
PHONE.................800 333-0483
Brandi Pedersen, *Prin*
EMP: 6 **EST:** 2011
SALES (est): 168.59K **Privately Held**
Web: www.smallbusinessproducts.com
SIC: 3577 Printers and plotters

(G-3398)
SMITH ELECTRO CHEMICAL CO
5936 Carthage Ct (45212-1103)
PHONE.................513 351-7227
Donald W Kifer, *Pr*
Robert Kifer, *
EMP: 26 **EST:** 1948
SQ FT: 25,000
SALES (est): 580.67K **Privately Held**
Web: www.smithelectrochemical.com
SIC: 3471 Electroplating of metals or formed products

(G-3399)
SMITHFIELD PACKAGED MEATS CORP (DH)
805 E Kemper Rd (45246-2515)
P.O. Box 405020 (45240-5020)
PHONE.................513 782-3800
Joseph B Sebring, *Pr*
Mike Corbett, *
Mark Dorsey, *
◆ **EMP:** 125 **EST:** 1957
SQ FT: 10,000
SALES (est): 1.72B **Privately Held**
SIC: 2011 Pork products, from pork slaughtered on site
HQ: Smithfield Foods, Inc.
200 Commerce St
Smithfield VA 23430
757 365-3000

(G-3400)
SOFFSEAL INC
11735 Chesterdale Rd (45246-3405)
PHONE.................513 934-0815
Gary Anderson, *Pr*
Donna Anderson, *Sec*
▲ **EMP:** 26 **EST:** 1973
SALES (est): 2.54MM
SALES (corp-wide): 2.54MM **Privately Held**
Web: www.soffseal.com
SIC: 3069 3061 3053 Rubber automotive products; Mechanical rubber goods; Gaskets; packing and sealing devices
PA: Alp Usa, Inc.
545 Johnson Ave Ste 4
Bohemia NY 11716
800 448-5188

Cincinnati - Hamilton County (G-3425)

(G-3401)
SOLID SURFACE CONCEPTS INC
7660 Production Dr (45237-3209)
P.O. Box 43335 (45243-0335)
PHONE..................................513 948-8677
Rob Butler, *Pr*
Kenneth Granger, *
Bill Butler, *
Steve Butler, *
EMP: 24 **EST:** 1989
SQ FT: 6,956
SALES (est): 1.94MM **Privately Held**
Web: www.solidsurfaceconcepts.com
SIC: 2431 3281 2541 1411 Millwork; Cut stone and stone products; Wood partitions and fixtures; Dimension stone

(G-3402)
SOLO PRODUCTS INC
838 Reedy St (45202-2216)
PHONE..................................513 321-7884
Steve Kunkemoeller, *CEO*
Doug Hearn, *CFO*
EMP: 12 **EST:** 1987
SALES (est): 3.03MM **Privately Held**
Web: www.soloproductsandcontainers.com
SIC: 5085 3086 Rubber goods, mechanical; Carpet and rug cushions, foamed plastics

(G-3403)
SOUTHERN GRAPHIC SYSTEMS LLC
9435 Waterstone Blvd Ste 300 (45249-8226)
PHONE..................................513 648-4641
Kerri Randolph, *Brnch Mgr*
EMP: 21
SALES (corp-wide): 998.42MM **Privately Held**
Web: www.sgsco.com
SIC: 2796 Platemaking services
HQ: Southern Graphic Systems, Llc
626 W Main St Ste 500
Louisville KY 40202
502 637-5443

(G-3404)
SOUTHERN OHIO PRINTING
2230 Gilbert Ave (45206-2531)
PHONE..................................513 241-5150
Robert Van Lear, *Owner*
EMP: 7 **EST:** 1998
SALES (est): 477.84K **Privately Held**
SIC: 2752 Offset printing

(G-3405)
SPECIALTY LITHOGRAPHING CO
1035 W 7th St (45203-1285)
PHONE..................................513 621-0222
Elmer A Babey, *CEO*
Mark Babey, *Pr*
James Babey, *VP*
Carol Evans, *Sec*
EMP: 17 **EST:** 1947
SQ FT: 20,000
SALES (est): 1.69MM **Privately Held**
Web: www.specialtylitho.com
SIC: 2752 Offset printing

(G-3406)
SPECTEX LLC
6156 Wesselman Rd (45248-1204)
PHONE..................................603 330-3334
Kelley Mckenzie, *Admn*
EMP: 17 **EST:** 2001
SALES (est): 2.1MM **Privately Held**
Web: www.sur-seal.com
SIC: 3554 Die cutting and stamping machinery, paper converting

(G-3407)
SPEEDPRO IMAGING
2888 E Kemper Rd (45241-1820)
PHONE..................................513 771-4776
Dave Sperry, *Prin*
EMP: 7 **EST:** 2006
SALES (est): 512.32K **Privately Held**
Web: www.speedpro.com
SIC: 3993 Signs and advertising specialties

(G-3408)
SPIKES BEVERAGE COMPANY INC
245 Northland Blvd Unit D (45246-8601)
PHONE..................................513 429-5134
Erik Murphy, *Dir*
Brian Gettelfinger, *Prin*
EMP: 9 **EST:** 2020
SALES (est): 133.41K **Privately Held**
SIC: 3699 Electrical equipment and supplies, nec

(G-3409)
SPORTSCO IMPRINTING
8277 Wicklow Ave (45236-1613)
PHONE..................................513 641-5111
Joe Eigel, *Pt*
Eric Kattus, *Pt*
EMP: 8 **EST:** 1993
SQ FT: 1,800
SALES (est): 423.62K **Privately Held**
SIC: 2262 2395 Screen printing: manmade fiber and silk broadwoven fabrics; Emblems, embroidered

(G-3410)
SPRING GROVE MANUFACTURING INC
Also Called: Cinncinati Bindery
2838 Spring Grove Ave (45225-2268)
PHONE..................................513 542-6900
Jeff Best, *Pr*
EMP: 10 **EST:** 1989
SALES (est): 505.12K **Privately Held**
Web: www.cincybindery.com
SIC: 2789 Binding only: books, pamphlets, magazines, etc.

(G-3411)
SPRINGDOT INC (PA)
Also Called: Springdot
2611 Colerain Ave (45214-1711)
PHONE..................................513 542-4000
Josh Deutsch, *Pr*
Jeff Deutsch, *
John Brenner, *
Thomas Deutsch, *Stockholder**
EMP: 60 **EST:** 1904
SQ FT: 70,000
SALES (est): 11.11MM
SALES (corp-wide): 11.11MM **Privately Held**
Web: www.springdot.com
SIC: 2752 4899 2759 2675 Offset printing; Data communication services; Commercial printing, nec; Die-cut paper and board

(G-3412)
SQUEAKY CLEAN CINCINNATI INC
Also Called: Squeaky Clean Off & Coml Clg
1500 Goodman Ave (45224-1005)
P.O. Box 31055 (45231-0055)
PHONE..................................513 729-2712
Larry Vaughan, *Pr*
EMP: 10 **EST:** 1986
SALES (est): 620K **Privately Held**
Web: floor-cleaning-services.cmac.ws
SIC: 3589 Commercial cleaning equipment

(G-3413)
STAC ENTERPRISES LLC
4211 Marcrest Dr (45211-2329)
PHONE..................................513 574-7822
EMP: 7 **EST:** 2014
SALES (est): 309.09K **Privately Held**
Web: www.staccard.com
SIC: 7372 Prepackaged software

(G-3414)
STANDARD PUBLISHING LLC
8805 Governors Hill Dr Ste 400 (45249-3314)
PHONE..................................513 931-4050
▲ **EMP:** 200 **EST:** 2004
SALES (est): 43.18MM **Privately Held**
Web: www.standardpub.com
SIC: 2721 Magazines: publishing only, not printed on site
PA: Cfm Religion Publishing Group Llc
8805 Governors Hill Dr # 40
Cincinnati OH 45249

(G-3415)
STANDARD TEXTILE CO INC (PA)
Also Called: Pridecraft Enterprises
1 Knollcrest Dr (45237-1608)
P.O. Box 371805 (45222-1805)
PHONE..................................513 761-9255
Gary Heiman, *CEO*
Alex Heiman, *
Edward Frankel, *CAO**
Norman Frankel, *SALES**
Chris Bopp, *CIO**
◆ **EMP:** 300 **EST:** 1940
SQ FT: 150,000
SALES (est): 393.56MM
SALES (corp-wide): 393.56MM **Privately Held**
Web: www.standardtextile.com
SIC: 2299 7389 5023 Linen fabrics; Textile designers; Linens and towels

(G-3416)
STARKS PLASTICS LLC
11236 Sebring Dr (45240-2715)
PHONE..................................513 541-4591
EMP: 10 **EST:** 1993
SQ FT: 1,400
SALES (est): 1.02MM **Privately Held**
Web: www.starksplastics.com
SIC: 3089 5046 Plastics processing; Store fixtures

(G-3417)
STARR SERVICES INC
3625 Spring Grove Ave (45223-2458)
PHONE..................................513 241-7708
Robert Meade, *Pr*
EMP: 7 **EST:** 1975
SQ FT: 5,000
SALES (est): 459.82K **Privately Held**
Web: www.starrprinting.net
SIC: 2752 2759 Offset printing; Letterpress printing

(G-3418)
STEEL IT LLC
250 Mccullough St (45226)
PHONE..................................513 253-3111
Craig Freeman, *Managing Member**
EMP: 34 **EST:** 2015
SALES (est): 6.34MM **Privately Held**
SIC: 3441 Fabricated structural metal

(G-3419)
STEEL QUEST INC
8180 Corporate Park Dr Ste 250 (45242)
PHONE..................................513 772-5000
Matthew S Kuhnell, *Pr*
EMP: 9 **EST:** 1993
SQ FT: 3,500
SALES (est): 4.68MM **Privately Held**
Web: www.steelquest.com
SIC: 3441 Fabricated structural metal

(G-3420)
STEGEMEYER MACHINE INC
212 Mccullough St (45226-2120)
PHONE..................................513 321-5651
Richard Stegemeyer, *Pr*
Deanna Stegemeyer, *Sec*
EMP: 7 **EST:** 1907
SQ FT: 4,500
SALES (est): 506.04K **Privately Held**
SIC: 3599 Machine shop, jobbing and repair

(G-3421)
STELLAR SYSTEMS INC
1944 Harrison Ave (45214-1176)
PHONE..................................513 921-8748
William L Spetz, *Pr*
EMP: 7 **EST:** 1980
SQ FT: 8,000
SALES (est): 757.49K **Privately Held**
Web: www.stellarsystems.com
SIC: 7371 3577 Computer software development; Computer peripheral equipment, nec

(G-3422)
STEVENSON COLOR INC
Also Called: SGS Cincinnati
535 Wilmer Ave (45226-1828)
PHONE..................................513 321-7500
Thomas Stevenson, *Pr*
EMP: 190 **EST:** 1926
SQ FT: 116,800
SALES (est): 45.31MM
SALES (corp-wide): 998.42MM **Privately Held**
Web: www.sgsco.com
SIC: 2796 2752 Color separations, for printing; Commercial printing, lithographic
HQ: Southern Graphic Systems, Llc
626 W Main St Ste 500
Louisville KY 40202
502 637-5443

(G-3423)
STONE STATEMENTS INCORPORATED
7451 Fields Ertel Rd (45241-0003)
PHONE..................................513 489-7866
Douglas R Beyersdoerfer, *Pr*
▲ **EMP:** 8 **EST:** 2004
SALES (est): 1.87MM **Privately Held**
Web: www.stonestatements.com
SIC: 1411 1799 Granite dimension stone; Counter top installation

(G-3424)
STREETPOPS INC
Also Called: Streetpops
4720 Vine St (45217-1267)
PHONE..................................513 446-7505
Sara Bornick, *CEO*
EMP: 7 **EST:** 2011
SALES (est): 231.29K **Privately Held**
Web: www.streetpops.com
SIC: 2024 Fruit pops, frozen

(G-3425)
STUART COMPANY
2160 Patterson St (45214-1844)
PHONE..................................513 621-9462
Philip G Gossard, *CEO*
EMP: 24 **EST:** 1953
SQ FT: 50,000
SALES (est): 463.14K **Privately Held**
Web: www.stuartcompany.net

Cincinnati - Hamilton County (G-3426)

GEOGRAPHIC SECTION

SIC: 2675 Die-cut paper and board

(G-3426)
STUDIO VERTU INC
1208 Central Pkwy # 1 (45202-7509)
PHONE 513 241-9038
◆ EMP: 8 EST: 1995
SQ FT: 18,000
SALES (est): 286.37K Privately Held
Web: www.studiovertu.com
SIC: 3253 3281 Ceramic wall and floor tile; Cut stone and stone products

(G-3427)
SUN CHEMICAL CORPORATION
General Printing Ink Division
12049 Centron Pl (45246-1789)
PHONE 513 671-0407
Pat Myers, Brnch Mgr
EMP: 49
SQ FT: 11,000
Web: www.sunchemical.com
SIC: 2893 2899 Printing ink; Ink or writing fluids
HQ: Sun Chemical Corporation
35 Waterview Blvd Ste 104
Parsippany NJ 07054
973 404-6000

(G-3428)
SUN CHEMICAL CORPORATION
Also Called: Sun Chemical US Rycoline
5020 Spring Grove Ave (45232-1988)
P.O. Box 16097 (45216-0097)
PHONE 513 681-5950
EMP: 27
Web: www.sunchemical.com
SIC: 2893 Printing ink
HQ: Sun Chemical Corporation
35 Waterview Blvd Ste 104
Parsippany NJ 07054
973 404-6000

(G-3429)
SUN CHEMICAL CORPORATION
Kohl & Madden Printing Ink Div
5020 Spring Grove Ave (45232-1988)
P.O. Box 32040 (45232-0040)
PHONE 513 681-5950
Lou Schulte, Mgr
EMP: 39
Web: www.sunchemical.com
SIC: 2893 Printing ink
HQ: Sun Chemical Corporation
35 Waterview Blvd Ste 104
Parsippany NJ 07054
973 404-6000

(G-3430)
SUN CHEMICAL CORPORATION
5000 Spring Grove Ave (45232-1926)
PHONE 513 830-8667
EMP: 46
Web: www.sunchemical.com
SIC: 2893 2865 Printing ink; Dyes and pigments
HQ: Sun Chemical Corporation
35 Waterview Blvd Ste 104
Parsippany NJ 07054
973 404-6000

(G-3431)
SUN CHEMICAL CORPORATION
Also Called: Pigments Division
4526 Chickering Ave (45232-1935)
PHONE 513 681-5950
Brian Leen, Brnch Mgr
EMP: 210
SQ FT: 91,671
Web: www.sunchemical.com
SIC: 2816 2865 Inorganic pigments; Cyclic crudes and intermediates
HQ: Sun Chemical Corporation
35 Waterview Blvd Ste 104
Parsippany NJ 07054
973 404-6000

(G-3432)
SUPER SYSTEMS INC (PA)
7205 Edington Dr (45249-1064)
PHONE 513 772-0060
EMP: 32 EST: 1993
SQ FT: 5,000
SALES (est): 9.9MM Privately Held
Web: www.supersystems.com
SIC: 3829 5084 Measuring and controlling devices, nec; Industrial machinery and equipment

(G-3433)
SUPERIOR PROPERTY RESTORATION
Also Called: Remodeling
2144 Schappelle Ln (45240-4602)
PHONE 513 509-6849
Roy Payne, Pr
EMP: 12 EST: 2000
SALES (est): 799.78K Privately Held
Web: www.superiorpropertyrestoration.com
SIC: 1389 1521 Construction, repair, and dismantling services; Single-family home remodeling, additions, and repairs

(G-3434)
SUR-SEAL LLC (PA)
6156 Wesselman Rd (45248-1204)
PHONE 513 574-8500
Dana Waterman, CEO
◆ EMP: 135 EST: 1965
SQ FT: 67,000
SALES (est): 115.03MM
SALES (corp-wide): 115.03MM Privately Held
Web: www.sur-seal.com
SIC: 3053 3069 Gaskets, all materials; Molded rubber products

(G-3435)
SURFACE ENHANCEMENT TECH LLC
3929 Virginia Ave (45227-3411)
PHONE 513 561-1520
EMP: 17 EST: 2000
SQ FT: 28,000
SALES (est): 2.01MM Privately Held
Web: www.lambdatechs.com
SIC: 3398 Brazing (hardening) of metal

(G-3436)
SURGICAL APPLIANCE INDS INC (PA)
3960 Rosslyn Dr (45209-1195)
PHONE 513 271-4594
L Thomas Applegate, Pr
▲ EMP: 200 EST: 1893
SQ FT: 225,000
SALES (est): 43.18MM
SALES (corp-wide): 43.18MM Privately Held
Web: www.saibrands.com
SIC: 3842 Surgical appliances and supplies

(G-3437)
SWEETS AND MEATS LLC
Also Called: Sweets & Meats Bbq
2249 Beechmont Ave (45230-5318)
PHONE 513 888-4227
Kristen Bailey, CEO
EMP: 12 EST: 2014

SALES (est): 600.53K Privately Held
Web: www.sweetsandmeatsbbq.com
SIC: 5812 2599 Restaurant, family: independent; Food wagons, restaurant

(G-3438)
T-N-T RGULATORY COMPLIANCE INC
731 Dorgene Ln (45244-1069)
PHONE 513 442-2464
Billy Tollett, Pr
EMP: 6 EST: 2017
SALES (est): 80.34K Privately Held
SIC: 1382 Oil and gas exploration services

(G-3439)
T-SHIRT CO
413 Northland Blvd (45240-3210)
PHONE 513 821-7100
EMP: 23 EST: 2017
SALES (est): 118.5K Privately Held
Web: www.cincytshirts.com
SIC: 2759 Screen printing

(G-3440)
TAMARRON TECHNOLOGY INC
8044 Montgomery Rd (45236-2919)
PHONE 800 277-3207
John Gill, VP
EMP: 10 EST: 2007
SQ FT: 4,000
SALES (est): 929.4K Privately Held
Web: www.tamarrontechnology.biz
SIC: 3272 5032 Building materials, except block or brick: concrete; Concrete building products

(G-3441)
TAMBRANDS SALES CORP (HQ)
Also Called: Tampax
1 Procter And Gamble Plz (45202-3315)
PHONE 513 983-1100
Wolfgang C Berndt, Pr
Erik G Nelson, VP Fin
▲ EMP: 130 EST: 1936
SQ FT: 100,000
SALES (est): 166.23MM
SALES (corp-wide): 82.01B Publicly Held
Web: www.tampax.com
SIC: 2676 Tampons, sanitary: made from purchased paper
PA: The Procter & Gamble Company
1 Procter & Gamble Plz
Cincinnati OH 45202
513 983-1100

(G-3442)
TAYLOR & MOORE CO
807 Wachendorf St (45215-4743)
PHONE 513 733-5530
George R Taylor Prestreas, Prin
George R Taylor, Pr
EMP: 25 EST: 1991
SQ FT: 11,898
SALES (est): 482.61K Privately Held
SIC: 3585 Air conditioning units, complete: domestic or industrial

(G-3443)
TECHNO ADHESIVES CO
12113 Mosteller Rd (45241-1591)
PHONE 513 771-1584
EMP: 6 EST: 1965
SALES (est): 2MM Privately Held
Web: www.technoadhesives.com
SIC: 2891 Adhesives

(G-3444)
TERRACOTTA INDUSTRIES LLC
5517 Fair Ln (45227-3401)

PHONE 513 313-6215
EMP: 6 EST: 2013
SALES (est): 128.44K Privately Held
Web: www.terracotta-industries.com
SIC: 3999 Manufacturing industries, nec

(G-3445)
TESTLINK USA INC
11445 Century Cir W (45246-3303)
PHONE 513 272-1081
Greg Hughes, CEO
Nick Beer, Ch
Simon Yeomans, Pr
EMP: 22 EST: 2013
SALES (est): 1.82MM Privately Held
Web: www.testlinkusa.com
SIC: 3578 Automatic teller machines (ATM)

(G-3446)
TEVA WOMENS HEALTH LLC (DH)
5040 Duramed Rd (45213-2520)
PHONE 513 731-9900
Druss L Downey, Prin
Lawrence A Glassman,
Timothy J Holt, *
EMP: 250 EST: 1982
SQ FT: 28,200
SALES (est): 113.88MM Privately Held
Web: www.duramed.com
SIC: 5122 2834 7389 Patent medicines; Pharmaceutical preparations; Packaging and labeling services
HQ: Teva Pharmaceuticals Usa, Inc.
400 Interpace Pkwy Bldg A
Parsippany NJ 07054
215 591-3000

(G-3447)
TH MAGNESIUM INC
9435 Waterstone Blvd Ste 290 (45249-8226)
PHONE 513 285-7568
Stephen Norris, Pr
Oliver Haun, VP Sls
EMP: 6 EST: 2015
SALES (est): 677.13K Privately Held
SIC: 3356 Magnesium

(G-3448)
THE F L EMMERT CO INC
Also Called: Emmert Grains
2007 Dunlap St (45214-2309)
PHONE 513 721-5808
EMP: 18 EST: 1881
SALES (est): 4.41MM Privately Held
Web: www.emmert.com
SIC: 2048 Prepared feeds, nec

(G-3449)
THE KORDENBROCK TOOL AND DIE CO
10250 Wayne Ave (45215-2299)
PHONE 513 326-4390
EMP: 12 EST: 1953
SALES (est): 1.63MM Privately Held
Web: www.kordenbrocktoolanddie.com
SIC: 3544 3469 3599 Special dies and tools; Stamping metal for the trade; Electrical discharge machining (EDM)

(G-3450)
THE PHOTO-TYPE ENGRAVING COMPANY (PA)
Also Called: Olberding Brand Family
2141 Gilbert Ave (45206-3021)
PHONE 513 281-0999
EMP: 60 EST: 1919
SALES (est): 43.97MM
SALES (corp-wide): 43.97MM Privately Held

GEOGRAPHIC SECTION
Cincinnati - Hamilton County (G-3475)

Web: www.phototype.com
SIC: **2754** 7336 7335 2796 Commercial printing, gravure; Commercial art and graphic design; Commercial photography; Platemaking services

(G-3451)
THERMO FISHER SCIENTIFIC INC
2110 E Galbraith Rd (45237-1625)
PHONE..................................800 955-6288
EMP: 8
SALES (corp-wide): 44.91B **Publicly Held**
Web: www.thermofisher.com
SIC: **3826** Analytical instruments
PA: Thermo Fisher Scientific Inc.
 168 3rd Ave
 Waltham MA 02451
 781 622-1000

(G-3452)
THIS IS L INC
1100 Sycamore St Ste 300 (45202-1376)
PHONE..................................415 630-5172
Talia Frenkel, *CEO*
EMP: 7 **EST:** 2011
SALES (est): 1.92MM
SALES (corp-wide): 82.01B **Publicly Held**
Web: www.thisisl.com
SIC: **2676** Tampons, sanitary: made from purchased paper
PA: The Procter & Gamble Company
 1 Procter & Gamble Plz
 Cincinnati OH 45202
 513 983-1100

(G-3453)
THOMAS PRODUCTS CO INC (PA)
3625 Spring Grove Ave (45223-2458)
PHONE..................................513 756-9009
Joseph Thomas, *CEO*
Paul Cecil Green, *Pr*
EMP: 25 **EST:** 1959
SQ FT: 25,000
SALES (est): 2.14MM
SALES (corp-wide): 2.14MM **Privately Held**
SIC: **2759** 3842 2761 2672 Flexographic printing; Surgical appliances and supplies; Manifold business forms; Paper; coated and laminated, nec

(G-3454)
TI MARIE CANDLE COMPANY LLC
311 Elm St Ste 270 (45202-2781)
PHONE..................................513 746-7798
Kimberly Jenkins, *CEO*
EMP: 12 **EST:** 2020
SALES (est): 469.31K **Privately Held**
Web: www.timariecandleco.com
SIC: **3999** 7389 Candles; Business Activities at Non-Commercial Site

(G-3455)
TIRES PLUS 7061
11994 Chase Plz (45240-1938)
PHONE..................................513 851-1900
Tony Micheal, *Prin*
EMP: 6 **EST:** 2010
SALES (est): 115.03K **Privately Held**
Web: local.tiresplus.com
SIC: **7534** Tire retreading and repair shops

(G-3456)
TITANIUM CONTRACTORS LTD
9400 Reading Rd (45215-3401)
PHONE..................................513 256-2152
Michael Postell, *Prin*
EMP: 8 **EST:** 2011
SALES (est): 223.94K **Privately Held**
SIC: **3356** Titanium

(G-3457)
TKF CONVEYOR SYSTEMS LLC
5298 River Rd (45233-1643)
PHONE..................................513 621-5260
EMP: 110 **EST:** 2011
SALES (est): 13.61MM **Privately Held**
Web: www.tkf.com
SIC: **3535** Conveyors and conveying equipment

(G-3458)
TPF INC
313 S Wayne Ave (45215-4522)
P.O. Box 15171 (45215-0171)
PHONE..................................513 761-9968
Charles Stiens, *Pr*
Robert Stiens, *Ch*
Kenneth Stiens, *VP*
Charlotte Stiens, *Sec*
EMP: 8 **EST:** 1969
SQ FT: 2,400
SALES (est): 849.41K **Privately Held**
Web: www.tpftherm.com
SIC: **3823** 7699 Thermometers, filled system: industrial process type; Industrial machinery and equipment repair

(G-3459)
TRANE TECHNOLOGIES COMPANY LLC
Also Called: Ingersoll-Rand
10300 Springfield Pike (45215-1118)
PHONE..................................513 459-4580
Brandon Gibbons, *Mgr*
EMP: 22
SQ FT: 10,000
Web: www.tranetechnologies.com
SIC: **3561** Pumps and pumping equipment
HQ: Ingersoll-Rand Industrial U.S., Inc.
 800 Beaty St Ste E
 Davidson NC 28036
 704 655-4000

(G-3460)
TRANE US INC
Also Called: Trane
10300 Springfield Pike (45215-1118)
PHONE..................................513 771-8884
Al Fullerton, *Mgr*
EMP: 71
Web: www.trane.com
SIC: **3585** Refrigeration and heating equipment
HQ: Trane U.S. Inc.
 800 Beaty St Ste E
 Davidson NC 28036
 704 655-4000

(G-3461)
TRANS ASH INC
Also Called: Gibbco
360 S Wayne Ave (45215-4523)
PHONE..................................859 341-1528
Brian Keplinger, *Mgr*
EMP: 10
SALES (corp-wide): 776.44MM **Privately Held**
Web: www.transash.com
SIC: **3295** Slag, crushed or ground
HQ: Trans Ash, Inc.
 617 Shepherd Dr
 Cincinnati OH 45215
 513 733-4770

(G-3462)
TRANSDUCERS DIRECT LLC
Also Called: Transducers Direct
12115 Ellington Ct (45249-1000)
PHONE..................................513 247-0601
◆ **EMP:** 16 **EST:** 1999
SALES (est): 3.96MM **Privately Held**
Web: www.transducersdirect.com
SIC: **3543** 5084 Industrial patterns; Industrial machine parts

(G-3463)
TREVED EXTERIORS
10235 Spartan Dr Ste T (45215-1243)
PHONE..................................513 771-3888
Eddie Oblinger, *Prin*
EMP: 7 **EST:** 2006
SALES (est): 522.06K **Privately Held**
Web: www.trevedexteriors.com
SIC: **2851** Paint removers

(G-3464)
TRI-STATE BEEF CO INC
2124 Baymiller St (45214-2208)
PHONE..................................513 579-1722
Yong Woo Koo, *Pr*
EMP: 11 **EST:** 1980
SALES (est): 576.51K **Privately Held**
SIC: **2011** 2013 5147 Meat packing plants; Sausages and other prepared meats; Meats and meat products

(G-3465)
TRILLIUM HEALTH CARE PRODUCTS
5177 Spring Grove Ave (45217-1050)
PHONE..................................513 242-2227
Alan Gropp, *Brnch Mgr*
EMP: 10
SALES (corp-wide): 109.59MM **Privately Held**
Web: www.trilliumhcp.com
SIC: **2841** Soap: granulated, liquid, cake, flaked, or chip
HQ: Trillium Health Care Products Inc
 2337 Parkdale Ave E
 Brockville ON K6V 5
 613 342-4436

(G-3466)
TRISTATE STEEL CONTRACTORS LLC
2508 Civic Center Dr Ste A (45231-1363)
PHONE..................................513 648-9000
EMP: 8 **EST:** 2004
SALES (est): 913.59K **Privately Held**
Web: www.tscsteel.com
SIC: **3441** Fabricated structural metal

(G-3467)
TROYKE MANUFACTURING COMPANY
11294 Orchard St (45241-1996)
PHONE..................................513 769-4242
Bernard R Froehlich, *Pr*
Eric N Froehlich, *VP*
EMP: 12 **EST:** 1952
SQ FT: 40,000
SALES (est): 2.42MM **Privately Held**
Web: www.troyke.com
SIC: **3545** Machine tool accessories

(G-3468)
TRU-TEX INTERNATIONAL CORP
11050 Southland Rd (45240-3713)
P.O. Box 40107 (45240-0107)
PHONE..................................513 825-8844
Harry G Henn, *Pr*
Ruth Henn, *CEO*
Chrisopher Henn, *VP*
Sandy Whitaker, *Off Mgr*
EMP: 21 **EST:** 1966
SQ FT: 8,000
SALES (est): 2.41MM **Privately Held**
Web: www.trutexint.com
SIC: **3544** Dies and die holders for metal cutting, forming, die casting

(G-3469)
TRUCK CAB MANUFACTURERS INC (PA)
2420 Anderson Ferry Rd (45238-3345)
P.O. Box 58400 (45258-8400)
PHONE..................................513 922-1300
▲ **EMP:** 35 **EST:** 1948
SALES (est): 4.84MM
SALES (corp-wide): 4.84MM **Privately Held**
Web: www.truckcab.com
SIC: **3713** 3441 Truck cabs, for motor vehicles; Fabricated structural metal

(G-3470)
TRUE DINERO RECORDS & TECH LLC
2611 Kemper Ln Uppr Level1 (45206-1220)
PHONE..................................513 428-4610
EMP: 8 **EST:** 2012
SALES (est): 274.24K **Privately Held**
Web: truedinerorecords.yolasite.com
SIC: **5735** 7336 2759 2752 Records; Commercial art and graphic design; Laser printing; Offset printing

(G-3471)
TRULOU HOLDINGS INC
5311 Robert Ave Ste A (45248-7200)
PHONE..................................513 347-0100
EMP: 22 **EST:** 1995
SQ FT: 12,000
SALES (est): 3.71MM **Privately Held**
Web: www.tristatetoolgrinding.com
SIC: **3599** Machine shop, jobbing and repair

(G-3472)
TS OAK INC
544 Mitchell Way Ct (45238-4783)
PHONE..................................513 252-7241
Adam Lorenz, *Prin*
EMP: 8 **EST:** 2016
SALES (est): 72K **Privately Held**
SIC: **2082** Malt beverages

(G-3473)
TSS ACQUISITION COMPANY
1201 Hill Smith Dr (45215-1228)
PHONE..................................513 772-7000
Bob Queen, *Brnch Mgr*
EMP: 6
SALES (corp-wide): 315.22MM **Privately Held**
Web: www.miqpartners.com
SIC: **3599** Machine shop, jobbing and repair
HQ: Tss Acquisition Company
 8800 Global Way
 West Chester OH

(G-3474)
TULKOFF FOOD PRODUCTS OHIO LLC
3015 E Kemper Rd (45241-1514)
PHONE..................................410 864-0523
Dawn Wade, *Managing Member*
EMP: 6 **EST:** 2020
SALES (est): 509.37K **Privately Held**
Web: www.tulkoff.com
SIC: **2035** Dressings, salad: raw and cooked (except dry mixes)

(G-3475)
TVONE NCSA
Also Called: Tvone Ncsa - N Centl & S Amer
621 Wilmer Ave (45226-1859)
PHONE..................................859 282-7303
EMP: 11 **EST:** 2017
SALES (est): 429.73K **Privately Held**
Web: www.tvone.com

Cincinnati - Hamilton County (G-3476)

SIC: 3651 Electronic kits for home assembly: radio, TV, phonograph

(G-3476)
UNCLE JAYS CAKES LLC
2516 Clifton Ave (45219-1004)
PHONE.................................513 882-3433
EMP: 6 EST: 2021
SALES (est): 221.85K **Privately Held**
SIC: 2051 Cakes, bakery: except frozen

(G-3477)
UNDERGROUND SPORTS SHOP INC
1233 Findlay St Ste Frnt (45214-2049)
PHONE.................................513 751-1662
Sean Mason, *Pr*
Jim Hebert, *Sec*
Andy Wolterman, *VP*
▲ EMP: 10 EST: 1992
SQ FT: 12,000
SALES (est): 1.22MM **Privately Held**
Web: www.undergroundsportsshop.com
SIC: 2759 7389 5199 Screen printing; Embroidery advertising; Advertising specialties

(G-3478)
UNITED - MAIER SIGNS INC
1030 Straight St (45214-1734)
PHONE.................................513 681-6600
Antony E Maier, *Pr*
Elvera Maier, *
EMP: 54 EST: 1964
SQ FT: 18,000
SALES (est): 4.68MM **Privately Held**
Web: www.united-maier.com
SIC: 3993 1799 Electric signs; Sign installation and maintenance

(G-3479)
UNITED DAIRY FARMERS INC (PA)
Also Called: U D F
3955 Montgomery Rd (45212-3798)
PHONE.................................513 396-8700
Brad Lindner, *Pr*
Marilyn Mitchell, *
EMP: 200 EST: 1940
SALES (est): 446.66MM
SALES (corp-wide): 446.66MM **Privately Held**
Web: www.udfinc.com
SIC: 5411 5143 2026 2024 Convenience stores, chain; Ice cream and ices; Milk processing (pasteurizing, homogenizing, bottling); Ice cream and ice milk

(G-3480)
UNITED ENVELOPE LLC
4890 Spring Grove Ave (45232-1933)
PHONE.................................513 542-4700
Stuart Grover, *Brnch Mgr*
EMP: 280
SALES (corp-wide): 113.71MM **Privately Held**
SIC: 2677 Envelopes
HQ: United Envelope, Llc
  65 Railroad Ave
  Ridgefield NJ 07657

(G-3481)
UNITED PRECISION SERVICES INC
Also Called: Union America
11183 Southland Rd (45240-3206)
PHONE.................................513 851-6900
Paul Kramer, *Pr*
▲ EMP: 9 EST: 2001
SQ FT: 10,000
SALES (est): 1.03MM **Privately Held**
Web: www.unitedprecisionservices.com
SIC: 3599 Machine shop, jobbing and repair

(G-3482)
UNITED STATES DRILL HEAD CO
5298 River Rd (45233-1688)
PHONE.................................513 941-0300
J H Nymberg Junior, *Pr*
Joseph E Bashor, *
EMP: 31 EST: 1915
SQ FT: 47,772
SALES (est): 3.88MM **Privately Held**
Web: www.usdrillhead.com
SIC: 3545 3363 3543 Cutting tools for machine tools; Aluminum die-castings; Industrial patterns

(G-3483)
UNIVERSAL PACKG SYSTEMS INC
Also Called: Paklab
470 Northland Blvd (45240-3211)
PHONE.................................513 674-9400
Jeff Topits, *Brnch Mgr*
EMP: 158
SALES (corp-wide): 379.38MM **Privately Held**
Web: www.paklab.com
SIC: 2844 7389 3565 2671 Cosmetic preparations; Packaging and labeling services; Bottling machinery: filling, capping, labeling; Plastic film, coated or laminated for packaging
PA: Universal Packaging Systems, Inc.
  14570 Monte Vista Ave
  Chino CA 91710
  909 517-2442

(G-3484)
UPRISING FOOD INC
4200 Plainville Rd (45227-3247)
PHONE.................................513 313-1087
William Schumacher, *CEO*
Kristen Schumacher, *Chief Brand Officer*
Mark Frommeyer, *Banker*
Sara Frommeyer, *Banker*
EMP: 9 EST: 2019
SALES (est): 506.66K **Privately Held**
Web: www.uprisingfood.com
SIC: 2051 Bread, cake, and related products

(G-3485)
UPSHIFT WORK LLC
Also Called: Upshift
2300 Montana Ave Ste 301 (45211-3890)
PHONE.................................513 813-5695
Steve Anevski, *CEO*
EMP: 201 EST: 2016
SALES (est): 3.28MM **Privately Held**
Web: www.upshift.work
SIC: 7372 7363 Application computer software; Temporary help service

(G-3486)
VALLEY ASPHALT CORPORATION (HQ)
Also Called: Asphalt
11641 Mosteller Rd (45241-1520)
PHONE.................................513 771-0820
EMP: 20 EST: 1934
SALES (est): 54.91MM
SALES (corp-wide): 225.16MM **Privately Held**
Web: www.jrjnet.com
SIC: 1611 2951 General contractor, highway and street construction; Asphalt and asphaltic paving mixtures (not from refineries)
PA: John R. Jurgensen Co.
  11641 Mosteller Rd
  Cincinnati OH 45241
  513 771-0820

(G-3487)
VAN-GRINER LLC
1009 Delta Ave (45208-3103)
PHONE.................................419 733-7951
EMP: 6 EST: 2010
SALES (est): 386.75K **Privately Held**
Web: www.van-griner.com
SIC: 2741 Miscellaneous publishing

(G-3488)
VARLAND METAL SERVICE INC
Also Called: Varland Plating Company
3231 Fredonia Ave (45229)
PHONE.................................513 861-0555
EMP: 48 EST: 1946
SALES (est): 6.13MM **Privately Held**
Web: www.varland.com
SIC: 3471 Electroplating of metals or formed products

(G-3489)
VENCO MANUFACTURING INC
Also Called: Collins & Venco Venturo
12110 Best Pl (45241-1569)
PHONE.................................513 772-8448
Larry R Collins, *Pr*
Ronald A Collins, *VP*
Mike Stritholt, *Treas*
Barbara Duke, *Sec*
▲ EMP: 13 EST: 1979
SQ FT: 35,000
SALES (est): 2.53MM
SALES (corp-wide): 23.07MM **Privately Held**
Web: www.venturo.com
SIC: 3714 Motor vehicle parts and accessories
PA: Venco Venturo Industries Llc
  12110 Best Pl
  Cincinnati OH 45241
  513 772-8448

(G-3490)
VENCO VENTURO INDUSTRIES LLC (PA)
Also Called: Venco/Venturo Div
12110 Best Pl (45241-1569)
PHONE.................................513 772-8448
Brett Collins, *Pr*
Mike Stritholt, *
Dave Foster, *
▲ EMP: 41 EST: 1952
SQ FT: 100,000
SALES (est): 23.07MM
SALES (corp-wide): 23.07MM **Privately Held**
Web: www.venturo.com
SIC: 3713 5012 3714 5084 Truck bodies (motor vehicles); Truck bodies; Motor vehicle parts and accessories; Cranes, industrial

(G-3491)
VENTILATION SYSTEMS JSC
Also Called: Vents - US
400 Murray Rd (45217-1013)
PHONE.................................513 348-3853
EMP: 19
Web: www.vents.ua
SIC: 3634 Fans, exhaust and ventilating, electric: household
HQ: Ventylyatsiini Systemy, At
  Bud. 1 Vul. Mykhaila Kotsyubynskogo
  Kyiv 01030

(G-3492)
VENTURO MANUFACTURING INC
12110 Best Pl (45241-1569)
PHONE.................................513 772-8448
Ronald A Collins, *VP*
Larry Collins, *Pr*
Mike Stritholt, *Treas*
Barbara Duke, *Sec*
EMP: 12 EST: 1952
SQ FT: 5,000
SALES (est): 4.66MM
SALES (corp-wide): 23.07MM **Privately Held**
Web: www.venturo.com
SIC: 3537 5084 Cranes, industrial truck; Industrial machinery and equipment
PA: Venco Venturo Industries Llc
  12110 Best Pl
  Cincinnati OH 45241
  513 772-8448

(G-3493)
VENUE LIFESTYLE & EVENT GUIDE
11959 Tramway Dr (45241-1666)
PHONE.................................513 405-6822
Kim Wanamaker, *Pr*
Steve Wanamaker, *VP*
EMP: 10 EST: 2010
SALES (est): 132.96K **Privately Held**
SIC: 2721 Magazines: publishing and printing

(G-3494)
VEOLIA WTS SYSTEMS USA INC
Also Called: General Ionics
11799 Enterprise Dr (45241-1510)
PHONE.................................513 794-1010
Dan Goins, *Mgr*
EMP: 8
Web: www.suezwatertechnologies.com
SIC: 3589 Water treatment equipment, industrial
HQ: Veolia Wts Systems Usa, Inc.
  3600 Horizon Blvd Ste 100
  Trevose PA 19053
  866 439-2837

(G-3495)
VERDIN ORGAN DIVISION
1118 Pendleton St Ste 410 (45202-8805)
PHONE.................................513 502-2333
EMP: 7 EST: 2018
SALES (est): 78.01K **Privately Held**
Web: www.verdinorgans.com
SIC: 3931 Musical instruments

(G-3496)
VERTIFLO PUMP COMPANY
7807 Redsky Dr (45249-1636)
PHONE.................................513 530-0888
Mark Werner, *Pr*
EMP: 17 EST: 1979
SQ FT: 18,000
SALES (est): 2.43MM **Privately Held**
Web: www.vertiflopump.com
SIC: 3594 3561 Fluid power pumps; Pumps and pumping equipment

(G-3497)
VESI INCORPORATED
Also Called: Vesi
7289 Kirkridge Dr (45233-4232)
PHONE.................................513 563-6002
Greg Visconti, *CEO*
Dale Davidson, *
Susan Litster, *
▲ EMP: 45 EST: 1992
SALES (est): 4.68MM **Privately Held**
Web: www.clublevelbrands.com
SIC: 2329 2339 Men's and boys' sportswear and athletic clothing; Sportswear, women's

(G-3498)
VICAS MANUFACTURING CO INC
8407 Monroe Ave (45236-1909)
P.O. Box 36310 (45236-0310)
PHONE.................................513 791-7741
Virginia Willoughby, *Pr*

Pon May, *
EMP: 47 EST: 1972
SQ FT: 25,600
SALES (est): 8.68MM **Privately Held**
Web: www.vi-cas.com
SIC: **3089** 3599 Injection molding of plastics; Machine shop, jobbing and repair

(G-3499)
VILLAGE CABINET SHOP INC
Also Called: Reynolds Cabinetry & Millwork
1820 Loisview Ln (45255-2617)
PHONE...................704 966-0801
Derrick A Reynolds, *Brnch Mgr*
EMP: 6
SIC: **2541** Cabinets, except refrigerated: show, display, etc.: wood
PA: The Village Cabinet Shop Inc
17746 93rd Pl N
Osseo MN 55311

(G-3500)
VINOKLET WINERY INC
11069 Colerain Rd (45252-1425)
PHONE...................513 385-9309
Kreso Mikulic, *CEO*
EMP: 21 EST: 2004
SALES (est): 1.16MM **Privately Held**
Web: www.vinokletwines.com
SIC: **2084** Wines

(G-3501)
VOLK CORPORATION
Also Called: Hathaway
635 Main St Ste 1 (45202-2524)
PHONE...................513 621-1052
Larry Schultz, *Brnch Mgr*
EMP: 8
SALES (corp-wide): 23.91MM **Privately Held**
Web: www.volkcorp.com
SIC: **3953** Marking devices
PA: Volk Corporation
455 E Cady St
Northville MI 48167
248 477-6700

(G-3502)
VULCAN CORPORATION
708 Walnut St (45202-4324)
PHONE...................513 621-2850
EMP: 69 EST: 1966
SALES (est): 854.67K
SALES (corp-wide): 9.95MM **Privately Held**
SIC: **3052** Rubber and plastics hose and beltings
PA: Vulcan International Corporation
300 Delaware Ave Ste 1704
Wilmington DE 19801
302 428-3181

(G-3503)
VULCAN INTERNATIONAL CORP
30 Garfield Pl Ste 1000 (45202-4308)
PHONE...................513 621-2850
Benjamin Gattler, *Brnch Mgr*
EMP: 9
SALES (corp-wide): 9.95MM **Privately Held**
SIC: **3069** Medical and laboratory rubber sundries and related products
PA: Vulcan International Corporation
300 Delaware Ave Ste 1704
Wilmington DE 19801
302 428-3181

(G-3504)
VURVEY LABS INC ✪
1008 Race St Ste 4 (45202-1091)
PHONE...................513 379-3595
EMP: 14 EST: 2022
SALES (est): 74.32K **Privately Held**
SIC: **7372** Application computer software

(G-3505)
VY INC
Also Called: Victor
3307 Clifton Ave Ste 2 (45220-2065)
PHONE...................513 421-8100
Victor Youkilis, *Ch Bd*
John Youkilis, *Pr*
EMP: 15 EST: 1946
SQ FT: 5,000
SALES (est): 1.5MM **Privately Held**
SIC: **3911** 5094 Jewelry apparel; Jewelry

(G-3506)
VYA INC
Also Called: Docustar
1325 Glendale Milford Rd (45215-1210)
P.O. Box 634015 (45263-4015)
PHONE...................513 772-5400
Jay Brokamp, *Pr*
Terry Brokamp, *
EMP: 41 EST: 1991
SQ FT: 56,000
SALES (est): 8.67MM **Privately Held**
Web: www.vyasystems.com
SIC: **2759** 2675 2752 Commercial printing, nec; Die-cut paper and board; Commercial printing, lithographic

(G-3507)
WALL COLMONOY CORPORATION
Aerobraze Division
940 Redna Ter (45215-1113)
PHONE...................513 842-4200
Ken Coldfelter, *Brnch Mgr*
EMP: 69
SALES (corp-wide): 98.07MM **Privately Held**
Web: www.wallcolmonoy.com
SIC: **3812** Search and navigation equipment
HQ: Wall Colmonoy Corporation
101 W Girard Ave
Madison Heights MI 48071
248 585-6400

(G-3508)
WAYGATE TECHNOLOGIES USA LP
1 Neumann Way (45215-1900)
PHONE...................866 243-2638
David Calhoun, *Brnch Mgr*
EMP: 89
SALES (corp-wide): 25.51B **Publicly Held**
Web: www.waygateinspectionacademy.com
SIC: **3829** 3844 Ultrasonic testing equipment ; Radiographic X-ray apparatus and tubes
HQ: Waygate Technologies Usa, Lp
721 Visions Dr
Skaneateles NY 13152
315 554-2000

(G-3509)
WCM HOLDINGS INC
11500 Canal Rd (45241-1862)
PHONE...................513 705-2100
David Herche, *CEO*
Tim Fogarty, *
Melvyn Fisher, *
▲ EMP: 120 EST: 1978
SALES (est): 10.63MM **Privately Held**
SIC: **5099** 2381 3842 Safety equipment and supplies; Gloves, work: woven or knit, made from purchased materials; Clothing, fire resistant and protective

(G-3510)
WELAGE CORPORATION
7712 Reinhold Dr (45237-2810)
P.O. Box 37665 (45222-0665)
PHONE...................513 681-2300
David Welage, *Pr*
Brad Ruter, *VP*
EMP: 15 EST: 1937
SQ FT: 15,000
SALES (est): 2.72MM **Privately Held**
Web: www.welagecorp.com
SIC: **3441** 3469 3544 Fabricated structural metal; Metal stampings, nec; Special dies, tools, jigs, and fixtures

(G-3511)
WELCH FOODS INC A COOPERATIVE
Also Called: Welch Foods
720 E Pete Rose Way (45202-3579)
PHONE...................513 632-5610
EMP: 60
SALES (corp-wide): 498.48MM **Privately Held**
Web: www.welchs.com
SIC: **2033** Canned fruits and specialties
HQ: Welch Foods Inc., A Cooperative
575 Virginia
Concord MA 01742
978 371-1000

(G-3512)
WELCH HOLDINGS INC
8953 E Miami River Rd (45247-2232)
PHONE...................513 353-3220
James R Welch, *Pr*
Ronnie L Welch, *
EMP: 29 EST: 1955
SQ FT: 3,400
SALES (est): 1.33MM **Privately Held**
Web: www.welchsand.com
SIC: **1442** Common sand mining

(G-3513)
WELCH SAND & GRAVEL INC
8953 E Miami River Rd (45247-2232)
P.O. Box 531700 (45253-1700)
PHONE...................513 353-3220
Chris Stalker, *Prin*
EMP: 14 EST: 2008
SALES (est): 2.4MM **Privately Held**
Web: www.welchsand.com
SIC: **1442** Construction sand and gravel

(G-3514)
WELDCO INC
2121 Spring Grove Ave (45214-1721)
PHONE...................513 744-9353
EMP: 33
SIC: **5084** 3264 Welding machinery and equipment; Porcelain electrical supplies

(G-3515)
WELLMAN CONTAINER CORPORATION
412 S Cooper Ave (45215-4555)
PHONE...................513 860-3040
Barbara J Wellman, *Pr*
Ronald J Wellman, *
EMP: 25 EST: 1981
SQ FT: 60,000
SALES (est): 3.8MM **Privately Held**
SIC: **2653** 2631 3993 2448 Boxes, corrugated: made from purchased materials ; Container, packaging, and boxboard; Displays and cutouts, window and lobby; Pallets, wood

(G-3516)
WEST CHESTER HOLDINGS LLC
Also Called: West Chester Protective Gear
11500 Canal Rd (45241-1862)
PHONE...................513 705-2100
Tim Fogarty, *CEO*
Jim Wilson, *
▲ EMP: 134 EST: 1995
SQ FT: 200,000
SALES (est): 31.5MM
SALES (corp-wide): 2.8B **Privately Held**
Web: www.westchesterclothing.com
SIC: **3842** 5099 2381 5137 Clothing, fire resistant and protective; Safety equipment and supplies; Gloves, work: woven or knit, made from purchased materials; Women's and children's clothing
HQ: Protective Industrial Products, Inc.
25 British American Blvd
Latham NY 12110
518 861-0133

(G-3517)
WESTERN & SOUTHERN LF INSUR CO (DH)
Also Called: Western-Southern Life
400 Broadway St Stop G (45202)
P.O. Box 1119 (45201)
PHONE...................513 629-1800
John F Barrett, *Pr*
James Vance, *
Danald J Wuebbling, *Sec*
EMP: 982 EST: 1888
SQ FT: 600,000
SALES (est): 62.71MM **Privately Held**
Web: www.westernsouthern.com
SIC: **6211** 6311 2511 Investment firm, general brokerage; Life insurance; Play pens, children's: wood
HQ: Western & Southern Financial Group, Inc.
400 Broadway
Cincinnati OH 45202
877 367-9734

(G-3518)
WHITE CASTLE SYSTEM INC
White Castle
3126 Exon Ave (45241-2548)
PHONE...................513 563-2290
Jarrett Cook, *Mgr*
EMP: 47
SALES (corp-wide): 538.44MM **Privately Held**
Web: www.whitecastle.com
SIC: **5812** 2099 Fast-food restaurant, chain; Sandwiches, assembled and packaged: for wholesale market
PA: White Castle System, Inc.
555 Edgar Waldo Way
Columbus OH 43215
614 228-5781

(G-3519)
WILLIAM POWELL COMPANY (PA)
Also Called: Powell Valve
3261 Spring Grove Ave (45225-1329)
PHONE...................513 852-2000
David R Cowart, *Pr*
Jeff Thompson, *
Brandy Cowart, *
◆ EMP: 70 EST: 1846
SALES (est): 48.03MM
SALES (corp-wide): 48.03MM **Privately Held**
Web: www.powellvalves.com
SIC: **3494** 3491 Valves and pipe fittings, nec; Pressure valves and regulators, industrial

(G-3520)
WILLIS MUSIC COMPANY
11700 Princeton Pike Unit E209 (45246-2535)
PHONE...................513 671-3288

Cincinnati - Hamilton County (G-3521)

Robert Mooney, *Mgr*
EMP: 10
SALES (corp-wide): 14.75MM **Privately Held**
Web: www.willismusic.com
SIC: 2741 5736 Music, sheet: publishing and printing; Musical instrument stores
PA: Willis Music Company
7567 Mall Rd
Florence KY 41042
859 283-2050

(G-3521)
WIN PLASTIC EXTRUSIONS LLC
Also Called: TMI
11502 Century Blvd (45246-3305)
PHONE............................330 929-1999
Patrick Mcmullen, *CFO*
EMP: 48 **EST:** 2007
SALES (est): 785.31K **Privately Held**
SIC: 2821 Polyvinyl chloride resins, PVC

(G-3522)
WINE CELLAR INNOVATIONS LLC
Also Called: Honeywell Authorized Dealer
4575 Eastern Ave (45226)
P.O. Box 8879 (45208)
PHONE............................513 321-3733
▼ **EMP:** 157 **EST:** 1978
SQ FT: 350,000
SALES (est): 22.96MM **Privately Held**
Web: www.winecellarinnovations.com
SIC: 2511 2541 Wood household furniture; Wood partitions and fixtures

(G-3523)
WJF ENTERPRISES LLC
Also Called: Specialty Wood Products
1347 Custer Ave (45208-2556)
PHONE............................513 871-7320
EMP: 8 **EST:** 1999
SQ FT: 32,000
SALES (est): 283.58K **Privately Held**
SIC: 2448 Wood pallets and skids

(G-3524)
WM LANG & SONS COMPANY
3280 Beekman St (45223-2423)
PHONE............................513 541-3304
Robert Schutte, *Pr*
Howard Schutte Junior, *Asst VP*
Joseph Schutte, *Corporate Secretary*
Jeffrey Tuttle, *VP*
EMP: 18 **EST:** 1892
SQ FT: 16,800
SALES (est): 2.48MM **Privately Held**
Web: www.langironworks.com
SIC: 3441 Building components, structural steel

(G-3525)
WOOD GRAPHICS INC (PA)
Also Called: United Engraving
8075 Reading Rd Ste 301 (45237-1416)
PHONE............................513 771-6300
Mark Richler, *Pr*
Gaylord H Fill, *
◆ **EMP:** 30 **EST:** 1972
SQ FT: 21,500
SALES (est): 2.44MM
SALES (corp-wide): 2.44MM **Privately Held**
SIC: 3555 7699 2796 Printing trades machinery; Industrial machinery and equipment repair; Platemaking services

(G-3526)
WORKS IN PROGRESS INC (PA)
3825 Edwards Rd Ste 800 (45209-1289)
PHONE............................802 658-3797
Larry Cain, *Pr*

Cara Cain V, *Pr*
EMP: 14 **EST:** 1993
SALES (est): 1.32MM **Privately Held**
Web: www.constructconnect.com
SIC: 2741 Miscellaneous publishing

(G-3527)
WRIGHT BROTHERS INC (PA)
1930 Losantiville Ave (45237-4106)
PHONE............................513 731-2222
Charles Wright, *Pr*
Denetria Wright, *Sec*
EMP: 15 **EST:** 1977
SQ FT: 15,000
SALES (est): 7.52MM
SALES (corp-wide): 7.52MM **Privately Held**
Web: www.wrightbros.com
SIC: 2813 3446 5084 Industrial gases; Architectural metalwork; Welding machinery and equipment

(G-3528)
WT ACQUISITION COMPANY LTD
Also Called: Waltek & Company
2130 Waycross Rd (45240-2719)
PHONE............................513 577-7980
EMP: 30
SIC: 3449 3211 Curtain wall, metal; Construction glass

(G-3529)
WULCO INC (PA)
Also Called: Jet Machine & Manufacturing
6899 Steger Dr Ste A (45237-3059)
PHONE............................513 679-2600
Richard G Wulfeck, *Pr*
Gary Wulfeck, *
Ken Wulfeck, *
▲ **EMP:** 100 **EST:** 1970
SQ FT: 100,000
SALES (est): 97.32MM **Privately Held**
Web: www.wulco.com
SIC: 5085 3599 Industrial supplies; Machine shop, jobbing and repair

(G-3530)
WULCO INC
Also Called: Jet Machine
6900 Steger Dr (45237-3096)
PHONE............................513 679-2600
Adam Wulfeck, *VP*
EMP: 99
SQ FT: 80,000
Web: www.jet-machine.com
SIC: 3599 Machine shop, jobbing and repair
PA: Wulco, Inc.
6899 Steger Dr Ste A
Cincinnati OH 45237

(G-3531)
XOMOX CORPORATION
Also Called: Crane Chempharma & Energy
4444 Cooper Rd (45242-5686)
PHONE............................936 271-6500
EMP: 20
SALES (corp-wide): 2.09B **Publicly Held**
Web: www.cranecpe.com
SIC: 3491 3593 3494 Boiler gauge cocks; Fluid power actuators, hydraulic or pneumatic; Plumbing and heating valves
HQ: Xomox Corporation
4526 Res Frest Dr Ste 400
The Woodlands TX 77381
936 271-6500

(G-3532)
XOMOX PFT CORP
4444 Cooper Rd (45242-0259)
PHONE............................936 271-6500
William Hayes, *Pr*

William Metz, *
Dale Friemoth, *
EMP: 418 **EST:** 2021
SALES (est): 69.88MM
SALES (corp-wide): 2.09B **Publicly Held**
SIC: 3491 3593 3494 Process control regulator valves; Fluid power cylinders and actuators; Valves and pipe fittings, nec
PA: Crane Company
100 1st Stmford Pl Ste 40
Stamford CT 06902
203 363-7300

(G-3533)
XS SMITH INC (PA)
5513 Vine St Ste 1 (45217-1022)
PHONE............................252 940-5060
Richard W Smith Junior, *Pr*
Scott Thompson, *Ex VP*
Cheryl Difiore, *Treas*
EMP: 20 **EST:** 1946
SQ FT: 40,000
SALES (est): 2.55MM
SALES (corp-wide): 2.55MM **Privately Held**
Web: www.structures-unlimited.com
SIC: 5191 3448 3231 Greenhouse equipment and supplies; Greenhouses, prefabricated metal; Products of purchased glass

(G-3534)
XTEK INC (PA)
11451 Reading Rd (45241-2283)
PHONE............................513 733-7800
Roger Miller, *Pr*
Frank Petrek, *
James J Raible, *
Albert Schreiver Iv, *VP Fin*
◆ **EMP:** 336 **EST:** 1909
SQ FT: 363,440
SALES (est): 131.6MM
SALES (corp-wide): 131.6MM **Privately Held**
Web: www.xtek.com
SIC: 3568 3547 3398 3312 Power transmission equipment, nec; Rolling mill machinery; Metal heat treating; Wheels, locomotive and car: iron and steel

(G-3535)
ZEDA INC
11560 Goldcoast Dr (45249-1640)
PHONE............................513 966-4633
Greg Morris, *CEO*
Greg Morris, *Prin*
Steve Rengers, *Prin*
EMP: 10 **EST:** 2019
SALES (est): 1.05MM **Privately Held**
Web: www.z8a.com
SIC: 3499 Fabricated metal products, nec

(G-3536)
ZIPSCENE LLC
Also Called: Zipscene
615 Main St Fl 5 (45202-2538)
PHONE............................513 201-5174
Rick Lamy, *
EMP: 62 **EST:** 2010
SQ FT: 2,000
SALES (est): 5.08MM **Privately Held**
Web: www.zipscene.com
SIC: 7372 Business oriented computer software

(G-3537)
ZOMIR LLC
895 Glendale Milford Rd (45215-1136)
P.O. Box 62655 (45262-0655)
PHONE............................513 771-1516
EMP: 7 **EST:** 2003

SALES (est): 218.16K **Privately Held**
SIC: 3231 Mirrors, truck and automobile: made from purchased glass

(G-3538)
ZTS INC
5628 Wooster Pike (45227-4121)
PHONE............................513 271-2557
Dave Zimmerman, *Pr*
Marge Zimmerman, *Sec*
Phil Zimmerman, *Prin*
▲ **EMP:** 10 **EST:** 1970
SQ FT: 8,000
SALES (est): 1.02MM **Privately Held**
Web: www.ztsinc.com
SIC: 3825 Battery testers, electrical

(G-3539)
ZYGO INC
Also Called: Cincy Deli & Carryout
2832 Jefferson Ave (45219-1920)
PHONE............................513 281-0888
Jim Powers, *CEO*
EMP: 8 **EST:** 1970
SQ FT: 1,500
SALES (est): 501.05K **Privately Held**
Web: www.zygo.com
SIC: 5411 2097 Delicatessen stores; Ice cubes

Circleville
Pickaway County

(G-3540)
ALL - DO WELD & FAB LLC
28155 River Dr (43113-9726)
PHONE............................740 477-2133
Sheng Stack, *Opers Mgr*
EMP: 6 **EST:** 2005
SALES (est): 529.7K **Privately Held**
SIC: 7692 Welding repair

(G-3541)
AMERICAN WOOD FIBERS INC
2500 Owens Rd (43113-8963)
PHONE............................740 420-3233
Mark Roth, *Mgr*
EMP: 32
Web: www.awf.com
SIC: 2499 Mulch or sawdust products, wood
PA: American Wood Fibers, Inc.
9740 Patuxent Woods Dr # 500
Columbia MD 21046

(G-3542)
BEAZER EAST INC
200 E Corwin St (43113-1906)
P.O. Box 268 (43113-0268)
PHONE............................740 474-3169
Leonard Mcferren, *Mgr*
EMP: 16
SALES (corp-wide): 23.02B **Privately Held**
SIC: 3273 3271 Ready-mixed concrete; Blocks, concrete or cinder: standard
HQ: Beazer East, Inc.
600 River Ave Ste 200
Pittsburgh PA 15212
412 428-9407

(G-3543)
CENTRAL COCA-COLA BTLG CO INC
Also Called: Coca-Cola
387 Walnut St (43113-2225)
PHONE............................740 474-2180
EMP: 29
SALES (corp-wide): 45.75B **Publicly Held**
Web: www.coca-cola.com
SIC: 2086 8741 Bottled and canned soft drinks; Management services

GEOGRAPHIC SECTION

Clayton - Montgomery County (G-3565)

HQ: Central Coca-Cola Bottling Company, Inc.
555 Taxter Rd Ste 550
Elmsford NY 10523
914 789-1100

(G-3544)
CIRCLEVILLE OIL CO
Also Called: Subway
224 Lancaster Pike (43113-1507)
P.O. Box 123 (43113-0123)
PHONE..................740 477-3341
Lori Whited, *Mgr*
EMP: 8
SALES (corp-wide): 2.48MM **Privately Held**
Web: www.subway.com
SIC: 1389 7539 5812 Construction, repair, and dismantling services; Brake services; Sandwiches and submarines shop
PA: Circleville Oil Co (Inc)
315 Town St
Circleville OH 43113
740 474-7544

(G-3545)
CLINE MACHINE AND AUTOMTN INC
Also Called: Suburban Metal Products
1050 Tarlton Rd (43113-9132)
PHONE..................740 474-4237
Joey R Cline, *Pr*
EMP: 22 **EST:** 2010
SALES (est): 1.24MM **Privately Held**
SIC: 3549 Metalworking machinery, nec

(G-3546)
DAN PATRICK ENTERPRISES INC
8564 Zane Trail Rd (43113-9745)
PHONE..................740 477-1006
Daniel E Patrick, *Pr*
Christine Patrick, *Sec*
EMP: 6 **EST:** 1985
SQ FT: 3,500
SALES (est): 508.18K **Privately Held**
Web: www.samson4x4.com
SIC: 3713 5013 7538 Truck bodies and parts ; Truck parts and accessories; General truck repair

(G-3547)
DUPONT SPECIALTY PDTS USA LLC
Also Called: Dupont Vespel Parts and Shapes
800 Dupont Rd (43113)
PHONE..................740 474-0635
Wayne Macdonald, *Mgr*
EMP: 75
SALES (corp-wide): 2.93B **Publicly Held**
Web: www.dupont.com
SIC: 2821 Plastics materials and resins
HQ: Dupont Specialty Products Usa, Llc
974 Centre Rd
Wilmington DE 19805
302 992-2941

(G-3548)
DUPONT SPECIALTY PDTS USA LLC
Also Called: Dupont
Rt 23 S Dupont Rd (43113)
P.O. Box 89 (43113-0089)
PHONE..................740 474-0220
Tony Eichstadt, *Mgr*
EMP: 50
SALES (corp-wide): 2.93B **Publicly Held**
Web: www.dupont.com
SIC: 2821 3861 3081 Polyesters; Photographic equipment and supplies; Unsupported plastics film and sheet
HQ: Dupont Specialty Products Usa, Llc
974 Centre Rd
Wilmington DE 19805
302 992-2941

(G-3549)
EPC-COLUMBIA INC
30627 Orr Rd (43113-9731)
PHONE..................740 420-5252
EMP: 92
Web: www.epcmfg.com
SIC: 3089 Injection molding of plastics
HQ: Epc-Columbia, Inc.
4000 Waco Rd
Columbia MO 65202
205 702-4166

(G-3550)
ERNIE GREEN INDUSTRIES INC
Also Called: Earnie Green Industries
30627 Orr Rd (43113-9731)
PHONE..................740 420-5252
Mark Sells, *Brnch Mgr*
EMP: 41
SALES (corp-wide): 338.9MM **Privately Held**
Web: www.epcmfg.com
SIC: 3714 Motor vehicle parts and accessories
PA: Ernie Green Industries, Inc.
1785 Big Hill Rd
Dayton OH 45439
614 219-1423

(G-3551)
FLORIDA PRODUCTION ENGRG INC
Also Called: Eg Industries
30627 Orr Rd (43113-9731)
PHONE..................740 420-5252
Chuck Reisinger, *Mgr*
EMP: 160
SALES (corp-wide): 338.9MM **Privately Held**
SIC: 3089 Injection molding of plastics
HQ: Florida Production Engineering, Inc.
2 E Tower Cir
Ormond Beach FL 32174
386 677-2566

(G-3552)
FPE INC
30627 Orr Rd (43113-9731)
PHONE..................740 420-5252
EMP: 200
SIC: 3089 Automotive parts, plastic

(G-3553)
GEORGIA-PACIFIC LLC
Also Called: Georgia-Pacific
2850 Owens Rd (43113-9079)
P.O. Box 379 (43113-0379)
PHONE..................740 477-3347
Terry Gaffney, *Mgr*
EMP: 130
SALES (corp-wide): 36.93B **Privately Held**
Web: www.gp.com
SIC: 2653 3412 2675 2671 Boxes, corrugated: made from purchased materials ; Metal barrels, drums, and pails; Die-cut paper and board; Paper; coated and laminated packaging
HQ: Georgia-Pacific Llc
133 Peachtree St Nw
Atlanta GA 30303
404 652-4000

(G-3554)
PPG INDUSTRIES INC
559 Pittsburgh Rd (43113-9436)
P.O. Box 457 (43113-0457)
PHONE..................740 474-3161
Dave Moss, *Brnch Mgr*
EMP: 203
SALES (corp-wide): 17.65B **Publicly Held**
Web: www.ppg.com

SIC: 2851 Paints and allied products
PA: Ppg Industries, Inc.
1 Ppg Pl
Pittsburgh PA 15272
412 434-3131

(G-3555)
RED BARN SCREEN PRINTING & EMB
Also Called: Red Barn, The
1144 Northridge Rd (43113-9396)
PHONE..................740 474-6657
Raymond Larry, *Pr*
Jerrilyn Stevens, *Pr*
EMP: 6 **EST:** 1983
SALES (est): 242.59K **Privately Held**
Web: www.redbarnonline.net
SIC: 2395 7336 Embroidery and art needlework; Silk screen design

(G-3556)
TANGENT AIR INC
127 Edison Ave (43113-2117)
PHONE..................740 474-1114
John Morehead, *Pr*
Jerry Jones, *
EMP: 38 **EST:** 1993
SQ FT: 17,000
SALES (est): 3.89MM **Privately Held**
Web: www.tangentairinc.com
SIC: 3321 3444 Cast iron pipe and fittings; Sheet metalwork

(G-3557)
TECHNICOLOR USA INC
Also Called: Circleville Glass Operations
24200 Us Highway 23 S (43113-7566)
PHONE..................614 474-8821
Chet Kucinski, *Mgr*
EMP: 1143
SQ FT: 325,000
SIC: 3651 3231 Household audio and video equipment; Products of purchased glass
HQ: Technicolor Usa, Inc.
6040 W Sunset Blvd
Hollywood CA 90028
317 587-4287

(G-3558)
TELESIS TECHNOLOGIES INC (DH)
Also Called: Telesis Marking Systems
28181 River Dr (43113-9726)
PHONE..................740 477-5000
Steve Sheng, *Pr*
Warren R Knipple, *
▲ **EMP:** 135 **EST:** 1971
SQ FT: 39,900
SALES (est): 36.87MM **Privately Held**
Web: www.telesis.com
SIC: 3953 Canceling stamps, hand: rubber or metal
HQ: Hitachi Industrial Equipment Systems Co., Ltd.
1-5-1, Sotokanda
Chiyoda-Ku TKY 101-0

(G-3559)
TRIMOLD LLC
200 Pittsburgh Rd (43113)
PHONE..................740 474-7591
Yoshimasa Okada, *Managing Member*
Yoshimasa Okada, *Managing Member*
Katsuya Kanda, *
EMP: 360 **EST:** 2005
SALES (est): 79.5MM **Privately Held**
Web: www.tstech.com
SIC: 3089 Injection molding of plastics
HQ: Ts Trim Industries Inc.
6380 Canal St
Canal Winchester OH 43110
614 837-4114

(G-3560)
TS TECH CO LTD (PA)
200 Pittsburgh Rd (43113-9288)
PHONE..................740 420-5617
EMP: 7 **EST:** 2018
SALES (est): 910.92K
SALES (corp-wide): 910.92K **Privately Held**
Web: www.tstech.co.jp
SIC: 3089 Plastics products, nec

(G-3561)
WYATT SPECIALTIES INC
4761 State Route 361 (43113-9736)
PHONE..................614 989-5362
James Wyatt, *Prin*
Deborah Wyatt, *Sec*
James Wyatt, *Pr*
EMP: 11 **EST:** 2010
SALES (est): 440.97K **Privately Held**
SIC: 3711 Automobile assembly, including specialty automobiles

Clarington
Monroe County

(G-3562)
AMERICAN HVY PLATE SLTIONS LLC
42722 State Route 7 Ste 12 (43915)
PHONE..................740 331-4620
Roxana Stoicea, *Managing Member*
Roxana Stoicea, *CFO*
EMP: 148 **EST:** 2017
SALES (est): 12.62MM **Privately Held**
Web: www.ahplates.com
SIC: 3312 Sheet or strip, steel, cold-rolled: own hot-rolled

Clayton
Montgomery County

(G-3563)
ANCHOR FABRICATORS INC
386 Talmadge Rd (45315-9621)
P.O. Box 99 (45315-0099)
PHONE..................937 836-5117
Tom Saldoff, *Pr*
Marshall Ruchman, *
Randee Saldoff, *Stockholder*
EMP: 43 **EST:** 1949
SQ FT: 60,000
SALES (est): 7.97MM **Privately Held**
Web: www.anchorfab.com
SIC: 3471 3599 3469 Buffing for the trade; Machine shop, jobbing and repair; Metal stampings, nec

(G-3564)
BLACKTHORN LLC
6113 Brookville Salem Rd (45315-9701)
PHONE..................937 836-9296
Greg Benedict, *Managing Member*
Sharon Yoakum, *VP*
Sharon Buehler, *Sec*
EMP: 10 **EST:** 1985
SQ FT: 20,000
SALES (est): 941.8K **Privately Held**
Web: www.blackthorn-inc.com
SIC: 3053 2899 3089 3296 Gaskets, all materials; Concrete curing and hardening compounds; Plastics hardware and building products; Fiberglass insulation

(G-3565)
HOFACKER PRCSION MACHINING LLC
7560 Jacks Ln (45315-8779)

Clayton - Montgomery County (G-3566)

PHONE..................................937 832-7712
EMP: 18 EST: 1997
SQ FT: 2,500
SALES (est): 2.25MM **Privately Held**
Web: www.hofackerprecision.com
SIC: **3599** 3544 Machine shop, jobbing and repair; Special dies and tools

(G-3566)
INDIAN LAKE RACEWAY LLC
6341 Silverbell Ct (45315-9750)
PHONE..................................937 837-7533
Brian C Petroziello, *Prin*
EMP: 6 EST: 2012
SALES (est): 135.89K **Privately Held**
SIC: **3644** Raceways

(G-3567)
KITTO KATSU INC
7445 Lockwood St (45315)
PHONE..................................818 256-6997
Hiran Jayasinghe, *Pr*
EMP: 7 EST: 2017
SALES (est): 238.18K **Privately Held**
SIC: **3999** 8742 Manufacturing industries, nec; Marketing consulting services

(G-3568)
SLUTERBECK TOOL & DIE CO INC
Also Called: Sluterbeck Tool Co
7540 Jacks Lane (45315-8779)
P.O. Box 87 (45315-0087)
PHONE..................................937 836-5736
Ronald Sluterbeck, *Pr*
Anne Goss, *Sec*
Steve Sluterbeck, *VP*
Greg Sluterbeck, *VP*
EMP: 10 EST: 1953
SQ FT: 6,000
SALES (est): 1.02MM **Privately Held**
SIC: **3544** Special dies and tools

Cleveland
Cuyahoga County

(G-3569)
17111 WATERVIEW PKWY LLC ◆
The Tower At Erieview 1301 East 9th St Ste 3000 (44114)
PHONE..................................216 706-2960
EMP: 12 EST: 2024
SALES (est): 316.48K
SALES (corp-wide): 6.58B **Publicly Held**
SIC: **3728** 5088 Aircraft parts and equipment, nec; Aircraft equipment and supplies, nec
PA: Transdigm Group Incorporated
1301 E 9th St Ste 3000
Cleveland OH 44114
216 706-2960

(G-3570)
1923 W 25TH ST INC
1923 W 25th St (44113-3418)
PHONE..................................216 696-7529
Richard Brown, *Prin*
EMP: 9 EST: 2001
SALES (est): 232.96K **Privately Held**
Web: www.natesohiocity.com
SIC: **2653** Corrugated and solid fiber boxes

(G-3571)
2 RETRIEVERS LLC
Also Called: Elugen Pharmaceuticals
2515 Jay Ave (44113-3091)
PHONE..................................216 200-9040
Kevin Lenahan, *CEO*
EMP: 8 EST: 2019
SALES (est): 938.11K **Privately Held**
Web: www.2retrievers.com
SIC: **2834** Pharmaceutical preparations

(G-3572)
4WALLSCOM LLC
4700 Lakeside Ave E Unit 173a (44114)
PHONE..................................216 432-1400
Gale Flanagan, *General Member*
EMP: 10 EST: 2004
SALES (est): 1.1MM **Privately Held**
Web: www.4walls.com
SIC: **2679** Wallpaper

(G-3573)
72 CHOCOLATE LLC
Also Called: 72 Chocolate Collection, The
1806 W 52nd St (44102-3394)
PHONE..................................216 672-6040
EMP: 6 EST: 2019
SALES (est): 310.71K **Privately Held**
Web: www.72chocolate.com
SIC: **2066** Chocolate and cocoa products

(G-3574)
A & A QUALITY PAVING & CEM LLC
13938a Cedar Rd Ste 250 (44118-3204)
PHONE..................................440 886-9595
Alfred E Edwards Senior, *Pr*
EMP: 6 EST: 2002
SALES (est): 113.35K **Privately Held**
SIC: **3241** Portland cement

(G-3575)
A & W TABLE PAD CO
Also Called: Pioneer Table Pad
6520 Carnegie Ave (44103-4697)
PHONE..................................800 541-0271
TOLL FREE: 800
Tamara Christman, *Pr*
EMP: 10 EST: 1915
SQ FT: 12,000
SALES (est): 870.61K **Privately Held**
Web: www.pioneertablepads.com
SIC: **2392** Table mats, plastic and textile

(G-3576)
A - Y MACHINING LLC
18504 Syracuse Ave (44110-2520)
PHONE..................................216 404-0400
Dennis Hager, *Prin*
EMP: 6 EST: 2007
SALES (est): 127.45K **Privately Held**
SIC: **3599** Machine shop, jobbing and repair

(G-3577)
A AABACO PLASTICS INC
Also Called: United Plastic Film
9520 Midwest Ave (44125-2463)
PHONE..................................216 663-9494
Daniel R Lee, *Pr*
Jonathan Lee, *VP*
David Lee, *Sec*
A R Mays, *Prin*
Elliott M Kaufman, *Prin*
EMP: 24 EST: 1968
SQ FT: 25,000
SALES (est): 2.12MM **Privately Held**
Web: www.aabacoplastics.com
SIC: **3089** Blister or bubble formed packaging, plastics

(G-3578)
A E F INC
Also Called: American Electric Furnace Co
24050 Commerce Park Fl 2 (44122-5833)
PHONE..................................216 360-9800
Robert Sords, *Pr*
Virginia Sords, *
Robert Sords Prestreas, *Prin*
EMP: 10 EST: 1920
SQ FT: 33,000
SALES (est): 202.96K **Privately Held**
SIC: **3567** Electrical furnaces, ovens, & heating devices, exc.induction

(G-3579)
A F KRAINZ CO
1364 E 47th St (44103-1220)
PHONE..................................216 431-4341
Andrew F Krainz Junior, *Owner*
EMP: 8 EST: 1974
SALES (est): 444.31K **Privately Held**
SIC: **2752** Offset printing

(G-3580)
A G INDUSTRIES INC
1 American Rd (44144-2354)
PHONE..................................216 252-7300
Jeff White, *Pr*
EMP: 99 EST: 1960
SQ FT: 30,000
SALES (est): 5.4MM
SALES (corp-wide): 14.52B **Privately Held**
SIC: **2541** Display fixtures, wood
HQ: American Greetings Corporation
1 American Blvd
Cleveland OH 44145
216 252-7300

(G-3581)
A JACKS MANUFACTURING CO
1441 Chardon Rd (44117-1510)
PHONE..................................216 531-1010
Charlie Crout, *Pr*
▲ EMP: 21 EST: 2003
SALES (est): 9.98MM
SALES (corp-wide): 1.66B **Publicly Held**
SIC: **3567** Industrial furnaces and ovens
HQ: Park-Ohio Industries, Inc.
6065 Parkland Blvd
Cleveland OH 44124
440 947-2000

(G-3582)
AA PALLETS LLC
4326 W 48th St (44144-1934)
PHONE..................................216 856-2614
Areli Arreaga, *Prin*
EMP: 6 EST: 2016
SALES (est): 696.84K **Privately Held**
Web: www.aapallets.com
SIC: **2448** Pallets, wood

(G-3583)
AAA STAMPING INC
4001 Pearl Rd Uppr (44109-3198)
PHONE..................................216 749-4494
Stan Gawor, *Pr*
EMP: 22 EST: 1985
SQ FT: 25,000
SALES (est): 2.31MM **Privately Held**
Web: www.aaastampinginc.com
SIC: **3469** Stamping metal for the trade

(G-3584)
AAJAJ HAIR COMPANY LLC
3905 W 18th St (44109-3074)
PHONE..................................216 309-0816
EMP: 10 EST: 2019
SALES (est): 283.15K **Privately Held**
SIC: **3999** Hair and hair-based products

(G-3585)
ABEL METAL PROCESSING INC
2105 E 77th St (44103-4990)
PHONE..................................216 881-4156
Eugene Schoenmeyer, *Pr*
Joan Kern, *VP*
EMP: 21 EST: 1975
SQ FT: 8,000
SALES (est): 684.14K **Privately Held**
Web: www.abelmetal.com
SIC: **3471** Electroplating of metals or formed products

(G-3586)
ABEONA THERAPEUTICS INC (PA)
Also Called: Abeona
6555 Carnegie Ave 4th Fl (44103-4637)
PHONE..................................646 813-4701
Vishwas Seshadri, *Pr*
Michael Amoroso, *Ch Bd*
Joseph Vazzano, *CFO*
Edward Carr, *CAO*
EMP: 27 EST: 1974
SQ FT: 45,705
SALES (est): 3.5MM
SALES (corp-wide): 3.5MM **Publicly Held**
Web: www.abeonatherapeutics.com
SIC: **2834** Pharmaceutical preparations

(G-3587)
ADI INC
Also Called: ABI
5350 Transportation Blvd Ste 18b (44125)
P.O. Box 389 (44286-0389)
PHONE..................................800 847-8950
Lloyd Ray Parr, *Pr*
Thomas L Feher, *Sec*
EMP: 10 EST: 1991
SALES (est): 992.41K **Privately Held**
Web: www.ultraclear.com
SIC: **2836** Biological products, except diagnostic

(G-3588)
ABL PRODUCTS INC
3726 Ridge Rd (44144-1182)
PHONE..................................216 281-2400
Athel Gicei, *Pr*
Leslie Gicei, *VP*
EMP: 13 EST: 1974
SALES (est): 450.67K **Privately Held**
Web: www.ablproducts.com
SIC: **3469** 3568 Stamping metal for the trade ; Sprockets (power transmission equipment)

(G-3589)
ACADEMY GRAPHIC COMM INC
1000 Brookpark Rd (44109-5824)
PHONE..................................216 661-2550
James M Champion, *Pr*
Elaine Champion, *
EMP: 22 EST: 1966
SQ FT: 1,400
SALES (est): 1MM **Privately Held**
Web: www.visitagc.com
SIC: **2752** 7336 Offset printing; Graphic arts and related design

(G-3590)
ACE RUBBER STAMP & OFF SUP CO
Also Called: Royal Acme
3110 Payne Ave (44114-4504)
PHONE..................................216 771-8483
Ted Cutts, *Pr*
EMP: 10 EST: 1935
SALES (est): 198.63K **Privately Held**
SIC: **3953** 5943 Embossing seals and hand stamps; Office forms and supplies

(G-3591)
ACME LIFTING PRODUCTS INC
Also Called: Universal Cargo
6892 W Snowville Rd Ste 2 (44141-3288)
PHONE..................................440 838-4430
Laura Davis, *Pr*
Arnold Davis, *VP*
EMP: 8 EST: 1986
SQ FT: 6,000
SALES (est): 880K **Privately Held**

GEOGRAPHIC SECTION

Cleveland - Cuyahoga County (G-3616)

SIC: 3536 Hoisting slings

(G-3592)
ACME SPIRALLY WOUND PAPER PDTS
Also Called: Acme Paper Tube
4810 W 139th St (44135-5036)
P.O. Box 35320 (44135-0320)
PHONE..................................216 267-2950
Dan Kobrak, *CEO*
Donald H Kobak Junior, *CEO*
EMP: 17 **EST:** 1953
SQ FT: 36,000
SALES (est): 2.29MM **Privately Held**
Web: www.acmespiral.com
SIC: 2655 Tubes, fiber or paper; made from purchased material

(G-3593)
ACOR ORTHOPAEDIC INC
Also Called: Cleveland Prosthetic Center
18700 S Miles Rd (44128-4242)
PHONE..................................440 532-0117
EMP: 14
SALES (corp-wide): 8.41MM **Privately Held**
Web: www.acor.com
SIC: 3842 Orthopedic appliances
PA: Acor Orthopaedic, Llc
    18530 S Miles Rd
    Cleveland OH 44128
    216 662-4500

(G-3594)
ACOR ORTHOPAEDIC LLC (PA)
18530 S Miles Rd (44128-4200)
PHONE..................................216 662-4500
Joseph Merolla, *Managing Member*
Greg Alaimo, *
Jeff Alaimo, *
▲ **EMP:** 34 **EST:** 1965
SQ FT: 35,000
SALES (est): 8.41MM
SALES (corp-wide): 8.41MM **Privately Held**
Web: www.acor.com
SIC: 3144 3143 3842 3086 Women's footwear, except athletic; Men's footwear, except athletic; Prosthetic appliances; Plastics foam products

(G-3595)
AD PISTON RING LLC
Also Called: Ad Piston Ring
3145 Superior Ave E (44114-4342)
PHONE..................................216 781-5200
Craig Duber, *Managing Member*
Bob Lee, *Managing Member*
Craig Duber, *Genl Mgr*
EMP: 10 **EST:** 1921
SQ FT: 12,000
SALES (est): 926.89K **Privately Held**
Web: www.adpistonring.com
SIC: 3592 Pistons and piston rings

(G-3596)
ADALET/SCOTT FETZER COMPANY
Also Called: Meriam Instrument
10920 Madison Ave (44102-2526)
PHONE..................................440 892-3074
Dave Thomas, *Prin*
EMP: 50 **EST:** 1987
SALES (est): 4.12MM **Privately Held**
Web: www.meriam.com
SIC: 3823 Process control instruments

(G-3597)
ADCHEM ADHESIVES INC
4111 E Royalton Rd (44147-2931)
PHONE..................................440 526-1976
Claude Dandurande, *Pr*
Brett Joint, *Mgr*
▲ **EMP:** 10 **EST:** 1996
SQ FT: 15,000
SALES (est): 715.49K **Privately Held**
SIC: 2891 Adhesives

(G-3598)
ADCRAFT DECALS INCORPORATED
7708 Commerce Park Oval (44131-2394)
PHONE..................................216 524-2934
Robert W Talion, *Pr*
Ciliox Rendina, *
EMP: 35 **EST:** 1961
SQ FT: 21,200
SALES (est): 4.9MM **Privately Held**
Web: www.adcraftdecals.com
SIC: 2759 3993 2752 2672 Screen printing; Signs and advertising specialties; Commercial printing, lithographic; Paper; coated and laminated, nec

(G-3599)
ADDED EDGE ASSEMBLY INC
26800 Fargo Ave Ste A (44146-1341)
PHONE..................................216 464-4305
Kurt Kodrich, *Pr*
Janet Kodrich, *Sec*
EMP: 15 **EST:** 1991
SQ FT: 3,000
SALES (est): 643.9K **Privately Held**
Web: www.addedge.com
SIC: 3549 Assembly machines, including robotic

(G-3600)
ADHEREX GROUP (PA) ✪
3100 Hamilton Ave (44114-3701)
PHONE..................................201 440-3806
Bob Marquette, *CEO*
EMP: 11 **EST:** 2023
SALES (est): 9.82MM
SALES (corp-wide): 9.82MM **Privately Held**
SIC: 2891 Adhesives

(G-3601)
ADMJ HOLDINGS LLC
Also Called: Advance Door Co.
5260 Commerce Pkwy W (44130-1271)
PHONE..................................216 588-0038
Jerry Oflanagan, *Prin*
Mary Oflanagan, *
EMP: 35 **EST:** 2019
SALES (est): 2.65MM **Privately Held**
Web: www.advance-door.com
SIC: 2381 Fabric dress and work gloves

(G-3602)
ADVANCE INDUSTRIES GROUP LLC
3636 W 58th St (44102-5641)
PHONE..................................216 741-1800
EMP: 20 **EST:** 2006
SQ FT: 35,000
SALES (est): 4.09MM **Privately Held**
Web: www.advanceindustriesgroup.com
SIC: 3441 3315 Fabricated structural metal; Wire and fabricated wire products

(G-3603)
ADVANCE MANUFACTURING CORP
6800 Madison Ave (44102-4099)
PHONE..................................216 333-1684
Herman Bredenbeck, *Pr*
Jon Bredenbeck, *
Kenneth Bailey, *
Doug Carlson, *
EMP: 48 **EST:** 1936
SQ FT: 64,000
SALES (est): 7.03MM **Privately Held**
Web: www.advancemanuf.com

SIC: 3599 3549 Machine shop, jobbing and repair; Metalworking machinery, nec

(G-3604)
ADVANCE METAL PRODUCTS INC
3636 W 58th St (44102-5641)
PHONE..................................216 741-1800
EMP: 19 **EST:** 1996
SQ FT: 30,000
SALES (est): 699.15K **Privately Held**
Web: www.advancewireforming.com
SIC: 3441 Fabricated structural metal

(G-3605)
ADVANCE WIRE FORMING INC
3636 W 58th St (44102-5641)
PHONE..................................216 432-3250
Jeff Stein, *Pr*
James Williams, *VP*
EMP: 10 **EST:** 2000
SQ FT: 30,000
SALES (est): 1.83MM **Privately Held**
Web: www.advancewireforming.com
SIC: 3496 Miscellaneous fabricated wire products

(G-3606)
ADVANCED KIFFER SYSTEMS INC
4905 Rocky River Dr (44135-3245)
PHONE..................................216 267-8181
Dale C Phillip, *Pr*
Lars Eriksson, *VP*
Susan Phillip, *Sec*
EMP: 24 **EST:** 1988
SQ FT: 85,000
SALES (est): 2.59MM
SALES (corp-wide): 9.17MM **Privately Held**
Web: www.akscutting.com
SIC: 3825 Test equipment for electronic and electric measurement
PA: Kiffer Industries, Inc.
    4905 Rocky River Dr
    Cleveland OH 44135
    216 267-1818

(G-3607)
ADVANCED NANOTHERAPIES INC
10000 Cedar Ave (44106-2119)
PHONE..................................415 517-0867
Philippe Urbain, *Pr*
Mehdi Shisheehbor, *VP*
Brandi Weekly, *Sec*
EMP: 19 **EST:** 2019
SALES (est): 4.01MM **Privately Held**
Web: www.advancednanotherapies.com
SIC: 3841 Surgical and medical instruments

(G-3608)
ADVANCED PAPER TUBE INC
1951 W 90th St (44102-2742)
PHONE..................................216 281-5691
Leon Lasky, *Pr*
Dorothy Lasky, *VP*
EMP: 19 **EST:** 1982
SQ FT: 27,000
SALES (est): 1.1MM **Privately Held**
Web: www.advancedpapertube.com
SIC: 2655 Tubes, fiber or paper; made from purchased material

(G-3609)
ADVANCED SURFACE TECHNOLOGY
12211 Sobieski Ave (44135-4857)
PHONE..................................216 476-8600
Joseph Lardner, *Pr*
James Mason, *VP*
EMP: 7 **EST:** 1991
SALES (est): 501.02K **Privately Held**
Web: www.advancedsurfaceinc.com

SIC: 3471 Electroplating of metals or formed products

(G-3610)
AERO-INSTRUMENTS CO LLC
Also Called: Aero Instruments
4223 Monticello Blvd (44121-2814)
P.O. Box 932066 (44193-0007)
PHONE..................................216 671-3133
EMP: 50
Web: www.aero-instruments.com
SIC: 3812 Search and navigation equipment

(G-3611)
AEROSCENA LLC
Also Called: Ascents
10000 Cedar Ave (44106-2119)
PHONE..................................800 671-1890
Mark Kohoot, *CEO*
EMP: 10 **EST:** 2010
SALES (est): 435.61K **Privately Held**
Web: www.aeroscena.com
SIC: 2844 Perfumes, natural or synthetic

(G-3612)
AETNA PLATING CO
6511 Morgan Ave (44127-1947)
PHONE..................................216 341-9111
Peter Sobey, *Pr*
Joel Newman, *Sec*
EMP: 15 **EST:** 1934
SQ FT: 55,000
SALES (est): 1.95MM **Privately Held**
Web: www.aetnaplating.com
SIC: 3471 Electroplating of metals or formed products

(G-3613)
AFFILIATED METAL INDUSTRIES
16110 Brookpark Rd (44135-3340)
PHONE..................................216 267-0155
James Land, *Pr*
EMP: 7 **EST:** 2017
SALES (est): 236.97K **Privately Held**
Web: www.affiliatedmetal.com
SIC: 3441 Fabricated structural metal

(G-3614)
AFFYMETRIX INC
26111 Miles Rd (44128-5933)
P.O. Box 68 (92018-0068)
PHONE..................................800 321-9322
EMP: 49
SALES (corp-wide): 44.91B **Publicly Held**
Web: www.affymetrix.com
SIC: 3826 Analytical instruments
HQ: Affymetrix, Inc.
    3380 Central Expy
    Santa Clara CA 95051

(G-3615)
AGMET LLC
5533 Dunham Rd (44137-3679)
PHONE..................................216 663-8200
Dave Crose, *Brnch Mgr*
EMP: 10
SALES (corp-wide): 21.96MM **Privately Held**
Web: www.agmet1.com
SIC: 5093 3341 Ferrous metal scrap and waste; Secondary nonferrous metals
PA: Agmet Llc
    7800 Medusa Rd
    Cleveland OH 44146
    440 439-7400

(G-3616)
AIN INDUSTRIES INC
13901 Aspinwall Ave (44110-2210)
P.O. Box 464 (44011-0464)

Cleveland - Cuyahoga County (G-3617)

PHONE..............................440 781-0950
Bill Kavila, *Pr*
Steve Misch, *VP*
Ted Black, *Sec*
EMP: 6 **EST:** 1986
SQ FT: 6,500
SALES (est): 378.9K **Privately Held**
SIC: 2841 5169 5087 Soap and other detergents; Chemicals and allied products, nec; Service establishment equipment

(G-3617)
AIR-RITE INC
Also Called: Air Rite Service Supply
1290 W 117th St (44107-3096)
PHONE..............................216 228-8200
TOLL FREE: 800
David Harris, *Pr*
Marilyn Harris, *
▼ **EMP:** 24 **EST:** 1951
SQ FT: 28,000
SALES (est): 3.87MM **Privately Held**
Web: www.airrite-supply.com
SIC: 7623 7699 5075 3564 Air conditioning repair; Boiler and heating repair services; Warm air heating equipment and supplies; Blowers and fans

(G-3618)
AIRCRAFT & AUTO FITTINGS CO
17120 Saint Clair Ave (44110-2531)
PHONE..............................216 486-0047
Martin Sexton, *Pr*
John Markulin, *Sec*
EMP: 8 **EST:** 1960
SQ FT: 4,800
SALES (est): 725.67K **Privately Held**
SIC: 3599 Machine shop, jobbing and repair

(G-3619)
AK-ISG STEEL COATING COMPANY
3531 Campbell Rd (44105-1017)
PHONE..............................216 429-6901
Wilbur Ross-chb, *Prin*
EMP: 13 **EST:** 1985
SQ FT: 500,000
SALES (est): 242.13K **Privately Held**
SIC: 3479 3471 Galvanizing of iron, steel, or end-formed products; Plating and polishing

(G-3620)
ALABAMA SLING CENTER INC
21000 Aerospace Pkwy (44142-1000)
PHONE..............................440 239-7000
Tony Mazzela, *Prin*
EMP: 20 **EST:** 2013
SALES (est): 990.56K **Privately Held**
SIC: 3496 Miscellaneous fabricated wire products

(G-3621)
ALBION MACHINE & TOOL CO INC
13200 Enterprise Ave (44135-5104)
PHONE..............................216 267-9627
EMP: 6 **EST:** 1987
SQ FT: 9,000
SALES (est): 484.53K **Privately Held**
SIC: 3599 Machine shop, jobbing and repair

(G-3622)
ALCAN CORPORATION (HQ)
6060 Parkland Blvd (44124-4225)
PHONE..............................440 460-3307
Tom Albanese, *Pr*
Eileen Burns Lerum, *VP*
Donald P Seberger, *Chief Counsel*
Robert J Mosesian, *VP*
Timothy Guerra, *VP*
◆ **EMP:** 22 **EST:** 2003
SQ FT: 11,000
SALES (est): 208.92MM
SALES (corp-wide): 54.04B **Privately Held**
SIC: 3351 3355 3496 3357 Wire, copper and copper alloy; Wire, aluminum: made in rolling mills; Miscellaneous fabricated wire products; Nonferrous wiredrawing and insulating
PA: Rio Tinto Plc
6 St. James's Square
London SW1Y
207 781-2000

(G-3623)
ALCHEMICAL TRANSMUTATION CORP
314 E 195th St (44119-1118)
PHONE..............................216 313-8674
James Stuart Koch, *Owner*
EMP: 8 **EST:** 2010
SALES (est): 210.51K **Privately Held**
Web: www.alcheminc.com
SIC: 3499 Fire- or burglary-resistive products

(G-3624)
ALCOHOL & DRUG ADDICTION SVCS
2012 W 25th St Ste 600 (44113-4119)
PHONE..............................216 348-4830
Russell Kaye, *Ex Dir*
EMP: 10 **EST:** 1991
SALES (est): 144.29K **Privately Held**
SIC: 2721 Periodicals

(G-3625)
ALCON INDUSTRIES INC
7990 Baker Ave (44102-1900)
PHONE..............................216 961-1100
Richard J Chalet, *Ch Bd*
Richard J Chalet, *Ch Bd*
▲ **EMP:** 100 **EST:** 1977
SQ FT: 130,000
SALES (est): 23.6MM **Privately Held**
Web: www.alconindustries.com
SIC: 3325 3441 3369 Alloy steel castings, except investment; Fabricated structural metal; Nonferrous foundries, nec

(G-3626)
ALERT SAFETY LITE PRODUCTS CO
24500 Solon Rd (44146-4716)
PHONE..............................440 232-5020
Alan Kovacik, *Pr*
Paul S Blanch, *Sec*
EMP: 12 **EST:** 1972
SQ FT: 40,000
SALES (est): 489.29K **Privately Held**
SIC: 3699 3643 Trouble lights; Outlets, electric: convenience

(G-3627)
ALFALIGHT INC
676 Alpha Dr (44143-2123)
PHONE..............................608 240-4800
Charlie Hoke, *Ch*
EMP: 9 **EST:** 2019
SALES (est): 169.41K **Privately Held**
Web: www.gandh.com
SIC: 3699 Electrical equipment and supplies, nec

(G-3628)
ALFRED MACHINE CO (HQ)
29500 Solon Rd (44139-3449)
PHONE..............................440 248-4600
Art Anton, *CEO*
EMP: 85 **EST:** 1964
SQ FT: 100,000
SALES (est): 18.35MM
SALES (corp-wide): 881.02MM **Privately Held**
SIC: 3599 Machine shop, jobbing and repair
PA: Swagelok Company
29500 Solon Rd
Solon OH 44139
440 248-4600

(G-3629)
ALKID CORPORATION
6035 Parkland Blvd (44124-4186)
PHONE..............................216 896-3000
Jon P Marten, *CEO*
EMP: 46 **EST:** 1953
SALES (est): 1.59MM
SALES (corp-wide): 19.07B **Publicly Held**
SIC: 3594 Fluid power pumps
PA: Parker-Hannifin Corporation
6035 Parkland Blvd
Cleveland OH 44124
216 896-3000

(G-3630)
ALL METAL FABRICATORS INC
15400 Commerce Park Dr (44142-2011)
PHONE..............................216 267-0033
William Yankovich, *Pr*
Mike Yankovich, *VP*
Carol Yankovich, *Sec*
EMP: 15 **EST:** 1978
SQ FT: 14,000
SALES (est): 1.74MM **Privately Held**
Web: www.all-metalfab.com
SIC: 3444 Sheet metal specialties, not stamped

(G-3631)
ALL OHIO COMPANIES INC
2735 Scranton Rd (44113-5181)
PHONE..............................216 420-9274
Paul Colletti, *Prin*
EMP: 11 **EST:** 2013
SQ FT: 5,088
SALES (est): 940.82K **Privately Held**
Web: www.allohiopressurewash.com
SIC: 3446 1721 1799 Gates, ornamental metal; Exterior residential painting contractor; Exterior cleaning, including sandblasting

(G-3632)
ALL OHIO THREADED ROD CO INC
5349 Saint Clair Ave (44103-1311)
PHONE..............................216 426-1800
James Wolford, *CEO*
Rick Fien, *
James Wolford, *VP*
▲ **EMP:** 28 **EST:** 1981
SQ FT: 40,000
SALES (est): 4.38MM **Privately Held**
Web: www.allohiorod.com
SIC: 3312 5085 3316 Bar, rod, and wire products; Industrial supplies; Cold finishing of steel shapes

(G-3633)
ALL STREETS AUTO LLC ✪
15317 Chatfield Ave (44111-4301)
PHONE..............................330 714-7717
Dalton Lindesmith, *Managing Member*
EMP: 12 **EST:** 2022
SALES (est): 1.35MM **Privately Held**
SIC: 2396 Automotive and apparel trimmings

(G-3634)
ALL TRADES CONTRACTORS LLC
9920 Olivet Ave (44108-3546)
PHONE..............................440 850-5693
EMP: 8 **EST:** 2020
SALES (est): 184.36K **Privately Held**
SIC: 1389 Construction, repair, and dismantling services

(G-3635)
ALL-TYPE WELDING & FABRICATION
7690 Bond St (44139-5351)
PHONE..............................440 439-3990
Mike Distaulo, *Pr*
Dennis Whitaker, *
EMP: 40 **EST:** 1974
SQ FT: 34,000
SALES (est): 7.64MM **Privately Held**
Web: www.atwf-inc.com
SIC: 3599 7692 1761 Machine and other job shop work; Welding repair; Sheet metal work, nec

(G-3636)
ALLEGION ACCESS TECH LLC
Stanley Assembly Technologies
5335 Avion Park Dr (44143-1916)
P.O. Box 50400 (46250-0400)
PHONE..............................440 461-5500
John E Turpin, *Brnch Mgr*
EMP: 32
SQ FT: 40,000
Web: www.stanleyaccess.com
SIC: 3423 3546 Hand and edge tools, nec; Power-driven handtools
HQ: Allegion Access Technologies Llc
65 Scott Swamp Rd
Farmington CT 06032

(G-3637)
ALLIED TOOL & DIE INC
16146 Puritas Ave (44135-2691)
PHONE..............................216 941-6196
Fred Montag, *Pr*
Walter Montag, *Stockholder*
EMP: 19 **EST:** 1946
SALES (est): 2.36MM **Privately Held**
Web: www.alliedtool-die.com
SIC: 3469 3544 Stamping metal for the trade; Special dies and tools

(G-3638)
ALPHA PACKAGING HOLDINGS INC
Also Called: Progressive Plastics
14801 Emery Ave (44135-1476)
PHONE..............................216 252-5595
EMP: 275
SALES (corp-wide): 868.81MM **Privately Held**
Web: www.pretiumpkg.com
SIC: 3089 3085 Molding primary plastics; Plastics bottles
HQ: Alpha Packaging Holdings, Inc.
1555 Page Industrial Blvd
Saint Louis MO 63132

(G-3639)
ALPHA TOOL & MOLD INC
83 Alpha Park (44143-2265)
PHONE..............................440 473-2343
Robert Pischel, *Pr*
Al Pischel, *Sec*
Alfred Pischel, *Prin*
Helen Pischel, *Prin*
William M Fumich, *Prin*
▲ **EMP:** 12 **EST:** 1976
SQ FT: 8,500
SALES (est): 2.21MM **Privately Held**
Web: www.alphatoolandmold.com
SIC: 3544 Special dies and tools

(G-3640)
ALPHA ZETA HOLDINGS INC (PA)
2981 Independence Rd (44115-3615)
PHONE..............................216 271-1601
Joseph T Turgeon, *CEO*
James B Krimmel, *Pr*
EMP: 6 **EST:** 2003
SALES (est): 24.62MM
SALES (corp-wide): 24.62MM **Privately Held**

GEOGRAPHIC SECTION

Cleveland - Cuyahoga County (G-3664)

SIC: **2819** 2869 6799 Industrial inorganic chemicals, nec; Industrial organic chemicals, nec; Investors, nec

(G-3641)
ALSHER APM
7601 Detour Ave (44103-1849)
PHONE..................................216 496-8288
Leon Polott, *Pr*
EMP: 8 **EST:** 2013
SALES (est): 207.85K **Privately Held**
Web: www.alsherapm.com
SIC: **3479** Coating of metals and formed products

(G-3642)
ALTHAR LLC
5432 Broadway Ave (44127-1509)
PHONE..................................216 408-9860
EMP: 10 **EST:** 2021
SALES (est): 419.08K **Privately Held**
Web: www.atssounds.com
SIC: **3651** Speaker systems

(G-3643)
ALUMINUM BEARING CO OF AMERICA
Also Called: Albeco
4775 W 139th St (44135-5033)
PHONE..................................216 267-8560
Jane Beyer, *Pr*
EMP: 9 **EST:** 1956
SQ FT: 3,000
SALES (est): 1.98MM **Privately Held**
Web: www.albeco.com
SIC: **5051** 3429 Aluminum bars, rods, ingots, sheets, pipes, plates, etc.; Hardware, nec

(G-3644)
ALUMINUM COATING MANUFACTURERS
Also Called: Alcm
7301 Bessemer Ave (44127-1817)
PHONE..................................216 341-2000
Richard Kaplan, *Pr*
EMP: 16 **EST:** 1970
SQ FT: 50,000
SALES (est): 613.19K **Privately Held**
Web: www.alcm.com
SIC: **2891** 2851 2952 2951 Sealants; Paints and paint additives; Asphalt felts and coatings; Asphalt paving mixtures and blocks

(G-3645)
AMAC ENTERPRISES INC
5925 W 130th St (44130-1076)
PHONE..................................216 362-1880
Dean Caimples, *Mgr*
EMP: 13
SQ FT: 160,000
SALES (corp-wide): 14.96MM **Privately Held**
Web: www.amacent.com
SIC: **3471** Anodizing (plating) of metals or formed products
PA: Amac Enterprises, Inc.
    5909 W 130th St
    Parma OH 44130
    216 362-1880

(G-3646)
AMANI VINES LLC
3100 E 45th St Ste 512 (44127-1095)
PHONE..................................440 335-5432
EMP: 10 **EST:** 2021
SALES (est): 283.41K **Privately Held**
SIC: **2084** Wines

(G-3647)
AMAROK INDUSTRIES LLC
6895 Dogwood Cir (44130-3506)
PHONE..................................216 898-1948
Kevin Snider, *Prin*
EMP: 15 **EST:** 2015
SALES (est): 90.97K **Privately Held**
SIC: **3599** Industrial machinery, nec

(G-3648)
AMECO USA MET FBRCTION SLTONS
4600 W 160th St (44135-2630)
PHONE..................................440 899-9400
EMP: 9 **EST:** 2010
SALES (est): 8.05MM **Privately Held**
Web: www.ameco-usa.com
SIC: **3441** Fabricated structural metal
PA: American Manufacturing And Engineering Company
    4600 W 160th St
    Cleveland OH 44135

(G-3649)
AMERICAN ALLOY CORPORATION
9501 Allen Dr (44125-4603)
PHONE..................................216 642-9638
▲ **EMP:** 37
SIC: **3531** Construction machinery

(G-3650)
AMERICAN BRASS MFG CO
5000 Superior Ave (44103-1299)
PHONE..................................216 431-6565
Robert Mc Conville Junior, *Ch*
▲ **EMP:** 12 **EST:** 1894
SQ FT: 40,000
SALES (est): 902.33K **Privately Held**
Web: www.rvfaucets.com
SIC: **3432** Plumbers' brass goods: drain cocks, faucets, spigots, etc.

(G-3651)
AMERICAN BRONZE CORPORATION
2941 Broadway Ave (44115-3692)
PHONE..................................216 341-7800
Gerald Goldstein, *Pr*
Joshua Goldstein, *
EMP: 25 **EST:** 1924
SQ FT: 50,000
SALES (est): 10MM **Privately Held**
Web: www.americanbronzecorp.com
SIC: **3366** Copper foundries

(G-3652)
AMERICAN GREETINGS CORPORATION (HQ)
Also Called: American Greetings
1 American Blvd (44145-8151)
PHONE..................................216 252-7300
Joe Arcuri, *CEO*
Aaron Siegel, *VP*
Chad Anderson, *Ex Dir*
Gregory M Steinberg, *CFO*
◆ **EMP:** 1700 **EST:** 1906
SQ FT: 1,194,414
SALES (est): 689.67MM
SALES (corp-wide): 14.52B **Privately Held**
Web: www.americangreetings.com
SIC: **2771** 2679 2656 2678 Greeting cards; Gift wrap, paper: made from purchased material; Cups, paper: made from purchased material; Stationery: made from purchased material
PA: Clayton, Dubilier & Rice, Inc.
    375 Park Ave Fl 18
    New York NY 10152
    212 407-5200

(G-3653)
AMERICAN IR MET CLEVELAND LLC
1240 Marquette St (44114-3920)
PHONE..................................216 266-0509
◆ **EMP:** 20 **EST:** 1983
SQ FT: 70,000
SALES (est): 30.8MM
SALES (corp-wide): 407.17MM **Privately Held**
Web: www.aimcleveland.com
SIC: **5051** 3441 Steel; Fabricated structural metal
HQ: American Iron & Metal (U.S.A.), Inc.
    25 Kenney Dr
    Cranston RI 02920
    401 463-5605

(G-3654)
AMERICAN METAL TREATING CO
1043 E 62nd St (44103-1094)
PHONE..................................216 431-4492
Richard Roenn, *Pr*
Carol Roenn, *Sec*
▲ **EMP:** 22 **EST:** 1926
SQ FT: 15,830
SALES (est): 2.42MM **Privately Held**
Web: www.americanmetaltreating.com
SIC: **3398** Brazing (hardening) of metal

(G-3655)
AMERICAN PRECISION SPINDLES
Also Called: SKF Machine Tools Service
670 Alpha Dr (44143-2123)
PHONE..................................267 436-6000
EMP: 8 **EST:** 1997
SQ FT: 10,000
SALES (est): 3.61MM
SALES (corp-wide): 9.24B **Privately Held**
Web: www.precisionspindleinc.com
SIC: **3552** Spindles, textile
HQ: Skf Usa Inc.
    890 Forty Foot Rd
    Lansdale PA 19446
    267 436-6000

(G-3656)
AMERICAN TANK & FABRICATING CO (PA)
Also Called: A T & F Co
12314 Elmwood Ave (44111)
PHONE..................................216 252-1500
Terry Ripich, *Ch Bd*
Michael Ripich, *
Kenneth Ripich, *
Brian Spitz, *
Michael Puleo, *HEAVY FABRICATING**
▲ **EMP:** 100 **EST:** 1940
SQ FT: 300,000
SALES (est): 57.84MM
SALES (corp-wide): 57.84MM **Privately Held**
Web: www.atfco.com
SIC: **5051** 3443 Metals service centers and offices; Weldments

(G-3657)
AMERICLEAN 2 LLC
2061 Gehring Ave (44113-4120)
PHONE..................................216 781-3720
Randy Zimmerman, *Brnch Mgr*
EMP: 15
SALES (corp-wide): 15.55MM **Privately Held**
Web: www.ejthomascompany.com
SIC: **3714** Cleaners, air, motor vehicle
PA: Americlean 2 Llc
    5101 Forrest Dr Ste C
    New Albany OH 43054
    614 294-3373

(G-3658)
AMIR FOODS INC
761 Beta Dr Ste A (44143-2329)
PHONE..................................440 646-9388
EMP: 10 **EST:** 1993
SQ FT: 7,100
SALES (est): 443.21K **Privately Held**
Web: www.amirfoods.com
SIC: **2099** Food preparations, nec

(G-3659)
AMROS INDUSTRIES INC
14701 Industrial Pkwy (44135-4547)
PHONE..................................216 433-0010
Gregory Shteyngarts, *Pr*
EMP: 28 **EST:** 1986
SQ FT: 65,000
SALES (est): 1.02MM **Privately Held**
Web: www.clamshellusa.com
SIC: **7389** 2821 Packaging and labeling services; Thermoplastic materials

(G-3660)
ANALIZA INC (PA)
3615 Superior Ave E Ste 4407b (44114-4139)
PHONE..................................216 432-9050
EMP: 9 **EST:** 1996
SQ FT: 5,000
SALES (est): 2.33MM **Privately Held**
Web: www.analiza.com
SIC: **2834** Pharmaceutical preparations

(G-3661)
ANCHOR INDUSTRIES INCORPORATED
30775 Solon Industrial Pkwy (44139-4338)
PHONE..................................440 473-1414
Doug Kaufman, *Pr*
▲ **EMP:** 47 **EST:** 1999
SALES (est): 5.45MM **Privately Held**
Web: www.anchor-online.com
SIC: **3462** Automotive forgings, ferrous: crankshaft, engine, axle, etc.

(G-3662)
ANCHOR METAL PROCESSING INC
12200 Brookpark Rd (44130-1146)
PHONE..................................216 362-6463
Fred Pfaff, *Brnch Mgr*
EMP: 15
Web: www.anchor-mfg.com
SIC: **3599** 1761 3444 Machine shop, jobbing and repair; Sheet metal work, nec; Sheet metalwork
PA: Anchor Metal Processing, Inc.
    11830 Brookpark Rd
    Cleveland OH 44130

(G-3663)
ANCHOR METAL PROCESSING INC (PA)
11830 Brookpark Rd (44130-1103)
PHONE..................................216 362-1850
Edward Pfaff, *Ch Bd*
Frederick Pfaff, *
Jeff Pfaff, *
Robert Pfaff, *
EMP: 30 **EST:** 1992
SQ FT: 46,000
SALES (est): 4.51MM **Privately Held**
Web: www.anchor-mfg.com
SIC: **3599** 1761 3444 Machine shop, jobbing and repair; Sheet metal work, nec; Sheet metalwork

(G-3664)
ANCHOR TOOL & DIE CO
Also Called: Anchor Manufacturing Group
12200 Brookpark Rd (44130-1146)

Cleveland - Cuyahoga County (G-3665)

PHONE....................216 362-1850
Edward Pfaff, *Ch*
Frederick A Pfaff, *Pr*
Jeff Pfaff, *Treas*
Jim Walker, *CFO*
Robert Pfaff, *Sec*
▲ **EMP:** 275 **EST:** 1970
SQ FT: 350,000
SALES (est): 45.25MM **Privately Held**
Web: www.anchor-mfg.com
SIC: 3465 3544 3469 Automotive stampings; Special dies, tools, jigs, and fixtures; Metal stampings, nec

(G-3665)
ANDEEN-HAGERLING INC
31200 Bainbridge Rd Ste 2 (44139-2298)
PHONE....................440 349-0370
Carl W Hagerling, *Pr*
Carl G Andeen, *VP*
EMP: 14 **EST:** 1982
SQ FT: 7,600
SALES (est): 1.74MM **Privately Held**
Web: www.andeen-hagerling.com
SIC: 3825 Bridges: Kelvin, Wheatstone, vacuum tube, megohm, etc.

(G-3666)
ANDERSON DOOR CO
18090 Miles Rd (44128-3435)
PHONE....................216 475-5700
James B Anderson Junior, *Pr*
James B Anderson Iii, *VP*
Virginia Anderson, *
EMP: 17 **EST:** 1920
SQ FT: 30,000
SALES (est): 1.37MM **Privately Held**
Web: www.andersondoor.com
SIC: 2431 3442 Garage doors, overhead, wood; Garage doors, overhead: metal

(G-3667)
ANDERSOUND PA SERVICE
15911 Harvard Ave (44128-2049)
PHONE....................216 401-4631
Clarence Anderson Junior, *Owner*
EMP: 6 **EST:** 1975
SALES (est): 229.2K **Privately Held**
SIC: 3651 Audio electronic systems

(G-3668)
ANGSTROM GRAPHICS INC (PA)
4437 E 49th St (44125-1005)
PHONE....................216 271-5300
Wayne R Angstrom, *CEO*
Rachel Malakoff, *
◆ **EMP:** 250 **EST:** 1989
SQ FT: 225,000
SALES (est): 90.03MM **Privately Held**
Web: www.angstromgraphics.com
SIC: 2721 2754 2752 Magazines: publishing and printing; Commercial printing, gravure; Commercial printing, lithographic

(G-3669)
ANGSTROM GRAPHICS INC MIDWEST (HQ)
4437 E 49th St (44125-1005)
PHONE....................216 271-5300
Wayne R Angstrom, *Ch Bd*
Rachel Malakoff, *
EMP: 249 **EST:** 1917
SQ FT: 230,000
SALES (est): 51.77MM **Privately Held**
Web: www.angstromgraphics.com
SIC: 2752 7331 Offset printing; Direct mail advertising services
PA: Angstrom Graphics Inc
4437 E 49th St
Cleveland OH 44125

(G-3670)
APEX ADVANCED TECHNOLOGIES LLC
4857 W 130th St A (44135-5137)
PHONE....................216 898-1595
Dennis Hammond, *Managing Member*
▲ **EMP:** 6 **EST:** 2000
SQ FT: 12,000
SALES (est): 545.09K **Privately Held**
Web: www.apexadvancedtechnologies.com
SIC: 2899 Corrosion preventive lubricant

(G-3671)
APPROVED PLUMBING CO
Also Called: Approved Plbg & Sewer Clg Co
770 Ken Mar Industrial Pkwy (44147-2920)
PHONE....................216 663-5063
Dennis Schlekie, *Pr*
EMP: 10 **EST:** 1940
SALES (est): 940.3K **Privately Held**
Web: www.approvedplumbing.com
SIC: 1711 2434 Plumbing contractors; Wood kitchen cabinets

(G-3672)
ARC DRILLING INC (PA)
9551 Corporate Cir (44125-4261)
PHONE....................216 525-0920
Jason Busse, *CEO*
Lee Trem, *
Kevin Trem, *
Will Houghtaling, *
Will Houghtaling, *
EMP: 31 **EST:** 1947
SQ FT: 5,000
SALES (est): 5.39MM
SALES (corp-wide): 5.39MM **Privately Held**
Web: www.arcdrilling.com
SIC: 3599 Machine shop, jobbing and repair

(G-3673)
ARCHITECTURAL FIBERGLASS INC
8300 Bessemer Ave (44127-1839)
PHONE....................216 641-8300
▲ **EMP:** 30 **EST:** 1990
SQ FT: 20,000
SALES (est): 4.85MM **Privately Held**
Web: www.fiberglassafi.com
SIC: 2221 Glass and fiberglass broadwoven fabrics

(G-3674)
ARISDYNE SYSTEMS INC
17830 Englewood Dr Ste 11 (44130-3485)
PHONE....................216 458-1991
Peter Reimers, *CEO*
Frederick W Clarke, *Ex VP*
Peter Reimers, *Pr*
Cheryl Petrencsik, *CFO*
Scott Incorvia, *COO*
EMP: 15 **EST:** 2006
SALES (est): 4.71MM **Privately Held**
Web: www.arisdyne.com
SIC: 3612 Saturable reactors

(G-3675)
ARMOUR SPRAY SYSTEMS INC
210 Hayes Dr Ste I (44131-1056)
PHONE....................216 398-3838
Michael J Mihna Junior, *Pr*
Michael J Mihna Iii, *VP*
▲ **EMP:** 10 **EST:** 1976
SQ FT: 5,000
SALES (est): 1.97MM **Privately Held**
Web: www.armourspray.com
SIC: 5084 3563 Pumps and pumping equipment, nec; Spraying outfits: metals, paints, and chemicals (compressor)

(G-3676)
ARROW INTERNATIONAL INC (PA)
9900 Clinton Rd (44144)
PHONE....................216 961-3500
John E Gallagher, *CEO*
◆ **EMP:** 145 **EST:** 1965
SALES (est): 75.87MM
SALES (corp-wide): 75.87MM **Privately Held**
Web: www.arrowinternational.com
SIC: 3944 Board games, puzzles, and models, except electronic

(G-3677)
ART GALVANIZING WORKS INC
3935 Valley Rd (44109-3092)
PHONE....................216 749-0020
James Klein, *Pr*
Adrienne Klein, *VP*
EMP: 17 **EST:** 1935
SQ FT: 9,775
SALES (est): 823.48K **Privately Held**
Web: www.artgalvanizing.com
SIC: 3479 Coating of metals and formed products

(G-3678)
ART-AMERICAN PRINTING PLATES
1138 W 9th St Fl 4 (44113-1007)
PHONE....................216 241-4420
John T Mc Sweeney, *Pr*
Lawrence Mc Sweeney, *VP*
EMP: 10 **EST:** 1928
SQ FT: 11,000
SALES (est): 427.32K **Privately Held**
SIC: 2796 7336 Platemaking services; Graphic arts and related design

(G-3679)
ARTISAN ALES LLC
17448 Lorain Ave (44111-4028)
PHONE....................216 544-8703
Richard Skains, *Pr*
EMP: 21 **EST:** 2016
SALES (est): 381.8K **Privately Held**
SIC: 5813 2082 Drinking places; Beer (alcoholic beverage)

(G-3680)
ARTISAN CONSTRUCTORS LLC
Also Called: Artisan Renovations
600 Superior Ave E (44114-2614)
PHONE....................216 800-7641
James Abrams, *Managing Member*
James Abrams, *Prin*
EMP: 25 **EST:** 2008
SALES (est): 1.52MM **Privately Held**
SIC: 1522 7299 1521 1389 Residential construction, nec; Home improvement and renovation contractor agency; Single-family home remodeling, additions, and repairs; Construction, repair, and dismantling services

(G-3681)
ARTISAN TOOL & DIE CORP
4911 Grant Ave (44125-1027)
PHONE....................216 883-2769
James Berkes, *Pr*
David Dross, *
▼ **EMP:** 74 **EST:** 1968
SQ FT: 65,000
SALES (est): 888.59K **Privately Held**
Web: www.alacriant.com
SIC: 3469 3544 Metal stampings, nec; Special dies and tools

(G-3682)
ARTISTIC METAL SPINNING INC
Also Called: Zoia
4700 Lorain Ave (44102-3443)
PHONE....................216 961-3336
Lorraine Hangauer, *Pr*
Donald E Hangauer, *Sec*
Ronald W Hangauer, *VP*
EMP: 6 **EST:** 1930
SQ FT: 12,000
SALES (est): 919.04K **Privately Held**
Web: www.artisticmetalspinning.com
SIC: 3469 Stamping metal for the trade

(G-3683)
ARTISTIC ROCK LLC
3786 Fairoaks Rd (44121-1923)
PHONE....................216 291-8856
Ronan Basler, *Prin*
EMP: 7 **EST:** 2011
SALES (est): 253.67K **Privately Held**
Web: www.artisticrock.net
SIC: 5999 3272 Concrete products, pre-cast; Art marble, concrete

(G-3684)
ARZEL TECHNOLOGY INC
Also Called: Arzel Zoning Technology
4801 Commerce Pkwy (44128-5905)
PHONE....................216 831-6068
Lenny Roth, *Sr VP*
Adam Bush, *
▼ **EMP:** 29 **EST:** 1983
SQ FT: 40,000
SALES (est): 4.09MM **Privately Held**
Web: www.arzelzoning.com
SIC: 3823 Process control instruments

(G-3685)
ASCO POWER TECHNOLOGIES LP
6255 Halle Dr (44125-4615)
PHONE....................216 573-7600
Bob Daniels, *Genl Mgr*
EMP: 113
SALES (corp-wide): 82.05MM **Privately Held**
Web: www.ascopower.com
SIC: 3613 3625 Switchgear and switchboard apparatus; Resistors and resistor units
HQ: Asco Power Technologies, L.P.
160 Park Ave
Florham Park NJ 07932

(G-3686)
ASCON TECNOLOGIC N AMER LLC
Also Called: Ascon Tecnologic
1111 Brookpark Rd (44109-5825)
PHONE....................216 485-8350
Steven Craig, *Genl Mgr*
EMP: 6 **EST:** 2012
SALES (est): 793.13K **Privately Held**
Web: www.ascontecnologic.com
SIC: 3823 Process control instruments

(G-3687)
ASG
15700 S Waterloo Rd (44110-3814)
PHONE....................216 486-6163
Bryon Schafer, *Mgr*
EMP: 19 **EST:** 2014
SALES (est): 363.8K **Privately Held**
Web: www.asg-jergens.com
SIC: 3423 Hand and edge tools, nec

(G-3688)
ASG DIVISION JERGENS INC
15700 S Waterloo Rd Jergens Way (44110-3814)
PHONE....................888 486-6163
EMP: 22 **EST:** 2015
SALES (est): 1.6MM **Privately Held**
Web: www.asg-jergens.com

GEOGRAPHIC SECTION

Cleveland - Cuyahoga County (G-3712)

SIC: 3423 3629 1731 Screw drivers, pliers, chisels, etc. (hand tools); Battery chargers, rectifying or nonrotating; Electric power systems contractors

(G-3689)
ASHLAND CHEMCO INC
Also Called: Ask Chemicals
2191 W 110th St (44102-3593)
PHONE..................216 961-4690
EMP: 14
SALES (corp-wide): 2.19B **Publicly Held**
SIC: 2899 Chemical preparations, nec
HQ: Ashland Chemco Inc.
1979 Atlas St
Columbus OH 43228
859 815-3333

(G-3690)
ASHTA ENTERPRISES LTD LBLTY CO
3001 W 121st St (44111-1638)
PHONE..................216 252-7620
EMP: 6 **EST:** 2019
SALES (est): 488.49K **Privately Held**
SIC: 3462 Iron and steel forgings

(G-3691)
ASHTA FORGE & MACHINE INC
3001 W 121st St (44111-1638)
PHONE..................216 252-7000
Wayne Phelps, *Pr*
Karen Mason, *Sec*
EMP: 19 **EST:** 1992
SALES (est): 220.52K **Privately Held**
Web: www.bulaforge.com
SIC: 3599 Machine shop, jobbing and repair

(G-3692)
ASPEN FASTENERS USA
1028 E 134th St (44110-2248)
PHONE..................800 479-0056
EMP: 6 **EST:** 2016
SALES (est): 134.07K **Privately Held**
SIC: 3965 Fasteners

(G-3693)
ASSEMBLY SPECIALTY PDTS INC
14700 Brookpark Rd (44135-5166)
PHONE..................216 676-5600
Erno Nagy, *Pr*
Attila Nagy, *VP*
EMP: 22 **EST:** 1971
SQ FT: 33,500
SALES (est): 4.35MM **Privately Held**
Web: www.assemblyspecialty.com
SIC: 3496 Cable, uninsulated wire: made from purchased wire

(G-3694)
AT HOLDINGS CORPORATION
23555 Euclid Ave (44117-1703)
PHONE..................216 692-6000
Michael S Lipscomb, *Ch Bd*
Frances S St Clair, *
David Scaife, *
EMP: 736 **EST:** 1990
SQ FT: 1,800,000
SALES (est): 187.9MM **Privately Held**
SIC: 3724 3728 6512 Pumps, aircraft engine ; Aircraft parts and equipment, nec; Commercial and industrial building operation
HQ: Eaton Corporation
1000 Eaton Blvd
Cleveland OH 44122
440 523-5000

(G-3695)
AT&F ADVANCED METALS LLC (PA)
12314 Elmwood Ave (44111-5906)
PHONE..................330 684-1122
▲ **EMP:** 23 **EST:** 2002
SQ FT: 15,000
SALES (est): 8.15MM
SALES (corp-wide): 8.15MM **Privately Held**
Web: www.atfco.com
SIC: 3446 3443 Railings, prefabricated metal ; Process vessels, industrial: metal plate

(G-3696)
ATELIERKOPII LLC ✣
11811 Shaker Blvd Ste 204 (44120-1927)
PHONE..................216 559-0815
Brianna Mitchell, *Prin*
EMP: 6 **EST:** 2023
SALES (est): 78.58K **Privately Held**
SIC: 2678 Stationery products

(G-3697)
ATHENS FOODS INC
13600 Snow Rd (44142-2546)
PHONE..................216 676-8500
Eric Moscahlaidis, *Ch Bd*
Robert Tansing, *
William Buckingham, *Marketing**
Jeff Swint, *
Sandy Sanders, *
EMP: 180 **EST:** 1958
SQ FT: 114,000
SALES (est): 26.64MM **Privately Held**
Web: www.athensfoods.com
SIC: 2038 2045 Frozen specialties, nec; Prepared flour mixes and doughs

(G-3698)
AUSTIN POWDER COMPANY (DH)
25800 Science Park Dr Ste 300 (44122-7386)
PHONE..................216 464-2400
William Jack Davis, *Ch Bd*
David M Gleason, *
Jason F Rawlings, *
Michael A Gleason, *
▲ **EMP:** 70 **EST:** 1833
SQ FT: 25,000
SALES (est): 721.82MM
SALES (corp-wide): 749.73MM **Privately Held**
Web: www.austinpowder.com
SIC: 2892 Explosives
HQ: Austin Powder Holdings Company
25800 Science Park Dr # 300
Cleveland OH 44122

(G-3699)
AUSTIN POWDER HOLDINGS COMPANY (HQ)
25800 Science Park Dr Ste 300 (44122-7311)
PHONE..................216 464-2400
◆ **EMP:** 60 **EST:** 1837
SQ FT: 25,000
SALES (est): 749.73MM
SALES (corp-wide): 749.73MM **Privately Held**
Web: www.austinpowder.com
SIC: 2892 Explosives
PA: Davis Mining & Manufacturing, Inc.
5957 Windswept Blvd
Wise VA 24293
276 395-3354

(G-3700)
AUTO BOLT COMPANY
Also Called: Auto Bolt and Nut Company, The
4740 Manufacturing Ave (44135-2640)
PHONE..................216 881-3913
Robert Kocian, *Pr*
EMP: 60 **EST:** 2005
SQ FT: 64,100
SALES (est): 11.4MM **Privately Held**
Web: www.autobolt.net
SIC: 3452 Bolts, metal

(G-3701)
AUTO-TAP INC
3317 W 140th St (44111-2428)
PHONE..................216 671-1043
Jim Sullivan, *Pr*
Mike Peteras, *Stockholder*
Frank Suarez, *Stockholder*
EMP: 9 **EST:** 1972
SQ FT: 18,000
SALES (est): 919.03K **Privately Held**
Web: www.auto-tap.net
SIC: 3559 Degreasing machines, automotive and industrial

(G-3702)
AUTOMATED PACKG SYSTEMS INC
Also Called: AUTOMATED PACKAGING SYSTEMS, INC.
13555 Mccracken Rd (44125-1993)
PHONE..................216 663-2000
Yates Brad, *Mgr*
EMP: 120
SALES (corp-wide): 5.49B **Publicly Held**
Web: www.autobag.com
SIC: 3081 2673 Packing materials, plastics sheet; Bags: plastic, laminated, and coated
HQ: Automated Packaging Systems, Llc
10175 Philipp Pkwy
Streetsboro OH 44241
330 528-2000

(G-3703)
AUTOMATED WHEEL LLC
8525 Clinton Rd (44144-1014)
PHONE..................216 651-9022
◆ **EMP:** 16 **EST:** 2005
SALES (est): 559.59K **Privately Held**
Web: www.arewaywheel.com
SIC: 3471 Plating of metals or formed products

(G-3704)
AUTOMATIC STAMP PRODUCTS INC
1822 Columbus Rd (44113-2472)
PHONE..................216 781-7933
Raymond L Haserodt, *VP*
EMP: 19 **EST:** 1946
SQ FT: 44,000
SALES (est): 2MM **Privately Held**
Web: www.automaticstamp.com
SIC: 3469 Stamping metal for the trade

(G-3705)
AUTOMATION FINISHING INC
Also Called: Automation Finishing
3206 W 121st St (44111-1720)
PHONE..................216 251-8805
Steve Star, *Pr*
EMP: 10 **EST:** 2000
SALES (est): 235.42K **Privately Held**
SIC: 3471 Plating of metals or formed products

(G-3706)
AUTOTX INC
4635 Northfield Rd (44128-4508)
PHONE..................216 510-6666
EMP: 9 **EST:** 2020
SALES (est): 227.09K **Privately Held**
Web: www.autotxinc.com
SIC: 3465 Body parts, automobile: stamped metal

(G-3707)
AVERY DENNISON CORPORATION
15939 Industrial Pkwy (44135-3321)
PHONE..................216 267-8700
EMP: 7
SALES (corp-wide): 8.36B **Publicly Held**
Web: www.averydennison.com
SIC: 2672 Adhesive papers, labels, or tapes: from purchased material
PA: Avery Dennison Corporation
8080 Norton Pkwy
Mentor OH 44060
440 534-6000

(G-3708)
AVILES CONSTRUCTION CO INC
7011 Clark Ave (44102-5316)
PHONE..................216 939-1084
Jose Aviles, *Pr*
Elisa E Velez, *Sec*
Maria Aviles, *Treas*
Alex Aviles, *VP*
Jose E Aviles, *Pr*
EMP: 11 **EST:** 1983
SALES (est): 960.8K **Privately Held**
Web: www.avilesenergysolutions.com
SIC: 2821 Cellulose acetate (plastics)

(G-3709)
AVTRON AEROSPACE INC
7900 E Pleasant Valley Rd (44131-5529)
PHONE..................216 750-5152
John Pesec, *Pr*
Joseph Flower, *
EMP: 117 **EST:** 1953
SQ FT: 65,000
SALES (est): 24.8MM **Privately Held**
Web: www.testek.com
SIC: 3351 3728 Bars and bar shapes, copper and copper alloy; Aircraft parts and equipment, nec

(G-3710)
AVTRON HOLDINGS LLC
7900 E Pleasant Valley Rd (44131-5529)
PHONE..................216 642-1230
James Ettamarna, *
Theodore A Laufik, *
Peter Taft, *
Karen Tuleta, *
EMP: 40 **EST:** 2007
SQ FT: 47,707
SALES (est): 1.8MM **Privately Held**
Web: www.testek.com
SIC: 3625 3825 Electric controls and control accessories, industrial; Instruments to measure electricity

(G-3711)
AVTRON LOADBANK INC
6255 Halle Dr (44125-4615)
P.O. Box 4100 (63136-8506)
PHONE..................216 573-7600
EMP: 109
SIC: 3613 3625 Switchgear and switchboard apparatus; Resistors and resistor units

(G-3712)
AWNING FABRI CATERS INC
10237 Lorain Ave (44111-5435)
P.O. Box 182 (44012-0182)
PHONE..................216 476-4888
TOLL FREE: 800
Todd Krupa, *Pr*
EMP: 7 **EST:** 1987
SALES (est): 421.87K **Privately Held**
Web: awning-and-canopy-dealers.cmac.ws
SIC: 2394 Awnings, fabric: made from purchased materials

Cleveland - Cuyahoga County (G-3713)

(G-3713)
B & B PAPER CONVERTERS INC
12500 Elmwood Ave Frnt (44111-5910)
PHONE..................216 941-8100
Jerry Jazwa, *Pr*
EMP: 17 **EST:** 1947
SQ FT: 120,000
SALES (est): 390.37K **Privately Held**
Web: www.bbpaper.com
SIC: 2621 Newsprint paper

(G-3714)
B & P SPRING PRODUCTION CO
19520 Nottingham Rd (44110-2730)
PHONE..................216 486-4260
Ken Godnavec, *Pr*
Lorraine Ray, *Sec*
EMP: 27 **EST:** 1952
SQ FT: 13,000
SALES (est): 2.16MM **Privately Held**
Web: www.bpspring.com
SIC: 3495 Precision springs

(G-3715)
B & R MACHINE CO
2216 W 65th St (44102-5302)
PHONE..................216 961-7370
William E Graham, *Pr*
Teala Graham, *Sec*
EMP: 18 **EST:** 1958
SQ FT: 12,000
SALES (est): 1.56MM **Privately Held**
Web: www.brmachineco.com
SIC: 3545 3599 Machine tool accessories; Machine shop, jobbing and repair

(G-3716)
B&A ISON STEEL INC
Also Called: Buckeye Metals Industries
3238 E 82nd St (44104-4338)
P.O. Box 31528 (44131-0528)
PHONE..................216 663-4300
Bruce Ison, *Pr*
EMP: 10 **EST:** 1997
SQ FT: 45,000
SALES (est): 4.92MM
SALES (corp-wide): 48.57MM **Privately Held**
Web: www.buckeye-metals.com
SIC: 3469 5051 Metal stampings, nec; Steel
PA: Paragon Steel Enterprises, Llc
4211 County Road 61
Butler IN 46721
260 868-1100

(G-3717)
B-R-O-T INCORPORATED
4730 Briar Rd (44135-2595)
PHONE..................216 267-5335
Kenneth Ott, *Pr*
Patricia Ott, *
Robert Ott, *
▲ **EMP:** 25 **EST:** 1946
SQ FT: 22,000
SALES (est): 4.35MM **Privately Held**
Web: www.brot-inc.com
SIC: 3444 2542 Sheet metalwork; Partitions and fixtures, except wood

(G-3718)
B2D SOLUTIONS INC
Also Called: Ballastshop
3558 Lee Rd (44120-5123)
PHONE..................855 484-1145
John Mahoney, *Pr*
EMP: 8 **EST:** 2000
SALES (est): 1.14MM **Privately Held**
Web: www.ballastshop.com
SIC: 5063 3648 Lighting fixtures; Decorative area lighting fixtures

(G-3719)
BARBS GRAFFITI INC (PA)
Also Called: Graffiti Co
3111 Carnegie Ave (44115-2632)
PHONE..................216 881-5550
Abe Miller, *Pr*
Barbara Miller, *
▲ **EMP:** 38 **EST:** 1984
SQ FT: 18,000
SALES (est): 9.07MM
SALES (corp-wide): 9.07MM **Privately Held**
Web: www.graffiticaps.com
SIC: 2353 2395 5136 5137 Baseball caps; Pleating and stitching; Sportswear, men's and boys'; Sportswear, women's and children's

(G-3720)
BARILE PRECISION GRINDING INC
12320 Plaza Dr (44130-1043)
PHONE..................216 267-6500
Michael Barile, *Pr*
EMP: 11 **EST:** 1977
SALES (est): 961.68K **Privately Held**
Web: www.barilegrinding.com
SIC: 3599 Machine shop, jobbing and repair

(G-3721)
BARKER PRODUCTS COMPANY
1028 E 134th St (44110-2248)
P.O. Box 10845 (44110-0845)
▲ **EMP:** 30 **EST:** 1945
SALES (est): 4.49MM **Privately Held**
Web: www.barkerplating.com
SIC: 3471 Electroplating of metals or formed products

(G-3722)
BARTH INDUSTRIES CO LLC (PA)
Also Called: Landis Machine Division
12650 Brookpark Rd (44130-1154)
PHONE..................216 267-1950
Richard Legan, *Pr*
Russ Lauer, *
▲ **EMP:** 22 **EST:** 2006
SQ FT: 120,700
SALES (est): 7.38MM
SALES (corp-wide): 7.38MM **Privately Held**
Web: www.barthindustries.com
SIC: 3541 3542 3535 3699 Machine tools, metal cutting type; Machine tools, metal forming type; Conveyors and conveying equipment; Electrical equipment and supplies, nec

(G-3723)
BASF CATALYSTS LLC
Also Called: BASF
23800 Mercantile Rd (44122-5908)
P.O. Box 22126 (44122-0126)
PHONE..................216 360-5005
John Ferek, *Brnch Mgr*
EMP: 117
SALES (corp-wide): 74.89B **Privately Held**
Web: catalysts.basf.com
SIC: 2819 8731 Catalysts, chemical; Commercial physical research
HQ: Basf Catalysts Llc
33 Wood Ave S
Iselin NJ 08830
732 205-5000

(G-3724)
BASIC CASES INC
19561 Miles Rd (44128-4111)
PHONE..................216 662-3900
Kenneth Wieder, *Pr*
Ruth Wieder, *VP*
EMP: 8 **EST:** 1980

SQ FT: 22,000
SALES (est): 621.92K **Privately Held**
Web: www.perfectdomain.com
SIC: 2511 2521 Wood household furniture; Wood office furniture

(G-3725)
BD LAPLACE LLC (PA)
Also Called: Bayou Steel Group
28026 Gates Mills Blvd (44124-4730)
PHONE..................985 652-4900
Robert Simon, *CEO*
Alton Davis, *
◆ **EMP:** 410 **EST:** 1979
SALES (est): 25MM
SALES (corp-wide): 25MM **Privately Held**
Web: www.stjohnig.com
SIC: 3312 Structural and rail mill products

(G-3726)
BEA-ECC APPARELS INC
1287 W 76th St (44102-2050)
PHONE..................216 650-6336
Siba Beavogui, *Prin*
EMP: 8 **EST:** 2002
SALES (est): 473.86K **Privately Held**
SIC: 2311 Men's and boy's suits and coats

(G-3727)
BEACON METAL FABRICATORS INC
5425 Hamilton Ave Ste D (44114-3983)
PHONE..................216 391-7444
Kenneth Grobolsek, *Pr*
Robert Grobolssek, *VP*
EMP: 13 **EST:** 1987
SQ FT: 11,000
SALES (est): 380.93K **Privately Held**
Web: www.beaconmetalfab.com
SIC: 3599 3444 3446 Machine and other job shop work; Bins, prefabricated sheet metal; Railings, prefabricated metal

(G-3728)
BECKETT-GREENHILL LLC
Also Called: Colony Hardware
1800 E 30th St (44114-4410)
PHONE..................216 861-5730
EMP: 15 **EST:** 2007
SQ FT: 40,000
SALES (est): 2.37MM **Privately Held**
Web: www.colonyhardware.com
SIC: 3965 Fasteners

(G-3729)
BELLAS JEWELS LLC
975 Parkwood Dr 10ste1 (44108-3052)
PHONE..................216 551-9593
Tyreka Williams, *Managing Member*
EMP: 8 **EST:** 2021
SALES (est): 306.7K **Privately Held**
SIC: 3961 Jewelry apparel, non-precious metals

(G-3730)
BERGSTROM COMPANY LTD PARTNR
Also Called: Weldon Pump
640 Golden Oak Pkwy (44146-6504)
PHONE..................440 232-2282
Tony Coletto, *CEO*
Blane Mckelvey, *Genl Pt*
Walter T Bergstrom, *Pt*
Jon Bergstrom, *Pt*
Barbara Bergstrom, *Pt*
EMP: 25 **EST:** 1918
SQ FT: 13,600
SALES (est): 3.33MM **Privately Held**
Web: www.weldonpumps.com

SIC: 3714 3594 3586 3561 Fuel pumps, motor vehicle; Fluid power pumps and motors; Measuring and dispensing pumps; Pumps and pumping equipment

(G-3731)
BERKSHIRE ROAD HOLDINGS INC
3344 E 80th St (44127-1851)
PHONE..................216 883-4200
James Lamantia, *Pr*
Jay E Irvin, *Ex VP*
EMP: 18 **EST:** 1958
SQ FT: 60,000
SALES (est): 4.53MM **Privately Held**
Web: www.genstlcorp.com
SIC: 5051 3398 3441 Steel; Metal heat treating; Fabricated structural metal

(G-3732)
BESTEN INC
4416 Lee Rd (44128-2902)
PHONE..................216 910-2880
Fred Floyd, *Prin*
EMP: 11 **EST:** 1998
SALES (est): 214.26K **Privately Held**
SIC: 3559 Special industry machinery, nec

(G-3733)
BEVERAGE MCH & FABRICATORS INC
13301 Lakewood Heights Blvd (44107-6219)
PHONE..................216 252-5100
John D Geiger, *Pr*
Nancy Geiger, *Sec*
EMP: 15 **EST:** 1932
SQ FT: 15,000
SALES (est): 1.26MM **Privately Held**
Web: www.bevmachine.com
SIC: 3599 Machine shop, jobbing and repair

(G-3734)
BHL INTERNATIONAL INC
10533 Baltic Rd (44102-1634)
PHONE..................216 458-8472
Emeka Iwenofu, *Prin*
EMP: 8 **EST:** 2018
SALES (est): 72.06K **Privately Held**
Web: www.bhlinternational.com
SIC: 1389 Oil field services, nec

(G-3735)
BIG GUS ONION RINGS INC
4500 Turney Rd (44105-6716)
PHONE..................216 883-9045
Peter George, *Pr*
Thomas George, *VP*
Angela George, *Sec*
EMP: 11 **EST:** 1968
SQ FT: 5,000
SALES (est): 582.95K **Privately Held**
Web: www.biggusonionrings.com
SIC: 2037 5148 2099 Vegetables, quick frozen & cold pack, excl. potato products; Fruits, fresh; Food preparations, nec

(G-3736)
BIG RIVER ONLINE
2509 Euclid Heights Blvd (44106-2709)
PHONE..................855 244-7487
EMP: 7 **EST:** 2014
SALES (est): 171.34K **Privately Held**
Web: www.gobigriver.com
SIC: 7372 Prepackaged software

(G-3737)
BIMBO BKRIES USA CLVLAND HTS D
4570 E 71st St (44105-5604)
PHONE..................216 641-5700

GEOGRAPHIC SECTION
Cleveland - Cuyahoga County (G-3759)

EMP: 6 **EST**: 2010
SALES (est): 157.46K **Privately Held**
SIC: 2051 Bakery: wholesale or wholesale/retail combined

(G-3738)
BIZALL INC
Also Called: Promote-U-Graphics
1935 W 96th St Ste H (44102-2600)
PHONE..........................216 939-9580
Brent White, *Pr*
Tyrone White, *VP*
EMP: 7 **EST**: 1992
SQ FT: 15,000
SALES (est): 620.09K **Privately Held**
SIC: 5734 2759 Printers and plotters: computers; Commercial printing, nec

(G-3739)
BLACK & DECKER CORPORATION
Also Called: Black & Decker
12100 Snow Rd Ste 1 (44130-9319)
PHONE..........................440 842-9100
Mark Konecek, *Brnch Mgr*
EMP: 6
SALES (corp-wide): 15.78B **Publicly Held**
Web: www.blackanddecker.com
SIC: 3546 Power-driven handtools
HQ: The Black & Decker Corporation
701 E Joppa Rd
Towson MD 21286
410 716-3900

(G-3740)
BLAINS FOLDING SERVICE INC
4103 Detroit Ave (44113-2721)
PHONE..........................216 631-4700
Edward Blain, *Pr*
Carol Blain, *Sec*
EMP: 7 **EST**: 1967
SALES (est): 516.77K **Privately Held**
SIC: 2789 Binding only: books, pamphlets, magazines, etc.

(G-3741)
BLASTER HOLDINGS LLC (PA)
Also Called: Gunk
8500 Sweet Valley Dr (44125-4214)
PHONE..........................216 901-5800
Randy Pindor, *Pr*
EMP: 9 **EST**: 2020
SALES (est): 9.85MM
SALES (corp-wide): 9.85MM **Privately Held**
Web: www.blasterproducts.com
SIC: 2911 2819 2842 Fuel additives; Catalysts, chemical; Automobile polish

(G-3742)
BLASTER LLC (PA)
8500 Sweet Valley Dr (44125-4214)
PHONE..........................216 901-5800
Randy Pindor, *Pr*
EMP: 39 **EST**: 1959
SQ FT: 20,000
SALES (est): 10.89MM
SALES (corp-wide): 10.89MM **Privately Held**
Web: www.blasterproducts.com
SIC: 2911 2819 2842 2992 Fuel additives; Catalysts, chemical; Automobile polish; Lubricating oils and greases

(G-3743)
BOARD OF PARK COMMISSIONERS
4101 Fulton Pkwy (44144-1923)
PHONE..........................216 635-3200
Dan T Moore, *Prin*
EMP: 10 **EST**: 2005
SALES (est): 230.66K **Privately Held**
Web: www.clevelandmetroparks.com

SIC: 3949 Shafts, golf club

(G-3744)
BODYCOTE THERMAL PROC INC
5475 Avion Park Dr (44143-1918)
PHONE..........................440 473-2020
Ron Perkins, *Brnch Mgr*
EMP: 42
SALES (corp-wide): 1B **Privately Held**
Web: www.bodycote.com
SIC: 3398 Metal heat treating
HQ: Bodycote Thermal Processing, Inc.
12750 Merit Dr Ste 1400
Dallas TX 75251
214 904-2420

(G-3745)
BOLGER
4200 W 229th St (44126-1835)
PHONE..........................440 979-9577
Roger Bolger, *Prin*
EMP: 7 **EST**: 2005
SALES (est): 94.7K **Privately Held**
Web: www.bolger.com
SIC: 2752 Offset printing

(G-3746)
BOMAT INC
19218 Redwood Rd (44110-2736)
PHONE..........................216 692-8382
EMP: 7 **EST**: 2016
SALES (est): 941.17K
SALES (corp-wide): 7.26B **Publicly Held**
SIC: 2899 Concrete curing and hardening compounds
PA: Rpm International Inc.
2628 Pearl Rd
Medina OH 44256
330 273-5090

(G-3747)
BONFOEY CO
1710 Euclid Ave (44115-2134)
PHONE..........................216 621-0178
Richard G Moore, *Pr*
Mina V Moore, *Sec*
Olga Merela, *Treas*
EMP: 15 **EST**: 1893
SQ FT: 9,300
SALES (est): 2.2MM **Privately Held**
Web: www.bonfoey.com
SIC: 2499 5719 8999 Picture and mirror frames, wood; Pictures, wall; Art restoration

(G-3748)
BORDEN DAIRY CO CINCINNATI LLC (DH)
Also Called: H. Meyer Dairy
3068 W 106th St (44111-1801)
PHONE..........................513 948-8811
EMP: 27 **EST**: 1976
SALES (est): 21.74MM **Privately Held**
Web: www.bordendairy.com
SIC: 2026 2086 5143 5144 Milk processing (pasteurizing, homogenizing, bottling); Bottled and canned soft drinks; Dairy products, except dried or canned; Poultry and poultry products
HQ: National Dairy, Llc
8750 N Central Expy # 400
Dallas TX 75231
214 459-1100

(G-3749)
BORMAN ENTERPRISES INC
Also Called: Cleveland Indus Training Ctr
1311 Brookpark Rd (44109-5829)
PHONE..........................216 459-9292
Donald Borman, *Pr*
Marybeth Borman, *Sec*
Joseph Scheall, *VP*

EMP: 10 **EST**: 1975
SQ FT: 13,000
SALES (est): 1.57MM **Privately Held**
Web: www.clevelandindustrialtraining.com
SIC: 3599 8222 Machine shop, jobbing and repair; Technical institute

(G-3750)
BOXIT CORPORATION (HQ)
5555 Walworth Ave (44102-4430)
PHONE..........................216 631-6900
Joel Zaas, *Pr*
Carole Holowecky, *
Donald Zaas, *
Mark Cassese, *
EMP: 12 **EST**: 1971
SQ FT: 100,000
SALES (est): 20.61MM
SALES (corp-wide): 23.99MM **Privately Held**
Web: www.boxit.com
SIC: 2652 2657 Setup paperboard boxes; Folding paperboard boxes
PA: The Apex Paper Box Company
5601 Walworth Ave
Cleveland OH 44102
216 631-4000

(G-3751)
BOXIT CORPORATION
3000 Quigley Rd B (44113-4591)
PHONE..........................216 416-9475
Mark Cassese, *Prin*
EMP: 88
SALES (corp-wide): 23.99MM **Privately Held**
Web: www.boxit.com
SIC: 2657 2652 Folding paperboard boxes; Setup paperboard boxes
HQ: Boxit Corporation
5555 Walworth Ave
Cleveland OH 44102
216 631-6900

(G-3752)
BPI EC LLC
127 Public Sq Ste 5110 (44114-1313)
PHONE..........................216 589-0198
EMP: 9
SALES (est): 5.84MM
SALES (corp-wide): 8.03B **Privately Held**
SIC: 3714 Motor vehicle brake systems and parts
HQ: Bpi Holdings International, Inc.
4400 Prime Pkwy
Mchenry IL 60050
815 363-9000

(G-3753)
BRAKE PARTS INC CHINA LLC (DH)
127 Public Sq Ste 5110 (44114-1313)
PHONE..........................216 589-0198
EMP: 6
SALES (est): 20.25MM
SALES (corp-wide): 8.03B **Privately Held**
SIC: 3714 Motor vehicle brake systems and parts
HQ: Bpi Holdings International, Inc.
4400 Prime Pkwy
Mchenry IL 60050
815 363-9000

(G-3754)
BRANTLEY PARTNERS IV LP
3550 Lander Rd Ste 160 (44124-5727)
PHONE..........................216 464-8400
Robert Pinkas, *Ch*
Michael J Finn, *Pr*
Tab A Keplinger, *VP*
EMP: 8 **EST**: 2000

SALES (est): 626.27K **Privately Held**
Web: www.brantleypartners.com
SIC: 6799 5141 2066 2099 Investors, nec; Groceries, general line; Chocolate and cocoa products; Food preparations, nec

(G-3755)
BREINING MECH SYSTEMS INC (PA)
883 Addison Rd (44103-1607)
PHONE..........................216 391-2400
John Sickle Junior, *Pr*
EMP: 8 **EST**: 1947
SALES (est): 734.2K
SALES (corp-wide): 734.2K **Privately Held**
Web: www.breiningmechanicalsystems.com
SIC: 3444 Sheet metalwork

(G-3756)
BRIDGESTONE RET OPERATIONS LLC
Also Called: Firestone
6874 Pearl Rd (44130-3615)
PHONE..........................440 842-3200
Sunil Rebello, *Mgr*
EMP: 8
Web: www.bridgestoneamericas.com
SIC: 5531 7534 Automotive tires; Tire repair shop
HQ: Bridgestone Retail Operations, Llc
333 E Lake St Ste 300
Bloomingdale IL 60108
630 259-9000

(G-3757)
BRIDGESTONE RET OPERATIONS LLC
Also Called: Firestone
5117 Wilson Mills Rd (44143-3005)
PHONE..........................440 461-4747
Zach Grashik, *Mgr*
EMP: 6
Web: www.bridgestoneamericas.com
SIC: 5531 7534 Automotive tires; Rebuilding and retreading tires
HQ: Bridgestone Retail Operations, Llc
333 E Lake St Ste 300
Bloomingdale IL 60108
630 259-9000

(G-3758)
BRIDGESTONE RET OPERATIONS LLC
Also Called: Firestone
12420 Cedar Rd (44106-3129)
PHONE..........................216 229-2550
Adam Coyle, *Mgr*
EMP: 8
SQ FT: 8,366
Web: www.bridgestoneamericas.com
SIC: 5531 7534 Automotive tires; Rebuilding and retreading tires
HQ: Bridgestone Retail Operations, Llc
333 E Lake St Ste 300
Bloomingdale IL 60108
630 259-9000

(G-3759)
BRIDGESTONE RET OPERATIONS LLC
Also Called: Firestone
700 Richmond Rd (44143-2918)
PHONE..........................216 382-8970
Stephen Park, *Mgr*
EMP: 7
SQ FT: 10,010
Web: www.bridgestoneamericas.com
SIC: 5531 7534 Automotive tires; Rebuilding and retreading tires
HQ: Bridgestone Retail Operations, Llc
333 E Lake St Ste 300

Cleveland - Cuyahoga County (G-3760)

Bloomingdale IL 60108
630 259-9000

(G-3760)
BRITTANY STAMPING LLC
50 Public Sq Ste 4000 (44113-2243)
PHONE..............................216 267-0850
Frederick W Clarke, *CEO*
Charles P Bolton, *Ch Bd*
Forrest D Hayes, *Vice Chairman*
Jerome R Gratry, *V Ch Bd*
Janet M Tilton, *Treas*
EMP: 1300 **EST:** 1978
SQ FT: 8,000
SALES (est): 35.54MM **Privately Held**
SIC: 3469 3321 3089 3269 Metal stampings, nec; Gray iron castings, nec; Thermoformed finished plastics products, nec; Stoneware pottery products

(G-3761)
BROCO PRODUCTS INC
8510 Bessemer Ave (44127-1843)
PHONE..............................216 531-0880
Barry Brown, *Pr*
Joyce Brown, *VP*
EMP: 9 **EST:** 1968
SALES (est): 2MM **Privately Held**
Web: www.brocoproducts.com
SIC: 3559 2899 Metal finishing equipment for plating, etc.; Metal treating compounds

(G-3762)
BROOKLYN MACHINE & MFG CO INC
5180 Grant Ave (44125-1065)
PHONE..............................216 341-1846
Walter Spann, *Pr*
Frederick Spann, *Sec*
EMP: 7 **EST:** 1923
SQ FT: 8,500
SALES (est): 968K **Privately Held**
Web: www.brooklynmachinemfg.com
SIC: 3599 Machine shop, jobbing and repair

(G-3763)
BROST FOUNDRY COMPANY (PA)
2934 E 55th St (44127-1207)
PHONE..............................216 641-1131
Tom Peretti, *Pr*
EMP: 28 **EST:** 1910
SQ FT: 45,000
SALES (est): 5.08MM
SALES (corp-wide): 5.08MM **Privately Held**
Web: www.brostfoundry.com
SIC: 3366 3365 3369 3325 Castings (except die), nec, bronze; Aluminum and aluminum-based alloy castings; Nonferrous foundries, nec; Steel foundries, nec

(G-3764)
BROTHERS PRINTING CO INC
2000 Euclid Ave (44115-2276)
PHONE..............................216 621-6050
Dotty Kaufman, *CEO*
Jay Kaufman, *Pr*
David Kaufman, *Treas*
EMP: 12 **EST:** 1925
SQ FT: 36,000
SALES (est): 760.93K **Privately Held**
Web: www.brosprintcle.com
SIC: 2752 2759 Offset printing; Letterpress printing

(G-3765)
BRUENING GLASS WORKS INC
Also Called: Konys, Mark Glass Design
20157 Lake Rd (44116-1514)
PHONE..............................440 333-4768
Marc Konys, *Pr*
Chris Konys, *VP*
EMP: 6 **EST:** 1945
SQ FT: 1,500
SALES (est): 588.61K **Privately Held**
Web: www.brueningglass.com
SIC: 3231 5719 5712 Mirrored glass; Mirrors; Furniture stores

(G-3766)
BRUSHES INC
5400 Smith Rd (44142-2025)
PHONE..............................216 267-8084
Mary Drews, *Pr*
EMP: 24 **EST:** 1958
SQ FT: 9,600
SALES (est): 474.47K **Privately Held**
Web: www.malinco.com
SIC: 3991 Brushes, household or industrial

(G-3767)
BRUSHES INC
Also Called: Malin Company
5400 Smith Rd (44142-2025)
PHONE..............................216 267-8084
▲ **EMP:** 18
SALES (est): 4.14MM **Privately Held**
Web: www.malinco.com
SIC: 3496 Miscellaneous fabricated wire products

(G-3768)
BUCKINGHAM SRC INC
Also Called: SRC Worldwide
3425 Service Rd (44111-2421)
PHONE..............................216 941-6115
◆ **EMP:** 10
SIC: 2899 Fluxes: brazing, soldering, galvanizing, and welding

(G-3769)
BUD MAY INC
Also Called: Maynard Company, The
16850 Hummel Rd (44142-2131)
PHONE..............................216 676-8850
John Maynard, *Pr*
Tom Maynard, *VP*
Joan Santoro, *Mgr*
EMP: 10 **EST:** 1974
SQ FT: 18,000
SALES (est): 720.79K **Privately Held**
SIC: 3541 Grinding, polishing, buffing, lapping, and honing machines

(G-3770)
BUFFEX METAL FINISHING INC
1935 W 96th St Ste L (44102-2600)
PHONE..............................216 631-2202
Orlando Joe R Quintana, *Pr*
Louis Quintana, *VP*
EMP: 15 **EST:** 1987
SQ FT: 10,000
SALES (est): 633.39K **Privately Held**
Web: www.buffex.net
SIC: 3471 Electroplating of metals or formed products

(G-3771)
BULA FORGE & MACHINE INC (PA)
Also Called: Bula Defense Systems
3001 W 121st St (44111-1638)
PHONE..............................216 252-7600
Wayne Phelps, *Pr*
Karen Mason, *VP*
EMP: 22 **EST:** 1973
SALES (est): 5.02MM
SALES (corp-wide): 5.02MM **Privately Held**
Web: www.bulaforge.com
SIC: 3462 Iron and steel forgings

(G-3772)
BULA FORGE MACHINE
12117 Berea Rd Ste 1 (44111-1600)
PHONE..............................216 252-7600
EMP: 9 **EST:** 2020
SALES (est): 2.18MM **Privately Held**
Web: www.bulaforge.com
SIC: 3599 Machine shop, jobbing and repair

(G-3773)
BUSCHMAN CORPORATION
1740 E 43rd St (44103-2314)
PHONE..............................216 431-6633
EMP: 8 **EST:** 1982
SALES (est): 115.93K **Privately Held**
SIC: 3312 Blast furnaces and steel mills

(G-3774)
BUSCHMAN CORPORATION
4100 Payne Ave Ste 1 (44103-2340)
PHONE..............................216 431-6633
Tom Buschman, *CEO*
Ross Defelice, *Pr*
▲ **EMP:** 19 **EST:** 1977
SQ FT: 90,000
SALES (est): 5K **Privately Held**
Web: www.buschman.com
SIC: 3312 2679 2295 Rods, iron and steel: made in steel mills; Paper products, converted, nec; Tape, varnished: plastic, and other coated (except magnetic)

(G-3775)
BUSH INC
15901 Industrial Pkwy (44135-3321)
PHONE..............................216 362-6700
H Russell Bush, *Pr*
EMP: 12 **EST:** 1999
SALES (est): 496.13K **Privately Held**
SIC: 2752 Offset printing

(G-3776)
BWXT NCLEAR OPRTIONS GROUP INC
24703 Euclid Ave (44117-1714)
PHONE..............................216 912-3000
Mary Salomone, *Brnch Mgr*
EMP: 1592
Web: www.bwxt.com
SIC: 3443 Fabricated plate work (boiler shop)
HQ: Bwxt Nuclear Operations Group, Inc.
2016 Mount Athos Rd
Lynchburg VA 24504

(G-3777)
BYG INDUSTRIES INC
Also Called: Guerin-Zimmerman Co
8003 Clinton Rd (44144-1004)
PHONE..............................216 961-5436
James R Brasty, *Pr*
John Brasty Senior, *VP*
EMP: 6 **EST:** 1934
SQ FT: 10,000
SALES (est): 974.12K **Privately Held**
Web: www.stressandpainclinic.com
SIC: 3444 3599 Sheet metalwork; Machine shop, jobbing and repair

(G-3778)
C A LITZLER CO INC
4800 W 160th St (44135-2689)
PHONE..............................216 267-8020
Matthew C Litzler, *Pr*
J H Rogers, *
P S Sprague, *
William J Urban, *
Julia Mayer, *
▲ **EMP:** 42 **EST:** 1953
SQ FT: 32,000
SALES (est): 11.41MM
SALES (corp-wide): 25.92MM **Privately Held**
Web: www.calitzler.com
SIC: 3567 3535 3552 3549 Industrial furnaces and ovens; Conveyors and conveying equipment; Textile machinery; Metalworking machinery, nec
PA: C.A. Litzler Holding Company
4800 W 160th St
Cleveland OH 44135
216 267-8020

(G-3779)
C P S ENTERPRISES INC
Also Called: Able One's Moving Company
9815 Reno Ave (44105-2723)
PHONE..............................216 441-7969
EMP: 7 **EST:** 1991
SALES (est): 120.87K **Privately Held**
SIC: 4212 2759 Moving services; Commercial printing, nec

(G-3780)
CA LITZLER HOLDING COMPANY (PA)
4800 W 160th St (44135-2634)
PHONE..............................216 267-8020
Matthew C Litzler, *CEO*
William J Urban, *
Juila L Mayer, *
▲ **EMP:** 59 **EST:** 1999
SALES (est): 25.92MM
SALES (corp-wide): 25.92MM **Privately Held**
Web: www.calitzler.com
SIC: 3567 Industrial furnaces and ovens

(G-3781)
CAILIN DEVELOPMENT LLC
896 E 70th St (44103-1706)
PHONE..............................216 408-6261
Louis Finucane, *Managing Member*
EMP: 10 **EST:** 1996
SALES (est): 847.22K **Privately Held**
Web: www.cailindev.com
SIC: 3523 3532 3965 3462 Farm machinery and equipment; Mining machinery; Straight pins: steel or brass; Iron and steel forgings

(G-3782)
CAKE HOUSE CLEVELAND LLC
1536 Saint Clair Ave Ne Ste 65 (44114-2004)
PHONE..............................216 870-4659
EMP: 10 **EST:** 2019
SALES (est): 929.32K **Privately Held**
SIC: 2051 Cakes, bakery: except frozen

(G-3783)
CAM-LEM INC
1768 E 25th St (44114-4418)
PHONE..............................216 391-7750
Brian Mathewson, *CEO*
Terrell Pin, *COO*
EMP: 9 **EST:** 1993
SQ FT: 1,100
SALES (est): 777.23K **Privately Held**
Web: www.camlem.com
SIC: 3559 3544 3264 Robots, molding and forming plastics; Special dies, tools, jigs, and fixtures; Porcelain electrical supplies

(G-3784)
CANARY HEALTH TECHNOLOGIES INC
5005 Rockside Rd Ste 600 (44131-6827)
PHONE..............................617 784-4021
Raj Reddy, *Pr*
EMP: 10 **EST:** 2018
SALES (est): 10MM **Privately Held**

GEOGRAPHIC SECTION
Cleveland - Cuyahoga County (G-3805)

SIC: 3845 Ultrasonic scanning devices, medical

(G-3785)
CANVAS SPECIALTY MFG CO
4045 Saint Clair Ave (44103-1117)
PHONE..................216 881-0647
Carl E Heilman, Pr
EMP: 7 EST: 1930
SQ FT: 8,500
SALES (est): 441.4K Privately Held
Web: www.canvasspecialty.com
SIC: 2394 7699 Awnings, fabric: made from purchased materials; Nautical repair services

(G-3786)
CAPCO AUTOMOTIVE PRODUCTS CORP
1111 Superior Ave Eaton Ctr (44114-2522)
PHONE..................216 523-5000
Francisco E Bertolaccina, Ch Bd
Cal E Cheesbrough, *
Jose Roberto Morato, *
EMP: 2300 EST: 1959
SQ FT: 226,270
SALES (est): 76.6MM Privately Held
SIC: 3714 Transmissions, motor vehicle
HQ: Eaton Corporation
1000 Eaton Blvd
Cleveland OH 44122
440 523-5000

(G-3787)
CAPITAL TOOL COMPANY
1110 Brookpark Rd (44109-5871)
PHONE..................216 661-5750
Richard Crane, Pr
EMP: 45 EST: 1962
SQ FT: 20,000
SALES (est): 3.71MM Privately Held
Web: www.capitaltoolco.com
SIC: 3544 3545 3443 Special dies and tools; Machine tool accessories; Fabricated plate work (boiler shop)

(G-3788)
CARAUSTAR INDUSTRIES INC
Also Called: Cleveland Recycling Plant
3400 Vega Ave (44113-4954)
PHONE..................216 961-5060
Richard Ryan, Mgr
EMP: 10
SALES (corp-wide): 5.22B Publicly Held
Web: www.caraustar.com
SIC: 2679 2611 Paperboard products, converted, nec; Pulp mills
HQ: Caraustar Industries, Inc.
5000 Astell Pwdr Sprng Rd
Austell GA 30106
770 948-3101

(G-3789)
CARAUSTAR INDUSTRIES INC
Also Called: Cleveland Digital Imaging Svcs
7960 Lorain Ave (44102-4256)
PHONE..................216 939-3001
Petrelli Tony, VP
EMP: 19
SALES (corp-wide): 5.22B Publicly Held
Web: www.greif.com
SIC: 2631 Paperboard mills
HQ: Caraustar Industries, Inc.
5000 Astell Pwdr Sprng Rd
Austell GA 30106
770 948-3101

(G-3790)
CARAVAN PACKAGING INC (PA)
6427 Eastland Rd (44142-1305)
PHONE..................440 243-4100
Fred Hitti, Pr
Chris Pisanelli, VP
Sue Hitti, Treas
▲ EMP: 9 EST: 1962
SQ FT: 40,000
SALES (est): 2.29MM
SALES (corp-wide): 2.29MM Privately Held
Web: www.caravanpackaging.com
SIC: 4783 2441 6512 Packing goods for shipping; Nailed wood boxes and shook; Commercial and industrial building operation

(G-3791)
CARCO AMERICA LLC
1100 Superior Ave E Ste 1100 (44114-2530)
PHONE..................216 928-5409
Daniel M Prendergast, Prin
EMP: 7 EST: 2014
SALES (est): 189.69K Privately Held
SIC: 3555 Printing trades machinery

(G-3792)
CARGILL INCORPORATED
Also Called: Cargill
2400 Ships Channel (44113-2673)
P.O. Box 6920 (44101-1920)
PHONE..................216 651-7200
Bob Soupko, Brnch Mgr
EMP: 205
SALES (corp-wide): 176.74B Privately Held
Web: www.cargill.com
SIC: 2048 2899 Prepared feeds, nec; Chemical preparations, nec
PA: Cargill, Incorporated
15407 Mcginty Rd W
Wayzata MN 55391
800 227-4455

(G-3793)
CARMENS INSTALLATION CO
2865 Mayfield Rd (44118-1633)
PHONE..................216 321-4040
Carmen T Montello, Pr
Salvatore Montello, VP
Rose Marie Montello, Sec
EMP: 12 EST: 1954
SQ FT: 4,500
SALES (est): 498.1K Privately Held
Web: www.carmenscwt.com
SIC: 1799 2211 Drapery track installation; Draperies and drapery fabrics, cotton

(G-3794)
CARR BROS BLDRS SUP & COAL CO
7177 Northfield Rd (44146-5403)
PHONE..................440 232-3700
Floyd E Carr Junior, Pr
Duane Carr, *
Michael Carr, *
Amy Rickleman, *
EMP: 35 EST: 1892
SQ FT: 3,000
SALES (est): 2.87MM Privately Held
Web: www.carrbros.net
SIC: 3273 Ready-mixed concrete

(G-3795)
CARRERA HOLDINGS INC
101 W Prospect Ave (44115-1093)
PHONE..................216 687-1711
James B Mooney, Prin
EMP: 28 EST: 1999
SALES (est): 991.21K
SALES (corp-wide): 38.24MM Privately Held
SIC: 2329 2339 Knickers, dress (separate): men's and boys'; Aprons, except rubber or plastic: women's, misses', juniors'
PA: Carrera Spa
Via Sant'irene 1
Caldiero VR 37042
045 232-0506

(G-3796)
CARTER CARBURETOR LLC ✪
127 Public Sq Ste 5300 (44114-1219)
PHONE..................216 314-2711
Shekhar Kumar, *
EMP: 1600 EST: 2023
SALES (est): 130MM
SALES (corp-wide): 8.03B Privately Held
SIC: 3621 Motors and generators
HQ: Carter Carburetor Holdings, Llc
127 Public Sq Ste 5300
Cleveland OH 44114
216 906-2744

(G-3797)
CASE OHIO BURIAL CO (PA)
1720 Columbus Rd (44113-2410)
P.O. Box 26020 (44126-0020)
PHONE..................440 779-1992
Grace Caffo, Pr
Ronald Caffo, VP
Wanda Armburger, Sec
EMP: 13 EST: 1944
SQ FT: 70,000
SALES (est): 1.17MM
SALES (corp-wide): 1.17MM Privately Held
SIC: 3995 5087 Burial caskets; Caskets

(G-3798)
CASTALLOY INC
7990 Baker Ave (44102-1903)
PHONE..................216 961-7990
Richard J Chalet, Prin
Michael Wood, *
Thomas Waldin, *
▲ EMP: 55 EST: 1977
SQ FT: 40,000
SALES (est): 4.99MM Privately Held
Web: www.alconindustries.com
SIC: 3324 Steel investment foundries

(G-3799)
CASTELLI MARBLE LLC (PA)
3958 Superior Ave E (44114-4130)
PHONE..................216 361-1222
Luigi Castelli, CEO
Luigi Castelli, Managing Member
Gina Vicio, Sec
▲ EMP: 7 EST: 1987
SQ FT: 10,000
SALES (est): 2.24MM
SALES (corp-wide): 2.24MM Privately Held
Web: www.castellimarbleinc.com
SIC: 5032 3281 Marble building stone; Cut stone and stone products

(G-3800)
CBTS TECHNOLOGY SOLUTIONS LLC
5910 Landerbrook Dr Ste 250 (44124-6508)
PHONE..................440 569-2300
Theodore H Torbeck, CEO
EMP: 270
SALES (corp-wide): 3.15B Privately Held
Web: www.cbts.com
SIC: 7379 7372 Computer related consulting services; Business oriented computer software
HQ: Cbts Technology Solutions Llc
25 Merchant St
Cincinnati OH 45246

(G-3801)
CCL LABEL INC
CCL Design
15939 Industrial Pkwy (44135-3321)
PHONE..................216 676-2703
Chief Anderson, Mgr
EMP: 58
SALES (corp-wide): 4.75B Privately Held
Web: www.cclind.com
SIC: 2672 3081 3497 2678 Adhesive papers, labels, or tapes: from purchased material; Unsupported plastics film and sheet; Metal foil and leaf; Stationery products
HQ: Ccl Label, Inc.
161 Worcester Rd Ste 403
Framingham MA 01701
508 872-4511

(G-3802)
CDI INDUSTRIES INC
Also Called: Coaxial Dynamics
6800 Lake Abrams Dr (44130-3455)
PHONE..................440 243-1100
Joseph D Kluha, Pr
EMP: 24 EST: 1969
SQ FT: 16,000
SALES (est): 2.47MM Privately Held
Web: www.coaxial.com
SIC: 3663 3825 3613 Receivers, radio communications; Instruments to measure electricity; Switchgear and switchboard apparatus

(G-3803)
CENTERLESS GRINDING SERVICE
Also Called: C G S
19500 S Miles Rd (44128-4251)
P.O. Box 535 (44202-0535)
PHONE..................216 251-4100
Jim Daso, Pr
Terry Daso, Treas
EMP: 8 EST: 1959
SQ FT: 3,632
SALES (est): 593.8K Privately Held
Web: www.myersprecision.com
SIC: 3999 3599 Grinding and pulverizing of materials, nec; Machine shop, jobbing and repair

(G-3804)
CERTIFIED WELDING CO
9603 Clinton Rd (44144-1083)
PHONE..................216 961-5410
John Salisbury, Pr
Doris Ann Salisbury, VP
EMP: 9 EST: 1950
SALES (est): 242.84K Privately Held
SIC: 7692 3599 Welding repair; Machine shop, jobbing and repair

(G-3805)
CHALFANT SEW FABRICATORS INC
Also Called: Chalfant Loading Dock Eqp
11525 Madison Ave (44102)
PHONE..................216 521-7922
Jeff Chalfant, Pr
Stephanie Chalfant, *
◆ EMP: 30 EST: 1940
SQ FT: 50,000
SALES (est): 4.8MM Privately Held
Web: www.chalfantusa.com
SIC: 3069 2394 Sponge rubber and sponge rubber products; Canvas and related products

Cleveland - Cuyahoga County (G-3806)

(G-3806)
CHAMPION PLATING INC
5200 Superior Ave (44103-1341)
PHONE.....................216 881-1050
Christine Sparano, *Pr*
Arthur Pasek Junior, *VP*
EMP: 15 **EST:** 1908
SQ FT: 25,000
SALES (est): 1.02MM **Privately Held**
SIC: 3471 Electroplating of metals or formed products

(G-3807)
CHARIZMA CORP
Also Called: National Screen Production
1400 E 30th St Ste 201 (44114-4050)
P.O. Box 33520 (44133-0520)
PHONE.....................216 621-2220
Marcy Szabados, *Pr*
EMP: 7 **EST:** 1980
SQ FT: 5,000
SALES (est): 409.21K **Privately Held**
Web: www.nsp-screenprinting.com
SIC: 2396 5199 Screen printing on fabric articles; Advertising specialties

(G-3808)
CHARLES C LEWIS COMPANY
1 W Interstate St Ste 200 (44146-4256)
PHONE.....................440 439-3150
Steve Mccoy, *Mgr*
EMP: 10
SALES (corp-wide): 11.44MM **Privately Held**
Web: www.charlesclewis.com
SIC: 3312 Blast furnaces and steel mills
PA: The Charles C Lewis Company
  209 Page Blvd
  Springfield MA 01104
  413 733-2121

(G-3809)
CHARLES MESSINA
Also Called: Joseph Industries
16645 Granite Rd (44137-4301)
PHONE.....................216 663-3344
Charles Messina, *Owner*
EMP: 17 **EST:** 1978
SQ FT: 170,000
SALES (est): 482.17K **Privately Held**
SIC: 2653 Corrugated and solid fiber boxes

(G-3810)
CHART ASIA INC
1 Infinity Corporate Centre Dr (44125-5369)
PHONE.....................440 753-1490
Samuel F Thomas, *Pr*
EMP: 140 **EST:** 1995
SALES (est): 8.7MM **Publicly Held**
Web: www.chartindustries.com
SIC: 3443 Heat exchangers, plate type
HQ: Chart Inc.
  407 7th St Nw
  New Prague MN 56071
  952 758-4484

(G-3811)
CHART INDUSTRIES INC
5885 Landerbrook Dr Ste 150 (44124-4045)
PHONE.....................440 753-1490
Samuel F Thomas, *Pr*
Arthur S Holmes, *
EMP: 381 **EST:** 1992
SALES (est): 11.21MM **Publicly Held**
Web: www.chartindustries.com
SIC: 3443 Heat exchangers, plate type
HQ: Chart Inc.
  407 7th St Nw
  New Prague MN 56071
  952 758-4484

(G-3812)
CHART INTERNATIONAL INC (HQ)
1 Infinity Corporate Centre Dr (44125-5369)
PHONE.....................440 753-1490
Samuel F Thomas, *Pr*
EMP: 67 **EST:** 1998
SALES (est): 22.41MM **Publicly Held**
Web: www.chartindustries.com
SIC: 3443 3317 3559 3569 Heat exchangers, plate type; Steel pipe and tubes; Cryogenic machinery, industrial; Separators for steam, gas, vapor, or air (machinery)
PA: Chart Industries, Inc.
  2200 Arprt Ind Dr Ste 1
  Ball Ground GA 30107

(G-3813)
CHARTER MANUFACTURING CO INC
Charter Steel Division
4300 E 49th St (44125-1004)
PHONE.....................216 883-3800
Kevin Burg, *Brnch Mgr*
EMP: 64
SALES (corp-wide): 570.48MM **Privately Held**
Web: www.chartermfg.com
SIC: 3312 Rods, iron and steel: made in steel mills
PA: Charter Manufacturing Company, Inc.
  12121 Corporate Pkwy
  Mequon WI 53092
  262 243-4700

(G-3814)
CHECK POINT SOFTWARE TECH INC
6100 Oak Tree Blvd Ste 200 (44131)
PHONE.....................440 748-0900
EMP: 37
SALES (corp-wide): 894.19MM **Privately Held**
Web: www.checkpoint.com
SIC: 7372 Prepackaged software
HQ: Check Point Software Technologies, Inc.
  100 Oracle Pkwy
  Redwood City CA 94065

(G-3815)
CHEF 2 CHEF FOODS LLC
1893 E 55th St (44103-3640)
PHONE.....................216 696-0080
EMP: 9 **EST:** 2016
SALES (est): 507.89K **Privately Held**
SIC: 2038 Frozen specialties, nec

(G-3816)
CHEMICAL SOLVENTS INC (PA)
3751 Jennings Rd (44109-2889)
PHONE.....................216 741-9310
Edward Pavlish, *Ch Bd*
E H Pavlish, *
Gerald J Schill, *
Patricia Pavlish, *
Thos A Mason, *
▲ **EMP:** 45 **EST:** 1970
SQ FT: 30,000
SALES (est): 99.45MM
SALES (corp-wide): 99.45MM **Privately Held**
Web: www.chemicalsolvents.com
SIC: 5169 7349 3471 2992 Detergents and soaps, except specialty cleaning; Chemical cleaning services; Cleaning and descaling metal products; Oils and greases, blending and compounding

(G-3817)
CHEMTRADE LOGISTICS INC
2545 W 3rd St (44113-2512)
PHONE.....................216 566-8070
EMP: 21 **EST:** 2019
SALES (est): 3.03MM **Privately Held**
Web: www.chemtradelogistics.com
SIC: 2819 Industrial inorganic chemicals, nec

(G-3818)
CHI CORPORATION (PA)
Also Called: CHI Storage Solutions Corp
5265 Naiman Pkwy Ste H (44139-1013)
PHONE.....................440 498-2300
John R Thome Senior, *Ch*
John Thome Junior, *Pr*
EMP: 9 **EST:** 1994
SALES (est): 5.96MM **Privately Held**
Web: www.chicorporation.com
SIC: 7373 3572 Systems software development services; Computer tape drives and components

(G-3819)
CHILCOTE COMPANY
Also Called: Tap Packaging Solutions
4600 Tiedeman Rd (44144-2332)
PHONE.....................216 781-6000
Jay Anthony Hyland, *CEO*
David B Chilcote, *
Daniel Malloy, *
Matthew Moir, *
◆ **EMP:** 140 **EST:** 1906
SALES (est): 23.48MM **Privately Held**
Web: www.oliverinc.com
SIC: 2675 2652 2657 Die-cut paper and board; Setup paperboard boxes; Folding paperboard boxes

(G-3820)
CHOCOLATE PIG INC (PA)
Also Called: Fantasy Candies
5338 Mayfield Rd (44124-2479)
PHONE.....................440 461-4511
Joel Fink, *Pr*
EMP: 6 **EST:** 1990
SQ FT: 3,500
SALES (est): 2.15MM **Privately Held**
Web: www.fantasycandies.com
SIC: 2064 5441 2066 Candy and other confectionery products; Candy, nut, and confectionery stores; Chocolate and cocoa products

(G-3821)
CHROMIUM CORPORATION
8701 Union Ave (44105-1611)
PHONE.....................216 271-4910
Richard Young, *Mgr*
EMP: 50
SALES (corp-wide): 6.27B **Privately Held**
SIC: 3443 3471 Fabricated plate work (boiler shop); Plating and polishing
HQ: Chromium Corporation
  14911 Quorum Dr Ste 600
  Dallas TX 75254
  972 851-0500

(G-3822)
CITY OF CLEVELAND
Also Called: Printing & Reproduction Div
1735 Lakeside Ave E (44114-1118)
PHONE.....................216 664-3013
Michael Hewett, *Commsnr*
EMP: 21
SALES (corp-wide): 972.69MM **Privately Held**
Web: www.clevelandohio.gov
SIC: 2752 9199 Commercial printing, lithographic; General government administration
PA: City Of Cleveland
  601 Lakeside Ave E Rm 210
  Cleveland OH 44114
  216 664-2000

(G-3823)
CITY OF CLEVELAND
Also Called: Parking Facilities
500 Lakeside Ave E (44114-1019)
PHONE.....................216 664-2711
Paul Bender, *Dir*
EMP: 313 **EST:** 2009
SALES (est): 5.79MM
SALES (corp-wide): 972.69MM **Privately Held**
Web: www.clevelandohio.gov
SIC: 3559 Parking facility equipment and supplies
PA: City Of Cleveland
  601 Lakeside Ave E Rm 210
  Cleveland OH 44114
  216 664-2000

(G-3824)
CITY PLATING AND POLISHING LLC
Also Called: City Plating
4821 W 130th St (44135-5137)
PHONE.....................216 267-8138
Randy Solganik, *Managing Member*
EMP: 7 **EST:** 2001
SQ FT: 20,000
SALES (est): 890.82K **Privately Held**
Web: www.cityplate.com
SIC: 3471 Electroplating of metals or formed products

(G-3825)
CLARKE-BOXIT CORPORATION
5601 Walworth Ave (44102-4432)
PHONE.....................716 487-1950
Donald Zaas, *CEO*
Joel Zaas, *Pr*
Mark Cassese, *VP*
Carole Halowecky, *CFO*
EMP: 43 **EST:** 1992
SALES (est): 2.34MM
SALES (corp-wide): 23.99MM **Privately Held**
SIC: 2652 Setup paperboard boxes
PA: The Apex Paper Box Company
  5601 Walworth Ave
  Cleveland OH 44102
  216 631-4000

(G-3826)
CLE PICKLES INC
6727 Bonnieview Rd (44143-3508)
PHONE.....................440 473-3740
Itini Spyrou, *Prin*
EMP: 7 **EST:** 2012
SALES (est): 173.63K **Privately Held**
SIC: 2035 Pickled fruits and vegetables

(G-3827)
CLEANLIFE ENERGY LLC
Also Called: Unibat
7620 Hub Pkwy (44125-5736)
PHONE.....................800 316-2532
Justin Miller, *CEO*
Jonathan Koslo, *VP*
▲ **EMP:** 15 **EST:** 2011
SALES (est): 4.19MM **Privately Held**
Web: www.cleanlifeled.com
SIC: 3356 3679 5063 Battery metal; Liquid crystal displays (LCD); Lighting fixtures

(G-3828)
CLEARVUE INSULATING GLASS CO
14735 Lorain Ave Ste 1 (44111-3175)
PHONE.....................216 651-1140
Jeffrey Fogel, *Pr*
EMP: 11 **EST:** 1970
SALES (est): 399.44K **Privately Held**
Web: www.clearvueig.com

GEOGRAPHIC SECTION
Cleveland - Cuyahoga County (G-3853)

SIC: 3211 5039 Insulating glass, sealed units ; Exterior flat glass: plate or window

(G-3829)
CLECORR INC
Also Called: Clecorr Packaging
10610 Berea Rd Rear (44102-2595)
PHONE.................................216 961-5500
Kevin L Smith, *Pr*
Christopher Dye, *
EMP: 29 EST: 1987
SQ FT: 67,000
SALES (est): 4.86MM **Privately Held**
Web: www.clecorrpackaging.com
SIC: 2653 Boxes, corrugated: made from purchased materials

(G-3830)
CLEVELAND ACTIVIST
1223 W 6th St (44113-1339)
PHONE.................................888 817-3777
EMP: 7 EST: 2018
SALES (est): 62.99K **Privately Held**
Web: www.clevescene.com
SIC: 2711 Newspapers, publishing and printing

(G-3831)
CLEVELAND AEC WEST LLC
14000 Keystone Pkwy (44135-5170)
PHONE.................................216 362-6000
Deepmala Agarwal, *Prin*
EMP: 6 EST: 2015
SALES (est): 165.78K **Privately Held**
SIC: 2835 Veterinary diagnostic substances

(G-3832)
CLEVELAND BEAN SPROUT INC
2675 E 40th St (44115-3508)
PHONE.................................216 881-2112
Casey Chiu, *Pr*
Judy Chiu, *VP*
EMP: 10 EST: 1991
SQ FT: 12,000
SALES (est): 230.88K **Privately Held**
SIC: 0139 0161 2052 Alfalfa farm; Pea and bean farms; Cookies

(G-3833)
CLEVELAND BLACK OXIDE INC
11400 Brookpark Rd (44130-1131)
PHONE.................................216 861-4431
Bob Mcelwee, *Pr*
Kim Elliott, *VP*
EMP: 11 EST: 2013
SALES (est): 1.03MM **Privately Held**
Web: www.clevelandblackoxide.com
SIC: 3471 Electroplating of metals or formed products

(G-3834)
CLEVELAND CABINETS LLC
19389 Lorain Rd (44126-1918)
PHONE.................................216 459-7676
EMP: 9 EST: 2018
SALES (est): 401.18K **Privately Held**
Web: www.clecabinets.com
SIC: 2434 Wood kitchen cabinets

(G-3835)
CLEVELAND CANVAS GOODS MFG CO
1960 E 57th St (44103-3804)
PHONE.................................216 361-4567
William Morton Iii, *Pr*
William J Morton Iii, *Pr*
Tyler Martinez, *
EMP: 26 EST: 1922
SQ FT: 29,500
SALES (est): 3MM **Privately Held**

Web: www.clevelandcanvas.com
SIC: 2394 2393 2326 2296 Canvas and related products; Textile bags; Men's and boy's work clothing; Tire cord and fabrics

(G-3836)
CLEVELAND CIRCUITS CORP
Also Called: Instrumatics
15516 Industrial Pkwy (44135-3314)
PHONE.................................216 267-9020
EMP: 25 EST: 1994
SQ FT: 18,500
SALES (est): 2.23MM **Privately Held**
SIC: 3672 Printed circuit boards

(G-3837)
CLEVELAND CONTROLS INC
1111 Brookpark Rd (44109-5825)
PHONE.................................216 398-0330
Steve Craig, *Pr*
EMP: 18 EST: 1942
SQ FT: 10,000
SALES (est): 1.05MM **Privately Held**
Web: www.clevelandcontrols.com
SIC: 3823 Combustion control instruments

(G-3838)
CLEVELAND DRAPERY STITCH INC
Also Called: Drapery Stitch
12890 Berea Rd (44111-1624)
PHONE.................................216 252-3857
George Beckmann, *Pr*
Wayne Monar, *VP*
EMP: 19 EST: 1978
SQ FT: 7,200
SALES (est): 492.62K **Privately Held**
Web: www.draperystitch.com
SIC: 2211 2221 Draperies and drapery fabrics, cotton; Draperies and drapery fabrics, manmade fiber and silk

(G-3839)
CLEVELAND E SPEEDPRO IMAGING
Also Called: Speedpro Imaging
26851 Miles Rd (44128-5991)
PHONE.................................216 342-4954
Ron Levine, *Owner*
EMP: 6 EST: 2013
SALES (est): 270.95K **Privately Held**
Web: www.speedpro.com
SIC: 3993 Signs and advertising specialties

(G-3840)
CLEVELAND GEAR COMPANY INC (DH)
3249 E 80th St (44104-4395)
P.O. Box 70100t (44190-0001)
PHONE.................................216 641-9000
▲ EMP: 96 EST: 1912
SALES (est): 23.82MM
SALES (corp-wide): 541.5MM **Privately Held**
Web: www.clevelandgear.com
SIC: 3566 3569 Speed changers, drives, and gears; Lubricating equipment
HQ: Industrial Manufacturing Company Llc
 8223 Brcksvlle Rd Ste 100
 Brecksville OH 44141
 440 838-4700

(G-3841)
CLEVELAND GRANITE & MARBLE LLC
4121 Carnegie Ave (44103-4336)
PHONE.................................216 291-7637
Kimberly K Lisboa, *Managing Member*
▲ EMP: 33 EST: 2000
SQ FT: 50,000
SALES (est): 2.42MM **Privately Held**
Web: www.clevelandgranite.com

SIC: 3291 1799 Abrasive metal and steel products; Home/office interiors finishing, furnishing and remodeling

(G-3842)
CLEVELAND IGNITION CO INC
600 Golden Oak Pkwy (44146-6504)
PHONE.................................440 439-3688
Walt Lemonovith, *Pr*
Charles O'toole, *Prin*
▲ EMP: 9 EST: 1917
SQ FT: 8,000
SALES (est): 1.72MM **Privately Held**
Web: www.clevelandignition.com
SIC: 3714 Motor vehicle parts and accessories

(G-3843)
CLEVELAND INDUS TRAINING CTR
706 E 163rd St (44110-2453)
PHONE.................................216 531-3446
Donald Borman, *Prin*
EMP: 6 EST: 2012
SALES (est): 121.58K **Privately Held**
Web: www.aspratechcenter.com
SIC: 3599 Machine shop, jobbing and repair

(G-3844)
CLEVELAND JEWISH PUBL CO
Also Called: Cleveland Jewish News
23880 Commerce Park Ste 1 (44122-5830)
PHONE.................................216 454-8300
Rob Certner, *CEO*
Cynthia Dettelbach, *
EMP: 38 EST: 1964
SQ FT: 9,000
SALES (est): 2.69MM **Privately Held**
Web: www.clevelandjewishnews.com
SIC: 2711 Newspapers, publishing and printing

(G-3845)
CLEVELAND LLC
13602 Kelso Ave (44110-2156)
PHONE.................................216 249-3098
Agnes Burris, *Prin*
EMP: 15 EST: 2010
SALES (est): 292.8K **Privately Held**
Web: www.clevelandplating.com
SIC: 3471 Electroplating and plating

(G-3846)
CLEVELAND MEDICAL DEVICES INC
Also Called: Clevemed
4415 Euclid Ave Ste 400 (44103-3757)
PHONE.................................216 619-5928
Robert N Schmidt, *Ch*
Hani Kayyali, *Pr*
Bryan Kolkowski, *VP*
EMP: 20 EST: 1991
SQ FT: 9,000
SALES (est): 4.05MM **Privately Held**
Web: www.clevemed.com
SIC: 3845 3842 Electromedical apparatus; Surgical appliances and supplies

(G-3847)
CLEVELAND MENU PRINTING INC
1441 E 17th St (44114-2012)
PHONE.................................216 241-5256
Tom Ramella, *Pr*
Jerry Ramella, *
Gerry Ramella, *
Daniel Payne, *
George Maxwell, *
▼ EMP: 25 EST: 1930
SQ FT: 15,000
SALES (est): 3.93MM **Privately Held**
Web: www.clevelandmenu.com
SIC: 2759 Menus: printing, nsk

(G-3848)
CLEVELAND METAL PROCESSING INC (PA)
20303 1st Ave (44130-2433)
PHONE.................................440 243-3404
Juan Chahda, *Pr*
Liliana Chahda, *
EMP: 114 EST: 1947
SQ FT: 119,000
SALES (est): 6.6MM
SALES (corp-wide): 6.6MM **Privately Held**
Web: www.clevelandmetroparks.com
SIC: 3465 3544 Automotive stampings; Special dies and tools

(G-3849)
CLEVELAND PLATING LLC
1028 E 134th St (44110-2248)
PHONE.................................216 249-0300
Elva Wade, *Managing Member*
EMP: 7 EST: 2015
SALES (est): 766.57K **Privately Held**
Web: www.clevelandplating.com
SIC: 3471 Plating of metals or formed products

(G-3850)
CLEVELAND PRESS
30628 Detroit Road (44145-5844)
PHONE.................................440 289-3227
EMP: 6 EST: 2014
SALES (est): 90.05K **Privately Held**
Web: www.clevelandpress.com
SIC: 2741 Miscellaneous publishing

(G-3851)
CLEVELAND PRESS
452 Bishop Rd (44143-1957)
PHONE.................................440 442-5101
Lynne Bolivar-wolford, *Prin*
EMP: 6 EST: 2010
SALES (est): 76.67K **Privately Held**
Web: www.clevelandmemory.org
SIC: 2741 Miscellaneous publishing

(G-3852)
CLEVELAND RANGE LLC (DH)
Also Called: Manitwoc Ovens Advnced Cooking
760 Beta Dr Ste G (44143-2334)
PHONE.................................216 481-4900
Robert Pritt, *Managing Member*
John Stevenson, *
▲ EMP: 209 EST: 1922
SALES (est): 29.72MM
SALES (corp-wide): 2.67MM **Privately Held**
Web: www.clevelandrange.com
SIC: 3589 3556 3634 Commercial cooking and foodwarming equipment; Food products machinery; Electric housewares and fans
HQ: Welbilt, Inc.
 2227 Welbilt Blvd
 Trinity FL 34655
 727 375-7010

(G-3853)
CLEVELAND REBABBITTING SVC INC
15593 Brookpark Rd (44142-1618)
PHONE.................................216 433-0123
Kenneth Roller, *Pr*
Bradford Roller, *VP*
EMP: 9
SQ FT: 15,000
SALES (est): 1MM **Privately Held**
Web: www.rebabbit.com
SIC: 3568 Bearings, bushings, and blocks

Cleveland - Cuyahoga County (G-3854)   GEOGRAPHIC SECTION

(G-3854)
CLEVELAND ROLL FORMING CO
3170 W 32nd St (44109-1529)
PHONE..................................216 281-0202
William P Ekey, *Pr*
Edward L Ekey, *VP*
EMP: 7 EST: 1947
SQ FT: 11,700
SALES (est): 874.75K Privately Held
Web: www.clevelandrollforming.com
SIC: 3544 Special dies and tools

(G-3855)
CLEVELAND SPECIALTY PDTS INC
2130 W 110th St (44102-3510)
PHONE..................................216 281-8300
Manuel P Glynias, *Pr*
EMP: 26 EST: 2009
SALES (est): 3.35MM Privately Held
Web: www.clevelandlumber.com
SIC: 3089 Extruded finished plastics products, nec

(G-3856)
CLEVELAND STEEL TOOL COMPANY
474 E 105th St (44108-1378)
PHONE..................................216 681-7400
Mark Dawson, *Pr*
Wayne Haas, *
◆ EMP: 26 EST: 1908
SQ FT: 25,000
SALES (est): 4.4MM Privately Held
Web: www.clevelandsteeltool.com
SIC: 3544 Punches, forming and stamping

(G-3857)
CLEVELAND SUPPLYONE INC (DH)
Also Called: Supplyone Retail
26801b Fargo Ave (44146-1338)
PHONE..................................216 514-7000
◆ EMP: 50 EST: 1914
SALES (est): 27.71MM
SALES (corp-wide): 838.82MM Privately Held
Web: www.supplyone.com
SIC: 5113 5162 5085 2653 Industrial and personal service paper; Plastics film; Glass bottles; Corrugated and solid fiber boxes
HQ: Supplyone, Inc.
    11 Campus Blvd Ste 150
    Newtown Square PA 19073
    484 582-5005

(G-3858)
CLEVELAND TOOL AND MACHINE INC
4717 Hinckley Industrial Pkwy (44109-6004)
PHONE..................................216 267-6010
Victor Bota, *Pr*
Maria Bota, *VP*
Douglas Neece, *VP*
◆ EMP: 15 EST: 1996
SALES (est): 2.82MM Privately Held
Web: www.clevtool.com
SIC: 3599 Machine shop, jobbing and repair

(G-3859)
CLEVELAND VIBRATOR COMPANY
4544 Hinckley Industrial Pkwy (44109-6010)
PHONE..................................800 221-3298
Jeffrey Chokel, *Ch Bd*
EMP: 12 EST: 2016
SALES (est): 1.11MM Privately Held
Web: www.clevelandvibrator.com
SIC: 3532 Mining machinery

(G-3860)
CLEVELAND WIND COMPANY LLC
4176 Hinsdale Rd (44121-2704)
PHONE..................................216 269-7667
Robert Parins, *Prin*
EMP: 6 EST: 2010
SALES (est): 104.19K Privately Held
SIC: 3621 Windmills, electric generating

(G-3861)
CLEVELAND WIRE CLOTH MFG LLC ✪
3573 E 78th St (44105-1517)
PHONE..................................216 341-1832
Nicholas A Reif, *Managing Member*
EMP: 26 EST: 2022
SALES (est): 5.55MM
SALES (corp-wide): 5.57MM Privately Held
Web: www.wirecloth.com
SIC: 3496 Hardware cloth, woven wire
PA: Freshwater Capital Llc
    1375 E 9th St Fl 29
    Cleveland OH

(G-3862)
CLEVELAND-CLIFFS INC (PA)
Also Called: Cliffs
200 Public Sq Ste 3300 (44114)
PHONE..................................216 694-5700
Lourenco Goncalves, *Ch Bd*
Celso Goncalves, *Ex VP*
James D Graham, *Legal*
Traci Forrester, *Environment Vice President*
Kimberly Floriani, *CAO*
◆ EMP: 175 EST: 1847
SALES (est): 22B
SALES (corp-wide): 22B Publicly Held
Web: www.clevelandcliffs.com
SIC: 3312 Blast furnaces and steel mills

(G-3863)
CLEVELAND-CLIFFS INTL HOLDG CO
1100 Superior Ave E Fl 18 (44114-2518)
PHONE..................................216 694-5700
EMP: 95 EST: 2008
SALES (est): 1.34MM
SALES (corp-wide): 22B Publicly Held
Web: www.clevelandcliffs.com
SIC: 1011 Iron ores
PA: Cleveland-Cliffs Inc.
    200 Public Sq Ste 3300
    Cleveland OH 44114
    216 694-5700

(G-3864)
CLEVELAND-CLIFFS STEEL CORP (DH)
Also Called: Cleveland-Cliffs
200 Public Sq Ste 3300 (44114-2315)
PHONE..................................216 694-5700
Lourenco Goncalves, *Pr*
◆ EMP: 90 EST: 1989
SQ FT: 136,000
SALES (est): 1.9B
SALES (corp-wide): 22B Publicly Held
Web: www.clevelandcliffs.com
SIC: 3312 Sheet or strip, steel, hot-rolled
HQ: Cleveland-Cliffs Steel Holding Corporation
    200 Public Sq Ste 3300
    Cleveland OH 44114

(G-3865)
CLEVELANDCOM
4800 Tiedeman Rd (44144-2336)
PHONE..................................216 862-7159
EMP: 71 EST: 2013
SALES (est): 619.47K Privately Held
Web: www.cleveland.com
SIC: 2711 Newspapers

(G-3866)
CLEVELND-CLFFS CLVLAND WRKS LL (HQ)
3060 Eggers Ave (44105-1012)
PHONE..................................216 429-6000
Dan Boone, *Pr*
▲ EMP: 248 EST: 2002
SQ FT: 40,000
SALES (est): 462.89MM
SALES (corp-wide): 22B Publicly Held
Web: www.intlsteel.com
SIC: 3312 Blast furnaces and steel mills
PA: Cleveland-Cliffs Inc.
    200 Public Sq Ste 3300
    Cleveland OH 44114
    216 694-5700

(G-3867)
CLEVELND-CLFFS CLVLAND WRKS LL
3100 E 4th St (44127)
PHONE..................................216 429-6000
Sylvia Gerkin, *Brnch Mgr*
EMP: 30
SALES (corp-wide): 22B Publicly Held
Web: www.clevelandcliffs.com
SIC: 3312 Blast furnaces and steel mills
HQ: Cleveland Cleveland-Cliffs Works Llc
    3060 Eggers Ave
    Cleveland OH 44105
    216 429-6000

(G-3868)
CLEVELND-CLIFFS STL HOLDG CORP (DH)
200 Public Sq Ste 3300 (44114-2315)
PHONE..................................216 694-5700
C Lourenco Goncalves, *Ch Bd*
C Lourenco Goncalves, *Ch Bd*
Terry G Fedor, *
R Christopher Cebula, *CAO*
Celso L Goncalves Junior, *VP*
◆ EMP: 300 EST: 1993
SALES (est): 6.36B
SALES (corp-wide): 22B Publicly Held
Web: www.cleveland-cliffs.com
SIC: 3312 Sheet or strip, steel, hot-rolled
HQ: Cliffs Steel Inc.
    200 Public Sq Ste 3300
    Cleveland OH 44114
    216 694-5700

(G-3869)
CLIFFS & ASSOCIATES LTD
1100 Superior Ave E Ste 1500 (44114-2530)
PHONE..................................216 694-5700
EMP: 6 EST: 1996
SQ FT: 65,000
SALES (est): 844.4K Privately Held
Web: www.clevelandcliffs.com
SIC: 1011 Iron ores

(G-3870)
CLIFFS EMPIRE INC
200 Public Sq Ste 3300 (44114-2315)
PHONE..................................216 694-5700
EMP: 8
SALES (est): 281.3K Privately Held
Web: www.clevelandcliffs.com
SIC: 1011 Iron ores

(G-3871)
CLIFFS LOGAN COUNTY COAL LLC
200 Public Sq Ste 3300 (44114-2315)
PHONE..................................216 694-5700
▼ EMP: 108 EST: 2010
SALES (est): 872.46K
SALES (corp-wide): 22B Publicly Held
SIC: 5989 1221 Coal; Coal preparation plant, bituminous or lignite
PA: Cleveland-Cliffs Inc.
    200 Public Sq Ste 3300
    Cleveland OH 44114
    216 694-5700

(G-3872)
CLIFFS MINING COMPANY
200 Public Sq Ste 3300 (44114-2315)
PHONE..................................216 694-5700
Lourenco Goncalves, *Ch Bd*
Celso Goncalves, *Ex VP*
Clifford Smith, *Ex VP*
EMP: 19 EST: 1883
SQ FT: 40,000
SALES (est): 10.04MM
SALES (corp-wide): 22B Publicly Held
SIC: 1011 Iron ores
PA: Cleveland-Cliffs Inc.
    200 Public Sq Ste 3300
    Cleveland OH 44114
    216 694-5700

(G-3873)
CLIFFS MINING HOLDING SUB CO
200 Public Sq Ste 3300 (44114-2315)
PHONE..................................216 694-5700
EMP: 17 EST: 2015
SALES (est): 540.77K Privately Held
SIC: 1011 Iron ore sintering at the mine

(G-3874)
CLIFFS MINING SERVICES COMPANY
1100 Superior Ave E Ste 1500 (44114)
PHONE..................................218 262-5913
EMP: 171 EST: 1991
SALES (est): 2.48MM
SALES (corp-wide): 22B Publicly Held
SIC: 1011 Iron ores
PA: Cleveland-Cliffs Inc.
    200 Public Sq Ste 3300
    Cleveland OH 44114
    216 694-5700

(G-3875)
CLIFFS NATURAL RESOURCES EXPLO
200 Public Sq Ste 3300 (44114-2315)
PHONE..................................216 694-5700
Lourenco Goncalves, *Prin*
EMP: 114 EST: 2013
SALES (est): 2.46MM
SALES (corp-wide): 22B Publicly Held
SIC: 1011 Iron ore mining
PA: Cleveland-Cliffs Inc.
    200 Public Sq Ste 3300
    Cleveland OH 44114
    216 694-5700

(G-3876)
CLIFFS STEEL INC (HQ)
200 Public Sq Ste 3300 (44114-2315)
PHONE..................................216 694-5700
Cliford T Smith, *Pr*
Celso L Goncalves Junior, *Ex VP*
James D Graham, *Ex VP*
Kimberly A Floriani, *Sr VP*
Denise M Caruso, *VP*
EMP: 21 EST: 2021
SALES (est): 6.38B
SALES (corp-wide): 22B Publicly Held
Web: www.clevelandcliffs.com
SIC: 3312 Blast furnaces and steel mills
PA: Cleveland-Cliffs Inc.
    200 Public Sq Ste 3300
    Cleveland OH 44114
    216 694-5700

▲ = Import ▼ = Export
◆ = Import/Export

GEOGRAPHIC SECTION

Cleveland - Cuyahoga County (G-3898)

(G-3877)
CLIFFS UTAC HOLDING LLC
200 Public Sq Ste 3300 (44114-2315)
PHONE..................216 694-5700
EMP: 57 **EST:** 2018
SALES (est): 4.19MM
SALES (corp-wide): 22B **Publicly Held**
SIC: 1081 Metal mining services
PA: Cleveland-Cliffs Inc.
200 Public Sq Ste 3300
Cleveland OH 44114
216 694-5700

(G-3878)
CLIMATE PROS LLC
5309 Hamilton Ave (44114-3909)
PHONE..................216 881-5200
Todd Ernest, *CEO*
EMP: 85
Web: www.climatepros.com
SIC: 1711 5078 2541 2434 Refrigeration contractor; Commercial refrigeration equipment; Cabinets, except refrigerated: show, display, etc.: wood; Wood kitchen cabinets
PA: Climate Pros, Llc
2190 Gladstone Ct Ste E
Glendale Heights IL 60139

(G-3879)
CO PAC SERVICES INC
3113 W 110th St (44111-2753)
PHONE..................216 688-1780
Craig Jaworski, *Pr*
Mike Marfeka, *VP*
Phil Puhala, *Sec*
▲ **EMP:** 15 **EST:** 1994
SQ FT: 65,000
SALES (est): 2.11MM **Privately Held**
Web: www.copac.com
SIC: 3993 Displays and cutouts, window and lobby

(G-3880)
COCHEM INC
Also Called: Clark Oil & Chemical Division
7555 Bessemer Ave (44127-1821)
PHONE..................216 341-8914
Tom Mesterhazy, *Pr*
Patrick J Amer, *
EMP: 29 **EST:** 1912
SQ FT: 18,000
SALES (est): 23.8MM **Privately Held**
Web: www.clarkoilandchemical.com
SIC: 2992 Lubricating oils and greases
PA: Mco, Inc.
7555 Bessemer Ave
Cleveland OH 44127

(G-3881)
CODONICS INC (PA)
17991 Englewood Dr Ste B (44130-3493)
PHONE..................800 444-1198
Peter Botten, *CEO*
◆ **EMP:** 208 **EST:** 1982
SALES (est): 35.16MM
SALES (corp-wide): 35.16MM **Privately Held**
Web: www.codonics.com
SIC: 3841 Surgical and medical instruments

(G-3882)
COLLINWOOD SHALE BRICK SUP CO (PA)
16219 Saranac Rd (44110-2435)
PHONE..................216 587-2700
Dorothy Strohm, *Ch Bd*
Scott Terhune, *Pr*
Cynthia S Terhune, *Treas*
EMP: 50 **EST:** 1921
SQ FT: 10,000
SALES (est): 40.72MM
SALES (corp-wide): 40.72MM **Privately Held**
SIC: 3273 5032 Ready-mixed concrete; Brick, stone, and related material

(G-3883)
COLOR BAR PRINTING CENTERS INC
4576 Renaissance Pkwy (44128-5702)
P.O. Box 1922 (44234-1922)
PHONE..................216 595-3939
Roger Perlmuter, *Pr*
Mary Ann Perlmuter, *VP*
EMP: 9 **EST:** 1992
SQ FT: 16,248
SALES (est): 488.36K **Privately Held**
Web: www.colorbar.net
SIC: 2752 Offset printing

(G-3884)
COLUMBIA INDUSTRIAL PDTS INC
4100 Payne Ave (44103-2346)
PHONE..................216 431-6633
Ross Defelice, *Pr*
EMP: 15 **EST:** 2001
SQ FT: 80,000
SALES (est): 1.5MM **Privately Held**
Web: www.buschman.com
SIC: 3561 Industrial pumps and parts

(G-3885)
COM-CORP INDUSTRIES INC
7601 Bittern Ave (44103-1060)
PHONE..................216 431-6266
Thomas Stanciu, *CEO*
William Beckwith, *
Kimberly Watroba, *
John Strazzanti, *Stockholder**
◆ **EMP:** 100 **EST:** 1980
SQ FT: 150,000
SALES (est): 23.52MM **Privately Held**
Web: www.ccioh.com
SIC: 3469 Stamping metal for the trade

(G-3886)
COMBER HOLDINGS INC
3304 W 67th Pl (44102-5243)
PHONE..................216 961-8600
Dean Comber, *Pr*
EMP: 40 **EST:** 1984
SQ FT: 30,000
SALES (est): 6.71MM **Privately Held**
Web: www.shakervalleyfoods.com
SIC: 5141 2011 Food brokers; Meat packing plants

(G-3887)
COMCORP INC (HQ)
Also Called: Sun Newspaper Div
1801 Superior Ave E (44114-2135)
PHONE..................718 981-1234
John Urbancich, *Pr*
Douglas J Lightner, *
EMP: 175 **EST:** 1969
SQ FT: 22,500
SALES (est): 16.33K
SALES (corp-wide): 2.88B **Privately Held**
SIC: 2711 Newspapers: publishing only, not printed on site
PA: Advance Publications, Inc.
1 World Trade Ctr Fl 43
New York NY 10007
718 981-1234

(G-3888)
COMEX NORTH AMERICA INC (HQ)
Also Called: Comex Group
101 W Prospect Ave Ste 1020 (44115-1093)
PHONE..................303 307-2100
Leon Cohen, *Pr*
Christopher Connor, *
◆ **EMP:** 90 **EST:** 2000
SQ FT: 2,900
SALES (est): 132.3MM
SALES (corp-wide): 22.15B **Publicly Held**
SIC: 2851 8742 5198 5231 Paints and paint additives; Corporation organizing consultant ; Paints; Paint
PA: The Sherwin-Williams Company
101 W Prospect Ave
Cleveland OH 44115
216 566-2000

(G-3889)
COMMERCIAL ELECTRIC PDTS CORP (PA)
1821 E 40th St (44103-3503)
PHONE..................216 241-2886
Roger Meyer, *Pr*
Kenneth Culp, *
EMP: 44 **EST:** 1927
SQ FT: 32,000
SALES (est): 17.02MM
SALES (corp-wide): 17.02MM **Privately Held**
Web: www.commercialelectric.com
SIC: 5085 3661 3824 7699 Power transmission equipment and apparatus; Telephones and telephone apparatus; Mechanical and electromechanical counters and devices; Industrial equipment services

(G-3890)
COMMUNITY CARE NETWORK INC (PA)
4614 Prospect Ave Ste 240 (44103-4365)
PHONE..................216 671-0977
David Lundeen, *Pr*
Christopher Cassidy, *CFO*
EMP: 49 **EST:** 2005
SALES (est): 2.18MM
SALES (corp-wide): 2.18MM **Privately Held**
Web: www.ccnms.org
SIC: 3825 Network analyzers

(G-3891)
COMPASS ENERGY LLC
17877 Saint Clair Ave Ste 1 (44110-2636)
PHONE..................866 665-2225
EMP: 10 **EST:** 2004
SQ FT: 238,000
SALES (est): 225.32K **Privately Held**
Web: www.compassinnovation.com
SIC: 2211 Broadwoven fabric mills, cotton

(G-3892)
COMPLIANT HEALTHCARE TECH LLC (PA)
Also Called: C H T
7123 Pearl Rd Ste 305 (44130-4944)
PHONE..................216 255-9607
EMP: 25 **EST:** 2006
SQ FT: 8,200
SALES (est): 13.12MM **Privately Held**
Web: www.chthealthcare.com
SIC: 7389 3826 Gas system conversion; Gas testing apparatus

(G-3893)
COMPONENT SYSTEMS INC
Also Called: A-Wall
5350 Tradex Pkwy (44102-5887)
PHONE..................216 252-9292
Tim Nelson, *Pr*
Thomas A Nelson, *VP*
Gineen Nelson, *Sec*
EMP: 20 **EST:** 1978
SALES (est): 3.41MM **Privately Held**
Web: www.a-wall.com
SIC: 2542 Partitions and fixtures, except wood

(G-3894)
COMTURN MANUFACTURING LLC
13704 Enterprise Ave (44135-5114)
PHONE..................219 267-6911
EMP: 9 **EST:** 2002
SALES (est): 103.66K **Privately Held**
Web: www.comturnmfg.com
SIC: 3599 Machine shop, jobbing and repair

(G-3895)
CONDOR TOOL & DIE INC
Also Called: Anchor Die Technologies
4541 Industrial Pkwy (44135-4598)
PHONE..................216 671-6000
Edward Pfaff, *Ch Bd*
Frederick Pfaff, *
Robert Pfaff, *
Jeff Pfaff, *
EMP: 35 **EST:** 1982
SQ FT: 25,000
SALES (est): 2.57MM **Privately Held**
SIC: 3544 Special dies and tools

(G-3896)
CONSOLIDATED GRAPHICS GROUP INC
Also Called: Consolidated Solutions
1614 E 40th St (44103-2319)
PHONE..................216 881-9191
▲ **EMP:** 170 **EST:** 1984
SQ FT: 75,000
SALES (est): 43.48MM **Privately Held**
Web: www.csinc.com
SIC: 2752 2759 7331 2791 Offset printing; Commercial printing, nec; Direct mail advertising services; Typesetting

(G-3897)
CONSOLDTED PRECISION PDTS CORP (PA)
Also Called: Cpp
1621 Euclid Ave Ste 1850 (44115-2126)
PHONE..................216 453-4800
James Stewart, *CEO*
Steve Clodfelter, *
Ali Ghavami, *
Debbie Comstock, *
Mel Crosier, *
▲ **EMP:** 250 **EST:** 1991
SQ FT: 10,000
SALES (est): 2.07B
SALES (corp-wide): 2.07B **Privately Held**
Web: www.cppcorp.com
SIC: 3365 3324 Aluminum foundries; Steel investment foundries

(G-3898)
CONSOLIDATED COATINGS CORP
3735 Green Rd (44122-5705)
PHONE..................216 514-7596
J K Milliken, *Genl Mgr*
Thomas C Sullivan, *
Paul A Granzier, *
EMP: 2047 **EST:** 1904
SQ FT: 4,000
SALES (est): 4.71MM
SALES (corp-wide): 7.26B **Publicly Held**
SIC: 5169 2891 2851 2842 Adhesives and sealants; Adhesives and sealants; Paints and allied products; Polishes and sanitation goods
HQ: Republic Powdered Metals, Inc.
2628 Pearl Rd
Medina OH 44256
330 225-3192

Cleveland - Cuyahoga County (G-3899)

(G-3899)
CONSOLIDATED FOUNDRIES INC (HQ)
Also Called: C P P
1621 Euclid Ave Ste 1850 (44115-2126)
PHONE.................909 595-2252
Steve Clodfelter, *Pr*
▲ **EMP:** 135 **EST:** 1991
SALES (est): 19.13MM
SALES (corp-wide): 2.07B **Privately Held**
Web: www.cppcorp.com
SIC: 3324 Aerospace investment castings, ferrous
PA: Consolidated Precision Products Corp.
1621 Euclid Ave Ste 1850
Cleveland OH 44115
216 453-4800

(G-3900)
CONSTRUCTION TECHNIQUES INC (HQ)
15007 Snow Rd Ste 100 (44142-2064)
P.O. Box 42067 (44142-0067)
PHONE.................216 267-7310
B J Akers, *Pr*
EMP: 10 **EST:** 1965
SQ FT: 1,500
SALES (est): 773.64K
SALES (corp-wide): 2.03MM **Privately Held**
Web: www.fabriform1.com
SIC: 2299 6794 Jute and flax textile products ; Patent buying, licensing, leasing
PA: Intrusion-Prepakt, Incorporated.
15910 Pearl Rd Ste 101
Cleveland OH 44136
440 238-6950

(G-3901)
CONTINENTAL METAL PROC CO (PA)
18711 Cleveland Ave (44110)
P.O. Box 18130 (44118-0130)
PHONE.................216 268-0000
Joseph Freund, *Pr*
Rubin Freund, *VP*
Mike Freund, *VP*
EMP: 19 **EST:** 1957
SQ FT: 328,000
SALES (est): 1.79MM
SALES (corp-wide): 1.79MM **Privately Held**
SIC: 3341 Aluminum smelting and refining (secondary)

(G-3902)
CONTINENTAL METAL PROC CO
14919 Saranac Rd (44110-2344)
PHONE.................216 268-0000
Michael Freund, *VP*
EMP: 22
SQ FT: 320,000
SALES (corp-wide): 1.79MM **Privately Held**
SIC: 3341 Aluminum smelting and refining (secondary)
PA: Continental Metal Processing Co (Inc)
18711 Cleveland Ave
Cleveland OH 44110
216 268-0000

(G-3903)
CONTROL LINE EQUIPMENT INC
14750 Industrial Pkwy (44135-4548)
PHONE.................216 433-7766
Mike Rotella, *CEO*
Robert May, *VP*
▲ **EMP:** 12 **EST:** 1979
SQ FT: 12,000
SALES (est): 2.58MM **Privately Held**
Web: www.control-line.com

SIC: 5084 3593 Hydraulic systems equipment and supplies; Fluid power cylinders and actuators

(G-3904)
COPERNICUS THERAPEUTICS INC
11000 Cedar Ave Ste 145 (44106-3060)
PHONE.................216 231-0227
EMP: 11 **EST:** 1997
SQ FT: 6,000
SALES (est): 2.37MM **Privately Held**
Web: www.cgsys.com
SIC: 2836 8731 Biological products, except diagnostic; Commercial physical research

(G-3905)
COPY KING INC
3333 Chester Ave (44114-4600)
PHONE.................216 861-3377
Margaret Walsh, *Pr*
John Schneeberger, *VP*
EMP: 28 **EST:** 1990
SQ FT: 15,000
SALES (est): 3.5MM **Privately Held**
Web: www.copy-king.com
SIC: 2752 Offset printing

(G-3906)
CORNER ALLEY LLC
402 Euclid Ave (44114-2215)
P.O. Box 14100 (44114-0100)
PHONE.................216 298-4070
Michael Grasso, *Genl Mgr*
EMP: 100 **EST:** 2010
SALES (est): 6.23MM **Privately Held**
Web: www.thecorneralley.com
SIC: 3949 Bowling alleys and accessories

(G-3907)
COSMO PLASTICS COMPANY (HQ)
Also Called: Cosmo
30201 Aurora Rd (44139-2745)
PHONE.................440 498-7500
▲ **EMP:** 150 **EST:** 1968
SALES (est): 37.71K
SALES (corp-wide): 37.71K **Privately Held**
Web: www.cosmocorp.com
SIC: 3082 3089 Unsupported plastics profile shapes; Plastics hardware and building products
PA: Marbeach Corp.
30201 Aurora Rd
Cleveland OH
440 498-7500

(G-3908)
COUNTRY PARLOUR ICE CREAM CO
12905 York Delta Dr Ste C (44133-3551)
PHONE.................440 237-4040
Jeri Hovanec, *Prin*
Craig Hovanec, *Sec*
EMP: 10 **EST:** 1988
SALES (est): 872.14K **Privately Held**
Web: www.countryparlouricecream.com
SIC: 2024 2099 5143 Ice cream, bulk; Food preparations, nec; Dairy products, except dried or canned

(G-3909)
COVENTRY STEEL SERVICES INC
4200 E 71st St Ste 1 (44105)
P.O. Box 25077 (44125)
PHONE.................216 883-4477
Brian Migchelbrink, *Pr*
Joseph Hustosky, *VP*
Jeff Migchelbrink, *Sec*
EMP: 16 **EST:** 1985
SQ FT: 35,000
SALES (est): 951.4K **Privately Held**
Web: www.coventrysteel.com

SIC: 3441 5051 Fabricated structural metal; Steel

(G-3910)
CPC HOLDING INC
2926 Chester Ave (44114-4414)
PHONE.................216 383-3932
Miriam Strebeck, *Ch Bd*
Emerson O Mcarthur Iii, *Pr*
EMP: 30 **EST:** 1916
SALES (est): 5.52MM **Privately Held**
Web: www.continentalprod.com
SIC: 2851 Paints and paint additives

(G-3911)
CPI GROUP LIMITED
Also Called: Puremonics
13858 Tinkers Creek Rd (44125-5661)
P.O. Box 25411 (44125-0411)
PHONE.................216 525-0046
EMP: 10 **EST:** 2005
SQ FT: 2,000
SALES (est): 471.18K **Privately Held**
Web: www.cpigroupltd.com
SIC: 3675 8711 Electronic capacitors; Electrical or electronic engineering

(G-3912)
CPP GROUP HOLDINGS LLC (PA)
1621 Euclid Ave Ste 1850 (44115-2126)
PHONE.................216 453-4800
James V Stewart, *CEO*
Timothy Trombetta I, *CFO*
EMP: 50 **EST:** 2019
SALES (est): 822.51MM
SALES (corp-wide): 822.51MM **Privately Held**
Web: www.cppcorp.com
SIC: 6719 3089 Investment holding companies, except banks; Automotive parts, plastic

(G-3913)
CPP-CLEVELAND INC (DH)
1621 Euclid Ave Ste 1850 (44115-2126)
PHONE.................216 453-4800
James V Stewart, *CEO*
EMP: 100 **EST:** 1979
SALES (est): 25.84MM
SALES (corp-wide): 822.51MM **Privately Held**
SIC: 3369 Lead castings, except die-castings
HQ: Cfhc Holdings, Inc.
1621 Euclid Ave Ste 1850
Cleveland OH

(G-3914)
CRAIN COMMUNICATIONS INC
Also Called: Crain's Cleveland Business
700 W Saint Clair Ave Ste 310 (44113-1230)
PHONE.................216 522-1383
Elizabeth Mcintyre, *Mgr*
EMP: 29
SALES (corp-wide): 249.16MM **Privately Held**
Web: www.crain.com
SIC: 2721 2711 Magazines: publishing only, not printed on site; Newspapers
PA: Crain Communications, Inc.
1155 Gratiot Ave
Detroit MI 48207
313 446-6000

(G-3915)
CRAWFORD ACQUISITION CORP
Also Called: Famous Kiss-N-Korn Shop
16130 Saint Clair Ave (44110-3029)
PHONE.................216 486-0702
Dan Crawford, *Pr*
EMP: 9 **EST:** 1973

SQ FT: 8,000
SALES (est): 211.53K **Privately Held**
SIC: 2064 Popcorn balls or other treated popcorn products

(G-3916)
CRAWFORD UNITED CORPORATION (PA)
10514 Dupont Ave (44108-1348)
PHONE.................216 541-8060
Brian E Powers, *Ch Bd*
Kelly J Marek, *VP Fin*
EMP: 52 **EST:** 1910
SQ FT: 37,000
SALES (est): 143.89MM
SALES (corp-wide): 143.89MM **Publicly Held**
Web: www.crawfordunited.com
SIC: 3823 3829 Industrial process measurement equipment; Measuring and controlling devices, nec

(G-3917)
CROWNE GROUP LLC (PA)
127 Public Sq Ste 5110 (44114)
PHONE.................216 589-0198
Robert Henderson, *Managing Member*
EMP: 14 **EST:** 2013
SALES (est): 208.02MM
SALES (corp-wide): 208.02MM **Privately Held**
SIC: 3559 8711 Degreasing machines, automotive and industrial; Industrial engineers

(G-3918)
CTS NATIONAL CORPORATION
101 W Prospect Ave Ste 1020 (44115-1093)
PHONE.................216 566-2000
EMP: 27 **EST:** 2019
SALES (est): 10.46MM
SALES (corp-wide): 22.15B **Publicly Held**
SIC: 2851 Paints and allied products
PA: The Sherwin-Williams Company
101 W Prospect Ave
Cleveland OH 44115
216 566-2000

(G-3919)
CUMMINS - ALLISON CORP
Also Called: Cummins
6777 Engle Rd Ste H (44130-7941)
PHONE.................440 824-5050
David Profera, *Brnch Mgr*
EMP: 8
SALES (corp-wide): 1.39MM **Publicly Held**
Web: www.cranepi.com
SIC: 5046 5087 5044 3519 Commercial equipment, nec; Shredders, industrial and commercial; Check writing, signing, and endorsing machines; Internal combustion engines, nec
HQ: Cummins-Allison Corp.
852 Feehanville Dr
Mount Prospect IL 60056
800 786-5528

(G-3920)
CURRENT LIGHTING SOLUTIONS LLC
Also Called: GE Current
1099 Ivanhoe Rd (44110-3232)
PHONE.................216 266-4416
Manish Bhandari, *Brnch Mgr*
EMP: 333
SALES (corp-wide): 1.6B **Privately Held**
Web: www.led.com
SIC: 3646 Commercial lighting fixtures
HQ: Current Lighting Solutions, Llc

25825 Science Pk Dr Ste 4
Beachwood OH 44122
216 462-4700

(G-3921)
CURTIS INDUSTIRES
1301 E 9th St Ste 700 (44114-1800)
PHONE....................216 430-5759
EMP: 8 **EST:** 2010
SALES (est): 428.26K Privately Held
SIC: 3531 Construction machinery

(G-3922)
CURTISS-WRIGHT FLOW CTRL CORP
Nova Machine Div
18001 Sheldon Rd (44130-2465)
PHONE....................216 267-3200
David Linton, *CEO*
EMP: 60
SALES (corp-wide): 2.85B Publicly Held
Web: www.curtisswright.com
SIC: 3452 3429 3369 3356 Bolts, metal; Hardware, nec; Nonferrous foundries, nec; Nonferrous rolling and drawing, nec
HQ: Curtiss-Wright Flow Control Corporation
1966 Broadhollow Rd Ste E
Farmingdale NY 11735
631 293-3800

(G-3923)
CUSTOM CLTCH JINT HYDRLICS INC (PA)
3417 Saint Clair Ave Ne (44114-4186)
PHONE....................216 431-1630
David Ballantyne, *CEO*
Donald Meintel, *Pr*
Patricia Beason, *Treas*
Scott Ballantyne, *Sec*
Elmer T Elbrecht, *Prin*
EMP: 11 **EST:** 1960
SQ FT: 52,000
SALES (est): 3.31MM
SALES (corp-wide): 3.31MM Privately Held
Web: www.customclutch.com
SIC: 3714 3594 3561 3492 Motor vehicle transmissions, drive assemblies, and parts; Fluid power pumps; Cylinders, pump; Hose and tube couplings, hydraulic/pneumatic

(G-3924)
CUSTOM CONNECTOR CORPORATION
1821 E 40th St (44103-3503)
PHONE....................216 241-1679
Roger Meyer, *Pr*
Robert Meyer, *Pr*
Larry Weider, *VP*
▲ **EMP:** 20 **EST:** 1969
SQ FT: 15,000
SALES (est): 4.73MM
SALES (corp-wide): 17.02MM Privately Held
Web: www.customconnector.com
SIC: 3678 Electronic connectors
PA: Commercial Electric Products Corporation
1821 E 40th St
Cleveland OH 44103
216 241-2886

(G-3925)
CUSTOM PAPER TUBES INC
6030 Carey Dr (44125-4260)
P.O. Box 35140 (44135-0140)
PHONE....................216 362-2964
EMP: 25 **EST:** 1962
SALES (est): 2.38MM Privately Held
Web: www.custompapertubes.com

SIC: 2655 Tubes, for chemical or electrical uses: paper or fiber

(G-3926)
CUSTOM RUBBER CORPORATION
1274 E 55th St (44103-1029)
PHONE....................216 391-2928
William Braun, *Pr*
◆ **EMP:** 75 **EST:** 1956
SQ FT: 70,000
SALES (est): 9.72MM Privately Held
Web: www.customrubbercorp.com
SIC: 3069 Molded rubber products

(G-3927)
CUTTERCROIX LLC
7251 Engle Rd Ste 350 (44130-3419)
PHONE....................330 289-6185
EMP: 16 **EST:** 2016
SALES (est): 285.4K Privately Held
Web: www.cuttercroix.com
SIC: 3652 Prerecorded records and tapes

(G-3928)
CUTTING EDGE TECHNOLOGIES INC
Also Called: Telos Systems
1241 Superior Ave E (44114-3204)
PHONE....................216 574-4759
Steve Church, *CEO*
Frank J Foti, *
Anthony Foti, *
EMP: 19 **EST:** 1988
SALES (est): 890.96K Privately Held
SIC: 3679 3661 Electronic circuits; Telephone and telegraph apparatus

(G-3929)
CUTTING SYSTEMS INC
15593 Brookpark Rd (44142)
PHONE....................216 928-0500
Kris Asadorian, *Pr*
George Asadorian, *VP*
Kevan Asadorian, *VP*
Sergey Edilyan, *VP*
▲ **EMP:** 16 **EST:** 1996
SQ FT: 44,500
SALES (est): 2.91MM Privately Held
Web: www.cuttingsystems.com
SIC: 3541 Plasma process metal cutting machines

(G-3930)
CUYAHOGA FENCE LLC
3100 E 45th St Ste 504 (44127-1095)
P.O. Box 43547 (44143-0547)
PHONE....................216 830-2200
Rita Samorezov, *Prin*
EMP: 15 **EST:** 2008
SALES (est): 1.3MM Privately Held
SIC: 1799 3446 Fence construction; Grillwork, ornamental metal

(G-3931)
CUYAHOGA REBUILDERS INC
5111 Brookpark Rd (44134-1047)
PHONE....................216 635-0659
Randolph Treudler, *Pr*
EMP: 6 **EST:** 1967
SQ FT: 2,500
SALES (est): 576.97K Privately Held
SIC: 3694 Alternators, automotive

(G-3932)
CW LIQUIDATION INC
1801 E 9th St Ste 1100 (44114-3103)
EMP: 100
SIC: 3441 Fabricated structural metal

(G-3933)
CWD LLC (DH)
Also Called: Centric Parts
127 Public Sq Ste 5110 (44114-1313)
PHONE....................310 218-1082
Marc Weinsweig, *Managing Member*
Henry Hippert, *
Jayme Farina, *
Jason Soika, *
Gary Nix, *
◆ **EMP:** 37 **EST:** 2000
SQ FT: 80,000
SALES (est): 44.31MM
SALES (corp-wide): 8.03B Privately Held
Web: www.centricparts.com
SIC: 3714 Motor vehicle parts and accessories
HQ: Cwd Intermediate Holdings Ii, Llc
127 Public Sq Ste 5110
Cleveland OH

(G-3934)
CYBERUTILITY LLC
1599 Maywood Rd (44121-4101)
PHONE....................216 291-8723
John Scott Minor, *Managing Member*
EMP: 8 **EST:** 1999
SALES (est): 702.88K Privately Held
SIC: 2911 Petroleum refining

(G-3935)
D INDUSTRIES INC
1350 Euclid Ave Ste 1500 (44115-1832)
PHONE....................216 535-4900
Paul Althoff, *Prin*
EMP: 7 **EST:** 2008
SALES (est): 175.21K Privately Held
SIC: 3999 Manufacturing industries, nec

(G-3936)
D JACOB INDUSTRIES LLC
13995 Enterprise Ave (44135-5117)
PHONE....................440 292-7277
Daniel Ganim, *Prin*
EMP: 11 **EST:** 2017
SALES (est): 521.2K Privately Held
SIC: 3999 Manufacturing industries, nec

(G-3937)
DAKOTA SOFTWARE CORPORATION (PA)
1375 Euclid Ave Ste 500 (44115-1808)
PHONE....................216 765-7100
Reginald C Shiverick, *Pr*
EMP: 61 **EST:** 1988
SALES (est): 7.48MM
SALES (corp-wide): 7.48MM Privately Held
Web: www.dakotasoft.com
SIC: 7372 Prepackaged software

(G-3938)
DAL-LITTLE FABRICATING INC
Also Called: Megna Plastics
11707 Putnam Ave (44105-5416)
P.O. Box 44067 (44144-0067)
PHONE....................216 883-3323
Betty J Massielle, *Pr*
Joe Massielle, *Pr*
EMP: 8 **EST:** 1991
SQ FT: 13,000
SALES (est): 512.62K Privately Held
Web: www.dallittle.com
SIC: 3229 3441 Glass fiber products; Fabricated structural metal

(G-3939)
DALAMER INDUSTRIES LLC
6701 Hubbard Ave (44127-1475)
PHONE....................440 855-1368

Mark Palik, *Prin*
EMP: 6 **EST:** 2012
SALES (est): 162.36K Privately Held
SIC: 3999 Manufacturing industries, nec

(G-3940)
DARLING INGREDIENTS INC
1002 Peltnine Ave (44109)
PHONE....................216 651-9300
Lorie Shorvath, *Mgr*
EMP: 7
SQ FT: 28,122
SALES (corp-wide): 6.53B Publicly Held
Web: www.darlingii.com
SIC: 2077 5191 Animal and marine fats and oils; Farm supplies
PA: Darling Ingredients Inc.
5601 N Macarthur Blvd
Irving TX 75038
972 717-0300

(G-3941)
DARLING INGREDIENTS INC
1002 Belt Line Ave (44109-2848)
PHONE....................216 351-3440
Howard Murray, *Mgr*
EMP: 7
SALES (corp-wide): 6.53B Publicly Held
Web: www.darlingii.com
SIC: 2077 Animal and marine fats and oils
PA: Darling Ingredients Inc.
5601 N Macarthur Blvd
Irving TX 75038
972 717-0300

(G-3942)
DARRAH ELECTRIC COMPANY (PA)
5914 Merrill Ave (44102-5699)
PHONE....................216 631-0912
David J Darrah, *Pr*
Robert J Darrah, *Ch Bd*
John A Darrah, *VP*
Neal A Darrah, *Sec*
EMP: 19 **EST:** 1960
SQ FT: 18,000
SALES (est): 6.63MM
SALES (corp-wide): 6.63MM Privately Held
Web: www.darrahelectric.com
SIC: 3679 3612 3674 Rectifiers, electronic; Power and distribution transformers; Semiconductors and related devices

(G-3943)
DAWN ENTERPRISES INC (PA)
Also Called: Sportwing
9155 Sweet Valley Dr (44125-4223)
PHONE....................216 642-5506
Robert Kovach, *Pr*
Lawrence De Laat, *General Vice President**
Lori M Kovach, *
▲ **EMP:** 40 **EST:** 1973
SQ FT: 69,900
SALES (est): 9.42MM
SALES (corp-wide): 9.42MM Privately Held
Web: www.sportwing.com
SIC: 3089 5521 Injection molding of plastics; Used car dealers

(G-3944)
DAY-GLO COLOR CORP (DH)
4515 Saint Clair Ave (44103-1268)
PHONE....................216 391-7070
Alice J Walker, *Prin*
Arthur A Sayre, *
John D Steele, *
Phil Rozick, *Research**
▲ **EMP:** 140 **EST:** 1931
SQ FT: 36,000
SALES (est): 98.96MM

Cleveland - Cuyahoga County (G-3945)

GEOGRAPHIC SECTION

SALES (corp-wide): 7.26B **Publicly Held**
Web: www.dayglo.com
SIC: **2816** 2851 Inorganic pigments; Lacquers, varnishes, enamels, and other coatings
HQ: Republic Powdered Metals, Inc.
2628 Pearl Rd
Medina OH 44256
330 225-3192

(G-3945)
DAY-GLO COLOR CORP
4518 Hamilton Ave (44114-3854)
PHONE..................216 391-7070
Steven Jackson, *Brnch Mgr*
EMP: 19
SALES (corp-wide): 7.26B **Publicly Held**
Web: www.dayglo.com
SIC: **2816** 2851 Inorganic pigments; Lacquers, varnishes, enamels, and other coatings
HQ: Day-Glo Color Corp.
4515 Saint Clair Ave
Cleveland OH 44103
216 391-7070

(G-3946)
DBHL INC (HQ)
4700 W 160th St (44135-2632)
PHONE..................216 267-7100
Gary A Oatey, *Pr*
Kevin Komar, *Contrlr*
▲ **EMP:** 54 **EST:** 2002
SALES (est): 2.48MM
SALES (corp-wide): 304.6MM **Privately Held**
Web: www.oatey.com
SIC: **5999** 3088 Plumbing and heating supplies; Plastics plumbing fixtures
PA: Oatey Co.
20600 Emerald Pkwy
Cleveland OH 44135
800 203-1155

(G-3947)
DCD TECHNOLOGIES INC
17920 S Waterloo Rd (44119-3222)
PHONE..................216 481-0056
Dave Hodgson, *Pr*
EMP: 41 **EST:** 1974
SQ FT: 18,000
SALES (est): 753.95K **Privately Held**
Web: www.dcdtech.com
SIC: **3544** Dies and die holders for metal cutting, forming, die casting

(G-3948)
DCM MANUFACTURING INC (HQ)
4540 W 160th St (44135-2628)
PHONE..................216 265-8006
◆ **EMP:** 50 **EST:** 1994
SQ FT: 68,000
SALES (est): 27.48MM
SALES (corp-wide): 61.53MM **Privately Held**
Web: www.dcm-mfg.com
SIC: **3621** 3433 3714 Motors, electric; Heating equipment, except electric; Motor vehicle parts and accessories
PA: Dreison International, Inc.
4540 W 160th St
Cleveland OH 44135
216 362-0755

(G-3949)
DCW ACQUISITION INC
Also Called: Regol-G Industries
10646 Leuer Ave (44108-1352)
P.O. Box 608957 (44108-0957)
PHONE..................216 451-0666
Dan Waite, *Pr*

EMP: 22 **EST:** 1986
SQ FT: 20,000
SALES (est): 525.32K **Privately Held**
Web: www.regol-g.com
SIC: **7389** 2394 2393 2392 Sewing contractor; Canvas and related products; Textile bags; Household furnishings, nec

(G-3950)
DEFENSE CO INC
600 Superior Ave E (44114-2614)
PHONE..................413 998-1637
Kent Rosenthal, *Pr*
EMP: 21 **EST:** 1976
SALES (est): 486.04K **Privately Held**
SIC: **3769** Guided missile and space vehicle parts and aux. equip., R&D

(G-3951)
DENIM6729 INC
6729 Denison Ave (44102-5438)
PHONE..................216 854-3634
EMP: 6 **EST:** 2018
SALES (est): 46.58K **Privately Held**
SIC: **2211** Denims

(G-3952)
DEPENDABLE STAMPING COMPANY
1160 E 222nd St (44117-1176)
PHONE..................216 486-5522
Jeffrey N Beres, *Pr*
Michael Beres, *General Vice President*
Roy Beres, *
EMP: 25 **EST:** 1981
SQ FT: 20,000
SALES (est): 4.45MM **Privately Held**
Web: www.dependablestamping.com
SIC: **3469** Stamping metal for the trade

(G-3953)
DERMA GLOW MED SPA CORP
22237 Lorain Rd (44126-3315)
PHONE..................440 641-1406
Hanin M Hamid, *Prin*
EMP: 6 **EST:** 2020
SALES (est): 62.35K **Privately Held**
Web: www.dermaglowcle.com
SIC: **2061** Raw cane sugar

(G-3954)
DETREX CORPORATION (DH)
Also Called: Research Technologies Intl
1000 Belt Line Ave (44109-2848)
PHONE..................216 749-2605
Thomas E Mark, *Pr*
Robert M Currie, *VP*
◆ **EMP:** 10 **EST:** 1920
SQ FT: 5,000
SALES (est): 321.27MM **Privately Held**
Web: www.detrexchemicals.com
SIC: **2819** 3589 Inorganic acids except nitric and phosphoric; Commercial cleaning equipment
HQ: Italmatch Chemicals Spa
Via Magazzini Del Cotone 17
Genova GE 16128

(G-3955)
DI IORIO SHEET METAL INC
5002 Clark Ave (44102-4552)
P.O. Box 602210 (44102-0210)
PHONE..................216 961-3703
Anthony Di Iorio, *Pr*
Anna Di Iorio, *Sec*
EMP: 12 **EST:** 1963
SQ FT: 34,000
SALES (est): 1.85MM **Privately Held**
SIC: **3444** Sheet metalwork

(G-3956)
DIAMOND MACHINERY LLC
Also Called: Diamond Machinery Company
19525 Hilliard Blvd Unit 16729 (44116-4750)
PHONE..................216 312-1235
William T Danicki, *Pr*
EMP: 8 **EST:** 2019
SALES (est): 350.02K **Privately Held**
Web: www.diamondmachineryco.com
SIC: **3553** 7699 Woodworking machinery; Industrial machinery and equipment repair

(G-3957)
DIASOME PHARMACEUTICALS INC
10000 Cedar Ave Ste 6 (44106-2119)
PHONE..................216 444-7110
Robert Geho, *CEO*
Todd Hobbs, *CMO*
Peter Tollman, *Ch Bd*
EMP: 17 **EST:** 2008
SALES (est): 6.09MM **Privately Held**
Web: www.diasome.com
SIC: **2834** Pharmaceutical preparations

(G-3958)
DIE-CUT PRODUCTS CO
Also Called: D C
1801 E 30th St (44114-4471)
PHONE..................216 771-6994
Ari Comet, *Pr*
Steve A Comet, *Pr*
Arlene R Comet, *VP*
EMP: 10 **EST:** 1944
SQ FT: 10,600
SALES (est): 1.41MM **Privately Held**
Web: www.diecut.com
SIC: **3069** 3452 3053 3499 Washers, rubber; Washers; Gaskets; packing and sealing devices; Shims, metal

(G-3959)
DIPS PUBLISHING INC
4229 E 124th St (44105-6301)
PHONE..................216 801-7886
David A Wright, *Prin*
EMP: 6 **EST:** 2016
SALES (est): 121.55K **Privately Held**
SIC: **2741** Miscellaneous publishing

(G-3960)
DIRECTCONNECTGROUP LTD
Also Called: D C G
5501 Cass Ave (44102-2121)
PHONE..................216 281-2866
Robert A Durham, *Pt*
Scott L Durham, *Pt*
James E Pinkin, *Pt*
Steven J Pinkin, *Pt*
Terry Storms, *Pt*
EMP: 10 **EST:** 2003
SALES (est): 497.43K **Privately Held**
Web: www.dcgone.com
SIC: **2752** 7331 Offset printing; Mailing service

(G-3961)
DISH ONE UP SATELLITE INC
3634 Euclid Ave Ste 100 (44115-2535)
PHONE..................216 482-3875
Firas Essa, *Pr*
EMP: 99 **EST:** 2001
SALES (est): 7.84MM **Privately Held**
Web: www.dish1up.com
SIC: **3679** 5731 Antennas, satellite: household use; Antennas, satellite dish

(G-3962)
DISTILLATA COMPANY (PA)
1608 E 24th St (44114-4212)

P.O. Box 93845 (44101-5845)
PHONE..................216 771-2900
TOLL FREE: 800
William E Schroeder, *Pr*
Herbert Buckman, *
J C Little, *
R M Egan, *
Dalphne Axline, *
EMP: 70 **EST:** 1897
SQ FT: 100,000
SALES (est): 15.25MM
SALES (corp-wide): 15.25MM **Privately Held**
Web: www.distillata.com
SIC: **2899** 5149 Distilled water; Mineral or spring water bottling

(G-3963)
DISTRIBUTOR GRAPHICS INC
6909 Engle Rd Ste 13 (44130-3484)
PHONE..................440 260-0024
Richard Doerr, *Pr*
James F Gottschalk, *VP*
Robert Wilson, *Treas*
EMP: 8 **EST:** 1985
SQ FT: 8,500
SALES (est): 725K **Privately Held**
Web: www.magicmkt.com
SIC: **2752** Offset printing

(G-3964)
DIVERSIFIED MOLD CASTINGS LLC
Also Called: Diversified Mold & Castings Co
19800 Miles Rd (44128-4118)
PHONE..................216 663-1814
Vince Costello, *Prin*
EMP: 37 **EST:** 2008
SALES (est): 4.21MM **Privately Held**
Web: www.diversifiedmolds.com
SIC: **3544** Special dies and tools

(G-3965)
DOAN/PYRAMID SOLUTIONS LLC
5069 Corbin Dr (44128-5413)
PHONE..................216 587-9510
EMP: 53 **EST:** 2004
SALES (est): 4.83MM **Privately Held**
SIC: **3822** Environmental controls

(G-3966)
DOLLARS N CENT INC
1057 S Belvoir Blvd (44121-2944)
PHONE..................971 381-0406
Roderick Byers, *CEO*
EMP: 11 **EST:** 2005
SALES (est): 374.23K **Privately Held**
SIC: **7389** 1389 Financial services; Construction, repair, and dismantling services

(G-3967)
DOMINION ENTERPRISES
26301 Curtiss Wright Pkwy (44143-4413)
PHONE..................216 472-1870
Michelle Dubblestyne, *Prin*
EMP: 9
Web: www.dominionenterprises.com
SIC: **2721** Periodicals
HQ: Dominion Enterprises
150 Granby St Ste 150 # 150
Norfolk VA 23510

(G-3968)
DOMINO FOODS INC
Also Called: Domino Sugar
2075 E 65th St (44103-4630)
PHONE..................216 432-3222
Jeffrey Bender, *Brnch Mgr*
EMP: 172
SALES (corp-wide): 2.16B **Privately Held**
Web: www.asr-group.com

▲ = Import ▼ = Export
◆ = Import/Export

GEOGRAPHIC SECTION

Cleveland - Cuyahoga County (G-3992)

SIC: 2099 7389 Sugar; Packaging and labeling services
HQ: Domino Foods Inc.
99 Wood Ave S Ste 901
Iselin NJ 08830
732 590-1173

(G-3969)
DORN COLOR LLC
11555 Berea Rd (44102)
PHONE..................................216 634-2252
▲ EMP: 118 EST: 1929
SALES (est): 20.73MM
SALES (corp-wide): 20.73MM Privately Held
Web: www.dorncolor.com
SIC: 2752 Cards, lithographed
PA: Signum Llc
32000 Aurora Rd Ste C
Solon OH 44139
440 248-2233

(G-3970)
DOVE DIE AND STAMPING COMPANY
15665 Brookpark Rd (44142-1668)
PHONE..................................216 267-3720
Gerald Wagner, *Pr*
Norma Wagner, *
EMP: 45 EST: 1952
SQ FT: 42,000
SALES (est): 9.74MM Privately Held
Web: www.dovedie.com
SIC: 3469 3544 Stamping metal for the trade; Special dies and tools

(G-3971)
DRABIK MANUFACTURING INC
15601 Commerce Park Dr (44142-2016)
PHONE..................................216 267-1616
James Drabik, *Pr*
EMP: 17 EST: 1962
SQ FT: 13,000
SALES (est): 1.82MM Privately Held
Web: www.drabikinc.com
SIC: 3599 7692 Machine shop, jobbing and repair; Welding repair

(G-3972)
DREISON INTERNATIONAL INC (PA)
4540 W 160th St (44135-2628)
PHONE..................................216 362-0755
John Berger Junior, *Pr*
Theodore Berger Junior, *Pr*
Theodore J Berger Senior, *Ch Bd*
Marilyn J Berger, *
Whitney Slaght, *
◆ EMP: 190 EST: 1986
SQ FT: 210,000
SALES (est): 61.53MM
SALES (corp-wide): 61.53MM Privately Held
Web: www.dreison.com
SIC: 3643 3621 3561 3564 Current-carrying wiring services; Motors, electric; Pumps and pumping equipment; Purification and dust collection equipment

(G-3973)
DRINK MODERN TECHNOLOGIES LLC ✪
4125 Lorain Ave 2nd Fl (44113-3718)
PHONE..................................216 577-1536
Mike Dougherty, *Managing Member*
EMP: 8 EST: 2022
SALES (est): 635.78K Privately Held
SIC: 3556 Beverage machinery

(G-3974)
DRUM PARTS INC
7580 Garfield Blvd (44125-1216)
PHONE..................................216 271-0702
Curtis Crowder, *Opers Mgr*
EMP: 14 EST: 1968
SALES (est): 73.45K Privately Held
Web: www.drumpartsinc.com
SIC: 3412 Drums, shipping: metal

(G-3975)
DUBLIN PLASTICS INC
9202 Reno Ave (44105-2125)
PHONE..................................216 641-5904
Donald R Newman, *Pr*
James Newman, *Sec*
EMP: 8 EST: 1983
SALES (est): 659.33K Privately Held
SIC: 3089 Injection molding of plastics

(G-3976)
DUCT FABRICATORS INC
Also Called: Fab3 Group
883 Addison Rd (44103-1607)
PHONE..................................216 391-2400
John Sickle, *Prin*
Steven Haydu, *Prin*
EMP: 8 EST: 2011
SALES (est): 1.52MM Privately Held
Web: www.tinshops.com
SIC: 3444 Sheet metalwork

(G-3977)
DUCTS INC
883 Addison Rd (44103-1607)
PHONE..................................216 391-2400
Charlotte Sickle, *Ch*
Patricia Sickle Mc Elroy, *
John E Sickle Junior, *Pr*
James Sickle, *
EMP: 18 EST: 1962
SQ FT: 30,000
SALES (est): 589.33K Privately Held
SIC: 1761 3444 Sheet metal work, nec; Sheet metalwork

(G-3978)
DUPONT SPECIALTY PDTS USA LLC
Also Called: Dupont Vespel Parts and Shapes
6200 Hillcrest Dr (44125-4624)
PHONE..................................216 901-3600
Anthony Adetayo, *Brnch Mgr*
EMP: 118
SALES (corp-wide): 2.93B Publicly Held
Web: www.dupont.com
SIC: 3366 3568 Bushings and bearings; Power transmission equipment, nec
HQ: Dupont Specialty Products Usa, Llc
974 Centre Rd
Wilmington DE 19805
302 992-2941

(G-3979)
DURABLE PLATING CO
4404 Saint Clair Ave (44103-1188)
PHONE..................................216 391-2132
Joe Akers, *Pr*
Tim Akers, *VP*
Shirley Akers, *Sec*
EMP: 7 EST: 1935
SQ FT: 6,500
SALES (est): 559.55K Privately Held
Web: www.renzettilaw.com
SIC: 3471 Electroplating of metals or formed products

(G-3980)
DURAY PLATING COMPANY INC
13701 Triskett Rd (44111-1520)
PHONE..................................216 941-5540
Kenneth R Roth, *Pr*
EMP: 25 EST: 1963
SQ FT: 6,000
SALES (est): 2.03MM Privately Held
Web: www.durayplatingco.com
SIC: 3471 Electroplating of metals or formed products

(G-3981)
DVUV LLC
4641 Hinckley Industrial Pkwy (44109-6002)
PHONE..................................216 741-5511
▼ EMP: 20 EST: 2005
SQ FT: 20,000
SALES (est): 4.09MM Privately Held
Web: www.dvuv.com
SIC: 2521 Wood office furniture

(G-3982)
DYNAMIC TOOL & MOLD INC
12126 York Rd Unit N (44133-3688)
PHONE..................................440 237-8665
EMP: 7 EST: 1996
SQ FT: 3,500
SALES (est): 763.2K Privately Held
Web: www.dynamictoolandmold.com
SIC: 3544 Special dies and tools

(G-3983)
E & K PRODUCTS CO INC
3520 Cesko Ave (44109-1487)
PHONE..................................216 631-2510
Lee Klimek, *Pr*
Lee Klimek, *Ch Bd*
David Klimek, *VP*
Joyce Klimek, *Sec*
EMP: 8 EST: 1966
SQ FT: 25,000
SALES (est): 687.84K Privately Held
Web: www.ekproducts.com
SIC: 3599 3444 Machine shop, jobbing and repair; Sheet metalwork

(G-3984)
E D M FASTAR INC
13410 Enterprise Ave (44135-5162)
PHONE..................................216 676-0100
Frank Star, *Pr*
EMP: 7 EST: 1999
SQ FT: 3,000
SALES (est): 681.79K Privately Held
Web: www.fastaredm.com
SIC: 3544 Special dies and tools

(G-3985)
E POMPILI SONS INC
Also Called: Pompili Precast Concrete
12307 Broadway Ave (44125-1847)
PHONE..................................216 581-8080
William Pompili, *Pr*
EMP: 8 EST: 1953
SQ FT: 14,500
SALES (est): 895.1K Privately Held
Web: www.pompiliprecastconcrete.com
SIC: 3272 Concrete products, precast, nec

(G-3986)
E-Z ELECTRIC MOTOR SVC CORP
8510 Bessemer Ave (44127-1843)
P.O. Box 22531 (44122-0531)
PHONE..................................216 581-8820
Demetrius Ledgyard, *Pr*
EMP: 29 EST: 1965
SQ FT: 15,000
SALES (est): 857.18K Privately Held
Web: www.ezelectricmotor.com
SIC: 7694 Electric motor repair

(G-3987)
EAGLE FAMILY FOODS GROUP LLC (PA)
1975 E 61st St (44103-3810)
PHONE..................................330 382-3725
Paul Smucker Wagstaff, *CEO*
Paul Smucker Wagstaff, *Managing Member*
Larry Herman, *
Jeff Boyle, *CAO**
Dan Gentile, *
EMP: 25 EST: 2015
SALES (est): 101.8MM
SALES (corp-wide): 101.8MM Privately Held
Web: www.eaglefoods.com
SIC: 2023 Condensed milk

(G-3988)
EAGLE INDUSTRIES
16911 Saint Clair Ave (44110-2536)
P.O. Box 361403 (44136-0024)
PHONE..................................440 376-3885
EMP: 6 EST: 2018
SALES (est): 238.25K Privately Held
Web: www.eagleindustries.com
SIC: 3999 Manufacturing industries, nec

(G-3989)
EAST WEST COPOLYMER LLC (PA)
Also Called: East West Copolymer
28026 Gates Mills Blvd (44124-4730)
PHONE..................................225 267-3400
Gregory Nelson, *Pr*
Celso Goncalves, *Sr VP*
Patrick Bowers, *VP*
Bobby Rikhoff, *VP*
◆ EMP: 54 EST: 2005
SALES (est): 17.98MM Privately Held
SIC: 2822 Synthetic rubber

(G-3990)
EAST WOODWORKING COMPANY
2044 Random Rd (44106-2392)
P.O. Box 221185 (44122-0995)
PHONE..................................216 791-5950
Zigmund T Hersh, *Pr*
Albert Hersh, *VP*
Coby Hersh, *Mgr*
Ken Hersh, *Mgr*
EMP: 8 EST: 1956
SQ FT: 12,400
SALES (est): 780.36K Privately Held
SIC: 1751 2521 2522 3261 Cabinet building and installation; Cabinets, office: wood; Office cabinets and filing drawers, except wood; Vitreous plumbing fixtures

(G-3991)
EATON AEROQUIP LLC (HQ)
Also Called: Eaton Global Hose
1000 Eaton Blvd (44122-6058)
PHONE..................................440 523-5000
Alexander M Cutler, *CEO*
E R Franklin, *
◆ EMP: 220 EST: 1940
SQ FT: 21,000
SALES (est): 489.85MM Privately Held
SIC: 3052 3492 3429 3069 Rubber hose; Hose and tube fittings and assemblies, hydraulic/pneumatic; Clamps and couplings, hose; Molded rubber products
PA: Eaton Corporation Public Limited Company
30 Pembroke Road
Dublin D04Y0

(G-3992)
EATON CORPORATION
Airflex Div
9919 Clinton Rd (44144-1077)
PHONE..................................216 281-2211

(PA)=Parent Co (HQ)=Headquarters
✪ = New Business established in last 2 years

Cleveland - Cuyahoga County (G-3993)

GEOGRAPHIC SECTION

James W Fisher, *Brnch Mgr*
EMP: 200
Web: www.dix-eaton.com
SIC: 3714 3625 3542 3568 Air brakes, motor vehicle; Electromagnetic clutches or brakes; Brakes, metal forming; Clutches, except vehicular
HQ: Eaton Corporation
1000 Eaton Blvd
Cleveland OH 44122
440 523-5000

(G-3993)
EATON CORPORATION
Also Called: NA Financial Service Center
6055 Rockside Woods Blvd N (44131-2301)
P.O. Box 818035 (44181-8035)
PHONE....................440 826-1115
EMP: 217
Web: www.dix-eaton.com
SIC: 3625 Relays and industrial controls
HQ: Eaton Corporation
1000 Eaton Blvd
Cleveland OH 44122
440 523-5000

(G-3994)
EATON CORPORATION (HQ)
Also Called: Eaton
1000 Eaton Blvd (44122-6058)
PHONE....................440 523-5000
Craig Arnold, *Ch*
Mark Mcguire, *Ex VP*
Thomas Moran, *Sr VP*
David Foster, *Senior Vice President Corporate Development*
Katrina R Redmond Scp, *CIO*
◆ **EMP:** 450 **EST:** 1911
SALES (est): 1.95B Privately Held
Web: www.dix-eaton.com
SIC: 3625 3714 3594 3559 Motor controls and accessories; Motor vehicle engines and parts; Pumps, hydraulic power transfer; Semiconductor manufacturing machinery
PA: Eaton Corporation Public Limited Company
30 Pembroke Road
Dublin D04Y0

(G-3995)
EATON ELECTRIC HOLDINGS LLC (HQ)
1000 Eaton Blvd (44122-6058)
PHONE....................440 523-5000
Kirk Hachigian, *Pr*
Bruce M Taten, *
David Barta, *
Tyler Johnson, *
▲ **EMP:** 406 **EST:** 1996
SALES (est): 2.02B Privately Held
Web: www.eaton.com
SIC: 3612 3613 3644 3536 Transformers, except electric; Panel and distribution boards and other related apparatus; Noncurrent-carrying wiring devices; Hoists, cranes, and monorails
PA: Eaton Corporation Public Limited Company
30 Pembroke Road
Dublin D04Y0

(G-3996)
EATON ELECTRICAL
23555 Euclid Ave (44117-1703)
P.O. Box 818021 (44181-8021)
PHONE....................787 257-4470
EMP: 16 **EST:** 2017
SALES (est): 6.05MM Privately Held
SIC: 3625 Motor controls and accessories

(G-3997)
EATON INDUSTRIAL CORPORATION
Also Called: Argo Tech Fluid Elec Dist Div
1000 Eaton Blvd (44122-6058)
PHONE....................216 692-5456
Heath Monesmith, *Brnch Mgr*
EMP: 101
SIC: 7699 3728 Pumps and pumping equipment repair; Aircraft parts and equipment, nec
HQ: Eaton Industrial Corporation
23555 Euclid Ave
Cleveland OH 44117
216 523-4205

(G-3998)
EATON INDUSTRIAL CORPORATION (HQ)
23555 Euclid Ave (44117-1703)
PHONE....................216 523-4205
Craig Arnold, *CEO*
Raul R Keen, *
John S Glover, *
Earl R Franklin, *
EMP: 433 **EST:** 1990
SQ FT: 1,800,000
SALES (est): 93.26MM Privately Held
SIC: 3724 3728 Pumps, aircraft engine; Aircraft parts and equipment, nec
PA: Eaton Corporation Public Limited Company
30 Pembroke Road
Dublin D04Y0

(G-3999)
ECONOMY FLAME HARDENING INC
896 E 70th St (44103-1706)
PHONE....................216 431-9333
Charles P Triplett, *Pr*
EMP: 11 **EST:** 1992
SALES (est): 211.94K Privately Held
SIC: 3356 Nonferrous rolling and drawing, nec

(G-4000)
EDGE 247 CORP
2765 E 55th St Ste 7 (44104-2856)
PHONE....................216 771-7000
Salina Jones, *Pr*
EMP: 6 **EST:** 2013
SALES (est): 123.89K Privately Held
SIC: 2759 Commercial printing, nec

(G-4001)
EG ENTERPRISE SERVICES INC
5000 Euclid Ave Ste 100 (44103-3752)
P.O. Box 18029 (44118-0029)
PHONE....................216 431-3300
EMP: 12 **EST:** 1993
SQ FT: 10,000
SALES (est): 293.87K Privately Held
SIC: 2752 7331 7334 Offset printing; Mailing service; Photocopying and duplicating services

(G-4002)
ELCO CORPORATION (DH)
Also Called: Elco
1000 Belt Line Ave (44109)
PHONE....................800 321-0467
Dave Millin, *CEO*
Bob Lunoe, *
◆ **EMP:** 33 **EST:** 1974
SQ FT: 72,000
SALES (est): 44.34MM Privately Held
Web: www.lubeperformanceadditives.com
SIC: 2869 Industrial organic chemicals, nec
HQ: Detrex Corporation
1000 Belt Line Ave
Cleveland OH 44109
216 749-2605

(G-4003)
ELECTRIC CORD SETS INC (PA)
Also Called: Happy Trails Rv
4700 Manufacturing Ave (44135)
PHONE....................216 261-1000
Thomas Benbow, *Ch Bd*
Cathy Gilmour, *Treas*
Edward Benbow, *VP Opers*
Tammy Liloie, *VP*
◆ **EMP:** 6 **EST:** 1947
SQ FT: 3,500
SALES (est): 7.21MM
SALES (corp-wide): 7.21MM Privately Held
Web: www.ecspremier.com
SIC: 3643 Current-carrying wiring services

(G-4004)
ELECTRO-MAGWAVE INC
Also Called: E M Wave
10221 Sweet Valley Dr Ste 1 (44125-4277)
PHONE....................216 453-1160
Frank Kim Goryance, *Pr*
Anthony Zupancic, *VP Opers*
EMP: 7 **EST:** 2007
SALES (est): 999.79K Privately Held
Web: www.emwaveinc.com
SIC: 3663 Antennas, transmitting and communications

(G-4005)
ELECTROLIZING CORP OF OHIO (PA)
1325 E 152nd St (44112-2075)
P.O. Box 12007 (44112-0007)
PHONE....................800 451-8655
Lawrence E Noble, *Pr*
Scott Noble, *Ex VP*
Todd Noble, *VP*
EMP: 20 **EST:** 1948
SQ FT: 20,000
SALES (est): 4.83MM
SALES (corp-wide): 4.83MM Privately Held
Web: www.ecofohio.com
SIC: 3471 Electroplating of metals or formed products

(G-4006)
ELECTROLIZING CORPORATION OHIO
Also Called: ELECTROLIZING CORPORATION OF OHIO
1655 Collamer Ave (44110-3201)
PHONE....................216 451-8653
EMP: 10
SQ FT: 12,342
SALES (corp-wide): 4.83MM Privately Held
Web: www.ecofohio.com
SIC: 3471 Electroplating of metals or formed products
PA: The Electrolizing Corporation Of Ohio
1325 E 152nd St
Cleveland OH 44112
800 451-8655

(G-4007)
ELMET TECHNOLOGIES INC
21801 Tungsten Rd (44117-1117)
PHONE....................216 692-3990
EMP: 36 **EST:** 1995
SQ FT: 150,000
SALES (est): 6.23MM Privately Held
Web: www.hcstarck.com
SIC: 3339 Primary nonferrous metals, nec

(G-4008)
EM ES BE COMPANY LLC
Also Called: M.S. Barkin Company
18210 Saint Clair Ave (44110-2610)
PHONE....................216 761-9500

EMP: 8 **EST:** 1966
SQ FT: 2,500
SALES (est): 457.26K Privately Held
Web: www.msbarkinco.com
SIC: 3911 5944 Jewelry, precious metal; Jewelry, precious stones and precious metals

(G-4009)
EM4 INC
676 Alpha Dr (44143-2123)
PHONE....................608 240-4800
Brian Engstrom, *Brnch Mgr*
EMP: 25
SALES (corp-wide): 187.38MM Privately Held
Web: www.gandh.com
SIC: 3674 Semiconductors and related devices
HQ: Em4 Inc
7 Oak Park Dr
Bedford MA 01730
701 276 7601

(G-4010)
EM4 INC
Also Called: G&H Baltimore
676 Alpha Dr (44143-2123)
PHONE....................410 987-5600
Mark Webster, *Brnch Mgr*
EMP: 25
SALES (corp-wide): 187.38MM Privately Held
Web: www.gandh.com
SIC: 3661 Fiber optics communications equipment
HQ: Em4 Inc
7 Oak Park Dr
Bedford MA 01730
781 275-7501

(G-4011)
EMERSON INDUSTRIAL AUTOMATION
7800 Hub Pkwy (44125-5711)
PHONE....................216 901-2400
EMP: 9 **EST:** 2015
SALES (est): 602.23K Privately Held
Web: www.emerson.com
SIC: 3823 Process control instruments

(G-4012)
EMPIRE BRASS CO
Also Called: American Brass
5000 Superior Ave (44103-1238)
PHONE....................216 431-6565
Robert Mc Connville, *Pr*
▲ **EMP:** 7 **EST:** 1903
SALES (est): 1.58MM Privately Held
Web: www.empirebrassfaucets.com
SIC: 5074 3432 3364 Plumbing fittings and supplies; Plumbing fixture fittings and trim; Nonferrous die-castings except aluminum

(G-4013)
EMX INDUSTRIES INC (HQ)
5660 Transportation Blvd (44125-5363)
PHONE....................216 518-9888
Joseph Williams, *Pr*
▲ **EMP:** 16 **EST:** 1987
SALES (est): 9.96MM
SALES (corp-wide): 9.96MM Privately Held
Web: www.emxinc.com
SIC: 3699 Security control equipment and systems
PA: Watervale Equity Partners Fund I G.P., Llc
29525 Chagrin Blvd
Beachwood OH 44122
216 926-7219

▲ = Import ▼ = Export
◆ = Import/Export

GEOGRAPHIC SECTION
Cleveland - Cuyahoga County (G-4035)

(G-4014)
ENAMELAC COMPANY
18103 Roseland Rd (44112-1001)
P.O. Box 5058 (44085-0258)
PHONE...................216 481-8878
John M Kanuch Junior, *Pr*
EMP: 10 **EST:** 1950
SQ FT: 10,000
SALES (est): 957.58K **Privately Held**
Web: www.enamelac.com
SIC: 3479 Enameling, including porcelain, of metal products

(G-4015)
ENERCO GROUP INC (PA)
Also Called: Mr Heater
4560 W 160th St (44135-2628)
P.O. Box 6660 (44101-1660)
PHONE...................216 916-3000
Franco Pozzi, *CEO*
Jeff Bush, *
Mark Przypyfz, *
Allen Haire, *
▲ **EMP:** 101 **EST:** 1957
SQ FT: 120,875
SALES (est): 46.82MM
SALES (corp-wide): 46.82MM **Privately Held**
Web: www.enerco.com
SIC: 3433 Gas infrared heating units

(G-4016)
ENERCO TECHNICAL PRODUCTS INC
Also Called: Mr. Heater
4560 W 160th St (44135-2628)
P.O. Box 6660 (44101-1660)
PHONE...................216 916-3000
Allen L Haire, *CEO*
John D Duross, *
Francis Verchick, *
▲ **EMP:** 54 **EST:** 1986
SQ FT: 48,000
SALES (est): 3.72MM
SALES (corp-wide): 46.82MM **Privately Held**
Web: www.heatstarbyenerco.com
SIC: 3433 Gas infrared heating units
PA: Enerco Group, Inc.
4560 W 160th St
Cleveland OH 44135
216 916-3000

(G-4017)
ENERSYS
12690 Elmwood Ave (44111-5912)
PHONE...................216 252-4242
Walter Sauerteig, *Genl Mgr*
EMP: 168
SALES (corp-wide): 3.71B **Publicly Held**
Web: www.enersys.com
SIC: 3691 Lead acid batteries (storage batteries)
PA: Enersys
2366 Bernville Rd
Reading PA 19605
610 208-1991

(G-4018)
ENESPRO LLC
15825 Industrial Pkwy (44135-3319)
PHONE...................630 332-2801
Chuck Grossman, *CEO*
Michael Enright, *Pr*
EMP: 8 **EST:** 2017
SALES (est): 989.63K **Privately Held**
Web: www.enesproppe.com
SIC: 3842 Gloves, safety
PA: National Safety Apparel, Inc.
15825 Industrial Pkwy
Cleveland OH 44135

(G-4019)
ENPROTECH INDUSTRIAL TECH LLC (DH)
Also Called: Enprotech Mechanical Services
4259 E 49th St (44125-1001)
PHONE...................216 883-3220
Chris Pascarella, *CEO*
▲ **EMP:** 23 **EST:** 1950
SQ FT: 96,000
SALES (est): 75.03MM **Privately Held**
Web: www.enprotech.com
SIC: 3547 3365 3599 8711 Rolling mill machinery; Machinery castings, aluminum; Custom machinery; Engineering services
HQ: Industrious Group Inc.
4259 E 49th St
Cleveland OH 44125
216 206-0080

(G-4020)
ENSIGN PRODUCT COMPANY INC
3528 E 76th St (44105-1510)
P.O. Box 27167 (44127-0167)
PHONE...................216 341-5911
Birney R Walker Iii, *Pr*
Christopher Walker, *VP*
Charles Snyder, *Sec*
EMP: 6 **EST:** 1920
SQ FT: 9,000
SALES (est): 616.73K **Privately Held**
SIC: 2992 2899 Lubricating oils; Chemical preparations, nec

(G-4021)
ENTERPRISE TOOL & DIE COMPANY
4940 Schaaf Ln (44131-1008)
PHONE...................216 351-1300
Robert C Schweikert, *Pr*
Richard W Schweikert, *VP*
Todd Schweikert, *Sec*
EMP: 10 **EST:** 1954
SQ FT: 10,000
SALES (est): 974.84K **Privately Held**
SIC: 3544 Dies and die holders for metal cutting, forming, die casting

(G-4022)
ENVIRI CORPORATION
Sherwood Divisions of Harsco
7900 Hub Pkwy (44125-5713)
PHONE...................216 961-1570
Tom Hensley, *Mgr*
EMP: 7
SALES (corp-wide): 2.07B **Publicly Held**
Web: www.enviri.com
SIC: 3443 Industrial vessels, tanks, and containers
PA: Enviri Corporation
100-120 N 18th St # 17
Philadelphia PA 19103
267 857-8715

(G-4023)
ENVIROFAB INC
7914 Lake Ave (44102-1933)
P.O. Box 602750 (44102-0750)
PHONE...................216 651-1767
Thomas J Rusnak, *Pr*
Richard Rusnak, *VP*
EMP: 15 **EST:** 1974
SQ FT: 42,000
SALES (est): 729.19K **Privately Held**
Web: www.envirofab.net
SIC: 3564 Dust or fume collecting equipment, industrial

(G-4024)
EOS TECHNOLOGY INC
8525 Clinton Rd (44144-1014)
PHONE...................216 281-2999
John Hadgis, *Pr*

Gregory Hadgis, *VP*
EMP: 17 **EST:** 1996
SALES (est): 581.96K **Privately Held**
SIC: 3599 Machine shop, jobbing and repair

(G-4025)
EPSILON MANAGEMENT CORPORATION
Also Called: Areway
8525 Clinton Rd (44144-1014)
PHONE...................216 634-2500
◆ **EMP:** 200
Web: www.epsilonmgmt.com
SIC: 2851 3471 Paints and allied products; Polishing, metals or formed products

(G-4026)
EQUIPMENT MFRS INTL INC
Also Called: E M I
16151 Puritas Ave (44135-2617)
P.O. Box 94725 (44101-4725)
PHONE...................216 651-6700
Jerry Senk, *Prin*
R T Mackin, *
Joe Mcfarland, *Prin*
Bill Vondriska, *Prin*
Dave Bowman, *Prin*
▲ **EMP:** 30 **EST:** 1982
SQ FT: 65,000
SALES (est): 7.51MM **Privately Held**
Web: www.emi-inc.com
SIC: 3559 5084 Foundry machinery and equipment; Industrial machinery and equipment

(G-4027)
ERICO PRODUCTS INC
Also Called: Erico
34600 Solon Rd (44139-2695)
PHONE...................440 248-0100
▲ **EMP:** 428
SIC: 3644 3441 3629 3643 Noncurrent-carrying wiring devices; Fabricated structural metal; Electronic generation equipment; Rail bonds, electric: for propulsion and signal circuits

(G-4028)
ERIE STREET THEA SVCS INC
1621 E 41st St (44103-2305)
PHONE...................216 426-0050
Angie Davis, *Pr*
EMP: 8 **EST:** 1993
SALES (est): 1.06MM **Privately Held**
Web: www.eriestreet.net
SIC: 5049 3999 Theatrical equipment and supplies; Theatrical scenery

(G-4029)
ERIEVIEW METAL TREATING CO
Also Called: Apex Metals
4465 Johnston Pkwy (44128-2998)
PHONE...................216 663-1780
Alex Kappos, *Pr*
Dennis Kappos, *
George Kappos Junior, *Sec*
EMP: 100 **EST:** 1961
SQ FT: 70,000
SALES (est): 11.91MM **Privately Held**
Web: www.erieviewmetal.com
SIC: 3471 Electroplating of metals or formed products

(G-4030)
ESSI ACOUSTICAL PRODUCTS
11750 Berea Rd Ste 1 (44111-1603)
P.O. Box 643 (44107-0943)
PHONE...................216 251-7888
Mark Essi, *Pr*
EMP: 10 **EST:** 1984
SQ FT: 6,000

SALES (est): 1.07MM **Privately Held**
Web: www.essiacoustical.com
SIC: 3296 Acoustical board and tile, mineral wool

(G-4031)
ESTERLINE TECHNOLOGIES CORP (HQ)
Also Called: Esterline
1301 E 9th St Ste 3000 (44114-1871)
PHONE...................216 706-2960
Curtis C Reusser, *Ch Bd*
Stephen M Nolan, *Ex VP*
Paul P Benson, *Chief Human Resources Officer*
Donald E Walther, *Ex VP*
▼ **EMP:** 35 **EST:** 1967
SALES (est): 1.54B
SALES (corp-wide): 6.58B **Publicly Held**
Web: www.esterline.com
SIC: 3728 3812 3429 Aircraft assemblies, subassemblies, and parts, nec; Aircraft control instruments; Aircraft hardware
PA: Transdigm Group Incorporated
1301 E 9th St Ste 3000
Cleveland OH 44114
216 706-2960

(G-4032)
EUCLID CHEMICAL COMPANY (DH)
19215 Redwood Rd (44110-2735)
PHONE...................800 321-7628
Thomas Gairing, *Pr*
◆ **EMP:** 20 **EST:** 1910
SALES (est): 111.09MM
SALES (corp-wide): 7.26B **Publicly Held**
Web: www.euclidchemical.com
SIC: 2899 4213 3272 Chemical preparations, nec; Trucking, except local; Concrete products, nec
HQ: Tremco Cpg Inc.
3735 Green Rd
Beachwood OH 44122
216 292-5000

(G-4033)
EUCLID COFFEE CO INC
17230 S Waterloo Rd (44110-3811)
PHONE...................216 481-3330
James M Repak, *Pr*
M J Repak, *CEO*
EMP: 8 **EST:** 1935
SQ FT: 10,000
SALES (est): 693.74K **Privately Held**
Web: www.euclidcoffee.com
SIC: 2095 Coffee roasting (except by wholesale grocers)

(G-4034)
EUCLID JALOUSIES INC
490 E 200th St (44119-1500)
PHONE...................440 953-1112
Timothy Huquila, *Pr*
Bob Dunmire, *VP*
EMP: 7 **EST:** 1954
SQ FT: 2,400
SALES (est): 527.78K **Privately Held**
Web: www.euclidjalousies.com
SIC: 3442 5211 Screen and storm doors and windows; Windows, storm: wood or metal

(G-4035)
EUCLID MEDIA GROUP LLC (PA)
Also Called: Do 210
737 Bolivar Rd (44115-1259)
P.O. Box 1028 (44096-1028)
PHONE...................216 241-7550
Daniel N Zelman, *Managing Member*
EMP: 10 **EST:** 1998
SALES (est): 5.02MM
SALES (corp-wide): 5.02MM **Privately Held**

Cleveland - Cuyahoga County (G-4036)

Web: www.chavagroup.com
SIC: **2711** Newspapers, publishing and printing

(G-4036)
EUREKA SCREW MACHINE PDTS CO
Also Called: Eureka Screw Machine Co
3960 E 91st St (44105-3964)
PHONE..................................216 883-1715
William Rubick, *Pr*
Irene Rubick, *Treas*
EMP: 6 EST: 1950
SQ FT: 5,136
SALES (est): 423.1K **Privately Held**
Web: www.eurekamachine.com
SIC: **3451** Screw machine products

(G-4037)
EVEN CUT ABRASIVE COMPANY
850 E 72nd St (44103-1007)
PHONE..................................216 881-9595
Art Ellison, *Pr*
EMP: 19 EST: 1932
SALES (est): 778.41K **Privately Held**
Web: www.evencut.com
SIC: **3291** Abrasive products

(G-4038)
EVEREADY PRINTING INC
Also Called: Weprintquick.com
20700 Miles Pkwy (44128-5506)
PHONE..................................216 587-2389
Roger Wolfson, *Prin*
Roger Wolfson, *Pr*
Scott Wolfson, *VP*
EMP: 21 EST: 1905
SALES (est): 2.45MM **Privately Held**
Web: www.evereadyprint.com
SIC: **2752** Offset printing

(G-4039)
EVERYTHING IN AMERICA
Also Called: Eia
4141 Stilmore Rd (44121-3129)
PHONE..................................347 871-6872
Patrick Hadley, *VP*
Renee Hawkins, *Asst VP*
EMP: 8 EST: 2013
SALES (est): 397.1K **Privately Held**
SIC: **5211** 2452 7389 Modular homes; Modular homes, prefabricated, wood; Business services, nec

(G-4040)
EXACT-TOOL & DIE INC
5425 W 140th St (44142-1704)
PHONE..................................216 676-9140
Frank K Chesek, *CEO*
John J Melnik, *
Mark S Klepper, *
Robert Matis, *
Ron Gunter, *
EMP: 35 EST: 1977
SQ FT: 60,000
SALES (est): 5.76MM **Privately Held**
Web: www.exact-tool.com
SIC: **3465** 3469 3544 3694 Automotive stampings; Metal stampings, nec; Special dies, tools, jigs, and fixtures; Engine electrical equipment

(G-4041)
EXCELLENT TOOL & DIE INC
10921 Briggs Rd (44111-5333)
PHONE..................................216 671-9222
John Kinsch, *Pr*
John Kinsch, *Pr*
Edith Burnside, *VP*
EMP: 6 EST: 1983
SQ FT: 4,800
SALES (est): 549.6K **Privately Held**

Web: www.excellent-tool.com
SIC: **3599** Machine shop, jobbing and repair

(G-4042)
EXPLORYS INC
1111 Superior Ave E (44114-2522)
PHONE..................................216 767-4700
Stephen Mchale, *CEO*
Charles Lougheed, *
Aaron Cornell, *
Thomas Chickerella, *
EMP: 26 EST: 2009
SALES (est): 10.8MM
SALES (corp-wide): 61.86B **Publicly Held**
Web: www.ibm.com
SIC: **7372** Application computer software
PA: International Business Machines Corporation
1 New Orchard Rd
Armonk NY 10504
914 499-1900

(G-4043)
EXPO PACKAGING INC
Also Called: Expo Machinery
4832 Ridge Rd (44144-3329)
PHONE..................................216 267-9700
Patricia Kaszas, *Pr*
Lorenz J Kaszas, *Genl Mgr*
Tim Kaszas Senior, *VP*
Jim Kaszas Junior, *VP*
EMP: 6 EST: 1982
SALES (est): 340K **Privately Held**
SIC: **7389** 3565 Packaging and labeling services; Packaging machinery

(G-4044)
EXPRESS GROUND SERVICES INC
Also Called: Eminent Transport
1241 E 172nd St (44119-3128)
PHONE..................................216 870-9374
Rashid Sharif, *Pr*
EMP: 6 EST: 2021
SALES (est): 502.18K **Privately Held**
SIC: **3537** 7389 Trucks: freight, baggage, etc.: industrial, except mining; Business services, nec

(G-4045)
EZ BRITE BRANDS INC
806 Sharon Dr Ste C (44145-7701)
P.O. Box 40025 (44140-0025)
PHONE..................................440 871-7817
Edmond Aghajanian, *Pr*
Marcia Meermans, *Ofcr*
EMP: 11 EST: 1989
SQ FT: 11,000
SALES (est): 957.67K **Privately Held**
SIC: **2842** Dusting cloths, chemically treated

(G-4046)
FABRICATING MACHINE TOOLS LTD
12360 Plaza Dr (44130-1043)
PHONE..................................440 666-9187
TOLL FREE: 800
EMP: 6 EST: 1997
SQ FT: 6,000
SALES (est): 496.21K **Privately Held**
SIC: **3599** Machine shop, jobbing and repair

(G-4047)
FALCON INNOVATIONS INC
3316 W 118th St (44111-1723)
PHONE..................................216 252-0676
Robert A Jewell Junior, *Pr*
EMP: 6 EST: 1964
SQ FT: 6,400
SALES (est): 503.99K **Privately Held**
Web: www.falconinnovations.com
SIC: **3599** Machine shop, jobbing and repair

(G-4048)
FALLON PHARAOHS
3911 Grosvenor Rd (44118-2315)
PHONE..................................216 990-2746
Lavelle Moore, *Pr*
EMP: 7 EST: 2019
SALES (est): 250K **Privately Held**
SIC: **2329** Men's and boy's clothing, nec

(G-4049)
FALLS STAMPING & WELDING CO
Also Called: Plant Two
1720 Fall St (44113-2416)
PHONE..................................216 771-9635
John Hall, *Frmn Supr*
EMP: 13
SALES (corp-wide): 23.36MM **Privately Held**
Web: www.falls-stamping.com
SIC: **3465** Automotive stampings
PA: Falls Stamping & Welding Company
2900 Vincent St
Cuyahoga Falls OH 44221
330 928-1191

(G-4050)
FARASEY STEEL FABRICATORS INC
4000 Iron Ct (44115-3582)
PHONE..................................216 641-1853
Don J Henderson, *Pr*
Don J Henderson, *Pr*
Robert L Henderson, *VP*
George R Henderson, *VP*
EMP: 15 EST: 1859
SQ FT: 14,000
SALES (est): 1.72MM **Privately Held**
Web: www.faraseysteelfab.com
SIC: **3441** Fabricated structural metal

(G-4051)
FBC CHEMICAL CORPORATION
7301 Bessemer Ave (44127-1817)
PHONE..................................216 341-2000
EMP: 21
SALES (corp-wide): 43.14MM **Privately Held**
Web: www.fbcchem.com
SIC: **3312** Chemicals and other products derived from coking
PA: Fbc Chemical Corporation
634 Route 228
Mars PA 16046
724 625-3116

(G-4052)
FCI INC
4801 W 160th St (44135-2633)
PHONE..................................216 251-5200
Kenneth Edgar, *Pr*
Irene Edgar, *
EMP: 80 EST: 1958
SALES (est): 6.33MM **Privately Held**
Web: www.jbtc.com
SIC: **3089** Injection molding of plastics

(G-4053)
FDI ENTERPRISES
17700 Saint Clair Ave (44110-2621)
PHONE..................................440 269-8282
EMP: 9 EST: 2016
SALES (est): 573.27K **Privately Held**
Web: www.tripolymer.com
SIC: **3089** Plastics products, nec

(G-4054)
FEDERAL HOSE MANUFACTURING LLC
10514 Dupont Ave (44108-1348)
PHONE..................................800 346-4673
EMP: 25 EST: 2021

SALES (est): 1.16MM **Privately Held**
Web: www.federalhose.com
SIC: **3599** Hose, flexible metallic

(G-4055)
FEDPRO INC (HQ)
Also Called: Gasoila Thred-Taper
4520 Richmond Rd (44128-5757)
PHONE..................................216 464-6440
Jon Outcalt Junior, *CEO*
Jon Outcalt Senior, *Ch*
Jon Outcalt Junior, *Pr*
▲ **EMP: 28 EST:** 1915
SQ FT: 4,000
SALES (est): 35.43MM
SALES (corp-wide): 35.43MM **Privately Held**
Web: www.fpcintl.com
SIC: **2891** Sealing compounds, synthetic rubber or plastic
PA: Fpc International, Inc.
4520 Richmond Rd
Cleveland OH 44128
216 464-6440

(G-4056)
FENCE ONE INC
Also Called: Great Lake Fence
11111 Broadway Ave (44125-1659)
PHONE..................................216 441-2600
Michael Ely, *Pr*
EMP: 14 EST: 1951
SQ FT: 12,000
SALES (est): 3MM **Privately Held**
Web: www.greatlakesfence.com
SIC: **1521** 1799 3496 General remodeling, single-family houses; Fence construction; Miscellaneous fabricated wire products

(G-4057)
FERRALLOY INC
28001 Ranney Pkwy (44145-1159)
PHONE..................................440 250-1900
William Habansky Junior, *Pr*
Sherri Habansky, *Sec*
▲ **EMP: 8 EST:** 1978
SQ FT: 15,000
SALES (est): 4.14MM **Privately Held**
Web: www.ferralloy.com
SIC: **5051** 3599 Castings, rough: iron or steel ; Machine shop, jobbing and repair

(G-4058)
FERROTHERM CORPORATION
4758 Warner Rd (44125-1117)
PHONE..................................216 883-9350
Haakon Egeland, *CEO*
Haakon Egeland, *Ch Bd*
Emery Ceo, *Pr*
Alf Egeland, *
Thor Egeland, *
▲ **EMP: 105 EST:** 1939
SQ FT: 90,000
SALES (est): 22.76MM **Privately Held**
Web: www.ferrotherm.com
SIC: **3462** 3724 3812 3694 Turbine engine forgings, ferrous; Aircraft engines and engine parts; Search and navigation equipment; Engine electrical equipment

(G-4059)
FIELDS PROCESS TECHNOLOGY INC
1849 W 24th St (44113-3513)
P.O. Box 91806 (44101-3806)
PHONE..................................216 781-4787
Joseph Fields, *Owner*
EMP: 6 EST: 2001
SALES (est): 527.87K **Privately Held**
SIC: **3089** Plastics containers, except foam

GEOGRAPHIC SECTION
Cleveland - Cuyahoga County (G-4083)

(G-4060)
FINE POINTS INC
Also Called: Tekus, L Sweater Design
12602 Larchmere Blvd (44120-1110)
PHONE.....................216 229-6644
Liz Tekus, *Pr*
Henry Roth, *VP*
EMP: 11 **EST:** 1984
SALES (est): 467.69K **Privately Held**
Web: www.finepoints.com
SIC: 2253 5949 Sweaters and sweater coats, knit; Sewing, needlework, and piece goods

(G-4061)
FINELLI ORNAMENTAL IRON CO
Also Called: Finelli Architectural Iron Co
30815 Solon Rd (44139-3485)
PHONE.....................440 248-0050
Frank Finelli, *Pr*
Angelo Finelli, *VP*
James Korosec, *VP*
EMP: 33 **EST:** 1962
SQ FT: 15,000
SALES (est): 3.45MM **Privately Held**
Web: www.finelliironworks.com
SIC: 3446 1751 Ornamental metalwork; Carpentry work

(G-4062)
FIRST BRANDS GROUP LLC (DH)
127 Public Sq Ste 5300 (44114)
PHONE.....................248 371-1700
Patrick James, *Managing Member*
EMP: 11 **EST:** 2013
SALES (est): 6.49B
SALES (corp-wide): 8.03B **Privately Held**
SIC: 3714 Windshield wiper systems, motor vehicle
HQ: First Brands Group Intermediate, Llc
    127 Public Sq Ste 5110
    Cleveland OH 44114
    216 589-0198

(G-4063)
FIRST BRNDS GROUP HOLDINGS LLC (PA)
127 Public Sq Ste 5110 (44114-1313)
PHONE.....................216 589-0198
Patrick James, *CEO*
EMP: 29 **EST:** 2020
SALES (est): 8.03B
SALES (corp-wide): 8.03B **Privately Held**
SIC: 3069 Tubing, rubber

(G-4064)
FIRST BRNDS GROUP INTRMDATE LL (HQ)
Also Called: Luberfiner
127 Public Sq Ste 5110 (44114-1313)
PHONE.....................216 589-0198
Patrick James, *Managing Member*
EMP: 11 **EST:** 2018
SALES (est): 6.49B
SALES (corp-wide): 8.03B **Privately Held**
SIC: 3069 Tubing, rubber
PA: First Brands Group Holdings, Llc
    127 Public Sq Ste 5110
    Cleveland OH 44114
    216 589-0198

(G-4065)
FIVES N AMERCN COMBUSTN INC (DH)
4455 E 71st St (44105-5601)
PHONE.....................216 271-6000
Luigi Russo, *Ch Bd*
Erik Paulhardt, *Pr*
Kathy E Ruekberg, *VP*
Philippe Guerreau, *Sec*

◆ **EMP:** 244 **EST:** 1917
SQ FT: 400,000
SALES (est): 104.64MM
SALES (corp-wide): 409.51MM **Privately Held**
Web: www.fivesgroup.com
SIC: 3433 Heating equipment, except electric
HQ: Fives Inc.
    23400 Halsted Rd
    Farmington Hills MI 48335
    248 477-0800

(G-4066)
FLAGSHIP TRADING CORPORATION
Also Called: Manufacturers Wholesale Lumber
734 Alpha Dr Ste J (44143-2135)
EMP: 35 **EST:** 1983
SALES (est): 4.96MM **Privately Held**
SIC: 2491 5031 Structural lumber and timber, treated wood; Lumber, plywood, and millwork

(G-4067)
FLASH INDUSTRIAL TECH LTD
30 Industry Dr (44146-4414)
PHONE.....................440 786-8979
Lawrence P Zajac, *Prin*
Mary Elizabeth Zajac, *Prin*
▲ **EMP:** 9 **EST:** 1995
SQ FT: 18,000
SALES (est): 1.85MM **Privately Held**
Web: www.flashindustrial.com
SIC: 3599 Machine shop, jobbing and repair

(G-4068)
FLEXNOVA INC (PA)
6100 Oak Tree Blvd Ste 200 (44131-2544)
PHONE.....................216 288-6961
Steve Rossi, *Pr*
EMP: 10 **EST:** 2003
SQ FT: 1,000
SALES (est): 2.99MM
SALES (corp-wide): 2.99MM **Privately Held**
Web: www.flexnova.com
SIC: 7372 Prepackaged software

(G-4069)
FLEXRACK BY QCELLS LLC (PA)
Also Called: NSM
23000 Harvard Rd Ste B (44122)
P.O. Box 270666 (06127-0666)
PHONE.....................216 998-5988
◆ **EMP:** 145 **EST:** 1986
SALES (est): 22.04MM
SALES (corp-wide): 22.04MM **Privately Held**
Web: www.extrusions.com
SIC: 3354 Aluminum rod and bar

(G-4070)
FLIGHT BRIGHT LTD
23100 Miles Rd (44128-5441)
P.O. Box 391718 (44139-8718)
PHONE.....................216 663-6677
Allen Warner, *Pr*
EMP: 15 **EST:** 2004
SALES (est): 910K **Privately Held**
Web: www.flitebrite.com
SIC: 3471 Cleaning, polishing, and finishing

(G-4071)
FLOWCRETE NORTH AMERICA INC
19218 Redwood Rd (44110-2736)
PHONE.....................936 539-6700
Mark Greaves, *Pr*
Edward W Moore, *
▲ **EMP:** 24 **EST:** 2004
SALES (est): 10.51MM
SALES (corp-wide): 7.26B **Publicly Held**

Web: www.flowcrete.in
SIC: 3996 Tile, floor: supported plastic
HQ: Flowcrete Group Limited
    1 Chamberlain Square
    Birmingham W MIDLANDS

(G-4072)
FLUID SYSTEM SERVICE INC
13825 Triskett Rd (44111-1523)
P.O. Box 771414 (44107-0057)
PHONE.....................216 651-2450
John C Balliett, *Pr*
D Thomas George, *Sec*
EMP: 8 **EST:** 1981
SALES (est): 965.11K **Privately Held**
Web: www.fluidsystemsohio.com
SIC: 3511 7699 Hydraulic turbines; Hydraulic equipment repair

(G-4073)
FLUKE ELECTRONICS CORPORATION
28775 Aurora Rd (44139-1837)
PHONE.....................800 850-4608
EMP: 40 **EST:** 2004
SALES (est): 1.45MM
SALES (corp-wide): 6.07B **Publicly Held**
Web: www.fluke.com
SIC: 3825 Instruments to measure electricity
PA: Fortive Corporation
    6920 Seaway Blvd
    Everett WA 98203
    425 446-5000

(G-4074)
FOAM SEAL INC
5109 Hamilton Ave (44114-3907)
PHONE.....................216 881-8111
Sarah Nash, *Ch Bd*
Ronald Moeller, *
EMP: 120 **EST:** 1977
SQ FT: 250,000
SALES (est): 14.28MM **Privately Held**
Web: www.novagard.com
SIC: 2891 2911 Adhesives and sealants; Greases, lubricating
PA: Novagard Solutions, Inc.
    5109 Hamilton Ave
    Cleveland OH 44114

(G-4075)
FOAM-TEX SOLUTIONS CORP
13981 W Parkway Rd (44135-4511)
PHONE.....................216 889-2702
Donald Abshire, *CEO*
Alan Abshire, *VP Prd*
▲ **EMP:** 6 **EST:** 1999
SQ FT: 6,700
SALES (est): 444.68K **Privately Held**
Web: www.foam-tex.com
SIC: 2841 Soap and other detergents

(G-4076)
FOIL TAPES LLC
1700 London Rd (44112-1201)
PHONE.....................216 255-6655
Adam Schlesinger, *Managing Member*
EMP: 6 **EST:** 2018
SALES (est): 186.31K **Privately Held**
SIC: 3497 Foil, laminated to paper or other materials

(G-4077)
FOLLOW PRINT CLUB ON FACEBOOK
11150 East Blvd (44106-1711)
PHONE.....................216 707-2579
EMP: 7 **EST:** 2011
SALES (est): 168.09K **Privately Held**

SIC: 2752 Commercial printing, lithographic

(G-4078)
FOOD DESIGNS INC
Also Called: Ohio City Pasta
5299 Crayton Ave (44104-2829)
PHONE.....................216 651-9221
Gary W Thomas, *Pr*
EMP: 10 **EST:** 1991
SALES (est): 1.03MM **Privately Held**
Web: www.ohiocitypasta.com
SIC: 2099 2032 Pasta, uncooked: packaged with other ingredients; Ravioli: packaged in cans, jars, etc.

(G-4079)
FOOTE PRINTING COMPANY INC
Also Called: Audit Forms
2800 E 55th St (44104-2862)
PHONE.....................216 431-1757
Michael Duhr, *Pr*
Karl-heinz Duhr, *Pr*
Steven Duhr, *VP*
Steven Duhhr, *CEO*
EMP: 15 **EST:** 1907
SQ FT: 16,000
SALES (est): 1.84MM **Privately Held**
Web: www.footeprinting.com
SIC: 2752 2759 Offset printing; Letterpress printing

(G-4080)
FORCE ROBOTS LLC
1768 E 25th St Ste 315 (44114-4418)
PHONE.....................216 881-8360
EMP: 8 **EST:** 2009
SALES (est): 138.55K **Privately Held**
Web: www.forcerobots.com
SIC: 3559 Robots, molding and forming plastics

(G-4081)
FOREST CITY COMPANIES INC
Also Called: Forest City Packaging
3607 W 56th St (44102-5739)
PHONE.....................216 586-5279
Anthony Galang, *Pr*
Dawn Galang, *
EMP: 23 **EST:** 2003
SQ FT: 42,000
SALES (est): 4.99MM **Privately Held**
Web: www.forestcityco.com
SIC: 4783 2441 2394 Packing goods for shipping; Boxes, wood; Canvas and related products

(G-4082)
FOREST HILL PUBLISHING LLC
13200 Forest Hill Ave (44112-4508)
PHONE.....................216 761-8316
Cedric Richardson, *Prin*
EMP: 6 **EST:** 2009
SALES (est): 87.24K **Privately Held**
Web: www.foresthillpublishing.com
SIC: 2741 Miscellaneous publishing

(G-4083)
FORGE PRODUCTS CORPORATION
Also Called: Forged Products
9503 Woodland Ave (44104-2487)
PHONE.....................216 231-2600
Charles E Thayer Ii, *Pr*
EMP: 50 **EST:** 1962
SQ FT: 31,600
SALES (est): 12.39MM **Privately Held**
Web: www.forgeproducts.com
SIC: 3312 3463 3462 Forgings, iron and steel; Nonferrous forgings; Iron and steel forgings

Cleveland - Cuyahoga County (G-4084)   GEOGRAPHIC SECTION

(G-4084)
FORMTEK INC (DH)
Also Called: Formtek International
4899 Commerce Pkwy (44128-5905)
PHONE..................................216 292-4460
Joe Mayer, *Pr*
▲ EMP: 60 EST: 1984
SQ FT: 56,000
SALES (est): 35.52MM
SALES (corp-wide): 689.94MM **Privately Held**
Web: www.formtekgroup.com
SIC: 3547 3549 3535 Pipe and tube mills; Coiling machinery; Conveyors and conveying equipment
HQ: Formtek Inc
   711 Ogden Ave
   Lisle IL 60532
   630 285-1500

(G-4085)
FORMTEK METAL FORMING INC
Yoder Manufacturing Division
4899 Commerce Pkwy (44128-5905)
PHONE..................................216 292-4460
Glenn Ertel, *Brnch Mgr*
EMP: 95
SALES (corp-wide): 689.94MM **Privately Held**
Web: www.formtekgroup.com
SIC: 3547 Rolling mill machinery
HQ: Formtek, Inc.
   4899 Commerce Pkwy
   Cleveland OH 44128
   216 292-4460

(G-4086)
FOUNDRY ARTISTS INC
Also Called: Studio Foundry
4404 Perkins Ave (44103-3544)
PHONE..................................216 391-9030
Mark Olitsky, *Pr*
Craig Horstman, *Treas*
John Ranally, *Sec*
Lisa Kenion, *VP*
EMP: 7 EST: 1988
SQ FT: 3,000
SALES (est): 981.61K **Privately Held**
Web: www.foundryshow.com
SIC: 3366 Bronze foundry, nec

(G-4087)
FOUNT LLC
2570 Superior Ave E Ste 504 (44114-4235)
PHONE..................................216 855-8751
EMP: 6 EST: 2013
SALES (est): 214.88K **Privately Held**
Web: www.fountleather.com
SIC: 3111 Bag leather

(G-4088)
FPT CLEVELAND LLC (DH)
Also Called: Ferrous Processing and Trading
8550 Aetna Rd (44105-1607)
PHONE..................................216 441-3800
Andrew M Luntz, *
▲ EMP: 105 EST: 1999
SALES (est): 59.34MM
SALES (corp-wide): 22B **Publicly Held**
Web: www.fptscrap.com
SIC: 4953 5051 5093 3341 Recycling, waste materials; Iron and steel (ferrous) products; Ferrous metal scrap and waste; Secondary nonferrous metals
HQ: Ferrous Processing And Trading Company
   1333 Brewery Park Blvd # 400
   Detroit MI 48207
   313 567-9710

(G-4089)
FRAM GROUP
127 Public Sq Ste 5110 (44114-1313)
PHONE..................................479 271-7934
Ike Peterson, *Owner*
EMP: 9 EST: 2012
SALES (est): 454.38K **Privately Held**
SIC: 3714 Motor vehicle parts and accessories

(G-4090)
FRANCK AND FRIC INCORPORATED
7919 Old Rockside Rd (44131-2300)
P.O. Box 31148 (44131-0148)
PHONE..................................216 524-4451
Donald R Skala Senior, *Pr*
David R Skala, *VP*
Donald C Skala Junior, *VP*
Stacey Carson, *Asst VP*
EMP: 51 EST: 1934
SQ FT: 20,000
SALES (est): 4.26MM **Privately Held**
Web: franck-fric-inc.business.site
SIC: 1711 1761 3441 3444 Ventilation and duct work contractor; Sheet metal work, nec; Fabricated structural metal; Sheet metalwork

(G-4091)
FREEWAY CORPORATION (PA)
9301 Allen Dr (44125-4688)
PHONE..................................216 524-9700
◆ EMP: 110 EST: 1944
SALES (est): 27.2MM
SALES (corp-wide): 27.2MM **Privately Held**
Web: www.freewaycorp.com
SIC: 3469 Metal stampings, nec

(G-4092)
FUNNY TIMES INC
2176 Lee Rd (44118-2908)
P.O. Box 18530 (44118-0530)
PHONE..................................216 371-8600
Raymond Lesser, *Pr*
Susan Wolpert, *Sec*
EMP: 6 EST: 1985
SALES (est): 661K **Privately Held**
Web: www.funnytimes.com
SIC: 2711 Newspapers, publishing and printing

(G-4093)
FURNITURE CONCEPTS INC
4925 Galaxy Pkwy Ste G (44128-5961)
PHONE..................................216 292-9100
Karyl Walker, *CEO*
EMP: 12 EST: 1991
SQ FT: 1,700
SALES (est): 5MM **Privately Held**
Web: www.furnitureconcepts.com
SIC: 2522 5021 7641 Office furniture, except wood; Office furniture, nec; Furniture repair and maintenance

(G-4094)
FX DIGITAL MEDIA INC
Also Called: Hot Cards.com
2400 Superior Ave E Ste 100 (44114-4236)
PHONE..................................216 241-4040
Columbus Woodruff, *Brnch Mgr*
EMP: 9
SIC: 2752 Offset printing
PA: Fx Digital Media, Inc.
   1600 E 23rs St Rs
   Cleveland OH 44114

(G-4095)
FX DIGITAL MEDIA INC (PA)
1600 E 23rd St (44114)
PHONE..................................216 241-4040
John Gadd, *CEO*
Columbus Woodruff, *Pr*
Nikki Woodruff, *Stockholder*
EMP: 17 EST: 1997
SQ FT: 15,000
SALES (est): 2.27MM **Privately Held**
SIC: 7336 2754 Commercial art and graphic design; Color printing: gravure

(G-4096)
G & S METAL PRODUCTS CO INC (PA)
3330 E 79th St (44127-1831)
P.O. Box 78510 (44105-8510)
PHONE..................................216 441-0700
◆ EMP: 165 EST: 1949
SALES (est): 39.36MM
SALES (corp-wide): 39.36MM **Privately Held**
Web: www.gsmetal.com
SIC: 3411 5023 5072 3556 Pans, tinned; Kitchenware; Hardware; Food products machinery

(G-4097)
G AND J AUTOMATIC SYSTEMS INC
Also Called: G & J Packaging
14701 Industrial Pkwy (44135-4547)
PHONE..................................216 741-6070
Gregory Shteyngarts, *Pr*
EMP: 30 EST: 1985
SQ FT: 23,000
SALES (est): 1.15MM **Privately Held**
SIC: 7389 3565 Packaging and labeling services; Packaging machinery

(G-4098)
G T METAL FABRICATORS INC
Also Called: Acromet Metal Fabricators
12126 York Rd Unit E (44133-3688)
PHONE..................................440 237-8745
Gary Callahan, *Pr*
Judy Callahan, *VP*
EMP: 12 EST: 1966
SQ FT: 9,000
SALES (est): 2.37MM **Privately Held**
Web: www.acromet.com
SIC: 3444 Sheet metal specialties, not stamped

(G-4099)
G W COBB CO
3914 Broadway Ave 16 (44115-3694)
PHONE..................................216 341-0100
George W Cobb Junior, *Pr*
EMP: 12 EST: 1940
SQ FT: 15,000
SALES (est): 1.69MM **Privately Held**
Web: www.gwcobb.com
SIC: 3411 5084 Food containers, metal; Industrial machinery and equipment

(G-4100)
G2 MATERIALS LLC
17325 Euclid Ave Ste 3038 (44112-1255)
PHONE..................................216 293-4211
Timothy Gascoigne, *Managing Member*
EMP: 6 EST: 2021
SALES (est): 321.03K **Privately Held**
Web: www.g2materials.com
SIC: 3444 Machine guards, sheet metal

(G-4101)
GARFIELD ALLOYS INC (PA)
4878 Chaincraft Rd (44125-1807)
PHONE..................................216 587-4843
Chuck Slovich, *Pr*
Mike Slovich Junior, *Sec*
◆ EMP: 12 EST: 1950
SQ FT: 60,000
SALES (est): 5.03MM
SALES (corp-wide): 5.03MM **Privately Held**
SIC: 3369 Magnesium and magnes.-base alloy castings, exc. die-casting

(G-4102)
GARICK LLC (HQ)
Also Called: Ogg Garick
8400 Sweet Valley Dr Ste 408 (44125-4244)
PHONE..................................216 581-0100
Gary P Trinetti, *Managing Member*
EMP: 20 EST: 1980
SALES (est): 61.11MM
SALES (corp-wide): 20.43B **Publicly Held**
Web: www.garick.com
SIC: 2875 0711 2499 5091 Potting soil, mixed; Soil preparation services; Mulch or sawdust products, wood; Athletic goods
PA: Waste Management, Inc.
   800 Capitol St Ste 3000
   Houston TX 77002
   713 512-6200

(G-4103)
GARLAND COMMERCIAL INDUSTRIES LLC
1333 E 179th St (44110)
PHONE..................................800 338-2204
◆ EMP: 47 EST: 1973
SALES (est): 1.46MM
SALES (corp-wide): 2.67MM **Privately Held**
SIC: 3556 3589 3631 3567 Ovens, bakery; Cooking equipment, commercial; Household cooking equipment; Industrial furnaces and ovens
HQ: Welbilt, Inc.
   2227 Welbilt Blvd
   Trinity FL 34655
   727 375-7010

(G-4104)
GARLAND INDUSTRIES INC (PA)
3800 E 91st St (44105-2103)
PHONE..................................216 641-7500
David Sokol, *Pr*
Melvin Chrostowski, *VP Mktg*
G Richard Olivier, *Admn Execs*
William Oley, *VP Sls*
Joe Orlando, *Sls Mgr*
EMP: 8 EST: 1895
SQ FT: 150,000
SALES (est): 715.07MM
SALES (corp-wide): 715.07MM **Privately Held**
Web: www.garlandco.com
SIC: 2952 6512 8712 Roofing materials; Commercial and industrial building operation; Architectural services

(G-4105)
GARLAND/DBS INC
3800 E 91st St (44105-2103)
PHONE..................................216 641-7500
Dave Sokol, *Pr*
Richard Debacco, *VP*
Melvin Chrostowski, *VP Mktg*
Chuck Ripepi, *CFO*
EMP: 250 EST: 2009
SALES (est): 41.27MM
SALES (corp-wide): 715.07MM **Privately Held**
Web: www.dbsgarland.com
SIC: 2952 6512 8712 Roofing materials; Commercial and industrial building operation; Architectural services
HQ: The Garland Company Inc
   3800 E 91st St
   Cleveland OH 44105
   216 641-7500

GEOGRAPHIC SECTION

Cleveland - Cuyahoga County (G-4129)

(G-4106)
GE LIGHTING INC
Also Called: GE
1975 Noble Rd (44112-1719)
Rural Route 1975 Noble Rd (44112)
PHONE..................216 266-2121
Bill Lacey, *CEO*
Ken Friesen, *
EMP: 80 **EST:** 1996
SALES (est): 54.41MM
SALES (corp-wide): 399.47MM **Privately Held**
Web: www.gelighting.com
SIC: 3646 Commercial lighting fixtures
PA: Savant Systems, Inc.
    45 Perseverance Way
    Hyannis MA 02601
    508 683-2500

(G-4107)
GEAR COMPANY OF AMERICA INC
14300 Lorain Ave (44111-2297)
PHONE..................216 671-5400
Edward Morel, *Pr*
EMP: 60 **EST:** 1946
SQ FT: 96,000
SALES (est): 8.32MM **Privately Held**
Web: www.gearcoa.com
SIC: 3462 3714 3566 Gears, forged steel; Gears, motor vehicle; Gears, power transmission, except auto

(G-4108)
GEBAUER COMPANY
4444 E 153rd St (44128-2955)
PHONE..................216 581-3030
John Giltinan, *CEO*
Margaret Giltinan, *
David O'halloran, *Pr*
Ted Kulak, *
▲ **EMP:** 34 **EST:** 1957
SQ FT: 16,000
SALES (est): 8.3MM **Privately Held**
Web: www.gebauer.com
SIC: 2834 Pharmaceutical preparations

(G-4109)
GEM TOOL LLC
17000 Saint Clair Ave Ste 102 (44110-2535)
PHONE..................216 771-8344
Nick Carlozzi, *Prin*
EMP: 8 **EST:** 2014
SALES (est): 495.32K **Privately Held**
Web: www.gemtoolmachining.com
SIC: 3545 Cutting tools for machine tools

(G-4110)
GEMCO PACIFIC ENERGY LLC
200 Public Sq (44114-2316)
PHONE..................216 937-1371
Joshua Gottlieb, *Brnch Mgr*
EMP: 17
SALES (corp-wide): 183.83K **Privately Held**
SIC: 3572 Computer storage devices
PA: Gemco Pacific Energy, Llc
    18 N Main St Ste 200
    Chagrin Falls OH 44022
    440 914-9677

(G-4111)
GENERAL AWNING COMPANY INC
1350 E Granger Rd (44131-1206)
P.O. Box 275 (44402-0275)
PHONE..................216 749-0110
Paul Gall, *Pr*
EMP: 13 **EST:** 1950
SQ FT: 10,000
SALES (est): 460.06K **Privately Held**
SIC: 3444 1751 1761 Awnings, sheet metal; Window and door (prefabricated) installation ; Siding contractor

(G-4112)
GENERAL ELECTRIC COMPANY
Also Called: GE
1814 E 45th St (44103-2321)
PHONE..................216 391-8741
Mike Kridle, *Mgr*
EMP: 48
SALES (corp-wide): 67.95B **Publicly Held**
Web: www.ge.com
SIC: 3641 Lamps, incandescent filament, electric
PA: General Electric Company
    1 Aviation Way
    Cincinnati OH 45215
    617 443-3000

(G-4113)
GENERAL ELECTRIC COMPANY
Also Called: GE
18683 S Miles Rd (44128-4297)
PHONE..................216 663-2110
Steve Hilgendorf, *Mgr*
EMP: 40
SQ FT: 53,462
SALES (corp-wide): 67.95B **Publicly Held**
Web: www.ge.com
SIC: 3844 Radiographic X-ray apparatus and tubes
PA: General Electric Company
    1 Aviation Way
    Cincinnati OH 45215
    617 443-3000

(G-4114)
GENERAL ELECTRIC COMPANY
Also Called: GE
1099 Ivanhoe Rd (44110-3293)
PHONE..................216 268-3846
James C Wiester, *Brnch Mgr*
EMP: 46
SALES (corp-wide): 67.95B **Publicly Held**
Web: www.ge.com
SIC: 2819 2899 2851 Industrial inorganic chemicals, nec; Chemical preparations, nec ; Paints and allied products
PA: General Electric Company
    1 Aviation Way
    Cincinnati OH 45215
    617 443-3000

(G-4115)
GENERAL ELECTRIC COMPANY
Also Called: GE
4477 E 49th St (44125-1097)
PHONE..................216 883-1000
Donald Mysliwiec, *Mgr*
EMP: 39
SQ FT: 12,000
SALES (corp-wide): 67.95B **Publicly Held**
Web: www.ge.com
SIC: 7629 3621 3613 3612 Electrical repair shops; Motors and generators; Switchgear and switchboard apparatus; Transformers, except electronic
PA: General Electric Company
    1 Aviation Way
    Cincinnati OH 45215
    617 443-3000

(G-4116)
GENERAL MOTORS LLC
General Motors
5400 Chevrolet Blvd (44130-1451)
PHONE..................216 265-5000
Al Maclauhlin, *Mgr*
EMP: 2028
Web: www.gm.com
SIC: 5511 3465 3714 2531 Automobiles, new and used; Body parts, automobile: stamped metal; Motor vehicle parts and accessories; Public building and related furniture
HQ: General Motors Llc
    300 Rnaissance Ctr Ste L1
    Detroit MI 48243

(G-4117)
GENERAL SHEAVE COMPANY INC
1335 Main Ave (44113-2389)
PHONE..................216 781-8120
Antun Bunjevac, *Pr*
EMP: 9 **EST:** 1951
SQ FT: 7,500
SALES (est): 724.96K **Privately Held**
Web: www.generalsheave.com
SIC: 3599 Machine shop, jobbing and repair

(G-4118)
GENERAL STEEL CORPORATION ✪
3344 E 80th St (44127-1851)
PHONE..................216 883-4200
James Grasso, *Pr*
EMP: 13 **EST:** 2022
SALES (est): 3.6MM
SALES (corp-wide): 17.81MM **Privately Held**
SIC: 5051 3398 3441 Steel; Metal heat treating; Fabricated structural metal
PA: Mcdonald Steel Corporation
    100 Ohio Ave
    Mc Donald OH 44437
    330 530-9118

(G-4119)
GENIE REPROS INC
2211 Hamilton Ave (44114-1154)
PHONE..................216 696-6677
Barry Bishop, *Pr*
EMP: 11 **EST:** 1968
SQ FT: 7,900
SALES (est): 459.95K **Privately Held**
Web: www.genierepros.com
SIC: 2752 Lithographing on metal

(G-4120)
GENT MACHINE COMPANY
12315 Kirby Ave (44108-1616)
PHONE..................216 481-2334
Richard W Gent Junior, *Pr*
Diane Gent, *
Richard W Gent Iv, *VP*
EMP: 50 **EST:** 1927
SALES (est): 9.64MM **Privately Held**
Web: www.gentmachine.com
SIC: 3451 Screw machine products

(G-4121)
GEON COMPANY
6100 Oak Tree Blvd (44131-2544)
PHONE..................216 447-6000
Thomas A Waltermire, *Pr*
Thomas A Waltermire, *Ch Bd*
Donald P Knechtges Senior, *Vice President Business*
Gregory L Rutman, *
W David Wilson, *
EMP: 3200 **EST:** 1993
SQ FT: 387,877
SALES (est): 112.76MM **Privately Held**
Web: www.geon.com
SIC: 2821 2869 2812 Polyvinyl chloride resins, PVC; Ethylene; Chlorine, compressed or liquefied

(G-4122)
GEROW EQUIPMENT COMPANY INC
706 E 163rd St (44110-2453)
PHONE..................216 383-8800
Robert L Gerow, *CEO*
EMP: 7 **EST:** 1943
SQ FT: 1,500
SALES (est): 762.01K **Privately Held**
Web: gerow-equipment-co.business.site
SIC: 3561 5084 Industrial pumps and parts; Heat exchange equipment, industrial

(G-4123)
GES AGM
12300 Snow Rd (44130-1001)
PHONE..................216 658-6505
EMP: 24 **EST:** 2017
SALES (est): 2.37MM **Privately Held**
Web: www.ges-agm.com
SIC: 3624 Fibers, carbon and graphite

(G-4124)
GEW INC
11941 Abbey Rd Ste X (44133-2663)
PHONE..................440 237-4439
Brian Wenger, *Pr*
▲ **EMP:** 9 **EST:** 1999
SALES (est): 1.61MM **Privately Held**
Web: www.gewuv.com
SIC: 3555 Printing trades machinery

(G-4125)
GIE MEDIA INC (PA)
5811 Canal Rd (44125-3430)
PHONE..................800 456-0707
Richard J W Foster, *CEO*
Chris Foster, *
Dan Moreland, *
EMP: 35 **EST:** 1980
SQ FT: 6,500
SALES (est): 24.01MM
SALES (corp-wide): 24.01MM **Privately Held**
Web: www.giemedia.com
SIC: 2721 2731 Magazines: publishing only, not printed on site; Books, publishing only

(G-4126)
GLASS BLOCK HEADQUARTERS INC
3535 W 140th St Ste B (44111-2419)
PHONE..................216 941-5470
Sophia Fernandez, *Pr*
Elias Fernandez, *VP*
EMP: 6 **EST:** 2004
SALES (est): 501.97K **Privately Held**
Web: www.glassblockhq.com
SIC: 3229 Blocks and bricks, glass

(G-4127)
GLF INTERNATIONAL INC (PA)
3690 Orange Pl Ste 495 (44122-4465)
PHONE..................216 621-6901
James Mcclurg, *Pr*
Gary Mcclurg, *Sec*
EMP: 10 **EST:** 1993
SQ FT: 20,000
SALES (est): 1.8MM **Privately Held**
SIC: 1479 Fluorspar mining

(G-4128)
GLOBAL MANUFACTURING ASSOC INC
1750 E 39th St (44114-4531)
PHONE..................216 938-9056
EMP: 6 **EST:** 2016
SALES (est): 112.33K **Privately Held**
Web: www.gmfga.com
SIC: 3999 Manufacturing industries, nec

(G-4129)
GLOBE PIPE HANGER PRODUCTS INC
14601 Industrial Pkwy (44135-4545)

Cleveland - Cuyahoga County (G-4130)

PHONE..................216 362-6300
◆ **EMP:** 20 **EST:** 1978
SQ FT: 30,000
SALES (est): 2.8MM **Privately Held**
Web: www.globepipehanger.com
SIC: 3569 Firefighting and related equipment

(G-4130)
GMR FURNITURE SERVICES LTD
Also Called: PDQ Installation Co
1801 E 9th St Ste 1100 (44114-3103)
PHONE..................216 244-5072
EMP: 6 **EST:** 2007
SALES (est): 495.19K **Privately Held**
SIC: 2542 Cabinets: show, display, or storage: except wood

(G-4131)
GMX
3800 E 91st St (44105-2103)
PHONE..................216 641-7502
Janis Manning Attorney, *Prin*
EMP: 7 **EST:** 2019
SALES (est): 198.65K **Privately Held**
Web: www.gmxco.com
SIC: 3999 Manufacturing industries, nec

(G-4132)
GOING MY WAY TRNSP SVCS LLC
4655 Queen Mary Dr (44121-3419)
PHONE..................423 623-3802
Michael Holmes, *Admn*
EMP: 6 **EST:** 2009
SALES (est): 81.49K **Privately Held**
SIC: 3599 Industrial machinery, nec

(G-4133)
GOLDEN DRAPERY SUPPLY INC
Also Called: Golden Window Fashions
2500 Brookpark Rd Unit 3 (44134-1450)
PHONE..................216 351-3283
Bernard Golden Junior, *Pr*
EMP: 28 **EST:** 1983
SQ FT: 25,000
SALES (est): 2.94MM **Privately Held**
SIC: 5023 2591 Window furnishings; Window blinds

(G-4134)
GRABO INTERIORS INC
3605 Perkins Ave (44114-4632)
PHONE..................216 391-6677
Joseph Grabo, *Pr*
Paul Grabo, *VP*
EMP: 6 **EST:** 1979
SQ FT: 4,400
SALES (est): 499.42K **Privately Held**
Web: www.grabointeriors.com
SIC: 2511 Wood household furniture

(G-4135)
GRAFTECH GLOBAL ENTPS INC
12900 Snow Rd (44130-1012)
PHONE..................216 676-2000
Joel Hawthorne, *Pr*
EMP: 10 **EST:** 2016
SALES (est): 886.22K **Publicly Held**
Web: graftech2022cr.q4web.com
SIC: 3629 Electrical industrial apparatus, nec
PA: Graftech International Ltd.
982 Keynote Cir
Brooklyn Heights OH 44131

(G-4136)
GRAFTECH INTL TRDG INC
12900 Snow Rd (44130-1012)
PHONE..................216 676-2000
EMP: 30
SALES (est): 760.92K **Privately Held**
Web: graftech2022cr.q4web.com

SIC: 3624 Carbon and graphite products

(G-4137)
GRAFTECH NY INC
12900 Snow Rd (44130-1012)
PHONE..................216 676-2000
EMP: 17 **EST:** 1967
SALES (est): 247.15K **Privately Held**
Web: graftech2022cr.q4web.com
SIC: 3624 Carbon and graphite products

(G-4138)
GRAND ARCHT ETRNL EYE 314 LLC
Also Called: Grand Architect
10413 Nelson Ave (44105-4250)
PHONE..................800 377-8147
EMP: 10 **EST:** 2021
SALES (est): 250K **Privately Held**
SIC: 1389 3531 0783 1731 Construction, repair, and dismantling services; Construction machinery attachments; Removal services, bush and tree; Electrical work

(G-4139)
GRAND HARBOR YACHT SALES & SVC
Also Called: Sneller Machine Tool Division
706 Alpha Dr (44143-2125)
PHONE..................440 442-2919
John Bennington, *Pr*
EMP: 6 **EST:** 1973
SQ FT: 7,000
SALES (est): 502.75K **Privately Held**
Web: www.snellermachine.com
SIC: 3599 5084 3537 3531 Machine shop, jobbing and repair; Industrial machinery and equipment; Industrial trucks and tractors; Construction machinery

(G-4140)
GRAPHIC ART SYSTEMS INC
Also Called: Grafix
5800 Pennsylvania Ave (44137-4331)
PHONE..................216 581-9050
Jordan Katz, *Pr*
Hayley Ann Prendergast, *
◆ **EMP:** 27 **EST:** 1963
SQ FT: 45,000
SALES (est): 6.98MM **Privately Held**
Web: www.grafixarts.com
SIC: 3089 Injection molding of plastics

(G-4141)
GREAT LAKES BREWING CO
1947 W 28th St (44113-3422)
PHONE..................216 771-4404
Robert Centa, *Admn*
EMP: 24
SALES (corp-wide): 37.83MM **Privately Held**
SIC: 2082 Malt beverages
PA: The Great Lakes Brewing Co
2516 Market Ave
Cleveland OH 44113
216 771-4404

(G-4142)
GREAT LAKES BREWING CO
2516 Market Ave (44113-3434)
PHONE..................216 771-4404
Patrick F Conway, *Pr*
Daniel J Conway, *Sec*
Steven Pauwels, *COO*
◆ **EMP:** 185 **EST:** 1988
SQ FT: 20,000
SALES (est): 41.41MM **Privately Held**
Web: www.greatlakesbrewing.com

SIC: 2082 5813 5812 Beer (alcoholic beverage); Bar (drinking places); American restaurant

(G-4143)
GREAT LAKES ETCHING FINSHG CO
7010 Krick Rd (44146-4445)
PHONE..................440 439-3624
Ronald Pool, *Owner*
Ronald Pool Senior, *Pr*
Ronald Pool Iii, *VP*
Joanne Marold, *VP*
EMP: 13 **EST:** 1962
SALES (est): 401.88K **Privately Held**
SIC: 3479 Etching on metals

(G-4144)
GREAT LAKES GRAPHICS INC
3354 Superior Ave E (44114-4123)
PHONE..................216 391-0077
Anthony R Lux, *Pr*
EMP: 13 **EST:** 1983
SQ FT: 15,000
SALES (est): 978.71K **Privately Held**
SIC: 3555 7336 Plates, offset; Graphic arts and related design

(G-4145)
GREAT LAKES GROUP
Also Called: Great Lakes Towing
4500 Division Ave (44102-2228)
PHONE..................216 621-4854
Sheldon Guren, *Ch Bd*
Ronald Rasmus, *
George Sogar, *
EMP: 120 **EST:** 1978
SQ FT: 6,000
SALES (est): 8.67MM **Privately Held**
Web: www.thegreatlakesgroup.com
SIC: 3731 4492 Shipbuilding and repairing; Marine towing services

(G-4146)
GREAT LAKES PUBLISHING COMPANY (PA)
Also Called: Cleveland Magazine
1422 Euclid Ave Ste 730 (44115-2001)
PHONE..................216 771-2833
Lute Harmon Senior, *Ch Bd*
Lute Harmon Junior, *Pr*
Christopher Valantasis, *
Nicole Stoner, *
Geli Valli, *
EMP: 75 **EST:** 1972
SQ FT: 19,000
SALES (est): 10.46MM
SALES (corp-wide): 10.46MM **Privately Held**
Web: www.glpublishing.com
SIC: 2721 7374 Magazines: publishing only, not printed on site; Computer graphics service

(G-4147)
GREAT LKES NROTECHNOLOGIES INC
6100 Rockside Woods Blvd N Ste 415 (44131-2366)
PHONE..................855 456-3876
EMP: 20 **EST:** 2010
SALES (est): 3.55MM **Privately Held**
Web: www.glneurotech.com
SIC: 3845 Electromedical apparatus

(G-4148)
GREATER CLEVE PIPE FTTING FUND
6305 Halle Dr (44125)
PHONE..................216 524-8334
Niel Ginley, *Pr*
EMP: 10 **EST:** 2002

SALES (est): 1.83MM **Privately Held**
Web: www.pipefitters120.org
SIC: 3494 Pipe fittings

(G-4149)
GREATER CLEVELAND FCC
4440 W 210th St (44126-2131)
PHONE..................440 333-5984
Nancy Williams, *Prin*
EMP: 8 **EST:** 2010
SALES (est): 245.44K **Privately Held**
SIC: 2711 Newspapers, publishing and printing

(G-4150)
GRIP SPRITZ LLC
5747 W 44th St (44134-2403)
PHONE..................440 888-7022
Thomas Rose, *Prin*
EMP: 6 **EST:** 2011
SALES (est): 103.98K **Privately Held**
Web: www.gripspritz.com
SIC: 3949 Golf equipment

(G-4151)
GROFF INDUSTRIES
2201 W 110th St (44102-3511)
PHONE..................216 634-9100
John Rusnak, *Managing Member*
EMP: 10 **EST:** 2006
SALES (est): 237.13K **Privately Held**
Web: www.groffind.com
SIC: 3999 7389 Manufacturing industries, nec; Packaging and labeling services

(G-4152)
GROUP INDUSTRIES INC (PA)
Also Called: Drum Parts
7580 Garfield Blvd (44125-1216)
P.O. Box 25409 (44125-0409)
PHONE..................216 271-0702
Martin Tiernan, *Ch Bd*
Lane A Zamin, *
Dale Zeleznik, *
Curtis Crowder, *
◆ **EMP:** 32 **EST:** 1968
SQ FT: 24,000
SALES (est): 8.94MM
SALES (corp-wide): 8.94MM **Privately Held**
Web: www.drumpartsinc.com
SIC: 3429 3592 3452 Hardware, nec; Carburetors, pistons, piston rings and valves; Bolts, nuts, rivets, and washers

(G-4153)
GROVER MUSICAL PRODUCTS INC (PA)
Also Called: Grover Trophy Musical Products
9287 Midwest Ave (44125-2415)
PHONE..................216 391-1188
Richard I Berger, *Pr*
Dann Skutt, *
Daniel Greene, *
▲ **EMP:** 22 **EST:** 1923
SQ FT: 60,000
SALES (est): 3.94MM
SALES (corp-wide): 3.94MM **Privately Held**
Web: www.grotro.com
SIC: 3931 Musical instruments

(G-4154)
GSI OF OHIO LLC
Also Called: Sidari's Italian Foods
3820 Lakeside Ave E (44114-3848)
PHONE..................216 431-3344
▲ **EMP:** 18
SIC: 2099 Pasta, rice, and potato, packaged combination products

GEOGRAPHIC SECTION   Cleveland - Cuyahoga County (G-4179)

(G-4155)
GUARANTEED FNSHG UNLIMITED INC
3200 W 121st St (44111-1720)
PHONE..................................216 252-8200
William Kozak, *CEO*
Joseph Janke, *
▲ **EMP:** 35 **EST:** 1983
SQ FT: 50,000
SALES (est): 4.61MM **Privately Held**
Web: www.gfuinc.com
SIC: 3471 Electroplating of metals or formed products

(G-4156)
GUARDIAN PUBLICATIONS INC
55 Public Sq Ste 2075 (44113-1974)
PHONE..................................216 621-5005
Eric Tayfel, *Prin*
EMP: 6 **EST:** 2008
SALES (est): 91K **Privately Held**
SIC: 2741 Miscellaneous publishing

(G-4157)
GUSTAVE JULIAN JEWELERS INC
7432 State Rd (44134-5858)
PHONE..................................440 888-1100
Jim Julian, *Pr*
Jayne Julian, *Sec*
Edward Julian, *VP*
EMP: 7 **EST:** 1948
SQ FT: 2,400
SALES (est): 760.24K **Privately Held**
Web: www.julianjeweler.com
SIC: 5944 7631 3911 Silverware; Jewelry repair services; Jewelry, precious metal

(G-4158)
GWJ LIQUIDATION INC
Also Called: Perfection Fine Products
16153 Libby Rd (44137-1219)
PHONE..................................216 475-5770
Jack M Goldberg, *Pr*
William Overton, *VP*
EMP: 18 **EST:** 1951
SQ FT: 30,000
SALES (est): 1.8MM **Privately Held**
Web: www.greatwesternjuice.com
SIC: 2033 2087 Fruit juices: fresh; Cocktail mixes, nonalcoholic

(G-4159)
H & B MACHINE & TOOL INC
1390 E 40th St (44103)
PHONE..................................216 431-3254
Frank Spisich, *Pr*
Geraldine Spisich, *VP*
EMP: 12 **EST:** 1962
SQ FT: 8,000
SALES (est): 479.16K **Privately Held**
Web: www.hb-machine.com
SIC: 3599 Machine shop, jobbing and repair

(G-4160)
H & H TRUCK PARTS LLC
5500s Cloverleaf Pkwy (44125-4802)
PHONE..................................216 642-4540
EMP: 30 **EST:** 2004
SQ FT: 12,000
SALES (est): 4.16MM **Privately Held**
Web: www.hhtruckparts.com
SIC: 3713 5531 Truck bodies and parts; Truck equipment and parts

(G-4161)
H P MANUFACTURING CO
3740 Prospect Ave E (44115-2706)
PHONE..................................216 361-6500
EMP: 8 **EST:** 2015
SALES (est): 194.23K **Privately Held**
Web: www.hpmanufacturing.com
SIC: 3089 Injection molding of plastics

(G-4162)
HAFCO-CASE INC
12212 Sprecher Ave (44135-5122)
PHONE..................................216 267-4644
Phyllis Tarnawsky, *Pr*
Bohdan Tarnawsky, *General Vice President*
Natalie Tarnawsky, *Sec*
EMP: 8 **EST:** 1951
SQ FT: 8,000
SALES (est): 934.78K **Privately Held**
SIC: 3599 Machine shop, jobbing and repair

(G-4163)
HAHN MANUFACTURING COMPANY
5332 Hamilton Ave (44114-3984)
PHONE..................................216 391-9300
Robert E Hahn, *Pr*
Laura L Hahn, *
Greg Hahn, *
EMP: 34 **EST:** 1916
SQ FT: 17,000
SALES (est): 6.22MM **Privately Held**
Web: www.hahnmfg.com
SIC: 3549 3599 Metalworking machinery, nec ; Machine shop, jobbing and repair

(G-4164)
HALO METAL PREP INC
5712 Brookpark Rd Unit C (44129-1208)
PHONE..................................216 741-0506
Dean M Mella, *Prin*
EMP: 6 **EST:** 2019
SALES (est): 437.34K **Privately Held**
Web: www.halometalprep.com
SIC: 3599 Machine shop, jobbing and repair

(G-4165)
HALVORSEN COMPANY
7500 Grand Division Ave Ste 1 (44125-1282)
P.O. Box 25625 (44125-0625)
PHONE..................................216 341-7500
Ross C Frick, *Pr*
Francis J Talty, *
John F Ray Junior, *Prin*
William Patrick Clyne, *
◆ **EMP:** 32 **EST:** 1954
SQ FT: 68,000
SALES (est): 5.25MM **Privately Held**
Web: www.halvorsenusa.com
SIC: 3441 3444 3443 Fabricated structural metal; Sheet metalwork; Fabricated plate work (boiler shop)

(G-4166)
HALVORSONS LLC
4780 W 220th St (44126-2664)
P.O. Box 26013 (44126-0013)
PHONE..................................440 503-1162
Sandra Lapohn, *Admn*
EMP: 7 **EST:** 2015
SALES (est): 64.3K **Privately Held**
Web: www.halvorsenusa.com
SIC: 3441 Fabricated structural metal

(G-4167)
HAMILTON MOLD & MACHINE CO
25016 Lakeland Blvd Rear (44132-2628)
PHONE..................................216 732-8200
Dale Fleming, *Pr*
Mark Fleming, *
John Fleming, *
EMP: 39 **EST:** 1917
SQ FT: 20,000
SALES (est): 4.61MM **Privately Held**
Web: www.hamiltonmold.com
SIC: 3544 Special dies and tools

(G-4168)
HANLON INDUSTRIES INC
Also Called: Fiberglass Engineering Co
1280 E 286th St (44132-2195)
PHONE..................................216 261-7056
Bernard M Hanlon, *Pr*
EMP: 10 **EST:** 1959
SALES (est): 968.02K **Privately Held**
Web: www.fiberglasshanlon.com
SIC: 3089 Injection molding of plastics

(G-4169)
HANSA BREWERY LLC
2717 Lorain Ave (44113-3414)
PHONE..................................216 631-6585
EMP: 6 **EST:** 2012
SALES (est): 226.02K **Privately Held**
Web: www.hansabrewery.com
SIC: 2082 Brewers' grain

(G-4170)
HARRIS CALORIFIC INC
22801 Saint Clair Ave (44117-2524)
PHONE..................................216 383-4107
EMP: 9 **EST:** 2014
SALES (est): 915.54K **Privately Held**
SIC: 3548 Welding apparatus

(G-4171)
HARTLINE PRODUCTS COINC
15035 Woodworth Rd Ste 3 (44110-3345)
PHONE..................................216 851-7189
Becky Hart, *Manager*
EMP: 9
SALES (corp-wide): 2.36MM **Privately Held**
Web: www.hartlineproducts.com
SIC: 2891 3241 Cement, except linoleum and tile; Cement, hydraulic
PA: Hartline Products Co.Inc.
    4568 Mayfield Rd Ste 202
    Cleveland OH 44121
    216 291-2303

(G-4172)
HARVARD COIL PROCESSING INC
5400 Harvard Ave (44105-4828)
PHONE..................................216 883-6366
EMP: 26 **EST:** 1996
SQ FT: 2,000
SALES (est): 2.05MM **Privately Held**
Web: www.harvardcoilprocessing.com
SIC: 3312 Blast furnaces and steel mills

(G-4173)
HCC HOLDINGS INC
4700 W 160th St (44135-2632)
PHONE..................................800 203-1155
EMP: 17 **EST:** 2011
SALES (est): 2.43MM
SALES (corp-wide): 304.6MM **Privately Held**
SIC: 3444 Metal roofing and roof drainage equipment
PA: Oatey Co.
    20600 Emerald Pkwy
    Cleveland OH 44135
    800 203-1155

(G-4174)
HEALTH AID OF OHIO INC (PA)
5230 Hauserman Rd Ste B (44130-1224)
P.O. Box 35107 (44135-0107)
PHONE..................................216 252-3900
Carol Gilligan, *Pr*
Cortney B Mcdowell, *VP*
Kristin O'neil, *Mgr*
David Tatka, *
Sheila Harrison, *
EMP: 50 **EST:** 1983
SQ FT: 18,000
SALES (est): 18.94MM
SALES (corp-wide): 18.94MM **Privately Held**
Web: www.healthaidofohio.com
SIC: 5999 7352 3821 Medical apparatus and supplies; Medical equipment rental; Incubators, laboratory

(G-4175)
HEALTH NUTS MEDIA LLC
4225 W 229th St (44126-1834)
PHONE..................................818 802-5222
EMP: 6 **EST:** 2012
SALES (est): 234.83K **Privately Held**
SIC: 7371 5999 7389 7372 Computer software writing services; Educational aids and electronic training materials; Business Activities at Non-Commercial Site; Educational computer software

(G-4176)
HEDALLOY DIE CORPORATION
3266 E 49th St (44127-1092)
PHONE..................................216 341-3768
John Susa, *Pr*
Joseph Susa, *Genl Mgr*
John Susa Junior, *VP*
EMP: 11 **EST:** 1991
SQ FT: 10,000
SALES (est): 407.36K **Privately Held**
SIC: 3544 Dies, steel rule

(G-4177)
HEILIND ELECTRONICS INC
Also Called: Maverick Electronics
5300 Avion Park Dr (44143-1917)
PHONE..................................440 473-9600
Rick Nemeth, *Mgr*
EMP: 20
SALES (corp-wide): 591.87MM **Privately Held**
Web: www.heilind.com
SIC: 5065 3315 Electronic parts; Cable, steel: insulated or armored
PA: Heilind Electronics, Inc.
    58 Jonspin Rd
    Wilmington MA 01887
    978 657-4870

(G-4178)
HELLAN STRAINER COMPANY
3249 E 80th St (44104-4341)
PHONE..................................216 206-4200
Philip Haynes, *Pr*
▲ **EMP:** 9 **EST:** 2000
SALES (est): 5.98MM
SALES (corp-wide): 541.5MM **Privately Held**
Web: www.hellanstrainer.com
SIC: 3569 Filters and strainers, pipeline
HQ: Industrial Manufacturing Company Llc
    8223 Brcksvlle Rd Ste 100
    Brecksville OH 44141
    440 838-4700

(G-4179)
HELLER MACHINE PRODUCTS INC
1971 W 90th St (44102-2742)
PHONE..................................216 281-2951
Jeff Evin, *Pr*
Mary Heller, *VP*
David Heller, *VP*
Eda Heller, *Dir*
Joyce Evin, *Dir*
EMP: 8 **EST:** 1953
SQ FT: 10,000
SALES (est): 758.83K **Privately Held**

Cleveland - Cuyahoga County (G-4180)

SIC: 3451 3812 3728 3429 Screw machine products; Search and navigation equipment; Aircraft parts and equipment, nec; Hardware, nec

(G-4180)
HENKEL US OPERATIONS CORP
Cleveland Manufacturing Fcilty
18731 Cranwood Pkwy (44128-4037)
PHONE..............................216 475-3600
Doug Karns, *Mgr*
EMP: 250
SALES (corp-wide): 23.39B **Privately Held**
Web: www.henkel.com
SIC: 2891 2851 2842 Adhesives; Paints and allied products; Polishes and sanitation goods
HQ: Henkel Us Operations Corporation
1 Henkel Way
Rocky Hill CT 06067
860 571-5100

(G-4181)
HENNINGS QUALITY SERVICE INC
3115 Berea Rd (44111-1505)
PHONE..............................216 941-9120
Herbert Morrow, *Pr*
James Brinker, *VP*
EMP: 17 EST: 1981
SQ FT: 20,000
SALES (est): 1.67MM **Privately Held**
Web: www.hqs1.com
SIC: 7694 Electric motor repair

(G-4182)
HENRY TOOLS INC
498 S Belvoir Blvd (44121-2351)
PHONE..............................216 291-1011
Clara Henry, *Ch Bd*
Richard Henry Senior, *Pr*
David Henry, *VP*
▲ EMP: 9 EST: 1973
SALES (est): 984.64K **Privately Held**
Web: www.henrytools.com
SIC: 3724 Aircraft engines and engine parts

(G-4183)
HEPHAESTUS TECHNOLOGIES LLC
Also Called: Gray Tech International
3811 W 150th St (44111-5806)
PHONE..............................216 252-0430
Helun Chahda, *CEO*
Helun Bachour Chahda, *
Eric Attel, *
Mario Chahda, *
EMP: 24 EST: 1987
SQ FT: 20,000
SALES (est): 4.57MM **Privately Held**
Web: www.graytechintl.com
SIC: 3599 Machine shop, jobbing and repair

(G-4184)
HERD MANUFACTURING INC
Also Called: Herd
9227 Clinton Rd (44144-1088)
PHONE..............................216 651-4221
Erich J Rock, *Pr*
Rita Laurenci, *Sec*
Erick M Rock Shdr, *Prin*
EMP: 40 EST: 1972
SQ FT: 25,000
SALES (est): 4.8MM **Privately Held**
Web: www.herdmfg.com
SIC: 3469 3544 3599 Stamping metal for the trade; Special dies and tools; Custom machinery

(G-4185)
HERMAN MANUFACTURING LLC
Also Called: Walsh Manufacturing
13825 Triskett Rd (44111-1523)
PHONE..............................216 251-6400
Martin Herman, *Managing Member*
EMP: 16 EST: 1963
SQ FT: 25,000
SALES (est): 4.58MM **Privately Held**
Web: www.walshmfg.com
SIC: 3564 3441 Dust or fume collecting equipment, industrial; Fabricated structural metal

(G-4186)
HEROLD SALADS INC
17512 Miles Ave (44128-3404)
PHONE..............................216 991-7500
Cathy L Herold, *Pr*
EMP: 23 EST: 1935
SQ FT: 20,000
SALES (est): 900.55K **Privately Held**
Web: www.heroldssalads.com
SIC: 2099 Salads, fresh or refrigerated

(G-4187)
HEXAGON INDUSTRIES INC
1135 Ivanhoe Rd (44110-3249)
PHONE..............................216 249-0200
Stephen R Jackson, *Pr*
Peter M Jackson, *
▲ EMP: 50 EST: 1979
SQ FT: 270,000
SALES (est): 9.5MM **Privately Held**
Web: www.hexagonindustries.com
SIC: 3452 Screws, metal

(G-4188)
HICKOK WAEKON LLC
10514 Dupont Ave (44108-1348)
PHONE..............................216 541-8060
EMP: 55 EST: 2018
SALES (est): 5.05MM **Privately Held**
Web: www.hickokwaekon.com
SIC: 3841 Diagnostic apparatus, medical

(G-4189)
HILITE INTL
7750 Hub Pkwy (44125-5709)
PHONE..............................216 641-9632
EMP: 8 EST: 2008
SALES (est): 185.94K **Privately Held**
SIC: 3714 Motor vehicle parts and accessories

(G-4190)
HINTERLAND COF STRATEGIES LLC
Also Called: Aviary
6515 Saint Clair Ave (44103-1635)
PHONE..............................440 829-5604
Christopher Feran, *Managing Member*
EMP: 8 EST: 2016
SALES (est): 60.01K **Privately Held**
SIC: 2095 Roasted coffee

(G-4191)
HITTI ENTERPRISES INC
6427 Eastland Rd (44142-1305)
PHONE..............................440 243-4100
Fred Hitti, *Pr*
EMP: 10 EST: 1989
SQ FT: 40,000
SALES (est): 1.66MM **Privately Held**
SIC: 3086 6531 Packaging and shipping materials, foamed plastics; Real estate agents and managers

(G-4192)
HK TECHNOLOGIES
4544 Hinckley Industrial Pkwy (44109-6010)
PHONE..............................330 337-9710
Micheal A Valore, *Prin*
EMP: 9 EST: 2010

SALES (est): 395.06K **Privately Held**
Web: www.clevelandvibrator.com
SIC: 3999 Vibrators, electric: designed for barber and beauty shops

(G-4193)
HKM DRECT MKT CMMNICATIONS INC (PA)
Also Called: H K M
5501 Cass Ave (44102-2121)
PHONE..............................800 860-4456
Rob Durham, *Pr*
Scott Durham, *
EMP: 140 EST: 1922
SQ FT: 86,000
SALES (est): 26.5MM
SALES (corp-wide): 26.5MM **Privately Held**
Web: www.hkmdirectmarket.com
SIC: 2752 7375 2791 2759 Commercial printing, lithographic; Information retrieval services; Typesetting; Commercial printing, nec

(G-4194)
HOLCIM (US) INC
2500 Elm St (44113-1114)
PHONE..............................216 781-9330
Thomas Peck, *Brnch Mgr*
EMP: 7
Web: www.holcim.us
SIC: 3241 Cement, hydraulic
HQ: Holcim (Us) Inc.
8700 W Bryn Mawr Ave Ste
Chicago IL 60631

(G-4195)
HOLCIM QUARRIES NY INC
Also Called: HOLCIM QUARRIES NY, INC.
560 Harrison Street (44113)
PHONE..............................216 566-0545
EMP: 27
SIC: 3241 Cement, hydraulic
HQ: Redland Quarries Ny Inc.
6211 N Ann Arbor Rd
Dundee MI

(G-4196)
HOLLY ROBAKOWSKI
641 E 185th St (44119-1764)
PHONE..............................440 854-9317
Holly Robakowski, *Owner*
EMP: 6
SALES (est): 130.75K **Privately Held**
SIC: 1389 7389 Construction, repair, and dismantling services; Business services, nec

(G-4197)
HOLMES MADE FOODS LLC
21315 Fairmount Blvd (44118-4805)
PHONE..............................216 618-5043
Bruce Holmes, *Prin*
EMP: 8 EST: 2011
SALES (est): 866.62K **Privately Held**
Web: www.holmesmouthwatering.com
SIC: 2099 Food preparations, nec

(G-4198)
HOME ASB & MOLD REMOVAL INC
4407 Brookpark Rd (44134-1163)
PHONE..............................216 661-6696
David R Meyer, *Prin*
EMP: 9 EST: 2011
SALES (est): 99.96K **Privately Held**
SIC: 3544 Industrial molds

(G-4199)
HOME STOR & OFF SOLUTIONS INC
Also Called: Closet Factory, The

5305 Commerce Pkwy W (44130-1274)
PHONE..............................216 362-4660
Kathy Pietrick, *Pr*
Robert J Pietrick Junior, *VP*
EMP: 27 EST: 1994
SQ FT: 5,000
SALES (est): 11.87MM **Privately Held**
Web: www.closetfactory.com
SIC: 5211 5712 2541 Closets, interiors and accessories; Furniture stores; Wood partitions and fixtures

(G-4200)
HORIZON GLOBAL CORPORATION (DH)
127 Public Sq (44114-1219)
PHONE..............................734 656-3000
Patrick James, *Pr*
Stephen Graham, *CFO*
EMP: 49 EST: 2015
SALES (est): 782.12MM
SALES (corp-wide): 8.03B **Privately Held**
Web: www.horizonglobal.com
SIC: 3714 3711 5531 Trailer hitches, motor vehicle; Wreckers (tow truck), assembly of; Auto and truck equipment and parts
HQ: Phnx Acquisition Corp
127 Public Sq Ste 5110
Cleveland OH

(G-4201)
HORIZONS INCORPORATED (PA)
Also Called: Panam Imaging Systems
18531 S Miles Rd (44128-4237)
PHONE..............................216 475-0555
Herbert A Wainer, *Pr*
Robert Miller, *
Micheal Rish, *
◆ EMP: 115 EST: 1967
SQ FT: 51,000
SALES (est): 32.87MM
SALES (corp-wide): 32.87MM **Privately Held**
Web: www.horizons-inc.com
SIC: 3861 Plates, photographic (sensitized)

(G-4202)
HORSBURGH & SCOTT CO (PA)
5114 Hamilton Ave (44114-3985)
PHONE..............................216 431-3900
Lloyd G Trotter, *Ch Bd*
Randy Burdick, *
Damian Thomas, *
Monty Yort, *
David Ottesen, *
◆ EMP: 167 EST: 2007
SQ FT: 240,000
SALES (est): 82.89MM
SALES (corp-wide): 82.89MM **Privately Held**
Web: www.horsburgh-scott.com
SIC: 3566 Gears, power transmission, except auto

(G-4203)
HOSE MASTER LLC (PA)
1233 E 222nd St (44117-1104)
PHONE..............................216 481-2020
◆ EMP: 275 EST: 1982
SALES (est): 71.25MM
SALES (corp-wide): 71.25MM **Privately Held**
Web: www.hosemaster.com
SIC: 3599 Hose, flexible metallic

(G-4204)
HP MANUFACTURING COMPANY INC (PA)
Also Called: House of Plastics
3705 Carnegie Ave (44115-2750)
PHONE..............................216 361-6500

GEOGRAPHIC SECTION
Cleveland - Cuyahoga County (G-4228)

John R Melchiorre, *Pr*
EMP: 62 **EST:** 1948
SQ FT: 110,000
SALES (est): 10MM
SALES (corp-wide): 10MM **Privately Held**
Web: www.hpmanufacturing.com
SIC: 3089 5162 3993 3082 Injection molding of plastics; Plastics sheets and rods; Signs and advertising specialties; Unsupported plastics profile shapes

(G-4205)
HR GRAPHICS
5246 E 98th St (44125-2475)
PHONE..................216 455-0534
Bob Roulan, *Owner*
EMP: 6 **EST:** 2008
SALES (est): 105.59K **Privately Held**
SIC: 2759 Commercial printing, nec

(G-4206)
HUBBELL MACHINE TOOLING INC
7507 Exchange St (44125-3305)
PHONE..................216 524-1797
Claude Petek, *CEO*
EMP: 22 **EST:** 1943
SQ FT: 16,000
SALES (est): 595.65K **Privately Held**
Web: www.hubbellmachine.com
SIC: 3599 Machine shop, jobbing and repair

(G-4207)
HUDSON SUPPLY COMPANY INC
4500 Lee Rd Ste 120 (44128-2959)
PHONE..................216 518-3000
Richard Kopittke, *Pr*
▲ **EMP:** 6 **EST:** 2005
SALES (est): 964.69K **Privately Held**
Web: www.hudsonsupply.com
SIC: 3545 Machine tool accessories

(G-4208)
HUMONGOUS HOLDINGS LLC
Also Called: Humongous Fan
23103 Miles Rd (44128)
PHONE..................216 663-8830
James Meskill, *Pr*
EMP: 11 **EST:** 2010
SALES (est): 3.36MM **Privately Held**
Web: www.humongousfan.com
SIC: 3564 Ventilating fans: industrial or commercial

(G-4209)
HUSQVARNA US HOLDING INC (HQ)
Also Called: Husqvarna Construction Pdts
20445 Emerald Pkwy Ste 205 (44135)
P.O. Box 35920 (44135)
PHONE..................216 898-1800
George Weigand, *Sr VP*
Ronald Zajaczkowski, *
Marie-louise Wingard, *Treas*
Richard Pietch, *
▲ **EMP:** 70 **EST:** 2001
SQ FT: 18,000
SALES (est): 135.59MM
SALES (corp-wide): 5.15B **Privately Held**
SIC: 3582 Dryers, laundry: commercial, including coin-operated
PA: Husqvarna Ab
   Drottninggatan 2
   Huskvarna 561 3
   36146500

(G-4210)
HY-GRADE CORPORATION (PA)
3993 E 93rd St (44105-4052)
PHONE..................216 341-7771
Michael Pemberton, *Pr*
EMP: 35 **EST:** 1951
SQ FT: 25,000
SALES (est): 3.82MM
SALES (corp-wide): 3.82MM **Privately Held**
Web: www.uniquepavingmaterials.com
SIC: 5032 2952 2951 Asphalt mixture; Asphalt felts and coatings; Asphalt paving mixtures and blocks

(G-4211)
HYSTER-YALE MATERIALS HDLG INC (PA)
Also Called: Hyster
5875 Landerbrook Dr Ste 300 (44124-4069)
PHONE..................440 449-9600
Alfred M Rankin Junior, *Ch Bd*
Rajiv K Prasad, *Pr*
Alfred M Rankin Junior, *Ex Ch Bd*
Scott A Minder, *Sr VP*
Dena R Mckee, *CAO*
EMP: 120 **EST:** 1989
SALES (est): 4.12B **Publicly Held**
Web: www.hyster-yale.com
SIC: 3537 Forklift trucks

(G-4212)
I JALCITE INC
25 W Prospect Ave (44115-1066)
PHONE..................216 622-5000
William H Bricker, *Pr*
George T Henning, *VP*
Glenn J Moran, *VP*
John C Skurek, *VP*
Richard J Hipple, *Dir*
EMP: 11 **EST:** 2000
SALES (est): 205.87K **Privately Held**
SIC: 3312 Blast furnaces and steel mills

(G-4213)
I-PLUS INC
4501 Lakeside Ave E (44114-3818)
PHONE..................216 432-9200
Richard Strozewski, *Pr*
Phyllis Mitchell, *VP*
EMP: 6 **EST:** 1988
SQ FT: 30,000
SALES (est): 849.56K **Privately Held**
SIC: 3089 Thermoformed finished plastics products, nec

(G-4214)
IM GREENBERG INC
Also Called: IMG
5470 Mayfield Rd (44124-2924)
PHONE..................440 461-4464
Steven Greenberg, *Pr*
EMP: 8 **EST:** 1968
SQ FT: 5,500
SALES (est): 171.88K **Privately Held**
Web: www.imgjewelers.com
SIC: 3911 7631 Jewelry, precious metal; Diamond setter

(G-4215)
IMAGE CONCEPTS INC
Also Called: AlphaGraphics Valley View
8200 Sweet Valley Dr Ste 107 (44125-4240)
PHONE..................216 524-9000
Patrick Delahunty, *VP*
Karey Zorv, *Pr*
EMP: 10 **EST:** 1998
SQ FT: 8,000
SALES (est): 1.64MM **Privately Held**
Web: www.imageconceptsprint.com
SIC: 2752 Offset printing

(G-4216)
IMALUX CORPORATION
11000 Cedar Ave Ste 250 (44106-3056)
PHONE..................216 502-0755
Michael Burke, *Pr*
Bill R Sanford, *Ch*
Thomas F Barnish, *VP*
Paul G Amazeen, *Ex VP*
Nancy J Tresser, *CMO*
EMP: 10 **EST:** 1996
SQ FT: 1,000
SALES (est): 1.36MM **Privately Held**
Web: www.imalux.com
SIC: 3845 Electromedical apparatus

(G-4217)
IMET CORPORATION
13400 Glenside Rd (44110-3528)
P.O. Box 10753 (44110-0753)
PHONE..................440 799-3135
Mehmet Gencer, *CEO*
Paul Zakriski, *Pr*
Carol Mills, *Treas*
EMP: 7 **EST:** 1997
SQ FT: 700
SALES (est): 737.89K **Privately Held**
Web: www.imet.net
SIC: 3589 Water treatment equipment, industrial

(G-4218)
IMPACT ARMOR TECHNOLOGIES LLC
17000 Saint Clair Ave Ste 106 (44110-2535)
PHONE..................216 706-2024
EMP: 10 **EST:** 2009
SALES (est): 485.79K **Privately Held**
SIC: 3297 Nonclay refractories

(G-4219)
IMPERIAL METAL SOLUTIONS LLC
2284 Scranton Rd (44113-4310)
PHONE..................216 781-4094
EMP: 18 **EST:** 2001
SQ FT: 23,000
SALES (est): 2.89MM **Privately Held**
Web: www.imspowder.net
SIC: 3479 Coating of metals and formed products

(G-4220)
IMPERIAL METAL SPINNING CO
7600 Exchange St (44125-3308)
PHONE..................216 524-5020
Christopher Bindel, *Pr*
Timothy Bindel, *VP*
EMP: 8 **EST:** 1954
SQ FT: 7,000
SALES (est): 964.43K **Privately Held**
Web: www.imperialmetalspinning.com
SIC: 3469 Stamping metal for the trade

(G-4221)
IMPRINT LLC
3654 W 104th St (44111-3817)
PHONE..................216 233-0066
Julia Garmon, *Prin*
EMP: 7 **EST:** 2014
SALES (est): 117.04K **Privately Held**
Web: www.precisionimprint.com
SIC: 2752 Commercial printing, lithographic

(G-4222)
INCORPRTED TRSTEES OF THE GSPL
1980 Brookpark Rd (44109-5810)
P.O. Box 6059 (44101-1059)
PHONE..................216 749-1428
Beryl Bidlen, *Pr*
EMP: 11 **EST:** 1991
SALES (est): 196.9K **Privately Held**
Web: www.uniongospelpress.com

SIC: 3555 2741 Printing presses; Miscellaneous publishing

(G-4223)
INDEPENDENT STAMPING INC
12025 Zelis Rd (44135-4699)
PHONE..................216 251-3500
William Nester, *Pr*
EMP: 30 **EST:** 1965
SQ FT: 11,000
SALES (est): 1.08MM **Privately Held**
Web: www.indstamping.com
SIC: 3469 3544 Stamping metal for the trade ; Special dies and tools

(G-4224)
INFINITE ENERGY MFG LLC
4517 Industrial Pkwy (44135-4541)
PHONE..................440 759-5920
Gilbert Sherman, *Pr*
EMP: 10
SALES (est): 600.28K **Privately Held**
SIC: 3499 Fabricated metal products, nec

(G-4225)
INFORMA MEDIA INC
1300 E 9th St (44114-1501)
PHONE..................216 696-7000
Bill Fallon, *Dir*
EMP: 650
SALES (corp-wide): 3.98B **Privately Held**
Web: www.informa.com
SIC: 2721 Magazines: publishing only, not printed on site
HQ: Informa Media, Inc.
   605 3rd Ave Fl 22
   New York NY 10158
   212 204-4200

(G-4226)
INK TECHNOLOGY CORPORATION
18320 Lanken Ave (44119-3216)
PHONE..................216 486-6720
Ian Walker, *Pr*
David Ringler, *
Ernest Walker, *
Ethel R Haff, *
Robert Jenson, *
◆ **EMP:** 26 **EST:** 1980
SQ FT: 20,000
SALES (est): 4.26MM **Privately Held**
Web: www.inktechnology.com
SIC: 2893 Printing ink

(G-4227)
INNOPLAST INC (PA)
5718 Transportation Blvd (44125-5343)
P.O. Box 23681 (44023-0681)
PHONE..................440 543-8660
Craig Mcconnell, *CEO*
Gary Bowling, *Pr*
Lisa Mcconnell, *VP*
Steve Budinsky, *Genl Mgr*
◆ **EMP:** 14 **EST:** 2006
SALES (est): 9.84MM **Privately Held**
Web: www.innoplast.com
SIC: 2822 3559 Ethylene-propylene rubbers, EPDM polymers; Parking facility equipment and supplies

(G-4228)
INNOVATIONS IN PLASTIC INC
1643 Eddy Rd (44112-4207)
PHONE..................216 541-6060
Charles Hazle, *Pr*
Mary Ann Hazle, *Sec*
EMP: 7 **EST:** 1972
SQ FT: 13,000
SALES (est): 888K **Privately Held**
Web: www.innovationsinplastic.com

Cleveland - Cuyahoga County (G-4229)

GEOGRAPHIC SECTION

SIC: 3089 Injection molding of plastics

(G-4229)
INNOVATIVE PRODUCTS INC
3201 E Royalton Rd Ste 5 (44147-2838)
P.O. Box 32935 (37930-2935)
PHONE.................................865 322-9715
Michael Tinter, *Dir*
Bryan Schreiber, *Dir*
EMP: 7 **EST:** 2011
SALES (est): 477.58K **Privately Held**
Web: www.magneticmic.com
SIC: 3812 Radio magnetic instrumentation

(G-4230)
INTEGRAL DESIGN INC
7670 Hub Pkwy (44125-5707)
P.O. Box 41031 (44141-0031)
PHONE.................................216 524-0555
Robert S Liptak, *Pr*
Richard M Liptak, *Sec*
EMP: 17 **EST:** 1071
SQ FT: 8,000
SALES (est): 685.41K **Privately Held**
SIC: 3089 3993 2542 2511 Thermoformed finished plastics products, nec; Signs and advertising specialties; Partitions and fixtures, except wood; Wood household furniture

(G-4231)
INTEGRATED POWER SERVICES LLC
Also Called: Monarch
5325 W 130th St (44130-1034)
PHONE.................................216 433-7808
Bridgette Gullatta, *Pr*
EMP: 100
Web: www.ips.us
SIC: 7694 Electric motor repair
PA: Integrated Power Services Llc
250 Exctive Ctr Dr Ste 20
Greenville SC 29615

(G-4232)
INTERIOR PRODUCTS CO INC
3615 Superior Ave E Ste 3104f (44114-4138)
PHONE.................................216 641-1919
Joseph J Frisse, *Pr*
EMP: 24 **EST:** 1971
SQ FT: 14,000
SALES (est): 1.92MM **Privately Held**
Web: www.reclaimedcleveland.com
SIC: 2521 Cabinets, office: wood

(G-4233)
INTERSTATE DIESEL SERVICE INC (PA)
Also Called: American Diesel
5300 Lakeside Ave E (44114-3916)
PHONE.................................216 881-0015
Alfred J Buescher, *CEO*
Ann Buescher, *
Brad Buescher, *
◆ **EMP:** 125 **EST:** 1947
SQ FT: 70,000
SALES (est): 25.56MM
SALES (corp-wide): 25.56MM **Privately Held**
Web: www.interstate-mcbee.com
SIC: 5013 3714 Automotive engines and engine parts; Fuel systems and parts, motor vehicle

(G-4234)
INTERSTATE TOOL CORPORATION
4538 W 130th St (44135-3574)
PHONE.................................216 671-1077
Warren Thompson, *Pr*

EMP: 20 **EST:** 1962
SQ FT: 22,000
SALES (est): 4.91MM **Privately Held**
Web: www.itctoolcorp.com
SIC: 5084 3545 3541 Machine tools and accessories; Cutting tools for machine tools; Machine tools, metal cutting type

(G-4235)
ION VACUUM IVAC TECH CORP
Also Called: Ion Vacuum Technologies
18678 Cranwood Pkwy (44128-4036)
PHONE.................................216 662-5158
Bela Fischer, *Pr*
George Fischer, *Sec*
EMP: 12 **EST:** 1987
SQ FT: 4,000
SALES (est): 909.17K **Privately Held**
Web: www.ivactech.com
SIC: 3479 8731 Coating of metals and formed products; Commercial physical research

(G-4236)
IONBOND LLC
24700 Highpoint Rd (44122-6005)
PHONE.................................216 831-0880
EMP: 11
Web: www.ionbond.com
SIC: 3479 Coating of metals and formed products
HQ: Ionbond, Llc
1823 E Whitcomb Ave
Madison Heights MI 48071

(G-4237)
IRONUNITS LLC
Also Called: Metallics
200 Public Sq Ste 3300 (44114-2315)
PHONE.................................216 694-5303
EMP: 25 **EST:** 2000
SALES (est): 31.32MM
SALES (corp-wide): 22B **Publicly Held**
SIC: 1011 Iron ore beneficiating
PA: Cleveland-Cliffs Inc.
200 Public Sq Ste 3300
Cleveland OH 44114
216 694-5700

(G-4238)
IRWIN ENGRAVING & PRINTING CO
5318 Saint Clair Ave Ste 1 (44103-1355)
PHONE.................................216 391-7300
TOLL FREE: 800
Milan L Nass, *Pr*
Milan L Nass, *CEO*
Martha Ness, *Sec*
EMP: 9 **EST:** 1922
SQ FT: 16,000
SALES (est): 796.93K **Privately Held**
Web: www.irwinengraving.com
SIC: 2759 2752 Engraving, nec; Offset printing

(G-4239)
ITALMATCH SC LLC
1000 Belt Line Ave (44109-2848)
PHONE.................................216 749-2605
Belinda Rosario, *CFO*
EMP: 13 **EST:** 2017
SALES (est): 1.61MM **Privately Held**
Web: www.italmatch.com
SIC: 2899 Chemical preparations, nec

(G-4240)
ITL CORP (HQ)
Also Called: Industrial Timber & Lumber Co
23925 Commerce Park (44122-5821)
PHONE.................................216 831-3140
Larry Evans, *Pr*
◆ **EMP:** 30 **EST:** 1957

SQ FT: 10,000
SALES (est): 18.4MM **Privately Held**
Web: www.itlcorp.com
SIC: 2421 2426 Kiln drying of lumber; Hardwood dimension and flooring mills
PA: Northwest Hardwoods, Inc.
2600 Network Blvd Ste 600
Frisco TX 75034

(G-4241)
ITT TORQUE SYSTEMS INC
Also Called: C M C
7550 Hub Pkwy (44125-5705)
PHONE.................................216 524-8800
▲ **EMP:** 230
SIC: 3625 3823 3566 Controls for adjustable speed drives; Process control instruments; Speed changers, drives, and gears

(G-4242)
J & C INDUSTRIES INC
4808 W 130th St (44135-5138)
PHONE.................................216 362-8867
Bruce Jasen, *Pr*
EMP: 14 **EST:** 1973
SQ FT: 16,000
SALES (est): 422.63K **Privately Held**
Web: www.jcindinc.com
SIC: 3599 Machine shop, jobbing and repair

(G-4243)
J & S TOOL CORPORATION
15330 Brookpark Rd (44135-3355)
PHONE.................................216 676-8330
Vernon Justice, *Pr*
Donald Justice, *
EMP: 18 **EST:** 1958
SQ FT: 10,000
SALES (est): 844.12K **Privately Held**
SIC: 3542 5084 3544 3541 Machine tools, metal forming type; Machine tools and accessories; Special dies, tools, jigs, and fixtures; Machine tools, metal cutting type

(G-4244)
J B STAMPING INC
7413 Associate Ave (44144-1190)
PHONE.................................216 631-0013
James Bailey, *Pr*
Stacy Zadar, *
EMP: 43 **EST:** 1973
SQ FT: 35,000
SALES (est): 4.85MM **Privately Held**
Web: www.jbstamping.com
SIC: 3469 Stamping metal for the trade

(G-4245)
J R M CHEMICAL INC
4881 Neo Pkwy (44128-3101)
PHONE.................................216 475-8488
Dave Czehut, *VP*
Scott Wiesler, *VP*
▲ **EMP:** 11 **EST:** 1988
SQ FT: 12,000
SALES (est): 2.23MM **Privately Held**
Web: www.soilmoist.com
SIC: 2819 Industrial inorganic chemicals, nec

(G-4246)
J SCHRADER COMPANY
4603 Fenwick Ave (44102-4597)
PHONE.................................216 961-2890
Len Gagnon, *Pr*
EMP: 17 **EST:** 1922
SQ FT: 34,000
SALES (est): 884.54K **Privately Held**
Web: www.jschraderco.com
SIC: 3469 3645 3646 Spinning metal for the trade; Table lamps; Commercial lighting fixtures

(G-4247)
J W HARWOOD CO (PA)
18001 Roseland Rd (44112-1109)
PHONE.................................216 531-6230
Walter B Harwood, *Pr*
Madeleine Harwood, *VP*
Marilyn Harwood, *Sec*
EMP: 12 **EST:** 1934
SQ FT: 12,000
SALES (est): 2.32MM
SALES (corp-wide): 2.32MM **Privately Held**
SIC: 3544 Special dies and tools

(G-4248)
JAE NAIL
3657 E 53rd St (44105-1180)
PHONE.................................216 225-3743
Jasmine M Spencer, *Owner*
EMP: 8 **EST:** 2020
SALES (est): 323.92K **Privately Held**
SIC: 3315 Nails, spikes, brads, and similar items

(G-4249)
JAKPRINTS INC
3133 Chester Ave (44114-4616)
PHONE.................................877 246-3132
Jacob Edwards, *Pr*
Dameon Guess, *
EMP: 127 **EST:** 1994
SQ FT: 32,000
SALES (est): 45.39MM **Privately Held**
Web: www.jakprints.com
SIC: 2752 Offset printing

(G-4250)
JAMESTOWN CONT CLEVELAND INC
4500 Renaissance Pkwy (44128-5702)
PHONE.................................216 831-3700
Glen Jenowsky, *Ch Bd*
Bruce Janowsky, *
Dick Weimer, *
EMP: 350 **EST:** 1961
SQ FT: 100,000
SALES (est): 53.09MM
SALES (corp-wide): 163.21MM **Privately Held**
Web: www.jamestowncontainer.com
SIC: 2653 Boxes, corrugated: made from purchased materials
PA: Jamestown Container Corp
14 Deming Dr
Falconer NY 14733
716 665-4623

(G-4251)
JASMINE DISTRIBUTING LTD
12117 Berea Rd (44111-1600)
PHONE.................................216 251-9420
Fady Chamoun, *Owner*
▲ **EMP:** 20 **EST:** 1986
SALES (est): 2.22MM **Privately Held**
Web: www.jasminebakery.com
SIC: 2051 Breads, rolls, and buns

(G-4252)
JBAR A/C INC
Also Called: Jbar
15501 Chatfield Ave (44111-4311)
PHONE.................................216 447-4294
Kevin R Keogh, *CEO*
Michael Pease, *Pr*
Kim Pease, *Sec*
▲ **EMP:** 25 **EST:** 2001
SQ FT: 21,000
SALES (est): 2.62MM **Privately Held**
Web: www.jbar-ac.com
SIC: 3714 3585 Heaters, motor vehicle; Air conditioning, motor vehicle

GEOGRAPHIC SECTION
Cleveland - Cuyahoga County (G-4277)

(G-4253)
JERGENS INC (PA)
Also Called: Tooling Components Division
15700 S Waterloo Rd (44110-3898)
PHONE..................................216 486-5540
Jack H Schron Junior, *Pr*
Sue Evans, *
Kurt Schron, *
▲ **EMP**: 195 **EST**: 1942
SQ FT: 104,000
SALES (est): 93.96MM
SALES (corp-wide): 93.96MM **Privately Held**
Web: www.jergensinc.com
SIC: 3443 3452 5084 3545 Fabricated plate work (boiler shop); Bolts, nuts, rivets, and washers; Machine tools and accessories; Drill bushings (drilling jig)

(G-4254)
JET DOCK SYSTEMS INC
9601 Corporate Cir (44125-4261)
PHONE..................................216 750-2264
▼ **EMP**: 30 **EST**: 1993
SQ FT: 30,000
SALES (est): 6.77MM **Privately Held**
Web: www.jetdock.com
SIC: 3448 Docks, prefabricated metal

(G-4255)
JET INC
750 Alpha Dr (44143-2146)
PHONE..................................440 461-2000
◆ **EMP**: 40 **EST**: 1959
SALES (est): 6.83MM **Privately Held**
Web: www.jetincorp.com
SIC: 3589 Sewage treatment equipment

(G-4256)
JIS DISTRIBUTION LLC (HQ)
15700 S Waterloo Rd (44110-3814)
PHONE..................................216 706-6552
Matt Schron, *Managing Member*
EMP: 13 **EST**: 2020
SALES (est): 10.05MM
SALES (corp-wide): 93.96MM **Privately Held**
Web: www.jergensinc.com
SIC: 5084 3443 Machine tools and accessories; Fabricated plate work (boiler shop)
PA: Jergens, Inc.
15700 S Waterloo Rd
Cleveland OH 44110
216 486-5540

(G-4257)
JMP INDUSTRIES
2906 Maplecrest Ave (44134-3620)
PHONE..................................216 749-6030
S Fiorentino, *Accounts Payable*
EMP: 8 **EST**: 1989
SALES (est): 189.59K **Privately Held**
Web: www.jmpind.com
SIC: 2819 Industrial inorganic chemicals, nec

(G-4258)
JOHN KRUSINSKI
Also Called: Krusinski's Meat Market
6300 Heisley Ave (44105-1226)
PHONE..................................216 441-0100
John Krusinski, *Owner*
EMP: 10 **EST**: 1952
SQ FT: 10,000
SALES (est): 948.69K **Privately Held**
SIC: 5147 5421 2099 2013 Meats, fresh; Meat markets, including freezer provisioners; Food preparations, nec; Sausages and other prepared meats

(G-4259)
JORDON AUTO SERVICE & TIRE INC
5201 Carnegie Ave (44103-4357)
PHONE..................................216 214-6528
Jordan Kaminsky, *Owner*
EMP: 7 **EST**: 2011
SALES (est): 796.63K **Privately Held**
SIC: 2653 7539 Pallets, corrugated: made from purchased materials; Automotive repair shops, nec

(G-4260)
JOSEPH T SNYDER INDUSTRIES INC
9210 Loren Ave (44105-2133)
PHONE..................................216 883-6900
Gregory Snyder, *Pr*
Robert Snyder, *VP*
EMP: 9 **EST**: 1969
SQ FT: 12,000
SALES (est): 987.79K **Privately Held**
Web: www.jtsnyder.com
SIC: 7389 2671 2653 Packaging and labeling services; Paper; coated and laminated packaging; Corrugated and solid fiber boxes

(G-4261)
JOSLYN HI-VOLTAGE COMPANY LLC
4000 E 116th St (44105-4310)
PHONE..................................216 271-6600
Jim Domo, *Pr*
▲ **EMP**: 103 **EST**: 1947
SQ FT: 100,000
SALES (est): 9.04MM **Privately Held**
SIC: 3613 Switchgear and switchboard apparatus
HQ: Abb Installation Products Inc.
860 Rdg Lake Blvd
Memphis TN 38120
901 252-5000

(G-4262)
JOY GLOBAL UNDERGROUND MIN LLC
6160 Cochran Rd (44139-3306)
PHONE..................................440 248-7970
Mark Sanders, *Brnch Mgr*
EMP: 21
SIC: 3535 Bucket type conveyor systems
HQ: Joy Global Underground Mining Llc
40 Pennwood Pl Ste 100
Warrendale PA 15086
724 779-4500

(G-4263)
JOYCE DAYTON LLC
6449 Wilson Mills Rd (44143-3443)
PHONE..................................440 449-3333
Lou D Amico, *Prin*
EMP: 10 **EST**: 2010
SALES (est): 74.19K **Privately Held**
SIC: 3569 General industrial machinery, nec

(G-4264)
JP CABINETS LLC
20910 Miles Pkwy (44128-5510)
PHONE..................................440 232-9780
EMP: 6 **EST**: 2002
SALES (est): 483.07K **Privately Held**
Web: www.jpcabinets.com
SIC: 2434 Wood kitchen cabinets

(G-4265)
JP SUGGINS MOBILE WLDG INC
2020 Saint Clair Ave Ne (44114-2013)
PHONE..................................216 566-7131
Jeffrey Hulligan, *Pr*
EMP: 18 **EST**: 1972
SQ FT: 3,600
SALES (est): 173.36K **Privately Held**
Web: www.cleveweld.com
SIC: 3441 7692 Fabricated structural metal; Welding repair

(G-4266)
JT PREMIER PRINTING CORP
Also Called: Premier Printing
18780 Cranwood Pkwy (44128-4038)
PHONE..................................216 831-8785
James Trombo, *Pr*
EMP: 16 **EST**: 1999
SALES (est): 413.94K **Privately Held**
Web: www.premierprintingcorp.com
SIC: 2752 Offset printing

(G-4267)
JUST NATURAL PROVISION COMPANY
4800 Crayton Ave (44104-2822)
PHONE..................................216 431-7922
Dennis Parker, *Pr*
EMP: 6 **EST**: 2001
SALES (est): 749.07K **Privately Held**
SIC: 2015 5144 Poultry slaughtering and processing; Poultry and poultry products

(G-4268)
K & G MACHINE COMPANY
26981 Tungsten Rd (44132-2992)
PHONE..................................216 732-7115
Monte Curtis, *Pr*
EMP: 15 **EST**: 1953
SQ FT: 24,000
SALES (est): 829.27K **Privately Held**
Web: www.kandgmachine.com
SIC: 3599 3743 Machine shop, jobbing and repair; Railroad equipment

(G-4269)
K S MACHINE INC
3215 Superior Ave E (44114-4344)
PHONE..................................216 687-0459
Thomas Wallace, *Pr*
EMP: 22 **EST**: 1931
SALES (est): 452.81K **Privately Held**
Web: www.ksmachineinc.com
SIC: 3599 Machine shop, jobbing and repair

(G-4270)
K&M AVIATION LLC
Also Called: Nextant Aerospace Holdings LLC
355 Richmond Rd (44143-4405)
PHONE..................................216 261-9000
Kenneth C Ricci, *CEO*
Jim Miller, *
Sean Mcgeough, *Pr*
Mark O' Donell, *
Michael A Rossi, *
EMP: 75 **EST**: 2007
SQ FT: 3,000
SALES (est): 24.2MM
SALES (corp-wide): 160.16MM **Privately Held**
Web: www.nextantaerospace.com
SIC: 3721 Aircraft
HQ: Flight Options International, Inc.
355 Richmond Rd
Richmond Heights OH 44143
216 261-3500

(G-4271)
K-SHA PRESS INC
13613 Tyler Ave (44111-4945)
PHONE..................................216 252-0037
Larry Rust, *Owner*
EMP: 6 **EST**: 2012
SALES (est): 44K **Privately Held**
SIC: 2741 Miscellaneous publishing

(G-4272)
KABAB-G INC
6676 Rochelle Blvd (44130-3977)
PHONE..................................216 476-3335
Ghazi Slailati, *Prin*
EMP: 6 **EST**: 2010
SALES (est): 217.91K **Privately Held**
SIC: 3421 Table and food cutlery, including butchers'

(G-4273)
KALIBURN INC
22801 Saint Clair Ave (44117-2524)
PHONE..................................843 695-4073
George Blankenship, *Prin*
EMP: 35 **EST**: 2013
SALES (est): 4.47MM
SALES (corp-wide): 4.19B **Publicly Held**
Web: www.lincolnelectriccutting.com
SIC: 3548 Welding and cutting apparatus and accessories, nec
PA: Lincoln Electric Holdings, Inc.
22801 St Clair Ave
Cleveland OH 44117
216 481-8100

(G-4274)
KARYALL-TELDAY INC
8221 Clinton Rd (44144-1008)
PHONE..................................216 281-4063
James Mindek, *Pr*
EMP: 18 **EST**: 1947
SQ FT: 43,000
SALES (est): 657.51K **Privately Held**
Web: www.karyalltelday.com
SIC: 2851 3499 Paints and paint additives; Boxes for packing and shipping, metal

(G-4275)
KASE EQUIPMENT CORPORATION
7400 Hub Pkwy (44125-5735)
PHONE..................................216 642-9040
Edward Hawkins, *Ch Bd*
Partick Hawkins, *
Dave Hodgson, *
◆ **EMP**: 100 **EST**: 1962
SQ FT: 68,360
SALES (est): 21.15MM **Privately Held**
Web: www.kaseequip.com
SIC: 3555 Printing trades machinery

(G-4276)
KAUFMAN CONTAINER COMPANY (PA)
1000 Keystone Pkwy Ste 100 (44135-5119)
P.O. Box 35902 (44135-0902)
PHONE..................................216 898-2000
Roger Seid, *Ch*
Ken Slater, *
Karen D Melton, *
Charles Borowiak, *
Anita Seid, *
◆ **EMP**: 118 **EST**: 1910
SQ FT: 180,000
SALES (est): 38.96MM
SALES (corp-wide): 38.96MM **Privately Held**
Web: www.kaufmancontainer.com
SIC: 5085 2759 Commercial containers; Screen printing

(G-4277)
KAVON FILTER PRODUCTS CO
837 E 79th St (44103-1807)
P.O. Box 1166 (07719-1166)
PHONE..................................732 938-3135
Douglas Von Bulow, *Pr*
Francis Cavanaugh, *VP*
Michael Cavanaugh, *VP*
Linda Von Bulow, *Ex Dir*
▼ **EMP**: 16 **EST**: 1962

Cleveland - Cuyahoga County (G-4278)

SALES (est): 396.74K **Privately Held**
Web: www.kavonfilter.com
SIC: **3599** 3569 Machine and other job shop work; Filters, general line: industrial

(G-4278)
KAWNEER COMPANY INC
4536 Industrial Pkwy (44135-4593)
PHONE..................................216 252-3203
Janice Gibson, *Genl Mgr*
EMP: 147
SALES (corp-wide): 8.96B **Privately Held**
Web: www.kawneer.us
SIC: **3442** Metal doors
HQ: Kawneer Company, Inc.
   555 Guthridge Ct
   Norcross GA 30092
   770 449-5555

(G-4279)
KEENE BUILDING PRODUCTS CO (PA)
2926 Chester Ave (44114-4414)
P.O. Box 241353 (44124-8353)
PHONE..................................440 605-1020
James Keene, *Pr*
▲ EMP: 67 EST: 2002
SALES (est): 29.15MM
SALES (corp-wide): 29.15MM **Privately Held**
Web: www.keenebuilding.com
SIC: **2677** 3625 Envelopes; Noise control equipment

(G-4280)
KEENER PRINTING INC
Also Called: Keener
401 E 200th St (44119-1594)
PHONE..................................216 531-7595
Duane Pecjak, *Pr*
EMP: 11 EST: 1976
SQ FT: 3,600
SALES (est): 422.28K **Privately Held**
Web: www.keenerprinting.com
SIC: **2752** 2791 Offset printing; Typesetting

(G-4281)
KELLY PLATING CO
10316 Madison Ave (44102-3594)
PHONE..................................216 961-1080
Donald J Kelly, *Pr*
James Kelly, *
Lauralee Paukert, *
EMP: 29 EST: 1932
SQ FT: 20,000
SALES (est): 2.8MM **Privately Held**
Web: www.kellyplating.com
SIC: **3471** Electroplating of metals or formed products

(G-4282)
KENCO PRODUCTS CO INC
3204 Sackett Ave (44109-2016)
PHONE..................................216 351-7610
John Kennedy, *Pr*
EMP: 9 EST: 1953
SQ FT: 32,000
SALES (est): 820K **Privately Held**
SIC: **3317** Steel pipe and tubes

(G-4283)
KEREK INDUSTRIES LTD LBLTY CO
750 Beta Dr Ste A (44143-2333)
EMP: 13 EST: 1986
SQ FT: 22,000
SALES (est): 2.2MM **Privately Held**
Web: www.kerekindustries.com
SIC: **3599** Machine shop, jobbing and repair

(G-4284)
KERN INC
755 Alpha Dr (44143-2124)
PHONE..................................440 930-7315
Thomas Brock, *Pr*
EMP: 144
SALES (corp-wide): 26.09MM **Privately Held**
Web: www.kerninc.com
SIC: **3579** 3577 Envelope stuffing, sealing, and addressing machines; Computer peripheral equipment, nec
HQ: Kern, Inc.
   3940 Gantz Rd Ste A
   Grove City OH 43123
   614 317-2600

(G-4285)
KEYSTONE BOLT & NUT COMPANY
Also Called: Keystone Threaded Products
7600 Hub Pkwy (44125-5707)
P.O. Box 31059 (44131-0059)
PHONE..................................216 524-9626
James W Krejci, *Pr*
Betsy Mitchell, *
▲ EMP: 60 EST: 1919
SQ FT: 30,000
SALES (est): 9.32MM **Privately Held**
Web: www.keystonethreaded.com
SIC: **3452** Bolts, metal

(G-4286)
KG63 LLC
Also Called: Multiple Products Company
15501 Chatfield Ave (44111-4311)
PHONE..................................216 941-7766
EMP: 10 EST: 2010
SALES (est): 923.51K **Privately Held**
Web: www.multipleproducts.com
SIC: **3469** Metal stampings, nec

(G-4287)
KG63 LLC
Also Called: Multiple Products Company
15501 Chatfield Ave (44111-4311)
PHONE..................................216 941-7766
William F Anderson, *Pr*
Joseph T Anderson, *VP*
Joel Newman, *Sec*
◆ EMP: 11 EST: 1945
SQ FT: 22,000
SALES (est): 1.33MM **Privately Held**
Web: www.multipleproducts.com
SIC: **3469** 3861 Stamping metal for the trade ; Photographic equipment and supplies

(G-4288)
KIFFER INDUSTRIES INC (PA)
4905 Rocky River Dr (44135-3245)
PHONE..................................216 267-1818
EMP: 36 EST: 1912
SALES (est): 9.17MM
SALES (corp-wide): 9.17MM **Privately Held**
Web: www.kiffer.com
SIC: **3544** 3599 3545 Special dies and tools; Custom machinery; Machine tool accessories

(G-4289)
KILROY COMPANY (PA)
Also Called: Trust Technologies
17325 Euclid Ave Ste 2042 (44112-1250)
PHONE..................................440 951-8700
Brett Jaffe, *Pr*
William S Kilroy Ii, *Ch Bd*
Paul Cardinale, *
Mark Plush, *
Frank Lamanna, *
EMP: 75 EST: 1967
SALES (est): 8.88MM

SALES (corp-wide): 8.88MM **Privately Held**
SIC: **3544** 3549 3545 3541 Jigs and fixtures; Metalworking machinery, nec; Machine tool accessories; Machine tools, metal cutting type

(G-4290)
KING MEDIA ENTERPRISES INC
Also Called: Call & Post
11800 Shaker Blvd (44120)
P.O. Box 22872 (44122)
PHONE..................................216 588-6700
Don King, *Pr*
Constance Harper, *Ex Dir*
EMP: 32 EST: 1998
SALES (est): 913.69K **Privately Held**
Web: www.callandpost.com
SIC: **2711** Commercial printing and newspaper publishing combined

(G-4291)
KINKOS INC
Also Called: Kinko's
4832 Ridge Rd (44144-3329)
PHONE..................................216 661-9950
Jim Wood, *Prin*
EMP: 14 EST: 2010
SALES (est): 237.26K **Privately Held**
SIC: **2752** Commercial printing, lithographic

(G-4292)
KINZUA ENVIRONMENTAL INC
1176 E 38th St Ste 1 (44114-3898)
PHONE..................................216 881-4040
Bradley R Waxman, *Pr*
EMP: 20 EST: 1974
SQ FT: 20,000
SALES (est): 4.5MM **Privately Held**
Web: www.kinzuachemical.com
SIC: **2842** Specialty cleaning

(G-4293)
KIP-CRAFT INCORPORATED (PA)
Also Called: Schoolbelles
4747 W 160th St (44135-2631)
PHONE..................................216 898-5500
Bruce J Carroll, *Pr*
Elaine Stephens, *
Mary Carroll, *
EMP: 60 EST: 1958
SALES (est): 11.34MM
SALES (corp-wide): 11.34MM **Privately Held**
Web: www.schoolbelles.com
SIC: **5699** 2339 2326 Uniforms; Women's and misses' outerwear, nec; Men's and boy's work clothing

(G-4294)
KIRKWOOD HOLDING INC (PA)
1239 Rockside Rd (44134)
PHONE..................................216 267-6200
L Thomas Koechley, *CEO*
Paul Hensen, *VP Opers*
Donna Ross, *VP*
Frederick Assini, *Sec*
EMP: 7 EST: 2004
SQ FT: 3,500
SALES (est): 39.18MM **Privately Held**
Web: www.toledocommutator.com
SIC: **3621** Commutators, electric motor

(G-4295)
KISS CUSTOM COATINGS LLC
4503 Fenwick Ave (44102-4532)
PHONE..................................440 941-5002
EMP: 6 EST: 2017
SALES (est): 81.52K **Privately Held**
Web: www.benkiss.com

SIC: **3479** Metal coating and allied services

(G-4296)
KNUTSEN MACHINE PRODUCTS INC
15020 Miles Ave (44128-2370)
PHONE..................................216 751-6500
Lee Downey, *Pr*
William Downey, *VP*
Paul E Landis, *Stockholder*
EMP: 6 EST: 1946
SQ FT: 20,000
SALES (est): 359.94K **Privately Held**
SIC: **3599** Machine shop, jobbing and repair

(G-4297)
KOWALSKI HEAT TREATING CO
3611 Detroit Ave (44113-2790)
PHONE..................................216 631-4411
Robert Kowalski, *Pr*
Carole Kowalski, *VP*
Stephen Kowalski, *VP*
Nancy Vermilye, *Sec*
EMP: 13 EST: 1975
SQ FT: 11,000
SALES (est): 3.62MM **Privately Held**
Web: www.khtheat.com
SIC: **3398** Metal heat treating

(G-4298)
KRAFTS EXOTIKA LLC
3553 Bosworth Rd (44111-6028)
PHONE..................................216 563-1178
Harry Larweh, *Prin*
EMP: 6 EST: 2016
SALES (est): 94.78K **Privately Held**
SIC: **2022** Natural cheese

(G-4299)
KROY LLC
Also Called: Buckeye Business Products
3830 Kelley Ave (44114-4534)
PHONE..................................216 426-5600
Stephen Kalette, *Managing Member*
Robert Kanner, *
▲ EMP: 177 EST: 1997
SQ FT: 110,000
SALES (est): 110.05MM
SALES (corp-wide): 121.85MM **Privately Held**
Web: www.buckeyebusiness.com
SIC: **2671** 3955 2761 Paper; coated and laminated packaging; Carbon paper and inked ribbons; Manifold business forms
PA: Pubco Corporation
   3830 Kelley Ave
   Cleveland OH 44114
   216 881-5300

(G-4300)
KRUMOR INC
7655 Hub Pkwy Ste 206 (44125-5739)
PHONE..................................216 328-9802
Robert Mikals, *Pr*
Herbert H Sher, *VP*
EMP: 10 EST: 1972
SALES (est): 1.4MM **Privately Held**
Web: www.krumor.com
SIC: **3829** Temperature sensors, except industrial process and aircraft

(G-4301)
KTRI HOLDINGS INC (HQ)
127 Public Sq Ste 5110 (44114)
PHONE..................................216 400-9308
Patrick James, *Pr*
Stephen Graham, *CFO*
EMP: 10 EST: 2007
SALES (est): 743.54MM
SALES (corp-wide): 8.03B **Privately Held**
Web: www.ktriholdings.com

GEOGRAPHIC SECTION
Cleveland - Cuyahoga County (G-4324)

SIC: 3714 Motor vehicle parts and accessories
PA: First Brands Group Holdings, Llc
127 Public Sq Ste 5110
Cleveland OH 44114
216 589-0198

(G-4302)
L J MINOR CORP
2621 W 25th St (44113-4708)
PHONE.................................216 861-8350
Engas Nitch, *Prin*
EMP: 11 **EST:** 2010
SALES (est): 1.39MM **Privately Held**
SIC: 2032 Canned specialties

(G-4303)
L T V STEEL COMPANY INC
200 Public Sq (44114-2316)
P.O. Box 6778 (44101-1778)
PHONE.................................216 622-5000
J Peter Kelly, *COO*
Richard Hipple, *Pr*
A Cole Tremain, *PUBLIC AFFAIRS*
John C Skurek, *VP*
Glen J Moran, *Sr VP*
EMP: 13500 **EST:** 1899
SQ FT: 315,000
SALES (est): 81.19MM **Privately Held**
SIC: 3312 Sheet or strip, steel, hot-rolled

(G-4304)
LACHINA CREATIVE INC
3791 Green Rd (44122-5705)
PHONE.................................216 292-7959
Jeff Lachina, *Pr*
EMP: 44 **EST:** 1978
SALES (est): 4.79MM **Privately Held**
Web: www.lachina.com
SIC: 2731 Book publishing

(G-4305)
LAIRD TECHNOLOGIES INC
4707 Detroit Ave (44102-2216)
PHONE.................................216 939-2300
Martin Rapp, *Pr*
EMP: 75
SALES (corp-wide): 2.93B **Publicly Held**
Web: www.lairdtech.com
SIC: 2891 Adhesives and sealants
HQ: Laird Technologies, Inc.
16401 Swingley Ridge Rd
Chesterfield MO 63017
636 898-6000

(G-4306)
LAKE BUILDING PRODUCTS INC
1361 Chardon Rd Ste 4 (44117-1557)
PHONE.................................216 486-1500
John Pogacnik, *Pr*
EMP: 24 **EST:** 1977
SQ FT: 34,000
SALES (est): 2.43MM **Privately Held**
Web: www.lbpsteel.com
SIC: 3441 1791 5051 Building components, structural steel; Structural steel erection; Metals service centers and offices

(G-4307)
LALAC ONE LLC
18451 Euclid Ave (44112-1016)
PHONE.................................216 432-4322
EMP: 31 **EST:** 2003
SQ FT: 30,000
SALES (est): 4.74MM **Privately Held**
Web: www.lefcoworthington.com
SIC: 4783 2441 4226 Packing and crating; Boxes, wood; Special warehousing and storage, nec

(G-4308)
LAM PRO INC
4701 Crayton Ave Ste A (44104-2819)
PHONE.................................216 426-0661
Kerry Stewart, *Pr*
Debbie Dragar, *Sec*
EMP: 13 **EST:** 1992
SQ FT: 33,000
SALES (est): 1.8MM **Privately Held**
Web: www.lampro.com
SIC: 3089 2789 2675 2672 Laminating of plastics; Bookbinding and related work; Die-cut paper and board; Paper; coated and laminated, nec

(G-4309)
LAMPORTS FILTER MEDIA INC
Also Called: Lamports Filter Media
837 E 79th St (44103-1807)
PHONE.................................216 881-2050
Walter Senney, *Pr*
Joyce Senney, *VP*
EMP: 9 **EST:** 1984
SQ FT: 25,000
SALES (est): 246.07K **Privately Held**
Web: www.lamports.com
SIC: 2393 Textile bags

(G-4310)
LANGENAU MANUFACTURING COMPANY
7306 Madison Ave (44102-4094)
PHONE.................................216 651-3400
W C Strangward, *Pr*
EMP: 24 **EST:** 1884
SQ FT: 40,000
SALES (est): 857.77K **Privately Held**
Web: www.langenau.com
SIC: 3432 3465 3469 3544 Plastic plumbing fixture fittings, assembly; Automotive stampings; Metal stampings, nec; Special dies, tools, jigs, and fixtures

(G-4311)
LANIER & ASSOCIATES INC
Also Called: Cleveland Black Pages
1814 E 40th St Ste 1c (44103-3500)
PHONE.................................216 391-7735
Bob Lanier, *Pr*
Linda Lanier, *VP*
EMP: 6 **EST:** 1991
SALES (est): 387.92K **Privately Held**
SIC: 2741 Directories, telephone: publishing only, not printed on site

(G-4312)
LANLY COMPANY
26201 Tungsten Rd (44132-2922)
PHONE.................................216 731-1115
Joe Vitale, *Pr*
Dennis W Hill, *
David Fowle, *
EMP: 44 **EST:** 1938
SQ FT: 68,000
SALES (est): 9.33MM **Privately Held**
Web: www.lanly.com
SIC: 3567 Heating units and devices, industrial: electric

(G-4313)
LARMCO WINDOWS INC (PA)
8400 Sweet Valley Dr Ste 404 (44125-4243)
PHONE.................................216 502-2832
William Simon, *Ch Bd*
Joe Talmon, *Pr*
EMP: 30 **EST:** 1959
SALES (est): 2.17MM
SALES (corp-wide): 2.17MM **Privately Held**
Web: www.larmco.com

(G-4314)
LAS AMERICAS INC
5722 Mayfield Rd (44124-2918)
PHONE.................................440 459-2030
Jefferson Evangelista, *Prin*
EMP: 6 **EST:** 2014
SALES (est): 62.38K **Privately Held**
SIC: 2099 Food preparations, nec

(G-4315)
LASER PRINTING SOLUTIONS INC
Also Called: L P S I
6040 Hillcrest Dr (44125-4620)
PHONE.................................216 351-4444
EMP: 14 **EST:** 1994
SQ FT: 5,000
SALES (est): 501.88K **Privately Held**
Web: www.laserprintingsolutions.com
SIC: 2759 Laser printing

(G-4316)
LAU HOLDINGS LLC (HQ)
16900 S Waterloo Rd (44110-3808)
PHONE.................................216 486-4000
Megan Fellinger, *Pr*
EMP: 79 **EST:** 2017
SQ FT: 50,000
SALES (est): 101.1MM
SALES (corp-wide): 184.04MM **Privately Held**
Web: www.lauparts.com
SIC: 3564 Ventilating fans: industrial or commercial
PA: Morrison Products, Inc.
16900 S Waterloo Rd
Cleveland OH 44110
216 486-4000

(G-4317)
LAWRENCE INDUSTRIES INC
Also Called: Arte Limited
4500 Lee Rd Ste 120 (44128-2959)
PHONE.................................216 518-1400
Robert Kopittke, *Brnch Mgr*
EMP: 101
SALES (est): 8.24MM **Privately Held**
Web: www.lawrenceindustriesinc.com
SIC: 3599 3541 Machine shop, jobbing and repair; Sawing and cutoff machines (metalworking machinery)
PA: Lawrence Industries, Inc.
4500 Lee Rd Ste 120
Cleveland OH 44128
216 518-7000

(G-4318)
LAWRENCE INDUSTRIES INC (PA)
4500 Lee Rd Ste 120 (44128-2959)
PHONE.................................216 518-7000
Lawrence A Kopittke Senior, *Pr*
Richard L Kopittke, *
Arthur Kopittke, *
◆ **EMP:** 50 **EST:** 1969
SQ FT: 160,000
SALES (est): 8.24MM
SALES (corp-wide): 8.24MM **Privately Held**
Web: www.lawrenceindustriesinc.com
SIC: 3599 3541 7699 5084 Machine shop, jobbing and repair; Sawing and cutoff machines (metalworking machinery); Tool repair services; Metalworking tools, nec (such as drills, taps, dies, files)

(G-4319)
LEIMKUEHLER INC (PA)
4625 Detroit Ave (44102-2295)
PHONE.................................440 899-7842
Robert Leimkuehler, *Pr*
EMP: 21 **EST:** 1948
SQ FT: 10,000
SALES (est): 2.74MM
SALES (corp-wide): 2.74MM **Privately Held**
Web: www.leimkuehlerinc.com
SIC: 5999 3842 Orthopedic and prosthesis applications; Surgical appliances and supplies

(G-4320)
LENNOX INDUSTRIES INC
Also Called: Lennox
4562 Hinckley Industrial Pkwy Unit 8 (44109-6025)
PHONE.................................216 739-1909
John Kelley, *Mgr*
EMP: 9
SALES (corp-wide): 4.98B **Publicly Held**
Web: www.lennox.com
SIC: 3585 Refrigeration and heating equipment
HQ: Lennox Industries Inc.
2100 Lake Park Blvd
Richardson TX 75080
972 497-5000

(G-4321)
LEWART PLASTICS LLC
3562 W 69th St (44102-5420)
PHONE.................................216 281-2333
EMP: 12 **EST:** 2018
SALES (est): 967.49K **Privately Held**
Web: www.lewartplastics.com
SIC: 3089 Injection molding of plastics

(G-4322)
LEXTECH INDUSTRIES LTD
6800 Union Ave (44105-1326)
PHONE.................................216 883-7900
David N Bortz, *Pr*
EMP: 6 **EST:** 1998
SQ FT: 143,000
SALES (est): 921.94K **Privately Held**
Web: www.lextechindustries.com
SIC: 3469 3568 3462 Stamping metal for the trade; Power transmission equipment, nec; Iron and steel forgings

(G-4323)
LICENSE AD PLATE COMPANY
13110 Enterprise Ave Side B (44135-5174)
PHONE.................................216 265-4200
Richard Russell, *Pr*
Loretta Patten, *Sec*
EMP: 10 **EST:** 1946
SQ FT: 6,000
SALES (est): 450.88K **Privately Held**
SIC: 3993 2759 Advertising novelties; Screen printing

(G-4324)
LINCOLN ELECTRIC COMPANY (HQ)
22801 Saint Clair Ave (44117)
PHONE.................................216 481-8100
Christopher L Mapes, *Ch Bd*
Frederick G Stueber, *
Anthony Battle, *
Geoffrey P Allman, *
◆ **EMP:** 3200 **EST:** 1895
SQ FT: 2,658,410
SALES (est): 1.39B
SALES (corp-wide): 4.19B **Publicly Held**
Web: www.lincolnelectric.com
SIC: 3548 Arc welding generators, a.c. and d.c.
PA: Lincoln Electric Holdings, Inc.
22801 St Clair Ave
Cleveland OH 44117
216 481-8100

Cleveland - Cuyahoga County (G-4325)

(G-4325)
LINCOLN ELECTRIC HOLDINGS INC (PA)
22801 Saint Clair Ave (44117)
PHONE..................216 481-8100
Christopher L Mapes, *Ch Bd*
Christopher L Mapes, *Ch Bd*
Gabriel Bruno, *Ex VP*
Jennifer I Ansberry, *Ex VP*
Michele R Kuhrt, *Chief Human Resources Officer*
EMP: 504 **EST:** 1895
SQ FT: 3,017,090
SALES (est): 4.19B
SALES (corp-wide): 4.19B **Publicly Held**
Web: www.lincolnelectric.com
SIC: 3548 Welding and cutting apparatus and accessories, nec

(G-4326)
LINCOLN FOODSERVICE PRODUCTS LLC
Also Called: Lincoln Foodservice Products
1333 E 179th St (44110)
PHONE..................260 459-8200
▲ **EMP:** 340
SIC: 3556 Ovens, bakery

(G-4327)
LINDE INC
Praxair
14788 York Rd (44133-4508)
PHONE..................440 237-8690
Brian Pasquerlo, *Superintnt*
EMP: 12
Web: www.lindeus.com
SIC: 2813 Industrial gases
HQ: Linde Inc.
10 Riverview Dr
Danbury CT 06810
203 837-2000

(G-4328)
LINEAR ACOUSTIC INC
1241 Superior Ave E (44114-3204)
PHONE..................717 735-3611
EMP: 7 **EST:** 2018
SALES (est): 203.92K **Privately Held**
Web: www.telosalliance.com
SIC: 3663 Radio and t.v. communications equipment

(G-4329)
LINESTREAM TECHNOLOGIES INC
1468 W 9th St Ste 435 (44113-1316)
PHONE..................216 862-7874
James G Dawson, *Prin*
Dave Neundorfer, *CEO*
EMP: 7 **EST:** 2008
SALES (est): 501.44K **Privately Held**
Web: www.linestream.com
SIC: 7372 Business oriented computer software

(G-4330)
LINSALATA CPITL PRTNERS FUND I
5900 Landerbrook Dr Ste 280 (44124-4020)
PHONE..................440 684-1400
Frank Linsalata, *Pt*
EMP: 9 **EST:** 1985
SALES (est): 856.09K **Privately Held**
Web: www.linsalatacapital.com
SIC: 6282 6799 3499 2676 Investment advisory service; Venture capital companies ; Safes and vaults, metal; Sanitary paper products

(G-4331)
LIQUID IMAGE CORP AMERICA
3700 Prospect Ave E (44115-2706)
PHONE..................216 458-9800
Lea Wiertel, *Pr*
Michael Wiertel, *VP*
EMP: 7 **EST:** 1997
SQ FT: 2,500
SALES (est): 980.01K **Privately Held**
SIC: 3663 Digital encoders

(G-4332)
LITURGICAL PUBLICATIONS INC
Also Called: LPI
4560 E 71st St (44105-5604)
PHONE..................216 325-6825
Lou Anthes, *Mgr*
EMP: 68
SALES (corp-wide): 47.85MM **Privately Held**
Web: www.4lpi.com
SIC: 2731 2789 2752 2721 Pamphlets: publishing and printing; Bookbinding and related work; Commercial printing, lithographic; Periodicals
PA: Liturgical Publications, Inc.
2875 S James Dr
New Berlin WI 53151
262 785-1188

(G-4333)
LKD AEROSPACE HOLDINGS INC (PA)
25101 Chagrin Blvd Ste 350 (44122-5643)
PHONE..................216 262-8481
Mark Chamberlain, *CEO*
Steven H Rosen, *Pr*
Jonathan Crandall, *VP*
EMP: 12 **EST:** 2016
SALES (est): 25.13MM
SALES (corp-wide): 25.13MM **Privately Held**
SIC: 3728 Aircraft parts and equipment, nec

(G-4334)
LOGAN CLUTCH CORPORATION
Also Called: Lc
28855 Ranney Pkwy (44145-1173)
PHONE..................440 808-4258
William A Logan, *Pr*
Madelon Logan, *
Elyse Logan, *
▲ **EMP:** 30 **EST:** 1975
SQ FT: 33,000
SALES (est): 8.06MM **Privately Held**
Web: www.loganclutch.com
SIC: 3568 5085 Clutches, except vehicular; Industrial supplies

(G-4335)
LOTUS PIPES & ROCKDRILLS USA
1700 E 12th St (44114)
PHONE..................516 209-6995
EMP: 10 **EST:** 2017
SALES (est): 524.09K **Privately Held**
Web: www.lotuspipesandrockdrills.com
SIC: 3089 Plastics processing

(G-4336)
LOUS SAUSAGE LTD
Also Called: Lou's Sausage
14723 Miles Ave (44128-2397)
PHONE..................216 752-5060
EMP: 24 **EST:** 1958
SQ FT: 7,500
SALES (est): 832.57K **Privately Held**
Web: www.loussausage.com
SIC: 2013 Sausages, from purchased meat

(G-4337)
LSC SERVICE CORP
20665 Lorain Rd (44126-2028)
PHONE..................440 331-1359
EMP: 6 **EST:** 2013
SALES (est): 56.97K **Privately Held**
Web: www.lsc.gov
SIC: 2752 Offset printing

(G-4338)
LUBRIQUIP INC
Also Called: Other Styles - See Operation
18901 Cranwood Pkwy (44128-4041)
P.O. Box 1441 (55440-1441)
PHONE..................216 581-2000
EMP: 300
SIC: 3714 Lubrication systems and parts, motor vehicle

(G-4339)
LUBRIZOL GLOBAL MANAGEMENT INC (OH)
Also Called: Lubrizol
9911 Brecksville Rd (44141-3201)
PHONE..................216 447-5000
Rebecca Liebert, *CEO*
Rick Tolin, *Pr*
Brian A Valentine, *VP*
John J King, *VP*
Leslie M Reynolds, *Sec*
◆ **EMP:** 10 **EST:** 1870
SQ FT: 380,000
SALES (est): 689.17MM
SALES (corp-wide): 364.48B **Publicly Held**
Web: www.lubrizol.com
SIC: 2899 2891 3088 2834 Chemical preparations, nec; Adhesives and sealants; Plastics plumbing fixtures; Pharmaceutical preparations
HQ: The Lubrizol Corporation
29400 Lakeland Blvd
Wickliffe OH 44092
440 943-4200

(G-4340)
LUCKY THIRTEEN INC
Also Called: Lucky Thirteen Laser
7413 Associate Ave (44144-1104)
PHONE..................216 631-0013
James Bailey, *Pr*
Francis J Dempsey, *Prin*
James P Bailey, *Prin*
Thomas G Scheiman, *Prin*
EMP: 8 **EST:** 2009
SALES (est): 1.33MM **Privately Held**
Web: www.jbstamping.com
SIC: 3699 Laser welding, drilling, and cutting equipment

(G-4341)
LUXCO INC
Also Called: Paramount Distillers
3116 Berea Rd (44111-1501)
PHONE..................216 671-6300
Paul A Lux, *Brnch Mgr*
EMP: 6
SALES (corp-wide): 836.52MM **Publicly Held**
Web: www.luxco.com
SIC: 2085 Bourbon whiskey
HQ: Luxco, Inc.
540 Mryvlle Cntre Dr Ste
Saint Louis MO 63141
314 772-2626

(G-4342)
M & M DIES INC
3502 Beyerle Rd (44105-1016)
PHONE..................216 883-6628
Donald Dostie, *Pr*
EMP: 7 **EST:** 1968
SQ FT: 2,940
SALES (est): 726.9K **Privately Held**
Web: www.mmdci.com
SIC: 3364 3544 Nonferrous die-castings except aluminum; Special dies and tools

(G-4343)
M & S EQUIPMENT LEASING CO
17700 Miles Rd (44128-3408)
PHONE..................216 662-8800
Lawrence Pace, *Ch Bd*
Paul Trapp, *CFO*
EMP: 11 **EST:** 1948
SQ FT: 60,000
SALES (est): 930K **Privately Held**
SIC: 5084 3519 3823 3612 Industrial machinery and equipment; Parts and accessories, internal combustion engines; Process control instruments; Transformers, except electric

(G-4344)
M ARGUESO & CO INC
Also Called: Paramelt
12651 Elmwood Ave (44111-5911)
PHONE..................216 252-4122
Rob Deck, *Genl Mgr*
EMP: 133
SALES (corp-wide): 982.03MM **Privately Held**
Web: www.paramelt.com
SIC: 2891 Adhesives and sealants
HQ: M. Argueso & Co., Inc.
2817 Mccracken St
Norton Shores MI 49441
231 759-7304

(G-4345)
M B SAXON CO INC
Also Called: Saxon Jewelers
47 Alpha Park (44143-2219)
PHONE..................440 229-5006
Michael B Saxon, *Pr*
EMP: 6 **EST:** 1979
SQ FT: 3,200
SALES (est): 484.01K **Privately Held**
Web: www.saxonjewelers.com
SIC: 3911 5944 5094 Jewelry, precious metal ; Jewelry, precious stones and precious metals; Jewelry

(G-4346)
M2M IMAGING CORPORATION
5427 Wilson Mills Rd (44143-3007)
PHONE..................440 684-9690
Jon T Devries, *Pr*
Joe Flicek, *CEO*
EMP: 8 **EST:** 1999
SQ FT: 2,500
SALES (est): 467.9K **Privately Held**
Web: www.m2mimaging.com
SIC: 3677 Coil windings, electronic

(G-4347)
M3 TECHNOLOGIES INC
13910 Enterprise Ave (44135-5118)
PHONE..................216 898-9936
Roger May, *Pr*
Danny May, *Sec*
Barry May, *Treas*
EMP: 10 **EST:** 2001
SALES (est): 1.82MM **Privately Held**
Web: www.m3techfab.com
SIC: 3444 Sheet metal specialties, not stamped

(G-4348)
MACE PERSONAL DEF & SEC INC (HQ)
4400 Carnegie Ave (44103-4342)

GEOGRAPHIC SECTION
Cleveland - Cuyahoga County (G-4370)

PHONE..................................440 424-5321
Carl Smith, *CFO*
◆ **EMP**: 30 **EST**: 2002
SQ FT: 30,000
SALES (est): 6.79MM
SALES (corp-wide): 37.02MM **Publicly Held**
Web: www.mace.com
SIC: 3999 5065 Self-defense sprays; Security control equipment and systems
PA: Mace Security International, Inc.
4400 Carnegie Ave
Cleveland OH 44103
440 424-5325

(G-4349)
MACE SECURITY INTL INC (PA)
Also Called: Mace
4400 Carnegie Ave (44103-4342)
PHONE..................................440 424-5325
Sanjay Singh, *Ch Bd*
Carl R Smith, *
Eric Crawford, *
Paul Hughes, *
Mark Barrus, *
◆ **EMP**: 52 **EST**: 1993
SQ FT: 5,000
SALES (est): 37.02MM
SALES (corp-wide): 37.02MM **Publicly Held**
Web: www.mace.com
SIC: 3699 3999 Security devices; Self-defense sprays

(G-4350)
MAGNESIUM REFINING TECHNOLOGIES INC
29695 Pettibone Rd (44139-5462)
PHONE..................................419 483-9199
▲ **EMP**: 90
SIC: 3339 Magnesium refining (primary)

(G-4351)
MAGNUM COMPUTERS INC
868 Montford Rd (44121-2012)
PHONE..................................216 781-1757
Dan Hanson, *Pr*
EMP: 10 **EST**: 1970
SQ FT: 3,000
SALES (est): 846.36K **Privately Held**
Web: www.magnuminc.com
SIC: 5045 1731 8748 7378 Computers, peripherals, and software; General electrical contractor; Business consulting, nec; Computer maintenance and repair

(G-4352)
MALIN WIRE CO
Also Called: Malin Co
5400 Smith Rd (44142-2081)
PHONE..................................216 267-9080
EMP: 25
Web: www.malinco.com
SIC: 3496 Miscellaneous fabricated wire products
HQ: Malin Wire Co
5400 Smith Rd
Cleveland OH 44142
216 267-9080

(G-4353)
MALLEYS CANDIES INC (PA)
Also Called: Malley's Chocolates
13400 Brookpark Rd (44135-5145)
PHONE..................................216 362-8700
Mike Malley, *Prin*
William Malley, *
Daniel Malley, *
▲ **EMP**: 62 **EST**: 1935
SQ FT: 60,000
SALES (est): 30.34MM

SALES (corp-wide): 30.34MM **Privately Held**
Web: www.malleys.com
SIC: 5441 5451 2064 2068 Candy; Ice cream (packaged); Candy bars, including chocolate covered bars; Nuts: dried, dehydrated, salted or roasted

(G-4354)
MAMECO INTERNATIONAL INC
4475 E 175th St (44128-3599)
PHONE..................................216 752-4400
Jeff Korach, *Prin*
EMP: 62 **EST**: 1913
SQ FT: 77,000
SALES (est): 1.74MM
SALES (corp-wide): 7.26B **Publicly Held**
SIC: 2891 2851 3069 Sealants; Paints and allied products; Floor coverings, rubber
PA: Rpm International Inc.
2628 Pearl Rd
Medina OH 44256
330 273-5090

(G-4355)
MANUFACTURERS SERVICE INC
11440 Brookpark Rd (44130-1131)
PHONE..................................216 267-3771
Carl C Jordan, *Pr*
Edward Jordan, *
David C Jordan, *
EMP: 25 **EST**: 1949
SQ FT: 40,000
SALES (est): 1.94MM **Privately Held**
Web: www.mobilewindshieldpro.com
SIC: 3469 3544 Metal stampings, nec; Special dies and tools

(G-4356)
MARADYNE CORPORATION (HQ)
4540 W 160th St (44135-2628)
PHONE..................................216 362-0755
▲ **EMP**: 58 **EST**: 1981
SALES (est): 12.55MM
SALES (corp-wide): 61.53MM **Privately Held**
Web: www.maradyne.com
SIC: 3714 Motor vehicle electrical equipment
PA: Dreison International, Inc.
4540 W 160th St
Cleveland OH 44135
216 362-0755

(G-4357)
MARCUS UPPE INC
Also Called: Clicks Document Management
815 Superior Ave E Ste 714 (44114-2706)
PHONE..................................216 263-4000
Mark Sukie, *Brnch Mgr*
EMP: 27
SIC: 2759 Commercial printing, nec
PA: Marcus Uppe Inc.
320 Fort Duquesne Blvd # 300
Pittsburgh PA 15222

(G-4358)
MARICH MACHINE AND TOOL CO
3815 Lakeside Ave E (44114-3843)
PHONE..................................216 391-5502
Andrew Marich, *Pr*
EMP: 9 **EST**: 1981
SQ FT: 10,000
SALES (est): 820.93K **Privately Held**
Web: www.marichmachine.com
SIC: 3599 Machine shop, jobbing and repair

(G-4359)
MARKING DEVICES INC
3110 Payne Ave (44114-4504)
PHONE..................................216 861-4498
Theodore Cutts, *Pr*

EMP: 8 **EST**: 1936
SALES (est): 957.75K
SALES (corp-wide): 3.1MM **Privately Held**
SIC: 3953 Embossing seals and hand stamps
PA: Royal Acme Corporation
3110 Payne Ave
Cleveland OH 44114
216 241-1477

(G-4360)
MARLIN MANUFACTURING CORP (PA)
12800 Corporate Dr (44130-9311)
PHONE..................................216 676-1340
John Tymkewicz, *Prin*
John H Breisch, *
Wallace B Heiser, *
Andy Gehrisch, *
◆ **EMP**: 64 **EST**: 1952
SQ FT: 42,000
SALES (est): 10.04MM
SALES (corp-wide): 10.04MM **Privately Held**
Web: www.marlinmfg.com
SIC: 3823 Pyrometers, industrial process type

(G-4361)
MARTIN PULTRUSION GROUP INC
20801 Miles Rd Ste B (44128-4530)
PHONE..................................440 439-9130
Jeff Martin, *Pr*
▼ **EMP**: 6 **EST**: 1993
SQ FT: 7,360
SALES (est): 990.01K **Privately Held**
Web: www.martinpultrusion.com
SIC: 3544 Special dies, tools, jigs, and fixtures

(G-4362)
MARTIN SHEET METAL INC
Also Called: Martin Cab Div
7108 Madison Ave (44102-4093)
PHONE..................................216 377-8200
Pauline Martin, *Ch Bd*
Robert P Martin Senior, *VP*
George F Voinovich, *
Frank Bendyck, *
EMP: 38 **EST**: 1920
SQ FT: 100,000
SALES (est): 11.6MM **Privately Held**
Web: www.martincab.com
SIC: 3537 3713 Cabs, for industrial trucks and tractors; Truck and bus bodies

(G-4363)
MARTINDALE ELECTRIC COMPANY
1375 Hird Ave (44107)
P.O. Box 72419 (44192)
PHONE..................................216 521-8567
Jim Satterthwaite, *Pr*
Jeffrey Snyder, *
F Z Marty, *
EMP: 48 **EST**: 1913
SQ FT: 33,000
SALES (est): 11.29MM **Privately Held**
Web: www.martindaleco.com
SIC: 3425 3541 Saw blades and handsaws; Machine tools, metal cutting type

(G-4364)
MARZANO INC
Also Called: Nunzios Cabinet Shop
4147 Pearl Rd (44109-3332)
PHONE..................................216 459-2051
Nunzio Marzano, *Pr*
Carlena Marzano, *Sec*
EMP: 8 **EST**: 1977
SQ FT: 10,000
SALES (est): 751.26K **Privately Held**

Web: www.nunzioscabinets.com
SIC: 2434 Wood kitchen cabinets

(G-4365)
MASTER CHROME SERVICE INC
5709 Herman Ave (44102-2195)
PHONE..................................216 961-2012
Gerald J Garver, *Pr*
Charloes Rowe, *
Micheal J Rowe, *
Zollie Dravez Stkldr, *Prin*
Theodore Rowe Stkldr, *Prin*
EMP: 10 **EST**: 1936
SQ FT: 10,000
SALES (est): 502.56K **Privately Held**
Web: www.masterchromeservice.com
SIC: 3471 Electroplating of metals or formed products

(G-4366)
MASTER CRAFT PRODUCTS INC
10621 Briggs Rd (44111-5329)
PHONE..................................216 281-5910
Jim Szente Junior, *Pr*
Cyndi Szente, *Treas*
EMP: 12 **EST**: 2002
SQ FT: 4,400
SALES (est): 1.13MM **Privately Held**
Web: www.mastercraftdies.com
SIC: 3544 Special dies and tools

(G-4367)
MASTER MFG CO INC
Also Called: Master Caster Company
9200 Inman Ave (44105-2110)
PHONE..................................216 641-0500
Iris Rubinfield, *Pr*
Penny Heinzmann, *
Pamela Vestal, *
◆ **EMP**: 34 **EST**: 1951
SQ FT: 10,000
SALES (est): 3.86MM **Privately Held**
Web: www.mastermfgco.com
SIC: 3429 2599 2392 3069 Furniture, builders' and other household hardware; Factory furniture and fixtures; Household furnishings, nec; Hard rubber and molded rubber products

(G-4368)
MASTER PRODUCTS COMPANY
6400 Park Ave (44105-4991)
PHONE..................................216 341-1740
R Jeffrey Walters, *Pr*
Greg Walters, *
David Mitskavich, *
Lisa Sparenga, *
EMP: 57 **EST**: 1919
SQ FT: 70,000
SALES (est): 9.71MM **Privately Held**
Web: www.masterproducts.com
SIC: 3452 3469 3568 Washers, metal; Stamping metal for the trade; Power transmission equipment, nec

(G-4369)
MAX - PRO TOOLS INC
8999 W Pleasant Valley Rd (44130-7644)
PHONE..................................800 456-0931
Steven Kurr, *Pr*
EMP: 10 **EST**: 2004
SALES (est): 670.4K **Privately Held**
SIC: 3541 Machine tools, metal cutting type

(G-4370)
MAXIM INTEGRATED PRODUCTS LLC
9000 Yale Ave (44108-2140)
PHONE..................................216 375-1057
EMP: 50 **EST**: 2019
SALES (est): 250K **Privately Held**

Cleveland - Cuyahoga County (G-4371)

GEOGRAPHIC SECTION

SIC: 3299 Architectural sculptures: gypsum, clay, papier mache, etc.

(G-4371)
MAY TOOL & DIE CO
9981 York Theta Dr Ste 1 (44133-3582)
PHONE..................440 237-8012
Gus May, *Engg Mgr*
EMP: 8 EST: 1980
SALES (est): 160.88K **Privately Held**
SIC: 3444 Sheet metalwork

(G-4372)
MAYFAIR GRANITE CO INC
Also Called: Mayfair Memorial
4202 Mayfield Rd (44121-3008)
PHONE..................216 382-8150
Michael J Johns Senior, *Pr*
Monica Johns, *VP*
Nicolette L Johns, *Sec*
Michael N Johns, *VP*
EMP: 7 EST: 1937
SALES (est): 509.22K **Privately Held**
Web: www.jcmemorials.com
SIC: 5999 5032 3993 Monuments, finished to custom order; Granite building stone; Signs and advertising specialties

(G-4373)
MAYFRAN INTERNATIONAL INC (HQ)
6650 Beta Dr (44143-2352)
PHONE..................440 461-4100
Naoshige Sakai, *Pr*
Steve Carlson, *
▲ EMP: 247 EST: 1983
SQ FT: 154,000
SALES (est): 37.68MM **Privately Held**
Web: www.mayfran.com
SIC: 3535 Belt conveyor systems, general industrial use
PA: Tsubakimoto Chain Co.
3-3-3, Nakanoshima, Kita-Ku
Osaka OSK 530-0

(G-4374)
MAZZELLA JHH COMPANY INC
Also Called: J Henry Holland
21000 Aerospace Pkwy (44142-1000)
PHONE..................440 239-7000
EMP: 87 EST: 2012
SALES (est): 1.92MM **Privately Held**
Web: www.mazzellacompanies.com
SIC: 3496 Miscellaneous fabricated wire products

(G-4375)
MAZZELLA LIFTING TECH INC (HQ)
Also Called: Rouster Lfting Rgging A Mzzlla
21000 Aerospace Pkwy (44142-1000)
PHONE..................440 239-7000
Anthony Mazzella, *CEO*
James J Mazzella, *
▲ EMP: 80 EST: 1959
SQ FT: 50,000
SALES (est): 60.44MM **Privately Held**
Web: www.mazzellacompanies.com
SIC: 3496 Miscellaneous fabricated wire products
PA: Mazzella Holding Company, Inc.
21000 Aerospace Pkwy
Cleveland OH 44142

(G-4376)
MAZZOLINI ARTCRAFT CO INC
1607 E 41st St (44103-2396)
PHONE..................216 431-7529
John Mazzolini, *Pr*
▲ EMP: 11 EST: 1904
SQ FT: 4,800
SALES (est): 947.85K **Privately Held**
Web: www.mazzoliniartcraft.com

SIC: 3299 5199 Statuary: gypsum, clay, papier mache, metal, etc.; Statuary

(G-4377)
MB DYNAMICS INC
25865 Richmond Rd (44146-1431)
PHONE..................216 292-5850
Richard Mccormick, *CEO*
▼ EMP: 29 EST: 1976
SQ FT: 25,000
SALES (est): 5.31MM **Privately Held**
Web: www.mbdynamics.com
SIC: 3829 Testing equipment: abrasion, shearing strength, etc.

(G-4378)
MC MACHINE LLC
9000 Brookpark Rd (44129-6832)
PHONE..................216 398-3666
▲ EMP: 25
SIC: 7539 7692 3444 3443 Machine shop, automotive; Welding repair; Sheet metalwork; Fabricated plate work (boiler shop)

(G-4379)
MCAFEE LLC
1050 Tollis Pkwy Apt 307 (44147-1897)
PHONE..................440 892-0173
Robert York, *Sls Mgr*
EMP: 7
SALES (corp-wide): 1.92B **Privately Held**
Web: www.mcafee.com
SIC: 7372 Prepackaged software
HQ: Mcafee, Llc
6220 America Center Dr
San Jose CA 95002

(G-4380)
MCHAEL D GORONOK STRING INSTRS
10823 Magnolia Dr (44106-1807)
PHONE..................216 421-4227
Michael D Goronok, *Owner*
EMP: 9 EST: 1992
SQ FT: 8,000
SALES (est): 394.8K **Privately Held**
SIC: 3931 5099 String instruments and parts ; Musical instruments

(G-4381)
MCKECHNIE AROSPC HOLDINGS INC
1301 E 9th St Ste 3000 (44114-1871)
PHONE..................216 706-2960
EMP: 48 EST: 2007
SALES (est): 7.86MM
SALES (corp-wide): 6.58B **Publicly Held**
SIC: 3728 Aircraft parts and equipment, nec
HQ: Transdigm, Inc.
1350 Euclid Ave
Cleveland OH 44115

(G-4382)
MCM IND CO INC (PA)
Also Called: McM Industries
22901 Millcreek Blvd Ste 250 (44122)
P.O. Box 284 (44065-0284)
PHONE..................216 292-4506
Gloria Reljanovic, *CEO*
Michael Reljanovic, *Pr*
◆ EMP: 12 EST: 1981
SQ FT: 1,000
SALES (est): 9.51MM **Privately Held**
Web: www.mcmindustries.com
SIC: 3496 Miscellaneous fabricated wire products

(G-4383)
MCM IND CO INC
7800 Finney Ave (44105-5125)
PHONE..................216 641-6300
Mike Zlojutro, *Brnch Mgr*
EMP: 16
SQ FT: 51,055
Web: www.mcmindustries.com
SIC: 3496 Miscellaneous fabricated wire products
PA: Mcm Ind. Co., Inc.
22901 Millcreek Blvd Ste 2
Cleveland OH 44122

(G-4384)
MCO INC (PA)
7555 Bessemer Ave (44127-1821)
PHONE..................216 341-8914
Tom Mesterhazy, *Pr*
EMP: 6 EST: 1989
SQ FT: 18,000
SALES (est): 23.8MM **Privately Held**
SIC: 2992 Lubricating oils and greases

(G-4385)
MDB FABRICATING INC
8600 E Pleasant Valley Rd (44131-5515)
PHONE..................216 799-7017
Mark Bender, *Pr*
EMP: 8 EST: 2011
SALES (est): 249.77K **Privately Held**
SIC: 3499 7692 Fabricated metal products, nec; Welding repair

(G-4386)
MEASUREMENT COMPUTING CORP (DH)
Also Called: Iotech
25971 Cannon Rd (44146)
PHONE..................440 439-4091
Mark Marini, *Pr*
EMP: 32 EST: 1982
SQ FT: 30,000
SALES (est): 9.98MM
SALES (corp-wide): 15.16B **Publicly Held**
SIC: 3823 Computer interface equipment, for industrial process control
HQ: National Instruments Corporation
11500 N Mopac Expy
Austin TX 78759
512 683-0100

(G-4387)
MEDCO LABS INC
Also Called: Medco Adhesive Coated Products
5156 Richmond Rd (44146-1331)
PHONE..................216 292-7546
Gary Fenton, *Pr*
Marvin Magar, *VP*
EMP: 27 EST: 1977
SQ FT: 15,000
SALES (est): 462.87K
SALES (corp-wide): 8.85MM **Privately Held**
Web: www.medcocoatedproducts.com
SIC: 3842 Adhesive tape and plasters, medicated or non-medicated
PA: Marlen Manufacturing And Development Co.
5150 Richmond Rd
Bedford OH 44146
216 292-7060

(G-4388)
MEDIVIEW XR INC
10000 Cedar Ave (44106-2119)
PHONE..................419 270-2774
John Black, *CEO*
EMP: 13 EST: 2019
SALES (est): 1.71MM **Privately Held**

Web: www.mediview.com
SIC: 3841 Medical instruments and equipment, blood and bone work

(G-4389)
MEDTRONIC INC
Also Called: Medtronic
5005 Rockside Rd Ste 1160 (44131-6801)
PHONE..................216 642-1977
Larry Saunders, *Brnch Mgr*
EMP: 14
Web: www.medtronic.com
SIC: 3841 Surgical and medical instruments
HQ: Medtronic, Inc.
710 Medtronic Pkwy
Minneapolis MN 55432
763 514-4000

(G-4390)
MEGA BRIGHT LLC
4979 W 130th St (44135-5139)
PHONE..................216 712-4689
Brad Du, *Prin*
EMP: 7 EST: 2013
SALES (est): 199.93K **Privately Held**
SIC: 3646 Commercial lighting fixtures

(G-4391)
MEGA TECHWAY INC (PA)
760 Beta Dr Ste F (44143-2334)
PHONE..................440 605-0700
Richard Sadler, *Pr*
Karl Weinfurtner, *
EMP: 125 EST: 2004
SQ FT: 3,500
SALES (est): 27.15MM
SALES (corp-wide): 27.15MM **Privately Held**
Web: www.megatechway.com
SIC: 3679 Harness assemblies, for electronic use: wire or cable

(G-4392)
MELIN TOOL COMPANY INC
5565 Venture Dr Ste C (44130-9302)
PHONE..................216 362-4200
Mike Wochna, *Pr*
Mildred Rathberger, *
John Stickney, *
EMP: 70 EST: 1938
SQ FT: 25,000
SALES (est): 16.03MM
SALES (corp-wide): 11.77B **Privately Held**
Web: www.melintool.com
SIC: 3545 3541 Cutting tools for machine tools; Machine tools, metal cutting type
HQ: Walter Ag
Derendinger Str. 53
Tubingen BW 72072
70717010

(G-4393)
MEMPHIS SMOKEHOUSE INC
Also Called: Tobacco Company
8463 Memphis Ave (44144-2126)
PHONE..................216 351-5321
EMP: 7 EST: 1995
SQ FT: 1,200
SALES (est): 994.61K **Privately Held**
SIC: 2111 Cigarettes

(G-4394)
MERIT BRASS CO (PA)
Also Called: Merit Brass
1 Merit Dr (44143-1457)
P.O. Box 43127 (44143-0127)
PHONE..................216 261-9800
▲ EMP: 236 EST: 1961
SALES (est): 44.19MM
SALES (corp-wide): 44.19MM **Privately Held**

GEOGRAPHIC SECTION
Cleveland - Cuyahoga County (G-4416)

Web: www.meritbrass.com
SIC: 3432 5051 5074 Plumbing fixture fittings and trim; Metals service centers and offices; Plumbing fittings and supplies

(G-4395)
MESSER LLC
6300 Halle Dr (44125-4618)
PHONE.....................216 533-7256
EMP: 20
SALES (corp-wide): 1.63B Privately Held
Web: www.messeramericas.com
SIC: 2813 Oxygen, compressed or liquefied
HQ: Messer Llc
  200 Smrst Corp Blvd # 7000
  Bridgewater NJ 08807
  800 755-9277

(G-4396)
METAL FABRICATING CORPORATION
10408 Berea Rd (44102-2506)
PHONE.....................216 631-8121
Bernard Golias Senior, *Ch*
Judy Kalski, *
Joseph Golias, *
Robert Golias, *
EMP: 87 EST: 1932
SQ FT: 150,000
SALES (est): 9.05MM Privately Held
Web: www.metalfabricatingcorp.com
SIC: 2542 3444 3469 3443 Cabinets: show, display, or storage: except wood; Bins, prefabricated sheet metal; Stamping metal for the trade; Fabricated plate work (boiler shop)

(G-4397)
MEYER PRODUCTS LLC
18513 Euclid Ave (44112-1084)
PHONE.....................216 486-1313
Louis Berkman, *Managing Member*
EMP: 48 EST: 2004
SALES (est): 11.64MM Privately Held
Web: www.meyerproducts.com
SIC: 3531 Construction machinery
HQ: Aebi Schmidt Holding Ag
  Schulstrasse 4
  Frauenfeld TG 8500

(G-4398)
MFH PARTNERS INC (PA)
6650 Beta Dr (44143-2352)
P.O. Box 43038 (44143-0045)
PHONE.....................440 461-4100
J D Sullivan, *Ch Bd*
Carron Redena, *
EMP: 279 EST: 2004
SQ FT: 4,000
SALES (est): 32.04MM
SALES (corp-wide): 32.04MM Privately Held
SIC: 5084 3535 3568 2296 Industrial machinery and equipment; Belt conveyor systems, general industrial use; Power transmission equipment, nec; Tire cord and fabrics

(G-4399)
MIC-RAY METAL PRODUCTS INC
9016 Manor Ave (44104-4524)
PHONE.....................216 791-2206
Michael Konicky Junior, *Pr*
Raymond Konicky, *Treas*
EMP: 10 EST: 1947
SQ FT: 5,000
SALES (est): 838.26K Privately Held
SIC: 3469 Metal stampings, nec

(G-4400)
MICELI DAIRY PRODUCTS CO (PA)
2721 E 90th St (44104-3396)
PHONE.....................216 791-6222
Joseph D Miceli, *CEO*
John J Miceli Junior, *Ex VP*
Joseph Lograsso, *
Charles Surace, *
Carol Lograsso, *
▲ EMP: 90 EST: 1946
SQ FT: 25,000
SALES (est): 42.47MM
SALES (corp-wide): 42.47MM Privately Held
Web: www.miceli-dairy.com
SIC: 2022 0241 Natural cheese; Milk production

(G-4401)
MICRO LAPPING & GRINDING CO
12320 Plaza Dr (44130-1060)
PHONE.....................216 267-6500
Ray Robaugh, *Pr*
John Dunmire, *
EMP: 10 EST: 1953
SQ FT: 25,000
SALES (est): 466.34K Privately Held
Web: www.microlapping.com
SIC: 3599 3471 Grinding castings for the trade; Plating and polishing

(G-4402)
MICROPURE FILTRATION INC
Also Called: Wfs Filter Co
837 E 79th St (44103-1807)
PHONE.....................952 472-2323
Trey Senney, *CEO*
Robert Pollmann, *Pr*
Marcy Pollmann, *Sec*
◆ EMP: 22 EST: 1980
SQ FT: 10,000
SALES (est): 985.45K Privately Held
Web: www.micropure.com
SIC: 3677 Filtration devices, electronic

(G-4403)
MICROSHEEN CORPORATION
1100 E 222nd St Ste 1 (44117-1127)
PHONE.....................216 481-5610
Lisa Habe, *Owner*
Mark Scanlon, *Genl Mgr*
Dan Roe, *Supervisor*
EMP: 10 EST: 1960
SQ FT: 30,000
SALES (est): 1.09MM
SALES (corp-wide): 24.2MM Privately Held
Web: www.microsheencorporation.com
SIC: 3471 Electroplating of metals or formed products
PA: Interlake Industries, Inc.
  4732 E 355th St
  Willoughby OH 44094
  440 942-0800

(G-4404)
MICROSOFT CORPORATION
Also Called: Microsoft
6050 Oak Tree Blvd Ste 300 (44131-6929)
PHONE.....................216 986-1440
Chris Caster, *Mgr*
EMP: 7
SALES (corp-wide): 211.91B Publicly Held
Web: www.microsoft.com
SIC: 7372 Application computer software
PA: Microsoft Corporation
  1 Microsoft Way
  Redmond WA 98052
  425 882-8080

(G-4405)
MID AMERICAN VENTURES INC
Also Called: Cookie Cupboard
7600 Wall St Ste 205 (44125-3358)
PHONE.....................216 524-0974
Richard A Pignatiello, *Pr*
Ellen Pignatiello, *VP*
EMP: 10 EST: 1983
SALES (est): 982.14K Privately Held
Web: www.cookiecupboard.com
SIC: 2045 2099 Doughs, frozen or refrigerated: from purchased flour; Food preparations, nec

(G-4406)
MID-AMERICA CHEMICAL CORP
4701 Spring Rd (44131-1025)
PHONE.....................216 749-0100
Frank J Martinek Junior, *Pr*
Julienne C Martinek, *VP*
Doris Hallaman, *Sec*
Debra Matrinek, *VP*
EMP: 9 EST: 1978
SQ FT: 19,000
SALES (est): 825K Privately Held
Web: www.midamericachem.com
SIC: 2851 2869 Paints and allied products; Solvents, organic

(G-4407)
MID-AMERICA STEEL CORP
Also Called: Mid-America Stainless
20900 Saint Clair Ave Rear (44117-1130)
PHONE.....................800 282-3466
EMP: 50
Web: www.masteel.com
SIC: 5051 3469 3316 3312 Steel; Metal stampings, nec; Cold finishing of steel shapes; Blast furnaces and steel mills

(G-4408)
MID-CONTINENT MINERALS CORP (PA)
20600 Chagrin Blvd Ste 850 (44122-5374)
PHONE.....................216 283-5700
Thomas G Gibbs, *Pr*
Harold Geiss, *Treas*
Mike Bakonyi, *CFO*
◆ EMP: 10 EST: 1975
SALES (est): 42.11MM
SALES (corp-wide): 42.11MM Privately Held
Web: www.midcontinentcoke.com
SIC: 3296 Insulation: rock wool, slag, and silica minerals

(G-4409)
MIDWEST BOX COMPANY
9801 Walford Ave Ste C (44102-4788)
PHONE.....................216 281-9021
Susan Hecht Remer, *CEO*
EMP: 20 EST: 1964
SQ FT: 150,000
SALES (est): 5.01MM Privately Held
Web: www.jamestowncontainer.com
SIC: 2653 Boxes, corrugated: made from purchased materials

(G-4410)
MIDWEST CURTAINWALLS INC
5171 Grant Ave (44125-1031)
PHONE.....................216 641-7900
Donald F Kelly Junior, *Pr*
EMP: 80 EST: 1986
SQ FT: 55,000
SALES (est): 20.39MM
SALES (corp-wide): 21.41MM Privately Held
Web: www.midwestcurtainwalls.com
SIC: 3449 3442 1751 Curtain wall, metal; Window and door frames; Window and door (prefabricated) installation
PA: Innovest Global, Inc.
  8834 Mayfield Rd
  Chesterland OH 44026
  216 815-1122

(G-4411)
MIDWEST MACHINE SERVICE INC
4700 Train Ave Ste 1 (44102-4591)
PHONE.....................216 631-8151
Kevin Klapcic, *Pr*
EMP: 7 EST: 1976
SQ FT: 6,000
SALES (est): 768.98K Privately Held
Web: www.midwestmachineservice.info
SIC: 3599 Machine shop, jobbing and repair

(G-4412)
MIDWEST RLWY PRSRVTION SOC INC
2800 W 3rd St (44113-2516)
PHONE.....................216 781-3629
Steven Korpos, *Ex Dir*
EMP: 7 EST: 1955
SALES (est): 291.87K Privately Held
Web: www.midwestrailway.org
SIC: 7699 3743 Antique repair and restoration, except furniture, autos; Railroad equipment

(G-4413)
MILES MIDPRINT INC
1215 W 10th St Ste B (44113-1291)
PHONE.....................216 860-4770
Nicholas Martin, *CEO*
EMP: 11 EST: 2018
SALES (est): 488.53K Privately Held
SIC: 7372 5045 7371 Business oriented computer software; Computer software; Computer software development and applications

(G-4414)
MILLCRAFT PURCHASING CORP
6800 Grant Ave (44105-5628)
PHONE.....................216 441-5505
Carol Braunschweig, *Prin*
EMP: 23 EST: 1998
SALES (est): 6.97MM Privately Held
Web: www.millcraft.com
SIC: 2631 Container, packaging, and boxboard
HQ: The Millcraft Paper Company
  9010 Rio Nero Dr
  Independence OH 44131

(G-4415)
MILLS CUSTOMS WOODWORKS
3950 Prospect Ave E (44115-2710)
PHONE.....................216 407-3600
Paul Mills, *Prin*
EMP: 9 EST: 2008
SALES (est): 453.76K Privately Held
SIC: 2431 Millwork

(G-4416)
MILLWOOD INC
Also Called: Cleveland Cstm Pallet & Crate
4201 Lakeside Ave E (44114-3814)
PHONE.....................216 881-1414
EMP: 20
Web: www.millwoodinc.com
SIC: 2448 Pallets, wood
PA: Millwood, Inc.
  3708 International Blvd
  Vienna OH 44473

Cleveland - Cuyahoga County (G-4417)

(G-4417)
MODERN INDUSTRIES INC
6610 Metta Ave (44103-1618)
PHONE..................................216 432-2855
Gregory Senn, *Pr*
Steve Seredick, *Ch Bd*
EMP: 7 **EST:** 1966
SQ FT: 22,000
SALES (est): 693.67K **Privately Held**
Web: www.modernindustriescleveland.com
SIC: 3599 Machine shop, jobbing and repair

(G-4418)
MODERN PIPE SUPPORTS CORP
4734 Commerce Ave (44103-3520)
P.O. Box 603544 (44103-0544)
PHONE..................................216 361-1666
Albert J Laufer, *Pr*
Cheryl A Laufer, *Sec*
EMP: 19 **EST:** 1906
SQ FT: 26,000
SALES (est): 472.27K **Privately Held**
Web: www.modernpipesupports.com
SIC: 3469 Metal stampings, nec

(G-4419)
MONACO PLATING INC
3555 E 91st St (44105-1601)
PHONE..................................216 206-2360
Louis C Monaco, *Pr*
EMP: 11 **EST:** 2008
SALES (est): 828.26K **Privately Held**
SIC: 3471 Plating of metals or formed products

(G-4420)
MONARCH STEEL COMPANY INC
Also Called: Monarch
4650 Johnston Pkwy (44128-3219)
PHONE..................................216 587-8000
Josh Kaufman, *CEO*
Robert L Meyer, *
Steve Lefkowitz, *
▲ **EMP:** 40 **EST:** 1934
SQ FT: 118,000
SALES (est): 16.75MM **Privately Held**
Web: www.monarchsteel.com
SIC: 5051 5049 3353 Steel; Precision tools; Coils, sheet aluminum
PA: American Consolidated Industries, Inc.
4650 Johnston Pkwy
Cleveland OH 44128

(G-4421)
MONROE TOOL AND MFG CO
3900 E 93rd St (44105-4094)
PHONE..................................216 883-7360
Herbert C Brosnan Junior, *Pr*
Herbert Brosnan Iii, *VP*
Anne Brosnan, *Treas*
EMP: 26 **EST:** 1940
SQ FT: 7,200
SALES (est): 442.52K **Privately Held**
Web: www.monroetoolmfg.com
SIC: 3599 Machine shop, jobbing and repair

(G-4422)
MORRISON PRODUCTS INC (PA)
16900 S Waterloo Rd (44110-3895)
PHONE..................................216 486-4000
▼ **EMP:** 131 **EST:** 1923
SALES (est): 184.04MM
SALES (corp-wide): 184.04MM **Privately Held**
Web: www.morrisonproducts.com
SIC: 3443 Heat exchangers, condensers, and components

(G-4423)
MORTON SALT INC
2100 W 3rd St (44113-2505)
PHONE..................................216 664-0728
EMP: 65
SALES (corp-wide): 1.22B **Privately Held**
Web: www.mortonsalt.com
SIC: 2899 Salt
HQ: Morton Salt, Inc.
444 W Lake St Ste 3000
Chicago IL 60606

(G-4424)
MPC INC
5350 Tradex Pkwy (44102-5887)
PHONE..................................440 835-1405
John Beverstock, *Pr*
EMP: 47 **EST:** 1975
SQ FT: 14,000
SALES (est): 2.04MM **Publicly Held**
Web: www.mpcsilentwall.com
SIC: 3296 5044 2493 Acoustical board and tile, mineral wool; Office equipment; Bulletin boards, cork
PA: Ceco Environmental Corp.
14651 Dallas Pkwy Ste 500
Dallas TX 75254

(G-4425)
MPC PLASTICS INC
1859 E 63rd St (44103-3832)
PHONE..................................216 881-7220
Albert Walcutt, *Pr*
EMP: 42 **EST:** 1984
SQ FT: 26,000
SALES (est): 2.21MM **Privately Held**
Web: www.mpcplating.com
SIC: 3471 Electroplating of metals or formed products

(G-4426)
MPC PLATING LLC
9921 Clinton Rd (44144-1035)
PHONE..................................216 881-7220
Albert N Walcutt, *Pr*
Rose Ann Walcutt, *
▲ **EMP:** 100 **EST:** 1980
SALES (est): 11.66MM **Privately Held**
Web: www.mpcplating.com
SIC: 3471 Electroplating of metals or formed products

(G-4427)
MR HEATER INC
Also Called: Heatstar
4560 W 160th St (44135-2628)
P.O. Box 44101 (44144-0101)
PHONE..................................216 916-3000
Allen L Haire, *Ch Bd*
John D Duross, *Vice Chairman*
Jeff Mack, *Pr*
Kevin Mcdonough, *VP Fin*
▲ **EMP:** 50 **EST:** 1986
SQ FT: 100,000
SALES (est): 1.62MM
SALES (corp-wide): 46.82MM **Privately Held**
Web: www.heatstarbyenerco.com
SIC: 3433 Gas infrared heating units
PA: Enerco Group, Inc.
4560 W 160th St
Cleveland OH 44135
216 916-3000

(G-4428)
MR O FFICIALS LLC
4408 Brooks Rd (44105-6087)
PHONE..................................216 240-2534
Sharmir Oglesby, *Prin*
EMP: 7 **EST:** 2016
SALES (est): 357.56K **Privately Held**

Web: www.mrofficials.com
SIC: 2759 Screen printing

(G-4429)
MRPICKER
595 Miner Rd (44143-2131)
PHONE..................................440 354-6497
Robert Blankenship, *CFO*
EMP: 9 **EST:** 2017
SALES (est): 334.18K **Privately Held**
SIC: 3845 Electromedical equipment

(G-4430)
MURRAY FABRICS INC (PA)
837 E 79th St (44103-1807)
PHONE..................................216 881-4041
Walter Senney, *Pr*
Joyce Senney, *Sec*
EMP: 10 **EST:** 1954
SALES (est): 2.77MM
SALES (corp-wide): 2.77MM **Privately Held**
Web: www.murrayfabrics.com
SIC: 2258 Net and netting products

(G-4431)
MURRAY MACHINE AND TOOL INC
17801 Sheldon Rd Side (44130-7992)
PHONE..................................216 267-1126
Frank P Ondercik Junior, *Pr*
EMP: 7 **EST:** 1927
SQ FT: 8,500
SALES (est): 504.45K **Privately Held**
SIC: 3599 3451 Machine shop, jobbing and repair; Screw machine products

(G-4432)
MYERS PRECISION GRINDING INC
19500 S Miles Rd (44128-4251)
P.O. Box 535 (44202-0535)
PHONE..................................216 587-3737
Joseph Tenebria, *Pr*
Gail Myers Tenebria, *Sec*
Ben Tenebria, *Treas*
EMP: 24 **EST:** 1973
SQ FT: 15,600
SALES (est): 855.69K **Privately Held**
Web: www.myersprecision.com
SIC: 3599 Machine shop, jobbing and repair

(G-4433)
MYSTIC CHEMICAL PRODUCTS CO
Also Called: Susan Products
3561 W 105th St (44111-3836)
PHONE..................................216 251-4416
John Gedeon Junior, *Pr*
John H Gedeon Senior, *Prin*
John H Gedeon Junior, *Prin*
R M Gedeon, *Prin*
EMP: 11 **EST:** 1970
SQ FT: 4,000
SALES (est): 188.62K **Privately Held**
SIC: 2879 Pesticides, agricultural or household

(G-4434)
NACCO INDUSTRIES INC (PA)
5875 Landerbrook Dr Ste 220 (44124)
PHONE..................................440 229-5151
J C Butler Junior, *Pr*
Alfred M Rankin Junior, *Non-Executive Chairman of the Board*
Elizabeth I Loveman, *VP*
Thomas A Maxwell, *VP*
John D Neumann, *VP*
EMP: 39 **EST:** 1913
SALES (est): 214.79MM
SALES (corp-wide): 214.79MM **Publicly Held**
Web: www.nacco.com

SIC: 3634 1221 5719 3631 Electric household cooking appliances; Surface mining, lignite, nec; Kitchenware; Household cooking equipment

(G-4435)
NATIONAL BIAS FABRIC CO
4516 Saint Clair Ave (44103-1288)
PHONE..................................216 361-0530
James R Engelbert, *Pr*
James R Engelbert, *Pr*
Keith Engelbert, *
Carol Ann Engelbert, *
EMP: 16 **EST:** 1902
SQ FT: 33,000
SALES (est): 462.61K **Privately Held**
Web: www.nationalbias.com
SIC: 2396 2631 2394 Bindings, bias: made from purchased materials; Paperboard mills; Canvas and related products

(G-4436)
NATIONAL ELECTRO-COATINGS INC
Also Called: National Office Services
15655 Brookpark Rd (44142-1619)
PHONE..................................216 898-0080
Robert W Schneider, *Ch*
Gregory R Schneider, *
Richard Corl, *
▲ **EMP:** 90 **EST:** 1967
SQ FT: 175,000
SALES (est): 19.87MM **Privately Held**
Web: www.natoffice.com
SIC: 2522 7641 1799 5021 Office furniture, except wood; Office furniture repair and maintenance; Office furniture installation; Office and public building furniture

(G-4437)
NATIONAL FOODS PACKAGING INC
8200 Madison Ave (44102-2727)
PHONE..................................216 622-2740
John Pallas, *Pr*
▲ **EMP:** 30 **EST:** 2001
SQ FT: 57,261
SALES (est): 9.1MM **Privately Held**
Web: www.nationalfoodsonline.com
SIC: 2099 2035 2045 5149 Seasonings and spices; Pickles, sauces, and salad dressings; Bread and bread type roll mixes: from purchased flour; Breakfast cereals

(G-4438)
NATIONAL PLATING CORPORATION
6701 Hubbard Ave Ste 1 (44127-1479)
PHONE..................................216 341-6707
Mark Palik, *Pr*
Sherrie Jezerinac, *
EMP: 48 **EST:** 1946
SQ FT: 100,000
SALES (est): 9.47MM **Privately Held**
Web: www.nationalplatingcorp.com
SIC: 3471 Electroplating of metals or formed products

(G-4439)
NATIONAL ROLLED THREAD DIE CO
7051 Krick Rd (44146-4497)
PHONE..................................440 232-8101
Paula Mau, *Pr*
Ronald D Mau, *VP Mfg*
Goetz Arndt, *Sec*
EMP: 11 **EST:** 1946
SQ FT: 18,000
SALES (est): 561.64K **Privately Held**
Web: www.nationaldie.com
SIC: 3545 Thread cutting dies

GEOGRAPHIC SECTION
Cleveland - Cuyahoga County (G-4465)

(G-4440)
NATIONAL SAFETY APPAREL INC (PA)
15825 Industrial Pkwy (44135-3319)
PHONE..................216 941-1111
◆ **EMP:** 60 **EST:** 1991
SALES (est): 22.21MM **Privately Held**
Web: www.thinknsa.com
SIC: 3842 Gloves, safety

(G-4441)
NAVIGATE CRDIAC STRUCTURES INC
9500 Euclid Ave (44195-0001)
PHONE..................949 482-5858
EMP: 8 **EST:** 2013
SALES (est): 533.37K **Privately Held**
Web: www.navigatecsi.com
SIC: 3841 Surgical and medical instruments

(G-4442)
NBW INC
4556 Industrial Pkwy (44135-4542)
PHONE..................216 377-1700
Burgess J Holt, *Ch*
Thomas Graves, *
Todd Holt, *
Buck L Holt, *
EMP: 48 **EST:** 1935
SQ FT: 25,000
SALES (est): 15.04MM **Privately Held**
Web: www.nbwinc.com
SIC: 1711 1796 7699 3443 Boiler setting contractor; Installing building equipment; Boiler and heating repair services; Fabricated plate work (boiler shop)

(G-4443)
NDI MEDICAL LLC (PA)
22901 Millcreek Blvd Ste 110 (44122)
PHONE..................216 378-9106
Geoff Thrope, *CEO*
◆ **EMP:** 15 **EST:** 2002
SALES (est): 3.85MM
SALES (corp-wide): 3.85MM **Privately Held**
Web: www.ndimedical.com
SIC: 3845 Electromedical equipment

(G-4444)
NEON
15201 Euclid Ave (44112-2803)
PHONE..................216 541-5600
EMP: 8 **EST:** 2010
SALES (est): 755.76K **Privately Held**
Web: www.neonhealth.org
SIC: 2813 Neon

(G-4445)
NEON CITY
11500 Madison Ave (44102-2326)
PHONE..................440 301-2000
EMP: 6 **EST:** 2017
SALES (est): 402.92K **Privately Held**
SIC: 2813 Neon

(G-4446)
NEON HEALTH SERVICES INC
4800 Payne Ave (44103-2443)
PHONE..................216 231-7700
Willie Austin, *Prin*
EMP: 40 **EST:** 2010
SALES (est): 9.59MM **Privately Held**
Web: www.neonhealth.org
SIC: 2813 Neon

(G-4447)
NERVIVE INC
Also Called: Nervive
5900 Landerbrook Dr Ste 350 (44124-4085)
PHONE..................847 274-1790
EMP: 10 **EST:** 2010
SALES (est): 267.16K **Privately Held**
Web: www.nervive.com
SIC: 3841 Medical instruments and equipment, blood and bone work

(G-4448)
NESCO INC (PA)
Also Called: Nesco Resource
6140 Parkland Blvd Ste 110 (44124-6106)
PHONE..................440 461-6000
Robert Tomsich, *Pr*
Frank Rzicznek, *VP*
◆ **EMP:** 20 **EST:** 1988
SQ FT: 55,000
SALES (est): 514.23MM
SALES (corp-wide): 514.23MM **Privately Held**
Web: www.nescoresource.com
SIC: 3535 3541 3544 8711 Conveyors and conveying equipment; Machine tools, metal cutting type; Special dies, tools, jigs, and fixtures; Engineering services

(G-4449)
NESTAWAY LLC
9100 Bank St Ste 1 (44125-3432)
PHONE..................216 587-1500
▲ **EMP:** 100
SIC: 1799 2392 Home/office interiors finishing, furnishing and remodeling; Household furnishings, nec

(G-4450)
NESTLE USA INC
Also Called: Nestle Food Service Factory
2621 W 25th St (44113-4708)
PHONE..................216 861-8350
Ingolf Nitsch, *Brnch Mgr*
EMP: 100
Web: www.nestleusa.com
SIC: 5499 2023 Health foods; Dry, condensed and evaporated dairy products
HQ: Nestle Usa, Inc.
1812 N Moore St
Arlington VA 22209
703 682-4600

(G-4451)
NEUROLOGIX TECHNOLOGIES INC
10000 Cedar Ave Ste 3-160 (44106-2119)
PHONE..................512 914-7941
Frank Carruba, *CEO*
EMP: 10 **EST:** 2015
SALES (est): 326.9K **Privately Held**
Web: www.neurologixtech.com
SIC: 3841 8742 7389 Diagnostic apparatus, medical; Management information systems consultant; Business services, nec

(G-4452)
NEURONOFF INC
11000 Cedar Ave Ste 290 (44106-3052)
PHONE..................216 505-1818
Shaher Ahmad, *Prin*
EMP: 15 **EST:** 2020
SALES (est): 2.12MM **Privately Held**
Web: www.neuronoff.com
SIC: 2833 Medicinals and botanicals

(G-4453)
NEW DAIRY OHIO LLC
3068 W 106th St (44111-1801)
PHONE..................214 258-1200
Gregg Engles, *CEO*
EMP: 89 **EST:** 2020
SALES (est): 2.15MM
SALES (corp-wide): 447.94MM **Privately Held**
SIC: 2021 Creamery butter
PA: New Dairy Opco, Llc
12400 Coit Rd Ste 200
Dallas TX 75251
214 258-1200

(G-4454)
NEW DAIRY OHIO TRANSPORT LLC
3068 W 106th St (44111-1801)
PHONE..................214 258-1200
Gregg Engles, *CEO*
EMP: 62 **EST:** 2020
SALES (est): 760.66K
SALES (corp-wide): 447.94MM **Privately Held**
SIC: 2023 Condensed, concentrated, and evaporated milk products
PA: New Dairy Opco, Llc
12400 Coit Rd Ste 200
Dallas TX 75251
214 258-1200

(G-4455)
NEWBURGH CRANKSHAFT INC
13304 Gilmore Ave (44135-2132)
PHONE..................440 502-6998
Bob Dillion, *Prin*
EMP: 7 **EST:** 2017
SALES (est): 47.35K **Privately Held**
Web: www.ohio-crankshaft.com
SIC: 3714 Motor vehicle parts and accessories

(G-4456)
NEXTANT AEROSPACE LLC
Also Called: Nextant Aerospace
18601 Cleveland Pkwy Dr (44135-3231)
PHONE..................216 898-4800
Jacqueline Disanto, *
EMP: 30 **EST:** 2012
SALES (est): 4.64MM **Privately Held**
Web: www.nextantaerospace.com
SIC: 3721 Aircraft

(G-4457)
NEXTANT AIRCRAFT LLC
355 Richmond Rd (44143-4404)
PHONE..................216 261-9000
Kenneth C Ricci, *Ch*
EMP: 7 **EST:** 2015
SALES (est): 104.16K **Privately Held**
Web: www.nextantaerospace.com
SIC: 3721 Aircraft

(G-4458)
NIDEC MOTOR CORPORATION
Also Called: Nidec Industrial Solutions
243 Tuxedo Ave (44131-1107)
PHONE..................216 642-1230
Anna Marie Kennedy, *Mgr*
EMP: 150
Web: www.nidec-industrial.com
SIC: 3823 Process control instruments
HQ: Nidec Motor Corporation
8050 W Florissant Ave
Saint Louis MO 63136

(G-4459)
NIDEC MOTOR CORPORATION
Also Called: Nidec Industrial Solutions
7555 E Pleasant Valley Rd (44131-5562)
PHONE..................216 642-1230
EMP: 30
Web: acim.nidec.com
SIC: 3823 3829 Process control instruments; Aircraft and motor vehicle measurement equipment
HQ: Nidec Motor Corporation
8050 W Florissant Ave
Saint Louis MO 63136

(G-4460)
NIPPON PAINT AUTO AMERICAS INC (DH)
Also Called: Nippon Paint America
11110 Berea Rd Ste 1 (44102-2540)
PHONE..................201 692-1111
Hiroaki Ueno, *CEO*
Hidefumi Morita, *Pr*
Joan P Daniels, *VP*
▲ **EMP:** 10 **EST:** 1990
SALES (est): 282.54MM **Privately Held**
Web: www.nipponpaintamericas.com
SIC: 2851 Paints and paint additives
HQ: Nippon Paint Holdings Co., Ltd.
2-1-2, Oyodokita, Kita-Ku
Osaka OSK 531-0

(G-4461)
NOBLE BEAST BREWING LLC
1864 W 45th St (44102-3406)
PHONE..................570 809-6405
Shaun Yasaki, *Prin*
EMP: 6 **EST:** 2015
SALES (est): 226.04K **Privately Held**
Web: www.noblebeastbeer.com
SIC: 2082 Malt beverages

(G-4462)
NOMAH NATURALS INC
200 Public Sq Ste 2300 (44114-2309)
PHONE..................330 212-8785
Michael Snyder, *Admn*
EMP: 6 **EST:** 2018
SALES (est): 267.49K **Privately Held**
SIC: 2833 Vitamins, natural or synthetic: bulk, uncompounded

(G-4463)
NOOK INDUSTRIES LLC (DH)
4950 E 49th St (44125-1016)
PHONE..................216 271-7900
Scott Benigni, *Managing Member*
Bradly Lodge, *
Todd Patriacca, *
Glenn E Deegan, *
▲ **EMP:** 256 **EST:** 2021
SQ FT: 110,000
SALES (est): 54.7MM
SALES (corp-wide): 6.25B **Publicly Held**
Web: www.nookindustries.com
SIC: 3451 Screw machine products
HQ: Altra Industrial Motion Corp.
300 Granite St Ste 201
Braintree MA 02184
781 917-0600

(G-4464)
NORMAN NOBLE INC
Also Called: N N I
5507 Avion Park Dr (44143-1921)
PHONE..................216 761-5387
Kevin Noble, *Prin*
EMP: 85
SALES (corp-wide): 86.29MM **Privately Held**
Web: www.nnoble.com
SIC: 3599 Machine shop, jobbing and repair
PA: Norman Noble, Inc.
5507 Avion Park Dr
Highland Heights OH 44143
216 761-5387

(G-4465)
NORTH COAST COMPOSITES INC
4605 Spring Rd (44131-1021)
PHONE..................216 398-8550
Richard L Petrovich, *Pr*
▲ **EMP:** 12 **EST:** 2003
SALES (est): 3.84MM
SALES (corp-wide): 189.21MM **Privately Held**

Cleveland - Cuyahoga County (G-4466)

Web: www.nctm.com
SIC: 2655 Cans, composite: foil-fiber and other: from purchased fiber
PA: Applied Composites Holdings, Llc
25692 Atlantic Ocean Dr
Lake Forest CA 92630
949 716-3511

(G-4466)
NORTH COAST CONTAINER LLC (HQ)
Also Called: Ncc
8806 Crane Ave (44105-1622)
PHONE..................................216 441-6214
EMP: 30 EST: 1930
SQ FT: 120,000
SALES (est): 27.47MM
SALES (corp-wide): 37.63MM Privately Held
Web: www.northcoastcontainer.com
SIC: 3412 Drums, shipping: metal
PA: General Steel Drum, Llc
4500 South Blvd
Charlotte NC 28209
704 525-7160

(G-4467)
NORTH COAST DUMPSTER SVCS LLC
3740 Carnegie Ave (44115-2755)
PHONE..................................216 644-5647
Gary Huddleston, Prin
EMP: 8 EST: 2016
SALES (est): 472.54K Privately Held
SIC: 3443 Dumpsters, garbage

(G-4468)
NORTH COAST EXOTICS INC
3159 W 68th St (44102-5305)
PHONE..................................216 651-5512
Earl Gibbs Junior, Pr
EMP: 6 EST: 1984
SQ FT: 15,000
SALES (est): 455.27K Privately Held
Web: north-coast-exotics-inc.business.site
SIC: 7699 3714 Miscellaneous automotive repair services; Motor vehicle parts and accessories

(G-4469)
NORTH COAST INSTRUMENTS INC
14615 Lorain Ave (44111-3166)
PHONE..................................216 251-2353
James Irwin, Pr
James Irwin, Pr
Charlotte G Irwin, Sec
Julia W Irwin, Treas
EMP: 9 EST: 2003
SQ FT: 20,000
SALES (est): 591.51K
SALES (corp-wide): 3.21MM Privately Held
SIC: 3593 Fluid power cylinders and actuators
PA: Ohio Pipe & Supply Company Incorporated
14615 Lorain Ave
Cleveland OH
216 251-2345

(G-4470)
NORTH COAST LITHO INC
4701 Manufacturing Ave (44135-2639)
PHONE..................................216 881-1952
Keith P Jaworski, Pr
EMP: 20 EST: 1993
SQ FT: 12,000
SALES (est): 2.4MM Privately Held
Web: www.northcoastlitho.com
SIC: 2752 Offset printing

(G-4471)
NORTH COAST MEDIA LLC
Also Called: NCM
1360 E 9th St Ste 1070 (44114-1754)
PHONE..................................216 706-3700
Kevin Stoltman, Pr
Kevin Stoltman, Pr
Steve Galperin, *
EMP: 62 EST: 2011
SALES (est): 10.82MM Privately Held
Web: www.northcoastmedia.net
SIC: 2731 Book publishing

(G-4472)
NORTH COAST MINORITY MEDIA LLC
Also Called: North Coast Publications
1360 E 9th St (44114-1737)
PHONE..................................216 407-4327
EMP: 9 EST: 2012
SALES (est): 436.49K Privately Held
Web: www.northcoastmedia.net
SIC: 2721 Magazines: publishing and printing

(G-4473)
NORTH COAST TIRE CO INC
7810 Old Rockside Rd (44131-2314)
P.O. Box 31273 (44131-0273)
PHONE..................................216 447-1690
Victor J Appenzeller, Pr
Julie A Appenzeller, VP
EMP: 8 EST: 1983
SQ FT: 8,500
SALES (est): 950.2K Privately Held
Web: www.northcoasttire.com
SIC: 7534 5014 Tire repair shop; Truck tires and tubes

(G-4474)
NORTHAST OHIO NGHBRHOOD HLTH S
Also Called: Southeast Health Center
13301 Miles Ave (44105-5521)
PHONE..................................216 751-3100
EMP: 31
SALES (corp-wide): 32.93MM Privately Held
Web: www.neonhealth.org
SIC: 2813 Neon
PA: Northcoast Ohio Neighborhood Health Services, Inc.
4800 Payne Ave
Cleveland OH 44103
216 231-7700

(G-4475)
NORTHEAST BLUEPRINT AND SUP CO
1230 E 286th St (44132-2138)
PHONE..................................216 261-7500
Timothy Yurick, Pr
James Yurick, Pr
EMP: 7 EST: 1962
SQ FT: 7,000
SALES (est): 857.28K Privately Held
Web: www.northeastblueprint.com
SIC: 7334 2752 Blueprinting service; Commercial printing, lithographic

(G-4476)
NORTHERN CHEM BLNDING CORP INC
360 Literary Rd (44113-4560)
PHONE..................................216 781-7799
John Zemaitis, Pr
▲ EMP: 9 EST: 1983
SQ FT: 35,000
SALES (est): 1.98MM Privately Held
Web: ncbcohio.lookchem.com

SIC: 2899 Metal treating compounds

(G-4477)
NORTHERN STAMPING CO
5900 Harvard Ave (44105-4850)
PHONE..................................216 883-8888
EMP: 10
SALES (corp-wide): 471.87MM Privately Held
Web: www.northernstamping.com
SIC: 3465 3469 Automotive stampings; Metal stampings, nec
HQ: Northern Stamping Co.
6600 Chapek Pkwy
Cleveland OH 44125
216 883-8888

(G-4478)
NORTHERN STAMPING CO (HQ)
Also Called: Northern Stamping, Inc.
6600 Chapek Pkwy (44125-1049)
PHONE..................................216 883-8888
Matthew Friedman, Pr
Scott Sheffield, VP
Ian Hessel, CFO
◆ EMP: 215 EST: 1989
SQ FT: 118,000
SALES (est): 404.06MM
SALES (corp-wide): 471.87MM Privately Held
Web: www.northernstamping.com
SIC: 3465 3469 Automotive stampings; Metal stampings, nec
PA: Bear Diversified, Inc.
4580 E 71st St
Cleveland OH 44125
216 883-8888

(G-4479)
NORTHERN STAMPING CO
Also Called: Northern Stamping Plant 2
7750 Hub Pkwy (44125-5709)
PHONE..................................216 642-8081
EMP: 10
SALES (corp-wide): 471.87MM Privately Held
Web: www.northernstamping.com
SIC: 3465 3714 Automotive stampings; Motor vehicle parts and accessories
HQ: Northern Stamping Co.
6600 Chapek Pkwy
Cleveland OH 44125
216 883-8888

(G-4480)
NORTHSHORE MOLD INC
2861 E Royalton Rd (44147-2827)
PHONE..................................440 838-8212
Joseph E Pajestka Junior, Pr
Vivian Pajestka, VP
EMP: 7 EST: 1985
SQ FT: 6,000
SALES (est): 676.15K Privately Held
Web: www.northshoremold.com
SIC: 3599 3089 Machine and other job shop work; Injection molding of plastics

(G-4481)
NORTHWIND INDUSTRIES INC
11324 Brookpark Rd (44130-1129)
PHONE..................................216 433-0666
Garry Patla, Pr
Christine Klukan, VP
EMP: 22 EST: 1985
SALES (est): 569.17K Privately Held
SIC: 3599 7692 3469 3444 Machine shop, jobbing and repair; Welding repair; Metal stampings, nec; Sheet metalwork

(G-4482)
NOSH BUTTERS LLC
1274 W 65th St (44102-2108)
P.O. Box 3672 (44223-7672)
PHONE..................................773 710-0668
Samuel Trohman, Prin
EMP: 8 EST: 2017
SALES (est): 247.78K Privately Held
Web: www.noshbutters.com
SIC: 5451 2068 Butter; Nuts: dried, dehydrated, salted or roasted

(G-4483)
NOVAGARD SOLUTIONS INC (PA)
Also Called: Foam Seal
5109 Hamilton Ave (44114-3907)
PHONE..................................216 881-8111
Sarah Nash, Ch Bd
Sarah Nash, Ch Bd
Ron Moeller, *
EMP: 104 EST: 2002
SQ FT: 250,000
SALES (est): 50MM Privately Held
Web: www.novagard.com
SIC: 5169 2822 2869 3567 Adhesives and sealants; Silicone rubbers; Silicones; Incinerators, thermal, fume & catalytic

(G-4484)
NOVAK J F MANUFACTURING CO LLC
Also Called: Cleveland Church Supply
2701 Meyer Ave (44109-1532)
PHONE..................................216 741-5112
Sharon Campbell, Mgr
EMP: 6 EST: 1932
SQ FT: 7,000
SALES (est): 380K Privately Held
Web: www.policesupplystorecleveland.com
SIC: 2395 5049 Emblems, embroidered; Religious supplies

(G-4485)
NOVOLYTE TECHNOLOGIES INC
Also Called: Novolyte Performance
8001 E Pleasant Valley Rd (44131-5526)
PHONE..................................216 867-1040
▲ EMP: 305
Web: www.novolyte.com
SIC: 2621 Specialty or chemically treated papers

(G-4486)
NPA COATINGS INC
Also Called: Npa Coatings
11110 Berea Rd Ste 1 (44102-2540)
PHONE..................................216 651-5900
▲ EMP: 180
Web: www.npacoatings.com
SIC: 2851 Paints and allied products

(G-4487)
NU-DI PRODUCTS CO INC
Also Called: Nu-Di
12730 Triskett Rd (44111-2529)
PHONE..................................216 251-9070
Kenneth Bihn, Pr
Tim Bihn, *
EMP: 85 EST: 1969
SQ FT: 38,000
SALES (est): 9.62MM Privately Held
Web: www.nu-di.com
SIC: 3825 5013 Engine electrical test equipment; Testing equipment, electrical: automotive

(G-4488)
NUTZ4COFFEE LTD
2800 Euclid Ave Ste 150 (44115-2430)

PHONE.................216 236-5292
Matthew Gorse, Prin
EMP: 7 EST: 2019
SALES (est): 492.77K **Privately Held**
Web: www.nutz4coffee.com
SIC: 2095 Roasted coffee

(G-4489)
OASIS CONSUMER HEALTHCARE LLC
Also Called: Ochc
425 Literary Rd Apt 100 (44113-4506)
PHONE.................216 394-0544
EMP: 6 EST: 2008
SALES (est): 409.87K **Privately Held**
Web: www.oasisbeautyrx.com
SIC: 2844 Mouthwashes

(G-4490)
OATEY CO (PA)
20600 Emerald Pkwy (44135)
P.O. Box 35906 (44135)
PHONE.................800 203-1155
▲ EMP: 300 EST: 1916
SALES (est): 304.6MM
SALES (corp-wide): 304.6MM **Privately Held**
Web: www.oatey.com
SIC: 3444 Metal roofing and roof drainage equipment

(G-4491)
OATEY SUPPLY CHAIN SVCS INC (HQ)
Also Called: Oatey
20600 Emerald Pkwy (44135-6022)
PHONE.................216 267-7100
John H Mcmillan, Ch
Neal Restivo, CEO
◆ EMP: 200 EST: 2001
SQ FT: 165,000
SALES (est): 85.03MM
SALES (corp-wide): 304.6MM **Privately Held**
Web: www.oatey.com
SIC: 3444 5074 Metal roofing and roof drainage equipment; Plumbing and hydronic heating supplies
PA: Oatey Co.
  20600 Emerald Pkwy
  Cleveland OH 44135
  800 203-1155

(G-4492)
OGLEBAY NORTON MAR SVCS CO LLC
1001 Lakeside Ave E 15th Fl (44114-1158)
PHONE.................216 861-3300
Michael D Lundin, Pr
EMP: 1500 EST: 1999
SALES (est): 22.31MM **Privately Held**
SIC: 1422 Crushed and broken limestone

(G-4493)
OHIO ALUMINUM INDUSTRIES INC
4840 Warner Rd (44125-1193)
PHONE.................216 641-8865
Kurt Blemaster, CEO
James E Herkner, *
Willem Der Velde, *
▲ EMP: 163 EST: 1970
SQ FT: 78,000
SALES (est): 23.58MM **Privately Held**
Web: www.ohioaluminum.com
SIC: 3363 Aluminum die-castings

(G-4494)
OHIO AWNING & MANUFACTURING CO
5777 Grant Ave (44105-5605)
PHONE.................216 861-2400
TOLL FREE: 800
Andrew Morse, Pr
Anne L Morse, *
▲ EMP: 30 EST: 1864
SQ FT: 80,000
SALES (est): 4.24MM **Privately Held**
Web: www.ohioawning.com
SIC: 2394 3993 Awnings, fabric: made from purchased materials; Electric signs

(G-4495)
OHIO BEVERAGE SYSTEMS INC
9200 Midwest Ave (44125-2416)
PHONE.................216 475-3900
James Rickon, Pr
EMP: 15 EST: 1983
SQ FT: 28,000
SALES (est): 2.47MM **Privately Held**
Web: www.ohiobev.net
SIC: 2086 Fruit drinks (less than 100% juice): packaged in cans, etc.

(G-4496)
OHIO BLOW PIPE COMPANY (PA)
Also Called: Ohio Blow Pipe
446 E 131st St (44108-1684)
PHONE.................216 681-7379
Edward Fakeris, Pr
William Roberts, *
Lisa Kern, *
EMP: 33 EST: 1967
SQ FT: 45,000
SALES (est): 24.37MM
SALES (corp-wide): 24.37MM **Privately Held**
Web: www.innoveyance.com
SIC: 8711 3564 3444 Engineering services; Blowers and fans; Sheet metalwork

(G-4497)
OHIO ENVELOPE MANUFACTURING CO
5161 W 164th St (44142-1592)
PHONE.................216 267-2920
David Rick Gould III, Pr
David Rick Gould Iii, Pr
Carol J Gould, *
EMP: 35 EST: 1936
SQ FT: 35,000
SALES (est): 5.14MM **Privately Held**
Web: www.ohioenvelope.com
SIC: 2759 2754 2677 Envelopes: printing, nsk; Envelopes: gravure printing; Envelopes

(G-4498)
OHIO IRISH AMERICAN NEWS
14615 Triskett Rd (44111-3123)
PHONE.................216 647-1144
EMP: 8 EST: 2014
SALES (est): 226.28K **Privately Held**
Web: www.iirish.us
SIC: 2711 Newspapers, publishing and printing

(G-4499)
OHIO MILLS CORPORATION (PA)
Also Called: Ohio Mill Supply
1719 E 39th St (44114-4530)
PHONE.................216 431-3979
Ronald Katz, Pr
EMP: 8 EST: 1983
SQ FT: 15,000
SALES (est): 1.51MM
SALES (corp-wide): 1.51MM **Privately Held**
Web: www.sodonate.com
SIC: 5651 2842 Unisex clothing stores; Dusting cloths, chemically treated

(G-4500)
OLYMPIC FOREST PRODUCTS CO
2280 W 11th St (44113-3662)
PHONE.................216 421-2775
Daniel Andrews, Pr
Howard A Steindler, *
EMP: 25 EST: 1980
SALES (est): 4.97MM **Privately Held**
Web: www.olyforest.com
SIC: 2448 Pallets, wood

(G-4501)
OM GROUP INC
127 Public Sq Ste 3900 (44114-1291)
PHONE.................216 781-0083
EMP: 12 EST: 2019
SALES (est): 1.13MM **Privately Held**
Web: www.omgroupinc.us
SIC: 2819 Industrial inorganic chemicals, nec

(G-4502)
OMCO SOLAR INC
1300 E 9th St (44114-1501)
PHONE.................216 621-6633
Robert C Heintel, Prin
EMP: 7 EST: 2010
SALES (est): 187.29K **Privately Held**
Web: www.omcoform.com
SIC: 3444 Sheet metalwork

(G-4503)
OMNI MEDIA CLEVELAND INC
1375 E 9th St Ste 1250 (44114-1789)
P.O. Box 1025 (44087-9025)
PHONE.................216 687-0077
EMP: 6 EST: 2018
SALES (est): 130.82K **Privately Held**
Web: www.omnimedia-usa.com
SIC: 3993 Signs and advertising specialties

(G-4504)
OMNI TECHNICAL PRODUCTS INC
Also Called: Wire Lab Company
15300 Industrial Pkwy (44135-3310)
PHONE.................216 433-1970
Robert J Fulop, Pr
Robert L Fulop, VP
EMP: 11 EST: 1980
SQ FT: 20,000
SALES (est): 1.97MM **Privately Held**
Web: www.wirelab.com
SIC: 3599 Machine shop, jobbing and repair

(G-4505)
ONCO WVA INC
1001 Lakeside Ave E 15th Fl (44114)
PHONE.................216 861-3300
EMP: 7 EST: 2004
SALES (est): 144.15K **Privately Held**
SIC: 1422 Crushed and broken limestone

(G-4506)
ONTEX INC
1001 Lakeside Ave E 15th Fl (44114)
PHONE.................216 861-3300
EMP: 10 EST: 2004
SALES (est): 349.03K **Privately Held**
Web: www.ontex.com
SIC: 1422 Crushed and broken limestone

(G-4507)
OPTOQUEST CORPORATION
10000 Cedar Ave (44106-2119)
PHONE.................216 445-3637
William J Dupps Junior, Prin
EMP: 10 EST: 2015
SALES (est): 194.97K **Privately Held**
Web: www.optoquest.net

(G-4508)
ORBYTEL PRINT AND PACKG INC
Also Called: Orbytel
4901 Johnston Pkwy (44128-3201)
PHONE.................216 267-8734
Albert Uvlin, Pr
Cynthia Uvlin, Sec
Mark Uvlin, COO
Clarence D Finke, Prin
James R Bingham, Prin
EMP: 8 EST: 1964
SQ FT: 12,300
SALES (est): 4.54MM **Privately Held**
Web: www.orbytel.com
SIC: 2679 5085 Tags and labels, paper; Industrial supplies

(G-4509)
ORLANDO BAKING COMPANY (PA)
Also Called: Orlando
7777 Grand Ave (44104-3061)
PHONE.................216 361-1872
TOLL FREE: 800
Chester Orlando, Pr
Joseph Orlando, *
Christine Brindle, *
Edna Rosenblum, *
Glenn W Eckert, *
▲ EMP: 253 EST: 1872
SQ FT: 80,000
SALES (est): 52.17MM
SALES (corp-wide): 52.17MM **Privately Held**
Web: www.orlandobaking.com
SIC: 2051 Bread, all types (white, wheat, rye, etc); fresh or frozen

(G-4510)
OSBORNE INC
26481 Cannon Rd (44146-1843)
PHONE.................440 232-1440
Patrick Donnelly, Genl Mgr
EMP: 10
SQ FT: 6,000
SALES (corp-wide): 14.18MM **Privately Held**
Web: www.osbornecompaniesinc.com
SIC: 3273 Ready-mixed concrete
PA: Osborne, Inc.
  7954 Reynolds Rd
  Mentor OH 44060
  440 942-7000

(G-4511)
OSTEOSYMBIONICS LLC
1768 E 25th St Ste 316 (44114-4418)
P.O. Box 128 (44202-0128)
PHONE.................216 881-8500
Cynthia Brogan, Managing Member
EMP: 10 EST: 2006
SALES (est): 744.37K **Privately Held**
Web: www.osteosymbionics.com
SIC: 3842 Implants, surgical

(G-4512)
OTIS ELEVATOR COMPANY
9800 Rockside Rd Ste 1200 (44125-6270)
PHONE.................216 573-2333
Gordy Sell, Mgr
EMP: 44
SALES (corp-wide): 14.21B **Publicly Held**
Web: www.otis.com
SIC: 5084 1796 3534 Elevators; Elevator installation and conversion; Elevators and equipment
HQ: Otis Elevator Company
  1 Carrier Pl

SIC: 8062 3841 General medical and surgical hospitals; Surgical and medical instruments

Cleveland - Cuyahoga County (G-4513)

Farmington CT 06032
860 674-3000

(G-4513)
OTTO KONIGSLOW MFG CO
13300 Coit Rd (44110-2285)
PHONE..................................216 851-7900
J P Lawson, *Pr*
Cofer Mcintosh, *CEO*
EMP: 15 **EST:** 1876
SQ FT: 72,500
SALES (est): 2.46MM **Privately Held**
Web: www.ottokonigslowmfg.com
SIC: 3724 3548 Aircraft engines and engine parts; Welding and cutting apparatus and accessories, nec

(G-4514)
P & P MACHINE TOOL INC
26189 Broadway Ave (44146-6512)
PHONE..................................440 232-7404
Wayne Pelcarsky, *Pr*
Thomas Pelcarsky, *VP*
EMP: 6 **EST:** 1980
SQ FT: 4,000
SALES (est): 481.12K **Privately Held**
SIC: 3599 Machine shop, jobbing and repair

(G-4515)
P L M CORPORATION
1400 Brookpark Rd (44109-5832)
PHONE..................................216 341-8008
Michael Dunn, *Pr*
EMP: 9 **EST:** 1994
SALES (est): 1.11MM **Privately Held**
Web: www.plmcorporation.net
SIC: 3272 Paving materials, prefabricated concrete

(G-4516)
P Q CORP
2380 W 3rd St (44113-2509)
PHONE..................................216 621-0840
EMP: 9 **EST:** 2020
SALES (est): 385.98K **Privately Held**
SIC: 2819 Industrial inorganic chemicals, nec

(G-4517)
P S C INC
21761 Tungsten Rd (44117-1116)
PHONE..................................216 531-3375
Matthew C Litzler, *Pr*
William J Urban, *COO*
▲ **EMP:** 8 **EST:** 1970
SQ FT: 12,000
SALES (est): 2.48MM
SALES (corp-wide): 25.92MM **Privately Held**
Web: www.pscrfheat.com
SIC: 3567 1731 Dielectric heating equipment ; General electrical contractor
PA: C.A. Litzler Holding Company
4800 W 160th St
Cleveland OH 44135
216 267-8020

(G-4518)
P2P MFG LLC
Also Called: P2p Manufacturing
4911 Grant Ave (44125-1027)
PHONE..................................216 282-4110
Ryan Fredmonsky, *Prin*
EMP: 10 **EST:** 2019
SALES (est): 233.74K **Privately Held**
Web: www.p2p-mfg.com
SIC: 3599 Machine shop, jobbing and repair

(G-4519)
PACK LINE CORP
22900 Miles Rd (44128-5445)
PHONE..................................212 564-0664
Michael Beilinson, *Prin*
▲ **EMP:** 45 **EST:** 2003
SALES (est): 1.02MM **Privately Held**
SIC: 3565 Packaging machinery
PA: Packline Ltd
59 Prof. Shor
Holon 58811

(G-4520)
PALISIN & ASSOCIATES INC (PA)
Also Called: Sup-R-Die
10003 Memphis Ave (44144-2031)
PHONE..................................216 252-3930
David L Palisin, *Pr*
Marilyn J Palisin, *VP*
EMP: 22 **EST:** 1956
SQ FT: 11,000
SALES (est): 4.99MM
SALES (corp-wide): 4.99MM **Privately Held**
Web: www.suprdie.com
SIC: 3544 Special dies and tools

(G-4521)
PARAMELT ARGUESO KINDT INC
Also Called: Paramelt
12651 Elmwood Ave (44111-5911)
PHONE..................................216 252-4122
David P Kindt, *Pr*
▲ **EMP:** 7 **EST:** 2010
SALES (est): 998.37K **Privately Held**
Web: www.paramelt.com
SIC: 2891 Adhesives

(G-4522)
PARAMOUNT DISTILLERS INC
Also Called: Lonz Winery
3116 Berea Rd (44111-1596)
PHONE..................................216 671-6300
▲ **EMP:** 337
SIC: 2084 2085 5182 5812 Wines; Distilled and blended liquors; Wine; Eating places

(G-4523)
PARK PLACE TECHNOLOGIES LLC (PA)
5910 Landerbrook Dr Ste 300 (44124)
PHONE..................................877 778-8707
Chris Adams, *Pr*
Hal Malstrom, *
Ted Rieple, *
Mike Knightly, *
Judy Collister, *
EMP: 161 **EST:** 1991
SQ FT: 41,000
SALES (est): 367.44MM **Privately Held**
Web: www.parkplacetechnologies.com
SIC: 7379 3571 7378 3572 Computer related consulting services; Electronic computers; Computer peripheral equipment repair and maintenance; Computer storage devices

(G-4524)
PARK-OHIO HOLDINGS CORP (PA)
6065 Parkland Blvd Ste 1 (44124-6145)
PHONE..................................440 947-2000
Matthew Crawford, *Ch*
Patrick Fogarty, *CFO*
◆ **EMP:** 18 **EST:** 1998
SQ FT: 20,150
SALES (est): 1.66B
SALES (corp-wide): 1.66B **Publicly Held**
Web: www.pkoh.com
SIC: 3069 3567 3363 3524 Molded rubber products; Induction heating equipment; Aluminum die-castings; Lawn and garden tractors and equipment

(G-4525)
PARK-OHIO INDUSTRIES INC (HQ)
Also Called: Park-Ohio
6065 Parkland Blvd Ste 1 (44124)
PHONE..................................440 947-2000
Matthew V Crawford, *Pr*
Patrick W Fogarty, *CAO*
EMP: 106 **EST:** 1984
SQ FT: 60,450
SALES (est): 1.66B
SALES (corp-wide): 1.66B **Publicly Held**
Web: www.pkoh.com
SIC: 3462 3069 3567 3363 Iron and steel forgings; Molded rubber products; Induction heating equipment; Aluminum die-castings
PA: Park-Ohio Holdings Corp.
6065 Parkland Blvd Ste 1
Cleveland OH 44124
440 947-2000

(G-4526)
PARK-OHIO PRODUCTS INC
7000 Denison Ave (44102-5247)
PHONE..................................216 961-7200
▲ **EMP:** 100 **EST:** 1995
SQ FT: 40,000
SALES (est): 35.64MM
SALES (corp-wide): 1.66B **Publicly Held**
Web: www.pkoh.com
SIC: 3069 Molded rubber products
HQ: Park-Ohio Industries, Inc.
6065 Parkland Blvd
Cleveland OH 44124
440 947-2000

(G-4527)
PARKER AEROSPACE
19600 Five Points Rd (44135-3109)
PHONE..................................216 225-2721
Cody Risker, *Mgr*
EMP: 9 **EST:** 2018
SALES (est): 234.12K **Privately Held**
SIC: 3812 Search and navigation equipment

(G-4528)
PARKER HANNIFIN PARTNER B LLC
6035 Parkland Blvd (44124-4186)
PHONE..................................216 896-3000
EMP: 20 **EST:** 2012
SALES (est): 4.15MM
SALES (corp-wide): 19.07B **Publicly Held**
SIC: 3594 Fluid power pumps and motors
PA: Parker-Hannifin Corporation
6035 Parkland Blvd
Cleveland OH 44124
216 896-3000

(G-4529)
PARKER ROYALTY PARTNERSHIP
6035 Parkland Blvd (44124-4186)
PHONE..................................216 896-3000
EMP: 48 **EST:** 2008
SALES (est): 3.25MM
SALES (corp-wide): 19.07B **Publicly Held**
SIC: 3594 Fluid power pumps and motors
PA: Parker-Hannifin Corporation
6035 Parkland Blvd
Cleveland OH 44124
216 896-3000

(G-4530)
PARKER RST-PROOF CLEVELAND INC
1688 Arabella Rd (44112-1418)
PHONE..................................216 481-6680
Frederick A Fruscella, *Ch Bd*
Sharon Bodine, *
EMP: 37 **EST:** 1935
SQ FT: 75,000
SALES (est): 4.85MM **Privately Held**
Web: www.parkerhq.com
SIC: 3479 3471 Rust proofing (hot dipping) of metals and formed products; Plating and polishing

(G-4531)
PARKER-HANNIFIN CORPORATION
Also Called: Flight Operations
19600 Five Points Rd (44135-3109)
PHONE..................................216 433-1795
Allen Maurer, *Dir*
EMP: 6
SALES (corp-wide): 19.07B **Publicly Held**
Web: www.parker.com
SIC: 5084 3822 Hydraulic systems equipment and supplies; Environmental controls
PA: Parker-Hannifin Corporation
6035 Parkland Blvd
Cleveland OH 44124
216 896-3000

(G-4532)
PARKER-HANNIFIN CORPORATION (PA)
Also Called: Parker
6035 Parkland Blvd (44124-4186)
PHONE..................................216 896-3000
Jennifer A Parmentier, *CEO*
Thomas L Williams, *
Andrew D Ross, *Pr*
Todd M Leombruno, *Ex VP*
▲ **EMP:** 4558 **EST:** 1918
SALES (est): 19.07B
SALES (corp-wide): 19.07B **Publicly Held**
Web: www.parker.com
SIC: 3593 3492 3594 Fluid power cylinders and actuators; Control valves, fluid power: hydraulic and pneumatic; Fluid power pumps

(G-4533)
PARKING & TRAFFIC CONTROL SEC
Also Called: Ptc Industries
13651 Newton Rd (44130-2735)
PHONE..................................440 243-7565
Donald Shorts, *CEO*
Lee Shorts, *Pr*
EMP: 15 **EST:** 1979
SQ FT: 20,000
SALES (est): 1.69MM **Privately Held**
Web: www.obardoorandgate.com
SIC: 3824 1799 8711 Parking meters; Parking facility equipment and maintenance ; Designing: ship, boat, machine, and product

(G-4534)
PARKOHIO WORLDWIDE LLC (HQ)
6065 Parkland Blvd Ste 1 (44124)
PHONE..................................440 947-2000
Matthew Crawford, *Ch*
EMP: 36 **EST:** 2018
SALES (est): 33.41MM
SALES (corp-wide): 1.66B **Publicly Held**
Web: www.pkoh.com
SIC: 3069 Molded rubber products
PA: Park-Ohio Holdings Corp.
6065 Parkland Blvd Ste 1
Cleveland OH 44124
440 947-2000

(G-4535)
PARMA HEIGHTS LICENSE BUREAU
6339 Olde York Rd (44130-3059)
PHONE..................................440 888-0388
Dan Hughes, *Owner*
EMP: 7 **EST:** 1999
SALES (est): 581.57K **Privately Held**
Web: bmv.ohio.gov
SIC: 3469 Automobile license tags, stamped metal

▲ = Import ▼ = Export
◆ = Import/Export

GEOGRAPHIC SECTION
Cleveland - Cuyahoga County (G-4557)

(G-4536)
PCC AIRFOILS LLC (DH)
3401 Enterprise Pkwy Ste 200 (44122)
PHONE..................216 831-3590
Peter Waite, *Managing Member*
◆ **EMP:** 29 **EST:** 2002
SQ FT: 14,000
SALES (est): 454.46MM
SALES (corp-wide): 364.48B **Publicly Held**
Web: www.pccairfoils.com
SIC: 3369 Nonferrous foundries, nec
HQ: Precision Castparts Corp.
  5885 Meadows Rd Ste 620
  Lake Oswego OR 97035
  503 946-4800

(G-4537)
PCC AIRFOILS LLC
Also Called: Sherwood Refractores
1781 Octavia Rd (44112-1410)
PHONE..................216 692-7900
Thomas Lenard, *Genl Mgr*
EMP: 250
SALES (corp-wide): 364.48B **Publicly Held**
Web: www.pccairfoils.com
SIC: 3369 3812 3677 3543 Castings, except die-castings, precision; Search and navigation equipment; Electronic coils and transformers; Foundry cores
HQ: Pcc Airfoils, Llc
  3401 Entp Pkwy Ste 200
  Cleveland OH 44122
  216 831-3590

(G-4538)
PEERLESS METAL PRODUCTS INC
6017 Superior Ave (44103-1447)
PHONE..................216 431-6905
EMP: 16 **EST:** 1996
SQ FT: 32,000
SALES (est): 463.24K **Privately Held**
Web: www.peerlessmetalproducts.com
SIC: 3469 Stamping metal for the trade

(G-4539)
PEMCO INC
5663 Brecksville Rd (44131-1593)
PHONE..................216 524-2990
William J Koteles, *Pr*
William John Koteles, *Pr*
Ivan Kovacs, *
Kathleen Koteles, *
EMP: 43 **EST:** 1942
SQ FT: 25,000
SALES (est): 4.98MM **Privately Held**
Web: www.pemcomedical.com
SIC: 3841 3599 3845 3545 Surgical and medical instruments; Machine shop, jobbing and repair; Electromedical equipment; Machine tool accessories

(G-4540)
PEMRO CORPORATION
Also Called: Pemro Distribution
125 Alpha Park (44143-2224)
PHONE..................800 440-5441
Jon C Raney, *Pr*
Shari Raney, *Sec*
Gregory J Dziak, *Prin*
Todd Chaston, *Sls Mgr*
Matt Raney, *Genl Mgr*
EMP: 10 **EST:** 2001
SQ FT: 3,500
SALES (est): 2.45MM **Privately Held**
Web: www.pemro.com
SIC: 5065 2899 5045 Electronic parts; Fluxes: brazing, soldering, galvanizing, and welding; Anti-static equipment and devices

(G-4541)
PERITEC BIOSCIENCES LTD
Also Called: Peritec Biosciences
3291 Bremerton Rd (44124-5346)
PHONE..................216 445-3756
Nancy Rubin, *CFO*
Naga Mallika Sattiraju, *Mgr*
EMP: 8 **EST:** 2005
SALES (est): 363.43K **Privately Held**
Web: www.peritecbio.com
SIC: 3841 Surgical and medical instruments

(G-4542)
PERSONNEL SELECTION SERVICES
31517 Walker Rd (44140-1415)
PHONE..................440 835-3255
Paul Michalko, *Pr*
EMP: 10 **EST:** 1990
SALES (est): 260.84K **Privately Held**
SIC: 1389 8071 Testing, measuring, surveying, and analysis services; Testing laboratories

(G-4543)
PETNET SOLUTIONS CLEVELAND LLC
2035 E 86th St Rm Jb-122 (44106-2963)
PHONE..................865 218-2000
EMP: 16
SALES (est): 544.94K
SALES (corp-wide): 89.68B **Privately Held**
SIC: 2835 Radioactive diagnostic substances
HQ: Petnet Solutions, Inc.
  810 Innovation Dr
  Knoxville TN 37932
  865 218-2000

(G-4544)
PETRO GEAR CORPORATION (PA)
3901 Hamilton Ave (44114-3831)
PHONE..................216 431-2820
EMP: 10 **EST:** 1917
SQ FT: 40,000
SALES (est): 4.87MM
SALES (corp-wide): 4.87MM **Privately Held**
Web: www.stahlgear.com
SIC: 3566 Gears, power transmission, except auto

(G-4545)
PG SQUARE LLC
6035 Parkland Blvd (44124-4186)
PHONE..................216 896-3000
EMP: 10 **EST:** 2008
SALES (est): 1.42MM
SALES (corp-wide): 19.07B **Publicly Held**
SIC: 3823 Process control instruments
PA: Parker-Hannifin Corporation
  6035 Parkland Blvd
  Cleveland OH 44124
  216 896-3000

(G-4546)
PHIL VEDDA & SONS INC
Also Called: Vedda Printing
12000 Berea Rd (44111-1608)
PHONE..................216 671-2222
Phillip Vedda, *Pr*
James Vedda, *VP*
Grace Vedda, *Sec*
EMP: 8 **EST:** 1956
SQ FT: 20,000
SALES (est): 2.74MM **Privately Held**
Web: www.veddaprinting.com
SIC: 2752 Offset printing

(G-4547)
PHILIPS MED SYSTEMS CLVLAND IN (HQ)
Also Called: Philips Healthcare
595 Miner Rd (44143-2131)
PHONE..................440 483-3000
David A Dripchak, *CEO*
Jerry C Cirino, *Ex VP*
William J Cull Senior, *VP*
Robert Blankenship, *CFO*
◆ **EMP:** 500 **EST:** 1970
SQ FT: 495,000
SALES (est): 665.76MM
SALES (corp-wide): 18.51B **Privately Held**
Web: www.emergin.com
SIC: 3844 5047 5137 3842 X-ray apparatus and tubes; X-ray film and supplies; Hospital gowns, women's and children's; Surgical appliances and supplies
PA: Koninklijke Philips N.V.
  High Tech Campus 52
  Eindhoven NB 5656
  853015541

(G-4548)
PHILLIPS ELECTRIC CO
Also Called: Phillips Electric
4126 Saint Clair Ave (44103-1120)
PHONE..................216 361-0014
Jennifer Marriott, *CEO*
Jennifer Marriott, *Pr*
EMP: 16 **EST:** 1946
SQ FT: 40,000
SALES (est): 5MM **Privately Held**
Web: www.redmondwaltz.com
SIC: 7694 5063 Electric motor repair; Motors, electric

(G-4549)
PHUNKENSHIP - PLATFORM BEER CO
3137 Sackett Ave (44109-2013)
PHONE..................216 417-7743
EMP: 10 **EST:** 2019
SALES (est): 396.94K **Privately Held**
SIC: 2082 Beer (alcoholic beverage)

(G-4550)
PIEDMONT WATER SERVICES LLC
21400 Lorain Rd (44126-2125)
P.O. Box 1369 (58702-1369)
PHONE..................216 554-4747
David Niederst, *Managing Member*
EMP: 10 **EST:** 2014
SALES (est): 891.46K **Privately Held**
SIC: 2834 Chlorination tablets and kits (water purification)

(G-4551)
PIERCE-WRIGHT PRECISION INC
13606 Enterprise Ave (44135-5112)
PHONE..................216 362-2870
David B Pierce, *Pr*
EMP: 7 **EST:** 1978
SQ FT: 10,000
SALES (est): 526.73K **Privately Held**
Web: www.conceptdesigns.com
SIC: 3599 Machine shop, jobbing and repair

(G-4552)
PIERRES ICE CREAM COMPANY INC ✪
6200 Euclid Ave (44103-3724)
PHONE..................216 432-1144
Doug Smith, *CEO*
Matthew J Anderson, *CFO*
EMP: 80 **EST:** 2022
SALES (est): 9.68MM **Privately Held**
Web: www.pierres.com
SIC: 2024 Ice cream and frozen deserts

(G-4553)
PINNACLE GRAPHICS IMAGING INC
Also Called: P G I
17920 S Waterloo Rd (44119-3222)
PHONE..................216 781-1800
Dan J Nugent, *Pr*
EMP: 9 **EST:** 1991
SALES (est): 489.88K **Privately Held**
Web: www.pgicolor.com
SIC: 2796 Color separations, for printing

(G-4554)
PIONEER CLDDING GLZING SYSTEMS
2550 Brookpark Rd (44134-1407)
PHONE..................216 816-4242
Michael Robinson, *Brnch Mgr*
EMP: 35
SALES (corp-wide): 50.25MM **Privately Held**
Web: www.pioneerglazing.com
SIC: 1793 1741 3448 Glass and glazing work; Masonry and other stonework; Prefabricated metal components
PA: Pioneer Cladding And Glazing Systems
  4074 Bethany Rd
  Mason OH 45040
  513 583-5925

(G-4555)
PIONEER MANUFACTURING INC (PA)
Also Called: Pioneer Athletics
4529 Industrial Pkwy (44135-4505)
PHONE..................216 671-5500
▲ **EMP:** 99 **EST:** 1906
SALES (est): 14.63MM
SALES (corp-wide): 14.63MM **Privately Held**
Web: www.pioneerathletics.com
SIC: 2952 5087 2842 2841 Asphalt felts and coatings; Cleaning and maintenance equipment and supplies; Polishes and sanitation goods; Soap and other detergents

(G-4556)
PJ BUSH ASSOCIATES INC
Also Called: Bush Integrated
15901 Industrial Pkwy (44135-3321)
PHONE..................216 362-6700
Kathleen Bush, *CEO*
Patrick J Bush, *Prin*
EMP: 43 **EST:** 1985
SQ FT: 40,000
SALES (est): 2.37MM **Privately Held**
Web: www.bushintegrated.com
SIC: 2759 Business forms: printing, nsk

(G-4557)
PLAIN DEALER PUBLISHING CO (HQ)
Also Called: Plain Dealer, The
4800 Tiedeman Rd (44144-2336)
P.O. Box 630504 (45263-0504)
PHONE..................216 999-5000
TOLL FREE: 800
Terrance C Z Egger, *Pr*
Robert M Long, *VP*
Virginia Wang, *Finance*
Joseph J Bowman, *Sr VP*
Robert A Perona, *Sr VP*
EMP: 6 **EST:** 1932
SQ FT: 210,000
SALES (est): 21.89MM
SALES (corp-wide): 40.16MM **Privately Held**
Web: www.plaindealer.com
SIC: 2711 Newspapers, publishing and printing
PA: Advance Digital Inc.
  3100 Hrbrside Fncl Ctr Pl
  Jersey City NJ 07311

Cleveland - Cuyahoga County (G-4558)   GEOGRAPHIC SECTION

201 459-2808

(G-4558)
PLASMAN AB LP
Also Called: Plasman Cleveland Mfg
3000 W 121st St (44111-1639)
PHONE.................................216 252-2995
David Wiskel, *Pt*
Hal Leitch, *Pt*
EMP: 112 **EST:** 1992
SQ FT: 58,000
SALES (est): 17.4MM
SALES (corp-wide): 1.3B **Privately Held**
Web: www.plasman.com
SIC: 3471 Electroplating of metals or formed products
HQ: Plasman Us Holdco Llc
1301 W Long Lake Rd # 255
Troy MI 48098
248 205-7004

(G-4559)
PLASTER PROCESS CASTINGS CO
Also Called: Diversified Mold and Castings
19800 Miles Rd (44128-4118)
PHONE.................................216 663-1814
Vince Costello, *Pr*
EMP: 30 **EST:** 1939
SQ FT: 7,500
SALES (est): 2.62MM **Privately Held**
Web: www.diversifiedmolds.com
SIC: 3363 3364 Aluminum die-castings; Zinc and zinc-base alloy die-castings

(G-4560)
PLASTIC WORKS INC
19851 Ingersoll Dr (44116-1817)
P.O. Box 369 (44839-0369)
PHONE.................................440 331-5575
Eric Kvame, *Mgr*
EMP: 12
SALES (corp-wide): 1.2MM **Privately Held**
SIC: 3086 2671 Packaging and shipping materials, foamed plastics; Paper; coated and laminated packaging
PA: The Plastic Works Inc
10502 Mudbrook Rd
Huron OH 44839
419 433-6576

(G-4561)
PLATFORM BEERS LLC
Also Called: Platform Beer
4125 Lorain Ave (44113-3718)
PHONE.................................440 539-3245
Paul Benner, *Managing Member*
EMP: 12 **EST:** 2013
SQ FT: 5,000
SALES (est): 5.45MM
SALES (corp-wide): 1.31B **Privately Held**
Web: www.platformbeer.co
SIC: 2082 Near beer
HQ: Anheuser-Busch, Llc
1 Busch Pl
Saint Louis MO 63118
800 342-5283

(G-4562)
PLUS MARK LLC
1 American Rd (44144-2354)
PHONE.................................216 252-6770
Kurt Schoen, *Pr*
Dick Gygi, *VP*
Stephen J Smith, *Treas*
Chris Haffke, *Sec*
Jim Kaiser, *Asst Tr*
◆ **EMP:** 100 **EST:** 1977
SQ FT: 1,600,000
SALES (est): 45.42MM
SALES (corp-wide): 14.52B **Privately Held**
SIC: 2621 2396 2771 Wrapping paper; Automotive and apparel trimmings; Greeting cards
HQ: American Greetings Corporation
1 American Blvd
Cleveland OH 44145
216 252-7300

(G-4563)
POLY PRODUCTS INC
837 E 79th St (44103-1807)
PHONE.................................216 391-7659
Walter Senney, *Pr*
Joyce Senney, *VP*
EMP: 6 **EST:** 1983
SQ FT: 12,000
SALES (est): 606.51K **Privately Held**
Web: www.poly-products.com
SIC: 3559 3568 Refinery, chemical processing, and similar machinery; Bearings, bushings, and blocks

(G-4564)
PORATH BUSINESS SERVICES INC
Also Called: Porath Printing
21000 Miles Pkwy (44128-5515)
PHONE.................................216 626-0060
Gerald A Engelhart, *Pr*
EMP: 17 **EST:** 1951
SQ FT: 5,000
SALES (est): 2.07MM **Privately Held**
Web: www.porathprintsource.com
SIC: 2752 7331 Offset printing; Mailing service

(G-4565)
POSTLE INDUSTRIES INC (PA)
Also Called: Cermet Technologies
5500 W 164th St (44142-1512)
PHONE.................................216 265-9000
John G Postle, *Pr*
Chris J Postle, *
▲ **EMP:** 20 **EST:** 1968
SQ FT: 15,000
SALES (est): 7.35MM
SALES (corp-wide): 7.35MM **Privately Held**
Web: www.hardbandingsolutions.com
SIC: 3548 2851 Welding and cutting apparatus and accessories, nec; Epoxy coatings

(G-4566)
POTTERS INDUSTRIES LLC
Potters Industries
2380 W 3rd St (44113-2509)
PHONE.................................216 621-0840
Bob Hooper, *Mgr*
EMP: 53
SALES (corp-wide): 406.19MM **Privately Held**
Web: www.pottersindustries.com
SIC: 3231 Reflector glass beads, for highway signs or reflectors
HQ: Potters Industries, Llc
3222 Phnxvlle Pike Ste 10
Malvern PA 19355
484 895-3200

(G-4567)
PPG INDUSTRIES INC
14800 Emery Ave (44135-1477)
PHONE.................................216 671-7793
Dian Lind, *Brnch Mgr*
EMP: 29
SALES (corp-wide): 17.65B **Publicly Held**
Web: www.ppg.com
SIC: 2851 Paints and allied products
PA: Ppg Industries, Inc.
1 Ppg Pl
Pittsburgh PA 15272
412 434-3131

(G-4568)
PPG INDUSTRIES OHIO INC (HQ)
Also Called: PPG Oak Creek
3800 W 143rd St (44111-4997)
PHONE.................................216 671-0050
Charles E Bunch, *CEO*
Bill Silvestri, *Pr*
J Rich Alexander, *VP*
Dennis N Taljan, *Sec*
◆ **EMP:** 602 **EST:** 1999
SQ FT: 439,551
SALES (est): 561.41MM
SALES (corp-wide): 17.65B **Publicly Held**
Web: www.ppg.com
SIC: 2851 Paints and paint additives
PA: Ppg Industries, Inc.
1 Ppg Pl
Pittsburgh PA 15272
412 434-3131

(G-4569)
PPG INDUSTRIES OHIO INC
Also Called: PPG Deco USA
P.O. Box 94995 (44101-4995)
PHONE.................................412 434-3888
EMP: 209
SALES (corp-wide): 17.65B **Publicly Held**
Web: www.ppg.com
SIC: 2851 Paints and paint additives
HQ: Ppg Industries Ohio, Inc.
3800 W 143rd St
Cleveland OH 44111
216 671-0050

(G-4570)
PPL HOLDING COMPANY
25201 Chagrin Blvd # 360 (44122-5600)
PHONE.................................216 514-1840
Mark Mansour, *Bd of Dir*
EMP: 9 **EST:** 2015
SALES (est): 124.89K **Privately Held**
SIC: 2821 Thermoplastic materials

(G-4571)
PRECIOUS MMORIES CSTM PRTG INC
7512 Lexington Ave (44103-4147)
PHONE.................................216 721-3909
Anthony Dlockum, *CEO*
Beverly Dlockum, *COO*
EMP: 6 **EST:** 2012
SALES (est): 171.8K **Privately Held**
SIC: 2752 Commercial printing, lithographic

(G-4572)
PRECISE TOOL & MFG CORP
5755 Canal Rd (44125-3429)
PHONE.................................216 524-1500
Ronald Volandt, *Pr*
EMP: 10 **EST:** 1950
SQ FT: 5,200
SALES (est): 867.03K **Privately Held**
SIC: 3545 Cutting tools for machine tools

(G-4573)
PRECISION COATINGS INC
Also Called: Precison Coating Technology
3289 E 80th St (44104-4341)
PHONE.................................216 441-0805
Dale Palik, *Pr*
Lucille Palik, *Sec*
Mike Palik, *VP*
EMP: 11 **EST:** 1981
SQ FT: 22,000
SALES (est): 923.8K **Privately Held**
Web: www.precisioncoatingscorp.com
SIC: 3479 Coating of metals and formed products

(G-4574)
PRECISION ENGINEERED PLAS INC
7000 Denison Ave (44102-5247)
PHONE.................................216 334-1105
EMP: 20 **EST:** 1997
SALES (est): 9.7MM
SALES (corp-wide): 1.66B **Publicly Held**
SIC: 3089 Automotive parts, plastic
HQ: Park-Ohio Industries, Inc.
6065 Parkland Blvd
Cleveland OH 44124
440 947-2000

(G-4575)
PRECISION METAL PRODUCTS INC
Also Called: Metal Stamping
5745 Canal Rd (44125-3402)
PHONE.................................216 447-1900
George Jacin, *Pr*
George A Jacin, *
Aaron Jason, *
Amber Jacon, *
EMP: 30 **EST:** 1961
SQ FT: 16,000
SALES (est): 5MM **Privately Held**
Web: www.pmpstamping.com
SIC: 3469 3549 Stamping metal for the trade; Assembly machines, including robotic

(G-4576)
PRECISION METAL PRODUCTS INC
9005 Bank St (44125-3425)
PHONE.................................216 447-1900
EMP: 10 **EST:** 2020
SALES (est): 2.46MM **Privately Held**
Web: www.pmpstamping.com
SIC: 3469 Stamping metal for the trade

(G-4577)
PRECISION WELDING CORPORATION
7900 Exchange St (44125-3334)
P.O. Box 25548 (44125-0548)
PHONE.................................216 524-6110
Dennis Nader, *Pr*
Randy Nader, *
EMP: 32 **EST:** 1946
SQ FT: 26,000
SALES (est): 2.31MM **Privately Held**
Web: www.precisionweldingcorp.net
SIC: 7692 3444 3441 Welding repair; Sheet metalwork; Fabricated structural metal

(G-4578)
PREDICOR LLC
2728 Euclid Ave Ste 300 (44115-2428)
PHONE.................................419 460-1831
Timothy Walker, *Managing Member*
Timothy Walker, *Prin*
Dhruv Seshadri, *Prin*
Evan Davies, *Prin*
EMP: 6 **EST:** 2019
SALES (est): 418.19K **Privately Held**
SIC: 3571 Electronic computers

(G-4579)
PREMIER CHEMICALS
7251 Engle Rd (44130-3443)
PHONE.................................440 234-4600
Robert Acord, *Prin*
EMP: 6 **EST:** 2010
SALES (est): 141.82K **Privately Held**
SIC: 2899 Chemical preparations, nec

(G-4580)
PREMIER CONTAINER INC (PA)
Also Called: Premier Container
4500 Crayton Ave (44104-2816)
PHONE.................................800 230-7132
Mike Hanzak, *Pr*

▲ = Import ▼ = Export
◆ = Import/Export

GEOGRAPHIC SECTION

Cleveland - Cuyahoga County (G-4603)

EMP: 23 EST: 2012
SALES (est): 4.6MM
SALES (corp-wide): 4.6MM **Privately Held**
Web: www.premier-container.com
SIC: **3537** Containers (metal), air cargo

(G-4581)
PREMIER MANUFACTURING CORP (HQ)
3003 Priscilla Ave (44134-4230)
PHONE..................................216 941-9700
Paul Kara, *Pr*
Steve Koss, *
Donald C Dawson, *
◆ EMP: 118 EST: 1962
SALES (est): 27.15MM
SALES (corp-wide): 482.27MM **Privately Held**
Web: www.sswtechnologies.com
SIC: **3496** 3296 Miscellaneous fabricated wire products; Mineral wool
PA: Ssw Advanced Technologies, Llc
3501 Tulsa St
Fort Smith AR 72903
479 646-1651

(G-4582)
PREMIER PRINTING CORPORATION
18780 Cranwood Pkwy (44128-4038)
PHONE..................................216 478-9720
James Trombo, *Pr*
Jeffrey Trombo, *VP*
EMP: 17 EST: 2000
SQ FT: 10,000
SALES (est): 543.65K **Privately Held**
Web: www.premierprintingcorp.com
SIC: **2752** Offset printing

(G-4583)
PRESQUE ISLE ORTHTICS PRSTHTIC
Also Called: Presque Isle Medical Tech
14055 Cedar Rd Ste 107 (44118-3333)
PHONE..................................216 371-0660
Solomon Heifetz, *Managing Member*
EMP: 8 EST: 2013
SALES (est): 634.83K **Privately Held**
Web: www.presqueislemedical.com
SIC: **8011** 5999 3842 Primary care medical clinic; Orthopedic and prosthesis applications; Prosthetic appliances

(G-4584)
PRESRITE CORPORATION (PA)
3665 E 78th St (44105-2048)
PHONE..................................216 441-5990
Donald J Diemer, *Ch Bd*
George Longhour, *VP*
William Berglund, *Ex VP*
Keith Vanderburg, *Sec*
Chris Carman, *Pr*
EMP: 300 EST: 1969
SQ FT: 180,000
SALES (est): 94.22MM
SALES (corp-wide): 94.22MM **Privately Held**
Web: www.presrite.com
SIC: **3462** Automotive and internal combustion engine forgings

(G-4585)
PRESSCO TECHNOLOGY INC (PA)
Also Called: Pressco
29200 Aurora Rd (44139-1847)
PHONE..................................440 498-2600
Don W Cochran, *Pr*
Thomas P O'brien, *SLS*
Ed Morgan, *
William C Holmes, *
James R Bridgeland Junior, *Prin*
▲ EMP: 90 EST: 1990
SQ FT: 60,000
SALES (est): 26.17MM
SALES (corp-wide): 26.17MM **Privately Held**
Web: www.pressco.com
SIC: **3829** 3825 Physical property testing equipment; Instruments to measure electricity

(G-4586)
PRESSURE WASHER MFRS ASSN INC
1300 Sumner Ave (44115-2851)
PHONE..................................216 241-7333
John H Addington, *Prin*
EMP: 6 EST: 2008
SALES (est): 80K **Privately Held**
Web: www.pwma.org
SIC: **3452** Washers

(G-4587)
PRINCE & IZANT LLC (PA)
12999 Plaza Dr (44130-1093)
P.O. Box 931247 (44193-0042)
PHONE..................................216 362-7000
▲ EMP: 22 EST: 1927
SALES (est): 18.99MM
SALES (corp-wide): 18.99MM **Privately Held**
Web: www.princeizant.com
SIC: **3915** 7692 3911 Jewelry soldering for the trade; Brazing; Jewel settings and mountings, precious metal

(G-4588)
PRINTING RESOURCES INC
4713 Manufacturing Ave (44135-2639)
PHONE..................................216 881-7660
Anthony Gamellia, *Prin*
EMP: 6
SALES (est): 98.8K **Privately Held**
SIC: **2752** Commercial printing, lithographic

(G-4589)
PRODUCTS CHEMICAL COMPANY LLC
4005 Clark Ave (44109-1128)
PHONE..................................216 218-1155
James Purcell, *CEO*
EMP: 15 EST: 2019
SALES (est): 726.58K **Privately Held**
Web: www.prod-chem.com
SIC: **2842** Polishes and sanitation goods

(G-4590)
PROFILE GRINDING INC
4593 Spring Rd (44131-1023)
PHONE..................................216 351-0600
Karen Homer, *Pr*
EMP: 23 EST: 1945
SQ FT: 20,000
SALES (est): 6.9MM **Privately Held**
Web: www.profilegrinding.com
SIC: **3451** 3599 Screw machine products; Machine shop, jobbing and repair

(G-4591)
PROGRESS RAIL SERVICES CORP
Also Called: Cleveland Track Material
6600 Bessemer Ave (44127-1804)
PHONE..................................216 641-4000
EMP: 260
SALES (corp-wide): 67.06B **Publicly Held**
SIC: **3743** Railroad equipment
HQ: Progress Rail Services Corporation
1600 Progress Dr
Albertville AL 35950
800 476-8769

(G-4592)
PROJITECH INC
2310 Superior Ave E Ste 200 (44114-4245)
PHONE..................................970 333-9727
EMP: 10 EST: 2013
SALES (est): 533.79K **Privately Held**
SIC: **7372** Application computer software

(G-4593)
PROPRESS INC
3135 Berea Rd Ste 1 (44111-1513)
PHONE..................................216 631-8200
EMP: 10 EST: 1995
SQ FT: 3,000
SALES (est): 993.12K **Privately Held**
Web: www.propressinc.com
SIC: **2741** 7311 Telephone and other directory publishing; Advertising agencies

(G-4594)
PROTECH POWDER COATINGS INC
11110 Berea Rd Ste 1 (44102-2540)
PHONE..................................216 244-2761
EMP: 17
SALES (corp-wide): 202.63K **Privately Held**
Web: www.theprotechgroup.com
SIC: **3479** Coating of metals and formed products
HQ: Protech Powder Coatings, Inc.
21 Audrey Pl
Fairfield NJ 07004

(G-4595)
PROTOTYPE FABRICATORS CO
10911 Briggs Rd (44111-5300)
PHONE..................................216 252-0080
Richard Poddubny, *Pr*
EMP: 10 EST: 1971
SQ FT: 7,200
SALES (est): 944.57K **Privately Held**
SIC: **3441** Fabricated structural metal

(G-4596)
PS SUPERIOR INC
Also Called: P S Awards
9257 Midwest Ave (44125-2415)
PHONE..................................216 587-1000
Elizabeth Sudyk, *Pr*
Joanne Sudyk, *Sec*
EMP: 23 EST: 1958
SQ FT: 10,000
SALES (est): 953.59K **Privately Held**
Web: www.psawards.com
SIC: **3499** 7389 5199 Trophies, metal, except silver; Lettering service; Advertising specialties

(G-4597)
PUBCO CORPORATION (PA)
3830 Kelley Ave (44114)
PHONE..................................216 881-5300
William Dillingham, *Pr*
Stephen R Kalette, *
Maria Szubski, *
◆ EMP: 85 EST: 1996
SQ FT: 312,000
SALES (est): 121.85MM
SALES (corp-wide): 121.85MM **Privately Held**
Web: www.buckeyebusiness.com
SIC: **3531** 3955 6512 Construction machinery; Carbon paper and inked ribbons; Nonresidential building operators

(G-4598)
PUCEL ENTERPRISES INC
1440 E 36th St (44114-4117)
PHONE..................................216 881-4604
Robert A Mlakar, *Pr*
Kathleen M Mlakar-cook, *VP*
Ann Marie Mlakar-leissa, *VP*
Anthony F Mlakar, *
Rita T Mlakar, *
EMP: 55 EST: 1949
SQ FT: 105,000
SALES (est): 8.21MM **Privately Held**
Web: www.pucelenterprises.com
SIC: **3499** 3441 3537 3443 Furniture parts, metal; Fabricated structural metal; Industrial trucks and tractors; Fabricated plate work (boiler shop)

(G-4599)
PUCEL ENTERPRISES INC
1401 E 34th St (44114-4136)
PHONE..................................800 336-4986
EMP: 6
SALES (est): 72K **Privately Held**
Web: www.pucelenterprises.com
SIC: **3499** Furniture parts, metal

(G-4600)
PULSAR ECOPRODUCTS LLC
Also Called: Pulsar Products
3615 Superior Ave E Ste 4402a (44114-4138)
PHONE..................................216 861-8800
Pj Kijinski, *Managing Member*
▲ EMP: 13 EST: 1998
SQ FT: 7,500
SALES (est): 6.04MM **Privately Held**
Web: www.pulsarproducts.com
SIC: **5112** 3861 3952 5947 Stationery and office supplies; Photographic equipment and supplies; Lead pencils and art goods; Gift, novelty, and souvenir shop

(G-4601)
PYRAMID PLASTICS INC
9202 Reno Ave (44105-2187)
PHONE..................................216 641-5904
Donald Newman, *Ch Bd*
Mike Dezort, *
James E Newman, *
EMP: 25 EST: 1931
SQ FT: 10,000
SALES (est): 651.59K **Privately Held**
SIC: **3089** Injection molding of plastics

(G-4602)
QCSM LLC
Also Called: Columbia Industries
9335 Mccracken Blvd (44125-2311)
PHONE..................................216 650-8731
EMP: 6 EST: 2013
SALES (est): 219.74K **Privately Held**
Web: www.columbiaind.com
SIC: **3451** 8711 3599 3593 Screw machine products; Mechanical engineering; Machine and other job shop work; Fluid power cylinders, hydraulic or pneumatic

(G-4603)
QUALITOR INC (DH)
127 Public Sq Ste 5300 (44114-1219)
PHONE..................................248 204-8600
Gary Cohen, *CEO*
Scott Gibaratz, *CFO*
▲ EMP: 6 EST: 1999
SQ FT: 2,500
SALES (est): 117.8MM
SALES (corp-wide): 8.03B **Privately Held**
SIC: **3714** 5013 Motor vehicle engines and parts; Motor vehicle supplies and new parts
HQ: Qualitor Acquisition Inc
127 Public Sq Ste 5110
Cleveland OH

(PA)=Parent Co (HQ)=Headquarters
✪ = New Business established in last 2 years

Cleveland - Cuyahoga County (G-4604)

(G-4604)
QUALITY BORATE CO LLC
3690 Orange Pl Ste 495 (44122-4465)
PHONE................................216 896-1949
▲ **EMP:** 10 **EST:** 2000
SQ FT: 3,500
SALES (est): 1.73MM **Privately Held**
Web: www.qualityborate.com
SIC: 5169 2879 Chemicals and allied products, nec; Agricultural chemicals, nec

(G-4605)
QUALITY CUTTER GRINDING CO
15501 Commerce Park Dr (44142-2014)
PHONE................................216 362-6444
Carl Scafuro, *Pr*
Debbie Ebert, *Sec*
EMP: 21 **EST:** 1978
SQ FT: 13,500
SALES (est): 1.23MM **Privately Held**
Web: www.qualitycuttergrinding.com
SIC: 3545 7000 Cutting tools for machine tools; Knife, saw and tool sharpening and repair

(G-4606)
QUALITY INDUSTRIES INC
3716 Clark Ave (44109-1142)
PHONE................................216 961-5566
Jerry Kaplan, *Pr*
Jim Kaplan, *VP*
EMP: 6 **EST:** 1945
SQ FT: 12,000
SALES (est): 506.02K **Privately Held**
Web: www.qualityindustries.com
SIC: 3599 Machine shop, jobbing and repair

(G-4607)
QUALITY PLATING CO
1443 E 40th St (44103-1182)
P.O. Box 603247 (44103-0247)
PHONE................................216 361-0151
Daniel Miller, *Pr*
▲ **EMP:** 9 **EST:** 1944
SQ FT: 11,895
SALES (est): 981.14K **Privately Held**
Web: www.qualityplatinginc.com
SIC: 3471 8711 Chromium plating of metals or formed products; Engineering services

(G-4608)
QUALITY SOLUTIONS INC
Also Called: QUALITY SOLUTIONS INC
P.O. Box 40147 (44140-0147)
PHONE................................440 933-9946
Francis P Toolan Junior, *Brnch Mgr*
EMP: 27
Web: www.firebrandtech.com
SIC: 2741 8742 8732 Business service newsletters: publishing and printing; Management consulting services; Market analysis or research
HQ: Quality Solutions, Inc.
  44 Merrimac St Ste 22
  Newburyport MA 01950

(G-4609)
QUALITY STAMPING PRODUCTS CO (PA)
5322 Bragg Rd (44127-1283)
PHONE................................216 441-2700
Alan Nayman, *Pr*
Kenneth Nayman, *VP*
Dorothy Nayman, *Sec*
Nan Nayman, *VP*
EMP: 16 **EST:** 1951
SQ FT: 20,000
SALES (est): 1.69MM
SALES (corp-wide): 1.69MM **Privately Held**
SIC: 3469 Stamping metal for the trade

(G-4610)
QUES INDUSTRIES INC
5420 W 140th St (44142-1703)
PHONE................................216 267-8989
Quentin Meng, *Pr*
▲ **EMP:** 16 **EST:** 1983
SQ FT: 50,000
SALES (est): 4.62MM **Privately Held**
Web: www.quesinc.com
SIC: 2899 Water treating compounds

(G-4611)
R & T ESTATE LLC
Also Called: Gray Area Bistro Ultra Lounge
17001 Euclid Ave (44112-1431)
PHONE................................216 862-0822
Willis Tabron, *Managing Member*
EMP: 15 **EST:** 2018
SQ FT: 2,600
SALES (est): 900K **Privately Held**
SIC: 5812 2084 Cafe; Wines

(G-4612)
R E MAY INC
1401 E 24th St (44114-2176)
PHONE................................216 771-6332
Betty D Pangrace, *Pr*
John E Pangrace, *VP*
EMP: 22 **EST:** 1973
SQ FT: 5,000
SALES (est): 446.43K **Privately Held**
Web: www.brandingsuite.com
SIC: 2796 Lithographic plates, positives or negatives

(G-4613)
RAM SENSORS INC
875 Canterbury Rd (44145-1488)
PHONE................................440 835-3540
Ron Miller, *Pr*
Caroline J Miller, *
EMP: 25 **EST:** 1981
SQ FT: 16,000
SALES (est): 2.5MM **Privately Held**
Web: www.ramsensors.com
SIC: 3823 3315 Temperature instruments: industrial process type; Wire, steel: insulated or armored

(G-4614)
RANDYS PICKLES LLC
2203 Superior Ave E (44114-4222)
PHONE................................440 864-6611
Andrew Rainey, *CEO*
EMP: 8 **EST:** 2013
SQ FT: 3,000
SALES (est): 258.83K **Privately Held**
Web: www.randysartisanal.com
SIC: 2035 Pickles, sauces, and salad dressings

(G-4615)
RANGE IMPACT INC (PA)
200 Park Ave Ste 400 (44122-4297)
PHONE................................216 304-6556
Michael Cavanaugh, *CEO*
Edward Feighan, *Ch Bd*
Richard Mckilligan, *CFO*
Brandon Zipp, *CSO*
EMP: 7 **EST:** 2007
SALES (est): 19.35MM
SALES (corp-wide): 19.35MM **Publicly Held**
Web: www.malachiteinnovations.com
SIC: 2833 8731 Medicinals and botanicals; Commercial physical research

(G-4616)
RAY FOGG CONSTRUCTION INC
981 Keynote Cir Ste 15 (44131-1842)
PHONE................................216 351-7976
Raymon B Fogg Senior, *Pr*
Richard Neiden, *VP*
Michael J Merle, *Ex VP*
Virginia Fogg, *Sec*
Raymon B Fogg Junior, *Ex VP*
EMP: 23 **EST:** 1980
SQ FT: 5,760
SALES (est): 604.26K **Privately Held**
Web: www.fogg.com
SIC: 2821 Plastics materials and resins

(G-4617)
RAYS SAUSAGE INC
3146 E 123rd St (44120-3179)
PHONE................................216 921-8782
Renee Cash, *Pr*
Raymond Cash, *VP*
Leslie Lester, *CFO*
EMP: 8 **EST:** 1952
SQ FT: 660
SALES (est): 821.04K **Privately Held**
Web: www.rayssausage.com
SIC: 2013 Sausages, from purchased meat

(G-4618)
REBIZ LLC
1925 Saint Clair Ave Ne (44114-2028)
PHONE................................844 467-3249
Jumaid Hasan, *Managing Member*
EMP: 50 **EST:** 2014
SALES (est): 5.08MM **Privately Held**
Web: www.rebiz.com
SIC: 7372 7374 Business oriented computer software; Optical scanning data service

(G-4619)
RECOB GREAT LAKES EXPRESS INC
20600 Sheldon Rd (44142-1312)
PHONE................................216 265-7940
Daniel S Recob, *Pr*
EMP: 8 **EST:** 2003
SALES (est): 119.98K **Privately Held**
SIC: 2741 Miscellaneous publishing

(G-4620)
RED SEAL ELECTRIC COMPANY
3835 W 150th St (44111-5891)
PHONE................................216 941-3900
Samuel Stryffeler, *Pr*
Daniel T Stryffeler, *
Judy Stryffeler, *
Jeff Stryffeler, *
▲ **EMP:** 38 **EST:** 1946
SQ FT: 28,000
SALES (est): 7.78MM **Privately Held**
Web: www.redseal.com
SIC: 3644 Insulators and insulation materials, electrical

(G-4621)
RED TIE GROUP INC (PA)
Also Called: Braden-Sutphin Ink Company
4521 Industrial Pkwy (44135-4541)
▲ **EMP:** 36 **EST:** 1913
SALES (est): 22.29MM
SALES (corp-wide): 22.29MM **Privately Held**
Web: www.bsink.com
SIC: 2893 Printing ink

(G-4622)
REFOCUS HOLDINGS INC
2310 Superior Ave E Ste 210 (44114-4244)
PHONE................................216 751-8384
Greg Shick, *Pr*
EMP: 19 **EST:** 2004
SALES (est): 2.43MM **Privately Held**
Web: www.lightspec.com
SIC: 3674 Light emitting diodes

(G-4623)
RELIABLE PATTERN WORKS INC
590 Golden Oak Pkwy (44146-6502)
PHONE................................440 232-8820
Stephanie Kapcio, *Pr*
Stephanie Kacio, *Sec*
EMP: 7 **EST:** 1913
SQ FT: 7,500
SALES (est): 726.18K **Privately Held**
Web: www.reliablepattern.com
SIC: 3543 Industrial patterns

(G-4624)
RENEGADE BRANDS LLC
3201 Enterprise Pkwy Ste 490 (44122-7330)
PHONE................................216 342-4347
Cathy Horton, *CEO*
EMP: 7 **EST:** 2012
SQ FT: 5,000
SALES (est): 906.53K **Privately Held**
Web: www.renegadebrands.com
SIC: 2841 Soap: granulated, liquid, cake, flaked, or chip

(G-4625)
REPKO MACHINE INC
5081 W 164th St (44142-1599)
PHONE................................216 267-1144
John Palmer Iii, *Pr*
Valentyna Palmer, *Sec*
EMP: 9 **EST:** 1951
SQ FT: 16,000
SALES (est): 867.76K **Privately Held**
Web: www.repko.com
SIC: 3599 Machine shop, jobbing and repair

(G-4626)
REPRO ACQUISITION COMPANY LLC
Also Called: Reprocenter, The
25001 Rockwell Dr (44117-1239)
PHONE................................216 738-3800
▲ **EMP:** 14 **EST:** 1999
SQ FT: 32,000
SALES (est): 785.38K **Privately Held**
Web: www.reprocenter.com
SIC: 2752 7375 2789 Offset printing; Information retrieval services; Bookbinding and related work

(G-4627)
REPUBLIC TECHNOLOGY CORP
200 Public Sq (44114-2316)
PHONE................................216 622-5000
Richard J Hipple, *Pr*
George T Henning, *VP*
Glenn J Moran, *VP*
John C Skurek, *VP*
N David Bleisch, *Sec*
EMP: 11 **EST:** 2000
SALES (est): 190.12K **Privately Held**
SIC: 3312 3448 Sheet or strip, steel, hot-rolled; Prefabricated metal buildings

(G-4628)
RESEARCH ORGANICS LLC
Also Called: Safc Cleveland
4353 E 49th St (44125)
PHONE................................216 883-8025
Rob Sternfeld, *Pr*
Fred Sternfeld, *
▲ **EMP:** 75 **EST:** 1966
SQ FT: 100,000
SALES (est): 24.9MM
SALES (corp-wide): 22.82B **Privately Held**
Web: resorg.lookchem.com

GEOGRAPHIC SECTION

Cleveland - Cuyahoga County (G-4653)

SIC: **2899** 2869 Chemical preparations, nec; Industrial organic chemicals, nec
HQ: Sigma-Aldrich Corporation
3050 Spruce St
Saint Louis MO 63103
314 771-5765

(G-4629)
RESILIENCE FUND III LP (PA)
25101 Chagrin Blvd Ste 350 (44122-5643)
PHONE..................................216 292-0200
David Glickman, *Pt*
Ki Mixon, *Pt*
William Tobin, *Pt*
EMP: **30** EST: 2010
SALES (est): 85.81MM
SALES (corp-wide): 85.81MM **Privately Held**
SIC: **6799** 3567 Investors, nec; Industrial furnaces and ovens

(G-4630)
REVOLUTION MACHINE WORKS INC
5613 Cloverleaf Pkwy (44125-4816)
P.O. Box 1063 (44021-1063)
PHONE..................................706 505-6525
Kris Fugate, *Pr*
EMP: **8** EST: 2018
SALES (est): 1.89MM **Privately Held**
Web: www.revolutionmw.net
SIC: **3599** Machine shop, jobbing and repair

(G-4631)
RFW HOLDINGS INC
Also Called: R F W
1200 Smith Ct (44116-1520)
PHONE..................................440 331-8300
Richard Wilber, *Pr*
EMP: **8** EST: 1984
SALES (est): 718.82K **Privately Held**
Web: www.sobstad.com
SIC: **2394** Sails: made from purchased materials

(G-4632)
RICHARD STEEL COMPANY INC
11110 Avon Ave (44105-4223)
P.O. Box 31516 (44131-0516)
PHONE..................................216 520-6390
Richard Jereb, *Pr*
EMP: **9** EST: 1981
SQ FT: 5,000
SALES (est): 745.09K **Privately Held**
SIC: **3441** Fabricated structural metal

(G-4633)
RICKING HOLDING CO
5800 Grant Ave (44105-5608)
PHONE..................................513 825-3551
Carl Ricking Junior, *Pr*
Joyce Ricking, *
Julie Ricking, *
Carla Droll, *
Preston M Simpson, *
EMP: **33** EST: 1974
SALES (est): 1.26MM **Privately Held**
Web: www.joshen.com
SIC: **5141** 2656 5113 Groceries, general line ; Cups, paper: made from purchased material; Bags, paper and disposable plastic

(G-4634)
RICOH USA INC
Also Called: Nightrider Overnite Copy Svc
5575 Venture Dr Ste A (44130-9304)
PHONE..................................412 281-6700
Bernie Chorba, *Mgr*
EMP: **10**
Web: www.ricoh-usa.com
SIC: **5044** 3579 Photocopy machines; Paper handling machines

HQ: Ricoh Usa, Inc.
300 Egleview Blvd Ste 200
Exton PA 19341
610 296-8000

(G-4635)
RING SNACK LLC
850 Euclid Ave Ste 819 (44114-3306)
PHONE..................................216 334-4356
Adedeji Tiamiyu, *Managing Member*
EMP: **7**
SALES (est): 78.58K **Privately Held**
SIC: **3581** Automatic vending machines

(G-4636)
RITIME INCORPORATED
6363 York Rd Ste 104 (44130-3031)
PHONE..................................330 273-3443
William E Avis, *Pr*
EMP: **9** EST: 1966
SQ FT: 10,000
SALES (est): 124.64K **Privately Held**
SIC: **3599** 3542 Machine shop, jobbing and repair; Machine tools, metal forming type

(G-4637)
RIVERSIDE DRIVES INC
Also Called: Riverside Drives
4509 W 160th St (44135-2627)
P.O. Box 35166 (44135-0166)
PHONE..................................216 362-1211
Bernard Dillemuth, *Pr*
David Dillemuth, *
Kathleen Dillemuth, *
▼ EMP: **28** EST: 1985
SQ FT: 7,500
SALES (est): 15.37MM **Privately Held**
Web: www.riversidedrives.com
SIC: **5063** 3699 Power transmission equipment, electric; Electrical equipment and supplies, nec

(G-4638)
RIVERSIDE MFG ACQUISITION LLC
5344 Bragg Rd (44127-1274)
PHONE..................................585 458-2090
Mike Hill, *Pr*
Gerard Shafer, *
EMP: **16** EST: 1973
SQ FT: 120,000
SALES (est): 751.28K **Privately Held**
SIC: **2789** Binding only: books, pamphlets, magazines, etc.

(G-4639)
RIVERSIDE TRANSPORTATION LLC
9718 Heath Ave (44104-5518)
PHONE..................................440 935-3120
EMP: **7**
SALES (est): 78.58K **Privately Held**
SIC: **3799** Transportation equipment, nec

(G-4640)
RJ CANVAS WORKS INC
3980 Jennings Rd (44109-2860)
PHONE..................................216 337-6099
Jim Fish, *Prin*
EMP: **6** EST: 2010
SALES (est): 126.47K **Privately Held**
SIC: **2211** Canvas

(G-4641)
ROBERTS DEMAND NO 3 CORP
Also Called: Electro-Plating & Fabricating
4008 E 89th St (44105-3919)
P.O. Box 605635 (44105-0635)
PHONE..................................216 641-0660
Les Demand, *Pr*
William Demand, *VP*
Don Paukert, *Stockholder*

EMP: **21** EST: 1939
SQ FT: 13,500
SALES (est): 554.36K **Privately Held**
SIC: **3471** Cleaning and descaling metal products

(G-4642)
ROCKPORT READY MIX INC
Also Called: Rockport Ready Mix
3092 Rockefeller Ave (44115-3612)
PHONE..................................216 432-9465
Ann Nock, *Pr*
EMP: **25** EST: 1993
SALES (est): 4.48MM **Privately Held**
Web: www.rockportreadymix.com
SIC: **3273** Ready-mixed concrete

(G-4643)
ROCKWELL AUTOMATION INC
6680 Beta Dr (44143-2352)
PHONE..................................440 646-7900
EMP: **10**
Web: www.rockwellautomation.com
SIC: **3625** Relays and industrial controls
PA: Rockwell Automation, Inc.
1201 S 2nd St
Milwaukee WI 53204

(G-4644)
ROCKWELL AUTOMATION INC
1 Allen Bradley Dr (44124-6118)
PHONE..................................440 646-5000
Sandra Klosowski, *Brnch Mgr*
EMP: **99**
SQ FT: 156,653
Web: www.rockwellautomation.com
SIC: **3625** Electric controls and control accessories, industrial
PA: Rockwell Automation, Inc.
1201 S 2nd St
Milwaukee WI 53204

(G-4645)
ROECHLING INDUS CLEVELAND LP (DH)
Also Called: Rochling Glastic Composites
4321 Glenridge Rd (44121-2805)
PHONE..................................216 486-0100
Jim Azzarello, *Pt*
◆ EMP: **200** EST: 1988
SQ FT: 127,000
SALES (est): 51.61MM
SALES (corp-wide): 2.7B **Privately Held**
Web: www.roechling.com
SIC: **3089** 2821 3083 3644 Thermoformed finished plastics products, nec; Molding compounds, plastics; Laminated plastics sheets; Noncurrent-carrying wiring devices
HQ: Rochling Industrial Se & Co. Kg
Rochlingstr. 1
Haren (Ems) NI 49733
59347010

(G-4646)
ROL- FAB INC
4949 Johnston Pkwy (44128-3201)
PHONE..................................216 662-2500
Robert Hansen, *Pr*
▼ EMP: **32** EST: 1969
SQ FT: 70,000
SALES (est): 5.06MM **Privately Held**
Web: www.rol-fab.com
SIC: **3441** Building components, structural steel

(G-4647)
ROSE METAL INDUSTRIES LLC
1155 Marquette St (44114-3919)
PHONE..................................216 426-8615
Robert Rose, *Pr*
EMP: **24**

SALES (corp-wide): 4.61MM **Privately Held**
Web: www.rosemetalindustries.com
SIC: **3441** Fabricated structural metal
PA: Rose Metal Industries, Llc
1536 E 43rd St
Cleveland OH 44103
216 881-3355

(G-4648)
ROSE METAL INDUSTRIES LLC (PA)
1536 E 43rd St (44103-2310)
PHONE..................................216 881-3355
Robert B Rose, *Managing Member*
EMP: **11** EST: 1904
SQ FT: 10,000
SALES (est): 4.61MM
SALES (corp-wide): 4.61MM **Privately Held**
Web: www.rosemetalindustries.com
SIC: **3441** 7692 3462 3443 Fabricated structural metal; Welding repair; Iron and steel forgings; Ladles, metal plate

(G-4649)
ROSE PROPERTIES INC
Also Called: Rose Metal Industries
1536 E 43rd St (44103-2310)
PHONE..................................216 881-6000
Robert Rose, *Pr*
EMP: **17** EST: 1952
SQ FT: 10,000
SALES (est): 802.71K **Privately Held**
Web: www.roseironworks.com
SIC: **3441** Fabricated structural metal

(G-4650)
ROSENFELD JEWELRY INC
5668 Mayfield Rd (44124-2916)
PHONE..................................440 446-0099
Henry Rosenfeld, *Pr*
Ruth Rosenfeld, *VP*
Arthur Rosenfeld, *Sec*
EMP: **8** EST: 1967
SQ FT: 1,350
SALES (est): 506.6K **Privately Held**
Web: www.rosenfeldjewelry.com
SIC: **3911** 5944 Jewelry, precious metal; Jewelry stores

(G-4651)
ROSSBOROUGH AUTOMOTIVE CORP
3425 Service Rd (44111-2421)
PHONE..................................216 941-6115
Chet Scholtz, *Prin*
EMP: **11** EST: 2006
SALES (est): 177.1K **Privately Held**
Web: www.src-worldwide.com
SIC: **2899** Fluxes: brazing, soldering, galvanizing, and welding

(G-4652)
ROSSBOROUGH SUPPLY CO
3425 Service Rd (44111-2421)
PHONE..................................216 941-6115
EMP: **12** EST: 2017
SALES (est): 365.17K **Privately Held**
Web: www.src-worldwide.com
SIC: **3369** Machinery castings, exc. die, nonferrous, exc. alum. copper

(G-4653)
ROTOPOLYMERS
26210 Emery Rd Ste 202 (44128-5770)
PHONE..................................216 645-0333
Jose A Gomez Godoy, *Prin*
EMP: **10** EST: 2016
SALES (est): 800.36K **Privately Held**
Web: www.rotopolymers.com

Cleveland - Cuyahoga County (G-4654)

SIC: 2821 Plastics materials and resins

(G-4654)
ROYAL ACME CORPORATION (PA)
Also Called: Adsetting Service
3110 Payne Ave (44114-4504)
PHONE..............................216 241-1477
Theodore D Cutts, Pr
▲ EMP: 22 EST: 1932
SALES (est): 3.1MM
SALES (corp-wide): 3.1MM Privately Held
Web: www.royalacme.com
SIC: 3953 2791 3993 3053 Embossing seals and hand stamps; Typesetting; Signs and advertising specialties; Gaskets; packing and sealing devices

(G-4655)
ROYAL APPLIANCE INTL CO
7005 Cochran Rd (44139-4303)
PHONE..............................440 996-2000
Chris Ourieri, Pr
Andy Klaus, CFO
Pat Sullivan, CEO
EMP: 10 EST: 1953
SALES (est): 5.04MM Privately Held
Web: www.dirtdevil.com
SIC: 3635 Household vacuum cleaners
HQ: Royal Appliance Mfg. Co.
8405 Ibm Dr
Charlotte NC 28262
440 996-2000

(G-4656)
ROYAL CABINET DESIGN CO INC
15800 Commerce Park Dr (44142-2019)
PHONE..............................216 267-5330
Joseph Estephan, Pr
Elie Estephan, VP
Georgette Estephan, Sec
EMP: 12 EST: 1982
SALES (est): 2.93MM Privately Held
Web: www.royalcabinetdesign.com
SIC: 2434 Wood kitchen cabinets

(G-4657)
ROYAL POWDER CORPORATION
4800 Briar Rd (44135-5040)
PHONE..............................216 898-0074
Kirit Patel, Pr
EMP: 6 EST: 2003
SQ FT: 1,300
SALES (est): 950.64K Privately Held
Web: www.royalpowder.com
SIC: 3399 Metal powders, pastes, and flakes

(G-4658)
RP HOSKINS INC
3033 W 44th St (44113-4817)
PHONE..............................216 631-1000
Christopher S Hoskins, Pr
Richard P Hoskins, *
Flo Roll, Finance*
EMP: 22 EST: 1978
SQ FT: 10,000
SALES (est): 1.85MM Privately Held
Web: www.truco-inc.com
SIC: 2899 2952 Waterproofing compounds; Roofing felts, cements, or coatings, nec

(G-4659)
RSB SPINE LLC
2530 Superior Ave E Ste 703 (44114-4200)
P.O. Box 250 (44070-0250)
PHONE..............................216 241-2804
John Redmond, Managing Member
EMP: 9 EST: 2001
SALES (est): 536.48K Privately Held
Web: www.rsbspine.com
SIC: 3841 Surgical instruments and apparatus

(G-4660)
RTI REMMELE ENGINEERING INC
5801 Postal Rd (44181-2184)
P.O. Box 81292 (44181-0292)
PHONE..............................651 635-4179
EMP: 98
SALES (corp-wide): 6.64B Publicly Held
Web: www.howmet.com
SIC: 3569 Gas generators
HQ: Rti Remmele Engineering, Inc.
10 Old Highway 8 Sw
Saint Paul MN 55112
651 635-4100

(G-4661)
RUBBERSET COMPANY
101 W Prospect Ave (44115-1093)
PHONE..............................800 345-4939
EMP: 7 EST: 2011
SALES (est): 232.57K Privately Held
Web: www.besttliebco.com
SIC: 3563 Robots for industrial spraying, painting, etc.

(G-4662)
RUDYS STRUDEL SHOP
Also Called: Rudy's Strudel & Bakery
5580 Ridge Rd (44129-2396)
PHONE..............................440 886-4430
Eugenia Polatajko, Owner
EMP: 6 EST: 1948
SQ FT: 7,900
SALES (est): 358.05K Privately Held
Web: www.rudysstrudel.com
SIC: 2051 2052 Bakery: wholesale or wholesale/retail combined; Cookies and crackers

(G-4663)
RUSH FIXTURE & MILLWORK CO
1978 W 3rd St (44113-2525)
PHONE..............................216 241-9100
Roger Solomon, Pr
EMP: 15 EST: 1999
SALES (est): 933.11K Privately Held
SIC: 2431 Millwork

(G-4664)
S & H INDUSTRIES INC
Also Called: Keysco Tools
5200 Richmond Rd (44146-1387)
PHONE..............................216 831-0550
John Turk, Pr
Steven Perney, *
Edward Clancy, *
▲ EMP: 24 EST: 1952
SQ FT: 23,000
SALES (est): 226.41K
SALES (corp-wide): 2.72MM Privately Held
Web: www.shindustries.com
SIC: 3423 Mechanics' hand tools
PA: S & H Industries Inc
5200 Richmond Rd
Bedford OH 44146
216 831-0550

(G-4665)
S & H INDUSTRIES INC
14577 Lorain Ave (44111-3156)
PHONE..............................216 831-0550
Sharon M Conrad, Prin
▲ EMP: 9 EST: 2010
SALES (est): 446.23K Privately Held
Web: www.shindustries.com
SIC: 3999 Manufacturing industries, nec

(G-4666)
S A LANGMACK COMPANY
Also Called: Niagara Custombilt Mfg
13400 Glenside Rd (44110-3528)
PHONE..............................216 541-0500
Chris Langmack, Pr
John C Langmack, Prin
Clark B Langmack, VP
Virginia Langmack, Sec
EMP: 16 EST: 1934
SQ FT: 25,000
SALES (est): 881.83K Privately Held
SIC: 3565 3569 Bottle washing and sterilizing machines; Filters, general line: industrial

(G-4667)
S R P M INC
30300 Bruce Industrial Pkwy Ste B (44139-3921)
PHONE..............................440 248-8440
Mark Steinmeyer, Pr
Craig Steinmeyer, *
EMP: 30 EST: 1953
SQ FT: 15,000
SALES (est): 3.96MM Privately Held
Web: www.srpm.com
SIC: 3599 Machine shop, jobbing and repair

(G-4668)
SAINT CTHERINES METALWORKS INC
1985 W 68th St (44102-3906)
PHONE..............................216 409-0576
Van Peplin, Pr
EMP: 9 EST: 2001
SQ FT: 20,000
SALES (est): 713.4K Privately Held
Web: www.scmetalworking.com
SIC: 2842 8661 Metal polish; Religious organizations

(G-4669)
SAINT-GOBAIN HYCOMP LLC
17960 Englewood Dr (44130-3438)
PHONE..............................440 234-2002
EMP: 120 EST: 1992
SQ FT: 48,600
SALES (est): 21.39MM
SALES (corp-wide): 397.78MM Privately Held
Web: www.omniseal-solutions.com
SIC: 3089 Injection molding of plastics
HQ: Saint Gobain Performance Plastics France
34 Rue Du Moulin Des Aulnaies
Charny Oree De Puisaye 89120
386637878

(G-4670)
SAMSEL ROPE & MARINE SUPPLY CO (PA)
Also Called: Samsel Supply Company
1285 Old River Rd Uppr (44113-1279)
PHONE..............................216 241-0333
Kathleen A Petrick, Pr
F Michael Samsel, *
Wentworth J Marshall, *
Scott Balser, *
Grace F Wilcox, *
▲ EMP: 32 EST: 1958
SQ FT: 100,000
SALES (est): 8.4MM
SALES (corp-wide): 8.4MM Privately Held
Web: www.samselsupply.com
SIC: 2394 5051 4959 5085 Canvas and related products; Rope, wire (not insulated); Environmental cleanup services; Industrial supplies

(G-4671)
SANDVIK ROCK PROC SLTONS N AME
1214 Marquette St (44114-3920)
PHONE..............................216 431-2600
Leo Matthews, Mgr
EMP: 10
SALES (corp-wide): 11.77B Privately Held
Web: www.rammer.com
SIC: 3531 Construction machinery
HQ: Sandvik Rock Processing Solutions North America, Llc
3900 Kelley Ave
Cleveland OH 44114
216 431-2600

(G-4672)
SANDVIK ROCK PROC SLTONS N AME (HQ)
3900 Kelley Ave (44114-4536)
PHONE..............................216 431-2600
Phil Paranic, Pr
Kathy Toth, CFO
◆ EMP: 47 EST: 1942
SQ FT: 110,000
SALES (est): 22.78MM
SALES (corp-wide): 11.77B Privately Held
Web: www.rammer.com
SIC: 3531 Bituminous batching plants
PA: Sandvik Ab
Hogbovagen 45
Sandviken 811 3
26260000

(G-4673)
SANSEI SHOWA CO LTD
31000 Bainbridge Rd (44139-2227)
PHONE..............................440 248-4440
Michihiko Kobayashi, Pr
Paul Biddlestone, VP
EMP: 27 EST: 1972
SQ FT: 12,500
SALES (est): 3.51MM Privately Held
Web: www.sanseishowa.com
SIC: 3823 Process control instruments
HQ: Sansei Denshi Co., Ltd.
1-11-8, Iwadokita
Komae TKY 201-0

(G-4674)
SCHOOL UNIFORMS AND MORE INC
13721 Lorain Ave (44111-3439)
PHONE..............................216 365-1957
Nadia Habeeb, Prin
EMP: 7 EST: 2008
SALES (est): 190K Privately Held
SIC: 2326 Work uniforms

(G-4675)
SCHUMANN ENTERPRISES INC
Also Called: E.C. Kitzel & Sons
12340 Plaza Dr (44130-1043)
PHONE..............................216 267-6850
Thomas Schumann, Pr
Meredith Schumann, Corporate Secretary*
EMP: 30 EST: 1927
SALES (est): 3.67MM Privately Held
Web: www.kitzel.com
SIC: 3545 3291 Diamond cutting tools for turning, boring, burnishing, etc.; Abrasive wheels and grindstones, not artificial

(G-4676)
SCHWEIZER DIPPLE INC
7227 Division St (44146-5405)
PHONE..............................440 786-8090
Michael J Kelley, Pr
Lynn E Ulrich, *
Peter A Mcgrogan, VP
Roy Page, *
Dennis J Clark, *
EMP: 55 EST: 1932
SQ FT: 27,000
SALES (est): 21.1MM
SALES (corp-wide): 40.19MM Privately Held

GEOGRAPHIC SECTION

Cleveland - Cuyahoga County (G-4698)

Web: www.schweizer-dipple.com
SIC: **1711** 3496 3444 3443 Mechanical contractor; Miscellaneous fabricated wire products; Sheet metalwork; Fabricated plate work (boiler shop)
PA: Kelley Steel Erectors, Inc.
7220 Division St
Cleveland OH 44146
440 232-1573

(G-4677)
SCOTT FETZER COMPANY
Cleveland Wood Products
3881 W 150th St (44111-5806)
PHONE.................................216 252-1190
Ryan Pereira, *Genl Mgr*
EMP: 45
SQ FT: 15,280
SALES (corp-wide): 226 **Privately Held**
Web: www.scottfetzer.com
SIC: **3635** Household vacuum cleaners
PA: The Scott Fetzer Company
28800 Clemens Rd
Westlake OH 44145
440 892-3000

(G-4678)
SCOTT FETZER COMPANY
Adalet
4801 W 150th St (44135-3301)
PHONE.................................216 267-9000
Fred Lemke, *Brnch Mgr*
EMP: 150
SALES (corp-wide): 226 **Privately Held**
Web: www.scottfetzer.com
SIC: **5063** 3469 3357 3613 Wire and cable; Metal stampings, nec; Nonferrous wiredrawing and insulating; Control panels, electric
PA: The Scott Fetzer Company
28800 Clemens Rd
Westlake OH 44145
440 892-3000

(G-4679)
SCOTT FRANCIS ANTIQUE PRINTS
2826 Franklin Blvd (44113-2978)
PHONE.................................216 737-0873
Scott Francis, *Prin*
EMP: 6 EST: 2009
SALES (est): 117.03K **Privately Held**
SIC: **2752** Commercial printing, lithographic

(G-4680)
SCOTTCARE CORPORATION (HQ)
Also Called: Scottcare Crdvscular Solutions
4791 W 150th St (44135-3301)
PHONE.................................216 362-0550
Deepak Malhotra, *Pr*
EMP: 30 EST: 1990
SALES (est): 604.22K
SALES (corp-wide): 226 **Privately Held**
Web: www.scottcare.com
SIC: **3841** Surgical instruments and apparatus
PA: The Scott Fetzer Company
28800 Clemens Rd
Westlake OH 44145
440 892-3000

(G-4681)
SCOVIL HANNA LLC
Also Called: Arrowhead Industries
4545 Johnston Pkwy (44128-2954)
PHONE.................................216 581-1500
▲ EMP: 40 EST: 1974
SALES (est): 16.97MM
SALES (corp-wide): 355.83K **Privately Held**
Web: www.bfc-profile.de

SIC: **3315** Wire and fabricated wire products
HQ: Bfcc U.S. Inc.
742 J A Cochran Byp
Chester SC 29706

(G-4682)
SDG INC
10000 Cedar Ave (44106-2119)
P.O. Box 91023 (44101-3023)
PHONE.................................440 893-0771
W Blair Geho, *Pr*
Robert Geho, *VP*
Hans C Geho, *Sec*
EMP: 13 EST: 1981
SQ FT: 12,000
SALES (est): 1.01MM **Privately Held**
Web: www.sdgpharma.com
SIC: **8733** 2869 Noncommercial research organizations; Industrial organic chemicals, nec

(G-4683)
SDO SPORTS LTD
10250 Brecksville Rd (44141-3342)
PHONE.................................440 546-9998
EMP: 7 EST: 1995
SQ FT: 3,000
SALES (est): 281.27K **Privately Held**
SIC: **2752** Commercial printing, lithographic

(G-4684)
SECURASTOCK LLC
11470 Euclid Ave (44106-3934)
PHONE.................................330 957-5711
Bill Warren, *COO*
EMP: 14 EST: 2016
SALES (est): 3.28MM **Privately Held**
Web: www.securastock.com
SIC: **3581** Automatic vending machines

(G-4685)
SEEMRAY LLC
261 Alpha Park (44143-2225)
PHONE.................................440 536-8705
Bogdan Glushko, *CEO*
EMP: 23 EST: 2017
SALES (est): 1.49MM **Privately Held**
Web: www.seemray.com
SIC: **2431** 1751 5211 Windows and window parts and trim, wood; Window and door installation and erection; Door and window products

(G-4686)
SERVICE STATION EQUIPMENT CO (PA)
Also Called: Sseco Solutions
1294 E 55th St (44103-1029)
PHONE.................................216 431-6100
TOLL FREE: 800
David Chrien, *Pr*
Diana Chrien, *VP*
EMP: 9 EST: 1960
SQ FT: 45,000
SALES (est): 2.6MM
SALES (corp-wide): 2.6MM **Privately Held**
Web: www.ssecosolutions.com
SIC: **5087** 3559 Carwash equipment and supplies; Petroleum refinery equipment

(G-4687)
SHALIX INC
10910 Briggs Rd (44111-5332)
PHONE.................................216 941-3546
David Schultheis, *Pr*
EMP: 10 EST: 1996
SALES (est): 852.51K **Privately Held**
SIC: **3544** Special dies and tools

(G-4688)
SHARP TOOL SERVICE INC
4735 W 150th St Unit H (44135-3352)
PHONE.................................330 273-4144
Richard Schirripa, *CEO*
Jeff Schirripa, *
Laura Schirripa, *.
Rick Schirripa, *Stockholder*
Joe Schirripa, *Stockholder*
EMP: 25 EST: 1985
SQ FT: 22,000
SALES (est): 2.38MM **Privately Held**
Web: www.sharptool-service.com
SIC: **3545** Cutting tools for machine tools

(G-4689)
SHEAR SERVICE INC
Also Called: Shear Service, The
3175 E 81st St (44104-4386)
PHONE.................................216 341-2700
Kim Curtis, *Pr*
EMP: 8 EST: 1972
SALES (est): 495.64K **Privately Held**
SIC: **7389** 3312 Metal slitting and shearing; Blast furnaces and steel mills

(G-4690)
SHEFFIELD BRONZE PAINT CORP
17814 S Waterloo Rd (44119-3295)
P.O. Box 19206 (44119-0206)
PHONE.................................216 481-8330
Mel Hart, *Pr*
EMP: 20 EST: 1925
SQ FT: 100,000
SALES (est): 2.32MM **Privately Held**
Web: www.sheffieldbronze.com
SIC: **2851** Paints and paint additives

(G-4691)
SHELLY COMPANY
4431 W 130th St (44135-3011)
PHONE.................................216 688-0684
EMP: 6
SALES (corp-wide): 32.72B **Privately Held**
Web: www.shellyco.com
SIC: **1422** Crushed and broken limestone
HQ: Shelly Company
80 Park Dr
Thornville OH 43076
740 246-6315

(G-4692)
SHERIDAN WOODWORKS INC
17801 S Miles Rd (44128-4249)
PHONE.................................216 663-9333
Edward Sheridan, *Pr*
EMP: 14 EST: 1985
SQ FT: 16,000
SALES (est): 522.23K **Privately Held**
Web: www.sheridanwoodworks.com
SIC: **2431** 1751 Millwork; Cabinet building and installation

(G-4693)
SHERWIN-WILLIAMS COMPANY (PA)
Also Called: Sherwin-Williams
101 W Prospect Ave Ste 1020 (44115)
PHONE.................................216 566-2000
Heidi Petz, *CEO*
John G Morikis, *
Allen J Mistysyn, *VP Fin*
Mary L Garceau, *Sr VP*
Gregory P Sofish, *Senior Vice President Human Resources*
EMP: 1200 EST: 1866
SALES (est): 22.15B
SALES (corp-wide): 22.15B **Publicly Held**
Web: www.sherwin-williams.com
SIC: **2851** 5231 Paints and allied products; Paint and painting supplies

(G-4694)
SHERWIN-WILLIAMS COMPANY
Also Called: Sherwin-Williams
6012 Orchard Grove Ave (44144-1533)
PHONE.................................216 566-2000
EMP: 6
SALES (corp-wide): 22.15B **Publicly Held**
Web: www.sherwin-williams.com
SIC: **2851** Paints and allied products
PA: The Sherwin-Williams Company
101 W Prospect Ave
Cleveland OH 44115
216 566-2000

(G-4695)
SHERWIN-WILLIAMS MFG CO
101 W Prospect Ave Ste 1020 (44115-1027)
PHONE.................................216 566-2000
Allen J Mistysyn, *VP*
Mary L Garceau, *VP*
Jeffrey J Miklich, *Asst VP*
Stephen J Perisutti, *Asst VP*
Lawrence J Boron, *Asst VP*
EMP: 10 EST: 2017
SALES (est): 9.21MM
SALES (corp-wide): 22.15B **Publicly Held**
Web: www.sherwin-williams.com
SIC: **2851** 5198 Paints and allied products; Paint or varnish thinner
PA: The Sherwin-Williams Company
101 W Prospect Ave
Cleveland OH 44115
216 566-2000

(G-4696)
SHERWN-WLLAMS AUTO FNSHES CORP (HQ)
4440 Warrensville Center Rd (44128-2837)
PHONE.................................216 332-8330
Christopher Connor, *CEO*
Thomas Havlitzel, *
◆ EMP: 30 EST: 1995
SALES (est): 102.84MM
SALES (corp-wide): 22.15B **Publicly Held**
Web: industrial.sherwin-williams.com
SIC: **5231** 2851 Paint; Paints and allied products
PA: The Sherwin-Williams Company
101 W Prospect Ave
Cleveland OH 44115
216 566-2000

(G-4697)
SHERWOOD VALVE LLC
7900 Hub Pkwy (44125-5713)
PHONE.................................216 264-5023
Richard Gravagna, *Brnch Mgr*
EMP: 35
Web: www.sherwoodvalve.com
SIC: **3491** Industrial valves
HQ: Sherwood Valve Llc
100 Business Center Dr # 400
Pittsburgh PA 15205

(G-4698)
SHORELINE MACHINE PRODUCTS CO (PA)
19301 Saint Clair Ave (44117-1087)
PHONE.................................216 481-8033
Robert Arth, *Pr*
Larry Arth, *VP*
John J Ewers, *Prin*
Joseph Frank Tekavic, *Prin*
Richard Kaufman, *Prin*
EMP: 11 EST: 1967
SQ FT: 15,000
SALES (est): 3.06MM
SALES (corp-wide): 3.06MM **Privately Held**
Web: www.shorelineproducts.com

Cleveland - Cuyahoga County (G-4699)

SIC: 3599 Machine shop, jobbing and repair

(G-4699)
SIFCO APPLIED SRFC CNCEPTS LLC (PA)
Also Called: Sifco ASC
5708 E Schaaf Rd (44131-1308)
PHONE..................................216 524-0099
Charles Allen, *Managing Member*
Norman Hay, *
EMP: 34 EST: 2012
SQ FT: 18,000
SALES (est): 10.03MM
SALES (corp-wide): 10.03MM **Privately Held**
Web: www.sifcoasc.com
SIC: 3471 Plating of metals or formed products

(G-4700)
SIFCO INDUSTRIES INC (PA)
Also Called: OIFCO
970 E 64th St (44103)
PHONE..................................216 881-8600
Peter W Knapper, *Pr*
Alayne L Reitman, *Ch Bd*
Thomas R Kubera, *CFO*
◆ EMP: 157 EST: 1916
SQ FT: 280,000
SALES (est): 87.02MM
SALES (corp-wide): 87.02MM **Publicly Held**
Web: www.sifco.com
SIC: 3724 3462 3471 Aircraft engines and engine parts; Aircraft forgings, ferrous; Anodizing (plating) of metals or formed products

(G-4701)
SIGMA-ALDRICH CORPORATION
Research Organics
4353 E 49th St (44125-1003)
P.O. Box 14508 (63178-4508)
PHONE..................................216 206-5424
EMP: 67
SALES (corp-wide): 22.82B **Privately Held**
Web: www.sigmaaldrich.com
SIC: 2899 5169 Chemical preparations, nec; Chemicals and allied products, nec
HQ: Sigma-Aldrich Corporation
3050 Spruce St
Saint Louis MO 63103
314 771-5765

(G-4702)
SIGNATURE SIGN CO INC
1776 E 43rd St (44103-2314)
PHONE..................................216 426-1234
Bruce Farkas, *Pr*
EMP: 15 EST: 1987
SQ FT: 10,000
SALES (est): 358.57K **Privately Held**
Web: www.signaturesigncompany.com
SIC: 1799 2499 Sign installation and maintenance; Signboards, wood

(G-4703)
SINGLETON CORPORATION
3280 W 67th Pl (44102-5241)
PHONE..................................216 651-7800
Raymund Singleton, *Pr*
Eric Singleton, *VP*
Carol Singleton, *Sec*
Laura Singleton, *Treas*
▼ EMP: 17 EST: 1947
SQ FT: 30,000
SALES (est): 4.67MM **Privately Held**
Web: www.singletoncorp.com
SIC: 3559 5169 Anodizing equipment; Anti-corrosion products

(G-4704)
SKF USA INC
Also Called: SKF Machine Tool Services
670 Alpha Dr (44143-2123)
PHONE..................................440 720-0275
David Rodgers, *Brnch Mgr*
EMP: 29
SQ FT: 4,000
SALES (corp-wide): 9.24B **Privately Held**
Web: www.skf.com
SIC: 3053 Gaskets; packing and sealing devices
HQ: Skf Usa Inc.
890 Forty Foot Rd
Lansdale PA 19446
267 436-6000

(G-4705)
SMART BUSINESS NETWORK INC (PA)
Also Called: Smart Business Magazine
835 Sharon Dr Ste 200 (44145-7703)
PHONE..................................440 250-7000
Fred Koury, *CEO*
EMP: 25 EST: 1988
SQ FT: 10,000
SALES (est): 9.06MM **Privately Held**
Web: www.sbnonline.com
SIC: 2711 Newspapers: publishing only, not printed on site

(G-4706)
SMART FORCE LLC
22801 Saint Clair Ave (44117-2524)
PHONE..................................216 481-8100
David J Nangle, *Prin*
EMP: 25 EST: 2003
SALES (est): 970.34K
SALES (corp-wide): 4.19B **Publicly Held**
SIC: 3548 Welding apparatus
PA: Lincoln Electric Holdings, Inc.
22801 St Clair Ave
Cleveland OH 44117
216 481-8100

(G-4707)
SMART SONIC CORPORATION
Also Called: Smart Snic Stencil Clg Systems
837 E 79th St (44103-1807)
PHONE..................................818 610-7900
William C Schreiber, *Pr*
EMP: 8 EST: 1993
SQ FT: 4,400
SALES (est): 1.14MM **Privately Held**
Web: www.smartsonic.com
SIC: 3699 2842 3589 Cleaning equipment, ultrasonic, except medical and dental; Polishes and sanitation goods; Sewage and water treatment equipment

(G-4708)
SMARTSODA HOLDINGS INC (PA)
6095 Parkland Blvd (44124-6139)
PHONE..................................888 998-9668
Lior Shafir, *CEO*
Julia Solooki, *Ch*
Solomon Sol Mayer, *Ofcr*
EMP: 20 EST: 2019
SALES (est): 3.02MM
SALES (corp-wide): 3.02MM **Privately Held**
Web: www.smartsoda.com
SIC: 2099 5963 Syrups; Beverage services, direct sales

(G-4709)
SNAP RITE MANUFACTURING INC
14300 Darley Ave (44110-2172)
PHONE..................................910 897-4080
EMP: 35
SALES (corp-wide): 8.58MM **Privately Held**
Web: www.snaprite.com
SIC: 3585 Air conditioning equipment, complete
PA: Snap Rite Manufacturing, Inc.
232 N Ida St
Coats NC 27521
910 897-4080

(G-4710)
SNOW DRAGON LLC
1441 Chardon Rd (44117-1510)
PHONE..................................440 295-0238
John Allin, *Managing Member*
EMP: 12 EST: 2005
SALES (est): 5.8MM
SALES (corp-wide): 1.66B **Publicly Held**
Web: www.snowdragonmelters.com
SIC: 3531 Snow plow attachments
HQ: Park-Ohio Industries, Inc.
6065 Parkland Blvd
Cleveland OH 44124
440 947-2000

(G-4711)
SNYDER INTL BREWING GROUP LLC (PA)
Also Called: Sibg
1940 E 6th St Ste 200 (44114-2202)
PHONE..................................216 619-7424
Dave Snyder, *Pt*
Christopher Livingston, *
EMP: 25 EST: 1998
SALES (est): 8.76MM
SALES (corp-wide): 8.76MM **Privately Held**
SIC: 2082 Beer (alcoholic beverage)

(G-4712)
SOBEL CORRUGATED CONTAINERS INC
Also Called: Miles Folding Box Co Div
1111 Superior Ave E Ste 1111 (44114-2522)
PHONE..................................216 475-2100
EMP: 200
Web: www.sobelcorr.com
SIC: 2653 Boxes, corrugated: made from purchased materials

(G-4713)
SOLON GLASS CENTER INC
Also Called: Solon Glass Ctr
33001 Station St (44139-2935)
PHONE..................................440 248-5018
Roy Kucia, *Pr*
EMP: 10 EST: 1962
SALES (est): 938.99K **Privately Held**
Web: www.solonglass.com
SIC: 1793 3231 Glass and glazing work; Products of purchased glass

(G-4714)
SONOGAGE INC
26650 Renaissance Pkwy Ste 3 (44128)
PHONE..................................216 464-1119
Alex Dybbs, *Pr*
EMP: 10 EST: 1985
SALES (est): 786.5K **Privately Held**
Web: www.sonogage.com
SIC: 3841 Diagnostic apparatus, medical

(G-4715)
SOUNDWICH INC
17000 Saint Clair Ave (44110-2535)
PHONE..................................216 249-4900
EMP: 20
SALES (corp-wide): 24.57MM **Privately Held**
Web: www.soundwich.com
SIC: 3714 Motor vehicle engines and parts
PA: Soundwich, Inc.
881 Wayside Rd
Cleveland OH 44110
216 486-2666

(G-4716)
SOUNDWICH INC (PA)
881 Wayside Rd (44110-2961)
PHONE..................................216 486-2666
Perry Peck, *CEO*
Kevin Cleary, *
Steve Tomoba, *
Jeff Kristofeld, *
J Patrick Morris, *
EMP: 80 EST: 1988
SQ FT: 46,974
SALES (est): 24.57MM
SALES (corp-wide): 24.57MM **Privately Held**
Web: www.soundwich.com
SIC: 3714 Motor vehicle engines and parts

(G-4717)
SOUTH SHORE FINISHERS INC
1720 Willey Ave (44113-4367)
PHONE..................................216 664-1792
Fran Dickson, *Pr*
Dom Dickson, *VP*
EMP: 6 EST: 1983
SQ FT: 25,000
SALES (est): 508.94K **Privately Held**
Web: www.southshorefinishers.com
SIC: 3471 Plating of metals or formed products

(G-4718)
SP MOUNT PRINTING COMPANY
1306 E 55th St (44103-1302)
PHONE..................................216 881-3316
Scott C Mc Gill, *Pr*
Gerald Mc Gill Senior, *Treas*
Gerald Mcgill Junior, *VP*
EMP: 22 EST: 1867
SQ FT: 45,000
SALES (est): 1.9MM **Privately Held**
Web: www.spmount.com
SIC: 2752 Offset printing

(G-4719)
SPARKS BELTING COMPANY INC
4653 Spring Rd (44131-1078)
PHONE..................................216 398-7774
Andy Balog, *Rgnl Mgr*
EMP: 6
SQ FT: 13,800
SALES (corp-wide): 1.02B **Privately Held**
Web: www.sparksbelting.com
SIC: 3535 Conveyors and conveying equipment
HQ: Sparks Belting Company, Inc.
5005 Kraft Ave Se
Grand Rapids MI 49512

(G-4720)
SPECIALTY HARDWARE INC
2200 Kerwin Rd Apt 710 (44118-3954)
PHONE..................................216 291-1160
Lisa Hayzlett, *Pr*
James Hayzlett, *VP*
◆ EMP: 8 EST: 1996
SALES (est): 616.93K **Privately Held**
SIC: 3429 3999 5072 Luggage hardware; Handles, handbag and luggage; Hardware

(G-4721)
SPOTLIGHT WRITING LLC
3344 Elsmere Rd (44120-3442)
PHONE..................................216 751-6889
Nicholi A Evans, *Prin*
EMP: 6 EST: 2010
SALES (est): 130K **Privately Held**
SIC: 3648 Spotlights

GEOGRAPHIC SECTION
Cleveland - Cuyahoga County (G-4744)

(G-4722)
SPRINGCO METAL COATINGS INC
12500 Elmwood Ave (44111-5910)
PHONE.....................216 941-0020
Paul W Springer, *Pr*
David Starn, *VP*
Jason Conn, *VP*
EMP: 250 **EST:** 1977
SQ FT: 140,000
SALES (est): 24.02MM **Privately Held**
Web: www.springcometalcoating.com
SIC: 3479 3471 Painting of metal products; Plating and polishing

(G-4723)
SRC WORLDWIDE INC (HQ)
3425 Service Rd (44111-2421)
PHONE.....................216 941-6115
Marc Pignataro, *CEO*
Cary Nordan, *Pr*
Brian Kucia, *CFO*
Jonathan Ward, *Sec*
▲ **EMP:** 15 **EST:** 2014
SQ FT: 70,000
SALES (est): 5.31MM **Publicly Held**
Web: www.src-worldwide.com
SIC: 2899 Fluxes: brazing, soldering, galvanizing, and welding
PA: Barings Bdc, Inc.
  300 S Tryon St Ste 2500
  Charlotte NC 28202

(G-4724)
SSR COMMUNITY DEV GROUP LLC
3957 Princeton Blvd (44121-2336)
PHONE.....................216 466-2674
Cedric White, *CEO*
EMP: 6 **EST:** 2010
SALES (est): 51.12K **Privately Held**
SIC: 1721 1521 1761 3271 Painting and paper hanging; General remodeling, single-family houses; Roofing and gutter work; Blocks, concrete: landscape or retaining wall

(G-4725)
STAHL GEAR & MACHINE CO
3901 Hamilton Ave (44114-3831)
PHONE.....................216 431-2820
Herman Bronstein, *Pr*
Joel Bronstein, *
Mike Kramer, *
EMP: 25 **EST:** 1917
SQ FT: 40,000
SALES (est): 1.03MM **Privately Held**
Web: www.stahlgear.com
SIC: 3566 3561 3462 Gears, power transmission, except auto; Pumps and pumping equipment; Iron and steel forgings

(G-4726)
STAINLESS AUTOMATION
1978 W 74th St (44102-2987)
PHONE.....................216 961-4550
Lois Martin, *Owner*
EMP: 7 **EST:** 1984
SQ FT: 3,000
SALES (est): 504.89K **Privately Held**
Web: www.stainlessautomation.com
SIC: 3549 3559 Metalworking machinery, nec ; Vibratory parts handling equipment

(G-4727)
STAMCO INDUSTRIES INC
26650 Lakeland Blvd (44132-2644)
PHONE.....................216 731-9333
William Sopko, *Pr*
◆ **EMP:** 38 **EST:** 1983
SQ FT: 130,000
SALES (est): 9.08MM **Privately Held**
Web: www.stamcoind.com
SIC: 3465 Automotive stampings

(G-4728)
STANDARD MACHINE INC
1952 W 93rd St (44102-2790)
PHONE.....................216 631-4440
Jim Dopoulos, *Pr*
Eli Manos, *
Linda S Kratky, *
Marion R Herrington, *
EMP: 32 **EST:** 1969
SQ FT: 31,000
SALES (est): 4.16MM **Privately Held**
Web: www.standardmachineinc.com
SIC: 3599 Machine shop, jobbing and repair

(G-4729)
STANDARD WELLNESS COMPANY LLC
425 Literary Rd Apt 100 (44113-4506)
PHONE.....................330 931-1037
Marc Deluca, *CEO*
Kyle Ciccarello, *
Emily Simmerly, *
EMP: 180 **EST:** 2017
SALES (est): 15.04MM **Privately Held**
Web: www.standardwellness.com
SIC: 2834 7389 Medicines, capsuled or ampuled; Business Activities at Non-Commercial Site

(G-4730)
STANLEY INDUSTRIES INC
19120 Cranwood Pkwy (44128-4088)
PHONE.....................216 475-4000
Jay Cusick, *Pr*
▼ **EMP:** 24 **EST:** 1946
SQ FT: 20,000
SALES (est): 1.31MM **Privately Held**
Web: www.stanley-industries.com
SIC: 3599 5084 Machine shop, jobbing and repair; Metal refining machinery and equipment

(G-4731)
STATE INDUSTRIAL PRODUCTS CORP (PA)
Also Called: State Chemical Manufacturing
5915 Landerbrook Dr Ste 300 (44124-4039)
PHONE.....................877 747-6986
Harold Uhrman, *Pr*
Robert M San Julian, *
William Barnett, *
Brian Limbert, *
Dan Prugar, *
◆ **EMP:** 300 **EST:** 1911
SQ FT: 240,000
SALES (est): 192.96MM
SALES (corp-wide): 192.96MM **Privately Held**
Web: www.stateindustrial.com
SIC: 2841 5072 2842 2992 Soap: granulated, liquid, cake, flaked, or chip; Bolts, nuts, and screws; Polishes and sanitation goods; Lubricating oils and greases

(G-4732)
STATUS ENTERTAINMENT GROUP LLC
17005 Larchwood Ave (44135-1223)
PHONE.....................216 252-2243
Greg Bonkowski, *CEO*
EMP: 6 **EST:** 2010
SALES (est): 86.04K **Privately Held**
Web: www.prittentertainmentgroup.com
SIC: 7929 2721 Entertainers and entertainment groups; Magazines: publishing only, not printed on site

(G-4733)
STEELTEC PRODUCTS LLC
13000 Saint Clair Ave (44108-2033)
PHONE.....................216 681-1114
John Bargar, *Managing Member*
EMP: 12 **EST:** 2002
SQ FT: 100,000
SALES (est): 997.01K **Privately Held**
Web: www.steeltecproducts.com
SIC: 3441 Fabricated structural metal

(G-4734)
STEIN LLC
2032 Campbell Rd (44105-1059)
P.O. Box 470548 (44147-0548)
PHONE.....................216 883-7444
Dave Bilek, *Brnch Mgr*
EMP: 75
Web: www.steininc.com
SIC: 3399 3549 Iron ore recovery from open hearth slag; Metalworking machinery, nec
HQ: Stein, Llc
  3 Summit Park Dr Ste 425
  Independence OH 44131
  440 526-9301

(G-4735)
STIBER FABRICATING INC
Also Called: Mailposts By Mike
1678 Leonard St (44113-2436)
P.O. Box 347175 (44134-7175)
PHONE.....................216 771-7210
Michael Stiber, *Pr*
Genmarie Stiber, *VP*
EMP: 13 **EST:** 1987
SQ FT: 10,000
SALES (est): 1.13MM **Privately Held**
SIC: 2542 5211 Counters or counter display cases, except wood; Lumber and other building materials

(G-4736)
STITCHGRRL LLC
10252 Berea Rd (44102-2502)
PHONE.....................216 269-4398
Shannon Okey, *Admn*
EMP: 6 **EST:** 2017
SALES (est): 267.77K **Privately Held**
SIC: 2395 Embroidery and art needlework

(G-4737)
STRETCHTAPE INC
3100 Hamilton Ave (44114-3701)
PHONE.....................216 486-9400
Alex F Mc Donald, *CEO*
Harry Mc Donald, *
Vonna Mc Donald, *
▲ **EMP:** 40 **EST:** 1984
SQ FT: 55,000
SALES (est): 9.82MM
SALES (corp-wide): 9.82MM **Privately Held**
Web: www.stretchtape.com
SIC: 2672 2671 3861 Adhesive papers, labels, or tapes: from purchased material; Paper; coated and laminated packaging; Sensitized film, cloth, and paper
PA: Adherex Group
  3100 Hamilton Ave
  Cleveland OH 44114
  201 440-3806

(G-4738)
STRICKER REFINISHING INC
2060 Hamilton Ave (44114-1115)
PHONE.....................216 696-2906
Tom Stricker, *Pr*
Greg Stricker, *Sec*
EMP: 7 **EST:** 1984
SQ FT: 4,000
SALES (est): 920.23K **Privately Held**
Web: www.srcplating.com
SIC: 3471 Electroplating of metals or formed products

(G-4739)
STRICTLY STITCHERY INC
Also Called: In Sttches Ctr For Ltrgcal Art
13801 Shaker Blvd Apt 4a (44120-5628)
PHONE.....................440 543-7128
Brenda Grauer, *Pr*
EMP: 10 **EST:** 1984
SQ FT: 800
SALES (est): 631.01K **Privately Held**
SIC: 3269 5999 Art and ornamental ware, pottery; Religious goods

(G-4740)
STRIPMATIC PRODUCTS INC
5301 Grant Ave Ste 200 (44125-1053)
PHONE.....................216 241-7143
William J Adler Junior, *Pr*
Elizabeth R Adler, *
▲ **EMP:** 29 **EST:** 1946
SQ FT: 42,000
SALES (est): 4.23MM **Privately Held**
Web: www.stripmatic.com
SIC: 3469 3465 3568 3498 Stamping metal for the trade; Automotive stampings; Power transmission equipment, nec; Fabricated pipe and fittings

(G-4741)
STRONG BINDERY INC
13015 Larchmere Blvd (44120-1147)
PHONE.....................216 231-0001
Ellen Strong, *Pr*
EMP: 9 **EST:** 1985
SALES (est): 723.07K **Privately Held**
Web: www.strongbindery.com
SIC: 2789 Binding only: books, pamphlets, magazines, etc.

(G-4742)
STUART-DEAN CO INC
2615 Saint Clair Ave Ne (44114-4014)
PHONE.....................412 765-2752
Aaron Wolk, *Mgr*
EMP: 6
SALES (corp-wide): 65.45MM **Privately Held**
Web: www.stuartdean.com
SIC: 1799 1743 3471 Ornamental metal work ; Terrazzo, tile, marble and mosaic work; Plating and polishing
PA: Stuart-Dean Co. Inc.
  43-50 10th St
  Long Island City NY 11101
  800 322-3180

(G-4743)
STUDGIONSGROUP LLC
10413 Way Ave (44105-2766)
PHONE.....................216 804-1561
EMP: 20 **EST:** 2020
SALES (est): 665.65K **Privately Held**
SIC: 2051 5999 Bakery: wholesale or wholesale/retail combined; Cosmetics

(G-4744)
SUBURBAN PRESS INCORPORATED
3818 Lorain Ave (44113-3785)
PHONE.....................216 961-0766
William C Mueller, *Pr*
Paul R Mueller, *VP*
Ellen Mueller, *Sec*
Richard M Mueller, *VP*
EMP: 20 **EST:** 1955
SALES (est): 2.72MM **Privately Held**
Web: www.suburbanpressinc.com

(PA)=Parent Co (HQ)=Headquarters
✿ = New Business established in last 2 years

Cleveland - Cuyahoga County (G-4745)

SIC: 2752 2791 2789 2759 Offset printing; Typesetting; Bookbinding and related work; Commercial printing, nec

(G-4745)
SUMMERS ACQUISITION CORP (DH)
Also Called: Summers Rubber Company
12555 Berea Rd (44111-1619)
PHONE...................................216 941-7700
Mike Summers, *Pr*
William M Summers, *
Gene Mayo, *
Gwendolyn M Summers, *
Eugene Mayo, *
▲ **EMP:** 26 **EST:** 1949
SQ FT: 63,000
SALES (est): 23.11MM
SALES (corp-wide): 4.71B **Privately Held**
Web: www.summersrubber.com
SIC: 5085 3429 Rubber goods, mechanical; Hardware, nec
HQ: Hampton Rubber Company
1669 W Pembroke Ave
Hampton VA 23661
757 722-9818

(G-4746)
SUN POLISHING CORP
13800 Progress Pkwy Ste E (44133-4354)
PHONE...................................440 237-5525
Frank Schumacher, *Pr*
EMP: 8 **EST:** 1978
SQ FT: 3,160
SALES (est): 500K **Privately Held**
Web: www.sunpolishcorp.com
SIC: 3471 Polishing, metals or formed products

(G-4747)
SUPERIOR FLUX & MFG CO
6615 Parkland Blvd (44139-4345)
PHONE...................................440 349-3000
Yehuda Baskin, *Pr*
Barbara Baskin, *VP Opers*
John Dunn, *Sec*
◆ **EMP:** 13 **EST:** 1932
SQ FT: 16,500
SALES (est): 4.38MM **Privately Held**
Web: www.superiorflux.com
SIC: 2899 Fluxes: brazing, soldering, galvanizing, and welding

(G-4748)
SUPERIOR HOLDING LLC (DH)
3786 Ridge Rd (44144-1127)
PHONE...................................216 651-9400
Thomas Farrel, *Pr*
EMP: 36 **EST:** 2009
SALES (est): 12MM
SALES (corp-wide): 8.44B **Publicly Held**
Web: www.superiorprod.com
SIC: 3494 5085 3492 Valves and pipe fittings, nec; Industrial supplies; Fluid power valves and hose fittings
HQ: Engineered Controls International, Llc
100 Rego Dr
Elon NC 27244

(G-4749)
SUPERIOR PRECISION PRODUCTS
968 E 69th Pl (44103-1760)
PHONE...................................216 881-3696
Zeljko Tokic, *Pr*
EMP: 6 **EST:** 1976
SQ FT: 16,000
SALES (est): 518.4K **Privately Held**
SIC: 3599 Machine shop, jobbing and repair

(G-4750)
SUPERIOR PRINTING INK CO INC
7655 Hub Pkwy Ste 205 (44125-5739)
PHONE...................................216 328-1720
Scott Allen, *Mgr*
EMP: 7
SALES (corp-wide): 54.32MM **Privately Held**
Web: www.superiorink.com
SIC: 2851 2893 Varnishes, nec; Gravure ink
PA: Superior Printing Ink Co Inc
10 York Ave
West Caldwell NJ 07006
201 478-5600

(G-4751)
SUPERIOR PRODUCTS LLC
3786 Ridge Rd (44144-1127)
PHONE...................................216 651-9400
Donald L Mottinger, *Pr*
Tim Giesse, *
Tim Austin *
Gregory K Gens, *
EMP: 65 **EST:** 2009
SQ FT: 75,000
SALES (est): 12MM
SALES (corp-wide): 8.44B **Publicly Held**
Web: www.superiorprod.com
SIC: 3494 5085 3492 Valves and pipe fittings, nec; Industrial fittings; Fluid power valves and hose fittings
HQ: Superior Holding, Llc
3786 Ridge Rd
Cleveland OH 44144
216 651-9400

(G-4752)
SUPERIOR TOOL CORPORATION
Also Called: Superior Tool Company
100 Hayes Dr Ste C (44131-1057)
PHONE...................................216 398-8600
◆ **EMP:** 50
Web: www.superiortool.com
SIC: 3423 Plumbers' hand tools

(G-4753)
SUPERIOR WELD AND FABG CO INC
15002 Woodworth Rd (44110-3310)
PHONE...................................216 249-5122
EMP: 6 **EST:** 1994
SQ FT: 7,000
SALES (est): 774.06K **Privately Held**
Web: www.superiorweldfab.com
SIC: 3442 7692 Metal doors, sash, and trim; Welding repair

(G-4754)
SUPERTRAPP INDUSTRIES INC
Also Called: Supertrapp
4540 W 160th St (44135-2628)
PHONE...................................216 265-8400
Kevin Berger, *Pr*
Theodore Berger, *
Whitney Slaght Iii, *Sec*
James M Smith, *
▲ **EMP:** 83 **EST:** 1988
SQ FT: 210,000
SALES (est): 21.5MM
SALES (corp-wide): 61.53MM **Privately Held**
Web: www.supertrapp.com
SIC: 3714 Mufflers (exhaust), motor vehicle
PA: Dreison International, Inc.
4540 W 160th St
Cleveland OH 44135
216 362-0755

(G-4755)
SUPPLY TECHNOLOGIES LLC (HQ)
Also Called: I L S
6065 Parkland Blvd Ste 1 (44124)
P.O. Box 248199 (44124)
PHONE...................................440 947-2100
Michael Justice, *Managing Member*
Brian Norris, *
◆ **EMP:** 150 **EST:** 1998
SQ FT: 7,000
SALES (est): 61.7MM
SALES (corp-wide): 1.66B **Publicly Held**
Web: www.supplytechnologies.com
SIC: 5085 3452 3469 Fasteners, industrial: nuts, bolts, screws, etc.; Bolts, nuts, rivets, and washers; Stamping metal for the trade
PA: Park-Ohio Holdings Corp.
6065 Parkland Blvd Ste 1
Cleveland OH 44124
440 947-2000

(G-4756)
SURE-FOOT INDUSTRIES CORP
Also Called: Skid Guard
20260 1st Ave (44130-2430)
P.O. Box 707 (44017-0707)
PHONE...................................440 234-4446
Clarence Haas, *Pr*
Raymond Buckley, *
Shirley Haas, *
▲ **EMP:** 32 **EST:** 1979
SQ FT: 7,000
SALES (est): 4.3MM **Privately Held**
Web: www.surefootcorp.com
SIC: 3291 Abrasive products

(G-4757)
SWAGELOK COMPANY
Also Called: Flight Operations
328 Bishop Rd (44143-1446)
PHONE...................................440 442-6611
Bob Parmelee, *Mgr*
EMP: 10
SALES (corp-wide): 881.02MM **Privately Held**
Web: www.aldvalve.com
SIC: 4581 3494 Hangar operation; Valves and pipe fittings, nec
PA: Swagelok Company
29500 Solon Rd
Solon OH 44139
440 248-4600

(G-4758)
SWAGELOK COMPANY
318 Bishop Rd (44143-1446)
PHONE...................................440 473-1050
William Cosgrove, *Mgr*
EMP: 48
SALES (corp-wide): 881.02MM **Privately Held**
Web: www.aldvalve.com
SIC: 3494 Pipe fittings
PA: Swagelok Company
29500 Solon Rd
Solon OH 44139
440 248-4600

(G-4759)
SWAGELOK COMPANY
358 Bishop Rd (44143-1446)
PHONE...................................440 461-7714
Robin Lavigne, *Mgr*
EMP: 39
SALES (corp-wide): 881.02MM **Privately Held**
Web: www.aldvalve.com
SIC: 3599 Machine shop, jobbing and repair
PA: Swagelok Company
29500 Solon Rd
Solon OH 44139
440 248-4600

(G-4760)
SWIGER COIL SYSTEMS LTD
4677 Manufacturing Ave (44135-2673)
PHONE...................................216 362-7500
Michael Aladjem, *Managing Member*
▲ **EMP:** 190 **EST:** 2010
SALES (est): 26.27MM **Privately Held**
Web: www.wabteccorp.com
SIC: 3621 3677 Electric motor and generator parts; Electronic coils and transformers

(G-4761)
SWIMMER PRINTING INC
Also Called: AlphaGraphics
1215 Superior Ave E Ste 110 (44114)
PHONE...................................216 623-1005
Judith Swimmer, *Pr*
Brad Swimmer, *VP*
EMP: 8 **EST:** 1990
SALES (est): 965.54K **Privately Held**
Web: www.alphagraphics.com
SIC: 2752 Commercial printing, lithographic

(G-4762)
SWITCHBACK GROUP INC (HQ)
Also Called: Mpac Switchback
5638 Transportation Blvd (44125)
PHONE...................................216 290-6040
David Shepherd, *Pr*
EMP: 25 **EST:** 2004
SALES (est): 22.1MM
SALES (corp-wide): 142.34MM **Privately Held**
Web: www.switchbackgroup.com
SIC: 3565 Packaging machinery
PA: Mpac Group Plc
Station Estate
Tadcaster LS24
247 642-1100

(G-4763)
SYSTEM SEALS INC (HQ)
9505 Midwest Ave (44125-2421)
PHONE...................................440 735-0200
▲ **EMP:** 22 **EST:** 1995
SQ FT: 10,000
SALES (est): 23.96MM
SALES (corp-wide): 1.01MM **Privately Held**
Web: www.systemseals.com
SIC: 3953 5084 Embossing seals and hand stamps; Hydraulic systems equipment and supplies
PA: System Seals Europe Ltd
Carlton House
Rushden NORTHANTS NN10
132 783-0954

(G-4764)
T & B FOUNDRY COMPANY
2469 E 71st St (44104-1967)
PHONE...................................216 391-4200
Edward Pruc, *Pr*
Ted Pruc, *
EMP: 29 **EST:** 1992
SQ FT: 275,000
SALES (est): 796.8K **Privately Held**
SIC: 3321 3369 3322 Gray iron castings, nec; Nonferrous foundries, nec; Malleable iron foundries

(G-4765)
T D DYNAMICS INC
Also Called: Morgan Litho
4101 Commerce Ave (44103-3507)
PHONE...................................216 881-0800
Dale Fellows, *Pr*
Thomas M Baginski, *VP*
EMP: 10 **EST:** 1961
SQ FT: 19,800
SALES (est): 956.8K **Privately Held**

GEOGRAPHIC SECTION

Cleveland - Cuyahoga County (G-4788)

Web: www.morganlitho.com
SIC: 2752 Offset printing

(G-4766)
TALAN PRODUCTS INC
18800 Cochran Ave (44110-2700)
PHONE..............................216 458-0170
Steve Peplin, *CEO*
Peter Accorti, *
Adam Snyder, *
▲ **EMP:** 60 **EST:** 1986
SQ FT: 100,000
SALES (est): 17.43MM **Privately Held**
Web: www.talanproducts.com
SIC: 3469 Stamping metal for the trade

(G-4767)
TATHAM SCHULZ INCORPORATED
Also Called: Cleveland Black Oxide
11400 Brookpark Rd (44130-1131)
PHONE..............................216 861-4431
David Tatham, *Pr*
Ken Schulz, *
Richard Tatham, *
EMP: 35 **EST:** 1981
SALES (est): 4.88MM **Privately Held**
Web: tatham.openfos.com
SIC: 3471 Electroplating of metals or formed products

(G-4768)
TBC RETAIL GROUP INC
Also Called: Ntb
5370 W 130th St (44142-1801)
PHONE..............................216 267-8040
Jim Zeuli, *Mgr*
EMP: 30
SALES (corp-wide): 1.8B **Privately Held**
Web: jobs.tbccorp.com
SIC: 7534 5531 Tire retreading and repair shops; Automotive tires
HQ: Tbc Retail Group, Inc.
4280 Prof Ctr Dr Ste 400
Palm Beach Gardens FL 33410
561 383-3000

(G-4769)
TEAM PLASTICS INC
3901 W 150th St (44111-5810)
PHONE..............................216 251-8270
EMP: 10 **EST:** 1994
SQ FT: 14,000
SALES (est): 2.21MM **Privately Held**
Web: teamplasticscom.homestead.com
SIC: 3089 Injection molding of plastics

(G-4770)
TEAM WENDY LLC
17000 Saint Clair Ave Bldg 1 (44110-2535)
PHONE..............................216 738-2518
Dan T Moore Iii, *Ch*
Thomas J Prodouz, *Pr*
▲ **EMP:** 60 **EST:** 1997
SQ FT: 60,000
SALES (est): 15.58MM **Privately Held**
Web: www.teamwendy.com
SIC: 3086 Padding, foamed plastics

(G-4771)
TECH INDUSTRIES INC
1313 Washington Ave (44113)
PHONE..............................216 861-7337
Bruno Aldons, *Pr*
James Weiskittel, *VP*
Arnold Lowe, *VP*
EMP: 19 **EST:** 1953
SQ FT: 10,000
SALES (est): 594.39K **Privately Held**
Web: www.tech-ind.com
SIC: 3544 Special dies and tools

(G-4772)
TECH READY MIX INC
5000 Crayton Ave (44104)
P.O. Box 5270 (44101)
PHONE..............................216 361-5000
Janice Knight, *Prin*
Mark F Perkins, *
EMP: 45 **EST:** 2008
SALES (est): 7.3MM **Privately Held**
Web: www.techreadymix.com
SIC: 3273 Ready-mixed concrete

(G-4773)
TECHNICAL MACHINE PRODUCTS INC
5500 Walworth Ave (44102-4431)
P.O. Box 920 (45356-0920)
▲ **EMP:** 10 **EST:** 1978
SALES (est): 2.79MM
SALES (corp-wide): 20.79MM **Privately Held**
SIC: 3559 3542 Rubber working machinery, including tires; Pressing machines
PA: The French Oil Mill Machinery Company
1035 W Greene St
Piqua OH 45356
937 773-3420

(G-4774)
TECHNLOGY INSTALL PARTNERS LLC
Also Called: Security Designs
13701 Enterprise Ave (44135-5113)
PHONE..............................888 586-7040
Erica Temple, *Pr*
Ryan Temple, *
EMP: 40 **EST:** 2014
SALES (est): 3.35MM **Privately Held**
Web: www.technologyinstallpartners.com
SIC: 3699 Security control equipment and systems

(G-4775)
TEMPCRAFT CORPORATION
3960 S Marginal Rd (44114-3835)
PHONE..............................216 391-3885
John Plant, *Ch Bd*
EMP: 763 **EST:** 1960
SQ FT: 100,000
SALES (est): 3.22MM
SALES (corp-wide): 6.64B **Publicly Held**
SIC: 3544 3543 Industrial molds; Industrial patterns
HQ: Howmet Corporation
3850 White Lake Dr
Whitehall MI 49461
231 894-5686

(G-4776)
TEMPEST INC
12750 Berea Rd (44111-1622)
PHONE..............................216 883-6500
Charles Ruebensaal, *Pr*
◆ **EMP:** 25 **EST:** 2000
SQ FT: 65,000
SALES (est): 7.77MM **Privately Held**
Web: www.tempest-eng.com
SIC: 3585 Refrigeration and heating equipment
PA: Great Lakes Management, Inc.
2700 E 40th St Ste 1
Cleveland OH 44115

(G-4777)
TERNION INC (PA)
Also Called: Skyline Trisource Exhibits
7635 Hub Pkwy Ste A (44125-5741)
PHONE..............................216 642-6180
Wendy Ressing-seitz, *Pr*

Kristie Jones-damalas, *Sec*
◆ **EMP:** 23 **EST:** 1989
SQ FT: 23,000
SALES (est): 5.23MM
SALES (corp-wide): 5.23MM **Privately Held**
SIC: 5046 3993 2542 Display equipment, except refrigerated; Signs and advertising specialties; Partitions and fixtures, except wood

(G-4778)
THE APEX PAPER BOX COMPANY (PA)
5601 Walworth Ave (44102-4432)
PHONE..............................216 631-4000
▼ **EMP:** 9 **EST:** 1932
SALES (est): 23.99MM
SALES (corp-wide): 23.99MM **Privately Held**
Web: www.boxit.com
SIC: 2652 2657 Setup paperboard boxes; Folding paperboard boxes

(G-4779)
THE BASIC ALUMINUM CASTINGS CO
1325 E 168th St (44110-2522)
PHONE..............................216 481-5606
EMP: 85 **EST:** 1946
SALES (est): 7.45MM **Privately Held**
Web: www.basicaluminum.com
SIC: 3363 3542 Aluminum die-castings; Die casting machines

(G-4780)
THE BLONDER COMPANY
Also Called: Blonder Home Accents
3950 Prospect Ave E (44115-2710)
PHONE..............................216 431-3560
◆ **EMP:** 245
Web: www.blonderhome.com
SIC: 5198 2679 5719 Wallcoverings; Wallpaper: made from purchased paper; Housewares, nec

(G-4781)
THE CLEVELAND-CLIFFS IRON CO
1100 Superior Ave E Ste 1500 (44114-2530)
PHONE..............................216 694-5700
J A Carrabba, *CEO*
D S Gallagher, *
W R Calfee, *
Laurie Brlas, *
EMP: 176 **EST:** 1847
SQ FT: 40,000
SALES (est): 26.54MM
SALES (corp-wide): 22B **Publicly Held**
Web: www.clevelandcliffs.com
SIC: 1011 Iron ore mining
PA: Cleveland-Cliffs Inc.
200 Public Sq Ste 3300
Cleveland OH 44114
216 694-5700

(G-4782)
THE FISCHER & JIROUCH COMPANY
4821 Superior Ave (44103-1233)
PHONE..............................216 361-3840
Robert Mattei, *Pr*
Salvatore Grandinetti, *Sec*
Carloina Cretoni, *Stockholder*
EMP: 8 **EST:** 1902
SQ FT: 30,000
SALES (est): 922.22K **Privately Held**
Web: www.fischerandjirouch.com
SIC: 3299 Architectural sculptures: gypsum, clay, papier mache, etc.

(G-4783)
THE GARLAND COMPANY INC (HQ)
3800 E 91st St (44105-2197)
PHONE..............................216 641-7500
EMP: 100 **EST:** 1988
SALES (est): 288.45MM
SALES (corp-wide): 715.07MM **Privately Held**
Web: www.garlandco.com
SIC: 2952 2851 Roofing materials; Epoxy coatings
PA: Garland Industries, Inc.
3800 E 91st St
Cleveland OH 44105
216 641-7500

(G-4784)
THE GREAT LAKES TOWING COMPANY (PA)
Also Called: Great Lakes Shipyard
4500 Division Ave (44102-2228)
PHONE..............................216 621-4854
EMP: 73 **EST:** 1899
SALES (est): 21.99MM
SALES (corp-wide): 21.99MM **Privately Held**
Web: www.thegreatlakesgroup.com
SIC: 4492 3731 Tugboat service; Shipbuilding and repairing

(G-4785)
THE HATTENBACH COMPANY
Also Called: Hattenbach
5309 Hamilton Ave (44114-3909)
PHONE..............................216 881-5200
EMP: 85
Web: www.hattenbach.com
SIC: 1711 5078 2541 2434 Refrigeration contractor; Commercial refrigeration equipment; Cabinets, except refrigerated: show, display, etc.: wood; Wood kitchen cabinets

(G-4786)
THE HOLTKAMP ORGAN CO
2909 Meyer Ave (44109-1536)
P.O. Box 609396 (44109-0396)
PHONE..............................216 741-5180
F Christian Holtkamp, *Pr*
Thomas Lucchesi, *Sec*
EMP: 12 **EST:** 1855
SQ FT: 15,700
SALES (est): 884.99K **Privately Held**
Web: www.holtkamporgan.com
SIC: 3931 Pipes, organ

(G-4787)
THE IDEAL BUILDERS SUPPLY & FUEL CO INC (PA)
4720 Brookpark Rd (44134-1014)
PHONE..............................216 741-1600
EMP: 12 **EST:** 1906
SALES (est): 2.01MM
SALES (corp-wide): 2.01MM **Privately Held**
Web: www.idealbuilders.com
SIC: 3271 5032 5211 Concrete block and brick; Brick, except refractory; Brick

(G-4788)
THE KINDT-COLLINS COMPANY LLC
12651 Elmwood Ave (44111-5994)
PHONE..............................216 252-4122
◆ **EMP:** 72
Web: www.kindt-collins.com
SIC: 5085 2999 3363 3364 Industrial supplies; Waxes, petroleum: not produced in petroleum refineries; Aluminum die-castings; Brass and bronze die-castings

Cleveland - Cuyahoga County (G-4789)

GEOGRAPHIC SECTION

(G-4789)
THE NATIONAL TELEPHONE SUPPLY COMPANY
5100 Superior Ave (44103-1284)
PHONE.................................216 361-0221
▼ **EMP:** 50 **EST:** 1910
SALES (est): 5.03MM **Privately Held**
Web: www.nicopress.com
SIC: 3643 Connectors and terminals for electrical devices

(G-4790)
THEB INC
Also Called: A Quick Copy Center
3700 Kelley Ave (44114-4533)
PHONE.................................216 391-4800
Rhonda Garcia, *Pr*
Tom Garcia, *Sec*
EMP: 7 **EST:** 1962
SQ FT: 4,000
SALES (est): 507.66K **Privately Held**
SIC: 2752 Offset printing

(G-4791)
THERMAGON INC
Also Called: Laird Technologies
4707 Detroit Ave (44102-2216)
PHONE.................................216 939-2300
▲ **EMP:** 75
Web: www.thermagon.com
SIC: 2891 Adhesives and sealants

(G-4792)
THERMO SYSTEMS TECHNOLOGY INC
2000 Auburn Dr Ste 200 (44122-4328)
PHONE.................................216 292-8250
Henry A Becker, *Pr*
EMP: 17 **EST:** 1990
SALES (est): 439.99K **Privately Held**
Web: www.thermosys.com
SIC: 3567 3433 Heating units and devices, industrial: electric; Heating equipment, except electric

(G-4793)
THERMOPRENE INC
5718 Transportation Blvd (44125-5343)
P.O. Box 23681 (44023-0681)
PHONE.................................440 543-8660
Richard K Raymond, *Pr*
Craig Mcconnell, *VP*
▲ **EMP:** 10 **EST:** 1997
SALES (est): 2.05MM **Privately Held**
Web: www.thermoprene.com
SIC: 3089 Injection molding of plastics

(G-4794)
THOMPSON ALUMINUM CASTING CO
Also Called: Thompson Castings
5161 Canal Rd (44125-1143)
PHONE.................................216 206-2781
Dave Oberg, *Prin*
▲ **EMP:** 81 **EST:** 1948
SQ FT: 60,000
SALES (est): 10.51MM **Privately Held**
Web: www.thompsoncasting.com
SIC: 3364 3369 3363 3365 Magnesium and magnesium-base alloy die-castings; Magnesium and magnes.-base alloy castings, exc. die-casting; Aluminum die-castings; Aluminum foundries

(G-4795)
THOSE CHRCTERS FROM CLVLAND LL
Also Called: T C F C
1 American Rd (44144-2354)
PHONE.................................216 252-7300
Ed Fructembaum, *Ch*
Thomas Schneider, *VP*
William Meyer, *VP*
Howard Weinshenker, *VP*
Dale A Cable, *Treas*
EMP: 18 **EST:** 1984
SQ FT: 5,000
SALES (est): 343.16K **Privately Held**
SIC: 8999 2771 Art related services; Greeting cards

(G-4796)
TILDEN MINING COMPANY LC (HQ)
200 Public Sq Ste 3300 (44114-2315)
PHONE.................................216 694-5700
Lourenco Goncalves, *Pr*
Terry Fedor, *Ex VP*
Timothy K Flanagan, *CFO*
James Graham, *CLO*
EMP: 580 **EST:** 1995
SALES (est): 369.3MM
SALES (corp-wide): 22B **Publicly Held**
SIC: 1011 Iron ore mining
PA: Cleveland-Cliffs Inc.
 200 Public Sq Ste 3300
 Cleveland OH 44114
 216 694-5700

(G-4797)
TINY FOOTPRINTS DAYCARE LLC
Also Called: Tiny Foot Prnts Child Enrchmen
1367 W 65th St (44102-2109)
PHONE.................................216 938-7306
EMP: 7 **EST:** 2019
SALES (est): 188.29K **Privately Held**
SIC: 2752 Commercial printing, lithographic

(G-4798)
TMS INTERNATIONAL LLC
4300 E 49th St (44125-1004)
PHONE.................................216 441-9702
Keith Kelley, *Prin*
EMP: 27
SIC: 3312 Blast furnaces and steel mills
HQ: Tms International, Llc
 Southside Wrks Bldg 1 3f
 Pittsburgh PA 15203
 412 678-6141

(G-4799)
TODD INDUSTRIES INC
7300 Northfield Rd Ste 1 (44146-6106)
PHONE.................................440 439-2900
Gerald Boehnlein Senior, *Pr*
Gerald Boehnlein Junior, *VP*
Judith A Boehnlein, *
EMP: 45 **EST:** 1972
SQ FT: 45,000
SALES (est): 3.39MM **Privately Held**
Web: www.allmachining.com
SIC: 3549 3599 Metalworking machinery, nec; Machine shop, jobbing and repair

(G-4800)
TOMLINSON INDUSTRIES LLC
4350 Renaissance Pkwy Ste A (44128-5793)
PHONE.................................216 587-3400
▲ **EMP:** 170
SALES (est): 41.71MM
SALES (corp-wide): 43.62MM **Privately Held**
Web: www.tomlinsonind.com
SIC: 3556 Food products machinery
PA: Crown Brands Llc
 799 Central Ave Ste 300
 Highland Park IL 60035
 224 513-2917

(G-4801)
TOOL SYSTEMS INCORPORATED
71 Alpha Park (44143-2202)
PHONE.................................440 461-6363
Joseph Fortunato, *Pr*
Lillian A Fortunato, *Sec*
EMP: 15 **EST:** 1973
SQ FT: 1,300
SALES (est): 962.86K **Privately Held**
Web: www.toolsystemsinc.com
SIC: 5084 3545 Machine tools and accessories; Cutting tools for machine tools

(G-4802)
TOOLBOLD CORPORATION
Leadfree Faucets Division
5330 Commerce Pkwy W (44130-1273)
PHONE.................................440 543-1660
Harry Eisengrein, *Brnch Mgr*
EMP: 10
SALES (corp-wide): 4.43MM **Privately Held**
Web: www.toolbold.com
SIC: 3432 Faucets and spigots, metal and plastic
PA: Toolbold Corporation
 5330 Commerce Pkwy W
 Cleveland OH 44130
 216 676-9840

(G-4803)
TOOLBOLD CORPORATION (PA)
5330 Commerce Pkwy W (44130-1273)
PHONE.................................216 676-9840
Harry Eisengrein, *CEO*
Barbara Blech, *Pr*
EMP: 20 **EST:** 1976
SQ FT: 14,000
SALES (est): 4.43MM
SALES (corp-wide): 4.43MM **Privately Held**
Web: www.toolbold.com
SIC: 3599 Machine shop, jobbing and repair

(G-4804)
TOP KNOTCH PRODUCTS INC
819 Colonel Dr (44109-3768)
PHONE.................................419 543-2266
Lance E Larson, *Pr*
EMP: 8 **EST:** 1990
SQ FT: 5,000
SALES (est): 888.68K **Privately Held**
Web: www.topknotchproducts.com
SIC: 3496 Miscellaneous fabricated wire products

(G-4805)
TOP TOOL & DIE INC
15500 Brookpark Rd (44135-3334)
PHONE.................................216 267-5878
Anton Schiro, *Pr*
Irma Schiro, *Treas*
Bob Schiro, *VP*
EMP: 14 **EST:** 1979
SQ FT: 12,000
SALES (est): 608.53K **Privately Held**
Web: www.toptoolanddie.com
SIC: 3544 Special dies and tools

(G-4806)
TOPPS PRODUCTS INC
3201 E 66th St (44127-1403)
P.O. Box 1632 (39046-1632)
PHONE.................................913 685-2500
▼ **EMP:** 18 **EST:** 1994
SQ FT: 8,500
SALES (est): 2.48MM **Privately Held**
Web: www.toppsproducts.com
SIC: 3069 Roofing, membrane rubber

(G-4807)
TORRMETAL LLC
12125 Bennington Ave (44135-3729)
PHONE.................................216 671-1616
EMP: 20 **EST:** 2021
SALES (est): 980.17K **Privately Held**
Web: www.torrmetal.com
SIC: 3469 3544 Stamping metal for the trade; Special dies, tools, jigs, and fixtures

(G-4808)
TORRMETAL CORPORATION
12125 Bennington Ave (44135-3729)
PHONE.................................216 671-1616
Patrick Sheehan, *Pr*
Lisa M Habe, *Mng Pt*
EMP: 21 **EST:** 1992
SQ FT: 25,000
SALES (est): 4.68MM
SALES (corp-wide): 24.2MM **Privately Held**
Web: www.torrmetal.com
SIC: 3469 3544 Stamping metal for the trade; Special dies, tools, jigs, and fixtures
PA: Interlake Industries, Inc.
 4732 E 355th St
 Willoughby OH 44094
 440 942-0800

(G-4809)
TORTILLERIA LA BAMBA LLC
12119 Bennington Ave (44135)
PHONE.................................216 515-1600
▼ **EMP:** 6 **EST:** 2012
SALES (est): 552.78K **Privately Held**
Web: www.labambagroup.com
SIC: 2099 Tortillas, fresh or refrigerated

(G-4810)
TOTAL PLASTICS RESOURCES LLC
17851 Englewood Dr Ste A (44130-3489)
PHONE.................................440 891-1140
TOLL FREE: 877
David Gabay, *Brnch Mgr*
EMP: 6
SALES (corp-wide): 209.13MM **Privately Held**
Web: www.totalplastics.com
SIC: 3089 5162 Injection molding of plastics; Plastics sheets and rods
HQ: Total Plastics Resources Llc
 2810 N Burdick St Ste A
 Kalamazoo MI 49004
 269 344-0009

(G-4811)
TOTAL TOUCH LLC
250 W Huron Rd Ste 400 (44113-1411)
PHONE.................................800 726-2117
EMP: 29 **EST:** 2018
SALES (est): 442.33K
SALES (corp-wide): 27.19MM **Privately Held**
Web: www.totaltouchpos.com
SIC: 3578 Point-of-sale devices
PA: Electronic Merchant Systems, Llc
 250 W Huron Rd Ste 300
 Cleveland OH 44113
 216 524-0900

(G-4812)
TOWER PRESS DEVELOPMENT
3030 E 63rd St (44127-1364)
PHONE.................................216 241-4069
EMP: 6 **EST:** 2019
SALES (est): 37.59K **Privately Held**
Web: www.towerpressdevelopment.com
SIC: 2741 Miscellaneous publishing

GEOGRAPHIC SECTION
Cleveland - Cuyahoga County (G-4834)

(G-4813)
TRACER SPECIALTIES INC
1842 Columbus Rd (44113-2412)
PHONE.....................216 696-2363
Tejinder Singh, *Pr*
EMP: 8 **EST:** 1969
SQ FT: 7,500
SALES (est): 727.65K **Privately Held**
SIC: 3599 Machine shop, jobbing and repair

(G-4814)
TRANE INC
Also Called: Trane Cleveland
9555 Rockside Rd Ste 350 (44125-6283)
PHONE.....................440 946-7823
EMP: 30
Web: www.trane.com
SIC: 3585 Refrigeration and heating equipment
HQ: Trane Inc.
1 Centennial Ave Ste 101
Piscataway NJ 08854
732 652-7100

(G-4815)
TRANSDIGM INC
Also Called: Aerocontrolex
4223 Monticello Blvd (44121-2814)
PHONE.....................216 291-6025
Cathy Leak, *Prin*
EMP: 19
SALES (corp-wide): 6.58B **Publicly Held**
Web: www.aerocontrolex.com
SIC: 3561 3492 3563 3625 Pumps and pumping equipment; Fluid power valves and hose fittings; Air and gas compressors; Relays and industrial controls
HQ: Transdigm, Inc.
1350 Euclid Ave
Cleveland OH 44115

(G-4816)
TRANSDIGM INC (HQ)
1350 Euclid Ave (44115-1840)
PHONE.....................216 706-2960
W Nicholas Howley, *Ch Bd*
Kevin Stein, *Pr*
Robert S Henderson, *Vice Chairman*
Jorge L Valladares Iii, *COO*
Michael Lisman, *CFO*
EMP: 8 **EST:** 1993
SALES (est): 1.29B
SALES (corp-wide): 6.58B **Publicly Held**
Web: www.aerocontrolex.com
SIC: 3812 Defense systems and equipment
PA: Transdigm Group Incorporated
1301 E 9th St Ste 3000
Cleveland OH 44114
216 706-2960

(G-4817)
TRANSDIGM GROUP INCORPORATED (PA)
Also Called: Transdigm
1301 E 9th St Ste 3000 (44114-1871)
PHONE.....................216 706-2960
Kevin Stein, *Pr*
W Nicholas Howley, *Ex Ch Bd*
Sarah Wynne, *CAO*
Michael Lisman, *Ex VP*
Joel Reiss, *Ex VP*
EMP: 283 **EST:** 1993
SQ FT: 20,100
SALES (est): 6.58B
SALES (corp-wide): 6.58B **Publicly Held**
Web: www.transdigm.com
SIC: 3728 5088 Aircraft parts and equipment, nec; Aircraft equipment and supplies, nec

(G-4818)
TRANZONIC COMPANIES
26301 Curtiss Wright Pkwy Ste 200 (44143)
PHONE.....................440 446-0643
EMP: 233
SALES (corp-wide): 465.45MM **Privately Held**
Web: www.tranzonic.com
SIC: 2211 2326 2842 2273 Scrub cloths; Work garments, except raincoats: waterproof; Sanitation preparations, disinfectants and deodorants; Mats and matting
PA: The Tranzonic Companies
26301 Curtiss Wright Pkwy # 200
Cleveland OH 44143
216 535-4300

(G-4819)
TREC INDUSTRIES INC
4713 Spring Rd (44131-1025)
PHONE.....................216 741-4114
James M Trecokas, *Pr*
Laurel Trecokas, *Sec*
EMP: 19 **EST:** 1979
SQ FT: 10,000
SALES (est): 1.07MM **Privately Held**
Web: www.trecindustries.com
SIC: 3599 Machine shop, jobbing and repair

(G-4820)
TREMONT ELECTRIC INCORPORATED
Also Called: Delaware Company
2112 W 7th St (44113-3622)
PHONE.....................888 214-3137
Aaron Lemieux, *Prin*
Charles Ames, *Pr*
Aaron Lemiuex, *CEO*
Jill Lemiuex, *VP*
Benjamin Brooks, *Dir*
EMP: 9 **EST:** 2007
SALES (est): 855.24K **Privately Held**
Web: www.greennpower.com
SIC: 3621 Motors and generators

(G-4821)
TRI COUNTY CONCRETE INC
Also Called: Tri County Ready Mixed Con Co
10155 Royalton Rd (44133-4426)
P.O. Box 665 (44087-0665)
PHONE.....................330 425-4464
EMP: 11
SQ FT: 23,282
SALES (corp-wide): 3.06MM **Privately Held**
Web: www.tricountyconcretecompany.com
SIC: 3273 Ready-mixed concrete
PA: Tri County Concrete Inc
9423 Darrow Rd
Twinsburg OH 44087
330 425-4464

(G-4822)
TRI-CRAFT INC
17941 Englewood Dr (44130-3488)
PHONE.....................440 826-1050
Kathleen Byrnes, *Pr*
Monica Hargis, *VP*
EMP: 34 **EST:** 1967
SQ FT: 30,000
SALES (est): 4.67MM **Privately Held**
Web: www.tc-tm.com
SIC: 3089 3544 3469 Injection molded finished plastics products, nec; Special dies, tools, jigs, and fixtures; Metal stampings, nec

(G-4823)
TRI-WELD INC
4411 Detroit Ave (44113-2761)
PHONE.....................216 281-6009
George Calogar, *Pr*
Betty Calogar, *Sec*
EMP: 9 **EST:** 1970
SQ FT: 5,800
SALES (est): 329.15K **Privately Held**
Web: www.tri-weld.com
SIC: 7692 Welding repair

(G-4824)
TRIANGLE MACHINE PRODUCTS CO
6055 Hillcrest Dr (44125-4687)
PHONE.....................216 524-5872
Robb Scherler, *Pr*
Raymond Scherler, *
Roy Scherler, *
Michael Rosegger, *
Randy Scherler, *
EMP: 35 **EST:** 1950
SQ FT: 42,000
SALES (est): 3.73MM
SALES (corp-wide): 27.2MM **Privately Held**
Web: www.freewaycorp.com
SIC: 3451 Screw machine products
PA: Freeway Corporation
9301 Allen Dr
Cleveland OH 44125
216 524-9700

(G-4825)
TRIBCO INCORPORATED
18901 Cranwood Pkwy (44128-4041)
P.O. Box 202148 (44120-8119)
PHONE.....................216 486-2000
David N Bortz, *Pr*
EMP: 40 **EST:** 1980
SALES (est): 4.3MM **Privately Held**
Web: www.tribco.com
SIC: 3499 Friction material, made from powdered metal

(G-4826)
TRIBOTECH COMPOSITES INC
7800 Exchange St (44125-3332)
PHONE.....................216 901-1300
Arnold Von, *Pr*
✦ **EMP:** 9 **EST:** 2012
SALES (est): 3.95MM
SALES (corp-wide): 1.01MM **Privately Held**
Web: www.tribotechcomposites.com
SIC: 2821 Plastics materials and resins
HQ: System Seals, Inc.
9505 Midwest Ave
Cleveland OH 44125

(G-4827)
TRICO HOLDING CORPORATION (DH)
127 Public Sq Ste 5110 (44114)
PHONE.....................216 589-0198
EMP: 6 **EST:** 1986
SALES (est): 42.06MM
SALES (corp-wide): 8.03B **Privately Held**
SIC: 3714 Motor vehicle parts and accessories
HQ: Trico Products Corporation
127 Public Sq
Cleveland OH 44114
248 371-1700

(G-4828)
TRICO MACHINE PRODUCTS CORP
5081 Corbin Dr (44128-5413)
PHONE.....................216 662-4194
Julius Szorady Junior, *Pr*
James Szorady, *VP*

Mark Szorady, *Treas*
EMP: 10 **EST:** 1953
SQ FT: 8,000
SALES (est): 953.12K **Privately Held**
Web: www.tricomachine.com
SIC: 3599 Machine and other job shop work

(G-4829)
TRICO PRODUCTS CORPORATION (DH)
Also Called: Trico
127 Public Sq (44114-1217)
PHONE.....................248 371-1700
Patrick James, *Pr*
◆ **EMP:** 150 **EST:** 1917
SALES (est): 161.69MM
SALES (corp-wide): 8.03B **Privately Held**
Web: www.tricoproducts.com
SIC: 8734 3714 3082 8731 Testing laboratories; Windshield wiper systems, motor vehicle; Tubes, unsupported plastics; Commercial physical research
HQ: Ktri Holdings, Inc.
127 Public Sq Ste 5110
Cleveland OH 44114
216 400-9308

(G-4830)
TRIM TOOL & MACHINE INC
3431 Service Rd (44111)
PHONE.....................216 889-1916
Dane Willis, *Pr*
EMP: 20 **EST:** 1998
SALES (est): 2.37MM **Privately Held**
Web: www.trimtoolmachine.com
SIC: 3544 Special dies and tools

(G-4831)
TRINEL INC
5251 W 137th St (44142-1800)
PHONE.....................216 265-9190
Jimmy M Martella, *Pr*
Thomas A Martella, *Asst VP*
Rose Martella, *Sec*
EMP: 15 **EST:** 1986
SQ FT: 22,000
SALES (est): 478.59K **Privately Held**
Web: www.trinelinc.com
SIC: 3599 Grinding castings for the trade

(G-4832)
TRIPLE A BUILDERS INC
540 E 105th St (44108-4301)
PHONE.....................216 249-0327
Cynthia Mumford, *Pr*
EMP: 7 **EST:** 2000
SQ FT: 1,800
SALES (est): 433.13K **Privately Held**
SIC: 0782 1751 1752 1761 Lawn and garden services; Carpentry work; Floor laying and floor work, nec; Roofing, siding, and sheetmetal work

(G-4833)
TRITON DURO WERKS INC
12200 Sprecher Ave (44135-5122)
PHONE.....................216 267-1117
Victor De Leon, *CEO*
EMP: 19 **EST:** 1967
SQ FT: 12,000
SALES (est): 2.74MM **Privately Held**
Web: www.ziptool.com
SIC: 3465 3469 Automotive stampings; Metal stampings, nec

(G-4834)
TRU FORM METAL PRODUCTS INC
12305 Grimsby Ave (44135-4843)
PHONE.....................216 252-3700
Ron Seith, *Pr*
EMP: 8 **EST:** 2001

Cleveland - Cuyahoga County (G-4835)

(G-4835)
TRUCK FAX INC
17700 S Woodland Rd (44120-1767)
PHONE....................216 921-8866
Brian Luntz, *Pr*
Melissa Beesley, *Ex Sec*
◆ **EMP:** 8 **EST:** 1996
SALES (est): 931.59K **Privately Held**
SIC: 3399 7371 3999 Iron, powdered; Computer software development; Atomizers, toiletry

(G-4836)
TUGZ INTERNATIONAL LLC
4500 Division Ave (44102-2228)
PHONE....................216 621-4854
George Sogor, *Pr*
EMP: 15 **EST:** 1001
SALES (est): 1.28MM **Privately Held**
Web: www.thegreatlakesgroup.com
SIC: 3732 7389 Boatbuilding and repairing; Design, commercial and industrial

(G-4837)
TURBINE ENG CMPNENTS TECH CORP
Also Called: Whitcraft Cleveland
23555 Euclid Ave (44117-1703)
PHONE....................216 692-5200
Doug Folsom, *Mgr*
EMP: 340
SALES (corp-wide): 109.67MM **Privately Held**
SIC: 3724 3728 3463 Airfoils, aircraft engine; Aircraft parts and equipment, nec; Nonferrous forgings
PA: Turbine Engine Components Technologies Corporation
1211 Old Albany Rd
Thomasville GA 31792
229 228-2600

(G-4838)
TW MANUFACTURING CO
Also Called: Production Pattern Company
6065 Parkland Blvd (44124-6119)
PHONE....................440 439-3243
David Drunelle, *Manager*
EMP: 38 **EST:** 2008
SALES (est): 1.87MM
SALES (corp-wide): 1.66B **Publicly Held**
Web: www.prodpatt.com
SIC: 3543 3544 Foundry cores; Industrial molds
HQ: Park-Ohio Industries, Inc.
6065 Parkland Blvd
Cleveland OH 44124
440 947-2000

(G-4839)
TYCO FIRE PRODUCTS LP
Also Called: Tyco Fire Protection Products
5565 Venture Dr Ste A (44130-9302)
PHONE....................216 265-0505
EMP: 7
Web: www.tyco-fire.com
SIC: 3569 Sprinkler systems, fire: automatic
HQ: Tyco Fire Products Lp
1467 Elmwood Ave
Cranston RI 02910
215 362-0700

(G-4840)
TYLOK INTERNATIONAL INC
1061 E 260th St (44132-2877)
PHONE....................216 261-7310
Carole Hahl, *Pr*
Sandy Carroll, *
▲ **EMP:** 55 **EST:** 1955
SQ FT: 72,000
SALES (est): 10.71MM **Privately Held**
Web: www.tylok.com
SIC: 3494 3492 3491 Valves and pipe fittings, nec; Hose and tube fittings and assemblies, hydraulic/pneumatic; Pressure valves and regulators, industrial

(G-4841)
TYMEX PLASTICS INC
5300 Harvard Ave (44105-4826)
PHONE....................216 429-8950
Michael Turkovich, *Pr*
EMP: 45 **EST:** 2001
SQ FT: 160,000
SALES (est): 9.36MM **Privately Held**
Web: www.tymexplastics.com
SIC: 3087 Custom compound purchased resins

(G-4842)
U S ALLOY DIE CORP
4007 Brookpark Rd (44134-1131)
PHONE....................216 749-9700
Anthony Corrao Senior, *Pr*
Dyann Corrao, *VP*
Rachelle Corrao, *VP*
Anthony Carrao Junior, *VP*
EMP: 19 **EST:** 1955
SQ FT: 12,000
SALES (est): 1.04MM **Privately Held**
Web: www.usalloydie.com
SIC: 3544 3599 3541 Special dies and tools; Electrical discharge machining (EDM); Machine tools, metal cutting type

(G-4843)
UCI CONTROLS INC (PA) ✪
Also Called: Cleveland Controls
1111 Brookpark Rd (44109-5825)
PHONE....................216 398-0330
Matthew Churchill, *Pr*
Jim Ransbury, *CFO*
EMP: 34 **EST:** 2022
SALES (est): 13.12MM
SALES (corp-wide): 13.12MM **Privately Held**
SIC: 3613 Power switching equipment

(G-4844)
UNION CARBIDE CORPORATION
11709 Madison Ave (44107-5230)
P.O. Box 1153 (44055-0153)
PHONE....................216 529-3784
Al Miller, *Prin*
EMP: 13
SALES (corp-wide): 44.62B **Publicly Held**
Web: www.unioncarbide.com
SIC: 2869 Industrial organic chemicals, nec
HQ: Union Carbide Corporation
7501 State Hwy 185 N
Seadrift TX 77983
361 553-2997

(G-4845)
UNISON UCI INC
Also Called: Hays Cleveland
1111 Brookpark Rd (44109-5825)
▲ **EMP:** 7
Web: www.clevelandcontrols.com
SIC: 3823 Combustion control instruments

(G-4846)
UNITED FINSHG & DIE CUTNG INC
3875 King Ave (44114-3727)
PHONE....................216 881-0239
Laurie Jacbec, *Pr*
Aaron Jacbec, *Admn Execs*
EMP: 15 **EST:** 2004
SALES (est): 701.02K **Privately Held**
Web: www.unitedfdc.com
SIC: 3544 Special dies and tools

(G-4847)
UNITED IGNITION WIRE CORP
15620 Industrial Pkwy (44135-3316)
PHONE....................216 898-1112
Richard L Maxwell, *Pr*
Marie Maxwell, *Sec*
▲ **EMP:** 8 **EST:** 1988
SQ FT: 20,000
SALES (est): 840.7K **Privately Held**
Web: www.unitedmotorproducts.com
SIC: 3694 5521 Ignition apparatus, internal combustion engines; Used car dealers

(G-4848)
UNIVERSAL AUTO FILTER LLC
127 Public Sq Ste 5110 (44114-1313)
PHONE....................216 589-0198
EMP: 7
SALES (est): 4.79MM
SALES (corp-wide): 8.03B **Privately Held**
SIC: 3714 Motor vehicle parts and accessories
HQ: Champion Laboratories, Inc.
200 S 4th St
Albion IL 62806
618 445-6011

(G-4849)
UNIVERSAL GRINDING CORPORATION
1234 West 78th St (44102-1914)
PHONE....................216 631-9410
Donald R Toth, *Pr*
Nancy Toth, *
Kevin Decaire, *
▼ **EMP:** 49 **EST:** 1940
SQ FT: 86,000
SALES (est): 5.17MM **Privately Held**
Web: www.universalgrinding.com
SIC: 3599 Machine shop, jobbing and repair

(G-4850)
UNIVERSAL MANUFACTURING
9900 Clinton Rd (44144-1034)
PHONE....................816 396-0101
EMP: 7 **EST:** 2016
SALES (est): 292.66K **Privately Held**
SIC: 3999 Manufacturing industries, nec

(G-4851)
UNIVERSAL OIL INC
265 Jefferson Ave (44113-2594)
PHONE....................216 771-4300
TOLL FREE: 800
John J Purcell, *Pr*
EMP: 30 **EST:** 1875
SQ FT: 25,000
SALES (est): 22.78MM **Privately Held**
Web: www.universaloil.com
SIC: 5171 2992 Petroleum bulk stations; Lubricating oils

(G-4852)
UNIVERSAL STEEL COMPANY
6600 Grant Ave (44105-5692)
PHONE....................216 883-4972
David P Miller, *Ch*
Richard W Williams, *Pr*
Stephen F Ruscher, *VP*
▲ **EMP:** 100 **EST:** 1925
SQ FT: 200,000
SALES (est): 25.69MM
SALES (corp-wide): 79.1MM **Privately Held**
Web: www.univsteel.com
SIC: 3444 5051 Sheet metalwork; Steel
PA: Columbia National Group, Inc.
6600 Grant Ave
Cleveland OH 44105
216 883-4972

(G-4853)
UPRIGHT STEEL LLC
1335 E 171st St (44110-2525)
PHONE....................216 923-0852
EMP: 20 **EST:** 2010
SALES (est): 2.29MM **Privately Held**
Web: www.uprightsteelfab.com
SIC: 3441 3446 1791 Fabricated structural metal; Stairs, fire escapes, balconies, railings, and ladders; Concrete reinforcement, placing of

(G-4854)
UPRIGHT STEEL FABRICATORS LLC
1335 E 171st St (44110-2525)
PHONE....................216 923-0852
EMP: 12 **EST:** 2018
SALES (est): 942.38K **Privately Held**
Web: www.uprightsteelfab.com
SIC: 3441 Fabricated structural metal

(G-4855)
URETHANE POLYMERS INTL (HQ)
Also Called: U P I
3800 E 91st St (44105-2103)
PHONE....................216 430-3655
Kevin Mcnulty, *CEO*
Charles Ripepi, *CFO*
EMP: 10 **EST:** 1989
SQ FT: 72,000
SALES (est): 11.19MM
SALES (corp-wide): 11.19MM **Privately Held**
Web: www.urethanepolymers.com
SIC: 2899 2851 2821 Waterproofing compounds; Paints and allied products; Plastics materials and resins
PA: O S L, Inc
1308 E Wakeham Ave
Santa Ana CA 92705
714 505-4923

(G-4856)
US COTTON LLC
15501 Industrial Pkwy (44135-3313)
PHONE....................216 676-6400
John Levinsky, *Mgr*
EMP: 93
SALES (corp-wide): 1.44B **Privately Held**
Web: www.uscotton.com
SIC: 2844 2241 Perfumes, cosmetics and other toilet preparations; Cotton narrow fabrics
HQ: U.S. Cotton, Llc
531 Cotton Blossom Cir
Gastonia NC 28054
216 676-6400

(G-4857)
USB CORPORATION
26111 Miles Rd (44128-5933)
P.O. Box 68 (92018-0068)
PHONE....................216 765-5000
Michael Lachman, *Pr*
Fred Leffler, *Marketing**
Frank Maenpa, *Quality Vice President**
Kathy Fortney, *
EMP: 91 **EST:** 1998
SQ FT: 60,000
SALES (est): 23.46MM
SALES (corp-wide): 44.91B **Publicly Held**
Web: usbcorporation.lookchem.com
SIC: 2833 2834 2835 Medicinals and botanicals; Pharmaceutical preparations; Radioactive diagnostic substances

GEOGRAPHIC SECTION

Cleveland - Cuyahoga County (G-4880)

HQ: Affymetrix, Inc.
3380 Central Expy
Santa Clara CA 95051

(G-4858)
UTILITY WIRE PRODUCTS INC
3302 E 87th St (44127-1849)
PHONE......................216 441-2180
Ronald F Anzells, *Pr*
Donald J Anzells, *Treas*
Marcia Anzells, *Sec*
EMP: 14 **EST:** 1953
SQ FT: 48,000
SALES (est): 515.25K **Privately Held**
Web: www.utilitywire.com
SIC: 3496 Woven wire products, nec

(G-4859)
VACONO AMERICA LLC
1163 E 40th St Ste 301 (44114-3869)
PHONE......................216 938-7428
▲ **EMP:** 29 **EST:** 2011
SALES (est): 2.2MM **Privately Held**
Web: www.vacono.com
SIC: 3479 Aluminum coating of metal products

(G-4860)
VARBROS LLC (PA)
16025 Brookpark Rd (44142-1612)
PHONE......................216 267-5200
Rick Vargo, *
Dave Gido, *
Ernest R Vargo Junior, *Treas*
Joseph G Corsaro, *
▼ **EMP:** 90 **EST:** 1951
SQ FT: 113,000
SALES (est): 22.16MM
SALES (corp-wide): 22.16MM **Privately Held**
Web: www.varbroscorp.com
SIC: 3469 3714 Stamping metal for the trade ; Motor vehicle parts and accessories

(G-4861)
VARMLAND INC
Also Called: All Cstom Fabricators Erectors
1200 Brookpark Rd (44109-5828)
PHONE......................216 741-1510
Erik V Schneider, *Pr*
Karl M Schneider, *VP*
Deborah Schneider, *Sec*
EMP: 12 **EST:** 1943
SQ FT: 20,000
SALES (est): 1.4MM **Privately Held**
SIC: 3444 Sheet metal specialties, not stamped

(G-4862)
VE GLOBAL VENDING INC
Also Called: Vegv
8700 Brookpark Rd (44129-6810)
PHONE......................216 785-2611
Aviel Dafna, *Pr*
Nate Stansell, *COO*
▲ **EMP:** 10 **EST:** 2003
SALES (est): 219.44K **Privately Held**
Web: www.vesolutions.co
SIC: 3581 Automatic vending machines

(G-4863)
VECTOR MECHANICAL LLC
10917 Dale Ave (44111-4846)
PHONE......................216 337-4042
Ildiko Sarai, *Managing Member*
EMP: 8 **EST:** 2017
SALES (est): 1MM **Privately Held**
SIC: 1711 1799 3564 Mechanical contractor; Dock equipment installation, industrial; Ventilating fans: industrial or commercial

(G-4864)
VERTIV GROUP CORPORATION
5900 Landerbrook Dr Ste 300 (44124-4020)
PHONE......................440 460-3600
Steven M Barto, *Brnch Mgr*
EMP: 6
SALES (corp-wide): 6.86B **Publicly Held**
Web: www.vertiv.com
SIC: 3661 1731 Telephone and telegraph apparatus; Communications specialization
HQ: Vertiv Group Corporation
505 N Cleveland Ave
Westerville OH 43082
614 888-0246

(G-4865)
VETERANS STEEL INC
900 E 69th St (44103-1736)
PHONE......................216 938-7476
Karen Black, *Pr*
EMP: 13 **EST:** 2014
SALES (est): 779.51K **Privately Held**
SIC: 3449 Bars, concrete reinforcing: fabricated steel

(G-4866)
VGS INC
2239 E 55th St (44103-4451)
PHONE......................216 431-7800
Robert Comben Junior, *Pr*
Donald E Carlton, *
Mick Latkovich, *
James Huduk, *
EMP: 200 **EST:** 1998
SQ FT: 36,000
SALES (est): 3.41MM **Privately Held**
Web: www.vgsjob.org
SIC: 8331 2326 2311 Job training and related services; Work uniforms; Military uniforms, men's and youths': purchased materials

(G-4867)
VGU INDUSTRIES INC
Also Called: Vinyl Graphics
4747 Manufacturing Ave (44135-2639)
PHONE......................216 676-9093
Brian Stransky, *Pr*
▲ **EMP:** 35 **EST:** 1973
SQ FT: 40,000
SALES (est): 4.63MM **Privately Held**
Web: www.mosoundmusic.com
SIC: 3993 2759 2396 Signs, not made in custom sign painting shops; Screen printing ; Automotive and apparel trimmings

(G-4868)
VIBRANTZ CORPORATION
Ferro Crmic Glaze Prcln Enl Di
4150 E 56th St (44105-4890)
P.O. Box 6550 (44101-1550)
PHONE......................216 875-6213
John V Belcastro, *Prin*
EMP: 250
SALES (corp-wide): 1.88B **Privately Held**
Web: www.vibrantz.com
SIC: 2899 2851 3264 2893 Frit; Lacquers, varnishes, enamels, and other coatings; Porcelain electrical supplies; Printing ink
HQ: Vibrantz Corporation
6060 Parkland Blvd # 250
Mayfield Heights OH 44124
216 875-5600

(G-4869)
VIBRANTZ CORPORATION
4150 E 56th St (44105-4890)
P.O. Box 519 (15301-0519)
PHONE......................724 207-2152
David Klimas, *Mgr*

EMP: 36
SALES (corp-wide): 1.88B **Privately Held**
Web: www.vibrantz.com
SIC: 2816 Color pigments
HQ: Vibrantz Corporation
6060 Parkland Blvd # 250
Mayfield Heights OH 44124
216 875-5600

(G-4870)
VIBRANTZ CORPORATION
6060 Parkland Blvd Ste 250 (44124-4225)
PHONE......................442 224-6100
Mike Steele, *Mgr*
EMP: 10
SALES (corp-wide): 1.88B **Privately Held**
Web: www.vibrantz.com
SIC: 2819 Industrial inorganic chemicals, nec
HQ: Vibrantz Corporation
6060 Parkland Blvd # 250
Mayfield Heights OH 44124
216 875-5600

(G-4871)
VIBRANTZ CORPORATION
Also Called: Porcelain Enamels
6060 Parkland Blvd (44124-4225)
PHONE......................216 875-5600
Robert Szabo, *Mgr*
EMP: 25
SALES (corp-wide): 1.88B **Privately Held**
Web: www.vibrantz.com
SIC: 2899 Chemical preparations, nec
HQ: Vibrantz Corporation
6060 Parkland Blvd # 250
Mayfield Heights OH 44124
216 875-5600

(G-4872)
VICS TURNING COINC
16911 Saint Clair Ave (44110-2536)
PHONE......................216 531-5016
John Lamovec, *Pr*
Ann Maher, *Sec*
EMP: 6 **EST:** 1972
SQ FT: 16,500
SALES (est): 612.52K **Privately Held**
Web: www.vicsturning.com
SIC: 3599 Machine shop, jobbing and repair

(G-4873)
VICTORY WHITE METAL COMPANY
Also Called: Vwm Republic Metals
7930 Jones Rd (44105-3908)
P.O. Box 605217 (44105-0217)
PHONE......................216 641-2575
Lynn Carlson, *Mgr*
EMP: 12
SALES (corp-wide): 10.66MM **Privately Held**
Web: www.victorywhitemetal.com
SIC: 5051 3356 Lead; Lead and zinc
PA: The Victory White Metal Company
6100 Roland Ave
Cleveland OH 44127
216 271-1400

(G-4874)
VICTORY WHITE METAL COMPANY (PA)
6100 Roland Ave (44127-1399)
P.O. Box 605187 (44105-0187)
PHONE......................216 271-1400
Alex J Stanwick, *Pr*
Jennifer Sturman, *
▲ **EMP:** 60 **EST:** 1920
SQ FT: 60,000
SALES (est): 10.66MM
SALES (corp-wide): 10.66MM **Privately Held**
Web: www.victorywhitemetal.com

SIC: 5085 3356 Valves and fittings; Solder: wire, bar, acid core, and rosin core

(G-4875)
VICTORY WHITE METAL COMPANY
3027 E 55th St (44127-1275)
P.O. Box 605187 (44105-0187)
PHONE......................216 271-1400
Tim Hess, *Mgr*
EMP: 19
SQ FT: 50,000
SALES (corp-wide): 10.66MM **Privately Held**
Web: www.victorywhitemetal.com
SIC: 3341 4941 4225 Lead smelting and refining (secondary); Water supply; General warehousing and storage
PA: The Victory White Metal Company
6100 Roland Ave
Cleveland OH 44127
216 271-1400

(G-4876)
VINYL MNG LLC DBA VINYLONE
8001 Krueger Ave (44105)
PHONE......................440 261-5799
Stephen Donnelly, *Managing Member*
EMP: 20 **EST:** 2019
SALES (est): 3.31MM **Privately Held**
SIC: 2821 Plastics materials and resins

(G-4877)
VIPER ACQUISITION I INC (DH) ✪
127 Public Sq Ste 5300 (44114-1219)
PHONE......................216 589-0198
Patrick James, *Pr*
Stephen Graham, *CFO*
Edward James, *Ex VP*
Michael Baker, *Corporate Secretary*
EMP: 79 **EST:** 2022
SALES (est): 6.6MM
SALES (corp-wide): 8.03B **Privately Held**
SIC: 3714 Motor vehicle wheels and parts
HQ: Bpi Acquisition Company, Llc
127 Public Sq Ste 5110
Cleveland OH 44114
216 589-0198

(G-4878)
VISI-TRAK WORLDWIDE LLC (PA)
8400 Sweet Valley Dr Ste 406 (44125-4244)
PHONE......................216 524-2363
Jack Vann, *Pr*
EMP: 13 **EST:** 2000
SQ FT: 8,050
SALES (est): 3.01MM
SALES (corp-wide): 3.01MM **Privately Held**
Web: www.visi-trak.com
SIC: 3823 Process control instruments

(G-4879)
VITEX CORPORATION
2960 Broadway Ave (44115-3606)
PHONE......................216 883-0920
Robert Vitek Senior, *Pr*
Robert Vitek Junior, *VP*
Marie Vitek, *Sec*
EMP: 15 **EST:** 1970
SQ FT: 60,000
SALES (est): 2.17MM **Privately Held**
Web: www.vitexcorporation.com
SIC: 2842 Cleaning or polishing preparations, nec

(G-4880)
VOCATIONAL SERVICES INC
2239 E 55th St (44103-4451)
PHONE......................216 431-8085
Robert Comben, *Pr*

(PA)=Parent Co (HQ)=Headquarters
✪ = New Business established in last 2 years

Cleveland - Cuyahoga County (G-4881)

Donald E Carlson, *
EMP: 48 **EST:** 1980
SQ FT: 17,541
SALES (est): 596.34K **Privately Held**
Web: www.vsiserve.org
SIC: 2391 2511 8331 Curtains and draperies; Wood household furniture; Job training and related services

(G-4881)
VOICE PRODUCTS INC
23715 Mercantile Rd Ste A200 (44122)
PHONE.................216 360-0433
EMP: 10 **EST:** 1992
SALES (est): 710K **Privately Held**
Web: www.vproducts.com
SIC: 3669 Smoke detectors

(G-4882)
VOLPE MILLWORK INC
4500 Lee Rd (44128-2963)
PHONE.................216 691-0200
John Volpe, *Pr*
Salvatore Volpe, *Sec*
William Roy Laubscher, *Stockholder*
Mary Ellen Volpe, *Stockholder*
EMP: 7 **EST:** 1988
SQ FT: 9,000
SALES (est): 1.09MM **Privately Held**
Web: www.volpemillworkinc.com
SIC: 1521 2431 General remodeling, single-family houses; Millwork

(G-4883)
VON ROLL USA INC
Also Called: Von Roll Isola
4853 W 130th St (44135-5137)
PHONE.................216 433-7474
Larry Schwener, *Bmch Mgr*
EMP: 72
SALES (corp-wide): 4.22B **Privately Held**
Web: www.vonroll.com
SIC: 3644 Insulators and insulation materials, electrical
HQ: Von Roll Usa, Inc.
200 Von Roll Dr
Schenectady NY 12306
518 344-7100

(G-4884)
VOSS INDUSTRIES LLC (DH)
2168 W 25th St (44113)
PHONE.................216 771-7655
Daniel W Sedor Senior, *Pr*
Mark Schodowski, *
Nicola Antonelli, *
John F Fritskey, *
◆ **EMP:** 101 **EST:** 1957
SQ FT: 240,000
SALES (est): 115.31MM
SALES (corp-wide): 15.78B **Publicly Held**
Web: www.camaerospace.com
SIC: 3429 3469 3369 3499 Clamps and couplings, hose; Machine parts, stamped or pressed metal; Aerospace castings, nonferrous: except aluminum; Strapping, metal
HQ: Consolidated Aerospace Manufacturing, Llc
1425 S Acacia Ave
Fullerton CA 92831
714 989-2797

(G-4885)
VOYALE MINORITY ENTERPRISE LLC
5855 Grant Ave (44105-5607)
PHONE.................216 271-3661
EMP: 20 **EST:** 2004
SQ FT: 116,000
SALES (est): 4.59MM **Privately Held**

Web: www.vmellc.com
SIC: 3499 Metal household articles

(G-4886)
VWM-REPUBLIC INC
Also Called: Republic Metals
7930 Jones Rd (44105-3908)
P.O. Box 605217 (44105-0217)
PHONE.................216 641-2575
EMP: 18 **EST:** 1924
SALES (est): 2.55MM **Privately Held**
Web: www.republicmetals.com
SIC: 2816 Lead pigments: white lead, lead oxides, lead sulfate

(G-4887)
WABTEC CORPORATION
4677 Manufacturing Ave (44135-2637)
PHONE.................216 362-7500
EMP: 10
Web: www.wabteccorp.com
SIC: 3621 3677 Electric motor and generator parts; Electronic coils and transformers
HQ: Wabtec Corporation
30 Isabella St Ste 300
Pittsburgh PA 15212

(G-4888)
WABUSH MNES CLFFS MIN MNGING A
200 Public Sq Ste 3300 (44114-2315)
PHONE.................216 694-5700
John Tuomi, *Managing Member*
Terrance Taridei, *CFO*
EMP: 463 **EST:** 1957
SALES (est): 1.73MM
SALES (corp-wide): 22B **Publicly Held**
SIC: 1011 Iron ore mining
PA: Cleveland-Cliffs Inc.
200 Public Sq Ste 3300
Cleveland OH 44114
216 694-5700

(G-4889)
WACO SCAFFOLDING & EQUIPMENT INC
4545 Spring Rd (44131-1023)
P.O. Box 318028 (44131-8028)
PHONE.................216 749-8900
EMP: 550
SIC: 7359 3446 5082 1799 Equipment rental and leasing, nec; Scaffolds, mobile or stationary: metal; Scaffolding; Scaffolding

(G-4890)
WADE DYNAMICS INC
1411 E 39th St (44114-4120)
PHONE.................216 431-8484
Dennis Wade, *Pr*
Denise Wade, *Treas*
Peter Wade, *VP*
EMP: 9 **EST:** 1963
SQ FT: 6,000
SALES (est): 845.61K **Privately Held**
Web: www.wadedynamics.net
SIC: 3599 Machine shop, jobbing and repair

(G-4891)
WAGNER RUSTPROOFING CO INC
7708 Quincy Ave (44104-2099)
P.O. Box 31156 (44131-0156)
PHONE.................216 361-4930
Gregory Spann, *Pr*
Mark Spann, *VP*
EMP: 24 **EST:** 1919
SQ FT: 15,000
SALES (est): 866.3K **Privately Held**
SIC: 3471 Electroplating of metals or formed products

(G-4892)
WALLSEYE CONCRETE CORP (PA)
Also Called: Avon
26000 Sprague Rd (44138-2743)
P.O. Box 38159 (44138-0159)
PHONE.................440 235-1800
Sandra Hill, *Sec*
Brock Walls, *VP*
EMP: 11 **EST:** 1992
SQ FT: 3,400
SALES (est): 874.59K **Privately Held**
Web: www.westviewconcrete.com
SIC: 3241 Portland cement

(G-4893)
WARREN CASTINGS INC
2934 E 55th St (44127-1207)
PHONE.................216 883-2520
Willie Warren, *Pr*
EMP: 30 **EST:** 1983
SALES (est): 444.82K **Privately Held**
SIC: 3369 Castings, except die-castings, precision

(G-4894)
WARWICK PRODUCTS COMPANY
5350 Tradex Pkwy (44102-5887)
PHONE.................216 334-1200
Matthew Beverstock, *Pr*
Mike Beverstock, *
John Beverstock, *
Kathryn Koz, *
▼ **EMP:** 30 **EST:** 1949
SQ FT: 17,000
SALES (est): 7.66MM **Privately Held**
Web: www.warwickproducts.com
SIC: 3089 Cases, plastics

(G-4895)
WATERLOO INDUSTRIES INC
12487 Plaza Dr (44130-1056)
P.O. Box 30382 (44130-0382)
PHONE.................800 833-8851
EMP: 7 **EST:** 2013
SALES (est): 202.57K **Privately Held**
SIC: 3999 Manufacturing industries, nec

(G-4896)
WATERLOX COATINGS CORPORATION
9808 Meech Ave (44105-4191)
PHONE.................216 641-4877
John Wilson Hawkins, *Pr*
Kellie Hawkins Schaffner, *VP*
▼ **EMP:** 13 **EST:** 1910
SQ FT: 40,000
SALES (est): 2.42MM **Privately Held**
Web: www.waterlox.com
SIC: 2851 Paints: oil or alkyd vehicle or water thinned

(G-4897)
WATTERS MANUFACTURING CO INC
1931 W 47th St (44102-3413)
PHONE.................216 281-8600
Charles D Watters, *Pr*
EMP: 6 **EST:** 1959
SQ FT: 2,500
SALES (est): 469.52K **Privately Held**
SIC: 3451 Screw machine products

(G-4898)
WDI GROUP INC
Also Called: Solid Surfaces Plus
4031 W 150th St (44135)
PHONE.................216 251-5509
EMP: 78 **EST:** 1979
SALES (est): 9MM **Privately Held**
Web: www.rocksolid-surfaces.com

SIC: 2541 Table or counter tops, plastic laminated

(G-4899)
WEDGEWORKS MCH TL BORING INC
3169 E 80th St (44104-4343)
PHONE.................216 441-1200
Bradford Braude, *Pr*
Sherry Braude, *Sec*
EMP: 6 **EST:** 1990
SQ FT: 20,000
SALES (est): 607.27K **Privately Held**
SIC: 3599 Machine shop, jobbing and repair

(G-4900)
WEIDMANN ELECTRICAL TECH INC
Also Called: Weidmann
1300 E 9th St (44114-1501)
P.O. Box 903 (05819-0903)
PHONE.................937 508-2112
Ulrich W Suter, *Ch*
Franziska A Tschudi Sauber, *CEO*
Oliver Kopp, *CFO*
Daniel J Tschudi, *Prin*
▲ **EMP:** 8 **EST:** 1877
SALES (est): 1.01MM **Privately Held**
Web: www.weidmann-electrical.com
SIC: 1731 3826 Electrical work; Analytical instruments

(G-4901)
WEISKOPF INDUSTRIES CORP
54 Alpha Park (44143-2208)
P.O. Box 24390 (44124-0390)
PHONE.................440 442-4400
Edward A Weiskopf, *Pr*
Geoffrey Weiskopf, *Ex VP*
Pam Keidel, *Sec*
EMP: 11 **EST:** 1981
SALES (est): 445.5K **Privately Held**
Web: www.wicwipers.com
SIC: 2211 Tracing cloth, cotton

(G-4902)
WELDED RING PRODUCTS CO (PA)
2180 W 114th St (44102-3582)
PHONE.................216 961-3800
James C Janosek, *Pr*
Gary Horvath, *
▲ **EMP:** 80 **EST:** 1960
SQ FT: 250,000
SALES (est): 8.76MM
SALES (corp-wide): 8.76MM **Privately Held**
Web: www.weldedring.com
SIC: 3724 Aircraft engines and engine parts

(G-4903)
WELDERS SUPPLY INC (HQ)
Also Called: Lake Erie Iron and Metal
2020 Train Ave (44113-4205)
PHONE.................216 241-1696
Richard Osborne, *Pr*
Martin Hathy, *VP*
EMP: 12 **EST:** 1946
SQ FT: 8,000
SALES (est): 11.76MM
SALES (corp-wide): 12.38MM **Privately Held**
SIC: 2813 5084 5999 Oxygen, compressed or liquefied; Welding machinery and equipment; Welding supplies
PA: Osair, Inc.
7001 Center St
Mentor OH 44060
440 974-6500

(G-4904)
WERNER G SMITH INC
1730 Train Ave (44113-4289)
PHONE.................216 861-3676

▼ EMP: 12 EST: 1950
SALES (est): 4.97MM Privately Held
Web: www.wernergsmith.com
SIC: 5088 2869 2077 Marine supplies; Amines, acids, salts, esters; Animal and marine fats and oils

(G-4905)
WEST-CAMP PRESS INC
1538 E 41st St (44103-2337)
PHONE..................................216 426-2660
EMP: 53
SALES (corp-wide): 20.26MM Privately Held
Web: www.westcamppress.com
SIC: 2261 Screen printing of cotton broadwoven fabrics
PA: West-Camp Press, Inc.
    39 Collegeview Rd
    Westerville OH 43081
    614 882-2378

(G-4906)
WHITEROCK PIGMENTS INC
1768 E 25th St (44114-4418)
PHONE..................................216 391-7765
Robert L Meyer, *CEO*
Thomas M Forman, *Ch*
EMP: 10 EST: 2013
SALES (est): 1.19MM Privately Held
SIC: 2816 Titanium dioxide, anatase or rutile (pigments)

(G-4907)
WHITNEY STAINED GL STUDIO INC
5939 Broadway Ave (44127-1718)
PHONE..................................216 348-1616
Peter Billington, *Pr*
Glenn Billington, *VP*
EMP: 9 EST: 1994
SQ FT: 12,000
SALES (est): 480.21K Privately Held
Web: www.whitneystainedglass.com
SIC: 8999 3231 Stained glass art; Stained glass: made from purchased glass

(G-4908)
WILD FIRE SYSTEMS
535 Ransome Rd (44143-1993)
PHONE..................................440 442-8999
James Berilla, *Owner*
EMP: 6 EST: 1975
SALES (est): 374.67K Privately Held
SIC: 3823 7379 Computer interface equipment, for industrial process control; Computer related consulting services

(G-4909)
WILLIAM EXLINE INC
12301 Bennington Ave (44135-3796)
PHONE..................................216 941-0800
William B Exline, *Pr*
August Tischer, *
Michael P Exline, *
EMP: 21 EST: 1929
SQ FT: 35,000
SALES (est): 483.62K Privately Held
Web: www.williamexline.com
SIC: 2782 Passbooks: bank, etc.

(G-4910)
WILLIAMS STEEL RULE DIE CO
1633 E 40th St (44103-2304)
P.O. Box 43518 (44143-0518)
PHONE..................................216 431-3232
Jeff Jazbec, *Pr*
EMP: 16 EST: 1961
SQ FT: 52,000
SALES (est): 507.77K Privately Held
Web: www.valve3.com

SIC: 3544 3953 2675 3993 Paper cutting dies; Embossing seals, corporate and official; Paper die-cutting; Signs and advertising specialties

(G-4911)
WINDSOR TOOL INC
10714 Bellaire Rd (44111-5324)
PHONE..................................216 671-1900
Marc Ravas, *Pr*
EMP: 10 EST: 1946
SQ FT: 5,000
SALES (est): 819.84K Privately Held
SIC: 3544 Special dies and tools

(G-4912)
WIRE PRODUCTS COMPANY INC
Also Called: WIRE PRODUCTS COMPANY, INC.
14700 Industrial Pkwy (44135-4548)
PHONE..................................216 267-0777
EMP: 7
SQ FT: 56,625
SALES (corp-wide): 14.65MM Privately Held
Web: www.wire-products.com
SIC: 3495 3315 3469 Mechanical springs, precision; Hangers (garment), wire; Metal stampings, nec
PA: Wire Products Company, Llc
    14601 Industrial Pkwy
    Cleveland OH 44135
    216 267-0777

(G-4913)
WIRE PRODUCTS COMPANY LLC (PA)
14601 Industrial Pkwy (44135-4595)
PHONE..................................216 267-0777
E Scot Kennedy, *Pr*
Winston Breeden Junior, *Ex VP*
Dale Zeleznik, *
Gail Breeden, *Stockholder*
Dan Collins, *
EMP: 103 EST: 1951
SQ FT: 43,000
SALES (est): 14.65MM
SALES (corp-wide): 14.65MM Privately Held
Web: www.wire-products.com
SIC: 3496 Miscellaneous fabricated wire products

(G-4914)
WLS STAMPING CO (PA)
Also Called: Wls Stamping & Fabricating
3292 E 80th St (44104-4392)
PHONE..................................216 271-5100
Robert Guy, *Dir*
Daniel C Cronin, *
Craig Kotnik, *
Susan Nash, *
▲ EMP: 74 EST: 1944
SQ FT: 30,000
SALES (est): 18.64MM
SALES (corp-wide): 18.64MM Privately Held
Web: www.wlsstamping.com
SIC: 3469 3544 Stamping metal for the trade; Special dies and tools

(G-4915)
WM PLOTZ MACHINE AND FORGE CO
Also Called: Peerless Pump Clveland Svc Ctr
2514 Center St (44113-1111)
PHONE..................................216 861-0441
James W Plotz, *Pr*
Thomas D Plotz, *Sec*
EMP: 32 EST: 1888
SQ FT: 21,000

SALES (est): 1.33MM Privately Held
SIC: 3599 7699 Machine shop, jobbing and repair; Pumps and pumping equipment repair

(G-4916)
WODIN INC
5441 Perkins Rd (44146)
PHONE..................................440 439-4222
R Grant Murphy, *Pr*
EMP: 35 EST: 1967
SQ FT: 30,000
SALES (est): 5.09MM Privately Held
Web: www.wodin.com
SIC: 3462 3463 3599 3965 Machinery forgings, ferrous; Nonferrous forgings; Machine shop, jobbing and repair; Fasteners

(G-4917)
WOLFORD INDUSTRIAL PARK
9801 Walford Ave (44102-4777)
PHONE..................................216 281-3980
Marvin Hecht, *Pr*
EMP: 8 EST: 2017
SALES (est): 340.89K Privately Held
SIC: 2653 Boxes, corrugated: made from purchased materials

(G-4918)
WOOD-SEBRING CORPORATION
13800 Enterprise Ave (44135-5116)
PHONE..................................216 267-3191
Joseph Kronander, *Pr*
Joseph Kronander, *Pr*
Mary Kronander, *Sec*
EMP: 7 EST: 1944
SQ FT: 10,000
SALES (est): 481.68K Privately Held
SIC: 3451 Screw machine products

(G-4919)
WOODGRAIN ENTERPRISES LLC
3755 E 154th St (44128-1113)
PHONE..................................216 854-8151
Don Marshall, *Prin*
EMP: 6 EST: 2017
SALES (est): 27.98K Privately Held
Web: www.woodgrain.com
SIC: 2431 Millwork

(G-4920)
WOODHILL PLATING WORKS COMPANY
9114 Reno Ave (44105-2123)
P.O. Box 605304 (44105-0304)
PHONE..................................216 883-1344
John W Sparano Senior, *Pr*
James Sparano, *
John W Sparano Junior, *VP*
Jeff Sparano, *
Jerry Sparano, *
EMP: 25 EST: 1932
SQ FT: 25,000
SALES (est): 2.57MM Privately Held
Web: www.woodhillplating.com
SIC: 3471 Electroplating of metals or formed products

(G-4921)
WOODSTOCK PRODUCTS INC
2914 Broadway Ave (44115-3606)
PHONE..................................216 641-3811
Terry Dunay, *Pr*
Clara Dunay, *Sec*
EMP: 6 EST: 1958
SQ FT: 5,000
SALES (est): 750.44K Privately Held
Web: www.woodstockproductsinc.com

SIC: 2048 Feed concentrates

(G-4922)
WORLD JOURNAL
1735 E 36th St (44114-4521)
PHONE..................................216 458-0988
Yu-chen Hsiao, *Prin*
EMP: 8 EST: 2010
SALES (est): 89.12K Privately Held
Web: www.wjgnet.com
SIC: 2711 Newspapers, publishing and printing

(G-4923)
WORTHINGTON MID-RISE CNSTR INC (HQ)
Also Called: Worthington Industries
3100 E 45th St Ste 400 (44127-1095)
PHONE..................................216 472-1511
Marybeth Bosko, *Pr*
Michael Whitticar, *
EMP: 40 EST: 2002
SQ FT: 14,000
SALES (est): 27.69MM
SALES (corp-wide): 4.92B Publicly Held
Web: www.worthingtonibs.com
SIC: 3446 Purlins, light gauge steel
PA: Worthington Enterprises, Inc.
    200 W Old Wlson Bridge Rd
    Worthington OH 43085
    614 438-3210

(G-4924)
WP CPP HOLDINGS LLC (DH)
1621 Euclid Ave Ste 1850 (44115-2126)
PHONE..................................216 453-4800
EMP: 6 EST: 2011
SALES (est): 822.51MM
SALES (corp-wide): 822.51MM Privately Held
Web: www.cppcorp.com
SIC: 3724 Turbines, aircraft type
HQ: Wp Cpp Holdings Ii Inc.
    1621 Euclid Ave Ste 1850
    Cleveland OH

(G-4925)
WYMAN-GORDON COMPANY
Also Called: Wyman Gordon
3097 E 61st St (44127-1312)
PHONE..................................216 341-0085
Tim Herron, *Brnch Mgr*
EMP: 48
SALES (corp-wide): 364.48B Publicly Held
Web: www.wyman.com
SIC: 3462 Iron and steel forgings
HQ: Wyman-Gordon Company
    244 Worcester St
    North Grafton MA 01536
    508 839-8252

(G-4926)
XAPC CO
Also Called: Avalon
15583 Brookpark Rd (44142-1618)
PHONE..................................216 362-4100
Doug Ciabotti, *CEO*
Lindsey Krauth, *Prs Mgr*
Tom Ward, *VP Sls*
▲ EMP: 238 EST: 1982
SQ FT: 36,000
SALES (est): 19.4MM Privately Held
SIC: 3324 Steel investment foundries

(G-4927)
XCELLENCE PUBLICATIONS INC
860 Eddy Rd (44108-2382)
PHONE..................................216 326-1891
Sharina George, *Prin*
EMP: 6 EST: 2008

Cleveland - Cuyahoga County (G-4928)

GEOGRAPHIC SECTION

SALES (est): 153.29K **Privately Held**
Web: www.xcellencemagazine.com
SIC: **2741** Miscellaneous publishing

(G-4928)
YLT RED CLEVELAND LLC
417 Prospect Ave E (44115-1105)
PHONE..................................216 664-0941
EMP: 9 EST: 2019
SALES (est): 491.19K **Privately Held**
Web: www.cleveland.com
SIC: **2711** Newspapers, publishing and printing

(G-4929)
YOUR CARPENTER INC
2403 Saint Clair Ave Ne (44114-4020)
P.O. Box 14519 (44114-0519)
PHONE..................................216 621-2166
Matt Howells, *Prin*
EMP: 8 EST: 2006
SALES (est): 709.00K **Privately Held**
SIC: **3423** Carpenters' hand tools, except saws: levels, chisels, etc.

(G-4930)
ZACLON LLC
2981 Independence Rd (44115-3699)
PHONE..................................216 271-1601
◆ EMP: 25 EST: 2003
SALES (est): 24.62MM
SALES (corp-wide): 24.62MM **Privately Held**
Web: www.zaclon.com
SIC: **2819** Industrial inorganic chemicals, nec
PA: Alpha Zeta Holdings, Inc.
    2981 Independence Rd
    Cleveland OH 44115
    216 271-1601

(G-4931)
ZAGAR INC
24000 Lakeland Blvd (44132-2618)
PHONE..................................216 731-0500
John F Zagar, *Pr*
David Arnold, *
◆ EMP: 25 EST: 1941
SQ FT: 50,000
SALES (est): 5.01MM **Privately Held**
Web: www.zagar.com
SIC: **3546** 3541 Power-driven handtools; Machine tools, metal cutting type

(G-4932)
ZEN INDUSTRIES INC
Also Called: American Mine Door
6200 Harvard Ave (44105)
PHONE..................................216 432-3240
Kim Zenisek, *Pr*
Ed Ebner, *
EMP: 35 EST: 1906
SQ FT: 70,000
SALES (est): 5.33MM **Privately Held**
Web: www.minedoor.com
SIC: **3532** Mining machinery

(G-4933)
ZF ACTIVE SAFETY & ELEC US LLC
8333 Rockside Rd (44125-6134)
PHONE..................................216 750-2400
Richard Rowan, *Mgr*
EMP: 122
SALES (corp-wide): 144.19K **Privately Held**
Web: www.exactcarepharmacy.com
SIC: **3714** Motor vehicle parts and accessories
HQ: Zf Active Safety & Electronics Us Llc
    34605 W 12 Mile Rd
    Farmington Hills MI 48335
    765 429-1936

(G-4934)
ZING PAC INC
30300 Solon Industrial Pkwy (44139-4378)
PHONE..................................440 248-7997
Daniel Mcbride, *Prin*
EMP: 6 EST: 2010
SALES (est): 78.53K **Privately Held**
Web: www.zingpac.com
SIC: **3086** Packaging and shipping materials, foamed plastics

(G-4935)
ZIPPITYCOM PRINT LLC
1600 E 23rd St (44114-4208)
PHONE..................................216 438-0001
J P Dell'aquila, *Managing Member*
Dennis Dimitrov, *COO*
EMP: 12 EST: 2017
SALES (est): 1.78MM **Privately Held**
Web: www.zippityprint.com
SIC: **2752** Offset printing

(G-4936)
ZIRCOA INC (PA)
31501 Solon Rd (44139-3526)
PHONE..................................440 248-0500
John Kaniuk, *Pr*
▲ EMP: 130 EST: 1956
SQ FT: 120,000
SALES (est): 23.37MM
SALES (corp-wide): 23.37MM **Privately Held**
Web: www.zircoa.com
SIC: **3339** 3297 2851 Zirconium metal, sponge and granules; Nonclay refractories; Paints and allied products

Cleveland Heights
Cuyahoga County

(G-4937)
AUGUSTE MOONE ENTERPRISES LTD
3355 Tullamore Rd (44118-2938)
PHONE..................................216 333-9248
Augustin Jackson, *CEO*
EMP: 25 EST: 2010
SALES (est): 192.51K **Privately Held**
SIC: **8299** 2731 5942 8999 Educational services; Books, publishing only; Children's books; Writing for publication

(G-4938)
CONTINENTAL COATINGS LLC
3007 E Overlook Rd (44118-2437)
PHONE..................................216 429-1843
James Keene, *Pr*
EMP: 9 EST: 2016
SALES (est): 200.16K **Privately Held**
SIC: **3479** Metal coating and allied services

(G-4939)
DATA COOLING TECHNOLOGIES LLC
3092 Euclid Heights Blvd (44118-2026)
PHONE..................................330 954-3800
Gregory Gyllstrom, *CEO*
William M Weber, *
EMP: 42 EST: 2005
SQ FT: 100,000
SALES (est): 2.57MM **Privately Held**
SIC: **3433** Heating equipment, except electric

(G-4940)
MADE MEN CIRCLE LLC
2883 Mayfield Rd Apt 2 (44118-1698)
PHONE..................................216 501-0414
EMP: 6 EST: 2020
SALES (est): 60K **Privately Held**

SIC: **3161** Clothing and apparel carrying cases

(G-4941)
MOMMA JS BLAZING KITCHEN LLC
2281 S Overlook Rd (44106-3141)
PHONE..................................216 551-8791
EMP: 8
SALES (est): 348.11K **Privately Held**
SIC: **2099** 7389 Food preparations, nec; Business services, nec

(G-4942)
PHO & RICE LLC
1780 Coventry Rd (44118-1630)
PHONE..................................216 563-1122
Wansiri Kulsaree, *Prin*
EMP: 6 EST: 2013
SALES (est): 175.44K **Privately Held**
Web: www.phoandricecoventry.com
SIC: **2098** Noodles (e.g. egg, plain, and water), dry

(G-4943)
TALUS RENEWABLES INC
3762 Bainbridge Rd (44118-2244)
PHONE..................................650 248-5374
Hiro Iwanaga, *CEO*
EMP: 20 EST: 2021
SALES (est): 833.31K **Privately Held**
SIC: **4911** 2873
; Anhydrous ammonia

(G-4944)
UNGER KOSHER BAKERY INC
Also Called: Ungers Bakery
1831 S Taylor Rd (44118-2101)
PHONE..................................216 321-7176
Marek Rosenberg, *Pr*
Magdalena Rosenberg, *Sec*
EMP: 12 EST: 1967
SQ FT: 12,000
SALES (est): 503.67K **Privately Held**
SIC: **5461** 5411 5149 2099 Bread; Grocery stores, independent; Bakery products; Food preparations, nec

Cleves
Hamilton County

(G-4945)
4D SCREENPRINTING LTD
5833 Hamilton Cleves Rd (45002-9529)
PHONE..................................513 353-1070
Chris Drew, *Prin*
EMP: 6 EST: 2005
SALES (est): 387.95K **Privately Held**
Web: www.4dscreenprinting.com
SIC: **2759** Screen printing

(G-4946)
BRUEWER WOODWORK MFG CO
10000 Cilley Rd (45002-9735)
PHONE..................................513 353-3505
Ralph H Bruewer, *Pr*
August Bruewer, *
Gary A Bruewer, *
Richard M Ruffing, *
▲ EMP: 55 EST: 1973
SQ FT: 155,000
SALES (est): 9.56MM **Privately Held**
Web: mail.bruewerwoodwork.com
SIC: **3083** 2541 2435 2434 Plastics finished products, laminated; Office fixtures, wood; Hardwood veneer and plywood; Wood kitchen cabinets

(G-4947)
CHARLES BRENT NICHOLS
5041 Tanglewood Park Dr (45002)
PHONE..................................513 772-7000
Charles B Nichols, *Prin*
EMP: 7 EST: 2009
SALES (est): 196.45K **Privately Held**
SIC: **3599** Machine shop, jobbing and repair

(G-4948)
CONVEYOR SOLUTIONS LLC
6705 Dry Fork Rd (45002-9732)
PHONE..................................513 367-4845
EMP: 10 EST: 2001
SQ FT: 6,200
SALES (est): 1.79MM **Privately Held**
Web: www.conveyorsolutionsllc.com
SIC: **3535** Belt conveyor systems, general industrial use

(G-4949)
CORNHOLE WORLDWIDE LLC
5007 Hamilton Cleves Rd (45002-7502)
PHONE..................................513 324-2777
EMP: 6 EST: 2010
SALES (est): 342.3K **Privately Held**
Web: www.cornholeworldwide.com
SIC: **3944** Games, toys, and children's vehicles

(G-4950)
EPOXY SYSTEMS BLSTG CATING INC
5640 Morgan Rd (45002-8720)
PHONE..................................513 924-1800
Ray Litmer, *Pr*
Barbara Ferneding, *Prin*
EMP: 15 EST: 2007
SALES (est): 2MM **Privately Held**
Web: www.epoxy-systems-blast-powder-paint.com
SIC: **2851** Epoxy coatings

(G-4951)
ERNST ENTERPRISES INC
Also Called: Ernst Concrete
7340 Dry Fork Rd (45002-9431)
PHONE..................................513 367-1939
EMP: 8
SALES (corp-wide): 240.08MM **Privately Held**
Web: www.ernstconcrete.com
SIC: **3273** Ready-mixed concrete
PA: Ernst Enterprises, Inc.
    3361 Successful Way
    Dayton OH 45414
    937 233-5555

(G-4952)
FDI CABINETRY LLC
Also Called: Fdi
5555 Dry Fork Rd (45002-9733)
P.O. Box 832 (45041-0832)
PHONE..................................513 353-4500
EMP: 9 EST: 2011
SQ FT: 12,000
SALES (est): 962.76K **Privately Held**
Web: www.fdicabinetry.com
SIC: **2434** 3993 1799 3083 Wood kitchen cabinets; Signs and advertising specialties; Home/office interiors finishing, furnishing and remodeling; Plastics finished products, laminated

(G-4953)
HANSON AGGREGATES EAST
7000 Dry Fork Rd (45002-9732)
PHONE..................................513 353-1100
Tom Rodurbush, *Prin*
EMP: 6 EST: 2004

GEOGRAPHIC SECTION

Clyde - Sandusky County (G-4977)

SALES (est): 456.86K **Privately Held**
SIC: **1442** Construction sand and gravel

(G-4954)
HEALTHWARES MANUFACTURING
5838b Hamilton Cleves Rd (45002-9529)
PHONE..................................513 353-3691
Greg Overman, *Pr*
Joe Overman, *VP*
EMP: 12 EST: 1996
SALES (est): 741.78K **Privately Held**
Web: www.healthwares.com
SIC: **3842** Wheelchairs

(G-4955)
JAMES BUNNELL INC
7000 Dry Fork Rd (45002-9732)
PHONE..................................513 353-1100
Jack Ernest, *Pr*
Vicki Earnst, *Sec*
EMP: 10 EST: 1955
SQ FT: 1,160
SALES (est): 792.78K **Privately Held**
SIC: **1442** Construction sand and gravel

(G-4956)
JOHNSON PRCISION MACHINING INC
5919 Hamilton Cleves Rd (45002-9051)
PHONE..................................513 353-4252
Mary C Hubbard, *Pr*
Ellis Hubbard, *VP*
EMP: 8 EST: 1983
SQ FT: 7,500
SALES (est): 651.69K **Privately Held**
SIC: **3599** Machine shop, jobbing and repair

(G-4957)
KINNEMYERS CORNERSTONE CAB INC
Also Called: Kinnemeyers Cornerstone Cab Co
6000 Hamilton Cleves Rd (45002-9530)
PHONE..................................513 353-3030
Ken Kinnemeyer, *Pr*
EMP: 6 EST: 2004
SALES (est): 414.63K **Privately Held**
Web: www.cornerstonecabinets.com
SIC: **2599** 2434 Cabinets, factory; Wood kitchen cabinets

(G-4958)
L & L ORNAMENTAL IRON CO
Also Called: L & L Railings
6024 Hamilton Cleves Rd (45002-9530)
PHONE..................................513 353-1930
Randy Seiler, *Pr*
Dean Seiler, *VP*
EMP: 25 EST: 1959
SQ FT: 8,000
SALES (est): 2.22MM **Privately Held**
Web: www.llrailings.com
SIC: **2431** 3446 3354 Railings, stair: wood; Ornamental metalwork; Aluminum extruded products

(G-4959)
METAL MAINTENANCE INC
Also Called: Architectural Metal Maint
322 N Finley St (45002-1005)
P.O. Box 41 (45001-0041)
PHONE..................................513 661-3300
Steve Campbell, *Pr*
EMP: 10 EST: 1997
SALES (est): 723.6K **Privately Held**
Web: www.metalmaintenance.com
SIC: **3446** Architectural metalwork

(G-4960)
MINI MIX INC
7432 Hamilton Cleves Rd (45002-9400)
PHONE..................................513 353-3811
Ken Warby, *Pr*
Pete Warby, *VP*
▲ EMP: 9 EST: 1990
SALES (est): 199.13K **Privately Held**
Web: www.educarejoliet.com
SIC: **3273** 5082 Ready-mixed concrete; Concrete processing equipment

(G-4961)
MODERN SHEET METAL WORKS INC
6037 State Rte 128 (45002)
P.O. Box 53187 (45253)
PHONE..................................513 353-3666
Dorothy Johnson, *Pr*
Cynthia Freppon, *
Pamela Rosenacher, *
William Freppon, *
Jennifer Sucher, *
EMP: 25 EST: 1936
SQ FT: 16,000
SALES (est): 4.47MM **Privately Held**
Web: www.modernsheetmetal.com
SIC: **3444** Sheet metalwork

(G-4962)
POHL MACHINING INC (PA)
Also Called: Miami Machine
4901 Hamilton Cleves Rd (45002-9753)
P.O. Box 10 (45002-0010)
PHONE..................................513 353-2929
Shawna Vanderpohl, *Pr*
Irvin Vanderpohl, *
EMP: 26 EST: 2013
SALES (est): 8.61MM
SALES (corp-wide): 8.61MM **Privately Held**
Web: www.miamimachine.com
SIC: **3599** Machine shop, jobbing and repair

(G-4963)
POWERCLEAN EQUIPMENT COMPANY
5945 Dry Fork Rd (45002-9794)
PHONE..................................513 202-0001
Tom Ossege, *Pr*
Gary Ossege, *VP*
EMP: 16 EST: 2005
SALES (est): 2.3MM **Privately Held**
Web: www.powercleanequipment.com
SIC: **7359** 3635 5084 Equipment rental and leasing, nec; Household vacuum cleaners; Cleaning equipment, high pressure, sand or steam

(G-4964)
SPURLINO MATERIALS LLC
6600 Dry Fork Rd (45002-9392)
PHONE..................................513 202-1111
Allan Roelle, *Mgr*
EMP: 9
SALES (corp-wide): 8.3MM **Privately Held**
Web: www.spurlino.net
SIC: **3273** Ready-mixed concrete
PA: Spurlino Materials, Llc
4000 Oxford State Rd
Middletown OH 45044
513 705-0111

(G-4965)
STOCK MFG & DESIGN CO INC (PA)
Also Called: Q M P
10040 Cilley Rd (45002-9735)
P.O. Box 68 (45002-0068)
PHONE..................................513 353-3600
William H Reyering, *Pr*

Dennis K Stock, *
Anthony Stock, *
EMP: 15 EST: 1974
SQ FT: 80,000
SALES (est): 20.91MM
SALES (corp-wide): 20.91MM **Privately Held**
Web: www.stockmfg.com
SIC: **3441** Fabricated structural metal

(G-4966)
TAKK INDUSTRIES INC
5838a Hamilton Cleves Rd (45002-9529)
PHONE..................................513 353-4306
Joseph Overman, *Pr*
Gregory Overman, *Ex VP*
▲ EMP: 16 EST: 1944
SALES (est): 2.37MM **Privately Held**
Web: www.takk.com
SIC: **3629** 3469 Static elimination equipment, industrial; Metal stampings, nec

(G-4967)
TISCH ENVIRONMENTAL INC (PA)
145 S Miami Ave (45002-1250)
PHONE..................................513 467-9000
Wilbur John Tisch, *Pr*
James Paul Tisch, *VP*
▲ EMP: 22 EST: 1998
SQ FT: 12,000
SALES (est): 10MM
SALES (corp-wide): 10MM **Privately Held**
Web: www.tisch-env.com
SIC: **3564** Blowers and fans

Clinton
Summit County

(G-4968)
COMMUNITY CARE ON WHEELS
2 Kauffmans Crk (44216-8658)
PHONE..................................330 882-5506
Cathy Jacobs, *Pr*
EMP: 6 EST: 2009
SALES (est): 193.91K **Privately Held**
SIC: **3312** Blast furnaces and steel mills

(G-4969)
J & M FABRICATIONS LLC
3000 S 1st St (44216-9110)
PHONE..................................330 860-4346
EMP: 9 EST: 2017
SALES (est): 440.98K **Privately Held**
SIC: **3441** Fabricated structural metal

Cloverdale
Putnam County

(G-4970)
JONASHTONS LLC
12485 State Route 634 (45827-9723)
PHONE..................................419 488-2363
EMP: 7 EST: 1994
SALES (est): 488.19K **Privately Held**
SIC: **3599** Machine shop, jobbing and repair

Clyde
Sandusky County

(G-4971)
CLYDE TOOL & DIE INC
Also Called: Clyde Foam
524 S Church St (43410-2100)
PHONE..................................419 547-9574
Bruce G Schrader, *Pr*
EMP: 18 EST: 1942

SQ FT: 30,000
SALES (est): 2.48MM **Privately Held**
Web: www.clydetool.com
SIC: **3544** 2821 Special dies and tools; Molding compounds, plastics

(G-4972)
EVERGREEN RECYCLING LLC (DH)
Also Called: Evergreen Midwest
202 Watertower Dr (43410-2154)
PHONE..................................419 547-1400
Greg Johnson, *Managing Member*
EMP: 22 EST: 1998
SALES (est): 11.54MM **Privately Held**
Web: www.evergreentogether.com
SIC: **2821** Polystyrene resins
HQ: Polychem, Llc
6277 Heisley Rd
Mentor OH 44060
440 357-1500

(G-4973)
J TEK TOOL & MOLD INC
304 Elm St (43410-2124)
PHONE..................................419 547-9476
John Cattano, *Pr*
EMP: 10 EST: 1989
SQ FT: 10,000
SALES (est): 951.61K **Privately Held**
Web: www.jtektool.com
SIC: **3544** Special dies and tools

(G-4974)
MIDWEST COMPOST INC
7250 State Route 101 E (43410-8519)
PHONE..................................419 547-7979
Eugene F Windau, *Pr*
Joseph Tauch, *VP*
John Steager, *Sec*
EMP: 14 EST: 1988
SQ FT: 2,432
SALES (est): 2.28MM **Privately Held**
SIC: **2875** Compost

(G-4975)
POLYCHEM LLC
Also Called: Evergreen Plastics
202 Watertower Dr (43410-2154)
PHONE..................................419 547-1400
Mark Jeckering, *Genl Mgr*
EMP: 75
Web: www.polychem.com
SIC: **3052** 4953 Plastic belting; Recycling, waste materials
HQ: Polychem, Llc
6277 Heisley Rd
Mentor OH 44060
440 357-1500

(G-4976)
REVERE PLAS SYSTEMS GROUP LLC (HQ)
401 Elm St (43410-2148)
PHONE..................................419 547-6918
EMP: 450 EST: 2005
SALES (est): 93.22MM **Privately Held**
Web: www.revereplasticssystems.com
SIC: **3089** Injection molding of plastics
PA: Old Rev, Llc
16855 Suthpark Dr Ste 100
Westfield IN 46074

(G-4977)
REVERE PLASTICS SYSTEMS LLC
401 Elm St (43410-2148)
PHONE..................................573 785-0871
Danny Neff, *Mgr*
EMP: 236
SALES (corp-wide): 28.58MM **Privately Held**
Web: www.revereplasticssystems.com

Clyde - Sandusky County (G-4978)

SIC: 3089 Injection molding of plastics
HQ: Revere Plastics Systems, Llc
39555 Orchard Hill Pl # 155
Novi MI 48375

(G-4978)
SANDCO INDUSTRIES
567 Premier Dr (43410-2157)
PHONE..............................419 547-3273
Donald Nalley, *Dir*
EMP: 42 **EST:** 1964
SALES (est): 1.39MM **Privately Held**
Web: www.sandcoind.com
SIC: 8331 3639 Sheltered workshop; Major kitchen appliances, except refrigerators and stoves

(G-4979)
WHIRLPOOL CORPORATION
Also Called: Whirlpool
119 Birdseye St (43410-1397)
PHONE..............................419 547 7711
Casey Drabik, *VP*
EMP: 240
SQ FT: 1,500,000
SALES (corp-wide): 19.45B **Publicly Held**
Web: www.whirlpoolcorp.com
SIC: 3632 3639 3582 3633 Freezers, home and farm; Dishwashing machines, household; Commercial laundry equipment; Washing machines, household; including coin-operated
PA: Whirlpool Corporation
2000 N M-63
Benton Harbor MI 49022
269 923-5000

(G-4980)
WHIRLPOOL CORPORATION
Also Called: Whirlpool
1081 W Mcpherson Hwy (43410-1001)
PHONE..............................419 547-2610
Tom Borro, *Mgr*
EMP: 6
SALES (corp-wide): 19.45B **Publicly Held**
Web: www.whirlpoolcorp.com
SIC: 3633 Household laundry equipment
PA: Whirlpool Corporation
2000 N M-63
Benton Harbor MI 49022
269 923-5000

Coldwater
Mercer County

(G-4981)
ALUMETAL MANUFACTURING COMPANY
4555 Sr 127 (45828)
P.O. Box 166 (45828-0166)
PHONE..............................419 268-2311
Lavern W Gross, *Pr*
Oliver Giere, *Sec*
EMP: 21 **EST:** 1950
SQ FT: 25,000
SALES (est): 1.5MM **Privately Held**
Web: www.alumetalmfg.com
SIC: 3444 Awnings, sheet metal

(G-4982)
BASIC GRAIN PRODUCTS INC
Also Called: Tastemorr Snacks
300 E Vine St 310 (45828-1354)
PHONE..............................419 678-2304
Carol Knapke, *Pr*
Amy Day, *Prin*
Ralph F Keister, *Prin*
EMP: 100 **EST:** 1994
SQ FT: 100,000
SALES (est): 9.74MM **Privately Held**
SIC: 2052 2099 2096 Rice cakes; Food preparations, nec; Potato chips and similar snacks

(G-4983)
CAMELOT MANUFACTURING INC
210 Butler St (45828-1103)
P.O. Box 44 (45828-0044)
PHONE..............................419 678-2603
Charles A Froning, *Pr*
EMP: 17 **EST:** 1981
SQ FT: 14,000
SALES (est): 554.62K **Privately Held**
SIC: 3441 7692 3469 Fabricated structural metal; Welding repair; Metal stampings, nec

(G-4984)
CASAD COMPANY INC
Also Called: Totally Promotional
450 S 2nd St (45828-1803)
PHONE..............................419 586-9457
▲ **EMP:** 15 **EST:** 1992
SQ FT: 7,000
SALES (est): 6.61MM **Privately Held**
Web: www.totallypromotional.com
SIC: 2759 3993 Screen printing; Signs and advertising specialties

(G-4985)
COLDWATER MACHINE COMPANY LLC
911 N 2nd St (45828-8736)
PHONE..............................419 678-4877
EMP: 113 **EST:** 1956
SALES (est): 18.01MM
SALES (corp-wide): 4.19B **Publicly Held**
Web: www.coldwatermachine.com
SIC: 3545 3544 Machine tool accessories; Special dies and tools
PA: Lincoln Electric Holdings, Inc.
22801 St Clair Ave
Cleveland OH 44117
216 481-8100

(G-4986)
DERUIJTER INTL USA INC
Also Called: Dri Rubber
120 Harvest Dr (45828)
P.O. Box 90 (45828)
PHONE..............................419 678-3909
◆ **EMP:** 10 **EST:** 1995
SQ FT: 35,000
SALES (est): 8.39MM **Privately Held**
Web: www.deruijterusa.com
SIC: 3069 Plumbers' rubber goods
HQ: De Ruijter International B.V.
Prof. Minckelersweg 1
Waalwijk NB 5144
416674000

(G-4987)
EXCEL MACHINE & TOOL INC
212 Butler St (45828-1103)
PHONE..............................419 678-3318
Timothy Moorman, *Pr*
Dale Kahlig, *VP*
EMP: 10 **EST:** 1991
SALES (est): 989.35K **Privately Held**
Web: www.tubebenders.com
SIC: 3599 Machine shop, jobbing and repair

(G-4988)
FORM MANUFACTURING LLC
149 Harvest Dr (45828-8748)
PHONE..............................419 678-1400
Kevin Myer, *Engr*
EMP: 10 **EST:** 2015
SALES (est): 512.5K **Privately Held**
Web: www.4mmfg.com

SIC: 2295 Plastic coated yarns or fabrics

(G-4989)
FORM MFG
149 Harvest Dr (45828-8748)
PHONE..............................419 763-1030
Bradley T Meyer, *Prin*
EMP: 6 **EST:** 2016
SALES (est): 245.89K **Privately Held**
SIC: 3999 Manufacturing industries, nec

(G-4990)
FORTY NINE DEGREES LLC
149 Harvest Dr (45828-8748)
PHONE..............................419 678-0100
EMP: 11 **EST:** 2003
SALES (est): 2.72MM **Privately Held**
Web: www.fortyninedegrees.com
SIC: 3993 Signs and advertising specialties

(G-4991)
HARDIN CREEK MACHINE & TL INC
200 Hardin St (45828-9794)
PHONE..............................419 678-4913
Joseph Wenning, *Pr*
Randy Schmitz, *VP*
EMP: 10 **EST:** 1984
SQ FT: 6,000
SALES (est): 915.17K **Privately Held**
SIC: 3544 3599 Special dies and tools; Machine and other job shop work

(G-4992)
HEALTH CARE PRODUCTS INC
410 Nisco St (45828-8750)
P.O. Box 116 (45828-0116)
PHONE..............................419 678-9620
Michael Bruns, *Pr*
▲ **EMP:** 38 **EST:** 2005
SQ FT: 50,000
SALES (est): 5.1MM **Privately Held**
Web: www.hcp3.com
SIC: 2676 Napkins, sanitary: made from purchased paper

(G-4993)
HOME BAKERY
109 W Main St (45828-1702)
PHONE..............................419 678-3018
Carl Brunson, *Owner*
Bruce A Fox, *Owner*
EMP: 10 **EST:** 1885
SQ FT: 3,000
SALES (est): 411.08K **Privately Held**
SIC: 2051 Bakery: wholesale or wholesale/ retail combined

(G-4994)
K VENTURES INC
Also Called: EMB Designs
211 E Main St (45828-1720)
P.O. Box 112 (45828-0112)
PHONE..............................419 678-2308
Michelle Ebbing, *Pr*
Mike Knapschaefer, *Sec*
EMP: 10 **EST:** 2003
SQ FT: 24,000
SALES (est): 879.13K **Privately Held**
Web: www.designsemb.com
SIC: 5099 5137 5699 2395 Signs, except electric; Women's and children's sportswear and swimsuits; Uniforms; Embroidery and art needlework

(G-4995)
LEFELD WELDING & STL SUPS INC (PA)
Also Called: Lefeld Supplies Rental
600 N 2nd St (45828-9777)
PHONE..............................419 678-2397

Stanley E Lefeld, *CEO*
Gary Lefeld, *
▲ **EMP:** 43 **EST:** 1953
SQ FT: 10,400
SALES (est): 17.78MM
SALES (corp-wide): 17.78MM **Privately Held**
Web: www.lefeld.com
SIC: 5084 7353 1799 3441 Welding machinery and equipment; Heavy construction equipment rental; Welding on site; Fabricated structural metal

(G-4996)
LINCOLN ELECTRIC AUTOMTN INC
911 N 2nd St (45828-8736)
PHONE..............................419 678-4877
John Campbell, *Brnch Mgr*
EMP: 115
SALES (corp-wide): 4.19B **Publicly Held**
Web: www.coldwatermachine.com
SIC: 3545 3544 Machine tool accessories; Special dies and tools
HQ: Lincoln Electric Automation, Inc.
407 S Main St
Fort Loramie OH 45845
937 295-2120

(G-4997)
LRP SOLUTIONS INC
120 Harvest Dr (45828-8733)
PHONE..............................419 678-3909
John M Deeds, *Prin*
EMP: 9 **EST:** 2017
SALES (est): 533.5K **Privately Held**
Web: www.drirubber.com
SIC: 3069 Rubber floorcoverings/mats and wallcoverings

(G-4998)
MERCER COLOR CORPORATION
425 Hardin St (45828-8742)
P.O. Box 113 (45828-0113)
PHONE..............................419 678-8273
Mark A Baumer, *Pr*
Patrick J Berger, *VP*
EMP: 9 **EST:** 1981
SQ FT: 12,000
SALES (est): 747.69K **Privately Held**
Web: www.mercercolor.com
SIC: 2752 Offset printing

(G-4999)
PAX STEEL PRODUCTS INC
104 E Vine St (45828-1246)
PHONE..............................419 678-1481
Bill Kramer, *Pr*
EMP: 6 **EST:** 2003
SALES (est): 159.77K **Privately Held**
SIC: 3523 Farm machinery and equipment

(G-5000)
RANDALL BEARINGS INC
821 Weis St (45828-9612)
PHONE..............................419 678-2486
Jeff Hager, *Brnch Mgr*
EMP: 12
Web: www.randallbearings.com
SIC: 3568 3624 3366 Bearings, bushings, and blocks; Carbon and graphite products; Copper foundries
HQ: Randall Bearings, Inc.
240 Jay Begg Pkwy
Lima OH 45804
419 223-1075

(G-5001)
SIGNATURE PARTNERS INC
Also Called: Signature 4 Image
149 Harvest Dr (45828-8748)
PHONE..............................419 678-1400

GEOGRAPHIC SECTION
Columbia Station - Lorain County (G-5024)

Bradley Meyer, *Pr*
Paul Meikemp, *
▲ **EMP:** 65 **EST:** 1992
SALES (est): 10MM **Privately Held**
Web: www.signature4.com
SIC: 3479 Name plates: engraved, etched, etc.

(G-5002)
TAYLOR COMMUNICATIONS INC
Also Called: Standard Register
515 W Sycamore St (45828-1663)
P.O. Box 109 (45828-0109)
PHONE..................................419 678-6000
Barry Paynter, *Brnch Mgr*
EMP: 33
SALES (corp-wide): 3.81B **Privately Held**
Web: www.taylor.com
SIC: 2759 Commercial printing, nec
HQ: Taylor Communications, Inc.
1725 Roe Crest Dr
North Mankato MN 56003
866 541-0937

(G-5003)
VAL-CO PAX INC (DH)
Also Called: Val Products
210 E Main St (45828-1751)
P.O. Box 117 (45828-0117)
PHONE..................................717 354-4586
Frederick Steudler, *CEO*
Steve Hough, *
William Kramer, *
▲ **EMP:** 67 **EST:** 1935
SQ FT: 130,000
SALES (est): 12.85MM
SALES (corp-wide): 63.95MM **Privately Held**
Web: www.val-co.com
SIC: 3523 3443 Hog feeding, handling, and watering equipment; Fabricated plate work (boiler shop)
HQ: Val Products, Inc.
2599 Old Philadelphia Pike
Bird In Hand PA 17505
717 392-3978

Collins
Huron County

(G-5004)
FACILITY SERVICE PROS LLC
3206 Townsend Angling Rd (44826-9723)
PHONE..................................419 577-6123
Misty Bainbridge, *CEO*
Michael Bainbridge, *Managing Member*
Misty Bainbridge, *Managing Member*
EMP: 6 **EST:** 2016
SALES (est): 508.23K **Privately Held**
Web: www.fs-pros.com
SIC: 7389 1542 8744 1389 Business Activities at Non-Commercial Site; Commercial and office buildings, renovation and repair; Facilities support services; Construction, repair, and dismantling services

Columbia Station
Lorain County

(G-5005)
AQUATIC TECHNOLOGY
26966 Royalton Rd (44028-9758)
PHONE..................................440 236-8330
Greg Smith, *Owner*
◆ **EMP:** 10 **EST:** 1991
SQ FT: 4,300
SALES (est): 628.9K **Privately Held**
Web: www.aquatictech.com
SIC: 5999 5199 3999 Aquarium supplies; Pets and pet supplies; Pet supplies

(G-5006)
ATOM BLASTING & FINISHING INC
24933 Sprague Rd (44028-9671)
PHONE..................................440 235-4765
Richard Ferry, *Pr*
Karen Widener, *VP*
▲ **EMP:** 6 **EST:** 1970
SALES (est): 587.41K **Privately Held**
SIC: 3471 Finishing, metals or formed products

(G-5007)
CAL SALES EMBROIDERY
13975 Station Rd (44028-9401)
PHONE..................................440 236-3820
Edward L Pete Houston, *Owner*
EMP: 6 **EST:** 1986
SQ FT: 1,800
SALES (est): 431.84K **Privately Held**
Web: www.calsalesembroidery.com
SIC: 2395 2396 5199 Embroidery products, except Schiffli machine; Screen printing on fabric articles; Advertising specialties

(G-5008)
CHOICE BALLAST SOLUTIONS LLC
11700 Station Rd (44028-9728)
P.O. Box 627 (44028-0627)
PHONE..................................440 973-9841
John Dooley, *Pr*
EMP: 7 **EST:** 2013
SALES (est): 140.55K **Privately Held**
Web: www.choiceballast.com
SIC: 3589 Water treatment equipment, industrial

(G-5009)
CINEEN INC
25011 Royalton Rd (44028-9404)
PHONE..................................440 236-3658
Yusra Suleiman, *Prin*
EMP: 7 **EST:** 2014
SALES (est): 149.23K **Privately Held**
SIC: 2082 5999 Beer (alcoholic beverage); Alcoholic beverage making equipment and supplies

(G-5010)
COLUMBIA STAMPING INC
Also Called: Total Automation
13676 Station Rd (44028-9538)
PHONE..................................440 236-6677
James D Galvin, *Pr*
Ken Dillinger, *Sec*
EMP: 32 **EST:** 1990
SQ FT: 37,000
SALES (est): 775.73K **Privately Held**
Web: www.totalautomationinc.com
SIC: 3544 3542 Die sets for metal stamping (presses); Die casting machines

(G-5011)
CONTROL ELECTRIC CO
12130 Eaton Commerce Pkwy (44028-9208)
PHONE..................................216 671-8010
Mike Vogt, *Pr*
EMP: 23 **EST:** 1963
SQ FT: 6,800
SALES (est): 4.81MM **Privately Held**
Web: www.controlelectric.com
SIC: 3625 8711 2542 Industrial electrical relays and switches; Engineering services; Partitions and fixtures, except wood

(G-5012)
DIMENSION INDUSTRIES INC
27335 Royalton Rd (44028-9159)
P.O. Box 1130 (44028-1130)
PHONE..................................440 236-3265
William Biljes, *Pr*
EMP: 11 **EST:** 1986
SQ FT: 7,200
SALES (est): 479.65K **Privately Held**
Web: www.dimensionindustries.com
SIC: 3599 Machine and other job shop work

(G-5013)
LA GANKE & SONS STAMPING CO
13676 Station Rd (44028-9538)
PHONE..................................216 451-0278
Charles Laganke, *Pr*
Kim Lorris, *Sec*
EMP: 10 **EST:** 1961
SQ FT: 18,500
SALES (est): 943.24K **Privately Held**
SIC: 3469 3544 Stamping metal for the trade ; Special dies and tools

(G-5014)
MODERN MOLD CORPORATION
27684 Royalton Rd (44028-9073)
PHONE..................................440 236-9600
David Bowes, *Pr*
EMP: 7 **EST:** 1984
SALES (est): 953.8K **Privately Held**
Web: www.tonerplastics.com
SIC: 3089 Injection molding of plastics

(G-5015)
OBHC INC
Also Called: Original Beverage Holder Co
33549 E Royalton Rd Unit 9 (44028-9306)
PHONE..................................440 236-5112
Tim Jenkins, *Pr*
EMP: 7 **EST:** 2007
SQ FT: 6,000
SALES (est): 950.41K **Privately Held**
Web: www.obhcinc.com
SIC: 3585 3993 5149 Soda fountain and beverage dispensing equipment and parts; Scoreboards, electric; Wine makers' equipment and supplies

(G-5016)
PERRONS PRINTING COMPANY
Also Called: Image Graphics
27500 Royalton Rd Ste D (44028-9713)
P.O. Box 669 (44028-0669)
PHONE..................................440 236-8870
Edward Perron Senior, *Pr*
Linda Perron, *VP*
George D Maurer Senior, *Prin*
EMP: 16 **EST:** 1982
SQ FT: 10,000
SALES (est): 525.85K **Privately Held**
Web: www.printdirectforless.com
SIC: 2752 7336 Offset printing; Graphic arts and related design

(G-5017)
PIER TOOL & DIE INC
27369 Royalton Rd (44028)
P.O. Box 452 (44028)
PHONE..................................440 236-3188
Mario J Pierzchala, *Pr*
Karen Pierzchala, *VP*
Randy Pierzchala, *Manager*
EMP: 24 **EST:** 1985
SQ FT: 15,000
SALES (est): 977.63K **Privately Held**
SIC: 3544 Special dies and tools

(G-5018)
PRINT DIRECT FOR LESS 2 INC
27500 Royalton Rd (44028-9713)
P.O. Box 669 (44028-0669)
PHONE..................................440 236-8870
Edward M Perron Junior, *Pr*
Linda Perron, *VP*
Edward M Perron Junior, *VP*
Nellie Akalp, *Prin*
▼ **EMP:** 15 **EST:** 2004
SALES (est): 2.44MM **Privately Held**
Web: www.printdirectforless.com
SIC: 2752 Offset printing

(G-5019)
ROLLER SOURCE INC
34100 E Royalton Rd (44028-9759)
PHONE..................................440 748-4033
Steve Leuschel, *Pr*
George Novak, *VP*
EMP: 10 **EST:** 1985
SALES (est): 915.71K **Privately Held**
Web: www.therollersource.com
SIC: 3069 Medical and laboratory rubber sundries and related products

(G-5020)
ROYALTON INDUSTRIES INC
12450 Eaton Commerce Pkwy Ste 1 (44028-9213)
PHONE..................................440 748-9900
William A Baltes Senior, *Ch Bd*
William A Baltes Junior, *Treas*
EMP: 10 **EST:** 1979
SQ FT: 10,000
SALES (est): 1.87MM **Privately Held**
SIC: 3599 Custom machinery

(G-5021)
SEAWAY BOLT AND SPECIALS COMPANY
Also Called: Seaway
11561 Station Rd (44028-9503)
P.O. Box 908 (44028-0908)
PHONE..................................440 236-5015
EMP: 84 **EST:** 1957
SALES (est): 5.37MM **Privately Held**
Web: www.seawaybolt.com
SIC: 3499 3399 Drain plugs, magnetic; Metal fasteners

(G-5022)
SUPERIOR ENERGY SYSTEMS LLC
13660 Station Rd (44028-9538)
PHONE..................................440 236-6009
Donald Fernald, *CEO*
Derek Rimko, *VP*
William J Young, *VP*
Mike Walters, *VP*
Philip J Lombardo, *Prin*
▼ **EMP:** 17 **EST:** 2002
SQ FT: 14,000
SALES (est): 3.95MM **Privately Held**
Web: www.superiornrg.com
SIC: 3714 Propane conversion equipment, motor vehicle

(G-5023)
TRIAD CAPITAL GROUP LLC
Also Called: Special Metal Stamping
13676 Station Rd (44028-9538)
PHONE..................................440 236-6677
EMP: 13 **EST:** 2011
SALES (est): 1.36MM **Privately Held**
Web: www.triadcg.com
SIC: 3441 Fabricated structural metal

(G-5024)
WILLISON WRED DEN INCORPORTATE

Columbiana - Columbiana County (G-5025)

GEOGRAPHIC SECTION

27852 Royalton Rd (44028-9161)
PHONE..................................440 236-9693
EMP: 6 EST: 2014
SALES (est): 425.32K Privately Held
Web: www.williamsonwireedm.com
SIC: 3496 Miscellaneous fabricated wire products

Columbiana
Columbiana County

(G-5025)
A PLUS POWDER COATERS INC
1384 Kauffman Ave (44408-9750)
PHONE..................................330 482-4389
Robert Bertelsen, CEO
EMP: 44 EST: 1996
SQ FT: 20,250
SALES (est): 3.98MM Privately Held
Web: www.apluspowder.com
SIC: 3479 Coating of metals and formed products

(G-5026)
ALLOY MACHINING AND FABG INC
1028 Lower Elkton Rd (44408-8427)
P.O. Box 49 (44408-0049)
PHONE..................................330 482-5543
Ed Keating, Pr
EMP: 19 EST: 2005
SALES (est): 497.19K Privately Held
SIC: 3599 Machine shop, jobbing and repair

(G-5027)
AMERICAN STEEL LLC
326 Blueberry Dr (44408-1414)
P.O. Box 62 (44408-0062)
PHONE..................................330 482-4299
Karen L Grant, Prin
EMP: 7 EST: 2015
SALES (est): 242.19K Privately Held
Web: www.americansteel-jds.com
SIC: 3441 Fabricated structural metal

(G-5028)
BOARDMAN STEEL INC
156 Nulf Dr (44408-9720)
PHONE..................................330 758-0951
Dave Deibel, Pr
EMP: 55 EST: 1963
SQ FT: 49,000
SALES (est): 4.46MM Privately Held
Web: workspaceupdates.googleblog.com
SIC: 3441 Building components, structural steel

(G-5029)
BUCKEYE COMPONENTS LLC
1340 State Route 14 (44408-9648)
PHONE..................................330 482-5163
EMP: 30 EST: 1993
SQ FT: 8,000
SALES (est): 2.47MM Privately Held
SIC: 5031 2439 Lumber, plywood, and millwork; Trusses, wooden roof

(G-5030)
CBC GLOBAL
Also Called: Columbiana Boiler Company, LLC
200 W Railroad St (44408-1281)
PHONE..................................330 482-3373
Michael J Sherwin, Pr
Thomas F Dougherty, *
Alan G Eckert, *
Gerianne Klepfer, *
Charles R Moore, *
◆ EMP: 45 EST: 1894

SQ FT: 50,000
SALES (est): 16.44MM
SALES (corp-wide): 16.44MM Privately Held
Web: www.cbco.com
SIC: 1791 3443 Storage tanks, metal: erection; Process vessels, industrial: metal plate
PA: Columbiana Holding Co Inc
200 W Railroad St
Columbiana OH 44408
330 482-3373

(G-5031)
CENTURY CONTAINER LLC
32 W Railroad St (44408-1203)
PHONE..................................330 457-2367
Don R Br, CEO
EMP: 25
Web: www.centurycontainercorporation.com
SIC: 3089 Plastics containers, except foam
HQ: Century Container, Llc
5331 State Route 7
New Waterford OH 44445
330 457-2367

(G-5032)
COBBLERS CORNER LLC
1115 Village Plz (44408-8480)
PHONE..................................330 482-4005
EMP: 13 EST: 1975
SQ FT: 8,000
SALES (est): 478.93K Privately Held
Web: www.cobblerscorner1.com
SIC: 5661 3021 7251 Men's boots; Rubber and plastics footwear; Footwear, custom made

(G-5033)
COL-PUMP COMPANY INC
131 E Railroad St (44408-1318)
PHONE..................................330 482-1029
Thomas Bowker, Pr
Paul Rance, *
EMP: 60 EST: 1882
SQ FT: 100,000
SALES (est): 8.41MM Privately Held
Web: www.col-pump.net
SIC: 3321 Gray iron castings, nec

(G-5034)
COLUMBIANA FOUNDRY COMPANY
501 Lisbon St (44408-1267)
P.O. Box 98 (44408-0098)
PHONE..................................330 482-3336
EMP: 130 EST: 1933
SALES (est): 10MM Privately Held
Web: www.columbianafoundry.com
SIC: 3321 3325 3369 3312 Gray iron castings, nec; Steel foundries, nec; Nonferrous foundries, nec; Blast furnaces and steel mills

(G-5035)
COMPCO COLUMBIANA COMPANY (HQ)
Also Called: Compco Industries
400 W Railroad St (44408-1213)
PHONE..................................330 482-0200
Gregory Smith, Ch Bd
Clarence Smith Senior, Ch Bd
Joel Sofranko, CFO
EMP: 63 EST: 1998
SALES (est): 18.58MM
SALES (corp-wide): 33.46MM Privately Held
Web: www.compco.com
SIC: 3469 3443 Metal stampings, nec; Tanks, standard or custom fabricated: metal plate
PA: S-P Company, Inc.

400 W Railroad St Ste 1
Columbiana OH 44408
330 782-5651

(G-5036)
COMPCO YOUNGSTOWN COMPANY
Also Called: Compco Industries
400 W Railroad St (44408-1213)
PHONE..................................330 482-6488
Gregory Smith, Ch Bd
Clarence R Smith Junior, Ch Bd
James B Greene, CCO*
EMP: 88 EST: 1952
SQ FT: 200,000
SALES (est): 14.88MM
SALES (corp-wide): 33.46MM Privately Held
Web: www.compco.com
SIC: 3443 3469 3444 Tanks, standard or custom fabricated: metal plate; Metal stampings, nec; Sheet metalwork
PA: S-P Company, Inc.
400 W Railroad St Ste 1
Columbiana OH 44408
330 782-5651

(G-5037)
E-1 (2012) HOLDINGS INC
Also Called: Envelope 1
41969 State Route 344 (44408-9421)
PHONE..................................330 482-3900
▲ EMP: 180
SIC: 2677 Envelopes

(G-5038)
ENVELOPE 1 INC (PA)
41969 State Route 344 (44408-9421)
PHONE..................................330 482-3900
Tarry Pidgeon, CEO
Cody Stokes, CFO
▲ EMP: 97 EST: 2012
SALES (est): 41.98MM
SALES (corp-wide): 41.98MM Privately Held
Web: www.envelope1.com
SIC: 2677 Envelopes

(G-5039)
FEDERAL IRON WORKS COMPANY
42082 State Route 344 (44408-9421)
P.O. Box 150 (44408-0150)
PHONE..................................330 482-5910
Edward M Sferra, Pr
Edward M Sferra Junior, Pr
Marcella A Sferra, VP
EMP: 22 EST: 1920
SALES (est): 2.16MM Privately Held
Web: www.cycomsolutions.com
SIC: 3446 1761 Architectural metalwork; Architectural sheet metal work

(G-5040)
GREEN HARVEST ENERGY LLC
1340 State Route 14 (44408-9648)
PHONE..................................330 716-3068
John J Monroe, Pr
Robert J Holmes, Ch
Jean Holt, Prin
EMP: 9 EST: 2009
SALES (est): 185.97K Privately Held
SIC: 2869 Industrial organic chemicals, nec

(G-5041)
HUMTOWN PATTERN COMPANY
Also Called: Humtown Products
44708 Columbiana Waterford Rd (44408-9605)
P.O. Box 367 (44408-0367)
PHONE..................................330 482-5555
Mark Lamoncha, Pr
Criss La Moncha, *

Brandon Lamoncha, *
Terrie Marshall, *
Sheri Lamoncha, *
EMP: 67 EST: 1959
SQ FT: 55,000
SALES (est): 14.73MM Privately Held
Web: www.humtown.com
SIC: 2759 3543 Commercial printing, nec; Foundry cores

(G-5042)
J & H MANUFACTURING LLC
Also Called: J & H Mfg
1652 Columbiana Lisbon Rd (44408-9443)
P.O. Box 12 (44408-0012)
PHONE..................................330 482-2636
John Kephart, Managing Member
▲ EMP: 13 EST: 2003
SQ FT: 41,000
SALES (est): 859.53K Privately Held
SIC: 3462 Iron and steel forgings

(G-5043)
J&J PRECISION FABRICATORS LTD
Also Called: J&J Precision Fabrication
1341 Heck Rd (44408-9599)
PHONE..................................330 482-4964
EMP: 10 EST: 2001
SQ FT: 11,500
SALES (est): 427.68K Privately Held
SIC: 7692 3599 Welding repair; Crankshafts and camshafts, machining

(G-5044)
MAHONING VALLEY TOOL & MCH LLC
1380 Wardingley Ave (44408-9727)
PHONE..................................330 482-0870
Tim Haldiman, Prin
EMP: 11 EST: 2008
SALES (est): 937.93K Privately Held
Web: www.mahoningvalleytool.com
SIC: 3544 Special dies and tools

(G-5045)
MILLER CASTINGS INC
1634 Lower Elkton Rd (44408-9404)
P.O. Box 440 (44408-0440)
PHONE..................................330 482-2923
Mike Miller, Pr
EMP: 52 EST: 1993
SALES (est): 1.59MM Privately Held
SIC: 3365 Aluminum foundries

(G-5046)
NEWELL - PSN LLC (PA)
235 E State Route 14 Ste 104 (44408-8494)
P.O. Box 48 (44408-0048)
PHONE..................................304 387-2700
Rick Stanley, Pr
▲ EMP: 6 EST: 2005
SALES (est): 1.33MM Privately Held
Web: www.newellporcelain.com
SIC: 3264 Insulators, electrical: porcelain

(G-5047)
OAKS WELDING INC
201 Prospect St (44408)
P.O. Box 23 (44408-0023)
PHONE..................................330 482-4216
Jack Guy, Pr
Jeff Guy, Pr
Maribell Guy, Sec
Geri Rubicky, Treas
EMP: 8 EST: 1927
SQ FT: 11,025
SALES (est): 889.31K Privately Held
Web: www.oakswelding.com

SIC: 3599 7692 7629 Machine shop, jobbing and repair; Welding repair; Electrical repair shops

(G-5048)
QFM STAMPING INC
400 W Railroad St Ste 1 (44408-1294)
PHONE.................................330 337-3311
EMP: 12 EST: 2016
SALES (est): 570.37K **Privately Held**
SIC: 3469 Stamping metal for the trade

(G-5049)
RANCE INDUSTRIES INC
1361 Heck Rd (44408-9599)
P.O. Box 325 (44408-0325)
PHONE.................................330 482-1745
John Rance, *Pr*
Karen Rance, *Treas*
EMP: 15 EST: 1997
SQ FT: 20,000
SALES (est): 2.23MM **Privately Held**
Web: www.ranceindustries.com
SIC: 3441 Fabricated structural metal

(G-5050)
S-P COMPANY INC (PA)
400 W Railroad St Ste 1 (44408-1294)
PHONE.................................330 782-5651
Gregory Smith, *CEO*
Clarence R Smith Junior, *Ch Bd*
Douglas Hagy, *
Richard Kamperman, *
EMP: 90 EST: 1946
SQ FT: 44,000
SALES (est): 33.46MM
SALES (corp-wide): 33.46MM **Privately Held**
SIC: 3469 3443 3498 6512 Metal stampings, nec; Tanks, standard or custom fabricated: metal plate; Tube fabricating (contract bending and shaping); Commercial and industrial building operation

(G-5051)
SPECIALTY CERAMICS INC
41995 State Route 344 (44408-9421)
PHONE.................................330 482-0800
Richard Ludwig, *Pr*
Richard F Wilk, *
EMP: 100 EST: 1990
SQ FT: 47,000
SALES (est): 10.28MM **Privately Held**
Web: www.scifibre.com
SIC: 3433 3255 Logs, gas fireplace; Clay refractories
PA: Unifrax Holding Co.
600 Riverwalk Pkwy
Tonawanda NY 14150

(G-5052)
STAR FAB INC
400 W Railroad St Ste 8 (44408-1294)
P.O. Box 553 (44406-0553)
PHONE.................................330 482-1601
John Zepernick, *Brnch Mgr*
EMP: 40
SALES (corp-wide): 15.54MM **Privately Held**
Web: www.starext.com
SIC: 3354 3711 Aluminum extruded products ; Automobile assembly, including specialty automobiles
PA: Star Fab, Inc.
7055 Herbert Rd
Canfield OH 44406
330 533-9469

(G-5053)
VARI-WALL TUBE SPECIALISTS INC
1350 Wardingsley Ave (44408-9727)
P.O. Box 340 (44408-0340)
PHONE.................................330 482-0000
Randall Alexoff, *Pr*
Peter Alexoff, *
Thomas Lodge, *
▲ EMP: 100 EST: 1985
SQ FT: 60,000
SALES (est): 9.93MM **Privately Held**
Web: www.vari-wall.com
SIC: 3354 3751 3714 Shapes, extruded aluminum, nec; Motorcycles, bicycles and parts; Motor vehicle parts and accessories

(G-5054)
VIVO BROTHERS LLC
1387 Columbiana Lisbon Rd (44408-9485)
PHONE.................................330 629-8686
Vince Vivo, *Prin*
EMP: 10 EST: 2000
SALES (est): 1.57MM **Privately Held**
Web: www.vivobrothers.com
SIC: 2599 Cabinets, factory

(G-5055)
VPL LLC
14101 Market St (44408-9788)
PHONE.................................330 549-0195
EMP: 10 EST: 2017
SALES (est): 260.49K **Privately Held**
SIC: 2084 Wines

(G-5056)
ZARBANA ALUM EXTRUSIONS LLC
41738 Esterly Dr (44408-9448)
P.O. Box 46 (44408-0046)
PHONE.................................330 482-5092
Billy Joe Miller, *Administration Finance*
EMP: 37 EST: 2005
SALES (est): 14.77MM
SALES (corp-wide): 395.23K **Privately Held**
Web: www.zarbana.com
SIC: 3354 Aluminum extruded products
HQ: Roccafranca Spa
Via Rudiana 4
Roccafranca BS 25030

(G-5057)
ZARBANA INDUSTRIES INC
41738 Esterly Dr (44408-9448)
P.O. Box 46 (44408-0046)
PHONE.................................330 482-5092
EMP: 37
Web: www.zarbana.com
SIC: 3354 Aluminum extruded products

(G-5058)
ZORICH INDUSTRIES INC
1400 Wardingsley Ave (44408-9727)
PHONE.................................330 482-9803
Frank Phillips, *Prin*
EMP: 9 EST: 2004
SALES (est): 335K **Privately Held**
Web: www.zorichind.com
SIC: 3999 Atomizers, toiletry

Columbus
Delaware County

(G-5059)
BREAKING BREAD PIZZA COMPANY
8824 Commerce Loop Dr (43240-2121)
PHONE.................................614 754-4777
Thomas Dumit, *Pr*
William York, *VP*
Micheal Scott, *VP*
EMP: 9 EST: 2006
SALES (est): 184.4K **Privately Held**
SIC: 2051 Bread, cake, and related products

(G-5060)
BRY AIR INC
8415 Pulsar Pl Ste 200 (43240-4032)
PHONE.................................614 839-0250
EMP: 6 EST: 2018
SALES (est): 62.7K **Privately Held**
Web: www.bry-air.com
SIC: 3585 Refrigeration and heating equipment

(G-5061)
CABINET SHOP
9075 Antares Ave (43240-2012)
PHONE.................................614 885-9676
Hans Jurawitz, *Owner*
EMP: 9 EST: 2007
SALES (est): 868.57K **Privately Held**
Web: www.thecabshop.com
SIC: 2434 Wood kitchen cabinets

(G-5062)
EXACT EQUIPMENT CORPORATION (HQ)
1900 Polaris Pkwy (43240-4035)
PHONE.................................215 295-2000
Robert C Enichan, *Pr*
EMP: 10 EST: 1986
SQ FT: 9,000
SALES (est): 6.14MM
SALES (corp-wide): 3.79B **Publicly Held**
SIC: 3565 3596 3824 Packaging machinery; Industrial scales; Fluid meters and counting devices
PA: Mettler-Toledo International Inc.
1900 Polaris Pkwy Fl 6
Columbus OH 43240
614 438-4511

(G-5063)
HEADLEE ENTERPRISES LTD
Also Called: AlphaGraphics
9015 Antares Ave (43240-2012)
PHONE.................................614 785-1476
Chad Headlee, *Pt*
Murray Headlee, *Pt*
EMP: 8 EST: 2001
SQ FT: 4,200
SALES (est): 972.06K **Privately Held**
Web: www.alphagraphics.com
SIC: 2752 Commercial printing, lithographic

(G-5064)
MCGRAW-HILL SCHL EDCATN HLDNGS
8787 Orion Pl (43240-4027)
PHONE.................................614 430-4000
Chris Wiggens, *Prin*
EMP: 750
Web: www.mheducation.com
SIC: 2731 Book publishing
HQ: Mcgraw-Hill School Education Holdings, Llc
2 Penn Plz Fl 20
New York NY 10121
646 766-2000

(G-5065)
METTLER-TOLEDO INTL FIN INC (DH)
1900 Polaris Pkwy (43240-4055)
PHONE.................................614 438-4511
EMP: 11 EST: 2008
SALES (est): 1.43MM
SALES (corp-wide): 3.79B **Publicly Held**
SIC: 3596 5049 7699 3821 Industrial scales; Analytical instruments; Professional instrument repair services; Pipettes, hemocytometer
HQ: Mettler-Toledo, Llc
1900 Polaris Pkwy Fl 6
Columbus OH 43240
614 438-4511

(G-5066)
METTLER-TOLEDO INTL INC (PA)
1900 Polaris Pkwy (43240-4055)
PHONE.................................614 438-4511
Patrick Kaltenbach, *Pr*
Robert F Spoerry, *Non-Executive Chairman of the Board*
Shawn P Vadala, *CFO*
◆ EMP: 2963 EST: 1991
SALES (est): 3.79B
SALES (corp-wide): 3.79B **Publicly Held**
Web: www.mt.com
SIC: 3826 3596 3821 3823 Analytical instruments; Industrial scales; Laboratory measuring apparatus; Process control instruments

(G-5067)
METTLER-TOLEDO LLC (HQ)
1900 Polaris Pkwy (43240-4055)
PHONE.................................614 438-4511
◆ EMP: 1000 EST: 1901
SALES (est): 2B
SALES (corp-wide): 3.79B **Publicly Held**
Web: www.mt.com
SIC: 3596 5049 7699 3821 Industrial scales; Analytical instruments; Professional instrument repair services; Pipettes, hemocytometer
PA: Mettler-Toledo International Inc.
1900 Polaris Pkwy Fl 6
Columbus OH 43240
614 438-4511

(G-5068)
METTLR-TLEDO GLOBL HLDNGS LLC (HQ)
1900 Polaris Pkwy (43240-4035)
PHONE.................................614 438-4511
Mary T Finnegan, *Treas*
EMP: 57 EST: 2010
SALES (est): 1.23MM
SALES (corp-wide): 3.79B **Publicly Held**
SIC: 3451 3826 Screw machine products; Analytical instruments
PA: Mettler-Toledo International Inc.
1900 Polaris Pkwy Fl 6
Columbus OH 43240
614 438-4511

(G-5069)
RAININ INSTRUMENT LLC
1900 Polaris Pkwy (43240-4035)
PHONE.................................510 564-1600
Ruben Rosso, *Prin*
EMP: 20 EST: 2008
SALES (est): 2.19MM **Privately Held**
Web: www.mt.com
SIC: 3596 Scales and balances, except laboratory

(G-5070)
RENEWAL BY ANDERSEN LLC
400 Lazelle Rd Ste 1 (43240-2077)
PHONE.................................614 781-9600
Jake Zahnow, *Prin*
EMP: 7
SALES (corp-wide): 1.78B **Privately Held**
Web: www.renewalbyandersen.com
SIC: 3442 2431 Screens, window, metal; Millwork
HQ: Renewal By Andersen Llc

Columbus - Delaware County (G-5071)

9900 Jamaica Ave S
Cottage Grove MN 55016
855 871-7377

(G-5071)
VEEAM GOVERNMENT SOLUTIONS LLC
8800 Lyra Dr Ste 350 (43240-2151)
PHONE.................................614 339-8200
William Largent, *Prin*
Ming Miranda, *
EMP: 25 **EST:** 2018
SALES (est): 1.35MM **Privately Held**
SIC: 7372 Prepackaged software

(G-5072)
VEEAM SOFTWARE CORPORATION (PA)
8800 Lyra Dr Ste 350 (43240)
PHONE.................................614 339-8200
William H Largent, *CEO*
Ratmir Timashev, *
Rick Hoffman, *WORLDWIDE CHANNELS ALLIANCES*
Carrie Reber, *WORLDWIDE Marketing*
Doug Hazelman, *Product Strategy Vice President*
EMP: 1274 **EST:** 2007
SALES (est): 963MM **Privately Held**
Web: www.veeam.com
SIC: 7372 Business oriented computer software

(G-5073)
VIAVI SOLUTIONS INC
8740 Orion Pl Ste 100 (43240-4063)
PHONE.................................316 522-4981
EMP: 8
SALES (corp-wide): 1.11B **Publicly Held**
Web: www.viavisolutions.com
SIC: 3826 3674 Analytical instruments; Optical isolators
PA: Viavi Solutions Inc.
1445 S Spectrum Blvd # 102
Chandler AZ 85286
408 404-3600

Columbus
Franklin County

(G-5074)
1ONE STOP PRINTING INC
1509 Blatt Blvd Ste 8303 (43230-6925)
PHONE.................................614 216-1438
Deon Pollard, *Pr*
EMP: 10 **EST:** 2019
SALES (est): 549.09K **Privately Held**
Web: www.1onestopinc.com
SIC: 2752 Commercial printing, lithographic

(G-5075)
2 TONES BREWING CO
145 N Hamilton Rd (43213-1308)
PHONE.................................740 412-0845
EMP: 6 **EST:** 2016
SALES (est): 488.62K **Privately Held**
Web: www.2tonesbrewingco.com
SIC: 2082 Malt beverages

(G-5076)
212 SCENT STUDIO LLC
950 Vernon Rd (43209-2469)
PHONE.................................614 906-3673
EMP: 7 **EST:** 2020
SALES (est): 64.31K **Privately Held**
Web: www.212scentstudio.com
SIC: 3999 Candles

(G-5077)
4MATIC VALVE AUTOMTN OHIO LLC
4993 Cleveland Ave (43231-4734)
PHONE.................................614 806-1221
EMP: 10 **EST:** 2021
SALES (est): 382.98K **Privately Held**
SIC: 3491 Industrial valves

(G-5078)
5TH ELEMENT FITNESS LLC
6124 Busch Blvd (43229-2579)
PHONE.................................614 537-6038
Paris Long, *Managing Member*
EMP: 8 **EST:** 2012
SALES (est): 395.86K **Privately Held**
Web: www.5thelement.fit
SIC: 2819 Industrial inorganic chemicals, nec

(G-5079)
614 MEDIA GROUP LLC
Also Called: 614 Magazine
160 E Main St (43215-5344)
PHONE.................................614 488-4400
EMP: 40 **EST:** 2008
SALES (est): 3.37MM **Privately Held**
Web: www.614mediagroup.com
SIC: 2721 Magazines: publishing and printing

(G-5080)
A L D PRECAST CORP (PA)
400 Frank Rd (43207-2423)
PHONE.................................614 449-3366
William E Anderson, *Prin*
EMP: 8 **EST:** 2007
SALES (est): 4.9MM **Privately Held**
Web: www.aldprecast.com
SIC: 3272 Concrete products, precast, nec

(G-5081)
A WESTLAKE AXIALL CO
1441 Universal Rd (43207-1730)
PHONE.................................614 754-3677
EMP: 6 **EST:** 2019
SALES (est): 104.97K **Privately Held**
Web: www.westlake.com
SIC: 2821 Plastics materials and resins

(G-5082)
A-DISPLAY SERVICE CORP
Also Called: Signature Store Fixtures
541 Dana Ave (43223-5202)
PHONE.................................614 469-1230
Anthony Grilli, *Pr*
Nancy Grilli, *Sec*
Mario Grilli, *CEO*
EMP: 10 **EST:** 1978
SQ FT: 8,500
SALES (est): 866.51K **Privately Held**
Web: www.signaturemillshop.com
SIC: 2434 Wood kitchen cabinets

(G-5083)
AAT USA LLC
Also Called: Able Applied Technologies
1850 Denune Ave (43211-1718)
P.O. Box 12515 (43212-0515)
PHONE.................................614 388-8866
Michael Mcnamara, *CEO*
Rob Sanpini, *
EMP: 32 **EST:** 1989
SQ FT: 150,000
SALES (est): 9.19MM **Privately Held**
Web: www.ableat.com
SIC: 3648 3699 Lighting equipment, nec; Electrical equipment and supplies, nec

(G-5084)
ABBOTT
923 Dennison Ave (43201-3400)
PHONE.................................608 931-1057
Stephanie Ferguson, *Prin*
EMP: 11 **EST:** 2015
SALES (est): 1.57MM **Privately Held**
SIC: 2834 Pharmaceutical preparations

(G-5085)
ABBOTT LABORATORIES
Also Called: Abbott Nutrition
585 Cleveland Ave (43215-1755)
P.O. Box 16546 (43216)
PHONE.................................614 624-3191
Eric Christensen, *Mgr*
EMP: 550
SQ FT: 378,500
SALES (corp-wide): 40.11B **Publicly Held**
Web: www.abbott.com
SIC: 2834 2087 2086 2032 Pharmaceutical preparations; Flavoring extracts and syrups, nec; Bottled and canned soft drinks; Canned specialties
PA: Abbott Laboratories
100 Abbott Park Rd
Abbott Park IL 60064
224 667-6100

(G-5086)
ABBOTT LABORATORIES
350 N 5th St (43215-2103)
PHONE.................................614 624-3192
EMP: 13
SALES (corp-wide): 40.11B **Publicly Held**
Web: www.abbott.com
SIC: 2834 Pharmaceutical preparations
PA: Abbott Laboratories
100 Abbott Park Rd
Abbott Park IL 60064
224 667-6100

(G-5087)
ABBOTT LABORATORIES
Also Called: Tobal Products
2900 Easton Square Pl (43219-6225)
PHONE.................................847 937-6100
Steven K Williams, *Brnch Mgr*
EMP: 51
SALES (corp-wide): 40.11B **Publicly Held**
Web: www.abbott.com
SIC: 2834 3841 2879 4226 Pharmaceutical preparations; Surgical and medical instruments; Insecticides, agricultural or household; Special warehousing and storage, nec
PA: Abbott Laboratories
100 Abbott Park Rd
Abbott Park IL 60064
224 667-6100

(G-5088)
ABBOTT LABORATORIES
625 Cleveland Ave (43215-1754)
P.O. Box 16718 (43216-6718)
PHONE.................................800 551-5838
EMP: 198
SALES (corp-wide): 40.11B **Publicly Held**
Web: www.abbott.com
SIC: 2834 Pharmaceutical preparations
PA: Abbott Laboratories
100 Abbott Park Rd
Abbott Park IL 60064
224 667-6100

(G-5089)
ABBOTT LABORATORIES
Abbott Nutrition
3300 Stelzer Rd (43219-3034)
PHONE.................................614 624-7677
Don Paton, *Brnch Mgr*
EMP: 3000
SALES (corp-wide): 40.11B **Publicly Held**
Web: www.abbott.com
SIC: 2834 Druggists' preparations (pharmaceuticals)
PA: Abbott Laboratories
100 Abbott Park Rd
Abbott Park IL 60064
224 667-6100

(G-5090)
ABITEC CORPORATION (HQ)
501 W 1st Ave (43215-1101)
PHONE.................................614 429-6464
◆ **EMP:** 20 **EST:** 1994
SQ FT: 12,000
SALES (est): 98.1MM
SALES (corp-wide): 25.28B **Privately Held**
Web: www.abiteccorp.com
SIC: 2844 2834 2869 2045 Perfumes, cosmetics and other toilet preparations; Pharmaceutical preparations; Industrial organic chemicals, nec; Prepared flour mixes and doughs
PA: Wittington Investments Limited
10 Grosvenor Street
London W1K 4
207 399-6565

(G-5091)
ABLE PALLET MFG & REPR
1271 Harmon Ave (43223-3306)
P.O. Box 23083 (43223-0083)
PHONE.................................614 444-2115
Charles O'hara, *Pr*
EMP: 8 **EST:** 1984
SQ FT: 5,089
SALES (est): 293.77K **Privately Held**
SIC: 7699 2448 Pallet repair; Wood pallets and skids

(G-5092)
ACCENT DRAPERY CO INC
Also Called: Accent Drapery Supply Co
1180 Goodale Blvd (43212-3793)
PHONE.................................614 488-0741
Patrick Casbarro, *Pr*
Brian Whiteside, *
EMP: 27 **EST:** 1967
SQ FT: 19,500
SALES (est): 2.35MM **Privately Held**
Web: www.accentdraperies.com
SIC: 5714 5023 2391 Draperies; Draperies; Curtains and draperies

(G-5093)
ACCLAIMD INC
1275 Kinnear Rd (43212-1180)
PHONE.................................614 219-9519
David Lyons, *Pr*
EMP: 15 **EST:** 2012
SALES (est): 801.63K
SALES (corp-wide): 94.93K **Privately Held**
Web: domains.squadhelp.com
SIC: 7372 Application computer software
PA: Eboss Online Recruitment Solutions (Eboss) Limited
Unit 13
Poole
207 183-0675

(G-5094)
ACCULON ENERGY INC ✪
1275 Kinnear Rd (43212-1180)
PHONE.................................614 259-7792
Andrew Thomas, *Pr*
EMP: 11 **EST:** 2022
SALES (est): 1.94MM **Privately Held**
SIC: 3691 Storage batteries

(G-5095)
ACCURATE INSULATION LLC
495 S High St Ste 50 (43215-5689)
PHONE.................................302 241-0940

GEOGRAPHIC SECTION

Columbus - Franklin County (G-5119)

EMP: 10 **EST:** 2016
SALES (est): 2.11MM **Privately Held**
Web:
www.accurateinsulationdelaware.com
SIC: 3571 Personal computers (microcomputers)

(G-5096)
ACCURATE MANUFACTURING COMPANY
1940 Lone Eagle St (43228-3626)
P.O. Box 28666 (43228-0666)
PHONE...................614 878-6510
Tom Lindblom, *CEO*
Angela Merrill, *VP*
EMP: 24 **EST:** 1943
SQ FT: 10,000
SALES (est): 2.18MM **Privately Held**
Web:
www.accuratemanufacturingco.com
SIC: 3542 3599 3548 Presses: hydraulic and pneumatic, mechanical and manual; Machine shop, jobbing and repair; Welding apparatus

(G-5097)
ACCUSCAN INSTRUMENTS INC
Also Called: Omni Tech Electronics
5098 Trabue Rd (43228-9391)
PHONE...................614 878-6644
R H Mandalaywala, *Pr*
R H, *Pr*
EMP: 10 **EST:** 1996
SQ FT: 10,000
SALES (est): 744.8K **Privately Held**
Web: www.omnitech-usa.com
SIC: 3821 Laboratory apparatus, except heating and measuring

(G-5098)
ACME HOME IMPROVEMENT CO INC
2909 E 4th Ave (43219-2827)
P.O. Box 13063 (43213-0063)
PHONE...................614 252-2129
Judith Hinckley, *Pr*
James Linthwaite, *VP*
Vicki Romanoff, *Sec*
EMP: 10 **EST:** 1958
SQ FT: 7,800
SALES (est): 1.02MM **Privately Held**
SIC: 1521 3441 1761 1751 General remodeling, single-family houses; Fabricated structural metal; Roofing, siding, and sheetmetal work; Carpentry work

(G-5099)
ACOUSTECH SYSTEMS LLC
1250 Arthur E Adams Dr (43221-3560)
PHONE...................270 796-5853
EMP: 9 **EST:** 2014
SALES (est): 400.45K **Privately Held**
Web: www.acoustechsystems.com
SIC: 3999 Manufacturing industries, nec

(G-5100)
ACTION EXPRESS INC
100 E Campus View Blvd Ste 250 (43235-4647)
PHONE...................929 351-3620
Levan Lomidze, *Pr*
EMP: 7 **EST:** 2018
SALES (est): 629.97K **Privately Held**
SIC: 2741 Miscellaneous publishing

(G-5101)
ACTUAL INDUSTRIES LLC
655 N James Rd (43219-1837)
PHONE...................614 379-2739
Fredrick Lee, *Prin*
EMP: 7 **EST:** 2012
SALES (est): 197.5K **Privately Held**

Web: www.actualindustries.com
SIC: 3999 Manufacturing industries, nec

(G-5102)
ADSR ENT LLC
1888 Noe Bixby Rd (43232-2675)
PHONE...................773 280-2129
EMP: 10
SALES (est): 413.11K **Privately Held**
SIC: 3537 7389 Trucks: freight, baggage, etc.: industrial, except mining; Business services, nec

(G-5103)
ADVANCED FUEL SYSTEMS INC
841 Alton Ave (43219-3710)
PHONE...................614 252-8422
Timothy L Thickstun, *Pr*
Steve Thickstun, *VP*
Joanne Thickstun, *Sec*
▼ **EMP:** 8 **EST:** 1998
SQ FT: 8,500
SALES (est): 2.1MM **Privately Held**
Web: www.advfuel.com
SIC: 3561 3728 Pumps and pumping equipment; Aircraft parts and equipment, nec

(G-5104)
ADVANTAGE PRINT SOLUTIONS LLC
79 Acton Rd (43214-3301)
PHONE...................614 519-2392
Debbie Smith, *Prin*
EMP: 6 **EST:** 2009
SALES (est): 443.28K **Privately Held**
Web: www.advantageprintsolutions.com
SIC: 2752 Offset printing

(G-5105)
AGRI COMMUNICATORS INC
Also Called: Ohio's Country Journal
280 N High St Fl 6 (43215-2594)
PHONE...................614 273-0465
Bart Johnson, *Pr*
Marilyn Johnson, *Sec*
EMP: 23 **EST:** 1972
SALES (est): 759.53K **Privately Held**
Web: www.ocj.com
SIC: 7313 2721 Radio, television, publisher representatives; Periodicals, publishing only

(G-5106)
AGRIUM ADVANCED TECH US INC
701 Kaderly Dr (43228-1031)
PHONE...................614 276-5103
Karl Creighton, *Brnch Mgr*
EMP: 7
SALES (corp-wide): 29.06B **Privately Held**
Web: www.nutrien.com
SIC: 2873 Nitrogenous fertilizers
HQ: Agrium Advanced Technologies (U.S.) Inc.
2915 Rocky Mountain Ave # 400
Loveland CO 80538

(G-5107)
AHMF INC (PA)
Also Called: Original Mattress Factory
2245 Wilson Rd (43228-9594)
PHONE...................614 921-1223
Ronald E Trzcinski, *Ch Bd*
Jeffrey C Merill, *VP*
Lawrence S Carlson, *VP*
Perry Doermann, *Sec*
Tony Dempsey, *VP*
EMP: 20 **EST:** 1992
SQ FT: 22,000
SALES (est): 2.42MM **Privately Held**
SIC: 2515 5712 5021 Mattresses and foundations; Bedding and bedsprings; Mattresses

(G-5108)
AIRBRUSH SUGAR SHACK INC
3480 Cleveland Ave (43224-2907)
PHONE...................614 735-4988
EMP: 7 **EST:** 2011
SALES (est): 34K **Privately Held**
SIC: 3952 Brushes, air, artists'

(G-5109)
AKRON BRASS COMPANY
Also Called: Weldon Technologies
3656 Paragon Dr (43228-9750)
PHONE...................614 529-7230
Sean Tillinghast, *Prin*
EMP: 23
SALES (corp-wide): 3.27B **Publicly Held**
Web: www.akronbrass.com
SIC: 3647 3699 3648 Vehicular lighting equipment; Electrical equipment and supplies, nec; Lighting equipment, nec
HQ: Akron Brass Company
343 Venture Blvd
Wooster OH 44691

(G-5110)
AKZO NOBEL COATINGS INC
1313 Windsor Ave Ste 1313 (43211-2851)
PHONE...................614 294-3361
Paul Hoelzer, *Genl Mgr*
EMP: 107
SALES (corp-wide): 11.26B **Privately Held**
SIC: 2851 Paints and allied products
HQ: Akzo Nobel Coatings Inc.
535 Marriott Dr Ste 500
Nashville TN 37214
440 297-5100

(G-5111)
ALL PRO OVRHD DOOR SYSTEMS LLC
1985 Oakland Park Ave (43224-3636)
P.O. Box 361478 (43236-1478)
PHONE...................614 444-3667
EMP: 8 **EST:** 2007
SALES (est): 918.36K **Privately Held**
Web: www.allprodoors.com
SIC: 3442 2431 Metal doors, sash, and trim; Door frames, wood

(G-5112)
ALLFAB INC
2273 Williams Rd (43207-5121)
PHONE...................614 491-4944
Lise S Roth, *Pr*
Russell W Roth, *VP*
EMP: 15 **EST:** 1985
SQ FT: 15,000
SALES (est): 2.98MM **Privately Held**
Web: www.allfabinc.com
SIC: 3444 Sheet metalwork

(G-5113)
ALLIED FABRICATING & WLDG CO
5699 Chantry Dr (43232-4731)
PHONE...................614 751-6664
Thomas Caminiti, *CEO*
Joseph Caminiti, *
Jack Burgoon, *
Raymond Cunningham, *
EMP: 34 **EST:** 1971
SQ FT: 30,000
SALES (est): 4.54MM **Privately Held**
Web: www.afaw.net
SIC: 3444 7692 3535 3441 Sheet metal specialties, not stamped; Welding repair; Conveyors and conveying equipment; Fabricated structural metal

(G-5114)
ALLIED MINERAL PRODUCTS LLC (PA)
2700 Scioto Pkwy (43221-4660)
PHONE...................614 876-0244
Jonathan R Tabor, *Pr*
Anthony S Disaia, *
John S Halsted Junior, *VP*
Paul D Jamieson, *
Douglas K Doza, *
◆ **EMP:** 290 **EST:** 1961
SQ FT: 450,000
SALES (est): 91.72MM
SALES (corp-wide): 91.72MM **Privately Held**
Web: www.alliedmineral.com
SIC: 3297 Nonclay refractories

(G-5115)
ALLIED SIGN CO
818 Marion Rd (43207-2553)
P.O. Box 7760 (43207-0760)
PHONE...................614 443-9656
Richard L Frost, *Pr*
EMP: 11 **EST:** 1955
SQ FT: 8,000
SALES (est): 417.74K **Privately Held**
Web: www.alliedsignco.com
SIC: 3993 Signs and advertising specialties

(G-5116)
ALRO STEEL CORPORATION
555 Hilliard Rome Rd (43228-9265)
PHONE...................614 878-7271
Steve White, *Mgr*
EMP: 32
SALES (corp-wide): 3.43B **Privately Held**
Web: www.alro.com
SIC: 5051 5085 5162 3444 Steel; Industrial supplies; Plastics materials, nec; Sheet metalwork
PA: Alro Steel Corporation
3100 E High St
Jackson MI 49203
517 787-5500

(G-5117)
ALTEC INDUSTRIES INC
1667 Watkins Rd (43207-3323)
PHONE...................614 295-4895
Christopher Anderson, *Brnch Mgr*
EMP: 6
SALES (corp-wide): 1.21B **Privately Held**
Web: www.altec.com
SIC: 3531 Construction machinery
HQ: Altec Industries, Inc.
210 Inverness Center Dr
Birmingham AL 35242
205 991-7733

(G-5118)
ALVITO CUSTOM IMPRINTS LLC
726 E Lincoln Ave (43229-5024)
PHONE...................614 207-1004
EMP: 6 **EST:** 2009
SALES (est): 200.84K **Privately Held**
Web: www.alvitoimprints.com
SIC: 2752 Commercial printing, lithographic

(G-5119)
AMATECH INC
1633 Woodland Ave (43219-1135)
PHONE...................614 252-2506
Rick Bittner, *Brnch Mgr*
EMP: 24
Web: www.amatechinc.com
SIC: 3086 7336 2671 Plastics foam products; Package design; Plastic film, coated or laminated for packaging
PA: Amatech, Inc.
1460 Grimm Dr

(PA)=Parent Co (HQ)=Headquarters
✿ = New Business established in last 2 years

2024 Harris Ohio Industrial Directory

Erie PA 16501

(G-5120)
AMERICAN BOTTLING COMPANY
Also Called: Dr. Pepper 7 Up Columbus
960 Stelzer Rd (43219-3740)
PHONE..................614 237-4201
Dan Grassbaugh, *Brnch Mgr*
EMP: 79
Web: www.drpepper.com
SIC: 2086 Soft drinks: packaged in cans, bottles, etc.
HQ: The American Bottling Company
6425 Hall Of Fame Ln
Frisco TX 75034

(G-5121)
AMERICAN BOTTLING COMPANY
Also Called: 7 Up / R C/Canada Dry Btlg Co
950 Stelzer Rd (43219-3740)
PHONE..................614 237-4201
Mike Stall, *Brnch Mgr*
EMP: 107
Web: www.keurigdrpepper.com
SIC: 2086 5149 Soft drinks: packaged in cans, bottles, etc.; Groceries and related products, nec
HQ: The American Bottling Company
6425 Hall Of Fame Ln
Frisco TX 75034

(G-5122)
AMERICAN COLORSCANS INC
Also Called: ACS Commercial Graphics
5178 Sinclair Rd (43229-5437)
PHONE..................614 895-0233
EMP: 22
SIC: 2752 Color lithography

(G-5123)
AMERICAN COMMUNITY NEWSPAPERS
5255 Sinclair Rd (43229-5042)
PHONE..................614 888-4567
EMP: 7 **EST:** 2009
SALES (est): 109.38K **Privately Held**
SIC: 2711 Newspapers, publishing and printing

(G-5124)
AMERICAN CORRUGATED PRODUCTS INC
4700 Alkire Rd (43228-3495)
PHONE..................614 870-2000
EMP: 220
SIC: 2653 3086 2671 2657 Boxes, corrugated: made from purchased materials; Plastics foam products; Paper; coated and laminated packaging; Folding paperboard boxes

(G-5125)
AMERICAN IMPRSSIONS SPORTSWEAR
Also Called: American Imprssions Sportswear
5523 Mercer St (43235-7596)
PHONE..................614 848-6677
EMP: 9 **EST:** 1992
SALES (est): 1MM **Privately Held**
SIC: 2396 2759 Screen printing on fabric articles; Promotional printing

(G-5126)
AMERICAN ISOSTATIC PRESSES INC
Also Called: A I P
1205 S Columbus Airport Rd (43207-4304)
PHONE..................614 497-3148
▲ **EMP:** 16 **EST:** 1992
SQ FT: 14,000
SALES (est): 4.43MM **Privately Held**

Web: www.aiphip.com
SIC: 3821 Furnaces, laboratory

(G-5127)
AMERICAN LED-GIBLE INC
Also Called: Led-Andon
1776 Lone Eagle St (43228-3655)
PHONE..................614 851-1100
Charles R Morrison, *Pr*
Robin L Morrison, *CFO*
▲ **EMP:** 10 **EST:** 1976
SQ FT: 7,000
SALES (est): 1.81MM **Privately Held**
Web: www.ledgible.com
SIC: 3993 Electric signs

(G-5128)
AMERICAN ORTHOPEDICS INC (PA)
1151 W 5th Ave (43212-2529)
PHONE..................614 291-6454
Richard F Nitsch, *Pr*
Ronald Kidd, *Pr*
Loretta Kidd, *Sec*
Zachary Ruhl, *VP*
Barbara Berndt, *Mgr*
EMP: 19 **EST:** 1970
SQ FT: 7,000
SALES (est): 2.49MM
SALES (corp-wide): 2.49MM **Privately Held**
Web: www.amerortho.com
SIC: 3842 Prosthetic appliances

(G-5129)
AMERICAN REGENT INC
960 Crupper Ave (43229-1109)
PHONE..................614 436-2222
Joseph Kenneth Keller, *CEO*
EMP: 100
Web: www.americanregent.com
SIC: 2834 Pharmaceutical preparations
HQ: American Regent, Inc.
5 Ramsay Rd
Shirley NY 11967
631 924-4000

(G-5130)
AMERICAN SCIENTIFIC LLC
6420 Fiesta Dr (43235-5208)
PHONE..................614 764-9002
Sanjay Sadana, *Managing Member*
▲ **EMP:** 7 **EST:** 1999
SALES (est): 1.03MM **Privately Held**
Web: www.american-scientific.com
SIC: 3826 Analytical instruments

(G-5131)
AMERISOURCE HEALTH SVCS LLC
Also Called: American Health Packaging
2550 John Glenn Ave Ste A (43217)
PHONE..................614 492-8177
▲ **EMP:** 89 **EST:** 1996
SQ FT: 153,000
SALES (est): 49.88MM
SALES (corp-wide): 262.17B **Publicly Held**
Web: www.americanhealthpackaging.com
SIC: 2064 4783 Cough drops, except pharmaceutical preparations; Packing goods for shipping
HQ: Amerisourcebergen Drug Corporation
1 West First Ave
Conshohocken PA 19428
610 727-7000

(G-5132)
AMERITECH PUBLISHING INC
Also Called: SBC
2550 Corporate Exchange Dr Ste 310 (43231-7659)

PHONE..................614 895-6123
David Lobdell, *Mgr*
EMP: 1328
SALES (corp-wide): 122.43B **Publicly Held**
SIC: 2741 Directories, telephone: publishing only, not printed on site
HQ: Ameritech Publishing, Inc.
23500 Northwestern Hwy
Southfield MI

(G-5133)
AMPSCO DIVISION
2301 Fairwood Ave (43207-2768)
PHONE..................614 444-2181
Dennis J Leukart, *Pr*
Matthew Leukart, *VP*
EMP: 170 **EST:** 1960
SQ FT: 250,000
SALES (est): 437.27K
SALES (corp-wide): 49.65MM **Privately Held**
Web: www.superior-dictool.com
SIC: 3599 Machine shop, jobbing and repair
PA: Superior Production Llc
2301 Fairwood Ave
Columbus OH 43207
614 444-2181

(G-5134)
AMT MACHINE SYSTEMS LIMITED
1760 Zollinger Rd Ste 2 (43221-2843)
PHONE..................740 965-2693
Dennis R Pugh, *Pt*
Howard Ubert, *Pt*
Gregory Knight, *Pt*
Eric Ribble, *Pt*
EMP: 10 **EST:** 1996
SQ FT: 2,000
SALES (est): 751.7K **Privately Held**
SIC: 3451 Screw machine products

(G-5135)
AMT MACHINE SYSTEMS LTD
50 W Broad St Ste 1200 (43215-3301)
PHONE..................614 635-8050
Dennis R Pugh, *CEO*
Howard Ubert, *Prin*
▲ **EMP:** 10 **EST:** 2009
SALES (est): 491.68K **Privately Held**
Web: www.amtmachinesystems.com
SIC: 3599 Machine shop, jobbing and repair

(G-5136)
AMTEKCO INDUSTRIES LLC (HQ)
Also Called: Amtekco
2300 Lockbourne Rd (43207-2167)
PHONE..................614 228-6590
Earl B Sisson, *Pr*
John Mccormick, *Pr*
Bruce Wasserstrom, *
Hugh E Kirkwood Junior, *Pr*
Ollie Rossman, *
EMP: 100 **EST:** 1962
SALES (est): 29.59MM
SALES (corp-wide): 378.09MM **Privately Held**
Web: www.amtekco.com
SIC: 3469 2541 Kitchen fixtures and equipment: metal, except cast aluminum; Cabinets, except refrigerated: show, display, etc.: wood
PA: The Wasserstrom Company
4500 E Broad St
Columbus OH 43213
614 228-6525

(G-5137)
AMTEKCO INDUSTRIES INC
Also Called: AMTEKCO INDUSTRIES INC
33 W Hinman Ave (43207-1809)

PHONE..................614 228-6525
Ron Bower, *Pr*
EMP: 50
SALES (corp-wide): 378.09MM **Privately Held**
Web: www.amtekco.com
SIC: 2541 3469 Wood partitions and fixtures; Metal stampings, nec
HQ: Amtekco Industries, Llc
2300 Lockbourne Rd
Columbus OH 43207
614 228-6590

(G-5138)
ANADEM INC
3620 N High St Ste 201 (43214-3643)
PHONE..................614 262-2539
EMP: 7 **EST:** 1977
SALES (est): 490.08M **Privately Held**
Web: www.anadem.com
SIC: 2741 Miscellaneous publishing

(G-5139)
ANCHOR HOCKING LLC (HQ)
Also Called: Anchor Hocking Company, The
1600 Dublin Rd Ste 200 (43215-2095)
PHONE..................740 687-2500
Mark Eichhorn, *Pr*
Mark Hedstrom, *
Joe Sundberg, *
Bert Filice, *
◆ **EMP:** 1200 **EST:** 1905
SALES (est): 529.62MM
SALES (corp-wide): 697.24MM **Privately Held**
Web: www.anchorhocking.com
SIC: 3089 3229 3411 3221 Cups, plastics, except foam; Tableware, glass or glass ceramic; Metal cans; Glass containers
PA: Anchor Hocking Holdings, Inc.
1600 Dublin Rd Ste 200
Columbus OH 43215
740 687-2500

(G-5140)
ANCHOR HOCKING CORPORATION
1600 Dublin Rd (43215-2095)
PHONE..................614 633-4247
EMP: 19 **EST:** 1928
SALES (est): 1.27MM **Privately Held**
Web: www.anchorhocking.com
SIC: 3229 Pressed and blown glass, nec

(G-5141)
ANCHOR HOCKING HOLDINGS INC (PA)
1600 Dublin Rd Ste 200 (43215)
PHONE..................740 687-2500
Mark Eichhorn, *Pr*
Bert Filice, *CSO*
Mike Hanson, *
Jamie Keller, *
EMP: 503 **EST:** 2011
SALES (est): 697.24MM
SALES (corp-wide): 697.24MM **Privately Held**
Web: www.theoneidagroup.com
SIC: 3089 3469 Plastics kitchenware, tableware, and houseware; Kitchen fixtures and equipment, porcelain enameled

(G-5142)
ANCHOR PATTERN COMPANY
748 Frebis Ave (43206-3709)
PHONE..................614 443-2221
Wilbur S Smith Iii, *Pr*
Barbara L Smith, *Sec*
EMP: 6 **EST:** 1967
SQ FT: 4,000
SALES (est): 966.32K **Privately Held**
Web: www.anchorpattern.com

GEOGRAPHIC SECTION

Columbus - Franklin County (G-5166)

SIC: **3543** Industrial patterns

(G-5143)
ANDELYN BIOSCIENCES INC (HQ)
1180 Arthur E Adams Dr (43221-3542)
PHONE.........................844 228-2366
Adam Lauber, *Admn*
Michael Osborne, *
Wade Macedone, *
EMP: 210 **EST:** 1998
SALES (corp-wide): 3.6B **Privately Held**
Web: www.andelynbio.com
SIC: **2834** Pharmaceutical preparations
PA: Nationwide Children's Hospital
   700 Childrens Dr
   Columbus OH 43205
   614 722-2000

(G-5144)
ANDERSON CONCRETE CORP
Also Called: Buckeye Ready Mix
400 Frank Rd (43207-2456)
P.O. Box 398 (43216-0398)
PHONE.........................614 443-0123
Douglas Anderson, *Pr*
Richard D Anderson, *
William Feltz, *Product Vice President*
John Mynes, *
William S Dunn, *
EMP: 150 **EST:** 1921
SALES (est): 31.48MM **Privately Held**
Web: www.andersonconcrete.com
SIC: **3273** Ready-mixed concrete

(G-5145)
ANDERSON GLASS CO INC
2816 Morse Rd (43231-6094)
PHONE.........................614 476-4877
Bradley Anderson, *Pr*
Helena Anderson, *
EMP: 26 **EST:** 1949
SQ FT: 32,000
SALES (est): 2.24MM **Privately Held**
Web: www.andersoncompanies.com
SIC: **5039** 3231 3229 Exterior flat glass; plate or window; Products of purchased glass; Pressed and blown glass, nec

(G-5146)
ANHEUSER-BUSCH LLC
Also Called: Anheuser-Busch
700 Schrock Rd (43229-1159)
PHONE.........................614 847-6213
Kevin Lee, *Mgr*
EMP: 500
SALES (corp-wide): 1.31B **Privately Held**
Web: www.budweisertours.com
SIC: **2082** Beer (alcoholic beverage)
HQ: Anheuser-Busch, Llc
   1 Busch Pl
   Saint Louis MO 63118
   800 342-5283

(G-5147)
ANTHONY-THOMAS CANDY COMPANY (PA)
Also Called: Anthony-Thomas Candy Shoppes
1777 Arlingate Ln (43228)
P.O. Box 21865 (43221)
PHONE.........................614 274-8405
Tom Zanetos, *CEO*
Joseph Zanetos, *
Gregory Zanetos, *
Agnes Zanetos, *
▲ **EMP:** 125 **EST:** 1907
SQ FT: 152,000
SALES (est): 23.3MM
SALES (corp-wide): 23.3MM **Privately Held**

Web: www.anthony-thomas.com
SIC: **2064** 5441 2068 2066 Candy and other confectionery products; Candy, nut, and confectionery stores; Salted and roasted nuts and seeds; Chocolate and cocoa products

(G-5148)
APERA INSTRUMENTS LLC
6656 Busch Blvd (43229-1125)
PHONE.........................614 285-3080
Qingxiang Wu, *Admn*
EMP: 8 **EST:** 2016
SALES (est): 1.17MM **Privately Held**
Web: www.aperainst.com
SIC: **3829** Measuring and controlling devices, nec

(G-5149)
APPIAN MANUFACTURING CORP
2025 Camaro Ave (43207-1716)
PHONE.........................614 445-2230
Fran A Vendetta, *Pr*
▲ **EMP:** 30 **EST:** 1990
SQ FT: 40,000
SALES (est): 6.64MM **Privately Held**
Web: www.appianmfg.com
SIC: **3441** 3498 Fabricated structural metal; Fabricated pipe and fittings
PA: Necco K.K.
   1-7-44, Namiki
   Kawaguchi STM 332-0

(G-5150)
APPLICATION LINK INCORPORATED
4449 Easton Way Fl 2 (43219-7005)
PHONE.........................614 934-1735
Michael Reed, *Pr*
EMP: 15 **EST:** 1979
SQ FT: 2,000
SALES (est): 769.45K **Privately Held**
Web: www.perfectdomain.com
SIC: **7372** 5045 7371 Business oriented computer software; Computers, peripherals, and software; Custom computer programming services

(G-5151)
AQUA SCIENCE INC
1877 E 17th Ave (43219-1006)
PHONE.........................614 252-5000
Dan L Smucker, *Pr*
Darrell L Miller Junior, *VP*
EMP: 34 **EST:** 1983
SQ FT: 28,000
SALES (est): 4.97MM **Privately Held**
Web: www.aquascience.com
SIC: **2899** Water treating compounds

(G-5152)
ARBENZ INC
Also Called: Edwards Steel
1777 Mckinley Ave (43222-1050)
PHONE.........................614 274-6800
EMP: 25 **EST:** 1932
SALES (est): 4.68MM **Privately Held**
Web: www.edwardssteel.com
SIC: **3441** 3444 Fabricated structural metal; Sheet metalwork

(G-5153)
ARIEZHAIR COLLECTION LLC
1747 Olentangy River Rd (43212-1453)
PHONE.........................614 964-5748
Alexis Whitfield, *Managing Member*
EMP: 10
SALES (est): 283.15K **Privately Held**
SIC: **3999** Hair and hair-based products

(G-5154)
ARMADA POWER LLC
230 West St Ste 150 (43215-2785)
PHONE.........................614 721-4844
Ray Pustinger, *Managing Member*
EMP: 8 **EST:** 2014
SQ FT: 2,000
SALES (est): 1.05MM **Privately Held**
Web: www.armadapower.com
SIC: **7371** 3663 Computer software systems analysis and design, custom; Light communications equipment

(G-5155)
ARMOR
2218 Bristol Rd (43221-1204)
PHONE.........................614 459-1414
EMP: 8 **EST:** 2016
SALES (est): 93.02K **Privately Held**
Web: www.highcomarmor.com
SIC: **3555** Printing trades machinery

(G-5156)
ASHLAND CHEMCO INC
Also Called: Ashland Distribution
1979 Atlas St (43228-9645)
P.O. Box 2219 (43216-2219)
PHONE.........................614 790-3333
Ted Harris, *Distribution Vice President*
EMP: 150
SALES (corp-wide): 2.19B **Publicly Held**
SIC: **2899** 5169 Chemical preparations, nec; Chemicals and allied products, nec
HQ: Ashland Chemco Inc.
   1979 Atlas St
   Columbus OH 43228
   859 815-3333

(G-5157)
ASHLAND SPCALTY INGREDIENTS GP
1979 Atlas St (43228-9645)
PHONE.........................614 529-3311
EMP: 151
SALES (corp-wide): 2.19B **Publicly Held**
Web: www.ashland.com
SIC: **2899** Chemical preparations, nec
HQ: Ashland Specialty Ingredients G.P.
   8145 Blazer Dr
   Wilmington DE 19808
   302 594-5000

(G-5158)
ASIST TRANSLATION SERVICES
Also Called: Asist Translation Services
4891 Sawmill Rd Ste 200 (43235-7266)
PHONE.........................614 451-6744
Elena Tsinman, *Pr*
EMP: 12 **EST:** 1983
SQ FT: 8,000
SALES (est): 2.48MM **Privately Held**
Web: www.asisttranslations.com
SIC: **7389** 2791 Translation services; Typesetting

(G-5159)
ASK CHEMICALS LP
4400 Easton Cmns (43219-6226)
P.O. Box 395 (43216-0395)
PHONE.........................614 763-0248
EMP: 8 **EST:** 2017
SALES (est): 218.39K **Privately Held**
Web: www.ask-chemicals.com
SIC: **2899** Chemical preparations, nec

(G-5160)
ASSEMBLY MACHINING WIRE PDTS
Also Called: A M W
2375 Refugee Park (43207-2173)
PHONE.........................614 443-1110

Gregory Allan Donovan, *Pr*
EMP: 7 **EST:** 1974
SQ FT: 10,000
SALES (est): 578.62K **Privately Held**
SIC: **3599** Machine shop, jobbing and repair

(G-5161)
AT&T CORP
Also Called: AT&T
150 E Gay St Ste 4a (43215-3130)
PHONE.........................614 223-8236
Connie Browning, *Pr*
EMP: 31
SALES (corp-wide): 122.43B **Publicly Held**
Web: www.att.com
SIC: **4812** 4813 2741 Cellular telephone services; Telephone communication, except radio; Miscellaneous publishing
HQ: At&T Enterprises, Llc
   208 S Akard St
   Dallas TX 75202
   800 403-3302

(G-5162)
ATCHLEY SIGNS & GRAPHICS LLC
Also Called: 360 Wrapz
1616 Transamerica Ct (43228-9332)
PHONE.........................614 421-7446
Derek Atchley, *Prin*
Christine Atchley, *Prin*
EMP: 13 **EST:** 2006
SALES (est): 991.95K **Privately Held**
Web: www.atchleysigns.com
SIC: **3993** 7389 Signs, not made in custom sign painting shops; Printed circuitry graphic layout

(G-5163)
ATLAS INDUSTRIAL CONTRS LLC (HQ)
Also Called: Atlas Industrial Contractors
5275 Sinclair Rd (43229-5042)
PHONE.........................614 841-4500
George Ghanem, *Pr*
Timothy Seils, *
EMP: 300 **EST:** 1923
SQ FT: 20,000
SALES (est): 95.55MM **Privately Held**
Web: www.atlascos.com
SIC: **1731** 3498 1796 Electrical work; Fabricated pipe and fittings; Machine moving and rigging
PA: Gmg Holdings, Llc
   5275 Sinclair Rd
   Columbus OH 43229

(G-5164)
ATM NERDS LLC
175 S 3rd St Ste 200 (43215-5194)
PHONE.........................614 983-3056
EMP: 10 **EST:** 2021
SALES (est): 750K **Privately Held**
SIC: **3578** Automatic teller machines (ATM)

(G-5165)
AULD CORPORATION
1569 Westbelt Dr (43228-3839)
P.O. Box 218373 (43221-8373)
PHONE.........................614 454-1010
Dan Auld, *CEO*
EMP: 9 **EST:** 2014
SALES (est): 837.19K **Privately Held**
SIC: **3446** 2752 Architectural metalwork; Commercial printing, lithographic

(G-5166)
AUTOBODY SUPPLY COMPANY INC
212 N Grant Ave (43215-2691)
PHONE.........................614 228-4328
EMP: 68

Columbus - Franklin County (G-5167)

GEOGRAPHIC SECTION

SIC: 3563 5013 5198 Air and gas compressors including vacuum pumps; Automotive supplies; Paints, varnishes, and supplies

(G-5167)
AVURE AUTOCLAVE SYSTEMS INC (DH)
Also Called: ABB Autoclave Systems
3721 Corp Dr (43231)
PHONE..............................614 891-2732
Jerry Toops, *Pr*
◆ **EMP:** 12 **EST:** 1986
SQ FT: 20,000
SALES (est): 1.06MM **Publicly Held**
SIC: 3823 5084 Pressure measurement instruments, industrial; Industrial machinery and equipment
HQ: Avure Technologies Incorporated
1830 Airport Exchange Blv
Erlanger KY 41018

(G-5168)
AWC TRANSITION CORPORATION
6540 Huntley Rd (43229-1087)
PHONE..............................614 846-2918
Kelly Davirro, *Pr*
▲ **EMP:** 14 **EST:** 1957
SQ FT: 5,000
SALES (est): 1.46MM **Privately Held**
Web: www.americanwhistle.com
SIC: 3949 Sporting and athletic goods, nec

(G-5169)
B & A HOLISTIC FD & HERBS LLC
Also Called: Holistic Foods Herbs and Books
4550 Heaton Rd Ste B7 (43229-6611)
PHONE..............................614 747-2200
EMP: 10 **EST:** 2011
SALES (est): 200K **Privately Held**
SIC: 2833 Drugs and herbs: grading, grinding, and milling

(G-5170)
B & G TOOL COMPANY
4832 Kenny Rd (43220-2793)
PHONE..............................614 451-2538
Michael Plahuta, *Pr*
Daniel Plahuta, *VP*
EMP: 7 **EST:** 1965
SQ FT: 8,800
SALES (est): 997.47K **Privately Held**
Web: www.b-gtool.com
SIC: 3599 3312 Machine shop, jobbing and repair; Tool and die steel

(G-5171)
B B BRADLEY COMPANY INC
2699 Scioto Pkwy (43221-4658)
PHONE..............................614 777-5600
EMP: 7
SALES (corp-wide): 5.06MM **Privately Held**
Web: www.bbbradley.com
SIC: 3086 5199 Packaging and shipping materials, foamed plastics; Packaging materials
PA: The B B Bradley Company Inc
7755 Crile Rd
Concord Township OH 44077
440 354-2005

(G-5172)
BAKELITE CHEMICALS LLC
1975 Watkins Rd (43207-3443)
PHONE..............................404 652-4000
Rick Urschel, *Pr*
EMP: 69
SALES (corp-wide): 1.29B **Privately Held**

SIC: 2821 Melamine resins, melamine-formaldehyde
HQ: Bakelite Chemicals Llc
1040 Crown Pointe Pkwy
Atlanta GA 30338

(G-5173)
BALL CORPORATION
Also Called: Ball Metal Food Container
2690 Charter St (43228-4600)
PHONE..............................614 771-9112
Gordan Freeman, *Brnch Mgr*
EMP: 65
SALES (corp-wide): 14.03B **Publicly Held**
Web: www.ball.com
SIC: 3411 Metal cans
PA: Ball Corporation
9200 W 108th Cir
Westminster CO 80021
303 469-3131

(G-5174)
BANNER METALS GROUP INC
1308 Holly Ave (43212-3115)
PHONE..............................614 291-3105
Bronson Jones, *CEO*
John E O'brien Iii, *CEO*
C Bronson Jones, *General Vice President**
F M Jaeger, *
James H Kennedy, *
EMP: 40 **EST:** 1921
SQ FT: 70,000
SALES (est): 6.28MM **Privately Held**
Web: www.bannermetalsgroup.com
SIC: 3469 3544 Stamping metal for the trade; Special dies and tools

(G-5175)
BARR ENGINEERING INCORPORATED (PA)
Also Called: National Engrg Archtctral Svcs
2800 Corporate Exchange Dr Ste 240 (43231-7628)
PHONE..............................614 714-0299
Jawdat Siddiqi, *Pr*
Enoch Chipukaizer, *
EMP: 35 **EST:** 1992
SQ FT: 1,500
SALES (est): 8.57MM **Privately Held**
SIC: 8711 8713 8734 1799 Civil engineering; Surveying services; Testing laboratories; Core drilling and cutting

(G-5176)
BASF CORPORATION
Also Called: Midwest Distribution Center
9565 Logistics Ct (43217-0001)
PHONE..............................614 662-5682
Larry Baker, *Brnch Mgr*
EMP: 70
SALES (corp-wide): 74.89B **Privately Held**
Web: www.basf.com
SIC: 2869 2819 2899 2843 Industrial organic chemicals, nec; Industrial inorganic chemicals, nec; Antifreeze compounds; Surface active agents
HQ: Basf Corporation
100 Park Ave
Florham Park NJ 07932
800 962-5781

(G-5177)
BEAM TECHNOLOGIES INC
80 E Rich St Ste 400 (43215-5286)
PHONE..............................800 648-1179
Alex Frommeyer, *CEO*
Alexander Curry, *
Daniel Dykes, *
EMP: 330 **EST:** 2012
SALES (est): 50.05MM **Privately Held**
Web: www.beambenefits.com

SIC: 3841 6411 Surgical and medical instruments; Insurance agents, brokers, and service

(G-5178)
BECKMAN XMO
376 Morrison Rd Ste D (43213-1447)
PHONE..............................614 864-2232
Tracy Beckman, *Prin*
EMP: 10 **EST:** 2010
SALES (est): 444.14K **Privately Held**
Web: www.beckmanxmo.com
SIC: 2752 Offset printing

(G-5179)
BEEHEX INC
1130 Gahanna Pkwy (43230-6615)
PHONE..............................512 633-5304
Benjamin Felnter, *COO*
EMP: 7 **EST:** 2016
SALES (est): 904.09K **Privately Held**
Web: www.beehex.com
SIC: 3555 Printing trades machinery

(G-5180)
BEEHEX LLC
1130 Gahanna Pkwy (43230-6615)
PHONE..............................512 633-5304
EMP: 11 **EST:** 2015
SALES (est): 889.93K **Privately Held**
Web: www.beehex.com
SIC: 2099 Baking powder and soda, yeast, and other leavening agents

(G-5181)
BELEM GROUP LLC
6012 E Main St (43213-3355)
PHONE..............................614 604-6870
Shad Bucher, *Pr*
EMP: 6 **EST:** 2019
SALES (est): 359.82K **Privately Held**
SIC: 2711 Commercial printing and newspaper publishing combined

(G-5182)
BENCHMARK ARCHTECTURAL SYSTEMS
Also Called: Kingspan Benchmark
720 Marion Rd (43207-2553)
PHONE..............................614 444-0110
Russel Shiels, *Pr*
Ilhan Eser, *
▲ **EMP:** 40 **EST:** 1997
SQ FT: 96,000
SALES (est): 20.76MM **Privately Held**
SIC: 3448 Prefabricated metal buildings and components
HQ: Kingspan Insulated Panels Inc.
726 Summerhill Dr
Deland FL 32724
386 626-6789

(G-5183)
BEST GRAPHICS
3760 Snouffer Rd Ste B (43235-3710)
PHONE..............................614 327-7929
Tom Howard, *Prin*
EMP: 7 **EST:** 2007
SALES (est): 94.51K **Privately Held**
Web: www.bestgraphicscompany.com
SIC: 3993 Signs and advertising specialties

(G-5184)
BEXLEY FABRICS INC
2476 E Main St (43209-2441)
P.O. Box 124 (43119-0124)
PHONE..............................614 231-7272
Edward E Goldin, *Owner*
EMP: 8 **EST:** 1939
SALES (est): 412.06K **Privately Held**

SIC: 2295 Sleeving, textile: saturated

(G-5185)
BEXLEY IMAGING
2222 Welcome Pl (43209-7813)
PHONE..............................614 533-6560
EMP: 7 **EST:** 2019
SALES (est): 247.94K **Privately Held**
Web: www.bexley.org
SIC: 3841 Surgical and medical instruments

(G-5186)
BIG MOUTH EGG ROLLS LLC
737 Parkwood Ave (43219-2517)
PHONE..............................614 404-3607
Linda Horne, *Mgr*
EMP: 14
SALES (corp-wide): 203.17K **Privately Held**
SIC: 2053 Frozen bakery products, except bread
PA: Big Mouth Egg Rolls Llc
11001 Converse Rd
Plain City OH 43064
614 404-3607

(G-5187)
BIG NOODLE LLC
687 Kenwick Rd (43209-2592)
PHONE..............................614 558-7170
Christina Providence, *Prin*
EMP: 7 **EST:** 2011
SALES (est): 201.1K **Privately Held**
Web: www.bodybuzzsystem.com
SIC: 2098 Noodles (e.g. egg, plain, and water), dry

(G-5188)
BILL DAVIS STADIUM
650 Borror Dr (43210-1135)
PHONE..............................614 292-2624
Bill Davis, *Prin*
EMP: 14 **EST:** 2010
SALES (est): 81.99K **Privately Held**
Web: www.ohiostatebuckeyes.com
SIC: 2531 Stadium seating

(G-5189)
BIO-BLOOD COMPONENTS INC
1393 N High St (43201-2459)
PHONE..............................614 294-3183
EMP: 103
SALES (corp-wide): 10.71MM **Privately Held**
SIC: 8099 2836 Blood bank; Biological products, except diagnostic
PA: Bio-Blood Components, Inc.
5700 Pleasant View Rd
Memphis TN 38134
901 384-6250

(G-5190)
BIOBENT HOLDINGS LLC
Also Called: Biobent Polymers
1275 Kinnear Rd Ste 239 (43212-1180)
PHONE..............................513 658-5560
Keith Masavage, *CEO*
Michele Cole, *Prin*
EMP: 6 **EST:** 2012
SALES (est): 474.36K **Privately Held**
SIC: 2821 Plastics materials and resins

(G-5191)
BISON BUILDERS LLC
Also Called: Cabinet Guys, The
6999 Huntley Rd Ste M (43229-1031)
PHONE..............................614 636-0365
EMP: 18
SALES (est): 1.68MM **Privately Held**

▲ = Import ▼ = Export
◆ = Import/Export

GEOGRAPHIC SECTION

Columbus - Franklin County (G-5217)

SIC: **1522** 2434 5031 Hotel/motel and multi-family home renovation and remodeling; Vanities, bathroom: wood; Kitchen cabinets

(G-5192)
BIZZY BEE PRINTING INC
Also Called: Innovative Computer Forms
1500 W 3rd Ave Ste 106 (43212-2887)
PHONE..................................614 771-1222
Chris Schmelzer, *Pr*
Rosemary Schmelzer, *Sec*
Rick Schmelzer, *Treas*
EMP: 6 **EST:** 1987
SALES (est): 828.9K **Privately Held**
Web: www.biggprint.com
SIC: **2752** Offset printing

(G-5193)
BJ EQUIPMENT LTD
Also Called: Rent-A-John
4522 Lockbourne Rd (43207-4231)
P.O. Box 753 (43216-0753)
PHONE..................................614 497-1188
William Reynolds Senior, *Pr*
William Reynolds Junior, *VP*
Bonnie Jean Reynolds, *Sec*
EMP: 24 **EST:** 1956
SALES (est): 1.54MM **Privately Held**
Web: www.potty4u.com
SIC: **7359** 3444 3443 3431 Portable toilet rental; Sheet metalwork; Fabricated plate work (boiler shop); Metal sanitary ware

(G-5194)
BJOND INC
1463 Briarmeadow Dr (43235-1612)
PHONE..................................614 537-7246
Kenneth Leachman, *CEO*
EMP: 8 **EST:** 2013
SALES (est): 328.23K **Privately Held**
Web: www.researchgermany.com
SIC: **7372** 7389 Business oriented computer software; Business services, nec

(G-5195)
BLACK & DECKER (US) INC
1948 Schrock Rd (43229-1563)
PHONE..................................614 895-3112
Dave Burica, *Mgr*
EMP: 7
SALES (corp-wide): 15.78B **Publicly Held**
Web: www.blackanddecker.com
SIC: **3546** Power-driven handtools
HQ: Black & Decker (U.S.) Inc.
    1000 Stanley Dr
    New Britain CT 06053
    860 225-5111

(G-5196)
BLACK GOLD CAPITAL LLC
2121 Bethel Rd Ste A (43220-1804)
PHONE..................................614 348-7460
Ernie Malas, *Managing Member*
Darshan Vyas, *Managing Member*
EMP: 20 **EST:** 2019
SALES (est): 4MM **Privately Held**
SIC: **3533** 5013 Oil and gas field machinery; Pumps, oil and gas

(G-5197)
BLACK RADISH CREAMERY LTD
59 Spruce St (43215-1622)
PHONE..................................614 517-9520
John Reese, *Managing Member*
EMP: 6 **EST:** 2011
SALES (est): 521.11K **Privately Held**
Web: www.blackradishcreamery.com
SIC: **2021** Creamery butter

(G-5198)
BLACKBURNS FABRICATION INC
2467 Jackson Pike (43223-3846)
PHONE..................................614 875-0784
Mark A Blackburn, *Pr*
Edsel L Blackburn Senior, *VP*
Carolyn Blackburn, *
Kim Green, *
EMP: 30 **EST:** 1995
SQ FT: 50,000
SALES (est): 9.2MM **Privately Held**
Web: www.blackburnsfab.com
SIC: **3441** 5051 Fabricated structural metal; Structural shapes, iron or steel

(G-5199)
BLACKSTAR INTERNATIONAL INC
361 Indian Mound Rd (43213-2629)
PHONE..................................917 510-5482
Robert Black, *Pr*
EMP: 7
SALES (est): 308.68K **Privately Held**
SIC: **3999** Manufacturing industries, nec

(G-5200)
BLACKWOOD SHEET METAL INC
844 Kerr St (43215-1499)
PHONE..................................614 291-3115
Diana Blackwood Newby, *Pr*
Charles Newby, *VP*
EMP: 8 **EST:** 1908
SQ FT: 10,000
SALES (est): 709.29K **Privately Held**
SIC: **7692** 3443 Welding repair; Fabricated plate work (boiler shop)

(G-5201)
BLOCKAMERICA CORPORATION
Also Called: Glass Block Warehouse, The
750 Kaderly Dr (43228-1032)
PHONE..................................614 274-0700
John Heisler, *Pr*
Carol Heisler, *VP*
John Heisler Ii, *VP*
EMP: 6 **EST:** 1987
SQ FT: 2,500
SALES (est): 502.71K **Privately Held**
Web: www.theglassblockwarehouse.com
SIC: **3229** 5031 5231 Blocks and bricks, glass; Windows; Glass

(G-5202)
BLU BIRD LLC (PA)
Also Called: Stone Center
1736 Mckinley Ave (43222-1051)
PHONE..................................614 276-3585
EMP: 9 **EST:** 2020
SALES: 2.34MM
SALES (corp-wide): 2.34MM **Privately Held**
Web: www.stonecenters.com
SIC: **3281** Cut stone and stone products

(G-5203)
BLUE CHIP MANUFACTURING & SALES INC
3155 Lamb Ave (43219-2344)
PHONE..................................614 475-3853
EMP: 36
SIC: **3441** Fabricated structural metal

(G-5204)
BOB SUMEREL TIRE CO INC
2807 International St (43228-4616)
PHONE..................................614 527-9700
EMP: 10
SALES (corp-wide): 97.34MM **Privately Held**
Web: www.bobsumereltire.com

SIC: **5014** 5015 7534 Tires and tubes; Batteries, used: automotive; Tire retreading and repair shops
PA: Bob Sumerel Tire Co., Inc.
    1257 Cox Ave
    Erlanger KY 41018
    859 283-2700

(G-5205)
BOSTIK INC
802 Harmon Ave (43223-2410)
PHONE..................................614 232-8510
Al Lombardi, *Brnch Mgr*
EMP: 35
SALES (corp-wide): 125.67MM **Privately Held**
Web: www.bostik.com
SIC: **2891** Adhesives and sealants
HQ: Bostik, Inc.
    11320 W Watertwn Plnk Rd
    Wauwatosa WI 53226
    414 774-2250

(G-5206)
BOYER SIGNS & GRAPHICS INC
3200 Valleyview Dr (43204-2080)
PHONE..................................216 383-7242
EMP: 20 **EST:** 1964
SQ FT: 22,000
SALES (est): 464.73K **Privately Held**
Web: www.boyersigns.com
SIC: **3993** 1799 Electric signs; Sign installation and maintenance

(G-5207)
BRATTIEGIRLZ LLC
175 S 3rd St Ste 200 (43215-5194)
PHONE..................................513 607-4757
EMP: 8 **EST:** 2020
SALES (est): 567.49K **Privately Held**
SIC: **3537** Trucks, tractors, loaders, carriers, and similar equipment

(G-5208)
BREKKIE SHACK GRANDVIEW LLC
2 Miranova Pl Ste 700 (43215-5098)
PHONE..................................614 306-5618
EMP: 7 **EST:** 2018
SALES (est): 471.71K **Privately Held**
Web: www.thebrekkieshack.com
SIC: **2711** Newspapers, publishing and printing

(G-5209)
BRENDONS FIBER WORKS
306 E Jeffrey Pl (43214-1714)
PHONE..................................614 353-6599
Laura K Brendon, *Prin*
EMP: 6 **EST:** 2010
SALES (est): 172.93K **Privately Held**
SIC: **3296** Mineral wool

(G-5210)
BREWERY REAL ESTATE PARTNR
467 N High St (43215-2007)
PHONE..................................614 224-9023
EMP: 6 **EST:** 2008
SALES (est): 120.07K **Privately Held**
SIC: **2082** Beer (alcoholic beverage)

(G-5211)
BREWPUB RESTAURANT CORPORATION
Also Called: Barley's Brewing Company
467 N High St (43215-2007)
PHONE..................................614 228-2537
Tiffany Jezerinac, *Pr*
EMP: 38 **EST:** 1992
SALES (est): 950.72K **Privately Held**
Web: www.smokehousebrewing.com

SIC: **5812** 2082 American restaurant; Malt beverages

(G-5212)
BRIDGE COMPONENTS INCORPORATED
3476 Millikin Ct (43228-9765)
P.O. Box 1228 (43017-6228)
PHONE..................................614 873-0777
Neil Spears, *Pr*
EMP: 7 **EST:** 2001
SALES (est): 734.5K **Privately Held**
Web: www.bridgecomponentsind.com
SIC: **2824** 3449 Elastomeric fibers; Bars, concrete reinforcing: fabricated steel

(G-5213)
BRIDGE COMPONENTS INDS INC
3476 Millikin Ct (43228-9765)
PHONE..................................614 873-0777
Tyler Spears, *Pr*
EMP: 15 **EST:** 2011
SALES (est): 1.96MM **Privately Held**
Web: www.bridgecomponentsind.com
SIC: **3312** Railroad crossings, steel or iron

(G-5214)
BRIDGESTONE RET OPERATIONS LLC
Also Called: Firestone
4015 E Broad St (43213-1130)
PHONE..................................614 864-3350
Brian Roper, *Mgr*
EMP: 10
Web: www.firestonecompleteautocare.com
SIC: **5531** 7534 Automotive tires; Rebuilding and retreading tires
HQ: Bridgestone Retail Operations, Llc
    333 E Lake St Ste 300
    Bloomingdale IL 60108
    630 259-9000

(G-5215)
BRIDGESTONE RET OPERATIONS LLC
Also Called: Firestone
35 Great Southern Blvd (43207-4001)
PHONE..................................614 491-8062
Tom Dummar, *Mgr*
EMP: 10
Web: www.bridgestoneamericas.com
SIC: **5531** 7534 7539 Automotive tires; Rebuilding and retreading tires; Brake services
HQ: Bridgestone Retail Operations, Llc
    333 E Lake St Ste 300
    Bloomingdale IL 60108
    630 259-9000

(G-5216)
BRIDGESTONE RET OPERATIONS LLC
Also Called: Firestone
180 N 3rd St (43215-2920)
PHONE..................................614 224-4221
Joe Struewing, *Mgr*
EMP: 8
SQ FT: 5,550
Web: www.bridgestoneamericas.com
SIC: **5531** 7534 Automotive tires; Rebuilding and retreading tires
HQ: Bridgestone Retail Operations, Llc
    333 E Lake St Ste 300
    Bloomingdale IL 60108
    630 259-9000

(G-5217)
BRILISTA FOODS COMPANY INC (PA)
Also Called: Krema Nut Co

1000 Goodale Blvd (43212-3827)
PHONE..............................614 299-4132
Michael Giunta, *Pr*
Peggy Giunta, *VP*
Brian Giunta, *VP*
David Block, *VP*
EMP: 8 EST: 1991
SQ FT: 8,500
SALES (est): 1.07MM **Privately Held**
Web: www.krema.com
SIC: 2038 Snacks, incl. onion rings, cheese sticks, etc.

(G-5218)
BRISKHEAT CORPORATION (DH)
4800 Hilton Corporate Dr (43232-4150)
PHONE..............................614 294-3376
Domenic Federico, *CEO*
▲ EMP: 159 EST: 1949
SQ FT: 40,000
SALES (est): 60.64MM
SALES (corp-wide): 3.82B **Privately Held**
Web: www.briskheat.com
SIC: 3585 Refrigeration and heating equipment
HQ: Backer Ehp Inc.
    4700 John Bragg Hwy
    Murfreesboro TN 37127

(G-5219)
BUCKEYE BOXES INC (PA)
601 N Hague Ave (43204-1498)
PHONE..............................614 274-8484
Craig Hoyt, *Pr*
Judd Hauenstein, *
Ken Churchill, *
▲ EMP: 60 EST: 1966
SQ FT: 100,000
SALES (est): 22.79MM
SALES (corp-wide): 22.79MM **Privately Held**
Web: www.buckeyeboxes.com
SIC: 2653 3993 2675 2631 Boxes, corrugated: made from purchased materials; Signs and advertising specialties; Die-cut paper and board; Paperboard mills

(G-5220)
BUCKEYE METAL WORKS INC
3240 Petzinger Rd (43232-3912)
PHONE..............................614 239-8000
EMP: 8 EST: 1994
SQ FT: 15,000
SALES (est): 2.35MM **Privately Held**
Web: www.buckeyemetal.com
SIC: 3444 Sheet metal specialties, not stamped

(G-5221)
BUNN-MINNICK CO
875 Michigan Ave (43215-1108)
PHONE..............................614 299-7934
Philip D Minnick, *Pr*
Robert W Bunn Junior, *VP*
Leo Klise, *Sec*
EMP: 8 EST: 1969
SQ FT: 26,000
SALES (est): 349.68K **Privately Held**
Web: www.bunnminnick.com
SIC: 7699 3931 Organ tuning and repair; Pipes, organ

(G-5222)
BURTON METAL FINISHING INC
Also Called: Burton Mtal Fnshg Inc Pwdr Cti
1711 Woodland Ave (43219-1137)
PHONE..............................614 252-9523
Daniel Burton, *Pr*
Scott Burton, *
Victoria Burton, *
EMP: 25 EST: 1987
SQ FT: 5,000
SALES (est): 3.99MM **Privately Held**
Web: www.burtonmetal.com
SIC: 3471 Electroplating of metals or formed products

(G-5223)
BUSINESS IDNTFCTION SYSTEMS IN
Also Called: Sign-A-Rama
6185 Huntley Rd Ste M (43229-1094)
PHONE..............................614 841-1255
Stephen M Thompson, *Pr*
EMP: 6 EST: 1993
SQ FT: 5,200
SALES (est): 497.81K **Privately Held**
Web: www.signarama.com
SIC: 3993 5999 Signs and advertising specialties; Banners, flags, decals, and posters

(G-5224)
BYBF INC
107 S High St (43215-3408)
PHONE..............................614 706-3050
EMP: 9 EST: 2017
SALES (est): 432.82K **Privately Held**
Web: www.bybe.com
SIC: 7372 Application computer software

(G-5225)
CADBURY SCHWEPPES BOTTLING
950 Stelzer Rd (43219-3740)
PHONE..............................614 238-0469
John Ferrante, *Prin*
EMP: 7 EST: 2007
SALES (est): 237.52K **Privately Held**
SIC: 2086 Bottled and canned soft drinks

(G-5226)
CALGON CARBON CORPORATION
835 N Cassady Ave (43219-2203)
PHONE..............................614 258-9501
EMP: 9
Web: www.calgoncarbon.com
SIC: 2819 Charcoal (carbon), activated
HQ: Calgon Carbon Corporation
    3000 Gsk Dr
    Moon Township PA 15108
    412 787-6700

(G-5227)
CALLAHAN CUTTING TOOLS INC
Also Called: Blade Manufacturing Co, The
915 Distribution Dr Ste A (43228-1009)
PHONE..............................614 294-1649
Marc A Callahan, *Pr*
◆ EMP: 7 EST: 2004
SQ FT: 10,000
SALES (est): 880.89K **Privately Held**
SIC: 3541 3425 Machine tools, metal cutting type; Saw blades and handsaws

(G-5228)
CALM DISTRIBUTORS LLC
1084 Rarig Ave (43219-2360)
PHONE..............................614 678-5554
Cesar Fuentes, *Prin*
EMP: 6 EST: 2014
SALES (est): 524.06K **Privately Held**
Web: www.calmdistributors.com
SIC: 2032 Canned specialties

(G-5229)
CAP & ASSOCIATES INC
Also Called: Cap Fixtures
445 Mccormick Blvd (43213-1526)
PHONE..............................614 863-3363
Charlene A Prosnik, *CEO*
Jason Prosnik, *
Joseph Chaulk, *
◆ EMP: 170 EST: 1981
SQ FT: 110,000
SALES (est): 49.7MM **Privately Held**
Web: www.capfixtures.com
SIC: 2541 2542 Store fixtures, wood; Fixtures, store: except wood

(G-5230)
CAPEHART ENTERPRISES LLC
Also Called: Minuteman Press
1724 Northwest Blvd Ste B (43212-2272)
PHONE..............................614 769-7746
Gerald C Capehart, *Managing Member*
EMP: 15 EST: 1998
SQ FT: 1,500
SALES (est): 934.13K **Privately Held**
Web: www.minuteman.com
SIC: 2752 5199 8742 Commercial printing, lithographic; Advertising specialties; Marketing consulting services

(G-5231)
CAPITAL CITY AWNING COMPANY
577 N 4th St (43215)
PHONE..............................614 221-5404
TOLL FREE: 800
Timothy Kellogg, *Pr*
Michael Mc Connell, *
Eugene E Mc Connell Junior, *Stockholder*
EMP: 50 EST: 1944
SQ FT: 25,600
SALES (est): 4.64MM **Privately Held**
Web: www.capitalcityawning.com
SIC: 2394 2393 Awnings, fabric: made from purchased materials; Canvas bags

(G-5232)
CAPITAL PRSTHTIC ORTHTIC CTR I (PA)
4678 Larwell Dr (43220-3621)
PHONE..............................614 451-0446
Lisa Crawford, *CEO*
Patricia W Kozersky, *Sec*
EMP: 12 EST: 1982
SQ FT: 3,200
SALES (est): 3MM
SALES (corp-wide): 3MM **Privately Held**
Web: www.capitalprosthetics.net
SIC: 3842 Limbs, artificial

(G-5233)
CAPITAL RESIN CORPORATION
324 Dering Ave (43207-2956)
PHONE..............................614 445-7177
Judithe Wensinger, *CEO*
▲ EMP: 76 EST: 1976
SQ FT: 6,000
SALES (est): 40.85MM **Privately Held**
Web: www.capitalresin.com
SIC: 2819 2821 Inorganic acids except nitric and phosphoric; Acrylic resins

(G-5234)
CAPITOL CITICOM INC
Also Called: Citicom
2225 Citygate Dr Ste A (43219-3651)
P.O. Box 361563 (43236-1563)
PHONE..............................614 472-2679
Kevin Oakes, *Pr*
Gail E Oakes, *VP*
Michael Oakes, *VP*
EMP: 20 EST: 1985
SQ FT: 11,500
SALES (est): 3.53MM **Privately Held**
Web: www.citicomprint.com
SIC: 7372 7389 7334 2752 Publisher's computer software; Printers' services: folding, collating, etc.; Photocopying and duplicating services; Offset and photolithographic printing

(G-5235)
CAPITOL SQUARE PRINTING INC
59 E Gay St (43215-3103)
PHONE..............................614 221-2850
Marilyn S Smith, *Pr*
Craig Poland, *VP*
EMP: 7 EST: 1975
SQ FT: 4,500
SALES (est): 659.93K **Privately Held**
Web: www.capitolsquareprinting.com
SIC: 2752 Offset printing

(G-5236)
CARDINAL BUILDERS INC
4409 E Main St (43213-3061)
PHONE..............................614 237-1000
Tim Coady, *Pr*
Tim Kane, *Stockholder*
EMP: 32 EST: 1965
SQ FT: 22,000
SALES (est): 679.54K **Privately Held**
SIC: 3541 1521 1522 1761 Machine tool replacement & repair parts, metal cutting types; General remodeling, single-family houses; Hotel/motel and multi-family home renovation and remodeling; Siding contractor

(G-5237)
CARDINAL BUILDING SUPPLY LLC
1000 Edgehill Rd Ste B (43212-3684)
PHONE..............................614 706-4499
Mark Gundling, *Managing Member*
EMP: 9 EST: 2014
SALES (est): 142.79K **Privately Held**
Web: www.carterlumber.com
SIC: 5211 2426 5031 Flooring, wood; Lumber, hardwood dimension; Lumber, plywood, and millwork

(G-5238)
CARDINAL OPERATING COMPANY
6677 Busch Blvd (43229-1101)
PHONE..............................614 846-5757
EMP: 6 EST: 2018
SALES (est): 4.51MM **Privately Held**
Web: www.cardinalopco.com
SIC: 1382 Oil and gas exploration services

(G-5239)
CAS LABORATORIES LLC
6361 Nicholas Dr (43235-5204)
PHONE..............................740 815-2440
EMP: 7 EST: 2017
SALES (est): 166.7K **Privately Held**
Web: www.cas-labs.com
SIC: 3999

(G-5240)
CATHOLIC DIOCESE OF COLUMBUS
Also Called: Catholic Times
197 E Gay St Ste 4 (43215-3229)
PHONE..............................614 224-5195
Teresa Ianaggi, *Mgr*
EMP: 9
SALES (corp-wide): 38.56MM **Privately Held**
Web: www.columbuscatholic.org
SIC: 2711 Newspapers
PA: Catholic Diocese Of Columbus
    198 E Broad St
    Columbus OH 43215
    614 224-2251

(G-5241)
CENTRAL COCA-COLA BTLG CO INC
Also Called: Coca-Cola
4500 Groves Rd (43232-4106)
PHONE..............................614 863-7200
Doug Davis, *Mgr*

EMP: 158
SQ FT: 150,000
SALES (corp-wide): 45.75B **Publicly Held**
Web: www.coca-cola.com
SIC: 2086 Bottled and canned soft drinks
HQ: Central Coca-Cola Bottling Company, Inc.
555 Taxter Rd Ste 550
Elmsford NY 10523
914 789-1100

(G-5242)
CENTRAL OIL ASPHALT CORP (PA)
8 E Long St Ste 400 (43215-2914)
PHONE..............................614 224-8111
F L Shafer, *Pr*
EMP: 7 **EST:** 1934
SQ FT: 4,600
SALES (est): 3.97MM
SALES (corp-wide): 3.97MM **Privately Held**
SIC: 2951 Asphalt and asphaltic paving mixtures (not from refineries)

(G-5243)
CERELIA USA CORP
430 N Yearling Rd (43213-1070)
PHONE..............................614 471-9994
M Guillaume Reveilhac, *CEO*
EMP: 31 **EST:** 2014
SALES (est): 1.6MM
SALES (corp-wide): 2.02MM **Privately Held**
Web: www.cerelia.com
SIC: 2052 Bakery products, dry
PA: Cerelia Bakery Canada L.P
6925 Invader Cres
Mississauga ON L5T 2
800 253-6844

(G-5244)
CERTIFIED WALK IN TUBS
Also Called: Home Pro
926 Freeway Dr N (43229-5424)
PHONE..............................614 436-4848
Skyler Alexander, *Pt*
Skyler Alexander, *Pt*
EMP: 6 **EST:** 2012
SALES (est): 85.47K **Privately Held**
SIC: 5999 3088 Plumbing and heating supplies; Plastics plumbing fixtures

(G-5245)
CEUTIX PHARMA INC
2041 Builders Pl (43204-4886)
PHONE..............................614 388-8800
Ye Deng, *Prin*
EMP: 8 **EST:** 2016
SALES (est): 153.24K **Privately Held**
SIC: 2834 Pharmaceutical preparations

(G-5246)
CGS LIQUIDATION COMPANY LLC
1875 Lone Eagle St (43228-3647)
PHONE..............................614 878-6041
EMP: 10 **EST:** 2013
SALES (est): 210.56K **Privately Held**
Web: www.columbusgasket.com
SIC: 3053 Gaskets, all materials

(G-5247)
CHAMPION STRAPPING PDTS INC
1819 Walcutt Rd Ste 13 (43228-9149)
PHONE..............................614 527-1454
Andrew Sandberg, *Prin*
EMP: 9 **EST:** 2010
SALES (est): 478.49K **Privately Held**
SIC: 3499 Strapping, metal

(G-5248)
CHEP (USA) INC
2130 New World Dr (43207-3433)
PHONE..............................614 497-9448
Matt Mallory, *Mgr*
EMP: 7
Web: www.chep.com
SIC: 2448 Pallets, wood
HQ: Chep (U.S.A.) Inc.
5897 Windward Pkwy
Alpharetta GA 30005
770 668-8100

(G-5249)
CHOICE MARKETING
5130 Transamerica Dr (43228-9269)
PHONE..............................614 638-8404
Cullan Laing, *Prin*
EMP: 6 **EST:** 2018
SALES (est): 118.54K **Privately Held**
Web: www.choice-marketing-partners.com
SIC: 2711 Newspapers

(G-5250)
CITI 2 CITI LOGISTICS
Also Called: Abacus Biodiesel Complex
6031 E Main St (43213-3590)
PHONE..............................614 306-4109
Kenneth Turner, *Prin*
EMP: 6 **EST:** 2009
SALES (est): 289.64K **Privately Held**
SIC: 2999 Petroleum and coal products, nec

(G-5251)
CLARK GRAVE VAULT COMPANY (PA)
Also Called: C.T.L. Steel Division
375 E 5th Ave (43201-2819)
P.O. Box 8250 (43201-0250)
PHONE..............................614 294-3761
David Beck, *Pr*
Mark Beck, *
David A Beck Ii, *VP*
Douglas A Beck, *Marketing* *
Nancy M Beck, *
EMP: 140 **EST:** 1898
SQ FT: 300,000
SALES (est): 23.5MM
SALES (corp-wide): 23.5MM **Privately Held**
Web: www.clarkvault.com
SIC: 3316 3272 Strip, steel, flat bright, cold-rolled: purchased hot-rolled; Precast terrazzo or concrete products

(G-5252)
CLASSIC STONE COMPANY INC
4090 Janitrol Rd (43228-1396)
PHONE..............................614 833-3946
R G Reitter, *Pr*
Steven Waits, *VP*
EMP: 10 **EST:** 1998
SQ FT: 20,000
SALES (est): 800.67K **Privately Held**
SIC: 3281 Cut stone and stone products

(G-5253)
CLEVELAND PLANT AND FLOWER CO
2370 Marilyn Park Ln (43219-1792)
P.O. Box 30837 (43230-0837)
PHONE..............................614 478-9900
Brian Davis, *Mgr*
EMP: 9
SQ FT: 3,000
SALES (corp-wide): 22.39MM **Privately Held**
Web: www.cpfco.com
SIC: 5193 5992 3999 Flowers, fresh; Flowers, fresh; Candles
PA: The Cleveland Plant And Flower Company
12920 Corporate Dr
Cleveland OH 44130
216 898-3500

(G-5254)
CLEVELAND-CLIFFS COLUMBUS LLC
4300 Alum Creek Dr (43207-4519)
PHONE..............................614 492-8287
Heather Paarlberg, *Brnch Mgr*
EMP: 25
SALES (corp-wide): 22B **Publicly Held**
SIC: 3312 Galvanized pipes, plates, sheets, etc.: iron and steel
HQ: Cleveland-Cliffs Columbus Llc
4020 Kinross Lakes Pkwy
Richfield OH 44286
614 492-6800

(G-5255)
CLOCKINGME LLC
3280 Morse Rd (43231-6175)
PHONE..............................614 400-9727
EMP: 10
SALES (est): 413.11K **Privately Held**
SIC: 3695 Computer software tape and disks: blank, rigid, and floppy

(G-5256)
CLUSTER SOFTWARE INC
2674 Billingsley Rd (43235-1924)
PHONE..............................614 760-9380
Kailasnath Murthy, *Pr*
Vishwa Vedula, *VP*
EMP: 12 **EST:** 1996
SALES (est): 463.82K **Privately Held**
Web: www.clustersoft.com
SIC: 7372 Business oriented computer software

(G-5257)
CMD MEDTECH LLC
3585 Interchange Rd (43204-1400)
PHONE..............................614 364-4243
EMP: 11 **EST:** 2016
SALES (est): 522.96K **Privately Held**
Web: www.cmdmedtech.com
SIC: 3841 Surgical and medical instruments

(G-5258)
COACHELLA TROTTING & PRTG LTD
1625 Bethel Rd (43220-2071)
PHONE..............................614 326-1009
V Dawn Falleur, *Prin*
EMP: 7 **EST:** 2010
SALES (est): 88.89K **Privately Held**
SIC: 2752 Commercial printing, lithographic

(G-5259)
COCA-COLA COMPANY
Also Called: Coca-Cola
2455 Watkins Rd (43207-3488)
P.O. Box 2589 (43216-2589)
PHONE..............................614 491-6305
Willi Pete, *Mgr*
EMP: 41
SALES (corp-wide): 45.75B **Publicly Held**
Web: www.coca-colacompany.com
SIC: 2086 Bottled and canned soft drinks
PA: The Coca-Cola Company
1 Coca-Cola Plz
Atlanta GA 30313
404 676-2121

(G-5260)
COLORTECH GRAPHICS & PRINTING (PA)
4000 Business Park Dr (43204-5023)
PHONE..............................614 766-2400
C Wayne Booker, *Pr*
EMP: 19 **EST:** 1985
SQ FT: 1,600
SALES (est): 873.83K
SALES (corp-wide): 873.83K **Privately Held**
Web: www.colortechdesign.com
SIC: 7334 2791 Photocopying and duplicating services; Typesetting

(G-5261)
COLUMBUS APPAREL STUDIO LLC
Also Called: Columbus Apparel Studio
757 Garden Rd Ste 110 (43214-2294)
PHONE..............................614 706-7292
Denise Falter, *CEO*
EMP: 10 **EST:** 2018
SALES (est): 598.45K **Privately Held**
Web: www.columbusapparelstudio.com
SIC: 2331 2339 2321 2329 Women's and misses' blouses and shirts; Women's and misses' athletic clothing and sportswear; Men's and boys' dress shirts; Men's and boy's clothing, nec

(G-5262)
COLUMBUS ART MEMORIAL INC
606 W Broad St (43215-2712)
PHONE..............................614 221-9333
Mel Lee, *Mgr*
EMP: 8
SQ FT: 5,000
SALES (corp-wide): 1.06MM **Privately Held**
Web: www.columbusartmemorial.com
SIC: 3272 Monuments, concrete
PA: Art Columbus Memorial Inc
766 Greenlawn Ave
Columbus OH 43223
614 443-5778

(G-5263)
COLUMBUS CANVAS PRODUCTS INC
Also Called: Columbus Canvas Products
577 N 4th St (43215-2101)
PHONE..............................614 375-1397
Janet M Kellogg, *Pr*
Michael Mcconnell, *VP*
Timothy Kellogg, *VP*
EMP: 10 **EST:** 1958
SQ FT: 10,000
SALES (est): 803.09K **Privately Held**
Web: www.columbuscanvasproducts.com
SIC: 2394 2393 3949 2392 Canvas and related products; Cushions, except spring and carpet: purchased materials; Sporting and athletic goods, nec; Household furnishings, nec

(G-5264)
COLUMBUS CONTROLS INC
3573 Johnny Appleseed Ct (43231-4985)
PHONE..............................614 882-9029
EMP: 30 **EST:** 1981
SALES (est): 4.64MM **Privately Held**
Web: www.columbuscontrols.com
SIC: 3822 3613 Environmental controls; Control panels, electric

(G-5265)
COLUMBUS HEATING & VENT CO
182 N Yale Ave (43222-1127)
PHONE..............................614 274-1177
Charles R Gulley, *Pr*

Columbus - Franklin County (G-5266) — GEOGRAPHIC SECTION

Greogy Yoak, *
Mikel Plythe, *
Michael Blythe, *
EMP: 135 **EST:** 1874
SALES (est): 9.26MM **Privately Held**
Web: www.columbusheat.com
SIC: 1711 3585 Warm air heating and air conditioning contractor; Furnaces, warm air: electric

(G-5266)
COLUMBUS INCONTACT
555 S Front St (43215-5668)
PHONE.................801 245-8369
EMP: 10 **EST:** 2017
SALES (est): 369.18K **Privately Held**
Web: www.nice.com
SIC: 7372 Prepackaged software

(G-5267)
COLUMBUS INSTRUMENTS LLC
950 N Hague Ave (43204-2121)
PHONE.................614 276-0861
EMP: 25 **EST:** 2020
SALES (est): 2.36MM **Privately Held**
Web: www.colinst.com
SIC: 3826 Analytical instruments

(G-5268)
COLUMBUS INSTRUMENTS INTL CORP
Also Called: Columbus Instruments
950 N Hague Ave (43204-2121)
PHONE.................614 276-0593
Jan A Czekajewski, *Pr*
Laura Damas, *
♦ **EMP:** 48 **EST:** 1970
SQ FT: 19,460
SALES (est): 9.57MM **Privately Held**
Web: www.colinst.com
SIC: 3826 Analytical instruments

(G-5269)
COLUMBUS INTERNATIONAL CORP (PA)
200 E Campus View Blvd Ste 200 (43235-4678)
PHONE.................614 323-1086
Rajeev Kumar, *Pr*
EMP: 8 **EST:** 2001
SQ FT: 2,000
SALES (est): 1.7MM
SALES (corp-wide): 1.7MM **Privately Held**
Web: www.columbuscorp.com
SIC: 7372 Business oriented computer software

(G-5270)
COLUMBUS KOMBUCHA COMPANY LLC
930 Freeway Dr N (43229-5424)
PHONE.................614 262-0000
EMP: 8 **EST:** 2011
SQ FT: 5,000
SALES (est): 768.68K **Privately Held**
SIC: 2082 Malt beverages

(G-5271)
COLUMBUS MACHINE WORKS INC
2491 Fairwood Ave (43207-2709)
PHONE.................614 409-0244
Michael Stacey, *Pr*
Diana Stacey, *Sec*
EMP: 11 **EST:** 1997
SQ FT: 3,729
SALES (est): 1.82MM **Privately Held**
Web: www.columbusmachine.com
SIC: 3599 Machine shop, jobbing and repair

(G-5272)
COLUMBUS MESSENGER COMPANY (PA)
Also Called: Madison Messenger
3500 Sullivant Ave (43204-1887)
PHONE.................614 272-5422
Phillip Daubel, *Owner*
EMP: 25 **EST:** 1972
SQ FT: 4,000
SALES (est): 2.01MM
SALES (corp-wide): 2.01MM **Privately Held**
Web: www.columbusmessenger.com
SIC: 2711 Newspapers, publishing and printing

(G-5273)
COLUMBUS PIPE AND EQUIPMENT CO
Also Called: Steel Warehouse Division
763 E Markison Ave (43207)
P.O. Box 07010 (13207)
PHONE.................614 444-7871
TOLL FREE: 800
Bruce Jay Silberstein, *Pr*
Jonathan Silberstein, *VP*
Mike Denoewer, *CFO*
Helen Silberstein, *Sec*
Roberta Silberstein, *Stockholder*
EMP: 15 **EST:** 1932
SQ FT: 50,000
SALES (est): 3.16MM **Privately Held**
Web: plumbing-equipment-dealers.cmac.ws
SIC: 5082 7692 5074 Construction and mining machinery; Welding repair; Plumbing fittings and supplies

(G-5274)
COLUMBUS PODCAST COMPANY LLC
105 N Cassingham Rd (43209-1459)
PHONE.................614 405-8298
Kerouac Smith, *Prin*
EMP: 6 **EST:** 2018
SALES (est): 100.11K **Privately Held**
Web: www.columbus.org
SIC: 2711 Newspapers, publishing and printing

(G-5275)
COLUMBUS PUBLIC SCHOOL DST
Also Called: COLUMBUS PUBLIC SCHOOL DISTRICT
300 E Livingston Ave (43215-5761)
PHONE.................614 365-6517
EMP: 10
SALES (corp-wide): 966.92MM **Privately Held**
Web: www.ccsoh.us
SIC: 2273 Finishers of tufted carpets and rugs
PA: Columbus City School District
270 E State St Fl 3
Columbus OH 43215
614 365-5000

(G-5276)
COLUMBUS ROOF TRUSSES INC (PA)
2525 Fisher Rd (43204-3588)
PHONE.................614 272-6464
TOLL FREE: 800
Tony Iacovetta, *Pr*
Eugene R Iacovetta, *
Rose A Pritchard, *
EMP: 30 **EST:** 1959
SQ FT: 51,000
SALES (est): 3.7MM
SALES (corp-wide): 3.7MM **Privately Held**
Web: www.columbusrooftruss.com
SIC: 2439 Trusses, wooden roof

(G-5277)
COLUMBUS SIGN COMPANY (PA)
1515 E 5th Ave (43219-2483)
PHONE.................614 252-3133
Michael Hoy, *Pr*
Michael S Hoy, *
EMP: 30 **EST:** 1911
SQ FT: 15,000
SALES (est): 2.57MM
SALES (corp-wide): 2.57MM **Privately Held**
Web: www.columbussign.com
SIC: 3993 Neon signs

(G-5278)
COLUMBUS STEEL CASTINGS CO
Also Called: Columbus Castings
2211 Parsons Ave (43207-2448)
PHONE.................614 444-2121
▲ **EMP:** 750
SIC: 3325 Steel foundries, nec

(G-5279)
COLUMBUS STEELMASTERS INC
660 Concrea Rd (43219-1822)
PHONE.................614 231-2141
Brenda Neale, *CEO*
Steven Neale, *Pr*
EMP: 12 **EST:** 1971
SQ FT: 17,000
SALES (est): 1.66MM **Privately Held**
SIC: 3444 Sheet metal specialties, not stamped

(G-5280)
COLUMBUS V&S GALVANIZING LLC
987 Buckeye Park Rd (43207-2596)
PHONE.................614 449-8281
Werner Niehaus, *Pr*
Brian Miller, *Managing Member*
EMP: 90 **EST:** 2001
SALES (est): 9.68MM **Privately Held**
Web: www.hotdipgalvanizing.com
SIC: 3479 Galvanizing of iron, steel, or end-formed products

(G-5281)
COLUMBUS WATER SECTION PERMIT
910 Dublin Rd (43215-1169)
PHONE.................614 645-8039
EMP: 6 **EST:** 2019
SALES (est): 240.52K **Privately Held**
Web: new.columbus.gov
SIC: 3542 Machine tools, metal forming type

(G-5282)
COLUMBUS-SPORTS PUBLICATIONS
Also Called: Buckeye Sports Bulletin
1200 Chambers Rd (43212-1703)
P.O. Box 12453 (43212-0453)
PHONE.................614 486-2202
Frank L Moskowitz, *Pr*
EMP: 11 **EST:** 1981
SALES (est): 456.63K **Privately Held**
Web: www.buckeyesports.com
SIC: 2711 Newspapers, publishing and printing

(G-5283)
COMMUNICATOR NEEDS
90 W Campus View Blvd (43235-1447)
P.O. Box 258 (43085-0258)
PHONE.................614 781-1160
EMP: 6 **EST:** 2012
SALES (est): 186.01K **Privately Held**
Web: www.communicatornewsohio.com
SIC: 2711 Newspapers, publishing and printing

(G-5284)
COMPUTER ALLIED TECHNOLOGY CO
3385 Somerford Rd (43221-1438)
PHONE.................614 457-2292
Mark Taylor, *Pr*
Pat Taylor, *Sec*
EMP: 7 **EST:** 1986
SALES (est): 469.9K **Privately Held**
SIC: 7371 3569 Computer software development; Robots, assembly line: industrial and commercial

(G-5285)
CONCEPT 9 INC
1604 Clara St (43211-2664)
PHONE.................614 294-3743
Kenneth J Nienkirchen, *Ch Bd*
Karl Nienkirchen, *Pr*
Kris Nienkirchen, *VP*
EMP: 6 **EST:** 1981
SQ FT: 5,000
SALES (est): 482.81K **Privately Held**
SIC: 2759 Screen printing

(G-5286)
CONNECT HOUSING BLOCKS LLC
577 W Nationwide Blvd Ste 600 (43215-2339)
PHONE.................614 503-4344
Brad Dehays, *Managing Member*
EMP: 25
SALES (est): 2.86MM **Privately Held**
Web: www.connecthousingblocks.com
SIC: 3448 Prefabricated metal buildings and components

(G-5287)
CONNS POTATO CHIP CO INC
1271 Alum Creek Dr (43209-2721)
PHONE.................614 252-2150
Nick Miller, *Mgr*
EMP: 45
SQ FT: 1,050
SALES (corp-wide): 8.79MM **Privately Held**
Web: www.connspotatochips.com
SIC: 2096 Potato chips and similar snacks
PA: Conn's Potato Chip Co., Inc.
1805 Kemper Ct
Zanesville OH 43701
740 452-4615

(G-5288)
CONQUEST MAPS LLC
5696 Westbourne Ave (43213-1487)
PHONE.................614 654-1627
Ross Worden, *Pr*
EMP: 11 **EST:** 2016
SALES (est): 1.63MM **Privately Held**
Web: www.conquestmaps.com
SIC: 2741 Miscellaneous publishing

(G-5289)
CONTRACT LUMBER INC
200 Schofield Dr (43213-3803)
PHONE.................614 751-1109
EMP: 13
SALES (corp-wide): 72.48MM **Privately Held**
Web: www.contractlumber.com
SIC: 7349 5211 5031 2421 Building maintenance services, nec; Lumber and other building materials; Lumber: rough, dressed, and finished; Lumber: rough, sawed, or planed
PA: Contract Lumber, Inc.
3245 Hazelton Etna Rd Sw

▲ = Import ▼ = Export
♦ = Import/Export

GEOGRAPHIC SECTION — Columbus - Franklin County (G-5315)

Pataskala OH 43062
740 964-3147

(G-5290)
CONTROL-X INC
3546 Rosburg Dr (43228-7089)
PHONE..............................614 777-9729
EMP: 7 **EST:** 1990
SALES (est): 490.92K **Privately Held**
SIC: 3844 X-ray apparatus and tubes

(G-5291)
CONVAULT OF OHIO INC
841 Alton Ave (43219-3710)
P.O. Box 89 (43068-0089)
PHONE..............................614 252-8422
Tim Thickstun, *Pr*
Steven Thickstun, *Sec*
Joanne Thickstun, *VP*
EMP: 9 **EST:** 1990
SALES (est): 764.09K **Privately Held**
Web: www.mastohio.com
SIC: 3443 Fuel tanks (oil, gas, etc.), metal plate

(G-5292)
CONVEYOR GUARD CORP
187 W Johnstown Rd (43230-5714)
PHONE..............................614 337-1727
EMP: 6 **EST:** 2012
SALES (est): 219.56K **Privately Held**
Web: www.conveyorguard.com
SIC: 3496 Miscellaneous fabricated wire products

(G-5293)
COOKIE BOUQUETS INC
Also Called: Cookie Bouquet
6665 Huntley Rd Ste F (43229-1045)
PHONE..............................614 888-2171
Christian Mccoy, *Pr*
EMP: 7 **EST:** 1984
SQ FT: 4,500
SALES (est): 523.69K **Privately Held**
Web: www.cookiebouquets.com
SIC: 5461 5947 2052 Cookies; Gift baskets; Cookies and crackers

(G-5294)
COOPER LIGHTING LLC
Also Called: Cooper Lighting Solutions
P.O. Box 182368 (43218-2368)
PHONE..............................800 334-6871
EMP: 10 **EST:** 2012
SALES (est): 1.2MM **Privately Held**
SIC: 3648 Lighting equipment, nec

(G-5295)
COPIER RESOURCES INC
Also Called: Cri Digital
4800 Evanswood Dr (43229)
P.O. Box 14824 (43214)
PHONE..............................614 268-1100
Scott Di Francesco, *Pr*
EMP: 6 **EST:** 1991
SQ FT: 4,000
SALES (est): 896.33K **Privately Held**
Web: www.cridigital.net
SIC: 7629 7359 5734 3575 Electrical repair shops; Office machine rental, except computers; Computer and software stores; Cathode ray tube (CRT), computer terminal

(G-5296)
CORE MOLDING TECHNOLOGIES INC (PA)
800 Manor Park Dr (43228-9762)
PHONE..............................614 870-5000
▲ **EMP:** 518 **EST:** 1988
SALES (est): 357.74MM **Publicly Held**

Web: www.coremt.com
SIC: 3089 Injection molding of plastics

(G-5297)
CORPORATE ELEVATOR LLC
35 E Gay St Ste 218 (43215-8128)
P.O. Box 538 (43054-0538)
PHONE..............................614 288-1847
Ivan Isreal, *Prin*
EMP: 9 **EST:** 2014
SALES (est): 267.9K **Privately Held**
Web: www.corporate-elevator.net
SIC: 8243 7372 7371 Repair training, computer; Application computer software; Custom computer programming services

(G-5298)
COSTUME SPECIALISTS INC
1801 Lone Eagle St (43228-3647)
PHONE..............................614 464-2115
Wendy C Goldstein, *Pr*
EMP: 36 **EST:** 1979
SALES (est): 5.43MM **Privately Held**
Web: www.costumespecialists.com
SIC: 2389 7299 Theatrical costumes; Costume rental

(G-5299)
COTT SYSTEMS INC
2800 Corporate Exchange Dr Ste 300 (43231-1678)
PHONE..............................614 847-4405
Deborah A Ball, *CEO*
Jodie Bare, *
Karen L Bailey, *
Drew Shepppared, *
Mike Sosh, *
EMP: 95 **EST:** 1888
SQ FT: 20,000
SALES (est): 16.43MM **Privately Held**
Web: www.cottsystems.com
SIC: 7373 7371 2789 Computer integrated systems design; Computer software development and applications; Beveling of cards

(G-5300)
COUNTERTOP SALES
5767 Westbourne Ave (43213-1488)
PHONE..............................614 626-4476
Phillip Holbrook, *Pr*
EMP: 11 **EST:** 2002
SALES (est): 247.19K **Privately Held**
Web: www.premierctscolumbus.com
SIC: 2541 Counter and sink tops

(G-5301)
COW INDUSTRIES INC (PA)
Also Called: Central Ohio Welding
1875 Progress Ave (43207-1781)
PHONE..............................614 443-6537
John Burns, *Pr*
Michael Netto, *
Gary Carter, *
Christina Bradford, *
EMP: 40 **EST:** 1911
SQ FT: 80,000
SALES (est): 8.62MM
SALES (corp-wide): 8.62MM **Privately Held**
Web: www.cowind.com
SIC: 3499 3444 Machine bases, metal; Sheet metalwork

(G-5302)
COX INTERIOR INC
Also Called: Cox's Interior Supply
2220 Citygate Dr (43219-3565)
PHONE..............................614 473-9169
Mick Householder, *Mgr*
EMP: 8

SALES (corp-wide): 119.76MM **Privately Held**
Web: www.coxinterior.com
SIC: 2431 Millwork
HQ: Cox Interior, Inc.
1751 Old Columbia Rd
Campbellsville KY 42718
270 789-3129

(G-5303)
COZMYK ENTERPRISES INC
3757 Courtright Ct (43227-2250)
PHONE..............................614 231-1370
Alan L Cozmyk, *Pr*
Christopher J Minnillo, *Prin*
EMP: 15 **EST:** 1986
SQ FT: 20,000
SALES (est): 2.41MM **Privately Held**
Web: www.americanbackflowcalibration.com
SIC: 3446 Ornamental metalwork

(G-5304)
CPMM SERVICES GROUP INC
3785 Indianola Ave (43214-3754)
PHONE..............................614 447-0165
Dan Dimitroff, *Pr*
EMP: 25 **EST:** 1984
SQ FT: 12,500
SALES (est): 570.9K **Privately Held**
Web: www.cpmmservicesinc.com
SIC: 7331 2752 7374 Mailing list compilers; Offset printing; Data processing service

(G-5305)
CRANE BLENDING CENTER
2141 Fairwood Ave (43207-1753)
P.O. Box 1058 (43216-1058)
PHONE..............................614 542-1199
Phil Stobart, *Pr*
EMP: 40 **EST:** 2000
SALES (est): 2.66MM **Privately Held**
SIC: 2821 Polyvinyl chloride resins, PVC

(G-5306)
CRAWFORD PRODUCTS INC
3637 Corporate Dr (43231-7997)
PHONE..............................614 890-1822
William A Crawford, *CEO*
Kevin P Crawford, *Pr*
Scott Stauch, *VP*
▲ **EMP:** 21 **EST:** 1970
SQ FT: 12,500
SALES (est): 9.83MM **Privately Held**
Web: www.crawfordproducts.com
SIC: 5085 3452 Fasteners, industrial: nuts, bolts, screws, etc.; Bolts, nuts, rivets, and washers

(G-5307)
CREATIVE NEST LLC
Also Called: Belocal
3885 Barley Cir (43207-4602)
PHONE..............................614 216-8102
Trent Soles, *Prin*
EMP: 6 **EST:** 2015
SALES (est): 55.85K **Privately Held**
Web: www.belocalpub.com
SIC: 2741 Miscellaneous publishing

(G-5308)
CRMD LLC
1190 N High St (43201-2411)
PHONE..............................440 225-7179
EMP: 8 **EST:** 2017
SALES (est): 832.31K **Privately Held**
Web: www.getcrmd.com
SIC: 2024 Ice cream and frozen deserts

(G-5309)
CSG SOFTWARE
700 Taylor Ave (43219-2527)
PHONE..............................614 986-2600
Rick Lueckel, *Prin*
EMP: 7 **EST:** 2007
SALES (est): 65.56K **Privately Held**
SIC: 7372 7699 Prepackaged software; Cleaning services

(G-5310)
CURVES AND MORE WOODWORKING
2002 Zettler Rd (43232-3834)
PHONE..............................614 239-7837
Steven Blake, *Prin*
EMP: 8 **EST:** 2007
SALES (est): 214.03K **Privately Held**
SIC: 2431 Millwork

(G-5311)
CUSTOM SIGN CENTER
400 N Wilson Rd (43204-1208)
PHONE..............................614 279-6035
EMP: 6 **EST:** 2018
SALES (est): 432.17K **Privately Held**
Web: www.customsigncenter.com
SIC: 3993 Signs and advertising specialties

(G-5312)
CUSTOMWORKS INC
330 Lenappe Dr (43214-3118)
PHONE..............................614 262-1002
Jon Fotis, *Pr*
EMP: 9 **EST:** 1946
SQ FT: 14,500
SALES (est): 837.36K **Privately Held**
Web: www.customworksinc.com
SIC: 2541 Table or counter tops, plastic laminated

(G-5313)
DABAR INDUSTRIES LLC
7630 Copper Glen St (43235-1637)
PHONE..............................614 873-3949
Cliff Baseler, *Pr*
EMP: 15 **EST:** 2015
SALES (est): 965.92K **Privately Held**
SIC: 3443 Tanks, standard or custom fabricated: metal plate

(G-5314)
DAILY FANTASY CIRCUIT INC
5 E Long St Ste 603 (43215-2931)
PHONE..............................614 989-8689
Justin Fox, *Prin*
EMP: 6 **EST:** 2016
SALES (est): 62.99K **Privately Held**
SIC: 2711 Newspapers, publishing and printing

(G-5315)
DAILY REPORTER
580 S High St Ste 316 (43215-5659)
PHONE..............................614 224-4835
Ed Frederickson, *Pr*
Dan Shillingburg, *
EMP: 24 **EST:** 1896
SQ FT: 5,500
SALES (est): 2.82MM
SALES (corp-wide): 13.77MM **Privately Held**
Web: www.thedailyreporteronline.com
SIC: 2711 Newspapers, publishing and printing
PA: Calcomco, Inc.
5544 S Red Pine Cir
Kalamazoo MI 49009
313 885-9228

Columbus - Franklin County (G-5316)

(G-5316)
DANITE HOLDINGS LTD
Also Called: Danite Sign Co
1640 Harmon Ave (43223-3321)
PHONE.................................614 444-3333
Tim Mccord, *Pr*
Shelley Mccord, *Sec*
Calvin Lutz, *Stockholder**
C William Klausman, *
EMP: 50 EST: 1954
SQ FT: 33,500
SALES (est): 9.83MM **Privately Held**
Web: www.danitesign.com
SIC: **3993** 1799 Electric signs; Sign installation and maintenance

(G-5317)
DAVIS CUMMINS INC
3679 E Livingston Ave (43227-2243)
PHONE.................................614 309-6077
EMP: 8 EST: 2010
SALES (est): 67.28K **Privately Held**
Web: www.cummins.com
SIC: **3714** Motor vehicle parts and accessories

(G-5318)
DAZPAK FLEXIBLE PACKAGING CORP (PA)
2901 E 4th Ave (43219)
PHONE.................................614 252-2121
James Rooney, *CEO*
Mike Mc Coy, *CFO*
▲ EMP: 102 EST: 1964
SQ FT: 50,000
SALES (est): 26.83MM
SALES (corp-wide): 26.83MM **Privately Held**
Web: www.dazpak.com
SIC: **2673** 5113 Plastic bags: made from purchased materials; Bags, paper and disposable plastic

(G-5319)
DC REPROGRAPHICS CO
Also Called: AlphaGraphics
1254 Courtland Ave (43201-2829)
PHONE.................................614 297-1200
Daniel R Cannell, *Pr*
EMP: 18 EST: 2012
SALES (est): 1.19MM **Privately Held**
Web: www.alphagraphics.com
SIC: **2752** Commercial printing, lithographic

(G-5320)
DEADBOLTS PLUS
1509 Lockbourne Rd (43206-3741)
PHONE.................................614 405-2117
EMP: 6 EST: 2012
SALES (est): 106K **Privately Held**
SIC: **3429** Keys, locks, and related hardware

(G-5321)
DECO CRETE SUPPLY
700 Harrison Dr (43204-3513)
PHONE.................................614 372-5142
EMP: 6 EST: 2018
SALES (est): 221.22K **Privately Held**
Web: www.deco-cretesupply.com
SIC: **3273** Ready-mixed concrete

(G-5322)
DEE PRINTING INC
4999 Transamerica Dr (43228-9381)
P.O. Box 85 (43026-0085)
PHONE.................................614 777-8700
Dorothy J Murnane, *Pr*
EMP: 14 EST: 1974
SQ FT: 4,000
SALES (est): 2.3MM **Privately Held**
Web: www.deeprinting.com
SIC: **2759** 7311 Letterpress printing; Advertising agencies

(G-5323)
DEFABCO INC
3765 E Livingston Ave (43227-2258)
PHONE.................................614 231-2700
EMP: 60 EST: 1972
SALES (est): 10.01MM **Privately Held**
Web: www.defabco.com
SIC: **1761** 3443 3535 3444 Sheet metal work, nec; Pipe, standpipe, and culverts; Conveyors and conveying equipment; Sheet metalwork

(G-5324)
DELILLE OXYGEN COMPANY (PA)
772 Marion Rd (43207-2595)
P.O. Box 7809 (43207-0809)
PHONE.................................614 444-1177
Richard F Carlile, *Prin*
Joseph R Smith, *
Tom Smith, *
Jim Smith, *
EMP: 40 EST: 1964
SQ FT: 20,000
SALES (est): 25.92MM
SALES (corp-wide): 25.92MM **Privately Held**
Web: www.delille.com
SIC: **2813** 5085 Acetylene; Welding supplies

(G-5325)
DELPHIA CONSULTING LLC
250 E Broad St Ste 1150 (43215-3773)
PHONE.................................614 421-2000
Brian Delphia, *Pr*
Brian Delphia, *CEO*
Alexander Main, *
EMP: 40 EST: 1999
SALES (est): 8.63MM **Privately Held**
Web: www.delphiaconsulting.com
SIC: **8742** 7372 Human resource consulting services; Business oriented computer software

(G-5326)
DIAMOND INNOVATIONS INC (PA)
Also Called: Hyperion
6325 Huntley Rd (43229-1007)
P.O. Box 568 (43085-0568)
PHONE.................................614 438-2000
Ron Voigt, *CEO*
◆ EMP: 406 EST: 1955
SALES (est): 96.53MM
SALES (corp-wide): 96.53MM **Privately Held**
Web: www.hyperionmt.com
SIC: **3291** Abrasive products

(G-5327)
DIRCKSEN AND ASSOCIATES INC
743 S Front St (43206-1905)
P.O. Box 13662 (43213-0662)
PHONE.................................614 238-0413
Daniel W Dircksen, *Pr*
EMP: 6 EST: 1983
SALES (est): 852.07K **Privately Held**
Web: www.dircksenassociates.com
SIC: **3728** 5088 Military aircraft equipment and armament; Transportation equipment and supplies

(G-5328)
DISCOVER PUBLICATIONS
6425 Busch Blvd (43229-1862)
PHONE.................................877 872-3080
Leo Zupam, *Prin*
EMP: 9 EST: 2009
SALES (est): 797.57K **Privately Held**
Web: www.discoverpubs.com
SIC: **2741** Miscellaneous publishing

(G-5329)
DISPATCH PRINTING COMPANY (PA)
62 E Broad St (43215-3503)
EMP: 600 EST: 1871
SQ FT: 200,000
SALES (est): 450.12MM
SALES (corp-wide): 450.12MM **Privately Held**
Web: www.dispatch.com
SIC: **2711** Newspapers, publishing and printing

(G-5330)
DISTINCTIVE SURFACES LLC
4600 Bridgeway Ave (43219-1893)
PHONE.................................614 431-0898
Jonathan Ruper, *Managing Member*
EMP: 18 EST: 2013
SALES (est): 2.59MM **Privately Held**
Web: www.distinctivekitchen.com
SIC: **2434** Wood kitchen cabinets

(G-5331)
DISTRICT BREWING COMPANY INC
Also Called: Columbus Brewing Company
2555 Harrison Rd (43204-3511)
PHONE.................................614 224-3626
Eric Bean, *Pr*
Susie Edwards, *
Ben Pridgeon, *
▲ EMP: 48 EST: 1988
SQ FT: 6,000
SALES (est): 5.7MM **Privately Held**
Web: www.columbusbrewing.com
SIC: **5813** 2082 Bars and lounges; Beer (alcoholic beverage)

(G-5332)
DLZ OHIO INC (HQ)
6121 Huntley Rd (43229-1003)
PHONE.................................614 888-0040
Vikram Raj Rajadhyaksha, *Ch*
A James Siebert, *
David Cutlip, *
Allan C Strange, *
P V Rajadhyaksha, *
EMP: 200 EST: 1950
SQ FT: 45,000
SALES (est): 18.43MM **Privately Held**
Web: www.dlz.com
SIC: **8711** 1382 8712 8713 Consulting engineer; Geophysical exploration, oil and gas field; Architectural services; Surveying services
PA: Dlz Corporation
6121 Huntley Rd
Columbus OH 43229

(G-5333)
DM PALLET SERVICE INC
2019 Rathmell Rd (43207-5012)
PHONE.................................614 491-0881
Dexter Mounts Ii, *Pr*
Dexter Mounts Senior, *Sec*
EMP: 15 EST: 1985
SQ FT: 800
SALES (est): 398.53K **Privately Held**
Web: www.dmpallet.com
SIC: **2448** Pallets, wood

(G-5334)
DNO INC
3650 E 5th Ave (43219-1805)
PHONE.................................614 231-3601
Anthony Dinovo, *Pr*
Carol Dinovo, *
EMP: 80 EST: 1989
SQ FT: 10,000
SALES (est): 16.73MM **Privately Held**
Web: www.dnoinc.com
SIC: **2099** 5148 Salads, fresh or refrigerated; Fruits, fresh

(G-5335)
DRAKE BROTHERS LTD
1215 Forsythe Ave (43201-3202)
PHONE.................................415 819-4941
EMP: 6 EST: 2008
SALES (est): 172.01K **Privately Held**
Web: www.brothersdrake.com
SIC: **2084** Wines

(G-5336)
DRIVELINE 1 INC
1369 Frank Rd (43223-3729)
P.O. Box 40 (43123-0040)
PHONE.................................614 279-7734
Bruce Hickman, *Pr*
EMP: 9 EST: 1993
SQ FT: 7,500
SALES (est): 868.73K **Privately Held**
Web: www.driveline1.com
SIC: **3714** Motor vehicle parts and accessories

(G-5337)
DURE FOODS US LLC
6967 Alum Creek Dr (43217-1244)
PHONE.................................614 409-9030
EMP: 15 EST: 2004
SQ FT: 50,000
SALES (est): 3.57MM
SALES (corp-wide): 13.48MM **Privately Held**
Web: www.durefoods.com
SIC: **2099** Food preparations, nec
PA: Dure Foods Limited
120 Roy Blvd
Brantford ON N3R 7
519 753-5504

(G-5338)
E BEE PRINTING INC
70 S 4th St (43215-4315)
PHONE.................................614 224-0416
Debbi Bussman, *Prin*
EMP: 7 EST: 2009
SALES (est): 223.89K **Privately Held**
SIC: **2752** Offset printing

(G-5339)
E RETAILING ASSOCIATES LLC
Also Called: Customized Girl
2282 Westbrooke Dr (43228-9416)
PHONE.................................614 300-5785
Taj Schaffnit, *Managing Member*
Kurt J Schmalz, *
EMP: 64 EST: 2004
SALES (est): 10.35MM **Privately Held**
Web: www.eretailing.com
SIC: **8748** 5961 2253 Business consulting, nec; Electronic shopping; T-shirts and tops, knit

(G-5340)
E-WASTE SYSTEMS (OHIO) INC
1033 Brentnell Ave Ste 300 (43219-2186)
PHONE.................................614 824-3057
George Pardos, *CEO*
Steve Hollinshead, *CFO*
EMP: 7 EST: 2010
SALES (est): 225.72K **Privately Held**
SIC: **3861** Photocopy machines

(G-5341)
EAGLE SPECIALTY MATERIALS LLC
233 Erie Rd (43214-3600)
PHONE.................................216 401-6075

GEOGRAPHIC SECTION
Columbus - Franklin County (G-5368)

EMP: 8 **EST:** 2019
SALES (est): 412.83K **Privately Held**
SIC: 3273 Ready-mixed concrete

(G-5342)
EARTHLEY WELLNESS
320 Outerbelt St Ste J (43213-1537)
PHONE...............614 625-1064
Benjamin Tietje, *CEO*
EMP: 10 **EST:** 2016
SALES (est): 1.49MM **Privately Held**
Web: www.earthley.com
SIC: 2833 Medicinals and botanicals

(G-5343)
ECLIPSE 3D/PI LLC
825 Taylor Rd (43230-6235)
PHONE...............614 626-8536
Jeff Burt, *CEO*
Sandra Burt, *
Scott Wolfe, *
EMP: 45 **EST:** 1994
SALES (est): 2.71MM **Privately Held**
Web: www.eclipsecreative.com
SIC: 7335 2621 Photographic studio, commercial; Printing paper

(G-5344)
EDDIES IRON LUNG LLC
2490 Eastcleft Dr (43221-1854)
PHONE...............614 493-3411
Douglas Curtis, *Prin*
EMP: 6 **EST:** 2017
SALES (est): 106.47K **Privately Held**
SIC: 3842 Iron lungs

(G-5345)
EDEN CRYOGENICS LLC
7630 Copper Glen St (43235-1637)
PHONE...............614 873-3949
Steve L Hensley, *Pr*
▲ **EMP:** 45 **EST:** 2006
SALES (est): 4.42MM **Privately Held**
Web: www.edencryogenics.com
SIC: 3559 Cryogenic machinery, industrial

(G-5346)
EDGE EXPONENTIAL LLC
1140 Gahanna Pkwy (43230-6615)
PHONE...............614 226-4421
Jim Droty, *Pr*
Craig Ryan Turner, *Dir*
EMP: 10 **EST:** 2020
SALES (est): 600.58K **Privately Held**
Web: www.edgeinnovationhub.com
SIC: 3556 Food products machinery

(G-5347)
EFCO CORP
Also Called: Economy Forms
3900 Zane Trace Dr (43228-3833)
PHONE...............614 876-1226
Jim Davis, *Mgr*
EMP: 6
SALES (corp-wide): 244.82MM **Privately Held**
Web: www.efcoforms.com
SIC: 5051 7353 4225 3444 Steel; Heavy construction equipment rental; General warehousing; Concrete forms, sheet metal
HQ: Efco Corp
1800 Ne Broadway Ave
Des Moines IA 50313
515 266-1141

(G-5348)
ELEMENTS HR INC
2845 Canterbury Ln (43221-3016)
PHONE...............614 488-6944
EMP: 6 **EST:** 2007

SALES (est): 103.56K **Privately Held**
SIC: 2819 Elements

(G-5349)
ELMERS PRODUCTS INC
180 E Broad St Fl 4 (43215-3763)
PHONE...............614 225-4000
Michael Endres, *Brnch Mgr*
EMP: 79
SALES (corp-wide): 8.13B **Publicly Held**
Web: www.elmers.com
SIC: 2891 Adhesives and sealants
HQ: Elmer's Products, Inc.
6655 Pachtree Dunwoody Rd
Atlanta GA 30328

(G-5350)
ELYTUS LTD
601 S High St (43215-5620)
PHONE...............614 824-4985
EMP: 11 **EST:** 2007
SALES (est): 1.65MM **Privately Held**
Web: www.rts.com
SIC: 7372 Utility computer software

(G-5351)
EMBROIDERY DESIGN GROUP LLC
2564 Billingsley Rd (43235-1990)
PHONE...............614 798-8152
Mary Bandeen, *Managing Member*
EMP: 10 **EST:** 1993
SALES (est): 419.91K **Privately Held**
Web: www.embroiderydesigngroup.com
SIC: 2395 Embroidery products, except Schiffli machine

(G-5352)
EMPRESS ROYALTY LTD
236 Fairway Dr (43214-1748)
PHONE...............614 943-1903
EMP: 6 **EST:** 2019
SALES (est): 741.66K **Privately Held**
Web: www.empressroyalty.com
SIC: 1382 Oil and gas exploration services

(G-5353)
ENDLESS HOME IMPROVEMENTS LLC
3897 Fergus Rd (43207-4253)
PHONE...............614 599-1799
EMP: 6
SALES (est): 149.99K **Privately Held**
SIC: 1389 7389 Construction, repair, and dismantling services; Business services, nec

(G-5354)
ENGINEERED MARBLE INC
4064 Fisher Rd (43228-1020)
PHONE...............614 308-0041
EMP: 6 **EST:** 1994
SQ FT: 6,100
SALES (est): 500K **Privately Held**
Web: www.engineeredmarbleinc.com
SIC: 3281 Marble, building: cut and shaped

(G-5355)
ENGINEERED PROFILES LLC
2141 Fairwood Ave (43207-1753)
PHONE...............614 754-3700
Mike Davis, *Pr*
Brian Davis, *
Adam Wachter, *
EMP: 328 **EST:** 1999
SQ FT: 300,000
SALES (est): 100.01MM **Privately Held**
Web: www.engineeredprofiles.com
SIC: 3089 Injection molding of plastics
HQ: The Crane Group Companies Limited
330 W Spring St Ste 200

Columbus OH 43215
614 754-3000

(G-5356)
ENTROCHEM INC
1245 Kinnear Rd (43212-1155)
PHONE...............614 946-7602
Jim Mcguire, *Pr*
EMP: 10 **EST:** 1999
SALES (est): 1.42MM **Privately Held**
Web: www.entrotech.com
SIC: 2891 Adhesives

(G-5357)
EP FERRIS & ASSOCIATES INC
2130 Quarry Trails Dr # 2 (43228-8981)
PHONE...............614 299-2999
Edward P Ferris, *Ch Bd*
Matthew Ferris, *Dir*
EMP: 40 **EST:** 1987
SALES (est): 10.01MM **Privately Held**
Web: www.epferris.com
SIC: 8742 8711 1389 Management consulting services; Construction and civil engineering; Testing, measuring, surveying, and analysis services

(G-5358)
ERNST ENTERPRISES INC
711 Stimmel Rd (43223-2905)
PHONE...............614 443-9456
John C Ernst Junior, *Brnch Mgr*
EMP: 34
SALES (corp-wide): 240.08MM **Privately Held**
Web: www.ernstconcrete.com
SIC: 5211 3273 Cement; Ready-mixed concrete
PA: Ernst Enterprises, Inc.
3361 Successful Way
Dayton OH 45414
937 233-5555

(G-5359)
ERNST ENTERPRISES INC
569 N Wilson Rd (43204-1459)
PHONE...............614 308-0063
EMP: 13
SALES (corp-wide): 240.08MM **Privately Held**
Web: www.ernstconcrete.com
SIC: 3273 Ready-mixed concrete
PA: Ernst Enterprises, Inc.
3361 Successful Way
Dayton OH 45414
937 233-5555

(G-5360)
ESPLINE LLC
1810 Grace Ln (43220-4957)
PHONE...............401 234-4520
EMP: 8 **EST:** 2009
SALES (est): 161.32K **Privately Held**
Web: www.espline.com
SIC: 7372 Application computer software

(G-5361)
ESSILOR LABORATORIES AMER INC
Also Called: Top Network
3671 Interchange Rd (43204-1499)
PHONE...............614 274-0840
Don Lepore, *Mgr*
EMP: 31
SALES (corp-wide): 2.55MM **Privately Held**
Web: www.essilorinstrumentsusa.com
SIC: 3851 5049 Eyeglasses, lenses and frames; Optical goods
HQ: Essilor Laboratories Of America, Inc.
13515 N Stemmons Fwy
Dallas TX 75234
972 241-4141

(G-5362)
EVANS ADHESIVE CORPORATION (HQ)
925 Old Henderson Rd (43220-3779)
PHONE...............614 451-2665
C Russell Thompson, *Pr*
EMP: 27 **EST:** 1900
SALES (est): 10.19MM
SALES (corp-wide): 84.16MM **Privately Held**
Web: www.evansadhesive.com
SIC: 2891 5085 Adhesives; Abrasives and adhesives
PA: Meridian Adhesives Group Llc
15720 Brixham Hill Ave # 500
Charlotte NC

(G-5363)
EVANS ADHESIVE CORPORATION LTD
925 Old Henderson Rd (43220-3779)
PHONE...............614 451-2665
◆ **EMP:** 39
SIC: 2891 2821 Adhesives; Plastics materials and resins

(G-5364)
EVANS CREATIVE GROUP LLC
Also Called: Columbus Underground
11 E Gay St (43215-3125)
PHONE...............614 657-9439
EMP: 9 **EST:** 2008
SQ FT: 2,600
SALES (est): 529.59K **Privately Held**
Web: www.columbusunderground.com
SIC: 2741 Internet publishing and broadcasting

(G-5365)
EXPONENTIA US INC (PA)
424 Beecher Rd Ste A (43230-3510)
PHONE...............614 944-5103
Giri Suvramani, *Pr*
Gira Suvramani, *Pr*
EMP: 6 **EST:** 2000
SQ FT: 5,200
SALES (est): 755.89K **Privately Held**
Web: www.exponentiaus.com
SIC: 7372 Publisher's computer software

(G-5366)
EXPRESS PHARMACY & DME LLC
2750 S Hamilton Rd Ste 19 (43232-5188)
PHONE...............210 981-9690
Daniel Winston Amoh Junior, *Managing Member*
EMP: 6 **EST:** 2019
SALES (est): 317.43K **Privately Held**
Web: www.expresspharmacyanddme.com
SIC: 5912 3069 Drug stores and proprietary stores; Medical and laboratory rubber sundries and related products

(G-5367)
EXTERIOR PORTFOLIO LLC
1441 Universal Rd (43207-1730)
P.O. Box 1058 (43216-1058)
PHONE...............614 754-3400
EMP: 250
SIC: 3089 Siding, plastics

(G-5368)
EYE SURGERY CENTER OHIO INC (PA)
Also Called: Arena Eye Surgeons
262 Neil Ave Ste 320 (43215-4624)
PHONE...............614 228-3937
TOLL FREE: 800
Peter Utrata, *Prin*

Columbus - Franklin County (G-5369) — GEOGRAPHIC SECTION

EMP: 25 EST: 1984
SQ FT: 2,200
SALES (est): 4.84MM
SALES (corp-wide): 4.84MM Privately Held
Web: www.arenaeyesurgeons.com
SIC: 3841 8011 Eye examining instruments and apparatus; Offices and clinics of medical doctors

(G-5369)
FABX LLC
1819 Walcutt Rd Ste 100 (43228-9149)
PHONE..................................614 565-5835
Todd Wurstner, Managing Member
EMP: 10 EST: 2020
SALES (est): 1.21MM Privately Held
SIC: 3441 Building components, structural steel

(G-5370)
FACILITIES MANAGEMENT FX LLC
800 Yard St Ste 115 (43212-3866)
PHONE..................................614 519-2186
Jeffery Wilkins, CEO
Brian Gregory, *
Jeffery Wilkins Ceojeffery Wilkins, CEO
EMP: 56 EST: 2014
SQ FT: 3,200
SALES (est): 5.13MM Privately Held
Web: www.gofmx.com
SIC: 7372 Application computer software

(G-5371)
FBG BOTTLING GROUP LLC
Also Called: Frostop
818 S Yearling Rd (43213-3056)
P.O. Box 9841 (43209-0841)
PHONE..................................614 580-7063
Mike Gutter, Pr
EMP: 11 EST: 2012
SALES (est): 455.64K Privately Held
Web: www.frostop.com
SIC: 2086 Bottled and canned soft drinks

(G-5372)
FCBDD
2879 Johnstown Rd (43219-1719)
PHONE..................................614 475-6440
EMP: 58 EST: 2014
SALES (est): 1.33MM Privately Held
Web: www.fcbdd.org
SIC: 3999

(G-5373)
FCX PERFORMANCE INC (HQ)
Also Called: Jh Instruments
3000 E 14th Ave (43219)
PHONE..................................614 253-1996
Thomas Cox, Ch
Russell S Frazee, *
Chris Hill, *
Theron Neese, *
Brian Miller, *
▲ EMP: 40 EST: 1999
SQ FT: 44,000
SALES (est): 544.13MM
SALES (corp-wide): 4.41B Publicly Held
Web: www.fcxperformance.com
SIC: 5084 5085 3494 Instruments and control equipment; Industrial supplies; Valves and pipe fittings, nec
PA: Applied Industrial Technologies, Inc.
 1 Applied Plz
 Cleveland OH 44115
 216 426-4000

(G-5374)
FEDERAL PARKWAY DIESEL CO LLC
1879 Federal Pkwy Ste 100 (43207-5712)
PHONE..................................614 571-0388
EMP: 6 EST: 2020
SALES (est): 236.7K Privately Held
SIC: 2911 Diesel fuels

(G-5375)
FINE LINE GRAPHICS CORP
Also Called: Fine Line Graphics
2364 Featherwood Dr (43228-8236)
P.O. Box 163370 (43216-3370)
PHONE..................................614 486-0276
James Basch, Pr
Mark Carro, *
Gregory Davis, *
▲ EMP: 170 EST: 1979
SALES (est): 12.15MM Privately Held
Web: www.perfectdomain.com
SIC: 2752 7331 Offset printing; Mailing service

(G-5376)
FIREHOUSE FOODS
917 F Whittier St (43206-1584)
PHONE..................................614 592-8115
EMP: 6
SALES (est): 425.67K Privately Held
SIC: 2099 Food preparations, nec

(G-5377)
FISHEL COMPANY
Johnson Brothers Construction
1600 Walcutt Rd (43228-9394)
PHONE..................................614 850-4400
Ed Evans, Mgr
EMP: 167
SALES (corp-wide): 758.31MM Privately Held
Web: www.teamfishel.com
SIC: 1623 8711 1731 3612 Telephone and communication line construction; Engineering services; Electrical work; Transformers, except electric
PA: The Fishel Company
 1366 Dublin Rd
 Columbus OH 43215
 614 274-8100

(G-5378)
FLAG LADY INC
Also Called: Flag Lady's Flag Store, The
4567 N High St (43214-2042)
PHONE..................................614 263-1776
Mary Leavitt, Pr
Lori Leavitt Watson, VP
EMP: 9 EST: 1979
SQ FT: 5,000
SALES (est): 966.45K Privately Held
Web: www.flagladyusa.com
SIC: 5999 2399 Flags; Flags, fabric

(G-5379)
FLEXSYS AMERICA LP
1658 Williams Rd (43207-5109)
PHONE..................................618 482-6371
EMP: 15
SALES (corp-wide): 105.28MM Privately Held
SIC: 3069 Reclaimed rubber and specialty rubber compounds
HQ: Flexsys America L.P.
 260 Springside Dr
 Akron OH 44333

(G-5380)
FLIGHTSAFETY INTERNATIONAL INC (HQ)
3100 Easton Square Pl Ste 100 (43219-6289)
PHONE..................................614 324-3500
Bradley Thress, Pr
Patricia Arundell-lampe, Sr VP
Diana Svp-teammate Resources Wheeler, Prin
Steve Gross, *
Brian Moore, *
▲ EMP: 110 EST: 1951
SQ FT: 36,000
SALES (est): 621.73MM
SALES (corp-wide): 364.48B Publicly Held
Web: www.flightsafety.com
SIC: 8249 3699 Aviation school; Flight simulators (training aids), electronic
PA: Berkshire Hathaway Inc.
 3555 Farnam St Ste 1440
 Omaha NE 68131
 402 346-1400

(G-5381)
FLOYD BELL INC (PA)
720 Dearborn Park Ln (43085-5703)
PHONE..................................614 294-4000
▲ EMP: 69 EST: 1971
SALES (est): 7.39MM
SALES (corp-wide): 7.39MM Privately Held
Web: www.floydbell.com
SIC: 3669 5065 3661 3651 Emergency alarms; Telephone equipment; Telephone and telegraph apparatus; Household audio and video equipment

(G-5382)
FORTERRA PIPE & PRECAST LLC
1500 Haul Rd (43207-1888)
PHONE..................................614 445-3830
Wayne Greene, Pr
EMP: 11 EST: 2016
SALES (est): 1.07MM Privately Held
Web: www.rinkerpipe.com
SIC: 3272 Concrete products, nec

(G-5383)
FORTIN WELDING & MFG INC
Also Called: Fortin Ironworks
944 W 5th Ave (43212-2657)
PHONE..................................614 291-4342
Joe Vangundy, Pr
Dan Fortin, *
Fred Fortin, *
John Fortin, *
Robert Fortin, *
EMP: 39 EST: 1946
SQ FT: 60,000
SALES (est): 5.24MM Privately Held
Web: www.fortinironworks.com
SIC: 3449 3446 Miscellaneous metalwork; Ornamental metalwork

(G-5384)
FORTNER UPHOLSTERING INC
2050 S High St (43207-2425)
PHONE..................................614 475-8282
David F Fortner Junior, Pr
Diana Orum, Sec
Glen Mcallister, Pr
David F Fortner Junior, Prin
Wanda L Fortner, Prin
▲ EMP: 16 EST: 1967
SQ FT: 7,000
SALES (est): 4.12MM Privately Held
Web: www.fortnerinc.com
SIC: 5712 2512 7641 3429 Furniture stores; Upholstered household furniture; Reupholstery and furniture repair; Furniture, builders' and other household hardware

(G-5385)
FRANKLIN ART GLASS STUDIOS
222 E Sycamore St (43206-2198)
PHONE..................................614 221-2972
Gary L Helf, Ch Bd
Andrea Reid, *
▲ EMP: 24 EST: 1900
SQ FT: 55,000
SALES (est): 4.22MM Privately Held
Web: www.franklinartglass.com
SIC: 3231 5231 5945 Stained glass: made from purchased glass; Glass, leaded or stained; Hobby, toy, and game shops

(G-5386)
FRANKLIN COMMUNICATIONS INC
Also Called: Wsny FM
4401 Carriage Hill Ln (43220-3837)
PHONE..................................614 459-9769
Edward K Christian, CEO
Alan Goodman, *
EMP: 35 EST: 1945
SQ FT: 10,000
SALES (est): 2.56MM Publicly Held
Web: www.rewindcolumbus.com
SIC: 4832 2711 Radio broadcasting stations; Newspapers
HQ: Saga Communications Of New England, Inc
 73 Kercheval Ave Ste 201
 Grosse Pointe Farms MI 48236
 313 886-7070

(G-5387)
FRANKLIN INTERNATIONAL INC (PA)
Also Called: Constrction Adhsves Slants Div
2020 Bruck St (43207-2382)
PHONE..................................614 443-0241
◆ EMP: 378 EST: 1935
SALES (est): 112.91MM
SALES (corp-wide): 112.91MM Privately Held
Web: www.franklininternational.com
SIC: 2891 2821 Adhesives; Plastics materials and resins

(G-5388)
FRED D PFENING COMPANY
Also Called: Plant 2
1075 W 5th Ave (43212-2691)
PHONE..................................614 294-5361
John Legg, Brnch Mgr
EMP: 7
SALES (corp-wide): 9.99MM Privately Held
Web: www.pfening.com
SIC: 3556 Bakery machinery
PA: The Fred D Pfening Company
 1075 W 5th Ave
 Columbus OH 43212
 614 294-5361

(G-5389)
FRED D PFENING COMPANY (PA)
1075 W 5th Ave (43212-2691)
PHONE..................................614 294-5361
Fred D Pfening Junior, CEO
Fred D Pfening Iii, Pr
Ed Brackman, VP
Timothy D Pfening, Sec
William F Kearns, VP
EMP: 41 EST: 1919
SQ FT: 55,000
SALES (est): 9.99MM
SALES (corp-wide): 9.99MM Privately Held
Web: pfening.openfos.com
SIC: 3535 3585 3556 Pneumatic tube conveyor systems; Air conditioning units, complete: domestic or industrial; Mixers, commercial, food

(G-5390)
FRIENDLY CANDLE LLC
1160 Corrugated Way (43201-2902)
PHONE..................................740 683-0312
Devin Dingey, Prin

EMP: 6 **EST:** 2016
SALES (est): 406.29K **Privately Held**
Web: www.friendlycandle.com
SIC: 3999 Candles

(G-5391)
FUTURE POLYTECH INC (PA)
2215 Citygate Dr Ste D (43219-3589)
PHONE..................................614 942-1209
Tony Durieux, *Pr*
EMP: 22 **EST:** 2011
SALES (est): 3.34MM
SALES (corp-wide): 3.34MM **Privately Held**
Web: www.futurepolytech.com
SIC: 2671 Plastic film, coated or laminated for packaging

(G-5392)
FUZZY TEN LLC
3375 En Joie Dr (43228-9430)
PHONE..................................614 276-4738
John Adams Adams, *Owner*
EMP: 6 **EST:** 2018
SALES (est): 61.18K **Privately Held**
SIC: 2621 Paper mills

(G-5393)
G & J PEPSI-COLA BOTTLERS INC
Also Called: Pepsico
870 N 22nd St (43219-2427)
PHONE..................................866 647-2734
EMP: 49
SALES (corp-wide): 404.54MM **Privately Held**
Web: www.gjpepsi.com
SIC: 2086 Carbonated soft drinks, bottled and canned
PA: G & J Pepsi-Cola Bottlers Inc
  9435 Waterstone Blvd # 390
  Cincinnati OH 45249
  513 785-6060

(G-5394)
G & J PEPSI-COLA BOTTLERS INC
Also Called: Pepsico
1241 Gibbard Ave (43219-2438)
PHONE..................................614 253-8771
Thomas Pendrey, *Brnch Mgr*
EMP: 550
SQ FT: 200,000
SALES (corp-wide): 404.54MM **Privately Held**
Web: www.gjpepsi.com
SIC: 2086 Carbonated soft drinks, bottled and canned
PA: G & J Pepsi-Cola Bottlers Inc
  9435 Waterstone Blvd # 390
  Cincinnati OH 45249
  513 785-6060

(G-5395)
GARDNER INC (PA)
3641 Interchange Rd (43204-1499)
PHONE..................................614 456-4000
John F Finn, *CEO*
James P Finn, *VP*
Michael L Finn, *VP*
John T Finn, *CFO*
◆ **EMP:** 222 **EST:** 1975
SQ FT: 204,000
SALES (est): 96.66MM
SALES (corp-wide): 96.66MM **Privately Held**
Web: www.gardnerinc.com
SIC: 3524 Lawn and garden equipment

(G-5396)
GAWA TRADERS WHOLESALE & DIST
250 West St (43215-7513)

PHONE..................................614 697-1440
EMP: 30 **EST:** 2020
SALES (est): 1.06MM **Privately Held**
Web: www.gawatraders.com
SIC: 2051 Bakery: wholesale or wholesale/retail combined

(G-5397)
GENERAL THEMING CONTRS LLC
Also Called: GTC Artist With Machines
3750 Courtright Ct (43227-2253)
P.O. Box 27173 (43227-0173)
PHONE..................................614 252-6342
Richard D Rogovin, *Prin*
Kim Schanzenbach, *
Rich Witherspoon, *
▲ **EMP:** 105 **EST:** 1999
SQ FT: 60,000
SALES (est): 18.37MM **Privately Held**
Web: www.artistswithmachines.com
SIC: 7389 7336 2759 2396 Sign painting and lettering shop; Commercial art and graphic design; Commercial printing, nec; Automotive and apparel trimmings

(G-5398)
GENERALS BOOKS
Also Called: The General's Books
522 Norton Rd (43228-2617)
P.O. Box 28685 (43228-0685)
PHONE..................................614 870-1861
David Roth, *Pr*
Robin Patricia Roth, *Pr*
EMP: 8 **EST:** 1983
SQ FT: 1,980
SALES (est): 673.97K **Privately Held**
Web: www.bluegraymagazine.com
SIC: 2721 Magazines: publishing only, not printed on site

(G-5399)
GENPAK LLC
845 Kaderly Dr (43228-1033)
PHONE..................................614 276-5156
Scott Wilson, *Mgr*
EMP: 50
Web: www.genpak.com
SIC: 3089 Plastics containers, except foam
HQ: Genpak Llc
  10601 Westlake Dr
  Charlotte NC 28273
  800 626-6695

(G-5400)
GEORGIA-PACIFIC LLC
Also Called: Georgia-Pacific
1975 Watkins Rd (43207-3443)
PHONE..................................614 491-9100
Kurt Miller, *Mgr*
EMP: 40
SALES (corp-wide): 36.93B **Privately Held**
Web: www.gp.com
SIC: 2621 Paper mills
HQ: Georgia-Pacific Llc
  133 Peachtree St Nw
  Atlanta GA 30303
  404 652-4000

(G-5401)
GFL ENVIRONMENTAL SVCS USA INC
Also Called: Heartland Petroleum
4001 E 5th Ave (43219-1812)
PHONE..................................614 441-4001
Sayed Atiyeah, *Manager*
EMP: 45
SALES (corp-wide): 5.03B **Privately Held**
SIC: 2911 5172 Mineral oils, natural; Fuel oil
HQ: Gfl Environmental Services Usa, Inc.
  18927 Hickory Creek Dr
  Mokena IL 60448
  866 579-6900

(G-5402)
GFS CHEMICALS INC
800 Kaderly Dr (43228-1034)
PHONE..................................614 351-5347
John Pringle, *Mgr*
EMP: 28
SALES (corp-wide): 48.46MM **Privately Held**
Web: www.gfschemicals.com
SIC: 2819 Industrial inorganic chemicals, nec
PA: Gfs Chemicals, Inc.
  155 Hidden Ravines Dr
  Powell OH 43065
  740 881-5501

(G-5403)
GFS CHEMICALS INC
851 Mckinley Ave (43222-1148)
P.O. Box 245 (43065-0245)
PHONE..................................614 224-5345
Robert Pierro, *Brnch Mgr*
EMP: 60
SALES (corp-wide): 48.46MM **Privately Held**
Web: www.gfschemicals.com
SIC: 2819 2899 2869 Chemicals, reagent grade: refined from technical grade; Chemical preparations, nec; Industrial organic chemicals, nec
PA: Gfs Chemicals, Inc.
  155 Hidden Ravines Dr
  Powell OH 43065
  740 881-5501

(G-5404)
GLISTER INC
Also Called: Kingswood Company, The
830 Harmon Ave (43223-2410)
PHONE..................................614 252-6400
Kristie Nicolosi, *Pr*
EMP: 49 **EST:** 2005
SALES (est): 5.03MM **Privately Held**
Web: www.thekingswoodcompany.com
SIC: 2842 Polishes and sanitation goods

(G-5405)
GLOBAL TRUCKING LLC
3723 Ellerdale Dr (43230-4086)
PHONE..................................614 598-6264
Ayan Hassan Abdinizak, *Admn*
Ayan Abdirizak, *Managing Member*
EMP: 10 **EST:** 2016
SALES (est): 500.2K **Privately Held**
SIC: 3537 Trucks, tractors, loaders, carriers, and similar equipment

(G-5406)
GOLDEN ANGLE ARCHTCTRAL GROUP
Also Called: General Contractor
4207 E Broad St Ste C (43213-1200)
PHONE..................................614 531-7932
Jermaine Wilson, *CEO*
EMP: 8 **EST:** 2014
SALES (est): 504.5K **Privately Held**
SIC: 1761 8712 1751 1521 Roofing, siding, and sheetmetal work; Architectural services; Window and door installation and erection; Patio and deck construction and repair

(G-5407)
GONGWER NEWS SERVICE INC (PA)
Also Called: Ohio Report
175 S 3rd St (43215-5188)
PHONE..................................614 221-1992
Alan A Miller, *Pr*
Scott Miller, *Asst VP*
EMP: 11 **EST:** 1906
SALES (est): 1.6MM
SALES (corp-wide): 1.6MM **Privately Held**
Web: www.gongwer-oh.com

SIC: 2721 8111 Magazines: publishing only, not printed on site; Legal services

(G-5408)
GRAFFITI FOODS LIMITED
333 Outerbelt St (43213-1529)
PHONE..................................614 759-1921
EMP: 13 **EST:** 2004
SQ FT: 7,600
SALES (est): 2.46MM
SALES (corp-wide): 57.51MM **Privately Held**
Web: www.graffitifoods.com
SIC: 2099 Food preparations, nec
PA: New Horizons Baking Company, Llc
  211 Woodlawn Ave
  Norwalk OH 44857
  419 668-8226

(G-5409)
GRAHAM ELECTRIC
2855 Banwick Rd (43232-3821)
PHONE..................................614 231-8500
EMP: 12 **EST:** 2015
SALES (est): 789.52K **Privately Held**
Web: www.graham-electric.com
SIC: 3699 1731 Electrical equipment and supplies, nec; Electrical work

(G-5410)
GRAMKE ENTERPRISES LTD
3021 E 4th Ave Ste B (43219-2888)
PHONE..................................614 252-8711
▲ **EMP:** 7 **EST:** 2001
SALES (est): 509.75K **Privately Held**
SIC: 3479 Painting, coating, and hot dipping

(G-5411)
GRASSROOTS STRATEGIES LLC
5990 E Livingston Ave (43232-2927)
PHONE..................................614 783-6515
EMP: 6 **EST:** 2012
SALES (est): 352.02K **Privately Held**
Web: www.grassrootsstrategiesllc.com
SIC: 2759 Commercial printing, nec

(G-5412)
GREEN ROOM BREWING LLC
Also Called: Seventh Son Brewing
1101 N 4th St (43201-3683)
PHONE..................................614 421-2337
EMP: 7 **EST:** 2010
SALES (est): 449.17K **Privately Held**
SIC: 5813 2082 Bars and lounges; Near beer

(G-5413)
GUITAMMER COMPANY
Also Called: Buttkicker
7099 Huntley Rd Ste 108 (43229-1068)
P.O. Box 82 (43086-0082)
PHONE..................................614 898-9370
Mark A Luden, *Pr*
Mark A Luden, *Ch Bd*
Lawrence L Lemoine, *COO*
Marvin Clamme, *VP Engg*
◆ **EMP:** 7 **EST:** 1990
SQ FT: 15,000
SALES (est): 1.55MM **Privately Held**
Web: www.guitammer.com
SIC: 3679 Transducers, electrical

(G-5414)
H Y O INC
Also Called: Pengywn
2550 W 5th Ave (43204-3815)
PHONE..................................614 488-2861
Jim Kime, *Pr*
Sheila Kime, *Sec*
EMP: 26 **EST:** 1986
SQ FT: 20,000

SALES (est): 4.47MM **Privately Held**
Web: www.pengwyn.com
SIC: **3531** 3594 Snow plow attachments; Fluid power pumps and motors

(G-5415)
HACKMAN FRAMES LLC
502 Schrock Rd (43229-1028)
PHONE..............................614 841-0007
EMP: **15** EST: 1991
SQ FT: 14,000
SALES (est): 615.1K **Privately Held**
Web: www.hackmanframes.com
SIC: **2499** Picture frame molding, finished

(G-5416)
HAKE HEAD LLC
Also Called: Maramor Chocolates
1855 E 17th Ave (43219-1006)
PHONE..............................614 291-2244
Michael Ryan, *Managing Member*
▲ **EMP: 16** EST: 2002
SQ FT: 30,000
SALES (est): 793.42K **Privately Held**
Web: www.maramor.com
SIC: **2064** Candy and other confectionery products

(G-5417)
HAMAN ENTERPRISES INC
Also Called: Haman Midwest
75 W Southington Ave (43085-3852)
PHONE..............................614 888-7574
Tod Haman, *Pr*
▲ **EMP: 19** EST: 1984
SALES (est): 2.33MM **Privately Held**
Web: www.hamanmidwest.com
SIC: **2752** 2759 Offset printing; Calendars: printing, nsk

(G-5418)
HAMILTON TANKS LLC
2200 Refugee Rd (43207-2898)
PHONE..............................614 445-8446
TOLL FREE: 800
EMP: **17** EST: 1915
SQ FT: 30,000
SALES (est): 5.12MM
SALES (corp-wide): 25.34MM **Privately Held**
Web: www.hamiltontanks.com
SIC: **3443** Tanks, lined: metal plate
PA: Meeker Equipment Co., Inc.
 4381 Front Mountain Rd
 Belleville PA 17004
 717 667-6000

(G-5419)
HARBOR WRAPS LLC
341 S 3rd St Ste 100 (43215-7426)
PHONE..............................614 725-0429
EMP: **6** EST: 2018
SALES (est): 297.7K **Privately Held**
Web: www.harborwraps.com
SIC: **3993** Signs and advertising specialties

(G-5420)
HARPER ENGRAVING & PRINTING CO (PA)
2626 Fisher Rd (43204-3561)
P.O. Box 426 (43216-0426)
PHONE..............................614 276-0700
Donald Mueller, *Pr*
EMP: **73** EST: 1891
SQ FT: 40,000
SALES (est): 9.41MM
SALES (corp-wide): 9.41MM **Privately Held**
Web: www.harperengraving.com

SIC: **2759** 2752 Commercial printing, nec; Offset printing

(G-5421)
HARRIS PAPER CRAFTS INC
266 E 5th Ave (43201-2818)
PHONE..............................614 299-2141
Richard Potts, *Pr*
EMP: **10** EST: 1983
SALES (est): 888.05K **Privately Held**
Web: www.harrispc.net
SIC: **2679** 2796 2789 2675 Paper products, converted, nec; Platemaking services; Bookbinding and related work; Die-cut paper and board

(G-5422)
HARROP INDUSTRIES INC
3470 E 5th Ave (43219-1797)
PHONE..............................614 231-3621
◆ EMP: **49** EST: 1919
SALES (est): 11MM **Privately Held**
Web: www.harropusa.com
SIC: **3567** Ceramic kilns and furnaces

(G-5423)
HAWTHORNE COLLECTIVE INC
4400 Easton Cmns Ste 125 (43219-6223)
PHONE..............................937 644-0011
See Attachment, *Prin*
EMP: **22** EST: 2021
SALES (est): 3.77MM
SALES (corp-wide): 3.55B **Publicly Held**
SIC: **2873** Nitrogenous fertilizers
PA: The Scotts Miracle-Gro Company
 14111 Scottslawn Rd
 Marysville OH 43040
 937 644-0011

(G-5424)
HAZELBAKER INDUSTRIES LTD
Also Called: Wellnitz
1661 Old Henderson Rd (43220-3617)
EMP: **17** EST: 1994
SQ FT: 2,500
SALES (est): 1.19MM **Privately Held**
Web: www.wellnitz.com
SIC: **3271** 5211 3272 Blocks, concrete or cinder: standard; Masonry materials and supplies; Concrete products, nec

(G-5425)
HEARTLAND GROUP HOLDINGS LLC
4001 E 5th Ave (43219-1812)
PHONE..............................614 441-4001
EMP: **90**
SIC: **3559** Refinery, chemical processing, and similar machinery

(G-5426)
HELENA AGRI-ENTERPRISES LLC
800 Distribution Dr (43228-1004)
PHONE..............................614 275-4200
Helena Cwu, *Brnch Mgr*
EMP: **9**
Web: www.helenaagri.com
SIC: **5191** 2819 Chemicals, agricultural; Chemicals, high purity: refined from technical grade
HQ: Helena Agri-Enterprises, Llc
 225 Schilling Blvd
 Collierville TN 38017
 901 761-0050

(G-5427)
HERITAGE MARBLE OF OHIO INC
Also Called: Heritage Marbles
7086 Huntley Rd (43229-1022)
PHONE..............................614 436-1464
Gene Daniels, *Pr*

EMP: **10** EST: 1976
SQ FT: 22,000
SALES (est): 417.71K **Privately Held**
SIC: **3281** 1411 Marble, building: cut and shaped; Dimension stone

(G-5428)
HEXION INC (PA)
Also Called: Hexion
180 E Broad St (43215-3707)
P.O. Box 1310 (43216-1310)
PHONE..............................888 443-9466
Michael Lefenfeld, *Pr*
Mark Bidstrup, *Ex VP*
Douglas A Johns, *Ex VP*
Matthew A Sokol, *Ex VP*
EMP: **243** EST: 1899
SALES (est): 1.26B
SALES (corp-wide): 1.26B **Privately Held**
Web: www.hexion.com
SIC: **8711** 2821 5169 4911 Chemical engineering; Epoxy resins; Chemicals, industrial and heavy

(G-5429)
HEXION LLC (HQ)
180 E Broad St Fl 26 (43215-3707)
PHONE..............................614 225-4000
William H Carter, *
George Knight, *
Mary N Jorgensen, *
◆ EMP: **100** EST: 2004
SQ FT: 200,000
SALES (est): 439.43MM **Privately Held**
Web: www.hexion.com
SIC: **2821** 2899 Thermosetting materials; Chemical preparations, nec
PA: Hexion Topco, Llc
 180 E Broad St
 Columbus OH 43215

(G-5430)
HEXION TOPCO LLC (PA)
180 E Broad St (43215)
PHONE..............................614 225-4000
▼ EMP: **68** EST: 2010
SALES (est): 439.43MM **Privately Held**
SIC: **2821** 2869 6719 Thermosetting materials; Silicones; Investment holding companies, except banks

(G-5431)
HEXION US FINANCE CORP
180 E Broad St (43215-3707)
PHONE..............................614 225-4000
Bill Klosterman, *Dir*
▼ EMP: **46** EST: 2009
SALES (est): 4.4MM
SALES (corp-wide): 1.26B **Privately Held**
SIC: **2821** Plastics materials and resins
PA: Hexion Inc.
 180 E Broad St
 Columbus OH 43215
 888 443-9466

(G-5432)
HI LITE PLASTIC PRODUCTS
Also Called: Capital Toe Grinding
3760 E 5th Ave (43219-1807)
PHONE..............................614 235-9050
Offie Bartley, *Owner*
EMP: **6** EST: 1977
SALES (est): 459.01K **Privately Held**
Web: www.hiliteplastics.com
SIC: **3089** Kitchenware, plastics

(G-5433)
HIGH RIDGE BRANDS CO
1654 Williams Rd (43207-5109)
PHONE..............................614 497-1660
EMP: **6** EST: 2018

SALES (est): 137.77K **Privately Held**
SIC: **2844** Perfumes, cosmetics and other toilet preparations

(G-5434)
HIGHCOM GLOBAL SECURITY INC (HQ)
Also Called: Blastwrap
2901 E 4th Ave Unit J (43219-2896)
PHONE..............................727 592-9400
Francis Michaud, *Ch Bd*
Francis Michaud, *Interim Chairman of the Board*
Michael L Bundy, *COO*
EMP: **7** EST: 1999
SQ FT: 32,155
SALES (est): 16.93MM
SALES (corp-wide): 1.5MM **Publicly Held**
Web: www.blastgardtech.com
SIC: **3699** Fire control or bombing equipment, electronic
PA: 2538093 Ontario Inc
 4400-101 Bay St
 Toronto ON M5J 2

(G-5435)
HIGHLIGHTS CONSUMER SVCS INC
1800 Watermark Dr (43215-1048)
P.O. Box 269 (43216-0269)
PHONE..............................570 253-1164
Kent Johnson, *CEO*
Lece Lohr, *Pr*
EMP: **15** EST: 2011
SALES (est): 2.65MM
SALES (corp-wide): 109.4MM **Privately Held**
Web: shop.highlights.com
SIC: **2731** Books, publishing only
PA: Highlights For Children, Inc.
 1800 Watermark Dr
 Columbus OH 43215
 614 486-0631

(G-5436)
HIGHLIGHTS FOR CHILDREN INC (PA)
Also Called: Highlights For Children Publr
1800 Watermark Dr (43215-1035)
P.O. Box 269 (43216-0269)
PHONE..............................614 486-0631
▲ EMP: **250** EST: 1946
SALES (est): 109.4MM
SALES (corp-wide): 109.4MM **Privately Held**
Web: shop.highlights.com
SIC: **2721** Magazines: publishing and printing

(G-5437)
HIKMA LABS INC
Also Called: Roxane Laboratories
1900 Arlingate Ln (43228-3175)
PHONE..............................614 276-4000
Chris Boneham, *Brnch Mgr*
EMP: **8**
SALES (corp-wide): 2.88B **Privately Held**
Web: www.roxane.com
SIC: **2834** Pharmaceutical preparations
HQ: Hikma Labs Inc.
 1809 Wilson Rd
 Columbus OH 43216

(G-5438)
HIKMA LABS INC (DH)
1809 Wilson Rd (43216)
P.O. Box 16532 (43216)
PHONE..............................614 276-4000
Michael Raya, *CEO*
Brian Hoffmann, *
Mohammed Obeidat, *
George J Muench Iii, *Treas*
David Berger, *

GEOGRAPHIC SECTION
Columbus - Franklin County (G-5461)

▲ **EMP:** 116 **EST:** 2005
SALES (est): 45.66MM
SALES (corp-wide): 2.88B **Privately Held**
Web: www.roxane.com
SIC: 2834 Druggists' preparations (pharmaceuticals)
HQ: West-Ward Holdings Limited
1 New Burlington Place
London W1S 2
207 399-2760

(G-5439)
HIKMA PHARMACEUTICALS USA INC
Also Called: Non-Injectable Manufacturing
1809 Wilson Rd (43228-9579)
PHONE..............................614 276-4000
EMP: 30
SALES (corp-wide): 2.88B **Privately Held**
Web: www.hikma.com
SIC: 2834 Pharmaceutical preparations
HQ: Hikma Pharmaceuticals Usa Inc.
200 Connell Dr Ste 4100
Berkeley Heights NJ 07922
908 673-1030

(G-5440)
HIKMA SPECIALTY USA INC
1900 Arlingate Ln (43228-3175)
PHONE..............................856 489-2110
Frank Savastano, *Pr*
George J Muench Iii, *Treas*
David Berger, *Sec*
Rebecca Jewell, *Sec*
EMP: 30 **EST:** 2013
SALES (est): 3.23MM
SALES (corp-wide): 2.88B **Privately Held**
Web: www.hikma
SIC: 2834 Pharmaceutical preparations
HQ: Eurohealth (U.S.A.), Inc
200 Connell Dr Fl 4
Berkeley Heights NJ 07922

(G-5441)
HIRSCHVOGEL INCORPORATED
2230 S 3rd St (43207-2431)
PHONE..............................614 445-6060
Arun Thandapani, *CEO*
Felix Schmieder, *
Mark Hoosier, *
Robert Hartwell, *
Charles Bentz, *
◆ **EMP:** 300 **EST:** 1988
SQ FT: 155,000
SALES (est): 81.55MM
SALES (corp-wide): 1.5B **Privately Held**
Web: www.hirschvogel.com
SIC: 3714 Motor vehicle parts and accessories
PA: Hirschvogel Holding Gmbh
Dr.-Manfred-Hirschvogel-Str. 6
Denklingen BY 86920
82432910

(G-5442)
HITE PARTS EXCHANGE INC
2235 Mckinley Ave (43204-3400)
PHONE..............................614 272-5115
Thomas A Blake, *Pr*
Dona Blake, *
EMP: 13 **EST:** 1937
SQ FT: 14,000
SALES (est): 805.57K **Privately Held**
Web: www.hiteparts.com
SIC: 5013 3714 3625 3594 Automotive supplies and parts; Motor vehicle engines and parts; Relays and industrial controls; Fluid power pumps and motors

(G-5443)
HJ SYSTEMS INC
230 N Central Ave (43222-1001)
PHONE..............................614 351-9777
James E Stang, *Pr*
EMP: 10 **EST:** 1993
SQ FT: 20,000
SALES (est): 913.07K **Privately Held**
Web: www.hjsystemsinc.com
SIC: 2431 Millwork

(G-5444)
HONEYWELL INTERNATIONAL INC
Also Called: Honeywell
2080 Arlingate Ln (43228-4112)
PHONE..............................302 327-8920
EMP: 54
SALES (corp-wide): 36.66B **Publicly Held**
Web: www.honeywell.com
SIC: 3829 3674 Pressure transducers; Semiconductors and related devices
PA: Honeywell International Inc.
855 S Mint St
Charlotte NC 28202
704 627-6200

(G-5445)
HONEYWELL LEBOW PRODUCTS
Also Called: Honeywell Senfopec
2080 Arlingate Ln (43228-4112)
PHONE..............................614 850-5000
Phil Geraffo, *VP*
▲ **EMP:** 200 **EST:** 2000
SALES (est): 52.82MM
SALES (corp-wide): 36.66B **Publicly Held**
SIC: 3724 Aircraft engines and engine parts
PA: Honeywell International Inc.
855 S Mint St
Charlotte NC 28202
704 627-6200

(G-5446)
HOSTER GRAPHICS COMPANY INC
Also Called: Advance Graphics
2580 Westbelt Dr (43228-3827)
PHONE..............................614 299-9770
Frank Hoster, *Pr*
EMP: 13 **EST:** 1929
SALES (est): 2.1MM **Privately Held**
Web: www.advancecolumbus.com
SIC: 2752 7334 Offset printing; Photocopying and duplicating services

(G-5447)
HOWARD INDUSTRIES INC
1840 Progress Ave (43207-1707)
PHONE..............................614 444-9900
EMP: 15 **EST:** 1964
SALES (est): 2.15MM **Privately Held**
Web: www.howardchem.com
SIC: 7389 2843 5051 3087 Packaging and labeling services; Emulsifiers, except food and pharmaceutical; Miscellaneous nonferrous products; Custom compound purchased resins

(G-5448)
HYPE SOCKS LLC
204 S Front St Apt 400 (43215-4753)
PHONE..............................855 497-3769
Josh M Wintermantel, *Managing Member*
EMP: 15 **EST:** 2015
SALES (est): 1.01MM **Privately Held**
Web: www.hypesocks.com
SIC: 2252 Socks

(G-5449)
HYPER TECH RESEARCH INC
539 Industrial Mile Rd (43228-2412)
PHONE..............................614 481-8050
Michael Tomsic, *Pr*
Lawrence Walley, *CFO*
Sarah Tomsic, *Stockholder*
Sherrie Cantu, *Stockholder*
David Doll, *Prin*
EMP: 16 **EST:** 2001
SQ FT: 50,000
SALES (est): 2.11MM **Privately Held**
Web: www.hypertechresearch.com
SIC: 3674 Semiconductors and related devices

(G-5450)
HYTEC-DEBARTOLO LLC
Also Called: Hytec Automotive
4419 Equity Dr (43228-3856)
PHONE..............................614 527-9370
▲ **EMP:** 7 **EST:** 2009
SQ FT: 34,600
SALES (est): 2.39MM
SALES (corp-wide): 28.51MM **Privately Held**
SIC: 3714 Water pump, motor vehicle
PA: Debartolo Holdings, Llc
3820 Northdale Blvd # 100
Tampa FL 33624
813 908-8400

(G-5451)
IABF INC
Also Called: Industrial Aluminum Foundry
1890 Mckinley Ave (43222-1004)
PHONE..............................614 279-4498
Andrew B Kientz, *Pr*
EMP: 8 **EST:** 1966
SQ FT: 7,500
SALES (est): 732.05K **Privately Held**
Web: www.iabfinc.com
SIC: 3365 3369 Aluminum and aluminum-based alloy castings; Nonferrous foundries, nec

(G-5452)
ICC SAFETY SERVICE INC
1070 Leona Ave (43201-3039)
PHONE..............................614 261-4557
Tiffany Adair, *Pr*
Christopher Duger, *VP*
EMP: 6 **EST:** 2004
SQ FT: 3,900
SALES (est): 930.23K **Privately Held**
Web: www.iccsafetysurfaces.com
SIC: 3271 Blocks, concrete: insulating

(G-5453)
IKE SMART CITY
250 N Hartford Ave (43222-1100)
PHONE..............................614 294-4898
Pete Scantland, *CEO*
EMP: 23 **EST:** 2017
SALES (est): 923.52K **Privately Held**
Web: www.ikesmartcity.com
SIC: 3993 7312 Signs and advertising specialties; Outdoor advertising services

(G-5454)
IMH LLC
160 Easton Town Ctr (43219-6074)
PHONE..............................513 800-9830
EMP: 10
SIC: 2844 Perfumes and colognes
PA: I.M.H. Llc
7020 Huntley Rd Ste C
Columbus OH 43229

(G-5455)
IMH LLC (PA)
7020 Huntley Rd Ste C (43229-1050)
PHONE..............................614 436-0991
EMP: 8 **EST:** 2011
SALES (est): 1.95MM **Privately Held**
SIC: 2844 Perfumes and colognes

(G-5456)
IMPACT PRINTING AND DESIGN LLC
4670 Groves Rd (43232-4164)
PHONE..............................833 522-6200
Jd Pitzer, *Prin*
EMP: 12 **EST:** 2008
SALES (est): 593.8K **Privately Held**
Web: www.impactprintanddesign.com
SIC: 7389 3953 5699 2759 Design services; Screens, textile printing; T-shirts, custom printed; Poster and decal printing and engraving

(G-5457)
INDUSTRIAL PATTERN & MFG CO
899 N 20th St (43219-2420)
PHONE..............................614 252-0934
Thomas C Birkefeld, *Pr*
Charles J Birkefeld, *VP*
Jay Hrun, *VP Engg*
EMP: 17 **EST:** 1947
SQ FT: 5,000
SALES (est): 958.17K **Privately Held**
Web: www.industrialpattern.com
SIC: 3543 Industrial patterns

(G-5458)
INEOS COMPOSITES US LLC (DH)
955 Yard St # 400 (43212-3915)
PHONE..............................614 790-9299
Jim Ratcliffe, *Managing Member*
EMP: 69 **EST:** 2019
SALES (est): 298.64MM
SALES (corp-wide): 917.38K **Privately Held**
Web: www.ineos.com
SIC: 2821 Plastics materials and resins
HQ: Ineos Enterprises Holdings Limited
15-19 Britten Street
London SW3 3
192 851-6948

(G-5459)
INHANCE TECHNOLOGIES LLC
6575 Huntley Rd Ste D (43229-1039)
PHONE..............................614 846-6400
Tom Gardener, *Mgr*
EMP: 35
SQ FT: 7,500
SALES (corp-wide): 98.81MM **Privately Held**
Web: www.inhancetechnologies.com
SIC: 3089 Injection molding of plastics
HQ: Inhance Technologies Llc
22008 N Berwick Dr
Houston TX 77095
800 929-1743

(G-5460)
INLAND PRODUCTS INC (PA)
599 Frank Rd (43223-3813)
P.O. Box 2228 (43216-2228)
PHONE..............................614 443-3425
Gary H Baas, *Pr*
EMP: 21 **EST:** 1867
SQ FT: 40,000
SALES (est): 3.83MM
SALES (corp-wide): 3.83MM **Privately Held**
SIC: 2077 5159 Grease rendering, inedible; Hides

(G-5461)
INNOVATIVE GRAPHICS LTD
2580 Westbelt Dr (43228-3827)
PHONE..............................877 406-3636
Michael Foley, *Pr*
EMP: 13 **EST:** 2018
SALES (est): 995.05K **Privately Held**
SIC: 2752 Commercial printing, lithographic

(PA)=Parent Co (HQ)=Headquarters
✪ = New Business established in last 2 years

Columbus - Franklin County (G-5462) — GEOGRAPHIC SECTION

(G-5462)
INSKEEP BROTHERS INC
Also Called: Inskeep Brothers Printers
3193 E Dublin Granville Rd (43231-4035)
PHONE.....................................614 898-6620
Jeff Inskeep, *Pr*
Paula Inskeep, *VP*
EMP: 12 **EST:** 1888
SQ FT: 11,000
SALES (est): 484.69K **Privately Held**
Web: www.inskeepbrothers.com
SIC: 2752 Offset printing

(G-5463)
INSTANTWHIP CONNECTICUT INC (PA)
2200 Cardigan Ave (43215-1092)
PHONE.....................................614 488-2536
Douglas A Smith, *Pr*
Clifton J Smith, *Ch Bd*
Robert Pavlick, *General Vice President*
G Frederick Smith, *Sec*
Thomas G Michaelides, *Treas*
EMP: 18 **EST:** 1946
SQ FT: 10,300
SALES (est): 3.66MM
SALES (corp-wide): 3.66MM **Privately Held**
Web: www.instantwhip.com
SIC: 2026 5143 Whipped topping, except frozen or dry mix; Dairy products, except dried or canned

(G-5464)
INSTANTWHIP FOODS INC (PA)
2200 Cardigan Ave (43215-1092)
PHONE.....................................614 488-2536
Douglas A Smith, *Pr*
Thomas G Michaelides, *VP*
EMP: 18 **EST:** 1934
SQ FT: 10,300
SALES (est): 97.42MM
SALES (corp-wide): 97.42MM **Privately Held**
Web: www.instantwhip.com
SIC: 6794 8741 2026 5143 Franchises, selling or licensing; Administrative management; Fluid milk; Dairy products, except dried or canned

(G-5465)
INSTANTWHIP PRODUCTS CO PA (HQ)
Also Called: Instantwhip of Pennsylvania
2200 Cardigan Ave (43215-1092)
PHONE.....................................614 488-2536
Douglas A Smith, *Pr*
EMP: 18 **EST:** 1940
SQ FT: 20,300
SALES (est): 4.68MM
SALES (corp-wide): 97.42MM **Privately Held**
Web: www.instantwhip.com
SIC: 2026 5143 Whipped topping, except frozen or dry mix; Dairy products, except dried or canned
PA: Instantwhip Foods, Inc.
2200 Cardigan Ave
Columbus OH 43215
614 488-2536

(G-5466)
INSTANTWHIP-BUFFALO INC (HQ)
2200 Cardigan Ave (43215-1092)
PHONE.....................................614 488-2536
Douglas A Smith, *Pr*
Thomas G Michaelides, *Treas*
G Frederick Smith, *Sec*
John Beck, *VP*
EMP: 10 **EST:** 1939
SQ FT: 10,300
SALES (est): 5.99MM
SALES (corp-wide): 97.42MM **Privately Held**
SIC: 2026 5143 Whipped topping, except frozen or dry mix; Dairy products, except dried or canned
PA: Instantwhip Foods, Inc.
2200 Cardigan Ave
Columbus OH 43215
614 488-2536

(G-5467)
INSTANTWHIP-CHICAGO INC (PA)
2200 Cardigan Ave (43215-1092)
PHONE.....................................614 488-2536
Douglas A Smith, *Pr*
Clifton J Smith, *
G Frederick Smith, *
Thomas G Michaelides, *
Jim Ring, *
EMP: 36 **EST:** 1946
SQ FT: 10,300
SALES (est): 5.51MM
SALES (corp-wide): 5.51MM **Privately Held**
Web: www.instantwhip.com
SIC: 2026 Cream, whipped

(G-5468)
INSTANTWHIP-SYRACUSE INC (PA)
2200 Cardigan Ave (43215-1092)
PHONE.....................................614 488-2536
Douglas A Smith, *Pr*
Raymond Winslow, *General Vice President*
Thomas G Michaelides, *Treas*
G Frederick Smith, *Sec*
Clifton J Smith, *Ch Bd*
EMP: 17 **EST:** 1940
SQ FT: 10,300
SALES (est): 3.17MM
SALES (corp-wide): 3.17MM **Privately Held**
SIC: 2026 Whipped topping, except frozen or dry mix

(G-5469)
INSULPRO INC
4650 Indianola Ave (43214-1884)
PHONE.....................................614 262-3768
Greg Freed, *Pr*
EMP: 10 **EST:** 1989
SALES (est): 912.19K **Privately Held**
SIC: 3494 Line strainers, for use in piping systems

(G-5470)
INTELLINETICS INC (PA)
2190 Dividend Dr (43228-3806)
PHONE.....................................614 388-8908
James F Desocio, *Pr*
Robert C Schroeder, *Ch Bd*
Matthew L Chretien, *CSO*
Joseph D Spain, *CFO*
EMP: 14 **EST:** 1996
SQ FT: 6,000
SALES (est): 16.89MM
SALES (corp-wide): 16.89MM **Publicly Held**
Web: www.intellinetics.com
SIC: 7372 Prepackaged software

(G-5471)
INTERBAKE FOODS LLC (HQ)
Also Called: Norse Dairy Systems
1740 Joyce Ave (43219-1026)
PHONE.....................................614 294-4931
Raymond Baxter, *Pr*
Paul M Desjardins, *
◆ **EMP:** 55 **EST:** 1972
SALES (est): 486.26MM
SALES (corp-wide): 42.47B **Privately Held**
Web: www.interbake.com
SIC: 2052 2051 Cookies; Bread, cake, and related products
PA: George Weston Limited
700-22 St Clair Ave E
Toronto ON M4T 2
226 271-5030

(G-5472)
INTERFACE LOGIC SYSTEMS INC
Also Called: Weighing Division
1020 Taylor Station Rd Ste F (43230-6675)
P.O. Box 30772 (43230-0772)
PHONE.....................................614 236-8388
James Gottliebson, *Pr*
Eli Sneward, *Pr*
EMP: 9 **EST:** 1986
SALES (est): 894.47K **Privately Held**
Web: www.interfacelogic.com
SIC: 7629 3596 Electrical measuring instrument repair and calibration; Scales and balances, except laboratory

(G-5473)
INTERIOR DNNAGE SPCIALITES INC
470 E Starr Ave (43201-3695)
PHONE.....................................614 291-0900
Georgina Stevenson, *Pr*
Scott Stevenson, *VP*
EMP: 20 **EST:** 2001
SQ FT: 35,000
SALES (est): 795.4K **Privately Held**
SIC: 3086 Plastics foam products

(G-5474)
INTERNATIONAL CONFECTIONS COMPANY LLC
Also Called: Maxfield Candy Company
1855 E 17th Ave (43219-1006)
PHONE.....................................800 288-8002
▼ **EMP:** 200
SIC: 2064 Chocolate candy, except solid chocolate

(G-5475)
INTERNTNAL PDTS SRCING GROUP I
Also Called: Ipsg
2701 Charter St Ste A (43228-4639)
PHONE.....................................614 334-1500
EMP: 244
SALES (corp-wide): 824.57MM **Privately Held**
SIC: 3571 Electronic computers
HQ: International Products Sourcing Group, Inc.
4119 Leap Rd
Hilliard OH 43026

(G-5476)
INTERNTNAL TCHNCAL CATINGS INC
Also Called: Itc Manufacturing
845 E Markison Ave (43207-1388)
PHONE.....................................800 567-6592
Judith Fernandez, *Brnch Mgr*
EMP: 187
Web: www.itcmfg.com
SIC: 3496 Shelving, made from purchased wire
PA: International Technical Coatings, Inc.
110 S 41st Ave
Phoenix AZ 85009

(G-5477)
INTERSTATE TRUCKWAY INC
5440 Renner Rd (43228-8941)
PHONE.....................................614 771-1220
Willy Walraven, *Brnch Mgr*
EMP: 15
Web: www.interstatetrailer.com
SIC: 3799 5012 Trailers and trailer equipment; Automobiles and other motor vehicles
PA: Interstate Truckway Inc
1755 Dreman Ave
Cincinnati OH 45223

(G-5478)
INVIRSA INC
1275 Kinnear Rd Ste 217 (43212-0017)
PHONE.....................................614 344-1765
Robert Shalwitz, *CEO*
EMP: 7 **EST:** 2016
SALES (est): 1.05MM **Privately Held**
Web: www.invirsa.com
SIC: 2834 Pharmaceutical preparations

(G-5479)
IPA LTD
Also Called: Zed Digital
199 Mckenna Creek Dr (43230-6127)
PHONE.....................................614 523-3974
Sumithra Jagannath, *Pr*
EMP: 13 **EST:** 2014
SQ FT: 1,500
SALES (est): 413.71K **Privately Held**
SIC: 7371 7373 2741 7374 Computer software development; Computer integrated systems design; Internet publishing and broadcasting; Computer graphics service

(G-5480)
IRONFAB LLC
1771 Progress Ave (43207-1749)
PHONE.....................................614 443-3900
EMP: 13 **EST:** 2003
SALES (est): 2.54MM **Privately Held**
Web: www.ironfabllc.com
SIC: 3441 Fabricated structural metal

(G-5481)
ISP CHEMICALS LLC
1979 Atlas St (43228-9645)
PHONE.....................................614 876-3637
Doctor Paul Taylor, *Dir*
EMP: 70
SALES (corp-wide): 23.98MM **Privately Held**
SIC: 2834 Pharmaceutical preparations
PA: Isp Chemicals Llc
455 N Main St
Calvert City KY 42029
270 395-4165

(G-5482)
J & E PUBLICATIONS LLC
3307 Kirkham Rd (43221-1313)
PHONE.....................................614 457-7989
David J Chakeres Esq, *Prin*
EMP: 6 **EST:** 2004
SALES (est): 52K **Privately Held**
SIC: 2741 Miscellaneous publishing

(G-5483)
J S C PUBLISHING
958 King Ave (43212-2655)
PHONE.....................................614 424-6911
Joe Paxton, *Owner*
EMP: 6 **EST:** 2000
SALES (est): 228.05K **Privately Held**
SIC: 2731 Pamphlets: publishing and printing

(G-5484)
J SOLUTIONS LLC
216 E Hinman Ave (43207-1182)
PHONE.....................................614 732-4857
Jennifer Williams, *Prin*
EMP: 7 **EST:** 2012
SALES (est): 79.66K **Privately Held**

▲ = Import ▼ = Export
◆ = Import/Export

GEOGRAPHIC SECTION
Columbus - Franklin County (G-5509)

Web: www.jsolutions.us
SIC: 2752 Commercial printing, lithographic

(G-5485)
JACOBI CARBONS INC
432 Mccormick Blvd (43213-1525)
PHONE..................215 546-3900
Bill Eubanks, *Pr*
◆ EMP: 79 EST: 2001
SALES (est): 45.17MM **Privately Held**
Web: www.jacobi.net
SIC: 2895 Carbon black
HQ: Jacobi Carbons Ab
Slojdaregatan 1
Kalmar 393 6
480417550

(G-5486)
JAIN AMERICA FOODS INC (HQ)
Also Called: Jain Americas
1819 Walcutt Rd Ste I (43228)
PHONE..................614 850-9400
Anil Jain, *CEO*
Nerinder Gupta, *COO*
John Donovan, *CFO*
◆ EMP: 7 EST: 1998
SQ FT: 30,000
SALES (est): 25.12MM **Privately Held**
Web: www.jainamericas.com
SIC: 3086 2821 3081 Plastics foam products; Molding compounds, plastics; Polyvinyl film and sheet
PA: Jain Irrigation Systems Limited
Jain Plastic Park, N.H. No. 6,
Jalgaon MH 42500

(G-5487)
JAMES K GREEN ENTERPRISES INC
Also Called: Columbus Gasket & Supply
1875 Lone Eagle St (43228-3647)
PHONE..................614 878-6041
James K Green, *Pr*
▲ EMP: 9 EST: 1976
SQ FT: 14,000
SALES (est): 892.9K **Privately Held**
Web: www.columbusgasket.com
SIC: 3053 3069 Gaskets, all materials; Molded rubber products

(G-5488)
JAPO INC
3902 Indianola Ave (43214-3156)
P.O. Box 630 (43216-0630)
PHONE..................614 263-2850
▼ EMP: 47
SIC: 5085 3089 Industrial supplies; Injection molding of plastics

(G-5489)
JAX WAX INC
3145 E 17th Ave (43219-2329)
PHONE..................614 476-6769
Jack Minor, *Pr*
EMP: 10 EST: 1993
SQ FT: 5,600
SALES (est): 827.16K **Privately Held**
Web: www.jaxwax.com
SIC: 2842 Automobile polish

(G-5490)
JBS INDUSTRIES LTD
1001 Atlantic Ave Apt 783 (43229-1777)
PHONE..................513 314-5599
EMP: 6 EST: 2005
SALES (est): 88.7K **Privately Held**
Web: www.jbsindustries.com
SIC: 3999 Manufacturing industries, nec

(G-5491)
JE GROTE COMPANY INC (PA)
Also Called: Grote
1160 Gahanna Pkwy (43230-6615)
PHONE..................614 868-8414
James E Grote, *Ch Bd*
Bob Grote, *
◆ EMP: 100 EST: 1969
SQ FT: 73,500
SALES (est): 56.95MM
SALES (corp-wide): 56.95MM **Privately Held**
Web: www.grotecompany.com
SIC: 3589 3556 Cooking equipment, commercial; Food products machinery

(G-5492)
JENIS SPLENDID ICE CREAMS LLC (PA)
401 N Front St Ste 300 (43215-2263)
PHONE..................614 488-3224
Charles Bauer, *Managing Member*
EMP: 23 EST: 2003
SALES (est): 22.12MM
SALES (corp-wide): 22.12MM **Privately Held**
Web: www.jenis.com
SIC: 5451 2024 Ice cream (packaged); Custard, frozen

(G-5493)
JENTGEN STEEL SERVICES LLC
611 E Weber Rd Ste 201 (43211-1097)
PHONE..................614 268-6340
EMP: 10 EST: 2011
SALES (est): 346.25K **Privately Held**
SIC: 3448 Trusses and framing, prefabricated metal

(G-5494)
JET CONTAINER COMPANY
1033 Brentnell Ave Ste 100 (43219-2186)
PHONE..................614 444-2133
Stephen J Schmitt, *Pr*
Richard Prohl, *Managing Member**
Mike Schmitt, *
EMP: 57 EST: 1977
SQ FT: 175,000
SALES (est): 9.38MM **Privately Held**
Web: www.jetcontainer.com
SIC: 2653 Boxes, corrugated: made from purchased materials

(G-5495)
JET FUEL TECH INC
100 E Broad St Fl 16 (43215-3684)
PHONE..................614 463-1986
Perry Jeter Junior, *Owner*
EMP: 8 EST: 2015
SALES (est): 164.47K **Privately Held**
Web: www.jetfuelathlete.com
SIC: 2911 Jet fuels

(G-5496)
JETCOAT LLC
Also Called: Jetcoat
472 Brehl Ave (43223-1973)
P.O. Box 23054 (43223-0054)
PHONE..................800 394-0047
David L Thorson, *Managing Member*
EMP: 20 EST: 2007
SQ FT: 5,000
SALES (est): 8.69MM **Privately Held**
Web: www.jetcoatinc.com
SIC: 2891 Sealants
PA: Thorworks Industries, Inc.
2520 Campbell St
Sandusky OH 44870

(G-5497)
JLS FUNERAL HOME
2322 Randy Ct (43232-8470)
PHONE..................614 625-1220
Jimmie Spurlock, *Prin*
EMP: 10
SALES (est): 180.06K **Privately Held**
SIC: 2396 5087 7389 Veils and veiling: bridal, funeral, etc.; Cemetery and funeral director's equipment and supplies; Business services, nec

(G-5498)
JMAC INC (PA)
200 W Nationwide Blvd Unit 1 (43215)
PHONE..................614 436-2418
John P Mcconnell, *Ch Bd*
Michael A Priest, *Pr*
George N Corey, *Prin*
▲ EMP: 28 EST: 1980
SQ FT: 6,000
SALES (est): 94.51MM
SALES (corp-wide): 94.51MM **Privately Held**
SIC: 3325 5198 7999 5511 Steel foundries, nec; Paints; Ice skating rink operation; Automobiles, new and used

(G-5499)
JOHN ADAMS
3375 En Joie Dr (43228-9430)
PHONE..................614 564-9307
John Adams Adams, *Owner*
EMP: 7 EST: 2016
SALES (est): 86K **Privately Held**
SIC: 2621 Paper mills

(G-5500)
JOHNSONS REAL ICE CREAM LLC
Also Called: Wilcoxon, James H Jr
2728 E Main St (43209-2534)
PHONE..................614 231-0014
James H Wilcoxon Junior, *Pr*
EMP: 109 EST: 1950
SQ FT: 4,600
SALES (est): 1.11MM **Privately Held**
Web: www.johnsonsrealicecream.com
SIC: 5812 5143 2024 Ice cream stands or dairy bars; Dairy products, except dried or canned; Ice cream and frozen deserts

(G-5501)
JUDITH LEIBER LLC (PA)
4300 E 5th Ave (43219-1816)
PHONE..................614 449-4217
EMP: 20 EST: 2000
SALES (est): 5.69MM
SALES (corp-wide): 5.69MM **Privately Held**
SIC: 3171 Women's handbags and purses

(G-5502)
KAMPS PALLETS
2132 Refugee Rd (43207-2841)
PHONE..................616 818-4323
EMP: 8 EST: 2018
SALES (est): 268.73K **Privately Held**
Web: www.kampspallets.com
SIC: 2448 Pallets, wood

(G-5503)
KANTNER INGREDIENTS INC
Also Called: AME Nutrition Ingredients
975 Worthington Woods Loop Rd (43085-5743)
PHONE..................614 766-3638
Douglas E Kantner, *Pr*
◆ EMP: 7 EST: 2004
SALES (est): 858.76K **Privately Held**
Web: www.kantnergroup.com
SIC: 2099 Food preparations, nec

(G-5504)
KARN MEATS INC
Also Called: Central Market Specialty Meats
922 Taylor Ave (43219-2558)
PHONE..................614 252-3712
Richard Karn, *Pr*
EMP: 50 EST: 1971
SQ FT: 50,000
SALES (est): 5.16MM **Privately Held**
Web: www.karnmeats.com
SIC: 2011 2013 Meat packing plants; Sausages and other prepared meats

(G-5505)
KEFFS INC
2117 S High St (43207-2428)
P.O. Box 1310 (43017-6310)
PHONE..................614 443-0586
K R Gay, *Pr*
Kenneth Robert Gay, *Pr*
Elizabeth Sue Gay, *VP*
EMP: 26 EST: 1962
SQ FT: 35,000
SALES (est): 852.5K **Privately Held**
Web: www.accredocbs.com
SIC: 3496 Shelving, made from purchased wire

(G-5506)
KENAN ADVANTAGE GROUP INC
Also Called: Advantage Truck Trailers
500 Manor Park Dr (43228-9396)
PHONE..................614 878-4050
Dan Peckinpaugh, *Mgr*
EMP: 8
SALES (corp-wide): 1.55B **Privately Held**
Web: www.thekag.com
SIC: 3715 Truck trailers
PA: The Kenan Advantage Group Inc
4366 Mt Pleasant St Nw
North Canton OH 44720
800 969-5419

(G-5507)
KENDALL HOLDINGS LTD (PA)
Also Called: Phpk Technologies
2111 Builders Pl (43204-4886)
PHONE..................614 486-4750
Richard Coleman, *Pt*
▲ EMP: 49 EST: 2004
SQ FT: 60,000
SALES (est): 9.51MM
SALES (corp-wide): 9.51MM **Privately Held**
Web: www.phpk.com
SIC: 3443 Fabricated plate work (boiler shop)

(G-5508)
KENWEL PRINTERS INC
4272 Indianola Ave (43214-2891)
PHONE..................614 261-1011
David G Starner, *Pr*
Mike Fisher, *
EMP: 36 EST: 1969
SQ FT: 15,000
SALES (est): 3.03MM **Privately Held**
Web: www.kenwelprinters.com
SIC: 2752 2789 2759 Offset printing; Bookbinding and related work; Commercial printing, nec

(G-5509)
KEURIG DR PEPPER INC
950 Stelzer Rd (43219-3740)
PHONE..................614 237-4201
David Gerics, *Brnch Mgr*
EMP: 57
Web: www.keurigdrpepper.com

Columbus - Franklin County (G-5510)

SIC: 2086 Soft drinks: packaged in cans, bottles, etc.
PA: Keurig Dr Pepper Inc.
53 South Ave
Burlington MA 01803

(G-5510)
KEY FINISHES LLC
727 Harrison Dr (43204-3507)
PHONE..................................614 351-8393
James H Mccurdy, *CFO*
▲ EMP: 9 EST: 2010
SALES (est): 1.47MM **Privately Held**
Web: www.keyfinishes.com
SIC: 3399 Powder, metal

(G-5511)
KISSICAKES-N-SWEETS LLC
7660 Silver Fox Dr (43235-1835)
PHONE..................................614 940-2779
George T Kissi, *Prin*
EMP: 0 EST: 2011
SALES (est): 90.76K **Privately Held**
Web: www.kissicakes.com
SIC: 2053 Cakes, bakery: frozen

(G-5512)
KNOX ENERGY INC
795 Old Woods Rd (43235-1248)
PHONE..................................614 885-4828
Mark Jordan, *Pr*
EMP: 6 EST: 2017
SALES (est): 99.73K **Privately Held**
Web: www.knoxenergy.com
SIC: 1382 Oil and gas exploration services

(G-5513)
KOKOSING MATERIALS INC
4755 S High St (43207-4028)
P.O. Box 334 (43019-0334)
PHONE..................................614 491-1199
Bill Burgett, *Pr*
Bob Bailey, *
EMP: 24 EST: 1996
SALES (est): 780.75K **Privately Held**
Web: www.kokosing.biz
SIC: 2951 Asphalt and asphaltic paving mixtures (not from refineries)

(G-5514)
KOLMER
3851 N High St Ste B (43214-3751)
PHONE..................................614 261-0190
J Kolmer, *Prin*
EMP: 6 EST: 2008
SALES (est): 187.26K **Privately Held**
SIC: 3826 Environmental testing equipment

(G-5515)
KRISPY KREME DOUGHNUT CORP
Also Called: Krispy Kreme 322
3690 W Dublin Granville Rd (43235-7987)
PHONE..................................614 798-0812
James Lewis, *Mgr*
EMP: 23
SQ FT: 2,158
SALES (corp-wide): 1.69B **Publicly Held**
Web: www.krispykreme.com
SIC: 5461 2051 Doughnuts; Pastries, e.g. danish: except frozen
HQ: Krispy Kreme Doughnut Corp
2116 Hawkins St Ste 102
Charlotte NC 28203
980 270-7117

(G-5516)
KRISPY KREME DOUGHNUT CORP
Also Called: Krispy Kreme
2557 Westbelt Dr (43228-3826)
PHONE..................................614 876-0058
Ron Snyder, *Mgr*
EMP: 70
SALES (corp-wide): 1.69B **Publicly Held**
Web: www.krispykreme.com
SIC: 5461 2051 Doughnuts; Pastries, e.g. danish: except frozen
HQ: Krispy Kreme Doughnut Corp
2116 Hawkins St Ste 102
Charlotte NC 28203
980 270-7117

(G-5517)
KYRON TOOL & MACHINE CO INC
2900 Banwick Rd (43232-3838)
PHONE..................................614 231-6000
Charles P Haueisen, *Pr*
Randal Hauesein, *VP*
Rosemary Hauesein, *Treas*
EMP: 10 EST: 1949
SQ FT: 50,000
SALES (est): 1.05MM **Privately Held**
Web: www.kyrontool.com
SIC: 3599 Machine shop, jobbing and repair

(G-5518)
LAMBERT SHEET METAL INC
Also Called: Lsmi
3776 E 5th Ave (43219-1807)
PHONE..................................614 237-0384
Carl Lambert, *Pr*
Betty Lambert, *VP*
EMP: 15 EST: 1969
SQ FT: 10,000
SALES (est): 1.96MM **Privately Held**
Web: www.lambertsheetmetal.com
SIC: 3444 Sheet metal specialties, not stamped

(G-5519)
LANDON VAULT COMPANY
1477 Frebis Ave (43206-3763)
PHONE..................................614 443-5505
Martin Pehrson, *Pr*
Autumn Epperson, *Sec*
EMP: 20 EST: 1920
SQ FT: 3,600
SALES (est): 2.17MM **Privately Held**
SIC: 3272 Burial vaults, concrete or precast terrazzo

(G-5520)
LANG STONE COMPANY INC (PA)
4099 E 5th Ave (43219-1812)
P.O. Box 360747 (43236-0747)
PHONE..................................614 235-4099
TOLL FREE: 800
E Dean Coffman, *Pr*
Joann Coffman, *
▲ EMP: 39 EST: 1856
SQ FT: 10,000
SALES (est): 18.28MM
SALES (corp-wide): 18.28MM **Privately Held**
Web: www.langstone.com
SIC: 5032 5211 3281 3272 Granite building stone; Lumber and other building materials; Cut stone and stone products; Concrete products, nec

(G-5521)
LAPHAM-HICKEY STEEL CORP
Lapham-Hickey
753 Marion Rd (43207-2554)
PHONE..................................614 443-4881
Eric Sattler, *Mgr*
EMP: 48
SQ FT: 110,000
SALES (corp-wide): 235.89MM **Privately Held**
Web: www.lapham-hickey.com
SIC: 5051 3443 3441 3398 Steel; Fabricated plate work (boiler shop); Fabricated structural metal; Metal heat treating
PA: Lapham-Hickey Steel Corp.
5500 W 73rd St
Bedford Park IL 60638
708 496-6111

(G-5522)
LARSEN CUSOTM CABINETRY
5660 Westbourne Ave (43213-1485)
PHONE..................................614 282-3929
Dean Lansen, *Prin*
EMP: 6 EST: 2008
SALES (est): 160K **Privately Held**
SIC: 2434 Wood kitchen cabinets

(G-5523)
LEHNER SIGNS INC
2983 Switzer Ave (43219-2315)
PHONE..................................614 258-0500
Robin Owens, *Pr*
EMP: 7 EST: 1990
SQ FT: 2,400
SALES (est): 754.43K **Privately Held**
Web: www.lehnersigns.com
SIC: 3993 Signs and advertising specialties

(G-5524)
LH MARSHALL COMPANY
1601 Woodland Ave (43219-1135)
PHONE..................................614 294-6433
Dorothy B Roberts, *Pr*
Cynthia R Padilla, *Sec*
Janet Forgue, *Treas*
Courtney Roberts, *VP*
▲ EMP: 18 EST: 1927
SALES (est): 2.22MM **Privately Held**
Web: www.lhmarshall.com
SIC: 3829 Measuring and controlling devices, nec

(G-5525)
LIFE SUPPORT DEVELOPMENT LTD
777 Dearborn Park Ln Ste R (43085-5716)
PHONE..................................614 221-1765
EMP: 8 EST: 2010
SALES (est): 668.98K **Privately Held**
Web: www.lifesupport.com
SIC: 2086 Fruit drinks (less than 100% juice): packaged in cans, etc.

(G-5526)
LIFETIME PRODUCTS INC
4364 Sullivant Ave (43228-2819)
PHONE..................................614 272-1255
Chris Roberts, *Mgr*
EMP: 8
SALES (corp-wide): 291.23MM **Privately Held**
Web: www.lifetime.com
SIC: 3949 Sporting and athletic goods, nec
PA: Lifetime Products Inc.
Freeport Ctr Bldg D11 # 11
Clearfield UT 84016
801 776-1532

(G-5527)
LINCOLN ELECTRIC AUTOMTN INC
1700 Jetway Blvd (43219-1675)
PHONE..................................614 471-5926
John Campbell, *Brnch Mgr*
EMP: 45
SALES (corp-wide): 4.19B **Publicly Held**
Web: www.rimrockcorp.com
SIC: 3563 3569 3443 3541 Spraying outfits: metals, paints, and chemicals (compressor); Robots, assembly line: industrial and commercial; Ladles, metal plate; Machine tools, metal cutting type
HQ: Lincoln Electric Automation, Inc.
407 S Main St
Fort Loramie OH 45845
937 295-2120

(G-5528)
LINDE GAS & EQUIPMENT INC
Also Called: Linde Gas North America
7029 Huntley Rd (43229-1099)
PHONE..................................614 846-7048
Cindy Fenton, *Brnch Mgr*
EMP: 6
Web: www.lindeus.com
SIC: 2813 Nitrogen
HQ: Linde Gas & Equipment Inc.
10 Riverview Dr
Danbury CT 06810
844 445-4633

(G-5529)
LINDE GAS & EQUIPMENT INC
Praxair
450 Greenlawn Ave (43223-2611)
PHONE..................................614 443-7687
Pratt Thompson, *Mgr*
EMP: 25
Web: www.lindeus.com
SIC: 2813 Industrial gases
HQ: Linde Gas & Equipment Inc.
10 Riverview Dr
Danbury CT 06810
844 445-4633

(G-5530)
LOAD32 LLC
265 N Oakley Ave (43204-3762)
PHONE..................................614 984-6648
Durrell Burgess, *Managing Member*
EMP: 10 EST: 2020
SALES (est): 489.82K **Privately Held**
SIC: 3537 Trucks: freight, baggage, etc.: industrial, except mining

(G-5531)
LOFT VIOLIN SHOP
4604 N High St (43214-2002)
PHONE..................................614 267-7221
David Schlub, *Owner*
Richard C Schlub, *Pt*
EMP: 11 EST: 1976
SALES (est): 863.88K **Privately Held**
Web: www.theloftviolinshop.com
SIC: 7699 5736 3931 7359 Musical instrument repair services; Musical instrument stores; Musical instruments; Musical instrument rental services

(G-5532)
LONG SIGN CO
979 E 5th Ave (43201-3064)
PHONE..................................614 294-1057
John Long, *Owner*
EMP: 6 EST: 2000
SALES (est): 136.53K **Privately Held**
SIC: 3993 Signs and advertising specialties

(G-5533)
LONOLIFE INC
432 W 2nd Ave (43201-3314)
PHONE..................................614 296-2250
EMP: 7 EST: 2015
SALES (est): 630.67K **Privately Held**
Web: www.lonolife.com
SIC: 2032 Soups and broths, canned, jarred, etc.

(G-5534)
LOTUS LOVE LLC
Also Called: Custom Dsign Chakra Reiki Jwly
1091 Fountain Ln Apt B (43213-4157)
P.O. Box 47 (43109-0047)

GEOGRAPHIC SECTION

Columbus - Franklin County (G-5558)

PHONE.................................614 964-8477
EMP: 25 EST: 2018
SALES (est): 855.91K **Privately Held**
SIC: 3911 Jewelry apparel

(G-5535)
LOUIS INSTANTWHIP-ST INC
2200 Cardigan Ave (43215-1092)
PHONE.................................614 488-2536
Douglas A Smith, *Pr*
G Frederick Smith, *Sec*
Thomas G Michaelides, *VP*
EMP: 18 EST: 1971
SQ FT: 10,300
SALES (est): 1.04MM **Privately Held**
Web: www.instantwhip.com
SIC: 2026 5143 Whipped topping, except frozen or dry mix; Dairy products, except dried or canned

(G-5536)
LUCKYS BOTTLES INC
2401 Mac Ct (43235-2811)
PHONE.................................614 447-9522
Nelson N Jeck Senior, *CEO*
Nelson N Jeck Junior, *Pr*
Jo Ann Jeck, *Sec*
EMP: 12 EST: 1977
SALES (est): 657.13K **Privately Held**
Web: www.goto-qsp.com
SIC: 3089 Injection molding of plastics

(G-5537)
LVD ACQUISITION LLC (HQ)
Also Called: Oasis International
222 E Campus View Blvd (43235-4634)
PHONE.................................614 861-1350
Jeff Chiarugi, *Pr*
Michael Leibold, *
◆ EMP: 69 EST: 1910
SQ FT: 15,000
SALES (est): 47.04MM
SALES (corp-wide): 652.75MM **Privately Held**
Web: www.oasiscoolers.com
SIC: 3585 3431 5078 Coolers, milk and water: electric; Drinking fountains, metal; Drinking water coolers, mechanical
PA: Culligan International Company
9399 W Higgins Rd # 1100
Rosemont IL 60018
847 430-2800

(G-5538)
MAC LEAN J S CO
5454 Alkire Rd (43228-3606)
PHONE.................................614 878-5454
J Bruce Lean Mac, *Pr*
M Richard Lean Mac, *Genl Mgr*
Richard Gomez, *
Mike Hunter, *
EMP: 23 EST: 1888
SQ FT: 86,000
SALES (est): 682.2K **Privately Held**
SIC: 2541 2542 2435 2434 Store fixtures, wood; Partitions and fixtures, except wood; Hardwood veneer and plywood; Wood kitchen cabinets

(G-5539)
MAGNEXT LTD
7100 Huntley Rd Ste 100 (43229-1076)
PHONE.................................614 433-0011
Dmitri Troianovski, *Managing Member*
EMP: 19 EST: 2005
SQ FT: 28,000
SALES (est): 3.07MM **Privately Held**
Web: www.magnext.com
SIC: 3572 Computer storage devices

(G-5540)
MARATHON AT SAWMILL
Also Called: Sawmill Marathon
7200 Sawmill Rd (43235-5964)
PHONE.................................614 734-0836
Donald Spangler, *Owner*
EMP: 10 EST: 1983
SALES (est): 808.97K **Privately Held**
SIC: 2421 Sawmills and planing mills, general

(G-5541)
MARFO COMPANY (PA)
Also Called: Trading Corp of America
799 N Hague Ave (43204-1424)
PHONE.................................614 276-3352
Bill Giovanello, *CEO*
Alan Johnson, *
EMP: 98 EST: 1977
SQ FT: 41,000
SALES (est): 9.97MM
SALES (corp-wide): 9.97MM **Privately Held**
Web: www.marsala.com
SIC: 5094 3911 Jewelry; Jewelry apparel

(G-5542)
MARK W THRUMAN
85 Mcnaughten Rd (43213-2174)
PHONE.................................614 754-5500
Mark W Thruman, *Prin*
EMP: 7 EST: 2010
SALES (est): 90.31K **Privately Held**
Web: www.ohiogastro.com
SIC: 3841 Gastroscopes, except electromedical

(G-5543)
MARSHALLTOWN PACKAGING INC
601 N Hague Ave (43204-1422)
PHONE.................................641 753-5272
Gary Bolar, *
▲ EMP: 9 EST: 1993
SQ FT: 54,000
SALES (est): 2.5MM
SALES (corp-wide): 22.79MM **Privately Held**
SIC: 2653 Boxes, corrugated: made from purchased materials
PA: Buckeye Boxes, Inc.
601 N Hague Ave
Columbus OH 43204
614 274-8484

(G-5544)
MARTINA METAL LLC
1575 Shawnee Ave (43211-2643)
PHONE.................................614 291-9700
EMP: 20
Web: www.martina-metal.com
SIC: 1761 3444 3441 3364 Sheet metal work, nec; Sheet metalwork; Fabricated structural metal; Nonferrous die-castings except aluminum

(G-5545)
MATERIALS SCIENCE INTL INC
1660 Georgesville Rd (43228-3613)
PHONE.................................614 870-0400
Neil Crabbe, *Pr*
William F Bailey, *
▲ EMP: 30 EST: 1987
SQ FT: 12,500
SALES (est): 4.51MM **Privately Held**
Web: www.msitarget.com
SIC: 3599 Machine shop, jobbing and repair

(G-5546)
MATHEWS PRINTING COMPANY
1250 S Front St (43206-3437)
P.O. Box 188 (43216-0188)
PHONE.................................614 444-1010
Robert Mathews, *Pr*
EMP: 11 EST: 1992
SQ FT: 15,000
SALES (est): 415.87K **Privately Held**
Web: www.mathews-printing.com
SIC: 2752 Offset printing

(G-5547)
MATTHEW WARREN INC
Also Called: Capital Spring
2000 Jetway Blvd (43219-1673)
PHONE.................................614 418-0250
William Hunsucker, *Prin*
EMP: 47
SALES (corp-wide): 1.05B **Privately Held**
Web: www.mwcomponents.com
SIC: 3493 3495 Steel springs, except wire; Wire springs
HQ: Matthew Warren, Inc.
3426 Toringdon Way # 100
Charlotte NC 28277
704 837-0331

(G-5548)
MB RENOVATIONS & DESIGNS LLC
4449 Easton Way Ste 200 (43219-7005)
PHONE.................................614 772-6139
Marcus Bryant, *Prin*
Meagan Sparks, *Prin*
EMP: 9 EST: 2017
SALES (est): 517.12K **Privately Held**
SIC: 1389 Construction, repair, and dismantling services

(G-5549)
MC ALISTER WOODWORKING
6035 Huntley Rd (43229-1001)
PHONE.................................614 989-6264
Jared Mcalister, *Prin*
EMP: 6 EST: 2011
SALES (est): 160.51K **Privately Held**
SIC: 2431 Millwork

(G-5550)
MCGILL AIRCLEAN LLC
Also Called: McGill Airclean
1777 Refugee Rd (43207-2119)
PHONE.................................614 829-1200
Paul R Hess, *Managing Member*
Jerry Childress, *
◆ EMP: 70 EST: 2004
SQ FT: 15,000
SALES (est): 18.29MM
SALES (corp-wide): 126.17MM **Privately Held**
Web: www.mcgillairclean.com
SIC: 3564 1796 Precipitators, electrostatic; Pollution control equipment installation
HQ: United Mcgill Corporation
1 Mission Park
Groveport OH 43125
614 829-1200

(G-5551)
MCGILL AIRFLOW LLC
2400 Fairwood Ave (43207-2708)
PHONE.................................614 829-1200
Ed Kromer, *Mgr*
EMP: 55
SALES (corp-wide): 126.17MM **Privately Held**
Web: www.mcgillairflow.com
SIC: 3444 Ducts, sheet metal
HQ: Mcgill Airflow Llc
1 Mission Park
Groveport OH 43125
614 829-1200

(G-5552)
MCGLENNON METAL PRODUCTS INC
940 N 20th St (43219-2423)
P.O. Box 188 (45315-0188)
PHONE.................................614 252-7114
Thomas Saldoff, *Pr*
EMP: 15 EST: 1988
SQ FT: 22,000
SALES (est): 2.41MM **Privately Held**
Web: www.mcglennonmetal.com
SIC: 3469 Stamping metal for the trade

(G-5553)
MCGRAW-HILL GLOBAL EDUCATN LLC
Also Called: McGraw-Hill Learning Group
4400 Easton Commons (43219-6226)
P.O. Box 182605 (43218-2605)
PHONE.................................800 338-3987
EMP: 88
Web: www.mheducation.com
SIC: 2731 Book publishing
HQ: Mcgraw-Hill Global Education, Llc
2 Penn Plz Fl 20
New York NY 10121
646 766-2000

(G-5554)
MCL INC
Also Called: McL Whitehall
5240 E Main St (43213-2501)
PHONE.................................614 861-6259
Jim Bell, *Mgr*
EMP: 37
SALES (corp-wide): 41.7MM **Privately Held**
Web: www.mclhomemade.com
SIC: 2051 Bakery: wholesale or wholesale/ retail combined
PA: Mcl, Inc.
2730 E 62nd St
Indianapolis IN 46220
317 257-5425

(G-5555)
MCLEOD BAR GROUP LLC
234 King Ave (43201-2776)
PHONE.................................614 299-2099
EMP: 15 EST: 2017
SALES (est): 574.85K **Privately Held**
SIC: 2599 Bar, restaurant and cafeteria furniture

(G-5556)
MCNEIL GROUP INC
Also Called: Pinnacle Metal Products
1701 Woodland Ave (43219-1137)
PHONE.................................614 298-0300
Susan Mcneil, *Pr*
Michael Mcneil, *VP*
EMP: 32 EST: 1992
SQ FT: 41,000
SALES (est): 5.39MM **Privately Held**
Web: www.pinnmetalstairs.com
SIC: 3499 Furniture parts, metal

(G-5557)
MCNEIL HOLDINGS LLC
1701 Woodland Ave (43219-1137)
PHONE.................................614 298-0300
EMP: 6 EST: 1998
SALES (est): 743.15K **Privately Held**
Web: www.pinnmetalstairs.com
SIC: 3441 Fabricated structural metal

(G-5558)
MEDRANO USA INC (PA)
Also Called: Medrano USA
4311 Janitrol Rd Ste 500 (43228-1390)

Columbus - Franklin County (G-5559) GEOGRAPHIC SECTION

PHONE..................614 272-5856
Gerardo Fernandez, *CEO*
Luis Fernandez, *CFO*
Gerardo Santiago, *Sec*
EMP: 29 **EST:** 2016
SQ FT: 700
SALES (est): 8.9MM
SALES (corp-wide): 8.9MM **Privately Held**
SIC: 3537 Platforms, stands, tables, pallets, and similar equipment

(G-5559)
MERISTEM CROP PRFMCE GROUP LLC
575 W 1st Ave Apt 100 (43215-5100)
PHONE..................833 637-4783
Jeff Troendle, *Pr*
EMP: 31 **EST:** 2020
SALES (est): 2.22MM **Privately Held**
Web: www.meristemag.com
SIC: 3523 Sprayers and spraying machines, agricultural

(G-5560)
METTLER-TOLEDO LLC
Toledo Scales & Systems
6600 Huntley Rd (43229-1048)
PHONE..................614 841-7300
Al Herold, *Mgr*
EMP: 170
SQ FT: 71,000
SALES (corp-wide): 3.79B **Publicly Held**
Web: www.mt.com
SIC: 3596 Industrial scales
HQ: Mettler-Toledo, Llc
1900 Polaris Pkwy Fl 6
Columbus OH 43240
614 438-4511

(G-5561)
MGF SOURCING US LLC (HQ)
Also Called: MGF Sourcing
4200 Regent St Ste 205 (43219-6229)
PHONE..................614 904-3300
Michael Yee, *CEO*
James Schwartz, *
Jennie Wilson, *
▲ **EMP:** 60 **EST:** 2011
SQ FT: 16,000
SALES (est): 435.85MM **Publicly Held**
Web: www.mgfsourcing.com
SIC: 2211 Twills, drills, denims and other ribbed fabrics: cotton
PA: Sycamore Partners Management, L.P.
9 W 57th St Ste 3100
New York NY 10019

(G-5562)
MICKES QUALITY MACHINING LLC
488 Trade Rd (43204-6241)
PHONE..................614 746-6639
Mickes Frank Junior, *Prin*
EMP: 7 **EST:** 2008
SALES (est): 244.09K **Privately Held**
Web: www.mqmcnc.com
SIC: 3599 Machine shop, jobbing and repair

(G-5563)
MID-OHIO ELECTRIC CO
1170 Mckinley Ave (43222-1113)
PHONE..................614 274-8000
Cynthia Langhirt, *Pr*
Bruce A Langhirt, *
Vince Langhirt, *
EMP: 26 **EST:** 1955
SQ FT: 13,800
SALES (est): 4.7MM **Privately Held**
Web: www.mid-ohioelectric.com
SIC: 7694 5063 7629 8711 Electric motor repair; Motors, electric; Circuit board repair; Electrical or electronic engineering

(G-5564)
MID-STATE SALES INC (PA)
Also Called: Mid-State Sales
1101 Gahanna Pkwy (43230-6600)
PHONE..................614 864-1811
▲ **EMP:** 56 **EST:** 1969
SALES (est): 13.73MM
SALES (corp-wide): 13.73MM **Privately Held**
Web: www.midstate-sales.com
SIC: 5084 3494 3492 Hydraulic systems equipment and supplies; Pipe fittings; Hose and tube fittings and assemblies, hydraulic/pneumatic

(G-5565)
MIDWEST MOTOR SUPPLY CO (PA)
Also Called: Kimball Midwest
4800 Roberts Rd (43228-9791)
P.O. Box 2470 (43216-2470)
PHONE..................800 233-1294
Patrick J Mccurdy Junior, *CEO*
Patrick J Mccurdy Junior, *Pr*
Ed Mccurdy, *VP*
David Mccurdy, *VP*
Charles Mccurdy, *VP*
▲ **EMP:** 200 **EST:** 1955
SQ FT: 85,000
SALES (est): 129.4MM
SALES (corp-wide): 129.4MM **Privately Held**
Web: www.kimballmidwest.com
SIC: 3965 3399 8742 Fasteners; Metal fasteners; Materials mgmt. (purchasing, handling, inventory) consultant

(G-5566)
MIDWEST QUALITY BEDDING INC
3860 Morse Rd (43219-3014)
PHONE..................614 504-5971
EMP: 45
SALES (corp-wide): 237.62K **Privately Held**
SIC: 2515 Mattresses and bedsprings
PA: Midwest Quality Bedding Inc
9036 Picardy Ct
Dublin OH

(G-5567)
MIDWEST STRAPPING PRODUCTS
1819 Walcutt Rd Ste 13 (43228-9149)
PHONE..................614 527-1454
EMP: 9 **EST:** 2000
SALES (est): 960K **Privately Held**
SIC: 3499 Strapping, metal

(G-5568)
MILATHAN WHOLESALERS
423 N Front St 237 (43215-2228)
PHONE..................614 697-1458
EMP: 30 **EST:** 2020
SALES (est): 1.16MM **Privately Held**
Web: www.milathan.com
SIC: 3613 Distribution boards, electric

(G-5569)
MILLENNIUM CELL INC
1250 Arthur E Adams Dr (43221-3560)
PHONE..................614 688-5160
Michelle Laverty, *Prin*
EMP: 8 **EST:** 2016
SALES (est): 211.62K **Privately Held**
Web: www.ewi.org
SIC: 3612 Transformers, except electric

(G-5570)
MILLER ENERGY LLC
3812 Zephyr Pl (43232-4245)
PHONE..................614 367-1812
Keith Miller, *Prin*

EMP: 9 **EST:** 2012
SALES (est): 121.97K **Privately Held**
Web: www.millerenergy.com
SIC: 1382 Oil and gas exploration services

(G-5571)
MILLWORK ELEMENTS LLC
6663 Huntley Rd Ste A (43229-1033)
PHONE..................614 905-8163
EMP: 7 **EST:** 2017
SALES (est): 312.47K **Privately Held**
Web: www.millworkelements.com
SIC: 2431 Millwork

(G-5572)
MINIMALLY INVASIVE DEVICES INC
Also Called: Mid
1275 Kinnear Rd (43212-1180)
PHONE..................614 484-5036
Wayne Poll, *CEO*
Caroline Crisafulli, *VP Opers*
Kenneth Jones, *CFO*
EMP: 8 **EST:** 2007
SALES (est): 1.04MM **Privately Held**
Web: www.floshield.com
SIC: 3841 Surgical and medical instruments

(G-5573)
MMF INC
Rainbow Custom Powder Coaters
1977 Mcallister Ave (43205-1614)
PHONE..................614 252-2522
EMP: 9
SALES (corp-wide): 1.5MM **Privately Held**
Web: www.millsmetal.net
SIC: 3471 Plating of metals or formed products
PA: Mmf Incorporated
1977 Mcallister Ave
Columbus OH 43205
614 252-0078

(G-5574)
MMF INCORPORATED (PA)
Also Called: Mills Metal Finishing
1977 Mcallister Ave (43205-1614)
PHONE..................614 252-0078
Brian L Mills, *Pr*
Cheryl Camp, *VP*
Foster Mills, *Dir*
Steven Mills, *Stockholder*
EMP: 11 **EST:** 1974
SQ FT: 9,400
SALES (est): 1.5MM
SALES (corp-wide): 1.5MM **Privately Held**
Web: www.millsmetaloh.com
SIC: 3479 Coating of metals and formed products

(G-5575)
MOBILE SOLUTIONS LLC
149 N Hamilton Rd (43213-1308)
PHONE..................614 286-3944
EMP: 10 **EST:** 2012
SQ FT: 2,500
SALES (est): 506.89K **Privately Held**
Web: www.mobilesolutions-usa.com
SIC: 3711 Cars, electric, assembly of

(G-5576)
MODE INDUSTRIES INC
3000 E Main St Ste 134 (43209-3717)
PHONE..................614 504-8008
EMP: 8 **EST:** 2019
SALES (est): 253.72K **Privately Held**
SIC: 3999 Manufacturing industries, nec

(G-5577)
MOK INDUSTRIES LLC
4449 Easton Way (43219-6093)

PHONE..................614 934-1734
EMP: 10 **EST:** 2003
SQ FT: 3,000
SALES (est): 210.74K **Privately Held**
Web: mokil.goldsupplier.com
SIC: 3674 Solar cells

(G-5578)
MOMENTIVE PERFORMANCE MTLS INC
180 E Broad St (43215-3707)
PHONE..................614 986-2495
Steve Delarge, *Opers Mgr*
EMP: 1500
Web: www.momentive.com
SIC: 2869 Silicones
HQ: Momentive Performance Materials Inc.
2750 Balltown Rd
Niskayuna NY 12309

(G-5579)
MONKS COPY SHOP INC
47 E Gay St (43215-3103)
PHONE..................614 461-6438
Edward M Smith, *Pr*
EMP: 18 **EST:** 1980
SQ FT: 15,718
SALES (est): 939.47K **Privately Held**
Web: www.monkscopyshop.com
SIC: 7334 2752 Photocopying and duplicating services; Commercial printing, lithographic

(G-5580)
MORI SHUJI
Also Called: Geodyne One
3755 Mountview Rd (43220-4801)
PHONE..................614 459-1296
Shuji Mori, *Owner*
EMP: 7 **EST:** 1992
SALES (est): 399.75K **Privately Held**
SIC: 1382 Oil and gas exploration services

(G-5581)
MORRISON MEDICAL LTD
3735 Paragon Dr (43228-9751)
PHONE..................800 438-6677
EMP: 7 **EST:** 1999
SALES (est): 158.52K **Privately Held**
SIC: 3841 Surgical and medical instruments

(G-5582)
MORRISON SIGN COMPANY INC
2757 Scioto Pkwy (43221-4658)
PHONE..................614 276-1181
David Morrison, *Pr*
Helen Morrison, *
EMP: 27 **EST:** 1979
SQ FT: 18,000
SALES (est): 4.24MM **Privately Held**
Web: www.morrisonsigns.com
SIC: 3993 2759 Signs, not made in custom sign painting shops; Screen printing

(G-5583)
MOVE EZ INC
Also Called: Moveeasy
855 Grandview Ave Ste 140 (43215-1189)
PHONE..................844 466-8339
Venkatesh Ganapathy, *CEO*
EMP: 57 **EST:** 2014
SALES (est): 1.52MM **Privately Held**
Web: www.moveeasy.com
SIC: 7372 6411 4212 Application computer software; Insurance agents, brokers, and service; Moving services

(G-5584)
MRS INDUSTRIAL INC
Also Called: M R S

2583 Harrison Rd (43204-3511)
PHONE..............................614 308-1070
Scott J Cosgrove, *Pr*
Scott Cosgrove, *
Kenneth Michael Cosgrove, *
Ronald L Belford, *
▲ **EMP**: 24 **EST**: 1997
SQ FT: 60,000
SALES (est): 4.96MM **Privately Held**
Web: www.mrsindustrial.com
SIC: 3444 Sheet metalwork

(G-5585)
MURPHY TRACTOR & EQP CO INC
Also Called: John Deere Authorized Dealer
2121 Walcutt Rd (43228-9575)
PHONE..............................614 876-1141
EMP: 8
Web: www.murphytractor.com
SIC: 3531 5082 Construction machinery; Construction and mining machinery
HQ: Murphy Tractor & Equipment Co., Inc.
5375 N Deere Rd
Park City KS 67219
855 246-9124

(G-5586)
MVP PHARMACY
1931 Parsons Ave (43207-2364)
PHONE..............................614 449-8000
EMP: 7 **EST**: 2013
SALES (est): 363.76K **Privately Held**
SIC: 2834 Pharmaceutical preparations

(G-5587)
N WASSERSTROM & SONS INC
Also Called: Select Seating
862 E Jenkins Ave (43207-1317)
PHONE..............................614 737-5410
Greg Pell, *Mgr*
EMP: 8
SALES (corp-wide): 378.09MM **Privately Held**
Web: www.wasserstrom.com
SIC: 2511 2531 Wood household furniture; Public building and related furniture
HQ: N. Wasserstrom & Sons, Inc.
2300 Lockbourne Rd
Columbus OH 43207
614 228-5550

(G-5588)
N WASSERSTROM & SONS INC (HQ)
Also Called: Wasserstrom Marketing Division
2300 Lockbourne Rd (43207-6111)
PHONE..............................614 228-5550
William Wasserstrom, *Pr*
John H Mc Cormick, *Sr VP*
Reid Wasserstrom, *Sec*
◆ **EMP**: 250 **EST**: 1933
SQ FT: 175,000
SALES (est): 100.47MM
SALES (corp-wide): 378.09MM **Privately Held**
Web: www.wasserstrom.com
SIC: 3556 5046 3444 Food products machinery; Restaurant equipment and supplies, nec; Sheet metalwork
PA: The Wasserstrom Company
4500 E Broad St
Columbus OH 43213
614 228-6525

(G-5589)
NATIONAL ELECTRIC COIL INC (PA)
Also Called: N E C Columbus
800 King Ave (43212-2644)
P.O. Box 370 (43216-0370)
PHONE..............................614 488-1151
◆ **EMP**: 300 **EST**: 1994
SQ FT: 500,000

SALES (est): 70.69MM **Privately Held**
Web: www.national-electric-coil.com
SIC: 7694 Electric motor repair

(G-5590)
NATIONAL FRT VGTABLE TECH CORP
Also Called: Fresh Vegetable Technology
250 Civic Center Dr (43215-5086)
PHONE..............................740 400-4055
Daniel Cashman, *CEO*
Mitch Adams, *
Keith Stoll, *
Richard Cashman, *Stockholder*
EMP: 25 **EST**: 1986
SQ FT: 150,000
SALES (est): 578.35K **Privately Held**
SIC: 2037 Fruits, quick frozen and cold pack (frozen)

(G-5591)
NBBI
1055 Crupper Ave (43229-1108)
PHONE..............................614 888-8320
EMP: 7 **EST**: 2009
SALES (est): 510.02K **Privately Held**
Web: www.nationalboard.org
SIC: 3433 Boilers, low-pressure heating: steam or hot water

(G-5592)
NELSON COMPANY
2160 Refugee Rd (43207-2841)
PHONE..............................614 444-1164
EMP: 6
SALES (corp-wide): 21.9MM **Privately Held**
Web: www.nelsoncompany.com
SIC: 2448 Pallets, wood
PA: The Nelson Company
4517 North Point Blvd
Baltimore MD 21219
410 477-3000

(G-5593)
NETWORK PRINTING & GRAPHICS
443 Crestview Rd (43202-2244)
PHONE..............................614 230-2084
Cathy Ann Dawson, *Pr*
EMP: 10 **EST**: 1989
SQ FT: 7,500
SALES (est): 663.49K **Privately Held**
SIC: 2752 7331 2791 2789 Offset printing; Direct mail advertising services; Typesetting; Bookbinding and related work

(G-5594)
NEW AQUA LLC
Also Called: NEW AQUA LLC
3707 Interchange Rd (43204-1435)
PHONE..............................614 265-9000
EMP: 13
SALES (corp-wide): 35.47MM **Privately Held**
Web: www.aquasystems.com
SIC: 3589 Water filters and softeners, household type
HQ: New Aqua, Llc
7785 E Us Hwy 36
Avon IN 46123
317 272-3000

(G-5595)
NEW HORIZONS FD SOLUTIONS LLC (PA)
3455 Millennium Ct (43219-5550)
PHONE..............................614 861-3639
Trina Bediako, *CEO*
EMP: 29 **EST**: 2021
SALES (est): 4.96MM

SALES (corp-wide): 4.96MM **Privately Held**
Web: www.coalescencellc.com
SIC: 2099 Baking powder and soda, yeast, and other leavening agents

(G-5596)
NEWALL ELECTRONICS INC
1803 Obrien Rd (43228-3866)
PHONE..............................614 771-0213
Martha Sullivan, *Pr*
Paul Vasington, *CFO*
▲ **EMP**: 14 **EST**: 1989
SQ FT: 7,000
SALES (est): 4.07MM
SALES (corp-wide): 4.03B **Privately Held**
Web: www.newall.com
SIC: 3829 Measuring and controlling devices, nec
HQ: Custom Sensors & Technologies, Inc.
1461 Lawrence Dr
Thousand Oaks CA 91320
805 716-0322

(G-5597)
NEWMAST MKTG & COMMUNICATIONS
Also Called: Printing Company, The
2060 Integrity Dr N (43209-2726)
PHONE..............................614 837-1200
Terry L Wike, *Pr*
EMP: 8 **EST**: 1898
SQ FT: 15,000
SALES (est): 168.15K **Privately Held**
SIC: 7336 2752 Silk screen design; Offset printing

(G-5598)
NHMF LLC
1701 Moler Rd (43207-1684)
PHONE..............................614 444-2184
John Orenchuk, *Prin*
EMP: 8 **EST**: 2019
SALES (est): 437.17K **Privately Held**
SIC: 3999 Manufacturing industries, nec

(G-5599)
NMN SPINCO INC
330 W Spring St Ste 303 (43215-2390)
PHONE..............................800 850-0335
Mike Swinford, *Pr*
EMP: 6
SALES (est): 79.71K **Privately Held**
SIC: 3842 Wheelchairs

(G-5600)
NORSE DAIRY SYSTEMS INC
1700 E 17th Ave (43219-1005)
P.O. Box 1869 (43216-1869)
PHONE..............................614 294-4931
EMP: 201 **EST**: 1995
SQ FT: 850
SALES (corp-wide): 42.47B **Privately Held**
SIC: 6719 3565 3556 2671 Investment holding companies, except banks; Packaging machinery; Food products machinery; Paper; coated and laminated packaging
PA: George Weston Limited
700-22 St Clair Ave E
Toronto ON M4T 2
226 271-5030

(G-5601)
NORSE DAIRY SYSTEMS LP
1740 Joyce Ave (43219-1026)
P.O. Box 1869 (43216-1869)
PHONE..............................614 294-4931
◆ **EMP**: 340 **EST**: 1995
SALES (est): 48.39MM
SALES (corp-wide): 42.47B **Privately Held**

Web: www.norse.com
SIC: 3556 2052 2656 Ice cream manufacturing machinery; Cones, ice cream; Ice cream containers: made from purchased material
HQ: Interbake Foods Llc
1740 Joyce Ave
Columbus OH 43219
614 294-4931

(G-5602)
NORTH COUNTRY CHARCUTERIE LLC
1145 Chesapeake Ave Ste E (43212-2286)
PHONE..............................614 670-5726
James Forbes, *Managing Member*
EMP: 10 **EST**: 2014
SALES (est): 600K **Privately Held**
Web: www.northcountrycharcuterie.com
SIC: 5421 2011 5147 2013 Meat markets, including freezer provisioners; Meat packing plants; Meats and meat products; Bacon, side and sliced: from purchased meat

(G-5603)
NORTHEAST CABINET CO LLC
6063 Taylor Rd (43230-3211)
PHONE..............................614 759-0800
James P Yankle, *Prin*
EMP: 8 **EST**: 2006
SALES (est): 615.32K **Privately Held**
Web: www.jyanklecompany.com
SIC: 2434 Wood kitchen cabinets

(G-5604)
NORTHWOOD ENERGY CORPORATION
941 Chatham Ln Ste 100 (43221-2471)
PHONE..............................614 457-1024
Ralph W Talmage, *Pr*
Dave Haid, *VP*
Frederick H Kennedy, *Prin*
Joan S Talmage, *Prin*
EMP: 21 **EST**: 1983
SQ FT: 5,000
SALES (est): 2.64MM **Privately Held**
Web: www.northwoodenergy.com
SIC: 1382 Oil and gas exploration services

(G-5605)
NOXGEAR LLC
2264 Green Island Dr (43228-9432)
PHONE..............................937 248-1860
Tom Walters, *CEO*
EMP: 6 **EST**: 2012
SALES (est): 194.78K **Privately Held**
Web: www.noxgear.com
SIC: 2329 Vests (suede, leatherette, etc.), sport: men's and boys'

(G-5606)
NTB NATIONAL TIRE AND BATTERY
1640 Holt Rd (43228-3649)
PHONE..............................614 870-8945
Roger Mengerinck, *Prin*
EMP: 7 **EST**: 2010
SALES (est): 149K **Privately Held**
SIC: 5531 7534 Automotive tires; Tire repair shop

(G-5607)
NUCON INTERNATIONAL INC (PA)
7000 Huntley Rd (43229-1035)
P.O. Box 29151 (43229-0151)
PHONE..............................614 846-5710
J Louis Kovach, *Pr*
Joseph C Enneking, *VP*
Paul E Kovach, *Sec*
▲ **EMP**: 11 **EST**: 1972

Columbus - Franklin County (G-5608)

SQ FT: 22,000
SALES (est): 13.69MM
SALES (corp-wide): 13.69MM **Privately Held**
Web: www.nucon-int.com
SIC: **5199** 8711 8734 3829 Charcoal; Pollution control engineering; Pollution testing; Nuclear radiation and testing apparatus

(G-5608)
NUTS ARE GOOD INC (PA)
Also Called: Buffalo Peanuts
Busch Blvd (43229)
PHONE..................586 619-2400
Daniel B Levy, *Pr*
EMP: 12 EST: 1989
SQ FT: 10,000
SALES (est): 1.8MM **Privately Held**
Web: www.freshroastedalmondco.com
SIC: **2068** 5145 Salted and roasted nuts and seeds; Nuts, salted or roasted

(G-5609)
O E MEYER CO
5677 Chantry Dr (43232-4731)
PHONE..................614 428-5656
EMP: 21
Web: www.oemeyer.com
SIC: **3548** Welding apparatus
PA: O. E. Meyer Co.
3303 Tiffin Ave Ste 1
Sandusky OH 44870

(G-5610)
OBERFIELDS LLC
1165 Alum Creek Dr (43209-2719)
PHONE..................614 252-0955
Chris Buttke, *Mgr*
EMP: 21
SALES (corp-wide): 21.04MM **Privately Held**
Web: www.oberfields.com
SIC: **3272** 3271 2531 Concrete products, nec; Concrete block and brick; Public building and related furniture
HQ: Oberfield's, Llc
528 London Rd
Delaware OH 43015
740 369-7644

(G-5611)
OCTSYS SECURITY CORP
Also Called: O S C
341 S 3rd St Ste 100-42 (43215-5463)
P.O. Box 1071 (43216-1071)
PHONE..................614 470-4510
Vincent King, *CEO*
EMP: 9 EST: 2013
SALES (est): 70.1K **Privately Held**
SIC: **3089** 3999 Identification cards, plastics; Stereographs, photographic

(G-5612)
OH ROAD LLC
2636 Berwyn Rd (43221-3208)
PHONE..................614 582-4765
EMP: 6 EST: 2018
SALES (est): 119.96K **Privately Held**
SIC: **2759** Commercial printing, nec

(G-5613)
OHIO COFFEE COLLABORATIVE LTD
Also Called: One Line Coffee
745 N High St (43215-1425)
PHONE..................614 564-9852
Ralph Miller, *Brnch Mgr*
EMP: 15
SALES (corp-wide): 4.82MM **Privately Held**
Web: www.onelinecoffee.com
SIC: **5812** 5149 5499 2095 Coffee shop; Coffee, green or roasted; Coffee; Roasted coffee
PA: Ohio Coffee Collaborative Ltd
2084 Taylor Ln
Newark OH 43055
614 289-2939

(G-5614)
OHIO DEPARTMENT TRANSPORTATION
1606 W Broad St (43223-1202)
PHONE..................614 351-2898
EMP: 20
SIC: **3669** 9621 Transportation signaling devices; Regulation, administration of transportation, State government
HQ: Ohio Department Of Transportation
1980 W Broad St
Columbus OH 43223

(G-5615)
OHIO DESIGNER CRAFTSMEN ENTPS (HQ)
Also Called: Columbus Winter Fair
1665 W 5th Ave (43212-2315)
PHONE..................614 486-7119
Sharon Kokot, *Dir*
EMP: 12 EST: 1963
SQ FT: 2,000
SALES (est): 899.93K **Privately Held**
Web: www.ohiocraft.org
SIC: **5947** 8741 2721 Artcraft and carvings; Management services; Periodicals, publishing only
PA: Ohio Designer-Craftsmen
1665 W 5th Ave
Columbus OH 43212

(G-5616)
OHIO DISTINCTIVE ENTERPRISES
Also Called: Ohio Distinctive Software
6500 Fiesta Dr (43235-5201)
PHONE..................614 459-0453
Stanford Apseloff, *Pr*
Glen Apseloff, *VP*
Timothy M Clark, *Sec*
EMP: 25 EST: 1986
SQ FT: 12,000
SALES (est): 1.95MM **Privately Held**
Web: ohiodistinctivebucket.s3-website-us-east-2.amazonaws.com
SIC: **7372** Prepackaged software

(G-5617)
OHIO ELECTRIC MOTOR SERVICE CENTER INC
1854 S High St (43207-2373)
PHONE..................614 444-1451
EMP: 12
SIC: **7694** 5063 Electric motor repair; Motors, electric

(G-5618)
OHIO ELECTRIC MOTOR SVC LLC (PA)
1909 E Livingston Ave (43209-2733)
PHONE..................614 444-1451
EMP: 11 EST: 2011
SALES (est): 1.93MM
SALES (corp-wide): 1.93MM **Privately Held**
Web: www.ohioelectricmotorservicecenter.com
SIC: **7694** Electric motor repair

(G-5619)
OHIO FOAM CORPORATION
1513 Alum Creek Dr (43209-2712)
PHONE..................614 252-4877
Phil Johnson, *Brnch Mgr*
EMP: 8
SALES (corp-wide): 7.68MM **Privately Held**
Web: www.ohiofoam.com
SIC: **3069** 3086 Foam rubber; Plastics foam products
PA: Ohio Foam Corporation
820 Plymouth St
Bucyrus OH 44820
419 563-0399

(G-5620)
OHIO LABEL INC
5005 Transamerica Dr (43228-9381)
PHONE..................614 777-0180
Stacy Graham, *CEO*
EMP: 13 EST: 1990
SQ FT: 12,000
SALES (est): 1.03MM **Privately Held**
Web: www.ohiolabel.com
SIC: **2759** Labels and seals: printing, nsk

(G-5621)
OHIO MODEL PRODUCTS LLC ✪
Also Called: Buddy RC
4180 Fisher Rd (43228-1024)
PHONE..................614 808-4488
EMP: 10 EST: 2022
SALES (est): 513.78K **Privately Held**
Web: www.ohiomodelplanes.com
SIC: **3944** Airplane models, toy and hobby

(G-5622)
OHIO NEWS NETWORK
Also Called: Ohio News Network
770 Twin Rivers Dr (43215-1127)
PHONE..................614 460-3700
Tom Greidorn, *Genl Mgr*
EMP: 20 EST: 1996
SALES (est): 235.68K **Privately Held**
Web: www.10tv.com
SIC: **7383** 2711 4841 News syndicates; Newspapers; Cable and other pay television services

(G-5623)
OHIO NEWSPAPER SERVICES INC
Also Called: Adohio
1335 Dublin Rd Ste 216b (43215-1000)
PHONE..................614 486-6677
Frank Deaner, *Ex Dir*
EMP: 8 EST: 1933
SALES (est): 234.11K
SALES (corp-wide): 321.9K **Privately Held**
Web: www.adohio.net
SIC: **7313** 2711 Newspaper advertising representative; Newspapers, publishing and printing
PA: Ohio News Media Association
1335 Dublin Rd Ste 216b
Columbus OH 43215
614 486-6677

(G-5624)
OHIO NEWSPAPERS FOUNDATION
1335 Dublin Rd Ste 216b (43215-1000)
PHONE..................614 486-6677
EMP: 7 EST: 2010
SALES (est): 261.06K **Privately Held**
SIC: **2711** Newspapers, publishing and printing

(G-5625)
OHIO PACKING COMPANY
1306 Harmon Ave (43223-3365)
P.O. Box 30961 (43230-0961)
PHONE..................614 445-0627
Walter Wilke Junior, *Pr*
Carla Jones, ✱
Edward Wilke Junior, *Sec*
James Wilke, ✱
EMP: 190 EST: 1907
SQ FT: 70,000
SALES (est): 9.19MM **Privately Held**
Web: www.ohiopacking.com
SIC: **2011** Pork products, from pork slaughtered on site

(G-5626)
OHIO RIGHTS GROUP
1021 E Broad St (43205-1357)
PHONE..................614 300-0529
Chad Callender, *Prin*
EMP: 8 EST: 2015
SALES (est): 205.94K **Privately Held**
Web: www.ohiorightsgroup.info
SIC: **2711** Newspapers, publishing and printing

(G-5627)
OHIO STATE PLASTICS
1917 Joyce Ave (43219-1029)
PHONE..................614 299-5618
Dwayne Margin, *Mgr*
EMP: 87 EST: 1998
SALES (est): 2.21MM
SALES (corp-wide): 15.9B **Publicly Held**
SIC: **2656** Food containers (liquid tight), including milk cartons
HQ: Altium Packaging Llc
2500 Windy Ridge Pkwy Se # 1400
Atlanta GA 30339
678 742-4600

(G-5628)
OHIO STEEL INDUSTRIES INC (PA)
2575 Ferris Rd (43224-2597)
PHONE..................614 471-4800
◆ EMP: 75 EST: 1958
SALES (est): 45.44MM
SALES (corp-wide): 45.44MM **Privately Held**
Web: www.osiplastics.com
SIC: **3441** Fabricated structural metal

(G-5629)
OHIO TRAILER SUPPLY INC
Also Called: Ots
2966 Westerville Rd (43224-4563)
PHONE..................614 471-9121
Jet Chrysler, *Pr*
EMP: 7 EST: 1980
SQ FT: 8,000
SALES (est): 912.64K **Privately Held**
Web: www.ohiotrailer.com
SIC: **7692** 5013 Welding repair; Trailer parts and accessories

(G-5630)
OHIO WIRE FORM & SPRING CO
2270 S High St (43207-2432)
PHONE..................614 444-3676
P E Van Horn Junior, *Ch*
Stephen A Van Horn, *Pr*
Samuel E Van Horn, *VP*
EMP: 30 EST: 1947
SQ FT: 43,800
SALES (est): 2.84MM **Privately Held**
Web: www.ohiowireform.com
SIC: **3496** 3495 Miscellaneous fabricated wire products; Wire springs

(G-5631)
OHIO WOOD RECYCLING INC
Also Called: Dm Pallet Service
2019 Rathmell Rd (43207-5012)
PHONE..................614 491-0881
Dexter Mounts, *Pr*
EMP: 8 EST: 1990
SALES (est): 197.44K **Privately Held**

GEOGRAPHIC SECTION
Columbus - Franklin County (G-5656)

SIC: 2448 Pallets, wood

(G-5632)
OHLHEISER CORP
1900 Jetway Blvd (43219-1681)
PHONE..............................860 953-7632
Robert Pelletier, *Owner*
EMP: 9 EST: 2017
SALES (est): 957.06K **Privately Held**
Web: www.otcindustrial.com
SIC: 3569 General industrial machinery, nec

(G-5633)
OHLINGER DEV & EDITORIAL CO
Also Called: Ohlinger Studios
28 W Henderson Rd (43214)
PHONE..............................614 261-5360
Monica Ohlinger, *Pr*
EMP: 52 EST: 2019
SALES (est): 2.7MM **Privately Held**
Web: www.ohlingerstudios.com
SIC: 2741 Miscellaneous publishing

(G-5634)
OHLINGER PUBLISHING SVCS INC
Also Called: Ohlinger Studios
28 W Henderson Rd (43214-2628)
PHONE..............................614 261-5360
Monica Ohlinger, *Pr*
EMP: 30 EST: 2001
SALES (est): 2.48MM **Privately Held**
Web: www.ohlingerstudios.com
SIC: 2741 Miscellaneous publishing

(G-5635)
OIL WORKS LLC
1611 Integrity Dr E (43209-2730)
PHONE..............................614 245-3090
EMP: 8 EST: 2011
SALES (est): 1.09MM **Privately Held**
Web: www.oilworksllc.com
SIC: 2911 5093 Oils, lubricating; Oil, waste

(G-5636)
OLD TRAIL PRINTING COMPANY
Also Called: Old Trail Printing Co
100 Fornoff Rd (43207-2475)
PHONE..............................614 443-4852
Mary Held, *Pr*
Michael Held, *Stockholder Principal**
Dave Held, *Stockholder Principal**
Susan Horn, *Stockholder Principal**
Jeff Lampert, *
EMP: 125 EST: 1924
SQ FT: 55,000
SALES (est): 22.57MM **Privately Held**
Web: www.oldtrailprinting.com
SIC: 2752 2791 2789 2759 Offset printing; Typesetting; Bookbinding and related work; Commercial printing, nec

(G-5637)
OMETEK INC
790 Cross Pointe Rd (43230-6685)
PHONE..............................614 861-6729
EMP: 90 EST: 1977
SALES (est): 20.48MM **Privately Held**
Web: www.ometek.com
SIC: 3599 Machine shop, jobbing and repair

(G-5638)
OMNITECH ELECTRONICS INC
5090 Trabue Rd (43228-9391)
PHONE..............................800 822-1344
Bogdan Zaleski, *Pr*
EMP: 10 EST: 1998
SQ FT: 22,500
SALES (est): 472.93K **Privately Held**
Web: www.omnitech-usa.com

SIC: 3826 Analytical instruments

(G-5639)
ONE ORIJIN LLC
4300 E 5th Ave (43219-1816)
PHONE..............................630 362-5291
Tod H Friedman, *Managing Member*
EMP: 6 EST: 2017
SALES (est): 325.38K **Privately Held**
SIC: 2833 Medicinals and botanicals

(G-5640)
ONE TORTILLA CO
1724 Northwest Blvd (43212-2246)
PHONE..............................614 570-9312
Shawn Korn, *Prin*
EMP: 8 EST: 2014
SALES (est): 397.65K **Privately Held**
SIC: 2099 Tortillas, fresh or refrigerated

(G-5641)
ONEIDA CONSUMER LLC
1600 Dublin Rd Ste 200 (43215-2095)
PHONE..............................740 687-2500
Mark Eichhorn, *CEO*
EMP: 13 EST: 2018
SALES (est): 346.58K **Privately Held**
SIC: 3089 3469 Plastics containers, except foam; Metal stampings, nec
PA: Lenox Corporation
    1414 Radcliffe St
    Bristol PA 19007

(G-5642)
OPC POLYMERS LLC
Also Called: OPC Polymers
1920 Leonard Ave (43219-2514)
P.O. Box 369004 (43236-9004)
PHONE..............................614 253-8511
EMP: 176 EST: 1919
SALES (est): 5.02MM **Privately Held**
Web: www.yenkin-majestic.com
SIC: 2851 2821 2869 Paints and paint additives; Plastics materials and resins; Plasticizers, organic: cyclic and acyclic

(G-5643)
ORANGE BARREL MEDIA LLC
250 N Hartford Ave (43222-1100)
PHONE..............................614 294-4898
Pete Scantland, *CEO*
Adam Borchers, *
EMP: 75 EST: 2004
SALES (est): 12.72MM **Privately Held**
Web: www.obm.com
SIC: 3993 7312 Signs and advertising specialties; Outdoor advertising services

(G-5644)
ORBIS RPM LLC
592 Claycraft Rd (43230-5319)
PHONE..............................419 307-8511
Chad Goodwin, *Brnch Mgr*
EMP: 8
SALES (corp-wide): 1.94B **Privately Held**
Web: www.orbiscorporation.com
SIC: 3081 Unsupported plastics film and sheet
HQ: Orbis Rpm, Llc
    1055 Corporate Center Dr
    Oconomowoc WI 53066
    262 560-5000

(G-5645)
OSI GLOBAL SOURCING LLC
2575 Ferris Rd (43224-2540)
PHONE..............................614 471-4800
Tom Martini, *Pr*
▲ EMP: 19 EST: 2008
SALES (est): 539.62K **Privately Held**

Web: www.ohiosteel.com
SIC: 2821 Plastics materials and resins

(G-5646)
OTC INDUSTRIAL TECHNOLOGIES (PA)
1900 Jetway Blvd (43219)
PHONE..............................800 837-6827
Bill Canady, *CEO*
EMP: 15 EST: 2021
SALES (est): 10.75MM
SALES (corp-wide): 10.75MM **Privately Held**
Web: www.otcindustrial.com
SIC: 3531 Construction machinery

(G-5647)
OUTFIT GOOD LLC
1145 Chesapeake Ave Ste G (43212-2284)
PHONE..............................419 565-3770
EMP: 6 EST: 2017
SALES (est): 249.67K **Privately Held**
Web: www.outfitgood.com
SIC: 2323 Men's and boy's neckwear

(G-5648)
OWENS CORNING
Also Called: 1-800-Usa-home.com
2050 Integrity Dr S (43209-2728)
PHONE..............................614 754-4098
Stephen Brooks, *Mgr*
EMP: 13
Web: www.owenscorning.com
SIC: 3296 Fiberglass insulation
PA: Owens Corning
    1 Owens Corning Pkwy
    Toledo OH 43659

(G-5649)
P S PLASTICS INC
2020 Britains Ln (43224-5612)
PHONE..............................614 262-7070
John Pyers, *Pr*
Rob Sutliff, *Sec*
EMP: 15 EST: 1985
SQ FT: 6,700
SALES (est): 469.44K **Privately Held**
SIC: 3089 Injection molding of plastics

(G-5650)
PACTIV LLC
2120 Westbelt Dr (43228-3820)
P.O. Box 28147 (43228-0147)
PHONE..............................614 771-5400
Joe Deal, *Opers Mgr*
EMP: 73
Web: www.pactivevergreen.com
SIC: 2631 7389 Paperboard mills; Packaging and labeling services
HQ: Pactiv Llc
    1900 W Field Ct
    Lake Forest IL 60045
    847 482-2000

(G-5651)
PAKRA LLC
449 E Mound St (43215-5514)
PHONE..............................614 477-6965
Rini Das, *Managing Member*
EMP: 10 EST: 2007
SQ FT: 900
SALES (est): 550.74K **Privately Held**
Web: www.pakragames.com
SIC: 7372 8331 8249 8742 Business oriented computer software; Job training and related services; Business training services; Management consulting services

(G-5652)
PANACEA PRODUCTS CORPORATION (PA)
Also Called: J-Mak Industries
2711 International St (43228)
PHONE..............................614 850-7000
Frank A Paniccia, *Pr*
Gregg Paniccia, *
Jim Fancelli, *
Fred Pagura, *
Louis Calderone, *
◆ EMP: 40 EST: 1967
SALES (est): 49.68MM
SALES (corp-wide): 49.68MM **Privately Held**
Web: www.panaceaproducts.com
SIC: 5051 2542 3496 Metals service centers and offices; Partitions and fixtures, except wood; Miscellaneous fabricated wire products

(G-5653)
PANACEA PRODUCTS CORPORATION
1825 Joyce Ave (43219-1027)
PHONE..............................614 429-6320
Frank Panancea, *Brnch Mgr*
EMP: 24
SALES (corp-wide): 49.68MM **Privately Held**
Web: www.panaceaproducts.com
SIC: 3496 3423 2542 Miscellaneous fabricated wire products; Hand and edge tools, nec; Partitions and fixtures, except wood
PA: Panacea Products Corporation
    2711 International St
    Columbus OH 43228
    614 850-7000

(G-5654)
PANTRYBAG
769 Sullivant Ave (43222-1678)
PHONE..............................614 927-8744
Chiahanam C Ani, *Pr*
EMP: 10 EST: 2019
SALES (est): 479.63K **Privately Held**
SIC: 2674 Shipping and shopping bags or sacks

(G-5655)
PAPEL COUTURE
Also Called: PC
6522 Singletree Dr (43229-1119)
PHONE..............................614 848-5700
Vadim Daskal, *Owner*
Scott Vogel, *Genl Mgr*
EMP: 6 EST: 2011
SQ FT: 600
SALES (est): 603.3K
SALES (corp-wide): 990.14K **Privately Held**
Web: www.papelcouture.com
SIC: 2759 Invitation and stationery printing and engraving
PA: Daskal Enterprise, Llc
    6522 Singletree Dr
    Columbus OH 43229
    614 848-5700

(G-5656)
PARKER-HANNIFIN CORPORATION
Also Called: Tube Fittings Division
3885 Gateway Blvd (43228-9723)
PHONE..............................614 279-7070
William Bowman, *Brnch Mgr*
EMP: 120
SALES (corp-wide): 19.07B **Publicly Held**
Web: www.parker.com
SIC: 3494 5074 Pipe fittings; Plumbing fittings and supplies

Columbus - Franklin County (G-5657)

PA: Parker-Hannifin Corporation
6035 Parkland Blvd
Cleveland OH 44124
216 896-3000

(G-5657)
PART 2 SCREEN PRTG DESIGN INC
935 King Ave (43212-2656)
PHONE..................614 294-4429
EMP: 6 **EST:** 1996
SQ FT: 5,000
SALES (est): 410K **Privately Held**
SIC: 2759 2395 Screen printing; Embroidery products, except Schiffli machine

(G-5658)
PATH ROBOTICS INC (PA)
528 Maier Pl (43215-3264)
PHONE..................330 808-2788
Andrew Lonsberry, *CEO*
EMP: 55 **EST:** 2018
SALES (est): 54.95MM
SALES (corp-wide): 54.95MM **Privately Held**
Web: www.path-robotics.com
SIC: 3599 Custom machinery

(G-5659)
PATH ROBOTICS INC
3950 Business Park Dr (43204-5008)
PHONE..................614 816-1991
EMP: 65
SALES (corp-wide): 54.95MM **Privately Held**
Web: www.path-robotics.com
SIC: 3599 Custom machinery
PA: Path Robotics, Inc.
528 Maier Pl
Columbus OH 43215
330 808-2788

(G-5660)
PAUL PETERSON COMPANY (PA)
950 Dublin Rd (43215-1169)
P.O. Box 1510 (43216-1510)
PHONE..................614 486-4375
Paul Peterson Junior, *Ch Bd*
Parr Peterson, *CEO*
Aaron Peterson, *Pr*
Colette Peterson, *Sec*
EMP: 13 **EST:** 1932
SQ FT: 2,000
SALES (est): 13.29MM
SALES (corp-wide): 13.29MM **Privately Held**
Web: www.ppco.net
SIC: 1611 1799 3669 5084 Guardrail construction, highways; Waterproofing; Traffic signals, electric; Safety equipment

(G-5661)
PAUL PETERSON SAFETY DIV INC
950 Dublin Rd (43215-1169)
P.O. Box 1510 (43216-1510)
PHONE..................614 486-4375
Paul Peterson Junior, *Pr*
Parr Peterson, *
Gary Boylan, *
Colette Peterson, *
EMP: 34 **EST:** 1975
SQ FT: 3,800
SALES (est): 995.53K
SALES (corp-wide): 13.29MM **Privately Held**
SIC: 3993 7359 5999 Signs, not made in custom sign painting shops; Work zone traffic equipment (flags, cones, barrels, etc.); Safety supplies and equipment
PA: The Paul Peterson Company
950 Dublin Rd
Columbus OH 43215

614 486-4375

(G-5662)
PAYDAY 124 INC
2246 Citygate Dr (43219-3588)
PHONE..................614 509-1080
EMP: 99 **EST:** 1982
SALES (est): 15.97MM **Privately Held**
Web: www.hopkinsprinting.com
SIC: 2752 Offset printing

(G-5663)
PEARSON EDUCATION INC
4350 Equity Dr (43228-4801)
PHONE..................614 876-0371
Sheila Hickle, *Brnch Mgr*
EMP: 6
SALES (corp-wide): 4.58B **Privately Held**
Web: www.pearson.com
SIC: 2721 Periodicals
HQ: Pearson Education, Inc.
221 River St
Hoboken NJ 07030
201 236-7000

(G-5664)
PEARSON EDUCATION INC
800 N High St (43215-1430)
PHONE..................614 841-3700
Bruce Johnson, *Mgr*
EMP: 25
SALES (corp-wide): 4.58B **Privately Held**
Web: www.pearson.com
SIC: 2721 Periodicals
HQ: Pearson Education, Inc.
221 River St
Hoboken NJ 07030
201 236-7000

(G-5665)
PEEBLES - HERZOG INC
50 Hayden Ave (43222-1019)
PHONE..................614 279-2211
Michael B Herzog, *Pr*
Michael Lauffer, *VP*
Molly Herzog, *Sec*
EMP: 7 **EST:** 1975
SQ FT: 6,500
SALES (est): 884K **Privately Held**
Web: www.peeblesherzog.com
SIC: 3931 7699 Pipes, organ; Organ tuning and repair

(G-5666)
PENNANT INC
Also Called: Pennant Manufacturing
401 N Front St Ste 350 (43215-2249)
PHONE..................937 584-5411
Mike Gaby, *CEO*
Jim Tighe, *CFO*
Mike Ryan, *VP*
Kathy Rupp, *Dir Opers*
EMP: 24 **EST:** 1998
SALES (est): 861.24K **Privately Held**
Web: www.pennant-us.com
SIC: 3496 Clips and fasteners, made from purchased wire

(G-5667)
PENNY FAB LLC
Also Called: Penny Fab
1055 Gibbard Ave (43201-3052)
PHONE..................740 967-3669
EMP: 12 **EST:** 1990
SQ FT: 50,000
SALES (est): 1.51MM **Privately Held**
Web: www.pennyfab.com
SIC: 3441 3499 Fabricated structural metal for ships; Fire- or burglary-resistive products

(G-5668)
PEPSI-COLA METRO BTLG CO INC
Also Called: Pepsico
2553 N High St (43202-2555)
PHONE..................614 261-8193
Al Vogt, *Mgr*
EMP: 16
SALES (corp-wide): 86.39B **Publicly Held**
Web: www.pepsico.com
SIC: 2086 Carbonated soft drinks, bottled and canned
HQ: Pepsi-Cola Metropolitan Bottling Company, Inc.
700 Anderson Hill Rd
Purchase NY 10577
914 767-6000

(G-5669)
PERCUVISION LLC
2030 Dividend Dr (43228-3847)
PHONE..................614 891-4800
Errol Singh Md Facs, *CEO*
Earl Singh J.d., *COO*
Rick Karr Mba, *VP Opers*
David Busick Mba M S Me, *Marketing Communication Director*
EMP: 16 **EST:** 2007
SQ FT: 7,500
SALES (est): 453.54K **Privately Held**
Web: www.percuvision.com
SIC: 3841 Surgical and medical instruments

(G-5670)
PERFORMANCE RESEARCH INC
Also Called: PRI Marine
3328 Westerville Rd (43224-3700)
PHONE..................614 475-8300
Robert M Proffit, *Pr*
EMP: 7 **EST:** 1953
SQ FT: 10,000
SALES (est): 731.33K **Privately Held**
SIC: 3519 Marine engines

(G-5671)
PHARMAFORCE INC
960 Crupper Ave (43229-1109)
EMP: 250
SIC: 2834 Adrenal pharmaceutical preparations

(G-5672)
PHILADELPHIA INSTANTWHIP INC
2200 Cardigan Ave (43215-1092)
PHONE..................614 488-2536
Douglas A Smith, *Pr*
G Frederick Smith, *Sec*
Thomas G Michaelides, *Treas*
Tom Willard, *Genl Mgr*
EMP: 14 **EST:** 1954
SALES (est): 4.06MM
SALES (corp-wide): 97.42MM **Privately Held**
Web: www.instantwhip.com
SIC: 2026 5143 Whipped topping, except frozen or dry mix; Dairy products, except dried or canned
PA: Instantwhip Foods, Inc.
2200 Cardigan Ave
Columbus OH 43215
614 488-2536

(G-5673)
PHILIP RADKE
1184 Bonham Ave (43211-2954)
PHONE..................614 475-6788
Philip Radke, *Prin*
EMP: 7 **EST:** 2017
SALES (est): 112.44K **Privately Held**
SIC: 7534 Tire repair shop

(G-5674)
PHOTO-TYPE ENGRAVING COMPANY
2500 Harrison Rd (43204-3510)
PHONE..................614 308-1900
Doug Rittenhouse, *Brnch Mgr*
EMP: 35
SALES (corp-wide): 43.97MM **Privately Held**
Web: www.phototype.com
SIC: 2791 Photocomposition, for the printing trade
PA: The Photo-Type Engraving Company
2141 Gilbert Ave
Cincinnati OH 45206
513 281-0999

(G-5675)
PITT PLASTICS INC (DH)
3980 Groves Rd Ste A (43232-4172)
PHONE..................614 868-8660
Terry Callow, *Parent*
EMP: 65 **EST:** 1972
SQ FT: 120,000
SALES (est): 50.06MM **Privately Held**
SIC: 2821 2673 Polyethylene resins; Bags: plastic, laminated, and coated
HQ: Pitt Plastics, Inc.
1400 E Atkinson Ave
Pittsburg KS 66762
620 231-4030

(G-5676)
PJS WHOLESALE INC
2551 Westbelt Dr (43228)
PHONE..................614 402-9363
Azmi Azzam Alhamouri, *Prin*
Mahmoud T Almahmoud, *Prin*
▲ **EMP:** 6 **EST:** 2009
SALES (est): 299.61K **Privately Held**
SIC: 2253 T-shirts and tops, knit

(G-5677)
PLASKOLITE LLC
Also Called: Retail Display Group
400 W Nationwide Blvd Ste 400 (43215-2394)
P.O. Box 1497 (43216-1497)
PHONE..................614 294-3281
James R Dunn, *Brnch Mgr*
EMP: 48
SALES (corp-wide): 443.48MM **Privately Held**
Web: www.plaskolite.com
SIC: 2821 3083 Acrylic resins; Laminated plastics plate and sheet
PA: Plaskolite, Llc
400 W Nationwide Blvd # 400
Columbus OH 43215
614 294-3281

(G-5678)
PLASKOLITE LLC (PA)
400 W Nationwide Blvd Ste 400 (43215-2394)
PHONE..................614 294-3281
Ryan Schroeder, *Pr*
Mark Grindley, *COO*
Peter Lynch, *CFO*
David Dennis, *Chief Strategy Officer*
♦ **EMP:** 238 **EST:** 1950
SQ FT: 650,000
SALES (est): 443.48MM
SALES (corp-wide): 443.48MM **Privately Held**
Web: www.plaskolite.com
SIC: 2821 Plastics materials and resins

GEOGRAPHIC SECTION
Columbus - Franklin County (G-5704)

(G-5679)
PLASTIC SUPPLIERS INC (PA)
2400 Marilyn Ln (43219-1721)
PHONE..................614 471-9100
George L Thomas, *Pr*
Peter Driscoll, *
Steve H Dudley, *
Erich Emhuff, *
◆ **EMP:** 29 **EST:** 1959
SQ FT: 7,500
SALES (est): 82.22MM
SALES (corp-wide): 82.22MM **Privately Held**
Web: www.earthfirstfilms.com
SIC: 2821 Plastics materials and resins

(G-5680)
PLASTICS FAMILY HOLDINGS INC
Also Called: Branch 49
2220 International St (43228-4630)
PHONE..................614 272-0777
Roger Plizga, *Mgr*
EMP: 10
Web: www.lairdplastics.com
SIC: 5162 3089 Plastics materials, nec; Windows, plastics
HQ: Plastics Family Holdings, Inc.
5800 Cmpus Circ Dr E Ste
Irving TX 75063
469 299-7000

(G-5681)
PMG CINCINNATI INC
570 N High St (43215-2052)
PHONE..................513 421-7275
Michael W Mercer, *Prin*
EMP: 10 **EST:** 2018
SALES (est): 442.92K **Privately Held**
Web: www.cincinnati.com
SIC: 2711 Newspapers, publishing and printing

(G-5682)
POPS PRINTED APPAREL LLC
1758 N High St Unit 2 (43201-4422)
PHONE..................614 372-5651
Austin Pence, *Managing Member*
EMP: 6 **EST:** 2014
SQ FT: 2,000
SALES (est): 367.41K **Privately Held**
Web: www.printedbypops.com
SIC: 2759 Screen printing

(G-5683)
PORCELAIN STEEL BUILDINGS COMPANY
Also Called: Psb Company
555 W Goodale St (43215-1104)
P.O. Box 1089 (43216-1089)
PHONE..................614 228-5781
▲ **EMP:** 80
SIC: 3479 3444 Coating of metals and formed products; Restaurant sheet metalwork

(G-5684)
POWER DISTRIBUTORS LLC (PA)
Also Called: Central Power Systems
3700 Paragon Dr (43228-9750)
PHONE..................614 876-3543
Matthew Finn, *Pr*
▲ **EMP:** 81 **EST:** 2012
SALES (est): 87.56MM
SALES (corp-wide): 87.56MM **Privately Held**
Web: www.powerdistributors.com
SIC: 5084 3524 Engines and parts, air-cooled; Lawn and garden equipment

(G-5685)
PPAFCO INC
1096 Ridge St (43215-1154)
PHONE..................614 488-7259
Laura Bowman, *Pr*
EMP: 23 **EST:** 1978
SQ FT: 15,000
SALES (est): 909.53K **Privately Held**
Web: www.ppafco.com
SIC: 3089 3069 5074 Fittings for pipe, plastics; Nipples, rubber; Pipes and fittings, plastic

(G-5686)
PRECISION DUCT FABRICATION LLC
182 N Yale Ave (43222-1127)
PHONE..................614 580-9385
EMP: 10 **EST:** 2020
SALES (est): 998.71K **Privately Held**
Web: www.precisionductandfab.com
SIC: 3444 Ducts, sheet metal

(G-5687)
PRECISION MACHINE TOOL
1625 W Mound St (43223-1809)
PHONE..................614 564-9360
Todd Wurstner, *Prin*
EMP: 6 **EST:** 2013
SALES (est): 144.57K **Privately Held**
SIC: 3599 Machine shop, jobbing and repair

(G-5688)
PREISSER INC
Also Called: PIP Printing
3560 Millikin Ct Ste A (43228-9765)
P.O. Box 827 (43017-6827)
PHONE..................614 345-0199
Gail Preisser, *Pr*
Thomas Preisser, *Sec*
EMP: 43 **EST:** 1974
SALES (est): 3.47MM **Privately Held**
Web: www.pip.com
SIC: 2752 2791 Offset printing; Typesetting

(G-5689)
PRESSURE CONNECTIONS CORP
610 Claycraft Rd (43230-5328)
PHONE..................614 863-6930
◆ **EMP:** 56 **EST:** 1981
SALES (est): 8.61MM **Privately Held**
Web: www.pressureconnections.com
SIC: 3498 5085 3494 3492 Tube fabricating (contract bending and shaping); Industrial supplies; Valves and pipe fittings, nec; Fluid power valves and hose fittings

(G-5690)
PRIME EQUIPMENT GROUP LLC
Also Called: Diversified Mch Pdts Gnsville GA
2001 Courtright Rd (43232-4480)
PHONE..................614 253-8590
Joseph Gasbarro, *Pr*
David Kreim, *CFO*
Nick Gasbarro, *
◆ **EMP:** 100 **EST:** 1986
SALES (est): 23.28MM **Publicly Held**
Web: www.jbtc.com
SIC: 3556 Poultry processing machinery
PA: John Bean Technologies Corporation
70 W Madison St Ste 4400
Chicago IL 60602

(G-5691)
PRINT SYNDICATE INC
2282 Westbrooke Dr (43228-9416)
PHONE..................617 290-9550
James Keller, *COO*
EMP: 23 **EST:** 2014
SALES (est): 1.23MM **Privately Held**
Web: www.printsyndicate.com
SIC: 2752 Commercial printing, lithographic

(G-5692)
PRINT SYNDICATE LLC
901 W 3rd Ave Ste A (43212-3108)
PHONE..................614 519-0341
Jarred Mullins, *Pr*
EMP: 14 **EST:** 2013
SALES (est): 552.64K **Privately Held**
Web: www.printsyndicate.com
SIC: 2752 Commercial printing, lithographic

(G-5693)
PRO TIRE INC
61 N Brice Rd (43213-1580)
PHONE..................614 864-8662
Thomas Geiger, *Pr*
Thomas Geiger Senior, *Sec*
EMP: 10 **EST:** 1997
SQ FT: 40,000
SALES (est): 807.5K **Privately Held**
Web: www.tirepros.com
SIC: 7534 5014 Tire retreading and repair shops; Automobile tires and tubes

(G-5694)
PROFORM GROUP INC
1715 Georgesville Rd (43228-3619)
PHONE..................614 332-9654
Joe Vannata, *Brnch Mgr*
EMP: 15
SALES (corp-wide): 3MM **Privately Held**
Web: www.proformtrailers.com
SIC: 3713 Truck bodies (motor vehicles)
PA: Proform Group, Inc.
4400 Don Cayo Dr
Muskogee OK 74403
918 682-8666

(G-5695)
PROGRESS RAIL SERVICES CORP
2351 Westbelt Dr (43228-3823)
PHONE..................614 850-1730
David Heatter, *Brnch Mgr*
EMP: 34
SALES (corp-wide): 67.06B **Publicly Held**
SIC: 3743 Railroad equipment
HQ: Progress Rail Services Corporation
1600 Progress Dr
Albertville AL 35950
800 476-8769

(G-5696)
PROVIDENCE REES INC
2111 Builders Pl (43204-4886)
P.O. Box 12535 (43212-0535)
PHONE..................614 833-6231
Leo Steger, *Sec*
Billy Parsley, *
Lee Nichols, *
EMP: 11 **EST:** 1982
SQ FT: 36,000
SALES (est): 407.69K **Privately Held**
SIC: 3496 8711 Wire winding; Engineering services

(G-5697)
PUBLISHING GROUP LTD
781 Northwest Blvd Ste 202 (43212-3874)
PHONE..................614 572-1240
Chuck Steie, *CEO*
Dave Prosser, *Pr*
Kathy Gillis, *VP Opers*
Chuck Stein, *CEO*
EMP: 10 **EST:** 1990
SALES (est): 962.88K **Privately Held**
Web: www.cityscenecolumbus.com
SIC: 2721 7389 2741 5199 Magazines: publishing and printing; Trade show arrangement; Art copy: publishing and printing; Advertising specialties

(G-5698)
PURPLE ORCHID BOUTIQUE LLC
1535 Cunard Rd (43227-3279)
PHONE..................614 554-7686
EMP: 7 **EST:** 2020
SALES (est): 60K **Privately Held**
SIC: 2335 Women's, junior's, and misses' dresses

(G-5699)
PYRAMID INDUSTRIES LLC
327 Briarwood Dr (43213-2055)
PHONE..................614 783-1543
Eric Joyner, *Prin*
EMP: 10 **EST:** 2017
SALES (est): 384.61K **Privately Held**
SIC: 3999 Manufacturing industries, nec

(G-5700)
Q T COLUMBUS LLC
1330 Stimmel Rd (43223-2917)
PHONE..................800 758-2410
EMP: 6 **EST:** 2005
SALES (est): 771.04K **Privately Held**
SIC: 7532 5531 3713 Body shop, trucks; Automotive tires; Utility truck bodies
PA: Q.T. Equipment Company
151 W Dartmore Ave
Akron OH 44301

(G-5701)
QAF TECHNOLOGIES INC
1212 E Dublin Granville Rd Ste 105 (43229-3302)
PHONE..................440 941-4348
Athar Ashraf, *Pr*
Aila Ashraf, *
EMP: 25 **EST:** 2012
SALES (est): 1.98MM **Privately Held**
Web: www.qaftech.com
SIC: 3621 Power generators

(G-5702)
QUALITY BAKERY COMPANY INC
Also Called: Mountain Top Frozen Pies Div
50 N Glenwood Ave (43222-1206)
P.O. Box 453 (43216-0453)
PHONE..................614 224-1424
Jeff Waller, *Mgr*
EMP: 135
SQ FT: 32,836
SALES (corp-wide): 1.82B **Publicly Held**
SIC: 2051 Bread, cake, and related products
HQ: The Quality Bakery Company Inc
380 Polaris Pkwy Ste 400
Westerville OH 43082
614 846-2232

(G-5703)
QUANTUM SOLUTIONS GROUP
1555 Bethel Rd (43220-2003)
PHONE..................614 442-0664
EMP: 6 **EST:** 2019
SALES (est): 289.93K **Privately Held**
Web: www.quantum-health.com
SIC: 3572 Computer storage devices

(G-5704)
QUIKRETE COMPANIES LLC
6225 Huntley Rd (43229-1005)
PHONE..................614 885-4406
Robert Miller, *Brnch Mgr*
EMP: 47
SQ FT: 10,000
Web: www.quikrete.com
SIC: 3272 3241 2899 Dry mixture concrete; Cement, hydraulic; Chemical preparations, nec
HQ: The Quikrete Companies Llc
5 Concourse Pkwy Ste 1900

Columbus - Franklin County (G-5705) — GEOGRAPHIC SECTION

Atlanta GA 30328
404 634-9100

(G-5705)
R & J BARDON INC
4676 Larwell Dr (43220-3621)
PHONE...........................614 457-5500
Chris Swearingen, *Pr*
Leslie Swearingen, *VP*
EMP: 9 **EST:** 1979
SQ FT: 3,000
SALES (est): 676.89K **Privately Held**
Web: www.rjbardon.com
SIC: 2752 Offset printing

(G-5706)
R & S MONITIONS INC
181 Rosslyn Ave (43214-1474)
PHONE...........................614 846-0597
Ron Herman, *Pr*
Sherry Herman, *VP*
EMP: 6 **EST:** 1996
SALES (est): 385.33K **Privately Held**
SIC: 3482 5941 Small arms ammunition; Firearms

(G-5707)
R HOLDINGS 2500 CO
Also Called: Renite Lubrication Engineers
2500 E 5th Ave (43219-2700)
P.O. Box 30830 (43230-0830)
PHONE...........................800 883-7876
Stephen M Halliday, *Ch Bd*
Francis E Cook, *VP Opers*
Leo L Harding, *VP Sls*
Eugene F Cook, *VP*
Doctor Rodger P Kampf, *Dir*
EMP: 20 **EST:** 1932
SALES (est): 1.9MM **Privately Held**
Web: www.renite.com
SIC: 2992 3569 Oils and greases, blending and compounding; Lubrication equipment, industrial

(G-5708)
R&R CANDLES LLC
6745 Mcvey Blvd (43235-2821)
PHONE...........................614 600-7729
EMP: 6 **EST:** 2018
SALES (est): 248.66K **Privately Held**
Web: www.rrcandles.com
SIC: 3999 Candles

(G-5709)
RAM PRODUCTS INC
1091 Stimmel Rd (43223-2911)
PHONE...........................614 443-4634
John Pelleriti, *Pr*
Richard Dawson, *VP*
Anne Pelleriti, *Treas*
EMP: 37 **EST:** 1980
SQ FT: 8,000
SALES (est): 950.97K **Privately Held**
Web: www.ramprocess.com
SIC: 3542 Presses: hydraulic and pneumatic, mechanical and manual

(G-5710)
RAMSEY STAIRS & WDWKG LLC
4134 Little Pine Dr (43230-1166)
PHONE...........................614 694-2101
Robert Ramsey, *Pr*
EMP: 6 **EST:** 2020
SALES (est): 250.02K **Privately Held**
Web: www.ramseystairs.com
SIC: 2431 Millwork

(G-5711)
RAPID MR INTERNATIONAL LLC
1500 Lake Shore Dr Ste 310 (43204-3936)
PHONE...........................614 486-6300
EMP: 7 **EST:** 2006
SALES (est): 550K **Privately Held**
Web: www.rapidmri.com
SIC: 3677 Electronic coils and transformers

(G-5712)
RAYMAR HOLDINGS CORPORATION
3700 Lockbourne Rd (43207-5133)
PHONE...........................614 497-3033
Charles Marcum, *Pr*
Mike Marcum, *
EMP: 50 **EST:** 1972
SQ FT: 29,000
SALES (est): 25.82MM **Privately Held**
Web: www.cardinalcontainer.com
SIC: 2653 Boxes, corrugated: made from purchased materials
HQ: Stronghaven, Incorporated
2727 Paces Ferry Rd Se 1-1850
Atlanta GA 30339
678 235-2713

(G-5713)
RCS CROSS WOODS MAPLE LLC
222 E Campus View Blvd (43235-4634)
PHONE...........................614 825-0670
EMP: 23
SALES (corp-wide): 178.5K **Privately Held**
SIC: 2499 Laundry products, wood
PA: Rcs Cross Woods Maple Llc
355 E Campus View Blvd
Columbus OH 43235
614 846-0091

(G-5714)
READY ROBOTICS CORPORATION
1080 Steelwood Rd (43212-1360)
PHONE...........................833 732-3967
Benjamin Gibbs, *CEO*
EMP: 38 **EST:** 2016
SALES (est): 5.2MM **Privately Held**
Web: www.ready-robotics.com
SIC: 3569 Robots, assembly line: industrial and commercial

(G-5715)
RED BARAKUDA LLC
4439 Shoupmill Dr (43230-1489)
PHONE...........................614 596-5432
EMP: 7 **EST:** 2009
SALES (est): 244.83K **Privately Held**
SIC: 3949 7389 Flies, fishing: artificial; Business Activities at Non-Commercial Site

(G-5716)
REGALIA PRODUCTS INC
2117 S High St (43207-2428)
P.O. Box 1310 (43017-6310)
PHONE...........................614 579-8399
Kenneth Gay, *Prin*
Jeffery Ferguson, *Prin*
EMP: 10 **EST:** 2013
SALES (est): 879.8K **Privately Held**
Web: www.regaliaproducts.com
SIC: 2541 Store and office display cases and fixtures

(G-5717)
REINKE COMPANY INC
1616 Tremont Rd (43212-1127)
PHONE...........................614 570-2578
EMP: 6 **EST:** 2016
SALES (est): 103.91K **Privately Held**
Web: www.reinke.com
SIC: 3523 Farm machinery and equipment

(G-5718)
RESILIENT HOLDINGS INC
Also Called: Magnum Press
6155 Huntley Rd Ste F (43229-1096)
PHONE...........................614 847-5600
David G Umbreit, *Prin*
Douglas J Conley, *Prin*
EMP: 10 **EST:** 1988
SALES (est): 981.88K **Privately Held**
Web: www.magnum-press.com
SIC: 2752 Offset printing

(G-5719)
RESPIRONICS NOVAMETRIX LLC
9570 Logistics Ct (43217-7500)
PHONE...........................800 345-6443
EMP: 1951
SALES (corp-wide): 18.51B **Privately Held**
SIC: 3841 3845 Surgical and medical instruments; Electromedical equipment
HQ: Respironics Novametrix, Llc
3000 Minuteman Rd
Andover MA 01810
724 882-4120

(G-5720)
RESTRICTED KEY
635 E Weber Rd (43211-1040)
PHONE...........................614 405-2109
EMP: 6 **EST:** 2013
SALES (est): 104.79K **Privately Held**
Web: www.goldenbearlock.com
SIC: 3429 Keys, locks, and related hardware

(G-5721)
RETAIL PROJECT MANAGEMENT INC ◆
Also Called: Innovative Displays
2580 Westbelt Dr (43228-3827)
PHONE...........................614 299-9880
EMP: 6 **EST:** 2022
SALES (est): 502.22K **Privately Held**
SIC: 2893 Printing ink

(G-5722)
RICKLY HYDROLOGICAL CO
1700 Joyce Ave (43219-1026)
P.O. Box 2817 (43086-2817)
PHONE...........................614 297-9877
Michael Rickly, *Owner*
EMP: 24 **EST:** 1925
SALES (est): 3.94MM **Privately Held**
Web: www.prph2o.com
SIC: 3823 Industrial process measurement equipment

(G-5723)
RIMROCK CORPORATION
1700 Jetway Blvd (43219-1675)
PHONE...........................614 471-5926
▲ **EMP:** 50
Web: www.rimrockcorp.com
SIC: 3563 3569 3443 3541 Spraying outfits: metals, paints, and chemicals (compressor); Robots, assembly line: industrial and commercial; Ladles, metal plate; Machine tools, metal cutting type

(G-5724)
RIMROCK HOLDINGS CORPORATION
1700 Jetway Blvd (43219-1675)
PHONE...........................614 471-5926
Tom Dejong, *Pr*
Tom Dejong, *Pr*
EMP: 150 **EST:** 1999
SALES (est): 17.48MM
SALES (corp-wide): 4.19B **Publicly Held**
Web: www.rimrockcorp.com
SIC: 3563 3569 3443 3541 Spraying outfits: metals, paints, and chemicals (compressor); Robots, assembly line: industrial and commercial; Ladles, metal plate; Machine tools, metal cutting type
PA: Lincoln Electric Holdings, Inc.
22801 St Clair Ave
Cleveland OH 44117
216 481-8100

(G-5725)
RJM STAMPING CO
1641 Universal Rd (43207-1704)
PHONE...........................614 443-1191
Laura L Lloyd, *Pr*
Floyd Lloyd, *VP*
EMP: 12 **EST:** 1983
SQ FT: 9,016
SALES (est): 1MM **Privately Held**
Web: www.rjmstamping.com
SIC: 3469 Stamping metal for the trade

(G-5726)
RNM HOLDINGS INC
2350 Refugee Park (43207-2173)
PHONE...........................614 444-5556
EMP: 17
Web: www.crane1.com
SIC: 7353 5084 3536 Cranes and aerial lift equipment, rental or leasing; Cranes, industrial; Cranes, overhead traveling
PA: Rnm Holdings, Inc.
550 Conover Dr
Franklin OH 45005

(G-5727)
ROACH STUDIOS LLC
Also Called: Ctc / Roach Studios
441 E Hudson St (43202-2704)
PHONE...........................614 725-1405
EMP: 10 **EST:** 2011
SALES (est): 474.28K **Privately Held**
Web: www.roach-studios.com
SIC: 2396 2211 Screen printing on fabric articles; Apparel and outerwear fabrics, cotton

(G-5728)
ROADSAFE TRAFFIC SYSTEMS INC
1350 Stimmel Rd (43223-2917)
PHONE...........................614 274-9782
Steve Fisher, *Mgr*
EMP: 6
Web: www.roadsafetraffic.com
SIC: 3531 Construction machinery
PA: Roadsafe Traffic Systems, Inc.
8750 W Bryn Mawr Ave
Chicago IL 60631

(G-5729)
ROBEY TOOL INC
1593 E 5th Ave (43219-2572)
PHONE...........................614 251-0412
Wilbur Robey, *Pr*
EMP: 6 **EST:** 2019
SALES (est): 73.35K **Privately Held**
SIC: 3599 Machine shop, jobbing and repair

(G-5730)
ROBINSON INC
2948 Granada Hills Dr (43231-2904)
PHONE...........................614 898-0654
EMP: 7 **EST:** 2010
SALES (est): 50.49K **Privately Held**
Web: www.obrienrobinson.com
SIC: 3441 Fabricated structural metal

(G-5731)
ROSE PRODUCTS AND SERVICES INC

GEOGRAPHIC SECTION
Columbus - Franklin County (G-5756)

545 Stimmel Rd (43223-2901)
PHONE..............................614 443-7647
Robert Roth, *Pr*
EMP: 19 **EST:** 1926
SQ FT: 50,000
SALES (est): 965.1K **Privately Held**
SIC: 5087 2842 Janitors' supplies; Specialty cleaning

(G-5732)
ROY RETRAC INCORPORATED
Also Called: Phyllis Ann's
100 E Campus View Blvd Ste 250 (43235-4647)
PHONE..............................740 564-5552
Katherine Carter, *CEO*
EMP: 6 **EST:** 2020
SALES (est): 700K **Privately Held**
SIC: 2099 Food preparations, nec

(G-5733)
RR DONNELLEY & SONS COMPANY
Also Called: Bowne of Columbus
41 S High St Ste 3750 (43215-6161)
PHONE..............................614 221-8385
FAX: 614 221-8427
EMP: 8
SALES (corp-wide): 6.9B **Publicly Held**
SIC: 2791 Typesetting
PA: R. R. Donnelley & Sons Company
35 W Wacker Dr Ste 3650
Chicago IL 60601
312 326-8000

(G-5734)
RUSSELL GROUP UNITED LLC
Also Called: Trg United
1250 Arthur E Adams Dr Ste 205 (43221-3560)
P.O. Box 1087 (43054-1087)
PHONE..............................614 353-6853
George Nelson, *CEO*
EMP: 10 **EST:** 2013
SALES (est): 999.46K **Privately Held**
Web: www.trgunited.com
SIC: 3679 8712 8742 8748 Harness assemblies, for electronic use: wire or cable ; Architectural engineering; Management consulting services; Business consulting, nec

(G-5735)
RV MOBILE POWER LLC
830 Kinnear Rd (43212-1442)
PHONE..............................855 427-7978
James Conroy Ii, *CEO*
EMP: 9 **EST:** 2018
SALES (est): 2.67MM **Privately Held**
Web: www.rvmp.co
SIC: 5063 3621 3674 3639 Generators; Generators and sets, electric; Solar cells; Hot water heaters, household

(G-5736)
S BECKMAN PRINT GRPHIC SLTONS
Also Called: Beckman Xmo
376 Morrison Rd Ste D (43213-1447)
PHONE..............................614 864-2232
Tracy Beckman, *Pr*
EMP: 20 **EST:** 1979
SQ FT: 4,100
SALES (est): 451.54K **Privately Held**
SIC: 2752 Offset printing

(G-5737)
S&S SIGN SERVICE
485 Ternstedt Ln (43228-2128)
PHONE..............................614 279-9722
Robert Sherry, *CEO*
EMP: 6 **EST:** 2005
SALES (est): 384.6K **Privately Held**
SIC: 3993 Signs and advertising specialties

(G-5738)
SAFECOR HEALTH LLC
4000 Business Park Dr (43204-5023)
PHONE..............................614 351-6117
EMP: 8
Web: www.safecorhealth.com
SIC: 7389 2834 Packaging and labeling services; Pharmaceutical preparations
PA: Safecor Health, Llc
4060 Business Park Dr B
Columbus OH 43204

(G-5739)
SAFECOR HEALTH LLC (PA)
Also Called: R S C
4060 Business Pk Dr Ste B (43204-5046)
PHONE..............................781 933-8780
EMP: 10 **EST:** 2008
SALES (est): 21.99MM **Privately Held**
Web: www.safecorhealth.com
SIC: 7389 2834 Packaging and labeling services; Pharmaceutical preparations

(G-5740)
SAFELITE GROUP INC (DH)
Also Called: Safelite Autoglass
7400 Safelite Way (43235)
P.O. Box 182827 (43218)
PHONE..............................614 210-9000
Renee Cacchillo, *Pr*
Douglas Herron, *
Tim Spencer, *
Dino Lano, *
Natalie Crede, *
◆ **EMP:** 1000 **EST:** 1947
SALES (est): 1.38B
SALES (corp-wide): 3.16B **Privately Held**
Web: www.safelite.com
SIC: 7536 3231 6411 Automotive glass replacement shops; Windshields, glass: made from purchased glass; Insurance claim processing, except medical
HQ: Belron Group Sa
Boulevard Prince Henri 9b
Luxembourg 1724
27478860

(G-5741)
SALEM MANUFACTURING & SLS INC
171 N Hamilton Rd (43213-1300)
PHONE..............................614 572-4242
W Thomas Goble, *Pr*
EMP: 6 **EST:** 1978
SQ FT: 5,000
SALES (est): 703.47K **Privately Held**
SIC: 3599 Machine shop, jobbing and repair

(G-5742)
SALINDIA LLC
2756 Eastland Mall (43232-4901)
PHONE..............................614 501-4799
EMP: 6 **EST:** 2008
SALES (est): 38.97K **Privately Held**
SIC: 2389 Men's miscellaneous accessories

(G-5743)
SAMMY S AUTO DETAIL
3514 Cleveland Ave (43224-2908)
PHONE..............................614 263-2728
Sam Cavin, *CEO*
EMP: 10 **EST:** 2003
SALES (est): 501.46K **Privately Held**
Web: www.sammysautospa.com
SIC: 3589 7538 Car washing machinery; General automotive repair shops

(G-5744)
SAMSON
772 N High St Ste 101 (43215-1457)
PHONE..............................614 504-8038
Nicholas Dwane Starns, *Prin*
EMP: 8 **EST:** 2015
SALES (est): 427.64K **Privately Held**
Web: www.samsonmensemporium.com
SIC: 2326 Men's and boy's work clothing

(G-5745)
SANDVIK INC
Also Called: Sandvik Hyperion
6325 Huntley Rd (43229-1007)
PHONE..............................614 438-6579
EMP: 132
SALES (corp-wide): 11.77B **Privately Held**
Web: www.home.sandvik
SIC: 3316 Strip, steel, cold-rolled, nec: from purchased hot-rolled,
HQ: Sandvik, Inc.
1483 Dogwood Way
Mebane NC 27302
919 563-5008

(G-5746)
SANTEC RESOURCES INC
2324 Myrtle Valley Dr (43228-8244)
PHONE..............................614 664-9540
Raghu Kondakrindhi, *Prin*
EMP: 15 **EST:** 2007
SQ FT: 1,300
SALES (est): 523.57K **Privately Held**
SIC: 1382 8742 7379 7371 Oil and gas exploration services; Management consulting services; Computer related consulting services; Computer software development

(G-5747)
SARAGA NORTHERN LIGHTS LLC
Also Called: Saraga International Food
3353 Cleveland Ave (43224-3644)
PHONE..............................614 928-3100
EMP: 10 **EST:** 2019
SALES (est): 429.02K **Privately Held**
SIC: 3496 Grocery carts, made from purchased wire

(G-5748)
SAWMILL COMMONS 4420
209 E State St (43215-4309)
P.O. Box 2050 (43216-2050)
PHONE..............................614 764-7878
EMP: 6 **EST:** 2008
SALES (est): 176.97K **Privately Held**
Web: www.sawmillcommons.com
SIC: 2421 Sawmills and planing mills, general

(G-5749)
SAWMILL ROAD MANAGEMENT CO LLC (PA)
370 S 5th St (43215-5433)
PHONE..............................937 342-9071
Judy Ross, *Managing Member*
EMP: 30 **EST:** 1996
SALES (est): 1.94MM
SALES (corp-wide): 1.94MM **Privately Held**
SIC: 6531 2421 Buying agent, real estate; Sawmills and planing mills, general

(G-5750)
SCAREFACTORY INC
350 Mccormick Blvd # C (43213-1550)
PHONE..............................614 565-3590
David Fachman, *Pr*
EMP: 15 **EST:** 1993
SQ FT: 38,000
SALES (est): 1.66MM **Privately Held**
Web: www.scarefactory.com
SIC: 3999 Theatrical scenery

(G-5751)
SCHODORF TRUCK BODY & EQP CO
885 Harmon Ave (43223-2411)
P.O. Box 23322 (43223-0322)
PHONE..............................614 228-6793
Joe Schodorf, *Pr*
Paul F Schodorf, *
EMP: 21 **EST:** 1882
SQ FT: 52,000
SALES (est): 3.4MM **Privately Held**
Web: www.schodorftruck.com
SIC: 5012 3713 3211 Truck bodies; Truck bodies (motor vehicles); Flat glass

(G-5752)
SCHOLZ & EY ENGRAVERS INC
1558 Parsons Ave (43207-1252)
PHONE..............................614 444-8052
Kevin Scholz, *Pr*
Stephen Scholz, *Prin*
EMP: 11 **EST:** 1950
SQ FT: 3,100
SALES (est): 348.02K **Privately Held**
SIC: 3479 5947 5094 5199 Engraving jewelry, silverware, or metal; Gift shop; Jewelry; Gifts and novelties

(G-5753)
SCHOOL PRIDE LIMITED
3511 Johnny Appleseed Ct (43231-4985)
PHONE..............................614 568-0697
Daren Brown, *Pr*
Janet Brown, *
EMP: 23 **EST:** 2000
SALES (est): 1.89MM **Privately Held**
Web: www.schoolpride.com
SIC: 2399 Banners, pennants, and flags

(G-5754)
SCI ENGINEERED MATERIALS INC
Also Called: SCI
2839 Charter St (43228-4607)
PHONE..............................614 486-0261
Jeremiah R Young, *Pr*
Laura F Shunk, *Ch Bd*
Gerald S Blaskie, *VP*
EMP: 23 **EST:** 1987
SQ FT: 32,000
SALES (est): 27.98MM **Privately Held**
Web: www.sciengineeredmaterials.com
SIC: 3674 Semiconductors and related devices

(G-5755)
SCORECARDS UNLIMITED LLC
Also Called: Golf Dsign Srecards Unlimited
1820 W Dublin Granville Rd (43085-3461)
PHONE..............................614 885-0796
Paul Filing, *Managing Member*
EMP: 8 **EST:** 1976
SALES (est): 882.85K **Privately Held**
Web: www.scorecardsunlimited.net
SIC: 2752 Offset printing

(G-5756)
SCRIPTEL CORPORATION
2222 Dividend Dr (43228-3808)
PHONE..............................877 848-6824
John Powers, *CEO*
Kristal Scott, *Mgr*
▲ **EMP:** 17 **EST:** 2001
SALES (est): 4.82MM **Privately Held**
Web: www.scriptel.com
SIC: 3577 Computer peripheral equipment, nec
PA: Sutisoft, Inc.
333 Camarillo Ter Ste 2

Sunnyvale CA 94085

(G-5757)
SEEKIRK INC
2420 Scioto Harper Dr (43204-3480)
PHONE.................................614 278-9200
Douglas Seeley, *CEO*
Pamela Seeley, *Treas*
EMP: 14 **EST:** 1982
SQ FT: 11,000
SALES (est): 2.16MM **Privately Held**
Web: www.seekirk.com
SIC: 3823 Annunciators, relay and solid state types

(G-5758)
SELECTEON CORPORATION
2041 Arlingate Ln (43228-4113)
PHONE.................................614 710-1132
Thomas J Ward, *Pr*
EMP: 26 **EST:** 2004
SQ FT: 20,000
SALES (est): 2.49MM **Privately Held**
Web: www.selecteon.com
SIC: 3599 Machine shop, jobbing and repair

(G-5759)
SENTEK CORPORATION
1300 Memory Ln N (43209-2736)
PHONE.................................614 586-1123
Niklas Almstedt, *Pr*
Ann Almstedt, *VP*
EMP: 7 **EST:** 1999
SQ FT: 9,000
SALES (est): 1.25MM **Privately Held**
Web: www.sentekcorp.com
SIC: 3547 8748 Ferrous and nonferrous mill equipment, auxiliary; Systems analysis and engineering consulting services

(G-5760)
SERMONIX PHARMACEUTICALS INC
250 E Broad St Ste 250 (43215-3778)
PHONE.................................614 864-4919
Miriam Portman, *CEO*
David Portman, *CEO*
Miriam Portman, *COO*
EMP: 10 **EST:** 2019
SALES (est): 1.76MM **Privately Held**
Web: www.sermonixpharma.com
SIC: 2834 Pills, pharmaceutical

(G-5761)
SHELLI R MCMURRAY
1360 Louvaine Dr Rear (43223-3445)
PHONE.................................614 275-4381
Shelli R Mcmurray, *Prin*
EMP: 6 **EST:** 2010
SALES (est): 87.75K **Privately Held**
SIC: 2891 Adhesives

(G-5762)
SHEMS INC
154 N Hague Ave (43204-2609)
PHONE.................................614 279-2342
EMP: 6 **EST:** 2011
SALES (est): 164.77K **Privately Held**
SIC: 3743 Railroad equipment

(G-5763)
SHINANO PNEUMATIC INDS USA INC
1571 Westbelt Dr (43228-3839)
PHONE.................................614 529-6600
Daisuke Yamamoto, *Admn*
EMP: 6 **EST:** 2015
SALES (est): 94.46K **Privately Held**
SIC: 3423 Hand and edge tools, nec

(G-5764)
SHOEMAKER ELECTRIC COMPANY
Also Called: Shoemaker Industrial Solutions
831 Bonham Ave (43211-2999)
PHONE.................................614 294-5626
Fred N Kletrovets, *Pr*
Betty Kletrovets, *
Teri Richardson, *
▲ **EMP:** 29 **EST:** 1935
SQ FT: 16,000
SALES (est): 5.16MM **Privately Held**
Web: www.shoemakerindustrial.com
SIC: 7694 5063 Electric motor repair; Motors, electric

(G-5765)
SHOUT OUT LOUD PRINTS
809 Phillipi Rd (43228-1041)
PHONE.................................614 432-8990
EMP: 6 **EST:** 2010
SALES (est): 215.87K **Privately Held**
Web: www.shoutoutloudprints.com
SIC: 2752 Commercial printing, lithographic

(G-5766)
SHOW READY PROFESSIONALS
7299 Fall Creek Ln (43235-2072)
PHONE.................................614 817-5849
Ashley Shears, *Prin*
EMP: 6 **EST:** 2015
SALES (est): 90.17K **Privately Held**
SIC: 3273 Ready-mixed concrete

(G-5767)
SIGNAL INTERACTIVE
401 W Town St # B (43215-4034)
PHONE.................................614 360-3938
EMP: 6 **EST:** 2017
SALES (est): 245.99K **Privately Held**
Web: www.signal-interactive.com
SIC: 7372 Application computer software

(G-5768)
SIGNATURE CABINETRY INC
1285 Alum Creek Dr (43209-2721)
PHONE.................................614 252-2227
Jack E Mc Vey, *Pr*
EMP: 15 **EST:** 1993
SALES (est): 2.47MM **Privately Held**
Web: www.signaturecabinetryinc.com
SIC: 2434 Wood kitchen cabinets

(G-5769)
SIGNATURE FLEXIBLE PACKG LLC
2901 E 4th Ave (43219-2896)
PHONE.................................614 252-2121
Adrian Backer, *Brnch Mgr*
EMP: 14
SALES (corp-wide): 22.97MM **Privately Held**
Web: www.dazpak.com
SIC: 2891 2673 Adhesives and sealants; Bags: plastic, laminated, and coated
PA: Signature Flexible Packaging, Llc
  19310 San Jose Ave
  City Of Industry CA 91748
  909 598-7844

(G-5770)
SIGNCOM INCORPORATED
527 W Rich St (43215-4903)
PHONE.................................614 228-9999
Jim Hartley, *Pr*
EMP: 10 **EST:** 1982
SALES (est): 787K **Privately Held**
Web: www.signcominc.com
SIC: 3993 Neon signs

(G-5771)
SIGNME LLC
Also Called: Binkley, Geoffrey
39 E Gay St (43215-3103)
PHONE.................................614 221-7803
Geoffrey M Binkley, *Prin*
EMP: 7 **EST:** 2006
SALES (est): 160K **Privately Held**
SIC: 2399 Fabricated textile products, nec

(G-5772)
SIMPLE TIMES LLC
750 Cross Pointe Rd Ste M (43230-6692)
P.O. Box 639 (43004-0639)
PHONE.................................614 504-3551
EMP: 9 **EST:** 2018
SALES (est): 1.03MM **Privately Held**
Web: www.simpletimesmixers.com
SIC: 2085 Cordials and premixed alcoholic cocktails

(G-5773)
SIMPSON STRONG-TIE COMPANY INC
2600 International St (43228-4617)
PHONE.................................614 876-8060
Dave Williams, *Brnch Mgr*
EMP: 239
SALES (corp-wide): 2.21B **Publicly Held**
Web: www.strongtie.com
SIC: 5082 3643 3452 Construction and mining machinery; Current-carrying wiring services; Bolts, nuts, rivets, and washers
HQ: Simpson Strong-Tie Company Inc.
  5956 W Las Positas Blvd
  Pleasanton CA 94588
  925 560-9000

(G-5774)
SIRAJ RECOVERY LLC
4088 Seigman Ave (43213-2324)
PHONE.................................614 893-3507
EMP: 6
SALES (est): 226.5K **Privately Held**
SIC: 3799 7389 Towing bars and systems; Business services, nec

(G-5775)
SOLIDSTATE CONTROLS LLC (HQ)
Also Called: Ametek Solidstate Controls
875 Dearborn Dr (43085-1596)
PHONE.................................614 846-7500
▲ **EMP:** 160 **EST:** 1962
SALES (est): 52.58MM
SALES (corp-wide): 6.6B **Publicly Held**
Web: www.solidstatecontrolsinc.com
SIC: 3629 Power conversion units, a.c. to d.c.: static-electric
PA: Ametek, Inc.
  1100 Cassatt Rd
  Berwyn PA 19312
  610 647-2121

(G-5776)
SOLLIS THERAPEUTICS INC
1274 Kinnear Rd (43212-1154)
PHONE.................................614 701-9894
Greg Fiore, *CEO*
Bryan Jones, *CEO*
EMP: 20 **EST:** 2017
SALES (est): 1.09MM **Privately Held**
Web: www.sollistx.com
SIC: 2834 Pharmaceutical preparations

(G-5777)
SOLSTICE SLEEP PRODUCTS INC (PA)
Also Called: Bel-Air Mattress Company
3720 W Broad St (43228-1443)
PHONE.................................614 279-8850
Steve Belford, *Pr*
◆ **EMP:** 21 **EST:** 2009
SALES (est): 54.23MM
SALES (corp-wide): 54.23MM **Privately Held**
Web: www.jamisonbedding.com
SIC: 2515 Mattresses and bedsprings

(G-5778)
SONOCO PRODUCTS COMPANY
444 Mccormick Blvd (43213-1525)
PHONE.................................614 759-8470
Greg Ickes, *Prin*
EMP: 26
SALES (corp-wide): 6.78B **Publicly Held**
Web: www.sonoco.com
SIC: 2631 2671 2653 2655 Paperboard mills ; Paper; coated and laminated packaging; Corrugated and solid fiber boxes; Fiber cans, drums, and similar products
PA: Sonoco Products Company
  1 N 2nd St
  Hartsville SC 29550
  843 383-7000

(G-5779)
SOONDOOK LLC
6344 Nicholas Dr (43235-5206)
PHONE.................................614 389-5757
EMP: 20 **EST:** 2018
SALES (est): 975.16K **Privately Held**
Web: www.soondook.net
SIC: 2752 Commercial printing, lithographic

(G-5780)
SPECIAL DESIGN PRODUCTS INC
520 Industrial Mile Rd (43228-2413)
P.O. Box 28126 (43228-0126)
PHONE.................................614 272-6700
Nancy Evanichko, *Pr*
Stan Evanichko, *
Suzette King, *Stockholder**
EMP: 45 **EST:** 1990
SALES (est): 9.26MM **Privately Held**
Web: www.sdpfab.com
SIC: 3086 Packaging and shipping materials, foamed plastics

(G-5781)
SPECIALTY AMERICA INC
8351 N High St Ste 285 (43235-1440)
PHONE.................................516 252-2438
EMP: 17 **EST:** 2014
SALES (est): 140.7K **Privately Held**
SIC: 2621 Wrapping and packaging papers
PA: Specialty Polyfilms (India) Private Limited
  F-89 Midc Area Waluj
  Aurangabad MH 43113

(G-5782)
SPECIALTY FILMS INC
2887 Johnstown Rd (43219-1719)
PHONE.................................614 471-9100
EMP: 100 **EST:** 1994
SQ FT: 7,500
SALES (est): 2.65MM
SALES (corp-wide): 82.22MM **Privately Held**
SIC: 3081 Plastics film and sheet
PA: Plastic Suppliers, Inc.
  2400 Marilyn Ln
  Columbus OH 43219
  614 471-9100

(G-5783)
SPECIALTY PRINTING AND PROC
4670 Groves Rd (43232-4164)
PHONE.................................614 322-9035
Frank Schreck, *Owner*
EMP: 17 **EST:** 2000

GEOGRAPHIC SECTION

Columbus - Franklin County (G-5808)

SALES (est): 2.14MM **Privately Held**
Web: www.specialty-printing.com
SIC: 2759 Screen printing

(G-5784)
SPECIALTY SVCS CABINETRY INC
1253 Essex Ave (43201-2927)
PHONE..................................614 421-1599
Michael Melton, *Pr*
Joann Melton, *Sec*
EMP: 8 EST: 1985
SALES (est): 770.84K **Privately Held**
Web: www.specialty-services.net
SIC: 2521 2511 Cabinets, office: wood; Wood household furniture

(G-5785)
SPECTRUM NEWS OHIO
580 N 4th St Ste 350 (43215-2159)
PHONE..................................614 384-2640
EMP: 20 EST: 2019
SALES (est): 228.06K **Privately Held**
Web: www.ohiotavernnews.com
SIC: 2711 Newspapers, publishing and printing

(G-5786)
SPIRIT AVIONICS LTD (PA)
Also Called: Spirit Aeronautics
465 Waterbury Ct Ste C (43230-5312)
PHONE..................................614 237-4271
Tony Bailey, *Pr*
EMP: 15 EST: 2000
SALES (est): 7.61MM **Privately Held**
Web: www.spiritaeronautics.com
SIC: 7629 4581 2396 3629 Aircraft electrical equipment repair; Aircraft servicing and repairing; Automotive trimmings, fabric; Electronic generation equipment

(G-5787)
SPLENDID LLC
1415 E Dublin Granville Rd Ste 219 (43229-3356)
P.O. Box 141528 (43214-6528)
PHONE..................................614 396-6481
Shurki Mire, *Managing Member*
Moe Lee, *Prin*
EMP: 14 EST: 2017
SALES (est): 1.36MM **Privately Held**
SIC: 3531 Crane carriers

(G-5788)
SPRING WORKS INCORPORATED
3201 Alberta St (43204-2029)
PHONE..................................614 351-9345
Edgar Weil, *CEO*
EMP: 20 EST: 1981
SQ FT: 27,000
SALES (est): 2.45MM **Privately Held**
Web: www.thespringworks.com
SIC: 3495 Mechanical springs, precision

(G-5789)
STAR JET LLC
4130 E 5th Ave (43219-1802)
PHONE..................................614 338-4379
EMP: 25 EST: 2005
SALES (est): 872.94K **Privately Held**
SIC: 3721 Aircraft

(G-5790)
STARECASING SYSTEMS INC
Also Called: Starecasing
2822 Fisher Rd (43204-3538)
PHONE..................................312 203-5632
EMP: 8 EST: 2008
SALES (est): 429.27K **Privately Held**
Web: www.starecasing.com

SIC: 2435 Hardwood plywood, prefinished

(G-5791)
STATE PRINTING
4200 Surface Rd (43228-1313)
PHONE..................................614 995-1740
EMP: 9 EST: 2019
SALES (est): 292.35K **Privately Held**
SIC: 2741 Miscellaneous publishing

(G-5792)
STAUFS COFFEE ROASTERS LIMITED
705 Hadley Dr (43228-1029)
PHONE..................................614 486-4479
EMP: 8
SALES (est): 561.37K **Privately Held**
Web: www.staufs.com
SIC: 2095 Coffee roasting (except by wholesale grocers)

(G-5793)
STEER & GEAR INC
Also Called: Steer & Geer
1000 Barnett Rd (43227-1188)
PHONE..................................614 231-4064
Gerald Ries, *Pr*
Susan Ries, *
EMP: 11 EST: 1979
SALES (est): 447.82K **Privately Held**
Web: www.steerandgear.com
SIC: 3714 Power steering equipment, motor vehicle

(G-5794)
STERLING PROCESS EQUIPMENT & SERVICES INC (PA)
333 Mccormick Blvd (43213-1526)
PHONE..................................614 868-5151
EMP: 24 EST: 1983
SALES (est): 6.5MM
SALES (corp-wide): 6.5MM **Privately Held**
Web: www.sterlingpe.com
SIC: 3556 1623 Food products machinery; Pipeline construction, nsk

(G-5795)
STEWARD EDGE BUS SOLUTIONS
23 N Westgate Ave (43204-1344)
PHONE..................................614 826-5305
Linda Steward, *Pr*
EMP: 10 EST: 2016
SALES (est): 322.53K **Privately Held**
SIC: 8741 7371 8721 7372 Business management; Computer software systems analysis and design, custom; Billing and bookkeeping service; Operating systems computer software

(G-5796)
STYLE-LINE INCORPORATED (PA)
Also Called: Chelsea House Fabrics
901 W 3rd Ave Ste A (43212-3131)
P.O. Box 2706 (43216-2706)
PHONE..................................614 291-0600
Laura R Prophater, *Pr*
William H Prophater, *
EMP: 35 EST: 1969
SQ FT: 54,000
SALES (est): 4.15MM
SALES (corp-wide): 4.15MM **Privately Held**
Web: www.lookhuman.com
SIC: 5023 5131 2391 1799 Venetian blinds; Drapery material, woven; Curtains, window: made from purchased materials; Drapery track installation

(G-5797)
SUBURBAN STL SUP CO LTD PARTNR
Also Called: Suburban Steel of Indiana
1900 Deffenbaugh Ct (43230-8604)
PHONE..................................317 783-6555
Mark Debellis, *Pr*
EMP: 8
SALES (corp-wide): 9.66MM **Privately Held**
Web: www.suburbansteelsupply.com
SIC: 3441 Fabricated structural metal
PA: Suburban Steel Supply Co. Limited Partnership
1900 Deffenbaugh Ct
Gahanna OH 43230
614 737-5501

(G-5798)
SUNRISE FOODS INC
Also Called: Sunrise Foods
2097 Corvair Blvd (43207-1701)
PHONE..................................614 276-2880
Mark Pi Junior, *Pr*
Mark Pi Senior Stk Hld, *Prin*
Men Ma Stk Hld, *Prin*
EMP: 48 EST: 1997
SQ FT: 38,000
SALES (est): 9.28MM **Privately Held**
Web: www.sunrisefoodsohio.com
SIC: 2038 2013 2035 2099 Ethnic foods, nec, frozen; Frozen meats, from purchased meat; Pickles, sauces, and salad dressings; Food preparations, nec

(G-5799)
SUPERIOR METAL WORX LLC
1239 Alum Creek Dr (43209-2721)
PHONE..................................614 879-9400
EMP: 15 EST: 2013
SALES (est): 1.8MM **Privately Held**
Web: www.superiormetalworx.com
SIC: 3441 Fabricated structural metal

(G-5800)
SUPERIOR PRODUCTION LLC (PA)
Also Called: Superior Die Tool & Machine Co
2301 Fairwood Ave (43207-2768)
PHONE..................................614 444-2181
▲ EMP: 200 EST: 1914
SALES (est): 49.65MM
SALES (corp-wide): 49.65MM **Privately Held**
Web: www.superior-dietool.com
SIC: 3714 3544 3469 5531 Bumpers and bumperettes, motor vehicle; Special dies and tools; Metal stampings, nec; Automotive accessories

(G-5801)
SUPERIOR WELDING CO
906 S Nelson Rd (43205-3098)
PHONE..................................614 252-8539
Steve Shipley, *Pr*
Sandra R Shipley, *VP*
EMP: 14 EST: 1947
SQ FT: 22,000
SALES (est): 432.37K **Privately Held**
Web: www.superior-welding.com
SIC: 3599 Machine shop, jobbing and repair

(G-5802)
SUPPLY TECHNOLOGIES LLC
590 Claycraft Rd (43230-5319)
PHONE..................................614 759-9939
Thomas Giscizinski, *Mgr*
EMP: 24
SALES (corp-wide): 1.66B **Publicly Held**
Web: www.supplytechnologies.com

SIC: 3452 Bolts, nuts, rivets, and washers
HQ: Supply Technologies Llc
6065 Parkland Blvd
Cleveland OH 44124
440 947-2100

(G-5803)
SUSTAINMENT ACTIONS LLC
20 S 3rd St Ste 210 (43215-4206)
PHONE..................................330 805-3468
Bradford Klusmann, *Prin*
EMP: 11 EST: 2021
SALES (est): 485.88K **Privately Held**
SIC: 3199 Leather goods, nec

(G-5804)
SWAPIL INC
2740 Airport Dr Ste 310 (43219-2295)
P.O. Box 4087 (60174-9081)
▼ EMP: 55 EST: 1986
SALES (est): 22.91MM
SALES (corp-wide): 1.15B **Privately Held**
SIC: 3089 Stock shapes, plastics
PA: New Enterprise Stone & Lime Co., Inc.
3912 Brumbaugh Rd
New Enterprise PA 16664
814 766-2211

(G-5805)
T E Q HI INC
1525 Alum Creek Dr (43209)
PHONE..................................877 448-3701
Satyen Prabhu, *Pr*
Fatyen Prabhu, *Pr*
EMP: 35 EST: 1988
SQ FT: 17,000
SALES (est): 7.5MM
SALES (corp-wide): 645.5MM **Privately Held**
SIC: 3567 Industrial furnaces and ovens
HQ: Inductotherm Corp.
10 Indel Ave
Rancocas NJ 08073
609 267-9000

(G-5806)
TAIKISHA USA INC
1939 Refugee Rd (43207)
PHONE..................................614 444-5602
Mark Swedni, *Brnch Mgr*
EMP: 65
Web: www.tksindustrial.com
SIC: 3559 Metal finishing equipment for plating, etc.
HQ: Taikisha Usa, Inc
901 Tower Dr Ste 300
Troy MI 48098
248 786-5000

(G-5807)
TALLY HO SLIPCOVERS
2019 Andover Rd (43212-1006)
PHONE..................................614 448-6170
EMP: 6 EST: 2012
SALES (est): 112.45K **Privately Held**
SIC: 2392 Slip covers: made of fabric, plastic, etc.

(G-5808)
TARAHILL INC
Also Called: Pet Goods Mfg
3985 Groves Rd (43232-4138)
PHONE..................................706 864-0808
Floyd E Seal, *Pr*
◆ EMP: 16 EST: 1972
SALES (est): 390.13K **Privately Held**
SIC: 3199 Dog furnishings: collars, leashes, muzzles, etc.: leather

---

(PA)=Parent Co (HQ)=Headquarters
✪ = New Business established in last 2 years

Columbus - Franklin County (G-5809)

(G-5809)
TARIGMA CORPORATION
Also Called: Ooteksofpak
6161 Busch Blvd Ste 110 (43229-2553)
PHONE..............................614 436-3734
J Declan Smith, *Pr*
Keith Sarbaugh, *Treas*
Winthrop Worcester, *Sec*
EMP: 10 **EST:** 1995
SQ FT: 1,000
SALES (est): 958.42K **Privately Held**
Web: www.tarigma.com
SIC: 7372 Prepackaged software

(G-5810)
TARRIER FOODS CORP
Also Called: Tarrier
2700 International St (43228-4640)
PHONE..............................614 876-8594
Timothy A Tarrier, *Pr*
Ann Tarrier, *
Julia A Creeme, *
EMP: 42 **EST:** 1978
SQ FT: 54,000
SALES (est): 35.34MM **Privately Held**
Web: www.tarrierfoods.com
SIC: 5149 5145 2099 Dried or canned foods; Nuts, salted or roasted; Food preparations, nec

(G-5811)
TARRIER STEEL COMPANY INC
1379 S 22nd St (43206)
P.O. Box 7885 (43207)
PHONE..............................614 444-4000
Todd Tarrier, *Pr*
EMP: 41 **EST:** 1920
SQ FT: 36,000
SALES (est): 8.75MM **Privately Held**
Web: www.tarrier.com
SIC: 3441 3446 Fabricated structural metal; Ornamental metalwork

(G-5812)
TAYLOR COMMUNICATIONS INC
3950 Business Park Dr (43204-5008)
PHONE..............................614 351-6868
EMP: 13
SALES (corp-wide): 3.81B **Privately Held**
Web: www.taylor.com
SIC: 2752 4225 Commercial printing, lithographic; General warehousing and storage
HQ: Taylor Communications, Inc.
1725 Roe Crest Dr
North Mankato MN 56003
866 541-0937

(G-5813)
TAYLOR METAL
6400 Huntley Rd Ste 102 (43229-1043)
PHONE..............................614 401-8007
EMP: 6 **EST:** 2017
SALES (est): 47.75K **Privately Held**
Web: www.taylormetalsohio.com
SIC: 3444 Sheet metalwork

(G-5814)
TDS CUSTOM CABINETS LLC
1819 Walcutt Rd Ste 9 (43228-9149)
P.O. Box 56 (43026-0056)
PHONE..............................614 517-2220
Dustin Sauer, *Pr*
Terry Sauer, *Managing Member*
EMP: 6 **EST:** 2006
SQ FT: 36,000
SALES (est): 2.43MM **Privately Held**
Web: www.tdsmanufacturingllc.com
SIC: 2434 Wood kitchen cabinets

(G-5815)
TEAM INC
Tsi Manufacturing
3005 Silver Dr (43224-3945)
PHONE..............................614 263-1808
Sam Dematteo, *VP*
EMP: 14
SALES (corp-wide): 862.62MM **Publicly Held**
Web: www.teaminc.com
SIC: 3398 Metal heat treating
HQ: Team, Inc.
5095 Paris St
Denver CO 80239

(G-5816)
TECH-SONIC INC
2710 Sawbury Blvd (43235-1821)
PHONE..............................614 792-3117
Byoung Ou, *Pr*
Hyun Ou, *Treas*
EMP: 14 **EST:** 2005
SALES (est): 2.2MM **Privately Held**
Web: www.tech-sonic.us
SIC: 3548 3699 Electric welding equipment; Generators, ultrasonic

(G-5817)
TECH4IMAGING LLC
1910 Crown Park Ct (43235-2404)
PHONE..............................614 214-2655
Qussai Marashdeh, *CEO*
EMP: 12 **EST:** 2007
SALES (est): 1.15MM **Privately Held**
Web: www.tech4imaging.com
SIC: 7371 8711 3826 5049 Computer software development; Consulting engineer; Laser scientific and engineering instruments; Scientific and engineering equipment and supplies

(G-5818)
TERRASMART LLC
1000 Buckeye Park Rd (43207-2509)
PHONE..............................239 362-0211
EMP: 20
SALES (corp-wide): 1.38B **Publicly Held**
Web: www.terrasmart.com
SIC: 3441 3317 1711 Fabricated structural metal; Boiler tubes (wrought); Solar energy contractor
HQ: Terrasmart Llc
14590 Global Pkwy
Fort Myers FL 33913

(G-5819)
TGS SYSTEMS LLC
1060 Kingsmill Pkwy (43229-1143)
PHONE..............................614 431-6927
EMP: 7 **EST:** 2017
SALES (est): 611.8K **Privately Held**
SIC: 1382 Oil and gas exploration services

(G-5820)
THE COLUMBUS SHOW CASE COMPANY
Also Called: CSC Worldwide
4401 Equity Dr (43228-3856)
P.O. Box 21205 (43221-0205)
▲ **EMP:** 170
SIC: 2541 3585 2522 Showcases, except refrigerated: wood; Counters and counter display cases, refrigerated; Panel systems and partitions, office: except wood

(G-5821)
THE CRANE GROUP COMPANIES LIMITED (HQ)
330 W Spring St Ste 200 (43215-2389)
P.O. Box 1047 (43216)
PHONE..............................614 754-3000
EMP: 28 **EST:** 1947
SALES (est): 117.63MM **Privately Held**
Web: www.cranegroup.com
SIC: 3089 Extruded finished plastics products, nec
PA: Crane Group Co.
330 W Spring St Ste 200
Columbus OH 43215

(G-5822)
THE HARTMAN CORP
Also Called: Hartman Trophies
3216 Morse Rd (43231-6132)
PHONE..............................614 475-5035
Larry Hartman, *Pr*
Linda Hartman, *Sec*
Gary Hartman, *VP*
EMP: 6 **EST:** 1968
SQ FT: 6,500
SALES (est): 887.68K **Privately Held**
Web: www.hartmancorporation.com
SIC: 5999 5941 5947 3993 Trophies and plaques; Bowling equipment and supplies; Trading cards: baseball or other sports, entertainment, etc.; Signs and advertising specialties

(G-5823)
THE OLEN CORPORATION (PA)
4755 S High St (43207-4080)
PHONE..............................614 491-1515
TOLL FREE: 800
EMP: 62 **EST:** 1951
SALES (est): 26.19MM
SALES (corp-wide): 26.19MM **Privately Held**
Web: www.kokosing.biz
SIC: 1442 Construction sand and gravel

(G-5824)
THERMAL SOLUTIONS INC
3005 Silver Dr (43224-3945)
PHONE..............................614 263-1808
EMP: 6
SALES (est): 14.37MM **Privately Held**
Web: www.thermalsolutionsinc.com
SIC: 3398 Metal heat treating
PA: Thermal Solutions, Inc.
9329 County Rd 107
Proctorville OH 45669
740 886-2861

(G-5825)
THURNS BAKERY & DELI
541 S 3rd St (43215-5721)
PHONE..............................614 221-9246
Marilyn Plank, *Pr*
Dan Plank, *
Chris Plank, *
Bill Plank, *
EMP: 11 **EST:** 1972
SQ FT: 2,100
SALES (est): 236.4K **Privately Held**
SIC: 5461 5149 2051 Retail bakeries; Bakery products; Bread, cake, and related products

(G-5826)
TIBA LLC (PA)
Also Called: Signature Control Systems
2228 Citygate Dr (43219-3565)
PHONE..............................614 328-2040
Jon Dawsher, *Managing Member*
EMP: 30 **EST:** 1987
SALES (est): 9.98MM
SALES (corp-wide): 9.98MM **Privately Held**
Web: www.tibaparking.com
SIC: 3559 Parking facility equipment and supplies

(G-5827)
TOK DAWGS CHICKEN LLC
1743 Quigley Rd (43227-3435)
PHONE..............................614 813-2698
EMP: 6
SALES (est): 78.58K **Privately Held**
SIC: 2499 Food handling and processing products, wood

(G-5828)
TORTILLAS LA REYNA LLC
2171 E Dublin Granville Rd (43229-3512)
PHONE..............................630 247-9453
Alfredo Flores, *Managing Member*
EMP: 7
SALES (est): 78.58K **Privately Held**
SIC: 2099 Tortillas, fresh or refrigerated

(G-5829)
TOTAL TENNIS INC
Also Called: TTI Sports Equipment
1733 Cardiff Rd (43221-3806)
PHONE..............................614 488-5004
James Lathrop, *Pr*
Sally Ann Lathrop, *VP*
EMP: 10 **EST:** 1979
SALES (est): 683.75K **Privately Held**
Web: www.totaltennisinc.com
SIC: 3949 5091 Tennis equipment and supplies; Sporting and recreation goods

(G-5830)
TRANE US INC
Trane
2300 Citygate Dr Ste 100 (43219-3664)
PHONE..............................614 473-3131
Al Fullerton, *Dist Mgr*
EMP: 150
Web: www.trane.com
SIC: 3585 Refrigeration and heating equipment
HQ: Trane U.S. Inc.
800 Beaty St Ste E
Davidson NC 28036
704 655-4000

(G-5831)
TRANE US INC
Also Called: Trane National Account Service
2300 Citygate Dr Ste 250 (43219-3664)
PHONE..............................614 473-8701
EMP: 6
Web: www.trane.com
SIC: 3585 Refrigeration and heating equipment
HQ: Trane U.S. Inc.
800 Beaty St Ste E
Davidson NC 28036
704 655-4000

(G-5832)
TRANSMET CORPORATION
4290 Perimeter Dr (43228-1036)
PHONE..............................614 276-5522
Douglas Shull, *Pr*
▼ **EMP:** 8 **EST:** 1979
SQ FT: 17,000
SALES (est): 2.68MM **Privately Held**
Web: www.transmet.com
SIC: 3399 Flakes, metal

(G-5833)
TRAXLER PRINTING
310 W Pacemont Rd Apt A (43202-1071)
PHONE..............................614 593-1270
Zachary Traxler, *CEO*
EMP: 8 **EST:** 2016

GEOGRAPHIC SECTION

Columbus - Franklin County (G-5860)

SALES (est): 204.72K **Privately Held**
Web: www.traxlerprinting.com
SIC: 2752 Offset printing

(G-5834)
TRAXLER TEES LLC
3029 Silver Dr (43224-3945)
PHONE.................................614 593-1270
EMP: 11
SALES (est): 507.9K **Privately Held**
SIC: 2759 Screen printing

(G-5835)
TREWBRIC III INC
1701 Moler Rd (43207)
P.O. Box 07847 (43207)
PHONE.................................614 444-2184
Ted Coons, *Ch*
Ted Coons, *CEO*
Don Mcnutt, *Pr*
Lynn Coons, *
◆ EMP: 34 EST: 1948
SQ FT: 37,000
SALES (est): 5MM **Privately Held**
Web: www.afinitas.com
SIC: 1771 5084 3446 Concrete work; Cement making machinery; Architectural metalwork

(G-5836)
TRI-STATE SUPPLY CO INC
3840 Fisher Rd (43228-1016)
PHONE.................................614 272-6767
Jim Bruce, *Prin*
EMP: 10 EST: 1950
SQ FT: 10,000
SALES (est): 626.3K **Privately Held**
SIC: 2493 5046 2531 Bulletin boards, wood; Partitions; Blackboards, wood

(G-5837)
TRI-W GROUP INC
Also Called: Military Spec Packaging
835 Goodale Blvd (43212-3824)
PHONE.................................614 228-5000
▲ EMP: 1241
SIC: 3694 7538 7537 Distributors, motor vehicle engine; Diesel engine repair: automotive; Automotive transmission repair shops

(G-5838)
TRIP TRANSPORT LLC
2905 Sunbury Sq (43219-3409)
PHONE.................................773 969-1402
Alibashi Maalin, *Admn*
EMP: 7 EST: 2012
SALES (est): 240.03K **Privately Held**
SIC: 3537 Trucks, tractors, loaders, carriers, and similar equipment

(G-5839)
TROY FILTERS LTD
1680 Westbelt Dr (43228-3812)
P.O. Box 21295 (43221-0295)
PHONE.................................614 777-8222
Cory Elliott, *Managing Member*
EMP: 20 EST: 1993
SQ FT: 16,000
SALES (est): 2.31MM **Privately Held**
Web: www.troyfiltersusa.com
SIC: 3564 Filters, air: furnaces, air conditioning equipment, etc.

(G-5840)
TRUTECH CABINETRY LLC
2121 S James Rd (43232-3829)
PHONE.................................614 338-0680
Nick Willis, *Owner*
EMP: 8 EST: 2007

SALES (est): 877.12K **Privately Held**
Web: www.trutechcabinetry.com
SIC: 2434 Wood kitchen cabinets

(G-5841)
TURN-KEY TUNNELING INC
1247 Stimmel Rd (43223-2915)
PHONE.................................614 275-4832
Christine Froehrlich, *Pr*
Deborah Tingler, *
Brian Froehrlich, *
Michael J Fusco, *
EMP: 35 EST: 2005
SALES (est): 9.44MM **Privately Held**
Web: www.turn-keytunneling.com
SIC: 3531 Tunneling machinery

(G-5842)
U S HAIR INC
3727 E Broad St (43213-1127)
PHONE.................................614 235-5190
Tom Jeon, *Pr*
EMP: 6 EST: 2001
SALES (est): 483.45K **Privately Held**
Web: www.ushairbeauty.com
SIC: 3999 Hair and hair-based products

(G-5843)
UNITED SECURITY SEALS INC (PA)
Also Called: United Seal Company
2000 Fairwood Ave (43207-1607)
P.O. Box 7852 (43207-0852)
PHONE.................................614 443-7633
Herbert Cook, *Pr*
Daniel P Sander, *
▲ EMP: 30 EST: 1900
SQ FT: 20,000
SALES (est): 7.81MM
SALES (corp-wide): 7.81MM **Privately Held**
Web: www.unitedsecurityseals.com
SIC: 3312 3089 Bar, rod, and wire products; Plastics processing

(G-5844)
UNITY ENTERPRISES INC
Also Called: Cozmyk Enterprises
3757 Courtright Ct (43227-2250)
PHONE.................................614 231-1370
Christopher J Minnillo, *Prin*
EMP: 8 EST: 2000
SALES (est): 170.66K **Privately Held**
SIC: 3565 Packaging machinery

(G-5845)
UNIVERSAL FABG CNSTR SVCS INC
Also Called: UNI-Facs
1241 Mckinley Ave (43222-1114)
PHONE.................................614 274-1128
Steve Finkel, *Pr*
Robert Watts, *
▲ EMP: 25 EST: 1987
SQ FT: 120,000
SALES (est): 3.82MM **Privately Held**
SIC: 1541 3441 3599 1799 Renovation, remodeling and repairs: industrial buildings; Building components, structural steel; Catapults; Sandblasting of building exteriors

(G-5846)
UNIVERSAL PALLETS INC
611 Marion Rd (43207-2552)
PHONE.................................614 444-1095
EMP: 27
SALES (corp-wide): 4.01MM **Privately Held**
Web: www.48forty.com
SIC: 5031 2448 Pallets, wood; Cargo containers, wood
PA: Universal Pallets Inc.
    659 Marion Rd

Columbus OH 43207
614 444-1095

(G-5847)
UNIVERSITY SPORTS
PUBLICATIONS
1265 Indianola Ave (43201-2838)
PHONE.................................614 291-6416
Michael Shavefels, *CEO*
EMP: 9 EST: 1991
SALES (est): 128.59K **Privately Held**
SIC: 2711 2721 Newspapers; Periodicals

(G-5848)
UPPER ARLINGTON CREW INC
5257 Sinclair Rd (43229-5042)
P.O. Box 211086 (43221-8086)
PHONE.................................614 485-0089
EMP: 12 EST: 2010
SALES (est): 441.76K **Privately Held**
Web: www.uacrew.org
SIC: 2711 Newspapers, publishing and printing

(G-5849)
UPRIGHT PRESS LLC
2060 S High St (43207-2425)
PHONE.................................614 619-7337
EMP: 6 EST: 2015
SALES (est): 231.42K **Privately Held**
Web: www.uprightpress.com
SIC: 2741 Miscellaneous publishing

(G-5850)
URBN TIMBER LLC
29 Kingston Ave (43207)
PHONE.................................614 981-3043
Tyler Sirak, *Managing Member*
Treg Sherman, *Managing Member*
Tyler Hillyard, *Managing Member*
EMP: 6 EST: 2016
SALES (est): 530.17K **Privately Held**
Web: www.urbntimber.com
SIC: 2491 2426 5712 5021 Structural lumber and timber, treated wood; Carvings, furniture: wood; Custom made furniture, except cabinets; Furniture

(G-5851)
USTEK INCORPORATED
4663 Executive Dr Ste 3 (43220-3627)
PHONE.................................614 538-8000
Robert M Simon, *Pr*
Wendy Simon, *Sec*
▲ EMP: 10 EST: 1986
SQ FT: 650
SALES (est): 983.89K **Privately Held**
Web: www.ustek.com
SIC: 3674 Semiconductors and related devices

(G-5852)
UVONICS CO
1078 Goodale Blvd (43212-3831)
PHONE.................................614 458-1163
George A Anderson, *Pr*
Jerome Margeson, *VP Engg*
Susan Hatfield, *Dir*
EMP: 15 EST: 1973
SQ FT: 9,000
SALES (est): 1.48MM **Privately Held**
SIC: 3672 3625 8711 3674 Printed circuit boards; Control equipment, electric; Engineering services; Semiconductors and related devices

(G-5853)
V & C ENTERPRISES CO
Also Called: Printed Image, The
41 S Grant Ave (43215-3979)

PHONE.................................614 221-1412
EMP: 7 EST: 1991
SALES (est): 786.13K **Privately Held**
SIC: 2752 Offset printing

(G-5854)
VALLEY VITAMINS II INC
4449 Easton Way Fl 2 (43219-7005)
PHONE.................................330 533-0051
Adam Crouch, *CEO*
EMP: 10 EST: 2008
SALES (est): 184.25K **Privately Held**
SIC: 2833 Medicinals and botanicals

(G-5855)
VECTRA INC
Also Called: Vectra Visual
3950 Business Park Dr (43204-5021)
PHONE.................................614 351-6868
◆ EMP: 200
Web: www.taylor.com
SIC: 2752 4225 Commercial printing, lithographic; General warehousing and storage

(G-5856)
VENGEANCE IS MINE LLC
4612 Sawmill Rd (43220-2247)
PHONE.................................614 670-4745
Sudhir Dubey, *Pr*
EMP: 7 EST: 2016
SALES (est): 86.05K **Privately Held**
Web: www.avsmithbooks.com
SIC: 2741 Miscellaneous publishing

(G-5857)
VERIFONE INC
Also Called: 2checkout
855 Grandview Ave Ste 110 (43215-1102)
PHONE.................................800 837-4366
EMP: 114
SALES (corp-wide): 695.17MM **Privately Held**
Web: www.2checkout.com
SIC: 3578 Point-of-sale devices
HQ: Verifone, Inc.
    2744 N University Dr
    Coral Springs FL 33065
    800 837-4366

(G-5858)
VERITIV
2344 Limestone Way (43228-9197)
P.O. Box 183028 (43218-3028)
PHONE.................................614 323-3335
EMP: 13 EST: 2019
SALES (est): 331.18K **Privately Held**
SIC: 2621 Paper mills

(G-5859)
VERTIV JV HOLDINGS LLC
1050 Dearborn Dr (43085-1544)
PHONE.................................614 888-0246
Eva M Kalawski, *Sec*
EMP: 6488 EST: 2016
SALES (est): 64.55MM **Privately Held**
SIC: 3679 3585 6719 Power supplies, all types: static; Air conditioning units, complete: domestic or industrial; Investment holding companies, except banks

(G-5860)
VIRGINIA AIR DISTRIBUTORS INC
2821 Silver Dr (43211-1052)
PHONE.................................614 262-1129
Ken Baker, *CEO*
EMP: 8
SALES (corp-wide): 104.5MM **Privately Held**

Columbus - Franklin County (G-5861)

Web: www.virginiaair.com
SIC: 3585 Parts for heating, cooling, and refrigerating equipment
PA: Virginia Air Distributors Inc
2501 Waterford Lake Dr
Midlothian VA 23112
804 608-3600

(G-5861)
VOIGT & SCHWEITZER LLC (HQ)
987 Buckeye Park Rd (43207-2596)
PHONE..................614 449-8281
Werner Niehaus, *Pr*
Brian Miller, *Sr VP*
▲ EMP: 12 EST: 1968
SQ FT: 55,000
SALES (est): 140.05MM
SALES (corp-wide): 1.03B **Privately Held**
Web: www.hotdipgalvanizing.com
SIC: 3479 Galvanizing of iron, steel, or end-formed products
PA: Hill & Smith Plc
Westhaven House
Solihull W MIDLANDS B90 4
121 704-7430

(G-5862)
WALKER NATIONAL INC
2195 Wright Brothers Ave (43217-1157)
PHONE..................614 492-1614
Richard Longo, *Pr*
Deborah Krikorian, *
◆ EMP: 30 EST: 1988
SALES (est): 7.2MM
SALES (corp-wide): 55.92MM **Privately Held**
SIC: 3499 7699 Magnets, permanent: metallic; Industrial equipment services
PA: Industrial Magnetics, Inc.
1385 M 75 S
Boyne City MI 49712
231 582-3100

(G-5863)
WARD ENGINEERING INC
2041 Arlingate Ln (43228-4113)
PHONE..................614 442-8063
EMP: 8 EST: 2019
SALES (est): 218.39K **Privately Held**
SIC: 3841 Surgical and medical instruments

(G-5864)
WASSERSTROM CO
1641 Harmon Ave (43223-3318)
PHONE..................614 737-8568
Tina Sparks, *Prin*
EMP: 8 EST: 2010
SALES (est): 181.89K **Privately Held**
SIC: 3469 Kitchen fixtures and equipment: metal, except cast aluminum

(G-5865)
WASSERSTROM COMPANY (PA)
Also Called: National Smallwares
4500 E Broad St (43213-1360)
PHONE..................614 228-6525
Rodney Wasserstrom, *Pr*
Reid Wasserstrom, *
Dennis Blank, *
Alan Wasserstrom, *
David A Tumen, *
◆ EMP: 395 EST: 1902
SQ FT: 250,000
SALES (est): 378.09MM
SALES (corp-wide): 378.09MM **Privately Held**
Web: www.wasserstrom.com
SIC: 5087 3566 5021 5046 Restaurant supplies; Speed changers, drives, and gears; Office furniture, nec; Commercial cooking and food service equipment

(G-5866)
WATERSHED DISTILLERY LLC
1145 Chesapeake Ave Ste D (43212-2284)
PHONE..................614 357-1936
EMP: 50 EST: 2010
SQ FT: 4,700
SALES (est): 6.9MM **Privately Held**
Web: www.watersheddistillery.com
SIC: 5182 2085 Wine; Distilled and blended liquors

(G-5867)
WATKINS PRINTING COMPANY
1401 E 17th Ave (43211-2815)
P.O. Box 11618 (43211-0618)
PHONE..................614 297-8270
Tamara Watkins Green, *Sec*
Eric Watkins, *
David Watkins, *
EMP: 45 EST: 1949
SQ FT: 35,000
SALES (est): 7.62MM **Privately Held**
Web: www.watkinsprinting.com
SIC: 2752 2791 2789 Offset printing; Typesetting; Bookbinding and related work

(G-5868)
WEEKEND LEARNING PUBLS LLC
5584 Boulder Crest St (43235-2510)
PHONE..................614 336-7711
Husain Nuri, *Prin*
▲ EMP: 9 EST: 2010
SALES (est): 897.24K **Privately Held**
Web: www.weekendlearning.com
SIC: 2741 Miscellaneous publishing

(G-5869)
WELCH PACKAGING GROUP INC
Also Called: Welch Packaging Columbus
4700 Alkire Rd (43228-3495)
PHONE..................614 870-2000
EMP: 110
SALES (corp-wide): 457.79MM **Privately Held**
Web: www.welchpkg.com
SIC: 2621 7389 Wrapping and packaging papers; Packaging and labeling services
PA: Welch Packaging Group, Inc.
1020 Herman St
Elkhart IN 46516
574 295-2460

(G-5870)
WELDING CONSULTANTS INC
889 N 22nd St (43219-2426)
PHONE..................614 258-7018
William A Svekric Senior, *Pr*
William Svekric Junior, *VP*
EMP: 6 EST: 1981
SQ FT: 4,800
SALES (est): 616.49K **Privately Held**
Web: welding-consultants-llc.myshopify.com
SIC: 8742 8734 8711 7692 Management consulting services; Testing laboratories; Engineering services; Welding repair

(G-5871)
WELDING CONSULTANTS LLC
889 N 22nd St (43219-2426)
PHONE..................614 258-7018
Richard Holdren, *Pr*
EMP: 7 EST: 2016
SALES (est): 229.93K **Privately Held**
Web: welding-consultants-llc.myshopify.com
SIC: 7692 Welding repair

(G-5872)
WEST-CAMP PRESS INC
Also Called: American Colorscans
5178 Sinclair Rd (43229-5437)
PHONE..................614 895-0233
EMP: 22
SALES (corp-wide): 20.26MM **Privately Held**
Web: www.westcamppress.com
SIC: 2752 Color lithography
PA: West-Camp Press, Inc.
39 Collegeview Rd
Westerville OH 43081
614 882-2378

(G-5873)
WEST-WARD COLUMBUS INC
Also Called: Hikma Pharmaceuticals
1809 Wilson Rd (43228-9579)
P.O. Box 16532 (43216-6532)
PHONE..................614 276-4000
◆ EMP: 1100 EST: 1890
SALES (est): 117.9MM
SALES (corp-wide): 2.88B **Privately Held**
SIC: 2834 Druggists' preparations (pharmaceuticals)
HQ: West-Ward Holdings Limited
1 New Burlington Place
London W1S 2
207 399-2760

(G-5874)
WESTLAKE CORPORATION
Also Called: Westlake Epoxy
180 E Broad St (43215-3707)
PHONE..................614 986-2497
EMP: 38
Web: www.westlake.com
SIC: 2821 Epoxy resins
PA: Westlake Corporation
2801 Post Oak Blvd Ste 60
Houston TX 77056

(G-5875)
WHEEL GROUP HOLDINGS LLC
Also Called: Wheel One
2901 E 4th Ave Ste 3 (43219-2896)
PHONE..................614 253-6247
Joseph Nantle, *Off Mgr*
EMP: 6
SALES (corp-wide): 51MM **Privately Held**
Web: www.thewheelgroup.com
SIC: 3714 3452 Wheel rims, motor vehicle; Nuts, metal
PA: Wheel Group Holdings, Llc
1050 N Vineyard Ave
Ontario CA 91764
888 399-8885

(G-5876)
WHITE CASTLE SYSTEM INC (PA)
Also Called: White Castle
555 Edgar Waldo Way (43215-3070)
P.O. Box 1498 (43216-1498)
PHONE..................614 228-5781
Edgar W Ingram Iii, *Ch Bd*
Russell J Meyer, *
Nicholas Zuk, *
Elizabeth Ingram, *
Andrew Prakel, *Corporate Controller*
◆ EMP: 275 EST: 1921
SQ FT: 143,000
SALES (est): 538.44MM
SALES (corp-wide): 538.44MM **Privately Held**
Web: www.whitecastle.com
SIC: 5812 5142 2051 2013 Fast-food restaurant, chain; Meat, frozen: packaged; Bread, cake, and related products; Sausages and other prepared meats

(G-5877)
WILD OHIO BREWING COMPANY
2025 S High St (43207-2426)
PHONE..................614 262-0000
Russell Pinto, *Prin*
EMP: 8 EST: 2017
SALES (est): 2.13MM **Privately Held**
Web: www.wildohiobrewing.com
SIC: 5181 2082 Beer and ale; Ale (alcoholic beverage)

(G-5878)
WILLIAMS SCOTSMAN INC
871 Buckeye Park Rd (43207-2586)
PHONE..................614 449-8675
Sean Roche, *Brnch Mgr*
EMP: 64
SALES (corp-wide): 2.36B **Publicly Held**
Web: www.mobilemini.com
SIC: 3448 3441 3412 7359 Buildings, portable: prefabricated metal; Fabricated structural metal; Metal barrels, drums, and pails; Equipment rental and leasing, nec
HQ: Williams Scotsman, Inc.
4646 E Van Buren St # 40
Phoenix AZ 85008
480 894-6311

(G-5879)
WOLF COMPOSITE SOLUTIONS
3991 Fondorf Dr (43228-1025)
PHONE..................614 219-6990
Alex Wolford, *Pr*
Bethany Wolford, *Off Mgr*
▼ EMP: 17 EST: 1999
SQ FT: 53,000
SALES (est): 2.33MM **Privately Held**
Web: www.wolfcomposites.com
SIC: 3624 Fibers, carbon and graphite

(G-5880)
WOLF METALS INC
1625 W Mound St (43223-1809)
PHONE..................614 461-6361
James Wolf, *Pr*
Donna Wolf, *VP*
Karen Gould, *Sec*
EMP: 6 EST: 1974
SQ FT: 10,000
SALES (est): 1.44MM **Privately Held**
Web: www.wolfmetals.com
SIC: 3444 Sheet metal specialties, not stamped

(G-5881)
WORLD WIDE RECYCLERS INC
3755 S High St (43207-4011)
PHONE..................614 554-3296
Jeffery May Senior, *Pr*
EMP: 9 EST: 2006
SALES (est): 240.99K **Privately Held**
SIC: 2611 5064 Pulp mills, mechanical and recycling processing; Electric household appliances, nec

(G-5882)
WORTHINGTON CYLINDER CORP
1085 Dearborn Dr (43085-1542)
PHONE..................614 438-7900
EMP: 196
SALES (corp-wide): 4.92B **Publicly Held**
Web: www.worthingtonenterprises.com
SIC: 3443 3593 Cylinders, pressure: metal plate; Fluid power cylinders, hydraulic or pneumatic
HQ: Worthington Cylinder Corporation
200 W Old Wlson Bridge Rd
Worthington OH 43085
614 840-3210

▲ = Import ▼ = Export
◆ = Import/Export

GEOGRAPHIC SECTION

Concord Township - Lake County (G-5904)

(G-5883)
WORTHINGTON INDUSTRIES INC
Worthington Industries, Inc.
1055 Dearborn Dr (43085-1542)
PHONE..................614 438-3028
Bruce Ruhl, *Mgr*
EMP: 45
SQ FT: 15,000
SALES (corp-wide): 4.92B **Publicly Held**
Web: www.worthingtonenterprises.com
SIC: 7692 3544 Welding repair; Special dies and tools
PA: Worthington Enterprises, Inc.
 200 W Old Wlson Bridge Rd
 Worthington OH 43085
 614 438-3210

(G-5884)
WORTHINGTON INDUSTRIES INC
Also Called: Worthington Steel Div
1127 Dearborn Dr (43085-4920)
P.O. Box 182038 (43218-2038)
PHONE..................614 438-3190
Frank Roberto, *Prin*
EMP: 50
SALES (corp-wide): 4.92B **Publicly Held**
Web: www.worthingtonenterprises.com
SIC: 3316 Cold finishing of steel shapes
PA: Worthington Enterprises, Inc.
 200 W Old Wlson Bridge Rd
 Worthington OH 43085
 614 438-3210

(G-5885)
WORTHINGTON INDUSTRIES INC
Also Called: WORTHINGTON INDUSTRIES, INC.
1818 West Case Rd # 101 (43235-7521)
PHONE..................614 438-3113
Paul Spreng, *Mgr*
EMP: 13
SALES (corp-wide): 4.92B **Publicly Held**
Web: www.worthingtonenterprises.com
SIC: 3316 Strip, steel, cold-rolled, nec: from purchased hot-rolled,
PA: Worthington Enterprises, Inc.
 200 W Old Wlson Bridge Rd
 Worthington OH 43085
 614 438-3210

(G-5886)
WORTHNGTON STELPAC SYSTEMS LLC (HQ)
1205 Dearborn Dr (43085-4769)
PHONE..................614 438-3205
Mark Russell, *CEO*
EMP: 250 **EST:** 1999
SALES (est): 53.23MM
SALES (corp-wide): 4.92B **Publicly Held**
Web: www.worthingtonenterprises.com
SIC: 3325 5051 Steel foundries, nec; Metals service centers and offices
PA: Worthington Enterprises, Inc.
 200 W Old Wlson Bridge Rd
 Worthington OH 43085
 614 438-3210

(G-5887)
WYANDOTTE WINERY LLC
4640 Wyandotte Dr (43230-1258)
PHONE..................614 357-7522
Robin Coolidge, *Prin*
EMP: 7 **EST:** 1977
SALES (est): 78.58K **Privately Held**
Web: www.wyandottewinery.com
SIC: 2084 Wines

(G-5888)
WYMAN WOODWORKING
389 Robinwood Ave (43213-1752)
PHONE..................614 338-0615

Marc Wyman, *Prin*
EMP: 6 **EST:** 2008
SALES (est): 148.87K **Privately Held**
SIC: 2431 Millwork

(G-5889)
YACHIYO OF AMERICA INC (DH)
Also Called: Yachiyo Manufacturing America
2285 Walcutt Rd (43228-9575)
PHONE..................614 876-3220
Toshihiko Ogawa, *Pr*
Poshio Yanada, *
▲ **EMP:** 160 **EST:** 1997
SALES (est): 127.89MM **Privately Held**
Web: www.yachiyo-of-america.com
SIC: 3465 3089 3714 Automotive stampings; Novelties, plastics; Acceleration equipment, motor vehicle
HQ: Yachiyo Industry Co., Ltd.
 393, Kashiwabara
 Sayama STM 350-1

(G-5890)
Z M O COMPANY (PA)
Also Called: Z M O Oil
2140 Eakin Rd (43223-6258)
P.O. Box 8587 (44906-8587)
PHONE..................614 875-0230
Philip Schaffner, *Pr*
Don Schaffner, *VP*
Marie Schaffner, *Sec*
Valerie Schaffner, *Treas*
EMP: 6 **EST:** 1965
SALES (est): 722.85K
SALES (corp-wide): 722.85K **Privately Held**
SIC: 2834 Liniments

(G-5891)
ZANE PETROLEUM INC
Also Called: Hopewell Oil and Gas
575 S 3rd St (43215-5755)
PHONE..................740 454-8779
Jerry S Henderson, *Pr*
EMP: 10 **EST:** 1982
SALES (est): 970.37K **Privately Held**
SIC: 1382 Oil and gas exploration services

(G-5892)
ZANER-BLOSER INC (HQ)
Also Called: Superkids Reading Program
1400 Goodale Blvd Ste 200 (43212-3777)
P.O. Box 16764 (43216-6764)
PHONE..................614 486-0221
Lisa Carmona, *Pr*
▲ **EMP:** 149 **EST:** 1972
SQ FT: 15,000
SALES (est): 49.81MM
SALES (corp-wide): 109.4MM **Privately Held**
Web: www.zaner-bloser.com
SIC: 5192 5049 8249 2731 Books; School supplies; Correspondence school; Book publishing
PA: Highlights For Children, Inc.
 1800 Watermark Dr
 Columbus OH 43215
 614 486-0631

(G-5893)
ZIP PUBLISHING
1091 W 1st Ave (43212-3601)
PHONE..................614 485-0721
EMP: 6 **EST:** 2019
SALES (est): 194.99K **Privately Held**
Web: www.zippublishing.com
SIC: 2752 Offset printing

(G-5894)
ZSHOT INC
6155 Huntley Rd Ste D (43229-1096)
PHONE..................800 385-8581
Wallace Lau, *Pr*
▲ **EMP:** 9 **EST:** 2011
SALES (est): 1.01MM **Privately Held**
Web: www.zshot.com
SIC: 3484 Rifles or rifle parts, 30 mm. and below

(G-5895)
ZYVEX PERFORMANCE MTLS INC (HQ)
Also Called: Zyvex Technologies
1255 Kinnear Rd Ste 100 (43212-1155)
PHONE..................614 481-2222
Lance Criscuolo, *Pr*
Doctor Nagesh Potluri, *Chief Scientist*
EMP: 7 **EST:** 2007
SALES (est): 2.13MM
SALES (corp-wide): 4.94MM **Privately Held**
Web: www.zyvextech.com
SIC: 3624 Carbon and graphite products
PA: Ocsial Llc
 950 Taylor Station Rd W
 Gahanna OH 43230
 415 906-5271

Columbus Grove
Putnam County

(G-5896)
BUCKEYE TRACTOR CORPORATION
11313 Slabtown Rd (45830-9302)
P.O. Box 97 (45830-0097)
PHONE..................419 659-2162
Lynn Graham, *Pr*
▼ **EMP:** 8 **EST:** 1972
SQ FT: 11,200
SALES (est): 719.45K **Privately Held**
Web: www.buctraco.com
SIC: 3523 5261 Farm machinery and equipment; Retail nurseries and garden stores

(G-5897)
CARPE DIEM INDUSTRIES LLC (PA)
Also Called: Colonial Surface Solutions
4599 Campbell Rd (45830-9403)
PHONE..................419 659-5639
Patricia Langhals, *Pr*
Darren Langhals, *
EMP: 55 **EST:** 1989
SQ FT: 750
SALES (est): 9.25MM
SALES (corp-wide): 9.25MM **Privately Held**
Web: www.colonialsurfacesolutions.com
SIC: 3479 3471 3398 1799 Painting of metal products; Cleaning and descaling metal products; Metal heat treating; Coating of metal structures at construction site

(G-5898)
GROVE ENGINEERED PRODUCTS
201 E Cross St (45830-1302)
PHONE..................419 659-5939
Larry Clymer, *Pr*
▲ **EMP:** 6 **EST:** 2002
SALES (est): 914.15K **Privately Held**
Web: www.groveengineeredproducts.com
SIC: 2241 3011 Spindle banding; Tire and inner tube materials and related products

(G-5899)
PRODUCTION PRODUCTS INC
200 Sugar Grove Ln (45830-9627)
PHONE..................734 241-7242
Sam Modica, *Pr*
Grace Viers, *VP*
◆ **EMP:** 76 **EST:** 2004
SQ FT: 20,000
SALES (est): 21.61MM **Privately Held**
Web: www.midwayproducts.com
SIC: 3469 3548 Metal stampings, nec; Electric welding equipment
PA: Midway Products Group, Inc.
 1 Lyman E Hoyt Dr
 Monroe MI 48161

Concord Township
Lake County

(G-5900)
ADDIVANT
10641 Buckingham Pl (44077-8140)
PHONE..................440 352-1719
Jeff De Werth, *Mgr*
EMP: 8 **EST:** 2015
SALES (est): 134.76K **Privately Held**
SIC: 2899 Chemical preparations, nec

(G-5901)
AVERY DENNISON CORPORATION
7600 Auburn Rd Bldg 18 (44077-9608)
PHONE..................440 358-4691
Martina Mcissac, *Mgr*
EMP: 213
SALES (corp-wide): 8.36B **Publicly Held**
Web: www.averydennison.com
SIC: 2672 2679 Adhesive papers, labels, or tapes: from purchased material; Building, insulating, and packaging paper
PA: Avery Dennison Corporation
 8080 Norton Pkwy
 Mentor OH 44060
 440 534-6000

(G-5902)
B B BRADLEY COMPANY INC (PA)
7755 Crile Rd (44077-9702)
PHONE..................440 354-2005
Bruce Beaty, *Pr*
EMP: 40 **EST:** 1977
SALES (est): 5.06MM
SALES (corp-wide): 5.06MM **Privately Held**
Web: www.bbbradley.com
SIC: 3086 Packaging and shipping materials, foamed plastics

(G-5903)
CEMCO CONSTRUCTION CORPORATION
10176 Page Dr (44060-6816)
PHONE..................440 567-7708
Gianmichele Bruno, *Pr*
EMP: 6 **EST:** 2004
SALES (est): 499.2K **Privately Held**
Web: www.cem-co.com
SIC: 3273 Ready-mixed concrete

(G-5904)
DE NORA HOLDINGS US INC
7590 Discovery Ln (44077-9190)
PHONE..................440 710-5300
Paolo Dellacha, *Pr*
Angelo Ferrari, *
Silvia Bertini, *
EMP: 370 **EST:** 2015
SALES (est): 63.48MM
SALES (corp-wide): 885.74MM **Privately Held**

Concord Township - Lake County (G-5905)

SIC: 3589 Water purification equipment, household type
HQ: De Nora Holding (Uk) Limited
C/O Pirola Pennuto Zei & Associati Ltd
London EC4N

(G-5905)
DE NORA TECH LLC (DH)
7590 Discovery Ln (44077-9190)
PHONE..............................440 710-5334
Paolo Dellacha, *CEO*
Frank J Mcgorty, *COO*
Assunta Rossi, *
Angelo Ferrari, *
◆ **EMP:** 80 **EST:** 1982
SQ FT: 20,000
SALES (est): 99.5MM
SALES (corp-wide): 885.74MM **Privately Held**
Web: business.painesvilleohchamber.org
SIC: 3624 3589 7359 Electrodes, thermal and electrolytic uses; carbon, graphite; Sewage and water treatment equipment; Equipment rental and leasing, nec
HQ: Industrie De Nora Spa
Via Leonardo Bistolfi 35
Milano MI 20134

(G-5906)
ELTECH SYSTEMS CORPORATION (PA)
7590 Discovery Ln (44077-9190)
PHONE..............................440 285-0380
Dennis L Baxendale, *Prin*
EMP: 6 **EST:** 2018
SALES (est): 215.32K
SALES (corp-wide): 215.32K **Privately Held**
SIC: 2812 Alkalies and chlorine

(G-5907)
INNOVATIVE STONEWORKS INC
6815 Edinboro Pl (44077-2366)
P.O. Box 884 (44077-0884)
PHONE..............................440 352-2231
Belinda G Grassi, *Prin*
EMP: 7 **EST:** 2010
SALES (est): 243.15K **Privately Held**
SIC: 3841 Surgical and medical instruments

(G-5908)
ISK AMERICAS INCORPORATED (HQ)
7474 Auburn Rd (44077-9703)
PHONE..............................440 357-4600
Fujio Tamara, *Ch Bd*
F O Hicks, *
Marvin Hosokawa, *
R C Andrews, *
EMP: 16 **EST:** 1997
SQ FT: 4,400
SALES (est): 44.56MM **Privately Held**
Web: www.iskbc.com
SIC: 2816 2491 Titanium dioxide, anatase or rutile (pigments); Wood preserving
PA: Ishihara Sangyo Kaisha,Ltd.
1-3-15, Edobori, Nishi-Ku
Osaka OSK 550-0

(G-5909)
LAD TECHNOLOGY INC
7830 Hermitage Rd (44077-9114)
PHONE..............................561 543-9858
Donna Marie Domanovics, *Pr*
Louis Domanovics, *VP*
EMP: 19 **EST:** 1988
SALES (est): 527.72K **Privately Held**
Web: www.ladtechnology.com
SIC: 3672 Printed circuit boards

(G-5910)
PRESSURE TECHNOLOGY OHIO INC
7996 Auburn Rd (44077-9180)
P.O. Box 357336 (32635-7336)
PHONE..............................215 628-1975
David Bowles, *Pr*
EMP: 20 **EST:** 2002
SALES (est): 2.06MM **Privately Held**
Web: www.pressuretechnology.com
SIC: 3398 Metal heat treating

(G-5911)
RANPAK HOLDINGS CORP (HQ)
7990 Auburn Rd (44077-9701)
PHONE..............................440 354-4445
Omar M Asali, *Ch Bd*
Trent Meyerhoefer, *Sr VP*
Bill Drew, *Sr VP*
EMP: 14 **EST:** 1972
SALES (est): 336.3MM
SALES (corp-wide): 502.08MM **Publicly Held**
Web: www.ranpak.com
SIC: 2657 Paperboard backs for blister or skin packages
PA: Js Capital Llc
888 7th Ave Fl 40
New York NY 10016
212 655-7160

(G-5912)
ROBERTSON MANUFACTURING CO
10150 Colton Ave (44077-2195)
PHONE..............................216 531-8222
John S Green, *Pr*
Shannon Catalano, *Dir*
Sandra Essick, *Treas*
EMP: 10 **EST:** 1948
SALES (est): 990.24K **Privately Held**
Web: www.robertsongears.com
SIC: 3568 3566 Sprockets (power transmission equipment); Gears, power transmission, except auto

(G-5913)
VAL-CON INC
7201 Hermitage Rd (44077-9718)
PHONE..............................440 357-1898
Richard Vertocnik, *Pr*
Jonell Vertocnik, *VP*
EMP: 7 **EST:** 1982
SALES (est): 750K **Privately Held**
SIC: 3825 Energy measuring equipment, electrical

(G-5914)
WATER STAR INC
7590 Discovery Ln (44077-9190)
P.O. Box 710 (44080-0710)
PHONE..............................440 996-0800
Dan Longhenry, *Pr*
Andrew Niksa, *VP*
▲ **EMP:** 14 **EST:** 2002
SALES (est): 5.05MM
SALES (corp-wide): 1.24B **Publicly Held**
Web: americas.denora.com
SIC: 3356 3479 Titanium; Coating of metals and formed products
PA: Tennant Company
10400 Clean St
Eden Prairie MN 55344
763 540-1200

(G-5915)
ZSI MANUFACTURING INC
Also Called: American Belleville
8059 Crile Rd (44077-9180)
PHONE..............................440 266-0701
Steve Fowler, *CEO*
Christopher P Blossom, *CFO*
EMP: 11 **EST:** 2016

SQ FT: 21,500
SALES (est): 3.59MM **Privately Held**
Web: www.americanbelleville.com
SIC: 3493 Steel springs, except wire

Conneaut
Ashtabula County

(G-5916)
CASCADE OHIO INC
Also Called: C W Ohio
1209 Maple Ave (44030-2120)
PHONE..............................440 593-5800
Nicholas N Noirot, *Pr*
Gary C Trapp, *
▲ **EMP:** 282 **EST:** 1991
SQ FT: 250,000
SALES (est): 42.06MM **Privately Held**
Web: www.cwohio.com
SIC: 2431 3442 Windows and window parts and trim, wood; Metal doors, sash, and trim

(G-5917)
EXOMET INC
1100 Maple Ave (44030-2119)
PHONE..............................440 593-1161
Roger Stanbridge, *Prin*
EMP: 23 **EST:** 2008
SALES (est): 853.86K
SALES (corp-wide): 2.47B **Privately Held**
SIC: 5084 3559 Industrial machinery and equipment; Foundry machinery and equipment
HQ: Foseco, Inc.
20200 Sheldon Rd
Cleveland OH 44142
440 826-4548

(G-5918)
GENERAL ALUMINUM MFG COMPANY
Also Called: GENERAL ALUMINUM MFG. COMPANY
1370 Chamberlain Blvd (44030-1100)
P.O. Box 28 (44030-0028)
PHONE..............................440 593-6225
EMP: 300
Web: www.generalaluminum.com
SIC: 3365 3369 Aluminum and aluminum-based alloy castings; Nonferrous foundries, nec
HQ: General Aluminum Mfg. Llc
5159 S Prospect St
Ravenna OH 44266
330 297-1225

(G-5919)
HARBOR INDUSTRIAL CORP
859 W Jackson St (44030-2255)
PHONE..............................440 599-8366
Michael D Legeza, *Pr*
Dale Hoskins, *Sec*
EMP: 18 **EST:** 1985
SQ FT: 92,000
SALES (est): 2.04MM **Privately Held**
Web: www.harborindustrialcorp.com
SIC: 3089 Plastics hardware and building products

(G-5920)
HEAVENLY CREAMERY INC
264 Sandusky St (44030-2568)
PHONE..............................440 593-6080
Joseph Ericksen, *Pr*
Christine Ericksen, *Sec*
John Ericksen, *Treas*
EMP: 6 **EST:** 2015
SALES (est): 496.71K **Privately Held**
Web: www.heavenlycreamery.com

SIC: 2021 3556 Creamery butter; Ice cream manufacturing machinery

(G-5921)
INDEPENDENT CAN COMPANY
1049 Chamberlain Blvd (44030-1168)
PHONE..............................440 593-5300
Nancy Kalinowski, *Brnch Mgr*
EMP: 14
SALES (corp-wide): 90.37MM **Privately Held**
Web: www.independentcan.com
SIC: 3411 Tin cans
PA: Independent Can Company
1300 Brass Mill Rd
Belcamp MD 21017
410 272-0090

(G-5922)
KELLYS WLDG & FABRICATION LTD
285 N Amboy Rd (44030-3098)
PHONE..............................440 593-6040
Herbert Kelly Junior, *Pr*
EMP: 8 **EST:** 1991
SALES (est): 883.99K **Privately Held**
SIC: 7692 3441 1799 1542 Welding repair; Fabricated structural metal; Welding on site ; Nonresidential construction, nec

(G-5923)
LEATHER RESOURCE OF AMERICA INC
Also Called: Cortina Leathers
494 E Main Rd (44030-8666)
PHONE..............................440 262-5761
▲ **EMP:** 49 **EST:** 2005
SALES (est): 2.77MM **Privately Held**
SIC: 3111 3199 Finishing of leather; Boxes, leather

(G-5924)
LIGHTNING MOLD & MACHINE INC
Also Called: Lightning Mold & Machine
509 W Main Rd (44030-2975)
PHONE..............................440 593-6460
Ronald R Newhart, *Pr*
Loretta Newhart, *Sec*
Erik Newhart, *VP*
EMP: 10 **EST:** 1992
SQ FT: 2,700
SALES (est): 899.13K **Privately Held**
SIC: 3544 3599 Industrial molds; Custom machinery

(G-5925)
LUKJAN METAL PDTS HOLDG CO INC
645 Industry Rd (44030-3045)
P.O. Box 357 (44030-0357)
PHONE..............................440 599-8127
EMP: 18 **EST:** 2017
SALES (est): 863.58K **Privately Held**
Web: www.lukjan.com
SIC: 3444 Sheet metalwork

(G-5926)
LUKJAN METAL PRODUCTS INC (PA)
645 Industry Rd (44030-3045)
P.O. Box 357 (44030-0357)
PHONE..............................440 599-8127
Daniel Korda, *Pr*
Elena Kelly, *
EMP: 140 **EST:** 1964
SQ FT: 100,000
SALES (est): 49.68MM
SALES (corp-wide): 49.68MM **Privately Held**
Web: www.lukjan.com

GEOGRAPHIC SECTION

SIC: 3312 3444 Blast furnaces and steel mills ; Ducts, sheet metal

(G-5927)
LYONDLLBSELL ADVNCED PLYMERS I
Also Called: A Schulman
3365 E Center St (44030-3333)
PHONE...................440 224-7291
EMP: 78
Web: www.lyondellbasell.com
SIC: 2869 Industrial organic chemicals, nec
HQ: Lyondellbasell Advanced Polymers Inc.
1221 Mckinney St Ste 300
Houston TX 77010
713 309-7200

(G-5928)
MODERN ENGINEERING INC
527 W Adams St (44030-2272)
PHONE...................440 593-5414
David Mc Laughlin, *Owner*
EMP: 6 EST: 1985
SALES (est): 573.97K **Privately Held**
SIC: 3469 3599 Machine parts, stamped or pressed metal; Machine shop, jobbing and repair

(G-5929)
OVERHEAD DOOR CORPORATION
Also Called: Wayne - Dalton Plastics
1001 Chamberlain Blvd (44030-1168)
PHONE...................440 593-5226
EMP: 10
Web: www.overheaddoor.com
SIC: 1751 3089 3083 Garage door, installation or erection; Extruded finished plastics products, nec; Laminated plastics plate and sheet
HQ: Overhead Door Corporation
2501 S State Hwy 121 Ste
Lewisville TX 75067
469 549-7100

(G-5930)
PREMIX-HADLOCK COMPOSITES LLC
Also Called: Premix-Hadlock Composites LLC
3365 E Center St (44030-3333)
PHONE...................440 335-4301
Terry Morgan, *Pr*
▲ EMP: 107 EST: 2008
SQ FT: 110,000
SALES (est): 23.09MM
SALES (corp-wide): 59.91MM **Privately Held**
SIC: 3089 Injection molding of plastics
HQ: Hpc Holdings, Llc
3637 Ridgewood Rd
Fairlawn OH 44333

(G-5931)
S AND S TOOL INC
576 Blair St (44030-1463)
P.O. Box 127 (44030-0127)
PHONE...................440 593-4000
Paul Sedmak, *Pr*
Joe Sedmak, *VP*
EMP: 8 EST: 1983
SQ FT: 5,000
SALES (est): 857.25K **Privately Held**
Web: www.sstool1inc.com
SIC: 3599 Machine shop, jobbing and repair

(G-5932)
SECONDARY MACHINING SVCS INC
539 Center Rd (44030-2308)
P.O. Box 296 (44030-0296)
PHONE...................440 593-3040

Art Distelrath Junior, *Pr*
Madelon L Distelrath, *Treas*
Amy Distelrath, *VP*
EMP: 7 EST: 1985
SALES (est): 547.32K **Privately Held**
SIC: 3599 Machine shop, jobbing and repair

(G-5933)
TEIJIN AUTOMOTIVE TECH INC
333 Gore Rd (44030-2909)
PHONE...................440 945-4800
Dave Murtha, *Brnch Mgr*
EMP: 197
Web: www.teijinautomotive.com
SIC: 3089 Injection molding of plastics
HQ: Teijin Automotive Technologies, Inc.
255 Rex Blvd
Auburn Hills MI 48326
248 237-7800

(G-5934)
THE GAZETTE PRINTING CO INC
Also Called: Gazette Publishing
218 Washington St (44030-2605)
P.O. Box 212 (44030-0212)
PHONE...................440 593-6030
John Lampson, *Prin*
EMP: 9
SALES (corp-wide): 7.8MM **Privately Held**
Web: www.visitashtabulacounty.com
SIC: 2752 2711 Offset printing; Newspapers
PA: The Gazette Printing Co Inc
46 W Jefferson St
Jefferson OH 44047
440 576-9125

Conover
Miami County

(G-5935)
CAVEN AND SONS MEAT PACKING CO
7850 E Us Rte 36 (45317)
P.O. Box 400 (45317-0400)
PHONE...................937 368-3841
Howard Caven, *Pr*
Victor Caven, *VP*
Helen Caven, *Sec*
Dean Caven, *Treas*
EMP: 15 EST: 1951
SALES (est): 830.75K **Privately Held**
SIC: 2011 5147 5421 2013 Meat packing plants; Meats, fresh; Meat markets, including freezer provisioners; Sausages and other prepared meats

(G-5936)
CONOVER LUMBER COMPANY INC
Also Called: Staely Custom Crating
7960 Alcony Conover Rd. Rt 36 (45317-3503)
P.O. Box 464 (45317-0464)
PHONE...................937 368-3010
EMP: 14 EST: 2000
SQ FT: 3,584
SALES (est): 2.34MM **Privately Held**
Web: www.conoverlumber.net
SIC: 5211 2421 Lumber products; Flooring (dressed lumber), softwood

Continental
Putnam County

(G-5937)
HELENA AGRI-ENTERPRISES LLC
200 N Main St (45831-9172)
PHONE...................419 596-3806
EMP: 6

Web: www.helenaagri.com
SIC: 2819 5191 Chemicals, high purity: refined from technical grade; Fertilizers and agricultural chemicals
HQ: Helena Agri-Enterprises, Llc
225 Schilling Blvd
Collierville TN 38017
901 761-0050

(G-5938)
SOCAR OF OHIO INC (PA)
21739 Road E16 (45831-9003)
PHONE...................419 596-3100
Ken Charles, *
Cary Andrews, *
Donald G Smith, *
John Morris, *
EMP: 89 EST: 1971
SQ FT: 90,000
SALES (est): 9.36MM
SALES (corp-wide): 9.36MM **Privately Held**
SIC: 3441 2439 Joists, open web steel: long-span series; Structural wood members, nec

(G-5939)
VERHOFF MACHINE & WELDING INC
7300 Road 18 (45831)
PHONE...................419 596-3202
Edward Verhoff, *Pr*
Joseph Verhoff, *
Leonard J Verhoff, *
EMP: 120 EST: 1955
SQ FT: 150,000
SALES (est): 21.66MM **Privately Held**
Web: www.verhoff.com
SIC: 3599 3469 3444 3443 Machine shop, jobbing and repair; Metal stampings, nec; Sheet metalwork; Fabricated plate work (boiler shop)

Convoy
Van Wert County

(G-5940)
SHELLY MATERIALS INC
2364 Richey Rd (45832-9643)
PHONE...................419 622-2101
Gary Ferguson, *CEO*
EMP: 18
SALES (corp-wide): 32.72B **Privately Held**
Web: www.shellyco.com
SIC: 2951 Asphalt paving mixtures and blocks
HQ: Shelly Materials, Inc.
80 Park Dr
Thornville OH 43076
740 246-6315

Coolville
Athens County

(G-5941)
MIDDLETON LLYD DOLLS INC (PA)
Also Called: Middlton Lloyd Doll Fctry Outl
23689 Mountain Bell Rd (45723-9463)
PHONE...................740 989-2082
Janice Middleston, *Pr*
Lloyd Middleton, *Pr*
Janice Middleton, *VP*
EMP: 7 EST: 1990
SQ FT: 8,000
SALES (est): 1.58MM **Privately Held**
SIC: 3942 5945 5092 Dolls, except stuffed toy animals; Hobby, toy, and game shops; Dolls

Copley
Summit County

(G-5942)
AKRON DISPERSIONS INC
3291 Sawmill Rd (44321-1637)
P.O. Box 4195 (44321-0195)
PHONE...................330 666-0045
Michael Giustino, *CEO*
James Finn, *
Diane Hunsicker, *
▲ EMP: 25 EST: 1958
SQ FT: 56,000
SALES (est): 9.94MM **Privately Held**
Web: www.akrondispersions.com
SIC: 2819 2899 Industrial inorganic chemicals, nec; Chemical preparations, nec

(G-5943)
ALL FIRED UP PNT YOUR OWN POT
30 Rothrock Loop (44321-1331)
PHONE...................330 865-5858
Janelle Wertz, *Owner*
EMP: 6 EST: 2002
SALES (est): 484.03K **Privately Held**
Web: www.allfiredupakron.com
SIC: 3269 5719 Art and ornamental ware, pottery; Pottery

(G-5944)
BKT USA INC
Also Called: Bkt
202 Montrose West Ave Ste 240 (44321-2903)
PHONE...................330 836-1090
▲ EMP: 15 EST: 2009
SALES (est): 2.58MM **Privately Held**
Web: www.bkt-tires.com
SIC: 5531 3011 Automotive tires; Tires and inner tubes
PA: Balkrishna Industries Limited
Bkt House, C/15,
Mumbai MH 40001

(G-5945)
BLOCH PRINTING COMPANY
3569 Copley Rd (44321-1646)
PHONE...................330 576-6760
David Bloch, *Pr*
Maria Bloch, *VP*
EMP: 6 EST: 1977
SALES (est): 983.04K **Privately Held**
Web: www.blochprinting.com
SIC: 5112 2752 Business forms; Commercial printing, lithographic

(G-5946)
CARAUSTAR INDUSTRIES INC
Also Called: Caraustar
202 Montrose West Ave Ste 315 (44321-2904)
PHONE...................330 665-7700
EMP: 22
SALES (corp-wide): 5.22B **Publicly Held**
Web: www.caraustar.com
SIC: 2679 2655 3275 3089 Paperboard products, converted, nec; Tubes, fiber or paper: made from purchased material; Gypsum products; Injection molded finished plastics products, nec
HQ: Caraustar Industries, Inc.
5000 Astell Pwdr Sprng Rd
Austell GA 30106
770 948-3101

(G-5947)
COPLEY FIRE & RESCUE ASSN
Also Called: Copley Township Fire Dept
1540 S Cleveland Massillon Rd (44321-1908)

Copley - Summit County (G-5948)

PHONE..................................330 666-6464
Chief Joseph Ezzi, *Prin*
Joseph Ezzi, *Prin*
EMP: 21 **EST:** 1977
SALES (est): 308.78K **Privately Held**
Web: www.copley.oh.us
SIC: 3711 Fire department vehicles (motor vehicles), assembly of

(G-5948)
DOWNING ENTERPRISES INC
Also Called: Downing Exhibits
1287 Centerview Cir (44321-1632)
PHONE..................................330 666-3888
William Downing Junior, *CEO*
Michael Carano, *
Karen Gallaher, *
Craig Marsall, *
◆ **EMP:** 100 **EST:** 1972
SQ FT: 144,000
SALES (est): 20MM **Privately Held**
Web: www.downingexhibits.com
SIC: 7389 3999 Trade show arrangement; Barber and beauty shop equipment

(G-5949)
GLAXOSMITHKLINE LLC
4273 Ridge Crest Dr (44321-3067)
PHONE..................................330 608-2365
EMP: 6
SALES (corp-wide): 37.8B **Privately Held**
Web: us.gsk.com
SIC: 2834 Pharmaceutical preparations
HQ: Glaxosmithkline Llc
    2929 Walnut St Ste 1700
    Philadelphia PA 19104
    888 825-5249

(G-5950)
MEECH STTIC ELMINATORS USA INC
1298 Centerview Cir (44321-1632)
PHONE..................................330 564-2000
▲ **EMP:** 15 **EST:** 1995
SALES (est): 2.57MM **Privately Held**
Web: www.meech.com
SIC: 3823 Industrial process measurement equipment

(G-5951)
MILLER EXPRESS INC
828 Dogwood Ter (44321-1406)
PHONE..................................330 714-6751
Douglas Miller, *Prin*
EMP: 7 **EST:** 2008
SALES (est): 231.06K **Privately Held**
SIC: 2741 Miscellaneous publishing

(G-5952)
MULTIBASE INC
3835 Copley Rd (44321-1671)
PHONE..................................330 666-0505
Brian Schell, *Pr*
Gifford Shearer, *
Thomas G Tangney, *
Paul A Marcela, *
Joseph Rinaldi, *
▲ **EMP:** 85 **EST:** 1988
SQ FT: 160,000
SALES (corp-wide): 2.93B **Publicly Held**
Web: multibase.lookchem.com
SIC: 2821 Plastics materials and resins
PA: Dupont De Nemours, Inc.
    974 Centre Rd Bldg 730
    Wilmington DE 19805
    302 295-5783

(G-5953)
PRCC HOLDINGS INC
Also Called: Preferred Compounding
175 Montrose West Ave Ste 200
(44321-3122)
PHONE..................................330 798-4790
EMP: 238 **EST:** 2010
SQ FT: 5,000
SALES (est): 205MM **Privately Held**
SIC: 3069 Custom compounding of rubber materials

(G-5954)
PRIMAL LIFE ORGANICS LLC
405 Rothrock Rd Ste 105 (44321-3146)
PHONE..................................800 260-4946
Trina Felber, *CEO*
EMP: 20 **EST:** 2012
SALES (est): 5MM **Privately Held**
Web: www.primallifeorganics.com
SIC: 2844 5999 Perfumes, cosmetics and other toilet preparations; Cosmetics

(G-5955)
PVS CHEMICAL SOLUTIONS INC
3149 Copley Rd (44321-2127)
P.O. Box 4143 (44321-0143)
PHONE..................................330 666-0888
Bob Vorhees, *Mgr*
EMP: 10
SQ FT: 27,596
SALES (corp-wide): 651.47MM **Privately Held**
Web: www.pvschemicals.com
SIC: 2819 5169 Sulfur chloride; Chemicals and allied products, nec
HQ: Pvs Chemical Solutions, Inc.
    10900 Harper Ave
    Detroit MI 48213

(G-5956)
SRT SALES & SERVICE LLC
2917 Reserve Ave (44321-1736)
P.O. Box 14569 (44321-4569)
PHONE..................................330 620-0681
Sarah Thomarios, *Prin*
EMP: 7 **EST:** 2012
SALES (est): 233.75K **Privately Held**
Web: www.srtsands.com
SIC: 3441 Fabricated structural metal

Corning
Perry County

(G-5957)
ALTIER BROTHERS INC
155 Walnut St (43730)
P.O. Box 430 (43730-0430)
PHONE..................................740 347-4329
Louis Altier, *Pr*
EMP: 16 **EST:** 1950
SQ FT: 5,000
SALES (est): 625.99K **Privately Held**
Web: altier-bros-inc.business.site
SIC: 1389 Oil field services, nec

(G-5958)
JT PLUS WELL SERVICE LLC
140 E Main St (43730-9550)
PHONE..................................740 347-0070
Patrick W Altier, *Prin*
EMP: 10 **EST:** 2001
SALES (est): 946.55K **Privately Held**
SIC: 1389 Oil field services, nec

(G-5959)
SERGEANT STONE INC
1425 State Route 555 Ne (43730-9532)
P.O. Box 2086 (43702-2086)
PHONE..................................740 452-7434
Claude Imler, *Pr*
EMP: 7 **EST:** 2014
SALES (est): 237.45K **Privately Held**
Web: www.sergeantstone.com

SIC: 1422 Crushed and broken limestone

Cortland
Trumbull County

(G-5960)
BORTNICK TRACTOR SALES INC
6192 Warren Rd (44410-9736)
PHONE..................................330 924-2555
Dana W Harju, *Prin*
EMP: 15 **EST:** 2013
SALES (est): 4.12MM **Privately Held**
Web: www.bortnicktractorsales.com
SIC: 5261 3541 5083 Lawn and garden equipment; Saws and sawing machines; Agricultural machinery and equipment

(G-5961)
CONTROL TRANSFORMER INC
Also Called: Geneva Rubber Company
3701 Warren Meadville Rd (44410-9423)
PHONE..................................330 637-6015
William J Martin, *Pr*
▲ **EMP:** 45 **EST:** 2002
SQ FT: 30,000
SALES (est): 12.99MM
SALES (corp-wide): 1.66B **Publicly Held**
Web: www.control-transformer.com
SIC: 3612 Power transformers, electric
HQ: Ajax Tocco Magnethermic Corporation
    1745 Overland Avenue Ne
    Warren OH 44483
    800 547-1527

(G-5962)
EXTREME CASTER SERVICES INC
3333 Niles Cortland Rd Ne (44410-1786)
PHONE..................................330 637-9030
John C Grundy, *Prin*
EMP: 9 **EST:** 2008
SALES (est): 141.53K **Privately Held**
SIC: 3562 Casters

(G-5963)
HIGH LIFE
2792 Ivy Hill Cir (44410-9376)
PHONE..................................330 978-4124
EMP: 6
SALES (est): 78.44K **Privately Held**
SIC: 2851 Removers and cleaners

(G-5964)
HOWLAND PRINTING INC
Also Called: Proforma
3117 Niles Cortland Rd Ne (44410-1737)
PHONE..................................330 637-8255
Norma Harned, *Pr*
EMP: 7 **EST:** 1994
SQ FT: 1,500
SALES (est): 514.39K **Privately Held**
Web: www.proforma.com
SIC: 2752 Offset printing

(G-5965)
LAWBRE CO
Also Called: Architechual Etc
3311 Warren Meadville Rd (44410-8808)
PHONE..................................330 637-3363
Christopher Riekert, *Pr*
EMP: 6 **EST:** 1974
SQ FT: 5,000
SALES (est): 493.85K **Privately Held**
Web: www.lawbre.com
SIC: 3944 Dollhouses and furniture

(G-5966)
NUFLUX LLC ⊙
2395 State Route 5 (44410-9217)
PHONE..................................330 399-1122

William M West, *Managing Member*
EMP: 7 **EST:** 2023
SALES (est): 1.37MM
SALES (corp-wide): 18.67MM **Privately Held**
Web: www.optagroupllc.com
SIC: 3399 3312 Metal powders, pastes, and flakes; Electrometallurgical steel
PA: Opta Group Llc
    300 Corporate Pkwy
    Amherst NY 14226
    716 446-8914

(G-5967)
QUANTUM INTEGRATION LLC
1980 Niles Cortland Rd Ne (44410-9405)
PHONE..................................330 609-0355
Andre Camelli, *Prin*
EMP: 6 **EST:** 2012
SALES (est): 92.8K **Privately Held**
Web: www.quantumintegration.com
SIC: 3572 Computer storage devices

Coshocton
Coshocton County

(G-5968)
ANNIN & CO INC
Annin Flagmakers
700 S 3rd St (43812-2062)
PHONE..................................740 622-4447
Vane Scott Iii, *Mgr*
EMP: 172
SQ FT: 15,000
SALES (corp-wide): 94.54MM **Privately Held**
Web: www.annin.com
SIC: 2399 5999 3446 3429 Flags, fabric; Banners, flags, decals, and posters; Architectural metalwork; Hardware, nec
PA: Annin & Co., Inc.
    430 Mountain Ave Ste 410
    New Providence NJ 07974
    973 228-9400

(G-5969)
ANSELL HEALTHCARE PRODUCTS LLC
Also Called: Ansell Edmont Div
925 Chestnut St (43812-1302)
PHONE..................................740 622-4369
Kendall Cranston, *Mgr*
EMP: 240
Web: www.ansell.com
SIC: 3842 2822 2259 Gloves, safety; Synthetic rubber; Gloves, knit, except dress and semidress gloves
HQ: Ansell Healthcare Products Llc
    111 Wood Ave S Ste 210
    Iselin NJ 08830
    732 345-5400

(G-5970)
ANSELL HEALTHCARE PRODUCTS LLC
925 Chestnut St (43812-1302)
PHONE..................................740 622-4311
Allan Roman, *Mgr*
EMP: 21
Web: www.ansell.com
SIC: 3842 3069 Gloves, safety; Rubber coated fabrics and clothing
HQ: Ansell Healthcare Products Llc
    111 Wood Ave S Ste 210
    Iselin NJ 08830
    732 345-5400

GEOGRAPHIC SECTION

Coshocton - Coshocton County (G-5993)

(G-5971)
ARMCO INC
17400 State Route 16 (43812-9268)
PHONE..............................740 829-3000
EMP: 6 EST: 2010
SALES (est): 197.57K Privately Held
SIC: 3315 Steel wire and related products

(G-5972)
BAIRD CONCRETE PRODUCTS INC
15 Locust St (43812-1136)
P.O. Box 1028 (43812-5028)
PHONE..............................740 623-8600
John Baird, Pr
Margie Baird, VP
Cynthia Albertson, Sec
Tom Albertson, VP
EMP: 10 EST: 1989
SQ FT: 13,700
SALES (est): 1.08MM Privately Held
Web: www.bairdconcrete.biz
SIC: 3273 Ready-mixed concrete

(G-5973)
BEACH COMPANY
Also Called: Standard Advertising Co
240 Browns Ln (43812-2067)
P.O. Box 518 (43812-0518)
PHONE..............................740 622-0905
James M Beach, Pr
Beverly M Beach, Treas
Mary Caneer, VP
Margret Beach, Sec
Esward Beach, VP
EMP: 20 EST: 1923
SQ FT: 24,000
SALES (est): 475.27K Privately Held
Web: www.mlinecalendars.com
SIC: 2752 Calendars, lithographed

(G-5974)
BRYDET DEVELOPMENT CORPORATION
16867 State Route 83 (43812-9460)
P.O. Box 199 (43811-0199)
PHONE..............................740 623-0455
Paul E Bryant, Pr
Ron Deeter, *
▼ EMP: 11 EST: 1987
SQ FT: 4,500
SALES (est): 907.83K Privately Held
Web: www.brydet.com
SIC: 3532 Auger mining equipment

(G-5975)
BUCKEYE FABRIC FINISHERS INC
Also Called: Buckeye Fabric Finishing Co
1260 E Main St (43812-1700)
PHONE..............................740 622-3351
▲ EMP: 18 EST: 1988
SALES (est): 2.37MM Privately Held
Web: www.be-fabric.com
SIC: 2295 2899 2851 Waterproofing fabrics, except rubberizing; Chemical preparations, nec; Paints and allied products

(G-5976)
COSHOCTON ETHANOL LLC
18137 County Road 271 (43812-9465)
PHONE..............................740 623-3046
Mike Fedor, Managing Member
EMP: 13 EST: 2004
SALES (est): 2.5MM Privately Held
Web: www.coshoctongrain.com
SIC: 2869 Ethyl alcohol, ethanol

(G-5977)
EXCELLO FABRIC FINISHERS INC
802 S 2nd St (43812-1916)
P.O. Box 848 (43812-0848)
PHONE..............................740 622-7444
Kevin Lee, Pr
Charles Milligan, Prin
Edward L Lee, Ch Bd
William J Stenner, VP
Eugene Weir, Prin
EMP: 6 EST: 1966
SQ FT: 1,000
SALES (est): 977.59K Privately Held
Web: www.be-fabric.com
SIC: 2295 Waterproofing fabrics, except rubberizing

(G-5978)
FRANCISCO JAUME
Also Called: Coshocton Orthopedic Center
311 S 15th St Ste 206 (43812-1875)
P.O. Box 490 (43812-0490)
PHONE..............................740 622-1200
Francisco Jaume, Owner
EMP: 6 EST: 1997
SALES (est): 248.27K Privately Held
SIC: 3842 8011 Surgical appliances and supplies; Offices and clinics of medical doctors

(G-5979)
GENERAL ELECTRIC COMPANY
Also Called: GE
1350 S 2nd St (43812-1980)
PHONE..............................740 623-5379
Bob Callahan, Mgr
EMP: 12
SALES (corp-wide): 67.95B Publicly Held
Web: www.ge.com
SIC: 3083 Plastics finished products, laminated
PA: General Electric Company
   1 Aviation Way
   Cincinnati OH 45215
   617 443-3000

(G-5980)
GRESS OIL & GAS INC
Also Called: Gress Gas & Oil
3984 County Road 271 (43812-9709)
PHONE..............................740 622-8356
Jeff Gress, Pr
Lisa Gress, Prin
EMP: 11 EST: 1994
SALES (est): 228.6K Privately Held
SIC: 2911 Oils, fuel

(G-5981)
ITM MARKETING INC
Also Called: Intellitarget Marketing Svcs
331 Main St (43812-1510)
PHONE..............................740 295-3575
EMP: 124 EST: 1996
SALES (est): 6.18MM Privately Held
Web: www.itmmarketing.com
SIC: 8742 7374 2741 7322 Marketing consulting services; Data processing and preparation; Telephone and other directory publishing; Adjustment and collection services

(G-5982)
KRAFT HEINZ FOODS COMPANY
Also Called: Heinz
1660 S 2nd St (43812-1977)
PHONE..............................740 622-0523
Carol Villa, Mgr
EMP: 93
SQ FT: 120,000
SALES (corp-wide): 26.64B Publicly Held
Web: www.kraftheinzcompany.com
SIC: 2013 Sausages and other prepared meats
HQ: Kraft Heinz Foods Company
   1 Ppg Pl Ste 3400
   Pittsburgh PA 15222
   412 456-5700

(G-5983)
MCWANE INC
Clow Water Systems Company
2266 S 6th St (43812-8906)
P.O. Box 6001 (43812-6001)
PHONE..............................740 622-6651
Jeff Otterstedt, Mgr
EMP: 400
SALES (corp-wide): 970.37MM Privately Held
Web: www.mcwaneductile.com
SIC: 3321 5085 5051 3444 Cast iron pipe and fittings; Industrial supplies; Pipe and tubing, steel; Sheet metalwork
PA: Mcwane, Inc.
   2900 Highway 280 S # 300
   Birmingham AL 35223
   205 414-3100

(G-5984)
MFM BUILDING PRODUCTS CORP
425 Brewer Ln (43812-8965)
PHONE..............................740 622-2645
EMP: 25
SALES (corp-wide): 17.49MM Privately Held
Web: www.mfmbp.com
SIC: 2952 Asphalt felts and coatings
PA: Mfm Building Products Corp
   525 Orange St
   Coshocton OH 43812
   740 622-2645

(G-5985)
MFM BUILDING PRODUCTS CORP (PA)
525 Orange St (43812-2178)
P.O. Box 340 (43812-0340)
PHONE..............................740 622-2645
◆ EMP: 43 EST: 1952
SALES (est): 17.49MM
SALES (corp-wide): 17.49MM Privately Held
Web: www.mfmbp.com
SIC: 2952 Roof cement: asphalt, fibrous, or plastic

(G-5986)
MUSKINGUM GRINDING AND MCH CO
2155 Otsego Ave (43812-9401)
P.O. Box 396 (43812-0396)
PHONE..............................740 622-4741
Jeff Mulett, Pr
Janel Richards, Sec
EMP: 15 EST: 1945
SQ FT: 14,000
SALES (est): 1.33MM Privately Held
SIC: 3599 Machine shop, jobbing and repair

(G-5987)
NGO DEVELOPMENT CORPORATION
Also Called: Energy Corportive
504 N 3rd St (43812-1113)
P.O. Box 662 (43812-0662)
PHONE..............................740 622-9560
Scott Kees, Mgr
EMP: 453
SALES (corp-wide): 24.14MM Privately Held
Web: www.myenergycoop.com
SIC: 1382 4923 5984 Oil and gas exploration services; Gas transmission and distribution; Propane gas, bottled
HQ: Ngo Development Corporation
   1500 Granville Rd
   Newark OH 43055
   740 344-3790

(G-5988)
NOVELTY ADVERTISING CO INC
Also Called: Kenyon Co
1148 Walnut St (43812-1769)
PHONE..............................740 622-3113
Gregory Coffman, Pr
James Mcconnel, VP
◆ EMP: 50 EST: 1895
SQ FT: 100,000
SALES (est): 4.39MM Privately Held
Web: www.noveltyadv.com
SIC: 2752 5199 Calendars, lithographed; Advertising specialties

(G-5989)
OFCO INC
Also Called: Ohio Fabricators
111 N 14th St (43812-1710)
P.O. Box 218 (43812-0218)
PHONE..............................740 622-5922
Michael Shaw, CEO
Harold R Shaw, *
▲ EMP: 65 EST: 1945
SQ FT: 50,000
SALES (est): 9.22MM Privately Held
Web: www.ohfab.com
SIC: 3496 Wire cloth and woven wire products

(G-5990)
OHIO FABRICATORS COMPANY
1321 Elm St (43812-2216)
PHONE..............................740 622-5922
Marcia Bush, CEO
EMP: 12 EST: 2008
SALES (est): 401.03K Privately Held
Web: www.ohfab.com
SIC: 3441 Fabricated structural metal

(G-5991)
OXFORD MINING COMPANY INC (DH)
544 Chestnut St (43812-1209)
P.O. Box 1027 (43812-5027)
PHONE..............................740 622-6302
Charles C Ungurean, Pr
Thomas T Ungurean, Sec
Jeffrey M Gutman, Sr VP
Gregory J Honish, Sr VP
Daniel M Maher, Sr VP
EMP: 6 EST: 1985
SQ FT: 3,200
SALES (est): 100.03MM
SALES (corp-wide): 814.89MM Privately Held
SIC: 1221 Bituminous coal and lignite-surface mining
HQ: Westmoreland Resource Partners, Lp
   9540 S Maroon Cir Ste 300
   Englewood CO 80112

(G-5992)
OXFORD MINING COMPANY LLC (DH)
544 Chestnut St (43812-1209)
PHONE..............................740 622-6302
EMP: 12 EST: 1985
SALES (est): 22.02MM
SALES (corp-wide): 814.89MM Privately Held
SIC: 1221 Bituminous coal and lignite-surface mining
HQ: Westmoreland Resource Partners, Lp
   9540 S Maroon Cir Ste 300
   Englewood CO 80112

(G-5993)
OXFORD MINING COMPANY - KY LLC
544 Chestnut St (43812-1209)
PHONE..............................740 622-6302

Coshocton - Coshocton County (G-5994)

EMP: 33 EST: 2010
SALES (est): 6.04MM
SALES (corp-wide): 814.89MM **Privately Held**
SIC: **1221** Strip mining, bituminous
HQ: Oxford Mining Company, Llc
544 Chestnut St
Coshocton OH 43812

(G-5994)
RICHARD WRIGHT
15345 County Road 274 (43812-9788)
PHONE..................740 829-2127
Richard Wright, *Prin*
EMP: 6 EST: 2011
SALES (est): 108.09K **Privately Held**
SIC: **2741** Miscellaneous publishing

(G-5995)
SANCAST INC
535 Clow Ln (43812-9782)
PHONE..................740 022-0000
Don Hutchins, *Prin*
Don Popernik, *
John Fox, *
Nancy Foster, *
Julie Starcher, *
EMP: 50 EST: 1975
SQ FT: 56,000
SALES (est): 11.88MM **Publicly Held**
SIC: **3321** 3322 Ductile iron castings; Malleable iron foundries
HQ: Wabtec Components Llc
30 Isabella St
Pittsburgh PA 15212
412 825-1000

(G-5996)
SHAWNE SPRINGS WINERY
20093 County Road 6 (43812-9149)
PHONE..................740 623-0744
Randy Hall, *Prin*
EMP: 7 EST: 2007
SALES (est): 161.01K **Privately Held**
Web: www.shawneespringswinery.com
SIC: **2084** Wines

(G-5997)
SPRINT PRINT INC
Also Called: Market Media Creations
520 Main St (43812-1612)
PHONE..................740 622-4429
Jeff Eikenberry, *Pr*
EMP: 9 EST: 1999
SQ FT: 6,000
SALES (est): 927.86K **Privately Held**
SIC: **2752** 7319 Offset printing; Poster advertising service, except outdoor

(G-5998)
THOMAS J WEAVER INC (PA)
Also Called: Coshocton Pallet & Door Co
1501 Kenilworth Ave (43812-2430)
P.O. Box 412 (43812-0412)
PHONE..................740 622-2040
Thomas J Weaver, *Pr*
EMP: 12 EST: 1963
SALES (est): 2.31MM
SALES (corp-wide): 2.31MM **Privately Held**
SIC: **1542** 1541 1521 2448 Commercial and office building, new construction; Industrial buildings, new construction, nec; New construction, single-family houses; Pallets, wood

(G-5999)
WESTMORELAND RESOURCES GP LLC
544 Chestnut St (43812-1209)
PHONE..................740 622-6302

Martin Purvis, *CEO*
EMP: 81 EST: 2007
SALES (est): 24.31MM
SALES (corp-wide): 814.89MM **Privately Held**
SIC: **1221** Bituminous coal and lignite-surface mining
PA: Westmoreland Mining Llc
10375 Pk Mdows Dr Ste 400
Lone Tree CO 80124
303 922-6463

(G-6000)
WILEY COMPANIES (PA)
Also Called: Organic Technologies
545 Walnut St (43812-1656)
P.O. Box 1665 (43812-6665)
PHONE..................740 622-0755
▲ EMP: 130 EST: 1981
SALES (est): 45.49MM
SALES (corp-wide): 45.49MM **Privately Held**
Web: www.wileyco.com
SIC: **2087** 8731 2869 Concentrates, flavoring (except drink); Commercial physical research; Industrial organic chemicals, nec

(G-6001)
WILEY ORGANICS INC
Also Called: Organic Technologies
1245 S 6th St (43812-2809)
PHONE..................740 622-0755
David Wiley, *Pr*
EMP: 200
SALES (corp-wide): 45.49MM **Privately Held**
Web: www.wileyco.com
SIC: **2087** Concentrates, flavoring (except drink)
PA: Wiley Companies
545 Walnut St
Coshocton OH 43812
740 622-0755

(G-6002)
WILEYS FINEST LLC (PA)
545 Walnut St Ste B (43812-1656)
P.O. Box 1665 (43812-6665)
PHONE..................740 622-1072
Sam Wiley, *Managing Member*
Shane Griffiths, *Prin*
EMP: 192 EST: 2013
SALES (est): 10.96MM
SALES (corp-wide): 10.96MM **Privately Held**
Web: www.wileysfinest.com
SIC: **2077** 2079 2023 5499 Animal fats, oils, and meals; Edible fats and oils; Dietary supplements, dairy and non-dairy based; Health foods

Coventry Township
Summit County

(G-6003)
ACCU-TECH MANUFACTURING CO
195 Olivet Ave (44319-2324)
PHONE..................330 848-8100
Slyster Downs, *Pr*
John Ellis, *VP*
EMP: 10 EST: 2004
SALES (est): 170.48K **Privately Held**
SIC: **3441** Fabricated structural metal

(G-6004)
AKRON DESIGN & COSTUME LLC
888 Tippecanoe Dr (44319-2140)
PHONE..................330 644-0425

Debbie Meridith, *Owner*
EMP: 8 EST: 1981
SALES (est): 781.91K **Privately Held**
Web: www.akrondesign.com
SIC: **2389** 7299 Costumes; Costume rental

(G-6005)
AKRON EQUIPMENT COMPANY
3522 Manchester Rd Ste B (44319-1451)
PHONE..................330 645-3780
Edward L Mc Cartt, *Ch Bd*
Gary A Hill, *
Andrea Friede, *
▼ EMP: 80 EST: 1917
SQ FT: 2,000
SALES (est): 5.53MM **Privately Held**
SIC: **3599** Machine shop, jobbing and repair

(G-6006)
AMERICAN CONFECTIONS CO LLC
90 Logan Pkwy (44319-1177)
PHONE..................614 888-8838
Bill Wilson, *Dir Opers*
EMP: 9 EST: 2012
SALES (est): 431.94K **Privately Held**
SIC: **2026** 2066 Yogurt; Chocolate candy, solid

(G-6007)
CHEMEQUIP SALES INC
Also Called: R & R Engine & Machine
1004 Swartz Rd (44319-1340)
PHONE..................330 724-8300
Jeanie Menke, *Pr*
EMP: 30 EST: 1968
SQ FT: 2,500
SALES (est): 4.18MM **Privately Held**
Web: www.rrengine.com
SIC: **3519** 3621 Diesel engine rebuilding; Motors and generators

(G-6008)
DEBORAH MEREDITH
3425 Manchester Rd (44319-1412)
PHONE..................330 644-0425
Debbie Meredith, *Prin*
EMP: 6 EST: 2009
SALES (est): 137.65K **Privately Held**
SIC: **2389** 5699 7299 Costumes; Costumes, masquerade or theatrical; Costume rental

(G-6009)
FRIESS WELDING INC
Also Called: Summit Trailer Sales & Svcs
3342 S Main St (44319-3099)
PHONE..................330 644-8160
Jeff Friess, *Pr*
Russell C Friess, *CEO*
Betty Friess, *Sec*
EMP: 9 EST: 1968
SQ FT: 7,000
SALES (est): 237.77K **Privately Held**
Web: www.summittraileronline.net
SIC: **7692** 7539 5511 Welding repair; Radiator repair shop, automotive; Trucks, tractors, and trailers: new and used

(G-6010)
GARDNER PIE COMPANY
191 Logan Pkwy (44319-1188)
PHONE..................330 245-2030
EMP: 140 EST: 1944
SALES (est): 39.11MM **Privately Held**
Web: www.gardnerpie.com
SIC: **2053** 2051 Pies, bakery; frozen; Bread, cake, and related products

(G-6011)
KEN-DAL CORPORATION
644 Killian Rd (44319-2599)

PHONE..................330 644-7118
William Keasling, *Pr*
Alan Place, *VP*
▲ EMP: 10 EST: 1962
SQ FT: 12,000
SALES (est): 766.2K **Privately Held**
Web: admiral.kendal.org
SIC: **3599** Machine shop, jobbing and repair

(G-6012)
KUHLMAN CORPORATION
Also Called: B&G Contractors Supply
999 Swartz Rd (44319-1335)
PHONE..................330 724-9900
Jeff Johnston, *Brnch Mgr*
EMP: 25
SALES (corp-wide): 42.49MM **Privately Held**
Web: www.gerkencompanies.com
SIC: **3273** Ready-mixed concrete
PA: Kuhlman Corporation
1845 Indian Wood Cir
Maumee OH 43537
419 897-6000

(G-6013)
L & S HOME IMPROVEMENT
549 Saunders Ave (44319-2270)
PHONE..................330 906-3199
Lezjon Mantz, *Owner*
EMP: 6 EST: 2019
SALES (est): 200K **Privately Held**
SIC: **1389** Construction, repair, and dismantling services

(G-6014)
OHIO HCKRY HRVEST BRND PDTS IN
Also Called: Hickory Harvest Foods
90 Logan Pkwy (44319-1177)
PHONE..................330 644-6266
Joe Swiatkowski, *Pr*
Michael Swiatkowski, *
EMP: 32 EST: 1972
SQ FT: 32,000
SALES (est): 15.78MM **Privately Held**
Web: www.hickoryharvest.com
SIC: **5145** 5149 2099 Nuts, salted or roasted ; Fruits, dried; Food preparations, nec

(G-6015)
PACKAGING CORPORATION AMERICA
Also Called: PCA/Akron 312
708 Killian Rd (44319-2559)
PHONE..................330 644-9542
Ralph Snyder, *Mgr*
EMP: 55
SALES (corp-wide): 8.48B **Publicly Held**
Web: www.packagingcorp.com
SIC: **2653** Boxes, corrugated: made from purchased materials
PA: Packaging Corporation Of America
1 N Field Ct
Lake Forest IL 60045
847 482-3000

Covington
Miami County

(G-6016)
AIRAM PRESS CO LTD
Also Called: Airam Press
2065 Industrial Ct (45318-1265)
P.O. Box 9 (45318-0009)
PHONE..................937 473-5672
Fredrick J Ratermann, *Pr*
EMP: 10 EST: 2004
SALES (est): 456.21K **Privately Held**

GEOGRAPHIC SECTION

Web: www.airam.com
SIC: **3542** Presses: hydraulic and pneumatic, mechanical and manual

(G-6017)
ARENS CORPORATION (PA)
395 S High St (45318-1121)
P.O. Box 69 (45318-0069)
PHONE.................................937 473-2028
Gary Godfrey Senior, *Pr*
Ginger Godfrey, *VP*
Gary Godfrey, *Sec*
EMP: 17 **EST:** 1954
SQ FT: 2,000
SALES (est): 1.81MM
SALES (corp-wide): 1.81MM **Privately Held**
Web: www.arenspub.com
SIC: **2711** 2721 2752 Newspapers: publishing only, not printed on site; Magazines: publishing only, not printed on site; Offset printing

(G-6018)
ARENS CORPORATION
Also Called: Arens Publications & Printing
22 N High St (45318-1306)
PHONE.................................937 473-2028
Connie Didier, *Mgr*
EMP: 6
SALES (corp-wide): 1.81MM **Privately Held**
Web: www.arenspub.com
SIC: **2711** 2721 2752 Newspapers: publishing only, not printed on site; Magazines: publishing only, not printed on site; Offset printing
PA: The Arens Corporation
395 S High St
Covington OH 45318
937 473-2028

(G-6019)
B K PLASTICS INC
1400 Mote Dr (45318-1217)
P.O. Box 250 (45318-0250)
PHONE.................................937 473-2087
Robert Robbins, *Pr*
Karen Robbins, *Treas*
EMP: 6 **EST:** 1983
SQ FT: 12,000
SALES (est): 533.33K **Privately Held**
Web: www.bkpi.net
SIC: **2673** Plastic bags: made from purchased materials

(G-6020)
CONCEPT MACHINE & TOOL INC
2065 Industrial Ct (45318-1265)
P.O. Box 9 (45318-0009)
PHONE.................................937 473-3334
EMP: 23 **EST:** 1993
SALES (est): 1.15MM **Privately Held**
Web: www.conceptmach.com
SIC: **3599** Machine shop, jobbing and repair

(G-6021)
D&D CLSSIC AUTO RSTORATION INC
Also Called: D&D Classic Restoration
2300 Mote Dr (45318-1200)
PHONE.................................937 473-2229
Dale Sotsing, *Pr*
Rodger James, *VP*
Mark Kennison, *Sec*
EMP: 18 **EST:** 1985
SQ FT: 8,000
SALES (est): 430.73K **Privately Held**
Web: www.happytailsgroomingspa.com

SIC: **7389** 3711 5521 7532 Automobile recovery service; Motor vehicles and car bodies; Automobiles, used cars only; Tops (canvas or plastic), installation or repair: automotive

(G-6022)
FUSION METAL FABRICATION LLC
974 E Broadway St (45318-1711)
P.O. Box 158 (45318-0158)
PHONE.................................937 753-1090
EMP: 6 **EST:** 2019
SALES (est): 226.62K **Privately Held**
SIC: **3499** Fabricated metal products, nec

(G-6023)
GENERAL FILMS INC
645 S High St (45318-1182)
PHONE.................................888 436-3456
Roy J Weikert, *Ch*
Tim Weikert, *Pr*
Marilyn Dennings, *Sec*
Tom Granata, *VP*
EMP: 80 **EST:** 1938
SQ FT: 55,000
SALES (est): 13.05MM **Privately Held**
Web: www.generalfilms.com
SIC: **3081** 2673 Polyethylene film; Plastic and pliofilm bags

(G-6024)
GM MECHANICAL INC (PA)
4263 N State Route 48 (45318)
P.O. Box 190 (45318)
PHONE.................................937 473-3006
EMP: 74 **EST:** 1975
SALES (est): 9.96MM
SALES (corp-wide): 9.96MM **Privately Held**
SIC: **1794** 1711 3498 3444 Excavation work; Plumbing contractors; Fabricated pipe and fittings; Sheet metalwork

(G-6025)
HITACHI AUTOMATION OHIO INC
Also Called: Kec America
2000 Industrial Ct (45318-1266)
PHONE.................................937 753-1148
Hiroshi Ichiki, *Pr*
EMP: 11 **EST:** 2011
SALES (est): 2.23MM **Privately Held**
Web: www.kec-corp.jp
SIC: **3569** Robots, assembly line: industrial and commercial
PA: Hitachi, Ltd.
1-6-6, Marunouchi
Chiyoda-Ku TKY 100-0

(G-6026)
J&I DUCT FAB LLC
7502 W State Route 41 (45318-9746)
P.O. Box 190 (45318-0190)
PHONE.................................937 473-2121
EMP: 12 **EST:** 2013
SALES (est): 1.1MM **Privately Held**
Web: www.jiductfab.com
SIC: **3585** Heating and air conditioning combination units

(G-6027)
MAGIC MOLDING INC
6460 W Piqua Clayton Rd (45318-8630)
PHONE.................................937 778-0836
Newell Williams, *Prin*
EMP: 7 **EST:** 2010
SALES (est): 71.31K **Privately Held**
SIC: **3089** Molding primary plastics

(G-6028)
NEW TECH PLASTICS INC
1300 Mote Dr (45318)
P.O. Box 99 (45318)
PHONE.................................937 473-3011
EMP: 87 **EST:** 1980
SALES (est): 30MM **Privately Held**
Web: www.newtechplastics.com
SIC: **3081** Polyethylene film

(G-6029)
PBM COVINGTON LLC
400 Hazel St (45318-1724)
PHONE.................................937 473-2050
Scott F Jamison, *Managing Member*
EMP: 11 **EST:** 2008
SALES (est): 1.38MM **Privately Held**
SIC: **2834** Vitamin, nutrient, and hematinic preparations for human use

(G-6030)
PERRIGO
400 Hazel St (45318-1724)
PHONE.................................937 473-2050
EMP: 12 **EST:** 2013
SALES (est): 5.76MM **Privately Held**
Web: www.perrigo.com
SIC: **2834** Pharmaceutical preparations

(G-6031)
ROSEBUDS RANCH AND GARDEN LLC
Also Called: Rosebud's Real Food
473 E Troy Pike (45318-1196)
PHONE.................................937 214-1801
EMP: 10 **EST:** 2016
SALES (est): 500.03K **Privately Held**
Web: www.rosebudsrealfood.com
SIC: **2099** 2033 2095 Seasonings and spices; Canned fruits and specialties; Roasted coffee

(G-6032)
TUSCARORA WOOD MIDWEST LLC
6506 W Us Route 36 (45318-9661)
PHONE.................................937 603-8882
Rodney Long, *Prin*
EMP: 6 **EST:** 2007
SALES (est): 433.93K **Privately Held**
Web: www.tuscarorawoodmidwest.com
SIC: **2431** Millwork

Crestline
Crawford County

(G-6033)
FOWLER PRODUCTS INC
810 Colby Rd (44827-1799)
PHONE.................................419 683-4057
Mark Fowler, *Pr*
Phyllis Fowler, *Ch*
Robert Stauffer, *Stockholder*
Jean E Cole, *Stockholder*
Marcia A Dishon, *Stockholder*
▲ **EMP:** 17 **EST:** 1976
SQ FT: 52,000
SALES (est): 867.47K **Privately Held**
Web: www.fowler-inc.com
SIC: **3089** 3829 3084 3083 Extruded finished plastics products, nec; Measuring and controlling devices, nec; Plastics pipe; Laminated plastics plate and sheet

(G-6034)
INTERSTATE SIGN PRODUCTS INC
432 E Main St (44827-1118)
P.O. Box 187 (44827-0187)
PHONE.................................419 683-1962
Robin Wittmer, *Pr*

EMP: 6 **EST:** 1985
SQ FT: 4,000
SALES (est): 1MM **Privately Held**
Web: www.interstate911.com
SIC: **5085** 3993 Signmaker equipment and supplies; Letters for signs, metal

(G-6035)
NIESE FARMS
7506 Cole Rd (44827-9742)
PHONE.................................419 347-1204
Patrick Niese, *Pt*
EMP: 7 **EST:** 1965
SQ FT: 2,150
SALES (est): 505.47K **Privately Held**
SIC: **2043** Oatmeal: prepared as cereal breakfast food

(G-6036)
R&R SANITATION
317 N Wiley St (44827-1628)
PHONE.................................419 561-8090
Dominique Ward, *CEO*
EMP: 12 **EST:** 2020
SALES (est): 100K **Privately Held**
SIC: **2842** Sanitation preparations, disinfectants and deodorants

(G-6037)
ROCK IRON CORPORATION
1221 Warehouse Dr (44827)
PHONE.................................419 529-9411
Thomas Morehead, *Pr*
Gerald Morehead, *VP*
EMP: 11 **EST:** 1996
SALES (est): 481.22K **Privately Held**
SIC: **3544** 7389 Die sets for metal stamping (presses); Business Activities at Non-Commercial Site

Creston
Wayne County

(G-6038)
ATLANTIC VEAL & LAMB LLC
2416 E West Salem Rd (44217-9650)
PHONE.................................330 435-6400
Phillip Peerless, *Managing Member*
EMP: 10 **EST:** 2008
SALES (est): 2.13MM
SALES (corp-wide): 48.61MM **Privately Held**
SIC: **2011** Veal, from meat slaughtered on site
PA: Atlantic Veal And Lamb, Inc.
275 Morgan Ave
Brooklyn NY 11211
718 599-6400

(G-6039)
FRANK CSAPO
Also Called: Frank Csapo Oil & Gas Producer
157 Myers St (44217-9704)
PHONE.................................330 435-4458
Frank Csapo, *Owner*
EMP: 6 **EST:** 1970
SALES (est): 499.24K **Privately Held**
SIC: **1381** Drilling oil and gas wells

(G-6040)
MELLOTT BRONZE INC
4634 E Sterling Rd (44217-9241)
PHONE.................................330 435-6304
Ron Mellott, *Pr*
Ed Mellott, *VP*
Linda Mellott, *Sec*
EMP: 13 **EST:** 1985
SQ FT: 11,800
SALES (est): 2.32MM **Privately Held**

Cridersville
Auglaize County

(G-6041)
HAWTHORNE-SEVING INC
320 W Main St (45806-2215)
PHONE.................................419 643-5531
Charles L Dale, *Pr*
EMP: 39 **EST:** 1950
SQ FT: 10,000
SALES (est): 1.02MM
SALES (corp-wide): 1.02MM **Privately Held**
Web: www.hawthornesystems.com
SIC: 3535 3556 Conveyors and conveying equipment; Food products machinery
PA: E.S. Industries, Inc.
110 Brookview Ct
Lima OH 45801
419 643-2625

(G-6042)
KATIES LIGHT HOUSE LLC
300 Dupler Ave (45806-2304)
PHONE.................................419 645-5451
EMP: 13 **EST:** 1978
SALES (est): 431.56K **Privately Held**
Web: www.katieshandcraftedlighting.com
SIC: 3229 Bulbs for electric lights

Crooksville
Perry County

(G-6043)
ALFMAN LOGGING LLC
4499 Township Road 448 Ne (43731-9740)
PHONE.................................740 982-6227
EMP: 12 **EST:** 2011
SALES (est): 472.24K **Privately Held**
SIC: 2411 Logging camps and contractors

(G-6044)
BEAUMONT BROS STONEWARE INC
Also Called: Beaumont Brothers Pottery
410 Keystone St (43731-1034)
PHONE.................................740 982-0055
Roger Beaumont, *Pr*
Margie Beaumont, *
EMP: 24 **EST:** 1989
SQ FT: 14,000
SALES (est): 1.16MM **Privately Held**
SIC: 3269 Stoneware pottery products

(G-6045)
CHRISTY CATALYTICS LLC
713 Keystone St (43731-1039)
PHONE.................................740 982-1302
EMP: 7
Web: www.christycatalytics.com
SIC: 2819 Catalysts, chemical
HQ: Christy Catalytics, Llc
4641 Mcree Ave
Saint Louis MO 63110

(G-6046)
FERRO CORP
416 Maple Ave (43731-1305)
P.O. Box 151 (43731-0151)
PHONE.................................800 245-8225
Mick Pease, *Manager*
EMP: 6 **EST:** 2017
SALES (est): 93.51K **Privately Held**
Web: www.vibrantz.com
SIC: 3255 Clay refractories

(G-6047)
I CERCO INC
416 Maple Ave (43731-1305)
P.O. Box 151 (43731-0151)
PHONE.................................740 982-2050
Mick Pease, *Brnch Mgr*
EMP: 220
SALES (corp-wide): 32.17MM **Privately Held**
Web: www.cercocorp.com
SIC: 3255 3567 3297 Clay refractories; Industrial furnaces and ovens; Nonclay refractories
PA: I Cerco Inc
453 W Mcconkey St
Shreve OH 44676
330 567-2145

(G-6048)
PCC AIRFOILS LLC
Also Called: PCC AIRFOILS LLC
101 China St (43731-1111)
P.O. Box 206 (43731-0206)
PHONE.................................740 982-6025
Ryan Thrush, *Brnch Mgr*
EMP: 307
SALES (corp-wide): 364.48B **Publicly Held**
Web: www.pccairfoils.com
SIC: 3369 3728 Castings, except diecastings, precision; Aircraft parts and equipment, nec
HQ: Pcc Airfoils, Llc
3401 Entp Pkwy Ste 200
Cleveland OH 44122
216 831-3590

(G-6049)
PETRO WARE INC
Also Called: Swingle Drilling
713 Keystone St (43731-1039)
P.O. Box 220 (43731-0220)
PHONE.................................740 982-1302
Mark B Swingle, *Pr*
James R Swingle, *
EMP: 24 **EST:** 1985
SQ FT: 2,000
SALES (est): 784.18K **Privately Held**
Web: www.christycatalytics.com
SIC: 3569 3264 Filters, general line: industrial; Porcelain electrical supplies

(G-6050)
TEMPLE OIL AND GAS LLC
Also Called: Speed-O-Print
6626 Ceramic Rd Ne (43731-9419)
P.O. Box 70 (43731-0070)
PHONE.................................740 452-7878
Robert Swingle, *Pr*
EMP: 8 **EST:** 1969
SQ FT: 8,000
SALES (est): 999.77K **Privately Held**
SIC: 1381 1311 Directional drilling oil and gas wells; Natural gas production

Croton
Licking County

(G-6051)
MULLER PIPE ORGAN CO
Also Called: Muller Pipe Organ Company
122 N High St (43013-9007)
P.O. Box 353 (43013-0353)
PHONE.................................740 893-1700
John W Muller, *Pr*
Mary J Muller, *Sec*
EMP: 10 **EST:** 1986
SQ FT: 8,650
SALES (est): 615K **Privately Held**
Web: www.mullerpipeorgan.com
SIC: 3931 Musical instruments

(G-6052)
OHIO FRESH EGGS LLC (PA)
11212 Croton Rd (43013-9725)
PHONE.................................740 893-7200
Gary Bethel, *Managing Member*
▲ **EMP:** 6 **EST:** 1984
SQ FT: 5,000
SALES (est): 25.27MM
SALES (corp-wide): 25.27MM **Privately Held**
SIC: 5144 2015 Eggs; Egg processing

Crown City
Gallia County

(G-6053)
JEFFERSON LOGGING COMPANY LLC
148 Wells Run Rd (45623-9102)
PHONE.................................304 634-9203
John Jefferson, *Mgr*
EMP: 6 **EST:** 2018
SALES (est): 230.54K **Privately Held**
SIC: 2411 Logging camps and contractors

Cumberland
Guernsey County

(G-6054)
CUMBERLAND LIMESTONE LLC
53681 Spencer Rd (43732-9709)
PHONE.................................740 638-3942
Cris Sidwell, *Managing Member*
EMP: 21 **EST:** 2010
SALES (est): 4.84MM **Privately Held**
Web: www.cumberlandlimestone.com
SIC: 1422 Crushed and broken limestone

(G-6055)
KING LIMESTONE INC
53681 Spencer Rd (43732-9709)
PHONE.................................740 638-3942
Duane King, *Pr*
EMP: 15 **EST:** 1986
SQ FT: 1,200
SALES (est): 500.2K **Privately Held**
SIC: 1422 Crushed and broken limestone

Curtice
Ottawa County

(G-6056)
BUDGET DUMPSTERS
120 N Howard Rd (43412-9489)
PHONE.................................419 690-9896
Nathan Ehmann, *Prin*
EMP: 6 **EST:** 2017
SALES (est): 106.32K **Privately Held**
Web: www.budgetdumpsterstoledo.com
SIC: 3443 Dumpsters, garbage

(G-6057)
OTTAWA PRODUCTS CO
1602 N Curtice Rd Ste A (43412-9507)
PHONE.................................419 836-5115
Jeffery Hepner, *Pr*
Bruce Miller, *Dir*
George F Wasmer, *Ch*
EMP: 20 **EST:** 1997
SQ FT: 19,000
SALES (est): 2.5MM **Privately Held**
Web: www.ottawaproducts.com
SIC: 3429 3469 Clamps, metal; Spinning metal for the trade

(G-6058)
RENO MACHINE
11532 Rachel Rd (43412-9715)
PHONE.................................419 836-3093
Ray Slomka, *Prin*
EMP: 9 **EST:** 2003
SALES (est): 74.07K **Privately Held**
Web: www.reno-machine.com
SIC: 3599 Machine shop, jobbing and repair

(G-6059)
TAT MACHINE & TOOL LTD
1313 S Cousino Rd (43412-9100)
P.O. Box 184 (43412-0184)
PHONE.................................419 836-7706
Thomas A Truman, *Pt*
Joan C Truman, *Pt*
EMP: 8 **EST:** 1983
SQ FT: 7,500
SALES (est): 637.56K **Privately Held**
SIC: 3599 Machine shop, jobbing and repair

Cuyahoga Falls
Summit County

(G-6060)
ADVANCED HOLDING DESIGNS INC
Also Called: Ahd
3332 Cavalier Trl (44224-4906)
PHONE.................................330 928-4456
Mark Smrekar, *Pr*
Anne Daugherty, *Mgr*
EMP: 13 **EST:** 1988
SQ FT: 12,000
SALES (est): 458.25K **Privately Held**
Web: www.ahd-flex-e-on.com
SIC: 3545 Collets (machine tool accessories)

(G-6061)
ALDEN SAND & GRAVEL CO INC
Also Called: Alden Excavating
2486 Northampton Rd (44223-2712)
PHONE.................................330 928-3249
Connie Ensign, *Pr*
Robert E Alden Iii, *Sec*
EMP: 7 **EST:** 1963
SQ FT: 1,200
SALES (est): 214.16K **Privately Held**
SIC: 1442 1794 Sand mining; Excavation work

(G-6062)
ALTEC INDUSTRIES INC
307 Munroe Falls Ave (44221-2827)
PHONE.................................205 408-2341
Tim Smith, *Brnch Mgr*
EMP: 10
SALES (corp-wide): 1.21B **Privately Held**
Web: www.altec.com
SIC: 3531 3536 3713 Derricks, except oil and gas field; Cranes, overhead traveling; Truck bodies (motor vehicles)
HQ: Altec Industries, Inc.
210 Inverness Center Dr
Birmingham AL 35242
205 991-7733

(G-6063)
AMERICAN DE ROSA LAMPARTS LLC (HQ)
Also Called: Luminance
370 Falls Commerce Pkwy (44224-1062)
◆ **EMP:** 85 **EST:** 1951
SALES (est): 29.4MM
SALES (corp-wide): 31.1MM **Privately Held**

GEOGRAPHIC SECTION
Cuyahoga Falls - Summit County (G-6085)

Web: luminance.us.com
SIC: 5063 3364 3229 Lighting fixtures; Brass and bronze die-castings; Bulbs for electric lights
PA: Luminance Acquisition, Llc
25101 Chagrin Blvd # 350
Cleveland OH

(G-6064)
AMERICHEM INC (PA)
2000 Americhem Way (44221-3303)
PHONE.................330 929-4213
Matthew Hellstern, *CEO*
Tom Gannon, *
John Volcheck, *
◆ EMP: 100 EST: 1941
SQ FT: 83,000
SALES (est): 188.64MM
SALES (corp-wide): 188.64MM Privately Held
Web: www.americhem.com
SIC: 2851 2865 2816 2819 Paints and allied products; Color pigments, organic; Inorganic pigments; Industrial inorganic chemicals, nec

(G-6065)
AMERICHEM INC
Also Called: Americhem
155 E Steels Corners Rd (44224-4919)
PHONE.................330 926-3185
Rod Manfull, *Mgr*
EMP: 50
SQ FT: 78,214
SALES (corp-wide): 188.64MM Privately Held
Web: www.americhem.com
SIC: 2865 2816 Color pigments, organic; Inorganic pigments
PA: Americhem, Inc.
2000 Americhem Way
Cuyahoga Falls OH 44221
330 929-4213

(G-6066)
AMH HOLDINGS II INC
3773 State Rd (44223-2603)
PHONE.................330 929-1811
Thomas N Chieffe, *CEO*
EMP: 500 EST: 2002
SALES (est): 45.18MM Privately Held
Web: www.alside.com
SIC: 3355 Coils, wire aluminum: made in rolling mills

(G-6067)
APPLIED VISION CORPORATION (PA)
2020 Vision Ln (44223-4706)
PHONE.................330 926-2222
Amir Novini, *CEO*
Manijeh Novini, *
EMP: 60 EST: 1997
SQ FT: 80,000
SALES (est): 20.26MM
SALES (corp-wide): 20.26MM Privately Held
Web: www.antaresvisiongroup.com
SIC: 3577 Magnetic ink and optical scanning devices

(G-6068)
ASCOT VALLEY FOODS LTD
205 Ascot Pkwy (44223-3701)
PHONE.................330 376-9411
Robert J Zab, *Prin*
EMP: 50 EST: 2017
SALES (est): 2.32MM Privately Held
Web: www.ascotvalleyfoods.com
SIC: 2099 Food preparations, nec

(G-6069)
ASSOCIATED MATERIALS LLC (PA)
Also Called: Alside Supply Center
3773 State Rd (44223-2603)
P.O. Box 2010 (44309-2010)
PHONE.................330 929-1811
James Drexinger, *CEO*
Erik D Ragatz, *
Brian C Strauss, *
Scott F Stephens, *
William L Topper, *
▲ EMP: 1003 EST: 1947
SQ FT: 63,000
SALES (est): 1.18B
SALES (corp-wide): 1.18B Privately Held
Web: www.associatedmaterials.com
SIC: 3089 5033 5031 3442 Plastics hardware and building products; Roofing and siding materials; Windows; Metal doors, sash, and trim

(G-6070)
ASSOCIATED MATERIALS GROUP INC (PA)
3773 State Rd (44223-2603)
PHONE.................330 929-1811
EMP: 183 EST: 2010
SALES (est): 542.5MM Privately Held
Web: www.associatedmaterials.com
SIC: 3089 5033 5031 3442 Plastics hardware and building products; Roofing and siding materials; Windows; Metal doors, sash, and trim

(G-6071)
ASSOCIATED MTLS HOLDINGS LLC
3773 State Rd (44223-2603)
P.O. Box 2010 (44309-2010)
PHONE.................330 929-1811
Ira D Kleinman, *Ch Bd*
EMP: 2000 EST: 1947
SALES (est): 139.53MM Privately Held
Web: www.associatedmaterials.com
SIC: 5033 5031 5063 3442 Roofing and siding materials; Windows; Wire and cable; Metal doors, sash, and trim
PA: Associated Materials Group, Inc.
3773 State Rd
Cuyahoga Falls OH 44223

(G-6072)
BARRY-WEHMILLER COMPANIES INC
4485 Allen Rd (44224-1033)
PHONE.................330 923-0491
Jim Foley, *Brnch Mgr*
EMP: 14
Web: www.barrywehmiller.com
SIC: 3565 Packaging machinery
HQ: Barry-Wehmiller Companies, Inc.
8020 Forsyth Blvd
Saint Louis MO 63105
314 862-8000

(G-6073)
BOURBON PLASTICS INC
111 Stow Ave Ste 100 (44221-2560)
P.O. Box 23 (46504-0023)
PHONE.................574 342-0893
EMP: 35
SIC: 3644 3089 Insulators and insulation materials, electrical; Injection molded finished plastics products, nec

(G-6074)
CIRCLE PRIME MANUFACTURING
2114 Front St (44221)
P.O. Box 112 (44221)
PHONE.................330 923-0019
James Mothersbaugh, *Pr*

Robert Mothersbaugh, *
EMP: 27 EST: 1989
SQ FT: 50,000
SALES (est): 6.28MM Privately Held
Web: www.circleprime.com
SIC: 3672 8731 3663 3812 Printed circuit boards; Commercial physical research; Radio broadcasting and communications equipment; Antennas, radar or communications

(G-6075)
CLEVELAND ELEVATOR INC
121 E Ascot Ln (44223-3769)
PHONE.................216 924-0505
EMP: 9 EST: 2019
SALES (est): 95.58K Privately Held
Web: www.gableelevator.com
SIC: 3534 Elevators and equipment

(G-6076)
CORTAPE INC
60 Marc Dr (44223-2628)
PHONE.................330 929-6700
Matthew Mc Clellan, *Pr*
Erik W Akins, *Ch Bd*
◆ EMP: 17 EST: 1976
SQ FT: 25,000
SALES (est): 2.6MM Privately Held
Web: www.cortape.com
SIC: 2672 Tape, pressure sensitive: made from purchased materials

(G-6077)
CRAIN COMMUNICATIONS INC
Also Called: Rubber & Plastics News
2291 Riverfront Pkwy Ste 1000 (44221-2580)
PHONE.................330 836-9180
Robert S Simmons, *VP*
EMP: 36
SALES (corp-wide): 249.16MM Privately Held
Web: www.tirebusiness.com
SIC: 2711 2721 7389 Newspapers: publishing only, not printed on site; Periodicals; Advertising, promotional, and trade show services
PA: Crain Communications, Inc.
1155 Gratiot Ave
Detroit MI 48207
313 446-6000

(G-6078)
DBCR INC
Also Called: G.S. Steel Company
3400 Cavalier Trl (44224-4908)
PHONE.................330 920-1900
Donald E Potoczek, *Pr*
Beth Potoczek, *Treas*
EMP: 20 EST: 2005
SALES (est): 3.3MM Privately Held
Web: www.gssteel.com
SIC: 3541 7389 7692 Plasma process metal cutting machines; Metal cutting services; Welding repair

(G-6079)
DE ANGELO INSTRUMENT INC
1431 Falls Ave (44223-2442)
PHONE.................330 929-7266
David De Angelo, *Prin*
EMP: 7 EST: 1991
SALES (est): 81.49K Privately Held
SIC: 3599 Machine shop, jobbing and repair

(G-6080)
DENTRONIX INC
235 Ascot Pkwy (44223-3701)
PHONE.................330 916-7300
Jerry Sullivan, *Pr*

Joseph Fasano, *
EMP: 53 EST: 1976
SQ FT: 16,000
SALES (est): 2.51MM Privately Held
Web: www.diatechusa.com
SIC: 3843 5047 3842 3841 Orthodontic appliances; Dental equipment and supplies; Surgical appliances and supplies; Surgical and medical instruments
HQ: Coltene/Whaledent Inc.
235 Ascot Pkwy
Cuyahoga Falls OH 44223

(G-6081)
EWART-OHLSON MACHINE COMPANY
1435 Main St (44221-4926)
P.O. Box 359 (44222-0359)
PHONE.................330 928-2171
David L Ewart, *Ch*
Brian L Ewart, *
Earl Norrod, *
Margaret Ewart, *
David Achauer, *
▲ EMP: 28 EST: 1942
SQ FT: 39,000
SALES (est): 4.31MM Privately Held
Web: www.ewart-ohlson.com
SIC: 3599 Machine shop, jobbing and repair

(G-6082)
FACTS INC
2737 Front St (44221-1904)
PHONE.................330 928-2332
Albert H Curry, *Pr*
Thomas W Fisher Iii, *VP*
EMP: 20 EST: 1992
SQ FT: 10,000
SALES (est): 2.24MM Privately Held
Web: www.facts-inc.com
SIC: 7371 3823 Computer software systems analysis and design, custom; Industrial process control instruments

(G-6083)
FALLS STAMPING & WELDING CO (PA)
2900 Vincent St (44221-1954)
PHONE.................330 928-1191
Rick Boettner, *Ch*
David Cesar, *
Jason Taft, *
EMP: 125 EST: 1919
SQ FT: 95,000
SALES (est): 23.36MM
SALES (corp-wide): 23.36MM Privately Held
Web: www.falls-stamping.com
SIC: 3465 3469 3544 3711 Automotive stampings; Stamping metal for the trade; Special dies, tools, jigs, and fixtures; Chassis, motor vehicle

(G-6084)
FLEX-E-ON INC
3332 Cavalier Trl (44224-4906)
PHONE.................330 928-4496
Mark Smrekar, *Pr*
EMP: 10 EST: 1965
SQ FT: 12,000
SALES (est): 856.35K Privately Held
Web: www.ahd-flex-e-on.com
SIC: 3545 Chucks: drill, lathe, or magnetic (machine tool accessories)

(G-6085)
FOX TOOL CO INC
1471 Main St (44221-4926)
PHONE.................330 928-3402
Nathan Fox, *Pr*
EMP: 14 EST: 1973

Cuyahoga Falls - Summit County (G-6086)

SQ FT: 5,120
SALES (est): 444.02K **Privately Held**
Web: www.foxtoolcompany.com
SIC: **7699** 3545 Knife, saw and tool sharpening and repair; Cutting tools for machine tools

(G-6086)
GENTEK BUILDING PRODUCTS INC (HQ)
Also Called: Revere Building Products
3773 State Rd (44223-2603)
PHONE..................................800 548-4542
▲ EMP: 18 EST: 1994
SQ FT: 8,000
SALES (est): 48.17MM
SALES (corp-wide): 1.18B **Privately Held**
Web: www.alside.com
SIC: **3444** 3089 Siding, sheet metal; Siding, plastics
PA: Associated Materials, Llc
    3773 State Rd
    Cuyahoga Falls OH 44223
    330 929-1811

(G-6087)
GOJO INDUSTRIES INC
Also Called: Production
3783 State Rd (44223-2698)
P.O. Box 991 (44309-0991)
PHONE..................................330 255-6000
Joseph Kanfer, *Brnch Mgr*
EMP: 9
SALES (corp-wide): 425.22MM **Privately Held**
Web: www.gojo.com
SIC: **2842** Polishes and sanitation goods
PA: Gojo Industries, Inc.
    1 Gojo Plz Ste 500
    Akron OH 44311
    330 255-6000

(G-6088)
GOJO INDUSTRIES INC
3783 State Rd (44223-2698)
PHONE..................................330 255-6527
Jeffrey Vengrow, *Brnch Mgr*
▼ EMP: 12
SALES (corp-wide): 425.22MM **Privately Held**
Web: www.gojo.com
SIC: **2842** Polishes and sanitation goods
PA: Gojo Industries, Inc.
    1 Gojo Plz Ste 500
    Akron OH 44311
    330 255-6000

(G-6089)
HARBOR CASTINGS INC (PA)
2508 Bailey Rd (44221-2585)
PHONE..................................330 499-7178
C Richard Lynham, *CEO*
EMP: 45 EST: 1992
SQ FT: 13,000
SALES (est): 15.26MM
SALES (corp-wide): 15.26MM **Privately Held**
Web: www.harborinvestmentcastings.com
SIC: **3324** 3369 3325 Steel investment foundries; Nonferrous foundries, nec; Steel foundries, nec

(G-6090)
HARWOOD ENTP HOLDINGS INC
1365 Orlen Ave (44221-2957)
PHONE..................................330 923-3256
Richard Harwood, *Pr*
John H Eblen, *VP*
Lundy Mills, *Sec*
Donald R Harwood, *Stockholder*

EMP: 18 EST: 1952
SQ FT: 22,000
SALES (est): 3.46MM **Privately Held**
Web: www.harwoodrubber.com
SIC: **3479** 3061 Coating of metals with plastic or resins; Mechanical rubber goods

(G-6091)
INNOVATED HEALTH LLC
2241 Front St 1st Fl (44221-2501)
P.O. Box 963 (44223-0963)
PHONE..................................330 858-0651
Fred Guerra, *Managing Member*
EMP: 9 EST: 2014
SQ FT: 2,000
SALES (est): 926.41K **Privately Held**
SIC: **2023** Dietary supplements, dairy and non-dairy based

(G-6092)
JAY-EM AEROSPACE CORPORATION
75 Marc Dr (44223)
PHONE..................................330 923-0333
Michael E Bell Senior, *CEO*
EMP: 25 EST: 1992
SQ FT: 34,000
SALES (est): 7.18MM **Privately Held**
SIC: **3728** 3599 Wheels, aircraft; Machine shop, jobbing and repair

(G-6093)
JJ&PL SERVICES-CONSULTING LLC
1474 Main St (44221-4927)
PHONE..................................330 923-5783
Hans R Leitner, *CEO*
EMP: 38 EST: 2010
SALES (est): 4.69MM **Privately Held**
Web: www.mach3machining.com
SIC: **3441** 7699 Building components, structural steel; Industrial machinery and equipment repair

(G-6094)
JULIUS ZORN INC
Also Called: Juzo USA
3690 Zorn Dr (44223-3580)
P.O. Box 1088 (44223-1088)
PHONE..................................330 923-4999
Anne Rose Zorn, *Pr*
Petra Zorn, *
Uwe Schettler, *
▲ EMP: 75 EST: 1980
SQ FT: 30,000
SALES (est): 27.4MM
SALES (corp-wide): 118.66MM **Privately Held**
Web: www.juzousa.com
SIC: **5047** 3842 Medical equipment and supplies; Hosiery, support
PA: Julius Zorn Gmbh
    Juliusplatz 1
    Aichach BY 86551
    82519010

(G-6095)
KEUCHEL & ASSOCIATES INC
Also Called: Spunfab
175 Muffin Ln (44223)
P.O. Box 3435 (44223)
PHONE..................................330 945-9455
Ken Keuchel, *Pr*
Herb Keuchel, *Stockholder**
Herbert W Keuchel, *
Richard W Staehle, *
◆ EMP: 50 EST: 1979
SQ FT: 40,000
SALES (est): 4.65MM **Privately Held**
Web: www.spunfab.com
SIC: **2241** 8711 Narrow fabric mills; Consulting engineer

(G-6096)
KOLPIN OUTDOORS CORPORATION
Also Called: Premier O.E.M.
3479 State Rd (44223-2553)
PHONE..................................330 328-0772
James Nagy, *Pr*
▲ EMP: 12 EST: 2015
SALES (est): 2.53MM **Privately Held**
Web: www.kolpin.com
SIC: **3799** All terrain vehicles (ATV)

(G-6097)
KYOCERA HARDCOATING TECH LTD
220 Marc Dr (44223-2651)
PHONE..................................330 686-2136
EMP: 17 EST: 1995
SALES (est): 1.19MM **Privately Held**
Web: www.kyocera-hardcoating.com
SIC: **3479** Coating of metals and formed products

(G-6098)
KYOCERA SGS PRECISION TLS INC (PA)
Also Called: Kyocera Precision Tools
150 Marc Dr (44223-2630)
P.O. Box 187 (44262-0187)
PHONE..................................330 688-6667
Thomas Haag, *Pr*
Jeff Burton, *Prin*
Aaron Holb, *
▲ EMP: 50 EST: 1961
SALES (est): 58.68MM
SALES (corp-wide): 58.68MM **Privately Held**
Web: www.kyocera-sgstool.com
SIC: **3545** 5084 Cutting tools for machine tools; Industrial machinery and equipment

(G-6099)
KYOCERA SGS PRECISION TLS INC
238 Marc Dr (44223-2651)
PHONE..................................330 922-1953
Richard G Tichon, *Brnch Mgr*
EMP: 86
SALES (corp-wide): 58.68MM **Privately Held**
Web: www.kyocera-sgstool.com
SIC: **3545** Cutting tools for machine tools
PA: Kyocera Sgs Precision Tools, Inc.
    150 Marc Dr
    Cuyahoga Falls OH 44223
    330 688-6667

(G-6100)
LINDEN-TWO INC
137 Ascot Pkwy (44223)
PHONE..................................330 928-4064
Peter Tilgner, *Pr*
Ken Erwin, *
Bob Hughey, *
EMP: 42 EST: 1985
SQ FT: 26,000
SALES (est): 8.48MM **Privately Held**
Web: www.lindenindustries.com
SIC: **3559** 5084 Plastics working machinery; Industrial machinery and equipment

(G-6101)
MAIN STREET GOURMET LLC
Also Called: Main Street Cambritt Cookies
170 Muffin Ln (44223-3358)
PHONE..................................330 929-0000
David Choe, *
Alex Schneider, *
Steven Marks, *
Harvey Nelson, *
EMP: 108 EST: 1987
SQ FT: 60,000
SALES (est): 23.7MM **Privately Held**
Web: www.mainstreetgourmet.com

SIC: **2053** 2099 2052 2051 Frozen bakery products, except bread; Food preparations, nec; Cookies and crackers; Bread, cake, and related products

(G-6102)
MASTER MARKING COMPANY INC
2260 Stone Creek Trl (44223-3605)
PHONE..................................330 688-6797
Raymond X Heller, *Pr*
Steve Heller, *VP*
EMP: 10 EST: 1978
SALES (est): 461.25K **Privately Held**
SIC: **3479** 3953 3549 3544 Etching on metals; Marking devices; Metalworking machinery, nec; Special dies, tools, jigs, and fixtures

(G-6103)
MCHALE GROUP LTD
338 Remington Rd (44224-4916)
PHONE..................................330 923-7070
EMP: 6 EST: 2001
SALES (est): 106.44K **Privately Held**
SIC: **2822** Fluoro rubbers

(G-6104)
MEGA BRIGHT LLC
2251 Front St Ste 200 (44221-2578)
PHONE..................................330 577-8859
Bill Wang, *Dir*
EMP: 10 EST: 2013
SQ FT: 5,000
SALES (est): 974.2K **Privately Held**
Web: www.megabrightlight.com
SIC: **3645** 3646 Residential lighting fixtures; Commercial lighting fixtures

(G-6105)
MOORE MC MILLEN HOLDINGS (PA)
1850 Front St (44221)
PHONE..................................330 745-3075
EMP: 35 EST: 1994
SQ FT: 19,240
SALES (est): 13.07MM **Privately Held**
SIC: **3398** Metal heat treating

(G-6106)
NANOTRONICS IMAGING INC (PA)
Also Called: Nanotronics
2251 Front St Ste 110 (44221-2577)
P.O. Box 306 (44222-0306)
PHONE..................................330 926-9809
Matthew Putman, *CEO*
Matthew Putman, *CEO*
John Putman, *Pr*
EMP: 6 EST: 2007
SQ FT: 2,000
SALES (est): 25.15MM
SALES (corp-wide): 25.15MM **Privately Held**
Web: www.nanotronics.co
SIC: **3826** 3825 Analytical instruments; Semiconductor test equipment

(G-6107)
NSK INDUSTRIES INC (PA)
150 Ascot Pkwy (44223-3354)
P.O. Box 1089 (44223-0089)
PHONE..................................330 923-4112
◆ EMP: 67 EST: 1980
SALES (est): 14.81MM
SALES (corp-wide): 14.81MM **Privately Held**
Web: www.nskind.com
SIC: **5085** 3479 3451 Fasteners, industrial: nuts, bolts, screws, etc.; Coating of metals and formed products; Screw machine products

GEOGRAPHIC SECTION

Dalton - Wayne County (G-6132)

(G-6108)
PLASTIC PALLET AND CONTAINER
2305 Chestnut Blvd (44223-1022)
PHONE.................................330 631-4664
Martin R Ackerman, *Pr*
EMP: 6 **EST:** 2017
SALES (est): 246.34K **Privately Held**
Web: www.plasticpalletandcontainer.com
SIC: 2448 Pallets, wood

(G-6109)
PNEUMATIC SCALE CORPORATION (DH)
Also Called: Pneumatic Scale Angelus
10 Ascot Pkwy (44223-3325)
PHONE.................................330 923-0491
Timothy J Sulllivan, *CEO*
William J Morgan, *Pr*
David M Gianini, *VP*
Robert H Chapman, *Ch*
Gregory L Coonrod Mr, *Dir*
◆ **EMP:** 225 **EST:** 1895
SQ FT: 102,000
SALES (est): 95.2MM **Privately Held**
Web: www.psangelus.com
SIC: 3535 3569 3565 Conveyors and conveying equipment; Centrifuges, industrial ; Bottling machinery: filling, capping, labeling
HQ: Barry-Wehmiller Companies, Inc.
   8020 Forsyth Blvd
   Saint Louis MO 63105
   314 862-8000

(G-6110)
POLYMERICS INC (PA)
2828 2nd St (44221-1953)
PHONE.................................330 928-2210
C Robert Samples, *Ch Bd*
Joe Arhar, *
▲ **EMP:** 50 **EST:** 1974
SQ FT: 24,000
SALES (est): 11.37MM
SALES (corp-wide): 11.37MM **Privately Held**
Web: www.polymericsinc.com
SIC: 3069 2819 2891 2865 Custom compounding of rubber materials; Industrial inorganic chemicals, nec; Adhesives and sealants; Cyclic crudes and intermediates

(G-6111)
PREMIER UV PRODUCTS LLC
1738 Front St (44221-4712)
PHONE.................................330 715-2452
EMP: 6 **EST:** 2004
SALES (est): 161.68K **Privately Held**
SIC: 3799 All terrain vehicles (ATV)

(G-6112)
QUALITY CRAFT MACHINE INC
137 Ascot Pkwy (44223-3355)
PHONE.................................330 928-4064
EMP: 8 **EST:** 1994
SQ FT: 8,900
SALES (est): 324.14K **Privately Held**
Web: www.qcraft.com
SIC: 3599 Machine shop, jobbing and repair

(G-6113)
RECYCLING EQP SOLUTIONS CORP
276 Remington Rd Ste C (44224-4900)
PHONE.................................330 920-1500
Gary Gaither, *Pr*
Mary Gaither, *VP*
▼ **EMP:** 8 **EST:** 2001
SALES (est): 880.13K **Privately Held**
Web: www.therescorp.com
SIC: 3542 Mechanical (pneumatic or hydraulic) metal forming machines

(G-6114)
REUTHER MOLD & MFG CO INC
Also Called: Reuther Mold & Manufacturing
1225 Munroe Falls Ave (44221-3598)
PHONE.................................330 923-5266
Karl A Reuther Ii, *Pr*
Jessica Rhodes, *
EMP: 60 **EST:** 1950
SQ FT: 61,000
SALES (est): 9.41MM **Privately Held**
Web: www.reuthermold.com
SIC: 3544 3599 Industrial molds; Machine shop, jobbing and repair

(G-6115)
RMS EQUIPMENT LLC
Also Called: RMS Equipment Company
1 Vision Ln (44223-4710)
PHONE.................................330 564-1360
Armand Massary, *Pr*
▲ **EMP:** 1527 **EST:** 1917
SQ FT: 50,000
SALES (est): 4.82MM
SALES (corp-wide): 1.21B **Privately Held**
Web: www.steelastic.com
SIC: 3559 Rubber working machinery, including tires
HQ: Pettibone L.L.C.
   27501 Bella Vista Pkwy
   Warrenville IL 60555
   630 353-5000

(G-6116)
SARAHS VINEYARD INC
1204 W Steels Corners Rd (44223-3115)
PHONE.................................330 929-8057
Micheal Lytz, *Pr*
EMP: 8 **EST:** 2007
SALES (est): 605.47K **Privately Held**
Web: www.sarahsvineyardwinery.com
SIC: 2084 Wines

(G-6117)
SILICONE SOLUTIONS INC
338 Remington Rd (44224-4916)
PHONE.................................330 920-3125
David M Brassard, *Pr*
Lorraine R Brassard, *Treas*
EMP: 10 **EST:** 1996
SQ FT: 10,000
SALES (est): 2.21MM **Privately Held**
Web: www.siliconesolutions.com
SIC: 2869 2891 Silicones; Adhesives and sealants

(G-6118)
SPECTRUM PLASTICS CORPORATION
99 E Ascot Ln (44223-3788)
PHONE.................................330 926-9766
Mohammad Malik, *Pr*
▲ **EMP:** 9 **EST:** 1988
SQ FT: 25,000
SALES (est): 1.03MM **Privately Held**
Web: www.splastics.com
SIC: 3089 Injection molding of plastics

(G-6119)
STEELASTIC COMPANY LLC
1 Vision Ln (44223-4710)
PHONE.................................330 633-0505
Jim Vogel, *Pr*
Brian Fetzer, *Managing Member*
▲ **EMP:** 46 **EST:** 1970
SQ FT: 34,500
SALES (est): 21.11MM
SALES (corp-wide): 1.21B **Privately Held**
Web: www.steelastic.com
SIC: 3559 Automotive related machinery
HQ: Pettibone L.L.C.
   27501 Bella Vista Pkwy
   Warrenville IL 60555
   630 353-5000

(G-6120)
SUMMIT MILLWORK LLC
1619 Main St (44221-4047)
PHONE.................................330 920-4000
EMP: 8 **EST:** 2003
SQ FT: 30,000
SALES (est): 1.13MM **Privately Held**
Web: www.summitmillwork.com
SIC: 2431 Millwork

(G-6121)
TECHNICOTE INC
70 Marc Dr (44223-2628)
PHONE.................................330 928-1476
Dave Bolanz, *Mgr*
EMP: 40
SALES (corp-wide): 53.61MM **Privately Held**
Web: www.technicote.com
SIC: 2891 Adhesives
PA: Technicote, Inc.
   222 Mound Ave
   Miamisburg OH 45342
   800 358-4448

(G-6122)
TRI-M BLOCK AND SUPPLY INC
111 Stow Ave Ste 100 (44221-2560)
P.O. Box 166 (44691-0166)
PHONE.................................330 264-8771
Donald Morrow Senior, *Pr*
Donald Morrow Junior, *VP*
Linda Morrow, *Sec*
EMP: 13 **EST:** 1982
SQ FT: 10,000
SALES (est): 2.03MM **Privately Held**
SIC: 3271 Concrete block and brick

(G-6123)
TRM MANUFACTURING INC
601 Munroe Falls Ave (44221)
PHONE.................................330 769-2600
Yong-chang Tang, *CEO*
EMP: 34 **EST:** 2011
SALES (est): 18.55MM **Privately Held**
Web: www.trmmfg.com
SIC: 3462 Iron and steel forgings

(G-6124)
TRU-BORE MACHINE CO INC
1220 Orlen Ave (44221-2956)
PHONE.................................330 928-6215
Michele Crandall, *Pr*
EMP: 6 **EST:** 1966
SQ FT: 10,000
SALES (est): 743.42K **Privately Held**
SIC: 3599 Custom machinery

(G-6125)
TUFFY MANUFACTURING
140 Ascot Pkwy (44223-3743)
PHONE.................................330 940-2356
Lewis Zimmerman, *Pr*
EMP: 15 **EST:** 2014
SALES (est): 3.23MM **Privately Held**
Web: www.tuffymfg.com
SIC: 5521 5013 3999 Automobiles, used cars only; Automotive servicing equipment; Manufacturing industries, nec

(G-6126)
ULTRA TECH MACHINERY INC
297 Ascot Pkwy (44223-3701)
PHONE.................................330 929-5544
Don Hagarty, *Pr*
Robert Hagarty, *
Jim Hagarty, *

▲ **EMP:** 30 **EST:** 1986
SQ FT: 11,000
SALES (est): 8.44MM **Privately Held**
Web: www.utmachinery.com
SIC: 3599 7389 Machine shop, jobbing and repair; Design, commercial and industrial

(G-6127)
ULTRATECH POLYMERS INC
280 Ascot Pkwy (44223-3346)
PHONE.................................330 945-9410
EMP: 17 **EST:** 1995
SQ FT: 4,000
SALES (est): 1.94MM **Privately Held**
Web: www.ultratechpolymers.com
SIC: 3089 Injection molding of plastics

(G-6128)
WEAVER PROPACK - MARC DRIVE
129 Marc Dr (44223-2629)
PHONE.................................330 379-3660
EMP: 7 **EST:** 2016
SALES (est): 70.58K **Privately Held**
Web: www.weaverindustries.org
SIC: 3999 Manufacturing industries, nec

(G-6129)
WIN CD INC
Also Called: Win Plex
3333 Win St (44223-3790)
PHONE.................................330 929-1999
David K Pulk, *Pr*
EMP: 16 **EST:** 1995
SQ FT: 42,000
SALES (est): 549.67K **Privately Held**
Web: www.chasedoors.com
SIC: 2821 Plastics materials and resins

Dalton
Wayne County

(G-6130)
DENDRATEC LTD
1417 Zuercher Rd (44618-9776)
PHONE.................................330 473-4878
Clarence Jennings, *Prin*
EMP: 6 **EST:** 2008
SALES (est): 571.49K **Privately Held**
Web: www.dendratec.com
SIC: 2431 Millwork

(G-6131)
EGR PRODUCTS COMPANY INC (PA)
55 Eckard Rd (44618-9664)
PHONE.................................330 833-6554
Jeffery Daley, *Pr*
Jerome T Daley, *Pr*
Mary Ann Daley, *VP*
EMP: 16 **EST:** 1975
SQ FT: 30,000
SALES (est): 1.66MM
SALES (corp-wide): 1.66MM **Privately Held**
SIC: 3694 3714 Generators, automotive and aircraft; Motor vehicle parts and accessories

(G-6132)
HRH DOOR CORP
Also Called: Wayne - Dalton Rolling Doors
14512 Lincoln Way E (44618-9014)
PHONE.................................330 828-2291
Bill Hammer, *Mgr*
EMP: 25
SALES (corp-wide): 467.98MM **Privately Held**
Web: www.wayne-dalton.com
SIC: 3442 3446 Garage doors, overhead: metal; Architectural metalwork
PA: Hrh Door Corp.

Dalton - Wayne County (G-6133)

1 Door Dr
Mount Hope OH 44660
850 208-3400

(G-6133)
J HORST MANUFACTURING CO
Also Called: 2cravealloys
279 E Main St (44618-9601)
PHONE.................................330 828-2216
Roland Horst, *Pr*
Richard Horst, *
Mary Steiner, *
Don E Flath, *
EMP: 53 **EST:** 1963
SQ FT: 78,000
SALES (est): 8.77MM **Privately Held**
Web: www.jhorst.com
SIC: 3599 3441 3549 3547 Machine shop, jobbing and repair; Fabricated structural metal; Metalworking machinery, nec; Rolling mill machinery

(G-6134)
LAKE REGION OIL INC
26 N Cochran St (44618-9808)
P.O. Box 1478 (44648-1478)
PHONE.................................330 828-8420
Robert Dervin Ii, *Pr*
EMP: 6 **EST:** 1979
SQ FT: 2,500
SALES (est): 1.8MM **Privately Held**
Web: www.lakeregionoilinc.com
SIC: 1382 Oil and gas exploration services

(G-6135)
MARS HORSECARE US INC
Also Called: Mars Horsecare
330 E Schultz St (44618)
P.O. Box 505 (44618)
PHONE.................................330 828-2251
EMP: 45 **EST:** 1943
SALES (est): 23.09MM
SALES (corp-wide): 42.84B **Privately Held**
Web: www.buckeyenutrition.com
SIC: 2048 Alfalfa or alfalfa meal, prepared as animal feed
PA: Mars, Incorporated
6885 Elm St Ste 1
Mc Lean VA 22101
703 821-4900

(G-6136)
MASSILLON MATERIALS INC (PA)
26 N Cochran St (44618-9808)
P.O. Box 499 (44618-0499)
PHONE.................................330 837-4767
Howard J Wenger, *Pr*
EMP: 16 **EST:** 1985
SQ FT: 6,000
SALES (est): 2.38MM **Privately Held**
Web: www.massillon-materials.com
SIC: 1442 Sand mining

(G-6137)
OHIO DERMATOLOGICAL ASSN
698 Dalton Fox Lake Rd (44618-9403)
PHONE.................................330 465-8281
Jill Hostetler, *Admn*
EMP: 7 **EST:** 2017
SALES (est): 219.65K **Privately Held**
Web: www.ohderm.org
SIC: 2834 Dermatologicals

(G-6138)
P GRAHAM DUNN INC
630 Henry St (44618-9280)
PHONE.................................330 828-2105
Patrick Helmuth, *CEO*
Joe Knutson, *
Leanna Dunn, *
Robert Shetler, *
▲ **EMP:** 300 **EST:** 1976
SQ FT: 100,000
SALES (est): 48.94MM **Privately Held**
Web: www.pgrahamdunn.com
SIC: 2499 Laundry products, wood

(G-6139)
PETER GRAHAM DUNN INC
1417 Zuercher Rd (44618-9776)
PHONE.................................330 816-0035
Peter G Dunn, *Pr*
Leanna Dunn, *
◆ **EMP:** 21 **EST:** 1987
SQ FT: 36,000
SALES (est): 901.19K **Privately Held**
Web: www.pgrahamdunn.com
SIC: 3499 5199 Novelties and giftware, including trophies; Advertising specialties

(G-6140)
PIONEER CORP
16875 Jericho Rd (44618-9657)
PHONE.................................330 857-0267
Daniel Wengerd, *Pr*
Leon Wengerd, *
◆ **EMP:** 55 **EST:** 1978
SALES (est): 8.12MM **Privately Held**
Web: www.ackermansequipment.com
SIC: 3315 3441 Steel wire and related products; Fabricated structural metal

(G-6141)
ROBURA INC (PA)
Also Called: Lehman's
4779 Kidron Rd (44618-9287)
P.O. Box 270 (44636-0270)
PHONE.................................800 438-5346
◆ **EMP:** 94 **EST:** 1954
SALES (est): 9.34MM
SALES (corp-wide): 9.34MM **Privately Held**
Web: www.lehmans.com
SIC: 3639 Major kitchen appliances, except refrigerators and stoves

(G-6142)
S LEHMAN CENTRAL WAREHOUSE
289 Kurzen Rd N (44618-9009)
PHONE.................................330 828-8828
EMP: 7 **EST:** 2014
SALES (est): 181.76K **Privately Held**
Web: www.crownplacebrands.com
SIC: 5251 3429 Hardware stores; Hardware, nec

(G-6143)
SPRINGHILL DIMENSIONS
4530 Mount Eaton Rd S (44618-9128)
PHONE.................................330 317-1926
EMP: 21 **EST:** 2019
SALES (est): 824.47K **Privately Held**
Web: www.springhilldimensions.com
SIC: 2434 Wood kitchen cabinets

(G-6144)
WAYNEDALE TRUSS AND PANEL CO
93 Lake Dr (44618-9720)
PHONE.................................330 683-4471
Dianne Fry, *Prin*
EMP: 8 **EST:** 2010
SALES (est): 105.8K **Privately Held**
SIC: 2439 Trusses, wooden roof

(G-6145)
WORLD CLASS CARRIAGES LLC
5090 Mount Eaton Rd S (44618-9643)
PHONE.................................330 857-7811
EMP: 8 **EST:** 2020
SALES (est): 443.43K **Privately Held**
Web: www.worldclasscarriages.com
SIC: 3799 Carriages, horse drawn

(G-6146)
ZIMMERMAN STEEL & SUP CO LLC
18543 Davis Rd (44618-9697)
PHONE.................................330 828-1010
EMP: 10 **EST:** 1995
SQ FT: 11,700
SALES (est): 2.59MM **Privately Held**
Web: www.zimmermansteel.com
SIC: 3441 Fabricated structural metal

Damascus
Mahoning County

(G-6147)
BUCKEYE TRAILER & FAB CO LLC
14779 French St (44619-2903)
P.O. Box 45 (44619-0045)
PHONE.................................330 501-9440
EMP: 7 **EST:** 2017
SALES (est): 641.46K **Privately Held**
Web: www.buckeyetrailerrepair.com
SIC: 3799 Trailers and trailer equipment

Danville
Knox County

(G-6148)
COUNTRY LANE CUSTOM BUILDINGS
Also Called: Countryside Construction
21318 Pealer Mill Rd (43014-9640)
PHONE.................................740 485-8481
Andrew C Nisley, *Owner*
EMP: 9 **EST:** 2017
SALES (est): 436.48K **Privately Held**
SIC: 3999 7389 Miniatures; Business services, nec

(G-6149)
VALLEY VIEW PALLETS LLC
Also Called: Valley View Pallets Partners
22414 Hostetler Rd (43014-9638)
PHONE.................................740 599-0010
Ephraim Yoder, *Managing Member*
EMP: 9 **EST:** 1996
SALES (est): 820.08K **Privately Held**
SIC: 2448 7389 Pallets, wood; Business Activities at Non-Commercial Site

(G-6150)
YOUNGS LOCKER SERVICE INC
Also Called: Youngs Locker Serv & Meat Proc
16201 Nashville Rd (43014-9738)
P.O. Box Y (43014-0625)
PHONE.................................740 599-6833
Lawrence Payne, *Pr*
EMP: 10 **EST:** 1945
SQ FT: 10,000
SALES (est): 704.74K **Privately Held**
Web: www.youngscountrymarket.com
SIC: 2011 4222 2013 Meat packing plants; Warehousing, cold storage or refrigerated; Sausages and other prepared meats

Dayton
Greene County

(G-6151)
AES BEAVER VALLEY LLC
1065 Woodman Dr (45432-1423)
▲ **EMP:** 62 **EST:** 1983
SALES (est): 30.28MM
SALES (corp-wide): 12.67B **Publicly Held**
Web: www.aes.com
SIC: 3612 Power transformers, electric
PA: The Aes Corporation
4300 Wilson Blvd Ste 1100
Arlington VA 22203
703 522-1315

(G-6152)
AMCO PRODUCTS INC
500 N Smithville Rd (45431-1069)
PHONE.................................937 433-7982
Joseph M Raby, *CEO*
Ronald J Raby, *Pr*
Karla Simmons, *VP*
EMP: 10 **EST:** 1966
SQ FT: 58,600
SALES (est): 1.6MM **Privately Held**
Web: www.amco-products.com
SIC: 3451 Screw machine products

(G-6153)
ANTHONY BUSINESS FORMS INC
3160 Plainfield Rd (45432-3713)
P.O. Box 24754 (45424-0754)
PHONE.................................937 253-0072
Katherine D Harrah, *Pr*
EMP: 9 **EST:** 1985
SQ FT: 6,000
SALES (est): 426.27K **Privately Held**
Web: www.anthonybusinessforms.com
SIC: 5112 2754 2759 2791 Business forms; Labels: gravure printing; Envelopes: printing, nsk; Typesetting

(G-6154)
CAPITAL PRECISION MACHINE & TL
1865 Radio Rd (45431-1034)
PHONE.................................937 258-1176
Paul Powers Senior, *Owner*
Cliff Smith, *Prin*
EMP: 8 **EST:** 1978
SQ FT: 10,000
SALES (est): 717.56K **Privately Held**
Web: www.cpmtool.com
SIC: 3544 Special dies and tools

(G-6155)
CASSADY WOODWORKS INC
446 N Smithville Rd (45431-1080)
PHONE.................................937 256-7948
Tom Joch, *Pr*
EMP: 24 **EST:** 1958
SQ FT: 12,000
SALES (est): 853.67K **Privately Held**
Web: www.cassadywoodworks.com
SIC: 2431 2441 2541 Millwork; Nailed wood boxes and shook; Display fixtures, wood

(G-6156)
CPM TOOL CO LLC
1865 Radio Rd (45431-1034)
PHONE.................................937 258-1176
EMP: 7 **EST:** 2020
SALES (est): 600K **Privately Held**
Web: www.cpmtool.com
SIC: 3312 Tool and die steel and alloys

(G-6157)
D & B INDUSTRIES INC
5031 Linden Ave Ste B (45432-1893)
PHONE.................................937 253-8658
Brent Gillott, *Pr*
EMP: 7 **EST:** 1973
SQ FT: 5,000
SALES (est): 525.31K **Privately Held**
Web: www.d-bindustries.com
SIC: 3599 Machine shop, jobbing and repair

(G-6158)
DEFENSE RESEARCH ASSOC INC
3915 Germany Ln Ste 102 (45431-1688)

▲ = Import ▼ = Export
◆ = Import/Export

GEOGRAPHIC SECTION
Dayton - Montgomery County (G-6181)

PHONE..................937 431-1644
Leroy E Anderson, *CEO*
Ray Trimmer, *
Jeanette Anderson, *
Rebecca Trimmer, *
EMP: 25 **EST:** 1973
SQ FT: 15,000
SALES (est): 3.8MM **Privately Held**
Web: www.dra-engineering.com
SIC: 8731 8748 3724 Commercial physical research; Systems analysis and engineering consulting services; Research and development on aircraft engines and parts

(G-6159)
DLA DOCUMENT SERVICES
4165 Communications Blvd, Ste 2, Bldg 281, Door 18 (45433-5601)
PHONE..................937 257-6014
Leonard Xavier, *Dir*
EMP: 14
Web: www.dla.mil
SIC: 2752 9711 Commercial printing, lithographic; National security
HQ: Dla Document Services
5450 Carlisle Pike Bldg 9
Mechanicsburg PA 17050
717 605-2362

(G-6160)
DOXIE INC
Also Called: Signs Now Dayton
3197 Beaver Vu Dr (45434-6366)
PHONE..................937 427-3431
James Jackson, *Pr*
Carol Jackson, *VP*
EMP: 7 **EST:** 2016
SALES (est): 524.32K **Privately Held**
Web: www.signsnow.com
SIC: 3993 Signs and advertising specialties

(G-6161)
GREEN MACHINE TOOL INC
1865 Radio Rd (45431-1034)
PHONE..................937 253-0771
Eugene Green, *Pr*
Mary Ann Green, *VP*
EMP: 15 **EST:** 1979
SQ FT: 12,000
SALES (est): 468K **Privately Held**
Web: www.greenmachinetool.com
SIC: 3599 3544 Machine shop, jobbing and repair; Forms (molds), for foundry and plastics working machinery

(G-6162)
GREENE COUNTY
Also Called: Green County Wtr Sup & Trtmnt
1122 Beaver Valley Rd (45434-7014)
PHONE..................937 429-0127
EMP: 8
SIC: 3589 4941 Sewage and water treatment equipment; Water supply
PA: Greene County
35 Greene St
Xenia OH 45385
937 562-5006

(G-6163)
ICAD INC
2689 Commons Blvd Ste 100 (45431)
PHONE..................866 280-2239
EMP: 10 **EST:** 1984
SALES (est): 72.6K **Privately Held**
Web: www.icadmed.com
SIC: 3841 Surgical and medical instruments

(G-6164)
INNOVATIVE MECH SYSTEMS LLC
Also Called: American Metal Fabricators
3100 Plainfield Rd Ste A (45432-3725)
PHONE..................937 813-8713
EMP: 8 **EST:** 1986
SQ FT: 37,000
SALES (est): 1.18MM **Privately Held**
SIC: 3444 Sheet metalwork

(G-6165)
L3 TECHNOLOGIES INC
Also Called: Raytheon
47 Alf/ Raythoen Arospace Bld 201 Area C 5 (45433)
PHONE..................937 257-8501
Dave Riegel, *Prin*
EMP: 6
SALES (corp-wide): 19.42B **Publicly Held**
Web: www.l3harris.com
SIC: 3663 Telemetering equipment, electronic
HQ: L3 Technologies, Inc.
600 3rd Ave Fl 34
New York NY 10016
321 727-9100

(G-6166)
LAU HOLDINGS LLC
4509 Springfield St (45431-1042)
PHONE..................937 476-6500
Daniel Hake, *Brnch Mgr*
EMP: 46
SALES (corp-wide): 184.04MM **Privately Held**
Web: www.lauparts.com
SIC: 3564 Ventilating fans: industrial or commercial
HQ: Lau Holdings, Llc
16900 S Waterloo Rd
Cleveland OH 44110
216 486-4000

(G-6167)
LAU INDUSTRIES INC
Also Called: Supreme Fan/Industrial Air
4509 Springfield St (45431-1042)
PHONE..................216 894-3903
Damian Macaluso, *Pr*
Christopher Wampler, *
Dan Disser, *
▼ **EMP:** 1865 **EST:** 1929
SQ FT: 50,000
SALES (est): 110.16MM **Privately Held**
SIC: 3564 Ventilating fans: industrial or commercial
HQ: Johnson Controls, Inc.
5757 N Green Bay Ave
Milwaukee WI 53209
920 245-6409

(G-6168)
MANTYCH METALWORKING INC
3175 Plainfield Rd (45432-3712)
PHONE..................937 258-1373
Kathleen Mantych, *CEO*
Colleen Mantych, *Pr*
Cristy Mantych, *VP*
EMP: 26 **EST:** 1971
SQ FT: 24,000
SALES (est): 1.53MM **Privately Held**
Web: www.mantych.net
SIC: 3599 3444 Machine shop, jobbing and repair; Sheet metalwork

(G-6169)
MARSH COMPOSITES LLC
1691 Spaulding Rd (45432-3723)
PHONE..................937 350-1214
EMP: 6 **EST:** 2017
SALES (est): 208.79K **Privately Held**

SIC: 2221 3089 Automotive fabrics, manmade fiber; Automotive parts, plastic

(G-6170)
MIAMI VALLEY LIGHTING LLC
1065 Woodman Dr (45432-1423)
PHONE..................937 224-6000
Joyce Reives, *Managing Member*
EMP: 7 **EST:** 2001
SQ FT: 1,500
SALES (est): 88.73K
SALES (corp-wide): 12.67B **Publicly Held**
Web: www.lightingsimplified.com
SIC: 3648 Street lighting fixtures
HQ: Dpl Inc.
1065 Woodman Dr
Dayton OH 45432
937 259-7215

(G-6171)
MIAMI VLY MFG & ASSEMBLY INC
1889 Radio Rd (45431-1034)
PHONE..................937 254-6665
Joseph S Rosenkranz, *Pr*
EMP: 12 **EST:** 1993
SQ FT: 5,000
SALES (est): 1MM **Privately Held**
Web: www.mvmainc.com
SIC: 3599 Machine shop, jobbing and repair

(G-6172)
RUSKIN MANUFACTURING
4509 Springfield St (45431-1042)
PHONE..................937 476-6500
EMP: 8 **EST:** 2019
SALES (est): 183.34K **Privately Held**
Web: www.ruskin.com
SIC: 3822 Environmental controls

(G-6173)
SELECT SIGNS
1755 Spaulding Rd (45432-3727)
PHONE..................937 262-7095
Jon Cowell, *Prin*
EMP: 22 **EST:** 2007
SALES (est): 2.44MM **Privately Held**
Web: www.selectsigns.com
SIC: 3993 Signs and advertising specialties

(G-6174)
TOASTMASTERS INTERNATIONAL
1854 Redleaf Ct (45432-4103)
PHONE..................937 429-2680
Dan Reeves, *Treas*
EMP: 10
SALES (corp-wide): 26.23MM **Privately Held**
Web: www.toastmasters.org
SIC: 8299 2721 Educational service, nondegree granting: continuing educ.; Magazines: publishing only, not printed on site
PA: Toastmasters International
9127 S Jamaica St Ste 400
Englewood CO 80112
949 858-8255

(G-6175)
UNISON INDUSTRIES LLC
2455 Dayton Xenia Rd (45434-7148)
PHONE..................904 667-9904
Belinda Kidwell, *Mgr*
EMP: 400
SALES (corp-wide): 67.95B **Publicly Held**
Web: www.unisonindustries.com
SIC: 3728 4581 3714 3498 Aircraft parts and equipment, nec; Aircraft servicing and repairing; Motor vehicle parts and accessories; Fabricated pipe and fittings
HQ: Unison Industries, Llc
7575 Baymeadows Way
Jacksonville FL 32256
904 739-4000

(G-6176)
YOUNGS PUBLISHING INC
4130 Linden Ave Ste 150 (45432-3088)
PHONE..................937 259-6575
Ronald K Young Senior, *Pr*
Ronald K Young Junior, *VP*
EMP: 8 **EST:** 1988
SALES (est): 470.54K **Privately Held**
Web: www.reforsale.org
SIC: 2721 Magazines: publishing and printing

Dayton
Montgomery County

(G-6177)
4 OVER LLC
7801 Technology Blvd (45424-1574)
PHONE..................937 610-0629
Frank Johnston, *VP*
EMP: 47
SALES (corp-wide): 172.36MM **Privately Held**
Web: www.4over.com
SIC: 2759 Commercial printing, nec
HQ: 4 Over, Llc
1225 Los Angeles St
Glendale CA 91204
818 246-1170

(G-6178)
A & B IRON & METAL CO INC
329 Washington St (45402-2541)
P.O. Box 123 (45301-0123)
PHONE..................937 228-1561
Greg Thoma, *Pr*
Joseph Caperna, *Pr*
Rosalia Caperna, *VP*
EMP: 9 **EST:** 1949
SQ FT: 500
SALES (est): 483.91K **Privately Held**
Web: www.abironmetal.com
SIC: 5093 4953 3341 3231 Metal scrap and waste materials; Refuse systems; Secondary nonferrous metals; Products of purchased glass

(G-6179)
ACCRO-CAST CORPORATION
4147 Gardendale Ave (45417-9509)
PHONE..................937 228-0497
Fred Luther, *Pr*
EMP: 20 **EST:** 1964
SQ FT: 5,000
SALES (est): 387.92K **Privately Held**
Web: www.accrocast.com
SIC: 3363 Aluminum die-castings

(G-6180)
ACCU-GRIND & MFG CO INC
272 Leo St (45404-1006)
P.O. Box 117 (45337-0117)
PHONE..................937 224-3303
Jeff Heisey, *Pr*
EMP: 43 **EST:** 1988
SQ FT: 39,500
SALES (est): 4.7MM **Privately Held**
Web: www.accugrind.net
SIC: 3599 Machine shop, jobbing and repair

(G-6181)
ACCUTECH PLASTIC MOLDING INC
5015 Kitridge Rd (45424-4433)
P.O. Box 24272 (45424-0272)
PHONE..................937 233-0017
William Stoddard Junior, *Pr*
EMP: 7 **EST:** 1977

Dayton - Montgomery County (G-6182)

SQ FT: 6,000
SALES (est): 523.02K **Privately Held**
SIC: 3089 Injection molding of plastics

(G-6182)
ACTION RUBBER CO INC
601 Fame Rd (45449-2355)
PHONE..................937 866-5975
Ron Mc Croson, *Pr*
EMP: 10 **EST:** 1984
SQ FT: 12,500
SALES (est): 1.05MM **Privately Held**
Web: www.actionrubber.com
SIC: 3069 Molded rubber products

(G-6183)
AD INDUSTRIES INC
6450 Poe Ave Ste 109 (45414-2646)
PHONE..................303 744-1911
◆ **EMP:** 7776
SIC: 3634 3564 3535 3714 Fans, exhaust and ventilating, electric: household; Ventilating fans: industrial or commercial; Conveyors and conveying equipment; Motor vehicle parts and accessories

(G-6184)
ADCURA MFG
1314 Farr Dr (45404-2736)
PHONE..................937 222-3800
Russel Phie, *Owner*
EMP: 6 **EST:** 2005
SALES (est): 793.1K **Privately Held**
Web: www.adcuramfg.com
SIC: 3496 Miscellaneous fabricated wire products

(G-6185)
ADEPT MANUFACTURING CORP
1710 E 1st St (45403-1128)
PHONE..................937 222-7110
Mike Mueller, *Pr*
Sandy Mueller, *Treas*
EMP: 10 **EST:** 1992
SALES (est): 1.33MM **Privately Held**
SIC: 3544 Special dies and tools

(G-6186)
AERO JET WASH LLC
450 Gargrave Rd (45449-2462)
PHONE..................866 381-7955
Shawn Tadayon, *Managing Member*
Mike Vahedy, *Managing Member*
EMP: 10 **EST:** 2006
SALES (est): 977.99K **Privately Held**
Web: www.aerojetwash.com
SIC: 3724 4581 Aircraft engines and engine parts; Aircraft cleaning and janitorial service

(G-6187)
AEROSEAL LLC
Also Called: Aerobarrier
1851 S Metro Pkwy (45459-2523)
PHONE..................937 428-9300
Amit Gupta, *Brnch Mgr*
EMP: 30
SALES (corp-wide): 31.78MM **Privately Held**
Web: www.aeroseal.com
SIC: 8748 3679 Energy conservation consultant; Hermetic seals, for electronic equipment
PA: Aeroseal Llc
225 Byers Rd 1
Miamisburg OH 45342
937 428-9300

(G-6188)
AFC STAMPING & PRODUCTION INC
4900 Webster St (45414-4831)
PHONE..................937 275-8700
EMP: 115 **EST:** 1971
SALES (est): 24.46MM
SALES (corp-wide): 49.44MM **Privately Held**
Web: www.afcstamping.com
SIC: 3469 Metal stampings, nec
PA: Fc Industries, Inc.
4900 Webster St
Dayton OH 45414
937 275-8700

(G-6189)
AFC TOOL CO INC
4900 Webster St (45414-4831)
PHONE..................937 275-8700
EMP: 30 **EST:** 1972
SALES (est): 13.3MM
SALES (corp-wide): 49.44MM **Privately Held**
Web: www.afctool.com
SIC: 3544 Special dies and tools
PA: Fc Industries, Inc.
4900 Webster St
Dayton OH 45414
937 275-8700

(G-6190)
AFS TECHNOLOGY LLC
6649 Deer Bluff Dr (45424)
PHONE..................937 545-0627
John Tiernan, *Pr*
EMP: 13 **EST:** 2005
SALES (est): 2.99MM **Privately Held**
Web: www.afstechnologyusa.com
SIC: 3523 Elevators, farm

(G-6191)
AGILE MANUFACTURING TECH LLC
220 N Jersey St (45403-1220)
PHONE..................937 258-3338
EMP: 10 **EST:** 2019
SALES (est): 780.48K **Privately Held**
SIC: 3999 Manufacturing industries, nec

(G-6192)
AIDA-AMERICA CORPORATION (HQ)
7660 Center Point 70 Blvd (45424-6365)
PHONE..................937 237-2382
◆ **EMP:** 65 **EST:** 1995
SALES (est): 23.08MM **Privately Held**
Web: www.aida-global.com
SIC: 3542 Presses: forming, stamping, punching, sizing (machine tools)
PA: Aida Engineering, Ltd.
2-10, Oyamacho, Midori-Ku
Sagamihara KNG 252-0

(G-6193)
ALLEY CAT DESIGNS INC
919 Senate Dr (45459-4017)
PHONE..................937 291-8803
EMP: 8 **EST:** 1996
SQ FT: 2,800
SALES (est): 871.17K **Privately Held**
Web: www.alleycatworldwide.com
SIC: 3552 2395 Printing machinery, textile; Embroidery products, except Schiffli machine

(G-6194)
ALLIED MOTION AT DAYTON
2275 Stanley Ave (45404-1226)
PHONE..................937 228-3171
EMP: 16 **EST:** 2018
SALES (est): 3.14MM **Privately Held**
SIC: 3621 Motors, electric

(G-6195)
ALLIED SILK SCREEN INC
2740 Thunderhawk Ct (45414-3464)
PHONE..................937 223-4921
Dennis Brzozowski, *Pr*
David Brzozowski, *VP*
EMP: 7 **EST:** 1970
SQ FT: 10,000
SALES (est): 439.51K **Privately Held**
Web: www.alliedsilkscreen.com
SIC: 2759 Screen printing

(G-6196)
ALRO STEEL CORPORATION
821 Springfield St (45403-1252)
PHONE..................937 253-6121
TOLL FREE: 800
Tim Elliott, *Mgr*
EMP: 40
SQ FT: 120,000
SALES (corp-wide): 3.43B **Privately Held**
Web: www.alro.com
SIC: 5051 3441 3317 3316 Steel; Fabricated structural metal; Steel pipe and tubes; Cold finishing of steel shapes
PA: Alro Steel Corporation
3100 E High St
Jackson MI 49203
517 787-5500

(G-6197)
AMERICAN AERO COMPONENTS LLC
2601 W Stroop Rd Ste 62 (45439-2030)
PHONE..................937 367-5068
Ajitesh Kakade, *Managing Member*
EMP: 7 **EST:** 2015
SQ FT: 50,000
SALES (est): 601.07K **Privately Held**
SIC: 3451 3599 3728 3724 Screw machine products; Machine and other job shop work; Aircraft parts and equipment, nec; Aircraft engines and engine parts

(G-6198)
AMERICAN BOTTLING COMPANY
7 Up Bottling Co of Dayton
3131 Transportation Rd (45404-2372)
PHONE..................937 236-0333
Michael Eichner, *Mgr*
EMP: 99
SQ FT: 100,000
Web: www.keurigdrpepper.com
SIC: 2086 Soft drinks: packaged in cans, bottles, etc.
HQ: The American Bottling Company
6425 Hall Of Fame Ln
Frisco TX 75034

(G-6199)
AMERICAN CITY BUS JOURNALS INC
Also Called: Dayton Business Journal
40 N Main St Ste 810 (45423-1053)
PHONE..................937 528-4400
EMP: 268
SALES (corp-wide): 2.88B **Privately Held**
Web: www.acbj.com
SIC: 2711 7313 Newspapers: publishing only, not printed on site; Newspaper advertising representative
HQ: American City Business Journals, Inc.
120 W Morehead St Ste 400
Charlotte NC 28202
704 973-1000

(G-6200)
AMERICAN CONCRETE PRODUCTS INC
Also Called: American Brick & Block
1433 S Euclid Ave (45417-3839)
PHONE..................937 224-1433
Lee Snyder, *Pr*
Lee E Snyder, *Treas*
EMP: 12 **EST:** 1987
SQ FT: 10,000
SALES (est): 1.08MM **Privately Held**
Web: www.snyderonline.com
SIC: 3271 5211 Blocks, concrete or cinder: standard; Brick

(G-6201)
AMERICAN INDUS MAINTANENCE
605 Springfield St (45403-1248)
PHONE..................937 254-3400
Marvin Price, *Pr*
Cari Price, *VP*
EMP: 8 **EST:** 1991
SQ FT: 19,000
SALES (est): 1.71MM **Privately Held**
Web: www.aimsandblasting.com
SIC: 5231 3471 Paint and painting supplies; Sand blasting of metal parts

(G-6202)
AMERICAN POWER LLC
Also Called: Apowermedia
1819 Troy St (45404-2400)
PHONE..................937 235-0418
Adil Baguirov, *CEO*
Adil Baguirov, *Managing Member*
EMP: 12 **EST:** 2013
SALES (est): 2.5MM **Privately Held**
Web: www.americanpowertransport.com
SIC: 5047 3842 5088 7379 Medical equipment and supplies; Surgical appliances and supplies; Transportation equipment and supplies; Computer related consulting services

(G-6203)
AMERICAN RESCUE TECHNOLOGY INC
2780 Culver Ave (45429-3724)
PHONE..................937 293-6240
Richard S Michalo, *Pr*
◆ **EMP:** 10 **EST:** 1993
SQ FT: 11,000
SALES (est): 2.34MM **Privately Held**
Web: www.art4rescue.com
SIC: 5084 3569 Safety equipment; Firefighting and related equipment

(G-6204)
AMERICAN WAY EXTERIORS LLC
7666 Mcewen Rd (45459-3908)
PHONE..................937 221-8860
Stephen Moad, *Pr*
EMP: 7 **EST:** 2014
SALES (est): 931K **Privately Held**
Web: www.americanwayexteriors.com
SIC: 3292 1761 1799 Roofing, asbestos felt roll; Roofing, siding, and sheetmetal work; Asbestos removal and encapsulation

(G-6205)
AMERIWATER LLC
3345 Stop 8 Rd (45414-3425)
PHONE..................937 461-8833
Greg Reny, *Pr*
James Baker, *
▲ **EMP:** 47 **EST:** 1992
SQ FT: 48,000
SALES (est): 13.23MM **Privately Held**
Web: www.ameriwater.com
SIC: 3589 Water treatment equipment, industrial

GEOGRAPHIC SECTION
Dayton - Montgomery County (G-6229)

(G-6206)
ANALYTICA USA INC (PA)
711 E Monument Ave Ste 309 (45402)
PHONE..................................513 348-2333
Vikram Seshadri, *CEO*
EMP: 14 **EST:** 2006
SALES (est): 1.69MM
SALES (corp-wide): 1.69MM **Privately Held**
Web: www.analytica.net
SIC: 7371 3825 Software programming applications; Radio apparatus analyzers, nec

(G-6207)
ANNARINO FOODS LTD
2787 Armstrong Ln (45414-4225)
PHONE..................................937 274-3663
Anthony Annarino, *Pt*
Leonard M Annarino, *Pt*
EMP: 10 **EST:** 1990
SQ FT: 6,000
SALES (est): 1.27MM **Privately Held**
Web: www.annarinofoods.com
SIC: 2033 2035 Spaghetti and other pasta sauce: packaged in cans, jars, etc; Dressings, salad: raw and cooked (except dry mixes)

(G-6208)
AOG INC
Also Called: Agents of Gaming
7672 Mcewen Rd (45459-3908)
P.O. Box 31571 (45437-0571)
PHONE..................................937 436-2412
Bruce Graw, *Pr*
Robert Glass, *VP*
Kelly Lofgren, *Treas*
EMP: 7 **EST:** 1997
SQ FT: 6,000
SALES (est): 395.69K **Privately Held**
Web: www.agentsofgaming.com
SIC: 3944 Games, toys, and children's vehicles

(G-6209)
APEX TOOL GROUP LLC
762 W Stewart St (45417-3971)
PHONE..................................937 222-7871
EMP: 128
SALES (corp-wide): 1.8MM **Privately Held**
Web: www.apextoolgroup.com
SIC: 3546 Power-driven handtools
HQ: Apex Tool Group, Llc
910 Ridgebrook Rd Ste 200
Sparks Glencoe MD 21152

(G-6210)
APS-MATERIALS INC (PA)
Also Called: A P S
4011 Riverside Dr (45405-2364)
P.O. Box 1106 (45401-1106)
PHONE..................................937 278-6547
Michael C Wilson, *Pr*
Joseph T Cheng, *
▲ **EMP:** 65 **EST:** 1975
SQ FT: 50,000
SALES (est): 26.45MM
SALES (corp-wide): 26.45MM **Privately Held**
Web: www.apsmaterials.com
SIC: 3479 2899 2851 Coating of metals and formed products; Chemical preparations, nec; Paints and allied products

(G-6211)
AQUA PRECISION LLC
165 Janney Rd (45404-1225)
PHONE..................................937 912-9582
Michael Witt, *Prin*
EMP: 11 **EST:** 2016

SALES (est): 712.44K **Privately Held**
Web: www.aquaprecision.net
SIC: 3599 Machine shop, jobbing and repair

(G-6212)
ARGROV BOX CO
6030 Webster St (45414-3434)
P.O. Box 305 (45042-0305)
PHONE..................................937 898-1700
Kenneth Eppich, *Pr*
Judith Eppich, *VP*
Dean Timmons, *COO*
EMP: 13 **EST:** 1969
SQ FT: 42,400
SALES (est): 232.48K **Privately Held**
Web: www.argrov.com
SIC: 2653 5113 Boxes, corrugated: made from purchased materials; Boxes and containers

(G-6213)
ARK OPERATIONS INC
2700 Kettg Tower 40n Main St (45423)
PHONE..................................419 871-1186
EMP: 6 **EST:** 2018
SALES (est): 147.78K **Privately Held**
Web: www.arkoperations.com
SIC: 3085 Plastics bottles

(G-6214)
ARTISAN GRINDING SERVICE INC
1300 Stanley Ave (45404-1092)
P.O. Box 131 (45404-0131)
PHONE..................................937 667-7383
Carolyn M Buechly, *Pr*
Jeryl L Yantis, *Sec*
Teresa Landers, *Asst VP*
EMP: 11 **EST:** 1977
SQ FT: 14,000
SALES (est): 970.04K **Privately Held**
Web: www.artisangrinding.com
SIC: 3599 Machine shop, jobbing and repair

(G-6215)
ASIDACO LLC (PA)
Also Called: Alterntive Sltons Innvtion Dev
400 Linden Ave Ste 95 (45403)
PHONE..................................800 204-1544
Andrea T Bashaw, *Managing Member*
EMP: 9 **EST:** 2008
SALES (est): 1.2MM
SALES (corp-wide): 1.2MM **Privately Held**
Web: www.asidaco.com
SIC: 1731 1711 4911 3694 Electric power systems contractors; Solar energy contractor; Battery charging alternators and generators

(G-6216)
ATI SOLUTIONS PROPERTIES LLC
8801 Sugarcreek Pt (45458-2833)
PHONE..................................937 609-7681
Mark Nagy, *Prin*
EMP: 6 **EST:** 2018
SALES (est): 176.51K **Privately Held**
SIC: 3312 Stainless steel

(G-6217)
AUTO-VALVE INC
1707 Guenther Rd (45417-9398)
PHONE..................................937 854-3037
Raymond C Clark, *Pr*
Beth Seall, *
EMP: 50 **EST:** 1948
SQ FT: 17,800
SALES (est): 8.81MM **Privately Held**
Web: www.autovalve.com
SIC: 3728 Aircraft parts and equipment, nec

(G-6218)
AUTOMATION SYSTEMS DESIGN INC
Also Called: A S D
3540 Vance Rd (45439-7939)
PHONE..................................937 387-0351
Sunny Kullar, *Prin*
Sukhi Kullar, *CFO*
EMP: 20 **EST:** 2000
SALES (est): 9.02MM **Privately Held**
Web: www.asddayton.com
SIC: 3535 Robotic conveyors

(G-6219)
AUTOMATION TECHNOLOGY INC
1900 Troy St (45404-2194)
PHONE..................................937 233-6084
Robert Storar, *CEO*
N Chris Storar, *
Jeff Storar, *
EMP: 25 **EST:** 1982
SQ FT: 20,000
SALES (est): 4.44MM **Privately Held**
Web: www.atidayton.com
SIC: 3625 3825 3829 3823 Actuators, industrial; Test equipment for electronic and electrical circuits; Measuring and controlling devices, nec; Process control instruments

(G-6220)
AVION TOOL CORPORATION
3620 Lenox Dr (45429-1516)
PHONE..................................937 278-0779
Paul Molnar, *Pr*
EMP: 16 **EST:** 1947
SQ FT: 11,000
SALES (est): 711.08K **Privately Held**
Web: www.countrybarnrestaurant.com
SIC: 3724 Aircraft engines and engine parts

(G-6221)
B & P COMPANY INC
97 Compark Rd (45459-4801)
P.O. Box 41184 (45441-0184)
PHONE..................................937 298-0265
Margaret Wright, *Pr*
EMP: 9 **EST:** 1889
SQ FT: 13,000
SALES (est): 1.54MM **Privately Held**
Web: www.frownies.com
SIC: 2844 Cosmetic preparations

(G-6222)
B S F INC (PA)
8895 N Dixie Dr (45414-1803)
P.O. Box 459 (45377-0459)
PHONE..................................937 890-6121
Kathryn Keel, *Pr*
Mike Coale, *VP*
Chris Bright, *Prin*
Eric Metzger, *Prin*
Jackie Frank, *Prin*
EMP: 10 **EST:** 1974
SQ FT: 2,000
SALES (est): 2.47MM
SALES (corp-wide): 2.47MM **Privately Held**
Web: www.bsfinc.net
SIC: 3498 3568 Couplings, pipe: fabricated from purchased pipe; Couplings, shaft: rigid, flexible, universal joint, etc.

(G-6223)
BARSPLICE PRODUCTS INC
4900 Webster St (45414-4831)
PHONE..................................937 275-8700
◆ **EMP:** 48 **EST:** 1988
SALES (est): 10.18MM
SALES (corp-wide): 49.44MM **Privately Held**
Web: www.barsplice.com

SIC: 3449 Bars, concrete reinforcing: fabricated steel
PA: Fc Industries, Inc.
4900 Webster St
Dayton OH 45414
937 275-8700

(G-6224)
BEELIGHTING INC
347 Leo St (45404-1007)
PHONE..................................937 296-4460
Janet Zheng, *Prin*
EMP: 6 **EST:** 2014
SALES (est): 429.9K **Privately Held**
Web: www.beelite-led.com
SIC: 3648 Lighting equipment, nec

(G-6225)
BEIJING WEST INDUSTRIES
3100 Research Blvd Ste 10 (45420-4032)
PHONE..................................937 455-5281
EMP: 19 **EST:** 2010
SALES (est): 2.2MM **Privately Held**
Web: www.bwigroup.com
SIC: 3714 Motor vehicle parts and accessories

(G-6226)
BELTON FOODS LLC
Also Called: Belton Foods
2701 Thunderhawk Ct (45414-3445)
P.O. Box 13605 (45413-0605)
PHONE..................................937 890-7768
David V Sipos, *Pr*
Cindy Gillespie, *
Ted Dorow, *
Barbara Berer, *
Eleanor Sipos, *Stockholder**
EMP: 36 **EST:** 1949
SQ FT: 24,800
SALES (est): 9.54MM **Privately Held**
Web: www.beltonfoods.com
SIC: 2087 2086 2035 Concentrates, drink; Bottled and canned soft drinks; Pickles, sauces, and salad dressings

(G-6227)
BETA INDUSTRIES INC (PA)
2860 Culver Ave (45429-3794)
PHONE..................................937 299-7385
William B Walcott, *Pr*
Kenneth Walcott, *Dev*
Phyllis Walcott, *Sec*
EMP: 12 **EST:** 1968
SQ FT: 12,600
SALES (est): 4.76MM
SALES (corp-wide): 4.76MM **Privately Held**
Web: www.betaindustries.net
SIC: 3599 3699 Machine shop, jobbing and repair; Electrical equipment and supplies, nec

(G-6228)
BF & CD ROBERTS RE IMPRV
3336 Highcrest Ct (45405-2020)
PHONE..................................937 277-2632
Cd Roberts, *Prin*
EMP: 6 **EST:** 2008
SALES (est): 138.12K **Privately Held**
SIC: 3011 Tires and inner tubes

(G-6229)
BIKE MIAMI VALLEY OHIO
929 S Perry St (45402-2526)
PHONE..................................937 496-3825
Laura Estandia, *Ex Dir*
EMP: 7
SALES (est): 115.93K **Privately Held**
SIC: 3751 Motorcycles, bicycles and parts

(PA)=Parent Co (HQ)=Headquarters
✿ = New Business established in last 2 years

Dayton - Montgomery County (G-6230)

(G-6230)
BLAIRS CNC TURNING INC
Also Called: Blair's Cnc
245 Leo St (45404-1005)
P.O. Box 2840 (45401-2840)
PHONE..................937 461-1100
James Trochelman, *Pr*
Marina Trochelman, *VP*
EMP: 7 **EST:** 1986
SQ FT: 13,100
SALES (est) 694.58K **Privately Held**
SIC: 3599 Machine shop, jobbing and repair

(G-6231)
BLANG ACQUISITION LLC
Also Called: Kap Signs
7464 Webster St (45414-5816)
PHONE..................937 223-2155
John D Blang, *Managing Member*
EMP: 19 **EST:** 1969
SQ FT: 12,000
SALES (est): 766.2K **Privately Held**
Web: www.kapsigns.com
SIC: 2499 5999 5199 3993 Signboards, wood; Banners; Decals; Signs and advertising specialties

(G-6232)
BLUE CREEK ENTERPRISES INC
Also Called: Tabtronics
2153 Winners Cir (45404-1150)
PHONE..................937 222-9969
EMP: 20
SALES (corp-wide): 23.68MM **Privately Held**
Web: www.miracllc.com
SIC: 3672 Printed circuit boards
PA: Blue Creek Enterprises, Inc.
316 N Main St
Lynchburg OH 45142
937 364-2920

(G-6233)
BOB SUMEREL TIRE CO INC
7711 Center Point 70 Blvd (45424-6368)
PHONE..................937 235-0062
Dennis Lavoie, *Mgr*
EMP: 15
SALES (corp-wide): 97.34MM **Privately Held**
Web: www.bobsumereltire.com
SIC: 5531 7534 Automotive tires; Tire retreading and repair shops
PA: Bob Sumerel Tire Co., Inc.
1257 Cox Ave
Erlanger KY 41018
859 283-2700

(G-6234)
BOOKFACTORY LLC
2302 S Edwin C Moses Blvd (45417-4662)
PHONE..................937 226-7100
Andrew Gilmore, *
▼ **EMP:** 30 **EST:** 2002
SQ FT: 20,000
SALES (est): 4.85MM **Privately Held**
Web: www.bookfactory.com
SIC: 5942 2678 2731 2789 Book stores; Memorandum books, notebooks, and looseleaf filler paper; Book publishing; Bookbinding and related work

(G-6235)
BRANCH & BONE ARTISAN ALES LLC
905 Wayne Ave (45410-1247)
PHONE..................937 723-7608
EMP: 14 **EST:** 2016
SALES (est): 600K **Privately Held**
Web: www.branchandboneales.com
SIC: 2082 Beer (alcoholic beverage)

(G-6236)
BRIDGITS BATH LLC
1226 Pursell Ave (45420-1974)
PHONE..................937 259-1960
EMP: 7 **EST:** 2008
SALES (est): 460.08K **Privately Held**
Web: www.bridgitsbath.com
SIC: 3261 7389 Soap dishes, vitreous china; Business Activities at Non-Commercial Site

(G-6237)
BROADWAY SAND AND GRAVEL LLC
130 W 2nd St Ste 2000 (45402-1502)
PHONE..................937 853-5555
Michael Marshall, *Prin*
EMP: 6 **EST:** 2016
SALES (est): 69.55K **Privately Held**
SIC: 1442 Construction sand and gravel

(G-6238)
BUCHER PRINTING
26 N Clinton St (45402-1327)
PHONE..................937 228-2022
Randy Keithley, *Pr*
EMP: 6 **EST:** 2018
SALES (est): 90.74K **Privately Held**
SIC: 2672 Paper; coated and laminated, nec

(G-6239)
BUCKEYE OIL EQUIPMENT CO
20 Innovation Ct (45414-3968)
PHONE..................937 387-0671
Tim Stovell, *Prin*
EMP: 10 **EST:** 1977
SALES (est): 717.99K **Privately Held**
Web: www.jfpetrogroup.com
SIC: 3533 Oil and gas drilling rigs and equipment

(G-6240)
BUDDE PRECISION MACHINING CORP
2608 Nordic Rd (45414-3424)
PHONE..................937 278-1962
Michael Budde, *Pr*
EMP: 15 **EST:** 2018
SALES (est): 1.4MM **Privately Held**
Web: www.buddeprecision.com
SIC: 3599 Machine shop, jobbing and repair

(G-6241)
BUDDE SHEET METAL WORKS INC (PA)
305 Leo St (45404-1083)
PHONE..................937 224-0868
Candice Budde, *Pr*
Thomas Budde, *
Stephen L Budde, *
William R Budde Junior, *Sec*
EMP: 25 **EST:** 1922
SQ FT: 20,000
SALES (est): 7.23MM
SALES (corp-wide): 7.23MM **Privately Held**
Web: www.buddesheetmetal.com
SIC: 1761 3444 1711 Sheet metal work, nec; Sheet metalwork; Plumbing, heating, air-conditioning

(G-6242)
C & M RUBBER CO INC
414 Littell Ave (45419-3608)
P.O. Box 185 (45401-0185)
PHONE..................937 299-2782
James Mccloskey, *Pr*
Eric Weber, *VP*
EMP: 14 **EST:** 1964
SQ FT: 10,000
SALES (est): 1.75MM **Privately Held**
Web: www.cmrubber.com
SIC: 3061 Mechanical rubber goods

(G-6243)
C B MFG & SLS CO INC
American Cutting Edge
4475 Infirmary Rd (45449)
PHONE..................937 866-5986
Charles Biehn, *Mgr*
EMP: 19
SALES (corp-wide): 22.18MM **Privately Held**
Web: www.americancuttingedge.com
SIC: 3423 Hand and edge tools, nec
PA: C. B. Manufacturing And Sales Company, Inc.
4455 Infirmary Rd
Miamisburg OH 45342
937 866-5986

(G-6244)
C-LINK ENTERPRISES LLC
Also Called: Southern Ohio Kitchens
1825 Webster St (45404-1147)
PHONE..................937 222-2829
EMP: 10 **EST:** 1968
SQ FT: 25,000
SALES (est): 1.13MM **Privately Held**
SIC: 1521 2514 5722 General remodeling, single-family houses; Kitchen cabinets: metal; Kitchens, complete (sinks, cabinets, etc.)

(G-6245)
CABCONNECT INC
714 E Monument Ave Ste 107 (45402)
PHONE..................773 282-3565
EMP: 11 **EST:** 2019
SALES (est): 444.09K **Privately Held**
Web: www.cabconnect.com
SIC: 3652 Prerecorded records and tapes

(G-6246)
CARGILL INCORPORATED
Also Called: Cargill
3201 Needmore Rd (45414-4321)
PHONE..................937 236-1971
Sheila Willhoite, *Brnch Mgr*
EMP: 49
SALES (corp-wide): 176.74B **Privately Held**
Web: www.cargill.com
SIC: 2046 2087 2041 Corn starch; Flavoring extracts and syrups, nec; Flour and other grain mill products
PA: Cargill, Incorporated
15407 Mcginty Rd W
Wayzata MN 55391
800 227-4455

(G-6247)
CARSON-SAEKS INC (PA)
Also Called: Karen Carson Creations
2601 Timber Ln (45414-4733)
P.O. Box 13297 (45413-0297)
PHONE..................937 278-5311
William Smith, *Ch Bd*
Terrence Mollaun, *
Jeff Smith, *
◆ **EMP:** 35 **EST:** 1985
SQ FT: 20,000
SALES (est): 5.52MM
SALES (corp-wide): 5.52MM **Privately Held**
Web: www.karencarson.com
SIC: 2869 Perfume materials, synthetic

(G-6248)
CASSANOS INC (PA)
Also Called: Cassano's Pizza & Subs
1700 E Stroop Rd (45429-5095)
PHONE..................937 294-8400
Vic Cassano Junior, *Ch Bd*
EMP: 45 **EST:** 1949
SQ FT: 37,500
SALES (est): 30.98K
SALES (corp-wide): 30.98K **Privately Held**
Web: www.cassanos.com
SIC: 5812 5149 6794 2045 Pizzeria, chain; Baking supplies; Franchises, selling or licensing; Pizza doughs, prepared: from purchased flour

(G-6249)
CASSIS PACKAGING CO
1235 Mccook Ave (45404-2812)
PHONE..................937 223-8868
TOLL FREE: 800
Sheila Cassis, *Pr*
Cassandra Cassis, *VP*
EMP: 13 **EST:** 1957
SQ FT: 26,000
SALES (est): 1.21MM **Privately Held**
Web: www.cassispackaging.com
SIC: 2449 4783 Rectangular boxes and crates, wood; Crating goods for shipping

(G-6250)
CERTIFIED HEAT TREATING INC (PA)
4475 Infirmary Rd (45449)
P.O. Box 354 (45449)
PHONE..................937 866-0245
Joseph Biehn, *Pr*
EMP: 13 **EST:** 1970
SQ FT: 20,000
SALES (est): 2.08MM
SALES (corp-wide): 2.08MM **Privately Held**
Web: www.heattreating.com
SIC: 3398 Metal heat treating

(G-6251)
CHAOS ENTERTAINMENT
Also Called: CD / Dvd Distribution
7570 Mount Whitney St (45424-6944)
PHONE..................937 520-5260
EMP: 8 **EST:** 2008
SALES (est): 456.88K **Privately Held**
SIC: 3561 Pumps and pumping equipment

(G-6252)
CHEF INK LLC
1131 Benfield Dr (45429-4450)
PHONE..................937 474-2032
Dominic Colaizzi, *Prin*
EMP: 6 **EST:** 2010
SALES (est): 50K **Privately Held**
SIC: 2893 Printing ink

(G-6253)
CHEMCORE INC (PA)
20 Madison St (45402-2106)
P.O. Box 802 (45401-0802)
PHONE..................937 228-6118
Mike Klaus, *CEO*
Reiff Lorenz, *Pr*
Geoffrey Lorenz, *VP*
EMP: 10 **EST:** 2000
SALES (est): 2.38MM
SALES (corp-wide): 2.38MM **Privately Held**
Web: www.chemstation.com
SIC: 5169 2869 Chemical additives; Industrial organic chemicals, nec

GEOGRAPHIC SECTION — Dayton - Montgomery County (G-6278)

(G-6254)
CHEMINEER INC
Also Called: Kenics
5870 Poe Ave (45414-3442)
P.O. Box 1123 (45401-1123)
PHONE..................937 454-3200
◆ **EMP:** 160
Web: www.nov.com
SIC: 3559 3556 3554 3531 Chemical machinery and equipment; Food products machinery; Paper industries machinery; Construction machinery

(G-6255)
CHROMALLOY CORPORATION
7425 Webster St (45414-5817)
PHONE..................937 890-3775
Pete Stodd, *Pr*
EMP: 11
SALES (corp-wide): 1.2B **Privately Held**
Web: www.chromalloy.com
SIC: 3569 Assembly machines, non-metalworking
PA: Chromalloy Corporation
3999 Rca Blvd
Palm Beach Gardens FL 33410
561 935-3571

(G-6256)
CIRCUIT CENTER
4738 Gateway Cir (45440-1724)
PHONE..................513 435-2131
Michael Kerr, *Prin*
EMP: 8 **EST:** 2004
SALES (est): 171.94K **Privately Held**
SIC: 3672 Printed circuit boards

(G-6257)
COCA-COLA CONSOLIDATED INC
Also Called: Coca-Cola
1000 Coca Cola Blvd (45424-6375)
PHONE..................937 878-5000
Bob Tiootson, *Mgr*
EMP: 355
SALES (corp-wide): 6.65B **Publicly Held**
Web: www.cokeconsolidated.com
SIC: 2086 Bottled and canned soft drinks
PA: Coca-Cola Consolidated, Inc.
4100 Coca-Cola Plz
Charlotte NC 28211
704 557-4400

(G-6258)
COLBY WOODWORKING INC
1912 Lucille Dr (45404-1109)
PHONE..................937 224-7676
Steven Colby, *Pr*
EMP: 20 **EST:** 1985
SALES (est): 1.16MM **Privately Held**
SIC: 2434 Wood kitchen cabinets

(G-6259)
COMMCONNECT
5747 Executive Blvd (45424-1448)
PHONE..................937 414-0505
Scott Dilworth, *Prin*
EMP: 10 **EST:** 2007
SALES (est): 1.94MM **Privately Held**
Web: www.comm-connect.com
SIC: 3351 Wire, copper and copper alloy

(G-6260)
COMMERCIAL MTAL FBRICATORS INC
150 Commerce Park Dr (45404-1273)
PHONE..................937 233-4911
Patrick Dakin, *Pr*
James D Utrecht, *
Molly Dakin, *
EMP: 40 **EST:** 1954
SALES (est): 6.14MM **Privately Held**
Web: www.commercialmetalfabricators.com
SIC: 3441 3444 3443 Fabricated structural metal; Sheet metalwork; Fabricated plate work (boiler shop)

(G-6261)
COMPONENT SOLUTIONS GROUP INC (HQ)
7755 Paragon Rd Ste 104 (45459-4052)
PHONE..................937 434-8100
Ernie Riling, *Pr*
Sam Pfabe, *CFO*
EMP: 12 **EST:** 1998
SQ FT: 3,500
SALES (est): 30.08MM **Privately Held**
Web: www.componentsolutionsgroup.com
SIC: 5031 3452 Pallets, wood; Bolts, nuts, rivets, and washers
PA: Bufab Ab (Publ)
Stenfalksvagen 1
VArnamo 331 4

(G-6262)
COMPOSITE TECHNOLOGIES CO LLC
401 N Keowee St (45404-1602)
PHONE..................937 228-2880
Mike Dematto, *Managing Member*
Jay Binder, *Managing Member*
EMP: 80 **EST:** 1998
SQ FT: 100,000
SALES (est): 16.24MM
SALES (corp-wide): 51.58MM **Privately Held**
Web: www.ctcplastics.com
SIC: 3089 Plastics containers, except foam
PA: Soin International, Llc
1129 Mmsburg Cntrvlle Rd Ste
Dayton OH 45449
937 427-7646

(G-6263)
CONTECH BRIDGE SOLUTIONS LLC
Also Called: Bridgetek
7941 New Carlisle Pike (45424-1507)
PHONE..................937 878-2170
Jim Feltner, *Mgr*
EMP: 9
Web: www.conteches.com
SIC: 3272 Concrete products, nec
HQ: Contech Bridge Solutions Llc
9025 Cntrpinte Dr Ste 400
West Chester OH 45069

(G-6264)
COUCH BUSINESS DEVELOPMENT INC
Also Called: Fordyce Custom Finishing
32 Bates St (45402-1326)
PHONE..................937 253-1099
David Couch, *Pr*
EMP: 15 **EST:** 2010
SQ FT: 49,250
SALES (est): 488.08K **Privately Held**
Web: www.artifexfinishing.com
SIC: 2541 2491 1751 Display fixtures, wood; Millwork, treated wood; Store fixture installation

(G-6265)
COX PUBLISHING HQ
1611 S Main St (45409-2547)
PHONE..................937 225-2000
Michael Joseph, *Prin*
EMP: 9 **EST:** 2007
SALES (est): 643.35K **Privately Held**
SIC: 2741 Miscellaneous publishing

(G-6266)
CREATIVE FOAM DAYTON MOLD
3337 N Dixie Dr (45414-5645)
PHONE..................937 279-9987
EMP: 14 **EST:** 2013
SALES (est): 2.75MM **Privately Held**
Web: www.creativefoam.com
SIC: 3086 Plastics foam products

(G-6267)
CRG PLASTICS INC
2661 Culver Ave (45429-3721)
PHONE..................937 298-2025
Jerry Wenzke, *Pr*
Nancy Wenzke, *VP*
▲ **EMP:** 10 **EST:** 1987
SQ FT: 8,000
SALES (est): 421.76K **Privately Held**
Web: www.vernonwhite.tv
SIC: 2821 3089 Polytetrafluoroethylene resins, teflon; Molding primary plastics

(G-6268)
CTC PLASTICS
Also Called: Ctc East
943 Woodley Rd (45403-1446)
PHONE..................937 281-4002
EMP: 242
SALES (corp-wide): 51.58MM **Privately Held**
Web: www.ctcplastics.com
SIC: 3089 Injection molding of plastics
HQ: Ctc Plastics
401 N Keowee St
Dayton OH 45404
937 228-9184

(G-6269)
CTC PLASTICS (HQ)
401 N Keowee St (45404-1602)
PHONE..................937 228-9184
Vishal Soin, *CEO*
Mike Dematto, *COO*
William R Senften, *CFO*
EMP: 23 **EST:** 2012
SALES (est): 26.87MM
SALES (corp-wide): 51.58MM **Privately Held**
Web: www.ctcplastics.com
SIC: 3089 Injection molding of plastics
PA: Soin International, Llc
1129 Mmsburg Cntrvlle Rd Ste
Dayton OH 45449
937 427-7646

(G-6270)
CUSTOM BLIND CORPORATION
Also Called: Castle Blinds and Draperies
2895 Culver Ave (45429-3725)
PHONE..................937 643-2907
FAX: 937 643-1119
EMP: 12
SQ FT: 6,000
SALES (est): 1.29MM **Privately Held**
SIC: 2591 5023 1521 Drapery hardware and window blinds and shades; Vertical blinds; Single-family home remodeling, additions, and repairs

(G-6271)
CUSTOM NICKEL LLC
45 N Clinton St (45402-1346)
PHONE..................937 222-1995
EMP: 6 **EST:** 1980
SALES (est): 553.97K **Privately Held**
Web: www.custom-nickel.com
SIC: 3471 Plating of metals or formed products

(G-6272)
DAY-HIO PRODUCTS INC
709 Webster St (45404-1527)
PHONE..................937 445-0782
John L Lenz, *Pr*
▲ **EMP:** 11 **EST:** 1953
SQ FT: 15,000
SALES (est): 260.18K **Privately Held**
SIC: 3451 Screw machine products

(G-6273)
DAYTON BAG & BURLAP CO
448 Huffman Ave (45403-2506)
PHONE..................937 253-1722
EMP: 10
SALES (corp-wide): 46.25MM **Privately Held**
Web: www.daybag.com
SIC: 4225 2299 General warehousing and storage; Burlap, jute
PA: The Dayton Bag & Burlap Co
322 Davis Ave
Dayton OH 45403
937 258-8000

(G-6274)
DAYTON BINDERY SERVICE INC
3757 Inpark Dr (45414-4417)
PHONE..................937 235-3111
FAX: 937 235-5070
EMP: 20
SALES (est): 2.15MM **Privately Held**
SIC: 2789 Bookbinding and related work

(G-6275)
DAYTON CITY PAPER GROUP LLC
Also Called: Impact Weekly
126 N Main St Ste 240 (45402-1766)
P.O. Box 10065 (45402-7065)
PHONE..................937 222-8855
Mehdi Adineh, *Managing Member*
EMP: 10 **EST:** 1993
SALES (est): 861.39K **Privately Held**
SIC: 2711 Newspapers, publishing and printing

(G-6276)
DAYTON CLUTCH & JOINT INC (PA)
2005 Troy St 1 (45404-2936)
P.O. Box 163 (45404-0163)
PHONE..................937 236-9770
Keith Knight, *Pr*
Nancy Knight, *Sec*
EMP: 16 **EST:** 1956
SQ FT: 16,000
SALES (est): 2.62MM
SALES (corp-wide): 2.62MM **Privately Held**
Web: www.daytonclutch.com
SIC: 3714 Motor vehicle parts and accessories

(G-6277)
DAYTON COATING TECH LLC
1926 E Siebenthaler Ave (45414-5334)
PHONE..................937 278-2060
EMP: 6 **EST:** 1999
SQ FT: 15,000
SALES (est): 1.05MM **Privately Held**
Web: www.toolgrindcoat.com
SIC: 3479 Coating of metals and formed products

(G-6278)
DAYTON FORGING HEAT TREATING
215 N Findlay St (45403-1200)
PHONE..................937 253-4126
Eric Wilson, *Pr*
Martha Todd Wilson, *
EMP: 65 **EST:** 1919

Dayton - Montgomery County (G-6279)

GEOGRAPHIC SECTION

SQ FT: 100,000
SALES (est): 9.71MM **Privately Held**
Web: www.daytonforging.com
SIC: **3398** 3462 Metal heat treating; Machinery forgings, ferrous

(G-6279)
DAYTON GEAR AND TOOL CO
500 Fame Rd (45449-2387)
PHONE..................937 866-4327
Thomas R Baird, *Pr*
EMP: 20 EST: 1946
SQ FT: 3,000
SALES (est): 4.88MM **Privately Held**
Web: www.daytongear.com
SIC: **3566** Gears, power transmission, except auto

(G-6280)
DAYTON LASER & AESTHETIC MEDIC
6611 Clyo Rd Ste E (45459-2705)
PHONE..................937 208-8282
Lisa Smith, *Prin*
EMP: 7 EST: 2007
SALES (est): 140.62K **Privately Held**
SIC: **2834** 8011 Medicines, capsuled or ampuled; Physicians' office, including specialists

(G-6281)
DAYTON LEGAL BLANK INC
Also Called: Signature Printing
875 Congress Park Dr (45459-4047)
P.O. Box 750788 (45475-0788)
PHONE..................937 435-4405
EMP: 11 EST: 1873
SALES (est): 487.14K **Privately Held**
SIC: **2791** 2759 2752 2789 Typesetting; Commercial printing, nec; Commercial printing, lithographic; Bookbinding and related work

(G-6282)
DAYTON MACHINE TOOL COMPANY
Also Called: M D Tool
1314 Webster St (45404-1568)
PHONE..................937 222-6444
EMP: 25 EST: 1950
SALES (est): 969.17K **Privately Held**
Web: www.firsttoolcorp.com
SIC: **3541** 3549 7699 Machine tools, metal cutting type; Metalworking machinery, nec; Industrial machinery and equipment repair

(G-6283)
DAYTON MOLDED URETHANES LLC
Also Called: D M U
3337 N Dixie Dr (45414-5645)
PHONE..................937 279-9987
William Palmer, *Pr*
EMP: 63 EST: 2001
SQ FT: 50,000
SALES (est): 3.53MM
SALES (corp-wide): 198.24MM **Privately Held**
SIC: **3089** Injection molding of plastics
PA: Creative Foam Corporation
300 N Alloy Dr
Fenton MI 48430
810 629-4149

(G-6284)
DAYTON MOLDED URETHANES LLC
6400 Sand Lake Rd (45414-2635)
PHONE..................937 279-1910
EMP: 36 EST: 2013
SALES (est): 4.79MM
SALES (corp-wide): 198.24MM **Privately Held**

SIC: **3061** Mechanical rubber goods
PA: Creative Foam Corporation
300 N Alloy Dr
Fenton MI 48430
810 629-4149

(G-6285)
DAYTON ONE LLC
212 Heid Ave (45404-1220)
PHONE..................937 265-0227
EMP: 6 EST: 2016
SALES (est): 313.95K **Privately Held**
Web: www.daytonone.com
SIC: **3599** Machine shop, jobbing and repair

(G-6286)
DAYTON PATTERN INC
5591 Wadsworth Rd (45414-3446)
P.O. Box 13779 (45413-0779)
PHONE..................937 277-0761
Erik Zimmer, *Pr*
Janice Zimmer, *Sec*
EMP: 6 EST: 1965
SQ FT: 7,000
SALES (est): 508.81K **Privately Held**
Web: www.daytonpattern.com
SIC: **3543** Industrial patterns

(G-6287)
DAYTON POLYMERIC PRODUCTS INC
3337 N Dixie Dr (45414-5645)
PHONE..................937 279-9987
EMP: 60 EST: 2001
SALES (est): 3.9MM **Privately Held**
SIC: **3086** Packaging and shipping materials, foamed plastics

(G-6288)
DAYTON PROGRESS CORPORATION (DH)
500 Progress Rd (45449-2351)
P.O. Box 39 (45449)
PHONE..................937 859-5111
David Turpin, *Pr*
Randy Wissinger, *VP Fin*
Sawato Hayashi, *Prin*
▲ EMP: 525 EST: 1946
SALES (est): 151.11MM **Privately Held**
Web: www.daytonprogress.com
SIC: **3544** 3545 3495 3493 Punches, forming and stamping; Machine tool accessories; Wire springs; Steel springs, except wire
HQ: Dayton Lamina Corporation
500 Progress Rd
Dayton OH 45449
937 859-5111

(G-6289)
DAYTON PROGRESS INTL CORP
500 Progress Rd (45449-2326)
PHONE..................937 859-5111
Alan Shaffer, *Pr*
David Turpin, *VP*
Randy S Wissinger, *VP Fin*
Bill Mills, *VP*
EMP: 57 EST: 1969
SALES (est): 1.78MM **Privately Held**
Web: www.daytonlamina.com
SIC: **3544** Special dies and tools
HQ: Dayton Progress Corporation
500 Progress Rd
Dayton OH 45449
937 859-5111

(G-6290)
DAYTON STENCIL WORKS COMPANY
Also Called: Datono Products

113 E 2nd St (45402-1753)
P.O. Box 126 (45401-0126)
PHONE..................937 223-3233
TOLL FREE: 800
Edward Jauch, *Pr*
Larry Horwath, *VP*
David Jauch, *Sec*
John Jauch, *Treas*
EMP: 19 EST: 1859
SQ FT: 18,000
SALES (est): 3.76MM **Privately Held**
Web: www.daytonstencil.com
SIC: **3949** 3953 3544 5085 Golf equipment; Marking devices; Special dies, tools, jigs, and fixtures; Industrial supplies

(G-6291)
DAYTON WIRE PRODUCTS INC
7 Dayton Wire Pkwy (45404-1282)
PHONE..................937 236-8000
David Leiser, *Pr*
Brian Schissler, *
EMP: 40 EST: 1965
SQ FT: 62,500
SALES (est): 4.36MM **Privately Held**
Web: www.ncttech.com
SIC: **3496** 3993 Miscellaneous fabricated wire products; Signs and advertising specialties

(G-6292)
DAYTON-PHOENIX GROUP INC (PA)
1619 Kuntz Rd (45404-1240)
PHONE..................937 496-3900
Gale Kooken, *Pr*
Roger Fleming, *
John Murphy, *
◆ EMP: 99 EST: 1992
SALES (est): 114.96MM **Privately Held**
Web: www.dayton-phoenix.com
SIC: **3621** 3743 Motors and generators; Railroad equipment

(G-6293)
DB UNLIMITED LLC
Also Called: Db Products USA
61 Marco Ln (45458-3818)
PHONE..................937 401-2602
John Sackett, *Genl Mgr*
EMP: 10 EST: 2013
SALES (est): 386.68K **Privately Held**
Web: www.dbunlimitedco.com
SIC: **3651** 5065 Audio electronic systems; Sound equipment, electronic

(G-6294)
DC PRINTING LLC
2149 N Gettysburg Ave (45406-3563)
PHONE..................937 640-1957
Shatyea Howard, *Owner*
EMP: 6 EST: 2017
SALES (est): 242.66K **Privately Held**
Web: www.dcprintcompany.com
SIC: **2752** Commercial printing, lithographic

(G-6295)
DCM SOUNDEX INC
Also Called: Soundex Communications Group
1901 E 5th St (45403-2347)
P.O. Box 1942 (45401-1942)
PHONE..................937 522-0371
Sam Nicolosi, *Pr*
EMP: 15 EST: 1974
SALES (est): 1.22MM **Privately Held**
SIC: **3678** 3679 Electronic connectors; Transducers, electrical

(G-6296)
DELMA CORP
Also Called: Dayton Manufacturing Company
3327 Elkton Ave (45403-1357)

PHONE..................937 253-2142
Robert J Davis, *Pr*
Lisa Davis, *
Ronald Connelly, *
Lisa D Houseman, *
Mary W Davis, *
EMP: 65 EST: 1991
SQ FT: 52,000
SALES (est): 9.81MM **Privately Held**
Web: www.daytonmanufacturing.com
SIC: **3444** Metal housings, enclosures, casings, and other containers

(G-6297)
DESIGN PATTERN WORKS INC
2312 E 3rd St (45403-2015)
PHONE..................937 252-0797
George Weckler, *Pr*
James Weckler, *VP*
EMP: 8 EST: 1977
SALES (est): 777.29K **Privately Held**
SIC: **3543** Industrial patterns

(G-6298)
DGL WOODWORKING INC
5931 Wolf Creek Pike (45426-2439)
PHONE..................937 837-7091
FAX: 937 854-7568
EMP: 10
SQ FT: 10,000
SALES (est): 820K **Privately Held**
Web: www.dglwoodworking.com
SIC: **2522** 2434 1751 Cabinets, office; except wood; Wood kitchen cabinets; Cabinet and finish carpentry

(G-6299)
DIMCO GRAY
8200 S Suburban Dr (45458-2709)
PHONE..................937 291-4720
Terry Tate, *Contrlr*
EMP: 9 EST: 2018
SALES (est): 224.41K **Privately Held**
SIC: **3089** Injection molding of plastics

(G-6300)
DOLING & ASSOC DNTL LAB INC
3318 Successful Way (45414-4318)
PHONE..................937 254-0075
Ted Doling, *Pr*
Joe Wiener, *VP*
EMP: 16 EST: 1986
SQ FT: 3,000
SALES (est): 531.42K **Privately Held**
Web: www.dalabllc.com
SIC: **3842** 8072 Surgical appliances and supplies; Crown and bridge production

(G-6301)
DONUT PLACE KINGS INC
100 N James H Mcgee Blvd (45402-6735)
PHONE..................937 829-9725
Mansour A Issa, *Admn*
EMP: 6 EST: 2017
SALES (est): 75.48K **Privately Held**
SIC: **2051** Doughnuts, except frozen

(G-6302)
DOUBLE D D MTLS INSTLLTION INC
Also Called: Double D D Mtls Instllation In
7733 N Main St (45415-2551)
PHONE..................937 898-2534
George Dahling, *Pr*
EMP: 8 EST: 1996
SQ FT: 2,000
SALES (est): 1.03MM **Privately Held**
SIC: **5211** 5031 1799 3699 Fencing; Fencing, wood; Fence construction; Door opening and closing devices, electrical

GEOGRAPHIC SECTION
Dayton - Montgomery County (G-6327)

(G-6303)
DRAGOON TECHNOLOGIES INC (PA)
Also Called: Dragoonitcn
900 Senate Dr (45459-4017)
PHONE.................................937 439-9223
Kathy Appenzeller, *CEO*
EMP: 6 **EST:** 1993
SQ FT: 51,000
SALES (est): 1.8MM
SALES (corp-wide): 1.8MM **Privately Held**
Web: www.dragoonitcn.com
SIC: 3812 Radar systems and equipment

(G-6304)
DRONE EXPRESS INC (PA) ✪
123 Webster St (45402-1391)
PHONE.................................513 577-5152
EMP: 18 **EST:** 2022
SALES (est): 2.57MM
SALES (corp-wide): 2.57MM **Privately Held**
Web: www.droneexpress.com
SIC: 3728 Target drones

(G-6305)
DRT HOLDINGS INC (PA)
618 Greenmount Blvd (45419-3271)
PHONE.................................937 298-7391
EMP: 60 **EST:** 2008
SALES (est): 177.41MM **Privately Held**
Web: www.drtholdingsllc.com
SIC: 6719 3599 3728 Investment holding companies, except banks; Machine shop, jobbing and repair; Aircraft parts and equipment, nec

(G-6306)
DRT MFG CO LLC
618 Greenmount Blvd (45419-3271)
PHONE.................................937 298-7391
EMP: 150 **EST:** 2019
SALES (est): 10.09MM **Privately Held**
Web: www.drtholdingsllc.com
SIC: 3599 Machine shop, jobbing and repair

(G-6307)
DRT MFG CO LLC (HQ)
Also Called: Drt
4201 Little York Rd (45414-2507)
PHONE.................................937 297-6670
Gregory S Martin, *VP Opers*
Stephen Barnes, *
◆ **EMP:** 63 **EST:** 1949
SALES (est): 26.38MM **Privately Held**
Web: mp.drtholdingsllc.com
SIC: 3544 3545 Special dies and tools; Machine tool accessories
PA: Drt Holdings, Inc.
        618 Greenmount Blvd
        Dayton OH 45419

(G-6308)
DUPONT ELECTRONIC POLYMERS LP
1515 Nicholas Rd (45417-6712)
PHONE.................................937 268-3411
Ellen Kullman, *Ch Bd*
Craig F Binetti, *Pr*
David G Bills, *Sr VP*
James C Borel, *Ex VP*
Benito Cachinero-snchez, *Sr VP*
EMP: 65 **EST:** 2001
SALES (est): 24.73MM
SALES (corp-wide): 17.23B **Publicly Held**
Web: www.dupont.com
SIC: 2819 Industrial inorganic chemicals, nec
HQ: Eidp, Inc.
        9330 Zionsville Rd
        Indianapolis IN 46268
        833 267-8382

(G-6309)
DYNAPOINT TECHNOLOGIES INC
475 Progress Rd (45449-2323)
P.O. Box 1447 (45501-1447)
PHONE.................................937 859-5193
Jeffrey G Beatty, *Pr*
EMP: 23 **EST:** 1969
SQ FT: 14,000
SALES (est): 493.9K **Privately Held**
Web: www.dynapointtech.com
SIC: 3599 Machine shop, jobbing and repair

(G-6310)
DYSINGER INCORPORATED (PA)
4316 Webster St (45414-4936)
PHONE.................................937 297-7761
EMP: 44 **EST:** 1973
SALES (est): 6MM
SALES (corp-wide): 6MM **Privately Held**
Web: www.dysinger.com
SIC: 3545 3544 3496 Cutting tools for machine tools; Special dies, tools, jigs, and fixtures; Miscellaneous fabricated wire products

(G-6311)
EASTMAN KODAK COMPANY
Also Called: Kodak
3000 Research Blvd (45420-4003)
PHONE.................................937 259-3000
Patty A Cord, *Brnch Mgr*
EMP: 20
SALES (corp-wide): 573MM **Publicly Held**
Web: www.kodak.com
SIC: 3355 3577 5043 Aluminum rolling and drawing, nec; Computer peripheral equipment, nec; Projection apparatus, motion picture and slide
PA: Eastman Kodak Company
        343 State St
        Rochester NY 14650
        585 724-4000

(G-6312)
ECO-GROUPE INC (PA)
6161 Ventnor Ave (45414-2651)
PHONE.................................937 898-2603
William Gaiser, *CEO*
Karin Gaiser, *Pr*
Kelly Ferguson, *VP*
EMP: 16 **EST:** 2011
SALES (est): 17.11MM
SALES (corp-wide): 17.11MM **Privately Held**
SIC: 3085 Plastics bottles

(G-6313)
EDFA LLC
Also Called: Martin-Palmer Tool
90 Vermont Ave (45404-1521)
PHONE.................................937 222-1415
Flem Messer, *Prin*
April Messer, *Prin*
EMP: 7 **EST:** 2019
SALES (est): 991.89K **Privately Held**
Web: www.martinpalmertool.com
SIC: 3544 Special dies and tools

(G-6314)
ELECTRO POLISH COMPANY
332 Vermont Ave (45404-1597)
PHONE.................................937 222-3611
Kent Kumbroch, *Pr*
Stuart Price, *
EMP: 34 **EST:** 1949
SQ FT: 8,000
SALES (est): 4.31MM **Privately Held**
Web: www.electro-polish.com
SIC: 3471 Electroplating of metals or formed products

(G-6315)
ELECTRO-LINE INC
118 S Terry St (45403-2312)
P.O. Box 1688 (45401-1688)
PHONE.................................937 461-5683
Bruce Jump, *Pr*
Bruce Jump, *Pr*
Jeffrey J Bucher, *VP*
Jeff Bucher, *VP*
EMP: 15 **EST:** 1958
SQ FT: 15,000
SALES (est): 1.91MM **Privately Held**
Web: www.rpaelect.com
SIC: 3679 5065 Electronic circuits; Electronic parts and equipment, nec

(G-6316)
ELECTROWIND
1960 Troy St (45404-2159)
PHONE.................................937 229-0101
EMP: 7 **EST:** 1997
SALES (est): 142.71K **Privately Held**
SIC: 3599 Industrial machinery, nec

(G-6317)
ELK TECHNOLOGIES LLC
390 Signalfire Dr (45458-3633)
PHONE.................................937 902-4165
Brad Robillard, *Prin*
EMP: 7 **EST:** 2017
SALES (est): 307.87K **Privately Held**
Web: www.elktechnologies.net
SIC: 3599 Machine shop, jobbing and repair

(G-6318)
ELLIOTT TOOL TECHNOLOGIES LTD (PA)
Also Called: Elliott
1760 Tuttle Ave (45403-3428)
PHONE.................................937 253-6133
EMP: 66 **EST:** 1892
SQ FT: 37,000
SALES (est): 11.87MM **Privately Held**
Web: www.elliott-tool.com
SIC: 7359 3542 5072 3541 Equipment rental and leasing, nec; Machine tools, metal forming type; Hand tools; Machine tools, metal cutting type

(G-6319)
EMERSON HELIX
40 W Stewart St (45409-2667)
PHONE.................................937 710-5771
EMP: 6 **EST:** 2018
SALES (est): 248.58K **Privately Held**
Web: www.emerson.com
SIC: 3823 Process control instruments

(G-6320)
ENCON INC
Also Called: Encon
6161 Ventnor Ave (45414-2651)
P.O. Box 13418 (45413-0418)
PHONE.................................937 898-2603
◆ **EMP:** 140
Web: www.anyon.info
SIC: 3085 3089 Plastics bottles; Plastics containers, except foam

(G-6321)
EPIX TUBE CO INC (PA)
5800 Wolf Creek Pike (45426-2438)
PHONE.................................937 529-4858
Paul Kasperski, *Pr*
Angela Salazar, *CFO*
EMP: 10 **EST:** 2009
SALES (est): 9.72MM
SALES (corp-wide): 9.72MM **Privately Held**
Web: www.epixtube.com
SIC: 2599 5531 Factory furniture and fixtures; Automotive accessories

(G-6322)
ERNST ENTERPRISES INC (PA)
Also Called: Ernst Concrete
3361 Successful Way (45414-4317)
PHONE.................................937 233-5555
John C Ernst Junior, *Pr*
David Ernst, *VP*
Dan Ernst, *Stockholder*
Bob Hines, *Prin*
EMP: 20 **EST:** 1946
SQ FT: 6,300
SALES (est): 240.08MM
SALES (corp-wide): 240.08MM **Privately Held**
Web: www.ernstconcrete.com
SIC: 3273 Ready-mixed concrete

(G-6323)
ESTEE 2 INC
612 Linden Ave (45403-2513)
PHONE.................................937 224-7853
Dan Rinehart, *Pr*
Werner Triftshouser, *Stockholder*
Gerhard Triftshouser, *Stockholder*
EMP: 21 **EST:** 1945
SQ FT: 28,000
SALES (est): 2.46MM **Privately Held**
Web: www.esteemold.com
SIC: 3544 Special dies and tools

(G-6324)
ESTHER PRICE CANDIES CORPORATION (PA)
Also Called: Esther Price Candies & Gifts
1709 Wayne Ave (45410-1711)
PHONE.................................937 253-2121
EMP: 25 **EST:** 1926
SALES (est): 19.47MM
SALES (corp-wide): 19.47MM **Privately Held**
Web: www.estherprice.com
SIC: 2064 5441 5145 Candy and other confectionery products; Candy, nut, and confectionery stores; Confectionery

(G-6325)
EUGENE STEWART
Also Called: Spectrum Printing & Design
5671 Webster St (45414-3518)
PHONE.................................937 898-1117
Eugene Stewart, *Owner*
EMP: 8 **EST:** 1991
SQ FT: 6,000
SALES (est): 588.86K **Privately Held**
SIC: 2791 7336 2789 2752 Typesetting; Art design services; Bookbinding and related work; Commercial printing, lithographic

(G-6326)
EVANS BAKERY INC
700 Troy St (45404-1851)
P.O. Box 64 (45404-0064)
PHONE.................................937 228-4151
Edward William Evans, *Pr*
Rose Mary Evans, *VP*
EMP: 8 **EST:** 1952
SQ FT: 1,600
SALES (est): 465.38K **Privately Held**
Web: www.evansbakery.com
SIC: 2051 5461 Bakery: wholesale or wholesale/retail combined; Doughnuts

(G-6327)
EVER SECURE SEC SYSTEMS INC
Also Called: Ess
5523 Salem Ave Ste 134 (45426-1451)
PHONE.................................937 369-8294
Victor Nwufoh, *Pr*

Dayton - Montgomery County (G-6328)

Victor Nwufoh, *Pr*
Robert Todd, *Ex VP*
EMP: 16 **EST:** 1998
SQ FT: 1,500
SALES (est): 681.12K **Privately Held**
SIC: 8711 3699 Civil engineering; Security devices

(G-6328)
FALCON TOOL & MACHINE INC
2795 Lance Dr (45409)
PHONE..................937 534-9999
EMP: 7 **EST:** 1994
SQ FT: 7,000
SALES (est): 550K **Privately Held**
Web: www.falcon-tool.com
SIC: 3541 3599 Machine tools, metal cutting type; Machine shop, jobbing and repair

(G-6329)
FASTSIGNS
Also Called: Fastsigns
6020 N Dixie Dr (45414-4018)
PHONE..................937 890-6770
EMP: 7 **EST:** 2018
SALES (est): 189.29K **Privately Held**
Web: www.fastsigns.com
SIC: 3993 Signs and advertising specialties

(G-6330)
FC INDUSTRIES INC (PA)
4900 Webster St (45414-4831)
PHONE..................937 275-8700
EMP: 46 **EST:** 1988
SALES (est): 49.44MM
SALES (corp-wide): 49.44MM **Privately Held**
Web: www.fcindinc.com
SIC: 3544 3469 3449 Special dies and tools; Metal stampings, nec; Miscellaneous metalwork

(G-6331)
FERNANDES ENTERPRISES LLC (PA)
Also Called: Fourjay Industries
2801 Ontario Ave (45414-5136)
PHONE..................937 890-6444
Vernon Fernandes, *Pr*
▲ **EMP:** 18 **EST:** 1956
SQ FT: 9,600
SALES (est): 2.35MM
SALES (corp-wide): 2.35MM **Privately Held**
Web: www.fourjay.com
SIC: 3699 Electric sound equipment

(G-6332)
FIDELITY ORTHOPEDIC INC
8514 N Main St (45415-1325)
PHONE..................937 228-0682
TOLL FREE: 800
Hillmo Hodzic, *Pr*
Adam Murka, *Dir*
Mark Murka, *Dir*
EMP: 6 **EST:** 1929
SQ FT: 4,000
SALES (est): 894.97K **Privately Held**
Web: www.fidelityorthopedic.com
SIC: 3842 Limbs, artificial

(G-6333)
FIRST TOOL CORP (PA)
612 Linden Ave (45403-2589)
PHONE..................937 254-6197
Robert J Davis, *Pr*
Lisa Davis, *
Ron Connelly, *
Pauline Miller, *
Seymour D Ramby, *
EMP: 40 **EST:** 1966

SQ FT: 60,000
SALES (est): 9.65MM
SALES (corp-wide): 9.65MM **Privately Held**
Web: www.firsttoolcorp.com
SIC: 3542 3544 Machine tools, metal forming type; Jigs and fixtures

(G-6334)
FIVE POINTS DISTILLERY LLC
122 Van Buren St (45402-2934)
PHONE..................937 776-4634
Murphy Laselle, *Prin*
EMP: 11 **EST:** 2012
SQ FT: 5,000
SALES (est): 588.81K **Privately Held**
Web: www.belleofdayton.com
SIC: 2085 Rye whiskey

(G-6335)
FLEET GRAPHICS INC
1701 Thomas Paine Pkwy (16160 2610)
PHONE..................937 252-2552
Scott Waggoner, *Pr*
Val R Waggoner, *VP*
Richard Brice, *Sec*
EMP: 9 **EST:** 1954
SQ FT: 6,000
SALES (est): 2.42MM **Privately Held**
Web: www.fltgfx.com
SIC: 3571 2752 Computers, digital, analog or hybrid; Commercial printing, lithographic

(G-6336)
FLOWERS BAKING CO OHIO LLC
1791 Stanley Ave (45404-1116)
PHONE..................937 260-4412
EMP: 47
SALES (corp-wide): 5.09B **Publicly Held**
SIC: 2051 Bread, cake, and related products
HQ: Flowers Baking Co. Of Ohio, Llc
  325 W Alexis Rd Ste 1
  Toledo OH 43612
  419 269-9202

(G-6337)
FLOWSERVE CORPORATION
Flowserve
2200 E Monument Ave (45402-1362)
PHONE..................937 226-4000
John Carano, *Brnch Mgr*
EMP: 41
SALES (corp-wide): 4.32B **Publicly Held**
Web: www.flowserve.com
SIC: 3561 Industrial pumps and parts
PA: Flowserve Corporation
  5215 N Ocnnor Blvd Ste 70 Connor
  Irving TX 75039
  972 443-6500

(G-6338)
FRANKLIN IRON & METAL CORP
1939 E 1st St (45403-1131)
PHONE..................937 253-8184
Jack Edelman, *Pr*
Debra Edelman, *
▲ **EMP:** 105 **EST:** 1961
SQ FT: 60,000
SALES (est): 22.21MM **Privately Held**
Web: www.franklin-iron.com
SIC: 5093 3341 3312 Ferrous metal scrap and waste; Secondary nonferrous metals; Blast furnaces and steel mills

(G-6339)
FRIENDS SERVICE CO INC
4604 Salem Ave (45416-1712)
PHONE..................800 427-1704
Kenneth J Schroeder, *Brnch Mgr*
EMP: 15
Web: www.friendsoffice.com

SIC: 5112 5021 5087 2752 Stationery and office supplies; Furniture; Service establishment equipment; Commercial printing, lithographic
PA: Friends Service Co., Inc.
  2300 Bright Rd
  Findlay OH 45840

(G-6340)
FRIES MACHINE & TOOL INC
5729 Webster St (45414-3520)
PHONE..................937 898-6432
Arland Fries, *CEO*
Tony E Fries, *Pr*
Lisa A Fries, *Sec*
EMP: 17 **EST:** 1999
SQ FT: 4,000
SALES (est): 469.88K **Privately Held**
Web: www.friesmachineandtool.com
SIC: 3599 Machine shop, jobbing and repair

(G-6341)
FUKUVI USA INC
7631 Progress Ct (45424-6378)
PHONE..................937 236-7288
▲ **EMP:** 65 **EST:** 1996
SQ FT: 84,000
SALES (est): 21.67MM **Privately Held**
Web: www.fukuvi-usa.com
SIC: 3089 Injection molding of plastics
PA: Fukuvi Chemical Industry Co.,Ltd.
  33-66, Sanjuhasshacho
  Fukui FKI 918-8

(G-6342)
FURNITURE BY OTMAR INC (PA)
301 Miamisburg Centerville Rd (45459)
PHONE..................937 435-2039
Josef Otmar Iv, *Pr*
Alberto Otmar, *VP*
▲ **EMP:** 12 **EST:** 1960
SQ FT: 10,000
SALES (est): 1.12MM
SALES (corp-wide): 1.12MM **Privately Held**
Web: www.furniturebyotmar.com
SIC: 2511 5712 Wood household furniture; Furniture stores

(G-6343)
FUYAO GLASS AMERICA INC (HQ)
2801 W Stroop Rd (45439-1502)
PHONE..................937 496-5777
Zuogui Xie, *Pr*
Tim Reynolds, *
EMP: 12 **EST:** 2014
SALES (est): 126.65MM **Privately Held**
Web: www.fuyaousa.com
SIC: 3231 5013 Products of purchased glass ; Automobile glass
PA: Fuyao Glass Industry Group Co., Ltd.
  Fuyao Industrial Area 1
  Fuqing FJ 35030

(G-6344)
GALAPAGOS INC (PA)
3345 Old Salem Rd (45415-1232)
PHONE..................937 890-3068
Onno Van De Stolpe, *CEO*
EMP: 25 **EST:** 2003
SALES (est): 7.64MM **Privately Held**
Web: www.glpg.com
SIC: 2833 2899 Medicinals and botanicals; Chemical preparations, nec

(G-6345)
GCI METALS INC
7660 W 3rd St (45417-7539)
PHONE..................937 835-7123
Kimberly Smallwood, *Pr*
EMP: 19 **EST:** 2013

SALES (est): 2.14MM **Privately Held**
Web: gcimetals.wixsite.com
SIC: 3499 Fabricated metal products, nec

(G-6346)
GDC INDUSTRIES LLC
170 Gracewood Dr (45458-2505)
PHONE..................937 367-7229
Louis Luedtke, *CEO*
EMP: 6 **EST:** 2015
SALES (est): 496.44K **Privately Held**
SIC: 3339 Tin-base alloys (primary)

(G-6347)
GE AVIATION SYSTEMS LLC
Also Called: Tech Development
6800 Poe Ave (45414-2530)
PHONE..................937 898-9600
EMP: 160
SALES (corp-wide): 67.95B **Publicly Held**
Web: www.tdi-airstarter.com
SIC: 3812 Aircraft control systems, electronic
HQ: Ge Aviation Systems Llc
  1 Neumann Way
  Cincinnati OH 45215
  937 898-9600

(G-6348)
GEM CITY ENGINEERING CO (DH)
Also Called: Libra Industries
401 Leo St (45404-1009)
PHONE..................937 223-5544
Jim Kircher, *CEO*
Luis Montiel, *
EMP: 120 **EST:** 1936
SQ FT: 250,000
SALES (est): 23.33MM
SALES (corp-wide): 144.38MM **Privately Held**
Web: www.libraindustries.com
SIC: 3679 3544 3569 3549 Antennas, receiving; Special dies and tools; Assembly machines, non-metalworking; Metalworking machinery, nec
HQ: Libra Industries, Llc
  7770 Division Dr
  Mentor OH 44060
  440 974-7770

(G-6349)
GEM CITY METAL TECH LLC
Also Called: Gem City
1825 E 1st St (45403-1129)
PHONE..................937 252-8998
Dennis Nystrom, *Managing Member*
Don Nystron, *Managing Member**
Norb Overla, *
Dennis Mc Wright, *
EMP: 49 **EST:** 1990
SQ FT: 53,000
SALES (est): 10MM **Privately Held**
Web: www.gcmetalspinning.com
SIC: 3356 3446 3444 3469 Nonferrous rolling and drawing, nec; Architectural metalwork; Sheet metalwork; Spinning metal for the trade

(G-6350)
GENERAL DYNMICS MSSION SYSTEMS
Also Called: Electronics & Communications
1900 Founders Dr Ste 106 (45420-4030)
PHONE..................937 723-2001
Jay Ebersohl, *Brnch Mgr*
EMP: 6
SALES (corp-wide): 42.27B **Publicly Held**
Web: www.gdmissionsystems.com
SIC: 3571 Electronic computers
HQ: General Dynamics Mission Systems, Inc.
  12450 Fair Lakes Cir

GEOGRAPHIC SECTION — Dayton - Montgomery County (G-6373)

Fairfax VA 22033
877 449-0600

(G-6351)
GENEVA GEAR & MACHINE INC
339 Progress Rd (45449-2321)
P.O. Box 292528 (45429-0528)
PHONE..................937 866-0318
Otto G Takacs Junior, *Pr*
EMP: 11 **EST:** 1960
SQ FT: 12,700
SALES (est): 354.78K **Privately Held**
SIC: 3568 3566 3462 Power transmission equipment, nec; Gears, power transmission, except auto; Iron and steel forgings

(G-6352)
GINKO VOTING SYSTEMS LLC
Also Called: Ginko Systems
600 Progress Rd (45449-2300)
PHONE..................937 291-4060
Franklin Dunkin, *CEO*
Lawrence Whitehead, *VP*
EMP: 21 **EST:** 2004
SQ FT: 12,000
SALES (est): 3.4MM **Privately Held**
Web: www.ginkosystemsllc.com
SIC: 3578 3695 Automatic teller machines (ATM); Computer software tape and disks: blank, rigid, and floppy

(G-6353)
GLEASON METROLOGY SYSTEMS CORP (HQ)
Also Called: Gleason M & M Precision
300 Progress Rd (45449-2322)
PHONE..................937 384-8901
Terry Turner, *Ex VP*
Douglas Beerck, *
◆ **EMP:** 49 **EST:** 1951
SQ FT: 68,000
SALES (est): 20.8MM
SALES (corp-wide): 469.63MM **Privately Held**
Web: www.gleason.com
SIC: 3829 3823 3769 3621 Measuring and controlling devices, nec; Process control instruments; Space vehicle equipment, nec; Motors and generators
PA: Gleason Corporation
1000 University Ave
Rochester NY 14607
585 473-1000

(G-6354)
GLEN D LALA
Also Called: Innovative Creations
2610 Willowburn Ave (45417-9434)
P.O. Box 328 (45066-0328)
PHONE..................937 274-7770
Glen D Lala, *Owner*
EMP: 6 **EST:** 1986
SQ FT: 12,000
SALES (est): 470.44K **Privately Held**
SIC: 2759 7699 Screen printing; Printing trades machinery and equipment repair

(G-6355)
GLOBAL MANUFACTURING SOLUTIONS
2001 Kuntz Rd (45404-1221)
PHONE..................937 236-8315
Charles M Woods, *Pr*
William Bankes, *VP*
EMP: 11 **EST:** 1995
SQ FT: 46,000
SALES (est): 551.47K **Privately Held**
Web: www.globalms.com
SIC: 3082 8734 5947 5199 Unsupported plastics profile shapes; Product testing laboratory, safety or performance; Gifts and novelties; Foams and rubber

(G-6356)
GLOBE MOTORS INC (HQ)
Also Called: Globe Motors
2275 Stanley Ave (45404-1226)
PHONE..................334 983-3542
Steven Mchenry, *CEO*
William Gillespie, *CFO*
▲ **EMP:** 150 **EST:** 1945
SALES (est): 85.01MM
SALES (corp-wide): 578.63MM **Publicly Held**
Web: www.alliedmotion.com
SIC: 3621 Motors, electric
PA: Allient Inc.
495 Commerce Dr Ste 3
Amherst NY 14228
716 242-8634

(G-6357)
GLOBE PRODUCTS INC (PA)
5051 Kitridge Rd (45424-4433)
P.O. Box 77 (45404-0077)
PHONE..................937 233-0233
Scott Kroencke, *Pr*
James E Kroencke, *CEO*
W Patrick Winton, *Stockholder*
▲ **EMP:** 19 **EST:** 1919
SQ FT: 100,000
SALES (est): 2.66MM
SALES (corp-wide): 2.66MM **Privately Held**
Web: www.globe-usa.com
SIC: 3599 Machine shop, jobbing and repair

(G-6358)
GLT INC (PA)
Also Called: Johnson Contrls Authorized Dlr
3341 Successful Way (45414-4317)
PHONE..................937 237-0055
Kevin Knight, *Pr*
Chris Knight, *VP*
◆ **EMP:** 12 **EST:** 1987
SQ FT: 75,000
SALES (est): 10.07MM
SALES (corp-wide): 10.07MM **Privately Held**
Web: www.gltonline.com
SIC: 3541 5075 Machine tools, metal cutting type; Warm air heating and air conditioning

(G-6359)
GMD INDUSTRIES LLC
Also Called: Production Screw Machine
1414 E 2nd St (45403-1023)
PHONE..................937 252-3643
▼ **EMP:** 65 **EST:** 2000
SQ FT: 35,000
SALES (est): 9.77MM **Privately Held**
Web: www.psmco.com
SIC: 3599 Machine shop, jobbing and repair

(G-6360)
GRB HOLDINGS INC
131 Janney Rd (45404-1225)
P.O. Box 173 (45404-0173)
PHONE..................937 236-3250
David Gitridge, *Pr*
David Gutridge, *
EMP: 53 **EST:** 1913
SQ FT: 50,000
SALES (est): 1.05MM **Privately Held**
SIC: 3295 3471 Minerals, ground or treated; Plating and polishing

(G-6361)
GREEN LEAF PRINTING AND DESIGN
1001 E 2nd St Ste 2485 (45402-1498)
PHONE..................937 222-3634
Larry Blevins, *Prin*
EMP: 8 **EST:** 2009
SALES (est): 471.63K **Privately Held**
Web: www.greenleafprinting.com
SIC: 2759 Screen printing

(G-6362)
GREEN TOKAI CO LTD
3700 Inpark Dr (45414-4418)
PHONE..................937 237-1630
Charlie Sapp, *Brnch Mgr*
EMP: 144
Web: www.greentokai.com
SIC: 3714 Motor vehicle parts and accessories
HQ: Green Tokai Co., Ltd.
55 Robert Wright Dr
Brookville OH 45309
937 833-5444

(G-6363)
GREGORY STONE CO INC
1860 N Gettysburg Ave (45417-9585)
PHONE..................937 275-7455
Thomas L Call, *Pr*
Jackie K Call, *VP*
EMP: 9 **EST:** 1936
SQ FT: 7,000
SALES (est): 1.1MM **Privately Held**
Web: www.gregorystonecompany.com
SIC: 5211 1411 Masonry materials and supplies; Limestone, dimension-quarrying

(G-6364)
H GERSTNER & SONS INC
Also Called: Gerstner International
20 Gerstner Way (45402-8408)
PHONE..................937 228-1662
John Campbell, *Pr*
Nancy Campbell, *Sec*
▲ **EMP:** 20 **EST:** 1906
SQ FT: 30,000
SALES (est): 2.49MM **Privately Held**
Web: www.gerstnerusa.com
SIC: 2441 Tool chests, wood

(G-6365)
HAM SIGNS LLC DBA FASTSIGNS
6020 N Dixie Dr (45414-4018)
PHONE..................937 890-6770
EMP: 12 **EST:** 1995
SALES (est): 682.15K **Privately Held**
SIC: 3993 7532 Signs and advertising specialties; Truck painting and lettering

(G-6366)
HEAT PRECISION MACHINING INC
2796 Culver Ave (45429-3724)
PHONE..................937 233-3140
Hans H Soltau, *Prin*
EMP: 11 **EST:** 2007
SALES (est): 189.39K **Privately Held**
Web: www.heatprecision.com
SIC: 3599 Machine shop, jobbing and repair

(G-6367)
HEC INVESTMENTS INC
4800 Wadsworth Rd (45414-4224)
PHONE..................937 278-9123
▲ **EMP:** 144 **EST:** 1975
SALES (est): 8.77MM **Privately Held**
Web: www.superiorabrasives.com
SIC: 3291 Abrasive products

(G-6368)
HESS ADVANCED SOLUTIONS LLC
7415 Chambersburg Rd (45424-3921)
P.O. Box 17669 (45417-0669)
PHONE..................937 829-4794
Frederick Edmonds, *CEO*
EMP: 8 **EST:** 2016
SQ FT: 15,000
SALES (est): 554.83K **Privately Held**
SIC: 3699 1731 8711 1711 Electrical equipment and supplies, nec; Electrical work; Heating and ventilation engineering; Heating and air conditioning contractors

(G-6369)
HINKLE FINE FOODS INC
4800 Wadsworth Rd (45414-4224)
PHONE..................937 836-3665
Benny S Hinkle, *Pr*
Marlene M Hinkle, *Sec*
Craig Frost, *Pt*
Micheal Beller, *Pt*
EMP: 10 **EST:** 1975
SQ FT: 8,200
SALES (est): 2.32MM **Privately Held**
Web: www.hinklefinefoods.com
SIC: 2035 Seasonings and sauces, except tomato and dry

(G-6370)
HOCKER TOOL AND DIE INC
5161 Webster St (45414-4227)
PHONE..................937 274-3443
Ronald S Hocker, *Pr*
William K Hocker, *VP*
EMP: 26 **EST:** 1972
SQ FT: 12,000
SALES (est): 9.08MM **Privately Held**
Web: www.hockertoolanddie.com
SIC: 3544 Special dies and tools

(G-6371)
HOME CITY ICE COMPANY
1020 Gateway Dr (45404-2281)
PHONE..................937 461-6028
Joel Heck, *Mgr*
EMP: 7
SALES (corp-wide): 100.42MM **Privately Held**
Web: www.homecityice.com
SIC: 2097 5999 Manufactured ice; Ice
PA: The Home City Ice Company
6045 Bridgetown Rd Ste 1
Cincinnati OH 45248
513 574-1800

(G-6372)
HONEYWELL FIRST RESPONDER PDTS
4978 Riverton Dr (45414-3964)
PHONE..................937 264-1726
EMP: 7 **EST:** 2015
SALES (est): 116.8K **Privately Held**
SIC: 2326 Men's and boy's work clothing

(G-6373)
HOUSE OF 10000 PICTURE FRAMES
2210 Wilmington Pike (45420-1433)
PHONE..................937 254-5541
William Heath, *Owner*
EMP: 9 **EST:** 1971
SQ FT: 4,000
SALES (est): 456.43K **Privately Held**
Web: www.houseof10kpictureframes.com
SIC: 5999 5719 2499 Picture frames, ready made; Pictures, wall; Picture frame molding, finished

---

(PA)=Parent Co (HQ)=Headquarters
✪ = New Business established in last 2 years

Dayton - Montgomery County (G-6374)

(G-6374)
HOWMEDICA OSTEONICS CORP
474 Windsor Park Dr (45459-4111)
PHONE.................................937 291-3900
Patrick Barnes, *Brnch Mgr*
EMP: 70
SALES (corp-wide): 20.5B **Publicly Held**
SIC: 3841 Surgical and medical instruments
HQ: Howmedica Osteonics Corp.
325 Corporate Dr
Mahwah NJ 07430
201 831-5000

(G-6375)
HR MACHINE LLC
1934 Stanley Ave (45404-1121)
P.O. Box 213 (45301-0213)
PHONE.................................937 222-7644
Jennifer Hudson, *Mgr*
Larry Hudson, *VP*
EMP: 8 **EST:** 2010
SQ FT: 7,000
SALES (est): 992.14K **Privately Held**
Web: www.hrmachine.net
SIC: 3441 3914 Fabricated structural metal; Trophies, stainless steel

(G-6376)
HTEC SYSTEMS INC
561 Congress Park Dr (45459-4036)
PHONE.................................937 438-3010
Phillip Hayden, *Ch*
Peter A Flaherty, *Pr*
Christopher Hayden, *Sec*
▼ **EMP:** 10 **EST:** 2005
SQ FT: 4,000
SALES (est): 935.88K **Privately Held**
Web: www.htecsystems.com
SIC: 8711 7389 1629 3599 Consulting engineer; Design services; Industrial plant construction; Custom machinery

(G-6377)
HYLAND MACHINE COMPANY
Also Called: Hyland Screw Machine Products
1900 Kuntz Rd (45404-1251)
P.O. Box 133 (45404-0133)
PHONE.................................937 233-8600
Forest Hyland, *Pr*
Dan Hyland, *
▲ **EMP:** 27 **EST:** 1928
SQ FT: 42,000
SALES (est): 4.56MM **Privately Held**
Web: www.hylandmach.com
SIC: 3451 Screw machine products

(G-6378)
IDX CORPORATION
2875 Needmore Rd (45414-4301)
PHONE.................................937 401-3225
David Mueller, *Genl Mgr*
EMP: 150
SALES (corp-wide): 7.22B **Publicly Held**
Web: www.idxcorporation.com
SIC: 3083 2521 3999 2511 Plastics finished products, laminated; Wood office furniture; Plaques, picture, laminated; Wood household furniture
HQ: Idx Corporation
2801 E Beltline Ave Ne
Grand Rapids MI 49525
844 249-4633

(G-6379)
IDX DAYTON LLC
Also Called: Universal Forest Products
2875 Needmore Rd (45414-4301)
PHONE.................................937 401-3460
Isaac Bokros, *Asst Mgr*
▲ **EMP:** 123 **EST:** 2012
SALES (est): 24.33MM

SALES (corp-wide): 7.22B **Publicly Held**
SIC: 2542 2541 Partitions and fixtures, except wood; Store and office display cases and fixtures
PA: Ufp Industries, Inc.
2801 E Beltline Ave Ne
Grand Rapids MI 49525
616 364-6161

(G-6380)
IGNYTE ASSURANCE PLATFORM
714 E Monument Ave (45402-1382)
PHONE.................................833 446-9831
Narinder Aulakh, *Prin*
EMP: 20 **EST:** 2018
SALES (est): 1.21MM **Privately Held**
Web: www.ignyteplatform.com
SIC: 7372 Prepackaged software

(G-6381)
INDOOR ENVMTL SPECIALISTS INC
Also Called: Environmental Doctor
438 Windsor Park Dr (45459-4111)
PHONE.................................937 433-5202
Brenden Gitzinger, *Pr*
Margie Gitzinger, *VP*
EMP: 22 **EST:** 2006
SQ FT: 3,000
SALES (est): 974.46K **Privately Held**
Web: www.envirodoc.com
SIC: 7349 5999 1799 3564 Air duct cleaning; Air purification equipment; Waterproofing; Air purification equipment

(G-6382)
INDUSTRIAL FIBERGLASS SPC INC
Also Called: Fiber Systems
351 Deeds Ave (45404)
PHONE.................................937 222-9000
Theodore Morton, *Ch Bd*
Janice Morton, *
Valerie Cline, *
Karen Ramsey, *
Melanie Shockey, *
EMP: 35 **EST:** 1978
SALES (est): 4.47MM **Privately Held**
Web: www.ifs-frp.com
SIC: 3229 1799 Glass fiber products; Service station equipment installation, maint., and repair

(G-6383)
INNOVATIVE VEND SOLUTIONS LLC
740 Royal Ridge Dr (45449-2334)
PHONE.................................866 931-9413
Patrick Mcdonald, *Prin*
EMP: 18 **EST:** 2008
SALES (est): 2.94MM **Privately Held**
Web: www.innovativevendingsolutions.com
SIC: 3581 Automatic vending machines

(G-6384)
INSTANTWHIP-DAYTON INC (PA)
Also Called: Tiller Foods
5820 Executive Blvd (45424-1451)
PHONE.................................937 235-5930
Donald Tiller Junior, *Pr*
Donald Tiller Junior, *Pr*
William B Tiller, *VP*
David Yost, *Sec*
▲ **EMP:** 9 **EST:** 1936
SQ FT: 15,000
SALES (est): 1.55MM
SALES (corp-wide): 1.55MM **Privately Held**
SIC: 2026 2023 5143 Half and half; Cream substitutes; Dairy products, except dried or canned

(G-6385)
INSTANTWHIP-DAYTON INC
Also Called: Tiller Foods
967 Senate Dr (45459-4017)
PHONE.................................937 435-4371
David Yost, *Genl Mgr*
EMP: 6
SALES (corp-wide): 1.55MM **Privately Held**
SIC: 2026 2023 Half and half; Cream substitutes
PA: Instantwhip-Dayton, Inc.
5820 Executive Blvd
Dayton OH 45424
937 235-5930

(G-6386)
INTEGRITY MANUFACTURING CORP
3723 Inpark Dr (45414-4417)
P.O. Box 312 (45404-0312)
PHONE.................................937 233-6792
Richard L Halderman, *Pr*
Gretchen Halderman, *VP*
EMP: 18 **EST:** 1977
SQ FT: 11,950
SALES (est): 933.54K **Privately Held**
Web: www.integrity-mfg.com
SIC: 3451 3599 Screw machine products; Machine shop, jobbing and repair

(G-6387)
JAMES C FREE INC (PA)
Also Called: James Free Jewelers
3100 Far Hills Ave (45429-2512)
PHONE.................................937 298-0171
Michael S Karaman, *Pr*
▲ **EMP:** 20 **EST:** 1940
SQ FT: 6,000
SALES (est): 3.45MM
SALES (corp-wide): 3.45MM **Privately Held**
Web: www.jamesfree.com
SIC: 3911 5944 Jewelry, precious metal; Jewelry, precious stones and precious metals

(G-6388)
JEFF BONHAM ELECTRIC INC
3647 Wright Way Rd (45424-5165)
PHONE.................................937 233-7662
Jeff Bonham, *Pr*
Bryan Farlow, *VP*
EMP: 22 **EST:** 1959
SQ FT: 1,500
SALES (est): 5.11MM **Privately Held**
Web: www.jeffbonhamelectric.com
SIC: 1731 3613 General electrical contractor; Panel and distribution boards and other related apparatus

(G-6389)
JET PRODUCTS INCORPORATED
535 E Dixie Dr (45449-1828)
PHONE.................................937 866-7969
Wayne Busdiecker, *Pr*
Lawrence Larsen, *VP*
▲ **EMP:** 9 **EST:** 1974
SQ FT: 7,500
SALES (est): 739.95K **Privately Held**
Web: www.sajetproducts.com
SIC: 3537 Lift trucks, industrial: fork, platform, straddle, etc.

(G-6390)
JOYCE/DAYTON CORP (HQ)
3300 S Dixie Dr Ste 101 (45439-2318)
P.O. Box 635789 (45263-5789)
PHONE.................................937 294-6261
Michael Harris, *Pr*
▲ **EMP:** 30 **EST:** 1893
SQ FT: 20,000

SALES (est): 28.45MM
SALES (corp-wide): 4.41B **Publicly Held**
Web: www.joycedayton.com
SIC: 3569 Jacks, hydraulic
PA: Graham Holdings Company
1812 North Moore Street
Rosslyn VA 22209
703 345-6362

(G-6391)
JOYCE/DAYTON CORP
P.O. Box 1630 (45401-1630)
PHONE.................................937 294-6261
Michael Harris, *Pr*
EMP: 35
SALES (corp-wide): 4.41B **Publicly Held**
Web: www.joycedayton.com
SIC: 3569 Filters
HQ: Joyce/Dayton Corp.
3300 S Dixie Dr Ste 101
Dayton OH 45439
937 294-6261

(G-6392)
JTL ENTERPRISES LLC (PA)
5700 Webster St (45414-3521)
P.O. Box 13027 (45413-0027)
PHONE.................................937 890-8189
EMP: 20 **EST:** 2001
SALES (est): 46.91MM
SALES (corp-wide): 46.91MM **Privately Held**
SIC: 5531 7534 Automotive tires; Tire recapping

(G-6393)
JUDO STEEL COMPANY INC
Also Called: Judo Steel
1526 Nicholas Rd (45417-6713)
P.O. Box 751586 (45475-1586)
EMP: 10 **EST:** 1994
SQ FT: 6,000
SALES (est): 1.46MM **Privately Held**
SIC: 3441 Building components, structural steel

(G-6394)
JULIE MAYNARD INC
Also Called: Consolidated Vehicle Converter
4991 Hempstead Station Dr (45429-5159)
PHONE.................................937 443-0408
▲ **EMP:** 10 **EST:** 1996
SQ FT: 20,000
SALES (est): 2.84MM **Privately Held**
SIC: 3714 3566 Motor vehicle parts and accessories; Speed changers, drives, and gears

(G-6395)
JUST BUSINESS INC
Also Called: Onstage Publications
1612 Prosser Ave Ste 100 (45409-2041)
PHONE.................................866 577-3303
Norman L Orlowski, *Pr*
Kyle Orlowski, *VP Sls*
Garett Orlowski, *VP Opers*
EMP: 14 **EST:** 2001
SQ FT: 2,000
SALES (est): 2.25MM **Privately Held**
Web: www.audienceaccess.co
SIC: 8742 2731 7311 Marketing consulting services; Book publishing; Advertising consultant

(G-6396)
K & B ACQUISITIONS INC
Also Called: Mehaffie Pie Company
3013 Linden Ave (45410-3028)
PHONE.................................937 253-1163
Greg Hay, *Pr*
Jim Columbus, *VP*

GEOGRAPHIC SECTION
Dayton - Montgomery County (G-6417)

Barb Columbus, *Treas*
Bruce Kouse, *VP*
EMP: 10 **EST:** 1930
SQ FT: 9,000
SALES (est): 968.45K **Privately Held**
SIC: 2051 5461 Pies, bakery: except frozen; Pies

(G-6397)
KBR INC ✪
2700 Indian Ripple Rd (45440-3638)
PHONE..................937 320-2731
EMP: 11 **EST:** 2022
SALES (est): 318.11K **Privately Held**
Web: www.kbr.com
SIC: 3728 Aircraft parts and equipment, nec

(G-6398)
KELLEY COMMUNICATION DEV
Also Called: Kelley Bible Books
2312 Candlewood Dr (45419-2825)
P.O. Box 292113 (45429-0113)
PHONE..................937 298-6132
Robert Kelley, *Owner*
EMP: 7 **EST:** 1979
SALES (est): 315.77K **Privately Held**
Web: www.kcdev.com
SIC: 2731 Books, publishing only

(G-6399)
KOLHFAB CSTM PLSTIC FBRICATION
2025 Webster St (45404-1143)
PHONE..................937 237-2098
Bernie Kohlbarg, *CEO*
EMP: 6 **EST:** 2011
SALES (est): 507.46K **Privately Held**
SIC: 3089 Injection molding of plastics

(G-6400)
L3 TECHNOLOGIES INC
3155 Research Blvd Ste 101 (45420)
PHONE..................937 223-3285
Walker Larimer, *Brnch Mgr*
EMP: 7
SALES (corp-wide): 19.42B **Publicly Held**
Web: www.l3harris.com
SIC: 3812 Navigational systems and instruments
HQ: L3 Technologies, Inc.
    600 3rd Ave Fl 34
    New York NY 10016
    321 727-9100

(G-6401)
LAHM-TROSPER INC
Also Called: Lahm Tool
1030 Springfield St (45403-1350)
P.O. Box 336 (45401-0336)
PHONE..................937 252-8741
James Trosper, *Pr*
EMP: 27 **EST:** 1997
SQ FT: 10,000
SALES (est): 2.77MM **Privately Held**
Web: www.lahmtool.com
SIC: 3541 3544 Machine tools, metal cutting type; Special dies, tools, jigs, and fixtures

(G-6402)
LEDBETTER PARTNERS LLC
214 W Monument Ave (45402-3015)
P.O. Box 10068 (45402-7068)
PHONE..................937 253-5311
Sean H Harmon, *Prin*
EMP: 6 **EST:** 2018
SALES (est): 168.82K **Privately Held**
SIC: 3471 Plating and polishing

(G-6403)
LEGRAND NORTH AMERICA LLC
Also Called: C2g
6500 Poe Ave (45414-2527)
PHONE..................937 224-0639
EMP: 420
Web: www.legrand.us
SIC: 1731 5063 5045 3643 Communications specialization; Cable conduit; Computer peripheral equipment; Current-carrying wiring services
HQ: Legrand North America, Llc
    60 Woodlawn St
    West Hartford CT 06110
    860 233-6251

(G-6404)
LENCO INDUSTRIES INC
3301 Klepinger Rd (45406-1823)
PHONE..................937 277-9364
John L Lenz, *Pr*
Robert Wagner, *
EMP: 19 **EST:** 1955
SQ FT: 15,000
SALES (est): 394.26K **Privately Held**
Web: www.swattrucks.com
SIC: 3451 Screw machine products

(G-6405)
LENZ INC
Also Called: Lenz Company
3301 Klepinger Rd (45406-1823)
P.O. Box 1044 (45401-1044)
PHONE..................937 277-9364
Robert Wagner, *Pr*
▲ **EMP:** 50 **EST:** 1955
SQ FT: 15,000
SALES (est): 6.28MM **Privately Held**
Web: www.lenzinc.com
SIC: 6531 3089 Real estate brokers and agents; Fittings for pipe, plastics

(G-6406)
LEWARK METAL SPINNING INC
2746 Keenan Ave (45414)
PHONE..................937 275-3303
Larry W Lewark, *Pr*
Pete Hagenbuch, *
EMP: 50 **EST:** 1993
SQ FT: 35,000
SALES (est): 9.05MM **Privately Held**
Web: www.lewarkmetalspinning.com
SIC: 3499 3469 Friction material, made from powdered metal; Spinning metal for the trade

(G-6407)
LIFE SCIENCES - VANDALIA LLC (HQ)
4201 Little York Rd (45414)
PHONE..................937 387-0880
Simon Newman, *CEO*
EMP: 138 **EST:** 2005
SALES (est): 24.64MM
SALES (corp-wide): 433.51MM **Privately Held**
Web: mp.drtholdingsllc.com
SIC: 3841 Surgical and medical instruments
PA: Asp Navigate Acquisition Corp.,
    3426 Torigndon Way # 100
    Charlotte NC 28277
    704 280-8875

(G-6408)
LION APPAREL INC (DH)
7200 Poe Ave Ste 400 (45414-2798)
PHONE..................937 898-1949
Steve Schwartz, *CEO*
Andrew Schwartz, *Legal*
Theodore Schwartz, *
Mark Berliant, *
Mark Jahnke, *
◆ **EMP:** 150 **EST:** 1930
SQ FT: 37,000
SALES (est): 108.19MM
SALES (corp-wide): 13.99MM **Privately Held**
Web: www.lionprotects.com
SIC: 2311 Firemen's uniforms: made from purchased materials
HQ: Lion Group, Inc.
    7200 Poe Ave Ste 400
    Dayton OH 45414
    937 898-1949

(G-6409)
LION APPAREL INC
Bodyguard
6450 Poe Ave Ste 300 (45414-2600)
P.O. Box 13576 (45413-0576)
PHONE..................937 898-1949
Richard Lapedes, *Pr*
EMP: 100
SALES (corp-wide): 13.99MM **Privately Held**
Web: www.lionprotects.com
SIC: 2311 Firemen's uniforms: made from purchased materials
HQ: Lion Apparel, Inc.
    7200 Poe Ave Ste 400
    Dayton OH 45414
    937 898-1949

(G-6410)
LION FIRST RESPONDER PPE INC
7200 Poe Ave Ste 400 (45414-2798)
PHONE..................937 898-1949
Steve Schwartz, *CEO*
David Cook, *
EMP: 57 **EST:** 2015
SALES (est): 24.98MM
SALES (corp-wide): 13.99MM **Privately Held**
SIC: 2311 3842 5047 Firemen's uniforms: made from purchased materials; Clothing, fire resistant and protective; Medical equipment and supplies
HQ: Lion Safety Resources Group, Inc.
    7200 Poe Ave Ste 400
    Dayton OH 45414
    937 898-1949

(G-6411)
LION GROUP INC (HQ)
7200 Poe Ave Ste 400 (45414)
PHONE..................937 898-1949
Steve Schwartz, *CEO*
Andrew Schwartz, *
James Disanto, *
Richard Musick, *
EMP: 90 **EST:** 2014
SQ FT: 3,700
SALES (est): 327.39MM
SALES (corp-wide): 13.99MM **Privately Held**
Web: www.lionprotects.com
SIC: 6719 2311 5047 Investment holding companies, except banks; Firemen's uniforms: made from purchased materials; Medical equipment and supplies
PA: Lion Protects B.V.
    Rheastraat 14
    Tilburg NB 5047
    135076800

(G-6412)
LITEFLEX DISC LLC
3251 Mccall St (45417)
P.O. Box 69 (45322)
PHONE..................937 836-7025
John Prikkel Iii, *Pr*
Daniel Chien, *
Ray Blatz, *
▲ **EMP:** 55 **EST:** 2001
SALES (est): 9.96MM **Privately Held**
Web: www.liteflexllc.com
SIC: 3493 Leaf springs: automobile, locomotive, etc.

(G-6413)
LITHO-PRINT LTD
848 E Monument Ave (45402-1312)
PHONE..................937 222-4351
Darrell Templeton, *Pt*
Sandra Templeton, *Pt*
Leanore Obelewicz, *Pt*
Paul Obolwicz, *Pt*
EMP: 16 **EST:** 1951
SQ FT: 15,500
SALES (est): 2.21MM **Privately Held**
Web: www.lithoprintco.com
SIC: 2752 Offset printing

(G-6414)
LOCK 27 BREWING LLC
Also Called: Dayton Brewery & Pub
1024 Quail Run Dr (45458-9619)
PHONE..................937 433-2739
Steve Barnhart, *Prin*
EMP: 14 **EST:** 2013
SALES (est): 1.24MM **Privately Held**
Web: www.lock27brewing.com
SIC: 5813 2082 Beer garden (drinking places); Beer (alcoholic beverage)

(G-6415)
LORD CORPORATION
Mechanical Products Division
4644 Wadsworth Rd (45414-4220)
PHONE..................937 278-9431
Janet Eastep, *Mgr*
EMP: 150
SQ FT: 30,000
SALES (corp-wide): 19.07B **Publicly Held**
Web: www.parker.com
SIC: 3545 3769 Machine tool accessories; Space vehicle equipment, nec
HQ: Lord Corporation
    111 Lord Dr
    Cary NC 27511
    919 468-5979

(G-6416)
LORENZ CORPORATION (PA)
Also Called: Show What You Know
501 E 3rd St (45402-2280)
P.O. Box 802 (45401-0802)
PHONE..................937 228-6118
Reiff Lorenz, *Pr*
Reiff Lorenz, *Ch Bd*
Geoffrey R Lorenz, *
John Schimtz, *
Kris Kropff, *
▲ **EMP:** 60 **EST:** 1890
SQ FT: 55,000
SALES (est): 9.68MM
SALES (corp-wide): 9.68MM **Privately Held**
Web: www.lorenz.com
SIC: 2759 5049 2721 2741 Music, sheet: printing, nsk; School supplies; Periodicals, publishing only; Music, sheet: publishing only, not printed on site

(G-6417)
M & J TOOLING LTD
Also Called: M & J Tooling
420 Davis Ave (45403-2912)
PHONE..................937 951-3527
Matthew Hemmerich, *Pt*
EMP: 10 **EST:** 2006
SALES (est): 906.36K **Privately Held**
Web: www.mjtoolingllc.com

(PA)=Parent Co (HQ)=Headquarters
✪ = New Business established in last 2 years

Dayton - Montgomery County (G-6418)

SIC: 3545 Machine tool accessories

(G-6418)
M T M MOLDED PRODUCTS COMPANY
3370 Obco Ct (45414-3500)
P.O. Box 13117 (45413-0117)
PHONE..................937 890-7461
Steve Minneman, *
Allen Minneman, *
◆ EMP: 25 EST: 1966
SQ FT: 92,000
SALES (est): 6.31MM Privately Held
Web: www.mtmcase-gard.com
SIC: 3089 Cases, plastics

(G-6419)
M21 INDUSTRIES LLC
Also Called: Module 21 Bldg Company
721 Springfield St (45403-1250)
P.O. Box 4044 (45401-4044)
PHONE..................937 701-1377
Jeffrey Levine, Managing Member
Wolfgang Dalichau, Managing Member
David Allen, VP
Don Carter, VP
Rusty Brown, VP
EMP: 25 EST: 1975
SQ FT: 230,000
SALES (est): 971.38K Privately Held
Web: www.m21industries.com
SIC: 2541 2431 Office fixtures, wood; Windows, wood

(G-6420)
MACHINE PRODUCTS COMPANY
5660 Webster St (45414-3596)
PHONE..................937 890-6600
Robert C Appenzeller, Pr
Rebecca A Cain, *
EMP: 36 EST: 1956
SQ FT: 40,000
SALES (est): 3.95MM Privately Held
Web: www.mpcdayton.com
SIC: 3599 3825 3694 Machine shop, jobbing and repair; Instruments to measure electricity; Engine electrical equipment

(G-6421)
MADSEN WIRE PRODUCTS INC
101 Madison St (45402-1711)
P.O. Box 98 (46776-0098)
PHONE..................937 829-6561
Gary Stephens, Pr
▲ EMP: 8 EST: 2001
SALES (est): 135.56K Privately Held
Web: www.madsenwire.com
SIC: 3315 Wire and fabricated wire products

(G-6422)
MAGNUM TOOL CORP
1407 Stanley Ave (45404-1110)
PHONE..................937 228-0900
Christopher S Grooms, Pr
Gregory S Grooms, Sec
◆ EMP: 10 EST: 1972
SQ FT: 6,000
SALES (est): 986.98K Privately Held
Web: www.magnumtoolcorp.com
SIC: 3544 Special dies and tools

(G-6423)
MAHLE BEHR DAYTON LLC
1720 Webster St (45404-1128)
PHONE..................937 369-2900
Rob Baker, Brnch Mgr
EMP: 676
SALES (corp-wide): 3.75MM Privately Held

SIC: 3714 Air conditioner parts, motor vehicle
HQ: Mahle Behr Dayton L.L.C.
1600 Webster St
Dayton OH 45404
937 369-2900

(G-6424)
MAHLE BEHR DAYTON LLC (DH)
1600 Webster St (45404-1144)
PHONE..................937 369-2900
Ing Heinz K Junker, Ch Bd
Willm Uhlenbecker, *
Wolf Hennig Scheider, *
Bruce Moorehouse, *
Milan Belans, *
◆ EMP: 93 EST: 2002
SALES (est): 498.08MM
SALES (corp-wide): 3.75MM Privately Held
SIC: 3714 Motor vehicle parts and accessories
HQ: Mahle Behr Gmbh & Co. Kg
Mauserstr. 3
Stuttgart BW
7115010

(G-6425)
MAHLE BEHR DAYTON LLC
1600 Webster St (45404-1144)
PHONE..................937 369-2000
EMP: 2000
SALES (corp-wide): 504.65K Privately Held
SIC: 3443 3585 Heat exchangers, condensers, and components; Refrigeration and heating equipment
HQ: Mahle Behr Dayton L.L.C.
1600 Webster St
Dayton OH 45404
937 369-2900

(G-6426)
MAHLE INDUSTRIES INCORPORATED
Also Called: Delphi-T - Vandalia Ptc
1600 Webster St (45404-1144)
PHONE..................937 890-2739
EMP: 30
SALES (corp-wide): 504.65K Privately Held
SIC: 3714 Motor vehicle parts and accessories
HQ: Mahle Industries, Incorporated
23030 Mahle Dr
Farmington Hills MI 48335
248 305-8200

(G-6427)
MANCOR OHIO INC (HQ)
1008 Leonhard St (45404-1666)
PHONE..................937 228-6141
Art Church, Ch Bd
Dale Harper, *
EMP: 50 EST: 2006
SALES (est): 79.25MM
SALES (corp-wide): 156.64MM Privately Held
Web: www.mancor.com
SIC: 3713 Truck bodies and parts
PA: Mancor Canada Inc
2485 Speers Rd
Oakville ON L6L 2
905 827-3737

(G-6428)
MANCOR OHIO INC
600 Kiser St (45404-1644)
PHONE..................937 228-6141
George Mcnight, Genl Mgr
EMP: 170
SALES (corp-wide): 156.64MM Privately Held

Web: www.mancor.com
SIC: 3713 Truck bodies and parts
HQ: Mancor Ohio Inc.
1008 Leonhard St
Dayton OH 45404

(G-6429)
MAR-VEL TOOL CO
858 Hall Ave (45404-1142)
PHONE..................937 223-2137
John G Glaser, Pr
Brett R Glaser, VP
EMP: 18 EST: 1984
SQ FT: 23,000
SALES (est): 587.45K Privately Held
Web: www.mar-veltool.com
SIC: 3544 Special dies and tools

(G-6430)
MARCO PRINTED PRODUCTS CO
Also Called: Marco's Papers
25 W Whipp Rd (45459-1811)
PHONE..................937 433-7030
Gary Ihle, Pr
David Ihle, Sec
Margaret Ihle, Treas
Karen Ihle, Mgr
EMP: 8 EST: 1971
SQ FT: 7,000
SALES (est): 216.85K Privately Held
Web: www.marcopaper.com
SIC: 2752 Offset printing

(G-6431)
MCBMRDD
5450 Salem Ave (45426-1585)
PHONE..................937 910-7301
Jake Hudson, Finance
EMP: 7 EST: 2017
SALES (est): 200.37K Privately Held
SIC: 2851 Paints and allied products

(G-6432)
MCINTOSH SAFE CORP
603 Leo St (45404-1507)
PHONE..................937 222-7008
John Mcintosh, Pr
EMP: 10 EST: 1996
SALES (est): 796.17K Privately Held
Web: www.mcintoshsafe.com
SIC: 3499 5044 Safes and vaults, metal; Vaults and safes

(G-6433)
MEASUREMENT SPECIALTIES INC
2670 Indian Ripple Rd (45440-3605)
PHONE..................937 427-1231
Brian Ream, Brnch Mgr
EMP: 38
Web: www.te.com
SIC: 3674 3676 Diodes, solid state (germanium, silicon, etc.); Thermistors, except temperature sensors
HQ: Measurement Specialties, Inc.
1000 Lucas Way
Hampton VA 23666
757 766-1500

(G-6434)
MEDICAL DEVICE BUS SVCS INC
2747 Armstrong Ln (45414-4225)
PHONE..................937 274-5850
EMP: 28
SALES (corp-wide): 85.16B Publicly Held
SIC: 3842 Orthopedic appliances
HQ: Medical Device Business Services, Inc.
700 Orthopaedic Dr
Warsaw IN 46582

(G-6435)
METALBRITE POLISHING LLC
2445 Neff Rd Unit 4 (45414-5067)
PHONE..................937 278-9739
Michael Barr, Owner
EMP: 11 EST: 1998
SALES (est): 506.94K Privately Held
Web: www.metal-britepolishing.com
SIC: 3471 Plating of metals or formed products

(G-6436)
METOKOTE CORPORATION
8040 Center Point 70 Blvd (45424-6373)
PHONE..................937 233-1565
EMP: 8
SALES (corp-wide): 17.65B Publicly Held
Web: www.ppgcoatingsservices.com
SIC: 3479 Coating of metals and formed products
HQ: Metokote Corporation
1340 Neubrecht Rd
Lima OH 45801
419 996-7800

(G-6437)
MEYERS PRINTING & DESIGN INC
254 Leo St (45404-1006)
PHONE..................937 461-6000
Gregory Meyers, Pr
EMP: 10 EST: 1999
SALES (est): 628.07K Privately Held
Web: www.mpdink.com
SIC: 2752 Offset printing

(G-6438)
MIAMI CONTROL SYSTEMS INC
4433 Interpoint Blvd (45424)
P.O. Box 96 (45383)
PHONE..................937 233-8146
Andy Minniear, Pr
EMP: 9 EST: 1994
SALES (est): 2.19MM Privately Held
Web: www.miamicontrol.com
SIC: 3625 Electric controls and control accessories, industrial

(G-6439)
MIAMI VALLEY MEALS INC
428 S Edwin C Moses Blvd (45402-8418)
PHONE..................937 938-7141
Amanda Delotelle, Prin
EMP: 8 EST: 2020
SALES (est): 1.97MM Privately Held
Web: www.miamivalleymeals.org
SIC: 2099 Food preparations, nec

(G-6440)
MIAMI VALLEY PUNCH & MFG
1540 Thomas Farm Ct (45458-4744)
PHONE..................937 237-0533
Kamlesh Trivedi, Pr
Sangita Trivedi, Treas
EMP: 13 EST: 1993
SALES (est): 425.65K Privately Held
SIC: 3544 7699 Punches, forming and stamping; Industrial equipment services

(G-6441)
MIAMI VLY PACKG SOLUTIONS INC
1752 Stanley Ave (45404-1117)
P.O. Box 296 (45404-0296)
PHONE..................937 224-1800
▲ EMP: 19 EST: 2009
SQ FT: 6,000
SALES (est): 2.55MM Privately Held
Web: www.mvpsohio.com
SIC: 2653 Boxes, corrugated: made from purchased materials

▲ = Import ▼ = Export
◆ = Import/Export

GEOGRAPHIC SECTION
Dayton - Montgomery County (G-6466)

(G-6442)
MICHELE CALDWELL
Also Called: MRC & Associates
3421 Olive Rd (45426-2655)
PHONE..................937 505-7744
F Michele Caldwell, *Owner*
Michele Caldwell, *Owner*
EMP: 6 **EST:** 1993
SALES (est): 225.69K **Privately Held**
SIC: 8742 7389 7372 7291 Management consulting services; Business oriented computer software; Tax return preparation services

(G-6443)
MICROSUN LAMPS LLC
7890 Center Point 70 Blvd (45424-6369)
PHONE..................888 328-8701
Bob Conner, *CEO*
▲ **EMP:** 8 **EST:** 2014
SALES (est): 1.14MM **Privately Held**
Web: www.microsunlamps.com
SIC: 5719 3645 Lighting, lamps, and accessories; Desk lamps

(G-6444)
MIDWEST SECURITY SERVICES
4050 Benfield Dr (45429-4651)
PHONE..................937 853-9000
Terry Rogers, *Pr*
Jeremy Filia, *Ex VP*
EMP: 20 **EST:** 2012
SALES (est): 1.98MM **Privately Held**
Web: www.mwsecurityservices.com
SIC: 3699 Security control equipment and systems

(G-6445)
MIDWEST TOOL & ENGINEERING CO
112 Webster St (45402-1363)
P.O. Box 481 (45409-0481)
EMP: 23 **EST:** 1920
SQ FT: 27,750
SALES (est): 832.91K **Privately Held**
Web: www.themidwesttool.com
SIC: 3544 3594 3545 Special dies and tools; Fluid power pumps and motors; Machine tool accessories

(G-6446)
MIKE-SELLS POTATO CHIP CO
Also Called: Mikesells Snack Fd Co Dist Ctr
1610 Stanley Ave (45404-1115)
PHONE..................937 228-9400
Lucas Mapp, *Prin*
EMP: 92 **EST:** 1947
SALES (est): 2.31MM **Privately Held**
Web: www.mikesells.com
SIC: 2096 Potato chips and similar snacks

(G-6447)
MIKE-SELLS POTATO CHIP CO (HQ)
333 Leo St (45404-1007)
P.O. Box 13749 (45413-0749)
PHONE..................937 228-9400
D W Mikesell, *
Martha J Mikesell, *
EMP: 30 **EST:** 1910
SQ FT: 95,000
SALES (est): 34.32MM
SALES (corp-wide): 47.84MM **Privately Held**
Web: www.mikesells.com
SIC: 2096 5145 Potato chips and other potato-based snacks; Snack foods
PA: Mike-Sell's West Virginia, Inc.
   333 Leo St
   Dayton OH 45404
   937 228-9400

(G-6448)
MIKE-SELLS WEST VIRGINIA INC (PA)
333 Leo St (45404)
P.O. Box 115 (45404)
PHONE..................937 228-9400
EMP: 75 **EST:** 1910
SALES (est): 47.84MM
SALES (corp-wide): 47.84MM **Privately Held**
SIC: 2096 5145 Potato chips and other potato-based snacks; Pretzels

(G-6449)
MILLAT INDUSTRIES CORP (PA)
4901 Croftshire Dr (45440-1721)
P.O. Box 931188 (44193-1449)
PHONE..................937 434-6666
Gregory Millat, *Pr*
Robert Millat, *
▲ **EMP:** 100 **EST:** 1969
SQ FT: 99,000
SALES (est): 35MM
SALES (corp-wide): 35MM **Privately Held**
Web: www.millatindustries.com
SIC: 3769 3599 3714 Space vehicle equipment, nec; Machine shop, jobbing and repair; Motor vehicle parts and accessories

(G-6450)
MILLAT INDUSTRIES CORP
7611 Center Point 70 Blvd (45424)
PHONE..................937 535-1500
EMP: 13
SALES (corp-wide): 35MM **Privately Held**
Web: www.millatindustries.com
SIC: 3714 Motor vehicle parts and accessories
PA: Millat Industries, Corp.
   4901 Croftshire Dr
   Dayton OH 45440
   937 434-6666

(G-6451)
MINCO TOOL AND MOLD INC (PA)
Also Called: Minco Group, The
5690 Webster St (45414-3519)
P.O. Box 13545 (45413-0545)
PHONE..................937 890-7905
EMP: 91 **EST:** 1956
SALES (est): 9.9MM
SALES (corp-wide): 9.9MM **Privately Held**
Web: www.mincogroup.com
SIC: 3544 Forms (molds), for foundry and plastics working machinery

(G-6452)
MINUTEMAN PRESS
2599 Needmore Rd (45414-4203)
PHONE..................937 701-7100
EMP: 7 **EST:** 2018
SALES (est): 225.96K **Privately Held**
Web: www.minutemanpress.com
SIC: 2752 Commercial printing, lithographic

(G-6453)
MKGS CORP
1712 Springfield St Ste 2 (45403-1447)
PHONE..................937 254-8181
Raymond P Horan, *Pr*
EMP: 13 **EST:** 1994
SQ FT: 25,000
SALES (est): 918.41K **Privately Held**
Web: www.intlam.com
SIC: 3083 Plastics finished products, laminated

(G-6454)
MODERN MACHINE DEVELOPMENT
400 Linden Ave Ste 3 (45403-2558)
PHONE..................937 253-4576
Bruce Vicory, *Pr*
David Wolfe, *VP*
Iva Nelson, *Sec*
EMP: 10 **EST:** 1968
SQ FT: 70,000
SALES (est): 830.56K **Privately Held**
SIC: 3599 5084 7692 Custom machinery; Welding machinery and equipment; Welding repair

(G-6455)
MOELLER BREW BARN LLC
416 E 1st St (45402-1220)
PHONE..................937 400-8628
EMP: 8
SALES (corp-wide): 4.38MM **Privately Held**
Web: www.moellerbrewbarn.com
SIC: 2082 Malt beverages
PA: Moeller Brew Barn, Llc
   8016 Marion Dr
   Maria Stein OH 45860
   419 925-3005

(G-6456)
MONAGHAN & ASSOCIATES INC
Also Called: Monaghan Tooling Group
30 N Clinton St (45402-1327)
P.O. Box 1012 (45401-1012)
PHONE..................937 253-7706
Scott Monaghan, *Pr*
EMP: 19 **EST:** 1986
SALES (est): 2.4MM **Privately Held**
Web: www.monaghantooling.com
SIC: 3545 5084 3541 Cutting tools for machine tools; Industrial machinery and equipment; Machine tools, metal cutting type

(G-6457)
MORNING PRIDE MFG LLC (HQ)
Also Called: Honeywell First Responder Pdts
1 Innovation Ct (45414)
PHONE..................937 264-2662
William L Grilliot, *Managing Member*
▲ **EMP:** 521 **EST:** 1998
SQ FT: 56,000
SALES (est): 256.89MM
SALES (corp-wide): 36.66B **Publicly Held**
SIC: 3842 2326 Respirators; Men's and boy's work clothing
PA: Honeywell International Inc.
   855 S Mint St
   Charlotte NC 28202
   704 627-6200

(G-6458)
MORNING PRIDE MFG LLC
4978 Riverton Dr (45414-3964)
PHONE..................937 264-1726
Patrick Walls, *Supervisor*
EMP: 521
SALES (corp-wide): 36.66B **Publicly Held**
SIC: 3842 Respirators
HQ: Morning Pride Mfg Llc
   1 Innovation Ct
   Dayton OH 45414
   937 264-2662

(G-6459)
MOUND MANUFACTURING CENTER INC
33 Commerce Park Dr (45404-1211)
PHONE..................937 236-8387
Albert J Hodapp Iii, *Pr*
Steve Priser, *VP*
EMP: 12 **EST:** 1994
SQ FT: 9,000
SALES (est): 2.37MM **Privately Held**
Web: www.moundmanufacturing.com

SIC: 8711 3599 Machine tool design; Machine shop, jobbing and repair

(G-6460)
MRS ELECTRONIC INC
6680 Poe Ave Ste 100 (45414-2855)
PHONE..................937 660-6767
Franz Hoffmann, *CEO*
Guenther Doergeloh, *COO*
EMP: 12 **EST:** 2015
SALES (est): 1.71MM **Privately Held**
Web: www.mrs-electronics.com
SIC: 3714 Motor vehicle electrical equipment

(G-6461)
MULLINS RUBBER PRODUCTS INC
2949 Valley Pike (45404-2693)
P.O. Box 24830 (45424-0830)
PHONE..................937 233-4211
William D Mullins, *Prin*
Dennis Mullins, *
William R Mullins Junior, *VP*
EMP: 52 **EST:** 1939
SQ FT: 75,000
SALES (est): 9.58MM **Privately Held**
Web: www.mullinsrubber.com
SIC: 3069 Molded rubber products

(G-6462)
MW METALS GROUP LLC
461 Homestead Ave (45417-3921)
P.O. Box 546 (45401-0546)
PHONE..................937 222-5992
Joel Frydman, *CEO*
Farley Frydman, *Pr*
EMP: 65 **EST:** 1955
SQ FT: 150,000
SALES (est): 18.57MM **Privately Held**
Web: www.mwmetals.com
SIC: 3341 5093 Secondary nonferrous metals; Scrap and waste materials

(G-6463)
NATIONAL CON BURIAL VLT ASSN
136 S Keowee St (45402-2241)
PHONE..................407 788-1996
EMP: 6 **EST:** 2019
SALES (est): 183.27K **Privately Held**
Web: ncbva.wildapricot.org
SIC: 3272 Burial vaults, concrete or precast terrazzo

(G-6464)
NATIONAL OILWELL VARCO LP
Also Called: Chemineer
5870 Poe Ave (45414-3442)
P.O. Box 1123 (45401-1123)
PHONE..................937 454-4660
Joel Staff, *Pt*
EMP: 99
SALES (corp-wide): 8.58B **Publicly Held**
Web: www.nov.com
SIC: 3556 3554 Food products machinery; Paper industries machinery
HQ: National Oilwell Varco, L.P.
   10353 Richmond Ave
   Houston TX 77042
   713 375-3700

(G-6465)
NATIONAL PALLET & MULCH LLC
3550 Intercity Dr (45424-5124)
PHONE..................937 237-1643
EMP: 10 **EST:** 2005
SALES (est): 967.4K **Privately Held**
SIC: 2448 Pallets, wood

(G-6466)
NCR TECHNOLOGY CENTER
1560 S Patterson Blvd (45409-2108)

Dayton - Montgomery County (G-6467)

PHONE..................937 445-1936
EMP: 9 **EST:** 2014
SALES (est): 351.86K
SALES (corp-wide): 3.83B **Publicly Held**
Web: www.ncr.com
SIC: 3578 7379 7374 7371 Point-of-sale devices; Computer related maintenance services; Data processing and preparation; Software programming applications
PA: Ncr Voyix Corporation
864 Spring St Nw
Atlanta GA 30308
937 445-1936

(G-6467)
ND PAPER INC
7777 Washington Village Dr Ste 210 (45459-3995)
PHONE..................937 528-3822
EMP: 251
Web: us.ndpaper.com
SIC: 2611 Pulp manufactured from waste or recycled paper
HQ: Nd Paper Inc.
2001 Spring Rd Ste 500
Oak Brook IL 60523
513 200-0908

(G-6468)
NDC TECHNOLOGIES INC
Also Called: Nordson MCS
8001 Technology Blvd (45424-1568)
PHONE..................937 233-9935
Bromley Beadle, *Pr*
EMP: 115
SALES (corp-wide): 2.63B **Publicly Held**
Web: www.ndc.com
SIC: 3826 Analytical instruments
HQ: Ndc Technologies, Inc.
8001 Technology Blvd
Dayton OH 45424
937 233-9935

(G-6469)
NDC TECHNOLOGIES INC (HQ)
Also Called: NDC Technologies
8001 Technology Blvd (45424-1568)
PHONE..................937 233-9935
Marti Nyman, *Pr*
▲ **EMP:** 105 **EST:** 1987
SQ FT: 45,000
SALES (est): 51.24MM
SALES (corp-wide): 2.63B **Publicly Held**
Web: www.ndc.com
SIC: 3829 Measuring and controlling devices, nec
PA: Nordson Corporation
28601 Clemens Rd
Westlake OH 44145
440 892-1580

(G-6470)
NEVCO SERVICES LTD
3620 Old Salem Rd (45415-1426)
PHONE..................937 603-1500
Daniel W Nevels, *Prin*
EMP: 7 **EST:** 2008
SALES (est): 51.16K **Privately Held**
SIC: 3993 Signs and advertising specialties

(G-6471)
NIOBIUM MICROSYSTEMS INC
444 E 2nd St (45402-1724)
PHONE..................937 203-8117
Rob Wiltbank, *CEO*
EMP: 177
SALES (corp-wide): 2.73MM **Privately Held**
Web: www.niobiummicrosystems.com
SIC: 3674 Semiconductors and related devices

PA: Niobium Microsystems, Inc.
421 Sw 6th Ave Ste 300
Portland OR 97204
503 626-6616

(G-6472)
NOBLE TOOL CORP
1535 Stanley Ave (45404-1112)
PHONE..................937 461-4040
Thomas Biegel, *Pr*
Nick Rosenkranz, *
EMP: 31 **EST:** 1980
SQ FT: 7,500
SALES (est): 4.88MM **Privately Held**
Web: www.nobletool.com
SIC: 3544 Special dies and tools

(G-6473)
NON-FERROUS CASTING COMPANY
736 Albany St (45417-3486)
P.O. Box 364 (45409-0364)
PHONE..................937 220-1102
James D Claffey, *Prin*
James D Claffey Junior Prinic, *Prin*
EMP: 6 **EST:** 1954
SQ FT: 12,000
SALES (est): 572.78K **Privately Held**
Web: www.nonferrouscasting.com
SIC: 3366 3365 Brass foundry, nec; Masts, cast aluminum

(G-6474)
NORTHROP GRMMN SPCE & MSSN SYS
1900 Founders Dr Ste 202 (45420-1182)
PHONE..................937 259-4956
EMP: 60
SIC: 7372 7374 Prepackaged software; Data processing and preparation
HQ: Northrop Grumman Space & Mission Systems Corp.
6379 San Ignacio Ave
San Jose CA 95119
703 280-2900

(G-6475)
NORTHWESTERN TOOLS INC
4800 Hempstead Station Dr (45429-3900)
PHONE..................937 298-9994
EMP: 16 **EST:** 1942
SALES (est): 1.98MM **Privately Held**
Web: www.northwesterntools.com
SIC: 3544 Jigs and fixtures

(G-6476)
NORWOOD MEDICAL LLC
2101 Winners Cir (45404-1176)
P.O. Box 3806 (45401-3806)
PHONE..................937 228-4101
Ken Hammelgarn, *Mgr*
EMP: 1061
SALES (corp-wide): 2.67MM **Privately Held**
Web: www.norwoodmedical.com
SIC: 3469 Metal stampings, nec
HQ: Norwood Medical Llc
2122 Winners Cir
Dayton OH 45404
937 228-4101

(G-6477)
NORWOOD MEDICAL LLC (DH)
Also Called: Norwood Medical
2122 Winners Cir (45404-1148)
P.O. Box 3806 (45401-3806)
PHONE..................937 228-4101
Kenneth Hemmelgarn Senior, *Pr*
Kenneth J Hemmelgarn Senior, *
Kenneth J Hemmelgarn Junior, *VP Fin*
Brian Hemmelgarn, *
EMP: 75 **EST:** 1926

SQ FT: 65,000
SALES (est): 159.92MM
SALES (corp-wide): 2.67MM **Privately Held**
Web: www.norwoodmedical.com
SIC: 3841 3845 Surgical and medical instruments; Electromedical apparatus
HQ: Heraeus Holding Gesellschaft Mit Beschrankter Haftung
Heraeusstr. 12-14
Hanau HE 63450
6181350

(G-6478)
NORWOOD TOOL COMPANY
Also Called: NORWOOD TOOL COMPANY
2055 Winners Cir (45404-1182)
PHONE..................937 228-4101
EMP: 7
SALES (corp-wide): 2.67MM **Privately Held**
Web: www.norwoodmedical.com
SIC: 3469 Metal stampings, nec
HQ: Norwood Medical Llc
2122 Winners Cir
Dayton OH 45404
937 228-4101

(G-6479)
NOV INC
Also Called: Chemineer
5870 Poe Ave (45414-3442)
PHONE..................937 454-3200
Daniel Margolien, *Genl Mgr*
EMP: 88
SALES (corp-wide): 8.58B **Publicly Held**
Web: www.nov.com
SIC: 3569 3531 Liquid automation machinery and equipment; Construction machinery
PA: Nov Inc.
10353 Richmond Ave
Houston TX 77042
346 223-3000

(G-6480)
NOV PROCESS & FLOW TECH US INC
5870 Poe Ave (45414-3442)
PHONE..................937 454-3300
EMP: 34
SALES (corp-wide): 8.58B **Publicly Held**
SIC: 3823 Industrial flow and liquid measuring instruments
HQ: Nov Process & Flow Technologies Us, Inc.
10353 Richmond Ave
Houston TX 77042
346 223-3000

(G-6481)
NTECH INDUSTRIES INC
5475 Kellenburger Rd (45424-1013)
PHONE..................707 467-3747
John Mayfield, *CEO*
EMP: 32 **EST:** 2001
SQ FT: 1,600
SALES (est): 1.39MM
SALES (corp-wide): 3.8B **Publicly Held**
SIC: 3523 Farm machinery and equipment
PA: Trimble Inc.
10368 Westmoor Dr
Westminster CO 80021
720 887-6100

(G-6482)
NU STREAM FILTRATION INC
1257 Stanley Ave (45404-1013)
PHONE..................937 949-3174
James Baker, *Pr*
EMP: 10 **EST:** 2017

SQ FT: 20,000
SALES (est): 1.23MM **Privately Held**
Web: www.nustreamfiltration.com
SIC: 3677 Filtration devices, electronic

(G-6483)
OAKLEY INC
1421 Springfield St Unit 2 (45403-1435)
P.O. Box 8302 (45040-5302)
PHONE..................949 672-6560
Sheila Oakley, *Brnch Mgr*
EMP: 10
SALES (corp-wide): 2.55MM **Privately Held**
Web: www.oakley.com
SIC: 3851 Ophthalmic goods
HQ: Oakley, Inc.
1 Icon
Foothill Ranch CA 92610
949 951-0991

(G-6484)
OERLIKON FRCTION SYSTEMS US IN
Also Called: Plant 5
240 Detrick St (45404-1699)
PHONE..................937 233-9191
Joe Caffano, *Brnch Mgr*
EMP: 38
Web: www.oerlikon.com
SIC: 3465 Automotive stampings
HQ: Oerlikon Friction Systems (Us) Inc.
240 Detrick St
Dayton OH 45404
937 449-4000

(G-6485)
OERLIKON FRICTION SYSTEMS
14 Heid Ave (45404-1216)
P.O. Box 745 (45401-0745)
PHONE..................937 449-4000
EMP: 38
Web: www.oerlikon.com
SIC: 3714 Acceleration equipment, motor vehicle
HQ: Oerlikon Friction Systems (Us) Inc.
240 Detrick St
Dayton OH 45404
937 449-4000

(G-6486)
OERLIKON FRICTION SYSTEMS (HQ)
240 Detrick St (45404-1699)
P.O. Box 745 (45401-0745)
PHONE..................937 449-4000
Eric A Schueler, *Pr*
John Parker, *
Mark Szporka, *
◆ **EMP:** 39 **EST:** 2002
SQ FT: 115,000
SALES (est): 49.66MM **Privately Held**
Web: www.oerlikon.com
SIC: 3714 Transmission housings or parts, motor vehicle
PA: Oc Oerlikon Corporation Ag, Pfaffikon
Churerstrasse 120
PfAffikon SZ 8808

(G-6487)
OHIO DEFENSE SERVICES INC
143 S Monmouth St (45403-2127)
PHONE..................937 608-2371
Michael Davis, *Prin*
EMP: 23 **EST:** 2017
SALES (est): 115.19K **Privately Held**
SIC: 3812 Defense systems and equipment

(G-6488)
OHIO METAL FABRICATING INC
6057 Milo Rd (45414-3417)
PHONE..................937 233-2400

GEOGRAPHIC SECTION
Dayton - Montgomery County (G-6514)

Gary Brandeberry, *Pr*
Leta Brandeberry, *Prin*
EMP: 17 **EST:** 2007
SQ FT: 18,000
SALES (est): 2.13MM **Privately Held**
Web: www.ohiometalfab.com
SIC: 3599 Machine shop, jobbing and repair

(G-6489)
OHIO METAL PRODUCTS COMPANY
35 Bates St (45402-1395)
PHONE.................937 228-6101
John D Moore, *Pr*
Janet A Simpson, *
▲ **EMP:** 24 **EST:** 1909
SQ FT: 32,000
SALES (est): 1.09MM **Privately Held**
Web: www.ohio-metal.com
SIC: 3451 3471 Screw machine products; Plating and polishing

(G-6490)
OHIO NEWSPAPERS INC (DH)
Also Called: Cox Media Group
1611 S Main St (45409-2547)
PHONE.................937 225-2000
Julia Wallace, *VP*
Charles D Shook, *
Edward L Shank, *
Sylvia J Planck, *
EMP: 550 **EST:** 1898
SQ FT: 150,000
SALES (est): 119.14MM
SALES (corp-wide): 2.85B **Privately Held**
Web: www.cmglocalsolutions.com
SIC: 2711 Commercial printing and newspaper publishing combined
HQ: Cox Newspapers, Inc.
6205 Pchtree Dnwody Rd N
Atlanta GA 30328

(G-6491)
OMNIPRESENCE CLEANING LLC
302 W Fairview Ave (45405-3304)
P.O. Box 20042 (45420-0042)
PHONE.................937 250-4749
EMP: 17 **EST:** 2009
SALES (est): 257.8K **Privately Held**
SIC: 7349 1389 8322 2741 Building maintenance services, nec; Construction, repair, and dismantling services; Senior citizens' center or association; Business service newsletters: publishing and printing

(G-6492)
OPEN ADDITIVE LLC
2750 Indian Ripple Rd (45440-3638)
PHONE.................937 306-6140
EMP: 11 **EST:** 2019
SALES (est): 1.17MM **Privately Held**
Web: www.arctos-us.com
SIC: 3552 8731 Textile machinery; Commercial physical research

(G-6493)
ORCHEM CORPORATION
130 W 2nd St Ste 2030 (45402-1502)
PHONE.................513 874-9700
EMP: 26 **EST:** 1996
SALES (est): 4.96MM **Privately Held**
Web: www.orchemcorp.com
SIC: 2842 Specialty cleaning

(G-6494)
OREGON VLG PRINT SHOPPE INC
Also Called: Oregon Printing
29 N June St (45403-1015)
PHONE.................937 222-9418
Judd Plattenburg, *Pr*
EMP: 15 **EST:** 1974
SQ FT: 5,300

SALES (est): 2.39MM **Privately Held**
Web: www.oregonprinting.com
SIC: 2752 Offset printing

(G-6495)
OUTLOOK TOOL INC
360 Fame Rd (45449-2313)
PHONE.................937 235-6330
Eric Staeuble, *Pr*
Ted Nevels, *Sec*
EMP: 6 **EST:** 1997
SQ FT: 3,200
SALES (est): 483.92K **Privately Held**
Web: www.outlooktool.com
SIC: 3599 Machine shop, jobbing and repair

(G-6496)
OVASE MANUFACTURING LLC
Also Called: Global Tool
1990 Berwyck Ave (45414-5556)
P.O. Box 3 (45066-0003)
PHONE.................937 275-0617
EMP: 10 **EST:** 2005
SALES (est): 535.91K **Privately Held**
SIC: 3599 Machine shop, jobbing and repair

(G-6497)
P J TOOL COMPANY INC
1115 Springfield St (45403-1420)
PHONE.................937 254-2817
Paul Hedrick, *Pr*
Jim Fedor, *Sec*
EMP: 6 **EST:** 1987
SQ FT: 2,600
SALES (est): 685.48K **Privately Held**
SIC: 3599 3544 Machine shop, jobbing and repair; Special dies, tools, jigs, and fixtures

(G-6498)
PAST PATTERNS
Also Called: Altman, Sandra L
128 Grafton Ave (45406-5420)
PHONE.................937 223-3722
Saundra Ros Altman, *Admn*
EMP: 6 **EST:** 2013
SALES (est): 165.85K **Privately Held**
SIC: 3543 Industrial patterns

(G-6499)
PAVE TECHNOLOGY CO
2751 Thunderhawk Ct (45414-3451)
PHONE.................937 890-1100
Walter D Wood, *Ch Bd*
Brad Boomershine, *
EMP: 45 **EST:** 1980
SQ FT: 20,000
SALES (est): 9.4MM **Privately Held**
Web: www.pavetechnologyco.com
SIC: 3643 3089 Current-carrying wiring services; Injection molding of plastics

(G-6500)
PENTAGEAR PRODUCTS LLC
6161 Webster St (45414-3435)
PHONE.................937 660-8182
EMP: 17 **EST:** 2005
SALES (est): 525.24K **Privately Held**
Web: www.pentagear.com
SIC: 3566 7389 Speed changers, drives, and gears; Business services, nec

(G-6501)
PEPSI-COLA METRO BTLG CO INC
Also Called: Pepsi-Cola
526 Milburn Ave (45404-1678)
PHONE.................937 461-4664
Tim Trant, *Genl Mgr*
EMP: 49
SQ FT: 115,000
SALES (corp-wide): 86.39B **Publicly Held**

Web: www.pepsico.com
SIC: 2086 5149 Soft drinks: packaged in cans, bottles, etc.; Groceries and related products, nec
HQ: Pepsi-Cola Metropolitan Bottling Company, Inc.
700 Anderson Hill Rd
Purchase NY 10577
914 767-6000

(G-6502)
PERMA EDGE PAVER EDGING
420 Davis Ave (45403-2912)
PHONE.................844 334-4464
EMP: 6 **EST:** 2018
SALES (est): 186.9K **Privately Held**
Web: www.permapaveredging.com
SIC: 2951 Asphalt paving mixtures and blocks

(G-6503)
PERMA-FIX OF DAYTON INC
300 Cherokee Dr (45417-8113)
PHONE.................937 268-6501
Brad Malatesta, *Pr*
Richard Kelecy, *VP*
EMP: 13 **EST:** 1941
SQ FT: 25,000
SALES (est): 3.93MM **Publicly Held**
Web: www.perma-fix.com
SIC: 4953 2992 Recycling, waste materials; Lubricating oils and greases
PA: Perma-Fix Environmental Services, Inc.
8302 Dunwoody Pl Ste 250
Atlanta GA 30350

(G-6504)
PHOENIX INKJET CLOUR SLTONS LL
707 Miamisburg Centerville Rd Ste 128 (45459)
PHONE.................937 602-8486
EMP: 7 **EST:** 2014
SALES (est): 546.3K **Privately Held**
Web: www.phoenixijc.com
SIC: 2893 Printing ink

(G-6505)
PIEDMONT CHEMICAL COMPANY INC
1516 Silver Lake Dr (45458-3529)
PHONE.................937 428-6640
Ed Kren, *Prin*
EMP: 9 **EST:** 2005
SALES (est): 239.13K **Privately Held**
SIC: 3471 Cleaning, polishing, and finishing

(G-6506)
PIETRA NATURALE INC
2425 Stanley Ave (45404-2728)
PHONE.................937 438-8882
Michael Carnevale Junior, *Pr*
Robert Carnevale, *VP*
Michael Ricky Carnevale, *Treas*
EMP: 12 **EST:** 1990
SALES (est): 2.44MM **Privately Held**
Web: www.pietranaturaleinc.com
SIC: 1799 3281 Counter top installation; Marble, building: cut and shaped

(G-6507)
PLATING TECHNOLOGY INC
1525 W River Rd (45417-6740)
PHONE.................937 268-6882
Jody Pollack Blazar, *Prin*
▲ **EMP:** 70 **EST:** 1953
SQ FT: 190,000
SALES (est): 9.89MM **Privately Held**
Web: www.platingtech.com

SIC: 3471 3469 Electroplating of metals or formed products; Machine parts, stamped or pressed metal

(G-6508)
PLUMB BUILDERS INC
2367 S Dixie Dr (45409-1858)
PHONE.................937 293-1111
Larry Freed, *Pr*
EMP: 10 **EST:** 1991
SALES (est): 997.74K **Privately Held**
SIC: 1521 5999 3999 Single-family housing construction; Technical aids for the handicapped; Wheelchair lifts

(G-6509)
PRATT INDUSTRIES INC
98 Quality Ln (45449-2141)
PHONE.................513 262-6253
EMP: 17
Web: www.prattindustries.com
SIC: 2653 Boxes, corrugated: made from purchased materials
PA: Pratt Industries, Inc.
1800 Sarasota Pkwy Ne C
Conyers GA 30013

(G-6510)
PRECISION AIRCRAFT COMPONENTS
2787 Armstrong Ln (45414-4225)
PHONE.................937 278-0265
Emsy Little Junior, *CEO*
Jonathan Hurlow, *Sec*
EMP: 24 **EST:** 1985
SQ FT: 17,500
SALES (est): 866.51K **Privately Held**
SIC: 3599 Machine shop, jobbing and repair

(G-6511)
PRECISION FINISHING SYSTEMS
6101 Webster St (45414-3435)
PHONE.................937 415-5794
Barbara Lipuma, *Pt*
EMP: 45 **EST:** 2012
SALES (est): 4MM **Privately Held**
Web: www.pfs-finishing.com
SIC: 3471 Cleaning, polishing, and finishing

(G-6512)
PRECISION GAGE & TOOL COMPANY
375 Gargrave Rd (45449-2465)
PHONE.................937 866-9666
Vicki Waltz, *Pr*
Leslie Heaton, *VP*
EMP: 20 **EST:** 1929
SQ FT: 16,000
SALES (est): 3.46MM **Privately Held**
Web: www.pgtgage.com
SIC: 3545 7699 Gauges (machine tool accessories); Caliper, gauge, and other machinists' instrument repair

(G-6513)
PRECISION MACHINING SERVICES
Also Called: Universal Tool Co
365 Leo St (45404-1007)
PHONE.................937 222-4608
Eric Kleinschmidt, *Pr*
Mike Farmer, *
EMP: 40 **EST:** 1936
SQ FT: 45,000
SALES (est): 801.09K **Privately Held**
Web: www.mccaytool.com
SIC: 3599 Machine shop, jobbing and repair

(G-6514)
PRECISION MANUFACTURING CO INC

Dayton - Montgomery County (G-6515)

GEOGRAPHIC SECTION

2149 Valley Pike (45404-2542)
PHONE..................937 236-2170
Faye Ledwick, *CEO*
EMP: 70 **EST:** 1967
SQ FT: 30,000
SALES (est): 9.36MM **Privately Held**
Web: www.precmfgco.com
SIC: 3679 Electronic circuits

(G-6515)
PRECISION MFG & ASSEMBLY LLC
2240 Richard St (45403-2551)
PHONE..................937 252-3507
William Bill Duckro, *Managing Member*
EMP: 65 **EST:** 2002
SALES (est): 6.3MM **Privately Held**
SIC: 3089 Automotive parts, plastic

(G-6516)
PRECISION MTAL FABRICATION INC (PA)
101 Heid Ave (45404-1217)
PHONE..................937 235-9261
Jim Hackenberger, *Pr*
John Limberg, *
EMP: 57 **EST:** 1984
SQ FT: 30,000
SALES (est): 9.02MM
SALES (corp-wide): 9.02MM **Privately Held**
Web: www.premetfab.com
SIC: 7692 3444 Welding repair; Sheet metalwork

(G-6517)
PRECISION PRESSED POWDERED MET
1522 Manchester Rd (45449-1933)
PHONE..................937 433-6802
Stephen G England, *Ch*
David Warner, *Pr*
EMP: 19 **EST:** 1983
SQ FT: 7,000
SALES (est): 1MM **Privately Held**
Web: www.precisionpressedpowderedmetals.com
SIC: 3469 Stamping metal for the trade

(G-6518)
PREMIER AEROSPACE GROUP LLC
Also Called: Jbk Manufacturing
2127 Troy St (45404-2162)
PHONE..................937 233-8300
Steve Olson, *Managing Member*
EMP: 35 **EST:** 2021
SALES (est): 2.55MM **Privately Held**
Web: www.jbkmfg.com
SIC: 3599 Machine shop, jobbing and repair

(G-6519)
PRIDE INVESTMENTS LLC
Also Called: American Heat Treating
1346 Morris Ave (45417-3829)
PHONE..................937 461-1121
Lawrence Gray, *Owner*
EMP: 15 **EST:** 2004
SQ FT: 32,000
SALES (est): 2.3MM **Privately Held**
Web: www.ahtdayton.com
SIC: 3398 Metal heat treating

(G-6520)
PRIMARY PDTS INGRDNTS AMRCAS L
5600 Brentlinger Dr (45414-3512)
PHONE..................937 236-5906
Dana Johnson, *Brnch Mgr*
EMP: 100
SALES (corp-wide): 1.16B **Privately Held**
Web: www.tateandlyle.com
SIC: 2899 2819 2087 Chemical preparations, nec; Industrial inorganic chemicals, nec; Flavoring extracts and syrups, nec
HQ: Primary Products Ingredients Americas Llc
2200 E Eldorado St
Decatur IL 62521
217 423-4411

(G-6521)
PRIMARY PDTS INGRDNTS AMRCAS L
Also Called: Tate & Lyle
5584 Webster St (45414-3517)
PHONE..................937 235-4074
EMP: 8
SALES (corp-wide): 1.16B **Privately Held**
Web: www.tateandlyle.com
SIC: 2046 Wet corn milling
HQ: Primary Products Ingredients Americas Llc
2200 E Eldorado St
Decatur IL 62521
217 423-4411

(G-6522)
PRIME PRINTING INC (PA)
8929 Kingsridge Dr (45458-1621)
P.O. Box 751591 (45475-1591)
PHONE..................937 438-3707
Gary Smith, *Pr*
Dan Cornelius, *
Tim Cox, *
EMP: 33 **EST:** 1991
SQ FT: 12,000
SALES (est): 2.19MM **Privately Held**
SIC: 2752 2796 2791 2789 Offset printing; Platemaking services; Typesetting; Bookbinding and related work

(G-6523)
PRINTING DIMENSIONS INC
500 N Irwin St (45403-1335)
PHONE..................937 256-0044
Michael E Feeley, *Pr*
Michael D Hornick, *VP*
John A Feeley, *Sec*
EMP: 12 **EST:** 1982
SALES (est): 1MM **Privately Held**
SIC: 2752 2759 Offset printing; Commercial printing, nec

(G-6524)
PRINTPOINT INC
150 S Patterson Blvd (45402-2421)
PHONE..................937 223-9041
Mike Munch, *Pr*
EMP: 7 **EST:** 1976
SQ FT: 13,000
SALES (est): 661.05K **Privately Held**
Web: www.printpointprinting.com
SIC: 2752 Offset printing

(G-6525)
PRO CHOICE CABINETRY LLC
5700 Far Hills Ave (45429-2242)
PHONE..................937 313-9297
Thomas Dement, *Prin*
EMP: 7 **EST:** 2014
SALES (est): 343.13K **Privately Held**
SIC: 2434 Wood kitchen cabinets

(G-6526)
PRO LINE COLLISION AND PNT LLC (PA)
Also Called: Proline Finishing
1 Armor Pl (45417-3443)
PHONE..................937 223-7611
EMP: 8 **EST:** 2005
SQ FT: 44,000
SALES (est): 2.49MM **Privately Held**
Web: www.carcpaint1.com
SIC: 3471 Finishing, metals or formed products

(G-6527)
PROCESS DEVELOPMENT CORP
6060 Milo Rd (45414-3418)
PHONE..................937 890-3388
Cliff Blacke, *Pr*
EMP: 22 **EST:** 1992
SQ FT: 42,000
SALES (est): 921.01K **Privately Held**
Web: www.adaptivedevcorp.com
SIC: 3559 3599 3582 3548 Automotive related machinery; Machine and other job shop work; Commercial laundry equipment; Welding apparatus

(G-6528)
PRODIGY PRINT INC
Also Called: Prodigy Print Ink
884 Valley St (45404-2066)
▲ **EMP:** 10 **EST:** 1982
SALES (est): 2.04MM **Privately Held**
SIC: 2759 2789 Screen printing; Bookbinding and related work

(G-6529)
PRODUCTION DESIGN SERVICES INC (PA)
Also Called: Pdsi Technical Services
313 Mound St (45402-8370)
PHONE..................937 866-3377
John H Schultz, *Pr*
John H Schultz, *Pr*
Jeffrey R Schultz, *
James A Schultz, *
EMP: 76 **EST:** 1978
SQ FT: 48,000
SALES (est): 19.25MM
SALES (corp-wide): 19.25MM **Privately Held**
Web: www.pdsitech.com
SIC: 3599 3559 Custom machinery; Sewing machines and hat and zipper making machinery

(G-6530)
PRODUCTION TUBE CUTTING INC
1100 S Smithville Rd (45403-3423)
PHONE..................937 254-6138
◆ **EMP:** 43 **EST:** 1959
SALES (est): 10.28MM **Privately Held**
Web: www.productiontubecutting.com
SIC: 3498 3559 3351 3083 Tube fabricating (contract bending and shaping); Refinery, chemical processing, and similar machinery ; Copper rolling and drawing; Laminated plastics plate and sheet

(G-6531)
PROFICIENT INFO TECH INC
Also Called: Pi-Tech
301 W 1st St (45402-3033)
PHONE..................937 470-1300
Tina Bustillo, *Pr*
EMP: 8 **EST:** 1994
SALES (est): 903.29K **Privately Held**
Web: www.pi-tech-inc.com
SIC: 7371 7372 7379 8742 Custom computer programming services; Application computer software; Computer related maintenance services; Marketing consulting services

(G-6532)
PROFOUND LOGIC SOFTWARE INC (PA)
396 Congress Park Dr (45459-4149)
P.O. Box 12559 (92658-5067)
PHONE..................937 439-7925
Alex Roytman, *CEO*
Alex Roytman, *Pr*
EMP: 20 **EST:** 2000
SALES (est): 6.38MM **Privately Held**
Web: www.profoundlogic.com
SIC: 7372 7379 7371 Prepackaged software ; Computer related consulting services; Software programming applications

(G-6533)
PROGRESSIVE PRINTERS INC
6700 Homestretch Rd (45414-2516)
PHONE..................937 222-1267
Dennis Livesay, *Pr*
Sharon L Staggs, *
Sheena Simmons, *
Dennis Livesay, *CEO*
Phil Bondi, *Genl Mgr*
EMP: 66 **EST:** 2001
SQ FT: 26,000
SALES (est): 9.73MM **Privately Held**
Web: www.progressiveprinters.com
SIC: 2752 2759 Offset printing; Commercial printing, nec

(G-6534)
PROJECTS UNLIMITED INC (PA)
6300 Sand Lake Rd (45414-2649)
PHONE..................937 918-2200
EMP: 170 **EST:** 1954
SALES (est): 38.25MM
SALES (corp-wide): 38.25MM **Privately Held**
Web: www.pui.com
SIC: 3672 3679 3643 3625 Printed circuit boards; Harness assemblies, for electronic use: wire or cable; Current-carrying wiring services; Relays and industrial controls

(G-6535)
PUTNAM PLASTICS INC
Also Called: Farm Products Division
255 S Alex Rd (45449-1910)
PHONE..................937 866-6261
Gary Spacht, *Mgr*
EMP: 8
SALES (corp-wide): 5.45MM **Privately Held**
Web: www.putnamplasticsinc.com
SIC: 5199 5113 3081 Packaging materials; Industrial and personal service paper; Polyethylene film
PA: Putnam Plastics Inc
30 W Stardust Rd
Cloverdale IN 46120
765 795-6102

(G-6536)
QUARTER CENTURY DESIGN LLC
2555 S Dixie Dr Ste 232 (45409-1518)
PHONE..................937 434-5127
EMP: 6 **EST:** 2006
SALES (est): 920.23K **Privately Held**
Web: www.quartercenturydesign.com
SIC: 3672 Printed circuit boards

(G-6537)
R D BAKER ENTERPRISES INC
Also Called: Alpha Water Conditioning Co
765 Liberty Ln (45449-2134)
PHONE..................937 461-5225
Bill Miller, *Brnch Mgr*
EMP: 6
SALES (corp-wide): 4.04MM **Privately Held**
Web: www.daytonsoftwater.com

SIC: 3589 8734 5074 Water purification equipment, household type; Water testing laboratory; Water softeners
PA: R. D. Baker Enterprises, Inc.
765 Liberty Ln
Dayton OH 45449
937 461-5225

(G-6538)
RAM PRECISION INDUSTRIES INC
Also Called: R A M Precision Tool
11125 Yankee St Ste A (45458-3698)
PHONE..................................937 885-7700
Richard Mount, CEO
▲ EMP: 85 EST: 1974
SQ FT: 55,000
SALES (est): 18.06MM Privately Held
Web: www.ramprecision.com
SIC: 3599 Machine shop, jobbing and repair

(G-6539)
RAM TOOL INC
1944 Neva Dr (45414-5525)
PHONE..................................937 277-0717
EMP: 7 EST: 1973
SQ FT: 4,000
SALES (est): 724.93K Privately Held
Web: www.ramtoolohio.com
SIC: 3544 Special dies and tools

(G-6540)
RAMBASEK REALTY INC
Also Called: Crystal Water Company
827 S Patterson Blvd (45402-2622)
PHONE..................................937 228-1189
Tom Rambasek, Pr
Nancy F Rambasek, VP
EMP: 19 EST: 1919
SQ FT: 16,000
SALES (est): 2.28MM Privately Held
SIC: 5149 5963 2899 7359 Water, distilled; Bottled water delivery; Distilled water; Equipment rental and leasing, nec

(G-6541)
RANDD ASSOC PRTG & PROMOTIONS
330 Progress Rd (45449-2322)
PHONE..................................937 294-1874
Rick Dobson, Pr
Rick Dobson, Pr
Pam Dobson, Sec
EMP: 7 EST: 1980
SQ FT: 3,200
SALES (est): 815.53K Privately Held
Web: www.randdassociates.com
SIC: 2752 5199 Offset printing; Advertising specialties

(G-6542)
RAYMOND ROBINSON
507 Jana Cir (45415-2127)
PHONE..................................937 890-1886
Raymond Robinson, Prin
EMP: 6 EST: 2009
SALES (est): 200.67K Privately Held
SIC: 2411 Logging

(G-6543)
RCT INDUSTRIES INC
Also Called: Adcura Mfg
1314 Farr Dr (45404-2736)
PHONE..................................937 602-1100
Russell Thie, Pr
EMP: 10 EST: 2000
SQ FT: 4,000
SALES (est): 1.05MM Privately Held
Web: www.adcuramfg.com
SIC: 3679 Electronic circuits

(G-6544)
READY TECHNOLOGY INC (HQ)
Also Called: Standard Die Supply
333 Progress Rd (45449-2490)
PHONE..................................937 866-7200
Michael Danly, Pr
▲ EMP: 14 EST: 1981
SQ FT: 10,000
SALES (est): 9.24MM Privately Held
Web: www.readytechnology.com
SIC: 5084 3544 3542 Metalworking tools, nec (such as drills, taps, dies, files); Special dies, tools, jigs, and fixtures; Bending machines
PA: Danly Corporation
3121 Commodore Plz Ph 5
Miami FL 33133

(G-6545)
RELY-ON MANUFACTURING INC
955 Springfield St (45403-1347)
PHONE..................................937 254-0118
Marsha Mosher, Pr
Peter T Mosher, VP
EMP: 6 EST: 1983
SALES (est): 992.4K Privately Held
SIC: 3451 Screw machine products

(G-6546)
RESPONSE METAL FABRICATORS
521 Kiser St (45404-1641)
PHONE..................................937 222-9000
Janice Morton, Pr
T R Morton, VP
EMP: 21 EST: 1998
SQ FT: 3,000
SALES (est): 712.42K Privately Held
Web: www.commercialmetalfabricators.com
SIC: 3441 Fabricated structural metal

(G-6547)
REX AMERICAN RESOURCES CORP (PA)
Also Called: Rex American Resources
7720 Paragon Rd (45459-4050)
PHONE..................................937 276-3931
Zafar Rizvi, Pr
Stuart A Rose, *
Douglas L Bruggeman, VP Fin
Edward M Kress, *
EMP: 102 EST: 1980
SQ FT: 7,500
SALES (est): 833.38MM
SALES (corp-wide): 833.38MM Publicly Held
Web: www.rexamerican.com
SIC: 2869 Fuels

(G-6548)
REYNOLDS MACHINERY INC
760 Liberty Ln (45449-2135)
PHONE..................................937 847-8121
Scott D Mays, Pr
Jeffrey J Jaske, CFO
Steve Mays, VP
Carl Mays, Prin
EMP: 14 EST: 1976
SQ FT: 12,500
SALES (est): 2.91MM Privately Held
Web: www.reynoldsmachinery.com
SIC: 3599 Machine shop, jobbing and repair

(G-6549)
RICHARD A SCOTT
8000 Allison Ave (45415-2205)
PHONE..................................937 898-1592
Richard A Scott, Prin
EMP: 6 EST: 2010
SALES (est): 84.53K Privately Held

SIC: 3566 Speed changers, drives, and gears

(G-6550)
RIXAN ASSOCIATES INC
7560 Paragon Rd (45459-5317)
PHONE..................................937 438-3005
Stephen Harris, Pr
Aaron Rick Harris, Ch
Beatrice Harris, Sec
EMP: 20 EST: 1959
SQ FT: 14,000
SALES (est): 5.4MM Privately Held
Web: www.rixan.com
SIC: 5084 3569 5065 Robots, industrial; Robots, assembly line: industrial and commercial; Electronic parts

(G-6551)
RMT CORPORATION
2552 Titus Ave (45414-4217)
PHONE..................................937 274-2121
Brent Shreiner, Pr
EMP: 10 EST: 1986
SQ FT: 1,267
SALES (est): 1.04MM Privately Held
Web: www.rmt-corp.com
SIC: 3599 Machine shop, jobbing and repair

(G-6552)
RONALD T DODGE CO
Also Called: Dodge Company
55 Westpark Rd (45459-4812)
PHONE..................................937 439-4497
Ronald J Versic, Pr
Ronald J Versic, Pr
Linda J Versic, VP
EMP: 10 EST: 1979
SQ FT: 8,000
SALES (est): 2.48MM Privately Held
Web: www.rtdodge.com
SIC: 2869 8731 High purity grade chemicals, organic; Commercial research laboratory

(G-6553)
RPA ELECTRONIC DISTRS INC
Also Called: R P A
122 S Terry St (45403-2340)
P.O. Box 1001 (45401-1001)
PHONE..................................937 223-7001
R Paul Perkins Junior, Prin
Sandy Strawser, Sec
EMP: 9 EST: 1971
SQ FT: 9,000
SALES (est): 957.34K Privately Held
Web: www.rpaelect.com
SIC: 5065 3679 Electronic parts; Electronic circuits

(G-6554)
RUBBER-TECH INC
5208 Wadsworth Rd (45414-3592)
PHONE..................................937 274-1114
Forest Back, Pr
L Irene Back, Sec
EMP: 22 EST: 1953
SQ FT: 10,000
SALES (est): 1.8MM Privately Held
Web: www.rubber-tech.com
SIC: 3069 3061 Molded rubber products; Mechanical rubber goods

(G-6555)
RYANWORKS INC
Also Called: Woodcraft
175 E Alex Bell Rd Ste 264 (45459-2701)
PHONE..................................937 438-1282
Alan Ryan, Pr
EMP: 10 EST: 1998
SALES (est): 1.12MM Privately Held

SIC: 5084 2499 Woodworking machinery; Decorative wood and woodwork

(G-6556)
S F MOCK & ASSOCIATES LLC
105 Westpark Rd (45459-4814)
PHONE..................................937 438-0196
EMP: 10 EST: 2016
SALES (est): 584.01K Privately Held
Web: www.safeguardmpg.com
SIC: 2761 5611 2759 Manifold business forms; Men's and boys' clothing stores; Business forms: printing, nsk

(G-6557)
SAFE-GRAIN INC
Also Called: Safe Grain Max Tronix
10522 Success Ln (45458-3561)
PHONE..................................513 398-2500
Greg Stevens, Dir
EMP: 8
SALES (corp-wide): 2.6MM Privately Held
Web: www.safegrain.com
SIC: 3523 Farm machinery and equipment
PA: Safe-Grain, Inc.
417 Wards Corner Rd Ste B
Loveland OH 45140
513 398-2500

(G-6558)
SAMPLE MACHINING INC
Also Called: Bitec
220 N Jersey St (45403-1220)
PHONE..................................937 258-3338
Beverly Bleicher, Pr
Kevin Bleicher, *
EMP: 45 EST: 1985
SQ FT: 19,000
SALES (est): 9.71MM Privately Held
Web: www.bitecsmi.com
SIC: 3599 8734 Custom machinery; Testing laboratories

(G-6559)
SCARLETT KITTY LLC
Also Called: Scarlett Ktty Bath Made Pretty
2786 Wilmington Pike (45419-2141)
PHONE..................................678 438-3796
Joy Coleman, CEO
EMP: 10 EST: 2014
SQ FT: 3,000
SALES (est): 625.1K Privately Held
SIC: 2844 Depilatories (cosmetic)

(G-6560)
SCENIC SOLUTIONS LTD LBLTY CO
355 Gargrave Rd (45449-2465)
PHONE..................................937 866-5062
Dan Mclaughlin, Managing Member
▲ EMP: 8 EST: 2000
SQ FT: 26,000
SALES (est): 1.89MM Privately Held
Web: www.scenicsolutions.com
SIC: 7922 2541 Scenery design, theatrical; Display fixtures, wood

(G-6561)
SCHUERHOLZ INC
3540 Marshall Rd (45429-4916)
PHONE..................................937 294-5218
Charles Schuerholz, Pr
EMP: 7 EST: 1961
SQ FT: 4,500
SALES (est): 665.5K Privately Held
Web: www.schuerholzprinting.com
SIC: 2752 7336 Offset printing; Graphic arts and related design

Dayton - Montgomery County (G-6562)

GEOGRAPHIC SECTION

(G-6562)
SCIENCE/ELECTRONICS INC
Also Called: Earth and Atmospheric Sciences
521 Kiser St (45404-1641)
PHONE..................937 224-4444
Ted Morton, *CEO*
Janice Morton, *CFO*
EMP: 18 **EST:** 1978
SQ FT: 90,000
SALES (est): 400.61K **Privately Held**
Web: www.se-one.com
SIC: 5049 3829 Scientific instruments; Measuring and controlling devices, nec

(G-6563)
SCOTTS COMPANY LLC
20 Innovation Ct (45414-3968)
PHONE..................937 454-2782
Kevin Laughlin, *Mgr*
EMP: 10
SALES (corp-wide): 3.55B **Publicly Held**
Web: www.scotts.com
SIC: 2873 Fertilizers: natural (organic), except compost
HQ: The Scotts Company Llc
14111 Scottslawn Rd
Marysville OH 43040
937 644-0011

(G-6564)
SCREEN WORKS INC (PA)
3970 Image Dr (45414-2524)
PHONE..................937 264-9111
Jeff Cottrell, *Prin*
Jeff Cottrell, *Prin*
Ron Witters, *Prin*
EMP: 48 **EST:** 1987
SQ FT: 42,000
SALES (est): 2.67MM
SALES (corp-wide): 2.67MM **Privately Held**
Web: www.screenworksinc.com
SIC: 7336 5199 7389 3993 Silk screen design; Advertising specialties; Embroidery advertising; Signs and advertising specialties

(G-6565)
SECURTEX INTERNATIONAL INC
Also Called: Sucurtex Digital
982 Senate Dr (45459-4017)
PHONE..................937 312-1414
Ted Humphrey, *Pr*
John Mccallum, *VP*
EMP: 10 **EST:** 2001
SQ FT: 12,500
SALES (est): 238.08K **Privately Held**
SIC: 3699 Security control equipment and systems

(G-6566)
SEEBACH INC
Also Called: Seebach Tools & Molds Mfg
2622 Keenan Ave (45414-4910)
PHONE..................937 275-3565
Mark Seebach, *CEO*
Carl Seebach, *VP*
James Seebach, *Pr*
EMP: 12 **EST:** 1940
SQ FT: 9,600
SALES (est): 208.53K **Privately Held**
Web: www.johncrane.com
SIC: 3599 Machine shop, jobbing and repair

(G-6567)
SELECT INDUSTRIES CORPORATION
60 Heid Ave (45404-1216)
P.O. Box 887 (45401-0887)
PHONE..................937 233-9191
Kelly Wogoman, *Ch*
Robert Whited, *Prin*
Mark Wogoman, *Pr*
◆ **EMP:** 200 **EST:** 1999
SQ FT: 250,000
SALES (est): 51.51MM **Privately Held**
Web: www.select.org
SIC: 3544 Special dies and tools
PA: Select International Corp.
60 Heid Ave
Dayton OH 45404

(G-6568)
SHAWN FLEMING IND TRCKG LLC
4982 Aquilla Dr (45415-3401)
PHONE..................937 707-8539
Shawn Fleming, *Managing Member*
EMP: 7 **EST:** 2015
SALES (est): 498.6K **Privately Held**
SIC: 4212 3537 4213 Local trucking, without storage; Trucks, tractors, loaders, carriers, and similar equipment; Trucking, except local

(G-6569)
SHILOH INDUSTRIES INC
5988 Executive Blvd Ste B (45424-1453)
PHONE..................937 236-5100
John Dixon, *Pr*
David W Dixon, *VP*
EMP: 18 **EST:** 1974
SQ FT: 18,000
SALES (est): 4.72MM **Privately Held**
SIC: 3679 3089 Electronic circuits; Injection molding of plastics

(G-6570)
SHORE TO SHORE INC (DH)
8170 Washington Village Dr (45458-1848)
PHONE..................937 866-1908
Howard Kurdin, *Pr*
John Lau, *
Chuck Rowland, *
◆ **EMP:** 100 **EST:** 1991
SQ FT: 30,000
SALES (est): 101.38MM
SALES (corp-wide): 4.75B **Privately Held**
SIC: 2679 2241 Labels, paper: made from purchased material; Labels, woven
HQ: Checkpoint Systems, Inc.
101 Wolf Dr
West Deptford NJ 08086
800 257-5540

(G-6571)
SHOUSHA TRUCKING LLC ○
3695 Barbarosa Dr (45416-1935)
PHONE..................937 270-4471
EMP: 7 **EST:** 2022
SALES (est): 523.04K **Privately Held**
SIC: 3537 7389 Trucks, tractors, loaders, carriers, and similar equipment; Business Activities at Non-Commercial Site

(G-6572)
SIGN CONNECTION INC
90 Compark Rd Ste B (45459-4967)
PHONE..................937 435-4070
Jane Fiehrer, *Pr*
EMP: 11 **EST:** 1997
SALES (est): 727.72K **Privately Held**
Web: www.signconnectioninc.com
SIC: 3993 Signs, not made in custom sign painting shops

(G-6573)
SIGN TECHNOLOGIES LLC
Also Called: Signetics
2001 Kuntz Rd (45404-1221)
PHONE..................937 439-3970
Shari Brown, *Finance*
EMP: 6 **EST:** 1960
SQ FT: 6,000
SALES (est): 491.67K **Privately Held**
Web: www.signetics1.com
SIC: 3993 Signs and advertising specialties

(G-6574)
SIGNWIRE WORLDWIDE INC
Also Called: Signwire.com
2781 Thunderhawk Ct (45414-3445)
PHONE..................937 428-6189
Jeffrey L Becht, *Pr*
EMP: 9 **EST:** 2008
SQ FT: 10,000
SALES (est): 133.58K **Privately Held**
SIC: 3993 Signs and advertising specialties

(G-6575)
SIMON ELLIS SUPERABRASIVES INC
501 Progress Rd (45449-2325)
P.O. Box 510 (28666-0510)
PHONE..................937 226-0683
David Rawson, *Pr*
Beverly Greene, *Sec*
Thomas Greene, *VP*
EMP: 9 **EST:** 1992
SQ FT: 5,000
SALES (est): 930.96K **Privately Held**
Web: www.simonellis.com
SIC: 3423 Hand and edge tools, nec

(G-6576)
SINEL COMPANY INC
4811 Pamela Sue Dr (45429-5349)
PHONE..................937 433-4772
Mitchell S Siler, *Pr*
EMP: 10 **EST:** 1934
SQ FT: 5,000
SALES (est): 561.92K **Privately Held**
Web: www.sinelcompany.com
SIC: 3543 Foundry cores

(G-6577)
SNYDER CONCRETE PRODUCTS INC
Also Called: Snyder Brick and Block
1433 S Euclid Ave (45417-3839)
PHONE..................937 224-1433
EMP: 9
SALES (corp-wide): 12.11MM **Privately Held**
Web: www.snyderonline.com
SIC: 5032 3271 Brick, except refractory; Blocks, concrete or cinder: standard
PA: Snyder Concrete Products, Inc.
2301 W Dorothy Ln
Moraine OH 45439
937 885-5176

(G-6578)
SOFTWARE SOLUTIONS INC (PA)
8534 Yankee St Ste 2b (45458-1889)
PHONE..................513 932-6667
John Rettig, *Pr*
EMP: 23 **EST:** 1978
SALES (est): 7.78MM
SALES (corp-wide): 7.78MM **Privately Held**
Web: www.mysoftwaresolutions.com
SIC: 5045 7372 7373 Computer software; Application computer software; Computer integrated systems design

(G-6579)
SOLVENT SOLUTIONS LLC
5014 Lausanne Dr (45458-3000)
PHONE..................937 648-4962
Frederick Willits, *Prin*
EMP: 7 **EST:** 2010
SALES (est): 130K **Privately Held**
SIC: 2911 Solvents

(G-6580)
SPAOS INC (PA)
Also Called: Quality Office Products
6012 N Dixie Dr (45414-4018)
P.O. Box 13661 (45413-0661)
PHONE..................937 890-0783
Jack Roberts, *Pr*
Bonnie Roberts, *Sec*
EMP: 6 **EST:** 1980
SALES (est): 699.39K
SALES (corp-wide): 699.39K **Privately Held**
Web: www.superiorprintingpromo.com
SIC: 2752 Offset printing

(G-6581)
SPECIALTY MACHINES INC
5370 Salem Ave (45426-1626)
PHONE..................937 837-8852
Donna Suess, *Pr*
Richard Suess, *VP*
William C Hoyer, *CEO*
EMP: 20 **EST:** 1947
SQ FT: 15,000
SALES (est): 2.63MM **Privately Held**
Web: www.specialtymachinesinc.com
SIC: 3599 Machine shop, jobbing and repair

(G-6582)
SPECTRACAM LTD
1112 East Race Dr (45404)
PHONE..................937 223-3805
Joseph Wendling, *Managing Member*
EMP: 7 **EST:** 1998
SQ FT: 6,300
SALES (est): 1.21MM **Privately Held**
Web: www.spectracam.com
SIC: 3544 3543 Special dies, tools, jigs, and fixtures; Industrial patterns

(G-6583)
SPECTRON INC
132 S Terry St (45403-2340)
P.O. Box 3518 (45401-3518)
PHONE..................937 461-5590
Betty Burnett, *Pr*
Jeff Bucher, *Pr*
EMP: 6 **EST:** 1966
SQ FT: 4,000
SALES (est): 737.38K **Privately Held**
Web: www.spectronus.com
SIC: 3679 Electronic circuits

(G-6584)
SPEEDLINE NORTH AMERICA INC
7887 Washington Village Dr (45459-3900)
PHONE..................937 291-7000
EMP: 7 **EST:** 2004
SALES (est): 11.19K **Privately Held**
SIC: 3714 Motor vehicle parts and accessories

(G-6585)
SPIEGLER BRAKE SYSTEMS USA LLC
Also Called: Spiegler Brake Systems USA
1699 Thomas Paine Pkwy (45459-2538)
PHONE..................937 291-1735
Matthias Schaub, *Managing Member*
▲ **EMP:** 6 **EST:** 1999
SQ FT: 3,500
SALES (est): 487.54K **Privately Held**
Web: www.spieglerusa.com
SIC: 3751 5571 Motorcycles, bicycles and parts; Motorcycle parts and accessories

(G-6586)
SRC LIQUIDATION LLC (PA)
111 W 1st St (45402-1154)
P.O. Box 1167 (45401-1167)

▲ = Import ▼ = Export
◆ = Import/Export

PHONE.....................937 221-1000
Landen Williams, *Pr*
F David Clarke Iii, *Ch Bd*
Diana Tullio, *CIO*
Benjamin T Cutting, *CFO*
James M Vaughn, *Treas*
◆ **EMP:** 600 **EST:** 1912
SALES (est): 447.06MM
SALES (corp-wide): 447.06MM **Privately Held**
Web: www.taylor.com
SIC: 2761 2672 2677 2759 Manifold business forms; Labels (unprinted), gummed: made from purchased materials; Envelopes; Promotional printing

(G-6587)
STACO ENERGY PRODUCTS CO
301 Gaddis Blvd (45403-1314)
PHONE.....................937 253-1191
EMP: 28
SALES (corp-wide): 52.28MM **Privately Held**
Web: www.stacoenergy.com
SIC: 3677 3612 Baluns; Instrument transformers (except portable)
HQ: Staco Energy Products Co.
2425 Technical Dr
Miamisburg OH 45342
937 253-1191

(G-6588)
STAFFORD GAGE & TOOL INC
4606 Webster St (45414-4826)
P.O. Box 433 (45377-0433)
PHONE.....................937 277-9944
Jeff Stafford, *Pr*
Judy Stafford, *Pr*
Jean Stafford, *VP*
Teresa Stafford, *VP*
EMP: 9 **EST:** 1947
SQ FT: 10,500
SALES (est): 943.58K **Privately Held**
Web: www.staffordgt.com
SIC: 3599 Machine shop, jobbing and repair

(G-6589)
STANCO PRECISION MFG INC
Also Called: Ss Industries
1 Walbrook Ave (45405-2341)
PHONE.....................937 274-1785
Stephen P Stanoikovich, *Pr*
Rhonda Stanoikovich, *Mgr*
▲ **EMP:** 9 **EST:** 1988
SQ FT: 8,000
SALES (est): 961.94K **Privately Held**
Web: www.stancoprecision.com
SIC: 3599 3544 Machine shop, jobbing and repair; Special dies and tools

(G-6590)
STANDARD REGISTER TECHNOLOGIES
600 Albany St (45417-3405)
PHONE.....................937 443-1000
Joseph P Morgan Junior, *CEO*
EMP: 9
SALES (est): 599.28K **Privately Held**
Web: www.taylor.com
SIC: 2759 Commercial printing, nec

(G-6591)
STARWIN INDUSTRIES LLC
3387 Woodman Dr (45429-4100)
PHONE.....................937 293-8568
Matthew Eberhardt, *CEO*
Rick Little, *
EMP: 50 **EST:** 1973
SQ FT: 30,000
SALES (est): 13.46MM
SALES (corp-wide): 18.89MM **Privately Held**

Web: www.starwin-ind.com
SIC: 7372 3728 3663 3599 Prepackaged software; Aircraft parts and equipment, nec; Radio and t.v. communications equipment; Machine and other job shop work
PA: Eti Mission Controls, Llc
3387 Woodman Dr
Dayton OH 45429
937 832-4200

(G-6592)
STATE OF OHIO DAYTON RACEWAY
777 Hollywood Blvd (45414-3698)
PHONE.....................937 237-7802
EMP: 29 **EST:** 2015
SALES (est): 209.91K **Privately Held**
Web: www.hollywooddaytonraceway.com
SIC: 3644 Raceways

(G-6593)
STAUB LASER CUTTING INC
Also Called: Staub Manufacturing Solutions
2501 Thunderhawk Ct (45414-3466)
PHONE.....................937 890-4486
Steve Staub, *Pr*
Sandy Keplinger, *
EMP: 40 **EST:** 1997
SQ FT: 15,000
SALES (est): 5.9MM **Privately Held**
Web: www.staubmfg.com
SIC: 3599 Machine shop, jobbing and repair

(G-6594)
STECK MANUFACTURING CO LLC
1200 Leo St (45404-1650)
PHONE.....................937 222-0062
Greg Carlson, *Pr*
▲ **EMP:** 13 **EST:** 1945
SALES (est): 11.21MM
SALES (corp-wide): 59.51MM **Privately Held**
Web: www.steckmfg.com
SIC: 3714 3599 Motor vehicle parts and accessories; Machine shop, jobbing and repair
PA: Cnl Strategic Capital, Llc
450 S Orange Ave Ste 1400
Orlando FL 32801
407 650-1000

(G-6595)
STEVENS INDUSTRIES LLC
2613 Millbridge Ct (45440-2223)
PHONE.....................937 266-8240
Michael Stevens, *Prin*
EMP: 6 **EST:** 2012
SALES (est): 147.73K **Privately Held**
SIC: 3999 Manufacturing industries, nec

(G-6596)
STOLLE MACHINERY COMPANY LLC
Also Called: Ultra Punch
7425 Webster St (45414-5817)
PHONE.....................937 497-5400
Keith Gilmore, *Mgr*
EMP: 113
SALES (corp-wide): 492.99MM **Privately Held**
Web: www.stollemachinery.com
SIC: 3544 3496 Punches, forming and stamping; Miscellaneous fabricated wire products
PA: Stolle Machinery Company, Llc
6949 S Potomac St
Centennial CO 80112
303 708-9044

(G-6597)
SUGAR CREEK PACKING CO
1241 N Gettysburg Ave (45417-9513)
PHONE.....................937 268-6601
Steve Shutte, *Mgr*
EMP: 6
SQ FT: 20,000
SALES (corp-wide): 700MM **Privately Held**
Web: www.sugarcreek.com
SIC: 2013 2011 Bacon, side and sliced: from purchased meat; Meat packing plants
PA: Sugar Creek Packing Co.
4350 Indeco Ct
Blue Ash OH 45241
740 335-3586

(G-6598)
SUPERIOR DIE
7796 John Elwood Dr (45459-5133)
PHONE.....................937 225-6369
Ben Adkins, *Prin*
EMP: 7 **EST:** 2016
SALES (est): 103.25K **Privately Held**
Web: www.superiordieset.com
SIC: 3544 Special dies and tools

(G-6599)
SUPERIOR MACHINING INC
2946 Lindale Ave (45414-5521)
PHONE.....................937 236-9619
Thomas Gilhooly, *CEO*
James Lewis, *
EMP: 32 **EST:** 2001
SQ FT: 16,764
SALES (est): 2.42MM **Privately Held**
SIC: 3541 Milling machines

(G-6600)
SUPPLIER INSPECTION SVCS INC (PA)
2941 S Gettysburg Ave (45439-7912)
PHONE.....................877 263-7097
Paul A Bowell, *Pr*
EMP: 11 **EST:** 1986
SQ FT: 50,000
SALES (est): 5.69MM
SALES (corp-wide): 5.69MM **Privately Held**
Web: www.sis-inspection.net
SIC: 3545 7389 Machine tool accessories; Inspection and testing services

(G-6601)
SUPPLY TECHNOLOGIES LLC
4704 Wadsworth Rd (45414-4222)
PHONE.....................937 898-5795
EMP: 8
SALES (corp-wide): 1.66B **Publicly Held**
Web: www.supplytechnologies.com
SIC: 5085 3452 3469 Fasteners, industrial: nuts, bolts, screws, etc.; Bolts, nuts, rivets, and washers; Stamping metal for the trade
HQ: Supply Technologies Llc
6065 Parkland Blvd
Cleveland OH 44124
440 947-2100

(G-6602)
SURE TOOL & MANUFACTURING CO
429 Winston Ave (45403-1400)
PHONE.....................937 253-9111
Jerrald Kuriger, *Pr*
Ruth Kuriger, *Sec*
Russell B Kuriger, *VP*
EMP: 23 **EST:** 1969
SQ FT: 14,000
SALES (est): 2.43MM **Privately Held**
Web: www.suretool.com

SIC: 3544 Special dies and tools

(G-6603)
SWIHART INDUSTRIES INC
5111 Webster St (45414-4227)
PHONE.....................937 277-4796
EMP: 30 **EST:** 1978
SALES (est): 2.72MM **Privately Held**
Web: www.swihartindustries.com
SIC: 3599 Machine shop, jobbing and repair

(G-6604)
SYSTEMAX MANUFACTURING INC
6450 Poe Ave Ste 200 (45414-2655)
PHONE.....................937 368-2300
Curt Rush, *Sec*
▲ **EMP:** 54 **EST:** 1980
SQ FT: 185,000
SALES (est): 6.18MM **Publicly Held**
SIC: 5961 7373 3577 3571 Computers and peripheral equipment, mail order; Systems integration services; Computer peripheral equipment, nec; Electronic computers
PA: Global Industrial Company
11 Harbor Park Dr
Port Washington NY 11050

(G-6605)
T & L CUSTOM SCREENING INC
3464 Successful Way (45414-4320)
PHONE.....................937 237-3121
EMP: 7 **EST:** 1996
SQ FT: 6,500
SALES (est): 596.41K **Privately Held**
Web: www.tlcustomtees.com
SIC: 2759 5199 2395 2396 Screen printing; Advertising specialties; Embroidery products, except Schiffli machine; Automotive and apparel trimmings

(G-6606)
T & R WELDING SYSTEMS INC
1 Janney Rd (45404-1263)
PHONE.....................937 228-7517
Mike Bozzo, *Pr*
▼ **EMP:** 15 **EST:** 1969
SQ FT: 15,000
SALES (est): 2.35MM **Privately Held**
Web: www.trwelding.com
SIC: 3496 7692 Miscellaneous fabricated wire products; Welding repair

(G-6607)
T E BROWN LLC (PA)
1205 Lamar St (45404-1658)
P.O. Box 89 (45404)
PHONE.....................937 223-2241
Teddy Brown, *Pr*
EMP: 12 **EST:** 2014
SQ FT: 10,000
SALES (est): 1.04MM
SALES (corp-wide): 1.04MM **Privately Held**
Web: www.instrulab.com
SIC: 7699 3823 Industrial equipment services ; Temperature measurement instruments, industrial

(G-6608)
TARGETED CMPUND MONITORING LLC
2790 Indian Ripple Rd Ste A (45440-3639)
PHONE.....................937 825-0842
Willie Steinecker, *CEO*
EMP: 6 **EST:** 2016
SALES (est): 308.62K **Privately Held**
Web: www.tcmglobalinc.com
SIC: 3826 Automatic chemical analyzers

Dayton - Montgomery County (G-6609)

GEOGRAPHIC SECTION

(G-6609)
TAYLOR COMMUNICATIONS INC
600 Albany St (45417-3405)
PHONE.................937 221-1000
Jim Miller, *Mgr*
EMP: 24
SALES (corp-wide): 3.81B **Privately Held**
Web: www.taylor.com
SIC: **2761** 2759 2752 8744 Manifold business forms; Commercial printing, nec; Commercial printing, lithographic; Facilities support services
HQ: Taylor Communications, Inc.
1725 Roe Crest Dr
North Mankato MN 56003
866 541-0937

(G-6610)
TAYLOR COMMUNICATIONS INC
7755 Paragon Road Ste 101 (45459-4052)
PHONE.................732 356-0081
Brian Clark, *Mgr*
EMP: 13
SALES (corp-wide): 3.81B **Privately Held**
Web: www.taylor.com
SIC: **2761** Manifold business forms
HQ: Taylor Communications, Inc.
1725 Roe Crest Dr
North Mankato MN 56003
866 541-0937

(G-6611)
TEC DESIGN & MANUFACTURING INC
4549 Gateway Cir (45440-1711)
PHONE.................937 435-2147
John A Hudock, *Pr*
EMP: 12 EST: 1968
SQ FT: 13,000
SALES (est): 144.34K **Privately Held**
SIC: **3542** 3469 Machine tools, metal forming type; Machine parts, stamped or pressed metal

(G-6612)
TECHMETALS INC (PA)
345 Springfield St (45403-1240)
P.O. Box 1266 (45401-1266)
PHONE.................937 253-5311
EMP: 93 EST: 1968
SALES (est): 13.81MM
SALES (corp-wide): 13.81MM **Privately Held**
Web: www.techmetals.com
SIC: **3471** Plating of metals or formed products

(G-6613)
TEKNOL INC (PA)
Also Called: Rubber Seal Products
5751 Webster St (45414-3520)
P.O. Box 13387 (45413-0387)
PHONE.................937 264-0190
Kent Von Behren, *Pr*
R Von Behren, *Stockholder**
▲ EMP: 57 EST: 1976
SQ FT: 60,000
SALES (est): 9.75MM
SALES (corp-wide): 9.75MM **Privately Held**
Web: www.medallionrefinish.com
SIC: **2899** 2891 5198 2851 Chemical preparations, nec; Sealants; Paints, varnishes, and supplies; Paints and allied products

(G-6614)
TERRA SURFACES LLC
6350 Frederick Pike (45414-2972)
PHONE.................937 836-1900
▲ EMP: 8 EST: 2004
SQ FT: 20,000
SALES (est): 920K **Privately Held**
SIC: **3281** Stone, quarrying and processing of own stone products

(G-6615)
TESSEC LLC
5621 Webster St (45414-3518)
PHONE.................937 576-0010
EMP: 70 EST: 2007
SALES (est): 9.45MM **Privately Held**
Web: www.tessec.com
SIC: **3721** 3599 3365 3724 Motorized aircraft ; Machine shop, jobbing and repair; Aerospace castings, aluminum; Aircraft engines and engine parts

(G-6616)
TESSEC MANUFACTURING SVCS LLC
Also Called: Tessec
5621 Webster St (45414)
PHONE.................937 985-3552
EMP: 21 EST: 2010
SALES (est): 3.29MM **Privately Held**
Web: www.tessec.com
SIC: **3452** 3544 3721 3761 Bolts, nuts, rivets, and washers; Special dies, tools, jigs, and fixtures; Aircraft; Guided missiles and space vehicles

(G-6617)
TESSEC TECHNOLOGY SERVICES LLC
5621 Webster St (45414-3518)
PHONE.................513 240-5601
David Evans, *Prin*
EMP: 38 EST: 2013
SALES (est): 2.49MM **Privately Held**
SIC: **3728** Aircraft parts and equipment, nec

(G-6618)
THE F A REQUARTH COMPANY
Also Called: Requarth Lumber Co.
447 E Monument Ave (45402-1226)
P.O. Box 38 (45401-0038)
PHONE.................937 224-1141
EMP: 30 EST: 1860
SALES (est): 4.98MM **Privately Held**
Web: www.requarth.com
SIC: **2431** 2491 5211 2421 Millwork; Wood preserving; Lumber and other building materials; Sawmills and planing mills, general

(G-6619)
THE MEAD CORPORATION
4751 Hempstead Station Dr (45429-5165)
PHONE.................937 495-6323
▲ EMP: 500
SIC: **2621** 2631 2653 2656 Printing paper; Corrugating medium; Boxes, corrugated: made from purchased materials; Sanitary food containers

(G-6620)
THE VULCAN TOOL COMPANY
730 Lorain Ave (45410-2400)
PHONE.................937 253-6194
▲ EMP: 7
Web: www.vulcantoolcompany.com
SIC: **3544** 3542 3541 3643 Special dies and tools; Machine tools, metal forming type; Machine tools, metal cutting type; Current-carrying wiring services

(G-6621)
THOMAS CABINET SHOP INC
321 Gargrave Rd (45449-2465)
PHONE.................937 847-8239
Jon Thomas, *Pr*
Don Thomas, *VP Opers*
Cherie Thomas, *Sec*
EMP: 10 EST: 1961
SQ FT: 11,800
SALES (est): 1.53MM **Privately Held**
SIC: **1542** 1751 2541 2434 Commercial and office buildings, renovation and repair; Cabinet building and installation; Wood partitions and fixtures; Wood kitchen cabinets

(G-6622)
THREE BOND INTERNATIONAL INC
101 Daruma Pkwy (45439-7908)
PHONE.................937 610-3000
EMP: 33
Web: www.threebond.com
SIC: **2891** Adhesives
HQ: Three Bond International, Inc.
6184 Schumacher Park Dr
West Chester OH 45069
513 779-7300

(G-6623)
THRIFT TOOL INC
5916 Milo Rd (45414-3416)
PHONE.................937 275-3600
Walter Jones, *Pr*
Jeff Jones, *VP*
EMP: 6 EST: 1990
SQ FT: 8,000
SALES (est): 656.76K **Privately Held**
Web: www.thrifttool.com
SIC: **3312** Tool and die steel and alloys

(G-6624)
THT PRESSES INC
Also Called: Tht Presses
7475 Webster St (45414-5817)
PHONE.................937 898-2012
Mike Thieman, *Pr*
▲ EMP: 25 EST: 1977
SQ FT: 51,000
SALES (est): 4.83MM **Privately Held**
Web: www.thtpresses.com
SIC: **3542** Die casting machines

(G-6625)
TIPP MACHINE & TOOL INC
4201 Little York Rd (45414-2507)
PHONE.................937 890-8428
EMP: 124
SIC: **3544** 3599 7389 Special dies and tools; Machine shop, jobbing and repair; Grinding, precision: commercial or industrial

(G-6626)
TOGA-PAK INC
2208 Sandridge Dr (45439)
P.O. Box Rr&Box363 (45409)
PHONE.................937 294-7311
EMP: 40 EST: 1981
SALES (est): 5.69MM **Privately Held**
Web: www.ipack.com
SIC: **3081** 5084 5199 Unsupported plastics film and sheet; Packaging machinery and equipment; Packaging materials

(G-6627)
TONEY TOOL MANUFACTURING INC
Also Called: Toney Tool
3488 Stop 8 Rd (45414-3428)
PHONE.................937 890-8535
EMP: 20 EST: 1982
SALES (est): 2.36MM **Privately Held**
Web: www.toneytool.com
SIC: **3559** 3544 7692 Automotive related machinery; Special dies and tools; Welding repair

(G-6628)
TOOLCRAFT PRODUCTS INC
1265 Mccook Ave (45404-2800)
P.O. Box 482 (45401-0482)
PHONE.................937 223-8271
Mark W Klug, *Pr*
Thomas W Thompson, ***
Henry Wagner Junior, *Treas*
Hugh E Wall Iii, *Sec*
Cherilynn M O'Malley, *CFO*
EMP: 40 EST: 1939
SQ FT: 56,000
SALES (est): 6.05MM **Privately Held**
Web: www.toolcraftproducts.com
SIC: **3544** Die sets for metal stamping (presses)

(G-6629)
TOOLRITE MANUFACTURING INC
2608 Nordic Rd (45414-3424)
PHONE.................937 278-1962
EMP: 12 EST: 1996
SALES (est): 1.39MM **Privately Held**
SIC: **3544** Special dies and tools

(G-6630)
TREADWAY MANUFACTURING LLC
8800 Frederick Pike (45414-1235)
PHONE.................937 266-3423
Kenny Treadway, *CEO*
EMP: 8 EST: 2005
SALES (est): 731.31K **Privately Held**
Web: www.treadwaymfg.com
SIC: **3599** Machine shop, jobbing and repair

(G-6631)
TRI-STATE PAPER INC
9000 Kenrick Rd (45458-5300)
P.O. Box 447 (45068-0447)
PHONE.................937 885-3365
EMP: 13 EST: 1979
SALES (est): 2.42MM **Privately Held**
SIC: **5199** 2653 Packaging materials; Boxes, corrugated: made from purchased materials

(G-6632)
TRIANGLE PRECISION INDUSTRIES
1650 Delco Park Dr (45420-1392)
PHONE.................937 299-6776
Gerald D Schriml, *Pr*
Paul S Holzinger, ***
EMP: 57 EST: 1982
SQ FT: 23,400
SALES (est): 6.55MM **Privately Held**
Web: www.triangleprecision.com
SIC: **3599** 7692 3446 3444 Machine shop, jobbing and repair; Welding repair; Architectural metalwork; Sheet metalwork

(G-6633)
TRIFECTA TOOL AND ENGRG LLC
4648 Gateway Cir (45440-1714)
PHONE.................937 291-0933
Bret West, *Managing Member*
▲ EMP: 9 EST: 2004
SQ FT: 15,000
SALES (est): 1.28MM **Privately Held**
SIC: **3089** Automotive parts, plastic

(G-6634)
TRIMBLE INC
Trimble Engineering
5475 Kellenburger Rd (45424-1013)
PHONE.................937 233-8921
Chris Shephard, *Brnch Mgr*
EMP: 11
SALES (corp-wide): 3.8B **Publicly Held**
Web: www.trimble.com
SIC: **3812** Navigational systems and instruments

GEOGRAPHIC SECTION
Dayton - Montgomery County (G-6659)

PA: Trimble Inc.
10368 Westmoor Dr
Westminster CO 80021
720 887-6100

(G-6635)
TROY ENGNRED CMPNNTS ASSMBLIES
Also Called: Teca
4900 Webster St (45414-4831)
PHONE.....................937 335-8070
Marvin Sauner, *Pr*
Jack Spencer, *VP*
Tony Vukufich, *AR Vice President*
Larry Ishmael, *Sec*
EMP: 8 **EST:** 2005
SALES (est): 879.56K **Privately Held**
Web: www.tecaassembly.com
SIC: 3011 Tire and inner tube materials and related products

(G-6636)
TROY VALLEY PETROLEUM
201 Valley St (45404-1864)
PHONE.....................937 604-0012
Amarjid Singh, *Prin*
EMP: 9 **EST:** 2007
SQ FT: 2,248
SALES (est): 385.1K **Privately Held**
SIC: 2911 Petroleum refining

(G-6637)
TRUSSCORE USA INC
6161 Ventnor Ave (45414-2651)
P.O. Box 695 (45377-0695)
PHONE.....................888 418-4679
Steve Bosman, *Dir*
David Caputo, *
Joel Koops, *
EMP: 45 **EST:** 2017
SALES (est): 30MM **Privately Held**
Web: www.trusscore.com
SIC: 3089 Plastics hardware and building products

(G-6638)
U S CHROME CORPORATION OHIO
Also Called: Production Plant
107 Westboro St (45417-4055)
PHONE.....................877 872-7716
Greg Santo, *Brnch Mgr*
EMP: 12
SQ FT: 8,000
SALES (corp-wide): 39.36MM **Privately Held**
Web: www.uschrome.com
SIC: 3471 Electroplating of metals or formed products
HQ: U.S. Chrome Corporation Of Ohio
175 Garfield Ave
Stratford CT
937 224-0548

(G-6639)
UGL INC
3118 Transportation Rd (45404-2359)
PHONE.....................630 250-1600
Jeounghui Ahn, *Prin*
EMP: 6 **EST:** 2013
SALES (est): 222.3K **Privately Held**
Web: www.uglinc.com
SIC: 3949 Boomerangs

(G-6640)
UNIVERSAL TOOL TECHNOLOGY LLC
3488 Stop 8 Rd (45414-3428)
P.O. Box 31249 (45437-0249)
PHONE.....................937 222-4608
Michael Farmer, *Managing Member*
EMP: 19 **EST:** 2001
SQ FT: 45,000
SALES (est): 407.28K **Privately Held**
Web: www.universal-systems.net
SIC: 3544 3599 Special dies and tools; Machine shop, jobbing and repair

(G-6641)
US AEROTEAM INC
2601 W Stroop Rd Ste 60 (45439-2030)
PHONE.....................937 458-0344
Suhas Kakde, *Pr*
Jeff Maag, *
EMP: 48 **EST:** 2005
SALES (est): 9.67MM **Privately Held**
Web: www.usaeroteam.com
SIC: 3728 Aircraft parts and equipment, nec

(G-6642)
VENTURE MFG CO
Also Called: Venture
3636 Dayton Park Dr (45414-4492)
PHONE.....................937 233-8792
▲ **EMP:** 25 **EST:** 1971
SALES (est): 4.99MM **Privately Held**
Web: www.venturemfgco.com
SIC: 3625 Actuators, industrial

(G-6643)
VENU ON 3RD
905 E 3rd St (45402-2248)
PHONE.....................937 222-2891
Jerry White, *Prin*
EMP: 7 **EST:** 2011
SALES (est): 291.7K **Privately Held**
SIC: 2599 Bar, restaurant and cafeteria furniture

(G-6644)
VIBRONIC
5208 Wadsworth Rd (45414-3508)
PHONE.....................937 274-1114
Leah Lach, *Brnch Mgr*
EMP: 6 **EST:** 2008
SALES (est): 173.3K **Privately Held**
SIC: 2822 Synthetic rubber

(G-6645)
VYRAL LLC
2078 E Dorothy Ln (45420-1112)
PHONE.....................937 993-7765
EMP: 12 **EST:** 2020
SALES (est): 1.21MM **Privately Held**
Web: www.vyralteq.com
SIC: 3577 Computer peripheral equipment, nec

(G-6646)
WALTER NORTH
900 Pimlico Dr Apt 2a (45459-8265)
PHONE.....................937 204-6050
Walter North, *Owner*
EMP: 11 **EST:** 2017
SALES (est): 448.3K **Privately Held**
SIC: 3571 7389 Electronic computers; Business services, nec

(G-6647)
WASCA LLC
750 Rosedale Dr (45402-5758)
PHONE.....................937 723-9031
EMP: 50
SIC: 3089 Plastics and fiberglass tanks

(G-6648)
WATSON HARAN & COMPANY INC
Also Called: Manoranjan Shaffer & Heidkamp
1500 Yankee Park Pl (45458-1878)
PHONE.....................937 436-1414
Angie Shaffer, *Mgr*
EMP: 6
Web: www.haranwatson.com
SIC: 8721 2759 Certified public accountant; Financial note and certificate printing and engraving
PA: Watson Haran & Company Inc
445 Hutchinson Ave # 695
Columbus OH 43235

(G-6649)
WELDMENTS INC
167 Heid Ave (45404-1217)
P.O. Box 320 (45404-0320)
PHONE.....................937 235-9261
James Hackenberger, *Pr*
John Limberg, *Sec*
Chuck Kraft, *VP*
EMP: 12 **EST:** 1985
SQ FT: 10,000
SALES (est): 939.44K
SALES (corp-wide): 9.02MM **Privately Held**
Web: www.weldments.com
SIC: 7692 1799 Welding repair; Welding on site
PA: Precision Metal Fabrication, Inc.
191 Heid Ave
Dayton OH 45404
937 235-9261

(G-6650)
WESTBROOK MFG INC
Also Called: Westbrook Manufacturing
600 N Irwin St (45403-1388)
PHONE.....................937 254-2004
▲ **EMP:** 270
Web: www.westbrookohio.com
SIC: 3599 3679 3714 3613 Machine and other job shop work; Harness assemblies, for electronic use: wire or cable; Motor vehicle parts and accessories; Switchgear and switchboard apparatus

(G-6651)
WESTROCK MWV LLC
Consumer & Office Products Div
10 W 2nd St (45402-1791)
PHONE.....................937 495-6323
Patricia B Robinson, *Mgr*
EMP: 61
SALES (corp-wide): 20.31B **Publicly Held**
Web: www.westrock.com
SIC: 2678 Stationery products
HQ: Westrock Mwv, Llc
3500 45th St Sw
Lanett AL 36863
804 444-1000

(G-6652)
WESTWOOD FBRCTION SHTMETAL INC
1752 Stanley Ave (45404-1117)
PHONE.....................937 837-0494
EMP: 27 **EST:** 1995
SQ FT: 25,000
SALES (est): 2.5MM **Privately Held**
Web: www.westwoodfabrication.com
SIC: 3441 Fabricated structural metal

(G-6653)
WESTWOOD FINISHING COMPANY
5881 Wolf Creek Pike (45426-2437)
PHONE.....................937 837-1488
Lavern Meyer, *Owner*
EMP: 13 **EST:** 1950
SALES (est): 629.35K **Privately Held**
Web: www.westwoodfinishingcompany.com
SIC: 3479 Coating of metals and formed products

(G-6654)
WFSR HOLDINGS LLC
220 E Monument Ave (45402-1287)
PHONE.....................877 735-4966
▲ **EMP:** 1254 **EST:** 2010
SALES (est): 2.06MM
SALES (corp-wide): 447.06MM **Privately Held**
SIC: 2752 2754 2759 2761 Commercial printing, lithographic; Commercial printing, gravure; Commercial printing, nec; Manifold business forms
PA: Src Liquidation Llc
111 W 1st St
Dayton OH 45402
937 221-1000

(G-6655)
WINKLER CO INC
Also Called: Oakwood Register, The
435 Patterson Rd (45419-4344)
P.O. Box 572 (45409-0572)
PHONE.....................937 294-2662
Dolores Winkler, *Pr*
Lance A Winkler, *VP*
Dana M Winkler, *Sec*
EMP: 6 **EST:** 1960
SQ FT: 2,700
SALES (est): 848.9K **Privately Held**
Web: www.oakwoodregister.com
SIC: 2711 2791 Newspapers: publishing only, not printed on site; Typesetting

(G-6656)
WINSTON HEAT TREATING INC
711 E 2nd St (45402-1319)
P.O. Box 1551 (45401-1551)
PHONE.....................937 226-0110
TOLL FREE: 800
John L Reger, *Pr*
EMP: 33 **EST:** 1967
SQ FT: 26,000
SALES (est): 4.67MM **Privately Held**
Web: www.winstonht.com
SIC: 3398 Metal heat treating

(G-6657)
WIS 1985 INC
1347 E 4th St (45402-2235)
P.O. Box 1415 (45401-1415)
PHONE.....................423 581-4916
Richard Carper, *Pr*
Scott Carper, *VP*
▲ **EMP:** 10 **EST:** 1985
SQ FT: 22,000
SALES (est): 414.95K **Privately Held**
Web: www.rscsales.com
SIC: 2752 5013 7336 Offset printing; Automotive supplies and parts; Silk screen design

(G-6658)
WISCO PRODUCTS INCORPORATED
109 Commercial St (45402-2297)
PHONE.....................937 228-2101
Mark Paxson, *Pr*
EMP: 30 **EST:** 1935
SQ FT: 23,000
SALES (est): 4.39MM **Privately Held**
Web: www.wiscoproducts.com
SIC: 3469 3089 Metal stampings, nec; Caps, plastics

(G-6659)
WOODBURN PRESS LTD
405 Littell Ave (45419-3609)
P.O. Box 329 (45409-0329)
PHONE.....................937 293-9245
EMP: 6 **EST:** 1996
SQ FT: 10,000
SALES (est): 824.08K **Privately Held**

Web: www.woodburnpress.com
SIC: 2731 2741 Book publishing; Posters: publishing and printing

(G-6660)
WORKER AUTOMATION INC
953 Belfast Dr (45440-3851)
PHONE..................................937 473-2111
Joe Hickey, *Pr*
Margrett Hickey, *Sec*
EMP: 8 EST: 1997
SQ FT: 14,000
SALES (est): 981.3K Privately Held
SIC: 3548 5084 7373 Welding apparatus; Robots, industrial; Computer integrated systems design

(G-6661)
WORKFLOWONE LLC
220 E Monument Ave (45402-1287)
P.O. Box 1167 (45401-1167)
PHONE..................................877 735-4966
♦ EMP: 2000
SIC: 2754 2791 4225 4731 Forms, business: gravure printing; Typesetting; General warehousing and storage; Freight transportation arrangement

(G-6662)
YODER INDUSTRIES INC (PA)
2520 Needmore Rd (45414-4204)
PHONE..................................937 278-5769
Charles W Slicer, *Ch*
Ron Zeverka, *
Pam Stewart, *
Charles W Slicer, *Prin*
J B Yoder, *
EMP: 110 EST: 1956
SQ FT: 32,000
SALES (est): 9.1MM
SALES (corp-wide): 9.1MM Privately Held
Web: www.yoderindustries.com
SIC: 3363 3369 3471 3365 Aluminum die-castings; Nonferrous foundries, nec; Plating and polishing; Aluminum foundries

(G-6663)
ZIMMER ENTERPRISES INC (PA)
Also Called: Kettering Monogramming
911 Senate Dr (45459-4017)
PHONE..................................937 428-1057
Jeffrey Zimmer, *Pr*
Patricia M Zimmer, *
▲ EMP: 24 EST: 1982
SALES (est): 2.43MM
SALES (corp-wide): 2.43MM Privately Held
Web: www.pbj-sport.com
SIC: 5137 2395 Women's and children's clothing; Embroidery products, except Schiffli machine

De Graff
Logan County

(G-6664)
ALAN BORTREE
Also Called: HI Standard Machine Co
8176 State Route 508 (43318-9624)
PHONE..................................937 585-6962
Alan Bortree, *Owner*
EMP: 6 EST: 1967
SQ FT: 5,500
SALES (est): 503.35K Privately Held
Web: www.hi-standardmachine.com
SIC: 3535 Conveyors and conveying equipment

(G-6665)
NATES NECTAR LLC
Also Called: Nate's Nectar
4684 Township Road 53 (43318-9669)
PHONE..................................937 935-3289
EMP: 7 EST: 2017
SALES (est): 375.05K Privately Held
Web: www.natesnectarandmore.com
SIC: 2099 Honey, strained and bottled

Deerfield
Portage County

(G-6666)
FOUNDERS SERVICE & MFG INC (PA)
Also Called: Founder's Service Co
879 State Route 14 (44411-9777)
P.O. Box 56 (44449-0056)
PHONE..................................330 584-7759
Doug Stanley, *Pr*
Thad Stanley, *Sec*
EMP: 6 EST: 1984
SQ FT: 8,000
SALES (est): 2.32MM
SALES (corp-wide): 2.32MM Privately Held
SIC: 3543 3544 Foundry cores; Forms (molds), for foundry and plastics working machinery

Defiance
Defiance County

(G-6667)
ADVANTAGE POWDER COATING INC (PA)
2090 E 2nd St Ste 102 (43512-8654)
PHONE..................................419 782-2363
Joellen Hornish, *Pr*
Sam Hornish, *
EMP: 70 EST: 1992
SQ FT: 51,000
SALES (est): 3.76MM Privately Held
Web: www.hornishgroup.com
SIC: 3479 Coating of metals and formed products

(G-6668)
AL-FE HEAT TREATING LLC
Aalberts Surface Technologies
2066 E 2nd St (43512-8654)
PHONE..................................419 782-7200
Ernie Lackner, *Brnch Mgr*
EMP: 19
SALES (corp-wide): 63.59MM Privately Held
Web: www.aalberts-ht.us
SIC: 3398 Metal heat treating
HQ: Al-Fe Heat Treating, Llc
209 W Mount Hope Ave
Lansing MI 48910
517 485-5090

(G-6669)
APACHE ACQUISITIONS LLC
1008 Jackson Ave (43512-2797)
PHONE..................................419 782-8003
Eric Westrick, *Prin*
EMP: 7 EST: 2008
SALES (est): 260.57K Privately Held
SIC: 1311 Crude petroleum production

(G-6670)
B & B MOLDED PRODUCTS INC
1250 Ottawa Ave (43512-3004)
P.O. Box 213 (43545-0213)
PHONE..................................419 592-8700
Donald V Gillett, *Pr*
▲ EMP: 40 EST: 1993
SQ FT: 55,000
SALES (est): 10.02MM Privately Held
Web: www.bbmolded.com
SIC: 3089 Injection molded finished plastics products, nec

(G-6671)
BAKER-SHINDLER CONTRACTING CO (PA)
Also Called: Baker-Shindler Builders Sup Co
525 Cleveland Ave (43512-3546)
P.O. Box 488 (43512-0488)
PHONE..................................419 782-5080
TOLL FREE: 800
Douglas Shindler, *Pr*
EMP: 20 EST: 1921
SQ FT: 8,500
SALES (est): 4.69MM
SALES (corp-wide): 4.69MM Privately Held
Web: www.baker-shindler.com
SIC: 1542 1541 3273 Specialized public building contractors; Industrial buildings, new construction, nec; Ready-mixed concrete

(G-6672)
CBS BORING AND MCH CO INC
2064 E 2nd St (43512-8654)
PHONE..................................419 784-9500
Dave Hodell, *Mgr*
EMP: 15
SALES (corp-wide): 24.88MM Privately Held
Web: www.cbsboring.com
SIC: 3599 Machine shop, jobbing and repair
PA: C.B.S. Boring And Machine Company, Inc.
33750 Riviera
Fraser MI 48026
586 294-7540

(G-6673)
CENTER CONCRETE INC
24187 Jewell Rd (43512-9135)
PHONE..................................419 782-2495
Don Pahl, *Brnch Mgr*
EMP: 9
Web: www.centerconcreteinc.com
SIC: 3273 Ready-mixed concrete
PA: Center Concrete, Inc.
8790 Us Rt 6
Edgerton OH 43517

(G-6674)
CLEMENS MOBILE WELDING LLC
25239 Commerce Dr (43512-1790)
PHONE..................................419 782-4220
Scott Clemens, *Managing Member*
Sherri Hammersmith, *
EMP: 25 EST: 1989
SALES (est): 1.54MM Privately Held
Web: www.clemensmobilewelding.com
SIC: 7692 Welding repair

(G-6675)
DECKED LLC
25401 Elliott Rd (43512-9003)
PHONE..................................208 806-0251
Bryan Perry, *Brnch Mgr*
EMP: 10
SALES (corp-wide): 34.7MM Privately Held
Web: www.decked.com
SIC: 3542 Machine tools, metal forming type
PA: Decked, L.L.C.
110 Lindsay Cir
Ketchum ID 83340
208 806-0251

(G-6676)
DEFIANCE METAL PRODUCTS CO (HQ)
21 Seneca St (43512-2274)
PHONE..................................419 784-5332
Stephen Mance, *CEO*
Sam Strausbaugh, *
Joellen Frederick, *
Don Johnson, *
Rick Creedmore, *
▲ EMP: 475 EST: 1939
SQ FT: 165,000
SALES (est): 186.76MM
SALES (corp-wide): 588.42MM Publicly Held
Web: www.mecinc.com
SIC: 3443 3544 Fabricated plate work (boiler shop); Special dies and tools
PA: Mayville Engineering Co Inc
135 S 84th St Ste 300
Milwaukee WI 53214
414 381-2860

(G-6677)
DEFIANCE PUBLISHING CO LTD
Also Called: Defiance Crescent News, The
624 W 2nd St (43512-2161)
P.O. Box 249 (43512-0249)
PHONE..................................419 784-5441
Mark Adams, *Pr*
EMP: 1034 EST: 1888
SQ FT: 9,000
SALES (est): 3.86MM
SALES (corp-wide): 467.21MM Privately Held
Web: www.crescent-news.com
SIC: 2711 Commercial printing and newspaper publishing combined
PA: Dix 1898, Inc.
212 E Liberty St
Wooster OH
330 264-3511

(G-6678)
GENERAL MOTORS LLC
Also Called: General Motors
26427 State Route 281 (43512-6781)
PHONE..................................419 782-7010
Thomas Gallther, *Mgr*
EMP: 309
Web: www.gm.com
SIC: 3321 3322 3365 3369 Gray iron castings, nec; Malleable iron foundries; Aluminum and aluminum-based alloy castings; Nonferrous foundries, nec
HQ: General Motors Llc
300 Rnaissance Ctr Ste L1
Detroit MI 48243

(G-6679)
GODFREY & WING INC
2066 E 2nd St (43512-8654)
PHONE..................................419 980-4616
John Horvath, *Brnch Mgr*
EMP: 10
SALES (corp-wide): 19.38MM Privately Held
Web: www.godfreywing.com
SIC: 3823 Absorption analyzers: infrared, x-ray, etc.: industrial
PA: Godfrey & Wing Inc.
220 Campus Dr
Aurora OH 44202
330 562-1440

(G-6680)
GT TECHNOLOGIES INC
Also Called: Defiance Operations
1125 Precision Way (43512-1919)

GEOGRAPHIC SECTION
Delaware - Delaware County (G-6703)

PHONE.................................419 782-8955
Joe Molnar, *Manager*
EMP: 52
SALES (corp-wide): 283.29MM **Privately Held**
Web: www.gttechnologies.com
SIC: 3714 3562 3599 3398 Motor vehicle engines and parts; Ball and roller bearings; Machine shop, jobbing and repair; Metal heat treating
PA Gt Technologies, Inc.
    5859 E Executive Dr
    Westland MI 48185
    734 467-8371

(G-6681)
HILLTOP PRINTING
1815 Baltimore St (43512-1913)
PHONE.................................419 782-9898
Verle L Harner, *Owner*
EMP: 6 **EST:** 1970
SQ FT: 5,000
SALES (est): 322.76K **Privately Held**
Web: www.hilltopprinting.net
SIC: 2752 Offset printing

(G-6682)
HUBBARD COMPANY
612 Clinton St (43512-2637)
P.O. Box 100 (43512-0100)
PHONE.................................419 784-4455
E Keith Hubbard, *Ch Bd*
Thomas K Hubbard, *
Stephen F Hubbard, *
Jean A Hubbard, *
EMP: 44 **EST:** 1906
SQ FT: 20,000
SALES (est): 2.24MM **Privately Held**
Web: www.friendsoffice.com
SIC: 5943 5192 2752 2732 Office forms and supplies; Books; Offset printing; Book printing

(G-6683)
INNOVATIVE FOOD PROCESSORS INC
136 Fox Run Dr (43512-1394)
PHONE.................................507 334-2730
EMP: 9 **EST:** 2019
SALES (est): 433.54K **Privately Held**
SIC: 2899 Chemical preparations, nec

(G-6684)
JOHNS MANVILLE CORPORATION
1410 Columbus Ave (43512-3181)
P.O. Box 7188 (43512-7188)
PHONE.................................419 782-0180
Randy Engel, *Genl Mgr*
EMP: 47
SALES (corp-wide): 364.48B **Publicly Held**
Web: www.jm.com
SIC: 3296 Mineral wool
HQ Johns Manville Corporation
    717 17th St
    Denver CO 80202
    303 978-2000

(G-6685)
JOHNS MANVILLE CORPORATION
925 Carpenter Rd (43512-1765)
PHONE.................................419 784-7000
Roger Snow, *Mgr*
EMP: 90
SALES (corp-wide): 364.48B **Publicly Held**
Web: www.jm.com
SIC: 3296 Fiberglass insulation
HQ Johns Manville Corporation
    717 17th St
    Denver CO 80202
    303 978-2000

(G-6686)
JOHNS MANVILLE CORPORATION
3rd And Perry (43512)
P.O. Box 158 (43512-0158)
PHONE.................................419 784-7000
Jerry Henry, *Pr*
EMP: 24
SALES (corp-wide): 364.48B **Publicly Held**
Web: www.jm.com
SIC: 3296 Fiberglass insulation
HQ Johns Manville Corporation
    717 17th St
    Denver CO 80202
    303 978-2000

(G-6687)
JOHNS MANVILLE CORPORATION
408 Perry St (43512)
PHONE.................................419 878-8111
Craig Mckibben, *Mgr*
EMP: 14
SALES (corp-wide): 364.48B **Publicly Held**
Web: www.jm.com
SIC: 3296 Fiberglass insulation
HQ Johns Manville Corporation
    717 17th St
    Denver CO 80202
    303 978-2000

(G-6688)
KOESTER MACHINED PRODUCTS CO
136 Fox Run Dr (43512-1394)
PHONE.................................419 782-0291
William C Koester, *Dir*
Jeanette Spiller, *Sec*
Michael Koester, *Pr*
EMP: 12 **EST:** 1990
SQ FT: 21,000
SALES (est): 157.85K **Privately Held**
SIC: 3599 Machine shop, jobbing and repair

(G-6689)
M W SOLUTIONS LLC
1802 Baltimore St Ste B (43512-2081)
PHONE.................................419 782-1611
Matthew Winzeler, *Managing Member*
EMP: 10 **EST:** 2010
SALES (est): 1.29MM **Privately Held**
Web: www.mwsolutionsllc.com
SIC: 3089 3694 3559 Automotive parts, plastic; Alternators, automotive; Automotive related machinery

(G-6690)
MANSFIELD INDUSTRIES
844 N Clinton St Lot C17 (43512-1699)
PHONE.................................419 785-4510
EMP: 7 **EST:** 2013
SALES (est): 53.49K **Privately Held**
Web: www.mansfieldec.com
SIC: 3999 Manufacturing industries, nec

(G-6691)
MARTIN DIESEL INC
27809 County Road 424 (43512-8147)
P.O. Box 1000 (43512-1000)
PHONE.................................419 782-9911
James M Martin Junior, *Pr*
Cliff Martin, *VP*
EMP: 21 **EST:** 1977
SQ FT: 17,500
SALES (est): 3.81MM **Privately Held**
Web: www.martindiesel.com
SIC: 3621 5013 5531 5084 Generators and sets, electric; Automotive supplies and parts ; Truck equipment and parts; Engines and parts, diesel

(G-6692)
MEEKS PASTRY SHOP
315 Clinton St (43512-2113)
PHONE.................................419 782-4871
William Meek, *Owner*
EMP: 6 **EST:** 1925
SQ FT: 2,500
SALES (est): 256.76K **Privately Held**
SIC: 2051 5461 Bread, cake, and related products; Pastries

(G-6693)
PREMIER PACKAGING SYSTEMS LLC
1711 Stonemore Dr (43512-3719)
PHONE.................................419 439-1900
Mike Kitchenmaster, *Admn*
EMP: 6 **EST:** 2016
SALES (est): 92.54K **Privately Held**
SIC: 2631 Container, packaging, and boxboard

(G-6694)
SENSORYFFCTS POWDR SYSTEMS INC
136 Fox Run Dr (43512-1394)
PHONE.................................419 783-5518
Charles A Nicolais, *CEO*
◆ **EMP:** 70 **EST:** 1870
SQ FT: 160,000
SALES (est): 32.54MM
SALES (corp-wide): 922.44MM **Publicly Held**
Web: www.balchem.com
SIC: 2099 Food preparations, nec
HQ Sensoryeffects, Inc.
    13723 Rverport Dr Ste 201
    Maryland Heights MO 63043

(G-6695)
STANDRIDGE COLOR CORPORATION
1122 Integrity Dr (43512-1948)
PHONE.................................770 464-3362
EMP: 16
SALES (corp-wide): 165.63MM **Privately Held**
Web: www.standridgecolor.com
SIC: 2865 Cyclic crudes and intermediates
PA Standridge Color Corporation
    1196 E Hightower Trl
    Social Circle GA 30025
    770 464-3362

(G-6696)
SUPERIOR BAR PRODUCTS INC
1710 Spruce St (43512-2457)
PHONE.................................419 784-2590
Mark Crandall, *Pr*
Deb Wittenmyer, *Treas*
EMP: 6 **EST:** 1988
SQ FT: 7,000
SALES (est): 483.76K **Privately Held**
Web: www.superiorbarproducts.com
SIC: 3451 Screw machine products

(G-6697)
TRESSLERS PLUMBING LLC
9170 State Route 15 (43512-8642)
P.O. Box 433 (43512-0433)
PHONE.................................419 784-2142
EMP: 7 **EST:** 1987
SALES (est): 486.86K **Privately Held**
SIC: 1481 Pumping or draining, nonmetallic mineral mines

(G-6698)
WERLOR INC
Also Called: Werlor Waste Control
1420 Ralston Ave (43512-1380)
PHONE.................................419 784-4285
Casey Wertz, *Pr*
Gerald Wertz, *
Mark Hageman, *
Tom Taylor, *
Casey Wertz, *VP*
EMP: 36 **EST:** 1969
SQ FT: 8,000
SALES (est): 3.57MM **Privately Held**
Web: www.werlor.com
SIC: 2875 4212 4953 Compost; Garbage collection and transport, no disposal; Recycling, waste materials

Delaware
Delaware County

(G-6699)
ACI INDUSTRIES LTD (PA)
970 Pittsburgh Dr Frnt (43015-3872)
PHONE.................................740 368-4160
Ralph Paglieri, *Pt*
Scott H Fischer, *
Helen Harper, *
◆ **EMP:** 49 **EST:** 1984
SQ FT: 225,000
SALES (est): 10MM
SALES (corp-wide): 10MM **Privately Held**
Web: www.aci-industries.com
SIC: 3341 5093 3339 Secondary nonferrous metals; Scrap and waste materials; Primary nonferrous metals, nec

(G-6700)
ACI INDUSTRIES CONVERTING LTD (HQ)
Also Called: J and J Sales
970 Pittsburgh Dr (43015-3872)
PHONE.................................740 368-4160
Mike Paglieri, *Genl Pt*
◆ **EMP:** 17 **EST:** 1990
SQ FT: 232,000
SALES (est): 10MM
SALES (corp-wide): 10MM **Privately Held**
Web: www.aci-industries.com
SIC: 2676 5113 Towels, napkins, and tissue paper products; Towels, paper
PA Aci Industries, Ltd.
    970 Pittsburgh Dr
    Delaware OH 43015
    740 368-4160

(G-6701)
ASSOCIATED HYGIENIC PDTS LLC
2332 Us Highway 42 S (43015-9502)
PHONE.................................770 497-9800
EMP: 560
SALES (corp-wide): 98.06MM **Privately Held**
Web: www.attindas.com
SIC: 2621 Paper mills
PA Associated Hygienic Products Llc
    1029 Old Creek Rd
    Greenville NC 27834
    770 497-9800

(G-6702)
ATKINS CUSTOM FRAMING LTD
3116 Troy Rd (43015-8799)
PHONE.................................740 816-1501
Mark A Atkins, *Prin*
EMP: 16 **EST:** 2015
SALES (est): 467K **Privately Held**
Web: www.atkinscustomframing.com
SIC: 2499 Picture frame molding, finished

(G-6703)
ATTENDS HEALTHCARE PDTS INC
Also Called: Attindas Hygiene Partners

Delaware - Delaware County (G-6704)

GEOGRAPHIC SECTION

2332 Us Highway 42 S (43015-9502)
PHONE..................................740 368-7880
EMP: 8
SALES (corp-wide): 103.92MM **Privately Held**
Web: www.attends.com
SIC: 2676 Sanitary paper products
PA: Attends Healthcare Products Inc.
8020 Arco Corp Dr Ste 200
Raleigh NC 27617
800 428-8363

(G-6704)
ATTIA APPLIED SCIENCES INC
Also Called: Taasi
548 W Central Ave (43015-1421)
PHONE..................................740 369-1891
Yosry Attia, *Pr*
Vera Attia, *VP*
EMP: 8 **EST:** 1985
SALES (est): 121.96K **Privately Held**
Web: www.taasi.com
SIC: 2899 Chemical preparations, nec

(G-6705)
BLACK WING SHOOTING CENTER LLC
3722 Marysville Rd (43015-9527)
PHONE..................................740 363-7555
Rex Gore, *Pr*
EMP: 9 **EST:** 2002
SALES (est): 2.36MM **Privately Held**
Web: www.blackwingsc.com
SIC: 7999 3949 Shooting range operation; Bases, baseball

(G-6706)
BUNS OF DELAWARE INC
Also Called: Buns Restaurant & Bakery
14 W Winter St (43015-1919)
PHONE..................................740 363-2867
Vasili Konstantinidis, *Pr*
EMP: 28 **EST:** 1864
SQ FT: 11,184
SALES (est): 471.15K **Privately Held**
Web: www.bunsrestaurant.com
SIC: 5812 5461 7299 2051 Eating places; Retail bakeries; Banquet hall facilities; Bread, cake, and related products

(G-6707)
CEDEE CEDAR INC (PA)
Also Called: Cedar Woodworking
3903 Us Highway 42 S (43015-9517)
PHONE..................................740 363-3148
Carl Reynolds, *CEO*
Kris Bargram, *Mgr*
EMP: 10 **EST:** 1985
SALES (est): 498.07K
SALES (corp-wide): 498.07K **Privately Held**
SIC: 2434 Wood kitchen cabinets

(G-6708)
CHARTER NEX FILMS - DELAWARE OH INC
Also Called: Charter Nex Films
1188 S Houk Rd (43015-3857)
PHONE..................................740 369-2770
EMP: 45
Web: www.cnginc.com
SIC: 3081 2673 Unsupported plastics film and sheet; Plastic and pliofilm bags

(G-6709)
CHARTER NEXT GENERATION INC
1188 S Houk Rd (43015-3857)
PHONE..................................740 369-2770
EMP: 128
SALES (corp-wide): 1.5B **Privately Held**
Web: www.cnginc.com
SIC: 2671 Plastic film, coated or laminated for packaging
PA: Charter Next Generation, Inc.
300 N La Salle Dr # 1575
Chicago IL 60654
608 868-5757

(G-6710)
CHROMA COLOR CORPORATION
100 Colomet Dr (43015-3846)
P.O. Box 690 (43015-0690)
PHONE..................................740 363-6622
Jeff Smik, *Brnch Mgr*
EMP: 30
SALES (corp-wide): 117.78MM **Privately Held**
Web: www.chromacolors.com
SIC: 2821 Plastics materials and resins
PA: Chroma Color Corporation
3900 W Dayton St
Mc Henry IL 60050
877 385-8777

(G-6711)
CONCRETE ONE CONSTRUCTION LLC ○
755 Us Highway 23 N Ste E (43015-6004)
PHONE..................................740 595-9680
Gerald Rowe Junior, *Managing Member*
EMP: 15 **EST:** 2023
SALES (est): 671.48K **Privately Held**
SIC: 1389 1771 Construction, repair, and dismantling services; Concrete work

(G-6712)
DELAWARE CITY VINEYARD
32 Troy Rd (43015-4503)
PHONE..................................740 362-6383
Robb Morgan, *Prin*
EMP: 9 **EST:** 2009
SALES (est): 231.11K **Privately Held**
Web: www.delawarecityvineyard.org
SIC: 2084 Wines

(G-6713)
DELAWARE DATA PRODUCTS
216 London Rd (43015-2584)
PHONE..................................740 369-5449
Christopher Bronstein, *Mgr*
EMP: 7 **EST:** 1989
SALES (est): 112.34K **Privately Held**
Web: www.ddpmailing.com
SIC: 2759 Commercial printing, nec

(G-6714)
DELAWARE GAZETTE COMPANY
Also Called: Mid Ohio Net
40 N Sandusky St Ste 202 (43015-1973)
PHONE..................................740 363-1161
Roy Brown, *Pr*
Walter D Thomson Ii, *Pr*
Thomas T Thomson, *
Henry C Thomson, *
EMP: 25 **EST:** 1818
SQ FT: 20,000
SALES (est): 1.76MM **Privately Held**
Web: www.delgazette.com
SIC: 2711 Commercial printing and newspaper publishing combined

(G-6715)
DELOHIO TECH
2061 State Route 521 (43015-8754)
PHONE..................................740 816-5628
Tom Davis, *Pr*
EMP: 6 **EST:** 2010
SALES (est): 210.98K **Privately Held**
SIC: 3571 Electronic computers

(G-6716)
DELOSCREW PRODUCTS
700 London Rd (43015-8638)
PHONE..................................740 363-1971
Mike Flora, *Pr*
Jay Egelski, *VP Fin*
Robi Dodadalltur, *OF ASSEMBLY*
Charles Oda, *Mgr*
EMP: 17 **EST:** 2008
SALES (est): 2.38MM **Privately Held**
Web: www.deloscrew.com
SIC: 3451 Screw machine products

(G-6717)
DIVERSE MFG SOLUTIONS LLC
970 Pittsburgh Dr Ste 22 (43015-3872)
PHONE..................................740 363-3600
EMP: 10 **EST:** 2010
SALES (est): 977.93K **Privately Held**
Web: www.dms-site.com
SIC: 3542 Sheet metalworking machines

(G-6718)
DOMESTIC CASTING COMPANY LLC
620 Liberty Rd (43015-9387)
PHONE..................................717 532-6615
Jerry Harmeyer, *Managing Member*
Tom James, *
Michael Heyne, *
EMP: 10 **EST:** 2003
SALES (est): 336.75K **Privately Held**
Web: www.domesticcasting.com
SIC: 3321 Gray iron castings, nec

(G-6719)
EMERSON CORP
975 Pittsburgh Dr (43015-2858)
PHONE..................................614 841-5498
EMP: 7 **EST:** 2019
SALES (est): 198.52K **Privately Held**
Web: www.emerson.com
SIC: 3823 Process control instruments

(G-6720)
ENGINEERED CONDUCTIVE MTL LLC
132 Johnson Dr (43015-8699)
PHONE..................................740 362-4444
Chuck Feeny, *Prin*
EMP: 8 **EST:** 2004
SALES (est): 122.96K **Privately Held**
SIC: 2891 Adhesives and sealants

(G-6721)
FEDERAL HEATH SIGN COMPANY LLC
1020 Pittsburgh Dr Ste A (43015-3878)
PHONE..................................740 369-0999
Ken Hermes, *Manager*
EMP: 57
Web: www.federalheath.com
SIC: 3993 Electric signs
HQ: Federal Heath Sign Company, Llc
1845 Prcnct Line Rd Ste 1
Hurst TX 76054

(G-6722)
FOUR NATURES KEEPERS INC
4651 Marysville Rd (43015-9528)
PHONE..................................740 363-8007
Willis J Whittaker, *Pr*
Nancy Pintavalli, *Sec*
EMP: 10 **EST:** 1997
SALES (est): 737.28K **Privately Held**
Web: www.natureskeepers.com
SIC: 2048 Bird food, prepared

(G-6723)
FRISCHCO INC
Also Called: Dairy Clean
715 Sunbury Rd (43015-9396)
PHONE..................................740 363-7537
Jim Frisch, *Mgr*
EMP: 10 **EST:** 2002
SALES (est): 387.97K **Privately Held**
SIC: 2052 Cones, ice cream

(G-6724)
GREIF INC (PA)
Also Called: Greif
425 Winter Rd (43015-8903)
P.O. Box 8014 (43015-8014)
PHONE..................................740 549-6000
Ole Rosgaard, *Pr*
Bruce Edwards, *
Lawrence A Hilsheimer, *Ex VP*
Gary R Martz, *Ex VP*
Bala V Sathyanarayanan, *Chief Human Resources Officer*
◆ **EMP:** 50 **EST:** 1926
SALES (est): 5.22B
SALES (corp-wide): 5.22B **Publicly Held**
Web: www.greif.com
SIC: 2449 2655 3412 3089 Shipping cases and drums, wood: wirebound and plywood; Fiber cans, drums, and similar products; Drums, shipping: metal; Plastics containers, except foam

(G-6725)
GREIF INC
Also Called: Grief Brothers
366 Greif Pkwy (43015-8260)
PHONE..................................740 657-6500
Kathy King, *Mgr*
EMP: 46
SALES (corp-wide): 5.22B **Publicly Held**
Web: www.deltacogroup.com
SIC: 2449 2655 3412 2653 Shipping cases and drums, wood: wirebound and plywood; Drums, fiber: made from purchased material; Drums, shipping: metal; Boxes, corrugated: made from purchased materials
PA: Greif, Inc.
425 Winter Rd
Delaware OH 43015
740 549-6000

(G-6726)
GREIF PACKAGING LLC (HQ)
Also Called: Corrchoice
366 Greif Pkwy (43015-8260)
PHONE..................................740 549-6000
Brian Dum, *CEO*
▲ **EMP:** 30 **EST:** 1983
SALES (est): 459.6MM
SALES (corp-wide): 5.22B **Publicly Held**
Web: www.greif.com
SIC: 3086 Packaging and shipping materials, foamed plastics
PA: Greif, Inc.
425 Winter Rd
Delaware OH 43015
740 549-6000

(G-6727)
GREIF USA LLC (DH)
366 Greif Pkwy (43015)
PHONE..................................740 549-6000
EMP: 96 **EST:** 2005
SALES (est): 100.09MM
SALES (corp-wide): 5.22B **Publicly Held**
Web: www.greif.com
SIC: 2655 Fiber cans, drums, and similar products
HQ: Greif Packaging Llc
366 Greif Pkwy
Delaware OH 43015

▲ = Import ▼ = Export
◆ = Import/Export

GEOGRAPHIC SECTION

Delaware - Delaware County (G-6749)

(G-6728)
HALLIDAY TECHNOLOGIES INC
105 Innovation Ct Ste F (43015-4351)
PHONE..............................614 504-4150
Don Halliday, *CEO*
Don Halliday, *Pr*
Patricia Halliday, *VP*
EMP: 7 **EST:** 1994
SQ FT: 400
SALES (est): 1.04MM **Privately Held**
Web: www.hallidaytech.com
SIC: 3829 8711 Measuring and controlling devices, nec; Consulting engineer

(G-6729)
HARRIS INSTRUMENT CORPORATION
155 Johnson Dr (43015-8500)
P.O. Box 982 (43015-7082)
PHONE..............................740 369-3580
Cathy Harris, *Pr*
David E Harris, *Stockholder*
Gary E Saum, *Stockholder*
John Harris, *Pr*
EMP: 9 **EST:** 1979
SQ FT: 10,000
SALES (est): 1.04MM **Privately Held**
Web: www.harris-instrument.com
SIC: 3829 3823 3625 Measuring and controlling devices, nec; Process control instruments; Relays and industrial controls

(G-6730)
HENKEL US OPERATIONS CORP
Also Called: Henkel Surface Technologies
421 London Rd (43015-2493)
P.O. Box 363 (43015-0363)
PHONE..............................740 363-1351
Tony Neal, *Brnch Mgr*
EMP: 218
SQ FT: 1,634
SALES (corp-wide): 23.39B **Privately Held**
Web: www.henkel.com
SIC: 2841 2842 Detergents, synthetic organic or inorganic alkaline; Polishes and sanitation goods
HQ: Henkel Us Operations Corporation
   1 Henkel Way
   Rocky Hill CT 06067
   860 571-5100

(G-6731)
HOME CITY ICE COMPANY
150 Johnson Dr (43015-8699)
PHONE..............................419 562-4953
TOLL FREE: 800
Bryan Stuckman, *Mgr*
EMP: 10
SALES (corp-wide): 100.42MM **Privately Held**
Web: www.homecityice.com
SIC: 2024 2097 Ice cream and frozen deserts; Manufactured ice
PA: The Home City Ice Company
   6045 Bridgetown Rd Ste 1
   Cincinnati OH 45248
   513 574-1800

(G-6732)
INTERNATIONAL PAPER COMPANY
International Paper
875 Pittsburgh Dr (43015-2860)
P.O. Box 8005 (43015-8005)
PHONE..............................740 369-7691
David Harbaugh, *Mgr*
EMP: 172
SALES (corp-wide): 18.92B **Publicly Held**
Web: www.internationalpaper.com
SIC: 2653 Boxes, corrugated: made from purchased materials
PA: International Paper Company
   6400 Poplar Ave
   Memphis TN 38197
   901 419-7000

(G-6733)
KHEMPCO BLDG SUP CO LTD PARTNR (PA)
Also Called: Arlington-Blaine Lumber Co
130 Johnson Dr (43015-8699)
PHONE..............................740 549-0465
James D Klingbeil Junior, *Genl Pt*
Richard Robinson, *Pt*
Donny Bowman, *Pt*
EMP: 100 **EST:** 1963
SALES (est): 22.54MM
SALES (corp-wide): 22.54MM **Privately Held**
Web: www.khempco.com
SIC: 5031 5211 2439 2431 Lumber: rough, dressed, and finished; Lumber and other building materials; Trusses, except roof: laminated lumber; Doors, wood

(G-6734)
LARCOM AND MITCHELL LLC
1800 Pittsburgh Dr (43015-3870)
PHONE..............................740 595-3750
Charles Mitchell, *Prin*
EMP: 9 **EST:** 2011
SALES (est): 864.16K **Privately Held**
Web: www.larcom-mitchell.com
SIC: 3599 Flexible metal hose, tubing, and bellows

(G-6735)
LIBERTY CASTING COMPANY LLC (PA)
550 Liberty Rd (43015-8670)
PHONE..............................740 363-1941
William B Shearer, *Managing Member*
Jerry Harmeyer, *
Tom James, *
Troy Fischer, *
Viera Maruli, *
▲ **EMP:** 70 **EST:** 2003
SQ FT: 400,000
SALES (est): 25.37MM
SALES (corp-wide): 25.37MM **Privately Held**
Web: www.libertycasting.com
SIC: 3321 Gray iron castings, nec

(G-6736)
LUVATA OHIO INC (HQ)
Also Called: Luvata
1376 Pittsburgh Dr (43015-3814)
PHONE..............................740 363-1981
Jussi Helavirta, *Ch Bd*
Jyrki Vesaluoma, *CEO*
Dirk Greywitt, *VP*
Carla Grispino, *Treas*
Robert Fleming, *Sec*
◆ **EMP:** 85 **EST:** 1946
SQ FT: 60,000
SALES (est): 26.31MM **Privately Held**
Web: www.luvata.com
SIC: 3548 Welding and cutting apparatus and accessories, nec
PA: Mitsubishi Materials Corporation
   3-2-3, Marunouchi
   Chiyoda-Ku TKY 100-0

(G-6737)
MIDWEST ACOUST-A-FIBER INC (PA)
Also Called: M. A. I.
759 Pittsburgh Dr (43015-2862)
PHONE..............................740 369-3624
Hardev Boucher, *Pr*
Thomas Gorzelski, *
EMP: 16 **EST:** 1979
SQ FT: 98,250
SALES (est): 52.95MM
SALES (corp-wide): 52.95MM **Privately Held**
Web: www.mwaaf.com
SIC: 3296 Mineral wool

(G-6738)
MSM FUNDRAISING LLC
2083 Klondike Rd (43015-8859)
PHONE..............................740 369-8160
EMP: 6 **EST:** 2010
SALES (est): 103.68K **Privately Held**
Web: www.msmfundraising.com
SIC: 7372 Application computer software

(G-6739)
NAGASE CHEMTEX AMERICA LLC
100 Innovation Ct (43015-7532)
PHONE..............................740 362-4444
Somari De Wet, *
▲ **EMP:** 49 **EST:** 1992
SQ FT: 20,000
SALES (est): 12.39MM **Privately Held**
Web: www.emsadhesives.com
SIC: 2891 Adhesives
HQ: Nagase Holdings America Corporation
   546 5th Ave Fl 19
   New York NY 10036
   212 703-1340

(G-6740)
NATIONAL LIME AND STONE CO
Also Called: National Lime Stone Clmbus Reg
2406 S Section Line Rd (43015-9518)
P.O. Box 537 (43015-0537)
PHONE..............................740 548-4206
Carolyn Coder, *Off Mgr*
EMP: 28
SALES (corp-wide): 167.89MM **Privately Held**
Web: www.natlime.com
SIC: 1422 Crushed and broken limestone
PA: The National Lime And Stone Company
   551 Lake Cascade Pkwy
   Findlay OH 45840
   419 422-4341

(G-6741)
NATIONAL METAL SHAPES INC
425 S Sandusky St Ste 1 (43015-3604)
PHONE..............................740 363-9559
John Vogel, *Pr*
▲ **EMP:** 25 **EST:** 1971
SQ FT: 85,000
SALES (est): 5.12MM **Privately Held**
Web: www.nationalmetalshapes.com
SIC: 3354 Aluminum extruded products

(G-6742)
OBERFIELDS LLC (HQ)
528 London Rd (43015-2850)
P.O. Box 362 (43015-0362)
PHONE..............................740 369-7644
Bruce Loris, *Pr*
EMP: 70 **EST:** 1961
SQ FT: 52,000
SALES (est): 21.04MM
SALES (corp-wide): 21.04MM **Privately Held**
Web: www.oberfields.com
SIC: 3272 Concrete products, precast, nec
PA: Oberfields Holdings Llc
   528 London Rd
   Delaware OH 43015
   740 369-7644

(G-6743)
PPG INDUSTRIES INC
Also Called: P P G Refinishing Group
760 Pittsburgh Dr (43015-3811)
PHONE..............................740 363-9610
Mike Tiehurst, *Mgr*
EMP: 6
SALES (corp-wide): 17.65B **Publicly Held**
Web: www.ppg.com
SIC: 2851 Paints and allied products
PA: Ppg Industries, Inc.
   1 Ppg Pl
   Pittsburgh PA 15272
   412 434-3131

(G-6744)
PPG INDUSTRIES OHIO INC
760 Pittsburgh Dr (43015-3811)
PHONE..............................740 363-9610
James Boyd, *Brnch Mgr*
EMP: 450
SALES (corp-wide): 17.65B **Publicly Held**
Web: www.ppg.com
SIC: 2851 Paints and allied products
HQ: Ppg Industries Ohio, Inc.
   3800 W 143rd St
   Cleveland OH 44111
   216 671-0050

(G-6745)
PRICE FARMS ORGANICS LTD
4838 Warrensburg Rd (43015-8589)
PHONE..............................740 369-1000
Tom Price, *Managing Member*
EMP: 17 **EST:** 1998
SQ FT: 1,000
SALES (est): 873.52K **Privately Held**
Web: www.pricefarms.org
SIC: 2875 Compost

(G-6746)
RJW TRUCKING COMPANY LTD
Also Called: Henderson Trucking
124 Henderson Ct (43015-8479)
PHONE..............................740 363-5343
Jack Henderson, *Managing Member*
EMP: 25 **EST:** 2000
SALES (est): 3.05MM **Privately Held**
Web: www.hendersontruckingohio.com
SIC: 1442 4212 Construction sand and gravel; Local trucking, without storage

(G-6747)
SAM DONG AMERICA INC
801 Pittsburgh Dr (43015-2860)
PHONE..............................740 363-1985
Ee Joo Lee, *Pr*
EMP: 10 **EST:** 2016
SALES (est): 228.23K **Privately Held**
Web: www.samdongamerica.com
SIC: 3357 Magnet wire, nonferrous

(G-6748)
SAM DONG OHIO INC
801 Pittsburgh Dr (43015-2860)
PHONE..............................740 363-1985
Ee Joo Lee, *Pr*
▲ **EMP:** 75 **EST:** 2009
SALES (est): 26.81MM **Privately Held**
Web: www.samdongamerica.com
SIC: 3331 Primary copper
PA: Sam Dong Co.,Ltd.
   816-41 Samyang-Ro, Daeso-Myeon
   Eumseong 27673

(G-6749)
SANDRA WEDDINGTON
Also Called: Blend of Seven Winery
1400 Stratford Rd (43015-2922)
PHONE..............................740 417-4286

Delaware - Delaware County (G-6750)   **GEOGRAPHIC SECTION**

Sandra Weddington, *Owner*
EMP: 15 **EST:** 2011
SALES (est): 967.71K **Privately Held**
Web: www.blendofsevenwinery.com
SIC: 2084 5182 5921 Wines; Wine; Wine

(G-6750)
SKY CLIMBER FABRICATING LLC
1600 Pittsburgh Dr (43015-3884)
PHONE..................................740 990-9430
EMP: 10 **EST:** 2016
SQ FT: 84,000
SALES (est): 1.03MM **Privately Held**
Web: www.skyclimber.com
SIC: 3449 7692 Bars, concrete reinforcing; fabricated steel; Welding repair

(G-6751)
SKY CLIMBER WIND SOLUTIONS LLC
1800 Pittsburgh Dr (43015-3870)
PHONE..................................740 203-3000
EMP: 24 **EST:** 2007
SALES (est): 1.1MM **Privately Held**
Web: www.skyclimber-re.com
SIC: 3446 Scaffolds, mobile or stationary: metal

(G-6752)
SOTERRA LLC
425 Winter Rd (43015-8903)
PHONE..................................740 549-6072
EMP: 8 **EST:** 2017
SALES (est): 2.14MM
SALES (corp-wide): 5.22B **Publicly Held**
Web: www.greif.com
SIC: 2631 3089 Container, packaging, and boxboard; Plastics containers, except foam
PA: Greif, Inc.
425 Winter Rd
Delaware OH 43015
740 549-6000

(G-6753)
STOVER INTERNATIONAL LLC
222 Stover Dr (43015-8601)
PHONE..................................740 363-5251
Dan Bloom, *Managing Member*
EMP: 25 **EST:** 2007
SALES (est): 2.4MM **Privately Held**
SIC: 3441 3549 3542 Fabricated structural metal; Assembly machines, including robotic ; Machine tools, metal forming type

(G-6754)
SUPPLY TECHNOLOGIES LLC
Also Called: Delo Screw Products
700 London Rd (43015-8637)
PHONE..................................740 363-1971
Jane Scroggins, *Contrlr*
EMP: 11
SALES (corp-wide): 1.66B **Publicly Held**
Web: www.supplytechnologies.com
SIC: 3451 Screw machine products
HQ: Supply Technologies Llc
6065 Parkland Blvd
Cleveland OH 44124
440 947-2100

(G-6755)
TJ CLARK INTERNATIONAL LLC
320 London Rd Ste 608 (43015-6407)
PHONE..................................614 388-8869
Eric Jenkusky, *Pr*
EMP: 8 **EST:** 2015
SQ FT: 2,200
SALES (est): 839.58K **Privately Held**
Web: www.tjclarkintl.com
SIC: 3561 3441 Pumps and pumping equipment; Fabricated structural metal

(G-6756)
WANNER METAL WORX INC
525 London Rd (43015)
P.O. Box 1004 (43015)
PHONE..................................740 369-4034
Craig Wanner, *Pr*
Richard Wanner Junior, *VP*
Rick Wanner, *
EMP: 50 **EST:** 1989
SQ FT: 250,000
SALES (est): 8.48MM **Privately Held**
Web: www.wannermetalworx.com
SIC: 3441 Fabricated structural metal

(G-6757)
WHITESIDE MANUFACTURING CO
309 Hayes St (43015-2189)
P.O. Box 322 (43015-0322)
PHONE..................................740 363-1179
Kirt Whiteside, *CEO*
Robert Whiteside, *
Terry Whiteside, *
▲ **EMP:** 40 **EST:** 1954
SQ FT: 75,000
SALES (est): 5.24MM **Privately Held**
Web: www.whitesidemfg.com
SIC: 3537 3429 Platforms, stands, tables, pallets, and similar equipment; Hardware, nec

Dellroy
Carroll County

(G-6758)
RNP INC
Also Called: Robert's Men's Shop
8014 Linden Dr Sw (44620-9747)
EMP: 7 **EST:** 1989
SALES (est): 680K **Privately Held**
SIC: 5661 5611 5699 2395 Men's shoes; Clothing accessories: men's and boys'; Formal wear; Embroidery products, except Schiffli machine

Delphos
Allen County

(G-6759)
A & J WOODWORKING INC
808 Ohio St (45833-1824)
PHONE..................................419 695-5655
Arnold Mohler, *Pr*
Jeff Mohler, *VP*
Jill Mohler, *Sec*
EMP: 8 **EST:** 1985
SALES (est): 862.9K **Privately Held**
Web: www.ajwoodworking.com
SIC: 1751 2541 2434 2431 Cabinet building and installation; Wood partitions and fixtures ; Wood kitchen cabinets; Millwork

(G-6760)
DELPHOS HERALD INC (PA)
Also Called: Eagle Print
405 N Main St (45833-1598)
PHONE..................................419 695-0015
Murray Cohen, *Ch Bd*
Ray Geary, *Asst Tr*
EMP: 83 **EST:** 1962
SQ FT: 14,000
SALES (est): 23.87MM
SALES (corp-wide): 23.87MM **Privately Held**
Web: www.delphosherald.com
SIC: 2711 2752 Newspapers, publishing and printing; Offset printing

(G-6761)
DELPHOS RUBBER COMPANY
1450 N Main St (45833-1150)
PHONE..................................419 692-3000
EMP: 20
SIC: 3069 Floor coverings, rubber
HQ: Delphos Rubber Company
715 Fountain Ave
Lancaster PA 17601
717 295-3400

(G-6762)
DELPHOS TENT AND AWNING INC
1454 N Main St (45833-1150)
PHONE..................................419 692-5776
TOLL FREE: 800
Andrew Wurst, *Pr*
Shellie Wurst, *VP*
Charlie Gerdeman, *Dir*
EMP: 16 **EST:** 1920
SQ FT: 5,000
SALES (est): 771.30K **Privately Held**
Web: www.delphostentawning.com
SIC: 2394 Canvas and related products

(G-6763)
DRAPERY STITCH OF DELPHOS
Also Called: Drapery Stitch
50 Summers Ln (45833-1791)
P.O. Box 307 (45833-0307)
PHONE..................................419 692-3921
Donald Beckman, *Pr*
Cheryl Beckman, *VP*
EMP: 10 **EST:** 1968
SQ FT: 18,000
SALES (est): 242.54K **Privately Held**
Web: www.draperystitch.com
SIC: 2391 Draperies, plastic and textile: from purchased materials

(G-6764)
DTR EQUIPMENT INC
1430 N Main St (45833-1150)
P.O. Box 163 (45853-0163)
PHONE..................................419 692-3000
Robert T Horstman, *Pr*
Richard A Horstman, *VP*
▲ **EMP:** 19 **EST:** 1996
SQ FT: 40,000
SALES (est): 226.45K **Privately Held**
SIC: 3069 Mats or matting, rubber, nec

(G-6765)
HYDROFRESH LTD
Also Called: Hydrofresh Hpp
1571 Gressel Dr (45833-9187)
PHONE..................................567 765-1010
Don Klausing, *Pr*
Mike Billig, *VP*
EMP: 7 **EST:** 2017
SQ FT: 36,616
SALES (est): 1.27MM
SALES (corp-wide): 57.53MM **Privately Held**
SIC: 2099 Food preparations, nec
HQ: Universal Pure, Llc
1601 Pioneers Blvd
Lincoln NE 68502
402 474-9500

(G-6766)
J & G GOECKE CLOTHING LLC ◘
Also Called: Lion Clothing
22877 Spieles Rd (45833-9549)
PHONE..................................419 692-9981
EMP: 6 **EST:** 2023
SALES (est): 78.58K **Privately Held**
SIC: 2311 7299 Tuxedos: made from purchased materials; Tuxedo rental

(G-6767)
KNIPPEN CHRYSLER DDGE JEEP INC
Also Called: Knippen Chrysler Dodge Jeep
800 W 5th St (45833-9212)
PHONE..................................419 695-4976
Ronald Knippen, *Pr*
John Klausing, *
Ronald Baumgarte, *
▲ **EMP:** 21 **EST:** 1981
SQ FT: 13,500
SALES (est): 2.78MM **Privately Held**
Web: www.knippenchryslerdodgejeep.com
SIC: 5511 5521 3714 7513 Automobiles, new and used; Used car dealers; Motor vehicle parts and accessories; Truck rental and leasing, no drivers

(G-6768)
KRENDL MACHINE COMPANY
1201 Spencerville Rd (45833-2381)
PHONE..................................419 692-3060
Joe Krendl, *Pr*
Jeffrey Krendl, *Plant Operator*
Joseph Krendl, *Vice President Business*
Lee Krendl, *
▼ **EMP:** 70 **EST:** 1958
SQ FT: 55,000
SALES (est): 11.07MM **Privately Held**
Web: www.krendlmachine.com
SIC: 3599 3432 3827 Machine shop, jobbing and repair; Plumbing fixture fittings and trim ; Optical instruments and lenses

(G-6769)
LAKEVIEW FARMS LLC (PA)
1600 Gressel Dr (45833-9153)
P.O. Box 98 (45833-0098)
PHONE..................................419 695-9925
Tom Davis, *CEO*
John Kopilchack, *
Martin Garlock, *
EMP: 140 **EST:** 2011
SQ FT: 36,250
SALES (est): 113.55MM
SALES (corp-wide): 113.55MM **Privately Held**
Web: www.lakeviewfarms.com
SIC: 2099 2026 2022 Dips, except cheese and sour cream based; Cream, sour; Cheese; natural and processed

(G-6770)
ORVAL KENT FOOD COMPANY LLC
1600 Gressel Dr (45833-9153)
P.O. Box 369 (45833-0369)
PHONE..................................419 695-5015
EMP: 29
SIC: 2099 Ready-to-eat meals, salads, and sandwiches

(G-6771)
RUBBER GRINDING INC
1430 N Main St (45833-1150)
P.O. Box 466 (45833-0466)
PHONE..................................419 692-3000
Ted Horstman, *Pr*
Rick Horstman, *VP*
◘ **EMP:** 100 **EST:** 1992
SQ FT: 50,000
SALES (est): 42.65MM
SALES (corp-wide): 4.59B **Publicly Held**
Web: www.rthprocessing.com
SIC: 3069 5941 Mats or matting, rubber, nec ; Exercise equipment
HQ: Ultimate Rb, Inc.
1430 N Main St
Delphos OH 45833
419 692-3000

▲ = Import ▼ = Export
◘ = Import/Export

(G-6772)
TOLEDO MOLDING & DIE LLC
900 Gressel Dr (45833-9154)
P.O. Box 393 (45833-0393)
PHONE..............................419 692-6022
Jack Ruhe, *Mgr*
EMP: 161
Web: www.tmdinc.com
SIC: 3089 3714 Injection molding of plastics; Motor vehicle parts and accessories
HQ: Toledo Molding & Die, Llc
  1429 Coining Dr
  Toledo OH 43612

(G-6773)
TOLEDO MOLDING & DIE LLC
Also Called: Delphos Plant 2
24086 State Route 697 (45833-9203)
P.O. Box 393 (45833-0393)
PHONE..............................419 692-6022
Keith Riegle, *Mgr*
EMP: 256
Web: www.tmdinc.com
SIC: 5031 3714 Molding, all materials; Motor vehicle parts and accessories
HQ: Toledo Molding & Die, Llc
  1429 Coining Dr
  Toledo OH 43612

(G-6774)
ULTIMATE RB INC (DH)
1430 N Main St (45833-1150)
PHONE..............................419 692-3000
Marvin Wool, *Pr*
EMP: 11 **EST:** 2014
SALES (est): 43.64MM
SALES (corp-wide): 4.59B **Publicly Held**
Web: www.ultimaterb.com
SIC: 3069 Mats or matting, rubber, nec
HQ: Accella Performance Materials Inc.
  2500 Adie Rd
  Maryland Heights MO
  314 432-3200

(G-6775)
ULTIMATE SYSTEMS LTD
1430 N Main St (45833-1150)
P.O. Box 465 (45833-0465)
PHONE..............................419 692-3005
◆ **EMP:** 50
Web: www.ultimatesystemsltd.com
SIC: 3069 Door mats, rubber

(G-6776)
US METALCRAFT INC
101 S Franklin St (45833-1936)
P.O. Box 308 (45833-0308)
PHONE..............................419 692-4962
Joel Birkmeier, *Pr*
Steve Birkmeier, *VP*
◆ **EMP:** 27 **EST:** 1959
SQ FT: 20,000
SALES (est): 5.86MM **Privately Held**
Web: www.usmetalcraft.com
SIC: 3365 Aluminum and aluminum-based alloy castings

(G-6777)
VAN WERT MACHINE INC
Also Called: Progressive Tool Division
210 E Cleveland St (45833-1941)
P.O. Box 40 (45833-0040)
PHONE..............................419 692-6836
Jesse F Hitchcock, *Pr*
Donald E Bechtol, *VP*
Gloria Bechtol, *Sec*
EMP: 13 **EST:** 1961
SQ FT: 18,600
SALES (est): 895.53K **Privately Held**
Web: www.progressive-tool.com

SIC: 3544 Special dies and tools

(G-6778)
VANAMATIC COMPANY
701 Ambrose Dr (45833-9179)
PHONE..............................419 692-6085
Jeffrey S Wiltsie, *Pr*
Perry J Wiltsie, *VP*
Patricia M Morris, *Sec*
EMP: 85 **EST:** 1954
SQ FT: 75,000
SALES (est): 15.68MM **Privately Held**
Web: www.vanamatic.com
SIC: 3451 Screw machine products

Delta
Fulton County

(G-6779)
AREA 419 FIREARMS LLC
Also Called: Area 419
4750 County Road 5 (43515-9262)
PHONE..............................419 830-8353
EMP: 12 **EST:** 2013
SALES (est): 773.45K **Privately Held**
Web: www.arca419.com
SIC: 5941 3489 Firearms; Artillery or artillery parts, over 30 mm.

(G-6780)
BEAVERSON MACHINE INC
11600 County Road 10 2 (43515-9748)
PHONE..............................419 923-8064
Ralph Beaverson, *Pr*
James Beaverson, *VP*
EMP: 6 **EST:** 1984
SQ FT: 3,000
SALES (est): 487.17K **Privately Held**
Web: www.beaversonmachine.com
SIC: 3599 Machine shop, jobbing and repair

(G-6781)
DELTA TOOL & DIE STL BLOCK INC
Also Called: Delta Tool & Die
5226 County Road 6 (43515-9648)
PHONE..............................419 822-5939
EMP: 28 **EST:** 1999
SQ FT: 27,500
SALES (est): 2.31MM **Privately Held**
Web: www.deltastamping.com
SIC: 3544 3469 Jigs and fixtures; Metal stampings, nec

(G-6782)
DESIGNER WINDOW TREATMENTS INC
302 Superior St (43515-1335)
P.O. Box 146 (43515-0146)
PHONE..............................419 822-4967
Leslie Zalecki, *Pr*
EMP: 8 **EST:** 1989
SALES (est): 657.91K **Privately Held**
SIC: 2591 Window blinds

(G-6783)
FULTON COUNTY PROCESSING LTD
7800 State Route 109 (43515-9335)
P.O. Box 67 (43515-0067)
PHONE..............................419 822-9266
James J Vanpoppel, *Managing Member*
▲ **EMP:** 125 **EST:** 2001
SALES (est): 23.11MM
SALES (corp-wide): 230.06MM **Privately Held**
Web: www.fcpltd.com
SIC: 3312 Stainless steel
HQ: Heidtman Steel Products, Inc.
  2401 Front St
  Toledo OH 43605
  419 691-4646

(G-6784)
GB MANUFACTURING COMPANY (PA)
Also Called: Gb
1120 E Main St (43515)
P.O. Box 8 (43515-0008)
PHONE..............................419 822-5323
Nelson U Reyes, *Pr*
Annette Y Petree, *
Michael Pechette, *
Mark Ries, *
▲ **EMP:** 53 **EST:** 2005
SQ FT: 50,000
SALES (est): 43.56MM
SALES (corp-wide): 43.56MM **Privately Held**
Web: www.gbmfg.com
SIC: 3469 Machine parts, stamped or pressed metal

(G-6785)
GLENN HUNTER & ASSOCIATES INC
1222 County Road 6 (43515-9644)
PHONE..............................419 533-0925
▼ **EMP:** 75 **EST:** 1993
SQ FT: 2,500
SALES (est): 24.81MM **Privately Held**
Web: www.glennhunterandassociates.com
SIC: 3559 Recycling machinery

(G-6786)
INDUSTRIAL REPAIR AND MFG
265 Rogers Rd (43515-9478)
PHONE..............................419 822-0314
EMP: 12
Web: www.irmworldwide.com
SIC: 7363 3443 Help supply services; Fabricated plate work (boiler shop)
PA: Industrial Repair And Manufacturing Inc
  1140 E Main St
  Delta OH 43515

(G-6787)
INDUSTRIAL REPAIR AND MFG (PA)
1140 E Main St (43515-9406)
PHONE..............................419 822-4232
TOLL FREE: 877
▲ **EMP:** 42 **EST:** 1995
SQ FT: 48,000
SALES (est): 4.92MM **Privately Held**
Web: www.irmworldwide.com
SIC: 7699 7363 3443 Industrial machinery and equipment repair; Truck driver services ; Containers, shipping (bombs, etc.): metal plate

(G-6788)
MESSER LLC
6744 County Road 10 (43515-9453)
PHONE..............................419 822-3909
EMP: 7
SALES (corp-wide): 1.63B **Privately Held**
Web: www.messeramericas.com
SIC: 2813 Industrial gases
HQ: Messer Llc
  200 Smrst Corp Blvd # 7000
  Bridgewater NJ 08807
  800 755-9377

(G-6789)
NATION TOOL & DIE LTD ✪
5226 County Road 6 (43515-9648)
PHONE..............................419 822-5939
Jerami Nation, *Pr*
Lynette Nation, *CFO*
EMP: 20 **EST:** 2022
SALES (est): 1.24MM **Privately Held**
SIC: 3544 3469 Jigs and fixtures; Metal stampings, nec

(G-6790)
NATION WELDING LLC
5226 County Road 6 (43515-9648)
PHONE..............................419 466-2241
Jerami Nation, *Prin*
EMP: 6 **EST:** 2019
SALES (est): 106.34K **Privately Held**
SIC: 7692 Welding repair

(G-6791)
TWIN POINT INC (PA)
Also Called: Workman Electronics
11955 County Road 10-2 (43515-9748)
PHONE..............................419 923-7525
Jerry Twining, *CEO*
▲ **EMP:** 7 **EST:** 1977
SALES (est): 1.33MM
SALES (corp-wide): 1.33MM **Privately Held**
SIC: 3679 Electronic circuits

(G-6792)
WORKMAN ELECTRONIC PDTS INC
Also Called: Electrical Insulation Company
11955 County Road 10-2 (43515-9748)
PHONE..............................419 923-7525
Jerry Twining, *Pr*
Judy Eyer, *Ch Bd*
James Twining, *Sr VP*
Thomas A Yoder, *Prin*
▲ **EMP:** 6 **EST:** 1936
SQ FT: 24,400
SALES (est): 472.84K
SALES (corp-wide): 1.33MM **Privately Held**
Web: www.workmanelectronics.com
SIC: 3679 Electronic circuits
PA: Twin Point Inc
  11955 County Road 10 2
  Delta OH 43515
  419 923-7525

Dennison
Tuscarawas County

(G-6793)
BLOOMS PRINTING INC
Also Called: Blooming Services
4792 N 4th Street Ext Se (44621-8929)
PHONE..............................740 922-1765
EMP: 12 **EST:** 1990
SALES (est): 447.68K **Privately Held**
Web: www.bloomsprinting.com
SIC: 2752 Commercial printing, lithographic

(G-6794)
CLAPP & HANEY BRAZED TL CO INC
901 Race St (44621-1509)
P.O. Box 105 (44621-0105)
PHONE..............................740 922-3515
Richard Liggett, *Pt*
Tom Benner, *Pt*
EMP: 18 **EST:** 1935
SALES (est): 1.85MM **Privately Held**
Web: www.clappandhaneybrazedtool.com
SIC: 3545 3599 Cutting tools for machine tools; Machine shop, jobbing and repair

(G-6795)
SERVICES ACQUISITION CO LLC
Also Called: Tank Services
4412 Pleasant Valley Rd Se (44621-9038)
P.O. Box 71 (44621-0071)
PHONE..............................330 479-9267
James Milano, *CEO*
EMP: 10 **EST:** 2014
SALES (est): 475.59K **Privately Held**
Web: www.tankservices.com

Dennison - Tuscarawas County (G-6796)   **GEOGRAPHIC SECTION**

SIC: **3731** Tankers, building and repairing

(G-6796)
UTICA EAST OHIO MIDSTREAM LLC
8349 Azalea Rd Sw (44621-9100)
PHONE.................................740 431-4168
EMP: 408 EST: 2012
SALES (est): 1.93MM
SALES (corp-wide): 10.91B **Publicly Held**
SIC: **1382** Oil and gas exploration services
HQ: Utica Gas Services, L.L.C.
   525 Central Park Dr # 1005
   Oklahoma City OK 73105
   877 413-1023

(G-6797)
VALLEY MINING INC
4412 Pleasant Valley Rd Se (44621-9038)
P.O. Box 152 (44683-0152)
PHONE.................................740 922-3942
EMP: 130
SIC: **1221** 1629 Auger mining, bituminous; Land preparation construction

Derwent
Guernsey County

(G-6798)
BI-CON SERVICES INC
Also Called: BSI Group, The
10901 Clay Pike Rd (43733-9900)
P.O. Box 10 (43733-0010)
PHONE.................................740 685-2542
EMP: 400 EST: 1971
SALES (est): 171.41MM **Privately Held**
Web: www.bi-conservices.com
SIC: **1623** 3498 3443 Water, sewer, and utility lines; Fabricated pipe and fittings; Fabricated plate work (boiler shop)

Deshler
Henry County

(G-6799)
CAST METALS INCORPORATED
104 W North St (43516-1164)
P.O. Box 87 (43516-0087)
PHONE.................................419 278-2010
Scott Ferguson, *Pr*
Tom Downer, *Pr*
EMP: 15 EST: 1946
SQ FT: 22,500
SALES (est): 1.38MM **Privately Held**
SIC: **3321** Gray iron castings, nec

(G-6800)
GRAMINEX LLC
2300 County Road C (43516-9756)
PHONE.................................419 278-1023
Justin Ritter, *Manager*
EMP: 15
SALES (corp-wide): 3.31MM **Privately Held**
Web: www.graminex.com
SIC: **2834** 2833 Extracts of botanicals: powdered, pilular, solid, or fluid; Medicinals and botanicals
PA: Graminex, L.L.C.
   95 Midland Rd
   Saginaw MI 48638
   989 797-5502

Dexter City
Noble County

(G-6801)
AMES COMPANIES INC
21460 Ames Ln (45727-9702)
P.O. Box 644 (13849-0644)
PHONE.................................740 783-2535
Jim Basham, *Brnch Mgr*
EMP: 25
SALES (corp-wide): 2.69B **Publicly Held**
Web: www.homebyames.com
SIC: **3423** Garden and farm tools, including shovels
HQ: The Ames Companies Inc
   13485 Veterans Way # 200
   Orlando FL 32827

(G-6802)
B&N COAL INC
38455 Marietta Rt (45727-6500)
P.O. Box 100 (45727-0100)
PHONE.................................740 783-3575
Carl Baker, *Pr*
Roger Osborne, *
Bob Cunningham, *
EMP: 36 EST: 1962
SQ FT: 21,000
SALES (est): 5.44MM **Privately Held**
SIC: **1221** 8711 Strip mining, bituminous; Engineering services

(G-6803)
WARREN DRILLING CO INC
Also Called: Warren Trucking
305 Smithson St (45727-9749)
P.O. Box 103 (45727-0103)
PHONE.................................740 783-2775
Dan R Warren, *Pr*
Randy C Warren, *
Emily Warren, *
Lewis D Warren, *
Paul H Warren, *
EMP: 110 EST: 1939
SALES (est): 12.53MM **Privately Held**
Web: www.warrendrillingandtrucking.com
SIC: **1381** Directional drilling oil and gas wells

Diamond
Portage County

(G-6804)
CEMEX MATERIALS LLC
4200 Universal Dr (44412-9700)
PHONE.................................330 654-2501
Chris Rowland, *Mgr*
EMP: 111
SIC: **3273** Ready-mixed concrete
HQ: Cemex Materials Llc
   1720 Cntrpark Dr E Ste 10
   West Palm Beach FL 33401
   561 833-5555

(G-6805)
DEANGELO INSTRUMENT INC
3200 Mcclintocksburg Rd (44412-9732)
PHONE.................................330 654-9264
Thomas A Clark, *Prin*
EMP: 7 EST: 2001
SALES (est): 207.82K **Privately Held**
SIC: **3599** Machine shop, jobbing and repair

Donnelsville
Clark County

(G-6806)
BEACH MANUFACTURING CO
118 N Hampton Rd (45319-5011)
P.O. Box 129 (45319-0129)
PHONE.................................937 882-6372
Ted Beach, *Pr*
Carrie M Ridenaur, *
Louis Beach, *
EMP: 120 EST: 1943
SQ FT: 20,000
SALES (est): 16.78MM **Privately Held**
Web: www.beachmfgco.com
SIC: **3714** 3231 Motor vehicle parts and accessories; Mirrors, truck and automobile: made from purchased glass

Dover
Tuscarawas County

(G-6807)
ALLIED MACHINE & ENGRG CORP (PA)
120 Deeds Dr (44622-9652)
P.O. Box 36 (44622-0036)
PHONE.................................330 343-4283
Bill Stokey, *CEO*
Michael A Stokey, *
Steve Stokey, *
Gary Kropf, *
Dave Triplett, *
▲ EMP: 219 EST: 1933
SALES (est): 66.08MM
SALES (corp-wide): 66.08MM **Privately Held**
Web: www.alliedmachine.com
SIC: **3545** Machine tool attachments and accessories

(G-6808)
BAERLOCHER USA LLC (DH)
Also Called: Baerlocher
3676 Davis Rd Nw (44622-9771)
PHONE.................................330 364-6000
Ray Buehler, *CEO*
David Keubel, *CFO*
▲ EMP: 10 EST: 1990
SQ FT: 10,000
SALES (est): 26.61MM
SALES (corp-wide): 591.42MM **Privately Held**
Web: www.baerlocher.com
SIC: **2819** Nonmetallic compounds
HQ: Baerlocher Gmbh
   Freisinger Str. 1
   UnterschleiBheim BY 85716
   89143730

(G-6809)
BFC INC (PA)
Also Called: Farmer Smiths Market
1213 E 3rd St (44622-1227)
PHONE.................................330 364-6645
William Barkett, *CEO*
James Barkett, *
Thomas Barkett, *
Ronald Barkett, *
EMP: 36 EST: 1924
SQ FT: 20,000
SALES (est): 3.71MM
SALES (corp-wide): 3.71MM **Privately Held**
Web: www.barkettfruit.com
SIC: **5148** 5143 5144 2099 Vegetables; Dairy products, except dried or canned; Eggs; Salads, fresh or refrigerated

(G-6810)
BREITENBACH WINE CELLARS INC
Also Called: Breitenbach Bed & Breakfast
5934 Old Route 39 Nw (44622-7787)
PHONE.................................330 343-3603
Cynthia Bixler, *Pr*
EMP: 8 EST: 1980
SALES (est): 854.35K **Privately Held**
Web: www.breitenbachwine.com
SIC: **2084** 5812 7011 Wines; Eating places; Bed and breakfast inn

(G-6811)
CHO BEDFORD INC (PA)
2997 Progress St (44622-9639)
PHONE.................................330 343-8896
Jeff Headlee, *Mgr*
Jeff Headlee, *Managing Member*
EMP: 60 EST: 1950
SALES (est): 9.77MM
SALES (corp-wide): 9.77MM **Privately Held**
Web: www.commercialfluidpower.com
SIC: **3492** Fluid power valves and hose fittings

(G-6812)
CHO BEDFORD INC
Commercial Fluid Power
2997 Progress St (44622-9639)
PHONE.................................330 343-8896
Melvin White, *Brnch Mgr*
EMP: 27
SALES (corp-wide): 9.77MM **Privately Held**
Web: www.commercialfluidpower.com
SIC: **3593** Fluid power cylinders, hydraulic or pneumatic
PA: Cho Bedford, Inc.
   2997 Progress St
   Dover OH 44622
   330 343-8896

(G-6813)
COMMERCIAL HONING LLC (DH)
Also Called: Commercial Fluid Power
2997 Progress St (44622-9639)
PHONE.................................330 343-8896
Jeff Headley, *Managing Member*
▲ EMP: 60 EST: 1946
SQ FT: 15,000
SALES (est): 14.08MM
SALES (corp-wide): 299.49MM **Privately Held**
Web: www.commercialfluidpower.com
SIC: **3599** 3471 3317 Machine shop, jobbing and repair; Plating and polishing; Steel pipe and tubes
HQ: National Tube Supply Company
   925 Central Ave
   University Park IL 60484

(G-6814)
DEFLECTO LLC
303 Oxford St Ste A (44622-1977)
PHONE.................................330 602-0840
EMP: 141
SALES (corp-wide): 475.79MM **Privately Held**
Web: www.deflecto.com
SIC: **3089** Plastics hardware and building products
HQ: Deflecto, Llc
   7035 E 86th St
   Indianapolis IN 46250
   317 849-9555

(G-6815)
DIRECT ACTION CO INC
Also Called: Dac
6668 Old Route 39 Nw (44622-7794)

P.O. Box 2205 (44622-1000)
PHONE..................................330 364-3219
EMP: 15 EST: 1997
SALES (est): 4.07MM **Privately Held**
Web: www.feeddac.com
SIC: 5122 2048 Vitamins and minerals; Feed supplements

(G-6816)
DORIS KIMBLE
Also Called: Red Hill Development Company
3596 State Route 39 Nw (44622-7232)
PHONE..................................330 343-1226
Doris Kimble, *Owner*
EMP: 9 EST: 1952
SALES (est): 629.76K **Privately Held**
Web: www.kimblecompanies.com
SIC: 1381 Drilling oil and gas wells

(G-6817)
DOVER CABINET INDUSTRIES INC
1568 State Route 39 Nw (44622-7346)
PHONE..................................330 343-9074
John A Perkowski, *Pr*
Lori Ann Perkowski, *VP*
EMP: 16 EST: 1982
SQ FT: 16,000
SALES (est): 2.19MM **Privately Held**
Web: www.dovercabinet.com
SIC: 2434 Wood kitchen cabinets

(G-6818)
DOVER CHEMICAL CORPORATION (HQ)
3676 Davis Rd Nw (44622-9771)
PHONE..................................330 343-7711
Jack Teat Junior, *Pr*
Chuck Fletcher, *
Darren Schwede, *
Don Stevenson, *
Tom Freeman, *
◆ EMP: 170 EST: 1975
SQ FT: 260,000
SALES (est): 202.07MM
SALES (corp-wide): 2.03B **Privately Held**
Web: www.doverchem.com
SIC: 2819 2869 2899 5169 Industrial inorganic chemicals, nec; Industrial organic chemicals, nec; Chemical preparations, nec; Chemicals and allied products, nec
PA: Icc Industries Inc.
    725 5th Ave
    New York NY 10022
    212 521-1700

(G-6819)
DOVER FABRICATION AND BURN INC (HQ)
2996 Progress St (44622-9639)
PHONE..................................330 339-1057
Robert Sensel, *Pr*
EMP: 7 EST: 2012
SALES (est): 980.98K
SALES (corp-wide): 12.58MM **Privately Held**
Web: www.doverhydraulics.com
SIC: 1799 7692 7353 Welding on site; Welding repair; Oil well drilling equipment, rental or leasing
PA: Dover Hydraulics, Inc.
    2996 Progress St
    Dover OH 44622
    330 364-1617

(G-6820)
DOVER HIGH PRFMCE PLAS INC
Also Called: Dhpp
140 Williams Dr Nw (44622-7662)
PHONE..................................330 343-3477
Mary L Schwab, *Pr*
George Maksim, *

EMP: 36 EST: 1990
SQ FT: 60,000
SALES (est): 9.17MM **Privately Held**
Web: www.dhpp.net
SIC: 3089 Injection molding of plastics

(G-6821)
DOVER MACHINE CO
2208 State Route 516 Nw (44622-7081)
PHONE..................................330 343-4123
Wayne Amistadi, *Pr*
EMP: 13 EST: 1955
SQ FT: 10,000
SALES (est): 239.01K **Privately Held**
Web: www.candbmachine.com
SIC: 3599 7692 3544 Machine shop, jobbing and repair; Welding repair; Special dies, tools, jigs, and fixtures

(G-6822)
DOVER TANK AND PLATE COMPANY
5725 Crown Rd Nw (44622-9649)
P.O. Box 70 (44622-0070)
PHONE..................................330 343-4443
David Lawless, *Pr*
Earl Lawless, *
Joseph Lawless, *
Luke Lawless, *
EMP: 45 EST: 1922
SQ FT: 40,000
SALES (est): 8.41MM **Privately Held**
Web: www.dovertank.com
SIC: 3441 3446 3444 3443 Fabricated structural metal; Architectural metalwork; Sheet metalwork; Fabricated plate work (boiler shop)

(G-6823)
E WARTHER & SONS INC
Also Called: Warther Cutlery
924 N Tuscarawas Ave (44622-2752)
PHONE..................................330 343-7513
Steve Cunningham, *Pr*
Joan Warther, *Sec*
EMP: 15 EST: 1946
SQ FT: 14,000
SALES (est): 1.45MM **Privately Held**
Web: www.warthercutlery.com
SIC: 3421 5947 Table cutlery, except with handles of metal; Gift shop

(G-6824)
FARSIGHT MANAGEMENT INC
6790 Middle Run Rd Nw (44622-7648)
PHONE..................................330 602-8338
Robert A Bennett, *Pr*
EMP: 10 EST: 2000
SALES (est): 847.22K **Privately Held**
Web: www.usefarsight.com
SIC: 1446 Molding sand mining

(G-6825)
GRAPHIC PUBLICATIONS INC
123 W 3rd St (44622-2968)
PHONE..................................330 343-4377
Hunter Bargin, *Prin*
Michael Mast, *
EMP: 8 EST: 2005
SALES (est): 228.27K **Privately Held**
SIC: 2711 Newspapers, publishing and printing

(G-6826)
HANNON COMPANY
Charles Rewinding Division
801 Commercial Pkwy (44622-3152)
P.O. Box 398 (44622-0398)
PHONE..................................330 343-7758
Timothy Welch, *Brnch Mgr*
EMP: 15
SQ FT: 12,200

SALES (corp-wide): 35.51MM **Privately Held**
Web: www.hanco.com
SIC: 7629 5063 7699 7694 Electrical repair shops; Motors, electric; Welding equipment repair; Electric motor repair
PA: The Hannon Company
    1605 Waynesburg Dr Se
    Canton OH 44707
    330 456-4728

(G-6827)
HVAC INC
Also Called: Dover Phila Heating & Cooling
133 W 3rd St (44622-2933)
PHONE..................................330 343-5511
Dana Moser, *Genl Mgr*
David Kinsey, *Pr*
James Moser, *Sec*
EMP: 16 EST: 1981
SQ FT: 10,000
SALES (est): 805.68K **Privately Held**
Web: www.doverphilahvac.com
SIC: 1711 3444 Warm air heating and air conditioning contractor; Sheet metalwork

(G-6828)
INCA PRESSWOOD-PALLETS LTD (PA)
3005 Progress St (44622-9640)
P.O. Box 248 (44622-0248)
PHONE..................................330 343-3361
Wolfgang Ketzer, *Ltd Pt*
Hans Inselkammer, *Ltd Pt*
▲ EMP: 35 EST: 1979
SQ FT: 45,000
SALES (est): 5.99MM
SALES (corp-wide): 5.99MM **Privately Held**
SIC: 2448 Pallets, wood

(G-6829)
J & J TOOL & DIE INC
203 W 4th St (44622-2905)
PHONE..................................330 343-4721
Scott Sherer, *Pr*
Carol Belt, *Sec*
EMP: 7 EST: 1966
SQ FT: 5,000
SALES (est): 604.1K **Privately Held**
Web: www.jjtooldie.com
SIC: 3544 Special dies and tools

(G-6830)
KIMBLE COMPANY (PA)
Also Called: Kimble Clay & Limestone
3596 State Route 39 Nw (44622-7232)
PHONE..................................330 343-1226
EMP: 160 EST: 1952
SALES (est): 78.85MM
SALES (corp-wide): 78.85MM **Privately Held**
Web: www.kimblecompanies.com
SIC: 1221 Bituminous coal and lignite-surface mining

(G-6831)
KRUZ INC
Also Called: Ravens Sales & Service
6332 Columbia Rd Nw (44622-7676)
PHONE..................................330 878-5595
Rufus Hall, *Mgr*
EMP: 30
SALES (corp-wide): 10.93MM **Privately Held**
Web: www.kruzinc.com
SIC: 3713 Dump truck bodies
PA: Kruz Inc.
    1201 W Culver Rd
    Knox IN 46534
    574 772-6673

(G-6832)
LLD GAS & OIL CORP
137 E Iron Ave (44622-2254)
P.O. Box 225 (44622-0225)
PHONE..................................330 364-6331
William Klopfer, *Pr*
EMP: 9 EST: 2005
SALES (est): 167.67K **Privately Held**
SIC: 1389 Pumping of oil and gas wells

(G-6833)
MARLITE INC (DH)
1 Marlite Dr (44622-2361)
PHONE..................................330 343 6621
Daryl Rosser, *Pr*
Greg Triplett, *
Kimberly Mcbride, *CFO*
Mark Jutte, *
Greg Leary, *
◆ EMP: 150 EST: 2004
SQ FT: 450,000
SALES (est): 68.12MM **Privately Held**
Web: www.marlite.com
SIC: 2542 Partitions and fixtures, except wood
HQ: Nudo Products, Inc.
    1500 Taylor Ave
    Springfield IL 62703
    217 528-5636

(G-6834)
MATERIALS PROCESSING INC
120 Deeds Dr (44622-9652)
P.O. Box 36 (44622-0036)
PHONE..................................330 730-5959
EMP: 7 EST: 2017
SALES (est): 156.3K **Privately Held**
SIC: 3089 Injection molding of plastics

(G-6835)
METEOR SEALING SYSTEMS LLC
Also Called: Meteor Automotive
400 S Tuscarawas Ave (44622-2342)
PHONE..................................330 343-9595
Joerg Busse, *VP*
▲ EMP: 155 EST: 1998
SALES (est): 44.93MM
SALES (corp-wide): 355.83K **Privately Held**
Web: www.meteor-sealingsystems.com
SIC: 3069 Tubing, rubber
HQ: Meteor Creative, Inc.
    1414 Commerce Park Dr
    Tipp City OH 45371
    800 273-1535

(G-6836)
MINTEQ INTERNATIONAL INC
5864 Crown Street Ext Nw (44622)
PHONE..................................330 343-8821
Ron Nanni, *Brnch Mgr*
EMP: 31
SQ FT: 150,000
Web: www.mineralstech.com
SIC: 3297 3255 3251 Brick refractories; Clay refractories; Brick and structural clay tile
HQ: Minteq International Inc.
    35 Highland Ave
    Bethlehem PA 18017

(G-6837)
NEXT SALES LLC
3258 Dogwood Ln Nw (44622-6822)
PHONE..................................330 704-4126
Michael R Ludwig, *Prin*
EMP: 12 EST: 2012
SALES (est): 161.57K **Privately Held**
Web: www.nextind.com
SIC: 3275 Acoustical plaster, gypsum

Dover - Tuscarawas County (G-6838) **GEOGRAPHIC SECTION**

(G-6838)
NORRIS MANUFACTURING LLC
317 E Broadway St (44622-1914)
PHONE...................................330 602-5005
EMP: 17 **EST:** 2002
SQ FT: 55,000
SALES (est): 1.4MM **Privately Held**
Web: www.cnorrismanufacturing.com
SIC: 3531 Construction machinery

(G-6839)
PERFORMANCE TANK SALES INC
424 W 3rd St (44622-3169)
EMP: 6 **EST:** 1998
SALES (est): 420.73K **Privately Held**
SIC: 3795 3799 Tanks and tank components; Trailers and trailer equipment

(G-6840)
REAM AND HAAGER LABORATORY INC
179 W Broadway St (44622-1916)
P.O. Box 706 (44622-0706)
PHONE...................................330 343-3711
Tim Levengood, Pr
EMP: 13 **EST:** 1960
SQ FT: 4,300
SALES (est): 1.4MM **Privately Held**
Web: www.rhlab.us
SIC: 8748 8734 0711 1389 Business consulting, nec; Water testing laboratory; Soil testing services; Pipe testing, oil field service

(G-6841)
ROGUE BOWSTRINGS
2140 Gordon Rd Nw (44622-7742)
P.O. Box 26 (44680-0026)
PHONE...................................330 749-9725
EMP: 6 **EST:** 2017
SALES (est): 127.69K **Privately Held**
Web: www.roguebowstrings.com
SIC: 3949 Sporting and athletic goods, nec

(G-6842)
SCHWAB INDUSTRIES INC (HQ)
2301 Progress St (44622-9641)
P.O. Box 400 (44622-0400)
PHONE...................................330 364-4411
Jerry A Schwab, Pr
David A Schwab, VP
Mary Lynn Hites, Treas
Donna Schwab, Sec
EMP: 15 **EST:** 1950
SQ FT: 2,500
SALES (est): 128.44MM
SALES (corp-wide): 32.72B **Privately Held**
SIC: 3273 5031 5032 Ready-mixed concrete; Lumber, plywood, and millwork; Concrete and cinder block
PA: Crh Public Limited Company
Stonemason S Way
Rathfarnham D16 K
14041000

(G-6843)
SMITH CONCRETE CO (PA)
Also Called: Division of Selling Materials
2301 Progress St (44622-9641)
P.O. Box 356 (45750-0356)
PHONE...................................740 373-7441
Mike Murphy, Genl Mgr
EMP: 50 **EST:** 1922
SQ FT: 2,000
SALES (est): 5.07MM
SALES (corp-wide): 5.07MM **Privately Held**
Web: www.shellyco.com

SIC: 3272 3273 1442 Dry mixture concrete; Ready-mixed concrete; Construction sand and gravel

(G-6844)
SNYDER MANUFACTURING INC
3001 Progress St (44622-9640)
P.O. Box 188 (44622-0188)
PHONE...................................330 343-4456
Dennis Snyder, Pr
Goerge Mokodean, *
▲ **EMP:** 60 **EST:** 1985
SQ FT: 50,000
SALES (est): 9.85MM **Privately Held**
Web: www.snyderman.com
SIC: 3083 Laminated plastics plate and sheet

(G-6845)
SUGARCREEK LIME SERVICE
Also Called: M B Trucking
2068 Gordon Rd Nw (44622-7741)
PHONE...................................330 364-4400
Matthew Beachy, Owner
EMP: 8 **EST:** 1979
SALES (est): 465.81K **Privately Held**
SIC: 3274 Lime

(G-6846)
SWISS HERITAGE WINERY
6011 Old Route 39 Nw (44622-7788)
PHONE...................................330 343-4108
EMP: 6 **EST:** 2019
SALES (est): 120.45K **Privately Held**
Web: www.broadruncheese.com
SIC: 2084 Wines

(G-6847)
TCB AUTOMATION LLC
601 W 15th St (44622-9763)
PHONE...................................330 556-6444
Joseph Dalessandro, Managing Member
EMP: 13 **EST:** 2013
SALES (est): 2MM **Privately Held**
Web: www.tcbautomation.com
SIC: 1731 3613 General electrical contractor; Control panels, electric

(G-6848)
TWIN CITIES CONCRETE CO (DH)
141 S Tuscarawas Ave (44622-1951)
PHONE...................................330 343-4491
Jerry Schwab, Pr
David Schwab, VP
Jerry Gwinn, Genl Mgr
Donna Schwab, Sec
Mary Lynn Schwab, Treas
EMP: 17 **EST:** 1949
SQ FT: 1,500
SALES (est): 86.63MM
SALES (corp-wide): 32.72B **Privately Held**
SIC: 3273 5072 Ready-mixed concrete; Builders' hardware, nec
HQ: Schwab Industries, Inc.
2301 Progress St
Dover OH 44622
330 364-4411

(G-6849)
UNION CAMP CORP
875 Harger St (44622-9441)
PHONE...................................330 343-7701
Gary Craig, Dir
▲ **EMP:** 7 **EST:** 2010
SALES (est): 169.67K **Privately Held**
SIC: 2819 Industrial inorganic chemicals, nec

(G-6850)
ZIEGLER TIRE AND SUPPLY CO
Also Called: Ziegler Oil Co
411 Commercial Pkwy (44622-3125)

PHONE...................................330 343-7739
Tom West, Mgr
EMP: 29
SQ FT: 100,000
SALES (corp-wide): 111.76MM **Privately Held**
Web: www.zieglertire.com
SIC: 5531 7534 Automotive tires; Rebuilding and retreading tires
PA: The Ziegler Tire And Supply Company
4150 Millennium Blvd Se
Massillon OH 44646
330 834-3332

(G-6851)
ZIMMER SURGICAL INC
Also Called: Zimmer Orthopaedic Surgical
200 W Ohio Ave (44622-9642)
PHONE...................................800 321-5533
Kenneth R Coonce, VP
James T Crines, *
▲ **EMP:** 300 **EST:** 2002
SALES (est): 101.05MM
SALES (corp-wide): 6.94B **Publicly Held**
Web: www.zimmerbiomet.com
SIC: 3842 Orthopedic appliances
PA: Zimmer Biomet Holdings, Inc.
345 E Main St
Warsaw IN 46580
574 267-6131

Doylestown
Wayne County

(G-6852)
ADAPT OIL
Also Called: Marathon Oil
188 N Portage St (44230-1370)
PHONE...................................330 658-1482
Clark Mowen, Prin
EMP: 6 **EST:** 2003
SALES (est): 122.28K **Privately Held**
Web: www.marathonoil.com
SIC: 1389 Oil and gas field services, nec

(G-6853)
COUNTER CONCEPTS INC
15535 Portage St (44230-1130)
PHONE...................................330 848-4848
EMP: 10 **EST:** 1993
SALES (est): 847.01K **Privately Held**
Web: www.counterconceptsinc.com
SIC: 2541 3083 5211 Counters or counter display cases, wood; Plastics finished products, laminated; Lumber and other building materials

(G-6854)
THE GALEHOUSE COMPANIES INC
Also Called: Galehouse Lumber
12667 Portage St (44230-9735)
P.O. Box 267 (44230-0267)
PHONE...................................330 658-2023
EMP: 30 **EST:** 1968
SALES (est): 10.79MM **Privately Held**
Web: www.galehouse.com
SIC: 5031 5211 1531 1521 Lumber: rough, dressed, and finished; Millwork and lumber; Condominium developers; New construction, single-family houses

Dresden
Muskingum County

(G-6855)
MINING AND RECLAMATION INC
15953 State Route 60 S (43821-9657)
P.O. Box 555 (43821-0555)

PHONE...................................740 327-5555
John Shupert, Pr
EMP: 7 **EST:** 1997
SALES (est): 200.07K **Privately Held**
SIC: 1081 Metal mining services

Dublin
Franklin County

(G-6856)
A GRADE NOTES INC (PA)
6385 Shier Rings Rd Ste 1 (43016-1261)
P.O. Box 4175 (43016-0617)
PHONE...................................614 299-9999
Gary V Stoep, CEO
Gary Vander Stoep, CEO
Kathy Gatton Eshelman, Pr
David Kiess, VP
Rita Wood, Sec
EMP: 8 **EST:** 1987
SQ FT: 1,000
SALES (est): 937.54K
SALES (corp-wide): 937.54K **Privately Held**
Web: www.gradeanotes.com
SIC: 2752 7334 Offset printing; Photocopying and duplicating services

(G-6857)
ADVANCED PRGRM RESOURCES INC (PA)
Also Called: Touchmark
2715 Tuller Pkwy (43017-2310)
PHONE...................................614 761-9994
EMP: 47 **EST:** 1989
SQ FT: 5,100
SALES (est): 3.62MM **Privately Held**
SIC: 7379 7373 8742 7372 Computer related consulting services; Systems integration services; Management consulting services; Application computer software

(G-6858)
ALKON CORPORATION
6750 Crosby Ct (43016-7644)
PHONE...................................614 799-6650
Mark Marino, Brnch Mgr
EMP: 21
SALES (corp-wide): 27.26MM **Privately Held**
Web: www.alkoncorp.com
SIC: 3491 3082 5084 5085 Industrial valves; Unsupported plastics profile shapes; Industrial machinery and equipment; Industrial supplies
PA: Alkon Corporation
728 Graham Dr
Fremont OH 43420
419 355-9111

(G-6859)
AMD SERVICES
6000 Buffalo Head Trl (43017-3598)
PHONE...................................614 571-7190
EMP: 6 **EST:** 2013
SALES (est): 193.65K **Privately Held**
SIC: 7372 Prepackaged software

(G-6860)
AMERICAN RODPUMP LTD
5201 Indian Hill Rd (43017-9708)
PHONE...................................440 987-9457
John Van Krevel, Pr
EMP: 6 **EST:** 2006
SALES (est): 240.88K **Privately Held**
SIC: 1311 Crude petroleum and natural gas

▲ = Import ▼ = Export
◆ = Import/Export

GEOGRAPHIC SECTION
Dublin - Franklin County (G-6883)

(G-6861)
ANDELYN BIOSCIENCES INC
Also Called: Andelyn Development Center
5185 Blazer Pkwy (43017-3308)
PHONE..................................614 332-0554
EMP: 8 **EST:** 1998
SALES (est): 115.47K **Privately Held**
SIC: 2834 Pharmaceutical preparations

(G-6862)
APPALACHIAN FUELS LLC (PA)
6375 Riverside Dr Ste 200 (43017-5045)
PHONE..................................606 928-0460
EMP: 247 **EST:** 2001
SALES (est): 19.87MM
SALES (corp-wide): 19.87MM **Privately Held**
SIC: 1241 Coal mining services

(G-6863)
ASK CHEMICALS LLC
495 Metro Pl S (43017-5331)
PHONE..................................800 848-7485
◆ **EMP:** 305 **EST:** 2010
SQ FT: 3,200
SALES (est): 105.13MM **Privately Held**
Web: www.ask-chemicals.com
SIC: 2899 Chemical preparations, nec
HQ: Ask Chemicals Gmbh
Reisholzstr. 16-18
Hilden NW 40721
211711030

(G-6864)
AUTOMATION AND CTRL TECH INC
Also Called: Act
6141 Avery Rd (43016)
P.O. Box 3667 (43016)
PHONE..................................614 495-1120
Charles Totel, *Pr*
Michael Iaquinta, *
Dave Pond, *
EMP: 26 **EST:** 1998
SQ FT: 21,000
SALES (est): 3.84MM **Privately Held**
Web: www.autocontroltech.com
SIC: 3829 3823 Measuring and controlling devices, nec; Process control instruments

(G-6865)
AVIDYNE
5980 Wilcox Pl Ste I (43016-6809)
PHONE..................................800 284-3963
Paul A Ryan, *Prin*
EMP: 8 **EST:** 2010
SALES (est): 229.3K **Privately Held**
Web: www.avidyne.com
SIC: 3724 Aircraft engines and engine parts

(G-6866)
BAMBERGER POLYMERS INC
9374 Culross Ct (43017-9685)
PHONE..................................614 718-9104
Larry Ubertini, *Pr*
EMP: 13
SALES (corp-wide): 8.01MM **Privately Held**
Web: www.bambergerpolymers.com
SIC: 2821 Plastics materials and resins
HQ: Bamberger Polymers, Inc.
Two Jericho Plaza Ste 109
Jericho NY 11753

(G-6867)
BIOSORTIA PHARMACEUTICALS INC
4266 Tuller Rd (43017-5007)
PHONE..................................614 636-4350
Ross O Youngs, *Pr*
Haiyin He, *
Guy T Carter, *
Michele H Cole, *
EMP: 16 **EST:** 2009
SALES (est): 2.51MM **Privately Held**
Web: www.biosortia.com
SIC: 2834 Pharmaceutical preparations

(G-6868)
BLACK BOX CORPORATION
5400 Frantz Rd Ste 240 (43016-6102)
PHONE..................................800 837-7777
Chris Tjotjos, *Brnch Mgr*
EMP: 8
Web: www.blackbox.com
SIC: 3577 Computer peripheral equipment, nec
HQ: Black Box Corporation
1000 Park Dr
Lawrence PA 15055
724 746-5500

(G-6869)
BOY RAD INC
Also Called: Goodyear
7742 Sawmill Rd (43016-8522)
PHONE..................................614 766-1228
EMP: 10 **EST:** 1989
SALES (est): 992.39K **Privately Held**
Web: www.boyradtire.com
SIC: 5531 7534 Automotive tires; Tire retreading and repair shops

(G-6870)
CAKE LLC
6724 Perimeter Loop Rd Unit 254 (43017-3202)
PHONE..................................614 592-7681
Lesley Blake, *Asst Sec*
EMP: 7 **EST:** 2013
SALES (est): 232.65K **Privately Held**
SIC: 7372 Home entertainment computer software

(G-6871)
CARDINAL HEALTH INC
7200 Cardinal Pl W (43017-1094)
PHONE..................................614 553-3830
EMP: 21
SALES (corp-wide): 205.01B **Publicly Held**
Web: www.cardinalhealth.com
SIC: 5122 5047 8741 3842 Pharmaceuticals; Surgical equipment and supplies; Management services; Surgical appliances and supplies
PA: Cardinal Health, Inc.
7000 Cardinal Pl
Dublin OH 43017
614 757-5000

(G-6872)
CARDINAL HEALTH INC (PA)
Also Called: Cardinalhealth
7000 Cardinal Pl (43017)
PHONE..................................614 757-5000
Jason M Hollar, *CEO*
Gregory B Kenny, *Non-Executive Chairman of the Board*
Aaron E Alt, *
Ola M Snow, *Chief Human Resources Officer*
Jessica L Mayer, *CLO CCO*
◆ **EMP:** 2800 **EST:** 1979
SALES (est): 205.01B
SALES (corp-wide): 205.01B **Publicly Held**
Web: www.cardinalhealth.com
SIC: 5122 5047 8741 3842 Pharmaceuticals; Surgical equipment and supplies; Management services; Surgical appliances and supplies

(G-6873)
CARDINAL HEALTH 414 LLC (HQ)
7000 Cardinal Pl (43017-1091)
PHONE..................................614 757-5000
Jason Hollar, *CEO*
Steve Mason Ceo Medical Segmen t, *Prin*
Debbie Weitzman Ceo Pharmaceut ical Segment, *Prin*
Ben Brinker, *
Brad Cochran, *
▲ **EMP:** 155 **EST:** 1971
SQ FT: 60,967
SALES (est): 1.04B
SALES (corp-wide): 205.01B **Publicly Held**
SIC: 2835 2834 8052 Radioactive diagnostic substances; Pharmaceutical preparations; Home for the mentally retarded, with health care
PA: Cardinal Health, Inc.
7000 Cardinal Pl
Dublin OH 43017
614 757-5000

(G-6874)
CARDINAL HEALTH TECH LLC (HQ)
Also Called: Cardinal Health
7000 Cardinal Pl (43017-1091)
PHONE..................................614 757-5000
EMP: 47 **EST:** 2002
SALES (est): 9.6MM
SALES (corp-wide): 205.01B **Publicly Held**
SIC: 3571 Electronic computers
PA: Cardinal Health, Inc.
7000 Cardinal Pl
Dublin OH 43017
614 757-5000

(G-6875)
COFFMAN MEDIA LLC
5995 Wilcox Pl Ste A (43016-9267)
PHONE..................................614 956-7015
Jason Ault, *COO*
EMP: 12 **EST:** 2010
SALES (est): 1.27MM **Privately Held**
Web: www.coffmanmedia.com
SIC: 3571 Computers, digital, analog or hybrid

(G-6876)
COMMAND ALKON INCORPORATED
6750 Crosby Ct (43016-7644)
PHONE..................................614 799-0600
Randy Willaman, *Brnch Mgr*
EMP: 40
SALES (corp-wide): 86.02MM **Privately Held**
Web: www.commandalkon.com
SIC: 3823 7371 3625 Industrial process measurement equipment; Custom computer programming services; Relays and industrial controls
PA: Command Alkon Incorporated
1800 Intl Pk Dr Ste 400
Birmingham AL 35243
205 879-3282

(G-6877)
COMPUTER WORKSHOP INC (PA)
5200 Upper Metro Pl Ste 140 (43017-5322)
PHONE..................................614 798-9505
Thelma Tippie, *Pr*
Terri Williams, *COO*
EMP: 20 **EST:** 1988
SALES (est): 5.33MM
SALES (corp-wide): 5.33MM **Privately Held**
Web: www.tcworkshop.com

SIC: 8243 7371 2741 Operator training, computer; Custom computer programming services; Miscellaneous publishing

(G-6878)
CRIMSON GATE CONSULTING CO (PA)
6457 Reflections Dr S200 (43017-2352)
PHONE..................................614 805-0897
Brent Dyke, *CEO*
Glenn Foote, *Dir Opers*
Brian Rogers, *Proj Mgr*
EMP: 9 **EST:** 2010
SQ FT: 300
SALES (est): 505.43K
SALES (corp-wide): 505.43K **Privately Held**
SIC: 8742 7372 Business management consultant; Business oriented computer software

(G-6879)
DIOCESAN PUBLICATIONS INC (PA)
6161 Wilcox Rd (43016)
PHONE..................................614 718-9500
Robert Zielke, *Pr*
Donald Zielke, *
EMP: 35 **EST:** 1972
SALES (est): 4.96MM
SALES (corp-wide): 4.96MM **Privately Held**
Web: www.diocesan.com
SIC: 2759 2741 Letterpress printing; Miscellaneous publishing

(G-6880)
DR DAVE SOLUTIONS LLC
Also Called: Software In Reach
6233 Riverside Dr (43017-5034)
PHONE..................................614 219-6543
David Keene, *Pt*
EMP: 6 **EST:** 2012
SALES (est): 140K **Privately Held**
Web: www.softwareinreach.com
SIC: 7372 Application computer software

(G-6881)
DUBLIN EMBROIDERER INC
7215 Sawmill Rd Ste 50 (43016-5013)
PHONE..................................614 789-1898
EMP: 6 **EST:** 2013
SALES (est): 80.07K **Privately Held**
SIC: 2395 Embroidery and art needlework

(G-6882)
DUBLIN MILLWORK CO INC
7575 Fishel Dr S (43016-8821)
PHONE..................................614 889-7776
Wilbur C Strait, *Ch Bd*
Scott Evisol, *Genl Mgr*
EMP: 6 **EST:** 1981
SQ FT: 100,000
SALES (est): 870.83K
SALES (corp-wide): 27.1MM **Privately Held**
Web: www.straitandlamp.com
SIC: 5031 2431 Trim, sheet metal; Millwork
PA: The Strait & Lamp Lumber Company Incorporated
269 National Rd Se
Hebron OH 43025
740 928-4501

(G-6883)
ECI MACOLA/MAX LLC (DH)
5455 Rings Rd Ste 100 (43017)
PHONE..................................978 539-6186
Alex Braverman, *
James A Workman, *
Lisa Wise, *
EMP: 170 **EST:** 1971

Dublin - Franklin County (G-6884)   **GEOGRAPHIC SECTION**

SQ FT: 30,000
SALES (est): 28.12MM **Privately Held**
Web: www.ecisolutions.com
SIC: 7371 7372 5045 2759 Computer software development; Prepackaged software; Computer software; Letterpress printing
HQ: Exact Holding B.V.
    Molengraaffsingel 33
    Delft ZH 2629
    157115000

(G-6884)
G M GRECO INC
6500 Emerald Pkwy Ste 100 (43016-6236)
PHONE..............................614 822-0522
George Greco, *Prin*
EMP: 6 **EST:** 2018
SALES (est): 235.28K **Privately Held**
SIC: 3732 Boatbuilding and repairing

(G-6885)
GCONSENT LLC
Also Called: Gconsent Logistics
5412 Talladega Dr (43016-7857)
PHONE..............................614 886-2416
Unyime Akpan, *CEO*
EMP: 12 **EST:** 2018
SALES (est): 1.04MM **Privately Held**
Web: www.gconsent.com
SIC: 3537 Trucks, tractors, loaders, carriers, and similar equipment

(G-6886)
GLOBAL COAL SALES GROUP LLC
6641 Dublin Center Dr (43017-5077)
P.O. Box 340290 (43234-0290)
PHONE..............................614 221-0101
Steven Read, *Pr*
Wayne M Boich, *Managing Member*
▼ **EMP:** 9 **EST:** 2008
SALES (est): 3.35MM
SALES (corp-wide): 7.47MM **Privately Held**
Web: www.globalcoalsales.com
SIC: 1241 Coal mining services
PA: Global Mining Holding Company, Llc
    41 S High St Ste 3750
    Columbus OH 43215
    614 221-0101

(G-6887)
GRACIE INTERNATIONAL CORP
6314 Olivia Ct (43016-8550)
PHONE..............................717 725-9138
Naomi Nafziger, *Prin*
EMP: 6 **EST:** 2011
SALES (est): 74.44K **Privately Held**
SIC: 2431 Millwork

(G-6888)
GUILD ASSOCIATES INC (PA)
5750 Shier Rings Rd (43016-1234)
PHONE..............................614 798-8215
Henry Berns, *CEO*
Dominic Dinovo, *
Dolores Dinovo, *
▲ **EMP:** 65 **EST:** 1981
SQ FT: 53,000
SALES (est): 24.49MM
SALES (corp-wide): 24.49MM **Privately Held**
Web: www.guildassociates.com
SIC: 3559 8731 Chemical machinery and equipment; Chemical laboratory, except testing

(G-6889)
GUILD ASSOCIATES INC
Also Called: Guild Biosciences
4412 Tuller Rd (43017-5033)

PHONE..............................843 573-0095
Nick Dinovo, *Mgr*
EMP: 7
SALES (corp-wide): 24.49MM **Privately Held**
Web: www.guildbiosciences.com
SIC: 8731 3559 Chemical laboratory, except testing; Chemical machinery and equipment
PA: Guild Associates, Inc.
    5750 Shier Rings Rd
    Dublin OH 43016
    614 798-8215

(G-6890)
HARTCO PRINTING COMPANY (PA)
Also Called: Hartco Products, The
4106 Delancy Park Dr (43016-7246)
PHONE..............................614 761-1292
Carlton W Hartley, *Pr*
Louann Hartley, *VP*
EMP: 8 **EST:** 1955
SQ FT: 9,900
SALES (est): 1.04MM
SALES (corp-wide): 1.04MM **Privately Held**
SIC: 2752 Offset printing

(G-6891)
HBD INDUSTRIES INC (PA)
5200 Upper Metro Pl Ste 110 (43017-5378)
PHONE..............................614 526-7000
◆ **EMP:** 25 **EST:** 1987
SALES (est): 241.4MM
SALES (corp-wide): 241.4MM **Privately Held**
Web: www.hbdindustries.com
SIC: 3052 3621 3566 3812 Rubber hose; Motors and generators; Speed changers (power transmission equipment), except auto; Magnetic field detection apparatus

(G-6892)
HBD/THERMOID INC (HQ)
Also Called: Thermoid
5200 Upper Metro Pl Ste 110 (43017-5378)
PHONE..............................614 526-7000
Randy Lady, *Genl Mgr*
▼ **EMP:** 56 **EST:** 2003
SALES (est): 39.34MM
SALES (corp-wide): 241.4MM **Privately Held**
Web: www.thermoid.com
SIC: 3429 3052 Hardware, nec; Rubber and plastics hose and beltings
PA: Hbd Industries, Inc.
    5200 Upper Metro Pl # 110
    Dublin OH 43017
    614 526-7000

(G-6893)
HIDAKA USA INC
5761 Shier Rings Rd (43016-1233)
PHONE..............................614 889-8611
Yoshihiro Hidaka, *Pr*
Mikihiro Hidaka, *
▲ **EMP:** 40 **EST:** 1989
SQ FT: 90,000
SALES (est): 10.54MM **Privately Held**
Web: www.hidakausainc.com
SIC: 3444 3469 Sheet metalwork; Machine parts, stamped or pressed metal
HQ: Hidaka Seiki Co., Ltd.
    3-28-5, Nishirokugo
    Ota-Ku TKY 144-0

(G-6894)
HUSKY MARKETING AND SUPPLY CO
Also Called: Husky Energy
5550 Blazer Pkwy Ste 200 (43017-3478)
PHONE..............................614 210-2300

Jonathan Mckenzie, *CFO*
EMP: 40 **EST:** 2007
SALES (est): 76.47MM
SALES (corp-wide): 40.39B **Privately Held**
Web: hmsc.huskyenergy.com
SIC: 1321 1382 Natural gasoline production; Oil and gas exploration services
PA: Cenovus Energy Inc
    225 6 Ave Sw
    Calgary AB T2P 1
    403 766-2000

(G-6895)
IMPERIAL STUCCO LLC
P.O. Box 1579 (43017-6579)
PHONE..............................614 787-5888
Jeffrey S Parenteau, *Prin*
EMP: 6 **EST:** 2010
SALES (est): 229.15K **Privately Held**
SIC: 3299 Stucco

(C 6806)
INEOS NEAL LLC
5220 Blazer Pkwy (43017-3494)
PHONE..............................610 790-3333
Ralston Skinner, *Pr*
EMP: 46 **EST:** 2019
SALES (est): 9.77MM
SALES (corp-wide): 2.19B **Publicly Held**
SIC: 2851 2821 2911 Paints and allied products; Plastics materials and resins; Heavy distillates
HQ: Ashland Chemco Inc.
    1979 Atlas St
    Columbus OH 43228
    859 815-3333

(G-6897)
INEOS SOLVENTS SALES US CORP
5220 Blazer Pkwy (43017-3494)
PHONE..............................614 790-3333
Ralston Skinner, *Pr*
EMP: 400 **EST:** 2019
SALES (est): 105.59MM
SALES (corp-wide): 2.19B **Publicly Held**
SIC: 2851 2821 Paints and allied products; Plastics materials and resins
HQ: Ashland Chemco Inc.
    1979 Atlas St
    Columbus OH 43228
    859 815-3333

(G-6898)
INNERDYNE HOLDINGS INC (HQ)
7000 Cardinal Pl (43017-1091)
PHONE..............................614 757-5000
Steve Mason, *CEO*
EMP: 52 **EST:** 1998
SALES (est): 35.49MM
SALES (corp-wide): 205.01B **Publicly Held**
SIC: 3841 Medical instruments and equipment, blood and bone work
PA: Cardinal Health, Inc.
    7000 Cardinal Pl
    Dublin OH 43017
    614 757-5000

(G-6899)
INSIGHTS SCCESS MEDIA TECH LLC
555 Metro Pl N Ste 100 (43017-1389)
PHONE..............................614 602-1754
Manish Bansal, *Managing Member*
EMP: 42 **EST:** 2016
SALES (est): 1.02MM **Privately Held**
Web: www.insightssuccess.com
SIC: 2721 Magazines: publishing and printing

(G-6900)
INTERSTATE GAS SUPPLY LLC (PA)
Also Called: Interstate Gas Supply
6100 Emerald Pkwy (43016-3248)
P.O. Box 9060 (43017-0960)
PHONE..............................877 995-4447
Scott White, *Pr*
Doug Austin, *
Jim Baich, *
Tami Wilson Cfro, *Prin*
EMP: 267 **EST:** 1989
SQ FT: 100,000
SALES (est): 302.94MM **Privately Held**
Web: www.igs.com
SIC: 1311 Natural gas production

(G-6901)
INVENTUS POWER (OHIO) INC (DH)
Also Called: Iccnexergy
5115 Parkcenter Ave Ste 275 (43017)
PHONE..............................614 351-2191
Patrick Trippel, *Pr*
▲ **EMP:** 10 **EST:** 1961
SQ FT: 46,000
SALES (est): 20.66MM
SALES (corp-wide): 1.04B **Privately Held**
SIC: 3692 Primary batteries, dry and wet
HQ: Inventus Power, Inc.
    1200 Internationale Pkwy # 101
    Woodridge IL 60517

(G-6902)
JASSTEK INC
555 Metro Pl N Ste 100 (43017-1389)
PHONE..............................614 808-3600
Sulakshana Singh, *Pr*
EMP: 11 **EST:** 2004
SQ FT: 1,200
SALES (est): 953.03K **Privately Held**
Web: www.jasstek.com
SIC: 7371 7372 7379 8748 Custom computer programming services; Business oriented computer software; Online services technology consultants; Systems engineering consultant, ex. computer or professional

(G-6903)
KASAI NORTH AMERICA INC
655 Metro Pl S Ste 560 (43017-3382)
PHONE..............................614 356-1494
EMP: 33
Web: www.kasai-na.com
SIC: 3089 3714 3429 Injection molded finished plastics products, nec; Motor vehicle parts and accessories; Hardware, nec
HQ: Kasai North America, Inc.
    1225 Garrison Dr
    Murfreesboro TN 37129
    615 546-6040

(G-6904)
KENTROX INC (HQ)
5800 Innovation Dr (43016-3271)
PHONE..............................614 798-2000
Richard S Cremona, *CEO*
Jeffrey S Estuesta, *
Charlie Vogt, *
Michael P Keegan, *
Eric Langille, *
▲ **EMP:** 100 **EST:** 2004
SALES (est): 12.37MM **Publicly Held**
Web: www.westell.com
SIC: 3661 Telephone central office equipment, dial or manual
PA: Westell Technologies, Inc.
    750 N Commons Dr
    Aurora IL 60504

▲ = Import   ▼ = Export   ◆ = Import/Export

GEOGRAPHIC SECTION
Dublin - Franklin County (G-6929)

(G-6905)
KINETICS NOISE CONTROL INC (PA)
Also Called: Hammond Kinetics
6300 Irelan Pl (43016-1278)
P.O. Box 655 (43017-0655)
PHONE..................................614 889-0340
♦ **EMP:** 135 **EST:** 1958
SALES (est): 38.42MM
SALES (corp-wide): 38.42MM **Privately Held**
Web: www.kineticsnoise.com
SIC: 3829 3625 3446 5084 Vibration meters, analyzers, and calibrators; Noise control equipment; Acoustical suspension systems, metal; Industrial machinery and equipment

(G-6906)
LANCASTER COLONY CORPORATION
Also Called: Lancaster Colony Design Group
280 Cramer Creek Ct (43017-2584)
PHONE..................................614 792-9774
EMP: 13
SALES (corp-wide): 1.22B **Publicly Held**
SIC: 2035 Dressings, salad: raw and cooked (except dry mixes)
PA: Lancaster Colony Corporation
380 Polaris Pkwy Ste 400
Westerville OH 43082
614 224-7141

(G-6907)
LSP TECHNOLOGIES INC
6161 Shamrock Ct (43016-1275)
PHONE..................................614 718-3000
Jeff L Dulaney, *Pr*
Mark O'loughlin, *VP*
David Lahrman, *VP*
Beth Mitchell, *Ex Sec*
EMP: 22 **EST:** 1994
SQ FT: 18,000
SALES (est): 7.13MM **Privately Held**
Web: www.lsptechnologies.com
SIC: 3724 Aircraft engines and engine parts

(G-6908)
MATRIX MEATS INC
5164 Blazer Pkwy (43017-1339)
PHONE..................................614 602-1846
Eric Jenkusky, *CEO*
EMP: 11 **EST:** 2019
SALES (est): 979.14K **Privately Held**
Web: www.matrixfood.tech
SIC: 2824 Protein fibers

(G-6909)
MEDINUTRA LLC
8050 Simfield Rd (43016-9062)
PHONE..................................614 292-6848
Robert Disilvestro, *Prin*
EMP: 6 **EST:** 2012
SALES (est): 191.83K **Privately Held**
SIC: 2048 Mineral feed supplements

(G-6910)
MIRUS ADAPTED TECH LLC
Also Called: Adapted Tech
288 Cramer Creek Ct (43017-2584)
PHONE..................................614 402-4585
Stephan Mertik, *Managing Member*
EMP: 20 **EST:** 2015
SALES (est): 1.8MM **Privately Held**
Web: www.adapted.tech
SIC: 1731 7372 Electrical work; Home entertainment computer software

(G-6911)
MIX MARKETING LLC
5675 Kentfield Dr (43016-3247)
PHONE..................................614 791-0489
Stacey Kuzda, *Prin*
EMP: 6 **EST:** 2010
SALES (est): 81.21K **Privately Held**
Web: www.mixmarketing.us
SIC: 3273 Ready-mixed concrete

(G-6912)
MODULAR ASSMBLY INNVATIONS LLC (PA)
600 Stonehenge Pkwy Ste 100 (43017-6026)
PHONE..................................614 389-4860
Billy R Vickers, *Pr*
EMP: 23 **EST:** 2010
SALES (est): 45.05MM
SALES (corp-wide): 45.05MM **Privately Held**
Web: www.modularai.com
SIC: 3559 Automotive related machinery

(G-6913)
NANOFIBER SOLUTIONS LLC
5164 Blazer Pkwy (43017-1339)
PHONE..................................614 319-3075
Ross Kayuha, *CEO*
John Lannutti, *CSO*
EMP: 12 **EST:** 2009
SQ FT: 20,000
SALES (est): 1.05MM **Privately Held**
Web: www.nanofibersolutions.com
SIC: 2835 2834 2821 Diagnostic substances; Liniments; Plasticizer/additive based plastic materials

(G-6914)
NATIONAL GLASS SVC GROUP LLC
Also Called: National Glass Service Group
5500 Frantz Rd Ste 120 (43017-3545)
PHONE..................................614 652-3699
EMP: 10 **EST:** 2008
SALES (est): 913.88K **Privately Held**
Web: www.nationalglassservicegroup.com
SIC: 2671 Paper; coated and laminated packaging

(G-6915)
NAVIDEA BIOPHARMACEUTICALS INC (PA)
Also Called: NAVIDEA
4995 Bradenton Ave Ste 240 (43017-3543)
PHONE..................................614 793-7500
Michael S Rosol, *CMO*
Alexander L Cappello, *Ch Bd*
John K Scott Junior, *V Ch Bd*
Michel Mikhail, *CRO*
Erika L Eves, *VP Fin*
EMP: 6 **EST:** 1983
SQ FT: 5,000
SALES (est): 65.65K
SALES (corp-wide): 65.65K **Publicly Held**
Web: www.navidea.com
SIC: 2834 2835 Pharmaceutical preparations; Diagnostic substances

(G-6916)
NORTH AMERICAN ASSEMBLIES LLC
600 Stonehenge Pkwy (43017-6026)
PHONE..................................843 420-5354
EMP: 27 **EST:** 2004
SALES (est): 4.84MM **Privately Held**
Web: www.modularai.com
SIC: 3011 Tires and inner tubes

(G-6917)
OHIO REFINING COMPANY LLC
5550 Blazer Pkwy Ste 200 (43017-3478)
PHONE..................................614 210-2300
Scott Howard, *Managing Member*
Daniel Syphard, *Sec*
EMP: 560 **EST:** 2008
SALES (est): 4B **Privately Held**
SIC: 2911 Petroleum refining

(G-6918)
ONGUARD SYSTEMS LLC
Also Called: Inneractiv
5992 Trafalgar Ct (43016-8310)
PHONE..................................614 325-0551
Jim Mazotas, *Mgr*
Jay Jayanthan, *CEO*
James Mazotas, *VP*
EMP: 10 **EST:** 2019
SALES (est): 440.67K **Privately Held**
SIC: 7372 Prepackaged software

(G-6919)
OSSID INC
5695 Avery Rd Ste E (43016-7907)
PHONE..................................724 463-3232
Kurt Woodall, *Prin*
EMP: 8 **EST:** 2018
SALES (est): 144.1K **Privately Held**
Web: www.ossid.com
SIC: 3565 Packaging machinery

(G-6920)
PARALLEL TECHNOLOGIES INC
4868 Blazer Pkwy (43017-3302)
PHONE..................................614 798-9700
Joseph Redman, *Pr*
Martin B Jacobs, *
EMP: 80 **EST:** 1984
SQ FT: 8,500
SALES (est): 34.75MM
SALES (corp-wide): 34.75MM **Privately Held**
Web: www.paralleltech.com
SIC: 1623 7372 Telephone and communication line construction; Business oriented computer software
PA: R C I Communications Inc
4868 Blazer Pkwy
Dublin OH 43017
614 798-9700

(G-6921)
PEERLESS-WINSMITH INC
Peerless Winsmith
5200 Upper Metro Pl Ste 110 (43017-5377)
PHONE..................................330 399-3651
Paul Petrich, *Mgr*
EMP: 328
SALES (corp-wide): 241.4MM **Privately Held**
SIC: 3621 Motors and generators
HQ: Peerless-Winsmith, Inc.
5200 Upper Metro Pl # 11
Dublin OH 43017
614 526-7000

(G-6922)
PENTAGON PROTECTION USA LLC
5500 Frantz Rd Ste 120 (43017-3545)
PHONE..................................614 734-7240
Sam Elzein, *Pr*
EMP: 10 **EST:** 2005
SALES (est): 801.51K **Privately Held**
Web: www.pentagonprotectionus.com
SIC: 1793 3699 Glass and glazing work; Security control equipment and systems

(G-6923)
PM POWER PRODUCTS LLC
4393 Tuller Rd Ste A (43017-5106)
PHONE..................................614 652-6509
EMP: 7 **EST:** 2017
SALES (est): 750K **Privately Held**
Web: www.pmpowerproducts.com
SIC: 3669 Communications equipment, nec

(G-6924)
POC HYDRAULIC TECHNOLOGIES LLC
5201 Indian Hill Rd (43017-9708)
PHONE..................................614 761-8555
John Van Krevel, *Prin*
EMP: 8 **EST:** 2018
SALES (est): 227.87K **Privately Held**
Web: www.pochydraulics.com
SIC: 3492 3593 Control valves, aircraft: hydraulic and pneumatic; Fluid power cylinders, hydraulic or pneumatic

(G-6925)
POWER ACQUISITION LLC (HQ)
5025 Bradenton Ave Ste 130 (43017-3506)
PHONE..................................614 228-5000
John B Simmons, *CEO*
J Michael Kirksey, *CFO*
EMP: 55 **EST:** 2016
SALES (est): 598.3MM
SALES (corp-wide): 1.47B **Privately Held**
SIC: 3694 7538 7537 Distributors, motor vehicle engine; Diesel engine repair: automotive; Automotiv e transmission repair shops
PA: Oep Capital Advisors, L.P.
510 Madison Ave Fl 19
New York NY 10022
212 277-1500

(G-6926)
PRECISION METAL PRODUCTS INC
5200 Upper Metro Pl (43017-5377)
PHONE..................................614 526-7000
Thomas Pozda, *CEO*
EMP: 108 **EST:** 2007
SALES (est): 17MM
SALES (corp-wide): 241.4MM **Privately Held**
Web: www.hbdindustries.com
SIC: 3444 Sheet metalwork
PA: Hbd Industries, Inc.
5200 Upper Metro Pl # 110
Dublin OH 43017
614 526-7000

(G-6927)
PRO ONCALL TECHNOLOGIES LLC
Also Called: Digital & Analog Design
4374 Tuller Rd Ste B (43017-5030)
PHONE..................................614 761-1400
David Myers, *Mgr*
EMP: 11
SALES (corp-wide): 24.76MM **Privately Held**
Web: www.prooncall.com
SIC: 5065 3661 Telephone equipment; Telephone and telegraph apparatus
PA: Pro Oncall Technologies, Llc
6902 E Kemper Road
Cincinnati OH 45249
513 489-7660

(G-6928)
PROFESSIONAL PLASTICS CORP
4863 Rays Cir (43016-6069)
PHONE..................................614 336-2498
Mark Casey, *VP Sls*
EMP: 7 **EST:** 2012
SALES (est): 127.24K **Privately Held**
SIC: 3089 Injection molding of plastics

(G-6929)
QUEST SOFTWARE INC
Aeilita Div
6500 Emerald Pkwy Ste 400 (43016-6234)
PHONE..................................614 336-9223
Ratmir Timashev, *Mgr*

Dublin - Franklin County (G-6930)

EMP: 46
SALES (corp-wide): 647.68MM **Privately Held**
Web: www.quest.com
SIC: **7372** Prepackaged software
PA: Quest Software Inc.
20 Enterprise Ste 100
Aliso Viejo CA 92656
949 754-8000

(G-6930)
QUESTLINE INC
5500 Frantz Rd Ste 156 (43017-3548)
PHONE..................614 255-3166
David Reim, CEO
Robert L Hines, *
EMP: 36 EST: 2011
SQ FT: 8,000
SALES (est): 3.65MM **Privately Held**
Web: www.questline.com
SIC: **2741** Business service newsletters: publishing and printing

(G-6931)
ROBERT W JOHNSON INC (PA)
Also Called: Diamond Cellar, The
6280 Sawmill Rd (43017-1470)
PHONE..................614 336-4545
R Andrew Johnson, CEO
Ron Croft, *
EMP: 70 EST: 1946
SQ FT: 23,000
SALES (est): 12.98MM
SALES (corp-wide): 12.98MM **Privately Held**
Web: www.diamondcellar.com
SIC: **5944 3911** Jewelry, precious stones and precious metals; Jewelry, precious metal

(G-6932)
RUSCILLI REAL ESTATE SERVICES
5100 Parkcenter Ave Ste 100 (43017)
PHONE..................614 923-6400
Timothy Kelton, Pr
Timothy D Kelton, Pr
David C Wade, Treas
EMP: 10 EST: 1978
SQ FT: 1,000
SALES (est): 887.9K **Privately Held**
Web: www.ruscillire.com
SIC: **6531 1389** Real estate agent, residential; Roustabout service

(G-6933)
SAINT-GOBAIN PRFMCE PLAS CORP
Also Called: Medex
6250 Shier Rings Rd (43016-1270)
PHONE..................614 889-2220
EMP: 100
SALES (corp-wide): 397.78MM **Privately Held**
Web: plastics.saint-gobain.com
SIC: **2821** Plastics materials and resins
HQ: Saint-Gobain Performance Plastics Corporation
20 Moores Rd
Malvern PA 19355
440 836-6900

(G-6934)
SALIENT SYSTEMS INC
4393 Tuller Rd Ste K (43017-5106)
PHONE..................614 792-5800
Robert Bower, CEO
EMP: 24 EST: 1984
SQ FT: 16,000
SALES (est): 4.58MM
SALES (corp-wide): 497.5MM **Publicly Held**
Web: www.salientsys.com

SIC: **3674 8742** Microprocessors; Business management consultant
HQ: L. B. Foster Rail Technologies, Inc.
415 Holiday Dr Ste 1
Pittsburgh PA 15220
412 928-3400

(G-6935)
SAREPTA THERAPEUTICS
5200 Blazer Pkwy (43017-3309)
PHONE..................614 766-3296
EMP: 14 EST: 2019
SALES (est): 1.86MM **Privately Held**
Web: www.sarepta.com
SIC: **2834** Pharmaceutical preparations

(G-6936)
SERTEK LLC
6399 Shier Rings Rd (43016-3213)
PHONE..................614 504-5828
EMP: 100 EST: 2009
SALES (est): 26.07MM **Privately Held**
Web: www.franke.com
SIC: **3312** Blast furnaces and steel mills
HQ: Franke Coffee Systems Americas Llc
800 Aviation Pkwy
Smyrna TN 37167
615 287-8200

(G-6937)
SMITHS MEDICAL ASD INC
5200 Upper Metro Pl Ste 200 (43017-5379)
P.O. Box 8106 (43016-2106)
PHONE..................800 796-8701
Eller Erock, Mgr
EMP: 23
SALES (corp-wide): 2.26B **Publicly Held**
SIC: **3841** Surgical and medical instruments
HQ: Smiths Medical Asd, Inc.
6000 Nathan Ln N
Plymouth MN 55442
763 383-3000

(G-6938)
SMITHS MEDICAL ASD INC
6250 Shier Rings Rd (43016-1270)
PHONE..................614 889-2220
Heather Wise, Mgr
EMP: 242
SALES (corp-wide): 2.26B **Publicly Held**
SIC: **3841** IV transfusion apparatus
HQ: Smiths Medical Asd, Inc.
6000 Nathan Ln N
Plymouth MN 55442
763 383-3000

(G-6939)
SMITHS MEDICAL NORTH AMERICA
5200 Upper Metro Pl Ste 200 (43017-5377)
PHONE..................614 210-7300
Srini Seshadri, Pr
Rob White, VP
EMP: 8 EST: 2019
SALES (est): 975.58K **Privately Held**
SIC: **3841 5047** Surgical and medical instruments; Medical and hospital equipment

(G-6940)
SMITHS MEDICAL PM INC (PA)
Also Called: BCI International
5200 Upper Metro Pl Ste 200 (43017-5379)
PHONE..................614 210-7300
Jeff Mccaulley, Pr
Walter Orme, Treas
Don Alexander, VP
Mark Sanderson, VP
Jeff Baker, VP
◆ EMP: 10 EST: 1976
SQ FT: 55,600
SALES (est): 23.51MM

SALES (corp-wide): 23.51MM **Privately Held**
SIC: **3841 5047** Diagnostic apparatus, medical; Electro-medical equipment

(G-6941)
SOLEO HEALTH INC
6190 Shamrock Ct Ste 100 (43016-1279)
PHONE..................844 467-8200
EMP: 22
Web: www.soleohealth.com
SIC: **2834 5912** Druggists' preparations (pharmaceuticals); Drug stores and proprietary stores
HQ: Soleo Health Inc.
950 Calcon Hook Rd Ste 19
Sharon Hill PA 19079
888 244-2340

(G-6942)
SOUTHEASTERN EMERGENCY EQP CO
5000 Tuttle Crossing Blvd (43016-1534)
PHONE..................919 556-1890
EMP: 10 EST: 2019
SALES (est): 369.22K **Privately Held**
SIC: **3841** Surgical and medical instruments

(G-6943)
STANLEY INDUSTRIAL & AUTO LLC
Also Called: Mac Tools
5195 Blazer Pkwy (43017-3308)
PHONE..................614 755-7089
Paul North, Mgr
EMP: 150
SALES (corp-wide): 15.78B **Publicly Held**
Web: www.mactools.com
SIC: **3469 3423 5251 2542** Boxes: tool, lunch, mail, etc.: stamped metal; Hand and edge tools, nec; Tools; Partitions and fixtures, except wood
HQ: Stanley Industrial & Automotive, Llc
5195 Blazer Pkwy
Dublin OH 43017
614 755-7000

(G-6944)
STANLEY INDUSTRIAL & AUTO LLC (HQ)
Also Called: Mac Tools
5195 Blazer Pkwy (43017-3308)
PHONE..................614 755-7000
James Ritter, *
Craig Douglas, *
Bruce Beatt, *
▲ EMP: 72 EST: 2013
SALES (est): 345.09MM
SALES (corp-wide): 15.78B **Publicly Held**
Web: www.mactools.com
SIC: **3546 5251 3423 3452** Power-driven handtools; Tools; Hand and edge tools, nec; Bolts, nuts, rivets, and washers
PA: Stanley Black & Decker, Inc.
1000 Stanley Dr
New Britain CT 06053
860 225-5111

(G-6945)
STANLEY STEEMER INTL INC (PA)
Also Called: Stanley Steemer Carpet Cleaner
5800 Innovation Dr (43016-3271)
P.O. Box 8004 (43016-2004)
PHONE..................614 764-2007
Wesley C Bates, CEO
Justin Bates, *
Eric Smith, *
Philip P Ryser, *
Mark Bunner C.p.a., VP
▲ EMP: 250 EST: 1947
SQ FT: 55,000
SALES (est): 263.72MM

SALES (corp-wide): 263.72MM **Privately Held**
Web: www.stanleysteemer.com
SIC: **7217 3635 6794 5713** Carpet and furniture cleaning on location; Household vacuum cleaners; Franchises, selling or licensing; Carpets

(G-6946)
STARRETT COMMUNICATIONS INC
7437 Christie Chapel Rd (43017-2416)
PHONE..................614 798-0606
Joe Starrett, Prin
EMP: 7 EST: 2009
SALES (est): 110K **Privately Held**
SIC: **3545** Machine tool accessories

(G-6947)
STERLING COMMERCE LLC
4600 Lakehurst Ct (43016-2248)
PHONE..................614 798-2192
EMP: 2500
SIC: **7372** Business oriented computer software

(G-6948)
SUBARU OF A
565 Metro Pl S Ste 150 (43017-7312)
PHONE..................614 793-2358
EMP: 6 EST: 2017
SALES (est): 197.72K **Privately Held**
Web: www.subaru.com
SIC: **5511 5012 3711** Automobiles, new and used; Automobile auction; Motor vehicles and car bodies

(G-6949)
SUTPHEN CORPORATION (PA)
Also Called: Sutphen
6450 Eiterman Rd (43016-8711)
P.O. Box 158 (43002-0158)
PHONE..................800 726-7030
Drew Sutphen, *
Thomas C Sutphen, *
Julie S Phelps, *
Robert M Sutphen, Stockholder*
Greg Mallon, *
▼ EMP: 180 EST: 1962
SQ FT: 90,000
SALES (est): 173.19MM
SALES (corp-wide): 173.19MM **Privately Held**
Web: www.sutphen.com
SIC: **3711 5087** Fire department vehicles (motor vehicles), assembly of; Firefighting equipment

(G-6950)
SYNSEI MEDICAL
6474 Weston Cir W (43016-7724)
PHONE..................609 759-1101
Dipanjan Nag, Pt
EMP: 7 EST: 2013
SALES (est): 143.31K **Privately Held**
SIC: **3845** Electrocardiographs

(G-6951)
TERRADYN CORPORATION
6457 Reflections Dr Ste 200 (43017-2352)
PHONE..................614 805-0897
Robert Shane Jones, CFO
EMP: 15 EST: 2019
SALES (est): 561.15K **Privately Held**
SIC: **1241** Coal mining services

(G-6952)
THA PRESIDENTIAL SUITE LLC
2957 Christopher John Dr Unit 308 (43017-2917)
PHONE..................216 338-7287

EMP: 7 EST: 2019
SALES (est): 293.04K **Privately Held**
SIC: 5999 2253 8742 Miscellaneous retail stores, nec; Lounge, bed, and leisurewear; Business management consultant

(G-6953)
TOUCH BIONICS INC (DH)
6640 Riverside Dr (43017-9531)
PHONE..................................800 233-6263
Ian Stevens, CEO
Melissa Peloquin, Sec
Jill Mcgregor, CFO
EMP: 7 EST: 2007
SQ FT: 6,200
SALES (est): 3.84MM
SALES (corp-wide): 718.65MM **Privately Held**
SIC: 3842 Prosthetic appliances
HQ: Ossur Europe B.V.
De Schakel 70
Eindhoven NB
499462840

(G-6954)
TRU COMFORT MATTRESS
8994 Mediterra Pl (43016-6098)
PHONE..................................614 595-8600
EMP: 6 EST: 2012
SALES (est): 123.33K **Privately Held**
SIC: 2515 Mattresses and foundations

(G-6955)
UNITED TRADE PRINTERS LLC
94 N High St Ste 290 (43017-1110)
PHONE..................................614 326-4829
▼ EMP: 20
SQ FT: 6,000
SALES (est): 5MM **Privately Held**
SIC: 2752 Commercial printing, lithographic

(G-6956)
UNIVAR SOLUTIONS USA LLC
6000 Parkwood Pl (43016-1213)
PHONE..................................800 531-7106
Dale Leachman, Brnch Mgr
EMP: 17
SALES (corp-wide): 11.48B **Privately Held**
Web: www.univarsolutions.com
SIC: 5169 5162 2821 Industrial chemicals; Plastics materials and basic shapes; Plastics materials and resins
HQ: Univar Solutions Usa Llc
3075 Hghland Pkwy Ste 200
Downers Grove IL 60515
331 777-6000

(G-6957)
VICTORY POSTCARDS INC
Also Called: Victory Postcards & Souvenirs
6129 Balmoral Dr (43017-8528)
PHONE..................................614 764-8975
Scott Armstrong, Pr
Kimberly Armstrong, VP
EMP: 6 EST: 1989
SALES (est): 501.3K **Privately Held**
Web: www.victorypostcards.com
SIC: 2759 5099 Post cards, picture: printing, nsk; Souvenirs

(G-6958)
W W WILLIAMS COMPANY LLC (DH)
400 Metro Pl N (43017-3577)
PHONE..................................614 228-5000
John Simmons, CEO
Andy Gasser, *
EMP: 60 EST: 2016
SALES (est): 522.02MM
SALES (corp-wide): 1.47B **Privately Held**
Web: www.wwwilliams.com

SIC: 3694 7538 7537 Distributors, motor vehicle engine; Diesel engine repair: automotive; Automotive transmission repair shops
HQ: Power Acquisition Llc
5025 Bradenton Ave # 130
Dublin OH 43017
614 228-5000

(G-6959)
WONDER-SHIRTS INC
7695 Crawley Dr (43017-8820)
PHONE..................................917 679-2336
Matthew Mohr, Pr
EMP: 6 EST: 2002
SALES (est): 374.43K **Privately Held**
Web: www.wonder-shirts.com
SIC: 2253 2211 T-shirts and tops, knit; Apparel and outerwear fabrics, cotton

(G-6960)
ZILLA
6728 Liggett Rd Ste 110 (43016-8306)
PHONE..................................614 763-5311
EMP: 8 EST: 2018
SALES (est): 938.7K **Privately Held**
Web: www.zillaexhibits.com
SIC: 3993 Signs and advertising specialties

Dunbridge
Wood County

(G-6961)
BLAKO INDUSTRIES INC
10850 Middleton Pike (43414-8004)
PHONE..................................419 246-6172
Ed Long, Pr
Charles Hansen, *
Paul J Leahy, *
EMP: 38 EST: 1970
SQ FT: 21,000
SALES (est): 571.05K **Privately Held**
Web: www.blako.com
SIC: 3081 Polyethylene film

Dundee
Tuscarawas County

(G-6962)
ALPINE CABINETS
7932 Township Road 662 (44624-9602)
PHONE..................................330 359-5724
EMP: 10 EST: 1995
SALES (est): 332.13K **Privately Held**
Web: www.alpinecabinets.com
SIC: 2434 Wood kitchen cabinets

(G-6963)
ALPINE DAIRY LLC
1658 Township Road 660 (44624-9601)
P.O. Box 209 (44690-0209)
PHONE..................................330 359-6291
Jon Solivan, Managing Member
EMP: 46 EST: 2012
SALES (est): 4.81MM **Privately Held**
SIC: 2022 Processed cheese

(G-6964)
CREATED HARDWOOD LTD
8454 State Route 93 Nw (44624-8722)
PHONE..................................330 556-1825
EMP: 8 EST: 2017
SALES (est): 487.5K **Privately Held**
Web: www.createdhardwood.com
SIC: 2426 Carvings, furniture: wood

(G-6965)
GALION-GODWIN TRUCK BDY CO LLC
Also Called: Galion Dump Bodies
7415 Township Road 666 (44624-9272)
PHONE..................................330 359-5495
▲ EMP: 10 EST: 2003
SALES (est): 3.44MM **Privately Held**
Web: www.galiongodwin.com
SIC: 3713 3711 5531 3441 Truck bodies (motor vehicles); Motor vehicles and car bodies; Truck equipment and parts; Fabricated structural metal

(G-6966)
L AND J WOODWORKING
9035 Senff Rd (44624-9414)
PHONE..................................330 359-3216
Ray Yoder Junior, Owner
EMP: 14 EST: 2003
SALES (est): 1.2MM **Privately Held**
SIC: 2431 Millwork

(G-6967)
MILLWOOD INC
Also Called: Millwood Pallet Co
18279 Dover Rd (44624-9425)
PHONE..................................330 359-5220
Jim Caughey, Mgr
EMP: 65
Web: www.millwoodinc.com
SIC: 2448 Pallets, wood
PA: Millwood, Inc.
3708 International Blvd
Vienna OH 44473

(G-6968)
MILLWOOD WHOLESALE INC
7969 Township Road 662 (44624-9602)
PHONE..................................330 359-6109
EMP: 10 EST: 2005
SALES (est): 765.47K **Privately Held**
Web: www.millwoodqualityfurniture.com
SIC: 1751 2431 2511 5021 Carpentry work; Millwork; Kitchen and dining room furniture; Chairs

(G-6969)
TRAIL CABINET
2270 Township Road 415 (44624-9654)
PHONE..................................330 893-3791
Robert Miller, Prin
EMP: 6 EST: 2008
SALES (est): 289.25K **Privately Held**
SIC: 2434 Wood kitchen cabinets

(G-6970)
TRAILWAY II
2261 County Road 168 (44624-9276)
PHONE..................................330 893-9195
Johanas Miller, Pr
EMP: 9 EST: 2013
SALES (est): 200.86K **Privately Held**
SIC: 2531 Chairs, table and arm

(G-6971)
TROYERS TRAIL BOLOGNA INC
6552 State Route 515 (44624-9226)
PHONE..................................330 893-2414
Dale Troyer, Pr
Greg Troyer, Pr
Kenneth Troyer, Sec
Darrin Troyer, VP
Kevin Troyer, VP
EMP: 12 EST: 1925
SQ FT: 1,050
SALES (est): 979.21K **Privately Held**
Web: www.troyerstrail.com

SIC: 2011 5411 Cured meats, from meat slaughtered on site; Grocery stores, independent

(G-6972)
WALNUT CREEK LUMBER CO LTD
10433 Pleasant Hill Rd Nw (44624)
P.O. Box 38 (44687)
PHONE..................................330 852-4559
Dennis A Raber, Pr
EMP: 10 EST: 1982
SQ FT: 864
SALES (est): 932.3K **Privately Held**
Web: www.walnutcreeklumber.com
SIC: 5031 2421 Lumber: rough, dressed, and finished; Custom sawmill

(G-6973)
WENGERD WOOD INC
1760 County Road 200 (44624-9694)
PHONE..................................330 359-4300
Wayne Wengerd, Pr
Dean Wengerd, Sec
Weyne Wengerd, Pr
EMP: 17 EST: 1998
SALES (est): 1.3MM **Privately Held**
Web: www.wengerdwood.com
SIC: 2431 Millwork

(G-6974)
WINESBURG HARDWOOD LBR CO LLC
2871 Us Route 62 (44624-9236)
PHONE..................................330 893-2705
Robert Coblentz, Pt
Owen Coblentz, Pt
Levi Coblentz, Pt
EMP: 18 EST: 1975
SQ FT: 4,000
SALES (est): 491.26K **Privately Held**
SIC: 2448 Pallets, wood

(G-6975)
YUTZY WOODWORKING LTD
2441 Us Route 62 (44624)
PHONE..................................330 359-6166
Dennis Yutzy, Owner
▲ EMP: 42 EST: 1999
SALES (est): 2.49MM **Privately Held**
Web: www.urbancollectionsohiousa.com
SIC: 2431 Millwork

Dunkirk
Hardin County

(G-6976)
NORTH COAST CUSTOM MOLDING INC
211 W Geneva St (45836-1008)
PHONE..................................419 905-6447
Jim Braeunig, Pr
Jane Miller, VP
Chad Erick Miller, VP
EMP: 15 EST: 1988
SQ FT: 9,700
SALES (est): 2.03MM **Privately Held**
Web: www.nccmolding.com
SIC: 3089 Molding primary plastics

East Canton
Stark County

(G-6977)
ABC TECHNOLOGIES DLHB INC
336 Wood St S (44730-1348)
P.O. Box 6030 (44706-0030)
PHONE..................................330 488-0716

East Canton - Stark County (G-6978)   GEOGRAPHIC SECTION

EMP: 31
SALES (corp-wide): 32.64B **Publicly Held**
Web: www.dlhbowles.com
SIC: 3089 3082 Injection molding of plastics; Tubes, unsupported plastics
HQ: Abc Technologies Dlhb, Inc
2422 Leo Ave Sw
Canton OH 44706
330 478-2503

(G-6978)
BARBCO INC
Also Called: Barbco
315 Pekin Dr Se (44730-9462)
P.O. Box 30189 (44730-0189)
PHONE.................................330 488-9400
Anthony R Barbera, *Prin*
Tony Barbera, *
David Barbera, *
John F Boggins, *
Richard C Kettler, *
▲ **EMP:** 46 **EST:** 1989
SQ FT: 15,000
SALES (est): 12.24MM **Privately Held**
Web: www.barbco.com
SIC: 3531 3541 Tunneling machinery; Drilling and boring machines

(G-6979)
KNIGHT MATERIAL TECH LLC (PA)
5385 Orchardview Dr Se (44730-9568)
P.O. Box 30070 (44730-0070)
PHONE.................................330 488-1651
Kevin Brooks, *Pr*
◆ **EMP:** 72 **EST:** 2001
SALES (est): 30.8MM
SALES (corp-wide): 30.8MM **Privately Held**
Web: www.knightmaterials.com
SIC: 2911 5172 5169 4922 Petroleum refining; Petroleum products, nec; Chemicals and allied products, nec; Natural gas transmission

(G-6980)
RECON SYSTEMS LLC
330 Wood St S (44730-1348)
P.O. Box 30100 (44730-0100)
PHONE.................................330 488-0368
Brandon Ballos, *Managing Member*
EMP: 6 **EST:** 2004
SALES (est): 700.15K **Privately Held**
Web: www.reconsystems.com
SIC: 3565 Packaging machinery

(G-6981)
RESCO PRODUCTS INC
6878 Osnaburg St Se (44730-9529)
P.O. Box 30169 (44730-0169)
PHONE.................................330 488-1226
Kurt Bletzacker, *Mgr*
EMP: 9
SQ FT: 1,500
SALES (corp-wide): 111.18MM **Privately Held**
Web: www.rescoproducts.com
SIC: 3255 Clay refractories
PA: Resco Products, Inc.
1 Robinson Plz Ste 300
Pittsburgh PA 15205
412 494-4191

(G-6982)
WORTHIGNTON PRODUCTS INC
1520 Wood Ave Se (44730-9591)
PHONE.................................330 452-7400
Paul Meeks, *Pr*
Jeffrey S Sanger, *VP*
▲ **EMP:** 6 **EST:** 2003
SALES (est): 677.5K **Privately Held**
Web: www.tuffboom.com

SIC: 3443 3429 3089 Buoys, metal; Marine hardware; Buoys and floats, plastics

East Cleveland
Cuyahoga County

(G-6983)
SAVANT TECHNOLOGIES LLC
Also Called: GE Lighting, A Savant Company
1975 Noble Rd (44112-1719)
PHONE.................................800 435-4448
Kathy Sterio, *Managing Member*
Royal Simmons, *
EMP: 927 **EST:** 1890
SALES (est): 112.44MM
SALES (corp-wide): 399.47MM **Privately Held**
Web: www.gelighting.com
SIC: 3641 Electric lamps
PA: Savant Systems, Inc.
45 Perseverance Way
Hyannis MA 02601
508 683-2500

East Liberty
Logan County

(G-6984)
C & F FABRICATIONS INC
3100 State St (43319-9453)
P.O. Box 258 (43319-0258)
PHONE.................................937 666-3234
William D Mercer, *CEO*
Betty J Mercer, *Pr*
Karen Lyon, *Contrlr*
W Douglas Mercer, *Treas*
EMP: 23 **EST:** 1959
SQ FT: 26,000
SALES (est): 904.85K **Privately Held**
Web: www.cffabcorp.com
SIC: 3496 Miscellaneous fabricated wire products

(G-6985)
CHEMTREAT
11000 State Route 347 (43319-9470)
PHONE.................................937 644-2525
Jack Juchcinski, *Pr*
EMP: 15 **EST:** 2017
SALES (est): 525.28K **Privately Held**
Web: www.chemtreat.com
SIC: 3589 Water treatment equipment, industrial

(G-6986)
GREAT LAKES ASSEMBLIES LLC
11590 Township Road 298 (43319-9487)
PHONE.................................937 645-3900
Billy R Vickers, *Pr*
EMP: 70 **EST:** 2004
SQ FT: 90,000
SALES (est): 9.55MM
SALES (corp-wide): 45.05MM **Privately Held**
Web: www.modularai.com
SIC: 3711 Automobile assembly, including specialty automobiles
PA: Modular Assembly Innovations Llc
600 Stonehenge Pkwy # 100
Dublin OH 43017
614 389-4860

(G-6987)
HARDING MACHINE ACQUISITION CO
Also Called: Global Precision Parts
13060 State Route 287 (43319-9489)
P.O. Box 752 (45891-0752)

PHONE.................................937 666-3031
Todd Kriegel, *
Dave Kriegel, *
Susan Mosier, *
EMP: 75 **EST:** 2006
SALES (est): 10MM **Privately Held**
Web: www.globalprecisionpartsinc.com
SIC: 3599 Machine shop, jobbing and repair

East Liverpool
Columbiana County

(G-6988)
C A JOSEPH CO (PA)
13712 Old Fredericktown Rd (43920-9531)
PHONE.................................330 385-6869
Charles Chuck Joseph, *Pr*
Mike Joseph, *VP*
Chris Joseph, *VP*
▲ **EMP:** 8 **EST:** 1974
SQ FT: 200,000
SALES (est): 4.51MM
SALES (corp-wide): 4.51MM **Privately Held**
Web: www.cajoseph.com
SIC: 3089 3599 Plastics processing; Machine shop, jobbing and repair

(G-6989)
CAMPBELL SIGNS & APPAREL LLC
47366 Y And O Rd (43920-8747)
PHONE.................................330 386-4768
EMP: 11 **EST:** 1989
SQ FT: 9,600
SALES (est): 921.9K **Privately Held**
Web: www.campbellsa.com
SIC: 3993 2759 2395 Signs, not made in custom sign painting shops; Screen printing; Embroidery and art needlework

(G-6990)
CF INDUSTRIES INC
425 River Rd (43920-3451)
PHONE.................................330 385-5424
Joe Palyan, *Brnch Mgr*
EMP: 128
Web: www.cfindustries.com
SIC: 2873 Anhydrous ammonia
HQ: Cf Industries, Inc.
2375 Waterview Dr
Northbrook IL 60062
847 405-2400

(G-6991)
COMMERCIAL DECAL OHIO INC
46686 Y And O Rd (43920-9710)
P.O. Box 2747 (43920-0747)
PHONE.................................330 385-7178
David Dunn, *Pr*
EMP: 14 **EST:** 1939
SQ FT: 11,000
SALES (est): 494.98K **Privately Held**
SIC: 2759 Decals: printing, nsk

(G-6992)
CUSTOM CRANKSHAFT INC
1730 Annesley Rd (43920-9410)
PHONE.................................330 382-1200
Scott Watson, *Pr*
EMP: 7 **EST:** 2003
SALES (est): 767.37K **Privately Held**
Web: www.customcrankshaft.net
SIC: 3599 Crankshafts and camshafts, machining

(G-6993)
DECARIA BROTHERS INC
104 E 5th St (43920-3031)
PHONE.................................330 385-0825

Erin Mccart, *Prin*
EMP: 6
SALES (corp-wide): 1.2MM **Privately Held**
Web: www.portersrx.com
SIC: 2836 Vaccines and other immunizing products
PA: Decaria Brothers, Inc.
4201 Sunset Blvd
Steubenville OH 43952
740 264-1669

(G-6994)
DELTA MANUFACTURING INC
Also Called: Twister Displays
49207 Calcutta Smithferry Rd (43920-9570)
P.O. Box 2704 (43920-0704)
PHONE.................................330 386-1270
Harry Smith, *Pr*
Jeff Smith, *VP*
EMP: 15 **EST:** 1972
SQ FT: 800,000
SALES (est): 2.22MM **Privately Held**
SIC: 3599 Amusement park equipment

(G-6995)
JOSEPH G PAPPAS
Also Called: J Pappas
3197 Forest Hills Dr (43920-1167)
PHONE.................................330 383-2917
Joseph G Pappas, *Prin*
EMP: 8 **EST:** 2011
SALES (est): 480.42K **Privately Held**
SIC: 1389 7389 Oil and gas field services, nec; Business Activities at Non-Commercial Site

(G-6996)
KENTAK PRODUCTS COMPANY
1308 Railroad St (43920-3430)
PHONE.................................330 386-3700
Doug Gomoll, *Pr*
EMP: 60
SALES (corp-wide): 14.46MM **Privately Held**
Web: www.kentak.com
SIC: 3082 3052 Tubes, unsupported plastics; Plastic hose
PA: Kentak Products Company
1230 Railroad St Ste 1
East Liverpool OH 43920
330 382-2000

(G-6997)
KENTAK PRODUCTS COMPANY (PA)
1230 Railroad St Ste 1 (43920-3406)
PHONE.................................330 382-2000
Douglas A Gomoll, *Pr*
Otto H Gomoll Junior, *Ch Bd*
William Mays, *
▲ **EMP:** 45 **EST:** 1969
SQ FT: 50,000
SALES (est): 14.46MM
SALES (corp-wide): 14.46MM **Privately Held**
Web: www.kentak.com
SIC: 3082 3052 Tubes, unsupported plastics; Plastic hose

(G-6998)
MASON COLOR WORKS INC
250 E 2nd St (43920-3110)
P.O. Box 76 (43920-5076)
PHONE.................................330 385-4400
▲ **EMP:** 16 **EST:** 1902
SALES (est): 2.16MM **Privately Held**
Web: www.masoncolor.com
SIC: 2816 Inorganic pigments

▲ = Import ▼ = Export
◆ = Import/Export

GEOGRAPHIC SECTION

(G-6999)
SH BELL COMPANY
2217 Michigan Ave (43920-3637)
PHONE............................412 963-9910
Rusty Davis, *Mgr*
EMP: 39
SALES (corp-wide): 20.28MM **Privately Held**
Web: www.shbellco.com
SIC: 3479 4226 4225 Aluminum coating of metal products; Special warehousing and storage, nec; General warehousing and storage
PA: S.H. Bell Company
644 Alpha Dr
Pittsburgh PA 15238
412 963-9910

(G-7000)
SMITH & THOMPSON ENTPS LLC
Also Called: Smith and Thompson Enterprise
46368 Y And O Rd (43920-3869)
PHONE............................330 386-9345
Diana Smith, *Managing Member*
Frank C Smith, *Owner*
EMP: 17 **EST:** 1972
SALES (est): 833.88K **Privately Held**
SIC: 0783 4959 0782 2951 Planting, pruning, and trimming services; Snowplowing; Lawn and garden services; Asphalt paving mixtures and blocks

(G-7001)
THE CHINA HALL COMPANY
Also Called: Hall Closet
1 Anna St (43920-3675)
P.O. Box 989 (43920-5989)
PHONE............................330 385-2900
◆ **EMP:** 120 **EST:** 1903
SALES (est): 14.94MM
SALES (corp-wide): 72.46MM **Privately Held**
Web: www.hallchina.com
SIC: 3262 China cookware
PA: The Fiesta Tableware Company
672 Fiesta Dr
Newell WV 26050
304 387-1300

(G-7002)
W C BUNTING CO INC
Also Called: Advertising Specialty Co
1425 Globe St (43920-2110)
PHONE............................330 385-2050
D Terrence O'hara, *Pr*
Tim O'hara, *VP*
EMP: 11 **EST:** 1880
SQ FT: 23,200
SALES (est): 311.99K **Privately Held**
Web: www.eastliverpoolchina.com
SIC: 3269 3993 Decalcomania work on china and glass; Advertising novelties

East Palestine
Columbiana County

(G-7003)
CARDINAL WELDING INC
895 E Taggart St (44413-2465)
P.O. Box 405 (44413-0405)
PHONE............................330 426-2404
Daniel Shofstahl, *Pr*
EMP: 6 **EST:** 1999
SQ FT: 25,000
SALES (est): 796.36K **Privately Held**
Web: www.cardinalwelding.com
SIC: 7692 3411 Welding repair; Metal cans

(G-7004)
E R ADVANCED CERAMICS INC
Also Called: US Group
600 E Clark St (44413-2430)
P.O. Box 270 (44413-0270)
PHONE............................330 426-9433
John Hayday, *Pr*
David A Early, *
Michael Dematteo, *
◆ **EMP:** 34 **EST:** 1990
SQ FT: 68,274
SALES (est): 4.21MM **Privately Held**
Web: www.usstoneware.com
SIC: 3531 3269 3547 3821 Construction machinery; Grinding media, pottery; Rolling mill machinery; Particle size reduction apparatus, laboratory

(G-7005)
EAST PALESTINE CHINA DCTG LLC
870 W Main St (44413-1328)
P.O. Box 109 (44413-0109)
PHONE............................330 426-9600
▲ **EMP:** 10 **EST:** 2006
SALES (est): 895.34K **Privately Held**
Web: www.eastpalestinechamber.com
SIC: 3231 Decorated glassware: chipped, engraved, etched, etc.

(G-7006)
LIQUID LUGGERS LLC
183 Edgeworth Ave (44413-1554)
PHONE............................330 426-2538
Lynn Neely, *Prin*
EMP: 50 **EST:** 2011
SALES (est): 4.79MM **Privately Held**
Web: www.liquidluggers.com
SIC: 3443 Tanks for tank trucks, metal plate

(G-7007)
RBS MANUFACTURING INC
145 E Martin St (44413-2337)
P.O. Box 430 (44413-0430)
PHONE............................330 426-9486
Dennis Garrett, *Prin*
George P Garrett, *
Rosemarie Garrett, *
EMP: 26 **EST:** 1977
SALES (est): 2.42MM **Privately Held**
Web: www.medartglobal.com
SIC: 3999 Dock equipment and supplies, industrial

(G-7008)
ROBERT MAYO INDUSTRIES
Also Called: Mayo, R A Industries
157 E Martin St (44413-2315)
PHONE............................330 426-2587
Robert A Mayo, *Owner*
EMP: 6 **EST:** 1963
SQ FT: 1,500
SALES (est): 489.23K **Privately Held**
SIC: 2512 7641 Upholstered household furniture; Reupholstery and furniture repair

(G-7009)
STROHECKER INCORPORATED
213 N Pleasant Dr (44413-2497)
PHONE............................330 426-9496
Richard Strohecker, *Pr*
Tony J Moran, *
◆ **EMP:** 40 **EST:** 1947
SQ FT: 4,000
SALES (est): 5.97MM **Privately Held**
Web: www.strohecker.com
SIC: 3567 3443 Industrial furnaces and ovens; Metal parts

(G-7010)
TEST MARK INDUSTRIES INC
995 N Market St (44413-1109)
PHONE............................330 426-2200
William F Tyger, *Pr*
Martin R Napolitano, *Sec*
William Quinlan, *Dir*
▼ **EMP:** 12 **EST:** 1991
SQ FT: 8,500
SALES (est): 1.98MM **Privately Held**
Web: www.testmark.net
SIC: 5049 3829 Laboratory equipment, except medical or dental; Physical property testing equipment

(G-7011)
TUBETECH INC (PA)
Also Called: Tubetech North America
900 E Taggart St (44413-2424)
P.O. Box 470 (44413-0470)
PHONE............................330 426-9476
Steve Oliphant, *CEO*
Stephen D Oliphant, *
Jon Roscow, *
Richard Downey, *
EMP: 6 **EST:** 1988
SQ FT: 80,000
SALES (est): 4.46MM
SALES (corp-wide): 4.46MM **Privately Held**
SIC: 3317 3471 Tubes, wrought: welded or lock joint; Plating of metals or formed products

(G-7012)
UNITY TUBE INC
1862 State Route 165 (44413-9737)
P.O. Box 425 (44413-0425)
PHONE............................330 426-4282
Robert Howe, *Pr*
EMP: 18 **EST:** 2003
SALES (est): 4.3MM **Privately Held**
Web: www.unitytube.com
SIC: 3498 Tube fabricating (contract bending and shaping)

East Sparta
Stark County

(G-7013)
CLARK SON ACTN LIQUIDATION INC
Also Called: Clark & Son
10233 Sandyville Ave Se (44626-9333)
PHONE............................330 866-9330
Clark J Barkheimer, *Pr*
▲ **EMP:** 8 **EST:** 2003
SALES (est): 1.07MM **Privately Held**
Web: www.clarkandsoninc.com
SIC: 2434 Wood kitchen cabinets

(G-7014)
LAND SPECIALTIES LLC
2293 Ullet St Sw (44626-9485)
PHONE............................330 663-6974
Tyler Cookson, *Prin*
EMP: 6 **EST:** 2019
SALES (est): 73.52K **Privately Held**
SIC: 3599 Machine shop, jobbing and repair

(G-7015)
WILLIAM NICCUM
Also Called: L.A.m Wldg & Met Fabrication
11882 Sandyville Ave Se (44626)
PHONE............................330 415-0154
William Niccum, *Owner*
EMP: 6 **EST:** 2014
SALES (est): 209.42K **Privately Held**
SIC: 3441 Fabricated structural metal

Eastlake
Lake County

(G-7016)
2-M MANUFACTURING COMPANY INC
34560 Lakeland Blvd (44095-5221)
PHONE............................440 269-1270
Mirko Cukelj, *Pr*
Katherine Cukelj, *
EMP: 25 **EST:** 1969
SALES (est): 1.9MM **Privately Held**
SIC: 3599 Machine shop, jobbing and repair

(G-7017)
AGILE SIGN & LTG MAINT INC
35280 Lakeland Blvd (44095-5359)
PHONE............................440 918-1311
Tim Ruff, *Pr*
EMP: 20 **EST:** 2007
SQ FT: 10,000
SALES (est): 2.47MM **Privately Held**
Web: www.agilesignohio.com
SIC: 3993 Signs and advertising specialties

(G-7018)
AGR CONSULTING INC
35400 Lakeland Blvd (44095-5304)
PHONE............................440 974-4030
EMP: 11 **EST:** 1994
SALES (est): 844.53K **Privately Held**
Web: www.absolutegrinding.com
SIC: 3599 Machine shop, jobbing and repair

(G-7019)
ASTRO MANUFACTURING & DESIGN INC (PA)
Also Called: Astro Manufacturing & Design
34459 Curtis Blvd (44095-4011)
PHONE............................888 215-1746
▲ **EMP:** 175 **EST:** 1977
SALES (est): 24.29MM
SALES (corp-wide): 24.29MM **Privately Held**
Web: www.astromfg.com
SIC: 3569 3599 3089 3444 Assembly machines, non-metalworking; Machine shop, jobbing and repair; Molding primary plastics; Sheet metalwork

(G-7020)
ASTRO MODEL DEVELOPMENT CORP
34459 Curtis Blvd (44095-4011)
PHONE............................440 946-8855
Ken Anderson, *Mgr*
EMP: 9 **EST:** 2018
SALES (est): 462.22K **Privately Held**
SIC: 3089 Injection molding of plastics

(G-7021)
ATS MACHINE & TOOL CO
37033 Lake Shore Blvd (44095-1103)
PHONE............................440 255-1120
Robert E Dutko, *Pr*
Denise Dutko, *VP*
EMP: 12 **EST:** 1981
SALES (est): 2MM **Privately Held**
Web: www.atsmachine.com
SIC: 3599 Machine shop, jobbing and repair

(G-7022)
BOND DISTRIBUTING LLC
Also Called: One Time
35585 Curtis Blvd Unit D (44095-4104)
PHONE............................440 461-7920
Scott Fishel, *Managing Member*
EMP: 6 **EST:** 2000

Eastlake - Lake County (G-7023)

GEOGRAPHIC SECTION

SALES (est): 504.57K **Privately Held**
Web: www.onetimewood.com
SIC: **2899** Chemical preparations, nec

(G-7023)
CONSOLDTED PRECISION PDTS CORP
Also Called: Cpp Cleveland
34000 Lakeland Blvd (44095-5215)
PHONE.................................440 953-0053
Carol Robinson, *Brnch Mgr*
EMP: 269
SALES (corp-wide): 2.07B **Privately Held**
Web: www.cppcorp.com
SIC: **3369** Castings, except die-castings, precision
PA: Consolidated Precision Products Corp.
   1621 Euclid Ave Ste 1850
   Cleveland OH 44115
   216 453-4800

(G-7024)
CPP-CLEVELAND INC
34000 Lakeland Blvd (44095-5215)
PHONE.................................440 953-0053
James Stewart, *CEO*
EMP: 200
SALES (corp-wide): 822.51MM **Privately Held**
SIC: **3369** Lead castings, except die-castings
HQ: Cpp-Cleveland, Inc.
   1621 Euclid Ave Ste 1850
   Cleveland OH 44115
   216 453-4800

(G-7025)
DIE CO INC
1889 E 337th St (44095-5231)
P.O. Box 5248 (44095-0248)
PHONE.................................440 942-8856
Donald G Hawk, *Pr*
Michael T Hawk, *
Donna Corrigan, *
▲ EMP: 48 EST: 1963
SQ FT: 35,000
SALES (est): 4.86MM **Privately Held**
Web: www.diecoinc.com
SIC: **3469 3496 3471 3429** Stamping metal for the trade; Miscellaneous fabricated wire products; Plating and polishing; Hardware, nec

(G-7026)
DIVERSIFIED MCH COMPONENTS LLC
34099 Melinz Pkwy Unit D (44095-4001)
PHONE.................................440 942-5701
Gregory J O'brien, *Managing Member*
EMP: 22 EST: 2005
SALES (est): 1.22MM **Privately Held**
Web: www.dmcparts.net
SIC: **3599** Machine shop, jobbing and repair

(G-7027)
EAGLEHEAD MANUFACTURING CO
35280 Lakeland Blvd Ste K (44095-5359)
PHONE.................................440 951-0400
Jeffery Cotman, *CEO*
Teresa Cotman, *VP*
EMP: 18 EST: 1996
SALES (est): 1.12MM **Privately Held**
Web: www.eaglehead.com
SIC: **3599** Machine shop, jobbing and repair

(G-7028)
ENPAC LLC
34355 Melinz Pkwy (44095-4033)
PHONE.................................440 975-0070
Timothy Reed, *Pt*
Timothy D Reed, *CFO*

▼ EMP: 80 EST: 2001
SQ FT: 66,500
SALES (est): 16.9MM **Privately Held**
Web: www.enpac.com
SIC: **3089** Plastics containers, except foam

(G-7029)
ENPRESS LLC
34899 Curtis Blvd (44095-4015)
PHONE.................................440 510-0108
Douglas Honer, *Managing Member*
Timothy Reid, *Managing Member*
▼ EMP: 40 EST: 2002
SALES (est): 9.79MM **Privately Held**
Web: www.enpress.com
SIC: **3089** Injection molding of plastics

(G-7030)
ESCO TURBINE TECH CLEVELAND
34000 Lakeland Blvd (44095-5215)
PHONE.................................440 953-0053
EMP: 12 EST: 2016
SALES (est): 487.78K **Privately Held**
Web: www.cppcorp.com
SIC: **3535** Conveyors and conveying equipment

(G-7031)
ESCO TURBINE TECHNOLOGIES - CLEVELAND INC
Also Called: Consolidated Precision Pdts
34000 Lakeland Blvd (44095-5215)
P.O. Box 10123 (97296-0123)
PHONE.................................440 953-0053
EMP: 170
Web: www.cppcorp.com
SIC: **3369** Castings, except die-castings, precision

(G-7032)
EUCLID PRECISION GRINDING CO
35400 Lakeland Blvd (44095-5304)
PHONE.................................440 946-8888
Eric Barbe, *Pr*
EMP: 6 EST: 1945
SQ FT: 9,600
SALES (est): 573.27K **Privately Held**
SIC: **3599** Machine shop, jobbing and repair

(G-7033)
H & R METAL FINISHING INC
1052 E 347th St (44095-2635)
PHONE.................................440 942-6656
Rosemarie Cruz, *Pr*
Rose Espendez, *Sec*
EMP: 6 EST: 1984
SALES (est): 495.4K **Privately Held**
Web: www.hrmetal.com
SIC: **3471** Electroplating of metals or formed products

(G-7034)
HEETER PRINTING COMPANY INC
33212 Lakeland Blvd (44095-5205)
PHONE.................................440 946-0606
Blake Laduc, *Mgr*
EMP: 50
SALES (corp-wide): 37.12MM **Privately Held**
Web: www.heeter.com
SIC: **2752** Offset printing
PA: Heeter Printing Company, Inc.
   441 Technology Dr
   Canonsburg PA 15317
   724 746-8900

(G-7035)
HI CARB CORP
1857 E 337th St # A (44095-5231)
PHONE.................................216 486-5000

John R Sonnie, *Pr*
EMP: 24 EST: 1955
SALES (est): 694.63K **Privately Held**
SIC: **3545** Tools and accessories for machine tools

(G-7036)
HIGH QUALITY TOOLS INC (PA)
Also Called: High Quality Tools
34940 Lakeland Blvd (44095-5226)
PHONE.................................440 975-9684
Mirko Cukelj, *Pr*
▲ EMP: 12 EST: 1983
SQ FT: 3,000
SALES (est): 2.74MM
SALES (corp-wide): 2.74MM **Privately Held**
Web: www.hqtinc.com
SIC: **5085 3545** Industrial tools; Tools and accessories for machine tools

(G-7037)
KRENGEL EQUIPMENT LLC
Also Called: Krengel Manufacturing
34580 Lakeland Blvd (44095-5221)
PHONE.................................440 946-3570
EMP: 140 EST: 2013
SALES (est): 10.12MM **Privately Held**
Web: www.krengelmfg.com
SIC: **3363 3544** Aluminum die-castings; Dies and die holders for metal cutting, forming, die casting

(G-7038)
KYNTROL HOLDINGS INC
34700 Lakeland Blvd (44095-5223)
PHONE.................................440 220-5990
Wayne Foley, *Pr*
EMP: 76 EST: 2010
SALES (est): 3.28MM **Privately Held**
Web: www.midwestllc.com
SIC: **3593** Fluid power actuators, hydraulic or pneumatic

(G-7039)
MICONVI PROPERTIES INC
Also Called: Bevcorp Properties
37200 Research Dr (44095-1869)
PHONE.................................440 954-3500
Michael Connelly, *Pr*
Vicki Connelly, *
◆ EMP: 20 EST: 1991
SALES (est): 875.16K **Privately Held**
Web: www.bevcorp.com
SIC: **3565** Bottling machinery: filling, capping, labeling

(G-7040)
MIDWEST PRECISION HOLDINGS INC (HQ)
34700 Lakeland Blvd (44095-5223)
PHONE.................................440 497-4086
Wayne Foley, *Pr*
EMP: 13 EST: 1953
SALES (est): 12.72MM
SALES (corp-wide): 71.94MM **Privately Held**
Web: www.midwestllc.com
SIC: **3812** Acceleration indicators and systems components, aerospace
PA: Tribus Aerospace Llc
   10 S Wacker Dr Ste 3300
   Chicago IL 60606
   312 876-7267

(G-7041)
MIDWEST PRECISION LLC
34700 Lakeland Blvd (44095-5223)
PHONE.................................440 951-2333
E Wayne Foley, *Managing Member*
William Marlowe, *

EMP: 52 EST: 2010
SQ FT: 38,000
SALES (est): 10.71MM
SALES (corp-wide): 71.94MM **Privately Held**
Web: www.midwestllc.com
SIC: **3451** Screw machine products
HQ: Midwest Precision Holdings Inc.
   34700 Lakeland Blvd
   Eastlake OH 44095
   440 497-4086

(G-7042)
MOLD MASTERS INTL LLC
34000 Melinz Pkwy (44095)
PHONE.................................440 953-0220
Jim Allen, *CEO*
George Goodrich, *
Robert Soltis, *
Vic Sirotek, *
Ron Kern, *
EMP: 170 EST: 1961
SQ FT: 54,000
SALES (est): 23.22MM **Privately Held**
Web: www.pccairfoils.com
SIC: **3324 2842** Steel investment foundries; Polishes and sanitation goods

(G-7043)
MRD SOLUTIONS LLC
34201 Melinz Pkwy Unit A (44095-4018)
PHONE.................................440 942-6969
EMP: 11 EST: 2005
SALES (est): 530.3K **Privately Held**
Web: www.mrd-s.net
SIC: **3541** Machine tools, metal cutting type

(G-7044)
PCC AIRFOILS LLC
Also Called: PCC AIRFOILS LLC
34300 Melinz Pkwy (44095-4026)
PHONE.................................440 585-8247
EMP: 303
SALES (corp-wide): 364.48B **Publicly Held**
Web: www.pccairfoils.com
SIC: **3369** Castings, except die-castings, precision
HQ: Pcc Airfoils, Llc
   3401 Entp Pkwy Ste 200
   Cleveland OH 44122
   216 831-3590

(G-7045)
POLYMER & STEEL TECH INC
34899 Curtis Blvd (44095-4015)
PHONE.................................440 510-0108
Douglas Horner, *Pr*
▼ EMP: 50 EST: 1988
SQ FT: 66,000
SALES (est): 5.25MM **Privately Held**
Web: polymer-steel-technologies-inc.sbcontract.com
SIC: **3089** Plastics containers, except foam

(G-7046)
REGENCY STEEL SUPPLY INC LLC
Also Called: Regency Steel Supplies
1662 E 361st St Unit 6a (44095-5341)
PHONE.................................440 306-0269
EMP: 7 EST: 2009
SALES (est): 510.18K **Privately Held**
SIC: **3315** Steel wire and related products

(G-7047)
RESZ FABRICATION INC
35280 Lakeland Blvd (44095-5359)
PHONE.................................440 207-0044
EMP: 6 EST: 2018
SALES (est): 763.45K **Privately Held**

▲ = Import ▼ = Export
◆ = Import/Export

Web: www.reszfab.com
SIC: 3714 Motor vehicle parts and accessories

(G-7048)
RVTRONIX CORPORATION
34099 Melinz Pkwy Unit E (44095)
PHONE..................................440 359-7200
EMP: 28 EST: 1998
SALES (corp-wide): 3.2MM Privately Held
Web: www.intellitronix.com
SIC: 3647 Automotive lighting fixtures, nec
PA: Evergreen Cooperative Corporation
4205 Saint Clair Ave
Cleveland OH 44103
216 268-5399

(G-7049)
STAINLESS SPECIALTIES INC
33240 Lakeland Blvd (44095-5205)
PHONE..................................440 942-4242
Dennis O'brien, Pr
Joan Podmore, *
EMP: 25 EST: 1993
SQ FT: 26,000
SALES (est): 2.71MM Privately Held
Web: www.hoodmart.com
SIC: 3441 3312 Fabricated structural metal; Blast furnaces and steel mills

(G-7050)
SUBURBAN MANUFACTURING CO
1924 E 337th St (44095-5229)
PHONE..................................440 953-2024
Richard E Grice, Pr
EMP: 60 EST: 1979
SQ FT: 31,000
SALES (est): 5.52MM Privately Held
Web: www.submfg.com
SIC: 3599 3546 3469 3561 Machine shop, jobbing and repair; Power-driven handtools; Metal stampings, nec; Pumps and pumping equipment

(G-7051)
T & D FABRICATING INC
Also Called: T & D Fabricating
1489 E 363rd St (44095-4137)
PHONE..................................440 951-5646
EMP: 20 EST: 1996
SALES (est): 2.25MM Privately Held
Web: www.tdfabricating.com
SIC: 3469 3498 3354 3351 Metal stampings, nec; Fabricated pipe and fittings; Aluminum extruded products; Copper rolling and drawing

(G-7052)
TYMOCA PARTNERS LLC
Also Called: Federal Gear
33220 Lakeland Blvd (44095-5205)
PHONE..................................440 946-4327
EMP: 10 EST: 2007
SALES (est): 2.1MM Privately Held
Web: www.fg-machine.com
SIC: 3462 Iron and steel forgings

(G-7053)
UNITED MACHINE AND TOOL INC
1956 E 337th St (44095-5229)
PHONE..................................440 946-7677
Martha Klatt, CEO
Harry Klatt, Pr
EMP: 8 EST: 1965
SQ FT: 10,000
SALES (est): 704.52K Privately Held
Web: www.unitedmachandtool.com
SIC: 3599 Machine shop, jobbing and repair

Eaton
Preble County

(G-7054)
AUKERMAN J F STEEL RULE DIE
5582 Ozias Rd (45320-9716)
P.O. Box 374 (45320-0374)
PHONE..................................937 456-4498
John F Aukerman Junior, Pr
EMP: 7 EST: 1975
SALES (est): 508.96K Privately Held
SIC: 3544 Dies, steel rule

(G-7055)
BRUBAKER METALCRAFTS INC
209 N Franklin St (45320-1819)
P.O. Box 353 (45320-0353)
PHONE..................................937 456-5834
Paul Brubaker, Pr
Wilma Brubaker, Sec
EMP: 7 EST: 1973
SQ FT: 3,000
SALES (est): 468.98K Privately Held
Web: www.brubakermetalcrafts.com
SIC: 3229 Lantern globes

(G-7056)
BULLEN ULTRASONICS INC
Also Called: Bullen
1301 Miller Williams Rd (45320-8507)
PHONE..................................937 456-7133
Mary A Bullen, Pr
Mary A Moreland, *
▲ EMP: 65 EST: 1969
SQ FT: 4,748
SALES (est): 15.4MM Privately Held
Web: www.bullentech.com
SIC: 3599 Machine shop, jobbing and repair

(G-7057)
CORNERSTONE MANUFACTURING INC
861 Us Route 35 (45320-8638)
P.O. Box 682 (45320-0682)
PHONE..................................937 456-5930
Ronnie J Kutter, Pr
Trisha Kutter, VP
EMP: 9 EST: 1980
SQ FT: 4,000
SALES (est): 896.87K Privately Held
Web: www.cornerstone-manufacturing.com
SIC: 3544 Special dies and tools

(G-7058)
ELECTRO-CAP INTERNATIONAL INC
1011 W Lexington Rd (45320-9290)
P.O. Box 87 (45320-0087)
PHONE..................................937 456-6099
W Nelson Hardin, Pr
Janet L Hardin, Sec
EMP: 18 EST: 1988
SQ FT: 10,000
SALES (est): 2.85MM Privately Held
Web: www.electro-cap.com
SIC: 3089 5047 Caps, plastics; Hospital equipment and furniture

(G-7059)
FIRST IMPRESSION WEAR LLC
120 E Main St (45320-1744)
PHONE..................................937 456-3900
Pat Taylor, Prin
EMP: 7 EST: 2005
SALES (est): 258.43K Privately Held
SIC: 2759 Screen printing

(G-7060)
HENNY PENNY CORPORATION (PA)
1219 U S 35 W (45320-8621)
P.O. Box 60 (45320-0060)
PHONE..................................937 456-8400
Steve Cobb, Ch
Rob Connelly, *
◆ EMP: 508 EST: 1986
SQ FT: 400,000
SALES (est): 128.51MM
SALES (corp-wide): 128.51MM Privately Held
Web: www.hennypenny.com
SIC: 3589 Cooking equipment, commercial

(G-7061)
I DREAM OF CAKES
995 Camden Rd (45320-9511)
PHONE..................................937 533-6024
Julie Rosfeld, Prin
EMP: 6 EST: 2006
SALES (est): 158.3K Privately Held
Web: www.idreamofcakes.net
SIC: 5461 2041 Cakes; Flour and other grain mill products

(G-7062)
INTERNATIONAL PAPER COMPANY
Also Called: International Paper
900 Us Route 35 (45320-8647)
PHONE..................................937 456-4131
John Winters, Brnch Mgr
EMP: 67
SALES (corp-wide): 18.92B Publicly Held
Web: www.internationalpaper.com
SIC: 2621 Paper mills
PA: International Paper Company
6400 Poplar Ave
Memphis TN 38197
901 419-7000

(G-7063)
KRAMER POWER EQUIPMENT CO
2388 State Route 726 N (45320-9217)
PHONE..................................937 456-2232
Joseph Kramer, Pr
C Jason Kramer, VP
EMP: 13 EST: 1975
SQ FT: 20,000
SALES (est): 236.49K Privately Held
Web: www.kramerusa.com
SIC: 3599 3444 3441 7692 Machine shop, jobbing and repair; Sheet metalwork; Fabricated structural metal; Welding repair

(G-7064)
LAM RESEARCH CORPORATION
Also Called: Lam Research
960 S Franklin St (45320-9421)
PHONE..................................937 472-3311
Mike Snell, Genl Mgr
EMP: 9
SALES (corp-wide): 17.43B Publicly Held
Web: www.lamresearch.com
SIC: 3674 Semiconductors and related devices
PA: Lam Research Corporation
4650 Cushing Pkwy
Fremont CA 94538
510 572-0200

(G-7065)
LEE PLASTIC COMPANY LLC
1100 Us Route 35 (45320-8620)
P.O. Box 271 (45320-0271)
PHONE..................................937 456-5720
EMP: 8 EST: 1990
SQ FT: 8,000
SALES (est): 931.67K Privately Held
Web: www.lee-plastic.com

SIC: 3089 Injection molding of plastics

(G-7066)
NEATON AUTO PRODUCTS MFG INC (HQ)
975 S Franklin St (45320-9400)
PHONE..................................937 456-7103
Naoki Horikawa, Pr
David Gulling, *
Kazuhiro Watanabe, *
▲ EMP: 26 EST: 1984
SQ FT: 500,000
SALES (est): 60.04MM Privately Held
Web: www.neaton.com
SIC: 3714 Motor vehicle engines and parts
PA: Nihon Plast Co.,Ltd.
3507-15, Yamamiya
Fujinomiya SZO 418-0

(G-7067)
PARKER-HANNIFIN CORPORATION
Tube Fittings Division
725 N Beech St (45320-1499)
PHONE..................................937 456-5571
William Bowman, Brnch Mgr
EMP: 71
SALES (corp-wide): 19.07B Publicly Held
Web: www.parker.com
SIC: 3494 5074 3498 3492 Pipe fittings; Plumbing fittings and supplies; Tube fabricating (contract bending and shaping); Fluid power valves and hose fittings
PA: Parker-Hannifin Corporation
6035 Parkland Blvd
Cleveland OH 44124
216 896-3000

(G-7068)
REGISTER HERALD OFFICE
200 Eaton Lewisburg Rd Ste 105 (45320-1190)
PHONE..................................937 456-5553
Darron Newman, Prin
EMP: 12 EST: 2002
SALES (est): 209.15K Privately Held
Web: www.registerherald.com
SIC: 2711 Commercial printing and newspaper publishing combined

(G-7069)
SEVEN MILE CREEK CORPORATION
315 S Beech St (45320-2311)
P.O. Box 155 (45320-0155)
PHONE..................................937 456-3320
William Cressell, Pr
William Cressell, Pr
Marqueeta Cressell, Sec
EMP: 7 EST: 1935
SQ FT: 3,850
SALES (est): 350K Privately Held
Web: www.sevenmilecreek.com
SIC: 2399 2392 2393 2326 Aprons, breast (harness); Shower curtains: made from purchased materials; Textile bags; Men's and boy's work clothing

(G-7070)
SILFEX INC (HQ)
950 S Franklin St (45320-9421)
PHONE..................................937 472-3311
▲ EMP: 54 EST: 2006
SALES (est): 141.32MM
SALES (corp-wide): 17.43B Publicly Held
Web: www.silfex.com
SIC: 3674 Semiconductors and related devices
PA: Lam Research Corporation
4650 Cushing Pkwy
Fremont CA 94538
510 572-0200

Edgerton - Williams County (G-7071) **GEOGRAPHIC SECTION**

Edgerton
Williams County

(G-7071)
ANDREW M FARNHAM
2112 County Road C60 (43517-9795)
PHONE..............................419 298-4300
Andrew M Farnham, *Prin*
EMP: 11 **EST:** 2001
SALES (est): 311.61K **Privately Held**
SIC: 2834 Pharmaceutical preparations

(G-7072)
BUILDING CONCEPTS INC (PA)
Also Called: Cardinal Truss & Components
444 N Michigan Ave (43517-9811)
P.O. Box 579 (43517-0579)
PHONE..............................419 298-2371
TOLL FREE: 800
William H Lutterbein, *Pr*
Dennis Imbrock, *VP*
Donald C Landel, *VP*
EMP: 16 **EST:** 1924
SQ FT: 14,000
SALES (est): 2.45MM
SALES (corp-wide): 2.45MM **Privately Held**
Web: www.lutterbein.com
SIC: 5211 1521 2439 Lumber and other building materials; Single-family housing construction; Trusses, wooden roof

(G-7073)
CENTER CONCRETE INC (PA)
8790 Us Highway 6 (43517)
P.O. Box 340 (43517-0340)
PHONE..............................800 453-4224
Don Pahl, *Pr*
Gary Weber, *Sec*
EMP: 10 **EST:** 1990
SQ FT: 800
SALES (est): 2.23MM **Privately Held**
Web: www.centerconcreteinc.com
SIC: 3273 Ready-mixed concrete

(G-7074)
EDGERTON FORGE INC (HQ)
257 E Morrison St (43517-9302)
PHONE..............................419 298-2333
Richard Horton, *CEO*
Skip Dietrick, *
Mark A Cluadio, *
Gordon Miller, *
EMP: 71 **EST:** 1972
SQ FT: 70,000
SALES (est): 13.27MM
SALES (corp-wide): 474.53MM **Privately Held**
Web: www.edgertonforge.com
SIC: 3462 3714 3423 Iron and steel forgings; Motor vehicle parts and accessories; Hand and edge tools, nec
PA: Avis Industrial Corporation
1909 S Main St
Upland IN 46989
765 998-8100

(G-7075)
FLEGAL BROTHERS INC
104 Industrial Dr (43517-9666)
PHONE..............................419 298-3539
Douglas Flegal, *Pr*
EMP: 20 **EST:** 1969
SALES (est): 375.11K **Privately Held**
SIC: 2611 4213 Pulp mills, mechanical and recycling processing; Trucking, except local

(G-7076)
MATCOR METAL FABRICATION INC
228 E Morrison St (43517-9389)
PHONE..............................419 298-2394
EMP: 6 **EST:** 2019
SALES (est): 25.09K **Privately Held**
Web: www.matcormetalfab.com
SIC: 7692 Welding repair

(G-7077)
MATSU OHIO INC
228 E Morrison St (43517-9389)
PHONE..............................419 298-2394
◆ **EMP:** 122 **EST:** 2009
SQ FT: 220,000
SALES (est): 50.62MM
SALES (corp-wide): 97.29MM **Privately Held**
Web: www.matcor-matsu.com
SIC: 3465 Body parts, automobile: stamped metal
PA: Matsu Manufacturing Inc
7657 Bramalea Rd
Brampton ON L6T 5
905 291-5000

(G-7078)
MIDWEST STAMPING & MFG CO
228 E Morrison St (43517-9389)
PHONE..............................419 298-2394
John Carney, *Prin*
EMP: 7 **EST:** 2008
SALES (est): 118.15K **Privately Held**
Web: www.matcor-matsu.com
SIC: 3999 Manufacturing industries, nec

(G-7079)
OREN ELLIOT PRODUCTS LLC
113 Industrial Dr (43517-9666)
PHONE..............................419 298-0015
Steven Elliott, *CEO*
EMP: 50 **EST:** 2021
SALES (est): 3.72MM **Privately Held**
Web: www.oepmachining.com
SIC: 3675 Electronic capacitors

(G-7080)
SOEMHEJEE INC
128 W Vine St (43517-8606)
P.O. Box 638 (43517-0638)
PHONE..............................419 298-2306
June Elliott, *Pr*
Oren Elliott, *
EMP: 45 **EST:** 1925
SQ FT: 24,000
SALES (est): 9.57MM **Privately Held**
Web: www.orenelliottproducts.com
SIC: 3675 3451 3469 Electronic capacitors; Screw machine products; Metal stampings, nec

(G-7081)
STAFFORD GRAVEL INC
4225 Co Rd 79 (43517)
P.O. Box 340 (43517-0340)
PHONE..............................419 298-2440
Gerry Weber, *Prin*
EMP: 11 **EST:** 2008
SALES (est): 1.01MM **Privately Held**
Web: www.staffordgravel.com
SIC: 1442 Construction sand and gravel

(G-7082)
STARK TRUSS COMPANY INC
400 Component Dr (43517)
P.O. Box 535 (43517-0535)
PHONE..............................419 298-3777
Duane Miller, *Brnch Mgr*
EMP: 57
SQ FT: 45,000
SALES (corp-wide): 99.05MM **Privately Held**
Web: www.starktruss.com
SIC: 2439 2511 2411 Trusses, wooden roof; Wood household furniture; Logging
PA: Stark Truss Company, Inc.
109 Miles Ave Sw
Canton OH 44710
330 478-2100

(G-7083)
WEBER SAND & GRAVEL INC
2702 County Road 3b (43517-9692)
PHONE..............................419 298-2388
Thomas B Weber, *Pr*
Judy Weber, *VP*
EMP: 9 **EST:** 1968
SQ FT: 2,000
SALES (est): 517.26K **Privately Held**
SIC: 1442 Common sand mining

Edison
Morrow County

(G-7084)
HORD ELEVATOR LLC
Also Called: Edison Branch
6775 Township Road 66 (43320-9767)
PHONE..............................419 562-1198
EMP: 101
Web: www.hordlivestock.com
SIC: 3523 Farm machinery and equipment
PA: Hord Elevator, Llc
1016 State Route 98
Bucyrus OH 44820

Edon
Williams County

(G-7085)
AGRIDRY LLC
3460 Us Highway 20 (43518-9733)
P.O. Box 336 (43518-0336)
PHONE..............................419 459-4399
Eli P Troyer, *Managing Member*
EMP: 10 **EST:** 2005
SALES (est): 1.68MM **Privately Held**
Web: www.agridrylink.com
SIC: 3567 1541 Driers and redriers, industrial process; Grain elevator construction

(G-7086)
DIMENSION HARDWOOD VENEERS INC
509 Woodville St (43518)
P.O. Box 59 (43518-0059)
PHONE..............................419 272-2245
Paul Horstman, *Pr*
▲ **EMP:** 50 **EST:** 1977
SQ FT: 56,000
SALES (est): 8.77MM **Privately Held**
Web: www.dimensionhardwoods.com
SIC: 2435 Hardwood veneer and plywood

(G-7087)
L & L MACHINE INC
2919 County Road 2l (43518-9771)
PHONE..............................419 272-5000
Laurie Lehman, *CEO*
Michael Lehman, *Pr*
EMP: 11 **EST:** 2002
SQ FT: 40,000
SALES (est): 1.07MM **Privately Held**
Web: www.landlmachine.com
SIC: 3599 Machine shop, jobbing and repair

(G-7088)
LINAMAR STRCTURES USA MICH INC
Also Called: Mobex Global
507 W Indiana St (43518-9644)
P.O. Box 77 (46701-0077)
PHONE..............................260 636-7030
EMP: 200
SALES (corp-wide): 5.89B **Privately Held**
Web: www.mobexglobal.com
SIC: 3714 Motor vehicle engines and parts
HQ: Linamar Structures Usa (Michigan) Inc.
32233 8 Mile Rd
Livonia MI 48152
248 477-6240

(G-7089)
LINAMAR STRCTURES USA MICH INC
Also Called: Mobex Global
201 Leanne St (43518)
PHONE..............................567 249-0838
EMP: 200
SALES (corp-wide): 5.89B **Privately Held**
Web: www.mobexglobal.com
SIC: 3714 Motor vehicle engines and parts
HQ: Linamar Structures Usa (Michigan) Inc.
32233 8 Mile Rd
Livonia MI 48152
248 477-6240

(G-7090)
NORTHWEST MOLDED PLASTICS
14372 County Road 4 (43518-9765)
PHONE..............................419 459-4414
Richard L Lemmon, *Owner*
EMP: 9 **EST:** 1976
SQ FT: 25,000
SALES (est): 722.49K **Privately Held**
SIC: 3089 Injection molding of plastics

(G-7091)
PLAS-TEC CORP
601 W Indiana St (43518-9645)
PHONE..............................419 272-2731
Kenneth Sharlow, *Genl Mgr*
Dennis Cox, *
EMP: 60 **EST:** 1970
SQ FT: 85,000
SALES (est): 9.43MM **Privately Held**
Web: www.plasteccorp.com
SIC: 3089 Injection molding of plastics

Eldorado
Preble County

(G-7092)
MIAMI VALLEY PLASTICS INC
310 S Main St (45321-9731)
PHONE..............................937 273-3200
George W Halderman, *CEO*
▲ **EMP:** 35 **EST:** 1967
SQ FT: 2,569
SALES (est): 2.6MM **Privately Held**
Web: www.miamivalleyplastics.com
SIC: 3089 Injection molding of plastics

Elida
Allen County

(G-7093)
A & D WOOD PRODUCTS INC (PA)
4220 Sherrick Rd (45807-9783)
PHONE..............................419 331-8859
EMP: 9 **EST:** 1991
SALES (est): 1.71MM **Privately Held**
SIC: 2448 Pallets, wood

GEOGRAPHIC SECTION

Elyria - Lorain County (G-7117)

(G-7094)
LIMA MILLWORK INC
4251 East Rd (45807-1534)
PHONE.................................419 331-3303
Mark Niemeyer, *Pr*
Thelma Neimeyer, *VP*
EMP: 18
SQ FT: 16,000
SALES (est): 808.07K **Privately Held**
Web: www.limamillwork.com
SIC: 2431 2511 2434 3281 Millwork; Wood household furniture; Wood kitchen cabinets ; Cut stone and stone products

(G-7095)
ORICK STAMPING INC
614 E Kiracofe Ave (45807-1034)
PHONE.................................419 331-0600
Paul Orick, *CEO*
Greg Orick, *
Monica Orick, *
EMP: 80 **EST:** 1969
SQ FT: 100,000
SALES (est): 12.98MM **Privately Held**
Web: www.orickstamping.com
SIC: 3469 3544 Stamping metal for the trade ; Special dies, tools, jigs, and fixtures

(G-7096)
PETERS FAMILY ENTERPRISES INC
5959 Allentown Rd (45807-9413)
P.O. Box 3133 (45807-0133)
PHONE.................................419 339-0555
Dave Peters, *Pr*
EMP: 8 **EST:** 2003
SALES (est): 868.46K **Privately Held**
SIC: 2499 Decorative wood and woodwork

(G-7097)
PRECISION TOOL GRINDING INC
216 S Greenlawn Ave Ste 5a (45807-1380)
PHONE.................................419 339-9959
Gary Schneer, *Pr*
EMP: 8 **EST:** 1988
SQ FT: 6,200
SALES (est): 748.47K **Privately Held**
Web: www.precisiontoolgrinding.com
SIC: 3599 Machine shop, jobbing and repair

(G-7098)
RANGE KLEEN MFG INC
4240 East Rd (45807-1533)
P.O. Box 696 (45802-0696)
PHONE.................................419 331-8000
Patrick O'connor, *Pr*
▲ **EMP:** 403 **EST:** 1971
SQ FT: 50,000
SALES (est): 49.74MM **Privately Held**
Web: www.rangekleen.com
SIC: 3365 3469 Cooking/kitchen utensils, cast aluminum; Metal stampings, nec

Elmore
Ottawa County

(G-7099)
ALVIN L ROEPKE
Also Called: Vision Quest
329 Rice St (43416-9404)
P.O. Box 197 (43416-0197)
PHONE.................................419 862-3891
Alvin L Roepke, *Owner*
EMP: 6 **EST:** 1989
SQ FT: 5,400
SALES (est): 378.64K **Privately Held**
SIC: 7336 2759 3993 2284 Silk screen design; Screen printing; Signs and advertising specialties; Embroidery thread

(G-7100)
CALVIN J MAGSIG
Also Called: Elmore Mfg Co
343 Clinton St (43416-7703)
P.O. Box 32 (43416-0032)
PHONE.................................419 862-3311
Calvin J Magsig, *Owner*
EMP: 7 **EST:** 1945
SQ FT: 15,000
SALES (est): 417.19K **Privately Held**
SIC: 3599 3494 Machine shop, jobbing and repair; Valves and pipe fittings, nec

(G-7101)
MACHINING TECHNOLOGIES INC (PA)
Also Called: M T
468 Maple St (43416-9423)
P.O. Box 287 (43416-0287)
PHONE.................................419 862-3110
William M Van Dorn, *CEO*
Thomas C Van Dorn, *
▲ **EMP:** 41 **EST:** 1985
SQ FT: 32,000
SALES (est): 10.48MM
SALES (corp-wide): 10.48MM **Privately Held**
Web: www.machiningtech.com
SIC: 3082 3545 Unsupported plastics profile shapes; Precision tools, machinists'

(G-7102)
MARTIN INDUSTRIES INC
473 Maple St (43416-9402)
P.O. Box 569 (43416-0569)
PHONE.................................419 862-2694
Tim Gerkensmeyer, *Pr*
EMP: 15 **EST:** 1985
SQ FT: 10,000
SALES (est): 494.79K **Privately Held**
SIC: 3069 3061 Hard rubber and molded rubber products; Mechanical rubber goods

(G-7103)
MATERION BRUSH INC
14710 W Portage River South Rd (43416-9500)
PHONE.................................419 862-2745
Art Tupper, *Brnch Mgr*
EMP: 700
SQ FT: 100,000
Web: www.materion.com
SIC: 3339 3369 3341 Beryllium metal; Nonferrous foundries, nec; Secondary nonferrous metals
HQ: Materion Brush Inc.
6070 Parkland Blvd Ste 1
Mayfield Heights OH 44124
216 486-4200

Elyria
Lorain County

(G-7104)
AEROWAVE INC
361 Windward Dr (44035-1633)
PHONE.................................440 731-8464
Bob Avon, *CEO*
EMP: 7 **EST:** 2012
SALES (est): 490.46K **Privately Held**
SIC: 3548 Welding apparatus

(G-7105)
ALCO MANUFACTURING CORP LLC (PA)
10584 Middle Ave (44035-7812)
PHONE.................................440 458-5165
Matt Dietrich, *CEO*
EMP: 22 **EST:** 2006

SALES (est): 37.94MM **Privately Held**
Web: www.alco.com
SIC: 3451 Screw machine products

(G-7106)
ALEXIS CONCRETE ENTERPRISE INC
672 Sugar Ln (44035-6310)
PHONE.................................440 366-0031
Edward Machovia, *Pr*
EMP: 15 **EST:** 2000
SALES (est): 963.21K **Privately Held**
Web: www.alexisconcrete.com
SIC: 3273 Ready-mixed concrete

(G-7107)
AMERICAN FLUID POWER INC
144 Reaser Ct (44035-6285)
PHONE.................................877 223-8742
Robert Weltman, *COO*
EMP: 7 **EST:** 2012
SALES (est): 619.4K **Privately Held**
Web: www.amerfluidpower.com
SIC: 3542 Bending machines

(G-7108)
AMERICAN METAL FABRICATING LLC
7516 W Ridge Rd (44035-1960)
PHONE.................................440 277-5600
Billy J Jackson, *Admn*
EMP: 6 **EST:** 2017
SALES (est): 117.68K **Privately Held**
SIC: 3499 Fabricated metal products, nec

(G-7109)
AMERICAN TURF RECYCLING LLC
860 Taylor St (44035-6232)
PHONE.................................440 323-0306
Daniel Macphee, *Pr*
EMP: 8 **EST:** 2014
SQ FT: 15,000
SALES (est): 590.06K **Privately Held**
SIC: 2821 Cellulose acetate (plastics)

(G-7110)
AMIDAC WIND CORPORATION
Also Called: Amidac Wind
151 Innovation Dr (44035-1675)
PHONE.................................213 973-4000
Ameer Alghusain, *CEO*
EMP: 7 **EST:** 2015
SALES (est): 116.84K **Privately Held**
Web: www.amidac.com
SIC: 3643 Lightning protection equipment

(G-7111)
APPLIED ENGNEERED SURFACES INC
535 Ternes Ln Rear (44035)
PHONE.................................440 366-0440
Lauren Yoakam, *Pr*
EMP: 20 **EST:** 1999
SALES (est): 1.18MM **Privately Held**
Web: www.uhpsurfaces.com
SIC: 3441 Building components, structural steel

(G-7112)
ARNCO CORPORATION
860 Garden St (44035)
PHONE.................................800 847-7661
Arlene P Tengel, *Prin*
William E Smith, *
◆ **EMP:** 71 **EST:** 1985
SALES (est): 11.57MM
SALES (corp-wide): 2.8B **Privately Held**
Web: www.duraline.com

SIC: 3661 3829 3644 3429 Telephones and telephone apparatus; Measuring and controlling devices, nec; Noncurrent-carrying wiring devices; Hardware, nec
PA: Audax Group Limited Partnership
101 Huntington Ave # 2450
Boston MA 02199
617 859-1500

(G-7113)
B&B DISTRIBUTORS LLC
Also Called: Builders Straight Edge
811 Taylor St (44035-6231)
PHONE.................................440 324-1293
George Hovanitz, *Managing Member*
EMP: 10 **EST:** 2004
SALES (est): 1.55MM **Privately Held**
Web: www.bandbdistributors.com
SIC: 3353 Aluminum sheet, plate, and foil

(G-7114)
BAKEMARK USA LLC
6325 Gateway Blvd S (44035-5447)
PHONE.................................440 323-5100
EMP: 12
SALES (corp-wide): 578.75MM **Privately Held**
Web: www.yourbakemark.com
SIC: 2045 Flours and flour mixes, from purchased flour
PA: Bakemark Usa Llc
7351 Crider Ave
Pico Rivera CA 90660
562 949-1054

(G-7115)
BASF CATALYSTS LLC
120 Pine St (44035-5228)
P.O. Box 4017 (44036-2017)
PHONE.................................440 322-3741
Randolph C Turk, *Brnch Mgr*
EMP: 117
SALES (corp-wide): 74.89B **Privately Held**
Web: catalysts.basf.com
SIC: 2819 Catalysts, chemical
HQ: Basf Catalysts Llc
33 Wood Ave S
Iselin NJ 08830
732 205-5000

(G-7116)
BASF CORPORATION
120 Pine St (44035-5228)
PHONE.................................440 329-2525
EMP: 42
SALES (corp-wide): 74.89B **Privately Held**
Web: www.basf.com
SIC: 2869 Industrial organic chemicals, nec
HQ: Basf Corporation
100 Park Ave
Florham Park NJ 07932
800 962-7831

(G-7117)
BRIDGESTONE RET OPERATIONS LLC
Also Called: Firestone
1951 Midway Blvd (44035-2480)
PHONE.................................440 324-3327
Ricargo Vega, *Mgr*
EMP: 8
Web: www.bridgestoneamericas.com
SIC: 5531 7534 Automotive tires; Rebuilding and retreading tires
HQ: Bridgestone Retail Operations, Llc
333 E Lake St Ste 300
Bloomingdale IL 60108
630 259-9000

Elyria - Lorain County (G-7118)

GEOGRAPHIC SECTION

(G-7118)
BRIDGESTONE RET OPERATIONS LLC
Also Called: Firestone
520 Abbe Rd S (44035-6302)
PHONE...................................440 365-8308
Richard Cerro, *Mgr*
EMP: 7
Web: www.bridgestoneamericas.com
SIC: 5531 7534 Automotive tires; Rebuilding and retreading tires
HQ: Bridgestone Retail Operations, Llc
333 E Lake St Ste 300
Bloomingdale IL 60108
630 259-9000

(G-7119)
BUCKEYE STATE WLDG & FABG INC
175 Woodford Ave (44035-5436)
P.O. Box 837 (44036-0837)
PHONE...................................440 322-0344
Chris Reddinger, *Owner*
EMP: 8
SALES (corp-wide): 2.74MM **Privately Held**
Web: www.buckeyeweldfab.com
SIC: 7692 Welding repair
PA: Buckeye State Welding & Fabricating, Inc.
131 Buckeye St
Elyria OH 44035
440 322-0319

(G-7120)
BUCKEYE STATE WLDG & FABG INC (PA)
131 Buckeye St (44035-5216)
P.O. Box 837 (44036-0837)
PHONE...................................440 322-0319
Kenneth E Reddinger, *Pr*
Patrick J Reddinger, *VP*
Christopher R Reddinger, *Sec*
EMP: 13 **EST:** 1957
SQ FT: 12,000
SALES (est): 2.74MM
SALES (corp-wide): 2.74MM **Privately Held**
Web: www.buckeyeweldfab.com
SIC: 3599 Machine shop, jobbing and repair

(G-7121)
CABLETEK WIRING PRODUCTS INC
1150 Taylor St (44035-6281)
PHONE...................................800 562-9378
Stan Leonowigh, *Pr*
EMP: 25 **EST:** 1998
SALES (est): 2.5MM **Privately Held**
Web: www.cable-tek.com
SIC: 3444 Metal housings, enclosures, casings, and other containers

(G-7122)
CASCADE PATTERN COMPANY INC
519 Ternes Ln (44035-6286)
PHONE...................................440 323-4300
Charles A Petek, *CEO*
Rick Petek,
Nick Petek,
EMP: 25 **EST:** 1972
SALES (est): 3.89MM **Privately Held**
Web: www.cascadepattern.com
SIC: 3543 Industrial patterns

(G-7123)
CASTCO INC
527 Ternes Ln (44035-6286)
P.O. Box 1368 (43015-8368)
PHONE...................................440 365-2333
Dan Petek, *CEO*
EMP: 15 **EST:** 1996

SALES (est): 477.75K **Privately Held**
SIC: 3321 Gray and ductile iron foundries

(G-7124)
CASTEK INC
527 Ternes Ln (44035-6286)
PHONE...................................440 365-2333
Daniel C Petek, *Pr*
EMP: 40 **EST:** 1921
SALES (est): 6.36MM **Privately Held**
Web: www.castekusa.com
SIC: 3365 Aluminum and aluminum-based alloy castings

(G-7125)
CENTRAL COCA-COLA BTLG CO INC
Also Called: Coca-Cola
1410 Lake Ave (44035-3124)
PHONE...................................440 324-3335
Scott Dickerhoff, *Mgr*
EMP: 41
SALES (corp-wide): 43.75B **Publicly Held**
Web: www.coca-cola.com
SIC: 2086 Bottled and canned soft drinks
HQ: Central Coca-Cola Bottling Company, Inc.
555 Taxter Rd Ste 550
Elmsford NY 10523
914 789-1100

(G-7126)
CHAPIN CUSTOMER MOLDING INC
635 Oberlin Elyria Rd (44035-7727)
PHONE...................................440 458-6550
EMP: 10 **EST:** 2019
SALES (est): 2.35MM **Privately Held**
Web: www.chapincustommolding.com
SIC: 3089 Injection molding of plastics

(G-7127)
CITY ELYRIA COMMUNICATION
851 Garden St (44035-4874)
PHONE...................................440 322-3329
EMP: 6
SALES (est): 369.14K **Privately Held**
SIC: 3669 Traffic signals, electric

(G-7128)
CONSUN FOOD INDUSTRIES INC
Also Called: Sunshine Farms Dairy
123 Gateway Blvd N (44035-4923)
PHONE...................................440 322-6301
Dennis Walter, *Pr*
EMP: 16
SALES (corp-wide): 9.28MM **Privately Held**
Web: www.myconvenient.com
SIC: 2026 Fluid milk
PA: Consun Food Industries, Inc.
123 Gateway Blvd N
Elyria OH 44035
440 322-6301

(G-7129)
DIAMOND PRODUCTS LIMITED
1111 Taylor St (44035-6245)
PHONE...................................440 323-4616
EMP: 8
SALES (corp-wide): 3.33B **Privately Held**
Web: www.diamondproducts.com
SIC: 3545 Machine tool accessories
HQ: Diamond Products, Limited
333 Prospect St
Elyria OH 44035
440 323-4616

(G-7130)
DIAMOND PRODUCTS LIMITED (DH)
333 Prospect St (44035-6154)
P.O. Box 1080 (44036-1080)

PHONE...................................440 323-4616
◆ **EMP:** 300 **EST:** 1945
SALES (est): 57.52MM
SALES (corp-wide): 3.33B **Privately Held**
Web: www.diamondproducts.com
SIC: 3545 Machine tool accessories
HQ: Tyrolit Limited
Eldon Close
Northampton NORTHANTS NN6 7
178 882-3738

(G-7131)
DIAMONDS PRODUCTS LLC
1250 E Broad St (44035-6311)
PHONE...................................440 323-4616
▲ **EMP:** 7 **EST:** 2003
SALES (est): 905.02K **Privately Held**
Web: www.diamondproducts.com
SIC: 3545 Diamond cutting tools for turning, boring, burnishing, etc.

(G-7132)
DIY HOLSTER LLC
Also Called: Diy Holster
781 Finwood Ct (44035-1616)
PHONE...................................419 921-2168
C Patrick, *Managing Member*
EMP: 8 **EST:** 2013
SALES (est): 973.14K **Privately Held**
Web: www.diyholster.com
SIC: 3199 5072 5961 Holsters, leather; Hardware; Tools and hardware, mail order

(G-7133)
DURA-LINE CORPORATION
Also Called: DURA-LINE CORPORATION
860 Garden St (44035-4826)
PHONE...................................440 322-1000
Steven Sminth, *Brnch Mgr*
EMP: 64
Web: www.duraline.com
SIC: 3084 Plastics pipe
HQ: Dura-Line Services Llc
11400 Parkside Dr Ste 300
Knoxville TN 37934
865 218-3460

(G-7134)
DURA-LINE SERVICES LLC
669 Sugar Ln (44035-6309)
PHONE...................................440 322-1000
Anette Fargo, *Plant Administrator*
EMP: 29
Web: www.duraline.com
SIC: 3084 Plastics pipe
HQ: Dura-Line Services Llc
11400 Parkside Dr Ste 300
Knoxville TN 37934
865 218-3460

(G-7135)
DYNATECH SYSTEMS INC
161 Reaser Ct (44035-6285)
P.O. Box 1589 (44036-1589)
PHONE...................................440 365-1774
Sue A Everett, *Pr*
EMP: 17 **EST:** 1984
SQ FT: 5,000
SALES (est): 908.01K **Privately Held**
Web: www.dynatech.com
SIC: 3425 5085 Saw blades and handsaws; Industrial supplies

(G-7136)
E C S CORP
Also Called: Elyria Concrete Step Company
8015 Murray Ridge Rd (44035-2071)
PHONE...................................440 323-1707
Betty Goad, *Pr*
Everett G Goad, *Pr*
Thomas R Goad, *VP*

Leanne Odel, *Sec*
Thomas Goad, *VP*
EMP: 8 **EST:** 1957
SQ FT: 9,300
SALES (est): 446.22K **Privately Held**
Web: www.elyriaconcretestep.com
SIC: 3446 3272 3271 Grillwork, ornamental metal; Steps, prefabricated concrete; Paving blocks, concrete

(G-7137)
E M SERVICE INC
600 Lowell St (44035-4841)
PHONE...................................440 323-3260
TOLL FREE: 800
EMP: 14 **EST:** 1918
SALES (est): 2.48MM **Privately Held**
Web: www.emserviceinc.com
SIC: 5999 7694 Motors, electric; Electric motor repair

(G-7138)
E P P INC
Also Called: Elyria Plastic Products
710 Taylor St (44035-6230)
PHONE...................................440 322-8577
James Reichlin, *Pr*
Jim Kastler, *VP*
R Stephen Laux, *Prin*
▲ **EMP:** 75 **EST:** 1988
SQ FT: 6,000
SALES (est): 18.23MM **Privately Held**
Web: www.elyriapp.com
SIC: 3089 Injection molding of plastics

(G-7139)
ELITE PROPERTY GROUP LLC
Also Called: 1st Choice Contractor
1036 N Pasadena Ave (44035-2966)
PHONE...................................216 356-7469
EMP: 12 **EST:** 2017
SALES (est): 436.85K **Privately Held**
SIC: 8742 8741 6531 1389 Construction project management consultant; Construction management; Real estate managers; Construction, repair, and dismantling services

(G-7140)
ELYRIA CONCRETE INC
400 Lowell St (44035-4837)
PHONE...................................440 322-2750
John Walls, *Pr*
Dave Walls, *VP*
Chad Walls, *VP*
EMP: 12 **EST:** 2004
SALES (est): 1.83MM **Privately Held**
Web: www.eci-concrete.com
SIC: 3273 Ready-mixed concrete

(G-7141)
ELYRIA FOUNDRY COMPANY LLC (PA)
120 Filbert St (44035)
PHONE...................................440 322-4657
EMP: 87 **EST:** 1905
SALES (est): 49.84MM
SALES (corp-wide): 49.84MM **Privately Held**
Web: www.elyriafoundry.com
SIC: 3321 3369 3325 2821 Gray iron castings, nec; Nonferrous foundries, nec; Steel foundries, nec; Plastics materials and resins

(G-7142)
ELYRIA MANUFACTURING CORP (PA)
Also Called: EMC Precision Machining
145 Northrup St (44035-6163)

GEOGRAPHIC SECTION

Elyria - Lorain County (G-7165)

P.O. Box 479 (44036-0479)
PHONE..............................440 365-4171
Bradley R Ohlemacher, *
Willim Ohlemacher, *
Bob Graney, *
▲ **EMP**: 53 **EST**: 1925
SQ FT: 86,000
SALES (est): 10.6MM
SALES (corp-wide): 10.6MM **Privately Held**
Web: www.emcprecision.com
SIC: 3451 Screw machine products

(G-7143)
ELYRIA METAL SPINNING FABG CO
Also Called: Metal Manufacturing
7511 W River Rd S (44035-6972)
P.O. Box 992 (44036-0992)
PHONE..............................440 323-8068
Donald Didomenico, *Pr*
EMP: 8 **EST**: 1962
SQ FT: 18,000
SALES (est): 962.3K **Privately Held**
Web: www.elyriametalspinning.com
SIC: 3469 3599 Spinning metal for the trade; Machine shop, jobbing and repair

(G-7144)
ELYRIA PATTERN CO INC
6785 W River Rd S (44035-7052)
PHONE..............................440 323-1526
James A Schroeder, *Pr*
James W Schroeder, *VP*
EMP: 7 **EST**: 1947
SALES (est): 696.35K **Privately Held**
Web: www.lorainmodern.com
SIC: 3543 Industrial patterns

(G-7145)
ELYRIA PLATING CORPORATION
118 Olive St (44035-4000)
PHONE..............................440 365-8300
Kevin J Flanigan, *CEO*
E F Gookins, *
EMP: 40 **EST**: 1937
SQ FT: 35,000
SALES (est): 3.32MM **Privately Held**
Web: www.elyriaplating.net
SIC: 3471 Electroplating of metals or formed products

(G-7146)
ELYRIA SPRING & SPECIALTY INC
123 Elbe St (44035-4879)
PHONE..............................440 323-5502
John Turk, *Pr*
EMP: 17 **EST**: 1999
SQ FT: 8,858
SALES (est): 2.12MM **Privately Held**
Web: www.elyriaspring.com
SIC: 3495 3496 3493 3469 Wire springs; Miscellaneous fabricated wire products; Steel springs, except wire; Metal stampings, nec

(G-7147)
ELYRIA SPRING SPCLTY HOLDG INC
123 Elbe St (44035-4879)
PHONE..............................440 323-5502
EMP: 12 **EST**: 2016
SALES (est): 979.09K **Privately Held**
Web: www.elyriaspring.com
SIC: 3469 5085 3495 Stamping metal for the trade; Springs; Wire springs

(G-7148)
EMC PRECISION MACHINING II LLC (PA)
145 Northrup St (44035-6147)
P.O. Box 479 (44036-0479)
PHONE..............................440 365-4171

EMP: 16 **EST**: 2010
SALES (est): 5.05MM
SALES (corp-wide): 5.05MM **Privately Held**
Web: www.emcprecision.com
SIC: 3599 Machine shop, jobbing and repair

(G-7149)
ENGELHARD CORP
120 Pine St (44035-5228)
PHONE..............................440 322-3741
Al Brightwell, *Prin*
▲ **EMP**: 6 **EST**: 2010
SALES (est): 238.74K **Privately Held**
Web: catalysts.basf.com
SIC: 2819 Industrial inorganic chemicals, nec

(G-7150)
ENVELOPE MART OF OHIO INC
1540 Lowell St (44035-4869)
PHONE..............................440 365-8177
Robert T Thompson, *Pr*
EMP: 19 **EST**: 2008
SALES (est): 1.17MM **Privately Held**
Web: www.emprintgroup.com
SIC: 5112 2677 Envelopes; Envelopes

(G-7151)
FELLER TOOL CO
6285 Lake Ave (44035-1021)
PHONE..............................440 324-6277
Doug Feller, *Pr*
Deborah Feller, *VP*
EMP: 10 **EST**: 1959
SALES (est): 931.7K **Privately Held**
SIC: 3544 3599 Special dies and tools; Machine shop, jobbing and repair

(G-7152)
FLORIDA INVACARE HOLDINGS LLC
1 Invacare Way (44035-4190)
P.O. Box 4028 (44036-2028)
PHONE..............................800 333-6900
EMP: 47 **EST**: 2005
SALES (est): 3.38MM
SALES (corp-wide): 741.73MM **Publicly Held**
Web: global.invacare.com
SIC: 3842 Surgical appliances and supplies
PA: Invacare Corporation
1 Invacare Way
Elyria OH 44035
440 329-6000

(G-7153)
GASFLUX COMPANY
32 Hawthorne St (44035-4008)
P.O. Box 1170 (44036-1170)
PHONE..............................440 365-1941
Robert C Farquhar, *Pr*
William K Farquhar, *Ch Bd*
Richard Hoffman, *VP*
Mary Ann Farquhar, *Treas*
◆ **EMP**: 8 **EST**: 1938
SQ FT: 20,000
SALES (est): 2.76MM **Privately Held**
Web: www.gasflux.com
SIC: 2899 Fluxes: brazing, soldering, galvanizing, and welding

(G-7154)
GATEWAY INDUSTRIAL PDTS INC
160 Freedom Ct (44035-2245)
P.O. Box 95 (44036-0095)
PHONE..............................440 324-4112
Peter Delaporte, *Pr*
Gayle Delaporte, *Genl Mgr*
▼ **EMP**: 20 **EST**: 1979
SQ FT: 25,000
SALES (est): 4.28MM **Privately Held**
Web: www.gatewayindustrial.com

SIC: 3089 2431 Window screening, plastics; Doors and door parts and trim, wood

(G-7155)
GEON PERFORMANCE SOLUTIONS LLC
835 Leo Bullocks Pkwy (44035-4895)
PHONE..............................440 987-4553
EMP: 53
SALES (corp-wide): 2.67MM **Privately Held**
Web: www.geon.com
SIC: 2821 Plastics materials and resins
HQ: Geon Performance Solutions, Llc
25777 Detroit Rd Ste 202
Westlake OH 44145
800 438-4366

(G-7156)
GREBER MACHINE TOOL INC
Also Called: Custom Powdr Coating By Greber
313 Clark St (44035-6105)
PHONE..............................440 322-3685
Ken Greber, *Pr*
Tammy Greber, *Treas*
EMP: 7 **EST**: 2004
SQ FT: 600
SALES (est): 896.66K **Privately Held**
Web: www.greberracing.com
SIC: 3479 7692 Coating of metals and formed products; Welding repair

(G-7157)
HONEYWELL INTERNATIONAL INC
Also Called: Honeywell
P.O. Box 419 (44036-0419)
PHONE..............................440 329-9000
EMP: 47
SALES (corp-wide): 36.66B **Publicly Held**
Web: www.honeywell.com
SIC: 3724 Aircraft engines and engine parts
PA: Honeywell International Inc.
855 S Mint St
Charlotte NC 28202
704 627-6200

(G-7158)
HYDRO-AIRE INC
Also Called: Lear Romec
241 Abbe Rd S (44035-6239)
P.O. Box 4014 (44036-2014)
PHONE..............................440 323-3211
Tazewell Rowe, *Treas*
EMP: 236
SALES (corp-wide): 2.09B **Publicly Held**
Web: www.craneae.com
SIC: 3728 Aircraft parts and equipment, nec
HQ: Hydro-Aire, Inc.
3000 Winona Ave
Burbank CA 91504

(G-7159)
HYDRO-AIRE AEROSPACE CORP (HQ)
249 Abbe Rd S (44035-6239)
PHONE..............................440 323-3211
Jay Higgs, *Pr*
EMP: 200 **EST**: 2011
SALES (est): 95.7MM
SALES (corp-wide): 2.09B **Publicly Held**
SIC: 3728 3369 Aircraft parts and equipment, nec; Aerospace castings, nonferrous: except aluminum
PA: Crane Company
100 1st Stmford Pl Ste 40
Stamford CT 06902
203 363-7300

(G-7160)
INTERTEK LLC
6805 W River Rd (44035-7054)
PHONE..............................440 323-3325
Dave W Dennis, *Pr*
EMP: 10 **EST**: 1969
SQ FT: 24,000
SALES (est): 2.45MM **Privately Held**
Web: www.intertekllc.com
SIC: 3599 Machine shop, jobbing and repair

(G-7161)
INVACARE CANADIAN HOLDINGS INC
1 Invacare Way (44035-4190)
PHONE..............................440 329-6000
EMP: 22 **EST**: 2003
SALES (est): 515.76K
SALES (corp-wide): 741.73MM **Publicly Held**
Web: global.invacare.com
SIC: 3842 Surgical appliances and supplies
PA: Invacare Corporation
1 Invacare Way
Elyria OH 44035
440 329-6000

(G-7162)
INVACARE CANADIAN HOLDINGS LLC
1 Invacare Way (44035-4190)
PHONE..............................440 329-6000
EMP: 18 **EST**: 2009
SALES (est): 503.11K
SALES (corp-wide): 741.73MM **Publicly Held**
Web: global.invacare.com
SIC: 3842 Surgical appliances and supplies
PA: Invacare Corporation
1 Invacare Way
Elyria OH 44035
440 329-6000

(G-7163)
INVACARE CONTINUING CARE INC
1 Invacare Way (44035-4190)
PHONE..............................800 668-2337
Matthew Monaghan, *Pr*
EMP: 8 **EST**: 2015
SALES (est): 163.79K **Privately Held**
Web: global.invacare.com
SIC: 3842 Surgical appliances and supplies

(G-7164)
INVACARE CORPORATION (PA)
Also Called: Invacare
1 Invacare Way (44035-4190)
P.O. Box 4028 (44036-2028)
PHONE..............................440 329-6000
Geoffrey P Purtill, *Pr*
Michael J Merriman Junior, *Non-Executive Chairman of the Board*
Kathleen P Leneghan, *Sr VP*
Anthony C Laplaca, *Sr VP*
Rick A Cassiday, *Chief Human Resources Officer*
◆ **EMP**: 662 **EST**: 1971
SALES (est): 741.73MM
SALES (corp-wide): 741.73MM **Publicly Held**
Web: global.invacare.com
SIC: 3842 2514 2813 Surgical appliances and supplies; Beds, including folding and cabinet, household: metal; Industrial gases

(G-7165)
INVACARE CORPORATION
1200 Taylor St (44035-6248)
PHONE..............................440 329-6000
John Dmytriw, *Brnch Mgr*

Elyria - Lorain County (G-7166)

EMP: 14
SQ FT: 13,000
SALES (corp-wide): 741.73MM **Publicly Held**
Web: global.invacare.com
SIC: 3842 Wheelchairs
PA: Invacare Corporation
1 Invacare Way
Elyria OH 44035
440 329-6000

(G-7166)
INVACARE CORPORATION
Also Called: Invacare It & Financial Svcs
1320 Taylor St (44035-6250)
PHONE..................800 333-6900
EMP: 8
SALES (corp-wide): 741.73MM **Publicly Held**
Web: global.invacare.com
SIC: 2514 2813 3842 Beds, including folding and cabinet, household: metal; Industrial gases; Wheelchairs
PA: Invacare Corporation
1 Invacare Way
Elyria OH 44035
440 329-6000

(G-7167)
INVACARE HCS LLC
Also Called: Bargmann Management, L.L.C.
1 Invacare Way (44035-4190)
PHONE..................330 634-9925
Lisa Bargmann, *Managing Member*
EMP: 27 EST: 2005
SALES (est): 2.64MM
SALES (corp-wide): 741.73MM **Publicly Held**
SIC: 3842 Surgical appliances and supplies
PA: Invacare Corporation
1 Invacare Way
Elyria OH 44035
440 329-6000

(G-7168)
INVACARE HOLDINGS LLC
1 Invacare Way (44035)
PHONE..................440 329-6000
EMP: 27 EST: 2001
SALES (est): 5.52MM
SALES (corp-wide): 741.73MM **Publicly Held**
Web: global.invacare.com
SIC: 3842 Surgical appliances and supplies
PA: Invacare Corporation
1 Invacare Way
Elyria OH 44035
440 329-6000

(G-7169)
INVACARE HOLDINGS CORPORATION
1 Invacare Way (44035-4190)
PHONE..................440 329-6000
Gerald Blouch, *CEO*
A Malachi Mixon Iii, *Ch Bd*
Joseph B Richey Ii, *Pr*
Anthony C Laplaca, *Sr VP*
Kai Zhu, *Sr VP*
▲ EMP: 115 EST: 1984
SALES (est): 10.29MM
SALES (corp-wide): 741.73MM **Publicly Held**
Web: global.invacare.com
SIC: 2514 3841 3842 Beds, including folding and cabinet, household: metal; Inhalation therapy equipment; Wheelchairs
HQ: Invacare International Corporation
1 Invacare Way
Elyria OH 44035

(G-7170)
J&M PRECISION DIE CASTING LLC
Also Called: J & M Precision Die Cast Inc
1329 Taylor St (44035-6249)
PHONE..................440 365-7388
Michael Prokop, *Pr*
EMP: 19 EST: 2015
SQ FT: 8,000
SALES (est): 503.25K
SALES (corp-wide): 11.75MM **Privately Held**
Web: www.jmdiecasting.com
SIC: 3599 Machine shop, jobbing and repair
PA: Rhenium Alloys, Inc.
38683 Taylor Pkwy
North Ridgeville OH 44039
440 365-7388

(G-7171)
JB ENTRPRSES PRTS DTAILING LLC
860 Taylor St (44035-6232)
PHONE..................440 300 4004
EMP: 8 EST: 2020
SALES (est): 723.59K **Privately Held**
Web: www.jbecustomcoaters.com
SIC: 3499 Fabricated metal products, nec

(G-7172)
JET FUEL STRATEGIES LLC
44050 Russia Rd (44035-6800)
PHONE..................440 323-4220
Josi U Ren, *Prin*
EMP: 8 EST: 2014
SALES (est): 758.05K **Privately Held**
Web: www.jetsfbo.com
SIC: 2911 Jet fuels

(G-7173)
LEAR MFG CO INC
147 Freedom Ct (44035-2245)
PHONE..................440 324-1111
Bonnie Lear, *Pr*
EMP: 15 EST: 2014
SALES (est): 480.8K **Privately Held**
Web: www.learmfg.com
SIC: 3452 Nuts, metal

(G-7174)
LORAIN MODERN PATTERN INC
159 Woodbury St (44035-4011)
PHONE..................440 365-6780
Todd R Roth, *Pr*
Sheila I Kelly-roth, *VP*
EMP: 10
SQ FT: 5,500
SALES (est): 809.2K **Privately Held**
Web: www.lorainmodern.com
SIC: 3543 Industrial patterns

(G-7175)
LOWER LIMB CENTERS LLC
1100 Abbe Rd N Ste D (44035-1667)
PHONE..................440 365-2502
Mark I Winters, *Prin*
EMP: 6 EST: 2008
SALES (est): 140.26K **Privately Held**
SIC: 3842 Limbs, artificial

(G-7176)
LTI POWER SYSTEMS INC
10800 Middle Ave Hngr B (44035-7893)
PHONE..................440 327-5050
▲ EMP: 20 EST: 1995
SQ FT: 35,000
SALES (est): 3.55MM **Privately Held**
Web: www.ltipowersystems.com
SIC: 3612 Specialty transformers

(G-7177)
MARATHON INDUSTRIAL CNTRS INC
100 Freedom Ct (44035-2245)
PHONE..................440 324-2748
Richard L Sipley, *Pr*
▼ EMP: 14 EST: 1999
SQ FT: 30,000
SALES (est): 765.63K **Privately Held**
Web: www.marathoncontainers.com
SIC: 3443 Industrial vessels, tanks, and containers

(G-7178)
MASTER BOLT LLC
811 Taylor St (44035-6231)
PHONE..................440 323-5529
EMP: 35 EST: 2020
SALES (est): 2.8MM **Privately Held**
Web: www.masterbolt.com
SIC: 3965 Fasteners

(G-7179)
MCCONNELL READY MIX
37500 Butternut Ridge Rd (44039-8466)
PHONE..................440 458-4325
EMP: 8 EST: 2014
SALES (est): 464.04K **Privately Held**
SIC: 3273 Ready-mixed concrete

(G-7180)
METAL BUILDING INTR PDTS CO
750 Adams St (44035)
PHONE..................440 322-6500
EMP: 16
SALES (corp-wide): 5.1MM **Privately Held**
Web: www.mbiproducts.com
SIC: 3296 Fiberglass insulation
PA: Metal Building Interior Products Co Inc
801 Bond St
Elyria OH
440 322-6500

(G-7181)
METRO DESIGN INC
10740 Middle Ave (44035-7816)
P.O. Box 248 (44036-0248)
PHONE..................440 458-4200
Jeffery Kraps, *Pr*
EMP: 29 EST: 1982
SQ FT: 10,000
SALES (est): 903.98K **Privately Held**
Web: www.metrodesigninc.com
SIC: 3599 7699 3844 Custom machinery; X-ray equipment repair; X-ray apparatus and tubes

(G-7182)
ML ERECTORS LLC
827 Walnut St (44035-3352)
PHONE..................440 328-3227
Matthew J Loftin, *Managing Member*
EMP: 7 EST: 2003
SQ FT: 26,000
SALES (est): 646.85K **Privately Held**
Web: www.mlerectors.com
SIC: 2759 Publication printing

(G-7183)
MULTILINK INC
Also Called: Multifab
580 Ternes Ln (44035-6252)
PHONE..................440 366-6966
Steven Kaplan, *Pr*
Kathy Kaplan, *
Steve Cannon, *
◆ EMP: 140 EST: 1983
SQ FT: 110,000
SALES (est): 51.75MM **Privately Held**
Web: www.gomultilink.com

SIC: 5063 3829 Wire and cable; Cable testing machines

(G-7184)
NELSON STUD WELDING INC (HQ)
7900 W Ridge Rd (44035-1952)
P.O. Box 4019 (44036-2019)
PHONE..................440 329-0400
Ken Caratelli, *Pr*
Debbie Hunnel, *
David Bubar, *
◆ EMP: 81 EST: 2000
SALES (est): 111.99MM
SALES (corp-wide): 15.78B **Publicly Held**
Web: www.stanleyengineeredfastening.com
SIC: 3452 3548 Bolts, nuts, rivets, and washers; Welding apparatus
PA: Stanley Black & Decker, Inc.
1000 Stanley Dr
New Britain CT 06053
860 225-5111

(G-7185)
NICE BODY AUTOMOTIVE LLC
Also Called: Nice Body Automotive
818 Cleveland St (44035-4108)
PHONE..................440 752-5568
Dezmon Lawrence, *CEO*
EMP: 7 EST: 2020
SALES (est): 222.28K **Privately Held**
SIC: 7539 7699 7538 3011 Automotive air conditioning repair; Miscellaneous automotive repair services; General automotive repair shops; Automobile tires, pneumatic

(G-7186)
NORTH AMERCN KIT SOLUTIONS INC (PA)
172 Reaser Ct (44035-6285)
PHONE..................800 854-3267
Steve Bersticker, *VP*
EMP: 37 EST: 2016
SALES (est): 6.25MM
SALES (corp-wide): 6.25MM **Privately Held**
Web: www.naksinc.com
SIC: 2511 Kitchen and dining room furniture

(G-7187)
NORTH COAST RIVET INC
700 Sugar Ln (44035-6312)
P.O. Box 1441 (44036-1441)
PHONE..................440 366-6829
Wesley L Shirley, *CEO*
Kathy Shirley, *Sec*
EMP: 12 EST: 1985
SQ FT: 6,000
SALES (est): 496.86K **Privately Held**
Web: www.valleyfastener.com
SIC: 3452 Rivets, metal

(G-7188)
OAK TREE INTL HOLDINGS INC
1209 Lowell St (44035-4803)
PHONE..................702 462-7295
EMP: 33
SALES (corp-wide): 1.07MM **Privately Held**
Web: www.oaktree-health.com
SIC: 2834 Pharmaceutical preparations
PA: Oak Tree International Holdings, Inc.
9550 S Eastrn Ave Ste 253
Las Vegas NV 89123
702 462-7295

(G-7189)
OHIO DISPLAYS INC
Also Called: Odi
825 Leona St (44035-2300)

GEOGRAPHIC SECTION

Elyria - Lorain County (G-7211)

PHONE..............................216 961-5600
Thomas R Mc Kay, *Ch Bd*
Judy Miller, *VP*
EMP: 15 **EST:** 1918
SQ FT: 70,000
SALES (est): 2.35MM **Privately Held**
Web: www.ohiodisplays.com
SIC: 3993 2542 Displays, paint process; Partitions and fixtures, except wood

(G-7190)
OHIO METALLURGICAL SERVICE INC
Also Called: Ohiomet
1033 Clark St (44035-6257)
P.O. Box 1228 (44036-1228)
PHONE..............................440 365-4104
Donald S Gaydosh, *Pr*
John Gaydosh, *
Glenn E Shoemaker, *
R E Baird, *
William D Latiano, *
EMP: 69 **EST:** 1947
SQ FT: 50,000
SALES (est): 9.05MM **Privately Held**
Web: www.ohiomet.com
SIC: 3398 Metal heat treating

(G-7191)
OHIO SCREW PRODUCTS INC
818 Lowell St (44035-4876)
P.O. Box 4027 (44036-2027)
PHONE..............................440 322-6341
Daniel Imbrogno, *Pr*
Dan Imbrogno, *
Edward N Imbrogno, *
Elmer Brown, *
Joseph Sullivan, *
EMP: 75 **EST:** 1945
SQ FT: 65,000
SALES (est): 10.98MM **Privately Held**
Web: www.ohioscrew.com
SIC: 3541 3451 Screw machines, automatic; Screw machine products

(G-7192)
PARKER-HANNIFIN CORPORATION
Fluid Systems Division
711 Taylor St (44035-6229)
P.O. Box 4032 (44036-4032)
PHONE..............................440 284-6277
Eric Mitchell, *Mgr*
EMP: 200
SALES (corp-wide): 19.07B **Publicly Held**
Web: www.parker.com
SIC: 3728 3724 Aircraft assemblies, subassemblies, and parts, nec; Aircraft engines and engine parts
PA: Parker-Hannifin Corporation
6035 Parkland Blvd
Cleveland OH 44124
216 896-3000

(G-7193)
PEPSI-COLA METRO BTLG CO INC
Also Called: Pepsi-Cola
925 Lorain Blvd (44035-2819)
PHONE..............................440 323-5524
Mike Schonberg, *Brnch Mgr*
EMP: 14
SALES (corp-wide): 86.39B **Publicly Held**
Web: www.pepsico.com
SIC: 2086 5149 Carbonated soft drinks, bottled and canned; Soft drinks
HQ: Pepsi-Cola Metropolitan Bottling Company, Inc.
700 Anderson Hill Rd
Purchase NY 10577
914 767-6000

(G-7194)
PERFECTION FABRICATORS INC
680 Sugar Ln (44035-6310)
PHONE..............................440 365-5850
James Ennes, *Pr*
David Ennes, *VP*
EMP: 10 **EST:** 1973
SQ FT: 27,000
SALES (est): 971.99K **Privately Held**
Web: www.perfectionfabricators.com
SIC: 3441 Fabricated structural metal

(G-7195)
PERSONAL PLUMBER SERVICE CORP
Also Called: Value-Rooter
42343 N Ridge Rd (44035-1130)
PHONE..............................440 324-4321
Russell Halstead, *Pr*
Russell A Halstead, *Owner*
Mellisa Holstead, *Treas*
Russel Halstead, *Pr*
EMP: 19 **EST:** 1997
SALES (est): 1.86MM **Privately Held**
SIC: 1711 2842 1794 Plumbing contractors; Drain pipe solvents or cleaners; Excavation work

(G-7196)
PLASTIC ENTERPRISES INC
Also Called: Bee Valve
1150 Taylor St (44035-6281)
PHONE..............................440 366-0220
Bill Kaatz, *Mgr*
EMP: 9
SALES (corp-wide): 4.63MM **Privately Held**
Web: www.plastic-enterprises.com
SIC: 3089 Injection molding of plastics
PA: Plastic Enterprises, Inc.
41520 Schadden Rd
Elyria OH 44035
440 324-3240

(G-7197)
PLASTIC ENTERPRISES INC (PA)
41520 Schadden Rd (44035-2227)
PHONE..............................440 324-3240
John Leonowich, *Pr*
William Kaatz, *VP*
▲ **EMP:** 22 **EST:** 1959
SQ FT: 35,000
SALES (est): 4.63MM
SALES (corp-wide): 4.63MM **Privately Held**
Web: www.plastic-enterprises.com
SIC: 3089 3544 Injection molding of plastics; Special dies, tools, jigs, and fixtures

(G-7198)
QUALITY BLOW MOLDING INC
635 Oberlin Elyria Rd (44035-7727)
PHONE..............................440 458-6550
EMP: 90 **EST:** 1994
SQ FT: 30,000
SALES (est): 9.42MM **Privately Held**
Web: www.qualityblowmolding.com
SIC: 3089 Injection molding of plastics

(G-7199)
REAL ALLOY SPECIALTY PDTS LLC
320 Huron St (44035-4829)
PHONE..............................440 322-0072
Erik Leith, *Brnch Mgr*
EMP: 20
SALES (corp-wide): 372.45MM **Privately Held**
Web: www.realalloy.com
SIC: 3355 Aluminum rolling and drawing, nec
HQ: Real Alloy Specialty Products, Llc
3700 Park East Dr Ste 300
Beachwood OH 44122
216 755-8836

(G-7200)
RECOGNITION ROBOTICS INC (PA)
141 Innovation Dr Pmb 306 (44035-1673)
PHONE..............................440 590-0499
Simon Melikian, *CEO*
Joe Cyrek, *VP*
EMP: 17 **EST:** 2006
SALES (est): 5.29MM
SALES (corp-wide): 5.29MM **Privately Held**
Web: www.recognitionrobotics.com
SIC: 3569 8742 Robots, assembly line: industrial and commercial; Automation and robotics consultant

(G-7201)
RIDGE TOOL COMPANY
321 Sumner St (44035-6125)
PHONE..............................440 329-4737
Ron Farkas, *Mgr*
EMP: 90
SALES (corp-wide): 15.16B **Publicly Held**
Web: www.ridgid.com
SIC: 3541 Machine tools, metal cutting type
HQ: Ridge Tool Company
400 Clark St
Elyria OH 44035
440 323-5581

(G-7202)
RIDGE TOOL COMPANY (HQ)
Also Called: Ridgid
400 Clark St (44035-6100)
P.O. Box 4023 (44036-2023)
PHONE..............................440 323-5581
B J Jones, *Pr*
◆ **EMP:** 800 **EST:** 1966
SQ FT: 600,000
SALES (est): 467.26MM
SALES (corp-wide): 15.16B **Publicly Held**
Web: www.ridgid.com
SIC: 3423 3547 3546 3541 Hand and edge tools, nec; Rolling mill machinery; Power-driven handtools; Pipe cutting and threading machines
PA: Emerson Electric Co.
8000 W Florissant Ave
Saint Louis MO 63136
314 553-2000

(G-7203)
RIDGE TOOL MANUFACTURING CO
400 Clark St (44035-6100)
P.O. Box 4023 (44036-2023)
PHONE..............................440 323-5581
Fred Pond, *Pr*
Scott Garfield, *
Ralph Shaw, *
EMP: 46 **EST:** 1989
SQ FT: 400,000
SALES (est): 15.55MM
SALES (corp-wide): 15.16B **Publicly Held**
Web: www.ridgid.com
SIC: 3541 3423 3547 3546 Machine tools, metal cutting type; Hand and edge tools, nec; Rolling mill machinery; Power-driven handtools
HQ: Ridge Tool Company
400 Clark St
Elyria OH 44035
440 323-5581

(G-7204)
SHALMET CORPORATION
164 Freedom Ct (44035-2245)
PHONE..............................440 236-8840
Hugh O Donnell, *Brnch Mgr*
EMP: 35
SALES (corp-wide): 2.55B **Publicly Held**
Web: www.carpentertechnology.com
SIC: 3471 Polishing, metals or formed products
HQ: Shalmet Corporation
116 Pinedale Indus Rd
Orwigsburg PA 17961
570 366-1414

(G-7205)
STANLEY ENGINEERED FASTEN
7900 W Ridge Rd (44035-1952)
PHONE..............................440 657-3537
EMP: 10 **EST:** 2019
SALES (est): 264.7K **Privately Held**
Web: www.stanleyengineeredfastening.com
SIC: 3965 Fasteners

(G-7206)
STAYS LIGHTING INC
Also Called: Best Fab Co.
936 Taylor St (44035-6234)
PHONE..............................440 328-3254
Joe Jingle, *Pr*
EMP: 8 **EST:** 2005
SQ FT: 9,200
SALES (est): 786.58K **Privately Held**
SIC: 3441 Fabricated structural metal

(G-7207)
STUD WELDING ASSOCIATES
101 Liberty Ct (44035-2238)
PHONE..............................216 392-7808
EMP: 6 **EST:** 2017
SALES (est): 215.92K **Privately Held**
SIC: 7692 Welding repair

(G-7208)
SUZIN L CHOCOLATIERS
230 Broad St (44035-5502)
PHONE..............................440 323-3372
Suzin Stefanelli, *Owner*
EMP: 8 **EST:** 1981
SQ FT: 26,000
SALES (est): 240.31K **Privately Held**
Web: www.suzinl.com
SIC: 2064 5441 5947 Chocolate candy, except solid chocolate; Candy; Gift shop

(G-7209)
SYMRISE INC
Also Called: Diana Food
110 Liberty Ct (44035-2237)
PHONE..............................440 324-6060
John Cassidy, *Brnch Mgr*
EMP: 116
Web: www.symrise.com
SIC: 2869 Perfume materials, synthetic
HQ: Symrise Inc.
300 North St
Teterboro NJ 07608
201 288-3200

(G-7210)
TEZ TOOL & FABRICATION INC
115 Buckeye St (44035-5216)
PHONE..............................440 323-2300
Matt Tezmer, *Pr*
EMP: 9 **EST:** 2001
SQ FT: 4,900
SALES (est): 172.23K **Privately Held**
SIC: 3089 Injection molded finished plastics products, nec

(G-7211)
THE RELIABLE SPRING WIRE FRMS
910 Taylor St (44035)
P.O. Box 58 (44036)
PHONE..............................440 365-7400

Elyria - Lorain County (G-7212) GEOGRAPHIC SECTION

Richard Mcbride, Pr
Sybil Mcbride, Sec
EMP: 41 **EST:** 1937
SALES (est): 4.6MM **Privately Held**
Web: www.reliablespring.com
SIC: 3469 3495 Stamping metal for the trade
; Mechanical springs, precision

(G-7212)
TOOL AND DIE SYSTEMS
38900 Taylor Pkwy (44035-6259)
PHONE..............................440 327-5800
William Flickinger, VP
EMP: 10 **EST:** 2020
SALES (est): 484.37K **Privately Held**
Web: www.tooldiesystems.com
SIC: 3444 Sheet metalwork

(G-7213)
TTR MANUFACTURING LLC
740 Sugar Ln (44035-6312)
P.O. Box 1060 (44036-1060)
PHONE..............................440 366-5005
EMP: 9 **EST:** 2010
SALES (est): 528.88K **Privately Held**
SIC: 3999 Manufacturing industries, nec

(G-7214)
ULTRA MACHINE INC
Also Called: Silver Machine Co
530 Lowell St (44035-4862)
PHONE..............................440 323-7632
Thomas C Guignette, Pr
EMP: 7 **EST:** 1977
SQ FT: 2,500
SALES (est): 557.74K **Privately Held**
SIC: 3599 Machine shop, jobbing and repair

(G-7215)
UNITED INITIATORS INC (HQ)
555 Garden St (44035-4870)
PHONE..............................440 323-3112
Ed Hoozemans, CEO
William Clements, *
Johannes Ziegler, *
◆ **EMP:** 63 **EST:** 2000
SQ FT: 40,000
SALES (est): 150.27MM
SALES (corp-wide): 254.57MM **Privately Held**
Web: www.degussa-initiators.com
SIC: 2819 2869 Catalysts, chemical;
Industrial organic chemicals, nec
PA: United Initiators Gmbh
Dr.-Gustav-Adolph-Str. 3
Pullach I. Isartal BY 82049
897 442-2237

(G-7216)
VECTRON INC
201 Perry Ct (44035-6149)
PHONE..............................440 323-3369
Robert Pustay, Pr
EMP: 23 **EST:** 1972
SQ FT: 48,000
SALES (est): 1.69MM **Privately Held**
Web: www.vectron.cc
SIC: 3599 3471 Machine shop, jobbing and
repair; Plating and polishing

(G-7217)
VTD SYSTEMS INC
7600 W River Rd S (44035-6934)
PHONE..............................440 323-4122
Robert Vilagi Junior, Pr
EMP: 20 **EST:** 1994
SQ FT: 5,100
SALES (est): 2.59MM **Privately Held**
Web: www.vtdsystems.com
SIC: 3599 Machine shop, jobbing and repair

(G-7218)
WESTVIEW CONCRETE CORP
Also Called: Avon Concrete
40105 Butternut Ridge Rd (44035-7903)
PHONE..............................440 458-5800
TOLL FREE: 800
John Walls, VP
EMP: 15
SQ FT: 1,202
SALES (corp-wide): 6.36MM **Privately Held**
Web: www.westviewconcrete.com
SIC: 3273 5211 Ready-mixed concrete;
Masonry materials and supplies
PA: Westview Concrete Corp.
26000 Sprague Rd
Olmsted Falls OH 44138
440 235-1800

(G-7219)
WOOSTER BRUSH COMPANY
070 Infirmary Rd (44035-4099)
PHONE..............................440 322-8081
Rick Dice, Brnch Mgr
EMP: 6
SALES (corp-wide): 51.67MM **Privately Held**
Web: www.woosterbrush.com
SIC: 3991 Paint and varnish brushes
PA: The Wooster Brush Company
604 Madison Ave
Wooster OH 44691
330 264-4440

(G-7220)
ZAYTRAN INC
41535 Schadden Rd (44035-2226)
P.O. Box 1660 (44036-1660)
PHONE..............................440 324-2814
Theodore Zajac Junior, Pr
Theodore Zajac Senior, Ch
Monica Parker, *
J C Wm Tattersall, *
EMP: 26 **EST:** 1980
SQ FT: 80,000
SALES (est): 1.81MM **Privately Held**
Web: www.zaytran.com
SIC: 3593 3492 Fluid power actuators,
hydraulic or pneumatic; Fluid power valves
and hose fittings

Englewood
Montgomery County

(G-7221)
AIMS-CMI TECHNOLOGY LLC
65 Haas Dr (45322-2842)
PHONE..............................937 832-2000
David A Delph, Pr
EMP: 17 **EST:** 2016
SQ FT: 12,000
SALES (est): 1.31MM **Privately Held**
Web: www.cmi-technology.com
SIC: 3599 3544 Machine shop, jobbing and
repair; Special dies, tools, jigs, and fixtures

(G-7222)
AIRBASE INDUSTRIES LLC
Also Called: Eaton Compressor & Fabrication
1000 Cass Dr (45315-8844)
PHONE..............................937 540-1140
Matthew Cain, Managing Member
◆ **EMP:** 10 **EST:** 2000
SQ FT: 60,000
SALES (est): 1.04MM **Privately Held**
Web: www.emaxcompressor.com
SIC: 3563 Air and gas compressors
including vacuum pumps

(G-7223)
ANGSTROM FIBER ENGLEWOOD LLC (PA) ✪
300 Lau Pkwy (45315-8826)
PHONE..............................734 756-1164
Nagesh Palakurthi, Managing Member
EMP: 34 **EST:** 2023
SALES (est): 5.57MM
SALES (corp-wide): 5.57MM **Privately Held**
SIC: 2273 Aircraft and automobile floor coverings

(G-7224)
C&W SWISS INC
100 Lau Pkwy (45315-8787)
PHONE..............................937 832-2889
Gregory Crabtree, Pr
Tammy Crabtree, VP
EMP: 18 **EST:** 1998
SALES (est): 1.55MM **Privately Held**
Web: www.cwswiss.com
SIC: 3599 Machine shop, jobbing and repair

(G-7225)
CMI TECHNOLOGY INC
65 Haas Dr (45322-2842)
PHONE..............................937 832-2000
EMP: 17
Web: www.cmi-technology.com
SIC: 3599 3544 Machine shop, jobbing and
repair; Special dies, tools, jigs, and fixtures

(G-7226)
CREATIVE COUNTERTOPS OHIO INC
Also Called: Creative Countertops
477 E Wenger Rd (45322-2831)
PHONE..............................937 540-9450
EMP: 10 **EST:** 2007
SQ FT: 10,000
SALES (est): 789.3K **Privately Held**
Web: www.creative-countertops.com
SIC: 3281 Granite, cut and shaped

(G-7227)
CREATIVE MICROSYSTEMS INC
Also Called: Civica CMI
52 Hillside Ct (45322-2745)
PHONE..............................937 836-4499
Lin Mallott, CEO
Arvind Kohli, *
EMP: 80 **EST:** 1979
SQ FT: 14,400
SALES (est): 9.46MM **Privately Held**
Web: www.civica.com
SIC: 7373 7372 Systems integration services
; Prepackaged software

(G-7228)
CROSSROADS MACHINE INC
65 Haas Dr (45322-2842)
PHONE..............................937 832-2000
John Howard, Prin
EMP: 6 **EST:** 2016
SALES (est): 142.59K **Privately Held**
Web: www.crossroadsmachine.com
SIC: 3599 Machine shop, jobbing and repair

(G-7229)
DISPLAY DYNAMICS INC
1 Display Point Dr (45315-8857)
P.O. Box 27 (45315-0027)
PHONE..............................937 832-2830
EMP: 22 **EST:** 1994
SQ FT: 40,000
SALES (est): 1.34MM **Privately Held**
Web: www.disdyn.com

SIC: 7389 2541 7319 1751 Exhibit
construction by industrial contractors; Store
fixtures, wood; Display advertising service;
Cabinet and finish carpentry

(G-7230)
EATON COMPRSR FABRICATION INC
Also Called: Polar Air
1000 Cass Dr (45315-8844)
PHONE..............................877 283-7614
◆ **EMP:** 25 **EST:** 2006
SQ FT: 50,000
SALES (est): 5.78MM **Privately Held**
Web: www.eatoncompressor.com
SIC: 3563 Air and gas compressors

(G-7231)
ENGLEWOOD PRECISION INC
375 Union Rd (45315-8802)
P.O. Box 399 (45322-0399)
PHONE..............................937 836-1910
EMP: 6 **EST:** 2014
SALES (est): 229.4K **Privately Held**
Web: www.epinei.com
SIC: 3469 Stamping metal for the trade

(G-7232)
HART & COOLEY LLC
1 Lau Pkwy (45315-8754)
PHONE..............................937 832-7800
EMP: 47
Web: www.hartandcooley.com
SIC: 3446 Registers (air), metal
HQ: Hart & Cooley Llc
4460 44th St Se Ste F
Grand Rapids MI 49512
616 656-8200

(G-7233)
IDEAL IMAGE INC
Also Called: Ideal Branding
115 Haas Dr (45322-2845)
PHONE..............................937 832-1660
Dale Paugh, Pr
J Belinda Paugh, *
Belinda Paugh, *
▲ **EMP:** 77 **EST:** 1993
SQ FT: 40,000
SALES (est): 18.92MM **Privately Held**
Web: www.idealimageinc.com
SIC: 3999 Barber and beauty shop equipment

(G-7234)
INTERNATIONAL BELLOWS
2 Ferrari Ct (45315-8988)
PHONE..............................937 294-6261
Thomas Armstrong, Pr
Tony Riggs, VP
Martin Sherry, VP
Tim Gockel, Treas
Greg Furlong, VP
EMP: 10 **EST:** 1993
SQ FT: 4,800
SALES (est): 998.41K **Privately Held**
Web: www.joycedayton.com
SIC: 3599 Bellows, industrial: metal

(G-7235)
KING KOLD INC
331 N Main St (45322-1333)
PHONE..............................937 836-2731
Douglas Smith, Pr
Robert L Smith, Sec
EMP: 31 **EST:** 1968
SQ FT: 5,210
SALES (est): 1.06MM **Privately Held**
Web: www.kingkoldinc.com

▲ = Import ▼ = Export
◆ = Import/Export

SIC: 2038 2013 2011 5142 Frozen specialties, nec; Cooked meats, from purchased meat; Meat packing plants; Fish, frozen: packaged

(G-7236)
LIPO TECHNOLOGIES INC
707 Harco Dr (45315-8854)
PHONE.................................937 264-1222
▲ **EMP:** 24
Web: www.lipotechnologies.com
SIC: 2869 Industrial organic chemicals, nec

(G-7237)
NANOLAP TECHNOLOGIES LLC
85 Harrisburg Dr (45322-2835)
PHONE.................................877 658-4949
EMP: 18 **EST:** 2007
SQ FT: 19,000
SALES (est): 484.63K **Privately Held**
Web: www.nanolapabrasives.com
SIC: 3291 Coated abrasive products

(G-7238)
NISSIN PRECISION N AMER INC
375 Union Rd (45315-8802)
P.O. Box 399 (45322 0399)
PHONE.................................937 836-1910
Todd Shimizu, *Pr*
Cathy Sayer, *
Mike Greer, *
Masatoshi Shimizu, *
Akio Adam Yamamoto, *VP*
▲ **EMP:** 80 **EST:** 1989
SALES (est): 19.4MM **Privately Held**
Web: www.nissinoh.com
SIC: 3663 3444 Television broadcasting and communications equipment; Sheet metalwork
PA: Nissin Kogyo Co., Ltd.
    1-1-1, Tsukinowa
    Otsu SGA 520-2

(G-7239)
PUZZLES & PLANESWALKERS LLC
7 N Main St (45322-1326)
PHONE.................................937 540-9047
EMP: 6 **EST:** 2012
SALES (est): 115.98K **Privately Held**
SIC: 3944 Puzzles

(G-7240)
RATLIFF METAL SPINNING COMPANY
40 Harrisburg Dr (45322-2834)
PHONE.................................937 836-3900
Michael K Ratliff, *Pr*
James D Ratliff, *VP*
Robin K Ratliff, *Treas*
EMP: 30 **EST:** 1967
SQ FT: 40,000
SALES (est): 3.96MM **Privately Held**
Web: www.ratliffmetal.com
SIC: 3469 Stamping metal for the trade

(G-7241)
SAMB LLC SERVICES
Also Called: Liberty Tax Service
504 Sorna Dr (45322-1453)
PHONE.................................937 660-0115
Abdou Samb, *Managing Member*
EMP: 7 **EST:** 2016
SALES (est): 296.94K **Privately Held**
Web: www.libertytax.com
SIC: 1389 7291 8721 5099 Construction, repair, and dismantling services; Tax return preparation services; Payroll accounting service; Durable goods, nec

(G-7242)
SK TECH INC
200 Metro Dr (45315-8700)
PHONE.................................937 836-3535
Nobuyoshi Saigusa, *Pr*
Hidki Kawase, *
Masatoshi Watanabe, *
Hideki Kawase, *
▲ **EMP:** 160 **EST:** 2002
SQ FT: 48,000
SALES (est): 22.64MM **Privately Held**
Web: www.sktechusa.com
SIC: 3694 Engine electrical equipment

(G-7243)
TCS SCHINDLER & CO LLC
Also Called: Yipes Stripes
36 Haas Dr (45322-2808)
PHONE.................................937 836-9473
Todd Schindler, *Managing Member*
EMP: 7 **EST:** 2012
SALES (est): 321.23K **Privately Held**
Web: www.yipesgraphics.com
SIC: 3993 Signs and advertising specialties

(G-7244)
TE-CO MANUFACTURING LLC
100 Quinter Farm Rd (45322-9705)
PHONE.................................937 836-0961
Richard Porter, *Managing Member*
▲ **EMP:** 76 **EST:** 1926
SQ FT: 40,000
SALES (est): 9.18MM **Privately Held**
Web: www.te-co.com
SIC: 3545 3829 3544 3429 Machine tool attachments and accessories; Measuring and controlling devices, nec; Special dies, tools, jigs, and fixtures; Hardware, nec

(G-7245)
TOM SMITH INDUSTRIES INC
Also Called: T S I
500 Smith Dr (45315-8788)
PHONE.................................937 832-1555
Annette H Smith, *CEO*
John A Shay, *
Steven D Good, *
Tarra E Enochs, *
▲ **EMP:** 85 **EST:** 1980
SQ FT: 108,000
SALES (est): 18.92MM **Privately Held**
Web: www.tomsmithindustries.com
SIC: 3544 3089 3714 Industrial molds; Injection molded finished plastics products, nec; Motor vehicle parts and accessories

(G-7246)
UNIFIED SCRNING CRSHING - OH I
Also Called: Ohio Wire Cloth
200 Cass Dr (45315-8834)
P.O. Box 280 (45322-0280)
PHONE.................................937 836-3201
Tom Lentsch, *Pr*
Michele Kleason, *Treas*
Devan Donalson, *Prin*
EMP: 6 **EST:** 1961
SQ FT: 10,000
SALES (est): 1.52MM
SALES (corp-wide): 22.5MM **Privately Held**
Web: www.unifiedscreening.com
SIC: 3496 5082 7699 Wire cloth and woven wire products; Mining machinery and equipment, except petroleum; Welding equipment repair
PA: Unified Screening & Crushing - Mn, Inc.
    3350 Hwy 149 S
    Eagan MN 55121
    651 454-8835

(G-7247)
VALUE ADDED PACKAGING INC
44 Lau Pkwy (45315-8777)
PHONE.................................937 832-9595
Jarod D Wenrick, *Pr*
▲ **EMP:** 15 **EST:** 1998
SQ FT: 20,000
SALES (est): 4.88MM **Privately Held**
Web: www.vapmanaged.com
SIC: 2653 Boxes, corrugated: made from purchased materials

(G-7248)
VANTAGE SPCLTY INGREDIENTS INC
707 Harco Dr (45315-8854)
PHONE.................................937 264-1222
Lou Frischling, *CEO*
EMP: 50 **EST:** 2012
SALES (est): 8.33MM **Privately Held**
Web: www.vantagegrp.com
SIC: 2869 Industrial organic chemicals, nec

(G-7249)
WOODBRIDGE ENGLEWOOD INC
Also Called: Hematite
300 Lau Pkwy (45315-8826)
P.O. Box 249 (45315-0249)
PHONE.................................937 540-9889
John C Pavanel, *Pr*
EMP: 25 **EST:** 2014
SALES (est): 19.36MM **Privately Held**
Web: www.englewood.oh.us
SIC: 3089 Automotive parts, plastic

Enon
Clark County

(G-7250)
HARDWOOD STORE INC
350 Enon Rd (45323-1004)
PHONE.................................937 864-2899
John B Clark, *Pr*
John B Clark, *Pr*
Lisa L Clark, *VP*
EMP: 6 **EST:** 1988
SQ FT: 16,000
SALES (est): 719.69K **Privately Held**
Web: www.thehardwoodstore.com
SIC: 2499 5211 Decorative wood and woodwork; Lumber products

(G-7251)
PROMAC INC
350 Conley Dr (45323-1002)
P.O. Box 158 (45323-0158)
PHONE.................................937 864-1961
Russell Foster, *Pr*
EMP: 14 **EST:** 1971
SQ FT: 22,000
SALES (est): 333.7K **Privately Held**
Web: www.promacinc.net
SIC: 3599 3544 Machine shop, jobbing and repair; Special dies, tools, jigs, and fixtures

(G-7252)
SEEPEX INC
511 Speedway Dr (45323)
P.O. Box 951454 (44193)
PHONE.................................937 864-7150
Mike Dillon, *Pr*
Ulrich Seeberger, *
◆ **EMP:** 115 **EST:** 1991
SQ FT: 35,000
SALES (est): 31.1MM
SALES (corp-wide): 6.88B **Publicly Held**
Web: www.seepex.com
SIC: 3586 3561 Measuring and dispensing pumps; Pumps and pumping equipment
HQ: Seepex Gmbh
    Scharnholzstr. 344
    Bottrop NW 46240
    20419960

Etna
Franklin County

(G-7253)
WAIBEL ELECTRIC CO INC
133 Humphries Dr (43068-6801)
PHONE.................................740 964-2956
Carl H Waibel Junior, *Pr*
Sherry Waibel, *Sec*
EMP: 16 **EST:** 1947
SQ FT: 5,200
SALES (est): 2.41MM **Privately Held**
Web: www.waibelelectric.com
SIC: 1731 3621 General electrical contractor ; Motors and generators

Etna
Licking County

(G-7254)
BEST LIGHTING PRODUCTS INC (HQ)
Also Called: Best Lighting Products
1213 Etna Pkwy (43062-8041)
PHONE.................................740 964-1198
Jeffrey S Katz, *CEO*
George Jue, *
◆ **EMP:** 55 **EST:** 1997
SQ FT: 60,000
SALES (est): 44.25MM **Privately Held**
Web: www.bestlighting.net
SIC: 5063 3646 Electrical apparatus and equipment; Commercial lighting fixtures
PA: Corinthian Capital Group, Llc
    601 Lexington Ave Rm 5901
    New York NY 10022

(G-7255)
JELD-WEN INC
Also Called: Jeld-Wen Millwork Masters
91 Heritage Dr (43062-9805)
PHONE.................................740 964-1431
Scott Farrington, *Brnch Mgr*
EMP: 107
Web: www.jeld-wen.com
SIC: 2431 Doors, wood
HQ: Jeld-Wen, Inc.
    2645 Silver Crescent Dr
    Charlotte NC 28273
    800 535-3936

(G-7256)
RIDGE CORPORATION (PA)
1201 Etna Pkwy (43062-8041)
PHONE.................................614 421-7434
Gary A Grandominico, *CEO*
▲ **EMP:** 98 **EST:** 1994
SALES (est): 31.14MM
SALES (corp-wide): 31.14MM **Privately Held**
Web: www.ridgecorp.com
SIC: 3443 Liners/lining

(G-7257)
YANKEE CANDLE COMPANY INC
Also Called: Polarpics
175 Heritage Dr (43062-9805)
PHONE.................................413 712-9416
EMP: 6
SALES (corp-wide): 8.13B **Publicly Held**
Web: www.yankeecandle.com
SIC: 3999 Candles
HQ: The Yankee Candle Company Inc
    16 Yankee Candle Way

Euclid
Cuyahoga County

(G-7258)
ADVANCED EQUIPMENT SYSTEMS LLC
22800 Lakeland Blvd (44132-2606)
PHONE..................216 289-6505
EMP: 8 **EST:** 2012
SQ FT: 65,000
SALES (est): 1.06MM **Privately Held**
Web: www.advancedequipmentsys.com
SIC: 3535 Conveyors and conveying equipment

(G-7259)
AJAX-CECO
1500 E 219th St (44117-1503)
PHONE..................440 295-0244
EMP: 11 **EST:** 2017
SALES (est): 330.53K **Privately Held**
Web: www.ajaxerie.com
SIC: 3599 Machine shop, jobbing and repair

(G-7260)
AMD PLASTICS INC (PA)
27600 Lakeland Blvd (44132-2152)
PHONE..................216 289-4862
Brian Coll, *Pr*
▲ **EMP:** 18 **EST:** 1984
SQ FT: 50,000
SALES (est): 4.97MM
SALES (corp-wide): 4.97MM **Privately Held**
Web: www.amdplastics.com
SIC: 3089 Thermoformed finished plastics products, nec

(G-7261)
AMERICAN METAL STAMPING CO LLC
20900 Saint Clair Ave (44117-1040)
PHONE..................216 531-3100
Diane Rodgers, *CFO*
EMP: 14 **EST:** 2003
SALES (est): 2.57MM **Privately Held**
Web: www.amstamping.com
SIC: 3441 Fabricated structural metal

(G-7262)
AMERICAN PUNCH CO
1655 Century Corners Pkwy (44132-3321)
PHONE..................216 731-4501
Robert Olson, *Pr*
David G Olson, *Sec*
EMP: 21 **EST:** 1990
SQ FT: 12,000
SALES (est): 3.79MM **Privately Held**
Web: www.americanpunchco.com
SIC: 3599 3544 3421 Machine shop, jobbing and repair; Special dies, tools, jigs, and fixtures; Cutlery

(G-7263)
BIC MANUFACTURING INC
Also Called: Brennan Inds Clvland Mfg Group
26420 Century Corners Pkwy (44132-3310)
PHONE..................216 531-9393
David D Carr, *Pr*
Tom Levicky, *
EMP: 26 **EST:** 1972
SQ FT: 42,000
SALES (est): 947.5K **Privately Held**
SIC: 3599 Machine shop, jobbing and repair

(G-7264)
BUCKEYE MACHINING INC
25020 Lakeland Blvd (44132)
PHONE..................216 731-9535
Jerry Mccarthy, *Pr*
Karen Mccarthy, *VP*
EMP: 8 **EST:** 1983
SQ FT: 7,500
SALES (est): 763.87K **Privately Held**
SIC: 3366 Bushings and bearings, bronze (nonmachined)

(G-7265)
CBD RELIEVE ME INC
22420 Tracy Ave (44123-3268)
PHONE..................216 544-1696
Claudio Gentile, *Prin*
EMP: 8 **EST:** 2018
SALES (est): 93.17K **Privately Held**
SIC: 2023 Dietary supplements, dairy and non-dairy based

(G-7266)
CUYAHOGA MOLDED PLASTICS CO (INC) (PA)
Also Called: Cuyahoga Plastics
1265 Babbitt Rd (44132-2798)
PHONE..................216 261-2744
EMP: 50 **EST:** 1960
SALES (est): 5.28MM
SALES (corp-wide): 5.28MM **Privately Held**
Web: www.cuyahogaplastics.com
SIC: 3089 2821 Molding primary plastics; Plastics materials and resins

(G-7267)
ELMET EUCLID LLC
21801 Tungsten Rd (44117-1117)
PHONE..................216 692-3990
Jacob Homiller, *Pr*
Paul Leblanc, *CFO*
EMP: 95 **EST:** 2021
SALES (est): 13.49MM
SALES (corp-wide): 77.73MM **Privately Held**
Web: www.hcstarcksolutions.com
SIC: 3339 Primary nonferrous metals, nec
PA: Elmet Technologies Llc
1560 Lisbon St
Lewiston ME 04240
207 333-6100

(G-7268)
EMMCO INC
19199 Saint Clair Ave (44117-1002)
PHONE..................216 429-2020
Eugene Mitocky, *Pr*
Loreen Mitocky, *Sec*
EMP: 6 **EST:** 1988
SALES (est): 883.38K **Privately Held**
Web: www.emmcoinc.com
SIC: 3593 Fluid power cylinders, hydraulic or pneumatic

(G-7269)
EUCLID HEAT TREATING CO
Also Called: E H T Company
1408 E 222nd St (44117-1108)
PHONE..................216 481-8444
TOLL FREE: 800
John Vanas, *Pr*
John H Vanas, *
EMP: 55 **EST:** 1946
SQ FT: 45,000
SALES (est): 9.25MM **Privately Held**
Web: www.euclidheattreating.com
SIC: 3398 Metal heat treating

(G-7270)
GUARDIAN TECHNOLOGIES LLC
Also Called: Germ Guardian
26251 Bluestone Blvd Ste 7 (44132-2826)
PHONE..................866 603-5900
Richard Farone, *
Ed Vlacich, *
◆ **EMP:** 36 **EST:** 2003
SQ FT: 72,000
SALES (est): 13.29MM
SALES (corp-wide): 132.35MM **Privately Held**
Web: www.lasko.com
SIC: 3564 3585 Air purification equipment; Humidifiers and dehumidifiers
PA: Lasko Group, Inc.
820 Lincoln Ave
West Chester PA 19380
610 692-7400

(G-7271)
H & W TOOL CO
1363 Chardon Rd Ste 3 (44117-1558)
PHONE..................216 795-5520
EMP: 8 **EST:** 2016
SALES (est): 490.25K **Privately Held**
Web: www.hwtool.com
SIC: 3599 Machine shop, jobbing and repair

(G-7272)
HANLON COMPOSITES LLC
21611 Tungsten Rd (44117-1115)
PHONE..................216 261-7056
Larry E Fulton, *CEO*
Larry E Fulton, *Managing Member*
EMP: 20 **EST:** 2018
SALES (est): 1.9MM **Privately Held**
Web: www.hanloncomposites.com
SIC: 3089 Plastics containers, except foam

(G-7273)
HICKMANS CONSTRUCTION CO LLC
21150 Morris Ave (44123-2922)
PHONE..................866 271-2565
EMP: 10 **EST:** 2021
SALES (est): 411.21K **Privately Held**
SIC: 3531 Construction machinery

(G-7274)
INDELCO CUSTOM PRODUCTS INC
25861 Tungsten Rd (44132-2817)
PHONE..................216 797-7300
Mitchell Opalich, *Pr*
Lorraine Simer, *VP*
EMP: 36 **EST:** 1964
SQ FT: 21,500
SALES (est): 917.12K **Privately Held**
Web: www.indelco.com
SIC: 3599 3498 3561 3089 Machine shop, jobbing and repair; Tube fabricating (contract bending and shaping); Pumps and pumping equipment; Fittings for pipe, plastics

(G-7275)
INFINITAIRE INDUSTRIES LLC
Also Called: Infinitaire Industries
24370 Hartland Dr (44123-2210)
PHONE..................216 600-2051
Alex Shorter, *CEO*
EMP: 6 **EST:** 2018
SALES (est): 155.13K **Privately Held**
SIC: 8748 8742 0139 2298 Economic consultant; Financial consultant; Cordage: abaca, sisal, henequen, hemp, jute, or other fiber

(G-7276)
IRONHAWK INDUSTRIAL DIST LLC
Also Called: Ironhawk Industrial
1261 Babbitt Rd Ste B (44132-2754)
PHONE..................216 502-3700
Patrick Hawkins, *Pr*
EMP: 8 **EST:** 2010
SALES (est): 896.3K **Privately Held**
Web: www.ironhawkindustrial.com
SIC: 8741 3531 Business management; Snow plow attachments

(G-7277)
JBJ TECHNOLOGIES INC
185 E 280th St (44132-1306)
PHONE..................216 469-7297
Michael Johnston, *Sr VP*
EMP: 6 **EST:** 2005
SALES (est): 242.78K **Privately Held**
SIC: 3599 Machine shop, jobbing and repair

(G-7278)
JSM EXPRESS INC
27301 Markbarry Ave (44132-2109)
PHONE..................216 272-4512
Jasmin Sakalic, *Prin*
EMP: 8 **EST:** 2006
SALES (est): 274.38K **Privately Held**
SIC: 3715 Truck trailers

(G-7279)
KEENE VILLAGE PLASTICS LTD
23610 Saint Clair Ave (44117-2515)
PHONE..................330 753-0100
EMP: 8 **EST:** 2017
SALES (est): 1.13MM **Privately Held**
Web: www.villageplastics.com
SIC: 3089 Injection molding of plastics

(G-7280)
KERR LAKESIDE INC
26841 Tungsten Rd (44132-2934)
P.O. Box 32220 (44132-0220)
PHONE..................216 261-2100
▲ **EMP:** 70 **EST:** 1948
SALES (est): 10.98MM **Privately Held**
Web: www.kerrlakeside.com
SIC: 3452 3451 Bolts, nuts, rivets, and washers; Screw machine products

(G-7281)
LAKE BUILDING PRODUCTS LTD
1361 Chardon Rd Ste 4 (44117-1557)
PHONE..................216 486-1500
John D Pogacnik, *Prin*
EMP: 10 **EST:** 2005
SALES (est): 966.76K **Privately Held**
Web: www.lbpsteel.com
SIC: 3441 Building components, structural steel

(G-7282)
MARIE NOBLE WINE COMPANY ✪
1891 Idlehurst Dr (44117-1878)
PHONE..................216 633-0025
Bertrim Bandy, *CEO*
EMP: 20 **EST:** 2022
SALES (est): 832.83K **Privately Held**
SIC: 2084 7389 Wines, brandy, and brandy spirits; Business services, nec

(G-7283)
MART PLUS FUEL
21820 Lake Shore Blvd (44123-1707)
PHONE..................216 261-0420
Anil Uppal, *Prin*
EMP: 9 **EST:** 2011
SALES (est): 181.57K **Privately Held**
Web: www.fuelmart.com
SIC: 2869 Fuels

GEOGRAPHIC SECTION
Euclid - Cuyahoga County (G-7306)

(G-7284)
MARVIN LEWIS ENTERPRISES LLC
27801 Euclid Ave (44132-3549)
PHONE..................216 785-8419
Marvin Lewis, *Pr*
EMP: 50 EST: 2021
SALES (est): 2.36MM **Privately Held**
SIC: 3728 Refueling equipment for use in flight, airplane

(G-7285)
MECHANICAL DYNAMICS ANALIS LLC
Also Called: Renewal Parts Maintenance
1250 E 222nd St (44117-1114)
PHONE..................440 946-0082
John L Vanderhoef, *CEO*
EMP: 21
Web: www.mdaturbines.com
SIC: 7699 3568 3053 Industrial machinery and equipment repair; Power transmission equipment, nec; Gaskets; packing and sealing devices
HQ: Mechanical Dynamics & Analysis Llc
19 British American Blvd
Latham NY 12110
518 399-3616

(G-7286)
MESOCOAT INC
Also Called: Mesocoat Advanced Coating Tech
24112 Rockwell Dr (44117-1252)
PHONE..................216 453-0866
Stephen Goss, *CEO*
▲ **EMP: 18 EST: 2007**
SALES (est): 5.2MM
SALES (corp-wide): 5.2MM **Privately Held**
Web: www.mesocoat.com
SIC: 3479 1799 5169 7699 Coating of metals and formed products; Corrosion control installation; Anti-corrosion products; Industrial equipment services
PA: Abakan Inc
2665 S Byshr Dr Ste 450
Miami FL 33133
786 206-5368

(G-7287)
NEWTON MATERION INC
21801 Tungsten Rd (44117-1117)
PHONE..................216 692-3990
Greg Fuller, *Dir Opers*
EMP: 300
Web: www.hcstarcksolutions.com
SIC: 3356 3313 3339 Tungsten, basic shapes; Molybdenum silicon, not made in blast furnaces; Rhenium refining (primary)
HQ: Newton Materion Inc
45 Industrial Pl
Newton MA 02461
617 630-5800

(G-7288)
NORAMCO INC
1400 E 222nd St (44117-1108)
PHONE..................216 531-3400
James M Popela, *CEO*
EMP: 51 EST: 1998
SALES (est): 363.31K
SALES (corp-wide): 21.15MM **Privately Held**
Web: www.noramcobag.com
SIC: 2673 Bags: plastic, laminated, and coated
PA: North American Plastics Chemicals Incorporated
1400 E 222nd St
Euclid OH 44117
216 531-3400

(G-7289)
NORMAN NOBLE INC
931 E 228th St (44123-3201)
PHONE..................216 851-4007
Lawrence Noble, *Pr*
EMP: 50
SALES (corp-wide): 86.29MM **Privately Held**
Web: www.nnoble.com
SIC: 3841 Instruments, microsurgical: except electromedical
PA: Norman Noble, Inc.
5507 Avion Park Dr
Highland Heights OH 44143
216 761-5387

(G-7290)
NORTH AMERICAN PLAS CHEM INC (PA)
Also Called: Noramco
1400 E 222nd St (44117-1108)
PHONE..................216 531-3400
James Popela, *Pr*
EMP: 35 EST: 1974
SQ FT: 25,000
SALES (est): 21.15MM
SALES (corp-wide): 21.15MM **Privately Held**
Web: www.noramcobag.com
SIC: 2673 2671 Plastic and pliofilm bags; Paper; coated and laminated packaging

(G-7291)
ORTHOTIC & PROSTHETIC SPC INC
20650 Lakeland Blvd (44119-3241)
PHONE..................216 531-2773
Richard Gaudio, *Pr*
Tom Heckman, *VP*
Jeff Gerl, *Sec*
EMP: 26 EST: 1972
SQ FT: 7,200
SALES (est): 1.26MM **Privately Held**
SIC: 3842 Orthopedic appliances

(G-7292)
PIONEER SOLUTIONS LLC
24800 Rockwell Dr (44117-1203)
PHONE..................216 383-3400
David Juba, *Managing Member*
EMP: 20 EST: 2004
SQ FT: 10,000
SALES (est): 2.69MM **Privately Held**
Web: www.pioneersolutionsllc.com
SIC: 3492 3542 8711 7389 Electrohydraulic servo valves, metal; Brakes, metal forming; Consulting engineer; Inspection and testing services

(G-7293)
POWDERMET INC (PA)
24112 Rockwell Dr (44117-1252)
PHONE..................216 404-0053
Andrew Sherman, *Pr*
EMP: 49 EST: 1996
SQ FT: 7,800
SALES (est): 9.51MM
SALES (corp-wide): 9.51MM **Privately Held**
Web: www.powdermetinc.com
SIC: 3399 Powder, metal

(G-7294)
POWDERMET POWDER PROD INC
24112 Rockwell Dr Ste D (44117-1252)
PHONE..................216 404-0053
Andrew Sherman, *CEO*
EMP: 10 EST: 2013
SALES (est): 674.95K **Privately Held**
Web: www.powdermetinc.com

SIC: 3821 Crushing and grinding apparatus, laboratory

(G-7295)
PPG INDUSTRIES OHIO INC
Also Called: Pretreatment & Specialty Pdts
23000 Saint Clair Ave (44117-2503)
PHONE..................412 434-1542
Jim Driddy, *Prin*
EMP: 66
SALES (corp-wide): 17.65B **Publicly Held**
Web: www.ppg.com
SIC: 2851 Paints and allied products
HQ: Ppg Industries Ohio, Inc.
3800 W 143rd St
Cleveland OH 44111
216 671-0050

(G-7296)
PRECISION HYDRLIC CNNCTORS INC
Also Called: PHC Divison Bic Manufacturing
26420 Century Corners Pkwy (44132-3310)
PHONE..................440 953-3778
Patrick De Capua, *Pr*
EMP: 15 EST: 1988
SQ FT: 12,000
SALES (est): 1.75MM **Privately Held**
SIC: 3599 Machine and other job shop work

(G-7297)
R & A SPORTS INC
Also Called: Adler Team Sports
23780 Lakeland Blvd (44132)
PHONE..................216 289-2254
John Domo, *Pr*
Richard Domo, *
Ruth Ann Domo, *
EMP: 25 EST: 1976
SQ FT: 16,000
SALES (est): 3.9MM **Privately Held**
Web: www.coachesonly.com
SIC: 5091 5136 5137 2396 Sporting and recreation goods; Sportswear, men's and boys'; Sportswear, women's and children's; Screen printing on fabric articles

(G-7298)
RALPHIE GIANNI MFG & CO LTD
250 E 271st St (44132-1606)
PHONE..................216 507-3873
EMP: 10 EST: 2018
SALES (est): 250.5K **Privately Held**
SIC: 2389 Apparel and accessories, nec

(G-7299)
RISHER & CO
27011 Tungsten Rd (44132-2990)
PHONE..................216 732-8351
William J Risher, *Pr*
EMP: 20 EST: 1942
SQ FT: 27,000
SALES (est): 444.05K **Privately Held**
Web: www.risherandcompany.com
SIC: 3599 Machine shop, jobbing and repair

(G-7300)
S C INDUSTRIES INC
24460 Lakeland Blvd (44132-2622)
P.O. Box 32307 (44132-0307)
PHONE..................216 732-9000
Earl Lauridsen, *Pr*
▲ **EMP: 20 EST: 1974**
SQ FT: 10,000
SALES (est): 4.68MM **Privately Held**
Web: www.scindustriesinc.com
SIC: 3366 7389 Bushings and bearings; Grinding, precision: commercial or industrial

(G-7301)
TECH-MED INC
Also Called: Shaker Numeric Mfg
1080 E 222nd St (44117-1101)
PHONE..................216 486-0900
Gary White, *Pr*
Carty White, *Sec*
EMP: 15 EST: 1953
SQ FT: 10,000
SALES (est): 2.05MM **Privately Held**
Web: www.shakernumeric.com
SIC: 3469 Machine parts, stamped or pressed metal

(G-7302)
TOMAHAWK ENTRMT GROUP LLC
26870 Drakefield Ave (44132-2009)
PHONE..................216 505-0548
Javon Bates, *CEO*
EMP: 10 EST: 2011
SALES (est): 852.31K **Privately Held**
SIC: 4832 2731 7389 8742 Radio broadcasting stations, music format; Book publishing; Music recording producer; Marketing consulting services

(G-7303)
TRI COUNTY DOOR SERVICE INC
21701 Tungsten Rd (44117-1116)
PHONE..................216 531-2245
Peter Look, *Pr*
Frank A Cigoy, *VP*
Mrs. Savage, *Bookkpr*
EMP: 10 EST: 1968
SQ FT: 10,000
SALES (est): 522.89K **Privately Held**
Web: www.tricountydoorservice.com
SIC: 3442 1751 Garage doors, overhead: metal; Carpentry work

(G-7304)
TRUST MANUFACTURING LLC (PA)
20080 Saint Clair Ave (44117-1015)
PHONE..................216 531-8787
EMP: 9 EST: 2004
SALES (est): 2.33MM
SALES (corp-wide): 2.33MM **Privately Held**
Web: www.trustmfg.com
SIC: 3599 Machine shop, jobbing and repair

(G-7305)
US LIGHTING GROUP INC
1148 E 222nd St (44117-1103)
PHONE..................216 896-7000
Paul Spivak, *CEO*
Susan Tubbs, *CFO*
EMP: 40 EST: 2013
SALES (est): 4.02MM **Privately Held**
Web: www.uslightinggroup.com
SIC: 3679 Electronic circuits

(G-7306)
VILLAGE PLASTICS CO
Also Called: 3d Systems
23610 Saint Clair Ave (44117-2515)
PHONE..................330 753-0100
Kevin Gerstenslager, *Prin*
EMP: 8 EST: 2004
SALES (est): 1.92MM
SALES (corp-wide): 29.15MM **Privately Held**
Web: www.villageplastics.com
SIC: 3544 Extrusion dies
PA: Keene Building Products Co.
2926 Chester Ave
Cleveland OH 44114
440 605-1020

Fairborn
Greene County

(G-7307)
ADAPT-A-PAK INC
678 Yellow Springs Fairfield Rd Ste 100 (45324)
PHONE..................937 845-0386
TOLL FREE: 800
EMP: 37 EST: 1987
SALES (est): 5.75MM **Privately Held**
Web: www.adaptapak.com
SIC: 2653 5113 Boxes, corrugated: made from purchased materials; Shipping supplies

(G-7308)
ALI INDUSTRIES LLC
Also Called: Abrasive Leaders & Innovators
747 E Xenia Dr (45324-8761)
PHONE..................937 878-3946
Terry Ali, *Pr*
Phillip Ali, *
Christopher Ali, *
Lee Kockentiet, *
◆ EMP: 283 EST: 1961
SQ FT: 260,360
SALES (est): 48.86MM
SALES (corp-wide): 7.26B **Publicly Held**
Web: www.gatorfinishing.com
SIC: 3291 Abrasive products
HQ: Rust-Oleum Corporation
11 E Hawthorn Pkwy
Vernon Hills IL 60061
847 367-7700

(G-7309)
ALL SRVICE PLASTIC MOLDING INC
611 Yellow Springs Fairfield Rd (45324)
PHONE..................937 415-3674
Keller Phillip, *Brnch Mgr*
EMP: 114
SALES (corp-wide): 27.09MM **Privately Held**
Web: www.mincogroup.com
SIC: 3089 Injection molding of plastics
PA: All Service Plastic Molding, Inc.
850 Falls Creek Dr
Vandalia OH 45377
937 890-0322

(G-7310)
APOGEE PLASTICS CORP
8300 Dayton Springfield Rd (45324-1911)
PHONE..................937 864-1966
Walter S Hoy, *Pr*
EMP: 11 EST: 2003
SALES (est): 135.97K **Privately Held**
SIC: 3089 Plastics processing

(G-7311)
CEMEX CEMENT INC
4410 State Rt 235 (45324-9773)
PHONE..................937 873-9858
EMP: 113
SIC: 3273 Ready-mixed concrete
HQ: Cemex Cement, Inc.
10100 Katy Fwy Ste 300
Houston TX 77043
713 650-6200

(G-7312)
CURTISS-WRIGHT CONTROLS
Also Called: Curtiss-Wright Controls
2600 Paramount Pl Ste 200 (45324-6816)
PHONE..................937 252-5601
EMP: 50
SALES (corp-wide): 2.85B **Publicly Held**
Web: www.curtisswright.com

SIC: 8711 8731 3769 3625 Consulting engineer; Commercial physical research; Space vehicle equipment, nec; Relays and industrial controls
HQ: Curtiss-Wright Controls Electronic Systems, Inc.
28965 Avenue Penn
Santa Clarita CA 91355
661 257-4430

(G-7313)
ERNST ENTERPRISES INC
Also Called: Valley Concrete Division
5325 Medway Rd (45324-9765)
PHONE..................937 878-9378
John Macfee, *Genl Mgr*
EMP: 21
SALES (corp-wide): 240.08MM **Privately Held**
Web: www.ernstconcrete.com
SIC: 3273 Ready-mixed concrete
PA: Ernst Enterprises, Inc
3361 Successful Way
Dayton OH 45414
937 233-5555

(G-7314)
FAIRBORN CEMENT PLANT
3250 Linebaugh Rd (45324)
PHONE..................937 879-8466
Bruce Moroz, *Prin*
EMP: 10 EST: 2010
SALES (est): 83.06K **Privately Held**
Web: www.fairborncement.com
SIC: 3273 Ready-mixed concrete

(G-7315)
FOX LITE INC
8300 Dayton Springfield Rd (45324-1911)
PHONE..................937 864-1966
Douglas Hoy, *Pr*
Walter Hoy, *
Mark Hopkins, *
▼ EMP: 30 EST: 1982
SQ FT: 74,000
SALES (est): 4.11MM **Privately Held**
Web: www.foxlite.com
SIC: 3089 Plastics hardware and building products

(G-7316)
GBR PROPERTY MAINTENANCE LLC
1260 Spangler Rd Bldg 1 (45324-9504)
PHONE..................937 879-0200
EMP: 10 EST: 2005
SALES (est): 609.62K **Privately Held**
SIC: 2951 Asphalt paving mixtures and blocks

(G-7317)
GLAWE MANUFACTURING CO INC
Also Called: Glawe Awnings
851 Zapata Dr (45324-5165)
PHONE..................937 754-0064
L Vernon Schaefer, *Pr*
Katherine Schaefer, *VP*
Thomas R Fridley, *VP*
EMP: 13 EST: 1877
SQ FT: 20,500
SALES (est): 353.96K **Privately Held**
Web: www.glaweawning.com
SIC: 2394 7359 Awnings, fabric: made from purchased materials; Equipment rental and leasing, nec

(G-7318)
LASERLINC INC
777 Zapata Dr (45324-5160)
PHONE..................937 318-2440
Dan Dixon, *Pr*

Jeff Kohler, *VP*
Jack Weiss, *VP*
▲ EMP: 20 EST: 1994
SQ FT: 19,000
SALES (est): 3.75MM **Privately Held**
Web: www.laserlinc.com
SIC: 3826 Analytical instruments

(G-7319)
MIAMI VALLEY PUBLISHING LLC
678 Yellow Springs Fairfield Rd (45324)
P.O. Box 681 (45324-0681)
PHONE..................937 879-5678
EMP: 143
Web: www.miamivalleypublishing.com
SIC: 2752 Offset printing

(G-7320)
MORRIS FURNITURE CO INC (PA)
Also Called: Morris Home Furnishing
2377 Commerce Center Blvd Ste A (45324-6378)
PHONE..................937 874-7100
▲ EMP: 150 EST: 1947
SALES (est): 88.44MM
SALES (corp-wide): 88.44MM **Privately Held**
Web: www.morrisathome.com
SIC: 2512 2511 5719 5712 Living room furniture: upholstered on wood frames; Kitchen and dining room furniture; Beddings and linens; Office furniture

(G-7321)
RAPISCAN SYSTEMS HIGH ENRGY IN
Also Called: Aracor
514 E Dayton Yellow Springs Rd (45324-6432)
PHONE..................937 879-4200
EMP: 30
SALES (est): 1.15B **Publicly Held**
Web: www.rapiscansystems.com
SIC: 3845 Electromedical equipment
HQ: Rapiscan Systems High Energy Inspection Corporation
520 Almanor Ave
Sunnyvale CA 94085
408 733-7780

(G-7322)
STADCO INC
Also Called: Stadco Automatics
632 Yellow Springs Fairfield Rd (45324)
PHONE..................937 878-0911
Dennis C Trammell, *Pr*
Kenneth Wilson, *
Jeffrey Lyon, *
EMP: 45 EST: 1948
SQ FT: 42,000
SALES (est): 7.59MM **Privately Held**
Web: www.stadcoprecision.com
SIC: 3451 3541 Screw machine products; Machine tools, metal cutting type

(G-7323)
SURFACE RECOVERY TECH LLC
833 Zapata Dr (45324-5165)
PHONE..................937 879-5864
Thomas Brooks, *Managing Member*
EMP: 15 EST: 2006
SQ FT: 20,000
SALES (est): 2.15MM **Privately Held**
Web: www.surfacerecovery.com
SIC: 3441 Fabricated structural metal

(G-7324)
TANGIBLE SOLUTIONS INC
678 Yellow Springs Fairfield Rd (45324)
PHONE..................937 912-4603
EMP: 23 EST: 2013

SALES (est): 5.23MM **Privately Held**
Web: www.tangiblesolutions3d.com
SIC: 8748 8711 3544 8299 Systems engineering consultant, ex. computer or professional; Engineering services; Special dies, tools, jigs, and fixtures; Educational services

(G-7325)
TEE CREATIONS
Also Called: Tca Graphics
701 N Broad St Ste C (45324-5262)
PHONE..................937 878-2822
Mike Brown, *Owner*
EMP: 9 EST: 1962
SQ FT: 5,000
SALES (est): 475.15K **Privately Held**
Web: www.tcagraphics.com
SIC: 2396 5699 Screen printing on fabric articles; Sports apparel

(G-7326)
VMETRO INC (DH)
Also Called: V Metro
2600 Paramount Pl Ste 200 (45324-6816)
PHONE..................281 584-0728
James H Gerberman, *Pr*
▲ EMP: 51 EST: 1987
SQ FT: 18,317
SALES (est): 938.06K
SALES (corp-wide): 2.85B **Publicly Held**
SIC: 3825 3672 3577 5065 Test equipment for electronic and electric measurement; Printed circuit boards; Computer peripheral equipment, nec; Electronic parts and equipment, nec
HQ: Curtiss-Wright Controls, Inc.
15801 Brixham Hill Ave # 200
Charlotte NC 28277
704 869-4600

(G-7327)
WCR INCORPORATED (PA)
Also Called: W C R
2377 Commerce Center Blvd Ste B (45324-6378)
PHONE..................937 223-0703
Kim Andreasen, *CEO*
Brad Stevens, *
Greg Pinasco, *
Ralene Stevens, *
◆ EMP: 32 EST: 1991
SQ FT: 54,000
SALES (est): 43.23MM
SALES (corp-wide): 43.23MM **Privately Held**
Web: www.wcrhx.com
SIC: 3443 Heat exchangers, condensers, and components

Fairfield
Butler County

(G-7328)
7 7 PRINT SOLUTIONS LLC
6601 Dixie Hwy Ste C (45014-5495)
PHONE..................513 600-4597
Benjamin Sasse, *Prin*
EMP: 10 EST: 2017
SALES (est): 486.61K **Privately Held**
SIC: 2752 Commercial printing, lithographic

(G-7329)
AAA LAMINATING AND BINDERY INC
Also Called: AAA Laminating & Bindery
7209 Dixie Hwy (45014-5544)
PHONE..................513 860-2680
Gerald Randall, *Pr*
EMP: 6 EST: 2005

GEOGRAPHIC SECTION

Fairfield - Butler County (G-7354)

SALES (est): 901.23K **Privately Held**
Web: www.aaalaminating.us
SIC: 2789 Bookbinding and related work

(G-7330)
AGFA CORPORATION
6104 Monastery Dr (45014-4460)
PHONE.................................513 829-6292
James Dixon, *Brnch Mgr*
EMP: 6
SALES (corp-wide): 431.66MM **Privately Held**
Web: www.agfa.com
SIC: 3861 Photographic equipment and supplies
HQ: Agfa Corporation
580 Gotham Pkwy
Carlstadt NJ 07072
800 540-2432

(G-7331)
AKRO TOOL CO INC
240 Donald Dr (45014-3007)
PHONE.................................513 858-1555
Ken Johnson, *Pr*
Donna Johnson, *Sec*
EMP: 8 EST: 1960
SQ FT: 10,000
SALES (est): 965.91K **Privately Held**
Web: www.akrotool.com
SIC: 3599 Machine shop, jobbing and repair

(G-7332)
ALBA MANUFACTURING INC
8950 Seward Rd (45011-9109)
PHONE.................................513 874-0551
Tom Moon, *Pr*
Thomas N Inderhees, *
Mike Kroger, *
EMP: 52 EST: 1973
SQ FT: 67,000
SALES (est): 11.39MM **Privately Held**
Web: www.albamfg.com
SIC: 3535 5084 3312 Conveyors and conveying equipment; Conveyor systems; Blast furnaces and steel mills

(G-7333)
AMERICAN FAN COMPANY
2933 Symmes Rd (45014-2099)
PHONE.................................513 874-2400
◆ EMP: 162
SIC: 3564 Exhaust fans: industrial or commercial

(G-7334)
AMERICAN INKS AND COATINGS CO
575 Quality Blvd (45014-2294)
PHONE.................................513 552-7200
George Sickinger, *Pr*
EMP: 6
SALES (corp-wide): 5.23MM **Privately Held**
Web: www.americaninksandcoatings.com
SIC: 2893 Printing ink
PA: American Inks And Coatings Company
3400 N Hutchison St
Pine Bluff AR 71602
870 247-2080

(G-7335)
AMERICAN MANUFACTURING & EQP
Also Called: Cincinnati Retread Systems
4990 Factory Dr (45014-1945)
PHONE.................................513 829-2248
Albert Penter, *Pr*
Carol Penter, *Treas*
Albert Penter Junior, *VP*
EMP: 9 EST: 1978
SQ FT: 12,000
SALES (est): 866.16K **Privately Held**
SIC: 3559 3714 3564 Tire retreading machinery and equipment; Motor vehicle parts and accessories; Blowers and fans

(G-7336)
BAYER
700 Nilles Rd (45014-3604)
PHONE.................................513 336-6600
Joe Bayer, *Admn*
EMP: 38 EST: 2017
SALES (est): 1.61MM **Privately Held**
SIC: 2834 Pharmaceutical preparations

(G-7337)
BCS TECHNOLOGIES LTD
1041 Tedia Way (45014-2004)
PHONE.................................513 829-4577
EMP: 10 EST: 1995
SQ FT: 8,000
SALES (est): 2.12MM **Privately Held**
Web: www.bcstechnologies.com
SIC: 3613 7373 Control panels, electric; Computer integrated systems design

(G-7338)
BIG OKI LLC
Also Called: Rnr Tire Express
6500 Dixie Hwy # 4 (45014-5424)
PHONE.................................513 874-1111
EMP: 36
SALES (corp-wide): 432.06K **Privately Held**
Web: www.rnrtires.com
SIC: 7534 Tire repair shop
PA: Big Oki Llc
7141 Manderlay Dr
Florence KY 41042
859 657-5200

(G-7339)
BK TOOL COMPANY INC
300 Security Dr (45014-4243)
PHONE.................................513 870-9622
Robert Reed Junior, *Treas*
EMP: 18 EST: 1972
SQ FT: 10,200
SALES (est): 750.26K **Privately Held**
Web: www.bktoolco.com
SIC: 3544 Special dies and tools

(G-7340)
BYRON PRODUCTS INC
3781 Port Union Rd (45014-2207)
PHONE.................................513 870-9111
Mark Byron, *Ch*
Rick Henry, *
▲ EMP: 70 EST: 1982
SQ FT: 44,000
SALES (est): 12.92MM **Privately Held**
Web: www.byronproducts.com
SIC: 7692 Welding repair

(G-7341)
BYRON PRODUCTS INC
250 Osborne Dr (45014-2246)
PHONE.................................513 870-9111
EMP: 6
SALES (est): 27.98K **Privately Held**
Web: www.byronproducts.com
SIC: 3999 Manufacturing industries, nec

(G-7342)
CALVARY INDUSTRIES INC (PA)
9233 Seward Rd (45014-5407)
PHONE.................................513 874-1113
John P Morelock Junior, *CEO*
Ivan Byers, *
Thomas Rielage, *
▲ EMP: 48 EST: 1983
SQ FT: 100,000
SALES (est): 200.07K
SALES (corp-wide): 200.07K **Privately Held**
Web: www.calvaryindustries.com
SIC: 2819 5169 Industrial inorganic chemicals, nec; Chemicals and allied products, nec

(G-7343)
CARR TOOL COMPANY
575 Security Dr (45014-4269)
PHONE.................................513 825-2900
Patricia Blum, *CEO*
Alex Blum, *
EMP: 21 EST: 1955
SQ FT: 13,000
SALES (est): 2.44MM **Privately Held**
Web: www.carrtool.com
SIC: 3532 Mining machinery

(G-7344)
CEMPLEX GROUP NC LLC
3195 Profit Dr (45014-4234)
PHONE.................................513 671-3300
EMP: 11 EST: 2012
SALES (est): 1.04MM **Privately Held**
Web: www.cemplexgroup.com
SIC: 2295 Waterproofing fabrics, except rubberizing

(G-7345)
CENT-ROLL PRODUCTS INC
4866 Factory Dr (45014-1915)
PHONE.................................513 829-5201
EMP: 33 EST: 1986
SALES (est): 3.61MM **Privately Held**
Web: www.cent-roll.com
SIC: 3069 Roll coverings, rubber

(G-7346)
CINCINNATI BABBITT INC
9217 Seward Rd (45014-5407)
PHONE.................................513 942-5088
Louis M Patterson, *Pr*
Dale A Frye, *Sec*
▲ EMP: 15 EST: 1990
SQ FT: 20,000
SALES (est): 503.47K **Privately Held**
Web: www.cinbab.com
SIC: 3599 Machine shop, jobbing and repair

(G-7347)
CINCINNATI GRINDING TECHNOLOGIES INC
Also Called: Cg Industries
300 Distribution Cir Ste G (45014-2239)
P.O. Box 47 (45040-0047)
PHONE.................................866 983-1097
EMP: 9
SIC: 3599 Grinding castings for the trade

(G-7348)
CKS SOLUTION INCORPORATED (PA)
4293 Muhlhauser Rd (45014-5450)
PHONE.................................513 947-1277
Peter Sung, *Pr*
James Braun, *CFO*
▲ EMP: 26 EST: 2008
SQ FT: 72,000
SALES (est): 4.91MM
SALES (corp-wide): 4.91MM **Privately Held**
Web: www.ckssolution.com
SIC: 3679 3674 Liquid crystal displays (LCD); Light emitting diodes

(G-7349)
COLOR RESOLUTIONS INTERNATIONAL LLC
Also Called: Cri
575 Quality Blvd (45014-2294)
PHONE.................................513 552-7200
EMP: 115
Web: new.colorresolutions.com
SIC: 2899 Ink or writing fluids

(G-7350)
DAMAK 1 LLC
Also Called: Teron Lighting
33 Donald Dr (45014-3025)
PHONE.................................513 858-6004
David Bellos, *CEO*
Micheal Bellos, *Pr*
▲ EMP: 45 EST: 1980
SQ FT: 51,100
SALES (est): 8.86MM
SALES (corp-wide): 8.86MM **Privately Held**
Web: www.teronlighting.com
SIC: 3646 Fluorescent lighting fixtures, commercial
PA: Tli, Llc
33 Donald Dr Uppr
Fairfield OH 45014
513 858-6004

(G-7351)
DEFFREN MACHINE TOOL SVC INC
Also Called: Akro Tool Company
240 Donald Dr (45014-3007)
PHONE.................................513 858-1555
Richard Deffren, *Pr*
EMP: 10 EST: 2003
SALES (est): 938.29K **Privately Held**
Web: www.akrotool.com
SIC: 3599 Machine shop, jobbing and repair

(G-7352)
DETROIT FLAME HARDENING CO
Also Called: Cincinnati Flame Hardening Co
375 Security Dr (45014-4250)
PHONE.................................513 942-1400
Allen Leach, *Mgr*
EMP: 10
SALES (corp-wide): 4.33MM **Privately Held**
Web: www.detroitflame.com
SIC: 3398 Metal heat treating
PA: Detroit Flame Hardening Company Inc
17644 Mount Elliott St
Detroit MI
313 891-2936

(G-7353)
DIXIE CONTAINER CORPORATION
Also Called: Pca/Fairfielde 329
3840 Port Union Rd (45014-2202)
PHONE.................................513 860-1145
EMP: 60
SIC: 2653 Corrugated and solid fiber boxes

(G-7354)
DIXON BAYCO USA
7280 Union Centre Blvd (45014-2344)
PHONE.................................513 874-8499
Robert Kettinger, *Pr*
▲ EMP: 8 EST: 2000
SALES (est): 5.45MM
SALES (corp-wide): 439.82MM **Privately Held**
Web: www.dixonvalve.com
SIC: 3823 Liquid level instruments, industrial process type
PA: Dvcc, Llc
1 Dixon Sq
Chestertown MD 21620
410 778-2000

Fairfield - Butler County (G-7355)

GEOGRAPHIC SECTION

(G-7355)
EDI CUSTOM INTERIORS INC
Also Called: Exhibit Design International
5648 Lindenwood Ln (45014-3563)
PHONE................513 829-3895
William H Snyder, *Pr*
Janice Snyder, *Stockholder*
EMP: 17 **EST:** 1981
SQ FT: 52,000
SALES (est): 899.55K **Privately Held**
SIC: 3999 Advertising display products

(G-7356)
EMPIRE PRINTING INC
9560 Le Saint Dr (45014-2253)
PHONE................513 242-3900
Dean Nieporte, *Pr*
EMP: 9 **EST:** 1956
SQ FT: 6,000
SALES (est): 601.49K **Privately Held**
Web: www.empireprintinginc.com
SIC: 2752 2760 Offset printing; Letterpress printing

(G-7357)
ENGRAVED IN USA LLC
93 Arndt Ct (45014-1943)
PHONE................513 301-7760
EMP: 8 **EST:** 2011
SALES (est): 558.86K **Privately Held**
SIC: 2499 Trophy bases, wood

(G-7358)
FAIRFIELD MANUFACTURING INC
8585 Seward Rd (45011-8652)
PHONE................513 642-0081
▲ **EMP:** 300
Web: www.takumistamping.com
SIC: 3469 Stamping metal for the trade

(G-7359)
FEINER PATTERN WORKS INC
7823 Seward Rd (45011-8638)
PHONE................513 851-9800
Kenneth Feiner, *Pr*
Jimmy Feiner, *VP*
EMP: 10 **EST:** 1957
SALES (est): 458.33K **Privately Held**
SIC: 3543 Industrial patterns

(G-7360)
FLINT GROUP US LLC
575 Quality Blvd (45014-2294)
PHONE................513 552-7232
EMP: 7
SALES (corp-wide): 1.91B **Privately Held**
Web: www.flintgrp.com
SIC: 2865 Color pigments, organic
PA: Flint Group Us Llc
   17177 N Laurel Park Dr # 300
   Livonia MI 48152
   734 781-4600

(G-7361)
FLOTURN INC (PA)
4236 Thunderbird Ln (45014-5482)
PHONE................513 860-8040
Michael North, *Pr*
Don Spillane, *
◆ **EMP:** 120 **EST:** 1962
SQ FT: 75,000
SALES (est): 41.23MM
SALES (corp-wide): 41.23MM **Privately Held**
Web: www.floturn.com
SIC: 3599 Machine shop, jobbing and repair

(G-7362)
FM AF LLC ✪
Also Called: American Fan
2933 Symmes Rd (45014-2001)
PHONE................866 771-6266
George Whittier, *CEO*
EMP: 147 **EST:** 2023
SALES (est): 25.25MM
SALES (corp-wide): 653.43MM **Privately Held**
SIC: 3564 Blowers and fans
HQ: Fairbanks Morse, Llc
   701 White Ave
   Beloit WI 53511
   800 356-6955

(G-7363)
FORCE CONTROL INDUSTRIES INC
3660 Dixie Hwy (45014-1105)
PHONE................513 868-0900
Robert Briede, *Prin*
James C Besl, *
Joseph E Besl, *
Eric Ferry, *
▲ **EMP:** 50 **EST:** 1969
SQ FT: 60,000
SALES (est): 9.43MM **Privately Held**
Web: www.forcecontrol.com
SIC: 3714 3594 3566 3568 Motor vehicle parts and accessories; Fluid power pumps and motors; Speed changers, drives, and gears; Clutches, except vehicular

(G-7364)
GWP HOLDINGS INC
8675 Seward Rd (45011-9716)
PHONE................513 860-4050
Wayde Hunker, *CEO*
Douglas Henderson, *
▲ **EMP:** 42 **EST:** 1968
SQ FT: 120,000
SALES (est): 936.55K **Privately Held**
SIC: 3441 3479 3446 3469 Floor posts, adjustable: metal; Painting, coating, and hot dipping; Architectural metalwork; Metal stampings, nec

(G-7365)
HARMON HOMES
5476 Camelot Dr Apt 40 (45014-4093)
PHONE................513 602-6896
Jackie Groves, *Prin*
EMP: 8 **EST:** 2018
SALES (est): 75.48K **Privately Held**
SIC: 2741 Miscellaneous publishing

(G-7366)
HI TECH PRINTING CO INC
3741 Port Union Rd (45014-2207)
PHONE................513 874-5325
EMP: 36
SIC: 2759 Flexographic printing

(G-7367)
HIPSY LLC
4951 Dixie Hwy (45014-3057)
PHONE................513 403-5333
Lerin Buggs, *Brnch Mgr*
EMP: 9
SALES (corp-wide): 874.19K **Privately Held**
Web: www.headbandsforwomen.com
SIC: 2339 Scarves, hoods, headbands, etc.: women's
PA: Hipsy Llc
   5321 Cleves Warsaw Pike
   Cincinnati OH 45238
   513 403-5333

(G-7368)
HONEYMOON PAPER PRODUCTS INC
7100 Dixie Hwy (45014-5543)
PHONE................513 755-7200
EMP: 70
Web: www.sctray.com
SIC: 2675 2653 Die-cut paper and board; Corrugated and solid fiber boxes

(G-7369)
HOWDEN NORTH AMERICA INC
Also Called: Howden North America
2933 Symmes Rd (45014-2001)
PHONE................513 874-2400
▲ **EMP:** 170 **EST:** 1996
SALES (est): 30.42MM
SALES (corp-wide): 3.44B **Privately Held**
Web: www.chartindustries.com
SIC: 3564 Blowers and fans
HQ: Howden North America Inc.
   2475 Grge Urban Blvd Ste
   Depew NY 14043
   330 867-8540

(G-7370)
HOWDEN USA COMPANY (DH)
Also Called: Howden
2933 Symmes Rd (45014-2001)
PHONE................513 874-2400
▲ **EMP:** 25 **EST:** 2013
SALES (est): 65.4MM **Privately Held**
Web: www.howden.com
SIC: 3564 Exhaust fans: industrial or commercial
HQ: Granite Holdings Global Limited
   1 Chamberlain Square
   Birmingham W MIDLANDS B3 3A

(G-7371)
HYO SEONG AMERICA CORPORATION
275 Northpointe Dr (45014-5445)
PHONE................513 682-6182
EMP: 10
SALES (est): 842.81K **Privately Held**
SIC: 3711 Motor vehicles and car bodies

(G-7372)
INNMARK COMMUNICATIONS LLC
375 Northpointe Dr (45014-5474)
PHONE................513 285-1040
EMP: 79
SALES (corp-wide): 96.09MM **Privately Held**
Web: www.innmarkcom.com
SIC: 2759 Commercial printing, nec
PA: Innmark Communications Llc
   420 Distribution Cir
   Fairfield OH 45014
   888 466-6627

(G-7373)
IVY VENTURES LLC
39 Citadel Dr Apt 2 (45014-8567)
PHONE................513 259-3307
EMP: 9 **EST:** 2008
SALES (est): 89.11K **Privately Held**
Web: www.centaurihs.com
SIC: 7372 Prepackaged software

(G-7374)
IWATA BOLT USA INC
102 Iwata Dr (45014-2298)
PHONE................513 942-5050
Nick Hiraga, *Brnch Mgr*
EMP: 14
SALES (corp-wide): 24.64MM **Privately Held**
Web: www.iwatabolt.co.jp
SIC: 3452 Bolts, metal
PA: Iwata Bolt Usa Inc.
   7131 Orangewood Ave
   Garden Grove CA 92841
   714 897-0800

(G-7375)
JOHNSON-NASH METAL PDTS INC
9265 Seward Rd (45014-5407)
PHONE................513 874-7022
Colleen Johnson, *Ch*
Charles Johnson, *Pr*
Craig Johnson, *CEO*
Carol Johnson Dreyer, *Sec*
EMP: 27 **EST:** 1936
SQ FT: 21,000
SALES (est): 2MM **Privately Held**
Web: www.johnsonnash.com
SIC: 3441 Fabricated structural metal

(G-7376)
JOURNAL NEWS
5120 Dixie Hwy (45014-3001)
PHONE................513 829-7900
EMP: 6 **EST:** 2014
SALES (est): 95.57K **Privately Held**
Web: www.journal-news.com
SIC: 2711 Newspapers, publishing and printing

(G-7377)
KAAA/HAMILTON ENTERPRISES INC
Also Called: K/H Enterprises
3143 Production Dr (45014-4227)
PHONE................513 874-5874
Mel Kaaa, *Pr*
Linda Deathrag, *
Bob Leslie, *
EMP: 30 **EST:** 1992
SQ FT: 20,000
SALES (est): 2.11MM **Privately Held**
SIC: 3211 Construction glass

(G-7378)
MACHINTEK CO
3721 Port Union Rd (45014-2200)
PHONE................513 551-1000
Roger Hasler, *Pr*
Louis Solimine, *
Vaughn Burckard, *
Andy Holbert, *Prin*
Chris Rubenacker, *Prin*
▲ **EMP:** 65 **EST:** 1985
SQ FT: 37,000
SALES (est): 10.26MM **Privately Held**
Web: www.machintek.com
SIC: 3599 Machine shop, jobbing and repair

(G-7379)
MASTER-HALCO INC
620 Commerce Center Dr (45011-8664)
PHONE................513 869-7600
Paul Smith, *Mgr*
EMP: 16
Web: www.masterhalco.com
SIC: 5051 3315 Steel; Fence gates, posts, and fittings: steel
HQ: Master-Halco, Inc.
   3010 Lyndon B Johnson Fwy
   Dallas TX 75234
   972 714-7300

(G-7380)
MASTERS PHARMACEUTICAL INC
8695 Seward Rd (45011-9716)
PHONE................513 290-2969
Ben Lazel, *Pr*
EMP: 8 **EST:** 2015
SALES (est): 263.17K **Privately Held**
Web: www.mastersrx.com
SIC: 2834 Pharmaceutical preparations

(G-7381)
MB MANUFACTURING CORP
2904 Symmes Rd (45014-2035)
PHONE................513 682-1461

GEOGRAPHIC SECTION

Fairfield - Butler County (G-7404)

Greg Kelley, *Prin*
EMP: 9 **EST:** 2003
SALES (est): 940.99K **Privately Held**
Web: www.mbveneer.com
SIC: 2421 Lumber: rough, sawed, or planed

(G-7382)
MCNEILUS TRUCK AND MFG INC
8997 Le Saint Dr (45014)
PHONE.................................513 874-2022
Ken Shurboff, *Brnch Mgr*
EMP: 25
SALES (corp-wide): 9.66B **Publicly Held**
Web: www.mcneilus.com
SIC: 3713 3531 Cement mixer bodies; Concrete plants
HQ: Mcneilus Truck And Manufacturing, Inc.
524 E Highway St
Dodge Center MN 55927
507 374-6321

(G-7383)
MENDENHALL TECHNICAL SERVICES INC
Also Called: M T S I
9175 Seward Rd (45014-5405)
PHONE.................................513 860-1280
◆ **EMP:** 22 **EST:** 1980
SALES (est): 5.4MM **Privately Held**
Web: www.mtsigt.com
SIC: 3511 8711 Turbines and turbine generator sets; Engineering services

(G-7384)
MIDWEST SPECIALTY PDTS CO INC
280 Northpointe Dr (45014-5443)
PHONE.................................513 874-7070
Michael Brunst, *Pr*
Thomas Brunst, *VP*
Steven Huesman, *Sec*
▲ **EMP:** 18 **EST:** 1965
SQ FT: 52,000
SALES (est): 3.33MM **Privately Held**
Web: www.tubesandcores.com
SIC: 2655 Fiber cans, drums, and similar products

(G-7385)
MT PLEASANT BLACKTOPPING INC
Also Called: Mt.pleasant Blacktopping
3199 Production Dr (45014-4227)
PHONE.................................513 874-3777
William House, *CEO*
Benjamin House, *Pr*
Anna House, *VP*
EMP: 8 **EST:** 1962
SQ FT: 3,200
SALES (est): 4.63MM **Privately Held**
Web: www.mtpleasantblacktopping.com
SIC: 1623 1771 2951 Sewer line construction ; Blacktop (asphalt) work; Asphalt and asphaltic paving mixtures (not from refineries)

(G-7386)
MULHERN BELTING INC
310 Osborne Dr (45014-2247)
PHONE.................................201 337-5700
George Ober, *Mgr*
EMP: 37
SQ FT: 10,000
SALES (corp-wide): 18.1MM **Privately Held**
Web: www.mulhernbelting.com
SIC: 3021 3535 Rubber and plastics footwear ; Conveyors and conveying equipment
PA: Mulhern Belting, Inc.
148 Bauer Dr
Oakland NJ 07436
201 337-5700

(G-7387)
NORTHERN PRECISION INC
3245 Production Dr (45014-4232)
PHONE.................................513 860-4701
Harold W Jarvis, *Pr*
Dane A Kerby, *Sr VP*
EMP: 15 **EST:** 1999
SQ FT: 5,000
SALES (est): 2.13MM **Privately Held**
Web: www.npswiss.com
SIC: 3599 Machine shop, jobbing and repair

(G-7388)
OCS INTELLITRAK INC
8660 Seward Rd (45011-9716)
PHONE.................................513 742-5600
▲ **EMP:** 12 **EST:** 1995
SQ FT: 14,500
SALES (est): 5.2MM **Privately Held**
Web: www.intellitrak.com
SIC: 3535 Conveyors and conveying equipment
PA: Lico, Inc.
9230 E 47th St
Kansas City MO 64133

(G-7389)
PACIFIC INDUSTRIES USA INC
8955 Seward Rd (45011-9109)
PHONE.................................513 860-3900
Toru Nishimura, *Pr*
◆ **EMP:** 25 **EST:** 1986
SQ FT: 53,000
SALES (est): 8.71MM **Privately Held**
SIC: 3714 Motor vehicle wheels and parts
PA: Pacific Industrial Co.,Ltd.
100, Kyutokucho
Ogaki GIF 503-0

(G-7390)
PACIFIC MANUFACTURING OHIO INC
8955 Seward Rd (45011-9109)
PHONE.................................513 860-3900
Toshiteru Ando, *Pr*
▲ **EMP:** 450 **EST:** 1999
SALES (est): 194.5MM **Privately Held**
Web: www.pacific-ind.co.jp
SIC: 3714 3469 Motor vehicle parts and accessories; Metal stampings, nec
PA: Pacific Industrial Co.,Ltd.
100, Kyutokucho
Ogaki GIF 503-0

(G-7391)
PACIFIC MANUFACTURING OHIO INC
8935 Seward Rd (45011-9109)
PHONE.................................513 860-3900
EMP: 46 **EST:** 2017
SALES (est): 194.06K **Privately Held**
SIC: 3999 Barber and beauty shop equipment

(G-7392)
PANELMATIC CINCINNATI INC
258 Donald Dr (45014-3007)
P.O. Box 141 (45071-0141)
PHONE.................................513 829-1960
Richard E Dooley, *Pr*
J P Stiffler Junior, *General Vice President*
David D Adamson, *
EMP: 24 **EST:** 1962
SQ FT: 21,300
SALES (est): 4.52MM
SALES (corp-wide): 56.9MM **Privately Held**
Web: www.panelmatic.com
SIC: 3613 8711 Control panels, electric; Designing: ship, boat, machine, and product
PA: Panelmatic, Inc.
6806 Willow Brook Park
Houston TX 77066

888 757-1957

(G-7393)
PEASE INDUSTIES INC
7100 Dixie Hwy (45014-5543)
PHONE.................................513 870-3600
David H Pease Junior, *Ch Bd*
Leonard W Cavens, *
Neil W Jackman, *National Account Vice President*
David A Aluise, *MFG*
EMP: 93 **EST:** 1892
SQ FT: 220,000
SALES (est): 2.48MM
SALES (corp-wide): 2.03B **Privately Held**
SIC: 3442 3089 2431 Metal doors; Doors, folding: plastics or plastics coated fabric; Doors, wood
PA: Pella Corporation
102 Main St
Pella IA 50219
641 621-1000

(G-7394)
PERFECTION PRINTING
9560 Le Saint Dr (45014-2253)
PHONE.................................513 874-2173
Steve Myers, *Pr*
Scott Myers, *VP*
Joe Myers, *Treas*
EMP: 13 **EST:** 1984
SQ FT: 10,000
SALES (est): 396.26K **Privately Held**
Web: www.perfectionprinting.com
SIC: 2752 Offset printing

(G-7395)
PREMIER CONSTRUCTION COMPANY
9361 Seward Rd (45014-5409)
PHONE.................................513 874-2611
Jan Gilkey, *Pr*
EMP: 11 **EST:** 1959
SQ FT: 10,000
SALES (est): 428.72K **Privately Held**
Web: www.premierconstructionco.com
SIC: 5031 1751 2452 Lumber: rough, dressed, and finished; Carpentry work; Panels and sections, prefabricated, wood

(G-7396)
PRESTIGE DISPLAY AND PACKAGING LLC
420 Distribution Cir (45014-5473)
PHONE.................................513 285-1040
▲ **EMP:** 16
SIC: 2653 Corrugated boxes, partitions, display items, sheets, and pad

(G-7397)
PRINTER COMPONENTS INC
4236 Thunderbird Ln (45014-5482)
PHONE.................................585 924-5190
◆ **EMP:** 9
SIC: 3861 5112 3955 5999 Printing equipment, photographic; Laser printer supplies; Print cartridges for laser and other computer printers; Photocopy machines

(G-7398)
PROMOSPARK INC
1120 Hicks Blvd Ste 201 (45014-2876)
P.O. Box 181147 (45018-1147)
PHONE.................................513 844-2211
Mark Johnston, *Pr*
EMP: 8
SALES (est): 529.51K **Privately Held**
Web: www.promospark.com
SIC: 2759 Screen printing

(G-7399)
PROMOSPARK INC
300 Osborne Dr (45014-2247)
P.O. Box 181147 (45018-1147)
PHONE.................................513 844-2211
Sarah Johnston, *Pr*
EMP: 12 **EST:** 2013
SALES (est): 773.93K **Privately Held**
Web: www.promospark.com
SIC: 2396 Apparel and other linings, except millinery

(G-7400)
QUALITY GOLD INC (PA)
Also Called: Quality Gold
500 Quality Blvd (45014-2292)
P.O. Box 18490 (45018-0490)
PHONE.................................513 942-7659
Michael Langhammer, *CEO*
Jason Langhammer, *
◆ **EMP:** 270 **EST:** 1979
SQ FT: 110,000
SALES (est): 51.26MM
SALES (corp-wide): 51.26MM **Privately Held**
Web: www.qgold.com
SIC: 3339 5944 Gold refining (primary); Clock and watch stores

(G-7401)
QUEEN CITY TOOL WORKS INC
125 Constitution Dr Ste 2 (45014-2256)
PHONE.................................513 874-0111
Martin Oehler, *Pr*
Tim Mayes, *VP*
EMP: 6 **EST:** 1998
SQ FT: 5,200
SALES (est): 499.74K **Privately Held**
Web: www.queencitytool.com
SIC: 3544 3599 Special dies and tools; Machine and other job shop work

(G-7402)
R K METALS LTD
3235 Homeward Way (45014-4237)
PHONE.................................513 874-6055
EMP: 30 **EST:** 1997
SQ FT: 45,000
SALES (est): 4.48MM **Privately Held**
Web: www.rkmetals.net
SIC: 3469 Stamping metal for the trade

(G-7403)
RIVER CITY PHARMA
8695 Seward Rd (45011-9716)
PHONE.................................513 870-1680
Danny Smith, *Pr*
Jason Smith, *VP*
EMP: 13 **EST:** 2012
SALES (est): 690.35K **Privately Held**
Web: www.mastersrx.com
SIC: 2834 5122 Pharmaceutical preparations ; Pharmaceuticals

(G-7404)
SAF-HOLLAND INC
105 Mercantile Dr (45014-3782)
PHONE.................................513 874-7888
EMP: 7
SALES (corp-wide): 2.29B **Privately Held**
Web: www.safholland.com
SIC: 3715 3568 3537 3452 Truck trailers; Power transmission equipment, nec; Industrial trucks and tractors; Bolts, nuts, rivets, and washers
HQ: Saf-Holland, Inc.
1950 Industrial Blvd
Muskegon MI 49442
231 773-3271

Fairfield - Butler County (G-7405)

GEOGRAPHIC SECTION

(G-7405)
SCHNEIDER AUTOMATION INC
5855 Union Centre Blvd (45014-2346)
PHONE..................612 426-0709
EMP: 177
SALES (corp-wide): 82.05K **Privately Held**
Web: www.schneider-electric.com
SIC: 3613 Switchgear and switchboard apparatus
HQ: Schneider Automation Inc.
800 Federal St
Andover MA 01810
978 794-0800

(G-7406)
SEA BIRD PUBLICATIONS INC
311 Nilles Rd Ste B (45014-2621)
PHONE..................513 869-2200
Ginger Byrd, *Owner*
EMP: 8 **EST:** 2013
SALES (est): 166.52K **Privately Held**
Web: www.seabirdpublications.com
SIC: 2741 Miscellaneous publishing

(G-7407)
SHAW INDUSTRIES INC
8580 Seward Rd Ste 400 (45011-8628)
PHONE..................513 942-3692
Jim Brown, *Brnch Mgr*
EMP: 752
SALES (corp-wide): 364.48B **Publicly Held**
Web: www.shawinc.com
SIC: 2273 Carpets and rugs
HQ: Shaw Industries, Inc.
616 E Walnut Ave
Dalton GA 30721

(G-7408)
SKYLINE CEM HOLDINGS LLC (PA)
Also Called: Skyline Chili
4180 Thunderbird Ln (45014-2235)
PHONE..................513 874-1188
Dick Williams, *Interim Chief Executive Officer*
▲ **EMP:** 137 **EST:** 1949
SQ FT: 42,000
SALES (est): 58.14MM
SALES (corp-wide): 58.14MM **Privately Held**
Web: www.skylinechili.com
SIC: 5812 2038 6794 5149 Restaurant, family: chain; Frozen specialties, nec; Franchises, selling or licensing; Groceries and related products, nec

(G-7409)
SKYWAY CEMENT COMPANY LLC
3155 Homeward Way (45014-4255)
PHONE..................513 478-0034
EMP: 26
SALES (corp-wide): 10.53MM **Privately Held**
Web: www.skywaycement.com
SIC: 3241 Cement, hydraulic
PA: Skyway Cement Company Llc
1717 N Naper Blvd Ste 111
Naperville IL 60563
800 643-1808

(G-7410)
SOUTHERN CHAMPION TRAY LP
Also Called: Southern Champion Tray, L.P.
7100 Dixie Hwy (45014-5543)
PHONE..................513 755-7200
John Zeiser, *Brnch Mgr*
EMP: 61
Web: www.sctray.com
SIC: 2675 2653 Die-cut paper and board; Corrugated and solid fiber boxes
PA: Southern Champion Tray, Llc

220 Compress St
Chattanooga TN 37405

(G-7411)
STANDEX ELECTRONICS INC (HQ)
Also Called: Standex-Meder Electronics
4150 Thunderbird Ln (45014-2235)
PHONE..................513 871-3777
John Meeks, *CEO*
Robert Lintz, *VP*
▲ **EMP:** 98 **EST:** 1999
SQ FT: 22,022
SALES (est): 43MM
SALES (corp-wide): 741.05MM **Publicly Held**
Web: www.standexelectronics.com
SIC: 3625 5065 Motor controls and accessories; Electronic parts and equipment, nec
PA: Standex International Corporation
23 Keewaydin Dr
Salem NH 03079
603 893-9701

(G-7412)
STANDEX INTERNATIONAL CORP
Standex Electronics
4150 Thunderbird Ln (45014-2235)
PHONE..................513 533-7171
Jim Suetholz, *Mgr*
EMP: 64
SALES (corp-wide): 741.05MM **Publicly Held**
Web: www.standex.com
SIC: 3675 3678 3644 Electronic capacitors; Electronic connectors; Noncurrent-carrying wiring devices
PA: Standex International Corporation
23 Keewaydin Dr
Salem NH 03079
603 893-9701

(G-7413)
TAKUMI STAMPING INC
8585 Seward Rd (45011-8652)
PHONE..................513 642-0081
Ken Naruse, *Pr*
EMP: 234 **EST:** 2016
SALES (est): 22.83MM **Privately Held**
Web: www.takumistamping.com
SIC: 3469 Stamping metal for the trade

(G-7414)
TEAMFG LLC
2052 Bohlke Blvd (45014-2017)
PHONE..................513 313-8855
Amy Mcfarland, *Prin*
EMP: 7 **EST:** 2016
SALES (est): 190.46K **Privately Held**
Web: www.the-fischer-group.com
SIC: 3999 Manufacturing industries, nec

(G-7415)
TECH/III INC
Also Called: Printing Plant
2594 Mack Rd (45014-5127)
PHONE..................513 482-7500
James E Oconnor, *Ch*
Carol S Horan, *
EMP: 42 **EST:** 1970
SALES (est): 4.97MM **Privately Held**
Web: www.printingplant.com
SIC: 2671 2759 Paper; coated and laminated packaging; Labels and seals: printing, nsk

(G-7416)
TEDIA COMPANY LLC
1000 Tedia Way (45014-2003)
PHONE..................513 874-5340
Hoon Choi, *Pr*

Elinora Park, *
Chris Dendy, *
John F Terbot Ii, *VP*
John L Muething, *
◆ **EMP:** 114 **EST:** 1974
SQ FT: 48,500
SALES (est): 52.13MM **Privately Held**
Web: www.tedia.com
SIC: 2869 Solvents, organic

(G-7417)
THE ELLENBEE-LEGGETT COMPANY INC
3765 Port Union Rd (45014-2207)
P.O. Box 8025 (45014)
PHONE..................513 874-3200
EMP: 110
Web: www.performancefoodservice.com
SIC: 5141 5147 5142 2015 Groceries, general line; Meats and meat products; Meat, frozen: packaged; Poultry slaughtering and processing

(G-7418)
THE WESTERN STATES MACHINE COMPANY
625 Commerce Center Dr (45011-1172)
P.O. Box 327 (45012-0327)
PHONE..................513 863-4758
◆ **EMP:** 57 **EST:** 1917
SALES (est): 9.22MM **Privately Held**
Web: www.westernstates.com
SIC: 3569 Centrifuges, industrial

(G-7419)
THE-FISCHER-GROUP
2028- 2052 Bohlke Blvd (45014)
PHONE..................513 285-1281
Vannessa Fisher, *Off Mgr*
EMP: 40 **EST:** 1997
SALES (est): 1.6MM **Privately Held**
Web: www.the-fischer-group.com
SIC: 3915 Lapidary work, contract or other

(G-7420)
TSR MACHINERY SERVICES INC
100 Security Dr (45014-4245)
PHONE..................513 874-9697
Todd Routh, *Pr*
Lisa Routh, *
EMP: 25 **EST:** 1989
SQ FT: 26,000
SALES (est): 741.68K **Privately Held**
Web: www.tsrmachinery.com
SIC: 3599 Machine shop, jobbing and repair

(G-7421)
USALCO FAIRFIELD PLANT LLC
3700 Dixie Hwy (45014-1106)
PHONE..................513 737-7100
EMP: 20 **EST:** 2009
SALES (est): 2.19MM **Privately Held**
Web: www.usalco.com
SIC: 2899 Water treating compounds

(G-7422)
USALCO MICHIGAN CITY PLANT LLC
Also Called: Usalco
3700 Dixie Hwy (45014-1106)
PHONE..................513 737-7100
Joseph Hickey, *Mgr*
EMP: 10
SALES (corp-wide): 243.29MM **Privately Held**
Web: www.usalco.com
SIC: 2819 Industrial inorganic chemicals, nec
PA: Usalco Michigan City Plant, Llc
2601 Cannery Ave
Baltimore MD 21226
410 918-2230

(G-7423)
VIBRA FINISH CO
8411 Seward Rd (45011-8651)
PHONE..................513 870-6300
Haskel Hall, *Pr*
EMP: 20
SALES (corp-wide): 4.63MM **Privately Held**
Web: www.vibrafinish.com
SIC: 3291 Abrasive products
PA: Vibra Finish Co.
2220 Shasta Way
Simi Valley CA 93065
805 578-0033

(G-7424)
VISTECH MFG SOLUTIONS LLC
Also Called: Vistech
4274 Thunderbird Ln (45014-5482)
PHONE..................513 860-1408
Terry Mclaughlin, *Brnch Mgr*
EMP: 13
SALES (corp-wide): 27.31MM **Privately Held**
Web: www.vistechmfg.com
SIC: 3999 Barber and beauty shop equipment
HQ: Vistech Manufacturing Solutions, Llc
1156 Scenic Dr Ste 120
Modesto CA 95350
209 544-9333

(G-7425)
WATCH-US INC
4450 Dixie Hwy (45014-1114)
PHONE..................513 829-8870
Dan Graf, *Pr*
▲ **EMP:** 20 **EST:** 1991
SQ FT: 90,000
SALES (est): 4.69MM **Privately Held**
Web: www.watchusinc.com
SIC: 3944 Automobile and truck models, toy and hobby

(G-7426)
WATERCO OF THE CENTRAL STATES
Also Called: Culligan
3215 Homeward Way (45014-4237)
PHONE..................937 294-0375
Jeffery Meyer, *Pr*
Nicole Duckworth, *
Jason Wesley, *
EMP: 25 **EST:** 2011
SALES (est): 1.94MM **Privately Held**
SIC: 3221 Water bottles, glass

(G-7427)
WHOLESALE BAIT CO INC
2619 Bobmeyer Rd (45014-1217)
PHONE..................513 863-2380
Gregory Fessel, *CEO*
Anthony G Fessel, *Pr*
Benjamin Fessel, *Dir*
EMP: 15 **EST:** 1950
SQ FT: 18,000
SALES (est): 9.41MM **Privately Held**
Web: www.wholesalebait.com
SIC: 5199 3949 Bait, fishing; Sporting and athletic goods, nec

(G-7428)
WORKSTREAM INC (HQ)
Also Called: Hamilton Casework Solutions
3158 Production Dr (45014-4228)
PHONE..................513 870-4400
Thadius Jaroszewicz, *CEO*
▼ **EMP:** 60 **EST:** 1988
SQ FT: 50,000
SALES (est): 25.86MM **Privately Held**
Web: www.myworkstream.com

▲ = Import ▼ = Export
◆ = Import/Export

SIC: 2521 2522 Panel systems and partitions (free-standing), office: wood; Panel systems and partitions, office: except wood
PA: H S Morgan Limited Partnership
3158 Production Dr
Fairfield OH 45014

(G-7429)
ZEBEC OF NORTH AMERICA INC
210 Donald Dr (45014-3007)
P.O. Box 181570 (45018-1570)
PHONE...................513 829-5533
Ed Synder, *Pr*
Scott Snyder, *
Chris Snyder, *
◆ **EMP:** 35 **EST:** 1992
SQ FT: 7,000
SALES (est): 4.02MM **Privately Held**
Web: www.zebec.com
SIC: 3949 5091 Sporting and athletic goods, nec; Sporting and recreation goods

Fairfield Township
Butler County

(G-7430)
BUTLER TECH
Also Called: Southwest Ohio Computer Assn
3611 Hamilton Middletown Rd
(45011-2241)
PHONE...................513 867-1028
Mike Crumley, *Superintnt*
EMP: 38
SALES (corp-wide): 78.28K **Privately Held**
Web: www.butlertech.org
SIC: 8211 7372 Public combined elementary and secondary school; Educational computer software
PA: Butler Technology & Career Development Schools
3603 Hmlton Middletown Rd
Hamilton OH 45011
513 868-1911

(G-7431)
INNOVATIVE CONTROL SYSTEMS
5870 Fairham Rd (45011-2035)
PHONE...................513 894-3712
Steven Saunders, *Pr*
Dave Edester, *VP*
EMP: 6 **EST:** 1992
SALES (est): 812.36K **Privately Held**
Web: www.icscarwashsystems.com
SIC: 3613 Control panels, electric

(G-7432)
SENSUS LLC
2991 Hamilton Mason Rd (45011-5355)
PHONE...................513 892-7100
Dan Wampler, *Managing Member*
▲ **EMP:** 12 **EST:** 1999
SQ FT: 25,000
SALES (est): 2.16MM **Privately Held**
Web: www.sensus.com
SIC: 2087 Pastes, flavoring
HQ: Synergy Flavors, Inc.
1500 Synergy Dr
Wauconda IL 60084
847 487-1011

Fairlawn
Summit County

(G-7433)
BEKAERT CORPORATION (DH)
3200 W Market St Ste 303 (44333-3326)
PHONE...................330 867-3325
Oswald Schmid, *CEO*
Beatriz Garcia-cos, *CFO*
Lieven Larmuseau, *
Curd Vandekerckhove, *
Piet Van Riet, *
◆ **EMP:** 30 **EST:** 1956
SQ FT: 10,771
SALES (est): 563.32MM
SALES (corp-wide): 609.87MM **Privately Held**
Web: fencing.bekaert.com
SIC: 3315 Wire and fabricated wire products
HQ: Bekaert North America Management Corporation
3200 W Market St Ste 303
Fairlawn OH 44333
330 867-3325

(G-7434)
BUCKEYE CORRUGATED INC (PA)
Also Called: B C I
822 Kumho Dr Ste 400 (44333-9298)
PHONE...................330 576-0590
Dale Sommer, *Pr*
Douglas A Bosnik, *Pr*
Mark A Husted, *CFO*
EMP: 9 **EST:** 1999
SQ FT: 11,000
SALES (est): 196.62MM
SALES (corp-wide): 196.62MM **Privately Held**
Web: www.bcipkg.com
SIC: 2653 Boxes, corrugated: made from purchased materials

(G-7435)
CONTITECH NORTH AMERICA INC (DH)
703 S Cleveland Massillon Rd (44333-3023)
PHONE...................330 664-7180
Jim Hill, *Pr*
▲ **EMP:** 17 **EST:** 1999
SALES (est): 1.52B
SALES (corp-wide): 45.02B **Privately Held**
Web: www.continental-industry.com
SIC: 3061 Mechanical rubber goods
HQ: Contitech Deutschland Gmbh
Continental-Plaza 1
Hannover NI 30173
51193802

(G-7436)
CONTITECH USA INC (DH)
Also Called: Continental Contitech
703 S Cleveland Massillon Rd (44333-3023)
PHONE...................330 664-7000
Cody Knauss, *Pr*
◆ **EMP:** 16 **EST:** 2007
SQ FT: 100,000
SALES (est): 493.8MM
SALES (corp-wide): 45.02B **Privately Held**
Web: www.continental-industry.com
SIC: 3069 Molded rubber products
HQ: Contitech North America, Inc.
703 S Clvlnd Massillon Rd
Fairlawn OH 44333

(G-7437)
EDUCATIONAL DIRECTION INC
Also Called: Emergency Training Inst Div
150 N Miller Rd Ste 200 (44333-3772)
PHONE...................330 836-8439
Alexander M Butman, *Pr*
Richard W Vomacka, *VP*
Warren Joblin, *Sec*
▼ **EMP:** 6 **EST:** 1967
SQ FT: 3,000
SALES (est): 340.16K **Privately Held**
SIC: 2741 5999 Technical manual and paper publishing; Audio-visual equipment and supplies

(G-7438)
ELIOKEM INC (DH)
175 Ghent Rd (44333-3330)
PHONE...................330 734-1100
John F Malloy, *Pr*
Robert Smith, *
Veronique Le Du, *
◆ **EMP:** 85 **EST:** 2001
SQ FT: 100,000
SALES (est): 53.61MM
SALES (corp-wide): 2.46B **Privately Held**
SIC: 2819 Industrial inorganic chemicals, nec
HQ: Synthomer Inc.
25435 Harvard Rd
Beachwood OH 44122
216 682-7000

(G-7439)
FRISBY PRINTING COMPANY
Also Called: Minuteman Press
3571 Brookwall Dr Unit C (44333-9295)
PHONE...................330 665-4565
Parris Frisby, *Pr*
EMP: 10 **EST:** 2008
SQ FT: 1,600
SALES (est): 980.08K **Privately Held**
Web: akron.minutemanpress.com
SIC: 2752 Commercial printing, lithographic

(G-7440)
GOT GRAPHIX LLC
3265 W Market St (44333-3337)
PHONE...................330 703-9047
Meeran Shafeer, *Managing Member*
EMP: 10 **EST:** 2011
SQ FT: 5,500
SALES (est): 778.71K **Privately Held**
SIC: 2759 2395 Screen printing; Embroidery and art needlework

(G-7441)
HGGC CITADEL PLAS HOLDINGS INC
Also Called: Citadel Plastics
3637 Ridgewood Rd (44333-3123)
PHONE...................330 666-3751
Mike Huff, *CEO*
Kevin Andrews, *OF ENGINEERED COMPOSITES*
Dennis Loughran, *CFO*
◆ **EMP:** 42 **EST:** 2012
SALES (est): 9.68MM **Privately Held**
SIC: 2821 Plastics materials and resins
HQ: Lyondellbassell Advanced Polymers Inc.
1221 Mckinney St Ste 300
Houston TX 77010
713 309-7200

(G-7442)
HPC HOLDINGS LLC (HQ)
Also Called: Composite Group, The
3637 Ridgewood Rd (44333-3123)
PHONE...................330 666-3751
EMP: 11 **EST:** 2008
SALES (est): 59.91MM
SALES (corp-wide): 59.91MM **Privately Held**
SIC: 2821 2655 Molding compounds, plastics ; Cans, composite: foil-fiber and other: from purchased fiber
PA: Bulk Molding Compounds, Inc.
1600 Powis Ct
West Chicago IL 60185
630 377-1065

(G-7443)
LEADER PUBLICATIONS INC
Also Called: West Side Leader
3075 Smith Rd Ste 204 (44333-4454)
PHONE...................330 665-9595
Clark Burns, *Genl Mgr*
EMP: 16 **EST:** 1984
SALES (est): 799.48K **Privately Held**
Web: www.akron.com
SIC: 2711 Newspapers: publishing only, not printed on site

(G-7444)
LITTLERN CORPORATION
1006 Bunker Dr Apt 207 (44333-3079)
PHONE...................330 848-8847
Ernest L Puskas Junior, *Pr*
EMP: 9 **EST:** 1980
SALES (est): 1.47MM **Privately Held**
Web: www.littlern.com
SIC: 2869 2819 4226 Industrial organic chemicals, nec; Industrial inorganic chemicals, nec; Special warehousing and storage, nec

(G-7445)
NEXT GENERATION PLASTICS LLC
3075 Smith Rd Ste 101 (44333-4453)
PHONE...................330 668-1200
EMP: 10 **EST:** 2016
SALES (est): 1.02MM **Privately Held**
Web: www.nextgenplastics.com
SIC: 2821 Plastics materials and resins

(G-7446)
PROFUSION INDUSTRIES LLC (PA)
822 Kumho Dr Ste 202 (44333-5105)
PHONE...................800 938-2858
Jack Woodyard, *VP*
Jon Golden, *
William Hatch, *
EMP: 8 **EST:** 2014
SALES (est): 20.85MM
SALES (corp-wide): 20.85MM **Privately Held**
Web: www.profusionindustries.com
SIC: 3081 3089 Unsupported plastics film and sheet; Extruded finished plastics products, nec

(G-7447)
RJF INTERNATIONAL CORPORATION
Also Called: Matting Products Div
3875 Embassy Pkwy (44333-8342)
PHONE...................330 668-2069
◆ **EMP:** 850
Web: www.rjfinternational.com
SIC: 3081 3089 3069 Floor or wall covering, unsupported plastics; Battery cases, plastics or plastics combination; Wallcoverings, rubber

(G-7448)
SANCTUARY SOFTWARE STUDIO INC
3090 W Market St Ste 300 (44333-3623)
PHONE...................330 666-9690
EMP: 49 **EST:** 1993
SALES (est): 2.15MM **Privately Held**
Web: www.sancsoft.com
SIC: 7372 7371 Application computer software; Computer software development

(G-7449)
SENTIENT STUDIOS LTD
2894 Chamberlain Rd Apt 6 (44333-3468)
P.O. Box 13141 (44334-8541)
PHONE...................330 204-8636
William Genkin, *Managing Member*
EMP: 41 **EST:** 2016

Fairlawn - Summit County (G-7450)

SALES (est): 1.04MM **Privately Held**
SIC: 7373 3569 Computer integrated systems design; Robots, assembly line: industrial and commercial

(G-7450)
SIGNET GROUP INC
375 Ghent Rd (44333-4601)
PHONE.................................330 668-5000
Charles E Scharff, *Prin*
EMP: 263 **EST:** 2000
SALES (est): 25.14MM **Privately Held**
Web: www.signetjewelers.com
SIC: 3911 Jewelry, precious metal
PA: Signet Jewelers Limited
C/O Conyers Corporate Services (Bermuda) Limited
Hamilton HM 11

(G-7451)
SIGNET GROUP SERVICES US INC
375 Ghent Rd (44333-4601)
PHONE.................................330 668-5000
EMP: 9 **EST:** 2021
SALES (est): 3.62MM **Privately Held**
SIC: 3911 Jewelry, precious metal
PA: Signet Jewelers Limited
C/O Conyers Corporate Services (Bermuda) Limited
Hamilton HM 11

(G-7452)
SSP INDUSTRIAL GROUP INC
3560 W Market St Ste 300 (44333-2687)
PHONE.................................330 665-2900
Richard M Hamlin, *Pr*
Mark Hamlin Junior, *Pr*
James Gaul, *Sec*
James D Van Tiem, *Sec*
▲ **EMP:** 9 **EST:** 1995
SALES (est): 967.58K **Privately Held**
SIC: 3465 3412 3411 8742 Automotive stampings; Metal barrels, drums, and pails; Food and beverage containers; Management consulting services

(G-7453)
TOTAL EDUCATION SOLUTIONS INC
Also Called: Tes Therapy
3428 W Market St (44333-3339)
PHONE.................................330 668-4041
Tawnia Novak, *Dir*
EMP: 99 **EST:** 2008
SALES (est): 2.8MM **Privately Held**
Web: www.tesidea.com
SIC: 3172 Personal leather goods, nec

Fairport Harbor
Lake County

(G-7454)
GEORGE WHALLEY COMPANY
Also Called: Cft Systems
1180 High St Ste 1 (44077-6921)
PHONE.................................216 453-0099
George M Whalley, *Pr*
Howard M Whalley, *VP*
EMP: 29 **EST:** 1937
SQ FT: 25,000
SALES (est): 900.76K **Privately Held**
Web: www.cftsystems.com
SIC: 3545 Tool holders

(G-7455)
LYONDELL CHEMICAL COMPANY
Also Called: Equistar
110 3rd St (44077-5837)
PHONE.................................440 352-9393
Michael Step, *Mgr*
EMP: 112
Web: www.lyondellbasell.com
SIC: 2821 Plastics materials and resins
HQ: Lyondell Chemical Company
1221 Mckinney St Ste 300
Houston TX 77010
713 309-7200

(G-7456)
MJM INDUSTRIES INC
1200 East St (44077-5571)
PHONE.................................440 350-1230
Eric Wachob, *CEO*
James E Heighway, *Vice Chairman*
Lois Roulston, *
▲ **EMP:** 110 **EST:** 1985
SQ FT: 35,500
SALES (est): 15MM **Privately Held**
Web: www.mjmindustries.com
SIC: 3679 Harness assemblies, for electronic use: wire or cable

(G-7457)
QUARTZ SCIENTIFIC INC (PA)
Also Called: Qsi
819 East St (44077-5596)
P.O. Box 1129 (44077-8129)
PHONE.................................360 574-6254
James R Atwell Junior, *Pr*
EMP: 22 **EST:** 1963
SQ FT: 44,000
SALES (est): 2.68MM
SALES (corp-wide): 2.68MM **Privately Held**
Web: www.qsiquartz.com
SIC: 3679 Quartz crystals, for electronic application

(G-7458)
RAMPE MANUFACTURING COMPANY
Also Called: Torque Transmission
1246 High St (44077-5536)
PHONE.................................440 352-8995
John N Rampe, *CEO*
John W Rampe, *Pr*
Willam Patrick, *Contrlr*
EMP: 17 **EST:** 1947
SQ FT: 40,000
SALES (est): 3.45MM **Privately Held**
Web: www.torquetrans.com
SIC: 3568 Power transmission equipment, nec

(G-7459)
US WELDING TRAINING LLC
518 5th St (44077-5663)
P.O. Box 1011 (44077-1011)
PHONE.................................440 669-9380
Michael Davison, *Prin*
EMP: 6 **EST:** 2012
SALES (est): 126.25K **Privately Held**
Web: www.uswedingtraining.com
SIC: 7692 Welding repair

Farmersville
Montgomery County

(G-7460)
QUALITY DURABLE INDUS FLOORS
Also Called: Q&D Industrial Floors
5005 Farmersville Germantn Pike (45325-9268)
PHONE.................................937 696-2833
Scott Carmack, *Pr*
Douglas Emrick, *VP*
Douglas A Emrick, *VP*
EMP: 14 **EST:** 2000
SALES (est): 1MM **Privately Held**
Web: www.qdifloors.com
SIC: 2851 7389 Epoxy coatings; Business services, nec

Fayette
Fulton County

(G-7461)
C & K MACHINE CO INC
604 N Park St (43521-9718)
P.O. Box 478 (43521-0478)
PHONE.................................419 237-3203
EMP: 7 **EST:** 1987
SALES (est): 597.61K **Privately Held**
SIC: 3599 Machine shop, jobbing and repair

(G-7462)
EAGLE MACHINING LLC
705 N Fayette St (43521-9586)
PHONE.................................419 237-1366
Nigel Crighton, *Managing Member*
EMP: 200 **EST:** 2021
SALES (est): 60MM **Privately Held**
SIC: 3621 Motors and generators

(G-7463)
ZF ACTIVE SAFETY US INC
705 N Fayette St (43521-9586)
PHONE.................................419 237-2511
Gary Predki, *Genl Mgr*
EMP: 16
SALES (corp-wide): 144.19K **Privately Held**
SIC: 3714 Motor vehicle parts and accessories
HQ: Zf Active Safety Us Inc.
12025 Tech Center Dr
Livonia MI 48150
734 855-2600

Fayetteville
Brown County

(G-7464)
DEUCE MACHINING LLC
3088 Us Highway 50 (45118-9012)
P.O. Box 57 (45118-0057)
PHONE.................................513 875-2291
EMP: 7 **EST:** 2008
SALES (est): 507.76K **Privately Held**
Web: www.deucemachining.com
SIC: 3599 Machine shop, jobbing and repair

(G-7465)
DR PEPPER/SEVEN UP INC
3943 Us Highway 50 (45118-1500)
PHONE.................................513 875-2466
Bill Hamann, *Dist Mgr*
EMP: 14
Web: www.drpepper.com
SIC: 2086 Soft drinks: packaged in cans, bottles, etc.
HQ: Dr Pepper/Seven Up, Inc.
6425 Hall Of Fame Ln
Frisco TX 75034
972 673-7000

(G-7466)
KILEY MACHINE COMPANY
4196 Anderson State Rd (45118-9777)
PHONE.................................513 875-3223
Dennis E Kiley, *Pr*
EMP: 8 **EST:** 1998
SALES (est): 643.15K **Privately Held**
SIC: 3599 Machine shop, jobbing and repair

Felicity
Clermont County

(G-7467)
FELICITY PLASTICS MACHINERY
892 Neville Penn Schoolhouse Rd (45120-9542)
P.O. Box 610 (45120-0610)
PHONE.................................513 876-7003
Craig Rigdon, *Pr*
EMP: 15 **EST:** 1987
SQ FT: 14,000
SALES (est): 535.01K **Privately Held**
SIC: 3089 Injection molding of plastics

(G-7468)
L C LIMING & SONS INC
Also Called: L & L Plastics
3200 State Route 756 (45120-9766)
PHONE.................................513 876-2555
James C Liming, *Pr*
Margaret Laubach, *Treas*
EMP: 8 **EST:** 1970
SQ FT: 9,250
SALES (est): 951.57K **Privately Held**
SIC: 3089 6515 Injection molding of plastics; Mobile home site operators

Findlay
Hancock County

(G-7469)
1 EMC LLC
1931 Tiffin Ave (45840-6752)
PHONE.................................216 990-2586
Paul Hadde, *Prin*
EMP: 6 **EST:** 2019
SALES (est): 245.28K **Privately Held**
SIC: 3572 Computer storage devices

(G-7470)
ACCENT SIGNAGE SYSTEMS INC
5409 Hamlet Dr (45840-6618)
PHONE.................................612 377-9156
Shereen Rahamim, *CEO*
EMP: 25 **EST:** 1984
SALES (est): 4.38MM **Privately Held**
Web: www.accentsignage.com
SIC: 3993 Signs and advertising specialties

(G-7471)
ADS
401 Olive St (45840-5358)
PHONE.................................419 422-6521
EMP: 8 **EST:** 2015
SALES (est): 230.48K **Privately Held**
Web: www.adspipe.com
SIC: 3084 Plastics pipe

(G-7472)
ADVANCE NOVELTY INCORPORATED
101 Stanford Pkwy (45840-1731)
PHONE.................................419 424-0363
Tom Heimann, *Prin*
EMP: 7 **EST:** 2007
SALES (est): 921.94K **Privately Held**
Web: www.advancenovelty2.com
SIC: 5092 3944 Toys, nec; Games, toys, and children's vehicles

(G-7473)
ADVANCED DRAINAGE SYSTEMS INC
12370 Hancock County Rd (45840)
PHONE.................................419 424-8222
EMP: 6

GEOGRAPHIC SECTION — Findlay - Hancock County (G-7497)

SALES (corp-wide): 3.07B **Publicly Held**
Web: www.adspipe.com
SIC: 3084 Plastics pipe
PA: Advanced Drainage Systems, Inc.
4640 Trueman Blvd
Hilliard OH 43026
614 658-0050

(G-7474)
ADVANCED DRAINAGE SYSTEMS INC
401 Olive St (45840-5358)
PHONE....................................419 424-8324
Bruce Rush, *Brnch Mgr*
EMP: 36
SALES (corp-wide): 3.07B **Publicly Held**
Web: www.adspipe.com
SIC: 3084 3083 Plastics pipe; Laminated plastics plate and sheet
PA: Advanced Drainage Systems, Inc.
4640 Trueman Blvd
Hilliard OH 43026
614 658-0050

(G-7475)
ALLEGRA PRINT & IMAGING
Also Called: Allegra Print
701 W Sandusky St (45840-2325)
P.O. Box 609 (45839-0609)
PHONE....................................419 427-8095
Karl Heminger, *Owner*
EMP: 8 EST: 2006
SALES (est): 117.23K **Privately Held**
Web: www.allegrafindlay.com
SIC: 2752 Offset printing

(G-7476)
AMERICAN PLASTICS LLC
Also Called: Centrex Plastics
814 W Lima St (45840-2312)
PHONE....................................419 423-1213
EMP: 240
SALES (corp-wide): 494.03MM **Privately Held**
Web: www.americanplasticsllc.com
SIC: 2673 3089 Food storage and trash bags (plastic); Plastics processing
HQ: American Plastics Llc
11840 Wstline Indus Dr St
Saint Louis MO 63146
800 325-1051

(G-7477)
ARCHIES TOO
2145 S Lake Ct (45840-1245)
PHONE....................................419 427-2663
Mike Miller, *Owner*
EMP: 8 EST: 2004
SALES (est): 212.97K **Privately Held**
Web: www.archiefans.com
SIC: 2024 Ice cream and frozen deserts

(G-7478)
AUSTIN POWDER COMPANY
Also Called: Austin Powder
3518 Township Road 142 (45840-9611)
PHONE....................................419 299-3347
Rita Whelchel, *Mgr*
EMP: 9
SALES (corp-wide): 749.73MM **Privately Held**
Web: www.austinpowder.com
SIC: 2892 Explosives
HQ: Austin Powder Company
25800 Science Park Dr # 300
Cleveland OH 44122
216 464-2400

(G-7479)
BACK IN BLACK CO
2100 Fostoria Ave (45840-8758)
P.O. Box 842 (45839-0842)
PHONE....................................419 425-5555
Michael Gardner, *Pr*
EMP: 40 EST: 2009
SALES (est): 1.65MM **Privately Held**
SIC: 3537 Industrial trucks and tractors

(G-7480)
BALL CORPORATION
1800 Production Dr (45840-5445)
PHONE....................................419 423-3071
EMP: 29
SALES (corp-wide): 14.03B **Publicly Held**
Web: www.ball.com
SIC: 3411 Food and beverage containers
PA: Ball Corporation
9200 W 108th Cir
Westminster CO 80021
303 469-3131

(G-7481)
BALL METAL BEVERAGE CONT CORP
Also Called: Ball Metal Beverage Cont Div
12340 Township Rd 99 E (45840)
PHONE....................................419 423-3071
Tom Martin, *Brnch Mgr*
EMP: 213
SALES (corp-wide): 14.03B **Publicly Held**
Web: www.ball.com
SIC: 3411 Beer cans, metal
HQ: Ball Metal Beverage Container Corp.
9300 W 108th Cir
Westminster CO 80021

(G-7482)
BALLINGER INDUSTRIES INC (PA)
2500 Fostoria Ave (45840-8732)
PHONE....................................419 422-4533
Jon Ballinger, *Pr*
▲ EMP: 12 EST: 1995
SALES (est): 66.9MM
SALES (corp-wide): 66.9MM **Privately Held**
SIC: 3531 Construction machinery

(G-7483)
BALLINGER INDUSTRIES INC
616 N Blanchard St (45840-5706)
PHONE....................................419 421-4704
EMP: 8
SALES (corp-wide): 66.9MM **Privately Held**
SIC: 3531 Buckets, excavating: clamshell, concrete, dragline, etc.
PA: Ballinger Industries, Inc.
2500 Fostoria Ave
Findlay OH 45840
419 422-4533

(G-7484)
BEST ONE TIRE & SVC LIMA INC
10456 W Us Route 224 Unit 1 (45840-1907)
PHONE....................................419 425-3322
Jason Myers, *Brnch Mgr*
EMP: 8
SALES (corp-wide): 14.67MM **Privately Held**
Web: www.bestonetire.com
SIC: 7534 5531 5014 Tire recapping; Automotive tires; Tires and tubes
PA: Best One Tire & Service Of Lima, Inc.
701 E Hanthorn Rd
Lima OH 45804
419 229-2380

(G-7485)
BOSSERMAN AUTOMOTIVE ENGRG LLC
Also Called: Aircraft-Refuelers.com
18919 Olympic Dr (45840-9453)
PHONE....................................419 722-2879
Terry Bosserman, *Pr*
▼ EMP: 6 EST: 2012
SALES (est): 359.89K **Privately Held**
SIC: 3713 Tank truck bodies

(G-7486)
BREAD KNEADS INC
510 S Blanchard St (45840-5951)
PHONE....................................419 422-3863
Kelley Smith, *Pr*
EMP: 9 EST: 1981
SALES (est): 725.32K **Privately Held**
Web: www.tarvinart.com
SIC: 5411 5149 2099 2051 Delicatessen stores; Groceries and related products, nec; Food preparations, nec; Bread, cake, and related products

(G-7487)
BRINKMAN TURKEY FARMS INC (PA)
Also Called: Brinkman's Country Corner
16314 State Route 68 (45840-9245)
PHONE....................................419 365-5127
Larry Brinkman, *Pr*
Joe Brinkman, *VP*
EMP: 18 EST: 1950
SQ FT: 6,000
SALES (est): 5.33MM
SALES (corp-wide): 5.33MM **Privately Held**
Web: www.brinkmanfarms.com
SIC: 5411 2015 2013 0115 Grocery stores, independent; Turkey, processed: canned; Prepared beef products, from purchased beef; Corn

(G-7488)
BROWN COMPANY OF FINDLAY LTD
225 Stanford Pkwy (45840-1733)
P.O. Box 1625 (45839-1625)
PHONE....................................419 425-3002
Melvin J Brown, *Pr*
EMP: 20 EST: 2007
SALES (est): 2.62MM **Privately Held**
Web: www.tbcfindlay.com
SIC: 3089 7389 Injection molding of plastics; Inspection and testing services

(G-7489)
BUCKMAN LTD
1413 Forest Park (45840-2991)
PHONE....................................419 420-1687
EMP: 7 EST: 2008
SALES (est): 64.78K **Privately Held**
Web: www.buckman.com
SIC: 2869 Industrial organic chemicals, nec

(G-7490)
C & H ENTERPRISES LTD
2121 Bright Rd (45840-5433)
PHONE....................................510 226-6083
Douglas D Hosey, *Prin*
EMP: 10 EST: 2009
SALES (est): 84.11K **Privately Held**
Web: www.candhenterprises.com
SIC: 3599 Machine shop, jobbing and repair

(G-7491)
CASCADE CORPORATION
2000 Production Dr (45840-5449)
P.O. Box 841 (45839-0841)
PHONE....................................419 425-3675
EMP: 32

Web: www.cascorp.com
SIC: 5084 3569 Materials handling machinery; Assembly machines, non-metalworking
HQ: Cascade Corporation
2201 Ne 201st Ave
Fairview OR 97024
503 669-6300

(G-7492)
CIRIGLIANO ENTERPRISES LLC
2410 Foxfire Ln (45840-7142)
PHONE....................................567 525-4571
Vincent Cirigliano, *CEO*
EMP: 9 EST: 1996
SALES (est): 720.97K **Privately Held**
SIC: 1521 1389 Single-family housing construction; Construction, repair, and dismantling services

(G-7493)
CITY APPAREL INC
116 E Main Cross St (45840-4817)
PHONE....................................419 434-1155
Andrea Kramer, *CEO*
Julie Weber, *Admn*
▲ EMP: 10 EST: 2007
SALES (est): 1.77MM **Privately Held**
Web: www.cityapparel.net
SIC: 5611 5621 5947 7389 Men's and boys' clothing stores; Women's clothing stores; Gifts and novelties; Embroidery advertising

(G-7494)
CLARK RM INC
400 Crystal Ave (45840-4770)
PHONE....................................419 425-9889
Marshall Clark, *Mgr*
EMP: 14
SIC: 2491 2449 2448 2441 Structural lumber and timber, treated wood; Wood containers, nec; Wood pallets and skids; Nailed wood boxes and shook
PA: Clark Rm Inc
1110 Summerlin Dr
Douglas GA

(G-7495)
CLASSIC SIGN COMPANY
3230 Township Road 232 (45840-9810)
PHONE....................................419 420-0058
EMP: 7 EST: 1994
SALES (est): 485.54K **Privately Held**
Web: www.classicsigncompany.com
SIC: 3993 Signs, not made in custom sign painting shops

(G-7496)
CONTROL INDUSTRIES INC
614 Central Ave (45840-5646)
P.O. Box 889 (43078-0889)
PHONE....................................937 653-7694
James Long, *Pr*
James B Long, *VP*
EMP: 6 EST: 1962
SQ FT: 3,200
SALES (est): 506.98K **Privately Held**
Web: www.controlindustriesinc.com
SIC: 3663 Receiver-transmitter units (transceiver)

(G-7497)
COOPER TIRE & RUBBER CO LLC (HQ)
Also Called: Cooper
701 Lima Ave (45840-2315)
P.O. Box 550 (45839-0550)
PHONE....................................419 423-1321
Bradley E Hughes, *Pr*
Gerald C Bialek, *Interim Vice President**
Paula S Whitesell, *Chief Human Resources Officer**

Findlay - Hancock County (G-7498)

Stephen Zamansky, *
◆ **EMP:** 1000 **EST:** 1930
SALES (est): 1.78B
SALES (corp-wide): 20.07B **Publicly Held**
Web: us.coopertire.com
SIC: 3011 Automobile tires, pneumatic
PA: The Goodyear Tire & Rubber Company
  200 Innovation Way
  Akron OH 44316
  330 796-2121

(G-7498)
COOPER TIRE VHCL TEST CTR INC (DH)
Also Called: Cooper
701 Lima Ave (45840-2315)
PHONE...................419 423-1321
Brad Hughes, *Pr*
Stephen O Schrooder, *Treas*
James E Kline, *Sec*
▲ **EMP:** 17 **EST:** 1984
SQ FT: 2,500
SALES (est): 11.41MM
SALES (corp-wide): 20.07B **Publicly Held**
SIC: 3011 4225 Automobile tires, pneumatic; General warehousing and storage
HQ: Cooper Tire & Rubber Company Llc
  701 Lima Ave
  Findlay OH 45840
  419 423-1321

(G-7499)
CROWLEY BLUE WTR PARTNERS LLC
539 S Main St (45840-3229)
PHONE...................419 422-2121
EMP: 14 **EST:** 2020
SALES (est): 1.52MM **Publicly Held**
SIC: 2911 Petroleum refining
PA: Marathon Petroleum Corporation
  539 S Main St
  Findlay OH 45840

(G-7500)
CUMMINS FILTRATION INC
2150 Industrial Dr (45840-5402)
P.O. Box 708 (45839-0708)
EMP: 250
SIC: 3569 3714 Filters; Motor vehicle parts and accessories

(G-7501)
DIETSCH BROTHERS INCORPORATED (PA)
400 W Main Cross St (45840-3317)
PHONE...................419 422-4474
Jeffery Dietsch, *Pr*
Richard Dietsch, *
Thomas Dietsch, *
EMP: 40 **EST:** 1937
SQ FT: 12,000
SALES (est): 4.5MM
SALES (corp-wide): 4.5MM **Privately Held**
Web: www.dietschs.com
SIC: 2066 2024 5441 Chocolate and cocoa products; Ice cream and frozen deserts; Confectionery

(G-7502)
DJM PLASTICS LTD
Also Called: DLM Plastics
1530 Harvard Ave (45840-1737)
PHONE...................419 424-5250
◆ **EMP:** 10 **EST:** 2005
SALES (est): 2.02MM **Privately Held**
Web: www.dlmplastics.com
SIC: 3089 3081 Injection molded finished plastics products, nec; Unsupported plastics film and sheet

(G-7503)
DS TECHSTAR INC
Also Called: Techstar
1219 W Main Cross St Ste 204 (45840-0707)
PHONE...................419 424-0888
D Steve Brown, *Pr*
D D Brown, *Sec*
Warren Brown, *Treas*
▲ **EMP:** 7 **EST:** 1990
SQ FT: 1,000
SALES (est): 1.01MM **Privately Held**
Web: www.techstar-inc.com
SIC: 3441 Bridge sections, prefabricated, highway

(G-7504)
FABCO INC (HQ)
2500 Fostoria Ave (45840-8732)
P.O. Box 1545 (45839-1545)
PHONE...................419 422-4533
Lynn Roeder, *CEO*
Timothy A Jones, *
▲ **EMP:** 50 **EST:** 1974
SQ FT: 35,000
SALES (est): 17.81MM
SALES (corp-wide): 66.9MM **Privately Held**
Web: www.fabco-inc.com
SIC: 3535 3444 3443 3441 Conveyors and conveying equipment; Sheet metalwork; Fabricated plate work (boiler shop); Fabricated structural metal
PA: Ballinger Industries, Inc.
  2500 Fostoria Ave
  Findlay OH 45840
  419 422-4533

(G-7505)
FINDLAY AMRCN PRSTHTIC ORTHTIC
12474 County Road 99 (45840-9736)
PHONE...................419 424-1622
TOLL FREE: 800
Jeremy Berman, *Pr*
Kenneth Berman Prosthetist, *Prin*
EMP: 6 **EST:** 1996
SALES (est): 444.43K **Privately Held**
Web: www.findlayprosthetic.com
SIC: 3842 3841 Braces, orthopedic; Medical instruments and equipment, blood and bone work

(G-7506)
FINDLAY MACHINE & TOOL LLC
Also Called: Fmt
2000 Industrial Dr (45840-5443)
P.O. Box 1562 (45839-1562)
PHONE...................419 434-3100
Joe Klein, *Pr*
Andrew Rill, *
George Hay, *
▲ **EMP:** 45 **EST:** 1940
SQ FT: 200,000
SALES (est): 12.65MM **Privately Held**
Web: www.fmtinc.com
SIC: 3089 Injection molding of plastics

(G-7507)
FINDLAY PALLET INC
300 Bell Ave (45840)
PHONE...................419 423-0511
Robert Reed, *Pr*
EMP: 9 **EST:** 1979
SALES (est): 913.94K **Privately Held**
SIC: 2448 Cargo containers, wood and wood with metal

(G-7508)
FINDLAY PALLET INC
102 Crystal Ave (45840-4734)
PHONE...................419 423-0511
David A Hackenberg, *Prin*
EMP: 8 **EST:** 1998
SALES (est): 143.77K **Privately Held**
SIC: 2448 Pallets, wood

(G-7509)
FINDLAY PRODUCTS CORPORATION
2045 Industrial Dr (45840-5444)
P.O. Box 1006 (45839-1006)
PHONE...................419 423-3324
◆ **EMP:** 130 **EST:** 1991
SQ FT: 224,000
SALES (est): 25.54MM **Privately Held**
Web: www.midwayproducts.com
SIC: 3465 3469 Automotive stampings; Metal stampings, nec
PA: Midway Products Group, Inc.
  1 Lyman E Hoyt Dr
  Monroe MI 48161

(G-7510)
FLEETMASTER EXPRESS INC
5250 Distribution Dr (45840-9814)
PHONE...................866 425-0666
Rob Mahlman, *Brnch Mgr*
EMP: 91
SALES (corp-wide): 81.91MM **Privately Held**
Web: www.fleetmasterexpress.com
SIC: 2741 Miscellaneous publishing
PA: Fleetmaster Express, Incorporated
  1814 Hollins Rd Ne Ste A
  Roanoke VA 24012
  540 344-8834

(G-7511)
FREUDENBERG-NOK GENERAL PARTNR
Also Called: Freudenberg-Nok Findlay
555 Marathon Blvd (45840-1790)
P.O. Box 269 (45839-0269)
PHONE...................419 427-5221
Roy Sehroeder, *Genl Mgr*
EMP: 170
SALES (corp-wide): 12.23B **Privately Held**
Web: www.freudenberg.com
SIC: 3053 3492 Gaskets, all materials; Fluid power valves and hose fittings
HQ: Freudenberg-Nok General Partnership
  47774 W Anchor Ct
  Plymouth MI 48170
  734 451-0020

(G-7512)
FRIENDS SERVICE CO INC (PA)
Also Called: Friends Business Source
2300 Bright Rd (45840-5432)
PHONE...................419 427-1704
Kenneth J Schroeder, *CEO*
Kenneth J Schroeder, *Pr*
Dale Alt, *CIO*
Margaret Schroeder, *
Dennis Mitchell, *
EMP: 73 **EST:** 1991
SQ FT: 65,000
SALES (est): 48.82MM **Privately Held**
Web: www.friendsoffice.com
SIC: 5021 5044 5087 2752 Furniture; Office equipment; Janitors' supplies; Photolithographic printing

(G-7513)
GILLIG CUSTOM WINERY INC
1720 Northridge Rd (45840-1905)
PHONE...................419 202-6057
EMP: 7 **EST:** 2015
SALES (est): 307.79K **Privately Held**
Web: www.gilligwinery.com
SIC: 2084 Wines

(G-7514)
GOULD FIRE PROTECTION INC
633 Bristol Dr (45840-6909)
PHONE...................419 957-2416
Arthur Gould, *Pr*
James Amos, *VP*
EMP: 6 **EST:** 1997
SALES (est): 621.79K **Privately Held**
SIC: 3569 Sprinkler systems, fire: automatic

(G-7515)
GRAHAM PACKG PLASTIC PDTS INC
170 Stanford Pkwy 7 (45840-1732)
PHONE...................419 421-8037
EMP: 180
SALES (corp-wide): 11.63B **Publicly Held**
SIC: 3085 Plastics bottles
HQ: Graham Packaging Plastic Products Inc.
  1 Seagate Ste 10
  Toledo OH 43604
  717 849-8500

(G-7516)
GSW MANUFACTURING INC (DH)
1801 Production Dr (45840)
P.O. Box 1045 (45839)
PHONE...................419 423-7111
Hiro Kojima, *Pr*
Yukinobu Ukai, *
▲ **EMP:** 412 **EST:** 1989
SQ FT: 72,000
SALES (est): 97.16MM **Privately Held**
Web: www.gswiring.com
SIC: 3714 3694 Automotive wiring harness sets; Engine electrical equipment
HQ: G.S. Wiring Systems, Inc.
  1801 Production Dr
  Findlay OH 45840

(G-7517)
GVS FILTRATION INC (DH)
2150 Industrial Dr (45840-5402)
PHONE...................419 423-9040
▲ **EMP:** 400 **EST:** 2011
SQ FT: 100,000
SALES (est): 101.14MM **Privately Held**
Web: www.kussfiltration.com
SIC: 3569 Filters, general line: industrial
HQ: Gvs Spa
  Via Roma 50
  Zola Predosa BO 40069
  051 617-6311

(G-7518)
HAMLET PROTEIN INC
5289 Hamlet Dr (45840)
PHONE...................567 525-5627
▼ **EMP:** 40 **EST:** 2011
SALES (est): 22.22MM
SALES (corp-wide): 2.67MM **Privately Held**
Web: www.hamletprotein.com
SIC: 2048 Prepared feeds, nec
HQ: Hamlet Protein A/S
  Saturnvej 51
  Horsens 8700
  75631020

(G-7519)
HANCOCK STRUCTURAL STEEL LLC
813 E Bigelow Ave (45840-4256)
P.O. Box 1546 (45839-1546)
PHONE...................419 424-1217
Charles G Wenner, *Managing Member*
Charles Weston Garrett Wenner, *CEO*
EMP: 10 **EST:** 2007
SQ FT: 15,000

GEOGRAPHIC SECTION

Findlay - Hancock County (G-7542)

SALES (est): 2.47MM **Privately Held**
Web: www.hancocksteel.com
SIC: 3441 Fabricated structural metal

(G-7520)
HANCOR INC
12370 Jackson Township Rd (45839)
P.O. Box 1047 (45839-1047)
PHONE.................................419 424-8222
Steve Ferell, *Mgr*
EMP: 45
SALES (corp-wide): 3.07B **Publicly Held**
Web: www.adspipe.com
SIC: 3084 Plastics pipe
HQ: Hancor, Inc.
  4640 Trueman Blvd
  Hilliard OH 43026
  614 658-0050

(G-7521)
HANCOR INC
Also Called: Hantech
433 Olive St (45840-5358)
P.O. Box 1047 (45839-1047)
PHONE.................................419 424-8225
Clark Inniger, *Mgr*
EMP: 45
SALES (corp-wide): 3.07B **Publicly Held**
Web: www.adspipe.com
SIC: 3089 3084 2821 Septic tanks, plastics; Plastics pipe; Plastics materials and resins
HQ: Hancor, Inc.
  4640 Trueman Blvd
  Hilliard OH 43026
  614 658-0050

(G-7522)
HIGH QUALITY PLASTICS INC
2000 Fostoria Ave (45840-9775)
P.O. Box 269 (45839-0269)
PHONE.................................419 422-8290
Frits Vanderklooster, *Prin*
EMP: 6 **EST:** 2006
SALES (est): 64.13K **Privately Held**
SIC: 3053 Gaskets; packing and sealing devices

(G-7523)
HITACHI ASTEMO AMERICAS INC
1901 Industrial Dr (45840-5442)
PHONE.................................419 425-1259
EMP: 218
SIC: 3714 Motor vehicle brake systems and parts
HQ: Hitachi Astemo Americas, Inc.
  955 Warwick Rd
  Harrodsburg KY 40330
  859 734-9451

(G-7524)
HOLTGREVEN SCALE & ELEC CORP
Also Called: Loadmaster Scale
420 E Lincoln St (45840-4945)
PHONE.................................419 422-4779
Leonard Holtgreven, *Pr*
Mark Holtgreven, *VP*
▲ **EMP:** 11 **EST:** 1958
SQ FT: 20,000
SALES (est): 1.86MM **Privately Held**
Web: www.loadmasterscale.com
SIC: 3596 Industrial scales

(G-7525)
HOUSE OF AWARDS INC
419 N Main St (45840-3378)
PHONE.................................419 422-7877
Jeff Crawford, *Pr*
Karen Crawford, *VP*
EMP: 7 **EST:** 1968
SQ FT: 3,500
SALES (est): 484.6K **Privately Held**

Web: www.hoashoes.com
SIC: 3949 5091 Sporting and athletic goods, nec; Sporting and recreation goods

(G-7526)
JK-CO LLC
16960 E State Route 12 (45840-9744)
PHONE.................................419 422-5240
Joseph L Kurtz, *Managing Member*
C Leon Thornton, *
▼ **EMP:** 45 **EST:** 2002
SQ FT: 40,000
SALES (est): 9.57MM **Privately Held**
Web: www.jk-co.com
SIC: 3743 4789 Railroad car rebuilding; Railroad car repair

(G-7527)
KREATE EXTRUSION LLC ✪
2000 Industrial Dr (45840)
PHONE.................................419 683-4057
Nickolas Reinhart, *Managing Member*
EMP: 6 **EST:** 2022
SALES (est): 442.48K **Privately Held**
SIC: 3089 Plastics containers, except foam

(G-7528)
LEGACY FARMERS COOPERATIVE (PA)
6566 County Road 236 (45840-9769)
PHONE.................................419 423-2611
Mark Sunderman, *Pr*
Dave Baer, *Sec*
Gary Herringshaw, *Treas*
Deborah Boger, *Contrlr*
EMP: 15 **EST:** 1989
SQ FT: 10,000
SALES (est): 336.16MM
SALES (corp-wide): 336.16MM **Privately Held**
Web: www.legacyfarmers.com
SIC: 5153 5191 5984 2875 Grains; Farm supplies; Liquefied petroleum gas dealers; Fertilizers, mixing only

(G-7529)
LFG SPECIALTIES LLC
16406 E Us Route 224 (45840-9772)
PHONE.................................419 424-4999
EMP: 50 **EST:** 1988
SQ FT: 3,000
SALES (est): 10.4MM
SALES (corp-wide): 4.32MM **Privately Held**
SIC: 3585 2899 Evaporative condensers, heat transfer equipment; Flares
HQ: Cb&I Group Inc.
  4171 Essen Ln
  Baton Rouge LA 70809
  337 685-4725

(G-7530)
MANUFCTRING BUS DEV SLTONS LLC
Also Called: Mbds
1950 Industrial Dr (45840-5441)
P.O. Box 1811 (45839-1811)
PHONE.................................419 294-1313
Brian Robertson, *Pr*
EMP: 60 **EST:** 2003
SQ FT: 50,000
SALES (est): 5.03MM **Privately Held**
Web: www.mbdsna.com
SIC: 3559 Automotive related machinery

(G-7531)
MARATHON OIL COMPANY
539 S Main St (45840-3229)
P.O. Box 151 (45839-0151)
PHONE.................................419 422-2121

EMP: 27
SALES (corp-wide): 8.04B **Publicly Held**
Web: www.marathonoil.com
SIC: 2911 Petroleum refining
HQ: Marathon Oil Company
  5555 San Felipe St B1
  Houston TX 77056
  713 629-6600

(G-7532)
MARATHON PETROLEUM COMPANY LP (HQ)
539 S Main St (45840)
P.O. Box 599500 (78259)
PHONE.................................419 422-2121
◆ **EMP:** 10 **EST:** 1997
SQ FT: 621,000
SALES (est): 161.44B **Publicly Held**
Web: www.marathonpetroleum.com
SIC: 5172 2951 2865 Gasoline; Asphalt paving mixtures and blocks; Cyclic crudes and intermediates
PA: Marathon Petroleum Corporation
  539 S Main St
  Findlay OH 45840

(G-7533)
MARATHON PETROLEUM CORPORATION (PA)
Also Called: Marathon Petroleum
539 S Main St (45840-3229)
PHONE.................................419 422-2121
▲ **EMP:** 1055 **EST:** 1887
SALES (est): 150.31B **Publicly Held**
Web: www.marathonpetroleum.com
SIC: 2911 5172 Petroleum refining; Gasoline

(G-7534)
MARATHON PTRO CNADA TRDG SUP U
539 S Main St (45840-3229)
PHONE.................................419 422-2121
Michael J Hennigan, *Pr*
EMP: 16 **EST:** 2020
SALES (est): 1.5MM **Publicly Held**
SIC: 2911 Petroleum refining
PA: Marathon Petroleum Corporation
  539 S Main St
  Findlay OH 45840

(G-7535)
MARBEE INC
Also Called: Marbee Printing & Graphic Art
2703 N Main St Ste 1 (45840-4039)
PHONE.................................419 422-9441
Randy Raymond, *Pr*
Teresa Raymond, *Sec*
EMP: 6 **EST:** 1991
SQ FT: 3,600
SALES (est): 555.47K **Privately Held**
Web: www.marbeeprinting.com
SIC: 2752 2759 Offset printing; Commercial printing, nec

(G-7536)
MC BROWN INDUSTRIES INC
10534 Township Road 128 (45840-9315)
PHONE.................................419 963-2800
Lester Brown, *Pr*
Dan Brown, *VP*
Lester John Brown Iii, *Sec*
EMP: 10 **EST:** 1971
SQ FT: 15,000
SALES (est): 845.65K **Privately Held**
SIC: 3441 3599 Fabricated structural metal; Machine shop, jobbing and repair

(G-7537)
MIDWAY PRODUCTS GROUP INC
2045 Industrial Drive (45840-5444)

PHONE.................................419 422-7070
Daryl Osburn, *Brnch Mgr*
EMP: 8
Web: www.midwayproducts.com
SIC: 3469 Metal stampings, nec
PA: Midway Products Group, Inc.
  1 Lyman E Hoyt Dr
  Monroe MI 48161

(G-7538)
MITEC POWERTRAIN INC
4000 Fostoria Ave (45840-8733)
PHONE.................................567 525-5606
▲ **EMP:** 232 **EST:** 2009
SQ FT: 100,000
SALES (est): 104.7MM
SALES (corp-wide): 230.9MM **Privately Held**
SIC: 3714 Motor vehicle parts and accessories
PA: Mtc Ag
  Rennbahn 25
  Eisenach TH 99817

(G-7539)
MOLTEN NORTH AMERICA CORP (DH)
1835 Industrial Dr (45840-5440)
P.O. Box 1451 (45839-1451)
PHONE.................................419 425-2700
Hiddaki Miyamoto, *Pr*
Toshikazu Yamate, *
▲ **EMP:** 189 **EST:** 1990
SQ FT: 100,814
SALES (est): 24.89MM **Privately Held**
Web: www.molten.co.jp
SIC: 3089 Automotive parts, plastic
HQ: Molten Corporation
  4-10-97-21, Kanonshinmachi, Nishi-Ku
  Hiroshima HIR 733-0

(G-7540)
MPLX GP LLC
539 S Main St (45840-3229)
PHONE.................................419 422-2121
Timothy T Griffith, *Sr VP*
Molly R Benson, *CCO*
Thomas Kaczynski, *VP Fin*
John J Quaid, *VP*
C Kristopher Hagedorn, *Ex VP*
EMP: 16 **EST:** 2012
SALES (est): 3.97MM **Publicly Held**
SIC: 2911 Petroleum refining
PA: Marathon Petroleum Corporation
  539 S Main St
  Findlay OH 45840

(G-7541)
NATIONAL LIME AND STONE CO
9860 County Road 313 (45840-9003)
P.O. Box 120 (45839-0120)
PHONE.................................419 423-3400
Denny Swick, *Brnch Mgr*
EMP: 19
SALES (corp-wide): 167.89MM **Privately Held**
Web: www.natlime.com
SIC: 3273 1422 Ready-mixed concrete; Crushed and broken limestone
PA: The National Lime And Stone Company
  551 Lake Cascade Pkwy
  Findlay OH 45840
  419 422-4341

(G-7542)
NICHIDAI AMERICA CORPORATION
Also Called: N A C
15630 E State Route 12 Ste 4 (45840-7771)
PHONE.................................419 423-7511

Yuzuru Mishimura, *Pr*
Kiyoshi Naaadawa, *VP*
EMP: 12 **EST:** 2006
SALES (est): 196.93K **Privately Held**
Web: www.nichidai.jp
SIC: 3312 Tool and die steel

(G-7543)
NICKOLAS PLASTICS LLC
814 W Lima St (45840)
PHONE..................419 423-1213
Terrence L Reinhart, *Pr*
◆ **EMP:** 240 **EST:** 2003
SALES (est): 57.43MM
SALES (corp-wide): 494.03MM **Privately Held**
Web: www.centrexplastics.com
SIC: 3089 Injection molding of plastics
HQ: American Plastics Llc
  11840 Wstline Indus Dr St
  Saint Louis MO 63146
  800 325-1051

(G-7544)
OGDEN NEWS PUBLISHING OHIO INC
Also Called: Courier, The
701 W Sandusky St (45840-2325)
PHONE..................419 422-5151
Jeremy Speer, *Publisher*
EMP: 75
Web: www.ogdennews.com
SIC: 2711 Newspapers: publishing only, not printed on site
HQ: Ogden News Publishing Of Ohio, Inc.
  314 W Market St
  Sandusky OH 44870
  419 625-5500

(G-7545)
OLDE MAN GRANOLA LLC
7227 W State Route 12 (45840-8802)
PHONE..................419 819-9576
Kelly Green, *Ex Dir*
Kelly Green, *Mgr*
Rebecca Green, *Mgr*
Mark Plaza, *Mgr*
Fay Plaza, *Dir Opers*
EMP: 10 **EST:** 2013
SALES (est): 616.39K **Privately Held**
Web: www.oldemangranola.com
SIC: 2043 7389 Granola and muesli, except bars and clusters; Business services, nec

(G-7546)
OLIVER RUBBER CO
701 Lima Ave (45840-2315)
PHONE..................419 420-6235
Larry Enders, *CEO*
EMP: 9 **EST:** 2019
SALES (est): 327.45K **Privately Held**
Web: www.oliverrubber.com
SIC: 3011 Tires and inner tubes

(G-7547)
OPERATIONAL SUPPORT SVCS LLC
1850 Industrial Dr (45840-5439)
P.O. Box 178 (45839-0178)
PHONE..................419 425-0889
EMP: 17 **EST:** 2002
SQ FT: 5,000
SALES (est): 1.36MM **Privately Held**
Web: www.operationalss.com
SIC: 2655 Fiber shipping and mailing containers

(G-7548)
OTTAWA OIL CO INC
Also Called: Findlay Party Mart
1100 Trenton Ave (45840-1920)
PHONE..................419 425-3301
EMP: 17
SALES (corp-wide): 126.95MM **Privately Held**
Web: www.ottawaoil.com
SIC: 1389 Pumping of oil and gas wells
HQ: Ottawa Oil Co., Inc.
  10305 State Route 224
  Ottawa OH
  419 523-6441

(G-7549)
P & A INDUSTRIES INC (HQ)
Also Called: Midway Products
600 Crystal Ave (45840)
P.O. Box 737 (48161)
PHONE..................419 422-7070
▲ **EMP:** 80 **EST:** 1983
SALES (est): 31.36MM **Privately Held**
Web: www.midwayproducts.com
SIC: 3465 Automotive stampings
PA: Midway Products Group, Inc.
  1 Lyman E Hoyt Dr
  Monroe MI 48161

(G-7550)
PARTITIONS PLUS INCORPORATED
12517 County Road 99 (45840-9771)
PHONE..................419 422-2600
Brian Robinson, *Admn*
EMP: 40 **EST:** 2011
SQ FT: 40,000
SALES (est): 5.1MM **Privately Held**
Web: www.partitions.plus
SIC: 5046 2541 5021 Partitions; Wood partitions and fixtures; Racks

(G-7551)
PIECO INC (PA)
Also Called: Superior Trim
2151 Industrial Dr (45840)
P.O. Box 118 (45839)
PHONE..................419 422-5335
Michael Gardner, *Pr*
EMP: 50 **EST:** 1997
SQ FT: 50,000
SALES (est): 37.77MM
SALES (corp-wide): 37.77MM **Privately Held**
Web: www.pieco.com
SIC: 2396 Automotive trimmings, fabric

(G-7552)
PRESSED PAPERBOARD TECH LLC
Also Called: Papertech
115 Bentley Ct (45840-1799)
PHONE..................419 423-4030
James Morgan, *Managing Member*
Randy Clifton, *
EMP: 160 **EST:** 1999
SALES (est): 29.03MM
SALES (corp-wide): 56.99MM **Privately Held**
Web: www.papertrays.com
SIC: 2679 Food dishes and utensils, from pressed and molded pulp
PA: May River Capital, Llc
  1 N Wacker Dr Ste 1920
  Chicago IL 60606
  312 750-1772

(G-7553)
PROSPIRA AMERICA CORPORATION (DH) ✪
2030 Production Dr (45839)
PHONE..................419 423-9552
Tatsuro Ishiyama, *CEO*
John Elliot, *CFO*
EMP: 18 **EST:** 2022
SALES (est): 125MM **Privately Held**
Web: www.prospira.us

SIC: 3826 Automatic chemical analyzers
HQ: Prospira Corporation
  580, Horikawacho, Saiwai-Ku
  Kawasaki KNG 212-0

(G-7554)
PUKKA INC (PA)
Also Called: Pukka Headwear
337 S Main St Fl 4 (45840-3373)
P.O. Box 773 (45839-0773)
PHONE..................419 429-7808
Shawn Rogers, *CEO*
Tate Miller, *
David Pruss, *
Andrea Rogers, *
◆ **EMP:** 37 **EST:** 2003
SALES (est): 10.2MM
SALES (corp-wide): 10.2MM **Privately Held**
Web: www.pukkainc.com
SIC: 2353 Caps: cloth, straw, and felt

(G-7555)
RADAR LOVE CO
Also Called: Superior Trim Formed Products
5500 Fostoria Ave (45840-8739)
P.O. Box 578 (45839-0578)
PHONE..................419 951-4750
Phillip D Gardner, *Pr*
Charles Henry, *Prin*
EMP: 21 **EST:** 1985
SQ FT: 12,000
SALES (est): 2.04MM **Privately Held**
SIC: 3089 3714 3713 Injection molding of plastics; Motor vehicle parts and accessories; Truck and bus bodies

(G-7556)
ROKI AMERICA CO LTD
2001 Production Dr (45840-5450)
P.O. Box 1044 (45839-1044)
PHONE..................419 424-9713
Takaya Shimada, *CEO*
Hiromitsu Shimada Junior, *Ch*
Toshifumi Sasamori, *
Bob Funkhouser, *
◆ **EMP:** 350 **EST:** 1989
SQ FT: 177,000
SALES (est): 68.84MM **Privately Held**
Web: www.roki-us.com
SIC: 3714 Filters: oil, fuel, and air, motor vehicle
PA: Roki Holdings Co.,Ltd.
  2396, Futamatachofutamata, Tenryu-Ku
  Hamamatsu SZO 431-3

(G-7557)
ROWMARK LLC (PA)
Also Called: Johnson Plastic Plus
5409 Hamlet Dr (45840-6618)
P.O. Box 1605 (45839-1605)
PHONE..................419 425-8974
Duane E Jebbett, *CEO*
Richard P Zydonik, *CCO*
◆ **EMP:** 100 **EST:** 2007
SQ FT: 65,000
SALES (est): 93.77MM
SALES (corp-wide): 93.77MM **Privately Held**
Web: www.rowmark.com
SIC: 3089 3083 Extruded finished plastics products, nec; Laminated plastics plate and sheet

(G-7558)
SANOH AMERICA INC (HQ)
1849 Industrial Dr (45840-5440)
P.O. Box 1626 (45839-1626)
PHONE..................419 425-2600
Masahiko Mizukami, *Pr*

Ryuichiro Harada, *
Hirohisa Nakamoto, *
Eric Carroll, *
Jeff Hook, *OK Vice President*
▲ **EMP:** 70 **EST:** 1986
SQ FT: 303,000
SALES (est): 280.4MM **Privately Held**
Web: www.sanoh-america.com
SIC: 3714 Motor vehicle parts and accessories
PA: Sanoh Industrial Co., Ltd.
  3-6-6, Shibuya
  Shibuya-Ku TKY 150-0

(G-7559)
SAUSSER STEEL COMPANY INC
230 Crystal Ave (45840-4796)
PHONE..................419 422-9632
Joe W Sausser, *Pr*
Larry Cherry, *VP*
Dorothy M Garlow, *Sec*
Donald Hutton, *VP*
▲ **EMP:** 18 **EST:** 1941
SQ FT: 500,000
SALES (est): 2.49MM **Privately Held**
Web: www.saussersteel.com
SIC: 3441 5084 5051 3446 Fabricated structural metal; Welding machinery and equipment; Steel; Architectural metalwork

(G-7560)
SHELVES WEST LLC
510 S Main St (45840-3230)
PHONE..................928 692-1449
EMP: 8
SALES (corp-wide): 494.03MM **Privately Held**
SIC: 3089 Injection molding of plastics
HQ: Shelves West, Llc
  4425 Windrose Ln
  Kingman AZ 86401
  928 692-1449

(G-7561)
SIMONA PMC LLC
2040 Industrial Dr (45840-5443)
P.O. Box 1123 (45839-1123)
PHONE..................419 429-0042
Duane Jebbett, *CEO*
EMP: 65 **EST:** 2003
SALES (est): 20.61MM
SALES (corp-wide): 739.55MM **Privately Held**
Web: www.simona-pmc.com
SIC: 3081 Plastics film and sheet
PA: Simona Ag
  Teichweg 16
  Kirn RP 55606
  6752140

(G-7562)
SKYMARK REFUELERS LLC
1525 Lima Ave (45840-1431)
PHONE..................419 957-1709
Joe Spoon, *Managing Member*
EMP: 81
SALES (corp-wide): 55.86MM **Privately Held**
Web: www.skymarkrefuelers.com
SIC: 3713 Truck and bus bodies
PA: Skymark Refuelers, Llc
  4001 E 149th St
  Kansas City MO 64147
  913 653-8100

(G-7563)
SMITHFIELD DIRECT LLC
4411 Township Road 142 (45840-9607)
PHONE..................419 422-2233
EMP: 93
Web: carando.sfdbrands.com

GEOGRAPHIC SECTION

Flushing - Belmont County (G-7586)

SIC: 2011 Meat packing plants
HQ: Smithfield Direct, Llc
4225 Naperville Rd # 600
Lisle IL 60532

(G-7564)
SMOKE RINGS INC
Also Called: Butt Hut
1928 Tiffin Ave (45840-6753)
PHONE.....................419 420-9966
Jean Dove, *Pr*
EMP: 7 EST: 1997
SALES (est): 691.95K **Privately Held**
Web: www.butthutohio.com
SIC: 2131 5993 Chewing and smoking tobacco; Tobacco stores and stands

(G-7565)
SONOCO PRTECTIVE SOLUTIONS INC
1900 Industrial Dr (45840-5441)
P.O. Box 714 (45839-0714)
PHONE.....................419 420-0029
EMP: 25
SQ FT: 100,000
SALES (corp-wide): 6.78B **Publicly Held**
Web: www.sonoco.com
SIC: 3089 3086 2821 Blister or bubble formed packaging, plastics; Plastics foam products; Plastics materials and resins
HQ: Sonoco Protective Solutions, Inc.
3930 N Ventura Dr
Arlington Heights IL 60004
847 398-0110

(G-7566)
SOUTHSIDE WOLFIES
546 6th St (45840-5148)
PHONE.....................419 422-5450
Shawn Lalji, *Owner*
EMP: 6 EST: 2012
SALES (est): 175.7K **Privately Held**
SIC: 2068 Salted and roasted nuts and seeds

(G-7567)
SQUARE ONE SOLUTIONS LLC
Also Called: Brown Box Company
130 Bentley Ct (45840-1779)
P.O. Box 965 (45839-0965)
PHONE.....................419 425-5445
Stephen Chan, *Pr*
EMP: 16 EST: 2012
SALES (est): 7.9MM **Privately Held**
Web: www.square1-solutions.com
SIC: 2653 Boxes, corrugated: made from purchased materials

(G-7568)
ST PAUL PARK REFINING CO
539 S Main St (45840-3229)
PHONE.....................419 422-2121
Gary R Heminger, *CEO*
EMP: 7 EST: 2010
SALES (est): 549.34K **Privately Held**
SIC: 1382 Oil and gas exploration services

(G-7569)
STONECO INC (DH)
1700 Fostoria Ave Ste 200 (45840-6218)
P.O. Box 865 (45839-0865)
PHONE.....................419 422-8854
John T Bearss, *Pr*
Don Weber, *VP*
Jack Zouhary, *Sec*
EMP: 33 EST: 1972
SQ FT: 34,000
SALES (est): 50.04MM
SALES (corp-wide): 32.72B **Privately Held**
Web: www.shellyco.com

SIC: 2951 1411 Asphalt and asphaltic paving mixtures (not from refineries); Limestone, dimension-quarrying
HQ: Shelly Company
80 Park Dr
Thornville OH 43076
740 246-6315

(G-7570)
STREAMSIDE MATERIALS LLC
Also Called: Streamside Materials
7440 Township Road 95 (45840-9659)
PHONE.....................419 423-1290
Randall Tucker, *CEO*
Brian Halm, *Dir Opers*
EMP: 6 EST: 2015
SALES (est): 310.53K **Privately Held**
Web: www.streamside.us
SIC: 8742 1442 Materials mgmt. (purchasing, handling, inventory) consultant; Construction sand and gravel

(G-7571)
SUPERIOR PLASTICS INTL INC
1116 Glen Meadow Dr (45840-6256)
PHONE.....................419 424-3113
EMP: 7 EST: 1992
SALES (est): 532.9K **Privately Held**
SIC: 3053 Gaskets and sealing devices

(G-7572)
SUPERIOR TRIM HOLDINGS LIMITED
2100 Fostoria Ave (45840-8758)
PHONE.....................419 425-5555
EMP: 6 EST: 2017
SALES (est): 371.74K **Privately Held**
Web: www.superiortrim.com
SIC: 3714 Motor vehicle parts and accessories

(G-7573)
TEXSTONE INDUSTRIES
433 Oak Ave (45840-4750)
P.O. Box 1126 (45839-1126)
PHONE.....................419 722-4664
EMP: 6 EST: 2012
SALES (est): 228.59K **Privately Held**
SIC: 3999 Manufacturing industries, nec

(G-7574)
TH PLASTICS INC
101 Bentley Ct (45840-1799)
PHONE.....................419 425-5825
EMP: 77
SALES (corp-wide): 94.97MM **Privately Held**
Web: www.thplastics.com
SIC: 3089 Aquarium accessories, plastics
PA: Th Plastics, Inc.
106 E Main St
Mendon MI 49072
269 496-8495

(G-7575)
THE NATIONAL LIME AND STONE COMPANY (PA)
551 Lake Cascade Pkwy (45840-1388)
P.O. Box 120 (45839-0120)
PHONE.....................419 422-4341
EMP: 30 EST: 1903
SALES (est): 167.89MM
SALES (corp-wide): 167.89MM **Privately Held**
Web: www.natlime.com
SIC: 1422 1442 3273 1423 Crushed and broken limestone; Sand mining; Ready-mixed concrete; Crushed and broken granite

(G-7576)
VALGROUP LLC
3441 N Main St (45840-4206)
PHONE.....................419 423-6500
Alberto Geronomi, *CEO*
EMP: 49 EST: 2014
SALES (est): 21.14MM
SALES (corp-wide): 29.24MM **Privately Held**
SIC: 3081 Plastics film and sheet
PA: Valgroup North America, Inc.
3441 N Main St
Findlay OH 45840
419 423-6500

(G-7577)
VALGROUP NORTH AMERICA INC (PA)
3441 N Main St (45840-4206)
PHONE.....................419 423-6500
Alberto Geronomi, *CEO*
EMP: 117 EST: 2014
SALES (est): 29.24MM
SALES (corp-wide): 29.24MM **Privately Held**
Web: www.valgroupco.com
SIC: 2671 Plastic film, coated or laminated for packaging

(G-7578)
VEONEER BRAKE SYSTEMS LLC
2001 Industrial Dr (45840-5444)
P.O. Box 886 (45839-0886)
PHONE.....................419 425-6725
EMP: 325 EST: 2015
SALES (est): 54.81MM
SALES (corp-wide): 54.81MM **Privately Held**
SIC: 3714 Motor vehicle brake systems and parts
HQ: Veoneer Us Safety Systems, Llc
26360 American Dr
Southfield MI 48034
248 223-0600

(G-7579)
WABASH NATIONAL CORPORATION
2000 Fostoria Ave (45840-9775)
PHONE.....................419 434-9409
EMP: 24
SALES (corp-wide): 2.54B **Publicly Held**
Web: www.onewabash.com
SIC: 3715 Truck trailers
PA: Wabash National Corporation
3900 Mccarty Ln
Lafayette IN 47905
765 771-5310

(G-7580)
WERK BRAU
Also Called: Werk Brau Co
4000 Fostoria Ave (45840-8733)
PHONE.....................419 421-4703
EMP: 6
SALES (est): 313.43K **Privately Held**
Web: www.werk-brau.com
SIC: 3531 Construction machinery

(G-7581)
WERK-BRAU COMPANY (HQ)
Also Called: Werk-Brau
2800 Fostoria Ave (45840-8757)
P.O. Box 1545 (45839-1545)
PHONE.....................419 422-2912
Paul Ballinger, *CEO*
Jon Ballinger, *
Jim Greulich, *
▲ EMP: 104 EST: 1947
SQ FT: 104,000
SALES (est): 49.09MM
SALES (corp-wide): 66.9MM **Privately Held**

Web: www.werk-brau.com
SIC: 3531 3412 Buckets, excavating: clamshell, concrete, dragline, etc.; Metal barrels, drums, and pails
PA: Ballinger Industries, Inc.
2500 Fostoria Ave
Findlay OH 45840
419 422-4533

(G-7582)
WERK-BRAU COMPANY
616 N Blanchard St (45840-5706)
PHONE.....................419 422-2912
EMP: 171
SALES (corp-wide): 66.9MM **Privately Held**
Web: www.werk-brau.com
SIC: 3531 Buckets, excavating: clamshell, concrete, dragline, etc.
HQ: Werk-Brau Company
2800 Fostoria Ave
Findlay OH 45840
419 422-2912

(G-7583)
WHIRLPOOL CORPORATION
Whirlpool
4901 N Main St (45840-8847)
PHONE.....................419 423-8123
John Haywood, *Div VP*
EMP: 100
SALES (corp-wide): 19.45B **Publicly Held**
Web: www.whirlpoolcorp.com
SIC: 3639 3632 Dishwashing machines, household; Household refrigerators and freezers
PA: Whirlpool Corporation
2000 N M-63
Benton Harbor MI 49022
269 923-5000

(G-7584)
ZF ACTIVE SAFETY US INC
1750 Production Dr (45840)
PHONE.....................734 812-6979
EMP: 7
SALES (corp-wide): 144.19K **Privately Held**
SIC: 3714 Motor vehicle engines and parts
HQ: Zf Active Safety Us Inc,
12025 Tech Center Dr
Livonia MI 48150
734 855-2600

Fleming
Washington County

(G-7585)
ANDERSON ENERGY INC
12959 State Route 550 (45729-5229)
P.O. Box 327 (45784-0327)
PHONE.....................740 678-8608
Den Anderson, *Pr*
EMP: 6 EST: 2006
SALES (est): 235.51K **Privately Held**
SIC: 1381 Drilling oil and gas wells

Flushing
Belmont County

(G-7586)
CREATIVE CANVAS LLC
132 Wood St (43977-9727)
PHONE.....................740 359-3173
EMP: 6 EST: 2014
SALES (est): 46.58K **Privately Held**
SIC: 2211 Canvas

Flushing - Belmont County (G-7587)

(G-7587)
GLENN MICHAEL BRICK
Also Called: Go For Broke Amusement
108 Wood St (43977-9727)
PHONE..................................740 391-5735
Glenn M Brick, *Owner*
EMP: 11 **EST:** 2007
SALES (est): 989.71K **Privately Held**
SIC: 4212 7993 7699 3578 Mail carriers, contract; Juke box; Automated teller machine (ATM) repair; Automatic teller machines (ATM)

(G-7588)
UNIONTOWN STONE
72607 Gun Club Rd (43977)
PHONE..................................740 968-4313
Jeff Sidwell, *Owner*
EMP: 8 **EST:** 1998
SALES (est): 290.44K **Privately Held**
Web: www.sidwellmaterials.com
SIC: 1422 Crushed and broken limestone

Forest
Hardin County

(G-7589)
AEROVATION TECH HOLDINGS LLC
11651 Township Rd 81 (45843)
PHONE..................................567 208-5525
EMP: 9 **EST:** 2011
SALES (est): 470K **Privately Held**
Web: www.aerovation.me
SIC: 8711 3721 Aviation and/or aeronautical engineering; Research and development on aircraft by the manufacturer

(G-7590)
BUCKEYE MCH FABRICATORS INC (PA)
610 E Lima St (45843-1182)
PHONE..................................419 273-2521
D Ray Marshall, *Pr*
Nancy Marshall, *Sec*
EMP: 50 **EST:** 1974
SQ FT: 65,000
SALES (est): 8.55MM
SALES (corp-wide): 8.55MM **Privately Held**
Web: www.buckeyemachine.com
SIC: 3599 Machine shop, jobbing and repair

(G-7591)
DUFF QUARRY INC
3798 State Route 53 (45843-9379)
PHONE..................................419 273-2518
James E Duff, *Pr*
EMP: 10
SALES (corp-wide): 3.38MM **Privately Held**
Web: www.duffquarry.com
SIC: 1422 Crushed and broken limestone
PA: Duff Quarry, Inc.
   9042 State Route 117
   Huntsville OH 43324
   937 686-2811

(G-7592)
SHELLY MATERIALS INC
3798 State Route 53 (45843-9379)
PHONE..................................419 273-2510
Norman Cochran, *Brnch Mgr*
EMP: 6
SALES (corp-wide): 32.72B **Privately Held**
Web: www.shellyco.com
SIC: 2951 Asphalt paving mixtures and blocks
HQ: Shelly Materials, Inc.
   80 Park Dr
   Thornville OH 43076
   740 246-6315

(G-7593)
TRIUMPH THERMAL SYSTEMS LLC (HQ)
200 Railroad St (45843-9193)
PHONE..................................419 273-2511
Michael Perhay, *Pr*
EMP: 56 **EST:** 2003
SQ FT: 125,000
SALES (est): 49.03MM **Publicly Held**
Web: www.triumph-thermal.com
SIC: 3728 3443 Aircraft parts and equipment, nec; Heat exchangers, condensers, and components
PA: Triumph Group, Inc.
   555 E Lancaster Ave # 400
   Radnor PA 19087

(G-7594)
VTS CO LTD
607 E Lima St (45843-1180)
PHONE..................................419 273-4010
Lloyd Swavel, *Pr*
EMP: 7 **EST:** 1996
SALES (est): 467.54K **Privately Held**
SIC: 3089 Extruded finished plastics products, nec

Fort Jennings
Putnam County

(G-7595)
G & S CUSTOM TOOLING LLC
18406 Road 20 (45844-9106)
PHONE..................................419 286-2888
German Darrin, *Admn*
EMP: 6 **EST:** 2014
SALES (est): 107.77K **Privately Held**
SIC: 3544 Special dies and tools

Fort Loramie
Shelby County

(G-7596)
CROWN EQUIPMENT CORPORATION
Also Called: Crown Lift Trucks
300 Tower Dr (45845)
P.O. Box 97 (45869-0097)
PHONE..................................937 295-4062
Sheryl Gray, *Brnch Mgr*
EMP: 47
SALES (corp-wide): 7.12B **Privately Held**
Web: www.crown.com
SIC: 3537 Lift trucks, industrial: fork, platform, straddle, etc.
PA: Crown Equipment Corporation
   44 S Washington St
   New Bremen OH 45869
   419 629-2311

(G-7597)
CUSTOM FOAM PRODUCTS INC (PA)
900 Tower Dr (45845-8712)
P.O. Box 288 (45845-0288)
PHONE..................................937 295-2700
Nick Fullenkamp, *Owner*
Steve Sherman, *VP*
EMP: 17 **EST:** 1998
SQ FT: 48,000
SALES (est): 5.49MM
SALES (corp-wide): 5.49MM **Privately Held**
Web: www.customfoaminc.com
SIC: 3086 Packaging and shipping materials, foamed plastics

(G-7598)
EDWARD D SEGEN & CO LLC
100 Enterprise Dr (45845-9407)
PHONE..................................937 295-3672
EMP: 11 **EST:** 2005
SALES (est): 251.51K **Privately Held**
Web: www.toolingtechgroup.com
SIC: 3599 Machine shop, jobbing and repair

(G-7599)
EDWARDS MACHINE SERVICE INC
8800 State Route 66 (45845-9806)
P.O. Box 33 (45845-0033)
PHONE..................................937 295-2929
Thomas Edwards, *Pr*
Ronald Edwards, *VP*
EMP: 10 **EST:** 1968
SQ FT: 7,500
SALES (est): 842.91K **Privately Held**
Web: www.edwardspressservice.com
SIC: 3599 Machine shop, jobbing and repair

(G-7600)
INDUSTRIAL MACHINING SERVICES
700 Tower Dr (45845)
P.O. Box 228 (45845)
PHONE..................................937 295-2022
EMP: 40 **EST:** 1996
SQ FT: 13,500
SALES (est): 9.96MM **Privately Held**
Web: www.ims-spi.com
SIC: 3599 Machine shop, jobbing and repair

(G-7601)
IRON WORKS INC
62 Elm St Ste A (45845-9411)
PHONE..................................937 420-2100
Bill Gelhaus, *Pr*
Dan Gelhaus, *VP*
EMP: 18 **EST:** 2016
SALES (est): 1.1MM **Privately Held**
SIC: 3537 3448 Engine stands and racks, metal; Prefabricated metal components

(G-7602)
KS WELDING & FABRICATION LLC
7820 Dawson Rd (45845-9765)
PHONE..................................937 420-2270
EMP: 6 **EST:** 2012
SALES (est): 61.73K **Privately Held**
SIC: 7692 Welding repair

(G-7603)
LINCOLN ELECTRIC AUTOMTN INC (HQ)
Also Called: Tennessee Rand
407 S Main St (45845-8716)
PHONE..................................937 295-2120
David M Knapke, *Pr*
EMP: 281 **EST:** 1962
SQ FT: 82,000
SALES (est): 137.07MM
SALES (corp-wide): 4.19B **Publicly Held**
Web: www.waynetrail.com
SIC: 3728 3599 7692 3544 Aircraft parts and equipment, nec; Tubing, flexible metallic; Welding repair; Special dies, tools, jigs, and fixtures
PA: Lincoln Electric Holdings, Inc.
   22801 St Clair Ave
   Cleveland OH 44117
   216 481-8100

(G-7604)
MJ BORNHORST ENTERPRISES LLC
400 Enterprise Dr (45845-9413)
P.O. Box 2 (45845-0002)
PHONE..................................937 295-3469
John Bornhorst, *Managing Member*
EMP: 25
SALES (est): 1.25MM **Privately Held**
Web: www.fortloramiechamber.com
SIC: 2752 Commercial printing, lithographic

(G-7605)
PARTNERS IN RECOGNITION INC
405 S Main St (45845-8716)
P.O. Box 27 (45845-0027)
PHONE..................................937 420-2150
Gregory Short, *Pr*
Angela Speelman, *
◆ **EMP:** 28 **EST:** 2001
SQ FT: 10,000
SALES (est): 3.42MM **Privately Held**
Web: www.gopir.com
SIC: 3999 Identification plates

(G-7606)
ROL - TECH INC
Also Called: Marwil
4814 Calvert Dr (45845)
P.O. Box 547 (32790-0547)
PHONE..................................214 905-8050
Roberto Diaz Del Castillo, *Pr*
Zachary Gillett, *VP*
Mark Lang, *Prin*
▲ **EMP:** 19 **EST:** 2002
SALES (est): 2.46MM **Privately Held**
SIC: 3545 Machine tool accessories

(G-7607)
SCHMITMEYER INC
Also Called: G W Tool & Die Co
195 Ben St (45845-9350)
P.O. Box 227 (45845-0227)
PHONE..................................937 295-2091
Jarett Schmitmeyer, *Pr*
Nicole Schmitmeyer, *VP*
EMP: 9 **EST:** 1946
SQ FT: 7,200
SALES (est): 973.55K **Privately Held**
Web: www.g-wtool.com
SIC: 3599 3544 Machine shop, jobbing and repair; Special dies and tools

(G-7608)
SELECT-ARC INC (PA)
600 Enterprise Dr (45845-9410)
P.O. Box 259 (45845-0259)
PHONE..................................937 295-5215
◆ **EMP:** 146 **EST:** 1996
SQ FT: 67,000
SALES (est): 26.63MM **Privately Held**
Web: www.select-arc.com
SIC: 3548 Welding apparatus

(G-7609)
SHARP ENTERPRISES INC
Also Called: A & B Printing
400 Enterprise Dr (45845-9413)
P.O. Box 2 (45845-0002)
PHONE..................................937 295-2965
James R Sharp, *Pr*
EMP: 19 **EST:** 1987
SQ FT: 8,000
SALES (est): 2.3MM **Privately Held**
Web: www.aandbprinting.com
SIC: 2752 Offset printing

(G-7610)
SOUTH SIDE DRIVE THRU
9204 Hilgefort Rd (45845-9717)
PHONE..................................937 295-2927
EMP: 6 **EST:** 1991
SALES (est): 305.1K **Privately Held**
SIC: 2082 Beer (alcoholic beverage)

(G-7611)
STUDIO ELEVEN INC (PA)
301 S Main St (45845-8755)

P.O. Box 315 (45845-0315)
PHONE..............................937 295-2225
Tom Barhorst, *Pr*
Maria Quinter, *Stockholder*
Frances A Barhorst, *Sec*
▲ **EMP**: 19 **EST**: 1992
SALES (est): 2.16MM **Privately Held**
Web: www.studioeleven.net
SIC: **2759** Screen printing

(G-7612)
TOOLING TECH HOLDINGS LLC (HQ)
100 Enterprise Dr (45845-9407)
PHONE..............................937 295-3672
Tony Seger, *CEO*
EMP: 19 **EST**: 2011
SALES (est): 48.44MM **Privately Held**
Web: www.toolingtechgroup.com
SIC: **3089** Thermoformed finished plastics products, nec
PA: Gennx360 Capital Partners, L.P.
208 W 122nd St
New York NY 10027

Fort Recovery
Mercer County

(G-7613)
BUCKEYE DESIGN & ENGR SVC LLC
2600 Wabash Rd (45846-9500)
P.O. Box 168 (45846-0168)
PHONE..............................419 375-4241
James Westgerdes, *Pt*
EMP: 6 **EST**: 2001
SALES (est): 998.85K **Privately Held**
SIC: **3089** Injection molding of plastics

(G-7614)
COOPER FARMS INC (PA)
2321 State Route 49 (45846-9501)
P.O. Box 339 (45846-0339)
PHONE..............................419 375-4116
James R Cooper, *Pr*
Gary A Cooper, *
Dianne L Cooper, *
Anada E Cooper, *
Neil Diller, *
EMP: 100 **EST**: 1940
SQ FT: 38,000
SALES (est): 106.74MM
SALES (corp-wide): 106.74MM **Privately Held**
Web: www.cooperfarms.com
SIC: **2048** 5191 Poultry feeds; Feed

(G-7615)
FORT RECOVERY EQUIPMENT INC
1201 Industrial Dr (45846-8046)
P.O. Box 646 (45846-0646)
PHONE..............................419 375-1006
Cyril G Le Fevre, *Pr*
Helen Le Fevre, *
Greg Le Fevre, *
◆ **EMP**: 10 **EST**: 1970
SQ FT: 30,000
SALES (est): 661.61K **Privately Held**
SIC: **5083** 3523 Livestock equipment; Barn, silo, poultry, dairy, and livestock machinery

(G-7616)
FORT RECOVERY EQUITY INC (PA)
2351 Wabash Rd (45846-9586)
PHONE..............................419 375-4119
William Glass, *CEO*
Arnie Sumner, *
EMP: 33 **EST**: 1919
SQ FT: 15,000
SALES (est): 10.47MM
SALES (corp-wide): 10.47MM **Privately Held**

(G-7617)
FORT RECOVERY INDUSTRIES INC (PA)
2440 State Route 49 (45846-9501)
P.O. Box 638 (45846-0638)
PHONE..............................419 375-4121
Wesley M Jetter, *Ch Bd*
Dean Jetter, *
Larry Holmes, *
◆ **EMP**: 199 **EST**: 1945
SQ FT: 120,000
SALES (est): 50.36MM
SALES (corp-wide): 50.36MM **Privately Held**
Web: www.fortrecoveryindustries.com
SIC: **3432** 3363 3429 Plumbing fixture fittings and trim; Aluminum die-castings; Hardware, nec

(G-7618)
FORT RECOVERY INDUSTRIES INC
1200 Industrial Park Dr (45846)
PHONE..............................419 375-3005
Randy Petit, *Mgr*
EMP: 58
SALES (corp-wide): 50.36MM **Privately Held**
Web: www.fortrecoveryindustries.com
SIC: **3432** Plumbing fixture fittings and trim
PA: Fort Recovery Industries, Inc.
2440 State Route 49
Fort Recovery OH 45846
419 375-4121

(G-7619)
HOME IDEA CENTER INC
1100 Commerce St (45846-8003)
P.O. Box 649 (45846-0649)
PHONE..............................419 375-4951
Dan Schoen, *Pr*
Travis Laux, *VP*
EMP: 15 **EST**: 1978
SQ FT: 12,000
SALES (est): 421.94K **Privately Held**
Web: www.ehomeidea.com
SIC: **2599** Cabinets, factory

(G-7620)
J & M MANUFACTURING CO INC
284 Railroad St (45846-8121)
P.O. Box 547 (45846-0547)
PHONE..............................419 375-2376
Michael Grieshop, *Pr*
Jeff Grieshop, *
◆ **EMP**: 200 **EST**: 1950
SQ FT: 400,000
SALES (est): 24.37MM **Privately Held**
Web: www.jm-inc.com
SIC: **3523** Farm machinery and equipment

(G-7621)
JR MANUFACTURING INC (PA)
900 Industrial Dr W (45846-8043)
P.O. Box 478 (45846-0478)
PHONE..............................419 375-8021
Chad Guggenbiller, *CFO*
Tomo Yamamoto, *
Jeff Roessner, *
Greg Lefevre, *
Cy Lefevre, *Stockholder*
▲ **EMP**: 130 **EST**: 1992
SQ FT: 48,000
SALES (est): 41.36MM
SALES (corp-wide): 41.36MM **Privately Held**
Web: www.jrmanufacturing.net

(G-7622)
JW MANUFACTURING LLC
317 Watkins Rd (45846-9125)
PHONE..............................419 375-5536
Josh Wuebker, *Prin*
EMP: 7 **EST**: 2014
SALES (est): 270.99K **Privately Held**
Web: www.jw-mfg.com
SIC: **3999** Manufacturing industries, nec

(G-7623)
MEL HEITKAMP BUILDERS LTD
635 Secret Judy Rd (45846)
P.O. Box 229 (45846-0229)
PHONE..............................419 375-0405
Joe Heitkamp, *Genl Pt*
Jack Heitkamp, *Pt*
Tony Heitkamp, *Pt*
Doug Heitkamp, *Pt*
EMP: 9 **EST**: 1990
SALES (est): 532.1K **Privately Held**
SIC: **8741** 2521 5712 Construction management; Cabinets, office: wood; Customized furniture and cabinets

(G-7624)
STEVE VORE WELDING AND STEEL
Also Called: Vores Steve Welding & Steel
3234 State Route 49 (45846-9507)
P.O. Box 37 (45846-0037)
PHONE..............................419 375-4087
Stephen Vore, *Pr*
EMP: 10 **EST**: 1974
SQ FT: 5,400
SALES (est): 978.57K **Privately Held**
SIC: **3312** 7692 1799 3444 Structural shapes and pilings, steel; Welding repair; Welding on site; Sheet metalwork

(G-7625)
SUSPENSION FEEDER CORPORATION
482 State Route 119 (45846-9563)
P.O. Box 369 (45883-0369)
PHONE..............................419 763-1377
Gregory G Baron, *Pr*
Roberta Baron, *Treas*
EMP: 10 **EST**: 1969
SQ FT: 12,000
SALES (est): 981.22K **Privately Held**
Web: www.suspensionfeeder.com
SIC: **3555** Printing trades machinery

(G-7626)
V H COOPER & CO INC (HQ)
Also Called: Cooper Foods
2321 State Route 49 (45846-9501)
P.O. Box 339 (45846-0339)
PHONE..............................419 375-4116
James R Cooper, *Pr*
Gary A Cooper, *
Dianne L Cooper, *
Anada E Cooper, *
Neil Diller, *
EMP: 150 **EST**: 1975
SQ FT: 4,400
SALES (est): 44.54MM
SALES (corp-wide): 93.22MM **Privately Held**
SIC: **0253** 2015 2011 Turkeys and turkey eggs; Chicken slaughtering and processing; Pork products, from pork slaughtered on site
PA: Cooper Hatchery, Inc.
22348 Road 140
Oakwood OH 45873
419 594-3325

Fostoria
Seneca County

(G-7627)
ALPHA COATINGS INC
622 S Corporate Dr W (44830-9447)
PHONE..............................419 435-5111
Terence White, *Pr*
EMP: 115 **EST**: 1994
SQ FT: 48,000
SALES (est): 39MM
SALES (corp-wide): 17.65B **Publicly Held**
SIC: **3479** 2891 Coating of metals and formed products; Adhesives and sealants
HQ: Whitford Worldwide Company, Llc
47 Park Ave
Elverson PA 19520

(G-7628)
ARCHER-DANIELS-MIDLAND COMPANY
Also Called: ADM
608 Findlay St (44830-1850)
P.O. Box 110 (44830-0110)
PHONE..............................419 435-6633
Dale Anderburry, *Mgr*
EMP: 25
SALES (corp-wide): 93.94B **Publicly Held**
Web: www.adm.com
SIC: **2041** 2077 2075 Flour and other grain mill products; Animal and marine fats and oils; Soybean oil mills
PA: Archer-Daniels-Midland Company
77 W Wacker Dr Ste 4600
Chicago IL 60601
312 634-8100

(G-7629)
B&D TRUCK PARTS SLS & SVCS LLC
1498 Perrysburg Rd (44830-1351)
PHONE..............................419 701-7041
EMP: 6 **EST**: 2010
SALES (est): 248.24K **Privately Held**
Web: www.banddtruckpartsstore.com
SIC: **8999** 3751 Artists and artists' studios; Motorcycle accessories

(G-7630)
CALLIES PERFORMANCE PRODUCTS INC
901 S Union St (44830-2561)
P.O. Box 926 (44830-0926)
PHONE..............................419 435-7448
▲ **EMP**: 60 **EST**: 1989
SALES (est): 9.59MM **Privately Held**
Web: www.callies.com
SIC: **3714** Crankshaft assemblies, motor vehicle

(G-7631)
FABRICATION SHOP INC
1395 Buckley St (44830-9459)
PHONE..............................419 435-7934
Bill Cronauer, *Pr*
Deborah Cronauer, *VP*
EMP: 18 **EST**: 1977
SQ FT: 15,000
SALES (est): 1.04MM **Privately Held**
Web: www.fabshop.com
SIC: **7692** 3443 3544 Welding repair; Fabricated plate work (boiler shop); Special dies and tools

(G-7632)
FILMTEC FABRICATIONS LLC
1120 Sandusky St (44830-2761)
P.O. Box 9040 (46899-9040)
PHONE..............................419 435-1819
Scott Glaze, *CEO*

Fostoria - Seneca County (G-7633) — GEOGRAPHIC SECTION

EMP: 24 EST: 2016
SALES (est): 1.17MM **Privately Held**
Web: www.filmtecfab.com
SIC: 3599 Machine shop, jobbing and repair

(G-7633)
FOSTORIA BSHNGS INSLATORS CORP
602 S Corporate Dr W Ste D (44830-9456)
P.O. Box 1064 (44830-1064)
PHONE..............................419 435-7514
Philip C John, *Pr*
▲ EMP: 6 EST: 2001
SALES (est): 696.6K **Privately Held**
Web: www.fostoriabushings.com
SIC: 3612 Transformers, except electric

(G-7634)
FOSTORIA BUSHINGS INC
Also Called: FB Ins
602 S Corporate Dr W (44830-9456)
P.O. Box 1064 (44830-1064)
PHONE..............................419 435-7514
▲ EMP: 9 EST: 1995
SALES (est): 1.02MM **Privately Held**
Web: www.fostoriabushings.com
SIC: 3612 Transformers, except electric

(G-7635)
FOSTORIA FOCUS INC
112 N Main St (44830-2223)
P.O. Box 1158 (44830-1158)
PHONE..............................419 435-6397
EMP: 7 EST: 1994
SALES (est): 150.05K **Privately Held**
SIC: 2711 Newspapers: publishing only, not printed on site

(G-7636)
FOSTORIA MT&F CORP
1401 Sandusky St (44830-2774)
PHONE..............................419 435-7676
Dick Kiser, *Pr*
EMP: 18 EST: 2007
SQ FT: 20,400
SALES (est): 1.78MM **Privately Held**
Web: www.machinetoolandfab.com
SIC: 3599 3441 3442 Custom machinery; Fabricated structural metal; Hangar doors, metal

(G-7637)
FRAM GROUP OPERATIONS LLC
Honeywell
1600 N Union St (44830-1958)
P.O. Box 880 (44830-0880)
PHONE..............................419 436-5827
Paul Humphrys, *Dir*
EMP: 29
SALES (corp-wide): 8.03B **Privately Held**
Web: www.fram.com
SIC: 3714 3264 Motor vehicle parts and accessories; Porcelain electrical supplies
HQ: Fram Group Operations Llc
2500 S Adams Rd
Rochester Hills MI 48309

(G-7638)
INLAND TARP & LINER LLC
1600 N Main St (44830-1941)
PHONE..............................419 436-6001
Ron Mackenzie, *Brnch Mgr*
EMP: 25
Web: www.inlandtarp.com
SIC: 1389 Oil field services, nec
PA: Inland Tarp & Liner, Llc
4172 N Frontage Rd E
Moses Lake WA 98837

(G-7639)
INNOVATION PLASTICS LLC
1150 State St (44830-3007)
PHONE..............................513 818-1771
EMP: 20 EST: 2015
SALES (est): 1.19MM **Privately Held**
SIC: 3089 4953 Casting of plastics; Recycling, waste materials

(G-7640)
KUZMA INDUSTRIES LLC
1541 N Township Road 101 (44830-9319)
PHONE..............................419 701-7005
Daniel Kuzma, *Pr*
EMP: 9 EST: 2021
SALES (est): 383.1K **Privately Held**
SIC: 3599 Machine shop, jobbing and repair

(G-7641)
MACHINE TOOL DESIGN & FAB LLC
1401 Sandusky St (44830-2774)
PHONE..............................419 435-7676
Christopher Eastman, *Managing Member*
EMP: 19 EST: 2016
SALES (est): 4.87MM
SALES (corp-wide): 5.08MM **Privately Held**
Web: www.machinetoolandfab.com
SIC: 7699 3544 3441 Metal reshaping and replating services; Special dies and tools; Fabricated structural metal
PA: Eastman Holding Llc
1185 W Parkway Blvd
Aurora OH 44202
419 435-7676

(G-7642)
MAMABEES HM GDS LIFESTYLE LLC
2186 Mccutchenville Rd (44830-9797)
PHONE..............................419 277-2914
EMP: 6 EST: 2021
SALES (est): 50K **Privately Held**
SIC: 2511 Wood household furniture

(G-7643)
MATERIAL PROCESSING & HDLG CO
1150 State St (44830)
PHONE..............................419 436-9562
James H Kenyon, *Pr*
EMP: 14 EST: 2019
SALES (est): 1.21MM **Privately Held**
Web: www.mphco.net
SIC: 2821 Plastics materials and resins

(G-7644)
MENNEL MILLING COMPANY
320 Findlay St (44830-1854)
PHONE..............................419 436-5130
Donald L Mennel, *Brnch Mgr*
EMP: 60
SALES (corp-wide): 211.12MM **Privately Held**
Web: www.mennel.com
SIC: 2041 Flour and other grain mill products
PA: The Mennel Milling Company
319 S Vine St
Fostoria OH 44830
419 435-8151

(G-7645)
MORGAN ADVANCED MATERIALS
200 N Town St (44830-2835)
PHONE..............................419 435-8182
Randy Bishop, *Manager*
▼ EMP: 160 EST: 2013
SALES (est): 25.07MM
SALES (corp-wide): 1.39B **Privately Held**
Web: www.morganadvancedmaterials.com

SIC: 3624 Carbon and graphite products
PA: Morgan Advanced Materials Plc
York House
Windsor BERKS SL4 1
175 383-7000

(G-7646)
MORGAN AM&T
200 N Town St (44830-2835)
PHONE..............................419 435-8182
EMP: 8 EST: 2019
SALES (est): 690.54K **Privately Held**
SIC: 3624 Carbon and graphite products

(G-7647)
NIPPON STL INTGRTED CRNKSHAFT
Also Called: Nsi Crankshaft
1815 Sandusky St (44830-2754)
PHONE..............................419 435-0411
Makoto Tsuruhara, *Pr*
Leslie P Lipski, *CFO*
Tim Hasegawa, *Ex VP*
EMP: 13 EST: 2007
SQ FT: 225,000
SALES (est): 9.61MM **Privately Held**
Web: www.nsicrankshaft.com
SIC: 3599 3714 Crankshafts and camshafts, machining; Crankshaft assemblies, motor vehicle
HQ: Nippon Steel North America, Inc.
920 Mmrial Cy Way Ste 700
Houston TX 77024
212 486-7150

(G-7648)
NORTON MANUFACTURING CO INC
455 W 4th St (44830-1864)
P.O. Box 1127 (44830-1127)
PHONE..............................419 435-0411
EMP: 11 EST: 2010
SALES (est): 356.32K **Privately Held**
Web: www.nsicrankshaft.com
SIC: 3714 Motor vehicle parts and accessories

(G-7649)
OK INDUSTRIES INC
2307 W Corporate Dr W (44830-9449)
PHONE..............................419 435-2361
James Kenyon, *Pr*
Jim Kenyon, *Pr*
EMP: 27 EST: 1992
SQ FT: 100,000
SALES (est): 936.14K **Privately Held**
Web: www.okindustriesinc.com
SIC: 2821 Plastics materials and resins

(G-7650)
POET BOREFINING - FOSTORIA LLC
Also Called: Poet Brfining- Fostoria 23200
2111 Sandusky St (44830-2790)
PHONE..............................419 436-0954
Art Thomas, *Genl Mgr*
Jeff Broin, *
EMP: 40 EST: 2007
SALES (est): 15.59MM **Privately Held**
Web: poetbiorefining-fostoria.aghost.net
SIC: 2869 Ethyl alcohol, ethanol
PA: Poet, Llc
4615 N Lewis Ave
Sioux Falls SD 57104

(G-7651)
ROPPE CORPORATION
1602 N Union St (44830-1958)
PHONE..............................419 435-8546
Donald P Miller, *Pr*
Judy R Miller, *Community Relations Vice President**
Bart Rogers, *Sales & Marketing**
Mark J Baker, *Finance Treasurer**

Angela K Briggs, *
◆ EMP: 300 EST: 1986
SALES (est): 135MM
SALES (corp-wide): 245.4MM **Privately Held**
Web: www.roppe.com
SIC: 3069 Flooring, rubber: tile or sheet
PA: Roppe Holding Company
1602 N Union St
Fostoria OH 44830
419 435-8546

(G-7652)
ROPPE HOLDING COMPANY
J Miller and Co
106 N Main St (44830-2223)
PHONE..............................419 435-6601
Jessica Sheridan, *Mgr*
EMP: 8
SALES (corp-wide): 245.4MM **Privately Held**
Web: www.roppeholdingcompany.com
SIC: 3089 3069 Extruded finished plastics products, nec; Rubber floorcoverings/mats and wallcoverings
PA: Roppe Holding Company
1602 N Union St
Fostoria OH 44830
419 435-8546

(G-7653)
ROPPE HOLDING COMPANY (PA)
1602 N Union St (44830-1958)
P.O. Box 1158 (44830-1158)
PHONE..............................419 435-8546
▲ EMP: 300 EST: 1955
SALES (est): 245.4MM
SALES (corp-wide): 245.4MM **Privately Held**
Web: www.roppeholdingcompany.com
SIC: 2426 3069 Hardwood dimension and flooring mills; Rubber floorcoverings/mats and wallcoverings

(G-7654)
SENECA MILLWORK INC
300 Court Pl (44830-2453)
P.O. Box 429 (44830-0429)
PHONE..............................419 435-6671
Donald Miller, *Pr*
Angela K Gillett, *
Donald Miller, *Prin*
Mark J Baker, *
Judy R Miller, *
▲ EMP: 50 EST: 1873
SQ FT: 120,000
SALES (est): 9.95MM
SALES (corp-wide): 245.4MM **Privately Held**
Web: www.senecamillwork.com
SIC: 2431 Moldings, wood: unfinished and prefinished
PA: Roppe Holding Company
1602 N Union St
Fostoria OH 44830
419 435-8546

(G-7655)
SENECA WIRE & MANUFACTURING CO INC (HQ)
Also Called: Seneca Wires
319 S Vine St (44830-1843)
PHONE..............................419 435-9261
EMP: 17 EST: 1905
SALES (est): 2.26MM **Privately Held**
Web: www.senecawire.com
SIC: 3315 Wire products, ferrous/iron: made in wiredrawing plants
PA: The Seneca Wire Group Inc
820 Willipie St
Wapakoneta OH 45895

▲ = Import ▼ = Export
◆ = Import/Export

(G-7656)
THE MENNEL MILLING COMPANY (PA)
319 S Vine St (44830-1843)
P.O. Box 806 (44830-0806)
PHONE..................................419 435-8151
▲ **EMP:** 24 **EST:** 1886
SALES (est): 211.12MM
SALES (corp-wide): 211.12MM **Privately Held**
Web: www.mennel.com
SIC: 2041 2048 4221 Flour; Prepared feeds, nec; Grain elevator, storage only

Frankfort
Ross County

(G-7657)
CONVEYOR METAL WORKS INC
2717 Bush Mill Rd (45628-9791)
PHONE..................................740 477-8700
Scott P Kadish, *Pr*
Christy Wolfe, *VP*
EMP: 20 **EST:** 2000
SQ FT: 30,000
SALES (est): 2.35MM **Privately Held**
Web: www.conveyormetalworks.com
SIC: 3535 Conveyors and conveying equipment

(G-7658)
ROCAL INC (PA)
3186 County Road 550 (45628-9503)
PHONE..................................740 998-2122
Robert Lightle, *CEO*
▲ **EMP:** 82 **EST:** 1962
SQ FT: 200,000
SALES (est): 9.49MM
SALES (corp-wide): 9.49MM **Privately Held**
Web: www.rocal.com
SIC: 3993 Signs, not made in custom sign painting shops

Franklin
Warren County

(G-7659)
3-D TECHNICAL SERVICES COMPANY
Also Called: 3-Dmed
255 Industrial Dr (45005-4429)
PHONE..................................937 746-2901
Robert Aumann, *Pr*
EMP: 25 **EST:** 1970
SQ FT: 15,000
SALES (est): 4.87MM **Privately Held**
Web: www.3-dtechnicalservices.com
SIC: 7389 2542 3999 Building scale models; Partitions and fixtures, except wood; Models, general, except toy

(G-7660)
A & B FOUNDRY LLC (PA)
835 N Main St (45005-1648)
PHONE..................................937 369-3007
EMP: 14 **EST:** 2018
SALES (est): 2.63MM
SALES (corp-wide): 2.63MM **Privately Held**
Web: www.abfoundry.com
SIC: 3599 Machine shop, jobbing and repair

(G-7661)
A&B FOUNDRY & MACHINING LLC
835 N Main St (45005-1697)
PHONE..................................937 746-3634
EMP: 35 **EST:** 1957
SALES (est): 4.32MM **Privately Held**
Web: www.abfoundry.com
SIC: 3599 Machine shop, jobbing and repair

(G-7662)
ADVANCED WELDING INC
901 N Main St (45005-1650)
PHONE..................................937 746-6800
EMP: 20 **EST:** 1991
SQ FT: 8,000
SALES (est): 912.55K **Privately Held**
SIC: 3443 3599 7692 3444 Fabricated plate work (boiler shop); Machine and other job shop work; Welding repair; Sheet metalwork

(G-7663)
ATLAS ROOFING CORPORATION
Gypsum & Roofing Div
675 Oxford Rd (45005-3678)
PHONE..................................937 746-9941
Eric Glowka, *Mgr*
EMP: 170
Web: www.atlasroofing.com
SIC: 3086 2951 2952 Insulation or cushioning material, foamed plastics; Asphalt paving mixtures and blocks; Asphalt felts and coatings
HQ: Atlas Roofing Corporation
    802 Highway 19 N Ste 190
    Meridian MS 39307
    601 484-8900

(G-7664)
BOND MACHINE COMPANY INC
921 N Main St (45005-1650)
P.O. Box 95 (45005-0095)
PHONE..................................937 746-4941
David Bond, *Pr*
Steve Bond, *Sec*
John Bond Junior, *VP*
Tom Bond, *Corporate Secretary*
EMP: 14 **EST:** 1968
SQ FT: 12,000
SALES (est): 2.09MM **Privately Held**
Web: www.bondmachineco.com
SIC: 3599 Machine shop, jobbing and repair

(G-7665)
CAST PLUS INC
415 Oxford Rd (45005-3639)
PHONE..................................937 743-7278
Maurice R Meeker, *Pr*
Richard Devaney, *
EMP: 14 **EST:** 1988
SQ FT: 40,000
SALES (est): 752.43K **Privately Held**
Web: www.legacyfinishing.com
SIC: 3479 Coating of metals and formed products

(G-7666)
CHENEY PULP AND PAPER COMPANY
1000 Anderson St (45005-2571)
P.O. Box 215 (45005-0215)
PHONE..................................937 746-9991
Mark Snyder, *Pr*
Donald A Davies, *
◆ **EMP:** 30 **EST:** 1924
SQ FT: 30,000
SALES (est): 4.33MM **Privately Held**
Web: www.dynosgroup.com
SIC: 2621 Paper mills

(G-7667)
CONTAINER GRAPHICS CORP
1 Miller St (45005-4455)
PHONE..................................937 746-5666
Steve Woods, *Brnch Mgr*
EMP: 19
SALES (corp-wide): 4MM **Privately Held**
Web: www.containergraphics.com
SIC: 3555 Printing trades machinery
PA: Container Graphics Corp.
    114 Ednbrgh S Dr Ste 104
    Cary NC 27511
    919 481-4200

(G-7668)
COUNTER-ADVICE INC
7002 State Route 123 (45005-2358)
PHONE..................................937 291-1600
Brian Donley, *Pr*
EMP: 11 **EST:** 1999
SQ FT: 13,000
SALES (est): 716.01K **Privately Held**
Web: www.counteradvice.com
SIC: 2434 Wood kitchen cabinets

(G-7669)
COX OHIO PUBLISHING
5000 Commerce Center Dr (45005-7200)
PHONE..................................937 743-6700
EMP: 24 **EST:** 2019
SALES (est): 501.79K **Privately Held**
Web: www.daytondailynews.com
SIC: 2731 Book publishing

(G-7670)
DLG WOODWORKS & FINISHING INC
330 Industry Dr (45005-6308)
PHONE..................................513 649-1245
Derreck Gatliff, *Prin*
EMP: 6 **EST:** 2018
SALES (est): 178.69K **Privately Held**
SIC: 2431 Millwork

(G-7671)
DRACOOL-USA INC (PA)
Also Called: Dracool
331 Industrial Dr (45005-4431)
PHONE..................................937 743-5899
Javier Avendano, *CEO*
◆ **EMP:** 24 **EST:** 1958
SALES (est): 4.97MM
SALES (corp-wide): 4.97MM **Privately Held**
Web: www.dracool-usa.com
SIC: 3441 Fabricated structural metal

(G-7672)
EMSSONS FAURECIA CTRL SYSTEMS
Also Called: Franklin Mfg Div
2301 Commerce Center Dr (45005-1896)
PHONE..................................937 743-0551
EMP: 400
SALES (corp-wide): 100.93MM **Privately Held**
Web: www.faurecia.com
SIC: 3714 3053 Exhaust systems and parts, motor vehicle; Gaskets; packing and sealing devices
HQ: Faurecia Emissions Control Systems Na, Llc
    543 Matzinger Rd
    Toledo OH 43612
    812 341-2000

(G-7673)
F & G TOOL AND DIE CO
130 Industrial Dr (45005-4428)
PHONE..................................937 746-3658
Dick Smith, *Brnch Mgr*
EMP: 6
SALES (corp-wide): 11.02MM **Privately Held**
Web: www.fgtool.com
SIC: 3542 3469 Machine tools, metal forming type; Metal stampings, nec
PA: F & G Tool And Die Co.
    3024 Dryden Rd
    Moraine OH 45439
    937 294-1405

(G-7674)
FERCO TECH LLC
291 Conover Dr (45005-1944)
P.O. Box 607 (45005-0607)
PHONE..................................937 746-6696
Bryan Perkins, *
Jim Clemons, *
EMP: 120 **EST:** 1984
SQ FT: 30,000
SALES (est): 22.48MM
SALES (corp-wide): 218.18MM **Privately Held**
Web: www.fercoaerospacegroup.com
SIC: 3728 Aircraft parts and equipment, nec
PA: Novaria Group, L.L.C.
    6685 Iron Horse Blvd
    North Richland Hills TX 76180
    214 707-8980

(G-7675)
FINZER ROLLER INC
Also Called: Rotadyne
315 Industrial Dr (45005-4431)
PHONE..................................937 746-4069
Pat Lakes, *Sec*
EMP: 10
SALES (corp-wide): 83.27MM **Privately Held**
Web: www.finzerroller.com
SIC: 3555 Printing trades machinery
PA: Finzer Roller, Inc.
    880 W Thorndale Ave
    Itasca IL 60143
    847 390-6200

(G-7676)
FRANKLIN CABINET COMPANY INC
2500 Commerce Center Dr (45005-1816)
PHONE..................................937 743-9606
Mark Duncan, *Pr*
EMP: 29 **EST:** 1991
SQ FT: 50,000
SALES (est): 2.15MM **Privately Held**
Web: www.franklincabinet.com
SIC: 3083 2541 2599 2531 Plastics finished products, laminated; Cabinets, lockers, and shelving; Bar, restaurant and cafeteria furniture; Public building and related furniture

(G-7677)
GENERAL ENGINE PRODUCTS LLC
2000 Watkins Glen Dr (45005-2392)
P.O. Box 488 (45005-0488)
PHONE..................................937 704-0160
Charles M Hall, *Pr*
James Armour, *
Daniel J Dell'orto, *
Jeffery Adams, *
▲ **EMP:** 80 **EST:** 2002
SALES (est): 14.55MM
SALES (corp-wide): 3.44B **Privately Held**
Web: www.amgeneral.com
SIC: 3519 Diesel engine rebuilding
HQ: Am General Llc
    105 N Niles Ave
    South Bend IN 46617
    574 237-6222

(G-7678)
GREENPOINT METALS INC
Also Called: GPM
301 Shotwell Dr (45005-4659)
P.O. Box 935 (45005-0935)
PHONE..................................937 743-4075
Brian D Williamson, *CEO*
Doug Everhart, *

Franklin - Warren County (G-7679) GEOGRAPHIC SECTION

Travis Hearn, *
Gary Mockabee, *
EMP: 35 **EST:** 2000
SQ FT: 150,000
SALES (est): 9.35MM **Privately Held**
Web: www.greenpointmetals.com
SIC: 3441 Fabricated structural metal

(G-7679)
H & W SCREW PRODUCTS INC
335 Industrial Dr (45005-4431)
PHONE.................................937 866-2577
Robert E Wray, *Pr*
Wendy Wray, *Treas*
Richard Carlisle, *Sec*
EMP: 15 **EST:** 1978
SQ FT: 10,000
SALES (est): 455.73K **Privately Held**
Web: www.h-wscrewproducts.com
SIC: 3451 Screw machine products

(G-7680)
HOMECARE MATTRESS INC
303 Conover Dr (45005-1957)
PHONE.................................937 746-2556
Debbie Lipps, *Pr*
P Scott Lipps, *VP*
EMP: 13 **EST:** 1991
SQ FT: 6,000
SALES (est): 2.39MM **Privately Held**
Web: www.sleeptitemattress.com
SIC: 3448 2515 5047 5712 Ramps, prefabricated metal; Mattresses and foundations; Medical and hospital equipment; Mattresses

(G-7681)
HUHTAMAKI INC
4000 Commerce Center Dr (45005-1897)
PHONE.................................937 746-9700
EMP: 65
SALES (corp-wide): 4.53B **Privately Held**
Web: www.huhtamaki.com
SIC: 3565 2656 Labeling machines, industrial ; Ice cream containers: made from purchased material
HQ: Huhtamaki, Inc.
 9201 Packaging Dr
 De Soto KS 66018
 913 583-3025

(G-7682)
IKO PRODUCTION INC
Also Called: Iko
1200 S Main St (45005-2781)
PHONE.................................937 746-4561
David Foulkes, *Brnch Mgr*
EMP: 20
SQ FT: 100,000
SALES (corp-wide): 1.26B **Privately Held**
SIC: 2952 3083 Roofing felts, cements, or coatings, nec; Laminated plastics plate and sheet
HQ: Iko Production, Inc.
 6 Denny Rd Ste 200
 Wilmington DE 19809

(G-7683)
LEGACY FINISHING INC
415 Oxford Rd (45005-3639)
P.O. Box 249 (45005-0249)
PHONE.................................937 743-7278
Tom Custer, *Prin*
EMP: 9 **EST:** 2011
SALES (est): 1.01MM **Privately Held**
Web: www.legacyfinishing.com
SIC: 3479 Coating of metals and formed products

(G-7684)
LIQUID MANUFACTURING SOLUTIONS
401 Shotwell Dr (45005-4660)
PHONE.................................937 401-0821
Steve Overdeck, *CEO*
♦ **EMP:** 36 **EST:** 2021
SQ FT: 45,000
SALES (est): 9.97MM **Privately Held**
Web: www.olivamed.net
SIC: 2079 Olive oil

(G-7685)
MARBLE ARCH PRODUCTS INC
263 Industrial Dr (45005-4429)
PHONE.................................937 746-8388
Keenan Beauchamp, *Pr*
EMP: 9 **EST:** 1990
SQ FT: 15,000
SALES (est): 1.38MM **Privately Held**
Web: www.marblearchproducts.com
SIC: 3088 5211 Bathroom fixtures, plastics; Bathroom fixtures, equipment and supplies

(G-7686)
MCS MIDWEST LLC (PA)
3876 Hendrickson Rd (45005-9726)
PHONE.................................513 217-0805
EMP: 7 **EST:** 2008
SALES (est): 4.82MM
SALES (corp-wide): 4.82MM **Privately Held**
Web: www.mcsmidwest.com
SIC: 3089 7699 Garbage containers, plastics ; Agricultural equipment repair services

(G-7687)
MIRACLE WELDING INC
Also Called: Miracle Air
141 Industrial Dr Ste 200 (45005-4427)
PHONE.................................937 746-9977
David Miracle, *Pr*
EMP: 6 **EST:** 1978
SQ FT: 12,000
SALES (est): 469.85K **Privately Held**
Web: www.miraclewelding.com
SIC: 3599 3441 Machine shop, jobbing and repair; Fabricated structural metal

(G-7688)
NC WORKS INC
3500 Commerce Center Dr (45005-7202)
PHONE.................................937 514-7781
Simon Chen, *Pr*
▲ **EMP:** 25 **EST:** 2020
SALES (est): 8.54MM **Privately Held**
Web: www.ncworksinc.com
SIC: 2299 Automotive felts
PA: Fehrer Enterprise Corporation.
 1, Miao-Pu Lane, Shau Shin Lee,
 Tainan-City 74100

(G-7689)
NIKTEC INC
127 Industrial Dr (45005-4427)
PHONE.................................513 282-3747
♦ **EMP:** 7 **EST:** 2007
SALES (est): 508.11K **Privately Held**
Web: www.niktec.com
SIC: 7629 3679 Electrical repair shops; Electronic circuits

(G-7690)
NOVOLEX HOLDINGS INC
Also Called: Burrrows Paper Corroc Div
2000 Commerce Center Dr (45005-1477)
PHONE.................................937 746-1933
Jef Hall, *Mgr*
EMP: 337
SQ FT: 106,000
SALES (corp-wide): 32.64B **Publicly Held**
Web: www.novolex.com
SIC: 2621 2656 2653 Tissue paper; Sanitary food containers; Boxes, corrugated: made from purchased materials
HQ: Novolex Holdings, Llc
 101 E Carolina Ave
 Hartsville SC 29550
 800 845-6051

(G-7691)
PFIZER INC
Also Called: Pfizer
160 Industrial Dr (45005-4428)
PHONE.................................937 746-3603
Fred Haller, *Mgr*
EMP: 18
SALES (corp-wide): 100.33B **Publicly Held**
Web: www.pfizer.com
SIC: 2833 2844 2099 2834 Antibiotics; Hair preparations, including shampoos; Cake fillings, except fruit; Drugs acting on the cardiovascular system, except diagnostic
PA: Pfizer Inc.
 66 Hudson Blvd E
 New York NY 10001
 800 879-3477

(G-7692)
PHARMACIA HEPAR LLC
160 Industrial Dr (45005-4428)
PHONE.................................937 746-3603
Fred J Haller, *Pr*
EMP: 49 **EST:** 1975
SQ FT: 35,000
SALES (est): 10.53MM
SALES (corp-wide): 100.33B **Publicly Held**
SIC: 2833 2834 Medicinal chemicals; Pharmaceutical preparations
PA: Pfizer Inc.
 66 Hudson Blvd E
 New York NY 10001
 800 879-3477

(G-7693)
PHE MANUFACTURING INC
Also Called: Phe Manufacturing
331 Industrial Dr (45005-4431)
PHONE.................................937 790-1582
Javier Avendano, *CEO*
EMP: 6 **EST:** 2013
SALES (est): 895.56K **Privately Held**
Web: www.phemfg.com
SIC: 3443 Heat exchangers, condensers, and components

(G-7694)
PRU INDUSTRIES INC
8401 Claude Thomas Rd Ste 57 (45005-1497)
PHONE.................................937 746-8702
James Riling, *Pr*
Marcie Marks, *VP*
Mark See, *VP*
EMP: 10 **EST:** 1990
SALES (est): 2.64MM **Privately Held**
SIC: 2448 Wood pallets and skids
HQ: Component Solutions Group, Inc.
 7755 Paragon Rd Ste 104
 Dayton OH 45459
 937 434-8100

(G-7695)
QUALITY ARCHITECTURAL AND FABR
8 Shotwell Dr (45005-4600)
PHONE.................................937 743-2923
Demida Davis, *Pr*
Theodosa L Davis, *VP*
EMP: 18 **EST:** 1997
SQ FT: 15,000
SALES (est): 1.61MM **Privately Held**
Web: www.qaf.cc
SIC: 3446 Architectural metalwork

(G-7696)
QUEST TECHNOLOGIES INC
Also Called: Quest Lasercut
600 Commerce Center Dr (45005-7205)
PHONE.................................937 743-1200
John Wenning, *Pr*
Mike Wolters, *VP*
EMP: 10 **EST:** 1995
SQ FT: 12,000
SALES (est): 2.01MM **Privately Held**
Web: www.questlasercut.com
SIC: 3599 3499 7389 Machine shop, jobbing and repair; Fire- or burglary-resistive products; Metal cutting services

(G-7697)
RITA OF MIAMISBURG LLC (PA)
6164 State Route 122 (45005-5202)
PHONE.................................937 247-5244
EMP: 6 **EST:** 2021
SALES (est): 63.4K
SALES (corp-wide): 63.4K **Privately Held**
SIC: 2024 Ice cream and frozen deserts

(G-7698)
RIVERVIEW PACKAGING INC
101 Shotwell Dr (45005-4653)
P.O. Box 155 (45005-0155)
PHONE.................................937 743-9530
Joan K Ferrell, *Pr*
Randal T Ferrell, *
Robert S Ferrell, *
Marshall D Ruchman, *
EMP: 40 **EST:** 1987
SQ FT: 75,000
SALES (est): 6.81MM **Privately Held**
SIC: 2653 Boxes, corrugated: made from purchased materials

(G-7699)
RNM HOLDINGS INC (PA)
550 Conover Dr (45005-1953)
PHONE.................................937 704-9900
Matt Milton, *Pr*
▲ **EMP:** 41 **EST:** 2007
SQ FT: 13,500
SALES (est): 23.8MM **Privately Held**
SIC: 3531 Crane carriers

(G-7700)
RTC CONVERTERS INC
300 Shotwell Dr (45005-4662)
PHONE.................................937 743-2300
Bonnie Vogel, *Pr*
EMP: 12 **EST:** 1994
SQ FT: 36,000
SALES (est): 1.06MM **Privately Held**
SIC: 3714 3566 Motor vehicle transmissions, drive assemblies, and parts; Speed changers, drives, and gears

(G-7701)
SERVING VETERANS MOBILITY INC
303 Conover Dr (45005-1957)
PHONE.................................937 746-4788
Debra Lipps, *VP*
EMP: 8
SALES (est): 558.44K **Privately Held**
Web: www.servingveteransmobility.com
SIC: 3999 Wheelchair lifts

(G-7702)
SHUR-FIT DISTRIBUTORS INC
Also Called: Shur-Form Laminates Division

221 N Main St (45005-1629)
PHONE.........................937 746-0567
Paul Gross, Pr
Hershal Nichol, *
Kent Gross, *
EMP: 11 EST: 1958
SQ FT: 58,000
SALES (est): 818.06K Privately Held
SIC: 2541 Table or counter tops, plastic laminated

(G-7703)
SRS MANUFACTURING CORP
395 Industrial Dr (45005-4431)
PHONE.........................937 746-3086
Carlos Robinson, Pr
EMP: 24 EST: 1978
SQ FT: 12,000
SALES (est): 805.07K Privately Held
Web: www.srsmfg.com
SIC: 3599 Machine shop, jobbing and repair

(G-7704)
SUNSTAR ENGRG AMERICAS INC
Also Called: Sunstar Sprockets
700 Watkins Glen Dr (45005-2394)
PHONE.........................937 743-9049
Naoki Achiwa, Prin
EMP: 73
Web: www.sunstar-engineering.com
SIC: 3751 Motorcycles, bicycles and parts
HQ: Sunstar Engineering Americas Inc.
85 S Pioneer Blvd
Springboro OH 45066

(G-7705)
TECH-WAY INDUSTRIES INC
301 Industrial Dr (45005-4458)
P.O. Box 517 (45005-0517)
PHONE.........................937 746-1004
Kenneth Parker, CEO
Robin Parker, *
Brian Kress, *
EMP: 55 EST: 1964
SQ FT: 90,000
SALES (est): 8.08MM Privately Held
Web: www.tech-wayindustries.com
SIC: 3089 Injection molding of plastics

(G-7706)
TOTAL QUALITY MACHINING INC
10 Shotwell Dr (45005-4600)
PHONE.........................937 746-7765
Theodosa Davis, Pr
Demida Davis, Treas
EMP: 12 EST: 1991
SQ FT: 25,000
SALES (est): 247.7K Privately Held
Web: www.totalqualitymachining.com
SIC: 3599 Machine shop, jobbing and repair

(G-7707)
TRI STATE PALLET INC (PA)
8401 Claude Thomas Rd (45005-1475)
PHONE.........................937 746-8702
John Sickinger, Pr
EMP: 24 EST: 2005
SALES (est): 2.4MM Privately Held
SIC: 2448 Pallets, wood

(G-7708)
VALUED RELATIONSHIPS INC
Also Called: My Alarm
1400 Commerce Center Dr Ste B (45005)
PHONE.........................800 860-4230
EMP: 331 EST: 1989
SQ FT: 10,000
SALES (est): 55.4MM
SALES (corp-wide): 2.75B Publicly Held
Web: www.vricares.com

SIC: 3845 Patient monitoring apparatus, nec
PA: Modivcare Inc.
4700 S Syrcuse St Ste 440
Denver CO 80237
404 888-5800

(G-7709)
WALTER F STEPHENS JR INC
415 South Ave (45005-3647)
PHONE.........................937 746-0521
Carla Baker, VP
Walter F Stephens Junior, Pr
Ruth Ann Stephens, Ch Bd
Diane Stephens Maloney, Sec
Patty Gleason, *
EMP: 50 EST: 1940
SQ FT: 45,000
SALES (est): 2.39MM Privately Held
Web: www.stephenscatalogs.com
SIC: 5999 2389 5122 5023 Police supply stores; Uniforms and vestments; Toiletries; Kitchenware

(G-7710)
WALTHER ENGRG & MFG CO INC
Also Called: Walther EMC
3501 Shotwell Dr (45005-4667)
PHONE.........................937 743-8125
Chris Walther, Pr
Phil Fensel, *
EMP: 49 EST: 1992
SQ FT: 35,000
SALES (est): 10.85MM Privately Held
Web: www.waltheremc.com
SIC: 3714 Motor vehicle parts and accessories

(G-7711)
WAYTEK CORPORATION
400 Shotwell Dr (45005-4661)
PHONE.........................937 743-6142
▲ EMP: 42
SIC: 2672 2891 Paper; coated and laminated, nec; Adhesives and sealants

Franklin Furnace
Scioto County

(G-7712)
G & J PEPSI-COLA BOTTLERS INC
Also Called: Pepsico
4587 Gallia Pike (45629-8777)
P.O. Box 299 (45629-0299)
PHONE.........................740 354-9191
Robert Ross, Brnch Mgr
EMP: 350
SALES (corp-wide): 404.54MM Privately Held
Web: www.pepsico.com
SIC: 2086 5149 Carbonated soft drinks, bottled and canned; Groceries and related products, nec
PA: G & J Pepsi-Cola Bottlers Inc
9435 Waterstone Blvd # 390
Cincinnati OH 45249
513 785-6060

(G-7713)
WOODWORKS UNLIMITED
330 Lambro Ln (45629-8994)
PHONE.........................740 574-0500
Gregory Chaffin, Owner
EMP: 6 EST: 2006
SALES (est): 188.43K Privately Held
SIC: 2431 Millwork

Frazeysburg
Muskingum County

(G-7714)
CALVARY CHRISTIAN CH OF OHIO
Also Called: Frazeysburg Restaurant & Bky
338 W 3rd St (43822-9785)
PHONE.........................740 828-9000
Reverend Scott Egbert, Pr
Robert Mcgraw, VP
Mari Anne Holbrook, *
EMP: 10 EST: 1968
SQ FT: 2,500
SALES (est): 55.47K Privately Held
SIC: 2051 8661 0241 5541 Bakery: wholesale or wholesale/retail combined; Christian and Reformed Church; Milk production; Filling stations, gasoline

(G-7715)
DK MANFCTURING FRAZEYSBURG INC (HQ)
Also Called: DK Manufacturing
119 W 2nd St (43822-9675)
P.O. Box 409 (43822-0409)
PHONE.........................740 828-3291
Allen L Handlan, Prin
Brad Williams, *
EMP: 14 EST: 2004
SALES (est): 27.91MM
SALES (corp-wide): 39.58MM Privately Held
Web: www.dkmanufacturing.com
SIC: 3089 Injection molding of plastics
PA: Dak Enterprises, Inc.
18062 Timber Trails Rd
Marysville OH 43040
740 828-3291

(G-7716)
TRAVIS COCHRAN
13065 Hamby Hill Rd (43822-9748)
PHONE.........................740 294-2368
Travis Cochran, Prin
EMP: 6 EST: 2015
SALES (est): 101.76K Privately Held
SIC: 2411 Logging

Fredericksburg
Wayne County

(G-7717)
A-1 RESOURCES LTD
8241 Tr 601 (44627)
PHONE.........................330 695-9351
John R Slater, CEO
▲ EMP: 10 EST: 2001
SQ FT: 6,700
SALES (est): 1.03MM Privately Held
SIC: 3469 Metal stampings, nec

(G-7718)
CABINET SPECIALTIES INC
10738 Criswell Rd (44627-9719)
PHONE.........................330 695-3463
Ivan Weaver, Pr
Robert Weaver, VP
EMP: 9 EST: 1988
SQ FT: 15,000
SALES (est): 492.79K Privately Held
Web: www.cabinetspecialties.co
SIC: 2434 Wood kitchen cabinets

(G-7719)
CHORE ANDEN
Also Called: Hickory Lane Welding
11461 Salt Creek Rd (44627-9755)

PHONE.........................330 695-2300
EMP: 10 EST: 1995
SALES (est): 408.5K Privately Held
SIC: 7692 Welding repair

(G-7720)
COUNTRY COMFORT WDWKG LLC
2 Mi Sw Of Mt Eaton (44627)
PHONE.........................330 695-4408
EMP: 6 EST: 2008
SALES (est): 138.54K Privately Held
SIC: 2431 Millwork

(G-7721)
CRA WELDING LLC
8728 Criswell Rd (44627-9813)
PHONE.........................330 317-2007
EMP: 6 EST: 2016
SALES (est): 215.34K Privately Held
Web: www.crawelding.com
SIC: 7692 Brazing

(G-7722)
CRISWELL FURNITURE LLC
8139 Criswell Rd (44627-9709)
PHONE.........................330 695-2082
Jonas Mast, Managing Member
Eli Mast, Managing Member
David Mast, Managing Member
EMP: 15 EST: 1997
SALES (est): 1.07MM Privately Held
SIC: 2511 Wood household furniture

(G-7723)
DOWEL YODER & MOLDING
4754 Township Road 613 (44627-9661)
PHONE.........................330 231-2962
Mark Miller, Pt
Roy Yoder, Pt
EMP: 9 EST: 1991
SALES (est): 938.35K Privately Held
SIC: 2431 5211 Moldings and baseboards, ornamental and trim; Lumber and other building materials

(G-7724)
HOLMES PRINTING SOLUTIONS LLC
8757 County Road 77 (44627-9446)
PHONE.........................330 234-9699
Phillip Holmes, Pr
EMP: 12 EST: 2010
SALES (est): 841.94K Privately Held
SIC: 2752 Offset printing

(G-7725)
HOLMVIEW WELDING LLC
4041 Township Road 606 (44627-9685)
PHONE.........................330 359-5315
Aaron Herscerger, Managing Member
EMP: 12 EST: 2014
SALES (est): 734.53K Privately Held
Web: www.novocollc.com
SIC: 7692 Welding repair

(G-7726)
MILLER CRIST
Also Called: Crosco Wood Products
10258 S Kansas Rd (44627-9754)
PHONE.........................330 359-7877
Cris Miller, Prin
Crist Miller, Owner
EMP: 7 EST: 1994
SQ FT: 8,000
SALES (est): 273.15K Privately Held
SIC: 2435 Hardwood plywood, prefinished

(G-7727)
MORRISON CUSTOM WELDING INC
4399 E Moreland Rd (44627-9513)
PHONE.........................330 464-1637

Fredericksburg - Wayne County (G-7728)

EMP: 7 **EST:** 2019
SALES (est): 152.35K **Privately Held**
Web: www.morrisonwelding.com
SIC: 7692 Welding repair

(G-7728)
MRS MLLERS HMMADE NOODLES LTD
9140 County Road 192 (44627-9436)
P.O. Box 289 (44627-0289)
PHONE.................................330 694-5814
Leon Miller, *Pt*
Esther Miller, *Pt*
Maria Miller, *Prin*
▲ **EMP:** 10 **EST:** 1973
SQ FT: 11,000
SALES (est): 2.25MM **Privately Held**
Web: www.mmhn.com
SIC: 2099 Food preparations, nec

(G-7729)
NOVOOO LLC ◐
4041 Township Road 606 (44627-9685)
PHONE.................................330 359-5315
David Miller, *Managing Member*
EMP: 24 **EST:** 2023
SALES (est): 1.04MM **Privately Held**
SIC: 3443 Fabricated plate work (boiler shop)

(G-7730)
OHIO CUSTOM DOOR LLC
Also Called: Diamond Door Limited
9141 County Road 201 (44627-9402)
PHONE.................................330 695-6301
EMP: 32 **EST:** 2003
SALES (est): 2.36MM **Privately Held**
Web: www.ohiodoorcompany.com
SIC: 2431 Doors and door parts and trim, wood

(G-7731)
QUALITY WOODPRODUCTS LLC
8216 Township Road 568 (44627-9409)
PHONE.................................330 279-2217
Herman Weaver, *Managing Member*
EMP: 8 **EST:** 2018
SALES (est): 440.14K **Privately Held**
SIC: 2431 Moldings, wood: unfinished and prefinished

(G-7732)
ROBIN INDUSTRIES INC
Also Called: Fredericksburg Facility
300 W Clay St (44627)
P.O. Box 242 (44627-0242)
PHONE.................................330 695-9300
Dave Wingett, *Prin*
EMP: 46
SALES (corp-wide): 74.78MM **Privately Held**
Web: www.robin-industries.com
SIC: 3069 3061 Molded rubber products; Mechanical rubber goods
PA: Robin Industries, Inc.
6500 Rockside Rd Ste 230
Independence OH 44131
216 631-7000

(G-7733)
SALT CREEK LUMBER COMPANY INC
11657 Salt Creek Rd (44627-9755)
P.O. Box 253 (44627-0253)
PHONE.................................330 695-3500
Norman Boerman, *Pr*
Shirley Boerman, *VP*
EMP: 6 **EST:** 1981
SQ FT: 8,000
SALES (est): 923.72K **Privately Held**

SIC: 5031 2421 Lumber: rough, dressed, and finished; Sawmills and planing mills, general

(G-7734)
WESTERN CUTTERHEADS LLC
4041 Township Road 606 (44627-9685)
PHONE.................................270 665-5302
David L Renfrow, *Admn*
EMP: 6 **EST:** 2015
SALES (est): 86.87K **Privately Held**
SIC: 3599 Machine shop, jobbing and repair

(G-7735)
YODER WINDOW & SIDING LTD (PA)
Also Called: Yoder Window and Siding
7846 Harrison Rd (44627-9798)
PHONE.................................330 695-6960
Jonas Yoder, *Pt*
Jonas M Yoder, *Pt*
Derryl R Troyer, *Pt*
EMP: 13 **EST:** 1992
SQ FT: 6,500
SALES (est): 2.02MM **Privately Held**
Web: www.yoderswindowandsiding.com
SIC: 2431 1751 1761 Windows, wood; Window and door (prefabricated) installation; Gutter and downspout contractor

(G-7736)
YODERS PRODUCE INC
Also Called: Quality Plastics
9599 S Apple Creek Rd (44627-9743)
PHONE.................................330 695-5900
Monroe Yoder, *Pr*
EMP: 22 **EST:** 1990
SALES (est): 2.67MM **Privately Held**
Web: www.yodersproduce.com
SIC: 2821 Molding compounds, plastics

(G-7737)
Z-KAN METAL PRODUCTS LLC
8724 County Road 235 (44627-9639)
PHONE.................................330 695-2397
EMP: 7 **EST:** 2020
SALES (est): 438.05K **Privately Held**
Web: www.zkanmetals.com
SIC: 3444 Sheet metalwork

Fredericktown
Knox County

(G-7738)
B&L SERVICES
28 Zent Ave (43019-1032)
PHONE.................................740 390-4272
Kyle Lybarger, *Prin*
EMP: 6 **EST:** 2019
SALES (est): 151.31K **Privately Held**
SIC: 1389 Oil field services, nec

(G-7739)
BENCHMARK-CABINETS LLC
97 Mount Vernon Ave (43019-7700)
PHONE.................................740 694-1144
Wesley Crum, *Owner*
EMP: 9 **EST:** 1994
SQ FT: 29,000
SALES (est): 360.08K **Privately Held**
Web: www.benchmark-cabinets.com
SIC: 2434 2541 Wood kitchen cabinets; Counter and sink tops

(G-7740)
COMPLETE METAL SERVICES
18581 Divelbiss Rd (43019-9740)
PHONE.................................740 694-0000
Barry Fluty, *Owner*
EMP: 6 **EST:** 2000

SQ FT: 3,600
SALES (est): 201.71K **Privately Held**
Web: www.peorialandscapingservice.com
SIC: 7692 Welding repair

(G-7741)
COUNTRY MANUFACTURING INC
333 Salem Ave Ext (43019-9186)
P.O. Box 104 (43019-0104)
PHONE.................................740 694-9926
Joe Chattin, *Pr*
Karen Gay Chattin, *Sec*
EMP: 17 **EST:** 1978
SQ FT: 15,000
SALES (est): 2.33MM **Privately Held**
Web: www.countrymfg.com
SIC: 3523 Farm machinery and equipment

(G-7742)
COUNTRYSIDE CABINETS
18720 Butler Rd (43019-9746)
PHONE.................................740 397-6488
John Martin Miller, *Prin*
EMP: 6 **EST:** 2010
SALES (est): 228.72K **Privately Held**
Web: www.countrysidecabinets.com
SIC: 2434 Wood kitchen cabinets

(G-7743)
DEE-JAYS CSTM BTCHRING PROC LL
17460 Ankneytown Rd (43019-8015)
PHONE.................................740 694-7492
Mike Jessee, *Managing Member*
Mike Jessee, *Owner*
EMP: 10 **EST:** 1978
SALES (est): 828.23K **Privately Held**
Web: www.deejayscustombutchering.com
SIC: 2011 5142 5421 Meat packing plants; Meat, frozen: packaged; Meat markets, including freezer provisioners

(G-7744)
DIVELBISS CORPORATION
9778 Mount Gilead Rd (43019-9161)
PHONE.................................800 245-2327
Terry L Divelbiss, *Pr*
Alan Divelbiss, *
EMP: 39 **EST:** 1974
SQ FT: 17,000
SALES (est): 8.12MM **Privately Held**
Web: www.divelbiss.com
SIC: 3625 Relays and industrial controls

(G-7745)
EDWARDS SHEET METAL WORKS INC
Also Called: Edwards Culvert Co
10439 Sparta Rd (43019-9025)
P.O. Box 239 (43019-0239)
PHONE.................................740 694-0010
Richard Well, *Pr*
Catherine Chris Well, *Sec*
EMP: 24 **EST:** 1907
SQ FT: 8,000
SALES (est): 742.41K **Privately Held**
SIC: 3444 Culverts, sheet metal

(G-7746)
FOOTE FOUNDRY LLC
283 N Main St (43019-1111)
PHONE.................................740 694-1595
Joseph E Locanti, *Managing Member*
Todd Colman, *
EMP: 24 **EST:** 1851
SQ FT: 70,000
SALES (est): 982.6K **Privately Held**
Web: www.footefoundry.com

SIC: 3321 Gray iron castings, nec

(G-7747)
FREDERICKTOWN TOMATO SHOW
P.O. Box 28 (43019-0028)
PHONE.................................740 694-4816
EMP: 7 **EST:** 2009
SALES (est): 120K **Privately Held**
Web: www.tomatoshow.com
SIC: 3599 Industrial machinery, nec

(G-7748)
FT PRECISION INC
Also Called: Ftp
9731 Mount Gilead Rd (43019-9167)
PHONE.................................740 694-1500
▲ **EMP:** 512 **EST:** 1994
SQ FT: 150,000
SALES (est): 104.97MM **Privately Held**
Web: www.ftprecision.com
SIC: 3714 Motor vehicle engines and parts
PA: Tanaka Seimitsu Kogyo Co.,Ltd.
328, Fuchumachishimada
Toyama TYM 939-2

(G-7749)
INDUSTRIAL AND MAR ENG SVC CO
Also Called: Imesco
13843 Armentrout Rd (43019-9717)
P.O. Box 247 (43019-0247)
PHONE.................................740 694-0791
Theresa C Chandler, *CEO*
EMP: 10 **EST:** 1974
SQ FT: 7,200
SALES (est): 717.58K **Privately Held**
Web: www.imescomfg.com
SIC: 3613 3625 3479 3993 Control panels, electric; Control circuit relays, industrial; Name plates: engraved, etched, etc.; Signs and advertising specialties

(G-7750)
KOKOSING MATERIALS INC
11624 Hyatt Rd (43019-9471)
PHONE.................................740 694-5872
John Gallucci Iii, *Prin*
EMP: 11
SALES (corp-wide): 1.17B **Privately Held**
Web: www.kokosing.biz
SIC: 2951 Asphalt and asphaltic paving mixtures (not from refineries)
HQ: Kokosing Materials, Inc.
17531 Waterford Rd
Fredericktown OH 43019
740 694-9585

(G-7751)
KOKOSING MATERIALS INC (HQ)
17531 Waterford Rd (43019-9159)
P.O. Box 334 (43019-0334)
PHONE.................................740 694-9585
EMP: 10 **EST:** 1980
SALES (est): 25.72MM
SALES (corp-wide): 1.17B **Privately Held**
Web: www.kokosing.biz
SIC: 2951 Asphalt and asphaltic paving mixtures (not from refineries)
PA: Kokosing, Inc.
6235 Wstrville Rd Ste 200
Westerville OH 43081
614 212-5700

(G-7752)
OPTIONS PLUS INCORPORATED
Also Called: Options Plus
143 Tuttle Ave (43019-1029)
PHONE.................................740 694-9811
Camilyn Jo Meleca, *Pr*
Melissa Chattin, *VP*
◆ **EMP:** 10 **EST:** 1976
SQ FT: 25,000

GEOGRAPHIC SECTION

Fremont - Sandusky County (G-7777)

SALES (est): 945.3K **Privately Held**
SIC: **3444** 3496 Sheet metalwork; Miscellaneous fabricated wire products

(G-7753)
SCHAFER DRIVELINE LLC (HQ)
Also Called: Schafer Industries
123 Phoenix Pl (43019-9162)
PHONE.................................740 694-2055
♦ EMP: 18 EST: 2012
SQ FT: 110,000
SALES (est): 22MM
SALES (corp-wide): 40.18MM **Privately Held**
Web: www.schaferindustries.com
SIC: **3714** Axles, motor vehicle
PA: Schafer Industries, Inc.
    4701 Nimtz Pkwy
    South Bend IN 46628
    574 234-4116

(G-7754)
TD LANDSCAPE INC
16780 Pinkley Rd (43019-9302)
P.O. Box 154 (43019-0154)
PHONE.................................740 694-0244
Teresa Huvler, *Pr*
Scott Huvler, *CEO*
EMP: 15 EST: 2016
SALES (est): 1.13MM **Privately Held**
Web: www.tdlandscape.net
SIC: **3523** Grounds mowing equipment

(G-7755)
TEXMASTER TOOLS INC
143 Tuttle Ave (43019-1029)
P.O. Box 132 (43019-0132)
PHONE.................................740 965-8778
John Capoccia, *Pr*
▲ EMP: 15 EST: 1990
SQ FT: 25,000
SALES (est): 2.16MM **Privately Held**
Web: www.texmaster.com
SIC: **5072** 3429 Hardware; Hardware, nec

(G-7756)
UMD AUTOMATED SYSTEMS INC
Also Called: U M D
9855 Salem Rd (43019-9301)
P.O. Box 317 (43019-0317)
PHONE.................................740 694-8614
EMP: 72 EST: 1996
SQ FT: 55,000
SALES (est): 17.67MM **Privately Held**
Web: www.umdautomatedsystems.com
SIC: **3441** Fabricated structural metal

(G-7757)
UMD CONTRACTORS INC
9855 Salem Rd (43019-9301)
P.O. Box 228 (43019-0228)
PHONE.................................740 694-8614
Don Rogers, *Pr*
EMP: 15 EST: 2003
SALES (est): 2.74MM **Privately Held**
Web: www.umdautomatedsystems.com
SIC: **3011** Tires and inner tubes

(G-7758)
VILLAGE WOODWORKING
8033 Ridge Rd (43019-9473)
PHONE.................................740 326-4361
Menno R Yoder, *Prin*
EMP: 6 EST: 2009
SALES (est): 135.94K **Privately Held**
SIC: **2431** Millwork

(G-7759)
WARD/KRAFT FORMS OF OHIO INC
700 Salem Ave Ext (43019-9188)
PHONE.................................740 694-0015
Robert A Horton, *VP*
Robert A Horton, *General Vice President*
Harold E Kraft, *
Fred Mitchelson, *
David Young, *
EMP: 36 EST: 1980
SQ FT: 41,400
SALES (est): 476.79K
SALES (corp-wide): 84.02MM **Privately Held**
SIC: **2759** Commercial printing, nec
HQ: Ward-Kraft, Inc.
    2401 Cooper St
    Fort Scott KS 66701
    800 821-4021

(G-7760)
WHITES LOGGING & LAND CLEARIN
197 Taylor St (43019-1054)
PHONE.................................419 921-9878
Jonathan White, *Prin*
EMP: 6 EST: 2018
SALES (est): 237.63K **Privately Held**
SIC: **2411** Logging camps and contractors

Freeport
Harrison County

(G-7761)
ROSEBUD MINING COMPANY
28490 Birmingham Rd (43973-9754)
PHONE.................................740 658-4217
EMP: 60
SALES (corp-wide): 221.86MM **Privately Held**
Web: www.rosebudmining.com
SIC: **1241** Coal mining services
PA: Rosebud Mining Company
    301 Market St
    Kittanning PA 16201
    724 545-6222

Fremont
Sandusky County

(G-7762)
ALKON CORPORATION (PA)
728 Graham Dr (43420-4073)
PHONE.................................419 355-9111
Mark Winter, *Pr*
▲ EMP: 60 EST: 1968
SQ FT: 40,000
SALES (est): 27.26MM
SALES (corp-wide): 27.26MM **Privately Held**
Web: www.alkoncorp.com
SIC: **3491** 3082 5084 5085 Valves, nuclear; Tubes, unsupported plastics; Industrial machinery and equipment; Hydraulic and pneumatic pistons and valves

(G-7763)
ATLAS INDUSTRIES INC
1750 E State St (43420-4056)
PHONE.................................419 355-1000
♦ EMP: 1001
Web: www.atlas-industries.com
SIC: **3599** Crankshafts and camshafts, machining

(G-7764)
AURIA FREMONT LLC
Also Called: Auria Solutions
400 S Stone St (43420-2658)
PHONE.................................419 332-1587
Brian Pour, *CEO*
EMP: 261 EST: 2007
SALES (est): 29.65MM **Privately Held**
Web: www.auriasolutions.com
SIC: **3714** Motor vehicle parts and accessories
HQ: Auria Solutions Usa Inc.
    26999 Centrl Pk Blvd # 30
    Southfield MI 48076
    248 728-8000

(G-7765)
BAP MANUFACTURING INC
601 N Stone St Ste 1 (43420-1566)
PHONE.................................419 332-5041
W Scott Brown, *Pr*
EMP: 25 EST: 1971
SQ FT: 10,000
SALES (est): 479.6K **Privately Held**
Web: www.bapman.com
SIC: **3545** Cutting tools for machine tools

(G-7766)
BENCHMARK PRINTS
2252 W State St (43420-1439)
PHONE.................................419 332-7640
Kenn Bower, *Owner*
EMP: 11 EST: 1981
SQ FT: 5,700
SALES (est): 403.86K **Privately Held**
Web: www.benchmarkprints.com
SIC: **2759** 5611 5199 Screen printing; Men's and boys' clothing stores; Advertising specialties

(G-7767)
BERLEKAMP PLASTICS INC
2587 County Road 99 (43420-9316)
PHONE.................................419 334-4481
Kenneth Berlekamp Junior, *Pr*
Sandra Berlekamp, *Sec*
EMP: 15 EST: 1929
SQ FT: 12,000
SALES (est): 2.29MM **Privately Held**
Web: www.berlekamp.com
SIC: **3089** Injection molding of plastics

(G-7768)
BLONDE SWAN
307 W State St (43420-2527)
PHONE.................................419 307-8591
Elizabeth Martin, *Owner*
Alex Poznanski, *Owner*
EMP: 11 EST: 2010
SALES (est): 718.66K **Privately Held**
Web: www.blondeswan.com
SIC: **2371** 2353 Hats, fur; Hats, caps, and millinery

(G-7769)
CARBO FORGE INC
150 State Route 523 (43420-9364)
PHONE.................................419 334-9788
Jeffrey Woitha, *Pr*
Jeffrey Witham, *
EMP: 44 EST: 1920
SQ FT: 90,000
SALES (est): 9.6MM **Privately Held**
Web: www.carboforge.com
SIC: **3462** Iron and steel forgings

(G-7770)
CD COMPANY LLC
215 N Stone St (43420)
PHONE.................................419 332-2693
EMP: 93 EST: 2011
SALES (est): 12.21MM **Privately Held**
Web: www.uniloy.com
SIC: **3544** Industrial molds

(G-7771)
CHRISTY MACHINE COMPANY
118 Birchard Ave (43420-3008)
P.O. Box 39 (43420-0039)
PHONE.................................419 332-6451
Randy Fielding, *Pr*
EMP: 15 EST: 1953
SQ FT: 7,000
SALES (est): 2.08MM **Privately Held**
Web: www.christymachine.com
SIC: **3556** Food products machinery

(G-7772)
CRESCENT MANUFACTURING COMPANY (PA)
Also Called: Crescent Blades
1310 Majestic Dr (43420-9142)
PHONE.................................419 332-6484
▲ EMP: 98 EST: 1898
SALES (est): 22.43MM
SALES (corp-wide): 22.43MM **Privately Held**
Web: www.crescentblades.com
SIC: **3421** 3425 Cutlery; Saw blades and handsaws

(G-7773)
CROWN BATTERY MANUFACTURING CO (PA)
Also Called: Crown Battery
1445 Majestic Dr (43420-9190)
P.O. Box 990 (43420-0990)
PHONE.................................419 334-7181
Hal Hawk, *Pr*
Tim Hack, *
♦ EMP: 450 EST: 1926
SQ FT: 220,000
SALES (est): 95.41MM
SALES (corp-wide): 95.41MM **Privately Held**
Web: www.crownbattery.com
SIC: **3691** Storage batteries

(G-7774)
CUTTING EDGE MANUFACTURING LLC
220 Sullivan Rd (43420-9671)
PHONE.................................419 355-0921
Joseph Fisher, *Prin*
EMP: 20 EST: 2016
SALES (est): 2.68MM **Privately Held**
Web: www.cuttingedgemanuf.com
SIC: **3599** Machine shop, jobbing and repair

(G-7775)
DECKER CUSTOM WOOD LLC
Also Called: Decker Custom Wood Working
505 W Mcgormley Rd (43420-8672)
PHONE.................................419 332-3464
EMP: 6 EST: 2004
SQ FT: 3,500
SALES (est): 532.04K **Privately Held**
Web: www.deckerwoodworking.com
SIC: **2431** Millwork

(G-7776)
ENERGY MANUFACTURING LTD
1830 Oak Harbor Rd (43420)
P.O. Box 1127 (44830-1127)
PHONE.................................419 355-9304
EMP: 6 EST: 2011
SQ FT: 40,000
SALES (est): 855.29K **Privately Held**
Web: www.energymanufacturing.com
SIC: **3586** Oil pumps, measuring or dispensing

(G-7777)
ENGLER PRINTING CO
808 W State St (43420-2538)

PHONE..............................419 332-2181
Jay Engler, *Owner*
EMP: 9 **EST:** 1952
SQ FT: 4,000
SALES (est): 530K **Privately Held**
Web: www.englerprinting.com
SIC: 2752 Offset printing

(G-7778)
FIRST CHOICE PACKAGING INC (PA)
Also Called: First Choice Packg Solutions
1501 W State St (43420-1629)
PHONE..............................419 333-4100
Paul W Tomick, *Ch*
Frank Wolfinger, *
▲ **EMP:** 105 **EST:** 1985
SALES (est): 23.18MM
SALES (corp-wide): 23.18MM **Privately Held**
Web: www.firstchoicepackaging.com
SIC: 3089 7389 Thermoformed finished plastics products, nec; Packaging and labeling services

(G-7779)
FLOWER MANUFACTURING LLC
423 Knapp St (43420-2512)
PHONE..............................888 241-9109
Kenneth F Flower, *Managing Member*
EMP: 8 **EST:** 2004
SALES (est): 922.99K **Privately Held**
Web: www.customfresheners.com
SIC: 3999 Sprays, artificial and preserved

(G-7780)
FREMONT COMPANY (PA)
Also Called: Fremont
802 N Front St (43420-1917)
PHONE..............................419 334-8995
Christopher Smith, *CEO*
Richard L Smith, *
Jeff Diehr, *
Christopher Smith, *VP*
Tom Smith, *
▼ **EMP:** 55 **EST:** 1905
SQ FT: 250,000
SALES (est): 51.18MM
SALES (corp-wide): 51.18MM **Privately Held**
Web: www.fremontcompany.com
SIC: 2033 Vegetables: packaged in cans, jars, etc.

(G-7781)
FREMONT CUTTING DIES INC
3179 Us 20 E (43420-9014)
PHONE..............................419 334-5153
Gregory Abdoo, *Pr*
EMP: 9 **EST:** 2000
SQ FT: 1,000
SALES (est): 1.37MM **Privately Held**
Web: www.fremontcuttingdies.com
SIC: 3544 Die springs

(G-7782)
FREMONT FLASK CO
1000 Wolfe Ave (43420-1670)
P.O. Box 594 (43420-0594)
PHONE..............................419 332-2231
Carl W Yeager Junior, *Pr*
James Yeager, *Sec*
John Yeager, *Treas*
EMP: 13 **EST:** 1938
SQ FT: 20,000
SALES (est): 951.87K **Privately Held**
Web: www.fremontflask.net
SIC: 3559 Foundry machinery and equipment

(G-7783)
FREMONT PLASTIC PRODUCTS INC
2101 Cedar St (43420-1015)
PHONE..............................419 332-6407
EMP: 250
SIC: 3089 3944 3714 3661 Blow molded finished plastics products, nec; Games, toys, and children's vehicles; Motor vehicle parts and accessories; Telephone and telegraph apparatus

(G-7784)
FREMONT PRINTING INC
1208 Dickinson St (43420-1647)
PHONE..............................480 272-3443
Dennis C Abdoo, *Pr*
EMP: 10 **EST:** 1950
SQ FT: 10,000
SALES (est): 710K **Privately Held**
SIC: 2752 2679 Commercial printing, lithographic; Paper products, converted, nec

(G-7785)
GANNETT STLLITE INFO NTWRK LLC
News Messenger, The
1800 E State St Ste B (43420-4083)
P.O. Box 1230 (43420-8230)
PHONE..............................419 334-1012
Cindy Bealer, *Admn*
EMP: 27
SQ FT: 2,792
SALES (corp-wide): 2.66B **Publicly Held**
Web: www.thenews-messenger.com
SIC: 2711 2752 Newspapers, publishing and printing; Commercial printing, lithographic
HQ: Gannett Satellite Information Network, Llc
7950 Jones Branch Dr
Mc Lean VA 22102
703 854-6000

(G-7786)
GENERAL CUTLERY INC (PA)
1918 N County Road 232 (43420-9595)
PHONE..............................419 332-2316
David Reitz, *Pr*
Carleton R Reitz, *VP*
Donna Shoemaker, *Sec*
EMP: 12 **EST:** 1945
SQ FT: 25,000
SALES (est): 1.26MM
SALES (corp-wide): 1.26MM **Privately Held**
SIC: 3421 Cutlery

(G-7787)
GLATFELTER CORPORATION
Glatfelter
2275 Commerce Dr (43420-1045)
PHONE..............................419 333-6700
Lloyd Tuskan, *Mgr*
EMP: 8
SALES (corp-wide): 1.39B **Publicly Held**
Web: www.glatfelter.com
SIC: 2761 2672 Manifold business forms; Paper; coated and laminated, nec
PA: Glatfelter Corporation
4350 Congress St Ste 600
Charlotte NC 28209
704 885-2555

(G-7788)
GRAHAM PACKAGING PET TECH INC
725 Industrial Dr (43420-8679)
PHONE..............................419 334-4197
Rick Van, *Mgr*
EMP: 27
Web: www.grahampackaging.com

SIC: 3085 3089 Plastics bottles; Plastics containers, except foam
HQ: Graham Packaging Pet Technologies Inc.
700 Indian Springs Dr # 100
Lancaster PA 17601

(G-7789)
GREEN BAY PACKAGING INC
Fremont Division
2323 Commerce Dr (43420-1052)
PHONE..............................419 332-5593
Paul Hasemeyer, *Mgr*
EMP: 129
SALES (corp-wide): 1.87B **Privately Held**
Web: www.gbpcoated.com
SIC: 2653 3412 Boxes, corrugated: made from purchased materials; Metal barrels, drums, and pails
PA: Green Bay Packaging Inc.
1700 N Webster Ave
Green Bay WI 54002
920 433-5111

(G-7790)
JS FABRICATIONS INC
1400 E State St (43420-4061)
PHONE..............................419 333-0323
Jack Swint, *Pr*
EMP: 8 **EST:** 1991
SALES (est): 1.09MM **Privately Held**
Web: www.jsfab1.com
SIC: 3441 1795 1721 Fabricated structural metal; Demolition, buildings and other structures; Industrial painting

(G-7791)
K DAVIS INC
Also Called: KDI Med Supply
206 Lynn St (43420-2375)
P.O. Box 162 (43431-0162)
PHONE..............................419 307-7051
Londa Davis, *Pr*
Kevin Davis, *Treas*
EMP: 6 **EST:** 1991
SALES (est): 958.62K **Privately Held**
SIC: 3822 3596 Appliance controls,except air-conditioning and refrigeration; Scales and balances, except laboratory

(G-7792)
KRAFT HEINZ FOODS COMPANY
Also Called: Heinz
1301 N River Rd (43420-9808)
PHONE..............................419 334-5724
EMP: 6
SALES (corp-wide): 26.64B **Publicly Held**
Web: www.kraftheinzcompany.com
SIC: 2033 Catsup: packaged in cans, jars, etc.
HQ: Kraft Heinz Foods Company
1 Ppg Pl Ste 3400
Pittsburgh PA 15222
412 456-5700

(G-7793)
KRAFT HEINZ FOODS COMPANY
Also Called: Quality Assurance
1200n N 5th St (43420-3935)
PHONE..............................419 332-7357
Bob Jurski, *Brnch Mgr*
EMP: 76
SALES (corp-wide): 26.64B **Publicly Held**
Web: www.kraftheinzcompany.com
SIC: 2099 Food preparations, nec
HQ: Kraft Heinz Foods Company
1 Ppg Pl Ste 3400
Pittsburgh PA 15222
412 456-5700

(G-7794)
LESHER PRINTERS INC
810 N Wilson Ave (43420-2271)
P.O. Box 565 (43420-0565)
PHONE..............................419 332-8253
Gary Cool, *Pr*
Emiel J Cool, *CEO*
Gary Cool, *Pr*
EMP: 11 **EST:** 1949
SQ FT: 24,000
SALES (est): 454.27K **Privately Held**
Web: www.lesherprinters.com
SIC: 2752 Offset printing

(G-7795)
LIGHT CRAFT MANUFACTURING INC
Also Called: Light Craft Direct
220 Sullivan Rd (43420-9671)
PHONE..............................419 332-0536
▲ **EMP:** 10 **EST:** 1987
SALES (est): 2.15MM **Privately Held**
Web: www.lightcraftmfg.com
SIC: 3646 Commercial lighting fixtures

(G-7796)
LUDLOW COMPOSITES CORPORATION
Also Called: Crown Mats & Mating
2100 Commerce Dr (43420-1048)
PHONE..............................419 332-5531
Vincent J Dephillips, *Pr*
B Randall Dobbs, *
Joann Northcott, *
Barry Payne, *
Chris Tricozzi, *
◆ **EMP:** 180 **EST:** 1943
SQ FT: 190,000
SALES (est): 24.58MM **Privately Held**
Web: www.ludlow-comp.com
SIC: 3069 3081 Mats or matting, rubber, nec ; Vinyl film and sheet

(G-7797)
MICHIGAN SUGAR COMPANY
1101 N Front St (43420-1922)
PHONE..............................419 332-9931
Mark Flegenheimer, *Mgr*
EMP: 10
SALES (corp-wide): 189.47MM **Privately Held**
Web: www.michigansugar.com
SIC: 2063 Beet sugar
PA: Michigan Sugar Company
122 Uptown Dr Unit 300
Bay City MI 48708
989 686-0161

(G-7798)
O E MEYER CO
1005 Everett Rd (43420-1432)
PHONE..............................419 332-6931
TOLL FREE: 800
Eric Wharton, *Brnch Mgr*
EMP: 8
Web: www.oemeyer.com
SIC: 3548 Welding and cutting apparatus and accessories, nec
PA: O. E. Meyer Co.
3303 Tiffin Ave Ste 1
Sandusky OH 44870

(G-7799)
ORBIS RPM LLC
2100 Cedar St (43420-1008)
PHONE..............................419 355-8310
Jay Neundorfer, *Brnch Mgr*
EMP: 10
SALES (corp-wide): 1.94B **Privately Held**
Web: www.orbiscorporation.com

SIC: 3081 Unsupported plastics film and sheet
HQ: Orbis Rpm, Llc
1055 Corporate Center Dr
Oconomowoc WI 53066
262 560-5000

(G-7800)
PALMER BROS TRANSIT MIX CON
210 N Stone St (43420)
PHONE..................................419 332-6363
Chuck Rapp, Mgr
EMP: 10
SALES (corp-wide): 5.86MM **Privately Held**
SIC: 3273 Ready-mixed concrete
PA: Palmer Bros Transit Mix Concrete Inc
12205 E Gypsy Lane Rd
Bowling Green OH 43402
419 352-4681

(G-7801)
PIXELLE SPCIALTY SOLUTIONS LLC
2275 Commerce Dr (43420-1045)
PHONE..................................419 333-6700
EMP: 221
SALES (corp-wide): 760.06MM **Privately Held**
Web: www.pixelle.com
SIC: 2621 Specialty or chemically treated papers
PA: Pixelle Specialty Solutions Llc
228 S Main St
Spring Grove PA 17362
717 225-4711

(G-7802)
PRAIRIE BUILDERS SUPPLY INC
2114 Hayes Ave (43420-2631)
P.O. Box 592 (43420-0592)
PHONE..................................419 332-7546
Richard A Adams, Pr
Jeffrey Adams, Sec
EMP: 7 EST: 1954
SQ FT: 15,000
SALES (est): 531.46K **Privately Held**
SIC: 5211 3271 Concrete and cinder block; Blocks, concrete or cinder: standard

(G-7803)
PROFESSIONAL SUPPLY INC
Also Called: Worthington Energy Innovations
504 Liberty St (43420-1929)
PHONE..................................419 332-7373
Thomas E Kiser, Pr
Dave Engeman, Treas
EMP: 18 EST: 1979
SQ FT: 9,600
SALES (est): 2.42MM **Privately Held**
Web: www.worldenergyinnovations.com
SIC: 3585 1711 Refrigeration and heating equipment; Plumbing, heating, air-conditioning

(G-7804)
ROOTS MEAT MARKET LLC
3721 W State St (43420-9771)
PHONE..................................419 332-0041
EMP: 23 EST: 2020
SALES (est): 1.48MM **Privately Held**
SIC: 2011 Meat packing plants

(G-7805)
ROOTS POULTRY INC
3721 W State St (43420-9771)
PHONE..................................419 332-0041
Mark Damschroder, CEO
Mike Damschroder, VP
EMP: 14 EST: 1980
SQ FT: 8,000
SALES (est): 1.14MM **Privately Held**
Web: www.rootspoultry.com
SIC: 2015 5144 5499 Chicken, processed: cooked; Poultry and poultry products; Eggs and poultry

(G-7806)
ROWEND INDUSTRIES INC
1035 Napoleon St Ste 101 (43420-2390)
PHONE..................................419 333-8300
Robert Jablonski, Pr
EMP: 8 EST: 2006
SALES (est): 475.88K **Privately Held**
Web: www.rowend.com
SIC: 3999 Barber and beauty shop equipment

(G-7807)
RUSTIC CHEESECAKE LLC
1029 Miller St (43420-2122)
PHONE..................................419 680-6156
Jacob Ollervides, Prin
EMP: 6 EST: 2017
SALES (est): 73.09K **Privately Held**
SIC: 2591 Window blinds

(G-7808)
SANDUSKY TECHNOLOGIES LLC
2107 Hayes Ave (43420-2630)
P.O. Box 1021 (44663-5121)
PHONE..................................419 332-8484
EMP: 8 EST: 2019
SALES (est): 487.68K **Privately Held**
Web: www.techniform-plastics.com
SIC: 3089 Injection molding of plastics

(G-7809)
SEAWIN INC
728 Graham Dr (43420-4073)
PHONE..................................419 355-9111
Prakash Jog, Pr
EMP: 49 EST: 1991
SALES (est): 609.68K
SALES (corp-wide): 27.26MM **Privately Held**
SIC: 3491 Industrial valves
PA: Alkon Corporation
728 Graham Dr
Fremont OH 43420
419 355-9111

(G-7810)
STANDARD TECHNOLOGIES LLC
Also Called: Standard Technologies
2641 Hayes Ave (43420-9715)
PHONE..................................419 332-6434
Max Valentine, Pr
EMP: 75 EST: 1916
SQ FT: 35,000
SALES (est): 16.89MM **Privately Held**
Web: www.standardtechn.com
SIC: 3444 Sheet metalwork

(G-7811)
STYLE CREST ENTERPRISES INC (PA)
2450 Enterprise St (43420)
P.O. Box A (43420)
PHONE..................................419 355-8586
Thomas L Kern, CEO
Phillip Burton, Pr
Henry Valle, *
Bryan T Kern, Operations*
Tyrone G Frantz, *
EMP: 58 EST: 1996
SQ FT: 40,000
SALES (est): 167.61MM
SALES (corp-wide): 167.61MM **Privately Held**
Web: www.stylecrestinc.com

SIC: 3089 5075 Plastics hardware and building products; Warm air heating and air conditioning

(G-7812)
THE FREMONT KRAUT COMPANY
724 N Front St (43420-1915)
PHONE..................................419 332-6481
Russell G Sorg, Pr
Orland H Hasselbach, General Vice President
Richard L Smith, *
Jan Sorg, Sec
EMP: 36 EST: 1906
SALES (est): 551.45K
SALES (corp-wide): 51.18MM **Privately Held**
Web: www.fremontcompany.com
SIC: 2033 Canned fruits and specialties
PA: The Fremont Company
802 N Front St
Fremont OH 43420
419 334-8995

(G-7813)
THE LOUIS G FREEMAN COMPANY LLC (DH)
Also Called: Freeman
911 Graham Dr (43420-4086)
PHONE..................................419 334-9709
▲ EMP: 60 EST: 1892
SALES (est): 12.22MM **Privately Held**
Web: www.brownmachinegroup.com
SIC: 3544 Special dies and tools
HQ: Brown Machine Group Intermediate Holdings, Inc.
330 N Ross St
Beaverton MI 48612
989 435-7741

(G-7814)
THERMO KING CORPORATION
Also Called: Thermo King Corporation
1750 E State St (43420-4056)
PHONE..................................567 280-9243
EMP: 7
Web: www.thermoking.com
SIC: 3823 Temperature measurement instruments, industrial
HQ: Thermo King Llc
314 W 90th St
Bloomington MN 55420
952 887-2200

(G-7815)
TI INC
2107 Hayes Ave (43420)
PHONE..................................419 332-8484
Clifford A Robinette, Pr
EMP: 30 EST: 1972
SQ FT: 16,000
SALES (est): 4.29MM **Privately Held**
Web: www.techniform-plastics.com
SIC: 3083 3599 Thermoplastics laminates: rods, tubes, plates, and sheet; Custom machinery

(G-7816)
UNILOY CENTURY LLC
215 N Stone St (43420-1505)
PHONE..................................419 332-2693
Scott Murphy, Brnch Mgr
EMP: 65
SALES (corp-wide): 103MM **Privately Held**
SIC: 2821 Molding compounds, plastics
HQ: Uniloy Century, Llc
5550 S Occidental Rd
Tecumseh MI 49286
517 424-8900

(G-7817)
UNIQUE FABRICATIONS INC
2520 Hayes Ave (43420)
PHONE..................................419 355-1700
Karl Skip Honsperger, Pr
Anthony Wayne Doble, VP
Madeline Doble, Sec
Ellen Honsperger, Treas
EMP: 17 EST: 1988
SQ FT: 12,000
SALES (est): 4.94MM **Privately Held**
Web: www.uniquefabinc.com
SIC: 3441 Building components, structural steel

(G-7818)
VALLEY ELECTRIC COMPANY
432 N Wood St (43420-2561)
PHONE..................................419 332-6405
Cynthia Auxter, Pr
Margaret Hoffman, VP
EMP: 6 EST: 1957
SALES (est): 994.71K **Privately Held**
Web: valley-electric-co.business.site
SIC: 1731 3679 General electrical contractor ; Electronic circuits

(G-7819)
WAHL REFRACTORY SOLUTIONS LLC (PA)
Also Called: Wahl
767 S State Route 19 (43420-9260)
PHONE..................................419 334-2658
Timothy M Albertson, Pr
Sarah Herman, *
◆ EMP: 64 EST: 2006
SALES (est): 11.04MM **Privately Held**
Web: www.wahlref.com
SIC: 3297 3255 Nonclay refractories; Mortars, clay refractory

(G-7820)
WOODBRIDGE GROUP
Also Called: Woodbridge
827 Graham Dr (43420-4075)
PHONE..................................419 334-3666
Mike Kohout, Mgr
EMP: 150
SALES (corp-wide): 10.66B **Publicly Held**
Web: www.woodbridgegroup.com
SIC: 3069 3714 Hard rubber and molded rubber products; Motor vehicle parts and accessories
HQ: The Woodbridge Company Limited
2400-65 Queen St W
Toronto ON M5H 2
416 364-8700

Fresno
Coshocton County

(G-7821)
BORDER LUMBER & LOGGING LTD
31181 County Road 10 (43824-9503)
PHONE..................................330 897-0177
John Hershberger, Prin
EMP: 8 EST: 2007
SALES (est): 125.68K **Privately Held**
SIC: 2411 Logging camps and contractors

(G-7822)
CF TOOLS LLC
52025 Township Road 509 (43824-9420)
PHONE..................................740 294-0419
Clinton Frye, Prin
EMP: 6 EST: 2015
SALES (est): 108.47K **Privately Held**
SIC: 3599 Industrial machinery, nec

Fresno - Coshocton County (G-7823) GEOGRAPHIC SECTION

(G-7823)
PEARL VALLEY CHEESE INC
54760 Township Road 90 (43824-9796)
P.O. Box 68 (43824-0068)
PHONE....................740 545-6002
W Charles Ellis, *Pr*
John E Stalder, *Pr*
Sally Ellis, *Sec*
EMP: 20 **EST:** 1928
SQ FT: 8,000
SALES (est): 3.82MM **Privately Held**
Web: www.pearlvalleycheese.com
SIC: 2022 Natural cheese

(G-7824)
PENWOOD MFG
30505 Township Road 212 (43824)
PHONE....................330 359-5600
Paul Nisley, *Owner*
EMP: 6 **EST:** 1999
SALES (est): 340.54K **Privately Held**
Web: www.penwoodbrands.com
SIC: 2511 Wood household furniture

(G-7825)
SUPERFINE MANUFACTURING INC
33715 County Road 10 (43824-9018)
PHONE....................330 897-9024
Dan Miller, *Prin*
EMP: 10 **EST:** 2000
SALES (est): 980.99K **Privately Held**
Web: www.superfineinc.com
SIC: 3599 Machine shop, jobbing and repair

(G-7826)
TJ OIL & GAS INC
27353 State Route 621 (43824-9747)
PHONE....................740 623-0190
EMP: 7 **EST:** 2011
SALES (est): 369.13K **Privately Held**
SIC: 1389 Construction, repair, and dismantling services

(G-7827)
TROYERS PALLET SHOP
31052 Township Road 227 (43824-8801)
PHONE....................330 897-1038
Atlee Troyer, *Owner*
EMP: 6 **EST:** 2001
SALES (est): 109.09K **Privately Held**
SIC: 2448 Pallets, wood and wood with metal

Gahanna
Franklin County

(G-7828)
ADB SAFEGATE AMERICAS LLC
Also Called: ADB
700 Science Blvd (43230-6641)
P.O. Box 30829 (43230-0829)
PHONE....................614 861-1304
Joe Pokoj, *Managing Member*
Michael Morrow, *
Gary Roser, *
◆ **EMP:** 220 **EST:** 2009
SALES (est): 87.13MM
SALES (corp-wide): 842.76K **Privately Held**
Web: www.adbsafegate.com
SIC: 3648 3812 Airport lighting fixtures: runway approach, taxi, or ramp; Search and navigation equipment
HQ: Adb Safegate
Leuvensesteenweg 585
Zaventem VBR 1930
27221711

(G-7829)
ADVANCED PLASTIC SYSTEMS INC
990 Gahanna Pkwy (43230-6613)
PHONE....................614 759-6550
Wolfgang Doerschlag, *Pr*
EMP: 17 **EST:** 1998
SQ FT: 25,000
SALES (est): 2.43MM **Privately Held**
Web: www.advancedplasticsystems.com
SIC: 3089 Injection molding of plastics

(G-7830)
ARCHITCTRAL IDENTIFICATION INC (PA)
1170 Claycraft Rd (43230-6640)
PHONE....................614 868-8400
William J Cooke, *Pr*
Barbara B Cooke, *Sec*
James W Cooke C O O, *Prin*
Robert C Barnhart Junior, *VP*
EMP: 18 **EST:** 1971
SQ FT: 5,000
SALES (est): 2.81MM
SALES (corp-wide): 2.81MM **Privately Held**
Web: www.archid.net
SIC: 8748 3993 Systems analysis or design; Electric signs

(G-7831)
BENCHMARK SHIELD LLC
950 Claycraft Rd (43230-6634)
PHONE....................614 695-6500
Mary P Walling, *Managing Member*
EMP: 9 **EST:** 2020
SALES (est): 388.56K **Privately Held**
Web: www.benchmarkinc.com
SIC: 3842 Personal safety equipment

(G-7832)
CDSS INC
Also Called: Embroidme
950 Taylor Station Rd Ste U (43230-6670)
PHONE....................614 626-8747
EMP: 8 **EST:** 2006
SALES (est): 408.56K **Privately Held**
Web: www.fullypromoted.com
SIC: 2395 Embroidery and art needlework

(G-7833)
DEEMSYS INC (PA)
800 Cross Pointe Rd Ste A (43230-6687)
PHONE....................614 322-9928
Vijiayarani Benjamin, *Ch Bd*
Jacob Benjamin, *
Dexter Benjamin, *
EMP: 52 **EST:** 2002
SQ FT: 5,100
SALES (est): 4.55MM
SALES (corp-wide): 4.55MM **Privately Held**
Web: www.deemsysinc.com
SIC: 8748 2741 7373 8299 Business consulting, nec; Internet publishing and broadcasting; Systems software development services; Educational service, nondegree granting: continuing educ.

(G-7834)
DIVERSITY-VUTEQ LLC
1015 Taylor Rd (43230-6202)
PHONE....................614 490-5034
EMP: 8 **EST:** 2015
SALES (est): 424.39K **Privately Held**
SIC: 3089 Plastics products, nec

(G-7835)
EXIDE TECHNOLOGIES LLC
861 Taylor Rd Unit G (43230-6275)
PHONE....................614 863-3866
Mark Patterson, *Mgr*
EMP: 7
SALES (corp-wide): 2.06B **Privately Held**
Web: www.exide.com
SIC: 5013 3629 Automotive batteries; Battery chargers, rectifying or nonrotating
PA: Exide Technologies, Llc
13000 Drfeld Pkwy Bldg 20
Milton GA 30004
678 566-9000

(G-7836)
GLOBAL REALMS LLC
81 Mill St Ste 300 (43230-1718)
PHONE....................614 828-7284
Devin Randolph, *Managing Member*
EMP: 6 **EST:** 2017
SALES (est): 366.99K **Privately Held**
Web: www.globalrealms.com
SIC: 8731 7371 3571 Computer (hardware) development; Computer software development; Electronic computers

(G-7837)
HEAT TREATING INC
675 Cross Pointe Rd (43230-6689)
PHONE....................614 759-9963
Rod Ingram, *VP*
EMP: 11 **EST:** 2009
SALES (est): 586.2K **Privately Held**
Web: www.heattreatinginc.com
SIC: 3398 Metal heat treating

(G-7838)
HOLLYWOOD IMPRINTS LLC
1000 Morrison Rd Ste D (43230-6669)
PHONE....................614 501-6040
EMP: 14 **EST:** 2006
SALES (est): 1.05MM **Privately Held**
Web: www.hollywoodimprints.com
SIC: 7336 2396 7319 Silk screen design; Fabric printing and stamping; Poster advertising service, except outdoor

(G-7839)
K PETROLEUM INC (PA)
905 Creekside Plz (43230-1718)
PHONE....................614 532-5420
Jam Khorrami, *Pr*
EMP: 10 **EST:** 1984
SQ FT: 3,000
SALES (est): 1.74MM
SALES (corp-wide): 1.74MM **Privately Held**
SIC: 1382 Oil and gas exploration services

(G-7840)
KAHIKI FOODS INC
Also Called: Kahiki
1100 Morrison Rd (43230)
PHONE....................614 322-3180
Alan L Hoover, *Pr*
Tim Tsao, *Marketing**
Frederick A Niebauer, *
▲ **EMP:** 160 **EST:** 1982
SQ FT: 119,000
SALES (est): 55.46MM **Privately Held**
Web: www.kahiki.com
SIC: 2038 Frozen specialties, nec
PA: Cj Corporation
12 Sowol-Ro 2-Gil, Jung-Gu
Seoul 04867

(G-7841)
KIC LTD
1129 Brookhouse Ln (43230-1973)
PHONE....................614 775-9570
Ian Downes, *Owner*
EMP: 7 **EST:** 2010
SALES (est): 99.63K **Privately Held**

SIC: 3714 Motor vehicle parts and accessories

(G-7842)
KONECRANES INC
1110 Claycraft Rd Ste C (43230-6630)
PHONE....................614 863-0150
Ashley Easter, *Mgr*
EMP: 27
Web: www.konecranes.com
SIC: 3536 Hoists, cranes, and monorails
HQ: Konecranes, Inc.
4401 Gateway Blvd
Springfield OH 45502

(G-7843)
LA BOIT SPECIALTY VEHICLES
700 Cross Pointe Rd (43230-6685)
PHONE....................614 231-7640
Gil Blais, *Pr*
Anne Blais, *Treas*
Samson Cheng, *
Ryan Depriest, *
EMP: 70 **EST:** 1980
SQ FT: 18,000
SALES (est): 10.88MM **Privately Held**
Web: www.laboit.com
SIC: 3711 3713 Ambulances (motor vehicles), assembly of; Ambulance bodies

(G-7844)
MCNEILUS TRUCK AND MFG INC
1130 Morrison Rd (43230-6646)
P.O. Box 30777 (43230-0777)
PHONE....................614 868-0760
Paul Ellingen, *Mgr*
EMP: 6
SALES (corp-wide): 9.66B **Publicly Held**
Web: www.mcneilusgarbagetrucks.com
SIC: 3713 5082 Cement mixer bodies; Concrete processing equipment
HQ: Mcneilus Truck And Manufacturing, Inc.
524 E Highway St
Dodge Center MN 55927
507 374-6321

(G-7845)
MIDDLETON PRINTING CO INC
81 Mill St Ste 300 (43230-1718)
PHONE....................614 294-7277
David H Stewart, *Pr*
Reno Camerucci, *VP*
EMP: 9 **EST:** 1950
SQ FT: 14,000
SALES (est): 813.83K **Privately Held**
Web: www.middletonprinting.com
SIC: 2752 2791 2759 Offset printing; Typesetting; Commercial printing, nec

(G-7846)
NIAGARA BOTTLING LLC
1700 Eastgate Pkwy (43230-8602)
PHONE....................614 751-7420
▲ **EMP:** 7
SALES (corp-wide): 120MM **Privately Held**
Web: www.niagarawater.com
SIC: 2086 Bottled and canned soft drinks
PA: Niagara Bottling, Llc
1440 Bridgegate Dr
Diamond Bar CA 91765
909 230-5000

(G-7847)
OCSIAL LLC (PA)
950 Taylor Station Rd Ste W (43230-6671)
PHONE....................415 906-5271
Yuri Koropachinsky, *Pr*
Peter Cuneo, *Ch Bd*
EMP: 11 **EST:** 2014
SALES (est): 4.94MM

SALES (corp-wide): 4.94MM **Privately Held**
Web: www.ocsial.com
SIC: 3624 Carbon and graphite products

(G-7848)
RIBBON TECHNOLOGY CORPORATION
Also Called: Ribtec
825 Taylor Station Rd (43230-6654)
P.O. Box 30758 (43230-0758)
PHONE..................................614 864-5444
Kevin Jackson, Pr
Scott Palmer, Sec
◆ EMP: 11 EST: 1971
SQ FT: 40,000
SALES (est): 5.54MM
SALES (corp-wide): 4.29MM **Privately Held**
Web: www.ribtec.com
SIC: 3357 Building wire and cable, nonferrous
HQ: Dynamic-Materials Limited
    Brookhill Industrial Estate
    Nottingham NOTTS NG16
    177 386-3100

(G-7849)
SNOW AVIATION INTL INC
949 Creek Dr (43230)
PHONE..................................614 588-2452
Harry T Snow, Pr
Bill Fergusson, *
Donald Smith, *
Richard Heybes, *
EMP: 20 EST: 1987
SQ FT: 28,000
SALES (est): 1.1MM **Privately Held**
SIC: 3721 3728 3724 Aircraft; Aircraft assemblies, subassemblies, and parts, nec; Aircraft engines and engine parts

(G-7850)
SUBURBAN STEEL SUPPLY CO LIMITED PARTNERSHIP (PA)
1900 Deffenbaugh Ct (43230-8604)
PHONE..................................614 737-5501
EMP: 65 EST: 1979
SALES (est): 9.66MM
SALES (corp-wide): 9.66MM **Privately Held**
Web: www.suburbansteelsupply.com
SIC: 3312 3498 3441 Sheet or strip, steel, cold-rolled: own hot-rolled; Fabricated pipe and fittings; Fabricated structural metal

(G-7851)
SURPLUS FREIGHT INC (PA)
501 Morrison Rd Ste 100 (43230-3541)
PHONE..................................614 235-7660
EMP: 7 EST: 2000
SALES (est): 5.48MM **Privately Held**
Web: www.surplusfurniture.com
SIC: 3537 Trucks: freight, baggage, etc.: industrial, except mining

(G-7852)
VICTORY DIRECT LLC
750 Cross Pointe Rd Ste M (43230-6692)
PHONE..................................614 626-0000
Joe King, Managing Member
EMP: 7 EST: 2008
SALES (est): 495.85K **Privately Held**
Web: www.victory-direct.com
SIC: 7331 2752 Mailing service; Business form and card printing, lithographic

Galena
Delaware County

(G-7853)
DITTY PRINTING LLC
6306 Crystal Valley Dr (43021-9588)
PHONE..................................614 893-7439
Brian Ditty, Owner
EMP: 6 EST: 2016
SALES (est): 336.07K **Privately Held**
Web: www.dittyprinting.com
SIC: 2752 Commercial printing, lithographic

(G-7854)
GALENA VAULT LTD
4909 Harlem Rd (43021-9302)
PHONE..................................740 965-2200
Marcia Jo M Eisenbrown, Owner
EMP: 6 EST: 2014
SALES (est): 121.88K **Privately Held**
Web: www.galenaohio.gov
SIC: 3272 Burial vaults, concrete or precast terrazzo

(G-7855)
K-O-K PRODUCTS INC
700 S 3 Bs And K Rd (43021-9725)
PHONE..................................740 548-0526
EMP: 15
Web: www.kokproducts.com
SIC: 2842 5087 Bleaches, household: dry or liquid; Service establishment equipment

(G-7856)
WAVEFLEX INC
5480 Roesland Dr (43021-9770)
PHONE..................................740 513-1334
Shawn Flannery, Pr
Jeremiah Friend, VP
EMP: 8 EST: 2017
SALES (est): 88.38K **Privately Held**
Web: www.wave-flex.com
SIC: 3669 Intercommunication systems, electric

Galion
Crawford County

(G-7857)
A & G MANUFACTURING CO INC
165 Gelsanliter Rd (44833)
PHONE..................................419 468-7433
Arvin Shifley, Brnch Mgr
EMP: 17
SALES (corp-wide): 9.98MM **Privately Held**
Web: www.agmercury.com
SIC: 3599 Machine shop, jobbing and repair
PA: A. & G. Manufacturing Co., Inc.
    280 Gelsanliter Rd
    Galion OH 44833
    419 468-7433

(G-7858)
A & G MANUFACTURING CO INC (PA)
Also Called: A G Mercury
280 Gelsanliter Rd (44833-2234)
P.O. Box 935 (44833-0935)
PHONE..................................419 468-7433
Arvin Shifley, Pr
Doug Shifley, *
Glen E Shifley Junior, Sec
Glen Shifley Senior, Prin
▲ EMP: 40 EST: 1970
SQ FT: 100,000
SALES (est): 9.98MM
SALES (corp-wide): 9.98MM **Privately Held**
Web: www.agmercury.com
SIC: 3599 7692 3446 3444 Machine shop, jobbing and repair; Welding repair; Architectural metalwork; Sheet metalwork

(G-7859)
ALEXANDER WILBERT VAULT CO (PA)
1263 State Hwy 598 (44833)
P.O. Box 177 (44833-0177)
PHONE..................................419 468-3477
C Phillip Longstreth, Pr
Sean Longstreth, VP
EMP: 9 EST: 1950
SALES (est): 884.15K
SALES (corp-wide): 884.15K **Privately Held**
Web: www.longstrethmemorials.com
SIC: 3272 Burial vaults, concrete or precast terrazzo

(G-7860)
AMERICAN STEEL GRAVE VAULT CO
799 Newberry Dr (44833-1146)
PHONE..................................419 468-6715
Brent Kingseed, Pr
Al Kingseed, VP
Mary Kingseed, Sec
EMP: 10 EST: 1908
SQ FT: 46,300
SALES (est): 457.99K **Privately Held**
Web: www.goibc.com
SIC: 3995 Grave vaults, metal

(G-7861)
BAILLIE LUMBER CO LP
3953 County Road 51 (44833-9630)
PHONE..................................419 462-2000
Russel Jones, Brnch Mgr
EMP: 40
SALES (corp-wide): 595.03MM **Privately Held**
Web: www.baillie.com
SIC: 5031 2426 2421 Lumber: rough, dressed, and finished; Hardwood dimension and flooring mills; Sawmills and planing mills, general
PA: Baillie Lumber Co., L.P.
    4002 Legion Dr
    Hamburg NY 14075
    800 950-2850

(G-7862)
BROTHERS BODY AND EQP LLC
352 South St Door 26 (44833)
P.O. Box 926 (44833-0926)
PHONE..................................419 462-1975
▲ EMP: 15 EST: 2006
SQ FT: 30,000
SALES (est): 1.7MM **Privately Held**
Web: www.brothersbande.com
SIC: 3713 Truck bodies and parts

(G-7863)
CASS FRAMES INC
6052 State Route 19 (44833-9771)
P.O. Box 625 (44833-0625)
PHONE..................................419 468-2863
James Cass, Pr
Bart Cass, VP
Delores Cass, Sec
EMP: 9 EST: 1990
SQ FT: 4,200
SALES (est): 940.18K **Privately Held**
SIC: 2499 Picture and mirror frames, wood

(G-7864)
CASS WOODWORKING INC
Also Called: Cass Woodworking
6052 State Route 19 (44833-9771)
P.O. Box 625 (44833-0625)
PHONE..................................800 589-8841
TOLL FREE: 800
James Cass, Pr
Brad Cass, VP
Delores J Cass, Sec
EMP: 10 EST: 1930
SQ FT: 7,500
SALES (est): 465.59K **Privately Held**
Web: www.casswoodinc.com
SIC: 2434 Wood kitchen cabinets

(G-7865)
CENTRAL STATE ENTERPRISES INC
1331 Freese Works Pl (Galion Indl Pk) (44833-9368)
PHONE..................................419 468-8191
Donald E Kuenzli Junior, Pr
Sandra Kuenzli, *
EMP: 37 EST: 1982
SQ FT: 28,000
SALES (est): 4.55MM **Privately Held**
Web: www.centralstateent.net
SIC: 3599 Machine shop, jobbing and repair

(G-7866)
CMI HOLDING COMPANY CRAWFORD
Also Called: CMI
1310 Freese Works Pl (44833-9368)
PHONE..................................419 468-9122
Kevin Hessey, Pr
Joy Hessey, *
Tonya Hoepf Cust Serv Prcng, Mgr
Keith Hummel, *
Brad Hessey, Acting Vice President*
◆ EMP: 70 EST: 2000
SALES (est): 11MM
SALES (corp-wide): 110MM **Privately Held**
SIC: 3714 Motor vehicle parts and accessories
HQ: Tramec Sloan, L.L.C.
    534 E 48th St
    Holland MI 49423
    800 336-7778

(G-7867)
COVERT MANUFACTURING INC
303 E Parson St (44833-3304)
PHONE..................................419 468-1761
EMP: 15
SALES (corp-wide): 44.67MM **Privately Held**
Web: www.covertmfg.com
SIC: 3599 Machine and other job shop work
PA: Covert Manufacturing, Inc.
    328 S East St
    Galion OH 44833
    419 468-1761

(G-7868)
COVERT MANUFACTURING INC (PA)
Also Called: Covert
328 S East St (44833-2729)
P.O. Box 608 (44833-0608)
PHONE..................................419 468-1761
Donald L Covert Senior, CEO
Kym Fox, *
Teri Williams, *
Donna Morrow, *
▲ EMP: 255 EST: 1971
SQ FT: 300,000
SALES (est): 44.67MM
SALES (corp-wide): 44.67MM **Privately Held**
Web: www.covertmfg.com
SIC: 3545 Machine tool accessories

Galion - Crawford County (G-7869)

(G-7869)
CRASE COMMUNICATIONS INC
120 Harding Way E Ste 104 (44833-1927)
PHONE..............................419 468-1173
Edward Crase, *Pr*
Linda Crase, *Sec*
EMP: 18 **EST:** 1986
SALES (est): 850.42K **Privately Held**
Web: www.crasecommunications.com
SIC: 1731 3661 Telephone and telephone equipment installation; Toll switching equipment, telephone

(G-7870)
DYENAMO DISTRIBUTING LLC
6124 State Route 19 (44833-8931)
P.O. Box 759 (44833-0759)
PHONE..............................419 462-9474
Ken Dye, *Owner*
EMP: 8 **EST:** 1993
SALES (est): 433.99K **Privately Held**
Web: www.tamaraheeierycompany.com
SIC: 2759 Promotional printing

(G-7871)
E & E NAMEPLATES INC
760 E Walnut St (44833-2133)
P.O. Box 756 (44833-0756)
PHONE..............................419 468-3617
EMP: 6 **EST:** 1976
SQ FT: 4,500
SALES (est): 264.13K **Privately Held**
Web: www.eenameplates.com
SIC: 2759 Screen printing

(G-7872)
EAGLE CRUSHER CO INC (PA)
525 S Market St (44833-2612)
P.O. Box 537 (44833-0537)
PHONE..............................419 468-2288
Susanne Cobey, *CEO*
Michael Tinkey, *
♦ **EMP:** 75 **EST:** 1915
SQ FT: 40,000
SALES (est): 39.86MM
SALES (corp-wide): 39.86MM **Privately Held**
Web: www.eaglecrusher.com
SIC: 3535 3532 3589 3531 Conveyors and conveying equipment; Crushing, pulverizing, and screening equipment; Sewage and water treatment equipment; Construction machinery

(G-7873)
ECLIPSE
126 N Union St (44833-1736)
PHONE..............................419 564-7482
Teresa Harris, *Prin*
EMP: 6 **EST:** 2016
SALES (est): 191.62K **Privately Held**
Web: www.eclipsecorp.us
SIC: 7372 Prepackaged software

(G-7874)
ELLIOTT MACHINE WORKS INC
1351 Freese Works Pl (44833-9368)
PHONE..............................419 468-4709
Richard Ekin, *Pr*
Brad Ekin, *
Brent Ekin, *
EMP: 48 **EST:** 1968
SQ FT: 54,000
SALES (est): 8.62MM **Privately Held**
Web: www.elliottmachine.com
SIC: 3713 3443 3537 Truck bodies (motor vehicles); Tanks for tank trucks, metal plate; Trucks: freight, baggage, etc.: industrial, except mining

(G-7875)
GALION LLC
515 N East St (44833)
P.O. Box 447 (44833)
PHONE..............................419 468-5214
EMP: 105 **EST:** 1994
SQ FT: 60,000
SALES (est): 21.94MM **Privately Held**
Web: www.galionllc.com
SIC: 3482 3444 Small arms ammunition; Sheet metalwork

(G-7876)
GALION CANVAS PRODUCTS (PA)
385 S Market St (44833-2608)
PHONE..............................419 468-5333
TOLL FREE: 800
Steve Siclair, *Owner*
Scott Goldsmith, *Prin*
EMP: 6 **EST:** 1958
SQ FT: 5,000
SALES (est): 785.43K
SALES (corp-wide): 785.43K **Privately Held**
Web: galioncanvasproducts.wordpress.com
SIC: 7359 2394 Tent and tarpaulin rental; Canvas and related products

(G-7877)
GEN-RUBBER LLC
352 South St (44833-2742)
P.O. Box 805 (44258-0805)
PHONE..............................440 655-3643
EMP: 6 **EST:** 2008
SALES (est): 645.32K **Privately Held**
Web: www.rubber-master.com
SIC: 3069 Custom compounding of rubber materials

(G-7878)
GLEDHILL ROAD MACHINERY CO
765 Portland Way S (44833)
P.O. Box P.O. Box 567 (44833)
PHONE..............................419 468-4400
Michael D Rarick, *Pr*
Garland Gledhill, *
Sherrie Dill, *
EMP: 50 **EST:** 1930
SQ FT: 57,000
SALES (est): 8.88MM **Privately Held**
Web: www.gledhillonline.com
SIC: 3531 Road construction and maintenance machinery

(G-7879)
GLEN-GERY CORPORATION
3785 Cardington Iberia Rd (44833-9101)
PHONE..............................419 468-4890
Joe Wishan, *Brnch Mgr*
EMP: 19
Web: www.glengery.com
SIC: 3251 Brick and structural clay tile
HQ: Glen-Gery Corporation
1166 Spring St
Reading PA 19610
610 374-4011

(G-7880)
HYDRANAMICS INC
Also Called: Hydranamics Div Carter Mch Co
820 Edward St (44833-2223)
PHONE..............................419 468-3530
Juanita Carter, *Ch*
Andrea Carter, *
EMP: 87 **EST:** 1941
SALES (est): 504.51K
SALES (corp-wide): 9.8MM **Privately Held**
Web: www.hydranamics.com

SIC: 3593 3547 Fluid power cylinders, hydraulic or pneumatic; Rolling mill machinery
PA: Carter Machine Company, Inc.
820 Edward St
Galion OH 44833
419 468-3530

(G-7881)
JUST PLASTICS INC
869 Smith St (44833-2761)
P.O. Box 645 (44833-0645)
PHONE..............................419 468-5506
Steve Eckstein, *Pr*
Judy Eckstein, *
EMP: 15 **EST:** 1986
SQ FT: 11,000
SALES (est): 630.49K **Privately Held**
SIC: 3089 Injection molding of plastics

(G-7882)
OTTERBACHER TRAILERS LLC
352 South St (44833-2742)
P.O. Box 129 (44827-0129)
PHONE..............................419 462-1975
EMP: 10 **EST:** 2002
SALES (est): 610K **Privately Held**
Web: www.brothersbande.com
SIC: 3799 Trailers and trailer equipment

(G-7883)
PRINTS & PAINTS FLR CVG CO INC
Also Called: My Floors By Prints and Paints
888 Bucyrus Rd (44833-1549)
PHONE..............................419 462-5663
Gary Frankhouse Senior, *Pr*
Sandra Frankhouse, *Ex VP*
Gary Frankhose Junior, *Treas*
Steve Frankhouse, *Sec*
EMP: 23 **EST:** 1977
SQ FT: 14,000
SALES (est): 2.12MM **Privately Held**
Web: www.myfloorsohiofa.com
SIC: 5231 2295 1743 5713 Paint; Laminating of fabrics; Tile installation, ceramic; Carpets

(G-7884)
SCHILLING GRAPHICS INC (PA)
275 Gelsanliter Rd (44833-2235)
P.O. Box 978 (44833-0978)
PHONE..............................419 468-1037
TOLL FREE: 800
Douglas Schilling, *Pr*
EMP: 33 **EST:** 1963
SQ FT: 20,000
SALES (est): 7.03MM
SALES (corp-wide): 7.03MM **Privately Held**
Web: www.schillinginc.com
SIC: 2752 3552 3555 2759 Decals, lithographed; Silk screens for textile industry; Printing trades machinery; Commercial printing, nec

(G-7885)
STARKEY MACHINERY INC
254 S Washington St (44833-2616)
P.O. Box 207 (44833-0207)
PHONE..............................419 468-2560
James D Starkey, *Pr*
Don Starkey, *VP*
EMP: 20 **EST:** 1881
SQ FT: 30,000
SALES (est): 2.48MM **Privately Held**
Web: www.starkeymachinery.com
SIC: 3559 5084 3594 3544 Clay working and tempering machines; Industrial machinery and equipment; Fluid power pumps and motors; Special dies, tools, jigs, and fixtures

(G-7886)
URBAN INDUSTRIES OF OHIO INC
Also Called: Urban Industries
525 King Ave (44833-1850)
P.O. Box 27 (44833-0027)
PHONE..............................419 468-3578
▲ **EMP:** 25 **EST:** 1947
SALES (est): 4.88MM **Privately Held**
Web: www.urbanindustries.com
SIC: 3446 3354 7389 1531 Architectural metalwork; Aluminum extruded products; Laminating service

(G-7887)
VULCAN PRODUCTS CO INC
208 S Washington St (44833-2616)
P.O. Box 216 (44833-0216)
PHONE..............................419 468-1039
Ralph Chamberlin, *Pr*
EMP: 16 **EST:** 1951
SALES (est): 494.56K **Privately Held**
Web: www.vulcanproducts.net
SIC: 3451 Screw machine products

Gallipolis
Gallia County

(G-7888)
BCMR PUBLICATIONS LLC
430 2nd Ave (45631-1130)
PHONE..............................740 441-7778
Christopher Rathburn, *Admn*
EMP: 9 **EST:** 2009
SQ FT: 2,080
SALES (est): 418.82K **Privately Held**
Web: www.bcmrpromo.com
SIC: 2741 Miscellaneous publishing

(G-7889)
BIG RIVER ELECTRIC INC
Also Called: Big River Electric
299 Upper River Rd (45631-1838)
P.O. Box 244 (45631-0244)
PHONE..............................740 446-4360
Kelly Counts, *Pr*
Geraldine Counts, *VP*
Debra Barcus, *Sec*
EMP: 6 **EST:** 1983
SQ FT: 8,500
SALES (est): 1MM **Privately Held**
Web: www.bigriverelec.com
SIC: 5999 7694 5063 Motors, electric; Electric motor repair; Motors, electric

(G-7890)
ELECTROCRAFT ARKANSAS INC
250 Mccormick Rd (45631-8745)
PHONE..............................501 268-4203
James Elsner, *CEO*
John Arico, *
Logan D Delany Junior, *Ch Bd*
▲ **EMP:** 56 **EST:** 2001
SQ FT: 50,000
SALES (est): 4.28MM **Privately Held**
Web: www.electrocraft.com
SIC: 3621 Electric motor and generator parts
HQ: Electrocraft, Inc.
2 Marin Way Ste 3
Stratham NH 03885

(G-7891)
ELECTROCRAFT OHIO INC
250 Mccormick Rd (45631-8745)
PHONE..............................740 441-6200
James Elsner, *Pr*
Mike Karsonovich, *Pr*
John Arico, *VP Fin*
Logan D Delany Junior, *Prin*
▲ **EMP:** 225 **EST:** 2002

SQ FT: 160,000
SALES (est): 46.85MM **Privately Held**
Web: www.electrocraft.com
SIC: 3625 Relays and industrial controls
HQ: Electrocraft, Inc.
  2 Marin Way Ste 3
  Stratham NH 03885

(G-7892)
FREEDOM HOMES
208 Upper River Rd (45631-1856)
PHONE...................................740 446-3093
EMP: 6 EST: 2018
SALES (est): 144.89K **Privately Held**
Web: www.freedomhomesohio.com
SIC: 2451 Mobile homes

(G-7893)
GKN PLC
Also Called: GKN Sinter Metals
2160 Eastern Ave (45631-1823)
PHONE...................................740 446-9211
Daniel Swannigan, *Brnch Mgr*
EMP: 9
SALES (corp-wide): 4.18B **Privately Held**
Web: www.gknaerospace.com
SIC: 3462 Iron and steel forgings
HQ: Gkn Limited
  2nd Floor, One Central Boulevard
  Solihull W MIDLANDS B90 8
  121 210-9800

(G-7894)
GKN SINTER METALS LLC
Also Called: Precision Forged Products
2160 Eastern Ave (45631-1823)
PHONE...................................740 441-3203
Greg Landis, *Brnch Mgr*
EMP: 139
SALES (corp-wide): 4.18B **Privately Held**
Web: www.gknpm.com
SIC: 3312 3568 3462 Sinter, iron; Power transmission equipment, nec; Iron and steel forgings
HQ: Gkn Sinter Metals, Llc
  1670 Opdyke Ct
  Auburn Hills MI 48326
  248 883-4500

(G-7895)
JM LOGGING INC
1624 Graham School Rd (45631-8002)
PHONE...................................740 441-0941
J M Clagg, *Owner*
EMP: 7 EST: 2010
SALES (est): 139.25K **Privately Held**
SIC: 2411 Logging camps and contractors

(G-7896)
KING KUTTER II INC
Also Called: Sfs Truck Sales & Parts
2150 Eastern Ave (45631)
P.O. Box 786 (45631)
PHONE...................................740 446-0351
James Phillip Fraley, *Pr*
Jeff Fraley, *
Deborah Swain, *
▲ EMP: 50 EST: 1982
SQ FT: 160
SALES (est): 23.24MM **Privately Held**
Web: www.kingkutter2.com
SIC: 5521 3713 Trucks, tractors, and trailers: used; Truck and bus bodies

(G-7897)
O-KAN MARINE REPAIR INC
267 Upper River Rd (45631-1838)
PHONE...................................740 446-4686
Tanya Wells, *Mgr*
Chris Preston, *Pr*
Jay Hall Junior, *VP*

Penny Preston, *Sec*
Sandra Neal, *Treas*
EMP: 22 EST: 1969
SALES (est): 453.21K **Privately Held**
Web: www.okanmarinerepair.com
SIC: 3732 3731 Boatbuilding and repairing; Barges, building and repairing

(G-7898)
PRECISION SIGNS & GRAPHICS LLC
161 Upper River Rd (45631-1836)
PHONE...................................740 446-1774
Hai Duong, *Prin*
EMP: 8 EST: 2010
SALES (est): 232.3K **Privately Held**
Web: www.1psg.net
SIC: 3993 Signs and advertising specialties

(G-7899)
RIVER CITY LEATHER INC
314 2nd Ave (45631-1103)
PHONE...................................740 645-5044
EMP: 8 EST: 2015
SALES (est): 431.35K **Privately Held**
Web: www.rivercityleather.com
SIC: 3199 Leather goods, nec

(G-7900)
RIVERVIEW PRODUCTIONS INC
Also Called: UNIQUE EXPRESSIONS
652 Jackson Pike (45631-1389)
P.O. Box 624 (45692-0624)
PHONE...................................740 441-1150
Thomas Meadows, *Ch*
EMP: 9 EST: 1991
SALES (est): 413.05K **Privately Held**
SIC: 5261 2611 Retail nurseries; Pulp mills, mechanical and recycling processing

(G-7901)
SANDS HILL MINING LLC
948 State Route 7 N (45631-9471)
P.O. Box 650 (45634-0650)
PHONE...................................740 384-4211
EMP: 6 EST: 2007
SALES (est): 225.75K **Privately Held**
SIC: 1429 Grits mining (crushed stone)

(G-7902)
SENTINEL DAILY
825 3rd Ave (45631-1624)
PHONE...................................740 992-2155
Charlene Hoeflich, *Prin*
EMP: 11 EST: 2009
SALES (est): 191.86K **Privately Held**
Web: www.wvnews.com
SIC: 2711 Commercial printing and newspaper publishing combined

(G-7903)
THOMAS DO-IT CENTER INC (PA)
Also Called: Thomas Rental
176 Mccormick Rd (45631-8745)
PHONE...................................740 446-2002
Autumn Thomas, *Ex Dir*
Jim Thomas, *
Marlene Hall, *
Lee Cyrus, *
Jay Hall, *
▲ EMP: 45 EST: 1988
SALES (est): 9.63MM
SALES (corp-wide): 9.63MM **Privately Held**
Web: www.thomasdoit.com
SIC: 7359 2439 5211 5251 Equipment rental and leasing, nec; Trusses, wooden roof; Lumber products; Hardware stores

Galloway
Franklin County

(G-7904)
EL NUEVO NARANJO
6142 Glenworth Ct (43119-8559)
PHONE...................................614 863-4212
James Diaz De Leon, *Prin*
EMP: 8 EST: 2008
SALES (est): 247.51K **Privately Held**
SIC: 3421 Table and food cutlery, including butchers'

(G-7905)
PETTITS PALLETS INC
1891 Dauphin Dr (43119-8513)
PHONE...................................614 351-4920
Brenda Pettit, *Pr*
Tim Pettit, *VP*
EMP: 7 EST: 1986
SALES (est): 767.08K **Privately Held**
SIC: 2448 Pallets, wood

Gambier
Knox County

(G-7906)
GHOST LOGGING LLC
Also Called: Andy McGough Tom Vantassel
17459 Glen Rd (43022-9710)
PHONE...................................740 504-1819
EMP: 7 EST: 2019
SALES (est): 310.32K **Privately Held**
SIC: 2411 Logging

(G-7907)
SMALL SAND & GRAVEL INC
10229 Killduff Rd (43022-9657)
P.O. Box 617 (43022-0617)
PHONE...................................740 427-3130
Michael W Small, *Pr*
William T Small, *
Carol Small, *
EMP: 35 EST: 1958
SALES (est): 4.15MM **Privately Held**
Web: www.smallssandandgravel.com
SIC: 3273 Ready-mixed concrete

(G-7908)
SMALLS ASPHALT PAVING INC
10229 Killduff Rd (43022-9657)
P.O. Box 552 (43022-0552)
PHONE...................................740 427-4096
Robert E Small, *Pr*
Michael Small, *VP*
William T Small, *Treas*
Carol Small, *Sec*
EMP: 15 EST: 1978
SALES (est): 516.59K **Privately Held**
Web: www.smallssandandgravel.com
SIC: 1771 2951 1611 Blacktop (asphalt) work; Asphalt paving mixtures and blocks; Highway and street construction

(G-7909)
SMALLS INC
Also Called: Small's Ready-Mixed Concrete
10229 Killduff Rd (43022-9657)
P.O. Box 503 (43022-0503)
PHONE...................................740 427-3633
Robert Small, *Pr*
Sharon Mills, *Sec*
EMP: 10 EST: 1994
SALES (est): 1.07MM **Privately Held**
Web: www.smallssandandgravel.com
SIC: 3273 Ready-mixed concrete

(G-7910)
YODERS FINE FOODS LLC
Also Called: Yoder's Cider Barn
3361 Martinsburg Rd (43022-9737)
PHONE...................................740 668-4961
Sheldon Yoder, *Managing Member*
▲ EMP: 10 EST: 1975
SALES (est): 928.72K **Privately Held**
Web: www.yodersfinefoods.com
SIC: 2023 2033 Condensed, concentrated, and evaporated milk products; Jams, including imitation: packaged in cans, jars, etc.

Garfield Heights
Cuyahoga County

(G-7911)
BJS DEMO&HAULING LLC ✪
4937 E 88th St (44125-2013)
P.O. Box 27211 (44127-0211)
PHONE...................................216 904-8909
EMP: 6 EST: 2022
SALES (est): 225.84K **Privately Held**
SIC: 3799 7389 Transportation equipment, nec; Business services, nec

Garrettsville
Portage County

(G-7912)
DCA CONSTRUCTION PRODUCTS LLC
10421 Industrial Dr (44231-9764)
PHONE...................................330 527-4308
EMP: 24 EST: 2002
SALES (est): 4MM **Privately Held**
Web: www.durajoint.com
SIC: 3272 Concrete products, nec

(G-7913)
DISKIN ENTERPRISES LLC
Also Called: Four Seasons Manufacturing
10421 Industrial Dr (44231-9764)
PHONE...................................330 527-4308
Michael E Diskin, *Pr*
Micheal A Diskin, *
EMP: 30 EST: 2016
SALES (est): 2.72MM **Privately Held**
Web: www.durajoint.com
SIC: 3089 Injection molding of plastics

(G-7914)
EDGEWELL PER CARE BRANDS LLC
10545 Freedom St (44231-9237)
PHONE...................................330 527-2191
Ronald R Taylor, *Brnch Mgr*
EMP: 11
SQ FT: 50,000
SALES (corp-wide): 2.25B **Publicly Held**
Web: www.edgewell.com
SIC: 3421 Cutlery
HQ: Edgewell Personal Care Brands, Llc
  6 Research Dr
  Shelton CT 06484
  203 944-5500

(G-7915)
GEAUGA COUNTING LOGGING LLC
12038 Prentiss Rd (44231-9694)
PHONE...................................440 478-7896
John Byler, *Admn*
EMP: 6 EST: 2015
SALES (est): 131.61K **Privately Held**
SIC: 2411 Logging

Garrettsville - Portage County (G-7916)

(G-7916)
HARRISON MCH & PLASTIC CORP (PA)
11614 State Route 88 (44231-9105)
P.O. Box 1826 (44234-1826)
PHONE.................................330 527-5641
Bryson Swanda, *Pr*
EMP: 25 **EST:** 1970
SQ FT: 30,000
SALES (est): 4.94MM
SALES (corp-wide): 4.94MM **Privately Held**
Web: www.harrisonplastic.com
SIC: 3089 3444 3084 Injection molding of plastics; Sheet metalwork; Plastics pipe

(G-7917)
JC ELECTRIC LLC
9717 State Route 88 (44231-9746)
P.O. Box 304 (44231-0304)
PHONE.................................330 760-2915
Jason Carmichael, *Owner*
EMP: 17 **EST:** 2001
SALES (est): 980.77K **Privately Held**
SIC: 1731 3699 1521 General electrical contractor; Door opening and closing devices, electrical; Single-family home remodeling, additions, and repairs

(G-7918)
KECAMM LLC
10404 Industrial Dr (44231-9764)
PHONE.................................330 527-2918
Cheryl A Macek, *CEO*
George Macek, *Pr*
EMP: 7 **EST:** 2003
SQ FT: 10,000
SALES (est): 744.01K **Privately Held**
Web: www.kecam.com
SIC: 3479 5084 Bonderizing of metal or metal products; Paint spray equipment, industrial

(G-7919)
KECOAT LLC
10610 Freedom St (44231-9763)
PHONE.................................330 527-0215
Darrin Macek, *Managing Member*
EMP: 13 **EST:** 2006
SQ FT: 10,000
SALES (est): 985.71K **Privately Held**
SIC: 3441 Fabricated structural metal

(G-7920)
LHPC INC (PA)
11964 State Route 88 (44231-9115)
P.O. Box 347 (44231-0347)
PHONE.................................330 527-2696
Larry Hermann, *Pr*
Ruth Hermann, *
EMP: 24 **EST:** 1967
SALES (est): 5.56MM
SALES (corp-wide): 5.56MM **Privately Held**
Web: www.hermannpicklecompany.com
SIC: 2035 Pickles, sauces, and salad dressings

(G-7921)
MACHINE TEK SYSTEMS INC
10400 Industrial Dr (44231-9764)
P.O. Box 187 (44231-0187)
PHONE.................................330 527-4450
Tim Paul, *Pr*
EMP: 33 **EST:** 1986
SQ FT: 22,000
SALES (est): 4.62MM **Privately Held**
Web: www.machineteksystemsinc.com
SIC: 3544 3599 3451 Special dies and tools; Machine shop, jobbing and repair; Screw machine products

(G-7922)
MEGA PLASTICS CO
10610 Freedom St (44231-9763)
PHONE.................................330 527-2211
Ronald Porter, *Pr*
Wendi Porter, *VP*
EMP: 20 **EST:** 1998
SQ FT: 25,000
SALES (est): 2.38MM **Privately Held**
Web: www.megaplastics.com
SIC: 3089 Plastics processing

(G-7923)
MODERN RETAIL SOLUTIONS LLC
10421 Industrial Dr (44231-9764)
PHONE.................................330 527-4308
▼ **EMP:** 24 **EST:** 1972
SQ FT: 100,000
SALES (est): 2.11MM **Privately Held**
Web: www.modern-retailsolutions.com
SIC: 2542 Partitions and fixtures, except wood

(G-7924)
PALLETS & CRATES INC
9294 State Route 305 (44231-9201)
P.O. Box 613 (44080-0613)
PHONE.................................330 527-4534
William Miller, *Pr*
EMP: 18 **EST:** 1992
SQ FT: 15,000
SALES (est): 628.45K **Privately Held**
SIC: 2448 Pallets, wood

(G-7925)
SUPERIOR QUALITY MACHINE CO
10500 Industrial Dr (44231-9250)
P.O. Box 303 (44231-0303)
PHONE.................................330 527-7146
Joe Kenesky, *Owner*
▲ **EMP:** 9 **EST:** 1988
SQ FT: 11,000
SALES (est): 400.54K **Privately Held**
Web: www.superiorqualitymachine.com
SIC: 3599 Machine shop, jobbing and repair

(G-7926)
THERM-O-LINK INC (PA)
10513 Freedom St (44231-9244)
PHONE.................................330 527-2124
Ronald M Krisher, *Ch Bd*
David Campbell, *
Thomas C B Letson, *
▲ **EMP:** 100 **EST:** 1978
SQ FT: 125,000
SALES (est): 23.71MM
SALES (corp-wide): 23.71MM **Privately Held**
Web: www.tolwire.com
SIC: 3357 3496 Nonferrous wiredrawing and insulating; Miscellaneous fabricated wire products

Gates Mills
Cuyahoga County

(G-7927)
ASSOCIATED PRESS REPAIR INC
7547 Brigham Rd (44040-9782)
PHONE.................................216 881-2288
Anthony Grbavac, *Pr*
Steve Grbavac, *VP*
EMP: 8 **EST:** 1985
SALES (est): 718.25K **Privately Held**

SIC: 3599 Machine shop, jobbing and repair

(G-7928)
LIMINAL ESPORTS LLC
Also Called: Liminal Data
1500 Chagrin River Rd Unit 361 (44040)
PHONE.................................440 423-5856
James Collins, *CEO*
EMP: 8 **EST:** 2019
SALES (est): 244.88K **Privately Held**
SIC: 7389 8732 7372 Business Activities at Non-Commercial Site; Research services, except laboratory; Educational computer software

Geneva
Ashtabula County

(G-7929)
ADRIA SCIENTIFIC GL WORKS CO
2683 State Route 534 S (44041)
P.O. Box 673 (44041-0673)
PHONE.................................440 474-6691
Milan Krmpotic, *Pr*
Brigitte Krmpotic, *Sec*
EMP: 6 **EST:** 1964
SQ FT: 18,000
SALES (est): 343.11K **Privately Held**
SIC: 3231 Products of purchased glass

(G-7930)
AITKEN PRODUCTS INC
Also Called: Aitken
566 N Eagle St (44041-1099)
P.O. Box 151 (44041-0151)
PHONE.................................440 466-5711
Suzanne Aitken Shannon, *Pr*
Louis J Doria, *Prin*
Thomas A Grabien, *Prin*
EMP: 8 **EST:** 1957
SQ FT: 50,000
SALES (est): 1.58MM **Privately Held**
Web: www.aitkenproducts.com
SIC: 3634 3433 Heating units, electric (radiant heat): baseboard or wall; Gas infrared heating units

(G-7931)
ARC RUBBER INC
100 Water St (44041-1192)
PHONE.................................440 466-4555
Robert Johnson Junior, *Pr*
Josephine Johnson, *Sec*
Robert Johnson Iii, *VP*
EMP: 10 **EST:** 1965
SQ FT: 20,000
SALES (est): 1.07MM **Privately Held**
Web: www.arcrubber.com
SIC: 3069 3061 Molded rubber products; Mechanical rubber goods

(G-7932)
BENNETT MACHINE & STAMPING CO
150 D Termination Ave (44041-1173)
PHONE.................................440 415-0401
EMP: 25 **EST:** 1969
SALES (est): 2.93MM **Privately Held**
Web: www.bennettmachine.com
SIC: 3469 Stamping metal for the trade

(G-7933)
BISCOTTI WINERY LLC
Also Called: Deer's Leap Winery
1520 Harpersfield Rd (44041-8308)
PHONE.................................440 466-1248
Robert Bostwick, *Mng Pt*
Jane Bostwick, *Mng Pt*
EMP: 16 **EST:** 2011
SALES (est): 878.92K **Privately Held**
Web: www.deersleapwine.com
SIC: 2084 Wines

(G-7934)
DWAYNE BENNETT INDUSTRIES
Also Called: Bennett Displays
6708 N Ridge Rd W (44041-7663)
PHONE.................................440 466-5724
Dwayne Bennett, *Owner*
EMP: 6 **EST:** 1991
SALES (est): 503.25K **Privately Held**
Web: www.bennettind.com
SIC: 2542 3441 Racks, merchandise display or storage: except wood; Fabricated structural metal

(G-7935)
ELSTER PERFECTION CORPORATION (DH)
Also Called: Honeywell Smart Energy
430 N Eagle St (44041-1157)
PHONE.................................440 428-1171
Barry O'connell, *Pr*
Timothy Stevens, *
◆ **EMP:** 100 **EST:** 1944
SQ FT: 75,000
SALES (est): 50.15MM
SALES (corp-wide): 36.66B **Publicly Held**
Web: automation.honeywell.com
SIC: 3498 3089 3429 3312 Fabricated pipe and fittings; Fittings for pipe, plastics; Hardware, nec; Blast furnaces and steel mills
HQ: Elster American Meter Company, Llc
855 S Mint St
Charlotte NC 28202
402 873-8200

(G-7936)
FERRANTE WINE FARM INC
5585 State Route 307 (44041)
PHONE.................................440 466-8466
Nicholas Ferrante, *Pr*
Nicholas Farrante, *Pr*
Mary Jo Ferrante, *Prin*
Peter Ferrante, *Prin*
Charles Rehor, *Prin*
EMP: 21 **EST:** 1979
SQ FT: 3,023
SALES (est): 945.63K **Privately Held**
Web: www.ferrantewinery.com
SIC: 0172 2084 5812 Grapes; Wines; Eating places

(G-7937)
H & H ENGINEERED MOLDED PDTS
436 N Eagle St (44041-1157)
PHONE.................................440 415-1814
Barry O Connell, *Pr*
Roy Sutterfield, *
Tim Stevens, *
EMP: 125 **EST:** 1971
SQ FT: 26,000
SALES (est): 3.31MM
SALES (corp-wide): 36.66B **Publicly Held**
SIC: 3089 Injection molding of plastics
HQ: Elster Perfection Corporation
436 N Eagle St
Geneva OH 44041
440 428-1171

(G-7938)
HDT EXPEDITIONARY SYSTEMS INC
5455 Route 307 West (44041)
PHONE.................................440 466-6640
James Maurer, *Pr*
EMP: 17
Web: www.hdtglobal.com

▲ = Import ▼ = Export
◆ = Import/Export

SIC: 3585 3564 3433 Air conditioning units, complete: domestic or industrial; Filters, air; furnaces, air conditioning equipment, etc.; Heating equipment, except electric
HQ: Hdt Expeditionary Systems, Inc.
30500 Aurora Rd Ste 100
Solon OH 44139
216 438-6111

(G-7939)
HONEYWELL SMART ENERGY
Also Called: Elster Perfection
436 N Eagle St (44041-1157)
P.O. Box 10 (44057-0010)
PHONE.................................440 415-1606
Tony Pallotta, *Mgr*
EMP: 75
SALES (corp-wide): 36.66B **Publicly Held**
Web: automation.honeywell.com
SIC: 3498 Fabricated pipe and fittings
HQ: Elster Perfection Corporation
436 N Eagle St
Geneva OH 44041
440 428-1171

(G-7940)
LOUIS ARTHUR STEEL COMPANY
Also Called: Arthur Louis Steel Co
200 North Ave E (44041-1166)
PHONE.................................440 997-5545
Andy Housel, *Genl Mgr*
EMP: 50
SALES (corp-wide): 8.07MM **Privately Held**
Web: www.arthurlouissteel.com
SIC: 3441 Fabricated structural metal
PA: The Louis Arthur Steel Company
185 Water St
Geneva OH 44041
440 997-5545

(G-7941)
LOUIS ARTHUR STEEL COMPANY (PA)
185 Water St (44041-1199)
P.O. Box 229 (44041-0229)
PHONE.................................440 997-5545
J Trombley Kanicki, *Pr*
J Matthew Kanicki, *Asst VP*
Sandra Kanicki, *VP*
James H Kanicki, *Stockholder*
J Barton Kanicki, *Stockholder*
EMP: 8 **EST:** 1949
SQ FT: 80,000
SALES (est): 8.07MM
SALES (corp-wide): 8.07MM **Privately Held**
Web: www.arthurlouissteel.com
SIC: 3441 5051 3444 3443 Building components, structural steel; Steel; Sheet metalwork; Fabricated plate work (boiler shop)

(G-7942)
LYONDLLBSELL ADVNCED PLYMERS I
Also Called: A Schulman Compression
110 N Eagle St (44041-1107)
PHONE.................................440 224-7544
EMP: 49
Web: www.lyondellbasell.com
SIC: 2821 Plastics materials and resins
HQ: Lyondellbasell Advanced Polymers Inc.
1221 Mckinney St Ste 300
Houston TX 77010
713 309-7200

(G-7943)
OLD FIREHOUSE WINERY INC
Also Called: Old Firehouse Cellars
5499 Lake Rd E (44041-9425)
P.O. Box 310 (44041-0310)
PHONE.................................440 466-9300
Joyce Otto, *Pr*
Dave Otto, *Sec*
Donald Woodward, *Treas*
EMP: 20 **EST:** 1988
SALES (est): 2.1MM **Privately Held**
Web: www.oldfirehousewinery.com
SIC: 5921 5182 2084 Wine; Wine; Wines, brandy, and brandy spirits

(G-7944)
OLD MILL WINERY INC
403 S Broadway (44041-1844)
PHONE.................................440 466-5560
Al Snyder, *Pt*
Joanne Snyder, *Pt*
EMP: 8 **EST:** 1995
SALES (est): 242.71K **Privately Held**
Web: www.theoldmillwinery.com
SIC: 2084 Wines

(G-7945)
TEGAM INC (HQ)
Also Called: Tegam
10 Tegam Way (44041-1144)
PHONE.................................440 466-6100
Andrew Brush, *Genl Mgr*
Adam Fleder, *
EMP: 43 **EST:** 1979
SQ FT: 28,600
SALES (est): 13.43MM
SALES (corp-wide): 1.66B **Publicly Held**
Web: www.tegam.com
SIC: 3829 7629 Measuring and controlling devices, nec; Electrical measuring instrument repair and calibration
PA: Advanced Energy Industries, Inc.
1595 Wynkoop St Ste 800
Denver CO 80202
970 407-6626

(G-7946)
WINERY AT SPRING HILL INC
6062 S Ridge Rd W (44041-8375)
P.O. Box 47 (44041-0047)
PHONE.................................440 466-0626
Richard Trice, *Prin*
Jeffrey Piotrowski, *CFO*
EMP: 6 **EST:** 2008
SALES (est): 250.67K **Privately Held**
Web: www.thewineryatspringhill.com
SIC: 2084 Wines

Genoa
Ottawa County

(G-7947)
GRAYMONT DOLIME (OH) INC
21880 State Route 163 (43430)
P.O. Box 158 (43430)
PHONE.................................419 855-8682
Stephane Godin, *Prin*
Mike Brown, *
Kenneth J Lahti, *Prin*
J Graham Weir, *
Kenneth J Lahti, *CFO*
▼ **EMP:** 54 **EST:** 1998
SALES (est): 10.83MM
SALES (corp-wide): 100.86MM **Privately Held**
Web: www.graymont.com
SIC: 3274 Lime
PA: Graymont, Inc.
301 S 700 E # 3950
Salt Lake City UT 84102
801 262-3942

(G-7948)
RCR PARTNERSHIP
Also Called: Paul Blausey Farms
424 N Martin Williston Rd (43430-9786)
PHONE.................................419 340-1202
EMP: 6 **EST:** 2013
SALES (est): 834.55K **Privately Held**
SIC: 3443 Farm storage tanks, metal plate

(G-7949)
RIVERSIDE MCH & AUTOMTN INC (PA)
Also Called: Riverside
1240 N Genoa Clay Center Rd (43430-1206)
PHONE.................................419 855-8308
Gerald Giesler, *CEO*
Jerry Giesler, *
Lester Meyer, *
EMP: 60 **EST:** 1989
SQ FT: 30,000
SALES (est): 9.54MM **Privately Held**
Web: www.riverside-machine.com
SIC: 3599 3549 Machine shop, jobbing and repair; Metalworking machinery, nec

Georgetown
Brown County

(G-7950)
BROWN CNTY BD MNTAL RTARDATION
325 W State St Bldg A (45121-1229)
PHONE.................................937 378-4891
Theresa Armstrong, *Prin*
Lena Bradford, *
EMP: 46 **EST:** 1966
SQ FT: 100,000
SALES (est): 322.86K **Privately Held**
Web: www.browncbdd.org
SIC: 8331 3993 2396 Sheltered workshop; Signs and advertising specialties; Automotive and apparel trimmings

Germantown
Montgomery County

(G-7951)
PROJECT ENGINEERING COMPANY
9874 Eby Rd (45327-9776)
PHONE.................................937 743-9114
John L Michael, *Pr*
EMP: 15 **EST:** 2002
SALES (est): 439.87K **Privately Held**
Web: www.projectengineeringcompany.com
SIC: 3544 Special dies and tools

(G-7952)
SMYRNA READY MIX CONCRETE LLC
9151 Township Park Dr (45327-8711)
PHONE.................................937 855-0410
Hank Ernst, *Brnch Mgr*
EMP: 37
SALES (corp-wide): 1.05B **Privately Held**
Web: www.smyrnareadymix.com
SIC: 5211 5032 3273 Cement; Concrete and cinder building products; Ready-mixed concrete
PA: Smyrna Ready Mix Concrete, Llc
1000 Hollingshead Cir
Murfreesboro TN 37129
615 355-1028

(G-7953)
THE DUPPS COMPANY (PA)
Also Called: Dupps
548 N Cherry St (45327-1185)
P.O. Box 189 (45327-0189)
PHONE.................................937 855-6555
◆ **EMP:** 41 **EST:** 1950
SALES (est): 200.24K
SALES (corp-wide): 200.24K **Privately Held**
Web: www.dupps.com
SIC: 2077 Rendering

(G-7954)
THOMAS D EPPERSON
Also Called: Epco
7440 Weaver Rd (45327-9390)
P.O. Box 19 (45327-0019)
PHONE.................................937 855-3300
Thomas D Epperson, *Owner*
EMP: 7 **EST:** 1981
SQ FT: 2,104
SALES (est): 461.97K **Privately Held**
Web: www.epcostainless.com
SIC: 3751 Motorcycle accessories

Gibsonburg
Sandusky County

(G-7955)
PROTECH PET LLC
3595 State Route 51 (43431-9746)
PHONE.................................419 552-4617
David Bryan, *Pr*
EMP: 16 **EST:** 2004
SALES (est): 1.35MM **Privately Held**
SIC: 2821 Plastics materials and resins

(G-7956)
TRI COUNTY TARP LLC (PA)
13100 Us Highway 23 (43431)
P.O. Box 600 (43406)
PHONE.................................419 288-3350
Gary L Harrison, *Managing Member*
EMP: 24 **EST:** 1977
SQ FT: 82,000
SALES (est): 2.54MM
SALES (corp-wide): 2.54MM **Privately Held**
Web: www.tritarp.com
SIC: 2394 2542 3354 Tarpaulins, fabric: made from purchased materials; Partitions for floor attachment, prefabricated: except wood; Aluminum extruded products

Gilboa
Putnam County

(G-7957)
HILLSIDE WINERY
221 Main St (45875-9757)
PHONE.................................419 456-3108
Lou Schaublin, *Prin*
EMP: 7 **EST:** 2008
SALES (est): 438.98K **Privately Held**
Web: www.thehillsidewinery.com
SIC: 2084 Wines

Girard
Trumbull County

(G-7958)
A J CONSTRUCTION CO
870 Shannon Rd (44420-2046)
PHONE.................................330 539-9544
EMP: 6 **EST:** 1993

Girard - Trumbull County (G-7959)

SALES (est): 489.98K **Privately Held**
SIC: **2541** Cabinets, except refrigerated: show, display, etc.: wood

(G-7959)
AIM SERVICES COMPANY
1500 Trumbull Ave (44420-3453)
PHONE..................................800 321-9038
EMP: **13** EST: 2017
SALES (est): 5.27MM **Privately Held**
Web: www.aimntls.com
SIC: **1389** Oil and gas field services, nec

(G-7960)
ALTRONIC LLC (DH)
712 Trumbull Ave (44420-3443)
PHONE..................................330 545-9768
Bruce R Beeghly, Pr
Joseph Lepley, VP
Alexander Steeb, Prin
Keith Brooks, Prin
David Boll, Prin
▲ EMP: **150** EST: 1955
SQ FT: 80,000
SALES (est): 49.53MM **Privately Held**
Web: www.altronic-llc.com
SIC: **3694** 3823 3613 3625 Ignition systems, high frequency; Temperature instruments: industrial process type; Control panels, electric; Relays and industrial controls
HQ: Hoerbiger Holding Ag
Baarerstrasse 18
Zug ZG 6302

(G-7961)
AMEX DIES INC
932 N State St (44420-1796)
PHONE..................................330 545-9766
Ted Dudzik, Pr
Sam Bates, Genl Mgr
EMP: **17** EST: 1961
SQ FT: 6,000
SALES (est): 1.09MM **Privately Held**
Web: www.amexdiesinc.com
SIC: **3544** Extrusion dies

(G-7962)
BARFECTIONS LLC (PA) ✧
1598 Motor Inn Dr (44420)
PHONE..................................330 759-3100
EMP: **15** EST: 2023
SALES (est): 2.67MM
SALES (corp-wide): 2.67MM **Privately Held**
SIC: **2064** Candy bars, including chocolate covered bars

(G-7963)
BRAINARD RIVET COMPANY
222 Harry St (44420-1759)
P.O. Box 30 (44420-0030)
PHONE..................................330 545-4931
Clyde Faust, CEO
Linda Kerekes, *
EMP: **30** EST: 1997
SQ FT: 61,000
SALES (est): 10MM
SALES (corp-wide): 46.16MM **Privately Held**
Web: www.brainardrivet.com
SIC: **3452** Bolts, nuts, rivets, and washers
PA: Fastener Industries, Inc.
1 Berea Cmns Ste 209
Berea OH 44017
440 243-0034

(G-7964)
CARDINAL PERCUSSION INC
1690 Tibbetts Wick Rd Ste 1 (44420-1276)
PHONE..................................330 707-4446
Mark Tirabassi, Prin

EMP: **7** EST: 2018
SALES (est): 245.84K **Privately Held**
Web: www.cardinalpercussion.com
SIC: **5736** 3931 Drums and related percussion instruments; Percussion instruments and parts

(G-7965)
CHECKERED EXPRESS INC
2501 W Liberty St (44420-3112)
PHONE..................................330 530-8169
Csaba Bujdoso, Pr
EMP: **15** EST: 2005
SALES (est): 1.61MM **Privately Held**
SIC: **2741** Miscellaneous publishing

(G-7966)
CRITICAL CTRL ENRGY SVCS INC
1688 Shannon Rd (44420-1121)
PHONE..................................330 539-4267
Bernie Vogel, Mgr
EMP: **15**
SALES (corp-wide): 19.99MM **Privately Held**
Web: www.gasana.com
SIC: **1389** Gas field services, nec
HQ: Critical Control Energy Services, Inc.
8444 Water St
Stonewood WV 26301
304 623-0020

(G-7967)
FIRE FAB CORP
999 Trumbull Ave (44420)
P.O. Box 128 (44410)
PHONE..................................330 759-9834
Ernie Nicholas, Pr
Mary Nicholas, Sec
Jamie Wilcox, Acctnt
EMP: **6** EST: 1987
SQ FT: 18,000
SALES (est): 715.22K **Privately Held**
Web: www.firefoe.com
SIC: **3569** Sprinkler systems, fire: automatic

(G-7968)
FIRE FOE CORP
999 Trumbull Ave (44420-3448)
P.O. Box 128 (44410-0128)
PHONE..................................330 759-9834
Earnest A Nicholas, Pr
Mary Nicholas, *
EMP: **35** EST: 1978
SQ FT: 18,000
SALES (est): 4.22MM **Privately Held**
Web: www.firefoe.com
SIC: **3569** 7699 Sprinkler systems, fire: automatic; Fire control (military) equipment repair

(G-7969)
GIRARD MACHINE COMPANY INC
700 Dot St (44420-1701)
P.O. Box 298 (44420-0298)
PHONE..................................330 545-9731
Carl Malito, Pr
Donald Malito, *
Robert Malito, *
EMP: **27** EST: 1946
SQ FT: 60,000
SALES (est): 1.23MM **Privately Held**
Web: www.morganengineering.com
SIC: **3559** 3599 Foundry, smelting, refining, and similar machinery; Machine shop, jobbing and repair

(G-7970)
KNIGHT LINE SIGNATURE AP CORP
16 W Liberty St (44420-2840)
PHONE..................................330 545-8108
EMP: **7** EST: 1994

SQ FT: 2,000
SALES (est): 780.16K **Privately Held**
Web: knight-line-signature-apparel-oh-1.hub.biz
SIC: **2759** Screen printing

(G-7971)
LIBERTY IRON & METAL INC
27 Furnace Ln (44420-3214)
P.O. Box 29 (44420-0029)
PHONE..................................724 347-4534
David P Miller, Ch Bd
EMP: **30**
SALES (corp-wide): 3.72MM **Privately Held**
SIC: **3312** Blast furnaces and steel mills
HQ: Liberty Iron & Metal, Inc.
2144 W Mcdowell Rd
Phoenix AZ 85009

(G-7972)
MARSH TECHNOLOGIES INC
30 W Main St Ste A (44420-2520)
PHONE..................................330 545-0085
Sandra G Marsh, Pr
EMP: **12** EST: 1985
SQ FT: 10,000
SALES (est): 1.13MM **Privately Held**
Web: www.gopwarrencounty.com
SIC: **3544** Special dies, tools, jigs, and fixtures

(G-7973)
MORGAN ENGINEERING SYSTEMS INC
Also Called: Morgan Mfg Plant No 3
700 Dot St (44420-1701)
PHONE..................................330 545-9731
Mark Fedor, CEO
EMP: **32**
SQ FT: 120,000
SALES (corp-wide): 33.18MM **Privately Held**
Web: www.morganengineering.com
SIC: **3559** 3599 Foundry, smelting, refining, and similar machinery; Machine shop, jobbing and repair
PA: Morgan Engineering Systems, Inc.
1049 S Mahoning Ave
Alliance OH 44601
330 823-6130

(G-7974)
ROCKY HINGE INC
1660 Harding Ave (44420-1514)
PHONE..................................330 539-6296
Rocky Shamlin, Owner
EMP: **6** EST: 2006
SQ FT: 3,072
SALES (est): 526.03K **Privately Held**
Web: www.rockyhinge.com
SIC: **5251** 3944 Hardware stores; Child restraint seats, automotive

(G-7975)
SOFT TOUCH WOOD LLC
Also Called: Soft Tuch Furn Repr Rfinishing
1560 S State St (44420-3315)
PHONE..................................330 545-4204
Terry Chudakoff, Pr
Bob Leer, *
EMP: **40** EST: 2000
SQ FT: 5,000
SALES (est): 4.83MM **Privately Held**
Web: www.softtouchfurniture.com
SIC: **7641** 2531 Furniture refinishing; Public building and related furniture

(G-7976)
VALLOUREC STAR LP
706 S State St (44420-3204)
PHONE..................................330 742-6227
EMP: **144**
SALES (corp-wide): 2.17MM **Privately Held**
Web: www.vallourec.com
SIC: **3317** Steel pipe and tubes
HQ: Vallourec Star, Lp
2669 Mrtin Lther King Jr
Youngstown OH 44510
330 742-6300

(G-7977)
YOUNGSTOWN BURIAL VAULT CO
316 Forsythe Ave (44420-2205)
PHONE..................................330 782-0015
Charles Phillips, Pr
EMP: **9** EST: 1945
SALES (est): 641.57K **Privately Held**
SIC: **3272** Burial vaults, concrete or precast terrazzo

Glandorf
Putnam County

(G-7978)
FIELD GYMMY INC
138-143 S Main St (45848)
P.O. Box 121 (45875-0121)
PHONE..................................419 538-6511
Melvin Nienberg, VP
Dennis Nienberg, Pr
Thomas Russell, Sec
EMP: **8** EST: 1974
SQ FT: 15,300
SALES (est): 735.77K **Privately Held**
SIC: **3523** 3713 3563 3531 Farm machinery and equipment; Truck and bus bodies; Air and gas compressors; Construction machinery

Glenford
Perry County

(G-7979)
SAND ROCK ENTERPRISES INC
14033 Sand Rock Rd (43739-9740)
PHONE..................................740 407-2735
Asami Agarle, Prin
EMP: **12** EST: 1995
SALES (est): 370.58K **Privately Held**
SIC: **1442** Construction sand and gravel

Glenmont
Holmes County

(G-7980)
BRIAR HILL STONE CO INC
12470 State Route 520 (44628)
P.O. Box 398 (44628-0398)
PHONE..................................216 377-5100
Toby Rosen, Trst
Bill W Alde, *
Eugene G Rosenthal, *
EMP: **60** EST: 1906
SQ FT: 4,000
SALES (est): 4.89MM **Privately Held**
Web: www.briarhillstone.com
SIC: **3281** Stone, quarrying and processing of own stone products

(G-7981)
BRIAR HILL STONE COMPANY
12470 State Route 520 (44628-9702)

▲ = Import ▼ = Export
✧ = Import/Export

P.O. Box 457 (44628-0457)
PHONE..............................330 377-5100
Frank Waller, *Pr*
Lowell M Shope, *Genl Mgr*
Connie D Scott, *VP*
EMP: 19 **EST:** 1917
SQ FT: 4,000
SALES (est): 456.95K **Privately Held**
Web: www.briarhillstone.com
SIC: 3281 Stone, quarrying and processing of own stone products

Glenwillow
Cuyahoga County

(G-7982)
STRIDE TOOL LLC
30333 Emerald Valley Pkwy (44139)
P.O. Box 2019 (30096)
PHONE..............................440 247-4600
Ron Ortiz, *CEO*
EMP: 150 **EST:** 2016
SALES (est): 50.71MM
SALES (corp-wide): 265.76MM **Privately Held**
Web: www.stridetool.com
SIC: 3423 Hand and edge tools, nec
PA: Diversitech Corporation
3039 Premiere Pkwy # 600
Duluth GA 30097
678 542-3600

Glouster
Athens County

(G-7983)
FROG RANCH FOODS LTD
5 S High St (45732-1051)
PHONE..............................740 767-3705
Craig Cornett, *Pr*
Kristi Hewitt, *CFO*
EMP: 10 **EST:** 1994
SQ FT: 10,000
SALES (est): 949.15K **Privately Held**
Web: www.frogranch.com
SIC: 2099 Food preparations, nec

Gnadenhutten
Tuscarawas County

(G-7984)
ALSCO METER
260 Echo Rd Sw (44629-9671)
PHONE..............................740 254-4500
Helen Miller, *Prin*
EMP: 6 **EST:** 2007
SALES (est): 97.05K **Privately Held**
SIC: 3829 Measuring and controlling devices, nec

(G-7985)
MILLWOOD LUMBER INC
Also Called: Millwood Logging
2400 Larson Rd Se (44629-9500)
P.O. Box 871 (44629-0871)
PHONE..............................740 254-4681
EMP: 22 **EST:** 1985
SALES (est): 3.53MM **Privately Held**
Web: www.millwoodlumberinc.com
SIC: 2421 Sawmills and planing mills, general

(G-7986)
PEMJAY INC
318 E Tuscarawas Ave (44629-5040)
P.O. Box 669 (44629-0669)
PHONE..............................740 254-4591
Yolanda Jagunic, *Ch Bd*
David Jagunic, *Pr*
Mark Dummermuth, *VP*
EMP: 18 **EST:** 1969
SQ FT: 8,000
SALES (est): 844.64K **Privately Held**
Web: www.pemjay.com
SIC: 3441 Fabricated structural metal

(G-7987)
PLYMOUTH FOAM LLC
1 Southern Gateway Dr (44629)
P.O. Box 177 (44629-0177)
PHONE..............................740 254-1188
Chris Coleman, *Mgr*
EMP: 72
Web: www.plymouthfoam.com
SIC: 3069 Medical and laboratory rubber sundries and related products
HQ: Plymouth Foam Llc
1800 Sunset Dr
Plymouth WI 53073
800 669-1176

(G-7988)
RIDGCO PALLET LLC
138 W Main St (44629-9689)
P.O. Box 56 (44629-0056)
PHONE..............................330 340-0048
Jacqueline D Ridgway, *Prin*
EMP: 10 **EST:** 2012
SALES (est): 349.35K **Privately Held**
SIC: 2448 Pallets, wood

(G-7989)
STOCKER CONCRETE COMPANY
7574 Us Hwy 36 Se (44629)
P.O. Box 176 (44629-0176)
PHONE..............................740 254-4626
Thomas Stocker, *Pr*
Bryan Stocker, *VP*
Jeffrey Stocker, *Sec*
William Stocker, *Stockholder*
EMP: 15 **EST:** 1933
SQ FT: 15,000
SALES (est): 1.8MM
SALES (corp-wide): 5MM **Privately Held**
Web: www.stockerconcrete.com
SIC: 3273 5032 5211 Ready-mixed concrete; Concrete building products; Masonry materials and supplies; Concrete block and brick
PA: Stocker Sand & Gravel Co.
Rr 36
Gnadenhutten OH 44629
740 254-4635

(G-7990)
STOCKER SAND & GRAVEL CO (PA)
Rte 36 (44629)
P.O. Box 176 (44629-0176)
PHONE..............................740 254-4635
Bill Stocker, *Pr*
Jeffrey Stocker, *Pr*
Bryan Stocker, *VP*
Thomas Stocker, *Sec*
EMP: 12 **EST:** 1933
SQ FT: 3,000
SALES (est): 5MM
SALES (corp-wide): 5MM **Privately Held**
Web: www.stockerconcrete.com
SIC: 1442 3271 Common sand mining; Blocks, concrete or cinder: standard

(G-7991)
TUSCO LIMITED PARTNERSHIP
Also Called: Tusco Display
239 S Chestnut St (44629-5005)
P.O. Box 175 (44629-0175)
PHONE..............................740 254-4343
EMP: 102 **EST:** 1949
SALES (est): 9.08MM **Privately Held**
Web: www.tuscomfg.com
SIC: 3993 2542 2541 Displays and cutouts, window and lobby; Partitions and fixtures, except wood; Wood partitions and fixtures

Goshen
Clermont County

(G-7992)
DANDY PRODUCTS INC (PA)
3314 State Route 131 (45122-8511)
PHONE..............................513 625-3000
Daniel R Reed, *Pr*
Colleen Reed, *VP*
EMP: 6 **EST:** 1989
SQ FT: 15,000
SALES (est): 979.82K **Privately Held**
Web: www.dandyproducts.net
SIC: 3069 Floor coverings, rubber

(G-7993)
LAB QUALITY MACHINING INC
6311 Roudebush Rd (45122-9571)
PHONE..............................513 625-0219
Linda A Brath, *Prin*
James Brath, *Pr*
EMP: 6 **EST:** 1985
SQ FT: 5,200
SALES (est): 469.44K **Privately Held**
Web: www.labqualitymachininginc.com
SIC: 3599 Machine shop, jobbing and repair

(G-7994)
ONESTOP SIGNS
2502 State Route 131 (45122-9415)
P.O. Box 275 (45158-0275)
PHONE..............................513 722-7867
EMP: 10
SALES (est): 444.6K **Privately Held**
Web: www.cincinnationestopsigns.com
SIC: 3993 Signs and advertising specialties

(G-7995)
TRIUMPHANT ENTERPRISES INC
7096 Hill Station Rd (45122-9728)
PHONE..............................513 617-1668
Richard G Hughes Senior, *Pr*
Jewell A Hughes, *VP*
EMP: 16 **EST:** 1993
SALES (est): 998.63K **Privately Held**
SIC: 3537 Trucks: freight, baggage, etc.: industrial, except mining

Grafton
Lorain County

(G-7996)
44STRONGER LLC
1019 Commerce Dr (44044-1279)
PHONE..............................440 371-6455
EMP: 7 **EST:** 2020
SALES (est): 35.37K **Privately Held**
Web: www.44stronger.com
SIC: 2759 Letterpress and screen printing

(G-7997)
BANKS MANUFACTURING COMPANY
40259 Banks Rd (44044-9750)
PHONE..............................440 458-8661
Tim Boyd, *Pr*
Sheila Boyd, *VP*
EMP: 10 **EST:** 1948
SQ FT: 10,000
SALES (est): 907.81K **Privately Held**
Web: www.banksmfgco.com
SIC: 1799 1721 3441 Sandblasting of building exteriors; Industrial painting; Fabricated structural metal

(G-7998)
EATON FABRICATING COMPANY INC
1009 Mcalpin Ct (44044-1322)
PHONE..............................440 926-3121
Ray D Roach Junior, *Pr*
Lloyd H Roach Senior, *Prin*
▲ **EMP:** 50 **EST:** 1963
SQ FT: 40,600
SALES (est): 9.21MM **Privately Held**
Web: www.eatonfab.com
SIC: 3599 3444 3443 Machine shop, jobbing and repair; Sheet metalwork; Fabricated plate work (boiler shop)

(G-7999)
ELITE INDUSTRIAL CONTROLS INC
38045 Crook St (44044-9605)
PHONE..............................440 477-6923
EMP: 6 **EST:** 2019
SALES (est): 149.23K **Privately Held**
Web: www.eliteindustrialcontrols.com
SIC: 3491 Automatic regulating and control valves

(G-8000)
GENERAL PLUG AND MFG CO (PA)
455 Main St (44044-1257)
P.O. Box 26 (44044-0026)
PHONE..............................440 926-2411
Kevin J Flanigan, *Pr*
▲ **EMP:** 125 **EST:** 1955
SQ FT: 70,000
SALES (est): 25.01MM
SALES (corp-wide): 25.01MM **Privately Held**
Web: www.generalplug.com
SIC: 3494 3599 3643 Pipe fittings; Machine shop, jobbing and repair; Current-carrying wiring services

(G-8001)
GRAFTON READY MIX CONCRET INC
1155 Elm St (44044-1303)
P.O. Box 823 (44052-0823)
PHONE..............................440 926-2911
Jeffrey Riddell, *Pr*
EMP: 120 **EST:** 1987
SQ FT: 15,000
SALES (est): 828.67K **Privately Held**
SIC: 3273 5032 5211 Ready-mixed concrete; Brick, stone, and related material; Masonry materials and supplies
PA: Consumeracq, Inc.
2509 N Ridge Rd E
Lorain OH 44055

(G-8002)
INSPYRE HEALTH SYSTEMS LLC
1004 Commerce Dr (44044-1273)
PHONE..............................440 412-7916
EMP: 8 **EST:** 2017
SALES (est): 359.65K **Privately Held**
Web: www.inspyrehs.com
SIC: 3841 Surgical and medical instruments

(G-8003)
JOE GONDA COMPANY INCORPORATED
Also Called: Gonda Wood Products
50000 Gondawood Dr (44044-9194)
P.O. Box 282 (44044-0282)
PHONE..............................440 458-6000
Michael Gonda, *Pr*
Patricia Marie Gonda, *Sec*
EMP: 8 **EST:** 1974
SQ FT: 7,500
SALES (est): 133.89K **Privately Held**

Grafton - Lorain County (G-8004)

SIC: 2448 2449 Pallets, wood; Wood containers, nec

(G-8004)
SATELLITE DATA INC
577 Main St (44044-1317)
PHONE..............................440 926-9300
EMP: 8 EST: 2009
SALES (est): 213.92K **Privately Held**
Web: www.satellitedataohio.com
SIC: 3663 Space satellite communications equipment

(G-8005)
SULO ENTERPRISES INC
Also Called: Magna Products
1017 Commerce Dr (44044-1279)
P.O. Box 247 (44044-0247)
PHONE..............................440 926-3322
Lowell L Snider, *Pr*
Suzanne Snider, *VP*
▲ EMP: 16 EST: 1984
SQ FT: 6,000
SALES (est): 789.44K **Privately Held**
SIC: 3499 Magnets, permanent: metallic

(G-8006)
VILLAGE OF GRAFTON
Also Called: Fire Department
1013 Chestnut St (44044-1406)
PHONE..............................440 926-2075
Randy Kimbro, *Chief*
EMP: 15
Web: www.villageofgrafton.org
SIC: 3711 Snow plows (motor vehicles), assembly of
PA: Village Of Grafton
    960 N Main St
    Grafton OH 44044

(G-8007)
WILLIS CNC
1008 Commerce Dr (44044-1275)
PHONE..............................440 926-0434
EMP: 10 EST: 2015
SALES (est): 453.87K **Privately Held**
Web: www.williscnc.com
SIC: 3599 Machine shop, jobbing and repair

Grand Rapids
Wood County

(G-8008)
A+ ENGINEERING FABRICATION INC
17562 Beech St (43522)
P.O. Box 470 (43522)
PHONE..............................419 832-0748
David Arno, *Pr*
Linda Arno, *VP*
EMP: 15 EST: 1989
SQ FT: 23,500
SALES (est): 2.41MM **Privately Held**
Web: www.aplusengineering.com
SIC: 3441 3599 8711 Fabricated structural metal; Machine shop, jobbing and repair; Engineering services

(G-8009)
Q S I FABRICATION
10333 S River Rd (43522-9350)
PHONE..............................419 832-1680
Tom Zitzelberger, *Pr*
EMP: 7 EST: 1998
SQ FT: 400
SALES (est): 728.07K **Privately Held**
Web: www.qsifab.com
SIC: 3441 Fabricated structural metal

(G-8010)
SAYLOR PRODUCTS CORPORATION
17484 Saylor Ln (43522-9792)
PHONE..............................419 832-2125
Douglas Mueller, *CEO*
EMP: 10 EST: 1902
SQ FT: 550
SALES (est): 1.55MM
SALES (corp-wide): 2.1MM **Privately Held**
Web: www.saylorproducts.com
SIC: 3644 Electric conduits and fittings
PA: Saylor Technical Products, Llc
    17484 Saylor Ln
    Grand Rapids OH 43522
    419 832-2125

Grand River
Lake County

(G-8011)
JED INDUSTRIES INC
320 River St (44045-8214)
P.O. Box 369 (44045-0369)
PHONE..............................440 639-9973
EMP: 17 EST: 1995
SQ FT: 27,000
SALES (est): 466.64K **Privately Held**
Web: www.jedindustries.com
SIC: 3599 5084 Machine shop, jobbing and repair; Industrial machinery and equipment

(G-8012)
KONGSBERG ACTATION SYSTEMS LLC
Also Called: Kongsberg Automotive
301 Olive St (44045-8221)
P.O. Box 98 (44045-0098)
PHONE..............................440 639-8778
Martin White, *Managing Member*
EMP: 35 EST: 2008
SALES (est): 16.78MM **Privately Held**
Web: www.kongsbergautomotive.com
SIC: 3714 Motor vehicle parts and accessories
PA: Kongsberg Automotive Asa
    Dyrmyrgata 48
    Kongsberg 3611

(G-8013)
SUMITOMO ELC CARBIDE MFG INC (DH)
210 River St (44045-8249)
P.O. Box 188 (44045-0188)
PHONE..............................440 354-0600
Yasuhisa Hashimoto, *Pr*
Takahiro Kimura, *Sec*
EMP: 10 EST: 1973
SQ FT: 25,000
SALES (est): 28.43MM **Privately Held**
Web: www.sumicarbide.com
SIC: 3541 3546 3545 3423 Machine tools, metal cutting type; Power-driven handtools; Machine tool accessories; Hand and edge tools, nec
HQ: Sumitomo Electric Carbide Inc
    1001 E Business Center Dr
    Mount Prospect IL 60056
    847 635-0044

Granville
Licking County

(G-8014)
ACUITY BRANDS LIGHTING INC
American Electric Lighting
3825 Columbus Rd Bldg A (43023-8604)
PHONE..............................800 754-0463
EMP: 121
SALES (corp-wide): 3.95B **Publicly Held**
Web: lithonia.acuitybrands.com
SIC: 3646 Commercial lighting fixtures
HQ: Acuity Brands Lighting, Inc.
    1170 Peachtree St Ne # 23
    Atlanta GA 30309

(G-8015)
CPIC AUTOMOTIVE INC
1226 Weaver Dr (43023-1257)
PHONE..............................740 587-3262
Cameron Cofer, *VP*
EMP: 8 EST: 2014
SQ FT: 15,000
SALES (est): 126.4K **Privately Held**
SIC: 3296 Fiberglass insulation

(G-8016)
ERATH VENEER CORP VIRGINIA
Also Called: Erath Veneer
2825 Hallie Ln # D (40020-9250)
P.O. Box 507 (24151-0507)
PHONE..............................540 483-5223
Michael G Erath, *Ch*
Michael G Erath, *Pr*
Rbobert C Moore, *Sec*
◆ EMP: 22 EST: 1952
SALES (est): 627.91K **Privately Held**
SIC: 2435 Veneer stock, hardwood

(G-8017)
HARVEST COMMISSARY LLC
3825 Columbus Rd Bldg J (43023-8614)
PHONE..............................513 706-1951
EMP: 23
SALES (corp-wide): 1.31MM **Privately Held**
SIC: 2099 2051 Food preparations, nec; Bread, cake, and related products
PA: Harvest Commissary Llc
    3579 Raccoon Valley Rd
    Granville OH 43023
    513 706-1951

(G-8018)
HOLOPHANE CORPORATION (HQ)
Also Called: Holophane
3825 Columbus Rd Bldg A (43023-8604)
PHONE..............................866 759-1577
Vernon J Nagel, *CEO*
◆ EMP: 128 EST: 1989
SALES (est): 205.25MM
SALES (corp-wide): 3.95B **Publicly Held**
Web: holophane.acuitybrands.com
SIC: 3646 3648 Commercial lighting fixtures; Outdoor lighting equipment
PA: Acuity Brands, Inc.
    1170 Peachtree St Ne # 23
    Atlanta GA 30309
    404 853-1400

(G-8019)
JAF USA LLC
Also Called: Jaf USA LLC Veneers
2825 Hallie Ln (43023-9256)
PHONE..............................919 935-2726
Tony Boothman, *VP*
EMP: 6 EST: 2018
SALES (est): 41.52K **Privately Held**
SIC: 2499 Furniture inlays (veneers)

(G-8020)
MERITOR INC
Also Called: Arvinmrtor Commerical Vhcl Sys
4009 Columbus Rd Unit 111 (43023-8613)
PHONE..............................740 348-3270
Mike Deep, *Mgr*
EMP: 154
SALES (corp-wide): 34.06B **Publicly Held**
Web: www.meritor.com
SIC: 3714 3713 Axles, motor vehicle; Truck and bus bodies
HQ: Meritor, Inc.
    2135 W Maple Rd
    Troy MI 48084

(G-8021)
MKFOUR INC
108 Hawks Cove Ct (43023-9031)
PHONE..............................620 629-1120
EMP: 7 EST: 2018
SALES (est): 326.35K **Privately Held**
SIC: 2911 Petroleum refining

(G-8022)
NUANCE COMPANY
17 Amanda Dr (43023-9190)
PHONE..............................740 964-0367
Scot Burdette, *Prin*
EMP: 10 EST: 2014
SALES (est): 52.44K **Privately Held**
Web: www.nuance.com
SIC: 7372 Prepackaged software

Gratis
Preble County

(G-8023)
TOLSON PALLET MFG INC
10240 State Rte 122 (45330)
P.O. Box 151 (45330-0151)
PHONE..............................937 787-3511
Keith Tolson, *Pr*
Brent Tolson, *VP*
EMP: 10 EST: 1969
SQ FT: 30,000
SALES (est): 996.46K **Privately Held**
SIC: 2448 Pallets, wood

Graysville
Washington County

(G-8024)
WHITACRE ENTERPRISES INC
35651 State Route 537 (45734-7002)
PHONE..............................740 934-2331
Koy Whitacre, *Pr*
EMP: 20 EST: 1900
SQ FT: 7,000
SALES (est): 921.72K **Privately Held**
Web: www.whitacrestore.com
SIC: 5411 1382 Convenience stores, independent; Oil and gas exploration services

Green
Summit County

(G-8025)
MODERN DESIGNS INC
310 Killian Rd (44232)
P.O. Box 247 (44232-0247)
PHONE..............................330 644-1771
Gregg Boyd, *Pr*
EMP: 9 EST: 1985
SALES (est): 490.56K **Privately Held**
Web: www.moderndesignsinc.com
SIC: 2434 Wood kitchen cabinets

Greenfield
Highland County

(G-8026)
ADIENT US LLC

GEOGRAPHIC SECTION

Greenville - Darke County (G-8049)

1147 N Washington St (45123-9782)
PHONE..............................937 981-2176
Joe Jones, *Prd Mgr*
EMP: 133
SQ FT: 65,000
Web: www.adient.com
SIC: 3714   Motor vehicle parts and accessories
HQ: Adient Us Llc
   49200 Halyard Dr
   Plymouth MI 48170
   734 254-5000

(G-8027)
AMERICAN MADE CORRUGATED PACKG
Also Called: A M C P
1100 N 5th St (45123)
P.O. Box 186 (45123-0186)
PHONE..............................937 981-2111
Arden Fife, *Pr*
Pat Mc Allister, *Sec*
EMP: 18 **EST:** 1987
SQ FT: 21,000
SALES (est): 693.37K **Privately Held**
SIC: 2653   5113   Boxes, corrugated: made from purchased materials; Corrugated and solid fiber boxes

(G-8028)
CORVAC COMPOSITES LLC
1025 N Washington St (45123-9780)
PHONE..............................248 807-0969
James Fitzell, *CEO*
EMP: 78
SALES (corp-wide): 144.97MM **Privately Held**
Web: www.corvaccomposites.com
SIC: 3089   Thermoformed finished plastics products, nec
HQ: Corvac Composites, Llc
   4450 36th St Se
   Kentwood MI 49512

(G-8029)
GMI COMPANIES INC
Woodware Furniture
512 S Washington St (45123-1645)
PHONE..............................937 981-0244
George L Leasure, *Pr*
EMP: 7
SALES (corp-wide): 23.2MM **Privately Held**
Web: www.ghent.com
SIC: 2531   2493   2599   2541   Blackboards, wood; Bulletin boards, cork; Boards: planning, display, notice; Showcases, except refrigerated: wood
PA: Gmi Companies, Inc.
   2999 Henkle Dr
   Lebanon OH 45036
   513 932-3445

(G-8030)
GMI COMPANIES INC
Also Called: Waddell A Div GMI Companies
512 S Washington St (45123-1645)
P.O. Box 18 (45123-0018)
PHONE..............................937 981-7724
Tom Septer, *Mgr*
EMP: 8
SALES (corp-wide): 23.2MM **Privately Held**
Web: www.ghent.com
SIC: 2541   Showcases, except refrigerated: wood
PA: Gmi Companies, Inc.
   2999 Henkle Dr
   Lebanon OH 45036
   513 932-3445

(G-8031)
GREENFIELD PRECISION PLAS LLC
175 Industrial Park Dr (45123-9000)
PHONE..............................937 803-0328
Thomas Karns, *VP*
EMP: 10 **EST:** 2018
SALES (est): 1.12MM **Privately Held**
Web: www.greenfieldprecisionplastics.com
SIC: 3089   Injection molding of plastics

(G-8032)
GREENFIELD RESEARCH INC (PA)
347 Edgewood Ave (45123-1149)
P.O. Box 239 (45123-0239)
PHONE..............................937 981-7763
Michael Penn, *Pr*
Robert Snider, *
▼ **EMP:** 150 **EST:** 1966
SQ FT: 60,000
SALES (est): 25.47MM
SALES (corp-wide): 25.47MM **Privately Held**
Web: www.greenfield-research.com
SIC: 2396   Screen printing on fabric articles

(G-8033)
SKYLINE MATERIAL SALES LLC
12325 Pommert Rd (45123-9275)
PHONE..............................937 661-1770
EMP: 8 **EST:** 2016
SALES (est): 850.95K **Privately Held**
Web: www.skylinematerial.com
SIC: 3444   Metal roofing and roof drainage equipment

Greentown
Stark County

(G-8034)
CANRON MANUFACTURING INC
3979 State Street N W (44630)
P.O. Box 356 (44630-0356)
PHONE..............................330 497-1131
John Kettering, *Pr*
Heidi Michel, *VP*
EMP: 10 **EST:** 1981
SQ FT: 15,000
SALES (est): 1MM **Privately Held**
Web: www.canronmfg.com
SIC: 3496   Miscellaneous fabricated wire products

Greenville
Darke County

(G-8035)
ALL ABOUT PLASTICS LLC
5339 State Route 571 (45331-9606)
PHONE..............................937 547-0098
EMP: 8 **EST:** 2003
SQ FT: 25,000
SALES (est): 530K **Privately Held**
SIC: 3089   Injection molding of plastics

(G-8036)
ANDERSONS MRATHON HOLDINGS LLC
5728 Sebring Warner Rd N (45331-9800)
PHONE..............................937 316-3700
EMP: 40
SALES (corp-wide): 14.75B **Publicly Held**
Web: www.andersonsinc.com
SIC: 2869   Ethyl alcohol, ethanol
HQ: The Andersons Marathon Holdings Llc
   1947 Briarfield Blvd
   Maumee OH 43537
   419 893-5050

(G-8037)
AVIENT CORPORATION
Also Called: Polyone
1050 Landsdowne Ave (45331-8382)
PHONE..............................800 727-4338
John Dimino, *Manager*
EMP: 17
Web: www.avient.com
SIC: 2821   Plastics materials and resins
PA: Avient Corporation
   33587 Walker Rd
   Avon Lake OH 44012

(G-8038)
BASF CORPORATION
1175 Martin St (45331-1886)
PHONE..............................937 547-6700
Jim Bero, *Brnch Mgr*
EMP: 150
SALES (corp-wide): 74.89B **Privately Held**
Web: www.basf.com
SIC: 2869   Industrial organic chemicals, nec
HQ: Basf Corporation
   100 Park Ave
   Florham Park NJ 07932
   800 962-7831

(G-8039)
BRIDGESTONE RET OPERATIONS LLC
Also Called: Firestone
425 Walnut St (45331-1920)
PHONE..............................937 548-1197
Mark Lacey, *Mgr*
EMP: 6
Web: www.bridgestoneamericas.com
SIC: 5531   7534   Automotive tires; Rebuilding and retreading tires
HQ: Bridgestone Retail Operations, Llc
   333 E Lake St Ste 300
   Bloomingdale IL 60108
   630 259-9000

(G-8040)
BROTHERS PUBLISHING CO LLC
Also Called: Early Bird, The
100 Washington Ave (45331-1515)
PHONE..............................937 548-3330
Keith Foutz, *Managing Member*
EMP: 25 **EST:** 1898
SALES (est): 412.7K **Privately Held**
Web: www.dailyadvocate.com
SIC: 2711   2791   7331   Newspapers: publishing only, not printed on site; Typesetting; Mailing list compilers

(G-8041)
CALMEGO SPECIALIZED PDTS LLC
1569 Martindale Rd (45331-9696)
PHONE..............................937 669-5620
EMP: 10 **EST:** 2011
SALES (est): 856.4K **Privately Held**
Web: www.calmegospecializedproducts.com
SIC: 3366   Copper foundries

(G-8042)
CLASSIC REPRODUCTIONS
5315 Meeker Rd (45331-9751)
P.O. Box 916 (45331-0916)
PHONE..............................937 548-9839
Thomas Jeffers, *Owner*
EMP: 8 **EST:** 1984
SQ FT: 48,000
SALES (est): 632.25K **Privately Held**
SIC: 3714   Motor vehicle body components and frame

(G-8043)
COMMERCIAL PRTG GREENVILLE INC
Also Called: Commercial Printing Co
314 S Broadway St (45331-1905)
PHONE..............................937 548-3835
Jeff Campbell, *Owner*
Joan Brante, *Prin*
Marian Campbell, *Sec*
EMP: 8 **EST:** 1923
SQ FT: 2,200
SALES (est): 482.71K **Privately Held**
SIC: 2752   Offset printing

(G-8044)
D A FITZGERALD CO INC
1045 Sater St (45331-1638)
P.O. Box 206 (45331-0206)
PHONE..............................937 548-0511
Don S Fitzgerald, *Pr*
Janice Fitzgerald, *Sec*
Scott Fitzgerald, *Sec*
EMP: 9 **EST:** 1967
SQ FT: 10,000
SALES (est): 921.63K **Privately Held**
Web: www.dafitzgerald.com
SIC: 3544   Special dies and tools

(G-8045)
FOUREMANS SAND & GRAVEL INC
2791 Wildcat Rd (45331-9453)
PHONE..............................937 547-1005
Gary B Foureman, *Pr*
Susan Foureman, *Sec*
John Foureman, *VP*
EMP: 6 **EST:** 1953
SQ FT: 14,000
SALES (est): 536.73K **Privately Held**
Web: www.fouremansgravel.com
SIC: 1442   1794   Gravel mining; Excavation and grading, building construction

(G-8046)
G S K INC
915 Front St (45331-1606)
P.O. Box 358 (45331-0358)
PHONE..............................937 547-1611
Jack Besecker, *CEO*
Chris Besecker, *Pr*
Patricia Besecker, *Sec*
EMP: 9 **EST:** 1977
SQ FT: 6,600
SALES (est): 970.33K **Privately Held**
SIC: 3089   2631   7389   Molding primary plastics; Paperboard mills; Packaging and labeling services

(G-8047)
JAFE DECORATING INC
1250 Martin St (45331-1870)
PHONE..............................937 547-1888
Randy O'dell, *Pr*
EMP: 120 **EST:** 1978
SQ FT: 36,000
SALES (est): 8.95MM **Privately Held**
Web: www.jafedecorating.com
SIC: 3231   Decorated glassware: chipped, engraved, etched, etc.

(G-8048)
JRB INDUSTRIES LLC
3425 State Route 571 (45331-3247)
PHONE..............................567 825-7022
EMP: 25 **EST:** 2017
SALES (est): 840.47K **Privately Held**
SIC: 3999   Atomizers, toiletry

(G-8049)
KITCHENAID INC
1700 Kitchen Aid Way (45331-8331)

Greenville - Darke County (G-8050)

PHONE..................................937 316-4782
EMP: 9 EST: 2017
SALES (est): 676.18K **Privately Held**
SIC: 3633 Household laundry equipment

(G-8050)
KNITTING MACHINERY CORP
Also Called: KNITTING MACHINERY CORP.
607 Riffle Ave (45331-1612)
P.O. Box 902 (45331-0902)
PHONE..................................937 548-2338
Chester Rice, *Mgr*
EMP: 10
SALES (corp-wide): 143.89MM **Publicly Held**
Web: www.knittingmachinerycorp.com
SIC: 3552 Knitting machines
HQ: Knitting Machinery Company Of America Llc
 15625 Saranac Rd
 Cleveland OH 44110
 216 851-9900

(G-8051)
MARKWITH TOOL COMPANY INC
Also Called: Millmcrawley
5261 S State Route 49 (45331-1035)
PHONE..................................937 548-6808
Merlin Miller, *Pr*
Maxine Miller, *VP*
EMP: 10 EST: 1968
SQ FT: 32,500
SALES (est): 487.87K **Privately Held**
Web: www.markwithtool.com
SIC: 3599 Custom machinery

(G-8052)
MONSANTO COMPANY
Also Called: Monsanto
1051 Landsdowne Ave (45331-8381)
PHONE..................................937 548-7858
Jim Larkin, *Mgr*
EMP: 10
SALES (corp-wide): 51.78B **Privately Held**
Web: www.monsanto.com
SIC: 2879 Agricultural chemicals, nec
HQ: Monsanto Technology Llc.
 800 N Lindbergh Blvd
 Saint Louis MO 63167
 314 694-1000

(G-8053)
NEFF MOTIVATION INC (DH)
645 Pine St (45331-1624)
P.O. Box 218 (45331-0218)
PHONE..................................937 548-3194
◆ EMP: 125 EST: 1902
SALES (est): 55.47MM
SALES (corp-wide): 8.13B **Publicly Held**
Web: www.neffco.com
SIC: 2399 3999 2329 2395 Emblems, badges, and insignia: from purchased materials; Plaques, picture, laminated; Jackets (suede, leatherette, etc.), sport: men's and boys'; Embroidery and art needlework
HQ: Visant Corporation
 3601 Minnesota Dr Ste 400
 Minneapolis MN 55435
 914 595-8200

(G-8054)
PAKFAB USA ENGNRED SLTIONS INC
5963 Jaysville Saint Johns Rd (45331-9398)
PHONE..................................937 547-0413
Kevin Wells, *Pr*
EMP: 14 EST: 2014
SALES (est): 1.17MM **Privately Held**
Web: www.pakfab.com

SIC: 3441 Fabricated structural metal

(G-8055)
PFI USA
5963 Jaysville Saint Johns Rd (45331-9398)
PHONE..................................937 547-0413
Albert Wiebe, *Prin*
EMP: 10 EST: 2014
SALES (est): 880.06K **Privately Held**
SIC: 3499 Automobile seat frames, metal

(G-8056)
RAMCO ELECTRIC MOTORS INC
5763 Jaysville Saint Johns Rd (45331-9678)
PHONE..................................937 548-2525
Dave Dunaway, *Pr*
Louis R Dunaway, *
EMP: 85 EST: 1986
SQ FT: 30,000
SALES (est): 28.85MM **Publicly Held**
Web: www.ramcoelectricmotors.com
SIC: 3621 3625 3363 Motors, electric; Relays and industrial controls; Aluminum die-castings
HQ: Arnold Magnetic Technologies Corporation
 770 Linden Ave
 Rochester NY 14625
 585 385-9010

(G-8057)
REBSCO INC
4362 Us Route 36 (45331-9754)
P.O. Box 370 (45331-0370)
PHONE..................................937 548-2246
EMP: 15 EST: 1965
SALES (est): 4.9MM **Privately Held**
Web: www.rebsco.com
SIC: 1542 2431 3448 3443 Commercial and office building, new construction; Millwork; Prefabricated metal buildings and components; Tanks, standard or custom fabricated: metal plate

(G-8058)
RUSSELL L GARBER (PA)
Also Called: Garber Farms
4891 Clark Station Rd (45331-9562)
PHONE..................................937 548-6224
Russell L Garber, *Owner*
EMP: 6 EST: 1954
SALES (est): 883.76K
SALES (corp-wide): 883.76K **Privately Held**
SIC: 2448 0161 Pallets, wood; Melon farms

(G-8059)
SPARTECH LLC
1050 Landsdowne Ave (45331-8382)
PHONE..................................937 548-1395
Julie A Mcalindon, *Mgr*
EMP: 119
SALES (corp-wide): 344.31MM **Privately Held**
Web: www.spartech.com
SIC: 3081 3089 Unsupported plastics film and sheet; Plastics containers, except foam
PA: Spartech Llc
 11650 Lkeside Crossing Ct
 Saint Louis MO 63146
 314 569-7400

(G-8060)
SPECIALIZED CASTINGS LTD
1569 Martindale Rd (45331-9696)
PHONE..................................937 669-5620
▼ EMP: 15 EST: 2003
SQ FT: 50,000
SALES (est): 2.23MM **Privately Held**

Web: www.spcastings.com
SIC: 3365 Aluminum and aluminum-based alloy castings

(G-8061)
ST HENRY TILE CO INC
Also Called: Wayne Builders Supply
5410 S State Route 49 (45331-1032)
PHONE..................................937 548-1101
Mike Homan, *Mgr*
EMP: 9
SALES (corp-wide): 24.3MM **Privately Held**
Web: www.sthenrytileco.com
SIC: 3271 5211 3272 Blocks, concrete or cinder: standard; Masonry materials and supplies; Concrete products, precast, nec
PA: The St Henry Tile Co Inc
 281 W Washington St
 Saint Henry OH 45883
 419 678-4841

(G-8062)
STATELINE POWER CORP
Also Called: Southeast Diesl Acquisition Sub
650 Pine St (45331-1625)
PHONE..................................937 547-1006
Tom Tracy Iii, *Pr*
EMP: 15 EST: 1978
SQ FT: 45,000
SALES (est): 6.46MM **Privately Held**
Web: www.statelinepower.com
SIC: 3569 3621 Gas producers, generators, and other gas related equipment; Motors and generators
HQ: Tradewinds Power Corp.
 5820 Nw 84th Ave
 Doral FL 33166

(G-8063)
VILLAGE OF ANSONIA
700 W Canal St (45331)
PHONE..................................937 337-5741
EMP: 21
Web: www.ansonia.k12.oh.us
SIC: 9199 3589 General government administration, Local government; Water treatment equipment, industrial
PA: Village Of Ansonia
 202 N Main St
 Ansonia OH 45303

(G-8064)
WHIRLPOOL CORPORATION
Whirlpool
1701 Kitchen Aid Way (45331-8331)
PHONE..................................937 548-4126
Eric Joiner, *Brnch Mgr*
EMP: 95
SALES (corp-wide): 19.45B **Publicly Held**
Web: www.whirlpoolcorp.com
SIC: 3634 Electric household cooking appliances
PA: Whirlpool Corporation
 2000 N M-63
 Benton Harbor MI 49022
 269 923-5000

(G-8065)
WOLF G T AWNING & TENT CO
3352 State Route 571 (45331-3229)
P.O. Box 248 (45331-0248)
PHONE..................................937 548-4161
Susan Miles, *Pr*
Maurie Miles, *VP*
EMP: 10 EST: 1896
SALES (est): 910.55K **Privately Held**
SIC: 7359 2394 Tent and tarpaulin rental; Canvas and related products

Greenwich
Huron County

(G-8066)
F SQUARED INC
9 Sunset Dr (44837-1020)
PHONE..................................419 752-7273
William Shipman, *Pr*
Patricia Shipman, *Sec*
EMP: 6 EST: 1981
SALES (est): 437.52K **Privately Held**
SIC: 3825 Electrical power measuring equipment

(G-8067)
JOHNSON BROS RUBBER CO INC
Also Called: Johnson Bros Greenwich
41 Center St (44837-1049)
PHONE..................................419 752-4814
Ken Bostic, *Mgr*
EMP: 30
SALES (corp-wide): 21.76MM **Privately Held**
Web: www.johnsonbrosrubbercompany.com
SIC: 5199 3743 3634 3545 Foams and rubber; Railroad equipment; Electric housewares and fans; Machine tool accessories
PA: Johnson Bros. Rubber Co.
 42 W Buckeye St
 West Salem OH 44287
 419 853-4122

(G-8068)
LAKEPARK INDUSTRIES INC
Also Called: Midway Products Group
40 Seminary St (44837-1040)
PHONE..................................419 752-4471
James Hoyt, *Pr*
Lloyd A Miller, *
EMP: 150 EST: 1985
SQ FT: 60,000
SALES (est): 63.43MM **Privately Held**
Web: www.midwayproducts.com
SIC: 3469 3465 Stamping metal for the trade; Automotive stampings
PA: Midway Products Group, Inc.
 1 Lyman E Hoyt Dr
 Monroe MI 48161

(G-8069)
NORVIN HILL MACHINERY LLC
4497 Edwards Rd (44837-9419)
PHONE..................................419 752-0278
Linda Zimmerman, *Prin*
EMP: 10 EST: 2016
SALES (est): 623.75K **Privately Held**
Web: www.norvinhillmachinery.com
SIC: 3599 Machine shop, jobbing and repair

(G-8070)
RICHLAND LAMINATED COLUMNS LLC
8252 State Route 13 (44837-9638)
PHONE..................................419 895-0036
EMP: 10 EST: 2004
SQ FT: 40,000
SALES (est): 1.8MM **Privately Held**
SIC: 2439 Arches, laminated lumber

Grove City
Franklin County

(G-8071)
3359 KINGSTON LLC
1111 London Groveport Rd (43123-9708)
PHONE..................................614 871-8989

EMP: 9 **EST:** 2007
SALES (est): 168.79K **Privately Held**
SIC: 2273 Carpets and rugs

(G-8072)
ADVANCE APEX INC (PA)
Also Called: Advance Cnc Machining
2375 Harrisburg Pike (43123-1057)
PHONE..........................614 539-3000
Jeremy J Hamilton, *Pr*
▲ **EMP:** 30 **EST:** 1987
SQ FT: 40,000
SALES (est): 5.35MM
SALES (corp-wide): 5.35MM **Privately Held**
Web: www.advancecnc.com
SIC: 3599 Machine shop, jobbing and repair

(G-8073)
ADVANCE INDUSTRIAL MFG INC
1996 Longwood Ave (43123-1218)
P.O. Box 1296 (43123-6296)
PHONE..........................614 871-3333
James Wintzer, *Pr*
James Wintzer, *Pr*
Cynthia T Wintzer, *
Doctor Christopher Wintzer, *Dir*
Gus Wintzer, *
EMP: 49 **EST:** 1993
SQ FT: 35,000
SALES (est): 9.04MM **Privately Held**
Web: www.advanceind.com
SIC: 3441 3443 3449 Fabricated structural metal; Fabricated plate work (boiler shop); Miscellaneous metalwork

(G-8074)
AFG INDUSTRIES INC
Also Called: AGC Automotive Americas
4000 Gantz Rd Ste A (43123-4844)
PHONE..........................614 322-4580
▲ **EMP:** 66
SIC: 7549 1793 1799 3231 Automotive customizing services, nonfactory basis; Glass and glazing work; Glass tinting, architectural or automotive; Products of purchased glass

(G-8075)
AIM ATTACHMENTS
1720 Feddern Ave (43123-1206)
PHONE..........................614 539-3030
Dennis Hamilton, *Owner*
▼ **EMP:** 8 **EST:** 2008
SALES (est): 424.01K **Privately Held**
Web: www.aimattachments.com
SIC: 3531 Construction machinery attachments

(G-8076)
ALL PACK SERVICES LLC
3442 Grant Ave (43123-2513)
PHONE..........................614 935-0964
EMP: 9 **EST:** 2013
SALES (est): 271.19K **Privately Held**
SIC: 7349 3613 Building maintenance services, nec; Time switches, electrical switchgear apparatus

(G-8077)
AMERICAN AWARDS INC
Also Called: Reynoldsburg Trophy
2380 Harrisburg Pike (43123-1058)
PHONE..........................614 875-1850
Steve Gibson, *Pr*
Gary Gibson, *Sec*
EMP: 11 **EST:** 1970
SQ FT: 6,500
SALES (est): 498.68K **Privately Held**
Web: www.awardsohio.com

SIC: 5999 3993 Trophies and plaques; Signs and advertising specialties

(G-8078)
AMERICAS MDULAR OFF SPECIALIST
4423 Broadway Ste A (43123-3078)
PHONE..........................614 277-0216
Ronald Mills, *Pr*
EMP: 7 **EST:** 1996
SALES (est): 534.96K **Privately Held**
Web: www.americasmodular.com
SIC: 2522 5712 Office furniture, except wood; Office furniture

(G-8079)
AMIR INTERNATIONAL FOODS INC
3504 Broadway (43123-1941)
PHONE..........................614 332-1742
Basel Said, *Prin*
EMP: 6 **EST:** 2011
SALES (est): 250.89K **Privately Held**
SIC: 2099 Food preparations, nec

(G-8080)
BOEHM INC (PA)
Also Called: Mammoth Labels & Packaging
2050 Hardy Pkwy St (43123-1214)
PHONE..........................614 875-9010
Stuart Reeve, *Pr*
Michael Hutchison, *
Jonda Lacy, *
▲ **EMP:** 30 **EST:** 1954
SQ FT: 12,000
SALES (est): 6.76MM
SALES (corp-wide): 6.76MM **Privately Held**
Web: www.boehminc.com
SIC: 2672 2759 Labels (unprinted), gummed: made from purchased materials; Decals: printing, nsk

(G-8081)
BUCK EQUIPMENT INC
1720 Feddern Ave (43123-1206)
PHONE..........................614 539-3039
Dennis Hamilton, *CEO*
◆ **EMP:** 35 **EST:** 1934
SQ FT: 60,000
SALES (est): 9.44MM **Privately Held**
Web: www.buckequipment.com
SIC: 3531 3743 3441 5088 Logging equipment; Railroad equipment; Fabricated structural metal; Railroad equipment and supplies

(G-8082)
CARE INDUSTRIES
6137 Enterprise Pkwy (43123-9539)
PHONE..........................614 584-6595
Jarrod Simmons, *Prin*
EMP: 6 **EST:** 2016
SALES (est): 129.27K **Privately Held**
SIC: 1389 Construction, repair, and dismantling services

(G-8083)
CONCORD FABRICATORS INC
6511 Seeds Rd (43123-8431)
PHONE..........................614 875-2500
Gary Hammel, *Pr*
Chuck Purdom, *VP*
EMP: 23 **EST:** 1988
SQ FT: 21,500
SALES (est): 5.27MM **Privately Held**
Web: www.concordfab.com
SIC: 1791 3441 Structural steel erection; Fabricated structural metal

(G-8084)
CROWN EQUIPMENT CORPORATION
Also Called: Crown Lift Trucks
2100 Southwest Blvd (43123-1898)
PHONE..........................614 274-7700
EMP: 71
SALES (corp-wide): 7.12B **Privately Held**
Web: www.crown.com
SIC: 3537 Lift trucks, industrial: fork, platform, straddle, etc.
PA: Crown Equipment Corporation
44 S Washington St
New Bremen OH 45869
419 629-2311

(G-8085)
CUMMINS INC
2297 Southwest Blvd Ste K (43123-1822)
P.O. Box 291989 (37229-1989)
PHONE..........................614 604-6004
Tammy Fawley, *Brnch Mgr*
EMP: 25
SALES (corp-wide): 34.06B **Publicly Held**
Web: www.cummins.com
SIC: 3519 3714 3694 3621 Internal combustion engines, nec; Motor vehicle parts and accessories; Engine electrical equipment; Generator sets: gasoline, diesel, or dual-fuel
PA: Cummins Inc.
500 Jackson St
Columbus IN 47201
812 377-5000

(G-8086)
CUSTOM INFORMATION SYSTEMS INC
Also Called: Clientrax Software
3347 Mcdowell Rd (43123-2907)
PHONE..........................614 875-2245
Michael Mantkowski, *Pr*
John Cantu, *VP*
EMP: 10 **EST:** 1987
SALES (est): 507.66K **Privately Held**
SIC: 7372 7389 Business oriented computer software; Business Activities at Non-Commercial Site

(G-8087)
DEERFIELD VENTURES INC
Also Called: Ink Well
2224 Stringtown Rd (43123-3926)
P.O. Box 305 (43123-0305)
PHONE..........................614 875-0688
David Keil, *Pr*
Anna Keil, *Sec*
EMP: 8 **EST:** 1982
SQ FT: 3,000
SALES (est): 995.28K **Privately Held**
Web: www.gcofficesupply.com
SIC: 2752 Offset printing

(G-8088)
DENNY PRINTING LLC ✪
3423 Mcginn Dr Apt 211 (43123-2673)
PHONE..........................417 825-4936
EMP: 6 **EST:** 2023
SALES (est): 78.58K **Privately Held**
SIC: 2752 Commercial printing, lithographic

(G-8089)
DYNAMP LLC
Also Called: Dynamp
3735 Gantz Rd Ste D (43123-4849)
PHONE..........................614 871-6900
▲ **EMP:** 27 **EST:** 2003
SQ FT: 16,000
SALES (est): 5.67MM **Privately Held**
Web: www.dynamp.com

SIC: 3825 Current measuring equipment, nec

(G-8090)
EDGE ADHESIVES INC
3709 Grove City Rd (43123-3020)
PHONE..........................614 875-6343
▲ **EMP:** 45 **EST:** 2010
SALES (est): 9.1MM **Privately Held**
Web: www.edgeadhesives.com
SIC: 2891 Adhesives

(G-8091)
EJ USA INC
1855 Feddern Ave (43123-1207)
PHONE..........................614 871-2436
Brian Hall, *Mgr*
EMP: 6
Web: www.ejco.com
SIC: 3321 Manhole covers, metal
HQ: Ej Usa, Inc.
301 Spring St
East Jordan MI 49727
800 874-4100

(G-8092)
ELECTR-GNRAL PLAS CORP CLUMBUS
6200 Enterprise Pkwy (43123-9286)
PHONE..........................614 871-2915
Patrick A Castro Senior, *Pr*
Patrick A Castro Junior, *VP*
EMP: 8 **EST:** 1961
SQ FT: 36,400
SALES (est): 3.77MM **Privately Held**
Web: www.electro-generalplastics.com
SIC: 3089 Injection molding of plastics

(G-8093)
FABCON COMPANIES LLC
3400 Jackson Pike (43123-8993)
PHONE..........................614 875-8601
Michael Lejeune, *CEO*
EMP: 100
SQ FT: 40,000
Web: www.fabconprecast.com
SIC: 3272 Prestressed concrete products
PA: Fabcon Companies, Llc
6111 Highway 13 W
Savage MN 55378

(G-8094)
FORGE BIOLOGICS INC
3900 Gantz Rd (43123-4834)
PHONE..........................216 401-7611
Timothy J Miller, *Pr*
EMP: 7 **EST:** 2020
SALES (est): 2.93MM **Privately Held**
Web: www.forgebiologics.com
SIC: 2836 Biological products, except diagnostic
HQ: Ajinomoto North America Holdings, Inc.
7124 N Marine Dr
Portland OR 97203
503 505-5783

(G-8095)
GATEKEEPER PRESS LLC
2167 Stringtown Rd Ste 109 (43123-2989)
PHONE..........................866 535-0913
EMP: 26 **EST:** 2019
SALES (est): 253.42K **Privately Held**
Web: www.gatekeeperpress.com
SIC: 2741 Miscellaneous publishing

(G-8096)
GREEN CORP MAGNETIC INC
4342 Mcdowell Rd (43123-4000)
PHONE..........................614 801-4000
Stephen Green, *Pr*
▲ **EMP:** 10 **EST:** 2003

Grove City - Franklin County (G-8097) — GEOGRAPHIC SECTION

SALES (est): 454.12K **Privately Held**
SIC: **3542** Magnetic forming machines

(G-8097)
HALCORE GROUP INC (HQ)
Also Called: Horton Emergency Vehicles
3800 Mcdowell Rd (43123-4022)
PHONE..................................614 539-8181
John Slawson, *Pr*
▼ EMP: 192 EST: 1997
SQ FT: 110,000
SALES (est): 82.98MM **Publicly Held**
Web: www.hortonambulance.com
SIC: **3711** Motor vehicles and car bodies
PA: Rev Group, Inc.
  245 S Exec Dr Ste 100
  Brookfield WI 53005

(G-8098)
INSTANTWHIP-COLUMBUS INC (HQ)
3855 Marlane Dr (43123-9224)
P.O. Box 249 (43120 0240)
PHONE..................................614 871-9447
Douglas A Smith, *Pr*
Vinson Lewis, *
Tom G Michaelides, *
G Fredrick Smith, *
EMP: 32 EST: 1936
SQ FT: 10,300
SALES (est): 6.32MM
SALES (corp-wide): 97.42MM **Privately Held**
Web: www.instantwhip.com
SIC: **2026** 5143 2023 8741 Whipped topping, except frozen or dry mix; Dairy products, except dried or canned; Dietary supplements, dairy and non-dairy based; Management services
PA: Instantwhip Foods, Inc.
  2200 Cardigan Ave
  Columbus OH 43215
  614 488-2536

(G-8099)
INTERCO DIVISION 10 OHIO INC
3600 Brookham Dr Ste D (43123-4851)
PHONE..................................614 875-2959
EMP: 9 EST: 2018
SALES (est): 500.82K **Privately Held**
SIC: **2844** Perfumes, cosmetics and other toilet preparations

(G-8100)
KIRK WILLIAMS COMPANY INC
2734 Home Rd (43123-1701)
PHONE..................................614 875-9023
James K Williams Junior, *Pr*
James K Williams Iii, *Sec*
EMP: 80 EST: 1949
SQ FT: 40,000
SALES (est): 22.21MM **Privately Held**
Web: www.kirkwilliamsco.com
SIC: **1711** 3564 3444 Mechanical contractor; Blowers and fans; Sheet metalwork

(G-8101)
LIBERTY TIRE RECYCLING LLC
Also Called: LIBERTY TIRE RECYCLING, LLC
3041 Jackson Pike (43123-9737)
PHONE..................................614 871-8097
EMP: 26
SALES (corp-wide): 302.95MM **Privately Held**
Web: www.libertytire.com
SIC: **7534** Tire retreading and repair shops
HQ: Liberty Tire Services, Llc
  600 River Ave Ste 3
  Pittsburgh PA 15212
  412 562-1700

(G-8102)
LOGITECH INC
6423 Seeds Rd (43123-9524)
PHONE..................................614 871-2822
Kirk Wallace, *Pr*
David W Ritchie Iii, *VP*
▲ EMP: 20 EST: 1990
SQ FT: 32,400
SALES (est): 2.16MM **Privately Held**
Web: www.logitechconveyor.com
SIC: **3535** 5084 Conveyors and conveying equipment; Conveyor systems

(G-8103)
MAGIC DRAGON MACHINE INC
3451 Grant Ave (43123-2512)
PHONE..................................614 539-8004
Richard Burket, *Pr*
EMP: 6 EST: 1993
SQ FT: 4,000
SALES (est): 490.49K **Privately Held**
SIC: **3711** Automobile assembly, including specialty automobiles

(G-8104)
MARNE PLASTICS LLC
3655 Brookham Dr Ste F (43123-4932)
PHONE..................................614 732-4666
EMP: 9 EST: 2013
SALES (est): 2.25MM **Privately Held**
Web: www.marneplastics.com
SIC: **3089** Injection molded finished plastics products, nec

(G-8105)
MESSER LLC
1699 Feddern Ave (43123-1205)
PHONE..................................614 539-2259
Judy Rogers, *Mgr*
EMP: 7
SALES (corp-wide): 1.63B **Privately Held**
Web: www.messeramericas.com
SIC: **2813** Industrial gases
HQ: Messer Llc
  200 Smrst Corp Blvd # 7000
  Bridgewater NJ 08807
  800 755-9277

(G-8106)
MID-OHIO SCREEN PRINT INC
4163 Kelnor Dr (43123-2960)
PHONE..................................614 875-1774
Mike Haughn, *Pr*
Steven Haughn, *VP*
EMP: 6 EST: 1977
SQ FT: 18,000
SALES (est): 465.39K **Privately Held**
SIC: **2759** Screen printing

(G-8107)
MIDWEST METAL PRODUCTS LLC
3945 Brookham Dr (43123-9741)
PHONE..................................614 539-7322
FAX: 614 539-7319
EMP: 25 EST: 1999
SALES (est): 2.58MM **Privately Held**
SIC: **3444** Sheet metalwork

(G-8108)
MOHAWK INDUSTRIES INC
3565 Urbancrest Industrial Dr (43123-1766)
PHONE..................................800 837-3812
Gary Miller, *Brnch Mgr*
EMP: 12
Web: www.mohawkind.com
SIC: **2273** 3253 Finishers of tufted carpets and rugs; Ceramic wall and floor tile
PA: Mohawk Industries, Inc.
  160 S Industrial Blvd
  Calhoun GA 30701

(G-8109)
MURRAY DISPLAY FIXTURES LTD
2300 Southwest Blvd (43123-4829)
PHONE..................................614 875-1594
Todd Murray, *CEO*
Kim Ellen Murray, *Treas*
Glenn Murray, *Pr*
Jonathan Murray, *VP*
EMP: 12 EST: 2006
SQ FT: 11,000
SALES (est): 1.66MM **Privately Held**
Web: www.mdfltd.com
SIC: **2541** 1751 Display fixtures, wood; Cabinet building and installation

(G-8110)
NATIONAL WLDG TANKER REPR LLC
Also Called: National Welding
2036 Hendrix Dr (43123-1215)
PHONE..................................614 875-3399
Bryan Baker, *Pr*
EMP: 9 EST: 2014
SALES (est): 479.12K **Privately Held**
Web: www.nationalweld.com
SIC: **7692** 7699 7389 9621 Welding repair; Tank repair and cleaning services; Inspection and testing services; Licensing, inspection: transportation facilities, services

(G-8111)
NEW SABINA INDUSTRIES INC
3650 Brookham Dr Ste A (43123-4929)
PHONE..................................937 584-2433
Ken Ferrell, *Brnch Mgr*
EMP: 6
Web: www.nippon-seiki.co.jp
SIC: **3714** Instrument board assemblies, motor vehicle
HQ: New Sabina Industries, Inc.
  12555 Us Highway 22 And 3
  Sabina OH 45169
  937 584-2433

(G-8112)
NEXUS VISION GROUP LLC
2156 Southwest Blvd (43123-1893)
PHONE..................................866 492-6499
▲ EMP: 11 EST: 2006
SALES (est): 457.97K **Privately Held**
SIC: **3851** Eyeglasses, lenses and frames

(G-8113)
OROURKE SALES CO
3319 Southwest Blvd (43123-2237)
PHONE..................................877 599-6548
EMP: 9 EST: 2018
SALES (est): 237.79K **Privately Held**
Web: www.orourkesales.com
SIC: **3639** Household appliances, nec

(G-8114)
OWENS CORNING SALES LLC
Also Called: Owens Corning
3750 Brookham Dr Ste K (43123-4850)
PHONE..................................614 539-0830
Anne Depaaew, *Mgr*
EMP: 16
Web: www.owenscorning.com
SIC: **3296** Fiberglass insulation
HQ: Owens Corning Sales, Llc
  1 Owens Corning Pkwy
  Toledo OH 43659
  419 248-8000

(G-8115)
PRECISE CUSTOM MILLWORK INC
6145 Enterprise Pkwy (43123-9539)
P.O. Box 1083 (43123-6083)
PHONE..................................614 539-7855
Charles Caudill, *Pr*
EMP: 8 EST: 2001
SQ FT: 6,000
SALES (est): 514.51K **Privately Held**
SIC: **2431** Millwork

(G-8116)
PRESTRESS SERVICES INDS LLC (PA)
3400 Southwest Blvd (43123)
P.O. Box 55436 (40555)
PHONE..................................859 299-0461
Martin Cohen, *Managing Member*
EMP: 250 EST: 2003
SALES (est): 79.57MM
SALES (corp-wide): 79.57MM **Privately Held**
Web: www.prestressservices.com
SIC: **3272** Concrete products, nec

(G-8117)
PVM INCORPORATED
3515 Grove City Rd (43123-3054)
PHONE..................................614 871-0302
Gary Curry, *Pr*
EMP: 8 EST: 1985
SQ FT: 10,000
SALES (est): 923.02K **Privately Held**
SIC: **3599** Machine shop, jobbing and repair

(G-8118)
RUBEX INC
Also Called: Edge Adhesives-Oh
3709 Grove City Rd (43123-3020)
PHONE..................................614 875-6343
Dave Burger, *CEO*
▼ EMP: 9 EST: 2005
SALES (est): 7.8MM
SALES (corp-wide): 7.8MM **Privately Held**
Web: www.rubex-us.com
SIC: **2891** Adhesives
PA: Edge Adhesives Holdings, Inc.
  5117 Northeast Pkwy
  Fort Worth TX 76106
  817 232-2026

(G-8119)
SHELLY MATERIALS INC
3300 Jackson Pike (43123-8875)
PHONE..................................614 871-6704
Craig Ferguson, *Brnch Mgr*
EMP: 26
SALES (corp-wide): 32.72B **Privately Held**
Web: www.shellyco.com
SIC: **3273** Ready-mixed concrete
HQ: Shelly Materials, Inc.
  80 Park Dr
  Thornville OH 43076
  740 246-6315

(G-8120)
SOUND COMMUNICATIONS INC
3474 Park St (43123-2530)
P.O. Box 1148 (43123-6148)
PHONE..................................614 875-8500
Darin Cooper, *CEO*
Garry Stephenson, *
Toni Vanhorn, *
Darin Cooper, *Sec*
EMP: 25 EST: 1983
SQ FT: 6,000
SALES (est): 4.93MM **Privately Held**
Web: www.soundcommunications.com
SIC: **3669** 7382 7338 Intercommunication systems, electric; Security systems services; Secretarial and court reporting

(G-8121)
TAYLOR COMMUNICATIONS INC
3545 Urbancrest Industrial Dr (43123-1766)
PHONE..................................937 221-3347

Wesley Thompson, *Mgr*
EMP: 13
SALES (corp-wide): 3.81B **Privately Held**
Web: www.taylor.com
SIC: 2761 Manifold business forms
HQ: Taylor Communications, Inc.
1725 Roe Crest Dr
North Mankato MN 56003
866 541-0937

(G-8122)
TIGERPOLY MANUFACTURING INC
6231 Enterprise Pkwy (43123-9271)
PHONE.................614 871-0045
Seiji Shiga, *Pr*
Michael S Crane, *
Yasuhiko Tomita, *
Reina Mito, *
▲ **EMP:** 350 **EST:** 1987
SQ FT: 196,000
SALES (est): 81.45MM **Privately Held**
Web: www.tigerpoly.com
SIC: 3089 3714 3621 3061 Blow molded finished plastics products, nec; Motor vehicle parts and accessories; Motors and generators; Mechanical rubber goods
PA: Tigers Polymer Corporation
1-4-1, Shinsenrihigashimachi
Toyonaka OSK 560-0

(G-8123)
TOOLTEX INC
6497 Seeds Rd (43123-9524)
PHONE.................614 539-3222
Paul Spurgeon, *Pr*
EMP: 15 **EST:** 1987
SALES (est): 4.28MM **Privately Held**
Web: www.tooltex.com
SIC: 5084 3559 Industrial machinery and equipment; Plastics working machinery

(G-8124)
TOSOH AMERICA INC (HQ)
3600 Gantz Rd (43123-1895)
PHONE.................614 539-8622
Jan Top, *Pr*
◆ **EMP:** 350 **EST:** 1989
SQ FT: 250,000
SALES (est): 687.43MM **Privately Held**
Web: www.tosohamerica.com
SIC: 5169 3564 5047 5052 Industrial chemicals; Blowers and fans; Diagnostic equipment, medical; Coal and other minerals and ores
PA: Tosoh Corporation
2-2-1, Yaesu
Chuo-Ku TKY 104-0

(G-8125)
TOSOH SMD INC (DH)
3600 Gantz Rd (43123-1895)
PHONE.................614 875-7912
Marten Blazic, *Pr*
▲ **EMP:** 121 **EST:** 1975
SQ FT: 250,000
SALES (est): 113.85MM **Privately Held**
Web: www.tosohsmd.com
SIC: 3674 Semiconductors and related devices
HQ: Tosoh America, Inc.
3600 Gantz Rd
Grove City OH 43123

(G-8126)
TRIMTEC SYSTEMS LTD
2455 Harrisburg Pike (43123-1453)
PHONE.................614 820-0340
EMP: 18
Web: www.trimtecfoam.com
SIC: 2431 Ornamental woodwork: cornices, mantels, etc.

(G-8127)
TURN-KEY INDUSTRIAL SVCS LLC
4512 Harrisburg Pike (43123)
PHONE.................614 274-1128
Gregory Less, *Managing Member*
EMP: 52 **EST:** 2017
SALES (est): 2.79MM **Privately Held**
Web: www.turn-keyind.com
SIC: 7692 3441 Automotive welding; Building components, structural steel

(G-8128)
VANDAVA INC
Also Called: Mob Apparel
4094 Broadway (43123-3025)
PHONE.................614 277-8003
William Chaffin, *Pr*
EMP: 8 **EST:** 2014
SALES (est): 551.64K **Privately Held**
SIC: 5999 2396 Miscellaneous retail stores, nec; Screen printing on fabric articles

Groveport
Franklin County

(G-8129)
AMSTED INDUSTRIES INCORPORATED
Griffin Wheel
3900 Bixby Rd (43125-9510)
PHONE.................614 836-2323
Joe Cuske, *Manager*
EMP: 54
SALES (corp-wide): 3.96B **Privately Held**
Web: www.amsted.com
SIC: 3321 5088 3743 3714 Railroad car wheels and brake shoes, cast iron; Railroad equipment and supplies; Railroad equipment; Motor vehicle parts and accessories
PA: Amsted Industries Incorporated
111 S Wacker Dr Ste 4400
Chicago IL 60606
312 645-1700

(G-8130)
AVT TECHNOLOGY SOLUTIONS LLC
5350 Centerpoint Pkwy (43125-2501)
PHONE.................727 539-7429
Robert M Dutkowsky, *CEO*
EMP: 92 **EST:** 2016
SALES (est): 10.12MM
SALES (corp-wide): 57.56B **Publicly Held**
SIC: 7372 Prepackaged software
HQ: Tech Data Corporation
5350 Tech Data Dr
Clearwater FL 33760
727 539-7429

(G-8131)
BECTON DICKINSON AND COMPANY
Also Called: Carefusion
2727 London Groveport Rd (43125-9304)
PHONE.................858 617-4272
EMP: 8 **EST:** 2016
SALES (est): 248.71K **Privately Held**
Web: www.bd.com
SIC: 3841 Surgical and medical instruments

(G-8132)
BENCHMARK EDUCATION CO LLC
6295 Commerce Center Dr Ste B (43125-1137)
PHONE.................845 215-9808
Tom Reycraft, *Pr*
EMP: 205
SALES (corp-wide): 105.99MM **Privately Held**
Web: www.benchmarkeducation.com
SIC: 2731 Book publishing
PA: Benchmark Education Company Llc
145 Huguenot St Fl 8
New Rochelle NY 10801
914 637-7200

(G-8133)
BOLTTECH MANNINGS INC
Also Called: Bolttech Mannings, Inc.
351 Lowery Ct Ste 3 (43125-9344)
PHONE.................614 836-0021
EMP: 6
SALES (corp-wide): 60.23MM **Privately Held**
Web: www.bolttechmannings.com
SIC: 3398 Metal heat treating
PA: Bolttech Mannings Llc
103 Equity Dr
Greensburg PA 15601
724 872-4873

(G-8134)
C & R INC (PA)
5600 Clyde Moore Dr (43125-1081)
PHONE.................614 497-1130
Ronald E Murphy, *Pr*
Phillip Lee Mc Kitrick, *
Christina M Murphy, *
EMP: 47 **EST:** 1972
SALES (est): 9.11MM
SALES (corp-wide): 9.11MM **Privately Held**
Web: www.crproducts.com
SIC: 3444 7692 3443 3312 Sheet metal specialties, not stamped; Welding repair; Fabricated plate work (boiler shop); Blast furnaces and steel mills

(G-8135)
CAREISMATIC BRANDS LLC
6625 Port Rd (43125-9101)
PHONE.................561 843-8727
EMP: 8
SALES (corp-wide): 204.35MM **Privately Held**
SIC: 3143 3144 5139 Men's footwear, except athletic; Women's footwear, except athletic; Shoes
HQ: Careismatic Brands, Llc
1119 Colorado Ave
Santa Monica CA 90401

(G-8136)
CREATIVE TOOL & DIE LLC
244 Main St (43125-1124)
PHONE.................614 836-0080
James Newman Junior, *Pt*
Anita Raisley, *Pt*
EMP: 6 **EST:** 1992
SQ FT: 2,600
SALES (est): 500.76K **Privately Held**
Web: www.creativetooldie.com
SIC: 3599 Machine shop, jobbing and repair

(G-8137)
DAVID MOORE
733 Blacklick St (43125-1209)
PHONE.................614 836-9331
David Moore, *Prin*
EMP: 6 **EST:** 2010
SALES (est): 120K **Privately Held**
SIC: 2273 Carpets and rugs

(G-8138)
EVOQUA WATER TECHNOLOGIES LLC
6300 Commerce Center Dr (43125-1183)
PHONE.................614 491-5917
Jim Campbell, *Mgr*
EMP: 6
Web: www.evoqua.com
SIC: 3589 7699 Water purification equipment, household type; Cleaning services
HQ: Evoqua Water Technologies Llc
210 6th Ave Ste 3300
Pittsburgh PA 15222
724 772-0044

(G-8139)
FINISHMASTER INC
Also Called: Autobody Supply Company
5830 Green Pointe Dr S (43125-1188)
PHONE.................614 228-4328
James Volpe, *Brnch Mgr*
EMP: 15
SALES (corp-wide): 13.87B **Publicly Held**
Web: www.finishmaster.com
SIC: 3563 5013 5198 Air and gas compressors including vacuum pumps; Automotive supplies; Paints, varnishes, and supplies
HQ: Finishmaster, Inc.
115 W Wa St Ste 700s
Indianapolis IN 46204
317 237-3678

(G-8140)
FLOOD HELIARC INC
Also Called: Flood Heliarc
4181 Venture Pl (43125-9207)
P.O. Box 237 (43125-0237)
PHONE.................614 835-3929
Robert Flood, *Pr*
Suzanne Flood, *Sec*
EMP: 10 **EST:** 1984
SQ FT: 7,000
SALES (est): 1.51MM **Privately Held**
Web: www.floodheliarc.com
SIC: 3444 3613 3469 Sheet metal specialties, not stamped; Switchgear and switchboard apparatus; Metal stampings, nec

(G-8141)
FLUVITEX USA INC
6510 Pontius Rd (43125-7505)
PHONE.................614 610-1199
Jaume Burgell, *CEO*
EMP: 118 **EST:** 2016
SQ FT: 123,588
SALES (est): 20.24MM **Privately Held**
Web: www.fluvitexusa.com
SIC: 2392 Blankets, comforters and beddings
HQ: Masias Maquinaria Sl
Calle Major De Santa Magdalena 1
Sant Joan Les Fonts GI 17857

(G-8142)
FRANK BRUNCKHORST COMPANY LLC
2225 Spiegel Dr (43125-9036)
PHONE.................614 662-5300
Alexander Morris, *Prin*
EMP: 8 **EST:** 2011
SALES (est): 1.97MM **Privately Held**
SIC: 5142 2013 Meat, frozen: packaged; Frozen meats, from purchased meat

(G-8143)
FRANKLIN EQUIPMENT LLC (HQ)
4141 Hamilton Square Blvd (43125-9084)
PHONE.................614 228-2014
EMP: 51 **EST:** 2007
SQ FT: 20,000
SALES (est): 52MM
SALES (corp-wide): 14.33B **Publicly Held**
Web: www.franklinequipmentllc.com
SIC: 3524 5083 Lawn and garden equipment ; Tractors, agricultural
PA: United Rentals, Inc.

Groveport - Franklin County (G-8144)

100 1st Stmford Pl Ste 70
Stamford CT 06902
203 622-3131

(G-8144)
GABRIEL LOGAN LLC (PA)
4141 Hamilton Square Blvd (43125-9084)
P.O. Box 446 (43123-0446)
PHONE..............................740 380-6809
Troy L Gabriel, *CEO*
Thomas Richardson, *
◆ **EMP:** 61 **EST:** 2002
SALES (est): 8.3MM
SALES (corp-wide): 8.3MM **Privately Held**
Web: www.gabriellogan.com
SIC: 2541 Display fixtures, wood

(G-8145)
GPI OHIO LLC
Also Called: Bell Ohio, Inc.
6300 Commerce Center Dr Ste 100
(43125-1183)
PHONE..............................605 332-6721
Benjamin Graham, *Pr*
EMP: 10 **EST:** 2015
SALES (est): 4.34MM **Publicly Held**
Web: www.bell-inc.com
SIC: 2657 Folding paperboard boxes
HQ: Gpi South Dakota Llc
617 W Algonquin St
Sioux Falls SD 57104
605 332-6721

(G-8146)
HOME CITY ICE COMPANY
4505 S Hamilton Rd (43125-9416)
PHONE..............................614 836-2877
Tony Bakes, *Brnch Mgr*
EMP: 11
SQ FT: 12,000
SALES (corp-wide): 100.42MM **Privately Held**
Web: www.homecityice.com
SIC: 5199 5999 2097 Ice, manufactured or natural; Ice; Manufactured ice
PA: The Home City Ice Company
6045 Bridgetown Rd Ste 1
Cincinnati OH 45248
513 574-1800

(G-8147)
IOSIL ENERGY CORPORATION
5700 Green Pointe Dr N Ste A
(43125-1082)
EMP: 10 **EST:** 2010
SALES (est): 1.26MM **Privately Held**
Web: www.iosilenergy.com
SIC: 3433 Solar heaters and collectors

(G-8148)
KDC US HOLDINGS INC (DH)
Also Called: Kdc Lynchburg
4400 S Hamilton Rd (43125-9559)
P.O. Box 10341 (24506-0341)
PHONE..............................434 845-7073
Ian Kalinosky, *Pr*
Ian Kalinoski, *
David Wardach, *General Vice President*
Nicholas Whitley, *
▲ **EMP:** 15 **EST:** 1991
SALES (est): 497.94MM
SALES (corp-wide): 1.7B **Privately Held**
SIC: 2844 2085 Cosmetic preparations; Grain alcohol for medicinal purposes
HQ: Kdc/One Development Corporation, Inc
375 Boul Roland-Therrien Bureau 210
Longueuil QC J4H 4
450 243-2000

(G-8149)
KRAFT ELECTRICAL CONTG INC
4407 Professional Pkwy (43125-9228)
PHONE..............................614 836-9300
EMP: 26
SALES (corp-wide): 22.8MM **Privately Held**
Web: www.kecc.com
SIC: 4813 3699 Telephone communication, except radio; Electrical equipment and supplies, nec
PA: Kraft Electrical Contracting, Inc.
5710 Hillside Ave
Cincinnati OH 45233
513 467-0500

(G-8150)
KUBOTA TRACTOR CORPORATION
6300 At One Kubota Way (43125-1186)
PHONE..............................614 835-3800
Ted Pederson, *Genl Mgr*
EMP: 26
Web: www.kubota.com
SIC: 3531 Construction machinery
HQ: Kubota Tractor Corporation
1000 Kubota Dr
Grapevine TX 76051
817 756-1171

(G-8151)
LOMAR ENTERPRISES INC
Also Called: Ecc Company
5905 Green Pointe Dr S Ste G
(43125-2007)
P.O. Box 55 (43125-0055)
PHONE..............................614 409-9104
Lou Onders, *Pr*
Mark Molnar, *VP*
EMP: 25 **EST:** 1981
SQ FT: 10,000
SALES (est): 1.68MM **Privately Held**
SIC: 3825 3544 Test equipment for electronic and electrical circuits; Special dies, tools, jigs, and fixtures

(G-8152)
LOPAUS POINT LLC
4395 Marketing Pl (43125-9556)
PHONE..............................614 302-7242
EMP: 10 **EST:** 2015
SALES (est): 1.04MM **Privately Held**
Web: www.lopauspoint.com
SIC: 2038 Ethnic foods, nec, frozen

(G-8153)
MCGILL CORPORATION (PA)
1 Mission Park (43125)
PHONE..............................614 829-1200
James D Mcgill, *Ch Bd*
Jayne F Mcgill, *Sec*
◆ **EMP:** 10 **EST:** 1986
SQ FT: 13,000
SALES (est): 126.17MM
SALES (corp-wide): 126.17MM **Privately Held**
Web: www.unitedmcgill.com
SIC: 3564 3444 5169 Precipitators, electrostatic; Ducts, sheet metal; Sealants

(G-8154)
METAL MAN INC
4681 Homer Ohio Ln Ste A (43125-9231)
PHONE..............................614 830-0968
Robert Posey, *Pr*
Ken Gilkerson, *VP*
EMP: 6 **EST:** 1989
SALES (est): 748.57K **Privately Held**
SIC: 3441 Fabricated structural metal

(G-8155)
NIFCO AMERICA CORPORATION
4485 S Hamilton Rd (43125-9334)
PHONE..............................614 836-8691
Allen Hofmann, *Prin*
EMP: 109
Web: www.nifcousa.com
SIC: 3089 Automotive parts, plastic
HQ: Nifco America Corporation
8015 Dove Pkwy
Canal Winchester OH 43110
614 920-6800

(G-8156)
PEERLESS LASER PROCESSORS INC
4353 Directors Blvd (43125-9504)
PHONE..............................614 836-5790
EMP: 15 **EST:** 1984
SQ FT: 35,000
SALES (est): 101.00K
SALES (corp-wide): 9.6MM **Privately Held**
Web: www.peerlesssaw.com
SIC: 3699 Laser welding, drilling, and cutting equipment
PA: The Peerless Saw Company
4353 Directors Blvd
Groveport OH 43125
614 836-5790

(G-8157)
PEERLESS SAW COMPANY (PA)
4353 Directors Blvd (43125-9350)
PHONE..............................614 836-5790
Steve Hartshorn, *Pr*
Tim Gase, *
Ken Lloyd, *
▲ **EMP:** 50 **EST:** 1931
SQ FT: 30,000
SALES (est): 9.6MM
SALES (corp-wide): 9.6MM **Privately Held**
Web: www.peerlesssaw.com
SIC: 3541 3425 Machine tools, metal cutting type; Saw blades, for hand or power saws

(G-8158)
PINNACLE DATA SYSTEMS INC
Also Called: Pdsi
6600 Port Rd (43125-9129)
PHONE..............................614 748-1150
▲ **EMP:** 148
SIC: 3575 3572 7378 7373 Computer terminals; Computer auxiliary storage units; Computer maintenance and repair; Systems software development services

(G-8159)
SHASTA BEVERAGES
3219 Rohr Rd (43125-9433)
PHONE..............................614 409-2965
EMP: 6 **EST:** 2018
SALES (est): 134.33K **Privately Held**
Web: www.shastapop.com
SIC: 2086 Soft drinks: packaged in cans, bottles, etc.

(G-8160)
STABER INDUSTRIES INC
4800 Homer Ohio Ln (43125-9390)
PHONE..............................614 836-5995
William Staber, *Pr*
▲ **EMP:** 35 **EST:** 1978
SQ FT: 55,000
SALES (est): 6MM **Privately Held**
Web: www.staber.com
SIC: 3633 3444 Household laundry equipment; Sheet metalwork

(G-8161)
TD SYNNEX CORPORATION
Also Called: Td Synnex Corporation
5350 Centerpoint Pkwy (43125-2501)
PHONE..............................614 669-6889
Charles Sims, *Prin*
EMP: 36
SALES (corp-wide): 57.56B **Publicly Held**
Web: www.tdsynnex.com
SIC: 3575 Computer terminals
HQ: Tech Data Corporation
5350 Tech Data Dr
Clearwater FL 33760
727 539-7429

(G-8162)
TIMKEN COMPANY
3782 Potomac St (43125-9472)
PHONE..............................614 836-3337
James Ferguson, *Brnch Mgr*
EMP: 10
SALES (corp-wide): 4.77B **Publicly Held**
Web: www.timken.com
SIC: 3562 Ball and roller bearings
PA: The Timken Company
4500 Mount Pleasant St Nw
North Canton OH 44720
234 262-3000

(G-8163)
TRANE US INC
Also Called: Trane
6600 Port Rd Ste 200 (43125-9129)
PHONE..............................614 497-6300
Sean Strane, *Brnch Mgr*
EMP: 7
Web: www.trane.com
SIC: 3585 Refrigeration and heating equipment
HQ: Trane U.S. Inc.
800 Beaty St Ste E
Davidson NC 28036
704 655-4000

(G-8164)
TRI-TECH LABORATORIES LLC (PA)
Also Called: Knowlton Packaging
4400 S Hamilton Rd (43125-9559)
PHONE..............................434 845-7073
EMP: 6 **EST:** 2017
SALES (est): 5.75MM
SALES (corp-wide): 5.75MM **Privately Held**
SIC: 2844 2085 Perfumes, cosmetics and other toilet preparations; Grain alcohol for medicinal purposes

(G-8165)
UNITED MCGILL CORPORATION (HQ)
1 Mission Park (43125-1100)
PHONE..............................614 829-1200
James D Mcgill, *Pr*
Jayne F Mcgill, *Sec*
▲ **EMP:** 30 **EST:** 1951
SQ FT: 13,000
SALES (est): 126.17MM
SALES (corp-wide): 126.17MM **Privately Held**
Web: www.unitedmcgill.com
SIC: 3444 3564 5169 3567 Ducts, sheet metal; Precipitators, electrostatic; Sealants; Industrial furnaces and ovens
PA: The Mcgill Corporation
One Mission Park
Groveport OH 43125
614 829-1200

(G-8166)
VERTIV CORPORATION
Also Called: Tech Data
5350 Centerpoint Pkwy (43125-2501)

▲ = Import ▼ = Export
◆ = Import/Export

PHONE..................614 491-9286
Giordano Albertazzi, *CEO*
EMP: 6
SALES (corp-wide): 6.86B **Publicly Held**
SIC: 3585 Refrigeration and heating equipment
HQ: Vertiv Corporation
505 N Cleveland Ave
Westerville OH 43082
614 888-0246

(G-8167)
WATTS WATER
6201 Green Pointe Dr S (43125-7501)
PHONE..................614 491-5143
EMP: 10 **EST:** 2017
SALES (est): 1.15MM **Privately Held**
Web: www.watts.com
SIC: 3491 Industrial valves

(G-8168)
WILLIAM R HAGUE INC
Also Called: Hague Quality Water Intl
4343 S Hamilton Rd (43125-9332)
PHONE..................614 836-2115
Robert Hague, *Pr*
◆ **EMP:** 100 **EST:** 1960
SQ FT: 90,000
SALES (est): 24.32MM
SALES (corp-wide): 3.85B **Publicly Held**
Web: www.haguewater.com
SIC: 5999 7389 3589 Water purification equipment; Water softener service; Water filters and softeners, household type
PA: A. O. Smith Corporation
11270 W Park Pl Ste 170
Milwaukee WI 53224
414 359-4000

Grover Hill
Paulding County

(G-8169)
FABSTAR TANKS INC
20302 Road 48 (45849-9324)
PHONE..................419 587-3639
Mark Sinn, *Pr*
EMP: 9 **EST:** 2011
SALES (est): 292.9K **Privately Held**
SIC: 3443 7389 Fuel tanks (oil, gas, etc.), metal plate; Business services, nec

(G-8170)
R & L TRUSS INC
17985 Road 60 (45849-9400)
P.O. Box 130 (45849-0130)
PHONE..................419 587-3440
Ron Treece, *CEO*
Larry Pressler, *Pr*
EMP: 10 **EST:** 1991
SQ FT: 3,360
SALES (est): 1.33MM **Privately Held**
Web: www.rltruss.com
SIC: 2439 Trusses, wooden roof

Gypsum
Ottawa County

(G-8171)
UNITED STATES GYPSUM COMPANY
121 S Lake St (43433)
P.O. Box 121 (43433-0121)
PHONE..................419 734-3161
Bill Steleger, *Brnch Mgr*
EMP: 350
SALES (corp-wide): 16B **Privately Held**
Web: www.usg.com

SIC: 3275 Gypsum products
HQ: United States Gypsum Company
550 W Adams St
Chicago IL 60661
312 606-4000

Hamden
Vinton County

(G-8172)
CORBETT R CAUDILL CHIPPING INC
35887 State Route 324 (45634-8824)
PHONE..................740 596-5984
Corbett R Caudill, *Pr*
Myrta Caudill, *Sec*
EMP: 8 **EST:** 1971
SALES (est): 930.36K **Privately Held**
Web: www.caudillchipping.com
SIC: 3546 4212 Hammers, portable: electric or pneumatic, chipping, etc.; Local trucking, without storage

(G-8173)
INDUSTRIAL TIMBER & LAND CO
35748 State Route 93 (45634-8872)
PHONE..................740 596-5294
Greg Mckinniss, *Prin*
EMP: 6 **EST:** 2007
SALES (est): 471.47K **Privately Held**
SIC: 2421 Sawmills and planing mills, general

Hamilton
Butler County

(G-8174)
ADS INTERNATIONAL
2650 Hamilton Eaton Rd (45011-9502)
PHONE..................513 896-2094
EMP: 7 **EST:** 2016
SALES (est): 525.95K
SALES (corp-wide): 3.07B **Publicly Held**
SIC: 3084 Plastics pipe
PA: Advanced Drainage Systems, Inc.
4640 Trueman Blvd
Hilliard OH 43026
614 658-0050

(G-8175)
ADVANCED DRAINAGE SYSTEMS INC
ADS Hancor
2650 Hamilton Eaton Rd (45011-9502)
P.O. Box 718 (45012-0718)
PHONE..................513 863-1384
Nathan Williams, *Brnch Mgr*
EMP: 100
SALES (corp-wide): 3.07B **Publicly Held**
Web: www.adspipe.com
SIC: 3084 Plastics pipe
PA: Advanced Drainage Systems, Inc.
4640 Trueman Blvd
Hilliard OH 43026
614 658-0050

(G-8176)
ALLMAND BOATS LLC
1000 Forest Ave (45015-1632)
PHONE..................513 805-4673
EMP: 6 **EST:** 2019
SALES (est): 687.59K **Privately Held**
Web: www.allmandboats.com
SIC: 3732 Boatbuilding and repairing

(G-8177)
AMERICAN PRINTING & LITHOG CO (PA)
528 S 7th St (45011-3619)
PHONE..................513 867-0602
Ronald Smith, *Pr*
Randolph Smith, *VP*
Richard Smith, *Sec*
EMP: 19 **EST:** 1959
SQ FT: 14,000
SALES (est): 1.67MM
SALES (corp-wide): 1.67MM **Privately Held**
SIC: 2791 2789 2752 2759 Typesetting; Bookbinding and related work; Commercial printing, lithographic; Commercial printing, nec

(G-8178)
AMERICAN RUGGED ENCLOSURES INC (PA)
4 Standen Dr (45015-2208)
PHONE..................513 942-3004
Raymond J Casey, *Pr*
Shawn Beckman, *Sec*
EMP: 12 **EST:** 1993
SQ FT: 13,500
SALES (est): 2.51MM **Privately Held**
Web: www.mlctechnologies.com
SIC: 3469 Electronic enclosures, stamped or pressed metal

(G-8179)
AMERICAN TOOL WORKS INC
Also Called: ATW
160 Hancock Ave (45011-4351)
PHONE..................513 844-6363
EMP: 19 **EST:** 1990
SALES (est): 1.26MM **Privately Held**
Web: www.americantoolworks.com
SIC: 3599 Machine shop, jobbing and repair

(G-8180)
ART TECHNOLOGIES LLC
Also Called: Art Metals Group
3795 Symmes Rd (45015-1373)
PHONE..................513 942-8800
▲ **EMP:** 60 **EST:** 1946
SQ FT: 40,000
SALES (est): 10.86MM **Privately Held**
Web: www.art-technologies.com
SIC: 3469 Stamping metal for the trade

(G-8181)
AT YOUR SERVICE
61 Betty Dr (45013-4408)
PHONE..................513 498-9392
Denise Goins, *Prin*
EMP: 6 **EST:** 2015
SALES (est): 43.01K **Privately Held**
Web: www.dispatch.com
SIC: 2711 Newspapers, publishing and printing

(G-8182)
ATLAS MACHINE AND SUPPLY INC
8556 Trade Center Dr # 250 (45011-9354)
PHONE..................502 584-7262
Sonny Welker, *Mgr*
EMP: 27
SALES (corp-wide): 52.44MM **Privately Held**
Web: www.atlasmachine.com
SIC: 5084 3599 Compressors, except air conditioning; Machine shop, jobbing and repair
PA: Atlas Machine And Supply, Inc.
7000 Global Dr
Louisville KY 40258
502 584-7262

(G-8183)
BARRETT PAVING MATERIALS INC (DH)
8590 Bilstein Blvd (45015-2206)
PHONE..................973 533-1001
Robert Doucet, *Pr*
Robert Pomton, *VP Opers*
Fred Shelton, *CFO*
◆ **EMP:** 20 **EST:** 1903
SALES (est): 377.18MM
SALES (corp-wide): 90.36MM **Privately Held**
Web: www.barrettpaving.com
SIC: 1611 2951 4213 1799 Highway and street paving contractor; Road materials, bituminous (not from refineries); Trucking, except local; Building site preparation
HQ: Barrett Industries Corporation
73 Hedqrters Plz N Towe F
Morristown NJ 07960

(G-8184)
BAXTER HOLDINGS INC
3370 Port Union Rd (45014-4491)
PHONE..................513 860-3593
Robert Kelly, *CEO*
EMP: 20 **EST:** 1923
SQ FT: 32,000
SALES (est): 392.97K **Privately Held**
SIC: 3272 3443 Steps, prefabricated concrete; Fabricated plate work (boiler shop)

(G-8185)
BETHART ENTERPRISES INC (PA)
Also Called: Bethart Printing Services
531 Main St (45013-3221)
PHONE..................513 863-6161
Richard Bethart, *Pr*
EMP: 14 **EST:** 1974
SQ FT: 4,400
SALES (est): 1.57MM
SALES (corp-wide): 1.57MM **Privately Held**
Web: www.bethart.com
SIC: 2752 7334 Offset printing; Photocopying and duplicating services

(G-8186)
BRIDGESTONE RET OPERATIONS LLC
Also Called: Firestone
33 N Brookwood Ave (45013-1209)
PHONE..................513 868-7399
Robert Johnson, *Mgr*
EMP: 7
SQ FT: 5,200
Web: www.bridgestoneamericas.com
SIC: 5531 7534 Automotive tires; Rebuilding and retreading tires
HQ: Bridgestone Retail Operations, Llc
333 E Lake St Ste 300
Bloomingdale IL 60108
630 259-9000

(G-8187)
BROOK & WHITTLE LIMITED
4000 Hamilton Middletown Rd (45011-2263)
PHONE..................513 860-2457
Mark Pollard, *CEO*
EMP: 25
Web: www.brookandwhittle.com
SIC: 2754 2759 Commercial printing, gravure ; Commercial printing, nec
PA: Brook & Whittle Limited
20 Carter Dr
Guilford CT 06437

Hamilton - Butler County (G-8188)

(G-8188)
BROWN DAVE PRODUCTS INC
4560 Layhigh Rd (45013-9200)
PHONE.................................513 738-1576
David Brown, *Pr*
EMP: 8 **EST:** 1979
SQ FT: 4,000
SALES (est): 185.73K **Privately Held**
Web: www.dbproducts.com
SIC: 3944 7371 Airplane models, toy and hobby; Custom computer programming services

(G-8189)
BUTLER CNTY SURGICAL PRPTS LLC
213 Dayton St (45011-1633)
PHONE.................................513 844-2200
Richard R Roebuck, *Prin*
EMP: 6 **EST:** 2009
SALES (est): 138.41K **Privately Held**
SIC: 3841 Surgical and medical instruments

(G-8190)
CHATTERBOX SPORTS LLC
Also Called: Media
6 S 2nd St Ste 205 (45011-2898)
PHONE.................................513 545-4754
Trace Fowler, *Managing Member*
EMP: 12 **EST:** 2020
SALES (est): 60.65K **Privately Held**
Web: www.chatterboxsports.com
SIC: 2741 7371 Internet publishing and broadcasting; Computer software development and applications

(G-8191)
CIMA INC
1010 Eaton Ave Ste B (45013-4684)
PHONE.................................513 382-8976
Thomas Uhl, *Prin*
EMP: 20 **EST:** 1994
SALES (est): 1.4MM **Privately Held**
Web: www.cimaohio.com
SIC: 2449 2448 Wood containers, nec; Pallets, wood

(G-8192)
CIMA INC
1010 Eaton Ave Ste B (45013-4684)
PHONE.................................513 382-8976
▲ **EMP:** 9 **EST:** 1992
SALES (est): 244.18K **Privately Held**
Web: www.cimaohio.com
SIC: 3561 7363 2449 Industrial pumps and parts; Temporary help service; Rectangular boxes and crates, wood

(G-8193)
CINCINNATI RADIATOR INC
3400 Port Union Rd (45014-4224)
PHONE.................................513 874-5555
Prasenjit Ray, *Genl Mgr*
Mark Epure, *Pr*
Phyllis Apure, *Sec*
▲ **EMP:** 13 **EST:** 1994
SQ FT: 11,000
SALES (est): 8MM
SALES (corp-wide): 8MM **Privately Held**
Web: www.cincyradiator.com
SIC: 7539 3541 3599 Radiator repair shop, automotive; Machine tools, metal cutting type; Machine and other job shop work
PA: Ohio Heat Holdings Llc
 945 Mckinney St Ste 572
 Houston TX 77002
 513 874-5555

(G-8194)
COLOR PRODUCTS INC
36 Standen Dr (45015-2210)
PHONE.................................513 860-2749
James K Krouse, *Pr*
EMP: 7 **EST:** 1993
SQ FT: 12,000
SALES (est): 870K **Privately Held**
SIC: 2865 Cyclic crudes and intermediates

(G-8195)
CONNAUGHTON WLDG & FENCE LLC
Also Called: Connaughton Welding & Fence
440 Vine St (45011-1777)
PHONE.................................513 867-0230
EMP: 6 **EST:** 1962
SQ FT: 5,000
SALES (est): 543.28K **Privately Held**
SIC: 1799 7692 3469 Fence construction; Welding repair; Ornamental metal stampings

(G-8196)
CRYOGENIC EQUIPMENT & SVCS INC
Also Called: Cesgroup
4583 Brate Dr (45011-3577)
PHONE.................................513 761-4200
Hans Vanackere, *CEO*
◆ **EMP:** 10 **EST:** 1998
SALES (est): 4.87MM **Privately Held**
Web: www.dsidantech.com
SIC: 3585 Refrigeration and heating equipment
PA: Dsi Dantech
 Vlaswaagplein 13
 Kortrijk VWV 8501

(G-8197)
CUSTOM FAB BY FISHER LLC
5009 Cincinnati Brookville Rd (45013-9210)
PHONE.................................513 738-4600
EMP: 11 **EST:** 2004
SALES (est): 208.4K **Privately Held**
SIC: 3599 Machine shop, jobbing and repair

(G-8198)
D B S STINLESS STL FABRICATORS
21 Standen Dr (45015-2209)
PHONE.................................513 856-9600
Nick Bauer, *Genl Mgr*
Russell Bowermaster, *Stockholder*
▲ **EMP:** 9 **EST:** 1985
SQ FT: 12,000
SALES (est): 911.11K **Privately Held**
SIC: 3444 Restaurant sheet metalwork

(G-8199)
DARANA HYBRID INC (PA)
903 Belle Ave (45015-1605)
PHONE.................................513 860-4490
▲ **EMP:** 92 **EST:** 1985
SQ FT: 20,000
SALES (est): 70MM **Privately Held**
Web: www.daranahybrid.com
SIC: 1731 3444 General electrical contractor; Sheet metalwork

(G-8200)
DUNN INDUSTRIAL SERVICES
5009 Cincinnati Brookville Rd (45013-9210)
P.O. Box 131 (45063-0131)
PHONE.................................513 738-4999
EMP: 6 **EST:** 2016
SALES (est): 390.43K **Privately Held**
SIC: 3499 3479 1522 Fabricated metal products, nec; Painting, coating, and hot dipping; Residential construction, nec

(G-8201)
DURO DYNE MIDWEST CORP
3825 Symmes Rd (45015-1376)
PHONE.................................513 870-6000
Randall Hinden, *Pr*
William Watman, *
▲ **EMP:** 119 **EST:** 1971
SQ FT: 51,000
SALES (est): 25.84MM
SALES (corp-wide): 210.44MM **Privately Held**
SIC: 3585 3564 3498 3469 Air conditioning equipment, complete; Ventilating fans: industrial or commercial; Fabricated pipe and fittings; Metal stampings, nec
HQ: Duro Dyne National Corp.
 81 Spence St
 Bay Shore NY 11706
 631 249-9000

(G-8202)
DYNAMAT INC (PA)
Also Called: Dynamat
3042 Symmes Rd (45015-1331)
PHONE.................................513 860-5094
Mark Seist, *CEO*
EMP: 14 **EST:** 2020
SALES (est): 1.25MM
SALES (corp-wide): 1.25MM **Privately Held**
Web: www.dynamat.com
SIC: 3443 Baffles

(G-8203)
DYNAMIC CONTROL NORTH AMER INC (PA)
Also Called: Dynamic Control
3042 Symmes Rd (45015-1331)
PHONE.................................513 860-5094
▲ **EMP:** 16 **EST:** 1989
SQ FT: 15,000
SALES (est): 3.93MM **Privately Held**
Web: www.dynamat.com
SIC: 3443 Baffles

(G-8204)
EAGLE CHEMICALS INC
2550 Bobmeyer Rd (45015-1366)
P.O. Box 713 (45012-0713)
PHONE.................................513 868-9662
EMP: 14
SIC: 2819 Industrial inorganic chemicals, nec

(G-8205)
EI CERAMICS
3 Standen Dr (45015-2209)
PHONE.................................513 881-2000
▲ **EMP:** 6 **EST:** 2013
SALES (est): 149.54K **Privately Held**
SIC: 3269 Pottery products, nec

(G-8206)
ELRA INDUSTRIES INC
550 S Erie Hwy (45011-4346)
PHONE.................................513 868-6228
Eldon Smith, *Pr*
EMP: 8 **EST:** 1977
SQ FT: 13,000
SALES (est): 750K **Privately Held**
Web: www.elra.com
SIC: 3089 Injection molding of plastics

(G-8207)
EXCEL LOADING SYSTEMS LLC
1051 Belle Ave (45015-1607)
PHONE.................................513 504-1069
EMP: 8 **EST:** 2016
SALES (est): 145.41K **Privately Held**
Web: www.excelloading.com

SIC: 3568 Joints, swivel and universal, except aircraft and auto

(G-8208)
FIN PAN INC (PA)
3255 Symmes Rd (45015-1361)
PHONE.................................513 870-9200
Elisa Schafer, *Pr*
Theodore Clear, *VP*
Louis A Beimford, *Prin*
Marsha G Rhodus, *Prin*
Theodore E Clear, *Prin*
◆ **EMP:** 18 **EST:** 1975
SQ FT: 40,000
SALES (est): 9.85MM
SALES (corp-wide): 9.85MM **Privately Held**
Web: www.finpan.com
SIC: 3272 Concrete products, precast, nec

(G-8209)
FUTURE FINISHES INC
40 Standen Dr (45015-2210)
PHONE.................................513 860-0020
Daniel L Brown, *Pr*
EMP: 15 **EST:** 1993
SQ FT: 25,000
SALES (est): 764.32K **Privately Held**
Web: www.futurefinishes.com
SIC: 3471 Plating of metals or formed products

(G-8210)
G & J PEPSI-COLA BOTTLERS INC
Also Called: Pepsi-Cola
2580 Bobmeyer Rd (45015-1394)
PHONE.................................513 896-3700
Don Chalfant, *Brnch Mgr*
EMP: 64
SQ FT: 50,000
SALES (corp-wide): 404.54MM **Privately Held**
Web: www.gjpepsi.com
SIC: 2086 Carbonated soft drinks, bottled and canned
PA: G & J Pepsi-Cola Bottlers Inc
 9435 Waterstone Blvd # 390
 Cincinnati OH 45249
 513 785-6060

(G-8211)
GERDAU AMERISTEEL US INC
2175 Schlichter Dr (45015-1481)
PHONE.................................513 869-7660
Mike Stanofer, *Mgr*
EMP: 10
SALES (corp-wide): 1.56B **Privately Held**
Web: gerdau.com
SIC: 3312 Blast furnaces and steel mills
HQ: Gerdau Ameristeel Us Inc.
 4221 W Boy Scout Blvd # 600
 Tampa FL 33607
 813 286-8383

(G-8212)
GL INDUSTRIES INC
Also Called: Climax Packaging Machinery
25 Standen Dr (45015-2209)
P.O. Box 18097 (45018-0097)
PHONE.................................513 874-1233
William George, *Pr*
EMP: 20 **EST:** 1959
SQ FT: 18,000
SALES (est): 3.54MM **Privately Held**
Web: www.climaxpackaging.com
SIC: 3565 7389 Packaging machinery; Packaging and labeling services

GEOGRAPHIC SECTION

(G-8213)
GLANCE SOFTWARE LLC
1340 Missy Ct (45013-7601)
PHONE..................................844 383-2500
Austin Klei, *Pr*
EMP: 10 **EST:** 2016
SALES (est): 299.59K **Privately Held**
Web: www.glancesoftware.com
SIC: 7372 7379 Prepackaged software; Computer related consulting services

(G-8214)
GVS INDUSTRIES INC
Also Called: Cadillac Papers
1030 Beissinger Rd (45013-9322)
PHONE..................................513 851-3606
Donald Gillespie, *Pr*
Sharon Sheppard, *Off Mgr*
Ronald Green, *Stockholder*
Donald Gillespie Ii, *Stockholder*
EMP: 6 **EST:** 1991
SALES (est): 499.29K **Privately Held**
Web: www.gvs.com
SIC: 2621 3861 5113 5112 Specialty or chemically treated papers; Toners, prepared photographic (not made in chemical plants); Industrial and personal service paper; Stationery and office supplies

(G-8215)
HACKER WOOD PRODUCTS INC
2144 Jackson Rd (45011-9534)
PHONE..................................513 737-4462
Chris Hacker, *Pr*
EMP: 6 **EST:** 1998
SQ FT: 2,200
SALES (est): 540.77K **Privately Held**
SIC: 2448 Pallets, wood

(G-8216)
HAMILTON BRASS & ALUM CASTINGS
706 S 8th St (45011-3753)
P.O. Box 657 (45012-0657)
EMP: 27 **EST:** 1918
SQ FT: 25,000
SALES (est): 812.49K **Privately Held**
Web: www.hamilton-ohio.com
SIC: 3364 3321 Brass and bronze die-castings; Gray and ductile iron foundries

(G-8217)
HAMILTON CUSTOM MOLDING INC
1365 Shuler Ave (45011-4567)
PHONE..................................513 844-6643
Ed White, *Pr*
Dorothy White, *Sec*
EMP: 7 **EST:** 1992
SQ FT: 20,000
SALES (est): 894.32K **Privately Held**
Web: www.hamiltoncm.com
SIC: 3089 3544 Plastics containers, except foam; Special dies, tools, jigs, and fixtures

(G-8218)
HAMILTON INDUSTRIAL GRINDING INC (PA)
Also Called: Carolina Knife Services
240 N B St (45013-3105)
PHONE..................................513 863-1221
▲ **EMP:** 20 **EST:** 1961
SALES (est): 4.63MM
SALES (corp-wide): 4.63MM **Privately Held**
Web: www.hamiltonknife.com
SIC: 3423 7699 Knives, agricultural or industrial; Knife, saw and tool sharpening and repair

(G-8219)
IMI-IRVING MATERIALS INC
600 Augspurger Rd (45011-6913)
PHONE..................................513 844-8444
Randy Jones, *Prin*
EMP: 7 **EST:** 2010
SALES (est): 187.96K **Privately Held**
SIC: 3273 Ready-mixed concrete

(G-8220)
INNOVTIVE LBLING SOLUTIONS INC
Also Called: I L S
4000 Hamilton Middletown Rd (45011-2263)
▲ **EMP:** 65 **EST:** 1996
SQ FT: 65,000
SALES (est): 9.05MM **Privately Held**
Web: www.brookandwhittle.com
SIC: 2759 Labels and seals: printing, nsk

(G-8221)
INTEGRATED POWER SERVICES LLC
2175a Schlichter Dr (45015-1482)
PHONE..................................513 863-8816
Jason Reynolds, *Brnch Mgr*
EMP: 28
SQ FT: 20,500
Web: www.ips.us
SIC: 7694 Electric motor repair
PA: Integrated Power Services Llc
250 Exctive Ctr Dr Ste 20
Greenville SC 29615

(G-8222)
IRVING MATERIALS INC
600 Augspurger Rd (45011-6913)
PHONE..................................513 844-8444
Randy Jones, *Brnch Mgr*
EMP: 10
SALES (corp-wide): 814.09MM **Privately Held**
Web: www.irvmat.com
SIC: 3273 Ready-mixed concrete
PA: Irving Materials, Inc.
8032 N State Road 9
Greenfield IN 46140
317 326-3101

(G-8223)
J R CUSTOM UNLIMITED INC
2620 Bobmeyer Rd (45015-1306)
PHONE..................................513 894-9800
James Riesenberg, *Pr*
EMP: 10 **EST:** 1999
SALES (est): 802.82K **Privately Held**
SIC: 2499 Decorative wood and woodwork

(G-8224)
JASON INCORPORATED
Also Called: Jacksonlea
3440 Symmes Rd (45015-1359)
PHONE..................................513 860-3400
Ron Locher, *Brnch Mgr*
EMP: 101
SALES (corp-wide): 834.99MM **Privately Held**
Web: www.osborn.com
SIC: 3446 3471 3291 2842 Ornamental metalwork; Plating and polishing; Abrasive products; Polishes and sanitation goods
PA: Jason Incorporated
833 E Michigan St Ste 900
Milwaukee WI 53202

(G-8225)
KAIVAC INC
Also Called: Kaivac
2680 Van Hook Ave (45015-1583)
PHONE..................................513 887-4600
Bob Robinson Senior, *Pr*
Carlene Robinson, *
Robert Toews, *
▲ **EMP:** 81 **EST:** 1998
SALES (est): 20.3MM **Privately Held**
Web: www.kaivac.com
SIC: 3589 Commercial cleaning equipment

(G-8226)
KUHLMANNS FABRICATION
1753 Millville Oxford Rd (45013-8931)
PHONE..................................513 967-4617
Mark Kuhlmann, *Prin*
EMP: 6 **EST:** 2008
SALES (est): 119.96K **Privately Held**
SIC: 3842 Welders' hoods

(G-8227)
LIBERTY SPORTSWEAR LLC
5573 Eureka Dr (45011-4267)
PHONE..................................513 755-8740
EMP: 6 **EST:** 1990
SALES (est): 463.02K **Privately Held**
Web: www.hofapparel.com
SIC: 2759 Screen printing

(G-8228)
LOUS MACHINE COMPANY INC
102 Hastings Ave (45011-4708)
PHONE..................................513 856-9199
G Danny Jackson, *Pr*
EMP: 10 **EST:** 1978
SQ FT: 10,000
SALES (est): 873.94K **Privately Held**
SIC: 3599 Machine shop, jobbing and repair

(G-8229)
MINUTEMAN PRESS
Also Called: Minuteman Press
223 Court St (45011-2827)
PHONE..................................513 454-7318
EMP: 7 **EST:** 2017
SALES (est): 98.02K **Privately Held**
Web: www.minutemanpress.com
SIC: 2752 Commercial printing, lithographic

(G-8230)
MUNICIPAL BREW WORKS LLC
306 Ashley Brook Dr (45013-6349)
PHONE..................................513 889-8369
James Goodman, *Prin*
EMP: 6 **EST:** 2014
SALES (est): 203.88K **Privately Held**
Web: www.municipal.beer
SIC: 2082 Malt beverages

(G-8231)
NETUREN AMERICA CORPORATION
2995 Moser Ct (45011-5430)
PHONE..................................513 863-1900
Etsla Yamamura, *CEO*
Makoto Nakahara, *Prin*
▲ **EMP:** 18 **EST:** 2007
SALES (est): 2.67MM **Privately Held**
Web: www.neturen-america.com
SIC: 3398 Metal heat treating

(G-8232)
NK MACHINE INC
1550 Pleasant Ave (45015-1035)
PHONE..................................513 737-8035
Nick Emenaker, *Pr*
Edward Emenaker, *Owner*
EMP: 7 **EST:** 1987
SQ FT: 6,000
SALES (est): 966.22K **Privately Held**
Web: www.nkmachine.com
SIC: 3599 Machine shop, jobbing and repair

(G-8233)
OHIO HEAT TRANSFER
3400 Port Union Rd (45014-4224)
PHONE..................................513 870-5323
EMP: 7
SALES (est): 451.18K **Privately Held**
Web: www.ohioheattransfer.com
SIC: 3443 Fabricated plate work (boiler shop)

(G-8234)
OLIVER HEALTHCARE PACKAGING CO
Also Called: Oliver-Tolas Healthcare Packg
3840 Symmes Rd (45015-1378)
PHONE..................................513 860-6880
Heather Fletcher, *Brnch Mgr*
EMP: 222
SALES (corp-wide): 2.13B **Privately Held**
Web: www.oliverhcp.com
SIC: 2672 Chemically treated papers, made from purchased materials
HQ: Oliver Healthcare Packaging Company
445 6th St Nw
Grand Rapids MI 49504
616 456-7711

(G-8235)
PLAS-TANKS INDUSTRIES INC (PA)
39 Standen Dr (45015-2209)
PHONE..................................513 942-3800
J Kent Covey, *Pr*
Connie Royse, *
EMP: 38 **EST:** 1976
SQ FT: 33,000
SALES (est): 5.41MM
SALES (corp-wide): 5.41MM **Privately Held**
Web: www.plastanks.com
SIC: 3089 3564 3444 3084 Tubs, plastics (containers); Blowers and fans; Sheet metalwork; Plastics pipe

(G-8236)
PRODUCTION MANUFACTURING INC
870 Hanover St Bldg A (45011-3790)
PHONE..................................513 892-2331
FAX: 513 892-0014
EMP: 25
SQ FT: 75,000
SALES (est): 6.2MM **Privately Held**
SIC: 3444 Sheet metalwork

(G-8237)
PVC INDUSTRIES INC
2921 Mcbride Ct (45011-5420)
PHONE..................................518 877-8670
Louis F Simonini, *Pr*
EMP: 30 **EST:** 1992
SALES (est): 4.49MM **Privately Held**
Web: www.vinylmax.com
SIC: 3089 Windows, plastics
PA: Sturbridge Associates Iii Llc
185 Union Ave
Providence RI 02909

(G-8238)
QLOG CORP
33 Standen Dr (45015-2209)
PHONE..................................513 874-1211
J Robert Warden, *Pr*
Thomas Rebel, *VP*
EMP: 9 **EST:** 1980
SQ FT: 7,500
SALES (est): 914.25K **Privately Held**
Web: www.qlog.com
SIC: 8748 3679 Systems analysis or design; Electronic circuits

Hamilton - Butler County (G-8239)

GEOGRAPHIC SECTION

(G-8239)
RUBBER DUCK 4X4 INC
1622 Smith Rd (45013-8629)
PHONE..................513 889-1735
Travis Depew, *Owner*
EMP: 6 **EST:** 2004
SALES (est): 500K **Privately Held**
Web: www.rubberduck4x4.com
SIC: 3714 Motor vehicle parts and accessories

(G-8240)
SAICA PACK US LLC
Also Called: Saica
2995 Mcbride Ct (45011-5420)
PHONE..................513 399-5602
Ramn Alejandro, *Pr*
EMP: 24 **EST:** 2020
SALES (est): 4.4MM **Privately Held**
SIC: 2657 2631 Folding paperboard boxes; Packaging board
HQ: Sociedad Anonima Industrias Celulosa Aragonesa
Calle San Juan De La Pela 144
Zaragoza Z

(G-8241)
SCHAEFER BOX & PALLET CO
11875 Paddys Run Rd (45013-9365)
PHONE..................513 738-2500
Stanley Schaefer, *CEO*
Tod Hollifield, *
EMP: 32 **EST:** 1968
SQ FT: 45,000
SALES (est): 3.44MM **Privately Held**
Web: www.schaeferboxandpallet.com
SIC: 2449 2448 2441 Rectangular boxes and crates, wood; Pallets, wood; Nailed wood boxes and shook

(G-8242)
SHAPE SUPPLY INC
700 S Erie Hwy (45011-3904)
PHONE..................513 863-6695
Eugene Lukjan, *Pr*
EMP: 7 **EST:** 1978
SQ FT: 16,000
SALES (est): 517.97K **Privately Held**
SIC: 3444 5075 Pipe, sheet metal; Warm air heating equipment and supplies

(G-8243)
SOAPYFLUFFS LLC
Also Called: Soapyfluffs
1600 Nw Washington Blvd (45013)
P.O. Box 1600 Nw (45013)
PHONE..................937 823-0015
Robert Sihto, *Managing Member*
EMP: 6
SALES (est): 75.6K **Privately Held**
SIC: 2841 Soap and other detergents

(G-8244)
SONOSITE INC
236 High St (45011-2711)
PHONE..................425 951-1200
EMP: 7 **EST:** 2018
SALES (est): 238.41K **Privately Held**
Web: www.sonosite.com
SIC: 3845 Electromedical equipment

(G-8245)
STAT INDUSTRIES INC
3269 Profit Dr (45014-4239)
PHONE..................513 860-4482
Robyn Kellough, *Mgr*
EMP: 6
Web: www.statindex.com
SIC: 2675 Index cards, die-cut: made from purchased materials

PA: Stat Industries, Inc.
137 Stone Rd
Chillicothe OH 45601

(G-8246)
STEIMEL METAL FAB LLC
2478 Morgan Ross Rd (45013-9416)
PHONE..................513 863-5310
Richard T Steimel, *Managing Member*
EMP: 6 **EST:** 2017
SALES (est): 176.43K **Privately Held**
Web: www.steimelmetalfab.com
SIC: 3441 Fabricated structural metal

(G-8247)
TERRY ASPHALT MATERIALS INC (DH)
8600 Bilstein Blvd (45015-2204)
PHONE..................513 874-6192
Dan Koeninger, *CEO*
EMP: 25 **EST:** 2013
SALES (est): 40.11MM
SALES (corp-wide): 90.36MM **Privately Held**
Web: www.terryasphalt.com
SIC: 5082 2952 Road construction and maintenance machinery; Asphalt felts and coatings
HQ: Barrett Industries Corporation
73 Hedqrters Plz N Towe F
Morristown NJ 07960

(G-8248)
THE HAMILTON CASTER & MFG COMPANY
1637 Dixie Hwy (45011-4087)
PHONE..................513 863-3300
▲ **EMP:** 68 **EST:** 1907
SALES (est): 9.52MM **Privately Held**
Web: www.hamiltoncaster.com
SIC: 3562 3312 Casters; Wheels

(G-8249)
THYSSENKRUPP BILSTEIN AMER INC (HQ)
8685 Bilstein Blvd (45015-2205)
PHONE..................513 881-7600
Fabian Schmahl, *Pr*
▲ **EMP:** 212 **EST:** 1972
SQ FT: 115,000
SALES (est): 510.8MM
SALES (corp-wide): 40.78B **Privately Held**
Web: www.bilsteinrocks.com
SIC: 3714 5013 Shock absorbers, motor vehicle; Springs, shock absorbers and struts
PA: Thyssenkrupp Ag
Thyssenkrupp Allee 1
Essen NW 45143
2018440

(G-8250)
TIPCO PUNCH INC
6 Rowe Ct (45015-2211)
PHONE..................513 874-9140
Jack Pickins, *CEO*
Scott Ellsworth, *VP*
EMP: 30 **EST:** 1973
SQ FT: 12,000
SALES (est): 7.67MM
SALES (corp-wide): 24.64MM **Privately Held**
Web: www.tipcopunch.com
SIC: 3544 Special dies and tools
HQ: Tipco Inc
1 Coventry Rd
Brampton ON L6T 4
905 791-9811

(G-8251)
TRI-MAC MFG & SVCS CO
Also Called: Tri-Mac Mfg & Serv
860 Belle Ave (45015-1151)
PHONE..................513 896-4445
William Bates, *Pr*
Bill Galster, *VP*
EMP: 13 **EST:** 1984
SQ FT: 40,000
SALES (est): 1.12MM **Privately Held**
Web: www.trimacmanufacturing.com
SIC: 3714 3554 5084 3549 Motor vehicle parts and accessories; Paper industries machinery; Trucks, industrial; Metalworking machinery, nec

(G-8252)
TRI-STATE HOBBIES RACEWAY LLC
3379 Dixie Hwy (45015-1655)
PHONE..................513 889-3954
Roger Hasler, *Dir*
EMP: 7 **EST:** 2007
SALES (est): 119.99K **Privately Held**
SIC: 3644 Raceways

(G-8253)
TRI-STATE JET MFG LLC
1480 Beissinger Rd (45013-1110)
PHONE..................513 896-4538
Jeff Pierson, *Pr*
EMP: 6 **EST:** 2012
SALES (est): 326.75K **Privately Held**
Web: www.tristatejet.com
SIC: 3812 Aircraft/aerospace flight instruments and guidance systems

(G-8254)
TRIANGLE SIGN CO LLC
221 N B St (45013-3195)
PHONE..................513 266-1009
Donald K Whittlesey, *Pt*
Everett Hoskins Junior, *Pt*
Tim Hoskins, *Pt*
EMP: 9 **EST:** 1920
SQ FT: 6,695
SALES (est): 698.44K **Privately Held**
Web: www.trianglesigncompany.com
SIC: 3993 7389 Neon signs; Sign painting and lettering shop

(G-8255)
ULTRAEDIT INC
Also Called: IDM Computer Solutions
5559 Eureka Dr Ste B (45011-4267)
PHONE..................216 464-7465
Derek Holder, *Dir*
EMP: 79
SALES (corp-wide): 284.59MM **Privately Held**
Web: www.ultraedit.com
SIC: 7372 Prepackaged software
HQ: Ultraedit, Inc.
10801 N Mpac Expy Bldg 1
Austin TX 78759
713 523-4433

(G-8256)
VALVSYS LLC
2 Rowe Ct (45015-2211)
PHONE..................513 870-1234
Brad Frank, *Pr*
▲ **EMP:** 8 **EST:** 2000
SALES (est): 991.59K **Privately Held**
Web: www.valvsys.com
SIC: 2812 Alkalies

(G-8257)
WALLOVER OIL HAMILTON INC
Also Called: National Oil Products
1000 Forest Ave (45015-1632)
PHONE..................513 896-6692
George Marquis, *Ch*
EMP: 43 **EST:** 1963
SQ FT: 15,000
SALES (est): 2.5MM
SALES (corp-wide): 1.95B **Publicly Held**
SIC: 2992 Re-refining lubricating oils and greases, nec
HQ: Wallover Enterprises Inc.
21845 Drake Rd
Strongsville OH 44149
440 238-9250

(G-8258)
WATSON GRAVEL INC (PA)
2728 Hamilton Cleves Rd (45013-9452)
PHONE..................513 863-0070
Ronald E Watson, *Pr*
Michael T Watson, *
Janet L Meyers, *
EMP: 37 **EST:** 1970
SQ FT: 2,000
SALES (est): 9.82MM
SALES (corp-wide): 9.82MM **Privately Held**
Web: www.watsongravel.com
SIC: 1442 Gravel mining

(G-8259)
WULCO INC
Also Called: Cima
1010 Eaton Ave Ste B # B (45013-4640)
PHONE..................513 379-6115
Richard G Wulfeck, *Pr*
EMP: 95
Web: www.wulco.com
SIC: 5085 3599 Industrial supplies; Machine shop, jobbing and repair
PA: Wulco, Inc.
6899 Steger Dr Ste A
Cincinnati OH 45237

Hamler
Henry County

(G-8260)
PRIGGE WOODWORKING
520 E Edgerton St (43524-9786)
PHONE..................419 274-1005
Kevin Prigge, *Prin*
EMP: 8 **EST:** 2008
SALES (est): 375.78K **Privately Held**
Web: www.priggewoodworking.com
SIC: 2431 Millwork

Hannibal
Monroe County

(G-8261)
ORMET CORPORATION
43840 State Rte 7 (43931)
PHONE..................740 483-1381
◆ **EMP:** 1250
Web: www.ormet.com
SIC: 3334 Primary aluminum

(G-8262)
ORMET PRIMARY ALUMINUM CORP
Also Called: Velvetflow
43840 State Rt 7 (43931)
PHONE..................740 483-1381
▲ **EMP:** 1100
Web: www.burnsideterminal.com
SIC: 3334 3297 Aluminum ingots and slabs; Nonclay refractories

Harrison
Hamilton County

(G-8263)
ABRA AUTO BODY & GLASS LP
Also Called: ABRA Autobody & Glass
10106 Harrison Ave (45030-1925)
PHONE..................................513 367-9200
EMP: 8
Web: www.abraauto.com
SIC: 7532 2851 Body shop, automotive; Paint removers
HQ: Abra Auto Body & Glass Lp
7225 Northland Dr N # 110
Brooklyn Park MN 55428
888 872-2272

(G-8264)
ALLIANCE KNIFE INC
124 May Dr (45030-2024)
P.O. Box 729 (45030-0729)
PHONE..................................513 367-9000
William L Keith, *Pr*
Sharon Keith, *Sec*
◆ **EMP:** 20 **EST:** 1985
SALES (est): 5.9MM **Privately Held**
Web: www.allianceknife.com
SIC: 5085 3545 Knives, industrial; Machine knives, metalworking

(G-8265)
BELL INDUSTRIES
9843 New Haven Rd (45030-1836)
PHONE..................................513 353-2355
Edward Vierling, *Owner*
EMP: 10 **EST:** 1933
SQ FT: 8,600
SALES (est): 889.68K **Privately Held**
Web: www.bell-ind.com
SIC: 3931 Bells (musical instruments)

(G-8266)
BRUENEMAN SALES INC
11583 Carolina Trace Rd (45030-9504)
PHONE..................................513 520-3377
EMP: 6 **EST:** 2008
SALES (est): 244.63K **Privately Held**
Web: www.bruenemansales.com
SIC: 3523 Greens mowing equipment

(G-8267)
CATEXEL NEASE LLC
Also Called: Nease Performance Chemicals
10740 Paddys Run Rd (45030-9251)
PHONE..................................513 738-1255
Frank Canepa, *Brnch Mgr*
EMP: 60
SALES (corp-wide): 355.83K **Privately Held**
Web: www.neaseco.com
SIC: 2869 Glycol ethers
HQ: Catexel Nease Llc
9774 Windisch Rd
West Chester OH 45069

(G-8268)
CINCINNATI CRANE & HOIST LLC
10860 Paddys Run Rd (45030-9252)
P.O. Box 1072 (45012-1072)
PHONE..................................513 202-1408
Richard Strobl, *CEO*
EMP: 13 **EST:** 2008
SQ FT: 36,000
SALES (est): 2.9MM **Privately Held**
Web: www.cincinnati-crane.com
SIC: 3536 1796 Hoists, cranes, and monorails; Installing building equipment

(G-8269)
CINCINNATI INCORPORATED (PA)
7420 Kilby Rd (45030-8915)
P.O. Box 11111 (45211-0111)
PHONE..................................513 367-7100
EMP: 244 **EST:** 1898
SALES (est): 52.23MM
SALES (corp-wide): 52.23MM **Privately Held**
Web: www.e-ci.com
SIC: 3549 Metalworking machinery, nec

(G-8270)
CINCINNATI TEST SYSTEMS INC (HQ)
10100 Progress Way (45030-1295)
PHONE..................................513 202-5100
Barbara A Jackson, *Prin*
Kevin Hansell, *
Joanna Moncivaiz, *
EMP: 51 **EST:** 1981
SQ FT: 25,000
SALES (est): 51.87MM
SALES (corp-wide): 287.07MM **Privately Held**
Web: www.cincinnati-test.com
SIC: 3823 Pressure measurement instruments, industrial
PA: Tasi Holdings, Inc.
40 Locke Dr Ste B
Marlborough MA 01752
513 202-5182

(G-8271)
COATING SYSTEMS INC
Also Called: C S I
150 Sales Ave (45030-1484)
PHONE..................................513 367-5600
Thomas W Ritter, *Pr*
John Ritter, *VP*
EMP: 17 **EST:** 1974
SQ FT: 20,000
SALES (est): 1.72MM **Privately Held**
Web: www.coatingsystems.com
SIC: 3479 Coating of metals and formed products

(G-8272)
CROWN PLASTICS CO LLC
116 May Dr (45030-2095)
PHONE..................................513 367-0238
Gary Ellerhorst, *Pr*
Gregg Ellerhorst, *
Ken Myers, *Stockholder*
Robert H Ellerhorst, *
▲ **EMP:** 52 **EST:** 1972
SQ FT: 56,000
SALES (est): 15.69MM **Privately Held**
Web: www.crownplastics.com
SIC: 2821 3081 Plastics materials and resins; Polypropylene film and sheet

(G-8273)
F & M MAFCO INC (HQ)
9149 Dry Fork Rd (45030-1901)
P.O. Box 11013 (45211-0013)
PHONE..................................513 367-2151
Gary Bernardez, *CEO*
◆ **EMP:** 186 **EST:** 1946
SQ FT: 85,000
SALES (est): 97.61MM
SALES (corp-wide): 180.37MM **Privately Held**
Web: www.ameco.com
SIC: 5085 5072 7353 5082 Welding supplies; Hardware; Heavy construction equipment rental; General construction machinery and equipment
PA: American Equipment Company, Inc.
2106 Anderson Rd
Greenville SC 29611

864 295-7800

(G-8274)
FEILHAUERS MACHINE SHOP INC
421 Industrial Dr (45030-2104)
PHONE..................................513 202-0545
Don Feilhauer, *Pr*
EMP: 11 **EST:** 1979
SQ FT: 8,000
SALES (est): 2.24MM **Privately Held**
SIC: 3599 Machine shop, jobbing and repair

(G-8275)
FRONTIER SIGNS & DISPLAYS INC
525 New Biddinger Rd (45030-1252)
P.O. Box 328 (45030-0328)
PHONE..................................513 367-0813
Jack S Wuesterfeld, *Pr*
Ruth Wuesterfeld, *Sec*
EMP: 7 **EST:** 1945
SQ FT: 17,000
SALES (est): 965.82K **Privately Held**
Web: www.frontiersigns.net
SIC: 2521 2522 3993 Wood office furniture; Office furniture, except wood; Signs and advertising specialties

(G-8276)
GEOGRAPH INDUSTRIES INC
475 Industrial Dr (45030-2104)
PHONE..................................513 202-9200
George Freudiger, *Pr*
Mark Freudiger, *
George Michael Freudiger, *
EMP: 26 **EST:** 1988
SQ FT: 25,000
SALES (est): 6.05MM **Privately Held**
Web: www.geograph-ind.com
SIC: 2541 3993 2521 2522 Wood partitions and fixtures; Signs and advertising specialties; Cabinets, office: wood; Chairs, office: padded or plain: except wood

(G-8277)
GREER & WHITEHEAD CNSTR INC (PA)
510 S State St Ste D (45030-1494)
PHONE..................................513 202-1757
Steven Whitehead, *Pr*
EMP: 8 **EST:** 1992
SALES (est): 397.38K
SALES (corp-wide): 397.38K **Privately Held**
SIC: 1711 1389 Mechanical contractor; Building oil and gas well foundations on site

(G-8278)
HALEX/SCOTT FETZER COMPANY (HQ)
Also Called: Halex, A Scott Fetzer Company
101 Production Dr (45030-1477)
PHONE..................................800 749-3261
Gary Heeman, *Pr*
◆ **EMP:** 25 **EST:** 1985
SALES (est): 23.61MM
SALES (corp-wide): 226 **Privately Held**
Web: www.halexco.com
SIC: 3699 Electrical equipment and supplies, nec
PA: The Scott Fetzer Company
28800 Clemens Rd
Westlake OH 44145
440 892-3000

(G-8279)
HOME CITY ICE COMPANY
5709 State Rte 128 (45030)
PHONE..................................513 353-9346
Cliff Riegler, *Mgr*
EMP: 10

SALES (corp-wide): 100.42MM **Privately Held**
Web: www.homecityice.com
SIC: 2097 Manufactured ice
PA: The Home City Ice Company
6045 Bridgetown Rd Ste 1
Cincinnati OH 45248
513 574-1800

(G-8280)
JTM PROVISIONS COMPANY INC (PA)
Also Called: Jtm Food Group
200 Sales Ave (45030-1485)
PHONE..................................513 367-4900
Anthony A Maas, *Pr*
John Maas Junior, *VP*
Jerome Maas, *
Joseph Maas, *
EMP: 400 **EST:** 1963
SQ FT: 96,000
SALES (est): 177.52MM
SALES (corp-wide): 177.52MM **Privately Held**
Web: www.jtmfoodgroup.com
SIC: 2038 Frozen specialties, nec

(G-8281)
JTM PROVISIONS COMPANY INC
Also Called: Jtm Food Group
270 Industrial Dr (45030)
PHONE..................................513 367-4900
Anthony A Maas, *Brnch Mgr*
EMP: 300
SALES (corp-wide): 177.52MM **Privately Held**
Web: www.jtmfoodgroup.com
SIC: 2038 Frozen specialties, nec
PA: Jtm Provisions Company, Inc.
200 Sales Ave
Harrison OH 45030
513 367-4900

(G-8282)
KAPLAN INDUSTRIES INC
Also Called: Midwest Cylinder
6255 Kilby Rd (45030-9440)
PHONE..................................856 779-8181
Dean Kaplan, *Pr*
Rita Kaplan, *
Jim Johnston, *
◆ **EMP:** 70 **EST:** 1959
SQ FT: 6,000
SALES (est): 22.87MM **Privately Held**
Web: www.kaplanindustries.com
SIC: 3491 8734 Compressed gas cylinder valves; Hydrostatic testing laboratory

(G-8283)
PCS PHOSPHATE COMPANY INC
10818 Paddys Run Rd (45030-9252)
PHONE..................................513 738-1261
Jack Sullivan, *Mgr*
EMP: 112
SALES (corp-wide): 29.06B **Privately Held**
SIC: 2819 Phosphates, except fertilizers: defluorinated and ammoniated
HQ: Pcs Phosphate Company, Inc.
1101 Skokie Blvd Ste 400
Northbrook IL 60062
847 849-4200

(G-8284)
POWEREX-IWATA AIR TECH INC
Also Called: Powerex
150 Production Dr (45030-1477)
PHONE..................................888 769-7979
Gary Heman, *Pr*
Charles Heman, *
Pruce Jacobs, *
▲ **EMP:** 70 **EST:** 1986

SQ FT: 75,000
SALES (est): 22.93MM
SALES (corp-wide): 226 Privately Held
Web: www.powerexinc.com
SIC: 3563 Air and gas compressors
PA: The Scott Fetzer Company
    28800 Clemens Rd
    Westlake OH 44145
    440 892-3000

(G-8285)
PRECISION FABRICATORS INC
707 Enterprise Dr (45030-1696)
PHONE..................................513 288-3358
Mike Geyer, Owner
EMP: 6 EST: 2018
SALES (est): 474.52K Privately Held
Web: www.precision-fab.com
SIC: 3443 Fabricated plate work (boiler shop)

(G-8286)
PREMIER INK SYSTEMS INC (PA)
10420 N State St (45030)
P.O. Box P.O. Box 670 (45030)
PHONE..................................513 367-2300
Thomas Farmer, Pr
EMP: 15 EST: 1984
SALES (est): 9.65MM
SALES (corp-wide): 9.65MM Privately Held
Web: www.premierink.com
SIC: 2851 2893 2899 Lacquers, varnishes, enamels, and other coatings; Printing ink; Chemical preparations, nec

(G-8287)
PUTTMANN INDUSTRIES INC
Also Called: Atlas Dowel & Wood Products Co
320 N State St (45030-1146)
P.O. Box 327 (45030-0327)
PHONE..................................513 202-9444
Peter Puttmann, Pr
▲ EMP: 15 EST: 1951
SQ FT: 65,000
SALES (est): 1.72MM Privately Held
Web: www.atlasdowel.com
SIC: 2499 Dowels, wood

(G-8288)
QUIKRETE COMPANIES LLC
Also Called: Quikrete Cincinnati
5425 Kilby Rd (45030-8910)
PHONE..................................513 367-6135
Glen Lainhart, Mgr
EMP: 38
SQ FT: 21,340
Web: www.quikrete.com
SIC: 3272 3273 Dry mixture concrete; Ready-mixed concrete
HQ: The Quikrete Companies Llc
    5 Concourse Pkwy Ste 1900
    Atlanta GA 30328
    404 634-9100

(G-8289)
R L TORBECK INDUSTRIES INC
Also Called: Torbeck Industries
355 Industrial Dr (45030-1483)
PHONE..................................513 367-0080
Richard L Torbeck Junior, Pr
EMP: 38 EST: 1975
SQ FT: 67,000
SALES (est): 2.73MM Privately Held
Web: www.torbeckind.com
SIC: 3441 3499 3448 3444 Fabricated structural metal; Metal household articles; Prefabricated metal buildings and components; Sheet metalwork

(G-8290)
SEKUWORKS LLC
Also Called: Northern Bank Note Company
9487 Dry Fork Rd (45030-2900)
PHONE..................................513 202-1210
EMP: 38
Web: www.sekuworks.com
SIC: 2754 2752 2759 Commercial printing, gravure; Commercial printing, lithographic; Commercial printing, nec

(G-8291)
SHIM SHACK
105 May Dr (45030-2023)
PHONE..................................877 557-3930
EMP: 7 EST: 2013
SALES (est): 239.91K Privately Held
Web: www.theshimshack.com
SIC: 3499 Shims, metal

(G-8292)
SIMPSON & SONS INC
10220 Harrison Ave (45030-1938)
PHONE..................................513 367-0152
Joseph A Simpson, Pr
James Simpson, VP
EMP: 12 EST: 1973
SQ FT: 10,500
SALES (est): 978.72K Privately Held
SIC: 4789 7692 Railroad maintenance and repair services; Welding repair

(G-8293)
STELTER AND BRINCK INC
201 Sales Ave (45030-1472)
PHONE..................................513 367-9300
Joseph A Brinck Ii, Pr
Henry Stelter, *
Larry Brinck, *
Mary B Turpen, *
EMP: 35 EST: 1940
SQ FT: 17,000
SALES (est): 9.16MM Privately Held
Web: www.stelterbrinck.com
SIC: 3564 3567 3494 3433 Blowers and fans ; Industrial furnaces and ovens; Valves and pipe fittings, nec; Heating equipment, except electric

(G-8294)
STOP STICK LTD
Also Called: Stop Stick, Liability Company
365 Industrial Dr (45030-1498)
PHONE..................................513 202-5500
Andrew Morrison, Pr
Louis M Groen, Managing Member
▲ EMP: 25 EST: 1993
SQ FT: 10,000
SALES (est): 4.3MM Privately Held
Web: www.stopstick.com
SIC: 3315 Nails, spikes, brads, and similar items

(G-8295)
SUPERIOR STRUCTURES INC
320 N State St (45030-1146)
P.O. Box 26 (45030-0026)
PHONE..................................513 942-5954
Tim Bischel, Prin
Charles Hatfield, Sec
EMP: 10 EST: 2000
SQ FT: 7,500
SALES (est): 2.18MM Privately Held
Web: www.superiorstructuresinc.com
SIC: 3448 1531 Greenhouses, prefabricated metal; Operative builders

(G-8296)
WAYNE/SCOTT FETZER COMPANY
Also Called: Wayne Water Systems
101 Production Dr (45030-1477)
PHONE..................................800 237-0987
Duane Johnson, Pr
▲ EMP: 200 EST: 1985
SQ FT: 160,000
SALES (est): 52.15MM
SALES (corp-wide): 226 Privately Held
Web: www.waynepumps.com
SIC: 3561 5074 Pumps, domestic: water or sump; Water purification equipment
PA: The Scott Fetzer Company
    28800 Clemens Rd
    Westlake OH 44145
    440 892-3000

(G-8297)
WHITEWATER PROCESSING LLC
10964 Campbell Rd (45030-8902)
PHONE..................................513 367-4133
Ryan Kopp, Pr
Kristin Feller, *
EMP: 100 EST: 1929
SQ FT: 7,500
SALES (est): 9.19MM Privately Held
SIC: 2015 Turkey, slaughtered and dressed

Hartford
Trumbull County

(G-8298)
STANWADE METAL PRODUCTS INC
Also Called: Stanwade Tanks and Equipment
6868 State Rt 305 (44424)
P.O. Box 10 (44424-0010)
PHONE..................................330 772-2421
EMP: 44 EST: 1947
SALES (est): 5.25MM Privately Held
Web: www.stanwade.com
SIC: 3443 5084 Fuel tanks (oil, gas, etc.), metal plate; Petroleum industry machinery

Hartville
Stark County

(G-8299)
CNB MACHINING AND MFG LLC
1052 Manning Rd Nw (44632-9505)
PHONE..................................330 877-2786
Richard Reaven, Prin
EMP: 10 EST: 2011
SALES (est): 382.85K Privately Held
SIC: 3999 Manufacturing industries, nec

(G-8300)
HARTVILLE CHOCOLATES INC
Also Called: Hartville Chocolate Factory
114 S Prospect Ave (44632-8906)
P.O. Box 1360 (44632-1360)
PHONE..................................330 877-1999
Mary L Barton, Pr
EMP: 17 EST: 1984
SQ FT: 3,200
SALES (est): 475.03K Privately Held
Web: www.hartvillechocolatefactory.com
SIC: 2066 5441 5999 Chocolate; Candy; Cake decorating supplies

(G-8301)
HERITAGE TRUCK EQUIPMENT INC
661 Powell Ave (44632-7800)
PHONE..................................330 699-4491
Eric Bontrager, Pr
Brian Bontrager, *
EMP: 85 EST: 2000
SALES (est): 16.37MM Privately Held
Web: www.heritagetruck.com
SIC: 3537 Trucks, tractors, loaders, carriers, and similar equipment

(G-8302)
L C F INC
Also Called: Love Chocolate Factory
114 S Prospect Ave (44632-8906)
P.O. Box 1360 (44632-1360)
PHONE..................................330 877-3322
Robert M Barton, Pr
▼ EMP: 9 EST: 1986
SQ FT: 12,000
SALES (est): 345.37K Privately Held
Web: www.strategicimpact.com
SIC: 2066 Chocolate candy, solid

(G-8303)
MITCHELL PIPING LLC
1101 Sunnyside St Sw (44632-9066)
PHONE..................................330 245-0258
EMP: 30 EST: 2010
SALES (est): 2.88MM Privately Held
Web: www.mitchell-piping.com
SIC: 3498 Fabricated pipe and fittings

(G-8304)
RANDOLPH TOOL COMPANY INC
750 Wales Dr (44632-8852)
PHONE..................................330 877-4923
Patrick Franze, Pr
Lisa M Franze, Treas
EMP: 12 EST: 1968
SQ FT: 5,800
SALES (est): 2.21MM Privately Held
Web: www.randolphtoolco.com
SIC: 3599 3423 Machine shop, jobbing and repair; Knives, agricultural or industrial

(G-8305)
ROCK SOLID CUT STONE & SUP INC
12989 Market Ave N (44632-9063)
PHONE..................................330 877-2775
Shawn Wittmer, Prin
EMP: 6 EST: 2015
SALES (est): 233.1K Privately Held
SIC: 3281 Paving blocks, cut stone

(G-8306)
SCANACON INCORPORATED
950 Wales Dr (44632-8856)
PHONE..................................330 877-7600
Kevin Wolf, Pr
Sven Hedman, Ch Bd
▲ EMP: 6 EST: 1995
SALES (est): 5.86MM
SALES (corp-wide): 249.37K Privately Held
Web: www.scanacon.com
SIC: 3565 Canning machinery, food
HQ: Scanacon Ab
    Fagerstagatan 18b
    SpAnga 163 5
    856482300

(G-8307)
SCOTT PROCESS SYSTEMS INC
Also Called: Spsi
1160 Sunnyside St Sw (44632-9098)
PHONE..................................330 877-2350
Andrew Hawranick, Pr
◆ EMP: 240 EST: 1983
SQ FT: 100,000
SALES (est): 40.1MM
SALES (corp-wide): 164.89MM Privately Held
Web: www.scottprocess.com
SIC: 3498 Pipe sections, fabricated from purchased pipe
PA: Ansgar Industrial, Llc
    6000 Fairview Rd Ste 1200
    Charlotte NC 28210
    866 284-1931

▲ = Import ▼ = Export
◆ = Import/Export

Haverhill
Scioto County

(G-8308)
ALTIVIA PETROCHEMICALS LLC
1019 Haverhill Ohio Furnace Rd (45636)
PHONE...................740 532-3420
Mark Tipton, *Mgr*
EMP: 50
SALES (corp-wide): 103.68MM **Privately Held**
Web: www.altivia.com
SIC: 2865 Phenol, alkylated and cumene
PA: Altivia Petrochemicals, Llc
  1100 La St Ste 4800
  Houston TX 77002
  713 658-9000

Haviland
Paulding County

(G-8309)
CUSTOM ASSEMBLY INC
2952 Road 107 (45851-9638)
PHONE...................419 622-3040
George Keysor, *Pr*
Sharon Keysor, *
Gus A Schlatter, *
Steven R Plummer, *
EMP: 50 **EST:** 1985
SQ FT: 60,000
SALES (est): 11.58MM **Privately Held**
Web: www.customassembly.net
SIC: 3751 Motorcycles, bicycles and parts

(G-8310)
DRAINAGE PRODUCTS INC
100 Main St (45851-8603)
P.O. Box 61 (45851-0061)
PHONE...................419 622-6951
Craig A Stoller, *Pr*
Thomas Coy, *Sec*
EMP: 19 **EST:** 1978
SALES (est): 2.46MM **Privately Held**
Web: www.haviland-drainage.com
SIC: 3084 Plastics pipe

(G-8311)
HAVILAND CULVERT COMPANY
100 Main St (45851-8603)
P.O. Box 97 (45851-0097)
PHONE...................419 622-6951
Russell W Stoller, *Pr*
Thomas A Gordon, *Sec*
EMP: 7 **EST:** 1972
SALES (est): 943.68K **Privately Held**
Web: www.haviland-drainage.com
SIC: 3272 Pipe, concrete or lined with concrete

(G-8312)
HAVILAND DRAINAGE PRODUCTS CO (PA)
100 Main St (45851-8603)
PHONE...................800 860-6294
Russell Stoller, *Pr*
Todd Stoller, *Sec*
EMP: 17 **EST:** 1924
SQ FT: 1,000
SALES (est): 5.24MM
SALES (corp-wide): 5.24MM **Privately Held**
Web: www.haviland-drainage.com
SIC: 3259 Drain tile, clay

(G-8313)
HAVILAND PLASTIC PRODUCTS CO
119 Main St (45851-8603)
P.O. Box 38 (45851-0038)
PHONE...................419 622-3110
▼ **EMP:** 26 **EST:** 1995
SALES (est): 4.36MM **Privately Held**
Web: www.havilandplastics.com
SIC: 3089 Injection molding of plastics

(G-8314)
MODERN PLASTICS RECOVERY INC
100 Main St (45851-8603)
P.O. Box 38 (45851-0038)
PHONE...................419 622-4611
Craig Stoller, *Pr*
EMP: 11 **EST:** 1990
SALES (est): 597.78K **Privately Held**
Web: www.havilandplastics.com
SIC: 2821 Plastics materials and resins

Hayesville
Ashland County

(G-8315)
COBURN INC (PA)
636 Ashland County Rd 30 A (44838)
P.O. Box 447 (44805-0447)
PHONE...................419 368-4051
Charles Zimmerman, *CEO*
Todd Zimmerman, *
EMP: 65 **EST:** 1966
SQ FT: 82,000
SALES (est): 9.07MM
SALES (corp-wide): 9.07MM **Privately Held**
Web: www.coburn-inc.com
SIC: 2631 Container, packaging, and boxboard

Heath
Licking County

(G-8316)
AMERICAN VENEER EDGEBANDING CO
Also Called: A.V.E.C.
1700 James Pkwy (43056-4027)
PHONE...................740 928-2700
Germany Heigtz, *Prin*
▲ **EMP:** 6 **EST:** 1997
SQ FT: 30,000
SALES (est): 2.41MM
SALES (corp-wide): 1.96B **Privately Held**
Web: www.avec-usa.com
SIC: 2435 2436 Veneer stock, hardwood; Veneer stock, softwood
HQ: Heitz International Beteiligungs Gmbh
  Maschweg 27
  Melle NI

(G-8317)
ATLANTIC INERTIAL SYSTEMS INC
781 Irving Wick Dr W Ste 01 (43056-9492)
PHONE...................740 788-3800
Al Bonacci, *Brnch Mgr*
EMP: 103
SALES (corp-wide): 68.92B **Publicly Held**
Web: www.atlanticinertial.com
SIC: 3812 Gyroscopes
HQ: Atlantic Inertial Systems Inc.
  250 Knotter Dr
  Cheshire CT 06410
  203 250-3500

(G-8318)
BOEING COMPANY
Also Called: Boeing
801 Irving Wick Dr W (43056-1199)
PHONE...................740 788-4000
Daniel Acassidy, *Brnch Mgr*
EMP: 25
SALES (corp-wide): 77.79B **Publicly Held**
Web: www.boeing.com
SIC: 3721 3812 Airplanes, fixed or rotary wing; Search and navigation equipment
PA: The Boeing Company
  929 Long Bridge Dr
  Arlington VA 22202
  703 465-3500

(G-8319)
DATA IMAGE
2345 Gratiot Rd Se (43056-9743)
PHONE...................740 763-7008
Dave Speelman, *Owner*
EMP: 6 **EST:** 1987
SALES (est): 230.65K **Privately Held**
Web: www.d-image.com
SIC: 2759 Laser printing

(G-8320)
GUSHEN AMERICA INC
701 International Dr (43056-1108)
PHONE...................708 664-2852
Shiwei Li, *Pr*
Shiwei Li, *Managing Member*
Zulin Shi, *Sec*
EMP: 6 **EST:** 2016
SALES (est): 933.21K **Privately Held**
SIC: 2869 Perfumes, flavorings, and food additives

(G-8321)
HARTMAN DISTRIBUTING LLC
1262 Bluejack Ln (43056-8228)
PHONE...................740 616-7764
EMP: 84 **EST:** 2012
SALES (est): 2.41MM **Privately Held**
SIC: 2759 Screen printing

(G-8322)
ISO TECHNOLOGIES INC
1870 James Pkwy (43056-4003)
PHONE...................740 928-0084
EMP: 20
SALES (corp-wide): 5.06MM **Privately Held**
Web: www.isotechfoam.com
SIC: 3086 Plastics foam products
PA: Iso Technologies, Inc.
  200 Milliken Dr
  Hebron OH 43025
  740 928-0084

(G-8323)
KAISER ALUMINUM FAB PDTS LLC
Also Called: Kaiser Aluminum Newark Works
600 Kaiser Dr (43056)
PHONE...................740 522-1151
Eric Angermeier, *Mgr*
EMP: 250
SALES (corp-wide): 3.09B **Publicly Held**
Web: www.kaiseraluminum.com
SIC: 3355 3334 Rods, rolled, aluminum; Primary aluminum
HQ: Kaiser Aluminum Fabricated Products, Llc
  1550 W Mcewen Dr Ste 500,
  Franklin TN 37067

(G-8324)
KLARITY MEDICAL PRODUCTS LLC
600 Industrial Pkwy Ste A (43056-1636)
PHONE...................740 788-8107
EMP: 10 **EST:** 2012
SALES (est): 2.23MM **Privately Held**
Web: www.klaritymedical.com
SIC: 3841 Surgical and medical instruments

(G-8325)
NAT2 INC
1675 James Pkwy (43056-4032)
PHONE...................614 270-2507
Shirley Bartee, *Mgr*
EMP: 21
SALES (corp-wide): 1.13MM **Privately Held**
SIC: 2099 Food preparations, nec
PA: Nat2, Inc.
  8754 Cotter St
  Lewis Center OH 43035
  614 270-2507

(G-8326)
PLANT PLANT CO ✪
630 Kaiser Dr (43056)
PHONE...................303 809-9588
Aaron Matthew Tullman, *CEO*
EMP: 25 **EST:** 2024
SALES (est): 985.44K **Privately Held**
SIC: 2099 Food preparations, nec

(G-8327)
POLYMER TECH & SVCS INC (HQ)
Also Called: Pts
1835 James Pkwy (43056-1092)
PHONE...................740 929-5500
Sharad Thakkar, *Pr*
EMP: 10 **EST:** 2002
SQ FT: 50,000
SALES (est): 5.12MM
SALES (corp-wide): 11.46MM **Privately Held**
Web: www.polymertechnologiesinc.com
SIC: 2611 2821 Pulp mills; Plastics materials and resins
PA: Niche Polymer Llc
  8815 Centre Park Dr # 400
  Columbia MD 21045
  304 273-1200

(G-8328)
R D HOLDER OIL CO INC
1000 Keller Dr (43056-8055)
PHONE...................740 522-3136
EMP: 18
SALES (corp-wide): 9.17MM **Privately Held**
Web: www.holderoil.com
SIC: 1311 Crude petroleum and natural gas
PA: R. D. Holder Oil Co., Inc.
  600 N Dayton Lakeview Rd
  New Carlisle OH 45344
  800 243-0432

(G-8329)
RAMP CREEK III LTD
1100 Thornwood Dr Lot 1 (43056-9501)
P.O. Box 240 (43068-0240)
PHONE...................740 522-0660
Roberto Ditommaso, *Prin*
EMP: 9 **EST:** 2001
SALES (est): 445.07K **Privately Held**
Web: www.rampcreek.com
SIC: 3272 Housing components, prefabricated concrete

(G-8330)
RTZ MANUFACTURING CO
12755 Fairview Rd (43056-9043)
P.O. Box 289 (43085-0289)
PHONE...................614 848-8366
Zoe Rosser, *Pr*
Ty Rosser, *VP*
EMP: 9 **EST:** 1994

Heath - Licking County (G-8331)

SALES (est): 981.99K **Privately Held**
SIC: **3599** Custom machinery

(G-8331)
SAMUEL SON & CO (USA) INC
Samuel Packaging Systems Group
1455 James Pkwy (43056-4007)
PHONE.................................740 522-2500
Jay Jones, *Mgr*
EMP: 100
SALES (corp-wide): 504.18MM **Privately Held**
Web: www.samuel.com
SIC: **3089** 5085 5084 5199 Plastics processing; Industrial supplies; Industrial machinery and equipment; Packaging materials
PA: Samuel, Son & Co. (Usa) Inc.
   1401 Davey Rd Ste 300
   Woodridge IL 60517
   800 323-4424

(G-8332)
UNDERGROUND EYES II LLC
2828 Ritchey Rd (43056-9063)
PHONE.................................352 601-1446
EMP: 6 **EST:** 2020
SALES (est): 301.62K **Privately Held**
SIC: **3732** Boatbuilding and repairing

(G-8333)
XPERION E & E USA LLC
1475 James Pkwy (43056-4007)
PHONE.................................740 788-9560
EMP: 25 **EST:** 2013
SQ FT: 50,000
SALES (est): 6.76MM **Privately Held**
SIC: **3624** Fibers, carbon and graphite
HQ: Hexagon Purus Gmbh
   Hannoversche Str. 1
   Kassel HE 34134
   561585490

Hebron
Licking County

(G-8334)
4W SERVICES
7901 Minecaster Rd (43025)
PHONE.................................614 554-5427
Donald White, *Owner*
EMP: 15 **EST:** 2011
SALES (est): 1.33MM **Privately Held**
SIC: **3715** 8999 Semitrailers for truck tractors ; Artists and artists' studios

(G-8335)
ALLIED TUBE & CONDUIT CORP
250 Capital Dr (43025-9489)
PHONE.................................740 928-1018
Scott Shipley, *Brnch Mgr*
EMP: 16
Web: www.atkore.com
SIC: **3644** Electric conduits and fittings
HQ: Allied Tube & Conduit Corporation
   16100 S Center Ave
   Harvey IL 60426
   708 339-1610

(G-8336)
ARMORSOURCE LLC
3600 Hebron Rd (43025-9664)
PHONE.................................740 928-0070
Yoav Kapah, *CEO*
Donald Blake, *Ex VP*
Tim Tallentire, *CFO*
▼ **EMP:** 20 **EST:** 2005
SQ FT: 120,000
SALES (est): 5.73MM **Privately Held**
Web: www.armorsource.com
SIC: **3469** Helmets, steel

(G-8337)
COVESTRO LLC
1111 O Neill Dr (43025-9409)
PHONE.................................740 929-2015
Lora Rand, *Mgr*
EMP: 150
SALES (corp-wide): 15.63B **Privately Held**
Web: www.covestro.com
SIC: **2822** 2821 Synthetic rubber; Plastics materials and resins
HQ: Covestro Llc
   1 Covestro Cir
   Pittsburgh PA 15205
   412 413-2000

(G-8338)
DIEBOLD NIXDORF INCORPORATED
Also Called: Self-Srvice PDT Dist Shipg Ctr
1050 O Neill Dr (43025)
PHONE.................................740 928-0200
EMP: 59
SALES (corp-wide): 1.63B **Publicly Held**
Web: www.dieboldnixdorf.com
SIC: **3578** Automatic teller machines (ATM)
PA: Diebold Nixdorf, Incorporated
   350 Orchard Ave Ne
   North Canton OH 44720
   330 490-4000

(G-8339)
DIEBOLD NIXDORF INCORPORATED
Also Called: Midwest Division
511 Milliken Dr (43025-9657)
PHONE.................................740 928-1010
Bob Brown, *Mgr*
EMP: 200
SALES (corp-wide): 1.63B **Publicly Held**
Web: www.dieboldnixdorf.com
SIC: **3499** 3578 Safes and vaults, metal; Banking machines
PA: Diebold Nixdorf, Incorporated
   350 Orchard Ave Ne
   North Canton OH 44720
   330 490-4000

(G-8340)
DJSC INC
1001 O Neill Dr (43025-9409)
P.O. Box 881 (43025-0881)
PHONE.................................740 928-2697
Christopher B Hollingshead, *Prin*
Debra Jean Dehmann, *Prin*
John M Hollingshead, *Prin*
Steven C Hollingshead, *Prin*
EMP: 38 **EST:** 1983
SQ FT: 22,500
SALES (est): 10.86MM **Privately Held**
SIC: **2752** 2759 Commercial printing, lithographic; Commercial printing, nec

(G-8341)
FOLDEDPAK INC
263 Milliken Dr (43025-9657)
PHONE.................................740 527-1090
EMP: 7 **EST:** 2015
SALES (est): 169.69K **Privately Held**
SIC: **2675** Die-cut paper and board

(G-8342)
FORCEONE LLC
3600 Hebron Rd (43025-9664)
PHONE.................................513 939-1018
EMP: 16 **EST:** 2000
SQ FT: 17,000
SALES (est): 384.05K **Privately Held**
SIC: **3842** Bulletproof vests

(G-8343)
HENDRICKSON INTERNATIONAL CORP
Also Called: Hendrickson Auxiliary Axles
277 N High St (43025-8008)
PHONE.................................740 929-5600
Mike Keeler, *Genl Mgr*
EMP: 78
SALES (corp-wide): 758.84MM **Privately Held**
Web: www.hendrickson-intl.com
SIC: **3714** 3493 3089 5084 Motor vehicle parts and accessories; Steel springs, except wire; Plastics containers, except foam; Industrial machinery and equipment
HQ: Hendrickson International Corporation
   840 S Frontage Rd
   Woodridge IL 60517

(G-8344)
HENDRICKSON USA LLC
277 N High St (43025-8008)
PHONE.................................740 929-5600
EMP: 382
SALES (corp-wide): 758.84MM **Privately Held**
Web: www.hendrickson-intl.com
SIC: **3714** Motor vehicle parts and accessories
HQ: Hendrickson Usa, L.L.C.
   840 S Frontage Rd
   Woodridge IL 60517

(G-8345)
INTEGRIS COMPOSITES INC
1051 O Neill Dr (43025)
PHONE.................................740 928-0326
Erick Johnson, *Brnch Mgr*
EMP: 65
Web: www.integriscomposites.com
SIC: **3229** 3795 8711 Yarn, fiberglass; Tanks and tank components; Engineering services
HQ: Integris Composites, Inc.
   8075 Leesburg Pike # 210
   Vienna VA 22182

(G-8346)
ISO TECHNOLOGIES INC (PA)
200 Milliken Dr (43025-9657)
PHONE.................................740 928-0084
Alan Benton, *Pr*
EMP: 10 **EST:** 1997
SQ FT: 20,000
SALES (est): 5.06MM
SALES (corp-wide): 5.06MM **Privately Held**
Web: www.isotechfoam.com
SIC: **3069** Foam rubber

(G-8347)
LEAR CORPORATION
Also Called: Renosol Seating
180 N High St (43025-9011)
P.O. Box 640 (43025-0640)
PHONE.................................740 928-4358
Jeff O'sickey, *Manager*
EMP: 103
SALES (corp-wide): 23.47B **Publicly Held**
Web: www.lear.com
SIC: **3714** Motor vehicle parts and accessories
PA: Lear Corporation
   21557 Telegraph Rd
   Southfield MI 48033
   248 447-1500

(G-8348)
MOLDING TECHNOLOGIES LTD
Also Called: Molding Technologies
85 N. High Street (43025)
PHONE.................................740 929-2065
EMP: 10 **EST:** 2017
SQ FT: 60,000
SALES (est): 864.05K **Privately Held**
SIC: **3089** Injection molding of plastics

(G-8349)
MOMENTIVE PERFORMANCE MTLS INC
611 O Neill Dr (43025-9680)
PHONE.................................740 928-7010
Cherly Glaton, *Mgr*
EMP: 760
Web: www.momentive.com
SIC: **2869** 3479 Silicones; Coating of metals with silicon
HQ: Momentive Performance Materials Inc.
   2750 Balltown Rd
   Niskayuna NY 12309

(G-8350)
MPW INDUSTRIAL SVCS GROUP INC (PA)
9711 Lancaster Rd (43025-9764)
PHONE.................................740 927-8790
Monte R Black, *CEO*
Jared Black,
Sarah D Pemberton,
EMP: 255 **EST:** 1972
SQ FT: 24,000
SALES (est): 213.53MM
SALES (corp-wide): 213.53MM **Privately Held**
Web: www.mpwservices.com
SIC: **7349** 8744 3589 Cleaning service, industrial or commercial; Facilities support services; Commercial cleaning equipment

(G-8351)
MTI ACQUISITION LLC
Also Called: Molding Technologies
85 N High St (43025)
P.O. Box 730 (43025-0730)
PHONE.................................740 929-2065
Jesse Downhour, *Managing Member*
EMP: 19 **EST:** 2000
SQ FT: 55,000
SALES (est): 457.55K **Privately Held**
Web: www.moldingtechnologies.com
SIC: **3089** Plastics hardware and building products

(G-8352)
NFI INDUSTRIES INC
111 Enterprise Dr (43025-9201)
PHONE.................................740 928-9522
EMP: 15 **EST:** 2006
SALES (est): 206.59K **Privately Held**
Web: www.nfiindustries.com
SIC: **3999** Manufacturing industries, nec

(G-8353)
OHIO METAL TECHNOLOGIES INC
470 John Alford Pkwy (43025-9437)
PHONE.................................740 928-8288
▲ **EMP:** 80 **EST:** 1996
SQ FT: 20,600
SALES (est): 10.27MM **Privately Held**
Web: www.ohiometal.net
SIC: **3441** Fabricated structural metal

(G-8354)
OWENS CORNING SALES LLC
Also Called: Owens Corning
341 O Neill Dr Bldg 6 (43025-9680)
P.O. Box 1477 (43025-1477)
PHONE.................................740 928-6620
Gary Jakubcin, *Brnch Mgr*
EMP: 50
SQ FT: 81,000

GEOGRAPHIC SECTION

Hicksville - Defiance County (G-8375)

SIC: 3296 Fiberglass insulation
HQ: Owens Corning Sales, Llc
1 Owens Corning Pkwy
Toledo OH 43659
419 248-8000

(G-8355)
PALMER DONAVIN MANUFACTURING
1120 O Neill Dr (43025-9409)
PHONE..................................740 527-1111
EMP: 12 **EST:** 2015
SALES (est): 814.74K **Privately Held**
Web: www.palmerdonavin.com
SIC: 3999 Manufacturing industries, nec

(G-8356)
PLASTIPAK PACKAGING INC
Also Called: Constar International
610 O Neill Dr Bldg 22 (43025-9680)
PHONE..................................740 928-4435
Brian Dunlap, Mgr
EMP: 103
SALES (corp-wide): 2.9B **Privately Held**
Web: www.plastipak.com
SIC: 3089 3085 Plastics containers, except foam; Plastics bottles
HQ: Plastipak Packaging, Inc.
41605 Ann Arbor Rd E
Plymouth MI 48170
734 455-3600

(G-8357)
POLYMERA INC
511 Milliken Dr (43025-9657)
PHONE..................................740 527-2069
Maan Said, Pr
Herbert Hutchison, Sr VP
Jeffrey Brandt, VP
Matthew Kollar, VP
Michael Skoff, CFO
EMP: 9 **EST:** 2010
SALES (est): 1.02MM **Privately Held**
Web: www.polymera.com
SIC: 3087 Custom compound purchased resins

(G-8358)
R R DONNELLEY & SONS COMPANY
Also Called: R R Donnelley
190 Milliken Dr (43025-9657)
PHONE..................................740 928-6110
Jeff Gebhart, Brnch Mgr
EMP: 280
SALES (corp-wide): 4.99B **Privately Held**
Web: www.rrd.com
SIC: 2759 Business forms: printing, nsk
HQ: R. R. Donnelley & Sons Company
35 W Wacker Dr
Chicago IL 60601
312 326-8000

(G-8359)
RESINOID ENGINEERING CORP (PA)
251 O Neill Dr (43025)
PHONE..................................740 928-6115
Clarence A Herbst Junior, Ch
Robert C Herbst, *
◆ **EMP:** 58 **EST:** 1939
SQ FT: 70,000
SALES (est): 17.45MM
SALES (corp-wide): 17.45MM **Privately Held**
Web: www.resinoid.com
SIC: 2821 3083 3089 Molding compounds, plastics; Laminated plastics plate and sheet ; Injection molding of plastics

(G-8360)
S R DOOR INC (PA)
Also Called: Seal-Rite Door
1120 O Neill Dr (43025-9409)
P.O. Box 2109 (43216-2109)
PHONE..................................740 927-3558
Scott A Miller, Pr
Glen Miller, *
EMP: 80 **EST:** 1980
SQ FT: 75,000
SALES (est): 9.96MM
SALES (corp-wide): 9.96MM **Privately Held**
Web: www.palmerdonavin.com
SIC: 2431 3442 3211 5031 Doors, wood; Metal doors; Construction glass; Lumber, plywood, and millwork

(G-8361)
SCHWEBEL BAKING COMPANY
121 O Neill Dr (43025-9680)
PHONE..................................330 783-2860
EMP: 7
SALES (corp-wide): 403.34MM **Privately Held**
Web: www.schwebels.com
SIC: 5461 2051 Bread; Bread, cake, and related products
PA: Schwebel Baking Company
965 E Midlothian Blvd
Youngstown OH 44502
330 783-2860

(G-8362)
SMARTBILL LTD
1050 O Neill Dr (43025-9409)
PHONE..................................740 928-6909
EMP: 17 **EST:** 2001
SQ FT: 10,000
SALES (est): 2.55MM **Privately Held**
Web: www.smartbillcorp.com
SIC: 2759 Business forms: printing, nsk

(G-8363)
STATE INDUSTRIAL PRODUCTS CORP
Also Called: State Chemical Manufacturing
383 N High St (43025-9436)
PHONE..................................740 929-6370
Kale Moberg, Brnch Mgr
EMP: 76
SALES (corp-wide): 192.96MM **Privately Held**
Web: www.stateindustrial.com
SIC: 2841 5072 Soap: granulated, liquid, cake, flaked, or chip; Bolts, nuts, and screws
PA: State Industrial Products Corporation
5915 Landerbrook Dr # 300
Cleveland OH 44124
877 747-6986

(G-8364)
SUNFIELD INC
116 Enterprise Dr (43025-9200)
PHONE..................................740 928-0405
Norio Hirotani, Pr
◆ **EMP:** 70 **EST:** 1993
SQ FT: 33,000
SALES (est): 24.48MM **Privately Held**
Web: www.sunfieldinc.com
SIC: 3469 Stamping metal for the trade
HQ: Ikeda Manufacturing Co., Ltd.
135-3, Nishishinmachi
Ota GNM 373-0

(G-8365)
THK MANUFACTURING AMERICA INC
471 N High St (43025-9012)
P.O. Box 759 (43025-0759)
PHONE..................................740 928-1415
▲ **EMP:** 160 **EST:** 1997
SQ FT: 400,000
SALES (est): 48.37MM **Privately Held**
SIC: 3823 3469 Process control instruments; Machine parts, stamped or pressed metal
HQ: Thk Holdings Of America, L.L.C.
200 Commerce Dr
Schaumburg IL 60173
847 310-1111

(G-8366)
TI GROUP AUTO SYSTEMS LLC
Bundy Tubing Div
3600 Hebron Rd (43025-9664)
PHONE..................................740 929-2049
Mark Lanancusa, Mgr
EMP: 40
SALES (corp-wide): 3.82B **Privately Held**
Web: www.tifluidsystems.com
SIC: 3317 3714 3498 Steel pipe and tubes; Motor vehicle parts and accessories; Fabricated pipe and fittings
HQ: Ti Group Automotive Systems, Llc
2020 Taylor Rd
Auburn Hills MI 48326
248 296-8000

(G-8367)
TRANSCENDIA INC
Also Called: Dow Chemical
3700 Hebron Rd (43025-9665)
PHONE..................................740 929-5100
Andy Maynard, Brnch Mgr
EMP: 110
SALES (corp-wide): 290.26MM **Privately Held**
Web: www.transcendia.com
SIC: 3081 Unsupported plastics film and sheet
PA: Transcendia, Inc.
9201 Belmont Ave
Franklin Park IL 60131
847 678-1800

(G-8368)
TRULITE GL ALUM SOLUTIONS LLC
160 N High St (43025-9011)
P.O. Box 220 (43025-0220)
PHONE..................................740 929-2443
EMP: 60
SIC: 3211 5039 3231 Tempered glass; Exterior flat glass: plate or window; Products of purchased glass
PA: Trulite Glass & Aluminum Solutions, Llc
403 Westpark Ct Ste 201
Peachtree City GA 30009

(G-8369)
UNIPAC INC
2109 National Rd Sw (43025-9639)
PHONE..................................740 929-2000
David L De Ment, Pr
Chris De Ment, Sec
EMP: 22 **EST:** 1973
SQ FT: 50,000
SALES (est): 4.77MM **Privately Held**
Web: www.unipacinc.com
SIC: 2657 2653 Folding paperboard boxes; Boxes, corrugated: made from purchased materials

Hicksville
Defiance County

(G-8370)
ADROIT THINKING INC
Also Called: 5-Acre Mill
10860 State Route 2 (43526-9366)
PHONE..................................419 542-9363
Tim Becker, Pr
Mary Becker, VP
EMP: 17 **EST:** 2004
SQ FT: 28,000
SALES (est): 2.42MM **Privately Held**
SIC: 2499 Laundry products, wood

(G-8371)
ARC SOLUTIONS INC
605 Industrial Dr (43526-1177)
P.O. Box 264 (43526-0264)
PHONE..................................419 542-9272
Dennis Vetter, Pr
EMP: 25 **EST:** 2001
SQ FT: 28,800
SALES (est): 3.62MM **Privately Held**
Web: www.arcsolinc.com
SIC: 7692 7699 5084 5999 Welding repair; Industrial machinery and equipment repair; Welding machinery and equipment; Welding supplies

(G-8372)
AVALIGN TECHNOLOGIES INC
801 Industrial Dr (43526-1174)
PHONE..................................419 542-7743
Forrest Whittaker, CEO
Kevin L Countryman, *
Kalli Countryman, *
John Rapes, *
EMP: 200 **EST:** 1993
SQ FT: 50,000
SALES (est): 15.11MM **Privately Held**
Web: www.nemcomed.com
SIC: 3842 3841 Splints, pneumatic and wood ; Surgical and medical instruments

(G-8373)
DL SCHWARTZ CO LLC
9737 State Route 49 (43526-9780)
PHONE..................................260 692-1464
EMP: 8 **EST:** 1935
SALES (est): 2.27MM **Privately Held**
SIC: 5072 3441 Hardware; Fabricated structural metal

(G-8374)
ENVIROKURE INCORPORATED
9408 Rosedale Rd (43526-9222)
PHONE..................................215 289-9800
David Mansfield, Mgr
EMP: 14
SALES (corp-wide): 4.99MM **Privately Held**
Web: www.envirokure.com
SIC: 2873 Fertilizers: natural (organic), except compost
PA: Envirokure, Incorporated
5222 Comly St
Philadelphia PA 19135
215 289-9800

(G-8375)
MST INC
Also Called: Modern Safety Techniques
11370 Breininger Rd (43526-9339)
P.O. Box 87 (43526-0087)
PHONE..................................419 542-6645
Charles Martin, Pr
James M Prickett, Prin
EMP: 7 **EST:** 1989

Hicksville - Defiance County (G-8376)

SQ FT: 10,000
SALES (est): 895.15K **Privately Held**
Web: www.modsafe.com
SIC: 3842 Respiratory protection equipment, personal

(G-8376)
NEMCO FOOD EQUIPMENT LTD (PA)
301 Meuse Argonne St (43526-1143)
P.O. Box 305 (43526-0305)
PHONE..................419 542-7751
Kenny Moffatt, *Ch Bd*
Stanley Guilliam, *
Larry Stewart, *
▼ **EMP:** 71 **EST:** 1976
SQ FT: 50,000
SALES (est): 26.28MM
SALES (corp-wide): 26.28MM **Privately Held**
Web: www.nemcofoodequip.com
SIC: 3556 Food products machinery

(G-8377)
PARKER-HANNIFIN CORPORATION
Hydraulic Valve Div
373 Meuse Argonne St (43526-1182)
PHONE..................419 542-6611
Andy Ross, *Brnch Mgr*
EMP: 29
SALES (corp-wide): 19.07B **Publicly Held**
Web: www.parker.com
SIC: 3492 3491 Valves, hydraulic, aircraft; Industrial valves
PA: Parker-Hannifin Corporation
6035 Parkland Blvd
Cleveland OH 44124
216 896-3000

(G-8378)
PEC BIOFUELS LLC
210 Wendell Ave (43526-1405)
PHONE..................419 542-8210
EMP: 6 **EST:** 2006
SALES (est): 495.96K **Privately Held**
SIC: 2836 2911 Biological products, except diagnostic; Diesel fuels

(G-8379)
SABRE INDUSTRIES INC
761 W High St (43526-1052)
PHONE..................419 542-1420
EMP: 11 **EST:** 2020
SALES (est): 544.76K **Privately Held**
Web: www.sabreindustries.com
SIC: 3441 Fabricated structural metal

(G-8380)
STEELES 5 ACRE MILL INC
10860 State Route 2 (43526-9366)
PHONE..................419 542-9363
Cathy Steele, *Pr*
EMP: 7 **EST:** 1992
SALES (est): 126.51K **Privately Held**
SIC: 2499 Decorative wood and woodwork

(G-8381)
TRI STATE DAIRY LLC
210 Wendell Ave (43526-1405)
P.O. Box 284 (43526-0284)
PHONE..................419 542-8788
EMP: 9
SALES (corp-wide): 1.19MM **Privately Held**
SIC: 2022 Natural cheese
PA: Tri State Dairy Llc
9946 Fiat Rd Sw
Baltic OH 43804
330 897-5555

(G-8382)
TRIBUNE PRINTING INC
Also Called: News Tribune
147 E High St (43526-1159)
P.O. Box 303 (43526-0303)
PHONE..................419 542-7764
Mary Ann Barth, *Pr*
EMP: 9 **EST:** 1970
SQ FT: 2,000
SALES (est): 897.81K **Privately Held**
Web: www.tribuneprintinginc.com
SIC: 2711 2752 Newspapers: publishing only, not printed on site; Commercial printing, lithographic

Highland Heights
Cuyahoga County

(G-8383)
C & S ASSOCIATES INC
Also Called: National Lien Digest
729 Miner Rd (44143-2117)
P.O. Box 24101 (44124-0101)
PHONE..................440 461-9661
Mary B Cowan, *Pr*
Delores A Cowan, *
Greg Powelson, *
Bernie Cowan, *
Bernard J Cowan, *
EMP: 50 **EST:** 1974
SQ FT: 9,000
SALES (est): 9.06MM **Privately Held**
Web: www.ncscredit.com
SIC: 7322 2721 Collection agency, except real estate; Periodicals, publishing only

(G-8384)
CAROLINA STAMPING COMPANY
5405 Avion Park Dr (44143-1918)
PHONE..................216 271-5100
EMP: 10 **EST:** 2019
SALES (est): 486.63K **Privately Held**
SIC: 3469 Stamping metal for the trade

(G-8385)
COTSWORKS INC (PA)
749 Miner Rd (44143-2145)
PHONE..................440 446-8800
Ken Applebaum, *CEO*
EMP: 94 **EST:** 2006
SQ FT: 6,000
SALES (est): 14.39MM **Privately Held**
Web: www.cotsworks.com
SIC: 3661 Fiber optics communications equipment

(G-8386)
GENVAC AEROSPACE INC
110 Alpha Park (44143-2215)
PHONE..................440 646-9986
Gerald T Mearini, *Prin*
Gerald Mearini, *Prin*
EMP: 11 **EST:** 2006
SALES (est): 502.95K **Privately Held**
Web: www.genvac.com
SIC: 3827 Optical instruments and lenses

(G-8387)
GOOCH & HOUSEGO (OHIO) LLC
Also Called: Clevelandcrystals
676 Alpha Dr (44143-2123)
PHONE..................216 486-6100
Gareth Jones, *CEO*
Jon Fowler, *Ex VP*
Terry Scribbins, *COO*
Andrew Boteler, *CFO*
EMP: 65 **EST:** 1973
SALES (est): 24.28MM
SALES (corp-wide): 146.6MM **Privately Held**
Web: www.gandh.com
SIC: 3823 3827 Process control instruments; Optical instruments and lenses
PA: Gooch & Housego Plc
Dowlish Ford
Ilminster TA19
146 025-6440

(G-8388)
HEICO AEROSPACE PARTS CORP (DH)
Also Called: Flight Specialties Components
375 Alpha Park (44143-2237)
PHONE..................954 987-6101
Luis J Morell, *Pr*
Elizabeth R Letendre, *
Carlos L Macau, *
Frank Stevens, *
EMP: 294 **EST:** 2001
SQ FT: 1,500
SALES (est): 47.93MM **Publicly Held**
Web: www.heico.com
SIC: 3724 Aircraft engines and engine parts
HQ: Heico Aerospace Corporation
3000 Taft St
Hollywood FL 33021
954 987-6101

(G-8389)
NORMAN NOBLE INC (PA)
5507 Avion Park Dr (44143-1921)
PHONE..................216 761-5387
Lawrence Noble, *Pr*
Chris Noble, *
Dan Stefano, *
▲ **EMP:** 450 **EST:** 1962
SQ FT: 20,000
SALES (est): 86.29MM
SALES (corp-wide): 86.29MM **Privately Held**
Web: www.nnoble.com
SIC: 3841 Instruments, microsurgical: except electromedical

(G-8390)
OPTICAL DISPLAY ENGRG INC
375 Alpha Park (44143-2237)
PHONE..................440 995-6555
Nicholas Wright, *Prin*
Jeremy Walker, *Prin*
EMP: 16 **EST:** 2018
SALES (est): 1.16MM **Privately Held**
Web: www.heico.com
SIC: 3724 Aircraft engines and engine parts

(G-8391)
PURE FOODS LLC
675 Alpha Dr Ste E (44143-2139)
PHONE..................303 358-8375
Anthony Stedillie, *Managing Member*
EMP: 9 **EST:** 2017
SALES (est): 667.81K **Privately Held**
SIC: 2099 Food preparations, nec

Hilliard
Franklin County

(G-8392)
ADS INTERNATIONAL INC
4640 Trueman Blvd (43026-2438)
PHONE..................614 658-0050
EMP: 36 **EST:** 1991
SALES (est): 1.8MM
SALES (corp-wide): 3.07B **Publicly Held**
Web: www.adspipe.com
SIC: 3084 Plastics pipe
PA: Advanced Drainage Systems, Inc.
4640 Trueman Blvd
Hilliard OH 43026
614 658-0050

(G-8393)
ADS VENTURES INC (HQ)
4640 Trueman Blvd (43026-2438)
PHONE..................614 658-0050
Joseph A Chlapaty, *Ch Bd*
EMP: 6 **EST:** 2003
SALES (est): 4.69MM
SALES (corp-wide): 3.07B **Publicly Held**
Web: www.adspipe.com
SIC: 3084 3086 Plastics pipe; Plastics foam products
PA: Advanced Drainage Systems, Inc.
4640 Trueman Blvd
Hilliard OH 43026
614 658-0050

(G-8394)
ADS WORLDWIDE INC (IIQ)
4640 Trueman Blvd (43026-2438)
PHONE..................614 658-0050
EMP: 6 **EST:** 2015
SALES (est): 965.35K
SALES (corp-wide): 3.07B **Publicly Held**
Web: www.adspipe.com
SIC: 3086 Plastics foam products
PA: Advanced Drainage Systems, Inc.
4640 Trueman Blvd
Hilliard OH 43026
614 658-0050

(G-8395)
ADVANCED DRAINAGE OF OHIO INC
4640 Trueman Blvd (43026-2438)
PHONE..................614 658-0050
Franklin E Eck, *CEO*
Joseph A Chlapaty, *
EMP: 65 **EST:** 1968
SALES (est): 2.46MM
SALES (corp-wide): 3.07B **Publicly Held**
Web: www.adspipe.com
SIC: 3084 Plastics pipe
PA: Advanced Drainage Systems, Inc.
4640 Trueman Blvd
Hilliard OH 43026
614 658-0050

(G-8396)
ADVANCED DRAINAGE SYSTEMS INC (PA)
Also Called: ADS
4640 Trueman Blvd (43026-2438)
PHONE..................614 658-0050
D Scott Barbour, *Pr*
Scott A Cottrill, *Ex VP*
Kevin C Talley, *Ex VP*
Darin S Harvey, *Executive Supply Chain Vice President*
Michael G Huebert, *VP Sls*
▼ **EMP:** 100 **EST:** 1966
SQ FT: 65,000
SALES (est): 3.07B
SALES (corp-wide): 3.07B **Publicly Held**
Web: www.adspipe.com
SIC: 3084 3086 Plastics pipe; Plastics foam products

(G-8397)
AMERICAN REGENT INC
4150 Lyman Dr (43026-1230)
PHONE..................614 436-2222
Joseph Kenneth Keller, *CEO*
EMP: 100
Web: www.americanregent.com
SIC: 2834 5122 Pharmaceutical preparations; Pharmaceuticals
HQ: American Regent, Inc.
5 Ramsay Rd
Shirley NY 11967
631 924-4000

GEOGRAPHIC SECTION

Hilliard - Franklin County (G-8422)

(G-8398)
ARES SPORTSWEAR LTD
3700 Lacon Rd Ste A (43026-2220)
PHONE..................614 767-1950
Michael Campbell, *Managing Member*
▲ **EMP:** 55 **EST:** 1994
SALES (est): 11.63MM **Privately Held**
Web: www.areswear.com
SIC: 2759 Screen printing

(G-8399)
ARMSTRONG WORLD INDUSTRIES INC
Also Called: Armstrong World
4241 Leap Rd Bldg A (43026-1125)
P.O. Box 580 (43026-0580)
PHONE..................614 771-9307
David G Haggerty, *Mgr*
EMP: 30
SQ FT: 225,000
SALES (corp-wide): 1.3B **Publicly Held**
Web: www.armstrong.com
SIC: 5713 3996 3251 Floor covering stores; Hard surface floor coverings, nec; Brick and structural clay tile
PA: Armstrong World Industries, Inc.
2500 Columbia Ave
Lancaster PA 17603
717 397-0611

(G-8400)
AXALT POWDE COATI SYSTE USA I
4150 Lyman Dr (43026-1230)
PHONE..................614 921-8000
Danielle Conner, *Mgr*
EMP: 8
SALES (corp-wide): 5.18B **Publicly Held**
Web: www.axalta.com
SIC: 2851 Paints and paint additives
HQ: Axalta Powder Coating Systems Usa, Inc.
9800 Genard Rd
Houston TX 77041

(G-8401)
AXALT POWDE COATI SYSTE USA I
4130 Lyman Dr (43026-1230)
PHONE..................614 600-4104
EMP: 8
SALES (corp-wide): 5.18B **Publicly Held**
Web: www.axalta.com
SIC: 2851 Paints and paint additives
HQ: Axalta Powder Coating Systems Usa, Inc.
9800 Genard Rd
Houston TX 77041

(G-8402)
BAESMAN GROUP INC (PA)
4477 Reynolds Dr (43026-1261)
PHONE..................614 771-2300
EMP: 91 **EST:** 1952
SALES (est): 22.34MM
SALES (corp-wide): 22.34MM **Privately Held**
Web: www.baesman.com
SIC: 2752 7331 2791 2789 Commercial printing, lithographic; Direct mail advertising services; Typesetting; Bookbinding and related work

(G-8403)
BALMAC INC
4010 Main St (43026-1423)
PHONE..................614 876-1295
Mark Slebodnik, *Prin*
EMP: 7 **EST:** 2010
SALES (est): 145.49K **Privately Held**
Web: www.jcccpa.com

SIC: 3829 Measuring and controlling devices, nec

(G-8404)
BENZLE PORCELAIN COMPANY
6100 Hayden Run Rd (43026-9456)
PHONE..................614 876-2159
Curtis M Benzle, *Pr*
EMP: 6 **EST:** 1979
SALES (est): 320K **Privately Held**
SIC: 3269 3961 Art and ornamental ware, pottery; Costume jewelry, ex. precious metal and semiprecious stones

(G-8405)
BLIND FACTORY SHOWROOM
Also Called: The Blind Factory
3670 Parkway Ln Ste M (43026-1237)
PHONE..................614 771-6549
Don Grove, *Pr*
Ann Grove, *Sec*
Andrew Grove, *VP*
EMP: 13 **EST:** 1977
SQ FT: 16,000
SALES (est): 828.89K **Privately Held**
Web: www.theblindfactoryohio.com
SIC: 2591 5719 5023 Blinds vertical; Vertical blinds; Vertical blinds

(G-8406)
CITYSCAPES INTERNATIONAL INC
4200 Lyman Ct (43026-1213)
PHONE..................614 850-2540
James Cullinan, *Pr*
EMP: 200 **EST:** 2004
SQ FT: 30,000
SALES (est): 21.64MM **Privately Held**
Web: www.cityscapesinc.com
SIC: 3531 Construction machinery

(G-8407)
COFFEE NEWS
3027 Landen Farm Rd W (43026-7191)
P.O. Box 659 (43026-0659)
PHONE..................614 679-2967
Nancy Slagle, *Mgr*
EMP: 6 **EST:** 2012
SALES (est): 117.08K **Privately Held**
Web: www.coffeenews.com
SIC: 2711 Newspapers, publishing and printing

(G-8408)
COLORAMICS LLC
Also Called: Mayco Colors
4077 Weaver Ct S (43026-1197)
PHONE..................614 876-1171
◆ **EMP:** 43 **EST:** 1989
SQ FT: 75,000
SALES (est): 9.98MM **Privately Held**
Web: www.maycocolors.com
SIC: 2851 Paints and paint additives

(G-8409)
CONNECT TELEVISION
4811 Northwest Pkwy (43026-1128)
PHONE..................614 876-4402
EMP: 6 **EST:** 2008
SALES (est): 176.83K **Privately Held**
SIC: 2298 Cable, fiber

(G-8410)
DECENT HILL PUBLISHERS LLC
Also Called: Decent Hill Press
2825 Wynneleaf St (43026-8144)
PHONE..................216 548-1255
EMP: 6 **EST:** 2010
SALES (est): 182.81K **Privately Held**
Web: www.decenthill.com

SIC: 2731 Book music: publishing only, not printed on site

(G-8411)
FAST SIGNS
Also Called: Fastsigns
4469 Cemetery Rd (43026-1120)
PHONE..................614 710-1312
EMP: 9 **EST:** 2019
SALES (est): 270.87K **Privately Held**
Web: www.fastsigns.com
SIC: 3993 Signs and advertising specialties

(G-8412)
FLUID POWER SOLUTIONS LLC (PA)
4400 Edgewyn Ave (43026-1221)
PHONE..................614 777-8954
Mike Rogers, *Managing Member*
EMP: 9 **EST:** 2000
SALES (est): 1.93MM
SALES (corp-wide): 1.93MM **Privately Held**
Web: www.fluid-power-solutions.com
SIC: 5084 3594 Hydraulic systems equipment and supplies; Fluid power pumps and motors

(G-8413)
HANCOR INC (HQ)
4640 Trueman Blvd (43026-2438)
PHONE..................614 658-0050
Steven A Anderson, *Pr*
Derek Kamp, *
William E Altermatt, *
Pat Ferren, *
John Maag, *
◆ **EMP:** 330 **EST:** 2002
SQ FT: 20,000
SALES (est): 159.96MM
SALES (corp-wide): 3.07B **Publicly Held**
Web: www.adspipe.com
SIC: 3084 3088 3089 3083 Plastics pipe; Plastics plumbing fixtures; Septic tanks, plastics; Laminated plastics plate and sheet
PA: Advanced Drainage Systems, Inc.
4640 Trueman Blvd
Hilliard OH 43026
614 658-0050

(G-8414)
INS ROBOTICS INC
3600 Parkway Ln (43026-1281)
PHONE..................888 293-5325
Beth Harkins, *Managing Member*
EMP: 6 **EST:** 2009
SALES (est): 732.28K **Privately Held**
Web: www.insrobotics.com
SIC: 3535 Conveyors and conveying equipment

(G-8415)
JACO PRODUCTS LLC
3659 Parkway Ln Ste A (43026-1214)
PHONE..................614 219-1670
Thomas Palmer, *Pr*
EMP: 7 **EST:** 2013
SALES (est): 524.27K **Privately Held**
Web: www.jacoproducts.com
SIC: 2821 3089 Plasticizer/additive based plastic materials; Plastics products, nec

(G-8416)
JD POWER SYSTEMS LLC
Also Called: John Deere Authorized Dealer
3979 Parkway Ln (43026-1250)
PHONE..................614 317-9394
Jeffrey D Mitchell, *Owner*
EMP: 12 **EST:** 2011
SALES (est): 1.48MM **Privately Held**
Web: www.jdpowersystems.com

SIC: 3621 5082 Motors and generators; Construction and mining machinery

(G-8417)
JIT COMPANY OHIO
5908 Heritage Lakes Dr (43026-7618)
PHONE..................614 529-8010
Marcy Wu, *Pr*
EMP: 8 **EST:** 1989
SALES (est): 224.61K **Privately Held**
Web: www.jitohio.com
SIC: 3599 Machine shop, jobbing and repair

(G-8418)
LASERFLEX CORPORATION (HQ)
Also Called: Laserflex
3649 Parkway Ln (43026-1214)
PHONE..................614 850-9600
Ken Kinkopf, *Pr*
EMP: 62 **EST:** 1992
SQ FT: 75,000
SALES (est): 22.35MM **Publicly Held**
Web: www.customlasercuttingservices.com
SIC: 7389 7699 7692 3599 Metal cutting services; Industrial machinery and equipment repair; Welding repair; Machine shop, jobbing and repair
PA: Ryerson Holding Corporation
227 W Monroe St Fl 27
Chicago IL 60606

(G-8419)
MARBLE CLIFF LIMESTONE INC
2650 Old Dublin Rd (43026)
PHONE..................614 488-3030
Paul D Rice, *Pr*
EMP: 7 **EST:** 2002
SQ FT: 1,884
SALES (est): 190.93K **Privately Held**
SIC: 1411 Limestone and marble dimension stone

(G-8420)
MOHAWK 11 INC
5529 Mirage Dr (43026-7963)
PHONE..................614 771-0327
Monjed Humelidan, *Prin*
EMP: 6 **EST:** 2015
SALES (est): 74.63K **Privately Held**
SIC: 2273 Carpets and rugs

(G-8421)
MORLAN & ASSOCIATES INC
Also Called: Flex Core Division
4970 Scioto Darby Rd Ste D (43026-1548)
P.O. Box 6047 (43026-6047)
PHONE..................614 889-6152
Teri Shaw, *Pr*
EMP: 11
SQ FT: 15,000
SALES (corp-wide): 5.23MM **Privately Held**
Web: www.flex-core.com
SIC: 3612 Transformers, except electric
PA: Morlan & Associates, Inc.
4970 Scioto Darby Rd D
Hilliard OH 43026
614 889-6152

(G-8422)
MORLAN & ASSOCIATES INC (PA)
Also Called: Flex-Core Division
4970 Scioto Darby Rd Ste D (43026-1548)
P.O. Box 6047 (43026-6047)
PHONE..................614 889-6152
Teri Shaw, *Pr*
Donald Morlan, *
Eric Whelan, *
Amy Mcnabb, *Corporate Secretary*
▼ **EMP:** 18 **EST:** 1977

Hilliard - Franklin County (G-8423)

GEOGRAPHIC SECTION

SQ FT: 15,000
SALES (est): 5.23MM
SALES (corp-wide): 5.23MM **Privately Held**
Web: www.flex-core.com
SIC: 3612 Transformers, except electric

(G-8423)
MXR IMAGING INC
Also Called: Baldwin
4770 Northwest Pkwy (43026-1131)
PHONE..........................614 219-2011
Eric Cole, *Mgr*
EMP: 6
SALES (corp-wide): 109.03MM **Privately Held**
Web: www.mxrimaging.com
SIC: 6411 2899 Medical insurance claim processing, contract or fee basis; Chemical supplies for foundries
PA: Mxr Imaging, Inc.
 4909 Murphy Canyon Rd # 120
 San Diego CA 92123
 858 565-4472

(G-8424)
NATIONAL SIGN SYSTEMS INC
Also Called: Advanced Visual Solutions
4200 Lyman Ct (43026-1213)
PHONE..........................614 850-2540
▼ **EMP:** 75 **EST:** 1987
SALES (est): 15.68MM **Privately Held**
Web: www.nationalsignsystems.com
SIC: 3993 3444 Signs and advertising specialties; Metal roofing and roof drainage equipment

(G-8425)
OGR PUBLISHING INC
Also Called: O Gauge Railroading
5825 Redsand Rd (43026-8057)
P.O. Box 218 (43026-0218)
PHONE..........................330 757-3020
Richard P Melvin, *Pr*
EMP: 7 **EST:** 2002
SQ FT: 4,000
SALES (est): 483.24K **Privately Held**
Web: www.ogaugerr.com
SIC: 2741 Miscellaneous publishing

(G-8426)
OHIO LAMINATING & BINDING INC
4364 Reynolds Dr (43026-1260)
PHONE..........................614 771-4868
Jim Ondecko, *Pr*
Jimmy R Ondecko, *
▲ **EMP:** 12 **EST:** 1987
SQ FT: 5,000
SALES (est): 391.16K **Privately Held**
Web: www.ohiolam.com
SIC: 7389 2789 2672 Laminating service; Bookbinding and related work; Paper; coated and laminated, nec

(G-8427)
OHIO SEMITRONICS INC
Also Called: OSI
4242 Reynolds Dr (43026-1260)
PHONE..........................614 777-1005
Warren E Bulman, *Ch Bd*
Robert A Shaw, *
◆ **EMP:** 88 **EST:** 1964
SQ FT: 49,000
SALES (est): 8.89MM **Privately Held**
Web: www.ohiosemitronics.com
SIC: 3674 3679 3663 3625 Semiconductors and related devices; Transducers, electrical ; Radio and t.v. communications equipment; Relays and industrial controls

(G-8428)
ON SITE SIGNS OHIO LTD
2970 Carlsbad Dr (43026-8876)
PHONE..........................614 496-9400
Kensler Todd, *Admn*
EMP: 8 **EST:** 2011
SALES (est): 159.7K **Privately Held**
Web: www.onsitesignsohio.com
SIC: 3993 Signs and advertising specialties

(G-8429)
OPEN TEXT INC
Also Called: Open Text
3671 Ridge Mill Dr (43026-7752)
PHONE..........................614 658-3588
Anik Ganguly, *Mgr*
EMP: 50
SALES (corp-wide): 832.31MM **Privately Held**
Web: www.opentext.com
SIC: 7372 Prepackaged software
HQ: Open Text Inc.
 2440 Sand Hill Rd Ste 302
 Menlo Park CA 94025
 650 645-3000

(G-8430)
PERDATUM INC
4098 Main St (43026-1437)
PHONE..........................614 761-1578
Mark Tochtenhagen, *Pr*
Leo Renner, *CFO*
EMP: 8 **EST:** 1993
SQ FT: 2,500
SALES (est): 633.24K **Privately Held**
SIC: 7372 Prepackaged software

(G-8431)
PHANTOM TECHNOLOGY LLC
Also Called: Pool Office Manager
4179 Lyman Dr (43026-1228)
P.O. Box 893 (34991-0893)
PHONE..........................614 710-0074
EMP: 6 **EST:** 2018
SALES (est): 476.62K **Privately Held**
Web: www.poolofficemanager.com
SIC: 7372 Business oriented computer software

(G-8432)
PHOENIX HYDRAULIC PRESSES INC
4329 Reynolds Dr (43026-1261)
P.O. Box 1048 (43065-1048)
PHONE..........................614 850-8940
Charles Sherman, *Pr*
EMP: 10 **EST:** 2003
SQ FT: 6,000
SALES (est): 1.85MM **Privately Held**
Web: www.phoenixhydraulic.com
SIC: 3542 Presses: hydraulic and pneumatic, mechanical and manual

(G-8433)
PRO LIGHTING LLC
5864 Hunting Haven Dr (43026-7992)
P.O. Box 1201 (43026-6201)
PHONE..........................614 561-0089
Jeffrey J Treadway, *Prin*
EMP: 7 **EST:** 2009
SALES (est): 212.5K **Privately Held**
SIC: 3648 Lighting equipment, nec

(G-8434)
PROTO PRCSION MFG SLUTIONS LLC
Also Called: Proto Precision Fabricators
4101 Leap Rd (43026-1117)
PHONE..........................614 771-0080
Sugu Suguness, *Prin*
EMP: 13 **EST:** 2018
SALES (est): 885.02K **Privately Held**
Web: www.protoprecision.com
SIC: 3999 Manufacturing industries, nec

(G-8435)
RAGE CORPORATION (PA)
Also Called: Rage Plastics
3949 Lyman Dr (43026-1274)
P.O. Box 159 (43026-0159)
PHONE..........................614 771-4771
George Saliaris, *Pr*
Dan Saliaris, *
▲ **EMP:** 68 **EST:** 1968
SQ FT: 65,000
SALES (est): 18.57MM
SALES (corp-wide): 18.57MM **Privately Held**
Web: www.rageplastics.com
SIC: 3089 3544 Injection molding of plastics; Special dies, tools, jigs, and fixtures

(G-8436)
RICH PRODUCTS CORPORATION
4600 Northwest Pkwy (43026-1130)
P.O. Box 490 (43026-0490)
PHONE..........................614 771-1117
Michael Callaway, *Mgr*
EMP: 150
SALES (corp-wide): 4.81B **Privately Held**
Web: www.richs.com
SIC: 2023 2099 2051 2045 Dry, condensed and evaporated dairy products; Food preparations, nec; Bread, cake, and related products; Prepared flour mixes and doughs
PA: Rich Products Corporation
 1 Robert Rich Way
 Buffalo NY 14213
 716 878-8000

(G-8437)
S & G MANUFACTURING GROUP LLC (PA)
Also Called: S&G Distribution
4830 Northwest Pkwy (43026-1131)
PHONE..........................614 529-0100
Bret Klisares, *Managing Member*
Eric Schmidlin, *
EMP: 132 **EST:** 1990
SQ FT: 105,500
SALES (est): 30.05MM **Privately Held**
Web: www.sgmgroup.com
SIC: 3441 3444 2435 2436 Fabricated structural metal; Sheet metalwork; Hardwood veneer and plywood; Softwood veneer and plywood

(G-8438)
SALSA RICA II LLC
3744 Fishinger Blvd (43026-8549)
PHONE..........................740 616-9918
Thais Moya, *Prin*
EMP: 6 **EST:** 2013
SALES (est): 176.8K **Privately Held**
Web: www.yummysalsarica.com
SIC: 2099 Dips, except cheese and sour cream based

(G-8439)
SEILER ENTERPRISES LLC
5397 Whispering Oak Blvd (43026-8968)
PHONE..........................614 330-2220
Jonathan W Seiler, *Prin*
EMP: 8 **EST:** 2017
SALES (est): 48.69K **Privately Held**
SIC: 3827 Optical instruments and lenses

(G-8440)
SENSOTEC LLC
Also Called: Sensorwerks
3450 Cemetery Rd (43026-8348)
PHONE..........................614 481-8616
EMP: 6 **EST:** 2004
SALES (est): 444.96K **Privately Held**
SIC: 3829 Pressure transducers

(G-8441)
SPIRAL PUBLISHING LLC
4149 Maystar Way (43026-3012)
PHONE..........................614 876-4347
Lesa Marie Mutters, *Prin*
EMP: 7 **EST:** 2010
SALES (est): 56K **Privately Held**
SIC: 2741 Miscellaneous publishing

(G-8442)
STAR DYNAMICS CORPORATION (PA)
Also Called: Aeroflex Powell
4455 Reynolds Dr (43026-1261)
PHONE..........................614 334-4510
Jerry Jost, *Pr*
▲ **EMP:** 65 **EST:** 1989
SQ FT: 20,000
SALES (est): 11.77MM
SALES (corp-wide): 11.77MM **Privately Held**
Web: www.stardynamics.com
SIC: 3812 Search and navigation equipment

(G-8443)
STATE METAL HOSE INC
4171 Lyman Dr (43026-1228)
PHONE..........................614 527-4700
Thomas Decamp, *CEO*
EMP: 7 **EST:** 2000
SALES (est): 1.1MM **Privately Held**
Web: www.statemetalhose.com
SIC: 3492 7692 Hose and tube fittings and assemblies, hydraulic/pneumatic; Welding repair

(G-8444)
SUTPHEN TOWERS INC
4500 Sutphen Ct (43026)
P.O. Box 158 (43002)
PHONE..........................614 876-1262
EMP: 81 **EST:** 1978
SALES (est): 19.23MM **Privately Held**
Web: www.sutphen.com
SIC: 3713 7538 Truck bodies and parts; Truck engine repair, except industrial

(G-8445)
TEACHERS PUBLISHING GROUP
Also Called: Essential Learning Products
4200 Parkway Ct (43026-1200)
PHONE..........................614 486-0631
Gary Meyers, *Pr*
Gary Meyers, *CEO*
Thomas Mason, *Treas*
▲ **EMP:** 10 **EST:** 1980
SQ FT: 36,000
SALES (est): 1.31MM
SALES (corp-wide): 109.4MM **Privately Held**
Web: www.primaryconcepts.com
SIC: 7371 2731 Custom computer programming services; Books, publishing only
PA: Highlights For Children, Inc.
 1800 Watermark Dr
 Columbus OH 43215
 614 486-0631

(G-8446)
TEXTILES INC
Also Called: Sales Office Rob Jordan Vp Sls
5892 Heritage Lakes Dr (43026-7617)
PHONE..........................614 529-8642
Rob Jordan, *Brnch Mgr*
EMP: 8
SALES (corp-wide): 9.37MM **Privately Held**

▲ = Import ▼ = Export
◆ = Import/Export

GEOGRAPHIC SECTION

Hillsboro - Highland County (G-8468)

SIC: **2511** 2599 Wood household furniture; Hotel furniture
PA: Textiles, Inc.
  23 Old Springfield Rd
  London OH 43140
  740 852-0782

(G-8447)
THE GUARDTOWER INC
Also Called: Shield Laminating
5514 Nike Dr (43026)
  PHONE.................................614 488-4311
  Lynn Bartells, *Pr*
  EMP: 10 **EST:** 1987
  SALES (est): 561.92K Privately Held
  Web: www.theguardtower.com
SIC: **3944** 5945 Games, toys, and children's vehicles; Models, toy and hobby

(G-8448)
THERMOPLASTIC ACCESSORIES CORP
Also Called: T A C
3949 Lyman Dr (43026-1209)
P.O. Box 159 (43026-0159)
  PHONE.................................614 771-4777
  George Saliaris, *Pr*
  Mary Lou Saliaris, *Sec*
  EMP: 11 **EST:** 1976
  SQ FT: 48,000
  SALES (est): 393.79K
  SALES (corp-wide): 18.57MM Privately Held
  Web: www.rageplastics.com
SIC: **3089** Blow molded finished plastics products, nec
PA: Rage Corporation
  3949 Lyman Dr
  Hilliard OH 43026
  614 771-4771

(G-8449)
TNEMEC CO INC
3974 Brown Park Dr Ste A (43026-1168)
  PHONE.................................614 850-8160
  Dan Haines, *Pr*
  EMP: 6 **EST:** 2018
  SALES (est): 135.14K Privately Held
  Web: www.tnemec.com
SIC: **2851** Paints and allied products

(G-8450)
TUBULAR TECHNIQUES INC
3025 Scioto Darby Executive Ct (43026-8990)
  PHONE.................................614 529-4130
  Steve Harman, *Pr*
  Amy Pope-harman, *Sec*
  Tracy Stamper, *Adm/Asst*
  EMP: 6 **EST:** 1972
  SQ FT: 7,500
  SALES (est): 2.12MM Privately Held
  Web: www.tubulartechniques.com
SIC: **5051** 3599 Tubing, metal; Tubing, flexible metallic

(G-8451)
VANNER HOLDINGS INC
Also Called: Vanner
4282 Reynolds Dr (43026-1260)
  PHONE.................................614 771-2718
  ◆ **EMP:** 55 **EST:** 2005
  SQ FT: 20,000
  SALES (est): 7.64MM Privately Held
  Web: www.vanner.com
SIC: **3629** 3823 3699 3648 Inverters, nonrotating: electrical; Process control instruments; Electrical equipment and supplies, nec; Lighting equipment, nec

(G-8452)
VICART PRCSION FABRICATORS INC
Also Called: Proto Precision Fabricators
4101 Leap Rd (43026-1117)
  PHONE.................................614 771-0080
  Arthur Handshy, *Pr*
  EMP: 35 **EST:** 1988
  SQ FT: 18,000
  SALES (est): 4.48MM Privately Held
  Web: www.protopresicion.com
SIC: **3444** Sheet metal specialties, not stamped

(G-8453)
VT INDUSTRIES LLC
1999 Friston Blvd (43026-6038)
  PHONE.................................614 804-6904
  EMP: 6 **EST:** 2011
  SALES (est): 84.89K Privately Held
SIC: **3999** Manufacturing industries, nec

(G-8454)
ZURN INDUSTRIES LLC
4501 Sutphen Ct (43026-1224)
  PHONE.................................814 455-0921
  Bob Armbrewster, *Mgr*
  EMP: 10
  Web: www.zurn.com
SIC: **5074** 3431 Plumbing and hydronic heating supplies; Sinks: enameled iron, cast iron, or pressed metal
HQ: Zurn Industries, Llc
  511 W Freshwater Way
  Milwaukee WI 53204
  855 663-9876

Hillsboro
Highland County

(G-8455)
BEAZER EAST INC
Plum Run Stone Division
4281 Roush Rd (45133-9147)
  PHONE.................................937 364-2311
  J Craig Morgan, *Mgr*
  EMP: 35
  SALES (corp-wide): 23.02B Privately Held
SIC: **3281** 3273 1422 Stone, quarrying and processing of own stone products; Ready-mixed concrete; Crushed and broken limestone
HQ: Beazer East, Inc.
  600 River Ave Ste 200
  Pittsburgh PA 15212
  412 428-9407

(G-8456)
CHAD ABBOTT SIGNS LLC
439 N West St (45133-1048)
  PHONE.................................937 393-8864
  Chad Abbott, *Prin*
  EMP: 6 **EST:** 2013
  SALES (est): 246.93K Privately Held
  Web: www.chadabbottsigns.com
SIC: **3993** Signs and advertising specialties

(G-8457)
G FORDYCE CO
210 Hobart Dr (45133-9487)
P.O. Box 309 (45133-0309)
  PHONE.................................937 393-3241
  Bob Wilson, *Owner*
  EMP: 6 **EST:** 1980
  SQ FT: 12,000
  SALES (est): 509.06K Privately Held
  Web: www.gfordyce.com
SIC: **3554** Folding machines, paper

(G-8458)
HIGGINS CONSTRUCTION & SUPPLY CO INC
Also Called: Higgins Tool Rental
3801 Us Highway 50 (45133-9178)
  PHONE.................................937 364-2331
  TOLL FREE: 800
  EMP: 12 **EST:** 1959
  SALES (est): 2.49MM Privately Held
SIC: **5211** 3444 5031 7359 Lumber and other building materials; Metal flooring and siding; Building materials, exterior; Equipment rental and leasing, nec

(G-8459)
HIGHLAND COMPUTER FORMS INC (PA)
Also Called: R & S Data Products
1025 W Main St (45133)
P.O. Box 831 (45133)
  PHONE.................................937 393-4215
  Robert D Wilson, *Pr*
  Philip D Wilson, *
  EMP: 56 **EST:** 1979
  SQ FT: 70,000
  SALES (est): 22.01MM
  SALES (corp-wide): 22.01MM Privately Held
  Web: www.hcf.com
SIC: **2752** 5112 Commercial printing, lithographic; Business forms

(G-8460)
JERRYS WELDING SUPPLY INC
Also Called: Jerry's Welding Supply ICN
5367 Us Highway 50 (45133-7532)
  PHONE.................................937 364-1500
  Gerald Bonnet, *Owner*
  EMP: 6 **EST:** 1998
  SALES (est): 209.83K Privately Held
SIC: **5084** 7692 5169 Welding machinery and equipment; Welding repair; Oxygen

(G-8461)
MID AMERICA TIRE OF HILLSBORO INC
Also Called: Best One Tire of Hillsboro
108 Willetsville Pike (45133-8461)
P.O. Box 728 (45133-0728)
  PHONE.................................937 393-3520
  EMP: 20
SIC: **5531** 7534 Automotive tires; Tire retreading and repair shops

(G-8462)
OHIO ASPHALTIC LIMESTONE CORP
8591 Mad River Rd (45133-9451)
  PHONE.................................937 364-2191
  TOLL FREE: 888
  Diana Jones, *Pr*
  William C Mason, *Pr*
  Dianna Jones, *VP*
  EMP: 10 **EST:** 1935
  SQ FT: 1,200
  SALES (est): 2.32MM
  SALES (corp-wide): 2.32MM Privately Held
  Web: www.ohio-asphaltic-limestone.com
SIC: **1422** Limestones, ground
PA: Miller-Mason Paving Co.
  8591 Mad River Rd
  Hillsboro OH
  937 364-2369

(G-8463)
OHIO VALLEY TRUSS COMPANY (PA)
6000 Us Highway 50 (45133-7546)
P.O. Box 365 (45133-0365)
  PHONE.................................937 393-3995
  Willard G Bohrer, *Pr*
  Joann Bohrer, *
  EMP: 35 **EST:** 1976
  SQ FT: 12,000
  SALES (est): 4.96MM
  SALES (corp-wide): 4.96MM Privately Held
SIC: **2439** Trusses, wooden roof

(G-8464)
PAS TECHNOLOGIES INC
Also Called: Standardaero
214 Hobart Dr (45133-9487)
  PHONE.................................937 840-1053
  Mark Greene, *Mgr*
  EMP: 100
  Web: www.standardaerocomponents.com
SIC: **3724** 7699 Aircraft engines and engine parts; Aircraft and heavy equipment repair services
HQ: Pas Technologies Inc.
  1234 Atlantic Ave
  North Kansas City MO 64116

(G-8465)
ROTARY FORMS PRESS INC (PA)
835 S High St (45133-9692)
  PHONE.................................937 393-3426
  Jon Cassner, *Pr*
  Brian Cassner, *Treas*
  EMP: 39 **EST:** 1952
  SQ FT: 24,500
  SALES (est): 223.27K
  SALES (corp-wide): 223.27K Privately Held
  Web: www.rotaryfp.com
SIC: **2761** 2752 Computer forms, manifold or continuous; Commercial printing, lithographic

(G-8466)
SEAL TITE LLC
Also Called: Seal Tite
120 Moore Rd (45133-8523)
  PHONE.................................937 393-4268
  EMP: 100 **EST:** 2003
  SQ FT: 120,000
  SALES (est): 23.97MM Privately Held
  Web: www.sealtitehvac.com
SIC: **3498** Fabricated pipe and fittings

(G-8467)
STANDARD AERO INC
214 Hobart Dr (45133-9487)
  PHONE.................................937 840-1053
  EMP: 10
  SALES (est): 1.5MM Privately Held
  Web: www.standardaerocomponents.com
SIC: **3599** Machine shop, jobbing and repair

(G-8468)
UNIT SETS INC
835 S High St (45133-9602)
  PHONE.................................937 840-6123
  Jon Cassner, *Pr*
  Jon H Cassner, *
  Kathy Cassner, *
  Brian Cassner, *
  EMP: 7 **EST:** 1972
  SQ FT: 25,000
  SALES (est): 31.26K
  SALES (corp-wide): 223.27K Privately Held
  Web: www.rotaryfp.com
SIC: **2761** Unit sets (manifold business forms)
PA: Rotary Forms Press, Inc.
  835 S High St
  Hillsboro OH 45133
  937 393-3426

Hillsboro - Highland County (G-8469)   GEOGRAPHIC SECTION

(G-8469)
WEASTEC INCORPORATED (HQ)
1600 N High St (45133-9400)
PHONE...................................937 393-6800
Yasusuke Sugino, *Pr*
Kiyoshi Koide, *
Bill Smith, *
Keigo Sakaguchi, *
▲ **EMP:** 222 **EST:** 1988
SQ FT: 190,000
SALES (est): 59.02MM **Privately Held**
Web: www.weastec.com
SIC: 3714 Motor vehicle electrical equipment
PA: Toyo Denso Co., Ltd.
    2-10-4, Shimbashi
    Minato-Ku TKY 105-0

(G-8470)
WILLIAMSON SAFE INC
5631 State Route 73 (45133-9005)
PHONE...................................937 393-9919
J Edgar Williamson, *Pr*
Bing C Williamson, *
EMP: 18 **EST:** 1979
SQ FT: 40,000
SALES (est): 442.45K **Privately Held**
SIC: 3499 Safe deposit boxes or chests, metal

Hinckley
Medina County

(G-8471)
A-KOBAK CONTAINER COMPANY INC
1701 W 130th St (44233-9586)
P.O. Box 490 (44233-0490)
PHONE...................................330 225-7791
Gerald H Dolph, *Pr*
Edward Clark, *VP*
EMP: 15 **EST:** 1963
SQ FT: 40,000
SALES (est): 1.81MM **Privately Held**
Web: www.akobak.com
SIC: 2653 Boxes, corrugated: made from purchased materials

(G-8472)
FWY MACHINE COMPANY LLC
2495 Stony Hill Rd (44233-9743)
PHONE...................................216 533-7515
B W Mcclain Authorized Represn t, *Prin*
EMP: 6 **EST:** 2005
SALES (est): 66.13K **Privately Held**
SIC: 3599 Machine shop, jobbing and repair

(G-8473)
GREAT LAKES STAIR & MLLWK CO
1545 W 130th St Ste A1 (44233-9168)
P.O. Box 125 (44233-0125)
PHONE...................................330 225-2005
Tim Noonan, *Pr*
Barb Noonan, *Sec*
EMP: 7 **EST:** 1990
SQ FT: 7,500
SALES (est): 774.75K **Privately Held**
Web: www.stair.com
SIC: 2431 5031 Staircases and stairs, wood; Doors and windows

(G-8474)
HINCKLEY WOOD PRODUCTS LTD
1545 W 130th St (44233-9121)
PHONE...................................330 220-9999
Tim Noonan, *Pr*
EMP: 12 **EST:** 2003
SALES (est): 488.07K **Privately Held**
SIC: 2431 Staircases and stairs, wood

(G-8475)
JAMAR PRECISION GRINDING CO
2661 Center Rd (44233-9562)
PHONE...................................330 220-0099
John Hatala, *Pr*
EMP: 48 **EST:** 1981
SALES (est): 5.18MM **Privately Held**
Web: web.jamargrinding.com
SIC: 3599 Machine shop, jobbing and repair

(G-8476)
L J PUBLISHING LLC
1287 Ridge Rd Ste B (44233-9288)
P.O. Box 425 (44280-0425)
PHONE...................................888 749-5994
EMP: 6 **EST:** 2011
SALES (est): 124.87K **Privately Held**
SIC: 2741 Miscellaneous publishing

(G-8477)
TARANTULA PERFORMANCE RACE LLC
Also Called: Tpr
1669 W 130th St Ste 301 (44233-9104)
PHONE...................................330 273-3456
◆ **EMP:** 7 **EST:** 2007
SQ FT: 15,000
SALES (est): 119.79K **Privately Held**
Web: www.tprusa.com
SIC: 3751 Motorcycles, bicycles and parts

(G-8478)
TURNWOOD INDUSTRY INC
365 State Rd (44233-9634)
PHONE...................................330 278-2421
Peter Svilar, *Pr*
Steve Svilar, *VP*
▲ **EMP:** 8 **EST:** 1982
SQ FT: 26,000
SALES (est): 304.36K **Privately Held**
SIC: 2434 2431 Wood kitchen cabinets; Interior and ornamental woodwork and trim

(G-8479)
WENTWORTH SOLUTIONS
1265 Ridge Rd (44233-9806)
P.O. Box 283 (44233-0283)
PHONE...................................440 212-7696
Sean Spigtle, *Pr*
Jessica Spittle, *Sec*
EMP: 10 **EST:** 2005
SALES (est): 1.8MM **Privately Held**
Web: www.wentinc.com
SIC: 7371 7372 Computer software writing services; Prepackaged software

(G-8480)
ZS CREAM & BEAN LLC
2706 Boston Rd (44233-9498)
PHONE...................................440 652-6369
Lawrence Zirker, *Prin*
EMP: 6 **EST:** 2010
SALES (est): 398.29K **Privately Held**
Web: www.zscreamandbean.com
SIC: 2024 Ice cream, bulk

Hiram
Portage County

(G-8481)
DUNSTONE COMPANY INC
17930 Great Lakes Pkwy (44234-9681)
PHONE...................................704 841-1380
John P Kryder, *Pr*
Keith Puckett, *VP*
EMP: 10 **EST:** 1956
SQ FT: 6,450
SALES (est): 1.01MM **Privately Held**
Web: www.shrinktape.com

SIC: 3089 Plastics processing

(G-8482)
DURAMAX GLOBAL CORP
Also Called: Duramax Marine
17990 Great Lakes Pkwy (44234-9681)
PHONE...................................440 834-5400
Richard Spangler, *Dir*
Tammy Simsa, *
EMP: 10 **EST:** 2015
SQ FT: 65,000
SALES (est): 994.4K **Privately Held**
Web: www.duramaxmarine.com
SIC: 3061 Mechanical rubber goods

(G-8483)
DURAMAX MARINE LLC
17990 Great Lakes Pkwy (44234-9681)
PHONE...................................440 834-5400
Richard Spangler, *Pr*
◆ **EMP:** 96 **EST:** 1000
SQ FT: 65,000
SALES (est): 18.85MM **Privately Held**
Web: www.duramaxmarine.com
SIC: 3069 Medical and laboratory rubber sundries and related products

(G-8484)
GEAUGA HIGHWAY CO
14126 Main Market Rd (44234-9604)
PHONE...................................440 834-4580
John Bojec, *Pr*
EMP: 10 **EST:** 2021
SALES (est): 526.03K **Privately Held**
SIC: 3531 7389 Asphalt plant, including gravel-mix type; Business Activities at Non-Commercial Site

(G-8485)
GREAT LAKES CHEESE CO INC (PA)
17825 Great Lakes Pkwy (44234-9677)
P.O. Box 1806 (44234-1806)
PHONE...................................440 834-2500
Gary Vanic, *Pr*
John Epprecht, *
Albert Z Meyers, *
Marcel Dasen, *
Hans Epprecht, *
◆ **EMP:** 500 **EST:** 1958
SQ FT: 218,000
SALES (est): 1.69B
SALES (corp-wide): 1.69B **Privately Held**
Web: www.greatlakescheese.com
SIC: 5143 2022 Cheese; Natural cheese

(G-8486)
MANTALINE CORPORATION
Also Called: Mantaline
6969 Constance Rd (44234-3402)
PHONE...................................330 569-3147
EMP: 6
SALES (corp-wide): 22.67MM **Privately Held**
Web: www.mantalinestandardseals.com
SIC: 3061 Mechanical rubber goods
PA: Mantaline Corporation
    4754 E High St
    Mantua OH 44255
    330 274-2264

(G-8487)
NES CORP
18031 Claridon Troy Rd (44234-9680)
P.O. Box 604252 (44104-0252)
PHONE...................................440 834-0438
John Bojec, *Pr*
EMP: 20 **EST:** 2000
SALES (est): 2.41MM **Privately Held**
SIC: 2951 1611 Asphalt and asphaltic paving mixtures (not from refineries); Surfacing and paving

(G-8488)
ROCKY MOUNTAIN LOGGING CO LLC
5880 State Route 82 (44234-9764)
PHONE...................................440 313-8574
Charles H Manning, *Prin*
EMP: 7 **EST:** 2010
SALES (est): 154.8K **Privately Held**
SIC: 2411 Logging camps and contractors

Holgate
Henry County

(G-8489)
MEDAL COMPONENTS LLC
515 Richholt St (43527-7731)
P.O. Box 125 (43527-0125)
PHONE...................................864 561-9464
EMP: 7 **EST:** 2019
SALES (est): 1.16MM **Privately Held**
Web: www.medalcomponents.com
SIC: 3089 Injection molding of plastics

(G-8490)
OHIO ROTATIONAL MOLDING LLC
503 Joe E Brown Ave (43527-9804)
PHONE...................................419 608-5040
EMP: 11 **EST:** 2017
SALES (est): 393.11K **Privately Held**
Web: www.ohiorotationalmolding.com
SIC: 2821 Molding compounds, plastics

(G-8491)
RANDALL BROTHERS LLC
30361 Defiance Ayersville (43527-9606)
PHONE...................................419 395-1764
Scott Randall, *Prin*
EMP: 8 **EST:** 2017
SALES (est): 749.36K **Privately Held**
Web: www.randallbros.biz
SIC: 3523 Farm machinery and equipment

Holland
Lucas County

(G-8492)
ADAMS ELEVATOR EQUIPMENT CO (DH)
Also Called: Schindler Logistics Center
1530 Timber Wolf Dr (43528-9129)
PHONE...................................847 581-2900
Robert Schreck, *CEO*
▲ **EMP:** 62 **EST:** 1930
SALES (est): 13.41MM **Privately Held**
Web: www.adamselevator.com
SIC: 3312 3825 3534 5084 Locomotive wheels, rolled; Signal generators and averagers; Elevators and equipment; Materials handling machinery
HQ: Schindler Enterprises Inc.
    20 Whippany Rd
    Morristown NJ 07960
    973 397-6500

(G-8493)
ADDITIVE METAL ALLOYS LTD
1421 Holloway Rd Ste B (43528-8647)
PHONE...................................800 687-6110
Richard Meklus, *Prin*
EMP: 8 **EST:** 2014
SQ FT: 1,100
SALES (est): 478.22K **Privately Held**
SIC: 3399 Powder, metal

(G-8494)
BOLLINGER TOOL & DIE INC
959 Hamilton Dr (43528-8211)

2024 Harris Ohio
Industrial Directory

▲ = Import ▼ = Export
◆ = Import/Export

GEOGRAPHIC SECTION

Holland - Lucas County (G-8517)

PHONE.................419 866-5180
Danny N Bollinger, *Pr*
Anne Bollinger, *VP*
EMP: 7 **EST:** 1985
SQ FT: 6,700
SALES (est): 666.97K Privately Held
SIC: 3544 Special dies and tools

(G-8495)
BUNTING BEARINGS LLC (PA)
1001 Holland Park Blvd (43528-9287)
P.O. Box 729 (43528-0729)
PHONE.................419 866-7000
Keith Brown, *Ch*
Thomas Kwiatkowski, *
George Mugford, *
Dale Kucaj, *
Rick Nelson, *
▲ **EMP:** 100 **EST:** 1907
SQ FT: 94,000
SALES (est): 39.8MM Privately Held
Web: www.buntingbearings.com
SIC: 3366 3566 Brass foundry, nec; Speed changers, drives, and gears

(G-8496)
CAMEO COUNTERTOPS INC (PA)
1610 Kieswetter Rd (43528-8678)
PHONE.................419 865-6371
Brian Hudock, *Pr*
Tim Sorokin, *
EMP: 20 **EST:** 1992
SQ FT: 22,000
SALES (est): 3.97MM Privately Held
Web: www.cameocountertops.com
SIC: 2541 5031 2821 Counter and sink tops; Lumber, plywood, and millwork; Plastics materials and resins

(G-8497)
CGS IMAGING INC
6950 Hall St (43528-9485)
PHONE.................419 897-3000
Chuck Stranc, *CEO*
Carol Stranc, *CFO*
▲ **EMP:** 14 **EST:** 2003
SQ FT: 14,000
SALES (est): 2.56MM Privately Held
Web: www.cgs-imaging.com
SIC: 3993 7319 Signs and advertising specialties; Display advertising service

(G-8498)
CLARIOS LLC
Also Called: Johnson Controls
10300 Industrial St (43528-9791)
PHONE.................419 865-0542
Aaron Byrne, *Mgr*
EMP: 600
Web: www.clarios.com
SIC: 3691 Batteries, rechargeable
HQ: Clarios, Llc
    5757 N Green Bay Ave
    Milwaukee WI 53209

(G-8499)
COLBURN PATTERSON LLC (PA)
1100 S Holland Sylvania Rd (43528)
PHONE.................419 866-5544
Tony J Colburn, *Managing Member*
EMP: 6 **EST:** 1994
SALES (est): 758.14K Privately Held
Web: www.colburnpatterson.com
SIC: 8721 7372 Accounting services, except auditing; Prepackaged software

(G-8500)
CREATIVE PRODUCTS INC
Also Called: CPI
1430 Kieswetter Rd (43528-9785)
PHONE.................419 866-5501

Marvin Smith, *Pr*
EMP: 9 **EST:** 1973
SQ FT: 26,000
SALES (est): 900.96K Privately Held
SIC: 5023 5211 2541 Kitchen tools and utensils, nec; Cabinets, kitchen; Wood partitions and fixtures

(G-8501)
D & J DISTRIBUTING & MFG
Also Called: Exotica Fresheners Co
1302 Holloway Rd (43528-9538)
PHONE.................419 865-2552
Adnan Elassir, *VP*
Adnan Elassir, *VP*
Oussama Elassir, *Pr*
◆ **EMP:** 27 **EST:** 1988
SQ FT: 45,000
SALES (est): 464.86K Privately Held
Web: www.exoticafresh.com
SIC: 2842 Sanitation preparations, disinfectants and deodorants

(G-8502)
DANA HEAVY VEHICLE SYSTEMS
Also Called: Dana Spicer Service Parts
6936 Airport Hwy (43528)
PHONE.................419 866-3900
Jim Wojciechowski, *Mgr*
EMP: 53
Web: www.dana.com
SIC: 3714 Motor vehicle parts and accessories
HQ: Dana Heavy Vehicle Systems Group, Llc
    3939 Technology Dr
    Maumee OH 43537

(G-8503)
DANA LIMITED
Also Called: Dana Supply Chain Mgmt
6201 Trust Dr (43528-8424)
PHONE.................419 866-7253
Ron Draheim, *Sls Dir*
EMP: 100
Web: www.dana.com
SIC: 3714 Motor vehicle parts and accessories
HQ: Dana Limited
    3939 Technology Dr
    Maumee OH 43537

(G-8504)
DESIGNETICS INC (PA)
1624 Eber Rd (43528-9776)
PHONE.................419 866-0700
Craig Williams, *Pr*
EMP: 73 **EST:** 1987
SQ FT: 20,000
SALES (est): 558K Privately Held
Web: www.designetics.com
SIC: 3559 3991 Automotive related machinery; Brooms and brushes

(G-8505)
DOYLE MANUFACTURING INC
Also Called: Shamrock Molded Products
1440 Holloway Rd (43528-8608)
PHONE.................419 865-2548
Michael A Doyle, *Pr*
Linda Doyle, *
Adrienne Sautter, *Prin*
Chad Doyle, *Prin*
Bryan Doyle, *Prin*
EMP: 70 **EST:** 1975
SQ FT: 100,000
SALES (est): 13.52MM Privately Held
Web: www.doyleshamrock.com
SIC: 3089 3544 Injection molding of plastics; Special dies, tools, jigs, and fixtures

(G-8506)
DREAMSCAPE MEDIA LLC
Also Called: Dreamscape Media
1417 Timber Wolf Dr (43528-8302)
PHONE.................877 983-7326
Bradley Rose, *Genl Mgr*
EMP: 8 **EST:** 2011
SALES (est): 1.09MM Privately Held
Web: www.dreamscapepublishing.com
SIC: 2731 Books, publishing only

(G-8507)
DYNAMIC DIES INC (PA)
1705 Commerce Rd (43528-9789)
P.O. Box 576 (43528-0576)
PHONE.................419 865-0249
EMP: 50 **EST:** 1971
SALES (est): 22.27MM
SALES (corp-wide): 22.27MM Privately Held
Web: www.dynamicdies.com
SIC: 3544 3555 2796 Special dies and tools; Printing plates; Platemaking services

(G-8508)
EDITENCOM LTD
7134 Railroad St (43528-9539)
P.O. Box 176 (43528-0176)
PHONE.................419 865-5877
Robert Disanza, *Pr*
▲ **EMP:** 40 **EST:** 1997
SQ FT: 30,000
SALES (est): 7.81MM Privately Held
Web: www.tencom.com
SIC: 3812 Antennas, radar or communications

(G-8509)
ELECTRONIC CONCEPTS ENGRG INC
Also Called: E C E
1465 Timber Wolf Dr (43528-8302)
PHONE.................419 861-9000
Karl W Swonger Junior, *CEO*
EMP: 16 **EST:** 1988
SQ FT: 17,900
SALES (est): 5.23MM Privately Held
Web: www.eceinc.com
SIC: 7371 8731 3728 7373 Computer software development; Electronic research; Aircraft assemblies, subassemblies, and parts, nec; Computer integrated systems design

(G-8510)
GENERIC SYSTEMS INC
10560 Geiser Rd (43528-8506)
P.O. Box 153 (43552-0153)
PHONE.................419 841-8460
EMP: 15 **EST:** 1996
SQ FT: 18,000
SALES (est): 1.06MM Privately Held
Web: www.genericfluidsystems.com
SIC: 3549 7373 7371 Assembly machines, including robotic; Systems integration services; Computer software development and applications

(G-8511)
HAMILTON MANUFACTURING CORP
1026 Hamilton Dr (43528-8210)
PHONE.................419 867-4858
Robin Ritz, *CEO*
Bonnie Osborne, *
Steve Alt, *
Laura Harris, *
▲ **EMP:** 45 **EST:** 1921
SQ FT: 32,000
SALES (est): 8.81MM Privately Held
Web: www.hamiltonmfg.com

SIC: 3172 8711 Coin purses; Designing: ship, boat, machine, and product

(G-8512)
HONEYBAKED FOODS INC
Also Called: Honeybaked
6145 Merger Dr (43528-8430)
P.O. Box 965 (43528-0965)
PHONE.................567 703-0002
Dan Kurz, *Pr*
Louis Schmidt Junior, *VP*
Mary Lou Anderson, *
Craig Kurz, *
EMP: 600 **EST:** 1984
SQ FT: 103,000
SALES (est): 36.06MM Privately Held
Web: www.honeybaked.com
SIC: 2013 Bacon, side and sliced: from purchased meat

(G-8513)
ICO PRODUCTS LLC
Also Called: Icomold By Fathom
6415 Angola Rd (43528-8501)
PHONE.................419 867-3900
EMP: 8
SALES (est): 309.05K Privately Held
Web: www.icomold.com
SIC: 3089 Injection molding of plastics

(G-8514)
IMAGE GROUP INC
1255 Corporate Dr (43528-9590)
PHONE.................419 866-3300
Jon M Levine, *CEO*
Joel A Levine, *
Tom Herman, *
Lisa Hoverson, *
Zack Ottenstein, *
◆ **EMP:** 44 **EST:** 1989
SQ FT: 29,400
SALES (est): 12.06MM Privately Held
Web: www.theimagegroup.com
SIC: 2261 Screen printing of cotton broadwoven fabrics

(G-8515)
JML HOLDINGS INC
Also Called: Bassett Nut Company
6210 Merger Dr (43528-9593)
PHONE.................419 866-7500
Jon M Levine, *Pr*
Larry J Robbins, *VP*
Jeff Williams, *COO*
◆ **EMP:** 33 **EST:** 1928
SQ FT: 12,000
SALES (est): 1.57MM Privately Held
Web: www.bassettnut.com
SIC: 5441 5145 2064 Nuts; Nuts, salted or roasted; Popcorn balls or other treated popcorn products

(G-8516)
KERN-LIEBERS TEXAS INC
1510 Albon Rd (43528-8684)
PHONE.................419 865-2437
Hannes Stein, *CEO*
EMP: 15 **EST:** 1988
SALES (est): 234.82K Privately Held
Web: www.kern-liebers-north-america.com
SIC: 3495 Wire springs

(G-8517)
KERN-LIEBERS USA INC (HQ)
1510 Albon Rd (43528-9159)
PHONE.................419 865-2437
Lothar Bauerle, *Pr*
Hans Jocheim Steim, *
Gert Wagner, *
▲ **EMP:** 60 **EST:** 1977

Holland - Lucas County (G-8518)

SQ FT: 40,000
SALES (est): 35.39MM
SALES (corp-wide): 802.75MM **Privately Held**
Web: www.kern-liebers-north-america.com
SIC: **3495** 3493 Mechanical springs, precision; Steel springs, except wire
PA: Hugo Kern Und Liebers Gmbh & Co. Kg Platinen- Und Federnfabrik Dr.-Kurt-Steim-Str. 35 Schramberg BW 78713 74225110

(G-8518)
MATHESON TRI-GAS INC
1720 Trade Rd (43528-8202)
PHONE..............................419 865-8881
Craig Morton, *Mgr*
EMP: 9
SQ FT: 18,120
Web: www.mathesongas.com
SIC: **5084** 2813 Welding machinery and equipment; Nitrogen
HQ: Matheson Tri-Gas, Inc. 3 Mountainview Rd Ste 3 # 3 Warren NJ 07059 908 991-9200

(G-8519)
NATIONAL COMPRESSOR SVCS LLC (PA)
10349 Industrial St (43528-9791)
P.O. Box 760 (43528-0760)
PHONE..............................419 868-4980
Erik E Babcock, *Pr*
Stan Kolev, *CFO*
Gregory Jones, *VP*
James Gordon, *VP*
Matthew Delong, *VP*
EMP: 39 EST: 2011
SQ FT: 60,000
SALES (est): 10.19MM
SALES (corp-wide): 10.19MM **Privately Held**
Web: www.national-compressor.com
SIC: **3563** Air and gas compressors

(G-8520)
NATIONAL ILLMINATION SIGN CORP
6525 Angola Rd (43528-9651)
P.O. Box 563 (43528-0563)
PHONE..............................419 866-1666
George L Jeakle, *Pr*
Neil Jeakle, *VP*
EMP: 9 EST: 1985
SQ FT: 18,200
SALES (est): 969.54K **Privately Held**
Web: www.nationalsignco.com
SIC: **3993** Electric signs

(G-8521)
OTTAWA RUBBER COMPANY (PA)
1600 Commerce Rd (43528-8689)
P.O. Box 553 (43528-0553)
PHONE..............................419 865-1378
Mike Bugert, *Pr*
EMP: 17 EST: 1945
SQ FT: 12,000
SALES (est): 5.33MM
SALES (corp-wide): 5.33MM **Privately Held**
Web: www.ottawarubber.com
SIC: **3069** Molded rubber products

(G-8522)
PATRIOT PRODUCTS INC
Also Called: Patriot Mobility
1133 Corporate Dr Ste B (43528-7405)
P.O. Box 88 (49771-0088)
PHONE..............................419 865-9712
Steven Grudzien, *Pr*
EMP: 15 EST: 2004
SALES (est): 1.91MM **Privately Held**
Web: www.dmetree.com
SIC: **3841** Surgical and medical instruments

(G-8523)
PETERSON AMERICAN CORPORATION
Peterson Spring - Maumee Plant
1625 Commerce Rd (43528-8689)
PHONE..............................419 867-8711
Geary Belzung, *Brnch Mgr*
EMP: 30
SQ FT: 41,400
SALES (corp-wide): 235.32MM **Privately Held**
Web: www.pspring.com
SIC: **3496** 3452 3592 3493 Miscellaneous fabricated wire products; Washers, metal; Carburetors, pistons, piston rings and valves; Steel springs, except wire
PA: Peterson American Corporation 3010 Lyndon B Johnson Fwy Dallas TX 75234 248 799-5400

(G-8524)
PRECISION CUTOFF LLC
7400 Airport Hwy (43528-9545)
P.O. Box 1040 (43528-1040)
PHONE..............................419 866-8000
Jim Cannaley, *Managing Member*
EMP: 28 EST: 1989
SQ FT: 150,000
SALES (est): 2.03MM **Privately Held**
Web: www.woodsage.com
SIC: **3441** Fabricated structural metal

(G-8525)
PRINCIPLED DYNAMICS INC
6920 Hall St (43528-9485)
PHONE..............................419 351-6303
Patricia Earl, *VP*
Gene Gunderson, *Prin*
James Swartz, *Prin*
Michael W Holmes, *Prin*
Robert E Holmes, *Prin*
EMP: 11 EST: 2012
SALES (est): 354.94K **Privately Held**
SIC: **2834** Pharmaceutical preparations

(G-8526)
QUALITY CARE PRODUCTS LLC
Also Called: Qcp
6920 Hall St (43528)
P.O. Box 1267 (43528)
PHONE..............................734 847-2704
James Swartz, *
EMP: 40 EST: 2001
SALES (est): 5.15MM **Privately Held**
Web: www.qcprx.com
SIC: **2834** Pharmaceutical preparations

(G-8527)
RENNCO AUTOMATION SYSTEMS INC
971 Hamilton Dr (43528-8211)
PHONE..............................419 861-2340
Mike E Owens, *Pr*
Dave Miklos, *
EMP: 30 EST: 1989
SQ FT: 15,000
SALES (est): 4.39MM **Privately Held**
Web: www.rennco automation.com
SIC: **3569** Robots, assembly line: industrial and commercial

(G-8528)
RNM HOLDINGS INC
1810 Eber Rd Ste C (43528-7898)
PHONE..............................419 867-8712
Matthew Milton, *Pr*
EMP: 11
SQ FT: 15,000
SIC: **5084** 3536 Cranes, industrial; Hoists, cranes, and monorails
PA: Rnm Holdings, Inc. 550 Conover Dr Franklin OH 45005

(G-8529)
SCHINDLER ELEVATOR CORPORATION
Also Called: Schindler Elevator
1530 Timber Wolf Dr Ste B (43528-9161)
P.O. Box 960 (43528-0960)
PHONE..............................419 861-5900
Mark Kershner, *Mgr*
EMP: 19
Web: www.schindler.com
SIC: **3534** 7699 Elevators and equipment; Elevators: inspection, service, and repair
HQ: Schindler Elevator Corporation 20 Whippany Rd Morristown NJ 07960 973 397-6500

(G-8530)
SELCO INDUSTRIES INC
1590 Albon Rd Ste 1 (43528-9410)
PHONE..............................419 861-0336
Seldon Hill, *Pr*
Ruby Hill, *
EMP: 24 EST: 1998
SQ FT: 17,000
SALES (est): 1.57MM **Privately Held**
Web: www.selcoindustries.com
SIC: **2678** Papeteries and writing paper sets

(G-8531)
SPONSELLER GROUP INC (PA)
1600 Timber Wolf Dr (43528-8303)
PHONE..............................419 861-3000
Harold P Sponseller, *Ch*
Keith Sponseller, *Pr*
David Nowak, *VP*
Kevin R Nevius, *VP*
EMP: 44 EST: 1973
SQ FT: 8,900
SALES (est): 11.2MM
SALES (corp-wide): 11.2MM **Privately Held**
Web: www.sponsellergroup.com
SIC: **8711** 3599 Consulting engineer; Machine shop, jobbing and repair

(G-8532)
TEKNI-PLEX INC
Also Called: Global Technology Center
1445 Timber Wolf Dr (43528-8302)
PHONE..............................419 491-2399
Paul J Young, *CEO*
Phil Bourgeois, *VP*
EMP: 41 EST: 1967
SALES (est): 5.16MM **Privately Held**
Web: www.tekni-plex.com
SIC: **2679** 7389 2672 Egg cartons, molded pulp: made from purchased material; Packaging and labeling services; Cloth lined paper: made from purchased paper

(G-8533)
TENCOM LTD
7134 Railroad St (43528)
PHONE..............................419 865-5877
Robert Disanza, *Prin*
Shannon Leach, *Off Mgr*
▲ EMP: 8 EST: 1997
SALES (est): 3.41MM **Privately Held**
Web: www.tencom.com
SIC: **3312** 3663 Bar, rod, and wire products; Antennas, transmitting and communications

(G-8534)
TRANE COMPANY
Also Called: Ingersoll Rand
1001 Hamilton Dr (43528-8210)
PHONE..............................419 491-2278
Dennis Goldsmith, *Brnch Mgr*
EMP: 17
Web: www.trane.com
SIC: **3585** Heating equipment, complete
HQ: The Trane Company 3600 Pammel Creek Rd La Crosse WI 54601 608 787-2000

(G-8535)
TURBINE STANDARD LTD (PA)
1750 Eber Rd Ste A (43528-7896)
PHONE..............................419 865-0355
David R Corwin, *Pr*
Patty Kops, *Contrlr*
▲ EMP: 9 EST: 2003
SALES (est): 4.88MM
SALES (corp-wide): 4.88MM **Privately Held**
Web: www.turbinestandard.com
SIC: **3724** Aircraft engines and engine parts

(G-8536)
VINYL DESIGN CORPORATION
7856 Hill Ave (43528-9181)
PHONE..............................419 283-4009
Patrick J Trompeter, *Pr*
EMP: 29 EST: 1988
SQ FT: 36,000
SALES (est): 4.72MM **Privately Held**
Web: www.vinyldesigncorp.com
SIC: **3089** 5033 2452 Windows, plastics; Siding, except wood; Prefabricated wood buildings

(G-8537)
WETTLE CORP
952 Holland Park Blvd (43528-9279)
PHONE..............................419 865-6923
Heather Wettle, *Prin*
EMP: 7 EST: 2013
SALES (est): 434.58K **Privately Held**
Web: www.wettlecorp.com
SIC: **3993** Signs and advertising specialties

(G-8538)
WOODSAGE INDUSTRIES LLC
7400 Airport Hwy (43528-9545)
P.O. Box 1040 (43528-1040)
PHONE..............................419 866-8000
Daniel Brown, *Managing Member*
EMP: 7 EST: 2000
SALES (est): 949.1K **Privately Held**
Web: www.woodsage.com
SIC: **3999** Atomizers, toiletry

(G-8539)
WOODSAGE LLC
Also Called: Proveyance Group
7400 Airport Hwy (43528-9545)
P.O. Box 1040 (43528-1040)
PHONE..............................419 866-8000
Daniel Brown, *CEO*
Curtis Bowers, *
EMP: 110 EST: 2014
SQ FT: 150,000
SALES (est): 13.97MM **Privately Held**
Web: www.woodsage.com
SIC: **3317** Steel pipe and tubes

GEOGRAPHIC SECTION

Hubbard - Trumbull County (G-8562)

(G-8540)
YONGHE PRECISION CASTINGS OHIO
1810 Eber Rd (43528-7897)
PHONE..................................330 447-6685
Shaosen Zhang, *Prin*
EMP: 8 **EST:** 2015
SALES (est): 111.09K **Privately Held**
SIC: 3469 Metal stampings, nec

Holmesville
Holmes County

(G-8541)
ACTION COUPLING & EQP INC
8248 County Road 245 (44633-9724)
P.O. Box 99 (44633-0099)
PHONE..................................330 279-4242
Scott Eliot, *Pr*
▲ **EMP:** 80 **EST:** 1991
SQ FT: 75,000
SALES (est): 10.74MM **Privately Held**
Web: www.actioncoupling.com
SIC: 3569 5087 3429 Firefighting and related equipment; Firefighting equipment; Hardware, nec

(G-8542)
AURIA HOLMESVILLE LLC
8281 County Road 245 (44633-9724)
PHONE..................................330 279-4505
Brian Pour, *Pr*
EMP: 271 **EST:** 2007
SALES (est): 58.89MM **Privately Held**
SIC: 3714 Motor vehicle parts and accessories
HQ: Auria Solutions Usa Inc.
  26999 Centrl Pk Blvd # 30
  Southfield MI 48076
  248 728-8000

(G-8543)
HEARTLAND STAIRWAYS INC
7964 Township Road 565 (44633-9702)
PHONE..................................330 279-2554
Roy Hostewtler, *Pr*
EMP: 6
SALES (corp-wide): 2.1MM **Privately Held**
Web: www.heartlandstairways.com
SIC: 2431 Millwork
PA: Heartland Stairways, Inc.
  8230 County Road 245
  Holmesville OH 44633
  330 279-2554

(G-8544)
HEARTLAND STAIRWAYS INC (PA)
8230 County Road 245 (44633-9724)
PHONE..................................330 279-2554
Roy Hostewtler, *Pr*
EMP: 9 **EST:** 2000
SQ FT: 17,000
SALES (est): 2.1MM
SALES (corp-wide): 2.1MM **Privately Held**
Web: www.heartlandstairways.com
SIC: 3534 Elevators and moving stairways

(G-8545)
HOLMES REDIMIX INC
7571 State Route 83 (44633-9633)
PHONE..................................330 674-0865
Daniel L Mathie, *Pr*
EMP: 25 **EST:** 2007
SALES (est): 4.43MM **Privately Held**
Web: www.melwaygroup.com
SIC: 1442 Construction sand and gravel

(G-8546)
HOLMES STAIR PARTS LTD
8614 Township Road 561 (44633-9706)
PHONE..................................330 279-2797
Ben R Hershberger, *Owner*
EMP: 20 **EST:** 1997
SALES (est): 2.1MM **Privately Held**
Web: www.holmesstair.cc
SIC: 3534 Elevators and moving stairways

(G-8547)
HOLMES SUPPLY CORP
7571 State Route 83 (44633-9633)
PHONE..................................330 279-2634
Steve Schlabach, *Pr*
EMP: 9 **EST:** 1997
SALES (est): 1.32MM **Privately Held**
Web: www.melwaygroup.com
SIC: 3299 2951 1442 Sand lime products; Asphalt paving mixtures and blocks; Construction sand and gravel

(G-8548)
HOLMES WHEEL SHOP INC
Also Called: American Stirrup
7969 County Road 189 (44633-9756)
P.O. Box 56 (44633-0056)
PHONE..................................330 279-2891
Ronald Clark, *Pr*
Paul Stutzman, *VP*
▲ **EMP:** 20 **EST:** 1970
SQ FT: 32,000
SALES (est): 1.56MM **Privately Held**
Web: www.holmeswheelshop.com
SIC: 2499 3199 Spools, reels, and pulleys: wood; Stirrups, wood or metal

(G-8549)
INTERNATIONAL AUTOMOTIVE COMPO
8281 County Road 245 (44633-9724)
PHONE..................................330 279-6557
Kim Landall, *Brnch Mgr*
EMP: 10
Web: www.iacgroup.com
SIC: 3069 Hard rubber products, nec
PA: International Automotive Components Group North America, Inc.
  27777 Franklin Rd # 2000
  Southfield MI 48034

(G-8550)
MILLER LOGGING INC
8373 State Route 83 (44633-9726)
P.O. Box 86 (44633-0086)
PHONE..................................330 279-4721
Roy A Miller Junior, *Pr*
Barbara Miller, *VP*
Levi Miller, *Sec*
EMP: 15 **EST:** 1962
SALES (est): 493.5K **Privately Held**
Web: www.millerlogging.com
SIC: 2421 1629 2411 Wood chips, produced at mill; Land clearing contractor; Logging

(G-8551)
ROTO SOLUTIONS INC
8300 County Rd 189 (44633)
PHONE..................................330 279-2424
Richard Cook, *Pr*
Ralph Kirkpatrick, *
Mark Scheibe, *
EMP: 24 **EST:** 2006
SALES (est): 390.27K **Privately Held**
Web: www.rotosolutions.com
SIC: 3089 Injection molding of plastics

Homer
Licking County

(G-8552)
OHIO STATE PALLET CORP
2175 Broehm Rd (43027)
PHONE..................................614 332-3961
Teresa Salyers, *Prin*
EMP: 6 **EST:** 2001
SALES (est): 225.46K **Privately Held**
Web: www.ohiostatepallet.com
SIC: 2448 Pallets, wood

Homerville
Medina County

(G-8553)
PRINT MARKETING INC
11820 Black River School Rd (44235-9716)
PHONE..................................330 625-1500
Robert Rodman, *Pr*
▲ **EMP:** 9 **EST:** 1983
SQ FT: 1,854
SALES (est): 210.15K **Privately Held**
SIC: 2752 Offset printing

Homeworth
Columbiana County

(G-8554)
HOMEWORTH FABRICATION MCH INC
23094 Georgetown Rd (44634)
P.O. Box 127 (44634-0127)
PHONE..................................330 525-5459
Ronald D Matz, *Pr*
Rocco Vizzuso, *VP*
EMP: 11 **EST:** 1986
SQ FT: 3,000
SALES (est): 1.21MM **Privately Held**
SIC: 3823 3544 Process control instruments; Jigs and fixtures

(G-8555)
OHIO DRILL & TOOL CO (PA)
Also Called: Homeworth Sales Service Div
23255 Georgetown Rd (44634)
P.O. Box 154 (44634)
PHONE..................................330 525-7717
Connie Hallman, *Pr*
George Sanor, *Ch Bd*
Daniel Matz, *VP*
Ronald D Matz, *Sec*
Dale Buckman, *Genl Mgr*
EMP: 20 **EST:** 1947
SQ FT: 5,000
SALES (est): 4.87MM
SALES (corp-wide): 4.87MM **Privately Held**
Web: www.ohiodrill.com
SIC: 5085 5261 3546 3545 Industrial tools; Lawn and garden equipment; Power-driven handtools; Machine tool accessories

(G-8556)
WAYNE A WHALEY
Also Called: Wayne Tire Service
4466 12th St (44634-9725)
PHONE..................................330 525-7779
Wayne Whaley, *Prin*
EMP: 6 **EST:** 1989
SALES (est): 62.16K **Privately Held**
SIC: 7534 5531 Tire repair shop; Automotive tires

Hopedale
Harrison County

(G-8557)
PRINTEESWEET
312 Blackburn Rd (43976-7712)
P.O. Box 456 (43976-0456)
PHONE..................................888 410-2160
Darin Heavilin, *Prin*
EMP: 6 **EST:** 2018
SALES (est): 206.17K **Privately Held**
Web: www.printeesweet.com
SIC: 2759 Screen printing

Howard
Knox County

(G-8558)
BAM FUEL INC
21191 Floralwood Dr (43028-9649)
PHONE..................................740 397-6674
Beth A Mickley, *Prin*
EMP: 6 **EST:** 2008
SALES (est): 144.45K **Privately Held**
SIC: 2869 Fuels

(G-8559)
PRECISION WELDING
123 Jonathon Dr (43028-9585)
PHONE..................................740 627-7320
Mark Vanhouten, *Prin*
EMP: 7 **EST:** 2017
SALES (est): 59.59K **Privately Held**
Web: www.precisionweldingcorp.net
SIC: 7692 Welding repair

(G-8560)
YODER MANUFACTURING
7679 Flack Rd (43028-9740)
PHONE..................................740 504-5028
Noah E Yoder, *Prin*
EMP: 8 **EST:** 2001
SALES (est): 306.59K **Privately Held**
SIC: 3999 Manufacturing industries, nec

Hubbard
Trumbull County

(G-8561)
BALL AROSOL SPECIALTY CONT INC
Also Called: Ball Aerosol And Specialty Container Inc.
644 Myron St (44425)
PHONE..................................330 534-1903
Bernie Grilli, *Brnch Mgr*
EMP: 36
SALES (corp-wide): 14.03B **Publicly Held**
Web: www.ball.com
SIC: 3411 Food and beverage containers
HQ: Ball Aerosol And Specialty Container Corporation
  9200 W 108th Cir
  Westminster CO 80021

(G-8562)
BARFECTIONS LLC
6105 W Liberty St (44425)
PHONE..................................330 759-3100
Mike Handel, *Contrlr*
EMP: 8
SALES (corp-wide): 2.67MM **Privately Held**
SIC: 2064 Candy and other confectionery products
PA: Barfections Llc

Hubbard - Trumbull County (G-8563)

1598 Motor Inn Dr
Girard OH 44420
330 759-3100

(G-8563)
ELLWOOD ENGINEERED CASTINGS CO
7158 Hubbard Masury Rd (44425-9756)
PHONE..................................330 568-3000
Pat Callihan, Pr
Lyda Force, *
Susan A Apel, *
◆ EMP: 135 EST: 1991
SALES (est): 22.72MM
SALES (corp-wide): 687.05MM Privately Held
Web: www.ellwoodengineeredcastings.com
SIC: 3321 3369 3322 Gray iron ingot molds, cast; Nonferrous foundries, nec; Malleable iron foundries
PA: Ellwood Group Inc
    600 Commercial Ave
    Ellwood City PA 16117
    724 752-3680

(G-8564)
INDEPENDENCE 2 LLC
Also Called: I2
623 W Liberty St (44425-1750)
P.O. Box 40 (44425-0040)
PHONE..................................800 414-0545
Ronald P Baldine, Mng Pt
Bonnie L Buchanan, Pt
Nick Ingoedue, Pt
▲ EMP: 10 EST: 2004
SQ FT: 10,000
SALES (est): 2.03MM Privately Held
Web: www.i2hardware.com
SIC: 3429 Door locks, bolts, and checks

(G-8565)
J & D STEEL SERVICE CENTER LLC
3030 Gale Dr (44425-1011)
PHONE..................................330 759-7430
EMP: 9 EST: 2003
SALES (est): 235.96K Privately Held
Web: www.jdsteelservice.com
SIC: 3599 Machine shop, jobbing and repair

(G-8566)
JET STREAM INTERNATIONAL INC
644 Myron St (44425-1466)
PHONE..................................330 505-9988
Edgar B Rumble Junior, CEO
Edgar B Rumble Junior, Pr
John Isbill, *
▲ EMP: 70 EST: 2000
SALES (est): 11.77MM Privately Held
Web: www.jetstr.cc
SIC: 3469 3272 Metal stampings, nec; Concrete structural support and building material

(G-8567)
KILAR MANUFACTURING INC
2616 N Main St (44425-3246)
PHONE..................................330 534-8961
Marilyn Kilar, Pr
EMP: 11 EST: 1988
SQ FT: 12,000
SALES (est): 519.21K Privately Held
Web: www.kilar.cc
SIC: 3713 3714 Car carrier bodies; Motor vehicle parts and accessories

(G-8568)
MS MURCKO & SONS LLC
8090 Chestnut Ridge Rd (44425-9718)
PHONE..................................724 854-4907
Thomas Murcko, Prin

Donald Murcko, Prin
EMP: 8 EST: 2020
SALES (est): 349.76K Privately Held
SIC: 3498 Fabricated pipe and fittings

(G-8569)
OHIO STEEL SHEET AND PLATE INC
7845 Chestnut Ridge Rd (44425-9702)
P.O. Box 1146 (44482-1146)
PHONE..................................800 827-2401
John Rebhan, Pr
Eric Rebhan, *
Mike Link, *
EMP: 45 EST: 1987
SQ FT: 320,000
SALES (est): 7.47MM Privately Held
Web: www.ohiosteelplate.com
SIC: 3312 5051 3444 Sheet or strip, steel, hot-rolled; Metals service centers and offices; Sheet metalwork

(G-8570)
PSK STEEL CORP
2960 Gale Dr (44425-1099)
P.O. Box 308 (44425-0308)
PHONE..................................330 759-1251
Jerry Kinast, Pr
Henry Kinast, *
Steven R Anderson, *
▲ EMP: 40 EST: 1962
SQ FT: 120,000
SALES (est): 9.8MM Privately Held
Web: www.psksteel.com
SIC: 3544 Special dies and tools

(G-8571)
TAYLOR - WINFIELD CORPORATION
Also Called: Denton & Anderson Mktg Div
3200 Innovation Place (44425)
PHONE..................................330 259-8500
John A Anderson Ii, Ch Bd
Michael G Marando, *
◆ EMP: 125 EST: 1882
SQ FT: 45,000
SALES (est): 10.23MM Privately Held
Web: www.taylor-winfield.com
SIC: 3548 3542 3567 Welding apparatus; Machine tools, metal forming type; Induction heating equipment

(G-8572)
WARREN FABRICATING CORPORATION (PA)
7845 Chestnut Ridge Rd (44425-9702)
PHONE..................................330 534-5017
Eric Rebhan, CEO
John C Rebhan, *
◆ EMP: 90 EST: 1967
SQ FT: 380,000
SALES (est): 26.11MM
SALES (corp-wide): 26.11MM Privately Held
Web: www.warfab.com
SIC: 3441 3599 3547 3532 Fabricated structural metal; Machine shop, jobbing and repair; Rolling mill machinery; Mining machinery

(G-8573)
WOODLAND CELLARS LLC
212 N Main St (44425-1656)
PHONE..................................330 240-4883
EMP: 6 EST: 2018
SALES (est): 345.33K Privately Held
Web: www.woodlandcellars.com
SIC: 2084 Wines

(G-8574)
YOUNGSTOWN-KENWORTH INC (PA)

Also Called: All-Line Truck Sales
7255 Hubbard Masury Rd (44425-9757)
PHONE..................................330 534-9761
Tomiel Mikes, Pr
Randall R Fiest, *
Geraldine Mikes, *
EMP: 18 EST: 1972
SQ FT: 14,900
SALES (est): 10.17MM
SALES (corp-wide): 10.17MM Privately Held
Web: www.youngstownkenworth.com
SIC: 5013 5012 7538 3713 Truck parts and accessories; Trucks, commercial; General automotive repair shops; Truck and bus bodies

Huber Heights
Montgomery County

(G-8575)
ENJET AERO LLC
Also Called: Enjet Aero Dayton
7700 New Carlisle Pike (45424-1512)
PHONE..................................937 878-3800
EMP: 11
SALES (est): 1.06MM Privately Held
Web: www.enjetaero.com
SIC: 3728 Aircraft parts and equipment, nec

(G-8576)
ENJET AERO DAYTON INC (DH)
Also Called: Enginetics Aero Space
7700 New Carlisle Pike (45424-1512)
PHONE..................................937 878-3800
Bruce Breckenridge, CEO
Christopher Ferraro, CFO
EMP: 39 EST: 1976
SQ FT: 57,000
SALES (est): 28.27MM
SALES (corp-wide): 78.96MM Privately Held
Web: www.enjetaero.com
SIC: 3724 3728 3812 3519 Aircraft engines and engine parts; Aircraft parts and equipment, nec; Search and navigation equipment; Jet propulsion engines
HQ: Enjet Aero Acquisitions Holding Inc.
    9401 Indian Creek Pkwy
    Overland Park KS 66210
    913 717-7396

(G-8577)
MJO INDUSTRIES INC (PA)
Also Called: Hughes-Peters
8000 Technology Blvd (45424-1573)
PHONE..................................800 590-4055
EMP: 88 EST: 1923
SALES (est): 42.32MM
SALES (corp-wide): 42.32MM Privately Held
Web: www.hughespeters.com
SIC: 5063 5065 3679 Wire and cable; Connectors, electronic; Electronic circuits

(G-8578)
MPE AEROENGINES INC
Also Called: Enginetics
7700 New Carlisle Pike (45424-1512)
PHONE..................................937 878-3800
Dale Pelfrey, CEO
EMP: 25 EST: 2010
SALES (est): 548.47K
SALES (corp-wide): 741.05MM Publicly Held
SIC: 3365 Aerospace castings, aluminum
PA: Standex International Corporation
    23 Keewaydin Dr
    Salem NH 03079
    603 893-9701

(G-8579)
PVS PLASTICS TECHNOLOGY CORP
6290 Executive Blvd (45424-1424)
PHONE..................................937 233-4376
Juerden Frank, Pr
▲ EMP: 20 EST: 2004
SQ FT: 25,000
SALES (est): 11.89MM
SALES (corp-wide): 355.83K Privately Held
Web: www.pvs-plastics.net
SIC: 3089 Injection molding of plastics
PA: Pvs Kunststofftechnik Beteiligungsges. Mbh
    Salzstr. 20
    Niedernhall BW
    794091260

(G-8580)
UPDIKE SUPPLY COMPANY
Also Called: Machine Tools Supply
8241 Expansion Way (45424-6381)
PHONE..................................937 482-4000
Steve Short, Pr
Jeff Butts, *
Trixi Myers, *
Shane Hannan, *
Rob Johnson, *
EMP: 36 EST: 1995
SALES (est): 4.98MM Privately Held
SIC: 3541 Machine tools, metal cutting type

Hudson
Summit County

(G-8581)
A JC INC
Also Called: A J C Hatchet Co
5145 Hudson Dr (44236-3735)
PHONE..................................800 428-2438
Mathew Crookston, Pr
Thomas Crookston, Sls Dir
Jim R Crookston, CFO
▲ EMP: 15 EST: 1968
SQ FT: 10,000
SALES (est): 2.32MM Privately Held
Web: www.ajctools.com
SIC: 3531 3423 3546 3429 Roofing equipment; Hand and edge tools, nec; Power-driven handtools; Hardware, nec

(G-8582)
ADVANCE MATERIALS PRODUCTS INC
Also Called: Adma Products
1890 Georgetown Rd (44236-4058)
PHONE..................................330 650-4000
Vladimir Moxson, Pr
Sophia Moxson, VP
▲ EMP: 6 EST: 1988
SQ FT: 20,000
SALES (est): 1.02MM Privately Held
Web: www.admaproducts.com
SIC: 3339 Titanium metal, sponge and granules

(G-8583)
ALPHA TECHNOLOGIES SVCS LLC (DH)
6279 Hudson Crossing Pkwy Ste 200 (44236)
PHONE..................................330 745-1641
◆ EMP: 60 EST: 1996
SALES (est): 48.18MM
SALES (corp-wide): 223.55MM Privately Held
Web: www.alpha-technologies.com
SIC: 3823 8748 Process control instruments; Testing services

GEOGRAPHIC SECTION
Hudson - Summit County (G-8607)

HQ: Dynisco Instruments Llc
38 Forge Pkwy
Franklin MA 02038
508 541-9400

(G-8584)
AMERICAN ULTRA SPECIALTIES INC
6855 Industrial Pkwy (44236-1158)
PHONE.................................330 656-5000
Christi Yacinski, *Pr*
William Stofey, *Stockholder*
Michaela M Stofey, *Sec*
Albert Sivillo, *Stockholder*
John Ningard Senior, *Stockholder*
EMP: 18 **EST:** 1979
SQ FT: 37,500
SALES (est): 2.33MM **Privately Held**
Web: www.ultraspecoil.com
SIC: 2992 5172 Re-refining lubricating oils and greases, nec; Lubricating oils and greases

(G-8585)
AMF BURNS
1797 Georgetown Rd (44236-4192)
PHONE.................................330 650-6500
EMP: 8 **EST:** 2015
SALES (est): 215.92K **Privately Held**
Web: www.amfbrunsamerica.com
SIC: 3443 Fabricated plate work (boiler shop)

(G-8586)
ARLINGTON VALLEY FARMS LLC (PA)
5369 Hudson Dr (44236-3739)
PHONE.................................216 426-5000
EMP: 25 **EST:** 2010
SALES (est): 4.62MM
SALES (corp-wide): 4.62MM **Privately Held**
Web: www.arlingtonvalleyfarms.com
SIC: 2051 Bread, cake, and related products

(G-8587)
BOXOUT LLC (PA)
Also Called: Meyerpt
6333 Hudson Crossing Pkwy (44236-4346)
PHONE.................................833 462-7746
Ron Harrington, *CEO*
◆ **EMP:** 219 **EST:** 1948
SQ FT: 50,000
SALES (est): 58.63MM
SALES (corp-wide): 58.63MM **Privately Held**
Web: www.meyerpt.com
SIC: 5122 5047 3843 8041 Vitamins and minerals; Medical and hospital equipment; Dental equipment and supplies; Offices and clinics of chiropractors

(G-8588)
CEIA USA LTD
Also Called: Ceia USA
6336 Hudson Crossing Pkwy (44236-4306)
PHONE.................................330 310-4741
Luca Cacioli, *CEO*
Alessandro Manneschi, *Managing Member**
Marco Manneschi, *Managing Member**
Luca Manneschi, *
Giovanni Manneschi, *
▲ **EMP:** 55 **EST:** 1997
SQ FT: 42,316
SALES (est): 19.99MM **Privately Held**
Web: www.ceia-usa.com
SIC: 3669 3812 3829 Metal detectors; Magnetic field detection apparatus; Magnetometers

(G-8589)
CLAFLIN CO
Also Called: Claflin Company
5270 Hudson Dr (44236-3738)
PHONE.................................330 650-0582
James C Claflin, *Pr*
Howard Claflin, *Pr*
EMP: 8 **EST:** 1973
SQ FT: 10,000
SALES (est): 748.06K **Privately Held**
Web: www.claflin.com
SIC: 3089 Injection molding of plastics

(G-8590)
CLEVELAND STEEL CONTAINER CORPORATION (PA)
100 Executive Pkwy (44236-1630)
PHONE.................................440 349-8000
◆ **EMP:** 24 **EST:** 1964
SALES (est): 138.41MM
SALES (corp-wide): 138.41MM **Privately Held**
Web: www.clevelandsteelcontainter.com
SIC: 3412 Pails, shipping: metal

(G-8591)
CLINICAL SPECIALTIES INC (HQ)
Also Called: Csi Infusion Services
6288 Hudson Crossing Pkwy (44236-4347)
PHONE.................................888 873-7888
Edward Rivalsky, *Pr*
EMP: 74 **EST:** 1988
SALES (est): 51.14MM **Publicly Held**
Web: www.clinicalspecialties.com
SIC: 2834 Intravenous solutions
PA: Option Care Health, Inc.
3000 Lakeside Dr Ste 300n
Bannockburn IL 60015

(G-8592)
CUTTER SOLUTINS INTL LLC
2614 Foxden (44236-2303)
PHONE.................................850 725-5600
Joseph Seme, *Mgr*
Nancy Seme, *Mgr*
EMP: 7 **EST:** 2011
SALES (est): 192.82K **Privately Held**
Web: www.tipdressercutter.com
SIC: 3545 Cutting tools for machine tools

(G-8593)
FLUID POWER INC
Also Called: Guardian Mfg.
1300 Hudson Gate Dr (44236-4401)
PHONE.................................330 653-5107
Matt Davis, *Pr*
Matthew Davis, *Ex VP*
Karen Voytek, *Off Mgr*
EMP: 12 **EST:** 1949
SQ FT: 12,000
SALES (est): 3.53MM
SALES (corp-wide): 5.67MM **Privately Held**
Web: www.fluidpowerohio.com
SIC: 3728 Oxygen systems, aircraft
PA: O2 Aero Acquisitions, Llc
8 Morgan Pl
Unionville CT

(G-8594)
GRIFFIN TECHNOLOGY INC
Also Called: Applied Collegiate Systems Div
50 Executive Pkwy (44236-1605)
PHONE.................................585 924-7121
Jonathan B Leiken, *Pr*
EMP: 190 **EST:** 1995
SALES (est): 69.35MM
SALES (corp-wide): 1.63B **Publicly Held**
SIC: 3571 3089 Mainframe computers; Identification cards, plastics
PA: Diebold Nixdorf, Incorporated
350 Orchard Ave Ne
North Canton OH 44720
330 490-4000

(G-8595)
HANDCRAFTED JEWELRY INC
Also Called: Jewelry Art
116 N Main St (44236-2827)
PHONE.................................330 650-9011
Georgianna Bojtos, *Pr*
Barbara Johnson, *VP*
EMP: 7 **EST:** 1977
SQ FT: 1,000
SALES (est): 873.46K **Privately Held**
Web: www.jewelryarthudson.com
SIC: 5944 5947 7699 2759 Jewelry, precious stones and precious metals; Gift shop; Customizing services; Engraving, nec

(G-8596)
HOWARD B CLAFLIN CO
Also Called: Claflin Co
5270 Hudson Dr (44236-3738)
PHONE.................................330 928-1704
Howard B Claflin, *Pr*
Bruce Claflin, *Sls Mgr*
EMP: 6 **EST:** 1957
SALES (est): 473.41K **Privately Held**
SIC: 2655 2599 Reels (fiber), textile: made from purchased material; Boards: planning, display, notice

(G-8597)
HUDSON EXTRUSIONS INC
1255 Norton Rd (44236-4403)
P.O. Box 255 (44236-0255)
PHONE.................................330 653-6015
Marylin Hansen, *Pr*
Dewey Hansen, *Stockholder**
EMP: 35 **EST:** 1956
SQ FT: 33,000
SALES (est): 5.12MM **Privately Held**
Web: www.hudsonextrusions.com
SIC: 3089 Injection molding of plastics

(G-8598)
IGNITION SYSTEMS INC
6751 Evergreen Rd (44236-3258)
PHONE.................................330 653-9674
David Wozencraft, *Prin*
EMP: 10 **EST:** 2010
SALES (est): 284.65K **Privately Held**
Web: www.csc-parts.com
SIC: 3612 Transformers, except electric

(G-8599)
IMPRINTS
77 Maple Dr (44236-3037)
PHONE.................................330 650-0467
William Stemple, *Owner*
EMP: 10 **EST:** 1983
SQ FT: 1,100
SALES (est): 547.5K **Privately Held**
SIC: 2791 Typesetting

(G-8600)
JAMES O EMERT JR
7920 Princewood Dr (44236-1576)
PHONE.................................330 650-6990
James O Emert, *Prin*
EMP: 7 **EST:** 2010
SALES (est): 93.83K **Privately Held**
SIC: 3317 Steel pipe and tubes

(G-8601)
KOBELCO STEWART BOLLING INC
1600 Terex Rd (44236-4086)
PHONE.................................330 655-3111
Atsushi Shigeno, *Pr*
Robert Mcdermott, *Sec*
Takehiko Fujioka, *
▲ **EMP:** 94 **EST:** 1923
SQ FT: 270,000
SALES (est): 21.03MM **Privately Held**
Web: www.ksbi.com
SIC: 3559 Rubber working machinery, including tires
HQ: Kobe Steel Usa Holdings Inc.
535 Madison Ave, 5th Fl
New York NY 10022

(G-8602)
LEAK FINDER INC
6583 Wooded View Dr (44236-1068)
PHONE.................................440 735-0130
EMP: 6 **EST:** 2009
SQ FT: 1,000
SALES (est): 396.69K **Privately Held**
Web: www.leakfinderinc.com
SIC: 1799 1389 7389 Gas leakage detection; Pipe testing, oil field service; Inspection and testing services

(G-8603)
MAGNUM ASSET ACQUISITION LLC
Also Called: Magnum Innovations
5675 Hudson Industrial Pkwy # 3 (44236-5012)
PHONE.................................330 915-2382
Ron Cozean, *Prin*
Maria Hughes, *
EMP: 28 **EST:** 2018
SALES (est): 2.49MM **Privately Held**
SIC: 3646 Fluorescent lighting fixtures, commercial

(G-8604)
MEGALIGHT INC
581 Boston Mills Rd Ste 500 (44236-1196)
PHONE.................................800 957-1797
Dillon Jiang, *Pr*
▲ **EMP:** 25 **EST:** 1999
SALES (est): 4.88MM **Privately Held**
Web: www.megalight.com
SIC: 5063 3645 3646 Lighting fixtures, commercial and industrial; Residential lighting fixtures; Commercial lighting fixtures

(G-8605)
METTLER FOOTWEAR INC
704 Westbrook Way (44236-5221)
PHONE.................................330 703-0079
Michael Mettler, *Pr*
EMP: 6
SALES (est): 258.8K **Privately Held**
SIC: 7389 3021 Business Activities at Non-Commercial Site; Rubber and plastics footwear

(G-8606)
NCRFORMSCOM
137 Owen Brown St (44236-2811)
PHONE.................................800 709-1938
EMP: 7 **EST:** 2013
SALES (est): 124.02K **Privately Held**
Web: www.ncrforms.com
SIC: 2759 Commercial printing, nec

(G-8607)
NCRX OPTICAL SOLUTIONS INC (PA)
105 Executive Pkwy Ste 401 (44236-1689)
P.O. Box 38004 (15238-8004)
PHONE.................................330 239-5353
John Traina, *CEO*
Patrick Cook, *Pr*
EMP: 6 **EST:** 2003
SALES (est): 194.54K
SALES (corp-wide): 194.54K **Privately Held**
Web: www.ncrxopticalsolutions.com

Hudson - Summit County (G-8608)

SIC: 3827 Optical test and inspection equipment

(G-8608)
PRINTERS DEVIL INC
77 Maple Dr (44236-3037)
PHONE..................330 650-1218
William Stemple, *Pr*
EMP: 27 EST: 1977
SQ FT: 800
SALES (est): 581.35K **Privately Held**
Web: www.printersdevilinc.com
SIC: 2752 7334 Offset printing; Photocopying and duplicating services

(G-8609)
RAMCO SPECIALTIES INC (PA)
5445 Hudson Industrial Pkwy (44236-3777)
PHONE..................330 653-5135
Richard Malson Ii, *Pr*
Mark Gamble, *
◆ EMP: 77 EST: 1077
SQ FT: 165
SALES (est): 27.75MM
SALES (corp-wide): 27.75MM **Privately Held**
Web: www.ramcospecialties.com
SIC: 3965 3452 3714 Fasteners; Nuts, metal ; Motor vehicle parts and accessories

(G-8610)
REZKEM CHEMICALS LLC
56 Milford Dr Ste 100 (44236-2760)
PHONE..................330 653-9104
Eric Gorze, *Pr*
▲ EMP: 10 EST: 2011
SALES (est): 826.9K **Privately Held**
Web: www.rezkemchemicals.com
SIC: 2869 Laboratory chemicals, organic

(G-8611)
SHERWIN-WILLIAMS COMPANY
Also Called: Sherwin-Williams
5860 Darrow Rd (44236-3864)
PHONE..................330 528-0124
EMP: 6
SALES (corp-wide): 22.15B **Publicly Held**
Web: www.sherwin-williams.com
SIC: 5231 2851 Paint; Paints and allied products
PA: The Sherwin-Williams Company
     101 W Prospect Ave
     Cleveland OH 44115
     216 566-2000

(G-8612)
SINTERED METAL INDUSTRIES INC
Also Called: Simet
1890 Georgetown Rd (44236-4058)
PHONE..................330 650-4000
Vladimir Moxson, *Pr*
Sophia Moxson, *VP*
EMP: 10 EST: 1985
SALES (est): 786.2K **Privately Held**
SIC: 3441 3568 Fabricated structural metal; Bearings, bushings, and blocks

(G-8613)
SPEARFYSH INC
60 W Streetsboro St Ste 5 (44236-2868)
PHONE..................330 487-0300
Marc Miller, *CEO*
Kim Lewis, *COO*
Rand Lennox, *Engr*
EMP: 9 EST: 2013
SQ FT: 1,900
SALES (est): 217.36K **Privately Held**
Web: www.spearfysh.com
SIC: 7372 Business oriented computer software

(G-8614)
SPECIALTY METALS PROC INC
837 Seasons Rd (44224-1027)
PHONE..................330 656-2767
▲ EMP: 47 EST: 1996
SQ FT: 170,000
SALES (est): 14.01MM **Publicly Held**
Web: www.specialtymetalspro.com
SIC: 3541 Machine tools, metal cutting type
PA: Ryerson Holding Corporation
     227 W Monroe St Fl 27
     Chicago IL 60606

(G-8615)
STARBRIGHT LIGHTING USA LLC
Also Called: Manufacturers Repdirect Distr
5136 Darrow Rd (44236-4004)
PHONE..................330 650-2000
Chris Bokash, *Managing Member*
EMP: 8 EST: 2013
SALES (est): 908.66K **Privately Held**
Web: www.starbrightlightingusa.com
SIC: 3648 Lighting equipment, nec

(G-8616)
THE LITTLE TIKES COMPANY (PA)
Also Called: Little Tikes
2180 Barlow Rd (44236-4199)
PHONE..................330 650-3000
◆ EMP: 1800 EST: 1967
SALES (est): 488.19MM
SALES (corp-wide): 488.19MM **Privately Held**
Web: www.littletikes.com
SIC: 3944 2519 Games, toys, and children's vehicles; Juvenile furniture, rattan or reed: padded or plain

(G-8617)
UNIVERSAL DRECT FLFLLMENT CORP
5581 Hudson Industrial Pkwy (44236-5019)
PHONE..................330 650-5000
Jared Florian, *Pr*
▲ EMP: 132 EST: 2005
SQ FT: 78,000
SALES (est): 21.21MM
SALES (corp-wide): 48.18MM **Privately Held**
Web: www.universalscreenarts.com
SIC: 5961 2741 2396 Catalog and mail-order houses; Miscellaneous publishing; Automotive and apparel trimmings
PA: Universal Screen Arts, Inc.
     5581 Hudson Indus Pkwy
     Hudson OH 44236
     330 650-5000

(G-8618)
UNIVERSAL SCREEN ARTS INC (PA)
Also Called: What On Earth
5581 Hudson Industrial Pkwy (44236-5019)
PHONE..................330 650-5000
◆ EMP: 45 EST: 1983
SALES (est): 48.18MM
SALES (corp-wide): 48.18MM **Privately Held**
Web: www.universalscreenarts.com
SIC: 5961 2396 2741 Catalog and mail-order houses; Automotive and apparel trimmings; Miscellaneous publishing

(G-8619)
WOLTERS KLUWER CLINICAL DRUG INFORMATION INC
1100 Terex Rd (44236-3771)
P.O. Box 1560 (21741-1560)
PHONE..................330 650-6506
EMP: 65
Web: www.wolterskluwer.com

SIC: 2731 2791 7379 Books, publishing only ; Typesetting, computer controlled; Computer related maintenance services

Huntsburg
Geauga County

(G-8620)
PRECISION SHEETROCK LLC
17080 Mayfield Rd (44046-9787)
PHONE..................440 477-7803
EMP: 6 EST: 2015
SALES (est): 170.38K **Privately Held**
SIC: 3599 Industrial machinery, nec

(G-8621)
WINDY KNOLL WOODWORKING LLC
15919 Mayfield Rd (44046-9777)
PHONE..................440 636-5092
David E Byler, *Prin*
EMP: 7 EST: 2016
SALES (est): 199.46K **Privately Held**
SIC: 2431 Millwork

Huntsville
Logan County

(G-8622)
DUFF QUARRY INC (PA)
Also Called: Duff Quarry
9042 State Route 117 (43324-9617)
P.O. Box 305 (43324-0305)
PHONE..................937 686-2811
James E Duff, *Pr*
Scott Duff, *VP*
Sandy Duff, *Sec*
EMP: 15 EST: 1953
SQ FT: 26,000
SALES (est): 3.38MM
SALES (corp-wide): 3.38MM **Privately Held**
Web: www.duffquarry.com
SIC: 1422 Crushed and broken limestone

(G-8623)
FIRE SAFETY SERVICES INC
6228 Township Road 95 (43324-9673)
PHONE..................937 686-2000
Steven Spath, *Pr*
Marcus Taylor, *VP*
Kay Spath, *Sec*
EMP: 18 EST: 1962
SQ FT: 6,400
SALES (est): 9.53MM **Privately Held**
Web: www.fssohio.com
SIC: 5099 5012 5087 3999 Fire extinguishers ; Fire trucks; Firefighting equipment; Fire extinguishers, portable

(G-8624)
RETENTION KNOB SUPPLY & MFG CO
4905 State Route 274 W (43324-9643)
P.O. Box 61 (43311-0061)
PHONE..................937 686-6405
Thomas E Christen, *Pr*
Carrie Christen, *Sec*
EMP: 10 EST: 1981
SQ FT: 100,000
SALES (est): 1.05MM **Privately Held**
Web: www.retentionknobsupply.com
SIC: 3545 Machine tool attachments and accessories

Huron
Erie County

(G-8625)
AKZO NOBEL COATINGS INC
300 Sprowl Rd (44839-2636)
PHONE..................419 433-9143
EMP: 26
SALES (corp-wide): 11.26B **Privately Held**
SIC: 2851 Paints and allied products
HQ: Akzo Nobel Coatings Inc.
     535 Marriott Dr Ste 500
     Nashville TN 37214
     440 297-5100

(G-8626)
AMERICAN PUBLISHERS LLC
Also Called: American Publishers
2401 Sawmill Pkwy (11830-2004)
PHONE..................419 626-0623
Steven Ester, *Pr*
John Rohan Junior, *Treas*
Catherine Bostron, *
John P Loughlin, *
EMP: 100 EST: 1918
SALES (est): 10.57MM
SALES (corp-wide): 4.29B **Privately Held**
Web: www.american-publishers.com
SIC: 2741 Miscellaneous publishing
PA: The Hearst Corporation
     300 W 57th St Fl 42
     New York NY 10019
     212 649-2000

(G-8627)
ARTHUR CORPORATION
1305 Huron Avery Rd (44839-2429)
PHONE..................419 433-7202
Charles Hensel, *Pr*
Mark Svancara, *
EMP: 65 EST: 1981
SQ FT: 65,000
SALES (est): 7.01MM **Privately Held**
Web: www.arthurcorp.com
SIC: 3089 3083 Thermoformed finished plastics products, nec; Laminated plastics plate and sheet

(G-8628)
ASSEMBLY WORKS INC
Also Called: Assembly Works Matrix Automtn
1705 Sawmill Pkwy (44839-2232)
PHONE..................419 433-5010
William E Kaman, *Pr*
Julie Smart, *Sec*
EMP: 8 EST: 1998
SQ FT: 10,200
SALES (est): 742.21K **Privately Held**
SIC: 3613 Panelboards and distribution boards, electric

(G-8629)
CENTRAL OHIO PAPER & PACKG INC (PA)
Also Called: Breckenridge Paper & Packaging
2350 University Dr E (44839-9173)
PHONE..................419 621-9239
Edward Pettegrew Junior, *Pr*
EMP: 15 EST: 1994
SQ FT: 12,000
SALES (est): 8.92MM **Privately Held**
SIC: 2671 Paper, coated or laminated for packaging

(G-8630)
CHEFS GARDEN INC
9009 Huron Avery Rd (44839-2448)
PHONE..................419 433-4947
Barbara Jones, *Pr*

▲ = Import ▼ = Export
◆ = Import/Export

Bob L Jones, *
Lee Jones, *
Robert N Jones, *
EMP: 130 **EST:** 1981
SQ FT: 1,684
SALES (est): 23.67MM **Privately Held**
Web: www.chefs-garden.com
SIC: 2099 5148 0161 Ready-to-eat meals, salads, and sandwiches; Fresh fruits and vegetables; Market garden

(G-8631)
DENTON ATD INC (PA)
900 Denton Dr (44839-8922)
PHONE.................................567 265-5200
Robert A Denton, *Ch*
David C Stein, *
Micheal Beebe, *
Craig Morgan, *Stockholder**
EMP: 29 **EST:** 1991
SQ FT: 16,000
SALES (est): 3.77MM **Privately Held**
Web: www.humaneticsgroup.com
SIC: 3999 3821 3829 Mannequins; Calibration tapes, for physical testing machines; Measuring and controlling devices, nec

(G-8632)
GEOCORP INC
9010 River Rd (44839-9523)
PHONE.................................419 433-1101
George Conrad, *Pr*
EMP: 46 **EST:** 1989
SQ FT: 6,000
SALES (est): 12.65MM **Privately Held**
Web: www.geocorpinc.com
SIC: 3823 Thermocouples, industrial process type

(G-8633)
HURON CEMENT PRODUCTS COMPANY (PA)
Also Called: H & C Building Supplies
617 Main St (44839-2593)
PHONE.................................419 433-4161
John Caporini, *Pr*
EMP: 38 **EST:** 1914
SQ FT: 37,800
SALES (est): 4.66MM
SALES (corp-wide): 4.66MM **Privately Held**
Web: www.terminalreadymix.com
SIC: 5032 3273 3546 3272 Cement; Ready-mixed concrete; Power-driven handtools; Concrete products, nec

(G-8634)
I 5S OF HURON INC
356 Main St (44839-1663)
PHONE.................................419 433-9075
Mike Glaser, *Prin*
EMP: 7 **EST:** 2006
SALES (est): 245.88K **Privately Held**
SIC: 2599 Bar, restaurant and cafeteria furniture

(G-8635)
LABEL AID INC
Also Called: Label Aid
608 Rye Beach Rd (44839-2064)
PHONE.................................419 433-2888
Darlene Crooks, *Pr*
Carl S Hanson, *
Lucille Hanson, *
Heather Feeney, *
▲ **EMP:** 32 **EST:** 1983
SQ FT: 40,000
SALES (est): 4.93MM **Privately Held**
Web: www.labelaidinc.com

SIC: 2759 2679 Labels and seals: printing, nsk; Labels, paper: made from purchased material

(G-8636)
LAKE ERIE AGGREGATES INC
720 Gloucester Dr (44839-1424)
P.O. Box 67 (44839-0067)
PHONE.................................419 541-0130
Jarret S Barnes, *Prin*
EMP: 6 **EST:** 2015
SALES (est): 75.31K **Privately Held**
SIC: 1442 Construction sand and gravel

(G-8637)
LAKEWAY MFG INC (PA)
730 River Rd (44839-2623)
P.O. Box 486 (44839-0486)
PHONE.................................419 433-3030
Jack Kenning, *Pr*
Barbara K Straka, *
EMP: 25 **EST:** 1977
SALES (est): 2.49MM
SALES (corp-wide): 2.49MM **Privately Held**
Web: www.lakewaymfg.com
SIC: 3567 3255 3446 3433 Industrial furnaces and ovens; Clay refractories; Architectural metalwork; Heating equipment, except electric

(G-8638)
LATANICK EQUIPMENT INC
720 River Rd (44839-2623)
PHONE.................................419 433-2200
Richard D Poorman, *Pr*
Richard Decker, *VP*
EMP: 20 **EST:** 1973
SQ FT: 32,000
SALES (est): 2.8MM **Privately Held**
Web: www.latanickequipment.com
SIC: 8711 3599 Designing: ship, boat, machine, and product; Custom machinery

(G-8639)
LUC ICE INC
10020 River Rd (44839-9768)
PHONE.................................419 734-2201
TOLL FREE: 800
Michael Luc, *Pr*
Paul Luc, *VP*
EMP: 7 **EST:** 1982
SALES (est): 465.19K **Privately Held**
Web: www.homecityice.com
SIC: 2097 Block ice

(G-8640)
MUDBROOK GOLF CTR AT THNDRBIRD
1609 Mudbrook Rd (44839-8905)
PHONE.................................419 433-2945
EMP: 6 **EST:** 2007
SALES (est): 399.62K **Privately Held**
Web: www.thunderbirdgolfcourses.com
SIC: 3949 Driving ranges, golf, electronic

(G-8641)
N2Y LLC
909 University Dr S (44839-9172)
P.O. Box 550 (44839-0550)
PHONE.................................419 433-9800
Christin Wostmann, *CEO*
David Swank, *
Steve Lubowicz, *
Don Wostmann, *
EMP: 135 **EST:** 1997
SQ FT: 16,800
SALES (est): 25.49MM **Privately Held**
Web: www.n2y.com

SIC: 3999 Education aids, devices and supplies

(G-8642)
ODYSSEY PRESS INC
913 Superior Dr (44839-1454)
PHONE.................................614 410-0356
David L Trotter, *Pr*
Mark Bober, *VP*
EMP: 12 **EST:** 1977
SQ FT: 10,000
SALES (est): 344.36K **Privately Held**
SIC: 2752 2759 Offset printing; Letterpress printing

(G-8643)
OPC CULTIVATION LLC
Also Called: Firelands Scientific
2300 University Dr E (44839-9173)
PHONE.................................419 616-5115
EMP: 10 **EST:** 2017
SALES (est): 496.08K **Privately Held**
Web: www.firelandsscientific.com
SIC: 3999

(G-8644)
PACER FLIGHT LLC
3306 Fox Rd (44839-2251)
PHONE.................................419 433-5562
EMP: 6 **EST:** 2001
SALES (est): 100K **Privately Held**
SIC: 3721 Airplanes, fixed or rotary wing

(G-8645)
SEVEN LAKEWAY REFRACTORIES LLC
730 River Rd (44839-2623)
PHONE.................................419 433-3030
Leanne Pate, *Managing Member*
EMP: 16 **EST:** 2021
SALES (est): 1.27MM **Privately Held**
SIC: 3255 Tile and brick refractories, except plastic

(G-8646)
YAKPADS INC
3504 Hull Rd (44839-2120)
PHONE.................................419 357-5684
Chester Dietrick, *Prin*
EMP: 6 **EST:** 2009
SALES (est): 105.58K **Privately Held**
Web: www.cascadecreek.com
SIC: 3949 Sporting and athletic goods, nec

Iberia
Morrow County

(G-8647)
COREWORTH HOLDINGS LLC
3396 Sr 309 (43325)
PHONE.................................419 468-7100
Rodney Whited, *Pt*
Randy Harper, *Pt*
▲ **EMP:** 8 **EST:** 2014
SALES (est): 418.4K **Privately Held**
Web: www.coreworth.com
SIC: 3469 Machine parts, stamped or pressed metal

(G-8648)
GLEN-GERY CORPORATION
County Rd 9 (43325)
P.O. Box 207 (43325-0207)
PHONE.................................419 468-5002
George Robinson, *Mgr*
EMP: 41
Web: www.glengery.com
SIC: 3251 3255 Structural brick and blocks; Clay refractories

HQ: Glen-Gery Corporation
1166 Spring St
Reading PA 19610
610 374-4011

(G-8649)
YIZUMI-HPM CORPORATION
Also Called: HPM North America Corp
3424 State Rt 309 (43325)
P.O. Box 210 (43325-0210)
PHONE.................................740 382-5600
Randy Clements, *Mgr*
▲ **EMP:** 27 **EST:** 2011
SALES (est): 19.36MM **Privately Held**
Web: www.hpmmachinery.com
SIC: 3542 Die casting machines
PA: Yizumi Holdings Co., Ltd.
No.22, Keyuan 3rd Road, High-Tech Zone, Shunde District
Foshan GD 52830

Independence
Cuyahoga County

(G-8650)
7SIGNAL INC (PA)
6155 Rockside Rd Ste 110 (44131-2217)
PHONE.................................216 777-2900
Thomas Barrett, *CEO*
Don Cook, *CMO**
EMP: 22 **EST:** 2011
SQ FT: 3,900
SALES (est): 3.17MM
SALES (corp-wide): 3.17MM **Privately Held**
Web: www.7signal.com
SIC: 3661 Telephone and telegraph apparatus

(G-8651)
ACCEL PERFORMANCE GROUP LLC (DH)
6100 Oak Tree Blvd Ste 200 (44131)
PHONE.................................216 658-6413
Robert Tobey, *CEO*
Robert Romanelli, *
Andrew Mazzarella, *
◆ **EMP:** 180 **EST:** 1993
SQ FT: 200,000
SALES (est): 53.05MM
SALES (corp-wide): 659.7MM **Publicly Held**
Web: www.airsoftswat.com
SIC: 3714 5013 3053 Motor vehicle parts and accessories; Automotive supplies and parts; Gaskets; packing and sealing devices
HQ: Msdp Group Llc
1350 Pullman Dr Dock #14
El Paso TX 79936
915 857-5200

(G-8652)
AGILE GLOBAL SOLUTIONS INC
5755 Granger Rd Ste 610 (44131-1458)
PHONE.................................916 655-7745
EMP: 29
SALES (corp-wide): 6.65MM **Privately Held**
Web: www.agileglobalsolutions.com
SIC: 7372 Business oriented computer software
PA: Agile Global Solutions, Inc.
193 Blue Ravine Rd # 160
Folsom CA 95630
916 353-1780

(G-8653)
ALCAN PRIMARY PRODUCTS CORP
6055 Rockside Woods Blvd N Ste 180 (44131-2301)

Independence - Cuyahoga County (G-8654) — GEOGRAPHIC SECTION

◆ **EMP:** 1949 **EST:** 2003
SALES (est): 2.01MM
SALES (corp-wide): 54.04B Privately Held
SIC: 3334 Primary aluminum
HQ: Alcan Corporation
6060 Parkland Blvd
Cleveland OH 44124
440 460-3307

(G-8654)
AW FABER-CASTELL USA INC
Also Called: Creativity For Kids
9000 Rio Nero Dr (44131-5502)
PHONE.................216 643-4660
▲ **EMP:** 79 **EST:** 1996
SALES (est): 46.1MM
SALES (corp-wide): 687.1MM Privately Held
Web: www.fabercastell.com
SIC: 5092 5112 3944 Arts and crafts equipment and supplies; Stationery and office supplies; Games, toys, and children's vehicles
HQ: Faber-Castell Ag
Nurnberger Str. 2
Stein BY 90547
91199650

(G-8655)
CARDIOINSIGHT TECHNOLOGIES INC
Also Called: Medtronic
3 Summit Park Dr Ste 400 (44131-2582)
PHONE.................216 274-2221
Patrick J Wethington, Pr
Charu Ramanathan, CSO
EMP: 9 **EST:** 2006
SALES (est): 1.94MM Privately Held
Web: www.cardioinsight.com
SIC: 3845 Electrocardiographs
PA: Medtronic Public Limited Company
20 Hatch Street Lower
Dublin D02 X

(G-8656)
CHALLENGER HARDWARE COMPANY
800 Resource Dr Ste 8 (44131-1875)
PHONE.................216 591-1141
Joe Ross, Pr
▲ **EMP:** 8 **EST:** 2005
SALES (est): 224.69K Privately Held
Web: www.challengercos.com
SIC: 3312 Stainless steel

(G-8657)
CHECKPOINT SURGICAL INC
Also Called: Checkpoint Surgical Instrs Inc
6050 Oak Tree Blvd Ste 360 (44131-6938)
PHONE.................216 378-9107
Leonard Cosentino, CEO
EMP: 55 **EST:** 2009
SALES (est): 8.64MM Privately Held
Web: www.checkpointsurgical.com
SIC: 3845 Electromedical equipment

(G-8658)
CHROMASCAPE LLC (PA)
Also Called: Amerimulch
7555 E Pleasant Valley Rd Ste 100 (44131-5557)
PHONE.................330 998-7574
Joseph Majewski, Pr
George Chase, *
Steve Lefkowitz, *
◆ **EMP:** 33 **EST:** 1998
SALES (est): 80.22MM
SALES (corp-wide): 80.22MM Privately Held
Web: www.chromascape.com

SIC: 2816 2895 Color pigments; Carbon black

(G-8659)
CONSTRCTION AGGRGTES CORP MICH
3 Summit Park Dr Ste 700 (44131-6901)
PHONE.................616 842-7900
Andrew D Eich, Prin
David Sensibar, Pr
Albert Fruend, Sec
EMP: 8 **EST:** 1982
SALES (est): 1.2MM Privately Held
SIC: 1442 Construction sand and gravel

(G-8660)
COVIA HOLDINGS LLC (PA)
3 Summit Park Dr Ste 700 (44131-6901)
PHONE.................800 255-7263
◆ **EMP:** 90 **EST:** 1970
SALES (est): 1.6B
SALES (corp-wide): 1.6B Privately Held
Web: www.coviacorp.com
SIC: 1446 Silica mining

(G-8661)
COVIA SOLUTIONS INC (HQ)
Also Called: Fairmount Minerals
3 Summit Park Dr Ste 700 (44131-6901)
P.O. Box 87 (44024-0087)
PHONE.................404 214-3200
Brian Richardson, Ex VP
Duncan Stuart, Ex VP
Rory O'donnell, Sr VP
Christopher Nagel, Ex VP
Russell Montgomery, Ex VP
▼ **EMP:** 9 **EST:** 1986
SALES (est): 426.94MM
SALES (corp-wide): 1.6B Privately Held
Web: www.coviacorp.com
SIC: 1442 Construction sand and gravel
PA: Covia Holdings Llc
3 Summit Park Dr Ste 700
Independence OH 44131
800 255-7263

(G-8662)
CRH US
6925 Granger Rd (44131-1407)
PHONE.................216 642-3920
EMP: 6 **EST:** 2018
SALES (est): 180.77K Privately Held
Web: www.ashgrove.com
SIC: 3531 Cement silos (batch plant)

(G-8663)
DUNHAM MACHINE INC
1311 E Schaaf Rd Bldg A (44131-1347)
PHONE.................216 398-4500
Ted Pawelec, Pr
EMP: 9 **EST:** 1988
SQ FT: 7,500
SALES (est): 953.81K Privately Held
Web: www.dunhammachine.com
SIC: 3599 Machine shop, jobbing and repair

(G-8664)
E VENTUS CORPORATION
5005 Rockside Rd (44131-2194)
PHONE.................216 643-6840
David Brennan, Mgr
EMP: 12 **EST:** 2010
SALES (est): 524.36K Privately Held
Web: www.e-ventus.com
SIC: 7372 Prepackaged software

(G-8665)
ECOPRO SOLUTIONS LLC
5617 E Schaaf Rd (44131-1305)
PHONE.................216 232-4040

Dennis B Angers, Pr
EMP: 50 **EST:** 2019
SALES (est): 3.43MM Privately Held
Web: www.ecopro.com
SIC: 3822 Hardware for environmental regulators

(G-8666)
EDGEWATER CAPITAL PARTNERS LP (PA)
5005 Rockside Rd Ste 840 (44131)
PHONE.................216 292-3838
Chris Childres, Mng Pt
Ryan J Meany, Pt
Richard Schwarz, Pt
EMP: 8 **EST:** 1998
SQ FT: 3,200
SALES (est): 80.2MM
SALES (corp-wide): 80.2MM Privately Held
Web: www.edgewatercapital.com
SIC: 6799 2899 Investors, nec; Chemical supplies for foundries

(G-8667)
EPIROC USA LLC
7171 E Pleasant Valley Rd (44131-5541)
PHONE.................844 437-4762
EMP: 14
SALES (corp-wide): 4.74B Privately Held
Web: www.epiroc.com
SIC: 3532 Drills, bits, and similar equipment
HQ: Epiroc Usa Llc
8001 Arista Pl Unit 400
Broomfield CO 80021
844 437-4762

(G-8668)
FIVE STAR TECHNOLOGIES LTD
6801 Brecksville Rd Ste 200 (44131-5032)
PHONE.................216 447-9422
EMP: 15 **EST:** 1995
SQ FT: 20,000
SALES (est): 1.51MM Privately Held
Web: www.fivestartech.com
SIC: 3823 Process control instruments

(G-8669)
GRAFTECH HOLDINGS INC
6100 Oak Tree Blvd Ste 300 (44131)
PHONE.................216 676-2000
Joel L Hawthorne, CEO
Erick R Asmussen, VP
John D Moran, VP
EMP: 98 **EST:** 1993
SALES (est): 9.13MM Publicly Held
Web: www.graftechaet.com
SIC: 1499 3624 Graphite mining; Carbon and graphite products
PA: Graftech International Ltd.
982 Keynote Cir
Brooklyn Heights OH 44131

(G-8670)
KOMATSU MINING CORP
981 Keynote Cir Ste 8 (44131-1842)
PHONE.................216 503-5029
Edward L Doheny, Brnch Mgr
EMP: 57
Web: www.joyglobal.com
SIC: 3532 Mining machinery
HQ: Komatsu Mining Corp.
311 E Greenfield Ave
Milwaukee WI 53204

(G-8671)
LIQUID DEVELOPMENT COMPANY (PA)
Also Called: L D C
5708 E Schaaf Rd (44131-1308)

PHONE.................216 641-9366
Doug Hutchinson, Pr
Beldon Hutchinson, VP
Dawn Hutchinson, Sec
Lynn Hutchinson, Treas
▲ **EMP:** 9 **EST:** 1978
SQ FT: 18,000
SALES (est): 835.5K
SALES (corp-wide): 835.5K Privately Held
Web: www.ldcbrushplate.com
SIC: 2899 3559 Chemical preparations, nec; Electroplating machinery and equipment

(G-8672)
MEDTRONIC INC
Also Called: Medtronic
3 Summit Park Dr Ste 400 (44131-2582)
PHONE.................763 526-2566
EMP: 8
Web: www.medtronic.com
SIC: 3841 Surgical and medical instruments
HQ: Medtronic, Inc.
710 Medtronic Pkwy
Minneapolis MN 55432
763 514-4000

(G-8673)
MILL & MOTION INC
5415 E Schaaf Rd (44131-1335)
PHONE.................216 524-4000
Daniel Hala, Pr
EMP: 12 **EST:** 1983
SQ FT: 18,000
SALES (est): 1.57MM Privately Held
Web: www.millmotion.com
SIC: 3599 8711 Machine shop, jobbing and repair; Designing: ship, boat, machine, and product

(G-8674)
MILL & MOTION PROPERTIES LTD
5415 E Schaaf Rd (44131-1335)
PHONE.................216 524-4000
Albert E Hala, Ch Bd
Daniel Hala, Pr
EMP: 12 **EST:** 1983
SALES (est): 830.95K Privately Held
SIC: 3824 Mechanical and electromechanical counters and devices

(G-8675)
MILLCRAFT GROUP LLC (PA)
Also Called: Deltacraft
9000 Rio Nero Dr (44131-5502)
PHONE.................216 441-5500
▲ **EMP:** 75 **EST:** 1995
SALES (est): 388.34MM Privately Held
Web: www.millcraft.com
SIC: 5111 5113 2679 Printing paper; Industrial and personal service paper; Paper products, converted, nec

(G-8676)
NAPROTEK HOLDINGS LLC
Also Called: Naprotek
5005 Rockside Rd Ste 840 (44131-6800)
PHONE.................408 830-5000
Daniel Everitt, CEO
Chris Springer, *
Peter Ostergard, *
EMP: 85 **EST:** 2020
SALES (est): 2.67MM Privately Held
SIC: 3672 Printed circuit boards

(G-8677)
NIDEC AVTRON AUTOMATION CORPORATION
Also Called: Avtron Industrial Automation
7555 E Pleasant Valley Rd (44131-5562)
PHONE.................216 642-1230
EMP: 150

GEOGRAPHIC SECTION

Ironton - Lawrence County (G-8699)

Web: www.nidec-avtron.com
SIC: 3823 3829 Process control instruments; Aircraft and motor vehicle measurement equipment

(G-8678)
OSRAM SYLVANIA INC
6400 Rockside Rd (44131-2309)
PHONE.................................800 463-9275
EMP: 59
SALES (corp-wide): 5B Privately Held
Web: www.sylvania-automotive.com
SIC: 3641 Electric lamps
HQ: Osram Sylvania Inc.
200 Ballardvale St Bldg 2
Wilmington MA 01887
978 570-3000

(G-8679)
PENINSULA PUBLISHING LLC
Also Called: Plastics Machinery Magazine
2 Summit Park Dr Ste 300 (44131-2560)
PHONE.................................330 524-3359
J A Lewellenc, CEO
EMP: 9 EST: 2015
SALES (est): 477.11K Privately Held
SIC: 2721 Magazines: publishing and printing

(G-8680)
POLYMER ADDITIVES HOLDINGS INC (PA)
Also Called: Valtris
7500 E Pleasant Valley Rd (44131-5536)
PHONE.................................216 875-7200
Paul Angus, Pr
Andy Gehrlein, *
Jim Mason, *
Steve Hughes, Comm Vice President*
EMP: 200 EST: 2014
SALES (est): 465.61MM
SALES (corp-wide): 465.61MM Privately Held
Web: www.valtris.com
SIC: 5169 2899 Chemicals and allied products, nec; Chemical preparations, nec

(G-8681)
PRECISION METALFORMING ASSN
6363 Oak Tree Blvd (44131-2556)
PHONE.................................216 901-8800
William E Gaskin, CEO
Doug Johnson, *
David C Klotz, *
Daniel E Ellashek, *
Bill Smith, *
▲ EMP: 41 EST: 1942
SQ FT: 20,000
SALES (est): 75.76K Privately Held
Web: www.pma.org
SIC: 8611 2731 Trade associations; Book publishing

(G-8682)
PREFERRED SOLUTIONS INC
5000 Rockside Rd Ste 230 (44131-2178)
PHONE.................................216 642-1200
John A Stahl, Pr
Jack Stahl, VP
EMP: 14 EST: 1992
SALES (est): 2.82MM Privately Held
Web: www.preferredsolutions.net
SIC: 3089 Plastics processing

(G-8683)
QUEZ MEDIA MARKETING INC
Also Called: Quez Media
6100 Oak Tree Blvd Ste 200 (44131-2544)
PHONE.................................216 910-0202
Jose A Vasquez, CEO
EMP: 14 EST: 2009
SALES (est): 1.11MM Privately Held

Web: www.quezmedia.com
SIC: 7374 2752 7336 7371 Computer graphics service; Offset printing; Commercial art and graphic design; Computer software systems analysis and design, custom

(G-8684)
ROBIN INDUSTRIES INC (PA)
Also Called: Elastotec Div
6500 Rockside Rd Ste 230 (44131-2319)
PHONE.................................216 631-7000
▲ EMP: 12 EST: 1947
SALES (est): 74.78MM
SALES (corp-wide): 74.78MM Privately Held
Web: www.robin-industries.com
SIC: 3069 3061 Molded rubber products; Mechanical rubber goods

(G-8685)
STEIN LLC (DH)
3 Summit Park Dr Ste 425 (44131-6902)
P.O. Box 470548 (44147-0548)
PHONE.................................440 526-9301
Donald Ries, CEO
Marc Glasgow, Pr
James Conlon, Sec
David Holvey, CFO
▲ EMP: 15 EST: 1945
SALES (est): 21.01MM Privately Held
Web: www.steininc.com
SIC: 7629 7699 3399 Electrical repair shops; Cleaning services; Iron ore recovery from open hearth slag
HQ: Tms International, Llc
Southside Wrks Bldg 1 3f
Pittsburgh PA 15203
412 678-6141

(G-8686)
STEIN HOLDINGS INC
3 Summit Park Dr Ste 425 (44131-6902)
PHONE.................................440 526-9301
EMP: 28 EST: 2016
SALES (est): 682.69K Privately Held
Web: www.steininc.com
SIC: 2542 Partitions and fixtures, except wood

(G-8687)
THYSSENKRUPP MATERIALS NA INC
6050 Oak Tree Blvd Ste 110 (44131-6927)
PHONE.................................216 883-8100
Randy Pacelli, Brnch Mgr
EMP: 60
SQ FT: 65,000
SALES (corp-wide): 40.78B Privately Held
Web: www.thyssenkrupp-materials-na.com
SIC: 5051 3341 Steel; Secondary nonferrous metals
HQ: Thyssenkrupp Materials Na, Inc.
22355 W 11 Mile Rd
Southfield MI 48033
248 233-5600

(G-8688)
TROYMILL LUMBER COMPANY
7000 Granger Rd Ste 1 (44131-1462)
PHONE.................................440 632-6353
Marvin Schaefer, Pr
Collen Satterlee, Mgr
EMP: 8 EST: 1992
SALES (est): 644.08K Privately Held
Web: www.troymill.com
SIC: 2448 Pallets, wood

(G-8689)
USER FRIENDLY PHONE BOOK LLC
2 Summit Park Dr Ste 105 (44131-2558)
PHONE.................................216 674-6500
Jack Nelson, Brnch Mgr
EMP: 46
SALES (corp-wide): 25.13MM Privately Held
Web: www.userfriendlymedia.com
SIC: 2741 Directories, telephone: publishing and printing
PA: User Friendly Phone Book, Llc
10200 Grogans Mill Rd # 440
The Woodlands TX 77380
281 465-5400

(G-8690)
WEDRON SILICA LLC
3 Summit Park Dr Ste 700 (44131)
P.O. Box 119 (60557)
PHONE.................................815 433-2449
William Conway, Ch
Charles Fowler, *
Jenniffer Deckard, *
Joseph Fodo, *
David Crandall, *
EMP: 90 EST: 1984
SQ FT: 4,500
SALES (est): 17.45MM
SALES (corp-wide): 1.6B Privately Held
SIC: 1446 Industrial sand
HQ: Covia Solutions Inc.
3 Summit Park Dr Ste 700
Independence OH 44131
404 214-3200

(G-8691)
WESTON BRANDS INC
7575 E Pleasant Valley Rd Ste 100 (44131-5567)
PHONE.................................800 814-4895
EMP: 9 EST: 2016
SALES (est): 229.55K Privately Held
Web: www.westonbrands.com
SIC: 2099 Food preparations, nec

(G-8692)
WISCONSIN INDUS SAND CO LLC
3 Summit Park Dr Ste 700 (44131-6901)
PHONE.................................715 235-0942
Jenniffer Deckard, Managing Member
William E Conway, *
Andrew D Eich, *
EMP: 26 EST: 1996
SALES (est): 16.31MM
SALES (corp-wide): 1.6B Privately Held
SIC: 2819 Silica compounds
HQ: Technisand, Inc.
3 Summit Park Dr Ste 700
Independence OH 44131

Irondale
Jefferson County

(G-8693)
C A JOSEPH CO
C A Joseph Machine Shop
170 Broadway St (43932)
P.O. Box 274 (43932-0274)
PHONE.................................330 532-4646
EMP: 17
SALES (corp-wide): 4.51MM Privately Held
Web: www.cajoseph.com
SIC: 3599 3444 3443 3441 Machine shop, jobbing and repair; Sheet metalwork; Fabricated plate work (boiler shop); Fabricated structural metal
PA: C. A. Joseph Co.

13712 Old Frdericktown Rd
East Liverpool OH 43920
330 385-6869

Ironton
Lawrence County

(G-8694)
ALLEN ENTERPRISES INC
Also Called: Tri-State Wilbert Vault Co
2900 S 9th St (45638-2844)
P.O. Box 231 (45638-0231)
PHONE.................................740 532-5913
Douglas M Allen, Pr
Ronald Keener, Sec
Gretchen A Allen, Dir
Robin Robison, Contrlr
EMP: 20 EST: 1928
SQ FT: 22,000
SALES (est): 2.53MM Privately Held
Web: www.tristatewilbert.com
SIC: 5039 3272 5087 Septic tanks; Septic tanks, concrete; Caskets

(G-8695)
AMERICAN HYDRAULIC SVCS INC
1912 S 1st St (45638-2478)
P.O. Box 624 (41129-0624)
PHONE.................................606 739-8680
Jeremiah Fulks, Pr
Randall Blankenship, *
▲ EMP: 41 EST: 2001
SALES (est): 9.14MM Privately Held
Web: www.americanhydraulic.net
SIC: 3593 7699 Fluid power cylinders, hydraulic or pneumatic; Hydraulic equipment repair

(G-8696)
AMERICAS STYRENICS LLC
925 County Road 1a (45638-8687)
PHONE.................................740 302-8667
EMP: 64
SALES (corp-wide): 7.42B Privately Held
Web: www.amsty.com
SIC: 2821 Plastics materials and resins
HQ: Americas Styrenics Llc
24 Waterway Ave Ste 1200
The Woodlands TX 77380

(G-8697)
EMERSON NETWORK POWER
3040 S 9th St (45638-2895)
PHONE.................................614 841-8054
Steve Hassell, Pr
EMP: 12 EST: 2016
SALES (est): 152.02K Privately Held
Web: www.emerson.com
SIC: 3613 3585 7629 Switchgear and switchboard apparatus; Refrigeration and heating equipment; Electrical repair shops

(G-8698)
ICON MACHINING LLC
987 Township Road 145 (45638-8403)
PHONE.................................740 532-6739
Kenneth Webb, Prin
EMP: 6 EST: 2004
SALES (est): 108.13K Privately Held
SIC: 3599 Machine shop, jobbing and repair

(G-8699)
PLATINUM INDUSTRIES LLC
Also Called: Platinum Industries
541 Private Road 908 (45638-8602)
PHONE.................................740 285-2641
Tim Price, Prin
Jim Price, Prin
Rob Marshall, Prin

Ironton - Lawrence County (G-8700)

EMP: 15 EST: 2019
SALES (est): 510.45K **Privately Held**
SIC: 3999 Manufacturing industries, nec

(G-8700)
PREMERE PRECAST PRODUCTS
317 Hecla St (45638-1370)
PHONE.............................740 533-3333
Evyian Terry, *Prin*
EMP: 7 EST: 2008
SALES (est): 138.08K **Privately Held**
Web: www.ohioprecast.org
SIC: 3272 Concrete products, precast, nec

(G-8701)
PRINTING EXPRESS INC
918b Center St (45638-1515)
P.O. Box 831 (45638-0831)
PHONE.............................740 533-9217
Mary Nenni, *Pr*
Mary Beth Nenni, *Pr*
Jennifer L Mayo, *VP*
EMP: 8 EST: 1985
SQ FT: 1,100
SALES (est): 374.99K **Privately Held**
Web: www.printingexpress.net
SIC: 2752 Offset printing

(G-8702)
RANEYS BEEF JERKY LLC
81 Township Road 1326 (45638-8345)
PHONE.............................606 694-1054
Deana L Raney, *Owner*
EMP: 7 EST: 2018
SALES (est): 219.42K **Privately Held**
SIC: 2013 Snack sticks, including jerky: from purchased meat

(G-8703)
ROACH WOOD PRODUCTS & PLAS INC
25 Township Road 328 (45638-8171)
PHONE.............................740 532-4855
Bruce Roach Senior, *CEO*
Bruce Roach Junior, *Pr*
EMP: 8 EST: 1984
SQ FT: 10,700
SALES (est): 1.39MM **Privately Held**
SIC: 3082 Unsupported plastics profile shapes

(G-8704)
SWIFT MANUFACTURING CO INC
700 Lorain St (45638-1088)
PHONE.............................740 237-4405
Michael Moore, *Pr*
Zachary Moore, *VP*
EMP: 6 EST: 2008
SALES (est): 994.16K **Privately Held**
Web: www.swiftmfg.net
SIC: 3339 Primary nonferrous metals, nec

(G-8705)
VERTIV CORPORATION
Also Called: Vertiv
3040 S 9th St (45638-2895)
PHONE.............................740 547-5100
Bob Walters, *Genl Mgr*
EMP: 124
SALES (corp-wide): 6.86B **Publicly Held**
Web: www.vertiv.com
SIC: 3823 Process control instruments
HQ: Vertiv Corporation
    505 N Cleveland Ave
    Westerville OH 43082
    614 888-0246

(G-8706)
WELLS GROUP LLC
487 Gallia Pike (45638-8080)
PHONE.............................740 532-9240
Kimberly Cole, *Brnch Mgr*
EMP: 10
SALES (corp-wide): 46.35MM **Privately Held**
Web: www.wellsgroupconcrete.com
SIC: 3273 Ready-mixed concrete
PA: The Wells Group Llc
    611 W Main St
    West Liberty KY 41472
    606 743-3485

Jackson
Jackson County

(G-8707)
AK READY MIX LLC
441 Dixon Run Rd (45640-8038)
PHONE.............................740 286-8900
EMP: 6 EST: 2007
SALES (est): 756.31K **Privately Held**
Web: www.akreadymix.net
SIC: 3273 Ready-mixed concrete

(G-8708)
ALUCHEM OF JACKSON INC
14782 Beaver Pike (45640-9661)
PHONE.............................740 286-2455
Ronald P Zapletal, *Pr*
Ronald L Bell, *
Edward L Butera, *
EMP: 34 EST: 1987
SALES (est): 2.95MM **Privately Held**
Web: www.aluchem.com
SIC: 2819 Industrial inorganic chemicals, nec

(G-8709)
BELLISIO
100 E Broadway St (45640-1347)
P.O. Box 550 (45640-0550)
PHONE.............................740 286-5505
◆ EMP: 13 EST: 2008
SALES (est): 183.18K **Privately Held**
Web: www.bellisiofoods.com
SIC: 2038 Frozen specialties, nec

(G-8710)
BELLISIO FOODS INC
100 E Bdwy (45640-1347)
P.O. Box 550 (45640-0550)
PHONE.............................740 286-5505
Jeff Wilson, *Brnch Mgr*
EMP: 110
Web: www.bellisiofoods.com
SIC: 2038 2033 Dinners, frozen and packaged; Spaghetti and other pasta sauce: packaged in cans, jars, etc
HQ: Bellisio Foods, Inc
    701 Washington Ave N # 400
    Minneapolis MN 55401

(G-8711)
BRENMAR CONSTRUCTION INC
900 Morton St (45640-1089)
PHONE.............................740 286-2151
Todd Ghearing, *Pr*
Tim Ousley, *
Andy Graham, *
EMP: 60 EST: 1988
SQ FT: 5,000
SALES (est): 22.06MM **Privately Held**
Web: www.brenmarconstruction.com
SIC: 1542 3312 Commercial and office building contractors; Structural shapes and pilings, steel

(G-8712)
BROWN PUBLISHING CO INC (PA)
Also Called: Brown Publishing
1 Acy Ave Ste D (45640-9563)
P.O. Box 270 (45640-0270)
PHONE.............................740 286-2187
Roy Brown, *Pr*
EMP: 15 EST: 1925
SQ FT: 5,250
SALES (est): 1MM
SALES (corp-wide): 1MM **Privately Held**
SIC: 2711 Newspapers: publishing only, not printed on site

(G-8713)
D G M INC
Also Called: Tow Path Ready Mix
1668 Kessinger School Rd (45640-9127)
PHONE.............................740 286-2131
Lonnie Lemaster, *Brnch Mgr*
EMP: 10
SALES (corp-wide): 8.76MM **Privately Held**
Web: www.towpathreadymix.com
SIC: 3273 Ready-mixed concrete
PA: D. G. M., Inc.
    1881 Adams Rd
    Beaver OH 45613
    740 226-1950

(G-8714)
ELEMETAL REFINING LLC
16064 Beaver Pike (45640-9659)
P.O. Box 605 (45640-0605)
PHONE.............................740 286-6457
EMP: 150 EST: 1974
SALES (est): 56.36MM
SALES (corp-wide): 103.18MM **Privately Held**
SIC: 3341 3356 3339 Secondary precious metals; Nonferrous rolling and drawing, nec ; Primary nonferrous metals, nec
PA: Elemetal, Llc
    15850 Dallas Pkwy
    Dallas TX 75248
    214 956-7600

(G-8715)
EQUIP BUSINESS SOLUTIONS CO (PA)
120 Twin Oaks Dr (45640-9828)
PHONE.............................614 854-9755
Craig Lund, *Pr*
EMP: 6 EST: 1997
SALES (est): 2.22MM
SALES (corp-wide): 2.22MM **Privately Held**
Web: www.equipbusinesssolutions.com
SIC: 2759 8742 5112 Commercial printing, nec; Management consulting services; Stationery and office supplies

(G-8716)
JACKSON MONUMENT INC
14 Fairmount St (45640-1409)
PHONE.............................740 286-1590
Stan Louis, *Pr*
Darryl Radliff, *Prin*
EMP: 8 EST: 1987
SALES (est): 760.36K **Privately Held**
Web: www.jacksonmonumentworks.com
SIC: 3272 5999 Monuments, concrete; Monuments, finished to custom order

(G-8717)
JALCO INDUSTRIES INC
330 Athens St (45640-9433)
P.O. Box 947 (45640-0947)
PHONE.............................740 286-3808
Randal L Ridge, *Pr*
Susan R Ridge, *Sec*
EMP: 10 EST: 1997
SQ FT: 10,000
SALES (est): 899.76K **Privately Held**
SIC: 3281 5032 Building stone products; Concrete building products

(G-8718)
MONTGOMERY MCH FABRICATION INC
206 Watts Blevins Rd (45640-9768)
P.O. Box 247 (45640-0247)
PHONE.............................740 286-2863
Carry E Montgomery, *Pr*
Bobbi D Montgomery, *
Jason Montgomery, *
Mary Montgomery, *
EMP: 35 EST: 1982
SQ FT: 20,000
SALES (est): 4.97MM **Privately Held**
Web: www.montgomerymachineshop.com
SIC: 3599 Machine shop, jobbing and repair

(G-8719)
OHIO METAL PROCESSING LLC
16064 Beaver Pike (45640-9659)
PHONE.............................740 912-2057
EMP: 8 EST: 2017
SQ FT: 70,000
SALES (est): 706.99K **Privately Held**
Web: www.greenelyonmetals.com
SIC: 3341 5051 Secondary precious metals; Copper products

(G-8720)
OSCO INDUSTRIES INC
165 Athens St (45640-1306)
P.O. Box 327 (45640-0327)
PHONE.............................740 286-5004
Keith Denny, *Brnch Mgr*
EMP: 86
SALES (corp-wide): 79.52MM **Privately Held**
Web: www.oscoind.com
SIC: 3321 3322 Gray iron castings, nec; Malleable iron foundries
PA: Osco Industries, Inc.
    734 11th St
    Portsmouth OH 45662
    740 354-3183

(G-8721)
PACIFIC MANUFACTURING TENN INC
555 Smith Ln (45640)
PHONE.............................513 900-7862
Hisaichi Seko, *Pr*
EMP: 6 EST: 2014
SQ FT: 189,000
SALES (est): 70.14K **Privately Held**
SIC: 3469 Ornamental metal stampings

(G-8722)
PHOENIX QUALITY MFG LLC
16064 Beaver Pike # 888 (45640-9659)
PHONE.............................705 279-0538
EMP: 30 EST: 2020
SALES (est): 2.37MM **Privately Held**
SIC: 3841 Surgical and medical instruments

(G-8723)
SPOT ON MAIN LLC
Also Called: Spot On Main Coffee Roastery
91 Harding Ave (45640)
P.O. Box 364 (45640)
PHONE.............................740 285-0441
EMP: 16
SALES (corp-wide): 730.82K **Privately Held**
SIC: 2095 Coffee roasting (except by wholesale grocers)
PA: The Spot On Main Llc
    298 E Main St
    Jackson OH 45640

GEOGRAPHIC SECTION

Jefferson - Ashtabula County (G-8744)

740 577-3327

(G-8724)
SPRING HLTHCARE DAGNOSTICS LLC ✪
16064 Beaver Pike (45640-9659)
PHONE...........................866 201-9503
I Amhed, *Managing Member*
EMP: 60 **EST:** 2022
SALES (est): 2.39MM **Privately Held**
Web: www.springdiagnostic.com
SIC: 3841 Surgical and medical instruments

(G-8725)
SUMMERS ORGANIZATION LLC
Also Called: Premium Wood & Garden Products
345 E Main St Ste H (45640-1789)
P.O. Box 527 (45640-0527)
PHONE...........................740 286-1322
EMP: 20 **EST:** 2001
SALES (est): 1.68MM **Privately Held**
SIC: 2873 Fertilizers: natural (organic), except compost

(G-8726)
SUPERIOR HARDWOODS OF OHIO
78 Jackson Hill Rd (45640-9301)
P.O. Box 166 (45640-0166)
PHONE...........................740 384-6862
Ammet Tonway, *Owner*
EMP: 28 **EST:** 2001
SALES (est): 281.07K **Privately Held**
SIC: 2411 2421 Timber, cut at logging camp; Sawmills and planing mills, general

(G-8727)
WATERLOO COAL COMPANY INC (PA)
Also Called: Madison Mine Supply Co
235 E Main St (45640-1715)
P.O. Box 626 (45640-0626)
PHONE...........................740 286-0004
EMP: 70 **EST:** 1934
SALES (est): 23.4MM
SALES (corp-wide): 23.4MM **Privately Held**
Web: www.waterloocoal.com
SIC: 1221 1411 1459 Strip mining, bituminous; Limestone, dimension-quarrying ; Clays (common) quarrying

(G-8728)
WINTERS PRODUCTS INC
Also Called: Winters Concrete
109 Athens St (45640-1306)
PHONE...........................740 286-4149
David R Michael, *Pr*
EMP: 10 **EST:** 1955
SQ FT: 800
SALES (est): 680K **Privately Held**
SIC: 3273 Ready-mixed concrete

Jackson Center
Shelby County

(G-8729)
AIRSTREAM INC (HQ)
1001 W Pike St (45334)
P.O. Box 629 (45334)
PHONE...........................937 596-6111
Robert Wheeler, *Pr*
Lawrence J Huttle, *
Peter B Orthwein, *
Wade F B Thompson, *
Dan Froehlich, *
◆ **EMP:** 350 **EST:** 1980
SQ FT: 286,000
SALES (est): 39.23K
SALES (corp-wide): 11.12B **Publicly Held**
Web: www.airstream.com
SIC: 3716 3792 3714 3713 Motor homes; Travel trailers and campers; Motor vehicle parts and accessories; Truck and bus bodies
PA: Thor Industries, Inc.
601 E Beardsley Ave
Elkhart IN 46514
574 970-7460

(G-8730)
CREATIVE PLASTICS INTL
18163 Snider Rd (45334-9734)
PHONE...........................937 596-6769
Gerald B Wurm, *Pr*
Keith Korn, *VP*
Randolph Korn, *VP*
Richard Wurm, *VP*
Valerie Sanderson, *Treas*
EMP: 17 **EST:** 1968
SQ FT: 40,000
SALES (est): 1.9MM **Privately Held**
Web: www.creativeplastics-thermoforming.com
SIC: 3089 Injection molding of plastics

(G-8731)
DESIGN ORIGINAL INC
402 Jackson St (45334-5057)
P.O. Box 727 (45334-0727)
PHONE...........................937 596-5121
Frank E Pusey, *Pr*
Glenn A Pusey, *VP*
EMP: 16 **EST:** 1971
SQ FT: 25,000
SALES (est): 2.38MM **Privately Held**
Web: www.design-original.com
SIC: 5136 5137 2396 2395 Sportswear, men's and boys'; Sportswear, women's and children's; Automotive and apparel trimmings; Pleating and stitching

(G-8732)
ELDORADO NATIONAL KANSAS INC
419 W Pike St (45334-9728)
PHONE...........................937 596-6849
Andrew Imanse, *CEO*
EMP: 210
Web: www.eldorado-bus.com
SIC: 3711 Buses, all types, assembly of
HQ: Eldorado National (Kansas), Inc.
2367 Century Dr
Goshen IN 46528

(G-8733)
EMI CORP (PA)
Also Called: E M I Plastic Equipment
801 W Pike St (45334-6037)
P.O. Box 590 (45334-0590)
PHONE...........................937 596-5511
James E Andraitis, *Pr*
Brad Wren, *
Linda Andraitis-varljen, *Treas*
▲ **EMP:** 85 **EST:** 1980
SQ FT: 80,000
SALES (est): 38.37MM
SALES (corp-wide): 38.37MM **Privately Held**
Web: www.emicorp.com
SIC: 3544 5084 Special dies, tools, jigs, and fixtures; Industrial machinery and equipment

(G-8734)
LACAL EQUIPMENT INC
901 W Pike St (45334-6024)
P.O. Box 757 (45334-0757)
PHONE...........................937 596-6106
Roger Dietrich, *Pr*
Tom Homan, *
Tony Niemeyer, *
Roger Detrick, *
Charles M Cole, *
▲ **EMP:** 50 **EST:** 1982
SQ FT: 14,000
SALES (est): 15.94MM
SALES (corp-wide): 94.51MM **Privately Held**
Web: www.lacal.com
SIC: 3714 Motor vehicle parts and accessories
PA: Jmac Inc.
200 W Ntnwide Blvd Unit 1
Columbus OH 43215
614 436-2418

(G-8735)
MASTER SWAGING INC
210 Washington St (45334-4010)
P.O. Box 550 (45334-0550)
PHONE...........................937 596-6171
Daniel Gilroy, *Pr*
Cindy Gilroy, *Prin*
EMP: 6 **EST:** 1960
SQ FT: 26,000
SALES (est): 632.13K **Privately Held**
Web: www.masterswaging.com
SIC: 3728 3599 Aircraft assemblies, subassemblies, and parts, nec; Machine shop, jobbing and repair

(G-8736)
PLASTIPAK PACKAGING INC
18015 State Route 65 (45334-9434)
P.O. Box 789 (45334-0789)
PHONE...........................937 596-6142
Willis Vetter, *Brnch Mgr*
EMP: 360
SALES (corp-wide): 2.9B **Privately Held**
Web: www.plastipak.com
SIC: 3085 2671 Plastics bottles; Paper; coated and laminated packaging
HQ: Plastipak Packaging, Inc.
41605 Ann Arbor Rd E
Plymouth MI 48170
734 455-3600

(G-8737)
PRECISION DETAILS INC
104 Washington St (45334-1101)
P.O. Box 696 (45334-0696)
PHONE...........................937 596-0068
Jeff Winemiller, *Pr*
Katie Winemiller, *VP*
EMP: 15 **EST:** 1981
SQ FT: 4,500
SALES (est): 1.74MM **Privately Held**
Web: www.precisiondetailsinc.com
SIC: 3544 Special dies and tools

(G-8738)
PRODEVA INC
100 Jerry Dr (45334-5075)
P.O. Box 729 (45334-0729)
PHONE...........................937 596-6713
Steve Bunke, *Pr*
Shirley Bunke, *Treas*
Frederick Bunke, *Sec*
EMP: 18 **EST:** 1957
SQ FT: 21,000
SALES (est): 823.57K **Privately Held**
Web: www.prodeva.com
SIC: 3599 3559 Machine shop, jobbing and repair; Recycling machinery

(G-8739)
THOR INDUSTRIES INC
419 W Pike St (45334-9728)
P.O. Box 629 (45334-0629)
PHONE...........................937 596-6111
EMP: 13
SALES (corp-wide): 11.12B **Publicly Held**
Web: www.thorindustries.com
SIC: 3799 3711 Recreational vehicles; Buses, all types, assembly of
PA: Thor Industries, Inc.
601 E Beardsley Ave
Elkhart IN 46514
574 970-7460

Jamestown
Greene County

(G-8740)
BALL JACKETS LLC
Also Called: Just-Ink-Tees
5120 Waynesville Jamestown Rd (45335)
P.O. Box 57 (45335-0057)
PHONE...........................937 572-1114
Jason Baker, *Prin*
Tara Allen, *
EMP: 25 **EST:** 2012
SALES (est): 2.26MM **Privately Held**
Web: www.justinktees.com
SIC: 2759 Screen printing

(G-8741)
CAESARCREEK PALLETS LTD
4392 Shawnee Trl (45335-1227)
PHONE...........................937 416-4447
Larry Payton, *Prin*
Steve Payton, *Prin*
Clarence Payton, *Prin*
EMP: 10 **EST:** 1987
SQ FT: 6,000
SALES (est): 285.29K **Privately Held**
SIC: 2448 Pallets, wood

(G-8742)
TWIST INC (PA)
47 S Limestone St (45335-9501)
P.O. Box 177 (45335-0177)
PHONE...........................937 675-9581
Joe W Wright, *Pr*
▲ **EMP:** 110 **EST:** 1972
SQ FT: 50,000
SALES (est): 45.56MM
SALES (corp-wide): 45.56MM **Privately Held**
Web: www.twistinc.com
SIC: 3495 3542 3469 3471 Mechanical springs, precision; Machine tools, metal forming type; Metal stampings, nec; Electroplating and plating

(G-8743)
TWIST INC
5100 Waynesville (45335)
PHONE...........................937 675-9581
J Smith, *Brnch Mgr*
EMP: 9
SALES (corp-wide): 45.56MM **Privately Held**
Web: www.twistinc.com
SIC: 3495 3542 3469 Mechanical springs, precision; Machine tools, metal forming type ; Metal stampings, nec
PA: Twist Inc.
47 S Limestone St
Jamestown OH 45335
937 675-9581

Jefferson
Ashtabula County

(G-8744)
ADA SOLUTIONS INC
901 Footville Richmond Rd E (44047)
PHONE...........................440 576-0423
David Chase, *Pr*

Jefferson - Ashtabula County (G-8745)

▼ **EMP:** 8 **EST:** 2012
SALES (est): 663.04K Privately Held
SIC: 2821 Molding compounds, plastics

(G-8745)
ALTERA POLYMERS LLC
222 S Sycamore St (44047-1434)
PHONE 864 973-7000
Barry Rhodes, *Managing Member*
EMP: 10 **EST:** 2011
SALES (est): 574.42K Privately Held
Web: www.alterapolymers.com
SIC: 2821 Plastics materials and resins

(G-8746)
CHUCK MEADORS PLASTICS CO
150 S Cucumber St (44047-1439)
PHONE 440 813-4466
Chuck Meadors, *Pr*
EMP: 10 **EST:** 2005
SALES (est): 853.18K Privately Held
SIC: 3089 Hardware, plastics

(G-8747)
JUBA INDUSTRIES INC
126 W Jefferson St (44047-1048)
PHONE 440 655-9960
Bruce Vance, *Prin*
EMP: 6 **EST:** 2010
SALES (est): 96.62K Privately Held
SIC: 3999 Manufacturing industries, nec

(G-8748)
KARLCO OILFIELD SERVICES INC
Also Called: Karlco
141 E Jefferson St (44047-1113)
P.O. Box 126 (44047-0126)
PHONE 440 576-3415
Clarence Tussel Junior, *Pr*
EMP: 15 **EST:** 1978
SQ FT: 3,000
SALES (est): 902.91K Privately Held
SIC: 1389 Oil field services, nec

(G-8749)
KEN FORGING INC
1049 Griggs Rd (44047-8772)
P.O. Box 277 (44047-0277)
PHONE 440 993-8091
Richard Kovach, *Pr*
Ken Kovach, *
EMP: 115 **EST:** 1970
SQ FT: 150,000
SALES (est): 17.45MM Privately Held
Web: www.kenforging.com
SIC: 3462 3544 Iron and steel forgings; Special dies and tools

(G-8750)
KING LUMINAIRE COMPANY INC (HQ)
Also Called: Stresscrete
1153 State Route 46 N (44047-8748)
P.O. Box 266 (44047-0266)
PHONE 440 576-9073
Greg Button, *Pr*
▲ **EMP:** 45 **EST:** 1984
SQ FT: 18,000
SALES (est): 21.16MM
SALES (corp-wide): 27.42MM Privately Held
Web: www.scgrp.com
SIC: 3646 Ornamental lighting fixtures, commercial
PA: Stress-Crete Holdings Inc
7-840 Walker's Line
Burlington ON L7N 2
905 632-9301

(G-8751)
LAKE CITY PLATING LLC
108 S Sycamore St (44047-1433)
PHONE 440 964-3555
EMP: 43
SALES (corp-wide): 22.53MM Privately Held
Web: www.lakecityplating.com
SIC: 3471 Electroplating of metals or formed products
PA: Lake City Plating, Llc
1701 Lake Ave
Ashtabula OH 44004
440 964-3555

(G-8752)
LAKE ERIE SHIP REPR FBRCTION L
1459 State Route 46 S (44047-9505)
PHONE 440 228-7110
Joseph Craine, *Managing Member*
EMP: 14 **EST:** 2012
SQ FT: 4,000
SALES (est): 847.78K Privately Held
SIC: 3731 3441 Shipbuilding and repairing; Fabricated structural metal

(G-8753)
METAL SALES MANUFACTURING CORP
352 E Erie St (44047-1406)
PHONE 440 319-3779
Bill Mako, *Mgr*
EMP: 13
SQ FT: 33,000
SALES (corp-wide): 347.39MM Privately Held
Web: metalsales.us.com
SIC: 3444 3449 3441 2952 Siding, sheet metal; Miscellaneous metalwork; Fabricated structural metal; Asphalt felts and coatings
HQ: Metal Sales Manufacturing Corporation
545 S 3rd St Ste 200
Louisville KY 40202
502 855-4300

(G-8754)
NEXT SURFACE INC
223 S Spruce St (44047-8321)
PHONE 440 576-0194
Rhine Blake, *CEO*
EMP: 52 **EST:** 2007
SALES (est): 9.74MM Privately Held
Web: www.ndci.biz
SIC: 3272 Concrete window and door components, sills and frames

(G-8755)
PICKENS PLASTICS INC
149 S Cucumber St (44047-1438)
PHONE 440 576-4001
EMP: 6
SALES (est): 229.94K Privately Held
SIC: 3089 Injection molding of plastics

(G-8756)
PRECISION WELD FAB
971 Footville Richmond Rd W (44047)
PHONE 440 576-5800
Brian Huffman, *Prin*
EMP: 6 **EST:** 2008
SALES (est): 142.72K Privately Held
SIC: 7692 Welding repair

(G-8757)
PRESRITE CORPORATION
322 S Cucumber St (44047-1423)
P.O. Box 550 (44047-0550)
PHONE 440 576-0015
Roy Stainfield, *Genl Mgr*
EMP: 58
SALES (corp-wide): 94.22MM Privately Held
Web: www.presrite.com
SIC: 3462 Iron and steel forgings
PA: Presrite Corporation
3665 E 78th St
Cleveland OH 44105
216 441-5990

(G-8758)
RMC USA INCORPORATION
149 S Cucumber St (44047-1438)
P.O. Box 127 (44047-0127)
PHONE 440 992-4906
EMP: 90
SIC: 3089 Molding primary plastics

(G-8759)
STRESS-CRETE COMPANY
Also Called: King Luminaire
1153 State Route 46 N (44047-8748)
P.O. Box 266 (44047-0266)
PHONE 440 576-9073
Jim Fultz, *Brnch Mgr*
EMP: 46
SALES (corp-wide): 27.42MM Privately Held
Web: www.scgrp.com
SIC: 3646 Commercial lighting fixtures
HQ: Stress-Crete Limited
7-840 Walker's Line
Burlington ON L7N 2
905 827-6901

(G-8760)
THE GAZETTE PRINTING CO INC (PA)
Also Called: Tribune, The
46 W Jefferson St (44047-1028)
P.O. Box 166 (44047-0166)
PHONE 440 576-9125
Jeffrey Lampson, *Pr*
John E Lampson, *
Marilyn Lampson, *
EMP: 62 **EST:** 1876
SQ FT: 8,600
SALES (est): 7.8MM
SALES (corp-wide): 7.8MM Privately Held
Web: www.visitashtabulacounty.com
SIC: 2711 Newspapers, publishing and printing

(G-8761)
TMD WEK NORTH LLC
Also Called: Wek Industries
1085 Jefferson Eagleville Rd (44047-1267)
P.O. Box 167 (44047-0167)
PHONE 440 576-6940
William Hylan, *CFO*
Kimberly Schaefer, *
EMP: 116 **EST:** 2014
SQ FT: 112,500
SALES (est): 20.53MM Privately Held
SIC: 3089 Blow molded finished plastics products, nec
HQ: Toledo Molding & Die, Llc
1429 Coining Dr
Toledo OH 43612

(G-8762)
TOD THIN BRUSHES INC
1152 State Route 46 N (44047-8748)
PHONE 440 576-6859
Michael R Oliver, *Pr*
Mildred Oliver, *Pr*
EMP: 10 **EST:** 1960
SQ FT: 2,500
SALES (est): 712.45K Privately Held
Web: www.todthinbrushesinc.com
SIC: 3991 Brushes, household or industrial

(G-8763)
WORTHINGTON CYLINDER CORP
863 State Route 307 E (44047-9668)
PHONE 440 576-5847
Dan Brubaker, *Brnch Mgr*
EMP: 181
SALES (corp-wide): 4.92B Publicly Held
Web: www.worthingtonenterprises.com
SIC: 3316 Cold finishing of steel shapes
HQ: Worthington Cylinder Corporation
200 W Wlson Bridge Rd
Worthington OH 43085
614 840-3210

Jeffersonville
Fayette County

(G-8764)
JFAB LLC
14514 State Route 729 (43128-9726)
PHONE 740 572-0227
Gregory Wright, *Prin*
EMP: 7 **EST:** 2016
SALES (est): 70.33K Privately Held
SIC: 3949 5961 Target shooting equipment; Electronic shopping

(G-8765)
L-H BATTERY COMPANY INC (PA) ◆
One Innovation Way (43128)
PHONE 937 613-3769
Bob Lee, *CEO*
EMP: 6 **EST:** 2023
SALES (est): 83.82K
SALES (corp-wide): 83.82K Privately Held
SIC: 3714 Motor vehicle engines and parts

(G-8766)
TFO TECH CO LTD
Also Called: T F O
221 State St (43128-1090)
PHONE 740 426-6381
Katsumasa Toya, *Ch*
Yoshio Saisharo, *
Kanji Endo, *
Curtis A Loveland, *
▲ **EMP:** 140 **EST:** 1988
SQ FT: 70,000
SALES (est): 28.56MM Privately Held
SIC: 3462 3465 3714 Automotive forgings, ferrous: crankshaft, engine, axle, etc.; Automotive stampings; Motor vehicle parts and accessories
PA: Tfo Corporation
2-16-4, Akabane
Kita-Ku TKY 115-0

Jewett
Harrison County

(G-8767)
MARKWEST UTICA EMG LLC
46700 Giacobbi Rd (43986-9553)
PHONE 740 942-4810
Frank M Semple, *Brnch Mgr*
EMP: 175
Web: www.markwest.com
SIC: 1321 Natural gas liquids
HQ: Markwest Utica Emg, L.L.C.
1515 Arapahoe St
Denver CO 80202
303 925-9200

GEOGRAPHIC SECTION

Kensington - Columbiana County (G-8790)

Johnstown
Licking County

(G-8768)
ALLIANCE CARPET CUSHION CO
143 Commerce Blvd (43031-9610)
PHONE..................................740 966-5001
Keith Anders, *Mgr*
EMP: 30
SIC: 2282 2273 Carpet yarn: twisting, winding, or spooling; Carpets and rugs
HQ: Alliance Carpet Cushion Co
180 Church St
Torrington CT 06790
860 489-4273

(G-8769)
APEKS LLC ✪
Also Called: Apeks Supercritical
31 Greenscape Ct (43031)
PHONE..................................740 809-1174
Andy Joseph, *Pr*
EMP: 20 **EST:** 2023
SQ FT: 10,000
SALES (est): 4.14MM
SALES (corp-wide): 10MM **Privately Held**
Web: www.apekssupercritical.com
SIC: 3542 Mechanical (pneumatic or hydraulic) metal forming machines
PA: Isolate Extraction Systems Inc.
1733 Majestic Dr Ste 104
Lafayette CO 80026
720 541-7301

(G-8770)
BUCKEYE READY-MIX LLC
7720 Johnstown Alexandria Rd (43031-9340)
PHONE..................................740 967-4801
EMP: 17
SALES (corp-wide): 48.26MM **Privately Held**
Web: www.buckeyereadymix.com
SIC: 3273 Ready-mixed concrete
PA: Buckeye Ready-Mix, Llc
7657 Taylor Rd Sw
Reynoldsburg OH 43068
614 575-2132

(G-8771)
BUD CORP
158 Commerce Blvd (43031-9011)
PHONE..................................740 967-9992
Kelton Brown, *Prin*
EMP: 8 **EST:** 2006
SALES (est): 1MM **Privately Held**
Web: www.budcorp.com
SIC: 1542 3444 5084 Nonresidential construction, nec; Sheet metalwork; Materials handling machinery

(G-8772)
CHAM COR INDUSTRIES INC
117 W Coshocton St (43031-1108)
PHONE..................................740 967-9015
Gary H Chambers Junior, *Pr*
Michael Chambers, *CEO*
Michael Bailey, *VP*
EMP: 8 **EST:** 1964
SQ FT: 6,000
SALES (est): 517.22K **Privately Held**
SIC: 2754 Job printing: gravure

(G-8773)
FORTRESS INDUSTRIES LLC
15710 Center Village Rd (43031-9264)
PHONE..................................614 402-3045
EMP: 6 **EST:** 2015
SALES (est): 344.37K **Privately Held**
Web: www.fortressindustriesllc.net
SIC: 3999 Manufacturing industries, nec

(G-8774)
MUNSON MACHINE COMPANY INC
80 E College Ave (43031-1204)
P.O. Box 304 (43031-0304)
PHONE..................................740 967-6867
Leroy Thacker, *Sec*
Todd Thacker, *Pr*
EMP: 7 **EST:** 1987
SQ FT: 4,500
SALES (est): 691.98K **Privately Held**
SIC: 3599 Machine shop, jobbing and repair

(G-8775)
MY SOAPS LLC
250 W Coshocton St (43031-1111)
PHONE..................................614 832-4634
EMP: 6 **EST:** 2010
SALES (est): 58.07K **Privately Held**
Web: www.my-soaps.com
SIC: 2844 Perfumes, cosmetics and other toilet preparations

(G-8776)
PUMPCO CONCRETE PUMPING LLC
7230 Johnstown Utica Rd (43031-9406)
PHONE..................................740 809-1473
Richard Miller, *Managing Member*
EMP: 12 **EST:** 2018
SALES (est): 718.95K **Privately Held**
Web: www.keimconcretepumping.com
SIC: 3462 Construction or mining equipment forgings, ferrous

(G-8777)
ROUTE 62
795 W Coshocton St (43031-9581)
PHONE..................................740 548-5418
EMP: 6 **EST:** 2010
SALES (est): 140.07K **Privately Held**
SIC: 3589 Car washing machinery

(G-8778)
STEEL CEILINGS INC
451 E Coshocton St (43031-9010)
PHONE..................................740 967-1063
▲ **EMP:** 24
SIC: 3324 Steel investment foundries

(G-8779)
TECHNICAL RUBBER COMPANY INC (PA)
Also Called: Tech International
200 E Coshocton St (43031)
P.O. Box 486 (43031)
PHONE..................................740 967-9015
Dan Layne, *Pr*
Robert Overs, *
Jeff Sellers, *
Gary Armstrong, *
Nikki Layne, *
◆ **EMP:** 197 **EST:** 1939
SQ FT: 10,000
SALES (est): 47.18MM
SALES (corp-wide): 47.18MM **Privately Held**
Web: www.trc4r.com
SIC: 3011 5014 2891 Tire sundries or tire repair materials, rubber; Tire and tube repair materials; Sealing compounds, synthetic rubber or plastic

(G-8780)
TRI-TECH LABORATORIES INC
Also Called: K D C
8825 Smiths Mill Rd N (43031)
PHONE..................................740 927-2817
EMP: 102 **EST:** 1991
SALES (est): 16.24MM **Privately Held**
SIC: 2834 Pharmaceutical preparations

(G-8781)
TRI-TECH LABORATORIES LLC
8825 Smiths Mill Rd N (43031)
PHONE..................................434 845-7073
EMP: 216
SALES (corp-wide): 5.75MM **Privately Held**
SIC: 2834 Pharmaceutical preparations
PA: Tri-Tech Laboratories Llc
4400 S Hamilton Rd
Groveport OH 43125
434 845-7073

(G-8782)
TRUFLEX RUBBER PRODUCTS CO
Also Called: Pang Rubber Company
200 E Coshocton St (43031-1096)
PHONE..................................740 967-9015
Pauline Chambers Yost, *Pr*
Mike Chambers, *
Cheryl Poulton, *
Robert Overs, *
EMP: 225 **EST:** 1964
SQ FT: 75,000
SALES (est): 13.33MM **Privately Held**
Web: www.pangindustrial.com
SIC: 3011 3069 Tire and inner tube materials and related products; Air-supported rubber structures

Junction City
Perry County

(G-8783)
K-MAR STRUCTURES LLC
Also Called: Mast Mini Barn
1825 Flagdale Rd S (43748-9792)
PHONE..................................231 924-5777
Marvin Mast, *Managing Member*
EMP: 10 **EST:** 2005
SQ FT: 17,000
SALES (est): 1.35MM **Privately Held**
Web: www.minibarnsonline.com
SIC: 3272 5999 Solid containing units, concrete; Sales barn

Kalida
Putnam County

(G-8784)
B-K TOOL & DESIGN INC
480 W Main St (45853-2024)
P.O. Box 416 (45853-0416)
PHONE..................................419 532-3890
Bob Kahle, *Pr*
Kevin M Kahle, *
EMP: 80 **EST:** 1987
SQ FT: 12,000
SALES (est): 19.96MM **Privately Held**
Web: www.bktool.com
SIC: 3544 Special dies and tools

(G-8785)
KALIDA MANUFACTURING INC
801 Ottawa St (45853)
P.O. Box P.O. Box 390 (45853)
PHONE..................................419 532-2026
Bruce R Henke, *Pr*
Tim Inoue, *
Sho Akimoto, *
▲ **EMP:** 250 **EST:** 1996
SQ FT: 300,000
SALES (est): 50.94MM **Privately Held**
Web: www.kalidamfg.com
SIC: 3714 Motor vehicle parts and accessories
HQ: Kth Parts Industries, Inc.
1111 State Route 235 N
Saint Paris OH 43072
937 663-5941

(G-8786)
SARKA BROS MACHINING INC
607 Ottawa St (45853)
P.O. Box 316 (45853-0316)
PHONE..................................419 532-2393
Bob Allen, *Pr*
Terry Burnett, *VP*
EMP: 8 **EST:** 1990
SQ FT: 24,000
SALES (est): 983.8K **Privately Held**
Web: www.sarkabros.com
SIC: 3556 Food products machinery

(G-8787)
UNVERFERTH MFG CO INC (PA)
Also Called: Unverferth
601 S Broad St (45853-2108)
P.O. Box 357 (45853-0357)
PHONE..................................419 532-3121
R Steven Unverferth, *Pr*
Richard A Unverferth, *
Gladys Unverferth, *
Dennis Kapcar, *
Daniel Fanger, *
◆ **EMP:** 249 **EST:** 1948
SQ FT: 828,501
SALES (est): 200.93MM
SALES (corp-wide): 200.93MM **Privately Held**
Web: www.unverferth.com
SIC: 3523 Farm machinery and equipment

Kelleys Island
Erie County

(G-8788)
KELLEYS ISLAND WINERY INC
418 Woodford Rd (43438-6616)
PHONE..................................419 746-2678
Kirt Zettler, *Pr*
Roberta Zettler, *Sec*
EMP: 8 **EST:** 1981
SQ FT: 7,000
SALES (est): 860.76K **Privately Held**
Web: www.kelleysislandwine.com
SIC: 2084 5921 Wines; Wine

(G-8789)
KELLSTONE INC
Also Called: Kellstone
Lake Shore Drive (43438)
P.O. Box 31 (43438-0031)
PHONE..................................419 746-2396
Ralph Kunar, *Mgr*
EMP: 40
SALES (corp-wide): 29.28MM **Privately Held**
SIC: 3281 1422 Cut stone and stone products; Crushed and broken limestone
HQ: Kellstone, Inc.
3203 Harvard Ave
Newburgh Heights OH 44105

Kensington
Columbiana County

(G-8790)
M3 MIDSTREAM LLC
Also Called: Kensington Plant
11543 State Route 644 (44427)
PHONE..................................330 223-2220

Kensington - Columbiana County (G-8791)

EMP: 34
SALES (corp-wide): 57MM **Privately Held**
Web: www.momentummidstream.com
SIC: 1382 Oil and gas exploration services
PA: M3 Midstream Llc
    600 Travis St Ste 5600
    Houston TX 77002
    713 783-3000

(G-8791)
WILLIAM S MILLER INC
11250 Montgomery Rd (44427-9702)
P.O. Box 145 (44423-0145)
PHONE 330 223-1794
George Miller, *Pr*
William Miller, *CEO*
Jane Todd, *Sec*
David W Miller, *VP*
EMP: 9 **EST:** 1985
SALES (est): 965.3K **Privately Held**
SIC: 1311 Crude petroleum production

Kent
Portage County

(G-8792)
ACCU-GRIND INC
4430 Crystal Pkwy (44240-8006)
PHONE 330 677-2225
Robert Sly, *Pr*
EMP: 8 **EST:** 1992
SQ FT: 4,000
SALES (est): 255.42K **Privately Held**
Web: www.maag.com
SIC: 7699 3421 Knife, saw and tool sharpening and repair; Knives: butchers', hunting, pocket, etc.

(G-8793)
ACCURATE PLASTICS LLC
4430 Crystal Pkwy (44240-8006)
PHONE 330 701-0019
John Satina, *Prin*
EMP: 11 **EST:** 2005
SALES (est): 513.41K **Privately Held**
Web: www.acculam.com
SIC: 2821 Plastics materials and resins

(G-8794)
ACS INDUSTRIES INC
Also Called: American Coupler Systems
2151 Mogadore Rd (44240-7261)
P.O. Box 810 (44240-0017)
PHONE 330 678-2511
▲ **EMP:** 95 **EST:** 1968
SALES (est): 21.96MM **Privately Held**
Web: www.acs-coupler.com
SIC: 3531 Construction machinery attachments

(G-8795)
ACTION SUPER ABRASIVE PDTS INC
945 Greenbriar Pkwy (44240-6478)
PHONE 330 673-7333
Joseph Haag, *Pr*
Dan Noonan, *VP*
EMP: 20 **EST:** 1985
SQ FT: 27,000
SALES (est): 2.34MM **Privately Held**
Web: www.actionsuper.com
SIC: 3291 Wheels, grinding: artificial

(G-8796)
AILES MILLWORK INC
1520 Enterprise Way (44240-7547)
PHONE 330 678-4300
Patrick Ailes, *Pr*
Ryan Ailes, *VP*
Margaret Ailes, *Sec*
EMP: 30 **EST:** 1975
SQ FT: 13,000
SALES (est): 859.43K **Privately Held**
Web: www.ailesmillwork.com
SIC: 2431 2434 Millwork; Wood kitchen cabinets

(G-8797)
AL-CAST MOLD & PATTERN
3865 Poplar Ln (44240-6893)
PHONE 330 968-4490
EMP: 6 **EST:** 2016
SALES (est): 43.43K **Privately Held**
Web: www.al-castmold.com
SIC: 3089 Injection molding of plastics

(G-8798)
ALLOY EXTRUSION COMPANY
4211 Karg Industrial Pkwy (44240)
PHONE 330 677-4946
EMP: 20
Web: www.alloyextrusion.com
SIC: 3061 8742 Mechanical rubber goods; Industrial consultant

(G-8799)
AMETEK TCHNICAL INDUS PDTS INC (HQ)
Also Called: Ametek Electromechanical Group
100 E Erie St Ste 130 (44240-3587)
PHONE 330 673-3451
David A Zapico, *Ch Bd*
Matt French, *
Peter Smith, *
Todd Schlegel, *
Kathryn E Sena, *
EMP: 65 **EST:** 2009
SALES (est): 85.66MM
SALES (corp-wide): 6.6B **Publicly Held**
Web: www.ametektip.com
SIC: 3621 5063 3566 Motors, electric; Motors, electric; Speed changers, drives, and gears
PA: Ametek, Inc.
    1100 Cassatt Rd
    Berwyn PA 19312
    610 647-2121

(G-8800)
ATLANTA ROTOMOLDING INC
4429 Crystal Pkwy (44240-8001)
PHONE 404 328-1004
EMP: 6 **EST:** 2018
SALES (est): 278.48K **Privately Held**
Web: www.dpiroto.com
SIC: 3089 Plastics products, nec

(G-8801)
BEEMER MACHINE COMPANY INC
1530 Enterprise Way (44240-7547)
PHONE 330 678-3822
Edward Burch, *Pr*
EMP: 8 **EST:** 1989
SALES (est): 739.23K **Privately Held**
Web: www.beemermachine.com
SIC: 3599 Machine shop, jobbing and repair

(G-8802)
BOYCE MACHINE INC
3609 Mogadore Rd (44240-7431)
PHONE 330 678-3210
Shelby C Boyce, *Pr*
Patricia Boyce, *Sec*
EMP: 9 **EST:** 1988
SQ FT: 5,400
SALES (est): 923.13K **Privately Held**
Web: www.boycemachine.com
SIC: 3599 Machine shop, jobbing and repair

(G-8803)
BRIDGESTONE RET OPERATIONS LLC
Also Called: Firestone
202 E Main St (44240-2527)
PHONE 330 673-1700
Thomas Shaw, *Mgr*
EMP: 7
Web: www.bridgestoneamericas.com
SIC: 5531 7534 Automotive tires; Rebuilding and retreading tires
HQ: Bridgestone Retail Operations, Llc
    333 E Lake St Ste 300
    Bloomingdale IL 60108
    630 259-9000

(G-8804)
COLONIAL MACHINE COMPANY INC
1041 Mogadore Rd (44240-7534)
P.O. Box 650 (44240-0012)
PHONE 330 673-5859
James Rankin, *Pr*
Roy Metcalf, *
EMP: 71 **EST:** 1945
SQ FT: 35,000
SALES (est): 9.06MM **Privately Held**
Web: www.colonial-machine.com
SIC: 3544 Special dies and tools

(G-8805)
COLONIAL PATTERNS INC
920 Overholt Rd (44240-7550)
PHONE 330 673-6475
Martin A Meluch, *Pr*
Valent Meluch, *
▲ **EMP:** 12 **EST:** 1952
SQ FT: 4,800
SALES (est): 755.07K **Privately Held**
Web: www.colonialpatt.com
SIC: 3543 3544 Industrial patterns; Special dies, tools, jigs, and fixtures

(G-8806)
D & J PRINTING INC
Also Called: Hess Print Solutions
3765 Sunnybrook Rd (44240-7443)
PHONE 330 678-5868
EMP: 324
SALES (corp-wide): 643.53MM **Privately Held**
Web: www.sheridan.com
SIC: 2752 Offset printing
HQ: D. & J. Printing, Inc.
    3323 Oak St
    Brainerd MN 56401
    218 829-2877

(G-8807)
DAVEY KENT INC
Also Called: Davey Drill
200 W Williams St (44240)
P.O. Box 400 (44240)
PHONE 330 673-5400
Tom Myers, *Pr*
J Thomas Myers Ii, *CEO*
David Myers, *VP*
J Gnandt, *Sec*
Chris Cooler, *Prin*
▲ **EMP:** 20 **EST:** 1981
SQ FT: 50,000
SALES (est): 3.61MM **Privately Held**
Web: newsite.daveykent.com
SIC: 3532 Drills and drilling equipment, mining (except oil and gas)

(G-8808)
DBH ASSCATES - OHIO LTD PARTNR
Also Called: Hess Print Solutions
3765 Sunnybrook Rd (44240-7443)
PHONE 330 676-2006
David B Hess, *Pt*

EMP: 7 **EST:** 2013
SALES (est): 350.33K **Privately Held**
SIC: 2759 Commercial printing, nec

(G-8809)
DERMAMED COATIN
271 Progress Blvd (44240-8055)
PHONE 330 474-3786
▲ **EMP:** 10 **EST:** 2012
SALES (est): 927.11K **Privately Held**
Web: www.dermamed.net
SIC: 2672 Paper; coated and laminated, nec

(G-8810)
DON WARTKO CONSTRUCTION CO
Also Called: Design Concrete Surfaces
975 Tallmadge Rd (44240-6474)
PHONE 330 673-5252
Thomas Wartko, *Pr*
David Wartko, *
Mike Wartko, *
Doris Wartko, *
Ron Wartko, *
EMP: 60 **EST:** 1967
SQ FT: 15,000
SALES (est): 12.73MM **Privately Held**
Web: www.donwartkoconstruction.com
SIC: 1623 1794 3732 Oil and gas line and compressor station construction; Excavation work; Boatbuilding and repairing

(G-8811)
EAST END WELDING LLC
357 Tallmadge Rd (44240-7201)
PHONE 330 677-6000
Tim Rosengarten, *CEO*
▲ **EMP:** 120 **EST:** 1967
SQ FT: 146,500
SALES (est): 16.96MM
SALES (corp-wide): 376.52MM **Privately Held**
Web: www.eastendwelding.com
SIC: 7692 3599 Welding repair; Custom machinery
PA: Connell Limited Partnership
    1 International Pl Fl 31
    Boston MA 02110
    617 737-2700

(G-8812)
ELBEX CORPORATION
Also Called: Elbex
300 Martinel Dr (44240-4369)
PHONE 330 673 3233
Edward L Bittle, *Pr*
EMP: 90 **EST:** 1991
SALES (est): 8.98MM **Privately Held**
Web: www.elbex-us.com
SIC: 3069 Medical and laboratory rubber sundries and related products

(G-8813)
EMBROIDERY NETWORK INC
Also Called: Do Duds
4693 Kent Rd (44240-5206)
PHONE 330 678-4887
Jennifer Cox, *Pr*
Susan W Ritchie, *VP*
Arch Ritchie, *VP*
EMP: 7 **EST:** 1990
SQ FT: 3,000
SALES (est): 972.56K **Privately Held**
Web: www.nnep.com
SIC: 2395 Embroidery products, except Schiffli machine

(G-8814)
EMERGENCY PRODUCTS & RES INC
Also Called: Epr
890 W Main St (44240-2284)
PHONE 330 673-5003

▲ **EMP:** 6 **EST:** 1992
SQ FT: 350,000
SALES (est): 959.36K **Privately Held**
Web: www.epandr.com
SIC: 2448 Pallets, wood

(G-8815)
FURUKAWA ROCK DRILL USA INC (HQ)
Also Called: Furukawa Rock Drill
805 Lake St (44240-2740)
PHONE..................................330 673-5826
Jeff Crane, *CEO*
Shoji Iguchi, *Dir*
◆ **EMP:** 15 **EST:** 1924
SQ FT: 240,000
SALES (est): 24.24MM **Privately Held**
Web: www.frdusa.com
SIC: 3533 3599 3546 Drilling tools for gas, oil, or water wells; Machine shop, jobbing and repair; Power-driven handtools
  PA: Furukawa Co., Ltd.
    2-6-4, Otemachi
    Chiyoda-Ku TKY 100-0

(G-8816)
FURUKAWA ROCK DRILL USA CO LTD (PA)
Also Called: Frd
711 Lake St (44240-2738)
PHONE..................................330 673-5826
Michael Sato, *Pr*
◆ **EMP:** 15 **EST:** 1956
SQ FT: 27,181
SALES (est): 2.4MM
SALES (corp-wide): 2.4MM **Privately Held**
Web: www.frdusa.com
SIC: 3545 3594 3546 3423 Tools and accessories for machine tools; Fluid power pumps and motors; Power-driven handtools ; Hand and edge tools, nec

(G-8817)
HAPCO INC
Also Called: Tarpco
390 Portage Blvd (44240-7283)
PHONE..................................330 678-9353
Charles George, *CEO*
Chuck George, *CEO*
Bernard Carpenter, *Pr*
John A Daily, *Prin*
◆ **EMP:** 11 **EST:** 1979
SQ FT: 23,000
SALES (est): 3.28MM **Privately Held**
Web: www.hapcoinc.com
SIC: 3545 5049 Diamond cutting tools for turning, boring, burnishing, etc.; Precision tools

(G-8818)
HUGO SAND COMPANY
7055 State Route 43 (44240-6198)
PHONE..................................216 570-1212
Dorothy Strohm, *Pr*
Sythnia Terhune, *VP*
Scott R Terhune, *VP*
EMP: 7 **EST:** 1928
SQ FT: 400
SALES (est): 877.82K **Privately Held**
SIC: 1442 Construction sand mining

(G-8819)
INDUSTRIAL MOLDED PLASTICS
425 1/2 W Grant St (44240-2311)
P.O. Box 726 (44240-0014)
PHONE..................................330 673-1464
Kelly Luli, *Pr*
Mary Ann Lewis, *VP*
EMP: 16 **EST:** 1973
SQ FT: 11,000
SALES (est): 385.79K **Privately Held**
SIC: 3083 Thermosetting laminates: rods, tubes, plates, and sheet

(G-8820)
J B MANUFACTURING INC
4465 Crystal Pkwy (44240-8005)
PHONE..................................330 676-9744
John L Anderson, *Pr*
EMP: 30 **EST:** 1976
SQ FT: 36,000
SALES (est): 458.37K **Privately Held**
SIC: 3599 Machine shop, jobbing and repair

(G-8821)
KENT ADHESIVE PRODUCTS CO
Also Called: K A P C O
1000 Cherry St (44240-7501)
P.O. Box 626 (44240-0011)
PHONE..................................330 678-1626
Edward Small, *Pr*
Philip M Zavracky, *
Jenifer Codrea, *
◆ **EMP:** 80 **EST:** 1974
SQ FT: 100,000
SALES (est): 23.36MM **Privately Held**
Web: www.kapco.com
SIC: 2679 2672 2675 7389 Paper products, converted, nec; Adhesive papers, labels, or tapes: from purchased material; Die-cut paper and board; Laminating service

(G-8822)
KENT DISPLAYS INC (PA)
Also Called: Improv Electronics
343 Portage Blvd (44240-9200)
PHONE..................................330 673-8784
Joel Domino, *
Asad Khan, *
▲ **EMP:** 90 **EST:** 1996
SQ FT: 42,000
SALES (est): 20.18MM **Privately Held**
Web: www.kentdisplays.com
SIC: 3679 Liquid crystal displays (LCD)

(G-8823)
KENT ELASTOMER PRODUCTS INC (HQ)
1500 Saint Clair Ave (44240-4364)
P.O. Box 668 (44240-0012)
PHONE..................................330 673-1011
Bob Oborn, *Pr*
▲ **EMP:** 140 **EST:** 1986
SQ FT: 42,000
SALES (est): 27.78MM
SALES (corp-wide): 331.16MM **Privately Held**
Web: www.kentelastomer.com
SIC: 3069 Medical and laboratory rubber sundries and related products
  PA: Meridian Industries, Inc.
    735 N Water St Ste 630
    Milwaukee WI 53202
    414 224-0610

(G-8824)
KENT INFORMATION SERVICES INC
6185 2nd Ave (44240-2991)
PHONE..................................330 672-2110
EMP: 6 **EST:** 1994
SALES (est): 354.87K **Privately Held**
Web: www.kentis.com
SIC: 2721 8721 Periodicals; Accounting, auditing, and bookkeeping

(G-8825)
KENT MOLD AND MANUFACTURING CO
1190 W Main St (44240-1942)
PHONE..................................330 673-3469
Paul Ferder, *Pr*
Henry Trivelli, *
EMP: 25 **EST:** 1944
SQ FT: 35,000
SALES (est): 1.81MM **Privately Held**
Web: www.kentmold.com
SIC: 3544 Special dies and tools

(G-8826)
KENT POST ACQUISITION INC
449 Dodge St (44240-3707)
PHONE..................................330 678-6343
Michael Pollard, *Pr*
Dennis Lyell, *Pr*
Gary Lyell, *VP*
EMP: 15 **EST:** 1983
SQ FT: 12,000
SALES (est): 4.26MM **Privately Held**
Web: www.kentautomation.com
SIC: 3599 Machine shop, jobbing and repair

(G-8827)
LAND OLAKES INC
Also Called: Land O'Lakes
2001 Mogadore Rd (44240-7296)
PHONE..................................330 678-1578
Steve Sehafer, *Mgr*
EMP: 60
SALES (corp-wide): 2.89B **Privately Held**
Web: www.landolakes-ingredients.com
SIC: 2022 Cheese; natural and processed
  PA: Land O'lakes, Inc.
    4001 Lexington Ave N
    Arden Hills MN 55112
    651 375-2222

(G-8828)
LINNEAS CANDY SUPPLIES INC (PA)
Also Called: Linnea's
4149 Karg Industrial Pkwy (44240-6425)
PHONE..................................330 678-7112
EMP: 20 **EST:** 1968
SALES (est): 26.91MM
SALES (corp-wide): 26.91MM **Privately Held**
Web: www.linneasinc.com
SIC: 5145 5441 2672 3089 Confectionery; Candy; Adhesive papers, labels, or tapes: from purchased material; Injection molding of plastics

(G-8829)
M N M MFG INC
449 Dodge St (44240-3707)
PHONE..................................330 256-5572
EMP: 11 **EST:** 2014
SALES (est): 761.47K **Privately Held**
SIC: 3999 Manufacturing industries, nec

(G-8830)
MAAG AUTOMATIK INC
Also Called: Maag Reduction Engineering .
235 Progress Blvd (44240-8055)
PHONE..................................330 677-2225
EMP: 35
SALES (corp-wide): 8.44B **Publicly Held**
Web: www.maag.com
SIC: 3532 5084 Crushing, pulverizing, and screening equipment; Pulverizing machinery and equipment
  HQ: Maag Reduction, Inc.
    9401 Sthrn Pine Blvd
    Charlotte NC 28273

(G-8831)
MAAG REDUCTION INC
235 Progress Blvd (44240-8055)
PHONE..................................704 716-9000
EMP: 15
SALES (corp-wide): 8.44B **Publicly Held**
Web: www.maag.com
SIC: 3561 Pumps and pumping equipment
  HQ: Maag Reduction, Inc.
    9401 Sthrn Pine Blvd
    Charlotte NC 28273

(G-8832)
MARK GRZIANIS ST TREATS EX INC (PA)
Also Called: Yaya's
1294 Windward Ln (44240-1895)
PHONE..................................330 414-6266
Mark Graziani, *Pr*
Wendy Graziani, *VP*
EMP: 12 **EST:** 2002
SALES (est): 577.59K
SALES (corp-wide): 577.59K **Privately Held**
SIC: 5812 2035 7389 Cafeteria; Dressings, salad: raw and cooked (except dry mixes); Business Activities at Non-Commercial Site

(G-8833)
MASTERS PRCISION MACHINING INC
4465 Crystal Pkwy (44240-8005)
PHONE..................................330 419-1933
Kenneth Rice, *Pr*
Charlotte Rice, *CFO*
EMP: 10 **EST:** 1979
SALES (est): 1.18MM **Privately Held**
Web: www.mpmachininginc.com
SIC: 3541 Numerically controlled metal cutting machine tools

(G-8834)
MERIDIAN INDUSTRIES INC
Also Called: Kent Elastomer Products
1500 Saint Clair Ave (44240-4364)
P.O. Box 668 (44240-0012)
PHONE..................................330 673-1011
Vann Epp Murray, *Pr*
EMP: 96
SALES (corp-wide): 331.16MM **Privately Held**
Web: www.meridiancompanies.com
SIC: 3069 3842 3083 3082 Tubing, rubber; Surgical appliances and supplies; Laminated plastics plate and sheet; Unsupported plastics profile shapes
  PA: Meridian Industries, Inc.
    735 N Water St Ste 630
    Milwaukee WI 53202
    414 224-0610

(G-8835)
METAL-MAX INC
1540 Enterprise Way (44240-7547)
PHONE..................................330 673-9926
EMP: 8 **EST:** 1999
SQ FT: 5,000
SALES (est): 937.33K **Privately Held**
SIC: 3444 Sheet metal specialties, not stamped

(G-8836)
MICHAEL KAUFMAN COMPANIES INC
Also Called: Educational Equipment
845 Overholt Rd (44240-7529)
P.O. Box 154 (44240-0003)
PHONE..................................330 673-4881
Michael Kaufman, *Pr*
John T Waller, *Prin*
◆ **EMP:** 12 **EST:** 1934
SQ FT: 60,000
SALES (est): 2.34MM **Privately Held**
SIC: 3281 2599 2493 2541 Blackboards, slate; Boards: planning, display, notice; Bulletin boards, cork; Store and office display cases and fixtures

Kent - Portage County (G-8837)

(G-8837)
MILLER BEARING COMPANY INC
420 Portage Blvd (44240-7285)
PHONE...................330 678-8844
Donald A Miller, *Pr*
Julie Miller, *
EMP: 28 EST: 1978
SQ FT: 75,000
SALES (est): 2.43MM Privately Held
Web: www.millerbearing.com
SIC: 3562 Ball bearings and parts

(G-8838)
MOLD SURFACE TEXTURES INC
Also Called: MST
4485 Crystal Pkwy Ste 300 (44240-8016)
PHONE...................330 678-8590
Joe Gendron, *Pr*
Aaron Pendergast, *Sec*
Kevin Gasaway, *Treas*
EMP: 6 EST: 2004
SALES (est): 502.13K Privately Held
Web: www.mstextures.com
SIC: 3544 Industrial molds

(G-8839)
NEWELL BRANDS INC
Also Called: Rubbermaid
212 Progress Blvd (44240-8015)
PHONE...................330 733-1184
Amy Smith, *Brnch Mgr*
EMP: 11
SALES (corp-wide): 8.13B Publicly Held
Web: www.newellbrands.com
SIC: 3069 Medical and laboratory rubber sundries and related products
PA: Newell Brands Inc.
  6655 Pachtree Dunwoody Rd
  Atlanta GA 30328
  770 418-7000

(G-8840)
OLIVE ROMANUM OIL INC
1881 Brady Lake Rd (44240-3003)
PHONE...................330 554-4102
EMP: 6 EST: 2017
SALES (est): 99.01K Privately Held
SIC: 2079 Olive oil

(G-8841)
ON US LLC
315 Gougler Ave (44240-2405)
PHONE...................330 286-3436
Ryan Cene, *Pr*
Ryan Cenc, *Managing Member*
EMP: 20 EST: 2017
SALES (est): 1.55MM Privately Held
Web: www.onus.co
SIC: 2086 Water, natural: packaged in cans, bottles, etc.

(G-8842)
P S P INC
Also Called: Petry Power Systems
7337 Westview Rd (44240-5911)
PHONE...................330 283-5635
Robert V Petry, *Pr*
EMP: 11 EST: 2007
SALES (est): 218.18K Privately Held
SIC: 2869 Fuels

(G-8843)
PODNAR PLASTICS INC
343 Portage Blvd Unit 3 (44240-9200)
PHONE...................330 673-2255
Scott Podnar, *Pr*
EMP: 6
SALES (corp-wide): 2.31MM Privately Held
Web: www.rez-tech-jars.com
SIC: 3089 Molding primary plastics
PA: Podnar Plastics, Inc.
  1510 Mogadore Rd
  Kent OH 44240
  330 673-2255

(G-8844)
PODNAR PLASTICS INC (PA)
1510 Mogadore Rd (44240-7599)
PHONE...................330 673-2255
Jack Podnar, *Pr*
Craig Podnar, *VP*
Scott Podnar V Press, *Prin*
EMP: 21 EST: 1977
SQ FT: 38,000
SALES (est): 2.31MM
SALES (corp-wide): 2.31MM Privately Held
Web: www.rez-tech-jars.com
SIC: 3089 Injection molding of plastics

(G-8845)
POLYMERICS INC
1540 Saint Clair Ave (44240-4364)
PHONE...................330 677-1131
Tony Bisesi, *Contrlr*
EMP: 20
SQ FT: 26,458
SALES (corp-wide): 11.37MM Privately Held
Web: www.polymericsinc.com
SIC: 2899 2821 Chemical preparations, nec; Plastics materials and resins
PA: Polymerics, Inc.
  2828 2nd St
  Cuyahoga Falls OH 44221
  330 928-2210

(G-8846)
POST PRODUCTS INC
1600 Franklin Ave (44240-4308)
P.O. Box 777 (44240-0015)
PHONE...................330 678-0048
Jay Mcelravy, *Pr*
Nancy Mcelravy, *Sec*
EMP: 7 EST: 1971
SQ FT: 6,000
SALES (est): 661.11K Privately Held
Web: www.postproductsinc.com
SIC: 3599 Machine shop, jobbing and repair

(G-8847)
PRESS OF OHIO INC
Also Called: Hess Print Solutions
3765 Sunnybrook Rd (44240-7443)
PHONE...................330 678-5868
Doug Mann, *Pr*
EMP: 20 EST: 2013
SALES (est): 3.81MM Privately Held
Web: www.pressofohio.com
SIC: 2759 Commercial printing, nec

(G-8848)
PRIMAL SCREEN INC
Also Called: Alpha Strike
1021 Mason Ave (44240)
PHONE...................330 677-1766
EMP: 10 EST: 1995
SQ FT: 10,000
SALES (est): 510.89K Privately Held
Web: www.primalscreenprinting.com
SIC: 2759 Screen printing

(G-8849)
PROTO MACHINE & MFG INC
2190 State Route 59 (44240-7142)
PHONE...................330 677-1700
Edward L Dias, *Pr*
Shelly Morgan, *Admn*
EMP: 15 EST: 1984
SQ FT: 10,000
SALES (est): 2MM Privately Held
Web: www.theprotoway.com
SIC: 3599 Machine shop, jobbing and repair

(G-8850)
PYRAMID MOLD & MACHINE CO INC
Also Called: Pyramid Mold & Machine Company
222 Martinel Dr (44240-4321)
P.O. Box 634 (44240-0011)
PHONE...................330 673-5200
Joan Siciliano, *Pr*
EMP: 13 EST: 1984
SQ FT: 10,000
SALES (est): 2.19MM Privately Held
Web: www.pyramidmold-machine.com
SIC: 3544 Special dies and tools

(G-8851)
QUICK SERVICE WELDING & MCH CO
117 E Summit St (44240-3556)
PHONE...................330 673-3818
Frank S Bowen, *Pr*
James M Bowen, *VP*
Wilma Bowen, *Sec*
EMP: 11 EST: 1919
SQ FT: 11,200
SALES (est): 943.72K Privately Held
SIC: 7692 3599 Welding repair; Machine shop, jobbing and repair

(G-8852)
REDUCTION ENGINEERING INC
Also Called: Accu Grind
235 Progress Blvd (44240-8055)
PHONE...................330 677-2225
◆ EMP: 45
Web: www.maag.com
SIC: 5084 3532 Industrial machinery and equipment; Crushing, pulverizing, and screening equipment

(G-8853)
REZ-TECH CORPORATION
1510 Mogadore Rd (44240-7531)
PHONE...................330 673-4009
Jack Podnar, *CEO*
Scott Podnar, *
Craig Podnar, *
Jeanette M Podnar, *
◆ EMP: 47 EST: 1981
SQ FT: 38,000
SALES (est): 6.64MM Privately Held
Web: www.rez-tech-jars.com
SIC: 3089 Injection molding of plastics

(G-8854)
ROBERT LONG MANUFACTURING CO
4192 Karg Industrial Pkwy (44240-6400)
PHONE...................330 678-0911
Robert Long, *Pr*
EMP: 8 EST: 1982
SQ FT: 7,200
SALES (est): 617.16K Privately Held
SIC: 3599 Machine shop, jobbing and repair

(G-8855)
RON-AL MOLD & MACHINE INC
1057 Mason Ave (44240)
P.O. Box 364 (44240)
PHONE...................330 673-7919
Ronald Siciliano, *Pr*
Alan Siciliano, *VP*
Rosalee Hodge, *Off Mgr*
EMP: 12 EST: 1980
SQ FT: 2,500
SALES (est): 1.82MM Privately Held
Web: www.ronalmold.com
SIC: 3544 Industrial molds

(G-8856)
ROTOLINE USA LLC
4429 Crystal Pkwy Ste B (44240-8001)
PHONE...................330 677-3223
Alain Stpierre, *Genl Mgr*
EMP: 6 EST: 2013
SALES (est): 1.17MM Privately Held
Web: www.rotoline.com
SIC: 3524 Rototillers (garden machinery)

(G-8857)
SAGE INTEGRATION HOLDINGS LLC (PA)
4075 Karg Industrial Pkwy Ste B (44240-6485)
P.O. Box 214 (44278-0214)
PHONE...................330 733-8183
Eric Frasier, *CEO*
Rod Bragg, *Prin*
EMP: 22 EST: 2001
SALES (est): 33.36MM
SALES (corp-wide): 33.36MM Privately Held
Web: www.sageintegration.com
SIC: 5065 3699 7382 Security control equipment and systems; Security devices; Security systems services

(G-8858)
SCHNELLER LLC (HQ)
Also Called: Polyplastex International
6019 Powdermill Rd (44240-7109)
PHONE...................330 676-7183
Richard Organ, *Managing Member*
John Schirra, *Managing Member**
Jeffrey Frye, *Managing Member**
◆ EMP: 112 EST: 2007
SQ FT: 125,000
SALES (est): 67.4MM
SALES (corp-wide): 6.58B Publicly Held
Web: www.schneller.com
SIC: 2295 Resin or plastic coated fabrics
PA: Transdigm Group Incorporated
  1301 E 9th St Ste 3000
  Cleveland OH 44114
  216 706-2960

(G-8859)
SCOTT MOLDERS INCORPORATED
7180 State Route 43 (44240-5940)
P.O. Box 645 (44240-0012)
PHONE...................330 673-5777
Scott Yahner, *Pr*
EMP: 70 EST: 1955
SQ FT: 23,000
SALES (est): 5.43MM Privately Held
Web: www.scottmolders.com
SIC: 3089 2821 Thermoformed finished plastics products, nec; Plastics materials and resins

(G-8860)
SEAL MASTER CORPORATION
Also Called: Sealmaster
340 Martinel Dr (44240-4369)
PHONE...................330 673-8410
Edward Bittle, *Brnch Mgr*
EMP: 50
SALES (corp-wide): 9.18MM Privately Held
Web: www.sealmaster.com
SIC: 2951 Asphalt paving mixtures and blocks
PA: Seal Master Corporation
  368 Martinel Dr
  Kent OH 44240
  330 673-8410

GEOGRAPHIC SECTION

Kenton - Hardin County (G-8884)

(G-8861)
SEAL MASTER CORPORATION (PA)
Also Called: Sealmaster
368 Martinel Dr (44240-4368)
PHONE..............................330 673-8410
EMP: 25 **EST:** 1974
SALES (est): 9.18MM
SALES (corp-wide): 9.18MM **Privately Held**
Web: www.sealmaster.com
SIC: 3053 Gaskets and sealing devices

(G-8862)
SELECT MACHINE INC
4125 Karg Industrial Pkwy (44240-6425)
PHONE..............................330 678-7676
EMP: 10 **EST:** 1994
SQ FT: 7,000
SALES (est): 993.34K **Privately Held**
SIC: 3544 3599 Special dies, tools, jigs, and fixtures; Machine shop, jobbing and repair

(G-8863)
SEW & SEW EMBROIDERY INC
881 Tallmadge Rd Ste C (44240-6451)
P.O. Box 333 (44278-0333)
PHONE..............................330 676-1600
Andrew Coufal, *Pr*
EMP: 12 **EST:** 1997
SALES (est): 779.81K **Privately Held**
Web: www.sewandsewemb.com
SIC: 2395 7389 5199 Embroidery products, except Schiffli machine; Advertising, promotional, and trade show services; Advertising specialties

(G-8864)
SMITHERS-OASIS COMPANY
Smithers-Oasis North America
919 Marvin St Bldg Dc (44240-2436)
P.O. Box 790 (44240-0016)
PHONE..............................330 673-5851
Robert Williams, *Brnch Mgr*
EMP: 11
SALES (corp-wide): 96.54MM **Privately Held**
Web: www.oasisfloral.com
SIC: 3086 Plastics foam products
PA: Smithers-Oasis Company
     295 S Water St Ste 201
     Kent OH 44240
     330 945-5100

(G-8865)
SMITHERS-OASIS COMPANY (PA)
Also Called: Smithersoasis North America
295 S Water St Ste 201 (44240-3591)
PHONE..............................330 945-5100
Charles F Walton, *CEO*
Robin M Kilbride, *Pr*
James Stull, *Treas*
◆ **EMP:** 15 **EST:** 1954
SQ FT: 7,500
SALES (est): 96.54MM
SALES (corp-wide): 96.54MM **Privately Held**
Web: www.oasisfloral.com
SIC: 3086 Packaging and shipping materials, foamed plastics

(G-8866)
SORBOTHANE INC (PA)
2144 State Route 59 (44240-7142)
PHONE..............................330 678-9444
Robert Whitlinger, *Prin*
David Church, *Pr*
EMP: 20 **EST:** 1982
SQ FT: 60,000
SALES (est): 3.63MM
SALES (corp-wide): 3.63MM **Privately Held**
Web: www.sorbothane.com
SIC: 3069 3545 3296 2821 Molded rubber products; Machine tool accessories; Mineral wool; Plastics materials and resins

(G-8867)
SOUND LABORATORY LLC ✪
109 S Water St (44240-3582)
PHONE..............................330 968-4060
EMP: 10 **EST:** 2023
SALES (est): 521.63K **Privately Held**
SIC: 3861 Sound recording and reproducing equipment, motion picture

(G-8868)
STEINERT INDUSTRIES INC
1507 Franklin Ave (44240-3770)
PHONE..............................330 678-0028
John J Steinert, *Pr*
Laura Cheges, *Sec*
EMP: 18 **EST:** 1976
SQ FT: 11,000
SALES (est): 2.44MM **Privately Held**
Web: www.steinertindustries.com
SIC: 3559 3599 Glass making machinery: blowing, molding, forming, etc.; Machine shop, jobbing and repair

(G-8869)
SUNNY BROOK PREST CONCRETE CO
3586 Sunnybrook Rd (44240-7448)
PHONE..............................330 673-7667
Joseph F Repasky Junior, *Pr*
EMP: 9 **EST:** 1979
SALES (est): 1.94MM **Privately Held**
Web: www.sunnybrookpressedconcrete.com
SIC: 3271 Architectural concrete: block, split, fluted, screen, etc.

(G-8870)
T-MAC MACHINE INC
924 Overholt Rd (44240-7551)
PHONE..............................330 673-0621
Ray Thompson, *Pr*
Ruth Thompson-asst, *Sec*
Gary Thompson, *Sec*
EMP: 7 **EST:** 1975
SQ FT: 10,400
SALES (est): 484.81K **Privately Held**
SIC: 3599 3069 Machine shop, jobbing and repair; Platens, except printers': solid or covered rubber

(G-8871)
TARPCO INC
390 Portage Blvd (44240-7283)
PHONE..............................330 677-8277
Chuck George, *Pr*
Harold A Neidlinger, *Pr*
Michael R Harrison, *VP*
EMP: 18 **EST:** 1938
SQ FT: 6,500
SALES (est): 1.59MM **Privately Held**
Web: www.tarpco.com
SIC: 2394 7359 3537 Tarpaulins, fabric: made from purchased materials; Tent and tarpaulin rental; Industrial trucks and tractors

(G-8872)
TECHNIDRILL SYSTEMS INC
429 Portage Blvd (44240-7286)
PHONE..............................330 678-9980
EMP: 36
Web: www.kays-dehoff.com
SIC: 3541 3546 3545 Drilling and boring machines; Power-driven handtools; Machine tool accessories

(G-8873)
TEMPRECISION INTL CORP (PA)
777 Stow St (44240-3429)
PHONE..............................855 891-7732
James Stull, *Pr*
EMP: 7 **EST:** 2018
SALES (est): 973.37K
SALES (corp-wide): 973.37K **Privately Held**
Web: www.temprecision.com
SIC: 3086 Plastics foam products

(G-8874)
THE D B HESS COMPANY
Also Called: Hess Print Solutions
3765 Sunnybrook Rd (44240-7443)
PHONE..............................330 678-5868
▲ **EMP:** 25
SIC: 2759 2789 Commercial printing, nec; Bookbinding and related work

(G-8875)
THE PRESS OF OHIO INC
Also Called: Hess Print Solutions - OH
3765 Sunnybrook Rd (44240-7443)
PHONE..............................330 678-5868
EMP: 400
SIC: 2732 Book printing

(G-8876)
TPO HESS HOLDINGS INC
Also Called: Hess Print Solutions
3765 Sunnybrook Rd (44240-7443)
PHONE..............................815 334-6140
Jerry Haywood, *CEO*
EMP: 30 **EST:** 2009
SALES (est): 4.95MM **Privately Held**
Web: www.hessprintsolutions.com
SIC: 2759 Commercial printing, nec

(G-8877)
TRAIL SPRAYER & SERVICE LLC
4211 Karg Industrial Pkwy (44240-6470)
PHONE..............................330 720-2966
EMP: 13 **EST:** 2015
SALES (est): 1.07MM
SALES (corp-wide): 12.49MM **Privately Held**
Web: www.trailsprayer.com
SIC: 3563 Spraying and dusting equipment
PA: Sprayworks Equipment Group, Llc
     2830 Cleveland Ave Nw
     Canton OH 44709
     330 587-4141

(G-8878)
TRANSDIGM INC
2146 State Route 59 (44240-7142)
PHONE..............................330 676-7147
Jeannette Selzer, *Brnch Mgr*
EMP: 10
SALES (corp-wide): 6.58B **Publicly Held**
Web: www.aerocontrolex.com
SIC: 2821 Plastics materials and resins
HQ: Transdigm, Inc.
     1350 Euclid Ave
     Cleveland OH 44115

(G-8879)
U S DEVELOPMENT CORP
Also Called: Akro-Plastics
900 W Main St (44240-2285)
PHONE..............................330 673-6900
Jerold Ramsey, *Pr*
EMP: 80 **EST:** 1985
SQ FT: 185,000
SALES (est): 10.75MM **Privately Held**
Web: www.rotomold.net
SIC: 3089 6512 Molding primary plastics; Commercial and industrial building operation

Kenton
Hardin County

(G-8880)
ATMOSPHERE ANNEALING LLC
Also Called: Aalberts Surface Technologies
1501 Raff Rd Sw (43326)
PHONE..............................330 478-0314
Saminathan Ramaswamy, *Mgr*
EMP: 65
SALES (corp-wide): 63.59MM **Privately Held**
Web: www.aalberts-ht.us
SIC: 3398 Annealing of metal
HQ: Atmosphere Annealing, Llc
     209 W Mount Hope Ave # 2
     Lansing MI 48910
     517 485-5090

(G-8881)
BAKELITE N SUMITOMO AMER INC
13717 Us Highway 68 (43326-9302)
PHONE..............................419 675-1282
Kurt Sandy, *Brnch Mgr*
EMP: 39
Web: www.sbhpp.com
SIC: 3089 Plastics containers, except foam
HQ: Sumitomo Bakelite North America, Inc.
     4400 Haggerty Hwy
     Commerce Township MI 48390

(G-8882)
DUREZ CORPORATION
Also Called: Durez
13717 Us Highway 68 (43326-9302)
PHONE..............................567 295-6400
Bill Bazell, *Mgr*
EMP: 48
SQ FT: 25,000
Web: resins.sbna-inc.com
SIC: 2891 2295 2821 Adhesives, plastic; Resin or plastic coated fabrics; Plastics materials and resins
HQ: Durez Corporation
     4400 Haggerty Hwy
     Commerce Township MI 48390
     248 313-7000

(G-8883)
GOLDEN GIANT INC
Also Called: Golden Giants Building System
13300 S Vision Dr (43326-9599)
P.O. Box 389 (43326-0389)
PHONE..............................419 674-4038
Gene A Good, *CEO*
Sharon J Good, *
Chris Richards, *
Paul N Mckinley, *Prin*
Wright Mccullough, *Prin*
EMP: 35 **EST:** 1971
SQ FT: 80,000
SALES (est): 9.28MM **Privately Held**
Web: www.goldengiant.us
SIC: 3448 Buildings, portable: prefabricated metal

(G-8884)
GRAPHIC PACKAGING INTL LLC
Also Called: International Paper
1300 S Main St (43326-2298)
PHONE..............................419 673-0711
Ted Riggs, *Brnch Mgr*
EMP: 375
Web: www.graphicpkg.com

Kenton - Hardin County (G-8885)

SIC: 2656 2621 Cups, paper: made from purchased material; Paper mills
HQ: Graphic Packaging International, Llc
1500 Riveredge Pkwy # 100
Atlanta GA 30328

(G-8885)
HARDIN COUNTY PUBLISHING CO (HQ)
Also Called: Kenton Times, The
201 E Columbus St (43326-1583)
P.O. Box 230 (43326-0230)
PHONE..................419 674-4066
Jeff Barnes, *Pr*
EMP: 36 EST: 1953
SQ FT: 9,600
SALES (est): 4.47MM
SALES (corp-wide): 9.48MM **Privately Held**
Web: www.kentontimes.com
SIC: 2711 Job printing and newspaper publishing combined
PA: Ray Barnes Newspaper Inc
201 E Columbus St 207
Kenton OH 43326
419 674-4066

(G-8886)
KENTON IRON PRODUCTS INC (PA)
13510 S Vision Dr (43326-1592)
PHONE..................419 674-4178
Jerry Harmeyer, *Pr*
Michael Heyne, *
EMP: 35 EST: 1974
SALES (est): 4.81MM
SALES (corp-wide): 4.81MM **Privately Held**
Web: www.kentoniron.com
SIC: 3321 3322 Gray iron ingot molds, cast; Malleable iron foundries

(G-8887)
KENTON STRL & ORN IR WORKS
100 Cleveland Ave (43326-1706)
P.O. Box 115 (43326-0115)
PHONE..................419 674-4025
O Bud A Winzenried, *Junior President*
O Bud A Winzenried Junior, *Pr*
Barbara E Winzenried, *
Anthony K Osbun, *
EMP: 70 EST: 1933
SQ FT: 22,000
SALES (est): 4.75MM **Privately Held**
SIC: 3449 3446 3444 3443 Miscellaneous metalwork; Architectural metalwork; Sheet metalwork; Fabricated plate work (boiler shop)

(G-8888)
MCCULLOUGH INDUSTRIES INC
13047 County Road 175 (43326-9022)
P.O. Box 222 (43326-0222)
PHONE..................419 673-0767
EMP: 25
SIC: 3537 Hoppers, end dump

(G-8889)
MCI INC
Also Called: Verizon Business
13047 County Road 175 (43326-9022)
PHONE..................800 245-9490
EMP: 19
SALES (corp-wide): 2.16B **Publicly Held**
Web: www.mcculloughind.com
SIC: 3537 Hoppers, end dump
HQ: Mci, Inc.
22901 Millcreek Blvd
Cleveland OH 44122
216 292-3800

(G-8890)
MCI INC
Also Called: McCullough Industries
13047 County Road 175 (43326-9022)
PHONE..................800 245-9490
EMP: 19
SALES (corp-wide): 2.16B **Publicly Held**
Web: www.mcculloughind.com
SIC: 3537 Hoppers, end dump
HQ: Mci, Inc.
22901 Millcreek Blvd
Cleveland OH 44122
216 292-3800

(G-8891)
MID OHIO WOOD RECYCLING INC
16289 State Route 31 (43326-8819)
PHONE..................419 673-8470
EMP: 8 EST: 1993
SQ FT: 30,000
SALES (est): 735.61K **Privately Held**
SIC: 2448 Pallets, wood

(G-8892)
MOLDMAKERS INC
13608 Us Highway 68 (43326-9302)
P.O. Box 372 (43326-0372)
PHONE..................419 673-0902
Gene R Longbrake, *Pr*
Shari K Longbrake, *Treas*
EMP: 10 EST: 1968
SQ FT: 12,000
SALES (est): 804.41K **Privately Held**
Web: www.moldmakersinc.com
SIC: 3544 3089 Special dies and tools; Injection molding of plastics

(G-8893)
MORTON BUILDINGS INC
14623 State Route 31 (43326-9021)
PHONE..................419 399-4549
Jeff Dawson, *Mgr*
EMP: 7
SALES (corp-wide): 213.04MM **Privately Held**
Web: www.mortonbuildings.com
SIC: 3448 Prefabricated metal buildings and components
PA: Morton Buildings, Inc.
252 W Adams St
Morton IL 61550
800 447-7436

(G-8894)
MORTON BUILDINGS INC
Also Called: Morton Buildings Plant
14483 State Route 31 (43326-9055)
P.O. Box 223 (43326-0223)
PHONE..................419 675-2311
EMP: 21
SALES (corp-wide): 213.04MM **Privately Held**
Web: www.mortonbuildings.com
SIC: 3448 5039 2452 Farm and utility buildings; Prefabricated structures; Prefabricated wood buildings
PA: Morton Buildings, Inc.
252 W Adams St
Morton IL 61550
800 447-7436

(G-8895)
OCCIDENTAL CHEMICAL DUREZ
13717 Us Highway 68 (43326-9590)
PHONE..................419 675-1310
Bill Bazell, *Prin*
▲ EMP: 10 EST: 2008
SALES (est): 252.67K **Privately Held**
SIC: 2819 Industrial inorganic chemicals, nec

(G-8896)
PLEASANT PRECISION INC
Also Called: Team Ppi
13840 Us Highway 68 (43326)
PHONE..................419 675-0556
EMP: 32 EST: 1977
SALES (est): 5.25MM **Privately Held**
Web: www.teamppi.com
SIC: 3544 3089 Forms (molds), for foundry and plastics working machinery; Injection molding of plastics

(G-8897)
PRECISION STRIP INC
190 Bales Rd (43326-8909)
PHONE..................419 674-4186
Don Bornhorst, *Brnch Mgr*
EMP: 52
SALES (corp-wide): 14.81B **Publicly Held**
Web: www.precision-strip.com
SIC: 4225 3341 General warehousing and storage; Secondary nonferrous metals
HQ: Precision Strip Inc.
86 S Ohio St
Minster OH 45865
419 628-2343

(G-8898)
ROBINSON FIN MACHINES INC
13670 Us Highway 68 (43326-9302)
PHONE..................419 674-4152
Sheryl Haushalter, *Pr*
Ruth A Haushalter, *
David Haushalter, *
Sheryl Haushalter, *VP*
▲ EMP: 46 EST: 1980
SQ FT: 27,000
SALES (est): 6.53MM **Privately Held**
Web: www.robfin.com
SIC: 3444 Sheet metalwork

(G-8899)
ROUND MATE SYSTEMS
13840 Us Highway 68 (43326-9302)
PHONE..................419 675-3334
Ron Pleasant, *Prin*
EMP: 7 EST: 2007
SALES (est): 249.13K **Privately Held**
Web: www.teamppi.com
SIC: 2431 Moldings and baseboards, ornamental and trim

(G-8900)
SCIOTO SIGN CO INC
6047 Us Highway 68 (43326-9218)
PHONE..................419 673-1261
Shawn Moore, *Pr*
Sandra A Pruden, *
EMP: 30 EST: 1897
SQ FT: 52,500
SALES (est): 4.81MM **Privately Held**
Web: www.sciotosigns.com
SIC: 3993 Signs, not made in custom sign painting shops

(G-8901)
SUPERIOR MACHINE TOOL INC
13606 Us Highway 68 (43326-9302)
PHONE..................419 675-2363
Bill Clum, *Pr*
EMP: 10 EST: 1968
SQ FT: 7,200
SALES (est): 885.78K **Privately Held**
Web: www.superiormachineinc.com
SIC: 3599 Machine shop, jobbing and repair

Kettering
Montgomery County

(G-8902)
BWI CHASSIS DYNAMICS NA INC
3100 Research Blvd (45420-4022)
PHONE..................937 455-5100
Jeff Zhao, *Brnch Mgr*
EMP: 13
Web: www.bwigroup.com
SIC: 3714 Motor vehicle parts and accessories
HQ: Bwi Chassis Dynamics (Na), Inc.
12501 Grand River Rd
Brighton MI 48116
937 455-5308

(G-8903)
BWI NORTH AMERICA INC
Ahg - Global Ride Dynamics
3100 Research Blvd Ste 210 (45420)
PHONE..................937 455-5190
Thomas P Gold, *Brnch Mgr*
EMP: 260
SALES (corp-wide): 32.41MM **Privately Held**
Web: www.bwigroup.com
SIC: 3714 Motor vehicle parts and accessories
HQ: Bwi North America Inc.
3100 Res Blvd Ste 240
Kettering OH 45420

(G-8904)
BWI NORTH AMERICA INC (DH)
Also Called: Bwi Group
3100 Research Blvd Ste 240 (45420)
PHONE..................937 253-1130
Zhong Wang, *Pr*
Zijian Zhao, *Dir*
▲ EMP: 20 EST: 2009
SQ FT: 60,000
SALES (est): 111.49MM
SALES (corp-wide): 32.41MM **Privately Held**
Web: www.bwigroup.com
SIC: 3714 5511 Motor vehicle parts and accessories; New and used car dealers
HQ: Beijingwest Industries Co., Ltd.
No.85 Puan Road, Doudian Town, Fangshan District
Beijing BJ 10242

(G-8905)
DAYTON BAG & BURLAP CO
4248 Display Ln (45429-5149)
PHONE..................419 733-7108
EMP: 21
SALES (corp-wide): 46.25MM **Privately Held**
Web: www.daybag.com
SIC: 2393 Textile bags
PA: The Dayton Bag & Burlap Co
322 Davis Ave
Dayton OH 45403
937 258-8000

(G-8906)
EASTMAN KODAK COMPANY
Also Called: Kodak
3100 Research Blvd Ste 250 (45420-4019)
PHONE..................937 259-3000
Bonnie Saravullo, *Brnch Mgr*
EMP: 45
SALES (corp-wide): 573MM **Publicly Held**
Web: www.kodak.com
SIC: 3861 Photographic equipment and supplies
PA: Eastman Kodak Company

343 State St
Rochester NY 14650
585 724-4000

(G-8907)
ETI TECH LLC
3387 Woodman Dr (45429-4131)
PHONE..................................937 832-4200
EMP: 13 **EST:** 1996
SQ FT: 23,000
SALES (est): 4.55MM
SALES (corp-wide): 18.89MM **Privately Held**
Web: www.etitechinc.com
SIC: 3812 3679 8711 3629 Search and navigation equipment; Electronic circuits; Engineering services; Electronic generation equipment
PA: Eti Mission Controls, Llc
3387 Woodman Dr
Dayton OH 45429
937 832-4200

(G-8908)
NANOSPERSE LLC
2000 Composite Dr (45420-1493)
PHONE..................................937 296-5030
▼ **EMP:** 9 **EST:** 2005
SQ FT: 10,000
SALES (est): 1.85MM **Privately Held**
Web: www.nanosperse.com
SIC: 3087 2891 2851 2821 Custom compound purchased resins; Epoxy adhesives; Epoxy coatings; Epoxy resins

(G-8909)
RESONETICS LLC
Also Called: Mound Laser Photonics Center
2941 College Dr (45420-1172)
PHONE..................................937 865-4070
EMP: 47
Web: www.resonetics.com
SIC: 3699 3841 Laser systems and equipment; Medical instruments and equipment, blood and bone work
PA: Resonetics Llc
26 Whipple St
Nashua NH 03060

(G-8910)
SEPMA TECHNOLOGIES LLC
Also Called: Sepmatech
2000 Composite Dr (45420-1493)
PHONE..................................937 660-3783
EMP: 6 **EST:** 2019
SALES (est): 178.02K **Privately Held**
Web: www.sepmatech.com
SIC: 3599 Machine shop, jobbing and repair

(G-8911)
XERION ADVANCED BATTERY CORP
3100 Research Blvd Ste 320 (45420)
PHONE..................................720 229-0697
John Busbee, *Pr*
Christopher Kolb, *Ex VP*
Paul Braun, *Prin*
EMP: 10 **EST:** 2012
SALES (est): 1.12MM **Privately Held**
Web: www.xerionbattery.com
SIC: 3691 Batteries, rechargeable

Kettlersville
Shelby County

(G-8912)
ROETTGER HARDWOOD INC
17066 Kettlersville Rd (45336)
P.O. Box 68 (45336-0068)
PHONE..................................937 693-6811
Viola Roettger, *Pr*
EMP: 12 **EST:** 1947
SQ FT: 74,000
SALES (est): 341.64K **Privately Held**
SIC: 2431 2434 Millwork; Wood kitchen cabinets

Kidron
Wayne County

(G-8913)
E P GERBER & SONS INC
Also Called: Gerber Lumber & Hardware
4918 Kidron Rd (44636)
P.O. Box 2 (44636-0002)
PHONE..................................330 857-2021
EMP: 65 **EST:** 1901
SALES (est): 20.06MM **Privately Held**
Web: www.gerberlumber.com
SIC: 5251 5211 3993 Hardware stores; Lumber and other building materials; Advertising novelties

(G-8914)
GERBER WOOD PRODUCTS INC
6075 Kidron Rd (44636)
P.O. Box 250 (44636-0250)
PHONE..................................330 857-9007
Steve Gerber, *Pr*
Eldon Gerber, *
EMP: 70 **EST:** 1946
SALES (est): 5.09MM **Privately Held**
Web: www.gerberwood.com
SIC: 3993 3999 Advertising novelties; Plaques, picture, laminated

(G-8915)
KIDRON INC
13442 Emerson Rd (44636)
P.O. Box 880 (27889-0880)
PHONE..................................330 857-3011
EMP: 500
Web: www.farmersbankgroup.com
SIC: 3713 3715 3444 Truck bodies (motor vehicles); Trailer bodies; Sheet metalwork

Killbuck
Holmes County

(G-8916)
BAKERWELL INC (PA)
10420 County Road 620 (44637-9728)
P.O. Box 425 (44637-0425)
PHONE..................................330 276-2161
W Rex Baker, *Pr*
Robert K Baker, *CFO*
EMP: 21 **EST:** 1980
SQ FT: 126,000
SALES (est): 7.61MM
SALES (corp-wide): 7.61MM **Privately Held**
Web: www.bakerwell.com
SIC: 1311 1389 Crude petroleum production; Servicing oil and gas wells

(G-8917)
BAKERWELL SERVICE RIGS INC (HQ)
10420 County Road 620 (44637-9728)
P.O. Box 425 (44637-0425)
PHONE..................................330 276-2161
W Rex Baker, *Pr*
Jeffrey Baker, *Sec*
Andrew Baker, *VP*
EMP: 18 **EST:** 1980
SALES (est): 4.82MM
SALES (corp-wide): 7.61MM **Privately Held**
Web: www.bakerwell.com
SIC: 1381 Service well drilling
PA: Bakerwell, Inc.
10420 County Road 620
Killbuck OH 44637
330 276-2161

(G-8918)
CROW WORKS LLC
9595 Us-62 (44637)
PHONE..................................888 811-2769
Belinda Hughes, *CFO*
Dennis Blankemeyer, *
Denise Blankemeyer, *
EMP: 50 **EST:** 2010
SQ FT: 4,800
SALES (est): 7.87MM **Privately Held**
Web: www.crowworks.com
SIC: 2521 2599 Wood office furniture; Bar, restaurant and cafeteria furniture

(G-8919)
DANIELS AMISH COLLECTION LLC
100 Straits Ln (44637-9549)
PHONE..................................330 276-0110
Christopher Karman, *Brnch Mgr*
EMP: 130
SALES (corp-wide): 19.12MM **Privately Held**
Web: www.danielsamish.com
SIC: 2519 Fiberglass furniture, household: padded or plain
PA: Daniel's Amish Collection, Llc
9190 Massillon Rd
Dundee OH 44624
330 359-0400

(G-8920)
JH WOODWORKING LLC
11259 Township Road 71 (44637-9444)
PHONE..................................330 276-7600
Joni Hostetler, *Prin*
EMP: 7 **EST:** 2011
SALES (est): 440.94K **Privately Held**
SIC: 2431 Millwork

(G-8921)
SHREINER COMPANY
50 Straits Ln (44637-9581)
P.O. Box 347 (44637-0347)
PHONE..................................800 722-9915
Justin Smith, *Pr*
EMP: 6 **EST:** 2019
SALES (est): 323.02K **Privately Held**
Web: www.shreinerco.com
SIC: 3069 Molded rubber products

(G-8922)
SHREINER SOLE COMPANY INC
1 Taylor Dr (44637)
P.O. Box 347 (44637-0347)
PHONE..................................330 276-6135
David Shreiner, *Pr*
▲ **EMP:** 10 **EST:** 1948
SQ FT: 56,750
SALES (est): 903.97K **Privately Held**
Web: www.shreinerco.com
SIC: 3069 3061 Soles, boot or shoe: rubber, composition, or fiber; Mechanical rubber goods

(G-8923)
SPERRY & RICE LLC
1088 N Main St (44637-9504)
PHONE..................................330 276-2801
Darrell Detzler, *Brnch Mgr*
EMP: 12
Web: www.sperryrice.com
SIC: 3061 Mechanical rubber goods
PA: Sperry & Rice, Llc
1088 N Main St
Killbuck OH 44637

(G-8924)
SPERRY & RICE LLC (PA)
Also Called: Sperry & Rice
1088 N Main St (44637-9504)
PHONE..................................765 647-4141
EMP: 8 **EST:** 2007
SALES (est): 4.84MM **Privately Held**
Web: www.sperryrice.com
SIC: 3061 Mechanical rubber goods

(G-8925)
WILSON CABINET CO
Straits Industrial Park (44637)
P.O. Box 305 (44637-0305)
PHONE..................................330 276-8711
Carl De Maria, *Pr*
Rebecca Stover, *
EMP: 8 **EST:** 1950
SQ FT: 75,000
SALES (est): 123.98K **Privately Held**
Web: www.wilsoncabinet.com
SIC: 2434 Vanities, bathroom: wood

(G-8926)
WILSONS COUNTRY CREATIONS INC
Also Called: Wilson's
13248 County Road 6 (44637 9434)
PHONE..................................330 377-4190
Tom Wilson, *Owner*
EMP: 9 **EST:** 1985
SQ FT: 3,500
SALES (est): 500.64K **Privately Held**
Web: www.wilsonscc.com
SIC: 5199 5261 3272 Statuary; Lawn ornaments; Concrete products, nec

Kimbolton
Guernsey County

(G-8927)
CALVIN W LAFFERTY
Also Called: Lafferty Chipping
72628 Hopewell Rd (43749-9586)
PHONE..................................740 498-6566
Calvin Lafferty, *Owner*
EMP: 8 **EST:** 1967
SALES (est): 963.27K **Privately Held**
SIC: 2421 Wood chips, produced at mill

(G-8928)
SIMONDS INTERNATIONAL LLC
76000 Old Twenty One Rd (43749-9610)
PHONE..................................978 424-0100
John Fogle, *Brnch Mgr*
EMP: 7
SALES (corp-wide): 206.09MM **Privately Held**
Web: www.simondsint.com
SIC: 3423 5251 Hand and edge tools, nec; Tools
HQ: Simonds International L.L.C.
135 Intervale Rd
Fitchburg MA 01420
978 424-0100

Kings Mills
Warren County

(G-8929)
SEVERN RIVER PUBLISHING LLC
P.O. Box 396 (45034-0396)
PHONE..................................703 819-4686
EMP: 9 **EST:** 2017
SALES (est): 127.92K **Privately Held**
Web: www.severnriverpublishing.com

SIC: 2741 Miscellaneous publishing

(G-8930)
WILSON CUSTOM WOODWORKING INC
1594 Saint John Pl (45034-9721)
PHONE..................513 233-5613
Holly Bejar, Prin
EMP: 8 EST: 2014
SALES (est): 54.13K Privately Held
SIC: 2431 Millwork

Kingston
Ross County

(G-8931)
KIPPS GRAVEL COMPANY INC
30464 Jackson Rd (45644-9626)
PHONE..................513 732-1024
Melvin M Kipp, Pr
Judy King, Sec
EMP: 8 EST: 1967
SALES (est): 440.92K Privately Held
SIC: 1442 1794 Gravel mining; Excavation work

Kingsville
Ashtabula County

(G-8932)
LYONS
5231 State Route 193 (44048-7713)
P.O. Box 554 (44048-0554)
PHONE..................440 224-0676
Elijah Lyons, Owner
EMP: 6 EST: 2008
SALES (est): 422.48K Privately Held
SIC: 3715 Truck trailers

(G-8933)
NELSON SAND & GRAVEL INC
5720 State Route 193 (44048-9715)
P.O. Box 466 (44048-0466)
PHONE..................440 224-0198
Thomas Nelson, Pr
Donna J Nelson, Sec
EMP: 10 EST: 1968
SQ FT: 6,000
SALES (est): 957.77K Privately Held
SIC: 1442 Common sand mining

(G-8934)
R W SIDLEY INC
3062 E Center St (44068)
PHONE..................440 224-2664
Robert Buescher, Pr
EMP: 20 EST: 1956
SALES (est): 183.41K Privately Held
Web: www.rwsidley.com
SIC: 3273 Ready-mixed concrete

Kinsman
Trumbull County

(G-8935)
BAYLOFF STMPED PDTS KNSMAN INC
8091 State Route 5 (44428-9628)
P.O. Box 289 (44428-0289)
PHONE..................330 876-4511
Richard Bayer, Pr
Kevin Jordan, *
Dan Moore, *
Dixon Morgan, *
M E Newcomer, *
EMP: 80 EST: 1948

SQ FT: 115,000
SALES (est): 6.4MM Privately Held
Web: www.bayloff.com
SIC: 3469 7692 3444 3315 Stamping metal for the trade; Welding repair; Sheet metalwork; Steel wire and related products

(G-8936)
MCGILL SEPTIC TANK CO
8913 State St (44428-9706)
PHONE..................330 876-2171
Charles Mcgill, Pr
James Mcelhinny, VP
EMP: 26 EST: 1958
SQ FT: 10,000
SALES (est): 1.03MM Privately Held
SIC: 3272 2531 Concrete products, precast, nec; Public building and related furniture

(G-8937)
R E H INC
Also Called: Hine Racing Equipment
St Rt 5 (44428)
P.O. Box 6 (44428-0006)
PHONE..................330 876-2775
EMP: 7 EST: 1991
SALES (est): 190.37K Privately Held
SIC: 3462 Automotive and internal combustion engine forgings

(G-8938)
STRATTON CREEK WOOD WORKS LLC
5915 Burnett East Rd (44428-9757)
PHONE..................330 876-0005
EMP: 11 EST: 2004
SALES (est): 1.68MM Privately Held
Web: www.strattoncreek.com
SIC: 2431 Millwork

Kirtland
Lake County

(G-8939)
ESSENTIALWARE
Also Called: Global Principals
7637 Euclid Chardon Rd (44094-8724)
PHONE..................888 975-0405
EMP: 8 EST: 2015
SALES (est): 262.51K Privately Held
Web: www.essentialware.com
SIC: 3999 Manufacturing industries, nec

(G-8940)
GRADEWORKS
7913 Euclid Chardon Rd Ste 10 (44094-9541)
PHONE..................440 487-4201
Matthew Clem, Prin
EMP: 6 EST: 2005
SALES (est): 231.97K Privately Held
Web: www.gradeworksinc.net
SIC: 3531 Road construction and maintenance machinery

(G-8941)
KIRTLAND PLASTICS INC
7955 Euclid Chardon Rd (44094-9014)
PHONE..................440 951-4466
Mark Di Lillo, Pr
EMP: 85 EST: 1961
SQ FT: 26,000
SALES (est): 5.4MM Privately Held
Web: www.endura.com
SIC: 3089 3544 Injection molded finished plastics products, nec; Special dies, tools, jigs, and fixtures

(G-8942)
WHOLESALE CHANNEL LETTERS
8603 Euclid Chardon Rd (44094-9586)
PHONE..................440 256-3200
Dale Heigley, Owner
EMP: 8 EST: 1990
SALES (est): 453.62K Privately Held
Web: www.wholesalesigns4u.com
SIC: 3993 Neon signs

Kitts Hill
Lawrence County

(G-8943)
DAVID ADKINS LOGGING
1260 Township Road 256 (45645-8885)
PHONE..................740 533-0297
David A Adkins, Sec
EMP: 6 EST: 2000
SALES (est): 329.21K Privately Held
SIC: 2411 Logging camps and contractors

(G-8944)
MILLWRGHT WLDG FBRICATION SVCS
1590 County Road 105 (45645-8632)
PHONE..................740 533-1510
Mike Moore, Pr
EMP: 6 EST: 1994
SALES (est): 118.71K Privately Held
SIC: 7692 Welding repair

La Rue
Marion County

(G-8945)
POWERMOUNT SYSTEMS INC
1602 Larue Marseilles Rd (43332-8928)
PHONE..................740 499-4330
Ronald Abbott, Prin
EMP: 9 EST: 2008
SALES (est): 168.51K Privately Held
Web: www.powermountsystems.com
SIC: 3355 Extrusion ingot, aluminum: made in rolling mills

Lagrange
Lorain County

(G-8946)
COLONIAL CABINETS INC
337 S Center St (44050-9014)
P.O. Box 62 (44050-0062)
PHONE..................440 355-9663
Jerry Duelley, Pr
Barry Ickes, VP
Kenneth Sooy, Sec
EMP: 7 EST: 1994
SQ FT: 10,000
SALES (est): 212.41K Privately Held
Web: www.colonialcabinets.com
SIC: 2434 Wood kitchen cabinets

(G-8947)
FINELY TUNED FABRICATIONS LLC
129 Commerce Dr (44050-9491)
PHONE..................216 513-6731
Marc Mercurio, Prin
EMP: 7 EST: 2010
SALES (est): 323.48K Privately Held
Web: www.finelytunedfabrications.com
SIC: 7692 Welding repair

(G-8948)
INSERVCO INC (DH)
Also Called: Staci Lagrange
110 Commerce Dr (44050)
P.O. Box 106 (44050)
PHONE..................847 855-9600
Frances Bernardic, Pr
Mike Nargi, VP
Greg Hebson, VP
Jere Simonson, Sec
▲ EMP: 71 EST: 1968
SQ FT: 26,300
SALES (est): 45.79MM Privately Held
Web: www.vexos.com
SIC: 3679 Electronic circuits
HQ: Vexos, Inc.
    60 E 42nd St Ste 1250
    New York NY 10165
    855 711-3227

(G-8949)
INTREPID CO
15815 Diagonal Rd (44050-9533)
PHONE..................440 355-6089
James M Knepper, Prin
EMP: 7 EST: 2001
SALES (est): 2.05MM Privately Held
Web: www.intrepidpotash.com
SIC: 2819 Industrial inorganic chemicals, nec

(G-8950)
LA GRANGE ELEC ASSEMBLIES CO
349 S Center St (44050-9014)
P.O. Box 555 (44050-0555)
PHONE..................440 355-5388
W Robin Mc Clain, Pr
Richard M Mc Clain, VP
EMP: 22 EST: 1971
SQ FT: 40,000
SALES (est): 2.99MM Privately Held
Web: www.lagrangeelectrical.com
SIC: 3679 Harness assemblies, for electronic use: wire or cable

(G-8951)
MADER MACHINE CO INC
Also Called: Mader Dampers
422 Commerce Dr E (44050-9316)
PHONE..................440 355-4505
Lon Zeager, Pr
Lon James Zeager, *
Nancy Zeager, *
EMP: 32 EST: 1963
SQ FT: 45,000
SALES (est): 3.93MM Privately Held
Web: www.maderdampers.com
SIC: 3822 Damper operators: pneumatic, thermostatic, electric

(G-8952)
MICRON MANUFACTURING INC
186 Commerce Dr (44050-8926)
PHONE..................440 355-4200
Mark A Zupan, Pr
Anne Zupan, *
EMP: 60 EST: 1992
SQ FT: 50,000
SALES (est): 11.13MM Privately Held
Web: www.micronmfg.com
SIC: 3599 Machine shop, jobbing and repair

(G-8953)
NEW AGE DESIGN & TOOL INC
162 Commerce Dr (44050-8926)
PHONE..................440 355-5400
Glen Allen, Pr
Donald Youngblood, Sec
EMP: 18 EST: 1993
SQ FT: 10,000
SALES (est): 893.59K Privately Held
Web: www.newagedesigntool.com

GEOGRAPHIC SECTION

Lakewood - Cuyahoga County (G-8978)

SIC: 3312   Tool and die steel

(G-8954)
PANEL MASTER LLC
191 Commerce Dr (44050-8926)
PHONE..................................440 355-4442
Ridley Watts, *Managing Member*
Cheryl Watts, *Finance*
EMP: 30   EST: 1985
SQ FT: 24,000
SALES (est): 9.52MM **Privately Held**
Web: www.panelmaster.com
SIC: 3613   3625   Control panels, electric; Relays and industrial controls

(G-8955)
STACI HOLDINGS INC
110 Commerce Dr (44050-9491)
PHONE..................................440 284-2500
Jim Thirkill, *Pr*
EMP: 7   EST: 2006
SALES (est): 113.3K **Privately Held**
SIC: 3679   Electronic circuits

(G-8956)
TRIMLINE DIE CORPORATION
421 Commerce Dr E (44050-9316)
P.O. Box 66 (44050-0066)
PHONE..................................440 355-6900
EMP: 20   EST: 1993
SQ FT: 10,000
SALES (est): 4.78MM
SALES (corp-wide): 22.16MM **Privately Held**
Web: www.varbroscorp.com
SIC: 3544   Special dies and tools
PA: Varbros, Llc
      16025 Brookpark Rd
      Cleveland OH 44142
      216 267-5200

(G-8957)
VEXOS INC
Also Called: Vexos Electronic Mfg Svcs
110 Commerce Dr (44050-9491)
PHONE..................................440 284-2500
John Wilkinson, *Sr VP*
EMP: 124
Web: www.vexos.com
SIC: 3672   Printed circuit boards
HQ: Vexos, Inc.
      60 E 42nd St Ste 1250
      New York NY 10165
      855 711-3227

Lakemore
Summit County

(G-8958)
ROBAN INC
1319 Main St (44250-9803)
P.O. Box 3483 (33572-1004)
PHONE..................................330 794-1059
Karen Medzi, *Pr*
EMP: 9   EST: 1972
SQ FT: 7,000
SALES (est): 621.19K **Privately Held**
Web: www.robansignage.com
SIC: 2796   7336   3479   Engraving platemaking services; Silk screen design; Etching on metals

Lakeside
Ottawa County

(G-8959)
CUSTOM CANVAS & BOAT REPR INC
Also Called: Custom Canvas & Upholstery
29 S Bridge Rd (43440-9483)
PHONE..................................419 732-3314
Shawn Harrison, *Pr*
Von Ellis, *VP*
David Walter, *Treas*
Carol Ellis, *Sec*
EMP: 9   EST: 1983
SQ FT: 4,800
SALES (est): 269.07K **Privately Held**
SIC: 2394   Liners and covers, fabric: made from purchased materials

Lakeside Marblehead
Ottawa County

(G-8960)
LAFARGE HOLCIM
831 S Quarry Rd (43440-2576)
PHONE..................................419 798-4866
EMP: 7   EST: 2018
SALES (est): 205.52K **Privately Held**
Web: www.holcim.us
SIC: 3241   Cement, hydraulic

Lakeview
Logan County

(G-8961)
UNITED TOOL AND MACHINE INC
490 N Main St (43331)
P.O. Box 307 (43331)
PHONE..................................937 843-5603
Claude Heintz, *Pr*
Sylvia Heintz, *Treas*
Chris Shrader, *Sec*
EMP: 13   EST: 1973
SQ FT: 41,000
SALES (est): 1.48MM **Privately Held**
Web: www.unitedtoolandmachineinc.com
SIC: 3599   Machine shop, jobbing and repair

Lakeville
Holmes County

(G-8962)
1200 FEET LIMITED
Also Called: Krin USA
41 County Road 2350 (44638-9614)
PHONE..................................419 827-6061
Deaunna F Morgan, *Admn*
EMP: 9   EST: 2013
SALES (est): 926.8K **Privately Held**
SIC: 3569   Filters, general line: industrial

(G-8963)
AXLE MACHINE SERVICES LTD
41 County Road 2350 (44638-9614)
P.O. Box 117 (44611-0117)
PHONE..................................419 827-2000
Dennis Morgan, *Pt*
EMP: 7   EST: 1997
SQ FT: 5,600
SALES (est): 514.85K **Privately Held**
SIC: 3599   Machine shop, jobbing and repair

(G-8964)
MID-OHIO FINISHING LLC
96 County Road 2575 (44638-9608)
PHONE..................................330 466-9117
Erwin E Hochstetler, *Owner*
EMP: 6   EST: 2018
SALES (est): 122.25K **Privately Held**
SIC: 3471   Electroplating of metals or formed products

Lakewood
Cuyahoga County

(G-8965)
717 INC
Also Called: 717 Ink
13000 Athens Ave Ste 110 (44107-6256)
PHONE..................................440 925-0402
EMP: 7   EST: 2010
SALES (est): 556.1K **Privately Held**
SIC: 2262   Screen printing: manmade fiber and silk broadwoven fabrics

(G-8966)
ASSOCIATED SOFTWARE CONS INC
Also Called: A S C
1101 Forest Rd (44107-1028)
PHONE..................................440 826-1010
Tim Liston, *Pr*
John H Liston, *Sec*
EMP: 17   EST: 1978
SALES (est): 2.36MM **Privately Held**
Web: www.powerlender.com
SIC: 7371   7372   Computer software systems analysis and design, custom; Prepackaged software

(G-8967)
BENSAN JEWELERS INC
Also Called: Broestl & Wallis Fine Jewelers
14410 Madison Ave (44107-4513)
PHONE..................................216 221-1434
Daniel D Wallis, *Pr*
Jeffery Broestl, *Sec*
EMP: 7   EST: 1946
SQ FT: 2,106
SALES (est): 999.55K **Privately Held**
Web: www.broestlwallis.com
SIC: 5944   3911   7631   Jewelry, precious stones and precious metals; Jewelry apparel; Jewelry repair services

(G-8968)
CAHILL SERVICES INC
13000 Athens Ave Ste 104e (44107-6256)
P.O. Box 811132 (44181-1132)
PHONE..................................216 410-5595
Christine M Cahill, *Prin*
EMP: 8   EST: 2012
SALES (est): 150.72K **Privately Held**
Web: www.cahillheatingrentals.com
SIC: 2851   Removers and cleaners

(G-8969)
CARE FUSION
14414 Detroit Ave Ste 205 (44107-4473)
PHONE..................................216 521-1220
EMP: 18   EST: 1992
SALES (est): 466.32K **Privately Held**
SIC: 3841   Surgical and medical instruments

(G-8970)
CLEVELAND MICA CO
1360 Hird Ave (44107-3091)
PHONE..................................216 226-1360
Bruce C Burton, *Pr*
Donna Brady, *Sec*
Kevin D Burton, *Stockholder*
EMP: 15   EST: 1932
SQ FT: 16,000
SALES (est): 1.23MM **Privately Held**
Web: www.clevelandmica.com
SIC: 3299   Mica products, built-up or sheet

(G-8971)
COLLECTIVE ARTS NETWORK
1372 Edwards Ave (44107-2346)
P.O. Box 771748 (44107-0067)
PHONE..................................216 235-3564
Michael Gill, *Sec*
EMP: 6   EST: 2015
SALES (est): 379.3K **Privately Held**
Web: www.canjournal.org
SIC: 2721   Periodicals

(G-8972)
COMPUTER ENTERPRISE INC
Also Called: Enterprise Electric
1530 Saint Charles Ave (44107-4341)
PHONE..................................216 228-7156
Vera Prete, *Pr*
Peter Prete, *VP*
EMP: 8   EST: 1991
SALES (est): 184.68K **Privately Held**
Web: www.computerenterprise.com
SIC: 1731   7372   Computerized controls installation; Business oriented computer software

(G-8973)
CREATIVE COATINGS LLC
1634 Waterbury Rd (44107-4977)
PHONE..................................216 226-9058
Michael P Mcguire, *Prin*
EMP: 15   EST: 2011
SALES (est): 81.52K **Privately Held**
Web: www.creativecoatings.com
SIC: 3479   Coating of metals and formed products

(G-8974)
EUCLID STEEL & WIRE INC
Also Called: ES&w
13000 Athens Ave Ste 101 (44107-6233)
PHONE..................................216 731-6744
Donald J Anzells, *Pr*
Donald J Anzells, *Prin*
Charles D Mc Bride, *Prin*
Daniel R Corcoran, *Prin*
T P Mc Mahon, *Prin*
EMP: 27   EST: 1978
SQ FT: 10,400
SALES (est): 485.69K **Privately Held**
Web: www.euclidsteel.com
SIC: 3315   Wire, steel: insulated or armored

(G-8975)
HAWTHORNE WIRE LTD
13000 Athens Ave Ste 101 (44107-6233)
PHONE..................................216 712-4747
Christopher Whiting, *Pr*
EMP: 14   EST: 2005
SALES (est): 543.02K **Privately Held**
Web: www.hawthornewire.com
SIC: 3315   Wire and fabricated wire products

(G-8976)
HEART HEALTHY HOMES CORP
11860 Clifton Blvd (44107-2000)
PHONE..................................216 521-6029
Keith R Jordan, *Pr*
EMP: 8   EST: 2020
SALES (est): 230.66K **Privately Held**
Web: www.owcenter.com
SIC: 2023   Dietary supplements, dairy and non-dairy based

(G-8977)
JOE THE PRINTER GUY LLC
1590 Parkwood Rd (44107-4739)
PHONE..................................216 651-3880
Joseph E Mchugh, *Prin*
EMP: 6   EST: 2008
SALES (est): 347.01K **Privately Held**
SIC: 2752   Commercial printing, lithographic

(G-8978)
LAKEWOOD OBSERVER INC
14900 Detroit Ave Ste 205 (44107-3922)

Lakewood - Cuyahoga County (G-8979)   **GEOGRAPHIC SECTION**

P.O. Box 770203 (44107-0017)
PHONE.................216 712-7070
Jim O'bryan, *Prin*
EMP: 9 **EST:** 2005
SALES (est): 215.12K **Privately Held**
Web: www.lakewoodobserver.com
SIC: 2711 Newspapers, publishing and printing

(G-8979)
NEOGRAF SOLUTIONS LLC
11709 Madison Ave (44107-5230)
PHONE.................216 529-3777
Natesh Krishnan, *CEO*
Drew Walker, *
Tony Glauser, *
Brian Bartos, *
EMP: 181 **EST:** 2016
SALES (est): 49.75MM **Privately Held**
Web: www.neograf.com
SIC: 3624 Electrodes, thermal and electrolytic uses; carbon, graphite

(G-8980)
NORTON INDUSTRIES INC
1366 W 117th St (44107-3011)
PHONE.................888 357-2345
Trisha Rhea, *Pr*
Alan Rhea, *VP*
EMP: 33 **EST:** 1967
SQ FT: 30,000
SALES (est): 3.23MM **Privately Held**
SIC: 3646 2541 Ceiling systems, luminous; Store fixtures, wood

(G-8981)
RAD-CON INC (PA)
Also Called: Entec International Systems
13001 Athens Ave Ste 300 (44107-6246)
PHONE.................440 871-5720
David R Blackman, *Pr*
Christopher Messina, *
Michael Mcdonald, *VP*
Sean Mcgreer, *VP*
▲ **EMP:** 23 **EST:** 1966
SQ FT: 6,000
SALES (est): 9MM
SALES (corp-wide): 9MM **Privately Held**
Web: www.rad-con.com
SIC: 8711 3567 Engineering services; Industrial furnaces and ovens

(G-8982)
RINGER LLC
12906 Arliss Dr (44107-2111)
PHONE.................216 228-1442
Shannon Salupo, *Prin*
EMP: 7 **EST:** 2010
SALES (est): 82.09K **Privately Held**
Web: www.theringer.com
SIC: 2711 Newspapers, publishing and printing

(G-8983)
TRICO ENTERPRISES LLC
17717 Hilliard Rd (44107-5332)
PHONE.................216 970-9984
EMP: 13
Web: www.tricoenterprises.com
SIC: 3553 Woodworking machinery
PA: Trico Enterprises Llc
   6430 Township Road 348
   Millersburg OH 44654

(G-8984)
WESTERN RESERVE DISTILLERS LLC
14221 Madison Ave (44107-4509)
PHONE.................330 780-9599
Kevin Thomas, *Managing Member*
Ann Thomas, *Managing Member*

EMP: 7 **EST:** 2014
SALES (est): 840.98K **Privately Held**
Web: www.westernreservedistillers.com
SIC: 2085 Distilled and blended liquors

Lancaster
Fairfield County

(G-8985)
ACCURATE MECHANICAL INC
566 Mill Park Dr (43130-7744)
PHONE.................740 681-1332
EMP: 58
SALES (corp-wide): 21.57MM **Privately Held**
Web: www.accuratehvac.com
SIC: 5074 5063 3499 1711 Heating equipment (hydronic); Electrical supplies, nec; Aerosol valves, metal; Septic system construction
PA: Accurate Mechanical, Inc.
   3001 River Rd
   Chillicothe OH
   740 775-5005

(G-8986)
ANCHI INC
Also Called: Anchor Hocking
1115 W 5th Ave (43130-2938)
PHONE.................740 653-2527
◆ **EMP:** 1500 **EST:** 2001
SALES (est): 171.52MM
SALES (corp-wide): 697.24MM **Privately Held**
SIC: 3231 Products of purchased glass
HQ: Anchor Hocking, Llc
   1600 Dublin Rd Bldg Ste
   Columbus OH 43215

(G-8987)
ANCHOR HOCKING CONSMR GL CORP
1115 W 5th Ave (43130-2900)
PHONE.................740 653-2527
Mark Eichorn, *Pr*
▼ **EMP:** 7 **EST:** 2006
SALES (est): 596.28K **Privately Held**
Web: www.anchorhocking.com
SIC: 3229 Glassware, art or decorative

(G-8988)
ANCHOR HOCKING GLASS COMPANY
1115 W 5th Ave (43130)
PHONE.................740 681-6025
Mark Eichorn, *Pr*
EMP: 7 **EST:** 2015
SALES (est): 11.15MM
SALES (corp-wide): 697.24MM **Privately Held**
Web: www.firekinggrill.com
SIC: 5023 3263 2821 Glassware; Commercial tableware or kitchen articles, fine earthenware; Plastics materials and resins
PA: Anchor Hocking Holdings, Inc.
   1600 Dublin Rd Ste 200
   Columbus OH 43215
   740 687-2500

(G-8989)
ANCHOR HOCKING GLASS CORP PA
519 N Pierce Ave (43130-2969)
PHONE.................740 681-6275
John Sheppard, *CEO*
EMP: 6 **EST:** 2014
SALES (est): 116.11K **Privately Held**
Web: www.anchorhocking.com

SIC: 3229 Pressed and blown glass, nec

(G-8990)
B & T WELDING AND MACHINE CO
423 S Mount Pleasant Ave (43130-3913)
P.O. Box 987 (43130-0987)
PHONE.................740 687-1908
Alvin R Brown, *Pr*
Patricia Brown, *VP*
Darlene Baker, *Treas*
EMP: 6 **EST:** 1973
SQ FT: 8,500
SALES (est): 474.12K **Privately Held**
SIC: 3599 Machine shop, jobbing and repair

(G-8991)
BABCOCK & WILCOX COMPANY
Also Called: Babcock & Wilcox Co
2600 E Main St (43130-8490)
P.O. Box 415 (43130-0415)
PHONE.................740 687-6500
Chris Mckeown, *Superintnt*
EMP: 99 **EST:** 1977
SALES (est): 44.36MM
SALES (corp-wide): 999.35MM **Publicly Held**
Web: www.babcock.com
SIC: 3511 Turbines and turbine generator sets
PA: Babcock & Wilcox Enterprises, Inc.
   1200 E Market St Ste 650
   Akron OH 44305
   330 753-4511

(G-8992)
BABCOCK & WILCOX ENTPS INC
2560 E Main St (43130-8490)
PHONE.................740 687-4370
EMP: 11
SALES (corp-wide): 999.35MM **Publicly Held**
Web: www.babcock.com
SIC: 3511 Turbines and turbine generator sets
PA: Babcock & Wilcox Enterprises, Inc.
   1200 E Market St Ste 650
   Akron OH 44305
   330 753-4511

(G-8993)
BAINTER MACHINING COMPANY (PA)
1230 Rainbow Dr Ne (43130-1137)
PHONE.................740 653-2422
Daniel A Bainter, *Pr*
Reda L Bainter, *Sec*
EMP: 9 **EST:** 1971
SQ FT: 2,000
SALES (est): 1.96MM
SALES (corp-wide): 1.96MM **Privately Held**
SIC: 3444 3599 Sheet metalwork; Machine shop, jobbing and repair

(G-8994)
BAINTER MACHINING COMPANY
842 N Columbus St (43130-2548)
PHONE.................740 756-4598
Dan Bainter, *Mgr*
EMP: 12
SALES (corp-wide): 1.96MM **Privately Held**
SIC: 3599 Machine shop, jobbing and repair
PA: Bainter Machining Company
   1230 Rainbow Dr Ne
   Lancaster OH 43130
   740 653-2422

(G-8995)
BUCKEYE READY-MIX LLC
Fairfield Concrete
1750 Logan Lancaster Rd Se (43130-9001)
PHONE.................740 654-4423
Jerry Culp, *Mgr*
EMP: 28
SALES (corp-wide): 48.26MM **Privately Held**
Web: www.buckeyereadymix.com
SIC: 3273 Ready-mixed concrete
PA: Buckeye Ready-Mix, Llc
   7657 Taylor Rd Sw
   Reynoldsburg OH 43068
   614 575-2132

(G-8996)
BWX TECHNOLOGIES INC
2600 E Main St (43130-8490)
PHONE.................740 687-4180
Dave Keller, *Brnch Mgr*
EMP: 51
Web: www.bwxt.com
SIC: 3621 Power generators
PA: Bwx Technologies, Inc.
   800 Main St Fl 4
   Lynchburg VA 24504

(G-8997)
C J KRAFT ENTERPRISES INC
Also Called: Bay Packing
301 S Maple St (43130-4406)
PHONE.................740 653-9606
Kathleen Kraft, *Pr*
David Kraft, *VP*
Karen Kraft, *Sec*
EMP: 9 **EST:** 1932
SQ FT: 2,000
SALES (est): 585.46K **Privately Held**
Web: www.bayfoodmarket.com
SIC: 5411 2011 5148 Grocery stores, independent; Meat packing plants; Fruits, fresh

(G-8998)
CAMERON INTERNATIONAL CORP
Also Called: Cameron Valve & Measurement
471 Quarry Rd Se (43130-8272)
PHONE.................740 654-4260
Bill Wingard, *Brnch Mgr*
EMP: 35
Web: www.slb.com
SIC: 3533 Oil and gas field machinery
HQ: Cameron International Corporation
   1333 West Loop S Ste 1700
   Houston TX 77027

(G-8999)
CARNAUDMETALBOX MACHINERY USA
Also Called: Crown Closures Machinery
1765 W Fair Ave (43130-2325)
PHONE.................740 681-6788
EMP: 6 **EST:** 2021
SALES (est): 88.79K **Privately Held**
SIC: 3542 Machine tools, metal forming type

(G-9000)
CIRBA SOLUTIONS US INC (PA)
Also Called: Lithchem
265 Quarry Rd Se (43130-8271)
PHONE.................740 653-6290
Steven Kinsbursky, *CEO*
▲ **EMP:** 29 **EST:** 2013
SALES (est): 46.81MM
SALES (corp-wide): 46.81MM **Privately Held**
Web: www.cirbasolutions.com

GEOGRAPHIC SECTION
Lancaster - Fairfield County (G-9023)

SIC: **2819** 4953 3341 Industrial inorganic chemicals, nec; Recycling, waste materials; Recovery and refining of nonferrous metals

(G-9001)
CIRBA SOLUTIONS US INC
265 Quarry Rd Se (43130-8271)
PHONE.................................740 653-6290
Ed Green, *Brnch Mgr*
EMP: 100
SALES (corp-wide): 46.81MM **Privately Held**
Web: www.cirbasolutions.com
SIC: **3691** Batteries, rechargeable
PA: Cirba Solutions Us, Inc.
   265 Quarry Rd Se
   Lancaster OH 43130
   740 653-6290

(G-9002)
CITY OF LANCASTER
Also Called: Lancaster Municipal Gas
1424 Campground Rd (43130-9503)
PHONE.................................740 687-6670
Michael R Pettit, *Superintnt*
EMP: 46
SALES (corp-wide): 52.07MM **Privately Held**
Web: ci.lancaster.oh.us
SIC: **1311** 4924 Crude petroleum and natural gas; Natural gas distribution
PA: City Of Lancaster
   104 E Main St
   Lancaster OH 43130
   740 687-6600

(G-9003)
CONSOLIDATED GRAPHICS INC
Also Called: Cyril-Scott Company, The
3950 Lancaster New Lexington Rd Se (43130-7899)
PHONE.................................740 654-2112
Chad Stephenson, *Pr*
EMP: 155
SALES (corp-wide): 4.99B **Privately Held**
Web: www.consolidatedgraphicsinc.com
SIC: **2752** Offset printing
HQ: Consolidated Graphics, Inc.
   5858 Westheimer Rd # 200
   Houston TX 77057

(G-9004)
CREATIVE CABINETS LTD
1807 Snoke Rd Sw (43130-8902)
PHONE.................................740 689-0603
EMP: 10 EST: 1996
SQ FT: 15,000
SALES (est): 933.68K **Privately Held**
SIC: **2434** Wood kitchen cabinets

(G-9005)
CROWN CLOSURES MACHINERY
1765 W Fair Ave (43130-2325)
PHONE.................................740 681-6593
John Conway, *CEO*
▲ EMP: 40 EST: 1996
SALES (est): 11.01MM
SALES (corp-wide): 12.01B **Publicly Held**
Web: www.crowncork.com
SIC: **3565** Packaging machinery
PA: Crown Holdings Inc.
   770 Township Line Rd # 100
   Yardley PA 19067
   215 698-5100

(G-9006)
CROWN CORK & SEAL USA INC
940 Mill Park Dr (43130-9786)
PHONE.................................740 681-3000
EMP: 90
SALES (corp-wide): 12.01B **Publicly Held**
Web: www.crowncork.com
SIC: **3089** 3466 3411 Closures, plastics; Closures, stamped metal; Metal cans
HQ: Crown Cork & Seal Usa, Inc.
   770 Township Line Rd
   Yardley PA 19067
   215 698-5100

(G-9007)
CROWN CORK & SEAL USA INC
1765 W Fair Ave (43130-2325)
PHONE.................................740 681-6593
EMP: 98
SALES (corp-wide): 12.01B **Publicly Held**
Web: www.crowncork.com
SIC: **3411** Metal cans
HQ: Crown Cork & Seal Usa, Inc.
   770 Township Line Rd
   Yardley PA 19067
   215 698-5100

(G-9008)
D K MANUFACTURING
2118 Commerce St (43130-9363)
PHONE.................................740 654-5566
Daniel Keifer, *Pr*
EMP: 25 EST: 2004
SALES (est): 960.16K **Privately Held**
Web: www.dkmanufacturing.com
SIC: **3089** Injection molding of plastics

(G-9009)
DEVAULT MACHINE & MOULD CO LLC
Also Called: General Machine and Mould Co
2294 Commerce St (43130-9363)
P.O. Box 785 (43130-0785)
PHONE.................................740 654-5925
Terris E Devault, *Managing Member*
EMP: 7 EST: 1966
SQ FT: 5,000
SALES (est): 725.66K **Privately Held**
Web: www.genmach.com
SIC: **3599** Machine shop, jobbing and repair

(G-9010)
DIAMOND ELECTRONICS INC
Also Called: Honeywell
1858 Cedar Hill Rd (43130-4178)
P.O. Box 415 (43130-0415)
PHONE.................................740 652-9222
George K Broady, *Ch Bd*
EMP: 51 EST: 1946
SQ FT: 72,000
SALES (est): 1.36MM **Privately Held**
SIC: **3663** Television closed circuit equipment

(G-9011)
DIAMOND POWER INTL INC
Also Called: Diamond Electronics
2530 E Main St (43130-8490)
PHONE.................................740 687-4001
Ron Burris, *Mgr*
EMP: 11
SALES (corp-wide): 999.35MM **Publicly Held**
Web: www.babcock.com
SIC: **3823** Process control instruments
HQ: Diamond Power International, Inc.
   2600 E Main St
   Lancaster OH 43130
   740 687-6500

(G-9012)
DIAMOND POWER INTL INC (DH)
Also Called: Diamond Power Specialty
2600 E Main St (43130-9366)
P.O. Box 415 (43130-0415)
PHONE.................................740 687-6500
Eileen M Competti, *Pr*
◆ EMP: 66 EST: 1903
SALES (est): 72.36MM
SALES (corp-wide): 999.35MM **Publicly Held**
Web: www.babcock.com
SIC: **3511** Turbines and turbine generator sets
HQ: The Babcock & Wilcox Company
   1200 E Market St Ste 650
   Akron OH 44305
   330 753-4511

(G-9013)
DISPATCH CONSUMER SERVICES
Also Called: Bag, The
3160 W Fair Ave (43130-9568)
PHONE.................................740 687-1893
Donna Holbrook, *Mgr*
EMP: 115
SALES (corp-wide): 450.12MM **Privately Held**
Web: www.dispatch.com
SIC: **2711** Newspapers, publishing and printing
HQ: Dispatch Consumer Services Inc
   5300 Crosswind Dr
   Columbus OH 43228
   740 548-5555

(G-9014)
DK MANUFACTURING LANCASTER INC
2118 Commerce St (43130-9363)
PHONE.................................740 654-5566
Daniel Keifer, *Pr*
EMP: 72 EST: 2004
SALES (est): 11.67MM
SALES (corp-wide): 39.58MM **Privately Held**
Web: www.dkmanufacturing.com
SIC: **3089** Injection molding of plastics
PA: Dak Enterprises, Inc.
   18062 Timber Trails Rd
   Marysville OH 43040
   740 828-3291

(G-9015)
FAIRFIELD WOOD WORKS LTD
1612 E Main St (43130-3472)
PHONE.................................740 689-1953
Ron Smith, *Pr*
Ben Smith, *VP*
Jed Smith, *VP*
EMP: 7 EST: 1998
SQ FT: 5,000
SALES (est): 811.47K **Privately Held**
Web: www.fairfieldwoodworks.com
SIC: **2434** 2431 Wood kitchen cabinets; Moldings and baseboards, ornamental and trim

(G-9016)
FIMM USA INC
4155 Brook Rd Nw (43130-8317)
PHONE.................................614 568-4874
◆ EMP: 19 EST: 2010
SALES (est): 2.46MM **Privately Held**
Web: www.fimmusa.com
SIC: **3991** Brooms and brushes

(G-9017)
GHP II LLC (DH)
Also Called: Anchor Hocking Indus GL Div
1115 W 5th Ave (43130-2938)
PHONE.................................740 687-2500
Mark Eichorn, *CEO*
Mark Hedstrom, *
George Hamilton, *
◆ EMP: 200 EST: 1905
SQ FT: 41,900
SALES (est): 136.26MM
SALES (corp-wide): 697.24MM **Privately Held**
SIC: **3229** 3089 3411 3221 Tableware, glass or glass ceramic; Cups, plastics, except foam; Metal cans; Glass containers
HQ: Anchor Hocking, Llc
   1600 Dublin Rd Bldg Ste
   Columbus OH 43215

(G-9018)
GHP II LLC
2893 W Fair Ave (43130-8993)
P.O. Box 600 (43130-0600)
PHONE.................................740 681-6825
Tom Gilligan, *Mgr*
EMP: 12
SQ FT: 1,300,000
SALES (corp-wide): 697.24MM **Privately Held**
SIC: **5023** 3231 China; Products of purchased glass
HQ: Ghp Ii, Llc
   1115 W 5th Ave
   Lancaster OH 43130
   740 687-2500

(G-9019)
INCESSANT SOFTWARE INC
8577 Ohio Wesleyan Ct Nw (43130-9329)
PHONE.................................614 206-2211
Al Pruden, *Pr*
EMP: 9 EST: 1997
SALES (est): 507.06K **Privately Held**
SIC: **7372** Prepackaged software

(G-9020)
LANCASTER METAL PRODUCTS INC
520 Slocum St (43130-2998)
PHONE.................................740 653-3421
Max Giles, *Pr*
Dorothy Giles, *VP*
Elizabeth Kilbarger, *VP*
EMP: 19 EST: 1950
SQ FT: 10,000
SALES (est): 2.32MM **Privately Held**
Web: www.lancastermetalproducts.com
SIC: **3599** Machine shop, jobbing and repair

(G-9021)
LANCASTER W SIDE COAL CO INC (PA)
700 Van Buren Ave (43130-2339)
PHONE.................................740 862-4713
Jerry H Fahrer, *Pr*
Mary K Cann, *VP*
Bruce Fahrer, *Treas*
William Cann, *Sec*
EMP: 1925
SQ FT: 1,600
SALES (est): 983.91K
SALES (corp-wide): 983.91K **Privately Held**
SIC: **3273** 5211 5032 Ready-mixed concrete; Lumber and other building materials; Brick, stone, and related material

(G-9022)
LITHCHEM INTL TOXCO INC
265 Quarry Rd Se (43130-8271)
PHONE.................................740 653-6290
Ed Green, *Prin*
EMP: 13 EST: 1998
SALES (est): 266.4K **Privately Held**
SIC: **3691** Storage batteries

(G-9023)
MARGO TOOL TECHNOLOGY INC
2616 Setter Ct Nw (43130-9151)
PHONE.................................740 653-8115
John Porter, *Pr*
Jeff Ellis, *Sec*
EMP: 10 EST: 1977
SQ FT: 7,500

(PA)=Parent Co (HQ)=Headquarters
✪ = New Business established in last 2 years

Lancaster - Fairfield County (G-9024)

SALES (est): 2.01MM **Privately Held**
Web: www.margotool.com
SIC: 3599 Machine shop, jobbing and repair

(G-9024)
MID-WEST FABRICATING CO
885 Mill Park Dr (43130-8061)
PHONE.................................740 277-7021
Ann Custer, *VP*
EMP: 20
SALES (corp-wide): 28.07MM **Privately Held**
Web: www.midwestfab.com
SIC: 3452 Bolts, metal
PA: Mid-West Fabricating Co.
313 N Johns St
Amanda OH 43102
740 969-4411

(G-9025)
MONDI PAKAGING
0105 Wilson Rd (43130-8144)
PHONE.................................541 686-2665
Dan Saunders, *Contrlr*
EMP: 7 **EST:** 2019
SALES (est): 247.56K **Privately Held**
SIC: 2611 Pulp mills

(G-9026)
MUSTER RDU INC
1450 E Walnut St (43130-4000)
PHONE.................................614 537-5440
Darin Hadinger, *CEO*
Al Burzynski, *Pr*
Sean Curran, *Prin*
Elizabeth Mallett, *Prin*
EMP: 8 **EST:** 2020
SALES (est): 454.53K **Privately Held**
SIC: 2451 Mobile buildings: for commercial use

(G-9027)
NEIL R SCHOLL INC
54 Snoke Hill Rd Ne (43130-9315)
PHONE.................................740 653-6593
Neil R Scholl, *Pr*
Betty Scholl, *VP*
EMP: 10 **EST:** 1954
SQ FT: 2,000
SALES (est): 577.71K **Privately Held**
SIC: 3599 5084 Custom machinery; Industrial machinery and equipment

(G-9028)
NEWELL HOLDINGS DELAWARE INC
1115 W 5th Ave (43130-2938)
PHONE.................................740 681-6461
◆ **EMP:** 61
SIC: 3211 Building glass, flat

(G-9029)
NICKLAUS GROUP LLC
1649 River Valley Cir N (43130-8401)
PHONE.................................740 277-5700
EMP: 10 **EST:** 2020
SALES (est): 788.92K **Privately Held**
Web: www.cabinetsbytng.com
SIC: 2434 Wood kitchen cabinets

(G-9030)
NORTH END PRESS INCORPORATED
235 S Columbus St (43130-4315)
PHONE.................................740 653-6514
Richard Benadum, *Pr*
Greg Benadum, *VP*
Brad A Benadum, *VP*
EMP: 17 **EST:** 1933
SQ FT: 55,000
SALES (est): 486.25K **Privately Held**
Web: krisnorthendpress.wixsite.com

SIC: 2789 Bookbinding and related work

(G-9031)
NORWESCO INC
3111 Wilson Rd (43130-8144)
PHONE.................................740 654-6402
Darrin Dittman, *Mgr*
EMP: 12
SQ FT: 15,000
Web: www.norwesco.com
SIC: 3089 Plastics and fiberglass tanks
HQ: Norwesco, Inc.
2200 Commerce Blvd
Mound MN 55364
952 446-1945

(G-9032)
PRECISION CNC LLC
1858 Cedar Hill Rd (43130-4178)
PHONE.................................740 689-9009
Paul Davis, *Managing Member*
Nathan Hawkins, *
EMP: 28 **EST:** 2006
SQ FT: 10,000
SALES (est): 4.45MM **Privately Held**
Web: www.precision-cnc.com
SIC: 3599 Machine shop, jobbing and repair

(G-9033)
PROFESSIONAL SCREEN PRINTING
731 N Pierce Ave (43130-2416)
PHONE.................................740 687-0760
Jeff Uhl, *Pr*
EMP: 8 **EST:** 1987
SQ FT: 3,000
SALES (est): 800K **Privately Held**
Web: www.professionalscreenprintinginc.com
SIC: 7336 2752 Silk screen design; Commercial printing, lithographic

(G-9034)
QUALITY RUBBER STAMP INC
1777 Victor Rd Nw (43130-0100)
PHONE.................................614 235-2700
John J Lawler, *Pr*
EMP: 8 **EST:** 1971
SALES (est): 865.8K **Privately Held**
Web: www.qrsohio.com
SIC: 3953 3083 2396 2395 Numbering stamps, hand: rubber or metal; Plastics finished products, laminated; Screen printing on fabric articles; Embroidery and art needlework

(G-9035)
R F I
276 Bremen Rd (43130-7873)
PHONE.................................740 654-4502
Don Eiferd, *Prin*
EMP: 6 **EST:** 2008
SALES (est): 119.1K **Privately Held**
SIC: 3699 Security control equipment and systems

(G-9036)
RABLE MACHINE INC
1858 Cedar Hill Rd (43130-4178)
PHONE.................................740 689-9009
Kris Porte, *Admn*
EMP: 45 **EST:** 2021
SALES (est): 2.37MM **Privately Held**
Web: www.rablemachineinc.com
SIC: 3999 Manufacturing industries, nec

(G-9037)
RD HOLDER OIL CO
238 N Pierce Ave (43130-3613)
PHONE.................................740 653-4031
EMP: 6 **EST:** 2019

SALES (est): 275.25K **Privately Held**
Web: www.holderoil.com
SIC: 2911 Road oils

(G-9038)
SHERIDAN ONE STOP CARRYOUT INC
1510 Sheridan Dr (43130-1303)
PHONE.................................740 687-1300
Eric Molzan, *Owner*
EMP: 7 **EST:** 1981
SALES (est): 666.67K **Privately Held**
SIC: 1311 Crude petroleum and natural gas

(G-9039)
SMITH RN SHEET METAL SHOP INC
1312 Campground Rd (43130-9503)
PHONE.................................740 653-5011
Patrick Smith, *Pr*
Sue Smith, *
Mary Jo Smith, *
EMP: 16 **EST:** 1922
SQ FT: 1,800
SALES (est): 2.21MM **Privately Held**
Web: www.rnsmith.net
SIC: 3444 Sheet metalwork

(G-9040)
SOUTHSTERN MCHNING FELD SVC IN (PA)
500 Lincoln Ave (43130-4243)
PHONE.................................740 689-1147
John Treitmaier, *Pr*
EMP: 37 **EST:** 1989
SQ FT: 6,500
SALES (est): 9.26MM **Privately Held**
Web: www.semohio.com
SIC: 3599 Machine shop, jobbing and repair

(G-9041)
SRI OHIO INC
1061 Mill Park Dr (43130-9577)
PHONE.................................740 653-5800
Bonnita Heston, *Prin*
▲ **EMP:** 40 **EST:** 2010
SALES (est): 7.85MM **Privately Held**
Web: www.serigraphierichford.com
SIC: 2759 Screen printing

(G-9042)
TED M FIGGINS
Also Called: Glass City Machining and Fab
347 S Columbus St Pmb 634 (43130-4329)
PHONE.................................740 277-3750
Ted M Figgins, *Owner*
EMP: 14 **EST:** 2015
SALES (est): 450K **Privately Held**
Web: www.glasscitymachining.com
SIC: 3441 3599 Fabricated structural metal; Machine shop, jobbing and repair

(G-9043)
THE CYRIL-SCOTT COMPANY
3950 Lancaster New Lexington Rd Se (43130-7899)
PHONE.................................740 654-2112
▲ **EMP:** 150
SIC: 2759 Commercial printing, nec

(G-9044)
THORWALD HOLDINGS INC
Also Called: Martins Partitions
866 Mill Park Dr (43130-2572)
P.O. Box 102 (43112-0102)
PHONE.................................740 756-9271
Tamara Miller, *Pr*
Bruce Miller, *Treas*
EMP: 15 **EST:** 2007
SALES (est): 1.04MM **Privately Held**

SIC: 2631 Packaging board

(G-9045)
TOXCO INC
265 Quarry Rd Se (43130-8271)
PHONE.................................740 653-6290
Ed Green, *Brnch Mgr*
EMP: 48
SALES (corp-wide): 23.94MM **Privately Held**
Web: www.toxco.com
SIC: 3691 Batteries, rechargeable
PA: Toxco, Inc.
125 E Commercial St Ste A
Anaheim CA 92801
714 738-8516

(G-9046)
TREEHOUSE PRIVATE BRANDS INC
Also Called: Ralston Food
3775 Lancaster New Lexington Rd Se (43130-9314)
PHONE.................................740 654-8880
Andy Rohrbach, *Brnch Mgr*
EMP: 258
SALES (corp-wide): 3.43B **Publicly Held**
Web: treehousefoods2023rb.q4web.com
SIC: 2043 Cereal breakfast foods
HQ: Treehouse Private Brands, Inc.
2021 Spring Rd Ste 600
Oak Brook IL 60523

(G-9047)
TREEHOUSE PRIVATE BRANDS INC
276 Bremen Rd (43130-7873)
PHONE.................................740 654-8880
Gary Rodkin, *CEO*
EMP: 32
SALES (corp-wide): 3.43B **Publicly Held**
Web: treehousefoods2023rb.q4web.com
SIC: 2043 Cereal breakfast foods
HQ: Treehouse Private Brands, Inc.
2021 Spring Rd Ste 600
Oak Brook IL 60523

(G-9048)
TRUE VISION
1726 E Main St (43130-9437)
PHONE.................................740 277-7550
EMP: 7 **EST:** 2019
SALES (est): 241.77K **Privately Held**
Web: www.drannahopkins.com
SIC: 8049 8042 5047 3827 Offices of health practitioner; Offices and clinics of optometrists; Medical and hospital equipment; Optical instruments and lenses

(G-9049)
ZEBCO INDUSTRIES INC
211 N Columbus St (43130-3006)
PHONE.................................740 654-4510
Kevin Stalter, *Pr*
Jill Stalter, *VP*
Madonna Christy, *Sec*
EMP: 19 **EST:** 1965
SQ FT: 128,000
SALES (est): 3.19MM **Privately Held**
Web: www.zebcoindustries.com
SIC: 3086 5113 2671 Packaging and shipping materials, foamed plastics; Industrial and personal service paper; Paper; coated and laminated packaging

Lansing
Belmont County

(G-9050)
VINO DI PICCIN LLC
55155 National Rd (43934)

▲ = Import ▼ = Export
◆ = Import/Export

GEOGRAPHIC SECTION

Lebanon - Warren County (G-9072)

P.O. Box 408 (43934-0408)
PHONE...................740 738-0261
Louis Piccin, *CEO*
John Piccin, *Pr*
Sharon Acosta, *Sec*
Steve Piccin, *VP*
Nina Lenz, *VP*
EMP: 14 **EST:** 2010
SQ FT: 3,600
SALES (est): 701K **Privately Held**
Web: www.vinodipiccin.com
SIC: 2084 Wine cellars, bonded: engaged in blending wines

Latham
Pike County

(G-9051)
LATHAM LIMESTONE LLC
6424 State Route 124 (45646-9703)
PHONE...................740 493-2677
EMP: 8 **EST:** 1960
SQ FT: 500
SALES (est): 562.7K **Privately Held**
Web: www.jrjnet.com
SIC: 1422 Limestones, ground

(G-9052)
LATHAM LUMBER & PALLET CO
9445 Street Rte 124 (45646)
P.O. Box 147 (45646-0147)
PHONE...................740 493-2707
Karen Chandler, *Pr*
EMP: 9 **EST:** 1973
SQ FT: 12,000
SALES (est): 255.59K **Privately Held**
SIC: 2499 Mulch, wood and bark

Latty
Paulding County

(G-9053)
AL-CO PRODUCTS INC
485 2nd St (45855)
P.O. Box 74 (45855-0074)
PHONE...................419 399-3867
Russell W Stoller, *Pr*
John F Kohler, *VP*
Trent Stoller, *Sec*
EMP: 9 **EST:** 1968
SQ FT: 11,000
SALES (est): 1.17MM
SALES (corp-wide): 5.24MM **Privately Held**
Web: www.al-coproducts.com
SIC: 3281 3949 2821 2434 Marble, building: cut and shaped; Sporting and athletic goods, nec; Plastics materials and resins; Wood kitchen cabinets
PA: Haviland Drainage Products Co.
    100 Main St
    Haviland OH 45851
    800 860-6294

Laurelville
Hocking County

(G-9054)
C & L ERECTORS & RIGGERS INC
16412 Thompson Ridge Rd (43135-9238)
P.O. Box 98 (43135-0098)
PHONE...................740 332-7185
Chris Riddle, *Pr*
Craig Riddle, *VP*
Dale W Riddle, *Stockholder*
EMP: 11 **EST:** 1967
SQ FT: 1,500

SALES (est): 688.08K **Privately Held**
SIC: 1629 2411 Land clearing contractor; Logging

(G-9055)
JACK PINE STUDIO LLC
21397 State Route 180 (43135-9307)
PHONE...................740 332-2223
EMP: 7 **EST:** 2017
SALES (est): 424.42K **Privately Held**
Web: www.jackpinestudio.com
SIC: 3229 Pressed and blown glass, nec

(G-9056)
T & D THOMPSON INC
Also Called: Hocking Hills Hardwoods
15952 State Route 56 E (43135-9741)
P.O. Box 88 (43135-0088)
PHONE...................740 332-8515
Terry L Thompson, *Pr*
David R Thompson, *
EMP: 31 **EST:** 1975
SQ FT: 50,000
SALES (est): 1.07MM **Privately Held**
Web: www.hardwoodproducts.com
SIC: 2448 2449 2431 2426 Pallets, wood; Wood containers, nec; Millwork; Hardwood dimension and flooring mills

Leavittsburg
Trumbull County

(G-9057)
DENMAN TIRE CORPORATION
400 Diehl South Rd (44430-9705)
PHONE...................330 675-4242
▲ **EMP:** 200
SIC: 3011 Pneumatic tires, all types

(G-9058)
LAURENCO SYSTEMS OF OHIO LLC
4255 W Market St (44430-9555)
P.O. Box 241 (44430-0241)
▲ **EMP:** 7 **EST:** 1992
SALES (est): 810K **Privately Held**
SIC: 2891 2295 Adhesives and sealants; Waterproofing fabrics, except rubberizing

Lebanon
Warren County

(G-9059)
ADDITION MANUFACTURING TECHNOLOGIES LLC
Also Called: Addisonmckee
1637 Kingsview Dr (45036-8395)
PHONE...................513 228-7000
▲ **EMP:** 175
Web: www.numalliance.com
SIC: 3542 3599 5084 3549 Bending machines; Machine shop, jobbing and repair ; Industrial machinery and equipment; Metalworking machinery, nec

(G-9060)
ADVICS MANUFACTURING OHIO INC
Also Called: Advics
1650 Kingsview Dr (45036-8390)
PHONE...................513 932-7878
Geoff Hearsum, *Pr*
Atsuo Matsumoto, *
◆ **EMP:** 625 **EST:** 2003
SQ FT: 323,000
SALES (est): 106.75MM **Privately Held**
Web: www.advics-ohio.com
SIC: 3714 Motor vehicle brake systems and parts

HQ: Advics North America, Inc.
    1650 Kingsview Dr
    Lebanon OH 45036
    513 696-5450

(G-9061)
ALLEN FIELDS ASSOC INC
3525 Grant Ave Ste D (45036-6431)
PHONE...................513 228-1010
Raymond Watson, *Owner*
EMP: 34 **EST:** 2004
SALES (est): 1.56MM **Privately Held**
Web: www.fieldselectric.com
SIC: 3699 5063 Electrical equipment and supplies, nec; Electrical apparatus and equipment

(G-9062)
AVID SIGNS PLUS LLC
495 Lakeside Dr (45036-1630)
PHONE...................513 932-7446
Greg L Davis, *Admn*
EMP: 6 **EST:** 2017
SALES (est): 156.18K **Privately Held**
Web: www.avidsignsplus.com
SIC: 3993 Signs and advertising specialties

(G-9063)
AWS INDUSTRIES INC
Also Called: Tomak Precision
2600 Henkle Dr (45036-8026)
PHONE...................513 932-7941
Alvin W Schaeper, *Pr*
Paul Balash, *
EMP: 45 **EST:** 1953
SQ FT: 20,000
SALES (est): 9.99MM **Privately Held**
Web: www.tomak.com
SIC: 3728 3841 Aircraft parts and equipment, nec; Surgical and medical instruments

(G-9064)
BIG CHIEF MANUFACTURING LTD
250 Harmon Ave (45036-8800)
PHONE...................513 934-3888
James Howe Junior, *Pt*
▲ **EMP:** 25 **EST:** 1998
SQ FT: 20,000
SALES (est): 5.42MM
SALES (corp-wide): 11.38MM **Privately Held**
Web: www.bigchiefmanufacturing.org
SIC: 3545 Machine tool accessories
HQ: Big Chief Supply Llc
    5150 Big Chief Dr
    Cincinnati OH 45227
    513 271-7411

(G-9065)
BUNNELL HILL CONSTRUCTION INC
3000g Henkle Dr (45036-9258)
PHONE...................513 932-6010
Kevin Scott, *Pr*
EMP: 12 **EST:** 1994
SALES (est): 1.01MM **Privately Held**
SIC: 1389 Construction, repair, and dismantling services

(G-9066)
CARL E OEDER SONS SAND & GRAV
Also Called: Sand & Gravel
1000 Mason Morrow Millgrove Rd (45036)
PHONE...................513 494-1555
Carl Edward Oeder, *Pr*
David Oeder, *
Verna Rae Oeder, *
Diane Browning, *
EMP: 10 **EST:** 1955
SQ FT: 23,600
SALES (est): 467.85K **Privately Held**

Web: www.oedersgravel.com
SIC: 1442 4212 7538 Sand mining; Dump truck haulage; Truck engine repair, except industrial

(G-9067)
CLOUTH SPRENGER LLC
1425 Kingsview Dr (45036-7591)
PHONE...................937 642-8390
▲ **EMP:** 13 **EST:** 2010
SALES (est): 1.14MM **Publicly Held**
Web: www.clouth.com
SIC: 3316 Strip, steel, razor blade, cold-rolled: purchased hot-rolled
PA: Kadant Inc.
    1 Technology Park Dr # 210
    Westford MA 01886

(G-9068)
CONTEMPRARY IMAGE LABELING INC
2034 Mckinley Blvd (45036-6425)
PHONE...................513 583-5699
EMP: 6 **EST:** 1994
SQ FT: 18,000
SALES (est): 965.69K **Privately Held**
SIC: 2759 Labels and seals: printing, nsk

(G-9069)
D & E MACHINE CO
962 S Us Route 42 (45036-7918)
PHONE...................513 932-2184
Kent P Coomer, *Pr*
Tim Wilkerson, *Opers Mgr*
Kimberly A Coomer, *VP*
EMP: 9 **EST:** 1990
SQ FT: 12,000
SALES (est): 1.64MM **Privately Held**
Web: www.demachine.com
SIC: 3599 Machine shop, jobbing and repair

(G-9070)
DUSTY DUCTZ LLC
518 Terrace Creek Ct (45036-8119)
PHONE...................317 462-9622
Aleena Taulbee-le, *Ofcr*
EMP: 7 **EST:** 2013
SALES (est): 87.26K **Privately Held**
SIC: 3714 Motor vehicle parts and accessories

(G-9071)
E-BEAM SERVICES INC
2775 Henkle Dr Unit B (45036-8256)
PHONE...................513 933-0031
Dave Keenan, *Brnch Mgr*
EMP: 24
SQ FT: 129,116
SALES (corp-wide): 11.85MM **Privately Held**
Web: www.ebeamservices.com
SIC: 3699 Electronic training devices
PA: E-Beam Services, Inc.
    270 Duffy Ave Ste H
    Hicksville NY 11801
    516 622-1422

(G-9072)
ECOLAB INC
726 E Main St Ste F (45036-1900)
PHONE...................513 932-0830
Dan Elam, *Dist Mgr*
EMP: 8
SALES (corp-wide): 15.32B **Publicly Held**
Web: www.ecolab.com
SIC: 2842 Sanitation preparations, disinfectants and deodorants
PA: Ecolab Inc.
    1 Ecolab Pl
    Saint Paul MN 55102
    800 232-6522

(PA)=Parent Co (HQ)=Headquarters
✪ = New Business established in last 2 years

Lebanon - Warren County (G-9073) — GEOGRAPHIC SECTION

(G-9073)
ERNST ENTERPRISES INC
4250 Columbia Rd (45036-9589)
PHONE..................513 874-8300
Robert Himes, *Mgr*
EMP: 28
SQ FT: 2,822
SALES (corp-wide): 240.08MM **Privately Held**
Web: www.ernstconcrete.com
SIC: 3273 Ready-mixed concrete
PA: Ernst Enterprises, Inc.
    3361 Successful Way
    Dayton OH 45414
    937 233-5555

(G-9074)
FB ACQUISITION LLC
2025 Mckinley Blvd (45036-8075)
PHONE..................513 459-7782
Alex Weaner, *Pr*
Alexander Weaner, *
EMP: 42 EST: 2021
SALES (est): 1.61MM **Privately Held**
SIC: 3398 3999 Annealing of metal; Manufacturing industries, nec

(G-9075)
FECON LLC
1087b Mane Way (45036-8049)
PHONE..................513 696-4430
John Heekin, *Pr*
EMP: 26
SIC: 3523 Farm machinery and equipment
PA: Fecon, Llc
    3460 Grant Ave
    Lebanon OH 45036

(G-9076)
FECON LLC (PA)
3460 Grant Ave (45036-6432)
PHONE..................513 696-4430
▲ EMP: 75 EST: 1992
SALES (est): 26.06MM **Privately Held**
Web: www.fecon.com
SIC: 3523 3531 Farm machinery and equipment; Construction machinery

(G-9077)
FLEXOPARTS COM
1054 Monroe Rd (45036-2889)
PHONE..................513 932-2060
EMP: 6 EST: 2016
SALES (est): 241.83K **Privately Held**
Web: www.flexoparts.com
SIC: 2759 Commercial printing, nec

(G-9078)
GENERGY
1623 Kirby Rd (45036-9205)
PHONE..................937 477-3628
Edward Heft, *Prin*
EMP: 6 EST: 2017
SALES (est): 217.19K **Privately Held**
Web: www.genergymfg.com
SIC: 3999 Manufacturing industries, nec

(G-9079)
GEORGE MANUFACTURING INC
160 Harmon Ave (45036-9511)
PHONE..................513 932-1067
EMP: 15 EST: 1995
SQ FT: 60,000
SALES (est): 385.1K **Privately Held**
SIC: 3312 3479 3444 Pipes and tubes; Painting, coating, and hot dipping; Sheet metalwork

(G-9080)
GEORGE STEEL FABRICATING INC
1207 Us Route 42 S (45036-8198)
PHONE..................513 932-2887
John George, *Pr*
Kevin Nickell, *
Brad Frost, *
EMP: 35 EST: 1960
SQ FT: 32,100
SALES (est): 5.02MM **Privately Held**
Web: www.georgesteel.com
SIC: 7692 3441 3599 Welding repair; Fabricated structural metal; Machine shop, jobbing and repair

(G-9081)
GEORGIA-PACIFIC PCPI INC
Also Called: Pax Corrugated Products, Inc.
1899 Kingsview Dr (45036-8397)
PHONE..................513 932-9855
Stan Bernard, *CEO*
James E Cory Ii, *Pr*
EMP: 100 EST: 1990
SQ FT: 119,457
SALES (est): 26.59MM
SALES (corp-wide): 36.93B **Privately Held**
Web: www.welchpkg.com
SIC: 2653 Boxes, corrugated: made from purchased materials
HQ: Georgia-Pacific Llc
    133 Peachtree St Nw
    Atlanta GA 30303
    404 652-4000

(G-9082)
GEYGAN ENTERPRISES INC
Also Called: Minuteman Press
101 Dave Ave Ste E (45036-2293)
PHONE..................513 932-4222
Michael Geygan, *Pr*
EMP: 15 EST: 1979
SALES (est): 324.42K **Privately Held**
Web: www.mmpressleb.com
SIC: 2752 7334 2759 5999 Commercial printing, lithographic; Photocopying and duplicating services; Labels and seals: printing, nsk; Rubber stamps

(G-9083)
GMI COMPANIES INC (PA)
Also Called: Ghent Manufacturing
2999 Henkle Dr (45036-9260)
PHONE..................513 932-3445
George L Leasure, *Ch*
Mary Alice Leasure, *
◆ EMP: 130 EST: 1970
SQ FT: 101,000
SALES (est): 23.2MM
SALES (corp-wide): 23.2MM **Privately Held**
Web: www.ghent.com
SIC: 2531 2493 2599 2541 Blackboards, wood; Bulletin boards, wood; Boards: planning, display, notice; Showcases, except refrigerated: wood

(G-9084)
GMI COMPANIES INC
Ghent A Division GMI Companies
2999 Henkle Dr (45036-9260)
PHONE..................513 932-3445
George L Leasure, *Pr*
EMP: 7
SALES (corp-wide): 23.2MM **Privately Held**
Web: www.ghent.com
SIC: 2531 2493 2599 2541 Blackboards, wood; Bulletin boards, wood; Boards: planning, display, notice; Showcases, except refrigerated: wood
PA: Gmi Companies, Inc.
    2999 Henkle Dr
    Lebanon OH 45036
    513 932-3445

(G-9085)
GOLDEN TURTLE CHOCOLATE FCTRY
120 S Broadway St Ste 1 (45036-1729)
P.O. Box 647 (45036-0647)
PHONE..................513 932-1990
Joy Kossouji, *Owner*
Ted Kossouji, *Pt*
EMP: 6 EST: 1982
SQ FT: 3,000
SALES (est): 474.32K **Privately Held**
SIC: 2066 5441 5947 Chocolate; Candy, nut, and confectionery stores; Gifts and novelties

(G-9086)
GRAFISK MASKINFABRIK AMER LLC
Also Called: Grafisk Msknfabrik-America LLC
603 Norgal Dr Ste F (45036-9382)
PHONE..................630 432-4370
▲ EMP: 11 EST: 2011
SALES (est): 509.11K
SALES (corp-wide): 11.09MM **Privately Held**
Web: www.gmfinishing.com
SIC: 2759 Commercial printing, nec
PA: Grafisk Maskinfabrik A/S
    Klintehoj Vange 12
    Birkerod
    45812300

(G-9087)
GREEN BAY PACKAGING INC
Cincinnati Division
760 Kingsview Dr (45036-9554)
PHONE..................513 489-8700
Wayne Petersen, *Mgr*
EMP: 71
SQ FT: 103,000
SALES (corp-wide): 1.87B **Privately Held**
Web: www.gbpcoated.com
SIC: 2653 3412 Boxes, corrugated: made from purchased materials; Metal barrels, drums, and pails
PA: Green Bay Packaging Inc.
    1700 N Webster Ave
    Green Bay WI 54302
    920 433-5111

(G-9088)
HEAT SENSOR TECHNOLOGIE LLC
Also Called: Heat & Sensor
627 Norgal Dr (45036-9275)
PHONE..................513 228-0481
Gary Shackeford, *Managing Member*
Michelle Shackeford, *
▲ EMP: 53 EST: 2002
SQ FT: 12,000
SALES (est): 9.33MM **Privately Held**
Web: www.heatandsensortech.com
SIC: 3567 Heating units and devices, industrial: electric

(G-9089)
INX INTERNATIONAL INK CO
Also Called: INX INTERNATIONAL INK CO
350 Homan Rd (45036-1181)
PHONE..................707 693-2990
EMP: 10
Web: www.inxinternational.com
SIC: 2893 Printing ink
HQ: Inx International Ink Co.
    150 N Martingale Rd # 700
    Schaumburg IL 60173
    630 382-1800

(G-9090)
JBM PACKAGING COMPANY
Also Called: Jbm Packaging
2850 Henkle Dr (45036-8894)
P.O. Box 828 (45036-0828)
PHONE..................513 933-8333
▲ EMP: 150 EST: 1985
SALES (est): 23.84MM **Privately Held**
Web: www.jbmpackaging.com
SIC: 2677 5112 Envelopes; Envelopes

(G-9091)
KADANT BLACK CLAWSON INC (HQ)
1425 Kingsview Dr (45036-7591)
PHONE..................513 229-8100
Jonathan W Painter, *Pr*
Thomas M Obrie, *
Sandra Lambert, *
◆ EMP: 75 EST: 1893
SQ FT: 20,000
SALES (est): 51.21MM **Publicly Held**
Web: fiberprocessing.kadant.com
SIC: 3554 Paper industries machinery
PA: Kadant Inc.
    1 Technology Park Dr # 210
    Westford MA 01886

(G-9092)
KANDO OF CINCINNATI INC
Also Called: Franklin Brazing Met Treating
2025 Mckinley Blvd (45036-8075)
PHONE..................513 459-7782
EMP: 50 EST: 1972
SQ FT: 53,000
SALES (est): 4.6MM **Privately Held**
Web: www.franklinbrazing.com
SIC: 3398 Brazing (hardening) of metal

(G-9093)
KIRBYS AUTO AND TRUCK REPR INC
Also Called: Warren Welding and Fabrication
875 Columbus Ave (45036-1692)
PHONE..................513 934-3999
Glen Kirby, *Pr*
Jennifer Kirby, *Sec*
EMP: 8 EST: 1996
SQ FT: 12,510
SALES (est): 946.88K **Privately Held**
Web: www.kirbysautorepair.com
SIC: 7538 7692 General automotive repair shops; Welding repair

(G-9094)
LUCAS SUMITOMO BRAKES INC
1650 Kingsview Dr (45036-8390)
PHONE..................513 934-0024
Paul C Hirt, *Prin*
EMP: 46 EST: 2005
SALES (est): 580.83K **Privately Held**
Web: www.advics-ohio.com
SIC: 3714 5013 5015 Motor vehicle brake systems and parts; Automotive brakes; Motor vehicle parts, used

(G-9095)
MAGGARD MMRALS LSER ART TECH L
19 N Sycamore St (45036-2041)
PHONE..................513 282-6969
EMP: 7 EST: 2006
SALES (est): 443.99K **Privately Held**
Web: www.maggardmemorials.com
SIC: 5999 3281 Monuments and tombstones; Monument or burial stone, cut and shaped

(G-9096)
MANE INC (DH)
Also Called: Mane Calafornia
2501 Henkle Dr (45036-7794)

GEOGRAPHIC SECTION
Lebanon - Warren County (G-9120)

PHONE..................513 248-9876
Jean Mane, *Ch Bd*
Brad Kelley, *
◆ **EMP:** 70 **EST:** 1998
SQ FT: 70,000
SALES (est): 105.12MM **Privately Held**
Web: www.mane.com
SIC: 2087 2099 Extracts, flavoring; Food preparations, nec
HQ: Mane Usa Inc.
60 Demarest Dr
Wayne NJ 07470
973 633-5533

(G-9097)
MIDWEST CONTAINER CORPORATION
1899 Kingsview Dr (45036)
PHONE..................513 870-3000
EMP: 20 **EST:** 1988
SALES (est): 2.54MM **Privately Held**
Web: www.midwestcontainercorporation.com
SIC: 2653 Boxes, corrugated: made from purchased materials

(G-9098)
NEWMAN DIAPHRAGMS LLC
964 W Main St (45036-9173)
PHONE..................513 932-7379
David Wj Newman, *Mgr*
EMP: 20 **EST:** 2021
SALES (est): 700K **Privately Held**
Web: www.newmangasket.com
SIC: 3053 Gaskets, all materials

(G-9099)
NEWMAN INTERNATIONAL INC
Also Called: Newman Sanitary Gasket
964 W Main St (45036-9173)
P.O. Box 222 (45036-0222)
PHONE..................513 932-7379
▲ **EMP:** 14 **EST:** 1988
SALES (est): 353.67K **Privately Held**
Web: www.newmangasket.com
SIC: 3053 Gaskets, all materials

(G-9100)
NEWMAN SANITARY GASKET COMPANY
964 W Main St (45036-9173)
P.O. Box 222 (45036-0222)
PHONE..................513 932-7379
David William Newman, *Pr*
Thomas Moore, *
EMP: 41 **EST:** 1973
SQ FT: 38,000
SALES (est): 4.52MM **Privately Held**
Web: www.newmangasket.com
SIC: 3053 Gaskets, all materials

(G-9101)
NICHOLSON MANUFACTURING CO LLC
1425 Kingsview Dr (45036-7591)
PHONE..................978 776-2000
Fatima Peeples, *Prin*
EMP: 6 **EST:** 2019
SALES (est): 443.66K **Publicly Held**
SIC: 3999 Manufacturing industries, nec
PA: Kadant Inc.
1 Technology Park Dr # 210
Westford MA 01886

(G-9102)
NORRENBROCK COMPANY INC
249 Wood Forge Cir (45036-8559)
PHONE..................513 316-1383
Gary Nottingham, *Prin*
EMP: 6 **EST:** 2018

SALES (est): 127.13K **Privately Held**
SIC: 3444 Sheet metalwork

(G-9103)
ONPOWER INC
3525 Grant Ave Ste A (45036)
PHONE..................513 228-2100
Larry D Davis, *Pr*
Tom Mergy, *
EMP: 27 **EST:** 2001
SQ FT: 41,350
SALES (est): 8MM **Privately Held**
Web: www.onpowerinc.com
SIC: 3511 8711 Gas turbines, mechanical drive; Consulting engineer

(G-9104)
OVERLY HAUTZ MOTOR BASE CO
Also Called: Overly Hautz Company
285 S West St (45036-2152)
P.O. Box 837 (45036-0837)
PHONE..................513 932-0025
Thomas Copanas, *Pr*
Edward Bees, *
Clara Mendez Dof, *Prin*
▲ **EMP:** 50 **EST:** 1984
SQ FT: 27,000
SALES (est): 9.44MM **Privately Held**
Web: www.overlyhautz.com
SIC: 3699 Electrical equipment and supplies, nec

(G-9105)
QUEEN CITY LASER
3460 Grant Ave (45036-6432)
PHONE..................513 696-4444
Solomon Gomez, *Pr*
EMP: 6 **EST:** 2017
SALES (est): 102.45K **Privately Held**
Web: www.queencitylaser.com
SIC: 3599 Machine shop, jobbing and repair

(G-9106)
R W LONG LUMBER & BOX CO INC
1840 Cornett Rd Ste 1 (45036-7511)
P.O. Box 678 (45036-0678)
PHONE..................513 932-5124
Marlene Long, *Pr*
Marlene Long, *Pr*
Rodney W Long, *VP*
EMP: 16 **EST:** 1979
SQ FT: 16,200
SALES (est): 1.06MM **Privately Held**
Web: www.rwlong.com
SIC: 5031 2448 Lumber, plywood, and millwork; Pallets, wood and wood with metal

(G-9107)
RACEWAY BEVERAGE LLC
11 S Broadway St (45036-1769)
PHONE..................513 932-2214
James P Smith Junior, *Prin*
EMP: 7 **EST:** 2008
SALES (est): 142.18K **Privately Held**
SIC: 3644 Raceways

(G-9108)
RESTORTION PARTS UNLIMITED INC (PA)
Also Called: Rpui
2175 Deerfield Rd (45036-6422)
PHONE..................513 934-0815
Mitch Williams, *CEO*
EMP: 10 **EST:** 2012
SALES (est): 10.76MM
SALES (corp-wide): 10.76MM **Privately Held**
Web: www.rpui.com
SIC: 3714 Motor vehicle parts and accessories

(G-9109)
RPMI PACKAGING INC
Also Called: Rpmi
3899 S Us Route 42 (45036-9530)
P.O. Box 105 (45040-0105)
PHONE..................513 398-4040
EMP: 10 **EST:** 1991
SALES (est): 1.4MM **Privately Held**
Web: www.rpmipackaging.com
SIC: 3565 Packaging machinery

(G-9110)
SCHMIDT PROGRESSIVE LLC
Also Called: Food Furniture
360 Harmon Ave (45036-8801)
P.O. Box 380 (45036-0380)
PHONE..................513 934-2600
Julia Rodenbeck, *Managing Member*
EMP: 23 **EST:** 1998
SQ FT: 55,000
SALES (est): 2.08MM **Privately Held**
Web: www.schmidtprogressive.com
SIC: 3089 Fiberglass doors

(G-9111)
SPECTRUM TEXTILES INC
5883 Casaway Rd (45036)
PHONE..................513 933-8346
Robin Steele, *Pr*
Jennifer Stenger, *VP*
EMP: 12 **EST:** 1995
SQ FT: 5,000
SALES (est): 880K **Privately Held**
SIC: 3728 Aircraft propellers and associated equipment

(G-9112)
STC INTERNATIONAL CO LTD (PA)
1499 Shaker Run Blvd (45036-4041)
PHONE..................561 308-6002
EMP: 8 **EST:** 2010
SALES (est): 1.99MM **Privately Held**
SIC: 3541 3545 2821 Machine tools, metal cutting type; Machine tool accessories; Plastics materials and resins

(G-9113)
TELEMPU N HAYASHI AMER CORP
1500 Kingsview Dr (45036-8389)
PHONE..................513 932-9319
EMP: 6
Web: www.htnanorthamerica.com
SIC: 2396 Automotive trimmings, fabric
HQ: Hayashi Telempu North America Corporation
14328 Genoa Ct
Plymouth MI 48170
734 456-5221

(G-9114)
TRAMONTE & SONS LLC
3850 Welden Dr (45036-8815)
PHONE..................513 770-5501
Michael R Tramonte Senior, *Managing Member*
EMP: 13 **EST:** 2002
SALES (est): 1.41MM **Privately Held**
Web: www.tramonteandsons.com
SIC: 8742 2084 Distribution channels consultant; Wines

(G-9115)
TRIM PARTS INC
2175 Deerfield Rd (45036-6422)
PHONE..................513 934-0815
Carl Chadwell, *Pr*
▲ **EMP:** 35 **EST:** 1982
SQ FT: 55,000
SALES (est): 10.76MM
SALES (corp-wide): 10.76MM **Privately Held**

Web: www.rpui.com
SIC: 3714 3544 3429 Motor vehicle parts and accessories; Special dies, tools, jigs, and fixtures; Hardware, nec
PA: Restoration Parts Unlimited, Inc.
2175 Deerfield Rd
Lebanon OH 45036
513 934-0815

(G-9116)
TRUE STEP LLC ✪
1105 S Us Route 42 (45036-9526)
PHONE..................513 933-0933
Jeff Kenny, *CEO*
Jerry Monnin, *Pr*
EMP: 16 **EST:** 2022
SALES (est): 330.97K **Privately Held**
Web: www.truestepllc.com
SIC: 3599 Machine shop, jobbing and repair

(G-9117)
TURTLECREEK TOWNSHIP
670 N State Route 123 (45036-7016)
PHONE..................513 932-4080
Steven Flint, *Chief*
EMP: 12
Web: www.turtlecreektownship.org
SIC: 9199 3621 General government administration; Generating apparatus and parts, electrical
PA: Turtlecreek Township
670 N State Route 123
Lebanon OH 45036
513 932-4902

(G-9118)
UGN INC
201 Exploration Dr (45036)
PHONE..................513 360-3500
Peter Anthony, *Pr*
EMP: 180
Web: www.ugn.com
SIC: 3714 Motor vehicle parts and accessories
HQ: U.G.N., Inc.
2650 Warrenville Rd # 300
Downers Grove IL 60515
773 437-2400

(G-9119)
VEGA AMERICAS INC (HQ)
Also Called: Ohmart Vega
3877 Mason Research Pkwy (45036-9435)
PHONE..................513 272-0131
Don Jackson, *Contrlr*
Shawn Little, *
Brian Oeder, *
◆ **EMP:** 200 **EST:** 1950
SALES (est): 134.55MM
SALES (corp-wide): 1.94MM **Privately Held**
Web: www.vega.com
SIC: 3823 Process control instruments
PA: Vega Grieshaber Kg
Am Hohenstein 113
Schiltach BW 77761
7836500

(G-9120)
VISTECH MFG SOLUTIONS LLC
265 S West St (45036-2152)
PHONE..................513 933-9300
Dylan Roundtree, *Manager*
EMP: 10
SALES (corp-wide): 27.31MM **Privately Held**
Web: www.vistechmfg.com
SIC: 3565 Packaging machinery
HQ: Vistech Manufacturing Solutions, Llc
1156 Scenic Dr Ste 120
Modesto CA 95350
209 544-9333

(PA)=Parent Co (HQ)=Headquarters
✪ = New Business established in last 2 years

Lebanon - Warren County (G-9121) — GEOGRAPHIC SECTION

(G-9121)
WRAY PRECISION PRODUCTS INC
3650 Turtlecreek Rd (45036-9685)
PHONE.................................513 228-5000
Steven Dorgan, *Pr*
EMP: 7 **EST:** 1997
SQ FT: 12,000
SALES (est): 615.78K **Privately Held**
SIC: 3599 Machine shop, jobbing and repair

Leesburg
Highland County

(G-9122)
CANDLE-LITE COMPANY LLC (HQ)
Also Called: Candle-Lite
250 Eastern Ave (45135-9783)
PHONE.................................937 780-2563
Calvin Johnston, *CEO*
EMP: 60 **EST:** 2014
SQ FT: 900,000
SALES (est): 157.86MM
SALES (corp-wide): 260.78MM **Privately Held**
Web: www.candle-lite.com
SIC: 3999 Candles
PA: Luminex Home Decor & Fragrance
  Holding Corporation
  10521 Millington Ct
  Blue Ash OH 45242
  513 563-1113

(G-9123)
CREATIVE FAB & WELDING LLC
Also Called: Valley Trailers
9691 Stafford Rd (45135-9464)
PHONE.................................937 780-5000
Cameron Dyck, *Pr*
Cameron Dyck, *Managing Member*
Mindy Wilson, *Sec*
EMP: 22 **EST:** 2008
SQ FT: 800
SALES (est): 4.91MM **Privately Held**
Web: www.cfwohio.com
SIC: 3441 7692 Fabricated structural metal; Welding repair

(G-9124)
DUTCH COUNTRY KETTLES LTD
6732 Pavey Rd (45135-9523)
PHONE.................................937 780-6718
Emma Troyer, *Prin*
EMP: 6 **EST:** 2008
SALES (est): 141K **Privately Held**
SIC: 2033 Canned fruits and specialties

(G-9125)
MASON COMPANY LLC
260 Depot Ln (45135-8438)
P.O. Box 365 (45135-0365)
PHONE.................................937 780-2321
Greg Taylor, *CEO*
EMP: 44 **EST:** 1892
SQ FT: 35,000
SALES (est): 8.56MM
SALES (corp-wide): 187.17K **Privately Held**
Web: www.masonco.com
SIC: 3496 Cages, wire
PA: Midmark Corporation
  10170 Penny Ln Ste 300
  Miamisburg OH 45342
  937 528-7500

(G-9126)
MM OUTSOURCING LLC
355 S South St (45135-9473)
P.O. Box 29 (45135-0029)
PHONE.................................937 661-4300

EMP: 10 **EST:** 2017
SALES (est): 475.73K **Privately Held**
SIC: 3052 3061 4212 Automobile hose, rubber; Automotive rubber goods (mechanical); Local trucking, without storage

Leetonia
Columbiana County

(G-9127)
LEETONIA TOOL COMPANY
142 Main St (44431-1181)
PHONE.................................330 427-6944
Robert L Holt, *Pr*
Dennis J Holt, *VP*
J W Holt, *Sec*
EMP: 11 **EST:** 1907
SQ FT: 25,000
SALES (est): 935.94K **Privately Held**
Web: www.lansingforge.com
SIC: 3429 Builders' hardware

(G-9128)
M K METALS
41659 Esterly Dr (44431-9676)
PHONE.................................330 482-3351
George Siembida, *Prin*
EMP: 7 **EST:** 2008
SALES (est): 96.7K **Privately Held**
SIC: 3441 Fabricated structural metal

(G-9129)
PENNEX ALUMINUM COMPANY LLC
1 Commerce Ave (44431-8720)
PHONE.................................330 427-6704
Thomas Hutchinson, *Brnch Mgr*
EMP: 95
SALES (corp-wide): 483.85MM **Privately Held**
Web: www.pennexaluminum.com
SIC: 3354 Aluminum extruded products
HQ: Pennex Aluminum Company Llc
  50 Community St
  Wellsville PA 17365

(G-9130)
QUAKER CITY CONCRETE PDTS LLC
290 E High St (44431-9653)
PHONE.................................330 427-2239
Jeff Foust, *Managing Member*
EMP: 8 **EST:** 1961
SQ FT: 4,000
SALES (est): 938.71K **Privately Held**
Web: www.quakercityseptictank.com
SIC: 3272 Septic tanks, concrete

(G-9131)
TOTAL WATER SOLUTIONS LLC
41562 Lodge Rd (44431-9630)
PHONE.................................234 567-5912
EMP: 6 **EST:** 2020
SALES (est): 248.56K **Privately Held**
SIC: 3589 Water treatment equipment, industrial

Leipsic
Putnam County

(G-9132)
DILLER METALS INC
507 S Eastom St (45856-1300)
PHONE.................................419 943-3364
EMP: 6 **EST:** 1994
SALES (est): 1.1MM **Privately Held**
SIC: 3443 Metal parts

(G-9133)
MARS PETCARE US INC
3700 State Route 65 (45856-9231)
PHONE.................................419 943-4280
Herminio Reynoso, *Mgr*
EMP: 17
SALES (corp-wide): 42.84B **Privately Held**
Web: www.marspetcare.com
SIC: 2047 Dog food
HQ: Mars Petcare Us, Inc.
  2013 Ovation Pkwy
  Franklin TN 37067
  615 807-4626

(G-9134)
PATRICK PRODUCTS INC
150 S Werner St (45856-1363)
PHONE.................................419 943-4137
Robert S Patrick, *Pr*
Thomas M Patrick, *
Roger Selhorst, *
▲ **EMP:** 145 **EST:** 1999
SQ FT: 300,000
SALES (est): 19.09MM **Privately Held**
SIC: 3089 Plastics containers, except foam

(G-9135)
POET BIOREFINING - LEIPSIC LLC
Also Called: Poet Biorefining-Leipsic
3875 State Route 65 (45856)
PHONE.................................419 943-7447
Jeff Lautt, *CEO*
Daniel Loveland, *
Mark Borer, *
EMP: 40 **EST:** 2005
SALES (est): 13.1MM **Privately Held**
Web: poetbiorefining-leipsic.aghost.net
SIC: 2869 Ethyl alcohol, ethanol
PA: Poet, Llc
  4615 N Lewis Ave
  Sioux Falls SD 57104

(G-9136)
PRECISION LASER & FORMING INC
6500 Road 5 (45856-9763)
PHONE.................................419 943-4350
Thomas Koenig, *CEO*
Howard Hermiller, *Treas*
EMP: 21 **EST:** 1998
SQ FT: 17,000
SALES (est): 2.37MM **Privately Held**
SIC: 3441 Fabricated structural metal

(G-9137)
PRO-TEC COATING COMPANY INC (PA)
5500 Protec Pkwy (45856-8215)
PHONE.................................419 943-1211
Richard E Veitch, *Pr*
Brent Rosebrook, *
▲ **EMP:** 230 **EST:** 1991
SQ FT: 725,000
SALES (est): 1.1B **Privately Held**
Web: www.proteccoating.com
SIC: 3479 Coating of metals and formed products

(G-9138)
PRO-TEC COATING COMPANY LLC
Also Called: Pro-tec Coating Company, Llc
4500 Protec Pkwy (45856)
PHONE.................................419 943-1100
Richard Veitch, *Pr*
EMP: 80
SALES (corp-wide): 21.07B **Publicly Held**
Web: www.proteccoating.com
SIC: 3479 Galvanizing of iron, steel, or end-formed products
HQ: Pro-Tec Coating Company, Inc.
  5500 Pro Tec Pkwy
  Leipsic OH 45856

(G-9139)
PRO-TEC COATING COMPANY LLC
Also Called: Pro-tec Coating Company, Llc
5000 Pro Tec Pkwy (45856-8212)
PHONE.................................419 943-1100
Richard Veitch, *Pr*
EMP: 80
SALES (corp-wide): 21.07B **Publicly Held**
Web: www.proteccoating.com
SIC: 3398 Annealing of metal
HQ: Pro-Tec Coating Company, Inc.
  5500 Pro Tec Pkwy
  Leipsic OH 45856

(G-9140)
RUHE SALES INC (PA)
5450 State Route 109 (45856-9438)
PHONE.................................419 943-3357
Marilyn Ruhe, *Pr*
Marilyn Ruhe, *Pr*
Robert G Ruhe, *VP*
EMP: 10 **EST:** 1963
SQ FT: 10,000
SALES (est): 828.59K
SALES (corp-wide): 828.59K **Privately Held**
Web: www.rsvpair.com
SIC: 0721 3721 4581 4512 Crop dusting services; Aircraft; Airports, flying fields, and services; Air transportation, scheduled

(G-9141)
WAGNER FARMS SAWMILL LTD LBLTY
13201 Road X (45856)
PHONE.................................419 653-4126
James Wagner, *Pt*
Thomas Wagner, *Pt*
Steven Wagner, *Pt*
Michael Wagner, *Pt*
EMP: 10 **EST:** 1940
SALES (est): 2.29MM **Privately Held**
Web: www.wagnersawmill.info
SIC: 2421 0191 2426 Sawmills and planing mills, general; General farms, primarily crop ; Hardwood dimension and flooring mills

(G-9142)
WARD CONSTRUCTION CO (PA)
385 Oak St (45856-1358)
PHONE.................................419 943-2450
Arnold W Rosebrock, *Pr*
Daniel A Rosebrock, *VP*
Barry A Rosebrock, *VP*
Patricia A Newell, *Sec*
EMP: 12 **EST:** 1967
SALES (est): 8.72MM
SALES (corp-wide): 8.72MM **Privately Held**
Web: www.wardcompanies.com
SIC: 1611 4212 1442 1771 General contractor, highway and street construction; Local trucking, without storage; Sand mining ; Concrete work

Lewis Center
Delaware County

(G-9143)
3D PRINTING
7139 Trillium Dr (43035-9670)
PHONE.................................501 248-0468
EMP: 6 **EST:** 2017
SALES (est): 83.91K **Privately Held**
Web: www.3dsystems.com
SIC: 2752 Commercial printing, lithographic

GEOGRAPHIC SECTION
Lewis Center - Delaware County (G-9166)

(G-9144)
ABRASIVE TECHNOLOGY LLC (PA)
8400 Green Meadows Dr N (43035-9453)
P.O. Box 545 (43035-0545)
PHONE..................740 548-4100
Loyal M Peterman Junior, *Pr*
Daryl L Peterman, *
▲ **EMP:** 200 **EST:** 1971
SQ FT: 100,000
SALES (est): 81.63MM
SALES (corp-wide): 81.63MM **Privately Held**
Web: www.abrasive-tech.com
SIC: 3291 Buffing or polishing wheels, abrasive or nonabrasive

(G-9145)
ABRASIVE TECHNOLOGY LAPIDARY
Also Called: Crystalite
8400 Green Meadows Dr N (43035-9453)
P.O. Box 545 (43035-0545)
PHONE..................740 548-4855
Loyal M Peterman, *Pr*
EMP: 22 **EST:** 1986
SQ FT: 50,000
SALES (est): 247.58K **Privately Held**
Web: www.abrasive-tech.com
SIC: 3291 Abrasive products

(G-9146)
ABSOLUTE IMPRESSIONS INC
281 Enterprise Dr (43035-9418)
PHONE..................614 840-0599
Keith Hamilton, *Pr*
Jeff Vigar, *VP*
EMP: 14 **EST:** 1997
SQ FT: 15,000
SALES (est): 1.57MM **Privately Held**
Web: www.absoluteimpressionsinc.com
SIC: 2759 Screen printing

(G-9147)
AIRWAVES LLC
7750 Green Meadows Dr Ste A (43035-8381)
PHONE..................740 548-1200
Kyle Kantner, *CEO*
Daniel Kaiser, *CFO*
◆ **EMP:** 250 **EST:** 2013
SQ FT: 50,000
SALES (est): 53.18MM
SALES (corp-wide): 252.15MM **Privately Held**
Web: www.airwavesinc.com
SIC: 2759 Screen printing
PA: Hybrid Promotions, Llc
    10700 Valley View St
    Cypress CA 90630
    714 952-3866

(G-9148)
AMERIHUA INTL ENTPS INC
707 Radio Dr (43035-7134)
PHONE..................740 549-0300
Stephen S Chen, *Ch Bd*
David W Chen, *VP Fin*
◆ **EMP:** 7 **EST:** 1984
SQ FT: 3,000
SALES (est): 1.47MM **Privately Held**
Web: www.reddestiny.com
SIC: 5149 8742 3231 Specialty food items; Management consulting services; Christmas tree ornaments: made from purchased glass

(G-9149)
ANIME PALACE
8185 Green Meadows Dr N Ste M (43035-8771)
PHONE..................408 858-1918
Jean Levin, *Prin*

▲ **EMP:** 7 **EST:** 2009
SALES (est): 466.2K **Privately Held**
Web: www.theanimepalace.com
SIC: 3944 5945 Games, toys, and children's vehicles; Toys and games

(G-9150)
APPLE & APPLE LLC
Also Called: Apple
1767 Westwood Dr (43035-7087)
PHONE..................740 972-2209
Brenda Applegate, *Prin*
EMP: 10 **EST:** 2015
SALES (est): 402.87K **Privately Held**
SIC: 3571 Electronic computers

(G-9151)
ATS OHIO INC
Also Called: Automation Tooling Systems
7115 Green Meadows Dr (43035-9445)
PHONE..................614 888-2344
Anthony Caputo, *CEO*
Carl Galloway, *
▼ **EMP:** 125 **EST:** 1974
SQ FT: 99,000
SALES (est): 42.54MM
SALES (corp-wide): 1.9B **Privately Held**
Web: www.atsautomation.com
SIC: 3563 Robots for industrial spraying, painting, etc.
PA: Ats Corporation
    730 Fountain St N Bldg 2
    Cambridge ON N3H 4
    604 332-2666

(G-9152)
ATS SYSTEMS OREGON INC
425 Enterprise Dr (43035-9424)
PHONE..................541 738-0932
Anthony Caputo, *CEO*
Maria Perrella, *
Stewart Mccrary, *Sec*
▲ **EMP:** 214 **EST:** 1966
SQ FT: 85,000
SALES (est): 4.13MM
SALES (corp-wide): 1.9B **Privately Held**
Web: www.atsautomation.com
SIC: 3569 5084 Robots, assembly line: industrial and commercial; Industrial machinery and equipment
PA: Ats Corporation
    730 Fountain St N Bldg 2
    Cambridge ON N3H 4
    604 332-2666

(G-9153)
BTC INC
8842 Whitney Dr (43035-8297)
PHONE..................740 549-2722
Sheldon Lambert, *Prin*
Jerold S Cook, *Prin*
EMP: 9 **EST:** 2010
SALES (est): 610.39K **Privately Held**
Web: www.btcgps.com
SIC: 3812 Search and navigation equipment

(G-9154)
BTC TECHNOLOGY SERVICES INC
617 Carle Ave (43035-8294)
PHONE..................740 549-2722
Sheldon Lambert, *CEO*
EMP: 8 **EST:** 2011
SALES (est): 110.35K **Privately Held**
SIC: 3812 Search and navigation equipment

(G-9155)
CARDINAL HEALTH INC
Also Called: Cardinal Hlth Nclear Prcsion H
850 Corduroy Rd Ste 100 (43035)
PHONE..................614 757-2863
EMP: 7

SALES (corp-wide): 205.01B **Publicly Held**
SIC: 5122 5047 8741 3842 Pharmaceuticals; Surgical equipment and supplies; Management services; Surgical appliances and supplies
PA: Cardinal Health, Inc.
    7000 Cardinal Pl
    Dublin OH 43017
    614 757-5000

(G-9156)
COLUMBUS INTERNATIONAL CORP
8876 Whitney Dr (43035-8297)
PHONE..................614 917-2274
Rajeev Kumar, *Brnch Mgr*
EMP: 10
SALES (corp-wide): 1.7MM **Privately Held**
Web: www.columbuscorp.com
SIC: 7372 Business oriented computer software
PA: Columbus International Corporation
    200 E Campus View Blvd
    Columbus OH 43235
    614 323-1086

(G-9157)
DINOL US INC
8520 Cotter St (43035-7138)
PHONE..................740 548-1656
Joe Renzi, *CEO*
EMP: 50 **EST:** 2014
SALES (est): 13.96MM
SALES (corp-wide): 20.7B **Privately Held**
SIC: 2899 Corrosion preventive lubricant
HQ: Wurth Group Of North America Inc.
    93 Grant St
    Ramsey NJ 07446

(G-9158)
DURACORP LLC (PA)
Also Called: Solut
7787 Graphics Way (43035-8000)
PHONE..................740 549-3336
Bill Shepard, *CEO*
Scott Rechel, *Managing Member*
Erik O Neil, *VP*
Jason Kauffman, *VP*
▼ **EMP:** 75 **EST:** 2005
SALES (est): 18.27MM **Privately Held**
Web: www.gosolut.com
SIC: 2621 2656 Packaging paper; Sanitary food containers

(G-9159)
ELECTRONIC IMAGING SVCS INC
Also Called: Vestcom Retail Solutions
8273 Green Meadows Dr N Ste 400 (43035-7373)
PHONE..................740 549-2487
EMP: 12
SALES (corp-wide): 8.36B **Publicly Held**
SIC: 8742 2759 Marketing consulting services; Commercial printing, nec
HQ: Electronic Imaging Services, Inc.
    2800 Cantrell Rd Ste 400
    Little Rock AR 72202
    501 663-0100

(G-9160)
EOI INC
Also Called: Medical Resources
8377 Green Meadows Dr N Ste C (43035-9506)
PHONE..................740 201-3300
Suzi Reichenbach, *CEO*
Randy Reichenbach, *VP*
Dianne Risch, *CFO*
▼ **EMP:** 16 **EST:** 1987
SQ FT: 18,000
SALES (est): 5.77MM **Privately Held**

Web: www.medicalresources.com
SIC: 5712 5021 5047 3841 Furniture stores; Office and public building furniture; Medical equipment and supplies; Diagnostic apparatus, medical

(G-9161)
GILSON COMPANY INC (PA)
7975 N Central Dr (43035-9409)
P.O. Box 200 (43035-0200)
PHONE..................740 548-7298
▲ **EMP:** 41 **EST:** 1939
SALES (est): 22.23MM
SALES (corp-wide): 22.23MM **Privately Held**
Web: www.globalgilson.com
SIC: 5049 3829 3821 Analytical instruments; Measuring and controlling devices, nec; Laboratory apparatus and furniture

(G-9162)
HEAT TREATING EQUIPMENT INC
8185 Green Meadows Dr N (43035-8770)
PHONE..................740 549-3700
EMP: 50 **EST:** 2004
SALES (est): 2.23MM **Privately Held**
SIC: 3398 Metal heat treating

(G-9163)
INDUSTRIAL SOLUTIONS INC
Also Called: I S I
8333 Green Meadows Dr N Ste A (43035-8497)
PHONE..................614 431-8118
James D Cooke, *Pr*
Susan Cooke, *VP*
EMP: 21 **EST:** 1987
SALES (est): 2.34MM **Privately Held**
Web: www.industrialsolutionsusa.com
SIC: 3613 Panelboards and distribution boards, electric

(G-9164)
INPOWER LLC
8311 Green Meadows Dr N (43035-9451)
P.O. Box 435 (43035-0435)
PHONE..................740 548-0965
Jim Sullivan, *Managing Member*
Patrick Sullivan, *OM*
EMP: 15 **EST:** 2000
SQ FT: 14,000
SALES (est): 4.33MM **Privately Held**
Web: www.inpowerelectronics.com
SIC: 3559 Electronic component making machinery

(G-9165)
INSIDE OUTFITTERS INC
Also Called: S O S Shades
8333 Green Meadows Dr N Ste B (43035-8497)
PHONE..................614 798-3500
▲ **EMP:** 46
SIC: 5023 2591 2221 2211 Draperies; Drapery hardware and window blinds and shades; Draperies and drapery fabrics, manmade fiber and silk; Draperies and drapery fabrics, cotton

(G-9166)
INTERNATIONAL NOODLE COMPANY
341 Enterprise Dr (43035-9418)
PHONE..................614 888-0665
Ridge Cheung, *Pr*
Jerry Cheung, *VP*
Ning Ho Cheung, *Sec*
▲ **EMP:** 15 **EST:** 1988
SQ FT: 12,000
SALES (est): 1.32MM **Privately Held**
SIC: 2098 Noodles (e.g. egg, plain, and water), dry

Lewis Center - Delaware County (G-9167)

(G-9167)
KDAE INC
7750 Green Meadows Dr Ste A (43035-8380)
PHONE..................844 543-8339
Donald L Feinstein, *Dir*
EMP: 7 **EST:** 1981
SALES (est): 46.58K **Privately Held**
SIC: 2211 Shirting fabrics, cotton

(G-9168)
KW ACQUISITION INC
Also Called: Karol-Warner
7975 N Central Dr (43035-9409)
PHONE..................740 548-7298
Trent Smith, *Pr*
EMP: 6 **EST:** 2016
SQ FT: 1,300
SALES (est): 584.81K **Privately Held**
Web: www.karolwarner.com
SIC: 3829 Physical property testing equipment

(G-9169)
LAPEL PINS UNLIMITED LLC
5649 Ketch St (43035-8233)
PHONE..................614 562-3218
Dean M Kuhn, *Prin*
EMP: 6 **EST:** 2008
SALES (est): 209.58K **Privately Held**
Web: www.lapelpinsunlimited.com
SIC: 3452 Pins

(G-9170)
LUMENOMICS INC
Also Called: Inside Outfitters
8333 Green Meadows Dr N Ste B (43035-8496)
PHONE..................614 798-3500
Carlee Swihart, *VP Opers*
EMP: 46
Web: www.insideoutfitters.com
SIC: 5023 2591 2221 2211 Draperies; Drapery hardware and window blinds and shades; Draperies and drapery fabrics, manmade fiber and silk; Draperies and drapery fabrics, cotton
PA: Lumenomics, Inc.
  7800 7th Ave S
  Seattle WA 98108

(G-9171)
MICROCOM CORPORATION
855 Corduroy Rd (43035-1550)
PHONE..................740 548-6262
Steven Wolfe, *CEO*
James R Larson, *
Steven Wolfe, *CFO*
David Dezse, *
▲ **EMP:** 24 **EST:** 1982
SALES (est): 5.23MM **Privately Held**
Web: www.microcomcorp.com
SIC: 3577 5111 5112 3953 Printers, computer ; Printing and writing paper; Inked ribbons; Marking devices

(G-9172)
MULTI-PLASTICS INC (PA)
7770 N Central Dr (43035-9404)
PHONE..................740 548-4894
John R Parsio, *Pr*
John Parsio Junior, *Ex VP*
Wesley Hall, *
Steven Parsio, *
Michael T Hickey, *
◆ **EMP:** 55 **EST:** 1979
SQ FT: 32,000
SALES (est): 107.83MM
SALES (corp-wide): 107.83MM **Privately Held**
Web: www.multi-plastics.com

SIC: 2821 Plastics materials and resins

(G-9173)
NAT2 INC (PA)
8754 Cotter St (43035-7104)
PHONE..................614 270-2507
Shirley Bartee, *Dir*
EMP: 7 **EST:** 2017
SALES (est): 1.13MM
SALES (corp-wide): 1.13MM **Privately Held**
SIC: 2099 Food preparations, nec

(G-9174)
NEXTECH MATERIALS LTD
Also Called: Nexceris
404 Enterprise Dr (43035-9423)
PHONE..................614 842-6606
EMP: 70 **EST:** 1994
SALES (est): 9.78MM **Privately Held**
Web: www.nexceris.com
SIC: 3823 3825 Industrial process measurement equipment; Energy measuring equipment, electrical

(G-9175)
PELTON ENVIRONMENTAL PDTS INC
8638 Cotter St (43035-7136)
PHONE..................440 838-1221
Edward Pelton, *VP*
EMP: 8 **EST:** 1992
SALES (est): 2.96MM **Privately Held**
Web: www.peltonenv.com
SIC: 5074 3589 Water purification equipment ; Sewage and water treatment equipment

(G-9176)
QUINTUS TECHNOLOGIES LLC
8270 Green Meadows Dr N (43035-9450)
PHONE..................614 891-2732
Ed Williams, *Managing Member*
EMP: 50 **EST:** 2014
SALES (est): 7.38MM **Privately Held**
Web: www.quintustechnologies.com
SIC: 7699 7389 3443 Industrial equipment services; Industrial and commercial equipment inspection service; Industrial vessels, tanks, and containers

(G-9177)
QXSOFT LLC
759 Carle Ave (43035-8293)
PHONE..................740 777-9609
Jian Shi, *Pr*
EMP: 6 **EST:** 2020
SALES (est): 454.51K **Privately Held**
Web: www.qxcmm.com
SIC: 7372 7371 Publisher's computer software; Software programming applications

(G-9178)
RETAIL MANAGEMENT PRODUCTS LTD
Also Called: Rxscan
8851 Whitney Dr (43035-7107)
PHONE..................740 548-1725
Max J Peoples, *Pt*
Bill Peoples, *Pt*
EMP: 14 **EST:** 1995
SALES (est): 2.05MM **Privately Held**
Web: www.rxscan.com
SIC: 7372 Business oriented computer software

(G-9179)
RUBBERTEC INDUSTRIAL PDTS CO
Elledge Gasket
7580 Commerce Ct (43035-9702)
PHONE..................740 657-3345

EMP: 8
SIC: 3053 Gaskets; packing and sealing devices
PA: Rubbertec Industrial Products Company
  7580 Commerce Ct
  Lewis Center OH 43035

(G-9180)
SARCOM INC
8337a Green Meadows Dr N (43035-9451)
PHONE..................614 854-1300
▲ **EMP:** 960
SIC: 5045 7373 7374 7372 Computers, peripherals, and software; Computer integrated systems design; Data processing and preparation; Prepackaged software

(G-9181)
TESA INC
544 Enterprise Dr Ste A (43035-9704)
PHONE..................614 847-8200
John Truitt, *Pr*
EMP: 7 **EST:** 1973
SALES (est): 1.03MM **Privately Held**
Web: www.tesa-inc.com
SIC: 3612 5063 Distribution transformers, electric; Electrical apparatus and equipment

(G-9182)
TRACEWELL SYSTEMS INC (PA)
567 Enterprise Dr (43035-9431)
PHONE..................614 846-6175
Larry Tracewell, *Pr*
Betty Tracewell, *
Matt Tracewell, *
EMP: 57 **EST:** 1973
SQ FT: 10,000
SALES (est): 23.74MM
SALES (corp-wide): 23.74MM **Privately Held**
Web: www.tracewell.com
SIC: 3572 3571 3728 Computer storage devices; Electronic computers; Aircraft parts and equipment, nec

(G-9183)
WIKA SENSOR TECHNLGY LP
6957 Green Meadows Dr (43035-3570)
PHONE..................614 430-0683
Bruce Yohr, *Pr*
EMP: 50 **EST:** 2008
SALES (est): 10.44MM
SALES (corp-wide): 645.98MM **Privately Held**
Web: www.wika.com
SIC: 3823 Process control instruments
HQ: Wika Holding, Lp
  1000 Wiegand Blvd
  Lawrenceville GA 30043
  770 513-8200

(G-9184)
YES MFG LLC
8919 Whitney Dr (43035-7105)
PHONE..................614 296-3553
EMP: 7 **EST:** 2013
SALES (est): 618.56K **Privately Held**
SIC: 3999 Manufacturing industries, nec

Lewisburg
Preble County

(G-9185)
ANDERSON PALLET & PACKG INC
Also Called: Anderson Pallet Service
210 Western Ave (45338-9584)
P.O. Box 669 (45338-0669)
PHONE..................937 962-2614

Ross Anderson, *Pr*
Grace Anderson, *Treas*
Marc Anderson, *VP*
EMP: 12 **EST:** 1983
SQ FT: 10,000
SALES (est): 442.54K **Privately Held**
SIC: 2448 Pallets, wood

(G-9186)
D M TOOL & PLASTICS INC (PA)
4140 Us Route 40 E (45338-9506)
P.O. Box 309 (45309-0309)
PHONE..................937 962-4140
Dennis Meyer, *Pr*
Bill Meyer, *VP*
Pat Meyer, *Treas*
EMP: 18 **EST:** 1977
SQ FT: 35,000
SALES (est): 4.78MM
SALES (corp-wide): 4.78MM **Privately Held**
SIC: 3089 3599 Injection molding of plastics; Machine shop, jobbing and repair

(G-9187)
LEWISBURG CONTAINER COMPANY (DH)
275 W Clay St (45338-8107)
P.O. Box 39 (45338-0039)
PHONE..................937 962-2681
Anthony Pratt, *Pr*
Davis Kyles, *
David Wiser, *
▲ **EMP:** 235 **EST:** 1955
SQ FT: 384,000
SALES (est): 51.78MM **Privately Held**
Web: www.prattindustries.com
SIC: 2653 Boxes, corrugated: made from purchased materials
HQ: Pratt Properties, Inc.
  1800 Sarasot Bus Pkwy Ne
  Conyers GA 30013
  770 918-5678

(G-9188)
MIAMI VALLEY SPRAY FOAM LLC
3428 Wysong Rd (45338-9762)
PHONE..................419 295-6536
James Zimmerman, *Prin*
EMP: 6 **EST:** 2013
SALES (est): 220.1K **Privately Held**
SIC: 2499 Decorative wood and woodwork

(G-9189)
PRATT INDUSTRIES INC
301 W Clay St (45338-8132)
P.O. Box 220 (45338-0220)
PHONE..................937 583-4990
EMP: 12
Web: www.prattindustries.com
SIC: 2621 2653 Paper mills; Corrugated and solid fiber boxes
PA: Pratt Industries, Inc.
  1800 Sarasota Pkwy Ne C
  Conyers GA 30013

(G-9190)
PROVIMI NORTH AMERICA INC (HQ)
Also Called: Cargill Premix and Nutrition
6571 State Route 503 N (45338-6713)
PHONE..................937 770-2400
Thomas Taylor, *Pr*
▲ **EMP:** 253 **EST:** 1973
SALES (est): 7.75MM
SALES (corp-wide): 176.74B **Privately Held**
Web: www.provimius.com
SIC: 5191 2048 Animal feeds; Prepared feeds, nec
PA: Cargill, Incorporated
  15407 Mcginty Rd W

Wayzata MN 55391
800 227-4455

(G-9191)
PROVIMI NORTH AMERICA INC
6531 State Route 503 N (45338-6713)
PHONE..................................937 770-2400
Dwight Armstrong, *Pr*
EMP: 32
SALES (corp-wide): 176.74B **Privately Held**
Web: www.provimius.com
SIC: 2048 Prepared feeds, nec
HQ: Provimi North America, Inc.
6571 State Route 503 N
Lewisburg OH 45338
937 770-2400

(G-9192)
PROVIMI NORTH AMERICA INC
6571 State Route 503 N (45338-6713)
PHONE..................................937 770-2400
EMP: 14
SALES (corp-wide): 176.74B **Privately Held**
Web: www.provimius.com
SIC: 2048 Prepared feeds, nec
HQ: Provimi North America, Inc.
6571 State Route 503 N
Lewisburg OH 45338
937 770-2400

(G-9193)
TWIN VALLEY MOLD & TOOL LLC
8725 Verona Rd (45338-9718)
PHONE..................................937 962-1403
Joyce S Myers, *Prin*
EMP: 6 **EST:** 2003
SALES (est): 95K **Privately Held**
SIC: 3544 Industrial molds

Lewistown
Logan County

(G-9194)
INDUSTRIAL FARM TANK INC
10676 Township Road 80 (43333-9759)
PHONE..................................937 843-2972
Pyllis Yazel, *CEO*
EMP: 25 **EST:** 1975
SQ FT: 10,000
SALES (est): 2.62MM **Privately Held**
Web: www.industrialfarmtankinc.com
SIC: 3089 3443 Molding primary plastics; Farm storage tanks, metal plate

Lexington
Richland County

(G-9195)
CHARTER NEXT GENERATION INC
165 Industrial Dr (44904-1338)
P.O. Box 809132 (60680-9132)
PHONE..................................419 884-8150
Apurva Shah, *Prin*
EMP: 128
SALES (corp-wide): 1.5B **Privately Held**
Web: www.cnginc.com
SIC: 2671 Plastic film, coated or laminated for packaging
PA: Charter Next Generation, Inc.
300 N La Salle Dr # 1575
Chicago IL 60654
608 868-5757

(G-9196)
CHARTER NEXT GENERATION INC
Also Called: CNG
1450 State Route 97 (44904-9321)
PHONE..................................419 884-8150
EMP: 128
SALES (corp-wide): 1.5B **Privately Held**
Web: www.nextgenfilms.com
SIC: 2671 Plastic film, coated or laminated for packaging
PA: Charter Next Generation, Inc.
300 N La Salle Dr # 1575
Chicago IL 60654
608 868-5757

(G-9197)
CHARTER NEXT GENERATION INC
235 Industrial Dr (44904-1347)
PHONE..................................419 884-8150
EMP: 128
SALES (corp-wide): 1.5B **Privately Held**
Web: www.cnginc.com
SIC: 2671 Plastic film, coated or laminated for packaging
PA: Charter Next Generation, Inc.
300 N La Salle Dr # 1575
Chicago IL 60654
608 868-5757

(G-9198)
CHARTER NEXT GENERATION INC
145 Frecka Dr (44904)
PHONE..................................419 884-8150
EMP: 128
SALES (corp-wide): 1.5B **Privately Held**
Web: www.cnginc.com
SIC: 2671 Plastic film, coated or laminated for packaging
PA: Charter Next Generation, Inc.
300 N La Salle Dr # 1575
Chicago IL 60654
608 868-5757

(G-9199)
CHARTER NEXT GENERATION INC
215 Industrial Dr (44904-1347)
PHONE..................................419 884-8150
David Frecka, *Mgr*
EMP: 128
SALES (corp-wide): 1.5B **Privately Held**
Web: www.nextgenfilms.com
SIC: 2671 Plastic film, coated or laminated for packaging
PA: Charter Next Generation, Inc.
300 N La Salle Dr # 1575
Chicago IL 60654
608 868-5757

(G-9200)
CONTACT INDUSTRIES INC
25 Industrial Dr (44904-1372)
P.O. Box 3086 (44904-0086)
PHONE..................................419 884-9788
James Arnholt, *Pr*
E R Mc Intyre, *Marketing**
EMP: 36 **EST:** 1988
SQ FT: 12,000
SALES (est): 4.73MM **Privately Held**
Web: www.contactindustriesinc.com
SIC: 3625 3825 3612 Switches, electronic applications; Instruments to measure electricity; Transformers, except electric

(G-9201)
ENGINEERED FILMS DIVISION INC
230 Industrial Dr (44904-1346)
PHONE..................................419 884-8150
▲ **EMP:** 100
SIC: 2673 2671 Plastic and pliofilm bags; Plastic film, coated or laminated for packaging

(G-9202)
STONERIDGE INC
Also Called: Hi-Stat A Stoneridge Co
345 S Mill St (44904-9573)
PHONE..................................419 884-1219
Tom Morell, *Manager*
EMP: 700
Web: www.stoneridge.com
SIC: 3714 Motor vehicle electrical equipment
PA: Stoneridge, Inc.
39675 Mackenzie Dr # 400
Novi MI 48377

(G-9203)
SUPPORT SVC LLC
Also Called: Support Service
25 Walnut St Ste 4 (44904-1260)
PHONE..................................419 617-0660
EMP: 7 **EST:** 2010
SQ FT: 450,000
SALES (est): 588.15K **Privately Held**
Web: www.supportsvc.com
SIC: 5531 7539 7536 8711 Auto and home supply stores; Alternators and generators, rebuilding and repair; Automotive glass replacement shops; Engineering services

Liberty Center
Henry County

(G-9204)
TRIPLE DIAMOND PLASTICS LLC
Also Called: Triple Diamond Plastics
405 N Pleasantview Dr (43532-9376)
P.O. Box 1967 (34274-1967)
PHONE..................................419 533-0085
N Berry Taylor, *CEO*
Kristine Taylor, *
EMP: 75 **EST:** 2012
SQ FT: 40,000
SALES (est): 9.35MM **Privately Held**
Web: www.tdplastics.com
SIC: 3089 Boxes, plastics

(G-9205)
VAN ORDERS PALLET COMPANY INC
5188 County Road 424 (43532-9549)
PHONE..................................419 875-6932
Casey Van Order, *Pr*
James Van Order, *Ch Bd*
Patricia Van Order, *Sec*
EMP: 10 **EST:** 1971
SALES (est): 242.21K **Privately Held**
SIC: 2448 2441 Pallets, wood; Nailed wood boxes and shook

Liberty Township
Butler County

(G-9206)
FASTSIGNS
Also Called: Fastsigns
6681 Woodland Trace Ct (45044-9175)
PHONE..................................513 226-6733
EMP: 6 **EST:** 2012
SALES (est): 176.93K **Privately Held**
Web: www.fastsigns.com
SIC: 3993 Signs and advertising specialties

(G-9207)
FLEXTRONICS INTL USA INC
6224 Windham Ct (45044-8659)
PHONE..................................513 755-2500
EMP: 25
Web: www.flex.com
SIC: 3672 Printed circuit boards
HQ: Flextronics International Usa, Inc.
6201 America Center Dr
San Jose CA 95002

(G-9208)
HAMILTON JOURNAL NEWS INC
7320 Yankee Rd (45044-9168)
PHONE..................................513 863-8200
Anne Hoffman, *Pr*
EMP: 24 **EST:** 1800
SALES (est): 471.56K **Privately Held**
Web: www.journal-news.com
SIC: 2711 Commercial printing and newspaper publishing combined

(G-9209)
PULSE JOURNAL
7320 Yankee Rd (45044-9168)
PHONE..................................513 829-7900
Ann Hoffman, *Prin*
EMP: 7 **EST:** 2003
SALES (est): 86.44K **Privately Held**
SIC: 2711 Newspapers, publishing and printing

(G-9210)
ROSE REMINGTON
7562 Bales St (45069-7516)
PHONE..................................513 755-1695
EMP: 6 **EST:** 2017
SALES (est): 80.23K **Privately Held**
Web: www.roseandremington.com
SIC: 2299 Jute and flax textile products

(G-9211)
ZELAYA STONEWORKS LLC
7590 Wyandot Ln Ste 1 (45044-9539)
PHONE..................................513 777-8030
EMP: 15 **EST:** 2006
SQ FT: 4,000
SALES (est): 1.8MM **Privately Held**
Web: www.zelayastoneworks.com
SIC: 3281 Granite, cut and shaped

Liberty Twp
Butler County

(G-9212)
COFFING CORPORATION (PA)
5336 Lesourdsville West Chester Rd (45011)
PHONE..................................513 919-2813
Chris Coffing, *Pr*
EMP: 24 **EST:** 1995
SQ FT: 5,000
SALES (est): 2.39MM
SALES (corp-wide): 2.39MM **Privately Held**
Web: www.coffingco.com
SIC: 7372 7389 Prepackaged software; Business Activities at Non-Commercial Site

(G-9213)
D M L STEEL TECH
6974 Zenith Ct (45011-7207)
PHONE..................................513 737-9911
Suguna Bommaraju, *Pt*
Rama Bommaraju, *Pt*
EMP: 6 **EST:** 2000
SALES (est): 209.01K **Privately Held**
Web: www.dmlsteeltech.com
SIC: 3315 8748 Steel wire and related products; Business consulting, nec

(G-9214)
DM2018 LLC
Also Called: Dalaco
4805 Hamilton Middletown Rd Ste A (45011-2686)
PHONE..................................513 893-5483
EMP: 13 **EST:** 1986

Liberty Twp - Butler County (G-9215)   GEOGRAPHIC SECTION

SQ FT: 120,000
SALES (est): 2.4MM **Privately Held**
SIC: 3272 Concrete products, nec

(G-9215)
FEATHER LITE INNOVATIONS INC
Also Called: Tuf-N-Lite
4805 Hamilton Middletown Rd
(45011-2686)
PHONE.................................513 893-5483
Randy Ledford, *Genl Mgr*
EMP: 11
Web: s532643390.onlinehome.us
SIC: 3444 Concrete forms, sheet metal
PA: Feather Lite Innovations, Inc.
650 Pleasant Valley Dr
Springboro OH 45066

(G-9216)
FIXTURE DIMENSIONS INC
5660 Liberty Woods Dr (45011-9783)
PHONE.................................513 360-7512
Linda F Schaffeld, *Pr*
▼ EMP: 30 EST: 1992
SALES (est): 1.88MM **Privately Held**
Web: www.fixturedimensions.com
SIC: 2541 2431 Store and office display cases and fixtures; Millwork

Lima
Allen County

(G-9217)
ADHESIVES LAB USA NORTH LLC
1040 Findlay Rd (45801-3102)
PHONE.................................567 825-2004
EMP: 10 EST: 2019
SALES (est): 898.71K **Privately Held**
Web: www.adhesiveslabusanorth.com
SIC: 2891 Adhesives

(G-9218)
AIRWAVE COMMUNICATIONS CONS
Also Called: Cell 4less
1209 Allentown Rd (45805-2432)
P.O. Box 5216 (45802-5216)
PHONE.................................419 331-1526
Dominic Sementelli, *Pr*
Jeff Lunguy, *Ex VP*
EMP: 8 EST: 1985
SQ FT: 2,700
SALES (est): 714.52K **Privately Held**
SIC: 4813 4812 3577 7371 Local and long distance telephone communications; Radio pager (beeper) communication services; Computer peripheral equipment, nec; Computer software systems analysis and design, custom

(G-9219)
ALLEN COUNTY FABRICATION INC
Also Called: A C F
999 Industry Ave (45804-4171)
PHONE.................................419 227-7447
Kevin E Hall, *Pr*
Ronald M Kennedy, *
Patricia Kennedy, *
EMP: 31 EST: 1992
SQ FT: 16,800
SALES (est): 4.99MM **Privately Held**
Web: www.allencountyohio.com
SIC: 3444 Sheet metal specialties, not stamped

(G-9220)
AMERICAN BOTTLING COMPANY
Also Called: 7 Up Bottling Co
2350 Central Point Pkwy (45804-3863)
PHONE.................................419 229-7777
Mike Hoenie, *Mgr*
EMP: 87
Web: www.keurigdrpepper.com
SIC: 2086 Soft drinks: packaged in cans, bottles, etc.
HQ: The American Bottling Company
6425 Hall Of Fame Ln
Frisco TX 75034

(G-9221)
AMERICAN TRIM LLC (HQ)
1005 W Grand Ave (45801-3429)
PHONE.................................419 228-1145
◆ EMP: 50 EST: 1948
SQ FT: 15,000
SALES (est): 275.58MM
SALES (corp-wide): 445.1MM **Privately Held**
Web: www.amtrim.com
SIC: 3469 Porcelain enameled products and utensils
PA: Superior Metal Products, Inc.
1005 W Grand Ave
Lima OH 45801
419 228-1145

(G-9222)
AMERIX NTRA-PHARMACEUTICAL INC
904 N Cable Rd (45805-1704)
PHONE.................................567 204-7756
EMP: 7 EST: 2014
SALES (est): 150K **Privately Held**
SIC: 2834 Pharmaceutical preparations

(G-9223)
BEST ONE TIRE & SVC LIMA INC (PA)
701 E Hanthorn Rd (45804-3823)
PHONE.................................419 229-2380
David Mitchell, *Pr*
Sheila Mitchell, *
▲ EMP: 45 EST: 1933
SQ FT: 100,000
SALES (est): 14.67MM
SALES (corp-wide): 14.67MM **Privately Held**
Web: www.bestonetire.com
SIC: 7534 5531 5014 Tire recapping; Automotive tires; Truck tires and tubes

(G-9224)
BRANDON SCREEN PRINTING
1755 Shawnee Rd (45805-3830)
PHONE.................................419 229-9837
Robert L Liddle, *Owner*
EMP: 10 EST: 1972
SALES (est): 447.43K **Privately Held**
Web: www.brandonscreenprinting.net
SIC: 2396 3993 2752 Screen printing on fabric articles; Signs and advertising specialties; Commercial printing, lithographic

(G-9225)
BRINKMAN LLC
Also Called: American Paint Recyclers
1524 Adak Ave (45805-3905)
PHONE.................................419 204-5934
Jeremy Brinkman, *Managing Member*
EMP: 10 EST: 2007
SALES (est): 783.23K **Privately Held**
SIC: 2851 5812 7359 Paints and paint additives; Pizzeria, independent; Equipment rental and leasing, nec

(G-9226)
BRP MANUFACTURING COMPANY
Also Called: Buckeye Rubber Products
637 N Jackson St (45801-4125)
PHONE.................................800 858-0482
Kendall House, *Pr*
Steve Pendergast, *
◆ EMP: 44 EST: 1997
SQ FT: 190,000
SALES (est): 5.05MM **Privately Held**
Web: www.brpmfg.com
SIC: 3069 3061 2822 Sheeting, rubber or rubberized fabric; Mechanical rubber goods ; Synthetic rubber

(G-9227)
CAMERON PACKAGING INC
250 E Hanthorn Rd (45804-2344)
PHONE.................................419 222-9404
Michael Cameron, *CEO*
Bridget Cribben, *Treas*
Grant Morgenstern, *Pr*
Diane Cameron, *Sec*
▲ EMP: 9 EST: 1969
SQ FT: 56,000
SALES (est): 1.03MM **Privately Held**
Web: www.cameronpackaging.com
SIC: 2653 Boxes, corrugated: made from purchased materials

(G-9228)
COCA-COLA CONSOLIDATED INC
Also Called: Coca-Cola
201 N Shore Dr (45801-4822)
P.O. Box 268 (45839-0268)
PHONE.................................419 422-3743
John Iafolla, *Brnch Mgr*
EMP: 9
SALES (corp-wide): 6.65B **Publicly Held**
Web: www.cokeconsolidated.com
SIC: 2086 Bottled and canned soft drinks
PA: Coca-Cola Consolidated, Inc.
4100 Coca-Cola Plz
Charlotte NC 28211
704 557-4400

(G-9229)
CONSOLIDATED BOTTLING COMPANY
Also Called: Pepsi Cola Bottling Co
1750 Greely Chapel Rd (45804-4122)
PHONE.................................419 227-3541
Louis A Cira, *General Vice President*
Kenneth Frankl, *
C A Carrature, *
EMP: 160 EST: 1901
SQ FT: 130,000
SALES (est): 11.01MM **Privately Held**
Web: www.pepsico.com
SIC: 2086 Carbonated soft drinks, bottled and canned

(G-9230)
CROWN GROUP CO (HQ)
Also Called: PPG Coating Services
1340 Neubrecht Rd (45801-3120)
PHONE.................................586 575-9800
Wayne Oliver, *CFO*
Jim Keena, *COO*
EMP: 28 EST: 2013
SALES (est): 158.55MM
SALES (corp-wide): 17.65B **Publicly Held**
Web: www.thecrowngrp.com
SIC: 3479 Coating of metals and formed products
PA: Ppg Industries, Inc.
1 Ppg Pl
Pittsburgh PA 15272
412 434-3131

(G-9231)
CSC
1161 Buckeye Rd (45804-1815)
PHONE.................................419 221-7037
EMP: 7 EST: 2019
SALES (est): 233.53K **Privately Held**
Web: www.dxc.com
SIC: 3795 Tanks and tank components

(G-9232)
CSS PUBLISHING COMPANY
5450 N Dixie Hwy (45807-9559)
P.O. Box 4503 (45802-4503)
PHONE.................................419 227-1818
Wesley T Runk, *Pr*
Elen Shockey, *
David Runk, *
Tim Runk, *VP Mktg*
EMP: 20 EST: 1970
SQ FT: 50,000
SALES (est): 659.42K **Privately Held**
Web: store.csspub.com
SIC: 2731 5192 Books, publishing only; Books

(G-9233)
CUSTOM BLAST & COAT INC
Also Called: Custom Blast
1511 S Dixie Hwy (45804-1844)
PHONE.................................419 225-6024
G J Gossard, *Pr*
Bruce Dukeman, *Sec*
EMP: 8 EST: 2007
SALES (est): 937.75K **Privately Held**
Web: www.customblastandcoat.com
SIC: 3312 Blast furnace and related products

(G-9234)
CYGNUS HOME SERVICE LLC
Also Called: Schwan's Home Service
2545 Saint Johns Rd (45804-4004)
PHONE.................................419 222-9977
Mark Cornwell, *Brnch Mgr*
EMP: 43
SALES (corp-wide): 448.71MM **Privately Held**
Web: www.yelloh.com
SIC: 5963 2024 2037 Food services, direct sales; Ice cream, packaged: molded, on sticks, etc.; Fruit juice concentrates, frozen
PA: Cygnus Home Service, Llc
115 W College Dr
Marshall MN 56258
507 532-3274

(G-9235)
DESTER CORPORATION (DH)
1200 E Kibby St Bldg 32 (45804-3163)
PHONE.................................419 362-8020
Stef Vandeperre, *Pr*
◆ EMP: 10 EST: 2006
SQ FT: 157,000
SALES (est): 11.86MM **Privately Held**
Web: www.desterjobs.com
SIC: 3089 Plastics containers, except foam
HQ: Gategroup Holding Ag
Sagereistrasse 20
Glattbrugg ZH 8152

(G-9236)
DESTER CORPORATION
1200 E Kibby St Bldg 6 (45804-3163)
PHONE.................................419 362-8020
Patricia Hopkins, *Pr*
EMP: 12 EST: 2017
SALES (est): 917.99K **Privately Held**
Web: www.dester.com
SIC: 3089 Plastics containers, except foam

(G-9237)
DR PEPPER SNAPPLE GROUP
Also Called: Dr Pepper
2480 Saint Johns Rd (45804-4003)
PHONE.................................419 223-0072
Larry Young, *Pr*
EMP: 11 EST: 2015
SALES (est): 166.36K **Privately Held**
Web: www.keurigdrpepper.com

▲ = Import ▼ = Export
◆ = Import/Export

GEOGRAPHIC SECTION
Lima - Allen County (G-9261)

SIC: **2086** Soft drinks: packaged in cans, bottles, etc.

(G-9238)
DR PEPPER/SEVEN UP INC
2350 Central Point Pkwy (45804-3806)
PHONE..............................419 229-7777
EMP: 14
Web: www.drpepper.com
SIC: **2086** Soft drinks: packaged in cans, bottles, etc.
HQ: Dr Pepper/Seven Up, Inc.
6425 Hall Of Fame Ln
Frisco TX 75034
972 673-7000

(G-9239)
DUBOSE STRAPPING INC
1221 Stewart Rd (45801-3223)
P.O. Box 819 (28329-0819)
PHONE..............................419 221-0626
EMP: 28
Web: www.dubosestrapping.com
SIC: **3499** 2671 Strapping, metal; Paper; coated and laminated packaging
PA: Dubose Strapping, Inc.
906 Industrial Dr
Clinton NC 28328

(G-9240)
ENERGY & CTRL INTEGRATORS INC (PA)
1130 E Albert St (45804-1614)
PHONE..............................419 222-0025
Richard M Lyons, *Pr*
Randy Alvis, *VP*
Michael Lawrence, *Sec*
EMP: 6 **EST:** 1994
SQ FT: 5,400
SALES (est): 1.07MM **Privately Held**
Web: www.ecilighting.ie
SIC: **3822** Temperature controls, automatic

(G-9241)
ERNST ENTERPRISES INC
Also Called: Ernst Ready Mix Division
377 S Central Ave (45804-1301)
PHONE..............................419 222-2015
Edward Bryam, *Mgr*
EMP: 20
SALES (corp-wide): 240.08MM **Privately Held**
Web: www.ernstconcrete.com
SIC: **5211** 3275 Concrete and cinder block; Gypsum products
PA: Ernst Enterprises, Inc.
3361 Successful Way
Dayton OH 45414
937 233-5555

(G-9242)
ES INDUSTRIES INC (PA)
110 Brookview Ct (45801-2070)
PHONE..............................419 643-2625
Charles Dale, *Pr*
Charles L Dale, *Pr*
EMP: 10 **EST:** 1971
SALES (est): 1.02MM
SALES (corp-wide): 1.02MM **Privately Held**
SIC: **3535** 3556 4221 Conveyors and conveying equipment; Food products machinery; Grain elevator, storage only

(G-9243)
FORD MOTOR COMPANY
Also Called: Ford
1155 Bible Rd (45801-3193)
PHONE..............................419 226-7000
Paul A Edwards, *Brnch Mgr*
EMP: 1949
SQ FT: 2,424,360
SALES (corp-wide): 176.19MM **Publicly Held**
Web: www.ford.com
SIC: **5511** 3519 Automobiles, new and used; Internal combustion engines, nec
PA: Ford Motor Company
1 American Rd
Dearborn MI 48126
313 322-3000

(G-9244)
GASDORF TOOL AND MCH CO INC
445 N Mcdonel St (45801-4266)
PHONE..............................419 227-0103
Richard R Rapp, *Pr*
Lynn Krohn, *
EMP: 21 **EST:** 1953
SQ FT: 20,000
SALES (est): 5.56MM **Privately Held**
Web: www.gasdorf.com
SIC: **3599** 3544 Custom machinery; Special dies and tools

(G-9245)
GENERAL DYNMICS LAND SYSTEMS I
Also Called: General Dynmics Lima Army Tank
1161 Buckeye Rd (45804-1815)
PHONE..............................419 221-7000
Hank Kennedy, *Mgr*
EMP: 400
SALES (corp-wide): 42.27B **Publicly Held**
Web: www.gdls.com
SIC: **3795** Tanks, military, including factory rebuilding
HQ: General Dynamics Land Systems Inc.
38500 Mound Rd
Sterling Heights MI 48310
586 825-4000

(G-9246)
GROSS & SONS CUSTOM MILLWORK
1219 Grant St (45801-3735)
PHONE..............................419 227-0214
James H Gross, *Pr*
Debra Gross, *Treas*
EMP: 6 **EST:** 1983
SQ FT: 8,000
SALES (est): 473.95K **Privately Held**
Web: www.gross-sons.com
SIC: **2431** 2541 2434 Millwork; Counter and sink tops; Wood kitchen cabinets

(G-9247)
GUARDIAN ENERGY HOLDINGS LLC
2485 Houx Pkwy (45804-3901)
PHONE..............................567 940-9500
EMP: 104
SALES (corp-wide): 2.48MM **Privately Held**
Web: www.guardiannrg.com
SIC: **2869** Ethyl alcohol, ethanol
PA: Guardian Energy Holdings, Llc
4745 380th Ave
Janesville MN 56048
507 234-5000

(G-9248)
GUARDIAN LIMA LLC
2485 Houx Pkwy (45804-3901)
PHONE..............................567 940-9500
Don Dales, *CEO*
EMP: 34 **EST:** 2010
SALES (est): 24.31MM
SALES (corp-wide): 40.93MM **Privately Held**
Web: www.guardianlima.com
SIC: **2869** Ethyl alcohol, ethanol
PA: Guardian Energy, Llc
4745 380th Ave
Janesville MN 56048
507 234-5000

(G-9249)
HEAT TREATING TECHNOLOGIES
1799 E 4th St (45804-2713)
PHONE..............................419 224-8324
Chester L Walthall, *CEO*
Richard W Deibel, *Pr*
Judith Walthall, *Sec*
EMP: 23 **EST:** 1993
SQ FT: 33,000
SALES (est): 3.25MM **Privately Held**
Web: www.httlima.com
SIC: **3398** Metal heat treating

(G-9250)
HEMMELRATH COATINGS INC
Also Called: Hemmelrath
1340 Neubrecht Rd (45801-3120)
▲ **EMP:** 10 **EST:** 2006
SALES (est): 6.46MM
SALES (corp-wide): 17.65B **Publicly Held**
SIC: **3479** Coating of metals and formed products
HQ: Ppg Hemmelrath Lackfabrik Gmbh
Jakob-Hemmelrath-Str. 1
Klingenberg A. Main BY 63911
93721360

(G-9251)
HESSELING & SONS LLC
2818 Elida Rd Ste 1 (45805-1248)
PHONE..............................419 642-0013
Philip Hesseling, *Prin*
EMP: 7 **EST:** 2016
SALES (est): 475.08K **Privately Held**
Web: www.hesselingandsons.com
SIC: **3732** Boatbuilding and repairing

(G-9252)
HIGH TECH METAL PRODUCTS LLC
1900 Garland Ave (45804-3922)
PHONE..............................419 227-9414
Jerry Neuman, *Owner*
EMP: 8 **EST:** 1992
SALES (est): 997.84K **Privately Held**
SIC: **3599** Machine shop, jobbing and repair

(G-9253)
HUSKY LIMA REFINERY
1150 S Metcalf St (45804-1145)
PHONE..............................419 226-2300
EMP: 54 **EST:** 2016
SALES (est): 7.24MM **Privately Held**
SIC: **2911** Oils, fuel

(G-9254)
IHEARTCOMMUNICATIONS INC
Also Called: Clear Channel
667 W Market St (45801-4603)
PHONE..............................419 223-2060
EMP: 7
Web: www.iheartmedia.com
SIC: **4832** 2711 Radio broadcasting stations; Newspapers
HQ: Iheartcommunications, Inc.
20880 Stone Oak Pkwy
San Antonio TX 78258
210 822-2828

(G-9255)
INEOS LLC (PA)
1900 Fort Amanda Rd (45804-1827)
P.O. Box 628 (45802-0628)
PHONE..............................419 226-1200
Dennis Seith, *Pr*
David Brackett, *
Gary Wallace, *
Mike Nagle, *
Tim Avery, *
▲ **EMP:** 76 **EST:** 2002
SALES (est): 86.8MM **Privately Held**
Web: www.ineos.com
SIC: **2821** Plastics materials and resins

(G-9256)
INEOS NITRILES USA LLC (DH)
1900 Fort Amanda Rd (45804)
PHONE..............................281 535-6600
▲ **EMP:** 10 **EST:** 2015
SALES (est): 93.67MM
SALES (corp-wide): 917.38K **Privately Held**
Web: www.ineos.com
SIC: **2821** Plastics materials and resins
HQ: Ineos Americas Llc
2600 S Shore Blvd Ste 400
League City TX 77573
281 535-4266

(G-9257)
ISP LIMA LLC
12220 S Metcalf St (45804)
PHONE..............................419 998-8700
▲ **EMP:** 36 **EST:** 2005
SALES (est): 5.8MM
SALES (corp-wide): 23.98MM **Privately Held**
SIC: **2911** Petroleum refining
PA: Isp Chemicals Llc
455 N Main St
Calvert City KY 42029
270 395-4165

(G-9258)
JM HAMILTON GROUP INC
Also Called: Metal Coating Company
1700 Elida Rd (45805-1511)
PHONE..............................419 229-4010
Howell D Glover Junior, *Pr*
Richard W Hussey, *VP*
James I Hunt, *Prin*
John H Romey, *Prin*
Marie L Glover, *Prin*
EMP: 28 **EST:** 1939
SQ FT: 25,000
SALES (est): 1.39MM **Privately Held**
Web: www.metalcoatingcompany.com
SIC: **3479** 3559 3471 Coating of metals and formed products; Glass making machinery: blowing, molding, forming, etc.; Plating and polishing

(G-9259)
KEITH O KING
4095 Pioneer Rd (45807-9784)
PHONE..............................419 339-5028
Keith King, *Prin*
EMP: 6 **EST:** 2021
SALES (est): 205.43K **Privately Held**
SIC: **2711** Newspapers, publishing and printing

(G-9260)
KETTLE CREATIONS LLC
651 Commerce Pkwy (45804-4033)
PHONE..............................567 940-9401
EMP: 40
SIC: **2034** Potato products, dried and dehydrated

(G-9261)
LIMA ARMATURE WORKS INC
Also Called: Double Eagle Golf
142 E Pearl St (45801-4149)
PHONE..............................419 222-4010
TOLL FREE: 800

(PA)=Parent Co (HQ)=Headquarters
✪ = New Business established in last 2 years

Lima - Allen County (G-9262)

Rick Smith, *Pr*
James W Smith, *Ch Bd*
Margaret E Smith, *Sec*
EMP: 7 **EST:** 1927
SQ FT: 41,000
SALES (est): 828.26K Privately Held
Web: www.limaarmature.com
SIC: 7694 5063   Electric motor repair; Motors, electric

(G-9262)
LIMA PALLET COMPANY INC
1470 Neubrecht Rd (45801-3122)
PHONE.................................419 229-5736
Tracie Sanchez, *Pr*
Kelly Sarno, *Pers/VP*
EMP: 21 **EST:** 1981
SQ FT: 25,000
SALES (est): 2.34MM Privately Held
Web: www.limapallet.com
SIC: 2448 2441   Pallets, wood; Nailed wood boxes and shook

(G-9263)
LIMA REFINING COMPANY (HQ)
1150 S Metcalf St (45804-1145)
P.O. Box 4505 (45802-4505)
PHONE.................................419 226-2300
William Kalsse, *CEO*
Gregory King, *
◆ **EMP:** 33 **EST:** 2006
SALES (est): 116.12MM
SALES (corp-wide): 40.39B Privately Held
SIC: 2911   Petroleum refining
PA: Cenovus Energy Inc
    225 6 Ave Sw
    Calgary AB T2P 1
    403 766-2000

(G-9264)
LIMA SHEET METAL MACHINE & MFG
Also Called: Lima Sheet Metal
1001 Bowman Rd (45804-3409)
PHONE.................................419 229-1161
Michael R Emerick, *Pr*
Thomas Emerick, *
Ann Emerick, *
EMP: 31 **EST:** 1974
SQ FT: 26,250
SALES (est): 2.49MM Privately Held
Web: www.limasheetmetal.com
SIC: 3589 3599 7349 7692   Commercial cooking and foodwarming equipment; Machine shop, jobbing and repair; Building maintenance, except repairs; Welding repair

(G-9265)
LIMA SPORTING GOODS INC
1404 Allentown Rd (45805-2204)
PHONE.................................419 222-1036
David Kirian, *Pr*
EMP: 20 **EST:** 1976
SQ FT: 12,900
SALES (est): 2.27MM Privately Held
Web: www.limasportinggoods.net
SIC: 2759 5941   Screen printing; Team sports equipment

(G-9266)
LRI POST-ACQUISITION INC (PA)
893 Shawnee Rd (45805-3437)
PHONE.................................419 227-2200
Gary Stanklus, *Pr*
Darlene Stanklus, *Sec*
▲ **EMP:** 19 **EST:** 1991
SQ FT: 12,000
SALES (est): 4.76MM Privately Held
Web: www.leadar-roll.com
SIC: 3599   Machine shop, jobbing and repair

(G-9267)
MENARD INC
2614 N Eastown Rd (45807-1601)
PHONE.................................419 998-4348
Timothy Bart, *Mgr*
EMP: 204
SALES (corp-wide): 1.7B Privately Held
Web: www.menards.com
SIC: 2431   Millwork
PA: Menard, Inc.
    5101 Menard Dr
    Eau Claire WI 54703
    715 876-2000

(G-9268)
MESSER LLC
961 Industry Ave (45804-4171)
PHONE.................................419 227-9585
EMP: 10
SALES (corp-wide): 1.63B Privately Held
Web: www.messeramericas.com
SIC: 2813   Industrial gases
HQ: Messer Llc
    200 Smrst Corp Blvd # 7000
    Bridgewater NJ 08807
    800 755-9277

(G-9269)
MESSER LLC
1680 Buckeye Rd (45804-1826)
PHONE.................................419 221-5043
Stuart Emmons, *Brnch Mgr*
EMP: 7
SALES (corp-wide): 1.63B Privately Held
Web: www.messeramericas.com
SIC: 2813   Nitrogen
HQ: Messer Llc
    200 Smrst Corp Blvd # 7000
    Bridgewater NJ 08807
    800 755-9277

(G-9270)
METOKOTE CORPORATION (HQ)
Also Called: Ppg-Metokote
1340 Neubrecht Rd (45801-3120)
PHONE.................................419 996-7800
Jeffrey J Oravitz, *Pr*
▲ **EMP:** 445 **EST:** 1969
SQ FT: 30,000
SALES (est): 397.04MM
SALES (corp-wide): 17.65B Publicly Held
Web: www.ppgcoatingsservices.com
SIC: 3479   Coating of metals and formed products
PA: Ppg Industries, Inc.
    1 Ppg Pl
    Pittsburgh PA 15272
    412 434-3131

(G-9271)
MIDWEST COMMERCIAL MLLWK INC
514 N Union St (45801-4159)
PHONE.................................419 224-5001
EMP: 12 **EST:** 1996
SQ FT: 15,200
SALES (est): 2.37MM Privately Held
Web: www.mwmill.com
SIC: 2431   Millwork

(G-9272)
MURPHY TRACTOR & EQP CO INC
Also Called: John Deere Authorized Dealer
3550 Saint Johns Rd (45804-4017)
PHONE.................................419 221-3666
EMP: 8
Web: www.murphytractor.com
SIC: 3531 5082   Construction machinery; Construction and mining machinery
HQ: Murphy Tractor & Equipment Co., Inc.
    5375 N Deere Rd
    Park City KS 67219
    855 246-9124

(G-9273)
NATIONAL LIME AND STONE CO
1314 Findlay Rd (45801-3106)
PHONE.................................419 228-3434
Nick Morris, *Mgr*
EMP: 28
SQ FT: 1,200
SALES (corp-wide): 167.89MM Privately Held
Web: www.natlime.com
SIC: 1422   Crushed and broken limestone
PA: The National Lime And Stone Company
    551 Lake Cascade Pkwy
    Findlay OH 45840
    419 422-4341

(G-9274)
NEWS GAZETTE PRINTING COMPANY
Also Called: Ngp Printing Professional
324 W Market St (45801-4714)
P.O. Box 1017 (45802-1017)
PHONE.................................419 227-2527
Dan Mills, *Pr*
James Honegger, *VP*
Peter Paulik, *VP*
EMP: 11 **EST:** 1900
SQ FT: 2,800
SALES (est): 686.19K Privately Held
Web: www.ngpco.com
SIC: 2752   Offset printing

(G-9275)
PCS NITROGEN INC
Also Called: Arcadian Ohio
1900 Fort Amanda Rd (45804-1827)
P.O. Box 628 (45802-0628)
PHONE.................................419 226-1200
Chuck Treloar, *Mgr*
EMP: 17
SALES (corp-wide): 29.06B Privately Held
Web: www.nutrien.com
SIC: 2873   Nitrogen solutions (fertilizer)
HQ: Pcs Nitrogen, Inc.
    500 Lake Cook Rd Ste 150
    Deerfield IL 60015

(G-9276)
PCS NITROGEN OHIO LP
2200 Fort Amanda Rd (45804-1801)
P.O. Box 628 (45802-0628)
PHONE.................................419 879-8989
Jochen Tilk, *Pr*
Wayne Brownlee, *Ex VP*
EMP: 70 **EST:** 1993
SALES (est): 12.57MM
SALES (corp-wide): 29.06B Privately Held
SIC: 2873   Nitrogenous fertilizers
HQ: Potash Corporation Of Saskatchewan Inc
    1700-211 19 St E
    Saskatoon SK S7K 5
    306 933-8500

(G-9277)
PPG INDUSTRIES INC
2599 Shawnee Industrial Dr (45804-2365)
PHONE.................................419 331-2011
EMP: 19
SALES (corp-wide): 17.65B Publicly Held
Web: www.ppg.com
SIC: 2851   Paints and allied products
PA: Ppg Industries, Inc.
    1 Ppg Pl
    Pittsburgh PA 15272
    412 434-3131

(G-9278)
PROCTER & GAMBLE MFG CO
Also Called: Procter & Gamble
3875 Reservoir Rd (45801-3310)
P.O. Box 1900 (45802-1900)
PHONE.................................419 226-5500
J G Boney, *Brnch Mgr*
EMP: 250
SALES (corp-wide): 82.01B Publicly Held
Web: us.pg.com
SIC: 2844   Perfumes, cosmetics and other toilet preparations
HQ: The Procter & Gamble Manufacturing Company
    1 Procter And Gamble Plz
    Cincinnati OH 45202
    513 983-1100

(G-9279)
PROFORMA SYSTEMS ADVANTAGE
Also Called: Systems Advantage
1207 Findlay Rd (45801-3103)
PHONE.................................419 224-8747
EMP: 6 **EST:** 1995
SALES (est): 807.64K Privately Held
SIC: 2759   Calendars: printing, nsk

(G-9280)
PUNCH COMPONENTS INC
505 N Cable Rd (45805-2132)
PHONE.................................419 224-1242
EMP: 30
SQ FT: 50,000
SALES (est): 1.96MM Privately Held
SIC: 3663 3827   Television broadcasting and communications equipment; Optical instruments and lenses
PA: Iep Invest Nv
    Noorderlaan 139
    Antwerpen 2030
    57226720

(G-9281)
QUICK AS A WINK PRINTING CO
321 W High St (45801-4701)
PHONE.................................419 224-9786
TOLL FREE: 800
David S Beck, *Pr*
Julie Kirk, *Mgr*
EMP: 8
SQ FT: 5,000
SALES (est): 491.92K Privately Held
Web: www.quickasawink.org
SIC: 2752 2791 7389 5099   Offset printing; Typesetting; Sign painting and lettering shop; Rubber stamps

(G-9282)
RANDALL BEARINGS INC (DH)
Also Called: Randall
240 Jay Begg Pkwy (45804-1901)
P.O. Box 1258 (45802-1258)
PHONE.................................419 223-1075
Erwin Mayr, *CEO*
▲ **EMP:** 78 **EST:** 1906
SALES (est): 18.42MM Privately Held
Web: www.randallbearings.com
SIC: 3568 3624 3366   Bearings, bushings, and blocks; Carbon and graphite products; Copper foundries
HQ: Wieland-Werke Ag
    Graf-Arco-Str. 36
    Ulm BW 89079
    7319440

(G-9283)
RECYCLED POLYMER SOLUTIONS LLC
750 Buckeye Rd (45804-1906)
P.O. Box 4687 (45365-4687)
PHONE.................................937 821-4020

▲ = Import ▼ = Export
◆ = Import/Export

EMP: 6 **EST:** 2018
SALES (est): 309.79K **Privately Held**
SIC: 2822 Ethylene-propylene rubbers, EPDM polymers

(G-9284)
REGAL BELOIT AMERICA INC
200 E Chapman Rd (45801-2012)
PHONE.................608 364-8800
William Conway, *Manager*
EMP: 40
SALES (corp-wide): 6.25B **Publicly Held**
SIC: 3621 3625 Motors and generators; Relays and industrial controls
HQ: Regal Beloit America, Inc.
111 W Michigan St
Milwaukee WI 53203
608 364-8800

(G-9285)
RESOURCE RECYCLING INC
1596 Neubrecht Rd (45801-3124)
PHONE.................419 222-2702
Micah Hollinger, *Pr*
EMP: 15 **EST:** 2008
SALES (est): 2.88MM **Privately Held**
Web: www.resourcemulch.com
SIC: 4953 3999 4214 Recycling, waste materials; Grinding and pulverizing of materials, nec; Local trucking with storage

(G-9286)
RMT HOLDINGS INC
1025 Findlay Rd (45801-3171)
P.O. Box 5183 (45802-5183)
PHONE.................419 221-1168
Richard Toth, *Pr*
Cathi Toth, *VP*
EMP: 15 **EST:** 1989
SQ FT: 15,000
SALES (est): 1.95MM **Privately Held**
SIC: 2789 Paper cutting

(G-9287)
RUDOLPH FOODS COMPANY INC (PA)
Also Called: Rudolph Foods
6575 Bellefontaine Rd (45804-4415)
P.O. Box 509 (45802-0509)
PHONE.................909 383-7463
James Rudolph, *Ch*
John E Rudolph Senior, *Ch*
Richard Rudolph, *
Barbara Snyder, *
Philip Rudolph, *
◆ **EMP:** 160 **EST:** 1987
SQ FT: 110,000
SALES (est): 131.1MM
SALES (corp-wide): 131.1MM **Privately Held**
Web: www.rudolphfoods.com
SIC: 2096 2099 Pork rinds; Food preparations, nec

(G-9288)
SEWER RODDING EQUIPMENT CO
Also Called: Sreco Flexible
3434 S Dixie Hwy (45804-3756)
PHONE.................419 991-2065
Larry Drain, *Mgr*
EMP: 140
SALES (corp-wide): 9.75MM **Privately Held**
SIC: 5032 3546 3423 Sewer pipe, clay; Power-driven handtools; Hand and edge tools, nec
PA: Sewer Rodding Equipment Co Inc
3217 Carter Ave
Marina Del Rey CA 90292
310 301-9009

(G-9289)
SIGNS OHIO INC
57 Town Sq (45801-4950)
PHONE.................419 228-7446
Bud Smith, *CEO*
Greg Smith, *Pr*
EMP: 6 **EST:** 2006
SALES (est): 523.08K **Privately Held**
Web: www.signsohio.com
SIC: 3993 Signs and advertising specialties

(G-9290)
SNOW PRINTING CO INC
1000 W Grand Ave Frnt (45801-3498)
PHONE.................419 229-7669
Donald L Kohl, *Pr*
Daniel Kohl, *VP*
Joyce Kohl, *Sec*
EMP: 10 **EST:** 1890
SQ FT: 4,200
SALES (est): 980K **Privately Held**
SIC: 2752 2759 Offset printing; Letterpress printing

(G-9291)
SPALLINGER MILLWRIGHT SVC CO
Also Called: Spallnger Atclave Systms/US MI
1155 E Hanthorn Rd (45804-3929)
PHONE.................419 225-5830
Scott Spallinger, *Pr*
▲ **EMP:** 42 **EST:** 1989
SQ FT: 80,000
SALES (est): 9.61MM **Privately Held**
Web: www.spallinger.com
SIC: 3446 1796 Stairs, staircases, stair treads: prefabricated metal; Machinery installation

(G-9292)
STEVE MULCAHY
1700 Shawnee Rd (45805-3838)
PHONE.................419 229-4801
Steve Mulcahy, *Prin*
EMP: 7 **EST:** 2011
SALES (est): 169.37K **Privately Held**
Web: www.shawneecountryclub.com
SIC: 3799 Golf carts, powered

(G-9293)
SUPERIOR FORGE & STEEL CORP (PA)
1820 Mcclain Rd (45804-1978)
PHONE.................419 222-4412
James C Markovitz, *CEO*
Keith Schwarz, *
◆ **EMP:** 104 **EST:** 1991
SQ FT: 350,000
SALES (est): 25.43MM **Privately Held**
Web: www.sfsrolls.com
SIC: 3316 3462 Cold finishing of steel shapes; Iron and steel forgings

(G-9294)
SUPERIOR METAL PRODUCTS INC (PA)
Also Called: American Trim
1005 W Grand Ave (45801-3400)
PHONE.................419 228-1145
Leo Hawk, *Ch*
Richard Pfeifer, *
Dana Morgan, *
◆ **EMP:** 50 **EST:** 1958
SQ FT: 15,000
SALES (est): 445.1MM
SALES (corp-wide): 445.1MM **Privately Held**
Web: www.amtrim.com
SIC: 3429 3469 Hardware, nec; Porcelain enameled products and utensils

(G-9295)
TELEDOOR LLC
1075 Prosperity Rd (45801-3127)
P.O. Box 316 (45853-0316)
PHONE.................419 227-3000
John Recker, *Managing Member*
EMP: 7 **EST:** 2005
SQ FT: 22,000
SALES (est): 719.12K **Privately Held**
Web: www.teledoormfg.com
SIC: 2431 Doors, wood

(G-9296)
TELEDOOR MANUFACTURING LLC
1075 Prosperity Rd (45801-3127)
P.O. Box 316 (45853-0316)
PHONE.................419 227-3000
EMP: 8 **EST:** 2017
SALES (est): 304.56K **Privately Held**
Web: www.teledoormfg.com
SIC: 3999 Manufacturing industries, nec

(G-9297)
TERRY & JACK NEON SIGN CO
225 S Collins Ave (45804-3001)
PHONE.................419 229-0674
Jack L Pisel Junior, *Pr*
Mike Strange, *
Patricia Woods, *
EMP: 7 **EST:** 1947
SQ FT: 40,000
SALES (est): 235.96K **Privately Held**
SIC: 3993 Electric signs

(G-9298)
THE419
201 W Market St (45801-4819)
PHONE.................855 451-1018
EMP: 6 **EST:** 2016
SALES (est): 49.41K **Privately Held**
Web: www.the419.com
SIC: 2741 Miscellaneous publishing

(G-9299)
UNITED STATES PLASTIC CORP
Also Called: Neatlysmart
1390 Neubrecht Rd (45801-3120)
PHONE.................419 228-2242
EMP: 100 **EST:** 1962
SALES (est): 4MM
SALES (corp-wide): 49.68MM **Privately Held**
Web: www.usplastic.com
SIC: 5162 3089 Plastics materials and basic shapes; Plastics processing
HQ: Stanita Foundation
941 Fry Rd
Greenwood IN 46142
317 881-6751

(G-9300)
VINO BELLISSIMO
2412 Cable Ct (45805-3406)
PHONE.................419 296-4267
EMP: 7 **EST:** 2018
SALES (est): 173.87K **Privately Held**
Web: www.vinobmo.com
SIC: 2084 Wines

(G-9301)
WAYNE MORGAN CORP
895 Shawnee Rd (45805-3437)
P.O. Box 943 (45802-0943)
PHONE.................419 222-4181
James Gideon, *Pr*
EMP: 6 **EST:** 2011
SALES (est): 212.88K **Privately Held**
SIC: 3569 Generators: steam, liquid oxygen, or nitrogen

(G-9302)
WHEMCO-OHIO FOUNDRY INC
Also Called: Whemco
1600 Mcclain Rd (45804-1979)
PHONE.................419 222-2111
Charles R Novelli, *Pr*
Robert J Peterson, *VP*
Carl Maskiewicz, *VP*
Robert Zabelsky, *Quality Vice President*
Anthony J Poli, *Prin*
EMP: 140 **EST:** 1990
SALES (est): 25.39MM
SALES (corp-wide): 367.37MM **Privately Held**
Web: www.whemco.com
SIC: 3321 3325 3322 Gray iron castings, nec ; Steel foundries, nec; Malleable iron foundries
HQ: Whemco Inc.
5 Hot Metal St Ste 300
Pittsburgh PA 15203
412 390-2700

Lima
Auglaize County

(G-9303)
ALPHA INC
3320 Fort Shawnee Industrial Dr (45806-1843)
PHONE.................419 996-7355
Frederick F Brower, *Prin*
EMP: 9 **EST:** 1983
SALES (est): 231.82K **Privately Held**
SIC: 3089 Blister or bubble formed packaging, plastics

(G-9304)
ALPLA INC
3320 Fort Shawnee Industrial Dr (45806-1843)
PHONE.................419 991-9484
▲ **EMP:** 15
SALES (corp-wide): 242.12K **Privately Held**
Web: www.alpla.com
SIC: 3089 Plastics containers, except foam
HQ: Alpla Inc.
289 Highway 155 S
Mcdonough GA 30253
770 305-7213

(G-9305)
PRECISON THRMPLSTIC CMPNNTS IN
Also Called: P T C
3765 Saint Johns Rd (45806-2629)
P.O. Box 1296 (45802-1296)
PHONE.................419 227-4500
Randy E Carter, *CEO*
◆ **EMP:** 100 **EST:** 1982
SQ FT: 62,000
SALES (est): 10.49MM **Privately Held**
Web: www.ptclima.com
SIC: 3089 Injection molding of plastics

(G-9306)
PROSTAR LLC
4610 S Dixie Hwy Ste D (45806-1821)
P.O. Box 536 (45802-0536)
PHONE.................419 225-8806
EMP: 16 **EST:** 2004
SQ FT: 10,000
SALES (est): 1.81MM **Privately Held**
Web: www.prostarusa.net
SIC: 3799 Trailers and trailer equipment

Lisbon
Columbiana County

(G-9307)
ALBCO FOUNDRY INC
230 Maple St (44432-1275)
PHONE................................330 424-7716
EMP: 23 EST: 1956
SALES (est): 2.2MM **Privately Held**
Web: www.albco.com
SIC: 3366 3369 3365 Castings (except die), nec, bronze; Zinc and zinc-base alloy castings, except die-castings; Masts, cast aluminum

(G-9308)
BRIGHTPET NUTRITION GROUP LLC (PA)
38251 Industrial Park Rd (44432-8325)
PHONE................................330 424-1431
Matthew Golladay, Pr
EMP: 20 EST: 2016
SALES (est): 50.33MM
SALES (corp-wide): 50.33MM **Privately Held**
Web: www.brightpet.com
SIC: 2048 Canned pet food (except dog and cat)

(G-9309)
BUCKEYE CUSTOM FABRICATION LLC
7573 State Route 45 (44432-8382)
PHONE................................330 831-5619
EMP: 8 EST: 2017
SALES (est): 966.72K **Privately Held**
SIC: 3441 Fabricated structural metal

(G-9310)
CCBDD
35947 State Route 172 (44432-9404)
PHONE................................330 424-0404
EMP: 10 EST: 2017
SALES (est): 207.86K **Privately Held**
Web: www.ccbdd.net
SIC: 3999

(G-9311)
D W DICKEY AND SON INC (PA)
Also Called: D W Dickey
7896 Dickey Dr (44432)
P.O. Box 189 (44432)
PHONE................................330 424-1441
Gary Neville, Pr
Timothy Dickey, *
David Dickey, *
Janet Blosser, *
EMP: 128 EST: 1948
SALES (est): 43.61MM
SALES (corp-wide): 43.61MM **Privately Held**
Web: www.dwdickey.com
SIC: 5169 3273 5172 Explosives; Ready-mixed concrete; Fuel oil

(G-9312)
GLOBAL-PAK INC (PA)
9636 Elkton Rd (44432-9575)
P.O. Box 89 (44415-0089)
PHONE................................330 482-1993
James Foster, Pr
▲ EMP: 26 EST: 1998
SQ FT: 75,000
SALES (est): 10MM
SALES (corp-wide): 10MM **Privately Held**
Web: www.global-pak.com
SIC: 5199 2393 Packaging materials; Textile bags

(G-9313)
GRANT STREET PALLET INC
39196 Grant St (44432-9781)
P.O. Box 268 (44432-0268)
PHONE................................330 424-0355
Kenneth Miller, Pr
EMP: 8 EST: 2013
SALES (est): 507.13K **Privately Held**
SIC: 2448 Pallets, wood

(G-9314)
HEIM SHEET METAL INC
905 N Market St (44432-1023)
PHONE................................330 424-7820
David Belaney, Pr
Melinda Belaney, Sec
EMP: 6 EST: 1928
SALES (est): 516K **Privately Held**
SIC: 3444 Sheet metalwork

(G-9315)
HOUSING & EMRGNCY LGSTCS PLNNR
36905 State Route 30 (44432-9413)
PHONE................................209 201-7511
EMP: 20 EST: 2008
SALES (est): 685.23K **Privately Held**
SIC: 3999 Manufacturing industries, nec

(G-9316)
J & J TIRE & ALIGNMENT
12649 State Route 45 (44432-9698)
PHONE................................330 424-5200
Braine Schafer, Owner
EMP: 7 EST: 1977
SQ FT: 2,500
SALES (est): 638.98K **Privately Held**
SIC: 5531 7538 7534 7539 Batteries, automotive and truck; General automotive repair shops; Tire retreading and repair shops; Automotive repair shops, nec

(G-9317)
J I T PALLETS INC
39196 Grant St (44432-9781)
P.O. Box 268 (44432-0268)
PHONE................................330 424-0355
Kenneth Miller, Pr
EMP: 6 EST: 2015
SALES (est): 120.47K **Privately Held**
SIC: 2448 Pallets, wood

(G-9318)
J P INDUSTRIAL PRODUCTS INC
State Rte 518 (44432)
PHONE................................330 424-3388
Beccy Brown, Mgr
EMP: 22
SALES (corp-wide): 15.95MM **Privately Held**
Web: www.jpindustrial.com
SIC: 3086 Padding, foamed plastics
PA: J. P. Industrial Products, Inc.
  11988 State Route 45
  Lisbon OH 44432
  330 424-1110

(G-9319)
J P INDUSTRIAL PRODUCTS INC (PA)
Also Called: JP Industrial
11988 State Route 45 (44432-8625)
PHONE................................330 424-1110
James E Pastore, Pr
▲ EMP: 8 EST: 1989
SQ FT: 5,000
SALES (est): 15.95MM
SALES (corp-wide): 15.95MM **Privately Held**
Web: www.jpindustrial.com
SIC: 2821 Plastics materials and resins

(G-9320)
JPI COASTAL LLC
11988 State Route 45 (44432-9615)
PHONE................................330 424-1110
EMP: 8 EST: 2014
SALES (est): 519.76K **Privately Held**
Web: www.jpindustrial.com
SIC: 3087 Custom compound purchased resins

(G-9321)
LISBON POWDER COATING
6191 Lisbon Rd (44432-9310)
PHONE................................234 567-1324
Gabriel W Miller, Admn
EMP: 6 EST: 2014
SALES (est): 88.61K **Privately Held**
SIC: 3479 Coating of metals and formed products

(G-9322)
OGDEN NEWSPAPERS OHIO INC (DH)
Also Called: Morning Journal
308 Maple St (44432-1205)
PHONE................................330 424-9541
Beth Todd, Contrlr
EMP: 20 EST: 1852
SQ FT: 13,000
SALES (est): 2.41MM **Privately Held**
Web: www.morningjournalnews.com
SIC: 2711 Job printing and newspaper publishing combined
HQ: The Ogden Newspapers Inc
  1500 Main St
  Wheeling WV 26003
  304 233-0100

(G-9323)
OHIO PET FOODS INC (HQ)
38251 Industrial Park Rd (44432)
PHONE................................330 424-1431
Jim Golladay, Pr
Matthew Golladay, *
Travis Golladay, *
◆ EMP: 27 EST: 1978
SQ FT: 50,000
SALES (est): 17.79MM
SALES (corp-wide): 50.33MM **Privately Held**
Web: www.brightpet.com
SIC: 2048 2047 Feeds, specialty: mice, guinea pig, etc.; Dog food
PA: Brightpet Nutrition Group Llc
  38251 Industrial Park Rd
  Lisbon OH 44432
  330 424-1431

(G-9324)
PAPER SERVICE INC
12022 Leslie Rd (44432-9531)
PHONE................................330 227-3546
Randy Barnard, Pr
Dean Barnard, VP
EMP: 24 EST: 1968
SQ FT: 20,000
SALES (est): 650.97K **Privately Held**
SIC: 2621 Paper mills

(G-9325)
RAY LEWIS ENTERPRISES LLC
7235 State Route 45 (44432-8314)
PHONE................................330 424-9585
Tad E Rose Authorized Represen t, Prin
EMP: 6 EST: 2007
SALES (est): 52.6K **Privately Held**
SIC: 3084 Plastics pipe

(G-9326)
RL CRAIG INC
6496 State Route 45 (44432-8357)
PHONE................................330 424-1525
EMP: 13 EST: 1993
SQ FT: 7,600
SALES (est): 2.35MM **Privately Held**
Web: www.rlcraig.com
SIC: 3599 Machine shop, jobbing and repair

(G-9327)
WELDING IMPROVEMENT COMPANY
Also Called: Wicom Services
10070 Stookesberry Rd (44432-8639)
PHONE................................330 424-9666
Tina Strong, Pr
Scott Strong, VP
EMP: 8 EST: 1978
SALES (est): 2.45MM **Privately Held**
Web: www.weldingimprovement.com
SIC: 3441 Fabricated structural metal

Litchfield
Medina County

(G-9328)
MEDINA FOODS INC
Also Called: Gold Rush Jerky
9706 Crow Rd (44253-9549)
PHONE................................330 725-1390
Abdalla Nimer, Pr
Cathy Fobes, *
EMP: 45 EST: 1945
SQ FT: 50,000
SALES (est): 5.08MM **Privately Held**
Web: www.goldrushjerky.com
SIC: 2011 Meat packing plants

(G-9329)
OLD WORLD STONES
4791 Richman Rd (44253-9798)
PHONE................................330 299-1128
Ryan Hurst, Prin
▲ EMP: 8 EST: 2010
SALES (est): 140.64K **Privately Held**
Web: www.oldworldstones.com
SIC: 3479 Etching and engraving

(G-9330)
PARKN MANUFACTURING LLC
8035 Norwalk Rd Ste 107 (44253-9135)
PHONE................................330 723-8172
Willard Robert Scandlon, CEO
EMP: 12 EST: 1992
SQ FT: 10,000
SALES (est): 1.3MM **Privately Held**
Web: www.parkn-mfg.com
SIC: 3599 Machine shop, jobbing and repair

Lithopolis
Fairfield County

(G-9331)
UNITED MCGILL CORPORATION
122 E Columbus St (43136-1006)
PHONE................................614 920-1267
EMP: 16
SALES (corp-wide): 126.17MM **Privately Held**
Web: www.unitedmcgill.com
SIC: 3589 Water filters and softeners, household type
HQ: United Mcgill Corporation
  1 Mission Park
  Groveport OH 43125
  614 829-1200

Little Hocking
Washington County

(G-9332)
AGE GRAPHICS LLC (PA)
678 Collins Rd (45742-5397)
PHONE.................................740 989-0006
EMP: 9 **EST:** 1997
SALES (est): 1.29MM
SALES (corp-wide): 1.29MM **Privately Held**
Web: www.decals-oem.com
SIC: 3577 Graphic displays, except graphic terminals

(G-9333)
AMERICAN BOTTLING COMPANY
871 State Route 618 (45742-5377)
PHONE.................................740 423-9230
Robert Deeds, *Prin*
EMP: 56
Web: www.keurigdrpepper.com
SIC: 2086 Soft drinks: packaged in cans, bottles, etc.
HQ: The American Bottling Company
6425 Hall Of Fame Ln
Frisco TX 75034

Lockbourne
Franklin County

(G-9334)
DELL INC
Also Called: Genco
3795 Creekside Pkwy (43137-8501)
PHONE.................................614 491-4603
EMP: 15 **EST:** 2019
SALES (est): 551.11K **Privately Held**
Web: www.dell.com
SIC: 3571 Personal computers (microcomputers)

(G-9335)
GR8 NEWS PACKAGING LLC
3657 Tradeport Ct (43137)
PHONE.................................314 739-1202
Patrick Mcswain, *Managing Member*
EMP: 15 **EST:** 2019
SALES (est): 1.02MM **Privately Held**
SIC: 2621 Molded pulp products

(G-9336)
HIKMA PHARMACEUTICALS USA INC
2130 Rohr Rd (43137-9323)
PHONE.................................732 542-1191
Michael Raya, *Mgr*
EMP: 13
SALES (corp-wide): 2.88B **Privately Held**
Web: www.hikma.com
SIC: 2834 Pharmaceutical preparations
HQ: Hikma Pharmaceuticals Usa Inc.
200 Connell Dr Ste 4100
Berkeley Heights NJ 07922
908 673-1030

(G-9337)
J P SAND & GRAVEL COMPANY
Also Called: Marble Cliff Block & Bldrs Sup
5911 Lockbourne Rd (43137-9256)
P.O. Box 2 (43137-0002)
PHONE.................................614 497-0083
Richard A Roberts, *Pr*
Herbert Hartshorn, *
Mike Craiglow, *
Joann Roberts, *
EMP: 15 **EST:** 1925
SQ FT: 6,200
SALES (est): 522.84K **Privately Held**
SIC: 3271 1442 Blocks, concrete or cinder: standard; Construction sand mining

(G-9338)
LUXOTTICA NORTH AMER DIST LLC
2150 Bixby Rd (43137-9273)
PHONE.................................614 492-5610
EMP: 7 **EST:** 2009
SALES (est): 93.71K **Privately Held**
SIC: 3851 Frames and parts, eyeglass and spectacle

(G-9339)
LUXOTTICA OF AMERICA INC
Also Called: Luxottica Rx Operations
2150 Bixby Rd (43137-9273)
PHONE.................................614 492-5610
Chip Sexton, *Brnch Mgr*
EMP: 11
SALES (corp-wide): 2.55MM **Privately Held**
Web: www.luxottica.com
SIC: 3851 Ophthalmic goods
HQ: Luxottica Of America Inc.
4000 Luxottica Pl
Mason OH 45040

(G-9340)
NATIONAL LIME AND STONE CO
5911 Lockbourne Rd (43137-9256)
PHONE.................................614 497-0083
Richard Roberts, *Brnch Mgr*
EMP: 19
SQ FT: 4,032
SALES (corp-wide): 167.89MM **Privately Held**
Web: www.natlime.com
SIC: 3271 1442 Blocks, concrete or cinder: standard; Construction sand mining
PA: The National Lime And Stone Company
551 Lake Cascade Pkwy
Findlay OH 45840
419 422-4341

(G-9341)
VERTIV CORPORATION
1595 London Groveport Rd (43137-9259)
PHONE.................................614 888-0246
Shawn Mitchell, *Mgr*
EMP: 6
SALES (corp-wide): 6.86B **Publicly Held**
SIC: 3613 3585 7629 Regulators, power; Air conditioning equipment, complete; Electronic equipment repair
HQ: Vertiv Corporation
505 N Cleveland Ave
Westerville OH 43082
614 888-0246

(G-9342)
VSP LAB COLUMBUS
2605 Rohr Rd (43137-9281)
PHONE.................................614 409-8900
Ed Morris, *Prin*
EMP: 13 **EST:** 2003
SALES (est): 864.87K **Privately Held**
Web: www.vspone.com
SIC: 3827 Optical instruments and lenses

(G-9343)
WHIRLPOOL CORPORATION
Also Called: Whirlpool
6241 Shook Rd (43137-9306)
PHONE.................................614 409-4340
EMP: 11
SALES (corp-wide): 19.45B **Publicly Held**
Web: www.whirlpoolcorp.com
SIC: 3585 3632 3633 Air conditioning units, complete: domestic or industrial; Refrigerators, mechanical and absorption; household; Household laundry machines, including coin-operated
PA: Whirlpool Corporation
2000 N M-63
Benton Harbor MI 49022
269 923-5000

Lodi
Medina County

(G-9344)
ABC PLASTICS INC
140 West Dr (44254)
P.O. Box 59 (44254)
PHONE.................................330 948-3322
Barbara Lohmier, *Pr*
EMP: 40 **EST:** 1986
SQ FT: 66,000
SALES (est): 6.67MM **Privately Held**
Web: www.abcplasticslodi.com
SIC: 3089 Injection molded finished plastics products, nec

(G-9345)
ADVANCE BRONZE INC (PA)
139 Ohio St (44254-1047)
P.O. Box 280 (44254-0280)
PHONE.................................330 948-1231
David Del Propost, *Pr*
Tohmas Seringer, *
Jerry Shapiro, *
▲ **EMP:** 12 **EST:** 1954
SQ FT: 150,000
SALES (est): 9.21MM
SALES (corp-wide): 9.21MM **Privately Held**
Web: www.advancebronze.com
SIC: 3568 3366 Power transmission equipment, nec; Bushings and bearings

(G-9346)
ADVANCE BRONZEHUBCO DIV (HQ)
139 Ohio St (44254-1047)
PHONE.................................304 232-4414
EMP: 20 **EST:** 1969
SALES (est): 5.22MM
SALES (corp-wide): 9.21MM **Privately Held**
Web: www.advancebronze.com
SIC: 3366 Bronze foundry, nec
PA: Advance Bronze, Inc.
139 Ohio St
Lodi OH 44254
330 948-1231

(G-9347)
ALLOY FABRICATORS INC
700 Wooster St (44254-1340)
P.O. Box 37 (44254-0037)
PHONE.................................330 948-3535
Lance Yurich, *Pr*
Dan Dietrick, *Genl Mgr*
Donna Yurich Stckhdlr, *Prin*
EMP: 24 **EST:** 1939
SQ FT: 15,000
SALES (est): 4.24MM **Privately Held**
Web: www.alloyfab.net
SIC: 3441 Fabricated structural metal

(G-9348)
CARBON POLYMERS COMPANY
104 Lee St (44254-1056)
PHONE.................................330 948-3007
Saquib Toor, *Pr*
Pavel Smyshyaev, *CFO*
Jay Jafar Ctrl, *Prin*
EMP: 59 **EST:** 2021
SALES (est): 8.66MM **Privately Held**
Web: www.carbonpolymersco.com
SIC: 3089 Pallets, plastics

(G-9349)
CROPKING INCORPORATED
134 West Dr (44254)
PHONE.................................330 302-4203
Paul Brentlinger, *Pr*
Marilyn Brentlinger, *Sec*
◆ **EMP:** 16 **EST:** 1982
SQ FT: 40,000
SALES (est): 2.46MM **Privately Held**
Web: www.cropking.com
SIC: 3448 3999 Greenhouses, prefabricated metal; Hydroponic equipment

(G-9350)
FASTFEED CORPORATION
124 S Academy St (44254-1345)
PHONE.................................330 948-7333
Dan Reed, *Pr*
EMP: 6 **EST:** 1997
SALES (est): 998.44K **Privately Held**
Web: www.fastfeedcorporation.com
SIC: 3441 Fabricated structural metal

(G-9351)
I-M-A ENTERPRISES INC
700 Wooster St (44254-1340)
PHONE.................................330 948-3535
Robert Yurich, *Pr*
Dennis Yurich, *VP*
Laurice Paultz, *Sec*
EMP: 10 **EST:** 1968
SQ FT: 1,600
SALES (est): 570K **Privately Held**
SIC: 3444 Sheet metal specialties, not stamped

(G-9352)
KNOTT BRAKE COMPANY
144 West Dr (44254-1062)
PHONE.................................800 566-8887
▲ **EMP:** 50 **EST:** 1987
SALES (est): 88MM **Privately Held**
Web: www.knottbrake.com
SIC: 3714 Motor vehicle brake systems and parts
PA: Knott Holding Gmbh
Obinger Str. 17
Eggstatt BY 83125

(G-9353)
MAGNACO INDUSTRIES INC
140 West Dr (44254-1062)
PHONE.................................216 961-3636
Ken Geith, *Pr*
Magdalaine Geith, *Sec*
EMP: 25 **EST:** 1974
SQ FT: 43,000
SALES (est): 2.35MM **Privately Held**
SIC: 3714 7389 Motor vehicle parts and accessories; Packaging and labeling services

(G-9354)
PETRITION LLC
705 Medina St (44254-1130)
PHONE.................................717 572-5665
Landry Walker, *Pr*
EMP: 6 **EST:** 2016
SALES (est): 311.12K **Privately Held**
SIC: 2047 Dog food

(G-9355)
PIONEER MACHINE INC
104 S Prospect St (44254-1313)
P.O. Box 277 (44254-0277)

Lodi - Medina County (G-9356)

PHONE..................330 948-6500
Don Gray, Pr
Sherry Gray, VP
EMP: 6 EST: 1987
SQ FT: 8,400
SALES (est): 494.79K **Privately Held**
Web: www.communitypsychassoc.com
SIC: 3441 3599 Fabricated structural metal; Machine shop, jobbing and repair

(G-9356)
SHILLING TRANSPORT INC
9718 Avon Lake Rd (44254-9639)
PHONE..................330 948-1105
Gary Frank, Pr
EMP: 7 EST: 2002
SALES (est): 580.21K **Privately Held**
SIC: 3715 Truck trailers

(G-9357)
STEPHEN ANDREWS INC
Also Called: Camelot Printing
7634 Lafayette Rd (44254-9607)
PHONE..................330 725-2672
Stephen Andrews, Pr
EMP: 7 EST: 1978
SQ FT: 1,700
SALES (est): 496.39K **Privately Held**
Web: www.camelotprinting.com
SIC: 2759 2752 Commercial printing, nec; Commercial printing, lithographic

Logan
Hocking County

(G-9358)
AMANDA BENT BOLT COMPANY
Also Called: Amanda Manufacturing
1120 C I C Dr (43138-9153)
P.O. Box 1027 (43138-4027)
PHONE..................740 385-6893
Robert Gruschow, Pr
▲ EMP: 212 EST: 1953
SQ FT: 139,000
SALES (est): 38.58MM
SALES (corp-wide): 62.95MM **Privately Held**
Web: www.abb1.com
SIC: 3496 3452 Miscellaneous fabricated wire products; Bolts, nuts, rivets, and washers
PA: Deshler Group, Inc.
    34450 Industrial Rd
    Livonia MI 48150
    734 525-9100

(G-9359)
AVT BECKETT ELEVATORS USA INC
30130 Industrial Park Dr (43138-3603)
PHONE..................844 360-0288
Barb Buchanan, Pr
EMP: 8 EST: 2017
SALES (est): 1.16MM **Privately Held**
Web: www.avtbeckett.com
SIC: 3534 Elevators and equipment

(G-9360)
CARBORUNDUM GRINDING WHEEL COMPANY
Also Called: Carborundum
1011 E Front St (43138-9791)
P.O. Box 759 (43138-0759)
PHONE..................740 385-2171
▲ EMP: 33 EST: 1984
SALES (est): 4.55MM **Privately Held**
Web: www.carborundum.net
SIC: 3291 Wheels, grinding: artificial

(G-9361)
CLAY LOGAN PRODUCTS COMPANY
Also Called: Logan Foundry & Machine
201 S Walnut St (43138-1376)
PHONE..................740 385-2184
Richard H Brandt, Ch Bd
William R Brandt, *
Donald Hoobler, *
William Heft, *
EMP: 80 EST: 1904
SQ FT: 266,000
SALES (est): 21.84MM **Privately Held**
Web: www.loganclay.com
SIC: 3259 Clay sewer and drainage pipe and tile

(G-9362)
COLUMBUS WASHBOARD COMPANY LTD
4 E Main St (43138-1221)
PHONE..................740 380-3828
Jacqueline M Barnett, Managing Member
▲ EMP: 8 EST: 1926
SALES (est): 694.18K **Privately Held**
Web: www.columbuswashboard.com
SIC: 2499 Washboards, wood and part wood

(G-9363)
GENERAL ELECTRIC COMPANY
Also Called: GE
State Route 93 N (43138)
PHONE..................740 385-2114
John Davis, Brnch Mgr
EMP: 41
SALES (corp-wide): 67.95B **Publicly Held**
Web: www.loganglassandwindow.com
SIC: 3231 3229 Products of purchased glass ; Pressed and blown glass, nec
PA: General Electric Company
    1 Aviation Way
    Cincinnati OH 45215
    617 443-3000

(G-9364)
HOCKING HLLS ENRGY WELL SVCS L
32919 Logan Horns Mill Rd (43138-8497)
PHONE..................740 385-6690
David Poling, Managing Member
EMP: 7 EST: 2015
SALES (est): 772.4K **Privately Held**
SIC: 1382 1381 Geophysical exploration, oil and gas field; Drilling oil and gas wells

(G-9365)
HOCKING VALLEY CONCRETE INC (PA)
35255 Hocking Dr (43138-9482)
PHONE..................740 385-2165
William Vaughn, Pr
Mark Vaughn, VP
David Vaughn, VP
EMP: 12 EST: 1956
SQ FT: 2,000
SALES (est): 3.78MM
SALES (corp-wide): 3.78MM **Privately Held**
Web: www.hockingvalleyconcrete.com
SIC: 3273 1442 Ready-mixed concrete; Construction sand mining

(G-9366)
KEYNES BROS INC
1 W Front St (43138-1825)
P.O. Box 628 (43138-0628)
PHONE..................740 385-6824
EMP: 65
Web: www.keynesbros.com
SIC: 2041 5191 Flour mills, cereal (except rice); Feed

(G-9367)
KILBARGER CONSTRUCTION INC
Also Called: C & L Supply
450 Gallagher Ave (43138-1893)
P.O. Box 946 (43138-0946)
PHONE..................740 385-6019
Edward Kilbarger, CEO
James E Kilbarger, *
Anthony Kilbarger, *
Ann Kilbarger, *
EMP: 120 EST: 1958
SQ FT: 2,500
SALES (est): 21.74MM **Privately Held**
Web: www.kilbarger.com
SIC: 1381 Drilling oil and gas wells

(G-9368)
LOGAN COATINGS LLC
2255 E Front St (43138-8637)
P.O. Box 202 (43138-0202)
PHONE..................740 380-0047
James M Johnson, Prin
EMP: 11 EST: 2014
SALES (est): 1.01MM **Privately Held**
Web: www.logancoatings.com
SIC: 3479 Coating of metals and formed products

(G-9369)
LOGAN GLASS TECHNOLOGIES LLC ◆
12680 State Route 93 N (43138-2503)
PHONE..................740 385-2114
EMP: 6 EST: 2022
SALES (est): 292.85K **Privately Held**
SIC: 2431 Louver windows, glass, wood frame

(G-9370)
LOGAN WELDING INC
37062 Hocking Dr (43138-9465)
PHONE..................740 385-9651
Tim Cordle, Off Mgr
Julie Cordle, Off Mgr
EMP: 6 EST: 1976
SQ FT: 5,100
SALES (est): 491.62K **Privately Held**
Web: www.loganweldinginc.com
SIC: 7692 Welding repair

(G-9371)
MENNEL MILLING COMPANY
Also Called: Mennel Milling Logan
1 W Front St (43138-1825)
PHONE..................740 385-6824
Larry Hawkins, Opers
EMP: 37
SALES (corp-wide): 211.12MM **Privately Held**
Web: www.mennel.com
SIC: 5191 2041 Feed; Flour mills, cereal (except rice)
PA: The Mennel Milling Company
    319 S Vine St
    Fostoria OH 44830
    419 435-8151

(G-9372)
OSBURN ASSOCIATES INC (PA)
9383 Vanatta Rd (43138-8719)
P.O. Box 912 (43138-0912)
PHONE..................740 385-5732
Harry Osburn, Dir
Donna Osburn, Dir
Charles A Gerken, Dir
▲ EMP: 16 EST: 1982
SQ FT: 39,360
SALES (est): 9.04MM
SALES (corp-wide): 9.04MM **Privately Held**
Web: www.osburns.com

SIC: 3089 5063 Fittings for pipe, plastics; Boxes and fittings, electrical

(G-9373)
PATTONS TRCK & HVY EQP SVC INC
Also Called: K & K Auto & Truck Parts
35640 Hocking Dr (43138-9467)
P.O. Box 963 (43138-0963)
PHONE..................740 385-4067
Paul Doug Patton, Pr
Troy Sanborn, Off Mgr
EMP: 20 EST: 1991
SQ FT: 3,400
SALES (est): 464.06K **Privately Held**
Web: www.pattonstruckandkkautoparts.com
SIC: 3599 7538 5531 Machine shop, jobbing and repair; General automotive repair shops ; Auto and home supply stores

(G-9374)
QUALITY CONCEPTS TELECOM LTD
19485 Harble Rd (43138-9772)
PHONE..................740 385-2003
EMP: 8 EST: 1987
SQ FT: 1,400
SALES (est): 157.9K **Privately Held**
SIC: 3452 Bolts, nuts, rivets, and washers

(G-9375)
RALPH ROBINSON INC
Also Called: Oil Enterprises
700 Ohio Ave (43138-8469)
P.O. Box 84 (43138-0084)
PHONE..................740 385-2747
Michael Robinson, Pr
EMP: 6 EST: 1962
SQ FT: 4,700
SALES (est): 669.95K **Privately Held**
SIC: 1389 5084 Oil and gas wells: building, repairing and dismantling; Oil refining machinery, equipment, and supplies

(G-9376)
SIGNS UNLMTED THE GRPHIC ADVNT (PA)
Also Called: Advent Designs
21313 State Route 93 S (43138-7508)
PHONE..................614 836-7446
Ed Zell, Pr
Judy Zell, Prin
EMP: 7 EST: 1972
SQ FT: 20,000
SALES (est): 482.21K **Privately Held**
SIC: 3993 7389 Signs and advertising specialties; Design services

(G-9377)
SMEAD MANUFACTURING COMPANY
Also Called: The Smead Manufacturing Company
851 Smead Rd (43138-9500)
PHONE..................740 385-5601
Arthur Tripp, Mgr
EMP: 194
SALES (corp-wide): 227.57MM **Privately Held**
Web: www.smead.com
SIC: 2675 Folders, filing, die-cut: made from purchased materials
PA: The Smead Manufacturing Company Llc
    600 Smead Blvd
    Hastings MN 55033
    651 437-4111

(G-9378)
WRIGHTS WELL SERVICE LLC
37940 Scout Rd (43138-8832)
PHONE..................740 380-9602

Ken Wright, *Owner*
EMP: 6 **EST:** 2002
SALES (est): 214.88K **Privately Held**
Web: wrightswellservicellc.business.site
SIC: 1389 Servicing oil and gas wells

London
Madison County

(G-9379)
ADVANCED DRAINAGE SYSTEMS INC
Also Called: ADS
400 E High St (43140-9501)
PHONE..............................740 852-2980
Robert Sensabaugh, *Brnch Mgr*
EMP: 109
SALES (corp-wide): 3.07B **Publicly Held**
Web: www.adspipe.com
SIC: 3084 Plastics pipe
PA: Advanced Drainage Systems, Inc.
    4640 Trueman Blvd
    Hilliard OH 43026
    614 658-0050

(G-9380)
ALL SEAL
141 Sharp Ave (43140-9043)
P.O. Box 285 (43140-0285)
PHONE..............................740 852-2628
EMP: 7 **EST:** 2017
SALES (est): 144.63K **Privately Held**
SIC: 2952 Asphalt felts and coatings

(G-9381)
ARMALY LLC
Also Called: Armaly Brands
110 W 1st St (43140-1484)
PHONE..............................740 852-3621
Annmarie Armaly, *Treas*
▼ **EMP:** 40 **EST:** 2010
SALES (est): 13.98MM
SALES (corp-wide): 14.92MM **Privately Held**
Web: www.armalybrands.com
SIC: 3089 5199 3086 Floor coverings, plastics; Sponges (animal); Plastics foam products
PA: Armaly Sponge Company
    1900 Easy St
    Commerce Township MI 48390
    248 669-2100

(G-9382)
BODYCOTE IMT INC
443 E High St (43140-9501)
PHONE..............................740 852-5000
Chris Gattie, *Mgr*
EMP: 17
SALES (corp-wide): 1B **Privately Held**
Web: www.bodycote.com
SIC: 3398 3269 Metal heat treating; Pottery household articles, except kitchen articles
HQ: Bodycote Imt, Inc.
    155 River St
    Andover MA 01810
    978 470-0876

(G-9383)
BODYCOTE THERMAL PROC INC
Also Called: Bodycote Kolsterising
443 E High St (43140-9501)
PHONE..............................740 852-4955
Doug Ridgeway, *Genl Mgr*
EMP: 7
SALES (corp-wide): 1B **Privately Held**
Web: www.bodycote.com
SIC: 3398 Metal heat treating
HQ: Bodycote Thermal Processing, Inc.
    12750 Merit Dr Ste 1400
    Dallas TX 75251
    214 904-2420

(G-9384)
CHURCH & DWIGHT CO INC
Also Called: Arm & Hammer
110 W 1st St (43140-1484)
PHONE..............................740 852-3621
Neil Parrish, *Brnch Mgr*
EMP: 11
SALES (corp-wide): 5.87B **Publicly Held**
Web: www.churchdwight.com
SIC: 2812 Sodium bicarbonate
PA: Church & Dwight Co., Inc.
    500 Charles Ewing Blvd
    Ewing NJ 08628
    609 806-1200

(G-9385)
CREAMER METAL PRODUCTS INC (PA)
77 S Madison Rd (43140-1444)
PHONE..............................740 852-1752
Kennison Sims, *Pt*
Scott Sims, *Pt*
EMP: 19 **EST:** 1945
SQ FT: 31,000
SALES (est): 2.78MM
SALES (corp-wide): 2.78MM **Privately Held**
Web: www.creamermetal.com
SIC: 3523 Farm machinery and equipment

(G-9386)
DEER CREEK HONEY FARMS LTD
551 E High St (43140-9304)
PHONE..............................740 852-0899
Christopher L Dunham, *Pt*
Mark L Dunham, *Pt*
Lee T Dunham, *Pt*
EMP: 8 **EST:** 1938
SQ FT: 22,000
SALES (est): 937.44K **Privately Held**
Web: www.deercreekhoney.com
SIC: 2099 0279 Honey, strained and bottled; Apiary (bee and honey farm)

(G-9387)
GARY I TEACH JR
4855 Rosedale Milford Center Rd (43140)
PHONE..............................614 582-7483
Gary L Teach, *Prin*
EMP: 7 **EST:** 2010
SALES (est): 93.59K **Privately Held**
SIC: 2672 Paper; coated and laminated, nec

(G-9388)
GRA-MAG TRUCK INTR SYSTEMS LLC (DH)
470 E High St (43140-9303)
PHONE..............................740 490-1000
Rick Chefer, *Managing Member*
▲ **EMP:** 30 **EST:** 1998
SQ FT: 60,000
SALES (est): 16.04MM
SALES (corp-wide): 37.84B **Privately Held**
Web: www.gramag.com
SIC: 3714 Motor vehicle parts and accessories
HQ: Magna International Of America, Inc.
    750 Tower Dr
    Troy MI 48098

(G-9389)
INTELLIGRATED PRODUCTS LLC
475 E High St (43140-9303)
P.O. Box 899 (43140-0899)
PHONE..............................740 490-0300
▲ **EMP:** 33 **EST:** 2001
SQ FT: 210,000
SALES (est): 8.27MM
SALES (corp-wide): 36.66B **Publicly Held**
SIC: 3535 Conveyors and conveying equipment
HQ: Intelligrated Systems, Inc.
    7901 Innovation Way
    Mason OH 45040
    866 936-7300

(G-9390)
KMAK GROUP LLC
480 E High St (43140-9303)
P.O. Box 496 (43140-0496)
PHONE..............................937 308-1023
Kevin Henry, *Managing Member*
EMP: 11 **EST:** 2009
SQ FT: 15,000
SALES (est): 1.73MM **Privately Held**
SIC: 2448 3089 Cargo containers, wood and wood with metal; Air mattresses, plastics

(G-9391)
NISSEN CHEMITEC AMERICA INC
Also Called: Nissen Chemitec America
350 E High St (43140-9773)
PHONE..............................740 852-3200
Shawn Hendrix, *Pr*
Shinya Kawakami, *
Richard Hendrix, *
Kunihiko Nagura, *
▲ **EMP:** 380 **EST:** 1988
SQ FT: 155,000
SALES (est): 53.45MM **Privately Held**
Web: www.nissenchemitec.com
SIC: 3089 Injection molding of plastics
PA: Nissen Chemitec Corporation
    2-4-34, Nishiharacho
    Niihama EHM 792-0

(G-9392)
O CONNOR OFFICE PDTS & PRTG
60 W High St (43140-1075)
PHONE..............................740 852-2209
Gary Feliks, *Owner*
EMP: 8 **EST:** 1942
SQ FT: 3,200
SALES (est): 386.63K **Privately Held**
SIC: 5943 2752 Office forms and supplies; Offset printing

(G-9393)
POUNCE SIGNS & PRINT WEAR
1040 Spring Valley Rd (43140-9554)
PHONE..............................408 377-4680
Rick Brenstuhl, *Prin*
EMP: 6 **EST:** 2009
SALES (est): 284.42K **Privately Held**
SIC: 2759 Screen printing

(G-9394)
STANLEY ELECTRIC US CO INC (HQ)
420 E High St (43140-9799)
PHONE..............................740 852-5200
Shinomiya Masahiro, *Pr*
Shinomiya Masahiro, *Pr*
▲ **EMP:** 53 **EST:** 1981
SQ FT: 733,000
SALES (est): 260.34MM **Privately Held**
Web: www.stanleyelectricus.com
SIC: 3647 3694 3089 Automotive lighting fixtures, nec; Automotive electrical equipment, nec; Injection molding of plastics
PA: Stanley Electric Co., Ltd.
    2-9-13, Nakameguro
    Meguro-Ku TKY 153-0

(G-9395)
TEXTILES INC (PA)
Also Called: Jordan Young International
23 Old Springfield Rd (43140-2033)
PHONE..............................740 852-0782
Phillip Jordan, *Pr*
Catherine Jordan, *VP*
Rob Jordan, *VP*
▲ **EMP:** 6 **EST:** 1989
SQ FT: 4,000
SALES (est): 9.37MM
SALES (corp-wide): 9.37MM **Privately Held**
SIC: 2511 Wood household furniture

(G-9396)
UNDER HILL WATER WELL
1789 Itawamba Trl (43140-8737)
PHONE..............................740 852-0858
Timothy Underhill, *Prin*
EMP: 6 **EST:** 1999
SALES (est): 226.74K **Privately Held**
SIC: 3533 Drilling tools for gas, oil, or water wells

(G-9397)
WHITE TIGER INC
Also Called: White Tiger Graphics
131 S Oak St (43140-1446)
PHONE..............................740 852-4873
George Peyton, *Pr*
EMP: 14 **EST:** 1988
SQ FT: 6,000
SALES (est): 933.27K **Privately Held**
Web: www.whitetigergraphics.com
SIC: 7336 2752 5199 Graphic arts and related design; Offset printing; Advertising specialties

Londonderry
Ross County

(G-9398)
DON PUCKETT LUMBER INC
31263 Beech Grove Rd (45647-8942)
PHONE..............................740 887-4191
Tim Puckett, *Pr*
Jeff Puckett, *VP*
EMP: 17 **EST:** 1965
SALES (est): 184.03K **Privately Held**
SIC: 2421 Sawmills and planing mills, general

Lorain
Lorain County

(G-9399)
A-1 WELDING & FABRICATION
4909 Oak Point Rd (44053-1937)
PHONE..............................440 233-8474
Kenneth J Balko, *Pr*
Wayne Balko, *VP*
Holly Herbert, *Sec*
EMP: 10 **EST:** 1966
SALES (est): 1.02MM **Privately Held**
Web: www.a1weldingandfabrication.net
SIC: 3443 3312 Weldments; Structural shapes and pilings, steel

(G-9400)
ABSOLUTE ZERO MCH & DESIGN LLC
6042 White Tail Ln (44053-1877)
PHONE..............................440 370-4172
EMP: 6 **EST:** 2017
SALES (est): 43.13K **Privately Held**
Web: www.absolutemachine.com
SIC: 3999 Manufacturing industries, nec

Lorain - Lorain County (G-9401) — GEOGRAPHIC SECTION

(G-9401)
ACKERMAN
1138 W 19th St (44052-3834)
PHONE..............................440 246-2034
David Selent, *Pr*
EMP: 7 **EST:** 2008
SALES (est): 73.72K **Privately Held**
SIC: 3711 Snow plows (motor vehicles), assembly of

(G-9402)
BCT ALARM SERVICES INC
5064 Oberlin Ave (44053-3432)
P.O. Box 216 (44001-0216)
PHONE..............................440 669-8153
Brian J Jankowski, *Pr*
EMP: 6 **EST:** 2007
SALES (est): 753.46K **Privately Held**
Web: www.security-ohio.com
SIC: 2752 Commercial printing, lithographic

(G-9403)
BODNAR PRINTING CO INC
3480 Colorado Ave (44052-2818)
PHONE..............................440 277-8295
Ralph Woodward, *Pr*
Bonnie Woodward, *Sec*
EMP: 19 **EST:** 1948
SQ FT: 5,000
SALES (est): 905.83K **Privately Held**
Web: www.bodnarprinting.com
SIC: 2752 Offset printing

(G-9404)
BOSCOWOOD VENTURES INC ○
7425 Industrial Parkway Dr (44053-2064)
PHONE..............................440 429-5669
EMP: 12 **EST:** 2022
SALES (est): 562.28K **Privately Held**
SIC: 2448 Wood pallets and skids

(G-9405)
CAMACO LLC
Also Called: Camaco Lorain
3400 River Industrial Park Rd (44052-2900)
PHONE..............................440 288-4444
Willie Gratzel, *Brnch Mgr*
EMP: 560
SALES (corp-wide): 494.73MM **Privately Held**
Web: www.camacollc.com
SIC: 3499 Automobile seat frames, metal
HQ: Camaco, Llc
 37000 W Twlve Mile Rd Ste
 Farmington Hills MI 48331
 248 442-6800

(G-9406)
CGI GROUP BENEFITS LLC
1374 E 28th St (44055-1602)
PHONE..............................440 246-6191
Roberto Alvarez, *Asst Sec*
EMP: 6 **EST:** 2019
SALES (est): 184.53K **Privately Held**
SIC: 3317 Steel pipe and tubes

(G-9407)
CLEVELAND RECLAIM INDS INC (PA)
Also Called: TURTLE PLASTICS
7400 Industrial Parkway Dr (44053-2064)
PHONE..............................440 282-4917
Thomas Norton, *Ch Bd*
Liz Demetriou, *Pr*
Carol Maier, *CFO*
Dennis Hildebrandt, *VP*
Karen Bradley, *Bd of Dir*
EMP: 9 **EST:** 1982
SQ FT: 15,000
SALES (est): 237.28K
SALES (corp-wide): 237.28K **Privately Held**
Web: www.turtleplastics.com
SIC: 3089 Floor coverings, plastics

(G-9408)
CONSUMERACQ INC (PA)
2509 N Ridge Rd E (44055-3772)
P.O. Box 823 (44052-0823)
PHONE..............................440 277-9305
Jeffrey Riddell, *Pr*
Jacqueline Riddell, *Sec*
EMP: 30 **EST:** 1982
SQ FT: 4,000
SALES (est): 8.81MM **Privately Held**
Web: www.consumersbuilderssupply.com
SIC: 3273 5211 Ready-mixed concrete; Lumber and other building materials

(G-9409)
CONSUMERS BUILDERS SUPPLY CO (PA)
2509 N Ridge Rd E (44055-3772)
P.O. Box 824 (44052-0824)
PHONE..............................440 277-9306
Jeffrey Riddell, *Pr*
Jacqueline Riddell, *Sec*
EMP: 6 **EST:** 1904
SALES (est): 2.91MM
SALES (corp-wide): 2.91MM **Privately Held**
Web: www.consumersbuilderssupply.com
SIC: 3273 5211 Ready-mixed concrete; Lumber and other building materials

(G-9410)
DAYTON HEIDELBERG DISTRG CO
Also Called: DAYTON HEIDELBERG DISTRIBUTING CO.
5901 Baumhart Rd (44053-2012)
PHONE..............................440 989-1027
Kevin Knight, *VP*
EMP: 157
SALES (corp-wide): 2.07B **Privately Held**
Web: www.heidelbergdistributing.com
SIC: 2082 Beer (alcoholic beverage)
HQ: Dayton Heidelberg Distributing Co., Llc
 3601 Dryden Rd
 Moraine OH 45439
 937 222-8692

(G-9411)
ERDIE INDUSTRIES INC
1205 Colorado Ave (44052-3313)
PHONE..............................440 288-0166
Jason Erdie, *Pr*
Jeffrey Erdie, *
EMP: 40 **EST:** 1983
SQ FT: 50,000
SALES (est): 6.89MM **Privately Held**
Web: www.erdie.com
SIC: 2655 Tubes, fiber or paper; made from purchased material

(G-9412)
GLOBAL PLASTIC TECH INC
1657 Bdwy Ave (44052-3439)
PHONE..............................440 879-6045
Makki Odeh, *Pr*
EMP: 9 **EST:** 2017
SALES (est): 326.8K **Privately Held**
Web: www.global-plastic.com
SIC: 2673 Food storage and frozen food bags, plastic

(G-9413)
H P NIELSEN INC
Also Called: Nielsen Jewelers
753 Broadway (44052-1805)
PHONE..............................440 244-4255
Carl G Nielsen, *Pr*
Krystina Nielsen, *VP*
EMP: 6 **EST:** 1877
SQ FT: 2,600
SALES (est): 762.41K **Privately Held**
Web: www.nielsenjewelers.com
SIC: 5944 3911 7631 Jewelry, precious stones and precious metals; Jewelry, precious metal; Jewelry repair services

(G-9414)
INGERSOLL RAND
2199 E 28th St (44055-1932)
PHONE..............................440 277-7100
Rand Ingersoll, *Prin*
EMP: 10 **EST:** 2014
SALES (est): 235.78K **Privately Held**
Web: www.ohiopowertool.com
SIC: 3563 Air and gas compressors

(G-9415)
JOHNSON METALL INC
1305 Oberlin Ave (44052-1559)
PHONE..............................440 245-6826
EMP: 65
SIC: 3366 Bushings and bearings, brass (nonmachined)

(G-9416)
JOURNAL REGISTER COMPANY
Also Called: Morning Journal, The
401 Broadway Ste B (44052-1749)
PHONE..............................440 245-6901
Jeff Sudbrook, *Branch*
EMP: 51
SALES (corp-wide): 293.08MM **Privately Held**
Web: www.morningjournal.com
SIC: 2711 5994 Newspapers, publishing and printing; Newsstand
PA: Journal Register Company
 5 Hanover Sq Fl 25
 New York NY 10004
 212 257-7212

(G-9417)
KTS MET-BAR PRODUCTS INC
967 G St (44052-3329)
PHONE..............................440 288-9308
Delvis Kerns, *Pr*
EMP: 9 **EST:** 1984
SQ FT: 8,500
SALES (est): 676.37K **Privately Held**
Web: www.ktsmet-bar.com
SIC: 3451 Screw machine products

(G-9418)
KUHN FABRICATING INC
1637 E 28th St (44055-1701)
P.O. Box 1203 (44055-0203)
PHONE..............................440 277-4182
Lewis Kuhn, *Pr*
Rosemary Kuhn, *VP*
EMP: 6 **EST:** 1958
SQ FT: 18,000
SALES (est): 937.87K **Privately Held**
Web: www.kuhnfab.com
SIC: 3444 Sheet metal specialties, not stamped

(G-9419)
LAKE SCREEN PRINTING INC
1924 Broadway (44052-3682)
PHONE..............................440 244-5707
Ben Zientarski Junior, *Pr*
Teresa Zientarski, *VP*
Annette Zientarski, *Sec*
EMP: 8 **EST:** 1976
SQ FT: 10,000
SALES (est): 975.49K **Privately Held**
Web: www.lakescreenprinting.com
SIC: 2759 Screen printing

(G-9420)
LORAIN APPLES
1051 Meister Rd (44052-5141)
PHONE..............................440 282-4471
EMP: 6 **EST:** 2019
SALES (est): 247.09K **Privately Held**
Web: www.applesmarket.com
SIC: 3571 Personal computers (microcomputers)

(G-9421)
LORAIN COUNTY AUTO SYSTEMS INC
3400 River Industrial Park Rd (44052-2900)
PHONE..............................248 442-6800
Thomas Rockwell, *CFO*
EMP: 1613
SALES (corp-wide): 494.73MM **Privately Held**
Web: www.camacollc.com
SIC: 3714 Motor vehicle engines and parts
HQ: Lorain County Automotive Systems, Inc.
 7470 Industrial Pkwy Dr
 Lorain OH 44053
 440 960-7470

(G-9422)
LORAIN COUNTY AUTO SYSTEMS INC (HQ)
Also Called: Lcas
7470 Industrial Parkway Dr (44053-2070)
PHONE..............................440 960-7470
Arvind Pradhan, *CEO*
Tom Rockwell, *
▲ **EMP:** 50 **EST:** 1987
SQ FT: 36,000
SALES (est): 227.2MM
SALES (corp-wide): 494.73MM **Privately Held**
Web: www.camacollc.com
SIC: 3714 Motor vehicle engines and parts
PA: P & C Group I, Inc.
 37000 W 12 Mile Rd Ste 10
 Farmington Hills MI 48331
 248 442-6800

(G-9423)
M/W INTERNATIONAL INC
Also Called: Mwi Dmntable Office Partitions
3839 Heron Dr (44053-1597)
P.O. Box 470115 (44147-0115)
PHONE..............................440 526-6900
◆ **EMP:** 18 **EST:** 1996
SQ FT: 1,500
SALES (est): 1.88MM **Privately Held**
Web: www.mwintl.net
SIC: 2522 Office furniture, except wood

(G-9424)
MARIOTTI PRINTING CO LLC
513 E 28th St (44055-1396)
PHONE..............................440 245-4120
Martin Mariotti, *Managing Member*
EMP: 6 **EST:** 1937
SQ FT: 15,000
SALES (est): 371.67K **Privately Held**
Web: www.mariottiprinting.com
SIC: 2752 2759 Offset printing; Letterpress printing

(G-9425)
NATIONAL BRONZE MTLS OHIO INC
Also Called: Aviva Metals
5311 W River Rd (44055-3735)
PHONE..............................440 277-1226
Michael Greathead, *Pr*
Norman M Lazarus, *
Jill Conyer, *
Phil Meehan, *Sr VP*

▲ = Import ▼ = Export
◆ = Import/Export

GEOGRAPHIC SECTION

Loudonville - Ashland County (G-9450)

▲ **EMP:** 27 **EST:** 1997
SALES (est): 11.02MM **Privately Held**
Web: www.avivametals.com
SIC: 3366 3341 5051 Copper foundries; Secondary nonferrous metals; Copper
PA: Metchem Anstalt
C/O Feger Treuunternehmen Reg.
Vaduz

(G-9426)
NORLAB INC
Also Called: Norlab
7465 Industrial Parkway Dr (44053-2079)
P.O. Box 380 (44001-0380)
PHONE.................................440 282-5265
John Azok, *VP*
Frank Azok, *VP*
EMP: 10 **EST:** 1974
SQ FT: 10,000
SALES (est): 1.33MM **Privately Held**
Web: www.norlabdyes.com
SIC: 2819 Industrial inorganic chemicals, nec

(G-9427)
NOVEX PRODUCTS INC
2707 Toledo Ave Ste A (44055-1465)
PHONE.................................440 244-3330
Peyman Pakdel, *Pr*
▲ **EMP:** 30 **EST:** 2001
SQ FT: 30,000
SALES (est): 8.03MM **Privately Held**
Web: www.novexproducts.com
SIC: 2676 Towels, napkins, and tissue paper products

(G-9428)
PC CAMPANA INC
3000 Leavitt Rd Frnt (44052-4167)
PHONE.................................800 321-0151
▲ **EMP:** 94
SALES (corp-wide): 24.69MM **Privately Held**
Web: www.pccampana.com
SIC: 3441 Fabricated structural metal
PA: P.C. Campana, Inc.
6155 Park Square Dr Ste 1
Lorain OH 44053
800 321-0151

(G-9429)
PC CAMPANA INC (PA)
6155 Park Square Dr Ste 1 (44053-4145)
PHONE.................................800 321-0151
Robert M Campana, *CFO*
Michael Marsico, *
▲ **EMP:** 35 **EST:** 1969
SQ FT: 250,000
SALES (est): 24.69MM
SALES (corp-wide): 24.69MM **Privately Held**
Web: www.pccampana.com
SIC: 3441 Boat and barge sections, prefabricated metal

(G-9430)
PERKINS MOTOR SERVICE LTD (PA)
Also Called: Standard Welding & Lift Truck
1864 E 28th St (44055-1804)
PHONE.................................440 277-1256
EMP: 18 **EST:** 1969
SQ FT: 10,200
SALES (est): 4.12MM
SALES (corp-wide): 4.12MM **Privately Held**
SIC: 5013 5531 7692 7539 Truck parts and accessories; Truck equipment and parts; Automotive welding; Radiator repair shop, automotive

(G-9431)
PRIME INDUSTRIES INC
1817 Iowa Ave (44052-3359)
EMP: 37 **EST:** 1984
SQ FT: 53,000
SALES (est): 2.02MM **Privately Held**
SIC: 3086 3544 2821 2671 Plastics foam products; Special dies, tools, jigs, and fixtures; Plastics materials and resins; Paper; coated and laminated packaging

(G-9432)
RACEWAY PETROLEUM INC
Also Called: Raceway
3040 Oberlin Ave (44052-4563)
PHONE.................................440 989-2660
Imran Nazir, *Prin*
EMP: 11 **EST:** 2009
SALES (est): 234.63K **Privately Held**
SIC: 3644 Raceways

(G-9433)
REFRACTORY COATING TECH INC
2421 E 28th St (44055-2113)
PHONE.................................800 807-7464
EMP: 20
Web: www.refcotec.com
SIC: 3299 Insulsleeves (foundry materials)
PA: Refractory Coating Technologies, Inc.
542 Collins Blvd
Orrville OH 44667

(G-9434)
REPUBLIC ENGINEERED PRODUCTS
Also Called: Republic Steel
1807 E 28th St (44055-1803)
PHONE.................................440 277-2000
Jim Kuntz, *Pr*
EMP: 17 **EST:** 2015
SALES (est): 1.56MM **Privately Held**
Web: www.republicsteel.com
SIC: 3312 Bars, iron: made in steel mills

(G-9435)
REPUBLIC STEEL
1807 E 28th St (44055-1803)
PHONE.................................440 277-2000
Joseph Lapinsky, *Bmch Mgr*
EMP: 26
Web: www.republicsteel.com
SIC: 3312 Blast furnaces and steel mills
HQ: Republic Steel
2633 8th St Ne
Canton OH 44704
330 438-5435

(G-9436)
ROCKWELL METALS COMPANY LLC
3709 W Erie Ave (44053-1237)
PHONE.................................440 242-2420
▲ **EMP:** 15 **EST:** 2010
SQ FT: 54,000
SALES (est): 8.56MM **Privately Held**
Web: www.rockwellmetals.com
SIC: 5051 3444 Sheets, metal; Sheet metalwork

(G-9437)
SENTINEL MANAGEMENT INC
Also Called: Semco Carbon
3000 Leavitt Rd Unit 1 (44052-4168)
PHONE.................................440 821-7372
Vincent L Thompson, *Pr*
Nancy Thompson, *
Matt Thompson, *
EMP: 28 **EST:** 1971
SALES (est): 4.91MM **Privately Held**
SIC: 3624 Carbon and graphite products

(G-9438)
SKYLIFT INC
3000 Leavitt Rd Ste 6 (44052-4166)
PHONE.................................440 960-2100
George Wojnowski, *Pr*
Nicholas Jarmoszuk, *
EMP: 52 **EST:** 2001
SQ FT: 6,000
SALES (est): 9.03MM **Privately Held**
Web: www.skyliftus.com
SIC: 3537 Cranes, industrial truck

(G-9439)
SOUNDWORKS INC
7951 W Erie Ave (44053-2093)
PHONE.................................408 219-5737
EMP: 7 **EST:** 2018
SALES (est): 498.93K **Privately Held**
SIC: 3699 Electrical equipment and supplies, nec

(G-9440)
SYSCO GUEST SUPPLY LLC
7395 Industrial Parkway Dr (44052)
PHONE.................................440 960-2515
Jeff Dubois, *Mgr*
EMP: 26
SALES (corp-wide): 76.32B **Publicly Held**
Web: www.guestsupply.com
SIC: 5122 2844 5131 5139 Drugs, proprietaries, and sundries; Perfumes, cosmetics and other toilet preparations; Piece goods and notions; Footwear
HQ: Sysco Guest Supply, Llc
300 Davidson Ave
Somerset NJ 08873
732 537-2297

(G-9441)
TERMINAL READY-MIX INC
524 Colorado Ave (44052-2198)
PHONE.................................440 288-0181
Theresa Pelton, *Pr*
John Falbo, *
Diane Gale, *
Pete Falbo, *
▲ **EMP:** 45 **EST:** 1954
SQ FT: 1,000
SALES (est): 9.12MM **Privately Held**
Web: www.terminalreadymix.com
SIC: 3273 1611 Ready-mixed concrete; Highway and street paving contractor

(G-9442)
V & A PROCESS INC
2345 E 28th St (44055-2003)
PHONE.................................440 288-8137
Albert Di Luciano, *Pr*
Gilbert Rothman, *VP*
EMP: 11 **EST:** 1965
SALES (est): 1.91MM **Privately Held**
Web: www.vaprocessinc.com
SIC: 2821 Plastics materials and resins

(G-9443)
VERTIV ENERGY SYSTEMS INC
Also Called: Vertiv
1510 Kansas Ave (44052-3364)
PHONE.................................440 288-1122
◆ **EMP:** 800
SIC: 3661 3644 7629 Telephone and telegraph apparatus; Noncurrent-carrying wiring devices; Telecommunication equipment repair (except telephones)

(G-9444)
VERTIV GROUP CORPORATION
1510 Kansas Ave (44052-3364)
PHONE.................................440 288-1122
Dave Smith, *Opers Mgr*
EMP: 9
SALES (corp-wide): 6.86B **Publicly Held**
Web: www.vertiv.com
SIC: 3661 3644 7629 Telephone and telegraph apparatus; Noncurrent-carrying wiring devices; Telecommunication equipment repair (except telephones)
HQ: Vertiv Group Corporation
505 N Cleveland Ave
Westerville OH 43082
614 888-0246

(G-9445)
WS THERMAL PROCESS TECH INC
8301 W Erie Ave (44053-2090)
PHONE.................................440 385-6829
Joachin G Wunning, *Pr*
EMP: 9 **EST:** 2006
SALES (est): 908.57K **Privately Held**
Web: www.thermalprocessing.com
SIC: 3433 Gas burners, industrial

Lore City
Guernsey County

(G-9446)
BOB SUMEREL TIRE CO INC
63303 Institute Rd (43755-9754)
PHONE.................................740 432-5200
James Olden, *Mgr*
EMP: 9
SALES (corp-wide): 97.34MM **Privately Held**
Web: www.bridgestonetire.com
SIC: 5531 7534 5014 Automotive tires; Tire retreading and repair shops; Tires and tubes
PA: Bob Sumerel Tire Co., Inc.
1257 Cox Ave
Erlanger KY 41018
859 283-2700

(G-9447)
VIKING WELL SERVICE INC
64201 Wintergreen Rd (43755-9704)
PHONE.................................681 205-1999
EMP: 9 **EST:** 2003
SALES (est): 1.86MM **Privately Held**
SIC: 1381 Service well drilling

Loudonville
Ashland County

(G-9448)
CHAD M MARSH
16104 State Route 39 (44842-9722)
PHONE.................................419 994-0587
EMP: 6 **EST:** 2016
SALES (est): 380.36K **Privately Held**
SIC: 2084 Wines, brandy, and brandy spirits

(G-9449)
HOCHSTETLER MILLING LLC
552 State Route 95 (44842-9611)
PHONE.................................419 368-0004
EMP: 22 **EST:** 1987
SQ FT: 13,000
SALES (est): 2.31MM **Privately Held**
Web: www.hochstetlerloghomes.com
SIC: 7389 2452 Log and lumber broker; Log cabins, prefabricated, wood

(G-9450)
OAKBRIDGE TIMBER FRAMING
9001 Township Road 461 (44842-9701)
P.O. Box 89 (44842-0089)
PHONE.................................419 994-1052
Johnny Miller, *Owner*
EMP: 6

Loudonville - Ashland County (G-9451)

Web: www.oakbridgetimberframing.com
SIC: 2411 Timber, cut at logging camp
PA: Oakbridge Timber Framing
20857 Earnest Rd
Howard OH 43028

(G-9451)
OHIO BIOSYSTEMS COOP INC
134 S Adams St (44842-1502)
P.O. Box 381 (44661-0381)
PHONE.............................419 980-7663
Glenn Chipner, *Pr*
EMP: 7 EST: 2009
SALES (est): 455.95K **Privately Held**
SIC: 2869 Industrial organic chemicals, nec

(G-9452)
TRUAX PRINTING INC
425 E Haskell St (44842-1312)
PHONE.............................419 994-4166
Tom Truax, *Pr*
Bruce Truax, *
Sally Truax, *
Dan Truax, *
Zack Truax, *
EMP: 45 EST: 1966
SQ FT: 56,000
SALES (est): 8.95MM **Privately Held**
Web: www.truaxprinting.com
SIC: 2752 Offset printing

(G-9453)
UGLY BUNNY WINERY LLC
16104 State Route 39 (44842-9722)
PHONE.............................330 988-9057
Chad Marsh, *Managing Member*
EMP: 14 EST: 2017
SALES (est): 542.85K **Privately Held**
Web: uglybunnywinery.wpcomstaging.com
SIC: 2084 Wines

(G-9454)
YOUNGS SAND & GRAVEL CO INC
689 State Route 39 (44842)
P.O. Box 117 (44842-0117)
PHONE.............................419 994-3040
Myron Oswalt, *Pr*
EMP: 14 EST: 1946
SQ FT: 2,400
SALES (est): 2.04MM **Privately Held**
Web: www.youngssandandgravel.com
SIC: 1442 Construction sand and gravel

Louisville
Stark County

(G-9455)
ATI FLAT RLLED PDTS HLDNGS LLC
Also Called: ATI Flat Rolled Products
1500 W Main St (44641-2325)
PHONE.............................330 875-2244
Tony Denoi, *Mgr*
EMP: 10
Web: www.atimaterials.com
SIC: 3312 3471 3398 3316 Stainless steel; Plating and polishing; Metal heat treating; Cold finishing of steel shapes
HQ: Ati Flat Rolled Products Holdings, Llc
1000 Six Ppg Pl
Pittsburgh PA 15222
412 394-3047

(G-9456)
BRADLEY ENTERPRISES INC (PA)
Also Called: Family Fun
3750 Beck Ave (44641-9455)
PHONE.............................330 875-1444
Scott Cook, *Pr*
Terry Mckimm, *VP*
Pamela Halgreen, *Sec*
EMP: 6 EST: 1958
SQ FT: 1,500
SALES (est): 7.91MM
SALES (corp-wide): 7.91MM **Privately Held**
Web: www.familyfunpools.com
SIC: 3949 5091 Swimming pools, except plastic; Swimming pools, equipment and supplies

(G-9457)
H & H QUICK MACHINE INC
7816 Edison St Ne (44641-8325)
PHONE.............................330 935-0944
Martin Hustead, *Pr*
Anthony Hustead, *VP*
EMP: 10 EST: 1997
SALES (est): 961.68K **Privately Held**
SIC: 3599 Machine shop, jobbing and repair

(G-9458)
H-P PRODUCTS INC
2000 W Main St (44641-2344)
PHONE.............................330 875-7193
Paul Bishop, *Brnch Mgr*
EMP: 172
SQ FT: 24,000
SALES (corp-wide): 46.06MM **Privately Held**
Web: www.h-pproducts.com
SIC: 3498 3635 Tube fabricating (contract bending and shaping); Household vacuum cleaners
PA: H-P Products, Inc.
512 W Gorgas St
Louisville OH 44641
330 875-5556

(G-9459)
H-P PRODUCTS INC (PA)
512 W Gorgas St (44641-1305)
P.O. Box 3912 (44641-3912)
PHONE.............................330 875-5556
◆ EMP: 200 EST: 1948
SALES (est): 46.06MM
SALES (corp-wide): 46.06MM **Privately Held**
Web: www.h-pproducts.com
SIC: 3498 3564 3494 3354 Tube fabricating (contract bending and shaping); Air cleaning systems; Valves and pipe fittings, nec; Aluminum extruded products

(G-9460)
HERITAGE GROUP INC
303 S Chapel St (44641-1612)
PHONE.............................330 875-5566
John M Falk, *Brnch Mgr*
EMP: 3272
SALES (corp-wide): 894.43MM **Privately Held**
Web: www.thgrp.com
SIC: 2951 Asphalt and asphaltic paving mixtures (not from refineries)
PA: Heritage Group Inc
6320 Intech Way
Indianapolis IN 46278
317 872-6010

(G-9461)
HOPPEL FABRICATION SPECIALTIES
9481 Columbus Rd Ne Ste 1 (44641-8546)
PHONE.............................330 823-5700
Steffon Hoppel, *Pr*
Sheryl Hoppel, *VP*
Renee Heilman, *Treas*
EMP: 10 EST: 1987
SALES (est): 914.07K **Privately Held**
Web: www.hoppelfab.com

SIC: 3441 Fabricated structural metal

(G-9462)
J & L SPECIALTY STEEL INC
1500 W Main St (44641-2325)
P.O. Box 3920 (44641-3920)
PHONE.............................330 875-6200
Victor Fusco, *Prin*
EMP: 7 EST: 2013
SALES (est): 212.52K **Privately Held**
SIC: 3441 Fabricated structural metal

(G-9463)
JOHANNINGS INC
3244 South Nickel Plate Street (44641-9654)
PHONE.............................330 875-1706
Curtis Bates, *Pr*
Christy Bates, *Off Mgr*
EMP: 9 EST: 1964
SALES (est): 932.08K **Privately Held**
Web: www.johanningsinc.com
SIC: 2434 Wood kitchen cabinets

(G-9464)
MIDLAKE PRODUCTS & MFG CO
819 N Nickelplate St (44641-2455)
PHONE.............................330 875-4202
Jeffrey Rich, *Pr*
Jane Pukys, *
Greg Duplin, *
EMP: 60 EST: 1986
SQ FT: 28,000
SALES (est): 9.86MM **Privately Held**
Web: www.midlake.com
SIC: 3429 Hardware, nec

(G-9465)
MY SPLASH PAD
9897 Byers Ave (44641-9742)
PHONE.............................330 705-1802
EMP: 6 EST: 2012
SALES (est): 125.61K **Privately Held**
Web: www.myportablesplashpad.com
SIC: 3999 Manufacturing industries, nec

(G-9466)
OHIO ROLL GRINDING INC
5165 Louisville St (44641-8630)
P.O. Box 7099 (44705-0099)
PHONE.............................330 453-1884
James P Robinson, *Pr*
Catherine Robinson, *
EMP: 26 EST: 1981
SQ FT: 14,000
SALES (est): 2.14MM **Privately Held**
Web: www.ohioroll.com
SIC: 3599 3471 Machine shop, jobbing and repair; Plating and polishing

(G-9467)
OTC SERVICES INC
1776 Constitution Ave (44641-1362)
P.O. Box 188 (44641-0188)
PHONE.............................330 871-2444
Robert Ganser Junior, *CEO*
▲ EMP: 80 EST: 2012
SQ FT: 98,000
SALES (est): 22MM **Privately Held**
Web: www.otcservices.com
SIC: 3612 Transformers, except electric

(G-9468)
PERFORMANCE TECHNOLOGIES LLC
3690 Tulane Ave (44641-7960)
PHONE.............................330 875-1216
Andy Connolly, *Brnch Mgr*
EMP: 52
SALES (corp-wide): 4.15B **Publicly Held**

Web: www.patenergy.com
SIC: 1389 Pumping of oil and gas wells
HQ: Performance Technologies Llc
3715 S Radio Rd
El Reno OK 73036

(G-9469)
RAM INNOVATIVE TECH LLC
3969 Jeffries Cir (44641-7923)
PHONE.............................330 956-4056
EMP: 10 EST: 2012
SALES (est): 295.9K **Privately Held**
Web: www.raminnovative.com
SIC: 3599 Machine shop, jobbing and repair

(G-9470)
SALCO MACHINE INC
3822 Victory Ave (44641-8601)
PHONE.............................330 456-8281
Annette Rosenverg, *Pr*
Susanna Saliola, *Treas*
John Saliol, *VP*
EMP: 23 EST: 1982
SQ FT: 8,900
SALES (est): 856.59K **Privately Held**
Web: www.salcomachine.com
SIC: 3599 Machine shop, jobbing and repair

(G-9471)
SHERWOOD RTM CORP
4043 Beck Ave (44641-9402)
P.O. Box 211 (44641-0211)
PHONE.............................330 875-7151
Ronald Brookes, *Pr*
EMP: 6 EST: 1967
SQ FT: 15,000
SALES (est): 968.41K **Privately Held**
Web: www.sherwoodcorp.com
SIC: 2821 3543 Plastics materials and resins; Industrial patterns

(G-9472)
UNIWALL MFG CO (HQ)
3750 Beck Ave (44641-9455)
PHONE.............................330 875-1444
Scott Cook, *Pr*
Terry Mckimm, *VP*
Pamala Hellgren, *Sec*
EMP: 10 EST: 1958
SQ FT: 4,500
SALES (est): 4.19MM
SALES (corp-wide): 7.91MM **Privately Held**
Web: www.familyfunpools.com
SIC: 3949 Swimming pools, except plastic
PA: Bradley Enterprises Inc
3750 Beck Ave
Louisville OH 44641
330 875-1444

(G-9473)
WASHITA VALLEY ENTERPRISES INC
3707 Tulane Ave Bldg 9 (44641-7949)
P.O. Box 409 (44641-0409)
PHONE.............................330 510-1568
Tiffany Midgett, *Pr*
EMP: 10
SALES (corp-wide): 41.81MM **Privately Held**
Web: www.wvei.com
SIC: 1389 Oil consultants
PA: Washita Valley Enterprises, Inc.
1705 Se 59th St
Oklahoma City OK 73129
405 670-5338

Loveland
Clermont County

(G-9474)
AMANO CINCINNATI INCORPORATED
130 Commerce Dr (45140-7726)
PHONE.................513 697-9000
Kash Gokli, *VP*
EMP: 10
SQ FT: 52,200
Web: www.amano.com
SIC: 3559 3873 3829 3625 Parking facility equipment and supplies; Watches, clocks, watchcases, and parts; Measuring and controlling devices, nec; Relays and industrial controls
HQ: Amano Cincinnati Incorporated
  29j Commerce Way
  Totowa NJ 07512
  973 403-1900

(G-9475)
AMANO USA HOLDINGS INC
130 Commerce Dr (45140-7726)
PHONE.................973 403-1900
EMP: 9 **EST:** 2018
SALES (est): 739.6K **Privately Held**
Web: www.amano.com
SIC: 3469 Metal stampings, nec

(G-9476)
ANDRITZ INC
6680 Miami Woods Dr (45140-6120)
PHONE.................513 677-5620
EMP: 66
SALES (corp-wide): 7.83B **Privately Held**
Web: www.andritz.com
SIC: 3554 Pulp mill machinery
HQ: Andritz Inc.
  5405 Windward Pkwy 100w
  Alpharetta GA 30004
  770 640-2500

(G-9477)
CEASARS CREEK MARINE
11840 Carter Grove Ln (45140-1896)
PHONE.................513 897-2912
Bob Hedburg, *Prin*
EMP: 6 **EST:** 2005
SALES (est): 200.98K **Privately Held**
SIC: 3732 5551 Boatbuilding and repairing; Boat dealers

(G-9478)
COLD JET INTERNATIONAL LLC (PA)
Also Called: Cold Jet
455 Wards Corner Rd (45140-9033)
PHONE.................513 831-3211
Eugene L Cooke Iii, *Managing Member*
EMP: 80 **EST:** 2004
SALES: 19.67MM
SALES (corp-wide): 19.67MM **Privately Held**
Web: www.coldjet.com
SIC: 3589 2813 Commercial cleaning equipment; Dry ice, carbon dioxide (solid)

(G-9479)
CURRENT ELEC & ENRGY SOLUTIONS
Also Called: Current Electrical & Lighting
1527 State Route 28 (45140-8413)
PHONE.................513 575-4600
Tim Driscoll, *Prin*
EMP: 7 **EST:** 2015
SALES (est): 106.9K **Privately Held**
SIC: 3229 3641 5063 Bulbs for electric lights ; Electric lamps; Lighting fittings and accessories

(G-9480)
FISCHER GLOBAL ENTERPRISES LLC
Also Called: Periflo/Px Pumps USA
155 Commerce Dr (45140-7727)
PHONE.................513 583-4900
▲ **EMP:** 10 **EST:** 2003
SALES (est): 198.72K **Privately Held**
Web: www.periflo.com
SIC: 3561 Industrial pumps and parts

(G-9481)
FLOWSERVE CORPORATION
Flowserve
422 Wards Corner Rd Unit F (45140-6964)
PHONE.................513 874-6990
Brad Harrellson, *Genl Mgr*
EMP: 6
SALES (corp-wide): 4.32B **Publicly Held**
Web: www.flowserve.com
SIC: 3561 Industrial pumps and parts
PA: Flowserve Corporation
  5215 N Ocnnor Blvd Ste 70 Connor
  Irving TX 75039
  972 443-6500

(G-9482)
GQ BUSINESS PRODUCTS INC
142 Commerce Dr (45140-7726)
PHONE.................513 792-4750
Diana Queen, *Pr*
Gordon Queen, *Treas*
EMP: 8 **EST:** 1987
SALES (est): 1.36MM **Privately Held**
Web: www.gqproducts.com
SIC: 5112 2759 5199 Business forms; Commercial printing, nec; Advertising specialties

(G-9483)
GREENLIGHT OPTICS LLC
8940 Glendale Milford Rd (45140-8908)
PHONE.................513 247-9777
Todd Rutherford, *Managing Member*
Michael Okeefe, *Managing Member*
Bill Phillips, *Managing Member*
EMP: 20 **EST:** 2009
SQ FT: 8,000
SALES (est): 4.54MM **Privately Held**
Web: www.greenlightoptics.com
SIC: 3827 3089 Optical instruments and apparatus; Lenses, except optical: plastics

(G-9484)
HAECO INC (PA)
6504 Snider Rd (45140-9228)
PHONE.................513 722-1030
Jerry Henline, *Pr*
▲ **EMP:** 8 **EST:** 1985
SQ FT: 7,200
SALES (est): 2.83MM
SALES (corp-wide): 2.83MM **Privately Held**
Web: www.haeco.us
SIC: 3559 Pack-up assemblies, wheel overhaul

(G-9485)
HEULE TOOL CORPORATION
131 Commerce Dr (45140-7727)
PHONE.................513 860-9900
Heinrich Heule, *Pr*
Ulf Heule, *
Gary Brown, *
EMP: 25 **EST:** 1988
SQ FT: 3,500
SALES (est): 3.07MM **Privately Held**
Web: www.heuletool.com
SIC: 3599 Machine shop, jobbing and repair
PA: Heule Werkzeug Ag
  Wegenstrasse 11
  Balgach SG 9436

(G-9486)
INNERWOOD & COMPANY
688 Elizabeth Ln (45140-9172)
PHONE.................513 677-2229
J V Melink-hueber, *Prin*
Janine V Melink-hueber, *CEO*
EMP: 11 **EST:** 1993
SALES (est): 416.08K **Privately Held**
Web: www.innerwood.com
SIC: 2517 2521 Wood television and radio cabinets; Wood office filing cabinets and bookcases

(G-9487)
INTELLIGENT SIGNAL TECH INTL
Also Called: Ist International
6318 Dustywind Ln (45140-7730)
PHONE.................614 530-4784
Sheldyn K Armstrong, *Pr*
Matthew Bolton, *CFO*
EMP: 8 **EST:** 1997
SQ FT: 2,500
SALES (est): 968.01K **Privately Held**
Web: www.intelligentsignals.com
SIC: 3669 Traffic signals, electric

(G-9488)
INTERNATIONAL PAPER COMPANY
Also Called: International Paper
6283 Tri Ridge Blvd (45140-8318)
PHONE.................513 248-6319
EMP: 27
SALES (corp-wide): 18.92B **Publicly Held**
Web: www.internationalpaper.com
SIC: 2621 Paper mills
PA: International Paper Company
  6400 Poplar Ave
  Memphis TN 38197
  901 419-7000

(G-9489)
KLEENLINE LLC
6279 Tri Ridge Blvd Ste 410 (45140-8396)
PHONE.................800 259-5973
William M Shult, *Prin*
EMP: 14 **EST:** 2015
SALES (est): 89.98K **Privately Held**
Web: www.kleenline.com
SIC: 3535 Conveyors and conveying equipment

(G-9490)
KMGRAFX INC
Also Called: Asi Sign Systems
394 Wards Corner Rd Ste 100 (45140-8339)
PHONE.................513 248-4100
Kimberly Moscarino, *Pr*
Kenneth Knarr, *Treas*
EMP: 8 **EST:** 1982
SQ FT: 2,700
SALES (est): 468.48K **Privately Held**
Web: www.asisignage.net
SIC: 3993 Signs and advertising specialties

(G-9491)
LOCKFAST LLC
107 Northeast Dr (45140-7145)
PHONE.................800 543-7157
Ed Packer, *Pr*
EMP: 9 **EST:** 1969
SALES (est): 834.16K **Privately Held**
Web: www.lockfast.com
SIC: 2396 3965 3069 2672 Automotive trimmings, fabric; Tape, hook-and-eye, and snap fastener; Tape, pressure sensitive: rubber; Tape, pressure sensitive: made from purchased materials

(G-9492)
MACPRO INC
Also Called: Machine Products
1456 Fay Rd Unit B (45140-9771)
PHONE.................513 575-3000
D Wayne Hughes, *Pr*
David Hughes, *VP*
EMP: 10 **EST:** 1967
SQ FT: 20,000
SALES (est): 817.82K **Privately Held**
Web: www.macpro1.com
SIC: 3599 Machine shop, jobbing and repair

(G-9493)
MAINSTREAM WATERJET LLC
108 Northeast Dr (45140-7144)
PHONE.................513 683-5426
Thomas Harbin, *CEO*
Jayson Daus, *Pr*
EMP: 22 **EST:** 2004
SQ FT: 25,000
SALES (est): 4.68MM **Privately Held**
Web: www.mainstreamwaterjet.com
SIC: 3599 Machine shop, jobbing and repair

(G-9494)
MATERIAL HOLDINGS INC
185 Commerce Dr (45140-7727)
PHONE.................513 583-5500
Winfield Scott, *Pr*
Thomas C Hamm, *Prin*
Joe Schuetz, *CFO*
▲ **EMP:** 20 **EST:** 1999
SALES (est): 4.95MM **Privately Held**
Web: www.bryantpro.com
SIC: 3535 Conveyors and conveying equipment

(G-9495)
MATTR US INC
Also Called: Dsg-Canusa
173 Commerce Dr (45140-7727)
P.O. Box 498830 (45249-8830)
PHONE.................513 683-7800
Jim Raussen N America, *Sls Mgr*
EMP: 25
SALES (corp-wide): 934.5MM **Privately Held**
Web: www.tenaris.com
SIC: 3317 Steel pipe and tubes
HQ: Mattr Us Inc.
  5875 N Sam Hston Pkwy E S
  Houston TX 77032
  281 886-2350

(G-9496)
MENARD INC
Also Called: Menards
3787 W State Route 22 3 (45140-3515)
PHONE.................513 583-1444
Bert Marsh, *Mgr*
EMP: 150
SALES (corp-wide): 1.7B **Privately Held**
Web: www.menards.com
SIC: 2431 5211 Millwork; Lumber and other building materials
PA: Menard, Inc.
  5101 Menard Dr
  Eau Claire WI 54703
  715 876-2000

(G-9497)
MICHAELS PRE-CAST CON PDTS
1917 Adams Rd (45140-7236)
PHONE.................513 683-1292

Vernon Michael, *Pr*
Donald Michael, *VP*
Mary Jane Micheal, *Sec*
Vernon Jim Michael, *VP*
EMP: 10 **EST:** 1950
SQ FT: 5,000
SALES (est): 1MM **Privately Held**
SIC: 5032 5999 3446 3272 Concrete building products; Concrete products, pre-cast; Architectural metalwork; Concrete products, nec

(G-9498)
PHOENIX INDS & APPARATUS INC
6466 Snider Rd Apt C (45140-9542)
PHONE.................513 722-1085
Sheri L Nause, *Pr*
Carl D Nause, *VP*
EMP: 15 **EST:** 1969
SQ FT: 8,550
SALES (est): 974.88K **Privately Held**
SIC: 7692 Welding repair

(G-9499)
POWDER ALLOY CORPORATION
101 Northeast Dr (45140-7145)
PHONE.................513 984-4016
E Stephen Payne, *Pr*
Darlene Payne, *
Kimberly R Gatto, *
▲ **EMP:** 40 **EST:** 1973
SQ FT: 20,000
SALES (est): 9.5MM **Privately Held**
Web: www.powderalloy.com
SIC: 3479 Coating of metals and formed products

(G-9500)
RAY MEYER SIGN COMPANY INC
8942 Glendale Milford Rd (45140-8908)
PHONE.................513 984-5446
Ray A Meyer, *Pr*
Michael A Meyer, *
John A Meyer, *
Barbara A Meyer, *
EMP: 25 **EST:** 1956
SQ FT: 12,000
SALES (est): 2.26MM **Privately Held**
Web: www.raymeyersigns.com
SIC: 3993 Signs and advertising specialties

(G-9501)
ROBERDS CONVERTING CO INC
113 Northeast Dr (45140-7145)
PHONE.................513 683-6667
James J Achberger, *Pr*
John M Achberger, *
William W Achberger, *
EMP: 38 **EST:** 1905
SQ FT: 72,000
SALES (est): 5.52MM **Privately Held**
Web: www.roberdsconverting.com
SIC: 2679 Paperboard products, converted, nec

(G-9502)
ROZZI COMPANY INC (PA)
Also Called: Rozzi Company
10059 Loveland Madeira Rd (45140-8956)
P.O. Box 5 (45140-0005)
PHONE.................513 683-0620
Joseph Rozzi, *Pr*
Arthur Rozzi, *
Nancy Rozzi, *
▲ **EMP:** 25 **EST:** 1931
SALES (est): 4.54MM
SALES (corp-wide): 4.54MM **Privately Held**
Web: www.rozzifireworks.com
SIC: 2899 Fireworks

(G-9503)
SAFE-GRAIN INC (PA)
417 Wards Corner Rd Ste B (45140-9083)
PHONE.................513 398-2500
Scott Chant, *Pr*
EMP: 7 **EST:** 1954
SALES (est): 2.6MM
SALES (corp-wide): 2.6MM **Privately Held**
Web: www.safegrain.com
SIC: 3829 1731 Temperature sensors, except industrial process and aircraft; Electronic controls installation

(G-9504)
SATCO INC
457 Wards Corner Rd (45140-9027)
PHONE.................513 707-6150
EMP: 60
SALES (corp-wide): 56.12MM **Privately Held**
Web: www.satco-inc.com
SIC: 2448 Pallets, wood and metal combination
PA: Satco, Inc.
1601 E El Segundo Blvd
El Segundo CA 90245
310 322-4719

(G-9505)
SIGNODE INDUSTRIAL GROUP LLC
Also Called: Angleboard
396 Wards Corner Rd Ste 100 (45140-9060)
PHONE.................513 248-2990
Shane Harrisson, *Mgr*
EMP: 100
SALES (corp-wide): 12.01B **Publicly Held**
Web: www.signode.com
SIC: 2679 2671 Paper products, converted, nec; Paper; coated and laminated packaging
HQ: Signode Industrial Group Llc
14025 Riveredge Dr Ste 500
Tampa FL

(G-9506)
SIRRUS INC
422 Wards Corner Rd (45140-6965)
P.O. Box 53130 (45253-0130)
PHONE.................513 448-0308
▲ **EMP:** 34 **EST:** 2009
SALES (est): 4.78MM **Privately Held**
Web: www.sirruschemistry.com
SIC: 2891 Adhesives and sealants

(G-9507)
VALVE RELATED CONTROLS INC
Also Called: Vrc
143 Commerce Dr (45140-7727)
PHONE.................513 677-8724
Fred Tasch, *CEO*
Ed Lester, *Pr*
▲ **EMP:** 12 **EST:** 1990
SQ FT: 12,000
SALES (est): 1.44MM **Privately Held**
Web: www.vrc-usa.com
SIC: 5084 3625 Industrial machinery and equipment; Positioning controls, electric

(G-9508)
VICTAULIC
3605 Springlake Cir (45140-4409)
PHONE.................513 479-1764
Larry Pullin, *Mgr*
EMP: 7 **EST:** 2018
SALES (est): 75.99K **Privately Held**
Web: www.victaulic.com
SIC: 3494 Valves and pipe fittings, nec

(G-9509)
WASHING SYSTEMS LLC (HQ)
167 Commerce Dr (45140-7727)
PHONE.................800 272-1974
John Walroth, *CEO*
Jonathan C Dill, *Ex VP*
▼ **EMP:** 110 **EST:** 1989
SALES (est): 49.48MM **Privately Held**
Web: www.washingsystems.com
SIC: 5169 2841 Detergents; Soap and other detergents
PA: Kao Corporation
1-14-10, Nihombashikayabacho
Chuo-Ku TKY 103-0

Lowellville
Mahoning County

(G-9510)
ALUMINUM COLOR INDUSTRIES INC (PA)
369 W Wood St (44436-1039)
PHONE.................330 536-6295
Trude Stoeckel-spinosa, *Pr*
Lorna Willard, *Sec*
Tina Spinosa, *Treas*
EMP: 43 **EST:** 1953
SQ FT: 30,000
SALES (est): 4.62MM
SALES (corp-wide): 4.62MM **Privately Held**
SIC: 3442 3471 3444 Moldings and trim, except automobile: metal; Finishing, metals or formed products; Sheet metalwork

(G-9511)
ARS RECYCLING SYSTEMS LLC (PA)
Also Called: Advanced Recycling Systems
4000 Mccartney Rd (44436-9413)
PHONE.................330 536-8210
Gus G Lyras, *Pr*
Elio Mussullo, *
Victor Pallotta, *
Patsy Pilorusso, *Stockholder**
EMP: 17 **EST:** 1991
SQ FT: 25,000
SALES (est): 10.56MM **Privately Held**
Web: www.arsrecycling.com
SIC: 7699 3559 Welding equipment repair; Recycling machinery

(G-9512)
ARS RECYCLING SYSTEMS 2019 LLC
4000 Mccartney Rd (44436-9413)
PHONE.................330 536-8210
EMP: 20 **EST:** 2019
SALES (est): 1.35MM **Privately Held**
Web: www.arsrecycling.com
SIC: 3999 Manufacturing industries, nec

(G-9513)
ERNEST INDUSTRIES INC
4000 Mccartney Rd (44436-9413)
PHONE.................937 325-9851
Michael T Stute, *Pr*
EMP: 50 **EST:** 1967
SALES (est): 10.56MM **Privately Held**
Web: www.ernestindustries.com
SIC: 3559 Concrete products machinery
PA: Ars Recycling Systems, Llc
4000 Mccartney Rd
Lowellville OH 44436

(G-9514)
FALCON FOUNDRY COMPANY
96 6th St (44436-1264)
P.O. Box 301 (44436-0301)
PHONE.................330 536-6221
Gary S Slaven, *Pr*
Lisa Mendozzi, *
William R Lopatta, *
John Lopatta, *
◆ **EMP:** 90 **EST:** 1953
SQ FT: 175,000
SALES (est): 13.32MM **Privately Held**
Web: www.falconfoundry.com
SIC: 3366 Castings (except die), nec, copper and copper-base alloy

(G-9515)
GARLAND WELDING CO INC
804 E Liberty St (44436-1266)
PHONE.................330 536-6506
Rose Del Signore, *Pr*
Vincent Del Signore, *Prin*
Ralph Signore, *VP*
Nick Del Signore, *Sec*
Joanne Del Signore, *Sec*
EMP: 12 **EST:** 1962
SQ FT: 6,880
SALES (est): 2.32MM **Privately Held**
Web: www.garlandwelding.com
SIC: 3441 7692 Fabricated structural metal; Welding repair

(G-9516)
HILCORP ENERGY CO
8066 S State Line Rd (44436-9596)
PHONE.................330 536-6406
EMP: 6 **EST:** 2014
SALES (est): 108.5K **Privately Held**
Web: www.hilcorp.com
SIC: 1382 Oil and gas exploration services

(G-9517)
LYCO CORPORATION
Also Called: Pilorusso Construction Div
1089 N Hubbard Rd (44436-9737)
PHONE.................412 973-9176
Patsy Pilorusso, *Pr*
Elio Massullo, *Owner*
W C Pilorusso, *VP*
Mike Pallotto, *VP*
EMP: 33 **EST:** 1947
SQ FT: 25,000
SALES (est): 1.15MM **Privately Held**
Web: www.lyco-mfg.com
SIC: 7699 3441 Welding equipment repair; Fabricated structural metal

(G-9518)
RAVANA INDUSTRIES INC
6170 Center Rd (44436-9521)
PHONE.................330 536-4015
Danette J St Vencent, *CEO*
William St Vincent, *Pr*
EMP: 8 **EST:** 1988
SALES (est): 748.28K **Privately Held**
SIC: 3541 3363 Machine tool replacement & repair parts, metal cutting types; Aluminum die-castings

Lower Salem
Washington County

(G-9519)
BLAIR LOGGING
30530 Lebanon Rd (45745-9733)
PHONE.................740 934-2730
Ronald Blair, *Owner*
EMP: 6 **EST:** 1998
SALES (est): 401.13K **Privately Held**
SIC: 2411 Logging camps and contractors

Lucas
Richland County

(G-9520)
WINDY HILLS WOODWORKING
1761 Leiter Rd (44843-9542)
PHONE.................................419 892-3389
Craig Maglott, *Prin*
EMP: 6 **EST:** 2008
SALES (est): 86.96K **Privately Held**
SIC: 2431 Millwork

Lucasville
Scioto County

(G-9521)
COX INC
Also Called: Cox Precast
11201 State Route 104 (45648-7512)
PHONE.................................740 858-4400
TOLL FREE: 800
Forest Arbaugh, *Pr*
Keith Gallimore, *Off Mgr*
EMP: 9 **EST:** 1976
SALES (est): 124.12K **Privately Held**
SIC: 3272 Concrete products, precast, nec

(G-9522)
E A COX INC
11201 State Route 104 (45648-7512)
P.O. Box 819 (45648-0819)
PHONE.................................740 858-4400
Forrest Arbaugh, *Pr*
EMP: 8 **EST:** 1970
SALES (est): 716.36K **Privately Held**
SIC: 3272 Septic tanks, concrete

(G-9523)
MAKO FINISHED PRODUCTS INC
708 Fairground Rd (45648-3507)
P.O. Box 1030 (45662-1030)
PHONE.................................740 357-0839
Mark Miller, *Pr*
EMP: 25 **EST:** 2014
SALES (est): 1.58MM **Privately Held**
Web: www.makofinishedproducts.com
SIC: 3999 Manufacturing industries, nec

(G-9524)
MARK ANDRONIS
50 Mcnamer Brown Rd (45648-8874)
PHONE.................................740 259-5613
Mark Andronis, *Owner*
EMP: 6 **EST:** 2001
SALES (est): 107.21K **Privately Held**
SIC: 2499 Decorative wood and woodwork

(G-9525)
MICHAEL W NEWTON
Also Called: Newton's Paint & Body
768 Fairground Rd (45648-8363)
PHONE.................................740 352-9334
Michael W Newton, *Owner*
Michael Newton, *Owner*
EMP: 7 **EST:** 1990
SQ FT: 20,000
SALES (est): 1.3MM **Privately Held**
SIC: 7532 3479 Paint shop, automotive; Painting of metal products

(G-9526)
R & D LOGGING LLC
2218 Cramer Rd (45648-8316)
PHONE.................................740 259-6137
EMP: 6 **EST:** 2014
SALES (est): 169.76K **Privately Held**
SIC: 2411 Logging camps and contractors

Luckey
Wood County

(G-9527)
NSG GLASS NORTH AMERICA INC
21705 Pemberville Rd (43443-9783)
PHONE.................................734 755-5816
EMP: 118
SALES (corp-wide): 10.44MM **Privately Held**
SIC: 3211 Flat glass
PA: Nsg Glass North America, Inc.
811 Madison Ave
Toledo OH 43604
419 247-4800

Ludlow Falls
Miami County

(G-9528)
LYLE TATE
5573 State Route 55 (45339-9744)
PHONE.................................937 698-6526
EMP: 9 **EST:** 2014
SALES (est): 50K **Privately Held**
Web: www.tateandlyle.com
SIC: 2099 Food preparations, nec

(G-9529)
MARMAX MACHINE CO
Also Called: Meiring Precision
2425 S State Route 48 (45339-9792)
P.O. Box 99 (45339-0099)
PHONE.................................937 698-9900
David M Shepherd, *Owner*
EMP: 7 **EST:** 1983
SQ FT: 7,200
SALES (est): 291.32K **Privately Held**
Web: www.marmaxmachine.com
SIC: 3599 Machine shop, jobbing and repair

(G-9530)
WALL POLISHING LLC
1953 S State Route 48 (45339-8760)
PHONE.................................937 698-1330
Kenneth Wall, *Prin*
EMP: 7 **EST:** 2011
SALES (est): 249.32K **Privately Held**
SIC: 3471 Polishing, metals or formed products

Lyons
Fulton County

(G-9531)
B W GRINDING CO
Also Called: Bw Supply Co.
15048 County Rd 10-3 (43533-9713)
P.O. Box 307 (43533-0307)
PHONE.................................419 923-1376
Martin Welch, *Pr*
EMP: 35 **EST:** 1978
SQ FT: 30,000
SALES (est): 7.64MM **Privately Held**
Web: www.bwsupplyco.com
SIC: 5085 3324 Industrial tools; Commercial investment castings, ferrous

(G-9532)
MCS MFG LLC
15210 County Road 10 3 (43533-9713)
PHONE.................................419 923-0169
Aaron R Call, *Prin*
EMP: 14 **EST:** 2008
SALES (est): 448.84K **Privately Held**
Web: www.mcsmfg.com
SIC: 3999 Manufacturing industries, nec

(G-9533)
RAY-TECH INDUSTRIES LLC
15210 County Road 10 3 (43533-9713)
PHONE.................................419 923-0169
Aaron Call, *Prin*
EMP: 8 **EST:** 2005
SALES (est): 251.66K **Privately Held**
Web: www.ray-tech-ind.com
SIC: 3599 Machine shop, jobbing and repair

Macedonia
Summit County

(G-9534)
AGS CUSTOM GRAPHICS INC
Also Called: A G S Ohio
8107 Bavaria Dr E (44056)
PHONE.................................330 963-7770
John Green, *Pr*
Mark Edgar, *
EMP: 74 **EST:** 1993
SQ FT: 70,000
SALES (est): 23.96MM
SALES (corp-wide): 4.99B **Privately Held**
Web: www.rrd.com
SIC: 2752 2721 7375 2791 Offset printing; Periodicals; Information retrieval services; Typesetting
HQ: R. R. Donnelley & Sons Company
35 W Wacker Dr
Chicago IL 60601
312 326-8000

(G-9535)
AMERICAN LIGHT METALS LLC
Also Called: Empire Die Casting Company
635 Highland Rd E (44056-2109)
PHONE.................................330 908-3065
Yogen Rahangdale, *Managing Member*
EMP: 200 **EST:** 2013
SQ FT: 200,000
SALES (est): 63.17MM
SALES (corp-wide): 63.17MM **Privately Held**
SIC: 3363 3364 Aluminum die-castings; Zinc and zinc-base alloy die-castings
HQ: Srs Die Casting Holdings, Llc
635 Highland Rd E
Macedonia OH 44056
330 467-0750

(G-9536)
AWU CORP
325 Huntsford Dr (44056-1744)
PHONE.................................740 504-8448
Carri Brown, *Prin*
EMP: 6 **EST:** 2015
SALES (est): 98.61K **Privately Held**
SIC: 3599 Industrial machinery, nec

(G-9537)
BGH SPECIALTY STEEL INC
8190 Roll And Hold Pkwy Ste A (44056)
PHONE.................................330 467-0324
Todd Clemens, *Pr*
EMP: 7 **EST:** 2000
SALES (est): 256.96K **Privately Held**
Web: www.bgh.de
SIC: 3441 Fabricated structural metal

(G-9538)
BILZ VIBRATION TECHNOLOGY INC
895 Highland Rd E Ste F (44056-2128)
P.O. Box 241305 (44124-8305)
PHONE.................................330 468-2459
Marc A Brower, *Pr*
Bill Granchi, *VP*
▲ **EMP:** 15 **EST:** 2005
SQ FT: 8,000
SALES (est): 2.44MM **Privately Held**
Web: www.bilz-usa.com
SIC: 5084 3829 Machinists' precision measuring tools; Vibration meters, analyzers, and calibrators

(G-9539)
BINDTECH LLC
Also Called: Finish Line Binderies
8212 Bavaria Dr E (44056-2248)
PHONE.................................615 834-0404
EMP: 57
SALES (corp-wide): 78.34MM **Privately Held**
Web: www.bindtechinc.com
SIC: 2789 Binding only: books, pamphlets, magazines, etc.
HQ: Bindtech, Llc
1232 Antioch Pike
Nashville TN 37211
615 834-0404

(G-9540)
BUDGET MOLDERS SUPPLY INC
8303 Corporate Park Dr (44056-2300)
PHONE.................................216 367-7050
Ed Kuchar Senior, *Pr*
Ed Kuchar Junior, *VP*
Francis E Kuchar, *Sec*
Raymond A Kuchar, *OK Vice President*
EMP: 18 **EST:** 1987
SALES (est): 432.64K **Privately Held**
Web: www.ppe.com
SIC: 3559 Plastics working machinery

(G-9541)
CHAMPION WIN CO CLEVELAND LLC
9011 Freeway Dr Ste 1 (44056-1524)
PHONE.................................440 899-2562
◆ **EMP:** 11 **EST:** 1997
SALES (est): 881.57K **Privately Held**
Web: www.championwindow.com
SIC: 3442 5031 Storm doors or windows, metal; Windows

(G-9542)
CONNELLY INDUSTRIES LLC
9651 N Bedford Rd (44056-1007)
PHONE.................................330 468-0675
M K Connelly, *Prin*
EMP: 6 **EST:** 2011
SALES (est): 160.65K **Privately Held**
SIC: 3999 Manufacturing industries, nec

(G-9543)
CUSTOM GRAPHICS INC
Also Called: AGS Custom Graphics
8107 Bavaria Dr E (44056-2252)
PHONE.................................330 963-7770
Stan Ritter, *Pr*
EMP: 225 **EST:** 1977
SQ FT: 85,000
SALES (est): 12.96MM
SALES (corp-wide): 4.99B **Privately Held**
Web: www.rrd.com
SIC: 2752 Offset printing
HQ: Consolidated Graphics, Inc.
5858 Westheimer Rd # 200
Houston TX 77057

(G-9544)
DESIGN MOLDED PRODUCTS LLC (PA) ✪
8220 Bavaria Dr E (44056)
PHONE.................................330 963-4400

Macedonia - Summit County (G-9545)

Brian Schroeder, *Pr*
EMP: 17 **EST:** 2023
SALES (est): 6.29MM
SALES (corp-wide): 6.29MM **Privately Held**
SIC: 3089 Injection molded finished plastics products, nec

(G-9545)
DESIGN MOLDED PRODUCTS LLC
8272 Bavaria Dr E (44056)
PHONE..................330 963-4400
EMP: 33
SALES (corp-wide): 6.29MM **Privately Held**
Web: www.designmolded.com
SIC: 3089 Injection molding of plastics
PA: Design Molded Products Llc
8220 Bavaria Rd
Macedonia OH 44056
330 963-4400

(G-9546)
DIEMASTER TOOL & MOLD INC
895 Highland Rd E # 5 (44056-2128)
PHONE..................330 467-4281
Paul Badovick, *Pr*
Dorothy Badovick, *Sec*
EMP: 17 **EST:** 1966
SQ FT: 7,200
SALES (est): 996.2K **Privately Held**
Web: www.diemaster.com
SIC: 3089 Injection molding of plastics

(G-9547)
DON BASCH JEWELERS INC
8210 Macedonia Commons Blvd Unit 36 (44056)
PHONE..................330 467-2116
Don Basch, *Pr*
Denise Basch, *Sec*
EMP: 24 **EST:** 1979
SALES (est): 1.47MM **Privately Held**
Web: www.donbaschjewelers.com
SIC: 3911 7631 Jewelry, precious metal; Watch, clock, and jewelry repair

(G-9548)
EDC LIQUIDATING INC
Also Called: Empire Die Casting Co
635 Highland Rd E (44056-2109)
PHONE..................330 467-0750
▼ **EMP:** 200
SIC: 3364 3363 Zinc and zinc-base alloy die-castings; Aluminum die-castings

(G-9549)
ETS SCHAEFER LLC
8050 Highland Pointe Pkwy (44056-2147)
PHONE..................330 468-6600
EMP: 15
SALES (corp-wide): 372.45MM **Privately Held**
Web: www.etsschaefer.com
SIC: 3297 3433 Nonclay refractories; Heating equipment, except electric
HQ: Ets Schaefer, Llc
3700 Park East Dr Ste 300
Beachwood OH 44122
330 468-6600

(G-9550)
FEITL MANUFACTURING CO INC
8406 Bavaria Dr E (44056-2275)
PHONE..................330 405-6600
Julius Feitl, *Pr*
EMP: 25 **EST:** 2021
SQ FT: 70,000
SALES (est): 3.2MM **Privately Held**
Web: www.pmd-inc.com

SIC: 3429 3544 3469 Hardware, nec; Special dies, tools, jigs, and fixtures; Metal stampings, nec

(G-9551)
FORTERRA PIPE & PRECAST LLC
7925 Empire Pkwy (44056-2144)
PHONE..................330 467-7890
Sue Waters, *Brnch Mgr*
EMP: 24
Web: www.forterrabp.com
SIC: 3272 Culvert pipe, concrete
HQ: Forterra Pipe & Precast, Llc
511 E John Crptr Fwy Ste
Irving TX 75062
469 458-7973

(G-9552)
FUNCTIONAL PRODUCTS INC
8282 Bavaria Dr E (44056-2248)
PHONE..................330 963-3060
David Devore, *Pr*
Diane Costas, *VP*
▼ **EMP:** 12 **EST:** 1984
SQ FT: 24,000
SALES (est): 3.05MM **Privately Held**
Web: www.functionalproducts.com
SIC: 2911 5172 Oils, lubricating; Lubricating oils and greases

(G-9553)
G W STEFFEN BOOKBINDERS INC
8212 Bavaria Dr E (44056-2248)
PHONE..................330 963-0300
William Turoczy, *Pr*
Elizabeth L Turoczy, *
EMP: 50 **EST:** 1904
SQ FT: 45,000
SALES (est): 4.3MM **Privately Held**
SIC: 2789 Binding only: books, pamphlets, magazines, etc.

(G-9554)
GASPAR SERVICES LLC
Also Called: Akland Printing
7791 Capital Blvd Ste 2 (44056-2186)
PHONE..................330 467-8292
EMP: 6 **EST:** 1984
SQ FT: 4,200
SALES (est): 471.54K **Privately Held**
SIC: 2752 Offset printing

(G-9555)
GREAT DAY IMPROVEMENTS LLC (HQ)
Also Called: Patio Enclsures Stanek Windows
700 Highland Rd E (44056-2160)
PHONE..................267 223-1289
EMP: 265 **EST:** 2010
SALES (est): 645.76MM **Privately Held**
Web: www.greatdayimprovements.com
SIC: 3231 3448 3444 5712 Products of purchased glass; Prefabricated metal buildings; Sheet metalwork; Outdoor and garden furniture
PA: Gdic Group, Llc
1300 E 9th St Fl 20
Cleveland OH 44114

(G-9556)
IER FUJIKURA INC (PA)
Also Called: I E R Industries
8271 Bavaria Dr E (44056)
PHONE..................330 425-7121
John Elsley, *Pr*
Athur E Lange, *
▲ **EMP:** 128 **EST:** 1958
SQ FT: 60,000
SALES (est): 22.25MM **Privately Held**
Web: www.ierfujikura.com

SIC: 3069 3061 3053 2821 Molded rubber products; Mechanical rubber goods; Gaskets; packing and sealing devices; Plastics materials and resins

(G-9557)
INOVENT ENGINEERING INC
8877 Freeway Dr (44056-1506)
P.O. Box 560314 (44056-0314)
PHONE..................330 468-0019
Brian Fenn, *Pr*
P Clark Hungerford Junior, *Pr*
Ron Fenn, *VP*
Jim Eucker, *Stockholder*
EMP: 7 **EST:** 1984
SQ FT: 7,000
SALES (est): 844.59K **Privately Held**
Web: www.inoventengineering.com
SIC: 3599 8711 Custom machinery; Professional engineer

(G-9558)
JAY DEE SERVICE CORPORATION
Also Called: Bearing & Transm Sup Co Div
1320 Highland Rd E (44056-2310)
P.O. Box 560185 (44056-0185)
PHONE..................330 425-1546
John Zimmerman Senior, *CEO*
Constance A Zimmerman, *Pr*
John Zimmerman Junior, *VP Sls*
Alfred Palay, *Prin*
Julia Zimmerman, *Prin*
▲ **EMP:** 8 **EST:** 1979
SQ FT: 13,000
SALES (est): 3.37MM **Privately Held**
SIC: 5084 3562 Hydraulic systems equipment and supplies; Ball bearings and parts

(G-9559)
JDH HOLDINGS INC
8220 Bavaria Dr E (44056-2248)
PHONE..................330 963-4400
▲ **EMP:** 160
SIC: 3089 Injection molded finished plastics products, nec

(G-9560)
JOSLYN MANUFACTURING COMPANY
9400 Valley View Rd (44056-2060)
PHONE..................330 467-8111
Bret Joslyn, *Pr*
Charles B Joslyn, *
Brain Joslyn, *
▲ **EMP:** 25 **EST:** 1946
SQ FT: 105,000
SALES (est): 5.04MM **Privately Held**
Web: www.joslyn-mfg.com
SIC: 3089 Injection molding of plastics

(G-9561)
KIMPTON PRINTING & SPC CO
Also Called: Kimpton Prtg & Specialities
400 Highland Rd E (44056-2133)
PHONE..................330 467-1640
Dale Kimpton, *Pr*
Helen Kimpton, *VP*
Don Kimpton, *VP*
EMP: 10 **EST:** 1987
SQ FT: 2,400
SALES (est): 1.01MM **Privately Held**
Web: www.kimptonprinting.com
SIC: 2752 7336 Offset printing; Silk screen design

(G-9562)
M & M CERTIFIED WELDING INC
556 Highland Rd E Ste 3 (44056-2162)
PHONE..................330 467-1729
Matthew B Mccann, *Pr*

EMP: 10 **EST:** 1982
SQ FT: 16,000
SALES (est): 2.24MM **Privately Held**
Web: www.mmcertifiedwelding.com
SIC: 1799 7692 Welding on site; Welding repair

(G-9563)
NALK WOODS LLC
832 Sioux Ln (44056-1636)
PHONE..................216 548-0994
Andres Pagan, *Prin*
EMP: 6 **EST:** 2010
SALES (est): 237.59K **Privately Held**
SIC: 2499 Wood products, nec

(G-9564)
PEI LIQUIDATION COMPANY
700 Highland Rd E (44056-2160)
PHONE..................330 467-4267
TOLL FREE: 800
▲ **EMP:** 160
Web: www.patioenclosures.com
SIC: 3231 3448 3444 5712 Products of purchased glass; Prefabricated metal buildings; Sheet metalwork; Outdoor and garden furniture

(G-9565)
PLASTIC MATERIALS INC
775 Highland Rd E (44056-2111)
PHONE..................330 468-5706
William Speaks, *Prin*
EMP: 21 **EST:** 2012
SALES (est): 4.66MM **Privately Held**
Web: www.plasticmaterialsinc.com
SIC: 2821 Plastics materials and resins

(G-9566)
PLASTIC PROCESS EQUIPMENT INC (PA)
Also Called: Ppe
8303 Corporate Park Dr (44056-2300)
PHONE..................216 367-7000
Edward Kuchar, *Pr*
◆ **EMP:** 20 **EST:** 1974
SALES (est): 8.63MM
SALES (corp-wide): 8.63MM **Privately Held**
Web: www.ppe.com
SIC: 3559 5085 5084 Plastics working machinery; Industrial supplies; Industrial machinery and equipment

(G-9567)
POLY-CARB INC
9456 Freeway Dr (44056-1000)
P.O. Box 39278 (44139-0278)
PHONE..................440 248-1223
Puneet Singh, *Pr*
▲ **EMP:** 89 **EST:** 1973
SQ FT: 55,000
SALES (est): 10.03MM
SALES (corp-wide): 44.62B **Publicly Held**
Web: www.olinpolycarb.com
SIC: 2821 Silicone resins
HQ: The Dow Chemical Company
2211 H H Dow Way
Midland MI 48642
989 636-1000

(G-9568)
POLYONE CORPORATION
POLYONE CORPORATION
775 Highland Rd E (44056-2111)
PHONE..................330 467-8108
Kurt Walker, *Mgr*
EMP: 100
SQ FT: 18,000
Web: www.avient.com

SIC: 2821 3087 Plastics materials and resins; Custom compound purchased resins
PA: Avient Corporation
33587 Walker Rd
Avon Lake OH 44012

(G-9569)
PRECISION REPLACEMENT LLC
9009 Freeway Dr Unit 7 (44056-1523)
PHONE....................330 908-0410
Joseph D Lukes, *Prin*
EMP: 6 EST: 2004
SQ FT: 5,500
SALES (est): 482.84K Privately Held
SIC: 3565 5999 Vacuum packaging machinery; Electronic parts and equipment

(G-9570)
REVAIR LLC
1333 Highland Rd E Ste E (44056-2398)
PHONE....................440 462-6100
Scott Thomason, *CEO*
Eric Hider, *CFO*
EMP: 14 EST: 2014
SALES (est): 2.98MM Privately Held
Web: www.myrevair.com
SIC: 3634 Hair dryers, electric

(G-9571)
ROYAL CHEMICAL COMPANY LTD (HQ)
8679 Freeway Dr (44056-1535)
PHONE....................330 467-1300
EMP: 70 EST: 1938
SALES (est): 70MM
SALES (corp-wide): 112.99MM Privately Held
Web: www.royalchemical.com
SIC: 2841 Soap: granulated, liquid, cake, flaked, or chip
PA: Chemical Services Group, Inc.
8679 Freeway Dr
Macedonia OH 44056
330 467-1300

(G-9572)
SC FIRE PROTECTION LTD
Also Called: S C Fastening Systems
8531 Freeway Dr (44056-1534)
PHONE....................330 468-3300
Scott Filips, *Pr*
Chuck Domonkos, *CEO*
▲ EMP: 7 EST: 1999
SALES (est): 646.05K Privately Held
SIC: 2899 Fire extinguisher charges

(G-9573)
SIGNARAMA
Also Called: Sign-A-Rama
9862 Freeway Dr (44056-1580)
PHONE....................330 468-0556
EMP: 6 EST: 2018
SALES (est): 137.34K Privately Held
Web: www.signarama.com
SIC: 3993 Signs and advertising specialties

(G-9574)
SILGAN DISPENSING SYSTEMS CORP
1244 Highland Rd E (44056-2308)
PHONE....................330 425-4260
Kent Houser, *Pr*
George Sehringer, *
◆ EMP: 100 EST: 1973
SQ FT: 95,000
SALES (est): 18.15MM Publicly Held
Web: www.silgandispensing.com
SIC: 3089 Injection molding of plastics
PA: Silgan Holdings Inc.
4 Landmark Sq Ste 400
Stamford CT 06901

(G-9575)
SOURCE3MEDIA INC
9085 Freeway Dr (44056-1508)
PHONE....................330 467-9003
Gary Began, *Pr*
Ronald S Marshek, *
◆ EMP: 35 EST: 1967
SQ FT: 17,000
SALES (est): 8.75MM Privately Held
Web: www.source3media.com
SIC: 2752 Offset printing

(G-9576)
SR PRODUCTS
1380 Highland Rd E (44056-2310)
PHONE....................330 998-6500
Steve Harnish, *Pr*
Stephen Duke, *CFO*
EMP: 13 EST: 2014
SALES (est): 3.16MM Privately Held
Web: www.simonroofingproducts.com
SIC: 2952 Asphalt felts and coatings

(G-9577)
SRS DIE CASTING HOLDINGS LLC (HQ)
Also Called: Empire Diecasting
635 Highland Rd E (44056-2109)
PHONE....................330 467-0750
EMP: 24 EST: 2013
SALES (est): 63.17MM
SALES (corp-wide): 63.17MM Privately Held
Web: www.empirecastingco.com
SIC: 3363 3364 Aluminum die-castings; Zinc and zinc-base alloy die-castings
PA: Srs Light Metals Inc.
635 Highland Rd E
Macedonia OH 44056
330 467-0750

(G-9578)
SRS LIGHT METALS INC (PA)
635 Highland Rd E (44056-2109)
PHONE....................330 467-0750
EMP: 14 EST: 2013
SALES (est): 63.17MM
SALES (corp-wide): 63.17MM Privately Held
SIC: 3363 3364 Aluminum die-castings; Zinc and zinc-base alloy die-castings

(G-9579)
STANDARD SIGNS INCORPORATED (PA)
Also Called: Lumacurve Airfield Signs
9115 Freeway Dr (44056-1543)
PHONE....................330 467-2030
John A Messner, *Pr*
EMP: 7 EST: 1936
SQ FT: 27,000
SALES (est): 4.31MM
SALES (corp-wide): 4.31MM Privately Held
Web: www.lumacurve.com
SIC: 3993 Signs, not made in custom sign painting shops

(G-9580)
STANEK E F AND ASSOC INC
Also Called: Stanek Windows
700 Highland Rd E (44056-2160)
PHONE....................216 341-7700
Mark Davis, *Pr*
Jerry Donatelli, *
Robert Van Schoonhaven, *
Ron Stanek, *
EMP: 120 EST: 1985
SQ FT: 35,000
SALES (est): 18.63MM Privately Held
Web: www.stanekwindows.com
SIC: 3089 Windows, plastics

(G-9581)
SUNLESS INC (PA)
Also Called: Sunless
8909 Freeway Dr Ste A (44056-1574)
PHONE....................440 836-0199
Peter Van Niekerk, *CEO*
▼ EMP: 64 EST: 2000
SQ FT: 68,000
SALES (est): 26.54MM
SALES (corp-wide): 26.54MM Privately Held
Web: www.sunlessinc.com
SIC: 3648 Sun tanning equipment, incl. tanning beds

(G-9582)
SUPERFINISHERS INC
380 Highland Rd E (44056-2139)
PHONE....................330 467-2125
Frank Bucar, *Pr*
EMP: 7 EST: 1958
SQ FT: 5,000
SALES (est): 698.41K Privately Held
Web: www.superfinishers.com
SIC: 3471 3599 Finishing, metals or formed products; Machine shop, jobbing and repair

(G-9583)
SYSTEMS PACK INC
649 Highland Rd E (44056-2109)
PHONE....................330 467-5729
Ray Attwell, *Pr*
Dennis Kay, *
Laurene Neval, *
EMP: 30 EST: 1977
SQ FT: 62,131
SALES (est): 8MM Privately Held
Web: www.systemspackinc.com
SIC: 5199 7389 5113 2653 Packaging materials; Packaging and labeling services; Shipping supplies; Corrugated and solid fiber boxes

(G-9584)
TIN WIZARD HEATING & COOLG INC
8853 Robinwood Ter (44056-2719)
PHONE....................330 467-9826
James Plush, *Prin*
EMP: 6 EST: 2010
SALES (est): 240.79K Privately Held
SIC: 3356 Tin

(G-9585)
VOLENS LLC
480 Highland Rd E (44056-2106)
PHONE....................216 544-1200
Myron Hadetskyy, *Admn*
EMP: 6 EST: 2015
SALES (est): 151.21K Privately Held
SIC: 3537 5012 Industrial trucks and tractors; Trailers for trucks, new and used

(G-9586)
WILLARD MACHINE & WELDING INC
556 Highland Rd E Ste 3 (44056-2162)
PHONE....................330 467-0642
Margaret Willard, *Pr*
George C Willard, *VP*
EMP: 10 EST: 1971
SQ FT: 9,600
SALES (est): 759.13K Privately Held
SIC: 3713 7532 Specialty motor vehicle bodies; Top and body repair and paint shops

Madison
Lake County

(G-9587)
ALLPASS CORPORATION
222 N Lake St (44057-3118)
P.O. Box 10 (44057-0010)
PHONE....................440 998-6300
Joseph Passerell, *CEO*
David Passerell, *CEO*
Joe Passerell, *Pr*
Steve Passerell, *COO*
Mike Passerell, *VP*
▲ EMP: 12 EST: 1992
SALES (est): 2.04MM Privately Held
SIC: 3443 Metal parts

(G-9588)
CHALET DEBONNE VINEYARDS INC
Also Called: Chalet Debonne
7840 Doty Rd (44057-9511)
PHONE....................440 466-3485
Anthony Paul Debevc, *Pr*
Tony J Debevc, *VP*
Beth Debevc, *Sec*
EMP: 15 EST: 1971
SQ FT: 14,000
SALES (est): 2.21MM Privately Held
Web: www.debonne.com
SIC: 2084 Wines

(G-9589)
CHEMMASTERS INC
300 Edwards St (44057-3112)
PHONE....................440 428-2105
Daniel Schodowski, *Pr*
Greg Myers, *VP*
Paul Murphy Cbh, *Prin*
◆ EMP: 20 EST: 1987
SQ FT: 25,000
SALES (est): 8.88MM Privately Held
Web: www.chemmasters.net
SIC: 2899 2891 5169 2851 Concrete curing and hardening compounds; Sealants; Chemicals and allied products, nec; Paints and allied products

(G-9590)
COMPETETIVE CARBIDE INC
Also Called: Competitive Carbide
5879 Shore Dr (44057-1801)
PHONE....................440 350-9393
Tom Cirino, *Pr*
▲ EMP: 40 EST: 1992
SALES (est): 3.32MM Privately Held
Web: www.archcuttingtools.com
SIC: 3541 Machine tools, metal cutting type

(G-9591)
COUNTY OF LAKE
Also Called: Waste Water Treatment Plant
7815 Cashen Rd (44057-1651)
PHONE....................440 428-1794
Terry Rascke, *Mgr*
EMP: 10
SQ FT: 650
SALES (corp-wide): 219.71MM Privately Held
Web: www.lakecountyohio.gov
SIC: 3589 Water treatment equipment, industrial
PA: County Of Lake
8 N State St Ste 215
Painesville OH 44077
440 350-2500

(G-9592)
FORZZA CORPORATION (PA)
222 N Lake St (44057-3118)

Madison - Lake County (G-9593)

P.O. Box 10 (44057-0010)
PHONE..........................440 998-6300
Joseph C Passerell, *Pr*
Steve Passerell, *COO*
EMP: 21 **EST:** 2010
SALES (est): 6.89MM
SALES (corp-wide): 6.89MM **Privately Held**
SIC: 3585 Parts for heating, cooling, and refrigerating equipment

(G-9593)
LAURENTIA WINERY
6869 River Rd (44057-9008)
PHONE..........................440 296-9170
EMP: 10 **EST:** 2015
SALES (est): 1.8MM **Privately Held**
Web: www.laurentiawinery.com
SIC: 2084 Wines

(G-9594)
TOPKOTE INC
404 N Lake St (44057-3151)
PHONE..........................440 428-0525
Shane Slattman, *Prin*
EMP: 9 **EST:** 2006
SALES (est): 755.87K **Privately Held**
Web: www.topkote.biz
SIC: 3479 Coating of metals and formed products

(G-9595)
UNIVERSAL SCIENTIFIC INC
6210 Campbell Dr (44057-2003)
PHONE..........................440 428-1777
Thomas W Heckman, *Pr*
Phoebe Heckman, *Sec*
EMP: 8 **EST:** 1985
SQ FT: 2,500
SALES (est): 648.73K **Privately Held**
Web: www.universalscientificinc.com
SIC: 3821 Laboratory equipment: fume hoods, distillation racks, etc.

Magnolia
Stark County

(G-9596)
OLDE WOOD LTD
7557 Willowdale Ave Se (44643-9718)
PHONE..........................330 866-1441
Thomas Sancic, *CEO*
EMP: 35 **EST:** 1996
SQ FT: 70,000
SALES (est): 6.26MM **Privately Held**
Web: www.oldewoodltd.com
SIC: 3272 Building materials, except block or brick: concrete

(G-9597)
PHOENIX ASPHALT COMPANY INC
18025 Imperial Rd (44643)
PHONE..........................330 339-4935
James R Demuth, *Pr*
EMP: 6 **EST:** 2002
SALES (est): 173.16K **Privately Held**
SIC: 1442 5032 Construction sand and gravel; Sand, construction

Maineville
Warren County

(G-9598)
ABCO BAR & TUBE CUTNG SVC INC
7685 S State Route 48 Ste 1 (45039-8802)
PHONE..........................513 697-9487
Kris Martin, *Pr*
Jason Martin, *

EMP: 30 **EST:** 1973
SQ FT: 40,000
SALES (est): 8.98MM **Privately Held**
Web: www.abcomachining.com
SIC: 3451 3452 3599 Screw machine products; Bolts, nuts, rivets, and washers; Machine and other job shop work

(G-9599)
EMPANADAS AQUI LLC
8749 Surrey Pl (45039-9519)
PHONE..........................513 312-9566
EMP: 20 **EST:** 2020
SALES (est): 836.95K **Privately Held**
Web: www.empanadasaqui.com
SIC: 2099 Food preparations, nec

(G-9600)
FABACRAFT INC
Also Called: Fabacraft Co
201 Grandin Rd (45039-9762)
PHONE..........................510 077-0500
Edward F Bavis, *Ch Bd*
William Sieber, *
Dolly Mattingly, *
Michael Brown, *
EMP: 35 **EST:** 1958
SQ FT: 44,000
SALES (est): 3.46MM **Privately Held**
Web: www.bavis.com
SIC: 3535 Conveyors and conveying equipment

(G-9601)
MARKET READY
1129 Avalon Dr (45039-9131)
PHONE..........................513 289-9231
Dan H Letzler, *Owner*
EMP: 6 **EST:** 2013
SALES (est): 143.01K **Privately Held**
Web: www.marketreadyhs.com
SIC: 3273 Ready-mixed concrete

(G-9602)
TODD PEAK WOODWORK LLC
208 Saddle Creek Ln (45039-8434)
PHONE..........................513 560-6760
EMP: 6 **EST:** 2012
SALES (est): 54.13K **Privately Held**
Web: www.toddpeakwoodwork.com
SIC: 2431 Millwork

(G-9603)
TRINITY MIDWEST AVIATION LLC
8123 S State Route 48 (45039-8812)
PHONE..........................513 583-0519
EMP: 7 **EST:** 2012
SALES (est): 273.2K **Privately Held**
Web: www.trinitymidwest.com
SIC: 3728 Aircraft parts and equipment, nec

Malinta
Henry County

(G-9604)
GILSON SCREEN INCORPORATED
8-810 K-2 Rd (43535)
P.O. Box 99 (43535-0199)
PHONE..........................419 256-7711
David A Cody, *Pr*
Steven J Roby, *
Trent Smith, *
James A Cody, *
Shelly Franz, *
EMP: 42 **EST:** 1961
SQ FT: 30,000
SALES (est): 9.22MM **Privately Held**
Web: www.gilsonscreen.com

SIC: 3829 3444 Testing equipment: abrasion, shearing strength, etc.; Sheet metalwork

(G-9605)
JAD MACHINE COMPANY INC
10620 County Road J (43535-9713)
PHONE..........................419 256-6332
EMP: 12 **EST:** 1992
SQ FT: 12,000
SALES (est): 1MM **Privately Held**
Web: www.jadmachine.com
SIC: 3451 Screw machine products

Malta
Morgan County

(G-9606)
E Z GROUT CORPORATION
Also Called: Ezg Manufacturing
1833 N Riverview Rd (43758-9303)
PHONE..........................740 749-3512
Damian Lang, *Pr*
Daniel Kern, *
Douglas Taylor, *
▲ **EMP:** 25 **EST:** 1998
SALES (est): 5.89MM **Privately Held**
Web: www.ezgmfg.com
SIC: 3423 3531 Masons' hand tools; Construction machinery

(G-9607)
EZ GROUT CORPORATION INC
Also Called: Ezg Manufacturing
1833 N Riverview Rd (43758-9303)
PHONE..........................740 962-2024
Damian Lang, *Owner*
EMP: 40 **EST:** 2007
SALES (est): 6.62MM **Privately Held**
Web: www.ezgmfg.com
SIC: 5082 3499 3549 Masonry equipment and supplies; Chests, fire or burglary resistive: metal; Wiredrawing and fabricating machinery and equipment, ex. die

Malvern
Carroll County

(G-9608)
AMERICAN AXLE & MFG INC
Also Called: AAM Mtal Frmng-Mlvern Opration
3255 Alliance Rd Nw (44644-9756)
PHONE..........................330 863-7500
EMP: 24
SALES (corp-wide): 6.08B **Publicly Held**
Web: www.aam.com
SIC: 3714 Motor vehicle parts and accessories
HQ: American Axle & Manufacturing, Inc.
One Dauch Dr
Detroit MI 48211

(G-9609)
CAMBRIDGE MILL PRODUCTS INC
6005 Alliance Rd Nw (44644)
P.O. Box 490 (44644)
PHONE..........................330 863-1121
Charles Lebeau Iii, *Pr*
Jerry W Morris Ii, *VP*
EMP: 7 **EST:** 1970
SQ FT: 2,400
SALES (est): 1.11MM **Privately Held**
Web: www.cambridgemillproducts.com
SIC: 2992 Oils and greases, blending and compounding

(G-9610)
COLFOR MANUFACTURING INC (DH)
3255 Alliance Rd Nw (44644-9756)
PHONE..........................330 470-6207
▲ **EMP:** 363 **EST:** 1996
SQ FT: 60,000
SALES (est): 900MM
SALES (corp-wide): 6.08B **Publicly Held**
Web: www.colformanufacturinginc.com
SIC: 3462 3599 3463 Iron and steel forgings; Machine shop, jobbing and repair; Nonferrous forgings
HQ: American Axle & Manufacturing, Inc.
One Dauch Dr
Detroit MI 48211

(G-9611)
FOR CALL INC
3255 Alliance Rd Nw (44644-9756)
PHONE..........................330 863-0404
Inacio Moriguchi, *Pr*
EMP: 23 **EST:** 1967
SALES (est): 280.52K **Privately Held**
SIC: 3462 Iron and steel forgings

(G-9612)
GBS CORP
Also Called: GBS Filing Solutions
224 Morges Rd (44644-9736)
P.O. Box 308 (44644-0308)
PHONE..........................330 863-1828
Michele Benson, *Brnch Mgr*
EMP: 116
SALES (corp-wide): 190.76MM **Privately Held**
Web: www.gbscorp.com
SIC: 2675 2752 2672 2761 Folders, filing, die-cut: made from purchased materials; Forms, business: lithographed; Adhesive papers, labels, or tapes: from purchased material; Manifold business forms
PA: Gbs Corp.
7233 Freedom Ave Nw
North Canton OH 44720
330 494-5330

(G-9613)
GORDONS GRAPHICS INC
123 S Reed Ave (44644-9496)
P.O. Box 586 (44644-0586)
PHONE..........................330 863-2322
Brad Lewis, *Pr*
Jerry Hinton, *Sec*
EMP: 7 **EST:** 1987
SQ FT: 1,500
SALES (est): 892.88K **Privately Held**
Web: www.gordonsgraphics.com
SIC: 2752 2759 5734 5943 Offset printing; Engraving, nec; Computer and software stores; Office forms and supplies

(G-9614)
PERFECT PRODUCTS COMPANY
Also Called: Aurora Balloon Company
265 Morges Rd (44644-9753)
EMP: 25 **EST:** 1971
SQ FT: 36,000
SALES (est): 2.09MM **Privately Held**
SIC: 3069 Balloons, advertising and toy: rubber

(G-9615)
PRECISION WORKS MACHINE LLC
6056 Alliance Rd Nw (44644-9445)
PHONE..........................330 863-0871
Ryan Dustman, *Prin*
EMP: 6 **EST:** 2015
SALES (est): 149.4K **Privately Held**
Web: www.precisionworksmachine.com

GEOGRAPHIC SECTION

Mansfield - Richland County (G-9638)

SIC: 3599 Machine shop, jobbing and repair

(G-9616)
STREAMLINE EXCAVATING LLC
6090 Citrus Rd Nw (44644-9731)
P.O. Box 118 (44644-0118)
PHONE..................................330 495-8617
Greggory J Macri, *Prin*
EMP: 6 **EST:** 2019
SALES (est): 284.13K **Privately Held**
SIC: 3531 Plows: construction, excavating, and grading

Manchester
Adams County

(G-9617)
HAMMER JAMMER LLC
700 Brush Creek Rd (45144-9243)
PHONE..................................937 549-4062
Ken Mccaw, *Prin*
EMP: 6 **EST:** 2015
SALES (est): 78.7K **Privately Held**
SIC: 3541 Machine tools, metal cutting type

(G-9618)
HEADWATERS INCORPORATED
745 Us Highway 52 (45144-8450)
PHONE..................................989 671-1500
Sam Jackson, *Mgr*
EMP: 14
Web: www.ecomaterial.com
SIC: 3272 Siding, precast stone
HQ: Headwaters Incorporated
10701 S River Front Pkwy # 300
South Jordan UT 84095

(G-9619)
HILLTOP RECREATION INC
Also Called: Hilltop Golf Course
1649 Brown Hill Rd (45144-9317)
PHONE..................................937 549-2904
Thomas D Kizer Senior, *Pr*
George Beckner, *VP*
EMP: 14 **EST:** 1970
SQ FT: 2,451,000
SALES (est): 292.54K **Privately Held**
Web: tf.click.com.cn
SIC: 7997 2099 Golf club, membership; Ready-to-eat meals, salads, and sandwiches

Mansfield
Richland County

(G-9620)
A L CALLAHAN DOOR SALES
35 Industrial Dr (44904-1372)
PHONE..................................419 884-3667
TOLL FREE: 800
Don Callahan, *Owner*
EMP: 7 **EST:** 1983
SQ FT: 3,000
SALES (est): 1.03MM **Privately Held**
Web: www.callahandoors.com
SIC: 5211 7699 3699 Garage doors, sale and installation; Garage door repair; Door opening and closing devices, electrical

(G-9621)
ABLEPRINT / TOUCAN INC
26 W 6th St (44902-1068)
PHONE..................................419 522-9742
Peter Boyko, *CEO*
Janice Boyko, *Pr*
Michelle Blackledege, *VP*
EMP: 19 **EST:** 1994
SALES (est): 2.17MM **Privately Held**
Web: www.ableprint.com
SIC: 2759 Imprinting

(G-9622)
AK MANSFIELD
913 Bowman St (44903-4109)
PHONE..................................419 755-3011
Randy Hartman, *Prin*
EMP: 13 **EST:** 2007
SALES (est): 345.91K **Privately Held**
SIC: 3999 Bleaching and dyeing of sponges

(G-9623)
AMAROQ INC
Also Called: Guetle Die & Stamping
648 N Trimble Rd (44906-2002)
PHONE..................................419 747-2110
R T Mong, *Pr*
EMP: 7 **EST:** 1967
SQ FT: 8,000
SALES (est): 607.3K **Privately Held**
Web: www.amaroqinc.com
SIC: 3469 3544 Stamping metal for the trade ; Special dies, tools, jigs, and fixtures

(G-9624)
AMERASCREW INC
653 Lida St (44903-1242)
P.O. Box 1407 (44901-1407)
PHONE..................................419 522-2232
John R Keith, *Pr*
EMP: 21 **EST:** 1920
SQ FT: 37,000
SALES (est): 2.48MM **Privately Held**
Web: www.amerascrew.com
SIC: 3451 Screw machine products

(G-9625)
AMERICAN TOOL & MFG CO
Also Called: American Tool & Manufacturing
211 Newman St (44902-1461)
P.O. Box 1242 (44901-1242)
PHONE..................................419 522-2452
Myron Brenner, *Pr*
EMP: 15 **EST:** 1966
SQ FT: 40,000
SALES (est): 438.23K **Privately Held**
SIC: 3469 Stamping metal for the trade

(G-9626)
AS AMERICA INC
Also Called: American Standard Brands
41 Cairns Rd (44903-8992)
PHONE..................................419 522-4211
Kevin Oak, *Mgr*
EMP: 43
Web: www.americanstandard-us.com
SIC: 3261 3431 3281 2541 Plumbing fixtures, vitreous china; Metal sanitary ware ; Cut stone and stone products; Wood partitions and fixtures
HQ: As America, Inc.
30 Knightsbridge Rd # 301
Piscataway NJ 08854

(G-9627)
AUTOMATIC PARTS
433 Springmill St (44903-7008)
P.O. Box 1505 (44901-1505)
PHONE..................................419 524-5841
Robert H Wittmer, *Pr*
David A Wittmer, *VP*
EMP: 20 **EST:** 1956
SQ FT: 17,000
SALES (est): 1.66MM **Privately Held**
Web: www.automaticparts.com
SIC: 3599 Machine shop, jobbing and repair

(G-9628)
BLACK RIVER GROUP INC (PA)
Also Called: Black River Display Group
195 E 4th St (44902-1519)
PHONE..................................419 524-6699
Terry Neff, *Pr*
EMP: 47 **EST:** 1960
SQ FT: 74,000
SALES (est): 11.55MM
SALES (corp-wide): 11.55MM **Privately Held**
Web: www.blackriverconnect.com
SIC: 7311 2752 2791 2789 Advertising agencies; Commercial printing, lithographic; Typesetting; Bookbinding and related work

(G-9629)
BLEVINS METAL FABRICATION INC
Also Called: Blevins Fabrication
288 Illinois Ave S (44905-2827)
PHONE..................................419 522-6082
Lloyd T Blevins, *Pr*
EMP: 25 **EST:** 1997
SQ FT: 13,000
SALES (est): 4.47MM **Privately Held**
Web: www.blevinsfabricationcorp.com
SIC: 7692 3446 3444 3443 Welding repair; Architectural metalwork; Sheet metalwork; Fabricated plate work (boiler shop)

(G-9630)
BRANDTS CUSTOM MACHINING LLC
1183 Stewart Rd N (44905-1551)
PHONE..................................419 566-3192
Benjamin Brandt, *Prin*
EMP: 7 **EST:** 2008
SALES (est): 573.43K **Privately Held**
Web: www.bcm101.com
SIC: 3599 Machine shop, jobbing and repair

(G-9631)
BREITINGER COMPANY
595 Oakenwaldt St (44905-1900)
PHONE..................................419 526-4255
Milo Breitinger, *Pr*
EMP: 120 **EST:** 1954
SQ FT: 106,000
SALES (est): 13.94MM **Privately Held**
Web: www.breitingercompany.com
SIC: 3441 3469 7692 3444 Fabricated structural metal; Metal stampings, nec; Welding repair; Sheet metalwork

(G-9632)
BROST FOUNDRY COMPANY
198 Wayne St (44902-1433)
PHONE..................................419 522-1133
EMP: 22
SALES (corp-wide): 5.08MM **Privately Held**
Web: www.brostfoundry.com
SIC: 3366 Brass foundry, nec
PA: Brost Foundry Company (Inc)
2934 E 55th St
Cleveland OH 44127
216 641-1131

(G-9633)
BUCKLER INDUSTRIES INC
Also Called: National Machine Company
861 Expressview Dr (44905-1535)
P.O. Box 2127 (44905-0127)
PHONE..................................419 589-6134
Robert Buckler, *Pr*
Marianne Buckler, *
EMP: 25 **EST:** 1972
SQ FT: 100,000
SALES (est): 1.21MM **Privately Held**

SIC: 2796 Platemaking services

(G-9634)
BUNTING BEARINGS LLC
153 E 5th St (44902-1407)
P.O. Box 1053 (44901-1053)
PHONE..................................419 522-3323
Kim J Keogh, *Brnch Mgr*
EMP: 41
SQ FT: 68,000
Web: www.buntingbearings.com
SIC: 3366 3568 3369 3356 Bushings and bearings, bronze (nonmachined); Power transmission equipment, nec; Nonferrous foundries, nec; Nonferrous rolling and drawing, nec
PA: Bunting Bearings, Llc
1001 Holland Park Blvd
Holland OH 43528

(G-9635)
CASE-MAUL MANUFACTURING CO
30 Harker St (44903-1395)
PHONE..................................419 524-1061
Craig Case, *Pr*
Sandra Collins, *Sec*
Debbie Johnson, *Mgr*
▲ **EMP:** 10 **EST:** 1953
SQ FT: 18,000
SALES (est): 1.3MM **Privately Held**
Web: www.casemaul.com
SIC: 3599 7692 Machine shop, jobbing and repair; Welding repair

(G-9636)
CEMENT PRODUCTS INC
389 Park Ave E (44905-2896)
PHONE..................................419 524-4342
TOLL FREE: 877
Dwight Schmitz, *Pr*
Douglas Schmitz, *
Daniel Schmitz, *
EMP: 26 **EST:** 1916
SQ FT: 82,778
SALES (est): 4.24MM **Privately Held**
Web: www.cementproductsinc.com
SIC: 3271 3273 3272 Blocks, concrete or cinder: standard; Ready-mixed concrete; Concrete products, nec

(G-9637)
CENTRAL COCA-COLA BTLG CO INC
Also Called: Coca-Cola
100 Industrial Pkwy (44903-8999)
PHONE..................................419 522-2653
Mike Dewalt, *Mgr*
EMP: 54
SALES (corp-wide): 45.75B **Publicly Held**
Web: www.coca-cola.com
SIC: 2086 Bottled and canned soft drinks
HQ: Central Coca-Cola Bottling Company, Inc.
555 Taxter Rd Ste 550
Elmsford NY 10523
914 789-1100

(G-9638)
CLEANING LADY INC
190 Stewart Rd N (44905-2639)
PHONE..................................419 589-5566
Suzanne Stewart, *Pr*
EMP: 9 **EST:** 1978
SQ FT: 7,360
SALES (est): 233.31K **Privately Held**
SIC: 7349 5169 2841 Janitorial service, contract basis; Detergents; Detergents, synthetic organic or inorganic alkaline

---

(PA)=Parent Co (HQ)=Headquarters
✪ = New Business established in last 2 years

Mansfield - Richland County (G-9639)

GEOGRAPHIC SECTION

(G-9639)
CLEVELAND-CLIFFS STEEL CORP
Also Called: Mansfield Operations
913 Bowman St (44903-4109)
P.O. Box 247 (44901-0247)
PHONE..............................419 755-3011
Robert J Pasquarelli, *Brnch Mgr*
EMP: 500
SALES (corp-wide): 22B **Publicly Held**
Web: www.clevelandcliffs.com
SIC: 3312 Stainless steel
HQ: Cleveland-Cliffs Steel Corporation
200 Public Sq Ste 3300
Cleveland OH 44114

(G-9640)
CLINE FIRE LLC
161 N Trimble Rd (44906-2630)
PHONE..............................419 571-4119
EMP: 8 **EST:** 2017
SALES (est): 538.43K **Privately Held**
Web: www.clinefire.com
SIC: 3569 Firefighting and related equipment

(G-9641)
CORPAD COMPANY INC
555 Park Ave E (44905-2871)
P.O. Box 1492 (44901-1492)
PHONE..............................419 522-7818
Dane Arlen Bonecutter, *Prin*
EMP: 55 **EST:** 1980
SQ FT: 97,500
SALES (est): 8.97MM **Privately Held**
Web: www.tavens.com
SIC: 2653 Boxes, corrugated: made from purchased materials

(G-9642)
CRANE PLUMBING LLC
41 Cairns Rd (44903-8992)
PHONE..............................419 522-4211
◆ **EMP:** 1300
SIC: 3261 3431 3088 Bathroom accessories/fittings, vitreous china or earthenware; Metal sanitary ware; Shower stalls, fiberglass and plastics

(G-9643)
CSM HORVATH LEDGEBROOK INC
Also Called: Rost Boundry
198 Wayne St (44902-1433)
PHONE..............................419 522-1133
Chuck Horvath, *Pr*
EMP: 6 **EST:** 2010
SALES (est): 199.16K **Privately Held**
SIC: 3363 Aluminum die-castings

(G-9644)
CYRPRESS WINE CELLARS
37 E 4th St (44902-1303)
PHONE..............................419 295-2124
EMP: 6 **EST:** 2018
SALES (est): 113.37K **Privately Held**
Web: www.cypresscellars.com
SIC: 2084 Wines

(G-9645)
DECA MFG CO
300 S Mill St (44904-8519)
PHONE..............................419 884-0071
Hansford R Williams, *Pr*
Karen M Cashell, *VP*
Carolyn Williams, *Sec*
EMP: 15 **EST:** 1976
SQ FT: 33,000
SALES (est): 2.51MM **Privately Held**
Web: www.decamanufacturing.com
SIC: 3679 3544 3672 Harness assemblies, for electronic use: wire or cable; Industrial molds; Printed circuit boards

(G-9646)
DND EMULSIONS INC
270 Park Ave E (44902-1849)
P.O. Box 1178 (44901-1178)
PHONE..............................419 525-4988
Delbert Dawson, *Pr*
EMP: 12 **EST:** 1981
SQ FT: 2,940
SALES (est): 200.49K **Privately Held**
Web: www.ddemulsionsinc.com
SIC: 2869 2952 2992 Industrial organic chemicals, nec; Coating compounds, tar; Cutting oils, blending: made from purchased materials

(G-9647)
DTE INC
110 Baird Pkwy (44903-7909)
PHONE..............................419 522-3428
Dean Russell, *Pr*
Burke Melching, *
Rob Nelson, *
EMP: 30 **EST:** 1990
SQ FT: 45,000
SALES (est): 2.43MM **Privately Held**
Web: www.dteinc.com
SIC: 7629 3661 Telephone set repair; Telephone and telegraph apparatus

(G-9648)
DYNAMIC MACHINE WORKS
139 Illinois Ave S (44905-2825)
PHONE..............................419 564-7925
EMP: 6 **EST:** 2019
SALES (est): 211.65K **Privately Held**
Web: www.dynamicmachineworks.org
SIC: 3599 Machine shop, jobbing and repair

(G-9649)
EAGLES NEST HOLDINGS LLC
Also Called: Sabin Robbins Paper Company
1111 N Main St (44903-9718)
PHONE..............................419 526-4123
Joe Talion, *Mgr*
EMP: 50
SIC: 2679 Paper products, converted, nec
PA: Eagles Nest Holdings, Llc
455 E 86th St
New York NY 10028

(G-9650)
ECO ENERGY INTERNATIONAL LLC
233 Park Ave E (44902-1845)
PHONE..............................419 544-5000
EMP: 35 **EST:** 2021
SALES (est): 2.63MM **Privately Held**
Web: www.ecoenergyinternational.com
SIC: 2813 Hydrogen

(G-9651)
EDGE PLASTICS INC (PA)
449 Newman St (44902-1123)
PHONE..............................419 522-6696
Shelley Fisher, *Pr*
▲ **EMP:** 150 **EST:** 1989
SQ FT: 146,000
SALES (est): 41.82MM **Privately Held**
Web: www.edgeplasticsinc.com
SIC: 3089 Injection molded finished plastics products, nec

(G-9652)
ELTOOL CORPORATION
1400 Park Ave E (44905-2989)
PHONE..............................513 723-1772
Edward Crotty, *Pr*
EMP: 7 **EST:** 1999
SALES (est): 551.56K **Privately Held**
Web: www.eltool.com

SIC: 8742 3599 5084 Marketing consulting services; Machine shop, jobbing and repair; Industrial machinery and equipment

(G-9653)
ENERGY TECHNOLOGIES INC
Also Called: E T I
219 Park Ave E (44902)
PHONE..............................419 522-4444
Paul C Madden, *Pr*
John S Madden, *
EMP: 80 **EST:** 1991
SQ FT: 30,000
SALES (est): 9.78MM **Privately Held**
Web: www.ruggedsystems.com
SIC: 3629 3625 3621 Electronic generation equipment; Relays and industrial controls; Motors and generators

(G-9654)
FANNIN MACHINE COMPANY LLC
76 Atenway St (44902-1025)
PHONE..............................419 524-9525
Bobby Lee Fannin, *Managing Member*
EMP: 6 **EST:** 2018
SALES (est): 266K **Privately Held**
SIC: 3451 Screw machine products

(G-9655)
FILL-RITE COMPANY (HQ) ◆
600 S Airport Rd (44903-7831)
PHONE..............................419 755-1011
Scott King, *Pr*
EMP: 27 **EST:** 2022
SALES (est): 38.93MM
SALES (corp-wide): 659.51MM **Publicly Held**
Web: www.fillrite.com
SIC: 3561 Pumps and pumping equipment
PA: Gorman-Rupp Company
600 S Airport Rd
Mansfield OH 44903
419 755-1011

(G-9656)
FIVE HANDICAP INC (PA)
Also Called: Mansfield Graphics
127 N Walnut St (44902)
P.O. Box 7 (44901)
PHONE..............................419 525-2511
Chuck B Mccartney, *Pr*
EMP: 10 **EST:** 1929
SQ FT: 20,000
SALES (est): 1.55MM
SALES (corp-wide): 1.55MM **Privately Held**
Web: www.mansfieldgraphics.com
SIC: 3469 Stamping metal for the trade

(G-9657)
FLEET RELIEF COMPANY
550 N Main St (44902-7322)
PHONE..............................419 525-2625
EMP: 8 **EST:** 1996
SALES (est): 914.42K **Privately Held**
SIC: 7534 Tire repair shop

(G-9658)
FORREST MACHINE PDTS CO LTD
Also Called: Forrest Scrw Machine
145 Industrial Dr (44904-1338)
P.O. Box 3648 (44907-0648)
PHONE..............................419 589-3774
EMP: 22 **EST:** 2009
SALES (est): 2.97MM **Privately Held**
Web: www.fmpcorp.com
SIC: 3549 3451 Metalworking machinery, nec; Screw machine products

(G-9659)
GENERAL TECHNOLOGIES INC
855 W Longview Ave (44906-2131)
P.O. Box 1726 (44901-1726)
PHONE..............................419 747-1800
Margaret Marlow, *VP*
Susan L Moran, *Prin*
▲ **EMP:** 20 **EST:** 1957
SQ FT: 40,000
SALES (est): 5.57MM **Privately Held**
Web: www.general-technologies.com
SIC: 3469 7692 3444 3443 Metal stampings, nec; Welding repair; Sheet metalwork; Fabricated plate work (boiler shop)

(G-9660)
GLOBAL ENERGY PARTNERS LLC
Also Called: Gofs
3401 State Route 13 (44904-9394)
PHONE..............................419 756-8027
Jim Jackson, *Pr*
Annette Jones, *Sec*
EMP: 27 **EST:** 2013
SALES (est): 15.22MM **Privately Held**
Web: www.globalenergypartnersllc.com
SIC: 1389 5082 1623 Oil field services, nec; Oil field equipment; Oil and gas line and compressor station construction

(G-9661)
GORMAN-RUPP COMPANY
Ipt Pumps Division
305 Bowman St (44903-1689)
P.O. Box 1217 (44901-1217)
PHONE..............................419 755-1011
James A Lomax, *Dir*
EMP: 500
SALES (corp-wide): 659.51MM **Publicly Held**
Web: www.gormanrupp.com
SIC: 3561 Industrial pumps and parts
PA: Gorman-Rupp Company
600 S Airport Rd
Mansfield OH 44903
419 755-1011

(G-9662)
GORMAN-RUPP COMPANY
Also Called: Warehouse
100 Rupp Rd (44903)
P.O. Box 1217 (44901-1217)
PHONE..............................419 755-1245
Jeffrey Gorman, *Pr*
EMP: 8
SALES (corp-wide): 659.51MM **Publicly Held**
Web: www.gormanrupp.com
SIC: 5084 3561 Pumps and pumping equipment, nec; Pumps and pumping equipment
PA: Gorman-Rupp Company
600 S Airport Rd
Mansfield OH 44903
419 755-1011

(G-9663)
GORMAN-RUPP COMPANY (PA)
600 S Airport Rd (44903)
P.O. Box 1217 (44901)
PHONE..............................419 755-1011
Jeffrey S Gorman, *Pr*
James C Gorman, *
James C Kerr, *CFO*
Brigette A Burnell, *Corporate Secretary*
EMP: 147 **EST:** 1933
SALES (est): 659.51MM
SALES (corp-wide): 659.51MM **Publicly Held**
Web: www.gormanrupp.com
SIC: 3594 3561 Fluid power pumps and motors; Industrial pumps and parts

GEOGRAPHIC SECTION

Mansfield - Richland County

(G-9664)
GRAYWACKE INC
300 S Mill St (44904-8519)
PHONE..............................419 884-7014
Scott Huffman, *Pr*
Mark Huffman, *VP*
EMP: 14 **EST:** 1999
SQ FT: 14,000
SALES (est): 1.91MM **Privately Held**
Web: www.graywacke.net
SIC: 3691 Batteries, rechargeable

(G-9665)
GROWCO INC
844 Kochheiser Rd (44904-8637)
PHONE..............................419 886-4628
Jeff Mason, *Prin*
EMP: 11 **EST:** 2009
SALES (est): 318.61K **Privately Held**
SIC: 3272 Concrete products, nec

(G-9666)
HAPPY GRAPE LLC
300 E Main St (44904-1300)
P.O. Box 3305 (44904-0305)
PHONE..............................419 884-9463
Paul Smith, *Prin*
EMP: 9 **EST:** 2010
SALES (est): 509.32K **Privately Held**
Web: www.myhappygrape.com
SIC: 2084 Wines

(G-9667)
HAYFORD TECHNOLOGIES INC
Also Called: Milark Industries
500 S Airport Rd (44903-8067)
PHONE..............................419 524-7627
Matt Breitinger, *Pr*
Mary Breitinger, *
Trisha Breitinger, *
Brooke Breitinger, *
EMP: 99 **EST:** 2016
SALES (est): 2.83MM **Privately Held**
SIC: 3465 3469 Automotive stampings; Metal stampings, nec

(G-9668)
HIGHPOINT FIREARMS
Also Called: Hi-Point Firearms
1015 Springmill St (44906-1571)
PHONE..............................419 747-9444
Tom Deeb, *Pr*
Shirley Deeb, *
EMP: 34 **EST:** 1988
SQ FT: 24,000
SALES (est): 2.29MM **Privately Held**
Web: www.hi-pointfirearms.com
SIC: 3484 5941 Guns (firearms) or gun parts, 30 mm. and below; Sporting goods and bicycle shops

(G-9669)
IDEAL ELECTRIC POWER CO
Also Called: Ideal Electric
330 E 1st St (44902-7756)
PHONE..............................419 522-3611
◆ **EMP:** 30 **EST:** 1903
SQ FT: 280,000
SALES (est): 12.84MM **Privately Held**
Web: www.theidealelectric.com
SIC: 3621 3613 3625 Generators and sets, electric; Switchgear and switchgear accessories, nec; Relays and industrial controls

(G-9670)
IDEX CORPORATION
800 N Main St (44902-4204)
PHONE..............................419 526-7222
EMP: 7 **EST:** 2019
SALES (est): 206.8K **Privately Held**
Web: www.sandpiperpump.com
SIC: 3561 Pumps and pumping equipment

(G-9671)
JAY INDUSTRIES INC
Also Called: Broshco Fabricated Products
1595 W Longview Ave (44906-1806)
PHONE..............................419 747-4161
Rick R Taylor, *Pr*
Josh Taylor, *VP*
Dave Benick, *Ex VP*
Rodger Loesch, *CFO*
R G Taylor, *Prin*
▲ **EMP:** 930 **EST:** 1946
SQ FT: 125,000
SALES (est): 127.46MM **Privately Held**
Web: www.jayindinc.com
SIC: 2531 3089 Seats, automobile; Injection molding of plastics

(G-9672)
JAY MID-SOUTH LLC
150 Longview Ave E (44903-4206)
PHONE..............................256 439-6600
Rick Taylor, *Managing Member*
◆ **EMP:** 49 **EST:** 2004
SQ FT: 65,000
SALES (est): 2.67MM **Privately Held**
SIC: 3499 Automobile seat frames, metal

(G-9673)
JOHN L GARBER MATERIALS CORP
2745 Gass Rd (44904-8715)
PHONE..............................419 884-1567
John L Garber, *Pr*
Matthew Garber, *VP*
Donna West, *Sec*
EMP: 10 **EST:** 1956
SQ FT: 500
SALES (est): 454.37K **Privately Held**
SIC: 1442 Gravel mining

(G-9674)
JONES POTATO CHIP CO (PA)
823 Bowman St (44903-4107)
PHONE..............................419 529-9424
Robert Jones, *Pr*
Regina Jones, *
Charles K Hellinger, *
Frederick W Jones, *
EMP: 46 **EST:** 1940
SQ FT: 50,000
SALES (est): 9.05MM
SALES (corp-wide): 9.05MM **Privately Held**
Web: www.joneschips.com
SIC: 2096 5145 Potato chips and other potato-based snacks; Potato chips

(G-9675)
JOTCO INC
1400 Park Ave E (44905-2989)
PHONE..............................513 721-4943
EMP: 6 **EST:** 1984
SQ FT: 100,000
SALES (est): 691.18K **Privately Held**
Web: www.eltool.com
SIC: 3471 8711 3599 Finishing, metals or formed products; Engineering services; Machine and other job shop work

(G-9676)
KARMA METAL PRODUCTS INC
556 Caldwell Ave (44905-1401)
PHONE..............................419 524-4371
Thomas Taska, *Pr*
Ron Kocher, *VP*
Judy Taska, *Sec*
EMP: 10 **EST:** 1952
SQ FT: 6,800
SALES (est): 998.11K **Privately Held**
Web: www.karmametalproducts.com
SIC: 3451 3545 Screw machine products; Measuring tools and machines, machinists' metalworking type

(G-9677)
KOKOSING MATERIALS INC
215 Oak St (44907-1439)
PHONE..............................419 522-2715
Bill Burgett, *Brnch Mgr*
EMP: 10
SALES (corp-wide): 1.17B **Privately Held**
Web: www.kokosing.biz
SIC: 2951 Asphalt and asphaltic paving mixtures (not from refineries)
HQ: Kokosing Materials, Inc.
   17531 Waterford Rd
   Fredericktown OH 43019
   740 694-9585

(G-9678)
LENNOX MACHINE INC
Also Called: Lennox Machine Shop
1471 Sprang Pkwy (44903-6531)
P.O. Box 1643 (44901-1643)
PHONE..............................419 525-1020
Terry L Eighinger, *Pr*
David Eighinger, *VP*
EMP: 13 **EST:** 1988
SALES (est): 449.77K **Privately Held**
SIC: 3599 Machine shop, jobbing and repair

(G-9679)
LEXINGTON CONCRETE & SUP INC (PA)
362 N Trimble Rd (44906-2541)
P.O. Box 1342 (44901-1342)
PHONE..............................419 529-3232
Martin F Moritz, *Pr*
EMP: 8 **EST:** 2008
SQ FT: 260,000
SALES (est): 2.15MM **Privately Held**
Web: www.lexingtonconcreteinc.com
SIC: 3273 Ready-mixed concrete

(G-9680)
LONG VIEW STEEL CORP
1555 W Longview Ave (44906)
P.O. Box P.O. Box 2839 (44906)
PHONE..............................419 747-1108
David Jacko, *Pr*
EMP: 12 **EST:** 1999
SALES (est): 3.46MM **Privately Held**
SIC: 3312 Blast furnaces and steel mills

(G-9681)
MAJOR METALS COMPANY
844 Kochheiser Rd (44904-8637)
PHONE..............................419 886-4600
Jeffrey C Mason, *Pr*
Wayne Riffe, *
EMP: 30 **EST:** 1973
SQ FT: 60,000
SALES (est): 10MM **Privately Held**
Web: www.majormetals.net
SIC: 3312 5051 3317 Plate, sheet and strip, except coated products; Iron or steel flat products; Steel pipe and tubes

(G-9682)
MALABAR PROPERTIES LLC
Also Called: Deca Manufacturing
300 S Mill St (44904-8519)
PHONE..............................419 884-0071
Cameron Haring, *Pr*
EMP: 10 **EST:** 2018
SQ FT: 33,000
SALES (est): 1.35MM **Privately Held**
Web: www.decamanufacturing.com
SIC: 3679 Harness assemblies, for electronic use: wire or cable

(G-9683)
MANAIRCO INC
28 Industrial Pkwy (44903-8999)
P.O. Box 111 (44901-0111)
PHONE..............................419 524-2121
Gayle Gorman Freeman, *Pr*
James C Gorman, *Ch Bd*
Joel Beinbrech, *VP*
Marjorie Gorman, *Sec*
EMP: 9 **EST:** 1953
SQ FT: 14,000
SALES (est): 1.04MM **Privately Held**
Web: www.manairco.com
SIC: 3648 3645 Airport lighting fixtures: runway approach, taxi, or ramp; Residential lighting fixtures

(G-9684)
MANSFIELD BREW WORKS LLC
Also Called: Phoenix Brewing
131 N Diamond St (44902-1331)
PHONE..............................419 631-3153
EMP: 15 **EST:** 2013
SALES (est): 494.72K **Privately Held**
Web: www.phoenixbrewing.com
SIC: 5813 2082 Bars and lounges; Beer (alcoholic beverage)

(G-9685)
MANSFIELD ENGINEERED COMPONENTS LLC
Also Called: Assembleis Co
1776 Harrington Memorial Rd (44903-8996)
P.O. Box 1602 (44901-1602)
PHONE..............................419 524-1331
◆ **EMP:** 160 **EST:** 1987
SALES (est): 24.93MM **Privately Held**
Web: www.mansfieldec.com
SIC: 3499 Furniture parts, metal

(G-9686)
MANSFIELD INDUSTRIES INC
1776 Harrington Memorial Rd (44903-8996)
PHONE..............................419 524-1300
Otis M Cummins, *Ch*
Barry Jackenheimer, *
EMP: 15 **EST:** 1994
SALES (est): 5.47MM **Privately Held**
Web: www.mansfieldec.com
SIC: 3469 Stamping metal for the trade

(G-9687)
MATERN METAL WORKS INC
210 N Adams St (44902-1449)
P.O. Box 1686 (44901-1686)
PHONE..............................419 529-3100
Joseph Matern, *Pr*
Reba Matern, *VP*
EMP: 10 **EST:** 1982
SQ FT: 3,600
SALES (est): 968.22K **Privately Held**
Web: www.maternmetalworks.com
SIC: 3444 Sheet metalwork

(G-9688)
MCDANIEL PRODUCTS INC (PA)
Also Called: Automatic Parts
50 Industrial Pkwy (44903-8999)
P.O. Box 1505 (44901-1505)
PHONE..............................419 524-5841
EMP: 6 **EST:** 2008
SALES (est): 1.37MM **Privately Held**
SIC: 3451 Screw machine products

(G-9689)
MCDANIEL PRODUCTS INC
Also Called: Automatic Parts

Mansfield - Richland County (G-9690)

433 Springmill St (44903-7008)
P.O. Box 1505 (44901-1505)
PHONE.............................419 524-5841
EMP: 10
SIC: 3451 Screw machine products
PA: Mcdaniel Products, Inc.
50 Mansfield Indus Pkwy
Mansfield OH 44903

(G-9690)
MERLE NORMAN COSMETICS INC
893 Park Ave W (44906-2971)
PHONE.............................419 282-0630
EMP: 37
SALES (corp-wide): 64MM **Privately Held**
Web: www.merlenorman.com
SIC: 2844 Cosmetic preparations
PA: Merle Norman Cosmetics, Inc.
9130 Bellanca Ave
Los Angeles CA 90045
310 641-3000

(G-9691)
MICHAEL BYRNE MANUFACTURING CO INC
1855 Earth Boring Rd (44903-9000)
P.O. Box 444 (44901-0444)
PHONE.............................419 525-1214
EMP: 25 **EST:** 1966
SALES (est): 4.91MM **Privately Held**
Web: www.byrnegroup.com
SIC: 3531 3599 3546 3541 Tunneling machinery; Custom machinery; Power-driven handtools; Machine tools, metal cutting type

(G-9692)
MIDWEST AIRCRAFT PRODUCTS CO
Also Called: Mapco
125 S Mill St (44904-9571)
P.O. Box 457 (44901-0457)
PHONE.............................419 884-2164
Jeffrey Miller, *CEO*
Jerry Miller, *CEO*
▼ **EMP:** 12 **EST:** 1986
SQ FT: 25,000
SALES (est): 1.79MM **Privately Held**
Web: www.midwestaircraft.com
SIC: 3728 Aircraft parts and equipment, nec

(G-9693)
MILARK INDUSTRIES INC
520 S Airport Rd (44903-8067)
PHONE.............................419 524-7627
EMP: 80
Web: www.milarkindustries.com
SIC: 3465 3469 3751 3714 Automotive stampings; Metal stampings, nec; Motorcycles, bicycles and parts; Motor vehicle parts and accessories
PA: Milark Industries, Inc.
536 S Airport Rd
Mansfield OH 44903

(G-9694)
MILARK INDUSTRIES INC (PA)
536 S Airport Rd (44903-8067)
PHONE.............................419 524-7627
EMP: 94 **EST:** 1986
SALES (est): 16.7MM **Privately Held**
Web: www.milarkindustries.com
SIC: 3465 3469 3751 3714 Automotive stampings; Metal stampings, nec; Motorcycles, bicycles and parts; Motor vehicle parts and accessories

(G-9695)
MILLER FABRICATION AND WELDING
125 S Mill St (44904-9571)

PHONE.............................419 884-0459
EMP: 6 **EST:** 2019
SALES (est): 618.37K **Privately Held**
SIC: 3599 Machine shop, jobbing and repair

(G-9696)
MINNICH MANUFACTURING CO INC
1444 State Route 42 (44903-9509)
P.O. Box 367 (44901-0367)
PHONE.............................419 903-0010
James R Minnich, *Pr*
▲ **EMP:** 25 **EST:** 1968
SQ FT: 43,000
SALES (est): 9.21MM **Privately Held**
Web: www.minnich-mfg.com
SIC: 3531 Vibrators for concrete construction

(G-9697)
MK METAL PRODUCTS ENTPS INC (PA)
Also Called: Mavericks Stainless
90 Sawyer Pkwy (44903-6514)
P.O. Box 878 (44901-0878)
PHONE.............................419 756-3644
Richard L Kemp, *CEO*
J Douglas Drusbal, *
David Cole, *
EMP: 20 **EST:** 1956
SQ FT: 39,000
SALES (est): 4.61MM
SALES (corp-wide): 4.61MM **Privately Held**
Web: www.mkmetalproducts.com
SIC: 3441 Fabricated structural metal

(G-9698)
MODERN BUILDERS SUPPLY INC
85 Smith Ave (44905-2854)
PHONE.............................419 526-0002
EMP: 25
SALES (corp-wide): 346.23MM **Privately Held**
Web: www.modernbuilderssupply.com
SIC: 5032 3089 5033 5031 Brick, stone, and related material; Doors, folding: plastics or plastics coated fabric; Roofing, asphalt and sheet metal; Kitchen cabinets
PA: Modern Builders Supply, Inc.
3500 Phillips Ave
Toledo OH 43608
419 241-3961

(G-9699)
MORITZ CONCRETE INC
362 N Trimble Rd (44906-2541)
P.O. Box 1342 (44901-1342)
PHONE.............................419 529-3232
Martin F Moritz Junior, *Pr*
James Moritz, *
Peter Moritz, *
Robert Moritz, *
Joe Moritz, *
EMP: 47 **EST:** 1950
SQ FT: 260,000
SALES (est): 4.85MM **Privately Held**
Web: www.moritzconcrete.com
SIC: 3273 Ready-mixed concrete

(G-9700)
MORITZ INTERNATIONAL INC
665 N Main St (44902-4201)
PHONE.............................419 526-5222
Frank Moritz, *Pr*
Thomas R Moritz, *
EMP: 37 **EST:** 1992
SQ FT: 50,000
SALES (est): 5.59MM **Privately Held**
Web: www.moritzinternational.com
SIC: 3715 Truck trailers

(G-9701)
NANOGATE NORTH AMERICA LLC
Crestline Paint
515 Newman St (44902-1160)
P.O. Box 1527 (44901-1527)
PHONE.............................419 522-7745
Steve Kunz, *Brnch Mgr*
EMP: 300
SALES (corp-wide): 193.63MM **Privately Held**
Web: www.jayindinc.com
SIC: 3714 Motor vehicle parts and accessories
HQ: Nanogate North America Llc
150 Longview Ave E
Mansfield OH 44903
419 524-3778

(G-9702)
NANOGATE NORTH AMERICA LLC
Rohr Manufacturing Div
1555 W Longview Ave (44906-1806)
PHONE.............................419 747-1096
EMP: 300
SALES (corp-wide): 193.63MM **Privately Held**
Web: www.jayindinc.com
SIC: 3312 Tubes, steel and iron
HQ: Nanogate North America Llc
150 Longview Ave E
Mansfield OH 44903
419 524-3778

(G-9703)
NATIONAL PRIDE EQUIPMENT INC
Also Called: National Pride Equipment
905 Hickory Ln Ste 101 (44905-2873)
P.O. Box 467 (44805-0467)
PHONE.............................419 289-2886
Charles Collins, *Pr*
Richard Walter, *Sec*
EMP: 9 **EST:** 1992
SALES (est): 4.22MM **Privately Held**
SIC: 5046 3589 5087 Commercial equipment, nec; Car washing machinery; Carwash equipment and supplies

(G-9704)
NEWMAN TECHNOLOGY INC (HQ)
100 Cairns Rd (44903-8990)
PHONE.............................419 525-1856
Takuji Shimizu, *Pr*
Stephen Rourke, *Sr VP*
Yukihisa Murata, *Ex VP*
▲ **EMP:** 576 **EST:** 1987
SQ FT: 450,000
SALES (est): 96.62MM **Privately Held**
SIC: 3714 3751 Mufflers (exhaust), motor vehicle; Motorcycle accessories
PA: Sankei Giken Co., Ltd.
1024-11, Niihori
Kawaguchi STM 334-0

(G-9705)
NEWSPAPER NETWORK CENTRAL OH
70 W 4th St (44903-1676)
PHONE.............................419 524-3545
Tom Brennan, *Prin*
EMP: 9 **EST:** 2006
SALES (est): 149.87K **Privately Held**
SIC: 2711 Newspapers, publishing and printing

(G-9706)
NPAS INC
2090 Harrington Memorial Rd (44903)
P.O. Box 20306 (43220)
PHONE.............................614 595-6916
Daniel Fusco, *CEO*
EMP: 11 **EST:** 2021

SALES (est): 1.21MM **Privately Held**
Web: www.npas.com
SIC: 3613 3677 3672 3625 Switchgear and switchboard apparatus; Electronic coils and transformers; Printed circuit boards; Relays and industrial controls

(G-9707)
OHIO VALLEY MANUFACTURING INC
1501 Harrington Memorial Rd (44903-8995)
PHONE.............................419 522-5818
Michael C Fanello, *Pr*
John Fanello, *
Jeff Fanello, *
Steven Fanello, *
Thom Weber, *
EMP: 80 **EST:** 1999
SQ FT: 131,300
SALES (est): 21.81MM **Privately Held**
Web: www.ohiovalleymfg.com
SIC: 3469 3399 Stamping metal for the trade; Flakes, metal

(G-9708)
OHIO VLY STMPNG-ASSEMBLIES INC
500 Newman St (44902-1122)
PHONE.............................419 522-0983
Todd J Flagel, *Prin*
EMP: 27 **EST:** 2002
SALES (est): 1.01MM **Privately Held**
SIC: 3297 Nonclay refractories

(G-9709)
PCR RESTORATIONS INC
Also Called: Lehr Awning Co
933 W Longview Ave (44906-2133)
PHONE.............................419 747-7957
EMP: 11 **EST:** 1932
SQ FT: 11,000
SALES (est): 243.45K **Privately Held**
Web: www.pcr-lehrawning.com
SIC: 2394 3089 2221 5999 Canvas awnings and canopies; Awnings, fiberglass and plastics combination; Upholstery, tapestry, and wall covering fabrics; Awnings

(G-9710)
POSM SOFTWARE LLC
2145 Millsboro Rd (44906-1336)
PHONE.............................859 274-0041
Robert Katter, *Prin*
EMP: 13 **EST:** 2013
SALES (est): 970.93K **Privately Held**
Web: www.posmsoftware.com
SIC: 7372 Prepackaged software

(G-9711)
PRINT CENTERS OF OHIO INC
36 W 3rd St (44902-1218)
PHONE.............................419 526-4139
Amy Zimmerman, *Pr*
EMP: 16 **EST:** 1975
SQ FT: 12,000
SALES (est): 822.63K **Privately Held**
SIC: 2752 Offset printing

(G-9712)
RICHLAND NEWHOPE INDS INC (PA)
150 E 4th St (44902-1520)
P.O. Box 916 (44901-0916)
PHONE.............................419 774-4400
Elizabeth Prather, *Ex Dir*
EMP: 250 **EST:** 1963
SQ FT: 63,000
SALES (est): 8.39MM
SALES (corp-wide): 8.39MM **Privately Held**
Web: www.rniinc.com

GEOGRAPHIC SECTION
Mantua - Portage County (G-9735)

SIC: 0782 2448 7349 8331 Lawn and garden services; Wood pallets and skids; Building maintenance services, nec; Job training and related services

(G-9713)
RICHLAND SCREW MCH PDTS INC
531 Grant St (44903-1213)
P.O. Box 696 (44901-0696)
PHONE.................419 524-1272
Randall L Schoenman, *Pr*
EMP: 22 **EST:** 1946
SQ FT: 15,000
SALES (est): 3.48MM **Privately Held**
Web: www.richlandscrewmachine.com
SIC: 3451 Screw machine products

(G-9714)
RICHLAND SOURCE
40 W 4th St (44902-1206)
PHONE.................419 610-2100
EMP: 20 **EST:** 2013
SALES (est): 986.23K **Privately Held**
Web: www.richlandsource.com
SIC: 2741 Miscellaneous publishing

(G-9715)
RUSH WOODWORKS
2116 Kings Corners Rd E (44904-9730)
PHONE.................419 569-2370
EMP: 6 **EST:** 2019
SALES (est): 240.67K **Privately Held**
Web: www.rushwoodworks.com
SIC: 2431 Millwork

(G-9716)
RUSSELL T BUNDY ASSOCIATES INC
Also Called: Pan-Glo
1711 N Main St (44903-8111)
PHONE.................419 526-4454
William Matzke, *Mgr*
EMP: 10
SALES (corp-wide): 50.03MM **Privately Held**
Web: www.bundybakingsolutions.com
SIC: 3479 Pan glazing
PA: Russell T. Bundy Associates, Inc.
   417 E Water St Ste 1
   Urbana OH 43078
   937 652-2151

(G-9717)
SHELLY FISHER
Also Called: P P C Greatstuff Co
449 Newman St (44902-1123)
PHONE.................419 522-6696
Shelley Fisher, *Prin*
EMP: 9 **EST:** 2006
SALES (est): 457.4K **Privately Held**
SIC: 3089 Injection molding of plastics

(G-9718)
SIR STEAK MACHINERY INC
40 Baird Pkwy (44903-7908)
PHONE.................419 526-9181
James Munroe, *Pr*
Dean Schlichting, *Treas*
Richard C Biro, *VP*
Michael J Biro, *VP*
Robert S Biro, *Clerk*
EMP: 20 **EST:** 1948
SQ FT: 37,500
SALES (est): 2.05MM
SALES (corp-wide): 11MM **Privately Held**
SIC: 3556 Food products machinery
PA: The Biro Manufacturing Company
   1114 W Main St
   Marblehead OH 43440
   419 798-4451

(G-9719)
SKYBOX PACKAGING LLC
Also Called: Mr Box
1275 Pollock Pkwy (44905-1374)
P.O. Box 1567 (44901-1567)
PHONE.................419 525-7209
Marc Miller, *Pr*
EMP: 152 **EST:** 2001
SALES (est): 27.06MM
SALES (corp-wide): 882.33MM **Privately Held**
Web: www.skyboxpackaging.com
SIC: 3086 5199 2653 5162 Packaging and shipping materials, foamed plastics; Packaging materials; Boxes, corrugated: made from purchased materials; Plastics materials and basic shapes
PA: Atlantic Packaging Products Ltd
   111 Progress Ave
   Scarborough ON
   416 298-8101

(G-9720)
SOLSYS INC
96 Vanderbilt Rd (44904-8603)
PHONE.................419 886-4683
Jeffrey C Mason, *Pr*
EMP: 8 **EST:** 2007
SALES (est): 231.92K **Privately Held**
Web: www.solsysinc.net
SIC: 3572 Computer storage devices

(G-9721)
STEIN INC
1490 Old Bowman St (44903-8805)
PHONE.................419 747-2611
EMP: 8 **EST:** 2010
SALES (est): 135.78K **Privately Held**
Web: www.steininc.com
SIC: 2431 Millwork

(G-9722)
STRASSELLS MACHINE INC
1015 Springmill St (44906-1571)
PHONE.................419 747-1088
Michael Strassell, *Pr*
Kimberly Strassell, *VP*
EMP: 10 **EST:** 1987
SQ FT: 1,600
SALES (est): 1.88MM **Privately Held**
Web: www.hi-pointfirearms.net
SIC: 3599 Machine shop, jobbing and repair

(G-9723)
SUBURBANITE INC
1552 W Cook Rd (44906-3625)
PHONE.................419 756-4390
Dan Pease, *Pr*
EMP: 6 **EST:** 1991
SALES (est): 502.5K **Privately Held**
SIC: 3469 5521 Automobile license tags, stamped metal; Used car dealers

(G-9724)
TAYLOR METAL PRODUCTS CO
700 Springmill St (44903-1199)
PHONE.................419 522-3471
Richard G Taylor, *Pr*
Helen F Taylor, *
Mark Taylor, *
▲ **EMP:** 155 **EST:** 1923
SQ FT: 160,000
SALES (est): 23.12MM **Privately Held**
Web: www.tmpind.com
SIC: 3469 3465 Stamping metal for the trade ; Automotive stampings

(G-9725)
TE CONNECTIVITY CORPORATION
Cii Technologies Hartman Pdts
175 N Diamond St (44902-1004)
PHONE.................419 521-9500
Kathy Castor, *Brnch Mgr*
EMP: 112
Web: www.te.com
SIC: 3613 3625 3812 3769 Power switching equipment; Relays, for electronic use; Search and navigation equipment; Space vehicle equipment, nec
HQ: Te Connectivity Corporation
   1050 Westlakes Dr
   Berwyn PA 19312
   610 893-9800

(G-9726)
THE MANSFIELD STRL & ERCT CO (PA)
Also Called: Mansfield Fabricated Products
429 Park Ave E (44905-2844)
P.O. Box 427 (44901-0427)
PHONE.................419 522-5911
Richard Gash, *Pr*
Barbara Gash, *Sec*
EMP: 16 **EST:** 1924
SQ FT: 60,000
SALES (est): 2.16MM
SALES (corp-wide): 2.16MM **Privately Held**
SIC: 3441 5051 Fabricated structural metal; Metals service centers and offices

(G-9727)
THORNTON POWDER COATINGS INC
2300 N Main St (44903-6703)
P.O. Box 1119 (44901-1119)
PHONE.................419 522-7183
James Thornton, *Pr*
Dawn Thornton, *VP*
EMP: 8 **EST:** 1989
SQ FT: 20,000
SALES (est): 452.75K **Privately Held**
Web: www.thorntonpowdercoating.com
SIC: 3479 Coating of metals and formed products

(G-9728)
TRI-R TOOLING INC
220 Piper Rd (44905-1370)
PHONE.................419 522-8665
Robert John, *Pr*
Rudy John, *VP*
Renee John, *Treas*
EMP: 12 **EST:** 1990
SQ FT: 6,500
SALES (est): 1.86MM **Privately Held**
Web: www.trirtooling.com
SIC: 3599 Machine shop, jobbing and repair

(G-9729)
UNIVERSAL CH DIRECTORIES LLC
Also Called: Photography and Publishing
1150 National Pkwy (44906-1911)
PHONE.................419 522-5011
Jeffrey Earl Bellew, *Managing Member*
EMP: 6 **EST:** 2003
SALES (est): 1.13MM **Privately Held**
Web: www.ucdir.com
SIC: 7335 2759 Commercial photography; Publication printing

(G-9730)
WARREN RUPP INC
Also Called: Sandpiper
800 N Main St (44902-4209)
P.O. Box 1568 (44901-1568)
PHONE.................419 524-8388
Joshua Stiever, *Pr*
John Carter, *
◆ **EMP:** 224 **EST:** 1986
SQ FT: 80,000
SALES (est): 47.47MM
SALES (corp-wide): 3.27B **Publicly Held**
Web: www.warrenruppinc.com
SIC: 3561 Industrial pumps and parts
PA: Idex Corporation
   3100 Sanders Rd Ste 301
   Northbrook IL 60062
   847 498-7070

(G-9731)
WATERSOURCE LLC
1225 W Longview Ave (44906-1907)
PHONE.................419 747-9552
EMP: 7
SALES (corp-wide): 899.54K **Privately Held**
Web: www.watersourceusa.com
SIC: 3261 Plumbing fixtures, vitreous china
PA: Watersource, L.L.C.
   6 Foxmoor Ct
   Norwalk OH 44857
   419 747-9552

(G-9732)
WEISS INDUSTRIES INC
Also Called: Weiss Metallurgical Services
2480 N Main St (44903-8555)
P.O. Box 157 (44901-0157)
PHONE.................419 526-2480
Rudolph Weiss, *Pr*
William Heichel, *
Phyllis B Weiss, *
Maria Weiss, *
Robert Nikolaus, *
EMP: 30 **EST:** 1954
SQ FT: 40,000
SALES (est): 5.3MM **Privately Held**
Web: www.weissind.com
SIC: 3469 3398 3544 Metal stampings, nec; Metal heat treating; Special dies and tools

(G-9733)
WESTINGHOUSE A BRAKE TECH CORP
Also Called: Wabtec Global Services
472 Rembrandt St (44902-7015)
PHONE.................419 526-5323
EMP: 6
Web: www.wabteccorp.com
SIC: 3743 Brakes, air and vacuum: railway
PA: Westinghouse Air Brake Technologies Corporation
   30 Isabella St
   Pittsburgh PA 15212

Mantua
Portage County

(G-9734)
ASSOCIATED ASSOCIATES INC
Also Called: Associated Ready Mix Concrete
9551 Elliman Rd (44255)
P.O. Box 670538 (44067)
PHONE.................330 626-3300
Harold Joslin, *Pr*
Sandra Riha, *Sec*
EMP: 20 **EST:** 1993
SQ FT: 2,700
SALES (est): 2.34MM **Privately Held**
Web: www.associatedreadymix.com
SIC: 3273 5211 Ready-mixed concrete; Masonry materials and supplies

(G-9735)
CREATIVE PROCESSING INC
17540 Rapids Rd (44255)
P.O. Box 708 (44021-0708)
PHONE.................440 834-4070
EMP: 15 **EST:** 1992
SQ FT: 10,000

Mantua - Portage County (G-9736)

SALES (est): 406.19K **Privately Held**
Web: www.creativeprocessinginc.com
SIC: 3599 Machine shop, jobbing and repair

(G-9736)
ETCHWORKS
9769 State Route 44 (44255-9704)
PHONE..................................330 274-8345
William Puleo, *Prin*
EMP: 6 EST: 2007
SALES (est): 107.44K **Privately Held**
Web: www.etchworks.com
SIC: 3479 Etching and engraving

(G-9737)
INDUSTRIAL CONNECTIONS INC
11730 Timber Point Trl (44255-9694)
PHONE..................................330 274-2155
Wendy Carlton, *Pr*
▼ EMP: 6 EST: 1992
SQ FT: 7,000
SALES (est): 833.08K **Privately Held**
Web: www.industrialconnectionsinc.com
SIC: 5085 3492 Industrial fittings; Hose and tube fittings and assemblies, hydraulic/pneumatic

(G-9738)
LAKESIDE SAND & GRAVEL INC
3498 Frost Rd (44255-9136)
PHONE..................................330 274-2569
Larry Kotkowski, *Pr*
Ronald Kotkowski, *Sec*
EMP: 26 EST: 1954
SQ FT: 4,200
SALES (est): 5.57MM **Privately Held**
Web: www.lakesidesandgravel.com
SIC: 1442 Construction sand mining

(G-9739)
MANTALINE CORPORATION
Also Called: Transportation Group
4754 E High St (44255-9201)
PHONE..................................330 274-2264
Bryan Fink, *Mgr*
EMP: 7
SALES (corp-wide): 22.67MM **Privately Held**
Web: www.mantalinestandardseals.com
SIC: 5169 3061 Synthetic rubber; Mechanical rubber goods
PA: Mantaline Corporation
4754 E High St
Mantua OH 44255
330 274-2264

(G-9740)
MANTALINE CORPORATION (PA)
4754 E High St (44255-9201)
PHONE..................................330 274-2264
EMP: 115 EST: 1964
SALES (est): 22.67MM
SALES (corp-wide): 22.67MM **Privately Held**
Web: www.mantalinestandardseals.com
SIC: 3061 2822 3069 Mechanical rubber goods; Synthetic rubber; Hard rubber and molded rubber products

(G-9741)
OK BRUGMANN JR & SONS INC
4083 Mennonite Rd (44255-9413)
PHONE..................................330 274-2106
Oscar Brugmann Junior, *Pr*
Gail Brugmann, *VP*
Mark Brugmann, *Prin*
EMP: 10 EST: 1981
SALES (est): 1.43MM **Privately Held**
Web: www.okbrugmann.com

SIC: 5032 5211 3273 3272 Concrete and cinder building products; Concrete and cinder block; Ready-mixed concrete; Concrete products, nec

(G-9742)
OSCAR BRUGMANN SAND & GRAVEL
3828 Dudley Rd (44255-9426)
PHONE..................................330 274-8224
Roy Brugmann, *Pr*
Olga Van Auken, *Sec*
Joan Martin, *Sec*
EMP: 22 EST: 1929
SQ FT: 1,000
SALES (est): 5.14MM **Privately Held**
Web: www.obsag.com
SIC: 1442 Construction sand mining

(G-9743)
STAMM CONTRACTING COMPANY INC
4566 Orchard St (44255-9701)
P.O. Box 450 (44255-0450)
PHONE..................................330 274-8230
Hal Stamm, *Pr*
Elva Novotny, *
EMP: 25 EST: 1913
SQ FT: 1,500
SALES (est): 3.46MM **Privately Held**
Web: www.stammcontracting.com
SIC: 3273 1541 1542 5211 Ready-mixed concrete; Industrial buildings and warehouses; Commercial and office building contractors; Lumber and other building materials

(G-9744)
T J DAVIES COMPANY INC
11823 State Route 44 (44255-9647)
PHONE..................................440 248-5510
EMP: 8 EST: 1965
SALES (est): 851.81K **Privately Held**
Web: www.tjdavies.com
SIC: 3999 Barber and beauty shop equipment

(G-9745)
VISUAL ART GRAPHIC SERVICES
5244 Goodell Rd (44255-9746)
PHONE..................................330 274-2775
EMP: 9 EST: 1989
SQ FT: 35,000
SALES (est): 267.96K **Privately Held**
SIC: 2752 7336 Offset printing; Commercial art and graphic design

Maple Heights
Cuyahoga County

(G-9746)
ALTERNATE DEFENSE LLC
19101 Watercrest Ave (44137-3152)
PHONE..................................216 225-5889
Ronald Mitchell, *Admn*
EMP: 6 EST: 2015
SALES (est): 160.08K **Privately Held**
SIC: 3812 Defense systems and equipment

(G-9747)
BARNES SERVICES LLC
20677 Centuryway Rd (44137-3116)
PHONE..................................440 319-2088
Leon Barnes, *Prin*
EMP: 6
SALES (est): 164.98K **Privately Held**
SIC: 1389 Construction, repair, and dismantling services

(G-9748)
CHARLES SVEC INC
Also Called: Rock Lite
5470 Dunham Rd (44137-3690)
PHONE..................................216 662-5200
Michael Svec, *Pr*
Dean Svec, *
EMP: 25 EST: 1906
SQ FT: 25,000
SALES (est): 2.84MM **Privately Held**
Web: www.chassvecinc.com
SIC: 3271 3272 Concrete block and brick; Concrete products, nec

(G-9749)
CLIFTON STEEL COMPANY (HQ)
16500 Rockside Rd (44137-4324)
PHONE..................................216 662-6111
Herbert C Neides, *Pr*
Howard Feldenkris, *
Bruce Goodman, *CUST SERVCS**
▼ EMP: 58 EST: 1971
SQ FT: 160,000
SALES (est): 49.36MM
SALES (corp-wide): 54.37MM **Privately Held**
Web: www.cliftonsteel.com
SIC: 5051 3441 3443 3398 Steel; Fabricated structural metal; Metal parts; Metal heat treating
PA: Clifton Capital Holdings, Llc
16500 Rockside Rd
Maple Heights OH 44137
330 562-9000

(G-9750)
DEWITT INC
Also Called: Non-Ferrous Heat Treating
14450 Industrial Ave N (44137-3249)
PHONE..................................216 662-0800
John Whittaker, *Pr*
Joe Frankhauser, *Treas*
EMP: 8 EST: 1957
SQ FT: 10,000
SALES (est): 580K **Privately Held**
Web: www.nonferrousheattreating.com
SIC: 3398 Metal heat treating

(G-9751)
DR Z AMPS INC
Also Called: Dr Z Amplification
17011 Broadway Ave (44137-3407)
PHONE..................................216 475-1444
Michael D Zaite, *Pr*
EMP: 10 EST: 1988
SQ FT: 3,500
SALES (est): 771.91K **Privately Held**
Web: www.drzamps.com
SIC: 3651 Amplifiers: radio, public address, or musical instrument

(G-9752)
INEZ ESSENTIALS LLC
5333 Cato St (44137-2627)
PHONE..................................216 701-8360
EMP: 10 EST: 2020
SALES (est): 283.15K **Privately Held**
SIC: 3999 Candles

(G-9753)
LAMINATED CONCEPTS INC
14300 Industrial Ave N (44137-3248)
PHONE..................................216 475-4141
Vera Dudley, *Pr*
Lisa Elliots, *VP*
EMP: 11 EST: 1987
SQ FT: 8,500
SALES (est): 830K **Privately Held**
Web: www.laminatedconcepts.com

SIC: 2541 2434 Table or counter tops, plastic laminated; Wood kitchen cabinets

(G-9754)
MAMMANA CUSTOM WOODWORKING INC
14400 Industrial Ave N (44137-3249)
PHONE..................................216 581-9059
Max Mammana, *Pr*
EMP: 20 EST: 1993
SQ FT: 18,000
SALES (est): 1.47MM **Privately Held**
SIC: 2434 Wood kitchen cabinets

(G-9755)
MCKINLEY PACKAGING COMPANY
16645 Granite Rd (44137-4301)
PHONE..................................216 663-3344
Charles Messina, *Brnch Mgr*
EMP: 15
Web: www.mckinleypackaging.com
SIC: 2653 Boxes, corrugated: made from purchased materials
HQ: Mckinley Packaging Company
1503 Lyndon B Johnson Fwy
Dallas TX 75234
972 354-3600

(G-9756)
OHIO MAGNETICS INC
5400 Dunham Rd (44137-3653)
PHONE..................................216 662-8484
Thomas J Pozda, *CEO*
Randy L Greely, *
▲ EMP: 36 EST: 1917
SQ FT: 140,000
SALES (est): 9.6MM
SALES (corp-wide): 241.4MM **Privately Held**
Web: www.ohiomagnetics.com
SIC: 3499 3559 3669 3625 Magnets, permanent: metallic; Separation equipment, magnetic; Metal detectors; Relays and industrial controls
HQ: Peerless-Winsmith, Inc.
5200 Upper Metro Pl # 11
Dublin OH 43017
614 526-7000

(G-9757)
OR-TEC INC
5445 Dunham Rd (44137-3673)
PHONE..................................216 475-5225
David Marriott, *Genl Mgr*
Ciaran O-mezia, *Pr*
▲ EMP: 9 EST: 1979
SALES (est): 2.23MM **Privately Held**
Web: www.or-tec.com
SIC: 3589 Water treatment equipment, industrial

(G-9758)
R & C MONUMENT COMPANY LLC
5146 Warrensville Center Rd (44137-1929)
PHONE..................................216 297-5444
Jajuan L Robinson, *Admn*
EMP: 7 EST: 2017
SALES (est): 197.23K **Privately Held**
Web: www.monumentsdoniphan.com
SIC: 3272 Monuments and grave markers, except terrazzo

(G-9759)
RACELITE SOUTHCOAST INC
16518 Broadway Ave (44137-2602)
P.O. Box 370076 (44137-9076)
PHONE..................................216 581-4600
James Sima, *Pr*
Maryann Sima, *Sec*
EMP: 10 EST: 1967
SQ FT: 5,000

GEOGRAPHIC SECTION

SALES (est): 720K **Privately Held**
Web: www.racelitehardware.com
SIC: **3429** 3732 3469 3312 Marine hardware; Boatbuilding and repairing; Metal stampings, nec; Blast furnaces and steel mills

(G-9760)
SALON STYLING CONCEPTS LTD
Also Called: One Styling
20900 Libby Rd (44137-2929)
PHONE................................216 539-0437
Eun Joo Park, *Pr*
▲ EMP: 10 EST: 2011
SALES (est): 387.59K **Privately Held**
SIC: **3999** Hair curlers, designed for beauty parlors

(G-9761)
ST LAWRENCE HOLDINGS LLC
16500 Rockside Rd (44137-4324)
PHONE................................330 562-9000
Herbert Neides, *Pr*
Jonh Zanin, *
EMP: 34 EST: 2017
SALES (est): 5.01MM
SALES (corp-wide): 54.37MM **Privately Held**
Web: www.stlawrencesteel.com
SIC: **5051** 3443 3441 Steel; Fabricated plate work (boiler shop); Fabricated structural metal
PA: Clifton Capital Holdings, Llc
    16500 Rockside Rd
    Maple Heights OH 44137
    330 562-9000

(G-9762)
ST LAWRENCE STEEL CORPORATION
16500 Rockside Rd (44137-4324)
PHONE................................330 562-9000
◆ EMP: 34
Web: www.stlawrencesteel.com
SIC: **5051** 3443 3441 Steel; Fabricated plate work (boiler shop); Fabricated structural metal

(G-9763)
UNITED METAL FABRICATORS INC
14301 Industrial Ave S (44137-3252)
PHONE................................216 662-2000
Stephen B Martis, *Pr*
James A Martis, *
EMP: 30 EST: 1945
SQ FT: 16,500
SALES (est): 4.75MM **Privately Held**
Web: www.unitedmetalfabricators.com
SIC: **3441** Fabricated structural metal

Marblehead
Ottawa County

(G-9764)
BIRO MANUFACTURING COMPANY (PA)
Also Called: Biro Manufacturing Company
1114 W Main St (43440-2099)
PHONE................................419 798-4451
Carl G Biro, *Prin*
Richard C Biro, *
Robert S Biro, *General Vice President*
Michael J Biro, *
Teresa Marez, *
◆ EMP: 57 EST: 1986
SQ FT: 76,000
SALES (est): 11MM
SALES (corp-wide): 11MM **Privately Held**
Web: www.birosaw.com

SIC: **3556** Choppers, commercial, food

(G-9765)
FRONTWATERS REST & BREWING CO
Also Called: Frontwaters Brewing Company
8660 E Bayshore Rd (43440-9526)
PHONE................................419 798-8058
EMP: 8 EST: 1996
SQ FT: 4,800
SALES (est): 108.74K **Privately Held**
SIC: **5812** 2082 5181 Chicken restaurant; Beer (alcoholic beverage); Beer and ale

Marengo
Morrow County

(G-9766)
DARPRO STORAGE SOLUTIONS LLC
1089 County Road 26 (43334-3503)
PHONE................................567 233-3190
EMP: 23 EST: 2020
SALES (est): 4.83MM
SALES (corp-wide): 6.53B **Publicly Held**
Web: www.mfsparts.com
SIC: **2599** Carts, restaurant equipment
PA: Darling Ingredients Inc.
    5601 N Macarthur Blvd
    Irving TX 75038
    972 717-0300

(G-9767)
FISHBURN TANK TRUCK SERVICE
5012 State Route 229 (43334-9634)
P.O. Box 278 (43334-0278)
PHONE................................419 253-6031
EMP: 10 EST: 1962
SALES (est): 293.27K **Privately Held**
SIC: **1389** Haulage, oil field

(G-9768)
GIUSEPPES CONCESSIONS LLC
5383 Township Road 187 (43334-9783)
PHONE................................614 554-2551
Christopher Leadbeater, *Managing Member*
EMP: 10 EST: 2019
SALES (est): 356.19K **Privately Held**
SIC: **7999** 3443 Concession operator; Dumpsters, garbage

(G-9769)
MORITZ READY MIX INC
4083 Bennington Way (43334-9536)
PHONE................................419 253-0001
Frank Moritz, *CEO*
EMP: 12 EST: 1933
SALES (est): 1.26MM **Privately Held**
Web: www.moritzreadymix.com
SIC: **3273** Ready-mixed concrete

(G-9770)
SELECT LOGGING
5739 Township Road 21 (43334-9710)
PHONE................................419 564-0361
Jason Pauley, *Prin*
EMP: 6 EST: 2010
SALES (est): 219.23K **Privately Held**
SIC: **2411** Logging

Maria Stein
Mercer County

(G-9771)
MANCO MANUFACTURING CO
2411 Rolfes Rd (45860-9708)
PHONE................................419 925-4152
Nancy Nieberding, *Pr*

Patrick R Nieberding, *VP*
Eric Nieberding, *Treas*
EMP: 8 EST: 1974
SQ FT: 14,000
SALES (est): 947.32K **Privately Held**
Web: www.manco-mfg-co.com
SIC: **3441** Fabricated structural metal

(G-9772)
MOELLER BREW BARN LLC (PA)
8016 Marion Dr (45860-8706)
PHONE................................419 925-3005
Nick Moeller, *Managing Member*
Tony Scott, *Managing Member*
Scott Kinney, *CFO*
EMP: 9 EST: 2015
SALES (est): 4.38MM
SALES (corp-wide): 4.38MM **Privately Held**
Web: www.moellerbrewbarn.com
SIC: **2082** Malt beverages

(G-9773)
MS WELDING LLC
8070 Flyer Dr (45860-9570)
PHONE................................419 925-4141
EMP: 9 EST: 1983
SALES (est): 469.32K **Privately Held**
Web: www.mswelding.com
SIC: **7692** Welding repair

Marietta
Washington County

(G-9774)
ALPHA OMEGA IMPORT EXPORT LLC
1135 Browns Rd (45750-9074)
PHONE................................740 885-9155
Gerry Dallimore, *Prin*
EMP: 6 EST: 2018
SALES (est): 242.25K **Privately Held**
SIC: **3089** Lamp bases and shades, plastics

(G-9775)
ANTERO RESOURCES CORPORATION
27841 State Route 7 (45750-9060)
PHONE................................740 760-1000
EMP: 60
Web: www.anteroresources.com
SIC: **1382** Oil and gas exploration services
PA: Antero Resources Corporation
    1615 Wynkoop St
    Denver CO 80202

(G-9776)
ARTEX ENERGY GROUP LLC
2337 State Route 821 (45750-5475)
PHONE................................740 373-3313
Joe Brooker, *Pr*
Mike Mooney, *Ex VP*
Bill Cassidy, *VP*
EMP: 8 EST: 2011
SALES (est): 208.8K **Privately Held**
Web: www.artexenergy.com
SIC: **1382** Oil and gas exploration services

(G-9777)
ARTEX OIL COMPANY
2337 State Route 821 (45750-5475)
PHONE................................740 373-3313
Arthur Rupe, *CEO*
Jerry James, *Pr*
Gene Huck, *VP*
EMP: 20 EST: 1995
SALES (est): 2.44MM **Privately Held**
Web: www.artexoil.com

SIC: **1381** Drilling oil and gas wells

(G-9778)
BD OIL GATHERING CORP
649 Mitchells Ln (45750-6865)
PHONE................................740 374-9355
EMP: 29 EST: 1993
SALES (est): 2.26MM **Privately Held**
Web: www.bdoil.com
SIC: **1382** Oil and gas exploration services

(G-9779)
BOB LANES WELDING INC
5151 Warren Chapel Rd (45750-6537)
PHONE................................740 373-3567
Robert Lane, *Pr*
Sandra Lane, *Sec*
EMP: 13 EST: 1976
SALES (est): 416.51K **Privately Held**
SIC: **1799** 1623 7692 3444 Welding on site; Pipe laying construction; Welding repair; Sheet metalwork

(G-9780)
C L W INC
1201 Gilman Ave (45750-9499)
PHONE................................740 374-8443
David Armstrong, *Pr*
Frederick L Burge, *Sec*
EMP: 9 EST: 1972
SQ FT: 7,500
SALES (est): 974.01K **Privately Held**
Web: www.clwrg.com
SIC: **3444** Concrete forms, sheet metal

(G-9781)
CARON PRODUCTS AND SVCS INC
27640 State Route 7 (45750)
P.O. Box 715 (45750)
PHONE................................740 373-6809
Jon F Bergen, *Prin*
Bob Beckelman, *Prin*
Spencer Krigsman, *Prin*
Paul Sereni, *Prin*
Sue Eckberg, *Prin*
▲ EMP: 22 EST: 1985
SQ FT: 12,000
SALES (est): 7.07MM **Privately Held**
Web: www.caronproducts.com
SIC: **3823** 3821 Temperature instruments: industrial process type; Laboratory apparatus, except heating and measuring

(G-9782)
CARPER WELL SERVICE INC
30745 State Route 7 (45750-5177)
P.O. Box 273 (45773-0273)
PHONE................................740 374-2567
Millard E Carper, *Pr*
Ryan Carper, *Treas*
EMP: 10 EST: 1979
SQ FT: 3,500
SALES (est): 2.04MM **Privately Held**
SIC: **1389** Construction, repair, and dismantling services

(G-9783)
CDK PERFORATING LLC
2167 State Route 821 (45750-1196)
PHONE................................817 862-9834
EMP: 59
SALES (corp-wide): 609.53MM **Publicly Held**
Web: www.nineenergyservice.com
SIC: **1389** Oil field services, nec
HQ: Cdk Perforating, Llc
    6500 West Fwy Ste 600
    Fort Worth TX 76116
    817 945-1051

Marietta - Washington County (G-9784)

(G-9784)
CLUTCH MOV
100 Dayton Rd (45750-8773)
PHONE..................740 525-5510
Sarah Arnold, *Prin*
EMP: 6 **EST:** 2017
SALES (est): 73.53K **Privately Held**
Web: www.clutchmov.com
SIC: 2721 Periodicals

(G-9785)
COIL SPECIALTY CHEMICALS LLC
2375 Glendale Rd (45750-8038)
PHONE..................740 236-2407
Robert Coil, *Managing Member*
EMP: 8 **EST:** 2007
SQ FT: 5,000
SALES (est): 1.03MM **Privately Held**
Web: www.coilchem.com
SIC: 2869 Glycerin

(G-9786)
COMMUNITY ACTION PROGRAM CORP
Also Called: Community Action Wic Hlth Svc
696 Wayne St (45750-3265)
PHONE..................740 374-8501
Kathleen Boersma, *Dir*
EMP: 10
SALES (corp-wide): 17.72MM **Privately Held**
Web: www.wmcap.org
SIC: 8399 8093 8011 2241 Community action agency; Family planning and birth control clinics; Offices and clinics of medical doctors; Wicking
PA: Community Action Program Corp, Of Washington-Morgan County Ohio, Inc
218 Putnam St
Marietta OH 45750
740 373-3745

(G-9787)
CRESCENT & SPRAGUE
1100 Greene St (45750-2413)
PHONE..................740 373-2331
EMP: 10 **EST:** 2019
SALES (est): 978.35K **Privately Held**
Web: www.crescentsprague.com
SIC: 3621 Motors and generators

(G-9788)
DIRECTIONAL ONE SVCS INC USA
2163a-1 Gwb Complex 2 Bldg 6 State Route 821 (45750)
PHONE..................740 371-5031
Kevin Onishenko, *CEO*
EMP: 6 **EST:** 2014
SALES (est): 430.19K **Privately Held**
Web: www.directional1services.com
SIC: 1381 Directional drilling oil and gas wells

(G-9789)
DIVERSIFIED PRODUCTION LLC
111 Industry Rd Unit 206 (45750-9315)
P.O. Box 141 (45773-0141)
PHONE..................740 373-8771
Martin Miller, *Brnch Mgr*
EMP: 142
SALES (corp-wide): 99.2MM **Privately Held**
Web: ir.div.energy
SIC: 1382 Oil and gas exploration services
HQ: Diversified Production Llc
4150 Belden Village St Nw
Canton OH 44718

(G-9790)
DOAK LASER
2801 Waterford Rd (45750-6910)
PHONE..................740 374-0090
Bill Doak, *Prin*
EMP: 6 **EST:** 2008
SALES (est): 103.41K **Privately Held**
SIC: 3479 Etching and engraving

(G-9791)
EDGEWELL PERSONAL CARE COMPANY
P.O. Box 300 (45750-0300)
PHONE..................740 374-1905
Stacy Parks, *Brnch Mgr*
EMP: 10
SALES (corp-wide): 2.25B **Publicly Held**
Web: www.edgewell.com
SIC: 3421 Razor blades and razors
PA: Edgewell Personal Care Company
6 Research Dr Ste 400
Shelton CT 06484
203 944-5500

(G-9792)
ERAMET MARIETTA INC
16705 State Route 7 (45750-8519)
P.O. Box 299 (45750-0299)
PHONE..................740 374-1000
Michel Masci, *CFO*
◆ **EMP:** 205 **EST:** 1950
SALES (est): 82.19MM
SALES (corp-wide): 1.24B **Privately Held**
Web: marietta.eramet.com
SIC: 3313 Ferroalloys
HQ: Eramet Holding Manganese
10 Boulevard De Grenelle
Paris

(G-9793)
FLEXMAG INDUSTRIES INC (DH)
Also Called: Arnold Magnetic Technologies
107 Industry Rd (45750-9355)
PHONE..................740 373-3492
Tim Wilson, *CEO*
◆ **EMP:** 100 **EST:** 1981
SQ FT: 84,619
SALES (est): 20.69MM **Publicly Held**
Web: www.arnoldmagnetics.com
SIC: 3499 Magnets, permanent: metallic
HQ: Arnold Magnetic Technologies Corporation
770 Linden Ave
Rochester NY 14625
585 385-9010

(G-9794)
GANNETT STLLITE INFO NTWRK LLC
Also Called: Marietta Times
700 Channel Ln (45750-2342)
P.O. Box 761 (26102-0761)
PHONE..................304 485-1891
Roger Watson, *Mgr*
EMP: 20
SALES (corp-wide): 2.66B **Publicly Held**
Web: www.mariettatimes.com
SIC: 2711 Newspapers, publishing and printing
HQ: Gannett Satellite Information Network, Llc
7950 Jones Branch Dr
Mc Lean VA 22102
703 854-6000

(G-9795)
GILLARD CONSTRUCTION INC
Also Called: Cypress Valley Log Homes
1308 Greene St (45750-9809)
PHONE..................740 376-9744
John Gillard, *Pr*
Debra Gillard, *VP*
Kelly Gillard, *Sec*
Jill Wright, *Treas*
EMP: 16 **EST:** 1991
SALES (est): 2.41MM **Privately Held**
Web: www.gillardscustomcabinets.com
SIC: 1521 2434 5211 2452 General remodeling, single-family houses; Wood kitchen cabinets; Cabinets, kitchen; Log cabins, prefabricated, wood

(G-9796)
GRAE-CON PROCESS PIPING LLC
300 Commerce Dr (45750-3524)
PHONE..................740 282-6830
William Blake Junior, *Managing Member*
EMP: 35 **EST:** 2014
SALES (est): 1.97MM
SALES (corp-wide): 25.46MM **Privately Held**
Web: www.graecon.com
SIC: 3317 Steel pipe and tubes
PA: Grae-Con Construction, Inc.
880 Kingsdale Rd
Steubenville OH 43952
740 282-6830

(G-9797)
GRIMM SCIENTIFIC INDUSTRIES
1403 Pike St (45750-5106)
P.O. Box 2143 (45750-7143)
PHONE..................740 374-3412
Joseph E Grimm, *Pr*
Edmund Dutton, *VP*
Jane Grimm, *Sec*
Walt Brothers, *Treas*
EMP: 10 **EST:** 1979
SQ FT: 5,000
SALES (est): 1.6MM **Privately Held**
Web: www.grimmscientific.com
SIC: 3841 Physiotherapy equipment, electrical

(G-9798)
HAESSLY LUMBER SALES CO (PA)
25 Sheets Run Rd (45750-5186)
PHONE..................740 373-6681
Norman E Haessly Junior, *Pr*
Steve Haessly, *
Julie Haessly, *
EMP: 55 **EST:** 1941
SQ FT: 160
SALES (est): 7.48MM
SALES (corp-wide): 7.48MM **Privately Held**
Web: www.haesslylumber.com
SIC: 2421 2449 2448 2435 Lumber: rough, sawed, or planed; Wood containers, nec; Wood pallets and skids; Hardwood veneer and plywood

(G-9799)
HI-VAC CORPORATION (PA)
117 Industry Rd (45750-9355)
PHONE..................740 374-2306
◆ **EMP:** 135 **EST:** 1969
SALES (est): 24.78MM
SALES (corp-wide): 24.78MM **Privately Held**
Web: www.hi-vac.com
SIC: 3589 Vacuum cleaners and sweepers, electric: industrial

(G-9800)
HUNTER EUREKA PIPELINE LLC
125 Putnam St (45750-2936)
PHONE..................740 374-2940
EMP: 23 **EST:** 2010
SALES (est): 1.03MM
SALES (corp-wide): 6.52B **Publicly Held**
Web: www.triadhunter.com
SIC: 1382 Oil and gas exploration services
HQ: Blue Ridge Mountain Resources, Inc.
122 W John Carpenter Fwy # 300
Irving TX 75039

(G-9801)
HYDE BROTHERS PRTG & MKTG LLC (PA)
2343 State Route 821 Ste A (45750-5464)
PHONE..................740 373-2054
Kulick Richard, *Pr*
Steve Flaughers, *VP*
EMP: 8 **EST:** 2014
SALES (est): 217.79K
SALES (corp-wide): 217.79K **Privately Held**
Web: www.hydebrothersprinting.com
SIC: 2752 Offset printing

(G-9802)
INLAND HARDWOOD CORPORATION
Also Called: Inland Wood Products
25 Sheets Run Rd (45750-5186)
PHONE..................740 373-7187
Norman E Haessly Junior, *Pr*
Julie Haessly, *Sec*
Mark Haessly, *VP*
Steve Haessly, *Treas*
EMP: 17 **EST:** 1966
SALES (est): 627.71K
SALES (corp-wide): 7.48MM **Privately Held**
SIC: 2448 Pallets, wood
PA: Haessly Lumber Sales Co.
25 Sheets Run Rd
Marietta OH 45750
740 373-6681

(G-9803)
JERRY OFFENBERGER CNSTR LLC
575 Bramblewood Heights Rd (45750-8209)
PHONE..................740 374-2578
Jerry Offenberger O, *Owner*
EMP: 8 **EST:** 2018
SALES (est): 306.63K **Privately Held**
SIC: 3272 Concrete products, nec

(G-9804)
KAYDEN INDUSTRIES
2167 State Route 821 (45750-1196)
PHONE..................740 336-7801
EMP: 6 **EST:** 2015
SALES (est): 195.39K **Privately Held**
Web: www.kaydenindustries.com
SIC: 3999 Manufacturing industries, nec

(G-9805)
MAGNUM MAGNETICS CORPORATION (PA)
Also Called: Magnum Inks & Coatings
801 Masonic Park Rd (45750-9357)
PHONE..................740 373-7770
Allen Love, *Pr*
Tom Love, *
▼ **EMP:** 82 **EST:** 1991
SQ FT: 30,000
SALES (est): 35.05MM **Privately Held**
Web: www.magnummagnetics.com
SIC: 3499 Magnets, permanent: metallic

(G-9806)
MARIETTA RESOURCES CORPORATION
704 Pike St (45750-3501)
PHONE..................740 373-6305
Lynn Foster, *Pr*
EMP: 10 **EST:** 1984
SALES (est): 376.37K **Privately Held**

SIC: 1311 Crude petroleum production

(G-9807)
MASTER MAGNETICS INC
Also Called: Magnetic Source
108 Industry Rd (45750-9355)
PHONE.................................740 373-0909
EMP: 10
SALES (corp-wide): 13.84MM **Privately Held**
Web: www.magnetsource.com
SIC: 3499 Fire- or burglary-resistive products
PA: Master Magnetics, Inc.
    1211 Atchison Ct
    Castle Rock CO 80109
    303 688-3966

(G-9808)
MC ALARNEY POOL SPAS AND BILLD
Also Called: McAlarney Pols Spas Billd More
908 Pike St (45750-3505)
PHONE.................................740 373-6698
Wayne Mc Alarney, *Ex VP*
Cheryl Mcalarney, *
EMP: 17 EST: 1975
SQ FT: 6,500
SALES (est): 946.34K **Privately Held**
Web: www.mcalarney.com
SIC: 5091 3949 Swimming pools, equipment and supplies; Sporting and athletic goods, nec

(G-9809)
MIDWAY MACHINING INC
1060 Gravel Bank Rd (45750-8370)
PHONE.................................740 373-8976
Robert L Casto, *Pr*
Gary Hendershot, *VP*
Katherine E Murphy, *Sec*
EMP: 11 EST: 1969
SQ FT: 3,000
SALES (est): 1.98MM **Privately Held**
Web: www.midwaymachiningincorporated.com
SIC: 3599 Machine shop, jobbing and repair

(G-9810)
MONDO POLYMER TECHNOLOGIES INC
27620 State Route 7 (45750-5146)
P.O. Box 250 (45773-0250)
PHONE.................................740 376-9396
EMP: 40 EST: 1999
SQ FT: 3,200
SALES (est): 12.11MM **Privately Held**
Web: www.mondopolymer.com
SIC: 4953 2822 Recycling, waste materials; Synthetic rubber

(G-9811)
NINE DOWNHOLE TECHNOLOGIES LLC (PA)
2345 State Route 821 (45750-5362)
PHONE.................................817 862-9834
EMP: 7 EST: 2019
SALES (est): 116.58K
SALES (corp-wide): 116.58K **Privately Held**
SIC: 1389 Oil field services, nec

(G-9812)
OHIO VALLEY ALLOY SERVICES INC
100 Westview Ave (45750-9403)
PHONE.................................740 373-1900
▲ EMP: 20 EST: 1994
SQ FT: 2,500
SALES (est): 2.19MM **Privately Held**
Web: www.ohiovalleyalloys.com

SIC: 3312 4225 3341 Blast furnaces and steel mills; General warehousing; Secondary nonferrous metals

(G-9813)
OHIO VALLEY SPECIALTY COMPANY
115 Industry Rd (45750-9355)
PHONE.................................740 373-2276
Larry G Hawkins, *Pr*
Frank D Mendicino, *VP*
EMP: 12 EST: 1966
SQ FT: 7,000
SALES (est): 2.49MM **Privately Held**
Web: www.ovsc.com
SIC: 3339 Silicon, pure

(G-9814)
PARDSON INC
Also Called: Bird Watcher's Digest
149 Acme St (45750-3402)
P.O. Box 3396 (47803-0396)
PHONE.................................740 373-5285
Andy Thompson, *Pr*
William Thompson Iii, *VP*
Elsa Thompson, *Treas*
EMP: 13 EST: 1978
SQ FT: 3,400
SALES (est): 2.37MM **Privately Held**
Web: www.birdwatcher.info
SIC: 2721 2731 5961 Magazines: publishing only, not printed on site; Book publishing; Mail order house, nec

(G-9815)
PAWNEE MAINTENANCE INC
101 Rathbone Rd (45750-1437)
P.O. Box 269 (45750-0269)
PHONE.................................740 373-6861
Ted R Szabo, *Pr*
EMP: 16 EST: 1990
SQ FT: 3,000
SALES (est): 2.27MM **Privately Held**
Web: www.pawneemaintenance.com
SIC: 1541 3272 Industrial buildings and warehouses; Concrete products, nec

(G-9816)
PEN-ANN CORPORATION
Also Called: Hyde Brothers Printing Co
2343 State Route 821 Ste A (45750-5464)
P.O. Box 586 (45750-0586)
PHONE.................................740 373-2054
TOLL FREE: 800
Lewis Camp, *Pr*
David Mccullough, *Sec*
EMP: 9 EST: 1991
SQ FT: 5,000
SALES (est): 637.72K **Privately Held**
SIC: 2752 Offset printing

(G-9817)
PIONEER PIPE INC
Also Called: Pioneer Group
2021 Hanna Rd (45750-8255)
PHONE.................................740 376-2400
David M Archer, *Pr*
Arlene M Archer, *
▲ EMP: 600 EST: 1981
SQ FT: 24,800
SALES (est): 79.66MM **Privately Held**
Web: www.pioneergroup.us
SIC: 3498 1711 3443 3441 Pipe sections, fabricated from purchased pipe; Plumbing contractors; Fabricated plate work (boiler shop); Fabricated structural metal

(G-9818)
PROFUSION INDUSTRIES LLC
700 Bf Goodrich Rd (45750-7849)
P.O. Box 657 (45750-0657)
PHONE.................................740 374-6400

Jon Golden, *Brnch Mgr*
EMP: 92
SALES (corp-wide): 20.85MM **Privately Held**
Web: www.profusionindustries.com
SIC: 3081 Unsupported plastics film and sheet
PA: Profusion Industries, Llc
    822 Kumho Dr Ste 202
    Fairlawn OH 44333
    800 938-2858

(G-9819)
RAMPP COMPANY (PA)
20445 State Route 550 Ofc (45750-6900)
P.O. Box 608 (45750-0608)
PHONE.................................740 373-7886
Mark E Fulton, *Pr*
Charles Hall, *
Charles D Fogle, *
David Fox, *
Martin J Ramp, *
EMP: 45 EST: 1950
SQ FT: 50,000
SALES (est): 10.2MM
SALES (corp-wide): 10.2MM **Privately Held**
Web: www.ramppco.com
SIC: 3533 3443 3325 Drilling tools for gas, oil, or water wells; Crane hooks, laminated plate; Alloy steel castings, except investment

(G-9820)
RICHARDSON PRINTING CORP (PA)
Also Called: Zip Center, The-Division
201 Acme St (45750-3404)
P.O. Box 663 (45750-0663)
PHONE.................................800 848-9752
TOLL FREE: 800
Dennis E Valentine, *Pr*
Charles E Schwab, *
Robert Richardson Junior, *Stockholder*
▲ EMP: 60 EST: 1944
SQ FT: 100,000
SALES (est): 2.1MM
SALES (corp-wide): 2.1MM **Privately Held**
Web: www.rpcprint.com
SIC: 7389 2752 Mailing and messenger services; Offset printing

(G-9821)
SCEPTER SUPPLY LLC
1500 Greene St (45750-8044)
P.O. Box 233 (82003-0233)
PHONE.................................307 634-6074
Yon Malkuch, *VP*
EMP: 6
Web: www.sceptersupply.com
SIC: 3546 Drills and drilling tools
HQ: Scepter Supply, Llc
    1912 Whitney Rd Ste B
    Cheyenne WY 82007
    307 634-6074

(G-9822)
SEWAH STUDIOS INC
190 Mill Creek Rd (45750-1381)
P.O. Box 298 (45750-0298)
PHONE.................................740 373-2087
Bradford Smith, *Pr*
David Smith, *VP*
EMP: 16 EST: 1927
SQ FT: 6,000
SALES (est): 2.06MM **Privately Held**
Web: www.sewahstudios.com
SIC: 3446 Architectural metalwork

(G-9823)
SILICON PROCESSORS INC
1988 Masonic Park Rd (45750-5402)

PHONE.................................740 373-2252
W Trent Elliott, *Pr*
David Downing, *CFO*
EMP: 6 EST: 2004
SALES (est): 950K **Privately Held**
SIC: 3339 Silicon refining (primary, over 99% pure)

(G-9824)
SILVESCO INC
2985 State Route 26 (45750-7586)
P.O. Box 161 (45750-0161)
PHONE.................................740 373-6661
Rodney Paxton, *Pr*
Michele Paxton, *VP*
EMP: 10 EST: 1964
SQ FT: 11,800
SALES (est): 875.16K **Privately Held**
SIC: 2448 2449 Pallets, wood; Rectangular boxes and crates, wood

(G-9825)
SKUTTLE MFG CO
Also Called: Skuttle Indoor Air Qulty Pdts
101 Margaret St (45750-9052)
PHONE.................................740 373-9169
Davis Powers, *Pr*
Debby Romick, *Sec*
▲ EMP: 14 EST: 1917
SQ FT: 96,500
SALES (est): 2.88MM **Privately Held**
Web: www.skuttle.com
SIC: 3634 3564 3822 Humidifiers, electric: household; Filters, air: furnaces, air conditioning equipment, etc.; Environmental controls

(G-9826)
SMITH BROTHERS ERECTION INC
101 Industry Rd (45750-9355)
PHONE.................................740 373-3575
Robert A Gribben Junior, *Pr*
Robert A Gribben Iii, *Board Director*
EMP: 7 EST: 2011
SALES (est): 95.53K **Privately Held**
SIC: 1791 3449 Structural steel erection; Bars, concrete reinforcing: fabricated steel

(G-9827)
SOLVAY ADVANCED POLYMERS LLC
17005 State Route 7 (45750-8248)
P.O. Box 446 (45750-0446)
PHONE.................................740 373-9242
Joseph D Greulich, *Pr*
EMP: 73 EST: 2001
SALES (est): 10.26MM **Privately Held**
SIC: 2819 Radium, luminous compounds

(G-9828)
SOLVAY SPCLTY POLYMERS USA LLC
17005 State Route 7 (45750-8248)
P.O. Box 446 (45750-0446)
PHONE.................................740 373-9242
Wally Kandell, *Brnch Mgr*
EMP: 10
SALES (corp-wide): 146.05MM **Privately Held**
Web: www.solvay.com
SIC: 2821 Plastics materials and resins
HQ: Solvay Specialty Polymers Usa, L.L.C.
    4500 Mcginnis Ferry Rd
    Alpharetta GA 30005
    770 772-8200

(G-9829)
SOMERVILLE MANUFACTURING INC
15 Townhall Rd (45750-5374)
PHONE.................................740 336-7847
Steve Somerville, *Pr*
Peggy Somerville, *VP*

Marietta - Washington County (G-9830)

GEOGRAPHIC SECTION

EMP: 20 **EST:** 2013
SALES (est): 1.83MM **Privately Held**
Web: www.somervilleindustries.com
SIC: 3441 3444 7692 Fabricated structural metal; Sheet metalwork; Welding repair

(G-9830)
STEEL DYNAMICS LLC
15 Townhall Rd (45750-5374)
EMP: 22 **EST:** 2005
SQ FT: 3,000
SALES (est): 533.39K **Privately Held**
Web: www.steeldynamics.com
SIC: 3291 Abrasive metal and steel products

(G-9831)
STEVENS OIL & GAS LLC
110 Lynch Church Rd (45750-7545)
PHONE..........................740 374-4542
EMP: 7 **EST:** 2006
SALES (est): 481.02K **Privately Held**
Web: www.stevensoilandgas.com
SIC: 1382 Oil and gas exploration services

(G-9832)
STEVES VANS ACC UNLIMITED LLC
Also Called: Steve's Vans Auto Sales
221 Pike St (45750-3320)
PHONE..........................740 374-3154
TOLL FREE: 800
EMP: 9 **EST:** 1983
SQ FT: 3,700
SALES (est): 2.06MM **Privately Held**
Web: www.mariettamobilityservices.com
SIC: 5511 7532 5531 5999 Vans, new and used; Van conversion; Automotive accessories; Technical aids for the handicapped

(G-9833)
STONEBRIDGE OILFIELD SVCS LLC
406 Colegate Dr (45750-9252)
P.O. Box 60 (45750-0060)
PHONE..........................740 373-6134
Eddy Biehl, *Mgr*
EMP: 6 **EST:** 2014
SALES (est): 315.53K **Privately Held**
SIC: 3533 Oil and gas drilling rigs and equipment

(G-9834)
STRATAGRAPH NE INC
116 Ellsworth Ave (45750-8607)
P.O. Box 59 (45773-0059)
PHONE..........................740 373-3091
Walt Teer, *Pr*
EMP: 10 **EST:** 1985
SQ FT: 2,400
SALES (est): 863.6K **Privately Held**
Web: www.strata-ne.com
SIC: 1389 1381 Oil field services, nec; Drilling oil and gas wells

(G-9835)
TEIKOKU USA INC
27881 State Route 7 (45750-9060)
PHONE..........................304 699-1156
John Cox, *Brnch Mgr*
EMP: 13
Web: www.teikokupumps.com
SIC: 3561 Pumps and pumping equipment
HQ: Teikoku Usa Inc.
  959 Mearns Rd
  Warminster PA 18974

(G-9836)
THERMO FSHER SCNTFIC ASHVLLE L
401 Mill Creek Rd (45750-4304)
P.O. Box 649 (45750-0649)
PHONE..........................740 373-4763
Jamie Keefer, *Brnch Mgr*
EMP: 592
SQ FT: 287
SALES (corp-wide): 44.91B **Publicly Held**
Web: www.thermofisher.com
SIC: 3826 Analytical instruments
HQ: Thermo Fisher Scientific (Asheville) Llc
  275 Aiken Rd
  Asheville NC 28804
  828 658-2711

(G-9837)
TKN OILFIELD SERVICES LLC
108 Woodcrest Dr (45750-1352)
PHONE..........................740 516-2583
EMP: 12 **EST:** 2018
SQ FT: 1,500
SALES (est): 654.53K **Privately Held**
Web: www.tknoilfieldservices.com
SIC: 1389 Oil field services, nec

(G-9838)
TRIAD ENERGY CORPORATION
125 Putnam St (45750-2936)
PHONE..........................740 374-2940
Kean Weaver, *Pr*
James R Bryden, *VP*
EMP: 19 **EST:** 1956
SALES (est): 725.49K **Privately Held**
SIC: 2992 1382 Lubricating oils and greases; Oil and gas exploration services

(G-9839)
TRIAD HUNTER LLC (DH)
125 Putnam St Ste 100 (45750-2936)
PHONE..........................740 374-2940
EMP: 12 **EST:** 2009
SALES (est): 10.19MM
SALES (corp-wide): 6.52B **Publicly Held**
SIC: 1311 Crude petroleum production
HQ: Blue Ridge Mountain Resources, Inc.
  122 W John Carpenter Fwy # 300
  Irving TX 75039

(G-9840)
UNITED CHART PROCESSORS INC
1461 Masonic Park Rd (45750-5393)
PHONE..........................740 373-5801
David Graham, *Pr*
Barbara Graham, *VP*
EMP: 8 **EST:** 1984
SALES (est): 964.74K **Privately Held**
Web: www.ucpgas.com
SIC: 1389 Oil field services, nec

(G-9841)
UNITED DAIRY INC
1701 Greene St (45750-7000)
PHONE..........................740 373-4121
Joseph L Carson, *Pr*
EMP: 260
SALES (corp-wide): 80.92MM **Privately Held**
Web: www.drinkunited.com
SIC: 5451 2024 2026 Dairy products stores; Ice cream, packaged: molded, on sticks, etc.; Cottage cheese
PA: United Dairy, Inc.
  300 N 5th St
  Martins Ferry OH 43935
  740 633-1451

(G-9842)
VANGUARD PAINTS AND FINISHES INC
1409 Greene St (45750-9807)
P.O. Box 654 (45750-0654)
PHONE..........................740 373-5261
EMP: 22 **EST:** 1939
SALES (est): 4.96MM **Privately Held**
Web: www.vanguardpaints.com
SIC: 2851 Paints and allied products

(G-9843)
VIKING FABRICATORS INC
2021 Hanna Rd (45750-8255)
PHONE..........................740 374-5246
David M Archer, *Pr*
Arlene M Archer, *
Matthew Hilverding, *
James S Huggins, *
EMP: 25 **EST:** 1988
SQ FT: 20,000
SALES (est): 913.68K **Privately Held**
Web: www.pioneergroup.us
SIC: 3441 7692 3446 3443 Fabricated structural metal; Welding repair; Architectural metalwork; Fabricated plate work (boiler shop)

(G-9844)
WESTLAKE DIMEX LLC
Also Called: Dimex LLC
28305 State Route 7 (45750-5151)
P.O. Box 337 (45773-0337)
PHONE..........................740 374-3100
Andy Antil, *CEO*
Dan Allan, *
▲ **EMP:** 160 **EST:** 1991
SQ FT: 224,000
SALES (est): 52.85MM **Publicly Held**
Web: www.dimexcorp.com
SIC: 6726 3089 3069 Investment offices, nec; Plastics hardware and building products; Mats or matting, rubber, nec
PA: Westlake Corporation
  2801 Post Oak Blvd Ste 60
  Houston TX 77056

(G-9845)
WINSTON OIL CO INC
1 Court House Ln Ste 3 (45750-2900)
P.O. Box 754 (45750-0754)
PHONE..........................740 373-9664
Deborah Cunningham, *Prin*
EMP: 7 **EST:** 2007
SALES (est): 429.29K **Privately Held**
SIC: 3569 Gas producers, generators, and other gas related equipment

(G-9846)
ZIDE SPORT SHOP OF OHIO INC
Also Called: Zide Screen Printing
118 Industry Rd (45750-9355)
PHONE..........................740 373-8199
Randy Schneeberger, *Mgr*
EMP: 17
SALES (corp-wide): 2.94MM **Privately Held**
Web: www.zides.com
SIC: 2396 Screen printing on fabric articles
PA: Zide Sport Shop Of Ohio, Inc.
  253 2nd St
  Marietta OH 45750
  740 373-6446

Marion
Marion County

(G-9847)
ALIN MACHINING COMPANY INC
Also Called: ALIN MACHINING COMPANY, INC.
875 E Mark St (43302-2748)
PHONE..........................740 223-0200
Ryan Dballinger, *Brnch Mgr*
EMP: 71
SALES (corp-wide): 62.16MM **Privately Held**
Web: www.ppsvcs.com
SIC: 3511 Turbines and turbine generator sets
PA: Alin Machining Company, Llc
  3131 W Soffel Ave
  Melrose Park IL 60160
  708 681-1043

(G-9848)
BENDER COMMUNICATIONS INC (PA)
1541 Harding Hwy E (43302-4567)
PHONE..........................740 382-0000
TOLL FREE: 800
Donald L Bender, *Pr*
Dustin Bender, *VP*
Kelesta Edwards, *Sec*
Karen Bender, *Treas*
EMP: 10 **EST:** 1975
SQ FT: 2,500
SALES (est): 2.94MM
SALES (corp-wide): 2.94MM **Privately Held**
Web: www.bendercomm.com
SIC: 3669 5731 Intercommunication systems, electric; Radios, two-way, citizens band, weather, short-wave, etc.

(G-9849)
CENTRAL MACHINERY COMPANY LLC
Also Called: Cenmac Metalworks
1339 E Fairground Rd (43302-8873)
PHONE..........................740 387-1289
Rod Galbreath, *Pr*
EMP: 17 **EST:** 1960
SQ FT: 25,000
SALES (est): 4.38MM **Privately Held**
Web: www.cenmacmetalworks.com
SIC: 3599 3499 Machine shop, jobbing and repair; Fire- or burglary-resistive products

(G-9850)
CENTRAL MACHINERY COMPANY LLC
116 S Main St (43302-3702)
PHONE..........................740 387-1289
Charlotte R Baldauf, *Prin*
EMP: 9 **EST:** 2001
SALES (est): 124.73K **Privately Held**
SIC: 3569 General industrial machinery, nec

(G-9851)
ENVIRI CORPORATION
Also Called: Patent Construction Systems
3477 Harding Hwy E (43302-8534)
PHONE..........................740 387-1150
Don Broadwater, *Brnch Mgr*
EMP: 10
SALES (corp-wide): 2.07B **Publicly Held**
Web: www.enviri.com
SIC: 3537 3536 3535 3531 Industrial trucks and tractors; Hoists, cranes, and monorails; Conveyors and conveying equipment; Construction machinery
PA: Enviri Corporation
  100-120 N 18th St # 17
  Philadelphia PA 19103
  267 857-8715

(G-9852)
FOLKS CREATIVE PRINTERS INC
101 E George St (43302-2304)
P.O. Box 521 (43301-0521)
PHONE..........................740 383-6326
Trudi E Maish, *Ch Bd*
James L Saiter, *Pr*
Linda M Maish, *Sec*
EMP: 14 **EST:** 1922
SALES (est): 461.75K **Privately Held**
Web: www.folksprinting.com

SIC: 2752 3993 2789 2759 Offset printing; Signs and advertising specialties; Bookbinding and related work; Commercial printing, nec

(G-9853)
FRONT AND CENTER MGT GROUP LLC
Also Called: Promo Costumes
381 W Center St (43302-3651)
PHONE...............................740 383-5176
Edward T Emerson, *Prin*
Edward Emerson, *Prin*
EMP: 6 **EST:** 2020
SALES (est): 248.78K **Privately Held**
SIC: 2389 Apparel and accessories, nec

(G-9854)
GENERAL MACHINE & SAW COMPANY
305 Davids St (43302-4713)
P.O. Box 587 (43301-0587)
PHONE...............................740 382-1104
Joseph Murphy, *Pr*
Matt Murphy, *
Beth Murphy, *
Jack Dean, *
EMP: 96 **EST:** 1980
SQ FT: 100,000
SALES (est): 9.76MM **Privately Held**
Web: www.gmsaw.com
SIC: 3441 Fabricated structural metal

(G-9855)
HIGHWAY SAFETY CORP
Also Called: HIGHWAY SAFETY CORP.
473 W Fairground St (43302-1701)
PHONE...............................740 387-6991
Jim Chick, *Mgr*
EMP: 15
SALES (corp-wide): 85.75MM **Privately Held**
Web: www.highwaysafety.net
SIC: 3444 3479 Guard rails, highway: sheet metal; Galvanizing of iron, steel, or end-formed products
HQ: Highway Safety Llc
239 Commerce St
Glastonbury CT 06033
860 633-9445

(G-9856)
HILDRETH MFG LLC
1657 Cascade Dr (43302-8509)
P.O. Box 905 (43301-0905)
PHONE...............................740 375-5832
EMP: 25 **EST:** 1999
SALES (est): 4.81MM **Privately Held**
Web: www.hildrethmfg.com
SIC: 3331 Blocks, copper

(G-9857)
INTERNATIONAL PAPER COMPANY
Also Called: International Paper
1600 Cascade Dr (43302-8509)
PHONE...............................740 383-4061
Ron Iden, *Prin*
EMP: 40
SALES (corp-wide): 18.92B **Publicly Held**
Web: www.internationalpaper.com
SIC: 2621 Paper mills
PA: International Paper Company
6400 Poplar Ave
Memphis TN 38197
901 419-7000

(G-9858)
KATHLEEN WILLIAMS
354 Pearl St (43302-4941)
PHONE...............................740 360-3515
Kathleen Williams, *Prin*
EMP: 6 **EST:** 2010
SALES (est): 92.96K **Privately Held**
SIC: 2844 5999 Perfumes, cosmetics and other toilet preparations; Toiletries, cosmetics, and perfumes

(G-9859)
LAIPPLYS PRTG MKTG SLTIONS INC
270 E Center St (43302-4124)
P.O. Box 777 (43301-0777)
PHONE...............................740 387-9282
Ronald E Laipply, *Pr*
Jacque Laipply, *VP*
Effie Laipply, *Sec*
EMP: 9 **EST:** 1973
SQ FT: 5,000
SALES (est): 962.82K **Privately Held**
Web: www.laipplyqprint.com
SIC: 2789 7336 7331 Bookbinding and related work; Graphic arts and related design; Direct mail advertising services

(G-9860)
MARION DOFASCO INC
686 W Fairground St (43302-1706)
PHONE...............................740 382-3979
D Pether, *Prin*
EMP: 7 **EST:** 2016
SALES (est): 174.74M **Privately Held**
Web: www.ltv-copperweld.com
SIC: 3312 Blast furnaces and steel mills

(G-9861)
MARION INDUSTRIES LLC
999 Kellogg Pkwy (43302-1791)
PHONE...............................740 223-0075
EMP: 753
SIC: 3714 Motor vehicle wheels and parts

(G-9862)
MIDWEST GLYCOL SERVICES LLC ✪
116 Lawrence Ave (43302-3346)
PHONE...............................419 946-3326
Gennifer Schaefer, *CEO*
EMP: 25 **EST:** 2022
SALES (est): 1.16MM **Privately Held**
SIC: 2899 Chemical preparations, nec

(G-9863)
MILLS PARTITION COMPANY LLC
3007 Harding Hwy E Bldg 201 (43302-2575)
PHONE...............................740 375-0770
Donald H Mullett, *Ch Bd*
John Kleczka, *Sec*
▲ **EMP:** 70 **EST:** 1921
SALES (est): 13.52MM
SALES (corp-wide): 2.06B **Publicly Held**
SIC: 2542 Partitions for floor attachment, prefabricated: except wood
HQ: Bradley Company, Llc
W142n9101 Fountain Blvd
Menomonee Falls WI 53051
262 251-6000

(G-9864)
NACHURS ALPINE SOLUTIONS LLC (HQ)
Also Called: Nachurs Alpine Solutions Corp
421 Leader St (43302-2225)
PHONE...............................740 382-5701
Jeffrey Barnes, *Pr*
Robert Hopp, *
Reiny Packull, *
David Rose, *
▲ **EMP:** 25 **EST:** 1946
SALES (est): 114.52MM
SALES (corp-wide): 3.23B **Privately Held**
Web: www.nachurs.com

(G-9865)
NATIONAL LIME AND STONE CO
700 Likens Rd (43302-8601)
P.O. Box 144 (43301-0144)
PHONE...............................740 387-3485
Scott Silver, *Mgr*
EMP: 28
SALES (corp-wide): 167.89MM **Privately Held**
Web: www.natlime.com
SIC: 1422 5999 Limestones, ground; Rock and stone specimens
PA: The National Lime And Stone Company
551 Lake Cascade Pkwy
Findlay OH 45840
419 422-4341

(G-9866)
NEWSAFE TRANSPORT SERVICE INC
979 Pole Lane Rd (43302-8524)
P.O. Box 749 (43301-0749)
PHONE...............................740 387-1679
Rachpal Sangh, *Pr*
EMP: 11 **EST:** 2003
SQ FT: 400
SALES (est): 253.71K **Privately Held**
Web: www.newsafetransport.com
SIC: 3537 Trucks: freight, baggage, etc.: industrial, except mining

(G-9867)
NUCOR STEEL MARION INC
Scrap Division
400 Bartram Ave (43302-2108)
P.O. Box 1217 (43301-1217)
PHONE...............................740 383-6068
Tim Bia, *Mgr*
EMP: 20
SALES (corp-wide): 34.71B **Publicly Held**
Web: www.nucorhighway.com
SIC: 3312 5051 5093 Sheet or strip, steel, cold-rolled: own hot-rolled; Metals service centers and offices; Metal scrap and waste materials
HQ: Nucor Steel Marion, Inc.
912 Cheney Ave
Marion OH 43302
740 383-4011

(G-9868)
NUCOR STEEL MARION INC (HQ)
912 Cheney Ave (43302-6208)
P.O. Box 1801 (43301-1801)
PHONE...............................740 383-4011
◆ **EMP:** 375 **EST:** 1981
SALES (est): 63.75MM
SALES (corp-wide): 34.71B **Publicly Held**
Web: www.nucorhighway.com
SIC: 3316 3441 3312 5051 Cold finishing of steel shapes; Fabricated structural metal; Iron and steel products, hot-rolled; Iron and steel (ferrous) products
PA: Nucor Corporation
1915 Rexford Rd
Charlotte NC 28211
704 366-7000

(G-9869)
OHIO GALVANIZING LLC
467 W Fairground St (43302-1701)
PHONE...............................740 387-6474
W Patric Gregory Iii, *CEO*
Robert J West, *
EMP: 50 **EST:** 1994
SQ FT: 57,000
SALES (est): 5.55MM
SALES (corp-wide): 85.75MM **Privately Held**
Web: www.ohgalv.com
SIC: 3479 Coating of metals and formed products
PA: Race Rock Gp, L.L.C.
1980 Post Oak Blvd # 2175
Houston TX 77056
832 920-1276

(G-9870)
OVERHEAD DOOR CORPORATION
Todco
1332 E Fairground Rd (43302-8505)
PHONE...............................740 383-6376
Daniel C Rengert, *Pr*
EMP: 100
Web: www.overheaddoor.com
SIC: 3442 2431 3441 Garage doors, overhead: metal; Doors, wood; Fabricated structural metal
HQ: Overhead Door Corporation
2501 S State Hwy 121 Ste
Lewisville TX 75067
469 549-7100

(G-9871)
PACIFIC HIGHWAY PRODUCTS LLC
324 Barnhart St (43302-3206)
PHONE...............................740 914-5217
EMP: 9 **EST:** 2018
SALES (est): 734.73K **Privately Held**
SIC: 3699 Electrical welding equipment

(G-9872)
PISTON AUTOMOTIVE LLC
999 Kellogg Pkwy (43302-1791)
PHONE...............................740 223-0075
Robert Holloway, *Pr*
EMP: 753
SALES (corp-wide): 2.3B **Privately Held**
Web: www.pistonautomotive.com
SIC: 3714 Motor vehicle wheels and parts
HQ: Piston Automotive, L.L.C.
12723 Telegraph Rd Ste 1
Redford MI 48239
313 541-8674

(G-9873)
POET BIOREFINING MARION LLC
Also Called: Poet Biorefining
1660 Hillman Ford Rd (43302-9475)
PHONE...............................740 383-4400
EMP: 45 **EST:** 2008
SALES (est): 144MM **Privately Held**
Web: poetbiorefining-marion.aghost.net
SIC: 2869 2046 Ethyl alcohol, ethanol; Corn oil products
PA: Poet, Llc
4615 N Lewis Ave
Sioux Falls SD 57104

(G-9874)
R ANTHONY ENTERPRISES LLC
2626 Whetstone River Rd S (43302-8937)
PHONE...............................419 341-0961
Rocco Piacentino, *Managing Member*
EMP: 10 **EST:** 2012
SQ FT: 10,000
SALES (est): 581.78K **Privately Held**
SIC: 1389 Construction, repair, and dismantling services

Marion - Marion County (G-9875)

(G-9875)
REX WELDING INC
1410 E Center St (43302-4593)
PHONE.................................740 387-1650
Joel Plough, *Pr*
Mary E Plough, *VP*
Chris Plough, *Sec*
EMP: 10 **EST:** 1944
SQ FT: 9,000
SALES (est): 1.22MM **Privately Held**
SIC: 5051 1791 7692 7389 Steel; Structural steel erection; Welding repair; Crane and aerial lift service

(G-9876)
RI ALTO MFG INC
1632 Cascade Dr (43302-8509)
PHONE.................................740 914-4230
Rick Mattix, *Pr*
Maryann Mattix, *Sec*
Sam Hawkins, *VP*
EMP: 19 **EST:** 1981
SQ FT: 9,000
SALES (est): 4.24MM **Privately Held**
Web: www.rialtomfg.com
SIC: 3599 7692 Machine shop, jobbing and repair; Welding repair

(G-9877)
ROY I KAUFMAN INC
1672 Marion Upper Sandusky Rd (43302-1531)
PHONE.................................740 382-0643
Martin T Kaufman Ii, *Dir*
Beth Kaufman, *Sec*
EMP: 8 **EST:** 1956
SQ FT: 12,000
SALES (est): 662.24K **Privately Held**
SIC: 3496 Woven wire products, nec

(G-9878)
SAKAMURA USA INC
970 Kellogg Pkwy (43302-1783)
PHONE.................................740 223-7777
Takayuki Nakano, *Pr*
Jun Kobayashi, *VP*
Naomi Taniguchi, *Treas*
▲ **EMP:** 14 **EST:** 1997
SQ FT: 10,000
SALES (est): 6.76MM **Privately Held**
Web: www.sakamura.net
SIC: 3462 Iron and steel forgings
PA: Sakamura Machine Co., Ltd.
  46, Tominojo, Shimotsuya,
  Kumiyamacho
  Kuse-Gun KYO 613-0

(G-9879)
SCHWARZ PARTNERS PACKAGING LLC
Also Called: Royal Group, The
2135 Innovation Dr (43302-8261)
PHONE.................................740 387-3700
Jeff Gorsuch, *Brnch Mgr*
EMP: 75
SALES (corp-wide): 573.33MM **Privately Held**
Web: theroyalgroup.wpengine.com
SIC: 2653 Boxes, corrugated: made from purchased materials
HQ: Schwarz Partners Packaging, Llc
  10 W Carmel Dr Ste 300
  Carmel IN 46032
  317 290-1140

(G-9880)
SEMCO INC
1025 Pole Lane Rd (43302-8524)
PHONE.................................800 848-5764
Leonard Furman, *Ch*
Brett Tennar, *

Shelby Furman, *
Randy Furman, *
J Douglass Schrim, *
▲ **EMP:** 60 **EST:** 1976
SQ FT: 40,000
SALES (est): 9.99MM **Privately Held**
Web: www.semcotips.com
SIC: 3599 3366 Machine shop, jobbing and repair; Copper foundries

(G-9881)
SILVER LINE BUILDING PDTS LLC
2549 Innovation Dr (43302-8721)
PHONE.................................740 382-5595
EMP: 1191
SALES (corp-wide): 5.58B **Privately Held**
Web: www.silverlinewindows.com
SIC: 3089 Composition stone, plastics
HQ: Silver Line Building Products Llc
  1 Silver Line Dr
  North Brunswick NJ 08902
  732 435 1000

(G-9882)
SIMCOTE INC
Also Called: Simcote of Ohio Division
250 N Greenwood St (43302-3177)
PHONE.................................740 382-5000
Art Tofte, *Brnch Mgr*
EMP: 13
SALES (corp-wide): 9.74MM **Privately Held**
Web: www.simcote.com
SIC: 3479 3449 Painting, coating, and hot dipping; Miscellaneous metalwork
PA: Simcote, Inc.
  1645 Red Rock Rd
  Saint Paul MN 55119
  651 735-9660

(G-9883)
SIMS BROS INC (PA)
Also Called: Sims Brothers Recycling
1011 S Prospect St (43302-6217)
P.O. Box 1170 (43301-1170)
PHONE.................................740 387-9041
TOLL FREE: 800
▲ **EMP:** 95 **EST:** 1965
SALES (est): 32.93MM
SALES (corp-wide): 32.93MM **Privately Held**
Web: www.simsbros.com
SIC: 5051 5013 5093 3341 Iron and steel (ferrous) products; Automotive supplies and parts; Waste paper; Secondary nonferrous metals

(G-9884)
STEAM TRBINE ALTRNTIVE RSRCES
Also Called: Star
370 W Fairground St (43302)
P.O. Box 862 (43301)
PHONE.................................740 387-5535
Sue B Flaherty, *Ch Bd*
Tammy Flaherty, *
Ken Kubinski, *
Donna Macgregor Rambin, *
EMP: 45 **EST:** 1988
SALES (est): 8.4MM **Privately Held**
Web: www.starturbine.com
SIC: 3511 5085 Steam turbines; Industrial supplies

(G-9885)
STORAD LABEL CO
126 Blaine Ave (43302-3612)
P.O. Box 493 (43301-0493)
PHONE.................................740 382-6440
Bob Hord, *Pr*
Ann Hord, *VP*
EMP: 10 **EST:** 1966

SQ FT: 7,000
SALES (est): 374.53K **Privately Held**
Web: www.storadlabel.com
SIC: 2759 Labels and seals: printing, nsk

(G-9886)
TODCO
1295 E Fairground Rd (43302-8503)
PHONE.................................740 223-2542
Dennis Stone, *CEO*
EMP: 10 **EST:** 2017
SALES (est): 5.3MM **Privately Held**
Web: www.todco.com
SIC: 2431 Millwork

(G-9887)
TREE FREE RESOURCES LLC
Also Called: Tfr Printing
175 Park Blvd (43302-3534)
PHONE.................................740 751-4844
EMP: 8 **EST:** 2010
SALES (est): 410.44K **Privately Held**
Web: www.tfrprinting.com
SIC: 2759 Commercial printing, nec

(G-9888)
US YACHIYO INC
1177 Kellogg Pkwy (43302-1779)
PHONE.................................740 375-4687
Hiroshi Sasamoto, *Pr*
Kazuyoshi Itai, *
Tsugio Motoori, *
Yasushi Ota, *
Kazuhiro Asabuki, *
◆ **EMP:** 232 **EST:** 1999
SQ FT: 125,000
SALES (est): 48.54MM **Privately Held**
Web: www.yachiyo-of-america.com
SIC: 3795 Tanks and tank components
HQ: Yachiyo Of America Inc.
  2285 Walcutt Rd
  Columbus OH 43228

(G-9889)
WHIRLPOOL CORPORATION
Whirlpool
1300 Marion Agosta Rd (43302-9577)
PHONE.................................740 383-7122
Stan Kenneth, *VP*
EMP: 45
SALES (corp-wide): 19.45B **Publicly Held**
Web: www.whirlpoolcorp.com
SIC: 3633 5064 3632 Laundry dryers, household or coin-operated; Washing machines; Household refrigerators and freezers
PA: Whirlpool Corporation
  2000 N M-63
  Benton Harbor MI 49022
  269 923-5000

(G-9890)
WILLIAMS LEATHER PRODUCTS INC
Also Called: McKinley Leather
1476 Likens Rd Ste 104 (43302-8788)
PHONE.................................740 223-1604
EMP: 6 **EST:** 1994
SQ FT: 8,000
SALES (est): 386.93K **Privately Held**
Web: www.mckinleyleather.com
SIC: 3172 Personal leather goods, nec

(G-9891)
WILSON BOHANNAN COMPANY
Also Called: W B
621 Buckeye St (43302-6121)
P.O. Box 504 (43301-0504)
PHONE.................................740 382-3639
Howard Smith, *Pr*
Pamela Smith, *
Randy Dawson, *

Mark Williams, *
Craig Stone, *
EMP: 72 **EST:** 1860
SQ FT: 40,000
SALES (est): 19.29MM **Privately Held**
Web: www.padlocks.com
SIC: 3429 Padlocks

(G-9892)
WYANDOT USA LLC (PA)
Also Called: Wyandot Snacks
135 Wyandot Ave (43302)
PHONE.................................740 383-4031
Ken Romanzi, *Managing Member*
Erich Fritz, *COO*
▲ **EMP:** 244 **EST:** 1936
SQ FT: 265,000
SALES (est): 74.16MM
SALES (corp-wide): 74.16MM **Privately Held**
Web: www.wyandotsnacks.com
SIC: 2099 Food preparations, nec

Marshallville
Wayne County

(G-9893)
MARSHALLVILLE PACKING CO INC
50 E Market St (44645-9468)
P.O. Box 276 (44645-0276)
PHONE.................................330 855-2871
Frank T Tucker, *Pr*
Jeannette Tucker, *
EMP: 12 **EST:** 1960
SQ FT: 35,000
SALES (est): 399.87K **Privately Held**
Web: www.marshallville-meats.com
SIC: 5421 5147 2013 2011 Meat markets, including freezer provisioners; Meats, fresh; Sausages and other prepared meats; Meat packing plants

(G-9894)
NANCYS DRAPERIES INC
57 S Main St (44645-9773)
P.O. Box 305 (44645-0305)
PHONE.................................330 855-7751
Nancy Yoder, *Owner*
EMP: 8 **EST:** 1982
SALES (est): 489.45K **Privately Held**
Web: www.nancysdraperies.com
SIC: 2211 5714 1799 Draperies and drapery fabrics, cotton; Draperies; Drapery track installation

Martins Ferry
Belmont County

(G-9895)
ARROWSTRIP INC
1st & Locust St S (43935)
P.O. Box 37 (43935)
PHONE.................................740 633-2609
Pete Mysliwic, *Pr*
W Quay Mull Ii, *Ch Bd*
Lisa M Leach, *VP Fin*
Gary A Butler, *Ex VP*
▼ **EMP:** 18 **EST:** 1985
SQ FT: 25,000
SALES (est): 964.25K **Privately Held**
Web: www.arrowstrip.com
SIC: 3312 Galvanized pipes, plates, sheets, etc.: iron and steel

(G-9896)
AYERS LIMESTONE QUARRY INC
2002 Colerain Pike (43935)
P.O. Box 67 (43935-0067)

GEOGRAPHIC SECTION

Marysville - Union County (G-9916)

PHONE.............................740 633-2958
Thomas E Ayers Junior, *Pr*
Patricia Ayers, *Sec*
John Ayers, *VP*
EMP: 10 **EST:** 1958
SQ FT: 8,000
SALES (est): 971.98K **Privately Held**
SIC: 1422 3274 Whiting mining, crushed and broken-quarrying; Lime

(G-9897)
DANOS AND CUROLE
305 N 1st St (43935-1739)
PHONE.............................740 609-3599
EMP: 7 **EST:** 2017
SALES (est): 174.7K **Privately Held**
Web: www.danos.com
SIC: 1389 Oil field services, nec

(G-9898)
EASTERN OHIO NEWSPAPERS INC
200 S 4th St (43935-1312)
PHONE.............................740 633-1131
G O Nutting, *Pr*
EMP: 9 **EST:** 2011
SALES (est): 196.89K **Privately Held**
SIC: 2711 Newspapers, publishing and printing

(G-9899)
LESCO INC
Also Called: Lesco Service Center
100 Picoma Rd (43935-9700)
PHONE.............................740 633-6366
Frank Damato, *Mgr*
EMP: 10
SALES (corp-wide): 4.3B **Publicly Held**
Web: www.lesco.com
SIC: 5191 2875 Limestone, agricultural; Fertilizers, mixing only
HQ: Lesco, Inc.
1385 E 36th St
Cleveland OH 44114
216 706-9250

(G-9900)
UNITED DAIRY INC (PA)
Also Called: United Dairy Company
300 N 5th St (43935-1647)
P.O. Box 280 (43935-0280)
PHONE.............................740 633-1451
Joseph M Carson Junior, *Ch*
Gary Cowell, *VP Opers*
Joseph L Carson, *Pr*
George Wood, *Sec*
James Carson, *VP Mktg*
EMP: 200 **EST:** 1903
SQ FT: 20,000
SALES (est): 80.92MM
SALES (corp-wide): 80.92MM **Privately Held**
Web: www.drinkunited.com
SIC: 2026 2024 Milk processing (pasteurizing, homogenizing, bottling); Ice cream, bulk

(G-9901)
WILSON BLACKTOP CORP
915 Carlisle St Rear (43935-1511)
P.O. Box 128 (43916-0128)
PHONE.............................740 635-3566
Dale M Wilson, *Pr*
Mark E Wilson, *VP*
Janice L Wilson, *Sec*
EMP: 17 **EST:** 1976
SQ FT: 1,000
SALES (est): 2.17MM **Privately Held**
Web: www.wilsonblacktop.com

SIC: 2951 1611 1771 Asphalt and asphaltic paving mixtures (not from refineries); Highway and street paving contractor; Blacktop (asphalt) work

Martinsville
Clinton County

(G-9902)
ROZZI COMPANY INC
6047 State Route 350 (45146-9539)
PHONE.............................513 683-0620
EMP: 15
SALES (corp-wide): 4.54MM **Privately Held**
Web: www.rozzifireworks.com
SIC: 2899 Chemical preparations, nec
PA: The Rozzi Company Inc
10059 Loveland Madeira Rd
Loveland OH 45140
513 683-0620

(G-9903)
WILLIAM OEDER READY MIX INC
8807 State Route 134 (45146-9533)
PHONE.............................513 899-3901
William Oeder, *Pr*
Ronald Oeder, *VP*
Robert Oeder, *VP*
Jo Ann Parker, *Sec*
Alma Oeder, *Treas*
EMP: 20 **EST:** 1939
SQ FT: 3,000
SALES (est): 745.83K **Privately Held**
SIC: 3273 Ready-mixed concrete

Marysville
Union County

(G-9904)
AMERICAN AGRITECH LLC
Also Called: Botanicare
14111 Scottslawn Rd (43040-7800)
PHONE.............................480 777-2000
◆ **EMP:** 30 **EST:** 1996
SQ FT: 21,000
SALES (est): 10.01MM
SALES (corp-wide): 3.55B **Publicly Held**
SIC: 3423 Garden and farm tools, including shovels
PA: The Scotts Miracle-Gro Company
14111 Scottslawn Rd
Marysville OH 43040
937 644-0011

(G-9905)
BUCKEYE READY-MIX LLC
838 N Main St (43040-9701)
P.O. Box 31 (43068-0031)
PHONE.............................937 642-2951
Larry Randels, *VP*
EMP: 23
SQ FT: 3,000
SALES (corp-wide): 48.26MM **Privately Held**
Web: www.buckeyereadymix.com
SIC: 3273 Ready-mixed concrete
PA: Buckeye Ready-Mix, Llc
7657 Taylor Rd Sw
Reynoldsburg OH 43068
614 575-2132

(G-9906)
CONTITECH USA INC
Also Called: Continental Contitech
13601 Industrial Pkwy (43040-8890)
PHONE.............................937 644-8900
Ken Kontely, *Mgr*

EMP: 78
SALES (corp-wide): 45.02B **Privately Held**
Web: www.continental-industry.com
SIC: 5084 3399 3496 Industrial machinery and equipment; Metal fasteners; Mats and matting
HQ: Contitech Usa, Inc.
703 S Clvland Mssillon Rd
Fairlawn OH 44333

(G-9907)
DAK ENTERPRISES INC (PA)
18062 Timber Trails Rd (43040-8158)
P.O. Box 409 (43822-0409)
PHONE.............................740 828-3291
Daniel Keifer, *Pr*
EMP: 13 **EST:** 2004
SALES (est): 39.58MM
SALES (corp-wide): 39.58MM **Privately Held**
Web: www.dkmanufacturing.com
SIC: 3089 Injection molding of plastics

(G-9908)
ENGINEERED MFG & EQP CO
Also Called: E M E C
11611 Industrial Pkwy (43040-9522)
PHONE.............................937 642-7776
EMP: 8 **EST:** 1995
SQ FT: 9,000
SALES (est): 895.91K **Privately Held**
Web: www.emec.us
SIC: 3544 3699 Special dies, tools, jigs, and fixtures; Electrical equipment and supplies, nec

(G-9909)
FILE 13 INC
232 N Main St Ste K (43040-1160)
P.O. Box 626 (43040-0626)
PHONE.............................937 642-4855
Mark Ropp, *Prin*
EMP: 10 **EST:** 1998
SALES (est): 435.44K **Privately Held**
Web: www.ucoindustries.com
SIC: 3559 Tire shredding machinery

(G-9910)
FRANKES WOOD PRODUCTS LLC
825 Collins Ave (43040-1330)
PHONE.............................937 642-0706
William Franke, *Pr*
Michelle R Franke, *Stockholder*
Kevin Franke, *Stockholder*
Christopher S Franke, *Stockholder*
EMP: 25 **EST:** 2001
SQ FT: 93,800
SALES (est): 5.04MM **Privately Held**
Web: www.frankeswoodproducts.com
SIC: 2448 2449 2493 3061 Cargo containers, wood; Shipping cases and drums, wood: wirebound and plywood; Fiberboard, wood; Mechanical rubber goods

(G-9911)
GRAPHIC STITCH INC
169 Grove St Rm A (43040-1342)
PHONE.............................937 642-6707
Todd M Hoge, *Pr*
Karen Valentino, *Off Mgr*
EMP: 9 **EST:** 1995
SQ FT: 2,800
SALES (est): 925.89K **Privately Held**
Web: www.graphicstitch.com
SIC: 2395 2759 Embroidery products, except Schiffli machine; Commercial printing, nec

(G-9912)
GREENVILLE TECHNIOLOGY INC
15000 Industrial Pkwy (43040-9547)
PHONE.............................937 642-6744
EMP: 8 **EST:** 2015
SALES (est): 196.98K **Privately Held**
SIC: 3089 Automotive parts, plastic

(G-9913)
HAWTHORNE GARDENING COMPANY (HQ)
Also Called: Hawthorne Gardening Co.
14111 Scottslawn Rd (43040-7800)
PHONE.............................360 883-8846
James Hagedorn, *CEO*
Christopher Hagedorn, *Genl Mgr*
Michael Lukemire, *COO*
Randy Coleman, *Ex VP*
Ivan Smith, *CCO*
EMP: 24 **EST:** 2014
SALES (est): 215.71MM
SALES (corp-wide): 3.55B **Publicly Held**
Web: www.hawthorne-gardening.com
SIC: 5083 7342 3524 Lawn and garden machinery and equipment; Pest control services; Lawn and garden tractors and equipment
PA: The Scotts Miracle-Gro Company
14111 Scottslawn Rd
Marysville OH 43040
937 644-0011

(G-9914)
HAWTHORNE HYDROPONICS LLC (DH)
Also Called: Hawthorne Hydrophonics Botanic
14111 Scottslawn Rd (43040-7800)
PHONE.............................888 478-6544
Christopher J Hagedorn, *Pr*
Mark Scheiwer, *
Dimiter Todorov, *
Ross Haley, *
▲ **EMP:** 19 **EST:** 1997
SALES (est): 44.39MM
SALES (corp-wide): 3.55B **Publicly Held**
Web: www.hawthorne-gardening.com
SIC: 2879 5083 5084 3674 Agricultural chemicals, nec; Hydroponic equipment and supplies; Water pumps (industrial); Light emitting diodes
HQ: The Hawthorne Gardening Company
14111 Scottslawn Rd
Marysville OH 43040
360 883-8846

(G-9915)
HONDA DEV & MFG AMER LLC
Also Called: Honda Support Office
19900 State Route 739 (43040-9256)
PHONE.............................937 644-0724
EMP: 200
Web: www.honda.com
SIC: 5511 3711 3465 8742 Automobiles, new and used; Motor vehicles and car bodies; Automotive stampings; Training and development consultant
HQ: Honda Development & Manufacturing Of America, Inc.
24000 Honda Pkwy
Marysville OH 43040
937 642-5000

(G-9916)
HONDA DEV & MFG AMER LLC (DH)
Also Called: Marysville Auto Plant
24000 Honda Pkwy (43040)
PHONE.............................937 642-5000
Mitsugu Matsukawa, *Pr*
Tomomi Kosaka, *
John Adams, *
◆ **EMP:** 750 **EST:** 1978

Marysville - Union County (G-9917)

SQ FT: 2,235,000
SALES (est): 1.06B **Privately Held**
Web: www.honda.com
SIC: **3711** Motor vehicles and car bodies
HQ: American Honda Motor Co., Inc.
    1919 Torrance Blvd
    Torrance CA 90501
    310 783-2000

(G-9917)
HONDA DEV & MFG AMER LLC
25000 Honda Pkwy (43040-9190)
PHONE..................937 642-5000
EMP: 500
Web: www.honda.com
SIC: **3711** Automobile assembly, including specialty automobiles
HQ: Honda Development & Manufacturing Of America, Llc
    24000 Honda Pkwy
    Marysville OH 43040
    937 642-5000

(G-9918)
HONDA ENGINEERING NORTH AMERICA LLC
Also Called: Honda Engineering N Amer Inc
24000 Honda Pkwy (43040-9251)
PHONE..................937 642-5000
▲ EMP: 350
Web: www.hondaengineering.com
SIC: **3544** Special dies and tools

(G-9919)
HONDA TRANSMISSION MANUFACTURI
25000 Honda Pkwy (43040-9190)
PHONE..................937 843-5555
EMP: 15 EST: 2019
SALES (est): 1.11MM **Privately Held**
Web: www.honda.com
SIC: **3999** Manufacturing industries, nec

(G-9920)
HYPONEX CORPORATION (DH)
Also Called: Scotts- Hyponex
14111 Scottslawn Rd (43040-7800)
PHONE..................937 644-0011
James Hagedorn, *Pr*
Christopher Nagel, *
David M Brockman, *
David C Evans, *
EMP: 100 EST: 1980
SQ FT: 73,000
SALES (est): 478.3MM
SALES (corp-wide): 3.55B **Publicly Held**
Web: www.suntreksolar.com
SIC: **2873** 2875 Fertilizers: natural (organic), except compost; Fertilizers, mixing only
HQ: The Scotts Company Llc
    14111 Scottslawn Rd
    Marysville OH 43040
    937 644-0011

(G-9921)
INDUSTRIAL CERAMIC PRODUCTS INC
14401 Suntra Way (43040-9579)
PHONE..................937 642-3897
◆ EMP: 60 EST: 1936
SALES (est): 4.98MM **Privately Held**
Web: www.industrialceramic.com
SIC: **3255** 3297 Clay refractories; Nonclay refractories

(G-9922)
INTERNATIONAL PAPER COMPANY
Also Called: International Paper
13307 Industrial Pkwy (43040-9589)
PHONE..................937 578-7718
EMP: 14
SALES (corp-wide): 18.92B **Publicly Held**
Web: www.internationalpaper.com
SIC: **2621** Paper mills
PA: International Paper Company
    6400 Poplar Ave
    Memphis TN 38197
    901 419-7000

(G-9923)
LARSEN PACKAGING PRODUCTS INC
Also Called: Alpha Container
16789 Square Dr (43040-8476)
PHONE..................937 644-5511
Bill Larsen, *Brnch Mgr*
EMP: 12
Web: www.larsenpackaging.com
SIC: **2653** Boxes, corrugated: made from purchased materials
PA: Larsen Packaging Products, Inc.
    1350 S River St
    Batavia IL 60510

(G-9924)
LINEAR IT SOLUTIONS LLC
639 Gallop Ln (43040-7072)
PHONE..................614 306-0761
Scott Verbus, *Prin*
EMP: 10 EST: 2017
SALES (est): 816.12K **Privately Held**
Web: mail1.linearit.net
SIC: **3429** Hardware, nec

(G-9925)
MAGNETIC SCREW MACHINE PDTS
23241 State Route 37 (43040-9749)
PHONE..................937 348-2807
Bryan Bayes, *Pr*
EMP: 7 EST: 1971
SQ FT: 16,000
SALES (est): 999.22K **Privately Held**
SIC: **3451** Screw machine products

(G-9926)
MARYSVILLE NEWSPAPER INC (PA)
Also Called: Richwood Gazette
207 N Main St (43040-1161)
P.O. Box 226 (43040-0226)
PHONE..................937 644-9111
Daniel Behrens, *Pr*
Kevin Behrens, *
EMP: 30 EST: 1859
SQ FT: 10,000
SALES (est): 2.38MM
SALES (corp-wide): 2.38MM **Privately Held**
Web: www.marysvillejt.com
SIC: **2711** 2731 Newspapers, publishing and printing; Books, publishing and printing

(G-9927)
MARYSVILLE STEEL INC
323 E 8th St (43040)
P.O. Box 383 (43040-0383)
PHONE..................937 642-5971
Steven J Clayman, *CEO*
EMP: 31 EST: 1951
SQ FT: 50,000
SALES (est): 4.09MM **Privately Held**
SIC: **3441** 1791 5039 Fabricated structural metal; Structural steel erection; Joists

(G-9928)
MORIROKU TECHNOLOGY N AMER INC (HQ)
15000 Industrial Pkwy (43040-9547)
P.O. Box 974 (45331-0974)
PHONE..................937 548-3217
Yaf Nakao, *Pr*
William Laframboise, *VP*
Akihiko Hirano, *VP*
James Heiser, *Ex VP*
◆ EMP: 672 EST: 1986
SQ FT: 300,000
SALES (est): 103.1MM **Privately Held**
SIC: **3089** Injection molded finished plastics products, nec
PA: Moriroku Holdings Company, Ltd.
    1-1-1, Minamiaoyama
    Minato-Ku TKY 107-0

(G-9929)
NEW REPUBLIC INDUSTRIES LLC (PA)
Also Called: My Second Home Early Lrng Schl
497 Bridle Dr (43040-1658)
PHONE..................614 580-9927
EMP: 7 EST: 2018
SALES (est): 523.23K
SALES (corp-wide): 523.23K **Privately Held**
Web: www.advantage-ela.com
SIC: **3999** Manufacturing industries, nec

(G-9930)
PARKER-HANNIFIN CORPORATION
Hydraulic Pump Division
14249 Industrial Pkwy (43040-9504)
PHONE..................937 644-3915
Ken Theiss, *Brnch Mgr*
EMP: 15
SALES (corp-wide): 19.07B **Publicly Held**
Web: www.parker.com
SIC: **3594** 3491 3679 Pumps, hydraulic power transfer; Industrial valves; Electronic circuits
PA: Parker-Hannifin Corporation
    6035 Parkland Blvd
    Cleveland OH 44124
    216 896-3000

(G-9931)
PRECISION COATINGS SYSTEMS
948 Columbus Ave (43040-9501)
PHONE..................937 642-4727
Fred Myers Junior, *Pr*
Sherry Myers, *VP*
Wendy Myers, *VP*
Mark Myers, *VP*
EMP: 20 EST: 1989
SQ FT: 26,000
SALES (est): 999.71K **Privately Held**
Web: www.precisioncoatingsystems.com
SIC: **3479** 7532 7549 7514 Painting of metal products; Paint shop, automotive; Towing services; Rent-a-car service

(G-9932)
PREMIER PRTG CENTL OHIO LTD
16710 Square Dr (43040-9616)
PHONE..................937 642-0988
John Hubbard, *Pt*
Dan Behren, *Pt*
Jeff Barnes, *Pt*
Tom Thompson, *Pt*
Kevin Vehrens, *Pt*
EMP: 30 EST: 2000
SALES (est): 1.7MM **Privately Held**
SIC: **2711** 2752 Newspapers, publishing and printing; Commercial printing, lithographic

(G-9933)
PRIMROSE SCHOOL OF MARYSVILLE
115 N Plum St (43040-1262)
PHONE..................937 642-2125
EMP: 6 EST: 2017
SALES (est): 127.52K **Privately Held**
Web: www.marysvillejt.com
SIC: **2711** Newspapers, publishing and printing

(G-9934)
SCOTTS COMPANY LLC (HQ)
Also Called: Scotts Miracle-Gro Products
14111 Scottslawn Rd (43040-7801)
P.O. Box 418 (43040-0418)
PHONE..................937 644-0011
Michael P Kelty, *
Christopher L Nagel, *
David M Aronowitz, *
◆ EMP: 143 EST: 1969
SALES (est): 1.59B
SALES (corp-wide): 3.55B **Publicly Held**
Web: www.scotts.com
SIC: **2873** 2874 2879 0782 Fertilizers: natural (organic), except compost; Phosphates; Fungicides, herbicides; Lawn services
PA: The Scotts Miracle-Gro Company
    14111 Scottslawn Rd
    Marysville OH 43040
    937 644-0011

(G-9935)
SCOTTS MIRACLE-GRO COMPANY (PA)
Also Called: Scotts Miracle-Gro
14111 Scottslawn Rd (43040-7801)
PHONE..................937 644-0011
James Hagedorn, *Ch Bd*
James Hagedorn, *Ch Bd*
Nate Baxter, *COO*
Matthew E Garth, *CAO*
Dimiter Todorov, *Corporate Secretary*
▲ EMP: 343 EST: 1868
SALES (est): 3.55B
SALES (corp-wide): 3.55B **Publicly Held**
Web: www.scottsmiraclegro.com
SIC: **2873** 7342 2879 Nitrogenous fertilizers; Pest control services; Insecticides and pesticides

(G-9936)
SCOTTS MIRACLE-GRO COMPANY
Also Called: East Chemical Plant
14101 Industrial Pkwy (43040-9591)
PHONE..................937 578-5065
Mike Henkel, *Brnch Mgr*
EMP: 26
SALES (corp-wide): 3.55B **Publicly Held**
Web: www.scottsmiraclegro.com
SIC: **2873** 2879 Fertilizers: natural (organic), except compost; Fungicides, herbicides
PA: The Scotts Miracle-Gro Company
    14111 Scottslawn Rd
    Marysville OH 43040
    937 644-0011

(G-9937)
SCOTTS TEMECULA OPERATIONS LLC
14111 Scottslawn Rd (43040-7801)
PHONE..................800 221-1760
EMP: 46 EST: 2001
SALES (est): 4.42MM
SALES (corp-wide): 3.55B **Publicly Held**
SIC: **3524** Lawn and garden equipment
PA: The Scotts Miracle-Gro Company
    14111 Scottslawn Rd
    Marysville OH 43040
    937 644-0011

(G-9938)
SMG GROWING MEDIA INC (HQ)
14111 Scottslawn Rd (43040-7800)
PHONE..................937 644-0011
EMP: 12 EST: 2005
SALES (est): 39.21MM
SALES (corp-wide): 3.55B **Publicly Held**

SIC: 3524 5083 Lawn and garden equipment; Farm and garden machinery
PA: The Scotts Miracle-Gro Company
14111 Scottslawn Rd
Marysville OH 43040
937 644-0011

(G-9939)
SMGM LLC
14111 Scottslawn Rd (43040-7800)
PHONE..................................937 644-0011
EMP: 48 EST: 2004
SALES (est): 5.8MM
SALES (corp-wide): 3.55B Publicly Held
SIC: 2873 Nitrogenous fertilizers
PA: The Scotts Miracle-Gro Company
14111 Scottslawn Rd
Marysville OH 43040
937 644-0011

(G-9940)
STRAIGHT 72 INC
Also Called: MAI Manufacturing
20078 State Route 4 (43040-9723)
PHONE..................................740 943-5730
EMP: 60 EST: 1995
SALES (est): 9.25MM Privately Held
Web: www.maimfg.com
SIC: 8711 3544 Acoustical engineering; Special dies, tools, jigs, and fixtures

(G-9941)
SUMITOMO ELC WIRG SYSTEMS INC
14800 Industrial Pkwy (43040-7507)
PHONE..................................937 642-7579
EMP: 20
Web: www.sewsus.com
SIC: 3714 5063 3694 Automotive wiring harness sets; Wire and cable; Engine electrical equipment
HQ: Sumitomo Electric Wiring Systems, Inc.
1018 Ashley St
Bowling Green KY 42103
270 782-7397

(G-9942)
TOOL TECHNOLOGIES VAN DYKE
639 Clymer Rd (43040-9502)
P.O. Box 256 (43045-0256)
PHONE..................................937 349-4900
EMP: 10 EST: 1991
SQ FT: 5,000
SALES (est): 1.64MM Privately Held
Web: www.tooltechohio.com
SIC: 3829 3544 Measuring and controlling devices, nec; Special dies, tools, jigs, and fixtures

(G-9943)
TRIPLE ARROW INDUSTRIES INC
Also Called: Arch Polymers
13311 Industrial Pkwy (43040-9589)
PHONE..................................614 437-5588
Howard Wei, Pr
George Wu, VP
◆ EMP: 7 EST: 2010
SALES (est): 925.53K Privately Held
Web: www.triplearrowohio.com
SIC: 2821 5093 Plastics materials and resins; Metal scrap and waste materials

(G-9944)
Z LINE KITCHEN AND BATH LLC (PA)
Also Called: Z Line Kitchen and Bath
916 Delaware Ave (43040-1726)
PHONE..................................614 777-5004
Andy Zuro, CEO
EMP: 8 EST: 2004
SQ FT: 13,000
SALES (est): 24.6MM
SALES (corp-wide): 24.6MM Privately Held

Web: www.zlinekitchen.com
SIC: 3444 5722 Hoods, range: sheet metal; Gas ranges

Mason
Warren County

(G-9945)
AERO FULFILLMENT SERVICES CORP (PA)
3900 Aero Dr (45040-8840)
PHONE..................................800 225-7145
Jon T Gimpel, Pr
Jon T Gimpel, Pr
Brenda Conaway, *
▲ EMP: 100 EST: 1986
SQ FT: 125,000
SALES (est): 47.77MM
SALES (corp-wide): 47.77MM Privately Held
Web: www.aerofulfillment.com
SIC: 4225 7374 7331 2759 General warehousing; Data processing service; Mailing service; Commercial printing, nec

(G-9946)
AEROSERV INC
201 Industrial Row Dr (45040-2600)
P.O. Box 48 (45040-0048)
PHONE..................................513 932-9227
Steve Michael, Pr
EMP: 10 EST: 1988
SQ FT: 14,000
SALES (est): 995.45K Privately Held
Web: www.aeroservinc.com
SIC: 3599 Machine shop, jobbing and repair

(G-9947)
AI LIFE LLC
Also Called: Ai Wellness
4680 Parkway Dr Ste 300 (45040-7979)
PHONE..................................513 605-1079
Adam Ross, Managing Member
EMP: 10 EST: 2018
SALES (est): 200K Privately Held
Web: www.aiwellness.com
SIC: 2023 Dietary supplements, dairy and non-dairy based

(G-9948)
ALPHAGRAPHICS
7288 Central Parke Blvd (45040-6776)
PHONE..................................513 204-6070
Patrick Crowley, Pdt Mgr
EMP: 7 EST: 2018
SALES (est): 173.81K Privately Held
Web: www.alphagraphics.com
SIC: 2752 Commercial printing, lithographic

(G-9949)
AMPACET CORP
4705 Duke Dr Ste 400 (45040-9502)
PHONE..................................513 247-5403
Morgan Gibbs, Mgr
EMP: 7 EST: 2016
SALES (est): 184.86K Privately Held
Web: www.ampacet.com
SIC: 3089 Plastics products, nec

(G-9950)
ANDRE CORPORATION
4600 N Mason Montgomery Rd (45040-9176)
PHONE..................................574 293-0207
David Andre, Pr
EMP: 20 EST: 1991
SQ FT: 50,000
SALES (est): 901K Privately Held

SIC: 3452 3469 5085 Washers, metal; Stamping metal for the trade; Fasteners, industrial: nuts, bolts, screws, etc.

(G-9951)
ARMOR AFTERMARKET INC
4600 N Mason Montgomery Rd Oh (45040-9176)
PHONE..................................513 923-5600
EMP: 6 EST: 2011
SALES (est): 55.22K Privately Held
Web: www.armoraftermarket.com
SIC: 3599 Industrial machinery, nec

(G-9952)
ARMOR CONSOLIDATED INC (PA)
4600 N Mason Montgomery Rd (45040-9176)
PHONE..................................513 923-5260
David K Schmitt, CEO
EMP: 510 EST: 1996
SALES (est): 23.51MM
SALES (corp-wide): 23.51MM Privately Held
Web: www.thearmorgroup.com
SIC: 3441 3446 3443 6719 Fabricated structural metal; Architectural metalwork; Fabricated plate work (boiler shop); Investment holding companies, except banks

(G-9953)
ARMOR METAL GROUP ELKHART INC
4600 N Mason Montgomery Rd (45040-9176)
PHONE..................................800 672-6373
Jeffrey G Stagaro, Prin
EMP: 11 EST: 2012
SALES (est): 1.19MM Privately Held
Web: www.armorcontract.com
SIC: 3444 Sheet metalwork

(G-9954)
ARMOR METAL GROUP MASON INC (HQ)
Also Called: Armormetal
4600 N Mason Montgomery Rd (45040-9176)
PHONE..................................513 769-0700
Jeffrey G Stagaro, Prin
David K Schmitt, *
Frank Ahaus, *
▲ EMP: 200 EST: 1927
SALES (est): 98.08MM Privately Held
Web: www.thearmorgroup.com
SIC: 3441 3446 3444 3443 Fabricated structural metal; Architectural metalwork; Sheet metalwork; Fabricated plate work (boiler shop)
PA: The Armor Group, Inc.
4600 N Masn Montgomery Rd
Mason OH 45040

(G-9955)
ASHLEY F WARD INC (PA)
Also Called: Precision Tek Manufacturing
7490 Easy St (45040-9423)
PHONE..................................513 398-1414
Bill Ward, Ch Bd
William H Ward, *
Terry Bien, *
Brian Scalf, *
Nate Ruhenkamp, *
▲ EMP: 116 EST: 1908
SQ FT: 150,000
SALES (est): 3.38K
SALES (corp-wide): 3.38K Privately Held
Web: www.ashleyward.com
SIC: 3451 Screw machine products

(G-9956)
ATRICURE INC (PA)
Also Called: Atricure
7555 Innovation Way (45040-9695)
PHONE..................................513 755-4100
Michael H Carrel, Pr
B Kristine Johnson, *
Douglas J Seith, COO
M Andrew Wade, Sr VP
EMP: 1089 EST: 2000
SQ FT: 92,000
SALES (est): 399.25MM
SALES (corp-wide): 399.25MM Publicly Held
Web: www.atricure.com
SIC: 3841 Surgical instruments and apparatus

(G-9957)
BASCO MANUFACTURING COMPANY (PA)
Also Called: Basco Shower Enclosures
7201 Snider Rd (45040-9601)
PHONE..................................513 573-1900
George Rohde Junior, Pr
George Rohde Junior, CEO
Steve Lotz, *
G William Rohde Senior, Ch
◆ EMP: 174 EST: 1946
SQ FT: 80,000
SALES (est): 51.43MM
SALES (corp-wide): 51.43MM Privately Held
Web: www.bascoshowerdoor.com
SIC: 3231 Doors, glass: made from purchased glass

(G-9958)
BEAUMONT MACHINE LLC
Also Called: Beaumont Machine
7697 Innovation Way Ste 1100 (45040-9605)
PHONE..................................513 701-0421
EMP: 15 EST: 1990
SQ FT: 21,000
SALES (est): 4.28MM Privately Held
Web: www.beaumontmachine.com
SIC: 3823 7699 Industrial process measurement equipment; Precision instrument repair

(G-9959)
BEELINE PURCHASING LLC
4454 N Mallard Cv (45040-9041)
PHONE..................................513 703-3733
Cathleen Holden, Pr
EMP: 6 EST: 2010
SALES (est): 462.71K Privately Held
Web: www.beelinepurchasing.com
SIC: 5999 5047 3842 Alarm and safety equipment stores; Industrial safety devices: first aid kits and masks; Personal safety equipment

(G-9960)
BERRY FILM PRODUCTS CO INC (DH)
Also Called: Clopay
8585 Duke Blvd (45040-3100)
P.O. Box 959 (47706-0959)
PHONE..................................800 225-6729
Alan H Koblin, Pr
Tom Givens, *
◆ EMP: 100 EST: 1992
SQ FT: 35,000
SALES (est): 74.81MM Publicly Held
Web: www.berryglobal.com
SIC: 3081 Plastics film and sheet
HQ: Berry Global, Inc.
101 Oakley St
Evansville IN 47710

Mason - Warren County (G-9961)

(G-9961)
BODYCOTE SRFC TECH PRPERTY LLC
8118 Corporate Way Ste 201 (45040)
PHONE.................513 770-4900
Stephen Harris, *CEO*
Thomas Gibbons, *
EMP: 215 **EST:** 2007
SALES (est): 11.4MM **Privately Held**
Web: www.bodycote.com
SIC: 3398 Metal heat treating

(G-9962)
BODYCOTE SRFC TECH WRTBURG INC (DH)
Also Called: Ellison Surfc Technologies-Tn
8093 Columbia Rd Ste 201 (45040-9560)
PHONE.................513 770-4900
Stephen Harris, *CEO*
Thomas Gibbons, *Pr*
EMP: 46 **EST:** 1982
SALES (est): 1.21MM
SALES (corp-wide): 1B **Privately Held**
SIC: 3398 Metal heat treating
HQ: Bodycote Surface Technology Group, Inc.
8118 Corp Way Ste 201
Mason OH 45040

(G-9963)
BODYCOTE SURFACE TECH INC (DH)
Also Called: Ellison Surface Technologies
8118 Corporate Way Ste 201 (45040)
PHONE.................513 770-4922
Stephen Harris, *CEO*
Thomas Gibbons, *Pr*
EMP: 15 **EST:** 1986
SQ FT: 27,000
SALES (est): 24.06MM
SALES (corp-wide): 1B **Privately Held**
Web: www.bodycote.com
SIC: 3479 Coating of metals and formed products
HQ: Bodycote Surface Technology Group, Inc.
8118 Corp Way Ste 201
Mason OH 45040

(G-9964)
BODYCOTE SURFC TECH GROUP INC (HQ)
8118 Corporate Way Ste 201 (45040)
PHONE.................513 770-4900
Stephen Harris, *CEO*
Thomas Gibbons, *Pr*
EMP: 15 **EST:** 2004
SALES (est): 73.12MM
SALES (corp-wide): 1B **Privately Held**
Web: www.bodycote.com
SIC: 3479 Coating of metals and formed products
PA: Bodycote Plc
Springwood Court
Macclesfield SK10
162 550-5300

(G-9965)
BODYCOTE SURFC TECH MEXICO LLC
8118 Corporate Way Ste 201 (45040)
PHONE.................513 770-4900
Stephen Harris, *CEO*
Thomas Gibbons, *
EMP: 130 **EST:** 2013
SQ FT: 13,000
SALES (est): 45.43MM
SALES (corp-wide): 1B **Privately Held**
SIC: 3398 Metal heat treating

HQ: Bodycote Surface Technology Group, Inc.
8118 Corp Way Ste 201
Mason OH 45040

(G-9966)
BOSTON SCNTFIC NRMDLATION CORP
4267 S Haven Dr (45040-8629)
PHONE.................513 377-6160
EMP: 14
SALES (corp-wide): 12.68B **Publicly Held**
SIC: 3841 Surgical and medical instruments
HQ: Boston Scientific Neuromodulation Corporation
25155 Rye Canyon Loop
Valencia CA 91355

(G-9967)
CARDEN DOOR COMPANY LLC
1224 Castle Dr (45040-9433)
PHONE.................513 459-2233
Bruce Carden, *Cncl Mbr*
John Jackson, *Cncl Mbr*
EMP: 7 **EST:** 1998
SQ FT: 10,000
SALES (est): 760K **Privately Held**
Web: www.cardendoor.com
SIC: 2431 Doors and door parts and trim, wood

(G-9968)
CARTER MANUFACTURING CO INC
4220 State Route 42 (45040-1931)
PHONE.................513 398-7303
Chris Carter, *Pr*
EMP: 26 **EST:** 1973
SALES (est): 1.33MM **Privately Held**
Web: www.carter-mfg.com
SIC: 3544 7692 3541 Dies and die holders for metal cutting, forming, die casting; Welding repair; Machine tools, metal cutting type

(G-9969)
CARTER SCOTT-BROWNE
4220 State Route 42 (45040-1931)
PHONE.................513 398-3970
Christopher Carter, *Pr*
Don Bullock, *VP*
EMP: 9 **EST:** 1985
SALES (est): 134.81K **Privately Held**
SIC: 3312 Tool and die steel

(G-9970)
CENGAGE LEARNING INC
770 Broadway (45036-1726)
PHONE.................513 234-5967
EMP: 143
Web: www.cengage.com
SIC: 2731 Book publishing
HQ: Cengage Learning, Inc.
5191 Natorp Blvd
Mason OH 45040

(G-9971)
CENGAGE LEARNING INC (HQ)
Also Called: Course Technology
5191 Natorp Blvd Lowr (45040-7104)
PHONE.................617 289-7700
Michael Hansen, *Pr*
Angela M Schilling, *
Henry Pierz, *
Kevin Stone, *Chief Sales & Marketing Officer*
Dean D Durbin, *
◆ **EMP:** 60 **EST:** 1994
SALES (est): 1.12B **Privately Held**
Web: www.cengage.com

SIC: 2731 Books, publishing only
PA: Cengage Learning Holdings Ii, Inc.
5191 Natorp Blvd
Mason OH 45040

(G-9972)
CENGAGE LEARNING INC
Also Called: Thomson Higher Education
5191 Natorp Blvd Lowr (45040-7599)
PHONE.................415 839-2300
Frank Talamantez, *Mgr*
EMP: 315
Web: www.cengage.com
SIC: 2731 Textbooks: publishing and printing
HQ: Cengage Learning, Inc.
5191 Natorp Blvd
Mason OH 45040

(G-9973)
CENGAGE LRNG HOLDINGS II INC (PA)
Also Called: Cengage Learning
5191 Natorp Blvd (45040)
PHONE.................617 289-7700
Michael Hansen, *CEO*
William Rieders, *
Dean D Durbin, *
Kenneth Carson, *
Brian Mulligan, *
EMP: 50 **EST:** 1994
SALES (est): 1.12B **Privately Held**
Web: www.cengagegroup.com
SIC: 2731 Textbooks: publishing and printing

(G-9974)
CINCINNATI FAN & VENTILATOR COMPANY INC (DH)
Also Called: Cincinnati Fan
7697 Snider Rd (45040-8821)
PHONE.................513 573-0600
EMP: 96 **EST:** 1983
SALES (est): 49.67MM
SALES (corp-wide): 1.74B **Publicly Held**
Web: www.cincinnatifan.com
SIC: 3564 Blowing fans: industrial or commercial
HQ: Canvas Sx, Llc
6325 Ardrey Kell Rd Ste 4
Charlotte NC 28277
980 474-3700

(G-9975)
CINCINNATI FTN SQ NEWS INC
Also Called: Fountain News
8739 S Shore Pl (45040-5044)
PHONE.................513 421-4049
Diane Witte, *Pr*
James Witte, *VP*
Wanda Mauge, *Sec*
Vido Patel, *Mgr*
EMP: 10 **EST:** 1992
SQ FT: 2,200
SALES (est): 602.81K **Privately Held**
Web: www.lynchandassociates.com
SIC: 2711 Newspapers, publishing and printing

(G-9976)
CINCINNATI HEAT EXCHANGERS INC
6404 Thornberry Ct Ste 440 (45040-3502)
PHONE.................513 770-0777
Timothy J Stillson, *Pr*
Elizabeth Stillson, *Sec*
▲ **EMP:** 6 **EST:** 1994
SQ FT: 2,121
SALES (est): 595.33K **Privately Held**
Web: www.cinheats.com
SIC: 3443 Fabricated plate work (boiler shop)

(G-9977)
CINCINNATI INDUSTRIAL MCHY INC
4600 N Mason Montgomery Rd (45040-9176)
PHONE.................513 923-5600
David Williams, *Pr*
▲ **EMP:** 250 **EST:** 1943
SQ FT: 200,000
SALES (est): 98.08MM **Privately Held**
Web: www.cinind.com
SIC: 3441 Fabricated structural metal
HQ: Armor Metal Group Mason, Inc.
4600 N Masn Montgomery Rd
Mason OH 45040

(G-9978)
CLOPAY BUILDING PDTS CO INC (DH)
Also Called: Ideal Door
8585 Duke Blvd (45040-3100)
PHONE.................513 770-4800
Gene Colleran, *Pr*
Dan Beckley, *
Mister Pat Lohse, *VP*
◆ **EMP:** 36 **EST:** 1859
SQ FT: 35,000
SALES (est): 436.93MM
SALES (corp-wide): 2.69B **Publicly Held**
Web: www.clopaydoor.com
SIC: 2436 2431 Plywood, softwood; Garage doors, overhead, wood
HQ: Clopay Corporation
8585 Duke Blvd
Mason OH 45040
800 282-2260

(G-9979)
CLOPAY CORPORATION (HQ)
8585 Duke Blvd (45040-3100)
PHONE.................800 282-2260
Franklin Smith Junior, *CFO*
Gary Abyad, *Sr VP*
Ellen Shoemaker, *Sr VP*
Eugene Colleran, *Sr VP*
◆ **EMP:** 231 **EST:** 1889
SQ FT: 130,587
SALES (est): 935.67MM
SALES (corp-wide): 2.69B **Publicly Held**
Web: www.clopaydoor.com
SIC: 3081 3442 2431 1796 Plastics film and sheet; Garage doors, overhead: metal; Garage doors, overhead, wood; Power generating equipment installation
PA: Griffon Corporation
712 5th Ave Fl 18
New York NY 10019
212 957-5000

(G-9980)
CM PAULA COMPANY (PA)
Also Called: Geocentral
6049 Hi Tek Ct (45040-2603)
PHONE.................513 759-7473
Charles W Mc Cullough, *Ch Bd*
Greg Ionna, *
William Creager Ii, *Ex VP*
Bill Creager, *
▲ **EMP:** 25 **EST:** 1958
SQ FT: 56,000
SALES (est): 12.7MM
SALES (corp-wide): 12.7MM **Privately Held**
Web: www.cmpaula.com
SIC: 3089 2678 2499 3999 Novelties, plastics; Stationery: made from purchased materials; Decorative wood and woodwork; Bric-a-brac

GEOGRAPHIC SECTION

Mason - Warren County (G-10004)

(G-9981)
COGNEX CORP
4178 Meadowbrook Ln (45040-4509)
PHONE.................................513 339-0402
EMP: 6 **EST:** 2019
SALES (est): 116.14K **Privately Held**
Web: www.cognex.com
SIC: 3823 Process control instruments

(G-9982)
DANONE US LLC
7577 Central Parke Blvd (45040-6810)
PHONE.................................513 229-0092
George Denmen, *Mgr*
EMP: 42
SALES (corp-wide): 718.68MM **Privately Held**
Web: www.danoneawayfromhome.com
SIC: 2024 Yogurt desserts, frozen
HQ: Danone Us, Llc
   1 Maple Ave
   White Plains NY 10605
   914 872-8400

(G-9983)
DEERFIELD MANUFACTURING INC
Also Called: Ice Industries Deerfield
320 N Mason Montgomery Rd
(45040-7528)
PHONE.................................513 398-2010
Howard Ice, *Pr*
Jeff Boger,   *
Paul Bishop,   *
EMP: 24 **EST:** 1946
SQ FT: 80,000
SALES (est): 10.67MM **Privately Held**
Web: www.iceindustries.com
SIC: 3469 Stamping metal for the trade
PA: Ice Industries, Inc.
   3810 Herr Rd
   Sylvania OH 43560

(G-9984)
DIGITEK CORP
3785 Marble Ridge Ln (45040)
PHONE.................................513 794-3190
Marc E Brown, *Pr*
EMP: 10 **EST:** 2000
SALES (est): 1.53MM **Privately Held**
Web: www.digitekcorp.net
SIC: 5136 5137 2253 Uniforms, men's and boys'; Uniforms, women's and children's; T-shirts and tops, knit

(G-9985)
DOWN-LITE INTERNATIONAL INC (PA)
Also Called: Downlite
8153 Duke Blvd (45040-8104)
PHONE.................................513 229-3696
Joe Crawford, *CEO*
Robert Altbaier, *VP*
Chad Altbaier, *VP*
John G Kuhnash, *CFO*
Marvin Werthaiser, *Sec*
▲ **EMP:** 230 **EST:** 1983
SQ FT: 20,000
SALES (est): 65.3MM
SALES (corp-wide): 65.3MM **Privately Held**
Web: www.downlite.com
SIC: 2392 5719 Pillows, bed: made from purchased materials; Bedding (sheets, blankets, spreads, and pillows)

(G-9986)
E5 CHEM LLC
4834 Socialville Foster Rd (45040-6827)
PHONE.................................513 204-0173
Andrew Conrad, *CEO*
EMP: 7 **EST:** 2019
SALES (est): 242.64K **Privately Held**
SIC: 3999

(G-9987)
EBSCO INDUSTRIES INC
Also Called: Imagen Brands
4680 Parkway Dr Ste 200 (45040-8173)
P.O. Box 497 (45040-0497)
PHONE.................................513 398-3695
Lori Kates, *Genl Mgr*
EMP: 15
SALES (corp-wide): 3.1B **Privately Held**
Web: www.ebscoind.com
SIC: 2741 Miscellaneous publishing
PA: Ebsco Industries, Inc.
   5724 Highway 280 E
   Birmingham AL 35242
   205 991-6600

(G-9988)
ELLISON SURFACE TECH - W LLC (DH)
8093 Columbia Rd Ste 201 (45040-9560)
PHONE.................................513 770-4900
C Michael Ellison, *Managing Member*
EMP: 44 **EST:** 2006
SALES (est): 2.42MM
SALES (corp-wide): 1B **Privately Held**
Web: www.bodycote.com
SIC: 3479 Coating of metals and formed products
HQ: Bodycote Surface Technology Group, Inc.
   8118 Corp Way Ste 201
   Mason OH 45040

(G-9989)
EMPIRE PACKING COMPANY LP
4780 Alliance Dr (45040-7832)
PHONE.................................901 948-4788
Din Kirk, *Brnch Mgr*
EMP: 800
SALES (corp-wide): 138.53MM **Privately Held**
Web: www.ledbetterfoods.com
SIC: 2011 Meat packing plants
PA: Empire Packing Company, L.P.
   1837 Harbor Ave
   Memphis TN 38113
   901 948-4788

(G-9990)
ENGSTROM MANUFACTURING INC
4503 State Route 42 Ste B (45040-2064)
PHONE.................................513 573-0010
EMP: 9 **EST:** 1992
SALES (est): 207.34K **Privately Held**
SIC: 3452 3451 Screws, metal; Screw machine products

(G-9991)
ESSILOR OF AMERICA INC
4000 Luxottica Pl (45040-8114)
PHONE.................................513 765-6000
EMP: 17
SALES (corp-wide): 2.55MM **Privately Held**
Web: www.essilor.com
SIC: 3851 Frames, lenses, and parts, eyeglass and spectacle
HQ: Essilor Of America, Inc.
   13555 N Stemmons Fwy
   Dallas TX 75234

(G-9992)
EVOKES LLC
8118 Corporate Way Ste 212 (45040)
PHONE.................................513 947-8433
Daniel Lincoln, *Pr*
Tony Leslie,   *
EMP: 50 **EST:** 2015
SQ FT: 900
SALES (est): 5.06MM **Privately Held**
Web: www.evokesllc.com
SIC: 3822 8011 Building services monitoring controls, automatic; Surgeon

(G-9993)
FORTE INDUSTRIAL EQUIPMENT SYSTEMS INC
Also Called: Forte Industries
6037 Commerce Ct (45040-8819)
PHONE.................................513 398-2800
EMP: 32
SIC: 5084 8711 3537 Materials handling machinery; Consulting engineer; Industrial trucks and tractors

(G-9994)
FRENCH TRANSIT LLC
7588 Central Parke Blvd Ste 220 (45040)
PHONE.................................650 431-3959
EMP: 6 **EST:** 2019
SALES (est): 244.53K **Privately Held**
SIC: 2844 Perfumes, cosmetics and other toilet preparations

(G-9995)
GATESAIR INC (HQ)
5300 Kings Island Dr Ste 101 (45040-2668)
PHONE.................................513 459-3400
Barbara Spicek, *CEO*
Joseph Mack,   *
Jeff Hills,   *
▲ **EMP:** 80 **EST:** 1922
SQ FT: 30,000
SALES (est): 43.1MM
SALES (corp-wide): 1.81B **Privately Held**
Web: www.gatesair.com
SIC: 1731 3663 Communications specialization; Radio broadcasting and communications equipment
PA: The Gores Group Llc
   9800 Wilshire Blvd
   Beverly Hills CA 90212
   310 209-3010

(G-9996)
GLOBAL LASER TEK LLC
7697 Innovation Way Ste 700 (45040-9605)
PHONE.................................513 701-0452
Dan Polto, *Dir*
EMP: 24 **EST:** 2014
SALES (est): 207.02K
SALES (corp-wide): 4.38MM **Privately Held**
Web: www.globallasertek.com
SIC: 3599 Machine shop, jobbing and repair
PA: Global Specialty Machines, Llc
   7697 Innovation Way # 700
   Mason OH 45040
   513 701-0452

(G-9997)
GLOBAL SPECIALTY MACHINES LLC (PA)
7697 Innovation Way Ste 700 (45040-9605)
PHONE.................................513 701-0452
Ramesh Malhotra, *Managing Member*
Dan Polto, *Managing Member*
▲ **EMP:** 15 **EST:** 2012
SQ FT: 3,000
SALES (est): 4.38MM
SALES (corp-wide): 4.38MM **Privately Held**
Web: www.globalsmsas.com
SIC: 3541 Electron-discharge metal cutting machine tools

(G-9998)
GRAHAM PACKAGING PET TECH INC
1225 Castle Dr (45040-9672)
PHONE.................................513 398-5000
Lee Banks, *Brnch Mgr*
EMP: 27
Web: www.grahampackaging.com
SIC: 3089 Buckets, plastics
HQ: Graham Packaging Pet Technologies Inc.
   700 Indian Springs Dr # 100
   Lancaster PA 17601

(G-9999)
GRAPHIC INFO SYSTEMS INC
7177 Central Parke Blvd (45040)
P.O. Box 37958 (45222)
PHONE.................................513 948-1300
Walter Theiss, *Pr*
John Lauck, *Sec*
Edward Reilly, *Treas*
EMP: 16 **EST:** 1984
SALES (est): 4.2MM **Privately Held**
Web: www.graphicinfo.com
SIC: 2752 Offset printing

(G-10000)
HAAG-STREIT USA INC (DH)
Also Called: Reliance Medical Products
3535 Kings Mills Rd (45040)
PHONE.................................513 398-3937
Ernest Cavin, *CEO*
◆ **EMP:** 85 **EST:** 1898
SQ FT: 100,000
SALES (est): 48.83MM **Privately Held**
Web: us.haag-streit.com
SIC: 3841 5048 Surgical and medical instruments; Ophthalmic goods
HQ: Haag-Streit Holding Ag
   Gartenstadtstrasse 10
   KOniz BE 3098

(G-10001)
HI-TEK MANUFACTURING INC
Also Called: System EDM of Ohio
6050 Hi Tek Ct (45040-2602)
PHONE.................................513 459-1094
Cletis Jackson, *Pr*
Teresa Stang, *VP*
▲ **EMP:** 180 **EST:** 1979
SQ FT: 71,000
SALES (est): 41.41MM **Privately Held**
Web: www.hitekmfg.com
SIC: 3599 7692 3724 3714 Machine shop, jobbing and repair; Welding repair; Aircraft engines and engine parts; Motor vehicle parts and accessories

(G-10002)
HONEYWELL INTERNATIONAL I
7901 Innovation Way (45040-9498)
PHONE.................................513 282-5519
EMP: 18 **EST:** 2018
SALES (est): 3.01MM **Privately Held**
SIC: 3724 Aircraft engines and engine parts

(G-10003)
HSM SOLUTIONS INC
4370 Ashfield Pl (45040-1284)
PHONE.................................513 898-9586
Anu G, *Prin*
EMP: 6 **EST:** 2019
SALES (est): 53.62K **Privately Held**
Web: www.hsmsolutions.com
SIC: 3069 Fabricated rubber products, nec

(G-10004)
IBIZA HOLDINGS INC
7901 Innovation Way (45040-9498)

Mason - Warren County (G-10005)   GEOGRAPHIC SECTION

PHONE..........................513 701-7300
Chris Cole, *
Derek Nemeth, *Crdt Mgr*
EMP: 7 **EST:** 2014
SALES (est): 155.98K **Privately Held**
SIC: 3535 Conveyors and conveying equipment

(G-10005)
ICE INDUSTRIES INC
320 N Mason Montgomery Rd (45040-7528)
PHONE..........................513 398-2010
Jene Swick, *Brnch Mgr*
EMP: 33
Web: www.iceindustries.com
SIC: 3469 Stamping metal for the trade
PA: Ice Industries, Inc.
3810 Herr Rd
Sylvania OH 43560

(G-10006)
IMAGINE COMMUNICATIONS CORP
Also Called: Harris Broadcast
5300 Kings Island Dr Ste 101 (45040-2668)
PHONE..........................513 459-3400
Rich Lohmueller, *Prin*
EMP: 6
SQ FT: 17,000
SALES (corp-wide): 1.81B **Privately Held**
Web: www.imaginecommunications.com
SIC: 3663 Radio broadcasting and communications equipment
HQ: Imagine Communications Corp.
6100 Tennyson Pkwy # 130
Plano TX 75024
469 803-4900

(G-10007)
INTELLIGRATED INC (HQ)
7901 Innovation Way (45040-9498)
PHONE..........................866 936-7300
Chris Cole, *CEO*
Jim Mccarthy, *Pr*
Edward Puisis, *
▲ **EMP:** 29 **EST:** 2001
SALES (est): 494.97MM
SALES (corp-wide): 36.66B **Publicly Held**
Web: sps.honeywell.com
SIC: 3535 Conveyors and conveying equipment
PA: Honeywell International Inc.
855 S Mint St
Charlotte NC 28202
704 627-6200

(G-10008)
INTELLIGRATED HEADQUARTERS LLC
7901 Innovation Way (45040-9498)
PHONE..........................866 936-7300
EMP: 23 **EST:** 2014
SALES (est): 7.32MM
SALES (corp-wide): 36.66B **Publicly Held**
SIC: 3535 Conveyors and conveying equipment
HQ: Intelligrated Systems, Inc.
7901 Innovation Way
Mason OH 45040
866 936-7300

(G-10009)
INTELLIGRATED SUB HOLDINGS INC
7901 Innovation Way (45040-9498)
PHONE..........................513 701-7300
Chris Cole, *CEO*
EMP: 99 **EST:** 2013
SQ FT: 250,000
SALES (est): 11.94MM **Privately Held**
SIC: 3535 Conveyors and conveying equipment

(G-10010)
INTELLIGRATED SYSTEMS INC (HQ)
Also Called: Honeywell Intelligrated
7901 Innovation Way (45040-9498)
PHONE..........................866 936-7300
Chris Cole, *CEO*
Jim Mccarthy, *Pr*
Ed Puisis, *CFO*
▲ **EMP:** 800 **EST:** 1996
SQ FT: 390,000
SALES (est): 1.69B
SALES (corp-wide): 36.66B **Publicly Held**
Web: sps.honeywell.com
SIC: 3535 5084 7371 Conveyors and conveying equipment; Industrial machinery and equipment; Computer software development
PA: Honeywell International Inc.
855 S Mint St
Charlotte NC 28202
704 627-6200

(G-10011)
INTELLIGRATED SYSTEMS LLC
7901 Innovation Way (45040-9498)
PHONE..........................513 701-7300
Bryan Jones, *
Ed Puisis, *
Jim Mcknight, *Sr VP*
EMP: 2300 **EST:** 2001
SQ FT: 260,000
SALES (est): 365.17MM
SALES (corp-wide): 36.66B **Publicly Held**
SIC: 3535 5084 3537 Conveyors and conveying equipment; Materials handling machinery; Computer software development
HQ: Intelligrated Systems, Inc.
7901 Innovation Way
Mason OH 45040
866 936-7300

(G-10012)
INTELLIGRATED SYSTEMS OHIO LLC (DH)
7901 Innovation Way (45040-9498)
PHONE..........................513 701-7300
TOLL FREE: 800
Jim Mccarthy, *Pr*
Stephen Ackerman, *
Stephen Causey, *
◆ **EMP:** 600 **EST:** 2010
SQ FT: 332,000
SALES (est): 528.2MM
SALES (corp-wide): 36.66B **Publicly Held**
SIC: 3535 5084 3537 Conveyors and conveying equipment; Industrial machinery and equipment; Palletizers and depalletizers
HQ: Intelligrated Systems, Inc.
7901 Innovation Way
Mason OH 45040
866 936-7300

(G-10013)
INTERSTATE CONTRACTORS LLC
Also Called: Ic Roofing
762 Reading Rd # G (45040-1362)
PHONE..........................513 372-5393
EMP: 40 **EST:** 2010
SALES (est): 2.37MM **Privately Held**
Web: www.ic-roofing.com
SIC: 8611 3444 Business associations; Metal roofing and roof drainage equipment

(G-10014)
J W HARRIS CO INC (HQ)
Also Called: Harris Products Group, The
4501 Quality Pl (45040-1971)
PHONE..........................513 754-2000
◆ **EMP:** 252 **EST:** 1914
SALES (est): 56.36MM
SALES (corp-wide): 4.19B **Publicly Held**
Web: www.harrisproductsgroup.com
SIC: 3356 3548 2899 Solder: wire, bar, acid core, and rosin core; Welding wire, bare and coated; Fluxes: brazing, soldering, galvanizing, and welding
PA: Lincoln Electric Holdings, Inc.
22801 St Clair Ave
Cleveland OH 44117
216 481-8100

(G-10015)
JPC LLC
215 Kings Mills Rd (45040-1804)
PHONE..........................513 310-1608
Thomas Brinkman, *Asst Sec*
EMP: 6 **EST:** 2018
SALES (est): 113.97K **Privately Held**
SIC: 2273 Carpets and rugs

(G-10016)
K & K PRECISION INC
5001 N Mason Montgomery Rd (45040-9148)
PHONE..........................513 336-0032
David J Kappes, *Pr*
Larry G Hixson, *
Melinda Kappes, *
EMP: 38 **EST:** 1991
SALES (est): 5.38MM **Privately Held**
Web: www.kkprec.com
SIC: 3599 Machine shop, jobbing and repair

(G-10017)
KLOSTERMAN BAKING CO
Also Called: KLOSTERMAN BAKING CO.
1130 Reading Rd (45040-9156)
PHONE..........................513 398-2707
Chip Klosterman, *Pr*
EMP: 13
SQ FT: 60,000
SALES (corp-wide): 190.57MM **Privately Held**
Web: www.klostermanbakery.com
SIC: 2051 4225 Bakery: wholesale or wholesale/retail combined; General warehousing
PA: Klosterman Baking Co., Llc
4760 Paddock Rd
Cincinnati OH 45229
513 242-1004

(G-10018)
L-3 CMMNCATIONS NOVA ENGRG INC
4393 Digital Way (45040-7604)
P.O. Box 16850 (84116-0850)
PHONE..........................877 282-1168
Mark Fischer, *Pr*
EMP: 101 **EST:** 1990
SQ FT: 80,000
SALES (est): 3.8MM
SALES (corp-wide): 19.42B **Publicly Held**
SIC: 8711 3663 Electrical or electronic engineering; Carrier equipment, radio communications
HQ: L3 Technologies, Inc.
600 3rd Ave Fl 34
New York NY 10016
321 727-9100

(G-10019)
L3HARRIS CINCINNATI ELEC CORP (DH)
Also Called: Space & Sensors
7500 Innovation Way (45040-9695)
PHONE..........................513 573-6100
Patrick J Sweeney, *Ch*
Russ Walker, *
Vance King, *
Mark Dapore, *
Ed English, *
EMP: 600 **EST:** 1972
SQ FT: 230,000
SALES (est): 139MM
SALES (corp-wide): 19.42B **Publicly Held**
SIC: 3812 3769 3823 Detection apparatus: electronic/magnetic field, light/heat; Space vehicle equipment, nec; Infrared instruments, industrial process type
HQ: L3 Technologies, Inc.
600 3rd Ave Fl 34
New York NY 10016
321 727-9100

(G-10020)
LANTEK SYSTEMS INC (DH)
5412 Courseview Dr Ste 205 (45040)
PHONE..........................877 805-1028
Juan Louis Larranaga, *Pr*
Adria Iles, *Dir*
Alberto Martinez, *VP*
EMP: 6 **EST:** 1998
SQ FT: 2,750
SALES (est): 2.5MM
SALES (corp-wide): 4.51B **Privately Held**
Web: www.lantek.com
SIC: 7372 7371 5734 7373 Business oriented computer software; Computer software development and applications; Computer software and accessories; Computer system selling services
HQ: Lantek Sheet Metal Solutions Slu
Calle Ferdinand Zeppelin 2
Vitoria-Gasteiz 01510

(G-10021)
LORDSTOWN MOTORS CORP
Also Called: Lordstown
7588 Central Parke Blvd Ste 321 (45040)
PHONE..........................312 925-2466
Edward T Hightower, *CEO*
Daniel A Ninivaggi, *Ex Ch Bd*
Donna L Bell, *Ex VP*
Adam B Kroll, *PAO*
EMP: 8 **EST:** 2018
SALES (est): 2.34MM **Privately Held**
Web: www.lordstownmotors.com
SIC: 3711 Truck and tractor truck assembly

(G-10022)
LOWER INVESTMENTS LLC
4072 Pimlico Ct (45040-1848)
PHONE..........................765 825-4151
Authorized Represent Da Lower, *Prin*
EMP: 6 **EST:** 2007
SALES (est): 54.1K **Privately Held**
SIC: 3541 Machine tools, metal cutting type

(G-10023)
LYNX PRECISION PRODUCTS CORP
6636 Rosemont Ln (45040-5733)
PHONE..........................866 305-9012
John Cullinan, *Pr*
▲ **EMP:** 11 **EST:** 1995
SALES (est): 484.86K **Privately Held**
Web: www.lynx-vietnam-manufacturer.com
SIC: 3312 Forgings, iron and steel

(G-10024)
MAKINO INC (HQ)
7680 Innovation Way (45040-9695)
P.O. Box 8003 (45040-8003)
PHONE..........................513 573-7200
Donald Lane, *Pr*
Bob Henry, *
F Matsubara, *
◆ **EMP:** 356 **EST:** 1887
SQ FT: 320,000
SALES (est): 164.64MM **Privately Held**
Web: www.makino.com

GEOGRAPHIC SECTION
Mason - Warren County (G-10046)

SIC: 3541 Machine tools, metal cutting type
PA: Makino Milling Machine Co., Ltd.
2-3-19, Nakane
Meguro-Ku TKY 152-0

(G-10025)
MARTIN MARIETTA MATERIALS INC
Also Called: Martin Marietta Aggregates
4900 Parkway Dr (45040-8430)
PHONE.................513 701-1120
Michael Hunt, *Prin*
EMP: 10
Web: www.martinmarietta.com
SIC: 1422 Crushed and broken limestone
PA: Martin Marietta Materials Inc
4123 Parklake Ave
Raleigh NC 27612

(G-10026)
MAUSER USA LLC
1229 Castle Dr (45040-9672)
P.O. Box 350 (45040-0350)
PHONE.................513 398-1300
Steve Haunert, *Manager*
EMP: 90
Web: www.mauserpackaging.com
SIC: 3412 Drums, shipping: metal
HQ: Mauser Usa, Llc
1515 W 22nd St Ste 1100
Oak Brook IL 60523

(G-10027)
MCC - MASON W&S (DH)
Also Called: Multi-Color
5510 Courseview Dr (45040-2366)
PHONE.................513 459-1100
Richard Spear, *CEO*
Randall Spear, *
Michael Henry, *
▲ EMP: 125 EST: 1999
SQ FT: 80,000
SALES (est): 52.25MM
SALES (corp-wide): 14.52B **Privately Held**
SIC: 2759 Screen printing
HQ: Multi-Color Corporation
4053 Clough Woods Dr
Batavia OH 45103
513 381-1480

(G-10028)
MCDONALDS
Also Called: McDonald's
5301 Kings Island Dr (45040-2354)
PHONE.................513 336-0820
EMP: 19 EST: 2020
SALES (est): 57.19K **Privately Held**
Web: www.mcdonalds.com
SIC: 5813 5812 5499 2038 Drinking places; Eating places; Miscellaneous food stores; Frozen specialties, nec

(G-10029)
MIDWEST BATH SALT COMPANY LLC
8251 Arbor Square Dr (45040-9509)
PHONE.................513 770-9177
Warren Watson, *Asst Sec*
EMP: 7 EST: 2012
SALES (est): 70.88K **Privately Held**
SIC: 2844 Bath salts

(G-10030)
MITSUBISHI ELC AUTO AMER INC (DH)
4773 Bethany Rd (45040-8344)
PHONE.................513 573-6614
Takeo Sasaki, *Pr*
Dave Stone, *
◆ EMP: 422 EST: 1987
SQ FT: 220,000
SALES (est): 269.33MM **Privately Held**
Web: www.meaa-mea.com
SIC: 5511 3651 3714 Automobiles, new and used; Household audio and video equipment; Motor vehicle parts and accessories
HQ: Mitsubishi Electric Us Holdings, Inc.
5900 Katella Ave Ste A
Cypress CA 90630
714 220-2500

(G-10031)
MORSE ENTERPRISES INC
Also Called: AlphaGraphics Cincinnati
6678 Tri Way Dr (45040-2605)
PHONE.................513 229-3600
Cinda Morse, *Prin*
Steven Morse, *Prin*
EMP: 7 EST: 2013
SQ FT: 3,200
SALES (est): 890.58K **Privately Held**
Web: www.alphagraphics.com
SIC: 2752 7334 7336 2732 Commercial printing, lithographic; Photocopying and duplicating services; Commercial art and graphic design; Pamphlets: printing and binding, not published on site

(G-10032)
MULTI-COLOR CORPORATION
5510 Courseview Dr (45040-2366)
PHONE.................513 459-3283
Bob Feldman, *Brnch Mgr*
EMP: 9
SALES (corp-wide): 14.52B **Privately Held**
Web: www.mcclabel.com
SIC: 2759 2679 2672 Labels and seals: printing, nsk; Labels, paper: made from purchased material; Labels (unprinted), gummed: made from purchased materials
HQ: Multi-Color Corporation
4053 Clough Woods Dr
Batavia OH 45103
513 381-1480

(G-10033)
NORITAKE CO INC
4990 Alliance Dr (45040-4516)
PHONE.................513 234-0770
Nori Kambayashi, *Brnch Mgr*
EMP: 7
Web: www.noritake-elec.com
SIC: 3291 Synthetic abrasives
HQ: Noritake Co., Inc.
15-22 Fair Lawn Ave
Fair Lawn NJ 07410
201 796-2222

(G-10034)
OAKLEY DIE & MOLD CO
Also Called: O D M
4393 Digital Way (45040-7604)
PHONE.................513 754-8500
Ernest Petrinowitsch, *CEO*
Harry Petrinowitsch, *
Peggy Braun, *
▲ EMP: 35 EST: 1948
SALES (est): 4.19MM **Privately Held**
Web: www.odm.com
SIC: 3599 3544 3545 Machine shop, jobbing and repair; Industrial molds; Tools and accessories for machine tools

(G-10035)
OMYA DISTRIBUTION LLC (DH)
4605 Duke Dr (45040-7626)
PHONE.................513 387-4600
Anthony Colak, *
EMP: 12 EST: 2010
SALES (est): 60.96MM **Privately Held**
SIC: 2819 Calcium compounds and salts, inorganic, nec
HQ: Omya Inc.
9987 Carver Rd Ste 300
Blue Ash OH 45242
513 387-4600

(G-10036)
OMYA INDUSTRIES INC (HQ)
Also Called: Omya
4605 Duke Dr (45040-7626)
PHONE.................513 387-4600
Rainer Seidler, *CEO*
Patrick Preussner, *
Athanasios Katsilometes, *
Paul Thimons, *
◆ EMP: 85 EST: 1977
SALES (est): 193.55MM **Privately Held**
SIC: 1422 Crushed and broken limestone
PA: Omya Ag
Baslerstrasse 42
Oftringen AG 4665

(G-10037)
PEPSICO
Also Called: Pepsico
5181 Natorp Blvd Ste 450 (45040-7946)
PHONE.................513 229-3046
EMP: 9 EST: 2018
SALES (est): 178.56K **Privately Held**
Web: www.pepsico.com
SIC: 2086 Carbonated soft drinks, bottled and canned

(G-10038)
PHANTOM SOUND
104 Reading Rd (45040-1634)
PHONE.................513 759-4477
Howard Mc Gurdy, *Owner*
◆ EMP: 9 EST: 2000
SALES (est): 466.15K **Privately Held**
Web: www.phantomsound.com
SIC: 3651 5731 Speaker systems; Radio, television, and electronic stores

(G-10039)
PORTION PAC INC (DH)
7325 Snider Rd (45040-9193)
PHONE.................513 398-0400
Timothy E Hoberg, *Prin*
Pete Jack, *
Jeffrey Berger, *
Leslie Boettcher, *
▼ EMP: 400 EST: 1973
SQ FT: 100,000
SALES (est): 110.71MM
SALES (corp-wide): 26.64B **Publicly Held**
Web: www.portionpac.com
SIC: 2033 2035 Catsup: packaged in cans, jars, etc.; Seasonings and sauces, except tomato and dry
HQ: Kraft Heinz Foods Company
1 Ppg Pl Ste 3400
Pittsburgh PA 15222
412 456-5700

(G-10040)
PRASCO LLC (PA)
Also Called: Prasco Laboratories
6125 Commerce Ct (45040-6723)
PHONE.................513 204-1100
Christopher H Arington, *CEO*
David Vucurevich, *Pr*
▲ EMP: 49 EST: 2002
SALES (est): 90.46MM
SALES (corp-wide): 90.46MM **Privately Held**
Web: www.prasco.com
SIC: 2834 Pharmaceutical preparations

(G-10041)
PRATT (TARGET CONTAINER) INC
4700 Duke Dr Ste 140 (45040-9507)
PHONE.................513 770-0851
EMP: 88
SALES (corp-wide): 405.29K **Privately Held**
SIC: 2653 Corrugated and solid fiber boxes
PA: Pratt (Target Container), Inc.
4004 Smmit Blvd Ne Ste 10
Atlanta GA 30319
470 704-6986

(G-10042)
PRECISION QUINCY INDS INC
4600 N Mason Montgomery Rd (45040-9176)
PHONE.................888 312-5442
Frank Ferguson, *Pr*
EMP: 300 EST: 2012
SQ FT: 315,000
SALES (est): 24.55MM **Privately Held**
Web: www.pqind.com
SIC: 3441 Fabricated structural metal

(G-10043)
PROCTER & GAMBLE COMPANY
Also Called: Procter & Gamble
8700 S Mason Montgomery Rd (45040-9760)
P.O. Box 8006 (45040-8006)
PHONE.................513 622-1000
EMP: 75
SALES (corp-wide): 82.01B **Publicly Held**
Web: us.pg.com
SIC: 2844 2676 3421 2842 Deodorants, personal; Towels, napkins, and tissue paper products; Razor blades and razors; Specialty cleaning
PA: The Procter & Gamble Company
1 Procter & Gamble Plz
Cincinnati OH 45202
513 983-1100

(G-10044)
PULSE WORLDWIDE LTD
7554 Central Parke Blvd (45040-6816)
PHONE.................513 234-7829
Julie Gutterman, *Prin*
EMP: 9 EST: 2014
SALES (est): 380K **Privately Held**
Web: www.pulseworldwide.com
SIC: 3841 Surgical and medical instruments

(G-10045)
QUEST DIAGNOSTICS INCORPORATED
Also Called: Quest Diagnostics
4690 Parkway Dr (45040-8172)
PHONE.................513 229-5500
EMP: 9
SALES (corp-wide): 9.25B **Publicly Held**
Web: www.questdiagnostics.com
SIC: 8071 2835 Testing laboratories; Diagnostic substances
PA: Quest Diagnostics Incorporated
500 Plaza Dr
Secaucus NJ 07094
973 520-2700

(G-10046)
R-K ELECTRONICS INC
7405 Industrial Row Dr (45040-1301)
PHONE.................513 204-6060
John L Keller, *Pr*
Carolyn R Keller, *Ex VP*
▲ EMP: 14 EST: 1949
SQ FT: 11,200
SALES (est): 2.29MM **Privately Held**
Web: www.rke.com

(PA)=Parent Co (HQ)=Headquarters
✪ = New Business established in last 2 years

2024 Harris Ohio Industrial Directory

Mason - Warren County (G-10047)

SIC: 3625 3672 Control equipment, electric; Wiring boards

(G-10047)
REMTEC ENGINEERING
Also Called: Mbs Acquisition
6049 Hi Tek Ct (45040-2603)
PHONE..................513 860-4299
Keith Rosnell, *CEO*
EMP: 30 **EST:** 1981
SQ FT: 25,000
SALES (est): 1.04MM **Privately Held**
Web: www.remtecautomation.com
SIC: 3569 5084 Assembly machines, non-metalworking; Robots, industrial

(G-10048)
RHINESTAHL CORPORATION (PA)
Also Called: Rhinestahl AMG
1111 Western Row Rd (45040-1365)
PHONE..................513 489-1317
Dieter Mueller, *P*
Chris Hanna, *VP*
Dave Rettenmaier, *VP*
Scott Crislip, *VP*
▲ **EMP:** 72 **EST:** 1967
SQ FT: 120,000
SALES (est): 53.91MM
SALES (corp-wide): 53.91MM **Privately Held**
Web: www.rhinestahl.com
SIC: 3523 Turf and grounds equipment

(G-10049)
RHINESTAHL CORPORATION
Also Called: Rhinestahl CTS
7687 Innovation Way (45040-9695)
PHONE..................513 229-5300
Tom Hohnston, *Brnch Mgr*
EMP: 25
SALES (corp-wide): 53.91MM **Privately Held**
Web: www.rhinestahl.com
SIC: 3544 Special dies, tools, jigs, and fixtures
PA: Rhinestahl Corporation
1111 Western Row Rd
Mason OH 45040
513 489-1317

(G-10050)
RICK ALAN CUSTOM WOODWORKS INC
4455 Bethany Rd (45040-9688)
PHONE..................513 394-6957
EMP: 6 **EST:** 2017
SALES (est): 128.79K **Privately Held**
SIC: 2431 Millwork

(G-10051)
RYSE AERO HOLDCO INC
6951 Cintas Blvd (45040-8923)
PHONE..................513 318-9907
Mick Kowitz, *CEO*
EMP: 20 **EST:** 2021
SALES (est): 1.45MM **Privately Held**
SIC: 3812 Aircraft/aerospace flight instruments and guidance systems

(G-10052)
S&M TRUCKING LLC
5700 Gateway Ste 400 (45040-1890)
PHONE..................661 310-2585
EMP: 12 **EST:** 2014
SQ FT: 5,000
SALES (est): 1.02MM **Privately Held**
SIC: 4212 3537 4424 Local trucking, without storage; Trucks: freight, baggage, etc.: industrial, except mining; Intercoastal transportation, freight

(G-10053)
SALUS NORTH AMERICA INC
Also Called: Salus Enterprises North Amer
4700 Duke Dr Ste 200 (45040-9507)
PHONE..................888 387-2587
Shen Owyang, *Pr*
Janine M Kinney, *Sec*
EMP: 13 **EST:** 2000
SALES (est): 5.06MM **Privately Held**
Web: shop.salusinc.com
SIC: 3822 Thermostats and other environmental sensors
HQ: Computime Group Limited
6/F Hong Kong Science Park Bldg 20e Ph 3
Sha Tin NT

(G-10054)
SARA WOOD PHARMACEUTICALS LLC
Also Called: Sara Wood Pharmaceuticals
4518 Margaret Ct (45040-2922)
PHONE..................513 833-5502
Mina Pathel, *Prin*
David Schultenover, *Ofcr*
Mina Pathel, *Ofcr*
Eileen Rogers, *Ofcr*
Thomas Docherty, *COO*
EMP: 8 **EST:** 2016
SALES (est): 427.47K **Privately Held**
SIC: 2834 Solutions, pharmaceutical

(G-10055)
SIEMENS AG
6693 Summer Field Dr (45040-7332)
PHONE..................513 576-2451
Sivarama Nalluri, *Ofcr*
EMP: 32 **EST:** 2018
SALES (est): 196.02K **Privately Held**
Web: www.siemens.com
SIC: 3661 Telephones and telephone apparatus

(G-10056)
SIGHTGAIN INC
Also Called: Sightgain
5325 Deerfield Blvd (45040-2511)
PHONE..................202 494-9317
Christian Sorensen, *CEO*
EMP: 10 **EST:** 2019
SALES (est): 664.96K **Privately Held**
Web: www.sightgain.com
SIC: 7372 7373 7374 7375 Application computer software; Computer systems analysis and design; Computer processing services; On-line data base information retrieval

(G-10057)
SOUNDTRACE INC
408 4th Ave (45040-1508)
PHONE..................513 278-5288
Matthew Reinhold, *Prin*
EMP: 7 **EST:** 2021
SALES (est): 398.07K **Privately Held**
SIC: 3842 Hearing aids

(G-10058)
SPEAR INC
Also Called: Spear Application Systems
5510 Courseview Dr (45040-2385)
PHONE..................513 459-1100
▲ **EMP:** 80
Web: www.spearsystem.com
SIC: 2759 Screen printing

(G-10059)
SPECIAL MACHINED COMPONENTS
7626 Easy St (45040-9424)
PHONE..................513 459-1113

Larry Johnson, *Owner*
EMP: 9 **EST:** 1989
SQ FT: 12,000
SALES (est): 583.39K **Privately Held**
SIC: 3599 Machine shop, jobbing and repair

(G-10060)
SRI HEALTHCARE LLC
7086 Industrial Row Dr (45040-1363)
PHONE..................513 398-6406
EMP: 8 **EST:** 1990
SALES (est): 118.46K **Privately Held**
Web: www.sri-healthcare.com
SIC: 3841 Surgical and medical instruments

(G-10061)
SUPERIOR LABEL SYSTEMS INC (DH)
Also Called: Superior Machine Systems
7500 Industrial Row Dr (45040-1307)
PHONE..................513 336-0825
Kenneth Kidd, *Ch Bd*
Thomas Braig, *
EMP: 275 **EST:** 1970
SQ FT: 30,000
SALES (est): 52.38MM
SALES (corp-wide): 14.52B **Privately Held**
SIC: 3565 2759 3993 3577 Labeling machines, industrial; Flexographic printing; Signs and advertising specialties; Computer peripheral equipment, nec
HQ: W/S Packaging Group, Inc.
2571 S Hemlock Rd
Green Bay WI 54229
800 818-5481

(G-10062)
TELEDYNE INSTRUMENTS INC
Also Called: Teledyne Leeman Labs
4736 Socialville Foster Rd (45040-8265)
PHONE..................603 886-8400
Peter Brown, *Mgr*
EMP: 65
SALES (corp-wide): 5.64B **Publicly Held**
Web: www.teledyne.com
SIC: 3826 Spectrometers
HQ: Teledyne Instruments, Inc.
16830 Chestnut St
City Of Industry CA 91748
626 934-1500

(G-10063)
TELEDYNE INSTRUMENTS INC
Also Called: Teledyne Tekmar
4736 Socialville Foster Rd (45040-8265)
PHONE..................513 229-7000
EMP: 28
SALES (corp-wide): 5.64B **Publicly Held**
Web: www.teledynelabs.com
SIC: 5049 3826 3829 3821 Laboratory equipment, except medical or dental; Analytical instruments; Measuring and controlling devices, nec; Laboratory apparatus and furniture
HQ: Teledyne Instruments, Inc.
16830 Chestnut St
City Of Industry CA 91748
626 934-1500

(G-10064)
TELEDYNE TEKMAR COMPANY (DH)
Also Called: Tekmar-Dohrmann
4736 Socialville Foster Rd (45040-8265)
PHONE..................513 229-7000
Robert Mehrabian, *Ch Bd*
EMP: 25 **EST:** 1972
SQ FT: 40,000
SALES (est): 36.27MM
SALES (corp-wide): 5.64B **Publicly Held**
Web: www.teledynelabs.com

SIC: 5049 3826 3829 3821 Laboratory equipment, except medical or dental; Analytical instruments; Measuring and controlling devices, nec; Laboratory apparatus and furniture
HQ: Teledyne Instruments, Inc.
16830 Chestnut St
City Of Industry CA 91748
626 934-1500

(G-10065)
THE ARMOR GROUP INC (PA)
4600 N Mason Montgomery Rd (45040-9176)
PHONE..................513 923-5260
▲ **EMP:** 102 **EST:** 1927
SALES (est): 365.25MM **Privately Held**
Web: www.armorcontract.com
SIC: 3441 3446 3444 3443 Fabricated structural metal; Architectural metalwork; Sheet metalwork; Fabricated plate work (boiler shop)

(G-10066)
TO SCALE SOFTWARE LLC
Also Called: Stack Constructyion Technology
6398 Thornberry Ct (45040-7816)
PHONE..................513 253-0053
Phillip Ogilby, *Managing Member*
Jane Baysore, *
EMP: 35 **EST:** 2007
SALES (est): 4.1MM **Privately Held**
Web: www.cloudtakeoff.com
SIC: 7372 Prepackaged software

(G-10067)
VELOCITY CONCEPT DEV GROUP LLC (PA)
4393 Digital Way (45040-7604)
PHONE..................513 204-2100
EMP: 6 **EST:** 2012
SALES (est): 6.17MM
SALES (corp-wide): 6.17MM **Privately Held**
Web: www.velocityfast.com
SIC: 3999 Atomizers, toiletry

(G-10068)
VNDLY LLC
4900 Parkway Dr Ste 125 (45040-8430)
PHONE..................513 572-2500
Shashank Saxena, *CEO*
EMP: 50 **EST:** 2017
SQ FT: 5,483
SALES (est): 11.56MM **Publicly Held**
Web: www.workday.com
SIC: 7372 7374 Application computer software; Data processing service
PA: Workday, Inc.
6110 Stoneridge Mall Rd
Pleasanton CA 94588

(G-10069)
W/S PACKAGING GROUP INC
7400 Industrial Row Dr (45040-1302)
PHONE..................513 459-8800
Klaus Kok, *Brnch Mgr*
EMP: 90
SALES (corp-wide): 14.52B **Privately Held**
SIC: 2759 Labels and seals: printing, nsk
HQ: W/S Packaging Group, Inc.
2571 S Hemlock Rd
Green Bay WI 54229
800 818-5481

(G-10070)
WAYLENS INC
108 W Main St Ste 1 (45040-1700)
PHONE..................513 445-8684
EMP: 6 **EST:** 2017
SALES (est): 30.77K **Privately Held**

Web: shop.waylens.com
SIC: 7372 Prepackaged software

(G-10071)
WITT INDUSTRIES INC (HQ)
Also Called: Witt Products
4600 N Mason Montgomery Rd
(45040-9176)
PHONE..............................513 871-5700
TOLL FREE: 800
Tim Harris, Pr
▼ EMP: 100 EST: 1974
SQ FT: 71,500
SALES (est): 24.72MM **Privately Held**
Web: www.witt.com
SIC: 3479 3469 3441 3412 Galvanizing of iron, steel, or end-formed products; Garbage cans, stamped and pressed metal; Fabricated structural metal; Metal barrels, drums, and pails
PA: The Armor Group, Inc.
4600 N Masn Montgomery Rd
Mason OH 45040

Massillon
Stark County

(G-10072)
3-D SERVICE LTD (PA)
Also Called: Magnetech
800 Nave Rd Se (44646-9476)
PHONE..............................330 830-3500
Bernie Dewees, Pr
▲ EMP: 120 EST: 2002
SQ FT: 85,000
SALES (est): 4.3MM
SALES (corp-wide): 4.3MM **Privately Held**
Web: www.magnetech.com
SIC: 7694 7699 Electric motor repair; Industrial equipment services

(G-10073)
A & R MACHINE CO INC
13212 Vega St Sw (44647-9200)
PHONE..............................330 832-4631
Rollin Shriner, Pr
Patsy Shriner, VP
EMP: 6 EST: 1986
SQ FT: 10,000
SALES (est): 591.27K **Privately Held**
SIC: 3599 Custom machinery

(G-10074)
A R E LOGISTICS LLC
400 Nave Rd Se (44646-8898)
PHONE..............................330 327-7315
EMP: 6 EST: 2018
SALES (est): 542.72K **Privately Held**
SIC: 2821 Plastics materials and resins

(G-10075)
ABP INDUCTION LLC (PA)
Also Called: A B P Induction
607 1st St Sw (44646-6729)
PHONE..............................262 878-6390
Paul Decker, Managing Member*
Frank Possinger, *
◆ EMP: 15 EST: 2005
SALES (est): 9.86MM **Privately Held**
Web: www.abpinduction.com
SIC: 3567 Industrial furnaces and ovens

(G-10076)
ARE INC
400 Nave Rd Sw (44646)
P.O. Box 1100 (44648-1100)
PHONE..............................330 830-7800
EMP: 518

SIC: 3713 3714 3792 5013 Truck bodies and parts; Motor vehicle body components and frame; Travel trailers and campers; Motor vehicle supplies and new parts

(G-10077)
AVIENT CORPORATION
1675 Navarre Rd Se (44646-9607)
PHONE..............................330 834-3812
Steve Strover, Mgr
EMP: 11
Web: www.avient.com
SIC: 2821 Plastics materials and resins
PA: Avient Corporation
33587 Walker Rd
Avon Lake OH 44012

(G-10078)
BATES PRINTING INC
150 23rd St Se (44646-7046)
PHONE..............................330 833-5830
Dan Bates, Pr
John Bates, Pr
Daniel Bates, VP
EMP: 10 EST: 1913
SQ FT: 3,000
SALES (est): 726.19K **Privately Held**
Web: www.batesprinting.com
SIC: 2752 2759 Offset printing; Commercial printing, nec

(G-10079)
BRINKLEY TECHNOLOGY GROUP LLC
Also Called: Hercules Engine
2770 Erie St S (44646-7943)
PHONE..............................330 830-2498
Douglas Brinkley, Pr
EMP: 17 EST: 2015
SQ FT: 34,000
SALES (est): 2.41MM **Privately Held**
Web: www.herculesmanufacturing.com
SIC: 3599 3519 3621 3694 Oil filters, internal combustion engine, except auto; Governors, diesel engine; Storage battery chargers, motor and engine generator type; Distributors, motor vehicle engine

(G-10080)
C-N-D INDUSTRIES INC
Also Called: Cnd Machine
359 State Rd Nw (44647-4269)
PHONE..............................330 478-8811
Clyde Shetler, Pr
Don Rossbach, *
EMP: 40 EST: 1989
SQ FT: 28,000
SALES (est): 2.36MM **Privately Held**
SIC: 3441 3599 7692 3444 Fabricated structural metal; Machine shop, jobbing and repair; Welding repair; Sheet metalwork

(G-10081)
CANTON CARNIVAL WHEELS INC
2407 Tanglewood Dr Ne (44646-5011)
PHONE..............................330 837-3878
Richard K Mautz, Prin
EMP: 6 EST: 2009
SALES (est): 89.74K **Privately Held**
Web: www.cantoncarnivalofwheels.com
SIC: 3312 Blast furnaces and steel mills

(G-10082)
CARBONLESS ON DEMANDCOM LLC
332 Erie St S (44646-6740)
PHONE..............................330 837-8611
David Mathis, Owner
EMP: 19 EST: 1989
SALES (est): 1.63MM **Privately Held**

Web: www.carbonlessondemand.com
SIC: 2752 Offset printing

(G-10083)
CASE FARMS LLC
Also Called: Massillon Feed Mill
4001 Millennium Blvd Se (44646-9606)
PHONE..............................330 832-0030
Thomas R Shelton, Brnch Mgr
EMP: 50
Web: www.casefarms.com
SIC: 2015 Poultry slaughtering and processing
PA: Case Farms, L.L.C.
385 Pilch Rd
Troutman NC 28166

(G-10084)
CHARTER NEXT GENERATION INC
8333 Navarre Rd Se (44646-9652)
PHONE..............................330 830-6030
Kathy Bolhous, CEO
EMP: 128
SALES (corp-wide): 1.5B **Privately Held**
Web: www.cnginc.com
SIC: 2671 Plastic film, coated or laminated for packaging
PA: Charter Next Generation, Inc.
300 N La Salle Dr # 1575
Chicago IL 60654
608 868-5757

(G-10085)
COLD HEADED FAS ASSEMBLIES INC
1875 Harsh Ave Se Ste 3 (44646-7182)
P.O. Box 547 (44648-0547)
PHONE..............................330 833-0800
Oscar Lee, Pr
Gwen Hemperly, Sec
▲ EMP: 12 EST: 1990
SQ FT: 30,000
SALES (est): 913.72K **Privately Held**
SIC: 3452 3599 Bolts, metal; Machine shop, jobbing and repair

(G-10086)
CORRCHOICE CINCINNATI
777 3rd St Nw (44647-4203)
PHONE..............................330 833-2884
EMP: 7 EST: 2019
SALES (est): 287.4K **Privately Held**
Web: www.greif.com
SIC: 2621 Wrapping and packaging papers

(G-10087)
CRACK CORN LTD
7993 Hills And Dales Rd Ne (44646)
PHONE..............................440 467-0108
James Alay, Managing Member
EMP: 10 EST: 2019
SALES (est): 536.94K **Privately Held**
SIC: 2096 Potato chips and similar snacks

(G-10088)
CROWN CORK & SEAL USA INC
700 16th St Se (44646-7152)
PHONE..............................330 833-1011
Bernard Baumann, Mgr
EMP: 300
SALES (corp-wide): 12.01B **Publicly Held**
Web: www.crowncork.com
SIC: 3411 Aluminum cans
HQ: Crown Cork & Seal Usa, Inc.
770 Township Line Rd
Yardley PA 19067
215 698-5100

(G-10089)
DAVID A AND MARY A MATHIS
Also Called: D & M Printing
332 Erie St S (44646-6740)
PHONE..............................330 837-8611
David A Mathis, Owner
EMP: 7 EST: 1993
SALES (est): 326.22K **Privately Held**
SIC: 2752 Offset printing

(G-10090)
DOTCENTRAL LLC
1650 Deerford Ave Sw (44647-9732)
PHONE..............................330 809-0112
Daniel Swartz, Managing Member
EMP: 10 EST: 2017
SALES (est): 205.83K **Privately Held**
SIC: 2741 Internet publishing and broadcasting

(G-10091)
DW HERCULES LLC
Also Called: Hercules Engine Components
2770 Erie St S (44646-7943)
P.O. Box 451 (44648-0451)
PHONE..............................330 830-2498
Doug Brinkley, Pr
▲ EMP: 19 EST: 1999
SQ FT: 22,000
SALES (est): 1.1MM **Privately Held**
Web: dwhercules.openfos.com
SIC: 3519 5999 Parts and accessories, internal combustion engines; Engine and motor equipment and supplies

(G-10092)
E-B DISPLAY COMPANY INC
1369 Sanders Ave Sw (44647-7632)
P.O. Box 650 (44648-0650)
PHONE..............................330 833-4101
▲ EMP: 110 EST: 1952
SALES (est): 17.14MM
SALES (corp-wide): 17.14MM **Privately Held**
Web: www.ebdisplay.com
SIC: 3993 2542 Signs, not made in custom sign painting shops; Office and store showcases and display fixtures
HQ: Rotolo Industries, Inc.
1369 Sanders Ave Sw
Massillon OH

(G-10093)
E-B WIRE WORKS INC
1350 Sanders Ave Sw (44647-7631)
P.O. Box 650 (44648-0650)
PHONE..............................330 833-4101
▲ EMP: 71 EST: 1989
SALES (est): 9.36MM **Privately Held**
Web: www.ebdisplay.com
SIC: 3399 Tacks, nonferrous metal or wire

(G-10094)
ENGRAVERS GALLERY & SIGN CO
10 Lincoln Way E (44646-6632)
P.O. Box 709 (44648-0709)
PHONE..............................330 830-1271
Bonnie Fall, Owner
EMP: 6 EST: 1987
SQ FT: 1,600
SALES (est): 452.83K **Privately Held**
Web: nilboglin.wix.com
SIC: 3993 7389 Letters for signs, metal; Engraving service

(G-10095)
FANTASIA ENTERPRISES LLC
625 Erie St S (44646-6711)
PHONE..............................330 400-8741
EMP: 10

Massillon - Stark County (G-10096)

SALES (corp-wide): 1.74MM **Privately Held**
Web: fantasia-mining.myshopify.com
SIC: **1041** Underground gold mining
PA: Fantasia Enterprises, Llc
3412 S Smith Rd
Fairlawn OH 44333
330 665-9959

(G-10096)
FIBERCORR MILLS LLC
670 17th St Nw (44647-5343)
P.O. Box 453 (44648-0453)
PHONE.................................330 837-5151
▲ EMP: 77
SIC: **2679** 2631 Paper products, converted, nec; Paperboard mills

(G-10097)
FRESH MARK INC (PA)
Also Called: Superior's Brand Meats
1888 Southway St Sw (44646-9429)
PHONE.................................330 832-7491
Neil Genshaft, *Ch*
Tim Cranor, *
Tom Cicarella, *
David Cochenour, *
◆ EMP: 500 EST: 1932
SQ FT: 80,000
SALES (est): 1.38B
SALES (corp-wide): 1.38B **Privately Held**
Web: www.freshmark.com
SIC: **2013** 5147 2011 Prepared beef products, from purchased beef; Meats and meat products; Meat packing plants

(G-10098)
GAMEDAY VISION
1147 Oberlin Ave Sw (44647-7665)
PHONE.................................330 830-4550
Krista Simcic, *Pr*
EMP: 10 EST: 2010
SALES (est): 678.62K **Privately Held**
Web: www.gamedayvision.com
SIC: **3577** Printers and plotters

(G-10099)
GARY LAWRENCE ENTERPRISES INC
Also Called: Lawrence Machine
21 Charles Ave Sw (44646-6621)
P.O. Box 727 (44648-0727)
PHONE.................................330 833-7181
Gary Lawrence, *Pr*
Christopher Lawrence, *VP*
Eric Lawrence, *Treas*
EMP: 8 EST: 1976
SQ FT: 15,000
SALES (est): 486.86K **Privately Held**
Web: www.lawrencemachine.com
SIC: **3993** 5199 Signs and advertising specialties; Advertising specialties

(G-10100)
GERSTENSLAGER CONSTRUCTION
Also Called: Gerstenslager Hardwood Pdts
343 16th St Se (44646-7177)
PHONE.................................330 832-3604
Mike Gerstenslager, *Owner*
Myron F Gerstenslager Junior, *Owner*
EMP: 6 EST: 1958
SQ FT: 12,000
SALES (est): 330K **Privately Held**
Web: www.gerstenslagerhardwood.com
SIC: **2431** Millwork

(G-10101)
GREEN MEADOWS PAPER COMPANY
670 17th St Nw (44647-5343)
PHONE.................................330 837-5151
Scott Welch, *Prin*
Jay Frem, *
EMP: 65 EST: 2021
SALES (est): 10.8MM **Privately Held**
Web: www.gmpaperco.com
SIC: **2679** Paper products, converted, nec

(G-10102)
GREIF INC
787 Warmington Rd Se (44646-8830)
P.O. Box 675 (44648-0675)
PHONE.................................330 879-2936
Matt Sullivan, *Mgr*
EMP: 52
SALES (corp-wide): 5.22B **Publicly Held**
Web: www.greif.com
SIC: **2655** Fiber cans, drums, and similar products
PA: Greif, Inc.
425 Winter Rd
Delaware OH 43015
740 549-6000

(G-10103)
GSDI SPECIALTY DISPERSIONS INC
Also Called: Gsdi
1675 Navarre Rd Se (44646)
PHONE.................................330 848-9200
▲ EMP: 20 EST: 1980
SALES (est): 10.05MM **Publicly Held**
SIC: **2816** Color pigments
PA: Avient Corporation
33587 Walker Rd
Avon Lake OH 44012

(G-10104)
H P E INC (PA)
2025 Harsh Ave Se (44646-7127)
P.O. Box 528 (44648-0528)
PHONE.................................330 833-3161
Robert Boley, *Pr*
Robert N Boley, *Pr*
Sandra Boley, *Sec*
EMP: 7 EST: 1979
SQ FT: 12,000
SALES (est): 1.25MM
SALES (corp-wide): 1.25MM **Privately Held**
Web: www.hpe--inc.com
SIC: **3533** 3569 3547 3494 Oil and gas field machinery; Gas separators (machinery); Rolling mill machinery; Valves and pipe fittings, nec

(G-10105)
HEINZ FOREIGN INVESTMENT CO
1301 Oberlin Ave Sw (44647-7669)
P.O. Box 15222 (15237-0222)
PHONE.................................330 837-8331
EMP: 12 EST: 2015
SALES (est): 714.77K
SALES (corp-wide): 26.64B **Publicly Held**
Web: www.kraftheinzcompany.com
SIC: **2037** Frozen fruits and vegetables
PA: The Heinz Kraft Company
1 Ppg Pl
Pittsburgh PA 15222
412 456-5700

(G-10106)
HENDRICKS VACUUM FORMING INC
Also Called: Hvfi
3500 17th St Sw (44647-9700)
PHONE.................................330 837-2040
Robin Hendricks, *Pr*
EMP: 17 EST: 1978
SQ FT: 40,000
SALES (est): 2.29MM **Privately Held**
Web: www.hvfi.com
SIC: **3993** Electric signs

(G-10107)
HJ HEINZ COMPANY LP (DH)
Also Called: Heinz Frozen Foods
1301 Oberlin Ave Sw (44647-7669)
PHONE.................................330 837-8331
Allan Briggs, *Mng Pt*
Mike Parks, *Mgr*
Rick Uriguem, *Manager*
▲ EMP: 56 EST: 2000
SALES (est): 106.05MM
SALES (corp-wide): 26.64B **Publicly Held**
SIC: **2037** Frozen fruits and vegetables
HQ: Kraft Heinz Foods Company
1 Ppg Pl Ste 3400
Pittsburgh PA 15222
412 456-5700

(G-10108)
HUTH READY MIX & SUPPLY CO
Also Called: Huth Ready-Mix & Supply Co
501 5th St Sw (44647-5473)
P.O. Box 524 (44648-0524)
PHONE.................................330 833-4191
Roger L Huth, *Pr*
Alice H Huth, *Sec*
EMP: 38 EST: 1880
SQ FT: 3,000
SALES (est): 791.28K **Privately Held**
SIC: **3273** 5211 Ready-mixed concrete; Brick

(G-10109)
HYDRO-DYNE INC
225 Wetmore Ave Se (44646-6788)
P.O. Box 318 (44648-0318)
PHONE.................................330 832-5076
Rose Ann Dare, *Pr*
Lynn Neel, *
Sherri Mcmillen, *Mgr*
Ken Yeaman, *
Jean Holiday, *
▲ EMP: 50 EST: 1967
SQ FT: 130,000
SALES (est): 1.46MM **Privately Held**
Web: www.hydrodyneinc.com
SIC: **3585** 8711 Evaporative condensers, heat transfer equipment; Engineering services

(G-10110)
HYDRO-THRIFT CORPORATION
Also Called: Hydrothrift
1301 Sanders Ave Sw (44647-7632)
P.O. Box 1037 (44648-1037)
PHONE.................................330 837-5141
T K Heston, *Pr*
Paul Heston, *Treas*
▼ EMP: 23 EST: 1973
SQ FT: 27,000
SALES (est): 4.92MM **Privately Held**
Web: www.hydrothrift.com
SIC: **3443** 3585 Heat exchangers, condensers, and components; Air conditioning equipment, complete

(G-10111)
IDENTITEK SYSTEMS INC
Also Called: Adams Signs
1100 Industrial Ave Sw (44647-7608)
P.O. Box 347 (44648-0347)
PHONE.................................330 832-9844
Joseph Pugliese, *Pr*
EMP: 53 EST: 1943
SQ FT: 70,000
SALES (est): 9.74MM **Privately Held**
Web: www.adamsigns.com
SIC: **1799** 3993 Sign installation and maintenance; Signs and advertising specialties

(G-10112)
J L R PRODUCTS INC
1212 Oberlin Ave Sw (44647-7668)
PHONE.................................330 832-9557
Matthew Radocaj, *Pr*
EMP: 16 EST: 1993
SALES (est): 443.75K **Privately Held**
Web: www.jlrproducts.com
SIC: **3429** 3568 Pulleys, metal; Pulleys, power transmission

(G-10113)
JACODAR INC
1212 Oberlin Ave Sw (44647-7668)
PHONE.................................330 832-9557
Matthew Radocaj, *Pr*
EMP: 10 EST: 1983
SQ FT: 24,000
SALES (est): 1.39MM
SALES (corp-wide): 358.52MM **Privately Held**
Web: www.jlrproducts.com
SIC: **3452** Bolts, metal
PA: Ojim, Inc.
1212 Oberlin Ave Sw
Massillon OH 44647
330 832-9557

(G-10114)
KARL KUEMMERLING INC
129 Edgewater Ave Nw (44646-3321)
EMP: 18
SIC: **5261** 5083 5699 3524 Lawn and garden equipment; Lawn and garden machinery and equipment; Work clothing; Lawn and garden equipment

(G-10115)
KENDEL WELDING & FABRICATION
1700 Navarre Rd Se (44646)
PHONE.................................330 834-2429
Bettina M Kendel, *Pr*
Donald R Kendel, *VP*
EMP: 8 EST: 1999
SALES (est): 497.09K **Privately Held**
SIC: **7692** Welding repair

(G-10116)
KENMORE CONSTRUCTION CO INC
Also Called: American Sand & Gravel Div
9500 Forty Corners Rd Nw (44647-9309)
PHONE.................................330 832-8888
Chris Scala, *Mgr*
EMP: 75
SALES (corp-wide): 44.06MM **Privately Held**
Web: www.kenmorecompanies.com
SIC: **1611** 1442 General contractor, highway and street construction; Construction sand and gravel
PA: Kenmore Construction Co., Inc.
700 Home Ave
Akron OH 44310
330 762-8936

(G-10117)
KING MACHINE AND TOOL CO
1237 Sanders Ave Sw (44647-7684)
PHONE.................................330 833-7217
William Kapper, *Pr*
Tracy Kapper, *VP*
Kelly Kapper, *Treas*
Judith A Kapper, *Sec*
▲ EMP: 18 EST: 1949
SQ FT: 22,000
SALES (est): 4.16MM **Privately Held**
Web: www.kmtco.com
SIC: **3599** Machine shop, jobbing and repair

GEOGRAPHIC SECTION
Massillon - Stark County (G-10140)

(G-10118)
KRAFT HEINZ COMPANY
Also Called: Kraft Heinz Company
1301 Oberlin Ave Sw (44647-7669)
PHONE..................330 837-8331
Ken Stiffler, *Manager*
EMP: 700
SQ FT: 1,196
SALES (corp-wide): 26.64B **Publicly Held**
Web: www.kraftheinzcompany.com
SIC: 2033 2099 Tomato sauce: packaged in cans, jars, etc.; Food preparations, nec
PA: The Heinz Kraft Company
1 Ppg Pl
Pittsburgh PA 15222
412 456-5700

(G-10119)
LAND OLAKES INC
Also Called: Land O'Lakes
8485 Navarre Rd Sw (44646-8814)
PHONE..................330 879-2158
Gary Hauenstin, *Mgr*
EMP: 24
SALES (corp-wide): 2.89B **Privately Held**
Web: www.landolakesinc.com
SIC: 2048 5191 2047 Livestock feeds; Animal feeds; Dog and cat food
PA: Land O'lakes, Inc.
4001 Lexington Ave N
Arden Hills MN 55112
651 375-2222

(G-10120)
LLC RING MASTERS
240 6th St Nw (44647-5413)
PHONE..................330 832-1511
EMP: 26 **EST:** 2003
SQ FT: 51,000
SALES (est): 5.73MM **Privately Held**
Web: www.ring-masters.net
SIC: 3316 Cold finishing of steel shapes

(G-10121)
MAGNETECH INDUSTRIAL SVCS INC (DH)
Also Called: Magnetech Industrial Services
800 Nave Rd Se (44646-9476)
PHONE..................330 830-3500
Michael P Moore, *Pr*
William Wisniewieski, *
James I Depew, *
▲ **EMP:** 80 **EST:** 2000
SALES (est): 74MM **Publicly Held**
Web: www.magnetech.com
SIC: 7694 Electric motor repair
HQ: les Subsidiary Holdings, Inc
5433 Westheimer Rd # 500
Houston TX 77056
713 860-1500

(G-10122)
MASSILLON MACHINE & DIE INC
3536 17th St Sw (44647-9211)
PHONE..................330 833-8913
Gary Burkholder, *Pr*
EMP: 9 **EST:** 2004
SQ FT: 7,000
SALES (est): 922.96K **Privately Held**
SIC: 3599 1799 Custom machinery; Welding on site

(G-10123)
MASSILLON METAPHYSICS
912 Amherst Rd Ne (44646-4568)
P.O. Box 1305 (44648-1305)
PHONE..................330 837-1653
Lena Fain, *Prin*
EMP: 8 **EST:** 2011
SALES (est): 116.56K **Privately Held**
Web: www.massillonmuseum.org

SIC: 1499 Gemstone and industrial diamond mining

(G-10124)
MATCH MOLD & MACHINE INC
1100 Nova Dr Se (44646-8867)
PHONE..................330 830-5503
Timothy V Lidderdale, *Pr*
Thomas Knipfer, *
Ruth Lidderdale, *
EMP: 14 **EST:** 1981
SALES (est): 331.51K **Privately Held**
SIC: 3544 Special dies and tools

(G-10125)
MATRIX SYS AUTO FINISHES LLC
600 Nova Dr Se (44646-8884)
PHONE..................248 668-8135
W Kent Gardner, *Pr*
Sean Hook, *Director of Information*
EMP: 412 **EST:** 1983
SQ FT: 26,000
SALES (est): 5.94MM
SALES (corp-wide): 60.04MM **Privately Held**
Web: www.matrixsystem.com
SIC: 5198 2851 Paints; Paints and allied products
PA: Quest Specialty Chemicals, Inc.
225 Sven Farms Dr Ste 204
Charleston SC 29492
800 966-7580

(G-10126)
MEL WACKER SIGNS INC
Also Called: Wacker Sign
13076 Barrs St Sw (44647-9746)
PHONE..................330 832-1726
TOLL FREE: 800
Bonnie Maier, *Pr*
Melville Maier, *VP*
EMP: 6 **EST:** 1975
SALES (est): 380.85K **Privately Held**
Web: www.wackersigns.com
SIC: 3993 1799 5999 Signs, not made in custom sign painting shops; Sign installation and maintenance; Flags

(G-10127)
MIDWESTERN INDUSTRIES INC (PA)
915 Oberlin Ave Sw (44647-7661)
P.O. Box 810 (44648-0810)
PHONE..................330 837-4203
David Weaver, *VP*
Gary A Cunningham, *
Harold J Painter, *
William J Crone, *
Laverne J Riesbeck, *
▼ **EMP:** 92 **EST:** 1961
SQ FT: 148,000
SALES (est): 18.84MM
SALES (corp-wide): 18.84MM **Privately Held**
Web: www.midwesternind.com
SIC: 3559 3496 3564 3443 Screening equipment, electric; Mesh, made from purchased wire; Blowers and fans; Fabricated plate work (boiler shop)

(G-10128)
MILLS CUSTOM COATINGS
2976 Kipling Ave Nw (44646-2418)
PHONE..................330 280-0633
Joshua Mills, *Prin*
EMP: 6 **EST:** 2016
SALES (est): 195.92K **Privately Held**
SIC: 3479 Metal coating and allied services

(G-10129)
MISCOR GROUP LTD
800 Nave Rd Se (44646-9476)
PHONE..................330 830-3500
▲ **EMP:** 269
SIC: 7629 7539 3519 Electrical equipment repair services; Electrical services; Diesel, semi-diesel, or duel-fuel engines, including marine

(G-10130)
MPI LOGISTICS AND SERVICE INC
Also Called: M P I Logistics
1414 Industrial Ave Sw (44647-7663)
PHONE..................330 832-5309
Richard D Miller, *Pr*
Judith A Miller, *VP*
EMP: 21 **EST:** 1980
SQ FT: 16,500
SALES (est): 4.93MM **Privately Held**
Web: www.martinpallet.com
SIC: 7699 2448 4213 7549 Pallet repair; Pallets, wood; Trucking, except local; Automotive maintenance services

(G-10131)
NFM/WELDING ENGINEERS INC (PA)
Also Called: N F M
577 Oberlin Ave Sw (44647-7820)
PHONE..................330 837-3868
Philip A Roberson, *Pr*
Ronald Pribich, *
Scott Swallen, *
Paul Roberson, *
John Roberson, *
▲ **EMP:** 140 **EST:** 1985
SQ FT: 150,000
SALES (est): 48.86MM
SALES (corp-wide): 48.86MM **Privately Held**
Web: www.nfm.net
SIC: 3599 Machine shop, jobbing and repair

(G-10132)
OMNI USA INC
1100 Nova Dr Se (44646-8867)
PHONE..................330 830-5500
Timothy V Lidderdale, *Pr*
Theodore Buss, *
EMP: 48 **EST:** 1982
SALES (est): 985.25K **Privately Held**
SIC: 3363 Aluminum die-castings

(G-10133)
OSTER SAND AND GRAVEL INC
Also Called: Oster Enterprises
1955 Riverside Dr Nw (44647-9300)
PHONE..................330 833-2649
Bruce Bickel, *Mgr*
EMP: 8
SALES (corp-wide): 2.5MM **Privately Held**
Web: www.ostersandandgravelnorthcantonoh.com
SIC: 1442 1422 Construction sand and gravel; Crushed and broken limestone
PA: Oster Sand And Gravel, Inc.
5947 Whipple Ave Nw
Canton OH 44720
330 494-5372

(G-10134)
PLASTIC FORMING COMPANY INC
201 Vista Ave Se (44646-7938)
PHONE..................330 830-5167
Mike Warth, *Mgr*
EMP: 25
SALES (corp-wide): 9.86MM **Privately Held**
Web: www.pfccases.com

SIC: 3089 3086 3161 Blow molded finished plastics products, nec; Plastics foam products; Luggage
PA: The Plastic Forming Company Inc
20 S Bradley Rd
Woodbridge CT 06525
203 397-1338

(G-10135)
POHLMAN PRECISION LLC
Also Called: Pohlman
999 Oberlin Ave Sw (44647-7661)
PHONE..................636 537-1909
Mark Winham, *Contrlr*
EMP: 40 **EST:** 2015
SALES (est): 3.52MM **Privately Held**
SIC: 3451 Screw machine products

(G-10136)
PREMIER BUILDING SOLUTIONS LLC (PA)
480 Nova Dr Se (44646-9597)
PHONE..................330 244-2907
▲ **EMP:** 35 **EST:** 2006
SALES (est): 22.87MM **Privately Held**
Web: www.premierbuildingsolutions.net
SIC: 2891 Adhesives

(G-10137)
R W SCREW PRODUCTS INC
999 Oberlin Ave Sw (44647-7698)
P.O. Box 310 (44648-0310)
PHONE..................330 837-9211
James Woolley, *CEO*
Larry Longworth, *Pr*
EMP: 240 **EST:** 1948
SQ FT: 180,000
SALES (est): 25.76MM **Privately Held**
Web: www.rwscrew.com
SIC: 3451 Screw machine products

(G-10138)
RAH INVESTMENT HOLDING INC
Also Called: Electra - Cord, Inc.
1320 Sanders Ave Sw (44647-7631)
P.O. Box 1197 (44648-1197)
PHONE..................330 832-8124
Randall A Hutsell, *Pr*
▲ **EMP:** 75 **EST:** 1980
SQ FT: 33,000
SALES (est): 14.75MM
SALES (corp-wide): 12.55B **Publicly Held**
Web: www.electracord.net
SIC: 3699 3357 Extension cords; Nonferrous wiredrawing and insulating
HQ: Tpc Wire & Cable Corp.
9600 Valley View Rd
Macedonia OH 44056

(G-10139)
RETAIN LOYALTY LLC
1250 Sanders Ave Sw (44647-7683)
P.O. Box 6088 (44706-0088)
PHONE..................330 830-0839
Nancy Schmidt, *Pt*
Karl Schmidt, *Pt*
EMP: 7 **EST:** 1995
SALES (est): 952.61K **Privately Held**
Web: www.momentsusa.com
SIC: 3993 7313 7331 3555 Signs and advertising specialties; Electronic media advertising representatives; Direct mail advertising services; Mats, advertising and newspaper

(G-10140)
ROYAL DOCKS BREWING CO LLC
5646 Wales Ave Nw (44646-9096)
PHONE..................330 353-9103
John Bikis, *Prin*
EMP: 57 **EST:** 2014

SALES (est): 3.49MM **Privately Held**
Web: www.docks.beer
SIC: 2082 Malt beverages

(G-10141)
RW SCREW LLC
999 Oberlin Ave Sw (44647-7661)
PHONE..................................330 837-9211
EMP: 21 **EST:** 2019
SALES (est): 4.29MM **Privately Held**
Web: www.rwscrew.com
SIC: 3599 Machine shop, jobbing and repair

(G-10142)
SHEARERS FOODS LLC (HQ)
Also Called: Shearer's Snacks
100 Lincoln Way E (44646)
PHONE..................................800 428-6843
Mark Mcneil, *CEO*
Montgomery Pooley, *
Fritz Kohmann, *
Alan Fritts, *Corporate Controller*
C J Fraleigh, *
◆ **EMP:** 700 **EST:** 1980
SQ FT: 200,000
SALES (est): 712.7MM
SALES (corp-wide): 14.52B **Privately Held**
Web: www.shearers.com
SIC: 2096 5145 Potato chips and similar snacks; Snack foods
PA: Clayton, Dubilier & Rice, Inc.
375 Park Ave Fl 18
New York NY 10152
212 407-5200

(G-10143)
SHEARERS FOODS LLC
Also Called: Millennium Plant
4100 Millennium Blvd Se (44646-7449)
PHONE..................................330 767-7969
EMP: 13
SALES (corp-wide): 14.52B **Privately Held**
Web: www.shearers.com
SIC: 2096 Potato chips and similar snacks
HQ: Shearer's Foods, Llc
100 Lincoln Way E
Massillon OH 44646
800 428-6843

(G-10144)
SHERWIN-WILLIAMS COMPANY
Sherwin-Williams
600 Nova Dr Se (44646-8884)
P.O. Box 709 (44648-0709)
PHONE..................................330 830-6000
Thomas M Perry, *Pr*
EMP: 192
SQ FT: 139,645
SALES (corp-wide): 22.15B **Publicly Held**
Web: www.sherwin-williams.com
SIC: 2851 3087 2842 2891 Paints and paint additives; Custom compound purchased resins; Stain removers; Adhesives and sealants
PA: The Sherwin-Williams Company
101 W Prospect Ave
Cleveland OH 44115
216 566-2000

(G-10145)
SMITHERS GROUP INC
1845 Harsh Ave Se (44646-7123)
PHONE..................................330 833-8548
Michael J Hochschwender, *CEO*
EMP: 60
SALES (corp-wide): 115.78MM **Privately Held**
Web: www.smithers.com

SIC: 3829 8734 8071 Testing equipment: abrasion, shearing strength, etc.; Product testing laboratory, safety or performance; Medical laboratories
PA: The Smithers Group Inc
121 S Main St Ste 300
Akron OH 44308
330 762-7441

(G-10146)
SNACK ALLIANCE INC (DH)
100 Lincoln Way E (44646-6634)
P.O. Box 70 (97838-0070)
PHONE..................................330 767-3426
◆ **EMP:** 400 **EST:** 1996
SALES (est): 211.45MM
SALES (corp-wide): 14.52B **Privately Held**
SIC: 2096 Potato chips and similar snacks
HQ: Shearer's Foods, Llc
100 Lincoln Way E
Massillon OH 44646
800 428-6843

(G-10147)
SOUZZA LLC
3315 Lincoln Way E (44646-3715)
PHONE..................................330 479-9500
EMP: 7 **EST:** 2013
SALES (est): 408.05K **Privately Held**
Web: www.souzza.com
SIC: 7372 Application computer software

(G-10148)
STERILITE CORPORATION
Also Called: Sterilite
4495 Sterilite St Se (44646-7400)
PHONE..................................330 830-2204
EMP: 309
SALES (corp-wide): 430.83MM **Privately Held**
Web: sterilite-annex.edan.io
SIC: 3089 Plastics kitchenware, tableware, and houseware
PA: Sterilite Corporation
30 Scales Ln
Townsend MA 01469
978 597-1000

(G-10149)
THE MASSILLON-CLEVELAND-AKRONSIGN COMPANY
Also Called: MCA Industries
681 1st St Sw (44646-6729)
PHONE..................................330 833-3165
EMP: 137
SIC: 3993 Signs and advertising specialties

(G-10150)
TIGER SAND & GRAVEL LLC
411 Oberlin Ave Sw (44647-7826)
PHONE..................................330 833-6325
Leenn Cush, *Off Mgr*
David M Dipietro, *Managing Member*
EMP: 10 **EST:** 2005
SALES (est): 2.46MM **Privately Held**
Web: www.massillonlogistics.com
SIC: 1442 Construction sand and gravel

(G-10151)
TOWER INDUSTRIES LTD
Also Called: Tower Countertops
2101 9th St Sw (44647-7651)
PHONE..................................330 837-2216
EMP: 43 **EST:** 1995
SQ FT: 15,000
SALES (est): 8.97MM **Privately Held**
Web: www.towersurfaces.com
SIC: 3088 Plastics plumbing fixtures

(G-10152)
U S CHEMICAL & PLASTICS
600 Nova Dr Se (44646-8884)
PHONE..................................330 830-6000
John Nelson, *Manager*
◆ **EMP:** 8 **EST:** 2015
SALES (est): 1.02MM **Privately Held**
Web: www.uschem.com
SIC: 2899 Chemical preparations, nec

(G-10153)
VEHICLE SYSTEMS INC
Also Called: V S I
7130 Lutz Ave Nw (44646-9343)
PHONE..................................330 854-0535
Ervin Van Denberg, *Pr*
Vivian Vandenberg, *Sec*
Scott Vandenberg, *VP*
EMP: 7 **EST:** 1989
SALES (est): 790.43K **Privately Held**
SIC: 3714 8742 8731 Motor vehicle brake systems and parts; Management consulting services; Commercial physical research

(G-10154)
WASHINGTON PRODUCTS INC (PA)
1875 Harsh Ave Se Ste 1 (44646-7182)
P.O. Box 644 (44648-0644)
PHONE..................................330 837-5101
John A Boring, *Pr*
EMP: 10 **EST:** 1972
SQ FT: 30,000
SALES (est): 965.18K
SALES (corp-wide): 965.18K **Privately Held**
Web: www.wpimass.com
SIC: 3443 3647 3429 2656 Fabricated plate work (boiler shop); Automotive lighting fixtures, nec; Hardware, nec; Sanitary food containers

Masury
Trumbull County

(G-10155)
16363 SCA INC
7800 Addison Rd (44438-1207)
PHONE..................................330 448-0000
William Bilske, *Mgr*
EMP: 6
Web: www.pipelinesinc.com
SIC: 3494 1794 Line strainers, for use in piping systems; Excavation work
PA: 16363 Sca, Inc.
16363 Saint Clair Ave
East Liverpool OH 43920

(G-10156)
CAPARO BULL MOOSE INC
1433 Standard Ave (44438-1558)
P.O. Box 67 (44438-0067)
PHONE..................................330 448-4878
Dave Thompson, *Mgr*
EMP: 8
SALES (corp-wide): 197.93MM **Privately Held**
Web: www.bullmoosetube.com
SIC: 3317 Steel pipe and tubes
PA: Caparo Bull Moose, Inc.
1819 Clarkson Rd Ste 100
Chesterfield MO 63017
636 537-1249

(G-10157)
PS PINCHOT-SWOGGER PUBG LLC
8122 Warren Sharon Rd (44438-1038)
PHONE..................................330 448-1742
Judith Swogger, *Prin*
EMP: 6 **EST:** 2018

SALES (est): 37.59K **Privately Held**
Web: www.newsonthegreen.com
SIC: 2741 Miscellaneous publishing

(G-10158)
ROEMER INDUSTRIES INC
1555 Masury Rd (44438-1702)
PHONE..................................330 448-2000
Joseph L O'toole, *Pr*
Faith Otoole, *
EMP: 71 **EST:** 1937
SQ FT: 52,000
SALES (est): 10.84MM **Privately Held**
Web: www.roemerind.com
SIC: 3479 3469 3993 3613 Name plates: engraved, etched, etc.; Metal stampings, nec; Signs and advertising specialties; Switchgear and switchboard apparatus

Maumee
Lucas County

(G-10159)
ADDITIVE METAL ALLOYS
427 W Dussel Dr (43537-4208)
PHONE..................................419 215-5800
Rich Meklus, *Prin*
EMP: 6 **EST:** 2016
SALES (est): 176.62K **Privately Held**
SIC: 3399 Powder, metal

(G-10160)
AFFYMETRIX INC
434 W Dussel Dr (43537-1685)
PHONE..................................419 887-1233
Kristin Yakimow, *Brnch Mgr*
EMP: 37
SALES (corp-wide): 44.91B **Publicly Held**
Web: www.affymetrix.com
SIC: 3826 Analytical instruments
HQ: Affymetrix, Inc.
3380 Central Expy
Santa Clara CA 95051

(G-10161)
ALSIDE INC
3510 Briarfield Blvd (43537-9504)
PHONE..................................419 865-0934
Todd Anderson, *Brnch Mgr*
EMP: 55
SALES (corp-wide): 1.18B **Privately Held**
Web: www.alside.com
SIC: 5211 5033 3089 1751 Windows, storm: wood or metal; Siding, except wood; Siding, plastics; Window and door (prefabricated) installation
HQ: Alside, Inc.
3773 State Rd
Cuyahoga Falls OH 44223
330 929-1811

(G-10162)
ALTON PRODUCTS INC
425 W Sophia St (43537-1845)
P.O. Box 1115 (43537-8115)
PHONE..................................419 893-0201
Marcia Janicki, *Pr*
Karen S Prala, *Treas*
Cindy Albright, *Sec*
Joseph M Albright, *VP*
EMP: 13 **EST:** 1949
SQ FT: 21,000
SALES (est): 471.95K **Privately Held**
Web: www.altonpm.com
SIC: 3599 Machine shop, jobbing and repair

(G-10163)
AMERICAN FRAME CORPORATION (PA)

GEOGRAPHIC SECTION
Maumee - Lucas County (G-10184)

400 Tomahawk Dr (43537)
PHONE..............................419 893-5595
Laura Jajko, *Pr*
Ronald J Mickel, *
Dana Dunbar, *
Larry Haddad, *
Michael Cromly, *
▲ **EMP:** 63 **EST:** 1967
SQ FT: 33,000
SALES (est): 10.36MM
SALES (corp-wide): 10.36MM **Privately Held**
Web: www.americanframe.com
SIC: 5961 5023 3444 7699 Mail order house, nec; Homefurnishings; Sheet metalwork; Picture framing, custom

(G-10164)
ANDERSONS INC
Also Called: Fabrication Division
415 Illinois Ave (43537-1705)
P.O. Box 119 (43537-0119)
PHONE..............................419 891-2930
Michael Andersons, *Brnch Mgr*
EMP: 31
SALES (corp-wide): 14.75B **Publicly Held**
Web: www.andersonsinc.com
SIC: 3599 Machine shop, jobbing and repair
PA: The Andersons Inc
1947 Briarfield Blvd
Maumee OH 43537
419 893-5050

(G-10165)
ANDERSONS INC (PA)
Also Called: Andersons, The
1947 Briarfield Blvd (43537-1690)
P.O. Box 119 (43537-0119)
PHONE..............................419 893-5050
Michael J Anderson Senior, *Ch Bd*
Patrick E Bowe, *Pr*
William E Krueger, *COO*
Brian A Valentine, *Ex VP*
Christine M Castellano, *Corporate Secretary*
EMP: 150 **EST:** 1947
SALES (est): 14.75B
SALES (corp-wide): 14.75B **Publicly Held**
Web: www.andersonsinc.com
SIC: 0723 5191 2874 4789 Crop preparation services for market; Farm supplies; Phosphatic fertilizers; Railroad car repair

(G-10166)
APPLIED ENERGY TECH INC
Also Called: A E T
1720 Indian Wood Cir Ste E (43537-4000)
PHONE..............................419 537-9052
Terence Seikel, *Ch Bd*
Craig Winn, *Pr*
John Harberts, *VP*
Aaron Faust, *VP*
Terrence Seikel, *CFO*
EMP: 19 **EST:** 2009
SQ FT: 16,100
SALES (est): 1.84MM **Privately Held**
Web: www.aetenergy.com
SIC: 3441 Fabricated structural metal

(G-10167)
B & B PRINTING GRAPHICS INC
Also Called: Printing Graphics
1689 Lance Pointe Rd (43537-1603)
PHONE..............................419 893-7068
Beth Stewart, *Pr*
Barney Stewart, *VP*
EMP: 10 **EST:** 1987
SQ FT: 6,000
SALES (est): 950.52K **Privately Held**
SIC: 2752 Offset printing

(G-10168)
BARNES GROUP INC
370 W Dussel Dr Ste A (43537)
PHONE..............................419 891-9292
Tracy Allison, *Contrlr*
EMP: 172
SALES (corp-wide): 1.26B **Publicly Held**
Web: www.onebarnes.com
SIC: 5072 3495 Hardware; Wire springs
PA: Barnes Group Inc.
123 Main St
Bristol CT 06010
860 583-7070

(G-10169)
BARTON-CAREY MEDICAL PDTS INC (PA)
1331 Conant St Ste 102 (43537-1665)
P.O. Box 421 (43552-0421)
PHONE..............................419 887-1285
John H Mays, *Pr*
EMP: 28 **EST:** 1985
SALES (est): 2.46MM
SALES (corp-wide): 2.46MM **Privately Held**
Web: www.bartoncarey.com
SIC: 3842 2339 2326 Clothing, fire resistant and protective; Women's and misses' outerwear, nec; Men's and boy's work clothing

(G-10170)
BAY CONTROLS LLC
6528 Weatherfield Ct (43537-9468)
PHONE..............................419 891-4390
Scott Parry, *Pt*
▼ **EMP:** 30 **EST:** 1983
SQ FT: 12,000
SALES (est): 4.99MM **Privately Held**
Web: www.baycontrols.com
SIC: 3625 Industrial controls: push button, selector switches, pilot

(G-10171)
BERRY GLOBAL INC
1695 Indian Wood Cir (43537-4003)
PHONE..............................419 887-1602
Estelle Berry, *Brnch Mgr*
EMP: 6
Web: www.berryglobal.com
SIC: 3089 3081 Bottle caps, molded plastics; Unsupported plastics film and sheet
HQ: Berry Global, Inc.
101 Oakley St
Evansville IN 47710

(G-10172)
BIONIX SAFETY TECHNOLOGIES LTD (HQ)
1670 Indian Wood Cir (43537-4004)
PHONE..............................419 727-0552
Andrew Milligan, *Pr*
Doctor James Huttner, *VP*
EMP: 41 **EST:** 1988
SALES (est): 10.55MM **Privately Held**
Web: www.bionix.com
SIC: 3825 3826 5084 3829 Test equipment for electronic and electric measurement; Analytical instruments; Industrial machinery and equipment; Measuring and controlling devices, nec
PA: M&H Medical Holdings, Inc.
1670 Indian Wood Cir
Maumee OH 43537

(G-10173)
CDC CORPORATION
1445 Holland Rd (43537-1617)
PHONE..............................715 532-5548
▲ **EMP:** 43 **EST:** 1971

SQ FT: 80,000
SALES (est): 920.2K **Privately Held**
SIC: 2542 Partitions and fixtures, except wood

(G-10174)
CDC FAB CO
1445 Holland Rd (43537-1617)
PHONE..............................419 866-7705
Peter A Dewhirst, *Prin*
EMP: 14 **EST:** 2016
SALES (est): 781.23K **Privately Held**
SIC: 3448 Prefabricated metal buildings and components

(G-10175)
DAN K WILLIAMS INC
1350 Ford St (43537-1733)
P.O. Box 147 (43537-0147)
PHONE..............................419 893-3251
Dan K Williams, *Pr*
EMP: 9 **EST:** 2006
SALES (est): 297.86K **Privately Held**
SIC: 3273 Ready-mixed concrete

(G-10176)
DANA AUTO SYSTEMS GROUP LLC (DH)
3939 Technology Dr (43537-9194)
PHONE..............................419 887-3000
◆ **EMP:** 28 **EST:** 2007
SALES (est): 1.02B **Publicly Held**
Web: www.dana.com
SIC: 3714 Motor vehicle parts and accessories
HQ: Dana Limited
3939 Technology Dr
Maumee OH 43537

(G-10177)
DANA AUTOMOTIVE MFG INC (HQ)
Also Called: Dana Automotive Aftermarket,
3939 Technology Dr (43537-9194)
PHONE..............................419 887-3000
James K Kamsickas, *CEO*
EMP: 96 **EST:** 2001
SALES (est): 277MM **Publicly Held**
Web: www.dana.com
SIC: 3714 Motor vehicle parts and accessories
PA: Dana Incorporated
3939 Technology Dr
Maumee OH 43537

(G-10178)
DANA BRAZIL HOLDINGS I LLC (DH)
3939 Technology Dr (43537-9194)
PHONE..............................419 887-3000
Roger Wood, *CEO*
EMP: 8 **EST:** 2004
SALES (est): 194.52MM **Publicly Held**
Web: www.dana.com
SIC: 3714 Motor vehicle parts and accessories
HQ: Dana World Trade Corporation
3939 Technology Dr
Maumee OH 43537

(G-10179)
DANA COMMERCIAL VHCL PDTS LLC (DH)
Also Called: Dana
3939 Technology Dr (43537-9194)
PHONE..............................419 887-3000
◆ **EMP:** 143 **EST:** 2007
SALES (est): 53.47MM **Publicly Held**
Web: www.spicerparts.com
SIC: 3714 Motor vehicle parts and accessories

HQ: Dana Heavy Vehicle Systems Group, Llc
3939 Technology Dr
Maumee OH 43537

(G-10180)
DANA DRIVESHAFT MFG LLC (DH)
Also Called: Dana Driveshaft Products
6515 Maumee Western Rd (43537-9367)
PHONE..............................419 887-3000
▲ **EMP:** 6 **EST:** 2007
SALES (est): 117.45MM **Publicly Held**
Web: www.dana.com
SIC: 3714 Motor vehicle parts and accessories
HQ: Dana Driveshaft Products, Llc
3939 Technology Dr
Maumee OH 43537

(G-10181)
DANA DRIVESHAFT PRODUCTS LLC (DH)
Also Called: Dana Driveshaft Products
3939 Technology Dr (43537-9194)
PHONE..............................419 887-3000
▲ **EMP:** 27 **EST:** 2007
SALES (est): 117.45MM **Publicly Held**
Web: www.dana.com
SIC: 3714 Motor vehicle parts and accessories
HQ: Dana Automotive Systems Group, Llc
3939 Technology Dr
Maumee OH 43537

(G-10182)
DANA GLOBAL PRODUCTS INC (DH)
3939 Technology Dr (43537-9194)
P.O. Box 1000 (43537-7000)
PHONE..............................419 887-3000
Rodney R Filcek, *Pr*
Jeffrey S Bowen, *VP*
Marc S Levin, *Sec*
Lillian Etzkorn, *Treas*
◆ **EMP:** 44 **EST:** 1999
SALES (est): 24.34MM **Publicly Held**
Web: www.dana.com
SIC: 3714 Motor vehicle parts and accessories
HQ: Dana Limited
3939 Technology Dr
Maumee OH 43537

(G-10183)
DANA HVY VHCL SYSTEMS GROUP LL (DH)
Also Called: Dana Heavy Vhcl Systems Group
3939 Technology Dr (43537)
PHONE..............................419 887-3000
Nick Cole, *Pr*
◆ **EMP:** 45 **EST:** 2007
SALES (est): 121.53MM **Publicly Held**
Web: www.dana.com
SIC: 3714 Motor vehicle parts and accessories
HQ: Dana Limited
3939 Technology Dr
Maumee OH 43537

(G-10184)
DANA INCORPORATED (PA)
Also Called: Dana
3939 Technology Dr (43537)
P.O. Box 1000 (43537)
PHONE..............................419 887-3000
James K Kamsickas, *Ch Bd*
Timothy R Kraus, *Sr VP*
Douglas H Liedberg, *Sr VP*
EMP: 783 **EST:** 1904
SALES (est): 10.55B **Publicly Held**
Web: www.dana.com

Maumee - Lucas County (G-10185)

SIC: **3714** Motor vehicle parts and accessories

(G-10185)
DANA LIGHT AXLE MFG LLC (DH)
Also Called: Dana Light Axle Products
3939 Technology Dr (43537-9194)
PHONE..............................419 346-4528
Mark Howard, *Managing Member*
▲ EMP: 6 EST: 2007
SALES (est): 51.74MM **Publicly Held**
Web: www.dana.com
SIC: **3714** Motor vehicle parts and accessories
HQ: Dana Light Axle Products, Llc
  2100 W State Blvd
  Fort Wayne IN 46808

(G-10186)
DANA LIMITED (HQ)
3939 Technology Dr (43537-9194)
P.O. Box 1000 (43537-7000)
PHONE..............................419 887-3000
James Sweetnam, *Pr*
John Devine, *
Gary Convis, *Vice Chairman**
Marc S Levin, *
James Yost, *
▲ EMP: 500 EST: 2007
SALES (est): 1.92B **Publicly Held**
Web: www.dana.com
SIC: **3714 3053 3593 3492** Motor vehicle parts and accessories; Gaskets and sealing devices; Fluid power cylinders, hydraulic or pneumatic; Control valves, fluid power: hydraulic and pneumatic
PA: Dana Incorporated
  3939 Technology Dr
  Maumee OH 43537

(G-10187)
DANA LIMITED
6515 Maumee Western Rd (43537-9367)
PHONE..............................419 887-3000
EMP: 50
Web: www.dana.com
SIC: **3714** Motor vehicle parts and accessories
HQ: Dana Limited
  3939 Technology Dr
  Maumee OH 43537

(G-10188)
DANA LIMITED
Also Called: Dana Automotive Systems
6515 Maumee Western Rd (43537-9367)
PHONE..............................419 887-3000
EMP: 10 EST: 2019
SALES (est): 3.3MM **Privately Held**
Web: www.dana.com
SIC: **3714** Motor vehicle parts and accessories

(G-10189)
DANA LIMITED
Also Called: Dana Information Technology
580 Longbow Dr (43537-1709)
P.O. Box 537 (43697-0537)
PHONE..............................419 482-2000
Al Henderson, *Mgr*
EMP: 100
Web: www.dana.com
SIC: **3714** Motor vehicle parts and accessories
HQ: Dana Limited
  3939 Technology Dr
  Maumee OH 43537

(G-10190)
DANA OFF HIGHWAY PRODUCTS LLC (DH)
Also Called: Dana
3939 Technology Dr (43537-9194)
P.O. Box 1000 (43537-7000)
PHONE..............................419 887-3000
Nick Stanage, *Pr*
◆ EMP: 49 EST: 2007
SALES (est): 28.34MM **Publicly Held**
Web: www.dana.com
SIC: **3714** Motor vehicle parts and accessories
HQ: Dana Heavy Vehicle Systems Group, Llc
  3939 Technology Dr
  Maumee OH 43537

(G-10191)
DANA SAC USA INC
Also Called: Dana
3939 Technology Dr (43537-9194)
PHONE..............................419 887-3550
EMP: 20 EST: 2019
SALES (est): 4.27MM **Publicly Held**
Web: www.dana.com
SIC: **3714** Motor vehicle parts and accessories
PA: Dana Incorporated
  3939 Technology Dr
  Maumee OH 43537

(G-10192)
DANA SEALING MANUFACTURING LLC (DH)
3939 Technology Dr (43537-9194)
▲ EMP: 72 EST: 2007
SALES (est): 77.86MM **Publicly Held**
Web: www.dana.com
SIC: **3714** Motor vehicle parts and accessories
HQ: Dana Sealing Products, Llc
  3939 Technology Dr
  Maumee OH 43537

(G-10193)
DANA SEALING PRODUCTS LLC (DH)
3939 Technology Dr (43537-9194)
P.O. Box 1000 (43537-7000)
PHONE..............................419 887-3000
▲ EMP: 18 EST: 2007
SALES (est): 154.52MM **Publicly Held**
Web: www.dana.com
SIC: **3714** Motor vehicle parts and accessories
HQ: Dana Automotive Systems Group, Llc
  3939 Technology Dr
  Maumee OH 43537

(G-10194)
DANA STRUCTURAL MFG LLC
Also Called: Dana Structural Products
3939 Technology Dr (43537-9194)
PHONE..............................419 887-3000
▼ EMP: 108 EST: 2007
SALES (est): 9.55MM **Publicly Held**
Web: www.dana.com
SIC: **3714** Motor vehicle parts and accessories
HQ: Dana Structural Products, Llc
  3939 Technology Dr
  Maumee OH 43537

(G-10195)
DANA STRUCTURAL PRODUCTS LLC (DH)
Also Called: Dana Structural Products
3939 Technology Dr (43537-9194)
PHONE..............................419 887-3000
EMP: 6 EST: 2007
SALES (est): 9.55MM **Publicly Held**
Web: www.dana.com
SIC: **3714** Motor vehicle parts and accessories
HQ: Dana Automotive Systems Group, Llc
  3939 Technology Dr
  Maumee OH 43537

(G-10196)
DANA THERMAL PRODUCTS LLC (DH)
Also Called: Dana Thermal Products
3939 Technology Dr (43537-9194)
PHONE..............................419 887-3000
▲ EMP: 11 EST: 2007
SALES (est): 50.71MM **Publicly Held**
Web: www.dana.com
SIC: **3714** Motor vehicle parts and accessories
HQ: Dana Automotive Systems Group, Llc
  3939 Technology Dr
  Maumee OH 43537

(G-10197)
DANA WORLD TRADE CORPORATION (DH)
3939 Technology Dr (43537-9194)
PHONE..............................419 887-3000
Kenneth A Hiltz, *CFO*
EMP: 14 EST: 2006
SALES (est): 199.33MM **Publicly Held**
Web: www.dana.com
SIC: **3714** Motor vehicle parts and accessories
HQ: Dana Limited
  3939 Technology Dr
  Maumee OH 43537

(G-10198)
DEFENSE SURPLUS LLC
706 Waite Ave (43537-3464)
PHONE..............................419 460-9906
Vincent Porter, *Prin*
EMP: 6 EST: 2012
SALES (est): 179.99K **Privately Held**
SIC: **3812** Defense systems and equipment

(G-10199)
DENTSPLY SIRONA INC
520 Illinois Ave (43537-1708)
PHONE..............................419 893-5672
Garyn Livecchi, *Genl Mgr*
EMP: 64
SQ FT: 4,000
SALES (corp-wide): 3.96B **Publicly Held**
Web: www.dentsplysirona.com
SIC: **3843** Teeth, artificial (not made in dental laboratories)
PA: Dentsply Sirona Inc.
  13320 Ballantyne Corp Pl
  Charlotte NC 28277
  844 848-0137

(G-10200)
DENTSPLY SIRONA INC
Ransom & Randolph
3535 Briarfield Blvd (43537-9383)
PHONE..............................419 865-9497
Dan Nixon, *Brnch Mgr*
EMP: 25
SALES (corp-wide): 3.96B **Publicly Held**
Web: www.dentsplysirona.com
SIC: **3844 2821 3915 3843** X-ray apparatus and tubes; Molding compounds, plastics; Jewelers' castings; Impression material, dental
PA: Dentsply Sirona Inc.
  13320 Ballantyne Corp Pl
  Charlotte NC 28277
  844 848-0137

(G-10201)
EATON AEROQUIP LLC
1660 Indian Wood Cir (43537-4004)
PHONE..............................419 891-7775
EMP: 1316
SIC: **3052 3594 3593 3561** Rubber hose; Fluid power pumps and motors; Fluid power cylinders and actuators; Pumps and pumping equipment
HQ: Eaton Aeroquip Llc
  1000 Eaton Blvd
  Cleveland OH 44122
  440 523-5000

(G-10202)
GENIUS SOLUTIONS ENGRG CO (HQ)
Also Called: Gs Engineering
6421 Monclova Rd (43537-9760)
PHONE..............................419 794-9914
Grigoriy Grinberg, *Pr*
Matthew Shade, *
EMP: 39 EST: 2004
SALES (est): 9.47MM
SALES (corp-wide): 741.05MM **Publicly Held**
Web: www.mold-tech.com
SIC: **8711 2821 7389** Mechanical engineering; Thermoplastic materials; Engraving service
PA: Standex International Corporation
  23 Keewaydin Dr
  Salem NH 03079
  603 893-9701

(G-10203)
HALL-TOLEDO INC
525 W Sophia St (43537-1847)
P.O. Box 1501 (43537-8501)
PHONE..............................419 893-4334
Andrew F Boesel, *Pr*
EMP: 10 EST: 1928
SQ FT: 5,000
SALES (est): 2.58MM **Privately Held**
Web: www.hall-toledo.com
SIC: **3546 3714** Power-driven handtools; Motor vehicle parts and accessories
PA: Michabo Inc
  525 W Sophia St
  Maumee OH 43537

(G-10204)
HAMMILL MANUFACTURING CO (PA)
Also Called: Impact Cutoff Div
360 Tomahawk Dr (43537-1612)
P.O. Box 1450 (43537-8450)
PHONE..............................419 476-0789
John Hammill, *Ch Bd*
John E Hammill Junior, *Pr*
Carl Barnard, *
Robert Doubler, *
EMP: 100 EST: 1955
SQ FT: 80,000
SALES (est): 25.62MM
SALES (corp-wide): 25.62MM **Privately Held**
Web: www.hammillmedical.com
SIC: **3842 3545** Implants, surgical; Chucks: drill, lathe, or magnetic (machine tool accessories)

(G-10205)
HELM INSTRUMENT COMPANY INC
361 W Dussel Dr (43537-1649)
PHONE..............................419 893-4356
Richard T Wilhelm, *Pr*
Nancy Wilhelm, *
Mary L Tice, *
Michael Wilhelm, *
Thomas Wilhelm, *
EMP: 34 EST: 1962

GEOGRAPHIC SECTION

Maumee - Lucas County (G-10228)

SQ FT: 12,500
SALES (est): 5.15MM **Privately Held**
Web: www.helminstrument.com
SIC: 3829 3825 3823 3822 Measuring and controlling devices, nec; Instruments to measure electricity; Process control instruments; Environmental controls

(G-10206)
HENRY-GRIFFITTS LIMITED (HQ)
Also Called: About Golf
352 Tomahawk Dr (43537-1612)
PHONE..................419 482-9095
Bill Bales, *CEO*
◆ **EMP:** 6 **EST:** 2008
SALES (est): 2.8MM
SALES (corp-wide): 9.71MM **Privately Held**
SIC: 3999 Atomizers, toiletry
PA: Aboutgolf, Limited
   352 Tomahawk Dr
   Maumee OH 43537
   419 482-9095

(G-10207)
IMAGE BY J & K LLC
Also Called: Image
1575 Henthorne Dr (43537-1372)
PHONE..................888 667-6929
James Land Iv, *Managing Member*
EMP: 19 **EST:** 2006
SQ FT: 10,000
SALES (est): 967.57K **Privately Held**
SIC: 3589 7217 7349 7342 Floor washing and polishing machines, commercial; Carpet and upholstery cleaning; Building and office cleaning services; Rest room cleaning service

(G-10208)
ISHIKAWA GASKET AMERICA INC
1745 Indian Wood Cir Ste 125 (43537-4167)
PHONE..................419 353-7300
Toshio Matsuzaki, *Pr*
▲ **EMP:** 10 **EST:** 1992
SQ FT: 3,000
SALES (est): 1.6MM **Privately Held**
Web: www.ishikawaamerica.com
SIC: 3053 Gaskets, all materials
PA: Ishikawa Gasket Co., Ltd.
   2-5-5, Toranomon
   Minato-Ku TKY 105-0

(G-10209)
JOHNS MANVILLE CORPORATION
1020 Ford St (43537-1820)
PHONE..................419 467-8189
EMP: 7
SALES (corp-wide): 364.48B **Publicly Held**
Web: www.jm.com
SIC: 3296 Fiberglass insulation
HQ: Johns Manville Corporation
   717 17th St
   Denver CO 80202
   303 978-2000

(G-10210)
KELLERMYER BERGENSONS SVCS LLC
1575 Henthorne Dr (43537-1372)
PHONE..................419 867-4300
Mark Minasian, *CEO*
EMP: 60
SALES (corp-wide): 620.83MM **Privately Held**
Web: www.kbs-services.com
SIC: 3589 Commercial cleaning equipment
PA: Kellermyer Bergensons Services, Llc
   3605 Ocean Ranch Blvd
   Oceanside CA 92056
   760 631-5111

(G-10211)
KEYSTONE AUTO GLASS INC
2255 Linden Ct (43537-2338)
PHONE..................419 509-0497
Neal Golding, *Pr*
Alan Golding, *
Andrew K Golding, *
Brian Silver, *
EMP: 100 **EST:** 1953
SQ FT: 20,000
SALES (est): 5.44MM **Privately Held**
SIC: 3714 7536 5531 5013 Motor vehicle parts and accessories; Automotive glass replacement shops; Auto and home supply stores; Motor vehicle supplies and new parts

(G-10212)
KLINGER AGENCY INC
1760 Manley Rd (43537-9400)
PHONE..................419 893-9759
Bruce Klinger, *Prin*
EMP: 6 **EST:** 2014
SALES (est): 87.98K **Privately Held**
SIC: 3053 Gaskets, all materials

(G-10213)
KUHLMAN CORPORATION (PA)
Also Called: Kuhlman Construction Products
1845 Indian Wood Cir (43537-4072)
P.O. Box 714 (43697-0714)
PHONE..................419 897-6000
Timothy L Goligoski, *Pr*
Kenneth Kuhlman, *
Terry Schaefer, *
▲ **EMP:** 32 **EST:** 1901
SQ FT: 18,000
SALES (est): 42.49MM
SALES (corp-wide): 42.49MM **Privately Held**
Web: www.gerkencompanies.com
SIC: 4226 5032 3273 Special warehousing and storage, nec; Brick, stone, and related material; Ready-mixed concrete

(G-10214)
LINE DRIVE SPORTZ-LCRC LLC
2901 Key St Ste 1 (43537-2421)
PHONE..................419 794-7150
EMP: 6 **EST:** 2009
SALES (est): 370.75K **Privately Held**
SIC: 3949 Sporting and athletic goods, nec

(G-10215)
M&H MEDICAL HOLDINGS INC (PA)
Also Called: Bionix Radiation Therapy
1670 Indian Wood Cir (43537-4004)
PHONE..................419 727-8421
Andrew J Milligan, *Pr*
James J Huttner, *
Dawn Hall, *
▲ **EMP:** 35 **EST:** 1984
SALES (est): 10.55MM **Privately Held**
Web: www.bionix.com
SIC: 3841 3829 Surgical and medical instruments; Measuring and controlling devices, nec

(G-10216)
MAGNESIUM PRODUCTS GROUP INC
Also Called: M P G
3928 Azalea Cir (43537-9191)
PHONE..................310 971-5799
Bradley A Hirou, *Pr*
Ronald W Banks, *Ex VP*
Steve Hubble, *COO*
EMP: 6 **EST:** 2008
SALES (est): 301.24K **Privately Held**
SIC: 3441 Fabricated structural metal

(G-10217)
MAUMEE ASSEMBLY & STAMPING LLC
920 Illinois Ave (43537-1716)
PHONE..................419 304-2887
EMP: 330 **EST:** 2009
SALES (est): 25.87MM **Privately Held**
Web: www.mastamping.com
SIC: 3469 Stamping metal for the trade

(G-10218)
MAUMEE HOSE & FITTING INC
Also Called: Maumee Hose & Belting Co
720 Illinois Ave Ste H (43537-1750)
PHONE..................419 893-7252
James C Walsh, *Pr*
Karen Walsh, *VP*
EMP: 7 **EST:** 1988
SQ FT: 10,000
SALES (est): 994.89K **Privately Held**
SIC: 3429 5085 Clamps, couplings, nozzles, and other metal hose fittings; Hose, belting, and packing

(G-10219)
MCALEAR WINERY LLC
Also Called: Urban Pine Winery
3415 Briarfield Blvd (43537-9503)
PHONE..................567 703-1281
EMP: 6 **EST:** 2019
SALES (est): 77.61K **Privately Held**
Web: www.urbanpinewinery.com
SIC: 2084 Wines

(G-10220)
METAL FORMING & COINING LLC (PA)
Also Called: Netform
1007 Illinois Ave (43537-1752)
PHONE..................419 893-8748
Tim Cripsey, *Pr*
Kurt Geisheimer, *CFO*
Paul Kessler, *Ex VP*
Diana Wienrich, *Sec*
EMP: 100 **EST:** 1953
SQ FT: 103,000
SALES (est): 20.68MM
SALES (corp-wide): 20.68MM **Privately Held**
Web: www.netform.com
SIC: 3462 Iron and steel forgings

(G-10221)
MIRROR
Also Called: Community Mirror, The
113 W Wayne St (43537-2150)
PHONE..................419 893-8135
Michael Mc Carthy, *Owner*
EMP: 8 **EST:** 1980
SQ FT: 5,000
SALES (est): 239.19K **Privately Held**
Web: www.themirrornewspaper.com
SIC: 2711 Newspapers: publishing only, not printed on site

(G-10222)
MIRROR PUBLISHING CO INC
Also Called: Mirror, The
113 W Wayne St (43537-2150)
PHONE..................419 893-8135
Michael Mccarthy, *Pr*
EMP: 10 **EST:** 2007
SQ FT: 3,000
SALES (est): 487.66K **Privately Held**
Web: www.themirrornewspaper.com
SIC: 2711 Newspapers: publishing only, not printed on site

(G-10223)
MITCHS WELDING & HITCHES
802 Kingsbury St (43537-1826)
PHONE..................419 893-3117
EMP: 8 **EST:** 1980
SQ FT: 5,000
SALES (est): 771.79K **Privately Held**
Web: www.mitchsweldingandhitches.com
SIC: 3537 5561 Industrial trucks and tractors; Recreational vehicle parts and accessories

(G-10224)
PRESTIGE STORE INTERIORS INC
427 W Dussel Dr # 209 (43537-4208)
PHONE..................419 476-2106
Jeffrey Simenski, *Pr*
Blain Stobinski, *VP*
EMP: 18 **EST:** 1993
SALES (est): 680.08K **Privately Held**
SIC: 2542 Partitions and fixtures, except wood

(G-10225)
PRO-PAK INDUSTRIES INC (PA)
1125 Ford St (43537-1703)
P.O. Box 1176 (43537-8176)
PHONE..................419 729-0751
Leo Deiger, *Pr*
Anthony Deiger, *
Charles M Deiger, *
EMP: 109 **EST:** 1948
SALES (est): 22.94MM
SALES (corp-wide): 22.94MM **Privately Held**
Web: www.pro-pakindustries.com
SIC: 2653 Boxes, corrugated: made from purchased materials

(G-10226)
PROTECTIVE COATING TECH LLC
3600 Boulder Ridge Dr (43537-9235)
PHONE..................419 340-8645
Mike Francis, *Prin*
EMP: 6 **EST:** 2008
SALES (est): 107.52K **Privately Held**
SIC: 3479 Coating of metals and formed products

(G-10227)
RANSOM & RANDOLPH LLC (PA)
3535 Briarfield Blvd (43537-9383)
PHONE..................419 865-9497
Daniel Nixon, *Pr*
EMP: 6 **EST:** 2021
SALES (est): 10.09MM
SALES (corp-wide): 10.09MM **Privately Held**
Web: www.ransom-randolph.com
SIC: 3365 Aerospace castings, aluminum

(G-10228)
S E JOHNSON COMPANIES INC (DH)
1360 Ford St (43537-1733)
PHONE..................419 893-8731
John T Bearss, *CEO*
Terry J Moore, *Treas*
Jack Zouhary, *Sec*
Donald Weber, *VP*
Mark W Karchner, *CFO*
EMP: 23 **EST:** 1924
SQ FT: 34,000
SALES (est): 8.91MM
SALES (corp-wide): 32.72B **Privately Held**
Web: www.sejohnson.com
SIC: 1611 1622 2951 1411 General contractor, highway and street construction; Bridge construction; Asphalt and asphaltic paving mixtures (not from refineries); Limestone, dimension-quarrying
HQ: Shelly Company

Maumee - Lucas County (G-10229)

80 Park Dr
Thornville OH 43076
740 246-6315

(G-10229)
SENATOR INTERNATIONAL INC (HQ)
Also Called: Allermuir
4111 N Jerome Rd (43537)
PHONE................419 887-5806
Mark Brettschneider, *Pr*
▲ **EMP:** 22 **EST:** 2007
SALES (est): 17.06MM
SALES (corp-wide): 258.04MM **Privately Held**
Web: www.allermuir.com
SIC: 5712 2522 2521 Office furniture; Office furniture, except wood; Wood office furniture
PA: Senator International Limited
Syke Side Drive
Accrington LANCS BB5 5
128 272-5088

(G-10230)
SERVICE SPRING CORP
6615 Maumee Western Rd (43537-9368)
PHONE................419 867-0212
Michael Mcalear, *Brnch Mgr*
EMP: 7
SALES (corp-wide): 25.11MM **Privately Held**
Web: www.servicespring.com
SIC: 5085 3493 Industrial supplies; Steel springs, except wire
PA: Service Spring Corp.
1703 Toll Gate Dr
Maumee OH 43537
419 838-6081

(G-10231)
SERVICE SPRING CORP (PA)
1703 Toll Gate Dr (43537-1673)
PHONE................419 838-6081
Michael Mcalear, *CEO*
Clarence J Veigel, *
Evelyn F Veigel, *
Allen Bishop, *
▼ **EMP:** 70 **EST:** 1962
SQ FT: 98,000
SALES (est): 25.11MM
SALES (corp-wide): 25.11MM **Privately Held**
Web: www.servicespring.com
SIC: 3493 Steel springs, except wire

(G-10232)
SMASHRAY LTD
6450 Weatherfield Ct (43537-9146)
P.O. Box 1034 (43537-8034)
PHONE................989 620-7507
EMP: 6 **EST:** 2011
SALES (est): 179.55K **Privately Held**
SIC: 3648 Lighting equipment, nec

(G-10233)
SOCCER CENTRE OWNERS LTD
1620 Market Place Dr Ste 1 (43537-4318)
PHONE................419 893-5425
Brant Smith, *Pr*
EMP: 8 **EST:** 2012
SQ FT: 300,000
SALES (est): 332.68K **Privately Held**
Web: www.maumeesoccercentre.com
SIC: 3949 7999 Pads: football, basketball, soccer, lacrosse, etc.; Indoor court clubs

(G-10234)
SPOSIE LLC
4064 Technology Dr (43537-9738)
PHONE................888 977-2229
Ryan Wright, *Managing Member*
EMP: 12 **EST:** 2015

SQ FT: 35,000
SALES (est): 1.4MM **Privately Held**
Web: www.sposie.com
SIC: 2676 Infant and baby paper products

(G-10235)
STEPPING STONE ENTERPRISES INC
Also Called: Minuteman Press
1689 Lance Pointe Rd (43537-1603)
PHONE................419 472-0505
Steven Heaney, *Pr*
Ronald R Kimler, *VP*
Vicki Kimler, *Sec*
EMP: 14 **EST:** 1982
SALES (est): 894.5K **Privately Held**
Web: www.mmptoledo.com
SIC: 2752 Commercial printing, lithographic

(G-10236)
STONECO INC
Also Called: Shelley Company
1360 Ford St (43537-1733)
PHONE................419 893-7645
Lee Wehner, *Mgr*
EMP: 40
SALES (corp-wide): 32.72B **Privately Held**
Web: www.shellyco.com
SIC: 1422 5032 Crushed and broken limestone; Stone, crushed or broken
HQ: Stoneco, Inc.
1700 Fostoria Ave Ste 200
Findlay OH 45840
419 422-8854

(G-10237)
SUN CHEMICAL CORPORATION
Ink & Plates
1380 Ford St (43537-1733)
PHONE................419 891-3514
Wes Lucas, *Mgr*
EMP: 71
SQ FT: 68,000
Web: www.sunchemical.com
SIC: 2893 Printing ink
HQ: Sun Chemical Corporation
35 Waterview Blvd Ste 104
Parsippany NJ 07054
973 404-6000

(G-10238)
SURFACE COMBUSTION INC (PA)
1700 Indian Wood Cir (43537-4067)
P.O. Box 428 (43537-0428)
PHONE................419 891-7150
William J Bernard Junior, *Pr*
Max Hoetzl, *
William B J Bernard, *Dir*
▲ **EMP:** 100 **EST:** 1987
SQ FT: 36,000
SALES (est): 22.27MM
SALES (corp-wide): 22.27MM **Privately Held**
Web: www.surfacecombustion.com
SIC: 3567 Industrial furnaces and ovens

(G-10239)
THE ANDERSONS CLYMERS ETHANOL LLC
1947 Briarfield Blvd (43537-1690)
P.O. Box 119 (43537-0119)
PHONE................574 722-2627
EMP: 33
SIC: 2869 Ethyl alcohol, ethanol

(G-10240)
TIAMA AMERICAS INC
6500 Weatherfield Ct (43537-9468)
PHONE................269 274-3107
EMP: 24 **EST:** 2015

SALES (est): 2.15MM **Privately Held**
Web: www.tiama.com
SIC: 3221 Glass containers
HQ: Tiama
215 Chemin Du Grand Revoyet
Saint Genis Laval 69230

(G-10241)
TILT-OR-LIFT INC (PA)
124 E Dudley St (43537-3366)
P.O. Box 8728 (43537-8728)
PHONE................419 893-6944
Dennis Rober, *Pr*
EMP: 6 **EST:** 1973
SQ FT: 1,400
SALES (est): 1.61MM
SALES (corp-wide): 1.61MM **Privately Held**
Web: www.tiltorlift.com
SIC: 3537 5084 Lift trucks, industrial: fork, platform, straddle, etc.; Industrial machinery and equipment

(G-10242)
TOLEDO TRANSDUCERS INC
Also Called: Toledo Integrated Systems
1345 Ford St (43537-1732)
PHONE................419 724-4170
Mark Storer, *Pr*
Daniel N Falcone, *
Randall W Seed, *
EMP: 40 **EST:** 1976
SALES (est): 8.18MM **Privately Held**
Web: www.ttoledo.com
SIC: 3823 3829 3625 3613 Process control instruments; Measuring and controlling devices, nec; Relays and industrial controls; Switchgear and switchboard apparatus

(G-10243)
US COEXCELL INC
640 Mingo Dr (43537-1704)
PHONE................419 897-9110
Christopher Nelson, *Pr*
Dennis Puening, *VP*
▲ **EMP:** 41 **EST:** 1991
SQ FT: 40,000
SALES (est): 10.37MM
SALES (corp-wide): 138.41MM **Privately Held**
Web: www.coexcellinc.com
SIC: 3089 Plastics containers, except foam
PA: Cleveland Steel Container Corporation
100 Executive Pkwy
Hudson OH 44236
440 349-8000

(G-10244)
VICKERS INTERNATIONAL INC
3000 Strayer Rd (43537-9529)
PHONE................419 867-2200
Darryl F Allen, *Pr*
James Oathout, *Sec*
Gary J Findling, *Treas*
EMP: 50 **EST:** 1984
SQ FT: 21,000
SALES (est): 2.49MM **Privately Held**
SIC: 3561 3594 3491 Pumps and pumping equipment; Motors, pneumatic; Industrial valves
HQ: Eaton Corporation
1000 Eaton Blvd
Cleveland OH 44122
440 523-5000

(G-10245)
WILLIAMS CONCRETE INC
1350 Ford St (43537-1733)
PHONE................419 893-3251
Mark Williams, *Pr*
Terry Schaefer, *VP Fin*

EMP: 50 **EST:** 2001
SALES (est): 953.46K
SALES (corp-wide): 42.49MM **Privately Held**
Web: www.gerkencompanies.com
SIC: 3273 Ready-mixed concrete
PA: Kuhlman Corporation
1845 Indian Wood Cir
Maumee OH 43537
419 897-6000

(G-10246)
YZ ENTERPRISES INC
Also Called: Almondina Brand Biscuits
1930 Indian Wood Cir Ste 100 (43537-4001)
PHONE................419 893-8777
Yuval N Zaliouk, *CEO*
Susan M Zaliouk, *Ex VP*
Jack Hunter, *VP*
Christopher Moody, *VP Opers*
EMP: 20 **EST:** 1990
SQ FT: 12,500
SALES (est): 4.25MM **Privately Held**
Web: www.almondina.com
SIC: 2052 Cookies

Mayfield Heights
Cuyahoga County

(G-10247)
BECK ALUMINUM ALLOYS LTD
6150 Parkland Blvd # 260 (44124-4103)
PHONE................216 861-4455
EMP: 63
SIC: 3341 Secondary nonferrous metals

(G-10248)
FERRO INTERNATIONAL SVCS INC (DH)
6060 Parkland Blvd Ste 250 (44124-4225)
PHONE................216 875-5600
EMP: 8 **EST:** 2007
SALES (est): 10.95MM
SALES (corp-wide): 1.88B **Privately Held**
Web: www.vibrantz.com
SIC: 2816 Color pigments
HQ: Vibrantz Corporation
6060 Parkland Blvd # 250
Mayfield Heights OH 44124
216 875-5600

(G-10249)
GANEDEN BIOTECH INC
Also Called: Ganeden
5800 Landerbrook Dr Ste 300 (44124-4083)
PHONE................440 229-5200
EMP: 21
Web: www.bc30probiotic.com
SIC: 2834 Pharmaceutical preparations

(G-10250)
MATERION BRUSH INC (HQ)
Also Called: Materion
6070 Parkland Blvd Ste 1 (44124-4191)
PHONE................216 486-4200
Michael C Hasychak, *Pr*
▲ **EMP:** 100 **EST:** 1931
SALES (est): 536.5MM **Publicly Held**
Web: www.materion.com
SIC: 3351 3356 3264 3339 Copper and copper alloy sheet, strip, plate, and products; Nickel and nickel alloy pipe, plates, sheets, etc.; Porcelain parts for electrical devices, molded; Beryllium metal
PA: Materion Corporation
6070 Parkland Blvd
Mayfield Heights OH 44124

(G-10251)
MATERION CORPORATION (PA)
6070 Parkland Blvd (44124-4191)
PHONE..................................216 486-4200
Jugal K Vijayvargiya, *Pr*
Vinod M Khilnani, *Non-Executive Chairman of the Board**
Shelly M Chadwick, *VP Fin*
Gregory R Chemnitz, *VP*
John Zaranec, *CAO*
◆ **EMP:** 150 **EST:** 1931
SQ FT: 79,130
SALES (est): 1.67B Publicly Held
Web: www.materion.com
SIC: 3339 3351 3356 3341 Beryllium metal; Copper and copper alloy sheet, strip, plate, and products; Nickel and nickel alloy pipe, plates, sheets, etc.; Secondary precious metals

(G-10252)
NATURAL BEAUTY HC EXPRESS
6809 Mayfield Rd Apt 550 (44124-2262)
PHONE..................................440 459-1776
Stacey Carlton, *Mgr*
EMP: 7 **EST:** 2010
SALES (est): 236.21K Privately Held
SIC: 3999 Furniture, barber and beauty shop

(G-10253)
ONX ACQUISITION LLC
Also Called: Onx Enterprise Solutions
5910 Landerbrook Dr Ste 250 (44124-6508)
PHONE..................................440 569-2300
EMP: 300
SIC: 7372 7379 Business oriented computer software; Computer related consulting services

(G-10254)
PRIEST SERVICES INC (PA)
1127 Linda St 5885 Landerbrook Dr Ste 140 (44124)
PHONE..................................440 333-1123
Howard E Priest, *Ch Bd*
Homer S Taft, *Pr*
Carol Kuehnle, *Prin*
Donald W Farley, *Prin*
Judy Oneacre, *Prin*
EMP: 8 **EST:** 1950
SQ FT: 40,000
SALES (est): 2.31MM
SALES (corp-wide): 2.31MM Privately Held
SIC: 3275 2891 2851 Gypsum products; Adhesives and sealants; Paints and allied products

(G-10255)
TRIMBLE TRNSP ENTP SLTIONS INC (HQ)
6085 Parkland Blvd (44124-4184)
PHONE..................................216 831-6606
David Wangler, *Pr*
David Mook, ***
Jeffrey Ritter, ***
Scott Vanselous, ***
David Schildmeyer, ***
EMP: 125 **EST:** 1986
SQ FT: 32,500
SALES (est): 93.8MM
SALES (corp-wide): 3.8B Publicly Held
Web: transportation.trimble.com
SIC: 7372 Business oriented computer software
PA: Trimble Inc.
  10368 Westmoor Dr
  Westminster CO 80021
  720 887-6100

(G-10256)
VIBRANTZ CORPORATION (DH)
Also Called: Ferro
6060 Parkland Blvd Ste 250 (44124-4225)
PHONE..................................216 875-5600
Glenn Fish, *Pr*
Mark Whitney, *Ex VP*
◆ **EMP:** 90 **EST:** 1919
SALES (est): 1.13B
SALES (corp-wide): 1.88B Privately Held
Web: www.vibrantz.com
SIC: 2851 2816 Paints and allied products; Color pigments
HQ: Vibrantz Technologies Inc.
  16945 Northchase Dr # 2000
  Houston TX 77060
  646 747-4222

Mayfield Hts
Cuyahoga County

(G-10257)
JAN S KLEINMAN
136 Stonecreek Dr (44143-3654)
PHONE..................................440 473-9776
Jan S Kleinman, *Prin*
EMP: 6 **EST:** 2010
SALES (est): 154.31K Privately Held
SIC: 2519 Household furniture, nec

Mayfield Village
Cuyahoga County

(G-10258)
AHKEO LABS LLC
6685 Beta Dr (44143-2320)
PHONE..................................216 406-1919
Brent Skoda, *Managing Member*
EMP: 6 **EST:** 2015
SALES (est): 116.23K Privately Held
SIC: 3699 Electronic training devices

(G-10259)
OMNI SYSTEMS INC (PA)
701 Beta Dr Ste 31 (44143-2330)
PHONE..................................216 377-5160
EMP: 100 **EST:** 1990
SALES (est): 31.7MM Privately Held
Web: www.omnisystem.com
SIC: 2759 Flexographic printing

(G-10260)
PREFORMED LINE PRODUCTS CO (PA)
660 Beta Dr (44143-2398)
P.O. Box 91129 (44101-3129)
PHONE..................................440 461-5200
Robert G Ruhlman, *Ch Bd*
J Ryan Ruhlman, ***
Dennis F Mckenna, *Ex VP*
J Cecil Curlee Junior, *Pers/VP*
Caroline S Vaccariello, *Corporate Secretary*
EMP: 503 **EST:** 1947
SALES (est): 669.68MM
SALES (corp-wide): 669.68MM Publicly Held
Web: www.plp.com
SIC: 3644 3661 Pole line hardware; Fiber optics communications equipment

(G-10261)
QUALITY ELECTRODYNAMICS LLC
6655 Beta Dr Ste 100 (44143-2380)
PHONE..................................440 638-5106
Michael P Esposito Junior, *Ch*
Albert B Ratner, *Ch*
Debbie Sun, *CFO*
EMP: 115 **EST:** 2005
SALES (est): 25.66MM Privately Held
Web: www.qedinnovations.com
SIC: 3841 Surgical and medical instruments
PA: Canon Inc.
  3-30-2, Shimomaruko
  Ota-Ku TKY 146-0

Mc Arthur
Vinton County

(G-10262)
AUSTIN POWDER COMPANY
Also Called: Red Diamond Plant
430 Powder Plant Rd (45651-8260)
P.O. Box 317 (45651-0317)
PHONE..................................740 596-5286
Keith Mills, *Mgr*
EMP: 225
SALES (corp-wide): 749.73MM Privately Held
Web: www.austinpowder.com
SIC: 2892 Explosives
HQ: Austin Powder Company
  25800 Science Park Dr # 300
  Cleveland OH 44122
  216 464-2400

(G-10263)
CROWNOVER LUMBER COMPANY INC (PA)
501 Fairview Ave (45651)
P.O. Box 301 (45651-0301)
PHONE..................................740 596-5229
Lundy Crownover, *Pr*
EMP: 60 **EST:** 1959
SQ FT: 2,000
SALES (est): 5.19MM
SALES (corp-wide): 5.19MM Privately Held
Web: www.crownoverlumber.com
SIC: 2421 2426 Lumber: rough, sawed, or planed; Hardwood dimension and flooring mills

(G-10264)
SUPERIOR HARDWOODS OF OHIO
62581 Us Highway 50 (45651-8414)
P.O. Box 320 (45651-0320)
PHONE..................................740 596-2561
Emmett Conway, *Pr*
Emmett Conway, *Pr*
Adam Conway, ***
EMP: 15 **EST:** 1979
SQ FT: 11,000
SALES (est): 469.43K Privately Held
Web: www.superiorhardwoodsofohio.com
SIC: 2421 2426 Sawmills and planing mills, general; Hardwood dimension and flooring mills

Mc Clure
Henry County

(G-10265)
C DCAP MODEM LINE
232 S East St (43534-9900)
PHONE..................................419 748-7409
Barry Connly, *Prin*
EMP: 6 **EST:** 2010
SALES (est): 154.95K Privately Held
SIC: 3661 Modems

(G-10266)
INDUSTRIAL FLUID MGT INC
2926 Us Highway 6 (43534-9730)
PHONE..................................419 748-7460
Richard Bennett, *Pr*
EMP: 19 **EST:** 1993
SALES (est): 6.62MM
SALES (corp-wide): 458.93MM Privately Held
Web: www.ifmenviro.com
SIC: 3589 Water treatment equipment, industrial
HQ: Poggemeyer Design Group, Inc.
  1168 N Main St
  Bowling Green OH 43402
  419 244-8074

(G-10267)
SECOND OIL LTD
N695 County Road 6 (43534-9794)
PHONE..................................419 830-4688
EMP: 6 **EST:** 2006
SALES (est): 81.86K Privately Held
Web: www.second-oil.com
SIC: 1382 Oil and gas exploration services

Mc Comb
Hancock County

(G-10268)
CONSOLIDATED BISCUIT COMPANY
312 Rader Rd (45858-9751)
PHONE..................................419 293-2911
EMP: 15 **EST:** 2005
SQ FT: 136,806
SALES (est): 1.7MM Privately Held
Web: www.hearthsidefoods.com
SIC: 2052 Biscuits, dry

(G-10269)
CRUSHPROOF TUBING CO
100 North St (45858-7539)
P.O. Box 668 (45858-0668)
PHONE..................................419 293-2111
Vance M Kramer Junior, *Pr*
Richard Hollington, ***
EMP: 35 **EST:** 1950
SQ FT: 28,000
SALES (est): 4.77MM Privately Held
Web: www.crushproof.com
SIC: 3052 2822 Rubber and plastics hose and beltings; Synthetic rubber

(G-10270)
HEARTHSIDE FOOD SOLUTIONS LLC
Also Called: Consolidated Biscuit Company
312 Rader Rd (45858-9751)
PHONE..................................419 293-2911
EMP: 2500
Web: www.hearthsidefoods.com
SIC: 2052 Cookies
PA: Hearthside Food Solutions, Llc
  333 Finley Rd Ste 800
  Downers Grove IL 60515

(G-10271)
K & L READY MIX INC
5511 State Route 613 (45858-9345)
PHONE..................................419 293-2937
EMP: 10
SALES (corp-wide): 4.97MM Privately Held
Web: www.kandlreadymix.com
SIC: 3273 Ready-mixed concrete
PA: K & L Ready Mix Inc
  10391 State Route 15
  Ottawa OH 45875
  419 523-4376

Mc Cutchenville
Wyandot County

(G-10272)
BUCKYS MACHINE AND FAB LTD
8376 S County Road 47 (44844-9620)
PHONE 419 981-5050
EMP: 7 EST: 1988
SQ FT: 5,500
SALES (est): 717.12K **Privately Held**
SIC: 3599 Machine shop, jobbing and repair

Mc Dermott
Scioto County

(G-10273)
A AND R LOGGING LLC
222 Enley Rd (45652-7500)
PHONE 740 352-6182
EMP: 6 EST: 2014
SALES (est): 250.42K **Privately Held**
SIC: 2411 Logging

(G-10274)
OHIO VALLEY STAVE INC
18253 State Route 73 (45652-8925)
P.O. Box 279 (45652-0279)
PHONE 740 259-6222
EMP: 6 EST: 2019
SALES (est): 342.49K **Privately Held**
Web: www.ohiovalleyveneer.com
SIC: 2421 Sawmills and planing mills, general

(G-10275)
WALLER BROTHERS STONE COMPANY
744 Mcdermott Rushtown Rd (45652-8906)
P.O. Box 157 (45652-0157)
PHONE 740 858-1948
Frank L Waller, *Pr*
Lowell M Shope, *
EMP: 23 EST: 1908
SQ FT: 5,175
SALES (est): 2.5MM **Privately Held**
Web: www.wallerbrothersstone.com
SIC: 3281 3821 2511 Stone, quarrying and processing of own stone products; Laboratory apparatus and furniture; Wood household furniture

Mc Donald
Trumbull County

(G-10276)
AMROD BRIDGE & IRON LLC
105 Ohio Ave (44437-1900)
P.O. Box 749 (44501-0749)
EMP: 24 EST: 2005
SALES (est): 2.61MM **Privately Held**
SIC: 3441 Fabricated structural metal

(G-10277)
GENERAL ELECTRIC COMPANY
Also Called: GE
3159 Wildwood Dr (44437-1354)
P.O. Box 688 (44030-0688)
PHONE 440 593-1156
Jeff Adams, *Mgr*
EMP: 46
SALES (corp-wide): 67.95B **Publicly Held**
Web: www.ge.com
SIC: 3641 5719 Electric lamps; Lighting, lamps, and accessories
PA: General Electric Company
1 Aviation Way
Cincinnati OH 45215
617 443-3000

(G-10278)
MANDREL GROUP LLC
105 Ohio Ave (44437-1900)
PHONE 330 881-1266
Tim Merlin, *Managing Member*
EMP: 10 EST: 2021
SALES (est): 1.16MM **Privately Held**
Web: www.themandrelgroup.com
SIC: 3499 Machine bases, metal

(G-10279)
MCDONALD STEEL CORPORATION (PA)
100 Ohio Ave (44437-1954)
P.O. Box 416 (44437-0416)
PHONE 330 530-9118
James Grasso, *Pr*
Bill Bresnahan, *Ch Bd*
Mark Pecchia, *CFO*
◆ EMP: 80 EST: 1980
SQ FT: 680,000
SALES (est): 17.81MM
SALES (corp-wide): 17.81MM **Privately Held**
Web: www.mcdonaldsteel.com
SIC: 3312 Bars and bar shapes, steel, hot-rolled

(G-10280)
STEEL & ALLOY UTILITY PDTS INC
110 Ohio Ave (44437-1900)
P.O. Box 354 (44437-0354)
PHONE 330 530-2220
Nathan Gallo, *Pr*
Nick Gallo, *
▼ EMP: 50 EST: 1946
SQ FT: 60,000
SALES (est): 8.55MM **Privately Held**
SIC: 3569 3443 3444 3441 Assembly machines, non-metalworking; Fabricated plate work (boiler shop); Sheet metalwork; Fabricated structural metal

Mcconnelsville
Morgan County

(G-10281)
HANN MANUFACTURING INC
4678 N State Route 60 Nw (43756)
P.O. Box 400 (43758)
PHONE 740 962-3752
EMP: 26 EST: 1995
SQ FT: 30,000
SALES (est): 2.8MM **Privately Held**
Web: www.hannmfg.com
SIC: 2531 2448 2441 Public building and related furniture; Wood pallets and skids; Nailed wood boxes and shook

(G-10282)
MIBA BEARINGS US LLC
5037 N State Route 60 Nw (43756-9218)
PHONE 740 962-4242
F Peter Mitterbauer, *Ch Bd*
Markus Hofer, *
▲ EMP: 300 EST: 2001
SQ FT: 182,000
SALES (est): 95.82MM
SALES (corp-wide): 242.12K **Privately Held**
Web: www.miba.com
SIC: 5085 3365 3471 3511 Bearings; Aluminum foundries; Plating and polishing; Turbines and turbine generator sets
HQ: Mitterbauer Beteiligungs Gmbh
Dr. Mitterbauer-StraBe 3
Laakirchen 4663
76132541

(G-10283)
MIBA SINTER USA LLC
5045 N State Route 60 Nw (43756-9640)
PHONE 740 962-4242
Steve Krise, *Managing Member*
▲ EMP: 10 EST: 2008
SALES (est): 5.41MM
SALES (corp-wide): 242.12K **Privately Held**
Web: www.miba.com
SIC: 3312 Sinter, iron
HQ: Mitterbauer Beteiligungs Gmbh
Dr. Mitterbauer-StraBe 3
Laakirchen 4663
76132541

(G-10284)
MORGAN COUNTY PUBLISHING CO
Also Called: Morgan County Herald
25 N 5th St (43756-1200)
P.O. Box 268 (43756-0268)
PHONE 740 962-3377
Jack Barnes, *Pr*
EMP: 9 EST: 1964
SALES (est): 884.27K **Privately Held**
Web: www.mchnews.com
SIC: 2711 Newspapers, publishing and printing

Mechanicsburg
Champaign County

(G-10285)
DIRECT TOOL LLC
5953 Pleasant Chapel Rd (43044-9622)
PHONE 614 687-3111
Julie Maurer, *Prin*
EMP: 10 EST: 2017
SALES (est): 350.27K **Privately Held**
SIC: 3599 Machine and other job shop work

(G-10286)
MECHANICSBURG SAND & GRAVEL
5734 State Route 4 (43044-9748)
PHONE 937 834-2606
James Cushman, *Pr*
Charles Wibright Junior, *Sec*
EMP: 18 EST: 1957
SQ FT: 3,400
SALES (est): 763.99K **Privately Held**
Web: www.mechanicsburgsandandgravel.com
SIC: 1442 Construction sand mining

Mechanicstown
Carroll County

(G-10287)
KINGS WELDING AND FABG INC
5259 Bane Rd Ne (44651-9020)
PHONE 330 738-3592
Glen Richard King Senior, *Pr*
Diane Garrett, *
EMP: 17 EST: 1974
SQ FT: 9,500
SALES (est): 271.37K **Privately Held**
Web: www.kingswelding.net
SIC: 3599 7692 3498 3441 Machine shop, jobbing and repair; Welding repair; Fabricated pipe and fittings; Fabricated structural metal

Medina
Medina County

(G-10288)
3M COMPANY
Also Called: 3M
1030 Lake Rd (44256-2450)
PHONE 330 725-1444
Tom Gregory, *Brnch Mgr*
EMP: 36
SALES (corp-wide): 32.68B **Publicly Held**
Web: www.3m.com
SIC: 2672 Tape, pressure sensitive: made from purchased materials
PA: 3m Company
3m Center
Saint Paul MN 55144
651 733-1110

(G-10289)
AGRATI - MEDINA LLC (DH)
941 Lake Rd 955 (44256)
PHONE 330 725-8853
Ashi Uppal, *CEO*
Jack Woodruff, *CFO*
◆ EMP: 146 EST: 1978
SALES (est): 46.08MM
SALES (corp-wide): 706.55MM **Privately Held**
Web: www.agrati.com
SIC: 3452 Screws, metal
HQ: Agrati, Inc.
24000 S Western Ave
Park Forest IL 60466
704 747-1200

(G-10290)
AI ROOT COMPANY
Also Called: Root Candles
234 S State Rd (44256-2697)
PHONE 330 725-6677
Brad Root, *Brnch Mgr*
EMP: 9
SALES (corp-wide): 53.25MM **Privately Held**
Web: www.rootcandles.com
SIC: 3999 3085 Candles; Plastics bottles
PA: The A I Root Company
623 W Liberty St
Medina OH 44256
330 723-4359

(G-10291)
AI ROOT COMPANY (PA)
Also Called: West Liberty Commons
623 W Liberty St (44256-2225)
PHONE 330 723-4359
John A Root, *Ch Bd*
Brad I Root, *
Stuart Root, *
William Fleming, *
▲ EMP: 190 EST: 1869
SQ FT: 182,000
SALES (est): 53.25MM
SALES (corp-wide): 53.25MM **Privately Held**
Web: www.rootcandles.com
SIC: 3999 3085 Candles; Plastics bottles

(G-10292)
ALCHEM CORPORATION
525 W Liberty St (44256-2223)
PHONE 330 725-2436
B George Buskin, *Pr*
▲ EMP: 8 EST: 1976
SQ FT: 28,000
SALES (est): 1.61MM **Privately Held**
Web: www.alchemcorp.com

GEOGRAPHIC SECTION

Medina - Medina County (G-10317)

SIC: 2819 Industrial inorganic chemicals, nec

(G-10293)
ALSATIAN LLC
Also Called: Sushi On The Roll
985 Boardman Aly (44256-1599)
PHONE..................................330 661-0600
EMP: 9 EST: 2007
SQ FT: 3,000
SALES (est): 462.19K **Privately Held**
Web: www.sushiontherollonline.com
SIC: 2048 5146 Fish food; Fish and seafoods

(G-10294)
AMERICAN WOOD REFACE INC (PA)
854 Medina Rd (44256-9615)
PHONE..................................440 944-3750
Jason Hicks, *Pr*
EMP: 6 EST: 1990
SALES (est): 457.15K
SALES (corp-wide): 457.15K **Privately Held**
Web: www.woodreface.com
SIC: 2434 Wood kitchen cabinets

(G-10295)
APEX SIGNS INC
Also Called: Fastsigns
2755 Medina Rd (44256-8284)
PHONE..................................330 952-2626
Ed Gonzalez, *Pr*
EMP: 6 EST: 2015
SALES (est): 210.03K **Privately Held**
Web: www.fastsigns.com
SIC: 3993 Signs and advertising specialties

(G-10296)
APEX SPECIALTY CO INC
620 E Smith Rd Ste E7 (44256-3650)
PHONE..................................330 725-6663
EMP: 7 EST: 1956
SQ FT: 3,000
SALES (est): 774.27K **Privately Held**
SIC: 3599 Machine shop, jobbing and repair

(G-10297)
ARCH ANGLE WINDOW AND DOOR LLC
6979 Wooster Pike (44256-8860)
PHONE..................................800 548-0214
Andrew Coleman, *Managing Member*
EMP: 10 EST: 2015
SALES (est): 787.33K **Privately Held**
Web: www.archangleohio.com
SIC: 3442 Window and door frames

(G-10298)
AUTOMTIVE RFNISH CLOR SLTONS I
2771 Sunburst Dr (44256-6494)
PHONE..................................330 461-6067
Strath Wood, *Pr*
EMP: 50 EST: 2016
SALES (est): 853.04K **Privately Held**
SIC: 3999 7538 Atomizers, toiletry; General automotive repair shops

(G-10299)
AXON MEDICAL LLC
1484 Medina Rd Ste 117 (44256-5378)
PHONE..................................216 276-0262
Christopher Hardin, *Prin*
Joel Hawley, *Prin*
EMP: 20 EST: 2015
SALES (est): 809.12K **Privately Held**
SIC: 3841 3842 5047 Surgical and medical instruments; Surgical appliances and supplies; Instruments, surgical and medical

(G-10300)
BANDAGES & BOO-BOOS PRESS LLC
4101 Williamsburg Ct (44256-8667)
PHONE..................................614 271-6193
Erika Kimble, *Prin*
EMP: 6 EST: 2012
SALES (est): 80K **Privately Held**
SIC: 2741 Miscellaneous publishing

(G-10301)
BIL-JAC FOODS INC (PA)
3337 Medina Rd (44256-9631)
PHONE..................................330 722-7888
William Kelly, *Ch*
Robert Kelly, *
James Kelly, *
Ray Kelly, *
EMP: 25 EST: 1947
SQ FT: 6,000
SALES (est): 23.34MM
SALES (corp-wide): 23.34MM **Privately Held**
Web: www.bil-jac.com
SIC: 2047 Dog food

(G-10302)
BLASTER CORPORATION
775 W Smith Rd (44256-3556)
PHONE..................................216 901-5800
EMP: 11 EST: 2017
SALES (est): 1.25MM **Privately Held**
Web: www.blasterproducts.com
SIC: 2911 Petroleum refining

(G-10303)
BOND CHEMICALS INC
1154 W Smith Rd (44256-2443)
PHONE..................................330 725-5935
Thomas Goslee Junior, *Pr*
Carol Goslee, *VP*
EMP: 13 EST: 1960
SQ FT: 24,000
SALES (est): 494.72K **Privately Held**
Web: www.bondchemicalsinc.com
SIC: 2899 2819 Water treating compounds; Industrial inorganic chemicals, nec

(G-10304)
BPR-RICO EQUIPMENT INC (PA)
691 W Liberty St (44256-2225)
PHONE..................................330 723-4050
EMP: 80 EST: 1980
SALES (est): 22.78MM
SALES (corp-wide): 22.78MM **Privately Held**
Web: www.ricoequipment.com
SIC: 3537 Lift trucks, industrial: fork, platform, straddle, etc.

(G-10305)
BPR-RICO MANUFACTURING INC
Also Called: Bpr/Rico
691 W Liberty St (44256-2225)
PHONE..................................330 723-4050
▲ EMP: 100 EST: 1987
SQ FT: 175,000
SALES (est): 21.06MM
SALES (corp-wide): 22.78MM **Privately Held**
SIC: 3537 Lift trucks, industrial: fork, platform, straddle, etc.
PA: Bpr-Rico Equipment, Inc.
     691 W Liberty St
     Medina OH 44256
     330 723-4050

(G-10306)
BREAKWALL PUBLISHING LLC
Also Called: Seaside Retailer
3593 Medina Rd # 117 (44256-8182)
PHONE..................................813 575-2570
EMP: 6 EST: 2019
SALES (est): 254.86K **Privately Held**
Web: www.seasideretailer.com
SIC: 2721 Magazines: publishing and printing

(G-10307)
BREW KETTLE STRONGSVILLE LLC
3520 Longwood Dr (44256-8400)
P.O. Box 360893 (44136-0015)
PHONE..................................440 915-7074
EMP: 12 EST: 2013
SALES (est): 373.65K **Privately Held**
Web: www.thebrewkettle.com
SIC: 2082 Malt beverages

(G-10308)
CHICK MASTER INCUBATOR COMPANY (PA)
Also Called: Jamesway Chick Mstr Incubator
1093 Medina Rd (44256-8352)
PHONE..................................330 722-5591
Robert Holzer, *CEO*
Alan Shandler, *
Michael Hurd, *
Chad Daniels, *
◆ EMP: 89 EST: 1944
SALES (est): 24.34MM
SALES (corp-wide): 24.34MM **Privately Held**
Web: www.chickmaster.com
SIC: 3523 1711 Incubators and brooders, farm; Plumbing, heating, air-conditioning

(G-10309)
CHRONICLE TELEGRAM
885 W Liberty St (44256-1312)
PHONE..................................330 725-4166
George Hudnutt, *Owner*
EMP: 8 EST: 2010
SALES (est): 108.88K **Privately Held**
Web: www.chroniclet.com
SIC: 2711 Newspapers, publishing and printing

(G-10310)
CMBF PRODUCTS INC (HQ)
Also Called: Cbf
920 Lake Rd (44256-2453)
PHONE..................................440 528-4000
Ted Messmer, *Pr*
▲ EMP: 239 EST: 1924
SALES (est): 451.02MM
SALES (corp-wide): 669.66MM **Privately Held**
Web: www.carlislecbf.com
SIC: 3751 Brakes, friction clutch and other: bicycle
PA: Engineered Components And Systems, Llc
     N19w24200 Rivrwood Dr
     Waukesha WI 53188
     262 754-7300

(G-10311)
COMMERCIAL GRINDING SVCS INC
Also Called: Cgs
1155 Industrial Pkwy Unit 1 (44258)
P.O. Box 1121 (44258)
PHONE..................................330 273-5040
Kevin Thies, *CEO*
Kevin T Butas, *Pr*
EMP: 20 EST: 1975
SQ FT: 3,600
SALES (est): 2.17MM **Privately Held**
Web: www.cgstool.com
SIC: 3541 3545 Machine tools, metal cutting type; End mills

(G-10312)
CONTROLS INC
5204 Portside Dr (44256-5966)
P.O. Box 368 (44274-0368)
PHONE..................................330 239-4345
Robert Cowen, *Pr*
Scott Izzo, *
EMP: 25 EST: 1990
SALES (est): 4.2MM **Privately Held**
Web: www.controlsinc.com
SIC: 3625 7389 1731 Control equipment, electric; Design services; Electronic controls installation

(G-10313)
CONVIBER INC
Also Called: Heintz Conveying Belt Service
1066 Industrial Pkwy (44256-2449)
PHONE..................................330 723-6006
EMP: 10
SALES (corp-wide): 10.98MM **Privately Held**
Web: www.conviber.com
SIC: 7699 3559 Rubber product repair; Rubber working machinery, including tires
PA: Conviber, Inc.
     644 Garfield St
     Springdale PA 15144
     724 274-6300

(G-10314)
CORRPRO COMPANIES INC
Also Called: Corrpro Waterworks
1055 W Smith Rd (44256-2444)
PHONE..................................330 725-6681
George Giannakos, *Brnch Mgr*
EMP: 20
SALES (corp-wide): 1.48B **Privately Held**
Web: www.corrpro.com
SIC: 3699 8711 Electrical equipment and supplies, nec; Engineering services
HQ: Corrpro Companies, Inc.
     580 Goddard Ave
     Chesterfield MO 63005
     636 530-8000

(G-10315)
CORRPRO COMPANIES INTL INC
1055 W Smith Rd (44256-2444)
PHONE..................................330 723-5082
EMP: 48 EST: 2013
SALES (est): 2.63MM
SALES (corp-wide): 1.48B **Privately Held**
Web: www.corrpro.com
SIC: 3699 Electrical equipment and supplies, nec
HQ: Insituform Technologies, Llc
     17988 Edison Ave
     Chesterfield MO 63005
     636 530-8000

(G-10316)
CUSTOM CHEMICAL PACKAGING LLC
4086 Watercourse Dr (44256-7897)
PHONE..................................330 331-7416
EMP: 6 EST: 2005
SALES (est): 261.49K **Privately Held**
SIC: 2842 Automobile polish

(G-10317)
DAIRY FARMERS AMERICA INC
1035 Medina Rd Ste 300 (44256-5398)
PHONE..................................330 670-7800
Glenn Wallace, *Chief*
EMP: 24
SALES (corp-wide): 24.52B **Privately Held**
Web: www.dfamilk.com

Medina - Medina County (G-10318)

SIC: **2022** 2026 2021 0211 Cheese; natural and processed; Fluid milk; Creamery butter; Beef cattle feedlots
PA: Dairy Farmers Of America, Inc.
    1405 N 98th St
    Kansas City KS 66111
    816 801-6455

(G-10318)
DIE GUYS INC
5238 Portside Dr (44256-5966)
PHONE.....................330 239-3437
Jeri Potts, *CEO*
Cathy Greenwald, *Pr*
Luke Darling, *Sec*
EMP: 19 **EST:** 2000
SQ FT: 14,000
SALES (est): 2.32MM **Privately Held**
Web: www.dieguys.com
SIC: **3544** Dies, steel rule

(G-10319)
ENGINEERED POLYMER SYSTEMS LLC
2600 Medina Rd (44256-8145)
P.O. Box 370 (44274-0370)
PHONE.....................216 255-2116
EMP: 8 **EST:** 2009
SALES (est): 315.29K **Privately Held**
Web: www.engpolysys.com
SIC: **2821** Plastics materials and resins

(G-10320)
ENI USA R&M CO INC
740 S Progress Dr (44256-1368)
PHONE.....................330 723-6457
EMP: 10
SQ FT: 6,000
SALES (corp-wide): 137.63B **Privately Held**
Web: www.eni.com
SIC: **2992** 5172 Lubricating oils and greases; Petroleum products, nec
HQ: Eni Usa R&M Co. Inc.
    299 Park Ave Rm 1603
    New York NY 10171

(G-10321)
FACULTATIEVE TECH AMERICAS INC
Also Called: Incinerator Specialists
940 Lake Rd (44256-2453)
PHONE.....................330 723-6339
▲ **EMP:** 39 **EST:** 1908
SALES (est): 3.34MM **Privately Held**
Web: www.facultatieve-technologies.com
SIC: **3567** Fuel-fired furnaces and ovens

(G-10322)
FALCON INDUSTRIES INC (PA)
Also Called: Falcon
180 Commerce Dr (44256-3949)
PHONE.....................330 723-0099
J Don Fitzgerald, *CEO*
EMP: 27 **EST:** 1970
SQ FT: 24,000
SALES (est): 9.44MM
SALES (corp-wide): 9.44MM **Privately Held**
Web: www.falconindustries.com
SIC: **3541** 3535 3444 3423 Machine tools, metal cutting type; Conveyors and conveying equipment; Sheet metalwork; Hand and edge tools, nec

(G-10323)
FASTSIGNS
Also Called: Fastsigns
2736 Medina Rd Ste 109 (44256-9660)
PHONE.....................330 952-2626
EMP: 7
SALES (est): 149.13K **Privately Held**
Web: www.fastsigns.com
SIC: **3993** Signs and advertising specialties

(G-10324)
FIRE-DEX LLC (PA)
Also Called: Gear Wash
780 S Progress Dr (44256-1368)
PHONE.....................330 723-0000
Bill Burke, *Managing Member*
Brett Jaffe, *CEO*
▲ **EMP:** 81 **EST:** 1983
SQ FT: 28,000
SALES (est): 25.25MM
SALES (corp-wide): 25.25MM **Privately Held**
Web: www.firedex.com
SIC: **2389** Uniforms and vestments

(G-10325)
FOM USA INCORPORATED
1065 Medina Rd Ste 800 (44256-5376)
PHONE.....................234 248-4400
Daniel Donafini, *Pr*
Scott Kochevar, *VP Sls*
▲ **EMP:** 9 **EST:** 2008
SQ FT: 9,000
SALES (est): 5.47MM **Privately Held**
SIC: **3354** Aluminum extruded products
HQ: F.O.M. Industrie Srl
    Via Mercadante 85/87
    Cattolica RN 47841
    054 183-2777

(G-10326)
FOUNDATIONS WORLDWIDE INC (PA)
Also Called: Foundations
5216 Portside Dr (44256-5966)
PHONE.....................330 722-5033
Joseph A Lawlor, *Pr*
Lisa Vanadia, *VP*
◆ **EMP:** 21 **EST:** 2002
SQ FT: 60,000
SALES (est): 11.16MM
SALES (corp-wide): 11.16MM **Privately Held**
Web: www.foundations.com
SIC: **5999** 2511 3944 Children's furniture, nec; Children's wood furniture; Strollers, baby (vehicle)

(G-10327)
FOUR ELEMENTS INC
4328 Remsen Rd (44256-9077)
PHONE.....................330 591-4505
Charles Harrison, *Prin*
EMP: 6 **EST:** 2011
SALES (est): 113.38K **Privately Held**
SIC: **2819** Elements

(G-10328)
FRICTION PRODUCTS CO
Also Called: Hawk Performance
920 Lake Rd (44256-2453)
PHONE.....................330 725-4941
Chris Disantis, *CEO*
Ronald E Weinberg, *
Thomas A Gilbride, *
◆ **EMP:** 266 **EST:** 1989
SQ FT: 176,000
SALES (est): 53.34MM
SALES (corp-wide): 669.66MM **Privately Held**
Web: www.hawkperformance.com
SIC: **3728** 3714 Aircraft landing assemblies and brakes; Motor vehicle brake systems and parts
HQ: Cmbf Products, Inc.
    920 Lake Rd
    Medina OH 44256

(G-10329)
FUSION SOFTWARE INC
5235 Linda Dr (44256-7816)
PHONE.....................330 723-2957
Edward R Wadel, *Prin*
EMP: 8 **EST:** 2002
SALES (est): 155.64K **Privately Held**
SIC: **7372** Prepackaged software

(G-10330)
GASKO FABRICATED PRODUCTS LLC (HQ)
4049 Ridge Rd (44256-8618)
P.O. Box 1050 (44062-1050)
PHONE.....................330 239-1781
Randy Guernsey, *Pr*
Gregory Nemecek, *Pr*
Ed Bosken, *VP*
EMP: 32 **EST:** 1998
SQ FT: 12,000
SALES (est): 3.44MM
SALES (corp-wide): 8.29MM **Privately Held**
SIC: **3053** Gaskets, all materials
PA: Cornerstone Industrial Holdings Inc
    100 Park Pl
    Chagrin Falls OH 44022
    440 893-9144

(G-10331)
GOLIAS PUBLISHING COMPANY INC
7271 Lonesome Pine Trl (44256-7160)
PHONE.....................330 425-4744
Bernie Golias, *Prin*
EMP: 6 **EST:** 2010
SALES (est): 53K **Privately Held**
Web: www.goliaspublishing.com
SIC: **2741** Miscellaneous publishing

(G-10332)
HEARINGAID MEDINA SERVICE
799 N Court St (44256-1765)
PHONE.....................330 725-1060
EMP: 6 **EST:** 2019
SALES (est): 245.17K **Privately Held**
Web: www.medinahearing.com
SIC: **3842** Hearing aids

(G-10333)
HERAEUS ELECTRO-NITE CO LLC
6469 Fenn Rd (44256-9463)
PHONE.....................330 725-1419
EMP: 6
SALES (corp-wide): 2.67MM **Privately Held**
Web: www.heraeus-electro-nite.com
SIC: **3829** 3674 Thermocouples; Semiconductors and related devices
HQ: Heraeus Electro-Nite Co., Llc
    541 S Industrial Dr
    Hartland WI 53029
    215 944-9000

(G-10334)
HOWDEN NORTH AMERICA INC
935 Heritage Dr (44256-2404)
PHONE.....................330 721-7374
Edward Biesiada, *Brnch Mgr*
EMP: 12
SALES (corp-wide): 3.44B **Privately Held**
Web: www.chartindustries.com
SIC: **3564** Blowers and fans
HQ: Howden North America Inc.
    2475 Grge Urban Blvd Ste
    Depew NY 14043
    330 867-8540

(G-10335)
HOWDEN NORTH AMERICA INC
411 Independence Dr (44256-2406)
PHONE.....................330 867-8540
Scott Burdett, *Mgr*
EMP: 22
SQ FT: 2,662
SALES (corp-wide): 3.44B **Privately Held**
Web: www.chartindustries.com
SIC: **3564** Blowing fans: industrial or commercial
HQ: Howden North America Inc.
    2475 Grge Urban Blvd Ste
    Depew NY 14043
    330 867-8540

(G-10336)
I V MILLER & SONS
940 Lafayette Rd (44256-2415)
PHONE.....................732 493-4040
George Miller, *Pr*
Jack Miller, *VP*
Juni Fraser, *Sec*
▲ **EMP:** 18 **EST:** 1949
SALES (est): 2.20MM **Privately Held**
Web: www.ivmiller.com
SIC: **3479** Painting, coating, and hot dipping

(G-10337)
INTERACTIVE ENGINEERING CORP
884 Medina Rd (44256-9615)
PHONE.....................330 239-6888
Ming Zhang, *Pr*
▲ **EMP:** 25 **EST:** 1995
SQ FT: 200,000
SALES (est): 2.73MM **Privately Held**
Web: www.4iec.com
SIC: **8748** 3672 Systems analysis and engineering consulting services; Printed circuit boards

(G-10338)
INTERNATIONAL METAL SUPPLY LLC
3995 Medina Rd Ste 200 (44256-5958)
PHONE.....................330 764-1004
EMP: 8 **EST:** 2016
SALES (est): 1.79MM **Privately Held**
Web: www.intmetalsupply.com
SIC: **3313** Ferroalloys

(G-10339)
JES FOODS INC (PA)
865 W Liberty St Ste 200 (44256-3938)
P.O. Box 367 (44258-0367)
PHONE.....................216 883-8987
Elaine R Freed, *Pr*
William Freed, *
EMP: 19 **EST:** 1992
SALES (est): 4.96MM **Privately Held**
Web: www.jesfoods.com
SIC: **2033** Canned fruits and specialties

(G-10340)
KANYA INDUSTRIES LLC
694 W Liberty St (44256-2226)
PHONE.....................330 722-5432
Paul Kanya, *Prin*
EMP: 8 **EST:** 2017
SALES (est): 488.37K **Privately Held**
SIC: **3999** Manufacturing industries, nec

(G-10341)
KATHYS KRAFTS AND KOLLECTIBLES
3303 Hamilton Rd (44256-7633)
PHONE.....................423 787-3709
Kathy Hayes, *Prin*
EMP: 6 **EST:** 2013
SALES (est): 190.37K **Privately Held**
SIC: **2022** Natural cheese

GEOGRAPHIC SECTION

Medina - Medina County (G-10365)

(G-10342)
KELLY FOODS CORPORATION (PA)
3337 Medina Rd (44256-9631)
PHONE..................330 722-8855
Robert Kelly, *Pr*
Jim Kelly, *Sec*
▼ **EMP:** 22 **EST:** 1987
SALES (est): 11.4MM
SALES (corp-wide): 11.4MM **Privately Held**
Web: www.bil-jac.com
SIC: 2048 2047 Dry pet food (except dog and cat); Dog and cat food

(G-10343)
KG MEDINA LLC
Also Called: Ken Ganley Kia
2925 Medina Rd (44256-9672)
PHONE..................256 330-4273
Kenneth G Ganley, *Mgr*
EMP: 20 **EST:** 2019
SALES (est): 1.75MM **Privately Held**
Web: www.kenganleykia.com
SIC: 3714 Motor vehicle parts and accessories

(G-10344)
LEITNER FABRICATION LLC
935 Heritage Dr (44256-2404)
PHONE..................330 721-7374
EMP: 22
SIC: 3441 Fabricated structural metal

(G-10345)
LSQ MANUFACTURING INC
1140 Industrial Pkwy (44256-2486)
PHONE..................330 725-4905
Richard L Rauckhorst III, *Pr*
Richard L Rauckhorst Iii, *Pr*
Judith L Coffman, *VP*
EMP: 10 **EST:** 1946
SQ FT: 8,000
SALES (est): 926.61K **Privately Held**
Web: www.arthurproducts.com
SIC: 3494 3563 3432 Valves and pipe fittings, nec; Air and gas compressors; Plumbing fixture fittings and trim

(G-10346)
MANSFIELD PAINT CO INC
525 W Liberty St (44256-2223)
PHONE..................330 725-2436
George Bufkin, *CEO*
EMP: 8 **EST:** 1945
SQ FT: 24,000
SALES (est): 923.88K **Privately Held**
Web: www.mansfieldpaint.com
SIC: 2851 Paints: oil or alkyd vehicle or water thinned

(G-10347)
MEDINA COUNTY
Also Called: Medina County Recorders
144 N Broadway St Ste 117 (44256-1928)
PHONE..................330 723-3641
Linda Hoffman, *Brnch Mgr*
EMP: 19
SALES (corp-wide): 162.22MM **Privately Held**
Web: www.medinaco.org
SIC: 3825 Recorders, oscillographic
PA: Medina County
144 N Broadway St Ste 201
Medina OH 44256
330 723-3641

(G-10348)
MEDINA HNTNGTON RE GROUP II LL
635 N Huntington St (44256-1871)
PHONE..................330 591-2777

Darrel L Seibert Ii, *Prin*
EMP: 20 **EST:** 2017
SALES (est): 805.38K **Privately Held**
SIC: 2711 Newspapers, publishing and printing

(G-10349)
MEDINA POWDER COATING CORP
930 Lafayette Rd Unit C (44256-3509)
PHONE..................330 952-1977
EMP: 8 **EST:** 2013
SALES (est): 204.16K **Privately Held**
Web: www.medinapowdercoatingcorp.com
SIC: 3479 Coating of metals and formed products

(G-10350)
MEDINA POWDER GROUP INC
910 Lake Rd Ste B (44256-2765)
PHONE..................330 952-2711
EMP: 6 **EST:** 2015
SALES (est): 217.11K **Privately Held**
SIC: 3479 Coating of metals and formed products

(G-10351)
MEDINA SUPPLY COMPANY
820 W Smith Rd (44256-2425)
PHONE..................330 364-4411
Daryl Albright, *Mgr*
EMP: 45
SALES (corp-wide): 32.72B **Privately Held**
Web: www.shellyco.com
SIC: 1429 Igneus rock, crushed and broken-quarrying
HQ: Medina Supply Company
230 E Smith Rd
Medina OH 44256
330 723-3681

(G-10352)
MEDINA SUPPLY COMPANY (DH)
230 E Smith Rd (44256-3616)
PHONE..................330 723-3681
Jerry A Schwab, *Pr*
David Schwab, *VP*
Donna L Schwab, *Sec*
Mary Lynn Schwab, *Treas*
EMP: 20 **EST:** 1974
SQ FT: 2,000
SALES (est): 32.84MM
SALES (corp-wide): 32.72B **Privately Held**
Web: www.shellyco.com
SIC: 1442 3273 3281 5211 Construction sand and gravel; Ready-mixed concrete; Cut stone and stone products; Brick
HQ: Shelly Materials, Inc.
80 Park Dr
Thornville OH 43076
740 246-6315

(G-10353)
METAL MERCHANTS USA INC
445 W Liberty St (44256-2273)
P.O. Box 302 (44258-0302)
PHONE..................330 723-3228
Jerry Moody, *Prin*
EMP: 10 **EST:** 2010
SALES (est): 178.4K **Privately Held**
SIC: 3356 Nonferrous rolling and drawing, nec

(G-10354)
MILLER PLATING LLC
940 Lafayette Rd (44256-2415)
PHONE..................330 952-2550
Adam Anderson, *Managing Member*
EMP: 20 **EST:** 2019
SALES (est): 1MM **Privately Held**

SIC: 3471 Electroplating of metals or formed products

(G-10355)
MSLS GROUP LLC
Also Called: Main Street Lighting Standards
1080 Industrial Pkwy (44256-2449)
PHONE..................330 723-4431
Bernard Mcrae, *Managing Member*
EMP: 39 **EST:** 2014
SALES (est): 3.88MM **Privately Held**
Web: www.mainstreetlighting.com
SIC: 3312 Fence posts, iron and steel

(G-10356)
NORTHSTAR PUBLISHING INC
437 Lafayette Rd Ste 310 (44256-2398)
P.O. Box 1166 (44258-1166)
PHONE..................330 721-9126
Rodney Auth, *Pr*
EMP: 7 **EST:** 1998
SQ FT: 500
SALES (est): 991.25K **Privately Held**
Web: www.northstarpubs.com
SIC: 2741 Miscellaneous publishing

(G-10357)
OFFICE MAGIC INC (PA)
Also Called: Electrocoat
2290 Wilbur Rd (44256-8496)
PHONE..................510 782-6100
Craig Codding, *Pr*
EMP: 14 **EST:** 1975
SALES (est): 1.67MM
SALES (corp-wide): 1.67MM **Privately Held**
Web: www.electrocoat.ws
SIC: 3479 2522 7641 2519 Painting, coating, and hot dipping; Office desks and tables, except wood; Reupholstery; Fiberglass and plastic furniture

(G-10358)
OPTIMUM SURGICAL
2524 Medina Rd Ste 600 (44256-5390)
PHONE..................216 870-8526
Eric Henning, *Pr*
EMP: 10 **EST:** 2017
SALES (est): 450.11K **Privately Held**
Web: www.optimumsi.com
SIC: 7699 3841 Surgical instrument repair; Surgical instruments and apparatus

(G-10359)
OVATION PLYMR TECH ENGNRED MTL
Also Called: Optem
1030 W Smith Rd (44256-2445)
PHONE..................330 723-5686
Delbert Henderson, *COO*
Asis Banerjie, *Pr*
▲ **EMP:** 23 **EST:** 2004
SQ FT: 55,000
SALES (est): 4.18MM **Privately Held**
Web: www.opteminc.com
SIC: 2821 Plastics materials and resins

(G-10360)
OWENS CORNING ROOFG & ASP LLC
Also Called: Owens-Corning Fibrgls Trumbull
890 W Smith Rd (44256-2484)
PHONE..................330 764-7800
Jerry Moore, *Brnch Mgr*
EMP: 32
SIC: 3296 Mineral wool
HQ: Owens Corning Roofing And Asphalt, Llc
1 Owens Corning Pkwy
Toledo OH 43659
877 858-3855

(G-10361)
PACKAGING SPECIALTIES INC
300 Lake Rd (44256-2459)
PHONE..................330 723-6000
Robert Syme, *Ch Bd*
James Munson, *
◆ **EMP:** 50 **EST:** 1959
SQ FT: 59,000
SALES (est): 10.46MM
SALES (corp-wide): 10.46MM **Privately Held**
Web: www.packspec.com
SIC: 3412 3411 Metal barrels, drums, and pails; Metal cans
PA: Syme, Inc.
300 Lake Rd
Medina OH 44256
330 723-6000

(G-10362)
PARK CORPORATION (PA)
Also Called: Charleston Ordnance Center
3555 Reserve Commons Dr (44256-5900)
P.O. Box 8678 (25303-0678)
PHONE..................216 267-4870
Raymond P Park, *Ch Bd*
Daniel K Park, *
Shelva J Davis, *
Tim Geharing, *
Ricky L Bertrem, *
◆ **EMP:** 300 **EST:** 1948
SALES (est): 367.37MM
SALES (corp-wide): 367.37MM **Privately Held**
Web: www.parkcorp.com
SIC: 5084 3547 6512 7999 Industrial machinery and equipment; Rolling mill machinery; Commercial and industrial building operation; Exposition operation

(G-10363)
PLASTI-KOTE CO INC
Also Called: Valspar
1000 Lake Rd (44256-3598)
PHONE..................330 725-4511
Richard Rompala, *Ch Bd*
◆ **EMP:** 250 **EST:** 1989
SQ FT: 145,000
SALES (est): 51.9MM
SALES (corp-wide): 22.15B **Publicly Held**
Web: www.plastikote.com
SIC: 2813 2992 2851 Industrial gases; Lubricating oils and greases; Paints and allied products
PA: The Sherwin-Williams Company
101 W Prospect Ave
Cleveland OH 44115
216 566-2000

(G-10364)
PLASTICS CNVRTING SLUTIONS LTD
5341 River Styx Rd (44256-8725)
P.O. Box 88 (44258-0088)
PHONE..................330 722-2537
EMP: 6 **EST:** 2004
SALES (est): 105.37K **Privately Held**
SIC: 3089 Injection molding of plastics

(G-10365)
PLATE ENGRAVING CORPORATION
2324 Sharon Copley Rd (44256-9773)
PHONE..................330 239-2155
James Brobeck, *Pr*
James Michael Brobeck, *Pr*
Von Brobeck, *VP*
EMP: 6 **EST:** 1968
SQ FT: 4,018
SALES (est): 472.84K **Privately Held**
Web: plateengravingcorp.godaddysites.com

Medina - Medina County (G-10366)

SIC: 2796 3089 Engraving on copper, steel, wood, or rubber: printing plates; Engraving of plastics

(G-10366)
PROGRESSIVE MOLDING TECH
5234 Portside Dr (44256-5966)
PHONE..................................330 220-7030
Laird Daubenspeck, *CEO*
EMP: 8 EST: 2002
SQ FT: 8,900
SALES (est): 1.1MM **Privately Held**
Web: www.promoldtech.com
SIC: 3089 Injection molding of plastics

(G-10367)
PUREBUTTONSCOM LLC
4930 Chippewa Rd Unit A (44256-8824)
PHONE..................................330 721-1600
EMP: 15 EST: 2005
SQ FT: 1,200
SALES (est): 2.52MM **Privately Held**
Web: www.purebuttons.com
SIC: 5131 3965 Buttons; Fasteners, buttons, needles, and pins

(G-10368)
RAVAGO AMERICAS LLC
Entec Polymers
5192 Lake Rd (44256-8809)
PHONE..................................330 825-2505
Mike Gasper, *Brnch Mgr*
EMP: 43
Web: www.amcopolymers.com
SIC: 2821 Plastics materials and resins
HQ: Ravago Americas Llc
  1900 Smmit Twr Blvd Ste 9
  Orlando FL 32810
  800 262-6685

(G-10369)
REALIZED MFG LLC
879 S Progress Dr Ste A (44256-3926)
PHONE..................................330 535-3887
EMP: 10 EST: 2018
SALES (est): 485.77K **Privately Held**
Web: www.realizedmfg.com
SIC: 3841 Surgical and medical instruments

(G-10370)
REPUBLIC POWDERED METALS INC (HQ)
2628 Pearl Rd (44256-9099)
P.O. Box 777 (44258-0777)
PHONE..................................330 225-3192
Thomas Sullivan, *Ch Bd*
Frank C Sullivan, *CEO*
◆ EMP: 61 EST: 1963
SQ FT: 20,000
SALES (est): 1.29B
SALES (corp-wide): 7.26B **Publicly Held**
Web: www.rpminc.com
SIC: 2851 2891 3069 2899 Paints and allied products; Adhesives and sealants; Roofing, membrane rubber; Waterproofing compounds
PA: Rpm International Inc.
  2628 Pearl Rd
  Medina OH 44256
  330 273-5090

(G-10371)
RPM CONSUMER HOLDING COMPANY (HQ)
2628 Pearl Rd (44256-7623)
P.O. Box 777 (44258-0777)
PHONE..................................330 273-5090
Frank C Sullivan, *Pr*
Ronald A Rice, *Asst VP*
Keith R Smiley, *Treas*
Edward W Moore, *Sec*
Ron Rice, *Pr*
EMP: 49 EST: 2002
SALES (est): 24.9MM
SALES (corp-wide): 7.26B **Publicly Held**
Web: www.rpminc.com
SIC: 2891 3089 3952 3944 Adhesives; Kits, plastics; Brushes, air, artists'; Games, toys, and children's vehicles
PA: Rpm International Inc.
  2628 Pearl Rd
  Medina OH 44256
  330 273-5090

(G-10372)
RPM INTERNATIONAL INC (PA)
2628 Pearl Rd (44256-7623)
P.O. Box 777 (44258-0777)
PHONE..................................330 273-5090
Frank C Sullivan, *Ch Bd*
Edward W Moore, *CCO*
Russell L Gordon, *VP*
Matthew T Ratajczak, *Global Vice President*
Michael J Laroche, *CAO*
◆ EMP: 61 EST: 1947
SALES (est): 7.26B
SALES (corp-wide): 7.26B **Publicly Held**
Web: www.rpminc.com
SIC: 2891 3069 2899 2865 Adhesives and sealants; Roofing, membrane rubber; Waterproofing compounds; Dyes and pigments

(G-10373)
S&V INDUSTRIES INC (PA)
5054 Paramount Dr (44256-5363)
PHONE..................................330 666-1986
Senthil K Sundarapandian, *CEO*
Joan Owens, *
Mahesh Douglas, *
▲ EMP: 35 EST: 1993
SQ FT: 1,618
SALES (est): 12.47MM **Privately Held**
Web: www.svindustries.com
SIC: 5049 3089 3312 Engineers' equipment and supplies, nec; Casting of plastics; Forgings, iron and steel

(G-10374)
SEALY MATTRESS MFG CO LLC
1070 Lake Rd (44256-2450)
PHONE..................................800 697-3259
Vicky Avans, *Mgr*
EMP: 18
SALES (corp-wide): 4.93B **Publicly Held**
Web: www.tempursealy.com
SIC: 2515 Mattresses, innerspring or box spring
HQ: Sealy Mattress Manufacturing Company, Llc
  1000 Tempur Way
  Lexington KY 40511
  859 455-1000

(G-10375)
SFS GROUP USA INC
Also Called: Sfs Intec
5201 Portside Dr (44256-5966)
PHONE..................................330 239-7100
Urs Langenauer, *Genl Mgr*
EMP: 186
Web: us.sfs.com
SIC: 3714 Motor vehicle parts and accessories
HQ: Sfs Group Usa, Inc.
  1045 Spring St
  Wyomissing PA 19610
  610 376-5751

(G-10376)
SFS INTEC INC
5201 Portside Dr (44256-5966)
PHONE..................................330 239-7100
Jens Breu, *CEO*
EMP: 20 EST: 2003
SALES (est): 3.24MM **Privately Held**
SIC: 3714 Motor vehicle parts and accessories

(G-10377)
SHELLY MATERIALS INC
820 W Smith Rd (44256-2425)
PHONE..................................330 723-3681
EMP: 17
SALES (corp-wide): 32.72B **Privately Held**
Web: www.shellyco.com
SIC: 3273 Ready-mixed concrete
HQ: Shelly Materials, Inc.
  80 Park Dr
  Thornville OH 43076
  740 246-6315

(G-10378)
SOLUTIONS IN POLYCARBONATE LLC
6353 Norwalk Rd (44256-9455)
PHONE..................................330 572-2860
Bruce Gold, *Pr*
EMP: 15 EST: 2016
SQ FT: 24,000
SALES (est): 2.48MM **Privately Held**
Web: www.solutionsinpc.com
SIC: 3089 Windows, plastics

(G-10379)
STANDARD WLDG & STL PDTS INC
260 S State Rd (44256-2474)
P.O. Box 297 (44258-0297)
PHONE..................................330 273-2777
Christopher Coleman, *Pr*
Jack Colman, *VP*
Jayne Coleman, *Sec*
Charles Coleman, *CEO*
EMP: 15 EST: 1939
SQ FT: 30,000
SALES (est): 2.25MM **Privately Held**
Web: www.stdwelding.com
SIC: 3441 Fabricated structural metal

(G-10380)
SUPRO SPRING & WIRE FORMS INC
6440 Norwalk Rd Ste N (44256-7154)
PHONE..................................330 722-5628
▲ EMP: 35 EST: 1996
SQ FT: 12,000
SALES (est): 3.58MM **Privately Held**
Web: www.suprospring.com
SIC: 3495 Wire springs

(G-10381)
SYMATIC INC
Also Called: Ancom Business Products
803 E Washington St Ste 200 (44256-3333)
P.O. Box 150 (44212-0150)
PHONE..................................330 225-1510
Walter H Tanner, *Pr*
Cindy Holton, *
EMP: 14 EST: 1961
SALES (est): 434.13K **Privately Held**
SIC: 3579 5044 2541 2521 Paper handling machines; Office equipment; Wood partitions and fixtures; Wood office furniture

(G-10382)
SYME INC (PA)
300 Lake Rd (44256-2459)
PHONE..................................330 723-6000
Robert P Syme, *CEO*
Jim L Munson, *Pr*
EMP: 21 EST: 1976
SQ FT: 58,000
SALES (est): 10.46MM
SALES (corp-wide): 10.46MM **Privately Held**
Web: www.packspec.com
SIC: 3412 Metal barrels, drums, and pails

(G-10383)
TAHOMA MACHINING LTD
950 Lake Rd (44256-2453)
PHONE..................................330 952-2410
John Norris, *Genl Mgr*
EMP: 10 EST: 2012
SALES (est): 239.03K **Privately Held**
Web: www.tahomamachining.com
SIC: 3599 Machine shop, jobbing and repair

(G-10384)
TFP CORPORATION (PA)
Also Called: Tru-Weld Stud Welding Div
460 Lake Rd (44256-2457)
PHONE..................................330 725-7741
◆ EMP: 50 EST: 1928
SALES (est): 25.86MM
SALES (corp-wide): 25.86MM **Privately Held**
Web: www.tfpcorp.com
SIC: 3965 Fasteners

(G-10385)
THEKEN SPINE LLC
1153 Medina Rd Ste 100 (44256-5402)
PHONE..................................330 773-7677
EMP: 10
SALES (corp-wide): 4.92MM **Privately Held**
SIC: 3842 Implants, surgical
PA: Theken Spine, Llc
  5770 Armada Dr
  Carlsbad CA

(G-10386)
THERMO VENT MANUFACTURING INC
Also Called: Therm-O-Vent
1213 Medina Rd (44256-5408)
PHONE..................................330 239-0239
▲ EMP: 14 EST: 1995
SQ FT: 6,800
SALES (est): 498.26K **Privately Held**
Web: www.glassblocksupply.com
SIC: 3444 3564 Ventilators, sheet metal; Blowers and fans

(G-10387)
TIGER GENERAL LLC
6867 Wooster Pike (44256-8859)
PHONE..................................330 239-4949
EMP: 19 EST: 2008
SQ FT: 18,000
SALES (est): 2.74MM **Privately Held**
Web: www.tigergeneral.com
SIC: 3533 5511 Oil and gas drilling rigs and equipment; Trucks, tractors, and trailers: new and used

(G-10388)
TRAILER ONE INC
1030 W Liberty St (44256-1326)
PHONE..................................330 723-7474
Kenneth Smith, *Pr*
Bradley Thomas, *VP*
▼ EMP: 10 EST: 1989
SALES (est): 4.45MM **Privately Held**
Web: www.traileroneinc.com
SIC: 5511 3715 7359 Trucks, tractors, and trailers: new and used; Truck trailers; Equipment rental and leasing, nec

GEOGRAPHIC SECTION
Mentor - Lake County (G-10413)

(G-10389)
TROGDON PUBLISHING INC
Also Called: Ohio Standard Bread
5164 Normandy Park Dr Ste 100
(44256-5903)
PHONE.................330 721-7678
Bruce Trogdon, *Pr*
Raymond Leroy, *
EMP: 42 **EST:** 1975
SQ FT: 6,200
SALES (est): 5.47MM **Privately Held**
Web: www.thepostnewspapers.com
SIC: 2741 2711 Guides: publishing and printing; Newspapers

(G-10390)
UNISAND INCORPORATED
1097 Industrial Pkwy (44256-2448)
PHONE.................330 722-0222
David W Bullock, *Pr*
Douglas Bullock, *
▲ **EMP:** 26 **EST:** 1990
SQ FT: 3,000
SALES (est): 4.52MM **Privately Held**
Web: www.unisand.com
SIC: 3291 Abrasive wheels and grindstones, not artificial

(G-10391)
UNITED SPORT APPAREL
229 Harding St Ste B (44256-1288)
PHONE.................330 722-0818
David A Bricker, *Owner*
EMP: 10 **EST:** 1984
SQ FT: 6,000
SALES (est): 659.64K **Privately Held**
Web: www.usacustomapparel.com
SIC: 2759 2395 Screen printing; Embroidery products, except Schiffli machine

(G-10392)
UNITED TUBE CORPORATION
960 Lake Rd (44256-2453)
PHONE.................330 725-4196
Frank J Sadowski, *Pr*
Angelina Chaplain, *
Harvey O Yoder, *
EMP: 54 **EST:** 1945
SALES (est): 7.9MM **Privately Held**
Web: www.unitedtube.com
SIC: 3317 Tubes, wrought: welded or lock joint

(G-10393)
WAN DYNAMICS INC
303 N Court St Unit 1758 (44258-5377)
P.O. Box 1758 (44258-1758)
PHONE.................877 400-9490
Jason Valore, *Pr*
Jason Gintert, *VP*
EMP: 10 **EST:** 2016
SALES (est): 3MM **Privately Held**
Web: www.wandynamics.com
SIC: 3661 Telephone and telegraph apparatus

(G-10394)
WERKS KRAFT ENGINEERING LLC
935 Heritage Dr (44256-2404)
PHONE.................330 721-7374
Kris Klingmann, *Pr*
EMP: 45 **EST:** 2018
SQ FT: 60,000
SALES (est): 4.63MM **Privately Held**
Web: www.kraftwerks.com
SIC: 8711 3566 3535 3441 Engineering services; Speed changers (power transmission equipment), except auto; Conveyors and conveying equipment; Fabricated structural metal

(G-10395)
WOODBINE PRODUCTS COMPANY
Also Called: Powrkleen
915 W Smith Rd (44256-2446)
PHONE.................330 725-0165
Phillip Navratil, *Pr*
Stephen A Kuzyk Junior, *Sec*
▲ **EMP:** 14 **EST:** 1961
SQ FT: 20,000
SALES (est): 2.08MM **Privately Held**
Web: www.woodbineproducts.com
SIC: 2842 2844 Cleaning or polishing preparations, nec; Perfumes, cosmetics and other toilet preparations

(G-10396)
YOUNGS SEALCOATING LLC
2445 Station Rd (44256-9428)
PHONE.................330 591-5446
Jason Young, *Owner*
EMP: 6 **EST:** 2018
SALES (est): 272.1K **Privately Held**
Web: www.youngssealcoating.com
SIC: 2952 Asphalt felts and coatings

Medway
Clark County

(G-10397)
DAYCOA INC
Also Called: Daycoa Lighting
50 Walnut Rd (45341-1268)
P.O. Box 8 (45341-0008)
PHONE.................937 849-1315
EMP: 13 **EST:** 1957
SALES (est): 791.87K **Privately Held**
Web: www.daycoa.com
SIC: 3646 5063 Commercial lighting fixtures; Light bulbs and related supplies

(G-10398)
R & D INDUSTRIES LLC
1313 Lakeshore Dr (45341-1517)
PHONE.................937 397-5836
Randy D Berry, *Admn*
EMP: 6 **EST:** 2014
SALES (est): 347.03M **Privately Held**
SIC: 3999 Manufacturing industries, nec

(G-10399)
SAMKAT ENTERPRISES INC
10811 Schiller Rd (45341-9743)
PHONE.................937 398-6704
Annette Triplett, *Prin*
EMP: 6 **EST:** 2011
SALES (est): 49.82K **Privately Held**
SIC: 3732 Boatbuilding and repairing

(G-10400)
WAYNE CONCRETE COMPANY LLC
223 Western Dr (45341-9521)
PHONE.................937 545-9919
Wayne Gibson, *Owner*
EMP: 10 **EST:** 1987
SALES (est): 681.28K **Privately Held**
SIC: 1442 Construction sand and gravel

Mentor
Lake County

(G-10401)
1 888 U PITCH IT
7176 Fillmore Ct (44060-4816)
PHONE.................440 796-9028
Frank A Jurkoshek Junior, *Prin*
EMP: 6 **EST:** 2010
SALES (est): 85.09K **Privately Held**

SIC: 3089 Garbage containers, plastics

(G-10402)
ACCURATE TECH INC
Also Called: Accurate Tech
7230 Industrial Park Blvd (44060-5316)
PHONE.................440 951-9153
Micheal Karcic Senior, *Pr*
Micheal Karcic Junior, *VP*
EMP: 6 **EST:** 1987
SQ FT: 3,000
SALES (est): 505.79K **Privately Held**
Web: www.accuratetechinc.net
SIC: 3599 Machine shop, jobbing and repair

(G-10403)
ACO INC (DH)
Also Called: Quartz
9470 Pinecone Dr (44060-1863)
PHONE.................440 639-7230
Derek Humphries, *CEO*
Kevin Taylor, *
Judy Brubaker, *
◆ **EMP:** 50 **EST:** 1978
SQ FT: 30,000
SALES (est): 85.24MM
SALES (corp-wide): 1.11B **Privately Held**
Web: www.acousa.com
SIC: 3272 3089 3312 Concrete products, precast, nec; Plastics and fiberglass tanks; Stainless steel
HQ: Severin Ahlmann Holding Gmbh
Am Ahlmannkai
Budelsdorf SH 24782
43313540

(G-10404)
ACTIVITIES PRESS INC
Also Called: AP Direct
7181 Industrial Park Blvd (44060-5327)
PHONE.................440 953-1200
Graydon Bullard, *Pr*
Leroy Bridges, *
Linda Bridges, *
Martin Hilston, *
▲ **EMP:** 28 **EST:** 1947
SQ FT: 24,000
SALES (est): 4.75MM **Privately Held**
Web: www.activitiespress.com
SIC: 2752 2791 2789 Offset printing; Typesetting; Bookbinding and related work

(G-10405)
ADVANCED FME PRODUCTS INC
9413 Hamilton Dr (44060-8709)
PHONE.................440 953-0700
Thomas Nalfi, *Pr*
EMP: 11 **EST:** 2005
SALES (est): 587.78K **Privately Held**
Web: www.advsts.com
SIC: 3462 Nuclear power plant forgings, ferrous

(G-10406)
AERO TECH TOOL & MOLD INC
7224 Industrial Park Blvd (44060-5316)
PHONE.................440 942-3327
Tom Murphy, *Pr*
EMP: 6 **EST:** 1979
SQ FT: 12,000
SALES (est): 616.13K **Privately Held**
SIC: 3544 3728 3462 Industrial molds; Aircraft parts and equipment, nec; Iron and steel forgings

(G-10407)
AEXCEL CORPORATION (PA)
7373 Production Dr (44060-4858)
PHONE.................440 974-3800
◆ **EMP:** 34 **EST:** 1963
SALES (est): 8.96MM

SALES (corp-wide): 8.96MM **Privately Held**
Web: www.aexcelcorp.com
SIC: 2851 Paints and paint additives

(G-10408)
AIR POWER DYNAMICS LLC
7350 Corporate Blvd (44060-4856)
PHONE.................440 701-2100
Boya Belasic, *
EMP: 200 **EST:** 2002
SQ FT: 73,000
SALES (est): 24.79MM **Privately Held**
Web: www.airpowerdynamics.com
SIC: 3543 Industrial patterns

(G-10409)
AIR TECHNICAL INDUSTRIES INC
7501 Clover Ave (44060-5297)
PHONE.................440 951-5191
Pero Novak, *CEO*
Vida Novak, *
◆ **EMP:** 40 **EST:** 1964
SQ FT: 80,000
SALES (est): 9.7MM **Privately Held**
Web: www.airtechnical.com
SIC: 3569 3536 3535 5084 Robots, assembly line: industrial and commercial; Hoists, cranes and monorails; Bulk handling conveyor systems; Materials handling machinery

(G-10410)
ALB TYLER HOLDINGS INC
7255 Industrial Park Blvd Ste A
(44060-5331)
PHONE.................440 946-7171
Art Bastulli, *Pr*
Jody Kamenshy, *VP*
Kathleen Potts, *Sec*
EMP: 9 **EST:** 1990
SQ FT: 7,500
SALES (est): 835.17K **Privately Held**
Web: www.coastaldiamond.com
SIC: 3291 5085 Abrasive products; Industrial supplies

(G-10411)
ALL STATE GL BLOCK FCTRY INC
8781 East Ave (44060-4303)
PHONE.................440 205-8410
EMP: 8 **EST:** 1995
SQ FT: 3,000
SALES (est): 703.26K **Privately Held**
SIC: 1793 5231 3229 Glass and glazing work ; Glass; Blocks and bricks, glass

(G-10412)
ALLOY PRECISION TECH INC
6989 Lindsay Dr (44060-4928)
PHONE.................440 266-7700
Michael Canty, *CEO*
Michael Canty, *Pr*
Michele Ponsart, *
◆ **EMP:** 90 **EST:** 1935
SALES (est): 24.72MM **Privately Held**
Web: www.alloyprecisiontech.com
SIC: 3599 3498 3494 Bellows, industrial: metal; Fabricated pipe and fittings; Valves and pipe fittings, nec

(G-10413)
AMERICAN HERITAGE BILLD LLC
9248 Headlands Rd (44060-1026)
PHONE.................877 998-0908
◆ **EMP:** 70 **EST:** 1999
SALES (est): 8.22MM **Privately Held**
Web: www.americanheritagebilliards.com
SIC: 3949 Billiard and pool equipment and supplies, general

Mentor - Lake County (G-10414)

(G-10414)
AMERICAN METAL COATINGS INC (PA)
7700 Tyler Blvd (44060-4964)
PHONE..................................216 451-3131
EMP: 40 EST: 1995
SQ FT: 180,000
SALES (est): 8.62MM **Privately Held**
Web: www.americanmetal.com
SIC: 3479 Coating of metals and formed products

(G-10415)
AMERICAN STERILIZER COMPANY (PA)
5960 Heisley Rd (44060-1834)
P.O. Box 960 (44061-0960)
PHONE..................................440 392-8328
▲ EMP: 46 EST: 2009
SALES (est): 33.12MM
SALES (corp-wide): 33.12MM **Privately Held**
Web: www.steris.com
SIC: 3821 Sterilizers

(G-10416)
AMY INDUSTRIES INC
8790 Twinbrook Rd (44060-4333)
PHONE..................................440 942-3478
EMP: 6 EST: 2010
SALES (est): 243.81K **Privately Held**
SIC: 3999 Manufacturing industries, nec

(G-10417)
ANGSTROM PRECISION METALS LLC
8229 Tyler Blvd (44060-4218)
PHONE..................................440 255-6700
▲ EMP: 19 EST: 2010
SALES (est): 1.44MM **Privately Held**
Web: www.w-pm.com
SIC: 3545 Precision tools, machinists'
PA: Angstrom Automotive Group, Llc
    2000 Town Ctr Ste 100
    Southfield MI 48075

(G-10418)
ANODIZING SPECIALISTS INC
7547 Tyler Blvd (44060-4869)
PHONE..................................440 951-0257
David J Pecjak, *Pr*
Michael T Pecjak, *VP*
EMP: 31 EST: 1977
SQ FT: 11,000
SALES (est): 1.42MM **Privately Held**
Web: www.anodizingspecialists.com
SIC: 3471 Finishing, metals or formed products

(G-10419)
APOLLO MANUFACTURING CO LLC
7911 Enterprise Dr (44060-5311)
PHONE..................................440 951-9972
Allen Sandy, *Managing Member*
Ronald Jack, *
Draga Marusic, *
EMP: 30 EST: 1989
SQ FT: 25,000
SALES (est): 5.64MM **Privately Held**
Web: www.apollo-mfg.com
SIC: 3599 Machine shop, jobbing and repair

(G-10420)
APOLLO PLASTICS INC
7555 Tyler Blvd Ste 11 (44060-4866)
PHONE..................................440 951-7774
Stanley Skrbis, *Pr*
Maria Skrbis, *Sec*
EMP: 10 EST: 1973
SQ FT: 8,000
SALES (est): 943.89K **Privately Held**
Web: www.apolloplastics.net
SIC: 3544 3089 Industrial molds; Plastics processing

(G-10421)
ARBOR INDUSTRIES INC
6830 Patterson Dr (44060-4344)
PHONE..................................440 255-4720
EMP: 100 EST: 1978
SALES (est): 9.11MM **Privately Held**
Web: www.arborindustriesinc.com
SIC: 3469 Stamping metal for the trade

(G-10422)
ARCH CUTTING TLS - MENTOR LLC
9332 Pinecone Dr (44060-1861)
PHONE..................................440 350-9393
EMP: 7
SALES (est): 692.2K **Privately Held**
Web: www.archcuttingtools.com
SIC: 3541 Machine tools, metal cutting type

(G-10423)
AREM CO
Also Called: Jaytee Division
7234 Justin Way (44060-4881)
PHONE..................................440 974-6740
Bob Myotte, *Pr*
Jack Kurant, *Sec*
Becky Uyesugi, *VP*
EMP: 19 EST: 1981
SALES (est): 968.93K **Privately Held**
Web: www.aremtube.com
SIC: 3498 3949 3354 3471 Fabricated pipe and fittings; Sporting and athletic goods, nec; Aluminum extruded products; Plating and polishing

(G-10424)
AVALIGN - INTEGRATED LLC
7124 Industrial Park Blvd (44060-5314)
PHONE..................................440 269-6984
EMP: 11 EST: 2019
SALES (est): 956.53K **Privately Held**
Web: www.avalign.com
SIC: 3841 Surgical and medical instruments

(G-10425)
AVERY DENNISON CORPORATION
8100 Tyler Blvd (44060-4865)
PHONE..................................440 534-6527
EMP: 11
SALES (corp-wide): 8.36B **Publicly Held**
Web: www.averydennison.com
SIC: 2672 Paper; coated and laminated, nec
PA: Avery Dennison Corporation
    8080 Norton Pkwy
    Mentor OH 44060
    440 534-6000

(G-10426)
AVERY DENNISON CORPORATION (PA)
Also Called: Avery Dennison
8080 Norton Pkwy (44060)
PHONE..................................440 534-6000
Deon M Stander, *Pr*
Mitchell R Butier, *
Gregory S Lovins, *Sr VP*
Ignacio J Walker, *CLO*
Deena Baker Nel, *Chief Human Resource Officer*
EMP: 407 EST: 1935
SALES (est): 8.36B
SALES (corp-wide): 8.36B **Publicly Held**
Web: www.averydennison.com
SIC: 2672 3081 3497 2678 Adhesive papers, labels, or tapes: from purchased material; Unsupported plastics film and sheet; Metal foil and leaf; Notebooks: made from purchased paper

(G-10427)
AVERY DENNISON CORPORATION
Avery Dnnson Fsson Flms Div US
5750 Heisley Rd (44060-1830)
P.O. Box 8008 (44077-8008)
PHONE..................................440 639-3900
Bruce J Wilson, *Brnch Mgr*
EMP: 70
SALES (corp-wide): 8.36B **Publicly Held**
SIC: 2672 2679 3081 3497 Adhesive papers, labels, or tapes: from purchased material; Building, insulating, and packaging paper; Packing materials, plastics sheet; Metal foil and leaf
PA: Avery Dennison Corporation
    8080 Norton Pkwy
    Mentor OH 44060
    440 534-6000

(G-10428)
AVERY DENNISON CORPORATION
7100 Lindsay Dr (44060-4923)
PHONE..................................440 358-2828
EMP: 126
SALES (corp-wide): 8.36B **Publicly Held**
Web: www.averydennison.com
SIC: 2672 Adhesive backed films, foams and foils
PA: Avery Dennison Corporation
    8080 Norton Pkwy
    Mentor OH 44060
    440 534-6000

(G-10429)
AVERY DNNISON G HOLDINGS I LLC
8080 Norton Pkwy (44060-5990)
PHONE..................................440 534-6000
EMP: 24 EST: 2007
SALES (est): 1.54MM
SALES (corp-wide): 8.36B **Publicly Held**
SIC: 2672 Adhesive papers, labels, or tapes: from purchased material
PA: Avery Dennison Corporation
    8080 Norton Pkwy
    Mentor OH 44060
    440 534-6000

(G-10430)
BESTLIGHT LED CORPORATION
8909 East Ave (44060-4305)
PHONE..................................440 205-1552
James Moll, *Pr*
EMP: 7 EST: 2016
SALES (est): 480.17K **Privately Held**
Web: www.bestlightled.com
SIC: 3674 Light emitting diodes

(G-10431)
BRIDGESTONE RET OPERATIONS LLC
Also Called: Firestone
7495 Mentor Ave (44060-5405)
PHONE..................................440 299-6126
Nathan Tokar, *Mgr*
EMP: 10
Web: www.bridgestoneamericas.com
SIC: 5531 7534 7538 Automotive tires; Tire retreading and repair shops; General automotive repair shops
HQ: Bridgestone Retail Operations, Llc
    333 E Lake St Ste 300
    Bloomingdale IL 60108
    630 259-9000

(G-10432)
BRUMALL MANUFACTURING CORP
7850 Division Dr (44060)
PHONE..................................440 974-2622
Rod Brumberg, *Pr*
Yvonne Brumberg, *
▲ EMP: 40 EST: 1968
SQ FT: 25,000
SALES (est): 3.07MM **Privately Held**
Web: www.brumall.com
SIC: 3643 Connectors and terminals for electrical devices

(G-10433)
BURTON INDUSTRIES INC
7875 Division Dr (44060-4877)
PHONE..................................440 974-1700
Christopher Burton, *Pr*
Linda Burton, *Sec*
EMP: 27 EST: 1983
SALES (est): 6.22MM **Privately Held**
Web: www.burtonems.com
SIC: 3599 Machine shop, jobbing and repair

(G-10434)
BUYERS PRODUCTS COMPANY
8120 Tyler Blvd (44060-4852)
PHONE..................................440 974-8888
James Kleinman, *Brnch Mgr*
EMP: 251
SALES (corp-wide): 128.77MM **Privately Held**
Web: www.buyersproducts.com
SIC: 3465 Body parts, automobile: stamped metal
PA: Buyers Products Company
    9049 Tyler Blvd
    Mentor OH 44060
    440 974-8888

(G-10435)
BUYERS PRODUCTS COMPANY (PA)
9049 Tyler Blvd (44060-4800)
PHONE..................................440 974-8888
Mark Saltzman, *Pr*
Rhonda Carder, *CFO*
◆ EMP: 150 EST: 1947
SQ FT: 172,000
SALES (est): 128.77MM
SALES (corp-wide): 128.77MM **Privately Held**
Web: www.buyersproducts.com
SIC: 5013 3714 Truck parts and accessories; Motor vehicle parts and accessories

(G-10436)
CAIRNS INDUSTRIES LLC
7667 Jenther Dr (44060-4872)
PHONE..................................440 255-1190
Lori Bastian, *Prin*
EMP: 6 EST: 2012
SALES (est): 342.16K **Privately Held**
SIC: 3999 Manufacturing industries, nec

(G-10437)
CHEMSULTANTS INTERNATIONAL INC (PA)
9079 Tyler Blvd (44060)
P.O. Box 1118 (44061)
PHONE..................................440 974-3080
Jennifer Raj Muny, *Dir*
Keith Muny, *VP*
Judith Muny, *Sec*
EMP: 9 EST: 1986
SQ FT: 10,000
SALES (est): 4.82MM
SALES (corp-wide): 4.82MM **Privately Held**
Web: www.chemsultants.com

SIC: 3821 8734 8742 Laboratory apparatus and furniture; Product testing laboratory, safety or performance; Industry specialist consultants

(G-10438)
CLARIOS LLC
Also Called: Johnson Controls
7780 Metric Dr (44060-4862)
PHONE..................................440 205-7221
George Ells, *Brnch Mgr*
EMP: 33
Web: www.clarios.com
SIC: 2531 Seats, automobile
HQ: Clarios, Llc
 5757 N Green Bay Ave
 Milwaukee WI 53209

(G-10439)
CLARK RUBBER & PLASTIC COMPANY
Also Called: Clark Rubber & Plastics
8888 East Ave (44060-4306)
P.O. Box 299 (44061-0299)
PHONE..................................440 255-9793
Gregory Clark, *Pr*
EMP: 130 EST: 1970
SALES (est): 24.89MM **Privately Held**
Web: www.clarkrandp.com
SIC: 3061 3069 3089 Mechanical rubber goods; Molded rubber products; Extruded finished plastics products, nec

(G-10440)
CLIMAX METAL PRODUCTS COMPANY
8141 Tyler Blvd (44060-4855)
PHONE..................................440 943-8898
Jerry Wheaton, *CEO*
Gerald R Wheaton, *
John T White, *
L G Knecht, *
▲ EMP: 65 EST: 1946
SQ FT: 25,000
SALES (est): 17.27MM
SALES (corp-wide): 1.47B **Publicly Held**
Web: www.climaxmetal.com
SIC: 3366 3568 Bushings and bearings; Couplings, shaft: rigid, flexible, universal joint, etc.
PA: Rbc Bearings Incorporated
 1 Tribiology Ctr
 Oxford CT 06478
 203 267-7001

(G-10441)
COMMERCIAL DOCK & DOOR INC
7653 Saint Clair Ave (44060-5235)
PHONE..................................440 951-1210
Allen A Kovar, *Pr*
Raymond M Strumbly, *VP*
Tom Liebhardt, *CFO*
EMP: 22 EST: 2004
SALES (est): 2.57MM **Privately Held**
Web: www.commercialdockanddoor.com
SIC: 3448 Docks, prefabricated metal

(G-10442)
CONCORD ROAD EQUIPMENT MFG LLC
8200 Tyler Blvd Ste H (44060-4250)
PHONE..................................440 357-5344
Jeffery Warfield, *Managing Member*
EMP: 40 EST: 2021
SALES (est): 5.99MM
SALES (corp-wide): 128.77MM **Privately Held**
Web: www.concordroadequipment.com
SIC: 3531 Road construction and maintenance machinery
PA: Buyers Products Company

9049 Tyler Blvd
Mentor OH 44060
440 974-8888

(G-10443)
CORE MANUFACTURING LLC
Also Called: Core Manufacturing
8878 East Ave (44060-4306)
PHONE..................................440 946-8002
Ted Wolf, *Pr*
David Sukenik, *Dir*
Theodore Wolf, *Dir*
Richard Stark, *Dir*
EMP: 9 EST: 2013
SALES (est): 1.52MM **Privately Held**
Web: www.coremfg.net
SIC: 3452 Bolts, nuts, rivets, and washers

(G-10444)
CORE-TECH ENTERPRISES LLC
7850 Enterprise Dr (44060-5310)
PHONE..................................440 946-8324
EMP: 6 EST: 2016
SALES (est): 552.67K **Privately Held**
Web: www.core-tech-inc.com
SIC: 3599 Machine shop, jobbing and repair

(G-10445)
CRESCENT METAL PRODUCTS INC (PA)
Also Called: Cres Cor
5925 Heisley Rd (44060-1833)
PHONE..................................440 350-1100
Clifford D Baggott, *Prin*
Rio Degennaro, *
Gregory D Baggott, *
Heather B Stewart, *
Anna Baggott, *Prin*
▲ EMP: 171 EST: 1936
SALES (est): 45.8MM
SALES (corp-wide): 45.8MM **Privately Held**
Web: www.crescor.com
SIC: 3556 3567 3537 2542 Food products machinery; Industrial furnaces and ovens; Industrial trucks and tractors; Partitions and fixtures, except wood

(G-10446)
CREST PRODUCTS INC
Also Called: Crest Aluminum Products
8287 Tyler Blvd (44060-4218)
PHONE..................................440 942-5770
John M Allin, *Pr*
Peter Antos, *Treas*
Timothy Antos, *VP*
Nancy Worden, *Sec*
EMP: 18 EST: 1966
SQ FT: 41,500
SALES (est): 2.27MM **Privately Held**
Web: www.crestaluminum.com
SIC: 3444 7389 Awnings, sheet metal; Metal slitting and shearing

(G-10447)
CUYAHOGA MOLDED PLASTICS CO
9351 Mercantile Dr (44060-4523)
PHONE..................................216 261-2744
Ed Zalar, *Brnch Mgr*
EMP: 7
SALES (corp-wide): 5.28MM **Privately Held**
Web: www.cuyahogaplastics.com
SIC: 3089 Injection molding of plastics
PA: Cuyahoga Molded Plastics Co (Inc)
 1265 Babbitt Rd
 Euclid OH 44132
 216 261-2744

(G-10448)
DMI MANUFACTURING INC
7177 Industrial Park Blvd (44060)
PHONE..................................800 238-5384
Timothy J Doney, *Prin*
EMP: 13 EST: 1998
SALES (est): 2.47MM **Privately Held**
Web: www.dmiparts.com
SIC: 3433 Burners, furnaces, boilers, and stokers

(G-10449)
DRUMMOND DOLOMITE INC
Also Called: Drummond Dolomite Quarry
7954 Reynolds Rd (44060-5334)
P.O. Box 658 (44061-0658)
PHONE..................................440 942-7000
Jerome T Osborne, *Pr*
Harold T Larned, *VP*
Ilda Hayden, *Sec*
EMP: 10 EST: 1988
SALES (est): 740K **Privately Held**
SIC: 1422 Dolomite, crushed and broken-quarrying

(G-10450)
DRYCAL INC
7355 Production Dr (44060-4858)
PHONE..................................440 974-1999
Margus Sweigard, *Pr*
Lembit Sweigard, *VP*
EMP: 8 EST: 1969
SQ FT: 14,500
SALES (est): 859.92K **Privately Held**
Web: www.decalsbydrycal.com
SIC: 2759 Screen printing

(G-10451)
ENTERPRISE WELDING & FABG INC
6257 Heisley Rd (44060-1887)
PHONE..................................440 354-4128
Ivan Katic, *Pr*
Slavko Katic, *
Albert R Amigoni, *
EMP: 170 EST: 1975
SQ FT: 100,000
SALES (est): 41.8MM **Privately Held**
Web: www.enterprisewelding.com
SIC: 3444 Sheet metalwork

(G-10452)
ENTERPRISE WELDING FBRCTN
9280 Pineneedle Dr (44060-1824)
PHONE..................................440 354-3868
Mike Katic, *Prin*
EMP: 11 EST: 2008
SALES (est): 505.82K **Privately Held**
Web: www.enterprisewelding.com
SIC: 3441 Fabricated structural metal

(G-10453)
FABTECH OHIO INC
5451 Grace Dr (44060-1504)
PHONE..................................308 532-1860
EMP: 6 EST: 2019
SALES (est): 102.84K **Privately Held**
SIC: 3444 Sheet metalwork

(G-10454)
FASTSIGNS
7538 Mentor Ave (44060-5418)
PHONE..................................440 954-9191
EMP: 6 EST: 2018
SALES (est): 149K **Privately Held**
Web: www.fastsigns.com
SIC: 3993 Signs and advertising specialties

(G-10455)
FISCHER SPECIAL TOOLING CORP
7219 Commerce Dr (44060-5307)

PHONE..................................440 951-8411
Kevin Johnson, *Pr*
Molly Johnson, *Sec*
EMP: 22 EST: 1959
SQ FT: 5,000
SALES (est): 776.36K **Privately Held**
Web: www.fischerspecialtooling.com
SIC: 3544 3541 3545 Special dies, tools, jigs, and fixtures; Machine tools, metal cutting: exotic (explosive, etc.); Machine tool accessories

(G-10456)
FORMASTERS CORPORATION
5959 Pinecone Dr (44060-1866)
PHONE..................................440 639-9206
John J Ferguson, *Pr*
EMP: 12 EST: 1993
SQ FT: 10,500
SALES (est): 2.37MM **Privately Held**
Web: www.formasters.com
SIC: 3469 3449 Metal stampings, nec; Custom roll formed products

(G-10457)
FRANTZ MEDICAL DEVELOPMENT LTD (PA)
7740 Metric Dr (44060)
PHONE..................................440 255-1155
Mark G Frantz, *Pr*
J Paul Hanson, *VP*
EMP: 8 EST: 1980
SQ FT: 3,750
SALES (est): 9.14MM
SALES (corp-wide): 9.14MM **Privately Held**
Web: www.frantzgroup.com
SIC: 3841 3089 Surgical and medical instruments; Injection molding of plastics

(G-10458)
FREDON CORPORATION
8990 Tyler Blvd (44060-5368)
P.O. Box 600 (44061-0600)
PHONE..................................440 951-5200
Roger J Sustar, *CEO*
Alyson Scott, *
Chris Sustar, *
Richard Ditto, *
▼ EMP: 80 EST: 1967
SQ FT: 70,000
SALES (est): 16.37MM **Privately Held**
Web: www.fredon.com
SIC: 3599 3541 Custom machinery; Grinding machines, metalworking

(G-10459)
FREPEG INDUSTRIES INC
8624 East Ave (44060-4365)
PHONE..................................440 255-8595
Fred Stout, *Pr*
Peggy Stout, *VP*
EMP: 10 EST: 1988
SQ FT: 8,000
SALES (est): 378.51K **Privately Held**
SIC: 3469 Stamping metal for the trade

(G-10460)
FULLY INVOLVED PRINTING CO LLC
9819 Johnnycake Ridge Rd (44060-6711)
PHONE..................................440 635-6858
Danielle Rodeheaver, *Prin*
EMP: 6 EST: 2015
SALES (est): 99.82K **Privately Held**
Web: www.fullyinvolvedprinting.com
SIC: 2752 Commercial printing, lithographic

(G-10461)
FULTON SIGN & DECAL INC
7144 Industrial Park Blvd (44060-5314)
PHONE..................................440 951-1515

Mentor - Lake County (G-10462)

Charles Fulton, *Pr*
Gertrude Fulton, *VP*
Robert B Fulton, *Treas*
Gary Fulton, *Genl Mgr*
EMP: 6 **EST:** 1969
SQ FT: 5,000
SALES (est): 714.15K **Privately Held**
Web: www.fultonsign.com
SIC: 2759   Screen printing

(G-10462)
G & T MANUFACTURING CO
6085 Pinecone Dr (44060-1866)
PHONE.................................440 639-7777
Gerald Cutts, *Pr*
Thomas B Cutts, *Pr*
Gerald Cutts, *VP*
Beverly Cutts, *Sec*
Pat Caticchio, *Prin*
EMP: 19 **EST:** 1979
SQ FT: 6,200
SALES (est): 2.73MM **Privately Held**
Web: www.gtmanufacturingco.com
SIC: 3531 3537   Aerial work platforms: hydraulic/elec. truck/carrier mounted; Industrial trucks and tractors

(G-10463)
GDJ INC
Also Called: Technology Explortation Pdts
7585 Tyler Blvd (44060-4869)
PHONE.................................440 975-0258
Jack Gilbert, *Pr*
Deborah Gilbert, *VP*
EMP: 6 **EST:** 1992
SQ FT: 6,500
SALES (est): 597.19K **Privately Held**
Web: www.gdjinc.com
SIC: 3821   Laboratory equipment: fume hoods, distillation racks, etc.

(G-10464)
GLO-QUARTZ ELECTRIC HTR CO INC
Also Called: Heatmax Heaters
7084 Maple St (44060-4932)
P.O. Box 358 (44061-0358)
PHONE.................................440 255-9701
George T Strokes, *Pr*
Thomas M Strokes, *
Nancy L Strokes, *
EMP: 25 **EST:** 1952
SQ FT: 22,000
SALES (est): 2.94MM **Privately Held**
Web: www.heatmaxheaters.com
SIC: 3567 3823 3634 3433   Heating units and devices, industrial: electric; Process control instruments; Electric housewares and fans; Heating equipment, except electric

(G-10465)
GREAT LAKES POWER PRODUCTS INC (PA)
Also Called: John Deere Authorized Dealer
7455 Tyler Blvd (44060-8389)
PHONE.................................440 951-5111
Harry Allen Junior, *CEO*
Harry L Allen Junior, *Ch Bd*
Richard J Pennza, *
David Bell, *
Sam Profio, *
▲ **EMP:** 60 **EST:** 1973
SQ FT: 55,000
SALES (est): 27.96MM
SALES (corp-wide): 27.96MM **Privately Held**
Web: www.glpower.com

SIC: 5085 5084 3566   Power transmission equipment and apparatus; Materials handling machinery; Speed changers (power transmission equipment), except auto

(G-10466)
HABCO TOOL AND DEV CO INC
7725 Metric Dr (44060-4863)
PHONE.................................440 946-5546
Steven Sanders, *Pr*
EMP: 23 **EST:** 1955
SQ FT: 24,000
SALES (est): 3.77MM **Privately Held**
Web: www.habcotool.com
SIC: 3599 7692   Machine shop, jobbing and repair; Welding repair

(G-10467)
HDWT HOLDINGS INC
7124 Industrial Park Blvd (44060-5314)
PHONE.................................440 269-6984
Lee Dwyer, *Prin*
Mike Watts, *
Ray Arnold, *Prin*
Gus Deangelo, *
EMP: 60 **EST:** 1998
SQ FT:
SALES (est): 5.12MM **Privately Held**
Web: www.avalign.com
SIC: 3841 3842   Diagnostic apparatus, medical; Surgical appliances and supplies

(G-10468)
HEISLEY TIRE & BRAKE INC
5893 Heisley Rd (44060-1831)
PHONE.................................440 357-9797
Ralph Gamber Junior, *Pr*
Ralph Gamber Senior, *VP*
Joan Gamber, *
Nancy Gamber, *Secretary of Treasurer*
EMP: 11 **EST:** 1991
SQ FT: 4,000
SALES (est): 793.75K **Privately Held**
Web: www.heisleytire.net
SIC: 7534 7538 7539   Tire repair shop; Engine repair; Brake repair, automotive

(G-10469)
HENKEL US OPERATIONS CORP
7405 Production Dr (44060-4876)
PHONE.................................440 255-8900
Robert Kern, *Brnch Mgr*
EMP: 119
SALES (corp-wide): 23.39B **Privately Held**
Web: www.henkel.com
SIC: 2891   Adhesives
HQ: Henkel Us Operations Corporation
1 Henkel Way
Rocky Hill CT 06067
860 571-5100

(G-10470)
HIGHLAND PRODUCTS CORP
9331 Mercantile Dr (44060-4523)
PHONE.................................440 352-4777
Mark Erickson, *Pr*
Jeanne Wojciechowicz, *Sec*
EMP: 10 **EST:** 1992
SQ FT: 11,000
SALES (est): 1.02MM **Privately Held**
Web: www.highlandproducts.com
SIC: 3599   Machine shop, jobbing and repair

(G-10471)
INDUSTRIAL QUARTZ CORPORATION
7552 Saint Clair Ave Ste D (44060-5201)
PHONE.................................440 942-0909
Richard Intihar, *Pr*
Robert Initihar, *Genl Mgr*
▲ **EMP:** 26 **EST:** 1967

SQ FT: 10,000
SALES (est): 837.21K **Privately Held**
Web: www.indquartz.com
SIC: 3295 3769 3677 3498   Minerals, ground or treated; Space vehicle equipment, nec; Electronic coils and transformers; Fabricated pipe and fittings

(G-10472)
INDUSTRIAL THERMOSET PLAS INC
Also Called: I.T. Plastics
7675 Jenther Dr (44060-4872)
PHONE.................................440 975-0411
Jack Schriner, *Pr*
EMP: 10 **EST:** 1982
SQ FT: 8,000
SALES (est): 911.21K **Privately Held**
Web: www.itplastics.com
SIC: 2821   Molding compounds, plastics

(G-10473)
INNOVATIVE SPORT SURFACING LLC
8425 Station St (44060-4924)
PHONE.................................440 205-0875
Kristen Rossi, *Managing Member*
EMP: 17 **EST:** 2020
SALES (est): 1.5MM **Privately Held**
Web: www.innovativesportsurfacing.com
SIC: 3069 0782   Rubber floorcoverings/mats and wallcoverings; Turf installation services, except artificial

(G-10474)
INTEGRA ENCLOSURES LIMITED
8989 Tyler Blvd (44060-2184)
PHONE.................................440 269-4966
EMP: 100
SALES (est): 8.77MM **Privately Held**
Web: www.integraenclosures.com
SIC: 2821   Thermoplastic materials

(G-10475)
INTERNATIONAL HYDRAULICS INC
Also Called: Ihi Connectors R
7700 Saint Clair Ave (44060-5238)
PHONE.................................440 951-7186
Charles Ridley, *Pr*
▲ **EMP:** 50 **EST:** 1981
SQ FT: 62,000
SALES (est): 12.05MM **Privately Held**
Web: www.ihiconnectors.com
SIC: 3643   Electric connectors

(G-10476)
INTERPAK INC
Also Called: Roto Mold
7278 Justin Way (44060-4881)
PHONE.................................440 974-8999
Mark Shaw, *Pr*
Tad Heyman, *
▼ **EMP:** 43 **EST:** 1993
SQ FT: 65,000
SALES (est): 5.47MM **Privately Held**
Web: www.rotomold.com
SIC: 3089   Injection molding of plastics

(G-10477)
J & C GROUP INC OF OHIO
6781 Hopkins Rd (44060-4311)
PHONE.................................440 205-9658
James Smolik, *Pr*
Christine Smolik, *Stockholder*
◆ **EMP:** 16 **EST:** 2002
SQ FT: 13,000
SALES (est): 466.71K **Privately Held**
SIC: 3651 5065   Speaker systems; TV parts and accessories, nec

(G-10478)
J & L MANAGEMENT CORPORATION
Also Called: Kramer Printing
8634 Station St (44060-4316)
PHONE.................................440 205-1199
Leonard Kramer, *Pt*
Gerald Kramer, *Pt*
EMP: 6 **EST:** 1986
SQ FT: 7,000
SALES (est): 932.29K **Privately Held**
Web: www.kramercolor.com
SIC: 2752 2732   Offset printing; Book printing

(G-10479)
J & M INDUSTRIES INC
7775 Division Dr (44060-4861)
PHONE.................................440 951-1985
David Martin, *Pr*
EMP: 8 **EST:** 2000
SQ FT: 8,000
SALES (est): 709.45K **Privately Held**
Web: www.jmdiecasting.com
SIC: 3544   Dies and die holders for metal cutting, forming, die casting

(G-10480)
J & P PRODUCTS INC
Also Called: Specialties Unlimited
8865 East Ave (44060-4305)
PHONE.................................440 974-2830
Paul Jonke, *Pr*
Dennis Jonke, *
EMP: 48 **EST:** 1971
SQ FT: 18,000
SALES (est): 977.75K **Privately Held**
SIC: 3599   Machine shop, jobbing and repair

(G-10481)
JACK WALKER PRINTING CO
Also Called: Walker Printing Co.
9517 Jackson St (44060-4515)
PHONE.................................440 352-4222
Jack G Walker, *Pr*
▲ **EMP:** 18 **EST:** 1987
SQ FT: 3,500
SALES (est): 2.12MM **Privately Held**
Web: www.walker-printing.com
SIC: 2752 2791 2789 2759   Offset printing; Typesetting; Bookbinding and related work; Commercial printing, nec

(G-10482)
JADE PRODUCTS INC
9309 Mercantile Dr (44060-4523)
PHONE.................................440 352-1700
John Erickson, *Pr*
Darcy Erickson, *Contrlr*
EMP: 17 **EST:** 1992
SQ FT: 5,500
SALES (est): 2.37MM **Privately Held**
Web: www.jadeproductsinc.com
SIC: 3599   Machine shop, jobbing and repair

(G-10483)
JJ SLEEVES INC
6850 Patterson Dr (44060-4331)
PHONE.................................440 205-1055
EMP: 8 **EST:** 1991
SALES (est): 553.7K **Privately Held**
SIC: 3599   Machine shop, jobbing and repair

(G-10484)
JOHN D OIL AND GAS COMPANY
7001 Center St (44060-4933)
P.O. Box 5069 (44061-5069)
PHONE.................................440 255-6325
EMP: 7 **EST:** 1999
SALES (est): 1.09MM **Privately Held**
Web: www.johndoilandgas.com

SIC: 1382 1311 4225 Oil and gas exploration services; Crude petroleum and natural gas production; Warehousing, self storage

(G-10485)
JOHNSTON MFG CO INC
Also Called: J M C Rollmasters
7611 Saint Clair Ave (44060-5235)
PHONE..................................440 269-1420
Dennis Johnston, *Pr*
Marsha Johnston, *Sec*
EMP: 8 **EST:** 1968
SQ FT: 8,500
SALES (est): 727.75K **Privately Held**
Web: www.jmcrolls.com
SIC: 3544 Special dies and tools

(G-10486)
KAEPER MACHINE INC
8680 Twinbrook Rd (44060-4341)
PHONE..................................440 974-1010
Kye Hwang, *Pr*
Mike Kidner, *Prin*
EMP: 20 **EST:** 1998
SALES (est): 2.19MM **Privately Held**
Web: www.kaeper.com
SIC: 3545 3484 Precision tools, machinists'; Small arms

(G-10487)
KISH COMPANY INC (PA)
8020 Tyler Blvd Ste 100 (44060-4825)
PHONE..................................440 205-9970
John R Kish, *Pr*
Brian Richards, *VP*
◆ **EMP:** 16 **EST:** 1986
SQ FT: 4,800
SALES (est): 14.82MM
SALES (corp-wide): 14.82MM **Privately Held**
Web: www.kishcompany.com
SIC: 2816 3295 Inorganic pigments; Minerals, ground or otherwise treated

(G-10488)
L J MANUFACTURING INC
9436 Mercantile Dr (44060-1889)
PHONE..................................440 352-1979
Michael Ball, *Pr*
Darlene Ball, *Sec*
EMP: 8 **EST:** 1988
SQ FT: 10,000
SALES (est): 705.34K **Privately Held**
Web: www.ljmfg.com
SIC: 3599 Machine shop, jobbing and repair

(G-10489)
LAKE COUNTY PLATING CORP
7790 Division Dr (44060-4860)
PHONE..................................440 255-8835
Charles H Dowling, *Pr*
Janet Dowling, *VP*
EMP: 10 **EST:** 1958
SQ FT: 20,000
SALES (est): 779.77K **Privately Held**
Web: www.lakecountyplating.com
SIC: 3471 Electroplating of metals or formed products

(G-10490)
LAKE PUBLISHING INC
Also Called: Callender Group, The
9853 Johnnycake Ridge Rd Ste 107 (44060-6700)
PHONE..................................440 299-8500
James S Callender Junior, *Prin*
Heidi Callender, *Ofcr*
EMP: 7 **EST:** 2009
SQ FT: 1,150
SALES (est): 535.73K **Privately Held**
Web: www.thecallendergroup.com

SIC: 2741 8748 Miscellaneous publishing; Business consulting, nec

(G-10491)
LANKO INDUSTRIES INC
7301 Industrial Park Blvd (44060-5317)
PHONE..................................440 269-1641
John Lanphier, *Pr*
Susan Lanphier, *Sec*
EMP: 8 **EST:** 1981
SQ FT: 9,000
SALES (est): 810.84K **Privately Held**
Web: www.allsaintsainslie.org.au
SIC: 3544 Wire drawing and straightening dies

(G-10492)
LIBRA GUAYMAS LLC
7770 Division Dr (44060-4860)
PHONE..................................440 974-7770
Rod Howell, *CEO*
EMP: 115 **EST:** 2019
SALES (est): 17.62MM
SALES (corp-wide): 144.38MM **Privately Held**
SIC: 3291 Abrasive metal and steel products
HQ: Libra Industries, Llc
    7770 Division Dr
    Mentor OH 44060
    440 974-7770

(G-10493)
LIBRA INDUSTRIES LLC (DH)
7770 Division Dr (44060)
PHONE..................................440 974-7770
Jim Kircher, *CEO*
Luis Montiel, *
EMP: 120 **EST:** 1980
SQ FT: 52,000
SALES (est): 128.48MM
SALES (corp-wide): 144.38MM **Privately Held**
Web: www.libraindustries.com
SIC: 3599 3672 Machine shop, jobbing and repair; Printed circuit boards
HQ: Gem Cw Holdings, Llc
    1100 Superior Ave E
    Cleveland OH

(G-10494)
LINTERN CORPORATION (PA)
8685 Station St (44060)
P.O. Box 90 (44061)
PHONE..................................440 255-9333
Richard K Lintern, *Pr*
Ray Ohler, *Development*
◆ **EMP:** 35 **EST:** 1903
SQ FT: 22,500
SALES (est): 6.23MM
SALES (corp-wide): 6.23MM **Privately Held**
Web: www.lintern.com
SIC: 3585 3714 3648 Air conditioning units, complete: domestic or industrial; Heaters, motor vehicle; Lanterns: electric, gas, carbide, kerosene, or gasoline

(G-10495)
LITTLE MOUNTAIN PRECISION LLC
8677 Tyler Blvd (44060-4346)
PHONE..................................440 290-2903
Keith R Kraus, *Prin*
EMP: 11 **EST:** 2019
SALES (est): 1.2MM **Privately Held**
Web: www.littlemountainprecision.com
SIC: 3566 3599 Gears, power transmission, except auto; Machine and other job shop work

(G-10496)
LJ MANFCTURING INC MENTOR OHIO
6345 Carnegie St (44060-4532)
PHONE..................................440 953-3726
EMP: 7 **EST:** 2015
SALES (est): 68.02K **Privately Held**
Web: www.ljmfg.com
SIC: 3599 Machine shop, jobbing and repair

(G-10497)
LUMINAUD INC
8688 Tyler Blvd (44060-4348)
PHONE..................................440 255-9082
Thomas Lennox, *Pr*
Dorothy Lennox, *VP*
EMP: 7 **EST:** 1964
SQ FT: 5,000
SALES (est): 567.97K **Privately Held**
Web: www.luminaud.com
SIC: 3842 Limbs, artificial

(G-10498)
MAG-NIF INC
8820 East Ave (44060)
P.O. Box 720 (44061)
PHONE..................................440 255-9366
William W Knox Junior, *Ch Bd*
Jim Weiss, *
Dennis Delaat, *
▲ **EMP:** 100 **EST:** 1963
SQ FT: 180,000
SALES (est): 8.15MM **Privately Held**
Web: www.magnif.com
SIC: 3944 3089 Banks, toy; Injection molding of plastics

(G-10499)
MALISH CORPORATION (PA)
Also Called: Malish
7333 Corporate Blvd (44060-4857)
PHONE..................................440 951-5356
Jeffery J Malish, *Pr*
Fred Lombardi, *
Mark Ray, *
◆ **EMP:** 100 **EST:** 1948
SQ FT: 82,000
SALES (est): 22.31MM
SALES (corp-wide): 22.31MM **Privately Held**
Web: www.malish.com
SIC: 3991 3089 Brushes, household or industrial; Extruded finished plastics products, nec

(G-10500)
MATRIX TOOL & MACHINE INC
7870 Division Dr (44060-4874)
PHONE..................................440 255-0300
Richard Wilson, *Pr*
George Maust, *
Alan Bockmuller, *
EMP: 24 **EST:** 1975
SQ FT: 20,000
SALES (est): 3.42MM **Privately Held**
Web: www.matrix-tool.com
SIC: 3599 3545 Custom machinery; Machine tool accessories

(G-10501)
MENTORBIO LLC
9122 Hendricks Rd (44060-2146)
PHONE..................................440 796-2995
Mattew Micchia, *Prin*
EMP: 6 **EST:** 2010
SALES (est): 80.81K **Privately Held**
Web: www.mentorbio.com
SIC: 2841 Soap and other detergents

(G-10502)
METAL SEAL & PRODUCTS INC
7333 Corporate Blvd (44060-4857)
PHONE..................................440 946-8500
EMP: 175
Web: www.metalseal.com
SIC: 3451 3471 Screw machine products; Plating and polishing

(G-10503)
METAL SEAL PRECISION LTD (PA)
8687 Tyler Blvd (44060-4346)
PHONE..................................440 255-8888
John L Habe Iv, *Pr*
Allan B Pirnat, *
Richard Sippola, *
▼ **EMP:** 72 **EST:** 2011
SQ FT: 158,000
SALES (est): 27.49MM
SALES (corp-wide): 27.49MM **Privately Held**
Web: www.metalseal.com
SIC: 3444 Sheet metalwork

(G-10504)
MILL ROSE LABORATORIES INC
7310 Corp Blvd (44060)
PHONE..................................440 974-6730
Paul M Miller, *Pr*
Stephen W Kovalcheck Junior, *CFO*
Lawrence W Miller, *
▲ **EMP:** 40 **EST:** 1977
SQ FT: 59,000
SALES (est): 6.27MM
SALES (corp-wide): 24.82MM **Privately Held**
Web: www.millroselabs.com
SIC: 3991 5047 Brooms and brushes; Medical equipment and supplies
PA: The Mill-Rose Company
    7995 Tyler Blvd
    Mentor OH 44060
    440 255-9171

(G-10505)
MILL-ROSE COMPANY (PA)
Also Called: Mill-Rose
7995 Tyler Blvd (44060-4896)
PHONE..................................440 255-9171
Paul M Miller, *Pr*
Lawrence W Miller, *
Diane Miller, *
▲ **EMP:** 160 **EST:** 1920
SQ FT: 61,000
SALES (est): 24.82MM
SALES (corp-wide): 24.82MM **Privately Held**
Web: www.millrose.com
SIC: 3841 5085 3991 3624 Surgical instruments and apparatus; Industrial supplies; Brushes, household or industrial; Carbon and graphite products

(G-10506)
MONODE MARKING PRODUCTS INC (PA)
Also Called: Lectroetch Company, The
9200 Tyler Blvd (44060-1882)
PHONE..................................440 975-8802
Tom Mackey, *Pr*
EMP: 45 **EST:** 1956
SQ FT: 15,000
SALES (est): 9.29MM
SALES (corp-wide): 9.29MM **Privately Held**
Web: www.monode.com
SIC: 3542 5084 Marking machines; Printing trades machinery, equipment, and supplies

Mentor - Lake County (G-10507)

(G-10507)
MONODE STEEL STAMP INC
7620 Tyler Blvd (44060-4853)
PHONE..............................440 975-8802
Chris Lillstrung, *Mgr*
EMP: 14
Web: www.monode.com
SIC: 3542 3469 Marking machines; Metal stampings, nec
PA: Monode Steel Stamp, Inc
149 High St
New London OH 44851

(G-10508)
MUM INDUSTRIES INC (PA)
8989 Tyler Blvd (44060-2184)
P.O. Box 1870 (44061-1870)
PHONE..............................440 269-4966
Jim Cooney, *Pr*
Chris Brizes, *
▲ EMP: 64 EST: 1996
SALES (est): 24.44MM
SALES (corp-wide): 24.44MM Privately Held
Web: www.mumindustries.com
SIC: 2821 Plasticizer/additive based plastic materials

(G-10509)
NHVS INTERNATIONAL INC
7600 Tyler Blvd (44060-4853)
PHONE..............................440 527-8610
Sherry Richcreek, *CEO*
EMP: 325 EST: 2010
SQ FT: 100,000
SALES (est): 20.93MM Privately Held
Web: www.nhvsinternational.com
SIC: 3812 Acceleration indicators and systems components, aerospace

(G-10510)
NICKEL PLATE RAILCAR LLC
6730 N Palmerston Dr (44060-3976)
PHONE..............................440 382-6580
Kip Curran, *Prin*
EMP: 6 EST: 2008
SALES (est): 206.94K Privately Held
SIC: 3356 Nickel

(G-10511)
NIFTECH INC
Also Called: Niftech Precision Race Pdts
5565 Wilson Dr (44060-1555)
PHONE..............................440 257-6018
Julie Knaus, *Pr*
Raymond Knaus, *VP*
EMP: 10 EST: 1983
SALES (est): 742.14K Privately Held
Web: www.niftech.com
SIC: 3699 Electrical equipment and supplies, nec

(G-10512)
NORTHCOAST VALVE AND GATE INC
9437 Mercantile Dr (44060-4524)
P.O. Box 901 (44096-0901)
PHONE..............................440 392-9910
Anthony Fistek, *Pr*
EMP: 8 EST: 1985
SALES (est): 965.04K Privately Held
Web: www.ncvg.net
SIC: 3494 Valves and pipe fittings, nec

(G-10513)
NOVA METAL PRODUCTS INC
Also Called: Nova Metal Products
7500 Clover Ave (44060-5214)
PHONE..............................440 269-1741
Dan Novak, *CEO*
EMP: 20 EST: 2004
SALES (est): 2.37MM Privately Held
Web: www.novametalproducts.com
SIC: 3599 Machine shop, jobbing and repair

(G-10514)
OE EXCHANGE LLC (PA)
7750 Tyler Blvd (44060-4802)
PHONE..............................440 266-1639
EMP: 7 EST: 2008
SALES (est): 1.42MM
SALES (corp-wide): 1.42MM Privately Held
Web: www.wheelcraft.com
SIC: 3714 Wheels, motor vehicle

(G-10515)
OMEGA MACHINE & TOOL INC
7590 Jenther Dr (44060-4872)
PHONE..............................440 946-6846
Dolf Litschel, *Pr*
Ema Litschel, *VP*
EMP: 10 EST: 1980
SQ FT: 9,000
SALES (est): 759.3K Privately Held
Web: www.omegamachine.com
SIC: 3599 Machine shop, jobbing and repair

(G-10516)
OSAIR INC (PA)
7001 Center St (44060-4933)
P.O. Box 1020 (44061-1020)
PHONE..............................440 974-6500
Richard Osborne, *Pr*
Jon Magnusson, *VP*
EMP: 9 EST: 1963
SQ FT: 4,000
SALES (est): 12.38MM
SALES (corp-wide): 12.38MM Privately Held
Web: www.osairinc.com
SIC: 1381 2813 Drilling oil and gas wells; Nitrogen

(G-10517)
OSBORNE INC (PA)
7954 Reynolds Rd (44060-5334)
P.O. Box 658 (44061-0658)
PHONE..............................440 942-7000
Jerome T Osborne, *Prin*
William Mackey, *
▲ EMP: 25 EST: 1947
SQ FT: 4,500
SALES (est): 14.18MM
SALES (corp-wide): 14.18MM Privately Held
Web: www.osbornecompaniesinc.com
SIC: 5211 3273 3271 Lumber and other building materials; Ready-mixed concrete; Blocks, concrete or cinder: standard

(G-10518)
OSBORNE CO
7954 Reynolds Rd (44060-5334)
P.O. Box 658 (44061-0658)
PHONE..............................440 942-7000
Jerome T Osborne, *Pr*
Gerald J Smith, *
EMP: 24 EST: 1956
SQ FT: 4,500
SALES (est): 267.65K Privately Held
Web: www.osbornecompaniesinc.com
SIC: 3273 Ready-mixed concrete

(G-10519)
PAKO INC
7615 Jenther Dr (44060-4872)
PHONE..............................440 946-8030
Paul Kosir, *Pr*
▲ EMP: 216 EST: 1973
SQ FT: 142,000
SALES (est): 22.36MM Privately Held
Web: www.pakoinc.com
SIC: 3714 3728 3724 Motor vehicle parts and accessories; Aircraft parts and equipment, nec; Aircraft engines and engine parts

(G-10520)
PARKER-HANNIFIN CORPORATION
Also Called: Gas Turbine Fuel Systems
8940 Tyler Blvd (44060-2185)
PHONE..............................440 266-2300
Mark Seidel, *Brnch Mgr*
EMP: 50
SALES (corp-wide): 19.07B Publicly Held
Web: www.parker.com
SIC: 3594 Fluid power pumps
PA: Parker-Hannifin Corporation
6035 Parkland Blvd
Cleveland OH 44124
216 896-3000

(G-10521)
PCC AIRFOILS LLC
Pcc Airfoils Llc
8607 Tyler Blvd (44060-4222)
PHONE..............................440 255-9770
Armand Lauzon, *Genl Mgr*
EMP: 108
SQ FT: 55,000
SALES (corp-wide): 364.48B Publicly Held
Web: www.pccairfoils.com
SIC: 3369 3324 3724 Castings, except die-castings, precision; Steel investment foundries; Airfoils, aircraft engine
HQ: Pcc Airfoils, Llc
3401 Entp Pkwy Ste 200
Cleveland OH 44122
216 831-3590

(G-10522)
PERFORMANCE MOTORSPORTS INC
7201 Industrial Park Blvd (44060-5315)
PHONE..............................440 951-6600
EMP: 19 EST: 1989
SALES (est): 470.42K Privately Held
Web: www.wiseco.com
SIC: 3714 Motor vehicle parts and accessories

(G-10523)
PERFORMANCE SUPERABRASIVES LLC
Also Called: Coastal Diamond
7255 Industrial Park Blvd Ste A (44060-5331)
PHONE..............................440 946-7171
Scott Kaplan, *Managing Member*
EMP: 9 EST: 2012
SQ FT: 5,200
SALES (est): 676.34K Privately Held
SIC: 3291 3545 Wheels, grinding: artificial; Wheel turning equipment, diamond point or other

(G-10524)
PLASTICS MENTOR LLC
6160 Brownstone Ct (44060-2168)
PHONE..............................440 352-1357
Roger R Rhoads, *Prin*
EMP: 6 EST: 2010
SALES (est): 148.78K Privately Held
SIC: 3089 Injection molding of plastics

(G-10525)
PLATING PROCESS SYSTEMS INC
7561 Tyler Blvd Ste 5 (44060-4867)
P.O. Box 808 (44061-0808)
▼ EMP: 9 EST: 1985
SQ FT: 9,880
SALES (est): 998.61K Privately Held
Web: www.platingprocess.com
SIC: 2899 Plating compounds

(G-10526)
POLYCHEM LLC (HQ)
Also Called: Greenbridge
6277 Heisley Rd (44060)
PHONE..............................440 357-1500
Brian Jeckering, *CEO*
Barry Clifford, *
◆ EMP: 180 EST: 1973
SQ FT: 165,000
SALES (est): 105.3MM Privately Held
Web: www.polychem.com
SIC: 2671 Plastic film, coated or laminated for packaging
PA: The Sterling Group L P
9 Greenway Plz Ste 2400
Houston TX 77046

(G-10527)
POLYMER CONCEPTS INC
7555 Tyler Blvd Ste 1 (44060-4866)
PHONE..............................440 953-9605
Chris Callsen, *Pr*
▼ EMP: 7 EST: 1999
SQ FT: 6,000
SALES (est): 744.61K Privately Held
Web: www.polymerconcept.com
SIC: 2821 Polyurethane resins

(G-10528)
PRECISION BENDING TECH INC (PA)
Also Called: Stam
7350 Production Dr (44060-4859)
PHONE..............................440 974-2500
William Lennon, *Pr*
EMP: 11 EST: 2017
SALES (est): 8.41MM
SALES (corp-wide): 8.41MM Privately Held
Web: www.precisionbending.com
SIC: 3498 Tube fabricating (contract bending and shaping)

(G-10529)
PRECISION DIE MASTERS INC
8724 East Ave (44060-4304)
P.O. Box 263 (44061-0263)
PHONE..............................440 255-1204
Frank E Carmichael, *Pr*
EMP: 15 EST: 1977
SQ FT: 16,000
SALES (est): 499.76K Privately Held
SIC: 3544 Special dies and tools

(G-10530)
PRECISION METALS GROUP LLC
8687 Tyler Blvd (44060-4346)
PHONE..............................440 255-8888
EMP: 13 EST: 2018
SALES (est): 409.15K Privately Held
Web: www.metalseal.com
SIC: 3599 Machine shop, jobbing and repair

(G-10531)
PRINCETON TOOL INC (PA)
Also Called: Princeton Precision Group
7830 Division Dr (44060)
P.O. Box 508 (44061)
PHONE..............................440 290-8666
Kenneth Bevington Iii, *CEO*
▲ EMP: 135 EST: 1997
SALES (est): 20.3MM
SALES (corp-wide): 20.3MM Privately Held
Web: www.princetontool.com

GEOGRAPHIC SECTION
Mentor - Lake County (G-10553)

SIC: **3599** 5084 Machine shop, jobbing and repair; Tool and die makers equipment

(G-10532)
PROFAC INC (PA)
Also Called: Merritt
7198 Industrial Park Blvd (44060-5328)
PHONE.................................440 942-0205
G Michael Merritt, *CEO*
Keith E Merritt, *
Stephanie Cherok, *
▲ **EMP:** 135 **EST:** 1972
SQ FT: 90,000
SALES (est): 25.05MM
SALES (corp-wide): 25.05MM **Privately Held**
Web: www.merrittwoodwork.com
SIC: **2431** Millwork

(G-10533)
PROFAC INC
Also Called: Merritt Woodwork
7171 Industrial Park Blvd (44060-5351)
PHONE.................................440 942-0205
EMP: 65
SALES (corp-wide): 25.05MM **Privately Held**
Web: www.merrittwoodwork.com
SIC: **2431** Millwork
PA: Profac, Inc.
   7198 Industrial Park Blvd
   Mentor OH 44060
   440 942-0205

(G-10534)
PROFICIENT MACHINING CO
7522 Tyler Blvd Unit B-G (44060-5450)
PHONE.................................440 942-4942
Kenneth Putman, *Pr*
Kenneth Putman Junior, *Ex VP*
Carol Putman, *Sec*
EMP: 22 **EST:** 1973
SQ FT: 15,000
SALES (est): 4.18MM **Privately Held**
Web: www.proficientmachining.com
SIC: **3599** Machine shop, jobbing and repair

(G-10535)
PROFICIENT PLASTICS INC
7777 Saint Clair Ave (44060-5237)
P.O. Box 5053 (44061-5053)
PHONE.................................440 205-9700
EMP: 10 **EST:** 1997
SQ FT: 1,500
SALES (est): 1.1MM **Privately Held**
Web: www.proficientplastics.com
SIC: **3089** Injection molding of plastics

(G-10536)
PROGAGE INC
Also Called: Progage
7555 Tyler Blvd Ste 6 (44060-4866)
PHONE.................................440 951-4477
Edward Vadakin, *Pr*
EMP: 19 **EST:** 1985
SQ FT: 14,000
SALES (est): 2.43MM **Privately Held**
Web: www.progage.com
SIC: **3544** Special dies and tools

(G-10537)
PROGRESSIVE POWDER COATING INC
7742 Tyler Blvd (44060-4802)
PHONE.................................440 974-3478
EMP: 25 **EST:** 1995
SQ FT: 24,024
SALES (est): 2.46MM **Privately Held**
Web: www.progressivepowdercoating.com

SIC: **3479** Coating of metals and formed products

(G-10538)
PYROMATICS CORP (PA)
9321 Pineneedle Dr (44060-1825)
PHONE.................................440 352-3500
Andre Ezis, *CEO*
EMP: 10 **EST:** 1975
SQ FT: 27,000
SALES (est): 884.91K
SALES (corp-wide): 884.91K **Privately Held**
Web: www.pyromatics.com
SIC: **3221** 3231 3297 Glass containers; Products of purchased glass; Nonclay refractories

(G-10539)
QUADREL INC
Also Called: Quadrel Labeling Systems
7670 Jenther Dr (44060-4872)
PHONE.................................440 602-4700
Lon Deckard, *Pr*
Charles Wepler, *
Joseph P Rouse, *
◆ **EMP:** 43 **EST:** 1962
SQ FT: 3,842
SALES (est): 10.04MM **Privately Held**
Web: www.quadrel.com
SIC: **3565** Labeling machines, industrial

(G-10540)
QUALITY COMPONENTS INC
8825 East Ave (44060-4305)
P.O. Box 956 (44061-0956)
PHONE.................................440 255-0606
William Dennison Senior, *Pr*
EMP: 15 **EST:** 1999
SQ FT: 10,000
SALES (est): 2.5MM
SALES (corp-wide): 639.81MM **Publicly Held**
Web: www.qccmfg.com
SIC: **7699** 3548 Welding equipment repair; Welding and cutting apparatus and accessories, nec
HQ: Stratos International, Inc.
   299 Johnson Ave Sw
   Waseca MN 56093
   507 833-8822

(G-10541)
QUALTEK ELECTRONICS CORP
7610 Jenther Dr (44060-4872)
PHONE.................................440 951-3300
John Hallums, *Pr*
▲ **EMP:** 120 **EST:** 1979
SQ FT: 20,000
SALES (est): 9.92MM **Privately Held**
Web: www.qualtekusa.com
SIC: **3634** 3643 3577 3612 Electric housewares and fans; Current-carrying wiring services; Computer peripheral equipment, nec; Transformers, except electric

(G-10542)
R J K ENTERPRISES INC
Also Called: Niftech
5565 Wilson Dr (44060-1555)
PHONE.................................440 257-6018
Raymond Knaus, *Pr*
Julie Knaus, *VP*
Ellen Cook, *VP*
EMP: 10 **EST:** 1977
SQ FT: 1,500
SALES (est): 511.36K **Privately Held**
SIC: **7389** 3599 Design, commercial and industrial; Custom machinery

(G-10543)
R T & T MACHINING CO INC
Also Called: R T & T Machining
8195 Tyler Blvd (44060-4854)
PHONE.................................440 974-8479
F Paul Thompson, *Pr*
Ellen Thompson, *VP*
EMP: 14 **EST:** 1982
SQ FT: 12,000
SALES (est): 1.1MM **Privately Held**
Web: www.rttmachining.com
SIC: **3451** 3599 3545 3544 Screw machine products; Machine shop, jobbing and repair; Machine tool accessories; Special dies, tools, jigs, and fixtures

(G-10544)
RACE WINNING BRANDS INC (PA)
Also Called: Wiseco
7201 Industrial Park Blvd (44060-5315)
PHONE.................................440 951-6600
Robert Bruegging, *Pr*
Josh Vogel, *CFO*
EMP: 290 **EST:** 2016
SQ FT: 150,000
SALES (est): 195.05MM
SALES (corp-wide): 195.05MM **Privately Held**
Web: www.racewinningbrands.com
SIC: **3592** 3714 Pistons and piston rings; Motor vehicle parts and accessories

(G-10545)
RB SIGMA LLC
6111 Heisley Rd (44060-1837)
PHONE.................................440 290-0577
EMP: 85 **EST:** 2016
SALES (est): 34.04MM **Privately Held**
Web: www.rbsigma.com
SIC: **8741** 5047 3999 5734 Management services; Medical equipment and supplies; Barber and beauty shop equipment; Software, business and non-game

(G-10546)
RKI INC (PA)
Also Called: Roll-Kraft
8901 Tyler Blvd (44060-2184)
PHONE.................................888 953-9400
George C Gehrisch Junior, *Pr*
Sanjay Singh, *
Dennis M Langer, *
Chuck Summerhill, *
Ken Fruscella, *
EMP: 121 **EST:** 1964
SQ FT: 100,000
SALES (est): 19.92MM
SALES (corp-wide): 19.92MM **Privately Held**
Web: www.roll-kraft.com
SIC: **3547** Primary rolling mill equipment

(G-10547)
ROGERS DISPLAY INC (HQ)
Also Called: Rogers Company, The
7550 Tyler Blvd (44060-4868)
PHONE.................................440 951-9200
EMP: 30 **EST:** 1956
SALES (est): 12.99MM
SALES (corp-wide): 514.23MM **Privately Held**
Web: www.therogersco.com
SIC: **3993** 2542 Displays and cutouts, window and lobby; Partitions and fixtures, except wood
PA: Nesco, Inc.
   6140 Parkland Blvd # 110
   Cleveland OH 44124
   440 461-6000

(G-10548)
ROYAL PLASTICS INC
9410 Pineneedle Dr (44060-1880)
PHONE.................................440 352-1357
Gary Mcconnell, *Pr*
Bruce Usnik, *
Patricia Garner, *
▲ **EMP:** 225 **EST:** 1966
SQ FT: 135,000
SALES (est): 44.31MM **Privately Held**
Web: www.royalplastics.com
SIC: **3089** 3643 Injection molding of plastics; Current-carrying wiring services

(G-10549)
RS MANUFACTURING INC
8878 East Ave (44060-4306)
PHONE.................................440 946-8002
Richard Stark Senior, *Pr*
Richard Stark Junior, *VP*
David Stark, *Stockholder*
Robyn Stark, *Stockholder*
Dee Ann Stark, *Stockholder*
EMP: 15 **EST:** 1975
SQ FT: 4,800
SALES (est): 415.27K **Privately Held**
SIC: **3452** Bolts, metal

(G-10550)
S T TOOL & DESIGN INC
9452 Mercantile Dr (44060-1889)
PHONE.................................440 357-1250
John Fifa, *Genl Mgr*
Tony Sisa, *Mgr*
EMP: 14 **EST:** 1982
SQ FT: 6,000
SALES (est): 1.34MM **Privately Held**
Web: www.st-tool.com
SIC: **3599** Machine shop, jobbing and repair

(G-10551)
SEABISCUIT MOTORSPORTS INC (HQ)
7201 Industrial Park Blvd (44060)
PHONE.................................440 951-6600
▲ **EMP:** 290 **EST:** 1980
SQ FT: 150,000
SALES (est): 53.23MM
SALES (corp-wide): 195.05MM **Privately Held**
Web: www.wiseco.com
SIC: **3592** 3714 Pistons and piston rings; Motor vehicle parts and accessories
PA: Race Winning Brands, Inc.
   7201 Industrial Park Blvd
   Mentor OH 44060
   440 951-6600

(G-10552)
SEMPER QUALITY INDUSTRY INC
Also Called: Mc Cartney Industries
9411 Mercantile Dr (44060-4524)
P.O. Box 1449 (44061-1449)
PHONE.................................440 352-8111
Dale B Mccartney, *Pr*
Duane Mccartney, *VP*
EMP: 8 **EST:** 1985
SQ FT: 12,000
SALES (est): 986.75K **Privately Held**
Web: www.semperquality.com
SIC: **1721** 3479 Industrial painting; Coating of metals and formed products

(G-10553)
SGM CO INC
9000 Tyler Blvd (44060-1897)
PHONE.................................440 255-1190
Laura L Gerboth, *Pr*
Patrick L Gerboth, *
EMP: 40 **EST:** 1967
SQ FT: 45,000

Mentor - Lake County (G-10554)

SALES (est): 4.43MM **Privately Held**
Web: www.sgmcoinc.com
SIC: 3433 Heating equipment, except electric

(G-10554)
SHEET METAL PRODUCTS CO INC
5950 Pinecone Dr (44060-1865)
PHONE.............................440 392-9000
Joseph J Mahovlic, *CEO*
James F Saxa, *
Steven H Sneiderman, *
EMP: 25 EST: 1998
SALES (est): 10.09MM **Privately Held**
Web: www.smpohio.com
SIC: 3444 3429 Sheet metal specialties, not stamped; Hardware, nec
PA: The Providence Group Inc
    9290 Metcalf Rd
    Willoughby OH

(G-10555)
OKRIDO TOOL AND DIE INC
Also Called: Apollo Plastic
7555 Tyler Blvd Ste 11 (44060-4866)
PHONE.............................440 951-7774
Stanley Skrbis, *Pr*
Stanley Skrbis Junior, *VP*
Maria Skrbis, *
EMP: 20 EST: 1973
SQ FT: 24,000
SALES (est): 401.2K **Privately Held**
SIC: 3544 3089 Forms (molds), for foundry and plastics working machinery; Injection molding of plastics

(G-10556)
SMP WELDING LLC
8171 Tyler Blvd (44060-4826)
PHONE.............................440 205-9353
EMP: 12 EST: 1988
SQ FT: 10,000
SALES (est): 4.34MM **Privately Held**
Web: www.smpwelding.com
SIC: 7692 Welding repair

(G-10557)
SOUTH SHORE CONTROLS INC
9395 Pinecone Dr (44060-1862)
PHONE.............................440 259-2500
John Ovsek, *VP*
Chris Langmack, *
EMP: 45 EST: 1995
SQ FT: 22,000
SALES (est): 10.23MM **Privately Held**
Web: www.southshorecontrols.com
SIC: 3549 5084 Metalworking machinery, nec; Instruments and control equipment

(G-10558)
SPANG & COMPANY
Spang Power Electronics
9305 Progress Pkwy (44060-1855)
PHONE.............................440 350-6108
Timothy J Lindey, *Div Pres*
EMP: 31
SALES (corp-wide): 99.4MM **Privately Held**
Web: www.spang.com
SIC: 3699 3625 3674 3566 Electron linear accelerators; Control equipment, electric; Semiconductors and related devices; Speed changers, drives, and gears
PA: Spang & Company
    110 Delta Dr
    Pittsburgh PA 15238
    412 963-9363

(G-10559)
SPORTSMASTER
9140 Lake Shore Blvd (44060-1637)
PHONE.............................440 257-3900

Ronald Micchia D.d.s., *Owner*
EMP: 6 EST: 1984
SQ FT: 1,800
SALES (est): 119.02K **Privately Held**
SIC: 2891 Adhesives and sealants

(G-10560)
SSC CONTROLS COMPANY
8909 East Ave (44060-4305)
PHONE.............................440 205-1600
▲ EMP: 25 EST: 1994
SQ FT: 8,500
SALES (est): 2.41MM **Privately Held**
Web: www.ssccontrols.com
SIC: 3625 Relays and industrial controls

(G-10561)
STAM INC
Also Called: Stam
7350 Production Dr (44060-4859)
P.O. Box 951108 (44193-0005)
PHONE.............................440 974-2500
Kent Marvin, *Pr*
Brendan Anderson, *
H James Sheedy, *
▲ EMP: 45 EST: 1973
SQ FT: 28,000
SALES (est): 8.41MM
SALES (corp-wide): 8.41MM **Privately Held**
Web: www.precisionbending.com
SIC: 3498 Tube fabricating (contract bending and shaping)
PA: Precision Bending Technology, Inc.
    7350 Production Dr
    Mentor OH 44060
    440 974-2500

(G-10562)
STERIS CORPORATION
Also Called: Research & Development II
5900 Heisley Rd (44060-1834)
PHONE.............................440 354-2600
EMP: 52
Web: www.steris.com
SIC: 3841 Surgical and medical instruments
HQ: Steris Corporation
    5960 Heisley Rd
    Mentor OH 44060
    440 354-2600

(G-10563)
STERIS CORPORATION (DH)
5960 Heisley Rd (44060-1834)
PHONE.............................440 354-2600
Walter Rosebrough Junior, *Pr*
Michael Tokich, *CFO*
Kathie Bardwell, *CCO*
Adam Zangerle, *Sec*
Loyal Wilson, *Prin*
◆ EMP: 843 EST: 1985
SALES (est): 1.97B **Privately Held**
Web: www.steris.com
SIC: 3842 3845 3841 Sterilizers, hospital and surgical; Endoscopic equipment, electromedical, nec; Diagnostic apparatus, medical
HQ: Steris Limited
    Rutherford House
    Derby DE21
    345 241-3588

(G-10564)
STERIS CORPORATION
6515 Hopkins Rd (44060-4307)
PHONE.............................330 696-9946
Les Vinney, *Mgr*
EMP: 103
Web: www.steris.com
SIC: 3842 Sterilizers, hospital and surgical
HQ: Steris Corporation

5960 Heisley Rd
Mentor OH 44060
440 354-2600

(G-10565)
STERIS CORPORATION
6100 Heisley Rd (44060-1838)
PHONE.............................440 392-8079
EMP: 219
Web: www.steris.com
SIC: 3842 Surgical appliances and supplies
HQ: Steris Corporation
    5960 Heisley Rd
    Mentor OH 44060
    440 354-2600

(G-10566)
STERIS CORPORATION
9325 Pinecone Dr (44060-1862)
P.O. Box 75044 (44101-2199)
PHONE.............................440 354-2600
EMP: 109
Web: www.steris.com
SIC: 3842 Surgical appliances and supplies
HQ: Steris Corporation
    5960 Heisley Rd
    Mentor OH 44060
    440 354-2600

(G-10567)
STRATEGIC TECHNOLOGY ENTP
5960 Heisley Rd (44060-1834)
PHONE.............................440 354-2600
Gerry Reis, *VP*
Gerry Reis, *Pr*
Les Binney, *Pr*
EMP: 18 EST: 2002
SALES (est): 211.54K **Privately Held**
Web: www.steris.com
SIC: 3821 Clinical laboratory instruments, except medical and dental

(G-10568)
STRATUS UNLIMITED LLC (PA)
Also Called: Mc Group
8959 Tyler Blvd (44060-2133)
PHONE.............................440 209-6200
Tim Eippert, *CEO*
Kurt Ripkey, *CRO*
Bryan Hartnett, *
▲ EMP: 185 EST: 1995
SALES (est): 119.9MM
SALES (corp-wide): 119.9MM **Privately Held**
Web: www.stratusunlimited.com
SIC: 3993 Signs and advertising specialties

(G-10569)
SULECKI PRECISION PRODUCTS INC
8785 East Ave (44060-4303)
PHONE.............................440 255-5454
Daniel Sulecki, *Pr*
John Sulecki, *VP*
David Sulecki, *Sec*
Ed Sulecki, *Pur/Dir*
EMP: 10 EST: 1988
SQ FT: 4,500
SALES (est): 995.68K **Privately Held**
Web: www.suleckiprecision.com
SIC: 3599 3544 3444 3441 Machine shop, jobbing and repair; Special dies, tools, jigs, and fixtures; Sheet metalwork; Fabricated structural metal

(G-10570)
SUNSET INDUSTRIES INC
7567 Tyler Blvd (44060)
PHONE.............................440 306-8284
Tony Hauptman, *Pr*
Ivan Hauptman, *

Tony Hauptman, *Sec*
Rudy Hren, *
Frank Hren, *Stockholder*
EMP: 26 EST: 1959
SQ FT: 14,500
SALES (est): 4.29MM **Privately Held**
Web: www.sunsetindustries.com
SIC: 3812 3594 3599 Search and navigation equipment; Fluid power pumps and motors; Machine shop, jobbing and repair

(G-10571)
SUTTERLIN MACHINE & TL CO INC
9445 Pineneedle Dr (44060-1827)
PHONE.............................440 357-0817
Claude Sutterlin, *Pr*
EMP: 17 EST: 1966
SQ FT: 6,000
SALES (est): 2.28MM **Privately Held**
Web: www.sutterlinmachine.com
SIC: 3544 Special dies and tools

(G-10572)
TECMARK CORPORATION
Also Called: North Shore Safety
7335 Production Dr (44060-4858)
PHONE.............................440 205-9188
EMP: 25
SALES (corp-wide): 11.1MM **Privately Held**
Web: www.nssltd.com
SIC: 3823 Process control instruments
PA: Tecmark Corporation
    7745 Metric Dr
    Mentor OH 44060
    440 205-7600

(G-10573)
TECMARK CORPORATION (PA)
7745 Metric Dr (44060-4863)
PHONE.............................440 205-7600
Walter Swick, *CEO*
Sean Swick, *
Chuck Stein, *
Adam Stein Ctrl, *Prin*
▲ EMP: 55 EST: 1999
SQ FT: 23,000
SALES (est): 11.1MM
SALES (corp-wide): 11.1MM **Privately Held**
Web: www.tecmarkcorp.com
SIC: 3629 3823 3643 Electronic generation equipment; Process control instruments; Current-carrying wiring services

(G-10574)
TEN MFG LLC
7675 Saint Clair Ave (44060-5235)
PHONE.............................440 487-1100
Angelo Pariza, *Sole Member*
EMP: 10 EST: 2017
SALES (est): 627.57K **Privately Held**
SIC: 3599 Machine and other job shop work

(G-10575)
TFI MANUFACTURING LLC
8989 Tyler Blvd (44060-2184)
PHONE.............................440 290-9411
EMP: 8 EST: 2018
SALES (est): 229.36K **Privately Held**
Web: www.tfi-manufacturing.com
SIC: 8711 3469 3542 Engineering services; Metal stampings, nec; Die casting and extruding machines

(G-10576)
THERMOTION CORP
Also Called: Thermotion-Madison
6520 Hopkins Rd (44060-4308)
PHONE.............................440 639-8325
Gary Swanson, *Pr*

GEOGRAPHIC SECTION

Mentor On The Lake - Lake County (G-10600)

EMP: 15 EST: 1964
SALES (est): 2.43MM Privately Held
Web: www.thermotion.com
SIC: 3625 Actuators, industrial

(G-10577)
TOP SHELF EMBROIDERY LLC
9254 Mentor Ave (44060-6412)
PHONE..................440 209-8566
Tim Ferrell, Prin
EMP: 7 EST: 2010
SALES (est): 245.96K Privately Held
Web: www.topshelfmentor.com
SIC: 2395 Embroidery products, except Schiffli machine

(G-10578)
TOTAL MANUFACTURING CO INC
7777 Saint Clair Ave (44060)
P.O. Box 5053 (44061)
PHONE..................440 205-9700
Robert W Wisen, Pr
EMP: 22 EST: 1990
SALES (est): 3.48MM Privately Held
SIC: 3599 Machine shop, jobbing and repair

(G-10579)
TQ MANUFACTURING COMPANY INC
7345 Production Dr (44060-4858)
PHONE..................440 255-9000
EMP: 15 EST: 1996
SQ FT: 10,000
SALES (est): 451.45K Privately Held
Web: www.tqmfg.com
SIC: 3599 Machine shop, jobbing and repair

(G-10580)
TRAILER COMPONENT MFG INC
8120 Tyler Blvd (44060-4852)
PHONE..................440 255-2888
James Kleinman, Pr
Mark Saltzman, *
Thomas Gries, *
▲ EMP: 30 EST: 1992
SQ FT: 42,000
SALES (est): 4.84MM Privately Held
SIC: 3714 3599 3537 Motor vehicle parts and accessories; Machine and other job shop work; Industrial trucks and tractors

(G-10581)
TRANSFER EXPRESS INC
7650 Tyler Blvd (44060-4853)
PHONE..................440 918-1900
Ted Stahl, Pr
Matt Cook, *
Jason Ziga, *
◆ EMP: 65 EST: 1990
SQ FT: 85,000
SALES (est): 22.37MM
SALES (corp-wide): 76.93MM Privately Held
Web: www.transferexpress.com
SIC: 2759 2752 Screen printing; Transfers, decalcomania or dry; lithographed
PA: Stahls' Inc.
 25901 Jefferson Ave
 Saint Clair Shores MI 48081
 586 772-6161

(G-10582)
TRAVELERS CUSTOM CASE INC
7444 Tyler Blvd Ste C (44060-5402)
PHONE..................216 621-8447
Kenneth Nosse, Pr
Elizabeth Nosse, Sec
EMP: 10 EST: 1946
SQ FT: 18,000
SALES (est): 759.42K Privately Held
Web: www.travelerscustomcase.com

SIC: 3161 Cases, carrying, nec

(G-10583)
TRENT MANUFACTURING COMPANY
7310 Corporate Blvd (44060-4856)
PHONE..................216 391-1551
Lynn Gallatin, Pr
EMP: 8 EST: 1958
SALES (est): 217.58K Privately Held
Web: www.trentmfg.com
SIC: 3991 5085 Brushes, household or industrial; Brushes, industrial

(G-10584)
TRIDELTA INDUSTRIES INC (PA)
Also Called: Tdi
7333 Corporate Blvd (44060-4857)
P.O. Box 780 (44061-0780)
PHONE..................440 255-1080
Larry L Carr, Pr
Robert L Weinberg, VP
EMP: 9 EST: 1976
SALES (est): 837.87K
SALES (corp-wide): 837.87K Privately Held
Web: www.tridelta.com
SIC: 3625 3822 3643 3621 Industrial electrical relays and switches; Environmental controls; Current-carrying wiring services; Motors and generators

(G-10585)
TYLER HAVER INC (DH)
Also Called: W S Tyler
8570 Tyler Blvd (44060-4232)
PHONE..................440 974-1047
Randy A Bakeberg, Pr
▲ EMP: 50 EST: 1998
SQ FT: 65,000
SALES (est): 21.96MM
SALES (corp-wide): 584.82MM Privately Held
Web: www.wstyler.com
SIC: 3496 Miscellaneous fabricated wire products
HQ: Tylinter, Inc.
 8570 Tyler Blvd
 Mentor OH 44060
 800 321-6188

(G-10586)
TYLER INDUSTRIES INC
7471 Tyler Blvd Ste C (44060-5413)
PHONE..................440 578-1104
EMP: 9 EST: 2016
SALES (est): 51.8K Privately Held
Web: www.mumindustries.com
SIC: 3999 Manufacturing industries, nec

(G-10587)
ULTRA TECH INTERNATIONAL INC
7278 Justin Way (44060-4881)
PHONE..................440 974-8999
EMP: 6 EST: 2016
SALES (est): 195.03K Privately Held
SIC: 3089 Injection molding of plastics

(G-10588)
UNIQUE PACKAGING & PRINTING
9086 Goldfinch Ct (44060-1810)
P.O. Box 417 (44045-0417)
PHONE..................440 785-6730
Robert F Bradach, Pr
Madeline Bradach, VP
EMP: 10 EST: 1972
SQ FT: 20,000
SALES (est): 394.95K Privately Held
SIC: 7389 3991 Packaging and labeling services; Brooms and brushes

(G-10589)
UNITED STTES ENDSCOPY GROUP IN (DH)
Also Called: US Endoscopy
5976 Heisley Rd (44060-1873)
PHONE..................440 639-4494
Tony Siracusa, CEO
Gretchen Younker Cohen, *
Lynda Younker, *
▲ EMP: 161 EST: 1991
SQ FT: 30,000
SALES (est): 99.91MM Privately Held
Web: www.steris.com
SIC: 3841 Surgical and medical instruments
HQ: Steris Corporation
 5960 Heisley Rd
 Mentor OH 44060
 440 354-2600

(G-10590)
V K C INC
Also Called: Fab Form
7667 Jenther Dr (44060-4872)
PHONE..................440 951-9634
Joseph Chmielewski, Pr
EMP: 19 EST: 1978
SQ FT: 10,000
SALES (est): 4.46MM Privately Held
Web: www.fabforminc.com
SIC: 3469 Stamping metal for the trade

(G-10591)
VECTOR INTERNATIONAL CORP
Also Called: Vector Screenprinting & EMB
7404 Tyler Blvd (44060-5402)
PHONE..................440 942-2002
Doug Anderson, Pr
EMP: 8 EST: 1988
SQ FT: 6,000
SALES (est): 937.29K Privately Held
Web: www.vectorpromo.com
SIC: 2396 2395 Screen printing on fabric articles; Embroidery and art needlework

(G-10592)
VICON FABRICATING COMPANY LTD
7200 Justin Way (44060-4881)
PHONE..................440 205-6700
Jeffrey Conforte, *
Anita R Seidemann, *
EMP: 35 EST: 1965
SQ FT: 40,000
SALES (est): 8.53MM Privately Held
Web: www.viconfab.com
SIC: 3441 3398 Fabricated structural metal; Metal heat treating

(G-10593)
VISTA CREATIONS LLC
Also Called: Fastsigns
7896 Tyler Blvd (44060-4878)
PHONE..................440 954-9191
EMP: 6 EST: 2019
SALES (est): 197.23K Privately Held
Web: www.vistaequitypartners.com
SIC: 3993 Signs and advertising specialties

(G-10594)
VOLK OPTICAL INC
Also Called: Volk Optical
7893 Enterprise Dr (44060-5309)
PHONE..................440 942-6161
Jyoti Gupta, Pr
Gary Webel, *
▲ EMP: 70 EST: 1974
SQ FT: 18,000
SALES (est): 19.28MM
SALES (corp-wide): 2.23B Privately Held
Web: www.volk.com

SIC: 8011 3851 3827 Offices and clinics of medical doctors; Lenses, ophthalmic; Optical instruments and lenses
HQ: Halma Holdings Inc.
 535 Sprngfeld Ave Ste 110
 Summit NJ 07901
 513 772-5501

(G-10595)
WILSON OPTICAL LABS INC
Also Called: North American Coating Labs
9450 Pineneedle Dr (44060-1828)
PHONE..................440 357-7000
John H Wilson, CEO
Brian Wilson, Pr
EMP: 50 EST: 1974
SQ FT: 30,000
SALES (est): 4.65MM Privately Held
Web: www.nacl.com
SIC: 3851 3827 3229 Lens coating, ophthalmic; Optical instruments and lenses; Pressed and blown glass, nec

(G-10596)
WIRE SHOP INC
5959 Pinecone Dr (44060-1866)
PHONE..................440 354-6842
John Ferguson, Pr
Howard Pindale, VP
EMP: 20 EST: 1984
SQ FT: 20,000
SALES (est): 2.76MM Privately Held
Web: www.thewireshop.com
SIC: 3544 3599 Special dies and tools; Machine and other job shop work

(G-10597)
WISMAR PRCSION TOLING PROD INC
7505 Tyler Blvd Ste 2 (44060-5416)
PHONE..................440 296-0487
Gerald Wisen, Prin
Noel Martinez, Prin
EMP: 12 EST: 1996
SALES (est): 804.35K Privately Held
Web: www.wismarptp.com
SIC: 3599 Machine shop, jobbing and repair

(G-10598)
WS TYLER SCREENING INC
8570 Tyler Blvd (44060-4232)
PHONE..................440 974-1047
EMP: 39 EST: 2009
SALES (est): 1.77MM
SALES (corp-wide): 584.82MM Privately Held
Web: www.wstyler.com
SIC: 3496 Miscellaneous fabricated wire products
PA: Haver & Boecker Ohg
 Carl-Haver-Platz 3
 Oelde NW 59302
 2522300

(G-10599)
YUKON INDUSTRIES INC
7665 Mentor Ave Ste 113 (44060-5409)
PHONE..................440 478-4174
Leonard Norwood, CEO
EMP: 25 EST: 2008
SALES (est): 1.07MM Privately Held
SIC: 3585 Heating equipment, complete

Mentor On The Lake
Lake County

(G-10600)
AQUA PENNSYLVANIA INC
Also Called: Aqua Ohio

Mentor On The Lake - Lake County (G-10601)

GEOGRAPHIC SECTION

7748 Twilight Dr (44060-2629)
PHONE..............................440 257-6190
EMP: 6
SALES (corp-wide): 2.05B **Publicly Held**
Web: www.aquawater.com
SIC: **5499** 4941 3589 Water: distilled mineral or spring; Water supply; Water treatment equipment, industrial
HQ: Aqua Pennsylvania, Inc.
762 W Lancaster Ave
Bryn Mawr PA 19010
610 525-1400

(G-10601)
BLINGFLINGFOREVER LLC
7383 Dahlia Dr (44060-3121)
PHONE..............................216 215-6955
Monica Koczan, *Owner*
EMP: 7 EST: 2019
SALES (est): 246.75K **Privately Held**
SIC: **2339** Women's and misses' accessories

(G-10602)
DIAMOND HARD CHROME CO INC
7536 Monterey Bay Dr Unit 1 (44060-9004)
PHONE..............................216 391-3618
John R Tankovich, *Pr*
Robert Tankovich, *VP*
EMP: 15 EST: 1952
SALES (est): 494.89K **Privately Held**
SIC: **3471** Electroplating of metals or formed products

Metamora
Fulton County

(G-10603)
PARKER-HANNIFIN CORPORATION
Hydraulic Filter Division
16810 County Road 2 (43540)
PHONE..............................419 644-4311
Dibyava Ghosh, *Brnch Mgr*
EMP: 150
SALES (corp-wide): 19.07B **Publicly Held**
Web: www.parker.com
SIC: **3594** Fluid power pumps and motors
PA: Parker-Hannifin Corporation
6035 Parkland Blvd
Cleveland OH 44124
216 896-3000

Miamisburg
Montgomery County

(G-10604)
A-1 SPRINKLER COMPANY INC
2383 Northpointe Dr (45342-2989)
PHONE..............................937 859-6198
Bill Hausmann, *CEO*
EMP: 68 EST: 1982
SQ FT: 15,000
SALES (est): 14.17MM **Privately Held**
Web: www.a1ssi.com
SIC: **3569** 5087 Firefighting and related equipment; Firefighting equipment

(G-10605)
ADVANCED INDUS MSRMENT SYSTEMS (PA)
Also Called: Measurement Specialties
2580 Kohnle Dr (45342-3669)
P.O. Box 341118 (45434-1118)
PHONE..............................937 320-4930
David A Delph, *Pr*
▲ EMP: 13 EST: 2009
SALES (est): 4.31MM **Privately Held**
Web: www.aimsmetrology.com

SIC: **3829** Measuring and controlling devices, nec

(G-10606)
ADVANTIC BUILDING GROUP LLC
511 Byers Rd (45342-5337)
PHONE..............................513 290-4796
EMP: 14 EST: 2021
SALES (est): 1.09MM **Privately Held**
Web: www.advanticllc.com
SIC: **1799** 3543 Special trade contractors, nec; Industrial patterns

(G-10607)
AEROSEAL LLC (PA)
225 Byers Rd # 1 (45342-3614)
PHONE..............................937 428-9300
Amit Gupta, *CEO*
Vijay Kollepara, *VP*
Daniel Crowe, *CFO*
Chris Gibson, *VP Mktg*
Tim Burnette, *Commercial Vice President*
▲ EMP: 32 EST: 2011
SALES (est): 24.7MM
SALES (corp-wide): 24.7MM **Privately Held**
Web: www.aeroseal.com
SIC: **8748** 3679 Energy conservation consultant; Hermetic seals, for electronic equipment

(G-10608)
ALDRICH CHEMICAL
Also Called: Sigma-Aldrich
3858 Benner Rd (45342-4304)
PHONE..............................937 859-1808
Diane Szydell, *Mgr*
EMP: 74
SQ FT: 30,000
SALES (corp-wide): 22.82B **Privately Held**
SIC: **2819** 5084 2899 2869 Isotopes, radioactive; Chemical process equipment; Chemical preparations, nec; Industrial organic chemicals, nec
HQ: Aldrich Chemical
3050 Spruce St
Saint Louis MO 63103
314 771-5765

(G-10609)
ALEGRE INC
Also Called: Alegre Global Supply Solutions
3101 W Tech Blvd (45342-0819)
PHONE..............................937 885-6786
Lilly Phillips, *Pr*
Don Phillips, *VP*
▲ EMP: 18 EST: 1992
SQ FT: 24,000
SALES (est): 2.34MM **Privately Held**
Web: www.sourcealegre.com
SIC: **4225** 3714 5013 General warehousing; Motor vehicle engines and parts; Automotive supplies and parts

(G-10610)
ALLITE INC
8889 Gander Creek Dr (45342-5432)
PHONE..............................937 200-0831
EMP: 7 EST: 2014
SALES (est): 311K **Privately Held**
Web: www.alliteinc.com
SIC: **3354** Aluminum extruded products

(G-10611)
AMSIVE OH LLC
3303 W Tech Blvd (45342)
PHONE..............................937 885-8000
Don Landrum, *Managing Member*
Jim Wisnionski, *Managing Member*
Gordon Anderson, *Managing Member*
Mike Dolan, *Managing Member*

EMP: 70 EST: 1965
SQ FT: 140,000
SALES (est): 25.06MM
SALES (corp-wide): 147.04MM **Privately Held**
Web: www.amsive.com
SIC: **7331** 7374 2752 Direct mail advertising services; Data processing service; Commercial printing, lithographic
HQ: Amsive Aq Llc
1224 Poinsett Hwy
Greenville SC 29609

(G-10612)
APPLEHEART INC
Also Called: Appleheart
2240 E Central Ave (45342-7601)
PHONE..............................937 384-0430
Tom Robbins, *Pr*
EMP: 6 EST: 1990
SQ FT: 4,500
SALES (est): 548.73K **Privately Held**
Web: www.appleheartbrandingsolutions.com
SIC: **5699** 2759 2395 Uniforms and work clothing; Commercial printing, nec; Embroidery products, except Schiffli machine

(G-10613)
AVERY DENNISON CORPORATION
200 Monarch Ln (45342-3639)
PHONE..............................937 865-2439
EMP: 13
SALES (corp-wide): 8.36B **Publicly Held**
Web: identificationsolutions.averydennison.com
SIC: **2672** Adhesive papers, labels, or tapes: from purchased material
PA: Avery Dennison Corporation
8080 Norton Pkwy
Mentor OH 44060
440 534-6000

(G-10614)
B EXTERIOR COATINGS LLC
515 Anthony Ln (45342-3570)
PHONE..............................937 561-2654
EMP: 6 EST: 2013
SALES (est): 318.9K **Privately Held**
SIC: **3479** Coating, rust preventive

(G-10615)
BELL VAULT AND MONU WORKS INC
1019 S Main St (45342-3148)
PHONE..............................937 866-2444
Timothy Bell, *Pr*
Greg Bell, *Sec*
EMP: 28 EST: 1928
SQ FT: 17,000
SALES (est): 3.44MM **Privately Held**
Web: www.bellvaultandmonument.com
SIC: **3272** 5999 7261 3281 Burial vaults, concrete or precast terrazzo; Monuments, finished to custom order; Funeral service and crematories; Cut stone and stone products

(G-10616)
BILLERUD AMERICAS CORPORATION (HQ)
8540 Gander Creek Dr (45342-5439)
PHONE..............................877 855-7243
Kevin M Kuznicki, *Sr VP*
Kevin M Kuznicki, *Sr VP*
Aaron D Haas, *
Terrance M Dyer, *Senior Vice President Human Resources*
EMP: 391 EST: 2006
SALES (est): 1.28B
SALES (corp-wide): 4.06B **Privately Held**

Web: www.billerud.com
SIC: **2621** Paper mills
PA: Billerud Ab (Publ)
Evenemangsgatan 17
Solna 169 7
855333500

(G-10617)
BILLERUD COMMERCIAL LLC
8540 Gander Creek Dr (45342-5439)
PHONE..............................877 855-7243
Tor Lundqvist, *Managing Member*
EMP: 15 EST: 2021
SALES (est): 11.58MM
SALES (corp-wide): 4.06B **Privately Held**
SIC: **2621** Specialty papers
HQ: Billerud Americas Corporation
8540 Gander Creek Dr
Miamisburg OH 45342

(G-10618)
BILLERUD ESCANABA LLC
8540 Gander Creek Dr (45342)
PHONE..............................877 855-7243
EMP: 11 EST: 2016
SALES (est): 487.06K
SALES (corp-wide): 4.06B **Privately Held**
SIC: **2621** Paper mills
PA: Billerud Ab (Publ)
Evenemangsgatan 17
Solna 169 7
855333500

(G-10619)
BILLERUD US PROD HOLDG LLC (DH)
8540 Gander Creek Dr (45342-5439)
PHONE..............................877 855-7243
Mike Jackson, *CEO*
Mark A Angelson, *
Daniel A Clark, *
Jay A Epstein, *
David L Santez, *
◆ EMP: 380 EST: 2005
SALES (est): 542.57MM
SALES (corp-wide): 4.06B **Privately Held**
Web: www.billerud.com
SIC: **2621** 2611 Fine paper; Pulp manufactured from waste or recycled paper
HQ: Billerud Americas Corporation
8540 Gander Creek Dr
Miamisburg OH 45342

(G-10620)
BMC GROWTH FUND LLC
2991 Newmark Dr (45342-5416)
PHONE..............................937 291-4110
David Brixey, *Prin*
EMP: 162 EST: 2015
SALES (est): 20.38MM **Privately Held**
SIC: **2672** Paper; coated and laminated, nec

(G-10621)
BMF DEVICES INC
510 S Riverview Ave (45342-3028)
P.O. Box 1414 (45343-1414)
PHONE..............................937 866-3451
Gregg A Layman, *Pr*
Gary S Layman, *VP*
Rodney G Layman, *CFO*
▲ EMP: 19 EST: 1997
SALES (est): 2.36MM **Privately Held**
Web: www.bmfdevices.com
SIC: **3089** Plastics processing

(G-10622)
BRAINERD INDUSTRIES INC (PA)
680 Precision Ct (45342-6138)
P.O. Box 755 (45066-0755)
PHONE..............................937 228-0488
Gregory W Fritz, *Pr*

Miamisburg - Montgomery County (G-10642)

Rhonda Reynolds, *
EMP: 49 **EST:** 1997
SQ FT: 72,000
SALES (est): 8.55MM
SALES (corp-wide): 8.55MM **Privately Held**
Web: www.brainerdindustries.com
SIC: 3469 3993 3442 Stamping metal for the trade; Name plates: except engraved, etched, etc.: metal; Metal doors, sash, and trim

(G-10623)
BROWN CNC MACHINING INC
433 E Maple Ave (45342-2343)
PHONE.............................937 865-9191
Mike Brown, *Pr*
Steve Brown, *Ex VP*
EMP: 17 **EST:** 1996
SQ FT: 20,000
SALES (est): 2.38MM **Privately Held**
SIC: 3599 Machine shop, jobbing and repair

(G-10624)
C B MFG & SLS CO INC (PA)
4455 Infirmary Rd (45342-1299)
PHONE.............................937 866-5986
Charles S Biehn Junior, *CEO*
Richard Porter, *
Merle Wilberding, *
Donald M Cain, *
▲ **EMP:** 67 **EST:** 1967
SQ FT: 90,000
SALES (est): 22.18MM
SALES (corp-wide): 22.18MM **Privately Held**
Web: www.americancuttingedge.com
SIC: 5085 3423 Knives, industrial; Knives, agricultural or industrial

(G-10625)
CERTIFIED TOOL & GRINDING INC
Also Called: Ctg
4455 Infirmary Rd (45342-1233)
PHONE.............................937 865-5934
Charles Biehn, *Pr*
Joseph Biehn, *VP*
▲ **EMP:** 7 **EST:** 1972
SALES (est): 1.18MM
SALES (corp-wide): 2.08MM **Privately Held**
Web: www.toolgrindcoat.com
SIC: 3479 Coating of metals and formed products
PA: Certified Heat Treating, Inc
  4475 Infirmary Rd
  Dayton OH 45449
  937 866-0245

(G-10626)
CESO INC (PA)
Also Called: Ceso
3601 Rigby Rd Ste 300 (45342-5047)
PHONE.............................937 435-8584
David Oakes, *Pr*
James I Weprin, *
Kathleen Cyphert, *
EMP: 29 **EST:** 1987
SALES (est): 26.41MM
SALES (corp-wide): 26.41MM **Privately Held**
Web: www.cesoinc.com
SIC: 8711 3674 8712 Civil engineering; Light emitting diodes; Architectural services

(G-10627)
CHRISTIAN BLUE PAGES (PA)
521 Byers Rd Ste 102 (45342-5379)
PHONE.............................937 847-2583
Darrel Geis, *Pr*
EMP: 8 **EST:** 1991
SALES (est): 911.25K
SALES (corp-wide): 911.25K **Privately Held**
Web: www.christianblue.com
SIC: 2741 Directories, telephone: publishing only, not printed on site

(G-10628)
CONNECTIVE DESIGN INCORPORATED
Also Called: C D I
3010 S Tech Blvd (45342-4860)
PHONE.............................937 746-8252
Danya A Chandler, *Pr*
Mike Chandler, *VP*
EMP: 11 **EST:** 1991
SQ FT: 8,500
SALES (est): 4.54MM **Privately Held**
Web: www.connectivedesign.com
SIC: 3678 3714 3679 Electronic connectors; Automotive wiring harness sets; Harness assemblies, for electronic use: wire or cable

(G-10629)
COX NEWSPAPERS LLC
Also Called: Miamisburg News
230 S 2nd St (45342-2925)
P.O. Box 108 (45343-0108)
PHONE.............................937 866-3331
Donald J Miller, *Pr*
EMP: 10
SALES (corp-wide): 2.85B **Privately Held**
Web: www.coxnewspapers.com
SIC: 2711 Newspapers, publishing and printing
HQ: Cox Newspapers, Inc.
  6205 Pchtree Dnwody Rd N
  Atlanta GA 30328

(G-10630)
CUSTOM SERVICES AND DESIGNS (PA)
7075 Jamaica Rd (45342-2101)
P.O. Box 82 (45343-0082)
PHONE.............................937 866-7636
Jerry Stiver, *Owner*
EMP: 6 **EST:** 1988
SALES (est): 196.13K **Privately Held**
SIC: 3567 7699 Industrial furnaces and ovens; Industrial machinery and equipment repair

(G-10631)
CUSTOMFORMED PRODUCTS INC
Also Called: Custom Formed Products
645 Precision Ct (45342-6138)
PHONE.............................937 388-0480
Michael Schindler, *Pr*
EMP: 15 **EST:** 1973
SQ FT: 15,000
SALES (est): 2.3MM **Privately Held**
Web: www.customformedproducts.com
SIC: 2789 3469 3544 Paper cutting; Metal stampings, nec; Dies, steel rule

(G-10632)
DAY-TEC TOOL & MFG INC
4900 Lyons Rd Unit A (45342-6417)
PHONE.............................937 847-0022
Gerald Whitehead, *Pr*
Dana Whitehead, *Pr*
Joseph Baylogh, *VP*
EMP: 12 **EST:** 1985
SQ FT: 15,000
SALES (est): 1.03MM **Privately Held**
Web: www.daytectool.com
SIC: 3599 Machine shop, jobbing and repair

(G-10633)
DAYTON SUPERIOR CORPORATION (DH)
1125 Byers Rd (45342-5765)
PHONE.............................937 866-0711
Mark D Carpenter, *Pr*
Daniel T Dolson, *Ex VP*
◆ **EMP:** 115 **EST:** 1924
SQ FT: 72,000
SALES (est): 467.72MM
SALES (corp-wide): 69.06B **Privately Held**
Web: www.daytonsuperior.com
SIC: 3315 3452 3462 3089 Steel wire and related products; Dowel pins, metal; Construction or mining equipment forgings, ferrous; Plastics hardware and building products
HQ: Oaktree Capital Management, L.P.
  333 S Grand Ave Fl 28
  Los Angeles CA 90071

(G-10634)
DAYTON SYSTEMS GROUP INC
3003 S Tech Blvd (45342-4864)
PHONE.............................937 885-5665
EMP: 24 **EST:** 1993
SQ FT: 23,000
SALES (est): 1.15MM **Privately Held**
Web: www.daytonsystemsgroup.com
SIC: 3599 Machine shop, jobbing and repair

(G-10635)
DAYTRONIC CORPORATION (HQ)
Also Called: Daytronic
965 Capstone Cir (45342-1000)
PHONE.............................937 866-3300
Robert Bob Hart, *Pr*
EMP: 9 **EST:** 1954
SALES (est): 1.97MM **Privately Held**
Web: www.daytronic.com
SIC: 3829 Measuring and controlling devices, nec
PA: Global Power Technology Inc.
  191 Talmadge Rd Ste 3
  Edison NJ 08817

(G-10636)
DOUBLE DIPPIN INC
949 Blanche Dr (45342-2027)
PHONE.............................937 847-2572
Don Smith, *Prin*
EMP: 8 **EST:** 2001
SALES (est): 242.85K **Privately Held**
Web: www.doubledippin.com
SIC: 2024 Ice cream and ice milk

(G-10637)
ESKO-GRAPHICS INC (HQ)
Also Called: Eskoartwork
8535 Gander Creek Dr (45342-5436)
PHONE.............................937 454-1721
Stefaan Deveen, *CEO*
Frank Mcfaden, *CFO*
James O'reilly, *Sec*
◆ **EMP:** 70 **EST:** 1997
SQ FT: 27,000
SALES (est): 78.44MM
SALES (corp-wide): 1.73B **Publicly Held**
Web: www.esko.com
SIC: 5084 7372 Printing trades machinery, equipment, and supplies; Prepackaged software
PA: Veralto Corporation
  225 Wyman St Ste 250
  Waltham MA 02451
  202 828-0850

(G-10638)
EVENFLO COMPANY INC (DH)
Also Called: Evenflo
3131 Newmark Dr Ste 300 (45342-5400)
PHONE.............................937 415-3300
Dave Taylor, *CEO*
Peter Banat, *
Josh Korth, *
David Mcgillivary, *Treas*
◆ **EMP:** 48 **EST:** 1920
SQ FT: 1,250,000
SALES (est): 272.16MM **Privately Held**
Web: www.evenflo.com
SIC: 5099 2531 Baby carriages, strollers and related products; Seats, automobile
HQ: Goodbaby International Holdings Limited
  Rm 2502 25/F Tung Chiu Coml Ctr
  Wan Chai HK

(G-10639)
EXCELITAS TECHNOLOGIES CORP
1100 Vanguard Blvd (45342-0312)
PHONE.............................866 539-5916
Doug Benner, *Brnch Mgr*
EMP: 120
SALES (corp-wide): 1.48B **Privately Held**
Web: www.excelitas.com
SIC: 3829 3489 Thermometers and temperature sensors; Ordnance and accessories, nec
HQ: Excelitas Technologies Corp.
  200 West St Ste 4
  Waltham MA 02451

(G-10640)
GAYSTON CORPORATION
Also Called: Mulch Masters of Ohio
721 Richard St (45342-1840)
P.O. Box 523 (45343-0523)
PHONE.............................937 743-6050
Adam Stone, *CEO*
Andrew Sheldrick, *
◆ **EMP:** 125 **EST:** 1951
SQ FT: 280,000
SALES (est): 23.81MM **Privately Held**
Web: www.gayston.com
SIC: 1794 3999 2819 2499 Excavation and grading, building construction; Military insignia; Aluminum compounds; Mulch, wood and bark

(G-10641)
HAHN AUTOMATION GROUP US INC
10909 Industry Ln (45342-0818)
PHONE.............................937 886-3232
John C Hanna, *CEO*
Thomas Hahn, *
EMP: 60 **EST:** 1993
SQ FT: 63,000
SALES (est): 24.97MM
SALES (corp-wide): 2.27B **Privately Held**
Web: www.invotec.com
SIC: 8711 3599 Machine tool design; Custom machinery
HQ: Hahn Automation Group Holding Gmbh
  Liebshausener Str. 3
  Rheinbollen RP 55494
  676490220

(G-10642)
HAMMELMANN CORPORATION (HQ)
436 Southpointe Dr (45342-6459)
PHONE.............................937 859-8777
Gisela Hammelmann, *VP*
Michael Goecke, *VP*
Peter Englehardt, *Sec*
▲ **EMP:** 16 **EST:** 1987
SQ FT: 10,000
SALES (est): 7.08MM **Privately Held**
Web: www.hammelmann.com
SIC: 5084 3443 Pumps and pumping equipment, nec; Fabricated plate work (boiler shop)
PA: Interpump Group Spa

Miamisburg - Montgomery County (G-10643)

GEOGRAPHIC SECTION

Via Enrico Fermi 25
Sant'ilario D'enza RE 42049

(G-10643)
HARTZELL MFG CO LLC
2533 Technical Dr (45342)
PHONE..............................937 859-5955
EMP: 36 **EST:** 1939
SQ FT: 35,000
SALES (est): 8MM **Privately Held**
Web: pm.drtholdingsllc.com
SIC: 3444 3479 3471 Sheet metal specialties, not stamped; Coating of metals and formed products; Plating and polishing
HQ: Drt Precision Mfg., Llc
 1985 Campbell Rd
 Sidney OH 45365
 937 507-4308

(G-10644)
HEARTH PRODUCTS CONTROLS CO
Also Called: Galaxy Outdoor
2225 Lyons Rd (45342-4465)
PHONE..............................937 436-9800
Sean Steimle, *CEO*
Greg Stech, *General Vice President*
▲ **EMP:** 18 **EST:** 1976
SALES (est): 5.51MM **Privately Held**
Web: www.hpcfire.com
SIC: 3491 Process control regulator valves

(G-10645)
HEARTLAND PUBLICATIONS LLC
Also Called: Civitas Media
4500 Lyons Rd (45342-6447)
PHONE..............................860 664-1075
EMP: 110
SIC: 2759 Publication printing

(G-10646)
HILLTOP BASIC RESOURCES INC
Also Called: Riverbend Sand Rock and Gravel
4710 Soldiers Home W Carrollton Rd (45342-1274)
PHONE..............................937 859-3616
Mike Oliver, *Mgr*
EMP: 14
SALES (corp-wide): 59.62MM **Privately Held**
Web: www.hilltopcompanies.com
SIC: 5032 1442 Gravel; Construction sand and gravel
PA: Hilltop Basic Resources, Inc.
 50 E Rvrcnter Blvd Ste 10
 Covington KY 41011
 513 651-5000

(G-10647)
HUFFY SPORTS WASHINGTON INC
Also Called: Gen X Sports
225 Byers Rd (45342-3614)
PHONE..............................937 865-2800
John Muskovich, *Prin*
EMP: 16 **EST:** 2004
SALES (est): 532.5K
SALES (corp-wide): 69.37MM **Privately Held**
SIC: 3949 Basketball equipment and supplies, general
PA: Huffy Corporation
 8877 Gander Creek Dr
 Miamisburg OH 45342
 800 872-2453

(G-10648)
INNOMARK COMMUNICATIONS LLC
3233 S Tech Blvd (45342-0843)
PHONE..............................937 454-5555
EMP: 105
SALES (corp-wide): 96.09MM **Privately Held**
Web: www.innomarkcom.com
SIC: 2752 2789 Offset printing; Bookbinding and related work
PA: Innomark Communications Llc
 420 Distribution Cir
 Fairfield OH 45014
 888 466-6627

(G-10649)
JATRODIESEL INC
Also Called: Jatrodiesel
845 N Main St (45342-1871)
◆ **EMP:** 17 **EST:** 2004
SALES (est): 2.01MM **Privately Held**
Web: www.jatrodiesel.com
SIC: 2869 3519 Industrial organic chemicals, nec; Diesel engine rebuilding

(G-10650)
JOHNSON MFG SYSTEMS LLC
4505 Infirmary Rd (45342-1235)
PHONE..............................937 800-4744
Tom Johnson, *Pt*
Tom Johnson, *Managing Member*
EMP: 11 **EST:** 2003
SQ FT: 2,500
SALES (est): 1.3MM **Privately Held**
Web: www.jms-tech.net
SIC: 3599 3499 8711 Machine shop, jobbing and repair; Machine bases, metal; Mechanical engineering

(G-10651)
KILLER BROWNIE LTD
650 Precision Ct (45342-6138)
P.O. Box 751568 (45475-1568)
PHONE..............................937 535-5690
Norman C Mayne, *Managing Member*
EMP: 75 **EST:** 2000
SALES (est): 5.7MM **Privately Held**
Web: www.killerbrownie.com
SIC: 2051 Bakery: wholesale or wholesale/retail combined

(G-10652)
KONGSBERG PRCSION CTNG SYSTEMS
1983 Byers Rd (45342-5777)
PHONE..............................937 800-2169
Matt Thackray, *General Vice President*
EMP: 29 **EST:** 2021
SALES (est): 5.42MM
SALES (corp-wide): 355.83K **Privately Held**
Web: www.kongsbergsystems.com
SIC: 3545 Machine tool accessories
HQ: Kongsberg Precision Cutting Systems Belgium
 Kortrijksesteenweg 1087
 Gent VOV 9051
 93966967

(G-10653)
LAB-PRO INC
845 N Main St (45342-1871)
PHONE..............................937 434-9600
Joseph Jobe, *Pr*
EMP: 9 **EST:** 2004
SALES (est): 2.36MM **Privately Held**
Web: www.lab-pro.com
SIC: 3448 5039 Prefabricated metal buildings and components; Prefabricated buildings

(G-10654)
LEXISNEXIS GROUP (DH)
Also Called: Lexisnexis Group
9443 Springboro Pike (45342)
PHONE..............................937 865-6800
Kurt Sanford, *CEO*
Joe Eberhardt Gcno, *Prin*
▲ **EMP:** 162 **EST:** 2004
SALES (est): 359.22MM
SALES (corp-wide): 11.42B **Privately Held**
Web: www.lexisnexis.co.in
SIC: 7375 2741 Data base information retrieval; Miscellaneous publishing
HQ: Relx Inc.
 230 Park Ave Ste 700
 New York NY 10169
 212 309-8100

(G-10655)
MATTHEW BENDER & COMPANY INC
Also Called: Matthew Bender & Company
9443 Springboro Pike (45342-4425)
PHONE..............................518 487-3000
George Bearse, *VP*
EMP: 240
SALES (corp-wide): 11.42B **Privately Held**
Web: www.lexisnexis.com
SIC: 2721 2731 Periodicals; Book publishing
HQ: Matthew Bender & Company, Inc.
 744 Broad St Fl 8
 Newark NJ 07102
 518 487-3000

(G-10656)
METAL SHREDDERS INC
5101 Farmersville W Carrollton Rd (45342-1207)
P.O. Box 244 (45449)
PHONE..............................937 866-0777
Wilbur Cohen, *Ch*
Ken Cohen, *
EMP: 15 **EST:** 1971
SQ FT: 8,000
SALES (est): 441.5K **Privately Held**
SIC: 7389 3341 Metal slitting and shearing; Secondary nonferrous metals

(G-10657)
MIAMI VALLEY PRECISION INC
1944 Byers Rd (45342-3249)
PHONE..............................937 866-1804
EMP: 11 **EST:** 1994
SALES (est): 1.3MM **Privately Held**
Web: www.miamivalleyprecision.com
SIC: 3599 Machine shop, jobbing and repair

(G-10658)
MIAMI VLY COUNTERS & SPC INC
8515 Dayton Cincinnati Pike (45342-3168)
PHONE..............................937 865-0562
EMP: 6 **EST:** 1997
SQ FT: 2,987
SALES (est): 964.97K **Privately Held**
Web: www.miamivalleycounters.com
SIC: 2434 Wood kitchen cabinets

(G-10659)
MIAMI-CAST INC
901 N Main St (45342-1873)
PHONE..............................937 866-2951
George Deckebach, *Pr*
C Thomas Koehler, *VP*
Charles Koehler, *Treas*
EMP: 17 **EST:** 1993
SQ FT: 20,000
SALES (est): 1.31MM **Privately Held**
Web: www.miami-cast.com
SIC: 3321 Gray iron castings, nec

(G-10660)
MIAMISBURG COATING
925 N Main St (45342-1873)
PHONE..............................937 866-1323
William Sizemore, *Pt*
Opal Sizemore, *Pt*
EMP: 10 **EST:** 1984
SQ FT: 15,000
SALES (est): 663.59K **Privately Held**
SIC: 3479 Coating of metals and formed products

(G-10661)
MIDMARK CORPORATION (PA)
10170 Penny Ln Ste 300 (45342-5014)
PHONE..............................937 528-7500
John Baumann, *Pr*
Robert Morris, *
Mike Walker, *
Sharyl Gardner, *CAO**
Jon Wells, *CCO**
◆ **EMP:** 600 **EST:** 1915
SQ FT: 400,000
SALES (est): 187.17K
SALES (corp-wide): 187.17K **Privately Held**
Web: www.midmark.com
SIC: 3648 3842 3843 2542 Lighting equipment, nec; Stretchers; Dental equipment and supplies; Partitions and fixtures, except wood

(G-10662)
MIL-MAR CENTURY CORPORATION
8641 Washington Church Rd (45342-4470)
PHONE..............................937 275-4860
Trib Tewari, *Pr*
▲ **EMP:** 15 **EST:** 1954
SALES (est): 2MM **Privately Held**
Web: www.mil-mar.net
SIC: 3599 Machine shop, jobbing and repair

(G-10663)
MJCJ HOLDINGS INC
2580 Kohnle Dr (45342-3669)
PHONE..............................937 885-0800
Mike Campbell, *Pr*
Sean Quinn, *VP*
EMP: 8 **EST:** 1992
SALES (est): 295.77K **Privately Held**
Web: www.msicmm.com
SIC: 7699 8734 3559 Industrial machinery and equipment repair; Calibration and certification; Screening equipment, electric
PA: Advanced Industrial Measurement Systems, Inc.
 2580 Kohnle Dr
 Miamisburg OH 45342

(G-10664)
MOUND PRINTING COMPANY INC
Also Called: Promotional Spring
2455 Belvo Rd (45342-3909)
PHONE..............................937 866-2872
Wade Riggs, *Pr*
Frances Riggs, *
EMP: 25 **EST:** 1955
SQ FT: 30,000
SALES (est): 4.61MM **Privately Held**
Web: www.promotionalspring.com
SIC: 2752 Offset printing

(G-10665)
NEW PAGE CORPORATION
8540 Gander Creek Dr (45342-5439)
PHONE..............................877 855-7243
David J Paterson, *Pr*
EMP: 44 **EST:** 2016
SALES (est): 26.67MM **Privately Held**
Web: www.billerud.com
SIC: 2621 Paper mills

(G-10666)
NEWPAGE GROUP INC
8540 Gander Creek Dr (45342-5439)
PHONE..............................937 242-9500
George F Martin, *Pr*
Chan W Galbato, *
James C Tyrone, *

Daniel A Clark, *
Douglas K Cooper, *
EMP: 4500 **EST:** 2007
SALES (est): 195.98MM
SALES (corp-wide): 4.06B **Privately Held**
Web: www.billerud.com
SIC: 2621 Paper mills
HQ: Billerud Americas Corporation
  8540 Gander Creek Dr
  Miamisburg OH 45342

(G-10667)
OCM LLC
Also Called: Ohio Community Media
4500 Lyons Rd (45342-6447)
PHONE..................................937 247-2700
EMP: 264
Web: www.ohcommedia.com
SIC: 2711 Newspapers: publishing only, not printed on site

(G-10668)
OHIO GRAVURE TECHNOLOGIES INC
Also Called: Ohio Gravure Technologies
4401 Lyons Rd (45342-6456)
PHONE..................................937 439-1582
Chris Winter, Pr
Eric Serenius, Pr
▲ **EMP:** 13 **EST:** 2007
SALES (est): 5.26MM
SALES (corp-wide): 147.06MM **Privately Held**
Web: www.ohiogt.com
SIC: 2754 Commercial printing, gravure
HQ: Heliograph Holding Gmbh
  Konrad-Zuse-Bogen 18
  Krailling BY 82152
  89785960

(G-10669)
ONEIL & ASSOCIATES INC (PA)
Also Called: Oneil
495 Byers Rd (45342-3798)
PHONE..................................937 865-0800
Hernan Olivas, CEO
Hernan Olivas, Pr
Joe Stevens, *
David Stackhouse, CIO*
Cindy Schneider Ctrl, Prin
EMP: 176 **EST:** 1947
SQ FT: 75,000
SALES (est): 39.18MM
SALES (corp-wide): 39.18MM **Privately Held**
Web: www.oneil.com
SIC: 2741 8999 7336 Technical manuals: publishing only, not printed on site; Technical manual preparation; Commercial art and illustration

(G-10670)
PIONEER AUTOMOTIVE TECH INC (DH)
10100 Innovation Dr (45342-4966)
PHONE..................................937 746-2345
◆ **EMP:** 175 **EST:** 1981
SALES (est): 90.78MM **Privately Held**
SIC: 5013 3714 3651 Automotive supplies and parts; Motor vehicle parts and accessories; Household audio and video equipment
HQ: Pioneer North America, Inc.
  970 W 190th St Ste 360
  Torrance CA 90502
  310 952-2000

(G-10671)
PRECISION IMPACTS LLC
721 Richard St (45342-1840)
PHONE..................................937 530-8254
EMP: 89 **EST:** 2021
SALES (est): 7.95MM **Privately Held**
SIC: 3449 1761 Miscellaneous metalwork; Sheet metal work, nec

(G-10672)
PRINTING SERVICE COMPANY
3233 S Tech Blvd (45342-0843)
PHONE..................................937 425-6100
William Fair, Pr
Paul Molyneaux, Executive Vice President Finance & Administration*
Gary Boens, *
Rob Jones, *
Kristen Kahut, *
EMP: 70 **EST:** 1933
SQ FT: 40,000
SALES (est): 16.4MM **Privately Held**
SIC: 2752 Offset printing

(G-10673)
RELX INC
4700 Lyons Rd (45342-6453)
PHONE..................................937 865-6800
Bill Wheeler, Mgr
EMP: 7
SALES (corp-wide): 11.42B **Privately Held**
Web: www.lexisnexis.com
SIC: 2721 Periodicals
HQ: Relx Inc.
  230 Park Ave Ste 700
  New York NY 10169
  212 309-8100

(G-10674)
RELX INC
Also Called: Lexisnexis
9333 Springboro Pike (45342-4424)
PHONE..................................937 865-6800
Doug Kaplan, Brnch Mgr
EMP: 128
SALES (corp-wide): 11.42B **Privately Held**
Web: www.lexisnexis.com
SIC: 2731 Books, publishing only
HQ: Relx Inc.
  230 Park Ave Ste 700
  New York NY 10169
  212 309-8100

(G-10675)
RENEGADE MATERIALS CORPORATION
3363 S Tech Blvd (45342-0826)
PHONE..................................937 350-5274
Matthew Trombly, Pr
Vicki Hoffman, *
▲ **EMP:** 52 **EST:** 2007
SQ FT: 25,000
SALES (est): 24.94MM **Privately Held**
Web: www.renegademateriales.com
SIC: 3081 2891 2821 Plastics film and sheet ; Epoxy adhesives; Epoxy resins
PA: Teijin Limited
  3-2-1, Kasumigaseki
  Chiyoda-Ku TKY 100-0

(G-10676)
RETALIX INC
2490 Technical Dr (45342-6136)
PHONE..................................937 384-2277
Barry Shaked, Pr
Karen Weaver, *
Barry Shake, *
EMP: 47 **EST:** 1979
SQ FT: 72,000
SALES (est): 2.32MM **Privately Held**
Web: www.ncr.com
SIC: 5734 7372 Software, business and non-game; Prepackaged software
HQ: Ncr Global Ltd
  9 Dafna
  Raanana 43662

(G-10677)
RITA OF MIAMISBURG LLC
726 N Heincke Rd (45342-2742)
PHONE..................................937 247-5244
EMP: 31
SALES (corp-wide): 63.4K **Privately Held**
SIC: 2024 Ice cream and frozen deserts
PA: Rita Of Miamisburg Llc
  6164 State Route 122
  Franklin OH 45005
  937 247-5244

(G-10678)
ROCONEX CORPORATION
2444 Sydneys Bend Dr (45342-6790)
PHONE..................................937 339-2616
Ty Spear, Pr
EMP: 15 **EST:** 1954
SALES (est): 392.12K **Privately Held**
Web: www.roconex.com
SIC: 3555 3444 Printing trades machinery; Sheet metalwork

(G-10679)
RTI SECUREX LLC
20 S 1st St (45342-2816)
P.O. Box 750354 (45475-0354)
PHONE..................................937 859-5290
Ted Humphprey, Prin
EMP: 15 **EST:** 1999
SALES (est): 964.03K **Privately Held**
SIC: 3861 Cameras and related equipment

(G-10680)
RUMFORD PAPER COMPANY
8540 Gander Creek Dr (45342-5439)
PHONE..................................937 242-9230
George F Martin, Pr
EMP: 7 **EST:** 2010
SALES (est): 130.15K **Privately Held**
SIC: 2621 Paper mills

(G-10681)
SGI MATRIX LLC (PA)
1041 Byers Rd (45342-5487)
PHONE..................................937 438-9033
James Young, *
Jeffrey S Young, *
John Schomburg, *
Joseph Jenkins, *
EMP: 68 **EST:** 1977
SQ FT: 12,000
SALES (est): 18.53MM
SALES (corp-wide): 18.53MM **Privately Held**
Web: www.matrixsys.com
SIC: 8711 7373 3873 Engineering services; Computer integrated systems design; Watches, clocks, watchcases, and parts

(G-10682)
SHUPERT MANUFACTURING INC
3660 Benner Rd (45342-4368)
PHONE..................................937 859-7492
Randy Shupert, Pr
Glenda Shupert, Stockholder
▼ **EMP:** 14 **EST:** 1976
SQ FT: 38,000
SALES (est): 2.38MM **Privately Held**
Web: www.empowermfg.com
SIC: 3564 Blowers and fans

(G-10683)
SIGNATURE TECHNOLOGIES INC (DH)
Also Called: Com-Net Software Specialists
3728 Benner Rd (45342-4302)
PHONE..................................937 859-6323
Elie Geva, Pr
David Michaels, *
EMP: 40 **EST:** 1985
SQ FT: 25,000
SALES (est): 21.07MM
SALES (corp-wide): 27.61MM **Privately Held**
Web: www.sigtechinc.com
SIC: 3669 3674 3577 Transportation signaling devices; Semiconductors and related devices; Computer peripheral equipment, nec
HQ: Sita Information Networking Computing Uk Limited
  1 London Gate
  Hayes MIDDX UB3 1

(G-10684)
SPINTECH HOLDINGS INC
Also Called: Spintech
1964 Byers Rd (45342-3249)
PHONE..................................937 912-3250
EMP: 21 **EST:** 2010
SALES (est): 4.56MM **Privately Held**
Web: www.smarttooling.com
SIC: 3544 Special dies, tools, jigs, and fixtures

(G-10685)
STACO ENERGY PRODUCTS CO (HQ)
2425 Technical Dr (45342-6137)
PHONE..................................937 253-1191
Cary M Maguire, Ch Bd
Jeff Hoffman, Pr
Jefferey Nick, VP
◆ **EMP:** 6 **EST:** 1944
SALES (est): 14.76MM
SALES (corp-wide): 52.28MM **Privately Held**
Web: www.stacoenergy.com
SIC: 3677 3612 3999 Electronic coils and transformers; Generator voltage regulators; Military insignia
PA: Components Corporation Of America
  5950 Berkshire Ln # 1500
  Dallas TX 75225
  214 969-0166

(G-10686)
STEINER EOPTICS INC (PA)
Also Called: Sensor Technology Systems
3475 Newmark Dr (45342-5426)
PHONE..................................937 426-2341
Alan Page, Dir
EMP: 80 **EST:** 1991
SQ FT: 50,000
SALES (est): 16.24MM **Privately Held**
Web: www.steiner-defense.com
SIC: 8731 3851 Electronic research; Ophthalmic goods

(G-10687)
SYNAGRO MIDWEST INC
4515 Infirmary Rd (45342-1235)
PHONE..................................937 384-0669
Jim Rosendall, VP
EMP: 10 **EST:** 1979
SALES (est): 4.19MM
SALES (corp-wide): 126.64MM **Publicly Held**
SIC: 4953 2873 Recycling, waste materials; Nitrogenous fertilizers
HQ: Synagro Technologies, Inc.
  435 Williams Ct Ste 100
  Baltimore MD 21220

(G-10688)
T&T GRAPHICS INC
2563 Technical Dr (45342-6108)
P.O. Box 690 (45343-0690)

Miamisburg - Montgomery County (G-10689)

PHONE..................937 847-6000
EMP: 80 EST: 1971
SALES (est): 10.26MM
SALES (corp-wide): 23.21MM **Privately Held**
Web: www.ttgraphics.com
SIC: 3993 2759 2679 Advertising artwork; Decals: printing, nsk; Labels, paper: made from purchased material
PA: Repacorp, Inc.
  31 Industry Park Ct
  Tipp City OH 45371
  937 667-8496

(G-10689)
TARK INC (PA)
9273 Byers Rd (45342-4349)
PHONE..................937 434-6766
Joe Mccarthy, *CEO*
Jim Mccarthy, *Pr*
Donna Mccarthy, *VP*
John Boonott, *VP*
John Koverman, *Treas*
EMP: 30 EST: 1961
SALES (est): 9.05MM
SALES (corp-wide): 9.05MM **Privately Held**
Web: www.tarkinc.com
SIC: 3561 Pumps and pumping equipment

(G-10690)
TECH PRODUCTS CORPORATION (DH)
2215 Lyons Rd (45342-4465)
PHONE..................937 438-1100
Dan Rork, *Pr*
A M Zimmerman, *
Hugh E Wall Junior, *Prin*
Peirce Wood, *
EMP: 11 EST: 1967
SQ FT: 25,000
SALES (est): 10.71MM
SALES (corp-wide): 1.32B **Privately Held**
Web: www.novibes.com
SIC: 3625 5084 3829 3651 Noise control equipment; Noise control equipment; Measuring and controlling devices, nec; Household audio and video equipment
HQ: Fabreeka International Holdings, Inc.
  1023 Turnpike St
  Stoughton MA 02072
  781 341-3655

(G-10691)
TECHNICOTE INC (PA)
Also Called: Technicote
222 Mound Ave (45342-2996)
P.O. Box 188 (45343-0188)
PHONE..................800 358-4448
Frank Gavrillos, *Pr*
Michelle Davis, *CFO*
◆ EMP: 46 EST: 1980
SQ FT: 35,000
SALES (est): 53.61MM
SALES (corp-wide): 53.61MM **Privately Held**
Web: www.technicote.com
SIC: 2672 Adhesive papers, labels, or tapes: from purchased material

(G-10692)
TECHNICOTE WESTFIELD INC
222 Mound Ave (45342-2996)
PHONE..................937 859-4448
Dirk Desanzo, *Pr*
John Petel, *
John L Mc Cormick, *
Douglas Garwood, *
EMP: 22 EST: 1982
SQ FT: 35,000
SALES (est): 461.54K **Privately Held**
Web: www.technicote.com
SIC: 2672 Adhesive papers, labels, or tapes: from purchased material

(G-10693)
TERADATA OPERATIONS INC
2461 Rosina Dr (45342-6431)
PHONE..................937 866-0032
EMP: 429
Web: www.teradata.com
SIC: 3571 Electronic computers
HQ: Teradata Operations, Inc.
  17095 Via Del Campo
  San Diego CA 92127

(G-10694)
THE HOOVEN - DAYTON CORP
Also Called: H D C
511 Byers Rd (45342-5337)
P.O. Box 507 (45040-0507)
PHONE..................937 233-4473
▲ EMP: 101
Web: www.hoovendayton.com
SIC: 2679 2672 2671 2759 Tags and labels, paper; Tape, pressure sensitive: made from purchased materials; Paper; coated and laminated packaging; Labels and seals: printing, nsk

(G-10695)
TOAST WITH CAKE LLC
9231 Towering Pine Dr Apt L (45342-5807)
PHONE..................937 554-5900
Sherlonda Campbell, *Managing Member*
EMP: 7
SALES (est): 299.46K **Privately Held**
SIC: 2051 Bakery products, partially cooked (except frozen)

(G-10696)
TRU-FAB INC
2225 Lyons Rd (45342-4465)
PHONE..................937 435-1733
Steven Dudley, *Pr*
Ed Parker, *VP*
EMP: 21 EST: 1977
SALES (est): 1.15MM **Privately Held**
Web: www.hpcfire.com
SIC: 3441 Fabricated structural metal

(G-10697)
VENTARI CORPORATION
8641 Washington Church Rd (45342-4470)
PHONE..................937 278-4269
EMP: 11 EST: 2010
SALES (est): 210.01K **Privately Held**
Web: www.mil-mar.net
SIC: 3449 Miscellaneous metalwork

(G-10698)
VERSO PAPER INC
8540 Gander Creek Dr (45342-5439)
PHONE..................901 369-4100
David J Paterson, *Pr*
EMP: 50
SALES (est): 5.39MM **Privately Held**
Web: www.billerud.com
SIC: 2621 Paper mills

(G-10699)
VERSO QUINNESEC REP LLC (DH)
8540 Gander Creek Dr (45342-5439)
PHONE..................901 369-4100
EMP: 231 EST: 2010
SALES (est): 6.52MM
SALES (corp-wide): 4.06B **Privately Held**
SIC: 2621 Paper mills
HQ: Billerud Americas Corporation
  8540 Gander Creek Dr
  Miamisburg OH 45342

(G-10700)
WALTER GRINDERS INC
510 Earl Blvd (45342-6411)
PHONE..................937 859-1975
Joe Szenay, *Prin*
EMP: 12 EST: 2010
SALES (est): 276.14K **Privately Held**
Web: www.walter-machines.com
SIC: 3541 Machine tools, metal cutting type

(G-10701)
WAXCO INTERNATIONAL INC
Also Called: Dacraft
727 Dayton Oxford Rd (45342)
P.O. Box 147 (45343-0147)
PHONE..................937 746-4845
Roger Wax, *Pr*
Bill Wax, *VP*
EMP: 10 EST: 1985
SALES (est): 1.86MM **Privately Held**
Web: www.waxcointl.com
SIC: 3355 1521 5211 1761 Structural shapes, rolled, aluminum; General remodeling, single-family houses; Door and window products; Siding contractor

(G-10702)
WOODWORKING SHOP LLC
1195 Mound Rd (45342-6715)
PHONE..................513 330-9663
Mark Sams, *Pr*
EMP: 15 EST: 2002
SQ FT: 1,300
SALES (est): 2.01MM **Privately Held**
Web: www.thewoodworkingshop.com
SIC: 2599 2511 3425 Cabinets, factory; Wood household furniture; Saws, hand: metalworking or woodworking

(G-10703)
WURTH ELECTRONICS ICS INC
Also Called: Wurth Elecktronik
1982 Byers Rd (45342-3249)
PHONE..................937 415-7700
Brad Weaver, *CEO*
EMP: 27 EST: 2010
SALES (est): 11.87MM
SALES (corp-wide): 20.7B **Privately Held**
Web: www.we-online.com
SIC: 5065 3672 Electronic parts; Printed circuit boards
HQ: Wurth Group Of North America Inc.
  93 Grant St
  Ramsey NJ 07446

(G-10704)
YASKAWA AMERICA INC
Motoman Robotics Division
100 Automation Way (45342-4962)
PHONE..................937 847-6200
Steve Barhorst, *Div Pres*
EMP: 180
SQ FT: 304,815
Web: www.yaskawa.com
SIC: 7694 Armature rewinding shops
HQ: Yaskawa America, Inc.
  2121 S Norman Dr
  Waukegan IL 60085
  847 887-7000

Miamitown
Hamilton County

(G-10705)
BICKERS METAL PRODUCTS INC
5825 State Rte128 (45041)
P.O. Box 648 (45041-0648)
PHONE..................513 353-4000
Robert C Graff, *Pr*
Roger Coffaro, *VP*
Charles Coffaro, *Stockholder*
EMP: 40 EST: 1964
SQ FT: 30,000
SALES (est): 4.64MM **Privately Held**
SIC: 3441 3444 Fabricated structural metal; Sheet metalwork

(G-10706)
BROTHERS TOOL AND MFG LTD
8300 Harrison Ave (45041)
P.O. Box 89 (45041-0089)
PHONE..................513 353-9700
EMP: 18 EST: 1994
SQ FT: 6,000
SALES (est): 869.04K **Privately Held**
SIC: 3544 Special dies and tools

(G-10707)
CHARGER PRESS INC
6088 Rte128 (45041)
P.O. Box 117 (45041-0117)
PHONE..................513 542-3113
Gerald J Laake, *Pr*
EMP: 8 EST: 1956
SALES (est): 176.72K **Privately Held**
SIC: 2752 Offset printing

(G-10708)
GATEWAY CON FORMING SVCS INC
5938 Hamilton-Cleves Rd (45041)
P.O. Box 130 (45041-0130)
PHONE..................513 353-2000
Robert Bilz, *Pr*
Tim Hughey, *
Brandon Erfman, *
Jean C Hughey, *
J Robert Hughey, *Stockholder**
EMP: 75 EST: 1960
SQ FT: 3,000
SALES (est): 8.8MM
SALES (corp-wide): 8.8MM **Privately Held**
Web: www.gatewayconcreteforming.com
SIC: 1771 3449 3496 3429 Foundation and footing contractor; Bars, concrete reinforcing: fabricated steel; Miscellaneous fabricated wire products; Hardware, nec
PA: Imcon Corp.
  5938 State Route 128
  Miamitown OH 45041
  513 353-2000

(G-10709)
SEILKOP INDUSTRIES INC
A-G Tool & Die Company
5927 State Route 128 (45041-2501)
P.O. Box 250 (45041-0250)
PHONE..................513 353-3090
Ken Seilkop, *Owner*
EMP: 14
SQ FT: 19,000
SALES (corp-wide): 19.44MM **Privately Held**
Web: www.agtool.com
SIC: 3312 3544 Tool and die steel; Special dies, tools, jigs, and fixtures
PA: Seilkop Industries, Inc.
  425 W North Bend Rd
  Cincinnati OH 45216
  513 761-1035

Miamiville
Clermont County

(G-10710)
AIM INTERNATIONAL
264 Center St (45147)
PHONE..................513 831-2938
EMP: 8 EST: 2013

SALES (est): 113.58K **Privately Held**
Web: www.aimmro.com
SIC: 3728 Aircraft parts and equipment, nec

(G-10711)
IRVINE WOOD RECOVERY INC (PA)
110 Glendale Milford Rd (45147)
P.O. Box 110 (45147-0110)
PHONE..................513 831-0060
Les Irvine, *Pr*
EMP: 49 **EST:** 1982
SQ FT: 15,000
SALES (est): 4.86MM **Privately Held**
Web: www.irvinewoodrecovery.com
SIC: 2499 Mulch, wood and bark

(G-10712)
MESSER LLC
Boc Gases
State Road 126160 Glendale-Milford Road (45147)
PHONE..................513 831-4742
John L Seibert, *Mgr*
EMP: 13
SALES (corp-wide): 1.63B **Privately Held**
Web: www.messeramericas.com
SIC: 2813 Nitrogen
HQ: Messer Llc
200 Smrst Corp Blvd # 7000
Bridgewater NJ 08807
800 755-9277

Middle Point
Van Wert County

(G-10713)
TRAVELING RECYCLE WD PDTS INC
Also Called: T&R Wood Products
19590 Bellis Rd (45863-9721)
P.O. Box 143 (45863-0143)
PHONE..................419 968-2649
Eddy Miller, *Pr*
Scott Miller, *VP*
EMP: 15 **EST:** 1963
SQ FT: 13,680
SALES (est): 441.95K **Privately Held**
SIC: 2441 2448 2449 Boxes, wood; Pallets, wood; Wood containers, nec

Middlebranch
Stark County

(G-10714)
HEIDELBERG MTLS US CEM LLC
8282 Middlebranch Rd (44652-9006)
PHONE..................330 499-9100
EMP: 17
SALES (corp-wide): 23.02B **Privately Held**
Web: www.heidelbergmaterials.us
SIC: 3273 Ready-mixed concrete
HQ: Heidelberg Materials Us Cement Llc
300 E John Carpenter Fwy
Irving TX 75062
877 534-4442

Middleburg Heights
Cuyahoga County

(G-10715)
AP SERVICES LLC
18001 Sheldon Rd (44130-2465)
PHONE..................216 267-3200
EMP: 85 **EST:** 2010
SALES (est): 23.42MM
SALES (corp-wide): 2.85B **Publicly Held**
Web: www.cwnuclear.com

SIC: 3053 Gaskets; packing and sealing devices
PA: Curtiss-Wright Corporation
130 Harbour Place Dr # 300
Davidson NC 28036
704 869-4600

(G-10716)
CLEVELAND DIE & MFG CO (PA)
Also Called: Cleveland Die & Mfg
20303 1st Ave (44130-2433)
PHONE..................440 243-3404
Juan Chahda, *Pr*
Liliana Chahda, *VP*
◆ **EMP:** 133 **EST:** 1973
SQ FT: 165,000
SALES (est): 16.5MM
SALES (corp-wide): 16.5MM **Privately Held**
Web: www.clevelanddie.com
SIC: 3469 3544 Stamping metal for the trade ; Special dies, tools, jigs, and fixtures

(G-10717)
COATING SYSTEMS GROUP INC
6909 Engle Rd Bldg C (44130-3473)
PHONE..................440 816-9306
Frank Popiel, *Pr*
Dawn Kaminski, *Prin*
EMP: 10 **EST:** 2013
SALES (est): 886.19K **Privately Held**
Web: www.csginconline.com
SIC: 8711 3535 Engineering services; Conveyors and conveying equipment

(G-10718)
DUBOSE NAT ENRGY FAS MCHNED PR
18737 Sheldon Rd (44130-2472)
PHONE..................216 362-1700
EMP: 18 **EST:** 2010
SALES (est): 2.51MM
SALES (corp-wide): 14.81B **Publicly Held**
Web: www.dubosenes.com
SIC: 3965 Fasteners
PA: Reliance, Inc.
16100 N 71st St Ste 400
Scottsdale AZ 85254
480 564-5700

(G-10719)
IEC INFRARED SYSTEMS INC
Also Called: IEC
7803 Freeway Cir (44130-6308)
PHONE..................440 234-8000
Rick Pettergrew, *Pr*
EMP: 25 **EST:** 1999
SQ FT: 2,300
SALES (est): 5.22MM **Privately Held**
Web: www.iecinfrared.com
SIC: 3812 Infrared object detection equipment

(G-10720)
IEC INFRARED SYSTEMS LLC
Also Called: IEC
7803 Freeway Cir (44130-6308)
PHONE..................440 234-8000
Richard Pettegrew, *Managing Member*
EMP: 22 **EST:** 2013
SALES (est): 1.32MM **Privately Held**
Web: www.iecinfrared.com
SIC: 7389 3826 Design services; Infrared analytical instruments

(G-10721)
INCORPRTED TRSTEES OF THE GSPL
Also Called: Union Gospel Press Division
19695 Commerce Pkwy (44130-2408)

P.O. Box 6059 (44101-1059)
PHONE..................216 749-2100
Beryl C Bidlen, *Pr*
Reverend Lanny C Akers, *VP*
Robert Andrews, *
Vera Mc Kinney, *
EMP: 90 **EST:** 1902
SQ FT: 60,000
SALES (est): 4.6MM **Privately Held**
Web: www.uniongospelpress.com
SIC: 2721 5942 5999 8661 Periodicals, publishing and printing; Books, religious; Religious goods; Nonchurch religious organizations

(G-10722)
KINETIC CONCEPTS INC
Also Called: Kci
6751 Engle Rd (44130-7951)
PHONE..................440 234-8590
EMP: 10
SALES (corp-wide): 32.68B **Publicly Held**
Web: www.acelity.com
SIC: 3841 Surgical and medical instruments
HQ: Kinetic Concepts, Inc.
12930 W Interstate 10
San Antonio TX 78249
800 531-5346

(G-10723)
METAL FINISHING NEEDS LTD
7550 Lucerne Dr Ste 400 (44130-6503)
PHONE..................216 561-6334
Thomas J Foley, *Prin*
EMP: 6 **EST:** 2008
SALES (est): 136.19K **Privately Held**
SIC: 3471 Cleaning, polishing, and finishing

(G-10724)
NOVA MACHINE PRODUCTS INC
Also Called: Nova
18001 Sheldon Rd (44130-2465)
PHONE..................216 267-3200
David Linton, *CEO*
Martin R Benante, *
▲ **EMP:** 115 **EST:** 2005
SALES (est): 17.76MM
SALES (corp-wide): 2.85B **Publicly Held**
Web: www.cwnuclear.com
SIC: 3452 3429 3359 3356 Bolts, metal; Hardware, nec; Nonferrous foundries, nec; Nonferrous rolling and drawing, nec
PA: Curtiss-Wright Corporation
130 Harbour Place Dr # 300
Davidson NC 28036
704 869-4600

(G-10725)
PRECISION REMOTES LLC
7803 Freeway Cir (44130-6308)
PHONE..................510 215-6474
Bob Whiteaker, *Off Mgr*
EMP: 10 **EST:** 1997
SQ FT: 5,000
SALES (est): 447.57K **Privately Held**
Web: www.iecinfrared.com
SIC: 3861 Tripods, camera and projector

(G-10726)
RIVALS SPORTS GRILLE LLC
6710 Smith Rd (44130-2656)
PHONE..................216 267-0005
EMP: 48 **EST:** 2007
SQ FT: 4,368
SALES (est): 1.81MM **Privately Held**
Web: www.rivalscleveland.com
SIC: 5812 7372 Grills (eating places); Application computer software

(G-10727)
SINICO MTM US INC
7007 Engle Rd Ste C (44130-3512)
PHONE..................216 264-8344
Marco Barban, *Pr*
EMP: 7 **EST:** 2017
SALES (est): 619.92K **Privately Held**
Web: www.sinico.com
SIC: 3541 Machine tools, metal cutting type

(G-10728)
VERANTIS CORPORATION (PA)
7251 Engle Rd Ste 300 (44130-3400)
PHONE..................440 243-0700
Don Day, *CEO*
William Jackson, *
▼ **EMP:** 30 **EST:** 2009
SALES (est): 25.41MM **Privately Held**
Web: www.verantis.com
SIC: 5075 3564 Air pollution control equipment and supplies; Blowers and fans

Middlefield
Geauga County

(G-10729)
A & M PALLET SHOP INC
14550 Madison Rd (44062-9499)
P.O. Box 765 (44062-0765)
PHONE..................440 632-1941
Andy A Miller, *Pr*
EMP: 7 **EST:** 1967
SQ FT: 4,200
SALES (est): 321.5K **Privately Held**
SIC: 2448 Pallets, wood

(G-10730)
ALL FOAM PRODUCTS CO (PA)
Also Called: All Foam Pdts Safety Foam Proc
15005 Enterprise Way (44062-9369)
PHONE..................330 849-3636
Darrell Mcnair, *Pr*
Marvin Steinlauf, *VP*
Debbie Irlbacker, *VP*
Shelly Silver, *Sec*
EMP: 6 **EST:** 1977
SQ FT: 3,200
SALES (est): 2.01MM
SALES (corp-wide): 2.01MM **Privately Held**
Web: www.allfoam.com
SIC: 3086 Plastics foam products

(G-10731)
AMERICAN PLASTIC TECH INC
Also Called: A P T
15229 S State Ave (44062)
P.O. Box 37 (44062)
PHONE..................440 632-5203
Joseph A Bergen, *Pr*
Duncan M Simpson Junior, *Sr VP*
Edd Hiksman, *
▲ **EMP:** 182 **EST:** 1950
SQ FT: 178,000
SALES (est): 18.46MM **Privately Held**
Web: www.universalplastics.com
SIC: 3089 3559 Injection molding of plastics; Plastics working machinery

(G-10732)
ARROWHEAD PALLET LLC
7851 Parkman Mespo Rd (44062-9328)
PHONE..................440 693-4241
EMP: 6 **EST:** 1992
SALES (est): 289.34K **Privately Held**
SIC: 2448 Wood pallets and skids

Middlefield - Geauga County (G-10733)   GEOGRAPHIC SECTION

(G-10733)
BASETEK LLC (PA)
14975 White Rd (44062-9216)
PHONE.............................877 712-2273
Scott Sapita, *Managing Member*
EMP: 16 **EST:** 2000
SALES (est): 2.43MM
SALES (corp-wide): 2.43MM **Privately Held**
Web: www.basetek.com
SIC: 3531 5032 Construction machinery; Concrete and cinder block

(G-10734)
BENTRONIX CORP
14999 Madison Rd (44062-8403)
P.O. Box 1297 (44062-1297)
PHONE.............................440 632-0606
Ludmilla Benins, *Pr*
Peter Benins, *VP*
Brian Lanstrum, *VP*
EMP: 7 **EST:** 1984
SQ FT: 2,500
SALES (est): 751.62K **Privately Held**
Web: www.bentronix.com
SIC: 3613 7629 Control panels, electric; Electronic equipment repair

(G-10735)
BURKHOLDER WOODWORKING LLC
15078 Georgia Rd (44062-8228)
PHONE.............................440 313-8203
Roy R Burkholder Junior, *Admn*
EMP: 8 **EST:** 2012
SALES (est): 72.04K **Privately Held**
SIC: 2431 Millwork

(G-10736)
C L WOODWORKING LLC
15841 Chipmunk Ln (44062-7209)
PHONE.............................440 487-7940
Erwin Slabaugh, *Prin*
EMP: 6 **EST:** 2014
SALES (est): 240.83K **Privately Held**
Web: www.clwoodworkingohio.com
SIC: 2431 Millwork

(G-10737)
CABINETWORKS GROUP MICH LLC
15535 S State Ave (44062)
PHONE.............................440 632-2547
EMP: 114
SALES (corp-wide): 1.6B **Privately Held**
Web: www.cabinetworksgroup.com
SIC: 2434 Wood kitchen cabinets
PA: Cabinetworks Group Michigan, Llc
       20000 Victor Pkwy
       Livonia MI 48152
       734 205-4600

(G-10738)
CABINTWRKS GROUP MDDLFIELD LLC (HQ)
Also Called: Kraftmaid Cabinetry
15535 S State Ave (44062)
P.O. Box 1055 (44062-1055)
PHONE.............................888 562-7744
Keith Scherzer, *Managing Member*
Andrew Rattray, *
◆ **EMP:** 2533 **EST:** 1969
SALES (est): 417.53MM
SALES (corp-wide): 2.54B **Privately Held**
Web: www.kraftmaid.com
SIC: 2511 2434 Wood household furniture; Wood kitchen cabinets
PA: Cabinetworks Group, Inc.
       20000 Victor Pkwy Ste 100
       Livonia MI 48152
       734 205-4600

(G-10739)
CARTER-JONES LUMBER COMPANY
Also Called: Carter Lumber
14601 Kinsman Rd (44062-9245)
PHONE.............................440 834-8164
Lenny Barciskoi, *Mgr*
EMP: 30
SALES (corp-wide): 2.57B **Privately Held**
Web: www.carterlumber.com
SIC: 2452 5074 5211 Prefabricated buildings, wood; Plumbing and hydronic heating supplies; Lumber products
HQ: The Carter-Jones Lumber Company
       601 Tallmadge Rd
       Kent OH 44240
       330 673-6100

(G-10740)
CHEM TECHNOLOGIES LTD
14875 Bonner Dr (44062-8493)
PHONE.............................440 632-9311
S James Schill, *CEO*
Randall Vancura, *COO*
EMP: 99 **EST:** 2001
SQ FT: 120,000
SALES (est): 48.69MM **Privately Held**
Web: www.chemtechnologiesltd.com
SIC: 2819 2899 Industrial inorganic chemicals, nec; Chemical preparations, nec

(G-10741)
CHEROKEE HARDWOODS INC (PA)
Also Called: Amish Heritg WD Floors & Furn
16741 Newcomb Rd (44062-8248)
PHONE.............................440 632-0322
Wallace D Byler, *Pr*
Bill W Byler, *VP*
EMP: 6 **EST:** 1997
SQ FT: 12,500
SALES (est): 1.1MM
SALES (corp-wide): 1.1MM **Privately Held**
Web: www.cherokeehardwoods.com
SIC: 2421 2426 Sawmills and planing mills, general; Hardwood dimension and flooring mills

(G-10742)
CLEAR SKIES AHEAD LLC (PA)
15626 W High St (44062-9293)
P.O. Box 100 (44062-0100)
PHONE.............................440 632-3157
EMP: 6 **EST:** 2014
SALES (est): 271.46K
SALES (corp-wide): 271.46K **Privately Held**
Web: www.clearskiesllc.com
SIC: 2834 Pharmaceutical preparations

(G-10743)
CROSSCREEK PALLET CO
14530 Madison Rd (44062-9499)
PHONE.............................440 632-1940
Michael Yoder, *Owner*
EMP: 7 **EST:** 2005
SALES (est): 184.25K **Privately Held**
SIC: 2448 Pallets, wood

(G-10744)
CT SPECIALTY POLYMERS LTD
14875 Bonner Dr (44062-8493)
PHONE.............................440 632-9311
James Schill, *Prin*
EMP: 7 **EST:** 2010
SALES (est): 150K **Privately Held**
Web: www.chemtechnologiesltd.com
SIC: 2241 Rubber and elastic yarns and fabrics

(G-10745)
CUSTOM PALET MANUFACTURING
9291 N Girdle Rd (44062-9531)
PHONE.............................440 693-4603
Lester Mullet, *Owner*
EMP: 7 **EST:** 1995
SALES (est): 394.87K **Privately Held**
Web: www.lkelectric.net
SIC: 2448 Pallets, wood

(G-10746)
D MARTONE INDUSTRIES INC
Also Called: Jaco Products
15060 Madison Rd (44062-9450)
PHONE.............................440 632-5800
Frank Defino, *Pr*
David B Cathcart, *
Samuel R Martillotta, *
EMP: 30 **EST:** 1991
SQ FT: 38,000
SALES (est): 4.04MM **Privately Held**
Web: www.jacoproducts.com
SIC: 3089 Injection molding of plastics
PA: A.J.D. Holding Co.
       2181 Enterprise Pkwy
       Twinsburg OH 44087

(G-10747)
D P PRODUCTS INC
14790 Berkshire Ind. Pkwy. (44062)
PHONE.............................440 834-9663
Ken Ashba, *Prin*
EMP: 6 **EST:** 2011
SALES (est): 207K **Privately Held**
Web: www.dpproducts.com
SIC: 2448 Wood pallets and skids

(G-10748)
DRUMMOND CORPORATION
14990 Berkshire Industrial Pkwy (44062-9390)
P.O. Box 389 (44021-0389)
PHONE.............................440 834-9660
Paul Spangler Senior, *Pr*
Paul Spangler Junior, *VP*
Joan Spangler, *VP*
EMP: 15 **EST:** 1980
SQ FT: 10,000
SALES (est): 2.03MM **Privately Held**
Web: www.drummondcorp.com
SIC: 3089 Injection molding of plastics

(G-10749)
EEI ACQUISITION CORP
Also Called: Engineered Endeavors
15175 Kinsman Rd (44062-9471)
PHONE.............................440 564-5484
Patrick Deloney, *Pr*
Gerry Truax, *
EMP: 45 **EST:** 1988
SALES (est): 4.53MM **Privately Held**
SIC: 3663 Mobile communication equipment

(G-10750)
FLAMBEAU INC
15981 Valplast Rd (44062-9399)
P.O. Box 97 (44062-0097)
PHONE.............................440 632-6131
Jason Sauey, *Pr*
EMP: 97
Web: www.flambeau.com
SIC: 3089 Plastics containers, except foam
HQ: Flambeau, Inc.
       801 Lynn Ave
       Baraboo WI 53913
       800 352-6266

(G-10751)
GAS ASSIST INJCTION MLDING EXP
15285 S State Ave (44062-9468)
PHONE.............................440 632-5203
EMP: 7 **EST:** 2018
SALES (est): 137.81K **Privately Held**
Web: www.universalplastics.com
SIC: 3089 Injection molding of plastics

(G-10752)
GOLD KEY PROCESSING INC
Also Called: Hexpol Middlefield
14910 Madison Rd (44062-8403)
PHONE.............................440 632-0901
Ken Bloom, *
▼ **EMP:** 185 **EST:** 1997
SQ FT: 160,000
SALES (est): 39.59MM
SALES (corp-wide): 2.12B **Privately Held**
Web: www.hexpol.com
SIC: 3069 2891 Reclaimed rubber and specialty rubber compounds; Adhesives and sealants
HQ: Hexpol Holding Inc.
       14330 Kinsman Rd
       Burton OH 44021
       440 834-4644

(G-10753)
HANS ROTHENBUHLER & SON INC
15815 Nauvoo Rd (44062-8501)
PHONE.............................440 632-6000
John Rothenbuhler, *Pr*
▲ **EMP:** 40 **EST:** 1956
SALES (est): 6.97MM **Privately Held**
Web: www.rothenbuhlercheesemakers.com
SIC: 2022 5451 5143 2023 Natural cheese; Dairy products stores; Dairy products, except dried or canned; Dry, condensed and evaporated dairy products

(G-10754)
HARDWOOD LUMBER COMPANY INC
13813 Station Rd (44062-8728)
PHONE.............................440 834-1891
EMP: 13 **EST:** 1958
SALES (est): 2.98MM **Privately Held**
Web: www.hardwood-lumber.com
SIC: 5713 1751 2511 Floor covering stores; Cabinet building and installation; Wood household furniture

(G-10755)
HAUSER SERVICES LLC
Also Called: Hauser Landscaping
15668 Old State Rd (44062)
P.O. Box 1161 (44062)
PHONE.............................440 632-5126
Dave Hauser Mng, *Mgr*
Monique Hauser, *Managing Member*
EMP: 20 **EST:** 1988
SQ FT: 10,000
SALES (est): 2.6MM **Privately Held**
SIC: 2499 0781 Mulch, wood and bark; Landscape services

(G-10756)
HEXPOL COMPOUNDING LLC
14910 Madison Rd (44062-8403)
PHONE.............................440 632-1962
EMP: 129
SALES (corp-wide): 2.12B **Privately Held**
Web: www.hexpol.com
SIC: 3087 Custom compound purchased resins
HQ: Hexpol Compounding Llc
       14330 Kinsman Rd
       Burton OH 44021
       440 834-4644

GEOGRAPHIC SECTION

Middlefield - Geauga County (G-10781)

(G-10757)
HK LOGGING & LUMBER LTD
16465 Farley Rd (44062-8290)
PHONE...............440 632-1997
Henry Kuhns, *Pr*
EMP: 7 **EST:** 2004
SALES (est): 1.02MM **Privately Held**
Web: www.hkloggingandlumber.com
SIC: 2411 Logging camps and contractors

(G-10758)
INDEX INC
16582 Kinsman Rd (44062-9591)
PHONE...............440 632-5400
Emy E Picard, *Prin*
EMP: 8 **EST:** 2000
SALES (est): 74.42K **Privately Held**
Web: www.index-group.com
SIC: 2822 Synthetic rubber

(G-10759)
J K PLASTICS CO
14135 Madison Rd (44062-9763)
PHONE...............440 632-1482
FAX: 440 632-1482
EMP: 6
SQ FT: 8,400
SALES (est): 626.67K **Privately Held**
SIC: 3089 3635 Injection molding of plastics; Household vacuum cleaners

(G-10760)
JOBAP ASSEMBLY INC
16090 Industrial Pkwy Unit 9 (44062-6302)
PHONE...............440 632-5393
Rebecca Portman, *Pr*
Judith Mellenger, *Treas*
▲ **EMP:** 14 **EST:** 1990
SQ FT: 6,000
SALES (est): 528.01K **Privately Held**
Web: www.jobapassembly.com
SIC: 3699 1731 Electrical equipment and supplies, nec; Electrical work

(G-10761)
JOHNSONITE INC
Also Called: Johnsonite Rubber Flooring
16035 Industrial Pkwy (44062-9386)
P.O. Box 880 (44062-0880)
PHONE...............440 632-3441
Jeff Buttitta, *Pr*
Tom Dowling, *
▲ **EMP:** 500 **EST:** 1895
SALES (est): 96.76MM
SALES (corp-wide): 250.72K **Privately Held**
Web: commercial.tarkett.com
SIC: 3086 Carpet and rug cushions, foamed plastics
HQ: Tarkett
   Tour Initiale
   Puteaux

(G-10762)
KRAFTMAID TRUCKING INC (PA)
16052 Industrial Pkwy (44062-9382)
P.O. Box 1055 (44062-1055)
PHONE...............440 632-2531
EMP: 100 **EST:** 1989
SQ FT: 12,000
SALES (est): 10.48MM
SALES (corp-wide): 10.48MM **Privately Held**
Web: www.kraftmaid.com
SIC: 4813 2517 Telephone communication, except radio; Wood television and radio cabinets

(G-10763)
LA ROSE PAVING CO
16590 Nauvoo Rd (44062-9408)
P.O. Box 146 (44062-0146)
PHONE...............440 632-0330
TOLL FREE: 888
Linda Rose, *Pr*
Jim Rose, *VP*
EMP: 8 **EST:** 1997
SALES (est): 840.64K **Privately Held**
Web: www.larosepaving.com
SIC: 2951 Paving blocks

(G-10764)
MERCURY PLASTICS LLC
15760 Madison Rd (44062-8408)
P.O. Box 989 (44062-0989)
PHONE...............440 632-5281
EMP: 155 **EST:** 2017
SALES (est): 23.52MM
SALES (corp-wide): 7.97B **Publicly Held**
Web: www.mercury-plastics.com
SIC: 3089 Injection molding of plastics
PA: Masco Corporation
   17450 College Pkwy
   Livonia MI 48152
   313 274-7400

(G-10765)
MIDDLEFIELD GLASS INCORPORATED
17447 Kinsman Rd (44062-9433)
P.O. Box 1266 (44062-1266)
PHONE...............440 632-5699
Michael Lyons, *Pr*
Carol Lyons, *VP*
EMP: 15 **EST:** 1992
SQ FT: 9,000
SALES (est): 468.66K **Privately Held**
Web: www.middlefieldglass.com
SIC: 3231 5231 Stained glass: made from purchased glass; Glass, leaded or stained

(G-10766)
MIDDLEFIELD PALLET INC
15940 Burton Windsor Rd (44062-9791)
PHONE...............440 632-0553
Robert J Troyer, *Pr*
John A Yoder, *
EMP: 42 **EST:** 1998
SQ FT: 30,000
SALES (est): 4.71MM **Privately Held**
Web: www.middlefieldpallet.com
SIC: 2448 Pallets, wood

(G-10767)
MIDDLEFIELD PLASTICS INC
15235 Burton Windsor Rd (44062-9784)
P.O. Box 708 (44062-0708)
PHONE...............440 834-4638
John D Fisher, *Pr*
Edward Minick, *
EMP: 45 **EST:** 1970
SQ FT: 44,000
SALES (est): 8.63MM **Privately Held**
Web: www.middlefieldplastics.com
SIC: 3089 3053 Extruded finished plastics products, nec; Gaskets; packing and sealing devices

(G-10768)
MIDDLEFELD ORIGINAL CHEESE COOP
Also Called: Das Deutsch Cheese
16942 Kinsman Rd (44062-9484)
P.O. Box 237 (44062-0237)
PHONE...............440 632-5567
Eli D L Miller, *Pr*
Nevin R Byler, *General Vice President*
EMP: 17 **EST:** 1956
SQ FT: 12,000
SALES (est): 596.95K **Privately Held**
Web: www.middlefieldohio.com
SIC: 2022 Natural cheese

(G-10769)
MILLER LOGGING
5327 Parks West Rd (44062-9352)
PHONE...............440 693-4001
Eli P Miller, *Prin*
EMP: 6 **EST:** 1998
SALES (est): 111.31K **Privately Held**
SIC: 2411 Logging camps and contractors

(G-10770)
MILLERS LINIMENTS LLC
17150 Bundysburg Rd (44062-9247)
PHONE...............440 548-5800
Albert Miller, *Prin*
EMP: 6 **EST:** 2010
SALES (est): 216.1K **Privately Held**
SIC: 2834 Liniments

(G-10771)
MOLTEN MTAL EQP INNVATIONS LLC
Also Called: Mmei
15510 Old State Rd (44062-8208)
PHONE...............440 632-9119
Paul Cooper, *Pr*
Kevin Doherty, *
▲ **EMP:** 28 **EST:** 2012
SALES (est): 4.4MM **Privately Held**
Web: www.mmei-inc.com
SIC: 3561 Industrial pumps and parts

(G-10772)
MULTI-WING AMERICA INC
15030 Berkshire Industrial Pkwy (44062-9390)
P.O. Box 425 (44021-0425)
PHONE...............440 834-9400
Jesper Bernhoft, *Ch Bd*
Jim Crowley, *
William Crowley, *
John Crowley, *
Terese Crowley, *
▲ **EMP:** 45 **EST:** 1972
SQ FT: 27,500
SALES (est): 10.49MM **Privately Held**
Web: www.multi-wing.com
SIC: 3564 Exhaust fans: industrial or commercial

(G-10773)
MVP PLASTICS INC (PA)
15005 Enterprise Way (44062-9369)
PHONE...............440 834-1790
Darrell Mcnair, *Pr*
EMP: 10 **EST:** 2009
SQ FT: 5,000
SALES (est): 7.49MM **Privately Held**
Web: www.mvpplastics.com
SIC: 3089 Injection molding of plastics

(G-10774)
MYERS INDUSTRIES INC
Also Called: Dillen Products
15150 Madison Rd (44062-9495)
P.O. Box 738 (44062-0738)
PHONE...............440 632-1006
Dexter Chumley, *Mgr*
EMP: 40
SALES (corp-wide): 813.07MM **Publicly Held**
Web: www.myersindustries.com
SIC: 3089 3423 Injection molded finished plastics products, nec; Hand and edge tools, nec
PA: Myers Industries, Inc.
   1293 S Main St
   Akron OH 44301
   330 253-5592

(G-10775)
NAUVOO MACHINE LLC
16254 Nauvoo Rd (44062-9731)
PHONE...............440 632-1990
Lester Byler, *Pr*
EMP: 9 **EST:** 2008
SALES (est): 388.05K **Privately Held**
SIC: 3599 Machine and other job shop work

(G-10776)
NEFF-PERKINS COMPANY (PA)
16080 Industrial Pkwy (44062-9382)
PHONE...............440 632-1658
▲ **EMP:** 89 **EST:** 1979
SALES (est): 44.5MM
SALES (corp-wide): 44.5MM **Privately Held**
Web: www.neff-perkins.com
SIC: 3069 3089 Molded rubber products; Thermoformed finished plastics products, nec

(G-10777)
NORMANDY PRODUCTS CO
16125 Industrial Pkwy (44062-9393)
P.O. Box 52 (44062-0052)
PHONE...............440 632-5050
Carl Arysiak, *Prin*
EMP: 60
SQ FT: 64,000
SALES (corp-wide): 8.73MM **Privately Held**
Web: www.normandyproducts.com
SIC: 3082 3498 Tubes, unsupported plastics; Fabricated pipe and fittings
HQ: Normandy Products Co.
   1150 Freeport Rd
   Pittsburgh PA 15238
   412 826-1825

(G-10778)
NORTHEAST LOGGING & LUMBER LLC
8641 Fletcher Rd (44062-9608)
PHONE...............440 272-5100
Paul Detweiler, *Admn*
EMP: 6 **EST:** 2018
SALES (est): 81.72K **Privately Held**
SIC: 2411 Logging

(G-10779)
PCKD ENTERPRISES INC
Also Called: Molten Metals
15510 Old State Rd (44062-8208)
PHONE...............440 632-9119
Paul Cooper, *Pr*
Kevin Doherty, *VP*
Mark Andes, *Prin*
Sarah Mikash, *Prin*
▲ **EMP:** 18 **EST:** 1990
SQ FT: 16,000
SALES (est): 956.93K **Privately Held**
Web: www.mmei-inc.com
SIC: 3561 Industrial pumps and parts

(G-10780)
PHELPS CREEK WOOD WORKS LLC
9445 State Route 534 (44062-9516)
PHONE...............440 693-4314
Raymond Slabaugh, *Prin*
EMP: 6 **EST:** 2008
SALES (est): 192.25K **Privately Held**
SIC: 2434 Wood kitchen cabinets

(G-10781)
PLASTIC EXTRUSION TECH LTD
15229 S State Ave (44062-9468)

Middlefield - Geauga County (G-10782)

P.O. Box 92 (44062-0092)
PHONE..............................440 632-5611
William E Spencer, Pr
Diane Spencer, Corporate Secretary*
▼ EMP: 25 EST: 1997
SQ FT: 38,500
SALES (est): 4.73MM Privately Held
Web: www.plasticextrusiontech.net
SIC: 3089 Extruded finished plastics products, nec

(G-10782)
POLYCHEM DISPERSIONS INC
16066 Industrial Pkwy (44062-9382)
PHONE..............................800 545-3530
William Nichols, CEO
Anthony Vanni, *
Jeff Nichols, *
EMP: 45 EST: 1981
SQ FT: 30,000
SALES (est): 15.32MM Privately Held
Web: www.dispersions.com
SIC: 2869 Industrial organic chemicals, nec

(G-10783)
RAYMOND J DETWEILER
16747 Nauvoo Rd (44062-8411)
PHONE..............................440 632-1255
Albert Detweiler, Prin
EMP: 6 EST: 2009
SALES (est): 113.21K Privately Held
SIC: 2431 Millwork

(G-10784)
RESOURCE MTL HDLG & RECYCL INC (PA)
14970 Berkshire Industrial Pkwy (44062-9390)
PHONE..............................440 834-0727
Josh Jones, Pr
Stacey Cremers, COO
▼ EMP: 20 EST: 1991
SQ FT: 50,000
SALES (est): 5.28MM
SALES (corp-wide): 5.28MM Privately Held
Web: www.extera.eco
SIC: 5099 3089 Containers: glass, metal or plastic; Plastics containers, except foam

(G-10785)
ROTHENBHLER WHEY INGRDENTS INC
15815 Nauvoo Rd (44062-8501)
PHONE..............................440 632-0157
John Rothenbuhler, Pr
EMP: 16 EST: 1989
SQ FT: 1,364
SALES (est): 996.54K Privately Held
Web: www.rothenbuhlercheesemakers.com
SIC: 2022 Natural cheese

(G-10786)
ROTHENBUHLER CHEESE CHALET LLC
15815 Nauvoo Rd (44062-8501)
PHONE..............................800 327-9477
EMP: 10 EST: 2012
SALES (est): 262.34K Privately Held
Web: www.rothenbuhlercheesemakers.com
SIC: 2022 Natural cheese

(G-10787)
ROTHENBUHLER HOLDING COMPANY
15815 Nauvoo Rd (44062-8501)
PHONE..............................440 632-6000
Ann Rothenbuhler, Prin
Hans Rothenbuhler, Prin
EMP: 24 EST: 1973
SALES (est): 987.52K Privately Held
Web: www.rothenbuhlercheesemakers.com
SIC: 2022 Natural cheese

(G-10788)
SCHNIDER PALLET LLC
9782 Bundysburg Rd (44062-9362)
PHONE..............................440 632-5346
EMP: 9 EST: 2007
SALES (est): 420.19K Privately Held
SIC: 2448 Pallets, wood

(G-10789)
SIMON DE YOUNG CORPORATION
15010 Berkshire Industrial Pkwy (44062-9390)
P.O. Box 217 (44062-0217)
PHONE..............................440 834-3000
Simon D Young, Pr
Margaret D Young, Sec
EMP: 8 EST: 1984
SALES (est): 925.59K Privately Held
SIC: 3552 3549 Braiding machines, textile; Wiredrawing and fabricating machinery and equipment, ex. die

(G-10790)
SPI LIQUIDATION INC
Also Called: Sajar Plastics, Inc.
15285 S State Ave (44062-9468)
P.O. Box 37 (44062-0037)
EMP: 100
SIC: 3089 Injection molding of plastics

(G-10791)
SUBURBAN COMMUNICATIONS INC
Also Called: Good News
14905 N State Ave (44062-9747)
P.O. Box 95 (44062-0095)
PHONE..............................440 632-0130
Thomas Henry, Pr
Don Cimorell, *
Neil Belcher, *
EMP: 12 EST: 1979
SALES (est): 284.69K Privately Held
Web: www.good-news.com
SIC: 2721 2741 Magazines: publishing only, not printed on site; Miscellaneous publishing

(G-10792)
TROY INNOVATIVE INSTRS INC
15111 White Rd (44062-9216)
P.O. Box 1328 (44062-1328)
PHONE..............................440 834-9567
Brett Crawford, Pr
Carol Cseplo, *
Randall Hampton, *
August Deangelo, *
EMP: 40 EST: 1992
SQ FT: 12,000
SALES (est): 5.32MM Privately Held
Web: www.troyinnovative.com
SIC: 3841 Medical instruments and equipment, blood and bone work

(G-10793)
TROYMILL MANUFACTURING INC (PA)
Also Called: Troymill Wood Products
17055 Kinsman Rd (44062-9485)
P.O. Box 306 (44062-0306)
PHONE..............................440 632-5580
Marvin Schaefer, Pr
Steven Belman, VP
Brian Schaefer, Prin
EMP: 12 EST: 1988
SQ FT: 19,500
SALES (est): 18.74MM Privately Held
Web: www.troymill.com
SIC: 5031 2448 Lumber, plywood, and millwork; Wood pallets and skids

(G-10794)
TRUMBULL COUNTY HARDWOODS
9446 Bundysburg Rd (44062-9300)
PHONE..............................440 632-0555
▼ EMP: 23 EST: 1989
SQ FT: 600
SALES (est): 2.47MM Privately Held
Web: www.tchardwoods.com
SIC: 2421 2426 Lumber: rough, sawed, or planed; Hardwood dimension and flooring mills

(G-10795)
UNIVERSAL POLYMER & RUBBER LTD (PA)
15730 Madison Rd (44062-8408)
P.O. Box 767 (44062-0767)
PHONE..............................440 632-1691
Joe Colebank, Pr
Andrew Cavanagh, *
▲ EMP: 109 EST: 1988
SQ FT: 56,000
SALES (est): 25.23MM
SALES (corp-wide): 25.23MM Privately Held
Web: www.universalpolymer.com
SIC: 3069 3089 Molded rubber products; Extruded finished plastics products, nec

(G-10796)
V & S SCHULER ENGINEERING INC
15175 Kinsman Rd (44062-9471)
PHONE..............................330 452-5200
Brian Miller, Pr
EMP: 66
SALES (corp-wide): 1.03B Privately Held
Web: www.vsschuler.com
SIC: 3441 Fabricated structural metal
HQ: V & S Schuler Engineering Inc
2240 Allen Ave Se
Canton OH 44707

(G-10797)
WINDSOR MILL LUMBER LLC
8506 Bundysburg Rd (44062-9359)
PHONE..............................440 272-5930
EMP: 8 EST: 2008
SALES (est): 354.45K Privately Held
SIC: 2421 Lumber: rough, sawed, or planed

(G-10798)
WOODCRAFT INDUSTRIES INC
Also Called: WOODCRAFT INDUSTRIES, INC.
15351 S State Ave (44062-9469)
P.O. Box 250 (44062-0250)
PHONE..............................440 632-9655
Dan Miller, Mgr
EMP: 63
Web: www.woodcraftind.com
SIC: 2434 2431 2426 Wood kitchen cabinets ; Millwork; Dimension, hardwood
HQ: Quanex Custom Components, Inc.
525 Lincoln Ave Se
Saint Cloud MN 56304
320 656-2345

(G-10799)
WOODWORKS DESIGN
9005 N Girdle Rd (44062-9502)
PHONE..............................440 693-4414
Todd Armfelt, Prin
EMP: 7 EST: 1998
SALES (est): 990.4K Privately Held
Web: www.woodworks-design.com
SIC: 2431 Millwork

Middletown
Butler County

(G-10800)
3D SALES & CONSULTING INC
Also Called: M R T
408 Vanderveer St (45044-4239)
PHONE..............................513 422-1198
Talbert Selby, Pr
David Poe, *
EMP: 25 EST: 2007
SQ FT: 25,000
SALES (est): 4.42MM Privately Held
Web: www.mrtinc.com
SIC: 3599 Machine shop, jobbing and repair

(G-10801)
ACCESS ENVELOPE INC
2903 Terry Dr (45042-1731)
PHONE..............................513 889-0888
Karen Teotorman, Pr
EMP: 15 EST: 1999
SALES (est): 843.5K Privately Held
SIC: 2677 Envelopes

(G-10802)
AKERS PACKAGING SERVICE INC (PA)
Also Called: Akers Packaging Service Group
2820 Lefferson Rd (45044-6999)
P.O. Box 610 (45042-0610)
PHONE..............................513 422-6312
James F Akers, Ch Bd
William C Akers Ii, Pr
Michael S Akey, *
Marilyn R Akey, *
▲ EMP: 140 EST: 1963
SQ FT: 220,000
SALES (est): 74.17MM
SALES (corp-wide): 74.17MM Privately Held
Web: www.akers-pkg.com
SIC: 2653 Boxes, corrugated: made from purchased materials

(G-10803)
AKERS PACKAGING SOLUTIONS INC (PA)
Also Called: Akers Packaging Service Group
2820 Lefferson Rd (45044-6999)
P.O. Box 610 (45042-0610)
PHONE..............................513 422-6312
James F Akers, Ch Bd
William C Akers, *
Michael Shannon Akey, *
Alfred J Pedicone, *
EMP: 75 EST: 2014
SALES (est): 13.4MM
SALES (corp-wide): 13.4MM Privately Held
Web: www.akers-pkg.com
SIC: 2653 Boxes, corrugated: made from purchased materials

(G-10804)
AKKO FASTENER INC (PA)
1225 Hook Dr (45042-1734)
PHONE..............................513 489-8300
Nancy Fernandez, Pr
Nestor Fernandez, VP
▲ EMP: 16 EST: 1960
SALES (est): 4.63MM
SALES (corp-wide): 4.63MM Privately Held
Web: www.akkofastener.com
SIC: 3452 5072 Screws, metal; Bolts

GEOGRAPHIC SECTION

Middletown - Butler County (G-10829)

(G-10805)
BACKYARD SCOREBOARDS LLC
Also Called: Nifty Promo Products
431 Kenridge Dr (45042-4930)
PHONE.................................513 702-6561
EMP: 9 **EST:** 2005
SQ FT: 11,000
SALES (est): 518.92K **Privately Held**
Web: www.backyardscoreboards.com
SIC: 3949 Team sports equipment

(G-10806)
CENTURY MOLD COMPANY INC
55 Wright Dr (45044-3287)
PHONE.................................513 539-9283
Ron Ricotta, *Brnch Mgr*
EMP: 83
SALES (corp-wide): 197.74MM **Privately Held**
Web: www.centurymold.com
SIC: 3089 Injection molding of plastics
PA: Century Mold Company, Inc.
25 Vantage Point Dr
Rochester NY 14624
585 352-8600

(G-10807)
CITY OF MIDDLETOWN
Also Called: Water Treatment
805 Columbia Ave (45042-1907)
PHONE.................................513 425-7781
Scott Belcher, *Mgr*
EMP: 68
SALES (corp-wide): 64.88MM **Privately Held**
Web: www.cityofmiddletown.org
SIC: 3589 4941 Water treatment equipment, industrial; Water supply
PA: City Of Middletown
1 Donham Plz
Middletown OH 45042
513 425-7766

(G-10808)
CLEVELAND-CLIFFS STEEL CORP
622 Box (45042)
PHONE.................................513 425-3593
EMP: 10
SALES (corp-wide): 22B **Publicly Held**
Web: www.clevelandcliffs.com
SIC: 3312 Blast furnaces and steel mills
HQ: Cleveland-Cliffs Steel Corporation
200 Public Sq Ste 3300
Cleveland OH 44114

(G-10809)
CLEVELAND-CLIFFS STEEL CORP
Also Called: Clevelnd-Clffs Middletown Works
1801 Crawford St (45044-4572)
PHONE.................................513 425-5000
Doctor Stephen W Gilby, *Dir*
EMP: 148
SALES (corp-wide): 22B **Publicly Held**
Web: www.clevelandcliffs.com
SIC: 3312 Blast furnaces and steel mills
HQ: Cleveland-Cliffs Steel Corporation
200 Public Sq Ste 3300
Cleveland OH 44114

(G-10810)
CLEVELAND-CLIFFS STEEL CORP
801 Crawford St (45044-4537)
PHONE.................................513 425-3694
Brian Nuelk, *Brnch Mgr*
EMP: 298
SALES (corp-wide): 22B **Publicly Held**
Web: www.clevelandcliffs.com
SIC: 3312 Stainless steel
HQ: Cleveland-Cliffs Steel Corporation
200 Public Sq Ste 3300
Cleveland OH 44114

(G-10811)
COHEN BROTHERS INC (PA)
1520 14th Ave (45044-5801)
P.O. Box 957 (45044-0957)
PHONE.................................513 422-3696
TOLL FREE: 800
Wilbur Cohen, *Ch Bd*
Kenneth Cohen, *
Donald Zulanch, *
Robert Dumes, *
Neil Cohen, *
EMP: 50 **EST:** 1924
SQ FT: 90,000
SALES (est): 138.63MM
SALES (corp-wide): 138.63MM **Privately Held**
Web: www.cohenusa.com
SIC: 5093 3441 3341 3312 Ferrous metal scrap and waste; Fabricated structural metal; Secondary nonferrous metals; Blast furnaces and steel mills

(G-10812)
COHEN BROTHERS INC
Also Called: Cohen Brothers Inc Lafayette
1300 Lafayette Ave (45044-5913)
PHONE.................................513 217-5200
EMP: 15
SALES (corp-wide): 138.63MM **Privately Held**
Web: www.cohenusa.com
SIC: 5093 3312 3341 Ferrous metal scrap and waste; Blast furnaces and steel mills; Secondary nonferrous metals
PA: Cohen Brothers, Inc.
1520 14th Ave
Middletown OH 45044
513 422-3696

(G-10813)
CORNERSTONE BLDG BRANDS INC
2400 Yankee Rd (45044-8301)
PHONE.................................937 584-3300
EMP: 164
SALES (corp-wide): 5.58B **Privately Held**
Web: www.cornerstonebuildingbrands.com
SIC: 3448 Prefabricated metal buildings
HQ: Cornerstone Building Brands, Inc.
5020 Weston Pkwy
Cary NC 27513
281 897-7788

(G-10814)
CRANE CONSUMABLES INC
155 Wright Dr (45044-3311)
PHONE.................................513 539-9980
Robert Crane, *CEO*
EMP: 45 **EST:** 2007
SALES (est): 5.47MM **Privately Held**
Web: www.craneconsumables.com
SIC: 7389 2241 Packaging and labeling services; Labels, woven

(G-10815)
CREATIVE PRODUCTS INC
2705 Carmody Blvd (45042-1723)
PHONE.................................513 727-9872
Dan Bettinger, *Pr*
Alan Hupke, *VP*
EMP: 8 **EST:** 1995
SQ FT: 5,500
SALES (est): 421.21K **Privately Held**
Web: www.creatingproducts.com
SIC: 3599 Machine and other job shop work

(G-10816)
CROWN ELECTRIC ENGRG & MFG LLC
175 Edison Dr (45044-3269)
PHONE.................................513 539-7394
Chad Shell, *Managing Member*
Bruce Hack, *
▲ **EMP:** 25 **EST:** 2005
SQ FT: 48,000
SALES (est): 4.69MM **Privately Held**
Web: www.crown-electric.com
SIC: 3643 3444 Bus bars (electrical conductors); Sheet metal specialties, not stamped

(G-10817)
DAUBENMIRES PRINTING CO LLC
1527 Central Ave (45044-4135)
PHONE.................................513 425-7223
Gary Daubenmire, *Owner*
EMP: 8 **EST:** 1982
SQ FT: 4,000
SALES (est): 978.61K **Privately Held**
Web: www.daubenmiresprinting.com
SIC: 2752 2791 Offset printing; Typesetting

(G-10818)
DMK INDUSTRIES INC
1801 Made Dr (45044-8948)
PHONE.................................513 727-4549
Dennis Kuna, *Pr*
EMP: 15 **EST:** 1996
SALES (est): 2.15MM **Privately Held**
SIC: 3369 Nonferrous foundries, nec

(G-10819)
DYNAMIC DIES INC
1310 Hook Dr (45042-1712)
PHONE.................................513 705-9524
EMP: 27
SALES (corp-wide): 22.27MM **Privately Held**
Web: www.dynamicdies.com
SIC: 3544 Special dies and tools
PA: Dynamic Dies, Inc.
1705 Commerce Rd
Holland OH 43528
419 865-0249

(G-10820)
ELECTRO-METALLICS CO
3004 Lefferson Rd (45044-6903)
PHONE.................................513 423-8091
Hamilton Watkins, *Pr*
Jane M Watkins, *Sec*
EMP: 8 **EST:** 1965
SQ FT: 2,500
SALES (est): 765.19K **Privately Held**
SIC: 3471 Electroplating of metals or formed products

(G-10821)
ERNST ENTERPRISES INC
2504 S Main St (45044-7446)
PHONE.................................513 422-3651
EMP: 13
SALES (corp-wide): 240.08MM **Privately Held**
Web: www.ernstconcrete.com
SIC: 3273 Ready-mixed concrete
PA: Ernst Enterprises, Inc.
3361 Successful Way
Dayton OH 45414
937 233-5555

(G-10822)
ESSITY OPERATIONS WAUSAU LLC
700 Columbia Ave (45042-1931)
PHONE.................................513 217-3644
Mark Hoton, *Purchasing*
EMP: 36
SIC: 2621 Paper mills
HQ: Essity Operations Wausau Llc
N434 Greenville Ctr
Appleton WI 54914
920 725-7031

(G-10823)
ESSITY PROF HYGIENE N AMER LLC
Also Called: ESSITY PROFESSIONAL HYGIENE NORTH AMERICA LLC
700 Columbia Ave (45042-1931)
PHONE.................................513 217-3644
EMP: 18
Web: www.torkusa.com
SIC: 2621 Paper mills
HQ: Essity Professional Hygiene North America Llc
2929 Arch St Ste 2600
Philadelphia PA 19104
920 727-3770

(G-10824)
EVERTZ TECHNOLOGY SVC USA INC
2601 S Verity Pkwy Bldg 102 (45044-7482)
PHONE.................................513 422-8400
Egon Evertz, *Pr*
▲ **EMP:** 17 **EST:** 2003
SALES (est): 2.2MM **Privately Held**
Web: www.evertz-group.com
SIC: 3325 Steel foundries, nec

(G-10825)
G & R WELDING SERVICE LLC
1350 Hook Dr (45042-1712)
P.O. Box 612 (45042-0612)
PHONE.................................937 245-2341
Martin C Netherton, *Prin*
EMP: 6 **EST:** 2014
SALES (est): 131.05K **Privately Held**
SIC: 7692 Welding repair

(G-10826)
GENOA HEALTHCARE LLC
Also Called: Qol Meds
1036 S Verity Pkwy (45044-5513)
PHONE.................................513 727-0471
EMP: 6
SALES (corp-wide): 371.62B **Publicly Held**
Web: www.genoahealthcare.com
SIC: 2834 Pharmaceutical preparations
HQ: Genoa Healthcare Llc
707 S Grady Way Ste 700
Renton WA 98057

(G-10827)
GRANGER PLASTICS CO THE
1600 Made Industrial Dr (45044-8957)
PHONE.................................513 424-1955
EMP: 20 **EST:** 1994
SALES (est): 4.91MM **Privately Held**
Web: www.grangerplastics.com
SIC: 3089 Injection molding of plastics

(G-10828)
GRAPHIC PACKAGING INTL LLC
Also Called: Altivity Packaging
407 Charles St (45042-2107)
PHONE.................................513 424-4200
Scott Lebeau, *Mgr*
EMP: 143
Web: www.graphicpkg.com
SIC: 2631 2657 Folding boxboard; Folding paperboard boxes
HQ: Graphic Packaging International, Llc
1500 Riveredge Pkwy # 100
Atlanta GA 30328

(G-10829)
HY-BLAST INC
70 Enterprise Dr (45044-8925)
P.O. Box 602 (45042-0602)
PHONE.................................513 424-0704
Robert Cunningham, *Pr*
Thomas Cunningham, *VP*
Betty Jane Cunningham, *Sec*

Middletown - Butler County (G-10830)

Donald Ray Cunningham, *VP*
EMP: 23 **EST:** 1981
SQ FT: 25,000
SALES (est): 1.04MM **Privately Held**
Web: www.hyblastinc.com
SIC: 1799 3471 7699 Epoxy application; Polishing, metals or formed products; Industrial equipment cleaning

(G-10830)
INJECTION ALLOYS INCORPORATED
2601 S Verity Pkwy Bldg 1 (45044)
PHONE....................513 422-8819
Chris Jackson, *CEO*
Manuel Franco, *CFO*
Michelle Shockley Ctrl, *Prin*
▲ **EMP:** 10 **EST:** 2005
SALES (est): 2.63MM **Privately Held**
Web: www.injectionalloys.com
SIC: 3315 Wire and fabricated wire products
HQ: Injection Alloys Limited
   The Way
   Royston HERTS

(G-10831)
INTERNATIONAL PAPER COMPANY
Also Called: International Paper
912 Nelbar St (45042-2529)
PHONE....................800 473-0830
EMP: 29
SALES (corp-wide): 18.92B **Publicly Held**
Web: www.internationalpaper.com
SIC: 2621 Paper mills
PA: International Paper Company
   6400 Poplar Ave
   Memphis TN 38197
   901 419-7000

(G-10832)
INTERSCOPE MANUFACTURING INC
2901 Carmody Blvd (45042)
PHONE....................513 423-8866
John Michael Brill, *CEO*
◆ **EMP:** 50 **EST:** 1988
SQ FT: 175,000
SALES (est): 8.72MM **Privately Held**
Web: www.interscopemfg.com
SIC: 3599 7389 Custom machinery; Repossession service

(G-10833)
JEFF LORI JED HOLDINGS INC
1500 S University Blvd (45044-5968)
PHONE....................513 423-0319
Jeff Pennington, *Pr*
Lori Combs, *
Jed Brubaker, *
EMP: 40 **EST:** 1982
SQ FT: 70,000
SALES (est): 9.89MM **Privately Held**
Web: www.n-stockbox.com
SIC: 2653 Boxes, corrugated: made from purchased materials

(G-10834)
JOHN H HOSKING CO
Also Called: Diamond Aluminum Co
4665 Emerald Way (45044-8966)
PHONE....................513 422-9425
James Hodde Junior, *Pr*
EMP: 6 **EST:** 1956
SQ FT: 6,725
SALES (est): 503.94K **Privately Held**
Web: www.diamond-aluminum.com
SIC: 3498 Fabricated pipe and fittings

(G-10835)
KATHOM MANUFACTURING CO INC
1301 Hook Dr (45042-3571)
PHONE....................513 868-8890
Thomas R Wells, *Pr*
EMP: 22 **EST:** 1983
SALES (est): 3.99MM **Privately Held**
Web: www.kathom.com
SIC: 3089 3643 2821 Injection molding of plastics; Current-carrying wiring services; Plastics materials and resins

(G-10836)
LUBRISOURCE INC
2900 Cincinnati Dayton Rd (45044-9313)
P.O. Box 750221 (45475-0221)
PHONE....................937 432-9292
Angela Morrow, *Pr*
Angela Morrow, *Pr*
Kevin Morrow, *VP*
EMP: 17 **EST:** 2001
SALES (est): 4.11MM **Privately Held**
Web: www.lubrisource.com
SIC: 5084 3561 1389 7699 Hydraulic systems equipment and supplies; Pumps and pumping equipment; Oil sampling service for oil companies; Industrial equipment services

(G-10837)
M-D BUILDING PRODUCTS INC
Also Called: M-D Metal Source
100 Westheimer Dr (45044-3242)
PHONE....................513 539-2255
Carrie Taylor, *Brnch Mgr*
EMP: 10
SALES (corp-wide): 216.18MM **Privately Held**
Web: www.mdmetalsource.com
SIC: 3354 5031 5051 3442 Aluminum extruded products; Doors, nec; Aluminum bars, rods, ingots, sheets, pipes, plates, etc.; Screens, window, metal
PA: M-D Building Products, Inc.
   4041 N Santa Fe Ave
   Oklahoma City OK 73118
   405 528-4411

(G-10838)
M-D BUILDING PRODUCTS INC
100 Westheimer Dr (45044-3242)
PHONE....................513 539-2255
Carrie Taylor-lane, *Prin*
EMP: 104
SALES (corp-wide): 216.18MM **Privately Held**
Web: www.mdteam.com
SIC: 3442 Weather strip, metal
PA: M-D Building Products, Inc.
   4041 N Santa Fe Ave
   Oklahoma City OK 73118
   405 528-4411

(G-10839)
MAGELLAN AROSPC MIDDLETOWN INC (HQ)
2320 Wedekind Dr (45042-2390)
PHONE....................513 422-2751
John Furbay, *Dir Fin*
James S Butyniec, *
EMP: 100 **EST:** 1928
SALES (est): 25.02MM
SALES (corp-wide): 569.19MM **Privately Held**
SIC: 3724 3728 Aircraft engines and engine parts; Aircraft body assemblies and parts
PA: Magellan Aerospace Corporation
   3160 Derry Rd E
   Mississauga ON L4T 1
   905 677-1889

(G-10840)
MAGNUM MAGNETICS CORPORATION
Magnum Inks & Coatings
355 Wright Dr (45044-3268)
PHONE....................513 360-0790
EMP: 39
Web: www.magnummagnetics.com
SIC: 2893 Printing ink
PA: Magnum Magnetics Corporation
   801 Masonic Park Rd
   Marietta OH 45750

(G-10841)
MANUFACTURERS EQUIPMENT CO
Also Called: Meco
35 Enterprise Dr (45044-8928)
PHONE....................513 424-3573
Adam W Miller, *Pr*
J Howard Sachs, *Dir*
Frank B Carraher, *VP*
◆ **EMP:** 14 **EST:** 1910
SQ FT: 16,000
SALES (est): 2.98MM **Privately Held**
Web: www.mecoservices.com
SIC: 3496 3535 Wire chain; Belt conveyor systems, general industrial use

(G-10842)
MATHESON TRI-GAS INC
Also Called: AK Steel Door 360
1801 Crawford St (45044-4572)
PHONE....................513 727-9638
John Green, *Brnch Mgr*
EMP: 6
Web: www.mathesongas.com
SIC: 5084 2813 Welding machinery and equipment; Nitrogen
HQ: Matheson Tri-Gas, Inc.
   3 Mountainview Rd Ste 3 # 3
   Warren NJ 07059
   908 991-9200

(G-10843)
MCINTOSH MANUFACTURING LLC
3350 Yankee Rd (45044-8927)
PHONE....................513 424-5307
▼ **EMP:** 55 **EST:** 1998
SQ FT: 60,000
SALES (est): 15.38MM
SALES (corp-wide): 24.1MM **Privately Held**
Web: www.triosim.com
SIC: 3554 3312 Paper industries machinery; Stainless steel
PA: Triosim Corporation
   2111 N Sandra St
   Appleton WI 54911
   920 968-0800

(G-10844)
MIDDLETOWN LICENSE AGENCY INC
3232 Roosevelt Blvd (45044-6424)
P.O. Box 546 (45042-0546)
PHONE....................513 422-7225
Cristy Gamble, *Pr*
EMP: 9 **EST:** 2004
SALES (est): 148.43K **Privately Held**
SIC: 3469 Automobile license tags, stamped metal

(G-10845)
MOORCHILD LLC
Also Called: Murphy's Landing Casual Dining
6 S Broad St (45044-4000)
PHONE....................513 649-8867
Linda Moorman, *Managing Member*
Nancy Fairchild, *Managing Member*
EMP: 10 **EST:** 2014
SALES (est): 456.78K **Privately Held**
Web: www.murphys-landing.com
SIC: 2599 Bar, restaurant and cafeteria furniture

(G-10846)
NATREEOLA SOAP COMPANY LLC
2367 Bendel Dr (45044-9448)
PHONE....................513 390-2247
Angela Smith, *CEO*
EMP: 6 **EST:** 2021
SALES (est): 27.98K **Privately Held**
SIC: 2841 Soap and other detergents

(G-10847)
NATURAL BEAUTY PRODUCTS INC
Also Called: Decaplus
104 Charles St (45042-2139)
P.O. Box 1566 (45042-7383)
PHONE....................513 420-9400
Kenneth Alsop, *Pr*
David Haddix, *VP*
James Webb, *Treas*
Michelle Randall, *Sec*
EMP: 10 **EST:** 1985
SALES (est): 880.89K **Privately Held**
Web: www.deccaplus.com
SIC: 5999 2844 Hair care products; Hair preparations, including shampoos

(G-10848)
PACKAGING CORPORATION AMERICA
Also Called: Pca/Middletown 353
1824 Baltimore St (45044-5902)
P.O. Box 127 (45042-0127)
PHONE....................513 424-3542
Tom Falvey, *Mgr*
EMP: 96
SQ FT: 200,000
SALES (corp-wide): 8.48B **Publicly Held**
Web: www.packagingcorp.com
SIC: 2653 Boxes, corrugated: made from purchased materials
PA: Packaging Corporation Of America
   1 N Field Ct
   Lake Forest IL 60045
   847 482-3000

(G-10849)
PERSONAL DEFENSE & TACTICS LLC
2200 Ernestine Dr (45042-2794)
PHONE....................513 571-7163
EMP: 6 **EST:** 2012
SALES (est): 136.09K **Privately Held**
SIC: 3812 Defense systems and equipment

(G-10850)
PHILLIPS TUBE GROUP INC
Also Called: Phillips Tube Group, LLC
2201 Trine St (45044)
P.O. Box 125 (44875)
PHONE....................205 338-4771
Angela Phillips, *Pr*
EMP: 44 **EST:** 2016
SQ FT: 50,000
SALES (est): 5.5MM
SALES (corp-wide): 37.42MM **Privately Held**
Web: www.phillipstube.com
SIC: 3312 Pipes and tubes
PA: Phillips Mfg. And Tower Co.
   5578 State Rte 61 N
   Shelby OH 44875
   419 347-1720

(G-10851)
PILOT CHEMICAL CORP
3439 Yankee Rd (45044-8931)
PHONE....................513 424-9700
Jeff Russell, *Brnch Mgr*
EMP: 217
SQ FT: 25,000
SALES (corp-wide): 175.88MM **Privately Held**

GEOGRAPHIC SECTION
Midvale - Tuscarawas County (G-10875)

Web: www.pilotchemical.com
SIC: 2841 2842 Detergents, synthetic organic or inorganic alkaline; Polishes and sanitation goods
HQ: Pilot Chemical Corp.
9075 Cntre Pnte Dr Ste 40
West Chester OH 45069
513 326-0600

(G-10852)
PROGRESSIVE RIBBON INC (PA)
1533 Central Ave (45044-4135)
P.O. Box 887 (45044-0887)
PHONE................................513 705-9319
Darryl Bowen, *Pr*
Darryl Bowen, *Pr*
Dan Bush, *VP*
EMP: 20 **EST:** 1983
SQ FT: 20,000
SALES (est): 9.97MM
SALES (corp-wide): 9.97MM **Privately Held**
SIC: 3955 Ribbons, inked: typewriter, adding machine, register, etc.

(G-10853)
QUAKER CHEMICAL CORPORATION (HQ)
Also Called: Quaker Houghton
3431 Yankee Rd (45044-8931)
PHONE................................513 422-9600
Michael Barry, *Pr*
Carl Mitchell, *Pdt Mgr*
Donald Biltz, *Prin*
Patrick Piccioni, *Prin*
D Jeffry Benoliel, *Sec*
▲ **EMP:** 31 **EST:** 1995
SALES (est): 19.49MM
SALES (corp-wide): 1.95B **Publicly Held**
Web: home.quakerhoughton.com
SIC: 2992 2899 Lubricating oils and greases; Chemical preparations, nec
PA: Quaker Chemical Corporation
901 E Hector St
Conshohocken PA 19428
610 832-4000

(G-10854)
REBILTCO INC
8775 Thomas Rd (45042-1233)
P.O. Box 936 (45044-0936)
PHONE................................513 424-2024
Larry Eckhardt, *Pr*
EMP: 6 **EST:** 1977
SQ FT: 25,000
SALES (est): 499.07K **Privately Held**
Web: www.rebiltcoincweldfab.com
SIC: 3554 Corrugating machines, paper

(G-10855)
RELIABLE COATING SVC CO INC
1301 Hook Dr (45042-3571)
PHONE................................513 217-4680
Roger Rosenbalm, *Pr*
EMP: 7 **EST:** 2021
SALES (est): 750K **Privately Held**
SIC: 3479 Coating of metals with plastic or resins

(G-10856)
ROAD APPLE MUSIC
65 S Main St (45044-4061)
PHONE................................513 217-4444
Edward Hall, *Owner*
EMP: 6 **EST:** 2006
SALES (est): 182.74K **Privately Held**
SIC: 2741 Music book and sheet music publishing

(G-10857)
ROSS HX LLC (PA)
Also Called: Ross Hx
2722 Cincinnati Dayton Rd (45044-8960)
PHONE................................513 217-1565
Richard Ross, *Pr*
EMP: 25 **EST:** 2018
SQ FT: 9,000
SALES (est): 3.3MM
SALES (corp-wide): 3.3MM **Privately Held**
Web: www.rosshx.com
SIC: 3443 Heat exchangers, plate type

(G-10858)
SPURLINO MATERIALS LLC (PA)
4000 Oxford State Rd (45044-8973)
PHONE................................513 705-0111
Jim Spurlino, *Pr*
EMP: 50 **EST:** 2000
SQ FT: 10,000
SALES (est): 8.3MM
SALES (corp-wide): 8.3MM **Privately Held**
Web: www.spurlino.net
SIC: 3273 Ready-mixed concrete

(G-10859)
START PRINTING CO LLC
3140 Cincinnati Dayton Rd (45044-8921)
PHONE................................513 424-2121
EMP: 7 **EST:** 2011
SALES (est): 472.53K **Privately Held**
SIC: 2752 Commercial printing, lithographic

(G-10860)
SUNCOKE ENERGY INC
Also Called: Mto Suncoke
3353 Yankee Rd (45044-8927)
PHONE................................513 727-5571
Frederick Henderson, *Brnch Mgr*
EMP: 40
Web: www.suncoke.com
SIC: 1241 Coal mining services
PA: Suncoke Energy, Inc.
1011 Wrrnville Rd Ste 600
Lisle IL 60532

(G-10861)
SUPERIOR CASTER INC
Also Called: Superior Casters
455 Wright Dr (45044-3264)
PHONE................................513 539-8980
Lilly Chang, *Pr*
EMP: 10 **EST:** 1998
SALES (est): 1.41MM **Privately Held**
SIC: 5072 3562 Hardware; Casters
PA: Durable U.S.A., Inc.
2801 E Abram St
Arlington TX 76010

(G-10862)
TEMPLE INLAND
912 Nelbar St (45042-2529)
PHONE................................513 425-0830
EMP: 9 **EST:** 2015
SALES (est): 265.04K **Privately Held**
SIC: 2653 Boxes, corrugated: made from purchased materials

(G-10863)
TMS INTERNATIONAL LLC
1801 Crawford St (45044-4572)
PHONE................................513 425-6462
EMP: 15
Web: www.tmsinternational.com
SIC: 3312 Blast furnaces and steel mills
HQ: Tms International, Llc
Southside Wrks Bldg 1 3f
Pittsburgh PA 15203
412 678-6141

(G-10864)
TMS INTERNATIONAL LLC
3018 Oxford State Rd (45044-8900)
PHONE................................513 422-4572
EMP: 25
Web: www.tmsinternational.com
SIC: 3312 Blast furnaces and steel mills
HQ: Tms International, Llc
Southside Wrks Bldg 1 3f
Pittsburgh PA 15203
412 678-6141

(G-10865)
TMS INTERNATIONAL CORP
2601 S Verity Pkwy Bldg 3 (45044-7481)
PHONE................................513 422-9497
EMP: 11
Web: www.tmsinternational.com
SIC: 3312 Blast furnaces and steel mills
PA: Tms International Corp.
2835 E Carson St Ste 300
Pittsburgh PA 15203

(G-10866)
TOMSON STEEL COMPANY
1400 Made Dr (45044-8936)
PHONE................................513 420-8600
Stephen Lutz, *Pr*
Thomas Lutz, *
EMP: 25 **EST:** 1981
SQ FT: 94,000
SALES (est): 14.49MM **Privately Held**
Web: www.tomsonsteel.com
SIC: 5051 3291 Steel; Abrasive metal and steel products

(G-10867)
TOOL AND DIE WELDING
6831 Franklin Madison Rd (45042-1103)
PHONE................................513 265-3095
EMP: 6 **EST:** 2013
SALES (est): 52.6K **Privately Held**
SIC: 3599 Machine shop, jobbing and repair

(G-10868)
TUF-N-LITE LLC
7649 Keister Rd (45042-1020)
PHONE................................513 472-8400
Gail Berry, *Managing Member*
EMP: 10 **EST:** 2019
SALES (est): 523.97K **Privately Held**
Web: www.tufnlite.com
SIC: 2899 Concrete curing and hardening compounds

(G-10869)
VAIL RUBBER WORKS INC
Also Called: Midwest Service
605 Clark St (45042-2117)
PHONE................................513 705-2060
Donald Bown, *Brnch Mgr*
EMP: 13
SALES (corp-wide): 19.37MM **Privately Held**
Web: www.vailrubber.com
SIC: 3554 Paper industries machinery
PA: Vail Rubber Works, Inc.
521 Langley Ave
Saint Joseph MI 49085
877 350-0441

(G-10870)
WATSON GRAVEL INC
2100 S Main St (45044-7345)
PHONE................................513 422-3781
Ron Price, *Mgr*
EMP: 6
SALES (corp-wide): 9.82MM **Privately Held**
Web: www.watsongravel.com

SIC: 1442 Gravel mining
PA: Watson Gravel, Inc.
2728 Hamilton Cleves Rd
Hamilton OH 45013
513 863-0070

(G-10871)
WAUSAU PAPER CORP
Also Called: Wausau Mosinee Paper
700 Columbia Ave (45042-1931)
PHONE................................513 217-3623
Douglas Zirbel, *Mgr*
EMP: 281
Web: www.torkusa.com
SIC: 2621 Paper mills
HQ: Wausau Paper Corp.
2929 Arch St Ste 2600
Philadelphia PA 19104
866 722-8675

(G-10872)
WHITT MACHINE INC
806 Central Ave (45044-1718)
PHONE................................513 423-7624
Dean Whitt, *Pr*
Wendy Whitt, *VP*
Angie Snarski, *Sec*
EMP: 17 **EST:** 1981
SQ FT: 35,000
SALES (est): 423.32K **Privately Held**
SIC: 3599 7692 Machine shop, jobbing and repair; Welding repair

(G-10873)
WIKOFF COLOR CORPORATION
1392 Oxford State Rd (45044-7580)
PHONE................................513 423-0727
Bill Dishman, *Mgr*
EMP: 9
SALES (corp-wide): 156.45MM **Privately Held**
Web: www.wikoff.com
SIC: 2893 Printing ink
PA: Wikoff Color Corporation
1886 Merrit Rd
Fort Mill SC 29715
803 548-2210

Midvale
Tuscarawas County

(G-10874)
AMERICAN BOTTLING COMPANY
Also Called: 7 Up Bottling Co
Old Rte #250 (44653)
P.O. Box 535 (44653-0535)
PHONE................................740 922-5253
Nick Kazocoff, *Mgr*
EMP: 48
Web: www.keurigdrpepper.com
SIC: 2086 Soft drinks: packaged in cans, bottles, etc.
HQ: The American Bottling Company
6425 Hall Of Fame Ln
Frisco TX 75034

(G-10875)
AMKO SERVICE COMPANY (DH)
Also Called: Dover Cryogenics
3211 Brightwood Rd (44653)
P.O. Box 280 (44653-0280)
PHONE................................330 364-8857
Darren Nippard, *Pr*
Duane R Yant, *Prin*
▲ **EMP:** 50 **EST:** 1965
SALES (est): 2.55MM **Privately Held**
Web: www.amkotech.com

Midvale - Tuscarawas County (G-10876)

GEOGRAPHIC SECTION

SIC: 7699 3443 7629 Tank repair and cleaning services; Cryogenic tanks, for liquids and gases; Electrical repair shops
HQ: Linde Inc.
10 Riverview Dr
Danbury CT 06810
203 837-2000

(G-10876)
DOVER CONVEYOR INC
3323 Brightwood Rd (44653-1901)
P.O. Box 300 (44653-0300)
PHONE.................................740 922-9390
Joseph Coniglio, Pr
EMP: 25 EST: 1962
SQ FT: 40,000
SALES (est): 2.05MM Privately Held
Web: www.doverconveyor.com
SIC: 3535 3441 3532 Conveyors and conveying equipment; Fabricated structural metal; Cages, mine shaft

(G-10877)
FIBA TECHNOLOGIES INC
Also Called: Amko Service Company
3211 Brightwood Road (44653)
P.O. Box 280 (44653-0280)
PHONE.................................330 602-7300
David Ohl, Brnch Mgr
EMP: 11
SALES (corp-wide): 97.7MM Privately Held
Web: www.fibatech.com
SIC: 3443 Cryogenic tanks, for liquids and gases
PA: Fiba Technologies, Inc.
53 Ayer Rd
Littleton MA 01460
508 887-7100

(G-10878)
FLEX TECHNOLOGIES INC (PA)
5479 Gundy Dr (44653)
P.O. Box 400 (44653-0400)
PHONE.................................740 922-5992
▼ EMP: 40 EST: 1964
SALES (est): 6MM
SALES (corp-wide): 6MM Privately Held
Web: www.flextechnologies.com
SIC: 3084 3083 3357 3087 Plastics pipe; Laminated plastics plate and sheet; Nonferrous wiredrawing and insulating; Custom compound purchased resins

(G-10879)
HYDRAULIC SPECIALISTS INC
5655 Gundy Dr (44653)
PHONE.................................740 922-3343
Dale Burkholder, Pr
Laraine Burkholder, Sec
EMP: 18 EST: 1990
SQ FT: 15,000
SALES (est): 479.49K Privately Held
SIC: 3443 7699 3593 Industrial vessels, tanks, and containers; Hydraulic equipment repair; Fluid power cylinders and actuators

(G-10880)
KLX ENERGY SERVICES LLC
3571 Brighwood Rd (44653)
PHONE.................................740 922-1155
EMP: 35
SALES (corp-wide): 888.4MM Publicly Held
Web: www.klx.com
SIC: 1389 Fishing for tools, oil and gas field
HQ: Klx Energy Services Llc
3040 Post Oak Blvd # 1500
Houston TX 77056
832 844-1015

(G-10881)
MAINTENANCE REPAIR SUPPLY INC
Also Called: Convertapax
5539 Gundy Dr (44653)
P.O. Box 540 (44653-0540)
PHONE.................................740 922-3006
Brad Mathias, Pr
▲ EMP: 18 EST: 1985
SQ FT: 48,000
SALES (est): 2.18MM Privately Held
Web: www.maintenancerepairsupply.com
SIC: 5085 2821 5084 Industrial supplies; Polyesters; Plastic products machinery

Milan
Erie County

(G-10882)
CERTAINTEED LLC
11519 Us Highway 250 N (44846-9708)
PHONE.................................419 499-2581
Mark Hyde, Mgr
EMP: 247
SALES (corp-wide): 397.78MM Privately Held
Web: www.certainteed.com
SIC: 2952 Roofing materials
HQ: Certainteed Llc
20 Moores Rd
Malvern PA 19355
610 893-5000

(G-10883)
FREUDENBERG-NOK SEALING TECH
11617 State Route 13 (44846-9725)
PHONE.................................877 331-8427
EMP: 13 EST: 2015
SALES (est): 2.35MM Privately Held
Web: www.transtec.com
SIC: 3714 Motor vehicle parts and accessories

(G-10884)
JOHNS MANVILLE CORPORATION
49 Lockwood Rd (44846-9734)
PHONE.................................419 499-1400
Brian Keyser, Genl Mgr
EMP: 49
SALES (corp-wide): 364.48B Publicly Held
Web: www.jm.com
SIC: 2952 Roofing materials
HQ: Johns Manville Corporation
717 17th St
Denver CO 80202
303 978-2000

(G-10885)
PULLMAN COMPANY
Also Called: Tenneco
33 Lockwood Rd (44846-9734)
PHONE.................................419 499-2541
Casey Mcelwain, Brnch Mgr
EMP: 232
SALES (corp-wide): 18.04B Privately Held
Web: www.tenneco.com
SIC: 3714 Shock absorbers, motor vehicle
HQ: The Pullman Company
1 International Dr
Monroe MI 48161
734 243-8000

(G-10886)
SCHLESSMAN SEED CO (PA)
11513 Us Highway 250 N (44846-9708)
PHONE.................................419 499-2572
Daryl Deering, Ch Bd
Dave Herzer,
EMP: 23 EST: 1915
SQ FT: 100,000
SALES (est): 4.89MM
SALES (corp-wide): 4.89MM Privately Held
Web: www.schlessman-seed.com
SIC: 5191 2075 0723 0116 Seeds: field, garden, and flower; Soybean oil mills; Crop preparation services for market; Soybeans

(G-10887)
TENNECO INC
Also Called: Tenneco
33 Lockwood Rd (44846-9734)
PHONE.................................419 499-2541
EMP: 10
SALES (corp-wide): 18.04B Privately Held
Web: www.tenneco.com
SIC: 3714 Motor vehicle parts and accessories
HQ: Tenneco Inc.
7160 Mccormick Blvd
Skokie IL 60076
847 482-5000

(G-10888)
TRU-CAL INC (PA)
11001 Us Highway 250 N Unit 12b (44846-9495)
PHONE.................................419 202-1296
Nathan Wright, Pr
EMP: 10 EST: 2009
SALES (est): 2.3MM
SALES (corp-wide): 2.3MM Privately Held
Web: www.tru-cal.com
SIC: 3312 Blast furnaces and steel mills

Milford
Clermont County

(G-10889)
4BLAR LLC
5948 Shallow Creek Dr (45150-1525)
PHONE.................................513 576-0441
EMP: 6 EST: 2008
SALES (est): 101.67K Privately Held
SIC: 2273 Carpets and rugs

(G-10890)
9729 FLAGSTONE WAY LLC
5425 Timber Trail Pl (45150-8020)
PHONE.................................513 239-1950
Elizabeth O Bumgarner, Prin
EMP: 8 EST: 2009
SALES (est): 120K Privately Held
SIC: 3281 Flagstones

(G-10891)
AB PLASTICS INC
1287 Us Route 50 (45150-9688)
PHONE.................................513 576-6333
Robert Basile, Pr
Kim Basille, Sec
EMP: 9 EST: 1989
SQ FT: 5,000
SALES (est): 954.27K Privately Held
Web: www.ab-plastics.com
SIC: 3089 Injection molding of plastics

(G-10892)
AMERICAN INSULATION TECH LLC
6071 Branch Hill Guinea Pike Ste A (45150-1567)
PHONE.................................513 733-4248
EMP: 12 EST: 2013
SALES (est): 744.73K Privately Held
Web: www.aitinsulation.com

SIC: 3296 3081 Fiberglass insulation; Film base, cellulose acetate or nitrocellulose plastics

(G-10893)
B & D MACHINISTS INC
1350 Us Route 50 (45150-9205)
PHONE.................................513 831-8588
Tonson Roy Boone Junior, Pr
Steven Boone, VP
Gary W Boone, VP
Velma Boone, Sec
EMP: 15 EST: 1980
SQ FT: 16,000
SALES (est): 408.55K Privately Held
Web: www.bdmachinists.com
SIC: 3599 Machine shop, jobbing and repair

(G-10894)
BEARING PRECIOUS SEED INTL INC (PA)
1369 Woodville Pike Unit B (45150-2260)
PHONE.................................513 575-1706
▼ EMP: 6 EST: 1973
SALES (est): 2MM Privately Held
Web: www.bpsmilford.org
SIC: 2731 Books, publishing and printing

(G-10895)
BECK STUDIOS INC
1001 Tech Dr (45150-9780)
PHONE.................................513 831-6650
Dan L Ilhardt, Pr
Matthew Mullen, VP
Cathie Haverkamp, Sec
EMP: 20 EST: 1856
SQ FT: 9,000
SALES (est): 4.92MM Privately Held
Web: www.beckstudios.net
SIC: 1799 3999 Rigging, theatrical; Stage hardware and equipment, except lighting

(G-10896)
BREWER COMPANY (PA)
Also Called: Brewercote
25 Whitney Dr Ste 104 (45150-8400)
PHONE.................................800 394-0017
Pinckney W Brewer, Pr
Michael T Dooley, VP Fin
Thomas P Matlock, VP Sls
▲ EMP: 8 EST: 1933
SALES (est): 12.34MM
SALES (corp-wide): 12.34MM Privately Held
Web: www.asphaltstore.com
SIC: 2952 0782 2951 Coating compounds, tar; Seeding services, lawn; Asphalt paving mixtures and blocks

(G-10897)
CALORPLAST USA LLC
1287 Us Route 50 (45150-9688)
PHONE.................................513 576-6333
Graham Tenbrink, Prin
EMP: 9 EST: 2017
SALES (est): 2MM
SALES (corp-wide): 2MM Privately Held
Web: www.calorplastusa.com
SIC: 3089 Plastics hardware and building products
PA: Magen Eco - Energy Usa, Inc
950 Sunshine Ln
Altamonte Springs FL

(G-10898)
CHRIS STEPP
Also Called: Stepp Sewing Service
927 Business 28 Unit B (45150-1948)
PHONE.................................513 248-0822
Chris Stepp, Owner
EMP: 6 EST: 1975

GEOGRAPHIC SECTION

Milford - Clermont County (G-10921)

SQ FT: 1,200
SALES (est): 215.62K Privately Held
SIC: 2395 5651 Embroidery and art needlework; Unisex clothing stores

(G-10899)
CINCI CNC LLC
1139 Fox Run Rd (45150-2822)
PHONE..............................513 722-6756
Joshua Hafner, *Prin*
EMP: 6 EST: 2019
SALES (est): 120.92K Privately Held
Web: www.cincicnc.com
SIC: 3599 Machine shop, jobbing and repair

(G-10900)
CINCINNATI PRINT SOLUTIONS LLC
2002 Ford Cir Ste G (45150-2748)
PHONE..............................513 943-9500
EMP: 6 EST: 2006
SALES (est): 1.02MM Privately Held
Web: www.shamrockcompanies.net
SIC: 2752 7334 2759 Offset printing; Photocopying and duplicating services; Commercial printing, nec
PA: The Shamrock Companies Inc
  24090 Detroit Rd
  Westlake OH 44145

(G-10901)
CINCY SAFE COMPANY
5372 Galley Hill Rd (45150-9713)
PHONE..............................513 900-9152
Gary Krug, *Pr*
EMP: 12 EST: 1974
SALES (est): 444.71K Privately Held
Web: www.tchm.org
SIC: 3499 Safes and vaults, metal

(G-10902)
COMMERCIAL CNSTR GROUP LLC
5902 Montclair Blvd (45150-2501)
PHONE..............................513 722-1357
Daniel Taylor, *Managing Member*
EMP: 7 EST: 2000
SALES (est): 911.03K Privately Held
Web: www.ccgmidwest.com
SIC: 1389 1542 1531 Construction, repair, and dismantling services; Commercial and office building contractors

(G-10903)
CONVEYOR TECHNOLOGIES LTD
501 Techne Center Dr Ste B (45150-2796)
PHONE..............................513 248-0663
Charles Mitchell, *Pr*
Tony Mitchell, *VP*
Tim Mitchell, *VP*
EMP: 8 EST: 1997
SQ FT: 7,000
SALES (est): 942K Privately Held
Web: www.conveyortechltd.com
SIC: 3535 Conveyors and conveying equipment

(G-10904)
CUSTOM BUILT CRATES INC
1700 Victory Park Dr (45150-1812)
EMP: 20 EST: 1997
SALES (est): 2.68MM Privately Held
Web: www.custombuiltcrates.com
SIC: 4213 2449 7389 Trucking, except local; Rectangular boxes and crates, wood; Business services, nec

(G-10905)
F & S HYDRAULICS INC
6071 Branch Hill Guinea Pike Ste B (45150-2253)
PHONE..............................513 575-1600

James M Foster, *Pr*
Howard E Sneed, *VP*
EMP: 7 EST: 1977
SQ FT: 4,000
SALES (est): 560K Privately Held
SIC: 3599 Machine shop, jobbing and repair

(G-10906)
FOUNTAIN SPECIALISTS INC
226 Main St (45150-1124)
PHONE..............................513 831-5717
Lois Sedacca, *Pr*
Mark Sedacca, *VP*
EMP: 8 EST: 1960
SQ FT: 5,000
SALES (est): 967.35K Privately Held
Web: www.fountainspecialist.com
SIC: 5261 3272 3499 3089 Fountains, outdoor; Fountains, concrete; Fountains (except drinking), metal; Plastics processing

(G-10907)
GB LIQUIDATING COMPANY INC
22 Whitney Dr (45150-9783)
PHONE..............................513 248-7600
EMP: 20 EST: 1946
SALES (est): 460.7K Privately Held
Web: www.gordonbernard.com
SIC: 7371 2759 2741 2752 Custom computer programming services; Commercial printing, nec; Miscellaneous publishing; Calendar and card printing, lithographic

(G-10908)
HAMILTON PRODUCTS GROUP INC (DH)
1030 Round Bottom Rd (45150-9740)
PHONE..............................800 876-6066
▲ EMP: 47 EST: 1986
SALES (est): 21.39MM
SALES (corp-wide): 1.42MM Privately Held
Web: www.hamiltonproductsgroup.com
SIC: 3499 Fire- or burglary-resistive products
HQ: Gunnebo Ab
  Johan Pa Gardas Gata 7
  GOteborg 412 5
  102008240

(G-10909)
HAMILTON SAFE CO (DH)
Also Called: Hamilton Safe Company
1030 Round Bottom Rd (45150-9740)
PHONE..............................513 874-3733
Robert C Deluse, *Pr*
David Vanschoik, *VP*
Greg Holbrock, *Prin*
John Stroia, *Pr*
▲ EMP: 19 EST: 1967
SALES (est): 21.39MM
SALES (corp-wide): 1.42MM Privately Held
Web: www.hamiltonsecuritysolutions.com
SIC: 3499 Safe deposit boxes or chests, metal
HQ: Hamilton Products Group, Inc.
  1030 Round Bottom Rd
  Milford OH 45150
  800 876-6066

(G-10910)
HAMILTON SECURITY PRODUCTS CO
Also Called: Hamilton Safe
1030 Round Bottom Rd (45150-9740)
PHONE..............................513 874-3733
Robert Leslie, *CEO*
John Haining, *
▲ EMP: 46 EST: 1974

SALES (est): 8.48MM
SALES (corp-wide): 1.42MM Privately Held
Web: www.hamiltonsecuritysolutions.com
SIC: 3499 Safe deposit boxes or chests, metal
HQ: Gunnebo Ab
  Johan Pa Gardas Gata 7
  GOteborg 412 5
  102008240

(G-10911)
INLAND PAPERBOARD PKG
P.O. Box 5383 (97228-5383)
PHONE..............................562 946-6127
EMP: 7 EST: 2012
SALES (est): 491.78K Privately Held
SIC: 2631 Paperboard mills

(G-10912)
JOURNEY SYSTEMS LLC
25 Whitney Dr Ste 100 (45150-8400)
PHONE..............................513 831-6200
EMP: 14 EST: 2006
SQ FT: 9,875
SALES (est): 2.27MM Privately Held
Web: gov.journeysystems.com
SIC: 3571 5045 5734 Electronic computers; Computers, peripherals, and software; Computer and software stores

(G-10913)
MELINK CORPORATION
5140 River Valley Rd (45150-9108)
PHONE..............................513 685-0958
Stephen K Melink, *Pr*
EMP: 68 EST: 1997
SQ FT: 36,000
SALES (est): 20.82MM Privately Held
Web: www.melinkcorp.com
SIC: 8711 8748 3822 Heating and ventilation engineering; Energy conservation consultant; Appliance controls,except air-conditioning and refrigeration

(G-10914)
MILFORD PRINTERS (PA)
317 Main St (45150-1125)
P.O. Box 123 (45131-0123)
PHONE..............................513 831-6630
Robert M Heichel, *Owner*
EMP: 20 EST: 1978
SQ FT: 8,000
SALES (est): 1.71MM
SALES (corp-wide): 1.71MM Privately Held
SIC: 2752 Offset printing

(G-10915)
ODOM INDUSTRIES INC
Also Called: Odom
1262 Us Hwy 50 (45150-9767)
PHONE..............................513 248-0287
EMP: 50
Web: www.odomindustries.com
SIC: 3443 Tanks, standard or custom fabricated: metal plate

(G-10916)
OVERHOFF TECHNOLOGY CORP
1160 Us Route 50 (45150-9517)
P.O. Box 182 (45150-0182)
PHONE..............................513 248-2400
Robert Goldstein, *Pr*
EMP: 14 EST: 1971
SQ FT: 8,000
SALES (est): 1.95MM
SALES (corp-wide): 2.23MM Publicly Held
Web: www.overhoff.com

SIC: 3829 3823 Nuclear instrument modules ; Controllers, for process variables, all types
PA: Us Nuclear Corp.
  7051 Eton Ave
  Canoga Park CA 91303
  818 296-0746

(G-10917)
PPG INDUSTRIES INC
Also Called: P P G
500 Techne Center Dr (45150-2763)
PHONE..............................513 576-0360
Greg Wagner, *Mgr*
EMP: 25
SALES (corp-wide): 17.65B Publicly Held
Web: www.ppg.com
SIC: 2851 Shellac (protective coating)
PA: Ppg Industries, Inc.
  1 Ppg Pl
  Pittsburgh PA 15272
  412 434-3131

(G-10918)
PREMIER BANDAG INC
5997 Meijer Dr (45150-2191)
PHONE..............................513 248-8850
EMP: 14 EST: 1996
SALES (est): 236.12K Privately Held
SIC: 7534 Rebuilding and retreading tires

(G-10919)
PRIMEX
400 Techne Center Dr Ste 104 (45150-2792)
PHONE..............................513 831-9959
Douglas Strief, *Pr*
Catherine Strief, *
EMP: 20 EST: 1983
SQ FT: 20,000
SALES (est): 565.03K Privately Held
Web: www.primexcontrols.com
SIC: 3613 3823 3699 3625 Control panels, electric; Process control instruments; Electrical equipment and supplies, nec; Relays and industrial controls

(G-10920)
REMINGTON ENGRG MACHINING INC
5105 River Valley Rd (45150-9117)
PHONE..............................513 965-8999
Dan Mallaley, *Pr*
Valerie Mallaley, *Sec*
EMP: 6 EST: 1996
SQ FT: 2,500
SALES (est): 838.16K
SALES (corp-wide): 53.68MM Privately Held
SIC: 3599 Machine shop, jobbing and repair
PA: Cold Jet, Llc
  6283 Tri Ridge Blvd
  Loveland OH 45140
  513 831-3211

(G-10921)
SARDINIA CONCRETE COMPANY (PA)
911 Us Route 50 (45150)
PHONE..............................513 248-0090
James Fraley, *Mng Pt*
James E Sauls Junior, *Mgr*
EMP: 40 EST: 2003
SQ FT: 12,500
SALES (est): 8.54MM
SALES (corp-wide): 8.54MM Privately Held
Web: www.sardiniaconcrete.com
SIC: 3273 Ready-mixed concrete

Milford - Clermont County (G-10922)

(G-10922)
SIEMENS INDUSTRY INC
2000 Eastman Dr (45150-2712)
PHONE...................................513 576-2088
EMP: 23
SALES (corp-wide): 84.48B **Privately Held**
Web: www.siemens.com
SIC: **5311** 3569 Department stores; Heaters, swimming pool: electric
HQ: Siemens Industry, Inc.
100 Technology Dr
Alpharetta GA 30005
847 215-1000

(G-10923)
SILER EXCAVATION SERVICES
6025 Catherine Dr (45150-2203)
PHONE...................................513 400-8628
EMP: 40 EST: 2007
SALES (est): 1.93MM **Privately Held**
SIC: **1794** 1389 Excavation work; Construction, repair, and dismantling services

(G-10924)
SPEEDPRO IMAGING
2000 Ford Cir Ste G (45150-2749)
PHONE...................................513 753-5600
Lee H Hobson, *Prin*
EMP: 6 EST: 2007
SALES (est): 221.05K **Privately Held**
Web: www.speedpro.com
SIC: **3993** Signs and advertising specialties

(G-10925)
TATA AMERICA INTL CORP
Also Called: Tata Consultancy Services
1000 Summit Dr Unit 1 (45150-2724)
PHONE...................................513 677-6500
Sumanta Roy, *Rgnl Mgr*
EMP: 300
Web: www.tcs.com
SIC: **7372** 7373 7371 Prepackaged software ; Computer integrated systems design; Custom computer programming services
HQ: Tata America International Corporation
101 Park Ave Fl 2603
New York NY 10178
212 557-8038

(G-10926)
TRIUMPH SIGNS & CONSULTING INC
480 Milford Pkwy (45150-9104)
PHONE...................................513 576-8090
William Downey, *Pr*
EMP: 21 EST: 2005
SALES (est): 4.61MM **Privately Held**
Web: www.triumphsigns.com
SIC: **3993** Signs and advertising specialties

Milford Center
Union County

(G-10927)
ADVANCED TECHNOLOGY PRODUCTS INC (PA)
Also Called: A T P
190 N Mill St (43045-9765)
PHONE...................................937 349-4055
♦ EMP: 58 EST: 1990
SALES (est): 9.25MM **Privately Held**
Web: www.atp4pneumatics.com
SIC: **3052** Rubber and plastics hose and beltings

(G-10928)
FORUM WORKS LLC
77 Brown St (43045-8900)
P.O. Box 1330 (43065-1330)
PHONE...................................937 349-8685
EMP: 30 EST: 2019
SALES (est): 2.85MM **Privately Held**
Web: www.forumwrks.com
SIC: **2431** Millwork

(G-10929)
NUTRIEN AG SOLUTIONS INC
9972 State Route 38 (43045-9760)
PHONE...................................614 873-4253
Jason Hess, *Prin*
EMP: 6
SALES (corp-wide): 29.06B **Privately Held**
Web: www.nutrienagsolutions.com
SIC: **5261** 5191 2875 Fertilizer; Fertilizers and agricultural chemicals; Fertilizers, mixing only
HQ: Nutrien Ag Solutions, Inc.
3005 Rocky Mountain Ave
Loveland CO 80538
970 685-3300

Millbury
Wood County

(G-10930)
DOUTHIT COMMUNICATIONS INC
Also Called: Metro Press
1550 Woodville Rd (43447-9619)
P.O. Box 169 (43447-0169)
PHONE...................................419 855-7465
John Szozda, *Genl Mgr*
EMP: 55
SALES (corp-wide): 10.81MM **Privately Held**
Web: www.adwriter.com
SIC: **2711** Job printing and newspaper publishing combined
PA: Douthit Communications, Inc.
520 Warren St
Sandusky OH 44870
419 625-5825

(G-10931)
ELECTRO PLASMA INCORPORATED
Also Called: Epi Global
4400 Moline Martin Rd (43447-8400)
PHONE...................................419 838-7365
EMP: 106
Web: www.epiglobal.com
SIC: **3699** Electrical equipment and supplies, nec

(G-10932)
FORMLABS OHIO INC
Also Called: Spectra Photopolymers
27800 Lemoyne Rd Ste J (43447-9683)
PHONE...................................419 837-9783
Alex Mejiritski, *Pr*
EMP: 45 EST: 2017
SALES (est): 10.33MM
SALES (corp-wide): 179.32MM **Privately Held**
Web: www.formlabs.com
SIC: **2899** 5169 Chemical preparations, nec; Chemicals and allied products, nec
PA: Formlabs Inc.
35 Medford St Ste 201
Somerville MA 02143
617 932-5227

(G-10933)
GUARDIAN FABRICATION LLC
Also Called: Guardian Millbury
24145 W Moline Martin Rd (43447-9568)
PHONE...................................419 855-7706
EMP: 125
SALES (corp-wide): 36.93B **Privately Held**
Web: www.guardian.com
SIC: **3211** 3231 Plate glass, polished and rough; Products of purchased glass
HQ: Guardian Fabrication, Llc
2300 Harmon Rd
Auburn Hills MI 48326
248 340-1800

(G-10934)
LAKE TOWNSHIP TRUSTEES
3800 Ayers Rd (43447-9745)
PHONE...................................419 836-1143
Dan Mclargin, *Mgr*
EMP: 30
Web: www.laketwpohio.com
SIC: **9111** 7997 3531 City and town managers' office; Baseball club, except professional and semi-professional; Road construction and maintenance machinery
PA: Lake Township Trustees
27975 Cummings Rd
Millbury OH 43447

(G-10935)
LEVISON ENTERPRISES LLC
Also Called: Epi Global
4470 Moline Martin Rd (43447-9201)
PHONE...................................419 838-7365
David Levison, *Pr*
EMP: 25 EST: 2008
SQ FT: 14,000
SALES (est): 5.04MM **Privately Held**
Web: www.levisonenterprises.com
SIC: **3672** Printed circuit boards

(G-10936)
SPECTRA GROUP LIMITED INC
Also Called: Spectra Photopolymers
27800 Lemoyne Rd Ste J (43447-9683)
PHONE...................................419 837-9783
Douglas C Neckers, *Ch Bd*
Alex Mejiritski, *Pr*
EMP: 7 EST: 1990
SQ FT: 5,680
SALES (est): 2.03MM **Privately Held**
Web: www.sglinc.com
SIC: **2891** Adhesives

Millersburg
Holmes County

(G-10937)
77 COACH SUPPLY LTD
7426 County Road 77 (44654-9279)
PHONE...................................330 674-1454
EMP: 8 EST: 1982
SALES (est): 234.04K **Privately Held**
SIC: **5099** 2499 Wood and wood by-products ; Decorative wood and woodwork

(G-10938)
AFFORDABLE BARN CO LTD
Also Called: Southern Wholesale
4260 Township Road 617 (44654-7913)
PHONE...................................330 674-3001
Robert Yoder, *Mgr*
EMP: 10 EST: 2012
SALES (est): 2.47MM **Privately Held**
Web: www.affordablebarncompanyltd.com
SIC: **3448** Buildings, portable: prefabricated metal

(G-10939)
AL YODER CONSTRUCTION CO
Also Called: Fairview Log Homes
3375 County Road 160 (44654-8366)
P.O. Box 275 (44690-0275)
PHONE...................................330 359-5726
Alvin A Yoder, *Pr*
Ruth Yoder, *Sec*
Sarah Troyer, *Sec*
EMP: 6
SALES (est): 851.59K **Privately Held**
Web: www.fairviewloghomes.net
SIC: **1521** 2452 New construction, single-family houses; Log cabins, prefabricated, wood

(G-10940)
ALONOVUS CORP
Also Called: Bargain Hunter
7368 County Road 623 (44654-9387)
P.O. Box 358 (44654-0358)
PHONE...................................330 674-2300
Michael Mast, *Pr*
Frances Mast, *
▲ EMP: 25 EST: 1973
SQ FT: 12,000
SALES (est): 4.48MM **Privately Held**
Web: www.alonovus.com
SIC: **2721** 7336 Periodicals, publishing only; Graphic arts and related design

(G-10941)
AMISH WEDDING FOODS INC
316 S Mad Anthony St (44654-1388)
PHONE...................................330 674-9199
EMP: 40
Web: www.liparifoods.com
SIC: **2022** 2099 2013 Cheese; natural and processed; Food preparations, nec; Sausages and other prepared meats

(G-10942)
BARKMAN PRODUCTS LLC
2550 Township Road 121 (44654-8909)
PHONE...................................330 893-2520
Albert Barkman, *Prin*
EMP: 9 EST: 2008
SALES (est): 435.35K **Privately Held**
Web: www.barkmanfurniture.com
SIC: **2499** Decorative wood and woodwork

(G-10943)
BENT WOOD SOLUTIONS LLC
7426 County Road 77 (44654-9279)
PHONE...................................330 674-1454
Atlee N Kaufman, *Prin*
EMP: 7 EST: 1999
SALES (est): 415.64K **Privately Held**
Web: www.bentwoodsolutions.com
SIC: **1542** 3553 Commercial and office building contractors; Woodworking machinery

(G-10944)
BERLIN TRUCK CAPS & TARPS LTD
Also Called: Berlin Parts
4560 State Route 39 (44654-9600)
PHONE...................................330 893-2811
Wayne Beachy Senior, *Pt*
Wayne Beachy Junior, *Pt*
James Beachy, *Pt*
EMP: 10 EST: 1970
SQ FT: 12,000
SALES (est): 1.14MM **Privately Held**
SIC: **5199** 3792 Tarpaulins; Pickup covers, canopies or caps

(G-10945)
BERLIN WOODWORKING LLC
4575 Township Road 366 (44654-9102)
PHONE...................................330 893-3234
Gary Troyer, *Prin*
EMP: 7 EST: 2007
SALES (est): 247.22K **Privately Held**
SIC: **2431** Millwork

GEOGRAPHIC SECTION

Millersburg - Holmes County (G-10969)

(G-10946)
BIJOE DEVELOPMENT INC
7188 State Rte 62 & 39 (44654)
PHONE..............................330 674-5981
William Baker, *Pr*
Joseph Cross, *
EMP: 40 **EST:** 1989
SQ FT: 4,000
SALES (est): 1.01MM **Privately Held**
SIC: 1389 1311 Oil field services, nec; Crude petroleum and natural gas production

(G-10947)
BUCKEYE SEATING LLC
6945 Co Rd 672 (44654-8350)
P.O. Box 128 (44610-0128)
PHONE..............................330 893-7700
EMP: 14 **EST:** 2009
SALES (est): 1.04MM **Privately Held**
Web: www.buckeyeseating.com
SIC: 2512 2521 Chairs: upholstered on wood frames; Chairs, office: padded, upholstered, or plain: wood

(G-10948)
BUCKEYE WELDING
2507 Township Road 110 (44654-9085)
PHONE..............................330 674-0944
Alvin Wengerd, *Prin*
EMP: 6 **EST:** 2008
SALES (est): 292.24K **Privately Held**
Web: www.buckeyeweldingsupply.com
SIC: 7692 Welding repair

(G-10949)
BUNKER HILL CHEESE CO INC
Also Called: Heinis Cheese Chalet
6005 County Road 77 (44654-9045)
PHONE..............................330 893-2131
Peter Dauwalder, *Pr*
P H C Dauwalder, *
T D Gindlesberger, *
EMP: 60 **EST:** 1935
SQ FT: 80,000
SALES (est): 10.97MM **Privately Held**
Web: www.bunkerhillcheese.com
SIC: 2022 5451 5812 Natural cheese; Cheese; Snack shop

(G-10950)
CARTER-JONES LUMBER COMPANY
Carter Lumber
6139 State Route 39 (44654-8845)
PHONE..............................330 674-9060
EMP: 12
SALES (corp-wide): 2.57B **Privately Held**
Web: www.carterlumber.com
SIC: 5031 5211 2439 2434 Lumber, plywood, and millwork; Lumber and other building materials; Structural wood members, nec; Wood kitchen cabinets
HQ: The Carter-Jones Lumber Company
   601 Tallmadge Rd
   Kent OH 44240
   330 673-6100

(G-10951)
CHEESE HOLDINGS INC
Also Called: Troyer Cheese, Inc.
6597 County Road 625 (44654-9071)
PHONE..............................330 893-2479
James A Troyer, *Pr*
John Troyer, *Sec*
EMP: 45 **EST:** 1959
SQ FT: 59,500
SALES (est): 21.22MM
SALES (corp-wide): 320.05MM **Privately Held**
Web: www.liparifoods.com
SIC: 5147 2032 5143 5149 Meats, cured or smoked; Ethnic foods, canned, jarred, etc.; Cheese; Specialty food items
PA: Lipari Foods Operating Company Llc
   26661 Bunert Rd
   Warren MI 48089
   586 447-3500

(G-10952)
COUNTY OF HOLMES
Also Called: Holmes County Gis
75 E Clinton St Ste 112 (44654-1283)
PHONE..............................330 674-2083
Erik Parker, *Dir*
EMP: 7
SALES (corp-wide): 53.92MM **Privately Held**
Web: www.holmescountyauditor.org
SIC: 3999 9111 Globes, geographical; Executive offices, Local government
PA: County Of Holmes
   2 Court St Ste 14
   Millersburg OH 44654
   330 674-1896

(G-10953)
DS WELDING LLC
3982 State Route 39 (44654-8382)
PHONE..............................330 893-4049
David Shetler, *Prin*
EMP: 6 **EST:** 2016
SALES (est): 88.73K **Privately Held**
SIC: 7692 Welding repair

(G-10954)
EUROCASE ARCHTCTRAL CBNETS MLL
6086 State Route 241 (44654-9170)
PHONE..............................330 674-0681
Garrett M Roach, *Managing Member*
EMP: 15 **EST:** 2006
SALES (est): 1.02MM **Privately Held**
Web: www.eurocase.biz
SIC: 3469 Architectural panels or parts, porcelain enameled

(G-10955)
FRYBURG DOOR INC
6086 State Route 241 (44654-9170)
PHONE..............................330 674-5252
EMP: 60 **EST:** 1988
SALES (est): 4.28MM **Privately Held**
Web: www.fryburgdoor.com
SIC: 2431 2435 Doors, wood; Hardwood veneer and plywood

(G-10956)
GUGGISBERG CHEESE INC (PA)
Also Called: Chalet In The Valley
5060 State Route 557 (44654-9266)
PHONE..............................330 893-2550
Richard Guggisberg, *Pr*
Diane Melloe, *
Paul A Miller, *
Rosanne Parrot, *
Cynthia Mellor, *
EMP: 25 **EST:** 1976
SQ FT: 10,000
SALES (est): 18.44MM
SALES (corp-wide): 18.44MM **Privately Held**
Web: www.babyswiss.com
SIC: 2022 5812 5961 5451 Natural cheese; Eating places; Cheese, mail order; Cheese

(G-10957)
HERSHBERGER LAWN STRUCTURES
Also Called: Play Mor
8990 State Route 39 (44654-9791)
PHONE..............................330 674-3900
Paul Hershberger, *Pt*
Amos Stoltzfus Junior, *Pt*
EMP: 17 **EST:** 1992
SQ FT: 21,000
SALES (est): 2.24MM **Privately Held**
Web: www.playmorswingsets.com
SIC: 3944 5941 5091 Structural toy sets; Playground equipment; Sporting and recreation goods

(G-10958)
HERSHY WAY LTD
5918 County Road 201 (44654-9294)
PHONE..............................330 893-2809
Aden Hershberger, *Pt*
Steven Hershberger, *Pt*
Jay Hershberger, *Pt*
EMP: 7 **EST:** 1972
SALES (est): 526.53K **Privately Held**
Web: www.hershywayltd.com
SIC: 2519 3523 Lawn furniture, except wood, metal, stone, or concrete; Cattle feeding, handling, and watering equipment

(G-10959)
HILLSIDE WOOD LTD
8413 Township Road 652 (44654-8343)
PHONE..............................330 359-5991
Aden Troyer, *Mgr*
EMP: 8 **EST:** 1997
SALES (est): 411.31K **Privately Held**
SIC: 2426 Chair seats, hardwood

(G-10960)
HOBBY HILL WOOD WORKING
6559 County Road 77 (44654-9128)
PHONE..............................330 893-4518
Mark A Miller, *Prin*
EMP: 6 **EST:** 2009
SALES (est): 207.9K **Privately Held**
SIC: 2431 Millwork

(G-10961)
HOCHSTETLER WOOD
Also Called: H W Chair Co
6291 County Road 77 (44654-9277)
PHONE..............................330 893-2384
Eli Hochstetler, *Pt*
Ivan Hochstetler, *Pt*
Wayne Hochstetler, *Pt*
Mark Hochstetler, *Pt*
David Hochstetler, *Pt*
EMP: 16 **EST:** 1978
SQ FT: 35,500
SALES (est): 483.57K **Privately Held**
SIC: 2426 2511 Hardwood dimension and flooring mills; Chairs, Bentwood

(G-10962)
HOCHSTETLER WOOD LTD
6791 County Road 77 (44654-7901)
PHONE..............................330 893-1601
Eli Hochstetler, *Pr*
EMP: 8 **EST:** 2000
SALES (est): 394.94K **Privately Held**
SIC: 2511 Wood household furniture

(G-10963)
HOLMES BY-PRODUCTS CO INC
3175 Township Road 411 (44654-9176)
PHONE..............................330 893-2322
Abe Miller, *Pr*
Brian Miller, *
Mary Miller, *
▲ **EMP:** 50 **EST:** 1958
SQ FT: 15,000
SALES (est): 4.46MM **Privately Held**
Web: www.holmesbyproducts.com
SIC: 2077 Animal and marine fats and oils

(G-10964)
HOLMES CHEESE CO
9444 State Route 39 (44654-9764)
PHONE..............................330 674-6451
Robert J Ramseyer, *Pr*
Walter P Ramseyer, *
▲ **EMP:** 35 **EST:** 1941
SQ FT: 42,000
SALES (est): 4.46MM **Privately Held**
Web: www.holmescheese.com
SIC: 2022 Natural cheese

(G-10965)
HOLMES COUNTY HUB INC
Also Called: Daily Record, The
6 W Jackson St Ste C (44654-1396)
PHONE..............................330 674-1811
Cindy Hinkle, *Mgr*
EMP: 9 **EST:** 1985
SALES (est): 428.04K **Privately Held**
SIC: 2711 Newspapers, publishing and printing

(G-10966)
HOLMES CUSTOM MOULDING LTD
5039 County Road 120 (44654-9281)
P.O. Box 161 (44610-0161)
PHONE..............................330 893-3598
Dan Hershberg, *Managing Member*
Wayne Hershburg, *Managing Member*
Linda Hershburg, *Managing Member**
▲ **EMP:** 45 **EST:** 1992
SQ FT: 250,000
SALES (est): 10MM **Privately Held**
Web: www.hcmohio.com
SIC: 2431 Millwork

(G-10967)
HOLMES LUMBER & BLDG CTR INC (PA)
Also Called: Holmes Lumber & Supply
6139 S R 39 (44654)
PHONE..............................330 674-9060
Paul Miller, *Pr*
Harry A Shaw, *Prin*
James H Estill, *Prin*
Elmo M Estill, *Prin*
EMP: 104 **EST:** 1952
SQ FT: 16,000
SALES (est): 32.18MM
SALES (corp-wide): 32.18MM **Privately Held**
Web: www.holmeslumber.com
SIC: 5031 5211 2439 2434 Lumber, plywood, and millwork; Lumber and other building materials; Structural wood members, nec; Wood kitchen cabinets

(G-10968)
HOLMES MANUFACTURING
6775 County Road 624 (44654-8840)
PHONE..............................330 231-6327
Todd W Kandel, *Owner*
EMP: 8 **EST:** 2015
SALES (est): 241.11K **Privately Held**
Web: www.holmesmanufacturing.com
SIC: 7299 3353 Home improvement and renovation contractor agency; Aluminum sheet, plate, and foil

(G-10969)
HOPEWOOD INC
8087 Township Road 652 (44654-8898)
PHONE..............................330 359-5656
EMP: 6 **EST:** 1985
SALES (est): 412.98K **Privately Held**
Web: www.hopewoodinc.com
SIC: 2512 2511 Upholstered household furniture; Wood household furniture

Millersburg - Holmes County (G-10970)

(G-10970)
INKSCAPE PRINT AND PROMOS LLC
5991 County Road 77 (44654-9258)
PHONE..................................330 893-0160
Mark Mast, *Prin*
EMP: 11 EST: 2017
SALES (est): 559.61K **Privately Held**
SIC: 2752 Commercial printing, lithographic

(G-10971)
KAUFFMAN LUMBER & SUPPLY
4051 Us Route 62 (44654-9190)
PHONE..................................330 893-9186
Ella Kauffman, *Pt*
Abe Kauffman, *Pt*
Raymond Kauffman, *Pt*
Roy Kauffman, *Pt*
Aden Kauffman, *Pt*
EMP: 15 EST: 1931
SQ FT: 15,000
SALES (est): 472.41K **Privately Held**
SIC: 2421 1711 2448 5074 Furniture dimension stock, softwood; Mechanical contractor; Pallets, wood; Plumbing and hydronic heating supplies

(G-10972)
LBC CLAY CO LLC
4501 Township Road 307 (44654-9656)
PHONE..................................330 674-0674
Larry L Clark, *Prin*
EMP: 9 EST: 2010
SALES (est): 360.84K **Privately Held**
SIC: 3251 Brick and structural clay tile

(G-10973)
LIPARI FOODS OPERATING CO LLC
Also Called: Troyer Manufacturing
6597 County Road 625 (44654-9071)
PHONE..................................330 893-2479
Jonas Yoder, *Brnch Mgr*
EMP: 40
SALES (corp-wide): 320.05MM **Privately Held**
Web: www.liparifoods.com
SIC: 8721 2022 2099 2013 Accounting, auditing, and bookkeeping; Cheese; natural and processed; Food preparations, nec; Sausages and other prepared meats
PA: Lipari Foods Operating Company Llc
26661 Bunert Rd
Warren MI 48089
586 447-3500

(G-10974)
LIPARI FOODS OPERATING CO LLC
Also Called: Troyer Manufacturing
316 S Mad Anthony St (44654-1388)
PHONE..................................330 674-9199
Jonas Yoder, *Brnch Mgr*
EMP: 40
SALES (corp-wide): 320.05MM **Privately Held**
Web: www.liparifoods.com
SIC: 2022 2099 2013 Cheese; natural and processed; Food preparations, nec; Sausages and other prepared meats
PA: Lipari Foods Operating Company Llc
26661 Bunert Rd
Warren MI 48089
586 447-3500

(G-10975)
LITTLE COTTAGE COMPANY (PA)
4070 State Route 39 (44654-8394)
P.O. Box 455 (44610-0455)
PHONE..................................330 893-4212
Daniel Schlabach, *Pr*
Lisa Schlabach, *VP*
EMP: 10 EST: 1994
SALES (est): 2.49MM

SALES (corp-wide): 2.49MM **Privately Held**
Web: www.cottagekits.com
SIC: 3944 5945 Games, toys, and children's vehicles; Hobby, toy, and game shops

(G-10976)
LLC BOWMAN LEATHER
6705 Private Road 387 (44654-8249)
PHONE..................................330 893-1954
EMP: 7 EST: 2008
SALES (est): 377.97K **Privately Held**
SIC: 3199 5699 Leather goods, nec; Leather garments

(G-10977)
M H WOODWORKING LLC
Also Called: Buckeye Rocker
2789 County Rd Ste 600 (44654)
PHONE..................................330 893-3929
EMP: 8 EST: 2004
SALES (est): 704.59K **Privately Held**
SIC: 2431 Millwork

(G-10978)
MAC OIL FIELD SERVICE INC
7861 Township Road 306 (44654-9666)
P.O. Box 211 (44654-0211)
PHONE..................................330 674-7371
Robert G Mc Vicker Junior, *Pr*
Patricia Mc Vicker, *VP*
EMP: 21 EST: 1978
SQ FT: 1,376
SALES (est): 1.03MM **Privately Held**
SIC: 1389 4212 Oil field services, nec; Liquid haulage, local

(G-10979)
MAPLE HILL WOODWORKING LLC
2726 Trl 128 (44654)
PHONE..................................330 674-2500
Mark Miller, *Prin*
EMP: 6 EST: 2008
SALES (est): 198.47K **Privately Held**
SIC: 2431 Millwork

(G-10980)
MIDDLEBURY CHEESE COMPANY LLC
5060 State Route 557 (44654)
PHONE..................................330 893-2500
EMP: 12
SALES (corp-wide): 18.44MM **Privately Held**
Web: www.mimilk.com
SIC: 2022 Cheese spreads, dips, pastes, and other cheese products
HQ: Middlebury Cheese Company, Llc
11275 W 250 N
Middlebury IN 46540
574 825-9511

(G-10981)
MILLER LUMBER CO INC
7101 State Route 39 (44654-8828)
PHONE..................................330 674-0273
Myron Miller, *Pr*
Scott Miller, *Treas*
EMP: 21 EST: 1949
SQ FT: 5,000
SALES (est): 498.89K **Privately Held**
SIC: 2421 Kiln drying of lumber

(G-10982)
MILLERS STORAGE BARNS LLC
4230 State Route 39 (44654-9682)
PHONE..................................330 893-3293
Owen Miller, *Managing Member*
EMP: 10 EST: 1979
SQ FT: 15,928

SALES (est): 951.88K **Privately Held**
Web: www.millerstoragebarns.com
SIC: 2452 Farm buildings, prefabricated or portable: wood

(G-10983)
MILLERSBURG ICE COMPANY
25 S Grant St (44654-1322)
PHONE..................................330 674-3016
TOLL FREE: 800
Lewis Ritchey, *Pr*
Phillip Ritchey, *VP*
EMP: 20 EST: 1936
SQ FT: 18,000
SALES (est): 1.12MM **Privately Held**
Web: www.sitestar.net
SIC: 2097 5921 Manufactured ice; Beer (packaged)

(G-10984)
MOUNT HOPE PLANING
Also Called: Mhp Flooring
7598 Tr652 (44654)
PHONE..................................330 359-0538
John Miller Junior, *Owner*
EMP: 6 EST: 1999
SQ FT: 36,000
SALES (est): 231.69K **Privately Held**
Web: www.mounthopeplaning.com
SIC: 2431 1771 Millwork; Flooring contractor

(G-10985)
MT EATON PALLET LTD
4761 County Road 207 (44654-9055)
PHONE..................................330 893-2986
Dwain Schlabach, *Pt*
EMP: 19 EST: 1991
SQ FT: 12,000
SALES (est): 1.18MM **Privately Held**
Web: www.mteatonpallet.com
SIC: 2448 Pallets, wood

(G-10986)
MULTI PRODUCTS COMPANY
7188 State Route 39 (44654-9204)
P.O. Box 1597 (76241-1597)
PHONE..................................330 674-5981
Jeff Berlin, *CEO*
William T Baker, *
Greg Guthrie, *
Bud Doty, *
◆ EMP: 29 EST: 1965
SQ FT: 30,000
SALES (est): 2.24MM **Privately Held**
Web: www.plungerlift.com
SIC: 3533 5084 Oil field machinery and equipment; Industrial machinery and equipment

(G-10987)
NJM FURNITURE OUTLET INC
6899 County Road 672 (44654-8349)
PHONE..................................330 893-3514
James Kandell, *Prin*
EMP: 10 EST: 1996
SALES (est): 627.54K **Privately Held**
SIC: 2512 Upholstered household furniture

(G-10988)
P & R MFG
5935 County Road 349 (44654-9721)
PHONE..................................330 674-1431
Paul Miller, *Prin*
EMP: 7 EST: 2008
SALES (est): 181.88K **Privately Held**
SIC: 3999 Manufacturing industries, nec

(G-10989)
PRECISION GEOPHYSICAL INC (PA)
2695 State Route 83 (44654-9455)

P.O. Box 152 (44654-0152)
PHONE..................................330 674-2198
Steven Mc Crossin, *Pr*
EMP: 32 EST: 1990
SALES (est): 4.77MM **Privately Held**
Web: www.precisiongeophysical.com
SIC: 1382 Oil and gas exploration services

(G-10990)
REXAM PLC
Rexam Prescription Products
5091 County Road 120 (44654-9231)
PHONE..................................330 893-2451
Paul Arsenault, *Mgr*
EMP: 10
SALES (corp-wide): 14.03B **Publicly Held**
Web: www.ball.com
SIC: 3085 Plastics bottles
HQ: Rexam Limited
100 Capability Green
Luton BEDS LU1 3

(G-10991)
ROCKWOOD PRODUCTS LTD
Also Called: Rockwood Door & Millwork
5264 Township Road 401 (44654-8740)
PHONE..................................330 893-2392
EMP: 30 EST: 1986
SALES (est): 3.1MM **Privately Held**
Web: www.rockwooddoor.com
SIC: 5211 2431 5031 Door and window products; Doors and door parts and trim, wood; Doors and windows

(G-10992)
SCHLABACH WOODWORKS LTD
6678 State Route 241 (44654-8826)
PHONE..................................330 674-7488
EMP: 25 EST: 1993
SALES (est): 1.31MM **Privately Held**
SIC: 3996 Hard surface floor coverings, nec

(G-10993)
SHEDS DIRECT INC
4260 Township Road 617 (44654-7913)
PHONE..................................330 674-3001
Japheth Yoder, *Prin*
EMP: 6 EST: 2013
SALES (est): 55.59K **Privately Held**
Web: www.shedsdirectinc.com
SIC: 3448 Prefabricated metal buildings and components

(G-10994)
STAR BRITE EXPRESS CAR WA
887 S Washington St (44654-1707)
PHONE..................................330 674-0062
Rodney J Starr, *Prin*
EMP: 9 EST: 2006
SALES (est): 425.34K **Privately Held**
SIC: 2741 Miscellaneous publishing

(G-10995)
STONY HILL MIXING LTD
5526 Township Road 127 (44654-9452)
PHONE..................................330 674-0814
Mahlon Yoder, *Mgr*
Levi Yoder, *Pt*
EMP: 7 EST: 2001
SALES (est): 506.24K **Privately Held**
SIC: 2048 5191 Bird food, prepared; Feed

(G-10996)
STUTZMAN MANUFACTURING LTD
7727 Township Road 604 (44654-8352)
PHONE..................................330 674-4359
Bert L Stutzman, *Managing Member*
EMP: 6 EST: 1995
SALES (est): 532.88K **Privately Held**

GEOGRAPHIC SECTION

Mineral City - Tuscarawas County (G-11018)

SIC: **3542** 7389 Nail heading machines; Business services, nec

(G-10997)
TGS INTERNATIONAL INC
4464 State Route 39 (44654-9677)
P.O. Box 355 (44610-0355)
PHONE..................................330 893-4828
David Troyer, *Ex Dir*
Paul Weaver, *
Roman Mullet, *
EMP: 50 **EST:** 1986
SALES (est): 6.43MM
SALES (corp-wide): 148.82MM **Privately Held**
Web: www.cambooks.org
SIC: **4731** 2731 Freight forwarding; Book publishing
PA: Christian Aid Ministries
   4464 State Route 39
   Millersburg OH 44654
   330 893-2428

(G-10998)
TH MANUFACTURING INC
4674 County Road 120 (44654-9280)
PHONE..................................330 893-3572
Jeff Tomshi, *Pr*
EMP: 9 **EST:** 1992
SQ FT: 60,000
SALES (est): 1.71MM **Privately Held**
Web: www.thcores.com
SIC: **3543** Industrial patterns

(G-10999)
TIGER WOOD CO LTD
4112 State Route 557 (44654-9476)
PHONE..................................330 893-2744
Dennis Raber, *Pr*
EMP: 6 **EST:** 2018
SALES (est): 235.09K **Privately Held**
SIC: **2421** Sawmills and planing mills, general

(G-11000)
TOPE PRINTING INC
1056 S Washington St (44654-9438)
PHONE..................................330 674-4993
John C Tope, *Pr*
Andrew P Tope, *VP*
Vanessa Tope, *Sec*
EMP: 7 **EST:** 1974
SQ FT: 6,000
SALES (est): 500.53K **Privately Held**
Web: topeprinting.embarqspace.com
SIC: **2752** 2759 Offset printing; Letterpress printing

(G-11001)
TROYRIDGE MFG
3998 County Road 168 (44654-7000)
PHONE..................................330 893-7516
Norman Troyer, *Prin*
EMP: 6 **EST:** 2008
SALES (est): 486K **Privately Held**
SIC: **3999** Manufacturing industries, nec

(G-11002)
UNIVERSAL WELL SERVICES INC
11 S Washington St (44654-1341)
PHONE..................................814 333-2656
EMP: 93
SALES (corp-wide): 4.15B **Publicly Held**
Web: www.patenergy.com
SIC: **1389** Oil field services, nec
HQ: Universal Well Services, Inc.
   13549 S Mosiertown Rd
   Meadville PA 16335
   814 337-1983

(G-11003)
URBAN HERSHBERGER
Also Called: Valleyview Wood Turning Co
8260 Township Road 652 (44654-8341)
PHONE..................................330 763-0407
Ervin Hershberger, *Owner*
Leon Hershberger, *Genl Mgr*
EMP: 6 **EST:** 1983
SQ FT: 15,000
SALES (est): 225.7K **Privately Held**
Web: www.valleyviewwoodturnings.com
SIC: **2426** Stock, chair, hardwood: turned, shaped, or carved

(G-11004)
W H PATTEN DRILLING CO INC
6336 County Road 207 (44654-9153)
P.O. Box 10 (44654-0010)
PHONE..................................330 674-3046
William H Patten Iii, *Pr*
Kim Mathie, *Sec*
William H Patten Junior, *Stockholder*
EMP: 8 **EST:** 1940
SQ FT: 1,200
SALES (est): 600K **Privately Held**
SIC: **1311** Crude petroleum production

(G-11005)
WALNUT CREEK PLANING LTD
5778 State Route 515 (44654-8807)
PHONE..................................330 893-3244
Dwight Kratzer, *Pr*
Ken Kratzer, *
Charles Kratzer, *
◆ **EMP:** 100 **EST:** 1988
SQ FT: 90,000
SALES (est): 21.59MM **Privately Held**
Web: www.wcplaning.com
SIC: **5211** 2421 2499 2426 Millwork and lumber; Planing mills, nec; Decorative wood and woodwork; Hardwood dimension and flooring mills

(G-11006)
WASTE PARCHMENT INC
4510 Township Road 307 (44654-9656)
PHONE..................................330 674-6868
Robert Smith, *Pr*
Elaine Smith, *
EMP: 12 **EST:** 1990
SQ FT: 80,000
SALES (est): 462.09K **Privately Held**
SIC: **4953** 2611 Recycling, waste materials; Pulp mills

(G-11007)
WEAVER LEATHER LLC (HQ)
7540 County Road 201 (44654-9296)
P.O. Box 68 (44660-0068)
PHONE..................................330 674-7548
▲ **EMP:** 86 **EST:** 1973
SALES (est): 44.29MM
SALES (corp-wide): 469.89MM **Privately Held**
Web: www.weaverleather.com
SIC: **3199** 5199 3172 3161 Harness or harness parts; Leather and cut stock; Personal leather goods, nec; Luggage
PA: Blue Point Capital Partners Llc
   127 Public Sq Ste 5100
   Cleveland OH 44114
   216 535-4700

(G-11008)
YODER LUMBER CO INC (PA)
4515 Township Road 367 (44654-8885)
PHONE..................................330 893-3121
Eli J Yoder, *Pr*
Roy Yoder, *
Melvin Yoder, *
Ken Grate, *
Nathan Yoder, *
▼ **EMP:** 55 **EST:** 1947
SQ FT: 15,000
SALES (est): 24.4MM
SALES (corp-wide): 24.4MM **Privately Held**
Web: www.yoderlumber.com
SIC: **2421** 2448 2499 2431 Lumber: rough, sawed, or planed; Pallets, wood; Mulch, wood and bark; Millwork

(G-11009)
YODER LUMBER CO INC
7100 County Road 407 (44654-9628)
PHONE..................................330 674-1435
Mel Yoder, *Mgr*
EMP: 51
SALES (corp-wide): 24.4MM **Privately Held**
Web: www.yoderlumber.com
SIC: **2421** 2448 Lumber: rough, sawed, or planed; Wood pallets and skids
PA: Yoder Lumber Co., Inc.
   4515 Township Road 367
   Millersburg OH 44654
   330 893-3121

Millersport
Fairfield County

(G-11010)
ATWOOD ROPE MANUFACTURING INC
2185 Refugee St (43046-9748)
PHONE..................................614 920-0534
Curtis Dale Atwood, *CEO*
EMP: 6 **EST:** 2006
SALES (est): 263.96K **Privately Held**
Web: www.atwoodrope.com
SIC: **2298** Ropes and fiber cables

(G-11011)
GRAVEL DOCTOR OF OHIO
2985 Canal Dr (43046-8044)
PHONE..................................844 472-8353
EMP: 9 **EST:** 2014
SALES (est): 232.79K **Privately Held**
SIC: **1442** Construction sand and gravel

(G-11012)
HEFTY HOIST INC
Also Called: Aqua Marine Supply
2397a Refugee St (43046-9748)
P.O. Box 44 (43046-0044)
PHONE..................................740 467-2515
Chet Hauck, *Pr*
▲ **EMP:** 20 **EST:** 1984
SQ FT: 14,000
SALES (est): 2.74MM **Privately Held**
Web: www.heftyhoist.com
SIC: **3566** Reduction gears and gear units for turbines, except auto

(G-11013)
SCHELL SCENIC STUDIO INC
2140 Refugee St (43046-9748)
PHONE..................................614 444-9550
Gustav Schell, *Pr*
Philip G Schell, *VP*
EMP: 7 **EST:** 1994
SQ FT: 20,000
SALES (est): 511.98K **Privately Held**
Web: www.schellscenic.com
SIC: **3999** 7922 Theatrical scenery; Scenery rental, theatrical

(G-11014)
SEE YA THERE INC
Also Called: See Ya There Vacation and Trvl
12710 W Bank Dr Ne (43046-9738)
PHONE..................................614 856-9037
John J Allen, *Pr*
George Lindsey, *Treas*
Michael Hatem, *VP*
EMP: 7 **EST:** 1998
SQ FT: 800
SALES (est): 526.16K **Privately Held**
SIC: **2741** Newsletter publishing

(G-11015)
WELDON ICE CREAM COMPANY
2887 Canal Dr (43046-9701)
PHONE..................................740 467-2400
David Pierce, *Prin*
Undet Er Mined, *Owner*
EMP: 8 **EST:** 1930
SQ FT: 10,800
SALES (est): 567.78K **Privately Held**
Web: www.weldons.com
SIC: **2024** Ice cream, bulk

Millersville
Sandusky County

(G-11016)
CARMEUSE LIME INC
Also Called: Carmeuse Lime & Stone
3964 County Road 41 (43435-9619)
PHONE..................................419 638-2511
Mike Klenda, *Brnch Mgr*
EMP: 19
SALES (corp-wide): 2.67MM **Privately Held**
Web: www.carmeuse.com
SIC: **1422** Crushed and broken limestone
HQ: Carmeuse Lime, Inc.
   11 Stanwix St Fl 21
   Pittsburgh PA 15222
   412 995-5500

Mineral City
Tuscarawas County

(G-11017)
EVOLUTION LAWN & LANDSCAPE LLC
4389 Tabor Ridge Rd Ne (44656-8882)
PHONE..................................330 268-5306
Richard Kohler, *Pr*
EMP: 7 **EST:** 2013
SALES (est): 422.73K **Privately Held**
SIC: **0781** 0782 3645 4959 Landscape services; Lawn care services; Garden, patio, walkway and yard lighting fixtures: electric; Snowplowing

(G-11018)
HILLTOP ENERGY INC
6978 Lindentree Rd Ne (44656-8973)
P.O. Box 395 (44656-0395)
PHONE..................................330 859-2108
Brandy Caterley, *Dir*
EMP: 16
SQ FT: 3,200
SALES (corp-wide): 43.61MM **Privately Held**
Web: www.hilltopenergy.com
SIC: **2892** 2819 Explosives; Industrial inorganic chemicals, nec
HQ: Hilltop Energy, Inc.
   7896 Dickey Dr
   Lisbon OH 44432
   330 424-1441

(PA)=Parent Co (HQ)=Headquarters
✪ = New Business established in last 2 years

Mineral Ridge
Trumbull County

(G-11019)
FBR INDUSTRIES INC
1336 Seaborn St Ste 7 (44440-9006)
PHONE..............................330 701-7425
Stephen Fbrown, *Prin*
EMP: 9 **EST:** 2014
SALES (est): 407.33K **Privately Held**
Web: www.fbrindustries.com
SIC: 3999 Manufacturing industries, nec

(G-11020)
J & K POWDER COATING
1336 Seaborn St (44440-9006)
PHONE..............................330 540-6145
Jeffrey A Christy, *Prin*
EMP: 6 **EST:** 2012
SALES (est): 136.25K **Privately Held**
SIC: 3399 Powder, metal

(G-11021)
JMB ENERGY INC
3729 Union St (44440-9004)
PHONE..............................330 505-9610
Martin G Solomon, *Pr*
Ben Z Post, *Sec*
EMP: 20 **EST:** 1980
SALES (est): 327.31K **Privately Held**
SIC: 1311 Crude petroleum and natural gas

(G-11022)
L B FOSTER COMPANY
Also Called: Relay Rail Div.
1193 Salt Springs Rd (44440-9318)
PHONE..............................330 652-1461
Scott Calahoun, *Mgr*
EMP: 11
SQ FT: 3,000
SALES (corp-wide): 497.5MM **Publicly Held**
Web: www.lbfoster.com
SIC: 1799 3743 Coating of metal structures at construction site; Railroad equipment
PA: L. B. Foster Company
  415 Holiday Dr Ste 1
  Pittsburgh PA 15220
  412 928-3400

(G-11023)
MASHEEN SPECIALTIES
3519 Union St (44440-9008)
PHONE..............................330 652-7535
EMP: 6 **EST:** 2005
SALES (est): 89.06K **Privately Held**
SIC: 3541 Die sinking machines

(G-11024)
VALLEY CONTAINERS INC
3515 Union St (44440-9007)
P.O. Box 171 (44440-0171)
PHONE..............................330 544-2244
Steve Hershfeldt, *Pr*
EMP: 14 **EST:** 1980
SQ FT: 15,000
SALES (est): 2.06MM **Privately Held**
Web: www.vcibox.com
SIC: 2653 Boxes, corrugated: made from purchased materials

Minerva
Stark County

(G-11025)
ABRASIVE SUPPLY COMPANY INC
25240 State Route 172 (44657-9430)
PHONE..............................330 894-2818
Rob Miller, *Pr*
▲ **EMP:** 16 **EST:** 1991
SQ FT: 16,000
SALES (est): 1.93MM **Privately Held**
Web: www.polyblast.com
SIC: 3291 Abrasive products

(G-11026)
AMERICAN AXLE & MFG INC
Also Called: Minerva Manufacturing Facility
461 Knox Ct (44657-1530)
PHONE..............................330 868-5761
EMP: 49
SALES (corp-wide): 6.08B **Publicly Held**
Web: www.aam.com
SIC: 3714 Rear axle housings, motor vehicle
HQ: American Axle & Manufacturing, Inc.
  One Dauch Dr
  Detroit MI 48211

(G-11027)
B & H MACHINE INC
15001 Lincoln St Se (44657-8900)
P.O. Box 96 (44657-0096)
PHONE..............................330 868-6425
J Timothy Bush, *Pr*
EMP: 36 **EST:** 1951
SQ FT: 70,000
SALES (est): 5.15MM **Privately Held**
Web: www.bhcylinders.com
SIC: 3593 3599 Fluid power cylinders, hydraulic or pneumatic; Machine shop, jobbing and repair

(G-11028)
CARAUSTAR INDUS CNSMR PDTS GRO
Also Called: Minerva Tube Plant
460 Knox Ct (44657-1528)
PHONE..............................330 868-4111
Steve Lacher, *Mgr*
EMP: 75
SQ FT: 45,000
SALES (corp-wide): 5.22B **Publicly Held**
SIC: 2655 Tubes, fiber or paper: made from purchased material
HQ: Caraustar Industrial And Consumer Products Group Inc
  5000 Austell Powder Ste
  Austell GA 30106
  803 548-5100

(G-11029)
COLFOR MANUFACTURING INC
Also Called: Minerva Operations
461 Knox Ct (44657-1530)
PHONE..............................330 863-0404
EMP: 328
SALES (corp-wide): 6.08B **Publicly Held**
Web: www.colformanufacturinginc.com
SIC: 3462 Iron and steel forgings
HQ: Colfor Manufacturing, Inc.
  3255 Alliance Rd Nw
  Malvern OH 44644

(G-11030)
DUTCHCRAFT TRUSS COMPONENT INC
2212 Fox Ave Se (44657-9146)
PHONE..............................330 862-2220
EMP: 13 **EST:** 2005
SALES (est): 2.42MM **Privately Held**
Web: www.dutchcrafttruss.com
SIC: 2439 Trusses, wooden roof

(G-11031)
GENERAL COLOR INVESTMENTS INC
Also Called: Plastic Color Division
250 Bridge St (44657-1509)
P.O. Box 7 (44657-0007)
PHONE..............................330 868-4161
Holly Gartner, *Pr*
Keith W Gartner, *
EMP: 100 **EST:** 1938
SQ FT: 142,800
SALES (est): 24.57MM **Privately Held**
Web: www.generalcolor.com
SIC: 2816 3087 Color pigments; Custom compound purchased resins

(G-11032)
KEPCOR INC
Also Called: Ssi Tiles
215 Bridge St (44657-1508)
P.O. Box 119 (44657-0119)
PHONE..............................330 868-6434
Robert B Keplinger, *Pr*
Connie Keplinger, *VP*
EMP: 10 **EST:** 1988
SQ FT: 121,500
SALES (est): 700K **Privately Held**
SIC: 3253 3251 Ceramic wall and floor tile; Brick and structural clay tile

(G-11033)
KMI PROCESSING LLC
15441 Lisbon St Ne (44657-9191)
PHONE..............................330 862-2185
EMP: 46
SALES (corp-wide): 528.78K **Privately Held**
Web: www.kmiprocessing.com
SIC: 3541 Sawing and cutoff machines (metalworking machinery)
PA: Kmi Processing, Llc
  15383 Lisbon St Ne
  Minerva OH 44657
  330 862-2185

(G-11034)
MCDANIEL ENVELOPE COMPANY INC
1400 Union Ave Se (44657-9171)
P.O. Box 355 (44619-0355)
PHONE..............................330 868-5929
James H Pidgeon, *Pr*
Barry Pidgeon, *VP*
Michael J Pidgeon, *Sec*
EMP: 9 **EST:** 1973
SALES (est): 437.76K **Privately Held**
Web: www.mcdanielenvelope.com
SIC: 2759 Envelopes: printing, nsk

(G-11035)
MINERVA DAIRY INC
Also Called: Minerva Maid
430 Radloff Ave (44657-1400)
P.O. Box 60 (44657-0060)
PHONE..............................330 868-4196
Phillip Muller, *CEO*
Phillip Muller, *Pr*
Adam Muller, *
Venae Watts, *
Steven H Lefkowitz, *
EMP: 65 **EST:** 1900
SQ FT: 53,000
SALES (est): 16.4MM **Privately Held**
Web: www.minervadairy.com
SIC: 2023 2021 2022 Dry, condensed and evaporated dairy products; Creamery butter ; Processed cheese

(G-11036)
MINERVA WELDING AND FABG INC
22133 Us Route 30 (44657-9401)
P.O. Box 369 (44657-0369)
PHONE..............................330 868-7731
James A Gram, *Pr*
Stephen J Gram, *
Daniel E Gram, *
EMP: 40 **EST:** 1949
SQ FT: 20,000
SALES (est): 9.72MM **Privately Held**
Web: www.minervawelding.com
SIC: 5084 3599 Industrial machinery and equipment; Machine shop, jobbing and repair

(G-11037)
MONARCH PRODUCTS CO
105 Short St (44657-1698)
P.O. Box 118 (44657-0118)
PHONE..............................330 868-7717
Gene Mercarelli, *VP*
EMP: 17 **EST:** 1947
SQ FT: 16,000
SALES (est): 506.04K **Privately Held**
SIC: 3544 Special dies and tools

(G-11038)
PCC AIRFOILS LLC
PCC Airfoils LLC
3860 Union Ave Se (44657-8944)
PHONE..............................330 868-6441
Ken Buck, *General Vice President*
EMP: 214
SQ FT: 300,000
SALES (corp-wide): 364.48B **Publicly Held**
Web: www.pccairfoils.com
SIC: 3369 3324 Nonferrous foundries, nec; Steel investment foundries
HQ: Pcc Airfoils, Llc
  3401 Entp Pkwy Ste 200
  Cleveland OH 44122
  216 831-3590

(G-11039)
REGAL METAL PRODUCTS CO (PA)
3615 Union Ave Se (44657-8972)
P.O. Box 207 (44657-0207)
PHONE..............................330 868-6343
J Ted Tomak Junior, *CEO*
Mark Righetti, *
Christian Tomack, *
EMP: 38 **EST:** 1965
SQ FT: 125,000
SALES (est): 16MM
SALES (corp-wide): 16MM **Privately Held**
Web: www.regalmetalproducts.com
SIC: 3465 3544 Automotive stampings; Special dies, tools, jigs, and fixtures

(G-11040)
SUMMITVILLE TILES INC
Also Called: Summitville Labs
81 Arbor Rd Ne (44657-8755)
P.O. Box 90 (44657-0090)
PHONE..............................330 868-6463
Joseph Dutt, *Mgr*
EMP: 30
SALES (corp-wide): 24.79MM **Privately Held**
Web: www.summitville.com
SIC: 2891 3255 2899 Epoxy adhesives; Clay refractories; Chemical preparations, nec
PA: Summitville Tiles, Inc
  15364 State Rte 644
  Summitville OH 43962
  330 223-1511

(G-11041)
SUMMITVILLE TILES INC
1310 Alliance Rd Nw (44657-9767)
P.O. Box 283 (44657-0283)
PHONE..............................330 868-6771
James A Miller, *Mgr*
EMP: 23
SALES (corp-wide): 24.79MM **Privately Held**

Web: www.summitville.com
SIC: 3253 Floor tile, ceramic
PA: Summitville Tiles, Inc
   15364 State Rte 644
   Summitville OH 43962
   330 223-1511

(G-11042)
WESTMONT INC
3035 Union Ave Ne (44657-8667)
PHONE.................................330 862-3080
Michael Zawaski, *Pr*
EMP: 8 EST: 1978
SQ FT: 5,000
SALES (est): 725.58K **Privately Held**
Web: www.westmontinc.com
SIC: 3824 Mechanical and electromechanical counters and devices

Minford
Scioto County

(G-11043)
SCIOTO INDUSTRIAL COATINGS INC
38 Burro St (45653-8805)
PHONE.................................740 352-1011
Lisa Shephard, *Prin*
EMP: 8 EST: 2009
SALES (est): 289.49K **Privately Held**
SIC: 3479 Etching and engraving

Mingo Junction
Jefferson County

(G-11044)
EASTERN AUTOMATED PIPING
424 State St (43938-1053)
P.O. Box 249 (43938-0249)
PHONE.................................740 535-8184
Ron Kleineke, *Owner*
▼ **EMP:** 6 EST: 2012
SALES (est): 427.96K **Privately Held**
Web: www.easternconstructionservicesllc.com
SIC: 3499 3312 1711 1623 Fabricated metal products, nec; Blast furnaces and steel mills ; Plumbing, heating, air-conditioning; Pipeline construction, nsk

(G-11045)
FEX LLC (PA)
Also Called: Fex Group
1058 Commercial St (43938-1007)
PHONE.................................412 604-0400
Michael Thomas, *Managing Member*
▼ **EMP:** 18 EST: 1998
SALES (est): 5.54MM
SALES (corp-wide): 5.54MM **Privately Held**
Web: www.fexgroup.com
SIC: 5093 8744 3341 Metal scrap and waste materials; Environmental remediation; Recovery and refining of nonferrous metals

(G-11046)
JSW STEEL USA OHIO INC
Also Called: Jsw USA
1500 Commercial St (43938-1096)
P.O. Box 99 (43938-0099)
PHONE.................................740 535-8172
Mark Bush, *CEO*
Cynthia L Woolheater, *
Jonathan Shank, *
Rahul Singh, *
EMP: 347 EST: 2016
SALES (est): 166.04MM **Privately Held**
Web: www.jswsteel.us

SIC: 5051 3312 Steel; Pipes, iron and steel
PA: Jsw Steel Limited
   Jsw Centre, Bandra Kurla Complex,
   Mumbai MH 40005

Minster
Auglaize County

(G-11047)
ALBERT FREYTAG INC
306 Executive Dr (45865)
P.O. Box 5 (45865-0005)
PHONE.................................419 628-2018
William Freytag, *Pr*
Joseph Freytag, *
EMP: 25 EST: 1943
SQ FT: 1,200
SALES (est): 4.11MM **Privately Held**
Web: www.albertfreytaginc.com
SIC: 3441 1741 Fabricated structural metal; Masonry and other stonework

(G-11048)
BENDCO MACHINE & TOOL INC
283 W 1st St (45865-1251)
P.O. Box 6 (45865-0006)
PHONE.................................419 628-3802
Norman Tidwell, *Pr*
Kenneth C Wolaver, *Pr*
Norman E Bud Tidwell, *Sec*
Jennifer Axe, *Mgr*
EMP: 12 EST: 1981
SQ FT: 19,500
SALES (est): 926.26K **Privately Held**
Web: www.bendcomachine.com
SIC: 3542 3547 Bending machines; Rolling mill machinery

(G-11049)
DANONE US LLC
216 Southgate (45865-9552)
P.O. Box 122 (45865-0122)
PHONE.................................419 628-1295
Didier Menu, *Mgr*
EMP: 390
SALES (corp-wide): 725.97MM **Privately Held**
Web: www.dannon.com
SIC: 2024 Yogurt desserts, frozen
HQ: Danone Us, Llc
   1 Maple Ave
   White Plains NY 10605
   914 872-8400

(G-11050)
DUCO TOOL & DIE INC
19 S Main St (45865-1349)
P.O. Box 76 (45865-0076)
PHONE.................................419 628-2031
Dale J Dues, *Pr*
Margaret Dues, *Sec*
EMP: 10 EST: 1985
SQ FT: 10,000
SALES (est): 741.43K **Privately Held**
Web: mail.nktelco.net
SIC: 3544 7692 Special dies and tools; Welding repair

(G-11051)
EGYPT STRUCTURAL STEEL PROC
480 Osterloh Rd (45865-9750)
P.O. Box 124 (45865-0124)
PHONE.................................419 628-2375
Kenneth Osterloh, *Pr*
Doris Osterloh, *
EMP: 11 EST: 1988
SQ FT: 36,360
SALES (est): 141.17K **Privately Held**

SIC: 3441 3312 Fabricated structural metal; Blast furnaces and steel mills

(G-11052)
FABCOR INC
350 S Ohio St (45865-1272)
P.O. Box 58 (45865-0058)
PHONE.................................419 628-4428
EMP: 19 EST: 1985
SALES (est): 4.42MM **Privately Held**
Web: www.fabcor.com
SIC: 3444 3544 5021 Sheet metalwork; Special dies, tools, jigs, and fixtures; Furniture

(G-11053)
GLOBUS PRINTING & PACKG CO INC (PA)
1 Exec Pkwy (45865-1274)
P.O. Box 114 (45865-0114)
PHONE.................................419 628-2381
Dennis Schmiesing, *Pr*
Tim Schmiesing, *
EMP: 68 EST: 1957
SQ FT: 100,000
SALES (est): 14.14MM
SALES (corp-wide): 14.14MM **Privately Held**
Web: www.globusprinting.com
SIC: 2752 Offset printing

(G-11054)
KARD WELDING INC
Also Called: Kard Bridge Products
480 Osterloh Rd (45865-9750)
P.O. Box 124 (45865-0124)
PHONE.................................419 628-2598
Ken Osterloh, *Owner*
Doris Osterloh, *Pr*
Kenneth H Osterloh, *VP*
EMP: 20 EST: 1983
SQ FT: 36,360
SALES (est): 2.4MM **Privately Held**
Web: www.kardwelding.com
SIC: 3499 3443 Machine bases, metal; Fabricated plate work (boiler shop)

(G-11055)
MACHINE CONCEPTS INC
2167 State Route 66 (45865-9401)
P.O. Box 127 (45865-0127)
PHONE.................................419 628-3498
▲ **EMP:** 32 EST: 1994
SQ FT: 30,000
SALES (est): 9.54MM **Privately Held**
Web: www.machineconcepts.com
SIC: 3599 Machine shop, jobbing and repair

(G-11056)
MINSTER FARMERS COOP EXCH
Also Called: Minster Farmers Co-Op Exchange
292 W 4th St (45865-1024)
P.O. Box 100 (45865-0100)
PHONE.................................419 628-4705
Kevin Doseck, *Genl Mgr*
EMP: 55 EST: 1920
SQ FT: 4,800
SALES (est): 8.89MM **Privately Held**
SIC: 5191 5153 5172 2041 Farm supplies; Grain elevators; Engine fuels and oils; Flour and other grain mill products

(G-11057)
NIDEC MINSTER CORPORATION (DH)
Also Called: Minster Machine
240 W 5th St (45865-1065)
P.O. Box 120 (45865-0120)
PHONE.................................419 628-2331
◆ **EMP:** 258 EST: 1901

SALES (est): 219.63MM **Privately Held**
Web: www.minster.com
SIC: 3542 3568 Presses: hydraulic and pneumatic, mechanical and manual; Clutches, except vehicular
HQ: Nidec Americas Holding Corporation
   8050 West Florissant Ave
   Saint Louis MO 63136
   314 595-8000

(G-11058)
POST PRINTING CO (PA)
205 W 4th St (45865-1062)
P.O. Box 101 (45865-0101)
PHONE.................................859 254-7714
Tim Thompson, *Pr*
Jane Thompson, *
Glenn Thompson Ii, *VP*
EMP: 54 EST: 1896
SQ FT: 14,400
SALES (est): 9MM
SALES (corp-wide): 9MM **Privately Held**
Web: www.postprinting.com
SIC: 2759 2752 Letterpress printing; Offset printing

(G-11059)
PROGRESS TOOL & STAMPING INC
Also Called: Progress Tool Co
207 Southgate (45865-9552)
P.O. Box 53 (45865-0053)
PHONE.................................419 628-2384
Lee H Westerheide, *Pr*
EMP: 20 EST: 1968
SQ FT: 22,000
SALES (est): 2.34MM **Privately Held**
Web: www.progresstoolandstamping.com
SIC: 3544 3469 Special dies and tools; Metal stampings, nec

(G-11060)
SECURCOM INC
Also Called: Securcom
307 W 1st St (45865-1210)
P.O. Box 116 (45865-0116)
PHONE.................................419 628-1049
Bill Bergman, *Pr*
Marlene Hoying, *Sec*
James R Shenk, *Prin*
EMP: 22 EST: 1997
SALES (est): 2.06MM **Privately Held**
Web: www.securcom.com
SIC: 5999 7382 3699 5065 Telephone and communication equipment; Security systems services; Security control equipment and systems; Communication equipment

(G-11061)
SHELTERVISION LLC
3584 Mercer Auglaize County Rd (45865-9717)
P.O. Box 188 (45865-0188)
PHONE.................................419 852-7788
Douglas Ruhenkamp, *Prin*
EMP: 6 EST: 2011
SALES (est): 196.85K **Privately Held**
SIC: 3448 Prefabricated metal buildings and components

(G-11062)
SUNRISE COOPERATIVE INC
Also Called: Minster Farmers
292 W 4th St (45865-1024)
P.O. Box 870 (43420-0870)
PHONE.................................419 628-4705
Mike Bensman, *Brnch Mgr*
EMP: 7
SALES (corp-wide): 515.25MM **Privately Held**

Minster - Auglaize County (G-11063)

GEOGRAPHIC SECTION

Web: www.sunriseco-op.com
SIC: 5191 5153 5172 2041 Feed; Grain elevators; Engine fuels and oils; Flour and other grain mill products
PA: Sunrise Cooperative, Inc.
2025 W State St
Fremont OH 43420
419 332-6468

(G-11063)
TRADEMARK DESIGNS INC
17 Jackson St (45865-1144)
PHONE.................................419 628-3897
Mark Nolan, *Pr*
Jerry Henkaline, *Sec*
EMP: 20 **EST:** 1989
SQ FT: 3,700
SALES (est): 1.5MM **Privately Held**
Web: www.tmdzinc.com
SIC: 3999 Identification plates

(G-11064)
VAN-GRINER LLC
1 Executive Pkwy (45865-1274)
PHONE.................................419 733-7951
EMP: 6 **EST:** 2019
SALES (est): 88.13K **Privately Held**
Web: www.van-griner.com
SIC: 2741 Miscellaneous publishing

Mogadore
Portage County

(G-11065)
AAA PLASTICS & PALLETS INC
246 N Cleveland Ave (44260-1205)
PHONE.................................330 844-2556
Dan A Hargrove, *Pr*
EMP: 8 **EST:** 2002
SALES (est): 652.57K **Privately Held**
Web: www.aaaplasticsandpallets.com
SIC: 2448 Pallets, wood

(G-11066)
AMERIMOLD INC
595 Waterloo Rd Ste A (44260-8710)
PHONE.................................800 950-8020
Bill Wensel, *Pr*
EMP: 6 **EST:** 1988
SQ FT: 2,000
SALES (est): 568.48K **Privately Held**
Web: www.amerimoldexpo.com
SIC: 3544 3599 Industrial molds; Machine shop, jobbing and repair

(G-11067)
BICO AKRON INC
Also Called: Bico Steel Service Centers
3100 Gilchrist Rd (44260-1246)
PHONE.................................330 794-1716
Michael A Ensminger, *Pr*
▲ **EMP:** 65 **EST:** 1988
SQ FT: 90,000
SALES (est): 23.91MM
SALES (corp-wide): 84.25MM **Privately Held**
Web: www.bicosteel.com
SIC: 5051 3443 Steel; Fabricated plate work (boiler shop)
PA: Bico Buyer, Inc.
3100 Gilchrist Rd
Mogadore OH 44260
330 794-1716

(G-11068)
CORNWELL QUALITY TOOLS COMPANY
Also Called: Cornwell Quality Tools
200 N Cleveland Ave (44260-1205)
PHONE.................................330 628-2627
Bill Nobley, *Brnch Mgr*
EMP: 77
SQ FT: 3,000
SALES (corp-wide): 55.65MM **Privately Held**
Web: www.cornwelltools.com
SIC: 3423 5085 Hand and edge tools, nec; Industrial supplies
PA: The Cornwell Quality Tools Company
667 Seville Rd
Wadsworth OH 44281
330 336-3506

(G-11069)
DNH MIXING INC
3939a Mogadore Industrial Pkwy (44260-1224)
PHONE.................................330 296-6327
▲ **EMP:** 50
SIC: 3069 Custom compounding of rubber materials

(G-11070)
DUMA MEATS INC
857 Randolph Rd (44260-9343)
P.O. Box 54 (44260-0054)
PHONE.................................330 628-3438
Dave Duma, *Pr*
Beverley Duma, *Sec*
EMP: 8 **EST:** 1972
SQ FT: 3,000
SALES (est): 1.01MM **Privately Held**
Web: www.dumameats.com
SIC: 5421 2013 Freezer provisioners, meat; Sausages and other prepared meats

(G-11071)
DUMAS DEER PROCESSING LLC
831 Waterloo Rd (44260-9503)
PHONE.................................330 805-3429
David Duma, *Genl Mgr*
EMP: 6 **EST:** 2014
SALES (est): 120.23K **Privately Held**
Web: www.dumadeerprocessing.com
SIC: 2011 Meat packing plants

(G-11072)
EXTRUDED SLCONE PDTS GSKETS IN
3300 Gilchrist Rd (44260-1254)
PHONE.................................330 733-0101
Joseph E Foreman, *Pr*
EMP: 48 **EST:** 1984
SALES (est): 3.83MM **Privately Held**
Web: www.esprubber.com
SIC: 3061 Mechanical rubber goods

(G-11073)
F M P INC
3555 Gilchrist Rd (44260-1240)
PHONE.................................330 628-1118
EMP: 6 **EST:** 2019
SALES (est): 239.49K **Privately Held**
Web: www.florencemeat.com
SIC: 3399 Primary metal products

(G-11074)
GEORGIA-PACIFIC LLC
Also Called: Georgia-Pacific
3265 Gilchrist Rd (44260-1247)
PHONE.................................330 794-4444
Craig Mcneil, *Mgr*
EMP: 90
SALES (corp-wide): 36.93B **Privately Held**
Web: www.gp.com
SIC: 2621 Paper mills
HQ: Georgia-Pacific Llc
133 Peachtree St Nw
Atlanta GA 30303
404 652-4000

(G-11075)
HUNTERS MANUFACTURING CO INC (PA)
Also Called: Tenpoint Crossbow Technologies
1325 Waterloo Rd (44260-9608)
PHONE.................................330 628-9245
Richard L Bednar, *CEO*
Joanna Rolenz, *
Cindy Shaffer, *Secretary IV**
Steve Bednar, *
Philip Bednar, *
▲ **EMP:** 30 **EST:** 1993
SALES (est): 10.4MM **Privately Held**
Web: www.tenpointcrossbows.com
SIC: 3949 3999 Crossbows; Cigarette lighters, except precious metal

(G-11076)
JANORPOT LLC
3175 Gilchrist Rd (44260-1245)
PHONE.................................330 564-0232
Norm Belliveau, *Pr*
Ron Vandiver, *
Charles Snyder, *
▲ **EMP:** 35 **EST:** 2001
SQ FT: 40,000
SALES (est): 4.52MM **Privately Held**
Web: www.janorpot.com
SIC: 3089 Flower pots, plastics

(G-11077)
KENT ELASTOMER PRODUCTS INC
3890 Mogadore Industrial Pkwy (44260-1223)
PHONE.................................800 331-4762
Murrey Vanepp, *Prin*
EMP: 10
SALES (corp-wide): 331.16MM **Privately Held**
Web: www.kentelastomer.com
SIC: 3052 Rubber and plastics hose and beltings
HQ: Kent Elastomer Products, Inc.
1500 Saint Clair Ave
Kent OH 44240
330 673-1011

(G-11078)
MOORE WELL SERVICES INC
246 N Cleveland Ave (44260-1205)
P.O. Box 1399 (44224-0399)
PHONE.................................330 650-4443
Jeff Moore, *Pr*
Jeita Moore, *VP*
EMP: 19 **EST:** 1964
SQ FT: 8,000
SALES (est): 4.9MM **Privately Held**
Web: www.moorewellservices.com
SIC: 1381 Drilling oil and gas wells

(G-11079)
NEWELL BRANDS INC
Also Called: Newell Rubbermaid
3200 Gilchrist Rd (44260-1248)
PHONE.................................330 733-7771
Joe Soldano, *Brnch Mgr*
EMP: 23
SALES (corp-wide): 8.13B **Publicly Held**
Web: www.newellbrands.com
SIC: 3089 Plastics kitchenware, tableware, and houseware
PA: Newell Brands Inc.
6655 Pachtree Dunwoody Rd
Atlanta GA 30328
770 418-7000

(G-11080)
RUBBERMAID HOME PRODUCTS
Also Called: Rubbermaid
3200 Gilchrist Rd (44260-1248)
P.O. Box 1257 (61032-1257)
PHONE.................................330 733-7771
EMP: 52 **EST:** 2017
SALES (est): 15.1MM
SALES (corp-wide): 8.13B **Publicly Held**
SIC: 3089 Thermoformed finished plastics products, nec
PA: Newell Brands Inc.
6655 Pachtree Dunwoody Rd
Atlanta GA 30328
770 418-7000

(G-11081)
RUBBERMAID INCORPORATED
Rubbermaid
3200 Gilchrist Rd (44260-1248)
PHONE.................................330 733-7771
EMP: 2237
SALES (corp-wide): 8.13B **Publicly Held**
Web: www.rubbermaid.com
SIC: 3089 Planters, plastics
HQ: Rubbermaid Incorporated
6655 Pachtree Dunwoody Rd
Atlanta GA 30328
888 895-2110

(G-11082)
S P E INC
Also Called: Extruded Silicone Products
3300 Gilchrist Rd (44260-1254)
P.O. Box 37 (44260-0037)
PHONE.................................330 733-0101
EMP: 33 **EST:** 1984
SALES (est): 2.46MM **Privately Held**
SIC: 3069 2822 Rubber automotive products; Silicone rubbers

(G-11083)
SAM AMERICAS INC
3555 Gilchrist Rd (44260-1240)
P.O. Box 8 (44260-0008)
PHONE.................................330 628-1118
Kenji Saito, *Pr*
Kaz Nakai, *
EMP: 33 **EST:** 2006
SQ FT: 60,000
SALES (est): 15.07MM **Privately Held**
Web: www.samamericas.com
SIC: 3369 Castings, except die-castings, precision
PA: Shinagawa Refractories Co., Ltd.
2-2-1, Otemachi
Chiyoda-Ku TKY 100-0

(G-11084)
SHINAGAWA INC
Also Called: Shinagawa
3555 Gilchrist Rd (44260-1240)
P.O. Box 8 (44260-0008)
PHONE.................................330 628-1118
Keiji Saito, *Pr*
◆ **EMP:** 28 **EST:** 1993
SQ FT: 28,800
SALES (est): 5.59MM **Privately Held**
SIC: 3399 Metal powders, pastes, and flakes
PA: Shinagawa Refractories Co., Ltd.
2-2-1, Otemachi
Chiyoda-Ku TKY 100-0

(G-11085)
SUMMIT MACHINE LTD
3991 Mogadore Rd (44260-1367)
P.O. Box 127 (44260-0127)
PHONE.................................330 628-2663
▲ **EMP:** 23 **EST:** 2001
SQ FT: 23,000
SALES (est): 1.52MM **Privately Held**
Web: www.summit-machine.com
SIC: 3599 Machine shop, jobbing and repair

▲ = Import ▼ = Export
◆ = Import/Export

(G-11086)
SUMMIT MACHINING CO LTD
3991 Mogadore Rd (44260-1367)
PHONE...................................330 628-2663
EMP: 13 **EST:** 2019
SALES (est): 896.99K **Privately Held**
Web: www.summit-machine.com
SIC: 3599 Machine shop, jobbing and repair

(G-11087)
SUMMIT PLASTIC COMPANY
3175 Gilchrist Rd (44260-1245)
P.O. Box 117 (44278-0117)
PHONE...................................330 633-3668
Norman Belliveau, *CEO*
Chuck Snyder, *
George Collins, *
Jim Pfeiffer, *
▲ **EMP:** 70 **EST:** 1990
SQ FT: 55,000
SALES (est): 15.47MM **Privately Held**
Web: www.summitplastic.com
SIC: 3081 Unsupported plastics film and sheet

(G-11088)
TPL HOLDINGS LLC
Also Called: Label Print Technologies, LLC
3380 Gilchrist Rd (44260-1254)
PHONE...................................800 475-4030
Jodi Westphal, *Pr*
▲ **EMP:** 25 **EST:** 2011
SALES (est): 5.06MM
SALES (corp-wide): 33.67MM **Privately Held**
Web: www.labelprinttech.com
SIC: 2752 Commercial printing, lithographic
PA: Western Shield Acquisitions Llc
3760 Kilroy Arprt Way
Long Beach CA 90806
310 527-6212

(G-11089)
VACUUM ELECTRIC SWITCH CO INC (PA)
3900 Mogadore Industrial Pkwy (44260-1201)
PHONE...................................330 374-5156
Cecil C Wristen, *Pr*
Sandra M Wristen, *VP*
EMP: 17 **EST:** 1998
SQ FT: 200
SALES (est): 2.41MM
SALES (corp-wide): 2.41MM **Privately Held**
Web: www.vesco.com
SIC: 3613 7629 Switchboards and parts, power; Electronic equipment repair

(G-11090)
VERTEX INC
3956 Mogadore Industrial Pkwy (44260-1201)
PHONE...................................330 628-6230
Salvatore Brugnano, *Ch*
Ronald Mayfield, *
James Westhoff, *
Mike Ferarra, *
◆ **EMP:** 30 **EST:** 1992
SQ FT: 20,000
SALES (est): 6.28MM **Privately Held**
Web: www.vertexseals.com
SIC: 3069 3061 3053 Valves, hard rubber; Mechanical rubber goods; Gaskets; packing and sealing devices

(G-11091)
VESCO LLC
3900 Mogadore Industrial Pkwy (44260-1201)
PHONE...................................330 374-5156
Lance Sabados, *Pr*
EMP: 20 **EST:** 2021
SALES (est): 1.09MM **Privately Held**
SIC: 3699 Electrical equipment and supplies, nec

Monclova
Lucas County

(G-11092)
AIRCRAFT GROUND SERVICES
4449 Weckerly Rd (43542-9483)
PHONE...................................419 356-5027
EMP: 6 **EST:** 2020
SALES (est): 212.19K **Privately Held**
Web: www.tronair.com
SIC: 3728 Aircraft parts and equipment, nec

Monroe
Butler County

(G-11093)
ALFREBRO LLC
1055 Reed Dr (45050-1725)
PHONE...................................513 539-7373
EMP: 14 **EST:** 1983
SALES (est): 5.57MM
SALES (corp-wide): 93.94B **Publicly Held**
Web: www.adm.com
SIC: 2499 2819 Food handling and processing products, wood; Industrial inorganic chemicals, nec
HQ: Wild Flavors, Inc.
1261 Pacific Ave
Erlanger KY 41018

(G-11094)
APPVION INC
1025 Logistics Way (45044-3218)
PHONE...................................717 731-7522
EMP: 7 **EST:** 2018
SALES (est): 62.15K **Privately Held**
SIC: 2621 Paper mills

(G-11095)
ARKAY INDUSTRIES INC (PA)
240 American Way (45050-1202)
PHONE...................................513 360-0390
EMP: 25
SQ FT: 19,000
SALES (est): 31.59MM
SALES (corp-wide): 31.59MM **Privately Held**
SIC: 3089 3086 Injection molding of plastics; Plastics foam products

(G-11096)
ARKAY PLASTICS ALABAMA INC (HQ)
220 American Way (45050-1202)
PHONE...................................513 360-0390
FAX: 513 539-8904
EMP: 15
SALES (est): 23.55MM
SALES (corp-wide): 31.59MM **Privately Held**
SIC: 3089 Injection molding of plastics
PA: Arkay Industries, Inc.
240 American Way
Monroe OH 45050
513 360-0390

(G-11097)
CHROME DEPOSIT CORPORATION
341 Lawton Ave (45050-1215)
P.O. Box 130 (45050-0130)
PHONE...................................513 539-8486
Dan Zimmerman, *Mgr*
EMP: 29
SALES (corp-wide): 21.07B **Publicly Held**
Web: www.chromedeposit.com
SIC: 3471 Chromium plating of metals or formed products
HQ: Chrome Deposit Corporation
6640 Melton Rd
Portage IN 46368
219 763-1571

(G-11098)
CIPTED CORP
301 Lawton Ave (45050-1215)
PHONE...................................412 829-2120
EMP: 75
SALES (est): 4.52MM **Privately Held**
SIC: 3713 5012 Truck bodies (motor vehicles); Trucks, noncommercial

(G-11099)
CSAFE LLC
Also Called: Csafe
675 Gateway Blvd (45050-2587)
PHONE...................................513 360-7189
Jeff Pepperworth, *CEO*
◆ **EMP:** 8 **EST:** 1979
SALES (est): 1.87MM **Privately Held**
Web: www.csafeglobal.com
SIC: 3585 Refrigeration and heating equipment

(G-11100)
DAYTON TECHNOLOGIES
351 N Garver Rd (45050-1292)
PHONE...................................513 539-5474
Darwin Brown, *Prin*
EMP: 13 **EST:** 2007
SALES (est): 695.49K **Privately Held**
SIC: 3082 Unsupported plastics profile shapes

(G-11101)
DECEUNINCK NORTH AMERICA LLC (HQ)
351 N Garver Rd (45050-1233)
PHONE...................................513 539-4444
Filip Geeraert, *Pr*
▲ **EMP:** 36 **EST:** 1969
SALES (est): 152.11MM
SALES (corp-wide): 275.49MM **Privately Held**
Web: www.deceuninckna.com
SIC: 3082 Unsupported plastics profile shapes
PA: Deceuninck
Bruggesteenweg 360
Hooglede VWV 8830
51239211

(G-11102)
DESHAZO
60 American Way Ste B (45050-1718)
PHONE...................................513 402-7466
Ricky Griffis, *Prin*
EMP: 10 **EST:** 2018
SALES (est): 273.28K **Privately Held**
SIC: 3536 Hoists, cranes, and monorails

(G-11103)
DIXIE MACHINERY INC
Also Called: Dixitech Cnc
845 Todhunter Rd (45050-1032)
PHONE...................................513 360-0091
Devin Flowers, *Pr*
EMP: 15 **EST:** 1984
SALES (est): 6.73MM
SALES (corp-wide): 6.73MM **Privately Held**
Web: www.dixitechcnc.com
SIC: 3541 Machine tools, metal cutting type
PA: Devin Flowers, Inc.
1300 Ridenour Blvd Nw
Kennesaw GA 30152
302 521-1182

(G-11104)
DOUBLEDAY ACQUISITIONS LLC (PA)
Also Called: Acutemp
675 Gateway Blvd (45050-2587)
PHONE...................................513 360-7189
Patrick Schafer, *CEO*
Nadine Siqueland, *
▲ **EMP:** 44 **EST:** 1979
SALES (est): 120.28MM
SALES (corp-wide): 120.28MM **Privately Held**
Web: www.csafeglobal.com
SIC: 3823 Temperature instruments: industrial process type

(G-11105)
DR JS PRINT SHOP LTD
21 East Ave (45050-1307)
PHONE...................................513 571-6553
Jay Junker, *Prin*
EMP: 6 **EST:** 2010
SALES (est): 179.67K **Privately Held**
Web: www.drjsprintshop.com
SIC: 2752 Offset printing

(G-11106)
FLEETCHEM LLC
651 N Garver Rd (45050-1207)
PHONE...................................513 539-1111
Tj Blakemor, *Brnch Mgr*
EMP: 10
Web: www.fleetchem.com
SIC: 2045 Blended flour: from purchased flour
PA: Fleetchem, Llc
1222 Brassie Ave Ste 19
Flossmoor IL 60422

(G-11107)
G3 PACKAGING LLC ✪
4273 Salzman Rd (45044-9741)
PHONE...................................334 799-0015
Tom Gruber, *Managing Member*
EMP: 6 **EST:** 2022
SALES (est): 1MM **Privately Held**
SIC: 3089 Plastics containers, except foam

(G-11108)
GLASS COATINGS & CONCEPTS LLC
Also Called: Gcc
300 Lawton Ave (45050-1216)
P.O. Box 130 (45050-0130)
PHONE...................................513 539-5300
Lee Shepherd, *Managing Member*
▲ **EMP:** 25 **EST:** 2003
SALES (est): 5.03MM
SALES (corp-wide): 149.59MM **Privately Held**
Web: www.gcconcepts.com
SIC: 2893 3479 Printing ink; Painting, coating, and hot dipping
PA: The Shepherd Color Company
4539 Dues Dr
West Chester OH 45246
513 874-0714

(G-11109)
HONEY CELL INC MID WEST
6480 Hamilton Lebanon Rd (45044-9285)
PHONE...................................513 360-0280
Rick Gillette, *Genl Mgr*
EMP: 27 **EST:** 1997
SQ FT: 40,000
SALES (est): 5.07MM **Privately Held**

Monroe - Butler County (G-11110)

Web: www.valleycontainer.com
SIC: 2621 Paper mills
PA: Honey Cell, Inc.
850 Union Ave
Bridgeport CT 06607

(G-11110)
HONEYCOMB MIDWEST
6480 Hamilton Lebanon Rd (45044-9285)
PHONE..................................513 360-0280
EMP: 30
SALES (est): 1.8MM Privately Held
Web: www.valleycontainer.com
SIC: 2621 Art paper

(G-11111)
INTERACTIVE PRODUCTS CORP
5346 Roden Park Dr (45050-2504)
PHONE..................................513 313-3397
Mark Comeaux, Pr
EMP: 6 EST: 1995
SQ FT: 5,000
SALES (est): 567.36K Privately Held
SIC: 3577 Computer peripheral equipment, nec

(G-11112)
JOURNEY ELECTRONICS CORP
902 N Garver Rd (45050-1241)
P.O. Box 465 (45050-0465)
PHONE..................................513 539-9836
Michael Gorden, Pr
EMP: 7 EST: 1983
SQ FT: 3,000
SALES (est): 1.77MM Privately Held
Web: www.journeyelectronics.com
SIC: 3672 3823 Printed circuit boards; Industrial process control instruments
PA: Gorden Inc.
3269 Blackberry Ln
Malvern PA 19355

(G-11113)
KERRY FLAVOR SYSTEMS US LLC
Also Called: Kerry Ingredients & Flavours
1055 Reed Dr (45050-1725)
PHONE..................................513 539-7373
David Moats, VP
EMP: 10
SIC: 2869 2819 Flavors or flavoring materials, synthetic; Industrial inorganic chemicals, nec
PA: Kerry Flavor Systems Us, Llc
10261 Chester Rd
Cincinnati OH 45215

(G-11114)
KLW PLASTICS INC (DH)
980 Deneen Ave (45050-1210)
PHONE..................................513 539-2673
Kenneth M Roessler, Pr
Don Pearson, CFO
▲ EMP: 6 EST: 2004
SQ FT: 37,000
SALES (est): 9.54MM Privately Held
SIC: 3089 5099 Blow molded finished plastics products, nec; Containers: glass, metal or plastic
HQ: Bway Corporation
1515 W 22nd St Ste 1100
Oak Brook IL 60523

(G-11115)
LAHLOUH INC
150 Lawton Ave (45050-1212)
PHONE..................................650 692-6600
EMP: 9
SALES (corp-wide): 48.85MM Privately Held
Web: www.lahlouh.com
SIC: 2752 Offset printing

PA: Lahlouh, Inc.
1649 Adrian Rd
Burlingame CA 94010
650 692-6600

(G-11116)
MOELLER BREW BARN LLC
6550 Hamilton Lebanon Rd (45044-9285)
PHONE..................................937 400-8626
EMP: 8
SALES (corp-wide): 4.38MM Privately Held
Web: www.moellerbrewbarn.com
SIC: 2082 Malt beverages
PA: Moeller Brew Barn, Llc
8016 Marion Dr
Maria Stein OH 45860
419 925-3005

(G-11117)
PAC WORLDWIDE CORPORATION
Also Called: Pac Manufacturing
575 Gateway Blvd (45050-2586)
PHONE..................................800 535-0039
EMP: 37
Web: www.pac.com
SIC: 5112 2677 Envelopes; Envelopes
HQ: Pac Worldwide Corporation
15435 Ne 92nd St
Redmond WA 98052
425 202-4000

(G-11118)
R & L SOFTWARE LLC (PA)
Also Called: Marz Direct
421 Breaden Dr Ste 3 (45050-1575)
PHONE..................................513 847-4942
EMP: 9
SQ FT: 2,500
SALES (est): 1.38MM
SALES (corp-wide): 1.38MM Privately Held
SIC: 7373 7372 Computer system selling services; Prepackaged software

(G-11119)
ROGER SCHWEITZER SONS
150 Breaden Dr (45050-1872)
PHONE..................................513 241-4423
Steve Schweitzer, Pr
EMP: 7 EST: 1976
SALES (est): 96.24K Privately Held
SIC: 3443 Fabricated plate work (boiler shop)

(G-11120)
SOFTBOX SYSTEMS INC
675 Gateway Blvd (45050-2587)
PHONE..................................864 630-7860
Edwin Tattam, Pr
Kevin Valentine, *
▼ EMP: 61 EST: 2007
SALES (est): 25.8MM
SALES (corp-wide): 120.28MM Privately Held
Web: www.softboxsystems.com
SIC: 2653 Pallets, corrugated: made from purchased materials
HQ: Softbox Systems Limited
1 Ridgeway
Aylesbury BUCKS HP18

(G-11121)
WORTHINGTON ENTERPRISES INC
350 Lawton Ave (45050-1216)
PHONE..................................513 539-9291
David Kleimeyer, Mgr
EMP: 97
SQ FT: 120,000
SALES (corp-wide): 4.92B Publicly Held
Web: www.worthingtonenterprises.com

SIC: 3325 5051 3471 3441 Steel foundries, nec; Metals service centers and offices; Plating and polishing; Fabricated structural metal
PA: Worthington Enterprises, Inc.
200 W Old Wlson Bridge Rd
Worthington OH 43085
614 438-3210

Monroeville
Huron County

(G-11122)
BERRY GLOBAL INC
Also Called: Berry Plastics
311 Monroe St (44847-9406)
PHONE..................................419 465-2291
Thomas Salmon, Brnch Mgr
EMP: 66
Web: www.berryglobal.com
SIC: 3089 3081 Bottle caps, molded plastics; Unsupported plastics film and sheet
HQ: Berry Global, Inc.
101 Oakley St
Evansville IN 47710

(G-11123)
BORES MANUFACTURING INC
Also Called: Bores, J F Mfg
300 Sandusky St (44847-9476)
P.O. Box 216 (44847-0216)
PHONE..................................419 465-2606
Kevin Bores, Pr
Shirley Bores, Sec
EMP: 19 EST: 1973
SQ FT: 9,200
SALES (est): 1.04MM Privately Held
Web: www.boresmfg.com
SIC: 3714 3713 Motor vehicle parts and accessories; Truck and bus bodies

(G-11124)
HBE MACHINE INCORPORATED
1100 State Route 61 N (44847-9202)
PHONE..................................419 668-9426
Thomas R Hedrick, Pr
EMP: 6 EST: 1985
SQ FT: 10,000
SALES (est): 505.59K Privately Held
SIC: 3599 Machine shop, jobbing and repair

(G-11125)
SCOTTRODS LLC
2512 Higbee Rd (44847-9617)
PHONE..................................419 499-2705
EMP: 7 EST: 2007
SALES (est): 487.88K Privately Held
Web: www.scottrodscustom.com
SIC: 3229 7389 3711 Glass fiber products; Business Activities at Non-Commercial Site; Automobile bodies, passenger car, not including engine, etc.

(G-11126)
SMS TECHNOLOGIES INC
3531 Everingin Rd (44847-9726)
PHONE..................................419 465-4175
Stanley Schug, Pr
Nickie Schug, VP
EMP: 10 EST: 1990
SALES (est): 873.64K Privately Held
SIC: 3646 Commercial lighting fixtures

(G-11127)
VENTURE PACKAGING INC
311 Monroe St (44847-9406)
PHONE..................................419 465-2534
Ira Boots, Pr
James Kratochuil, *

John Rathbun, *
EMP: 90 EST: 1976
SQ FT: 112,000
SALES (est): 5.7MM Publicly Held
SIC: 3089 Injection molded finished plastics products, nec
HQ: Berry Global, Inc.
101 Oakley St
Evansville IN 47710

(G-11128)
VENTURE PACKAGING MIDWEST INC
311 Monroe St (44847-9406)
P.O. Box 246 (44847-0246)
PHONE..................................419 465-2534
EMP: 41 EST: 1997
SALES (est): 2.71MM Publicly Held
SIC: 3089 Bottle caps, molded plastics
HQ: Berry Global, Inc.
101 Oakley St
Evansville IN 47710

Montgomery
Hamilton County

(G-11129)
D J KLINGLER INC
Also Called: Montgomery License Bureau
9999 Montgomery Rd (45242-5311)
PHONE..................................513 891-2284
Donna Klingler, Pr
EMP: 6 EST: 1993
SALES (est): 489.69K Privately Held
SIC: 3469 7299 Automobile license tags, stamped metal; Personal appearance services

(G-11130)
KEMPF SURGICAL APPLIANCES INC
10567 Montgomery Rd (45242-4416)
PHONE..................................513 984-5758
Steven Kempf, Pr
Susan Kempf, Treas
EMP: 11 EST: 1963
SALES (est): 661.48K Privately Held
Web: www.kempfsurgical.com
SIC: 5999 5047 7352 3842 Hospital equipment and supplies; Hospital equipment and supplies, nec; Medical equipment rental; Surgical appliances and supplies

(G-11131)
SPICY OLIVE LLC
9901 Montgomery Rd (45242-5311)
PHONE..................................513 376-9061
EMP: 16
SALES (corp-wide): 949.38K Privately Held
Web: www.thespicyolive.com
SIC: 2079 Olive oil
PA: Spicy Olive Llc
7671 Cox Ln
West Chester OH 45069
513 847-4397

(G-11132)
VENTI-NOW
9891 Montgomery Rd Ste 302 (45242-6424)
PHONE..................................513 334-3375
John Molander, Pr
EMP: 8 EST: 2020
SALES (est): 94.54K Privately Held
Web: www.venti-now.org
SIC: 3444 Ventilators, sheet metal

Montpelier
Williams County

(G-11133)
20/20 CUSTOM MOLDED PLAS LLC (PA)
14620 Selwyn Dr (43543-9237)
PHONE.............................419 485-2020
EMP: 51 EST: 2000
SALES (est): 26.24MM
SALES (corp-wide): 26.24MM **Privately Held**
Web: www.2020cmp.com
SIC: 3089 Injection molding of plastics

(G-11134)
AMP PLASTICS OF OHIO LLC
1815 Magda Dr (43543-9208)
EMP: 20 EST: 2007
SALES (est): 1.92MM **Privately Held**
SIC: 3089 Injection molding of plastics

(G-11135)
CREATIVE LIQUID COATINGS INC
Also Called: CK Technologies
1701 Magda Dr (43543-9368)
PHONE.............................419 485-1110
EMP: 250
Web: www.creativeliquidcoatings.com
SIC: 3089 Injection molding of plastics
PA: Creative Liquid Coatings, Inc.
2620 Marion Dr
Kendallville IN 46755

(G-11136)
DECO PLAS PROPERTIES LLC
700 Randolph St (43543-1464)
PHONE.............................419 485-0632
EMP: 10 EST: 2005
SALES (est): 912.43K **Privately Held**
SIC: 2851 Paints and allied products

(G-11137)
DYCO MANUFACTURING INC
12708 State Route 576 (43543-9242)
PHONE.............................419 485-5525
Alan M Dye, Pr
Wes Dye, VP
Crystal Tyre, Sec
EMP: 14 EST: 1968
SALES (est): 2.74MM **Privately Held**
Web: www.dycomfg.com
SIC: 3469 3544 Stamping metal for the trade; Special dies and tools

(G-11138)
KIMBLE MACHINES INC
124 S Jonesville St (43543-1337)
PHONE.............................419 485-8449
Robert J Kimble, Pr
Margaret Kimble, Sec
EMP: 14 EST: 1989
SQ FT: 8,200
SALES (est): 459.33K **Privately Held**
Web: www.kimblemachines.com
SIC: 3599 Custom machinery

(G-11139)
MOORE INDUSTRIES INC
1317 Henricks Dr (43543-1951)
P.O. Box 316 (43543-0216)
PHONE.............................419 485-5572
Michael Moore, Pr
Rebecca Moore, *
▲ EMP: 65 EST: 1980
SQ FT: 40,000
SALES (est): 8.26MM **Privately Held**
Web: www.moore-industries.com

SIC: 3089 Injection molding of plastics

(G-11140)
POWERS AND SONS LLC (DH)
Also Called: Pioneer Frge A Div Pwers Sons
1613 Magda Dr (43543-9359)
PHONE.............................419 485-3151
▲ EMP: 220 EST: 2002
SQ FT: 200,000
SALES (est): 49.5MM **Privately Held**
Web: www.powersandsonsllc.com
SIC: 3714 Motor vehicle parts and accessories
HQ: Wanxiang (Usa) Holdings Corporation
88 Airport Rd Ste 100
Elgin IL 60123
847 622-8838

(G-11141)
RANTEK PRODUCTS LLC
1826 Magda Dr Ste A (43543-9366)
PHONE.............................419 485-2421
EMP: 6 EST: 2001
SALES (est): 813.99K **Privately Held**
Web: www.rantekproducts.com
SIC: 3199 Harness or harness parts

(G-11142)
RICHMOND MACHINE CO
1528 Travis Dr (43543-9524)
PHONE.............................419 485-5740
Lee Richmond, Pr
Robert Richmond, *
EMP: 32 EST: 1965
SQ FT: 60,000
SALES (est): 4.97MM **Privately Held**
Web: www.richmondmachinecompany.com
SIC: 3599 3535 Custom machinery; Conveyors and conveying equipment

(G-11143)
TOMAHAWK TOOL SUPPLY
1604 Magda Dr (43543-9206)
PHONE.............................419 485-8737
Jeff Thomas, Pr
EMP: 9 EST: 2003
SALES (est): 675.05K **Privately Held**
Web: www.tomahawk-tool.com
SIC: 3544 Special dies and tools

(G-11144)
VILLAGE REPORTER
115 Broad St (43543-1325)
PHONE.............................419 485-4851
Forrest Church, Prin
EMP: 8 EST: 2013
SALES (est): 171.69K **Privately Held**
Web: www.thevillagereporter.com
SIC: 2711 Newspapers, publishing and printing

(G-11145)
W C HELLER & CO INC
Also Called: Heller Sports Center
201 W Wabash St (43543-1840)
PHONE.............................419 485-3176
Robert L Heller, Pr
Patricia Heller, Treas
Andrew Heller, General Vice President
EMP: 10 EST: 1891
SQ FT: 25,500
SALES (est): 282.25K **Privately Held**
Web: www.wcheller.com
SIC: 2531 School furniture

(G-11146)
WINZELER COUPLINGS & MTLS LLC ✪
910 E Main St (43543-1260)

PHONE.............................419 485-3147
Joseph Folkman, Ch Bd
David Rauch, CEO
EMP: 88 EST: 2022
SALES (est): 4.91MM **Privately Held**
SIC: 3466 Closures, stamped metal

(G-11147)
WINZELER STAMPING CO (HQ)
129 W Wabash St (43543)
P.O. Box 226 (43543)
PHONE.............................419 485-3147
▲ EMP: 50 EST: 1919
SALES (est): 17.95MM
SALES (corp-wide): 17.95MM **Privately Held**
Web: www.winzelerstamping.com
SIC: 3429 3465 3469 3714 Clamps and couplings, hose; Automotive stampings; Metal stampings, nec; Motor vehicle parts and accessories
PA: Winzeler Manufacturing Company
129 W Wabash St
Montpelier OH 43543
419 485-8147

Montville
Geauga County

(G-11148)
5 S INC
9755 Plank Rd (44064-9712)
P.O. Box 188 (44064-0188)
PHONE.............................440 968-0212
Tom Sparks, Pr
EMP: 7 EST: 2005
SALES (est): 838.05K **Privately Held**
Web: www.5scomponents.com
SIC: 3599 Machine shop, jobbing and repair

(G-11149)
LINDEV INVESTORS GROUP INC
9215 Madison Rd (44064-8720)
PHONE.............................440 856-9201
David Devlin, Prin
EMP: 8 EST: 2013
SALES (est): 139.17K **Privately Held**
SIC: 1389 Construction, repair, and dismantling services

Moraine
Montgomery County

(G-11150)
3249 INC
3249 Dryden Rd (45439-1423)
PHONE.............................937 294-5692
Lisa S Pierce, Prin
EMP: 18 EST: 2005
SALES (est): 335.1K **Privately Held**
Web: www.empowermfg.com
SIC: 3599 Machine shop, jobbing and repair

(G-11151)
3JD INC
Also Called: Stone Center of Dayton
2823 Northlawn Ave (45439-1645)
PHONE.............................513 324-9655
Jerry Berkemeyer, Prin
▲ EMP: 15 EST: 2011
SALES (est): 1.91MM **Privately Held**
SIC: 2541 Counter and sink tops

(G-11152)
ACUTEMP THERMAL SYSTEMS
2900 Dryden Rd (45439-1618)
PHONE.............................937 312-0114
Marshall Griffin, CFO

EMP: 13 EST: 2012
SALES (est): 465.44K **Privately Held**
Web: www.csafeglobal.com
SIC: 3822 Temperature controls, automatic

(G-11153)
AEROSPACE LLC
Also Called: Aerospace Logistics
3300 Encrete Ln (45439-1944)
PHONE.............................937 561-1104
EMP: 10 EST: 2015
SALES (est): 511.98K **Privately Held**
SIC: 3728 Aircraft parts and equipment, nec

(G-11154)
AIRGAS USA LLC
2400 Sandridge Dr (45439-1849)
PHONE.............................937 222-8312
EMP: 6
SALES (corp-wide): 101.26MM **Privately Held**
Web: www.airgas.com
SIC: 5169 5084 5085 2813 Industrial gases; Welding machinery and equipment; Welding supplies; Industrial gases
HQ: Airgas Usa, Llc
259 N Radnor Chester Rd
Radnor PA 19087
216 642-6600

(G-11155)
ALLIED SHIPPING AND PACKAGING SUPPLIES INC
Also Called: ASAP
3681 Vance Rd (45439-7940)
PHONE.............................937 222-7422
EMP: 13 EST: 1981
SALES (est): 2.75MM **Privately Held**
Web: www.asapi.com
SIC: 5085 5162 7822 3086 Industrial supplies; Plastics materials and basic shapes; Video tapes, recorded: wholesale; Plastics foam products

(G-11156)
AMERICAN THERMAL INSTRS INC (PA)
2400 E River Rd (45439-1530)
PHONE.............................937 429-2114
Marvin L Kidd, CEO
Timothy Riazzi, *
Trent Matthews, *
EMP: 25 EST: 1981
SALES (est): 8.28MM
SALES (corp-wide): 8.28MM **Privately Held**
Web: www.americanthermal.com
SIC: 3829 Measuring and controlling devices, nec

(G-11157)
ANDRIN ENTERPRISES INC
Also Called: Mmp Printing
3350 Kettering Blvd (45439-2011)
PHONE.............................937 276-7794
Gary Luther, Pr
Shannon Luther, VP
EMP: 12 EST: 1979
SQ FT: 5,000
SALES (est): 900K **Privately Held**
SIC: 2752 2791 2789 Offset printing; Typesetting; Bookbinding and related work

(G-11158)
ANGELS LANDING INC
Also Called: Compass
3430 S Dixie Dr Ste 301 (45439-2316)
PHONE.............................513 687-3681
John Riedl, Prin
Dan Jackson, CFO

Moraine - Montgomery County (G-11159)

▲ EMP: 6 EST: 2004
SQ FT: 2,000
SALES (est): 471.35K **Privately Held**
SIC: 2514 Juvenile furniture, household; metal

(G-11159)
BARRETT PAVING MATERIALS INC
2701 W Dorothy Ln (45439-1864)
PHONE..................................937 293-9033
Jim Shaver, *Brnch Mgr*
EMP: 10
SALES (corp-wide): 90.36MM **Privately Held**
Web: www.barrettpaving.com
SIC: 3273 Ready-mixed concrete
HQ: Barrett Paving Materials Inc.
8590 Bilstein Blvd # 100
Hamilton OH 45015
973 533-1001

(G-11160)
BAYARD INC
2621 Dryden Rd Ste 300 (45439-1600)
PHONE..................................937 293-1415
John P Koize, *Prin*
EMP: 81
Web: www.bayardinc.com
SIC: 2759 Publication printing
HQ: Bayard, Inc.
1 Montauk Ave Ste 200
New London CT 06320

(G-11161)
BDS PACKAGING INC
3155 Elbee Rd Ste 201 (45439-2046)
PHONE..................................937 643-0530
▲ EMP: 15 EST: 1995
SQ FT: 78,264
SALES (est): 666.46K **Privately Held**
Web: www.bdspackaging.com
SIC: 2653 3993 7389 Boxes, corrugated: made from purchased materials; Displays and cutouts, window and lobby; Packaging and labeling services

(G-11162)
BERRY INVESTMENTS INC
3055 Kettering Blvd Ste 418 (45439-1900)
PHONE..................................937 293-0398
John W Berry Junior, *CEO*
William T Lincoln, *Pr*
EMP: 6 EST: 1983
SQ FT: 2,500
SALES (est): 899.97K **Privately Held**
SIC: 5091 3679 Sporting and recreation goods; Microwave components

(G-11163)
BRAVO LLC (HQ) ◆
Also Called: Bravo Pet Foods
2425 W Dorothy Ln (45439-1827)
PHONE..................................866 922-9222
David J Bogner, *Managing Member*
EMP: 17 EST: 2022
SALES (est): 11.29MM
SALES (corp-wide): 50.33MM **Privately Held**
Web: www.bravorawdiet.com
SIC: 2047 Dog food
PA: Brightpet Nutrition Group Llc
38251 Industrial Park Rd
Lisbon OH 44432
330 424-1431

(G-11164)
BRONT MACHINING INC
2601 W Dorothy Ln (45439-1831)
PHONE..................................937 228-4551
Gary Warlaumont, *Pr*
Brian Warlaumont, *VP*
EMP: 32 EST: 1975
SQ FT: 25,000
SALES (est): 2.59MM **Privately Held**
Web: www.brontmachine.com
SIC: 3451 3599 Screw machine products; Machine shop, jobbing and repair

(G-11165)
CARAUSTAR INDUSTRIES INC
2601 E River Rd (45439-1533)
PHONE..................................937 298-9969
Bill Theado, *Genl Mgr*
EMP: 38
SALES (corp-wide): 5.22B **Publicly Held**
Web: www.greif.com
SIC: 2655 Fiber cans, drums, and similar products
HQ: Caraustar Industries, Inc.
5000 Astell Pwdr Sprng Rd
Austell GA 30106
770 948-3101

(G-11166)
CHEMSTATION INTERNATIONAL INC (PA)
Also Called: Chemstation
3400 Encrete Ln (45439-1946)
PHONE..................................937 294-8265
EMP: 45 EST: 1982
SALES (est): 59.59MM
SALES (corp-wide): 59.59MM **Privately Held**
Web: www.chemstation.com
SIC: 6794 2842 2899 2841 Franchises, selling or licensing; Cleaning or polishing preparations, nec; Chemical preparations, nec; Soap and other detergents

(G-11167)
CROWN CORK & SEAL USA INC
5005 Springboro Pike (45439-2974)
PHONE..................................937 299-2027
Robert Mason, *Mgr*
EMP: 102
SQ FT: 50,000
SALES (corp-wide): 12.01B **Publicly Held**
Web: www.crowncork.com
SIC: 3411 Metal cans
HQ: Crown Cork & Seal Usa, Inc.
770 Township Line Rd
Yardley PA 19067
215 698-5100

(G-11168)
DADDY KATZ LLC
3250 Kettering Blvd (45439-1926)
PHONE..................................937 296-0347
William Winger Junior, *Prin*
EMP: 9 EST: 2008
SALES (est): 478.67K **Privately Held**
Web: www.daddykatz.com
SIC: 3089 Automotive parts, plastic

(G-11169)
DAPSCO
3110 Kettering Blvd (45439-1972)
PHONE..................................937 294-5331
Richard Schwartz, *Prin*
EMP: 10 EST: 2010
SALES (est): 851.26K **Privately Held**
SIC: 3571 Electronic computers

(G-11170)
DAYTON ARMOR LLC
2360 W Dorothy Ln Ste 107 (45439-1861)
PHONE..................................937 723-8675
Dean Slapak, *Pt*
EMP: 7 EST: 2010
SALES (est): 470.48K **Privately Held**
Web: www.daytonarmor.com

SIC: 3999 Barber and beauty shop equipment

(G-11171)
DAYTON BRICK COMPANY INC
Also Called: D & M Welding
2300 Arbor Blvd (45439-1724)
PHONE..................................937 293-4189
Jeffrey Mccarroll, *Pr*
Jeffrey Mc Carroll, *Pr*
Brian Mc Carroll, *Sec*
Justin Mccarroll, *Opers Mgr*
EMP: 15 EST: 1921
SQ FT: 15,000
SALES (est): 3.1MM **Privately Held**
Web: www.dmweldingusa.com
SIC: 7692 Welding repair

(G-11172)
DMAX LTD (DH)
Also Called: Dmax
3100 Dryden Rd (45439-1622)
PHONE..................................937 425-9700
Lawrence R Sessoms, *Prin*
Susumu Hosoi, *
◆ EMP: 98 EST: 1998
SQ FT: 700,000
SALES (est): 52.17MM **Publicly Held**
Web: www.dmaxengines.com
SIC: 3519 Engines, diesel and semi-diesel or dual-fuel
HQ: General Motors Llc
300 Rnaissance Ctr Ste L1
Detroit MI 48243

(G-11173)
DRYDEN SHAFTS LLC
3249 Dryden Rd (45439-1423)
PHONE..................................937 365-7420
Eli Liechty, *Managing Member*
EMP: 30 EST: 2017
SALES (est): 5.89MM **Privately Held**
Web: www.empowermfg.com
SIC: 3568 Power transmission equipment, nec

(G-11174)
ELECTRIPACK INC
2985 Springboro W (45439-1713)
PHONE..................................937 433-2602
Jeanne Wright, *CEO*
◆ EMP: 40 EST: 2002
SALES (est): 7.31MM **Privately Held**
Web: www.electripack.com
SIC: 3694 Harness wiring sets, internal combustion engines

(G-11175)
ENTING WATER CONDITIONING INC (PA)
Also Called: Superior Water Conditioning Co
3211 Dryden Rd Frnt (45439-1400)
PHONE..................................937 294-5100
TOLL FREE: 800
Mel Entingh, *CEO*
Dan Entingh, *
Doris Entingh, *
Karen Entingh, *
▲ EMP: 31 EST: 1965
SQ FT: 43,440
SALES (est): 2.89MM
SALES (corp-wide): 2.89MM **Privately Held**
Web: www.enting.com
SIC: 3589 5999 5074 Water filters and softeners, household type; Water purification equipment; Water purification equipment

(G-11176)
ERNST AMERICA INC
2920 Kreitzer Rd (45439-1644)
PHONE..................................937 434-3133
Neil Cordonnier, *Pr*
EMP: 13 EST: 2005
SALES (est): 2.04MM
SALES (corp-wide): 126.62MM **Privately Held**
Web: www.ernst.de
SIC: 3469 3312 Stamping metal for the trade; Tool and die steel and alloys
HQ: Ernst Umformtechnik Gmbh
Am Wiesenbach 1
Oberkirch BW 77704
78054060

(G-11177)
ERNST METAL TECHNOLOGIES LLC
3031 Dryden Rd (45439-1619)
PHONE..................................937 434-3133
Neil Cordonnier, *Pr*
EMP: 82
SALES (corp-wide): 126.62MM **Privately Held**
Web: www.ernst.de
SIC: 3469 Stamping metal for the trade
HQ: Ernst Metal Technologies Llc
2920 Kreitzer Rd
Moraine OH 45439

(G-11178)
ERNST METAL TECHNOLOGIES LLC (DH)
2920 Kreitzer Rd (45439-1644)
PHONE..................................937 434-3133
James Burt, *Managing Member*
▲ EMP: 44 EST: 2005
SALES (est): 53.26MM
SALES (corp-wide): 126.62MM **Privately Held**
Web: www.ernst.de
SIC: 3469 3312 Stamping metal for the trade; Tool and die steel and alloys
HQ: Ernst Umformtechnik Gmbh
Am Wiesenbach 1
Oberkirch BW 77704
78054060

(G-11179)
EXTREME MICROBIAL TECH LLC
Also Called: Extreme Microbial Technologies
2800 E River Rd (45439-1538)
PHONE..................................844 885-0088
Randall Mount, *Managing Member*
EMP: 21 EST: 2016
SALES (est): 2.25MM **Privately Held**
Web: www.extrememicrobial.com
SIC: 1799 3564 Decontamination services; Air purification equipment

(G-11180)
F & G TOOL AND DIE CO (PA)
3024 Dryden Rd (45439-1690)
PHONE..................................937 294-1405
Jeff Johnson, *Pr*
Gary M Fischer, *
Ed Scharer, *
EMP: 44 EST: 1948
SQ FT: 60,000
SALES (est): 11.02MM
SALES (corp-wide): 11.02MM **Privately Held**
Web: www.fgtool.com
SIC: 3544 3599 Special dies and tools; Custom machinery

(G-11181)
FORGELINE MOTORSPORTS LLC
Also Called: Forgeline Motorsports
3522 Kettering Blvd (45439-2000)

PHONE..........................800 886-0093
EMP: 25 EST: 1994
SQ FT: 5,600
SALES (est): 3.01MM Privately Held
Web: www.forgeline.com
SIC: 3714 Wheels, motor vehicle

(G-11182)
GRAY AMERICA CORP (PA)
3050 Dryden Rd (45439-1620)
PHONE..........................937 293-9313
◆ EMP: 23 EST: 1946
SALES (est): 56.46MM
SALES (corp-wide): 56.46MM Privately Held
Web: www.grayamerica.com
SIC: 3312 3452 Blast furnaces and steel mills ; Bolts, metal

(G-11183)
HARCO MANUFACTURING GROUP LLC (PA)
3535 Kettering Blvd (45439-2014)
PHONE..........................937 528-5000
Christina Harris, *
▲ EMP: 150 EST: 2006
SQ FT: 300,000
SALES (est): 44.11MM Privately Held
Web: www.harcoonline.com
SIC: 3714 Motor vehicle brake systems and parts

(G-11184)
HARCO MANUFACTURING GROUP LLC
3535 Kettering Blvd # 200 (45439-2014)
PHONE..........................937 528-5000
Tom Mc Nulty, *Brnch Mgr*
EMP: 150
Web: www.harcoonline.com
SIC: 3714 Motor vehicle brake systems and parts
PA: Harco Manufacturing Group, Llc
3535 Kettering Blvd
Moraine OH 45439

(G-11185)
HEADING4WARD INVESTMENT CO (PA)
Also Called: Miracle
2425 W Dorothy Ln (45439-1827)
PHONE..........................937 293-9994
William M Sherk Junior, *Pr*
◆ EMP: 66 EST: 1988
SQ FT: 11,500
SALES (est): 17.01MM Privately Held
Web: www.bngmiraclepet.com
SIC: 3999 0752 5999 Pet supplies; Animal specialty services; Pet supplies

(G-11186)
INSIGNIA SIGNS INC
2265 Dryden Rd (45439-1737)
PHONE..........................937 866-2341
Rick Dobson, *Pr*
Dan Mcbride, *Prin*
EMP: 8 EST: 2009
SALES (est): 1.1MM Privately Held
Web: www.imagineinsignia.com
SIC: 3993 7336 Electric signs; Graphic arts and related design

(G-11187)
JENA TOOL INC
5219 Springboro Pike (45439-2970)
PHONE..........................937 296-1122
George J Derr, *Ch*
EMP: 74 EST: 1968
SQ FT: 45,000
SALES (est): 9.11MM Privately Held
Web: www.jenatool.com
SIC: 3544 Special dies and tools

(G-11188)
KRAMER GRAPHICS INC
2408 W Dorothy Ln (45439-1828)
PHONE..........................937 296-9600
Mary Lou Kramer, *Ch*
John Kramer Junior, *Pr*
Kelley Kramer, *
▲ EMP: 50 EST: 1978
SALES (est): 9.59MM
SALES (corp-wide): 10.95MM Privately Held
Web: www.outdoorimagepop.com
SIC: 2752 Offset printing
PA: Outdoor Image, Llc
3400 Rivergreen Ct # 100
Duluth GA 30096
770 817-9517

(G-11189)
L&H THREADED RODS CORP
3050 Dryden Rd (45439-1620)
PHONE..........................937 294-6666
John C Gray, *Pr*
Jeff Schroder, *
▲ EMP: 125 EST: 1986
SQ FT: 45,000
SALES (est): 26.76MM
SALES (corp-wide): 56.46MM Privately Held
Web: www.lhrods.com
SIC: 3312 Rods, iron and steel: made in steel mills
PA: Gray America Corp.
3050 Dryden Rd
Moraine OH 45439
937 293-9313

(G-11190)
LASTAR INC
3555 Kettering Blvd (45439-2014)
PHONE..........................937 224-0639
▲ EMP: 420
SIC: 3678 Electronic connectors

(G-11191)
MAR-CON TOOL COMPANY
2301 Arbor Blvd (45439-1788)
PHONE..........................937 299-2244
Gene A Hamrick, *Pr*
Gene A Hamrick, *Pr*
Jeff Hamrick, *
Jim Hamrick, *
Gene Hamrick, *
EMP: 25 EST: 1959
SQ FT: 15,500
SALES (est): 2.95MM Privately Held
Web: www.marcontool.com
SIC: 3599 3728 3544 Machine shop, jobbing and repair; Aircraft parts and equipment, nec; Special dies, tools, jigs, and fixtures

(G-11192)
MCON INDS INC (HQ)
Also Called: Miller Consolidated Inds Inc
2221 Arbor Blvd (45439-1521)
PHONE..........................937 294-2681
Thomas Miller, *CEO*
Kelly Henderson, *
EMP: 49 EST: 1982
SQ FT: 55,000
SALES (est): 44.45MM
SALES (corp-wide): 44.45MM Privately Held
Web: www.millerconsolidated.com
SIC: 5051 3398 Steel; Metal heat treating
PA: Wilse, Inc.
938 W County Road 250 S
Greensburg IN

(G-11193)
METALLURGICAL SERVICE INC
2221 Arbor Blvd (45439-1575)
PHONE..........................937 294-2681
William R Miller, *Ch Bd*
Robert Miller, *VP*
Thomas Miller, *VP*
Alice L Miller, *Sec*
EMP: 12 EST: 1942
SQ FT: 45,000
SALES (est): 2.38MM
SALES (corp-wide): 44.45MM Privately Held
SIC: 3398 Metal heat treating
HQ: Mcon Inds, Inc.
2221 Arbor Blvd
Moraine OH 45439
937 294-2681

(G-11194)
METRO FLEX INC
3304 Encrete Ln (45439-1944)
PHONE..........................937 299-5360
Scot Terry, *CEO*
Charleston Cline, *Sec*
EMP: 8 EST: 2003
SALES (est): 605.82K Privately Held
Web: www.mfplates.com
SIC: 2759 Screen printing

(G-11195)
MIDWEST MUFFLER PROS & MORE
3061 Dryden Rd (45439-1619)
PHONE..........................937 293-2450
Brian Madden, *Pr*
EMP: 6 EST: 2014
SALES (est): 336.68K Privately Held
Web: www.midwestmufflerpros.com
SIC: 7539 3714 Automotive repair shops, nec ; Mufflers (exhaust), motor vehicle

(G-11196)
PERFORMNCE PLYMR SOLUTIONS INC
Also Called: Proof RES Advnced Cmpsites Div
2711 Lance Dr (45409-1519)
PHONE..........................937 298-3713
Larry Murphy, *CEO*
David B Curliss, *Pr*
Jason Lincoln, *VP*
▲ EMP: 14 EST: 2002
SQ FT: 25,000
SALES (est): 4.36MM Privately Held
SIC: 8733 8731 8711 2821 Scientific research agency; Commercial research laboratory; Mechanical engineering; Plastics materials and resins
PA: Proof Research, Inc.
10 Western Village Ln
Columbia Falls MT 59912

(G-11197)
PFLAUM PUBLISHING GROUP
3055 Kettering Blvd Ste 100 (45439-1989)
PHONE..........................937 293-1415
EMP: 13 EST: 2010
SALES (est): 178.84K Privately Held
Web: www.pflaum.com
SIC: 2741 Miscellaneous publishing

(G-11198)
PJL ENTERPRISE INC
2019 Springboro W (45439-1665)
PHONE..........................937 293-1415
Peter Li, *Pr*
EMP: 11
SIC: 2721 Magazines: publishing only, not printed on site
HQ: Pjl Enterprise, Inc.
3055 Kettering Blvd # 100
Moraine OH 45439
937 293-1415

(G-11199)
PJL ENTERPRISE INC (DH)
Also Called: Peter LI Education Group
3055 Kettering Blvd Ste 100 (45439-1989)
PHONE..........................937 293-1415
Peter J Li, *Pr*
EMP: 65 EST: 1971
SQ FT: 17,500
SALES (est): 8.21MM Privately Held
SIC: 2741 Miscellaneous publishing
HQ: Bayard, Inc.
1 Montauk Ave Ste 200
New London CT 06320

(G-11200)
PLACECRETE INC
2475 Arbor Blvd (45439-1776)
PHONE..........................937 298-2121
Donald L Phlipot, *Pr*
EMP: 26 EST: 1966
SQ FT: 17,000
SALES (est): 518.32K Privately Held
SIC: 3273 Ready-mixed concrete

(G-11201)
POLAR INC
2297 N Moraine Dr (45439-1507)
P.O. Box 2995 (46515-2995)
PHONE..........................937 297-0911
Robert J Crawford, *Pr*
Shaery Eilon, *Acctg Mgr*
▼ EMP: 10 EST: 1955
SQ FT: 3,000
SALES (est): 1.17MM Privately Held
SIC: 5169 5172 2841 Industrial chemicals; Petroleum products, nec; Soap and other detergents

(G-11202)
PREMIER INV CAST GROUP LLC
3034 Dryden Rd (45439-1620)
PHONE..........................937 299-7333
Harry Greenhouse, *Pt*
Peter Tur, *
EMP: 35 EST: 2017
SALES (est): 3.8MM Privately Held
Web: www.bimac.com
SIC: 3325 Steel foundries, nec

(G-11203)
PRINTING EXPRESS
3350 Kettering Blvd (45439-2011)
PHONE..........................937 276-7794
James Armstrong, *Owner*
EMP: 6 EST: 1989
SALES (est): 374.91K Privately Held
Web: www.printingexpressdayton.com
SIC: 2752 Offset printing

(G-11204)
PRODUCTION CONTROL UNITS INC
2280 W Dorothy Ln (45439-1892)
PHONE..........................937 299-5594
Thomas Hoge, *Pr*
Fred Bayer, *
▼ EMP: 100 EST: 1946
SQ FT: 58,000
SALES (est): 20.34MM Privately Held
Web: www.pcuinc.com
SIC: 3829 3823 Measuring and controlling devices, nec; Industrial process control instruments

(G-11205)
PROMATCH SOLUTIONS LLC
2251 Arbor Blvd (45439-1521)
PHONE..........................877 299-0185

Moraine - Montgomery County (G-11206)

Jeffrey R Relick, *Pr*
EMP: 15 **EST:** 1992
SQ FT: 11,500
SALES (est): 1.6MM **Privately Held**
SIC: 2741 7375 2789 2752 Micropublishing; Information retrieval services; Bookbinding and related work; Commercial printing, lithographic

(G-11206)
RACK PROCESSING COMPANY INC (PA)
2350 Arbor Blvd (45439-1760)
PHONE.................................937 294-1911
Craig Coy, *Pr*
Kevyn Coy, *
H Singer, *Prin*
EMP: 50 **EST:** 1948
SQ FT: 24,000
SALES (est): 14.75MM
SALES (corp-wide): 14.75MM **Privately Held**
Web: www.rackprocessing.com
SIC: 2542 3471 Partitions and fixtures, except wood; Plating and polishing

(G-11207)
RACK PROCESSING COMPANY INC
Also Called: Pique Stripping Division
2350 Arbor Blvd (45439-1760)
PHONE.................................937 294-1911
Dan Grammer, *Brnch Mgr*
EMP: 35
SALES (corp-wide): 14.75MM **Privately Held**
Web: www.rackprocessing.com
SIC: 3471 3479 2542 Electroplating of metals or formed products; Coating of metals with plastic or resins; Racks, merchandise display or storage: except wood
PA: Rack Processing Company, Inc.
2350 Arbor Blvd
Moraine OH 45439
937 294-1911

(G-11208)
ROLLING ENTERPRISES INC
Also Called: Cat-Wood Metalworks
2701 Lance Dr (45409-1519)
PHONE.................................937 866-4917
August Rolling, *Pr*
August Jay Rolling, *
EMP: 36 **EST:** 1994
SALES (est): 5.34MM **Privately Held**
Web: www.cat-wood.com
SIC: 3599 Machine shop, jobbing and repair

(G-11209)
ROTO TECH INC
2651 E River Rd (45439-1533)
PHONE.................................937 859-8503
David Millat, *Pr*
Natalie A Millat, *
EMP: 11 **EST:** 1979
SQ FT: 20,000
SALES (est): 262.42K **Privately Held**
Web: www.roto-techinc.com
SIC: 3545 3829 3823 3541 Rotary tables; Measuring and controlling devices, nec; Process control instruments; Machine tools, metal cutting type

(G-11210)
SANTOS INDUSTRIAL LTD (PA)
Also Called: Bimac
3034 Dryden Rd (45439-1620)
PHONE.................................937 299-7333
Roberto Santos, *Pr*
▲ **EMP:** 19 **EST:** 1958
SQ FT: 33,280
SALES (est): 5.28MM
SALES (corp-wide): 5.28MM **Privately Held**
Web: www.bimac.com
SIC: 3366 Copper foundries

(G-11211)
SNYDER CONCRETE PRODUCTS INC (PA)
Also Called: Snyder Brick and Block
2301 W Dorothy Ln (45439-1825)
PHONE.................................937 885-5176
Lee E Snyder, *CEO*
Mark Snyder, *
Julie Flory, *
▲ **EMP:** 25 **EST:** 1949
SQ FT: 50,000
SALES (est): 12.11MM
SALES (corp-wide): 12.11MM **Privately Held**
Web: www.snyderonline.com
SIC: 5032 3271 3272 Brick, except refractory; Blocks, concrete or cinder: standard; Concrete products, nec

(G-11212)
SOUTHPAW ENTERPRISES INC
2350 Dryden Rd (45439)
P.O. Box 1047 (45401)
PHONE.................................937 252-7676
Frank Howard, *Pr*
Paul Lauzau, *
▼ **EMP:** 34 **EST:** 1975
SQ FT: 37,500
SALES (est): 7.25MM **Privately Held**
Web: www.southpaw.com
SIC: 3842 Technical aids for the handicapped

(G-11213)
TAILORED SYSTEMS INC
Also Called: Vibrodyne Division
2853 Springboro W (45439-2045)
PHONE.................................937 299-3900
Joseph Riess, *Pr*
John Riess, *VP*
Ron Logan, *Sec*
Karen Berry, *Asst Tr*
EMP: 7 **EST:** 1982
SQ FT: 12,000
SALES (est): 992.74K **Privately Held**
Web: www.vibrodyne.com
SIC: 3541 3599 Deburring machines; Machine shop, jobbing and repair

(G-11214)
THE WAGNER-SMITH COMPANY
3201 Encrete Ln (45439-1903)
P.O. Box 127 (45401-0127)
PHONE.................................866 338-0398
EMP: 490 **EST:** 1917
SALES (est): 28MM
SALES (corp-wide): 4.66B **Publicly Held**
Web: www.wagnersmith.com
SIC: 1731 3531 5082 7353 General electrical contractor; Construction machinery; Construction and mining machinery; Heavy construction equipment rental
HQ: Mdu Construction Services Group, Inc.
1150 W Century Ave
Bismarck ND 58503
701 530-1000

(G-11215)
TKO MFG SERVICES INC
2360 W Dorothy Ln Ste 111 (45439-1861)
P.O. Box 2246 (45401-2246)
PHONE.................................937 299-1637
Gary Keithley, *Pr*
Agripina Boettcher, *VP*
EMP: 22 **EST:** 1982

SQ FT: 10,000
SALES (est): 189.33K **Privately Held**
SIC: 3714 7389 Motor vehicle parts and accessories; Packaging and labeling services

(G-11216)
TUF-TUG INC
3434 Encrete Ln (45439-1946)
PHONE.................................937 299-1213
Joseph F Deuer Junior, *Pr*
Louise Deuer, *Treas*
▲ **EMP:** 18 **EST:** 1987
SQ FT: 27,000
SALES (est): 5.06MM **Privately Held**
Web: www.tuf-tug.com
SIC: 3544 7539 Special dies, tools, jigs, and fixtures; Machine shop, automotive

(G-11217)
TYLER TECHNOLOGIES INC
1 Tyler Way (45439-7503)
PHONE.................................800 800-2581
EMP: 19
SALES (corp-wide): 1.95B **Publicly Held**
Web: www.tylertech.com
SIC: 7372 Prepackaged software
PA: Tyler Technologies, Inc.
5101 Tennyson Pkwy
Plano TX 75024
972 713-3700

Moreland Hills
Cuyahoga County

(G-11218)
BOWS BARRETTES & BAUBLES
4180 Chagrin River Rd (44022-1111)
PHONE.................................440 247-2697
Cherrie Miller, *Owner*
EMP: 10 **EST:** 1985
SALES (est): 331.24K **Privately Held**
SIC: 2353 Hats, trimmed: women's, misses', and children's

(G-11219)
FLOUR MANAGEMENT LLC (PA)
Also Called: Flour Pasta Company
34205 Chagrin Blvd (44022-1030)
PHONE.................................216 910-9019
EMP: 6 **EST:** 2011
SALES (est): 406.59K
SALES (corp-wide): 406.59K **Privately Held**
Web: www.flourestaurant.com
SIC: 2098 Macaroni and spaghetti

(G-11220)
PRECISION POLYMER CASTING LLC
140 Greentree Rd (44022-2424)
PHONE.................................440 343-0461
Terry Capuano, *Prin*
EMP: 8 **EST:** 2011
SALES (est): 1.06MM **Privately Held**
Web: www.precisionpolymercasting.com
SIC: 3325 Alloy steel castings, except investment

Morral
Marion County

(G-11221)
J-LENCO INC
664 N High St (43337)
P.O. Box 346 (43332)
PHONE.................................740 499-2260
Edward P Murphy, *Pr*
Nancy Murphy, *

Thomas A Frericks, *
▲ **EMP:** 22 **EST:** 1973
SALES (est): 2.44MM **Privately Held**
Web: www.jlenco.com
SIC: 3543 Industrial patterns

Morristown
Belmont County

(G-11222)
BUCKEYE BRAKE MFG INC
40168 National Rd W (43759)
P.O. Box 676 (43950-0676)
PHONE.................................740 782-1379
Greg Beckett, *Pr*
EMP: 10 **EST:** 1996
SALES (est): 791.13K **Privately Held**
SIC: 3714 Motor vehicle brake systems and parts

Morrow
Warren County

(G-11223)
ACTION MACHINE & MFG INC
6788 E Us Highway 22 And 3 (45152-9713)
PHONE.................................513 899-3889
Delores Nadine Hartman, *Pr*
Daryl Hartman, *VP*
Nick Hartman, *Sec*
EMP: 8 **EST:** 1963
SQ FT: 14,000
SALES (est): 582.97K **Privately Held**
SIC: 3599 Machine shop, jobbing and repair

(G-11224)
MILLER AND SLAY WDWKG LLC
4140 E Foster Maineville Rd (45152-8503)
PHONE.................................513 265-3816
Jon Miller, *Prin*
EMP: 7 **EST:** 2011
SALES (est): 245.18K **Privately Held**
SIC: 2431 Millwork

(G-11225)
SPEAR STONE PRESS
2691 Blackgold Ct (45152-5017)
PHONE.................................513 899-7337
Jacquelyn Ruiz, *Admn*
EMP: 6 **EST:** 2015
SALES (est): 72.14K **Privately Held**
Web: www.spearstonepress.com
SIC: 2741 Miscellaneous publishing

(G-11226)
VALLEY ASPHALT CORPORATION
Also Called: Morrow Gravel
4850 Stubbs Mills Rd (45152-8340)
PHONE.................................513 381-0652
Bob Ftayton, *Mgr*
EMP: 8
SALES (corp-wide): 225.16MM **Privately Held**
Web: www.jrjnet.com
SIC: 2951 Asphalt paving mixtures and blocks
HQ: Valley Asphalt Corporation
11641 Mosteller Rd
Cincinnati OH 45241
513 771-0820

(G-11227)
VALLEY MACHINE TOOL INC
9773 Morrow Cozaddale Rd (45152-8589)
PHONE.................................513 899-2737
Larry R Wilson, *Pr*
Ralph Wilson, *
Douglas Wilson, *

EMP: 40 EST: 1967
SQ FT: 11,000
SALES (est): 3.03MM Privately Held
SIC: 3599 7692 Machine shop, jobbing and repair; Welding repair

Mount Cory
Hancock County

(G-11228)
SNAPS INC
2557 Township Road 35 (45868-9701)
PHONE.................................419 477-5100
Nancy Ruppright, Pr
Gary Ruppright, VP
EMP: 6 EST: 1993
SALES (est): 553.85K Privately Held
Web: www.costumers.com
SIC: 2389 Theatrical costumes

Mount Eaton
Wayne County

(G-11229)
DUTCH QUALITY STONE INC
18012 Dover Rd (44659)
P.O. Box 308 (44659-0308)
PHONE.................................877 359-7866
▲ EMP: 100 EST: 1996
SQ FT: 40,000
SALES (est): 23.1MM Privately Held
Web: www.dutchqualitystone.com
SIC: 3281 Cut stone and stone products
HQ: Headwaters Incorporated
   10701 S Rver Front Pkwy
   South Jordan UT 84095

(G-11230)
FLEX TECHNOLOGIES INC
Also Called: Mount Eaton Division
16183 East Main St (44659)
P.O. Box 223 (44659-0223)
PHONE.................................330 359-5415
Jim Eichel, Mgr
EMP: 52
SALES (corp-wide): 6MM Privately Held
Web: www.flextechnologies.com
SIC: 3089 3714 3694 3564 Injection molding of plastics; Motor vehicle parts and accessories; Engine electrical equipment; Blowers and fans
PA: Flex Technologies, Inc.
   5479 Gundy Dr
   Midvale OH 44653
   740 922-5992

(G-11231)
QUALITY BLOCK & SUPPLY INC (DH)
Rte 250 (44659)
PHONE.................................330 364-4411
Jerry A Schwab, Pr
David Schwab, *
Donna Schwab, *
Mary Lynn Hites, Treas
EMP: 27 EST: 1973
SQ FT: 4,000
SALES (est): 5.91MM
SALES (corp-wide): 32.72B Privately Held
SIC: 3271 3273 5032 Blocks, concrete or cinder: standard; Ready-mixed concrete; Concrete and cinder block
HQ: Schwab Industries, Inc.
   2301 Progress St
   Dover OH 44622
   330 364-4411

Mount Gilead
Morrow County

(G-11232)
CONSOLIDATED GAS COOP INC
5255 State Route 95 (43338-9763)
P.O. Box 111 (43338-0111)
PHONE.................................419 946-6600
Nancy Salyer, CFO
EMP: 6 EST: 2001
SALES (est): 794.14K Privately Held
Web: www.consolidated.coop
SIC: 1321 Propane (natural) production

(G-11233)
GERICH FIBERGLASS INC
7004 Us Highway 42 (43338-9638)
PHONE.................................419 362-4591
Anton J Gerich, Pr
Lila S Gerich, *
EMP: 12 EST: 1975
SQ FT: 20,000
SALES (est): 1.01MM Privately Held
Web: www.fibrecore.com
SIC: 3714 3713 3715 3792 Motor vehicle body components and frame; Bus bodies (motor vehicles); Trailer bodies; Travel trailers and campers

(G-11234)
HIRT PUBLISHING CO INC
Also Called: Marrow County Sentinel
245 Neal Ave Ste A (43338-9372)
P.O. Box 149 (43338-0149)
PHONE.................................419 946-3010
Vicki Taylor, Mgr
EMP: 38
SALES (corp-wide): 4.2MM Privately Held
Web: www.putnamsentinel.com
SIC: 2711 5999 Newspapers, publishing and printing; Rubber stamps
PA: Hirt Publishing Co, Inc
   224 E Main St
   Ottawa OH 45875
   419 523-5709

(G-11235)
LILLY INDUSTRIES INC (PA)
Also Called: Lightning Bolt Fastners
6437 County Road 20 (43338-9624)
PHONE.................................419 946-7908
Phil Lilly, Pr
Alvin Lilly, VP
EMP: 20 EST: 1972
SQ FT: 8,000
SALES (est): 4.6MM
SALES (corp-wide): 4.6MM Privately Held
Web: 1gj.7ec.myftpupload.com
SIC: 3441 Fabricated structural metal

(G-11236)
WOODWORKS ZANESVILLE
7079 County Road 121 (43338-9396)
PHONE.................................740 624-3396
Norman Yoder, Prin
EMP: 7 EST: 2007
SALES (est): 243.66K Privately Held
SIC: 2431 Millwork

Mount Hope
Holmes County

(G-11237)
GMI HOLDINGS INC (DH)
Also Called: Genie Company, The
1 Door Dr (44660-2503)
P.O. Box 67 (44660-0067)
PHONE.................................800 354-3643
Mike Kridel, Pr
Craig Smith, *
◆ EMP: 350 EST: 1990
SQ FT: 230,000
SALES (est): 142.14MM Privately Held
Web: www.geniecompany.com
SIC: 5064 3699 Vacuum cleaners, nec; Door opening and closing devices, electrical
HQ: Overhead Door Corporation
   2501 S State Hwy 121 Ste
   Lewisville TX 75067
   469 549-7100

(G-11238)
HRH DOOR CORP (PA)
One Door Dr (44660-2503)
PHONE.................................850 208-3400
Willis Mullet, CEO
Thomas B Bennett Iii, Pr
Alma Mullet, *
E E Muller, *
W C Pyers, *
◆ EMP: 650 EST: 1954
SQ FT: 1,000,000
SALES (est): 467.98MM
SALES (corp-wide): 467.98MM Privately Held
Web: www.wayne-dalton.com
SIC: 3442 2431 Garage doors, overhead: metal; Garage doors, overhead, wood

Mount Orab
Brown County

(G-11239)
CINCINNATI DOWEL & WD PDTS CO
135 Oak St (45154-9090)
PHONE.................................937 444-2502
William Streight, Pr
◆ EMP: 25 EST: 1925
SQ FT: 2,400
SALES (est): 2.25MM Privately Held
Web: www.cincinnatidowel.com
SIC: 2499 Dowels, wood

(G-11240)
CINDOCO WOOD PRODUCTS CO
Also Called: Craftwood
410 Mount Clifton Dr (45154-9353)
PHONE.................................937 444-2504
Melissa Hacker, Pr
EMP: 10 EST: 2006
SALES (est): 904.29K Privately Held
Web: www.cindoco.com
SIC: 5099 2431 Wood and wood by-products ; Millwork

(G-11241)
HAWKLINE NEVADA LLC
200 Front St (45154-8964)
PHONE.................................937 444-4295
Larry Danna, *
▲ EMP: 8 EST: 2006
SQ FT: 150,000
SALES (est): 682.77K Privately Held
SIC: 3523 3799 Cabs, tractors, and agricultural machinery; Trailers and trailer equipment

(G-11242)
LUXUS PRODUCTS LLC
Also Called: Luxus Arms
222 Homan Way (45154-8269)
P.O. Box 11 (45154-0011)
PHONE.................................937 444-6500
EMP: 6 EST: 2009
SALES (est): 695.56K Privately Held
Web: www.hmdefense.com

SIC: 2491 Structural lumber and timber, treated wood

(G-11243)
MOYER VINEYARDS INC
Also Called: Moyer Winery & Restaurant
16765 Malady Rd (45154-9570)
P.O. Box 235 (45144-0235)
PHONE.................................937 549-2957
Carol White, Pr
EMP: 10 EST: 1973
SALES (est): 420.43K Privately Held
Web: www.moyerwineryrestaurant.com
SIC: 2084 5812 Wines; Restaurant, family: independent

(G-11244)
NET BRAZE LLC
351 Apple St (45154-8565)
PHONE.................................937 444-1444
▲ EMP: 18
SIC: 2899 Fluxes: brazing, soldering, galvanizing, and welding

(G-11245)
PRECISION WELDING & MFG INC (PA)
101 Day Rd (45154-8924)
P.O. Box 369 (45154-0369)
PHONE.................................937 444-6925
Daniel L Fischer, Pr
EMP: 10 EST: 1994
SQ FT: 20,000
SALES (est): 1.45MM Privately Held
Web: www.precisionweldingcorp.net
SIC: 7692 Welding repair

(G-11246)
PRO-TECH MANUFACTURING INC
14944 Hillcrest Rd (45154-8513)
PHONE.................................937 444-6484
EMP: 10 EST: 1994
SQ FT: 9,000
SALES (est): 925.02K Privately Held
SIC: 3544 Special dies and tools

(G-11247)
WEDCO LLC
Also Called: Bardwell Winery
716 N High St (45154-8349)
P.O. Box 391 (45154-0391)
PHONE.................................513 309-0781
Roy R Weddle, Managing Member
Roy R Weddle, Pr
Gayle Weddle, VP
EMP: 6 EST: 2005
SALES (est): 422.7K Privately Held
SIC: 6531 2082 5182 Real estate brokers and agents; Brewers' grain; Wine

(G-11248)
X-MIL INC
220 Homan Way (45154-8269)
P.O. Box 452 (45154-0452)
PHONE.................................937 444-1323
Steven E Seibert, Pr
Joel Scott Dalton, VP
Angie Kreidler, Sec
EMP: 20 EST: 1998
SALES (est): 2.29MM Privately Held
Web: www.x-mil.com
SIC: 3599 Machine shop, jobbing and repair

Mount Perry
Perry County

(G-11249)
B & D COMMISSARYS LLC
5705 State Route 204 Ne (43760-9734)

Mount Perry - Perry County (G-11250)

PHONE..................740 743-3890
William Dugas, *Pt*
David Dugas, *Pt*
EMP: 8 **EST:** 1998
SALES (est): 217.84K **Privately Held**
SIC: 2045 Pizza doughs, prepared: from purchased flour

(G-11250)
MAYSVILLE MATERIALS LLC
6535 Old Town Rd (43760-1100)
PHONE..................740 849-0474
EMP: 6 **EST:** 2013
SALES (est): 227.76K **Privately Held**
SIC: 1422 Crushed and broken limestone

(G-11251)
MT PERRY FOODS INC
5705 State Route 204 Ne (43760-9734)
P.O. Box 404 (43086-0404)
PHONE..................740 743-3890
Rey Martin, *Pr*
EMP: 75 **EST:** 2000
SALES (est): 8.68MM **Privately Held**
Web: www.mtperryfoods.com
SIC: 2499 Food handling and processing products, wood

(G-11252)
SCHEIDERS FOODS LLC (PA)
5705 State Route 204 (43760-9734)
PHONE..................740 404-6641
Jeff Cormell, *Managing Member*
EMP: 10 **EST:** 2021
SALES (est): 937.47K
SALES (corp-wide): 937.47K **Privately Held**
SIC: 2051 Bakery: wholesale or wholesale/retail combined

Mount Sterling
Madison County

(G-11253)
BLESCO SERVICES
8905 Mckendree Rd (43143-9120)
PHONE..................614 871-4900
Brian Spangler, *Pr*
EMP: 6 **EST:** 2016
SALES (est): 297.79K **Privately Held**
SIC: 3444 Sheet metalwork

(G-11254)
BROKE BOYS SEALCOATING LLC ◉
10698 Baldwin Rd (43143-9624)
PHONE..................614 477-0322
Jimmie Caudill, *Managing Member*
EMP: 7 **EST:** 2022
SALES (est): 75.6K **Privately Held**
SIC: 2952 Asphalt felts and coatings

(G-11255)
CPI INDUSTRIAL CO
299 Yankeetown St (43143-9410)
P.O. Box 235 (43143-0235)
PHONE..................614 445-0800
Mark Owens, *Pr*
Mark T Owens, *Pr*
Susan Flannigan, *Sec*
EMP: 22 **EST:** 1988
SALES (est): 5.16MM **Privately Held**
Web: www.epoxyfloors.com
SIC: 2851 Epoxy coatings

(G-11256)
MAHLE BEHR MT STERLING INC
10500 Oday Harrison Rd (43143-9474)
PHONE..................740 869-3333
◆ **EMP:** 367 **EST:** 2011
SALES (est): 94.17MM
SALES (corp-wide): 3.75MM **Privately Held**
SIC: 5013 3714 Automotive engines and engine parts; Motor vehicle engines and parts
HQ: Mahle Behr Japan K.K.
1-9-12, Kitaotsuka
Toshima-Ku TKY 170-0

(G-11257)
STEPHENS PIPE & STEEL LLC
10732 Schadel Ln (43143-9731)
P.O. Box 237 (43143-0237)
PHONE..................740 869-2257
Rick Redman, *Prin*
EMP: 135
Web: www.spsfence.com
SIC: 3523 3496 3494 3446 Farm machinery and equipment; Miscellaneous fabricated wire products; Valves and pipe fittings, nec; Architectural metalwork
HQ: Stephens Pipe & Steel, Llc
2224 E Highway 619
Russell Springs KY 42642
270 866-3331

(G-11258)
WATERSHED MANGEMENT LLC
Also Called: Nancy Blanket
10460 State Route 56 Se (43143-9429)
P.O. Box 126 (43143-0126)
PHONE..................740 852-5607
EMP: 10 **EST:** 1998
SALES (est): 1.12MM **Privately Held**
Web: www.nancysblankets.com
SIC: 5023 2399 Blankets; Aprons, breast (harness)

(G-11259)
WILLOWWOOD GLOBAL LLC
Also Called: Ohio Willow Wood Company, The
15441 Scioto Darby Rd (43143-9036)
P.O. Box 130 (43143-0130)
PHONE..................740 869-3377
Ryan Arbogast, *Pr*
Robert E Arbogast, *
C Joseph Arbogast, *
John Robertson, *
◆ **EMP:** 205 **EST:** 1907
SQ FT: 90,000
SALES (est): 43.73MM **Privately Held**
Web: www.willowwood.com
SIC: 3842 Limbs, artificial

Mount Vernon
Knox County

(G-11260)
AMG INDUSTRIES INC
300 Commerce Dr (43050-4642)
PHONE..................740 397-4044
EMP: 9 **EST:** 2018
SALES (est): 496.31K **Privately Held**
Web: www.amgindustries.com
SIC: 3999 Manufacturing industries, nec

(G-11261)
AMG INDUSTRIES LLC
200 Commerce Dr (43050-4699)
PHONE..................740 397-4044
David J Mcelroy, *Pr*
Mike Miller, *
Kim Rose, *
Dennis Mcelroy, *Ex VP*
EMP: 100 **EST:** 1904
SQ FT: 120,000
SALES (est): 25.3MM **Privately Held**
Web: www.amgindustries.com
SIC: 3469 Metal stampings, nec
PA: Reserve Group Management Company
3560 W Market St Ste 300
Fairlawn OH 44333

(G-11262)
AMG PRODUCTS LLC ◉
1375 Newark Rd (43050-4779)
PHONE..................614 507-7749
Douglas Spangler, *Managing Member*
EMP: 16 **EST:** 2023
SALES (est): 836.54K **Privately Held**
SIC: 3053 Gaskets; packing and sealing devices

(G-11263)
ARIEL CORPORATION
8405 Blackjack Rd (43050-2781)
PHONE..................740 397-0311
EMP: 14
SALES (corp-wide): 105.04MM **Privately Held**
Web: www.arielcorp.com
SIC: 3563 Air and gas compressors
PA: Ariel Corporation
35 Blackjack Road Ext
Mount Vernon OH 43050
740 397-0311

(G-11264)
ARIEL CORPORATION (PA)
35 Blackjack Road Ext (43050-9482)
PHONE..................740 397-0311
◆ **EMP:** 198 **EST:** 1966
SALES (est): 105.04MM
SALES (corp-wide): 105.04MM **Privately Held**
Web: www.arielcorp.com
SIC: 3563 Air and gas compressors including vacuum pumps

(G-11265)
BRIDGESTONE RET OPERATIONS LLC
Also Called: Firestone
855 Coshocton Ave Ste 21 (43050-1975)
PHONE..................740 397-5601
Robert Stauffer, *Mgr*
EMP: 10
SQ FT: 9,200
Web: www.bridgestoneamericas.com
SIC: 5531 7534 Automotive tires; Tire repair shop
HQ: Bridgestone Retail Operations, Llc
333 E Lake St Ste 300
Bloomingdale IL 60108
630 259-9000

(G-11266)
CAPITAL CITY OIL INC
Also Called: American Energy Pdts Inc Ind
375 Columbus Rd (43050-4427)
PHONE..................740 397-4483
EMP: 6 **EST:** 1995
SALES (est): 750K **Privately Held**
Web: www.capitalcityusedoil.com
SIC: 2911 4953 Oils, fuel; Refuse systems

(G-11267)
CENTRAL OHIO FABRICATORS LLC
105 Progress Dr (43050-4772)
PHONE..................740 393-3892
EMP: 25 **EST:** 1984
SQ FT: 22,000
SALES (est): 2.6MM **Privately Held**
Web: www.centralohiofab.com
SIC: 3441 Fabricated structural metal

(G-11268)
CITY OF MOUNT VERNON
Also Called: Water & Waste Water Dept.
1550 Old Delaware Rd (43050-8631)
PHONE..................740 393-9508
Judie Scott, *Admn*
EMP: 8
Web: www.mountvernonohio.org
SIC: 2899 Water treating compounds
PA: City Of Mount Vernon
40 Public Sq Ste 206
Mount Vernon OH 43050
740 393-9520

(G-11269)
COYNE GRAPHIC FINISHING INC
Also Called: Coyne Finishing
1301 Newark Rd (43050-4730)
PHONE..................740 397-6232
Robert Coyne, *Ch*
Kevin Coyne, *
Alice Ann Coyne, *
EMP: 28 **EST:** 1926
SQ FT: 57,000
SALES (est): 2.95MM **Privately Held**
Web: www.coynefinishing.com
SIC: 7336 2752 Graphic arts and related design; Commercial printing, lithographic

(G-11270)
DIVERSIFIED PRODUCTS & SVCS
1250 Vernonview Dr (43050-1447)
PHONE..................740 393-6202
EMP: 16 **EST:** 1982
SALES (est): 261.46K **Privately Held**
SIC: 5199 2541 2511 Packaging materials; Wood partitions and fixtures; Wood household furniture

(G-11271)
DOWN HOME
Also Called: Down Home Leather
9 N Main St (43050-3203)
PHONE..................740 393-1186
Laurel Lee Wagoner, *Owner*
EMP: 8 **EST:** 1971
SQ FT: 5,000
SALES (est): 410.32K **Privately Held**
Web: www.downhomeleather.com
SIC: 5947 3172 Gift shop; Personal leather goods, nec

(G-11272)
ELLIS BROTHERS INC UPG
14220 Parrott Ext (43050-4500)
PHONE..................740 397-9191
EMP: 9 **EST:** 2019
SALES (est): 740.43K **Privately Held**
Web: www.ellisbros.net
SIC: 3273 Ready-mixed concrete

(G-11273)
INTERNATIONAL PAPER COMPANY
International Paper
8800 Granville Rd (43050-9192)
PHONE..................740 397-5215
Mark Smith, *Brnch Mgr*
EMP: 53
SALES (corp-wide): 18.92B **Publicly Held**
Web: www.internationalpaper.com
SIC: 2621 Paper mills
PA: International Paper Company
6400 Poplar Ave
Memphis TN 38197
901 419-7000

(G-11274)
JELD-WEN INC
Also Called: Jeld-Wen Windows
1201 Newark Rd (43050-4728)

PHONE..................740 397-1144
Brad Hunter, *Mgr*
EMP: 189
Web: www.jeld-wen.com
SIC: 2431 Doors, wood
HQ: Jeld-Wen, Inc.
  2645 Silver Crescent Dr
  Charlotte NC 28273
  800 535-3936

(G-11275)
JELD-WEN INC
335 Commerce Dr (43050-4643)
PHONE..................740 397-3403
Ted Schnormeier, *Brnch Mgr*
EMP: 8
Web: www.jeld-wen.com
SIC: 2431 Doors, wood
HQ: Jeld-Wen, Inc.
  2645 Silver Crescent Dr
  Charlotte NC 28273
  800 535-3936

(G-11276)
KNOX MACHINE & TOOL
250 Columbus Rd (43050-4428)
PHONE..................740 392-3133
Korby Bricker, *Pr*
Trent Hauke, *Sec*
EMP: 9 **EST:** 1994
SALES (est): 706.41K **Privately Held**
SIC: 3599 Machine shop, jobbing and repair

(G-11277)
MACK INDUSTRIES INC
400 Howard St (43050-3547)
PHONE..................740 393-1121
EMP: 9
SALES (corp-wide): 134.58MM **Privately Held**
Web: www.mackconcrete.com
SIC: 3272 Burial vaults, concrete or precast terrazzo
PA: Mack Industries, Inc.
  1321 Industrial Pkwy N # 500
  Brunswick OH 44212
  330 460-7005

(G-11278)
MARKT LLC
314 W Burgess St (43050-2353)
PHONE..................740 397-5900
Taylor Todd, *Admn*
EMP: 7 **EST:** 2012
SALES (est): 764.04K **Privately Held**
Web: www.marktapparel.com
SIC: 5699 2395 2759 Uniforms and work clothing; Embroidery and art needlework; Screen printing

(G-11279)
MOHAWK MANUFACTURING INC
306 E Gambier St (43050-3514)
PHONE..................860 632-2345
Walter Nacey, *Pr*
EMP: 8 **EST:** 1996
SALES (est): 626.5K **Privately Held**
SIC: 3469 Stamping metal for the trade

(G-11280)
MOUNT VERNON PACKAGING INC
135 Progress Dr (43050-4772)
P.O. Box 950 (43050-0950)
PHONE..................740 397-3221
Donald Nuce, *Pr*
Margo Nuce, *VP*
EMP: 10 **EST:** 1971
SALES (est): 2.2MM **Privately Held**
Web: www.mountvernonpackaging.com
SIC: 2653 Boxes, corrugated: made from purchased materials

(G-11281)
MT VERNON CY WASTEWATER TRTMNT
3 Cougar Dr Unit 3 (43050-3866)
PHONE..................740 393-9502
Judi Scott, *Admn*
EMP: 6 **EST:** 2002
SALES (est): 253.96K **Privately Held**
Web: www.mountvernonohio.org
SIC: 3589 Water treatment equipment, industrial

(G-11282)
MT VERNON MACHINE & TOOL INC
Also Called: Mount Vernon Steel
8585 Blackjack Road Ext (43050-2782)
PHONE..................740 397-0311
EMP: 50
Web: www.mltwmachine.com
SIC: 3599 5999 Machine shop, jobbing and repair; Welding supplies

(G-11283)
OHIO TRUCK EQUIPMENT LLC
8920 Columbus Rd (43050-4405)
PHONE..................740 830-6488
EMP: 10 **EST:** 2015
SALES (est): 647.22K **Privately Held**
Web: www.robertsontruckgroup.com
SIC: 5531 3537 Auto and truck equipment and parts; Trucks, tractors, loaders, carriers, and similar equipment

(G-11284)
OWENS CORNING SALES LLC
Also Called: Owens Corning
100 Blackjack Road Ext (43050-9194)
PHONE..................614 399-3915
Bob Demory, *Mgr*
EMP: 12
SIC: 2621 3296 Building paper, insulation; Mineral wool
HQ: Owens Corning Sales, Llc
  1 Owens Corning Pkwy
  Toledo OH 43659
  419 248-8000

(G-11285)
PACS INDUSTRIES INC
8405 Blackjack Rd (43050-2781)
PHONE..................740 397-5021
▲ **EMP:** 100
SIC: 3613 3823 Switchgear and switchgear accessories, nec; Process control instruments

(G-11286)
PAGE ONE GROUP
10 E Vine St Ste C (43050-3244)
PHONE..................740 397-4240
Jana Burson, *Pt*
EMP: 7 **EST:** 1944
SQ FT: 800
SALES (est): 650.24K **Privately Held**
Web: www.pageonegroup.net
SIC: 2752 8742 Offset printing; Marketing consulting services

(G-11287)
PERFORMACE DIESEL INC
16901 Mcvay Rd (43050)
PHONE..................740 392-3693
Stephen Harsany, *Pr*
Angel Harsany, *Sec*
EMP: 10 **EST:** 1991
SQ FT: 7,000
SALES (est): 994.86K **Privately Held**
Web: www.purrformancediesel.com
SIC: 3519 Diesel engine rebuilding

(G-11288)
POTEMKIN INDUSTRIES INC (PA)
8043 Columbus Rd (43050-9358)
PHONE..................740 397-4888
Horst Krajenski, *Pr*
Debbie Hamilton, *
EMP: 19 **EST:** 1980
SQ FT: 14,000
SALES (est): 3.13MM
SALES (corp-wide): 3.13MM **Privately Held**
Web: www.global-compression.com
SIC: 3563 Air and gas compressors including vacuum pumps

(G-11289)
PRINTING ARTS PRESS INC
8028 Newark Rd (43050-8155)
P.O. Box 431 (43050-0431)
PHONE..................740 397-6106
Robert Vogt, *Pr*
Rhonda Gherman, *Ex Dir*
Charles Gherman, *Mgr*
EMP: 10 **EST:** 1945
SQ FT: 15,000
SALES (est): 981.41K **Privately Held**
Web: www.printingartspress.com
SIC: 2752 2791 Offset printing; Typesetting

(G-11290)
PROGRSSIVE COMMUNICATIONS CORP
Also Called: Mount Vernon News
18 E Vine St (43050-3226)
P.O. Box 791 (43050-0791)
PHONE..................740 397-5333
Kay H Culbertson, *Pr*
Michelle L Hartman, *
Elizabeth Lutwick, *
EMP: 51 **EST:** 1838
SQ FT: 30,000
SALES (est): 974.85K **Privately Held**
Web: www.mountvernonnews.com
SIC: 2711 2752 2791 Commercial printing and newspaper publishing combined; Offset printing; Typesetting

(G-11291)
REPLEX MIRROR COMPANY
Also Called: Replex Plastics
11 Mount Vernon Ave (43050-4163)
PHONE..................740 397-5535
Mark Schuetz, *Pr*
◆ **EMP:** 21 **EST:** 1991
SQ FT: 100,000
SALES (est): 4.77MM **Privately Held**
Web: www.replex.com
SIC: 3089 Thermoformed finished plastics products, nec

(G-11292)
ROLLS-ROYCE ENERGY SYSTEMS INC
105 N Sandusky St (43050-2447)
PHONE..................703 834-1700
◆ **EMP:** 1000
SIC: 3511 5084 8711 Turbines and turbine generator sets; Compressors, except air conditioning; Engineering services

(G-11293)
ROYAL METAL PRODUCTS LLC
Also Called: Heating & Cooling Products
325 Commerce Dr (43050-4643)
PHONE..................740 397-8842
EMP: 160
SALES (corp-wide): 3.83B **Privately Held**
Web: www.johnsoncontrols.com
SIC: 3444 3585 3312 Sheet metalwork; Refrigeration and heating equipment; Blast furnaces and steel mills
HQ: Royal Metal Products, Llc
  100 Royal Way
  Temple GA 30179

(G-11294)
SIEMENS ENERGY INC
607 W Chestnut St (43050-2335)
PHONE..................740 393-8200
EMP: 32
SALES (corp-wide): 33.81B **Privately Held**
Web: www.siemens.com
SIC: 3661 Telephones and telephone apparatus
HQ: Siemens Energy, Inc.
  4400 N Alafaya Trl
  Orlando FL 32826
  407 736-2000

(G-11295)
SIEMENS ENERGY INC
105 N Sandusky St (43050-2447)
PHONE..................740 393-8897
EMP: 32
SALES (corp-wide): 33.81B **Privately Held**
Web: www.siemens.com
SIC: 1629 1731 3511 Power plant construction; Energy management controls; Turbines and turbine generator sets
HQ: Siemens Energy, Inc.
  4400 N Alafaya Trl
  Orlando FL 32826
  407 736-2000

(G-11296)
SIEMENS ENERGY INC
Also Called: Siemens Power and Gas
105 N Sandusky St (43050-2447)
PHONE..................740 504-1947
Steven Charles Conner, *CEO*
EMP: 39
SALES (corp-wide): 33.81B **Privately Held**
Web: www.siemens.com
SIC: 3511 Steam turbines
HQ: Siemens Energy, Inc.
  4400 N Alafaya Trl
  Orlando FL 32826
  407 736-2000

(G-11297)
STRAWSER STEEL DRUM OHIO LTD
219 Commerce Dr (43050-4645)
PHONE..................614 856-5982
Brad Strawser, *Genl Pt*
EMP: 25 **EST:** 1985
SQ FT: 70,000
SALES (est): 4.94MM **Privately Held**
SIC: 3412 Metal barrels, drums, and pails

(G-11298)
UNITED PRECAST INC
400 Howard St (43050-3547)
PHONE..................740 393-1121
TOLL FREE: 800
John P Ellis, *Genl Mgr*
John D Ellis, *
George Ellis, *Stockholder*
Linda Ellis, *Stockholder*
EMP: 226 **EST:** 1970
SQ FT: 4,000
SALES (est): 18.92MM **Privately Held**
Web: www.unitedprecast.net
SIC: 3272 Concrete products, precast, nec

(G-11299)
VER-MAC INDUSTRIES INC
100 Progress Dr (43050-4700)
PHONE..................740 397-6511
Dennis Mcelroy, *Pr*

Mount Vernon - Knox County (G-11300)

Mitch Durbin, *
William D Heichel, *
▲ **EMP:** 40 **EST:** 1985
SQ FT: 26,000
SALES (est): 9.44MM **Privately Held**
Web: www.ver-macindustries.com
SIC: 3599 3496 3449 Machine shop, jobbing and repair; Miscellaneous fabricated wire products; Miscellaneous metalwork

(G-11300)
WEYERHAEUSER CO CONTAINEERBOAR
8800 Granville Rd (43050-9192)
PHONE.................................740 397-5215
Larry Tignor, *Prin*
EMP: 10 **EST:** 2009
SALES (est): 169.74K **Privately Held**
SIC: 2653 Boxes, corrugated: made from purchased materials

Mount Victory
Hardin County

(G-11301)
NATURES HEALTH FOOD LLC
21561 County Road 190 (43340-8827)
PHONE.................................419 260-9265
Tony Siebeneck, *Managing Member*
EMP: 11 **EST:** 2016
SALES (est): 500K **Privately Held**
SIC: 5149 2099 7389 Honey; Maple syrup; Business Activities at Non-Commercial Site

(G-11302)
RAVENWORKS DEER SKIN
34477 Shertzer Rd (43340-9615)
P.O. Box 6 (43340-0006)
PHONE.................................937 354-5151
Charles Harris, *Pt*
Nina Harris, *Pt*
EMP: 6 **EST:** 1970
SALES (est): 317.31K **Privately Held**
SIC: 3171 3172 Women's handbags and purses; Personal leather goods, nec

Munroe Falls
Summit County

(G-11303)
M S B MACHINE INC
36 Castle Dr (44262-1602)
PHONE.................................330 686-7740
Jim Burkart, *Pr*
EMP: 6 **EST:** 2004
SQ FT: 3,880
SALES (est): 464.52K **Privately Held**
SIC: 3599 Machine shop, jobbing and repair

(G-11304)
PHOENIX GRPHICS COMMUNICATIONS
99 Laurel Blvd (44262-1677)
PHONE.................................330 697-4171
Robert Rohrich, *Prin*
EMP: 8 **EST:** 2010
SALES (est): 162.71K **Privately Held**
SIC: 2752 Offset printing

(G-11305)
SONOCO PRODUCTS COMPANY
59 N Main St (44262-1064)
P.O. Box 217 (44262-0217)
PHONE.................................330 688-8247
John Parman, *Mgr*
EMP: 49
SALES (corp-wide): 6.78B **Publicly Held**

Web: www.sonoco.com
SIC: 2631 2655 Paperboard mills; Fiber cans, drums, and similar products
PA: Sonoco Products Company
1 N 2nd St
Hartsville SC 29550
843 383-7000

(G-11306)
SUPERIOR MOLD & DIE CO
449 N Main St (44262-1007)
PHONE.................................330 688-8251
Richard Yamokoski, *Pr*
Richard Yamokoski, *Pr*
Gale Young, *
Jeffery Yamokoski, *
EMP: 15 **EST:** 1943
SQ FT: 43,000
SALES (est): 2.73MM **Privately Held**
Web: www.s-m-d.us
SIC: 3544 3599 Industrial molds; Machine shop, jobbing and repair

(G-11307)
VADOSE SYN FUELS INC
323 S Main St (44262-1658)
PHONE.................................330 564-0545
EMP: 8 **EST:** 2008
SALES (est): 135.79K **Privately Held**
SIC: 2869 Fuels

Napoleon
Henry County

(G-11308)
ADVANCED DRAINAGE SYSTEMS INC
1075 Independence Dr (43545-9717)
PHONE.................................419 599-9565
Jason Hartland, *Mgr*
EMP: 23
SQ FT: 14,000
SALES (corp-wide): 3.07B **Publicly Held**
Web: www.adspipe.com
SIC: 3084 3083 Plastics pipe; Laminated plastics plate and sheet
PA: Advanced Drainage Systems, Inc.
4640 Trueman Blvd
Hilliard OH 43026
614 658-0050

(G-11309)
C&C FABRICATION LLC
13226 County Road R (43545-5966)
PHONE.................................419 592-1408
EMP: 13 **EST:** 2017
SALES (est): 2.09MM **Privately Held**
SIC: 3441 Fabricated structural metal

(G-11310)
CARSON INDUSTRIES LLC
1675 Industrial Dr (43545-9734)
PHONE.................................419 592-2309
Rich Gordinier, *Prin*
EMP: 8 **EST:** 2009
SALES (est): 219.22K **Privately Held**
SIC: 3089 Injection molding of plastics

(G-11311)
CUSTAR STONE CO
9072 County Road 424 (43545)
P.O. Box 607 (43545)
PHONE.................................419 669-4327
Brent Gerken, *Pr*
Mike Gerken, *VP*
Jon Myers, *Sec*
Julian Gerken, *Stockholder*
EMP: 33 **EST:** 1994
SQ FT: 3,000

SALES (est): 1.15MM **Privately Held**
Web: www.gerkencompanies.com
SIC: 1422 Crushed and broken limestone

(G-11312)
DEFIANCE STAMPING CO
800 Independence Dr (43545-9192)
PHONE.................................419 782-5781
Tony Stuart, *Pr*
Joe Harmon, *
Dennis Maude, *
Brian Callan, *
▲ **EMP:** 65 **EST:** 1927
SQ FT: 60,000
SALES (est): 10.45MM **Privately Held**
Web: www.defiancestamping.com
SIC: 3469 Stamping metal for the trade

(G-11313)
FORKLIFT SOLUTIONS LLC
425 Oxford St (43545-2068)
PHONE.................................419 717-9490
Ernie Franz, *Prin*
EMP: 7 **EST:** 2016
SALES (est): 62.68K **Privately Held**
SIC: 3537 Forklift trucks

(G-11314)
GAZETTE PUBLISHING COMPANY
Also Called: Fulton County Expositor
595 E Riverview Ave (43545-1865)
P.O. Box 376 (43567-0376)
PHONE.................................419 335-2010
Janice May, *Mgr*
EMP: 69
SALES (corp-wide): 4.39MM **Privately Held**
Web: www.northwestsignal.net
SIC: 7313 5994 2711 Newspaper advertising representative; Newsstand; Newspapers
PA: The Gazette Publishing Company
42 S Main St
Oberlin OH

(G-11315)
GERKEN MATERIALS INC (PA)
9072 County Road 424 (43545-9732)
P.O. Box 607 (43545-0607)
PHONE.................................419 533-2421
EMP: 50 **EST:** 1959
SALES (est): 46.53MM
SALES (corp-wide): 46.53MM **Privately Held**
Web: www.gerkencompanies.com
SIC: 1611 2951 Highway and street paving contractor; Asphalt and asphaltic paving mixtures (not from refineries)

(G-11316)
GILSON MACHINE & TOOL CO INC
529 Freedom Dr (43545-5945)
PHONE.................................419 592-2911
William E Gilson Junior, *Pr*
Glen Gilson, *Sec*
EMP: 20 **EST:** 1946
SQ FT: 11,000
SALES (est): 2.47MM **Privately Held**
Web: www.gilsonmachine.com
SIC: 3599 7692 3549 3544 Machine shop, jobbing and repair; Welding repair; Metalworking machinery, nec; Special dies, tools, jigs, and fixtures

(G-11317)
HIGH PRODUCTION TECHNOLOGY LLC
13068 County Road R (43545-5964)
PHONE.................................419 599-1511
Marlow Witt, *Brnch Mgr*
EMP: 8
Web: www.automaticfeed.com

SIC: 3542 Machine tools, metal forming type
HQ: High Production Technology, Llc
476 E Riverview Ave
Napoleon OH 43545
419 591-7000

(G-11318)
HIGH PRODUCTION TECHNOLOGY LLC (DH)
476 E Riverview Ave (43545-1855)
PHONE.................................419 591-7000
EMP: 15 **EST:** 1997
SQ FT: 6,000
SALES (est): 10.2MM **Privately Held**
Web: www.automaticfeed.com
SIC: 3542 3441 Presses: hydraulic and pneumatic, mechanical and manual; Fabricated structural metal
HQ: Automatic Feed Co.
476 E Riverview Ave
Napoleon OH 43545
419 592-0050

(G-11319)
HOLGATE METAL FAB INC
555 Independence Dr (43545-9656)
PHONE.................................419 599-2000
Jeff Spangler, *Pr*
Denise Spangler, *VP*
EMP: 15 **EST:** 1987
SQ FT: 16,000
SALES (est): 2.03MM **Privately Held**
Web: www.holgatemetalfab.com
SIC: 1711 1761 3444 3441 Boiler maintenance contractor; Sheet metal work, nec; Sheet metalwork; Fabricated structural metal

(G-11320)
INNOVATIVE TOOL & DIE INC
1700 Industrial Dr (43545-9282)
PHONE.................................419 599-0492
EMP: 8 **EST:** 1992
SQ FT: 5,000
SALES (est): 961.92K **Privately Held**
Web: www.innovative-tool.com
SIC: 3544 3599 Special dies and tools; Machine and other job shop work

(G-11321)
ISOFOTON NORTH AMERICA INC
800 Independence Dr (43545-9192)
PHONE.................................419 591-4330
▲ **EMP:** 10 **EST:** 2011
SALES (est): 957.32K **Privately Held**
SIC: 3674 Solar cells

(G-11322)
KOESTER CORPORATION (PA)
813 N Perry St (43545-1521)
PHONE.................................419 599-0291
Michael Koester, *Pr*
Jeanette Spiller, *
EMP: 40 **EST:** 1970
SQ FT: 40,000
SALES (est): 9.39MM
SALES (corp-wide): 9.39MM **Privately Held**
Web: www.koester-corp.com
SIC: 3569 3823 3613 Lubricating equipment; Pressure measurement instruments, industrial; Control panels, electric

(G-11323)
M & S AG SOLUTIONS LLC
Also Called: Paul Martin and Sons
755 American Rd (43545-6301)
PHONE.................................419 598-8675
Doug Martin, *Managing Member*
EMP: 13 **EST:** 2015
SALES (est): 1.47MM **Privately Held**

Web: www.martinequipment.net
SIC: 5999 3523 Farm equipment and supplies; Farm machinery and equipment

(G-11324)
MIDWEST WOOD TRIM INC
1650 Commerce Dr (43545-6726)
PHONE..................................419 592-3389
Brad Westhoven, *Pr*
Eugene Westhoven, *
EMP: 35 EST: 1984
SQ FT: 40,000
SALES (est): 2.82MM **Privately Held**
SIC: 2431 Moldings, wood: unfinished and prefinished

(G-11325)
MUSTANG PRINTING
Also Called: Turkeyfoot Printing
119 W Washington St (43545-1739)
P.O. Box 413 (43567-0413)
PHONE..................................419 592-2746
Jerry Dehnbostel, *Pr*
EMP: 10
SQ FT: 4,800
SALES (est): 1.44MM **Privately Held**
SIC: 2759 Commercial printing, nec
HQ: Mustang Corporation
    229 N Fulton St
    Wauseon OH
    419 335-9070

(G-11326)
NAPOLEON INC
Also Called: Northwest Signal
595 E Riverview Ave (43545-1865)
P.O. Box 567 (43545-0567)
PHONE..................................419 592-5055
Christopher Cullis, *Pr*
EMP: 19 EST: 1852
SQ FT: 7,200
SALES (est): 462.54K **Privately Held**
Web: www.northwestsignal.net
SIC: 2711 Newspapers, publishing and printing

(G-11327)
NAPOLEON MACHINE LLC
476 E Riverview Ave (43545-1855)
PHONE..................................419 591-7010
EMP: 35 EST: 2010
SALES (est): 5.59MM **Privately Held**
Web: www.napoleonmachine.com
SIC: 1721 3599 Commercial painting; Machine and other job shop work

(G-11328)
OKOLONA IRON & METAL LLC
18641 County Rd N (43545-6722)
PHONE..................................419 758-3701
Kevin Moore, *Mgr*
EMP: 12 EST: 2011
SALES (est): 1.02MM **Privately Held**
SIC: 3446 Ornamental metalwork

(G-11329)
OLDCASTLE INFRASTRUCTURE INC
1675 Industrial Dr (43545-9734)
PHONE..................................419 592-2309
EMP: 35
SALES (corp-wide): 32.72B **Privately Held**
Web: www.oldcastleinfrastructure.com
SIC: 3272 Concrete products, nec
HQ: Oldcastle Infrastructure, Inc.
    7000 Central Pkwy Ste 800
    Atlanta GA 30328
    770 270-5000

(G-11330)
PANDROL INC
25 Interstate Dr (43545-9714)
P.O. Box 69 (43545-0069)
PHONE..................................419 592-5050
David C Barrett Junior, *Prin*
◆ EMP: 61 EST: 1983
SQ FT: 60,000
SALES (est): 26.79MM
SALES (corp-wide): 2.67MM **Privately Held**
Web: www.railtechboutet.com
SIC: 3355 Rails, rolled and drawn, aluminum
HQ: Delachaux Sa
    307 Rue D Estienne D Orves
    Colombes 92700
    146881500

(G-11331)
PULLMAN COMPANY
Also Called: Tenneco
11800 County Road 424 (43545-5778)
PHONE..................................419 592-2055
Tom Weaver, *Bmch Mgr*
EMP: 204
SQ FT: 220,000
SALES (corp-wide): 18.04B **Privately Held**
Web: www.tenneco.com
SIC: 3714 Motor vehicle engines and parts
HQ: The Pullman Company
    1 International Dr
    Monroe MI 48161
    734 243-8000

(G-11332)
RAILTECH MATWELD INC
15 Interstate Dr (43545-9714)
PHONE..................................419 592-5055
Oliver Dolder, *Pr*
EMP: 41
SALES (corp-wide): 2.67MM **Privately Held**
Web: www.matweld.com
SIC: 2899 Chemical preparations, nec
HQ: Railtech Matweld, Inc.
    25 Interstate Dr
    Napoleon OH 43545

(G-11333)
RSV WLDING FBRCTION MCHNING IN
M063 County Road 12 (43545-9366)
P.O. Box 430 (43545-0430)
PHONE..................................419 592-0993
Ralph F Vocke, *Pr*
Randy Vocke, *VP*
Steve Vocke, *Sec*
EMP: 10 EST: 1979
SQ FT: 10,400
SALES (est): 734.28K **Privately Held**
SIC: 3441 7692 Fabricated structural metal; Welding repair

(G-11334)
SCOTT PORT-A-FOLD INC
5963 State Route 110 (43545-9332)
P.O. Box 177 (43502-0177)
PHONE..................................419 748-8880
James Lammy Junior, *Pr*
James E Lammy Junior, *Pr*
▲ EMP: 16 EST: 1949
SQ FT: 45,000
SALES (est): 270.25K **Privately Held**
SIC: 3086 3531 Plastics foam products; Construction machinery

Nashport
Muskingum County

(G-11335)
BDP SERVICES INC
Also Called: Sports Art
8255 Blackrun Rd (43830-9774)
PHONE..................................740 828-9685
Stephen Baum, *Pr*
Vince Paul, *Sec*
EMP: 8 EST: 1990
SQ FT: 28,000
SALES (est): 418.47K **Privately Held**
Web: www.sportsart-online.com
SIC: 2396 2395 Screen printing on fabric articles; Embroidery products, except Schiffli machine

(G-11336)
DARIN JORDAN
3460 Gorsuch Rd (43830-9492)
PHONE..................................740 819-3525
Darin Jordan, *Prin*
EMP: 9 EST: 2010
SALES (est): 602.88K **Privately Held**
SIC: 1389 Oil field services, nec

(G-11337)
HANBY FARMS INC
10790 Newark Rd (43830-9066)
P.O. Box 97 (43830-0097)
PHONE..................................740 763-3554
Ralph Hanby, *Pr*
Doug Hanby, *
David R Hanby, *
Carol Hanby, *
EMP: 40 EST: 1960
SQ FT: 10,000
SALES (est): 5.16MM **Privately Held**
Web: www.performancefeed.com
SIC: 2048 5153 5191 Livestock feeds; Corn; Fertilizer and fertilizer materials

(G-11338)
HERITAGE COOPERATIVE INC
10790 Newark Rd (43830-9066)
PHONE..................................740 828-2215
EMP: 12
Web: www.heritagecooperative.com
SIC: 2032 2099 Canned specialties; Food preparations, nec
PA: Heritage Cooperative, Inc.
    59 Greif Pkwy Ste 200
    Delaware OH 43015

(G-11339)
MUSCLE FEAST LLC (PA)
1320 Boston Rd (43830-9603)
PHONE..................................740 877-8808
▲ EMP: 10 EST: 2009
SQ FT: 16,000
SALES (est): 3.52MM **Privately Held**
Web: www.musclefeast.com
SIC: 5149 2023 Health foods; Dietary supplements, dairy and non-dairy based

Navarre
Stark County

(G-11340)
B & S TRANSPORT INC (PA)
11325 Lawndell Rd Sw (44662-8804)
P.O. Box 2678 (44720-0678)
PHONE..................................330 767-4319
Ronald Harris, *Pr*
Irvin Jackson, *VP*
EMP: 9 EST: 1977
SQ FT: 6,000
SALES (est): 1.55MM
SALES (corp-wide): 1.55MM **Privately Held**
SIC: 3011 5014 5052 5045 Tires and inner tubes; Tires and tubes; Coal and other minerals and ores; Computers, peripherals, and software

(G-11341)
FAR CORNER
13189 Mount Eaton St Sw (44662-9476)
P.O. Box 92 (44613-0092)
PHONE..................................330 767-3734
EMP: 6
SALES (est): 452.61K **Privately Held**
Web: www.farcorner-online.com
SIC: 2752 Commercial printing, lithographic

(G-11342)
GENCRAFT DESIGNS LLC
7412 Massillon Rd Sw (44662-9318)
PHONE..................................330 359-6251
Paul Swartzentruber, *Prin*
EMP: 27 EST: 1988
SQ FT: 7,200
SALES (est): 1.06MM **Privately Held**
Web: www.gencraftdesigns.com
SIC: 2511 7389 Wood household furniture; Design services

(G-11343)
GOJO INDUSTRIES INC
4676 Erie Ave Sw (44662-9658)
PHONE..................................330 255-6000
EMP: 7
SALES (corp-wide): 425.22MM **Privately Held**
Web: www.gojo.com
SIC: 2842 Polishes and sanitation goods
PA: Gojo Industries, Inc.
    1 Gojo Plz Ste 500
    Akron OH 44311
    330 255-6000

(G-11344)
IMAGINE THIS RENOVATIONS
4220 Alabama Ave Sw (44662-9618)
PHONE..................................330 833-6739
EMP: 8 EST: 2009
SALES (est): 369.2K **Privately Held**
SIC: 2759 Commercial printing, nec

(G-11345)
MASSILLON CONTAINER CO
49 Ohio St Sw (44662-1183)
PHONE..................................330 879-5653
EMP: 46 EST: 1949
SALES (est): 18.03MM
SALES (corp-wide): 18.03MM **Privately Held**
Web: www.vailpkg.com
SIC: 2653 Corrugated and solid fiber boxes
PA: Vail Industries, Inc.
    49 Ohio St Sw
    Navarre OH
    330 879-5653

(G-11346)
MILLER WELDMASTER CORPORATION (PA)
4220 Alabama Ave Sw (44662-9618)
PHONE..................................330 833-6739
Brent Nussbaum, *Pr*
Jeff Dimos, *
◆ EMP: 88 EST: 1973
SQ FT: 20,000
SALES (est): 18.64MM
SALES (corp-wide): 18.64MM **Privately Held**
Web: www.weldmaster.com

Navarre - Stark County (G-11347)

(G-11347)
MYSTA EQUIPMENT CO
6434 Werstler Ave Sw (44662-9140)
PHONE..................................330 879-5353
Stanley Josefczyk, *Owner*
EMP: 6 **EST:** 1983
SALES (est): 352.51K **Privately Held**
SIC: 3599 Machine and other job shop work

(G-11348)
OWENS CORNING
9318 Erie Ave Sw (44662-9448)
PHONE..................................419 248-8000
Jeannie Bender, *VP*
EMP: 6
Web: www.owenscorning.com
SIC: 3296 Fiberglass insulation
PA: Owens Corning
1 Owens Corning Pkwy
Toledo OH 43659

(G-11349)
PERENNIAL VINEYARDS LLC
11877 Poorman St Sw (44662-9683)
PHONE..................................330 832-3677
Damon Leeman, *Owner*
EMP: 10 **EST:** 2002
SQ FT: 10,000
SALES (est): 564.88K **Privately Held**
Web: www.thewineryatperennialvineyards.com
SIC: 2084 Wines

(G-11350)
PREMIER PALLET AND RECYCL INC
11361 Lawndell Ave Sw (44662)
P.O. Box 31 (44613)
PHONE..................................330 767-2221
Pete Grove, *Pr*
EMP: 11 **EST:** 2004
SALES (est): 356.64K **Privately Held**
Web: www.premierpallet.net
SIC: 2448 Pallets, wood

(G-11351)
PT METALS LLC
10384 Navarre Rd Sw (44662-9462)
PHONE..................................330 767-3003
Paul Miller, *
EMP: 25 **EST:** 2019
SALES (est): 1.02MM **Privately Held**
SIC: 3699 Laser welding, drilling, and cutting equipment

(G-11352)
RC INDUSTRIES INC
Also Called: Mid's Spaghetti Sauce
620 Main St N (44662-8556)
P.O. Box 5 (44662-0005)
PHONE..................................330 879-5486
Scott Ricketts, *Pr*
Steve Cress, *
EMP: 25 **EST:** 1964
SQ FT: 10,000
SALES (est): 4.93MM **Privately Held**
Web: www.midssauce.com
SIC: 2033 2035 Spaghetti and other pasta sauce: packaged in cans, jars, etc; Pickles, sauces, and salad dressings

(G-11353)
TERYDON INC
7260 Erie Ave Sw (44662-8807)
PHONE..................................330 879-2448
EMP: 40 **EST:** 1994
SQ FT: 800
SALES (est): 2.14MM

SALES (corp-wide): 24.28MM **Privately Held**
Web: www.stoneagetools.com
SIC: 3599 Custom machinery
PA: Stoneage, Inc.
466 S Skylane Dr Unit A
Durango CO 81303
970 259-2869

Negley
Columbiana County

(G-11354)
MAGNECO/METREL INC
51365 State Route 154 (44441-9728)
P.O. Box 176 (44441-0176)
PHONE..................................330 426-9468
Paul Painter, *Bmch Mgr*
EMP: 97
SALES (corp-wide): 52.06MM **Privately Held**
Web: www.magneco-metrel.com
SIC: 3255 3297 Clay refractories; Nonclay refractories
PA: Magneco/Metrel, Inc.
740 Waukegan Rd Ste 212
Deerfield IL 60015
630 543-6660

(G-11355)
X L SAND AND GRAVEL CO
9289 Jackman Rd (44441)
P.O. Box 255 (44441-0255)
PHONE..................................330 426-9876
Raymond Lansberry, *Pr*
James Lansberry, *Treas*
EMP: 26 **EST:** 1969
SQ FT: 1,000
SALES (est): 2.4MM **Privately Held**
Web: www.xlsandandgravel.com
SIC: 1442 Common sand mining

Nelsonville
Athens County

(G-11356)
GEORGIA-BOOT INC
Also Called: Durango Boot
39 E Canal St (45764-1247)
PHONE..................................740 753-1951
Gerald M Cohn, *CEO*
Thomas R Morrison, *Pr*
EMP: 100 **EST:** 1937
SALES (est): 16.82MM **Privately Held**
Web: www.georgiaboot.com
SIC: 5139 3144 3143 3021 Shoes; Women's footwear, except athletic; Men's footwear, except athletic; Rubber and plastics footwear

(G-11357)
MIDWEST FUEL LLC
1155 Chestnut St (45764)
PHONE..................................740 753-5960
EMP: 6 **EST:** 2011
SALES (est): 132.11K **Privately Held**
SIC: 2869 Fuels

(G-11358)
MILOS WHOLE WORLD GOURMET LLC
296 S Harper St (45764-1600)
PHONE..................................740 589-6456
Jonathan Leal, *Managing Member*
EMP: 9 **EST:** 2003
SALES (est): 2.31MM **Privately Held**
Web: www.miloswholeworld.com

SIC: 1541 2033 Food products manufacturing or packing plant construction; Canned fruits and specialties

(G-11359)
ROCKY BRANDS INC (PA)
39 E Canal St (45764-1247)
PHONE..................................740 753-9100
Jason Brooks, *Ch Bd*
Thomas D Robertson, *CFO*
Curtis A Loveland, *
EMP: 257 **EST:** 1932
SQ FT: 24,400
SALES (est): 461.83MM
SALES (corp-wide): 461.83MM **Publicly Held**
Web: www.rockybrands.com
SIC: 3143 3144 2329 2331 Men's footwear, except athletic; Women's footwear, except athletic; Men's and boys' sportswear and athletic clothing; Women's and misses' blouses and shirts

(G-11360)
US FOOTWEAR HOLDINGS LLC
39 E Canal St (45764-1247)
PHONE..................................740 753-9100
Jason S Brooks, *Managing Member*
EMP: 121 **EST:** 2020
SALES (est): 47.44MM
SALES (corp-wide): 461.83MM **Publicly Held**
SIC: 5139 3021 Footwear; Rubber and plastics footwear
PA: Rocky Brands, Inc.
39 E Canal St
Nelsonville OH 45764
740 753-9100

Nevada
Wyandot County

(G-11361)
SHOOT-A-WAY INC
7157 County Highway 134 (44849-9753)
PHONE..................................419 294-4654
John Joseph, *Pr*
EMP: 10 **EST:** 1990
SALES (est): 2.11MM **Privately Held**
Web: www.shootaway.com
SIC: 5699 3949 7389 Sports apparel; Team sports equipment; Advertising, promotional, and trade show services

(G-11362)
STIGER PRE CAST INC
17793 State Highway 231 (44849)
PHONE..................................740 482-2313
TOLL FREE: 800
Jim Riedlinger, *Pr*
Eva Mae Riedlinger, *VP*
Cathy Scheffler, *Sec*
EMP: 8 **EST:** 1943
SQ FT: 2,200
SALES (est): 931.2K **Privately Held**
Web: www.stigerprecast.com
SIC: 3272 3271 Septic tanks, concrete; Blocks, concrete or cinder: standard

New Albany
Franklin County

(G-11363)
614 CUPCAKES LLC
4045 Chelsea Grn W (43054-6027)
PHONE..................................614 245-8800
EMP: 6 **EST:** 2012
SALES (est): 529.93K **Privately Held**

SIC: 2051 Bread, cake, and related products

(G-11364)
ALENE CANDLES MIDWEST LLC
8860 Smiths Mill Rd Ste 100 (43054-6654)
PHONE..................................614 933-4005
EMP: 14 **EST:** 2011
SALES (est): 2.06MM **Privately Held**
Web: www.alene.com
SIC: 3999 Candles

(G-11365)
AMERICAN REGENT INC
6610 New Albany Rd E (43054-8730)
PHONE..................................614 436-2222
Joseph Kenneth Keller, *CEO*
EMP: 98
Web: www.americanregent.com
SIC: 2834 Pharmaceutical preparations
HQ: American Regent, Inc.
5 Ramsay Rd
Shirley NY 11967
631 924-4000

(G-11366)
ANOMATIC CORPORATION (DH)
Also Called: Anomatic Opportunity
8880 Innovation Campus Way (43054-6651)
PHONE..................................740 522-2203
William B Rusch, *Pr*
Scott L Rusch, *VP*
◆ **EMP:** 42 **EST:** 1974
SQ FT: 65,000
SALES (est): 100.5MM
SALES (corp-wide): 783.05MM **Privately Held**
Web: www.anomatic.com
SIC: 3471 3469 2396 Anodizing (plating) of metals or formed products; Metal stampings, nec; Automotive and apparel trimmings
HQ: Thyssen'sche Handelsgesellschaft Mit Beschrankter Haftung
Dohne 54
Mulheim An Der Ruhr NW 45468
208992180

(G-11367)
ARCHITECTURAL BUSSTRUT CORP
4311 Brompton Ct (43054-8982)
PHONE..................................614 933-8695
EMP: 10
Web: www.busstrut.com
SIC: 3648 5063 Lighting fixtures, except electric: residential; Lighting fixtures
PA: Architectural Busstrut Corp.
4787 Roberts Rd
Columbus OH 43228

(G-11368)
AROMAIR FINE FRAGRANCE COMPANY
8860 Smiths Mill Rd Ste 500 (43054-6653)
PHONE..................................614 984-2900
Nicholas Whitley, *CEO*
Richard Nihei, *
EMP: 500 **EST:** 2010
SALES (est): 54.85MM
SALES (corp-wide): 1.7B **Privately Held**
Web: www.aromair.com
SIC: 2842 Cleaning or polishing preparations, nec
HQ: Kdc Us Holdings, Inc.
4400 S Hamilton Rd
Groveport OH 43125

(G-11369)
AXIUM PACKAGING LLC (PA)
Also Called: Axium Plastics
9005 Smiths Mill Rd (43054-6650)

GEOGRAPHIC SECTION

New Albany - Franklin County (G-11394)

PHONE.................614 706-5955
EMP: 685 **EST:** 2011
SALES (est): 218.65MM **Privately Held**
Web: www.axiumpackaging.com
SIC: 3089 Plastics containers, except foam

(G-11370)
BOCCHI LABORATORIES OHIO LLC
9200 Smiths Mill Rd N (43054-6703)
PHONE.................614 741-7458
Edward Gotch, *CEO*
Wayne Byrne, *
EMP: 300 **EST:** 2014
SQ FT: 125,000
SALES (est): 78.23MM
SALES (corp-wide): 299.2MM **Privately Held**
Web: www.bocchilabs.com
SIC: 2844 Toilet preparations
PA: Bright Holdco, Llc
9002 Smiths Mill Rd
New Albany OH 43054
614 741-7458

(G-11371)
BRIGHT HOLDCO LLC (PA)
Also Called: Bright Innovation Labs
9002 Smith's Mill Rd N (43054-6647)
PHONE.................614 741-7458
Edward Gotch, *CEO*
Wayne Byrne, *CFO*
EMP: 44 **EST:** 2018
SALES (est): 299.2MM
SALES (corp-wide): 299.2MM **Privately Held**
Web: www.bringhtinnovationlabs.com
SIC: 2844 Face creams or lotions

(G-11372)
CCL LABEL INC
8600 Innovation Campus Way W (43054-7550)
PHONE.................856 273-0700
EMP: 59
SALES (corp-wide): 4.75B **Privately Held**
Web: www.cclind.com
SIC: 2759 Labels and seals: printing, nsk
HQ: Ccl Label, Inc.
161 Worcester Rd Ste 403
Framingham MA 01701
508 872-4511

(G-11373)
CENTRAL OHIO MET STMPING FBRCT
4361 Brompton Ct (43054)
P.O. Box 307776 (43230)
PHONE.................614 861-3332
John Davidson, *Pr*
Lawrence Davidson, *
Pennie Davidson, *
EMP: 25 **EST:** 1986
SALES (est): 4.55MM **Privately Held**
Web: www.centralohiometalstamping.com
SIC: 3469 Stamping metal for the trade

(G-11374)
COMMERCIAL VEHICLE GROUP INC (PA)
7800 Walton Pkwy (43054-8482)
PHONE.................614 289-5360
James Ray, *Pr*
Robert Griffin, *Ch Bd*
Douglas F Bowen, *Sr VP*
Christopher H Bohnert, *CFO*
Kristin Mathers, *Chief Human Resources Officer*
EMP: 391 **EST:** 2000
SALES (est): 994.68MM
SALES (corp-wide): 994.68MM **Publicly Held**

Web: www.cvgrp.com
SIC: 3694 2531 Automotive electrical equipment, nec; Seats, automobile

(G-11375)
COSMETIC TECHNOLOGIES LLC
8825 Smiths Mill Rd (43054-6649)
PHONE.................614 656-1130
Ian Kalinosky, *Prin*
EMP: 6 **EST:** 2015
SALES (est): 141.12K **Privately Held**
SIC: 2844 Depilatories (cosmetic)

(G-11376)
CUSTOM METAL PRODUCTS INC
Also Called: Do All Sheet Metal
5037 Babbitt Rd (43054-8301)
P.O. Box 149 (43054-0149)
PHONE.................614 855-2263
EMP: 10 **EST:** 2007
SQ FT: 24,000
SALES (est): 918.85K **Privately Held**
SIC: 3444 Metal housings, enclosures, casings, and other containers

(G-11377)
CVG NATIONAL SEATING CO LLC
Also Called: C V G
7800 Walton Pkwy (43054-8482)
PHONE.................219 872-7295
▲ **EMP:** 10 **EST:** 1976
SALES (est): 10.58MM
SALES (corp-wide): 994.68MM **Publicly Held**
Web: www.cvgrp.com
SIC: 3714 Motor vehicle parts and accessories
PA: Commercial Vehicle Group, Inc.
7800 Walton Pkwy
New Albany OH 43054
614 289-5360

(G-11378)
DESCO CORPORATION (PA)
7795 Walton Pkwy Ste 175 (43054-0002)
PHONE.................614 888-8855
Arnold B Siemer, *Pr*
Thomas Villano, *VP*
Russell M Gertmenian, *Sec*
Roger Bailey, *Treas*
Barbara J Siemer, *Sec*
EMP: 9 **EST:** 1975
SQ FT: 5,500
SALES (est): 180.13MM
SALES (corp-wide): 180.13MM **Privately Held**
Web: www.descocorporation.com
SIC: 3442 3825 3643 3531 Window and door frames; Instruments to measure electricity; Current-carrying wiring services; Construction machinery

(G-11379)
FORM5 PROSTHETICS INC
6560 New Albany Condit Rd (43054-9734)
PHONE.................614 226-1141
Aaron Westbrook, *CEO*
EMP: 11 **EST:** 2017
SALES (est): 273.93K **Privately Held**
Web: www.form5.org
SIC: 3842 Prosthetic appliances

(G-11380)
ISOCHEM INCORPORATED
3 Highgrove (43054-1106)
PHONE.................614 775-9328
Kevin E Klingerman, *Pr*
▲ **EMP:** 9 **EST:** 2000
SALES (est): 244.28K **Privately Held**
Web: isochemkautschuk.jimdo.com

SIC: 2821 Plastics materials and resins

(G-11381)
JANOVA LLC
7570 N Goodrich Sq (43054-8983)
PHONE.................614 638-6785
Brian Lusenhop, *Product Management Vice-President*
EMP: 6 **EST:** 2010
SALES (est): 230.54K **Privately Held**
Web: www.janova.us
SIC: 7372 Application computer software

(G-11382)
KDC ONE
8825 Smiths Mill Rd (43054-6649)
PHONE.................614 984-2871
EMP: 9
SALES (est): 518.28K **Privately Held**
Web: www.kdc-one.com
SIC: 2844 Cosmetic preparations

(G-11383)
MALIK MEDIA LLC
7591 Lambton Park Rd (43054-8513)
PHONE.................614 933-0328
Samuel Malik, *Prin*
EMP: 10 **EST:** 2016
SALES (est): 391.84K **Privately Held**
Web: www.thinknotable.com
SIC: 7319 2752 8742 7336 Advertising, nec; Commercial printing, lithographic; Marketing consulting services; Commercial art and graphic design

(G-11384)
MUELLER ELECTRIC COMPANY INC
7795 Walton Pkwy Ste 175 (43054-0002)
PHONE.................614 888-8855
Rodger Bailey, *CEO*
EMP: 14 **EST:** 2011
SALES (est): 187.25K **Privately Held**
Web: www.muellerelectric.com
SIC: 3679 3678 3825 Harness assemblies, for electronic use: wire or cable; Electronic connectors; Test equipment for electronic and electric measurement

(G-11385)
NPK LLC
13390 Morse Rd Sw (43054-7916)
P.O. Box 233 (43062-0233)
PHONE.................740 927-2801
Larry A Woodruff, *Prin*
EMP: 7 **EST:** 2009
SALES (est): 325.87K **Privately Held**
Web: www.npkusa.com
SIC: 3556 Smokers, food processing equipment

(G-11386)
OHIO CRAFTED MALT HOUSE LLC
8000 Walton Pkwy Ste 200 (43054-6014)
PHONE.................614 961-7805
EMP: 10 **EST:** 2019
SALES (est): 699.27K **Privately Held**
SIC: 2083 Barley malt

(G-11387)
OHIO HD VIDEO
1355 Bingham Mills Dr (43054-9414)
PHONE.................614 656-1162
Scott Handle, *Owner*
EMP: 11 **EST:** 2010
SALES (est): 486.46K **Privately Held**
SIC: 7841 3651 3861 Video tape rental; Household audio and video equipment; Photographic equipment and supplies

(G-11388)
OWENS FOODS INC
8111 Smiths Mill Rd (43054-1183)
EMP: 290
SIC: 2013 Sausages and related products, from purchased meat

(G-11389)
PWI INC
Also Called: Privacyware
5195 Hampsted Village Center Way (43054-8331)
PHONE.................732 212-8110
Gregory Salvato, *CEO*
EMP: 8 **EST:** 1987
SALES (est): 424.14K **Privately Held**
Web: www.pwiinc.com
SIC: 7372 7371 8742 Prepackaged software; Software programming applications; Corporation organizing consultant

(G-11390)
STICKTITE LENSES LLC ✪
5195 Hampsted Vlg Ctr Way (43054-8331)
PHONE.................571 276-9508
EMP: 10 **EST:** 2022
SALES (est): 555.23K **Privately Held**
SIC: 3851 3827 Lenses, ophthalmic; Optical instruments and lenses

(G-11391)
TRI-TECH LABORATORIES LLC
Also Called: Kdc/One
8825 Smiths Mill Rd (43054-6649)
PHONE.................614 656-1130
Nicholas Whitley, *CEO*
EMP: 173 **EST:** 2017
SALES (est): 21.28MM **Privately Held**
SIC: 2844 Cosmetic preparations

(G-11392)
TRIM SYSTEMS OPERATING CORP (HQ)
Also Called: Cvg Trim Systems
7800 Walton Pkwy (43054-8482)
PHONE.................614 289-5360
Gerald L Armstrong, *Pr*
▲ **EMP:** 80 **EST:** 1997
SALES (est): 106.15MM
SALES (corp-wide): 994.68MM **Publicly Held**
Web: www.cvgrp.com
SIC: 3714 Motor vehicle parts and accessories
PA: Commercial Vehicle Group, Inc.
7800 Walton Pkwy
New Albany OH 43054
614 289-5360

(G-11393)
VEEPAK OH LLC
Also Called: Voyant Beauty
9040 Smiths Mill Rd (43054-6647)
PHONE.................740 927-9002
Gene Sturino, *Prin*
EMP: 11 **EST:** 1991
SALES (est): 1.41MM **Privately Held**
Web: www.voyantbeauty.com
SIC: 2844 Cosmetic preparations

(G-11394)
VERIANO FINE FOODS SPIRITS LTD
5175 Zarley St Ste A (43054)
P.O. Box 617 (43054-0617)
PHONE.................614 745-7705
EMP: 15 **EST:** 2009
SQ FT: 10,000
SALES (est): 732.89K **Privately Held**
Web: www.buytessora.com

(PA)=Parent Co (HQ)=Headquarters
✪ = New Business established in last 2 years

SIC: 2085 5182 Distilled and blended liquors; Liquor

(G-11395)
VETGRAFT LLC
7590 Brandon Rd (43054-9059)
PHONE..................................614 203-0603
EMP: 9 EST: 2017
SALES (est): 190.54K **Privately Held**
Web: www.vetgraft.com
SIC: 2835 Veterinary diagnostic substances

New Boston
Scioto County

(G-11396)
A & M REFRACTORIES INC
202 West Ave (45662-4946)
PHONE..................................740 456-8020
Michael Cartee, Pr
Richard Bobst, VP
EMP: 20 EST: 1991
SQ FT: 60,000
SALES (est): 2.5MM **Privately Held**
Web: 212571.refwin.com
SIC: 3297 Nonclay refractories

(G-11397)
MARTIN MOHR
3521 Rhodes Ave (45662-4917)
PHONE..................................740 727-2233
Martin Mohr, Prin
EMP: 11 EST: 2013
SALES (est): 317.83K **Privately Held**
Web: www.martin-mohr.com
SIC: 3556 Food products machinery

New Bremen
Auglaize County

(G-11398)
AUGLAIZE ERIE MACHINE COMPANY
07148 Quellhorst Rd (45869-9632)
P.O. Box 72 (45869-0072)
PHONE..................................419 629-2068
Tom W Slife, Pr
Elaine Slife, *
EMP: 30 EST: 1978
SQ FT: 7,500
SALES (est): 2.87MM **Privately Held**
Web: www.aemcnc.com
SIC: 3599 Machine shop, jobbing and repair

(G-11399)
CROWN CREDIT COMPANY
44 S Washington St (45869-1288)
P.O. Box 640352 (45264-0352)
PHONE..................................419 629-2311
James Dicke Iii, Pr
EMP: 17 EST: 1980
SQ FT: 2,492
SALES (est): 4.5MM
SALES (corp-wide): 7.12B **Privately Held**
SIC: 3537 Lift trucks, industrial: fork, platform, straddle, etc.
PA: Crown Equipment Corporation
44 S Washington St
New Bremen OH 45869
419 629-2311

(G-11400)
CROWN EQUIPMENT CORPORATION (PA)
Also Called: Crown Lift Trucks
44 S Washington St (45869-1288)
PHONE..................................419 629-2311
James F Dicke Ii, Ch
James F Dicke Iii, Pr
Craig D Seitz, VP
Bradley L Smith, Asst Tr
John Tate, Sr VP
◆ EMP: 5434 EST: 1947
SQ FT: 25,000
SALES (est): 7.12B
SALES (corp-wide): 7.12B **Privately Held**
Web: www.crown.com
SIC: 3537 5531 Industrial trucks and tractors; Truck equipment and parts

(G-11401)
CROWN EQUIPMENT CORPORATION
Also Called: Crown Lift Trucks
624 W Monroe St (45869-1351)
PHONE..................................419 629-2311
David Obringer, Brnch Mgr
EMP: 48
SALES (corp-wide): 7.12B **Privately Held**
Web: www.crown.com
SIC: 3537 Lift trucks, industrial: fork, platform, straddle, etc.
PA: Crown Equipment Corporation
44 S Washington St
New Bremen OH 45869
419 629-2311

(G-11402)
CROWN EQUIPMENT CORPORATION
Also Called: Crown Lift Trucks
510 W Monroe St (45869-1300)
PHONE..................................419 629-2311
EMP: 20
SALES (corp-wide): 7.12B **Privately Held**
Web: www.crown.com
SIC: 3537 Lift trucks, industrial: fork, platform, straddle, etc.
PA: Crown Equipment Corporation
44 S Washington St
New Bremen OH 45869
419 629-2311

(G-11403)
KINNINGER PROD WLDG CO INC
710 Kuenzel Dr (45869-9699)
P.O. Box 33 (45869-0033)
PHONE..................................419 629-3491
Kevin Thobe, Pr
Cheryl Thobe, *
Donna Thobe, *
EMP: 53 EST: 1966
SQ FT: 54,000
SALES (est): 2.9MM **Privately Held**
Web: www.kinningerwelding.com
SIC: 7692 Welding repair

(G-11404)
MARKETING ESSENTIALS LLC
14 N Washington St (45869-1150)
P.O. Box 114 (45869-0114)
PHONE..................................419 629-0080
EMP: 41 EST: 2009
SALES (est): 893.65K **Privately Held**
Web: www.mktgessentials.com
SIC: 8743 2741 2721 2711 Public relations and publicity; Internet publishing and broadcasting; Magazines: publishing only, not printed on site; Newspapers: publishing only, not printed on site

(G-11405)
NEW BREMEN MACHINE & TOOL CO
705 Kuenzel Dr (45869-8600)
PHONE..................................419 629-3295
Joan Leffel, CEO
Jay Bergman, *
Randy Bergman, *
Robert Roth, *
EMP: 25 EST: 1928
SQ FT: 45,000
SALES (est): 4.05MM **Privately Held**
Web: www.newbremenmachine.com
SIC: 3469 3544 Metal stampings, nec; Special dies and tools

(G-11406)
NUPCO INC
06561 County Road 66a (45869-9800)
PHONE..................................419 629-2259
Luke Wilker, Pr
Virginia Dickie, VP
EMP: 6 EST: 1946
SQ FT: 3,750
SALES (est): 670.5K **Privately Held**
Web: www.nupcoplastictubing.com
SIC: 3084 Plastics pipe

(G-11407)
PRECISION REFLEX INC
710 Streine Dr (45869-8608)
P.O. Box 95 (45869-0095)
PHONE..................................419 629-2603
N David Dunlap, Pr
Mary Dunlap, Sec
EMP: 15 EST: 1978
SQ FT: 2,100
SALES (est): 502.53K **Privately Held**
Web: www.precisionreflex.com
SIC: 3599 2796 7692 Machine shop, jobbing and repair; Engraving on copper, steel, wood, or rubber: printing plates; Welding repair

(G-11408)
SAFEWAY PACKAGING INC (PA)
300 White Mountain Dr (45869-8621)
PHONE..................................419 629-3200
Kevin Manor, Pr
Ralph Stoner, *
EMP: 29 EST: 1984
SQ FT: 100,000
SALES (est): 18.29MM
SALES (corp-wide): 18.29MM **Privately Held**
Web: www.opuspkg.com
SIC: 2653 2673 2671 2631 Boxes, corrugated: made from purchased materials; Bags: plastic, laminated, and coated; Paper; coated and laminated packaging; Paperboard mills

(G-11409)
THIEMAN QUALITY METAL FAB INC
05140 Dicke Rd (45869-9750)
P.O. Box 45 (45869-0045)
PHONE..................................419 629-2612
Terry Marsee, Contrlr
EMP: 80 EST: 1951
SQ FT: 90,000
SALES (est): 9.79MM **Privately Held**
Web: www.thieman.com
SIC: 3441 Fabricated structural metal

(G-11410)
VISIONMARK NAMEPLATE CO LLC
100 White Mountain Dr (45869-8626)
P.O. Box 280 (45871-0280)
PHONE..................................419 977-3131
Jerry Merges, Pr
Mark Nolan, *
EMP: 27 EST: 2014
SQ FT: 20,000
SALES (est): 2.53MM **Privately Held**
Web: www.vmnameplate.com
SIC: 3479 Name plates: engraved, etched, etc.

New Carlisle
Clark County

(G-11411)
BEACH MFG PLASTIC MOLDING DIV
7816 W National Rd (45344-8272)
PHONE..................................937 882-6400
Theodore Beach, Pr
EMP: 8 EST: 2002
SALES (est): 197.26K **Privately Held**
SIC: 3089 Molding primary plastics

(G-11412)
CARLISLE PLASTICS COMPANY
320 Ohio Ave (45344-1630)
P.O. Box 146 (45344-0146)
PHONE..................................937 845-9411
Cynthia A Thomas, Pr
James Thomas, Sec
EMP: 7 EST: 1958
SQ FT: 12,000
SALES (est): 974.04K **Privately Held**
Web: www.carlisleplastics.com
SIC: 2821 3089 Polyvinyl chloride resins, PVC; Injection molding of plastics

(G-11413)
CUSTOM THREADING SYSTEMS LLC
Also Called: A Plus Machining & Tooling
1833 N Dayton Lakeview Rd (45344-9501)
PHONE..................................937 846-1405
EMP: 7 EST: 2007
SALES (est): 866.01K **Privately Held**
SIC: 3554 Paper industries machinery

(G-11414)
CUSTOM WAY WELDING INC
2217 N Dayton Lakeview Rd (45344-9578)
PHONE..................................937 845-9469
Brian Bonham, Pr
Amy Bonham, Sec
EMP: 10 EST: 1961
SQ FT: 12,052
SALES (est): 441.67K **Privately Held**
Web: www.customway.com
SIC: 1799 7692 5599 Ornamental metal work; Welding repair; Utility trailers

(G-11415)
GRIFFITHS MOBILE WELDING
411 S Dayton Lakeview Rd (45344-2128)
PHONE..................................937 750-3711
Carson Griffith, Prin
EMP: 6 EST: 2018
SALES (est): 25.09K **Privately Held**
SIC: 7692 Welding repair

(G-11416)
HIGH TECH CASTINGS
12170 Milton Carlisle Rd (45344-9701)
P.O. Box 486 (45344-0486)
PHONE..................................937 845-1204
Stephanie Partlow, Prin
EMP: 12 EST: 2012
SALES (est): 910.84K **Privately Held**
Web: www.htc-inc.com
SIC: 3366 Copper foundries

(G-11417)
HTCI CO
12170 Milton Carlisle Rd (45344-9701)
P.O. Box 486 (45344-0486)
PHONE..................................937 845-1204
Kevin King, Pr
Deborah Jenkins, Sec
EMP: 18 EST: 2003
SALES (est): 2.54MM **Privately Held**
Web: www.htc-inc.com

GEOGRAPHIC SECTION

New Franklin - Summit County (G-11441)

SIC: 3365 Aerospace castings, aluminum

(G-11418)
KAFFENBARGER TRUCK EQP CO
(PA)
10100 Ballentine Pike (45344-9534)
PHONE.................937 845-3804
Larry Kaffenbarger, *Pr*
Edward W Dunn, *
Everett L Kaffenbarger, *
◆ EMP: 110 EST: 1961
SQ FT: 30,000
SALES (est): 22.65MM
SALES (corp-wide): 22.65MM **Privately Held**
Web: www.knapheide.com
SIC: 3713 5013 Truck bodies (motor vehicles); Truck parts and accessories

(G-11419)
KRAM PRECISION MACHINING INC
1751 Dalton Dr (45344-2309)
PHONE.................937 849-1301
Greg Flory, *Pr*
Douglas Flory, *Treas*
▲ EMP: 6 EST: 1984
SQ FT: 6,000
SALES (est): 501.52K **Privately Held**
Web: www.kramprecision.com
SIC: 3599 Machine shop, jobbing and repair

(G-11420)
MAD RIVER STEEL LTD
Also Called: Mad River Steel Company
2141 N Dayton Lakeview Rd (45344-9578)
P.O. Box 411 (45344-0411)
PHONE.................937 845-4046
EMP: 8 EST: 1994
SQ FT: 10,200
SALES (est): 951.03K **Privately Held**
SIC: 3441 Building components, structural steel

(G-11421)
NCT TECHNOLOGIES GROUP INC
(PA)
Also Called: Nct Technologies Group
7867 W National Rd (45344-8292)
P.O. Box 37 (45344-0237)
PHONE.................937 882-6800
Andrew Flora, *Pr*
Curtis Flora, *VP*
EMP: 13 EST: 1951
SQ FT: 7,500
SALES (est): 5.06MM
SALES (corp-wide): 5.06MM **Privately Held**
Web: www.ncttech.com
SIC: 3441 Fabricated structural metal

(G-11422)
NO-BULL TACTICAL & MACHINE LLC
444 Lammes Ln (45344-9209)
PHONE.................937 470-7687
Stephan Shell, *Prin*
EMP: 6 EST: 2016
SALES (est): 98.61K **Privately Held**
Web: www.nobulltactical.com
SIC: 3599 Machine and other job shop work

(G-11423)
NUMERICS UNLIMITED INC
1700 Dalton Dr (45344-2307)
PHONE.................937 849-0100
Wayne Atkins, *Pr*
EMP: 22 EST: 1970
SQ FT: 15,000
SALES (est): 2.35MM **Privately Held**
Web: www.numericsunlimited.com
SIC: 3544 Industrial molds

(G-11424)
PATTON ALUMINUM PRODUCTS INC
65 Quick Rd (45344)
PHONE.................937 845-9404
Edward E Patton, *Pr*
EMP: 15 EST: 1965
SQ FT: 14,000
SALES (est): 2.22MM **Privately Held**
Web: www.pattonaluminum.com
SIC: 3354 3448 Shapes, extruded aluminum, nec; Screen enclosures

(G-11425)
PFI PRECISION INC
Also Called: Pfi Precision Machining
2011 N Dayton Lakeview Rd (45344-9550)
PHONE.................937 845-3563
Colleen Janek, *Pr*
▲ EMP: 30 EST: 1966
SQ FT: 16,000
SALES (est): 5.31MM **Privately Held**
Web: www.pfiprecision.com
SIC: 3451 Screw machine products

(G-11426)
STONYRIDGE INC
570 S Dayton Lakeview Rd (45344-2129)
PHONE.................937 845-9482
James B Gastineau, *Pr*
Kathy K Abney, *Sec*
EMP: 10 EST: 1984
SQ FT: 2,000
SALES (est): 633.12K **Privately Held**
Web: www.stonyridge.com
SIC: 6531 6552 3089 Real estate brokers and agents; Subdividers and developers, nec; Plastics hardware and building products

(G-11427)
TAYLOR TOOL & DIE INC
306 N Main St (45344-1839)
PHONE.................937 845-1491
Michael L Taylor, *Pr*
Jim Elrod, *VP*
Vern Young, *Sec*
EMP: 7 EST: 1982
SQ FT: 3,900
SALES (est): 917.14K **Privately Held**
SIC: 3544 Special dies and tools

(G-11428)
TETRA MOLD & TOOL INC
51 Quick Rd (45344-9294)
PHONE.................937 845-1651
Brent Hughes, *Pr*
Ronald L Hughes, *
Arleen Hughes, *
EMP: 25 EST: 1966
SQ FT: 10,000
SALES (est): 5.59MM **Privately Held**
Web: www.tetramold.com
SIC: 3089 3544 3714 Injection molding of plastics; Special dies, tools, jigs, and fixtures; Motor vehicle parts and accessories

(G-11429)
VANSCOYK SHEET METAL CORP
475 Quick Rd (45344-9255)
PHONE.................937 845-0581
David Van Scoyk, *Pr*
Wilma Van Skoyk, *VP*
David Van Skoyk, *Sec*
EMP: 7 EST: 1960
SQ FT: 10,000
SALES (est): 937.51K **Privately Held**
Web: www.vanscoyksheetmetal.com
SIC: 3441 Fabricated structural metal

New Concord
Muskingum County

(G-11430)
3-B WELDING LTD
2580 Holmes Rd (43762-9537)
PHONE.................740 819-4329
Wilmer Knowlton Iii, *Managing Member*
EMP: 9 EST: 2001
SALES (est): 434.85K **Privately Held**
Web: www.3-bwelding.com
SIC: 7692 Welding repair

(G-11431)
CARBONLESS CUT SHEET FORMS INC
1948 John Glenn Hwy (43762-9485)
PHONE.................740 826-1700
EMP: 18 EST: 1991
SQ FT: 6,000
SALES (est): 2.29MM **Privately Held**
Web: www.cacsf.com
SIC: 2759 5722 Business forms: printing, nsk ; Vacuum cleaners

(G-11432)
CERNER CORPORATION
Also Called: Resource Systems
140 S Friendship Dr (43762-9453)
PHONE.................740 826-7678
EMP: 76
SALES (corp-wide): 49.95B **Publicly Held**
Web: www.oracle.com
SIC: 7372 7371 Home entertainment computer software; Custom computer programming services
HQ: Cerner Corporation
   8779 Hillcrest Rd
   Kansas City MO 64138
   816 221-1024

(G-11433)
ROBERT BARR
Also Called: Big Sky Petroleum
1245 Friendship Dr (43762-1023)
PHONE.................740 826-7325
Robert Barr, *Prin*
EMP: 7 EST: 1981
SALES (est): 1.26MM **Privately Held**
SIC: 1311 5812 Crude petroleum production; Restaurant, family: independent

(G-11434)
TK GAS SERVICES INC
2303 John Glenn Hwy (43762-9310)
PHONE.................740 826-0303
Ted Korte, *Pr*
Jill Pattison, *
EMP: 50 EST: 1991
SQ FT: 4,000
SALES (est): 5.17MM **Privately Held**
Web: www.tkgasservices.com
SIC: 1389 4212 4213 Oil field services, nec; Local trucking, without storage; Trucking, except local

New Franklin
Summit County

(G-11435)
CLINTON MACHINE CO INC
6270 Van Buren Rd (44216-9743)
P.O. Box 280 (44216-0280)
PHONE.................330 882-2060
Joe Podnar, *CEO*
Delores C Gregory, *Prin*
John D Judge, *Prin*
Ashley Podnar, *Dir*
Mark Podnar, *Managing Member*
▲ EMP: 10 EST: 1969
SALES (est): 1.3MM **Privately Held**
Web: www.clintonmachineco.com
SIC: 3599 Machine shop, jobbing and repair

(G-11436)
G & J EXTRUSIONS INC
1580 Turkeyfoot Lake Rd (44203-4852)
P.O. Box 275 (49745-0275)
PHONE.................330 753-0162
Garry Dumbauld, *Pr*
Julie Dumbauld, *VP*
EMP: 6 EST: 1987
SQ FT: 10,000
SALES (est): 500.18K **Privately Held**
Web: www.gjextrude.com
SIC: 3089 Injection molding of plastics

(G-11437)
J MCCAMAN ENTERPRISES INC
Also Called: J M Machinery
3032 Franks Rd (44216-9327)
P.O. Box 378 (44282-0378)
PHONE.................330 825-2401
Michael L Dyer, *Pr*
EMP: 9 EST: 1990
SQ FT: 2,500
SALES (est): 452.77K **Privately Held**
Web: www.jmmachinery.com
SIC: 3559 5084 Plastics working machinery; Industrial machinery and equipment

(G-11438)
JCI JONES CHEMICALS INC
2500 Vanderhoof Rd (44203-4650)
PHONE.................330 825-2531
Dan Casmey, *Mgr*
EMP: 19
SQ FT: 22,848
SALES (corp-wide): 196.9MM **Privately Held**
Web: www.jcichem.com
SIC: 2812 8734 Chlorine, compressed or liquefied; Testing laboratories
PA: Jci Jones Chemicals, Inc.
   1765 Ringling Blvd
   Sarasota FL 34236
   941 330-1537

(G-11439)
MARTINS STEEL FABRICATION INC
2115 Center Rd (44216-8807)
PHONE.................330 882-4311
Jason Darrah, *Pr*
Beverly Martin, *VP*
EMP: 20 EST: 1990
SQ FT: 6,000
SALES (est): 4.71MM **Privately Held**
Web: www.martins-steel.com
SIC: 3441 Fabricated structural metal

(G-11440)
OHIO PLASTICS & BELTING CO LLC
6140 Manchester Rd (44319-4615)
P.O. Box 593 (44028-0593)
PHONE.................330 882-6764
EMP: 6 EST: 1995
SALES (est): 492.92K **Privately Held**
Web: www.ohioplastics.us
SIC: 2821 Plastics materials and resins

(G-11441)
PHILLIPS MCH & STAMPING CORP
5290 S Main St (44319-4997)
PHONE.................330 882-6714
Wilda Phillips, *Pr*
Craig Phillips, *VP*
EMP: 8 EST: 1939
SQ FT: 16,000

New Franklin - Summit County (G-11442)

SALES (est): 914.13K **Privately Held**
Web: www.phillipsstamping.com
SIC: 3469 3544 Stamping metal for the trade ; Special dies and tools

(G-11442)
PORTABLE CRUSHING LLC
4237 State Park Dr (44319-3444)
PHONE..................................330 618-5251
Timothy D Carr, *Prin*
EMP: 11 EST: 2013
SALES (est): 2.13MM **Privately Held**
SIC: 1442 Construction sand and gravel

(G-11443)
RUBBER ASSOCIATES INC
1522 Turkeyfoot Lake Rd (44203-4898)
PHONE..................................330 745-2186
Eugene Fiocca, *Pr*
Ronald Allan, *
Kris Fiocca, *
◆ **EMP: 100 EST:** 1952
SQ FT: 76,000
SALES (est): 9.56MM **Privately Held**
Web: www.rubberassociates.com
SIC: 3069 Molded rubber products

(G-11444)
TEMPERATURE CONTROLS CO INC
5729 Dailey Rd (44319-5111)
P.O. Box 7665 (44306-0665)
PHONE..................................330 773-6633
John Kerr, *Ch*
Robert J Kerr Senior, *Ch*
John Kerr, *Pr*
James Mc Clarnon, *VP*
Laura Kerr, *Sec*
EMP: 15 EST: 1952
SALES (est): 928.89K **Privately Held**
Web: www.tempcontrolco.com
SIC: 1711 7692 Mechanical contractor; Welding repair

New Hampshire
Auglaize County

(G-11445)
BETHEL ENGINEERING AND EQP INC
Also Called: Bethel Engineering
13830 Mcbeth Rd (45870)
P.O. Box 67 (45870-0067)
PHONE..................................419 568-1100
EMP: 35 EST: 1996
SQ FT: 51,000
SALES (est): 6.84MM **Privately Held**
Web: www.bethelengr.com
SIC: 3559 3441 Paint making machinery; Fabricated structural metal

New Holland
Pickaway County

(G-11446)
BEVERLY DOVE INC
43 E Front St (43145-9662)
P.O. Box 125 (43145-0125)
PHONE..................................740 495-5200
EMP: 7 EST: 1993
SQ FT: 7,000
SALES (est): 565.06K **Privately Held**
Web: www.gutterhangers.net
SIC: 3469 3541 Metal stampings, nec; Machine tools, metal cutting type

New Knoxville
Auglaize County

(G-11447)
HOGE LUMBER COMPANY (PA)
Also Called: Hoge Brush
701 S Main St State (45871)
PHONE..................................419 753-2263
John H Hoge, *Pr*
Bruce L Hoge, *
Clark T Froning, *
Jack R Hoge, *
▲ **EMP: 34 EST:** 1904
SQ FT: 400,000
SALES (est): 4.71MM
SALES (corp-wide): 4.71MM **Privately Held**
Web: www.hoge.com
SIC: 3448 1521 2521 Prefabricated metal buildings and components; New construction, single-family houses; Cabinets, office: wood

New Lebanon
Montgomery County

(G-11448)
B & B GEAR AND MACHINE CO INC
440 W Main St (45345-1426)
PHONE..................................937 687-1771
Jennifer Brinson, *Pr*
Kevin Brinson, *Pr*
Jennifer Brinson, *Owner*
EMP: 22 EST: 1976
SQ FT: 15,000
SALES (est): 5.99MM **Privately Held**
Web: www.bbgearmachine.com
SIC: 3566 3599 Gears, power transmission, except auto; Machine shop, jobbing and repair

(G-11449)
H DUANE LEIS ACQUISITIONS
Also Called: Micro Tool Service
443 S Diamond Mill Rd (45345-9146)
PHONE..................................937 835-5621
H Duane Leis, *Pr*
H Duane Leis Junior, *VP*
EMP: 11 EST: 2009
SALES (est): 497.6K **Privately Held**
SIC: 3545 Cutting tools for machine tools

(G-11450)
MARTIN WELDING LLC (PA)
1472 W Main St (45345-9772)
PHONE..................................937 687-3602
EMP: 10 EST: 1989
SALES (est): 1MM **Privately Held**
Web: www.martinwelding.com
SIC: 7692 Welding repair

New Lexington
Perry County

(G-11451)
COOPER-STANDARD AUTOMOTIVE INC
Cooper
2378 State Route 345 Ne (43764-9617)
PHONE..................................740 342-3523
Mister B Dickens, *Brnch Mgr*
EMP: 83
SQ FT: 80,000
SALES (corp-wide): 2.82B **Publicly Held**
Web: www.cooperstandard.com
SIC: 3714 3443 Motor vehicle brake systems and parts; Heat exchangers, condensers, and components
HQ: Cooper-Standard Automotive Inc.
40300 Traditions Dr
Northville MI 48168
248 596-5900

(G-11452)
HOCKING VALLEY CONCRETE INC
1500 Commerce Dr (43764-9432)
PHONE..................................740 342-1948
William Laughn, *Prin*
EMP: 8
SALES (corp-wide): 3.78MM **Privately Held**
Web: www.hockingvalleyconcrete.com
SIC: 3273 Ready-mixed concrete
PA: Hocking Valley Concrete, Inc.
35255 Hocking Dr
Logan OH 43138
740 385 2155

(G-11453)
LORI HOLDING CO (PA)
Also Called: Siemer Distributing
1400 Commerce Dr (43764-9500)
PHONE..................................740 342-3230
Joseph A Siemer Iii, *Pr*
EMP: 30 EST: 1980
SALES (est): 4.77MM
SALES (corp-wide): 4.77MM **Privately Held**
Web: www.siemermeats.com
SIC: 5147 5143 5199 5142 Meats, fresh; Cheese; Ice, manufactured or natural; Packaged frozen goods

(G-11454)
LUDOWICI ROOF TILE INC
4757 Tile Plant Rd Se (43764-9630)
P.O. Box 69 (43764-0069)
PHONE..................................740 342-1995
Herve Gastinel, *Pr*
Guillaume Latil, *
◆ **EMP: 80 EST:** 1989
SQ FT: 100,000
SALES (est): 21.07MM
SALES (corp-wide): 4.94MM **Privately Held**
Web: www.ludowici.com
SIC: 3272 Concrete products, nec
HQ: Terreal
13 17
Suresnes 92150

(G-11455)
PERRY COUNTY TRIBUNE
Also Called: Tribune Shopping News, The
399 Lincoln Park Dr Ste A (43764-1078)
P.O. Box 312 (43764-0312)
PHONE..................................740 342-4121
Deb Hutmire, *Genl Mgr*
EMP: 10 EST: 1975
SALES (est): 610.65K **Privately Held**
Web: www.perrytribune.com
SIC: 2711 6512 Newspapers, publishing and printing; Property operation, retail establishment

(G-11456)
R & D HILLTOP LUMBER INC
2126 State Route 93 Se (43764-9666)
PHONE..................................740 342-3051
Russell Howdyshell, *Pr*
Polly Howdyshell, *VP*
EMP: 26 EST: 1952
SQ FT: 8,000
SALES (est): 1.57MM **Privately Held**
SIC: 2421 Lumber: rough, sawed, or planed

(G-11457)
SOUTHEASTERN SHAFTING MFG INC
402 W Broadway St (43764-1007)
P.O. Box 168 (43764-0168)
PHONE..................................740 342-4629
Scott Jones Senior, *Pr*
Theresa M Jones, *Sec*
EMP: 18 EST: 1983
SALES (est): 2.27MM **Privately Held**
Web: www.seshafting.com
SIC: 3568 3599 Collars, shaft (power transmission equipment); Machine shop, jobbing and repair

(G-11458)
STAR-TJCM INC
701 Madison St (43764)
P.O. Box 71 (43764)
PHONE..................................740 342-3514
Bill Mooney, *CEO*
Christopher Mooney, *
William J Mooney, *
Daniel P Mooney, *
John Mooney, *
EMP: 35 EST: 1941
SQ FT: 36,000
SALES (est): 9.9MM **Privately Held**
Web: www.starengineering.com
SIC: 3567 Ceramic kilns and furnaces

(G-11459)
TERREAL NORTH AMERICA LLC
4757 Tile Plant Rd Se (43764-9630)
P.O. Box 309 (43764-0309)
PHONE..................................888 582-9052
Herve Gastinel, *Managing Member*
EMP: 175 EST: 2007
SALES (est): 8.96MM **Privately Held**
Web: www.terrealna.com
SIC: 3259 Roofing tile, clay

New London
Huron County

(G-11460)
APPLIED AUTOMATION ENTP INC
24 Cedar St (44851-1218)
PHONE..................................419 929-2428
Timothy Hedrick, *Pr*
Vaughn Lucal, *Treas*
Stephan Pabst, *Sec*
EMP: 23 EST: 2000
SQ FT: 15,000
SALES (est): 2MM **Privately Held**
Web: www.automationent.com
SIC: 3541 Chucking machines, automatic

(G-11461)
FIRELANDS FABRICATION
201 N Main St (44851-1015)
PHONE..................................419 929-0680
EMP: 14 EST: 2013
SALES (est): 2.41MM **Privately Held**
Web: www.firelandsfab.com
SIC: 3441 Fabricated structural metal

(G-11462)
FITCHVILLE EAST CORP
Also Called: Fitchville East Storage
1732 Us Highway 250 S (44851-9372)
PHONE..................................419 929-1510
EMP: 7 EST: 1981
SALES (est): 108.3K **Privately Held**
SIC: 3799 Trailers and trailer equipment

(G-11463)
KENT WATER SPORTS LLC (PA)
Also Called: Kent Water Sports
433 Park Ave (44851-1177)
PHONE.................................419 929-7021
Ken Meidell, *CEO*
J Robert Tipton, *
John Clark, *
Brian Zaletel, *
Marlene Sipp, *
▲ **EMP:** 100 **EST:** 1959
SQ FT: 25,000
SALES (est): 92.97MM
SALES (corp-wide): 92.97MM **Privately Held**
Web: www.kentoutdoors.com
SIC: 3949 Water sports equipment

(G-11464)
MONODE MARKING PRODUCTS INC
Also Called: Waldorf Marking Devices
149 High St (44851-1118)
PHONE.................................419 929-0346
Thomas Mackey, *Pr*
EMP: 10
SALES (corp-wide): 9.29MM **Privately Held**
Web: www.monode.com
SIC: 3542 3953 Marking machines; Marking devices
  PA: Monode Marking Products, Inc.
    9200 Tyler Blvd
    Mentor OH 44060
    440 975-8802

(G-11465)
NEW LONDON REGALIA MFG CO
1 Harmony Pl (44851-1248)
P.O. Box 125 (44851-0125)
PHONE.................................419 929-1516
Glen Hammersmith, *Pr*
S George Kurz, *Sec*
EMP: 7 **EST:** 1981
SQ FT: 7,500
SALES (est): 247.66K **Privately Held**
Web: www.newlondonregalia.com
SIC: 2389 Regalia

(G-11466)
RANKIN MFG INC
201 N Main St (44851-1015)
PHONE.................................419 929-8338
Eric Rankine, *Pr*
Michael Rankine, *Sec*
EMP: 23 **EST:** 1987
SQ FT: 52,500
SALES (est): 789.03K **Privately Held**
SIC: 3441 3799 3599 Fabricated structural metal; Trailers and trailer equipment; Machine and other job shop work

(G-11467)
ROERIG MACHINE
27348 State Route 511 (44851-9667)
PHONE.................................440 647-4718
EMP: 6 **EST:** 1986
SALES (est): 448.48K **Privately Held**
SIC: 3599 Machine shop, jobbing and repair

(G-11468)
SDG NEWS GROUP INC
Also Called: Firelands Farmer, The
43 E Main St (44851-1213)
P.O. Box 647 (44875-0647)
PHONE.................................419 929-3411
EMP: 10 **EST:** 1970
SALES (est): 491.27K **Privately Held**
Web: www.sdgnewsgroup.com
SIC: 2711 2752 Newspapers: publishing only, not printed on site; Commercial printing, lithographic

(G-11469)
SEWLINE PRODUCTS INC
30 S Railroad St (44851-1243)
PHONE.................................419 929-1114
Duane E Mills, *Pr*
Alana Mills, *Sec*
EMP: 8 **EST:** 1983
SQ FT: 30,980
SALES (est): 163.18K **Privately Held**
Web: www.sewline-product.com
SIC: 2392 2399 Blankets, comforters and beddings; Infant carriers

(G-11470)
THOMAS CREATIVE APPAREL INC
1 Harmony Pl (44851-1248)
PHONE.................................419 929-1506
Vickie Hall, *Pr*
EMP: 11 **EST:** 1972
SQ FT: 14,000
SALES (est): 423.99K **Privately Held**
Web: www.thomasrobes.com
SIC: 2384 2389 2353 Robes and dressing gowns; Lodge costumes; Hats, caps, and millinery

(G-11471)
TIERRA-DERCO INTERNATIONAL LLC
40 S Main St (44851-1138)
PHONE.................................419 929-2240
Heath White, *Mgr*
EMP: 7
Web: www.tdibrands.com
SIC: 3524 Lawn and garden equipment
  PA: Tierra-Derco International, Llc
    1000 S Saint Charles St
    Jasper IN 47546

(G-11472)
TIP PRODUCTS INC
106 Industrial Dr (44851-9111)
PHONE.................................216 252-2535
Dave Finley, *CEO*
Rhonda Gielow, *
Michelle Pellerin, *
EMP: 23 **EST:** 1965
SQ FT: 10,000
SALES (est): 2.49MM **Privately Held**
Web: www.tipproducts.com
SIC: 3643 3699 Cord connectors, electric; Electrical equipment and supplies, nec

New Madison
Darke County

(G-11473)
ERNIE GREEN INDUSTRIES INC
Also Called: Eg Industries
1855 State Rd Ste 121n (45346)
PHONE.................................614 219-1423
EMP: 16
SALES (corp-wide): 338.9MM **Privately Held**
Web: www.epcmfg.com
SIC: 3714 Motor vehicle wheels and parts
  PA: Ernie Green Industries, Inc.
    1785 Big Hill Rd
    Dayton OH 45439
    614 219-1423

(G-11474)
FLORIDA PRODUCTION ENGRG INC
Ernie Green Industries
1855 State Route 121 N (45346-9716)
PHONE.................................937 996-4361
Eric Opicka, *Mgr*
EMP: 90
SALES (corp-wide): 338.9MM **Privately Held**
SIC: 3465 3714 3429 Moldings or trim, automobile: stamped metal; Motor vehicle parts and accessories; Hardware, nec
  HQ: Florida Production Engineering, Inc.
    2 E Tower Cir
    Ormond Beach FL 32174
    386 677-2566

(G-11475)
LUDY GREENHOUSE MFG CORP (PA)
122 Railroad St (45346-5016)
P.O. Box 141 (45346-0141)
PHONE.................................800 255-5839
Stephan A Scantland, *Pr*
Deborah Scantland, *
EMP: 58 **EST:** 1957
SQ FT: 2,500
SALES (est): 10.14MM
SALES (corp-wide): 10.14MM **Privately Held**
Web: www.ludy.com
SIC: 1542 3448 Greenhouse construction; Greenhouses, prefabricated metal

New Matamoras
Washington County

(G-11476)
CONDEVCO INC
44403 State Route 7 (45767-6150)
P.O. Box 280 (45773-0280)
PHONE.................................740 373-5302
Carl Heinrich, *Prin*
EMP: 6 **EST:** 2009
SALES (est): 386.35K **Privately Held**
SIC: 1321 Natural gas liquids

(G-11477)
CREIGHTON SPORTS CENTER INC (PA)
205 Broadway Ave (45767-1193)
P.O. Box 400 (45767-0400)
PHONE.................................740 865-2521
Bill Creighton, *Pr*
Chris Creighton, *VP*
Pam Creighton, *Sec*
EMP: 7 **EST:** 1984
SQ FT: 2,400
SALES (est): 733.04K
SALES (corp-wide): 733.04K **Privately Held**
SIC: 3949 Sporting and athletic goods, nec

New Middletown
Mahoning County

(G-11478)
HITCH-HIKER MFG INC
10065 Rapp Rd (44442-9753)
PHONE.................................330 542-3052
Jeffrey Swartz, *Pr*
Holly Swartz, *VP*
EMP: 11 **EST:** 1973
SQ FT: 38,000
SALES (est): 2.17MM **Privately Held**
Web: www.hitch-hikermfg.com
SIC: 3799 Boat trailers

(G-11479)
PARAGON PLASTICS
5551 E Calla Rd (44442-9768)
P.O. Box 22 (44442-0022)
PHONE.................................330 542-9825
Michelle Rothrauff, *Prin*
EMP: 9 **EST:** 2004
SALES (est): 488.94K **Privately Held**
Web: www.paragonplastics.us
SIC: 3089 Injection molding of plastics

New Paris
Preble County

(G-11480)
ARNETT TOOL INC
217 W Main St (45347-1109)
P.O. Box 40 (45347-0040)
PHONE.................................937 437-0361
M James Arnett, *Pr*
Leatrice J Arnett, *Sec*
EMP: 7 **EST:** 1979
SQ FT: 4,800
SALES (est): 535.3K **Privately Held**
SIC: 3544 Special dies and tools

(G-11481)
DYNAMIC PLASTICS INC
Also Called: H & H Sailcraft
8207 H W Rd (45347-9241)
PHONE.................................937 437-7261
Paul Hemker, *Pr*
Heide Hemker, *Sec*
EMP: 8 **EST:** 1969
SQ FT: 20,000
SALES (est): 690.68K **Privately Held**
Web: dynamicplasticsinc.centurylinksite.net
SIC: 3089 3732 3531 5551 Injection molding of plastics; Sailboats, building and repairing; Construction machinery; Boat dealers

(G-11482)
H & S PRECISION SCREW PDTS INC
8205 H W Rd (45347)
PHONE.................................937 437-0316
Jerry J Winkle, *Pr*
EMP: 16 **EST:** 1978
SQ FT: 10,000
SALES (est): 269.28K **Privately Held**
Web: www.handspsp.com
SIC: 3451 Screw machine products

(G-11483)
MIDWEST STEEL FABRICATORS INC
8155 State Route 121 N (45347-9222)
P.O. Box 55 (45347-0055)
PHONE.................................937 437-0371
Ronald L Sprenkel, *Prin*
EMP: 6 **EST:** 2019
SALES (est): 92.74K **Privately Held**
Web: www.mideastmachinerymovers.com
SIC: 3441 Fabricated structural metal

New Philadelphia
Tuscarawas County

(G-11484)
AQUABLUE INCORPORATED
1776 Tech Park Dr Ne (44663-9410)
P.O. Box 446 (44663-0446)
PHONE.................................330 343-0220
Don Whittingham, *Pr*
EMP: 8 **EST:** 2005
SALES (est): 897.16K **Privately Held**
Web: www.aquabluechemical.com
SIC: 2899 5169 Water treating compounds; Chemicals and allied products, nec

(G-11485)
ATLAS AMERICA INC
1026a Cookson Ave Se (44663-9500)
PHONE.................................330 339-3155
Rich Weber, *Pr*
EMP: 10 **EST:** 2004
SALES (est): 854.02K **Privately Held**

New Philadelphia - Tuscarawas County (G-11486)

SIC: **1382** Oil and gas exploration services

(G-11486)
BATTLE MOTORS INC
1951 Reiser Ave Se (44663-3348)
PHONE..................................888 328-5443
Michael W Patterson, *CEO*
Oliver F Weilandt, *
Jill Cilmi, *
EMP: 126 **EST:** 2020
SALES (est): 27.38MM **Privately Held**
SIC: **3621** 5999 Motors and generators; Engine and motor equipment and supplies

(G-11487)
BRIDGES SHEET METAL
2244 Goshen Valley Dr Se (44663-6779)
PHONE..................................330 339-3185
EMP: 6 **EST:** 2008
SALES (est): 127.75K **Privately Held**
SIC: **3444** Sheet metalwork

(G-11488)
BROWN WOOD PRODUCTS COMPANY
7783 Crooked Run Rd Sw (44663-6411)
PHONE..................................330 339-8000
Todd Dennison, *Mgr*
EMP: 8
SALES (corp-wide): 4.1MM **Privately Held**
Web: www.brownwoodinc.com
SIC: **2499** Decorative wood and woodwork
PA: Brown Wood Products Company
   7040 N Lawndale Ave
   Lincolnwood IL 60712
   847 673-4780

(G-11489)
BULK CARRIER TRNSP EQP CO
2743 Brightwood Rd Se (44663-6773)
PHONE..................................330 339-3333
Richard S Hartrick, *Pr*
Marcia Hartrick, *
EMP: 22 **EST:** 1976
SALES (est): 1.2MM **Privately Held**
Web: www.bcte.com
SIC: **5012** 2519 Trailers for trucks, new and used; Household furniture, except wood or metal: upholstered

(G-11490)
BULK CARRIERS SERVICE INC
Also Called: Bcte
2743 Brightwood Rd Se (44663-6773)
PHONE..................................330 339-3333
Richard Hartrick, *Pr*
Doug Milburn, *VP*
EMP: 10 **EST:** 1995
SALES (est): 317.36K **Privately Held**
Web: www.bcte.com
SIC: **3799** 4789 5084 Recreational vehicles; Passenger train services; Engines and transportation equipment

(G-11491)
CASTINGS USA INC
2061 Brightwood Rd Se (44663-7724)
P.O. Box 202 (44653-0202)
PHONE..................................330 339-3611
Gregory M Dean, *Pr*
Terry Yahard, *Sec*
EMP: 7 **EST:** 1974
SQ FT: 8,000
SALES (est): 929.31K **Privately Held**
Web: www.reymondproducts.com
SIC: **3321** 3325 Gray iron castings, nec; Steel foundries, nec

(G-11492)
CHEMSPEC LTD
419 Tuscarawas Ave Nw (44663-1538)
PHONE..................................330 364-4422
EMP: 18
SALES (corp-wide): 166.77K **Privately Held**
Web: www.safic-alcan.com
SIC: **2891** Adhesives and sealants
HQ: Chemspec, Ltd.
   4450 Belden Village St Nw
   Canton OH 44718
   330 896-0355

(G-11493)
COPLEY OHIO NEWSPAPERS INC
Also Called: Times Reporter/Midwest Offset
629 Wabash Ave Nw (44663-4145)
P.O. Box 9901 (44711-0901)
PHONE..................................330 364-5577
Kevin Kampman, *Publisher*
EMP: 177
SALES (corp-wide): 2.66B **Publicly Held**
Web: www.cantonrep.com
SIC: **2711** 2752 7313 2791 Commercial printing and newspaper publishing combined; Offset printing; Newspaper advertising representative; Typesetting
HQ: Copley Ohio Newspapers Inc
   500 Market Ave S
   Canton OH 44702
   585 598-0030

(G-11494)
CRAFTED ELEMENTS LLC
742 Oak St Nw (44663-1841)
PHONE..................................816 739-1307
Todd Dennison, *Prin*
EMP: 6 **EST:** 2018
SALES (est): 186.8K **Privately Held**
Web: www.craftedelements.business
SIC: **2426** Carvings, furniture: wood

(G-11495)
CRANE CARRIER COMPANY LLC (HQ)
1951 Reiser Ave Se (44663-3348)
PHONE..................................918 286-2889
Randy Rollins, *Pr*
EMP: 145 **EST:** 1973
SALES (est): 47.9MM
SALES (corp-wide): 50.87MM **Privately Held**
Web: www.cranecarrier.com
SIC: **5013** 3713 Truck parts and accessories; Truck bodies and parts
PA: Battle Motors, Inc.
   612 Hampton Dr Ste B
   Venice CA 90291
   562 536-3614

(G-11496)
CRANE CARRIER HOLDINGS LLC
1951 Reiser Ave Se (44663-3348)
PHONE..................................918 286-2889
EMP: 150 **EST:** 2018
Web: www.cranecarrier.com
SIC: **6719** 5013 3713 Investment holding companies, except banks; Truck parts and accessories; Truck bodies and parts

(G-11497)
CUSTOM NEEDLE-PRINT LLC
670 Orchard Ave Nw (44663-1142)
PHONE..................................330 432-5506
Christopher Harmon, *Prin*
EMP: 6 **EST:** 2015
SALES (est): 400.98K **Privately Held**
Web: www.customneedleprint.com

SIC: **2752** Commercial printing, lithographic

(G-11498)
DENNEY PLASTICS MACHINING LLC
149 Stonecreek Rd Nw (44663-6902)
PHONE..................................330 308-5300
EMP: 18 **EST:** 1988
SALES (est): 2.7MM **Privately Held**
Web: www.denneyplastics.com
SIC: **3089** Injection molding of plastics

(G-11499)
DRJ WELDING SERVICES LLC
936 Front Ave Sw (44663-2090)
PHONE..................................740 229-7428
Dillon Cox, *Prin*
EMP: 10 **EST:** 2017
SALES (est): 303.37K **Privately Held**
SIC: **7692** Welding repair

(G-11500)
ELLIS LAUNDRY AND LIN SUP INC
213 8th Street Ext Sw (44663-2088)
PHONE..................................330 339-4941
Katherine Ellis, *Pr*
Jerry Ellis, *Sec*
EMP: 6 **EST:** 2003
SALES (est): 506.83K **Privately Held**
SIC: **3582** Ironers, commercial laundry and drycleaning

(G-11501)
FENTON BROS ELECTRIC CO
Also Called: Fenton's Festival of Lights
235 Ray Ave Ne (44663-2813)
P.O. Box 996 (44663-0996)
PHONE..................................330 343-0093
Tom Fenton, *Pr*
Dennis Fenton, *
Chris Fenton, *
Brian Fenton, *
Harold E Fenton, *Stockholder*
EMP: 30 **EST:** 1947
SQ FT: 37,000
SALES (est): 12.09MM **Privately Held**
SIC: **5063** 7694 Electrical supplies, nec; Electric motor repair

(G-11502)
FRANTZ GRINDING CO
1879 E High Ave (44663-3238)
P.O. Box 408 (44663-0408)
PHONE..................................330 343-8689
Joe M Frantz, *Pr*
Kay Frantz, *Sec*
EMP: 6 **EST:** 1946
SQ FT: 11,400
SALES (est): 474.01K **Privately Held**
SIC: **3599** Machine shop, jobbing and repair

(G-11503)
FREEPORT PRESS INC (PA)
2127 Reiser Ave Se (44663-3331)
P.O. Box 198 (43973-0198)
PHONE..................................330 308-3300
David G Pilcher, *Pr*
EMP: 149 **EST:** 1880
SQ FT: 36,000
SALES (est): 55.1MM
SALES (corp-wide): 55.1MM **Privately Held**
Web: www.freeportpress.com
SIC: **2752** Offset printing

(G-11504)
GRADALL INDUSTRIES LLC (DH)
Also Called: Gradall
406 Mill Ave Sw (44663)
PHONE..................................330 339-2211
Joseph H Keller, *

Daniel Kaltenbaugh, *
▲ **EMP:** 132 **EST:** 1992
SQ FT: 429,320
SALES (est): 99.6MM
SALES (corp-wide): 1.69B **Publicly Held**
Web: www.gradall.com
SIC: **3537** 3531 Industrial trucks and tractors; Construction machinery
HQ: Alamo Group (Usa) Inc.
   1627 E Walnut St
   Seguin TX 78155
   830 379-1480

(G-11505)
HYDRAULIC PARTS STORE INC
145 1st Dr Ne (44663-2857)
P.O. Box 808 (44663-0807)
PHONE..................................330 364-6667
Robert M Henning Senior, *Pr*
EMP: 42 **EST:** 1983
SQ FT: 25,000
SALES (est): 1.66MM **Privately Held**
SIC: **5084** 3594 3593 3492 Hydraulic systems equipment and supplies; Fluid power pumps and motors; Fluid power cylinders and actuators; Fluid power valves and hose fittings

(G-11506)
J & D MINING INC
3497 University Dr Ne (44663-6711)
PHONE..................................330 339-4935
John R Demuth, *Pr*
James R Demuth, *
EMP: 21 **EST:** 1981
SQ FT: 1,000
SALES (est): 1.35MM **Privately Held**
SIC: **1221** Bituminous coal surface mining

(G-11507)
KAY-ZEE INC
1279 Crestview Ave Sw (44663-9642)
P.O. Box 95 (44663-0095)
PHONE..................................330 339-1268
John Stratton, *Pr*
Kathryn Stratton, *VP*
EMP: 7 **EST:** 1962
SALES (est): 853.66K **Privately Held**
Web: www.kayzeeinc.net
SIC: **3861** Lens shades, camera

(G-11508)
KIMBLE CUSTOM CHASSIS COMPANY
Also Called: Kimble Manufacturing Company
1951 Reiser Ave Se (44663-3348)
PHONE..................................877 546-2537
James C Cahill, *Pr*
Jim Moberg, *
Gregory Stohler, *
Philip Keegan, *
Brian Shepherd, *
▲ **EMP:** 100 **EST:** 2006
SQ FT: 100,000
SALES (est): 21.71MM
SALES (corp-wide): 195.64MM **Privately Held**
SIC: **3713** Truck bodies and parts
PA: Hines Corporation
   1218 E Pontaluna Rd Ste B
   Spring Lake MI 49456
   231 799-6240

(G-11509)
KIMBLE MIXER COMPANY
Also Called: Hines Specialty Vehicle Group
1951 Reiser Ave Se (44663-3348)
PHONE..................................330 308-6700
▲ **EMP:** 75 **EST:** 1995
SQ FT: 100,000
SALES (est): 26.41MM

GEOGRAPHIC SECTION
New Philadelphia - Tuscarawas County (G-11532)

SALES (corp-wide): 195.64MM **Privately Held**
SIC: 3713 Cement mixer bodies
PA: Hines Corporation
1218 E Pontaluna Rd Ste B
Spring Lake MI 49456
231 799-6240

(G-11510)
LAUREN INTERNATIONAL LTD (PA)
143 Garland Dr Sw (44663-6300)
PHONE..............................234 303-2400
Kevin E Gray, *Pr*
David Gingrich, *
◆ **EMP:** 200 **EST:** 1965
SALES (est): 44.54MM
SALES (corp-wide): 44.54MM **Privately Held**
Web: www.laureninternational.com
SIC: 3069 Molded rubber products

(G-11511)
LIGHTNING SIGNS AND DECALS LLC
205 S Broadway St (44663-3830)
PHONE..............................304 403-1290
EMP: 6 **EST:** 2020
SALES (est): 415.37K **Privately Held**
Web: www.lightningsign.com
SIC: 3993 Signs and advertising specialties

(G-11512)
M R TRAILER SALES INC
1565 Steel Hill Rd Nw (44663-6503)
P.O. Box 562 (44622-0562)
PHONE..............................330 339-7701
Roger Rostad, *Pr*
Sharon Rostad, *Pr*
Don Rostad, *Dir*
Roger Rostad, *VP*
EMP: 8 **EST:** 1993
SALES (est): 897.31K **Privately Held**
Web: www.mrtrailersales.com
SIC: 5012 5599 3441 3715 Trailers for passenger vehicles; Utility trailers; Fabricated structural metal; Trailers or vans for transporting horses

(G-11513)
MANSFIELD JOURNAL CO
Also Called: Times Reporter
629 Wabash Ave Nw (44663-4145)
P.O. Box 9901 (44711-0901)
PHONE..............................330 364-8641
Brent Kettlewell, *Contrlr*
EMP: 173 **EST:** 1930
SQ FT: 65,000
SALES (est): 2.12MM
SALES (corp-wide): 293.08MM **Privately Held**
Web: www.timesreporter.com
SIC: 2711 2752 Newspapers, publishing and printing; Offset printing
PA: Journal Register Company
5 Hanover Sq Fl 25
New York NY 10004
212 257-7212

(G-11514)
MARATHON MFG & SUP CO
5165 Main St Ne (44663-8802)
P.O. Box 701 (44663-0701)
PHONE..............................330 343-2656
Emory Brumit, *Pr*
Peggy Brumit, *
EMP: 10 **EST:** 1969
SALES (est): 497.2K **Privately Held**
Web: www.marathonmfg.com
SIC: 5199 3953 Advertising specialties; Screens, textile printing

(G-11515)
MARSH INDUSTRIES INC
Marsh Chalk Board Co Div
1117 Bowers Ave Nw (44663-4129)
P.O. Box 1000 (44663-5100)
PHONE..............................330 308-8667
Brian Marsh, *Mgr*
EMP: 32
SALES (corp-wide): 7.5MM **Privately Held**
Web: www.polyvision.com
SIC: 2431 5211 5943 3281 Millwork; Planing mill products and lumber; School supplies; Cut stone and stone products
PA: Marsh Industries, Inc.
2301 E High Ave
New Philadelphia OH 44663
800 426-4244

(G-11516)
MARSH INDUSTRIES INC (PA)
2301 E High Ave (44663)
P.O. Box 1000 (44663)
PHONE..............................800 426-4244
▲ **EMP:** 68 **EST:** 1914
SALES (est): 7.5MM
SALES (corp-wide): 7.5MM **Privately Held**
Web: www.polyvision.com
SIC: 2431 2531 2493 Trim, wood; Blackboards, wood; Bulletin boards, wood

(G-11517)
MID-AMERICA PACKAGING LLC
2127 Reiser Ave Se (44663-3331)
PHONE..............................330 963-4199
▲ **EMP:** 650
SIC: 2674 Bags: uncoated paper and multiwall

(G-11518)
MILLER PRODUCTS INC
Also Called: Beech Engineering & Mfg
642 Wabash Ave Nw (44663-4146)
P.O. Box 947 (44663-0947)
PHONE..............................330 308-5934
Naomi Downend, *Genl Mgr*
EMP: 35
SALES (corp-wide): 70.41MM **Privately Held**
Web: www.mpilabels.com
SIC: 3537 3535 Industrial trucks and tractors ; Conveyors and conveying equipment
PA: Miller Products, Inc.
450 Courtney Rd
Sebring OH 44672
330 938-2134

(G-11519)
MILLER STUDIO INC
734 Fair Ave Nw (44663-1589)
P.O. Box 997 (44663-0997)
PHONE..............................330 339-1100
Naomi Downend, *Pr*
Jeff Miller, *
John A Basiletti, *
▲ **EMP:** 20 **EST:** 1934
SALES (est): 10.62MM
SALES (corp-wide): 70.41MM **Privately Held**
Web: www.miller-studio.com
SIC: 2672 3452 3429 Adhesive papers, labels, or tapes: from purchased material; Bolts, nuts, rivets, and washers; Hardware, nec
PA: Miller Products, Inc.
450 Courtney Rd
Sebring OH 44672
330 938-2134

(G-11520)
OAKTREE WIRELINE LLC
1825 E High Ave (44663-3280)
PHONE..............................330 352-7250
EMP: 9 **EST:** 2013
SQ FT: 3,000
SALES (est): 381.73K **Privately Held**
SIC: 1389 Well logging

(G-11521)
OHIO VALLEY SAND LLC
513 Mill Ave Se (44663-3864)
PHONE..............................740 661-4240
Mark Ogg, *Owner*
EMP: 8 **EST:** 2013
SALES (est): 839.59K **Privately Held**
SIC: 1442 Construction sand and gravel

(G-11522)
PARAMONT MACHINE COMPANY LLC
963 Commercial Ave Se (44663-2355)
PHONE..............................330 339-3489
Brian D Farley, *Pr*
EMP: 11 **EST:** 1999
SQ FT: 11,000
SALES (est): 741.4K **Privately Held**
Web: www.paramontmachinecompany.com
SIC: 3599 3451 3053 Machine shop, jobbing and repair; Screw machine products; Gaskets; packing and sealing devices
HQ: Plastics Family Holdings, Inc.
5800 Cmpus Circ Dr E Ste
Irving TX 75063
469 299-7000

(G-11523)
PRO A V OF OHIO
Also Called: Better Banner Printing
120 6th Dr Sw (44663-2020)
PHONE..............................877 812-5350
EMP: 6
SALES (est): 440.96K **Privately Held**
Web: www.proavofohio.com
SIC: 3993 Signs and advertising specialties

(G-11524)
R & J CYLINDER & MACHINE INC
464 Robinson Dr Se (44663-3336)
PHONE..............................330 364-8263
Ronald Sandy, *Pr*
Jeffrey Shepherd, *
Don Sandy, *Stockholder*
EMP: 53 **EST:** 1990
SQ FT: 33,500
SALES (est): 9.45MM **Privately Held**
Web: www.rjcylinder.com
SIC: 3593 3599 Fluid power cylinders, hydraulic or pneumatic; Machine and other job shop work

(G-11525)
REYMOND PRODUCTS INTL INC
2066 Brightwood Rd Se (44663-7724)
P.O. Box 202 (44653-0202)
PHONE..............................330 339-3583
Greg Dean, *Pr*
▲ **EMP:** 20 **EST:** 1948
SQ FT: 15,000
SALES (est): 3.47MM **Privately Held**
Web: www.reymondproducts.com
SIC: 3599 3544 Machine shop, jobbing and repair; Special dies, tools, jigs, and fixtures

(G-11526)
RICH INDUSTRIES INC
2384 Brightwood Rd Se (44663-6772)
PHONE..............................330 339-4113
William Arnold, *VP*
Jeffrey Contini, *
Anthony Contini, *
Scott Trammell, *
Rita Contini, *
▲ **EMP:** 50 **EST:** 1971
SQ FT: 28,000
SALES (est): 9.66MM **Privately Held**
Web: www.richindustriesinc.com
SIC: 2389 2393 2326 Disposable garments and accessories; Textile bags; Men's and boy's work clothing

(G-11527)
T A W INC
2565 Mathias Raceway Rd Sw (44663-6968)
P.O. Box 2449 (72921-2449)
PHONE..............................330 339-1212
Timothy A Woody, *Prin*
EMP: 6 **EST:** 2009
SALES (est): 142.82K **Privately Held**
SIC: 1389 Oil field services, nec

(G-11528)
TGS INDUSTRIES INC
406 Mill Ave Sw (44663-3835)
PHONE..............................330 339-2211
▼ **EMP:** 33
SIC: 3531 Excavators: cable, clamshell, crane, derrick, dragline, etc.

(G-11529)
TOLLOTI PIPE LLC
102 Barnhill Rd Se (44663-8864)
P.O. Box 129 (44683-0129)
PHONE..............................330 364-6627
Kyle Miller, *Prin*
EMP: 15 **EST:** 2011
SALES (est): 2.39MM **Privately Held**
Web: www.zuwy.com
SIC: 3084 Plastics pipe

(G-11530)
TOLLOTI PLASTIC PIPE INC (PA)
102 Barnhill Rd Se (44663-8864)
P.O. Box 508 (44663-0508)
PHONE..............................330 364-6627
Theodore Tolloti, *Pr*
Doris Tolloti, *
John Tolloti, *
EMP: 38 **EST:** 1963
SQ FT: 5,000
SALES (est): 4.8MM
SALES (corp-wide): 4.8MM **Privately Held**
SIC: 3084 Plastics pipe

(G-11531)
UNDER PRESSURE SYSTEMS INC
322 North Ave Ne (44663-2714)
P.O. Box 266 (43021-0266)
PHONE..............................330 602-4466
Cynthia J Valentine, *Pr*
EMP: 9 **EST:** 1998
SQ FT: 10,000
SALES (est): 2.4MM **Privately Held**
Web: www.underpressuresystemsllc.com
SIC: 3589 Water treatment equipment, industrial

(G-11532)
WELL SERVICE GROUP INC
1490 Truss Rd Sw (44663-7530)
PHONE..............................330 308-0880
Bil Woessner, *Genl Mgr*
EMP: 8 **EST:** 2013
SALES (est): 219.11K **Privately Held**
SIC: 1389 Oil field services, nec

New Plymouth
Vinton County

(G-11533)
ON GUARD DEFENSE LLC
66211 Bethel Rd (45654-8934)
PHONE..................740 596-1984
EMP: 6 **EST:** 2017
SALES (est): 165.71K **Privately Held**
Web: www.onguarddefense.com
SIC: 3812 Defense systems and equipment

New Riegel
Seneca County

(G-11534)
B M MACHINE
27 S Perry St (44853-9778)
PHONE..................419 595-2898
Robert Mathias, *Pr*
EMP: 41
SALES (corp-wide): 904.52K **Privately Held**
Web: www.bmmachine.com
SIC: 7699 3499 4213 Industrial machinery and equipment repair; Aerosol valves, metal ; Heavy machinery transport
PA: B M Machine
11722 W County Road 6
Alvada OH 44802
419 595-2898

(G-11535)
F & F SHTMTL & FABRICATION LLC
3601 County Road 14 (44853-9617)
PHONE..................419 618-3171
Jeff Fox, *Prin*
EMP: 6 **EST:** 2018
SALES (est): 54.36K **Privately Held**
SIC: 3499 Fabricated metal products, nec

(G-11536)
JUNO ENTERPRISES LLC
Also Called: Lucius Fence and Decking
8146 Us Highway 224 (44853-9729)
PHONE..................419 448-9350
EMP: 6 **EST:** 2020
SALES (est): 523.83K **Privately Held**
SIC: 2499 Fencing, docks, and other outdoor wood structural products

(G-11537)
SCHREINER MANUFACTURING LLC
1997 Township Road 66 (44853-9728)
PHONE..................419 937-0300
Brandan Schreiner, *Prin*
EMP: 7 **EST:** 2012
SALES (est): 437.38K **Privately Held**
SIC: 3999 Barber and beauty shop equipment

(G-11538)
TR BOES HOLDINGS INC
Also Called: Boes, Wilbert J
14 N Perry St (44853-9776)
P.O. Box 237 (44853-0237)
PHONE..................419 595-2255
Wilbert J Boes, *Pr*
Hildegarde Boes, *Prin*
Tom Boes, *VP*
Richard Boes, *Sec*
EMP: 26 **EST:** 1953
SQ FT: 4,500
SALES (est): 239.39K **Privately Held**
Web: www.newriegelcafe.com
SIC: 5812 2011 Barbecue restaurant; Meat packing plants

New Springfield
Mahoning County

(G-11539)
B V MFG INC
13426 Woodworth Rd (44443-9789)
P.O. Box 176 (44443-0176)
PHONE..................330 549-5331
Robert Maine, *Pr*
EMP: 13 **EST:** 1975
SQ FT: 6,200
SALES (est): 365.32K **Privately Held**
SIC: 3544 Extrusion dies

(G-11540)
D & D MINING CO INC
3379 E Garfield Rd (44443-9743)
PHONE..................330 549-3127
Donald Thompson, *Pr*
David Thompson, *VP*
EMP: 10 **EST:** 1972
SQ FT: 1,000
SALES (est): 989.25K **Privately Held**
SIC: 1221 Bituminous coal and lignite-surface mining

(G-11541)
EXTENDIT COMPANY
14150 Beaver Springfield Rd (44443-9773)
PHONE..................330 743-4343
Henry M Garlick, *Pr*
EMP: 6 **EST:** 1966
SALES (est): 709.09K **Privately Held**
Web: www.extenditco.com
SIC: 2951 Asphalt paving mixtures and blocks

(G-11542)
THOMPSON BROS MINING CO
Also Called: Thompson Brothers Mining
3379 E Garfield Rd (44443-9743)
PHONE..................330 549-3979
Don Thompson, *Pr*
Dave Thompson, *VP*
EMP: 10 **EST:** 1947
SQ FT: 1,000
SALES (est): 770K **Privately Held**
SIC: 1221 Strip mining, bituminous

New Vienna
Clinton County

(G-11543)
PALM HARBOR HOMES INC
11004 State Route 28 (45159-9516)
PHONE..................937 725-9465
Mike Schmitzer, *Prin*
EMP: 6 **EST:** 2011
SALES (est): 117.89K **Privately Held**
SIC: 2451 Mobile homes, personal or private use

(G-11544)
WELLS MANUFACTURING LLC
280 W Main St (45159-5024)
P.O. Box 325 (45159-0325)
PHONE..................937 987-2481
Glenn Douglas, *VP Opers*
Grant Douglas, *Pr*
James J Hughes Iii, *Prin*
EMP: 10 **EST:** 1945
SQ FT: 100,000
SALES (est): 631.61K **Privately Held**
Web: www.wellsmfgco.com
SIC: 3944 Games, toys, and children's vehicles

New Washington
Crawford County

(G-11545)
C E WHITE CO (HQ)
417 N Kibler St (44854)
P.O. Box 308 (44854)
PHONE..................419 492-2157
Tony Everett, *Pr*
Bob Knapp, *
▲ **EMP:** 54 **EST:** 1937
SQ FT: 65,000
SALES (est): 8.9MM
SALES (corp-wide): 430.3MM **Privately Held**
Web: www.hsmtransportation.com
SIC: 2531 Seats, miscellaneous public conveyances
PA: Hickory Springs Manufacturing Company
235 2nd Ave Nw
Hickory NC 28601
828 328-2201

(G-11546)
CREST BENDING INC
108 John St (44854-9702)
P.O. Box 458 (44854-0458)
PHONE..................419 492-2108
Robert E Studer, *Pr*
EMP: 45 **EST:** 1966
SQ FT: 50,000
SALES (est): 4.59MM **Privately Held**
Web: www.crestbending.com
SIC: 3312 7692 3498 3317 Tubes, steel and iron; Welding repair; Fabricated pipe and fittings; Steel pipe and tubes

(G-11547)
HERALD INC
625 S Kibler St (44854-9541)
P.O. Box 367 (44854-0367)
PHONE..................419 492-2133
EMP: 35 **EST:** 2010
SALES (est): 5.73MM **Privately Held**
Web: www.theheraldinc.com
SIC: 2752 Offset printing

(G-11548)
MANSFIELD BRASS & ALUMINUM CORPORATION
Also Called: Mansfield Castings
636 S Center St (44854-9417)
PHONE..................419 492-2154
EMP: 55
Web: www.mansfield-castings.com
SIC: 3365 Aluminum foundries

(G-11549)
NEW MANSFIELD BRASS & ALUM CO
636 S Center St (44854-9711)
PHONE..................419 492-2166
Russell Nelson, *Pr*
EMP: 12 **EST:** 2013
SALES (est): 433.15K **Privately Held**
Web: www.mansfield-castings.com
SIC: 3365 Aluminum and aluminum-based alloy castings

(G-11550)
OHIO FOAM CORPORATION
529 S Kibler St (44854-9524)
P.O. Box 61 (44820-0061)
PHONE..................419 492-2151
Diane Swartzmiller, *Prin*
EMP: 10
SQ FT: 15,000
SALES (corp-wide): 7.68MM **Privately Held**
Web: www.ohiofoam.com
SIC: 3069 2821 Foam rubber; Plastics materials and resins
PA: Ohio Foam Corporation
820 Plymouth St
Bucyrus OH 44820
419 563-0399

(G-11551)
STUMPS CONVERTING INC
742 W Mansfield St (44854-9449)
PHONE..................419 492-2542
Suzanne Stump, *Pr*
Dave Q Stump, *VP*
EMP: 10 **EST:** 1991
SALES (est): 500K **Privately Held**
SIC: 2679 5149 Paper products, converted, nec; Syrups, except for fountain use

(G-11552)
WURMS WOODWORKING COMPANY
Also Called: Gr Golf
725 W Mansfield St (44854)
P.O. Box 275 (44854)
PHONE..................419 492-2184
Gerald B Wurm, *Pr*
Richard Wurm, *
Mary Wurm, *
Valerie Sanderson, *
EMP: 44 **EST:** 1947
SQ FT: 60,000
SALES (est): 7.54MM **Privately Held**
Web: www.wurmsproducts.com
SIC: 2499 2531 3082 3083 Furniture inlays (veneers); Vehicle furniture; Unsupported plastics profile shapes; Laminated plastics plate and sheet

New Waterford
Columbiana County

(G-11553)
BARCON LLC
47161 State Route 558 (44445-9628)
PHONE..................866 883-4804
EMP: 8 **EST:** 2018
SALES (est): 262.75K **Privately Held**
Web: www.barcon.co
SIC: 3599 Machine shop, jobbing and repair

(G-11554)
CENTURY CONTAINER LLC (HQ)
5331 State Route 7 (44445-9787)
PHONE..................330 457-2367
Mark Brothers, *Pr*
EMP: 10 **EST:** 2014
SALES (est): 17.63MM **Privately Held**
Web: www.centurycontainercorporation.com
SIC: 3089 Plastics containers, except foam
PA: Thorworks Industries, Inc.
2520 Campbell St
Sandusky OH 44870

(G-11555)
CENTURY CONTAINER CORPORATION
5331 State Route 7 (44445-9787)
PHONE..................330 457-2367
▼ **EMP:** 155
SIC: 3089 Plastics containers, except foam

(G-11556)
CENTURY INDUSTRIES CORPORATION
5331 State Route 7 (44445-9787)
PHONE..................330 457-2367
Don R Brothers, *CEO*
Jill Brothers, *

GEOGRAPHIC SECTION

Roland Brothers, *
William G Houser, *
Budd Brothers, *
EMP: 25 **EST:** 1944
SQ FT: 100,000
SALES (est): 2.27MM **Privately Held**
Web:
www.centuryindustriescorporation.com
SIC: 2891 2952 Sealants; Asphalt felts and coatings

(G-11557)
LONNY EUGENE HORST
2239 Waterford Rd (44445-9793)
PHONE................................330 846-0057
Horst Lonny, *Prin*
EMP: 7 **EST:** 2014
SALES (est): 232.94K **Privately Held**
SIC: 7534 Tire retreading and repair shops

(G-11558)
MAJESTIC MANUFACTURING INC
4536 State Route 7 (44445-9785)
P.O. Box 128 (44445-0128)
PHONE................................330 457-2447
Vince Kudler, *Pr*
Jeff Kudler, *VP*
Chris Kudler, *Prin*
Linda Kudler, *Prin*
◆ **EMP:** 20 **EST:** 1971
SQ FT: 68,000
SALES (est): 2.05MM **Privately Held**
Web: www.majesticrides.com
SIC: 3599 5087 Carnival machines and equipment, amusement park, nec; Carnival and amusement park equipment

(G-11559)
SAINT JOHNSBURY PERFECT SCENTS
3324 State Route 7 (44445-9708)
PHONE................................330 846-0175
Tami Harris, *Prin*
EMP: 6 **EST:** 2013
SALES (est): 124.93K **Privately Held**
Web: www.stjohnsburycandles.com
SIC: 3999 Candles

Newark
Licking County

(G-11560)
ACUITY BRANDS LIGHTING INC
214 Oakwood Ave (43055-6716)
PHONE................................740 349-4343
Steve Hummel, *Manager*
EMP: 60
SALES (corp-wide): 3.95B **Publicly Held**
Web: lithonia.acuitybrands.com
SIC: 3646 3648 3645 3612 Commercial lighting fixtures; Lighting equipment, nec; Residential lighting fixtures; Transformers, except electric
HQ: Acuity Brands Lighting, Inc.
1170 Peachtree St Ne # 23
Atlanta GA 30309

(G-11561)
AMPACET CORPORATION
1855 James Pkwy (43056-1092)
PHONE................................740 929-5521
Jim Edge, *Brnch Mgr*
EMP: 87
SALES (corp-wide): 455.35MM **Privately Held**
Web: www.ampacet.com
SIC: 2869 2816 Industrial organic chemicals, nec; Inorganic pigments
PA: Ampacet Corporation
660 White Plins Rd Ste 36
Tarrytown NY 10591
914 631-6600

(G-11562)
AMY ELECTRIC
46 N 4th St (43055-5025)
P.O. Box 4247 (43058-4247)
PHONE................................740 349-9484
EMP: 6 **EST:** 2007
SALES (est): 27.72K **Privately Held**
SIC: 3699 Electrical equipment and supplies, nec

(G-11563)
ANDROM INDUSTRIES INC
9960 Butler Rd (43055-9794)
PHONE................................614 408-9067
Trace Joseph Johnson, *Prin*
EMP: 6 **EST:** 2015
SALES (est): 122.77K **Privately Held**
SIC: 3599 Air intake filters, internal combustion engine, except auto

(G-11564)
ANOMATIC CORPORATION
1650 Tamarack Rd (43055-1359)
PHONE................................740 522-2203
Chris Wilson, *Brnch Mgr*
EMP: 500
SALES (corp-wide): 783.05MM **Privately Held**
Web: www.anomatic.com
SIC: 3471 Anodizing (plating) of metals or formed products
HQ: Anomatic Corporation
8880 Innvation Campus Way
New Albany OH 43054
740 522-2203

(G-11565)
ARBORIS LLC
1780 Tamarack Rd (43055-1359)
PHONE................................740 522-9350
Tom Lindow, *Brnch Mgr*
EMP: 29
SALES (corp-wide): 24.02MM **Privately Held**
Web: www.arboris-us.com
SIC: 2819 Chemicals, high purity: refined from technical grade
PA: Arboris, Llc
1101 W Lathrop Ave
Savannah GA 31415
912 238-6355

(G-11566)
ASHCRAFT MACHINE & SUPPLY INC
185 Wilson St (43055-4099)
PHONE................................740 349-8110
Larry G Ashcraft, *Pr*
Jerry Ashcraft, *Pr*
John Balster, *Off Mgr*
Mike Ashcraft, *VP*
EMP: 12 **EST:** 1949
SQ FT: 15,000
SALES (est): 2.17MM **Privately Held**
Web: www.ashcraftmachine.com
SIC: 3599 Machine shop, jobbing and repair

(G-11567)
BOWERSTON SHALE COMPANY
1329 Seven Hills Rd (43055-8964)
PHONE................................740 763-3921
Beth Hillyer, *Mgr*
EMP: 150
SQ FT: 100,000
SALES (corp-wide): 23.2MM **Privately Held**
Web: www.bowerstonshale.com
SIC: 3251 Brick clay: common face, glazed, vitrified, or hollow
PA: Bowerston Shale Company (Inc)
515 Main St
Bowerston OH 44695
740 269-2921

(G-11568)
BTR ENTERPRISES LLC
7371 Stewart Rd (43055-9667)
PHONE................................740 975-2526
EMP: 6 **EST:** 2008
SALES (est): 92.2K **Privately Held**
SIC: 3482 Small arms ammunition

(G-11569)
BURDENS MACHINE & WELDING INC
94 S 5th St (43055-5302)
P.O. Box 177 (43058-0177)
PHONE................................740 345-9246
Donald Burden Senior, *Pr*
Donald Burden Junior, *VP*
Darrell Burden, *VP*
Robert Burden, *Sec*
EMP: 12 **EST:** 1977
SQ FT: 4,400
SALES (est): 424.99K **Privately Held**
SIC: 1799 3599 Welding on site; Machine shop, jobbing and repair

(G-11570)
CITY OF NEWARK
Also Called: Newark Water Plant
164 Waterworks Rd (43055-6057)
PHONE................................740 349-6765
Steve Rhodes, *Mgr*
EMP: 37
SALES (corp-wide): 54.01MM **Privately Held**
Web: www.buckeyeaxethrowing.com
SIC: 3561 Pumps, domestic: water or sump
PA: City Of Newark
40 W Main St
Newark OH 43055
740 670-7512

(G-11571)
COLUMBUS ROOF TRUSSES INC
Also Called: Central Ohio Bldg Components
400 Marne Dr (43055-8817)
PHONE................................740 763-3000
EMP: 10
SALES (corp-wide): 4.12MM **Privately Held**
SIC: 2439 Trusses, wooden roof
PA: Columbus Roof Trusses, Inc.
2525 Fisher Rd
Columbus OH 43204
614 272-6464

(G-11572)
CONTOUR FORMING INC
215 Oakwood Ave (43055-6751)
P.O. Box 727 (43058-0727)
PHONE................................740 345-9777
Terrie Lee Hill, *Pr*
Garrie Hill, *VP Mfg*
Tracie Hill, *VP Sls*
EMP: 18 **EST:** 1955
SQ FT: 100,000
SALES (est): 2.53MM **Privately Held**
SIC: 3356 3315 3444 3469 Nonferrous rolling and drawing, nec; Steel wire and related products; Sheet metalwork; Metal stampings, nec

(G-11573)
CP INDUSTRIES INC
Also Called: Pilot Chemical
11047 Lambs Ln (43055-9779)
PHONE................................740 763-2886
Kent Pitcher, *Pr*
Jeff Pitcher, *VP*
Martin Solomon, *VP*
Brian Pitcher, *Sec*
▲ **EMP:** 12 **EST:** 1999
SALES (est): 498.11K **Privately Held**
Web: www.cpadhesives.com
SIC: 2891 Adhesives

(G-11574)
ELKHEAD GAS & OIL CO
12163 Marne Rd (43055-8810)
PHONE................................740 763-3966
Maurice Dale Chapin, *Pr*
Michael Chapin, *VP*
James Chapin, *Sec*
EMP: 6 **EST:** 1964
SQ FT: 1,000
SALES (est): 841.11K **Privately Held**
Web: www.elkheadgasandoilco.com
SIC: 1382 1311 Oil and gas exploration services; Crude petroleum production

(G-11575)
EQUIPMENT GUYS INC
185 Westgate Dr (43055-9313)
PHONE................................614 871-9220
Matthew A Purdy, *Pr*
EMP: 11 **EST:** 1995
SALES (est): 2.31MM **Privately Held**
Web: www.equipmentguys.com
SIC: 3949 5084 Dumbbells and other weightlifting equipment; Industrial machinery and equipment

(G-11576)
FGS-WI LLC
37 S Park Pl (43055-5505)
PHONE................................630 375-8597
Michael Mumphrey, *Prin*
EMP: 21
SALES (corp-wide): 101.33MM **Privately Held**
Web: www.fgs.com
SIC: 2752 Offset printing
HQ: Fgs-Wi, Llc
1101 S Janesville St
Milton WI 53563
608 373-6500

(G-11577)
GOLF GALAXY GOLFWORKS INC
Also Called: Golfworks, The
4820 Jacksontown Rd (43056-9377)
P.O. Box 3008 (43058-3008)
PHONE................................740 328-4193
Mark Mccormick, *CEO*
Jerry Datz, *
Mark Wilson, *
Richard C Nordvoid, *
▲ **EMP:** 150 **EST:** 1974
SQ FT: 80,000
SALES (est): 20.39MM
SALES (corp-wide): 12.98B **Publicly Held**
Web: www.golfworks.com
SIC: 5091 2731 3949 5941 Golf equipment; Books, publishing only; Golf equipment; Golf, tennis, and ski shops
HQ: Golf Galaxy, Llc
345 Ct St
Coraopolis PA 15108

(G-11578)
GRANVILLE MILLING CO
Also Called: Granville Milling Drive-Thru
145 N Cedar St (43055-6705)
PHONE................................740 345-1305
Trent Smith, *Mgr*
EMP: 6
SALES (corp-wide): 4.55MM **Privately Held**

Newark - Licking County (G-11579) — GEOGRAPHIC SECTION

Web: www.granvillemilling.net
SIC: 2048 5191 Prepared feeds, nec; Animal feeds
PA: Granville Milling Co.
400 S Main St
Granville OH 43023
740 587-0221

(G-11579)
HOLOPHANE CORPORATION
Also Called: Unique Solutions
515 Mckinley Ave (43055-6737)
PHONE..................................740 349-4194
Richard Peterson, Mgr
EMP: 10
SALES (corp-wide): 3.95B Publicly Held
Web: holophane.acuitybrands.com
SIC: 3646 Commercial lighting fixtures
HQ: Holophane Corporation
3825 Columbus Rd Bldg A
Granville OH 43023

(G-11580)
HOPE TIMBER & MARKETING GROUP (PA)
Also Called: Wood Recovery
141 Union St (43055-3976)
P.O. Box 502 (43023-0502)
PHONE..................................740 344-1788
Thomas J Harvey, Pr
Deborah L Harvey, Ch
EMP: 18 EST: 1993
SQ FT: 40,000
SALES (est): 2.41MM Privately Held
Web: www.hopetimbermulch.com
SIC: 2499 2448 Mulch or sawdust products, wood; Pallets, wood

(G-11581)
HOPE TIMBER MULCH LLC
141 Union St (43055-3976)
P.O. Box 502 (43023-0502)
PHONE..................................740 344-1788
EMP: 6 EST: 2005
SQ FT: 20,000
SALES (est): 742.42K Privately Held
Web: www.hopetimbermulch.com
SIC: 2499 Mulch or sawdust products, wood

(G-11582)
HOPE TIMBER PALLET RECYCL LLC
Also Called: Hope Timber
141 Union St (43055-3976)
P.O. Box 502 (43023-0502)
PHONE..................................740 344-1788
▼ EMP: 36 EST: 2005
SALES (est): 2.72MM Privately Held
Web: www.hopetimbermulch.com
SIC: 2448 4953 Pallets, wood; Recycling, waste materials

(G-11583)
I G BRENNER INC
Also Called: Brenner International
1806 Stonewall Dr (43055-1652)
PHONE..................................740 345-8845
Robert M Fitzgerald, Pr
Jennifer Fitzgerald, Sec
EMP: 10 EST: 1950
SALES (est): 968K Privately Held
Web: www.igbint.com
SIC: 3599 Machine shop, jobbing and repair

(G-11584)
INNS HOLDINGS LTD
29 W Locust St (43055-5510)
PHONE..................................740 345-3700
EMP: 12 EST: 2017
SALES (est): 32.59K Privately Held
SIC: 7011 3571 Inns; Personal computers (microcomputers)

(G-11585)
KREAGER CO LLC
1045 Brice St (43055-6890)
PHONE..................................740 345-1605
Judson Kreager, Owner
EMP: 7 EST: 1983
SQ FT: 2,000
SALES (est): 715.81K Privately Held
Web: www.kreagercompany.com
SIC: 2434 Wood kitchen cabinets

(G-11586)
L & T COLLINS INC
Also Called: Minuteman of Heath
44 S 4th St (43055-5436)
PHONE..................................740 345-4494
Timothy M Collins, Pr
Laura Collins, CFO
EMP: 6 EST: 2003
SQ FT: 12,500
SALES (est): 703.86K Privately Held
Web: www.mpnewark.com
SIC: 2752 Offset printing

(G-11587)
M & H SCREEN PRINTING
1486 Hebron Rd (43056-1035)
PHONE..................................740 522-1957
Douglas Moore, Pt
Laurie Moore, Pt
Stan Hall, Pt
EMP: 6 EST: 1988
SQ FT: 4,000
SALES (est): 459.04K Privately Held
Web: www.mandhscreenprinting.com
SIC: 2759 Screen printing

(G-11588)
M & R PHILLIPS ENTERPRISES
Also Called: Scrappers Gallery
6242 Jacksontown Rd (43056-8303)
PHONE..................................740 323-0580
Mary Phillips, Pr
Rick Phillips, Sec
EMP: 10 EST: 2006
SALES (est): 398.22K Privately Held
SIC: 2782 Scrapbooks, albums, and diaries

(G-11589)
MARION STAR
22 N 1st St (43055-5608)
PHONE..................................740 328-8542
EMP: 6 EST: 2019
SALES (est): 67.98K Privately Held
Web: www.marionstar.com
SIC: 2711 Newspapers, publishing and printing

(G-11590)
MICHALEK MANUFACTURING LLC ◆
160 Obannon Ave (43055-6743)
PHONE..................................740 763-0910
EMP: 9 EST: 2022
SALES (est): 516.36K Privately Held
SIC: 3599 Machine shop, jobbing and repair

(G-11591)
MID OHIO WOOD PRODUCTS INC
535 Franklin Ave (43056-1610)
PHONE..................................740 323-0427
Jay Parkinson, Pr
Nancy Parkinson,
EMP: 20 EST: 1982
SQ FT: 16,000
SALES (est): 454.87K Privately Held
SIC: 2448 2426 Pallets, wood; Hardwood dimension and flooring mills

(G-11592)
MIDWEST MENU MATE INC
Also Called: Midwest Marketing
1065 Lizabeth Cir (43056-1626)
PHONE..................................740 323-2599
EMP: 10 EST: 1992
SALES (est): 580K Privately Held
SIC: 2741 7336 Atlas, map, and guide publishing; Commercial art and graphic design

(G-11593)
MODERN WELDING CO OHIO INC
1 Modern Way (43055-3921)
P.O. Box 4430 (43058-4430)
PHONE..................................740 344-9425
TOLL FREE: 800
John W Jones, Pr
Doug Rothert, VP
Jerry Waller, VP
James M Ruth, Ex VP
EMP: 30 EST: 1932
SQ FT: 52,000
SALES (est): 9.06MM
SALES (corp-wide): 130.45MM Privately Held
Web: www.modweldco.com
SIC: 3443 5051 Tanks, lined: metal plate; Metals service centers and offices
PA: Modern Welding Company, Inc.
2880 New Hartford Rd
Owensboro KY 42303
270 685-4400

(G-11594)
MOUNDBUILDERS BABE RUTH BASBAL
429 Ohio St (43055-6255)
PHONE..................................740 345-6830
EMP: 8 EST: 1995
SALES (est): 98.16K Privately Held
Web: www.baberuthleague.org
SIC: 2064 2024 Candy and other confectionery products; Ice cream and frozen desserts

(G-11595)
MYFOOTSHOPCOM LLC
1159 Cherry Valley Rd Se (43055-9321)
P.O. Box 456 (43023-0456)
PHONE..................................740 522-5681
Jeff A Oster, Pr
Thalia Oster, CEO
EMP: 6 EST: 2001
SALES (est): 704.52K Privately Held
Web: www.myfootshop.com
SIC: 3842 Braces, elastic

(G-11596)
NATIONAL GAS & OIL CORPORATION (DH)
Also Called: Permian Oil & Gas Division
1500 Granville Rd (43055-1500)
P.O. Box 4970 (43058-4970)
PHONE..................................740 344-2102
William Sullivan Junior, Ch Bd
Patrick J Mc Gonagle, Pr
Todd P Ware, VP
Gordon M King, VP
EMP: 36 EST: 1941
SQ FT: 10,000
SALES (est): 53.77MM
SALES (corp-wide): 130.87MM Privately Held
Web: www.theenergycoop.com
SIC: 4922 4924 4932 4911 Natural gas transmission; Natural gas distribution; Gas and other services combined; Electric services
HQ: National Gas & Oil Company Inc
1500 Granville Rd
Newark OH 43055
740 344-2102

(G-11597)
NEW WORLD ENERGY RESOURCES (PA)
1500 Granville Rd (43055-1536)
PHONE..................................740 344-4087
John Manczak, CEO
EMP: 13 EST: 2001
SALES (est): 24.14MM
SALES (corp-wide): 24.14MM Privately Held
SIC: 1382 Geological exploration, oil and gas field

(G-11598)
NGO DEVELOPMENT CORPORATION (HQ)
Also Called: National Production
1500 Granville Rd (43055-1536)
P.O. Box 4970 (43058-4970)
PHONE..................................740 344-3790
Dave Potter, Pr
Daniel S Mc Vey, VP
Todd P Ware, VP
▲ EMP: 22 EST: 1975
SALES (est): 11.43MM
SALES (corp-wide): 24.14MM Privately Held
Web: www.theenergycoop.com
SIC: 4922 1381 Pipelines, natural gas; Directional drilling oil and gas wells
PA: New World Energy Resources Inc
1500 Granville Rd
Newark OH 43055
740 344-4087

(G-11599)
OHIO RIVER VALLEY CABINET
4 Waterworks Rd (43055-6060)
PHONE..................................740 975-8846
Bob Bachmann, Owner
EMP: 6 EST: 1994
SALES (est): 248.34K Privately Held
SIC: 2434 Wood kitchen cabinets

(G-11600)
OWENS CRNING INSLTING SYSTM
400 Case Ave (43055-5805)
P.O. Box 3012 (43058-3012)
PHONE..................................740 328-2300
Fred Ramquist, Brnch Mgr
EMP: 762
SIC: 3296 Fiberglass insulation
HQ: Owens Corning Insulating Systems, Llc
1 Owens Corning Pkwy
Toledo OH 43659
419 248-8000

(G-11601)
PACKAGING CORPORATION AMERICA
Also Called: PCA/Newark 365
205 S 21st St (43055-3879)
P.O. Box 4610 (43058-4610)
PHONE..................................740 344-1126
Pom Watson, Brnch Mgr
EMP: 115
SALES (corp-wide): 8.48B Publicly Held
Web: www.packagingcorp.com
SIC: 2653 Boxes, corrugated: made from purchased materials
PA: Packaging Corporation Of America
1 N Field Ct

GEOGRAPHIC SECTION

Newbury - Geauga County (G-11625)

Lake Forest IL 60045
847 482-3000

(G-11602)
PRESTON
42 Sandalwood Dr (43055-9233)
PHONE..................................740 788-8208
Judith Preston, *Prin*
EMP: 10 **EST:** 2011
SALES (est): 723.62K **Privately Held**
SIC: 3545   Collars (machine tool accessories)

(G-11603)
PUGHS DESIGNER JEWELERS INC
12 W Main St (43055-5504)
PHONE..................................740 344-9259
Kevin Pugh, *Pr*
EMP: 8 **EST:** 1990
SALES (est): 653.84K **Privately Held**
Web: www.pughsdesignerjewelers.com
SIC: 5944 3961 7389 7631   Jewelry, precious stones and precious metals; Costume jewelry; Appraisers, except real estate; Jewelry repair services

(G-11604)
QUANTUM
400 Case Ave (43055-5805)
PHONE..................................740 328-2548
EMP: 18 **EST:** 2012
SALES (est): 345.84K **Privately Held**
SIC: 3572   Computer storage devices

(G-11605)
SHAMROCK PRINTING LLC
82 S 3rd St (43055-5312)
PHONE..................................740 349-2244
EMP: 8 **EST:** 2016
SALES (est): 83.91K **Privately Held**
Web: www.shamrockprinting.com
SIC: 2752   Offset printing

(G-11606)
SPECTRUM ADHESIVES INC
11047 Lambs Ln (43055-9779)
PHONE..................................740 763-2886
EMP: 7
SALES (corp-wide): 10.19MM **Privately Held**
Web: www.spectrumadhesives.com
SIC: 2891   Glue
PA: Spectrum Adhesives, Inc.
       5611 Universal Dr
       Memphis TN 38118
       901 795-1943

(G-11607)
STRATEGIC MATERIALS INC
101 S Arch St (43055-6202)
P.O. Box 816 (43058-0816)
PHONE..................................740 349-9523
Michael Back, *Brnch Mgr*
EMP: 6
SALES (corp-wide): 2.19B **Privately Held**
Web: www.smi.com
SIC: 3231   Products of purchased glass
HQ: Strategic Materials, Inc.
       17220 Katy Fwy Ste 150
       Houston TX 77094

(G-11608)
TECTUM INC
105 S 6th St (43055)
P.O. Box 3002 (43058)
PHONE..................................740 345-9691
Michael Massaro, *Pr*
Wayne Chester, *Marketing**
Stephen M Mihaly, *Stockholder**
John M Scott, *Stockholder**
◆ **EMP:** 120 **EST:** 1979

SQ FT: 100,000
SALES (est): 23.02MM
SALES (corp-wide): 1.3B **Publicly Held**
Web: www.tectum.com
SIC: 2493 3444 3296   Fiberboard, wood; Sheet metalwork; Mineral wool
PA: Armstrong World Industries, Inc.
       2500 Columbia Ave
       Lancaster PA 17603
       717 397-0611

(G-11609)
TRAFFIC CNTRL SGNLS SIGNS & MA
Also Called: City of Newark
1195 E Main St (43055-8869)
PHONE..................................740 670-7763
Gary Snavely, *Dir*
EMP: 7 **EST:** 2007
SALES (est): 443.64K **Privately Held**
Web: www.newarkohio.gov
SIC: 3993   Signs and advertising specialties

(G-11610)
UNIVERSAL PRODUCTION CORP
1776 Tamarack Rd (43055-1359)
PHONE..................................740 522-1147
◆ **EMP:** 24 **EST:** 1993
SQ FT: 98,000
SALES (est): 2.12MM **Privately Held**
Web: www.alink.com
SIC: 2436   Softwood veneer and plywood

(G-11611)
UNIVERSAL VENEER MILL CORP
1776 Tamarack Rd (43055-1384)
PHONE..................................740 522-1147
Klaus Krajewski, *Pr*
William Cooper, ***
EMP: 180 **EST:** 1978
SQ FT: 75,000
SALES (est): 9.26MM **Privately Held**
Web: www.alink.com
SIC: 2435   Hardwood veneer and plywood

(G-11612)
UNIVERSAL VENEER SALES CORP (PA)
1776 Tamarack Rd (43055-1384)
PHONE..................................740 522-1147
◆ **EMP:** 186 **EST:** 1993
SQ FT: 75,000
SALES (est): 9.29MM **Privately Held**
Web: www.alink.com
SIC: 2435   Veneer stock, hardwood

Newburgh Heights
Cuyahoga County

(G-11613)
DOREX LLC
4420 Gamma Ave (44105-3160)
PHONE..................................216 271-7064
Roman Lasocinski, *Prin*
EMP: 6 **EST:** 2010
SALES (est): 101.3K **Privately Held**
Web: www.dorex.com
SIC: 2392   Cushions and pillows

(G-11614)
FIRTH RIXSON INC
1616 Harvard Ave Ste 53 (44105-3040)
PHONE..................................860 760-1040
▲ **EMP:** 63
SIC: 3462   Iron and steel forgings

(G-11615)
HOWMET AEROSPACE INC
Also Called: HOWMET AEROSPACE INC
1600 Harvard Ave (44105-3040)

PHONE..................................216 641-3600
Ian Murray, *Mgr*
EMP: 1200
SALES (corp-wide): 6.64B **Publicly Held**
Web: www.howmet.com
SIC: 3463 3321   Aluminum forgings; Gray and ductile iron foundries
PA: Howmet Aerospace Inc.
       201 Isabella St Ste 200
       Pittsburgh PA 15212
       412 553-1950

(G-11616)
HOWMET ALUMINUM CASTING INC (HQ)
Also Called: Sigma Div
1600 Harvard Ave (44105-3040)
PHONE..................................216 641-4340
Raymond B Mitchell, *Pr*
EMP: 50 **EST:** 1989
SQ FT: 10,000
SALES (est): 103.56MM
SALES (corp-wide): 6.64B **Publicly Held**
Web: www.howmet.com
SIC: 3365   Aerospace castings, aluminum
PA: Howmet Aerospace Inc.
       201 Isabella St Ste 200
       Pittsburgh PA 15212
       412 553-1950

(G-11617)
HUNT PRODUCTS INC
3982 E 42nd St (44105-3165)
PHONE..................................440 667-2457
Jo Ann Hunt, *Pr*
Laura Hunt, ***
EMP: 9 **EST:** 1970
SQ FT: 30,000
SALES (est): 235.3K **Privately Held**
SIC: 7389 3544 3053 2675   Packaging and labeling services; Special dies, tools, jigs, and fixtures; Gaskets; packing and sealing devices; Die-cut paper and board

(G-11618)
MCGEAN-ROHCO INC
2910 Harvard Ave (44105-3010)
PHONE..................................216 441-4900
Kerry May, *Brnch Mgr*
EMP: 12
SQ FT: 350,000
SALES (corp-wide): 41.26MM **Privately Held**
Web: www.mcgean.com
SIC: 2899 2819 3471 2842   Chemical preparations, nec; Industrial inorganic chemicals, nec; Plating and polishing; Polishes and sanitation goods
PA: Mcgean-Rohco, Inc.
       2910 Harvard Ave
       Newburgh Heights OH 44105
       216 441-4900

(G-11619)
MCGEAN-ROHCO INC (PA)
Also Called: McGean
2910 Harvard Ave (44105-3010)
PHONE..................................216 441-4900
◆ **EMP:** 75 **EST:** 1929
SALES (est): 41.26MM
SALES (corp-wide): 41.26MM **Privately Held**
Web: www.mcgean.com
SIC: 2899 2819 3471   Chemical preparations, nec; Industrial inorganic chemicals, nec; Plating and polishing

(G-11620)
PARK-OHIO INDUSTRIES INC
Also Called: Ohio Crankshaft Div
3800 Harvard Ave (44105-3208)

PHONE..................................216 341-2300
Felix Parorick, *Prin*
EMP: 150
SQ FT: 427,000
SALES (corp-wide): 1.66B **Publicly Held**
Web: www.pkoh.com
SIC: 3714   Camshafts, motor vehicle
HQ: Park-Ohio Industries, Inc.
       6065 Parkland Blvd
       Cleveland OH 44124
       440 947-2000

Newbury
Geauga County

(G-11621)
CREATIVE MOLD AND MACHINE INC
10385 Kinsman Rd (44065-9701)
P.O. Box 323 (44065-0323)
PHONE..................................440 338-5146
Ray Lyons, *Pr*
Greg Davis, ***
Mishal Dedeck, *General Vice President**
EMP: 25 **EST:** 1987
SQ FT: 39,000
SALES (est): 2.61MM **Privately Held**
Web: www.creativemoldandmachine.com
SIC: 7692 3599   Welding repair; Machine shop, jobbing and repair

(G-11622)
DAN ALLEN SURGICAL LLC
Also Called: D. A. Surgical
11110 Kinsman Rd Unit 10 (44065-8604)
P.O. Box 189 (44065-0189)
PHONE..................................800 261-9953
EMP: 14 **EST:** 2014
SALES (est): 3.12MM **Privately Held**
Web: www.da-surgical.com
SIC: 8062 3842   General medical and surgical hospitals; Surgical appliances and supplies

(G-11623)
ENGINEERED ENDEAVORS INC
10975 Kinsman Rd (44065-9787)
PHONE..................................440 564-5484
EMP: 21
SIC: 3663   Mobile communication equipment

(G-11624)
GEAUGA CONCRETE INC
10509 Kinsman Rd (44065-9803)
P.O. Box 249 (44045-0249)
PHONE..................................440 338-4915
Hal Larned, *Pr*
EMP: 10 **EST:** 1981
SALES (est): 1.38MM
SALES (corp-wide): 3.62MM **Privately Held**
Web: geauga.oh.gov
SIC: 3273   Ready-mixed concrete
PA: Osborne Concrete & Stone Co.
       1 Williams St
       Grand River OH 44045
       440 357-5562

(G-11625)
GREEN VISION MATERIALS INC
11220 Kinsman Rd (44065-9676)
PHONE..................................440 564-5500
Beau Gibney, *Owner*
EMP: 15 **EST:** 2010
SALES (est): 2.5MM **Privately Held**
Web: www.greenvisionmaterials.com
SIC: 4953 3271   Recycling, waste materials; Blocks, concrete: landscape or retaining wall

Newbury - Geauga County (G-11626)

(G-11626)
HOT BRASS INC
15140 Munn Rd (44065-9728)
PHONE..................440 564-5179
Frank Karl Renovich, *Prin*
EMP: 7 **EST:** 2011
SALES (est): 52.31K **Privately Held**
SIC: 3366 Copper foundries

(G-11627)
INTELACOMM INC
12375 Kinsman Rd (44065-9684)
P.O. Box 332 (44065-0332)
PHONE..................888 610-9250
Robert Ruckstuh, *CEO*
Robert R Ruckstuhl, *CEO*
EMP: 6 **EST:** 2016
SALES (est): 150K **Privately Held**
Web: www.intelacomm.com
SIC: 2741 Internet publishing and broadcasting

(G-11628)
KINETICO INCORPORATED (HQ)
10845 Kinsman Rd (44065-8702)
PHONE..................440 564-9111
◆ **EMP:** 287 **EST:** 1970
SALES (est): 91.57MM
SALES (corp-wide): 635.39MM **Privately Held**
Web: www.kinetico.com
SIC: 3589 5074 6799 Water treatment equipment, industrial; Water heaters and purification equipment; Investors, nec
PA: Axel Johnson Inc.
    155 Spring St Fl 6
    New York NY 10012
    646 291-2445

(G-11629)
KKR LLC
14905 Cross Creek Pkwy (44065-9788)
P.O. Box 375 (44065-0375)
PHONE..................440 564-7168
J Casey Mcnicholas, *Prin*
EMP: 8 **EST:** 2001
SALES (est): 223.44K **Privately Held**
SIC: 2992 Oils and greases, blending and compounding

(G-11630)
MINUS G LLC
12300 Kinsman Rd Unit A-1 (44065)
P.O. Box 22 (44065)
PHONE..................440 817-0338
Katherine Gardner, *Managing Member*
EMP: 8 **EST:** 2016
SALES (est): 253.18K **Privately Held**
Web: www.minusg.com
SIC: 5461 2045 Retail bakeries; Prepared flour mixes and doughs

(G-11631)
NEWBURY SNDBLST & PNTG INC
Also Called: Newbury Sandblasting & Pntg
9992 Kinsman Rd (44065)
P.O. Box 378 (44065)
PHONE..................440 564-7204
Nelson Peterson, *Pr*
Pamela Peterson, *Sec*
EMP: 7 **EST:** 1976
SQ FT: 25,000
SALES (est): 657.43K **Privately Held**
SIC: 3471 7532 Sand blasting of metal parts; Paint shop, automotive

(G-11632)
NEWBURY WOODWORKS
10958 Kinsman Rd Unit 2 (44065-8602)
PHONE..................440 564-5273
EMP: 7 **EST:** 1996
SQ FT: 8,000
SALES (est): 250.64K **Privately Held**
SIC: 5712 2499 Cabinet work, custom; Decorative wood and woodwork

(G-11633)
OREILLY EQUIPMENT LLC
14555 Ravenna Rd (44065)
PHONE..................440 564-1234
EMP: 6 **EST:** 2002
SQ FT: 6,000
SALES (est): 2.25MM **Privately Held**
Web: www.oreillyequipment.com
SIC: 5599 3714 Utility trailers; Ice scrapers and window brushes, motor vehicle

(G-11634)
PADCO INDUSTRIES LLC
Also Called: Dem Manufacturing
10357 Kinsman Rd (44065-8700)
PHONE..................440 564-7160
Craig Padula, *Managing Member*
▲ **EMP:** 19 **EST:** 2005
SALES (est): 2.46MM **Privately Held**
Web: www.dem-mfg.com
SIC: 3999 Manufacturing industries, nec

(G-11635)
R W SIDLEY INCORPORATED
10688 Kinsman Rd (44065-9761)
P.O. Box 208 (44065-0208)
PHONE..................440 564-2221
Dan Craver, *Brnch Mgr*
EMP: 8
SALES (corp-wide): 83.57MM **Privately Held**
Web: www.rwsidley.com
SIC: 3273 3272 3271 1442 Ready-mixed concrete; Concrete products, nec; Concrete block and brick; Construction sand and gravel
PA: R. W. Sidley Incorporated
    436 Casement Ave
    Painesville OH 44077
    440 352-9343

(G-11636)
RALSTON INSTRUMENTS LLC
15035 Cross Creek Pkwy (44065-9726)
P.O. Box 340 (44072-0340)
PHONE..................440 564-1430
Griffin Ralston, *CEO*
Douglas Ralston, *Managing Member*
Corey Ralston, *
EMP: 25 **EST:** 1968
SALES (est): 3.74MM **Privately Held**
Web: www.ralstoninst.com
SIC: 3829 Measuring and controlling devices, nec

(G-11637)
SAINT-GOBAIN CERAMICS PLAS INC
Also Called: Saint Gobain Crystals
12359 Kinsman Rd (44065-9620)
PHONE..................440 542-2712
Tom Kinisky, *Pr*
EMP: 500 **EST:** 1951
SALES (est): 52.62MM
SALES (corp-wide): 397.78MM **Privately Held**
SIC: 3674 Semiconductors and related devices
PA: Compagnie De Saint-Gobain
    Tour Saint Gobain
    Courbevoie 92400

(G-11638)
UNITED ROLLER CO LLC
14910 Cross Creek Pkwy (44065-9788)
PHONE..................440 564-9698
EMP: 14 **EST:** 2002
SQ FT: 13,500
SALES (est): 1.22MM **Privately Held**
Web: www.united-roller.com
SIC: 3069 Rolls, solid or covered rubber

(G-11639)
WATEROPOLIS CORP
12361 Kinsman Rd (44065-8810)
PHONE..................440 564-5061
Kelly A Slattery, *Prin*
EMP: 6 **EST:** 2014
SALES (est): 500.99K **Privately Held**
Web: www.wateropolis.com
SIC: 3589 Water purification equipment, household type

Newcomerstown
Tuscarawas County

(G-11640)
31 INC
Also Called: Extra Seal
100 Enterprise Dr (43832-9242)
P.O. Box 278 (43832-0278)
PHONE..................740 498-8324
Charles Muhs, *Pr*
Robert Hendry, *
◆ **EMP:** 100 **EST:** 1961
SQ FT: 130,000
SALES (est): 21.65MM **Privately Held**
Web: www.31inc.com
SIC: 3011 3714 Tire sundries or tire repair materials, rubber; Tire valve cores

(G-11641)
ACCURATE PRODUCTS COMPANY
98 Elizabeth St (43832-1432)
P.O. Box 106 (43832-0106)
PHONE..................740 498-7202
Clark H Smith, *Pr*
R Clark Smith, *VP*
EMP: 6 **EST:** 1946
SALES (est): 600K **Privately Held**
SIC: 3366 Castings (except die), nec, brass

(G-11642)
ANNIN & CO
Also Called: ANNIN & CO.
100 State Route 258 (43832-8831)
PHONE..................740 498-5008
Vane Scott, *Mgr*
EMP: 31
SALES (corp-wide): 94.54MM **Privately Held**
Web: www.annin.com
SIC: 2399 Banners, pennants, and flags
PA: Annin & Co., Inc.
    430 Mountain Ave Ste 410
    New Providence NJ 07974
    973 228-9400

(G-11643)
BUCKEYE BOP LLC
Also Called: Buckeye Blow Out Preventer
401 Enterprise Dr (43832-9239)
PHONE..................740 498-9898
EMP: 9 **EST:** 2011
SALES (est): 816.34K **Privately Held**
Web: www.buckbop.com
SIC: 3564 3592 5719 Blowers and fans; Valves; Brushes

(G-11644)
H3D TOOL CORPORATION
Also Called: High Definition Tooling
295 Enterprise Dr (43832-8954)
P.O. Box 314 (43832-0314)
PHONE..................740 498-5181
EMP: 48 **EST:** 1994
SQ FT: 20,000
SALES (est): 7.12MM **Privately Held**
Web: www.h3dtool.com
SIC: 3545 5085 Diamond cutting tools for turning, boring, burnishing, etc.; Industrial supplies

(G-11645)
HERCO INC
295 Enterprise Dr (43832-8954)
P.O. Box 314 (43832-0314)
PHONE..................740 498-5181
Gary Dyer, *Pr*
Chris Dyer, *
EMP: 17 **EST:** 1968
SQ FT: 20,000
SALES (est): 463.37K **Privately Held**
Web: www.h3dtool.com
SIC: 3541 Machine tools, metal cutting type

(G-11646)
HV COIL
700 Newport St (43832-1279)
PHONE..................330 260-4126
EMP: 10 **EST:** 2018
SALES (est): 1.03MM **Privately Held**
Web: www.hvcoilusa.com
SIC: 3621 Motors and generators

(G-11647)
KURZ-KASCH INC (DH)
Also Called: Kurz-Kasch
199 E State St (43832-1468)
PHONE..................740 498-8343
Chad Merkel, *CEO*
Jack Senn, *
▲ **EMP:** 30 **EST:** 1916
SQ FT: 6,000
SALES (est): 12.5MM
SALES (corp-wide): 476.37MM **Privately Held**
Web: www.kurz-kasch.com
SIC: 3089 3677 Thermoformed finished plastics products, nec; Electronic coils and transformers
HQ: Prettl Manufacturing Corporation
    1721 White Horse Rd
    Greenville SC 29605
    864 220-1010

(G-11648)
OAK POINTE LLC
96 New Pace Rd (43832-1287)
PHONE..................740 498-9820
EMP: 26 **EST:** 2007
SALES (est): 1.49MM **Privately Held**
Web: www.stairpartsandmore.com
SIC: 2431 Millwork

(G-11649)
OHIO VALLEY SAND LLC
100 E State St (43832-1453)
PHONE..................330 440-6495
Gary Mcrill, *Mgr*
EMP: 8 **EST:** 2012
SALES (est): 234.47K **Privately Held**
Web: www.ohiovalleysandllc.com
SIC: 1442 Construction sand and gravel

(G-11650)
PARAGON INTGRTED SVCS GROUP LL
Also Called: Paragon Integrated Svcs Group
200 Enterprise Dr (43832-8954)
PHONE..................724 639-5126
EMP: 20
SALES (corp-wide): 21.87MM **Privately Held**
Web: www.paragonisg.com

SIC: 1389 Oil field services, nec
PA: Paragon Integrated Services Group Llc
825 Town And Country Ln # 120
Houston TX 77024
740 492-0190

(G-11651)
SIMONA BOLTARON INC
Also Called: A Simona Group Company
1 General St (43832-1230)
PHONE..............................740 498-5900
Lawrence J Schorr, *CEO*
Dean Li, *CFO*
◆ **EMP:** 100 **EST:** 2004
SQ FT: 175,000
SALES (est): 47.72MM **Privately Held**
Web: www.boltaron.com
SIC: 3081 2891 Film base, cellulose acetate or nitrocellulose plastics; Adhesives and sealants

Newton Falls
Trumbull County

(G-11652)
AMERICAN MOLDED PLASTICS INC
3876 Newton Falls Bailey Rd (44444-9746)
P.O. Box 434 (44444-0434)
PHONE..............................330 872-3838
Ray Allen, *Pr*
Bertha Allen, *VP*
EMP: 10 **EST:** 1989
SQ FT: 6,000
SALES (est): 977.37K **Privately Held**
Web: www.americanmoldedplastic.com
SIC: 3089 Injection molding of plastics

(G-11653)
BAR PROCESSING CORPORATION
1000 Windham Rd (44444-9586)
P.O. Box 280 (44444-0280)
PHONE..............................330 872-0914
Jack Stacky, *Mgr*
EMP: 14
SALES (corp-wide): 39.93MM **Privately Held**
Web: www.barprocessingcorp.com
SIC: 3471 3316 Finishing, metals or formed products; Cold finishing of steel shapes
HQ: Bar Processing Corporation
26601 W Huron River Dr
Flat Rock MI 48134
734 782-4454

(G-11654)
LUXAIRE CUSHION CO
2410 S Center St (44444-9408)
P.O. Box 156 (44444-0156)
PHONE..............................330 872-0995
Alan E Rathbun Junior, *Pr*
Steve Fackelman, *VP*
EMP: 10 **EST:** 1946
SQ FT: 55,000
SALES (est): 506.82K **Privately Held**
Web: www.luxairecushion.com
SIC: 2393 Cushions, except spring and carpet: purchased materials

(G-11655)
QUALITY SWITCH INC
715 Arlington Blvd (44444-8765)
P.O. Box 250 (44444-0250)
PHONE..............................330 872-5707
Russell Sewell, *Pr*
Rick Sewell, *
Laura Whitmore, *
EMP: 29 **EST:** 1974
SQ FT: 31,200
SALES (est): 4.41MM **Privately Held**
Web: www.qualityswitch.com
SIC: 3679 Electronic switches

(G-11656)
RS IMPRINTS LLC
5 S Milton Blvd (44444-1780)
PHONE..............................330 872-5905
Ross Sherlock, *Prin*
EMP: 7 **EST:** 2016
SALES (est): 210.15K **Privately Held**
Web: www.rsimprints.com
SIC: 2752 Commercial printing, lithographic

(G-11657)
S & S WLDG FABG MACHINING INC
2587 Miller Graber Rd (44444-9724)
PHONE..............................330 392-7878
R Saxton, *CEO*
Jonathan Saxton, *
Steven Saxton, *
EMP: 15 **EST:** 1969
SALES (est): 245.41K **Privately Held**
SIC: 3315 Welded steel wire fabric

(G-11658)
STONER GLASS ACT STUDIO LLC ✪
30 W Broad St (44444-1605)
PHONE..............................330 360-3294
Ronald Stoner, *Prin*
EMP: 7 **EST:** 2023
SALES (est): 78.58K **Privately Held**
SIC: 3231 Decorated glassware: chipped, engraved, etched, etc.

(G-11659)
TRANSCO RAILWAY PRODUCTS INC
2310 S Center St (44444-9406)
PHONE..............................330 872-0934
Robert Ewing, *Mgr*
EMP: 40
SQ FT: 100,000
SALES (corp-wide): 364.48B **Publicly Held**
Web: www.transcorailway.com
SIC: 3441 3743 Fabricated structural metal; Railroad equipment
HQ: Transco Railway Products Inc.
200 N La Salle St Lbby 5
Chicago IL 60601
312 427-2818

(G-11660)
VENTURE PLASTICS INC (PA)
Also Called: V P
4000 Warren Rd (44444)
P.O. Box 249 (44444-0249)
PHONE..............................330 872-5774
Kenneth M Groff, *CEO*
J Stephen Trapp, *
Bryon Osborne, *
James Smith, *
Gary Flattum, *
◆ **EMP:** 115 **EST:** 1969
SQ FT: 60,000
SALES (est): 40.38MM
SALES (corp-wide): 40.38MM **Privately Held**
Web: www.ventureplastics.com
SIC: 3089 Injection molding of plastics

Newtown
Hamilton County

(G-11661)
BRAIN BREW VENTURES 30 INC
3849 Edwards Rd (45244-2408)
PHONE..............................513 310-6374
Doug Hall, *CEO*
EMP: 10 **EST:** 2012
SALES (est): 1.01MM **Privately Held**
Web: www.brainbrewwhiskey.com
SIC: 6799 2085 Venture capital companies; Bourbon whiskey

Niles
Trumbull County

(G-11662)
BRT EXTRUSIONS INC
Also Called: Building Rlationships Together
1818 N Main St Unit 1 (44446-1285)
P.O. Box 309 (44446-0309)
PHONE..............................330 544-0177
Roy Smith, *Pr*
William Fusco, *
EMP: 220 **EST:** 2004
SQ FT: 92,000
SALES (est): 36MM **Privately Held**
Web: www.brtextrusions.com
SIC: 3354 Aluminum extruded products

(G-11663)
CHESTNUT LAND COMPANY
Also Called: Auntie Anne's
5555 Youngstown Warren Rd Unit 637 (44446-4804)
PHONE..............................330 652-1939
Debra Barbara, *Brnch Mgr*
EMP: 7
Web: www.auntieannes.com
SIC: 5461 2051 5812 Pretzels; Bread, cake, and related products; Eating places
PA: Chestnut Land Company
100 Debartolo Pl Ste 300
Youngstown OH 44512

(G-11664)
CHIEFFOS FROZEN FOODS INC
406 S Main St (44446-1454)
PHONE..............................330 652-1222
Richard Yannucci, *Pr*
EMP: 8 **EST:** 1970
SQ FT: 7,200
SALES (est): 701.63K **Privately Held**
Web: www.chieffopasta.com
SIC: 2099 Food preparations, nec

(G-11665)
CLEVELAND STEEL CONTAINER CORP
412 Mason St (44446-2349)
PHONE..............................330 544-2271
Chistopher Page, *Owner*
EMP: 40
SALES (corp-wide): 138.41MM **Privately Held**
Web: www.cscpails.com
SIC: 3412 Barrels, shipping: metal
PA: Cleveland Steel Container Corporation
100 Executive Pkwy
Hudson OH 44236
440 349-8000

(G-11666)
DINESOL PLASTICS INC
Also Called: Dinesol Plastics
195 E Park Ave (44446-2352)
P.O. Box 470 (44446-0470)
PHONE..............................330 544-7171
Robert Hendricks Junior, *Pr*
Kenneth Fibus, *
Kenneth Leonard, *
Michael Janak, *
▲ **EMP:** 150 **EST:** 1976
SQ FT: 380,000
SALES (est): 150MM **Privately Held**
Web: www.dinesol.com
SIC: 3089 Injection molding of plastics

(G-11667)
DURSO BAKERY INC
212 S Cedar Ave (44446-2308)
P.O. Box 605 (44446-0605)
PHONE..............................330 652-4741
Dominic D' Urso, *Pr*
Tony D'urso, *Sec*
Anthony D'urso, *Stockholder*
EMP: 10 **EST:** 1959
SQ FT: 7,000
SALES (est): 497.02K **Privately Held**
SIC: 2051 Bakery: wholesale or wholesale/retail combined

(G-11668)
FAULL & SON LLC
515 Holford Ave (44446-1796)
P.O. Box 627 (44446-0627)
PHONE..............................330 652-4341
James K Faull, *Prin*
EMP: 10 **EST:** 1949
SQ FT: 16,000
SALES (est): 905.62K **Privately Held**
Web: www.faullandson.com
SIC: 3469 3544 3498 3429 Stamping metal for the trade; Special dies and tools; Fabricated pipe and fittings; Hardware, nec

(G-11669)
GATEWAYS INDUSTRIES INC
1200 Youngstown Warren Rd (44446-4612)
PHONE..............................330 505-0479
EMP: 7 **EST:** 2016
SALES (est): 52.17K **Privately Held**
Web: www.gatewaystbl.com
SIC: 3999 Manufacturing industries, nec

(G-11670)
HOWLAND MACHINE CORP
947 Summit Ave (44446-3612)
PHONE..............................330 544-4029
Bruce V Dewey, *Pr*
EMP: 20 **EST:** 1989
SQ FT: 22,000
SALES (est): 4.21MM **Privately Held**
Web: www.hmcmachinetech.com
SIC: 3599 Machine shop, jobbing and repair

(G-11671)
HOWMET AEROSPACE INC
Also Called: HOWMET AEROSPACE INC
1000 Warren Ave (44446-1168)
PHONE..............................330 544-7633
EMP: 48
SALES (corp-wide): 6.64B **Publicly Held**
Web: www.howmet.com
SIC: 3355 3353 3463 Aluminum rolling and drawing, nec; Aluminum sheet and strip; Aluminum forgings
PA: Howmet Aerospace Inc.
201 Isabella St Ste 200
Pittsburgh PA 15212
412 553-1950

(G-11672)
INTERNTNAL TCHNCAL PLYMR SYSTE
Also Called: Itps
852 Ann Ave (44446-2924)
P.O. Box 111 (44446-0111)
PHONE..............................330 505-1218
▲ **EMP:** 23 **EST:** 1994
SQ FT: 5,000
SALES (est): 4.13MM **Privately Held**
Web: www.itps-inc.com
SIC: 2821 Plastics materials and resins

Niles - Trumbull County (G-11673)

(G-11673)
IRONICS INC
750 S Main St (44446-1372)
P.O. Box 292 (44446-0292)
PHONE.................................330 652-0583
Pete Tominey Junior, *Pr*
Mary Jane Tominey, *Stockholder*
EMP: 9 **EST:** 1974
SQ FT: 10,000
SALES (est): 1.18MM **Privately Held**
SIC: 2816 3295 Iron oxide pigments (ochers, siennas, umbers); Blast furnace slag

(G-11674)
J A MCMAHON INCORPORATED
6 E Park Ave (44446-5020)
PHONE.................................330 652-2588
John A Mcmahon Iii, *Pr*
EMP: 26 **EST:** 1945
SQ FT: 32,000
SALES (est): 3.33MM **Privately Held**
Web: www.jamcmahon.com
SIC: 3441 Building components, structural steel

(G-11675)
KRONER PUBLICATIONS INC (PA)
1123 W Park Ave (44446-1188)
P.O. Box 150 (44446-0150)
PHONE.................................330 544-5500
EMP: 30 **EST:** 1994
SALES (est): 2.64MM **Privately Held**
Web: www.thereviewnewspapers.com
SIC: 2711 Commercial printing and newspaper publishing combined

(G-11676)
MICHAELS STORES INC
Also Called: Michaels 9837
5555 Youngstown Warren Rd Unit 914 (44446-4804)
PHONE.................................330 505-1168
Paul Rockenfelder, *Brnch Mgr*
EMP: 11
SALES (corp-wide): 32.64B **Publicly Held**
Web: www.michaels.com
SIC: 3944 5945 Craft and hobby kits and sets ; Hobby, toy, and game shops
HQ: Michaels Stores, Inc.
    8000 Bent Branch Dr
    Irving TX 75063
    972 409-1300

(G-11677)
NILES BUILDING PRODUCTS COMPANY (PA)
1600 Hunter Ave (44446-1644)
P.O. Box 662 (44446-0662)
PHONE.................................330 544-0880
EMP: 16 **EST:** 1973
SALES (est): 5.3MM
SALES (corp-wide): 5.3MM **Privately Held**
Web: www.nilesbldg.com
SIC: 3441 3442 Building components, structural steel; Metal doors, sash, and trim

(G-11678)
NILES MANUFACTURING & FINSHG
465 Walnut St (44446-2374)
PHONE.................................330 544-0402
Robert Hendricks, *Pr*
EMP: 110 **EST:** 1984
SQ FT: 150,000
SALES (est): 10.49MM **Privately Held**
SIC: 3469 3479 3471 3444 Stamping metal for the trade; Coating of metals and formed products; Plating and polishing; Sheet metalwork

(G-11679)
NILES MIRROR & GLASS INC
234 Robbins Ave Ste 1 (44446-1769)
PHONE.................................330 652-6277
Robert Leonard, *CEO*
Rick Leonard, *Pr*
Laurie Paden, *Sec*
EMP: 20 **EST:** 1997
SQ FT: 17,000
SALES (est): 1.58MM **Privately Held**
SIC: 5231 1793 3211 Glass; Glass and glazing work; Insulating glass, sealed units

(G-11680)
NILES ROLL SERVICE INC (PA)
704 Warren Ave (44446-1643)
P.O. Box 86 (44446-0086)
PHONE.................................330 544-0026
Timothy L Boggs, *Pr*
Beverly Boggs, *Sec*
EMP: 11 **EST:** 1993
SQ FT: 4,964
SALES (est): 1.67MM **Privately Held**
Web: www.nilesrollservice.com
SIC: 3069 Roll coverings, rubber

(G-11681)
NMC METALS INC (PA)
Also Called: Niles Expanded Metals & Plas
310 N Pleasant Ave (44446-1173)
P.O. Box 231 (44446-0231)
PHONE.................................330 652-2501
▲ **EMP:** 48 **EST:** 1985
SALES (est): 8.78MM
SALES (corp-wide): 8.78MM **Privately Held**
Web: www.nilesexpandedmetals.com
SIC: 3449 Lath, expanded metal

(G-11682)
PHILLIPS MANUFACTURING CO
504 Walnut St (44446-2961)
PHONE.................................330 652-4335
Steve Dalrymple, *Brnch Mgr*
EMP: 60
SALES (corp-wide): 43.4MM **Privately Held**
Web: www.phillipsmfg.com
SIC: 3442 3444 3541 Metal doors, sash, and trim; Sheet metalwork; Machine tools, metal cutting type
PA: Phillips Manufacturing Co.
    4949 S 30th St
    Omaha NE 68107
    402 339-3800

(G-11683)
RMI TITANIUM COMPANY LLC
Also Called: Rti
2000 Warren Ave (44446-1148)
PHONE.................................330 544-9470
EMP: 63
SALES (corp-wide): 6.64B **Publicly Held**
Web: www.howmet.com
SIC: 3441 Fabricated structural metal
HQ: Rmi Titanium Company, Llc
    1000 Warren Ave
    Niles OH 44446
    330 652-9952

(G-11684)
RMI TITANIUM COMPANY LLC (HQ)
Also Called: Rti Niles
1000 Warren Ave (44446-1168)
PHONE.................................330 652-9952
Dawn S Hickton, *Pr*
John H Odle, *Ex VP*
Lawrence W Jacobs, *VP*
◆ **EMP:** 20 **EST:** 1998
SQ FT: 677,605
SALES (est): 628.66MM
SALES (corp-wide): 6.64B **Publicly Held**
SIC: 3399 3356 1741 3533 Powder, metal; Titanium; Masonry and other stonework; Oil and gas drilling rigs and equipment
PA: Howmet Aerospace Inc.
    201 Isabella St Ste 200
    Pittsburgh PA 15212
    412 553-1950

(G-11685)
RMI TITANIUM COMPANY LLC
Rti Hermitage
1000 Warren Ave (44446-1168)
PHONE.................................330 652-9955
Paul Mandell, *Brnch Mgr*
EMP: 9
SALES (corp-wide): 6.64B **Publicly Held**
SIC: 3356 Titanium
HQ: Rmi Titanium Company, Llc
    1000 Warren Ave
    Niles OH 44446
    330 652-9952

(G-11686)
RTI ALLOYS
1000 Warren Ave (44446-1168)
PHONE.................................330 652-9952
Robert G Helwig, *Admn*
▲ **EMP:** 9 **EST:** 2013
SALES (est): 221.44K **Privately Held**
SIC: 3312 Blast furnaces and steel mills

(G-11687)
RTI INTERNATIONAL METALS INC
Also Called: Alcoa Titanium Engineered Pdts
1000 Warren Ave (44446-1168)
◆ **EMP:** 2575
SIC: 3356 3441 Titanium; Fabricated structural metal

(G-11688)
RYMAN GRINDERS INC
704 Warren Ave (44446-1643)
P.O. Box 86 (44446-0086)
PHONE.................................330 652-5080
Timothy L Boggs, *Pr*
Tim L Boggs, *Pr*
EMP: 8 **EST:** 1996
SALES (est): 168.49K **Privately Held**
Web: www.rymangrinders.com
SIC: 3531 Grinders, stone: portable

(G-11689)
TRAICHAL CONSTRUCTION COMPANY (PA)
Also Called: Warren Door
332 Plant St (44446-1895)
P.O. Box 70 (44446-0070)
PHONE.................................800 255-3667
Edward Traichal, *Pr*
EMP: 26 **EST:** 1937
SQ FT: 15,000
SALES (est): 8.64MM
SALES (corp-wide): 8.64MM **Privately Held**
Web: www.warrendoor.com
SIC: 3442 1751 5199 5031 Metal doors; Window and door installation and erection; Advertising specialties; Doors and windows

(G-11690)
VANEX TUBE CORPORATION
301 Mckees Ln Ste 2 (44446-1374)
PHONE.................................330 544-9500
EMP: 70 **EST:** 1985
SALES (est): 3.33MM **Privately Held**
Web: www.vanextubecorp.com
SIC: 3498 3321 Tube fabricating (contract bending and shaping); Gray and ductile iron foundries

(G-11691)
WEST & BARKER INC
950 Summit Ave (44446-3693)
PHONE.................................330 652-9923
Samuel M Barker Iii, *Pr*
Suzanne Leone, *VP*
June Barker, *Sec*
EMP: 30 **EST:** 1971
SQ FT: 106,000
SALES (est): 1.89MM **Privately Held**
Web: www.westandbarker.com
SIC: 3089 2396 3069 3714 Plastics hardware and building products; Automotive and apparel trimmings; Thread, rubber; Motor vehicle parts and accessories

(G-11692)
WHEATLAND TUBE LLC
Also Called: Wheatland Tube Company
1800 Hunter Ave (44446-1671)
PHONE.................................724 342-6851
Mark Bahrey, *Brnch Mgr*
EMP: 133
Web: www.wheatland.com
SIC: 3317 3312 5051 Steel pipe and tubes; Blast furnaces and steel mills; Iron and steel (ferrous) products
HQ: Wheatland Tube, Llc
    1 Council Ave
    Wheatland PA 16161
    800 257-8182

(G-11693)
YAR CORPORATION
406 S Main St (44446-1454)
PHONE.................................330 652-1222
Richard A Yannucci, *Pr*
EMP: 7 **EST:** 2005
SALES (est): 405.75K **Privately Held**
SIC: 2098 Macaroni and spaghetti

North Baltimore
Wood County

(G-11694)
AUTOMATED BLDG COMPONENTS INC (PA)
2359 Grant Rd (45872-9662)
PHONE.................................419 257-2152
Harold L Mccarty, *CEO*
Marshal Mccarty, *Pr*
Jennifer Buckingham, *Stockholder**
EMP: 30 **EST:** 1973
SQ FT: 10,000
SALES (est): 8.87MM
SALES (corp-wide): 8.87MM **Privately Held**
Web: www.abctruss.com
SIC: 2421 2439 2541 2435 Building and structural materials, wood; Trusses, wooden roof; Wood partitions and fixtures; Hardwood veneer and plywood

(G-11695)
KEYSTONE FOODS LLC
Equity Group-Ohio Div
2208 Grant Rd (45872-9663)
P.O. Box 307 (45872-0307)
PHONE.................................419 257-2341
Steven Alberts, *Mgr*
EMP: 250
SQ FT: 60,000
SALES (corp-wide): 52.88B **Publicly Held**
Web: www.tysonfoods.com
SIC: 2013 Sausages and other prepared meats
HQ: Keystone Foods Llc
    905 Airport Rd Ste 400
    West Chester PA 19380
    610 667-6700

GEOGRAPHIC SECTION

(G-11696)
MID-WOOD INC
Also Called: True Value
101 E State St (45872-1358)
PHONE.................................419 257-3331
Joe Smith, *Mgr*
EMP: 10
SALES (corp-wide): 16.88MM **Privately Held**
Web: www.mid-wood.com
SIC: 5153 5261 5251 5531 Grains; Fertilizer; Hardware stores; Automotive tires
PA: Mid-Wood, Inc.
12965 Defiance Pike
Cygnet OH
419 352-5231

(G-11697)
NATIONAL BEEF OHIO LLC
2208 Grant Rd (45872-9663)
PHONE.................................800 449-2333
Bret G Wilson, *Managing Member*
EMP: 68 **EST:** 2018
SALES (est): 1.09MM
SALES (corp-wide): 2.12B **Privately Held**
SIC: 2011 Boxed beef, from meat slaughtered on site
PA: National Beef Packing Company, L.L.C.
12200 N Ambassador Dr # 101
Kansas City MO 64163
800 449-2333

(G-11698)
NATIONAL BEEF PACKING CO LLC
2208 Grant Rd (45872-9663)
PHONE.................................419 257-5500
EMP: 315
SALES (corp-wide): 2.12B **Privately Held**
Web: www.nationalbeef.com
SIC: 2011 Meat packing plants
PA: National Beef Packing Company, L.L.C.
12200 N Ambassador Dr # 101
Kansas City MO 64163
800 449-2333

(G-11699)
OHIO BEEF USA LLC
2208 Grant Rd (45872-9663)
PHONE.................................419 257-5536
EMP: 10 **EST:** 2019
SALES (est): 739.65K **Privately Held**
Web: www.nationalbeef.com
SIC: 2011 Meat packing plants

(G-11700)
TEIJIN AUTOMOTIVE TECH INC
Also Called: CSP North Baltimore
100 S Poe Rd (45872-9551)
PHONE.................................419 257-2231
Gary Dickson, *Brnch Mgr*
EMP: 251
Web: www.teijinautomotive.com
SIC: 3089 3714 Injection molding of plastics; Motor vehicle parts and accessories
HQ: Teijin Automotive Technologies, Inc.
255 Rex Blvd
Auburn Hills MI 48326
248 237-7800

(G-11701)
THE D S BROWN COMPANY (HQ)
300 E Cherry St (45872-1227)
P.O. Box 158 (45872-0158)
PHONE.................................419 257-3561
◆ **EMP:** 220 **EST:** 1992
SALES (est): 49.1MM
SALES (corp-wide): 1.38B **Publicly Held**
Web: www.dsbrown.com
SIC: 3061 3441 5032 Mechanical rubber goods; Fabricated structural metal for bridges; Paving materials

PA: Gibraltar Industries, Inc.
3556 Lake Shore Rd # 100
Buffalo NY 14219
716 826-6500

(G-11702)
TRUCK STOP EMBROIDERY
Also Called: Innovative Stiching
12906 Deshler Rd (45872-9650)
PHONE.................................419 257-2860
Jen Fackler, *Mgr*
EMP: 10
SALES (corp-wide): 234.07K **Privately Held**
SIC: 2395 Embroidery products, except Schiffli machine
PA: Truck Stop Embroidery
12906 Deshler Rd
North Baltimore OH 45872
419 257-2860

North Bend
Hamilton County

(G-11703)
AMERICAN STIRWAYS CSTM RAILING
2991 Triplecrown Dr (45052-9709)
PHONE.................................513 367-6700
Steve Bunnell, *Prin*
EMP: 8 **EST:** 2012
SALES (est): 296.08K **Privately Held**
SIC: 2431 Staircases, stairs and railings

(G-11704)
HAMMERSMITH BROS INVSTMNTS INC
Also Called: Baleco International
3200 State Line Rd (45052-9731)
P.O. Box 11331 (45211-0331)
PHONE.................................513 353-3000
E Bernard Haviland, *Pr*
▲ **EMP:** 20 **EST:** 1958
SQ FT: 72,000
SALES (est): 16.19MM
SALES (corp-wide): 214.48MM **Privately Held**
Web: www.baleco.com
SIC: 5091 3589 Swimming pools, equipment and supplies; Swimming pool filter and water conditioning systems
PA: Haviland Enterprises, Inc.
421 Ann St Nw
Grand Rapids MI 49504
616 361-6691

(G-11705)
NUTRIEN AG SOLUTIONS INC
10743 Brower Rd (45052-9761)
PHONE.................................513 941-4100
Bill Chokran, *Mgr*
EMP: 8
SALES (corp-wide): 29.06B **Privately Held**
Web: www.nutrienagsolutions.com
SIC: 2873 2875 2819 Nitrogenous fertilizers; Fertilizers, mixing only; Industrial inorganic chemicals, nec
HQ: Nutrien Ag Solutions, Inc.
3005 Rocky Mountain Ave
Loveland CO 80538
970 685-3300

(G-11706)
ROYSTER-CLARK INC
10743 Brower Rd (45052-9761)
P.O. Box 158 (45052-0158)
PHONE.................................513 941-4100
Bill Chockran, *Prin*
EMP: 7 **EST:** 2010

SALES (est): 130K **Privately Held**
Web: www.trammo.com
SIC: 2873 Nitrogenous fertilizers

(G-11707)
SUPER SIGNS INC
9890 Mount Nebo Rd (45052-9480)
PHONE.................................480 968-2200
EMP: 6 **EST:** 1990
SQ FT: 1,500
SALES (est): 98.64K **Privately Held**
Web: www.supersigns.biz
SIC: 3993 Signs and advertising specialties

(G-11708)
WERNKE WLDG & STL ERECTION CO
3150 State Line Rd (45052-9731)
PHONE.................................513 353-4173
Jeff Wernke, *Pr*
James Wernke, *Ch*
Jerry Wernke, *VP*
John Wernke, *Sec*
EMP: 14 **EST:** 1968
SQ FT: 4,800
SALES (est): 2.21MM **Privately Held**
Web: www.wernkesteel.com
SIC: 1791 3441 Iron work, structural; Fabricated structural metal

North Benton
Portage County

(G-11709)
BELOIT FUEL LLC
9379 First East St (44449-9631)
PHONE.................................330 584-1915
Charles R Pierce, *Prin*
EMP: 7 **EST:** 2008
SALES (est): 282.39K **Privately Held**
SIC: 2869 Fuels

(G-11710)
PAUL J TATULINSKI LTD
1595 W Main St (44449)
P.O. Box 382 (44449-0382)
PHONE.................................330 584-8251
Paul J Tatulinski, *Pr*
EMP: 10 **EST:** 1999
SQ FT: 4,704
SALES (est): 467K **Privately Held**
SIC: 3053 Gaskets, all materials

(G-11711)
THEISS UAV SOLUTIONS LLC
10881 Johnson Rd (44449-9652)
P.O. Box 1086 (44460-8086)
PHONE.................................330 584-2070
Chad Kapper, *Pr*
Richard Theiss, *Pdt Mgr*
EMP: 8 **EST:** 1992
SQ FT: 4,600
SALES (est): 883K
SALES (corp-wide): 44.54MM **Privately Held**
Web: www.theissuav.com
SIC: 3721 7363 Aircraft; Pilot service, aviation
PA: Lauren International, Ltd.
143 Garland Dr Sw
New Philadelphia OH 44663
234 303-2400

North Bloomfield
Trumbull County

(G-11712)
NORDEN MFG LLC
4210 Kinsman Rd Nw (44450-9710)
PHONE.................................440 693-4630
EMP: 37 **EST:** 1992
SALES (est): 4.89MM **Privately Held**
Web: www.nordenmfg.com
SIC: 3523 Farm machinery and equipment

North Canton
Stark County

(G-11713)
A STUCKI COMPANY
5335 Mayfair Rd (44720-1532)
PHONE.................................412 424-0560
Tom Seccombe, *Genl Mgr*
EMP: 8
SALES (corp-wide): 628.86MM **Privately Held**
Web: www.stucki.com
SIC: 3743 Railroad equipment
HQ: A. Stucki Company
360 Wright Brothers Dr
Coraopolis PA 15108
412 424-0560

(G-11714)
AIRSOURCES INC
950 Honeysuckle Cir Ne (44720-9838)
PHONE.................................610 983-0102
EMP: 6 **EST:** 1989
SALES (est): 429.81K **Privately Held**
SIC: 3444 Sheet metalwork

(G-11715)
ASC INDUSTRIES INC (DH)
Also Called: ASC
2100 International Pkwy (44720-1373)
PHONE.................................800 253-6009
David Peace, *CEO*
◆ **EMP:** 95 **EST:** 1976
SQ FT: 200,000
SALES (est): 49.86MM
SALES (corp-wide): 8.03B **Privately Held**
Web: www.ascindustries.com
SIC: 3714 Water pump, motor vehicle
HQ: Specialty Pumps Group, Inc.
127 Public Sq Ste 5110
Cleveland OH 44114
216 589-0198

(G-11716)
BALL CORPORATION
3075 Brookline Rd (44720-1526)
PHONE.................................330 244-2313
EMP: 16
SALES (corp-wide): 14.03B **Publicly Held**
Web: www.ball.com
SIC: 3411 Food and beverage containers
PA: Ball Corporation
9200 W 108th Cir
Westminster CO 80021
303 469-3131

(G-11717)
BIRO MANUFACTURING COMPANY
6658 Promway Ave Nw (44720-7316)
PHONE.................................419 798-4451
Sharon Edwards, *Mgr*
EMP: 10
SALES (corp-wide): 11MM **Privately Held**
Web: www.birosaw.com

North Canton - Stark County (G-11718)

SIC: 3556 Food products machinery
PA: The Biro Manufacturing Company
1114 W Main St
Marblehead OH 43440
419 798-4451

(G-11718)
CALVERT WIRE & CABLE CORP
4276 Strausser Street, Applegrove Ext (44720-7114)
PHONE..................................330 494-3248
Steve Hilson, *Mgr*
EMP: 26
Web: www.wesco.com
SIC: 3357 Nonferrous wiredrawing and insulating
HQ: Calvert Wire & Cable Corporation
17909 Clvland Pkwy Ste 18
Cleveland OH 44142
216 433-7600

(C 11710)
CANTON ELEVATOR INC
2575 Greensburg Rd (44720-1419)
PHONE..................................330 833-3600
Robert A Kazar, *CEO*
Michael J Paschke, *
◆ **EMP:** 75 **EST:** 2018
SQ FT: 80,000
SALES (est): 19.31MM **Privately Held**
Web: acim.nidec.com
SIC: 3534 3537 Elevators and equipment; Industrial trucks and tractors
HQ: Nidec Motor Corporation
8050 W Florissant Ave
Saint Louis MO 63136

(G-11720)
DELTA MEDIA GROUP INC
7015 Sunset Strip Ave Nw (44720-7078)
PHONE..................................330 493-0350
Noel England, *Pr*
EMP: 65 **EST:** 2000
SALES (est): 3.88MM **Privately Held**
Web: www.deltagroup.com
SIC: 7372 Application computer software

(G-11721)
DIEBOLD NIXDORF INCORPORATED
Also Called: Diebold
334 Orchard Ave Ne (44720-2556)
P.O. Box 3077 (44720-8077)
PHONE..................................336 662-1115
EMP: 28
SALES (corp-wide): 1.63B **Publicly Held**
Web: www.dieboldnixdorf.com
SIC: 3578 Calculating and accounting equipment
PA: Diebold Nixdorf, Incorporated
350 Orchard Ave Ne
North Canton OH 44720
330 490-4000

(G-11722)
DIEBOLD NIXDORF INCORPORATED (PA)
Also Called: Diebold Nixdorf
350 Orchard Ave Ne (44720)
P.O. Box 3077 (44720)
PHONE..................................330 490-4000
Octavio Marquez, *Pr*
Patrick J Byrne, *Non-Executive Chairman of the Board*
James A Barna, *Ex VP*
Elizabeth C Radigan, *CLO*
Jonathan B Myers, *Global Vice President*
EMP: 900 **EST:** 1859
SALES (est): 1.63B
SALES (corp-wide): 1.63B **Publicly Held**
Web: www.dieboldnixdorf.com

SIC: 3578 3699 3499 Automatic teller machines (ATM); Security control equipment and systems; Safes and vaults, metal

(G-11723)
DOCUMENT CONCEPTS INC
Also Called: Office Furniture Solution
607 S Main St # A (44720-3002)
PHONE..................................330 575-5685
Tim Barr, *Pr*
Terry A Moore, *
EMP: 22 **EST:** 2002
SQ FT: 15,000
SALES (est): 856.99K **Privately Held**
Web: www.document-concepts.com
SIC: 2752 Offset printing

(G-11724)
DUNCAN PRESS CORPORATION
5122 Strausser St Nw (44720-5545)
PHONE..................................330 477-4529
Richard Kempthorn, *Pr*
Scott Duncan, *VP*
Jed Parker, *VP*
EMP: 19 **EST:** 1958
SALES (est): 718.66K **Privately Held**
Web: www.duncanpress-inc.com
SIC: 2752 Offset printing

(G-11725)
ENVIRONMENTAL SAMPLING SUP INC (DH)
Also Called: E S S
4101 Shuffel St Nw (44720-6900)
PHONE..................................330 497-9396
Rachel Brydon Jannetta, *Pr*
Heather Collins Villemaire, *CFO*
Jenny L Stewart, *Sec*
▲ **EMP:** 67 **EST:** 1987
SALES (est): 14.07MM
SALES (corp-wide): 220.81K **Privately Held**
SIC: 3089 3231 Plastics containers, except foam; Products of purchased glass
HQ: Testamerica Holdings, Inc.
4101 Shuffel St Nw # 100
North Canton OH 44720
330 497-9396

(G-11726)
FANNIE MAY CONFECTIONS INC
5353 Lauby Rd (44720-1572)
PHONE..................................330 494-0833
Terry Michell, *Pr*
EMP: 800 **EST:** 2004
SALES (est): 97.35MM
SALES (corp-wide): 347.05MM **Privately Held**
Web: www.fanniemay.com
SIC: 5441 2066 Candy; Chocolate bars, solid
HQ: Fannie May Confections Brands, Inc.
9 W Washington St
Chicago IL 60602
330 494-0833

(G-11727)
FIVES BRONX INC
Also Called: Bronx Taylor Wilson
8817 Pleasantwood Ave Nw (44720-4759)
PHONE..................................330 244-1960
Brian Lombardi, *CEO*
Dave Macneilll, *
Curt Sabin, *
◆ **EMP:** 70 **EST:** 1988
SQ FT: 10,000
SALES (est): 21.89MM
SALES (corp-wide): 409.51MM **Privately Held**
Web: www.fivesgroup.com

SIC: 3547 Finishing equipment, rolling mill
HQ: Fives
3 Rue Drouot
Paris 75009
145237575

(G-11728)
FLUID AUTOMATION INC
8400 Port Jackson Ave Nw (44720-5464)
PHONE..................................248 912-1970
Lance H Daby, *Pr*
Leon L Daby, *VP*
Beverly Daby, *Sec*
EMP: 29 **EST:** 1974
SQ FT: 16,000
SALES (est): 534.95K **Privately Held**
Web: www.graco.com
SIC: 3561 3569 Industrial pumps and parts; Liquid automation machinery and equipment

(G-11729)
GBS CORP (PA)
Also Called: GBS Filing Solutions
7233 Freedom Ave Nw (44720-7123)
P.O. Box 2340 (44720-0340)
PHONE..................................330 494-5330
Eugene Calabria, *CEO*
Eugene Calabria, *Pr*
Laurence Merriman, *
Michele Benson, *
Michael Merriman, *
▲ **EMP:** 150 **EST:** 1971
SQ FT: 115,000
SALES (est): 190.76MM
SALES (corp-wide): 190.76MM **Privately Held**
Web: www.gbscorp.com
SIC: 2675 2672 2761 2759 Folders, filing, die-cut: made from purchased materials; Labels (unprinted), gummed: made from purchased materials; Manifold business forms; Commercial printing, nec

(G-11730)
GGB US HOLDCO LLC (HQ)
4500 Mount Pleasant St Nw (44720-5450)
PHONE..................................234 262-3000
Richard G Kyle, *Managing Member*
EMP: 13 **EST:** 2001
SALES (est): 283.13K
SALES (corp-wide): 4.77B **Publicly Held**
SIC: 3562 Ball and roller bearings
PA: The Timken Company
4500 Mount Pleasant St Nw
North Canton OH 44720
234 262-3000

(G-11731)
GLASCRAFT INC
8400 Port Jackson Ave Nw (44720-5464)
PHONE..................................330 966-3000
Morris Wheeler, *Pr*
Byron Bradley, *
EMP: 103 **EST:** 1959
SQ FT: 51,200
SALES (est): 4.09MM
SALES (corp-wide): 2.2B **Publicly Held**
Web: www.graco.com
SIC: 3563 Spraying outfits: metals, paints, and chemicals (compressor)
PA: Graco Inc.
88 11th Ave Ne
Minneapolis MN 55413
612 623-6000

(G-11732)
GOODRICH CORPORATION
6051 N Airport Dr (44720)
PHONE..................................330 374-2358
Jeremy Henry, *Brnch Mgr*
EMP: 6

SALES (corp-wide): 68.92B **Publicly Held**
Web: www.collinsaerospace.com
SIC: 3728 Aircraft parts and equipment, nec
HQ: Goodrich Corporation
2730 W Tyvola Rd
Charlotte NC 28217
704 423-7000

(G-11733)
GRACO OHIO INC (HQ)
Also Called: Liquid Control
8400 Port Jackson Ave Nw (44720-5464)
PHONE..................................330 494-1313
William C Schiltz, *Ch Bd*
Kenneth Jacobs, *
Barbara Schiltz, *
Ronald W Dougherty, *
▲ **EMP:** 100 **EST:** 1978
SQ FT: 73,000
SALES (est): 49.14MM
SALES (corp-wide): 2.2B **Publicly Held**
Web: www.graco.com
SIC: 3824 3586 5251 Predetermining counters; Measuring and dispensing pumps; Pumps and pumping equipment
PA: Graco Inc.
88 11th Ave Ne
Minneapolis MN 55413
612 623-6000

(G-11734)
GUTTER LOGIC CHARLOTTE LLC
7901 Cleveland Ave Nw Ste A (44720-8386)
PHONE..................................833 714-5479
EMP: 7 **EST:** 2019
SALES (est): 291.95K **Privately Held**
SIC: 3444 Gutters, sheet metal

(G-11735)
HAINES CRISS CROSS (PA)
8050 Freedom Ave Nw (44720-6912)
P.O. Box 900820 (84090-0820)
PHONE..................................330 494-9111
John Segherd, *Prin*
EMP: 6 **EST:** 2010
SALES (est): 481.32K
SALES (corp-wide): 481.32K **Privately Held**
Web: www.haines.com
SIC: 2741 Miscellaneous publishing

(G-11736)
HARRY LONDON CANDIES INC (DH)
Also Called: Harry London Chocolates
5353 Lauby Rd (44720-1572)
PHONE..................................330 494-0833
Terry Michell, *Pr*
Ed Seibolt, *
Matthew J Anderson, *
▲ **EMP:** 27 **EST:** 1922
SQ FT: 200,000
SALES (est): 45.64MM
SALES (corp-wide): 347.05MM **Privately Held**
SIC: 2066 5441 Chocolate and cocoa products; Candy
HQ: Fannie May Confections Brands, Inc.
9 W Washington St
Chicago IL 60602
330 494-0833

(G-11737)
HENDRICKSON USA LLC
9260 Pleasantwood Ave Nw (44720-9006)
PHONE..................................630 910-2800
EMP: 62
SALES (corp-wide): 758.84MM **Privately Held**
Web: www.hendrickson-intl.com

SIC: **3714** Motor vehicle parts and accessories
HQ: Hendrickson Usa, L.L.C.
840 S Frontage Rd
Woodridge IL 60517

(G-11738)
IMPERIAL ELECTRIC COMPANY
2575 Greensburg Rd (44720)
PHONE..................330 734-3600
David Molnar, *Pr*
Mark Schoolcraft, *
◆ EMP: **270** EST: **1889**
SALES (est): **25.22MM** Privately Held
Web: acim.nidec.com
SIC: **3621** Motors, electric
HQ: Nidec Motor Corporation
8050 W Florissant Ave
Saint Louis MO 63136

(G-11739)
J M SMUCKER FLIGHT DEPT
5430 Lauby Rd Bldg 7 (44720-1509)
PHONE..................330 497-0073
Hallie Mc Gonigal, *Prin*
EMP: **6** EST: **2013**
SALES (est): **146.03K** Privately Held
SIC: **2033** Canned fruits and specialties

(G-11740)
KIRK KEY INTERLOCK COMPANY LLC
9048 Meridian Cir Nw (44720-8387)
PHONE..................330 833-8223
James G Owens, *Managing Member*
▼ EMP: **47** EST: **1932**
SQ FT: **26,000**
SALES (est): **12.16MM**
SALES (corp-wide): **2.23B** Privately Held
Web: www.sentricsafetygroup.com
SIC: **3429** 5063 Keys, locks, and related hardware; Electrical apparatus and equipment
PA: Halma Public Limited Company
Misbourne Court Rectory Way
Amersham BUCKS HP7 0
149 472-1111

(G-11741)
LT ENTERPRISES OF OHIO LLC
334 Orchard Ave Ne (44720-2556)
PHONE..................330 526-6908
▲ EMP: **24** EST: **2005**
SALES (est): **2.36MM** Privately Held
SIC: **3444** Sheet metalwork

(G-11742)
MCF INDUSTRIES
1206 N Main St (44720-1926)
P.O. Box 2747 (44720-0747)
PHONE..................330 526-6337
Jon Graham, *Pr*
EMP: **12** EST: **2017**
SALES (est): **506.08K** Privately Held
Web: www.mcf-ind.com
SIC: **3599** Machine shop, jobbing and repair

(G-11743)
MICROPLEX INC
7568 Whipple Ave Nw (44720-6921)
PHONE..................330 498-0600
Valerie Walters, *Pr*
John Walters, *
Jon Harst, *
Susan Harst, *
EMP: **30** EST: **1985**
SQ FT: **12,000**
SALES (est): **5.29MM** Privately Held
Web: www.microplex-inc.com

SIC: **3496** 3679 5045 Cable, uninsulated wire: made from purchased wire; Harness assemblies, for electronic use: wire or cable; Computer peripheral equipment

(G-11744)
MOHLER LUMBER COMPANY
4214 Portage St Nw (44720-7399)
PHONE..................330 499-5461
Jennifer Hamilton, *Ch Bd*
Richard Rohrer, *Ch Bd*
Willidam Leed, *Pr*
Jed Rohrer, *VP*
Gary Leed, *Sec*
EMP: **20** EST: **1911**
SQ FT: **8,320**
SALES (est): **3.33MM** Privately Held
Web: www.mohlerlumber.com
SIC: **2435** 5211 2421 2426 Hardwood veneer and plywood; Millwork and lumber; Sawmills and planing mills, general; Hardwood dimension and flooring mills

(G-11745)
MOTION MOBILITY & DESIGN INC
6490 Promler St Nw (44720-7625)
PHONE..................330 244-9723
Paul V Pettini, *Pr*
Steve Williams, *VP*
EMP: **11** EST: **1999**
SQ FT: **12,000**
SALES (est): **2.04MM** Privately Held
Web: www.motionmobility.com
SIC: **3842** Braces, elastic

(G-11746)
MRO BUILT LLC
Also Called: Mro Built, Inc.
6410 Promway Ave Nw (44720-7622)
PHONE..................330 526-0555
Alfred A Olivieri, *Pr*
Dean Olivieri, *
Virginia Olivieri, *
Timothy Feller, *
EMP: **75** EST: **1977**
SQ FT: **55,000**
SALES (est): **12.25MM**
SALES (corp-wide): **48.19MM** Privately Held
Web: www.mrobuilt.com
SIC: **2599** 2542 2434 Cabinets, factory; Partitions and fixtures, except wood; Wood kitchen cabinets
PA: Fred Olivieri Construction Company
6315 Promway Ave Nw
North Canton OH 44720
330 494-1007

(G-11747)
MYERS POWER PRODUCTS INC (PA)
Also Called: Myers FSI
219 E Maple St Ste 100/200e (44720)
PHONE..................330 834-3200
Diana Grootonk, *CEO*
◆ EMP: **130** EST: **2003**
SQ FT: **40,000**
SALES (est): **172.09MM**
SALES (corp-wide): **172.09MM** Privately Held
Web: www.myerspower.com
SIC: **3613** Switchgear and switchboard apparatus

(G-11748)
NATIONAL LIME AND STONE CO
5377 Lauby Rd (44720-1523)
PHONE..................330 966-4836
Dave Webere, *Prin*
EMP: **9**
SALES (corp-wide): **167.89MM** Privately Held

Web: www.natlime.com
SIC: **1422** Crushed and broken limestone
PA: The National Lime And Stone Company
551 Lake Cascade Pkwy
Findlay OH 45840
419 422-4341

(G-11749)
PAARLO PLASTICS INC
7720 Tim Ave Nw (44720)
P.O. Box 2556 (44720)
PHONE..................330 494-3798
James D Park, *Pr*
▲ EMP: **65** EST: **1981**
SQ FT: **80,000**
SALES (est): **9.34MM** Privately Held
Web: www.paarloplastics.com
SIC: **3089** Blow molded finished plastics products, nec

(G-11750)
POLYCHEM OMS SYSTEMS LLC
5555 Massillon Rd (44720-1339)
PHONE..................330 427-1230
EMP: **12** EST: **2019**
SALES (est): **739.19K** Privately Held
SIC: **3553** Woodworking machinery

(G-11751)
POLYMER PACKAGING INC (PA)
7755 Freedom Ave Nw (44720-6905)
PHONE..................330 832-2000
Larry L Lanham, *CEO*
Chris Thomazin, *
William D Lanham, *
Jeffrey S Davis, *
◆ EMP: **86** EST: **1986**
SALES (est): **48.95MM**
SALES (corp-wide): **48.95MM** Privately Held
Web: www.polymerpkg.com
SIC: **5113** 5162 2621 2821 Paper, wrapping or coarse, and products; Plastics products, nec; Wrapping and packaging papers; Plastics materials and resins

(G-11752)
PORTAGE ELECTRIC PRODUCTS INC
Also Called: Pepi
7700 Freedom Ave Nw (44720)
P.O. Box 2170 (44720)
PHONE..................330 499-2727
Brandon Wehl, *Ch Bd*
Omar R Givler, *
Allyson Wehl, *
Ray Kolesar, *
Edward J Zink, *
▲ EMP: **220** EST: **1963**
SQ FT: **11,000**
SALES (est): **23.77MM** Privately Held
Web: www.pepiusa.com
SIC: **3822** 3829 Appliance controls,except air-conditioning and refrigeration; Measuring and controlling devices, nec

(G-11753)
POWELL ELECTRICAL SYSTEMS INC
Also Called: Pemco North Canton Division
8967 Pleasantwood Ave Nw (44720-4761)
PHONE..................330 966-1750
Bob Gens, *Brnch Mgr*
EMP: **92**
SQ FT: **41,600**
SALES (corp-wide): **699.31MM** Publicly Held
Web: www.powellind.com
SIC: **3678** 5063 3699 Electronic connectors; Electrical apparatus and equipment; Electrical equipment and supplies, nec

HQ: Powell Electrical Systems, Inc.
8550 Mosley Rd
Houston TX 77075
713 944-6900

(G-11754)
R R R DEVELOPMENT CO (PA)
8817 Pleasantwood Ave Nw (44720-4759)
PHONE..................330 966-8855
Ronald Dillard, *Pr*
Thomas Dillard, *
Robert Irwin, *
▲ EMP: **80** EST: **1982**
SALES (est): **19.38MM**
SALES (corp-wide): **19.38MM** Privately Held
Web: www.rrrdev.com
SIC: **3599** Machine shop, jobbing and repair

(G-11755)
RADON ELIMINATOR LLC
5046 Stoney Creek Ln (44720-1000)
PHONE..................330 844-0703
EMP: **11** EST: **2015**
SALES (est): **956.36K** Privately Held
Web: www.radoneliminator.com
SIC: **1389** 8744 8748 1731 Construction, repair, and dismantling services; Environmental remediation; Environmental consultant; Environmental system control installation

(G-11756)
RAIL BEARING SERVICE LLC
Also Called: Rail Bearing Service Inc
4500 Mount Pleasant St Nw (44720-5450)
P.O. Box 6929 (44706-0929)
PHONE..................234 262-3000
Mervyn Cronje, *Contrlr*
EMP: **350** EST: **1973**
SQ FT: **6,000**
SALES (est): **75.03MM**
SALES (corp-wide): **4.77B** Publicly Held
SIC: **3568** Railroad car journal bearings
PA: The Timken Company
4500 Mount Pleasant St Nw
North Canton OH 44720
234 262-3000

(G-11757)
RTX CORPORATION
6051 W Airport Dr (44720-1447)
PHONE..................330 784-5477
EMP: **268**
SALES (corp-wide): **68.92B** Publicly Held
Web: www.rtx.com
SIC: **3585** Refrigeration and heating equipment
PA: Rtx Corporation
1000 Wilson Blvd
Arlington VA 22209
781 522-3000

(G-11758)
SCHWEBEL BAKING COMPANY
Also Called: Schwebel Bkg Co N Canton Agcy
7382 Whipple Ave Nw (44720-7140)
PHONE..................330 926-9410
EMP: **7**
SALES (corp-wide): **403.34MM** Privately Held
Web: www.schwebels.com
SIC: **2051** Bread, cake, and related products
PA: Schwebel Baking Company
965 E Midlothian Blvd
Youngstown OH 44502
330 783-2860

North Canton - Stark County (G-11759)

(G-11759)
SECO MACHINE INC
5335 Mayfair Rd (44720-1532)
PHONE..................330 499-2150
Mary Seccombe, *Pr*
Delano F Rossio, *
Richard Seccombe, *
Annette M Rossio, *
EMP: 30 EST: 1985
SALES (est): 4.73MM **Privately Held**
Web: www.secomachine.com
SIC: 3599 Machine shop, jobbing and repair

(G-11760)
SEMTEC INC
7750 Strausser St Nw (44720-5258)
PHONE..................330 497-7224
EMP: 6 EST: 2010
SALES (est): 49.39K **Privately Held**
SIC: 3399 Primary metal products

(G-11761)
SIGMAN CLADDING INC
7630 Freedom Ave Nw (44720-6904)
PHONE..................330 497-5200
Delilah Volpe, *Prin*
EMP: 8 EST: 2016
SALES (est): 50.56K **Privately Held**
Web: www.foxenterpriseservices.com
SIC: 3444 Sheet metalwork

(G-11762)
STANDARD ENGINEERING GROUP INC
3516 Highland Park Nw (44720-4532)
PHONE..................330 494-4300
Ronald Schlemmer, *Pr*
William Simmons, *VP*
◆ EMP: 6 EST: 2000
SQ FT: 15,000
SALES (est): 731.77K **Privately Held**
Web: www.standardengineeringgroup.com
SIC: 3544 Special dies and tools

(G-11763)
STARK INDUSTRIAL LLC
5103 Stoneham Rd (44720-1540)
P.O. Box 3030 (44720-8030)
PHONE..................330 966-8108
Samuel Wilkof, *Pr*
Ray Wilkof, *
▼ EMP: 40 EST: 1959
SQ FT: 25,000
SALES (est): 5.26MM **Privately Held**
Web: www.starkindustrial.com
SIC: 3599 Machine shop, jobbing and repair

(G-11764)
TEST MEASUREMENT SYSTEMS INC
9073 Pleasantwood Ave Nw (44720-4763)
PHONE..................888 867-4872
John W Jobe, *Prin*
EMP: 9 EST: 2015
SALES (est): 300.31K **Privately Held**
Web: www.tmsi-usa.com
SIC: 3569 General industrial machinery, nec

(G-11765)
THERMTROL CORPORATION
Also Called: Thermtrol
8914 Pleasantwood Ave Nw (44720-4762)
PHONE..................330 497-4148
Mark Jeffries Senior, *Pr*
Mark Jeffries Senior, *Pr*
Mark A Jeffries Junior, *Ex VP*
John Komer, *
David Lett, *
◆ EMP: 800 EST: 1986
SQ FT: 24,000
SALES (est): 64.28MM **Privately Held**
Web: www.thermtrol.com
SIC: 3679 3822 Harness assemblies, for electronic use: wire or cable; Thermostats and other environmental sensors

(G-11766)
TIMKEN COMPANY (PA)
Also Called: TIMKEN
4500 Mount Pleasant St Nw (44720-5450)
P.O. Box 6929 (44706-0929)
PHONE..................234 262-3000
Richard G Kyle, *Pr*
John M Timken Junior, *Ch Bd*
Philip D Fracassa, *Ex VP*
Christopher A Coughlin, *Group President*
Hansal N Patel, *VP*
◆ EMP: 1335 EST: 1899
SALES (est): 4.77B
SALES (corp-wide): 4.77B **Publicly Held**
Web: www.timken.com
SIC: 3562 5085 Ball and roller bearings; Bearings, bushings, wheels, and gears

(G-11767)
TIMKEN NEWCO I LLC
4500 Mount Pleasant St Nw (44720-5450)
PHONE..................234 262-3000
EMP: 24 EST: 2016
SALES (est): 1.56MM
SALES (corp-wide): 4.77B **Publicly Held**
Web: www.timken.com
SIC: 3562 3566 3568 Ball and roller bearings; Gears, power transmission, except auto; Power transmission equipment, nec
PA: The Timken Company
    4500 Mount Pleasant St Nw
    North Canton OH 44720
    234 262-3000

(G-11768)
TIMKEN RECEIVABLES CORPORATION
4500 Mount Pleasant St Nw (44720-5450)
PHONE..................234 262-3000
EMP: 31 EST: 2010
SALES (est): 4.55MM
SALES (corp-wide): 4.77B **Publicly Held**
Web: www.timken.com
SIC: 3312 Blast furnaces and steel mills
PA: The Timken Company
    4500 Mount Pleasant St Nw
    North Canton OH 44720
    234 262-3000

(G-11769)
TMSI LLC
Also Called: Tmsi
8817 Pleasantwood Ave Nw (44720-4759)
P.O. Box 5414 (44334-0414)
PHONE..................888 867-4872
Gerald R Potts, *Pr*
◆ EMP: 14 EST: 1991
SALES (est): 8.26MM **Privately Held**
Web: www.tmsi-usa.com
SIC: 5013 3825 Testing equipment, electrical: automotive; Instruments to measure electricity
PA: Mesnac Co., Ltd.
    No.43, Zhengzhou Rd., Shibei District
    Qingdao SD 26604

(G-11770)
TRI - FLEX OF OHIO INC (PA)
2701 Applegrove St Nw (44720-6213)
PHONE..................330 705-7084
Paul R Lioi, *Prin*
Paul Lili, *Pr*
EMP: 6 EST: 2011
SALES (est): 2.24MM
SALES (corp-wide): 2.24MM **Privately Held**
SIC: 3365 Machinery castings, aluminum

(G-11771)
TRISTAN RUBBER MOLDING INC (PA)
7255 Whipple Ave Nw (44720-7137)
PHONE..................330 499-4055
EMP: 15 EST: 1995
SQ FT: 20,000
SALES (est): 3.96MM **Privately Held**
SIC: 3069 Molded rubber products

(G-11772)
UCI INTERNATIONAL LLC (DH)
2100 International Pkwy (44720-1373)
PHONE..................330 899-0340
Bruce Zorich, *CEO*
Nathan Iles, *CFO*
Keith A Zar, *VP*
Curtis Draper, *S&M/VP*
Mike Malady, *Pers/VP*
▲ EMP: 22 EST: 2000
SALES (est): 1.54B
SALES (corp-wide): 8.03B **Privately Held**
Web: www.uciholdings.com
SIC: 3714 Motor vehicle parts and accessories
HQ: Uci International Holdings, Inc.
    2100 International Pkwy
    North Canton OH 44720
    330 899-0340

(G-11773)
UPL INTERNATIONAL INC
Also Called: Universal Plastics
7661 Freedom Ave Nw (44720-6903)
PHONE..................330 433-2860
Jeffrey Scarpitti, *Pr*
Wade Scarpitti, *
EMP: 22 EST: 1976
SQ FT: 18,000
SALES (est): 4.6MM **Privately Held**
SIC: 3089 5162 Injection molding of plastics; Plastics products, nec

(G-11774)
W3 ULTRASONICS LLC
5288 Huckleberry St Nw (44720-6876)
PHONE..................330 284-3667
Scott Miller, *Pr*
EMP: 6 EST: 2013
SQ FT: 5,000
SALES (est): 237.48K **Privately Held**
SIC: 3589 Commercial cleaning equipment

(G-11775)
WILLIAMS PARTNERS LP
7235 Whipple Ave Nw (44720-7101)
PHONE..................330 414-6201
Travis Bonine, *Brnch Mgr*
EMP: 19
SALES (corp-wide): 10.91B **Publicly Held**
Web: www.williams.com
SIC: 1311 Natural gas production
HQ: Williams Partners L.P.
    1 Williams Ctr Bsmt 2
    Tulsa OK 74172

North Fairfield
Huron County

(G-11776)
FLY RACE FUELS LLC
1905 Maple Ridge Rd (44855-9653)
PHONE..................419 744-9402
Brenda Ooten, *Prin*
EMP: 6 EST: 2012
SALES (est): 180.45K **Privately Held**
SIC: 2869 Fuels

North Jackson
Mahoning County

(G-11777)
AMERICAN PLASTECH LLC
11635 Mahoning Ave (44451-9688)
P.O. Box 399 (44451-0399)
PHONE..................330 538-0576
Rick Amato, *Managing Member*
EMP: 6 EST: 2016
SALES (est): 499.74K **Privately Held**
SIC: 2431 Windows and window parts and trim, wood

(G-11778)
BCI AND V INVESTMENTS INC
11675 Mahoning Ave (44451-9688)
P.O. Box 698 (44451-0698)
PHONE..................330 538-0660
Harold Bartels, *Pr*
Randy Vegso, *
EMP: 19 EST: 1987
SQ FT: 26,000
SALES (est): 778.46K **Privately Held**
SIC: 2821 3356 Vinyl resins, nec; Nonferrous rolling and drawing, nec

(G-11779)
BLUE RIBBON TRAILERS LTD
12800 Leonard Pkwy (44451-8611)
PHONE..................330 538-4114
Clint Leonard, *Pr*
EMP: 8 EST: 2006
SALES (est): 342.58K **Privately Held**
Web: www.blueribbontrailers.com
SIC: 3799 Trailers and trailer equipment

(G-11780)
CANFIELD MANUFACTURING CO INC
Also Called: Wilson Specialties
489 Rosemont Rd (44451-9717)
PHONE..................330 533-3333
M J Stewart, *CEO*
Mary Mc Mahon, *Off Mgr*
EMP: 7 EST: 1800
SQ FT: 20,000
SALES (est): 601.71K **Privately Held**
SIC: 2426 2499 Lumber, hardwood dimension; Handles, wood

(G-11781)
CLEVELAND CORETEC INC
Also Called: Ttm
12080 Debartolo Dr (44451-9642)
P.O. Box 216 (44451-0216)
PHONE..................314 727-2087
Jonathan Schofield, *Prin*
EMP: 7 EST: 2012
SALES (est): 227.78K **Privately Held**
SIC: 3672 Printed circuit boards

(G-11782)
DDI NORTH JACKSON CORP
12080 Debartolo Dr (44451-9642)
P.O. Box 216 (44451-0216)
PHONE..................330 538-3900
Mark Curry, *CEO*
EMP: 8 EST: 2014
SALES (est): 425.73K **Privately Held**
SIC: 3672 Printed circuit boards

(G-11783)
EXTRUDEX ALUMINUM INC
12051 Mahoning Ave (44451-9617)
P.O. Box 697 (44451-0697)
PHONE..................330 538-4444
Andrew Gucciardi, *Pr*
▲ EMP: 120 EST: 1998
SQ FT: 110,000

SALES (est): 48.97MM **Privately Held**
Web: www.extrudex.com
SIC: 3354 Aluminum extruded products

(G-11784)
INNOVAR SYSTEMS LIMITED
12155 Commissioner Dr (44451-9640)
P.O. Box 486 (44451-0486)
PHONE..................330 538-3942
John Frano, *CEO*
Paul Graff, *
Scott Yakubek, *
EMP: 35 **EST:** 2003
SQ FT: 15,000
SALES (est): 6.26MM **Privately Held**
Web: www.innovarsystems.com
SIC: 3699 Laser welding, drilling, and cutting equipment

(G-11785)
JOHN ZIDIAN COMPANY
382 Rosemont Rd (44451-9631)
PHONE..................330 965-8455
EMP: 16
SALES (corp-wide): 4.74MM **Privately Held**
Web: www.summergardenfood.com
SIC: 2032 Italian foods, nec: packaged in cans, jars, etc.
PA: John Zidian Company
   574 Mcclurg Rd
   Youngstown OH 44512
   330 743-6050

(G-11786)
LIBERTY STEEL PRESSED PDTS LLC
11650 Mahoning Ave (44451-9688)
PHONE..................330 538-2236
Jim Grasso, *Pr*
EMP: 9 **EST:** 2015
SALES (est): 479.54K **Privately Held**
Web: www.libertysteelproducts.com
SIC: 3399 Primary metal products

(G-11787)
OHIO CUSTOM DIES LLC
293 Rosemont Rd (44451-9632)
P.O. Box 428 (44451-0428)
PHONE..................330 538-3396
EMP: 15 **EST:** 2020
SALES (est): 1.16MM **Privately Held**
Web: www.ohiocustomdies.com
SIC: 3544 Special dies and tools

(G-11788)
OHIO SPECIALTY DIES LLC
293 Rosemont Rd (44451-9632)
P.O. Box 428 (44451-0428)
PHONE..................330 538-3396
Joseph P Baco, *Managing Member*
EMP: 16 **EST:** 2011
SQ FT: 4,000
SALES (est): 1.33MM **Privately Held**
Web: www.ohiospecialtydies.com
SIC: 3544 Special dies and tools

(G-11789)
PMC SYSTEMS LIMITED
12155 Commissioner Dr (44451-9640)
P.O. Box 486 (44451-0486)
PHONE..................330 538-2268
John Frano, *Pr*
Paul Graff, *
EMP: 30 **EST:** 1983
SQ FT: 3,000
SALES (est): 4.55MM **Privately Held**
Web: www.pmcsystems.com
SIC: 3625 8711 Electric controls and control accessories, industrial; Electrical or electronic engineering

(G-11790)
SOVEREIGN CIRCUITS INC
12080 Debartolo Dr (44451-9642)
P.O. Box 216 (44451-0216)
PHONE..................330 538-3900
Robert Buss, *Prin*
EMP: 8 **EST:** 2014
SALES (est): 473.3K **Privately Held**
Web: www.sovereign-circuits.com
SIC: 3679 Electronic circuits

(G-11791)
STAMPED STEEL PRODUCTS INC
151 S Bailey Rd (44451-9636)
P.O. Box 5224 (44514-0224)
PHONE..................330 538-3951
William Robinson Junior, *Pr*
Micheal D Geiger, *Sec*
EMP: 11 **EST:** 2001
SQ FT: 59,000
SALES (est): 2.66MM **Privately Held**
SIC: 3469 5051 Stamping metal for the trade ; Stampings, metal

(G-11792)
TTM TECHNOLOGIES INC
12080 Debartolo Dr (44451-9642)
P.O. Box 216 (44451-0216)
PHONE..................330 538-3900
EMP: 118
SALES (corp-wide): 2.23B **Publicly Held**
Web: www.ttm.com
SIC: 3672 Printed circuit boards
PA: Ttm Technologies, Inc.
   200 Sndpointe Ave Ste 400
   Santa Ana CA 92707
   714 327-3000

(G-11793)
TTM TECHNOLOGIES NORTH AMERICA LLC
Also Called: Ttm Technologies
12080 Debartolo Dr (44451-9642)
P.O. Box 216 (44451-0216)
PHONE..................330 572-3400
EMP: 60
SIC: 3672 Printed circuit boards

(G-11794)
VINYL PROFILES ACQUISITION LLC
11675 Mahoning Ave (44451-9688)
P.O. Box 698 (44451-0698)
PHONE..................330 538-0660
Randy Vegso, *Pr*
EMP: 36 **EST:** 2009
SALES (est): 9.88MM **Privately Held**
Web: www.vinylprofilesinc.com
SIC: 3089 Injection molding of plastics

(G-11795)
VINYLTECH INC
11635 Mahoning Ave (44451-9688)
P.O. Box 127 (44451-0127)
PHONE..................330 538-0369
EMP: 22 **EST:** 1995
SALES (est): 949.87K **Privately Held**
SIC: 3544 Forms (molds), for foundry and plastics working machinery

North Kingsville
Ashtabula County

(G-11796)
HPC HOLDINGS LLC
3365 East Center St (44068)
P.O. Box 281 (44068-0281)
PHONE..................440 224-7204
Ken Lazo, *Prin*
EMP: 715

SALES (corp-wide): 59.91MM **Privately Held**
SIC: 2821 Molding compounds, plastics
HQ: Hpc Holdings, Llc
   3637 Ridgewood Rd
   Fairlawn OH 44333

(G-11797)
WHOLESALE IMPRINTS INC
Also Called: Ringer Screen Print
6259 Hewitt Ln (44068)
P.O. Box 507 (44068-0507)
PHONE..................440 224-3527
John Ringer, *Prin*
EMP: 40 **EST:** 2013
SALES (est): 3.04MM **Privately Held**
Web: www.ringer-wholesaleimprints.net
SIC: 2395 2396 Embroidery and art needlework; Fabric printing and stamping

North Lawrence
Stark County

(G-11798)
KELBLYS RIFLE RANGE INC
Also Called: Kelbly's
7222 Dalton Fox Lake Rd (44666-9543)
PHONE..................330 683-4674
George Kelbly Senior, *Pr*
James Kelbly, *VP*
George Kelbly Junior, *VP*
Karen Kelbly, *Sec*
EMP: 8 **EST:** 1970
SALES (est): 996.52K **Privately Held**
Web: www.kelbly.com
SIC: 3484 7999 Rifles or rifle parts, 30 mm. and below; Shooting range operation

(G-11799)
SJK MACHINE LLC
Also Called: McGuire Machine,
1862 Ben Fulton Rd (44666-9722)
PHONE..................330 868-3072
EMP: 14 **EST:** 2019
SALES (est): 994.81K **Privately Held**
SIC: 3545 Precision tools, machinists'

(G-11800)
US TUBULAR PRODUCTS INC
Also Called: Benmit Division
14852 Lincoln Way W (44666)
PHONE..................330 832-1734
Jeffrey J Cunningham, *Pr*
Brian Cunningham, *
Connye Cunningham, *
EMP: 60 **EST:** 1973
SQ FT: 100,000
SALES (est): 4.83MM **Privately Held**
Web: www.benmit.com
SIC: 8734 3498 Hydrostatic testing laboratory ; Tube fabricating (contract bending and shaping)

North Lima
Mahoning County

(G-11801)
BIRD EQUIPMENT LLC
Also Called: Specialty Fab
11950 South Ave (44452-9744)
PHONE..................330 549-1004
EMP: 28 **EST:** 1995
SQ FT: 49,500
SALES (est): 4.33MM
SALES (corp-wide): 180.13MM **Privately Held**
Web: www.birdequipmentllc.com

SIC: 3441 Fabricated structural metal
PA: Desco Corporation
   7795 Walton Pkwy Ste 175
   New Albany OH 43054
   614 888-8855

(G-11802)
COBRA MOTORCYCLES MFG
11511 Springfield Rd (44452-9755)
PHONE..................330 207-3844
▲ **EMP:** 11 **EST:** 1994
SALES (est): 376.53K **Privately Held**
SIC: 3751 Motorcycles and related parts

(G-11803)
COMMERCIAL MINERALS INC
10900 South Ave (44452-9792)
P.O. Box 217 (44452-0217)
PHONE..................330 549-2165
Thomas Mackall, *Pr*
Melanie Dunn, *Treas*
EMP: 6 **EST:** 1981
SQ FT: 6,000
SALES (est): 628.79K **Privately Held**
SIC: 1221 Bituminous coal surface mining

(G-11804)
DUO-CORP
280 Miley Rd (44452-8581)
P.O. Box 313 (44452-0313)
PHONE..................330 549-2149
William G Kinkade, *CEO*
Bradley W Kinkade, *
Stephen De Capua, *
Diane Kinkade, *
EMP: 17 **EST:** 1977
SQ FT: 70,000
SALES (est): 3.26MM **Privately Held**
Web: www.duo-corp.com
SIC: 3089 3442 Windows, plastics; Screen and storm doors and windows

(G-11805)
FRAMEWORK INDUSTRIES LLC
80 Eastgate Industrial Dr (44452)
PHONE..................234 759-2080
EMP: 6 **EST:** 2016
SALES (est): 54.13K **Privately Held**
Web: www.frameworkindustries.com
SIC: 2431 Door frames, wood

(G-11806)
INDUSTRIAL PAPER SHREDDERS INC
12037 South Ave (44452-9742)
PHONE..................888 637-4733
EMP: 14 **EST:** 1983
SALES (est): 198.57K **Privately Held**
Web: www.industrial-shredders.com
SIC: 3541 Machine tools, metal cutting type

(G-11807)
J AND N INCORPORATED
80 Eastgate Dr (44452-8563)
PHONE..................234 759-3741
Joseph Tesiz, *Pr*
EMP: 12 **EST:** 2004
SALES (est): 292.88K **Privately Held**
Web: www.jninternationalinc.com
SIC: 2679 Plates, pressed and molded pulp: from purchased material

(G-11808)
KTSDI LLC
801 E Middletown Rd (44452-9761)
PHONE..................330 783-2000
Ken Timmings, *Prin*
Bryon Gotham, *Acctnt*
EMP: 7 **EST:** 2009
SALES (est): 896.47K **Privately Held**

North Lima - Mahoning County (G-11809)

Web: www.ktsdi.com
SIC: **8748** 3714 Business consulting, nec; Axle housings and shafts, motor vehicle

(G-11809)
PRECISION ASSEMBLIES INC
Also Called: Firestone Machine
11233 South Ave (44452-9731)
PHONE..........................330 549-2630
David Mcdevitt, *Pr*
David Mc Devitt, *Pr*
EMP: 10 EST: 1968
SQ FT: 12,200
SALES (est): 611.14K **Privately Held**
SIC: **3599** 7692 7629 3523 Machine shop, jobbing and repair; Welding repair; Electrical repair shops; Farm machinery and equipment

(G-11810)
PRINT FACTORY PLL
Also Called: Poland Print Shop
11471 South Ave (44452-9772)
P.O. Box 312 (44452-0312)
PHONE..........................330 549-9640
John Primm, *Pt*
Doris Primm, *Pt*
EMP: 7 EST: 1999
SALES (est): 937.71K **Privately Held**
Web: www.printfactorypll.com
SIC: **2752** Offset printing

(G-11811)
QC LLC
730 Miley Rd (44452-8587)
PHONE..........................847 682-9072
Renato Prestes, *Mgr*
EMP: 20
SALES (corp-wide): 4.71B **Privately Held**
SIC: **2819** Iron (ferric/ferrous) compounds or salts
HQ: Qc Llc
1001 Winstead Dr Ste 480
Cary NC 27513
800 883-0010

(G-11812)
R A M PLASTICS CO INC
11401 South Ave (44452-9772)
P.O. Box 402 (44452-0402)
PHONE..........................330 549-3107
Richard Mallory, *Pr*
EMP: 24 EST: 1975
SQ FT: 20,000
SALES (est): 938.31K **Privately Held**
SIC: **3089** Injection molding of plastics

(G-11813)
STEEL VLY INDUS COATINGS LLC
558 Thornberry Trl (44452-8504)
PHONE..........................330 519-4348
Anthony Gialousis, *Owner*
EMP: 7 EST: 2017
SALES (est): 113.29K **Privately Held**
SIC: **3479** Metal coating and allied services

(G-11814)
STERLING MINING CORPORATION (HQ)
10900 South Ave (44452-9792)
P.O. Box 217 (44452-0217)
PHONE..........................330 549-2165
W Thomas Mackall, *Pr*
Denise Mackall, *Treas*
EMP: 12 EST: 1991
SQ FT: 6,000
SALES (est): 23.82MM
SALES (corp-wide): 23.82MM **Privately Held**
Web: www.efccfamily.com

SIC: **1222** Bituminous coal-underground mining
PA: The East Fairfield Coal Co
10900 South Ave
North Lima OH
330 549-2165

(G-11815)
TRAVIS PRODUCTS MFG INC
80 Eastgate Dr (44452-8563)
PHONE..........................234 759-3741
Joseph Soltesiz, *Prin*
EMP: 7 EST: 2007
SALES (est): 252.08K **Privately Held**
SIC: **3999** Manufacturing industries, nec

North Olmsted
Cuyahoga County

(G-11816)
AMERICAN RAMP SYSTEMS
4327 Coe Ave (44070-2820)
PHONE..........................440 336-4988
Martha Wright, *Prin*
EMP: 7 EST: 2005
SALES (est): 134.28K **Privately Held**
SIC: **3448** Prefabricated metal buildings and components

(G-11817)
ANAHEIM MANUFACTURING COMPANY
Also Called: Waste King
25300 Al Moen Dr (44070-5619)
P.O. Box 4146 (92803-4146)
PHONE..........................800 767-6293
Steve Lattman, *Pr*
Robert A Schneider, *VP*
▲ EMP: 50 EST: 1991
SALES (est): 20.79MM
SALES (corp-wide): 4.63B **Publicly Held**
Web: www.wasteking.com
SIC: **3639** Garbage disposal units, household
HQ: Moen Incorporated
25300 Al Moen Dr
North Olmsted OH 44070
800 289-6636

(G-11818)
BIANCHI USA INC
Also Called: Keyline
31336 Industrial Pkwy Ste 3 (44070)
PHONE..........................440 801-1083
Scott Hinton, *Pr*
▲ EMP: 15 EST: 2002
SALES (est): 4.29MM
SALES (corp-wide): 516.77K **Privately Held**
Web: www.bianchi1770usa.com
SIC: **3429** Keys and key blanks
HQ: Keyline Spa
Via Camillo Bianchi 2
Conegliano TV 31015

(G-11819)
BIOTHANE COATED WEBBING CORP
31393 Industrial Pkwy Bldg 2 (44070-4764)
PHONE..........................440 327-0485
EMP: 9 EST: 1977
SALES (est): 220.47K **Privately Held**
Web: www.biothane.us
SIC: **2821** Plastics materials and resins

(G-11820)
BREW CLEVELAND LLC
23489 Greenwood Ln (44070-1133)
PHONE..........................440 455-9218
Fredric Coffey, *Prin*
EMP: 7 EST: 2015

SALES (est): 415.75K **Privately Held**
SIC: **2082** Malt beverages

(G-11821)
BTA OF MOTORCARS INC
27500 Lorain Rd (44070-4038)
PHONE..........................440 716-1000
Gary Tamerlano, *Prin*
EMP: 12 EST: 2007
SALES (est): 427.86K **Privately Held**
Web: www.btacollision.com
SIC: **3479** Painting of metal products

(G-11822)
CLASSIC COATINGS
6074 Pebblebrook Ln (44070-4566)
PHONE..........................330 421-3703
EMP: 6 EST: 2012
SALES (est): 101.23K **Privately Held**
SIC: **3479** Coating of metals and formed products

(G-11823)
FRAGAPANE BAKERIES INC (PA)
Also Called: Fragapane Bakery & Deli
28625 Lorain Rd (44070-4009)
PHONE..........................440 779-6050
John Fragapane, *Pr*
Nick Fragapane, *VP*
Rose Fragapane, *Sec*
Victoria Fragapane, *Treas*
EMP: 8 EST: 1971
SQ FT: 4,000
SALES (est): 2.16MM
SALES (corp-wide): 2.16MM **Privately Held**
Web: www.fragapanebakeries.com
SIC: **5411** 5461 2051 Delicatessen stores; Retail bakeries; Bread, cake, and related products

(G-11824)
MOEN INCORPORATED (HQ)
Also Called: Moen
25300 Al Moen Dr (44070-5619)
PHONE..........................800 289-6636
◆ EMP: 20 EST: 1969
SALES (est): 462.51MM
SALES (corp-wide): 4.63B **Publicly Held**
Web: www.moen.com
SIC: **3432** Plumbers' brass goods: drain cocks, faucets, spigots, etc.
PA: Fortune Brands Innovations, Inc.
520 Lake Cook Rd
Deerfield IL 60015
847 484-4400

(G-11825)
PWA GREAT NORTHERN CORP CTR LP
25050 Country Club Blvd Ste 200 (44070)
PHONE..........................412 415-1177
EMP: 7 EST: 2011
SALES (est): 122.55K **Privately Held**
SIC: **3999** Stage hardware and equipment, except lighting

North Ridgeville
Lorain County

(G-11826)
ALANOD WESTLAKE METAL IND INC
36696 Sugar Ridge Rd (44039-3832)
PHONE..........................440 327-8184
John R Johnston Junior, *Pr*
Franke Lee, *Pr*
Greg Seeley, *Sec*
James Gula, *VP*
◆ EMP: 21 EST: 1970

SQ FT: 80,000
SALES (est): 22.96MM
SALES (corp-wide): 87.73MM **Privately Held**
Web: www.alanod-westlake.com
SIC: **5051** 3354 Aluminum bars, rods, ingots, sheets, pipes, plates, etc.; Aluminum extruded products
PA: Alanod Gmbh & Co. Kg
Egerstr. 12
Ennepetal NW 58256
233 398-6500

(G-11827)
ALLEN INDUSTRIAL COMPANY
7650 Race Rd (44039-3612)
PHONE..........................440 327-4100
Allen Retay, *Pr*
Marilyn Hoskinson, *Sec*
EMP: 14 EST: 1973
SQ FT: 28,000
SALES (est): 321.66K **Privately Held**
SIC: **3443** 3441 Fabricated plate work (boiler shop); Fabricated structural metal

(G-11828)
AMERICAN EGLE PRPRTY PRSRVTION
Also Called: 1 & 1 Property Preservation
39050 Center Ridge Rd (44039-2742)
PHONE..........................855 440-6938
John Davis, *Ex Dir*
Jodi Sanders, *Prin*
John Davis, *Prin*
EMP: 8 EST: 2012
SALES (est): 326.67K **Privately Held**
Web: www.americaneaglepropertypreservation.com
SIC: **1389** 1522 7299 8742 Construction, repair, and dismantling services; Residential construction, nec; Home improvement and renovation contractor agency; Management consulting services

(G-11829)
BECKETT AIR INCORPORATED (PA)
Also Called: PM Motor Fan Blade Company
37850 Taylor Pkwy (44039-3600)
P.O. Box 1236 (44036-1236)
PHONE..........................440 327-9999
Jonathan M Beckett, *CEO*
John D Beckett, *
▲ EMP: 88 EST: 1988
SALES (est): 24.31MM
SALES (corp-wide): 24.31MM **Privately Held**
Web: www.beckettair.com
SIC: **3433** 3585 3564 Heating equipment, except electric; Refrigeration and heating equipment; Blowers and fans

(G-11830)
BECKETT GAS INC (HQ)
Also Called: Beckett Thermal Solutions
38000 Taylor Pkwy (44039-3645)
P.O. Box 4037 (44036-4037)
PHONE..........................440 327-3141
Morrison J Carter, *Pr*
John D Beckett, *
Kevin A Beckett, *
▼ EMP: 63 EST: 1988
SQ FT: 140,000
SALES (est): 77.04MM
SALES (corp-wide): 100.07MM **Privately Held**
Web: www.beckettgas.com
SIC: **3433** Burners, furnaces, boilers, and stokers
PA: R.W. Beckett Corporation
38251 Center Ridge Rd
North Ridgeville OH 44039

GEOGRAPHIC SECTION

North Ridgeville - Lorain County (G-11855)

440 327-1060

(G-11831)
BINDERY TECH INC
35205 Center Ridge Rd (44039-3013)
PHONE..............................440 934-3247
Dave Sexton, *Prin*
EMP: 7 **EST:** 1995
SALES (est): 370.05K **Privately Held**
Web: www.binderytech.com
SIC: 2789 Binding only: books, pamphlets, magazines, etc.

(G-11832)
BIOTHANE COATED WEBBING CORP
34655 Mills Rd (44039-1843)
PHONE..............................440 327-0485
Frank Boron, *Pr*
▲ **EMP:** 35 **EST:** 1976
SQ FT: 25,000
SALES (est): 7.96MM **Privately Held**
Web: www.biothane.us
SIC: 2295 3083 2821 Resin or plastic coated fabrics; Laminated plastics plate and sheet; Plastics materials and resins

(G-11833)
BRACEMART LLC
36097 Westminister Ave (44039-4537)
PHONE..............................440 353-2830
William Hagy, *Prin*
Aaron Dibucci, *Pr*
EMP: 6 **EST:** 2015
SALES (est): 191.31K **Privately Held**
Web: www.brace-mart.com
SIC: 3842 3949 Braces, orthopedic; Sporting and athletic goods, nec

(G-11834)
BRG SPORTS INC
7501 Performance Ln (44039-2765)
PHONE..............................217 891-1429
EMP: 8 **EST:** 2019
SALES (est): 610.57K **Privately Held**
SIC: 3949 Sporting and athletic goods, nec

(G-11835)
C & S INDUSTRIAL LTD
5120 Mills Industrial Pkwy (44039-1958)
PHONE..............................440 327-2360
William Nestor, *Prin*
EMP: 8 **EST:** 2001
SQ FT: 7,250
SALES (est): 108.91K **Privately Held**
SIC: 3469 3544 5063 Metal stampings, nec; Special dies, tools, jigs, and fixtures; Electrical apparatus and equipment

(G-11836)
CONTOUR TOOL INC
38830 Taylor Pkwy (44035-6254)
PHONE..............................440 365-7333
Paul Reichlin, *Pr*
Yvonne D Reichlin, *
R Stephen Laux, *
EMP: 25 **EST:** 1986
SQ FT: 11,000
SALES (est): 2.56MM **Privately Held**
Web: www.contourprecisionmilling.com
SIC: 3545 3544 Machine tool accessories; Special dies and tools

(G-11837)
CUYAHOGA VENDING CO INC
Also Called: Cuyahoga Group, The
39405 Taylor Pkwy (44035-6264)
PHONE..............................440 353-9595
TOLL FREE: 800
EMP: 128
SALES (corp-wide): 22.36MM **Privately Held**
Web: www.cuyahogagroup.com
SIC: 7359 2099 Vending machine rental; Food preparations, nec
PA: Cuyahoga Vending Co., Inc.
14250 Industrial Ave S # 104
Maple Heights OH 44137
216 663-1457

(G-11838)
DRECO INC
7887 Root Rd (44039-4013)
P.O. Box 39328 (44039-0328)
PHONE..............................440 327-6021
H T Ammerman, *Prin*
Christopher A Draudt, *Pr*
Russell Draudt, *Pr*
Harry Miller, *Dir Fin*
Harold F Ellsworth, *Prin*
▲ **EMP:** 130 **EST:** 1932
SQ FT: 135,000
SALES (est): 18.75MM **Privately Held**
Web: www.drecoinc.com
SIC: 3089 Injection molding of plastics

(G-11839)
FATE INDUSTRIES INC
36682 Sugar Ridge Rd (44039-3832)
PHONE..............................440 327-1770
Rick Fate, *Pr*
Julie Fate, *Sec*
EMP: 8 **EST:** 1987
SQ FT: 2,800
SALES (est): 617.42K **Privately Held**
SIC: 3599 Machine shop, jobbing and repair

(G-11840)
FROHOCK-STEWART INC
39400 Taylor Pkwy (44035-6263)
PHONE..............................440 329-6000
Gerald B Blouch, *Pr*
▲ **EMP:** 40 **EST:** 1954
SALES: 4.14MM
SALES (corp-wide): 741.73MM **Publicly Held**
SIC: 3842 Surgical appliances and supplies
PA: Invacare Corporation
1 Invacare Way
Elyria OH 44035
440 329-6000

(G-11841)
GORSKI WELDING LLC
37190 Sugar Ridge Rd (44039-3630)
PHONE..............................440 412-7910
EMP: 6 **EST:** 2019
SALES (est): 225.99K **Privately Held**
Web: www.gorskiwelding.com
SIC: 7692 Welding repair

(G-11842)
GREENFIELD SOLAR CORP
7881 Root Rd (44039-4013)
PHONE..............................216 535-9200
Neil Sater, *Pr*
EMP: 7 **EST:** 2009
SALES (est): 950K **Privately Held**
Web: www.greenfieldsolar.com
SIC: 3674 Semiconductors and related devices

(G-11843)
H & S DISTRIBUTING INC
Also Called: Team Cobra Products
35478 Lorain Rd (44039-4461)
PHONE..............................800 336-7784
Robert Shaffer, *Ch Bd*
▲ **EMP:** 8 **EST:** 1980
SQ FT: 11,000
SALES (est): 823.88K **Privately Held**
Web: www.cobraproducts.com

SIC: 5091 3949 Bowling equipment; Bowling equipment and supplies

(G-11844)
HOISTECH LLC
32960 Fern Tree Ln (44039-2304)
PHONE..............................440 327-5379
EMP: 6 **EST:** 2010
SALES (est): 412.57K **Privately Held**
Web: www.hoistech.ie
SIC: 3949 Sporting and athletic goods, nec

(G-11845)
IMPACT INDUSTRIES INC
5120 Mills Industrial Pkwy (44039-1958)
PHONE..............................440 327-2360
William Nestor, *Pr*
Leslie Nestor, *
EMP: 25 **EST:** 1977
SQ FT: 25,000
SALES (est): 2.08MM **Privately Held**
Web: www.impactindustries.com
SIC: 3469 3544 Stamping metal for the trade; Special dies and tools

(G-11846)
INVACARE CORPORATION
Also Called: Invacare Hme
38683 Taylor Pkwy (44035-6200)
PHONE..............................440 329-6000
Brad Kushner, *Brnch Mgr*
EMP: 10
SALES (corp-wide): 741.73MM **Publicly Held**
Web: global.invacare.com
SIC: 3842 Surgical appliances and supplies
PA: Invacare Corporation
1 Invacare Way
Elyria OH 44035
440 329-6000

(G-11847)
JBC TECHNOLOGIES INC (PA)
7887 Bliss Pkwy (44039-3475)
PHONE..............................440 327-4522
Joe Bliss, *
▲ **EMP:** 66 **EST:** 1986
SALES (est): 47.53MM **Privately Held**
Web: www.jbc-tech.com
SIC: 3053 Gaskets, all materials

(G-11848)
KALT MANUFACTURING COMPANY
36700 Sugar Ridge Rd (44039-3800)
PHONE..............................440 327-2102
Joseph W Kalt, *Pr*
Jeanne M Kalt, *Treas*
Ann C Kalt, *Asst Tr*
Gayle A Bangs, *Sec*
▲ **EMP:** 54 **EST:** 1967
SQ FT: 60,000
SALES (est): 10.03MM **Privately Held**
Web: www.kaltmfg.com
SIC: 3544 3545 3549 3599 Special dies and tools; Machine tool accessories; Metalworking machinery, nec; Machine shop, jobbing and repair

(G-11849)
LORAIN RLED DIE PDTS INDUS SUP
6287 Lear Nagle Rd Ste 4 (44039-3369)
PHONE..............................440 281-8607
EMP: 6 **EST:** 1995
SQ FT: 2,800
SALES (est): 600K **Privately Held**
Web: www.lorainindie.com
SIC: 3544 Dies, steel rule

(G-11850)
METAL MARKER MANUFACTURING CO
Also Called: Metal Marker Manufacturing
6225 Lear Nagle Rd (44039-3223)
PHONE..............................440 327-2300
David Primrose, *Pr*
William Primrose, *Pr*
EMP: 10 **EST:** 1923
SQ FT: 16,000
SALES (est): 2.49MM **Privately Held**
Web: www.metalmarkermfg.com
SIC: 3953 Marking devices

(G-11851)
NORLAKE MANUFACTURING COMPANY (PA)
Also Called: Norlake
39301 Taylor Pkwy (44035-6272)
P.O. Box 215 (44036-0215)
PHONE..............................440 353-3200
James Markus, *Pr*
Daryl Jackson, *
▼ **EMP:** 80 **EST:** 1963
SQ FT: 50,000
SALES (est): 24.93MM
SALES (corp-wide): 24.93MM **Privately Held**
Web: www.norlakemfg.com
SIC: 3677 3714 3612 Transformers power supply, electronic type; Motor vehicle parts and accessories; Transformers, except electric

(G-11852)
P M MOTOR COMPANY
Also Called: P M Motor -Fan Blade Company
37850 Taylor Pkwy (44039-3643)
PHONE..............................440 327-9999
Michael Macken, *Pr*
Catherine E Macken, *Sec*
Joan B Macken, *VP*
EMP: 10 **EST:** 1952
SQ FT: 10,000
SALES (est): 215.72K **Privately Held**
SIC: 3469 Machine parts, stamped or pressed metal

(G-11853)
PLEXTRUSIONS INC
38870 Taylor Pkwy (44035-6254)
P.O. Box 4290 (44321-0290)
PHONE..............................330 668-2587
Eve Gribble, *Prin*
EMP: 13 **EST:** 2012
SALES (est): 1.63MM **Privately Held**
Web: www.plextrusions.com
SIC: 3083 Thermoplastics laminates: rods, tubes, plates, and sheet

(G-11854)
PROTECTIVE INDUSTRIAL POLYMERS
7875 Bliss Pkwy (44039)
PHONE..............................440 327-0015
EMP: 10 **EST:** 2008
SALES (est): 2.52MM **Privately Held**
Web: www.protectiveindustrialpolymers.com
SIC: 1771 2515 2822 8741 Flooring contractor; Mattresses, containing felt, foam rubber, urethane, etc.; Ethylene-propylene rubbers, EPDM polymers; Construction management

(G-11855)
PURITAS METAL PRODUCTS INC
39097 Center Ridge Rd (44039-3614)
PHONE..............................440 353-1917
Richard Cook, *CEO*

North Ridgeville - Lorain County (G-11856)

EMP: 6 EST: 1950
SQ FT: 15,000
SALES (est): 1.05MM Privately Held
Web: www.puritasmetal.com
SIC: 3441 Fabricated structural metal

(G-11856)
RAVEN CONCEALMENT SYSTEMS LLC
7889 Root Rd (44039-4013)
PHONE.................................440 508-9000
Michael Goerlick, *Managing Member*
John Chapman, *
Dotson Burton, *
Kelly Laurence, *
EMP: 45 EST: 2008
SALES (est): 4.98MM Privately Held
Web: www.rcsgear.com
SIC: 5399 3949 3089 Army-Navy goods stores; Cases, gun and rod (sporting equipment); Injection molding of plastics

(G-11857)
REFURB-WORLD LLC
33888 Center Ridge Rd (44039-3257)
PHONE.................................440 471-9030
EMP: 32 EST: 2017
SALES (est): 2.46MM Privately Held
SIC: 3549 Assembly machines, including robotic

(G-11858)
RHENIUM ALLOYS INC (PA)
Also Called: Rhenium Alloys
38683 Taylor Pkwy (44035-6200)
PHONE.................................440 365-7388
Mike Prokop, *Pr*
▲ EMP: 41 EST: 1994
SQ FT: 35,500
SALES (est): 11.75MM
SALES (corp-wide): 11.75MM Privately Held
Web: www.rhenium.com
SIC: 3313 3356 3498 3339 Electrometallurgical products; Tungsten, basic shapes; Fabricated pipe and fittings; Primary nonferrous metals, nec

(G-11859)
ROCK HARD INDUSTRIES LLC
Also Called: New Stone Age
34555 Mills Rd (44039-1841)
PHONE.................................440 327-3077
Matt Kerns, *CEO*
Krissy Kerns, *Pr*
EMP: 9 EST: 2019
SALES (est): 1.01MM Privately Held
SIC: 3441 Fabricated structural metal

(G-11860)
RW BECKETT CORPORATION (PA)
38251 Center Ridge Rd (44039-2895)
P.O. Box 1289 (44036-1289)
PHONE.................................440 327-1060
Kevin Beckett, *Pr*
Peter Duffield, *
▲ EMP: 193 EST: 1937
SQ FT: 40,000
SALES (est): 100.07MM
SALES (corp-wide): 100.07MM Privately Held
Web: www.beckettcorp.com
SIC: 3433 Oil burners, domestic or industrial

(G-11861)
TANGO ECHO BRAVO MFG INC
4915 Mills Industrial Pkwy (44039-1953)
PHONE.................................440 353-2605
Timothy E Bennett, *Pr*
EMP: 6 EST: 2005
SQ FT: 2,800

SALES (est): 482.85K Privately Held
Web: www.teb-mfg.com
SIC: 3999 Barber and beauty shop equipment

(G-11862)
TDS-BF/LS HOLDINGS INC
38900 Taylor Industrial Pkwy (44039)
PHONE.................................440 327-5800
Leonard Sikora, *Pr*
William T Flickinger, *
EMP: 28 EST: 1976
SQ FT: 60,000
SALES (est): 2.25MM Privately Held
SIC: 3444 3469 3599 3479 Sheet metalwork; Metal stampings, nec; Machine shop, jobbing and repair; Painting of metal products

(G-11863)
US REFRACTORY PRODUCTS LLC
7660 Race Rd (44039-3612)
PHONE.................................440 386-4580
Gary M Demarco, *Managing Member*
William Drake, *
◆ EMP: 25 EST: 2009
SQ FT: 30,000
SALES (est): 4.91MM Privately Held
Web: www.usrefractory.com
SIC: 3297 Nonclay refractories

(G-11864)
WOLFF BROS SUPPLY INC
38777 Taylor Industrial Pkwy (44035)
PHONE.................................440 327-1650
EMP: 15
SALES (corp-wide): 119.09MM Privately Held
Web: www.wolffbros.com
SIC: 3432 5074 5722 Plumbing fixture fittings and trim; Plumbing fittings and supplies; Air conditioning room units, self-contained
PA: Wolff Bros. Supply, Inc.
6078 Wolff Rd
Medina OH 44256
330 725-3451

North Royalton
Cuyahoga County

(G-11865)
5PD COATINGS LLC
12650 N Star Dr (44133-5947)
PHONE.................................216 235-6086
John Turnbull, *Prin*
EMP: 7 EST: 2008
SALES (est): 238.21K Privately Held
Web: www.5pdcoatings.com
SIC: 3714 Cleaners, air, motor vehicle

(G-11866)
ALLIED WITAN COMPANY
Also Called: Alwitco
13805 Progress Pkwy (44133-4391)
PHONE.................................440 237-9630
EMP: 16 EST: 1947
SALES (est): 3.87MM Privately Held
Web: www.alwitco.com
SIC: 3714 Mufflers (exhaust), motor vehicle

(G-11867)
AMCLO GROUP INC
Also Called: Amclo
9721 York Alpha Dr (44133-3505)
PHONE.................................216 791-8400
William Harkins, *Pr*
Karl Morganthaler, *
EMP: 22 EST: 1985

SQ FT: 39,000
SALES (est): 4.33MM Privately Held
Web: www.amclo.com
SIC: 3469 3089 Stamping metal for the trade; Injection molding of plastics

(G-11868)
BEST EQUIPMENT CO INC
12620 York Delta Dr (44133-3559)
PHONE.................................440 237-3515
Mike Dahlman, *Managing Member*
EMP: 20
SALES (corp-wide): 18.48MM Privately Held
Web: www.bestequipmentco.com
SIC: 3589 Sewer cleaning equipment, power
PA: Best Equipment Co Inc
5550 Poindexter Dr
Indianapolis IN 46235
317 823-3050

(G-11869)
CARDINAL AIR DESIGN LLC
8527 Ridge Rd (44133-1875)
PHONE.................................440 638-4717
EMP: 7 EST: 2016
SALES (est): 245.08K Privately Held
Web: www.cardinalairdesign.com
SIC: 3564 Blowers and fans

(G-11870)
CARDINAL PRODUCTS INC
11929 Abbey Rd Ste D (44133-2664)
PHONE.................................440 237-8280
Janet Stanley, *Pr*
EMP: 8 EST: 1989
SQ FT: 10,000
SALES (est): 761.7K Privately Held
Web: www.cardinalproductsinc.com
SIC: 3089 Injection molding of plastics

(G-11871)
COMM STEEL INC
8043 Corporate Cir Ste 2 (44133-1279)
PHONE.................................216 881-4600
Eddie B Perkins, *Pr*
Michael Ciofani, *
Robert J Ciofani, *
EMP: 50 EST: 1991
SQ FT: 130,000
SALES (est): 7.52MM Privately Held
SIC: 3441 Fabricated structural metal

(G-11872)
CONWAY GREENE CO INC
17325 Parkside Dr (44133-5413)
PHONE.................................440 230-2627
Barry Conway, *Pr*
Evalyn Greene, *Prin*
EMP: 7 EST: 1994
SALES (est): 898.99K Privately Held
Web: www.conwaygreene.com
SIC: 2731 Book publishing

(G-11873)
EAGLE PRECISION PRODUCTS LLC
13800 Progress Pkwy Ste J (44133-4354)
PHONE.................................440 582-9393
Bruce Reger, *Managing Member*
Joshua Reger, *VP*
EMP: 9 EST: 1979
SQ FT: 18,000
SALES (est): 2.36MM Privately Held
Web: www.eagleprecisionproducts.com
SIC: 3469 3544 Stamping metal for the trade; Special dies and tools

(G-11874)
ENVIRNMNTAL CMPLIANCE TECH LLC

Also Called: Ect
13953 Progress Pkwy (44133-4305)
PHONE.................................216 634-0400
Sendos Mohammad, *Mgr*
EMP: 10 EST: 2004
SALES (est): 1.11MM Privately Held
Web: www.ecttesting.com
SIC: 1799 4959 3826 Petroleum storage tanks, pumping and draining; Environmental cleanup services; Environmental testing equipment

(G-11875)
G & P CONSTRUCTION LLC
10139 Royalton Rd Ste D (44133-4473)
PHONE.................................855 494-4830
Nicholas Gorey, *Managing Member*
EMP: 50 EST: 2019
SALES (est): 4.97MM Privately Held
SIC: 5046 5084 1791 2542 Shelving, commercial and industrial; Industrial machinery and equipment; Structural steel erection; Shelving angles or slotted bars, except wood

(G-11876)
GARDELLA JEWELRY LLC
Also Called: Earth Dreams Jewelry
7432 Julia Dr (44133-3715)
PHONE.................................440 877-9261
Jacqueline Magyar, *COO*
EMP: 6 EST: 2011
SALES (est): 395.01K Privately Held
Web: www.naturedevajewelry.com
SIC: 3961 Jewelry apparel, non-precious metals

(G-11877)
GRABER METAL WORKS INC
9664 Akins Rd Ste 1 (44133-4595)
PHONE.................................440 237-8422
Steve M Graber Senior, *Pr*
Michael R Horvath, *
Katherine Graber, *
EMP: 10 EST: 1965
SQ FT: 25,000
SALES (est): 258.23K Privately Held
SIC: 3599 5051 3446 3444 Machine shop, jobbing and repair; Metals service centers and offices; Architectural metalwork; Sheet metalwork

(G-11878)
H & D STEEL SERVICE INC
Also Called: H & D Steel Service Center
9960 York Alpha Dr (44133-3588)
PHONE.................................800 666-3390
Raymond Gary Schreiber, *Ch Bd*
Joseph Bubba, *Pr*
James P Schreiber, *VP Opers*
Joseph A Cachat, *Prin*
R G Schreiber, *Prin*
▲ EMP: 50 EST: 1972
SQ FT: 125,000
SALES (est): 24.75MM Privately Held
Web: www.hdsteel.com
SIC: 5051 3541 5085 Iron or steel flat products; Home workshop machine tools, metalworking; Industrial tools

(G-11879)
INDUCTION TOOLING INC
12510 York Delta Dr (44133-3543)
PHONE.................................440 237-0711
William Stuehr, *Pr*
EMP: 15 EST: 1976
SQ FT: 25,000
SALES (est): 2.39MM Privately Held
Web: www.inductiontooling.com
SIC: 3567 Induction heating equipment

(G-11880)
INDUSTRIAL PARTS DEPOT LLC
Also Called: I P D
11266 Royalton Rd (44133-4474)
PHONE...................................440 237-9164
Jeff Guiliano, *Brnch Mgr*
EMP: 6
SALES (corp-wide): 77.26MM **Privately Held**
Web: www.ipdparts.com
SIC: 3519 5084 Parts and accessories, internal combustion engines; Engines and parts, diesel
HQ: Industrial Parts Depot, Llc
1550 Charles Willard St
Carson CA 90746
310 530-1900

(G-11881)
KENT CORPORATION
9601 York Alpha Dr (44133-3503)
PHONE...................................440 582-3400
Dean Costello, *CEO*
David Tsai, *
Mark Costello, *
◆ **EMP:** 31 **EST:** 1971
SQ FT: 22,000
SALES (est): 8.13MM **Privately Held**
Web: www.kentcorporation.com
SIC: 3549 Coiling machinery

(G-11882)
KRENZ PRECISION MACHINING INC
9801 York Alpha Dr (44133-3507)
PHONE...................................440 237-1800
Richard Krenz Junior, *Pr*
Alfred Krist, *
Paul Krenz, *
Adam Krenz, *
EMP: 65 **EST:** 1967
SQ FT: 35,000
SALES (est): 4.49MM **Privately Held**
Web: www.krenzkristmachine.com
SIC: 3599 Machine shop, jobbing and repair

(G-11883)
LASZERAY TECHNOLOGY LLC
12315 York Delta Dr (44133-3544)
PHONE...................................440 582-8430
Greg Clark, *CEO*
Steve Patton, *
▲ **EMP:** 81 **EST:** 1997
SQ FT: 60,000
SALES (est): 24.47MM **Privately Held**
Web: www.laszeray.com
SIC: 3089 3544 Injection molding of plastics; Special dies, tools, jigs, and fixtures

(G-11884)
LUNAR TOOL & MOLD INC
9860 York Alpha Dr (44133-3586)
PHONE...................................440 237-2141
Friedrich Hoffman Junior, *Pr*
EMP: 28 **EST:** 1965
SQ FT: 20,000
SALES (est): 906.38K **Privately Held**
Web: www.lunarmold.com
SIC: 3544 7692 Special dies and tools; Welding repair

(G-11885)
MAY CONVEYOR INC
9981 York Theta Dr (44133-3545)
PHONE...................................440 237-8012
Leonard May, *Pr*
Matias Dost, *VP*
▲ **EMP:** 17 **EST:** 1973
SQ FT: 55,000
SALES (est): 927.59K **Privately Held**
Web: www.mayconveyor.com
SIC: 3496 Conveyor belts

(G-11886)
MAY INDUSTRIES OF OHIO INC
9981 York Theta Dr (44133-3545)
PHONE...................................440 237-8012
EMP: 35 **EST:** 1973
SALES (est): 4.55MM **Privately Held**
Web: www.mayind.com
SIC: 3544 3469 3444 Special dies and tools; Stamping metal for the trade; Sheet metalwork

(G-11887)
MDF TOOL CORPORATION
Also Called: Mdf Tool
10166 Royalton Rd (44133-4427)
PHONE...................................440 237-2277
John Bunjevac, *CEO*
Larry Jackson, *Pr*
EMP: 18 **EST:** 1980
SQ FT: 8,000
SALES (est): 1.07MM **Privately Held**
Web: www.mdftool.com
SIC: 3544 3545 Special dies and tools; Machine tool accessories

(G-11888)
NEXT GERENATION CRIMPING
Also Called: N G C
9880 York Alpha Dr (44133-3508)
PHONE...................................440 237-6300
Fred Krist, *Pt*
EMP: 8 **EST:** 1999
SALES (est): 677.87K **Privately Held**
SIC: 3432 Plumbing fixture fittings and trim

(G-11889)
OAK INDUSTRIAL INC
12955 York Delta Dr Ste G (44133-3550)
PHONE...................................440 263-2780
Michael Johns, *CEO*
Russ Karla, *COO*
EMP: 7 **EST:** 2010
SQ FT: 5,000
SALES (est): 628.26K **Privately Held**
SIC: 3599 Machine and other job shop work

(G-11890)
OSI ENVIRONMENTAL LLC
Also Called: Oil Skimmers
12800 York Rd (44133-3683)
P.O. Box 33092 (44133-0092)
PHONE...................................440 237-4600
William R Townsend, *Pr*
William R Townsend, *Pr*
Jim Petrucci, *VP*
EMP: 22 **EST:** 1964
SQ FT: 100,000
SALES (est): 3.85MM **Privately Held**
Web: www.oilskim.com
SIC: 3569 3564 3533 3443 Filters; Blowers and fans; Oil and gas field machinery; Fabricated plate work (boiler shop)

(G-11891)
PRECISION CUT FABRICATING INC
9921 York Alpha Dr (44133-3509)
PHONE...................................440 877-1260
Brian Wendling, *Pr*
EMP: 14 **EST:** 1999
SALES (est): 957.28K **Privately Held**
SIC: 7389 3312 Scrap steel cutting; Sheet or strip, steel, hot-rolled

(G-11892)
ROYAL WIRE PRODUCTS INC (PA)
13450 York Delta Dr (44133-3584)
PHONE...................................440 237-8787
William F Peshina, *Pr*
Paige Peshina, *
William Nelson, *
▲ **EMP:** 60 **EST:** 1953
SQ FT: 35,000
SALES (est): 18.79MM
SALES (corp-wide): 18.79MM **Privately Held**
Web: www.royalwire.com
SIC: 3496 Cages, wire

(G-11893)
ROYALTON ARCHTCTRAL FBRICATION
13155 York Delta Dr (44133-3522)
PHONE...................................440 582-0400
Stefan Winkler, *Pr*
EMP: 13 **EST:** 1992
SQ FT: 10,000
SALES (est): 1.66MM **Privately Held**
Web: www.rafpanels.com
SIC: 3444 3446 Sheet metalwork; Architectural metalwork

(G-11894)
ROYALTON FOODSERVICE EQP CO
9981 York Theta Dr (44133-3545)
PHONE...................................440 237-0806
Leonhard May, *Pr*
Hannelore May, *Sec*
EMP: 14 **EST:** 1986
SQ FT: 40,000
SALES (est): 624.82K **Privately Held**
Web: www.royaltonfoodservice.com
SIC: 3556 3631 Food products machinery; Household cooking equipment

(G-11895)
RUSS JR ENTERPRISES INC
6165 Royalton Rd (44133-4918)
PHONE...................................440 237-4642
Russell J Sposit Junior, *CEO*
EMP: 11 **EST:** 2007
SALES (est): 400K **Privately Held**
SIC: 3589 Car washing machinery

(G-11896)
S & D ARCHITECTURAL METALS
12955 York Delta Dr (44133-3534)
PHONE...................................440 582-2560
Cynthia Blessing, *Pr*
Keith Blessing, *VP*
EMP: 7 **EST:** 2001
SALES (est): 832.53K **Privately Held**
SIC: 3444 Sheet metalwork

(G-11897)
SYMBOL TOOL & DIE INC
11000 Industrial First Ave (44133-2678)
PHONE...................................440 582-5989
Jon Ardelian, *Pr*
EMP: 6 **EST:** 1992
SQ FT: 4,000
SALES (est): 463.29K **Privately Held**
SIC: 3544 Special dies and tools

(G-11898)
TRAVELERS VACATION GUIDE
10143 Royalton Rd (44133-4470)
P.O. Box 33547 (44133-0547)
PHONE...................................440 582-4949
Pam Voigt, *Pr*
EMP: 7 **EST:** 1984
SQ FT: 1,400
SALES (est): 622.3K **Privately Held**
Web: www.guestquest.com
SIC: 2711 Newspapers: publishing only, not printed on site

(G-11899)
UNIVERSAL NORTH INC
Also Called: Universal Creative Concepts
10143 Royalton Rd Ste E (44133-4463)
PHONE...................................440 230-1366
John P Yurik, *CEO*
Jeffrey Yurik, *Pr*
Amy Ehrbar, *VP*
EMP: 11 **EST:** 1991
SQ FT: 1,800
SALES (est): 1.2MM **Privately Held**
Web: www.uccpromo.com
SIC: 2759 Commercial printing, nec

(G-11900)
VALLEY TOOL & DIE INC
Also Called: Valco Division
10020 York Theta Dr (44133-3581)
PHONE...................................440 237-0160
Adolf Eisenloeffel, *Pr*
Phillip S Eisenloeffel, *
Ernst Peters, *
Helmut Eisenloeffel, *
EMP: 65 **EST:** 1968
SQ FT: 54,000
SALES (est): 9.35MM **Privately Held**
Web: www.valcocleve.com
SIC: 3465 3451 3452 3542 Automotive stampings; Screw machine products; Bolts, nuts, rivets, and washers; Machine tools, metal forming type

(G-11901)
WHEELSKINS INC ✪
10589 Kings Way (44133-1970)
PHONE...................................800 755-2128
Russell A Karla, *Prin*
EMP: 6 **EST:** 2022
SALES (est): 60.98K **Privately Held**
Web: www.wheelskins.com
SIC: 3714 Motor vehicle parts and accessories

(G-11902)
WHITE MACHINE INC
9621 York Alpha Dr Side (44133-3594)
PHONE...................................440 237-3282
Larry White, *Pr*
Ronald White, *Ex VP*
Ruth White, *VP*
EMP: 8 **EST:** 1971
SQ FT: 7,600
SALES (est): 962.65K **Privately Held**
SIC: 3599 3728 3544 Machine shop, jobbing and repair; Aircraft parts and equipment, nec; Special dies, tools, jigs, and fixtures

(G-11903)
X-TREME FINISHES INC
Also Called: Line-X of Akron/Medina
4821 Brookhaven Dr (44133-6486)
PHONE...................................330 474-0614
Tawny R Zajc, *Prin*
EMP: 10 **EST:** 2013
SALES (est): 751.33K **Privately Held**
Web: www.x-tremefinishes.com
SIC: 3479 2851 1752 7549 Etching and engraving; Epoxy coatings; Access flooring system installation; Undercoating/rustproofing cars

Northfield
Summit County

(G-11904)
BULK HANDLING EQUIPMENT CO
28 W Aurora Rd (44067-2073)
P.O. Box 670855 (44067-0855)
PHONE...................................330 468-5703
Joseph Stakes, *Pr*
Joanne Stakes, *VP*
Mary Anne Stakes, *Sec*
EMP: 7 **EST:** 1985

Northfield - Summit County (G-11905)

SALES (est): 745.65K **Privately Held**
Web: www.bulkhand.com
SIC: 3535 Bulk handling conveyor systems

(G-11905)
CLEVELAND COATINGS INC
51 Meadow Ln (44067-1474)
PHONE..................................330 467-4326
EMP: 6 EST: 2016
SALES (est): 136.25K **Privately Held**
SIC: 3479 Metal coating and allied services

(G-11906)
GENERAL DIE CASTERS INC
6212 Akron Peninsula Rd (44067)
PHONE..................................330 467-6700
Tom Lenin, *Brnch Mgr*
EMP: 55
SQ FT: 45,136
SALES (corp-wide): 26.52MM **Privately Held**
Web: www.generaldie.com
SIC: 3363 3364 Aluminum die-castings; Zinc and zinc-base alloy die-castings
HQ: General Die Casters, Inc.
  2150 Highland Rd
  Twinsburg OH 44087
  330 678-2528

(G-11907)
HY-KO PRODUCTS COMPANY LLC
60 Meadow Ln (44067-1415)
PHONE..................................330 467-7446
Michael Bass, *Pr*
EMP: 36 EST: 2020
SALES (est): 929.74K
SALES (corp-wide): 51.35MM **Privately Held**
Web: www.hy-ko.com
SIC: 3993 Signs and advertising specialties
PA: Midwest Fastener Corp.
  9031 Shaver Rd
  Portage MI 49024
  269 327-6917

(G-11908)
NOR-FAB INC
Also Called: Metalcraft Industries
231 Beechwood Dr (44067-1905)
PHONE..................................330 467-6580
Gerald C Papile, *Pr*
EMP: 7 EST: 1974
SQ FT: 7,500
SALES (est): 225K **Privately Held**
SIC: 2542 Partitions for floor attachment, prefabricated: except wood

(G-11909)
PACIFIC ATLANTIC PROVS INC
8051 Vesta Ave (44067-2080)
PHONE..................................330 467-0150
David D Star, *Pr*
EMP: 7 EST: 1982
SALES (est): 151.53K **Privately Held**
SIC: 2092 Fish, fresh: prepared

(G-11910)
SMARTRONIX INC
416 Apple Hill Dr (44067-1107)
PHONE..................................216 378-3300
EMP: 10 EST: 1994
SQ FT: 4,500
SALES (est): 225.12K **Privately Held**
Web: www.smartronix-inc.com
SIC: 3571 5045 7373 7378 Electronic computers; Computers, peripherals, and software; Systems integration services; Computer peripheral equipment repair and maintenance

(G-11911)
STEVES SPORTS INC
10333 Northfield Rd Unit 136 (44067)
PHONE..................................440 735-0044
Steve Baraona, *Owner*
EMP: 6 EST: 2010
SALES (est): 501.69K **Privately Held**
SIC: 2759 Screen printing

(G-11912)
TERMINAL EQUIPMENT INDS INC
64 Privet Ln (44067-2883)
PHONE..................................330 468-0322
Ernest Pugh, *Pr*
Priscilla Pugh, *Treas*
EMP: 6 EST: 1977
SQ FT: 1,100
SALES (est): 485.1K **Privately Held**
Web: www.accucutinc.com
SIC: 3542 Machine tools, metal forming type

(G-11913)
TERRA COAT LLC
500 W Aurora Rd Ste 140 (44067-2164)
PHONE..................................216 254-8157
Dennis M Trusnik, *Prin*
EMP: 11 EST: 2010
SALES (est): 936.01K **Privately Held**
Web: www.terracoatllc.com
SIC: 3479 Coating of metals and formed products

(G-11914)
WEATHER KING HEATING & AC
51 Meadow Ln Ste E (44067-1475)
PHONE..................................330 908-0281
Raj Rai, *Pr*
EMP: 6 EST: 2000
SALES (est): 957.54K **Privately Held**
Web: www.weatherking1.com
SIC: 1711 3433 5075 3564 Warm air heating and air conditioning contractor; Boilers, low-pressure heating: steam or hot water; Air conditioning and ventilation equipment and supplies; Filters, air: furnaces, air conditioning equipment, etc.

(G-11915)
WEST 6TH PRODUCTS COMPANY (PA)
60 Meadow Ln (44067-1415)
PHONE..................................330 467-7446
▲ EMP: 92 EST: 1949
SALES (est): 22.71MM
SALES (corp-wide): 22.71MM **Privately Held**
Web: www.hy-ko.com
SIC: 3993 3822 Signs and advertising specialties; Hardware for environmental regulators

Northwood
Wood County

(G-11916)
ADIENT US LLC
7560 Arbor Dr (43619-7500)
PHONE..................................419 662-4900
Jeffrey Ryan Arnold, *Brnch Mgr*
EMP: 250
Web: www.adient.com
SIC: 3714 Motor vehicle parts and accessories
HQ: Adient Us Llc
  49200 Halyard Dr
  Plymouth MI 48170
  734 254-5000

(G-11917)
AMERICAN COLD FORGE LLC
5650 Woodville Rd (43619-2322)
PHONE..................................419 836-1062
Dave Huber, *Pr*
Jeffrey Leverenz, *
EMP: 29 EST: 2009
SALES (est): 3.1MM **Privately Held**
Web: www.americancoldforge.com
SIC: 5531 3462 3463 Automotive parts; Automotive and internal combustion engine forgings; Automotive forgings, nonferrous

(G-11918)
FAB-STEEL CO INC
240 W Andrus Rd (43619-1206)
PHONE..................................419 666-5100
Harold M Kowalka, *Pr*
Sharon A Kowalka, *VP*
Thomas Balyat, *Sec*
EMP: 14 EST: 1976
SQ FT: 10,000
SALES (est): 599.27K **Privately Held**
Web: www.fab-steel.com
SIC: 3441 Fabricated structural metal

(G-11919)
HIRZEL CANNING COMPANY (PA)
Also Called: Dei Fratelli
411 Lemoyne Rd (43619-1699)
PHONE..................................419 693-0531
Karl A Hirzel Junior, *Pr*
Joseph R Hirzel, *
William J Hirzel, *
▲ EMP: 25 EST: 1923
SQ FT: 250,000
SALES (est): 60.4MM
SALES (corp-wide): 60.4MM **Privately Held**
Web: www.deifratelli.com
SIC: 2033 8611 2034 Tomato products, packaged in cans, jars, etc.; Business associations; Dried and dehydrated fruits, vegetables and soup mixes

(G-11920)
HOT GRAPHIC SERVICES INC
Also Called: H.O.t
2595 Tracy Rd (43619-1004)
P.O. Box 307 (43697-0307)
PHONE..................................419 242-7000
Gregory D Shapiro, *Pr*
Flora I Shapiro, *
Myron Shapiro, *
Norman Shapiro, *
EMP: 30 EST: 1976
SQ FT: 11,000
SALES (est): 4.51MM **Privately Held**
Web: www.hotgraphics.us
SIC: 2791 2752 Photocomposition, for the printing trade; Offset printing

(G-11921)
JOBSKIN DIV OF TORBOT GROUP
3461 Curtice Rd (43619-1639)
PHONE..................................419 724-1475
Angie Zablocki, *Mgr*
EMP: 10 EST: 2004
SALES (est): 216.39K **Privately Held**
Web: www.bio-con.com
SIC: 3842 Bandages and dressings

(G-11922)
NORPLAS INDUSTRIES INC (DH)
Also Called: Magna
7825 Caple Blvd (43619-1070)
PHONE..................................419 662-3200
Seetarama Kotagiri, *CEO*
Graham Burrow, *
Patrick W D Mccann, *CFO*
Bruce R Cluney, *CLO*▼
◆ EMP: 267 EST: 1997
SQ FT: 450,000
SALES (est): 370.48MM
SALES (corp-wide): 37.84B **Privately Held**
Web: www.norplas.com
SIC: 3714 Motor vehicle parts and accessories
HQ: Magna Exteriors Of America, Inc.
  750 Tower Dr
  Troy MI 48098
  248 631-1100

(G-11923)
OAKLEY INDS SUB ASSMBLY DIV IN
6317 Fairfield Dr (43619-7508)
PHONE..................................419 661-8888
Dick Schmeltz, *Pr*
EMP: 13
SALES (corp-wide): 48.13MM **Privately Held**
Web: www.oakleysubassembly.com
SIC: 3714 Motor vehicle body components and frame
PA: Oakley Industries Sub Assembly Division, Inc.
  4333 Matthew
  Flint MI 48507
  810 720-4444

(G-11924)
OBR COOLING TOWERS INC
2845 Crane Way (43619-1098)
PHONE..................................419 243-3443
Peter Poll, *Pr*
John Hall, *
Philip Poll, *
Debra Haas, *
EMP: 45 EST: 1984
SALES (est): 10.62MM **Privately Held**
Web: www.obrcoolingtowers.com
SIC: 7699 3444 Industrial equipment services; Cooling towers, sheet metal

(G-11925)
PAWS & REMEMBER NW OHIO LLC
2121 Tracy Rd (43619-1324)
PHONE..................................419 662-9000
Kenny Chan, *Admn*
EMP: 8 EST: 2011
SALES (est): 230.12K **Privately Held**
SIC: 3272 Burial vaults, concrete or precast terrazzo

(G-11926)
PCHEM LLC
2533 Tracy Rd (43619-1083)
PHONE..................................419 699-1582
EMP: 7 EST: 2011
SALES (est): 373.75K **Privately Held**
Web: www.pchemllc.com
SIC: 2899 Chemical preparations, nec

(G-11927)
PILKINGTON NORTH AMERICA INC
2401 E Broadway St (43619-1318)
PHONE..................................800 547-9280
Dan Lubelski, *Brnch Mgr*
EMP: 125
Web: www.pilkington.com
SIC: 3211 Flat glass
HQ: Pilkington North America, Inc.
  811 Madison Ave Fl 3
  Toledo OH 43604
  419 247-3731

(G-11928)
QUALITY EXTRACTIONS GROUP LLC
2533 Tracy Rd (43619-1083)
PHONE..................................567 698-9802
James J Avolt, *Owner*

EMP: 7 **EST:** 2018
SALES (est): 1.23MM **Privately Held**
Web: www.qualityextractions.com
SIC: 2869 Fluorinated hydrocarbon gases

(G-11929)
TOLEDO METAL FINISHING INC
Also Called: Toledo Deburring Co
7880 Caple Blvd (43619-1099)
PHONE.................................419 661-1422
Robert E Van Schoick Junior, *Pr*
EMP: 8 **EST:** 1962
SQ FT: 18,000
SALES (est): 686.37K **Privately Held**
Web: www.deburringcompany.com
SIC: 3471 Finishing, metals or formed products

(G-11930)
TORBOT GROUP INC
Also Called: Jobskin Division
3461 Curtice Rd (43619-1639)
PHONE.................................419 724-1475
Greg Johnson, *Brnch Mgr*
EMP: 12
SALES (corp-wide): 6.3MM **Privately Held**
Web: www.torbot.com
SIC: 3841 Surgical and medical instruments
PA: Torbot Group, Inc.
1367 Elmwood Ave
Cranston RI 02910
401 780-8737

(G-11931)
TURNER CONCRETE PRODUCTS
2121 Tracy Rd (43619-1324)
PHONE.................................419 662-9007
Steve Turner, *Pr*
EMP: 10 **EST:** 2005
SALES (est): 243.84K **Privately Held**
Web: www.turnerconcreteproducts.com
SIC: 3273 Ready-mixed concrete

(G-11932)
TURNER VAULT CO
2121 Tracy Rd (43619-1324)
PHONE.................................419 537-1133
Steven Turner, *Pr*
EMP: 23 **EST:** 1958
SALES (est): 6.05MM **Privately Held**
Web: www.turnervault.com
SIC: 3272 Burial vaults, concrete or precast terrazzo

(G-11933)
WESCO DISTRIBUTION INC
Also Called: Wesco Distribution
6519 Fairfield Dr (43619-7507)
PHONE.................................419 666-1670
Chad Marrison, *Brnch Mgr*
EMP: 13
Web: www.wesco.com
SIC: 5085 3699 Industrial supplies; Electrical equipment and supplies, nec
HQ: Wesco Distribution, Inc.
225 W Station Square Dr # 700
Pittsburgh PA 15219

(G-11934)
WHITAKER FINISHING LLC
2707 Tracy Rd (43619-1050)
PHONE.................................419 666-7746
Greg Heminger, *Pr*
▲ **EMP:** 15 **EST:** 2009
SALES (est): 2.13MM **Privately Held**
Web: www.whitakerfinishing.com
SIC: 3471 Electroplating of metals or formed products

(G-11935)
YANFENG US AUTO INTR SYSTEMS I
Also Called: Johnson Contrls Authorized Dlr
7560 Arbor Dr (43619-7500)
PHONE.................................419 662-4905
Keith Wandell, *Pr*
EMP: 46
Web: www.johnsoncontrols.com
SIC: 2531 5075 Public building and related furniture; Warm air heating and air conditioning
HQ: Yanfeng International Automotive Technology Us I Llc
41935 W 12 Mile Rd
Novi MI 48377
248 319-7333

Norton
Summit County

(G-11936)
ACCENT MANUFACTURING INC (PA)
Also Called: Accent Showroom & Design Ctr
1026 Gardner Blvd (44203-6670)
PHONE.................................330 724-7704
Timothy Bush, *CEO*
Tim Bush, *Pr*
Anthony Piatko, *Sls Mgr*
Tom Baum, *Manager*
Betty Bush, *Sec*
EMP: 18 **EST:** 1962
SQ FT: 12,500
SALES (est): 1.38MM
SALES (corp-wide): 1.38MM **Privately Held**
Web: www.accentcustommarble.com
SIC: 1751 3433 3431 3261 Cabinet building and installation; Heating equipment, except electric; Metal sanitary ware; Vitreous plumbing fixtures

(G-11937)
ACE READY MIX CONCRETE CO INC
3826 Summit Rd (44203-5380)
PHONE.................................330 745-8125
EMP: 10 **EST:** 1995
SALES (est): 802.38K **Privately Held**
Web: www.esticocomputerservice.com
SIC: 3273 Ready-mixed concrete

(G-11938)
ALBERTS SCREEN PRINT INC
Also Called: Albert Screenprint
3704 Summit Rd (44203-5378)
P.O. Box 1041 (44203-9441)
PHONE.................................330 753-7559
Albert Falkenstein Senior, *Ch Bd*
Margaret Falkenstein, *
Albert S Falkenstein, *
▲ **EMP:** 115 **EST:** 1962
SQ FT: 103,000
SALES (est): 17.99MM **Privately Held**
Web: www.albertinc.com
SIC: 2759 3993 2752 Screen printing; Signs and advertising specialties; Commercial printing, lithographic

(G-11939)
CJ DANNEMILLER CO
5300 S Hametown Rd (44203-6126)
PHONE.................................330 825-7808
EMP: 21 **EST:** 1935
SALES (est): 10.22MM **Privately Held**
Web: www.cjdannemiller.com
SIC: 5113 5145 2099 2096 Industrial and personal service paper; Nuts, salted or roasted; Food preparations, nec; Potato chips and similar snacks

(G-11940)
COMPASS SYSTEMS & SALES LLC
Also Called: Compass S&S
5185 New Haven Cir (44203-4672)
PHONE.................................330 733-2111
Robert S Sherrod, *Pr*
Mark Rubin, *
Phil Hart, *
Brenda Pavlantos, *
▼ **EMP:** 56 **EST:** 2014
SQ FT: 43,500
SALES (est): 11.48MM **Privately Held**
Web: www.compasssystems.com
SIC: 3542 0724 Mechanical (pneumatic or hydraulic) metal forming machines; Cotton ginning

(G-11941)
E L STONE COMPANY
Also Called: Stonecote
2998 Eastern Rd (44203-3902)
P.O. Box 1012 (44203-9412)
PHONE.................................330 825-4565
Elma Micire, *VP*
Mark Micire, *
EMP: 50 **EST:** 1955
SQ FT: 135,000
SALES (est): 7.54MM **Privately Held**
Web: www.elstone.com
SIC: 3479 3471 Aluminum coating of metal products; Plating and polishing

(G-11942)
ETKO MACHINE INC
2796 Barber Rd (44203-1002)
P.O. Box 710 (44203-0710)
PHONE.................................330 745-4033
Julius J Koroshazi, *Pr*
George J Koroshazi, *VP*
Etelka Koroshazi, *Sec*
EMP: 9 **EST:** 1969
SQ FT: 4,000
SALES (est): 680.16K **Privately Held**
Web: www.etko.com
SIC: 3599 Machine shop, jobbing and repair

(G-11943)
FISHER SAND & GRAVEL INC
Also Called: Flesher Sand & Gravel
3322 Clark Mill Rd (44203-1028)
PHONE.................................330 745-9239
James Fisher, *Pr*
EMP: 7 **EST:** 1968
SQ FT: 3,888
SALES (est): 763.83K **Privately Held**
SIC: 1442 Construction sand and gravel

(G-11944)
ICP ADHESIVES AND SEALANTS INC (HQ)
2775 Barber Rd (44203-1001)
P.O. Box 1078 (44203-9478)
PHONE.................................330 753-4585
Stefan Miczka, *Ch*
Stefan Gantenbein, *Pr*
Ron Kozak, *Treas*
▲ **EMP:** 50 **EST:** 1985
SQ FT: 45,000
SALES (est): 47.08MM
SALES (corp-wide): 923.49MM **Privately Held**
Web: www.icpadhesives.com
SIC: 3086 2891 3296 2821 Plastics foam products; Sealants; Mineral wool; Plastics materials and resins
PA: Innovative Chemical Products Group, Llc
150 Dascomb Rd
Andover MA 01810
978 623-9980

(G-11945)
J E DOYLE COMPANY
Also Called: Doyle Systems
5186 New Haven Cir (44203-4671)
PHONE.................................330 564-0743
Joseph M Lynch, *Pr*
▲ **EMP:** 17 **EST:** 1922
SQ FT: 10,000
SALES (est): 1.14MM **Privately Held**
Web: www.doylesystems.com
SIC: 3554 Paper industries machinery

(G-11946)
JRP SOLUTIONS LLC
3764 Golf Course Dr (44203-5402)
PHONE.................................330 825-5989
John Pfeiffer, *Prin*
EMP: 6 **EST:** 2010
SALES (est): 93.4K **Privately Held**
SIC: 3541 Machine tool replacement & repair parts, metal cutting types

(G-11947)
KDA MANUFACTURING LLC
5221 S Cleveland Massillon Rd (44203-7819)
PHONE.................................330 590-7431
EMP: 15 **EST:** 2011
SALES (est): 1.73MM **Privately Held**
Web: www.kdamanufacturing.com
SIC: 3312 7692 3599 Stainless steel; Welding repair; Machine and other job shop work

(G-11948)
SDK ASSOCIATES INC
Also Called: Custom Control Specialists
2044 Wadsworth Rd Unit B (44203-5306)
P.O. Box 4054 (44321-0054)
PHONE.................................330 745-3648
Scott Fausneaucht, *Pr*
Deborah Fausneaucht, *VP*
EMP: 7 **EST:** 1996
SQ FT: 2,700
SALES (est): 554.64K **Privately Held**
SIC: 3625 Motor control centers

(G-11949)
SPZ MACHINE COMPANY INC
2871 Newpark Dr (44203-1047)
PHONE.................................330 848-3286
Peter Zarkovacki, *Owner*
David Scott Zarkovacki, *VP*
EMP: 8 **EST:** 1978
SQ FT: 50,000
SALES (est): 921.69K **Privately Held**
Web: www.spzmachine.net
SIC: 3599 Machine shop, jobbing and repair

(G-11950)
STARPOINT 20 LLC
3985 Eastern Rd Ste C (44203-6212)
PHONE.................................330 825-2373
▲ **EMP:** 6 **EST:** 2012
SALES (est): 227.19K **Privately Held**
SIC: 3069 Hard rubber and molded rubber products

(G-11951)
WAGNER MACHINE INC
5151 Wooster Rd W (44203-6261)
PHONE.................................330 706-0700
Michael Wagner, *CEO*
Michael Wagner, *Pr*
Courtney Wagner, *
▲ **EMP:** 35 **EST:** 1957
SQ FT: 20,000
SALES (est): 5.01MM **Privately Held**
Web: www.wagnermachine.com

Norwalk - Huron County (G-11952)   GEOGRAPHIC SECTION

SIC: 3599 Machine shop, jobbing and repair

Norwalk
Huron County

(G-11952)
ALLIED PDSTAL BOOM SYSTEMS LLC
405 Industrial Pkwy (44857-3101)
PHONE.................................419 663-0279
EMP: 6 **EST:** 2019
SALES (est): 465.52K **Privately Held**
Web: www.allied-pbs.com
SIC: 3599 Machine shop, jobbing and repair

(G-11953)
ALLIED PEDESTAL BOOM SYS LLC
75 Norwalk Commons Dr (44857-2637)
PHONE.................................419 663-0279
EMP: 8 **EST:** 2016
SALES (est): 445.61K **Privately Held**
Web: www.fabriweldcorporation.com
SIC: 3599 Machine shop, jobbing and repair

(G-11954)
AMERICRAFT CARTON INC
201 Republic St (44857-1157)
PHONE.................................419 668-1006
EMP: 8 **EST:** 2020
SALES (est): 212.12K **Privately Held**
Web: www.americraft.com
SIC: 2657 Folding paperboard boxes

(G-11955)
AVIENT CORPORATION
80 N West St (44857-1239)
PHONE.................................419 668-4844
Gary Weaver, *Brnch Mgr*
EMP: 50
Web: www.avient.com
SIC: 2865 3087 2851 2816 Dyes and pigments; Custom compound purchased resins; Paints and allied products; Inorganic pigments
PA: Avient Corporation
    33587 Walker Rd
    Avon Lake OH 44012

(G-11956)
BENNETT ELECTRIC INC
211 Republic St (44857-1157)
PHONE.................................800 874-5405
Daniel L Stewart, *Pr*
Charles Avarello, *VP*
Jean Stewart, *Sec*
EMP: 14 **EST:** 1925
SQ FT: 15,000
SALES (est): 4.57MM **Privately Held**
Web: www.bennett-electric.com
SIC: 5063 7694 Motors, electric; Electric motor repair

(G-11957)
BROOKER BROS FORGING CO INC
102 Jefferson St (44857-1969)
P.O. Box 498 (44857-0498)
PHONE.................................419 668-2535
Rickard E Brooker, *Pr*
EMP: 20 **EST:** 1946
SQ FT: 16,000
SALES (est): 1.96MM **Privately Held**
Web: www.brookerbrosforgings.com
SIC: 3462 Iron and steel forgings

(G-11958)
CASE MAUL CLAMPS INC
69 N West St (44857-1213)
P.O. Box 605 (44857-0605)
PHONE.................................419 668-6563
▲ **EMP:** 12 **EST:** 1994
SALES (est): 477.19K **Privately Held**
Web: www.case-maul.com
SIC: 3429 Clamps, metal

(G-11959)
CUSTOM METAL WORKS INC (PA)
193 Akron Rd (44857-1665)
PHONE.................................419 668-7831
Lawrence A Skinn, *Pr*
Cynthia Skinn, *Sec*
L Andrew Skinn, *VP*
Bradley Skinn, *VP*
EMP: 14 **EST:** 1981
SQ FT: 19,400
SALES (est): 1.12MM
SALES (corp-wide): 1.12MM **Privately Held**
Web: www.custommetal-inc.com
SIC: 7699 3599 3429 Industrial machinery and equipment repair; Machine shop, jobbing and repair; Hardware, nec

(G-11960)
CUSTOM SIGN & DESIGN LLC
911 Meadow Ln N (44857-9391)
PHONE.................................419 202-3633
EMP: 6 **EST:** 2019
SALES (est): 248.47K **Privately Held**
Web: www.customsignanddesign.com
SIC: 3993 Signs and advertising specialties

(G-11961)
DAN-MAR COMPANY INC
Also Called: Danmarco
200 Bluegrass Dr E (44857-1169)
PHONE.................................419 660-8830
James D Heckelman, *Pr*
Margaret Heckelman, *
Nancy Heckelman, *
EMP: 26 **EST:** 1972
SQ FT: 50,000
SALES (est): 9.58MM **Privately Held**
Web: www.danmarco.com
SIC: 3674 3629 Solid state electronic devices, nec; Blasting machines, electrical

(G-11962)
DURABLE CORPORATION
75 N Pleasant St (44857-1218)
P.O. Box 290 (44857-0290)
PHONE.................................800 537-1603
Jon M Anderson, *CEO*
Tom Secor, *
Marcia Norris, *
▲ **EMP:** 60 **EST:** 1923
SQ FT: 3,000
SALES (est): 9.9MM **Privately Held**
Web: www.durablecorp.com
SIC: 3069 2273 5013 Mats or matting, rubber, nec; Mats and matting; Bumpers

(G-11963)
EXTOL OF OHIO INC (PA)
208 Republic St (44857-1185)
PHONE.................................419 668-2072
Robin L Degraff, *Pr*
Mergie Simon, *
◆ **EMP:** 17 **EST:** 1990
SQ FT: 45,000
SALES (est): 7.4MM **Privately Held**
Web: www.extolohio.com
SIC: 3296 Insulation: rock wool, slag, and silica minerals

(G-11964)
EXTOL OF OHIO INC
208 Republic St (44857-1185)
PHONE.................................419 668-2072
Robin L Degraff, *Pr*
Brian Eisenhower, *
Robert Baldwin, *
Margie Simon, *
EMP: 18 **EST:** 1985
SQ FT: 45,000
SALES (est): 1.13MM **Privately Held**
Web: www.extolohio.com
SIC: 3086 Plastics foam products
PA: Extol Of Ohio, Inc.
    208 Republic St
    Norwalk OH 44857

(G-11965)
FABRIWELD CORPORATION
360 Eastpark Dr (44857-9500)
PHONE.................................419 663-0279
EMP: 203
Web: www.fabriweldcorporation.com
SIC: 3599 Machine shop, jobbing and repair
PA: Fabriweld Corporation
    405 Industrial Pkwy
    Norwalk OH 44857

(G-11966)
FABRIWELD CORPORATION (PA)
405 Industrial Pkwy (44857-3101)
PHONE.................................419 668-3358
Christopher C Price, *Pr*
Faith A Price, *
R David Smith, *
▲ **EMP:** 21 **EST:** 1989
SQ FT: 100,000
SALES (est): 23.02MM **Privately Held**
Web: www.fabriweldcorporation.com
SIC: 3599 Machine shop, jobbing and repair

(G-11967)
FAIR PUBLISHING HOUSE INC
15 Schauss Ave (44857-1851)
P.O. Box 350 (44857-0350)
PHONE.................................419 668-3746
Charles Doyle, *Pr*
Kevin F Doyle, *
EMP: 27 **EST:** 1880
SQ FT: 25,000
SALES (est): 873.8K
SALES (corp-wide): 4.84MM **Privately Held**
Web: www.fairpublishing.com
SIC: 2759 3993 2752 Imprinting; Signs and advertising specialties; Commercial printing, lithographic
PA: Rotary Printing Company
    15 Schauss Ave
    Norwalk OH 44857
    419 668-4821

(G-11968)
FOGHORN DESIGNS
98 E Main St (44857-1714)
PHONE.................................419 706-3861
Trevor Rood, *Owner*
EMP: 8 **EST:** 2010
SALES (est): 424.7K **Privately Held**
Web: www.foghorndesigns.com
SIC: 2759 Screen printing

(G-11969)
GFL ENVIRONMENTAL SVCS USA INC
4376 State Route 601 (44857-9128)
PHONE.................................281 486-4182
Patrick Dovigi, *Brnch Mgr*
EMP: 46
SALES (corp-wide): 5.03B **Privately Held**
SIC: 2911 Petroleum refining
HQ: Gfl Environmental Services Usa, Inc.
    18927 Hickory Creek Dr
    Mokena IL 60448
    866 579-6900

(G-11970)
GRAPHIC PACKAGING INTL LLC
209 Republic St (44857-1157)
PHONE.................................419 668-1006
Darrin Carlson, *Mgr*
EMP: 40
Web: www.americraft.com
SIC: 2657 Food containers, folding: made from purchased material
HQ: Graphic Packaging International, Llc
    1500 Riveredge Pkwy # 100
    Atlanta GA 30328

(G-11971)
GYRUS ACMI LP
Also Called: Olympus Surgical Technologies
93 N Pleasant St (44857-1218)
PHONE.................................419 668-8201
Tom Motta, *Brnch Mgr*
EMP: 153
SQ FT: 55,000
Web: medical.olympusamerica.com
SIC: 3841 3845 Surgical and medical instruments; Electromedical equipment
HQ: Gyrus Acmi, L.P.
    9600 Louisiana Ave N
    Minneapolis MN 55445
    763 416-3000

(G-11972)
HART ADVERTISING INC
69 E Seminary St 75 (44857)
P.O. Box 499 (44857-0499)
PHONE.................................419 668-1194
W Taylor Hart, *Pr*
Gay Hart-sanders, *Sec*
EMP: 10 **EST:** 1951
SALES (est): 482.66K **Privately Held**
Web: www.hartbillboards.com
SIC: 7312 3993 Billboard advertising; Signs and advertising specialties

(G-11973)
HEN HOUSE INC
Also Called: Ditz Designs
100 N West St (44857)
P.O. Box 586 (44857)
PHONE.................................419 663-3377
Robert Ludwig, *Pr*
Joyce Ditz, *
Jon Ditz, *
Deborah Ludwig, *
◆ **EMP:** 16 **EST:** 1980
SQ FT: 37,000
SALES (est): 947.36K **Privately Held**
Web: www.ditzdesigns.com
SIC: 2511 Stools, household: wood

(G-11974)
HERALD REFLECTOR INC (PA)
Also Called: Norwalk Reflector
61 E Monroe St (44857-1532)
P.O. Box 71 (44857-0071)
PHONE.................................419 668-3771
David Rau, *Pr*
Alice Rau, *
EMP: 50 **EST:** 1829
SQ FT: 10,000
SALES (est): 4.7MM
SALES (corp-wide): 4.7MM **Privately Held**
Web: www.norwalkreflector.com
SIC: 2711 Commercial printing and newspaper publishing combined

(G-11975)
INTELLIWORKS HT LLC
61 Saint Marys St (44857-1841)
P.O. Box 899 (44857-0899)
PHONE.................................419 660-9050
Dave Nunez, *Prin*
▲ **EMP:** 6 **EST:** 2007

GEOGRAPHIC SECTION

SALES (est): 984.84K **Privately Held**
Web: www.intelliworksht.com
SIC: **3559** Sewing machines and attachments, industrial, nec

(G-11976)
KUHLMAN INSTRUMENT COMPANY
54 Summit St (44857-2134)
P.O. Box 468 (44857-0468)
PHONE..................................419 668-9533
Mark Lacy, *CEO*
EMP: **6 EST:** 1959
SQ FT: 5,000
SALES (est): 940.85K **Privately Held**
Web: www.kuhlmaninstrument.com
SIC: **3823** Process control instruments

(G-11977)
LESCH BOAT COVER CANVAS CO LLC
43 1/2 Saint Marys St (44857-1809)
PHONE..................................419 668-6374
Daniel Lesch, *Prin*
EMP: **6 EST:** 1968
SQ FT: 3,000
SALES (est): 501.63K **Privately Held**
Web: www.leschcanvas.com
SIC: **2394** 2396 Tarpaulins, fabric: made from purchased materials; Automotive trimmings, fabric

(G-11978)
LINK TO SUCCESS INC
Also Called: Harknesservices
52 Summit St Ste 3 (44857-2171)
PHONE..................................888 959-4203
EMP: **6 EST:** 2010
SALES (est): 409.41K **Privately Held**
Web: www.harknesservices.com
SIC: **7349** 8742 2899 7389 Exhaust hood or fan cleaning; Management consulting services; Fire extinguisher charges; Business Activities at Non-Commercial Site

(G-11979)
MCR OF NORWALK INC
Also Called: Maple City Rubber Co
55 Newton St (44857-1200)
PHONE..................................419 668-8261
Michael Kilbane, *Pr*
Paul Bennett, *
Willam Chandler, *
▲ EMP: **44 EST:** 1915
SQ FT: 104,000
SALES (est): 5.27MM **Privately Held**
Web: www.tuftexballoons.com
SIC: **3069** Balloons, advertising and toy: rubber

(G-11980)
NEW HORIZONS BAKING CO LLC (PA)
211 Woodlawn Ave (44857-2276)
PHONE..................................419 668-8226
Ronald Jones, *Pr*
Tilmon F Brown, *
Trina Bediako, *
Robert Creighton, *
John Widman, *
EMP: **220 EST:** 1965
SQ FT: 4,526
SALES (est): 57.51MM
SALES (corp-wide): 57.51MM **Privately Held**
Web: www.newhorizonsbaking.com
SIC: **2051** Buns, bread type: fresh or frozen

(G-11981)
NORTH RIDGE ENTERPRISES INC
62 Firelands Blvd (44857-2423)
PHONE..................................440 965-5300
William Bodde, *CEO*
David Bodde, *
Robert Bodde, *VP*
EMP: **17 EST:** 1983
SALES (est): 1.93MM **Privately Held**
SIC: **3599** Machine shop, jobbing and repair

(G-11982)
NORWALK CONCRETE INDS INC (PA)
80 Commerce Dr (44857-9003)
P.O. Box 563 (44857-0563)
PHONE..................................419 668-8167
TOLL FREE: 800
John A Lendrum, *Pr*
Jeffrey S Malcolm, *
Edward Cierszewski, *
Kathleen Leak, *
▲ EMP: **40 EST:** 1906
SALES (est): 12.18MM
SALES (corp-wide): 12.18MM **Privately Held**
Web: www.nciprecast.com
SIC: **3272** Concrete products, precast, nec

(G-11983)
NORWALK WASTEWATER EQP CO
Also Called: Norweco
220 Republic St (44857-1156)
P.O. Box 410 (44857-0410)
PHONE..................................419 668-4471
Gregory Graves, *Pr*
Jan Graves, *
Michele Graves, *
◆ EMP: **71 EST:** 1906
SQ FT: 70,000
SALES (est): 24.79MM **Privately Held**
Web: www.norweco.com
SIC: **3589** Water treatment equipment, industrial

(G-11984)
OGDEN NEWS PUBLISHING OHIO INC
Also Called: Norwalk Reflector
34 E Main St (44857-1515)
PHONE..................................567 743-9843
Joe Centers, *Brnch Mgr*
EMP: **45**
Web: www.ogdennews.com
SIC: **2711** Newspapers: publishing only, not printed on site
HQ: Ogden News Publishing Of Ohio, Inc.
314 W Market St
Sandusky OH 44870
419 625-5500

(G-11985)
PALLET SOURCE INC
55 N Garfield St (44857-2008)
PHONE..................................419 660-8882
EMP: **14 EST:** 2004
SALES (est): 619.45K **Privately Held**
Web: www.palletsource.com
SIC: **2448** Pallets, wood

(G-11986)
PRECAST PRODUCTS LLC
Also Called: Norwalk Precast Molds, Inc.
205 Industrial Pkwy (44857-3105)
P.O. Box 293 (44857-0293)
PHONE..................................419 668-1639
Jan Graves, *Pr*
Gregory D Graves, *Pr*
EMP: **20 EST:** 1984
SQ FT: 75,000
SALES (est): 1.7MM **Privately Held**
Web: www.norwalkprecastmolds.com
SIC: **3544** Industrial molds

(G-11987)
R & D EQUIPMENT INC
206 Republic St (44857-1185)
PHONE..................................419 668-8439
George Gilbert, *Pr*
Chuck Plumb, *VP*
▲ EMP: **43 EST:** 1977
SQ FT: 18,000
SALES (est): 2.57MM **Privately Held**
SIC: **3555** Printing trades machinery

(G-11988)
SC STRATEGIC SOLUTIONS LLC
600 Industrial Pkwy (44857-3103)
PHONE..................................567 424-6054
Chad Stein, *Managing Member*
EMP: **151 EST:** 2007
SALES (est): 12.5MM **Privately Held**
Web: www.scstrategicsolutions.com
SIC: **7372** 7374 Application computer software; Data processing and preparation

(G-11989)
SOLID DIMENSIONS INC
Also Called: Solid Dimensions Line
720 Townline Road 151 (44857-9535)
PHONE..................................419 663-1134
Tim Parcher, *Pr*
Darla Parcher, *VP*
▲ EMP: **9 EST:** 1994
SALES (est): 935.68K **Privately Held**
Web: www.soliddimensions.com
SIC: **2499** Engraved wood products

(G-11990)
WESTCOTT WOODWORKS HM SVCS LLC
21 N Hester St (44857-1416)
PHONE..................................419 706-2250
Bryan Westcott, *Prin*
EMP: **6 EST:** 2016
SALES (est): 229.11K **Privately Held**
Web: www.westcottwoodworks.com
SIC: **2499** Wood products, nec

(G-11991)
WILLIAM DAUCH CONCRETE COMPANY (PA)
84 Cleveland Rd (44857-9020)
P.O. Box 204 (44857-0204)
PHONE..................................419 668-4458
William Dauch, *Pr*
Mona E Dauch, *Sec*
EMP: **15 EST:** 1966
SQ FT: 2,000
SALES (est): 9.78MM
SALES (corp-wide): 9.78MM **Privately Held**
Web: www.dauchconcrete.com
SIC: **5032** 3273 3272 3271 Brick, stone, and related material; Ready-mixed concrete; Concrete products, nec; Concrete block and brick

Norwich
Muskingum County

(G-11992)
LUMI-LITE CANDLE COMPANY
Also Called: Lumi Craft
102 Sundale Rd (43767-9717)
P.O. Box 97 (43767-0097)
PHONE..................................740 872-3248
William W Wilson, *Ch*
George Pappas, *
Tina Bales, *
Pete Pappas, *
▲ EMP: **100 EST:** 1957
SQ FT: 50,000
SALES (est): 8.51MM **Privately Held**
Web: www.cakecandle.com
SIC: **3999** Candles

(G-11993)
UNITED CANDLE COMPANY LLC
102 N Sundale Rd (43767-9766)
PHONE..................................740 872-3248
EMP: **8 EST:** 2019
SALES (est): 657.03K **Privately Held**
SIC: **3999** Candles

Norwood
Hamilton County

(G-11994)
COX INTERIOR INC
4080 Webster Ave (45212-2706)
PHONE..................................270 789-3129
Robert Mears, *Brnch Mgr*
EMP: **10**
SALES (corp-wide): 119.76MM **Privately Held**
Web: www.coxinterior.com
SIC: **2431** Moldings, wood: unfinished and prefinished
HQ: Cox Interior, Inc.
1751 Old Columbia Rd
Campbellsville KY 42718
270 789-3129

(G-11995)
EMD MILLIPORE CORPORATION
2909 Highland Ave (45212-2411)
PHONE..................................513 631-0445
Michael Mulligan, *VP*
EMP: **150**
SQ FT: 100,000
SALES (corp-wide): 22.82B **Privately Held**
Web: www.emdmillipore.com
SIC: **8731** 3295 2899 2842 Biotechnical research, commercial; Minerals, ground or treated; Chemical preparations, nec; Polishes and sanitation goods
HQ: Emd Millipore Corporation
400 Summit Dr
Burlington MA 01803
800 645-5476

(G-11996)
NAMOH OHIO HOLDINGS INC (PA)
Also Called: Neider, F A Co
5612 Carthage Ave (45212-1028)
P.O. Box 76548 (41076-0548)
◆ EMP: **22 EST:** 1916
SQ FT: 170,000
SALES (est): 5.13MM
SALES (corp-wide): 5.13MM **Privately Held**
Web: www.auveco.com
SIC: **3465** 5013 3714 3452 Automotive stampings; Automotive stampings; Motor vehicle parts and accessories; Bolts, nuts, rivets, and washers

(G-11997)
PALLET SPECS PLUS LLC
1701 Mills Ave (45212-2825)
P.O. Box 15236 (45215-0236)
PHONE..................................513 351-3200
EMP: **10 EST:** 2015
SQ FT: 20,000
SALES (est): 956.64K **Privately Held**
Web: www.palletspecsplus.com
SIC: **2448** Pallets, wood

(G-11998)
SHEPHERD MATERIAL SCIENCE CO (PA)

Norwood - Hamilton County (G-11999)

4900 Beech St (45212-2316)
PHONE...................513 731-1110
Thomas L Shepherd, Pr
EMP: 19 EST: 2010
SALES (est): 90MM
SALES (corp-wide): 90MM Privately Held
Web: www.shepchem.com
SIC: 2819 2869 Metal salts and compounds except sodium, potassium, aluminum; Industrial organic chemicals, nec

(G-11999)
SHEPHERD WIDNES LTD
4900 Beech St (45212-2316)
PHONE...................513 731-1110
▲ EMP: 55
SIC: 2819 Industrial inorganic chemicals, nec

(G-12000)
SIEMENS INDUSTRY INC
Also Called: Motors & Drives Division
4620 Forest Ave (45212-3306)
PHONE...................513 841-3100
Joerg Ernst, Mgr
EMP: 200
SQ FT: 550,000
SALES (corp-wide): 84.48B Privately Held
Web: new.siemens.com
SIC: 3621 Motors, electric
HQ: Siemens Industry, Inc.
    100 Technology Dr
    Alpharetta GA 30005
    847 215-1000

(G-12001)
THE SHEPHERD CHEMICAL COMPANY (HQ)
4900 Beech St (45212-2398)
PHONE...................513 731-1110
◆ EMP: 175 EST: 1916
SALES (est): 90MM
SALES (corp-wide): 90MM Privately Held
Web: www.shepchem.com
SIC: 2819 2869 Metal salts and compounds except sodium, potassium, aluminum; Industrial organic chemicals, nec
PA: The Shepherd Material Science Company
    4900 Beech St
    Norwood OH 45212
    513 731-1110

Nova
Ashland County

(G-12002)
AMPTECH MACHINING & WELDING
910 County Road 40 (44859-9723)
PHONE...................419 652-3444
Dana White, Owner
EMP: 9 EST: 2005
SALES (est): 190.07K Privately Held
Web: www.amptechwelding.com
SIC: 7692 Welding repair

(G-12003)
GRAPHITE SALES INC (PA)
220 Township Road 791 (44859-9703)
P.O. Box 23009 (44023-0009)
PHONE...................419 652-3388
Kevin Burmeister, CEO
Michael Slabe, CFO
◆ EMP: 15 EST: 1979
SQ FT: 16,000
SALES (est): 20.56MM
SALES (corp-wide): 20.56MM Privately Held
Web: www.graphitesales.com

SIC: 3624 Electrodes, thermal and electrolytic uses: carbon, graphite

(G-12004)
NOVA GOLF CORP
63 State Route 511 (44859-9728)
P.O. Box 150 (44233-0150)
PHONE...................419 652-3160
Brad T Ruminski, Prin
EMP: 6 EST: 2005
SALES (est): 228.42K Privately Held
SIC: 3949 Shafts, golf club

(G-12005)
ULTRABUILT PLAY SYSTEMS INC
1114 Us Highway 224 (44859-9773)
PHONE...................419 652-2294
Stephen Bennet, Pr
EMP: 10 EST: 1995
SQ FT: 6,200
SALES (est): 599.88K Privately Held
Web: www.ultrabuilt.com
SIC: 3949 2541 Playground equipment; Display fixtures, wood

Novelty
Geauga County

(G-12006)
ARROW FABRICATING CO
7355 Calley Ln (44072-9585)
PHONE...................216 641-0490
Ramesh Gavhane, Pr
Gaye Gavhane, *
EMP: 10 EST: 1974
SQ FT: 40,000
SALES (est): 372.08K Privately Held
SIC: 3441 Fabricated structural metal

(G-12007)
ASM INTERNATIONAL
9639 Kinsman Rd (44073-0002)
PHONE...................440 338-5151
Thomas Dudley, CEO
▲ EMP: 80 EST: 1913
SQ FT: 55,000
SALES (est): 7.42MM Privately Held
Web: www.asminternational.org
SIC: 2731 2721 7389 7999 Books, publishing only; Periodicals, publishing only; Advertising, promotional, and trade show services; Exhibition operation

(G-12008)
BAMF WELDING & FABRICATION LLC
9988 Kinsman Rd (44072-9316)
P.O. Box 335 (44065-0335)
PHONE...................440 862-8286
Connor Roberts, Managing Member
EMP: 7 EST: 2020
SALES (est): 82.17K Privately Held
Web: www.arc-houndwelding.com
SIC: 7692 Welding repair

Oak Harbor
Ottawa County

(G-12009)
ACPO LTD
Also Called: Acpo
8035 W Lake Winds Dr (43449)
P.O. Box 418 (43449)
PHONE...................419 898-8273
▲ EMP: 85 EST: 1988
SALES (est): 16.6MM
SALES (corp-wide): 8.36B Publicly Held

Web: label.averydennison.com
SIC: 2672 Adhesive papers, labels, or tapes: from purchased material
PA: Avery Dennison Corporation
    8080 Norton Pkwy
    Mentor OH 44060
    440 534-6000

(G-12010)
AVERY DENNISON CORPORATION
8035 W Lake Winds Dr (43449-8903)
PHONE...................419 898-8273
EMP: 10
SALES (est): 2.44MM Privately Held
Web: www.averydennison.jobs
SIC: 2672 Paper; coated and laminated, nec

(G-12011)
AYLING AND REICHERT CO CONSENT
411 S Railroad St (43449-1053)
P.O. Box 389 (43449-0389)
PHONE...................419 898-2471
Robert G Wilson, Pr
Robert G Wilson, Pr
Evelyn Wilson, *
EMP: 20 EST: 1926
SQ FT: 23,000
SALES (est): 875.34K Privately Held
Web: www.aylingreichert.com
SIC: 3469 3561 3443 Metal stampings, nec; Industrial pumps and parts; Floating covers, metal plate

(G-12012)
C NELSON MFG CO
Also Called: Nelson
265 N Lake Winds Pkwy (43449-9012)
PHONE...................419 898-3305
Kelley Smith, Pr
◆ EMP: 36 EST: 1898
SQ FT: 1,200
SALES (est): 6.3MM Privately Held
Web: www.cnelson.com
SIC: 3585 Refrigeration and heating equipment

(G-12013)
DAVIS FABRICATORS INC
15765 W State Route 2 (43449-9488)
PHONE...................419 898-5297
Todd Davis, CEO
Walter Davis, Pr
Sandra Davis, VP
EMP: 20 EST: 1983
SQ FT: 25,000
SALES (est): 2.3MM Privately Held
Web: www.davisfabricators.com
SIC: 3441 Fabricated structural metal

(G-12014)
NORTHERN MANUFACTURING CO INC
150 N Lake Winds Pkwy (43449-8921)
PHONE...................419 898-2821
Quintin Smith, Pr
Harry Bethel, *
Joe Bodner, *
Paul Schmitt, *
▲ EMP: 145 EST: 1951
SQ FT: 120,000
SALES (est): 37.7MM Privately Held
Web: www.northernmfg.com
SIC: 3441 Fabricated structural metal

(G-12015)
SURENERGY LLC
9500 W Moonlight Bay Ln (43449-9217)
PHONE...................419 626-8000
▲ EMP: 9 EST: 2009

SALES (est): 676.81K Privately Held
Web: www.surenergy.us
SIC: 3621 Windmills, electric generating

Oak Hill
Jackson County

(G-12016)
ANTHONY W HILDERBRANT
1701 Monroe Hollow Rd (45656-8931)
PHONE...................740 682-1035
Anthony W Hilderbrant, Prin
EMP: 8 EST: 2005
SALES (est): 147.24K Privately Held
SIC: 2411 Logging

(G-12017)
DALE R ADKINS
Also Called: Adkins, Dale Logging
106 Smith St (45656-0706)
P.O. Box 151 (45656-0151)
PHONE...................740 682-7312
Dale R Adkins, Owner
Dale Adkins, Owner
EMP: 6 EST: 1973
SALES (est): 340.77K Privately Held
SIC: 2411 4212 7389 Logging; Lumber (log) trucking, local; Log and lumber broker

(G-12018)
DENVER ADKINS
Also Called: Adkins & Sons
642 Phillip Kuhn Rd (45656-9645)
PHONE...................740 682-3123
Denver Adkins, Pt
EMP: 9 EST: 1972
SALES (est): 238.56K Privately Held
SIC: 2411 Logging camps and contractors

(G-12019)
H & H INDUSTRIES INC
5400 State Route 93 (45656-8552)
PHONE...................740 682-7721
Noah Hickman, Pr
Lisa Hickman, *
EMP: 70 EST: 2000
SALES (est): 9.57MM Privately Held
Web: www.hhindustriesinc.com
SIC: 3011 Retreading materials, tire

(G-12020)
KCS CLEANING SERVICE
7550 State Route 93 (45656-9359)
PHONE...................740 418-5479
Kathleen Strickland, Prin
EMP: 10 EST: 2009
SALES (est): 271.94K Privately Held
SIC: 2842 Polishes and sanitation goods

(G-12021)
LEE SAYLOR LOGGING LLC
565 Cress Rd (45656-9423)
PHONE...................740 682-0479
Garrett Saylor, Prin
EMP: 8 EST: 2016
SALES (est): 402.16K Privately Held
Web: www.saylorlogging.com
SIC: 2411 Wooden logs

(G-12022)
NOCK AND SON COMPANY
4138 Monroe Hollow Rd (45656-8995)
P.O. Box 196 (45656-0196)
PHONE...................740 682-7741
Hayden Hammond, Mgr
EMP: 15
SALES (corp-wide): 2.66MM Privately Held
Web: www.nockandson.com

SIC: 3255 Clay refractories
PA: The Nock And Son Company
    27320 W Oviatt Rd
    Cleveland OH 44140
    440 871-5525

(G-12023)
PLIBRICO COMPANY LLC
1627 Pyro Rd (45656-9311)
PHONE................................740 682-7755
Patrick Barry, *CEO*
EMP: 11
Web: www.plibrico.com
SIC: 3297 Brick refractories
PA: Plibrico Company, Llc
    1935 Techny Rd Ste 16
    Northbrook IL 60062

(G-12024)
RESCO PRODUCTS INC
Cedar Heights Clay Division
3542 State Route 93 (45656-8548)
P.O. Box 295 (45656-0295)
PHONE................................740 682-7794
Linda Simpson, *Mgr*
EMP: 6
SALES (corp-wide): 111.18MM **Privately Held**
Web: www.rescoproducts.com
SIC: 3255 3297 3251 Ladle brick, clay; Nonclay refractories; Brick and structural clay tile
PA: Resco Products, Inc.
    1 Robinson Plz Ste 300
    Pittsburgh PA 15205
    412 494-4491

(G-12025)
ROMAR METAL FABRICATING INC
201 Zane Oak Rd (45656-9742)
PHONE................................740 682-7331
Wayne R Newsom, *Pr*
EMP: 6 **EST:** 1983
SQ FT: 3,700
SALES (est): 557.54K **Privately Held**
SIC: 3441 7692 3444 Fabricated structural metal; Welding repair; Sheet metalwork

Oakwood
Montgomery County

(G-12026)
AQUAPRO SYSTEMS LLC
223 Telford Ave (45419-3222)
PHONE................................877 278-2797
Charles Murphy, *Pr*
EMP: 15 **EST:** 2004
SALES (est): 2.53MM **Privately Held**
Web: www.intermatic.com
SIC: 3589 3569 Swimming pool filter and water conditioning systems; Heaters, swimming pool: electric

(G-12027)
EAGLE SOFTWARE CORP
1201 Hathaway Rd (45419-3538)
PHONE................................937 630-4548
Kathy Huizenga, *COO*
EMP: 7 **EST:** 1997
SALES (est): 63.88K **Privately Held**
Web: www.emscheduler.com
SIC: 7372 Prepackaged software

(G-12028)
JONES OLD RUSTIC SIGN COMPANY
Also Called: Jones Signs
343 Beverly Pl (45419-3515)
PHONE................................937 643-1695
EMP: 8 **EST:** 1996

SALES (est): 234.2K **Privately Held**
Web: www.jonesrusticsigns.com
SIC: 3993 Signs, not made in custom sign painting shops

(G-12029)
PRODUCTION TUBE CUTTING
43 Briar Hill Rd (45419-3429)
PHONE................................937 299-7144
EMP: 8 **EST:** 2018
SALES (est): 70.15K **Privately Held**
Web: www.productiontubecutting.com
SIC: 3599 Machine shop, jobbing and repair

Oakwood
Paulding County

(G-12030)
COOPER HATCHERY INC (PA)
Also Called: Cooper Farms
22348 Rd 140 (45873-9303)
PHONE................................419 594-3325
James R Cooper, *CEO*
Gary A Cooper, *
Dianne Cooper, *
Anada E Cooper, *
Janice Fiely, *
EMP: 225 **EST:** 1934
SQ FT: 47,000
SALES (est): 93.22MM
SALES (corp-wide): 93.22MM **Privately Held**
SIC: 0254 0253 2015 5153 Poultry hatcheries; Turkey farm; Turkey, processed, nsk; Grains

(G-12031)
MANSFIELD WELDING SERVICE LLC
20027 State Route 613 (45873-9437)
PHONE................................419 594-2738
Randy Mansfield, *Managing Member*
EMP: 7 **EST:** 1990
SALES (est): 785.16K **Privately Held**
Web: www.mansfieldwelding.com
SIC: 3499 3548 Machine bases, metal; Welding apparatus

(G-12032)
ROBERTS MANUFACTURING CO INC
24338 Road 148 (45873-9115)
PHONE................................419 594-2712
Brian Bauer, *Pr*
Chuck Behrens, *
Brian Miller, *
Margaret Hopkins, *Stockholder**
Ronald E Bauer, *Stockholder**
▲ **EMP:** 50 **EST:** 1952
SQ FT: 15,000
SALES (est): 7.37MM **Privately Held**
Web: www.robertsmanufacturing.net
SIC: 3599 Machine shop, jobbing and repair

(G-12033)
STONECO INC
13762 Road 179 (45873-9012)
PHONE................................419 393-2555
Rick Welch, *Superintnt*
EMP: 45
SALES (corp-wide): 32.72B **Privately Held**
Web: www.shellyco.com
SIC: 1422 2951 Crushed and broken limestone; Asphalt paving mixtures and blocks
HQ: Stoneco, Inc.
    1700 Fostoria Ave Ste 200
    Findlay OH 45840
    419 422-8554

(G-12034)
TOOLING CONNECTION INC
State Rte 66 N Ste 12603 (45873)
P.O. Box 238 (45873-0238)
PHONE................................419 594-3339
Klee Dangler, *Pr*
EMP: 9 **EST:** 1981
SQ FT: 12,000
SALES (est): 974.56K **Privately Held**
Web: www.toolingconnection.com
SIC: 3541 3544 Machine tools, metal cutting type; Special dies and tools

Oakwood Village
Cuyahoga County

(G-12035)
AGMET METALS INC
7800 Medusa Rd (44146-5549)
PHONE................................440 439-7400
Dana J Cassidy, *CEO*
Timothy A Andel, *CFO*
EMP: 31 **EST:** 1981
SALES (est): 3.92MM **Privately Held**
Web: www.agmetmetals.com
SIC: 3559 Recycling machinery

(G-12036)
CABINET CONCEPTS INC
Also Called: Custom Millwork Designs
590 Golden Oak Pkwy Unit B (44146-6502)
PHONE................................440 232-4644
Karen Torrence, *Pr*
James Torrence, *VP*
EMP: 7 **EST:** 1989
SQ FT: 4,000
SALES (est): 688.23K **Privately Held**
Web: www.custommillworkcmd.com
SIC: 2434 Wood kitchen cabinets

(G-12037)
CLASSIC LAMINATIONS INC
7703 First Pl Ste B (44146-6730)
PHONE................................440 735-1333
James Tidd, *Pr*
Donna Tidd, *Sec*
EMP: 25 **EST:** 1976
SQ FT: 3,800
SALES (est): 2.43MM **Privately Held**
Web: www.classiclaminations.com
SIC: 3089 2789 Laminating of plastics; Bookbinding and related work

(G-12038)
EXECUTIVE SWEETS EAST INC
7603 First Pl (44146-6703)
PHONE................................440 359-9866
Jeffrey Williamson, *Pr*
Sandy Williamson, *Treas*
EMP: 7 **EST:** 1979
SQ FT: 1,300
SALES (est): 525.43K **Privately Held**
Web: www.executivesweets.com
SIC: 2064 2066 Chocolate candy, except solid chocolate; Chocolate and cocoa products

(G-12039)
GOOD NUTRITION LLC
Also Called: Good Greens
7710 First Pl (44146-6717)
PHONE................................216 534-6617
John Huff, *CEO*
Bill Ross, *Ch*
Natalie Alesci, *Treas*
EMP: 10 **EST:** 2015
SQ FT: 3,000
SALES (est): 509.81K **Privately Held**

SIC: 2064 Granola and muesli, bars and clusters

(G-12040)
N-MOLECULAR INC
Also Called: Sofie
7650 First Pl Ste B (44146)
PHONE................................440 439-5356
Kenneth Smithmier, *CEO*
EMP: 15
SALES (corp-wide): 2.52MM **Privately Held**
SIC: 2834 Pharmaceutical preparations
PA: N-Molecular, Inc.
    21000 Atl Blvd Ste 730
    Dulles VA 20166
    703 547-8161

(G-12041)
OAKWOOD LABORATORIES LLC (PA)
7670 First Pl Ste A (44146-6721)
PHONE................................440 359-0000
Edward C Smith, *Managing Member*
Edward C Smith, *Ch Bd*
Mark T Smith, *Pr*
Bc Thanoo, *VP*
EMP: 20 **EST:** 1997
SQ FT: 15,000
SALES (est): 13.9MM
SALES (corp-wide): 13.9MM **Privately Held**
Web: www.oakwoodlabs.com
SIC: 2834 Pharmaceutical preparations

(G-12042)
STATUS MENS ACCESSORIES
7650 First Pl Ste F (44146-6732)
PHONE................................440 786-9394
Scott Weger, *Pr*
Lee Schloss, *VP*
Mark Schloss, *VP*
▲ **EMP:** 6 **EST:** 2004
SALES (est): 416.84K **Privately Held**
SIC: 2389 Men's miscellaneous accessories

(G-12043)
SWIFT FILTERS INC (PA)
24040 Forbes Rd (44146-5650)
PHONE................................440 735-0995
Edwin C Swift Junior, *Pr*
Charles C Swift, *
EMP: 37 **EST:** 1995
SQ FT: 6,000
SALES (est): 6.21MM
SALES (corp-wide): 6.21MM **Privately Held**
Web: www.swiftfilters.com
SIC: 3569 5075 Filters; Air filters

(G-12044)
THERMO FISHER SCIENTIFIC INC
Also Called: Remel Products
1 Thermo Fisher Way (44146-6536)
PHONE................................800 871-8909
EMP: 27
SALES (corp-wide): 44.91B **Publicly Held**
Web: www.thermofisher.com
SIC: 5047 2835 3841 Diagnostic equipment, medical; Diagnostic substances; Surgical and medical instruments
PA: Thermo Fisher Scientific Inc.
    168 3rd Ave
    Waltham MA 02451
    781 622-1000

(G-12045)
VIEWRAY INC (PA)
2 Thermo Fisher Way (44146-6536)
PHONE................................440 703-3210
Paul Ziegler, *CEO*

Daniel Moore, *Ch Bd*
Cassie Mahar, *Interim Chief Financial Officer*
Martin Fuzz, *CMO*
James F Dempsey, *CSO*
▲ **EMP:** 52 **EST:** 2004
SALES (est): 102.21MM
SALES (corp-wide): 102.21MM **Publicly Held**
Web: www.viewray.com
SIC: 3845 5047 Electromedical equipment; Therapy equipment

(G-12046)
VIEWRAY TECHNOLOGIES INC (HQ)
2 Thermo Fisher Way (44146-6536)
PHONE...................................440 703-3210
Scott Drake, *CEO*
William W Wells, *Pr*
Shar Matin, *COO*
James Alecxih, *Chief Commercial Officer*
EMP: 15 **EST:** 2007
SALES (est): 22.91MM
SALES (corp-wide): 102.21MM **Publicly Held**
Web: www.viewray.com
SIC: 3845 Electromedical equipment
PA: Viewray, Inc.
    2 Thermo Fisher Way
    Oakwood Village OH 44146
    440 703-3210

(G-12047)
WELDON PUMP LLC
Also Called: Weldon Pump
640 Golden Oak Pkwy (44146-6504)
PHONE...................................440 232-2282
Kent Kelly, *CEO*
Jeffrey Kelly, *
Jennifer Kelly, *
EMP: 28 **EST:** 2015
SQ FT: 16,000
SALES (est): 2.5MM **Privately Held**
Web: www.weldonpumps.com
SIC: 3694 3728 3795 9661 Distributors, motor vehicle engine; R and D by manuf., aircraft parts and auxiliary equipment; Tanks and tank components; Space research and technology

Oberlin
Lorain County

(G-12048)
ATLAS MACHINE PRODUCTS CO
Also Called: Atlas Portable Space Solutions
44800 Us Highway 20 (44074-9702)
PHONE...................................216 228-3688
N Medley, *Pr*
William Slabe, *VP Mfg*
Ed Medley, *Sec*
EMP: 7 **EST:** 1952
SALES (est): 521.98K **Privately Held**
SIC: 3451 Screw machine products

(G-12049)
BIG PRODUCTIONS INC
45300b Us Highway 20 (44074-9262)
PHONE...................................440 775-0015
Joanne Douglas, *Pr*
EMP: 6 **EST:** 1997
SQ FT: 7,000
SALES (est): 497.01K **Privately Held**
Web: www.bigproductionsinc.com
SIC: 2299 Jute and flax textile products

(G-12050)
EAST OBERLIN CABINETS LLC
13184 Hale Rd (44074-9741)
PHONE...................................440 775-1166
Dennis Luttrell, *Owner*
EMP: 7 **EST:** 1976
SALES (est): 694.1K **Privately Held**
Web: www.eastoberlincabinets.com
SIC: 2511 2434 Silverware chests: wood; Vanities, bathroom: wood

(G-12051)
GIBSON BROS INC
Also Called: Gibson Bakery
23 W College St (44074-1543)
PHONE...................................440 774-2401
Allyn Gibson, *Pr*
David Gibson, *VP*
Melba Gibson, *Sec*
EMP: 11 **EST:** 1885
SQ FT: 3,010
SALES (est): 651.46K **Privately Held**
Web: www.oumousangareofficial.com
SIC: 5411 2051 2064 2024 Grocery stores, independent; Bakery, wholesale or wholesale/retail combined; Candy and other confectionery products; Ice cream and ice milk

(G-12052)
HYDRO TUBE ENTERPRISES INC (PA)
137 Artino St (44074-1265)
PHONE...................................440 774-1022
Mike Prokop, *Pr*
Thomas E Hamel, *
Richard Cooks, *
▲ **EMP:** 70 **EST:** 1922
SQ FT: 67,000
SALES (est): 22.56MM
SALES (corp-wide): 22.56MM **Privately Held**
Web: www.hydrotube.com
SIC: 3498 Tube fabricating (contract bending and shaping)

(G-12053)
JB POLYMERS INC
55 S Main St Ste 204 (44074-1626)
PHONE...................................216 941-7041
EMP: 9 **EST:** 1995
SQ FT: 40,000
SALES (est): 916.7K **Privately Held**
Web: www.jbpolymers.com
SIC: 2821 Plastics materials and resins

(G-12054)
KIPTON PROPERTIES INC
14647 State Route 511 (44074-9460)
PHONE...................................440 315-3699
Terry Johnson, *Pr*
EMP: 17 **EST:** 2013
SALES (est): 1.15MM **Privately Held**
Web: www.kiptonquarry.com
SIC: 3281 Stone, quarrying and processing of own stone products

(G-12055)
R R DONNELLEY & SONS COMPANY
Also Called: R & S Label
450 Sterns Rd (44074-1209)
PHONE...................................440 774-2101
EMP: 100
SQ FT: 23,141
SALES (corp-wide): 4.99B **Privately Held**
Web: www.rrd.com
SIC: 2752 2759 2672 2761 Commercial printing, lithographic; Letterpress printing; Paper; coated and laminated, nec; Continuous forms, office and business
HQ: R. R. Donnelley & Sons Company
    35 W Wacker Dr
    Chicago IL 60601
    312 326-8000

(G-12056)
RAY MURO
Also Called: Linda & Ray's Machine Service
176 N Main St (44074-1118)
PHONE...................................440 984-8845
Ray Muro, *Owner*
EMP: 6 **EST:** 2019
SALES (est): 106.06K **Privately Held**
SIC: 3559 Sewing machines and hat and zipper making machinery

Obetz
Franklin County

(G-12057)
CENTRAL ALUMINUM COMPANY LLC
2045 Broehm Rd (43207-5206)
P.O. Box 624 (43023-0624)
PHONE...................................614 491-5700
Lee Grove, *Genl Mgr*
EMP: 50 **EST:** 1963
SQ FT: 94,000
SALES (est): 15.06MM **Privately Held**
Web: www.centralaluminum.com
SIC: 3354 3479 Aluminum extruded products; Painting, coating, and hot dipping
PA: Gdic Group, Llc
    1300 E 9th St Fl 20
    Cleveland OH 44114

(G-12058)
CHERYL & CO
4465 Industrial Center Dr (43207-4589)
PHONE...................................614 776-1500
Jodi Dixon, *Brnch Mgr*
EMP: 13
Web: www.cheryls.com
SIC: 2052 2066 Cookies and crackers; Chocolate and cocoa products
HQ: Cheryl & Co.
    646 Mccorkle Blvd
    Westerville OH 43082
    614 776-1500

(G-12059)
DAYTON ROGERS OF OHIO INC
2309 Mcgaw Rd W (43207-4806)
PHONE...................................614 491-1477
EMP: 60 **EST:** 1973
SALES (est): 23.04MM
SALES (corp-wide): 66.05MM **Privately Held**
Web: www.daytonrogers.com
SIC: 3469 Stamping metal for the trade
PA: Dayton Rogers Manufacturing Co.
    8401 W 35w Service Dr Ne
    Minneapolis MN 55449
    763 717-6450

(G-12060)
LEMON GROUP LLC
Also Called: Mid-America Store Fixtures
2195 Broehm Rd (43207-5206)
PHONE...................................614 409-9850
EMP: 32 **EST:** 2011
SALES (est): 5.52MM **Privately Held**
Web: www.midasf.com
SIC: 6153 2541 Factoring services; Wood partitions and fixtures

(G-12061)
LIFELINE MOBILE INC
2050 Mcgaw Rd (43207-4800)
PHONE...................................614 497-8300
▼ **EMP:** 65 **EST:** 1991
SALES (est): 9.9MM **Privately Held**
Web: www.lifelinemobile.com

SIC: 3713 Specialty motor vehicle bodies

(G-12062)
MASONS SAND AND GRAVEL CO
2385 Rathmell Rd (43207-4835)
PHONE...................................614 491-3611
George C Smith, *Pr*
EMP: 9 **EST:** 1951
SQ FT: 3,000
SALES (est): 1.08MM **Privately Held**
Web: www.masonssandandgravel.com
SIC: 1442 Construction sand mining

(G-12063)
NATIONAL BEVERAGE CORP
Also Called: Shasta Beverges
4685 Groveport Rd (43207-5216)
PHONE...................................614 491-5415
Monte Hale, *Mgr*
EMP: 9
SALES (corp-wide): 1.17B **Publicly Held**
Web: www.nationalbeverage.com
SIC: 2086 Soft drinks: packaged in cans, bottles, etc.
PA: National Beverage Corp.
    8100 Sw 10th St Ste 4000
    Plantation FL 33324
    954 581-0922

(G-12064)
SHASTA BEVERAGES INC
Also Called: National Beverage
4685 Groveport Rd (43207-5295)
PHONE...................................614 491-5415
Monty Hale, *Mgr*
EMP: 52
SALES (corp-wide): 1.17B **Publicly Held**
Web: www.shastapop.com
SIC: 2086 Soft drinks: packaged in cans, bottles, etc.
HQ: Shasta Beverages, Inc.
    26901 Indl Blvd
    Hayward CA 94545
    954 581-0922

(G-12065)
ZENNI USA LLC
4531 Industrial Center Dr (43207-4589)
PHONE...................................614 439-9850
EMP: 100 **EST:** 2020
SALES (est): 14.8MM
SALES (corp-wide): 112.11MM **Privately Held**
SIC: 3851 5995 Eyeglasses, lenses and frames; Optical goods stores
PA: Zenni Optical, Inc.
    448 Ignacio Blvd Ste 332
    Novato CA 94949
    800 211-2105

Okeana
Butler County

(G-12066)
CUSTOM FABRICATION BY FISHER
100 Weaver Rd (45053-9711)
PHONE...................................513 738-4600
Rodney Fisher, *Prin*
EMP: 7 **EST:** 2008
SALES (est): 489.63K **Privately Held**
SIC: 3499 Novelties and giftware, including trophies

(G-12067)
D & E ELECTRIC INC
7055 Okeana Drewersburg Rd (45053-9651)
PHONE...................................513 738-1172
EMP: 9 **EST:** 1995

SALES (est): 381.77K **Privately Held**
SIC: 1731 3643 General electrical contractor
; Current-carrying wiring services

(G-12068)
WAVY TICKET LLC
3748 State Line Rd (45053)
PHONE.................................513 827-0886
Stephen Mann, *Managing Member*
EMP: 40 **EST:** 2020
SALES (est): 1.19MM **Privately Held**
SIC: 3599 Amusement park equipment

(G-12069)
WHITMAN CORPORATION
2530 Joyce Ln (45053-9746)
PHONE.................................513 541-3223
TOLL FREE: 888
James Erhardt, *Pr*
Susan Erhardt, *VP*
EMP: 6 **EST:** 1931
SQ FT: 8,016
SALES (est): 957.98K
SALES (corp-wide): 86.39B **Publicly Held**
Web: www.whitcorp.com
SIC: 3161 3199 Cases, carrying, nec;
 Saddles or parts
PA: Pepsico, Inc.
 700 Anderson Hill Rd
 Purchase NY 10577
 914 253-2000

(G-12070)
ZAENKERT SURVEYING
ESSENTIALS
7461a Cincinnati Brookville Rd
(45053-9780)
PHONE.................................513 738-2917
Robert Zaenkert, *Pr*
Michelle Zaenkert, *VP*
EMP: 8 **EST:** 1986
SQ FT: 2,100
SALES (est): 930.54K **Privately Held**
Web: www.hardwoodstakes.com
SIC: 2499 5049 5211 Surveyors' stakes,
 wood; Surveyor's instruments; Lumber and
 other building materials

Okolona
Henry County

(G-12071)
REPUBLIC MILLS INC
Also Called: Hudson Feeds
888 School St (43545-9246)
PHONE.................................419 758-3511
▼ **EMP:** 21 **EST:** 1995
SQ FT: 30,000
SALES (est): 3.94MM **Privately Held**
Web: www.republicmills.com
SIC: 2048 5191 Livestock feeds; Feed

Old Fort
Seneca County

(G-12072)
CHURCH & DWIGHT CO INC
2501 E County Rd 34 (44861)
P.O. Box 122 (44861-0122)
PHONE.................................419 992-4244
Bruce Neeley, *Brnch Mgr*
EMP: 14
SALES (corp-wide): 5.87B **Publicly Held**
Web: www.churchdwight.com
SIC: 2812 Sodium bicarbonate
PA: Church & Dwight Co., Inc.
 500 Charles Ewing Blvd
 Ewing NJ 08628
 609 806-1200

(G-12073)
M & B ASPHALT COMPANY INC
Also Called: Maple Grove Stone
1525 W County Road 42 (44861)
P.O. Box 136 (44861-0136)
PHONE.................................419 992-4236
EMP: 9
SALES (corp-wide): 7.66MM **Privately Held**
Web: www.mgqinc.com
SIC: 3273 Ready-mixed concrete
PA: M. & B. Asphalt Company, Inc.
 1525 W Seneca Cnty Rd 42
 Tiffin OH 44883
 419 992-4235

Olmsted Falls
Cuyahoga County

(G-12074)
ADAMS AUTOMATIC INC
26070 N Depot St (44138-1647)
P.O. Box 38156 (44138-0156)
PHONE.................................440 235-4416
Edward Bond, *Pr*
Eric Dales, *Pr*
Adria Bond, *VP*
EMP: 10 **EST:** 1952
SQ FT: 7,200
SALES (est): 1.1MM **Privately Held**
Web: www.adamsautomaticinc.com
SIC: 3451 Screw machine products

(G-12075)
AFFILIATED METAL INDUSTRIES INC
Also Called: A M I
25600 Chapin St (44138-2782)
PHONE.................................440 235-3345
EMP: 12 **EST:** 1959
SALES (est): 2.35MM **Privately Held**
Web: www.affiliatedmetal.com
SIC: 1791 3444 Structural steel erection;
 Sheet metalwork

(G-12076)
BELL TIRE CO (PA)
Also Called: Almira Tire & Supply Div
27003 Oakwood Cir Apt 107 (44138-3507)
PHONE.................................440 234-8022
Charles Russo, *VP*
Geraldine Russo, *Pr*
Joseph Russo, *Sec*
EMP: 11 **EST:** 1964
SQ FT: 75,000
SALES (est): 1.05MM
SALES (corp-wide): 1.05MM **Privately Held**
SIC: 5014 5531 7534 Automobile tires and
 tubes; Automotive tires; Rebuilding and
 retreading tires

(G-12077)
BLUE RIDGE PAPER PRODUCTS LLC
Also Called: Dairy Pak Div
7920 Mapleway Dr (44138-1626)
PHONE.................................440 235-7200
Dave Lewallen, *Brnch Mgr*
EMP: 83
SQ FT: 161,146
Web: www.pactivevergreen.com
SIC: 2621 Fine paper
HQ: Blue Ridge Paper Products Llc
 41 Main St
 Canton NC 28716
 828 454-0676

(G-12078)
BROCK CORPORATION (PA)
26000 Sprague Rd (44138-2743)
P.O. Box 38159 (44138-0159)
PHONE.................................440 235-1806
Brock Walls, *Pr*
Linda D Walls, *VP*
EMP: 8 **EST:** 1979
SQ FT: 3,400
SALES (est): 1.65MM
SALES (corp-wide): 1.65MM **Privately Held**
SIC: 3273 Ready-mixed concrete

(G-12079)
CHAMPION INTERNATIONAL
7920 Mapleway Dr (44138-1626)
PHONE.................................440 235-7200
David Kibler, *Prin*
EMP: 7 **EST:** 2011
SALES (est): 157.78K **Privately Held**
SIC: 2656 Sanitary food containers

(G-12080)
GERGEL-KELLEM COMPANY INC
Also Called: Watt Printers
8707 Forest View Dr (44138-2347)
P.O. Box 38381 (44138-0381)
PHONE.................................216 398-2000
John Gergel, *Pr*
Mike Nakonek, *
EMP: 60 **EST:** 1893
SALES (est): 8.9MM **Privately Held**
SIC: 2752 Offset printing

(G-12081)
MILLWORK ENTERPRISES LLC (PA)
25418 Tyndall Falls Dr (44138-2769)
PHONE.................................216 644-1481
EMP: 6 **EST:** 2017
SALES (est): 96.53K
SALES (corp-wide): 96.53K **Privately Held**
SIC: 2431 Millwork

(G-12082)
THERMAFAB ALLOY INC
25367 Water St (44138-2015)
PHONE.................................216 861-0540
George M Donnelly, *CEO*
Gilbert Sherman, *
Daniel P Conway, *
EMP: 15 **EST:** 1930
SQ FT: 58,000
SALES (est): 1.37MM **Privately Held**
SIC: 3087 Custom compound purchased
 resins

(G-12083)
VITA-MIX MANUFACTURING
CORPORATION (PA)
Also Called: Vitamix
8615 Usher Rd (44138)
PHONE.................................440 235-4840
◆ **EMP:** 237 **EST:** 1921
SALES (est): 145.56MM
SALES (corp-wide): 145.56MM **Privately Held**
Web: www.vitamix.com
SIC: 3634 Electric housewares and fans

(G-12084)
WESTVIEW CONCRETE CORP (PA)
26000 Sprague Rd (44138-2743)
P.O. Box 38159 (44138-0159)
PHONE.................................440 235-1800
EMP: 50 **EST:** 1957
SALES (est): 6.36MM
SALES (corp-wide): 6.36MM **Privately Held**
Web: www.westviewconcrete.com

SIC: 3273 5211 Ready-mixed concrete;
 Masonry materials and supplies

Olmsted Twp
Cuyahoga County

(G-12085)
AMERICAN WIRE & CABLE
COMPANY (PA)
7951 Bronson Rd (44138-1088)
PHONE.................................440 235-1140
Richard M Mcclain, *Pr*
Kim R Mcclain, *VP*
▲ **EMP:** 30 **EST:** 1955
SQ FT: 80,000
SALES (est): 20.2MM
SALES (corp-wide): 20.2MM **Privately Held**
Web: www.americanwireandcable.com
SIC: 3357 3351 3315 Nonferrous
 wiredrawing and insulating; Wire, copper
 and copper alloy; Steel wire and related
 products

(G-12086)
ATX NETWORKS
27036 Waterside Dr (44138-3228)
PHONE.................................440 427-9036
Ryan Caudill, *Prin*
EMP: 6 **EST:** 2018
SALES (est): 88.38K **Privately Held**
Web: www.atx.com
SIC: 3661 Telephone and telegraph
 apparatus

(G-12087)
HOME CITY ICE COMPANY
8131 Bronson Rd (44138-1032)
PHONE.................................513 598-3000
EMP: 6 **EST:** 1948
SALES (est): 62.38K **Privately Held**
SIC: 2097 Manufactured ice

(G-12088)
JONES INDUSTRIES LLC
Also Called: Holding Company
8543 Evergreen Trl (44138-8126)
PHONE.................................440 810-1251
Dina Jones, *CEO*
EMP: 12 **EST:** 2008
SALES (est): 368.8K **Privately Held**
SIC: 3999 Manufacturing industries, nec

(G-12089)
NEBULATRONICS INC
24542 Nobottom Rd (44138-1540)
PHONE.................................440 243-2370
Kenneth Rados, *Pr*
Steve Harris, *VP Mktg*
Mike Panfil, *VP*
EMP: 10 **EST:** 1985
SQ FT: 5,000
SALES (est): 120.62K **Privately Held**
SIC: 3825 3829 Transducers for volts,
 amperes, watts, vars, frequency, etc.;
 Measuring and controlling devices, nec

Ontario
Richland County

(G-12090)
COLE TOOL & DIE COMPANY
Also Called: Oil Tooling and Stamping
466 State Rte 314 N (44903-6555)
P.O. Box 150 (44862-0150)
PHONE.................................419 522-1272
Alan D Cole, *CEO*

Ontario - Richland County (G-12091)　　　　　　　　　　　　　　　　　　　　　　　　　　　GEOGRAPHIC SECTION

Dave Harmon, *
EMP: 40 **EST:** 1953
SQ FT: 28,000
SALES (est): 4.72MM **Privately Held**
Web: www.coletool.com
SIC: 3544 3469 3465 Special dies and tools; Metal stampings, nec; Automotive stampings

(G-12091)
EMERSON PROCESS MANAGEMENT
Also Called: Shafer Valve Company
2500 Park Ave W (44906-1235)
PHONE....................................419 529-4311
EMP: 121
SALES (corp-wide): 15.16B **Publicly Held**
Web: www.emersonprocess.com
SIC: 3594 3593 Fluid power pumps and motors; Fluid power actuators, hydraulic or pneumatic
HQ: Emerson Process Management Valve Automation, Inc.
8100 West Florissant Ave
Saint Louis MO 63136
314 553-2000

(G-12092)
OHIO ESC PRINT SHOP
890 W 4th St (44906-2565)
PHONE....................................419 774-2512
EMP: 6 **EST:** 2014
SALES (est): 195.96K **Privately Held**
Web: www.moesc.net
SIC: 2752 Offset printing

(G-12093)
OXYRASE INC
3000 Park Ave W (44906-1050)
P.O. Box 1345 (44901-1345)
PHONE....................................419 589-8800
Casey Zace, *Pr*
EMP: 10 **EST:** 1986
SQ FT: 7,000
SALES (est): 3.49MM **Privately Held**
Web: www.oxyrase.com
SIC: 2869 Enzymes

(G-12094)
P R MACHINE WORKS INC
1825 Nussbaum Pkwy (44906-2360)
PHONE....................................419 529-5748
Mark Romanchuk, *Pr*
Mark J Romanchuk, *
▲ **EMP:** 75 **EST:** 1964
SQ FT: 14,100
SALES (est): 9.18MM **Privately Held**
Web: www.prmachineworks.com
SIC: 3599 1531 Machine shop, jobbing and repair

(G-12095)
RAVEN PERSONAL DEFENSE SYSTEMS
1237 W 4th St (44906-1825)
PHONE....................................419 631-0573
Al Johnson, *Prin*
EMP: 6 **EST:** 2017
SALES (est): 137.91K **Privately Held**
SIC: 3812 Defense systems and equipment

(G-12096)
UNISPORT INC
Also Called: Johnny Johnson Sports
2254 Stumbo Rd (44906-3804)
PHONE....................................419 529-4727
H Kim Baird, *Pr*
Todd Baird, *VP*
EMP: 10 **EST:** 1987
SALES (est): 1.22MM **Privately Held**
Web: www.uni-sport.com
SIC: 5136 5137 5699 2759 Sportswear, men's and boys'; Sportswear, women's and children's; Sports apparel; Screen printing

(G-12097)
WHITE MULE COMPANY
2420 W 4th St (44906-1207)
PHONE....................................740 382-9008
Steve Ritchey, *Pr*
Debby Ritchey, *Sec*
EMP: 21 **EST:** 1925
SQ FT: 15,000
SALES (est): 2.31MM **Privately Held**
Web: www.whitemuleco.com
SIC: 3714 1791 Trailer hitches, motor vehicle; Iron work, structural

Oregon
Lucas County

(G-12098)
A & L INDUSTRIES
Also Called: A & L Inds Machining & Repr
2054 Grange St (43616-4442)
PHONE....................................419 698-3733
EMP: 7
SALES (est): 464.45K **Privately Held**
SIC: 3599 Machine shop, jobbing and repair

(G-12099)
ABC APPLIANCE INC
Also Called: ABC
3012 Navarre Ave (43616-3308)
PHONE....................................419 693-4414
J R Pruss, *Mgr*
EMP: 21
SALES (corp-wide): 400.19MM **Privately Held**
Web: www.abcwarehouse.com
SIC: 3639 5722 5731 5065 Major kitchen appliances, except refrigerators and stoves; Vacuum cleaners; High fidelity stereo equipment; Telephone equipment
PA: Abc Appliance, Inc.
1 W Silverdome Indus Park
Pontiac MI 48342
248 335-4222

(G-12100)
AD CHOICE INC
1532 Bury Rd (43616-5736)
PHONE....................................419 697-8889
Kathy Keel, *VP*
EMP: 8 **EST:** 2009
SALES (est): 258.48K **Privately Held**
SIC: 2752 Offset printing

(G-12101)
AECOM ENERGY & CNSTR INC
Also Called: Washington Group
4001 Cedar Point Rd (43616-1310)
P.O. Box 696 (43697-0696)
PHONE....................................419 698-6277
EMP: 8
SALES (corp-wide): 14.38B **Publicly Held**
Web: www.aecom.com
SIC: 1542 2911 Nonresidential construction, nec; Petroleum refining
HQ: Aecom Energy & Construction, Inc.
106 Newberry St Sw
Aiken SC 29801
213 593-8100

(G-12102)
AUTONEUM NORTH AMERICA INC
4131 Spartan Dr (43616-1300)
PHONE....................................419 690-8924
EMP: 70
Web: www.autoneum.com
SIC: 3714 Motor vehicle parts and accessories
HQ: Autoneum North America, Inc.
34705 W 12 Mile Rd Ste 10
Farmington Hills MI 48331
248 848-0100

(G-12103)
AUTONEUM NORTH AMERICA INC
Also Called: Rieter Automotive-Oregon Plant
645 N Lallendorf Rd (43616-1334)
PHONE....................................419 693-0511
Gordon Shaw, *Brnch Mgr*
EMP: 350
SQ FT: 150,000
Web: www.autoneum.com
SIC: 3625 3714 3444 3296 Relays and industrial controls; Motor vehicle parts and accessories; Sheet metalwork; Mineral wool
HQ: Autoneum North America, Inc.
34705 W 12 Mile Rd Ste 10
Farmington Hills MI 48331
248 848-0100

(G-12104)
BP PRODUCTS NORTH AMERICA INC
4001 Cedar Point Rd (43616-1310)
PHONE....................................419 698-6400
EMP: 17 **EST:** 1922
SALES (est): 10.38MM **Privately Held**
SIC: 1311 Crude petroleum and natural gas

(G-12105)
FOUTY & COMPANY INC
5003 Bayshore Rd (43616-4478)
P.O. Box 167544 (43616-7544)
PHONE....................................419 693-0017
Marion L Fouty, *Pr*
Ken Fouty, *Pr*
▲ **EMP:** 20 **EST:** 1966
SQ FT: 20,000
SALES (est): 4.36MM **Privately Held**
Web: www.foutywaterjet.com
SIC: 5085 3053 Rubber goods, mechanical; Gaskets, all materials

(G-12106)
LINDE INC
Also Called: Praxair
3742 Cedar Point Rd (43616-1302)
PHONE....................................419 698-8005
Bill Engberg, *Mgr*
EMP: 8
Web: www.lindeus.com
SIC: 2813 Industrial gases
HQ: Linde Inc.
10 Riverview Dr
Danbury CT 06810
203 837-2000

(G-12107)
MARSULEX INC
1400 Otter Creek Rd (43616-1232)
PHONE....................................419 698-8181
EMP: 28
SIC: 2819 Sulfuric acid, oleum

(G-12108)
MR EMBLEM INC
3209 Navarre Ave (43616-3311)
PHONE....................................419 697-1888
Pat Slygh, *CEO*
EMP: 7 **EST:** 1987
SQ FT: 3,600
SALES (est): 959.65K **Privately Held**
Web: www.mremblem.com
SIC: 2395 2396 5199 Embroidery and art needlework; Screen printing on fabric articles; Advertising specialties

(G-12109)
PSC 272 TRC PBF
1819 Woodville Rd (43616-3159)
PHONE....................................419 466-7129
EMP: 24 **EST:** 2019
SALES (est): 3.21MM **Privately Held**
Web: www.pbfenergy.com
SIC: 2911 Petroleum refining

(G-12110)
RBM ENVIRONMENTAL & CNSTR INC
4526 Bayshore Rd (43616-1035)
PHONE....................................419 693-5840
Bob J Petty, *Pr*
Mike S Petty, *
EMP: 14 **EST:** 1989
SALES (est): 642.83K **Privately Held**
SIC: 1794 7699 7692 3498 Excavation and grading, building construction; Tank and boiler cleaning service; Welding repair; Fabricated pipe and fittings

(G-12111)
SNOWS WOOD SHOP INC (PA)
7220 Brown Rd (43616-5805)
PHONE....................................419 836-3805
Vernon Snow, *Pr*
Minda Snow, *Sec*
Kurt Snow, *VP*
EMP: 21 **EST:** 1983
SQ FT: 10,380
SALES (est): 1.2MM **Privately Held**
Web: www.snowswoodshop.com
SIC: 2434 1751 Wood kitchen cabinets; Cabinet and finish carpentry

(G-12112)
TOLEDO ALFALFA MILLS INC
861 S Stadium Rd (43616-5898)
PHONE....................................419 836-3705
Kathryn Lumbrezes, *Pr*
Becky Lumbrezer-box, *Sec*
Gary Lumbrezer, *VP*
EMP: 8 **EST:** 1940
SQ FT: 6,000
SALES (est): 977.9K **Privately Held**
SIC: 2048 Alfalfa or alfalfa meal, prepared as animal feed

Orient
Pickaway County

(G-12113)
B & B INDUSTRIES INC
7001 Harrisburg Pike (43146-9468)
PHONE....................................614 871-3883
Bernard Harwood, *Owner*
EMP: 24 **EST:** 2016
SALES (est): 4.97MM **Privately Held**
Web: www.bandbindustries.com
SIC: 3799 Golf carts, powered

(G-12114)
DUPONT
15804 Matville Rd (43146-9186)
PHONE....................................740 412-9752
EMP: 6 **EST:** 2019
SALES (est): 172.03K **Privately Held**
Web: www.dupont.com
SIC: 2879 Agricultural chemicals, nec

(G-12115)
KMJ LEASING LTD
Also Called: B & B Industries
7001 Harrisburg Pike (43146-9468)
PHONE....................................614 871-3883
Mary A Harwood, *
EMP: 16 **EST:** 1971
SQ FT: 5,000

SALES (est): 1.02MM **Privately Held**
SIC: 4213 3799 Contract haulers; Golf carts, powered

Orrville
Wayne County

(G-12116)
ACCURATE ELECTRONICS INC
169 S Main St (44667-1801)
P.O. Box 900 (44667-0900)
PHONE....................330 682-7015
Jeffrey Evans, *CEO*
EMP: 102 **EST:** 1952
SQ FT: 6,000
SALES (est): 607.65K
SALES (corp-wide): 62.58MM **Privately Held**
SIC: 3679 3621 3812 3672 Electronic circuits; Generators and sets, electric; Search and navigation equipment; Printed circuit boards
PA: The Will-Burt Company
  401 Collins Blvd
  Orrville OH 44667
  330 682-7015

(G-12117)
AT&F ADVANCED METALS LLC
95 N Swinehart Rd (44667-9532)
PHONE....................330 684-1122
Michael Ripich, *Pr*
EMP: 12
SALES (corp-wide): 8.15MM **Privately Held**
Web: www.atfco.com
SIC: 3446 Railings, prefabricated metal
PA: At&F Advanced Metals Llc
  12314 Elmwood Ave
  Cleveland OH 44111
  330 684-1122

(G-12118)
BEKAERT CORPORATION
Also Called: Bekaert Orrville
510 Collins Blvd (44667-9796)
PHONE....................330 683-5060
Andrew Whited, *Manager*
EMP: 15
SALES (corp-wide): 609.87MM **Privately Held**
Web: fencing.bekaert.com
SIC: 3496 Miscellaneous fabricated wire products
HQ: Bekaert Corporation
  3200 W Market St Ste 303
  Fairlawn OH 44333
  330 867-3325

(G-12119)
BEKAERT CORPORATION
Also Called: Contours
322 E Pine St (44667-1853)
PHONE....................330 683-5060
Otto Simmerman, *Prin*
EMP: 49
SQ FT: 260,000
SALES (corp-wide): 609.87MM **Privately Held**
Web: fencing.bekaert.com
SIC: 3315 3316 3398 3479 Wire and fabricated wire products; Cold-rolled strip or wire; Metal heat treating; Coating of metals and formed products
HQ: Bekaert Corporation
  3200 W Market St Ste 303
  Fairlawn OH 44333
  330 867-3325

(G-12120)
CHEMSPEC USA LLC
9287 Smucker Rd (44667-9795)
PHONE....................330 669-8512
Ron Snow, *Pr*
Michael Hall, *
▼ **EMP:** 60 **EST:** 2016
SALES (est): 14.76MM
SALES (corp-wide): 5.18B **Publicly Held**
SIC: 2851 Paints and paint additives
HQ: Axalta Coating Systems, Llc
  50 Applied Bank Blvd # 300
  Glen Mills PA 19342
  855 547-1461

(G-12121)
CHEMSPEC USA INC
9287 Smucker Rd (44667-9795)
PHONE....................330 669-8512
▲ **EMP:** 54 **EST:** 1975
SALES (est): 27.83MM
SALES (corp-wide): 5.18B **Publicly Held**
SIC: 2819 2851 2891 5013 Catalysts, chemical; Lacquer: bases, dopes, thinner; Adhesives; Motor vehicle supplies and new parts
PA: Axalta Coating Systems Ltd.
  50 Applied Bnk Blvd Ste 3
  Glen Mills PA 19342
  855 547-1461

(G-12122)
COUNTRY SALES & SERVICE LLC
255 Tracy Bridge Rd (44667-9383)
PHONE....................330 683-2500
EMP: 15 **EST:** 2004
SALES (est): 1.42MM **Privately Held**
Web: www.countrysalesandservice.com
SIC: 3519 5999 5084 Engines, diesel and semi-diesel or dual-fuel; Engine and motor equipment and supplies; Industrial machinery and equipment

(G-12123)
DC ORRVILLE INC
229 W Market St (44667-1848)
P.O. Box 603 (44667-0603)
PHONE....................330 683-0646
Andrew Hamsher, *Pr*
Creg Rohr, *
EMP: 18 **EST:** 1987
SQ FT: 12,000
SALES (est): 472.2K **Privately Held**
Web: www.dutchcountryapple.com
SIC: 2051 Bread, cake, and related products

(G-12124)
FERRO CORPORATION
FERRO CORPORATION
1560 N Main St (44667-9170)
P.O. Box 602 (44667-0602)
PHONE....................330 682-8015
Kenneth Ackerman, *Brnch Mgr*
EMP: 47
SALES (corp-wide): 1.88B **Privately Held**
Web: www.vibrantz.com
SIC: 2865 Cyclic crudes and intermediates
HQ: Vibrantz Corporation
  6060 Parkland Blvd # 250
  Mayfield Heights OH 44124
  216 875-5600

(G-12125)
FOLGER COFFEE COMPANY (HQ)
Also Called: Folgers
1 Strawberry Ln (44667-1241)
PHONE....................800 937-9745
Susan Arnold, *Pr*
Alan G Lafley, *Pr*
Joseph H Etter, *Sr VP*
C C Daley Junior, *VP*
G W Price, *VP*
▲ **EMP:** 15 **EST:** 1850
SQ FT: 1,600,000
SALES (est): 211.29MM
SALES (corp-wide): 8.53B **Publicly Held**
Web: www.folgerscoffee.com
SIC: 2095 Coffee roasting (except by wholesale grocers)
PA: The J M Smucker Company
  1 Strawberry Ln
  Orrville OH 44667
  330 682-3000

(G-12126)
GERBER FARM DIVISION INC
133 Collins Blvd (44667-9074)
P.O. Box 206 (44636-0206)
PHONE....................800 362-7381
John R Metzger, *Pr*
EMP: 13 **EST:** 2012
SALES (est): 786.32K **Privately Held**
Web: www.gerbers.com
SIC: 2015 Chicken, processed: fresh

(G-12127)
HEARTLAND EDUCATION CMNTY INC
200 N Main St (44667-1640)
P.O. Box 280 (44667-0280)
PHONE....................330 684-3034
EMP: 9 **EST:** 2011
SALES (est): 322.45K **Privately Held**
Web: www.heartlandorrville.com
SIC: 2711 Newspapers, publishing and printing

(G-12128)
HEAT EXCHANGE APPLIED TECH INC
150 B Allen Ave (44667-9021)
PHONE....................330 682-4328
Bharat Patel, *Pr*
EMP: 10 **EST:** 1983
SQ FT: 19,000
SALES (est): 2.29MM **Privately Held**
Web: www.heat-voss.com
SIC: 3443 Fabricated plate work (boiler shop)

(G-12129)
J M SMUCKER COMPANY (PA)
Also Called: SMUCKER'S
1 Strawberry Ln (44667)
PHONE....................330 682-3000
Mark T Smucker, *Ch Bd*
John P Brase, *COO*
Tucker H Marshall, *CFO*
Jeannette L Knudsen, *Legal*
Tim Wayne, *Sr VP*
◆ **EMP:** 1700 **EST:** 1897
SALES (est): 8.53B
SALES (corp-wide): 8.53B **Publicly Held**
Web: www.jmsmucker.com
SIC: 2033 2099 2023 2087 Jams, jellies, and preserves, packaged in cans, jars, etc.; Syrups; Canned milk, whole; Beverage bases, concentrates, syrups, powders and mixes

(G-12130)
JLG INDUSTRIES INC
2927 E Paradise Street Ext (44667-9628)
PHONE....................330 684-0132
EMP: 50
SALES (corp-wide): 9.66B **Publicly Held**
Web: www.jlg.com
SIC: 3531 Construction machinery
HQ: Jlg Industries, Inc.
  1 Jlg Dr
  Mc Connellsburg PA 17233
  717 485-5161

(G-12131)
JLG INDUSTRIES INC
600 E Chestnut St (44667-1951)
PHONE....................330 684-0200
Wade Jones, *Brnch Mgr*
EMP: 52
SALES (corp-wide): 9.66B **Publicly Held**
Web: www.jlg.com
SIC: 3531 Construction machinery
HQ: Jlg Industries, Inc.
  1 Jlg Dr
  Mc Connellsburg PA 17233
  717 485-5161

(G-12132)
JM SMUCKER LLC (HQ)
1 Strawberry Ln (44667-1298)
PHONE....................330 682-3000
Mark T Smucker, *CEO*
EMP: 51 **EST:** 2002
SALES (est): 753.48MM
SALES (corp-wide): 8.53B **Publicly Held**
Web: www.smuckers.com
SIC: 5149 2047 Specialty food items; Dog food
PA: The J M Smucker Company
  1 Strawberry Ln
  Orrville OH 44667
  330 682-3000

(G-12133)
KNUDSEN & SONS INC
1 Strawberry Ln (44667-1241)
PHONE....................330 682-3000
EMP: 6
SALES (est): 870.01K
SALES (corp-wide): 8.53B **Publicly Held**
SIC: 2033 Fruit juices: concentrated, hot pack
PA: The J M Smucker Company
  1 Strawberry Ln
  Orrville OH 44667
  330 682-3000

(G-12134)
LAST ARROW MANUFACTURING LLC
8991 Lincoln Way E (44667-9336)
PHONE....................330 683-7777
EMP: 67 **EST:** 1974
SALES (est): 12.1MM **Privately Held**
Web: www.lastarrowmfg.com
SIC: 3599 Custom machinery

(G-12135)
LETTERGRAPHICS INC
400 W Market St (44667-1823)
P.O. Box 613 (44667-0613)
PHONE....................330 683-3903
Frank Wessels, *Pr*
Jim R Webster, *CEO*
EMP: 8 **EST:** 1976
SQ FT: 1,500
SALES (est): 965.87K **Privately Held**
Web: www.lettergraphicsinc.com
SIC: 3993 Electric signs

(G-12136)
MILOS KITCHEN LLC
1 Strawberry Ln (44667-1241)
PHONE....................330 682-3000
EMP: 6 **EST:** 2019
SALES (est): 2.54MM
SALES (corp-wide): 8.53B **Publicly Held**
Web: www.miloskitchen.com
SIC: 2047 Dog food
PA: The J M Smucker Company
  1 Strawberry Ln
  Orrville OH 44667
  330 682-3000

Orrville - Wayne County (G-12137)

GEOGRAPHIC SECTION

(G-12137)
MONARCH PLASTIC INC
516 Jefferson Ave (44667-1811)
P.O. Box 262 (44667-0262)
PHONE.................................330 683-0822
Larry R Caskey, *Pr*
Debra Caskey, *VP*
EMP: 12 **EST:** 1979
SQ FT: 10,000
SALES (est): 970.86K **Privately Held**
SIC: 3711 3714 Automobile bodies, passenger car, not including engine, etc.; Motor vehicle parts and accessories

(G-12138)
MOOG INC
1701 N Main St (44667-9172)
PHONE.................................330 682-0010
James King, *Prin*
EMP: 29
SALES (corp-wide): 3.32B **Publicly Held**
Web: www.moog.com
SIC: 3625 Actuators, industrial
PA: Moog Inc.
400 Jamison Rd
Elma NY 14059
716 652-2000

(G-12139)
MSF ACRES LLC
2600 Kidron Rd (44667-9645)
PHONE.................................330 857-0257
EMP: 10 **EST:** 2002
SALES (est): 549.97K **Privately Held**
Web: www.spdkidron.com
SIC: 2448 Pallets, wood

(G-12140)
NATIONAL PATTERN MFGCO
1200 N Main St (44667-1017)
P.O. Box 58 (44667-0058)
PHONE.................................330 682-6871
Anthony J Yonto, *Pr*
Anthony A Nicholas, *Pr*
Robert C Nicholas, *Sec*
EMP: 10 **EST:** 1952
SALES (est): 1.29MM
SALES (corp-wide): 40.99MM **Privately Held**
Web: www.qcfoundry.com
SIC: 3544 3543 Dies, plastics forming; Foundry patternmaking
PA: Quality Castings Company
1200 N Main St
Orrville OH 44667
330 682-6010

(G-12141)
NORTHFIELD PROPANE LLC
10355 Lincoln Way E (44667-9305)
P.O. Box 670236 (44067-0236)
PHONE.................................330 854-4320
EMP: 6 **EST:** 2019
SALES (est): 233.25K **Privately Held**
Web: www.northfieldpropane.com
SIC: 1389 Oil field services, nec

(G-12142)
NU PET COMPANY (HQ)
1 Strawberry Ln (44667-1241)
PHONE.................................330 682-3000
Barry C Dunaway, *Pr*
EMP: 18 **EST:** 2018
SALES (est): 72.48MM
SALES (corp-wide): 8.53B **Publicly Held**
SIC: 2099 2033 2023 2087 Syrups; Jams, jellies, and preserves, packaged in cans, jars, etc.; Canned milk, whole; Beverage bases, concentrates, syrups, powders and mixes
PA: The J M Smucker Company
1 Strawberry Ln
Orrville OH 44667
330 682-3000

(G-12143)
ORRVILLE BRONZE & ALUMINUM CO
Central Ct (44667)
P.O. Box 216 (44667-0216)
PHONE.................................330 682-4015
Robert R Cairnie II, *Pr*
Robert R Cairnie Ii, *Pr*
Hillary Cairnie, *VP*
Mark Cairnie, *VP*
EMP: 20 **EST:** 1934
SQ FT: 27,000
SALES (est): 1.71MM **Privately Held**
Web: www.orrville.com
SIC: 3366 Castings (except die), nec, copper and copper-base alloy

(C 12111)
ORRVILLE TRUCKING & GRADING CO (PA)
475 Orr St (44667-9764)
P.O. Box 220 (44667-0220)
PHONE.................................330 682-4010
Auvil Richmond, *Pr*
John H Wilson, *
EMP: 50 **EST:** 1953
SQ FT: 15,000
SALES (est): 7.15MM
SALES (corp-wide): 7.15MM **Privately Held**
Web: www.orrvilletrucking.com
SIC: 3273 3272 5031 Ready-mixed concrete; Concrete products, nec; Building materials, exterior

(G-12145)
ORRVILON INC
1400 Dairy Ln (44667-2505)
PHONE.................................330 684-9400
K P Singh, *Pr*
Alan Soler, *
Frank Bongrazio, *
▲ **EMP:** 110 **EST:** 2009
SQ FT: 350,000
SALES (est): 25.9MM
SALES (corp-wide): 681.48MM **Privately Held**
Web: www.holtecinternational.com
SIC: 3354 3442 Aluminum extruded products; Metal doors
PA: Holtec International
1001 N Us Highway 1
Jupiter FL 33477
561 745-7772

(G-12146)
PURINA MILLS LLC
Also Called: Purina Mills
635 Collins Blvd (44667-9796)
PHONE.................................330 682-1951
EMP: 9
SALES (corp-wide): 2.89B **Privately Held**
Web: www.purina.com
SIC: 2048 Prepared feeds, nec
HQ: Purina Mills, Llc
555 Mryvlle Univ Dr Ste 2
Saint Louis MO 63141

(G-12147)
QUALITY CASTINGS COMPANY (PA)
1200 N Main St (44667-1017)
P.O. Box 58 (44667-0058)
PHONE.................................330 682-6010
Matt Nicholas, *Pr*
Di Ck Nicholas, *CEO*
Richard Nicholas, *
David Yonto, *

Anthony A Nicholas, *
EMP: 290 **EST:** 1927
SALES (est): 40.99MM
SALES (corp-wide): 40.99MM **Privately Held**
Web: www.qcfoundry.com
SIC: 3321 Gray iron castings, nec

(G-12148)
ROBURA INC
3328 S Kohler Rd (44667-9604)
PHONE.................................330 857-7404
Albert Lehman, *Brnch Mgr*
EMP: 6
SALES (corp-wide): 9.34MM **Privately Held**
Web: www.lehmans.com
SIC: 2431 Exterior and ornamental woodwork and trim
PA: Robura, Inc.
4779 Kidron Rd
Dalton OH 44618
800 438-5346

(G-12149)
S & W EXPRESS INC
8849 Lincoln Way E (44667-9335)
PHONE.................................330 683-2747
Ivan Hoshstetler, *Pr*
EMP: 8 **EST:** 1988
SALES (est): 845.86K **Privately Held**
Web: www.swoodpallet.com
SIC: 2448 Pallets, wood

(G-12150)
SCHANTZ ORGAN COMPANY (PA)
Also Called: Schantz Custom Woodworking
626 S Walnut St (44667-2238)
P.O. Box 156 (44667-0156)
PHONE.................................330 682-6065
Victor B Schantz, *Pr*
Jeff Dexter, *
Eric Gastier, *
EMP: 19 **EST:** 1873
SQ FT: 45,600
SALES (est): 40.91K
SALES (corp-wide): 40.91K **Privately Held**
Web: www.schantzorgan.com
SIC: 3931 Organs, all types: pipe, reed, hand, electronic, etc.

(G-12151)
SMITHFOODS INC (PA)
1381 Dairy Ln (44667-2503)
P.O. Box 87 (44667-0087)
PHONE.................................330 683-8710
Nathan Schmid, *CEO*
Amy Miller, *Sec*
EMP: 35 **EST:** 2016
SALES (est): 198.42MM
SALES (corp-wide): 198.42MM **Privately Held**
Web: www.smithfoods.com
SIC: 2026 2024 Fluid milk; Ice cream and frozen deserts

(G-12152)
SMITHFOODS ORRVILLE INC
1381 Dairy Ln (44667-2503)
P.O. Box 87 (44667-0087)
PHONE.................................330 683-8710
◆ **EMP:** 204 **EST:** 1909
SALES (est): 8.79MM
SALES (corp-wide): 198.42MM **Privately Held**
Web: www.smithfoods.com
SIC: 2086 Carbonated beverages, nonalcoholic: pkged. in cans, bottles
PA: Smithfoods Inc.
1381 Dairy Ln
Orrville OH 44667

330 683-8710

(G-12153)
SMUCKER FOODSERVICE INC
1 Strawberry Ln (44667-1241)
PHONE.................................877 858-3855
EMP: 15 **EST:** 2019
SALES (est): 2.19MM
SALES (corp-wide): 8.53B **Publicly Held**
Web: www.smuckerawayfromhome.com
SIC: 2033 Jams, jellies, and preserves, packaged in cans, jars, etc.
PA: The J M Smucker Company
1 Strawberry Ln
Orrville OH 44667
330 682-3000

(G-12154)
SMUCKER INTERNATIONAL INC
Also Called: Smucker's
1 Strawberry Ln (44667-1241)
PHONE.................................330 682-3000
Tim Smucker, *Ch Bd*
Richard Smucker, *CEO*
Vince Byrd, *VP*
▼ **EMP:** 25 **EST:** 1988
SALES (est): 2.53MM
SALES (corp-wide): 8.53B **Publicly Held**
Web: www.smuckers.com
SIC: 2033 2099 2086 Canned fruits and specialties; Syrups; Bottled and canned soft drinks
PA: The J M Smucker Company
1 Strawberry Ln
Orrville OH 44667
330 682-3000

(G-12155)
SMUCKER MANUFACTURING INC
1 Strawberry Ln (44667-1241)
P.O. Box 280 (44667-0280)
PHONE.................................888 550-9555
Peter Farah, *Pr*
EMP: 16 **EST:** 2012
SALES (est): 5.94MM
SALES (corp-wide): 8.53B **Publicly Held**
Web: www.smuckers.com
SIC: 2033 Jams, jellies, and preserves, packaged in cans, jars, etc.
PA: The J M Smucker Company
1 Strawberry Ln
Orrville OH 44667
330 682-3000

(G-12156)
SMUCKER NATURAL FOODS INC
Strawberry Lane (44667)
P.O. Box 280 (44667-0280)
PHONE.................................330 682-3000
H Wagstaff, *Brnch Mgr*
EMP: 923
SALES (corp-wide): 8.53B **Publicly Held**
Web: www.smuckers.com
SIC: 2086 Bottled and canned soft drinks
HQ: Smucker Natural Foods, Inc.
37 Speedway Ave
Chico CA 95928
530 899-5000

(G-12157)
SMUCKER RETAIL FOODS INC
1 Strawberry Ln (44667-1241)
PHONE.................................330 682-3000
Peter Farah, *Pr*
EMP: 25 **EST:** 2012
SALES (est): 6.38MM
SALES (corp-wide): 8.53B **Publicly Held**
SIC: 2033 Jams, jellies, and preserves, packaged in cans, jars, etc.
PA: The J M Smucker Company
1 Strawberry Ln

▲ = Import ▼ = Export
◆ = Import/Export

Orrville OH 44667
330 682-3000

(G-12158)
SOUTHWOOD PALLET LLC ✪
8849 Lincoln Way E (44667-9335)
PHONE...............................330 682-3747
EMP: 65 **EST:** 2022
SALES (est): 2.79MM **Privately Held**
SIC: 2448 7389 Wood pallets and skids; Log and lumber broker

(G-12159)
TIMBER FRAMING LLC
10864 Ely Rd (44667-9512)
PHONE...............................330 749-7837
Abe Troyer, *Prin*
EMP: 6 **EST:** 2005
SALES (est): 313.62K **Privately Held**
SIC: 2431 Jalousies, glass, wood frame

(G-12160)
VENTURE PRODUCTS INC
500 Venture Dr (44667-2508)
P.O. Box 148 (44667-0148)
PHONE...............................330 683-0075
▲ **EMP:** 70 **EST:** 1988
SALES (est): 25.08MM
SALES (corp-wide): 4.55B **Publicly Held**
Web: www.ventrac.com
SIC: 3524 Lawn and garden tractors and equipment
PA: The Toro Company
8111 Lyndale Ave S
Bloomington MN 55420
952 888-8801

(G-12161)
VIBRANTZ TECHNOLOGIES INC
1560 N Main St (44667-9170)
P.O. Box 602 (44667-0602)
PHONE...............................330 765-4378
EMP: 7
SALES (corp-wide): 1.88B **Privately Held**
SIC: 2869 Industrial organic chemicals, nec
HQ: Vibrantz Technologies Inc.
16945 Northchase Dr # 2000
Houston TX 77060
646 747-4222

(G-12162)
WILL-BURT COMPANY
312 Collins Blvd (44667-9727)
P.O. Box 900 (44667-0900)
PHONE...............................330 682-7015
Jeffrey O Evans, *Mgr*
EMP: 16
SALES (corp-wide): 62.58MM **Privately Held**
Web: www.willburt.com
SIC: 3443 3449 3599 5039 Fabricated plate work (boiler shop); Miscellaneous metalwork; Machine shop, jobbing and repair; Prefabricated structures
PA: The Will-Burt Company
401 Collins Blvd
Orrville OH 44667
330 682-7015

(G-12163)
WILL-BURT COMPANY (PA)
401 Collins Blvd (44667-9752)
P.O. Box 900 (44667-0900)
PHONE...............................330 682-7015
Richard Lewin, *CEO*
Jeffrey Evans, *
Bruce Inzetta, *
Dan Plumly, *
▲ **EMP:** 105 **EST:** 1918
SALES (est): 62.58MM
SALES (corp-wide): 62.58MM **Privately Held**
Web: www.willburt.com
SIC: 3599 5039 3443 3449 Machine shop, jobbing and repair; Prefabricated structures ; Fabricated plate work (boiler shop); Miscellaneous metalwork

Orwell
Ashtabula County

(G-12164)
GVR WAREHOUSE AND PACKG LLC
4814 State Route 322 (44076)
PHONE...............................440 272-1005
Randy S Steffy, *Prin*
EMP: 7 **EST:** 2008
SALES (est): 75K **Privately Held**
SIC: 2621 Wrapping and packaging papers

(G-12165)
HSP BEDDING SOLUTIONS LLC
243 Staley Rd (44076-8381)
P.O. Box 459 (44076-0459)
PHONE...............................440 437-4425
Eli Schnucker, *Managing Member*
EMP: 26 **EST:** 2015
SALES (est): 2.45MM **Privately Held**
SIC: 2515 Mattresses and bedsprings

(G-12166)
KENNAMETAL INC
180 Penniman Rd (44076-9500)
PHONE...............................440 437-5131
David Orth, *Mgr*
EMP: 57
SALES (corp-wide): 2.08B **Publicly Held**
Web: www.kennametal.com
SIC: 3545 Cutting tools for machine tools
PA: Kennametal Inc.
525 William Penn Pl # 3300
Pittsburgh PA 15219
412 248-8000

(G-12167)
LOCK JOINT TUBE OHIO LLC
Also Called: Welded Tubes
135 Penniman Rd (44076-9557)
PHONE...............................210 278-3757
Ted Lerman, *Pr*
Joe Frandanisa, *
Peter Modelski, *
EMP: 172 **EST:** 2020
SALES (est): 29.66MM **Privately Held**
Web: www.weldedtubes.com
SIC: 3317 Welded pipe and tubes
HQ: Lock Joint Tube Llc
515 W Ireland Rd
South Bend IN 46614

(G-12168)
LSP TUBES INC
Also Called: Welded Tubes, Inc.
135 Penniman Rd (44076-9557)
P.O. Box 175 (44076-0175)
PHONE...............................216 378-2092
▲ **EMP:** 92
Web: www.weldedtubes.com
SIC: 3317 Tubes, wrought: welded or lock joint

(G-12169)
QUALITY DESIGN MACHINING INC
64 Penniman Rd (44076-9557)
PHONE...............................440 352-7290
Robert Fletcher, *Pr*
EMP: 8 **EST:** 1990
SALES (est): 961.74K **Privately Held**
Web: www.qualitydesignmachining.com
SIC: 3599 Machine and other job shop work

(G-12170)
SY LOGGING LLC
3104 Winters Rd (44076-9710)
PHONE...............................440 437-5744
Sam Yoder, *Prin*
EMP: 6 **EST:** 2014
SALES (est): 115.38K **Privately Held**
SIC: 2411 Logging

(G-12171)
WOODCRAFT INDUSTRIES INC
Also Called: WOODCRAFT INDUSTRIES, INC.
131 Grand Valley Ave (44076-9420)
P.O. Box 128 (44076-0128)
PHONE...............................440 437-7811
Brain Richie, *Brnch Mgr*
EMP: 135
Web: www.woodcraftind.com
SIC: 2434 2426 2431 Wood kitchen cabinets ; Dimension, hardwood; Millwork
HQ: Quanex Custom Components, Inc.
525 Lincoln Ave Se
Saint Cloud MN 56304
320 656-2345

(G-12172)
Y&B LOGGING
3647 Montgomery Rd (44076-9742)
PHONE...............................440 437-1053
Urie Yoder, *Prin*
EMP: 6 **EST:** 2013
SALES (est): 145.63K **Privately Held**
SIC: 2411 Logging camps and contractors

Osgood
Darke County

(G-12173)
DYNAMIC WELD CORPORATION
Also Called: Dynamic Weld
242 N St (45351)
P.O. Box 127 (45351)
PHONE...............................419 582-2900
Harry Heitkamp, *Pr*
Gene Niekamp, *Prin*
Ernie Davenport, *Prin*
Steve Wilker, *Prin*
Sue Heitkamp, *Prin*
EMP: 44 **EST:** 1981
SQ FT: 35,000
SALES (est): 5.97MM **Privately Held**
Web: www.dynamicweld.com
SIC: 3444 7692 Sheet metalwork; Welding repair

Ostrander
Delaware County

(G-12174)
K L M MANUFACTURING COMPANY
56 Huston St (43061-9618)
PHONE...............................740 666-5171
K Leroy Moore, *Pr*
EMP: 6 **EST:** 1971
SQ FT: 5,000
SALES (est): 583.69K **Privately Held**
SIC: 3541 Machine tools, metal cutting type

(G-12175)
MYRIAD INDUSTRIES INC
6011 Houseman Rd (43061-9626)
PHONE...............................619 232-6700
Thomas Brady Kingery Iii, *Prin*
EMP: 6 **EST:** 2012
SALES (est): 142.16K **Privately Held**
SIC: 3999 Manufacturing industries, nec

(G-12176)
SHELLY MATERIALS INC
8328 Watkins Rd (43061-9311)
PHONE...............................740 666-5841
Keith Siler, *VP*
EMP: 43
SALES (corp-wide): 32.72B **Privately Held**
Web: www.shellyco.com
SIC: 2951 1611 3274 1422 Asphalt and asphaltic paving mixtures (not from refineries); Surfacing and paving; Lime; Crushed and broken limestone
HQ: Shelly Materials, Inc.
80 Park Dr
Thornville OH 43076
740 246-6315

Ottawa
Putnam County

(G-12177)
CUSTOM WOODWORKING INC
214 S Main St (45875-9416)
PHONE...............................419 456-3330
EMP: 9 **EST:** 1991
SALES (est): 764.54K **Privately Held**
Web: www.customwoodworking214.com
SIC: 2434 Wood kitchen cabinets

(G-12178)
D 4 INDUSTRIES INC
685 Woodland Dr (45875-8627)
PHONE...............................419 523-9555
Jim Bibler, *Pr*
EMP: 9 **EST:** 2004
SALES (est): 796.4K **Privately Held**
SIC: 3599 Machine shop, jobbing and repair

(G-12179)
DRAINAGE PIPE & FITTINGS LLC
450 Tile Company St (45875-9217)
PHONE...............................419 538-6337
Floyd T Meyer, *Admn*
Crystal Solano, *Prin*
Floyd Tony Meyer, *Prin*
EMP: 8 **EST:** 2012
SALES (est): 459.6K **Privately Held**
SIC: 3494 Pipe fittings

(G-12180)
HIRZEL CANNING COMPANY
Ottawa Foods, Div of
325 E Williamstown Rd (45875-1802)
PHONE...............................419 523-3225
Karl E Hirzel, *Manager*
EMP: 7
SALES (corp-wide): 60.4MM **Privately Held**
Web: www.deifratelli.com
SIC: 2033 Tomato products, packaged in cans, jars, etc.
PA: Hirzel Canning Company
411 Lemoyne Rd
Northwood OH 43619
419 693-0531

(G-12181)
INDUSTRIAL MILLWRIGHT SVCS LLC
1024 Heritage Trl (45875-8521)
PHONE...............................419 523-9147
Duane Greear, *Managing Member*
Lisa Greear, *
EMP: 28 **EST:** 2003
SALES (est): 1.73MM **Privately Held**
Web: www.industrialmillwrightservices.com

Ottawa - Putnam County

(G-12182)
JB MACHINING CONCEPTS LLC
995 Sugar Mill Dr (45875-8526)
PHONE..............................419 523-0096
John Blankemeyer, *Sole Member*
Alexander Blankemeyer, *Engg Mgr*
EMP: 8 **EST:** 2007
SQ FT: 18,000
SALES (est): 881.47K **Privately Held**
Web: www.jbmachiningconcepts.com
SIC: 3646 3645 Commercial lighting fixtures; Residential lighting fixtures

(G-12183)
K & L READY MIX INC (PA)
10391 State Route 15 (45875-8641)
P.O. Box 325 (45875-0325)
PHONE..............................419 523-4376
Ron Kahle Junior, *Pr*
EMP: 19 **EST:** 1975
SQ FT: 12,000
SALES (est): 4.97MM
SALES (corp-wide): 4.97MM **Privately Held**
Web: www.kandlreadymix.com
SIC: 3273 Ready-mixed concrete

(G-12184)
MC ELWAIN INDUSTRIES INC
17941 Road L (45875-9455)
PHONE..............................419 532-3126
Amelia Mcelwain, *Pr*
EMP: 14 **EST:** 1983
SALES (est): 898.77K **Privately Held**
Web: www.mcelwainind.com
SIC: 7692 3441 Welding repair; Building components, structural steel

(G-12185)
NELSON MANUFACTURING COMPANY
6448 State Route 224 (45875-9789)
PHONE..............................419 523-5321
Anthony Niese, *Pr*
Chad Stall, *
Amy Niese, *
▼ **EMP:** 80 **EST:** 1947
SQ FT: 46,000
SALES (est): 15MM **Privately Held**
Web: www.nelsontrailers.com
SIC: 3715 7539 Semitrailers for truck tractors; Trailer repair

(G-12186)
OTTAWA DEFENSE LOGISTICS LLC
804 N Pratt St (45875-1556)
P.O. Box 468 (45875-0468)
PHONE..............................419 596-3202
Barb Rieman, *Managing Member*
EMP: 10 **EST:** 2006
SALES (est): 168.26K **Privately Held**
Web: www.ottawadefenselogistics.com
SIC: 7692 Welding repair

(G-12187)
PALPAC INDUSTRIES INC
610 N Agner St (45875-1533)
P.O. Box 109 (45875-0109)
PHONE..............................419 523-3230
Danny E Meyer, *Pr*
Mike Meyer, *Treas*
EMP: 18 **EST:** 1968
SQ FT: 62,000
SALES (est): 2.59MM **Privately Held**
Web: www.palpacindustries.com
SIC: 3089 3086 Molding primary plastics; Plastics foam products

(G-12188)
PHANTASM DSGNS SPRTSN MORE LTD
112 W Main St (45875-1722)
PHONE..............................419 538-6737
Don Huber, *Owner*
EMP: 9 **EST:** 1978
SALES (est): 744.25K **Privately Held**
Web: www.phantasmdesigns.com
SIC: 2262 2261 2395 7336 Screen printing: manmade fiber and silk broadwoven fabrics; Screen printing of cotton broadwoven fabrics; Embroidery and art needlework; Graphic arts and related design

(G-12189)
PUTNAM AGGREGATES CO
7053 Road M (45875-9754)
PHONE..............................419 523-6004
Barbara Shroyer, *Technical Staff*
EMP: 6 **EST:** 2012
SALES (est): 218.69K **Privately Held**
Web: www.putnamaggregates.com
SIC: 1442 Construction sand and gravel

(G-12190)
R K INDUSTRIES INC
725 N Locust St (45875-1466)
P.O. Box 306 (45875-0306)
PHONE..............................419 523-5001
Ann Woodyard, *Pr*
Barry Woodyard, *
Joe Maag, *
Kimberly French, *
▲ **EMP:** 85 **EST:** 1983
SQ FT: 45,000
SALES (est): 15.37MM **Privately Held**
Web: www.rkindustries.org
SIC: 7692 3465 Automotive welding; Automotive stampings

(G-12191)
SILGAN PLASTICS LLC
Also Called: Silgan
690 Woodland Dr (45875-8627)
PHONE..............................419 523-3737
Russ Zervais, *Pr*
EMP: 199
Web: www.silganplastics.com
SIC: 3089 Plastics containers, except foam
HQ: Silgan Plastics Llc
14515 North Outer 40 Rd # 21
Chesterfield MO 63017
800 274-5426

(G-12192)
STEEL TECHNOLOGIES LLC
740 E Williamstown Rd (45875-1873)
PHONE..............................419 523-5199
Rick Furber, *Mgr*
EMP: 50
Web: www.steeltechnologies.com
SIC: 3312 Sheet or strip, steel, cold-rolled: own hot-rolled
HQ: Steel Technologies Llc
700 N Hurstbourne Pkwy # 400
Louisville KY 40222
502 245-2110

(G-12193)
STERLING INDUSTRIES INC
740 E Main St (45875-2029)
PHONE..............................419 523-3788
Marilyn Kuhlman, *Pr*
Keith Kuhlman, *VP*
EMP: 10 **EST:** 1967
SQ FT: 9,600
SALES (est): 696.83K **Privately Held**
Web: www.sterlingindustries.com

SIC: 2441 2448 Boxes, wood; Pallets, wood

(G-12194)
STOEPFEL DRILLING CO
12245 State Route 115 (45875-9488)
PHONE..............................419 532-3307
John H Stoepfel Junior, *Pt*
Roger Winkle, *Pt*
EMP: 7 **EST:** 1954
SQ FT: 6,000
SALES (est): 515.67K **Privately Held**
SIC: 1481 1781 Mine and quarry services, nonmetallic minerals; Water well drilling

(G-12195)
VERHOFF ALFALFA MILLS INC (PA)
Also Called: Alfa Green Supreme
1188 Sugar Mill Dr (45875-8518)
PHONE..............................419 523-4767
Scott Verhoff, *Pr*
Donald Verhoff, *Pt*
Judith Fullenkamp, *Sec*
Darwin Verhoff, *VP*
▼ **EMP:** 7 **EST:** 1940
SQ FT: 500
SALES (est): 802.96K
SALES (corp-wide): 802.96K **Privately Held**
Web: www.alfagreensupreme.com
SIC: 0723 2048 Crop preparation services for market; Alfalfa or alfalfa meal, prepared as animal feed

(G-12196)
WARREN PRINTING & OFF PDTS INC
250 E Main St (45875-1944)
P.O. Box 229 (45875-0229)
PHONE..............................419 523-3635
Robert E Warren Junior, *Pr*
EMP: 10 **EST:** 1966
SALES (est): 972.38K **Privately Held**
Web: www.warrenprint.com
SIC: 2752 2759 5943 2679 Offset printing; Flexographic printing; Office forms and supplies; Tags and labels, paper

Ottoville
Putnam County

(G-12197)
ACME MACHINE AUTOMATICS INC
Also Called: Global Precision Parts
111 Progressive Dr (45876)
P.O. Box 579 (45876-0579)
PHONE..............................419 453-0010
Randy Mueller, *Pr*
▲ **EMP:** 20 **EST:** 1993
SQ FT: 62,500
SALES (est): 8.3MM **Privately Held**
Web: www.globalprecisionpartsinc.com
SIC: 3451 3484 Screw machine products; Small arms
PA: Kriegel Holding Company, Inc.
7600 Us Route 127
Van Wert OH 45891

(G-12198)
CREATIVE EDGE CBNETS WDWKG LLC
188 Nw Canal St (45876-8743)
P.O. Box 330 (45876-0330)
PHONE..............................419 453-3416
Craig Brinkman, *Managing Member*
EMP: 6 **EST:** 2014
SALES (est): 422.73K **Privately Held**
Web: www.creativeedgecabinets.com
SIC: 2434 Wood kitchen cabinets

(G-12199)
H & M MACHINE SHOP INC
290 State Route 189 (45876-8802)
P.O. Box 207 (45876-0207)
PHONE..............................419 453-3414
Todd Horstman, *Pr*
Diane Horstman, *VP*
Roger A Horstman, *Sec*
EMP: 16 **EST:** 1975
SQ FT: 50,000
SALES (est): 2.45MM **Privately Held**
Web: www.hmmachineshop.com
SIC: 3599 Machine shop, jobbing and repair

(G-12200)
J L WANNEMACHER SLS SVC INC
26992 Us 224 W (45876)
P.O. Box 265 (45876-0265)
PHONE..............................419 453-3445
James P Wannemacher, *Pr*
Lisa Wannemacher, *VP*
Ruth Wannemacher, *Sec*
EMP: 13 **EST:** 1867
SQ FT: 10,000
SALES (est): 2.38MM **Privately Held**
SIC: 5083 7699 2452 Farm and garden machinery; Farm machinery repair; Modular homes, prefabricated, wood

(G-12201)
M & W TRAILERS INC
525 East Main St (45876)
P.O. Box 519 (45876-0519)
PHONE..............................419 453-3331
Kenneth Markward, *Pr*
Thomas Markward, *VP*
Scott Markward, *Sec*
Elenor Wannemacher, *Prin*
Elmer A Markward, *Prin*
EMP: 10 **EST:** 1956
SQ FT: 10,000
SALES (est): 833.76K **Privately Held**
Web: www.mandwtrailersohio.com
SIC: 7539 3715 5012 7538 Trailer repair; Truck trailers; Trailers for trucks, new and used; General truck repair

(G-12202)
MILLER PRECISION MANUFACTURING INDUSTRIES INC
131 Progressive Dr (45876)
P.O. Box 489 (45876-0489)
PHONE..............................419 453-3251
EMP: 100 **EST:** 1988
SALES (est): 17.03MM **Privately Held**
Web: www.millerprecision.com
SIC: 3599 Machine shop, jobbing and repair

(G-12203)
PROGRESSIVE STAMPING INC
200 Progressive Dr (45876)
P.O. Box 549 (45876-0549)
PHONE..............................419 453-1111
Lloyd Miller, *Pr*
◆ **EMP:** 250 **EST:** 1999
SALES (est): 46.06MM **Privately Held**
Web: www.midwayproducts.com
SIC: 3469 Metal stampings, nec
PA: Midway Products Group, Inc.
1 Lyman E Hoyt Dr
Monroe MI 48161

(G-12204)
SCHNIPKE ENGRAVING CO INC (PA)
14223 Rd 24 (45876)
P.O. Box 278 (45876-0278)
PHONE..............................419 453-3376
EMP: 155 **EST:** 1962
SALES (est): 43.59MM
SALES (corp-wide): 43.59MM **Privately Held**

Web: www.schnipke.com
SIC: **3089** 3544 3479 Injection molding of plastics; Special dies, tools, jigs, and fixtures; Etching and engraving

Otway
Scioto County

(G-12205)
BLANKENSHIP LOGGING LLC
433 Curtis Smith Rd (45657-8936)
PHONE.................................740 372-3833
EMP: 6 EST: 2000
SALES (est): 400K **Privately Held**
SIC: **2411** Logging camps and contractors

(G-12206)
COX WOOD PRODUCT INC
5715 State Route 348 (45657-9231)
PHONE.................................740 372-4735
Shelby Kratzer, *Pr*
Eric Kratzer, *VP*
EMP: 10 EST: 1950
SALES (est): 492.55K **Privately Held**
SIC: **2448** 5211 Pallets, wood; Planing mill products and lumber

(G-12207)
POWELL LOGGING
7593 State Route 348 (45657-9078)
PHONE.................................740 372-6131
Russell Powell, *Prin*
EMP: 7 EST: 2008
SALES (est): 177.73K **Privately Held**
SIC: **2411** Logging

Overpeck
Butler County

(G-12208)
MIAMI ICE MACHINE INC
4251 Riverside Dr (45055)
P.O. Box 145 (45055-0145)
PHONE.................................513 863-6707
EMP: 9 EST: 2019
SALES (est): 330.11K **Privately Held**
Web: www.miamimachine.com
SIC: **3541** Milling machines

(G-12209)
MIAMI MACHINE CORPORATION
4251 Riverside Dr (45055)
P.O. Box 145 (45055-0145)
PHONE.................................513 863-6707
▲ EMP: 17
Web: www.miamimachine.com
SIC: **3554** Paper mill machinery: plating, slitting, waxing, etc.

Oxford
Butler County

(G-12210)
LETTERMAN PRINTING INC
316 S College Ave (45056-2225)
PHONE.................................513 523-1111
Jon C Rupel, *Pr*
Rhonda Rupel, *Sec*
EMP: 8 EST: 1991
SQ FT: 1,500
SALES (est): 582.63K **Privately Held**
Web: www.oxfordcopy.com
SIC: **2752** 2759 Offset printing; Commercial printing, nec

(G-12211)
MOONSHINE SCREEN PRINTING INC
23 N College Ave (45056-1108)
PHONE.................................513 523-7775
John Brosier, *Pr*
EMP: 8 EST: 1982
SQ FT: 7,500
SALES (est): 237.02K **Privately Held**
Web: www.moonshineprinting.com
SIC: **2759** 3993 Screen printing; Neon signs

(G-12212)
RELEVIUM LABS INC (PA)
4663 Katie Ln Ste O (45056-9525)
P.O. Box 800 (45056-0800)
PHONE.................................614 568-7000
Brent Reider, *Pr*
EMP: 7 EST: 2015
SALES (est): 241.28K
SALES (corp-wide): 241.28K **Privately Held**
Web: www.yarlap.com
SIC: **5047** 5999 3845 Electro-medical equipment; Medical apparatus and supplies ; Electromedical apparatus

(G-12213)
SCHNEIDER ELECTRIC USA INC
Also Called: Schneider Electric
5735 College Corner Pike (45056-9715)
PHONE.................................513 523-4171
Thomsa Mcdonald, *Brnch Mgr*
EMP: 500
SALES (corp-wide): 82.05K **Privately Held**
Web: www.se.com
SIC: **3699** 3677 3612 3357 Electrical equipment and supplies, nec; Electronic coils and transformers; Transformers, except electric; Nonferrous wiredrawing and insulating
HQ: Schneider Electric Usa, Inc.
    One Boston Pl Ste 2700
    Boston MA 02108
    978 975-9600

(G-12214)
WILD BERRY INCENSE INC
Also Called: Wild Berry Incense Factory
5475 College Corner Pike (45056-1010)
PHONE.................................513 523-8583
Mark Biales, *Pr*
Roger Atkin, *VP*
▲ EMP: 19 EST: 1992
SQ FT: 20,000
SALES (est): 3.32MM **Privately Held**
Web: www.wild-berry.com
SIC: **2899** 5947 Incense; Novelties

Painesville
Lake County

(G-12215)
ACCURATE METAL MACHINING INC
Also Called: Accurate
882 Callendar Blvd (44077-1218)
PHONE.................................440 350-8225
John Racic, *Pr*
Eva Szantho, *
Gabriel Loiczly, *
Thomas Loiczly, *
EMP: 250 EST: 1976
SQ FT: 15,000
SALES (est): 47.77MM **Publicly Held**
Web: www.accuratemetalmachining.com
SIC: **3599** Machine shop, jobbing and repair
HQ: Heico Flight Support Corp.
    3000 Taft St
    Hollywood FL 33021
    954 987-4000

(G-12216)
ATRA METAL SPINNING INC
572 S Saint Clair St (44077-3637)
P.O. Box 731 (44077-0731)
PHONE.................................440 354-9525
Carl Dixon, *Pr*
Greg Shirk, *VP*
James Dixon, *Sec*
EMP: 10 EST: 1981
SQ FT: 22,000
SALES (est): 963.94K **Privately Held**
SIC: **3469** Stamping metal for the trade

(G-12217)
AVERY DENNISON CORPORATION
670 Hardy Rd (44077-4573)
PHONE.................................440 358-3466
Linda E Chandler, *Brnch Mgr*
EMP: 152
SALES (corp-wide): 8.36B **Publicly Held**
Web: www.averydennison.com
SIC: **2672** Paper; coated and laminated, nec
PA: Avery Dennison Corporation
    8080 Norton Pkwy
    Mentor OH 44060
    440 534-6000

(G-12218)
AVERY DENNISON CORPORATION
Avery Dennison - Pff
250 Chester St Bldg 3 (44077-4129)
PHONE.................................440 358-2564
Rick Olszewski, *Brnch Mgr*
EMP: 300
SALES (corp-wide): 8.36B **Publicly Held**
Web: www.averydennison.com
SIC: **2672** 2891 Adhesive papers, labels, or tapes: from purchased material; Adhesives and sealants
PA: Avery Dennison Corporation
    8080 Norton Pkwy
    Mentor OH 44060
    440 534-6000

(G-12219)
BRUCE HIGH PERFORMANCE TRAN
1 High Tech Ave (44077-3701)
PHONE.................................440 357-8964
Laurie Dibiase, *Prin*
EMP: 14 EST: 2013
SALES (est): 4.99MM **Privately Held**
Web: www.brucetransporters.com
SIC: **3715** Truck trailers

(G-12220)
C DL SERVICES LLC
831 Callendar Blvd (44077-1218)
PHONE.................................440 354-1433
Kelly Hotchkiss, *Prin*
EMP: 6 EST: 2010
SALES (est): 88.88K **Privately Held**
SIC: **3679** Electronic circuits

(G-12221)
CASCADE UNLIMITED LLC
2510 Hale Rd (44077-4926)
PHONE.................................440 352-7995
EMP: 6 EST: 2016
SALES (est): 492.82K **Privately Held**
Web: www.cascadeunlimited.com
SIC: **3599** Machine shop, jobbing and repair

(G-12222)
CASHEN READY MIX
225 W Prospect St (44077-3257)
PHONE.................................440 354-3227
EMP: 6 EST: 2019
SALES (est): 264.3K **Privately Held**
Web: www.cashenreadymix.com

SIC: **3273** Ready-mixed concrete

(G-12223)
CONCORD ROAD EQUIPMENT MFG INC
348 Chester St (44077-4154)
P.O. Box 772 (44077-0772)
PHONE.................................440 357-5344
Glen Warfield, *Pr*
Jeffrey Warfield, *
EMP: 31 EST: 1975
SALES (est): 4.77MM **Privately Held**
Web: www.concordroadequipment.com
SIC: **3531** Road construction and maintenance machinery

(G-12224)
CONNECTORS UNLIMITED INC (PA)
1359 W Jackson St (44077-1341)
PHONE.................................440 357-1161
Martin Ignasiak, *Pr*
Don Barber, *Sec*
Ralph Victor, *Treas*
▲ EMP: 22 EST: 1997
SALES (est): 2.46MM
SALES (corp-wide): 2.46MM **Privately Held**
Web: my.connectorsunlimited.com
SIC: **3357** 3678 Nonferrous wiredrawing and insulating; Electronic connectors

(G-12225)
CUSTOM DESIGN CABINETS & TOPS
Also Called: Custom Design Kitchen & Bath
379 Fountain Ave (44077-1209)
PHONE.................................440 639-9900
George Lehtonen, *Pr*
Kaarina Lehtonen, *VP*
EMP: 8
SQ FT: 11,000
SALES (est): 910.04K **Privately Held**
SIC: **5031** 2541 Kitchen cabinets; Cabinets, except refrigerated: show, display, etc.: wood

(G-12226)
DE NORA NORTH AMERICA INC
7590 Discovery Ln (44077)
PHONE.................................440 357-4000
Lucieno Iacopepti, *CEO*
▲ EMP: 32 EST: 1998
SQ FT: 70,000
SALES (est): 1.58MM
SALES (corp-wide): 885.74MM **Privately Held**
SIC: **3589** Water treatment equipment, industrial
HQ: Oronzio De Nora International B.V.
    Basisweg 10
    Amsterdam NH 1043
    205214777

(G-12227)
DE NORA TECH LLC
Also Called: Warehouse
7661 Crile Rdunit 1 Bldg 2 (44077)
PHONE.................................440 285-0368
Karen Farinatzi, *Superintnt*
EMP: 7
SALES (corp-wide): 885.74MM **Privately Held**
Web: business.painesvilleohchamber.org
SIC: **3589** Water treatment equipment, industrial
HQ: De Nora Tech, Llc
    7590 Discovery Ln
    Concord Township OH 44077
    440 710-5334

(G-12228)
DESIGNER CNTEMPORARY LAMINATES
1700 Sheffield Ter (44077-4765)
PHONE..................................440 946-8207
Robert Krauss, *Pr*
EMP: 8 **EST:** 1985
SALES (est): 795.1K **Privately Held**
Web: www.dclweb.net
SIC: 3083 2541 Plastics finished products, laminated; Cabinets, except refrigerated: show, display, etc.: wood

(G-12229)
DUKES AEROSPACE INC
Also Called: Aero Fluid Products
313 Gillett St (44077-2918)
PHONE..................................818 998-9811
EMP: 79 **EST:** 2009
SALES (est): 19.92MM
SALES (corp-wide): 6.58B **Publicly Held**
Web: www.aerofluidproducts.com
SIC: 3728 Aircraft parts and equipment, nec
HQ: Transdigm, Inc.
   1350 Euclid Ave
   Cleveland OH 44115

(G-12230)
DYNA-FLEX INC
1000 Bacon Rd (44077-4637)
PHONE..................................440 946-9424
▲ **EMP:** 10 **EST:** 1995
SALES (est): 1MM **Privately Held**
Web: www.dynaflexinc.com
SIC: 3492 Hose and tube couplings, hydraulic/pneumatic

(G-12231)
ECKART AMERICA CORPORATION (DH)
Also Called: Eckart Aluminum
830 E Erie St (44077-4453)
P.O. Box 747 (44077-0747)
PHONE..................................440 954-7600
Anthony J Ameo Junior, *Pr*
Thomas Meola, *
◆ **EMP:** 100 **EST:** 1997
SALES (est): 124.14MM
SALES (corp-wide): 4.22B **Privately Held**
Web: www.eckart.net
SIC: 3399 2893 2816 Powder, metal; Printing ink; Inorganic pigments
HQ: Eckart Beteiligungs Gmbh
   Guntersthal 4
   Hartenstein BY 91235
   9152770

(G-12232)
ELEMENT 41 INC
1932 Pinewood Ln (44077-6148)
PHONE..................................440 579-5531
EMP: 15
SALES (corp-wide): 932.76K **Privately Held**
Web: www.element41chardon.com
SIC: 2819 Elements
PA: Element 41 Inc
   141 Main St
   Chardon OH 44024
   216 410-5646

(G-12233)
EVOLVE SOLUTIONS LLC
1 High Tech Ave (44077-3701)
PHONE..................................440 357-8964
EMP: 25 **EST:** 2019
SALES (est): 3.05MM **Privately Held**
SIC: 3312 Plate, steel

(G-12234)
EXECUTIVE WINGS INC
13550 Carter Rd (44077-9171)
PHONE..................................440 254-1812
Michael Toman, *Owner*
EMP: 8 **EST:** 2001
SALES (est): 502.76K **Privately Held**
SIC: 3721 Aircraft

(G-12235)
EXTRUDEX LIMITED PARTNERSHIP (PA)
Also Called: Extrudex
310 Figgie Dr (44077-3028)
PHONE..................................440 352-7101
George Humphrey, *Genl Pt*
George Humphrey, *Pr*
Tod Oliva, *Pt*
EMP: 27 **EST:** 1980
SQ FT: 27,120
SALES (est): 5.92MM **Privately Held**
Web: www.extrudex.net
SIC: 3089 3524 3431 Extruded finished plastics products, nec; Lawn and garden equipment; Metal sanitary ware

(G-12236)
FARETEC INC
1610 W Jackson St Unit 6 (44077-1388)
PHONE..................................440 350-9510
Tod C R Sackett, *Pr*
George Sackett, *Sec*
Constance Sackett, *Treas*
▲ **EMP:** 10 **EST:** 1991
SQ FT: 7,000
SALES (est): 991.9K **Privately Held**
Web: www.faretec.com
SIC: 3842 5047 Braces, orthopedic; Medical equipment and supplies

(G-12237)
FIRST FRANCIS COMPANY INC (HQ)
Also Called: Federal Hose Manufacturing
25 Florence Ave (44077-1103)
PHONE..................................440 352-8927
Ron George, *Pr*
EMP: 25 **EST:** 1997
SALES (est): 9.55MM
SALES (corp-wide): 143.89MM **Publicly Held**
Web: www.federalhose.com
SIC: 5085 3599 3444 3429 Hose, belting, and packing; Hose, flexible metallic; Sheet metalwork; Hardware, nec
PA: Crawford United Corporation
   10514 Dupont Ave
   Cleveland OH 44108
   216 541-8060

(G-12238)
FJR INDUSTRIES INC
5436 Stoney Ln (44077-9021)
PHONE..................................859 277-8207
John Hartman, *Owner*
EMP: 6 **EST:** 2009
SALES (est): 77.25K **Privately Held**
Web: www.yesterdayoutdoors.com
SIC: 3949 Sporting and athletic goods, nec

(G-12239)
GENESIS LAMP CORP
375 N Saint Clair St (44077-4053)
PHONE..................................440 354-0095
Edward C Zukowski, *Pr*
Margaret Zukowski, *Sec*
Donna Williams, *Sec*
▲ **EMP:** 15 **EST:** 1979
SQ FT: 6,400
SALES (est): 2.53MM **Privately Held**
Web: www.genesislamp.com

SIC: 3646 3648 Commercial lighting fixtures; Lighting equipment, nec

(G-12240)
GRAND-ROCK COMPANY INC
395 Fountain Ave (44077-1209)
PHONE..................................440 639-2000
William H Stoneman, *Pr*
Gerard Arth, *
▲ **EMP:** 50 **EST:** 1972
SQ FT: 52,000
SALES (est): 10.53MM **Privately Held**
Web: www.grandrock.com
SIC: 3714 3621 2531 Motor vehicle parts and accessories; Motors and generators; Public building and related furniture

(G-12241)
GREAT LAKES GLASSWERKS INC
360 W Prospect St (44077-3258)
PHONE..................................440 358-0460
Richard Chaykowsky, *Pr*
Julie Patterson, *VP*
John Wolfe, *Sec*
▲ **EMP:** 7 **EST:** 1997
SQ FT: 10,000
SALES (est): 768.94K **Privately Held**
Web: www.quartzsupply.com
SIC: 3679 Electronic circuits

(G-12242)
GUYER PRECISION INC
280 W Prospect St (44077-3256)
PHONE..................................440 354-8024
Thomas Guyer, *Pr*
EMP: 11 **EST:** 1997
SQ FT: 12,500
SALES (est): 2.39MM **Privately Held**
Web: www.guyerprecision.com
SIC: 3599 Machine shop, jobbing and repair

(G-12243)
HARDY INDUSTRIAL TECH LLC
Also Called: H I T
679 Hardy Rd (44077-4574)
PHONE..................................440 350-6300
Eric Lofquist, *CEO*
Scott Forster, *
▲ **EMP:** 71 **EST:** 2002
SALES (est): 23.27MM
SALES (corp-wide): 23.47MM **Privately Held**
SIC: 2869 Fuels
PA: Magnus International Group, Inc.
   679 Hardy Rd
   Painesville OH 44077
   216 592-8355

(G-12244)
HEALTH SENSE INC
Also Called: Healthsense
433 S State St (44077-3533)
PHONE..................................440 354-8057
Stephen Musgrave, *Pr*
EMP: 8 **EST:** 1982
SQ FT: 2,500
SALES (est): 141.94K **Privately Held**
SIC: 8299 8742 2711 Educational services; Hospital and health services consultant; Newspapers: publishing only, not printed on site

(G-12245)
HIGH TECH PRFMCE TRLRS INC
1 High Tech Ave (44077-3701)
PHONE..................................440 357-8964
Bruce C Hanusosky, *Pr*
Judy Hanusosky, *
Caity Hanusosky, *
Steve Lewis, *
Adam Olenchick, *

EMP: 72 **EST:** 1982
SQ FT: 84,000
SALES (est): 4MM **Privately Held**
Web: www.hightechtrailers.com
SIC: 3715 Truck trailers

(G-12246)
IMAX INDUSTRIES INC
117 W Walnut Ave (44077-2925)
PHONE..................................440 639-0242
Mike Miller, *Pr*
EMP: 10 **EST:** 1994
SALES (est): 2.2MM **Privately Held**
Web: www.imaxindustries.com
SIC: 8711 3548 Engineering services; Welding apparatus

(G-12247)
LBL LITHOGRAPHERS INC (PA)
Also Called: L B L Printing
365 W Prospect St (44077-3259)
PHONE..................................440 350-0106
Lawrence Gidley, *CEO*
Brian Gidley, *Pr*
Lois Gidley, *Sec*
EMP: 7 **EST:** 1975
SQ FT: 4,500
SALES (est): 2.1MM
SALES (corp-wide): 2.1MM **Privately Held**
Web: www.lblprinting.com
SIC: 2752 Offset printing

(G-12248)
MAGNUS INTERNATIONAL GROUP INC (PA)
679 Hardy Rd (44077-4574)
PHONE..................................216 592-8355
Eric Lofquist, *Prin*
Theresa M Paicic, *Pr*
Scott Forster, *VP*
John Malloy, *CFO*
Sharon Stefan, *Contrlr*
▲ **EMP:** 8 **EST:** 2007
SALES (est): 23.47MM
SALES (corp-wide): 23.47MM **Privately Held**
Web: www.magnusig.com
SIC: 4953 2048 2992 Recycling, waste materials; Prepared feeds, nec; Rust arresting compounds, animal or vegetable oil base

(G-12249)
MANUVIS CORP
1 Victoria Pl Ste 309 (44077-3482)
PHONE..................................440 352-6261
EMP: 6 **EST:** 2004
SALES (est): 116.06K **Privately Held**
Web: galaxy3.manuvis.com
SIC: 7372 Prepackaged software

(G-12250)
MATPLUS LTD
Also Called: Matplus
76 Burton St (44077-3011)
PHONE..................................440 352-7201
Jeffrey M Bednar, *Pr*
▲ **EMP:** 8 **EST:** 2004
SALES (est): 1.46MM **Privately Held**
Web: www.matplusinc.com
SIC: 3842 Orthopedic appliances

(G-12251)
MCNEIL INDUSTRIES INC
835 Richmond Rd Ste 2 (44077-1143)
PHONE..................................440 951-7756
Randall J Mcneil, *Pr*
▲ **EMP:** 30 **EST:** 1986
SQ FT: 18,000
SALES (est): 5.02MM **Privately Held**
Web: www.mcneilindustries.com

GEOGRAPHIC SECTION

Painesville - Lake County (G-12272)

SIC: **3366** 5085 Bushings and bearings; Seals, industrial

(G-12252)
OBRON ATLANTIC CORPORATION
Also Called: Eckart America
830 E Erie St (44077-4453)
P.O. Box 747 (44077-0747)
PHONE..................................440 954-7600
Anthony Ameo, *Pr*
Mark Wallace, *
EMP: 72 **EST:** 1912
SALES (est): 3.74MM
SALES (corp-wide): 4.22B Privately Held
SIC: **2816** 3399 Metallic and mineral pigments, nec; Powder, metal
HQ: Eckart America Corporation
830 E Erie St
Painesville OH 44077
440 954-7600

(G-12253)
OHIO ASSOCIATED ENTPS LLC
Also Called: Meritech
72 Corwin Dr (44077-1802)
PHONE..................................440 354-3148
John T Venaleck, *Brnch Mgr*
EMP: 17
SALES (corp-wide): 77.3MM Privately Held
Web: www.meritec.com
SIC: **3678** 3544 3469 3357 Electronic connectors; Special dies, tools, jigs, and fixtures; Metal stampings, nec; Communication wire
PA: Ohio Associated Enterprises Llc
97 Corwin Dr
Painesville OH 44077
440 354-2106

(G-12254)
OHIO ASSOCIATED ENTPS LLC
Also Called: Omnitec
1359 W Jackson St (44077-1341)
P.O. Box 110 (44077-0110)
PHONE..................................440 354-3148
James T Walch, *Brnch Mgr*
EMP: 34
SQ FT: 25,000
SALES (corp-wide): 77.3MM Privately Held
Web: www.meritec.com
SIC: **3643** Electric connectors
PA: Ohio Associated Enterprises Llc
97 Corwin Dr
Painesville OH 44077
440 354-2106

(G-12255)
PATH TECHNOLOGIES INC
437 W Prospect St (44077-3269)
PHONE..................................440 358-1500
David Princic, *Pr*
Mike Princic, *Stockholder*
Dorothy Princic, *Stockholder*
Barbara Sespico, *Stockholder*
EMP: 8 **EST:** 1986
SQ FT: 7,000
SALES (est): 894.62K Privately Held
Web: www.path-tech.com
SIC: **3599** Machine shop, jobbing and repair

(G-12256)
PCC AIRFOILS LLC
Also Called: PCC AIRFOILS LLC
870 Renaissance Pkwy (44077-1287)
PHONE..................................440 350-6150
EMP: 81
SALES (corp-wide): 364.48B Publicly Held
Web: www.pccairfoils.com

SIC: **3369** Nonferrous foundries, nec
HQ: Pcc Airfoils, Llc
3401 Entp Pkwy Ste 200
Cleveland OH 44122
216 831-3590

(G-12257)
PET PROCESSORS LLC
1350 Bacon Rd (44077-4781)
PHONE..................................440 354-4321
Gary Laughlin, *Dir*
▲ **EMP:** 77 **EST:** 1986
SQ FT: 350,000
SALES (est): 18.21MM Privately Held
Web: www.petus.com
SIC: **2821** Polyesters
PA: Diefenthal Holdings, Llc
1750 South Ln Ste 1
Mandeville LA 70471

(G-12258)
PRECISION CASTPARTS CORP
Also Called: PCC
870 Renaissance Pkwy (44077-1287)
PHONE..................................440 350-6150
EMP: 17
SALES (corp-wide): 364.48B Publicly Held
Web: www.precast.com
SIC: **3324** 3369 3724 3511 Steel investment foundries; Nonferrous foundries, nec; Aircraft engines and engine parts; Turbines and turbine generator sets
HQ: Precision Castparts Corp.
5885 Meadows Rd Ste 620
Lake Oswego OR 97035
503 946-4800

(G-12259)
QNNECT LLC (PA) ✪
1382 W Jackson St (44077-1306)
PHONE..................................864 275-8970
Kevin Perhamus, *Managing Member*
EMP: 12 **EST:** 2022
SALES (est): 6.93MM
SALES (corp-wide): 6.93MM Privately Held
Web: www.qnnectnow.com
SIC: **3678** Electronic connectors

(G-12260)
R W SIDLEY INCORPORATED (PA)
Also Called: R. W. Sidley
436 Casement Ave (44077-3817)
P.O. Box 150 (44077-0150)
PHONE..................................440 352-9343
Robert C Sidley, *Ch Bd*
Robert J Buescher, *
Dan Kennedy, *
Kevin Campany, *
Iola Black, *
▲ **EMP:** 30 **EST:** 1933
SQ FT: 10,000
SALES (est): 83.57MM
SALES (corp-wide): 83.57MM Privately Held
Web: www.rwsidley.com
SIC: **1771** 3299 Concrete work; Blocks and brick, sand lime

(G-12261)
R W SIDLEY INCORPORATED
Mining & Materials Division
436 Casement Ave (44077-3817)
P.O. Box 150 (44077-0150)
PHONE..................................440 352-9343
Bob Buscher, *Pr*
EMP: 10
SALES (corp-wide): 83.57MM Privately Held
Web: www.rwsidley.com

SIC: **1422** Cement rock, crushed and broken-quarrying
PA: R. W. Sidley Incorporated
436 Casement Ave
Painesville OH 44077
440 352-9343

(G-12262)
ROPAMA INC
Also Called: Roco Industries
380 W Prospect St (44077-3258)
PHONE..................................440 358-1304
Ron Mahoney, *Pr*
Pat Mahoney, *VP*
EMP: 10 **EST:** 1986
SALES (est): 430.39K Privately Held
Web: www.roco.com
SIC: **3398** Metal heat treating

(G-12263)
RUFF NEON & LIGHTING MAINT INC
295 W Prospect St (44077-3257)
PHONE..................................440 350-6267
Thomas A Ruff, *Pr*
EMP: 10 **EST:** 1991
SALES (est): 2.37MM Privately Held
Web: www.ruffneonsign.com
SIC: **3993** Neon signs

(G-12264)
STAFAST PRODUCTS INC (PA)
Also Called: Stafast West
505 Lakeshore Blvd (44077-1197)
PHONE..................................440 357-5546
Donald S Selle, *Pr*
Joan Selle, *
Stephen Selle, *
Christian Selle, *
Daniel Selle, *
◆ **EMP:** 40 **EST:** 1958
SQ FT: 20,600
SALES (est): 24.8MM
SALES (corp-wide): 24.8MM Privately Held
Web: shop.stafast.com
SIC: **5085** 3452 Fasteners, industrial: nuts, bolts, screws, etc.; Bolts, nuts, rivets, and washers

(G-12265)
T&T MACHINE INC
892 Callendar Blvd (44077-1218)
PHONE..................................440 354-0605
Tony Padovic, *Pr*
Dan Padovic, *VP*
EMP: 14 **EST:** 1993
SQ FT: 13,000
SALES (est): 3.03MM
SALES (corp-wide): 3.03MM Privately Held
Web: www.tandtmachineinc.com
SIC: **3599** Machine shop, jobbing and repair
PA: Precision Manufacturing Enterprise, Llc
3645 Sw 4th St
Miami FL

(G-12266)
TASYD INDUSTRIES LLC
466 W Jackson St (44077-3148)
PHONE..................................440 352-8019
EMP: 6 **EST:** 2000
SALES (est): 8.75MM Privately Held
SIC: **3999** Manufacturing industries, nec

(G-12267)
TECHNICAL GLASS PRODUCTS INC (PA)
881 Callendar Blvd (44077)
PHONE..................................440 639-6399
Jim Horvath, *Pr*
Robert Singer, *VP*

Halle Ricciardo, *Sec*
▲ **EMP:** 12 **EST:** 1990
SQ FT: 10,500
SALES (est): 2.23MM Privately Held
Web: www.technicalglass.com
SIC: **3229** Pressed and blown glass, nec

(G-12268)
TEKRAFT INDUSTRIES INC
244 Latimore St (44077-3903)
PHONE..................................440 352-8321
Terrence Tekavec, *Pr*
Victor Tekavec, *Stockholder*
EMP: 8 **EST:** 1988
SQ FT: 3,500
SALES (est): 778.8K Privately Held
SIC: **3599** Machine shop, jobbing and repair

(G-12269)
TESSA PRECISION PRODUCT INC
850 Callendar Blvd (44077-1218)
PHONE..................................440 392-3470
Paul Battaglia, *Pr*
Erika Battaglia, *
EMP: 50 **EST:** 1981
SQ FT: 25,000
SALES (est): 9.82MM Privately Held
Web: www.tessaprecision.com
SIC: **3599** 3545 Machine shop, jobbing and repair; Precision tools, machinists'

(G-12270)
THE LUBRIZOL CORPORATION
Also Called: Lubrizol Production Plant
155 Freedom Rd (44077-1234)
PHONE..................................440 357-7064
Tanya Travis, *Mgr*
EMP: 127
SQ FT: 1,524
SALES (corp-wide): 364.48B Publicly Held
Web: www.lubrizol.com
SIC: **2899** 2992 Chemical preparations, nec; Rust arresting compounds, animal or vegetable oil base
HQ: The Lubrizol Corporation
29400 Lakeland Blvd
Wickliffe OH 44092
440 943-4200

(G-12271)
THIRION BROTHERS EQP CO LLC
Also Called: Tbec
340 W Prospect St (44077-3258)
P.O. Box 1392 (44077-7317)
PHONE..................................440 357-8004
EMP: 6 **EST:** 2005
SQ FT: 1,015
SALES (est): 374.47K Privately Held
SIC: **3694** 7699 5082 Distributors, motor vehicle engine; Pumps and pumping equipment repair; General construction machinery and equipment

(G-12272)
TRANSDIGM INC
Aero Fluid Products
313 Gillett St (44077-2918)
PHONE..................................440 352-6182
Jennifer Griffin Managing, *Brnch Mgr*
EMP: 39
SALES (corp-wide): 6.58B Publicly Held
Web: www.transdigm.com
SIC: **3561** Pumps and pumping equipment
HQ: Transdigm, Inc.
1350 Euclid Ave
Cleveland OH 44115

(PA)=Parent Co (HQ)=Headquarters
✪ = New Business established in last 2 years

Painesville - Lake County (G-12273)

(G-12273)
TWIN RVERS TECH - PNSVILLE LLC
Also Called: Twin Rivers Technologies Mfg
679 Hardy Rd (44077-4574)
PHONE..................440 350-6300
Paul J Angelico, *Managing Member*
EMP: 21 **EST:** 2003
SALES (est): 1.25MM **Privately Held**
SIC: 2869 Industrial organic chemicals, nec

(G-12274)
VERSITEC MANUFACTURING INC
152 Elevator Ave (44077-3610)
PHONE..................440 354-4283
Royce Reinhart, *Pr*
Mark Neal, *VP*
EMP: 25 **EST:** 2000
SQ FT: 3,600
SALES (est): 747.86K **Privately Held**
Web: www.versitecinc.com
SIC: 3672 Printed circuit boards

(G-12275)
VISION PRESS INC
1634 W Jackson St (44077-1312)
P.O. Box 1308 (44077-8308)
PHONE..................440 357-6362
EMP: 6 **EST:** 1995
SALES (est): 750K **Privately Held**
Web: www.provisionimpressions.com
SIC: 2752 Offset printing

(G-12276)
WAYS CSTM WLDG & FABRICATION
1580 N Ridge Rd (44077-4423)
PHONE..................440 354-1350
EMP: 7 **EST:** 2019
SALES (est): 448.13K **Privately Held**
SIC: 7692 Welding repair

(G-12277)
WESTERN RESERVE LUBRICANTS
13981 Leroy Center Rd (44077-9782)
PHONE..................440 951-5700
EMP: 7 **EST:** 2008
SALES (est): 176.77K **Privately Held**
SIC: 2992 Lubricating oils

(G-12278)
WMG WOOD MORE
51 Johnnycake Ridge Rd (44077-2420)
PHONE..................440 350-3970
William Gubanyar, *Mgr*
EMP: 7 **EST:** 2018
SALES (est): 161.52K **Privately Held**
Web: www.wmgwood.com
SIC: 5211 2499 Lumber and other building materials; Wood products, nec

(G-12279)
XPONET INC
Also Called: Mold Tech
20 Elberta Rd (44077-1231)
PHONE..................440 354-6617
Ralph Victor, *Ch Bd*
Don Barber, *
EMP: 36 **EST:** 1984
SQ FT: 25,000
SALES (est): 829.53K **Privately Held**
Web: www.moldtech.com
SIC: 3357 3678 3643 3577 Communication wire; Electronic connectors; Current-carrying wiring services; Computer peripheral equipment, nec

(G-12280)
YOKOHAMA INDS AMRICAS OHIO INC
474 Newell St (44077-1254)
P.O. Box 1370 (44077-7309)
PHONE..................440 352-3321
Yosahisa Makabayopshi, *Pr*
Don Patt, *
Larry Tremaglio, *
▲ **EMP:** 92 **EST:** 1937
SQ FT: 132,000
SALES (est): 27.44MM **Privately Held**
Web: www.yokohamaiaohio.com
SIC: 3069 Molded rubber products
HQ: Yokohama Corporation Of North America
1 Macarthur Pl
Santa Ana CA 92707

(G-12281)
YOKOHAMA TIRE CORPORATION
Also Called: S A S Rubber
474 Newell St (44077-1254)
PHONE..................440 352-3321
Donald A Patt, *Prin*
EMP: 89
SQ FT: 50,000
Web: www.y-yokohama.com
SIC: 3061 Mechanical rubber goods
PA: Yokohama Rubber Company, Limited, The
2-1, Oiwake
Hiratsuka KNG 254-0

Paris
Stark County

(G-12282)
STALLION OILFIELD CNSTR LLC
3361 Baird Ave Se (44669-9769)
PHONE..................330 868-2083
Chrysta Dansby, *Brnch Mgr*
EMP: 54
Web: www.stallionis.com
SIC: 1389 Oil field services, nec
PA: Stallion Oilfield Construction, Llc
950 Corbindale Rd Ste 400
Houston TX 77024

Parkman
Geauga County

(G-12283)
CNC PRECISION MACHINE INC
18360 Industrial Cir (44080)
P.O. Box 739 (44080)
PHONE..................440 548-3880
Alex Szkoe, *Pr*
EMP: 63 **EST:** 2003
SALES (est): 8.08MM **Privately Held**
Web: www.cncprecisionmachineinc.com
SIC: 3599 Machine shop, jobbing and repair

(G-12284)
MONTVILLE PLASTICS & RBR LLC
Also Called: Iron Horse Engineering
15567 Main Market Rd (44080)
P.O. Box 527 (44080)
PHONE..................440 548-2005
Jay Roberts, *Managing Member*
Tracie Roberts, *
EMP: 55 **EST:** 2014
SQ FT: 50,000
SALES (est): 8.89MM **Privately Held**
Web: www.montvilleplastics.com
SIC: 3089 Injection molding of plastics

(G-12285)
MONTVILLE PLASTICS & RUBBER INC
Also Called: Montville Plastics
15567 Main Market Rd (44080)
P.O. Box 527 (44080-0527)
PHONE..................440 548-3211
EMP: 45
SIC: 3089 Extruded finished plastics products, nec

Parma
Cuyahoga County

(G-12286)
AMAC ENTERPRISES INC (PA)
5909 W 130th St (44130-1040)
PHONE..................216 362-1880
George Chimples, *Ch Bd*
Constantine Chimples, *
Thomas Chimples, *
Janet Chimples, *
Lee Lettie,, *
▲ **EMP:** 112 **EST:** 1951
SQ FT: 190,000
SALES (est): 14.96MM
SALES (corp-wide): 14.90MM **Privately Held**
Web: www.amacent.com
SIC: 3398 3471 Metal heat treating; Finishing, metals or formed products

(G-12287)
CROCHET KITTY LLC
Also Called: Crochet Kitty
12100 Snow Rd Ste 1 (44130)
PHONE..................440 340-5152
EMP: 8 **EST:** 2016
SALES (est): 117.89K **Privately Held**
Web: www.crochetkitty.com
SIC: 3999 Pet supplies

(G-12288)
FDC MACHINE REPAIR INC
5585 Venture Dr (44130-9300)
PHONE..................216 362-1082
Fred Di Censo, *Pr*
Ferdinando Di Censo, *
Maria Di Censo, *
EMP: 30 **EST:** 1985
SQ FT: 32,000
SALES (est): 5.02MM **Privately Held**
Web: www.fdcmachine.com
SIC: 3599 Machine shop, jobbing and repair

(G-12289)
FERGUSON ENTERPRISES LLC
2415 Brookpark Rd (44134-1404)
PHONE..................216 635-2493
EMP: 6
SALES (corp-wide): 29.73B **Privately Held**
Web: www.ferguson.com
SIC: 5074 3432 Plumbing fittings and supplies; Plumbing fixture fittings and trim
HQ: Ferguson Enterprises, Llc
751 Lakefront Cmns
Newport News VA 23606
757 969-4011

(G-12290)
GES GRAPHITE INC (PA)
Also Called: G E S
12300 Snow Rd (44130-1001)
PHONE..................216 658-6660
Keith Kearney, *CEO*
Baker Kearney, *
Hunter Kearney, *
◆ **EMP:** 31 **EST:** 1985
SQ FT: 100,000
SALES (est): 10.16MM **Privately Held**
Web: www.ges-agm.com
SIC: 5085 3624 Industrial supplies; Carbon and graphite products

(G-12291)
HYFAST AEROSPACE LLC
12313 Plaza Dr (44130-1044)
PHONE..................216 712-4158
Henry Ford, *Prin*
EMP: 7 **EST:** 2014
SALES (est): 511.12K **Privately Held**
Web: www.hyfast.com
SIC: 3728 Aircraft parts and equipment, nec

(G-12292)
OSG-STERLING DIE INC
12502 Plaza Dr (44130-1045)
PHONE..................216 267-1300
Denise L Lucas, *Prin*
▲ **EMP:** 51 **EST:** 2004
SALES (est): 4.05MM **Privately Held**
SIC: 3545 Cutting tools for machine tools
HQ: Osg Usa, Inc.
620 Stetson Ave
Saint Charles IL 60174
800 837-2223

(G-12293)
PAULIN INDUSTRIES INC
12400 Plaza Dr U1 (44130-1057)
PHONE..................216 433-7633
▲ **EMP:** 23
SIC: 5072 3452 Hardware; Bolts, nuts, rivets, and washers

(G-12294)
SAIRAM OIL INC
4610 Milford Ave (44134-2122)
PHONE..................440 289-8232
Himal Patel, *Prin*
EMP: 6 **EST:** 2016
SALES (est): 87.69K **Privately Held**
SIC: 1311 Crude petroleum and natural gas

(G-12295)
SEAL MASTERS LLC
5935 State Rd (44134-2864)
PHONE..................216 860-7710
Gino Miller, *Prin*
EMP: 6 **EST:** 2016
SALES (est): 72.76K **Privately Held**
Web: www.sealmaster.com
SIC: 2951 Asphalt paving mixtures and blocks

Pataskala
Licking County

(G-12296)
DENNELLI CUSTOM WDWKG INC
1886 Ivywood Ct (43062-8073)
PHONE..................740 927-1900
Danny J Iulianelli, *Prin*
EMP: 7 **EST:** 2009
SALES (est): 168K **Privately Held**
SIC: 2431 Millwork

(G-12297)
EXCELSIOR PRINTING CO
1014 Putnam Rd Sw (43062-9754)
PHONE..................740 927-2934
David Fannon, *Pr*
Melissa Fannon, *VP*
EMP: 9 **EST:** 1986
SQ FT: 8,200
SALES (est): 613.17K **Privately Held**
SIC: 2752 Offset printing

(G-12298)
GT TIRE SERVICE INC
Also Called: G T Automotive Service Center
15 W Broad St (43062-9647)

GEOGRAPHIC SECTION
Paulding - Paulding County (G-12320)

P.O. Box 296 (43062-0296)
PHONE.................................740 927-7226
Gary Townsend, *Pr*
EMP: 7 EST: 1988
SALES (est): 741.64K **Privately Held**
Web: www.gttires.net
SIC: 7534 5014 Tire repair shop; Tires and tubes

(G-12299)
JOULES ANGSTROM UV PRTG INKS C (PA)
104 Heritage Dr (43062)
PHONE.................................740 964-9113
Patrick T Carlisle, *Pr*
Richard Klonowski, *Stockholder**
Norris Duncan, *Stockholder**
EMP: 24 EST: 1999
SQ FT: 30,000
SALES (est): 4.58MM
SALES (corp-wide): 4.58MM **Privately Held**
Web: www.joulesangstrom.com
SIC: 2893 Printing ink

(G-12300)
KARS OHIO LLC
6359 Summit Rd Sw (43062-8763)
P.O. Box 34 (43073-0034)
PHONE.................................614 655-1099
EMP: 8 EST: 2014
SALES (est): 405.31K **Privately Held**
SIC: 2851 3479 1721 1629 Undercoatings, paint; Painting of metal products; Industrial painting; Blasting contractor, except building demolition

(G-12301)
KNOX ENERGY INC (PA)
11872 Worthington Rd Nw (43062-9770)
P.O. Box 705 (43054-0705)
PHONE.................................740 927-6731
Mark Jordan, *Pr*
EMP: 17 EST: 1998
SALES (est): 2.52MM
SALES (corp-wide): 2.52MM **Privately Held**
Web: www.knoxenergy.com
SIC: 1382 Oil and gas exploration services

(G-12302)
OHIO STEEL INDUSTRIES INC
Also Called: Structural Steel Fabrication
13792 Broad St Sw (43062-9189)
P.O. Box 197 (43073-0197)
PHONE.................................740 927-9500
Robet Eaton, *Brnch Mgr*
EMP: 75
SQ FT: 200,000
SALES (corp-wide): 45.44MM **Privately Held**
Web: www.osiplastics.com
SIC: 3441 Fabricated structural metal
PA: Ohio Steel Industries, Inc.
   2575 Ferris Rd
   Columbus OH 43224
   614 471-4800

(G-12303)
PATASKALA POST
Also Called: Heartland Communications Div
190 E Broad St Ste 2 # E (43062-7131)
P.O. Box 722 (43062-0722)
PHONE.................................740 964-6226
Randall Almendinger, *Owner*
EMP: 10 EST: 1999
SALES (est): 381.34K **Privately Held**
Web: www.hayesoffices.com
SIC: 2711 Newspapers, publishing and printing

(G-12304)
PROGRAMMABLE CONTROL SVC INC
Also Called: P C S
6900 Blacks Rd Sw (43062-9512)
PHONE.................................740 927-0744
Phil Fraley, *Pr*
EMP: 9 EST: 1982
SALES (est): 366.3K **Privately Held**
Web: www.programmablecontrol.com
SIC: 3569 5084 7378 Robots, assembly line: industrial and commercial; Robots, industrial; Computer maintenance and repair

(G-12305)
REDHAWK ENERGY SYSTEMS LLC
10340 Palmer Rd Sw (43062-9449)
P.O. Box 36 (43018-0036)
PHONE.................................740 927-8244
Thomas J Ulrich, *Managing Member*
EMP: 6 EST: 2003
SQ FT: 5,000
SALES (est): 1.14MM **Privately Held**
Web: www.redhawkenergy.net
SIC: 3674 Solar cells

(G-12306)
RONA ENTERPRISES INC
30 W Broad St (43062-8180)
P.O. Box 1498 (43062-1498)
PHONE.................................740 927-9971
Ronald A Thomas, *Pr*
EMP: 9 EST: 1969
SQ FT: 1,500
SALES (est): 986.52K **Privately Held**
Web: www.ronahomes.com
SIC: 2452 6531 Prefabricated wood buildings; Real estate agents and managers

(G-12307)
RYDER ENGRAVING INC
1029 Hazelton Etna Rd Sw (43062-8528)
PHONE.................................740 927-7193
Jill Gosnell, *Pr*
Chris Gosnell, *Sec*
EMP: 6 EST: 1972
SALES (est): 489.46K **Privately Held**
Web: www.ryderengraving.com
SIC: 3479 7389 Name plates: engraved, etched, etc.; Engraving service

(G-12308)
SCIOTO READY MIX LLC
6214 Taylor Rd Sw (43062-8885)
PHONE.................................740 924-9273
Steve Edmond, *
EMP: 60 EST: 2005
SALES (est): 11.3MM **Privately Held**
Web: www.sciotoreadymix.com
SIC: 5211 3273 Cement; Ready-mixed concrete

(G-12309)
SMI HOLDINGS INC
Also Called: Screen Machine
10685 Columbus Pkwy (43062-7421)
PHONE.................................740 927-3464
Bernard Cohen, *Ch*
Steven Cohen, *
Douglas Cohen, *
La June Cohen, *
◆ **EMP: 100 EST:** 1966
SALES (est): 9.84MM **Privately Held**
Web: www.screenmachine.com
SIC: 2752 Offset and photolithographic printing

(G-12310)
TRACTOR SUPPLY COMPANY
11309 Broad St Sw (43062-9257)
PHONE.................................740 963-8023
EMP: 8 EST: 1982
SALES (est): 115.93M **Privately Held**
SIC: 3523 Farm machinery and equipment

Paulding
Paulding County

(G-12311)
BAUGHMAN TILE COMPANY
8516 Road 137 (45879-9753)
PHONE.................................800 837-3160
TOLL FREE: 800
Gene A Baughman, *Pr*
Eric Baughman, *
Brad Baughman, *
Mary A Baughman, *
EMP: 100 EST: 1883
SQ FT: 100,000
SALES (est): 9.72MM **Privately Held**
Web: www.baughmantile.com
SIC: 3084 3259 Plastics pipe; Clay sewer and drainage pipe and tile

(G-12312)
DELPHOS HERALD INC
Paulding Progress
113 S Williams St (45879-1429)
P.O. Box 180 (45879-0180)
PHONE.................................419 399-4015
Doug Nutter, *Mgr*
EMP: 7
SQ FT: 7,000
SALES (corp-wide): 23.87MM **Privately Held**
Web: www.delphosherald.com
SIC: 2711 Newspapers, publishing and printing
PA: Herald Delphos Inc
   405 N Main St
   Delphos OH 45833
   419 695-0015

(G-12313)
HERBERT E ORR COMPANY INC
335 W Wall St (45879-1163)
P.O. Box 209 (45879-0209)
PHONE.................................419 399-4866
Greg Johnson, *Pr*
Donna J Garman, *Treas*
Ken Metzger, *
EMP: 125 EST: 1952
SQ FT: 48,000
SALES (est): 17.41MM **Privately Held**
Web: www.heorr.com
SIC: 5013 3479 Wheels, motor vehicle; Painting of metal products

(G-12314)
HOLCIM (US) INC
11435 Road 176 (45879-8834)
P.O. Box 160 (45879-0160)
PHONE.................................419 399-4861
Geoff Fehr, *Mgr*
EMP: 105
Web: www.holcim.us
SIC: 3241 Cement, hydraulic
HQ: Holcim (Us) Inc.
   8700 W Bryn Mawr Ave Ste
   Chicago IL 60631

(G-12315)
INNOVATIVE ASSEMBLY SVCS LLC
400 W Wall St (45879)
P.O. Box 301 (45879-0301)
PHONE.................................419 399-3886
Phillip Hall, *Managing Member*
EMP: 6 EST: 2001
SALES (est): 146.7K **Privately Held**
SIC: 3569 Assembly machines, non-metalworking

(G-12316)
INSOURCE TECH INC
12124 Road 111 (45879-9000)
PHONE.................................419 399-3600
Roger Manz, *Prin*
Ken Manz, *Prin*
EMP: 13 EST: 1997
SQ FT: 11,500
SALES (est): 359.78K **Privately Held**
Web: www.insource.tech
SIC: 3585 Heating and air conditioning combination units

(G-12317)
LAPHAM-HICKEY STEEL CORP
815 W Gasser Rd (45879-8765)
PHONE.................................419 399-4803
Douglas Fiske, *Brnch Mgr*
EMP: 53
SQ FT: 400,000
SALES (corp-wide): 235.89MM **Privately Held**
Web: www.lapham-hickey.com
SIC: 3316 3398 Cold finishing of steel shapes; Metal heat treating
PA: Lapham-Hickey Steel Corp.
   5500 W 73rd St
   Bedford Park IL 60638
   708 496-6111

(G-12318)
OHIO MIRROR TECHNOLOGIES INC (PA)
114 W Jackson St (45879-1264)
P.O. Box 223 (45879-0223)
PHONE.................................419 399-5903
Dennis R Krick, *Pr*
Tom Krick, *Treas*
Janet Krick Prein, *Prin*
EMP: 14 EST: 1975
SQ FT: 2,700
SALES (est): 703.76K
SALES (corp-wide): 703.76K **Privately Held**
SIC: 3231 Products of purchased glass

(G-12319)
P C WORKSHOP INC
900 W Caroline St (45879-1381)
P.O. Box 390 (45879-0390)
PHONE.................................419 399-4805
Megan Sierra, *CEO*
Brenda Miller, *Dir*
EMP: 10 EST: 1977
SALES (est): 1.47MM **Privately Held**
Web: www.pcworkshop.org
SIC: 7389 3711 Document and office record destruction; Automobile assembly, including specialty automobiles

(G-12320)
SPARTECH LLC
Also Called: Spartech Plastics
925 W Gasser Rd (45879-8765)
P.O. Box 420 (45879-0420)
PHONE.................................419 399-4050
EMP: 54
SALES (corp-wide): 344.31MM **Privately Held**
Web: www.spartech.com
SIC: 3081 3089 3083 Unsupported plastics film and sheet; Extruded finished plastics products, nec; Laminated plastics plate and sheet
PA: Spartech Llc
   11650 Lkeside Crossing Ct
   Saint Louis MO 63146
   314 569-7400

Payne
Paulding County

(G-12321)
GORDON TOOL INC
1301 State Route 49 (45880-9727)
PHONE...............................419 263-3151
William J Gordon, *Pr*
Lori Gordon, *Sec*
EMP: 15 **EST:** 1988
SQ FT: 15,625
SALES (est): 2.38MM **Privately Held**
Web: www.gordontool.com
SIC: 5251 3544 Tools; Special dies, tools, jigs, and fixtures

(G-12322)
TAYLOR PRODUCTS INC
230 S Laura St (45880-9094)
P.O. Box 77 (45880-0077)
PHONE...............................419 263-2313
Denise Reed, *Prin*
EMP: 21
SALES (corp-wide): 200K **Privately Held**
Web: www.taylormadeproducts.com
SIC: 3231 Products of purchased glass
PA: Taylor Products Inc
66 Kingsboro Ave
Gloversville NY 12078
518 773-9312

(G-12323)
TAYLOR PRODUCTS INC
Also Called: Taylor Made Glass Systems
407 N Maple St (45880-9021)
PHONE...............................419 263-2313
John Ori, *Mgr*
EMP: 21
SALES (corp-wide): 200K **Privately Held**
Web: www.taylormadeproducts.com
SIC: 3231 3211 Products of purchased glass; Flat glass
PA: Taylor Products Inc
66 Kingsboro Ave
Gloversville NY 12078
518 773-9312

(G-12324)
WILDCAT CREEK FARMS INC
Also Called: Wildcat Creek Popcorn
4633 Road 94 (45880-9124)
PHONE...............................419 263-2549
Don Benschneider, *Pr*
Dave Yenser, *VP*
Marge Yenser, *Sec*
EMP: 11 **EST:** 1980
SQ FT: 4,320
SALES (est): 403.69K **Privately Held**
Web: www.wildcatcreekpopcorn.com
SIC: 2099 0111 0119 0115 Popcorn, packaged: except already popped; Wheat; Popcorn farm; Corn

Peebles
Adams County

(G-12325)
BLACK GATE BLINDS LLC
1053 Purcell Rd (45660-9224)
PHONE...............................937 402-6158
Jeffrey Ryan Lawwell, *Prin*
EMP: 7 **EST:** 2019
SALES (est): 229.07K **Privately Held**
Web: www.blackgatehunting.com
SIC: 2591 Window blinds

(G-12326)
G P MANUFACTURING INC
376 Buckeye St (45660-1114)
P.O. Box 265 (45660-0265)
PHONE...............................937 544-3190
EMP: 6
SQ FT: 7,500
SALES (est): 302.5K **Privately Held**
SIC: 3537 Containers (metal), air cargo

(G-12327)
HEIDELBERG MATERIALS US INC
Also Called: Hanson Aggrgates Plum Run Quar
848 Plum Run Rd (45660-9706)
Rural Route 1 Box 11a (45660)
PHONE...............................937 587-2671
EMP: 28
SALES (corp-wide): 23.02B **Privately Held**
Web: www.heidelbergmaterials.us
SIC: 3273 Ready-mixed concrete
HQ: Heidelberg Materials Us, Inc.
300 E John Carpenter Fwy
Irving TX 75062

(G-12328)
J MCCOY LUMBER CO LTD (PA)
6 N Main St (45660-1243)
P.O. Box 306 (45660-0306)
PHONE...............................937 587-3423
Jack Mccoy, *Owner*
EMP: 13 **EST:** 1978
SQ FT: 2,400
SALES (est): 6.07MM
SALES (corp-wide): 6.07MM **Privately Held**
Web: www.jmccoylumber.com
SIC: 5031 2426 2431 Lumber: rough, dressed, and finished; Dimension, hardwood; Moldings, wood: unfinished and prefinished

(G-12329)
PEEBLES MESSENGER NEWSPAPER
58 S Main St (45660-1189)
PHONE...............................937 587-1451
Pamela Syroney, *Owner*
EMP: 8 **EST:** 2003
SALES (est): 357.59K **Privately Held**
Web: peeblesmessenger.weebly.com
SIC: 2711 Newspapers: publishing only, not printed on site

(G-12330)
QUEEN BEANERY COFFEEHOUSE LLC ◊
25675 State Route 41 (45660)
PHONE...............................937 798-4023
EMP: 6 **EST:** 2023
SALES (est): 60.98K **Privately Held**
SIC: 2095 Coffee extracts

(G-12331)
RYAN DEVELOPMENT CORPORATION
1 Ryan Rd (45660)
P.O. Box 336 (45660-0336)
PHONE...............................937 587-2266
G William Ryan, *Pr*
W Mark Ryan, *VP*
EMP: 11 **EST:** 1973
SQ FT: 20,000
SALES (est): 422.48K **Privately Held**
SIC: 3089 Extruded finished plastics products, nec

(G-12332)
SCHROCK JOHN
Also Called: Wheat Ridge Pallet & Lumber
99 Fugate Rd (45660-9144)
PHONE...............................937 544-8457
John Schrock, *Owner*
Melissa Black, *Acctnt*
EMP: 9 **EST:** 1984
SALES (est): 701.25K **Privately Held**
SIC: 2448 Pallets, wood

(G-12333)
SOUTHERN OHIO LUMBER LLC
Also Called: Southern Ohio Lumber
11855 State Route 73 (45660)
P.O. Box 145 (43085)
PHONE...............................614 436-4472
EMP: 13 **EST:** 1995
SQ FT: 25,000
SALES (est): 516.04K **Privately Held**
Web: www.southernohiolumber.com
SIC: 2448 Pallets, wood

Pemberville
Wood County

(G-12334)
COUNTYLINE CO-OP INC (PA)
425 E Front St (43450-7039)
P.O. Box C (43450-0430)
PHONE...............................419 287-3241
Donald Kline, *Pr*
Robert Schroder, *VP*
Thomas Sieving, *Sec*
Robert Rahrig, *Genl Mgr*
EMP: 10 **EST:** 1916
SQ FT: 10,000
SALES (est): 5.05MM
SALES (corp-wide): 5.05MM **Privately Held**
Web: www.countylinecoop.com
SIC: 5153 5191 2875 2041 Grains; Farm supplies; Fertilizers, mixing only; Flour and other grain mill products

(G-12335)
JA ACQUISITION CORP
Also Called: Hercules Stamping Co
850 W Front St (43450-9703)
P.O. Box F (43450-0433)
PHONE...............................419 287-3223
Wes Walters, *Pr*
James Gale, *Pr*
James Akers, *Ch Bd*
EMP: 15 **EST:** 1992
SQ FT: 30,000
SALES (est): 975.85K **Privately Held**
Web: www.universalmetalproducts.com
SIC: 3465 3469 Automotive stampings; Metal stampings, nec

(G-12336)
UNIVERSAL METAL PRODUCTS INC
850 W Front St (43450-9703)
P.O. Box F (43450-0433)
PHONE...............................419 287-3223
EMP: 41
SALES (corp-wide): 47.27MM **Privately Held**
Web: www.universalmetalproducts.com
SIC: 3469 Stamping metal for the trade
PA: Universal Metal Products, Inc.
29980 Lakeland Blvd
Wickliffe OH 44092
440 943-3040

Peninsula
Summit County

(G-12337)
A & C WELDING INC
80 Cuyahoga Falls Industrial Pkwy (44264-9568)
PHONE...............................330 762-4777
Carl Lamancusa, *Pr*
Michael Lamancusa, *
Timothy Gorbach, *
EMP: 25 **EST:** 1980
SALES (est): 4.59MM **Privately Held**
Web: www.acweld.com
SIC: 3444 7692 Sheet metalwork; Welding repair

(G-12338)
ANSCO MACHINE COMPANY
60 Cuyahoga Falls Industrial Pkwy (44264-9568)
PHONE...............................330 929-8181
Michael D Sterling, *Pr*
▲ **EMP:** 45 **EST:** 1991
SQ FT: 48,000
SALES (est): 6.28MM **Privately Held**
Web: www.anscomachine.com
SIC: 3599 Machine shop, jobbing and repair

(G-12339)
CENTER FOR INQUIRY INC
6413 Riverview Rd (44264-9624)
PHONE...............................330 671-7192
Bill Stalker, *Prin*
EMP: 6 **EST:** 2005
SALES (est): 68.74K **Privately Held**
SIC: 2721 Periodicals

(G-12340)
EAGLE ELASTOMER INC
70 Cuyahoga Falls Industrial Pkwy (44264-9568)
P.O. Box 939 (44223-0939)
PHONE...............................330 923-7070
Gene H Mckenna, *Prin*
Neil X Mc Hale, *
Regan Mc Hale, *
Vertina Ashling, *
EMP: 45 **EST:** 1983
SQ FT: 26,000
SALES (est): 8.61MM **Privately Held**
Web: www.eagleelastomer.com
SIC: 3069 2821 Tubing, rubber; Plastics materials and resins

(G-12341)
PREFORMED LINE PRODUCTS CO
Also Called: Pilot Plastics
200 Cuyahoga Falls Industrial Pkwy (44264-9572)
PHONE...............................330 920-1718
Robert G Ruhlman, *Pr*
EMP: 14
SALES (corp-wide): 669.68MM **Publicly Held**
Web: www.plp.com
SIC: 3089 Injection molding of plastics
PA: Preformed Line Products Company
660 Beta Dr
Mayfield Village OH 44143
440 461-5200

(G-12342)
TERRY LUMBER AND SUPPLY CO
1710 Mill St W (44264-9701)
P.O. Box 216 (44264-0216)
PHONE...............................330 659-6800
James Montaquilla, *VP*
Judy Lahoski, *Sec*
John Lahoski, *Mgr*
EMP: 11 **EST:** 1940
SQ FT: 20,000
SALES (est): 1.64MM **Privately Held**
Web: www.terrylumbersupply.com
SIC: 5251 5211 2448 2449 Hardware stores; Lumber and other building materials; Pallets, wood; Rectangular boxes and crates, wood

GEOGRAPHIC SECTION

(G-12343)
TRAIL MIX
1565 Boston Mills Rd W (44264-9617)
PHONE..................................330 657-2277
Pamela Good, *Mgr*
EMP: 8 **EST:** 2013
SALES (est): 191.39K **Privately Held**
Web: www.conservancyforcvnp.org
SIC: 3273 Ready-mixed concrete

(G-12344)
WCCV FLOOR COVERINGS LLC (PA)
4535 State Rd (44264-9799)
PHONE..................................330 688-0114
John F Martin, *Pr*
EMP: 16 **EST:** 1994
SALES (est): 4.97MM
SALES (corp-wide): 4.97MM **Privately Held**
Web: www.wccv.com
SIC: 5713 3253 Floor covering stores; Ceramic wall and floor tile

(G-12345)
WHOLECYCLE INC
Also Called: State 8 Motorcycle & Atv
100 Cuyahoga Falls Industrial Pkwy (44264-9569)
PHONE..................................330 929-8123
◆ **EMP:** 40 **EST:** 1990
SQ FT: 25,000
SALES (est): 7.78MM **Privately Held**
Web: www.state8.com
SIC: 5012 5571 3799 Motorcycles; Motorcycles; All terrain vehicles (ATV)

(G-12346)
WINE MILL
4964 Akron Cleveland Rd (44264-9513)
PHONE..................................234 571-2594
P Cunningham, *Genl Pt*
Patrick Cunningham, *Genl Pt*
EMP: 7 **EST:** 2014
SALES (est): 157.96K **Privately Held**
Web: www.thewinemill.com
SIC: 2084 Wines

(G-12347)
X44 CORP
Also Called: MBA Design
1601 Mill St W (44264-9798)
PHONE..................................330 657-2335
Steve Phillips, *Pr*
EMP: 10 **EST:** 1990
SQ FT: 2,800
SALES (est): 659.93K **Privately Held**
Web: www.mbadesigngroup.com
SIC: 2434 Wood kitchen cabinets

Pennsville
Morgan County

(G-12348)
JASPER PAULA
2425 Ervin Ln (43787-9545)
PHONE..................................740 559-3983
Paula Jasper, *CEO*
EMP: 6 **EST:** 2001
SALES (est): 169.2K **Privately Held**
SIC: 3648 Area and sports luminaries

Perry
Lake County

(G-12349)
ALL WRIGHT ENTERPRISES LLC
Fidanza Performance
4285 Main St (44081-9635)
PHONE..................................440 259-5656
Jeffrey Jenkins, *Pr*
EMP: 9
SALES (corp-wide): 988.27K **Privately Held**
Web: www.fidanza.com
SIC: 5013 3714 Clutches; Gears, motor vehicle
PA: All Wright Enterprises, Llc
5 Bisbee Ct Ste 109-313
Santa Fe NM 87508
440 259-5656

(G-12350)
CHEROKEE MANUFACTURING LLC
3891 Shepard Rd (44081-9633)
PHONE..................................800 777-5030
EMP: 14 **EST:** 2011
SALES (est): 1.12MM **Privately Held**
SIC: 3315 Baskets, steel wire

(G-12351)
GREAT LAKES POWER SERVICE CO
Also Called: John Deere Authorized Dealer
3691 Shepard Rd (44081-9694)
PHONE..................................440 259-0025
Harry Allen, *Owner*
EMP: 7
SALES (corp-wide): 23.26MM **Privately Held**
Web: www.glpower.com
SIC: 3699 5082 Laser welding, drilling, and cutting equipment; Construction and mining machinery
PA: Great Lakes Power Service Co.
7455 Tyler Blvd
Mentor OH 44060
440 951-5111

(G-12352)
JOINING METALS INC
3314 Blackmore Rd (44081-9320)
PHONE..................................440 259-1790
Jeff Beckwith, *Pr*
EMP: 12 **EST:** 2007
SALES (est): 2.38MM **Privately Held**
SIC: 3444 Sheet metalwork

(G-12353)
LUTHER MACHINE INC
4604 Davis Rd (44081-9667)
PHONE..................................440 259-5014
EMP: 6 **EST:** 1995
SALES (est): 388.44K **Privately Held**
SIC: 3545 Machine tool accessories

(G-12354)
MACDIVITT RUBBER COMPANY LLC
3291 Center Rd (44081-9589)
P.O. Box 129 (44081-0129)
PHONE..................................440 259-5937
Bob Mcdivitt, *Pr*
EMP: 20 **EST:** 1993
SQ FT: 20,000
SALES (est): 4.78MM **Privately Held**
Web: www.macdivittrubber.com
SIC: 3061 3069 Mechanical rubber goods; Molded rubber products

(G-12355)
MASTER CARBIDE TOOLS COMPANY
Also Called: Mastertech Diamond Products Co
3529 Lane Rd Ext (44081-9549)
PHONE..................................440 352-1112
Thomas Frakes, *Pr*
Cynthia Frakes, *VP*
EMP: 16 **EST:** 1946
SALES (est): 3.19MM **Privately Held**
Web: www.mastertechdiamond.com
SIC: 3545 Cutting tools for machine tools

(G-12356)
PRECISION POLYMER CASTING
4304 Maple St Ste 3 (44081-8659)
PHONE..................................440 205-1900
Terry Capuano, *Owner*
David Rabatin, *Prin*
▼ **EMP:** 10 **EST:** 1988
SQ FT: 24,000
SALES (est): 719.65K **Privately Held**
Web: www.precisionpolymercasting.com
SIC: 3089 Casting of plastics

(G-12357)
TT ELECTRONICS INTEGRATED MANUFACTURING SERVICES INC
Also Called: TT Electronics IMS
3700 Lane Rd Ext (44081-9563)
PHONE..................................440 352-8961
◆ **EMP:** 300 **EST:** 1976
SALES (est): 101.64MM
SALES (corp-wide): 765.19MM **Privately Held**
Web: www.ttelectronics.com
SIC: 3625 5731 Motor controls, electric; Consumer electronic equipment, nec
PA: Tt Electronics Plc
4th Floor St. Andrews House
Woking GU21
193 282-5300

Perrysburg
Wood County

(G-12358)
ACADIA SCIENTIFIC LLC
27100 Oakmead Dr (43551-2670)
PHONE..................................267 980-1644
Depu Chen, *Prin*
EMP: 8 **EST:** 2012
SALES (est): 226.38K **Privately Held**
SIC: 3312 Chemicals and other products derived from coking

(G-12359)
ADR FUEL INC
353 Elm St (43551-2177)
PHONE..................................419 872-2178
Glen Hefflinger, *Prin*
EMP: 8 **EST:** 2010
SALES (est): 137.28K **Privately Held**
SIC: 2869 Fuels

(G-12360)
ALL OHIO READY MIX CONCRETE
622 Eckel Rd (43551-1202)
PHONE..................................419 841-3838
Rick Stanley, *Prin*
EMP: 9 **EST:** 2007
SALES (est): 209.62K **Privately Held**
SIC: 3273 Ready-mixed concrete

(G-12361)
AMERICAN STEEL TREATING INC
29200 Glenwood Rd (43551-3025)
PHONE..................................419 874-2044
Roy Waits, *CEO*
Jeff Blanker, *
EMP: 65 **EST:** 1988
SALES (est): 5.5MM **Privately Held**
Web: www.americansteeltreating.com
SIC: 3398 Metal heat treating

(G-12362)
AMPP INCORPORATED
Also Called: Ampp
28271 Cedar Park Blvd Ste 5 (43551-4883)
PHONE..................................419 666-4747
Daniel A Worline, *Prin*
▲ **EMP:** 200 **EST:** 1984
SQ FT: 53,000
SALES (est): 26.83MM
SALES (corp-wide): 30.97MM **Privately Held**
SIC: 3444 Sheet metalwork
PA: T.L. Industries, Inc.
28271 Cedar Park Blvd # 8
Perrysburg OH 43551
419 666-8144

(G-12363)
B & B BOX COMPANY INC
26490 Southpoint Rd (43551-1370)
PHONE..................................419 872-5600
Gregory B Hammer, *Pr*
EMP: 18 **EST:** 1959
SQ FT: 32,500
SALES (est): 2.48MM **Privately Held**
Web: www.b-n-bbox.com
SIC: 2653 Boxes, corrugated: made from purchased materials

(G-12364)
BOTTOMLINE INK CORPORATION
Also Called: Blink Marketing Logistics
7829 Ponderosa Rd (43551-4854)
PHONE..................................419 897-8000
Nicholas J Cron, *Prin*
Mike Davison, *
▲ **EMP:** 29 **EST:** 1991
SQ FT: 58,000
SALES (est): 8.37MM **Privately Held**
Web: www.alwaysblink.com
SIC: 2759 5199 Advertising literature: printing, nsk; Advertising specialties

(G-12365)
BPREX HALTHCARE BROOKVILLE INC (DH)
Also Called: Rexam Closure Systems
1899 N Wilkinson Way (43551-1685)
PHONE..................................847 541-9700
Steve Wirrig, *CEO*
◆ **EMP:** 135 **EST:** 1987
SALES (est): 194.35MM **Publicly Held**
SIC: 3089 Caps, plastics
HQ: Berry Global, Inc.
101 Oakley St
Evansville IN 47710

(G-12366)
BUTT KICKN CREAMERY INC
26383 Carronade Dr (43551-6370)
PHONE..................................419 482-6610
Jerry A Benford, *Prin*
EMP: 6 **EST:** 2005
SALES (est): 171.34K **Privately Held**
SIC: 2021 Creamery butter

(G-12367)
CAMEO INC
995 3rd St - Ampoint (43551-4355)
P.O. Box 535 (43697-0535)
PHONE..................................419 661-9611
E Lee Ison, *Pr*
Brandon Ison, *
◆ **EMP:** 28 **EST:** 1940
SALES (est): 485.77K **Privately Held**
Web: www.cameo.com
SIC: 2844 Perfumes, cosmetics and other toilet preparations

(G-12368)
CARDINAL AGGREGATE INC
8026 Fremont Pike (43551-9733)
PHONE..................................419 872-4380
Mark Murray, *CEO*
Philip Bisel, *VP Opers*

Perrysburg - Wood County (G-12369)

EMP: 13 **EST:** 2005
SALES (est): 1.99MM **Privately Held**
Web: www.cardinalaggregate.com
SIC: 3281 Stone, quarrying and processing of own stone products

(G-12369)
CENTOR INC (HQ)
1899 N Wilkinson Way (43551-1685)
P.O. Box 446 (43552-0446)
PHONE..................567 336-8094
Ben Scheu, *Pr*
EMP: 13 **EST:** 1987
SALES (est): 96.51MM
SALES (corp-wide): 2.1B **Privately Held**
Web: www.centorrx.com
SIC: 2631 Container, packaging, and boxboard
PA: Gerresheimer Ag
Klaus-Bungert-Str. 4
Dusseldorf NW 40468
211619100

(G-12370)
CHAMPION WINDOW CO OF TOLEDO
7546 Ponderosa Rd Ste A (43551-5637)
PHONE..................419 841-0154
Toby Tokes, *Pr*
Ed Levine, *
EMP: 20 **EST:** 1953
SALES (est): 402.5K **Privately Held**
Web: www.championwindow.com
SIC: 5211 3444 3442 3231 Doors, storm: wood or metal; Sheet metalwork; Metal doors, sash, and trim; Products of purchased glass

(G-12371)
COOL SEAL USA LLC
232 J St (43551-4416)
PHONE..................419 666-1111
Mike Jaeck, *CFO*
Tim Wisnewski, *CFO*
Tab Hinkle, *Managing Member*
EMP: 16 **EST:** 2009
SALES (est): 4.94MM **Privately Held**
Web: www.coolsealusa.com
SIC: 3081 3083 Packing materials, plastics sheet; Laminated plastics plate and sheet

(G-12372)
CUTTING EDGE COUNTERTOPS INC
1300 Flagship Dr (43551-1375)
PHONE..................419 873-9500
Doug Heerdegen, *Pr*
Jeff Erickson, *
Jon Cousino, *
Rob Loughridge, *
◆ **EMP:** 32 **EST:** 2004
SQ FT: 24,000
SALES (est): 6.17MM **Privately Held**
Web: www.cectops.com
SIC: 3281 1743 Granite, cut and shaped; Marble installation, interior

(G-12373)
DCO LLC (DH)
900 E Boundary St Ste 8a (43551-2406)
PHONE..................419 931-9086
Joe Stancati, *Managing Member*
Bricy Stringham, *
◆ **EMP:** 31 **EST:** 1904
SALES (est): 45.51MM **Privately Held**
SIC: 3751 8741 Motor scooters and parts; Financial management for business
HQ: Enstar Holdings (Us) Llc
150 2nd Ave N Fl 3
Saint Petersburg FL 33701
727 217-2900

(G-12374)
DELAFOIL PENNSYLVANIA INC
Also Called: Delafoil
1775 Progress Dr (43551-2014)
PHONE..................610 327-9565
James Cash, *Pr*
EMP: 21 **EST:** 1979
SQ FT: 35,000
SALES (est): 391.57K **Privately Held**
SIC: 3444 3469 Sheet metalwork; Metal stampings, nec

(G-12375)
DEPOT DIRECT INC
Also Called: Kenakore Solutions
487 J St (43551-4303)
PHONE..................419 661-1233
▲ **EMP:** 42
Web: www.kenakoresolutions.com
SIC: 5084 7389 2741 Hydraulic systems equipment and supplies; Printing broker; Miscellaneous publishing

(G-12376)
DILLIN ENGINEERED SYSTEMS CORP
8030 Broadstone Rd (43551-4856)
PHONE..................419 666-6789
David A Smith, *Pr*
EMP: 50 **EST:** 2000
SQ FT: 40,000
SALES (est): 8.98MM **Privately Held**
Web: www.dillin.net
SIC: 8711 3535 Mechanical engineering; Conveyors and conveying equipment

(G-12377)
DRIFTER MARINE INC
28271 Cedar Park Blvd Ste 6 (43551-3846)
PHONE..................419 666-8144
Jon B Liebenthal, *Prin*
▲ **EMP:** 8 **EST:** 2010
SALES (est): 898.13K **Privately Held**
Web: www.driftermarine.com
SIC: 2399 Fishing nets

(G-12378)
ENCOMPASS ATMTN ENGRG TECH LLC
622 Eckel Rd (43551-1202)
P.O. Box 2912 (43606-0912)
PHONE..................419 873-0000
EMP: 10 **EST:** 2001
SQ FT: 3,200
SALES (est): 1.98MM **Privately Held**
SIC: 3823 Process control instruments

(G-12379)
EPRAD INC
Also Called: EPRAD
28271 Cedar Park Blvd Ste 1 (43551)
PHONE..................419 666-3266
Ham-hi Lee, *Pr*
Theodore Steschulte, *VP*
Joseph L Young, *VP*
EMP: 8 **EST:** 1985
SQ FT: 2,000
SALES (est): 8.92K **Privately Held**
Web: www.eprad.com
SIC: 3861 3651 Motion picture apparatus and equipment; Household audio and video equipment

(G-12380)
FCA NORTH AMERICA HOLDINGS LLC
Toledo Machining Plant
8000 Chrysler Dr (43551-4813)
PHONE..................419 661-3500
David Arndt, *Prin*
EMP: 120
Web: www.stellantis.com
SIC: 3714 Motor vehicle transmissions, drive assemblies, and parts
HQ: Fca Us Llc
1000 Chrysler Dr
Auburn Hills MI 48326

(G-12381)
FINALE PRODUCTS INC
Also Called: Car Brite
301 Walnut St (43551-1456)
PHONE..................419 874-2662
Alex Deedis, *Pr*
Robert Gibson, *VP*
Sharon Gibson, *VP*
Tim Gibson, *VP*
EMP: 8 **EST:** 1980
SQ FT: 25,600
SALES (est): 893.2K **Privately Held**
SIC: 2842 5013 5531 5169 Polishes and sanitation goods; Automotive supplies; Auto and home supply stores; Chemicals and allied products, nec

(G-12382)
FIRST SOLAR INC
Also Called: First Solar Electric
28101 Cedar Park Blvd (43551-4871)
P.O. Box 1032 (43697-1032)
PHONE..................419 661-1478
Michele Youngdale, *Brnch Mgr*
EMP: 22
Web: www.firstsolar.com
SIC: 3674 3433 Solar cells; Heating equipment, except electric
PA: First Solar, Inc.
350 W Washington St # 600
Tempe AZ 85288

(G-12383)
FRAZIER MACHINE AND PROD INC
26489 Southpoint Rd (43551-1371)
PHONE..................419 874-7321
Jeffrey B Frazier, *Pr*
Boyd M Frazier Junior, *CEO*
EMP: 23 **EST:** 1971
SQ FT: 18,000
SALES (est): 3.02MM **Privately Held**
Web: www.fraziermachine.com
SIC: 3599 3541 Machine shop, jobbing and repair; Machine tools, metal cutting type

(G-12384)
FRESH PRODUCTS LLC
30600 Oregon Rd (43551-4544)
PHONE..................419 531-9741
Robert B Brown, *
Doug Brown, *
◆ **EMP:** 55 **EST:** 1971
SQ FT: 48,000
SALES (est): 21.98MM **Privately Held**
Web: www.freshproducts.com
SIC: 2842 Deodorants, nonpersonal

(G-12385)
GLASSLINE CORPORATION (PA)
Also Called: Secure Pak
28905 Glenwood Rd (43551-3020)
P.O. Box 147 (43552-0147)
PHONE..................419 666-9712
Tom S Ziems, *Pr*
◆ **EMP:** 40 **EST:** 1970
SQ FT: 90,125
SALES (est): 24.85MM
SALES (corp-wide): 24.85MM **Privately Held**
Web: www.glassline.com

SIC: 3545 3565 3535 3541 Diamond dressing and wheel crushing attachments; Bottling machinery: filling, capping, labeling; Conveyors and conveying equipment; Machine tools, metal cutting type

(G-12386)
GLASSTECH INC (PA)
995 4th St (43551-4321)
PHONE..................419 661-9500
Mark D Christman, *Pr*
Ken Wetmore, *
Diane Tymiak, *
◆ **EMP:** 112 **EST:** 1971
SQ FT: 80,000
SALES (est): 23.45MM
SALES (corp-wide): 23.45MM **Privately Held**
Web: www.glasstech.com
SIC: 3211 3229 3231 Tempered glass; Glass tubes and tubing; Glass sheet bent: made from purchased glass

(G-12387)
GREENWAY HOME PRODUCTS INC
1270 Flagship Dr (43551-1381)
◆ **EMP:** 12 **EST:** 2005
SALES (est): 1.41MM **Privately Held**
SIC: 5023 2511 Homefurnishings; Wood household furniture

(G-12388)
HIAB USA INC (HQ)
12233 Williams Rd (43551-6802)
PHONE..................419 482-6000
Roland Sunden, *Pr*
Lennart Brelin, *
Doug Heerdegen, *
◆ **EMP:** 70 **EST:** 1962
SQ FT: 56,000
SALES (est): 138.21MM **Privately Held**
Web: www.hiab.com
SIC: 5084 3536 Cranes, industrial; Cranes, industrial plant
PA: Cargotec Oyj
Porkkalankatu 5
Helsinki 00180

(G-12389)
HINKLE MANUFACTURING INC
348 5th St (43551-4922)
P.O. Box 60210 (43460-0210)
PHONE..................419 666-5550
EMP: 96
SIC: 3086 2653 Packaging and shipping materials, foamed plastics; Corrugated boxes, partitions, display items, sheets, and pad

(G-12390)
IMCO CARBIDE TOOL INC
Also Called: Toledo Cutting Tools
28170 Cedar Park Blvd (43551-4872)
PHONE..................419 661-6313
Perry L Osburn, *Ch Bd*
Matthew S Osburn, *
Julie Whitlow, *
EMP: 90 **EST:** 1977
SQ FT: 25,000
SALES (est): 22.45MM **Privately Held**
Web: www.imcousa.com
SIC: 5084 3545 Machine tools and accessories; Tools and accessories for machine tools

(G-12391)
INDUSTRIAL HARDWOOD INC
Also Called: AAA
521 F St (43551-4313)
PHONE..................419 666-2503
Ashvin Shah, *Pr*

▲ = Import ▼ = Export
◆ = Import/Export

GEOGRAPHIC SECTION

Perrysburg - Wood County (G-12413)

EMP: 7 **EST:** 1973
SQ FT: 8,300
SALES (est): 992.97K **Privately Held**
SIC: 2448 Pallets, wood

(G-12392)
INNERAPPS LLC
Also Called: Identity Syncronizer
28350 Kensington Ln Ste 200 (43551-4174)
PHONE..............................419 467-3110
EMP: 8 **EST:** 2009
SALES (est): 513.65K **Privately Held**
Web: www.idsync.com
SIC: 7372 Business oriented computer software

(G-12393)
IRON BEAN INC
25561 Fort Meigs Rd Ste E (43551-5633)
PHONE..............................518 641-9917
EMP: 17 **EST:** 2017
SALES (est): 230.36K **Privately Held**
Web: www.ironbeancoffee.com
SIC: 5812 2095 5149 1541 Coffee shop; Roasted coffee; Coffee, green or roasted; Food products manufacturing or packing plant construction

(G-12394)
JERL MACHINE INC
11140 Avenue Rd (43551-2825)
PHONE..............................419 873-0270
Carol Coe, *CEO*
Linda Hetrick, *
Kristi Coe, *
Jayson Coy, *
EMP: 61 **EST:** 1974
SQ FT: 76,000
SALES (est): 10.96MM **Privately Held**
Web: www.jerl.com
SIC: 7692 3599 Welding repair; Machine shop, jobbing and repair

(G-12395)
KIEMLE-HANKINS COMPANY (PA)
Also Called: Kiemle-Hankins
94 H St (43551-4497)
P.O. Box 507 (43697-0507)
PHONE..............................419 661-2430
Stephen Martindale, *Ch*
Tim Martindale, *
Jeffrey Lee, *
EMP: 50 **EST:** 1928
SQ FT: 50,000
SALES (est): 14.06MM
SALES (corp-wide): 14.06MM **Privately Held**
Web: www.kiemlehankins.com
SIC: 7694 7629 3699 Electric motor repair; Electrical equipment repair services; Electrical equipment and supplies, nec

(G-12396)
LAKO TOOL & MANUFACTURING INC
7400 Ponderosa Rd (43551-4857)
P.O. Box 425 (43552-0425)
PHONE..............................419 662-5256
Larry E Smith, *Pr*
▲ **EMP:** 15 **EST:** 1974
SQ FT: 6,500
SALES (est): 3.2MM **Privately Held**
Web: www.lakotool.com
SIC: 3544 Special dies and tools

(G-12397)
LYONDLLBSELL ADVNCED PLYMERS I
12600 Eckel Rd (43551-1204)
PHONE..............................419 872-1408
EMP: 64

Web: www.lyondellbasell.com
SIC: 2821 Plastics materials and resins
HQ: Lyondellbasell Advanced Polymers Inc.
1221 Mckinney St Ste 300
Houston TX 77010
713 309-7200

(G-12398)
MARSHAS BUCKEYES LLC
25631 Fort Meigs Rd Ste E (43551-2098)
PHONE..............................419 872-7666
Marsha E Smith, *Managing Member*
EMP: 22 **EST:** 1985
SALES (est): 2.16MM **Privately Held**
Web: www.marshasbuckeyes.com
SIC: 2064 Candy and other confectionery products

(G-12399)
MASTER CHEMICAL CORPORATION (PA)
Also Called: Master Fluid Solutions
501 W Boundary St (43551-1200)
PHONE..............................419 874-7902
Mike Mchenry, *CEO*
Joe H Wright, *
Kyle R Stoffer, *
◆ **EMP:** 92 **EST:** 1951
SQ FT: 100,000
SALES (est): 85.33MM
SALES (corp-wide): 85.33MM **Privately Held**
Web: www.masterfluids.com
SIC: 2899 Chemical preparations, nec

(G-12400)
MICC MANUFACTURING CORPORATION
26695 Eckel Rd (43551-1209)
PHONE..............................567 331-0101
Fadi Nahhas, *CEO*
EMP: 6 **EST:** 2016
SALES (est): 551.34K **Privately Held**
Web: www.micccorp.com
SIC: 3443 Fabricated plate work (boiler shop)

(G-12401)
NATIONWIDE CHEMICAL PRODUCTS
24851 E Broadway Rd (43551-8947)
PHONE..............................419 714-7075
Joe Bassett, *Prin*
EMP: 6 **EST:** 2012
SALES (est): 204.61K **Privately Held**
Web: www.ncpprokill.com
SIC: 2869 Laboratory chemicals, organic

(G-12402)
NEW WASTE CONCEPTS INC
26624 Glenwood Rd (43551-4846)
PHONE..............................877 736-6924
Milton F Knight, *CEO*
Allan Wolf, *VP*
EMP: 10 **EST:** 1987
SQ FT: 5,000
SALES (est): 1.62MM **Privately Held**
Web: www.nwci.com
SIC: 2842 Sanitation preparations

(G-12403)
NEXT WAVE AUTOMATION LLC
600 W Boundary St (43551-1264)
PHONE..............................419 491-4520
Tim Owens, *Pr*
▲ **EMP:** 23 **EST:** 2007
SALES (est): 9.32MM **Privately Held**
Web: www.nextwaveautomation.com
SIC: 3599 Machine and other job shop work

(G-12404)
NORTHWOOD INDUSTRIES INC
7650 Ponderosa Rd (43551-4861)
PHONE..............................419 666-2100
Kurt Miller, *Pr*
EMP: 18 **EST:** 1968
SALES (est): 3.82MM **Privately Held**
Web: www.nwindustries.com
SIC: 3469 3541 7699 8711 Machine parts, stamped or pressed metal; Machine tools, metal cutting type; Industrial equipment services; Designing: ship, boat, machine, and product

(G-12405)
O-I GLASS INC (PA)
Also Called: O-I
1 Michael Owens Way (43551-2999)
PHONE..............................567 336-5000
Andres A Lopez, *Pr*
John H Walker, *Ch Bd*
John A Haudrich, *Sr VP*
Arnaud Aujouannet, *Chief Sales & Marketing Officer*
Darrow A Abrahams, *Corporate Secretary*
EMP: 155 **EST:** 1903
SALES (est): 7.11B
SALES (corp-wide): 7.11B **Publicly Held**
Web: www.o-i.com
SIC: 3221 Glass containers

(G-12406)
ODYSSEY MACHINE COMPANY LTD
26675 Eckel Rd # 5 (43551-1209)
PHONE..............................419 455-6621
Ronald Leroux, *Pr*
EMP: 7 **EST:** 2005
SALES (est): 567.26K **Privately Held**
Web: www.omc-xtd.com
SIC: 3599 7699 Custom machinery; Industrial machinery and equipment repair

(G-12407)
OHIO TABLE PAD COMPANY (PA)
Also Called: Ohio Table Pad Co Georgia Div
350 3 Meadows Dr (43551-3138)
P.O. Box 914 (43552-0914)
PHONE..............................419 872-6400
Christopher P Krauser, *Pr*
Jeffrey Lavoy, *VP*
Stephen R Krauser, *Stockholder*
Della B Bricker, *Prin*
N E Bricker, *Prin*
▲ **EMP:** 12 **EST:** 1923
SQ FT: 15,000
SALES (est): 5.58MM
SALES (corp-wide): 5.58MM **Privately Held**
SIC: 2299 5712 3949 2392 Felts and felt products; Furniture stores; Sporting and athletic goods, nec; Household furnishings, nec

(G-12408)
OHIO TABLE PAD COMPANY
Also Called: Southern Division
350 3 Meadows Dr (43551-3138)
P.O. Box 914 (43552-0914)
PHONE..............................419 872-6400
Don Unger, *Brnch Mgr*
EMP: 7
SALES (corp-wide): 5.58MM **Privately Held**
SIC: 2392 Pads and padding, table: except asbestos, felt, or rattan
PA: The Ohio Table Pad Company
350 3 Meadows Dr
Perrysburg OH 43551
419 872-6400

(G-12409)
OHIO TABLE PAD OF INDIANA
350 3 Meadows Dr (43551-3138)
PHONE..............................419 872-6400
Stephen Krauser, *Pr*
Christopher Krauser, *
Jeffrey Lavoy, *
▲ **EMP:** 56 **EST:** 1963
SQ FT: 15,000
SALES (est): 485.42K
SALES (corp-wide): 5.58MM **Privately Held**
SIC: 2299 Wool felts, pressed or needle loom
PA: The Ohio Table Pad Company
350 3 Meadows Dr
Perrysburg OH 43551
419 872-6400

(G-12410)
OI CALIFORNIA CONTAINERS INC (HQ)
1 Michael Owens Way (43551-2999)
PHONE..............................567 336-5000
EMP: 16
SALES (est): 1.02MM
SALES (corp-wide): 7.11B **Publicly Held**
Web: www.o-i.com
SIC: 3221 Glass containers
PA: O-I Glass, Inc.
1 Michael Owens Way
Perrysburg OH 43551
567 336-5000

(G-12411)
OLDCASTLE BUILDINGENVELOPE INC
291 M St (43551-4409)
PHONE..............................800 537-4064
Scott Switzer, *Brnch Mgr*
EMP: 88
SALES (corp-wide): 1.88B **Privately Held**
Web: www.obe.com
SIC: 3231 5231 Tempered glass: made from purchased glass; Glass
PA: Oldcastle Buildingenvelope, Inc.
5005 Lyndon B Johnson Fwy
Dallas TX 75244
214 273-3400

(G-12412)
ONIX CORPORATION
27100 Oakmead Dr (43551-2670)
PHONE..............................800 844-0076
Richard Allen, *Pr*
Charles Verhoff, *
Todd Mroczkowski, *
John Halderman, *
▲ **EMP:** 37 **EST:** 2006
SALES (est): 3.58MM **Privately Held**
Web: www.theonixcorp.com
SIC: 3433 Heating equipment, except electric

(G-12413)
ORBIS CORPORATION
Also Called: Hinkle Manufacturing
232 J St (43551-4416)
PHONE..............................262 560-5000
Jeff Wolens, *Brnch Mgr*
EMP: 96
SALES (corp-wide): 1.94B **Privately Held**
Web: www.orbiscorporation.com
SIC: 3086 2653 Packaging and shipping materials, foamed plastics; Corrugated boxes, partitions, display items, sheets, and pad
HQ: Orbis Corporation
1055 Corporate Center Dr
Oconomowoc WI 53066
262 560-5000

Perrysburg - Wood County (G-12414)

(G-12414)
OWENS-BROCKWAY GLASS CONT INC (DH)
Also Called: Owens-Brockway Glass Cntrs
1 Michael Owens Way (43551-2999)
PHONE..................567 336-8449
Mister Albert P L Stroucken, *Ch*
Steve Mccracken, *CEO*
Mathew Longthorne, *Pr*
Steve Bramlage, *Sr VP*
Jim Baehren, *Sr VP*
◆ EMP: 250 EST: 1987
SQ FT: 900,000
SALES (est): 1.02B
SALES (corp-wide): 7.11B **Publicly Held**
Web: www.owens-brockway.com
SIC: 3221 Glass containers
HQ: Owens-Brockway Packaging, Inc.
    1 Michael Owens Way
    Perrysburg OH 43551

(G-12415)
OWENS-ILLINOIS GENERAL INC
Also Called: O-1
1 Michael Owens Way (43551-2999)
PHONE..................567 336-5000
Al Stroucken, *CEO*
Thomas L Young, *
Ed Snyder, *
David G Van Hooser, *
Jim Baehren, *
▲ EMP: 550 EST: 1987
SQ FT: 900,000
SALES (est): 144.68MM
SALES (corp-wide): 7.11B **Publicly Held**
Web: www.o-i.com
SIC: 3221 Glass containers
HQ: Paddock Enterprises, Llc
    1 Michael Owens Way
    Perrysburg OH 43551
    567 336-5000

(G-12416)
OWENS-ILLINOIS GROUP INC (HQ)
1 Michael Owens Way (43551-2999)
PHONE..................567 336-5000
Albert P L Stroucken, *Ch Bd*
Stephen P Bramlage Junior, *CAO*
James W Baehren, *
Paul A Jarrell, *
◆ EMP: 60 EST: 1903
SALES (est): 1.32B
SALES (corp-wide): 7.11B **Publicly Held**
Web: www.o-i.com
SIC: 3221 Glass containers
PA: O-I Glass, Inc.
    1 Michael Owens Way
    Perrysburg OH 43551
    567 336-5000

(G-12417)
OWENS-ILLINOIS INC
Also Called: Oi
1 Michael Owens Way (43551-2999)
PHONE..................567 336-5000
EMP: 26500
SIC: 3221 Glass containers

(G-12418)
PADDOCK ENTERPRISES LLC (HQ)
1 Michael Owens Way 2 (43551-2999)
PHONE..................567 336-5000
Andres A Lopez, *Pr*
EMP: 31 EST: 2019
SALES (est): 185.99MM
SALES (corp-wide): 7.11B **Publicly Held**
SIC: 3221 Glass containers
PA: O-I Glass, Inc.
    1 Michael Owens Way
    Perrysburg OH 43551
    567 336-5000

(G-12419)
PALLET WORLD INC
8272 Fremont Pike (43551-9705)
PHONE..................419 874-9333
EMP: 26 EST: 1992
SQ FT: 3,000
SALES (est): 5.46MM **Privately Held**
Web: www.palletworldinc.com
SIC: 2448 Pallets, wood

(G-12420)
PRECISION BUSINESS SOLUTIONS
668 1st St (43551-4480)
PHONE..................419 661-8700
EMP: 10 EST: 2021
SALES (est): 981.46K **Privately Held**
Web: www.precisionbussol.com
SIC: 2759 Commercial printing, nec

(G-12421)
PRINTING UNLIMITED INC
325 W Indiana Ave Rear (43551-1528)
PHONE..................419 874-9828
Kevin Rantanen, *Prin*
EMP: 6 EST: 1994
SALES (est): 108.94K **Privately Held**
SIC: 2759 Commercial printing, nec

(G-12422)
QUANEX SCREENS LLC
7597 Broadmoor Rd (43551-4875)
PHONE..................419 662-5001
EMP: 23
Web: www.quanex.com
SIC: 3442 Screen and storm doors and windows
HQ: Quanex Screens Llc
    945 Bunker Hill Rd
    Houston TX 77024
    713 961-4600

(G-12423)
REACTIVE RESIN PRODUCTS CO
327 5th St (43551-4919)
PHONE..................419 666-6119
Jeff Freiburger, *Pr*
Robert L Hinkle, *
Joe Leonard, *
▲ EMP: 21 EST: 1988
SQ FT: 150,000
SALES (est): 4.05MM **Privately Held**
Web: www.rrp-mfg.com
SIC: 3565 3714 3089 Packaging machinery; Motor vehicle parts and accessories; Synthetic resin finished products, nec

(G-12424)
SATELYTICS INC
6330 Levis Commons Blvd (43551-7272)
PHONE..................419 372-0160
Jim Harpen, *Genl Mgr*
Milt Baker, *Pr*
Gail Nader, *Mgr*
EMP: 8 EST: 2009
SALES (est): 1.08MM **Privately Held**
Web: www.satelytics.com
SIC: 3826 Environmental testing equipment

(G-12425)
SCHUTZ CONTAINER SYSTEMS INC
2105 S Wilkinson Way (43551-1599)
PHONE..................419 872-2477
Pat Gillespe, *Brnch Mgr*
EMP: 80
SALES (corp-wide): 2.83B **Privately Held**
Web: www.schuetz-packaging.net
SIC: 2448 Cargo containers, wood and metal combination
HQ: Schutz Container Systems, Inc.
    200 Aspen Hill Rd
    Branchburg NJ 08876

(G-12426)
SHRADER TIRE & OIL INC
Also Called: Shrader Tire Oil Fleet Tire S
3511 Genoa Rd (43551-9703)
PHONE..................419 420-8435
Bryan Fields, *Mgr*
EMP: 6
SALES (corp-wide): 97.58MM **Privately Held**
Web: www.shradertireandoil.com
SIC: 5531 7534 Automotive tires; Tire retreading and repair shops
PA: Shrader Tire & Oil, Inc.
    2045 W Sylvania Ave # 51
    Toledo OH 43613
    419 472-2128

(G-12427)
SYSTEM PACKAGING OF GLASSLINE
28905 Glenwood Rd (43551-3020)
P.O. Box 147 (43552-0147)
PHONE..................419 666-9712
EMP: 91 EST: 1992
SALES (est): 1.54MM
SALES (corp-wide): 24.85MM **Privately Held**
Web: www.glassline.com
SIC: 3565 Packaging machinery
PA: Glassline Corporation
    28905 Glenwood Rd
    Perrysburg OH 43551
    419 666-9712

(G-12428)
TARPSTOP LLC (PA)
12000 Williams Rd (43551-6809)
P.O. Box 5760 (43613-0760)
PHONE..................419 873-7867
Andrew M Knepper, *Managing Member*
Ken Weschae, *
▲ EMP: 18 EST: 2001
SALES (est): 8.75MM
SALES (corp-wide): 8.75MM **Privately Held**
Web: www.tarpstop.com
SIC: 3713 Truck and bus bodies

(G-12429)
TBK HOLDINGS LLC (PA)
232 J St (43551-4416)
PHONE..................313 584-0400
EMP: 8 EST: 1971
SALES (est): 1.63MM
SALES (corp-wide): 1.63MM **Privately Held**
SIC: 3089 Plastics containers, except foam

(G-12430)
TECH DYNAMICS INC
361 D St Ste B (43551-5645)
PHONE..................419 666-1666
John W Zimmerman, *Pr*
David G Fielding, *VP*
EMP: 20 EST: 1984
SQ FT: 18,000
SALES (est): 2.59MM **Privately Held**
Web: www.techdynamics.us
SIC: 3441 Fabricated structural metal

(G-12431)
TECHNEGLAS INC
Also Called: TECHNEGLAS, INC.
25875 Dixie Hwy Bldg 52 (43551-1918)
PHONE..................419 873-2000
Leyshon Townsend, *Brnch Mgr*
EMP: 49
Web: www.techneglas.com
SIC: 3229 Glass tubes and tubing
HQ: Techneglas Llc
    2100 N Wilkinson Way
    Perrysburg OH 43551
    419 873-2000

(G-12432)
TECHNEGLAS LLC (HQ)
2100 N Wilkinson Way (43551-1598)
PHONE..................419 873-2000
Jeffrey T Lowry, *Pr*
▲ EMP: 10 EST: 1988
SQ FT: 18,000
SALES (est): 14.83MM **Privately Held**
Web: www.techneglas.com
SIC: 3479 3674 Coating of metals with plastic or resins; Silicon wafers, chemically doped
PA: Nippon Electric Glass Co., Ltd.
    2-7-1, Seiran
    Otsu SGA 520-0

(G-12433)
TECHNICAL GLASS PRODUCTS INC
7460 Ponderosa Rd (43551-4857)
PHONE..................425 396-8420
Joseph Murray, *Pr*
EMP: 10 EST: 2013
SALES (est): 2.41MM **Privately Held**
Web: www.fireglass.com
SIC: 3229 Scientific glassware

(G-12434)
TEREX UTILITIES INC
Also Called: Toledo Division
25661 Fort Meigs Rd Ste A (43551-2018)
PHONE..................419 470-8408
Don Elliott, *Brnch Mgr*
EMP: 10
SALES (corp-wide): 5.15B **Publicly Held**
Web: www.terex.com
SIC: 3531 Construction machinery
HQ: Terex Utilities, Inc.
    45 Glover Ave Ste 2
    Norwalk CT 06850
    203 222-7170

(G-12435)
TINY LION MUSIC GROUPS
Also Called: Groovemaster Music
144 E 5th St (43551-2235)
PHONE..................419 874-7353
Gaylord Richardson, *Owner*
EMP: 8 EST: 1992
SALES (est): 325.87K **Privately Held**
SIC: 2741 7389 Miscellaneous publishing; Music recording producer

(G-12436)
TL INDUSTRIES INC (PA)
28271 Cedar Park Blvd Ste 8 (43551-4883)
PHONE..................419 666-8144
Joseph Young, *Pr*
Joseph Young, *VP*
Theodore Stetschulte, *
EMP: 105 EST: 1970
SALES (est): 24.11MM
SALES (corp-wide): 24.11MM **Privately Held**
Web: www.tlindustries.com
SIC: 8711 3444 3629 3679 Electrical or electronic engineering; Sheet metalwork; Battery chargers, rectifying or nonrotating; Loads, electronic

(G-12437)
TMT INC
Also Called: Tmt Logistics
655 D St (43551-4908)
P.O. Box 408 (43552-0408)
PHONE..................419 592-1041

GEOGRAPHIC SECTION

Pickerington - Fairfield County (G-12459)

Tony Marks, *Pr*
EMP: 11 **EST:** 2000
SALES (est): 204.56K **Privately Held**
SIC: 4789 3999 Railroad maintenance and repair services; Dock equipment and supplies, industrial

(G-12438)
TOLEDO ELECTROMOTIVE INC
28765 White Rd (43551-3657)
PHONE.................................419 874-7751
Tony Palumbo, *Pr*
EMP: 6 **EST:** 1995
SALES (est): 466.8K **Privately Held**
SIC: 3625 Motor controls, electric

(G-12439)
TOLEDO SOLAR INC
1775 Progress Dr (43551)
PHONE.................................567 202-4145
Mark Hartel, *CEO*
Mark Haddad, *CFO*
EMP: 12 **EST:** 2019
SQ FT: 300,000
SALES (est): 2.52MM **Privately Held**
Web: www.toledo-solar.com
SIC: 3674 Solar cells

(G-12440)
TOLEDO TARP SERVICE INC
Also Called: Wilcox Awning & Sign
3273 Genoa Rd (43551-9703)
PHONE.................................419 837-5098
EMP: 20
Web: www.toledotarp.com
SIC: 2394 5085 Tarpaulins, fabric: made from purchased materials; Industrial supplies

(G-12441)
TWISTY TREAT LLC
750 W Boundary St (43551-1644)
PHONE.................................419 873-8033
Keena Amstutz, *Prin*
EMP: 8 **EST:** 2006
SALES (est): 167.54K **Privately Held**
SIC: 2024 Ice cream and frozen deserts

(G-12442)
UNIVERSAL HYDRAULIK USA CORP
25651 Fort Meigs Rd (43551-2076)
PHONE.................................419 873-6340
Michael Uhl, *CEO*
Ral Uhl, *CFO*
EMP: 7 **EST:** 2014
SQ FT: 4,500
SALES (est): 2.54MM
SALES (corp-wide): 16.81MM **Privately Held**
Web: www.universalhydraulik-usa.com
SIC: 3443 Heat exchangers: coolers (after, inter), condensers, etc.
PA: "universal Hydraulik Gmbh"
Siemensstr. 33
Neu-Anspach HE 61267
608194180

(G-12443)
WALKER TOOL & MACHINE COMPANY
7700 Ponderosa Rd (43551-4851)
PHONE.................................419 661-8000
Tarry F Beard, *Pr*
Larry L Beard, *Sec*
EMP: 13 **EST:** 1941
SQ FT: 18,500
SALES (est): 2.36MM **Privately Held**
Web: www.walkertoolandmachine.com
SIC: 3544 Special dies and tools

(G-12444)
WELCH PUBLISHING CO (PA)
Also Called: Perrysburg Messenger-Journal
117 E 2nd St (43551-2102)
P.O. Box 267 (43552-0267)
PHONE.................................419 874-2528
Matt H Welch, *Pr*
EMP: 20 **EST:** 1852
SQ FT: 6,000
SALES (est): 2.43MM
SALES (corp-wide): 2.43MM **Privately Held**
Web: www.perrysburg.com
SIC: 2711 2721 7375 2752 Job printing and newspaper publishing combined; Periodicals; Information retrieval services; Commercial printing, lithographic

(G-12445)
WHELCO INDUSTRIAL LTD
28210 Cedar Park Blvd (43551-4865)
PHONE.................................419 385-4627
EMP: 51 **EST:** 1992
SQ FT: 12,000
SALES (est): 7.31MM **Privately Held**
Web: www.whelco.com
SIC: 7694 Electric motor repair

(G-12446)
WONDERLY TRUCKING & EXCVTG LLC
3939 Fremont Pike (43551-9176)
PHONE.................................419 837-6294
Chad Wonderly, *Managing Member*
EMP: 10 **EST:** 2012
SALES (est): 530.37K **Privately Held**
SIC: 4212 3531 Timber trucking, local; Plows: construction, excavating, and grading

Perrysville
Ashland County

(G-12447)
MANSFIELD PLUMBING PDTS LLC (HQ)
150 E 1st St (44864-9421)
P.O. Box 334 (44805-0334)
PHONE.................................419 938-5211
Jim Morando, *Pr*
◆ **EMP:** 600 **EST:** 1929
SQ FT: 700,000
SALES (est): 97.96MM **Privately Held**
Web: www.mansfieldplumbing.com
SIC: 3261 3463 3088 3431 Vitreous plumbing fixtures; Plumbing fixture forgings, nonferrous; Plastics plumbing fixtures; Bathtubs: enameled iron, cast iron, or pressed metal
PA: Organizacion Corona S A
Calle 100 8 A 55 Torre C Piso 9
Bogota

(G-12448)
S & S AGGREGATES INC
Also Called: Shelly & Sands Zanesville OH
4540 State Route 39 (44864-9600)
PHONE.................................419 938-5604
EMP: 288
SALES (corp-wide): 433.35MM **Privately Held**
Web: www.shellyandsands.com
SIC: 1442 Construction sand mining
HQ: S & S Aggregates, Inc
3570 S River Rd
Zanesville OH 43701
740 453-0721

(G-12449)
STEP2 COMPANY LLC
2 Step 2 Dr (44864-9733)
P.O. Box 300 (44864-0300)
PHONE.................................419 938-6343
EMP: 400
Web: www.step2.com
SIC: 3089 3944 3423 Molding primary plastics; Games, toys, and children's vehicles; Hand and edge tools, nec
HQ: The Step2 Company Llc
10010 Aurora Hudson Rd
Streetsboro OH 44241

Petersburg
Mahoning County

(G-12450)
SUBTROPOLIS MINING CO
Also Called: Subtropolis Mine
5455 E Garfield Rd (44454)
PHONE.................................330 549-2165
EMP: 48
SALES (corp-wide): 2.38MM **Privately Held**
Web: www.efccfamily.com
SIC: 1221 Bituminous coal and lignite-surface mining
PA: Subtropolis Mining Co.
10900 South Ave
North Lima OH 44452
330 549-2165

Pettisville
Fulton County

(G-12451)
M & R REDI MIX INC (PA)
521 Commercial St (43553-6016)
P.O. Box 53273 (43553-0273)
PHONE.................................419 445-7771
Kurt Nofziger, *Pr*
Connie Nofziger, *
EMP: 20 **EST:** 1966
SQ FT: 2,000
SALES (est): 2.5MM
SALES (corp-wide): 2.5MM **Privately Held**
Web: www.gerkencompanies.com
SIC: 3273 4212 Ready-mixed concrete; Local trucking, without storage

(G-12452)
PETTISVILLE GRAIN CO (PA)
Also Called: Pgc Feeds
18251 County Road D-E (43553)
P.O. Box 53009 (43553-0009)
PHONE.................................419 446-2547
Neil E Rupp, *Pr*
James L Rufenacht, *Prin*
Corwin D Rufenacht, *Prin*
EMP: 21 **EST:** 1953
SALES (est): 21.22K
SALES (corp-wide): 21.22K **Privately Held**
Web: www.pettisvillegrain.com
SIC: 5153 5999 2048 2041 Grain elevators; Feed and farm supply; Prepared feeds, nec ; Flour and other grain mill products

(G-12453)
PETTISVILLE MEATS INCORPORATED
3082 Main St (43553)
P.O. Box 53148 (43553-0148)
PHONE.................................419 445-0921
Steve Mc Intosh, *Pr*
EMP: 11 **EST:** 1967
SQ FT: 7,500
SALES (est): 433.45K **Privately Held**
SIC: 2013 4222 5421 Sausages and other prepared meats; Storage, frozen or refrigerated goods; Meat markets, including freezer provisioners

Pickerington
Fairfield County

(G-12454)
ABOUT TIME SOFTWARE INC (PA)
12790 Pickerington Rd (43147-9457)
PHONE.................................614 759-6295
Mark Miller, *Pr*
EMP: 6 **EST:** 1999
SALES (est): 214.52K **Privately Held**
Web: www.abouttimesoftware.com
SIC: 7372 Prepackaged software

(G-12455)
ASHTON LLC
Also Called: Ashton Custom Prtg & Gift Sp
77 E Columbus St (43147-1382)
PHONE.................................614 833-4165
EMP: 11
SALES (corp-wide): 2.14MM **Privately Held**
Web: www.ashtonus.com
SIC: 2759 Screen printing
PA: Ashton Llc
309 Bethel St
Gibsonville NC 27249
336 447-4951

(G-12456)
BAGGALLINI INC
13405 Yarmouth Dr (43147-8493)
PHONE.................................800 448-8753
Devon Pike, *Pr*
▼ **EMP:** 16 **EST:** 2011
SALES (est): 3.61MM
SALES (corp-wide): 192.68MM **Privately Held**
Web: www.baggallini.com
SIC: 2393 5199 5948 Bags and containers, except sleeping bags: textile; Bags, textile; Luggage and leather goods stores
HQ: R. G. Barry Corporation
13405 Yarmouth Dr
Pickerington OH 43147
614 864-6400

(G-12457)
BRAND5 LLC
106 Cool Spring Ct (43147-8094)
PHONE.................................614 920-9254
EMP: 11 **EST:** 2006
SALES (est): 401.19K **Privately Held**
SIC: 2844 Perfumes, cosmetics and other toilet preparations

(G-12458)
CBUS INC
Also Called: N2 Publishing
13799 Nantucket Ave (43147-9315)
PHONE.................................614 327-6971
Mike Matheny, *Prin*
EMP: 10 **EST:** 2017
SALES (est): 229.3K **Privately Held**
Web: www.strollmag.com
SIC: 2741 Miscellaneous publishing

(G-12459)
CLEMENS LICENSE AGENCY
12825 Wheaton Ave (43147-8591)
PHONE.................................614 288-8007
Jennifer Clemens, *Owner*
EMP: 7 **EST:** 1993
SALES (est): 531.02K **Privately Held**

Pickerington - Fairfield County (G-12460)

(G-12460)
ECHO MOBILE SOLUTIONS LLC
108 Leasure Dr (43147-8001)
PHONE.................................614 282-3756
Trent Mcmurray, *CEO*
EMP: 6 **EST:** 2012
SALES (est): 203.54K **Privately Held**
Web: www.echocardreader.com
SIC: 7372 7389 Business oriented computer software; Business services, nec

(G-12461)
EVOQUA WATER TECHNOLOGIES LLC
Also Called: US Filter
1154 Hill Rd N (43147-8876)
PHONE.................................614 861-5440
Tim Swansonsn, *Mgr*
EMP: 6
Web: www.evoqua.com
SIC: 3569 Filters
HQ: Evoqua Water Technologies Llc
210 6th Ave Ste 3300
Pittsburgh PA 15222
724 772-0044

(G-12462)
FP HOLDCO INC
13405 Yarmouth Dr (43147)
PHONE.................................614 729-7205
Greg A Tunney, *Pr*
EMP: 9 **EST:** 1969
SALES (est): 224.1K **Privately Held**
Web: www.footpetals.com
SIC: 3144 Dress shoes, women's

(G-12463)
LOVE YUEH LLC
9126 Calverton Ter (43147-8178)
PHONE.................................614 408-8677
Erica King, *Managing Member*
EMP: 7
SALES (est): 242.16K **Privately Held**
SIC: 3942 7389 Clothing, doll; Business services, nec

(G-12464)
MIRION TECHNOLOGIES IST CORP
12954 Stonecreek Dr Ste C (43147-8840)
PHONE.................................614 367-2050
Daniel Messer, *Brnch Mgr*
EMP: 85
SALES (corp-wide): 800.9MM **Publicly Held**
SIC: 3559 Kilns
HQ: Mirion Technologies (Ist) Corporation
315 Dniel Zenker Dr # 204
Horseheads NY 14845
607 562-4300

(G-12465)
OHIO HOME & LEISURE PRODUCTS I
569 Pickerington Hills Dr (43147-1368)
P.O. Box 363 (43147-0363)
PHONE.................................614 833-4144
Daniel Digiannantoni, *Owner*
EMP: 7 **EST:** 2005
SALES (est): 180K **Privately Held**
SIC: 3699 8051 Security devices; Skilled nursing care facilities

(G-12466)
POLYSHIELD CORPORATION
8643 Chateau Dr (43147-9072)
PHONE.................................614 755-7674
Richard Allen, *CEO*
EMP: 10 **EST:** 2010
SALES (est): 487.4K **Privately Held**
SIC: 2822 Ethylene-propylene rubbers, EPDM polymers

(G-12467)
PRECISION CNC
192 Fox Glen Dr E (43147-7896)
PHONE.................................614 496-1048
EMP: 6 **EST:** 2018
SALES (est): 44.06K **Privately Held**
Web: www.proficientmachining.com
SIC: 3599 Machine shop, jobbing and repair

(G-12468)
R G BARRY CORPORATION
Also Called: Dearfoams Div
13405 Yarmouth Dr (43147-8493)
PHONE.................................212 244-3145
Howard Eisenberg, *Mgr*
EMP: 10
SALES (corp-wide): 192.68MM **Privately Held**
Web: www.rgbarry.com
SIC: 3142 House slippers
HQ: R. G. Barry Corporation
13405 Yarmouth Dr
Pickerington OH 43147
614 864-6400

(G-12469)
READY 2 RIDE TRNSP LLC
12435 Thoroughbred Dr (43147-8343)
PHONE.................................614 207-2683
Latarsha Bratton, *Pr*
Latarsha Pritchard, *Managing Member*
EMP: 9 **EST:** 2019
SALES (est): 575.1K **Privately Held**
SIC: 3743 Freight cars and equipment

(G-12470)
SHACKS STOP N GO LLC
107 Fox Glen Dr W (43147-8099)
PHONE.................................614 296-9292
EMP: 8 **EST:** 2021
SALES (est): 90.74K **Privately Held**
SIC: 2911 Petroleum refining

(G-12471)
SWEET PERSUASIONS LLC
9636 Circle Dr (43147-9650)
PHONE.................................614 216-9052
Melissa Lewis, *Prin*
EMP: 8 **EST:** 2010
SALES (est): 376.92K **Privately Held**
SIC: 2051 Bakery: wholesale or wholesale/retail combined

(G-12472)
VAN DYKE CUSTOM IRON INC
700 Janice Ln (43147-2034)
PHONE.................................614 860-9300
John Van Dyke, *Pr*
Darrell Van Dyke, *VP*
Michael Van Dyke, *VP Opers*
EMP: 6 **EST:** 1970
SALES (est): 878.96K **Privately Held**
SIC: 1521 3446 General remodeling, single-family houses; Architectural metalwork

Pierpont
Ashtabula County

(G-12473)
A W TAYLOR LUMBER INCORPORATED
1114 State Route 7 S (44082-9643)
PHONE.................................440 577-1889
EMP: 12 **EST:** 1983
SALES (est): 416.22K **Privately Held**
Web: www.robertsfabrication.com
SIC: 2448 Pallets, wood

(G-12474)
COMPLETE ENERGY SERVICES INC
7338 Us Route 6 (44082-9725)
PHONE.................................440 577-1070
Gary Lauer, *Pt*
EMP: 14 **EST:** 2012
SALES (est): 2.25MM **Privately Held**
Web: www.cesinc.com
SIC: 1389 Oil field services, nec

Piketon
Pike County

(G-12475)
ARTCO LLC
1729 Jasper Rd (45661-9738)
PHONE.................................740 493-2901
EMP: 7 **EST:** 2017
SALES (est): 244.13K **Privately Held**
SIC: 2752 Offset printing

(G-12476)
GLATFELTER CORPORATION
200 Schuster Rd (45661-9687)
PHONE.................................740 289-5100
Robert Browm, *Brnch Mgr*
EMP: 7
SALES (corp-wide): 1.39B **Publicly Held**
Web: www.glatfelter.com
SIC: 2621 Paper mills
PA: Glatfelter Corporation
4350 Congress St Ste 600
Charlotte NC 28209
704 885-2555

(G-12477)
JIM NIER CONSTRUCTION INC (PA)
Also Called: Jnc,
340 Bailey Chapel Rd (45661-9673)
PHONE.................................740 289-3925
Della Nier, *Pr*
Jim Nier, *VP*
EMP: 20 **EST:** 1984
SQ FT: 7,000
SALES (est): 1.93MM **Privately Held**
SIC: 1761 3444 1542 1541 Sheet metal work, nec; Sheet metalwork; Nonresidential construction, nec; Industrial buildings and warehouses

(G-12478)
LANSING BROS SAWMILL
897 Chenoweth Fork Rd (45661-9565)
PHONE.................................937 588-4291
Lloyd Lansing, *Prin*
EMP: 8 **EST:** 2010
SALES (est): 229.53K **Privately Held**
SIC: 2421 Sawmills and planing mills, general

(G-12479)
NO NAME LUMBER LLC
165 No Name Rd (45661-9736)
PHONE.................................740 289-3722
Marty Moore, *Prin*
EMP: 6 **EST:** 2006
SALES (est): 765.27K **Privately Held**
SIC: 2421 Sawmills and planing mills, general

(G-12480)
OHIO VALLEY VENEER INC (PA)
Also Called: Ohio Valley Veneer Co
16523 State Route 124 (45661-9728)
PHONE.................................740 493-2901
Gregory P Bergethon, *Pr*
▼ **EMP:** 47 **EST:** 1990
SALES (est): 8.4MM **Privately Held**
Web: www.ohiovalleyveneer.com
SIC: 2426 2435 2421 Lumber, hardwood dimension; Hardwood veneer and plywood; Sawmills and planing mills, general

(G-12481)
OVERHEAD DOOR OF PIKE COUNTY
Also Called: Custom Hitch & Trailer
4237 Us Highway 23 (45661-9703)
PHONE.................................740 289-3925
James Nier, *Owner*
Della Nier, *Owner*
EMP: 7 **EST:** 1994
SALES (est): 463.77K **Privately Held**
Web: www.overheaddoorpike.com
SIC: 3442 5531 5031 1751 Garage doors, overhead: metal; Trailer hitches, automotive; Lumber, plywood, and millwork; Carpentry work

(G-12482)
PARADIGM INTERNATIONAL INC
4239 Us Highway 23 (45661-9703)
PHONE.................................740 370-2428
Jeff Humble, *Pr*
EMP: 7 **EST:** 2005
SALES (est): 329.96K **Privately Held**
SIC: 2385 Gowns, plastic: made from purchased materials

(G-12483)
RHK HARDWOODS LLC
9188 Chenoweth Fork Rd (45661-9630)
PHONE.................................740 835-1097
Ryan Knight, *Prin*
EMP: 8 **EST:** 2016
SALES (est): 202.57K **Privately Held**
SIC: 2499 Wood products, nec

(G-12484)
S&R LUMBER LLC
207 Sugar Run Rd (45661-9740)
P.O. Box 275 (45642-0275)
PHONE.................................740 352-6135
Paul Henderson, *Managing Member*
EMP: 16 **EST:** 2018
SQ FT: 1,524,600
SALES (est): 1.7MM **Privately Held**
SIC: 2421 Lumber: rough, sawed, or planed

(G-12485)
SYNERGY MANUFACTURING LLC
4239 Us Highway 23 (45661-9703)
PHONE.................................740 352-5933
EMP: 25 **EST:** 2016
SALES (est): 3.23MM **Privately Held**
SIC: 3089 Injection molding of plastics

(G-12486)
TAYLOR LUMBER WORLDWIDE INC
Also Called: Taylor Lumber
16523 State Route 124 (45661-9728)
P.O. Box 279 (45652-0279)
PHONE.................................740 259-6222
Edward Robbins, *Pr*
Greg Lute, *
Shery Spriggs, *
▼ **EMP:** 132 **EST:** 1882
SALES (est): 17.7MM **Privately Held**
SIC: 2421 Sawmills and planing mills, general

(G-12487)
WOOLDRIDGE LUMBER CO
3264 Laurel Ridge Rd (45661-9620)
PHONE.................................740 289-4912
Mick Wooldridge, *Pt*
Dora Ransey, *Sec*

Mick Woodridge, *Pt*
EMP: 46 **EST:** 1971
SQ FT: 6,000
SALES (est): 648.71K **Privately Held**
SIC: 2421 Sawmills and planing mills, general

Pioneer
Williams County

(G-12488)
ACTION PRECISION PRODUCTS INC
100 E North Ave (43554-7808)
P.O. Box 188 (43554-0188)
PHONE.................................419 737-2348
Linda Heisler, *Pr*
Vonnie Beggs, *Treas*
Gary Beggs, *VP*
EMP: 16 **EST:** 1972
SQ FT: 9,000
SALES (est): 463.49K **Privately Held**
Web: www.actionprecision.com
SIC: 3599 Machine shop, jobbing and repair

(G-12489)
ALTENLOH BRINCK & CO US INC
302 Clark St (43554-7962)
PHONE.................................419 737-2381
EMP: 38
SALES (corp-wide): 380.76MM **Privately Held**
Web: www.spax.us
SIC: 3452 Screws, metal
HQ: Altenloh, Brinck & Co. Us, Inc.
  2105 Williams Co Rd 12 C
  Bryan OH 43506

(G-12490)
ARTESIAN OF PIONEER INC (PA)
50 Industrial Ave (43554)
P.O. Box 247 (43554-0247)
PHONE.................................419 737-2352
EMP: 15 **EST:** 1960
SALES (est): 6.22MM
SALES (corp-wide): 6.22MM **Privately Held**
Web: www.aopwater.com
SIC: 1629 3589 Waste water and sewage treatment plant construction; Sewage and water treatment equipment

(G-12491)
DONGAN ELECTRIC MFG CO
Pioneer Transformer Company
500 Cedar St (43554-7874)
PHONE.................................419 737-2304
EMP: 6
SALES (corp-wide): 9.5MM **Privately Held**
Web: www.dongan.com
SIC: 3612 Machine tool transformers
PA: Dongan Electric Manufacturing Co Inc
  34760 Garfield Rd
  Fraser MI 48026
  313 567-8500

(G-12492)
FINISHING DEPARTMENT
201 Ohio St (43554-7934)
PHONE.................................419 737-3334
EMP: 7 **EST:** 2015
SALES (est): 85.9K **Privately Held**
Web: www.finishingdepartment.com
SIC: 3479 Coating of metals and formed products

(G-12493)
NN METAL STAMPINGS LLC (PA)
Also Called: Pennant
510 S Maple St (43554-7956)
P.O. Box 248 (43554-0248)
PHONE.................................419 737-2311
Rob Harger, *Pr*
Nelson Melillo, *
Larry Martin, *
EMP: 25 **EST:** 1976
SQ FT: 60,000
SALES (est): 4.82MM
SALES (corp-wide): 4.82MM **Privately Held**
Web: www.nnmetalstampings.com
SIC: 3469 3544 3465 Electronic enclosures, stamped or pressed metal; Special dies, tools, jigs, and fixtures; Automotive stampings

(G-12494)
PIONEER CUSTOM COATING LLC
255 Industrial Ave Bldg D (43554-9510)
P.O. Box 337 (43554-0337)
PHONE.................................419 737-3152
Deniss Sentle, *Managing Member*
Dennis Sentle, *Managing Member*
Merry Sentle, *Managing Member*
EMP: 9 **EST:** 2001
SQ FT: 2,400
SALES (est): 738.12K **Privately Held**
SIC: 3479 Coating of metals and formed products

(G-12495)
PIONEER CUSTOM MOLDING INC
3 Kexon Dr (43554-9200)
P.O. Box 463 (43554-0463)
PHONE.................................419 737-3252
Terry Hendricks, *CEO*
David Roth, *
Bill Peterson, *
EMP: 23 **EST:** 1997
SQ FT: 22,500
SALES (est): 2.36MM **Privately Held**
SIC: 3089 Injection molding of plastics

(G-12496)
PREMIERE CON SOLUTIONS LLC
Also Called: Con-Cure
508 Cedar St (43554-7874)
P.O. Box 157 (43554-0157)
PHONE.................................419 737-9808
EMP: 13 **EST:** 2004
SQ FT: 100,000
SALES (est): 2.84MM **Privately Held**
Web: www.concure.com
SIC: 3272 Concrete products, nec

(G-12497)
RAPID MACHINE INC
610 N State St (43554-9506)
P.O. Box 365 (43554-0365)
PHONE.................................419 737-2377
Jim F Spangler, *Pr*
Jennifer Wines, *Sec*
EMP: 12 **EST:** 1978
SQ FT: 10,000
SALES (est): 1.01MM **Privately Held**
Web: www.rapidmachineinc.com
SIC: 3544 3541 3469 3444 Special dies, tools, jigs, and fixtures; Grinding, polishing, buffing, lapping, and honing machines; Metal stampings, nec; Sheet metalwork

(G-12498)
REIFEL INDUSTRIES INC
201 Ohio St (43554)
P.O. Box 909 (43554)
PHONE.................................419 737-2138
Thomas Reifel, *Pr*
M Kathleen Reifel, *
Louis Reifel, *
▲ **EMP:** 65 **EST:** 1984
SQ FT: 60,000
SALES (est): 9.89MM **Privately Held**
Web: www.finishingdepartment.com
SIC: 3479 3471 Coating of metals and formed products; Plating and polishing

(G-12499)
RELIABLE METAL BUILDINGS LLC
16570 Us Highway 20ns (43554-9614)
PHONE.................................419 737-1300
EMP: 6 **EST:** 2017
SALES (est): 1.07MM **Privately Held**
Web: www.reliablemetalbuildingsllc.com
SIC: 3448 Prefabricated metal buildings and components

(G-12500)
UNIVERSAL INDUSTRIAL PDTS INC
1 Coreway Dr (43554)
P.O. Box 628 (43554-0628)
PHONE.................................419 737-9584
Neil Marko, *Pr*
Randy Herriman, *Treas*
▲ **EMP:** 18 **EST:** 1947
SQ FT: 86,000
SALES (est): 7.22MM **Privately Held**
Web: www.universalindustrialproducts.com
SIC: 3429 Hardware, nec

Piqua
Miami County

(G-12501)
AESTHETIC FINISHERS INC
1502 S Main St (45356-8319)
PHONE.................................937 778-8777
Sally Coomer, *CEO*
William Coomer Iii, *VP*
EMP: 35 **EST:** 1992
SQ FT: 72,000
SALES (est): 3.12MM **Privately Held**
Web: www.afipowder.com
SIC: 3479 Coating of metals and formed products

(G-12502)
ALLIED COATING CORPORATION
220 Fox Dr (45356-9271)
PHONE.................................937 615-0391
Greg Flanary, *Pr*
Karen Flanary, *VP*
EMP: 10 **EST:** 1994
SALES (est): 913.42K **Privately Held**
Web: www.alliedcoating.net
SIC: 3479 Coating of metals and formed products

(G-12503)
APEX ALUMINUM DIE CAST CO INC
8877 Sherry Dr (45356-9111)
P.O. Box 617 (45356-0617)
PHONE.................................937 773-0432
EMP: 50 **EST:** 1980
SALES (est): 9.31MM **Privately Held**
Web: www.apexdiecasting.com
SIC: 3363 3369 Aluminum die-castings; Nonferrous foundries, nec

(G-12504)
ARKANSAS FACE VENEER CO INC (HQ)
1025 S Roosevelt Ave (45356-3713)
P.O. Box 919 (45356-0919)
PHONE.................................937 773-6295
Jeffery A Bannister, *CEO*
James Robert Hartzell, *Ch Bd*
Jon Snyder, *Pr*
Michael Bardo, *VP Fin*
Randi Pearson, *Treas*
▲ **EMP:** 12 **EST:** 1956
SQ FT: 20,000
SALES (est): 3.61MM
SALES (corp-wide): 11.08MM **Privately Held**
Web: www.arkansasface.com
SIC: 2435 Veneer stock, hardwood
PA: Hartzell Industries, Inc.
  1025 S Roosevelt Ave
  Piqua OH 45356
  937 773-6295

(G-12505)
ATLANTIC WELDING LLC
1708 Commerce Dr (45356-2602)
PHONE.................................937 570-5094
Zachary Walker, *Managing Member*
EMP: 11 **EST:** 2021
SALES (est): 2.4MM **Privately Held**
Web: www.atlanticweldingservices.com
SIC: 7389 1629 3317 1791 Business Activities at Non-Commercial Site; Oil refinery construction; Welded pipe and tubes; Structural steel erection

(G-12506)
ATLANTIS SPORTSWEAR INC
Also Called: College Issue
344 Fox Dr (45356-8298)
PHONE.................................937 773-0680
David Scott Reardon, *
David Scott Reardon, *
Gail Reardon, *
▲ **EMP:** 35 **EST:** 1985
SQ FT: 65,000
SALES (est): 4.49MM **Privately Held**
Web: www.atlantissports.com
SIC: 2261 2395 2396 Screen printing of cotton broadwoven fabrics; Emblems, embroidered; Automotive and apparel trimmings

(G-12507)
BORNHORST MOTOR SERVICE INC
Also Called: Electric Motor Service
8270 N Dixie Dr (45356-8636)
P.O. Box 110 (45356-0110)
PHONE.................................937 773-0426
Regina Owen, *Pr*
EMP: 8 **EST:** 1955
SQ FT: 6,000
SALES (est): 649.51K **Privately Held**
SIC: 7694 5063 Electric motor repair; Motors, electric

(G-12508)
CRANE PUMPS & SYSTEMS INC
Also Called: Pacific Valve
420 3rd St (45356-3918)
PHONE.................................937 773-2442
Allan Oak, *Brnch Mgr*
EMP: 175
SALES (corp-wide): 2.09B **Publicly Held**
Web: www.cranepumps.com
SIC: 5085 3494 Valves and fittings; Valves and pipe fittings, nec
HQ: Crane Pumps & Systems, Inc.
  420 3rd St
  Piqua OH 45356
  937 773-2442

(G-12509)
CRANE PUMPS & SYSTEMS INC (HQ)
420 3rd St (45356-3918)
PHONE.................................937 773-2442
Jim Lavish, *Pr*
◆ **EMP:** 328 **EST:** 1946
SQ FT: 120,000
SALES (est): 49.24MM
SALES (corp-wide): 2.09B **Publicly Held**

Piqua - Miami County (G-12510)

Web: www.cranepumps.com
SIC: 3561 Industrial pumps and parts
PA: Crane Company
100 1st Stmford Pl Ste 40
Stamford CT 06902
203 363-7300

(G-12510)
CRANE PUMPS & SYSTEMS INC
1950 Covington Ave (45356-2636)
PHONE..................................937 778-8947
Roy Speigle, *Brnch Mgr*
EMP: 166
SALES (corp-wide): 2.09B **Publicly Held**
Web: www.cranepumps.com
SIC: 3561 Pumps, domestic: water or sump
HQ: Crane Pumps & Systems, Inc.
420 3rd St
Piqua OH 45356
937 773-2442

(G-12511)
CRAYEX CORPORATION (PA)
1747 Commerce Dr (45356-2601)
P.O. Box 1673 (45356-4673)
PHONE..................................937 773-7000
▼ EMP: 65 EST: 1972
SALES (est): 19.86MM
SALES (corp-wide): 19.86MM **Privately Held**
Web: www.crayex.com
SIC: 2671 2673 3081 Plastic film, coated or laminated for packaging; Plastic bags: made from purchased materials; Unsupported plastics film and sheet

(G-12512)
DARKE PRECISION INC
291 Fox Dr (45356-9265)
P.O. Box 746 (45331-0746)
PHONE..................................937 548-2232
Harold Young, *Pr*
Randy Young, *Sec*
Roger Young, *Prin*
EMP: 17 EST: 1984
SQ FT: 4,800
SALES (est): 826.13K **Privately Held**
SIC: 3544 Special dies and tools

(G-12513)
DENIZEN INC
130 Fox Dr (45356-9269)
PHONE..................................937 615-9561
◆ EMP: 12 EST: 1996
SQ FT: 21,000
SALES (est): 4.82MM **Privately Held**
Web: www.denizenbracelet.com
SIC: 2241 5033 Electric insulating tapes and braids, except plastic; Insulation materials

(G-12514)
DYNA-VAC PLASTICS INC
921 S Downing St (45356-3823)
P.O. Box 614 (45356-0614)
PHONE..................................937 773-0092
Scott Lade, *Pr*
Richard Lade, *Prin*
Sandra Lade, *Sec*
EMP: 6 EST: 1985
SQ FT: 18,000
SALES (est): 594K **Privately Held**
SIC: 3089 Injection molding of plastics

(G-12515)
EPSILYTE HOLDINGS LLC
Also Called: Compounded Eps
555 E Statler Rd (45356-9227)
PHONE..................................937 778-9500
Matt Cox, *Brnch Mgr*
EMP: 75
SALES (corp-wide): 9.52MM **Privately Held**

Web: www.epsilyte.com
SIC: 2821 5162 Polystyrene resins; Resins
PA: Epsilyte Holdings Llc
1330 Lake Robbins Dr # 310
The Woodlands TX 77380
815 224-1525

(G-12516)
FORREST ENTERPRISES INC
Also Called: Forre Sports Accessories
510 W Statler Rd (45356-8281)
P.O. Box 244 (45356-0244)
PHONE..................................937 773-1714
James C Reynolds, *Pr*
Staton C Reynolds, *Pr*
Curtis Reynolds, *Treas*
▲ EMP: 11 EST: 1955
SQ FT: 6,500
SALES (est): 1.22MM **Privately Held**
Web: www.4sportsus.com
SIC: 4783 3949 3089 Packing and crating; Sporting and athletic goods, nec; Blister or bubble formed packaging, plastics

(G-12517)
FRENCH OIL MILL MACHINERY CO (PA)
Also Called: French USA
1035 W Greene St (45356-1855)
P.O. Box 920 (45356-0920)
PHONE..................................937 773-3420
Tayte French Lutz, *V Ch Bd*
Daniel P French, *
Irvin G Bieser Junior, *Sec*
Jason P Mcdaniel, *COO*
Dennis D Bratton, *
▲ EMP: 74 EST: 1900
SQ FT: 210,000
SALES (est): 20.79MM
SALES (corp-wide): 20.79MM **Privately Held**
Web: www.frenchoil.com
SIC: 3559 3542 3556 3554 Rubber working machinery, including tires; Presses: hydraulic and pneumatic, mechanical and manual; Presses, food: cheese, beet, cider, and sugarcane; Pulp mill machinery

(G-12518)
HAMPSHIRE CO
9225 State Route 66 (45356-8700)
P.O. Box 1195 (45356-1195)
PHONE..................................937 773-3493
Thomas F Hampshire, *Pr*
Robert Mikolajewski, *
Dorothy M Hampshire, *
EMP: 17 EST: 1957
SQ FT: 50,000
SALES (est): 3.05MM **Privately Held**
Web: www.hampshirecabinetry.com
SIC: 2434 Vanities, bathroom: wood

(G-12519)
HARMONY SYSTEMS AND SVC INC
1711 Commerce Dr (45356-2601)
PHONE..................................937 778-1082
▲ EMP: 70 EST: 1994
SQ FT: 110,000
SALES (est): 22.32MM **Privately Held**
Web: www.harmonysysandsvc.com
SIC: 3089 Injection molding of plastics

(G-12520)
HARTZELL FAN INC (PA)
910 S Downing St (45356-3824)
PHONE..................................937 773-7411
James Robert Hartzell, *Ch Bd*
Jeff Bannister Hartzell, *CEO*
George Atkinson, *Pr*
Thomas Gustafson, *VP*
Jane Farley, *Sec*

◆ EMP: 145 EST: 1927
SQ FT: 196,000
SALES (est): 40.53MM
SALES (corp-wide): 40.53MM **Privately Held**
Web: www.hartzellairmovement.com
SIC: 3564 3433 Blowers and fans; Heating equipment, except electric

(G-12521)
HARTZELL HARDWOODS INC (PA)
1025 S Roosevelt Ave (45356)
P.O. Box 919 (45356)
PHONE..................................937 773-7054
James Robert Hartzell, *Ch Bd*
Jeffery Bannister, *
Kelly Hostetter, *
Jane Osborn, *
▼ EMP: 65 EST: 1928
SQ FT: 275,000
SALES (est): 20.89MM
SALES (corp-wide): 20.89MM **Privately Held**
Web: www.hartzellhardwoods.com
SIC: 5031 2421 2426 Lumber: rough, dressed, and finished; Sawmills and planing mills, general; Hardwood dimension and flooring mills

(G-12522)
HARTZELL INDUSTRIES INC (PA)
1025 S Roosevelt Ave (45356-3713)
P.O. Box 919 (45356-0919)
PHONE..................................937 773-6295
James Robert Hartzell, *Ch Bd*
Jeff Bannister, *CEO*
Chris Oliss, *CFO*
Michael Bardo, *Pr*
Jane Farley, *Sec*
EMP: 13 EST: 1964
SQ FT: 20,000
SALES (est): 11.08MM
SALES (corp-wide): 11.08MM **Privately Held**
Web: www.hartzellairmovement.com
SIC: 2435 6719 Veneer stock, hardwood; Personal holding companies, except banks

(G-12523)
HARTZELL PROPELLER INC
1 Propeller Pl (45356-2656)
PHONE..................................937 778-4200
Joseph Brown, *Pr*
James Brown Iii, *Prin*
Jj Frigge, *
Bruce C Hanke, *
Robert G Allenbaugh, *
◆ EMP: 285 EST: 1917
SQ FT: 175,000
SALES (est): 52.83MM
SALES (corp-wide): 653.43MM **Privately Held**
Web: www.hartzellprop.com
SIC: 3728 Aircraft propellers and associated equipment
PA: Arcline Investment Management Lp
4 Embrcadero Ctr Ste 3460
San Francisco CA 94111
415 801-4570

(G-12524)
HOBART BROTHERS LLC
8585 Industry Park Dr (45356-9511)
PHONE..................................937 332-5953
Jim Schwepeji, *Prin*
EMP: 7
SALES (corp-wide): 16.11B **Publicly Held**
Web: www.hobartbrothers.com
SIC: 3548 Welding apparatus
HQ: Hobart Brothers Llc
101 Trade Sq E

Troy OH 45373
937 332-5439

(G-12525)
HOBART LLC
Also Called: P M I Food Equipment Group
8515 Industry Park Dr (45356-9511)
P.O. Box 702 (45356-0702)
PHONE..................................937 332-2797
EMP: 31
SALES (corp-wide): 16.11B **Publicly Held**
Web: www.hobartcorp.com
SIC: 3589 3556 3596 3585 Dishwashing machines, commercial; Food products machinery; Weighing machines and apparatus; Refrigeration equipment, complete
HQ: Hobart Llc
701 S Ridge Ave
Troy OH 45373

(G-12526)
INDUSTRY PRODUCTS CO (PA)
500 W Statler Rd (45356-8281)
PHONE..................................937 778-0585
Linda Cleveland, *Pr*
▲ EMP: 366 EST: 1966
SQ FT: 335,000
SALES (est): 44.52MM
SALES (corp-wide): 44.52MM **Privately Held**
Web: www.industryproductsco.com
SIC: 7692 3053 3714 3544 Automotive welding; Gaskets, all materials; Motor vehicle parts and accessories; Special dies, tools, jigs, and fixtures

(G-12527)
ISAIAH INDUSTRIES INC (PA)
Also Called: Classic Metal Roofing Systems
8510 Industry Park Dr (45356-8535)
P.O. Box 701 (45356-0701)
PHONE..................................937 773-9840
Todd Miller, *CEO*
◆ EMP: 55 EST: 1980
SQ FT: 5,000
SALES (est): 10.07MM
SALES (corp-wide): 10.07MM **Privately Held**
Web: www.isaiahindustries.com
SIC: 3354 3444 2952 Aluminum extruded products; Sheet metalwork; Asphalt felts and coatings

(G-12528)
J & D WOOD LTD
Also Called: J&D Wood Enterprises
401 S College St (45356-3429)
PHONE..................................937 778-9663
Joe A Kinsella, *Pr*
Douglas Kinsella, *VP*
EMP: 7 EST: 1982
SQ FT: 12,000
SALES (est): 550K **Privately Held**
Web: www.qualitypinebedding.com
SIC: 2499 Trophy bases, wood

(G-12529)
J M MOLD INC
1707 Commerce Dr (45356-2601)
PHONE..................................937 778-0077
Kriss Scheer, *Pr*
Robert P Scheer, *Pr*
EMP: 8 EST: 1966
SQ FT: 9,600
SALES (est): 952.75K **Privately Held**
Web: www.jmmoldinc.com
SIC: 3544 Industrial molds

GEOGRAPHIC SECTION
Piqua - Miami County (G-12553)

(G-12530)
JACKSON TUBE SERVICE INC (PA)
8210 Industry Park Dr (45356-8536)
P.O. Box 1650 (45356-4650)
PHONE.....................937 773-8550
Robert W Jackson, *CEO*
Marcus Sergy, *
▲ **EMP:** 127 **EST:** 1972
SQ FT: 75,000
SALES (est): 22.55MM
SALES (corp-wide): 22.55MM **Privately Held**
Web: www.jackson-tube.com
SIC: 3317 Steel pipe and tubes

(G-12531)
K B MACHINE & TOOL INC
1500 S Main St (45356-8319)
P.O. Box 426 (45356-0426)
PHONE.....................937 773-1624
Kenneth G Bricker, *Pr*
Joyce K Bricker, *Sec*
Miki Bricker, *VP*
EMP: 9 **EST:** 1972
SQ FT: 9,500
SALES (est): 947.51K **Privately Held**
SIC: 3544 Special dies and tools

(G-12532)
LITTLE PRINTING COMPANY
Also Called: Quality Forms
4317 W Us Route 36 (45356-9334)
P.O. Box 1176 (45356-1176)
PHONE.....................937 773-4595
Tom Kinnison, *Pr*
L J Bertke, *VP*
EMP: 14 **EST:** 1953
SQ FT: 54,000
SALES (est): 424.64K **Privately Held**
Web: www.qualforms.com
SIC: 2752 Offset printing

(G-12533)
LOSTCREEK TOOL & MACHINE INC
1150 S Main St (45356-9357)
PHONE.....................937 773-6022
Steve Rowe, *Pr*
Donald Rowe, *VP*
Shelby Rowe, *Sec*
EMP: 11 **EST:** 1978
SQ FT: 15,500
SALES (est): 413.7K **Privately Held**
SIC: 3599 7692 3544 Machine shop, jobbing and repair; Welding repair; Special dies, tools, jigs, and fixtures

(G-12534)
MAKERS SUPPLY LLC
6665 N Spiker Rd (45356-9333)
PHONE.....................937 203-8245
Garrett Burgoon, *Managing Member*
EMP: 6 **EST:** 2021
SALES (est): 530.13K **Privately Held**
SIC: 5093 2448 Scrap and waste materials; Wood pallets and skids

(G-12535)
MARK KNUPP MUFFLER & TIRE INC
950 S College St (45356-3700)
PHONE.....................937 773-1334
Mark Knupp, *Pr*
Rosemary Knupp, *Sec*
EMP: 21 **EST:** 1987
SQ FT: 9,000
SALES (est): 487.73K **Privately Held**
Web: www.markknupp.com
SIC: 5531 7533 7534 7539 Automotive parts; Muffler shop, sale or repair and installation; Tire repair shop; Brake repair, automotive

(G-12536)
MIAMI SPECIALTIES INC
Also Called: M C D Plastics & Manufacturing
172 Robert M Davis Pkwy (45356-8338)
PHONE.....................937 778-1850
Joann Howell, *Pr*
Robb Howell Iii, *VP*
EMP: 7 **EST:** 1993
SQ FT: 10,000
SALES (est): 869.12K **Privately Held**
SIC: 3089 Injection molding of plastics

(G-12537)
MINUTEMAN PRESS
120 W Water St (45356-2326)
PHONE.....................937 451-8222
EMP: 10 **EST:** 1975
SALES (est): 83.91K **Privately Held**
Web: www.minutemanpress.com
SIC: 2752 Commercial printing, lithographic

(G-12538)
NICKS PLATING CO
6980 Free Rd (45356-9279)
P.O. Box 337 (45356-0337)
PHONE.....................937 773-3175
Duane Penrod, *Pr*
EMP: 10 **EST:** 1973
SQ FT: 4,500
SALES (est): 921.46K **Privately Held**
Web: www.nicksplating.com
SIC: 3471 Electroplating of metals or formed products

(G-12539)
NITTO INC
220 Fox Dr (45356-9271)
PHONE.....................937 773-4820
EMP: 11
Web: www.nitto.com
SIC: 3714 Motor vehicle parts and accessories
HQ: Nitto, Inc.
400 Frank W Burr Blvd # 66
Teaneck NJ 07666
732 901-7905

(G-12540)
NITTO INC
1620 S Main St (45356-8320)
PHONE.....................937 773-4820
▲ **EMP:** 13
Web: www.nitto.com
SIC: 3714 Motor vehicle parts and accessories
HQ: Nitto, Inc.
400 Frank W Burr Blvd # 66
Teaneck NJ 07666
732 901-7905

(G-12541)
P & R SPECIALTY INC
1835 W High St (45356-9399)
P.O. Box 741 (45356-0741)
PHONE.....................937 773-0263
Greg Blankenship, *Pr*
Pat Kiernan, *
Alissa Blankenship, *
Mike Koon, *
Vincent Reidy, *
▲ **EMP:** 35 **EST:** 1982
SQ FT: 47,500
SALES (est): 5.26MM **Privately Held**
Web: www.prspecialty.com
SIC: 2499 3053 2675 2631 Spools, wood; Gaskets, all materials; Paper die-cutting; Paperboard mills

(G-12542)
PERFECTO INDUSTRIES INC
1729 W High St (45356-9300)
PHONE.....................937 778-1900
EMP: 45
SALES (corp-wide): 12.96MM **Privately Held**
Web: www.perfectoindustries.com
SIC: 3547 3549 3599 3537 Rolling mill machinery; Coiling machinery; Custom machinery; Industrial trucks and tractors
PA: Perfecto Industries, Inc.
1567 Calkins Dr
Gaylord MI 49735
989 732-2941

(G-12543)
PIQUA CHAMPION FOUNDRY INC
Also Called: Piqua
918 S Main St (45356-3858)
P.O. Box 716 (45356-0716)
PHONE.....................937 773-1234
EMP: 53 **EST:** 1974
SQ FT: 35,000
SALES (est): 1.15MM **Privately Held**
Web: www.championfoundry.com
SIC: 3321 Gray iron castings, nec

(G-12544)
PIQUA CHOCOLATE COMPANY INC (PA)
Also Called: Winans Chocolate and Coffee
124 N Main St (45356-2312)
PHONE.....................937 773-1981
Joe Reiser, *Pr*
EMP: 9 **EST:** 1993
SQ FT: 2,000
SALES (est): 5.3MM
SALES (corp-wide): 5.3MM **Privately Held**
Web: www.winanschocolate.com
SIC: 5441 5947 2064 Candy; Greeting cards ; Candy and other confectionery products

(G-12545)
PIQUA EMERY CUTTER & FNDRY CO
Also Called: Piqua Emery Foundry
821 S Downing St (45356-3821)
PHONE.....................937 773-4134
Stephen Mikolajewski, *Pr*
Helen Mikolajewski, *
Roger Mclain, *VP*
EMP: 54 **EST:** 1934
SQ FT: 54,000
SALES (est): 4.84MM **Privately Held**
Web: www.piquaemery.com
SIC: 3365 3369 3366 Aluminum and aluminum-based alloy castings; Nonferrous foundries, nec; Castings (except die), nec, bronze

(G-12546)
PIQUA GRANITE & MARBLE CO INC (PA)
Also Called: Classic Monuments
123 N Main St (45356-2311)
PHONE.....................937 773-2000
TOLL FREE: 800
Pat Obara, *Pr*
Steve Supinger, *VP*
EMP: 9 **EST:** 1882
SQ FT: 18,000
SALES (est): 896.15K
SALES (corp-wide): 896.15K **Privately Held**
Web: www.classicmonuments.com
SIC: 5999 5032 3281 Monuments, finished to custom order; Granite building stone; Marble, building: cut and shaped

(G-12547)
PIQUA MATERIALS INC
Also Called: Piqua Mineral Division
1750 W Statler Rd (45356-9264)
PHONE.....................937 773-4824
John Harris, *Brnch Mgr*
EMP: 79
SQ FT: 16,808
Web: www.piquamaterials.com
SIC: 1422 3274 Limestones, ground; Lime
PA: Piqua Materials, Inc.
11641 Mosteller Rd Ste 1
Cincinnati OH 45241

(G-12548)
PIQUA PAPER BOX COMPANY
616 Covington Ave (45356-3205)
P.O. Box 814 (45356-0814)
PHONE.....................937 773-0313
TOLL FREE: 800
Brian T Gleason, *Pr*
Frank J Gleason Junior, *Ch Bd*
Eugene Elsass, *
▲ **EMP:** 35 **EST:** 1908
SQ FT: 85,000
SALES (est): 3.87MM **Privately Held**
Web: www.piquapaperbox.com
SIC: 2653 Boxes, corrugated: made from purchased materials

(G-12549)
POLYSOURCE LLC
Also Called: Epsilyte
555 E Statler Rd (45356-9227)
PHONE.....................937 778-9500
David Shainberg, *Pr*
EMP: 40 **EST:** 2021
SALES (est): 8.53MM **Privately Held**
Web: www.polysource.net
SIC: 3089 Injection molding of plastics

(G-12550)
PROTO-MOLD PRODUCTS CO INC
1750 Commerce Dr (45356-2699)
PHONE.....................937 778-1959
Graig Flintcraft, *Pr*
Craig Flitcraft, *
EMP: 25 **EST:** 1979
SQ FT: 50,000
SALES (est): 2.31MM **Privately Held**
Web: www.protomoldproducts.com
SIC: 3089 Injection molding of plastics

(G-12551)
QUEEN EXHIBITS LLC
1707 Commerce Dr (45356-2601)
PHONE.....................937 615-6051
Walter Foster Queen, *Prin*
EMP: 9 **EST:** 2019
SALES (est): 415.69K **Privately Held**
Web: www.queenexhibits.com
SIC: 3993 Signs and advertising specialties

(G-12552)
RETTERBUSH FIBERGLASS CORP
719 Long St (45356-9262)
P.O. Box 207 (45356-0207)
PHONE.....................937 778-1936
Bryan Retterbush, *Pr*
EMP: 25 **EST:** 1976
SQ FT: 32,000
SALES (est): 2.51MM **Privately Held**
Web: www.retterbushfiberglass.com
SIC: 3089 Injection molding of plastics

(G-12553)
RV XPRESS INC
501 East St (45356-3930)
PHONE.....................937 418-0127
Michael T Mcgahan, *Prin*

Piqua - Miami County (G-12554) GEOGRAPHIC SECTION

Glenn Mckinney, *Pr*
EMP: 8 **EST:** 2007
SALES (est): 424.46K **Privately Held**
SIC: 3799 Recreational vehicles

(G-12554)
SMYRNA READY MIX CONCRETE LLC
Also Called: Srm Concrete
8395 Piqua Lockington Rd (45356-9701)
PHONE..................................937 773-0841
Dick Hoying, *Brnch Mgr*
EMP: 77
SALES (corp-wide): 1.05B **Privately Held**
Web: www.smyrnareadymix.com
SIC: 3273 Ready-mixed concrete
PA: Smyrna Ready Mix Concrete, Llc
1000 Hollingshead Cir
Murfreesboro TN 37129
615 355-1028

(G-12555)
TAILWIND TECHNOLOGIES INC (PA)
1 Propeller Pl (45356-2655)
PHONE..................................937 778-4200
James W Brown Iii, *Pr*
Matthew L Jesch, *CFO*
Joseph W Brown, *Prin*
Michael J Piscatella, *Prin*
EMP: 569 **EST:** 1988
SALES (est): 78.76MM **Privately Held**
Web: www.tailwindtechnologiesinc.com
SIC: 3356 Titanium

(G-12556)
TEMPO MANUFACTURING COMPANY
Also Called: Tempo Trophy Mfg
727 E Ash St (45356-2411)
P.O. Box 718 (45356-0718)
PHONE..................................937 773-6613
Robert Elrod, *Pr*
Patricia Elrod, *VP*
EMP: 8 **EST:** 1946
SQ FT: 30,000
SALES (est): 710.26K **Privately Held**
SIC: 3914 Trophies, nsk

(G-12557)
US KONDO CORPORATION
233 1st St (45356-4005)
PHONE..................................937 916-3045
Koshin Shimasaki, *Pr*
▲ **EMP:** 12 **EST:** 2009
SALES (est): 2.29MM **Privately Held**
Web: www.uskondo.com
SIC: 3714 Motor vehicle parts and accessories

Plain City
Madison County

(G-12558)
44TOOLSCOM
7640 Commerce Pl (43064-9222)
PHONE..................................614 873-4800
EMP: 6 **EST:** 2011
SALES (est): 656.03K **Privately Held**
Web: www.44tools.com
SIC: 3861 Motion picture film

(G-12559)
ACTIVE AERATION SYSTEMS INC
7245 Industrial Pkwy (43064-9487)
PHONE..................................614 873-3626
Deborah Wade, *CEO*
John Graves, *Pr*
Patty Hoke, *VP*
EMP: 6 **EST:** 1985
SALES (est): 735.85K **Privately Held**

SIC: 5046 5039 3589 Commercial equipment, nec; Septic tanks; Sewage treatment equipment

(G-12560)
ADVANCED GREEN TECH INC
8059 Corporate Blvd Ste A (43064-8070)
PHONE..................................614 397-8130
Christopher Brossia, *VP*
EMP: 6 **EST:** 2012
SALES (est): 210K **Privately Held**
SIC: 8999 3589 2096 5084 Scientific consulting; Water treatment equipment, industrial; Potato chips and other potato-based snacks; Pulp (wood) manufacturing machinery

(G-12561)
ALTRASERV LLC
Also Called: Brio Coffee Co
8495 Estates Ct (43064-8083)
P.O. Box 355 (43017-0355)
PHONE..................................614 889-2500
Dorothy Moran, *Pr*
Tom Moran, *VP*
EMP: 6 **EST:** 2008
SALES (est): 658.68K **Privately Held**
Web: www.altraserv.com
SIC: 2095 Roasted coffee

(G-12562)
APPLIED EXPERIENCE LLC
7780 Corporate Blvd (43064-3598)
PHONE..................................614 943-2970
Matthew Schrader, *Prin*
George Catlin, *Prin*
Christopher Brandon, *Prin*
Kedar Kapoor, *Prin*
Michael Krull, *Prin*
EMP: 7 **EST:** 2015
SALES (est): 691.28K **Privately Held**
Web: www.appliedxp.com
SIC: 7389 7373 8711 3599 Drafting service, except temporary help; Computer integrated systems design; Engineering services; Machine and other job shop work

(G-12563)
AUTOTOOL INC
7875 Corporate Blvd (43064-8045)
PHONE..................................614 733-0222
Bassam Homsi, *Pr*
EMP: 38 **EST:** 1994
SQ FT: 40,000
SALES (est): 6.34MM **Privately Held**
Web: www.autotoolinc.com
SIC: 3559 Automotive related machinery

(G-12564)
BAHLER MEDICAL INC
Also Called: Venture Medical
8910 Warner Rd (43064-9467)
PHONE..................................614 873-7600
Michael Bahler, *Pr*
EMP: 10 **EST:** 1987
SALES (est): 250.4K **Privately Held**
SIC: 3842 Implants, surgical

(G-12565)
BEACHY BARNS LTD
8720 Amish Pike (43064-9538)
PHONE..................................614 873-4193
TOLL FREE: 800
EMP: 12 **EST:** 1981
SQ FT: 7,500
SALES (est): 1.76MM **Privately Held**
Web: www.beachybarns.com
SIC: 2452 1542 Prefabricated wood buildings ; Garage construction

(G-12566)
BINDERY & SPC PRESSWORKS INC
Also Called: Pressworks
351 W Bigelow Ave (43064-1152)
PHONE..................................614 873-4623
Dick Izzard, *Pr*
Betty Izzard, *
Mark Izzard, *
Doug Izzard, *
Tami Roberts, *
EMP: 74 **EST:** 1978
SQ FT: 42,000
SALES (est): 18.97MM **Privately Held**
Web: www.pressworks.us
SIC: 2791 7331 2759 2789 Typesetting; Mailing service; Commercial printing, nec; Bookbinding and related work

(G-12567)
BROOKS PASTRIES INC
8205 Estates Pkwy Ste F (43064-8018)
PHONE..................................614 274-4880
Donald Wess Senior, *Pr*
Margret Wess, *VP*
EMP: 8
SALES (est): 475.5K **Privately Held**
SIC: 2051 5461 Bread, all types (white, wheat, rye, etc); fresh or frozen; Bread

(G-12568)
BUILDING BLOCK PERFORMANCE LLC
7920 Corporate Blvd Ste C (43064-9275)
PHONE..................................614 918-7476
Kamyron A White, *Managing Member*
EMP: 6 **EST:** 2014
SALES (est): 125.21K **Privately Held**
SIC: 7999 7372 Physical fitness instruction; Application computer software

(G-12569)
CALZUROCOM
8055 Corporate Blvd Unit B (43064)
PHONE..................................800 257-9472
Katherine Wesney, *Pr*
EMP: 7 **EST:** 2015
SALES (est): 226.14K **Privately Held**
Web: www.calzuro.com
SIC: 3021 Protective footwear, rubber or plastic

(G-12570)
CAMELOT CELLARS WINERY
7780 Corporate Blvd (43064-3598)
PHONE..................................614 441-8860
Charles Frobose, *Prin*
EMP: 10 **EST:** 2007
SALES (est): 360.24K **Privately Held**
Web: www.camelotcellars.com
SIC: 2084 Wines

(G-12571)
COM-FAB INC
4657 Price Hilliards Rd (43064-8838)
PHONE..................................740 857-1107
Jim Sheehy, *Pr*
EMP: 22 **EST:** 1970
SQ FT: 20,000
SALES (est): 2.65MM **Privately Held**
Web: www.comfab-inc.com
SIC: 3441 Fabricated structural metal

(G-12572)
DAILY NEEDS ASSISTANCE INC
Also Called: D N A
340 W Main St (43064-1198)
P.O. Box 211 (43064-0211)
PHONE..................................614 824-8340
Tamara Reed, *Dir*
EMP: 6 **EST:** 2013

SALES (est): 526.17K **Privately Held**
Web: www.dnaplaincity.org
SIC: 2711 Newspapers, publishing and printing

(G-12573)
DARBY CREEK MILLWORK LLC
10001 Plain City Georgesville Rd Ne (43064)
PHONE..................................614 873-3267
EMP: 7 **EST:** 1990
SQ FT: 8,000
SALES (est): 716.95K **Privately Held**
Web: www.darbymillworks.com
SIC: 2431 Doors, wood

(G-12574)
DELAWARE PAINT COMPANY LTD
Also Called: Ohio Brush Works
8455 Rausch Dr (43064-8064)
PHONE..................................740 368-9981
Pete Newton, *Pr*
Phillip Hopkins, *VP*
EMP: 15 **EST:** 2001
SQ FT: 12,000
SALES (est): 3.6MM **Privately Held**
Web: www.delawarepaintco.com
SIC: 3991 Brooms

(G-12575)
DISTINCTIVE MARBLE & GRAN INC
7635 Commerce Pl (43064-9223)
PHONE..................................614 760-0003
Chris Schnetzler, *Pr*
Kathy Schnetzler, *Prin*
▲ **EMP:** 10 **EST:** 2001
SALES (est): 1.54MM **Privately Held**
Web: www.distinctivemarbleandgranite.com
SIC: 1743 3281 Marble installation, interior; Curbing, granite or stone

(G-12576)
DRIVETRAIN USA INC
Also Called: Cryogenic Technical Services
8445 Rausch Dr (43064-8064)
P.O. Box 3787 (43016-0406)
PHONE..................................614 733-0940
John Canfield, *Pr*
EMP: 10 **EST:** 2008
SQ FT: 40,000
SALES (est): 937.03K **Privately Held**
SIC: 3679 Cryogenic cooling devices for infrared detectors, masers

(G-12577)
ECOCHEM ALTERNATIVE FUELS LLC
7304 Town St (43064-9483)
PHONE..................................614 764-3835
Joshua Koch, *Pt*
Joshua Koch, *CEO*
EMP: 35 **EST:** 2011
SALES (est): 4.66MM **Privately Held**
Web: www.hpcdfuel.com
SIC: 2869 Fuels

(G-12578)
ELASTOSTAR RUBBER CORP
8475 Rausch Dr (43064-8064)
PHONE..................................614 841-4400
Ghanshyam Dungarani, *Sls Mgr*
EMP: 20 **EST:** 2013
SALES (est): 1.61MM **Privately Held**
Web: www.elastostar.com
SIC: 3069 Medical and laboratory rubber sundries and related products

GEOGRAPHIC SECTION

Plain City - Madison County (G-12604)

(G-12579)
FRIESEN TRANSFER LTD
9280 Iams Rd (43064-9108)
PHONE..............................614 873-5672
Klaas Friesen, *Pr*
EMP: 6 **EST:** 1979
SALES (est): 460K **Privately Held**
SIC: 3713 0115 0111 Dump truck bodies; Corn; Wheat

(G-12580)
GOLF CAR COMPANY INC
8899 Memorial Dr (43064-8636)
PHONE..............................614 873-1055
William Mead, *Pr*
EMP: 12 **EST:** 2000
SALES (est): 656.55K **Privately Held**
Web: www.nationalcarts.com
SIC: 3949 7359 5599 Sporting and athletic goods, nec; Stores and yards equipment rental; Golf cart, powered

(G-12581)
HYRADIX INC
8445 Rausch Dr (43064-8064)
PHONE..............................847 391-1200
David M Cepla, *Pr*
▲ **EMP:** 20 **EST:** 2002
SALES (est): 499.07K **Privately Held**
SIC: 3569 Gas producers, generators, and other gas related equipment
PA: Eden Innovations Ltd
  L 15 197 St Georges Tce
  Perth WA 6000

(G-12582)
KML ACQUISITIONS LTD
10325 Spicebrush Dr (43064-2608)
PHONE..............................614 732-9777
EMP: 6 **EST:** 2001
SALES (est): 278.06K **Privately Held**
SIC: 2711 Commercial printing and newspaper publishing combined

(G-12583)
KNB TOOLS OF AMERICA INC
8440 Rausch Dr (43064-8047)
PHONE..............................614 733-0400
Toshihiko Kawanobe, *CEO*
▲ **EMP:** 20 **EST:** 2003
SALES (est): 658.79K **Privately Held**
Web: www.knb-tools.co.jp
SIC: 3545 Cutting tools for machine tools

(G-12584)
KREMA GROUP INC
Also Called: Crazy Richards
8415 Rausch Dr (43064-8064)
P.O. Box 715 (43017-0815)
PHONE..............................614 889-4824
Kimberly Wernli, *Pr*
Craig Sonksen, *Pr*
Joanna Carroll, *CFO*
Chris Wernli, *CEO*
Richard Sonksen, *Prin*
EMP: 10 **EST:** 2001
SALES (est): 2.43MM
SALES (corp-wide): 2.43MM **Privately Held**
Web: www.crazyrichards.com
SIC: 2099 Peanut butter
PA: Krema Products Inc.
  45 N High St
  Dublin OH 43017
  614 889-4824

(G-12585)
KTH INDUSTRIES
8205 Business Way (43064-7539)
PHONE..............................614 733-2020
EMP: 6 **EST:** 2016
SALES (est): 192.5K **Privately Held**
Web: www.kth.net
SIC: 3999 Manufacturing industries, nec

(G-12586)
MILLER CABINET LTD
6217 Converse Huff Rd (43064-9185)
PHONE..............................614 873-4221
TOLL FREE: 800
EMP: 12 **EST:** 2006
SALES (est): 1.94MM **Privately Held**
Web: www.millercabinets.com
SIC: 5722 2541 2521 2511 Kitchens, complete (sinks, cabinets, etc.); Cabinets, except refrigerated: show, display, etc.: wood; Wood office furniture; Wood household furniture

(G-12587)
OHIO LASER LLC
8260 Estates Pkwy (43064)
PHONE..............................614 873-7030
Gregg P Simpson, *Managing Member*
EMP: 20 **EST:** 1995
SQ FT: 30,000
SALES (est): 8MM **Privately Held**
Web: www.ohiolaser.com
SIC: 3499 Welding tips, heat resistant: metal

(G-12588)
OTP HOLDING LLC
Also Called: Pk Controls
8000 Corporate Blvd (43064-9220)
PHONE..............................614 733-0979
Matthew Patel, *Brnch Mgr*
EMP: 43
SALES (corp-wide): 1.04B **Privately Held**
Web: www.otcindustrial.com
SIC: 3625 Relays and industrial controls
HQ: Otp Holding Llc
  1900 Jetway Blvd
  Columbus OH 43219
  614 342-6123

(G-12589)
OXFORD RESOURCES INC
7858 Industrial Pkwy (43064-9468)
PHONE..............................614 873-7955
Randall J Asmo, *Prin*
EMP: 8 **EST:** 2013
SALES (est): 240.36K **Privately Held**
SIC: 2731 Book publishing

(G-12590)
PC MOLDING LLC
7680 Commerce Pl (43064-9222)
PHONE..............................614 873-7712
Gene J Kuzma, *Prin*
Bob Kellerman, *Mgr*
EMP: 8 **EST:** 2011
SALES (est): 271.5K
SALES (corp-wide): 23.81MM **Privately Held**
SIC: 3085 Plastics bottles
PA: Gk Packaging, Inc.
  7680 Commerce Pl
  Plain City OH 43064
  614 873-3900

(G-12591)
QUILTING INC (PA)
Also Called: Mattress Mart
7600 Industrial Pkwy (43064-9468)
PHONE..............................614 504-5971
Ben Tiburzio, *Pr*
▲ **EMP:** 55 **EST:** 1984
SQ FT: 85,000
SALES (est): 6.43MM **Privately Held**
SIC: 2515 Mattresses, innerspring or box spring

(G-12592)
STI LIQUIDATION INC
7710 Corporate Blvd (43064-9214)
PHONE..............................614 733-0099
Carrie Perini, *Pr*
EMP: 20 **EST:** 1979
SQ FT: 6,000
SALES (est): 4.06MM **Privately Held**
Web: www.silverthreadsinc.com
SIC: 2211 7389 2392 2391 Draperies and drapery fabrics, cotton; Interior designer; Household furnishings, nec; Curtains and draperies

(G-12593)
SUPERIOR PLASTICS INC
8163 Business Way (43064-9216)
PHONE..............................614 733-0307
EMP: 15
SALES (corp-wide): 6.34MM **Privately Held**
Web: www.superiorplasticsinc.com
SIC: 3089 Molding primary plastics
PA: Superior Plastics Inc.
  8175 Business Way
  Plain City OH 43064
  614 733-0307

(G-12594)
SUPERIOR PLASTICS INC (PA)
8175 Business Way (43064-9216)
PHONE..............................614 733-0307
◆ **EMP:** 20 **EST:** 1997
SALES (est): 6.34MM
SALES (corp-wide): 6.34MM **Privately Held**
Web: www.superiorplasticsinc.com
SIC: 3089 Injection molding of plastics

(G-12595)
TOTAL TENNIS INC
321 W Bigelow Ave (43064-7101)
PHONE..............................614 504-7446
EMP: 6 **EST:** 2017
SALES (est): 446.16K **Privately Held**
Web: www.totaltennisinc.com
SIC: 3949 Sporting and athletic goods, nec

(G-12596)
TUFFCO SAND AND GRAVEL INC
8195 Old State Route 161 (43064-8991)
P.O. Box 399 (43040-0399)
PHONE..............................614 873-3977
EMP: 6 **EST:** 1989
SALES (est): 843.3K **Privately Held**
SIC: 1442 Construction sand and gravel

(G-12597)
UNITED ROTARY BRUSH INC
8150 Business Way (43064-9209)
PHONE..............................937 644-3515
Bruce Davis, *Mgr*
EMP: 23
SQ FT: 63,820
SALES (corp-wide): 48.68MM **Privately Held**
Web: www.united-rotary.com
SIC: 3991 Brushes, household or industrial
PA: United Rotary Brush Corporation
  510 W Frontier Ln
  Olathe KS 66061
  913 888-8450

(G-12598)
VAPOR PIN ENTERPRISES INC
7750 Corporate Blvd (43064-9214)
PHONE..............................614 504-6915
Laurie Chilcote, *Prin*
EMP: 6 **EST:** 2017
SALES (est): 175.27K **Privately Held**
Web: www.vaporpin.com
SIC: 3452 Bolts, nuts, rivets, and washers

(G-12599)
VELOCYS INC
8520 Warner Rd (43064-3561)
PHONE..............................614 733-3300
David Pummell, *CEO*
Susan Robertson, *
Doctor Paul F Schubert, *COO*
EMP: 60 **EST:** 2000
SALES (est): 16.38MM
SALES (corp-wide): 290.16K **Privately Held**
Web: www.velocys.com
SIC: 8731 3559 Commercial physical research; Sewing machines and hat and zipper making machinery
PA: Velocys Plc
  Robert Robinson Avenue The Oxford
  Science Park
  Oxford OXON
  186 580-0821

(G-12600)
VISTA COMMUNITY CHURCH
8500 Memorial Dr Ste C (43064-8051)
P.O. Box 3278 (43016-0128)
PHONE..............................614 718-2294
EMP: 11 **EST:** 2006
SALES (est): 553.8K **Privately Held**
Web: www.vistacommunitychurch.org
SIC: 7372 8661 Application computer software; Religious organizations

(G-12601)
W OF OHIO INC (PA)
Also Called: Skiff Craft
225 Guy St (43064-1160)
P.O. Box 115 (43064-0115)
PHONE..............................614 873-4664
Gabriel Jabbour, *Pr*
EMP: 6 **EST:** 1996
SALES (est): 593.1K
SALES (corp-wide): 593.1K **Privately Held**
SIC: 3732 Boatbuilding and repairing

(G-12602)
WHITMER WOODWORKS INC
8490 Carters Mill Rd (43064-9116)
PHONE..............................614 873-1196
EMP: 7 **EST:** 1990
SALES (est): 944.03K **Privately Held**
Web: www.whitmerwoodworks.com
SIC: 2431 Millwork

(G-12603)
WORLD RESOURCE SOLUTONS CORP
8485 Estates Ct (43064-8015)
PHONE..............................614 733-3737
Thomas Warner, *Pr*
▲ **EMP:** 7 **EST:** 2002
SQ FT: 3,750
SALES (est): 996.67K **Privately Held**
Web: www.wrstool.biz
SIC: 3089 Injection molding of plastics

(G-12604)
WRIGHT ENRICHMENT INCORPORATED
Also Called: Wright Group, The
8000 Memorial Dr (43064-9007)
PHONE..............................337 783-3096
EMP: 12
SALES (corp-wide): 49.27MM **Privately Held**
Web: www.thewrightgroup.net
SIC: 2834 Vitamin preparations
PA: Wright Enrichment, Incorporated

Plain City - Madison County (G-12605) GEOGRAPHIC SECTION

201 Energy Pkwy Ste 100
Lafayette LA 70508
337 783-3096

(G-12605)
YONEZAWA USA INC
7920 Corporate Blvd Ste A (43064-9275)
PHONE..............................614 799-2210
Shunichi Aoki, *Pr*
EMP: 12 **EST:** 2014
SALES (est): 445.77K **Privately Held**
SIC: 3577 Computer peripheral equipment, nec

Pleasant Hill
Miami County

(G-12606)
CD SOLUTIONS INC
100 W Monument St (45359)
P.O. Box 536 (45359)
PHONE..............................937 676-2376
Jerald Warner, *Pr*
EMP: 8 **EST:** 1992
SQ FT: 10,000
SALES (est): 2.22MM **Privately Held**
Web: www.cds.com
SIC: 7374 3695 5099 Service bureau, computer; Magnetic and optical recording media; Compact discs

Pleasant Plain
Warren County

(G-12607)
HARTZ MOUNTAIN CORPORATION
Also Called: L M Animal Farms
5374 Long Spurling Rd (45162-9256)
P.O. Box 57 (45162-0057)
PHONE..............................513 877-2131
Larry Mohrfield, *Brnch Mgr*
EMP: 75
Web: www.hartz.com
SIC: 2047 3999 2048 Cat food; Pet supplies; Prepared feeds, nec
HQ: The Hartz Mountain Corporation
400 Plaza Dr Ste 400 # 400
Secaucus NJ 07094
800 275-1414

Plymouth
Huron County

(G-12608)
FIRELANDS MANUFACTURING LLC
500 Industrial Park Dr (44865)
P.O. Box 45 (44865-0045)
PHONE..............................419 687-8237
EMP: 8 **EST:** 2011
SALES (est): 264.87K **Privately Held**
Web: www.firelandsmfg.com
SIC: 3999 3548 Barber and beauty shop equipment; Welding and cutting apparatus and accessories, nec

(G-12609)
POWER SHELF LLC
500 Industrial Park Dr (44865)
PHONE..............................419 775-6125
EMP: 8 **EST:** 2008
SQ FT: 15,000
SALES (est): 641.59K **Privately Held**
Web: www.buypowershelf.com
SIC: 3644 Noncurrent-carrying wiring devices

Poland
Mahoning County

(G-12610)
CULTURED MARBLE INC
213 N Main St (44514-1662)
PHONE..............................330 549-2282
Todd Worsencroft, *Pr*
David Worsencroft, *Pr*
Arthur D Worsencroft, *Sec*
EMP: 8 **EST:** 1970
SALES (est): 711.58K **Privately Held**
SIC: 3299 3088 Synthetic stones, for gem stones and industrial use; Plastics plumbing fixtures

(G-12611)
GREAT LAKE PORT CORPORATION
Also Called: Grand River Railway Company
213 Diana Dr (44514-3714)
PHONE..............................330 718-3727
EMP: 8 **EST:** 2011
SALES (est): 442.64K **Privately Held**
Web: www.grandriverrailway.com
SIC: 3743 Railroad equipment

(G-12612)
US CONTROLS ACQUISITION LTD
Also Called: United States Controls
8511 Foxwood Ct (44514-4302)
PHONE..............................330 758-1147
Daniel Elliot Baun, *Pr*
EMP: 9 **EST:** 2014
SALES (est): 644.34K **Privately Held**
SIC: 3585 3492 3625 Parts for heating, cooling, and refrigerating equipment; Hose and tube fittings and assemblies, hydraulic/pneumatic; Controls for adjustable speed drives

Pomeroy
Meigs County

(G-12613)
FACEMYER LUMBER CO INC (PA)
31940 Bailey Run Rd (45769-9301)
P.O. Box 227 (45760-0227)
PHONE..............................740 992-5965
Eugene Facemyer, *Ch Bd*
Dennis Facemyer Junior, *VP*
Leslie Facemyer, *Sec*
▼ **EMP:** 18 **EST:** 1967
SQ FT: 1,500
SALES (est): 4.99MM
SALES (corp-wide): 4.99MM **Privately Held**
Web: www.facemyerlumber.com
SIC: 2421 2411 Custom sawmill; Veneer logs

(G-12614)
SNOWVILLE CREAMERY LLC
32623 State Route 143 (45769-9695)
PHONE..............................740 698-2301
Warren Taylor, *Managing Member*
EMP: 20 **EST:** 2003
SALES (est): 5.68MM **Privately Held**
Web: www.snowvillecreamery.com
SIC: 5143 2026 Dairy products, except dried or canned; Fluid milk

Port Clinton
Ottawa County

(G-12615)
ARES INC
818 Front St Lake Erie Business Park (43452)
PHONE..............................419 635-2175
Herb Roder, *Pr*
Ann Yamrick, *
EMP: 56 **EST:** 1971
SQ FT: 60,000
SALES (est): 7.83MM **Privately Held**
Web: www.aresinc.net
SIC: 3443 3482 3484 3489 Fabricated plate work (boiler shop); Small arms ammunition; Small arms; Ordnance and accessories, nec

(G-12616)
D & L EXCAVATING LTD
969 N Rymers Rd (43452-9437)
PHONE..............................419 271-0635
Darryl Trent, *Prin*
EMP: 6 **EST:** 2016
SALES (est): 479.56K **Privately Held**
SIC: 3531 Buckets, excavating: clamshell, concrete, dragline, etc.

(G-12617)
FELLHAUER MECHANICAL SYSTEMS
Also Called: Fellhauer In-Focus
2435 E Gill Rd (43452-2555)
PHONE..............................419 734-3674
John Fellhauer, *Pr*
EMP: 40 **EST:** 2003
SALES (est): 4MM **Privately Held**
SIC: 1711 7382 3651 Mechanical contractor; Security systems services; Household audio and video equipment

(G-12618)
FENNER DUNLOP PORT CLINTON LLC
Also Called: Fenner Dnlop Engnred Cnvyor Sl
5225 W Lakeshore Dr Ste 320 (43452)
PHONE..............................419 635-2191
Cassandra Pan, *Pr*
Bill Mooney, *CFO*
Ben Ficklen, *Sec*
▲ **EMP:** 115 **EST:** 1985
SQ FT: 200,000
SALES (est): 19.55MM
SALES (corp-wide): 1.05B **Privately Held**
SIC: 3535 Bucket type conveyor systems
HQ: Fenner Dunlop Americas, Llc
200 Crprate Ctr Dr Ste 22
Coraopolis PA 15108

(G-12619)
GABEL WELDING INC
2400 W Sandy Ln (43452-9791)
PHONE..............................567 201-8217
Cody Gabel, *Prin*
EMP: 6 **EST:** 2018
SALES (est): 25.09K **Privately Held**
SIC: 7692 Welding repair

(G-12620)
GREAT LAKES POPCORN COMPANY
60 Madison St (43452-1102)
PHONE..............................419 732-3080
Bill Yuhasz, *Pr*
EMP: 6 **EST:** 2000
SQ FT: 4,000
SALES (est): 444.46K **Privately Held**
Web: www.greatlakespopcorn.com
SIC: 2099 2064 5441 Popcorn, packaged: except already popped; Nuts, glace; Candy, nut, and confectionery stores

(G-12621)
LAKECRAFT INC (PA)
Also Called: Lakecraft
1010 W Lakeshore Dr (43452-9564)
PHONE..............................419 734-2828
Samuel J Conte, *Pr*
EMP: 6 **EST:** 1940
SQ FT: 15,000
SALES (est): 1.01MM
SALES (corp-wide): 1.01MM **Privately Held**
Web: www.lakecraft.com
SIC: 3599 7692 3561 Machine shop, jobbing and repair; Welding repair; Pumps, domestic: water or sump

(G-12622)
LOADMASTER TRAILER COMPANY LTD
Also Called: Loadmaster Trailers Mfg
2354 East Harbor Rd (43452-1517)
PHONE..............................419 732-3434
Gary Straw, *Pr*
Diane Straw, *Pr*
EMP: 13 **EST:** 1983
SQ FT: 12,000
SALES (est): 1MM **Privately Held**
Web: www.loadmasterboattrailer.com
SIC: 3799 7699 Boat trailers; Nautical repair services

(G-12623)
PORT CLINTON MANUFACTURING LLC
328 W Perry St (43452-1035)
P.O. Box 220 (43452-0220)
PHONE..............................419 734-2141
Daniel Stott, *Pr*
Jane Stott, *
EMP: 25 **EST:** 1928
SQ FT: 67,000
SALES (est): 3.16MM **Privately Held**
Web: www.pcmfg.net
SIC: 3451 Screw machine products

(G-12624)
PRECISION MACHINE & TOOL CO
142 W Wilcox Rd (43452-2366)
PHONE..............................419 334-8405
Ken Ambrozy, *Pr*
Carolyn Ambrozy, *Sec*
EMP: 10 **EST:** 1979
SALES (est): 480.95K **Privately Held**
Web: www.pmtcompany.com
SIC: 3599 Machine shop, jobbing and repair

(G-12625)
QUIKSTIR INC
Also Called: Quikspray
2105 W Lakeshore Dr (43452-9485)
P.O. Box 327 (43452-0327)
PHONE..............................419 732-2601
Thomas P Mc Ritchie, *Pr*
T Park Mc Ritchie, *Sec*
EMP: 23 **EST:** 1954
SQ FT: 6,000
SALES (est): 1.08MM **Privately Held**
Web: www.quikspray.com
SIC: 3561 3563 3531 Pumps and pumping equipment; Spraying outfits: metals, paints, and chemicals (compressor); Mixers, nec: ore, plaster, slag, sand, mortar, etc.

(G-12626)
QUINAMI LLC
Also Called: Gideon Owen Wine
3845 E Wine Cellar Rd (43452-3704)
PHONE..............................419 797-4445
EMP: 8 **EST:** 2019
SALES (est): 222.14K **Privately Held**
Web: www.gideonowenwine.com
SIC: 2084 Wines

(G-12627)
REXLES INC
Also Called: Plastiform Tool & Die

GEOGRAPHIC SECTION

Portsmouth - Scioto County (G-12648)

1850 W Lakeshore Dr (43452-9091)
P.O. Box 26 (43452-0026)
PHONE..............................419 732-8188
Rex Montgomery, *Pr*
Leslie Rister, *Sec*
EMP: 6 **EST:** 1988
SQ FT: 1,122
SALES (est): 591.57K **Privately Held**
SIC: 3089 Plastics processing

(G-12628)
SCRAMBL-GRAM INC
Also Called: Last Word, The
5225 W Lakeshore Dr Ste 340 (43452)
P.O. Box 2311 (44871-2311)
PHONE..............................419 635-2321
Scott Bowers, *Pr*
EMP: 7 **EST:** 1978
SQ FT: 5,500
SALES (est): 211.05K **Privately Held**
SIC: 3944 5945 2741 Board games, puzzles, and models, except electronic; Hobby, toy, and game shops; Miscellaneous publishing

(G-12629)
TACK-ANEW INC
Also Called: Brands' Marina
451 W Lakeshore Dr (43452-9478)
PHONE..............................419 734-4212
Dalton Brand, *Pr*
EMP: 17 **EST:** 1971
SQ FT: 15,000
SALES (est): 446.98K **Privately Held**
Web: www.brandsmarina.com
SIC: 4493 3731 Boat yards, storage and incidental repair; Shipbuilding and repairing

Port Jefferson
Shelby County

(G-12630)
MCCRARY METAL POLISHING CO INC
Also Called: McCrary
207 Pasco Montra Rd (45360)
P.O. Box 190 (45360-0190)
PHONE..............................937 492-1979
James P Mccrary Junior, *Pr*
Shirley Mc Crary, *VP*
▲ **EMP:** 12 **EST:** 1967
SQ FT: 4,800
SALES (est): 2.38MM **Privately Held**
Web: www.mccrarymetalpolishing.com
SIC: 3599 4225 2842 Machine shop, jobbing and repair; Warehousing, self storage; Metal polish

Port Washington
Tuscarawas County

(G-12631)
BATES METAL PRODUCTS INC
403 E Mn St (43837)
P.O. Box 68 (43837-0068)
PHONE..............................740 498-8371
James A Bates, *Pr*
Terry L Bates, *
Betty Bates, *
EMP: 60 **EST:** 1956
SQ FT: 106,500
SALES (est): 11.93MM **Privately Held**
Web: www.batesmetal.com
SIC: 4783 2542 3993 3469 Packing and crating; Racks, merchandise display or storage: except wood; Signs and advertising specialties; Metal stampings, nec

(G-12632)
DESIGNER STONE CO
303 E Main St (43837-9704)
PHONE..............................740 492-1300
Darren Galbraith, *Pr*
Lisa Massner, *Sec*
▲ **EMP:** 8 **EST:** 2006
SALES (est): 738.77K **Privately Held**
Web: www.thedesignerstoneco.com
SIC: 1411 Granite dimension stone

Portage
Wood County

(G-12633)
J D HYDRAULIC INC
Rte 25 (43451)
P.O. Box 188 (43451-0188)
PHONE..............................419 686-5234
James Simon, *Pr*
EMP: 10 **EST:** 1974
SQ FT: 12,000
SALES (est): 467.6K **Privately Held**
SIC: 3593 Fluid power cylinders, hydraulic or pneumatic

(G-12634)
LABORIE ENTERPRISES LLC
Also Called: Laborie Enterprises
10892 S Dixie Hwy (43451-9798)
PHONE..............................419 686-6245
Larry C Smith, *Pt*
Douglas Laborie, *Pt*
Ronald Laborie, *Pt*
Edith Laborie, *Pt*
EMP: 7 **EST:** 1991
SQ FT: 10,000
SALES (est): 959.54K **Privately Held**
Web: www.laborieenterprises.com
SIC: 5211 2431 Millwork and lumber; Moldings, wood: unfinished and prefinished

(G-12635)
MORLOCK ASPHALT LTD
9362 Merrill Rd (43451-9729)
PHONE..............................419 686-4601
Tony Morlock, *Managing Member*
EMP: 10 **EST:** 1995
SALES (est): 1.31MM **Privately Held**
Web: www.morlockasphaltltd.com
SIC: 1611 3541 Surfacing and paving; Milling machines

(G-12636)
PALMER BROS TRANSIT MIX CON
Also Called: Precision Aggregates
12580 Greensburg Pike (43451-9755)
PHONE..............................419 686-2366
EMP: 10
SALES (corp-wide): 5.86MM **Privately Held**
SIC: 3273 5032 Ready-mixed concrete; Stone, crushed or broken
PA: Palmer Bros Transit Mix Concrete Inc
   12205 E Gypsy Lane Rd
   Bowling Green OH 43402
   419 352-4681

(G-12637)
STONECO INC
11580 S Dixie Hwy (43451-9756)
PHONE..............................419 686-3311
Lee Wehner, *Mgr*
EMP: 7
SALES (corp-wide): 32.72B **Privately Held**
Web: www.shellyco.com
SIC: 1422 Crushed and broken limestone
HQ: Stoneco, Inc.
   1700 Fostoria Ave Ste 200
   Findlay OH 45840
   419 422-8854

Portland
Meigs County

(G-12638)
CRAIG SAYLOR
53020 State Route 124 (45770-9768)
PHONE..............................740 352-8363
EMP: 7 **EST:** 2013
SALES (est): 144.94K **Privately Held**
Web: www.saylorlogging.com
SIC: 2411 Logging camps and contractors

(G-12639)
MORNINGSTAR CSTM WOODWORKS LLC
53611 Sandy Desert Rd (45770-9765)
PHONE..............................740 508-7178
Adam Bullington, *Prin*
EMP: 6 **EST:** 2017
SALES (est): 89.43K **Privately Held**
SIC: 2431 Millwork

Portsmouth
Scioto County

(G-12640)
AIM MEDIA MIDWEST OPER LLC
1437 Layton Dr (45662-2315)
PHONE..............................740 354-6621
Zach Mccoy, *Brnch Mgr*
EMP: 6
SALES (corp-wide): 3.39MM **Privately Held**
Web: www.portsmouth-dailytimes.com
SIC: 2711 Newspapers, publishing and printing
PA: Aim Media Midwest Operating, Llc
   1001 N County Road 25a
   Troy OH 45373
   937 247-2700

(G-12641)
BICKETT MACHINE AND GAS SUPPLY
1411 Robinson Ave (45662-3508)
P.O. Box 698 (45662-0698)
PHONE..............................740 353-5710
TOLL FREE: 800
Frank M Coburn, *Pr*
Maureen Coburn, *VP*
Eric Lewis, *Mgr*
EMP: 8 **EST:** 1948
SQ FT: 7,500
SALES (est): 1.5MM **Privately Held**
Web: www.bicketts.com
SIC: 5084 3599 Welding machinery and equipment; Machine shop, jobbing and repair

(G-12642)
COCA-COLA CONSOLIDATED INC
Also Called: Coca-Cola
5050 Old Scioto Trl (45662-6461)
PHONE..............................740 353-3133
Tony Burns, *Prin*
EMP: 104
SALES (corp-wide): 6.65B **Publicly Held**
Web: www.cokeconsolidated.com
SIC: 2086 Bottled and canned soft drinks
PA: Coca-Cola Consolidated, Inc.
   4100 Coca-Cola Plz
   Charlotte NC 28211
   704 557-4400

(G-12643)
EVANS FOOD GROUP LTD
406 Barklow Extension Rd (45662-3599)
PHONE..............................626 636-8110
Byron Hernandez, *Mgr*
EMP: 11
SALES (corp-wide): 136.76MM **Privately Held**
Web: www.benestarbrands.com
SIC: 2096 Pork rinds
HQ: Evans Food Group Ltd.
   4118 S Halsted St
   Chicago IL 60609
   773 254-7400

(G-12644)
EVANS FOOD GROUP LTD
2310 8th St (45662-4740)
PHONE..............................740 285-3078
EMP: 9
SALES (corp-wide): 136.76MM **Privately Held**
Web: www.benestarbrands.com
SIC: 2096 Pork rinds
HQ: Evans Food Group Ltd.
   4118 S Halsted St
   Chicago IL 60609
   773 254-7400

(G-12645)
GRACIE PLUM INVESTMENTS INC
Also Called: Gracie Plum Investments
609 2nd St Unit 2 (45662-3974)
PHONE..............................740 355-9029
Francesca G Hartop, *CEO*
▼ **EMP:** 27 **EST:** 1999
SQ FT: 3,150
SALES (est): 4.67MM **Privately Held**
Web: www.atp4health.com
SIC: 7372 7374 7371 Application computer software; Data processing and preparation; Custom computer programming services

(G-12646)
K-J KUSTOM POWDER COAT
3015 Scioto Trl (45662-2213)
PHONE..............................740 961-5267
EMP: 6 **EST:** 2019
SALES (est): 241.51K **Privately Held**
Web: www.kjkustompowdercoating.com
SIC: 3479 Coating of metals and formed products

(G-12647)
KSA LIMITED PARTNERSHIP
6501 Pershing Ave (45662-7502)
PHONE..............................740 776-3238
Frank Anderson Iii, *Pt*
Tom Lodeman, *Pt*
EMP: 16 **EST:** 1992
SALES (est): 183.62K **Privately Held**
SIC: 3272 Ties, railroad: concrete

(G-12648)
MCGOVNEY READY MIX INC
Also Called: McGovney River Terminal
55 River Ave (45662-4712)
P.O. Box 510 (45662-0510)
PHONE..............................740 353-4111
TOLL FREE: 800
Carolyn Kegley, *Pr*
David Kegley, *VP*
Debra Coburn, *Sec*
EMP: 25 **EST:** 1964
SQ FT: 1,200
SALES (est): 911.13K **Privately Held**
Web: www.mcgovney.com
SIC: 3273 Ready-mixed concrete

Portsmouth - Scioto County (G-12649)

(G-12649)
MITCHELL BROS TIRE RTREAD SVC
Also Called: Mitchell Brothers Retread Svc
1205 Findlay St (45662-3449)
P.O. Box 1506 (45662-1506)
PHONE..................................740 353-1551
Mark Mitchell, *Pt*
Dennis Mitchell, *Pt*
Randy Mitchell, *Pt*
EMP: 7 **EST:** 1961
SALES (est): 498.71K **Privately Held**
SIC: 7534 5531 Tire recapping; Automotive tires

(G-12650)
MITCHELLACE INC (PA)
830 Murray St (45662-4515)
P.O. Box 89 (45662-0089)
PHONE..................................740 354-2813
Steven Keating, *Pr*
Kerry W Keating, *
Tom Keating, *
Mitchell Keating, *
◆ **EMP:** 74 **EST:** 1902
SQ FT: 365,000
SALES (est): 9.07MM
SALES (corp-wide): 9.07MM **Privately Held**
Web: www.mitchellace.com
SIC: 2241 Shoe laces, except leather

(G-12651)
NORTH SHORE PRINTING LLC
1105 Gallia St (45662-4142)
PHONE..................................740 876-9066
Jason Whisman, *Managing Member*
EMP: 6 **EST:** 2020
SALES (est): 246.04K **Privately Held**
Web: www.northshoreohio.com
SIC: 2752 7389 Commercial printing, lithographic; Business Activities at Non-Commercial Site

(G-12652)
OSCO INDUSTRIES INC (PA)
Also Called: Portsmouth Division
734 11th St (45662-3407)
P.O. Box 1388 (45662-1388)
PHONE..................................740 354-3183
William J Burke, *Ch Bd*
John M Burke, *Pr*
Jeffrey A Burke, *Sr VP*
Philip L Vetter, *VP*
Keith Denny, *VP*
◆ **EMP:** 285 **EST:** 1872
SQ FT: 150,000
SALES (est): 79.52MM
SALES (corp-wide): 79.52MM **Privately Held**
Web: www.oscoind.com
SIC: 3321 Gray iron castings, nec

(G-12653)
PORTSMOUTH BLOCK INC
Also Called: Portsmouth Block & Brick
2700 Gallia St (45662-4807)
PHONE..................................740 353-4113
Glenn Coriell, *Pr*
Mildred Coriell, *Sec*
Kevin Coriell, *VP*
EMP: 20 **EST:** 1930
SQ FT: 100,000
SALES (est): 2.19MM **Privately Held**
Web: www.portsmouthblock.com
SIC: 3271 5211 Blocks, concrete or cinder: standard; Lumber and other building materials

(G-12654)
ROCLA CONCRETE TIE INC
Also Called: ROCLA CONCRETE TIE, INC
6501 Pershing Ave (45662-7502)
PHONE..................................740 776-3238
EMP: 30
SALES (corp-wide): 2.67MM **Privately Held**
Web: www.vossloh-north-america.com
SIC: 3272 Concrete products, nec
HQ: Rocla Concrete Tie, Inc.
     1819 Denver W Dr Ste 450
     Lakewood CO 80401

(G-12655)
SAVORY FOODS INC
2240 6th St (45662-4787)
P.O. Box 1604 (45662-1604)
PHONE..................................740 354-6655
James Speak, *Pr*
EMP: 58 **EST:** 1946
SQ FT: 40,000
SALES (est): 4.85MM
SALES (corp-wide): 136.76MM **Privately Held**
Web: www.savoryfoods.com
SIC: 2099 Food preparations, nec
HQ: Evans Food Group Ltd.
     4118 S Halsted St
     Chicago IL 60609
     773 254-7400

(G-12656)
SOLE CHOICE INC
2415 Scioto Trl (45662-2536)
P.O. Box 89 (45662-0089)
PHONE..................................740 354-2813
Nelson K Smith, *Ch*
Ryan B Bouts, *
Bryan K Davis, *
Mark Harner, *Stockholder**
David Kuhn, *Stockholder**
▲ **EMP:** 30 **EST:** 2009
SALES (est): 4.85MM **Privately Held**
Web: www.solechoiceinc.com
SIC: 2241 Shoe laces, except leather

(G-12657)
SOUTHERN OHIO VAULT CO INC
Also Called: Sovac
502 Shale Dr (45662)
P.O. Box 418 (45662-0418)
PHONE..................................740 456-5898
Jerry Russell Senior, *Pr*
EMP: 9 **EST:** 1984
SALES (est): 939.62K **Privately Held**
SIC: 3272 Burial vaults, concrete or precast terrazzo

(G-12658)
SYMMES CREEK MINING LLC
538 6th St (45662-3843)
PHONE..................................740 353-1509
Justin Carter, *Prin*
EMP: 6 **EST:** 2014
SALES (est): 66.08K **Privately Held**
SIC: 1221 Bituminous coal surface mining

(G-12659)
TOM BARBOUR AUTO PARTS INC (PA)
Also Called: Barbour Auto Parts
915 11th St (45662-3410)
PHONE..................................740 354-4654
Josephine Keating, *Pr*
EMP: 12 **EST:** 1956
SQ FT: 12,000
SALES (est): 2.37MM
SALES (corp-wide): 2.37MM **Privately Held**
Web: www.barbourauto.com
SIC: 5531 3599 Automotive parts; Machine shop, jobbing and repair

(G-12660)
WHITE GRAVEL MINES PRODUCTIONS
1160 Simon Miller Rd (45662-8959)
PHONE..................................740 776-0510
Tom Martin, *Prin*
EMP: 6 **EST:** 2016
SALES (est): 70.17K **Privately Held**
Web: www.whitegravelmines.com
SIC: 1442 Construction sand and gravel

(G-12661)
YOST LABS INC
630 2nd St (45662-3902)
PHONE..................................740 876-4936
Lowell Morrison, *CFO*
Greg Merril, *Prin*
EMP: 10 **EST:** 2016
SALES (est): 949.02K **Privately Held**
Web: www.yostlabs.com
SIC: 3812 Search and navigation equipment

Powell
Delaware County

(G-12662)
ADVANCED INDUS MACHINING INC (PA)
3982 Powell Rd Ste 218 (43065-7662)
PHONE..................................614 596-4183
Morgan Koth, *Pr*
EMP: 15 **EST:** 2003
SQ FT: 3,600
SALES (est): 1.71MM
SALES (corp-wide): 1.71MM **Privately Held**
Web: www.aimmach.com
SIC: 1629 3599 Industrial plant construction; Amusement park equipment

(G-12663)
ATAMA TECH LLC
9485 Gibson Dr (43065-8018)
PHONE..................................614 763-0399
Amy Fickell, *Prin*
EMP: 6 **EST:** 2010
SALES (est): 55.6K **Privately Held**
SIC: 3544 Special dies and tools

(G-12664)
BRAND PRINTER LLC
7260 Cook Rd (43065-8599)
PHONE..................................614 404-2615
Cheryl Ramirez, *Prin*
EMP: 8 **EST:** 2015
SALES (est): 165.27K **Privately Held**
SIC: 2752 Offset printing

(G-12665)
BUILDING CTRL INTEGRATORS LLC (PA)
Also Called: B C I
383 N Liberty St (43065-8388)
PHONE..................................614 334-3300
EMP: 31 **EST:** 2000
SQ FT: 20,000
SALES (est): 11.3MM
SALES (corp-wide): 11.3MM **Privately Held**
Web: www.bcicontrols.com
SIC: 3822 Temperature controls, automatic

(G-12666)
CARBONKLEAN LLC
24 Village Pointe Dr (43065-7760)
PHONE..................................614 980-9515
EMP: 7 **EST:** 2015
SQ FT: 5,000
SALES (est): 519.05K **Privately Held**
Web: www.carbonklean.com
SIC: 2842 Specialty cleaning

(G-12667)
CARDIAC ANALYTICS LLC
5683 Liberty Rd N (43065-8996)
PHONE..................................614 314-1332
EMP: 10 **EST:** 2010
SALES (est): 584.95K **Privately Held**
SIC: 3845 Electromedical equipment

(G-12668)
CHARQUI JERKY CO
130 E Olentangy St (43065-9069)
PHONE..................................614 286-2938
Matt Salts, *Prin*
EMP: 6 **EST:** 2017
SALES (est): 171.07K **Privately Held**
Web: www.charquijerky.com
SIC: 2013 Snack sticks, including jerky: from purchased meat

(G-12669)
CONTINENTAL GL SLS & INV GROUP
Also Called: Continental Group
315 Ashmoore Cir W (43065-7486)
P.O. Box 1764 (43065-1764)
PHONE..................................614 679-1201
Sean Snyder, *Pt*
Chris Snyder, *Pt*
▲ **EMP:** 24 **EST:** 1998
SQ FT: 100,000
SALES (est): 2.21MM **Privately Held**
Web: www.cgsi.co
SIC: 3441 7011 3211 Fabricated structural metal; Hotels; Structural glass

(G-12670)
D-TERRA SOLUTIONS LLC
35 Clairedan Dr (43065-8064)
PHONE..................................614 450-1040
Denis Bruncak, *CEO*
▲ **EMP:** 7 **EST:** 2012
SALES (est): 1.44MM **Privately Held**
Web: www.dterrasolutions.com
SIC: 3714 Motor vehicle parts and accessories

(G-12671)
EMBLEM ATHLETIC LLC
106 Gainsway Ct (43065-9140)
PHONE..................................614 743-6955
EMP: 9 **EST:** 2017
SALES (est): 446.76K **Privately Held**
Web: www.emblemathletic.com
SIC: 2369 Girl's and children's outerwear, nec

(G-12672)
ENGLISH OAK LLC
8280 Lariat Ct (43065-7201)
PHONE..................................614 600-8038
Ryan Mecum, *Prin*
EMP: 9 **EST:** 2013
SALES (est): 302.32K
SALES (corp-wide): 18.92B **Publicly Held**
SIC: 2621 2631 Paper mills; Linerboard
PA: International Paper Company
     6400 Poplar Ave
     Memphis TN 38197
     901 419-7000

(G-12673)
EYESCIENCE LABS LLC
Also Called: Eyescience
493 Village Park Dr (43065-6605)

GEOGRAPHIC SECTION

PHONE..............................614 885-7100
Jeffrey Northup, *Managing Member*
EMP: 7 **EST:** 2007
SQ FT: 7,000
SALES (est): 827.39K **Privately Held**
Web: www.basicbrandsinc.com
SIC: 2834 Vitamin preparations

(G-12674)
GFS CHEMICALS INC (PA)
Also Called: GFS Chemicals
155 Hidden Ravines Dr (43065-9928)
P.O. Box 245 (43065-0245)
PHONE..............................740 881-5501
J Steel Hutchinson, *CEO*
J Steel Hutchinson, *Pr*
Darrell A Hutchinson, *Dir*
M Robert Pierron, *VP*
Edward Reusch, *CFO*
◆ **EMP:** 20 **EST:** 1928
SQ FT: 125,000
SALES (est): 48.46MM
SALES (corp-wide): 48.46MM **Privately Held**
Web: www.gfschemicals.com
SIC: 2819 2899 2869 2812 Chemicals, reagent grade: refined from technical grade; Chemical preparations, nec; Industrial organic chemicals, nec; Alkalies and chlorine

(G-12675)
IKIRISKA LLC
16 Village Pointe Dr (43065-7760)
PHONE..............................614 389-8994
EMP: 10 **EST:** 2020
SALES (est): 575.09K **Privately Held**
Web: ikiriska-custom-curtains.business.site
SIC: 2391 Curtains and draperies

(G-12676)
LEPD INDUSTRIES LTD
2292 Clairborne Dr (43065-8630)
PHONE..............................614 985-1470
Eric S Delbert, *Prin*
EMP: 6 **EST:** 2010
SALES (est): 220.17K **Privately Held**
SIC: 3999 Manufacturing industries, nec

(G-12677)
METAL PRODUCTS COMPANY (PA)
Also Called: Stamtex Metal Stampings
9455 Concord Rd (43065-8968)
PHONE..............................330 652-2558
Philip Frankle, *Pr*
EMP: 40 **EST:** 1921
SALES (est): 5.12MM
SALES (corp-wide): 5.12MM **Privately Held**
Web: www.stamtexmp.com
SIC: 3469 Stamping metal for the trade

(G-12678)
MORGAN WOOD PRODUCTS INC
9761 Fairway Dr (43065-6947)
P.O. Box 177 (43065-0177)
PHONE..............................614 336-4000
Luke Reinstetle, *Pr*
◆ **EMP:** 12 **EST:** 2002
SQ FT: 4,000
SALES (est): 5.98MM
SALES (corp-wide): 5.98MM **Privately Held**
Web: www.morganwood.org
SIC: 2448 Pallets, wood
PA: Evening Post Group, Llc
174 Meeting St Ste 200
Charleston SC 29401
843 867-2990

(G-12679)
NEW PATH INTERNATIONAL LLC
1476 Manning Pkwy Ste A (43065-7295)
PHONE..............................614 410-3974
Damon Canfield, *Managing Member*
Neil Macivor, *
◆ **EMP:** 25 **EST:** 1989
SQ FT: 13,000
SALES (est): 746.73K **Privately Held**
Web: www.npi.com
SIC: 3639 8711 7389 Major kitchen appliances, except refrigerators and stoves; Engineering services; Design, commercial and industrial

(G-12680)
SAWMILL 9721 LLC
9721 Sawmill Rd (43065-6613)
PHONE..............................614 937-4400
Jason Lusk, *Prin*
EMP: 6 **EST:** 2017
SALES (est): 105.64K **Privately Held**
SIC: 2421 Sawmills and planing mills, general

(G-12681)
STELLA LOU LLC
Also Called: Coldstone Creamery
3939 Hickory Rock Dr (43065-7333)
PHONE..............................937 935-9536
Joshua Klinger, *Managing Member*
EMP: 23 **EST:** 2014
SQ FT: 1,200
SALES (est): 183.32K **Privately Held**
Web: www.coldstonecreamery.com
SIC: 5812 2024 Ice cream stands or dairy bars; Ice cream and frozen deserts

(G-12682)
SUMMIT ONLINE PRODUCTS LLC
Also Called: Massageblocks.com
3982 Powell Rd Ste 137 (43065-7662)
PHONE..............................800 326-1972
Thomas W Turner, *Managing Member*
EMP: 6 **EST:** 2011
SALES (est): 307.6K **Privately Held**
Web: www.summitonlineproducts.com
SIC: 3841 Surgical and medical instruments

(G-12683)
TROGDAN PUBLISHING
1635 Strathshire Hall Pl (43065-9436)
PHONE..............................614 880-0178
EMP: 7 **EST:** 2018
SALES (est): 257.55K **Privately Held**
SIC: 2741 Miscellaneous publishing

Powhatan Point
Belmont County

(G-12684)
COAL SERVICES INC
Also Called: Coal Services Group
155 Highway 7 S (43942-1033)
PHONE..............................740 795-5220
Don Gentry, *Pr*
Robert Moore, *
Michael O Mckown, *Prin*
EMP: 471 **EST:** 1999
SALES (est): 3.24MM
SALES (corp-wide): 4.34B **Privately Held**
SIC: 8741 8711 1231 1222 Management services; Engineering services; Anthracite mining; Bituminous coal-underground mining
HQ: The American Coal Company
9085 Highway 34 N
Galatia IL 62935
618 268-6311

(G-12685)
UTAHAMERICAN ENERGY INC
153 Highway 7 S (43942-1033)
P.O. Box 910 (84520-0910)
PHONE..............................435 888-4000
David Hibbs, *Brnch Mgr*
EMP: 138
SALES (corp-wide): 4.34B **Privately Held**
SIC: 1222 Bituminous coal-underground mining
HQ: Utahamerican Energy, Inc.
45 W Sego Lily Dr Ste 401
Sandy UT 84070
435 888-4000

Proctorville
Lawrence County

(G-12686)
JOE FULLER INC
1132 Tinker Ln (45669-7819)
PHONE..............................740 886-6182
Norma Fuller, *Prin*
EMP: 6 **EST:** 2008
SALES (est): 68.22K **Privately Held**
SIC: 3599 Machine shop, jobbing and repair

(G-12687)
SUPERIOR MARINE WAYS INC
5852 County Rd 1 Suoth Pt (45669)
P.O. Box 519 (45669-0519)
PHONE..............................740 894-6224
Dale Manns, *Mgr*
EMP: 130
SALES (corp-wide): 21.4MM **Privately Held**
Web: www.superiormarineinc.com
SIC: 3731 7699 Barges, building and repairing; Boat repair
PA: Superior Marine Ways, Inc.
5852 County Road 1
South Point OH 45680
740 894-6224

(G-12688)
TRI-STATE PLATING & POLISHING
187 Township Road 1204 (45669-8688)
PHONE..............................304 529-2579
Edison Adkins, *Pr*
Laura L Adkins, *VP*
Joseph Adkins, *Genl Mgr*
EMP: 6 **EST:** 1963
SQ FT: 300
SALES (est): 646.95K **Privately Held**
SIC: 3471 7692 Electroplating of metals or formed products; Welding repair

Prospect
Marion County

(G-12689)
FLEMING CONSTRUCTION CO
Also Called: Scioto Sand & Gravel
5298 Marion Marysville Rd (43342-9342)
P.O. Box 31 (43301-0031)
PHONE..............................740 494-2177
Gerald E Fleming, *Pr*
Sonya Fleming, *
EMP: 15 **EST:** 1965
SQ FT: 2,400
SALES (est): 865.9K **Privately Held**
Web: www.flemingconstructioncompany.com
SIC: 1542 1541 1623 1442 Commercial and office building, new construction; Industrial buildings, new construction, nec; Sewer line construction; Gravel mining

(G-12690)
HERCULES INDUSTRIES INC
7194 Prospect Delaware Rd (43342-7505)
P.O. Box 197 (43342-0197)
PHONE..............................740 494-2620
Keith Popovich, *Pr*
Jean Meyer, *VP*
▲ **EMP:** 23 **EST:** 1969
SQ FT: 18,380
SALES (est): 5.69MM **Privately Held**
Web: www.herculock.com
SIC: 3429 Padlocks
PA: Scientific Forming Technologies Corporation
2545 Farmers Dr Ste 200
Columbus OH 43235

Quaker City
Guernsey County

(G-12691)
B&D WATER INC
69478 Fairground Rd (43773-2501)
P.O. Box 329 (81323-0329)
PHONE..............................330 771-3318
Tabitha Lassen, *Prin*
EMP: 11 **EST:** 2017
SALES (est): 565.73K **Privately Held**
Web: bd-water-inc.business.site
SIC: 2842 Sweeping compounds, oil or water absorbent, clay or sawdust

(G-12692)
BARNEYS HOT SHOT SERVICE LLC
22905 Caldwell Rd (43773-9769)
PHONE..............................740 517-9593
Brandon Barnhart, *Prin*
EMP: 6 **EST:** 2021
SALES (est): 542.73K **Privately Held**
Web: barneys-hot-shot-service-llc.business.site
SIC: 1389 Hot shot service

Racine
Meigs County

(G-12693)
J D DRILLING COMPANY
107 S 3rd St (45771-9552)
P.O. Box 369 (45771-0369)
PHONE..............................740 949-2512
James E Diddle, *Pr*
EMP: 12 **EST:** 1975
SQ FT: 6,000
SALES (est): 911.1K **Privately Held**
SIC: 1381 Drilling oil and gas wells

(G-12694)
MARIETTA MARTIN MATERIALS INC
Also Called: Martin Marietta Aggregates
50427 State Route 124 (45771-9082)
PHONE..............................740 247-2211
John Bentz, *Genl Mgr*
EMP: 6
Web: www.martinmarietta.com
SIC: 1422 Crushed and broken limestone
PA: Martin Marietta Materials Inc
4123 Parklake Ave
Raleigh NC 27612

(G-12695)
SHELLY MATERIALS INC
49947 State Route 338 (45771)
PHONE..............................740 247-2311
Michael Gard, *Mgr*
EMP: 10
SALES (corp-wide): 32.72B **Privately Held**
Web: www.shellyco.com

SIC: **4492** 1442 Tugboat service; Construction sand and gravel
HQ: Shelly Materials, Inc.
 80 Park Dr
 Thornville OH 43076
 740 246-6315

Radnor
Delaware County

(G-12696)
ULTERIOR PRODUCTS LLC
3142 N Section Line Rd (43066-9774)
P.O. Box 759 (43026-0759)
PHONE..................................614 441-9465
Kurt Nienberg, *Pr*
EMP: 6 **EST:** 2013
SALES (est): 500K **Privately Held**
Web: www.ulteriorproducts.com
SIC: **3535** Unit handling conveying systems

Randolph
Portage County

(G-12697)
EAST MANUFACTURING CORPORATION (PA)
1871 State Rte 44 (44265)
P.O. Box 277 (44265-0277)
PHONE..................................330 325-9921
Howard D Booher, *CEO*
David De Poincy, *Pr*
Robert J Bruce, *VP*
Donald C Pecano, *CFO*
Mark T Tate, *Sec*
▼ **EMP:** 266 **EST:** 1968
SQ FT: 350,000
SALES (est): 83.89MM
SALES (corp-wide): 83.89MM **Privately Held**
Web: www.eastmfg.com
SIC: **3715** 5013 7539 Trailer bodies; Truck parts and accessories; Automotive repair shops, nec

(G-12698)
EAST MANUFACTURING CORPORATION
3865 Waterloo Rd (44265-9802)
PHONE..................................330 325-9921
Torie Tollman, *Mgr*
EMP: 12
SALES (corp-wide): 83.89MM **Privately Held**
Web: www.eastmfg.com
SIC: **3715** Trailer bodies
PA: East Manufacturing Corporation
 1871 State Rte 44
 Randolph OH 44265
 330 325-9921

Ravenna
Portage County

(G-12699)
A C WILLIAMS CO INC (PA)
Also Called: Lake Metals
700 N Walnut St (44266-2300)
PHONE..................................330 296-6110
Dale E Mccoy, *Pr*
Barbara Cramer, *
EMP: 23 **EST:** 1944
SQ FT: 65,000
SALES (est): 8.36MM
SALES (corp-wide): 8.36MM **Privately Held**
Web: www.litemetals.com
SIC: **3369** 3321 Magnesium and magnes.-base alloy castings, exc. die-casting; Gray iron castings, nec

(G-12700)
ACE PRODUCTS & CONSULTING LLC
6800 N Chestnut St Ste 3 (44266-3927)
PHONE..................................330 577-4088
EMP: 10 **EST:** 2014
SALES (est): 1.01MM **Privately Held**
Web: www.ace-laboratories.com
SIC: **3069** Acid bottles, rubber

(G-12701)
AIR CRAFT WHEELS LLC
700 N Walnut St (44266-2372)
PHONE..................................440 937-7903
Dale Mccoy, *Pr*
EMP: 9 **EST:** 2004
SALES (est): 977.28K **Privately Held**
SIC: **3356** 3365 3369 Magnesium; Aluminum foundries; Nonferrous foundries, nec

(G-12702)
ALLEN AIRCRAFT PRODUCTS INC
312 E Lake St (44266-3428)
P.O. Box 951146 (44193-0005)
PHONE..................................330 296-9621
Kevin Barbeck, *Brnch Mgr*
EMP: 44
SALES (corp-wide): 17MM **Privately Held**
Web: www.allenaircraft.com
SIC: **3728** 3471 Aircraft parts and equipment, nec; Plating and polishing
PA: Allen Aircraft Products, Inc.
 6168 Woodbine Rd
 Ravenna OH 44266
 330 296-9621

(G-12703)
ALLEN AIRCRAFT PRODUCTS INC
Also Called: Metal Finishing Divison
4879 Newton Falls Rd (44266-9673)
P.O. Box 1211 (44266-1211)
PHONE..................................330 296-1531
EMP: 44
SALES (corp-wide): 17MM **Privately Held**
Web: www.allenaircraft.com
SIC: **3471** Finishing, metals or formed products
PA: Allen Aircraft Products, Inc.
 6168 Woodbine Rd
 Ravenna OH 44266
 330 296-9621

(G-12704)
ALLEN AIRCRAFT PRODUCTS INC (PA)
6168 Woodbine Rd (44266-9665)
P.O. Box 1211 (44266-1211)
PHONE..................................330 296-9621
▲ **EMP:** 60 **EST:** 1947
SALES (est): 17MM
SALES (corp-wide): 17MM **Privately Held**
Web: www.allenaircraft.com
SIC: **3728** 3471 5531 Aircraft parts and equipment, nec; Anodizing (plating) of metals or formed products; Auto and home supply stores

(G-12705)
AMERICAN QUALITY DOOR CO
6193 Courtesy Blvd (44266-3323)
PHONE..................................330 296-0393
Greg Miller, *Owner*
EMP: 7 **EST:** 2002
SALES (est): 114.7K **Privately Held**
SIC: **5211** 3699 Doors, wood or metal, except storm; Door opening and closing devices, electrical

(G-12706)
BECK ENERGY CORPORATION
160 N Chestnut St (44266-2256)
P.O. Box 1070 (44266-1070)
PHONE..................................330 297-6891
Raymond Beck, *Pr*
EMP: 25 **EST:** 1971
SQ FT: 4,000
SALES (est): 5.9MM **Privately Held**
Web: www.beckenergycorp.com
SIC: **1382** Oil and gas exploration services

(G-12707)
BECK SAND & GRAVEL INC
2820 Webb Rd (44266)
PHONE..................................330 626-3863
Rod Wenrich, *Pr*
Dan Lostoski, *VP*
EMP: 9 **EST:** 1950
SQ FT: 3,200
SALES (est): 1.08MM **Privately Held**
Web: www.becksand.com
SIC: **1442** Gravel mining

(G-12708)
BOLLARI/DAVIS INC
5292 S Prospect St (44266-9032)
P.O. Box 609 (44266-0609)
PHONE..................................330 296-4445
David Stonestreet, *Pr*
EMP: 10 **EST:** 1958
SQ FT: 13,000
SALES (est): 687.02K **Privately Held**
Web: www.bollaridavis.com
SIC: **3599** Machine shop, jobbing and repair

(G-12709)
CATACEL CORP
785 N Freedom St (44266-2469)
EMP: 11
Web: www.catacel.com
SIC: **3823** Combustion control instruments

(G-12710)
CITY OF RAVENNA
Also Called: Waste Water Plant, The
3722 Hommon Rd (44266-3543)
PHONE..................................330 296-5214
Michael Lacivita, *Mgr*
EMP: 9
Web: www.ravennaoh.gov
SIC: **4952** 3589 Sewerage systems; Sewage treatment equipment
PA: City Of Ravenna
 210 Park Way
 Ravenna OH 44266
 330 296-3864

(G-12711)
COLONIAL RUBBER COMPANY (PA)
706 Oakwood St (44266-2138)
P.O. Box 111 (44266-0111)
PHONE..................................330 296-2831
Dale P Fosnight, *Pr*
Wayne Slack, *
Wayne H Wise, *
Alan D Fosnight, *
EMP: 50 **EST:** 1937
SQ FT: 55,000
SALES (est): 5.02MM
SALES (corp-wide): 5.02MM **Privately Held**
SIC: **3061** 3069 Mechanical rubber goods; Hard rubber and molded rubber products

(G-12712)
DURACOTE CORPORATION
350 N Diamond St (44266-2155)
P.O. Box 1209 (44266-1209)
PHONE..................................330 296-9600
Jack Pallay, *Pr*
▼ **EMP:** 40 **EST:** 1947
SQ FT: 143,000
SALES (est): 7.75MM **Privately Held**
Web: www.duracote.com
SIC: **3083** 2295 3082 2261 Laminated plastics plate and sheet; Resin or plastic coated fabrics; Unsupported plastics profile shapes; Finishing plants, cotton

(G-12713)
ENDURO RUBBER COMPANY
685 S Chestnut St (44266-3068)
P.O. Box 752 (44266-0752)
PHONE..................................330 296-9603
Jerry Stuver, *Pr*
Neal A Stuver, *VP*
Luanne Stuver, *VP*
EMP: 9 **EST:** 1946
SQ FT: 24,000
SALES (est): 915.27K **Privately Held**
Web: www.endurorubber.com
SIC: **3069** Molded rubber products

(G-12714)
FIFE SERVICES LLC
9004 Emily Ct (44266-8352)
PHONE..................................614 829-6285
Donald R Russell Junior, *Owner*
EMP: 6 **EST:** 2013
SALES (est): 148.28K **Privately Held**
SIC: **3732** Boatbuilding and repairing

(G-12715)
FINE LINE EXCVTG & LDSCPG LLC
9251 Newton Falls Rd (44266-9285)
PHONE..................................330 541-0590
Amanda Huffman, *Prin*
EMP: 6 **EST:** 2017
SALES (est): 70.28K **Privately Held**
SIC: **1794** 0781 1629 3271 Excavation work; Landscape services; Drainage system construction; Blocks, concrete: landscape or retaining wall

(G-12716)
G GRAFTON MACHINE & RUBBER
640 Cleveland Rd (44266-2021)
PHONE..................................330 297-1062
Montgomery Grafton, *Pr*
EMP: 10 **EST:** 1969
SQ FT: 17,500
SALES (est): 981.72K **Privately Held**
Web: www.graftonmachine.com
SIC: **3599** 3069 Machine shop, jobbing and repair; Hard rubber and molded rubber products

(G-12717)
GENERAL ALUMINUM MFG COMPANY
5159 S Prospect St (44266-9031)
PHONE..................................330 297-1020
EMP: 20
SALES (corp-wide): 1.44B **Publicly Held**
Web: www.generalaluminum.com
SIC: **3365** 3369 Aluminum and aluminum-based alloy castings; Nonferrous foundries, nec
HQ: General Aluminum Mfg. Company
 5159 S Prospect St
 Ravenna OH 44266
 330 297-1225

GEOGRAPHIC SECTION
Ravenna - Portage County (G-12741)

(G-12718)
GENERAL ALUMINUM MFG LLC (HQ)
Also Called: Gamco
5159 S Prospect St (44266-9031)
PHONE.................................330 297-1225
Steve Case, *Pr*
Kevin Kaminsky, *Dir Fin*
Craig Schlauch, *Dir Opers*
Gary Mclaughlin, *Sls Dir*
◆ **EMP:** 132 **EST:** 1981
SALES (est): 130.2MM **Privately Held**
Web: www.generalaluminum.com
SIC: 3365 3369 Aluminum and aluminum-based alloy castings; Nonferrous foundries, nec
PA: Angstrom Automotive Group, Llc
2000 Town Ctr Ste 100
Southfield MI 48075

(G-12719)
H&H MACHINE SHOP RAVENNA LL
5292 S Prospect St (44266-9032)
PHONE.................................330 296-4445
EMP: 6 **EST:** 2016
SALES (est): 109.69K **Privately Held**
Web: www.hhmachine.com
SIC: 3599 Machine shop, jobbing and repair

(G-12720)
HYTECH SILICONE PRODUCTS INC
6112 Knapp Rd (44266-8876)
PHONE.................................330 297-1888
John Roberts, *Pr*
EMP: 6 **EST:** 1987
SQ FT: 2,450
SALES (est): 861.82K **Privately Held**
Web: www.hytechproducts.com
SIC: 3069 Molded rubber products

(G-12721)
LAAD SIGN & LIGHTING INC
3097 State Route 59 (44266-1653)
PHONE.................................330 379-2297
Linda Nichols, *Pr*
EMP: 10 **EST:** 2013
SALES (est): 864.57K **Privately Held**
Web: www.laadsignandlighting.com
SIC: 3993 Signs and advertising specialties

(G-12722)
LANGSTONS ULTMATE CLG SVCS INC
3764 Summit Rd (44266-3515)
PHONE.................................330 298-9150
Blake Langston, *Pr*
EMP: 10 **EST:** 1999
SALES (est): 209.4K **Privately Held**
Web: www.langstonscleaning.com
SIC: 3354 7699 Aluminum extruded products ; Cleaning services

(G-12723)
LG CHEM OHIO PETROCHEMICAL INC
310 Rayann Pkwy (44266)
PHONE.................................470 792-5127
Samantha Ritter, *CEO*
EMP: 7 **EST:** 2021
SALES (est): 851.5K **Privately Held**
SIC: 2899 Oils and essential oils

(G-12724)
LITE METALS COMPANY
700 N Walnut St (44266-2372)
PHONE.................................330 296-6110
Dale E Mc Coy, *Pr*
Barbara Cramer, *
EMP: 35 **EST:** 1973
SQ FT: 65,000
SALES (est): 8.36MM
SALES (corp-wide): 8.36MM **Privately Held**
Web: www.litemetals.com
SIC: 3369 3356 3365 Nonferrous foundries, nec; Magnesium; Aluminum foundries
PA: A C Williams Co Inc
700 N Walnut St
Ravenna OH 44266
330 296-6110

(G-12725)
MONTGOMERYS PALLET SERVICE INC
7937 State Route 44 (44266-9781)
PHONE.................................330 297-6677
Teresa Montgomery, *Pr*
William Montgomery, *VP*
EMP: 7 **EST:** 1992
SALES (est): 993.26K **Privately Held**
Web:
www.montgomerspalletservice.com
SIC: 2448 4953 Pallets, wood; Refuse collection and disposal services

(G-12726)
NICHOLS MOLD INC
222 W Lake St (44266-3651)
PHONE.................................330 297-9719
Edward Nichols, *Pr*
Nancy Nichols, *Sec*
EMP: 6 **EST:** 1972
SQ FT: 4,000
SALES (est): 605K **Privately Held**
Web: www.nicholsmold.com
SIC: 3544 3599 Industrial molds; Machine shop, jobbing and repair

(G-12727)
PERFORMANCE ELASTOMERS CORPORATION
Also Called: Performance Elastomers
7162 State Route 88 (44266-9189)
PHONE.................................330 297-2255
EMP: 81 **EST:** 1992
SALES (est): 14.36MM
SALES (corp-wide): 1.05B **Privately Held**
Web: www.performanceelastomers.com
SIC: 3061 Mechanical rubber goods
HQ: Pexco, Llc
1600 Birchwood Ave
Des Plaines IL 60018
847 296-5511

(G-12728)
PETTIGREW PUMPING INC
4171 Sandy Lake Rd (44266-9390)
P.O. Box 809 (44266-0809)
PHONE.................................330 297-7900
Matthew Pettigrew, *Prin*
EMP: 10 **EST:** 2007
SALES (est): 1.16MM **Privately Held**
Web: www.pettigrewpumping.com
SIC: 1389 Oil field services, nec

(G-12729)
QUIKRETE COMPANIES LLC
Also Called: Quikrete of Cleveland
2693 Lake Rockwell Rd (44266-8041)
PHONE.................................330 296-6080
Tim Ryon, *Mgr*
EMP: 30
SQ FT: 48,000
Web: www.quikrete.com
SIC: 3272 5211 3273 3241 Dry mixture concrete; Masonry materials and supplies; Ready-mixed concrete; Cement, hydraulic
HQ: The Quikrete Companies Llc
5 Concourse Pkwy Ste 1900
Atlanta GA 30328
404 634-9100

(G-12730)
R W MACHINE & TOOL INC
7944 State Route 44 (44266-9781)
PHONE.................................330 296-5211
Alan Wilbur, *CEO*
Michael Jenkins, *
Karen Wilbur, *
Mike Jenkins, *
▲ **EMP:** 17 **EST:** 1983
SQ FT: 17,500
SALES (est): 918.04K **Privately Held**
Web: www.rwmachinetool.com
SIC: 3599 Machine shop, jobbing and repair

(G-12731)
SAINT-GOBAIN PRFMCE PLAS CORP
335 N Diamond St (44266-2153)
PHONE.................................330 296-9948
Ron Bauer, *Genl Mgr*
EMP: 130
SALES (corp-wide): 397.78MM **Privately Held**
Web: plastics.saint-gobain.com
SIC: 2821 Plastics materials and resins
HQ: Saint-Gobain Performance Plastics Corporation
20 Moores Rd
Malvern PA 19355
440 836-6900

(G-12732)
SCHAEFFER METAL PRODUCTS INC
357 Commerce St (44266-2422)
PHONE.................................330 296-6226
Jack W Schaeffer Junior, *Pr*
Patricia Nock, *Sec*
EMP: 7 **EST:** 1971
SQ FT: 42,000
SALES (est): 499.26K **Privately Held**
Web: www.schaeffermetal.com
SIC: 7699 3443 Tank repair; Fabricated plate work (boiler shop)

(G-12733)
SCIENTIFIC PLASTICS LTD
7154 State Route 88 (44266-9189)
PHONE.................................305 557-3737
Bernardo Perafan, *Mgr*
◆ **EMP:** 10 **EST:** 2001
SALES (est): 629.8K **Privately Held**
Web: www.astraproductsltd.com
SIC: 3089 Injection molded finished plastics products, nec

(G-12734)
SIX C FABRICATION INC
5245 S Prospect St (44266-9032)
PHONE.................................330 296-5594
EMP: 305
SALES (corp-wide): 45MM **Privately Held**
Web: www.sixcfab.com
SIC: 3495 Wire springs
PA: Six C Fabrication, Inc.
349 Thomas Mill Rd
Winnfield LA 71483
318 628-2764

(G-12735)
SPRINGSEAL INC
800 Enterprise Pkwy (44266-8061)
PHONE.................................330 626-0673
Mark Knapp, *Pr*
EMP: 12 **EST:** 2004
SQ FT: 10,000
SALES (est): 4.86MM **Privately Held**
Web: www.springsealinc.com
SIC: 3089 Injection molding of plastics

(G-12736)
STA-WARM ELECTRIC COMPANY
553 N Chestnut St (44266)
P.O. Box 150 (44266)
PHONE.................................330 296-6461
John Snell, *Pr*
Brian Borthwick, *VP*
Linda Barns, *Mgr*
EMP: 10 **EST:** 1920
SQ FT: 25,000
SALES (est): 1.95MM **Privately Held**
Web: www.sta-warm.com
SIC: 3443 Fabricated plate work (boiler shop)

(G-12737)
T&A PALLETS INC
2849 Denny Rd (44266-9419)
PHONE.................................330 968-4743
Tony Rodriguez, *Prin*
EMP: 6 **EST:** 2009
SALES (est): 66.53K **Privately Held**
SIC: 2448 Pallets, wood and wood with metal

(G-12738)
TARPED OUT INC
Also Called: Mountain Tarp
4442 State Route 14 (44266-8741)
PHONE.................................330 325-7722
Marc Campitelli, *Brnch Mgr*
EMP: 26
Web: www.mountaintarp.com
SIC: 2394 Awnings, fabric: made from purchased materials
HQ: Tarped Out, Inc.
1002 N 15th St
Middlesboro KY 40965

(G-12739)
TREXLER RUBBER CO INC (PA)
503 N Diamond St (44266-2113)
P.O. Box 667 (44266-0667)
PHONE.................................330 296-9677
Jack W Schaefer, *Pr*
EMP: 20 **EST:** 1953
SQ FT: 26,000
SALES (est): 2.32MM
SALES (corp-wide): 2.32MM **Privately Held**
Web: www.trexlerrubber.com
SIC: 3069 2851 3544 Latex, foamed; Polyurethane coatings; Special dies, tools, jigs, and fixtures

(G-12740)
TRUE INDUSTRIES INC
Also Called: Cleveland Punch and Die
666 Pratt St (44266-3161)
P.O. Box 769 (44266-0769)
PHONE.................................330 296-4342
Kyle Brown, *Pr*
Dan Brown, *
Ryan Brodie, *
EMP: 50 **EST:** 1880
SQ FT: 70,000
SALES (est): 9.9MM **Privately Held**
Web: www.clevelandpunch.com
SIC: 3544 Special dies and tools

(G-12741)
W POLE CONTRACTING INC
4188 State Route 14 (44266-8739)
PHONE.................................330 325-7177
Wade Pol, *Pr*
Christine Pol, *Treas*
EMP: 10 **EST:** 1987
SALES (est): 934.15K **Privately Held**
SIC: 1389 Oil field services, nec

Ravenna - Portage County (G-12742)

(G-12742)
WESCO MACHINE INC
2304 Roberts Journey (44266-7809)
PHONE.................................330 688-6973
De Etta Connelly, Pr
Ronald Connelly, VP Opers
EMP: 17 **EST:** 1974
SALES (est): 2.46MM **Privately Held**
Web: www.wesco-machine.com
SIC: 3599 3559 Machine shop, jobbing and repair; Plastics working machinery

Rawson
Hancock County

(G-12743)
DNC HYDRAULICS LLC
5219 County Road 313 (45881-9650)
PHONE.................................419 963-2800
EMP: 12 **EST:** 1991
SALES (est): 2.52MM **Privately Held**
Web: www.dnchydraulics.com
SIC: 7699 3492 Industrial machinery and equipment repair; Control valves, fluid power: hydraulic and pneumatic

Ray
Vinton County

(G-12744)
TERRY G SICKLES
2207 Boy Scout Rd (45672-9672)
PHONE.................................740 286-8880
Terry G Sickles, Prin
EMP: 6 **EST:** 2010
SALES (est): 213.29K **Privately Held**
SIC: 2411 Logging

Rayland
Jefferson County

(G-12745)
SHELLY AND SANDS INC
Also Called: Tri-State Asphalt Co
1731 Old State Route 7 (43943-7962)
P.O. Box 66 (43943-0066)
PHONE.................................740 859-2104
TOLL FREE: 800
Mark Haverty, Genl Mgr
EMP: 6
SALES (corp-wide): 433.35MM **Privately Held**
Web: www.shellyandsands.com
SIC: 2951 1542 Asphalt paving mixtures and blocks; Nonresidential construction, nec
PA: Shelly And Sands, Inc.
3570 S River Rd
Zanesville OH 43701
740 453-0721

Raymond
Union County

(G-12746)
NATURE PURE LLC (PA)
26586 State Route 739 (43067-9763)
PHONE.................................937 358-2364
Kurt Lausecker, Managing Member
EMP: 15 **EST:** 2007
SALES (est): 2.57MM **Privately Held**
Web: www.naturepure.us
SIC: 0252 2048 Started pullet farm; Poultry feeds

Reading
Hamilton County

(G-12747)
POST
312 Elm St (45215-5540)
PHONE.................................513 768-8000
Margaret Buchanan, Prin
EMP: 10 **EST:** 2010
SALES (est): 83.68K **Privately Held**
Web: www.postconsumerbrands.com
SIC: 2711 Newspapers

Reynoldsburg
Franklin County

(G-12748)
ADVANCED INTEGRATION LLC
Also Called: Advint
6880 Tussing Rd (43068-4101)
PHONE.................................614 863-2433
Paul Salopek, CEO
Paul R Salopek, *
John C Albert, *
EMP: 32 **EST:** 1999
SQ FT: 6,000
SALES (est): 7.76MM **Privately Held**
Web: www.advint.com
SIC: 3825 Test equipment for electronic and electric measurement

(G-12749)
AFRAMIAN PARTNERSHIP LLC
7719 Taylor Rd Sw (43068-9626)
P.O. Box 91031 (43209-7031)
PHONE.................................614 868-8634
M Aframian Authorized Represen t, Prin
EMP: 6 **EST:** 2001
SALES (est): 81.49K **Privately Held**
SIC: 3599 Industrial machinery, nec

(G-12750)
ALBANY SCREEN PRINTING LLC
7049 Trillium Ln (43068-4832)
P.O. Box 80 (43004-0080)
PHONE.................................614 585-3279
Winter Adams, Pr
EMP: 15 **EST:** 2006
SALES (est): 529.5K **Privately Held**
SIC: 2759 2395 Screen printing; Embroidery and art needlework

(G-12751)
AMERICAN AIRLESS INC
7095 Americana Pkwy (43068-4118)
PHONE.................................614 552-0146
Jimmy Yang, Pr
Charles Lee, Dir
Lonnie Wells, Genl Mgr
EMP: 10 **EST:** 2008
SALES (est): 459.07K **Privately Held**
SIC: 3011 Tire and inner tube materials and related products

(G-12752)
B B & H TOOL COMPANY
7719 Taylor Rd Sw (43068-9626)
P.O. Box 100 (43026-0100)
PHONE.................................614 868-8634
Mousa Aframian, Owner
EMP: 8 **EST:** 1971
SQ FT: 8,000
SALES (est): 993.75K **Privately Held**
Web: www.bbhtool.com
SIC: 3599 Machine shop, jobbing and repair

(G-12753)
BATH & BODY WORKS LLC (HQ)
Also Called: Bath & Body Works
7 Limited Pkwy E (43068-5300)
PHONE.................................614 856-6000
◆ **EMP:** 336 **EST:** 1990
SALES (est): 1.06B
SALES (corp-wide): 7.43B **Publicly Held**
Web: www.bathandbodyworks.com
SIC: 5999 2844 Toiletries, cosmetics, and perfumes; Perfumes, cosmetics and other toilet preparations
PA: Bath & Body Works, Inc.
3 Limited Pkwy
Columbus OH 43230
614 415-7000

(G-12754)
BEAUTYAVENUES LLC (HQ)
Also Called: Bath and Body Works
7 Limited Pkwy E (43068-5300)
PHONE.................................614 856-6000
Charles Mcguigan, CEO
◆ **EMP:** 147 **EST:** 2005
SALES (est): 95.74MM
SALES (corp-wide): 7.43B **Publicly Held**
SIC: 5999 5122 2844 Toiletries, cosmetics, and perfumes; Perfumes; Face creams or lotions
PA: Bath & Body Works, Inc.
3 Limited Pkwy
Columbus OH 43230
614 415-7000

(G-12755)
BOB SUMEREL TIRE COMPANY INC
67 Klema Dr N Ste D (43068-6814)
PHONE.................................740 927-2811
Todd Sumerel, Pr
Bob Sumerel, CEO
EMP: 6 **EST:** 1993
SQ FT: 4,000
SALES (est): 621.13K **Privately Held**
Web: www.bobsumereltire.com
SIC: 5531 5014 7534 Automotive tires; Tires and tubes; Tire repair shop

(G-12756)
BRIDGESTONE RET OPERATIONS LLC
Also Called: Firestone
7085 E Main St (43068-2011)
PHONE.................................614 861-7994
James Thompson, Mgr
EMP: 7
Web: www.bridgestoneamericas.com
SIC: 5531 7534 Automotive tires; Rebuilding and retreading tires
HQ: Bridgestone Retail Operations, Llc
333 E Lake St Ste 300
Bloomingdale IL 60108
630 259-9000

(G-12757)
BUCKEYE READY-MIX LLC (PA)
Also Called: Buckeye Building Products
7657 Taylor Rd Sw (43068-9626)
P.O. Box 164119 (43216-4119)
PHONE.................................614 575-2132
Tom Murphy, *
Larry Randels, *
EMP: 50 **EST:** 1999
SQ FT: 10,000
SALES (est): 48.26MM
SALES (corp-wide): 48.26MM **Privately Held**
Web: www.buckeyereadymix.com
SIC: 3273 Ready-mixed concrete

(G-12758)
CHRISTIAN MISSIONARY ALLIANCE (PA)
Also Called: Alliance, The
6421 E Main St (43068-2378)
P.O. Box 35000 (80935-3500)
PHONE.................................380 208-6200
John Stumbo, Pr
Gary Benedict, *
Kenneth Baldes, *
EMP: 150 **EST:** 1880
SQ FT: 59,000
SALES (est): 88.61MM
SALES (corp-wide): 88.61MM **Privately Held**
Web: www.cmalliance.org
SIC: 8661 2731 5942 Miscellaneous denomination church; Books, publishing only; Books, religious

(G-12759)
COLUMBUS GRAPHICS INC
7295 Rickly St (43068-2513)
PHONE.................................614 577-9360
William Stewart Iii, Pr
EMP: 11 **EST:** 1981
SQ FT: 8,000
SALES (est): 257.33K **Privately Held**
Web: www.columbusgraphics.net
SIC: 3993 Signs and advertising specialties

(G-12760)
DAIFUKU AMERICA CORPORATION (DH)
6700 Tussing Rd (43068-5083)
PHONE.................................614 863-1888
Satoru Otani, Pr
Tatsuo Inoue, *
John Doychich, *
Ken Hamel, *
Akihiko Nishimura, *
▲ **EMP:** 150 **EST:** 1983
SQ FT: 70,000
SALES (est): 95.87MM **Privately Held**
Web: www.daifukuamerica.com
SIC: 3535 Conveyors and conveying equipment
HQ: Daifuku North America Holding Company
30100 Cabot Dr
Novi MI 48377
248 553-1000

(G-12761)
DIMENSIONAL METALS INC (PA)
Also Called: D M I
58 Klema Dr N (43068-9691)
PHONE.................................740 927-3633
Stephen C Wissman, CEO
Phillip Gastaldo, *
Steven Gastaldo, *
EMP: 43 **EST:** 1988
SQ FT: 34,000
SALES (est): 15.64MM **Privately Held**
Web: www.dmimetals.com
SIC: 1761 3444 3531 Sheet metal work, nec; Sheet metalwork; Roofing equipment

(G-12762)
DYNALAB EMS INC
555 Lancaster Ave (43068-1128)
PHONE.................................614 866-9999
Gary James, Pr
Charles Arbuckle, *
▲ **EMP:** 92 **EST:** 2008
SALES (est): 11.2MM
SALES (corp-wide): 53.76MM **Privately Held**
Web: www.dynalabems.com
SIC: 3679 Electronic circuits
PA: Dynalab, Inc.

555 Lancaster Ave
Reynoldsburg OH 43068
614 866-9999

(G-12763)
DYNALAB FF INC
555 Lancaster Ave (43068-1128)
PHONE..............................614 866-9999
Gary James, *Pr*
Charles Arbuckle, *Sec*
▲ **EMP:** 80 **EST:** 2008
SALES (est): 4.91MM
SALES (corp-wide): 53.76MM **Privately Held**
Web: www.dynalabems.com
SIC: 3679 Electronic circuits
PA: Dynalab, Inc.
    555 Lancaster Ave
    Reynoldsburg OH 43068
    614 866-9999

(G-12764)
DYNALAB INC (PA)
555 Lancaster Ave (43068-1128)
PHONE..............................614 866-9999
▲ **EMP:** 96 **EST:** 1984
SALES (est): 53.76MM
SALES (corp-wide): 53.76MM **Privately Held**
Web: www.dynalabems.com
SIC: 3679 3678 3672 3661 Harness assemblies, for electronic use: wire or cable ; Electronic connectors; Printed circuit boards; Telephone and telegraph apparatus

(G-12765)
FRAME WAREHOUSE
7502 E Main St (43068-1208)
PHONE..............................614 861-4582
Jeff Christian, *Owner*
EMP: 6 **EST:** 1964
SALES (est): 499.37K **Privately Held**
Web: www.theoriginalframewarehouse.com
SIC: 2499 2752 3499 Picture and mirror frames, wood; Posters, lithographed; Picture frames, metal

(G-12766)
FREDRICK WELDING & MACHINING
6840 Americana Pkwy (43068-4113)
PHONE..............................614 866-9650
Fred Williams, *Pr*
Tammy Corriveau, *VP*
John Corriveau, *VP*
Lillian Joyce Williams, *Sec*
EMP: 11 **EST:** 1973
SQ FT: 18,750
SALES (est): 433.8K **Privately Held**
Web: www.fredrickwelding.com
SIC: 3599 7692 Machine shop, jobbing and repair; Welding repair

(G-12767)
INTEGRITY GROUP CONSULTING INC
Also Called: Igc Software
6432 E Main St Ste 201 (43068-2369)
PHONE..............................614 759-9148
Brian Ferguson, *Pr*
EMP: 10 **EST:** 1999
SALES (est): 2.2MM
SALES (corp-wide): 19.28MM **Privately Held**
SIC: 7372 Business oriented computer software
HQ: Movehq Inc.
    3440 Hollenberg Dr
    Bridgeton MO 63044
    614 759-9148

(G-12768)
KENYETTA BAGBY ENTERPRISE LLC
6629 Penick Dr (43068-2836)
PHONE..............................614 584-3426
Kenyetta Bagby, *Pr*
EMP: 10 **EST:** 2007
SALES (est): 407.75K **Privately Held**
SIC: 2754 8741 6531 7929 Business form and card printing, gravure; Management services; Real estate agents and managers ; Entertainment service

(G-12769)
MULCH MANUFACTURING INC (HQ)
Also Called: Cypress Court
6747 Taylor Rd Sw (43068-9649)
PHONE..............................614 864-4004
▲ **EMP:** 40 **EST:** 1985
SALES (est): 56.54MM
SALES (corp-wide): 59.21MM **Privately Held**
Web: www.mulchmfg.com
SIC: 2499 Mulch, wood and bark
PA: Sustainablegreen Team, Ltd.
    24200 County Road 561
    Astatula FL 34705
    407 886-8733

(G-12770)
OHIO STATE INSTITUTE FIN INC
Also Called: Ohio Select Imprinted Fabrics
7394 E Main St (43068-2166)
PHONE..............................614 861-8811
Eleanor J Martin, *CEO*
Robert Martin, *Pr*
EMP: 8 **EST:** 1970
SQ FT: 1,600
SALES (est): 516.98K **Privately Held**
Web: www.ohioselect.com
SIC: 2396 5199 Screen printing on fabric articles; Advertising specialties

(G-12771)
OHIOS BEST JUICE COMPANY LLC
299 Pathfinder Dr Ste 103 (43068-4804)
PHONE..............................440 258-0834
EMP: 11 **EST:** 2020
SALES (est): 547.86K **Privately Held**
SIC: 2037 Frozen fruits and vegetables

(G-12772)
PRECISION POLYMERS INC
6919 Americana Pkwy (43068-4116)
PHONE..............................614 322-9951
Andrew Wood, *Pr*
EMP: 20 **EST:** 2000
SQ FT: 17,500
SALES (est): 2.43MM **Privately Held**
Web: www.precisionpolymers.com
SIC: 3089 Injection molding of plastics

(G-12773)
READY RIGS LLC
2321 Taylor Park Dr (43068-8052)
PHONE..............................740 963-9203
EMP: 10 **EST:** 2021
SALES (est): 571.29K **Privately Held**
SIC: 3537 Trucks: freight, baggage, etc.: industrial, except mining

(G-12774)
STREAMLINE MEDIA & PUBG LLC
2699 Prendergast Pl (43068-5218)
PHONE..............................614 822-1817
EMP: 6 **EST:** 2020
SALES (est): 50K **Privately Held**
SIC: 2711 Newspapers, publishing and printing

(G-12775)
TOWN CNTRY TECHNICAL SVCS INC
Also Called: Keytel Systems
6200 Eastgreen Blvd (43068-3442)
PHONE..............................614 866-7700
Kristopher Haley, *Pr*
EMP: 10 **EST:** 1983
SQ FT: 4,000
SALES (est): 2.14MM **Privately Held**
Web: www.keytelsystems.com
SIC: 7629 5999 1731 7373 Telecommunication equipment repair (except telephones); Telephone equipment and systems; Computer installation; Local area network (LAN) systems integrator

(G-12776)
TS TECH AMERICAS INC (HQ)
8458 E Broad St (43068-9749)
PHONE..............................614 575-4100
Minoru Maeda, *Pr*
Jason J Ma, *Ex VP*
Takayuki Taniuchi, *
Hiroshi Suzuki, *
▲ **EMP:** 350 **EST:** 2013
SALES (est): 915.06MM **Privately Held**
Web: www.tstech.com
SIC: 5099 2396 Child restraint seats, automotive; Automotive trimmings, fabric
PA: Ts Tech Co., Ltd.
    3-7-27, Sakaecho
    Asaka STM 351-0

(G-12777)
TS TECH USA CORPORATION (DH)
8400 E Broad St (43068-9749)
PHONE..............................614 577-1088
▲ **EMP:** 281 **EST:** 1994
SQ FT: 244,000
SALES (est): 90.78MM **Privately Held**
Web: www.tstech.com
SIC: 3714 Motor vehicle body components and frame
HQ: Ts Tech Americas, Inc.
    8458 E Broad St
    Reynoldsburg OH 43068
    614 575-4100

(G-12778)
TWO GRNDMTHERS GOURMET KIT LLC
9127 Firstgate Dr (43068-9596)
PHONE..............................614 746-0888
Vicky Moore, *Owner*
Ven Jackson, *Owner*
EMP: 6 **EST:** 2009
SALES (est): 289.54K **Privately Held**
SIC: 2033 Canned fruits and specialties

(G-12779)
UNIFI LLC
341 Cheyenne Way (43068-5125)
PHONE..............................614 288-9217
Pete Gonzales, *Prin*
EMP: 7 **EST:** 2014
SALES (est): 51.53K **Privately Held**
Web: www.unifiservice.com
SIC: 2281 Yarn spinning mills

(G-12780)
VS SERVICE COMPANY LLC
Also Called: Victorias Secret Service Co
4 Limited Pkwy E (43068-5300)
PHONE..............................614 415-2348
EMP: 1084 **EST:** 1986
SALES (est): 11.33MM
SALES (corp-wide): 6.18B **Publicly Held**
SIC: 2341 Women's and children's underwear
PA: Victoria's Secret & Co.
    4 Limited Pkwy E
    Reynoldsburg OH 43068
    614 577-7000

Richfield
Summit County

(G-12781)
ALLEGA CONCRETE CORP
5146 Allega Way (44286-9817)
PHONE..............................216 447-0814
John Allega, *Pr*
Joe Allega, *
Jim Allega, *
Jeffrey Wallis, *
EMP: 35 **EST:** 1990
SALES (est): 5.75MM **Privately Held**
Web: www.allega.com
SIC: 3273 Ready-mixed concrete

(G-12782)
CENTER FOR EXCPTONAL PRACTICES
3404 Brecksville Rd (44286-9662)
PHONE..............................330 523-5240
Robyn Reis, *Prin*
EMP: 7 **EST:** 2008
SALES (est): 155.21K **Privately Held**
Web: www.thecenteratdentalceramics.com
SIC: 3821 Clinical laboratory instruments, except medical and dental

(G-12783)
CISCO SYSTEMS INC
Also Called: Cisco Systems
4125 Highlander Pkwy (44286-9085)
PHONE..............................330 523-2000
Michael Wyss, *Brnch Mgr*
EMP: 7
SALES (corp-wide): 57B **Publicly Held**
Web: www.cisco.com
SIC: 3577 Data conversion equipment, media-to-media: computer
PA: Cisco Systems, Inc.
    170 W Tasman Dr
    San Jose CA 95134
    408 526-4000

(G-12784)
CLEVELAND-CLIFFS COLUMBUS LLC (DH)
4020 Kinross Lakes Pkwy Ste 101 (44286-9084)
PHONE..............................614 492-6800
▲ **EMP:** 96 **EST:** 2003
SALES (est): 47.11MM
SALES (corp-wide): 22B **Publicly Held**
SIC: 3479 3471 3398 Galvanizing of iron, steel, or end-formed products; Plating and polishing; Metal heat treating
HQ: Cleveland-Cliffs Steel Llc
    1 S Dearborn St Fl 19
    Chicago IL 60603
    312 346-0300

(G-12785)
DENTAL CERAMICS INC
3404 Brecksville Rd (44286-9662)
PHONE..............................330 523-5240
John Lavicka, *Pr*
EMP: 27 **EST:** 1963
SALES (est): 5.43MM **Privately Held**
Web: www.dentalceramicsusa.com
SIC: 8072 3843 Crown and bridge production ; Dental equipment and supplies

(G-12786)
EXIT 11 TRUCK TIRE SERVICE
5219 Brecksville Rd Ste B (44286-9697)

Richfield - Summit County (G-12787)

PHONE.................................330 659-6372
James Smith Junior, *Pr*
EMP: 9 **EST:** 1981
SQ FT: 8,000
SALES (est): 1.92MM **Privately Held**
Web: www.exit11trucktire.com
SIC: 5531 7534 Automotive tires; Tire repair shop

(G-12787)
FAWCETT CO INC
3863 Congress Pkwy (44286-9745)
PHONE.................................330 659-4187
Jack Grace, *Pr*
EMP: 7 **EST:** 1946
SQ FT: 16,000
SALES (est): 939.33K **Privately Held**
Web: www.fawcettco.com
SIC: 3559 7699 Paint making machinery; Industrial machinery and equipment repair

(G-12788)
FRONTIER TANK CENTER INC
3800 Congress Pkwy (44286-9745)
P.O. Box 460 (44286-0460)
PHONE.................................330 659-3888
James S Hollabaugh, *Pr*
Mary Hollabaugh, *
EMP: 14 **EST:** 1988
SQ FT: 25,000
SALES (est): 1.03MM **Privately Held**
Web: www.frontiertrailersales.com
SIC: 7699 5013 3714 Tank repair; Trailer parts and accessories; Motor vehicle body components and frame

(G-12789)
GOPOWERX INC
3850 Sawbridge Dr Unit 24 (44286-9260)
PHONE.................................440 707-6029
Neil Sater, *Pr*
EMP: 11 **EST:** 2010
SALES (est): 601.79K **Privately Held**
SIC: 5211 3674 Solar heating equipment; Semiconductors and related devices
PA: Mh Gopower Company Limited
6-2, Luke 3rd Rd.,
Kaohsiung City

(G-12790)
KINGSCOTE CHEMICALS INC
3778 Timberlake Dr (44286-9187)
PHONE.................................330 523-5300
EMP: 7 **EST:** 2013
SALES (est): 784.14K **Privately Held**
Web: www.kingscotechemicals.com
SIC: 2819 Industrial inorganic chemicals, nec

(G-12791)
MOREL LANDSCAPING LLC
3684 Forest Run Dr (44286-9408)
P.O. Box 41420 (44141-0420)
PHONE.................................216 551-4395
EMP: 11 **EST:** 2012
SQ FT: 9,000
SALES (est): 532.61K **Privately Held**
Web: www.morellandscaping.com
SIC: 1771 0783 3645 0781 Patio construction, concrete; Planting services, ornamental bush; Garden, patio, walkway and yard lighting fixtures: electric; Landscape services

(G-12792)
PAK MASTER LLC
3778 Timberlake Dr (44286-9187)
PHONE.................................330 523-5319
Peter Biierg, *Managing Member*
EMP: 50 **EST:** 2016
SQ FT: 100,000
SALES (est): 13.62MM

SALES (corp-wide): 142.34MM **Privately Held**
SIC: 3565 Packaging machinery
HQ: Switchback Group, Inc.
5638 Transportation Blvd
Cleveland OH 44125

(G-12793)
PREMIER FARNELL CORP (HQ)
4180 Highlander Pkwy (44286-9352)
PHONE.................................330 659-0459
♦ **EMP:** 55 **EST:** 1996
SALES (est): 1.39B
SALES (corp-wide): 26.54B **Publicly Held**
Web: www.farnell.com
SIC: 3451 Screw machine products
PA: Avnet, Inc.
2211 S 47th St
Phoenix AZ 85034
480 643-2000

(G-12794)
PREMIER FARNELL HOLDING INC (DH)
4180 Highlander Pkwy (44286-9352)
PHONE.................................330 523-4273
Dan Hill, *Pr*
Joseph R Daprile, *VP*
Paul M Barlak, *Treas*
Steven Webb, *VP*
♦ **EMP:** 20 **EST:** 1998
SQ FT: 35,000
SALES (est): 218.59MM
SALES (corp-wide): 26.54B **Publicly Held**
SIC: 5065 3429 Electronic parts and equipment, nec; Nozzles, fire fighting
HQ: Element14 Us Holdings Inc
4180 Highlander Pkwy
Richfield OH 44286
330 523-4280

(G-12795)
RAYHAVEN GROUP INC
Also Called: Rayhaven Group
3842 Congress Pkwy Ste A (44286-9745)
PHONE.................................330 659-3183
Robert Rickenbacker, *Mgr*
EMP: 6
Web: www.rayhaven.com
SIC: 3448 5046 5084 Prefabricated metal buildings; Commercial equipment, nec; Heat exchange equipment, industrial
PA: Rayhaven Group, Inc.
35901 Schoolcraft Rd
Livonia MI 48150

(G-12796)
SCRIPTYPE PUBLISHING INC
Also Called: Broadview Journal, The
4300 W Streetsboro Rd (44286-9796)
PHONE.................................330 659-0303
Sue Serdinak, *Pr*
EMP: 20 **EST:** 1978
SQ FT: 5,708
SALES (est): 367.39K **Privately Held**
Web: www.scriptype.com
SIC: 2741 Miscellaneous publishing

(G-12797)
SENSIBLE PRODUCTS INC
3857 Brecksville Rd (44286-9634)
PHONE.................................330 659-4212
EMP: 9 **EST:** 1984
SALES (est): 904.13K **Privately Held**
Web: www.senpro.net
SIC: 3429 Nozzles, fire fighting

(G-12798)
SMC CORPORATION OF AMERICA
4160 Highlander Pkwy Ste 200 (44286-9082)

PHONE.................................330 659-2006
Scott Chonko, *Brnch Mgr*
EMP: 13
Web: www.smcusa.com
SIC: 3625 3492 Actuators, industrial; Control valves, fluid power: hydraulic and pneumatic
HQ: Smc Corporation Of America
10100 Smc Blvd
Noblesville IN 46060
317 899-4440

(G-12799)
SNAP-ON BUSINESS SOLUTIONS INC (HQ)
4025 Kinross Lakes Pkwy (44286-9371)
PHONE.................................330 659-1600
Timothy Chambers, *Pr*
Jarry Baracz, *
Michael Maddison, *
EMP: 300 **EST:** 1987
SQ FT: 88,000
SALES (est): 126.89MM
SALES (corp-wide): 4.73B **Publicly Held**
Web: sbs.snapon.com
SIC: 7372 Business oriented computer software
PA: Snap-On Incorporated
2801 80th St
Kenosha WI 53143
262 656-5200

(G-12800)
TAYLOR COMMUNICATIONS INC
4125 Highlander Pkwy Ste 230 (44286-9085)
PHONE.................................216 265-1800
Ray Taylor, *Mgr*
EMP: 13
SALES (corp-wide): 3.81B **Privately Held**
Web: www.taylor.com
SIC: 2761 Manifold business forms
HQ: Taylor Communications, Inc.
1725 Roe Crest Dr
North Mankato MN 56003
866 541-0937

(G-12801)
TIMBERLAKE AUTOMATION INC
3778 Timberlake Dr (44286-9187)
PHONE.................................330 523-5300
Robert A Ciulla, *Pr*
EMP: 10 **EST:** 2008
SALES (est): 881.72K **Privately Held**
Web: www.herschal.com
SIC: 3823 Process control instruments

Richmond
Jefferson County

(G-12802)
MC CONNELLS MARKET
Also Called: McConnell's Farm Market
2189 State Route 43 (43944-7980)
PHONE.................................740 765-4300
Kenneth Mc Connell, *Pt*
James Mc Connell, *Pt*
EMP: 6 **EST:** 1953
SALES (est): 453.84K **Privately Held**
Web: www.mcconnellsmarket.com
SIC: 2011 5421 Meat packing plants; Meat markets, including freezer provisioners

(G-12803)
SIGN AMERICA INCORPORATED
3887 State Route 43 (43944-7912)
P.O. Box 396 (43944-0396)
PHONE.................................740 765-5555
Judith A Hilty, *Pr*
Scott Hilty Junior, *VP*

John Bray, *Sec*
EMP: 16 **EST:** 1986
SQ FT: 6,000
SALES (est): 2.53MM **Privately Held**
Web: www.signamericainc.com
SIC: 5046 3993 Signs, electrical; Signs and advertising specialties

Richmond Dale
Ross County

(G-12804)
APPALACHIA FREEZE DRY CO LLC ✪
659 Jackson St (45673-9705)
PHONE.................................740 412-0169
Kristen Howard, *Admn*
Kristen Howard, *Managing Member*
EMP: 10 **EST:** 2023
SALES (est): 413.11K **Privately Held**
SIC: 2034 2064 7389 Dried and dehydrated fruits, vegetables and soup mixes; Candy and other confectionery products; Business services, nec

Richmond Heights
Cuyahoga County

(G-12805)
AVIATION CMPNENT SOLUTIONS INC
26451 Curtiss Wright Pkwy Ste 106 (44143-4410)
PHONE.................................440 295-6590
Joe Klinehamer, *Pr*
EMP: 15 **EST:** 2006
SALES (est): 2.91MM **Privately Held**
Web: www.acs-parts.com
SIC: 3728 Aircraft parts and equipment, nec

(G-12806)
BODIED BEAUTIES LLC
4820 Geraldine Rd (44143-2832)
PHONE.................................216 971-1155
EMP: 9 **EST:** 2020
SALES (est): 490.77K **Privately Held**
SIC: 2339 Women's and misses' athletic clothing and sportswear

(G-12807)
CCP INDUSTRIES INC
Also Called: Ccp Industries
26301 Curtiss Wright Pkwy Ste 200 (44143-1454)
P.O. Box 6500 (44101-1500)
PHONE.................................216 535-4227
▼ **EMP:** 400
SIC: 5169 2392 2297 2273 Specialty cleaning and sanitation preparations; Household furnishings, nec; Nonwoven fabrics; Carpets and rugs

(G-12808)
JC CARTER LLC (DH)
Also Called: JC Carter Nozzles
26451 Curtiss Wright Pkwy Ste 106 (44143-4410)
PHONE.................................440 569-1818
▲ **EMP:** 8 **EST:** 2007
SALES (est): 4.69MM
SALES (corp-wide): 13.47B **Privately Held**
Web: www.jccarternozzles.com
SIC: 3559 Cryogenic machinery, industrial
HQ: Atlas Copco Mafi-Trench Company Llc
3037 Industrial Pkwy
Santa Maria CA 93455

(G-12809)
MOMENTIVE PERFORMANCE MTLS INC
Also Called: Momentive Performance Mtls
24400 Highland Rd (44143-2503)
PHONE...................440 878-5705
EMP: 147
Web: www.momentive.com
SIC: 2869 3479 Silicones; Coating of metals with silicon
HQ: Momentive Performance Materials Inc.
2750 Balltown Rd
Niskayuna NY 12309

(G-12810)
R & H ENTERPRISES LLC
Also Called: Rh Enterprises
4933 Karen Isle Dr (44143-1412)
PHONE...................216 702-4449
Ryan Hoover, *Managing Member*
EMP: 6 **EST:** 2008
SALES (est): 252.71K **Privately Held**
SIC: 7372 7389 Application computer software; Business Activities at Non-Commercial Site

(G-12811)
TRANZONIC COMPANIES
Also Called: Hospeco
26301 Curtiss Wright Pkwy Ste 200 (44143)
PHONE...................216 535-4300
Mike Blanchard, *Brnch Mgr*
EMP: 82
SALES (corp-wide): 465.45MM **Privately Held**
Web: www.tranzonic.com
SIC: 2676 3581 3842 3586 Napkins, sanitary: made from purchased paper; Automatic vending machines; Surgical appliances and supplies; Measuring and dispensing pumps
PA: The Tranzonic Companies
26301 Curtiss Wright Pkwy # 200
Cleveland OH 44143
216 535-4300

(G-12812)
TZ ACQUISITION CORP
Also Called: Tranzonic Companies
26301 Curtiss Wright Pkwy 2nd Fl (44143-4413)
PHONE...................216 535-4300
Kenneth Vuylsteke, *Prin*
Thomas S Friedl, *
◆ **EMP:** 25 **EST:** 1997
SQ FT: 22,000
SALES (est): 2.1MM **Privately Held**
SIC: 2211 2326 2842 2262 Scrub cloths; Work garments, except raincoats: waterproof; Sanitation preparations, disinfectants and deodorants; Napping: manmade fiber and silk broadwoven fabrics

Richwood
Union County

(G-12813)
CREATIVE FABRICATION LTD
20110 Predmore Rd (43344-9014)
PHONE...................740 262-5789
John Hughes, *Managing Member*
EMP: 7 **EST:** 2009
SALES (est): 443.58K **Privately Held**
Web: www.creativefabrication.org
SIC: 7692 7389 Welding repair; Business services, nec

(G-12814)
DP ASSEMBLY LLC
113 N Franklin St (43344-1060)
PHONE...................740 225-4591
EMP: 7 **EST:** 2018
SALES (est): 110.82K **Privately Held**
Web: www.dpassemblyllc.com
SIC: 3999 Manufacturing industries, nec

Ridgeville Corners
Henry County

(G-12815)
NASG AUTO-SEAT TEC LLC
19911 County Rd T (43555)
PHONE...................419 359-5954
David Vondeylen, *Managing Member*
EMP: 30 **EST:** 2013
SALES (est): 1.63MM **Privately Held**
SIC: 3469 Stamping metal for the trade

(G-12816)
NASG STING RDGVLLE CORNERS LLC (HQ)
Also Called: Alex Products, Inc.
19911 County Rd T (43555)
P.O. Box 326 (43555-0326)
PHONE...................419 267-5240
Dave Von Deylen, *Pr*
Gary Crider, *
▲ **EMP:** 300 **EST:** 1973
SQ FT: 150,000
SALES (est): 97.03MM
SALES (corp-wide): 250.69MM **Privately Held**
Web: www.nasg.net
SIC: 3599 Machine shop, jobbing and repair
PA: North American Stamping Group, Llc
119 Kirby Dr
Portland TN 37148
615 323-0500

(G-12817)
NASG TOOLING AND AUTOMTN LLC
19963 County Rd T (43555)
PHONE...................419 359-5954
EMP: 10 **EST:** 2013
SALES (est): 399.76K **Privately Held**
Web: www.nasg.net
SIC: 3599 Machine shop, jobbing and repair

Rio Grande
Gallia County

(G-12818)
INLAND PRODUCTS INC
Also Called: Galipols Reduction Co
P.O. Box 337 (45674-0337)
PHONE...................740 245-5514
Mark Dickson, *Mgr*
EMP: 15
SALES (corp-wide): 3.83MM **Privately Held**
SIC: 2077 Grease rendering, inedible
PA: Inland Products, Inc.
599 Frank Rd
Columbus OH 43223
614 443-3425

Ripley
Brown County

(G-12819)
RIPLEY METALWORKS LLC
111 Waterworks Rd (45167)
PHONE...................937 392-4992
Michael Walkup, *Genl Pt*
EMP: 45 **EST:** 1992
SQ FT: 75,000
SALES (est): 9.3MM **Privately Held**
Web: www.ripleymetalworks.com
SIC: 3441 Fabricated structural metal

Risingsun
Wood County

(G-12820)
WELLS INC
8176 Us Highway 23 (43457-9629)
P.O. Box 9 (43457-0009)
PHONE...................419 457-2611
Steffen Wellstein, *Pr*
Steffen R Wellstein, *Pr*
EMP: 10 **EST:** 1967
SQ FT: 15,000
SALES (est): 1.45MM **Privately Held**
Web: www.wellsfargoadvisors.com
SIC: 3494 Well adapters

Rittman
Wayne County

(G-12821)
FASTFORMINGCOM LLC
300 Morning Star Dr (44270-9644)
PHONE...................330 927-3277
James Reedy, *Pr*
EMP: 12 **EST:** 1999
SQ FT: 12,000
SALES (est): 1.87MM **Privately Held**
Web: www.fastforming.com
SIC: 3089 Injection molding of plastics

(G-12822)
IMPERIAL FAMILY INC
80 Industrial St (44270-1508)
P.O. Box 375 (44270-0375)
PHONE...................330 927-5065
Walter Staiger, *Pr*
John Klein, *
Genevieve Staiger, *
Eugene Staiger, *
Susan Klein, *
EMP: 55 **EST:** 1960
SQ FT: 60,000
SALES (est): 7.62MM **Privately Held**
Web: www.ip-inc.com
SIC: 3089 Injection molding of plastics

(G-12823)
J & O PLASTICS INC
12475 Sheets Rd (44270-9730)
PHONE...................330 927-3169
Oscar Gross, *Pr*
Edgar Gross, *
Christine Gross, *
EMP: 50 **EST:** 1982
SQ FT: 90,000
SALES (est): 10.12MM **Privately Held**
Web: www.jandoplastics.com
SIC: 3089 Injection molding of plastics

(G-12824)
LUKE ENGINEERING & MFG CORP
11 Pipestone Rd (44270-9729)
PHONE...................330 925-3344
Pam Craig, *Mgr*
EMP: 20
SALES (corp-wide): 8.71MM **Privately Held**
Web: www.lukeeng.com
SIC: 3471 Electroplating of metals or formed products
PA: Luke Engineering & Mfg Corp

456 South Blvd
Wadsworth OH 44281
330 335-1501

(G-12825)
MORTON SALT INC
151 Industrial Ave (44270-1593)
PHONE...................330 925-3015
Mark Wallace, *Brnch Mgr*
EMP: 150
SALES (corp-wide): 1.22B **Privately Held**
Web: www.mortonsalt.com
SIC: 5149 2899 Salt, edible; Chemical preparations, nec
HQ: Morton Salt, Inc.
444 W Lake St Ste 3000
Chicago IL 60606

(G-12826)
PFI DISPLAYS INC (PA)
Also Called: Promotional Fixtures
40 Industrial St (44270-1525)
P.O. Box 508 (44270-0508)
PHONE...................330 925-9015
Vincent Tricomi, *Ch Bd*
Anthony R Tricomi, *
James Tricomi, *
Carol Tricomi, *
Robert J Kapitan, *
EMP: 39 **EST:** 1970
SQ FT: 70,000
SALES (est): 5.02MM
SALES (corp-wide): 5.02MM **Privately Held**
Web: www.pfidisplays.com
SIC: 3993 2541 2542 Displays and cutouts, window and lobby; Store and office display cases and fixtures; Partitions and fixtures, except wood

(G-12827)
RITTMAN INC
Also Called: Mull Iron
10 Mull Dr (44270-9777)
PHONE...................330 927-6855
Chester Mull Junior, *Pr*
William Mull, *
Beth Mull, *
Richard J Wendelken, *
Robert A O'neil, *Prin*
EMP: 60 **EST:** 1983
SQ FT: 34,000
SALES (est): 9.33MM **Privately Held**
Web: www.mulliron.net
SIC: 3441 1791 Fabricated structural metal; Structural steel erection

(G-12828)
SWISS WOODCRAFT INC
15 Industrial St (44270-1507)
PHONE...................330 925-1807
Ken Maibach, *Pr*
Dave Rufener, *
EMP: 30 **EST:** 1981
SQ FT: 45,000
SALES (est): 4.02MM **Privately Held**
Web: www.swisswoodcraft.com
SIC: 2431 Doors, wood

(G-12829)
WIL-MARK FROYO LLC
124 Joshua Dr (44270-2001)
PHONE...................330 421-6043
Mark Hotes, *Prin*
EMP: 10 **EST:** 2013
SALES (est): 232.23K **Privately Held**
SIC: 2024 Yogurt desserts, frozen

Roaming Shores
Ashtabula County

(G-12830)
CCS INTERNATIONAL CIRCUITS LLC
2593 Cardinal Dr (44084-9542)
PHONE..................................440 563-3462
Curtis Payne, *Brnch Mgr*
EMP: 7
Web: www.ccsintlcircuits.com
SIC: 3679 Electronic circuits
PA: Ccs International Circuits Llc
523 S Paula Dr
Dunedin FL 34698

Rock Creek
Ashtabula County

(G-12831)
DAVID BIXEL
Also Called: Hartsgrove Machine
2683 State Route 534 (44084-9340)
PHONE..................................440 474-4410
David Bixel, *Owner*
EMP: 14 **EST:** 2001
SALES (est): 2.19MM **Privately Held**
Web: www.hartsgrovemachine.com
SIC: 3599 Machine shop, jobbing and repair

(G-12832)
REAL ALLOY SPECIALTY PDTS LLC
2639 E Water St (44084-9601)
PHONE..................................440 563-3487
Nancy Kern, *Mgr*
EMP: 841
SALES (corp-wide): 112.7MM **Publicly Held**
Web: www.realalloy.com
SIC: 3341 Aluminum smelting and refining (secondary)
HQ: Real Alloy Specialty Products, Llc
3700 Park East Dr Ste 300
Beachwood OH 44122

Rockford
Mercer County

(G-12833)
FREMONT COMPANY
Also Called: Fremont
150 Hickory St (45882-9264)
PHONE..................................419 363-2924
James Gibson, *Mgr*
EMP: 40
SALES (corp-wide): 51.18MM **Privately Held**
Web: www.fremontcompany.com
SIC: 2033 2099 2035 Fruit juices: packaged in cans, jars, etc.; Food preparations, nec; Pickles, sauces, and salad dressings
PA: The Fremont Company
802 N Front St
Fremont OH 43420
419 334-8995

(G-12834)
TRUSS WORX LLC
12412 Frysinger Rd (45882-9520)
PHONE..................................419 363-2100
Kimberly Green, *Prin*
EMP: 8 **EST:** 2009
SALES (est): 437.78K **Privately Held**
SIC: 2439 Trusses, wooden roof

(G-12835)
WORLD CONNECTIONS CORPS
10803 Erastus Durbin Rd (45882-9654)
PHONE..................................419 363-2681
Llloyd Linton, *Pr*
EMP: 13 **EST:** 2001
SALES (est): 161.74K **Privately Held**
SIC: 3081 Vinyl film and sheet

Rocky River
Cuyahoga County

(G-12836)
CANVUS INC ◆
18500 Lake Rd (44116-1744)
PHONE..................................216 340-7500
Alex Kowalski, *Pr*
EMP: 50 **EST:** 2022
SALES (est): 6.35MM **Privately Held**
SIC: 3611 Turbines and turbine generator sets

(G-12837)
CRUISIN TIMES MAGAZINE
20545 Center Ridge Rd Ste Ll40 (44116-3441)
P.O. Box 27247 (19118-0247)
PHONE..................................440 331-4615
John Shapiro, *Prin*
EMP: 6 **EST:** 2008
SALES (est): 189.86K **Privately Held**
Web: www.cruisintimesmagazine.com
SIC: 5994 2721 Magazine stand; Magazines: publishing and printing

(G-12838)
GREAT LAKES MFG GROUP LTD
19035 Old Detroit Rd (44116-1710)
PHONE..................................440 391-8266
Andrew E Drumm, *Pt*
Thomas Mc Neill, *Pt*
EMP: 7 **EST:** 2016
SALES (est): 511.05K **Privately Held**
Web: www.glmfg.com
SIC: 3312 8748 Stainless steel; Systems analysis and engineering consulting services

(G-12839)
OPAL DIAMOND LLC
20033 Detroit Rd N Ridge Annex 2nd Fl (44116-2400)
PHONE..................................330 653-5876
William Mitchell, *Pr*
Michael Reilly, *Ex VP*
Henry Ng, *VP*
EMP: 7 **EST:** 2015
SQ FT: 2,000
SALES (est): 611.59K **Privately Held**
SIC: 2875 Compost

(G-12840)
P S GRAPHICS INC
20284 Orchard Grove Ave (44116-3527)
PHONE..................................440 356-9656
Nancy Vedda, *Pr*
Phil Vedda, *VP*
EMP: 6 **EST:** 1969
SQ FT: 4,000
SALES (est): 432.8K **Privately Held**
SIC: 2759 Screen printing

(G-12841)
PAMEE LLC
18500 Lake Rd (44116-1744)
PHONE..................................216 232-9255
EMP: 50 **EST:** 2020
SALES (est): 2.07MM **Privately Held**
Web: www.pamee.com

SIC: 7372 Prepackaged software

(G-12842)
ROCKY RIVER BREWING CO
21290 Center Ridge Rd (44116-3204)
PHONE..................................440 895-2739
Gary Cintron, *Owner*
EMP: 12 **EST:** 1997
SQ FT: 4,000
SALES (est): 624.71K **Privately Held**
Web: www.rockyriverbrewco.com
SIC: 2082 5813 5812 Malt beverages; Drinking places; Eating places

(G-12843)
SCRATCH OFF WORKS LLC
19537 Lake Rd (44116-1858)
PHONE..................................440 333-4302
EMP: 8 **EST:** 1993
SALES (est): 808.89K **Privately Held**
Web: www.scratchoffworks.com
SIC: 2752 Offset printing

(G-12844)
SPECIALTY POLYMER PRODUCT
P.O. Box 16894 (44116-0894)
PHONE..................................216 281-8300
EMP: 7 **EST:** 2010
SALES (est): 52.75K **Privately Held**
SIC: 2821 Plastics materials and resins

(G-12845)
SYNTEC LLC
20525 Center Ridge Rd Ste 512 (44116-3447)
PHONE..................................440 229-6262
Maximillian Fisher, *Managing Member*
EMP: 11 **EST:** 2010
SALES (est): 2.37MM **Privately Held**
Web: www.syntecdental.com
SIC: 7372 7373 7379 Business oriented computer software; Computer integrated systems design; Computer related maintenance services

(G-12846)
ZULLIX LLC
18500 Lake Rd (44116-1744)
PHONE..................................440 536-9300
EMP: 30 **EST:** 2021
SALES (est): 2.68MM **Privately Held**
SIC: 7372 Application computer software

Rogers
Columbiana County

(G-12847)
PAUL R LIPP & SON INC
47563 Pancake Clarkson Rd (44455-9723)
PHONE..................................330 227-9614
Gregory A Lipp, *Pr*
Paul R Lipp, *VP*
Lauren Lipp, *Sec*
EMP: 10 **EST:** 1964
SALES (est): 892.27K **Privately Held**
Web: www.prlipp.com
SIC: 1794 3273 Excavation and grading, building construction; Ready-mixed concrete

Rome
Ashtabula County

(G-12848)
J AARON WEAVER
Also Called: Indian Creek Structures
5759 Us Highway 6 (44085-9634)
PHONE..................................440 474-9185

J Aaron Weaver, *Owner*
EMP: 6 **EST:** 2015
SQ FT: 2,400
SALES (est): 363.58K **Privately Held**
SIC: 2452 Prefabricated wood buildings

(G-12849)
MSC INDUSTRIES INC
5131 Ireland Rd (44085-9812)
P.O. Box 200 (44064-0200)
PHONE..................................440 474-8788
John M Husek, *Pr*
Mary C Husek, *Sec*
EMP: 6 **EST:** 1987
SQ FT: 4,000
SALES (est): 726K **Privately Held**
SIC: 3545 3469 Tools and accessories for machine tools; Machine parts, stamped or pressed metal

Rootstown
Portage County

(G-12850)
A TO Z PAPER BOX COMPANY
4477 Tallmadge Rd (44272-9610)
PHONE..................................330 325-8722
Douglas Eatinger, *Pr*
EMP: 9 **EST:** 1962
SQ FT: 3,600
SALES (est): 767.52K **Privately Held**
SIC: 2652 5113 2759 Filing boxes, paperboard: made from purchased materials; Bags, paper and disposable plastic; Commercial printing, nec

(G-12851)
BARREL RUN CRSSING WNERY VNYRD
Also Called: Brx
3272 Industry Rd (44272-9775)
PHONE..................................330 325-1075
EMP: 6 **EST:** 2010
SALES (est): 459.75K **Privately Held**
Web: www.barrelrunwinery.com
SIC: 2084 Wines

(G-12852)
EDINBURG FIXTURE AND MCH INC
3101 State Route 14 (44272-9791)
PHONE..................................330 947-1700
Terri Tomazin, *Pr*
EMP: 10 **EST:** 1990
SALES (est): 477.37K **Privately Held**
Web: www.efmautoclutch.com
SIC: 3599 Machine shop, jobbing and repair

(G-12853)
JET RUBBER COMPANY
4457 Tallmadge Rd (44272-9610)
PHONE..................................330 325-1821
Franklin R Brubaker, *Prin*
Karen Crooks, *
EMP: 43 **EST:** 1954
SQ FT: 20,000
SALES (est): 5.46MM **Privately Held**
Web: www.jetrubber.com
SIC: 3069 3053 3533 5085 Molded rubber products; Gaskets; packing and sealing devices; Gas field machinery and equipment ; Rubber goods, mechanical

(G-12854)
MINERS TRACTOR SALES INC (PA)
Also Called: Miner's Bishop Tractor Sales
6941 Tallmadge Rd (44272-9758)
PHONE..................................330 325-9914
Stephen Miner, *CEO*
Craig M Stephens, *Pr*

EMP: 10 EST: 2006
SALES (est): 2MM
SALES (corp-wide): 2MM Privately Held
Web: www.edinburgtractor.com
SIC: 3537 5999 Industrial trucks and tractors
; Farm tractors

(G-12855)
MONITOR MOLD & MACHINE CO
3393 Industry Rd (44272-9505)
P.O. Box 396 (44272-0396)
PHONE..................................330 697-7800
Phillip Warlop, *Pr*
EMP: 10 EST: 1980
SQ FT: 12,000
SALES (est): 860.2K Privately Held
SIC: 3544 Industrial molds

(G-12856)
NUEVUE SOLUTIONS INC
4209 State Route 44 D-134 (44272-9698)
PHONE..................................440 836-4772
William Mccroskey, *Pr*
James Sacher, *Prin*
EMP: 6 EST: 2016
SALES (est): 228.76K Privately Held
Web: www.nuevuesolutions.com
SIC: 3841 Surgical and medical instruments

(G-12857)
SINGLETON REELS INC
4612 Lynn Rd (44272-9710)
PHONE..................................330 274-2961
Scott Hamilton, *Pr*
EMP: 20 EST: 1972
SALES (est): 2.18MM Privately Held
Web: www.singletonreels.com
SIC: 2499 Reels, plywood

(G-12858)
WRONG TURN FABRICATION LLC
2792 Hartville Rd (44272-9659)
PHONE..................................330 802-8686
Dennis Eugene Siciliano, *Prin*
EMP: 6 EST: 2019
SALES (est): 124.72K Privately Held
SIC: 3599 Machine shop, jobbing and repair

Roseville
Muskingum County

(G-12859)
CLAY BURLEY PRODUCTS CO (PA)
455 Gordon St (43777-1110)
P.O. Box 35 (43777-0035)
PHONE..................................740 452-3633
Peter Petratsas, *Pr*
▲ EMP: 50 EST: 1922
SQ FT: 180,000
SALES (est): 4.82MM
SALES (corp-wide): 4.82MM Privately Held
Web: www.burleyclay.com
SIC: 3269 5032 Stoneware pottery products; Ceramic wall and floor tile, nec

(G-12860)
TRADEWINDS PRIN TWEAR
35 E Athens Rd (43777-1212)
P.O. Box 813 (43702-0813)
PHONE..................................740 214-5005
Tom Erdico, *Owner*
EMP: 6 EST: 2011
SALES (est): 249.38K Privately Held
Web: www.tradewindsprintwear.com
SIC: 2752 Offset printing

Rossburg
Darke County

(G-12861)
CAL-MAINE FOODS INC
3078 Washington Rd (45362-9500)
PHONE..................................937 337-9576
EMP: 61
SALES (corp-wide): 3.15B Publicly Held
Web: www.calmainefoods.com
SIC: 0252 2015 Chicken eggs; Poultry slaughtering and processing
PA: Cal-Maine Foods, Inc.
1052 Hghland Clny Pkwy St
Ridgeland MS 39157
601 948-6813

(G-12862)
FORT RECOVERY EQUITY EXCHANGE
Also Called: S & R Egg
13243 Cochran Rd (45362-9753)
PHONE..................................937 338-8901
Lou Daniels, *Mgr*
Greag Fortkamp, *
EMP: 7 EST: 2000
SALES (est): 97.65K Privately Held
SIC: 2015 Egg processing

Rossford
Wood County

(G-12863)
ELECTRO PRIME ASSEMBLY INC
63 Dixie Hwy Ste 7 (43460-1264)
PHONE..................................419 476-0100
Fred Busch, *Pr*
John Lauffer, *VP Fin*
James E Wilson, *VP Mfg*
Kevin Meade, *VP*
EMP: 11 EST: 1997
SALES (est): 147.64K Privately Held
Web: www.electroprime.com
SIC: 3471 Electroplating of metals or formed products

(G-12864)
ELECTRO PRIME GROUP LLC
63 Dixie Hwy Ste 7 (43460-1264)
PHONE..................................419 666-5000
Kavin Meade, *Brnch Mgr*
EMP: 80
Web: www.electroprime.com
SIC: 3471 Plating and polishing
PA: Electro Prime Group Llc
4510 Lint Ave Ste B
Toledo OH 43612

(G-12865)
HUNGER HYDRAULICS CC LTD
Also Called: Hunger Industrial Complex
63 Dixie Hwy Ste 1 (43460-1270)
P.O. Box 37 (43460-0037)
PHONE..................................419 666-4510
Walter Hunger, *Pr*
▲ EMP: 12 EST: 1996
SALES (est): 4.44MM Privately Held
Web: www.hunger-hydraulics.com
SIC: 3593 7699 Fluid power cylinders, hydraulic or pneumatic; Hydraulic equipment repair
HQ: Walter Hunger International Gesellschaft Mit Beschrankter Haftung
Alfred-Nobel-Str. 26
Wurzburg BY 97080
931900970

(G-12866)
IC-FLUID POWER INC
63 Dixie Hwy (43460-1269)
PHONE..................................419 661-8811
Bernd Hunger, *Pr*
Armin Hunger, *Pr*
▲ EMP: 10 EST: 1989
SQ FT: 15,000
SALES (est): 2.48MM Privately Held
Web: www.icfluid.com
SIC: 5084 3593 7699 3492 Hydraulic systems equipment and supplies; Fluid power cylinders and actuators; Hydraulic equipment repair; Fluid power valves and hose fittings

(G-12867)
INDUSTRIAL POWER SYSTEMS INC
Also Called: I P S
146 Dixie Hwy (43460-1215)
PHONE..................................419 531-3121
Kevin Gray, *CEO*
Kevin D Gray, *
Jeremiah Johnson, *
Tim Grosteffon, *
Mike Williams, *
EMP: 300 EST: 1985
SQ FT: 20,000
SALES (est): 60.52MM Privately Held
Web: www.ipscontractor.com
SIC: 1711 3498 1731 1796 Mechanical contractor; Coils, pipe: fabricated from purchased pipe; General electrical contractor; Millwright

(G-12868)
NAPTIME PRODUCTIONS LLC
107 Hidden Cove St (43460-1027)
P.O. Box 7 (43460-0007)
PHONE..................................419 662-9521
Lisa Sattler, *Prin*
EMP: 6 EST: 1995
SALES (est): 479.67K Privately Held
Web: www.naptimecards.com
SIC: 2771 5947 Greeting cards; Greeting cards

(G-12869)
PILKINGTON NORTH AMERICA INC
Also Called: Pilington Libbey-Owens-Ford Co
140 Dixie Hwy (43460-1215)
PHONE..................................419 247-3211
Dick Altman, *Mgr*
EMP: 360
SQ FT: 3,000,000
Web: www.pilkington.com
SIC: 3211 3231 Float glass; Products of purchased glass
HQ: Pilkington North America, Inc.
811 Madison Ave Fl 3
Toledo OH 43604
419 247-3731

(G-12870)
RADOCY INC
30652 East River Rd (43551-3441)
P.O. Box 67 (43460-0067)
PHONE..................................419 666-4400
Thomas Bradley, *Pr*
Paul F Radocy, *Stockholder*
EMP: 15 EST: 1940
SQ FT: 18,000
SALES (est): 2.11MM Privately Held
Web: www.radocy.com
SIC: 3536 3594 3566 Cranes, industrial plant ; Fluid power pumps and motors; Speed changers, drives, and gears

(G-12871)
RSW TECHNOLOGIES LLC
135 Dixie Hwy (43460-1241)
PHONE..................................419 662-8100
▲ EMP: 17 EST: 2007
SALES (est): 2.32MM Privately Held
Web: www.rswtechnologies.com
SIC: 3823 Process control instruments

(G-12872)
SASHA ELECTRONICS INC
Also Called: Digital Technologies
135 Dixie Hwy (43460-1241)
PHONE..................................419 662-8100
William R Wumer Junior, *Pr*
▲ EMP: 16 EST: 1982
SQ FT: 20,000
SALES (est): 784K Privately Held
Web: www.rswtechnologies.com
SIC: 7629 3822 Electronic equipment repair; Energy cutoff controls, residential or commercial types

(G-12873)
WELCH PUBLISHING CO
215 Osborne St (43460-1238)
PHONE..................................419 666-5344
John Welch, *VP*
EMP: 7
SQ FT: 1,167
SALES (corp-wide): 2.43MM Privately Held
Web: www.perrysburg.com
SIC: 2711 Newspapers: publishing only, not printed on site
PA: Welch Publishing Co.
117 E 2nd St
Perrysburg OH 43551
419 874-2528

Rushsylvania
Logan County

(G-12874)
DAYTON SUPERIOR CORPORATION
Also Called: Roberts Screw Products
270 Rush St (43347-2502)
PHONE..................................937 682-4015
Allan Kerns, *Brnch Mgr*
EMP: 19
SALES (corp-wide): 69.06B Privately Held
Web: www.daytonsuperior.com
SIC: 3429 Hardware, nec
HQ: Dayton Superior Corporation
1125 Byers Rd
Miamisburg OH 45342
937 866-0711

(G-12875)
ROBERTS MACHINE PRODUCTS LLC
270 Rush St (43347-2502)
P.O. Box 210 (43347-0210)
PHONE..................................937 682-4015
Mike Stapleton, *Prin*
Kelli Phillips, *Mgr*
EMP: 12 EST: 2010
SALES (est): 2.48MM Privately Held
Web: www.robertsmachineproducts.com
SIC: 3559 3599 Ammunition and explosives, loading machinery; Machine shop, jobbing and repair

Russells Point
Logan County

(G-12876)
HONDA DEV & MFG AMER LLC
6964 State Route 235 N (43348-9703)
PHONE..................937 843-5555
EMP: 823
Web: www.honda.com
SIC: 3714 Motor vehicle parts and accessories
HQ: Honda Development & Manufacturing Of America, Llc
24000 Honda Pkwy
Marysville OH 43040
937 642-5000

(G-12877)
HONDA TRANSMISSION MANUFACTURING OF AMERICA INC
6964 State Route 235 N (43348-9703)
P.O. Box 2200 (90509-2200)
PHONE..................937 843-5555
▲ **EMP:** 1200
Web: www.honda.com
SIC: 3714 Wheels, motor vehicle

(G-12878)
INDIAN LAKE SHOPPERS EDGE
204 1/2 Lincoln Blvd (43348-9681)
P.O. Box 38 (43348-0038)
PHONE..................937 843-6600
Art Shellenbarger, *Pt*
Miriam Shellenbarger, *Pt*
EMP: 9 **EST:** 1988
SALES (est): 488.16K **Privately Held**
Web: www.myshoppersedge.com
SIC: 2711 Newspapers: publishing only, not printed on site

(G-12879)
WEST OHIO TOOL CO
7311 World Class Dr (43348-9593)
P.O. Box 1457 (43348-1457)
PHONE..................937 842-6688
Kerry Buchenroth, *Pr*
EMP: 18 **EST:** 1989
SALES (est): 1.15MM **Privately Held**
Web: www.westohiotool.com
SIC: 3541 Machine tools, metal cutting type

(G-12880)
WORLD CLASS PLASTICS INC
7695 State Route 708 (43348-9506)
PHONE..................937 843-3003
▲ **EMP:** 80 **EST:** 1994
SQ FT: 42,000
SALES (est): 23.02MM **Privately Held**
Web: www.worldclassplastics.com
SIC: 3089 Injection molding of plastics

Russia
Shelby County

(G-12881)
A & M PALLET
3860 Rangeline Rd (45363-9784)
PHONE..................937 295-3093
Andy Meyer, *Mng Pt*
Mike Monnin, *Pt*
EMP: 8 **EST:** 1984
SQ FT: 700
SALES (est): 246.22K **Privately Held**
Web: www.aandmpallet.com
SIC: 2448 Pallets, wood

(G-12882)
ABRASIVE SOURCE INC
211 W Main St (45363-9678)
P.O. Box 369 (45363-0369)
PHONE..................937 526-9753
EMP: 10 **EST:** 1994
SQ FT: 1,600
SALES (est): 1.31MM **Privately Held**
Web: www.abrasivesource.com
SIC: 3291 Abrasive products

(G-12883)
FRANCIS MANUFACTURING COMPANY
500 E Mn St (45363)
P.O. Box 400 (45363-0400)
PHONE..................937 526-4551
William T Francis, *Pr*
Thomas V Francis, *
William T Francis, *Pr*
David J Francis, *
EMP: 125 **EST:** 1946
SQ FT: 145,000
SALES (est): 13.89MM **Privately Held**
Web: www.francismanufacturing.com
SIC: 3369 3365 Nonferrous foundries, nec; Aluminum foundries

(G-12884)
FRANCIS-SCHULZE CO
3880 Rangeline Rd (45363-9711)
P.O. Box 245 (45363-0245)
PHONE..................937 295-3941
Ralph Schulze, *Pr*
Rita Schulze, *
EMP: 29 **EST:** 1943
SQ FT: 50,000
SALES (est): 5.15MM **Privately Held**
Web: www.francisschulze.com
SIC: 3442 5031 Metal doors; Building materials, exterior

(G-12885)
L & J CABLE INC
102 Industrial Dr (45363-7501)
P.O. Box 61 (45363-0061)
PHONE..................937 526-9445
Doug Francis, *
Linda Francis, *VP*
▲ **EMP:** 20 **EST:** 1980
SALES (est): 1.31MM **Privately Held**
SIC: 3679 Harness assemblies, for electronic use: wire or cable

(G-12886)
OREILLY PRECISION PDTS INC
Also Called: O'Reilly Precision Tool
560 E Main St (45363-9806)
PHONE..................937 526-4677
Jeffrey O'reilly, *Pr*
Craig Martin, *
Shane Borchers, *
EMP: 35 **EST:** 1984
SALES (est): 3.85MM **Privately Held**
Web: www.oreillymts.com
SIC: 3312 3599 3541 Tool and die steel; Amusement park equipment; Grinding machines, metalworking

Sabina
Clinton County

(G-12887)
MIKE-SELLS POTATO CHIP CO
155 N College St (45169-1103)
PHONE..................937 228-9400
Barry Wilson, *Admn*
EMP: 69
SALES (corp-wide): 47.84MM **Privately Held**
Web: www.mikesells.com
SIC: 2096 Potato chips and similar snacks
HQ: Mike-Sell's Potato Chip Co.
333 Leo St
Dayton OH 45404
937 228-9400

(G-12888)
NEW SABINA INDUSTRIES INC (HQ)
12555 Us Highway 22 And 3 (45169-9463)
P.O. Box 8 (45169-0008)
PHONE..................937 584-2433
Kazu Kishi, *Pr*
▲ **EMP:** 37 **EST:** 1986
SQ FT: 150,000
SALES (est): 89.92MM **Privately Held**
Web: www.nippon-seiki.co.jp
SIC: 3714 Instrument board assemblies, motor vehicle
PA: Nippon Seiki Co., Ltd.
2-2-34, Higashizao
Nagaoka NIG 940-0

(G-12889)
PENNANT COMPANIES (PA)
12381 Us Highway 22 And 3 (45169-9304)
PHONE..................614 451-1782
Chuck Foster, *CEO*
Chuck Foster, *Ch Bd*
Larry Martin, *
EMP: 24 **EST:** 1999
SALES (est): 44.42MM
SALES (corp-wide): 44.42MM **Privately Held**
SIC: 3465 Moldings or trim, automobile: stamped metal

(G-12890)
PENNANT MOLDINGS INC
12381 Us Highway 22 And 3 (45169-9304)
PHONE..................937 584-5411
Kurt Walterhouse, *Pr*
Charles E Foster, *
Larry R Martin, *
EMP: 200 **EST:** 1966
SALES (est): 43.58MM
SALES (corp-wide): 44.42MM **Privately Held**
Web: www.pennant-us.com
SIC: 3469 3444 Stamping metal for the trade; Sheet metalwork
PA: Pennant Companies
12381 Us Highway 22 And 3
Sabina OH 45169
614 451-1782

(G-12891)
PREMIER FEEDS LLC (HQ)
292 N Howard St (45169-1110)
PHONE..................937 584-2411
Christopher V Meter, *Sec*
EMP: 7 **EST:** 1955
SQ FT: 60,000
SALES (est): 10.41MM
SALES (corp-wide): 10.11MM **Privately Held**
Web: www.premiersolutions.net
SIC: 2048 5261 5153 2041 Prepared feeds, nec; Fertilizer; Grains; Flour and other grain mill products
PA: Sabina Farmers Exchange, Inc.
292 N Howard St
Sabina OH 45169
937 584-6528

(G-12892)
PREMIER GRAIN LLC (PA)
1 Solutions Ave (45169-7500)
PHONE..................937 584-6552
John Heinz, *VP*
EMP: 6
SALES (est): 184.39K
SALES (corp-wide): 184.39K **Privately Held**
Web: www.premiergrainllc.com
SIC: 2048 Prepared feeds, nec

Sagamore Hills
Summit County

(G-12893)
POLYQUEST INC
762 Valley Brook Cir (44067-2241)
PHONE..................330 888-9448
Matthew Kerns, *Pr*
EMP: 15 **EST:** 1997
SQ FT: 12,000
SALES (est): 316.48K **Privately Held**
Web: www.polyquest.com
SIC: 3089 Injection molding of plastics

Saint Clairsville
Belmont County

(G-12894)
AMERICAN CNSLD NTRAL RSRCES IN (PA)
46226 National Rd (43950-8742)
PHONE..................740 338-3100
EMP: 22 **EST:** 2020
SALES (est): 140.95MM
SALES (corp-wide): 140.95MM **Privately Held**
Web: www.acnrinc.com
SIC: 1241 Coal mining services

(G-12895)
AMERICAN COAL COMPANY
46226 National Rd (43950-8742)
PHONE..................740 338-3334
Chris Newport, *Brnch Mgr*
EMP: 13
SALES (corp-wide): 4.34B **Privately Held**
SIC: 1241 Coal mining services
HQ: The American Coal Company
9085 Highway 34 N
Galatia IL 62935
618 268-6311

(G-12896)
AUSTIN POWDER COMPANY
74200 Edwards Rd (43950-9510)
PHONE..................740 968-1555
Dave Ferri, *Mgr*
EMP: 8
SALES (corp-wide): 749.73MM **Privately Held**
Web: www.austinpowder.com
SIC: 2892 Explosives
HQ: Austin Powder Company
25800 Science Park Dr # 300
Cleveland OH 44122
216 464-2400

(G-12897)
BELCO WORKS INC
Also Called: BELCO WORKS
68425 Hammond Rd (43950-8783)
PHONE..................740 695-0500
Anne Haning, *CEO*
EMP: 94 **EST:** 1966
SQ FT: 5,000
SALES (est): 4.19MM **Privately Held**
Web: www.belcoworks.com
SIC: 8331 3993 3931 2448 Sheltered workshop; Signs and advertising specialties; Musical instruments; Wood pallets and skids

GEOGRAPHIC SECTION

Saint Clairsville - Belmont County (G-12920)

(G-12898)
CLCB LLC
66920 S Ray Rd (43950-9457)
PHONE..................................316 284-0401
Allie Baugh, *Admn*
EMP: 8 **EST:** 2013
SALES (est): 70.88K **Privately Held**
SIC: 2099 Food preparations, nec

(G-12899)
COAL RESOURCES INC (PA)
46226 National Rd (43950-8742)
PHONE..................................216 765-1240
EMP: 37 **EST:** 1988
SALES (est): 95.36MM **Privately Held**
SIC: 1221 Bituminous coal and lignite-surface mining

(G-12900)
CRIMSON OAK GROVE RSOURCES LLC
46226 National Rd (43950-8742)
PHONE..................................740 338-3100
EMP: 11 **EST:** 2020
SALES (est): 2.86MM **Privately Held**
Web: www.acnrinc.com
SIC: 1241 Coal mining services

(G-12901)
D LEWIS INC
Also Called: Bill's Counter Tops
52235 National Rd (43950-9306)
PHONE..................................740 695-2615
David Lewis, *Pr*
EMP: 6 **EST:** 1971
SQ FT: 5,000
SALES (est): 761.26K **Privately Held**
Web: www.dlewis.com
SIC: 2542 2541 2434 Cabinets: show, display, or storage: except wood; Wood partitions and fixtures; Wood kitchen cabinets

(G-12902)
EMERY CNTY COAL RESOURCES INC
46226 National Rd (43950-8742)
PHONE..................................740 338-3100
Martin Reed, *Pr*
EMP: 6 **EST:** 2020
SALES (est): 230.59K **Privately Held**
SIC: 1241 Coal mining services

(G-12903)
EQUITRANS MIDSTREAM CORPO
252 W Main St Ste D (43950-1065)
P.O. Box 299 (43950-0299)
PHONE..................................304 626-7934
EMP: 6 **EST:** 2019
SALES (est): 67.91K **Privately Held**
Web: www.equitransmidstream.com
SIC: 1382 Oil and gas exploration services

(G-12904)
FORTIS ENERGY SERVICES INC
66999 Executive Dr (43950-7402)
PHONE..................................248 283-7100
EMP: 51
SALES (corp-wide): 41.09MM **Privately Held**
Web: www.fortisenergyservices.com
SIC: 1381 Drilling oil and gas wells
PA: Fortis Energy Services, Inc.
2844 Livernois Rd
Troy MI 48099
248 283-7100

(G-12905)
FRANKLIN COUNTY COAL COMPANY
46226 National Rd (43950-8742)
PHONE..................................740 338-3100
Robert E Murray, *CEO*
EMP: 301 **EST:** 2019
SALES (est): 12.22MM
SALES (corp-wide): 4.34B **Privately Held**
SIC: 1221 Bituminous coal and lignite-surface mining
HQ: Murray American Energy, Inc.
46226 National Rd
Saint Clairsville OH 43950
740 338-3100

(G-12906)
HARRISON COUNTY COAL COMPANY (HQ)
46226 National Rd (43950-8742)
PHONE..................................740 338-3100
Robert E Murray, *CEO*
EMP: 11 **EST:** 2014
SALES (est): 98.86MM
SALES (corp-wide): 140.95MM **Privately Held**
SIC: 1221 Bituminous coal and lignite-surface mining
PA: American Consolidated Natural Resources, Inc.
46226 National Rd
Saint Clairsville OH 43950
740 338-3100

(G-12907)
KENAMERICAN RESOURCES INC
46226 National Rd (43950-8742)
PHONE..................................740 338-3100
Bob Sandidge, *Pr*
Robert E Murray, *Dir*
Randy L Wiles, *VP*
James R Turner, *Treas*
Michael O Mckown, *Sec*
EMP: 165 **EST:** 1994
SALES (est): 46.9MM **Privately Held**
SIC: 1222 Bituminous coal-underground mining
HQ: Mill Creek Mining Company
46226 National Rd
Saint Clairsville OH 43950

(G-12908)
MARIETTA COAL CO (PA)
67705 Friends Church Rd (43950-9500)
P.O. Box 2 (43950-0002)
PHONE..................................740 695-2197
George Nicolozakes, *Ch*
Paul Gill, *
John Nicolozakes, *
EMP: 50 **EST:** 1946
SQ FT: 4,300
SALES (est): 9.66MM
SALES (corp-wide): 9.66MM **Privately Held**
SIC: 1221 Surface mining, bituminous, nec

(G-12909)
MARION CNTY COAL RESOURCES INC
46226 National Rd (43950-8742)
PHONE..................................740 338-3100
Robert Putsock, *Dir*
EMP: 10 **EST:** 2020
SALES (est): 437.25K **Privately Held**
SIC: 3312 Coal gas, derived from chemical recovery coke ovens

(G-12910)
MARION COUNTY COAL COMPANY
46226 National Rd (43950-8742)
PHONE..................................740 338-3100
Robert E Murray, *Pr*
EMP: 27 **EST:** 2013
SALES (est): 9.65MM
SALES (corp-wide): 140.95MM **Privately Held**
SIC: 3312 2865 Coal tar crudes, derived from chemical recovery coke ovens; Coal tar: crudes, intermediates, and distillates
PA: American Consolidated Natural Resources, Inc.
46226 National Rd
Saint Clairsville OH 43950
740 338-3100

(G-12911)
MCELROY COAL COMPANY (DH)
46226 National Rd (43950-8742)
PHONE..................................724 485-4000
Robert D Moore, *CEO*
P B Lilly, *Pr*
J N Magro, *VP*
EMP: 12 **EST:** 1987
SQ FT: 150,000
SALES (est): 155.54MM
SALES (corp-wide): 4.34B **Privately Held**
SIC: 1221 Bituminous coal surface mining
HQ: Consolidation Coal Company Inc
1000 Horizon Vue Dr
Canonsburg PA 15317
740 338-3100

(G-12912)
MEIGS COUNTY COAL COMPANY
46226 National Rd (43950-8742)
PHONE..................................740 338-3100
Robert E Murray, *CEO*
EMP: 358 **EST:** 2013
SALES (est): 9.18MM
SALES (corp-wide): 4.34B **Privately Held**
SIC: 1221 Bituminous coal and lignite-surface mining
HQ: Murray American Energy, Inc.
46226 National Rd
Saint Clairsville OH 43950
740 338-3100

(G-12913)
MILL CREEK MINING COMPANY (HQ)
Also Called: Energy Resources
46226 National Rd W (43950-8742)
PHONE..................................216 765-1240
Charles Shestac, *Pr*
EMP: 6 **EST:** 1981
SQ FT: 50,000
SALES (est): 56.57MM **Privately Held**
SIC: 1231 Underground mining, anthracite
PA: Coal Resources, Inc.
46226 National Rd
Saint Clairsville OH 43950

(G-12914)
MUHLENBERG COUNTY COAL CO LLC
46226 National Rd (43950-8742)
PHONE..................................740 338-3100
Robert E Murray, *CEO*
EMP: 55 **EST:** 2018
SALES (est): 22.49MM
SALES (corp-wide): 4.34B **Privately Held**
SIC: 1221 Bituminous coal and lignite-surface mining
HQ: Western Kentucky Consolidated Resources, Llc
46226 National Rd
Saint Clairsville OH 43950
740 338-3100

(G-12915)
MURRAY AMERICAN ENERGY INC (DH)
46226 National Rd (43950)
PHONE..................................740 338-3100
Robert E Murray, *Pr*
Robert D Moore, *VP*
Jason D Witt, *Sec*
Michael D Loiacono, *Treas*
EMP: 129 **EST:** 2013
SALES (est): 799.53MM
SALES (corp-wide): 4.34B **Privately Held**
SIC: 1221 Bituminous coal surface mining
HQ: Ohio Valley Resources, Inc.
29325 Chgrin Blvd Ste 300
Beachwood OH 44122
216 765-1240

(G-12916)
NOMAC DRILLING LLC
67090 Executive Dr (43950-8473)
PHONE..................................724 324-2205
EMP: 139
SALES (corp-wide): 4.15B **Publicly Held**
Web: www.patenergy.com
SIC: 1381 Drilling oil and gas wells
HQ: Nomac Drilling, L.L.C.
3400 S Radio Rd
El Reno OK 73036
405 422-2754

(G-12917)
OHIO HEAT TRANSFER LTD
66721 Executive Dr (43950-8474)
PHONE..................................740 695-0635
Mark E Epure, *Managing Member*
▲ **EMP:** 13 **EST:** 2003
SALES (est): 1.22MM **Privately Held**
Web: www.ohioheattransfer.com
SIC: 3443 Heat exchangers: coolers (after, inter), condensers, etc.

(G-12918)
OHIO VALLEY COAL COMPANY
46226 National Rd (43950-8742)
PHONE..................................740 926-1351
Robert E Murray, *CEO*
Robert D Moore, *
Michael O Mckown, *Sr VP*
John R Forrelli, *
Ryan M Murray C, *Pr*
EMP: 400 **EST:** 1969
SQ FT: 40,380
SALES (est): 95.82MM
SALES (corp-wide): 4.34B **Privately Held**
SIC: 1241 Coal mining services
HQ: Ohio Valley Resources, Inc.
29325 Chgrin Blvd Ste 300
Beachwood OH 44122
216 765-1240

(G-12919)
PROSPECT ROCK LLC
98 N Market St Ste 4 (43950-1274)
PHONE..................................740 512-0542
EMP: 10 **EST:** 2021
SALES (est): 150K **Privately Held**
SIC: 1389 7389 Roustabout service; Business Activities at Non-Commercial Site

(G-12920)
RAYLE COAL CO
67705 Friends Church Rd (43950-9500)
P.O. Box 2 (43950-0002)
PHONE..................................740 695-2197
George Nicolozakes, *Ch*
John Nicolozakes, *Pr*
EMP: 15 **EST:** 1974
SQ FT: 4,300
SALES (est): 902.52K **Privately Held**

Saint Clairsville - Belmont County (G-12921)

GEOGRAPHIC SECTION

SIC: 1221 4491 Surface mining, bituminous, nec; Marine cargo handling

(G-12921)
RIESBECK FOOD MARKETS INC
Also Called: Reisbeck Fd Mkts St Clirsville
104 Plaza Dr (43950-8736)
P.O. Box 707 (43950-0707)
PHONE..............................740 695-3401
Dennis Kasprowski, Brnch Mgr
EMP: 112
SALES (corp-wide): 105.41MM **Privately Held**
Web: www.riesbeckfoods.com
SIC: 5411 5912 5421 2051 Supermarkets, chain; Drug stores and proprietary stores; Meat and fish markets; Bread, cake, and related products
PA: Riesbeck Food Markets, Inc.
48661 National Rd
Saint Clairsville OH 43950
740 695-7050

(G-12922)
ROUGHCUT LLC
117 Pinecrest Dr (43950-1446)
PHONE..............................505 686-3615
EMP: 13 EST: 2011
SALES (est): 1.02MM **Privately Held**
Web: www.roughcutllc.com
SIC: 1381 Drilling oil and gas wells

(G-12923)
SIDWELL MATERIALS INC
72607 Gun Club Rd (43950-8637)
PHONE..............................740 968-4313
Jeffrey Sidwell, Pr
EMP: 15 EST: 2013
SALES (est): 933.82K **Privately Held**
Web: www.sidwellmaterials.com
SIC: 3273 Ready-mixed concrete

(G-12924)
ST CLAIRSVILLE DAIRY QUEEN
178 E Main St (43950-1534)
PHONE..............................740 635-1800
Pat Weisal, Prin
Cindy Byrd, Mgr
EMP: 7 EST: 2006
SALES (est): 168.48K **Privately Held**
SIC: 2024 Ice cream and frozen deserts

(G-12925)
STEIN-PALMER PRINTING CO
1 Westwood Dr Unit 202 (43950-1053)
PHONE..............................740 633-3894
Thomas R Palmer, Owner
EMP: 8 EST: 1916
SQ FT: 2,500
SALES (est): 380.74K **Privately Held**
SIC: 2752 Offset printing

(G-12926)
STRATA MINE SERVICES INC
68000 Bayberry Dr Unit 103 (43950-8102)
PHONE..............................740 695-6880
Jeff Hamrick, VP
EMP: 10 EST: 2006
SALES (est): 949.1K **Privately Held**
SIC: 3532 Mining machinery

(G-12927)
STRATA MINE SERVICES LLC
67925 Bayberry Dr (43950-9132)
PHONE..............................740 695-0488
EMP: 13
SALES (est): 1.04MM **Privately Held**
SIC: 1241 Mine preparation services

(G-12928)
WASHINGTON COUNTY COAL COMPANY
46226 National Rd (43950-8742)
PHONE..............................740 338-3100
Robert D Moore, CEO
EMP: 330 EST: 2013
SALES (est): 13.36MM
SALES (corp-wide): 4.34B **Privately Held**
SIC: 1221 Bituminous coal surface mining
HQ: Murray American Energy, Inc.
46226 National Rd
Saint Clairsville OH 43950
740 338-3100

(G-12929)
WESTERN KENTUCKY COAL CO LLC
46226 National Rd (43950-8742)
PHONE..............................740 338-3334
EMP: 50 EST: 2018
SALES (est): 4.92MM
SALES (corp-wide): 4.34B **Privately Held**
SIC: 1081 Metal mining services
HQ: Western Kentucky Consolidated Resources, Llc
46226 National Rd
Saint Clairsville OH 43950
740 338-3100

(G-12930)
WESTERN KY CNSLD RESOURCES LLC (DH)
46226 National Rd (43950-8742)
PHONE..............................740 338-3100
EMP: 8 EST: 2018
SALES (est): 47.15MM
SALES (corp-wide): 4.34B **Privately Held**
SIC: 1241 Coal mining services
HQ: Western Kentucky Resources Financing, Llc
46226 National Rd
Saint Clairsville OH 43950
740 338-3100

(G-12931)
WESTERN KY COAL RESOURCES LLC (DH)
46226 National Rd (43950)
PHONE..............................740 338-3100
EMP: 40 EST: 2018
SALES (est): 209.36MM
SALES (corp-wide): 4.34B **Privately Held**
SIC: 1222 Bituminous coal-underground mining
HQ: Murray Kentucky Energy, Inc.
46226 National Rd W
Saint Clairsville OH 43950
740 338-3100

(G-12932)
WESTERN KY RESOURCES FING LLC (DH)
46226 National Rd (43950-8742)
PHONE..............................740 338-3100
EMP: 8 EST: 2018
SALES (est): 47.15MM
SALES (corp-wide): 4.34B **Privately Held**
SIC: 1241 Coal mining services
HQ: Western Kentucky Coal Resources, Llc
46226 National Rd
Saint Clairsville OH 43950
740 338-3100

(G-12933)
WHEELING COFFEE & SPICE CO
117 Pinecrest Dr (43950-1446)
PHONE..............................304 232-0141
Mary Ann Lokmer, Pr
Stephanie Ann Lokmer, VP
EMP: 10 EST: 1914
SALES (est): 986.18K **Privately Held**
Web: www.wheelingcoffeeco.com
SIC: 2095 5149 Coffee roasting (except by wholesale grocers); Canned goods: fruit, vegetables, seafood, meats, etc.

Saint Henry
Mercer County

(G-12934)
BECKMAN & GAST COMPANY (PA)
282 W Kremer Hoying Rd (45883-9617)
P.O. Box 307 (45883-0307)
PHONE..............................419 678-4195
William C Gast, Pr
Karl J Gast, VP
Paul Moorman, Sec
EMP: 15 EST: 1927
SQ FT: 65,000
SALES (est): 5.61MM
SALES (corp-wide): 5.61MM **Privately Held**
Web: www.beckmangast.com
SIC: 2032 2033 Beans, without meat: packaged in cans, jars, etc.; Tomato products, packaged in cans, jars, etc.

(G-12935)
HI-TECH WIRE INC
631 E Washington St (45883-9683)
PHONE..............................419 678-8376
Bill Hemmelgarn, Pr
Susan Hemmelgarn, *
EMP: 57 EST: 1987
SQ FT: 30,000
SALES (est): 9.5MM **Privately Held**
Web: www.hi-techwire.com
SIC: 3544 Special dies and tools

(G-12936)
HOMESTRETCH SPORTSWEAR INC
491 S Eastern Ave (45883-9585)
P.O. Box 379 (45883-0379)
PHONE..............................419 678-4282
Don H Hess, Pr
Donna Hess, Ex VP
Kelly Hess, VP
Kim Hess, Sec
EMP: 9 EST: 1991
SQ FT: 1,920
SALES (est): 492.42K **Privately Held**
Web: www.homestretchsportswear.com
SIC: 2759 Screen printing

(G-12937)
R & R FABRICATIONS INC
601 E Washington St (45883)
P.O. Box P.O. Box 500 (45883)
PHONE..............................419 678-4831
EMP: 21 EST: 1986
SALES (est): 2.39MM **Privately Held**
Web: www.rrfabrications.com
SIC: 2541 Wood partitions and fixtures

(G-12938)
ST HENRY TILE CO INC (PA)
Also Called: Richmond Builders Supply
281 W Washington St (45883-9663)
P.O. Box 318 (45883-0318)
PHONE..............................419 678-4841
Bob Homan, Pr
Robert Homan, *
Eugene Subler, *
Mike Homan, *
Robert Bruns, Stockholder*
EMP: 35 EST: 1960
SQ FT: 7,600
SALES (est): 24.3MM
SALES (corp-wide): 24.3MM **Privately Held**
Web: www.sthenrytileco.com
SIC: 3271 5211 3273 Blocks, concrete or cinder: standard; Masonry materials and supplies; Ready-mixed concrete

(G-12939)
TEGR INC
191 N Eastern Ave (45883-9707)
P.O. Box 310 (45883-0310)
PHONE..............................419 678-4991
EMP: 24 EST: 1996
SQ FT: 20,000
SALES (est): 5.5MM **Publicly Held**
Web: www.tru-edge.com
SIC: 3599 Machine shop, jobbing and repair
HQ: Bis (Oh) Incorporated.
3989 Groves Rd
Columbus OH 43232
614 864-8400

(G-12940)
V H COOPER & CO INC
Also Called: Cooper Farms
1 Cooper Farm Dr (45883-9556)
PHONE..............................419 678-4853
Jim Cooper, Prin
EMP: 625
SALES (corp-wide): 93.22MM **Privately Held**
Web: www.cooperfarms.com
SIC: 2011 Sausages, from meat slaughtered on site
HQ: V. H. Cooper & Co, Inc
2321 State Route 49
Fort Recovery OH 45846

(G-12941)
V H COOPER & CO INC
Cooper Processing of St Henry
1 Cooper Farm Dr (45883-9556)
PHONE..............................419 678-4853
Dale Hart, Mgr
EMP: 625
SALES (corp-wide): 93.22MM **Privately Held**
SIC: 2015 2011 Turkey, processed, nsk; Meat packing plants
HQ: V. H. Cooper & Co, Inc
2321 State Route 49
Fort Recovery OH 45846

Saint Louisville
Licking County

(G-12942)
C GREEN & SONS INCORPORATED
Also Called: 64 Metals
9020 Mount Vernon Rd (43071-9672)
PHONE..............................740 745-2998
EMP: 18 EST: 1998
SALES (est): 3.34MM **Privately Held**
Web: www.lifespanbuildings.com
SIC: 2952 3448 Siding materials; Trusses and framing, prefabricated metal

(G-12943)
KOKOSING MATERIALS INC
9134 Mount Vernon Rd (43071-9637)
PHONE..............................740 745-3341
Tom Nethers, Prin
EMP: 11
SALES (corp-wide): 1.17B **Privately Held**
Web: www.kokosing.biz
SIC: 2951 Asphalt and asphaltic paving mixtures (not from refineries)
HQ: Kokosing Materials, Inc.
17531 Waterford Rd
Fredericktown OH 43019
740 694-9585

Saint Marys
Auglaize County

(G-12944)
ADIENT US LLC
1111 Mckinley Rd (45885-1816)
PHONE..................419 394-7800
EMP: 51
Web: www.adient.com
SIC: 3714 Motor vehicle parts and accessories
HQ: Adient Us Llc
  49200 Halyard Dr
  Plymouth MI 48170
  734 254-5000

(G-12945)
BEHRCO INC
Also Called: Unique Awards & Signs
1865 Celina Rd (45885-1219)
PHONE..................419 394-1612
Gerry Schetter, Pr
Julia Haehn, VP
Tom Crast, Sec
EMP: 6 EST: 1991
SQ FT: 3,000
SALES (est): 453.13K Privately Held
Web: www.uniqueas.org
SIC: 3914 3993 5094 5046 Trophies, plated (all metals); Electric signs; Trophies; Neon signs

(G-12946)
BEST INC
State Rte 116 (45885)
P.O. Box 775 (45885-0775)
PHONE..................419 394-2745
Richard Brock, Pr
Kaye Brock, Sec
EMP: 6 EST: 1981
SQ FT: 12,050
SALES (est): 504.5K Privately Held
SIC: 3599 Machine shop, jobbing and repair

(G-12947)
BEST PERFORMANCE INC
14381 State Route 116 (45885-9226)
P.O. Box 238 (45885-0238)
PHONE..................419 394-2299
EMP: 6 EST: 1984
SQ FT: 34,000
SALES (est): 800K Privately Held
Web: www.bestperformanceinc.com
SIC: 3599 Machine shop, jobbing and repair

(G-12948)
BRW TOOL INC
502 Scott St (45885-1862)
P.O. Box 417 (45885-0417)
PHONE..................419 394-3371
Ray Barber, Pr
EMP: 14 EST: 1966
SQ FT: 50,000
SALES (est): 1.02MM Privately Held
Web: www.brwtool.com
SIC: 3469 3544 Metal stampings, nec; Special dies and tools

(G-12949)
CARGILL INCORPORATED
Also Called: Cargill
1400 Mckinley Rd (45885-1821)
P.O. Box B (45885)
PHONE..................419 394-3374
EMP: 25
SALES (corp-wide): 176.74B Privately Held
Web: www.cargill.com
SIC: 2047 2048 Dog and cat food; Prepared feeds, nec
PA: Cargill, Incorporated
  15407 Mcginty Rd W
  Wayzata MN 55391
  800 227-4455

(G-12950)
CONAG INC
Also Called: Con-AG
16672 County Road 66a (45885-9212)
PHONE..................419 394-8870
Robert Hirschfeld, Pr
Lee Kuck, *
John Hirschfeld, *
EMP: 18 EST: 1979
SALES (est): 1.42MM Privately Held
Web: www.conag.com
SIC: 1422 Limestones, ground

(G-12951)
EXPRESS TRADING PINS LLC
105 Marbello Ct (45885-9548)
PHONE..................419 394-2550
Jeff Steininger, Prin
EMP: 6 EST: 2010
SALES (est): 91.17K Privately Held
SIC: 3452 Pins

(G-12952)
FLUIDPOWER ASSEMBLY INC
313 S Park Dr (45885-9689)
PHONE..................419 394-7486
Ronald E Langston, Pr
Eric Langston, Sec
Ruth Langston, VP
Mark Langston, VP
EMP: 6 EST: 1984
SQ FT: 6,000
SALES (est): 524.79K Privately Held
Web: www.hypowerequipment.com
SIC: 3542 3511 Riveting machines; Turbines and turbine generator sets

(G-12953)
HORIZON OHIO PUBLICATIONS INC (HQ)
Also Called: Evening Leader, The
102 E Spring St (45885-2310)
PHONE..................419 394-7414
Todd Boit, Pr
Roland Mc Bride, Ex VP
EMP: 17 EST: 1905
SQ FT: 8,000
SALES (est): 5.93MM
SALES (corp-wide): 47.1MM Privately Held
Web: www.theeveningleader.com
SIC: 2711 Commercial printing and newspaper publishing combined
PA: Horizon Publications, Inc.
  1120 N Carbon St Ste 100
  Marion IL 62959
  618 993-1711

(G-12954)
JOHNSON CONTROLS INC
Also Called: Johnson Controls
1111 Mckinley Road (45885-1816)
PHONE..................414 524-1200
Rob Luebke, Prin
EMP: 38 EST: 2016
SALES (est): 485.6K Privately Held
SIC: 3714 Motor vehicle parts and accessories

(G-12955)
KOSEI ST MARYS CORPORATION
1100 Mckinley Rd (45885-1815)
PHONE..................419 394-7840
Tomonori Okuyama, Pr
Douglas Kramer, VP
Shunkichi Kamiya, Prin
Bruce Sakamoto, Ch
Randy Wendel, Pr
▲ EMP: 681 EST: 1987
SQ FT: 470,000
SALES (est): 96.79MM Privately Held
Web: www.koseina.com
SIC: 3714 Wheels, motor vehicle
PA: Gyoseishoshi Okuda Tomiko Jimusho
  3-5-5, Sayamadai
  Sayama STM

(G-12956)
LIETTE L & S EXPRESS LLC
2286 Celina Rd (45885-1226)
P.O. Box 726 (45885-0726)
PHONE..................419 394-7077
Gregory D Liette, Prin
EMP: 6 EST: 2004
SQ FT: 4,910
SALES (est): 465.94K Privately Held
SIC: 2741 Miscellaneous publishing

(G-12957)
MERCER TOOL CORPORATION
311 S Park Dr (45885-9689)
PHONE..................419 394-7277
Donald Gladish, Pr
EMP: 25 EST: 1989
SQ FT: 21,000
SALES (est): 2.72MM Privately Held
SIC: 3312 Tool and die steel and alloys

(G-12958)
MUROTECH OHIO CORPORATION
Also Called: M T O
550 Mckinley Rd (45885-1803)
P.O. Box 716 (45885-0716)
PHONE..................419 394-6529
Naonobu Kemmoku, Pr
▲ EMP: 120 EST: 1998
SQ FT: 30,000
SALES (est): 25.16MM Privately Held
Web: www.murotech.com
SIC: 3465 Body parts, automobile: stamped metal
PA: Muro Corporation
  7-1, Kiyoharakogyodanchi
  Utsunomiya TCG 321-3

(G-12959)
OLD CLASSIC DELIGHT INC
Also Called: Classic Delight
310 S Park Dr (45885)
P.O. Box 367 (45885)
PHONE..................419 394-7955
Jim Clough, Pr
EMP: 55 EST: 1987
SQ FT: 18,800
SALES (est): 9.94MM Privately Held
Web: www.classicdelight.com
SIC: 2099 Food preparations, nec

(G-12960)
OLD SMO INC
323 S Park Dr (45885-9689)
PHONE..................419 394-3346
EMP: 7
SALES (corp-wide): 14.52MM Privately Held
Web: www.stmfoundry.com
SIC: 3321 Gray and ductile iron foundries
PA: Old Smo, Inc.
  405 E South St
  Saint Marys OH 45885
  419 394-3346

(G-12961)
OLD SMO INC (PA)
405 E South St (45885-2540)
PHONE..................419 394-3346
Angela Dine Molaskey, CEO
Colston L Dine, *
Mark Dine, *
Ronald S Stumphauzer, *
James Perts, *
EMP: 127 EST: 1984
SQ FT: 180,000
SALES (est): 14.52MM
SALES (corp-wide): 14.52MM Privately Held
Web: www.stmfoundry.com
SIC: 3321 3369 3322 Gray iron castings, nec; Nonferrous foundries, nec; Malleable iron foundries

(G-12962)
OMNI MANUFACTURING INC (PA)
901 Mckinley Rd (45885-1812)
P.O. Box 179 (45885-0179)
PHONE..................419 394-7424
Wayne L Freewalt, Pr
▲ EMP: 100 EST: 1982
SQ FT: 190,000
SALES (est): 23.03MM
SALES (corp-wide): 23.03MM Privately Held
Web: www.omnimfg.com
SIC: 3469 3479 3544 Stamping metal for the trade; Coating of metals and formed products; Special dies and tools

(G-12963)
OMNI MANUFACTURING INC
220 Cleveland Ave (45885-1706)
PHONE..................419 394-7424
EMP: 13
SALES (corp-wide): 23.03MM Privately Held
Web: www.omnimfg.com
SIC: 3469 3479 3544 Stamping metal for the trade; Coating of metals and formed products; Special dies and tools
PA: Omni Manufacturing, Inc.
  901 Mckinley Rd
  Saint Marys OH 45885
  419 394-7424

(G-12964)
PRO-PET LLC
1601 Mckinley Rd (45885-1864)
P.O. Box 369 (45885-0369)
PHONE..................419 394-3374
◆ EMP: 93 EST: 1996
SQ FT: 5,000
SALES (est): 106.04K
SALES (corp-wide): 176.74B Privately Held
SIC: 2047 2048 4212 7389 Cat food; Prepared feeds, nec; Animal and farm product transportation services; Packaging and labeling services
PA: Cargill, Incorporated
  15407 Mcginty Rd W
  Wayzata MN 55391
  800 227-4455

(G-12965)
QUALITY READY MIX INC (PA)
16672 County Road 66a (45885-9212)
PHONE..................419 394-8870
TOLL FREE: 800
Robert E Hirschfeld, Pr
John Hirschfeld, VP
Lee Kuck, Sec
EMP: 10 EST: 1931
SQ FT: 2,000
SALES (est): 2.93MM

Saint Marys - Auglaize County (G-12966)

SALES (corp-wide): 2.93MM **Privately Held**
Web: www.qrmconcrete.com
SIC: 3273 Ready-mixed concrete

(G-12966)
RELIABLE PRODUCTS CO
315 S Park Dr (45885-9689)
PHONE..................419 394-5854
Wayne Steineman, *Pr*
Kristine Ranly, *Sec*
EMP: 8 EST: 1973
SQ FT: 10,000
SALES (est): 907.1K **Privately Held**
SIC: 3541 Machine tools, metal cutting type

(G-12967)
SETEX INC
1111 Mckinley Rd (45885-1816)
PHONE..................419 394-7800
Mister Yamada, *Pr*
Shinichirou Shirahama, *Pr*
Robert Bowlin, *CFO*
▲ EMP: 470 EST: 1987
SQ FT: 168,000
SALES (est): 45.89MM **Privately Held**
Web: www.setexinc.net
SIC: 2531 Seats, automobile

(G-12968)
TAIYO AMERICA INC (HQ)
1702 E Spring St (45885-2460)
PHONE..................419 300-8811
Takuji Maekawa, *Pr*
▲ EMP: 10 EST: 1986
SQ FT: 50,000
SALES (est): 5.28MM **Privately Held**
Web: www.taiyo-america.com
SIC: 5084 3492 Hydraulic systems equipment and supplies; Fluid power valves for aircraft
PA: Taiyo,Ltd.
   2-6-8, Bingomachi, Chuo-Ku
   Osaka OSK 541-0

(G-12969)
WEBER READY MIX INC
16672 County Road 66a (45885-9212)
PHONE..................419 394-9097
Marc Bader, *VP*
EMP: 25 EST: 2016
SALES (est): 2.29MM **Privately Held**
SIC: 3273 Ready-mixed concrete

Saint Paris
Champaign County

(G-12970)
ALL OHIO WELDING INC
3833 State Route 235 N (43072-9536)
PHONE..................937 663-7116
Charles Grimes, *Pr*
Julie A Grimes, *Prin*
EMP: 7 EST: 2015
SALES (est): 590.05K **Privately Held**
SIC: 1799 3499 7692 Welding on site; Fire- or burglary-resistive products; Welding repair

(G-12971)
BHI TRANSITION INC
8801 Us Highway 36 (43072-9358)
PHONE..................937 663-4152
Bryce Hill, *Mgr*
EMP: 47
Web: www.brycehill.com
SIC: 3273 Ready-mixed concrete
PA: Bhi Transition, Inc.
   2301 Sheridan Ave
   Springfield OH 45505

(G-12972)
CAM MACHINE INC
513 S Springfield St (43072-9410)
PHONE..................937 663-5000
Douglas Macy, *Pr*
EMP: 29 EST: 1980
SALES (est): 3.02MM **Privately Held**
SIC: 3599 Machine shop, jobbing and repair

(G-12973)
KTH PARTS INDUSTRIES INC (HQ)
1111 N State Rte 235 (43072-9680)
P.O. Box 940 (43072-0940)
PHONE..................937 663-5941
Toshio Inoue, *Pr*
Sanichi Kanai, *
Fumio Takeuchi, *
◆ EMP: 770 EST: 1984
SQ FT: 811,500
SALES (est): 205.04MM **Privately Held**
Web: www.kth.net
SIC: 3714 Motor vehicle parts and accessories
PA: H-One Co.,Ltd.
   1-11-5, Sakuragicho, Omiya-Ku
   Saitama STM 330-0

(G-12974)
RUNKLES SAWMILL LLC
2534 Dialton Rd (43072-9423)
PHONE..................937 663-0115
Steve Runkle, *Managing Member*
EMP: 7 EST: 2004
SALES (est): 447.6K **Privately Held**
SIC: 2421 Sawmills and planing mills, general

Salem
Columbiana County

(G-12975)
ACCU-TEK TOOL & DIE INC
1390 Allen Rd Bldg 1 (44460-1003)
PHONE..................330 726-1946
James A Kutchel, *Pr*
Gary Sebrell, *VP*
EMP: 8 EST: 1990
SQ FT: 12,000
SALES (est): 902.63K **Privately Held**
Web: www.accutektoolanddie.com
SIC: 3544 3354 Special dies and tools; Aluminum extruded products

(G-12976)
ADVANTAGE MACHINE SHOP
777 S Ellsworth Ave (44460-3781)
PHONE..................330 337-8377
Vic Jones, *Owner*
EMP: 6 EST: 2005
SALES (est): 492.36K **Privately Held**
SIC: 3599 Machine shop, jobbing and repair

(G-12977)
AS AMERICA INC
605 S Ellsworth Ave (44460-3743)
PHONE..................330 332-9954
Jay Gould, *Pr*
EMP: 14
Web: www.americanstandard-us.com
SIC: 3261 3432 Vitreous plumbing fixtures; Plumbing fixture fittings and trim
HQ: As America, Inc.
   30 Knightsbridge Rd # 301
   Piscataway NJ 08854

(G-12978)
BUTECH INC
633 S Broadway Ave (44460)
PHONE..................330 337-0000
Matt Joing, *Prin*
EMP: 151
SALES (corp-wide): 42.17MM **Privately Held**
Web: www.butechbliss.com
SIC: 3541 Machine tools, metal cutting type
PA: Butech Inc.
   550 S Ellsworth Ave
   Salem OH 44460
   330 337-0000

(G-12979)
BUTECH INC (PA)
Also Called: Butech Bliss
550 S Ellsworth Ave (44460-3067)
PHONE..................330 337-0000
▲ EMP: 97 EST: 1985
SALES (est): 42.17MM
SALES (corp-wide): 42.17MM **Privately Held**
Web: www.butechbliss.com
SIC: 3541 Machine tools, metal cutting type

(G-12980)
CALL SIGN ALPHA LLC
2789 E State St Ste 10 (44460-9327)
PHONE..................330 842-6200
Timothy Snyder, *Owner*
EMP: 6 EST: 2017
SALES (est): 238.89K **Privately Held**
SIC: 3993 Signs and advertising specialties

(G-12981)
CARDINAL PUMPS EXCHANGERS INC (DH)
Also Called: Unifin Chesapeake
1425 Quaker Ct (44460-1008)
PHONE..................330 332-8558
Manny A Agostinho, *Pr*
Ed Shapiro, *Genl Mgr*
Matthew Flamini, *VP*
Jeanne R Hernandez, *Treas*
▲ EMP: 15 EST: 2007
SALES (est): 5.08MM **Publicly Held**
Web: www.wabteccorp.com
SIC: 3443 Heat exchangers, condensers, and components
HQ: Wabtec Components Llc
   30 Isabella St
   Pittsburgh PA 15212
   412 825-1000

(G-12982)
CASTRUCTION COMPANY INC
1588 Salem Pkwy (44460-1071)
PHONE..................330 332-9622
Benjamine R Brown, *Pr*
Shannon Brown, *VP*
EMP: 12 EST: 1965
SQ FT: 9,600
SALES (est): 921.47K **Privately Held**
Web: www.castruction.com
SIC: 3297 Cement refractories

(G-12983)
CHURCH BUDGET MONTHLY INC
157 W Pershing St (44460-2746)
P.O. Box 420 (44460-0420)
PHONE..................330 337-1122
EMP: 7 EST: 1996
SALES (est): 915.9K **Privately Held**
Web: www.churchbudget.com
SIC: 2677 Envelopes

(G-12984)
CHURCH-BUDGET ENVELOPE COMPANY
271 S Ellsworth Ave (44460-3071)
P.O. Box 420 (44460-0420)
PHONE..................800 446-9780
James A Pidgeon Junior, *Pr*
EMP: 48 EST: 1917
SQ FT: 60,000
SALES (est): 4.38MM **Privately Held**
Web: www.churchbudget.com
SIC: 2677 Envelopes

(G-12985)
CMI INDUSTRY AMERICAS INC (HQ)
435 W Wilson St (44460-2767)
PHONE..................330 332-4661
Rob Johnson, *Ch Bd*
Patricia Simonsic, *
▲ EMP: 100 EST: 1923
SQ FT: 250,000
SALES (est): 55.15MM
SALES (corp-wide): 4.57MM **Privately Held**
SIC: 3567 Metal melting furnaces, industrial: electric
PA: John Cockerill Traction
   Avenue Georges Pirson 12
   Manage 7170
   64521631

(G-12986)
COMPCO QUAKER MFG INC
187 Georgetown Rd (44460-2009)
PHONE..................330 482-0200
Gregory Smith, *Ch Bd*
Richard Kamperman, *
Richard Fryda, *
Joe Irwin, *
EMP: 37 EST: 2017
SALES (est): 5.1MM
SALES (corp-wide): 33.46MM **Privately Held**
Web: www.cqlmfg.com
SIC: 3469 3544 3465 3599 Metal stampings, nec; Special dies and tools; Automotive stampings; Machine and other job shop work
HQ: Compco Columbiana Company
   400 W Railroad St Ste 1
   Columbiana OH 44408
   330 482-0200

(G-12987)
CQL MFG LLC
187 Georgetown Rd (44460-2009)
PHONE..................330 482-5846
EMP: 100 EST: 2021
SALES (est): 25MM **Privately Held**
SIC: 3469 Ornamental metal stampings

(G-12988)
CTM INTEGRATION INCORPORATED
1318 Quaker Cir (44460-1051)
P.O. Box 589 (44460-0589)
PHONE..................330 332-1800
Thomas C Rumsey, *Pr*
Dan Mc Laughlin, *
EMP: 36 EST: 1980
SQ FT: 30,000
SALES (est): 4.91MM **Privately Held**
Web: www.ctmlabelingsystems.com
SIC: 3565 5084 3549 Packaging machinery; Industrial machinery and equipment; Metalworking machinery, nec

(G-12989)
CTM LABELING SYSTEMS
1318 Quaker Cir (44460-1051)
PHONE..................330 332-1800
EMP: 31 EST: 2018

SALES (est): 9.98MM **Privately Held**
Web: www.ctmlabelingsystems.com
SIC: **3565** Packaging machinery

(G-12990)
DANNY L BOYLE
14156 Duck Creek Rd (44460-9600)
PHONE...................330 206-1448
Danny Boyle, *Prin*
EMP: 6 EST: 2017
SALES (est): 156.42K **Privately Held**
SIC: **7692** Welding repair

(G-12991)
DILCO INDUSTRIES INC
300 Benton Rd (44460-2029)
PHONE...................330 337-6732
Robert Dillon Junior, *Pr*
Kathy Dillion, *Sec*
EMP: 22 EST: 1987
SQ FT: 14,000
SALES (est): 783.32K **Privately Held**
Web: www.dilcoind.com
SIC: **3599** Machine shop, jobbing and repair

(G-12992)
ETL PERFORMANCE PRODUCTS INC
1717 Pennsylvania Ave (44460-2781)
PHONE...................234 575-7226
Xiangdong Liu, *Pr*
EMP: 8 EST: 2017
SQ FT: 4,000
SALES (est): 859.58K **Privately Held**
Web: www.etlperformance.com
SIC: **3429** Clamps, metal

(G-12993)
EVERFLOW EASTERN PARTNERS LP
Also Called: Strawn Oil Field Service
29093 Salem Alliance Rd (44460-9706)
PHONE...................330 537-3863
Richard Strawn, *Brnch Mgr*
EMP: 6
SIC: **1389** Oil field services, nec
PA: Everflow Eastern Partners, L.P.
    585 W Main St
    Canfield OH 44406

(G-12994)
FIRESTONE LASER AND MFG LLC
14000 W Middletown Rd (44460-9184)
PHONE...................330 337-9551
Richard Kamperman, *Managing Member*
Gregory Smith, *Managing Member**
Rick Fryda, *Managing Member**
Tom Spivak, *Managing Member**
EMP: 25 EST: 1954
SALES (est): 2.16MM **Privately Held**
SIC: **3444** Sheet metalwork

(G-12995)
FLATIRON CRANE OPER CO LLC
Also Called: Simmers Crane Design & Svcs
1134 Salem Pkwy (44460-1063)
PHONE...................330 332-3300
Mark Bilali, *Pr*
Jill Mastandrea, *
EMP: 234 EST: 2021
SALES (est): 24.76MM **Privately Held**
Web: www.simmerscrane.com
SIC: **3536** Hoists, cranes, and monorails

(G-12996)
FRESH MARK INC
1735 S Lincoln Ave (44460-4203)
PHONE...................330 332-8508
Steve Smith, *Brnch Mgr*
EMP: 650
SQ FT: 125,000
SALES (corp-wide): 1.38B **Privately Held**
Web: www.freshmark.com
SIC: **2011** 2013 Meat packing plants; Sausages and other prepared meats
PA: Fresh Mark, Inc.
    1888 Southway St Sw
    Massillon OH 44646
    330 832-7491

(G-12997)
GORDON BROTHERS BTLG GROUP INC
776 N Ellsworth Ave (44460-1600)
P.O. Box 63 (44436-0063)
PHONE...................330 337-8754
Edward P Ned Jones Iii, *Ch*
Frank Tombo, *Prin*
Scott P Jones, *Pr*
EMP: 8 EST: 2004
SALES (est): 243.25K **Privately Held**
Web: www.gordonbroswater.com
SIC: **2086** Bottled and canned soft drinks

(G-12998)
GRID INDUSTRIAL HEATING INC
1108 Salem Pkwy (44460-1063)
P.O. Box 950 (44460-0950)
PHONE...................330 332-9931
Donald Stamp, *Pr*
EMP: 7 EST: 1985
SQ FT: 20,000
SALES (est): 649.89K **Privately Held**
Web: www.gridheating.com
SIC: **3433** 1711 Steam heating apparatus; Plumbing, heating, air-conditioning

(G-12999)
HALTEC CORPORATION
32585 N Price Rd (44460-9513)
P.O. Box 1180 (44460-8180)
PHONE...................330 222-1501
Thomas Moyer, *Pr*
Edward Russell, *
Mike Russell, *
David Caruso, *
Frank Bezon, *
◆ EMP: 116 EST: 1971
SQ FT: 65,000
SALES (est): 42.87MM **Privately Held**
Web: www.haltec.com
SIC: **3714** Tire valve cores

(G-13000)
HAZENSTAB MACHINE INC
1575 Salem Pkwy (44460-1072)
PHONE...................330 337-1865
James Hazenstab Junior, *Pr*
▲ EMP: 13 EST: 1977
SQ FT: 12,000
SALES (est): 472.73K **Privately Held**
Web: www.hazenstabmachine.com
SIC: **3599** Machine shop, jobbing and repair

(G-13001)
HOOVER FABRICATION LTD
1789 N Lincoln Ave (44460-1342)
PHONE...................330 575-1118
EMP: 7 EST: 2001
SALES (est): 219K **Privately Held**
SIC: **3291** Abrasive metal and steel products

(G-13002)
HOWMET AEROSPACE INC
Also Called: Howmet Aerospace Inc
32585 N Price Rd (44460-9513)
P.O. Box 1180 (44460-8180)
PHONE...................330 222-1501
Edward Russell, *Brnch Mgr*
EMP: 70
SALES (corp-wide): 6.64B **Publicly Held**
Web: www.howmet.com
SIC: **3353** Aluminum sheet and strip
PA: Howmet Aerospace Inc.
    201 Isabella St Ste 200
    Pittsburgh PA 15212
    412 553-1950

(G-13003)
HUNT VALVE ACTUATOR LLC
1913 E State St (44460-2491)
PHONE...................330 337-9535
Charles Ferrer, *
EMP: 80 EST: 2017
SQ FT: 50,000
SALES (est): 4.64MM **Privately Held**
Web: www.fairbanksmorsedefense.com
SIC: **3593** Fluid power actuators, hydraulic or pneumatic

(G-13004)
HUNT VALVE COMPANY INC (DH)
1913 E State St (44460-2491)
PHONE...................330 337-9535
▲ EMP: 72 EST: 1919
SALES (est): 48.27MM
SALES (corp-wide): 653.43MM **Privately Held**
Web: www.fairbanksmorsedefense.com
SIC: **3492** Control valves, fluid power: hydraulic and pneumatic
HQ: Valveco Inc.
    251 Little Falls Dr
    Wilmington DE 19808

(G-13005)
INTERSTATE PUMP COMPANY INC (PA)
33370 Winona Rd (44460-9011)
P.O. Box 109 (44460-0109)
PHONE...................330 222-1006
EMP: 7 EST: 1939
SALES (est): 2.02MM **Privately Held**
Web: www.interstatepump.com
SIC: **5084** 5085 3561 Pumps and pumping equipment, nec; Filters, industrial; Pumps and pumping equipment

(G-13006)
JOHN KRIZAY INC
1777 Pennsylvania Ave (44460-2781)
P.O. Box 974 (44460-0974)
PHONE...................330 332-5607
William Stratton, *Pr*
Linda Horsall, *
▲ EMP: 22 EST: 1968
SQ FT: 12,000
SALES (est): 2.05MM **Privately Held**
Web: www.jkrizay.com
SIC: **3229** Art, decorative and novelty glassware

(G-13007)
JOSEPH SABATINO
Also Called: Sabatino Cabinet
1834 Depot Rd (44460-4359)
PHONE...................330 332-5879
EMP: 6 EST: 1990
SQ FT: 8,500
SALES (est): 484.61K **Privately Held**
Web: www.sabatinocabinet.com
SIC: **1751** 2491 Carpentry work; Millwork, treated wood

(G-13008)
KORFF HOLDINGS LLC
Also Called: Quaker City Casting
310 E Euclid Ave (44460-3778)
PHONE...................330 332-1566
Geoffrey Korff, *Pr*
Jason Korff, *
Ronald H Lasko, *
▲ EMP: 120 EST: 1932
SALES (est): 20.76MM **Privately Held**
Web: www.quakercitycastings.com
SIC: **3325** 3321 Steel foundries, nec; Gray and ductile iron foundries

(G-13009)
L M EQUIPMENT & DESIGN INC
11000 Youngstown Salem Rd (44460-9654)
PHONE...................330 332-9951
Dave Hrovatic, *Pr*
Sue Lease, *CFO*
EMP: 10 EST: 2001
SALES (est): 233.38K **Privately Held**
Web: www.lmequipment.com
SIC: **7699** 3541 Industrial equipment services; Milling machines

(G-13010)
LASENOR USA LLC
600 Snyder Rd (44460-4260)
PHONE...................800 754-1228
Jeff Simmons, *Mgr*
EMP: 11 EST: 2019
SALES (est): 1.17MM **Privately Held**
Web: www.lasenor.com
SIC: **2099** Emulsifiers, food
HQ: Lasenor Emul Sl
    Carretera Abrera-Manresa
    Olesa De Montserrat B

(G-13011)
LIFT-TECH INTERNATIONAL INC
240 Pennsylvania Ave (44460-2733)
PHONE...................330 424-7248
▲ EMP: 345
SIC: **3536** Hoists

(G-13012)
LOWRY TOOL & DIE INC
986 Salem Pkwy (44460)
PHONE...................330 332-1722
Robert Lowry, *Pr*
EMP: 14 EST: 1966
SQ FT: 10,000
SALES (est): 2.15MM **Privately Held**
Web: www.lowrysupply.com
SIC: **3544** Special dies and tools

(G-13013)
LYLE PRINTING & PUBLISHING CO (PA)
Also Called: Farm & Dairy
185 E State St (44460-2842)
P.O. Box 38 (44460-0038)
PHONE...................330 337-3419
Scot Darling, *CEO*
Tom Darling, *
EMP: 50 EST: 1890
SQ FT: 12,500
SALES (est): 4.56MM
SALES (corp-wide): 4.56MM **Privately Held**
Web: www.lyleprinting.com
SIC: **2721** 2752 2759 Trade journals: publishing only, not printed on site; Offset printing; Letterpress printing

(G-13014)
MAC MANUFACTURING INC
1453 Allen Rd (44460-1004)
PHONE...................330 829-1680
Cora Mcdonald, *Brnch Mgr*
EMP: 104
Web: www.mactrailer.com
SIC: **3715** 5012 Truck trailers; Trailers for trucks, new and used
HQ: Mac Manufacturing, Inc.
    14599 Commerce St
    Alliance OH 44601

Salem - Columbiana County (G-13015)

(G-13015)
METAL & WIRE PRODUCTS COMPANY
1069 Salem Pkwy (44460-1062)
PHONE..............................330 332-1015
EMP: 14
Web: www.metalandwire.com
SIC: 3469 Stamping metal for the trade
PA: Metal & Wire Products Company Inc
1065 Salem Pkwy
Salem OH 44460

(G-13016)
METAL & WIRE PRODUCTS COMPANY (PA)
1065 Salem Pkwy (44460-1062)
PHONE..............................330 332-9448
EMP: 50 EST: 1981
SQ FT: 62,000
SALES (est): 9.31MM Privately Held
Web: www.metalandwire.com
SIC: 3469 3542 3544 Stamping metal for the trade; Machine tools, metal forming type; Special dies, tools, jigs, and fixtures

(G-13017)
MILLER-HOLZWARTH INC
450 W Pershing St (44460-2752)
PHONE..............................330 342-7224
EMP: 60 EST: 1955
SALES (est): 4.44MM Privately Held
Web: www.millerholzwarth.com
SIC: 3827 3861 3231 Periscopes; Photographic equipment and supplies; Products of purchased glass

(G-13018)
MILSEK FURNITURE POLISH INC
1351 Quaker Cir (44460-1006)
PHONE..............................330 542-2700
Chris Herubin, CEO
Chris Ruben, Pr
Dan Bender, Sec
EMP: 6 EST: 2006
SQ FT: 2,080
SALES (est): 517.9K Privately Held
Web: www.milsek.com
SIC: 2842 Polishes and sanitation goods

(G-13019)
MM INDUSTRIES INC
Also Called: Vorti-Siv
36135 Salem Grange Rd (44460-9442)
P.O. Box 720 (44460-0720)
PHONE..............................330 332-5947
Barbara Maroscher, Pr
Victor Maroscher, *
Art Maroscher, *
▲ EMP: 30 EST: 1967
SQ FT: 10,000
SALES (est): 3.79MM Privately Held
Web: www.vorti-siv.com
SIC: 3559 Screening equipment, electric

(G-13020)
MOORE MR SPECIALTY COMPANY
1050 Pennsylvania Ave (44460)
P.O. Box 107 (44460-0107)
PHONE..............................330 332-1229
Robert N Moore, Pr
Martha Moore, VP
EMP: 8 EST: 1966
SQ FT: 5,000
SALES (est): 852.24K Privately Held
SIC: 3443 Fabricated plate work (boiler shop)

(G-13021)
PETROLEUM HOLDINGS LLC
445 Prospect St (44460-2618)
PHONE..............................443 676-0150
EMP: 7 EST: 2017
SALES (est): 90.74K Privately Held
SIC: 2911 Petroleum refining

(G-13022)
PIMA VALVE LLC
1913 E State St (44460-2422)
PHONE..............................330 337-9535
George Whittier, Pr
EMP: 59 EST: 1967
SQ FT: 38,000
SALES (est): 9.52MM
SALES (corp-wide): 653.43MM Privately Held
Web: www.fairbanksmorsedefense.com
SIC: 3494 3491 3492 Valves and pipe fittings, nec; Industrial valves; Fluid power valves and hose fittings
HQ: Hunt Valve Company, Inc.
1913 E State St
Salem OH 44460
330 337-9535

(G-13023)
POLLOCK RESEARCH & DESIGN INC
Simmers Crane Design & Svc Co
1134 Salem Pkwy (44460-1063)
PHONE..............................330 332-3300
Randy L Stull, Mgr
EMP: 45
SALES (corp-wide): 49.18MM Privately Held
Web: www.readingcrane.com
SIC: 8711 7389 7353 3537 Civil engineering; Crane and aerial lift service; Heavy construction equipment rental; Industrial trucks and tractors
PA: Pollock Research & Design, Inc.
11 Vanguard Dr
Reading PA 19606
610 582-7203

(G-13024)
QUAKER MFG CORP
Also Called: Quaker Mfg
187 Georgetown Rd (44460-2009)
PHONE..............................330 332-4631
▲ EMP: 115
Web: www.cqlmfg.com
SIC: 3469 3544 3465 3599 Metal stampings, nec; Special dies and tools; Automotive stampings; Machine and other job shop work

(G-13025)
QUALITY FABRICATED METALS INC
14000 W Middletown Rd (44460-9184)
PHONE..............................330 332-7008
EMP: 38 EST: 1987
SQ FT: 42,000
SALES (est): 863K Privately Held
Web: www.fabricatedmetals.com
SIC: 3469 1799 Stamping metal for the trade ; Welding on site

(G-13026)
REDEX INDUSTRIES INC (PA)
Also Called: Udderly Smooth
1176 Salem Pkwy (44460-1063)
P.O. Box 939 (44460-0939)
PHONE..............................800 345-7339
William C Kennedy, Pr
William C Kennedy, Pr
Margaret Kennedy, Sec
EMP: 16 EST: 1976
SQ FT: 24,000
SALES (est): 4.83MM
SALES (corp-wide): 4.83MM Privately Held
Web: www.udderlysmooth.com

SIC: 2844 Face creams or lotions

(G-13027)
RIPPED VINYL
550 Fair Ave (44460-3317)
PHONE..............................330 332-5004
Ryan Mccoy, Prin
EMP: 6 EST: 2008
SALES (est): 71.26K Privately Held
Web: www.rippedvinyl.net
SIC: 3993 Signs and advertising specialties

(G-13028)
SALEM MILL & CABINET CO
1455 Quaker Cir (44460-1054)
P.O. Box 1072 (44460-8072)
PHONE..............................330 337-9568
Steven W Kastenhuber, Pr
EMP: 6 EST: 1986
SQ FT: 6,000
SALES (est): 906.04K Privately Held
SIC: 5211 2431 2434 Lumber products; Millwork; Wood kitchen cabinets

(G-13029)
SALEM WELDING & SUPPLY COMPANY
475 Prospect St (44460-2618)
P.O. Box 386 (44460-0386)
PHONE..............................330 332-4517
Frederick Baker Senior, Pr
Frederick Baker Junior, VP
Anna Baker, Sec
EMP: 9 EST: 1975
SQ FT: 15,200
SALES (est): 2.27MM Privately Held
Web: www.salemweldingco.com
SIC: 7692 5084 Welding repair; Welding machinery and equipment

(G-13030)
SAVI CORPORATION INC
31257 Salem Alliance Rd (44460-9746)
PHONE..............................330 277-3300
EMP: 7 EST: 2009
SALES (est): 61.98K Privately Held
Web: www.savi.com
SIC: 7372 Business oriented computer software

(G-13031)
SIMMONS FEED & SUPPLY LLC
Also Called: Simmons Grain Company
600 Snyder Rd (44460-4260)
PHONE..............................800 754-1228
Jeffrey Simmons, Pr
▲ EMP: 20 EST: 1982
SQ FT: 10,000
SALES (est): 17.75MM Privately Held
Web: www.simmonsgrain.com
SIC: 5153 3556 Grains; Oilseed crushing and extracting machinery

(G-13032)
SLATER ROAD MILLS INC
11000 Youngstown Salem Rd (44460-9654)
P.O. Box 1083 (44460-8083)
PHONE..............................330 332-9951
EMP: 25 EST: 1986
SALES (est): 2.41MM Privately Held
Web: www.lehmannmills.com
SIC: 3541 7699 3552 Milling machines; Industrial equipment services; Textile machinery

(G-13033)
THE LABEL TEAM INC
1251 Quaker Cir (44460-1050)
PHONE..............................330 332-1067
Dean J Mcdaniel, Pr

Paula Mcdaniel, VP
EMP: 15 EST: 1998
SQ FT: 11,400
SALES (est): 2.14MM Privately Held
Web: www.thelabelteam.net
SIC: 2759 Labels and seals: printing, nsk

(G-13034)
TRI-FAB INC
10372 W South Range Rd (44460-9621)
P.O. Box 310 (44460-0310)
PHONE..............................330 337-3425
Samuel Lippiatt, Pr
EMP: 32 EST: 1979
SQ FT: 44,000
SALES (est): 2.35MM Privately Held
SIC: 3644 3441 3444 Fuse boxes, electric; Fabricated structural metal; Sheet metalwork

(G-13035)
TURNER MACHINE CO
1433 Salem Pkwy (44460-1070)
PHONE..............................330 332-5821
Jacob O Kamm, Pr
Patricia Simonsic, Treas
EMP: 11 EST: 1943
SALES (est): 503.21K Privately Held
Web: www.turnermachineco.com
SIC: 3599 3547 3542 Machine shop, jobbing and repair; Rolling mill machinery; Machine tools, metal forming type

(G-13036)
VIC MAROSCHER
36135 Salem Grange Rd (44460-9442)
P.O. Box 720 (44460-0720)
PHONE..............................330 332-4958
Vic Maroscher, Owner
EMP: 10 EST: 2009
SALES (est): 396.61K Privately Held
Web: www.vorti-siv.com
SIC: 3999 Manufacturing industries, nec

Salineville
Columbiana County

(G-13037)
ACCESS MIDSTREAM
10 E Main St (43945-1134)
PHONE..............................330 679-2019
EMP: 7 EST: 2016
SALES (est): 184.82K Privately Held
SIC: 1382 Oil and gas exploration services

(G-13038)
BAILEE LOGGING LLC
36575 Dinch Rd (43945-9733)
PHONE..............................330 881-4688
Jeff Beadnell, Prin
EMP: 6 EST: 2016
SALES (est): 81.72K Privately Held
SIC: 2411 Logging

(G-13039)
M3 MIDSTREAM LLC
Also Called: Salineville Office
10 E Main St (43945-1134)
PHONE..............................330 679-5580
EMP: 34
SALES (corp-wide): 57MM Privately Held
Web: www.momentummidstream.com
SIC: 1382 Oil and gas exploration services
PA: M3 Midstream Llc
600 Travis St Ste 5600
Houston TX 77002
713 783-3000

Sandusky
Erie County

(G-13040)
ACH LLC
Also Called: Ach Sandusky Plastics
3020 Tiffin Ave (44870-5352)
PHONE.................................419 621-5748
Andy Short, *Prin*
▲ **EMP:** 8 **EST:** 2008
SALES (est): 915.24K **Privately Held**
SIC: 3714 Motor vehicle parts and accessories

(G-13041)
ACME PRINTING CO INC
2143 Sherman St (44870-4714)
P.O. Box 2311 (44871-2311)
PHONE.................................419 626-4426
Dean Everson, *Pr*
Fred Everson, *VP*
James Kellam, *Sec*
EMP: 6 **EST:** 1968
SQ FT: 10,000
SALES (est): 450K **Privately Held**
SIC: 2752 2796 2759 Offset printing; Embossing plates, for printing; Letterpress printing

(G-13042)
AHNER FABRICATING & SHTMTL INC
2001 E Perkins Ave (44870-5130)
PHONE.................................419 626-6641
Mark Ahner, *Pr*
Timothy Ahner, *
EMP: 24 **EST:** 1984
SQ FT: 7,000
SALES (est): 6.78MM **Privately Held**
Web: www.ahner-industrial.com
SIC: 3444 3914 5049 Sheet metal specialties, not stamped; Carving sets, stainless steel; Precision tools

(G-13043)
AMERICAN COLORS INC (PA)
4602 Timber Commons Dr (44870-7189)
P.O. Box 397 (44871-0397)
PHONE.................................419 621-4000
◆ **EMP:** 50 **EST:** 1975
SALES (est): 27.4MM
SALES (corp-wide): 27.4MM **Privately Held**
Web: www.americancolors.com
SIC: 2816 Color pigments

(G-13044)
AMERICAN QUALITY STRIPPING INC
1750 5th St (44870-1301)
PHONE.................................419 625-6288
Tim Finneran, *Pr*
Richard Finneran, *
EMP: 30 **EST:** 1987
SQ FT: 16,000
SALES (est): 4.51MM **Privately Held**
Web: www.americanqualitystripping.com
SIC: 3471 3398 Finishing, metals or formed products; Metal heat treating

(G-13045)
BRIDGESTONE RET OPERATIONS LLC
Also Called: Firestone
4320 Milan Rd (44870-5836)
PHONE.................................419 625-6571
Richard Oliver, *Mgr*
EMP: 6
Web: www.bridgestoneamericas.com
SIC: 5531 7534 7538 Automotive tires; Tire retreading and repair shops; General automotive repair shops
HQ: Bridgestone Retail Operations, Llc
333 E Lake St Ste 300
Bloomingdale IL 60108
630 259-9000

(G-13046)
BUDERER DRUG COMPANY INC (PA)
633 Hancock St (44870-3603)
PHONE.................................419 627-2800
Matthew Buderer, *VP*
James Buderer, *Pr*
EMP: 25 **EST:** 2014
SQ FT: 5,000
SALES (est): 4.98MM
SALES (corp-wide): 4.98MM **Privately Held**
Web: www.budererdrug.com
SIC: 5122 2834 Drugs and drug proprietaries; Proprietary drug products

(G-13047)
BUSCH & THIEM INC
1316 Cleveland Rd (44870-4271)
P.O. Box 1088 (44871-1088)
PHONE.................................419 625-7515
C A Busch, *Pr*
James R Kellam, *Sec*
EMP: 20 **EST:** 1926
SQ FT: 45,000
SALES (est): 2.53MM **Privately Held**
Web: www.buschthiem.com
SIC: 2542 3993 3496 3444 Racks, merchandise display or storage: except wood; Signs and advertising specialties; Miscellaneous fabricated wire products; Sheet metalwork

(G-13048)
CANTELLI BLOCK AND BRICK INC
1602 Milan Rd (44870-4116)
PHONE.................................419 433-0102
Raymond J Cantelli, *Pr*
Anita Cantelli, *
Adriana Cantelli, *
Ray A Cantelli, *
EMP: 25 **EST:** 1923
SALES (est): 2.51MM **Privately Held**
SIC: 3271 Blocks, concrete or cinder: standard

(G-13049)
DAISYFIELD PORK LLC
4413 W Bogart Rd (44870-9648)
PHONE.................................419 626-2251
Thomas M Routh, *Prin*
EMP: 6 **EST:** 2018
SALES (est): 325.66K **Privately Held**
Web: www.routhpacking.com
SIC: 2011 Meat packing plants

(G-13050)
DECKO PRODUCTS INC (PA)
2105 Superior St (44870-1891)
PHONE.................................419 626-5757
Bill Niggemyer, *Pr*
▲ **EMP:** 65 **EST:** 1930
SQ FT: 20,000
SALES (est): 18.41MM
SALES (corp-wide): 18.41MM **Privately Held**
Web: www.decko.com
SIC: 2064 Cake ornaments, confectionery

(G-13051)
DOUTHIT COMMUNICATIONS INC (PA)
Also Called: Photo Journals
520 Warren St (44870-2958)
P.O. Box 760 (44870-0760)
PHONE.................................419 625-5825
H Kenneth Iii, *Pr*
Harold K Douthit, *
Joanne Kraine, *
EMP: 75 **EST:** 1956
SQ FT: 12,000
SALES (est): 10.81MM
SALES (corp-wide): 10.81MM **Privately Held**
Web: www.adwriter.com
SIC: 2711 2741 Job printing and newspaper publishing combined; Miscellaneous publishing

(G-13052)
EDSAL SANDUSKY CORPORATION
Also Called: EDSAL SANDUSKY CORPORATION
117 E Washington Row (44870-2629)
PHONE.................................419 626-5465
EMP: 34
SALES (corp-wide): 19.34MM **Privately Held**
Web: www.sanduskycabinets.com
SIC: 2522 Cabinets, office: except wood
PA: Edsal Sandusky Llc
1555 W 44th St
Chicago IL 60609
773 475-3000

(G-13053)
ENCORE INDUSTRIES INC
319 Howard Dr (44870-8607)
PHONE.................................419 626-8000
Timothy Rathbun, *Brnch Mgr*
EMP: 125
SALES (corp-wide): 816.52K **Privately Held**
SIC: 3089 3559 3841 3411 Injection molded finished plastics products, nec; Plastics working machinery; Surgical and medical instruments; Metal cans
HQ: Encore Industries, Inc.
725 Water St
Cambridge OH 43725
419 626-8000

(G-13054)
ENCORE PLASTICS SOUTHEAST LLC
319 Howard Dr (44870-8607)
PHONE.................................419 626-8000
EMP: 10 **EST:** 2011
SALES (est): 147.21K **Privately Held**
SIC: 3089 Plastics products, nec

(G-13055)
ENTRATECH SYSTEMS LLC (PA)
Also Called: Entratech Systems
202 Fox Rd (44870-8363)
PHONE.................................419 433-7683
EMP: 9 **EST:** 1982
SQ FT: 14,000
SALES (est): 1.32MM
SALES (corp-wide): 1.32MM **Privately Held**
Web: www.entratech.com
SIC: 7539 3714 Electrical services; Filters: oil, fuel, and air, motor vehicle

(G-13056)
EQUINOX ENTERPRISES LLC
Also Called: A & L Metal Processing
1920 George St (44870-1739)
P.O. Box 1367 (44871-1367)
PHONE.................................419 627-0022
EMP: 12 **EST:** 1991
SQ FT: 25,000
SALES (est): 781.23K **Privately Held**
Web: www.almetalprocessing.com
SIC: 3471 Electroplating of metals or formed products

(G-13057)
ETHIMA INC
Also Called: Universal Clay Products
1528 First St (44870-3902)
PHONE.................................419 626-4912
Doctor Vimal Kumar, *Pr*
EMP: 55 **EST:** 1993
SQ FT: 80,000
SALES (est): 2.37MM **Privately Held**
SIC: 3264 3255 3295 3444 Insulators, electrical: porcelain; Foundry refractories, clay; Minerals, ground or treated; Sheet metalwork

(G-13058)
FANCY ME BOUTIQUE LLC
133 E Market St (44870-2507)
PHONE.................................419 357-8927
EMP: 6 **EST:** 2015
SALES (est): 254.7K **Privately Held**
Web: www.fancymeboutique.com
SIC: 5651 5641 5621 2389 Family clothing stores; Children's and infants' wear stores; Women's clothing stores; Apparel and accessories, nec

(G-13059)
GARY L GAST
Also Called: Ohio Wood Fabrication
2024 Campbell St (44870-4890)
PHONE.................................419 626-5915
Gary L Gast, *Owner*
EMP: 6 **EST:** 1991
SQ FT: 3,600
SALES (est): 425K **Privately Held**
SIC: 2541 Cabinets, except refrigerated: show, display, etc.: wood

(G-13060)
GEAUGA PUBLISHING COMPANY LTD
520 Warren St (44870-2958)
PHONE.................................419 625-5825
Harold Douthit, *Prin*
Dana R Andrassy, *Prin*
EMP: 9 **EST:** 1998
SALES (est): 167.37K **Privately Held**
SIC: 2711 Newspapers: publishing only, not printed on site

(G-13061)
GENERAL FABRICATIONS CORP
7777 Milan Rd (44870-9705)
P.O. Box 2461 (44871-2461)
PHONE.................................419 625-6055
Chester Boraski, *Pr*
Carol Boraski, *
EMP: 42 **EST:** 1982
SQ FT: 10,000
SALES (est): 7.55MM **Privately Held**
Web: www.gfcfinishing.com
SIC: 3559 3563 Paint making machinery; Air and gas compressors

(G-13062)
GUNDLACH SHEET METAL WORKS INC (PA)
Also Called: Honeywell Authorized Dealer
910 Columbus Ave (44870-3594)
PHONE.................................419 626-4525
Terry W Gundlach, *Ch*
Roger M Gundlach, *
Terry Kette, *
Andrew Gundluch, *
EMP: 33 **EST:** 1889

Sandusky - Erie County (G-13063)

SQ FT: 17,000
SALES (est): 17.84MM
SALES (corp-wide): 17.84MM Privately Held
Web: www.gundlachsheetmetal.com
SIC: 1711 3444 Warm air heating and air conditioning contractor; Sheet metalwork

(G-13063)
HK COOPERATIVE INC
Also Called: HK Coprative Inc/J H Routh Pkg
4413 W Bogart Rd (44870-9648)
PHONE..................419 626-2551
Jeff Wall, *Prin*
Paul Kalmbach, *Prin*
Blake Holden, *Prin*
EMP: 12 EST: 2020
SALES (est): 597.64K Privately Held
Web: www.routhpacking.com
SIC: 2011 Meat packing plants

(G-13064)
HULL READY MIX CONCRETE INC
Also Called: Hull Builders Supply
4419 Tiffin Ave (44870-9645)
P.O. Box 432 (44089-0432)
PHONE..................419 625-8070
Jeffery Riddell, *Pr*
EMP: 10 EST: 1999
SALES (est): 733.58K Privately Held
Web: www.buildersupply.com
SIC: 3273 4212 1611 7359 Ready-mixed concrete; Truck rental with drivers; Highway and street construction; Industrial truck rental

(G-13065)
INDISPENSER LTD
520 Warren St (44870-2958)
P.O. Box 760 (44871-0760)
PHONE..................419 625-5825
Harold Douthit, *Prin*
EMP: 45 EST: 1999
SALES (est): 2.71MM Privately Held
SIC: 3999 Advertising display products

(G-13066)
INDUSTRIAL NUT CORP
1425 Tiffin Ave (44870-2054)
PHONE..................419 625-8543
William Springer, *Pr*
John E Moffitt, *
James B Springer, *
John William Springer Iii, *VP*
▲ EMP: 54 EST: 1908
SQ FT: 100,000
SALES (est): 9.21MM Privately Held
Web: www.industrialnut.com
SIC: 3452 Nuts, metal

(G-13067)
ISAAC FOSTER MACK CO (PA)
Also Called: Sandusky Newspaper Group
314 W Market St (44870-2410)
PHONE..................419 625-5500
Dudley A White Junior, *Ch Bd*
David A Rau, *
Susan E White, *
EMP: 140 EST: 1822
SQ FT: 45,000
SALES (est): 92.2MM
SALES (corp-wide): 92.2MM Privately Held
Web: www.sanduskyregister.com
SIC: 4832 2711 2752 Radio broadcasting stations; Newspapers; Commercial printing, lithographic

(G-13068)
J H ROUTH PACKING COMPANY
4413 W Bogart Rd (44870)
P.O. Box 2253 (44871)
PHONE..................419 626-2251
EMP: 300 EST: 1947
SALES (est): 49.44MM Privately Held
Web: www.routhpacking.com
SIC: 2011 Meat packing plants

(G-13069)
JAMAC INC
422 Buchanan St (44870-4700)
PHONE..................419 625-9790
Mark Mc Gory, *Pr*
Elaine Mc Gory, *VP*
Blake Mc Gory, *Sec*
James G Mc Gory Junior, *Treas*
James G Mc Gory Senior, *Stockholder*
▼ EMP: 28 EST: 1983
SQ FT: 10,000
SALES (est): 733.58K Privately Held
Web: www.jamac.com
SIC: 2759 Labels and seals: printing, nsk

(G-13070)
JOHN BEAN TECHNOLOGIES CORP
Also Called: Jbt Foodtech
1622 First St (44870-3902)
PHONE..................419 626-0304
Larry Martin, *Brnch Mgr*
EMP: 260
Web: www.jbtc.com
SIC: 3556 Food products machinery
PA: John Bean Technologies Corporation
70 W Madison St Ste 4400
Chicago IL 60602

(G-13071)
KITCHENS BY JAVA
1903 Cleveland Rd (44870-4308)
PHONE..................419 621-7677
Jeff Hessler, *Owner*
EMP: 6 EST: 2002
SALES (est): 231.82K Privately Held
SIC: 2434 Wood kitchen cabinets

(G-13072)
KYKLOS BEARING INTERNATIONAL LLC
Also Called: K B I
2509 Hayes Ave (44870-5359)
PHONE..................419 627-7000
▲ EMP: 900
SIC: 3714 Bearings, motor vehicle

(G-13073)
LAKE SHORE GRAPHIC INDS INC
2111 Cleveland Rd (44870-4412)
PHONE..................419 626-8631
Craig H Stahl, *CEO*
William E Stahl, *Ch*
EMP: 17 EST: 1979
SALES (est): 423.48K Privately Held
SIC: 2752 Offset printing

(G-13074)
LEWCO INC (PA)
706 Lane St (44870-3846)
PHONE..................419 625-4014
Ronald Guerra, *Pr*
Gerald Guerra, *
◆ EMP: 187 EST: 1917
SQ FT: 135,000
SALES (est): 101.57MM
SALES (corp-wide): 101.57MM Privately Held
Web: www.lewcoinc.com

SIC: 3535 3567 Bulk handling conveyor systems; Industrial furnaces and ovens

(G-13075)
LONZ WINERY LLC
Also Called: Specialty Wine-Spirits
917 Bardshar Rd (44870-1507)
PHONE..................419 625-5474
Claudio Salvador, *Pr*
▲ EMP: 16 EST: 2002
SALES (est): 2.61MM Privately Held
Web: www.firelandswinery.com
SIC: 2084 Wines

(G-13076)
MAAGS AUTOMOTIVE & MCH INC
Also Called: Maag's Automotive
1640 Columbus Ave (44870-3542)
PHONE..................419 626-1539
Robert Maag, *Pr*
EMP: 9 EST: 1976
SQ FT: 1,500
SALES (est): 926.3K Privately Held
SIC: 3519 7538 7539 3714 Diesel engine rebuilding; Engine rebuilding: automotive; Automotive repair shops, nec; Motor vehicle parts and accessories

(G-13077)
MACHINE APPLICATIONS CORP
Also Called: Mac Instruments
3410 Tiffin Ave (44870-9752)
PHONE..................419 621-2322
James G Weit, *Pr*
Karen Weit, *Sec*
EMP: 7 EST: 1990
SQ FT: 1,672
SALES (est): 979.06K Privately Held
Web: www.macinstruments.com
SIC: 3823 Process control instruments

(G-13078)
MACK IRON WORKS COMPANY
124 Warren St (44870-2823)
PHONE..................419 626-3712
John O Bacon, *Pr*
Peter P Kowalski Junior, *VP*
EMP: 40 EST: 1901
SQ FT: 63,000
SALES (est): 9.42MM Privately Held
Web: www.mackiron.com
SIC: 3494 3444 3443 3446 Valves and pipe fittings, nec; Sheet metalwork; Fabricated plate work (boiler shop); Stairs, staircases, stair treads: prefabricated metal

(G-13079)
MARK ADVERTISING AGENCY INC
1600 5th St (44870-1300)
P.O. Box 413 (44871-0413)
PHONE..................419 626-9000
Joe Wesnitzer, *CEO*
Shelly Cook, *Pr*
Shirley Wesnitzer, *VP*
EMP: 15 EST: 1965
SQ FT: 8,000
SALES (est): 1.83MM Privately Held
Web: www.markadvertising.com
SIC: 2752 7311 Offset printing; Advertising agencies

(G-13080)
MECCAS LOUNGE LLC
2614 Pioneer Trl Apt 606 (44870-5148)
PHONE..................419 239-6918
EMP: 7 EST: 2021
SALES (est): 150K Privately Held
SIC: 2599 Food wagons, restaurant

(G-13081)
METALTEK INTERNATIONAL INC
Also Called: Metaltek International
615 W Market St (44870-2413)
PHONE..................419 626-5340
EMP: 90
Web: www.metaltek.com
SIC: 3366 Copper foundries
PA: Metaltek International, Inc.
905 E Saint Paul Ave
Waukesha WI 53188

(G-13082)
MIELKE FURNITURE REPAIR INC
3209 Columbus Ave (44870-5595)
PHONE..................419 625-4572
Daniel H Mielke, *Pr*
Allan R Mielke, *VP*
Christine Mielke, *Sec*
EMP: 8 EST: 1947
SQ FT: 2,800
SALES (est): 378.53K Privately Held
Web: www.mielkefurniture.com
SIC: 7641 2511 Furniture refinishing; Wood household furniture

(G-13083)
OGDEN NEWS PUBLISHING OHIO INC (DH)
Also Called: Courier, The
314 W Market St (44870-2410)
PHONE..................419 625-5500
Bob Nutting, *CEO*
EMP: 30 EST: 1997
SALES (est): 11.42MM Privately Held
Web: www.ogdennews.com
SIC: 2711 Newspapers: publishing only, not printed on site
HQ: The Ogden Newspapers Inc
1500 Main St
Wheeling WV 26003
304 233-0100

(G-13084)
OKAMOTO SANDUSKY MFG LLC
Also Called: Okamoto USA
3130 W Monroe St (44870-1811)
PHONE..................419 626-1633
Yoshiyuki Okamoto, *Pr*
▲ EMP: 100 EST: 2007
SALES (est): 19.41MM Privately Held
Web: www.okamotosandusky.com
SIC: 3069 Bibs, vulcanized rubber or rubberized fabric

(G-13085)
P & T PRODUCTS INC
472 Industrial Pkwy (44870-5883)
PHONE..................419 621-1966
Paul Todd, *Pr*
Jennifer Fildley, *VP*
Susan K Todd, *Sec*
EMP: 20 EST: 1988
SQ FT: 20,000
SALES (est): 4.93MM Privately Held
Web: www.p-tproductsinc.com
SIC: 2891 Sealants

(G-13086)
PARK PRESS DIRECT
2143 Sherman St (44870-4714)
P.O. Box 2311 (44871-2311)
PHONE..................419 626-4426
Slate Kessler, *Prin*
Scott Bowlers, *Prin*
EMP: 9 EST: 2015
SALES (est): 402.45K Privately Held
SIC: 2752 7389 Offset printing; Business Activities at Non-Commercial Site

GEOGRAPHIC SECTION

(G-13087)
PEERLESS STOVE & MFG CO
Also Called: Peerless Prof Cooking Eqp
334 Harrison St (44870)
P.O. Box 859 (44871-0859)
PHONE..............................419 625-4514
Brian R Huntley, *Pr*
EMP: 10 **EST:** 1916
SQ FT: 40,000
SALES (est): 2.24MM **Privately Held**
Web: www.peerlessovens.com
SIC: 3556 Food products machinery

(G-13088)
POLYNT COMPOSITES USA INC
1321 First St (44870-3901)
PHONE..............................816 391-6000
Scott Bechtel, *Mgr*
EMP: 25
SALES (corp-wide): 3.09B **Privately Held**
Web: www.polynt.com
SIC: 2834 2842 2851 2821 Emulsions, pharmaceutical; Polishes and sanitation goods; Paints and allied products; Polyesters
HQ: Polynt Composites Usa Inc.
99 E Cottage Ave
Carpentersville IL 60110

(G-13089)
SANDUSKY FABRICATING & SLS INC (PA)
Also Called: San-Fab Conveyor and Automtn
2000 Superior St (44870-1824)
P.O. Box 2190 (44871-2190)
PHONE..............................419 626-4465
Timothy H Shenigo, *Pr*
EMP: 23 **EST:** 1954
SQ FT: 85,000
SALES (est): 2.25MM
SALES (corp-wide): 2.25MM **Privately Held**
Web: www.sanfab.com
SIC: 3535 Conveyors and conveying equipment

(G-13090)
SANDUSKY INTERNATIONAL INC
Also Called: CARONDELET FOUNDRY
510 W Water St (44870)
PHONE..............................419 626-5340
Edward R Ryan, *CEO*
Richard A Hargrave, *
◆ **EMP:** 200 **EST:** 1904
SQ FT: 500,000
SALES (est): 81.06M **Privately Held**
Web: www.metaltek.com
SIC: 3325 3369 Alloy steel castings, except investment; Castings, except die-castings, precision
PA: Metaltek International, Inc.
905 E Saint Paul Ave
Waukesha WI 53188

(G-13091)
SANDUSKY MACHINE & TOOL INC
2223 Tiffin Ave (44870-1994)
PHONE..............................419 626-8359
Walter Schaufler, *Ch Bd*
James Schaufler, *Pr*
EMP: 26 **EST:** 1966
SQ FT: 17,600
SALES (est): 473.85K **Privately Held**
SIC: 3599 Machine shop, jobbing and repair

(G-13092)
SANDUSKY PACKAGING CORPORATION
2016 George St (44870-1797)
P.O. Box 2217 (44871-2217)
PHONE..............................419 626-8520
Randall A Johnson, *Pr*
Greg Norman, *
Connie Turinsky, *
EMP: 49 **EST:** 1965
SQ FT: 75,000
SALES (est): 10MM **Privately Held**
Web: www.sanduskypackaging.com
SIC: 2652 2657 Setup paperboard boxes; Folding paperboard boxes

(G-13093)
SCHWAB MACHINE INC
3120 Venice Rd (44870-1886)
PHONE..............................419 626-0245
Robert Schwab, *Pr*
James Mcmahon, *VP*
EMP: 6 **EST:** 1946
SQ FT: 9,600
SALES (est): 487.69K **Privately Held**
Web: www.schwabmachine.com
SIC: 3599 Machine shop, jobbing and repair

(G-13094)
SPOERR PRECAST CONCRETE INC
2020 Caldwell St (44870-4874)
PHONE..............................419 625-9132
William R Shank, *Pr*
William Shank, *Pr*
Robert Shank, *Research Vice President*
EMP: 15 **EST:** 1933
SQ FT: 18,000
SALES (est): 484.24K **Privately Held**
Web: www.spoerrprecast.com
SIC: 3272 Concrete products, precast, nec

(G-13095)
THERMOCOLOR LLC (DH)
Also Called: Rhetech Colors
2901 W Monroe St (44870-1810)
PHONE..............................419 626-5677
EMP: 25 **EST:** 1986
SQ FT: 30,000
SALES (est): 11.62MM
SALES (corp-wide): 2.12B **Privately Held**
Web: www.rhetechcolors.com
SIC: 2821 Plastics materials and resins
HQ: Hexpol Holding Inc.
14330 Kinsman Rd
Burton OH 44021
440 834-4644

(G-13096)
THORWORKS INDUSTRIES INC (PA)
Also Called: Sealmaster
2520 Campbell St (44870-5309)
P.O. Box 2218 (44871-2218)
PHONE..............................419 626-4375
David Thorson, *Pr*
Larry Mullins, *
◆ **EMP:** 110 **EST:** 1985
SQ FT: 80,000
SALES (est): 99.44MM **Privately Held**
Web: www.thorworks.com
SIC: 2951 3531 2952 2891 Asphalt paving mixtures and blocks; Construction machinery; Asphalt felts and coatings; Adhesives and sealants

(G-13097)
TOFT DAIRY INC
3717 Venice Rd (44870-1640)
P.O. Box 2558 (44871-2558)
PHONE..............................419 625-4376
TOLL FREE: 800
Eugene H Meisler, *Pr*
Carl Meisler, *
Nicholas Catri, *
Thomas E Meisler, *
Charles M Meisler, *
EMP: 52 **EST:** 1900
SQ FT: 94,000
SALES (est): 9.5MM **Privately Held**
Web: www.toftdairy.com
SIC: 2026 2024 Milk processing (pasteurizing, homogenizing, bottling); Ice cream and ice milk

(G-13098)
TUNE TOWN CAR AUDIO
Also Called: Tune Town
2345 E Perkins Ave (44870-5176)
PHONE..............................419 627-1100
TOLL FREE: 877
EMP: 7 **EST:** 1994
SQ FT: 4,800
SALES (est): 438.2K **Privately Held**
Web: www.tune-town.com
SIC: 5731 3651 High fidelity stereo equipment; Household audio and video equipment

(G-13099)
UNION FABRICATING AND MCH CO
3427 Venice Rd (44870-1766)
PHONE..............................419 626-5963
TOLL FREE: 800
Alden V Lake, *CEO*
Mary Lake, *Sec*
Daniel Lake, *Pr*
Jeffrey Lake, *VP*
EMP: 7 **EST:** 1965
SALES (est): 737.43K **Privately Held**
SIC: 3441 Fabricated structural metal

(G-13100)
UNITED WHEEL AND HUB LLC
214 Marshall Ave (44870-5499)
P.O. Box 595 (44811-0595)
PHONE..............................419 483-2639
Mark Blakely, *Prin*
▲ **EMP:** 7 **EST:** 2010
SALES (est): 162.49K **Privately Held**
Web: unitedwheel.wordpress.com
SIC: 3312 Wheels

(G-13101)
UNIVERSAL DSIGN FBRICATION LLC
Also Called: Fabrication and Welding
7319 Portland Rd (44870-9672)
PHONE..............................419 202-5269
John Eckhardt, *Managing Member*
EMP: 10 **EST:** 2018
SALES (est): 475.3K **Privately Held**
Web: www.universaldesignandfabrication.com
SIC: 7389 1531 1799 3443 Design services; Welding on site; Weldments

(G-13102)
US TSUBAKI POWER TRANSM LLC
Also Called: Engineering Chain Div
1010 Edgewater Ave (44870-1601)
PHONE..............................419 626-4560
Myron Timmer, *VP*
EMP: 180
Web: www.ustsubaki.com
SIC: 5049 3568 3714 3462 Engineers' equipment and supplies, nec; Chain, power transmission; Motor vehicle parts and accessories; Iron and steel forgings
HQ: U.S. Tsubaki Power Transmission Llc
301 E Marquardt Dr
Wheeling IL 60090
847 459-9500

(G-13103)
VENTRA SANDUSKY LLC
3020 Tiffin Ave (44870-5352)
PHONE..............................419 627-3600
▲ **EMP:** 263 **EST:** 2007
SALES (est): 26.65MM
SALES (corp-wide): 1.56B **Privately Held**
Web: www.ventra.com
SIC: 3822 3714 Environmental controls; Motor vehicle parts and accessories
PA: Flex-N-Gate Llc
1306 E University Ave
Urbana IL 61802
217 384-6600

(G-13104)
WAGNER QUARRIES COMPANY
Also Called: Hanson Aggregates
4203 Milan Rd (44870-5880)
PHONE..............................419 625-8141
Chuck Cashan, *Mgr*
EMP: 24 **EST:** 1912
SQ FT: 2,400
SALES (est): 2.71MM **Privately Held**
Web: www.wagnerquarry.com
SIC: 1422 Limestones, ground

Sarahsville
Noble County

(G-13105)
BIEDENBACH LOGGING
48443 Seneca Lake Rd (43779-9732)
PHONE..............................740 732-6477
John Biedenbach, *Pt*
EMP: 6 **EST:** 1978
SALES (est): 459.58K **Privately Held**
SIC: 2411 1629 Logging camps and contractors; Earthmoving contractor

Sardinia
Brown County

(G-13106)
COCA-COLA
Also Called: Coca-Cola
136 Fairview Ave (45171-9354)
PHONE..............................937 446-4644
EMP: 7 **EST:** 2011
SALES (est): 137.63K **Privately Held**
Web: www.coca-cola.com
SIC: 2086 Bottled and canned soft drinks

(G-13107)
MANNINGS PACKING CO
100 College Ave (45171-7500)
P.O. Box 23 (45171-0023)
PHONE..............................937 446-3278
Gregory Thomas Manning, *Pt*
Robert Manning, *Pt*
EMP: 8 **EST:** 1950
SQ FT: 5,000
SALES (est): 866.61K **Privately Held**
Web: www.manningpacking.com
SIC: 2011 Meat packing plants

(G-13108)
SARDINIA READY MIX INC
9 Oakdale Ave (45171)
P.O. Box 53 (45171-0053)
PHONE..............................937 446-2523
David Taylor, *Pr*
Charles Taylor, *VP*
Cheryl Taylor, *Sec*
EMP: 22 **EST:** 1951
SQ FT: 2,000
SALES (est): 3.71MM **Privately Held**
Web: www.sardiniareadymix.com
SIC: 3273 Ready-mixed concrete

Sardinia - Brown County (G-13109)

(G-13109)
SEAN ISON LOGGING LLC
1740 State Route 321 (45171-8462)
PHONE......................740 835-7222
Sean Ison, *Prin*
EMP: 7 EST: 2016
SALES (est): 236.75K Privately Held
SIC: 2411 Logging camps and contractors

Sardis
Monroe County

(G-13110)
APPALACHIAN OILFIELD SVCS LLC
34602 State Route 7 (43946-8704)
P.O. Box 430 (45767-0430)
PHONE......................337 216-0066
EMP: 13 EST: 2015
SALES (est): 2.59MM Privately Held
SIC: 1389 Oil field services, nec

Scio
Harrison County

(G-13111)
M3 MIDSTREAM LLC
Also Called: Harrison Hub
37950 Crimm Rd (43988-8761)
PHONE......................740 945-1170
EMP: 34
SALES (corp-wide): 57MM Privately Held
Web: www.momentummidstream.com
SIC: 1382 Oil and gas exploration services
PA: M3 Midstream Llc
    600 Travis St Ste 5600
    Houston TX 77002
    713 783-3000

(G-13112)
SCIO LAMINATED PRODUCTS INC
117 Fowler Ave (43988-9779)
P.O. Box 6561 (26003-0627)
PHONE......................740 945-1321
W Quay Mull Ii, *Ch Bd*
Terry Call, *
Michael Piazza, *
Wqm Industries, *Stockholder*
Charles J Kaiser Junior, *Prin*
EMP: 10 EST: 1946
SQ FT: 70,000
SALES (est): 116.54K Privately Held
SIC: 2541 Table or counter tops, plastic laminated

(G-13113)
UTICA EAST OHIO MIDSTREAM LLC
117 Fowler Ave (43988-9779)
PHONE......................740 945-2226
EMP: 7 EST: 2013
SALES (est): 854.01K Privately Held
SIC: 1382 Oil and gas exploration services

Seaman
Adams County

(G-13114)
ALL WAYS GREEN LAWN & TURF LLC
1856 Greenbrier Rd (45679-9552)
PHONE......................937 763-4766
EMP: 7 EST: 2008
SALES (est): 569.94K Privately Held
SIC: 2875 0781 Fertilizers, mixing only; Landscape services

(G-13115)
RJS MACHINE SHOP SERVICES LLC
720 Pondlick Rd (45679-9504)
PHONE......................937 927-0137
Richard Jones, *Prin*
EMP: 7 EST: 2004
SALES (est): 241.82K Privately Held
SIC: 3599 Machine shop, jobbing and repair

Sebring
Mahoning County

(G-13116)
AMERICANA GLASS CO INC
356 E Maryland Ave (44672-1518)
P.O. Box 310 (44672-0310)
PHONE......................330 938-6135
Joan Mercer, *Pr*
James Puckett, *Sec*
EMP: 10 EST: 1988
SQ FT: 7,500
SALES (est): 836.71K
SALES (corp-wide): 3.92MM Privately Held
SIC: 3231 3262 Decorated glassware: chipped, engraved, etched, etc.; Vitreous china table and kitchenware
PA: Americana Art China Co., Inc.
    316 Manito Trl
    Mercer PA 16137
    330 938-6133

(G-13117)
APEX CONTROL SYSTEMS INC
751 N Johnson Rd (44672-1011)
P.O. Box 66 (44672-0066)
PHONE......................330 938-2588
EMP: 65 EST: 1992
SALES (est): 12MM Privately Held
Web: www.apexcontrol.com
SIC: 3625 8748 3676 3643 Electric controls and control accessories, industrial; Business consulting, nec; Electronic resistors; Current-carrying wiring services

(G-13118)
BINOS INC
700 W Ohio Ave (44672-1003)
PHONE......................330 938-0888
Bryan Rohrer, *CEO*
EMP: 8
SALES (est): 803.63K Privately Held
SIC: 3556 5812 Food products machinery; Pizza restaurants

(G-13119)
CIRCLE MACHINE ROLLS INC
245 W Kentucky Ave (44672-1909)
PHONE......................330 938-9010
Peter Kuhlmann, *Pr*
Ken Kuhlmann, *
Brenda Reed, *
▲ EMP: 27 EST: 1965
SQ FT: 15,000
SALES (est): 3.08MM Privately Held
Web: www.rollsbycircle.com
SIC: 3599 3547 Machine shop, jobbing and repair; Rolling mill machinery

(G-13120)
FOUNDRY SAND SERVICE LLC
20455 Lake Park Blvd (44672-1771)
P.O. Box 262 (44672-0262)
PHONE......................330 823-6152
Jim Budd, *Dir*
EMP: 13 EST: 2015
SALES (est): 1.26MM Privately Held
Web: www.foundrysands.com
SIC: 1442 Construction sand and gravel

(G-13121)
M PI LABEL SYSTEMS
450 Courtney Rd (44672-1339)
P.O. Box 70 (44672-0070)
PHONE......................330 938-2134
Randy Kocher, *Pr*
Carson Mc Neely, *Pr*
Donald J Mcdanial, *Pr*
Joe Skiba, *Treas*
EMP: 6 EST: 1991
SALES (est): 290.4K Privately Held
Web: www.mpilabels.com
SIC: 2759 2754 3565 Labels and seals: printing, nsk; Labels: gravure printing; Labeling machines, industrial

(G-13122)
MILLER PRODUCTS INC (PA)
Also Called: M P I Label Systems
450 Courtney Rd (44672-1339)
P.O. Box 70 (44672-0070)
PHONE......................330 938-2134
EMP: 160 EST: 1968
SALES (est): 70.41MM
SALES (corp-wide): 70.41MM Privately Held
Web: www.mpilabels.com
SIC: 2672 Adhesive papers, labels, or tapes: from purchased material

(G-13123)
MODERN CHINA COMPANY INC (PA)
550 E Ohio Ave (44672-1642)
P.O. Box 309 (44672-0309)
PHONE......................330 938-6104
Debbie Grindley, *Pr*
EMP: 35 EST: 1959
SQ FT: 27,000
SALES (est): 2.39MM
SALES (corp-wide): 2.39MM Privately Held
Web: www.modernchinasouv.com
SIC: 5947 3229 3263 Souvenirs; Glassware, art or decorative; Semivitreous table and kitchenware

(G-13124)
MPI LABELS OF BALTIMORE INC (HQ)
Also Called: Mpi Label Systems.
450 Courtney Rd (44672-1339)
P.O. Box 70 (44672-0070)
PHONE......................330 938-2134
EMP: 47 EST: 2010
SQ FT: 110,000
SALES (est): 10.64MM
SALES (corp-wide): 70.41MM Privately Held
Web: www.mpilabels.com
SIC: 2759 2754 3565 Labels and seals: printing, nsk; Labels: gravure printing; Labeling machines, industrial
PA: Miller Products, Inc.
    450 Courtney Rd
    Sebring OH 44672
    330 938-2134

(G-13125)
REFRACTORY SPECIALTIES INC
Also Called: Unifrax Sebring S Operations
230 W California Ave (44672-1920)
PHONE......................330 938-2101
Richard F Wilk Junior, *Pr*
Suhas Patil, *
Jim Vaughn, *
▲ EMP: 49 EST: 1992
SQ FT: 55,000
SALES (est): 12.83MM Privately Held
Web: www.rsifibre.com

SIC: 3296 3823 3297 Mineral wool; Process control instruments; Graphite refractories: carbon bond or ceramic bond
PA: Unifrax Holding Co.
    600 Riverwalk Pkwy
    Tonawanda NY 14150

(G-13126)
SEBRING FLUID POWER CORP
513 N Johnson Rd (44672-1007)
P.O. Box 6 (44672-0006)
PHONE......................330 938-9984
Paul Mc Guire, *Pr*
Stan Ware, *Treas*
EMP: 7 EST: 1986
SQ FT: 10,000
SALES (est): 482.72K Privately Held
SIC: 3599 3593 Machine shop, jobbing and repair; Fluid power cylinders and actuators

(G-13127)
TRUCUT INCORPORATED (PA)
1145 Allied Dr (44672-1355)
PHONE......................330 938-9806
David Gano, *Pr*
Larry Grossi, *Ex VP*
▲ EMP: 53 EST: 1968
SQ FT: 85,000
SALES (est): 11.86MM
SALES (corp-wide): 11.86MM Privately Held
Web: www.trucut.com
SIC: 3544 3542 3469 3613 Special dies and tools; Machine tools, metal forming type; Metal stampings, nec; Control panels, electric

(G-13128)
UNITED DIE & MFG SALES CO
100 S 17th St (44672-1914)
P.O. Box 38 (44672-0038)
PHONE......................330 938-6141
Gary Close, *Pr*
Dennis Close, *
EMP: 30 EST: 1951
SQ FT: 40,000
SALES (est): 2.44MM Privately Held
Web: www.uniteddiemfg.com
SIC: 3429 3469 Hardware, nec; Stamping metal for the trade

(G-13129)
VACUFORM INC
500 Courtney Rd (44672-1349)
P.O. Box 117 (44672-0117)
PHONE......................330 938-9674
Michael Hubbs, *VP*
▲ EMP: 35 EST: 1998
SQ FT: 50,000
SALES (est): 5.09MM Privately Held
Web: www.vacuforminc.com
SIC: 3297 Nonclay refractories
HQ: Unifrax I Llc
    600 Riverwalk Pkwy Ste 120
    Tonawanda NY 14150

Senecaville
Guernsey County

(G-13130)
PAUL YODER
13051 Deerfield Rd (43780-9406)
PHONE......................740 439-5811
Paul Yoder, *Owner*
EMP: 6 EST: 1998
SQ FT: 6,500
SALES (est): 487.83K Privately Held
Web: www.yoderbuilding.com

SIC: 2542 Cabinets: show, display, or storage: except wood

Seven Hills
Cuyahoga County

(G-13131)
RENT-A-MOM INC
4531 Hillside Rd (44131-4611)
PHONE...................................216 901-9599
Linda Delaney, Pr
EMP: 6 EST: 1998
SALES (est): 117.47K Privately Held
Web: www.rentamominc.com
SIC: 3635 Household vacuum cleaners

Seven Mile
Butler County

(G-13132)
ENCORE PRECAST LLC
416 W Ritter (45062)
P.O. Box 380 (45062-0380)
PHONE...................................513 726-5678
Charles Ehlers, Prin
EMP: 35 EST: 2001
SALES (est): 11.23MM Privately Held
Web: www.encoreprecastllc.com
SIC: 3272 5032 5211 Septic tanks, concrete; Concrete and cinder building products; Concrete and cinder block

Seville
Medina County

(G-13133)
4-B WOOD SPECIALTIES INC
Also Called: 4-B Wood Custom Cabinets
255 W Greenwich Rd (44273-8876)
PHONE...................................330 769-2188
Kurt E Grassell, Pr
Tracy Romanotto, Off Mgr
EMP: 14 EST: 1976
SQ FT: 17,000
SALES (est): 392.95K Privately Held
Web: www.4bwood.com
SIC: 2434 Wood kitchen cabinets

(G-13134)
ALLIED POLYMERS
21 Mill St (44273-9164)
P.O. Box 154 (44273-0154)
PHONE...................................330 975-4200
Edward Jospeh, Pt
Edward Jospeh, Pt
EMP: 8 EST: 1992
SALES (est): 870.12K Privately Held
SIC: 2822 Ethylene-propylene rubbers, EPDM polymers

(G-13135)
BENCHMARK CRAFTSMAN INC
Also Called: Benchmark Craftsmen
4700 Greenwich Rd (44273-8848)
PHONE...................................866 313-4700
Nathan Sublett, Pr
EMP: 30 EST: 2002
SALES (est): 4.49MM Privately Held
Web: benchmark.us.com
SIC: 7389 3993 Exhibit construction by industrial contractors; Displays and cutouts, window and lobby

(G-13136)
BIG WHEELS LEASING LLC
4970 Park Ave W (44273-9376)
PHONE...................................330 769-1594
EMP: 7 EST: 2011
SALES (est): 373.12K Privately Held
SIC: 3312 Blast furnaces and steel mills

(G-13137)
BLAIR RUBBER COMPANY
5020 Enterprise Pkwy (44273)
PHONE...................................330 769-5583
John M Glenn, CEO
◆ EMP: 65 EST: 1981
SQ FT: 50,000
SALES (est): 13.43MM
SALES (corp-wide): 1.26B Privately Held
Web: www.blairrubber.com
SIC: 3069 3535 Linings, vulcanizable rubber; Belt conveyor systems, general industrial use
HQ: Goldis Enterprises, Inc.
   120 Hay Rd
   Wilmington DE 19809
   302 764-3100

(G-13138)
BLAIR SALES INC
Also Called: Blair Rubber
5020 Enterprise Pkwy (44273-8960)
PHONE...................................330 769-5586
Yedidia Koschitzky, Pr
EMP: 67 EST: 2017
SALES (est): 3.91MM Privately Held
Web: www.blairrubber.com
SIC: 2822 Silicone rubbers

(G-13139)
BLEACHTECH LLC
320 Ryan Rd (44273-9109)
PHONE...................................216 921-1980
Richard Immerman, Managing Member
Richard Immerman, Pr
Benjamin Calkins, *
EMP: 25 EST: 2002
SALES (est): 9.96MM Privately Held
Web: www.bleachtech.com
SIC: 7349 2819 5169 Chemical cleaning services; Bleaching powder, lime bleaching compounds; Chemicals and allied products, nec

(G-13140)
BOB SUMEREL TIRE CO INC
8692 Lake Rd (44273-9000)
PHONE...................................330 769-9092
Jason Negray, Brnch Mgr
EMP: 11
SALES (corp-wide): 97.34MM Privately Held
Web: www.bobsumereltire.com
SIC: 5531 7534 7537 7538 Automotive tires; Tire retreading and repair shops; Automotive transmission repair shops; General automotive repair shops
PA: Bob Sumerel Tire Co., Inc.
   1257 Cox Ave
   Erlanger KY 41018
   859 283-2700

(G-13141)
COMDESS COMPANY INC
8733 Wooster Pike Rd (44273-9363)
P.O. Box 91 (44273-0091)
PHONE...................................330 769-2094
Sam Mandich, Pr
▲ EMP: 21 EST: 1981
SQ FT: 25,000
SALES (est): 835.64K Privately Held
Web: www.comdess.com
SIC: 3089 Thermoformed finished plastics products, nec

(G-13142)
HYLOAD INC (DH)
5020 Enterprise Pkwy (44273-8960)
PHONE...................................330 336-6604
Dave Jentzsch, Pr
▼ EMP: 7 EST: 1982
SQ FT: 40,000
SALES (est): 5.82MM
SALES (corp-wide): 1.26B Privately Held
Web: www.hyload.com
SIC: 3069 2952 Roofing, membrane rubber; Asphalt felts and coatings
HQ: Iko Holdings Plc
   Carthusian Ct
   London EC1M

(G-13143)
ISLAND DELIGHTS INC
240 W Greenwich Rd (44273-8878)
P.O. Box 187 (44273-0187)
PHONE...................................866 887-4100
James Murray, Pr
Greg Miller, VP
EMP: 8 EST: 2009
SQ FT: 12,000
SALES (est): 943.59K Privately Held
Web: www.islanddelights.com
SIC: 5441 2064 Candy; Candy and other confectionery products

(G-13144)
JJ SEVILLE LLC
Also Called: Seville Bronze
22 Milton St (44273-9316)
P.O. Box 45 (44273-0045)
PHONE...................................330 769-2071
EMP: 17 EST: 2009
SALES (est): 11.94MM Privately Held
Web: www.sevillebronze.com
SIC: 3351 Bronze rolling and drawing

(G-13145)
STELLAR GROUP INC
4935 Enterprise Pkwy (44273-8930)
PHONE...................................330 769-8484
Dennis Rowbotham, Contrlr
EMP: 17 EST: 2017
SALES (est): 2.3MM Privately Held
Web: www.stellargroupinc.com
SIC: 2899 Corrosion preventive lubricant

Shadyside
Belmont County

(G-13146)
KNIGHT MANUFACTURING CO INC
Also Called: Belmont Stamping
E 40th St (43947)
P.O. Box 98 (43947-0098)
PHONE...................................740 676-5516
EMP: 6
SALES (corp-wide): 2.37MM Privately Held
SIC: 3444 3469 3589 Sheet metalwork; Metal stampings, nec; Garbage disposers and compactors, commercial
PA: Knight Manufacturing Co Inc
   399 E 40th St
   Shadyside OH 43947
   740 676-9532

(G-13147)
KNIGHT MANUFACTURING CO INC (PA)
399 E 40th St (43947-1206)
P.O. Box 27 (43947-0027)
PHONE...................................740 676-9532
David Knight, Pr
EMP: 10 EST: 1935
SQ FT: 140,000
SALES (est): 2.37MM
SALES (corp-wide): 2.37MM Privately Held
SIC: 3599 3469 Machine shop, jobbing and repair; Boxes: tool, lunch, mail, etc.: stamped metal

(G-13148)
NEW CUT TOOL AND MFG CORP
1 New Cut Road (43947)
P.O. Box 8 (43947-0008)
PHONE...................................740 676-1666
Michael Koonce, Pr
Cynthia Badia, VP
EMP: 10 EST: 1979
SQ FT: 2,700
SALES (est): 858.37K Privately Held
SIC: 3599 Machine shop, jobbing and repair

Shaker Heights
Cuyahoga County

(G-13149)
ACORN TECHNOLOGY CORPORATION
3176 Morley Rd (44122)
PHONE...................................216 663-1244
Lalana Green, Pr
Robert Green, VP
EMP: 20 EST: 1993
SALES (est): 2.2MM Privately Held
Web: www.perfectdomain.com
SIC: 3613 5063 3634 3429 Panel and distribution boards and other related apparatus; Electrical apparatus and equipment; Ceiling fans; Aircraft & marine hardware, inc. pulleys & similar items

(G-13150)
BAKER STORE EQUIPMENT COMPANY
23449 Laureldale Rd (44122-2106)
EMP: 10 EST: 1956
SALES (est): 1.19MM Privately Held
Web: www.bakerstorequip.com
SIC: 2541 Store fixtures, wood

(G-13151)
C-MOLD INC
22251 Mccauley Rd (44122-2713)
EMP: 25 EST: 1993
SQ FT: 21,500
SALES (est): 844.91K Privately Held
Web: www.cmold.net
SIC: 3089 Injection molding of plastics

(G-13152)
CELLULAR TECHNOLOGY LIMITED
Also Called: Ctl Analyzers
20521 Chagrin Blvd Ste 200 (44122-5350)
PHONE...................................216 791-5084
EMP: 40 EST: 1998
SQ FT: 30,000
SALES (est): 8.75MM Privately Held
Web: www.immunospot.com
SIC: 8071 3821 Medical laboratories; Clinical laboratory instruments, except medical and dental

(G-13153)
CTL ANALYZERS LLC (PA)
Also Called: Cellular Technology Ltd
20521 Chagrin Blvd Ste 200 (44122-5350)
PHONE...................................216 791-5084
EMP: 47 EST: 1999
SALES (est): 5MM Privately Held
Web: www.immunospot.com

Shaker Heights - Cuyahoga County (G-13154)

SIC: 3845 Electromedical equipment

(G-13154)
FULLGOSPEL PUBLISHING
16781 Chagrin Blvd Ste 134 (44120-3721)
P.O. Box 201331 (44120-8105)
PHONE...................................216 339-1973
Kathy Brown, *Owner*
EMP: 10 EST: 2018
SALES (est): 423.86K **Privately Held**
Web: www.fullgospelpublishing.com
SIC: 2741 Miscellaneous publishing

(G-13155)
LEGATUM PROJECT INC
15820 Van Aken Blvd # 102 (44120-5343)
PHONE...................................216 533-8843
Erika Neeson, *Pr*
EMP: 6 EST: 2017
SALES (est): 76.15K **Privately Held**
SIC: 2741 Internet publishing and broadcasting

(G-13156)
MODEL MEDICAL LLC
3429 Lee Rd Apt 12 (44120-3652)
PHONE...................................216 972-0573
EMP: 10 EST: 2020
SALES (est): 397.72K **Privately Held**
SIC: 2326 Medical and hospital uniforms, men's

(G-13157)
MOLD MASTERS INC
18224 Fernway Rd (44122-3434)
PHONE...................................216 561-6653
Igor Rae, *Prin*
EMP: 7 EST: 2005
SALES (est): 188.14K **Privately Held**
Web: www.moldmastersneo.com
SIC: 3543 Industrial patterns

(G-13158)
PURUSHEALTH LLC
3558 Lee Rd (44120-5123)
PHONE...................................800 601-0580
John Huff, *CEO*
EMP: 11 EST: 2011
SALES (est): 792.27K **Privately Held**
SIC: 2099 Food preparations, nec

Shandon
Butler County

(G-13159)
CARTESSA CORP
4825 Cincinnati Brookville Rd (45063-5000)
P.O. Box 190 (45063-0190)
PHONE...................................513 738-4477
Darryl Kristof, *Pr*
Kathleen Kristof, *VP*
▼ EMP: 17 EST: 1975
SQ FT: 5,000
SALES (est): 3.15MM **Privately Held**
Web: www.cartessa.com
SIC: 3672 5065 Printed circuit boards; Electronic parts and equipment, nec

(G-13160)
DIAMOND TRAILERS INC
Also Called: Diamond Heavy Haul
5045 Cincinnati-Brookville Rd (45063)
P.O. Box 146 (45063-0146)
PHONE...................................513 738-4500
Tonya Engel, *Pr*
Steven J Engel, *Pr*
EMP: 13 EST: 1997
SQ FT: 92,000
SALES (est): 759.62K **Privately Held**
Web: www.diamondheavyhaul.com
SIC: 3715 Truck trailers

(G-13161)
TRI STATE EQUIPMENT COMPANY
5009 Cincinnati-Brookville Rd (45063)
P.O. Box 155 (45063-0155)
PHONE...................................513 738-7227
Kevin Hughes, *Pr*
EMP: 6 EST: 1973
SQ FT: 5,000
SALES (est): 635K **Privately Held**
SIC: 5084 7699 7359 3563 Industrial machinery and equipment; Aircraft and heavy equipment repair services; Equipment rental and leasing, nec; Spraying outfits: metals, paints, and chemicals (compressor)

Sharon Center
Medina County

(G-13162)
ATC LEGACY INC
Also Called: Aerotorque Corporation
1441 Wolf Creek Trail (44274)
P.O. Box 305 (44274-0305)
PHONE...................................330 590-8105
David Heidenreich, *Pr*
Doug Herr, *Genl Mgr*
EMP: 6 EST: 2007
SALES (est): 2.78MM
SALES (corp-wide): 4.77B **Publicly Held**
Web: www.pttech.com
SIC: 3566 Speed changers, drives, and gears
HQ: Ebog Legacy, Inc.
1441 Wolf Creek Trl
Sharon Center OH 44274
330 239-4933

(G-13163)
BEAUFORT RFD INC
1420 Wolf Creek Trl (44274)
P.O. Box 359 (44274-0359)
PHONE...................................330 239-4331
▲ EMP: 17 EST: 1996
SQ FT: 62,000
SALES (est): 12.19MM **Privately Held**
Web: www.rfdbeaufortmarine.com
SIC: 3842 Life preservers, except cork and inflatable
HQ: Survitec Group (Usa), Inc.
1420 Wolfcreek Trl
Sharon Center OH 44274

(G-13164)
CAREY COLOR INC
6835 Ridge Rd (44274)
PHONE...................................330 239-1835
Gary Moravcik, *Pr*
Russell Kotalac, *VP*
Ebert Libbey, *Quality Control*
EMP: 60 EST: 1978
SQ FT: 19,000
SALES (est): 9.31MM **Privately Held**
Web: www.careyweb.com
SIC: 2759 Commercial printing, nec

(G-13165)
CELL-O-CORE CO
6935 Ridge Rd (44274)
P.O. Box 342 (44274-0342)
PHONE...................................330 239-4370
Lino Abram, *CEO*
David C Nelson, *
Craig Cook, *
Tom Allen, *
▲ EMP: 50 EST: 1941
SQ FT: 50,000
SALES (est): 9.8MM **Privately Held**
Web: www.cellocore.com
SIC: 3089 Extruded finished plastics products, nec

(G-13166)
EBOG LEGACY INC (HQ)
Also Called: Ebo Group, Inc.
1441 Wolf Creek Trail (44274)
P.O. Box 305 (44274-0305)
PHONE...................................330 239-4933
Keith Nichols, *CEO*
David Given, *Ch Bd*
EMP: 96 EST: 1977
SQ FT: 12,200
SALES (est): 24.61MM
SALES (corp-wide): 4.77B **Publicly Held**
Web: www.ebogroupinc.com
SIC: 3568 3542 3714 3566 Clutches, except vehicular; Brakes, metal forming; Motor vehicle parts and accessories; Speed changers, drives, and gears
PA: The Timken Company
4500 Mount Pleasant St Nw
North Canton OH 44720
234 262-3000

(G-13167)
SHARON MANUFACTURING INC
6867 Ridge Rd (44274)
P.O. Box 119 (44274-0119)
PHONE...................................330 239-1561
John Beres, *Pr*
Tom Klimchak, *Opers Mgr*
EMP: 20 EST: 1970
SQ FT: 22,000
SALES (est): 2.4MM **Privately Held**
Web: www.sharonmfg.net
SIC: 3443 3441 Metal parts; Fabricated structural metal

(G-13168)
SURVITEC GROUP (USA) INC (DH)
1420 Wolfcreek Trl (44274)
P.O. Box 359 (44274-0359)
PHONE...................................330 239-4331
David Abbott, *Pr*
Gerald Chunat, *
Roseann Ziraks, *
D J Wilman, *Asst VP*
Doug Baxter, *
▼ EMP: 9 EST: 2006
SALES (est): 31.34MM **Privately Held**
SIC: 3069 Pontoons, rubber
HQ: Survitec Group Limited
Aviator Industrial Park
Ellesmere Port CH65
151 670-9009

(G-13169)
TILT 15 INC
1440 Wolf Creek Trl (44274)
PHONE...................................330 239-4192
James Ankoviak, *Pr*
Tom Lorick, *
Dan Sharpe, *
Kc Corbett-chaney, *CFO*
▲ EMP: 97 EST: 1993
SALES (est): 14.26MM **Privately Held**
SIC: 3842 Surgical appliances and supplies
PA: Winco Mfg., Llc
5516 Sw 1st Ln
Ocala FL 34474

Sharonville
Hamilton County

(G-13170)
ARI PHOENIX INC (PA)
11163 Woodward Ln (45241-1856)
PHONE...................................513 229-3750
Gareth Hudson, *CEO*
James Mock, *
EMP: 27 EST: 2015
SALES (est): 9.33MM
SALES (corp-wide): 9.33MM **Privately Held**
Web: www.ari-hetra.com
SIC: 3536 3564 Hoists; Exhaust fans: industrial or commercial

(G-13171)
KUTOL PRODUCTS COMPANY INC (PA)
100 Partnership Way (45241-1571)
PHONE...................................513 527-5500
Joseph W Rhodenbaugh, *Pr*
Tom Rhodenbaugh, *VP*
▲ EMP: 96 EST: 1912
SQ FT: 160,000
SALES (est): 23.86MM
SALES (corp-wide): 23.86MM **Privately Held**
Web: www.kutol.com
SIC: 2841 Soap: granulated, liquid, cake, flaked, or chip

(G-13172)
KUTOL PRODUCTS COMPANY INC
11955 Enterprise Dr (45241-1513)
PHONE...................................513 527-5500
EMP: 44
SALES (corp-wide): 23.86MM **Privately Held**
Web: www.kutol.com
SIC: 2841 Soap: granulated, liquid, cake, flaked, or chip
PA: Kutol Products Company, Inc.
100 Partnership Way
Sharonville OH 45241
513 527-5500

(G-13173)
SAFRAN USA INC
300 E Business Way (45241-2384)
PHONE...................................513 247-7000
EMP: 207
SALES (corp-wide): 781.02MM **Privately Held**
Web: www.safran-group.com
SIC: 3621 Motors and generators
HQ: Safran Usa, Inc.
700 S Washington St # 320
Alexandria VA 22314
703 351-9898

(G-13174)
USUI INTERNATIONAL CORPORATION
88 Partnership Way (45241-1507)
PHONE...................................513 448-0410
Haruyasu Ito, *Pr*
EMP: 230
Web: www.usuiusa.com
SIC: 3714 Connecting rods, motor vehicle engine
HQ: Usui International Corporation
44780 Helm St
Plymouth MI 48170
734 354-3626

GEOGRAPHIC SECTION

Shelby - Richland County (G-13195)

(G-13175)
WORKHORSE GROUP INC (PA)
Also Called: Workhorse
3600 Park 42 Dr Ste 160e (45241-4039)
PHONE..................................888 646-5205
EMP: 64 **EST:** 2007
SALES (est): 13.09MM **Publicly Held**
Web: www.workhorse.com
SIC: 3714 Motor vehicle parts and accessories

(G-13176)
WORKHORSE TECHNOLOGIES INC
3600 Park 42 Dr Ste 160 (45241-4039)
PHONE..................................888 646-5205
Richard Dauch, *CEO*
Martin J Rucidlo, *Pr*
Julio C Rodriguez, *CFO*
EMP: 45 **EST:** 2007
SALES (est): 1.98MM **Publicly Held**
SIC: 3711 3714 Motor vehicles and car bodies; Motor vehicle parts and accessories
PA: Workhorse Group Inc.
  3600 Park 42 Dr Ste 160e
  Sharonville OH 45241

Shawnee
Perry County

(G-13177)
SUPERIOR FIBERS INC
9702 Iron Point Rd Se (43782-9723)
P.O. Box 478 (26547-0478)
PHONE..................................740 394-2491
Robert Williams, *Dir*
EMP: 332
SALES (corp-wide): 27.53MM **Privately Held**
Web: www.superiorfibers.com
SIC: 3089 Awnings, fiberglass and plastics combination
PA: Superior Fibers, Inc.
  1333 Corporate Dr #250
  Irving TX 75038
  972 600-9953

Sheffield Lake
Lorain County

(G-13178)
ADVANCED WLDG FABRICATION INC (PA)
821 Lafayette Blvd (44054-1432)
PHONE..................................440 724-9165
Scott J Cornelius Senior, *Pr*
Scott J Cornelius Junior, *VP*
EMP: 11 **EST:** 2004
SALES (est): 600.93K
SALES (corp-wide): 600.93K **Privately Held**
SIC: 7692 Welding repair

Sheffield Village
Lorain County

(G-13179)
ADI MACHINING INC
Also Called: Advanced Design Industries
4686 French Creek Rd (44054-2716)
PHONE..................................440 277-4141
Leonard Jungbluth, *Pr*
Jerome R Winiasz, *Prin*
EMP: 21 **EST:** 1980
SQ FT: 2,500
SALES (est): 506K **Privately Held**

Web:
www.advanceddesignindustries.com
SIC: 3599 Machine shop, jobbing and repair

(G-13180)
ADVANCED DESIGN INDUSTRIES INC
Also Called: ADI
4686 French Creek Rd (44054-2716)
PHONE..................................440 277-4141
Jerome Winiasz, *Pr*
Thomas Winiasz, *
Edward J Winiasz, *
R G Brooks Junior, *Prin*
▲ **EMP:** 38 **EST:** 1955
SQ FT: 27,000
SALES (est): 2.41MM **Privately Held**
Web:
www.advanceddesignindustries.com
SIC: 3569 3599 8711 Robots, assembly line: industrial and commercial; Machine shop, jobbing and repair; Designing: ship, boat, machine, and product

(G-13181)
BENKO PRODUCTS INC
Also Called: Environmental Products Div
5350 Evergreen Pkwy (44054-2446)
PHONE..................................440 934-2180
John Benko, *Pr*
Robert Benko, *VP*
▼ **EMP:** 23 **EST:** 1983
SQ FT: 30,000
SALES (est): 7.92MM **Privately Held**
Web: www.benkoproducts.com
SIC: 3534 3567 3448 2542 Elevators and moving stairways; Industrial furnaces and ovens; Prefabricated metal buildings and components; Partitions and fixtures, except wood

(G-13182)
GREEN IMPRESSIONS LLC
842 Abbe Rd (44054-2302)
PHONE..................................440 240-8508
Joseph Schill, *Prin*
Joseph Schill, *Pr*
James P Louth, *
EMP: 62 **EST:** 2011
SALES (est): 6.46MM **Privately Held**
Web: www.mygreenimpressions.com
SIC: 7349 0782 0781 4959 Building maintenance services, nec; Lawn and garden services; Landscape services; Snowplowing

(G-13183)
HKM DRECT MKT CMMNICATIONS INC
Also Called: H K M Drect Mktg Cmmunications
2931 Abbe Rd (44054-2424)
PHONE..................................440 934-3060
Joann Tomasheski, *Mgr*
EMP: 20
SALES (corp-wide): 23.74MM **Privately Held**
Web: www.hkmdirectmarket.com
SIC: 2759 Commercial printing, nec
PA: Hkm Direct Market Communications, Inc.
  5501 Cass Ave
  Cleveland OH 44102
  800 860-4456

(G-13184)
J D INDOOR COMFORT INC
Also Called: J D Indoor Comfort Duct Clg
4040 Colorado Ave (44054-2512)
PHONE..................................440 949-8758
James Sustersic, *Pr*

EMP: 14 **EST:** 1994
SALES (est): 2.44MM **Privately Held**
Web: www.jdindoorcomfort.com
SIC: 3585 1711 Air conditioning equipment, complete; Plumbing, heating, air-conditioning

(G-13185)
MAGNA INTERNATIONAL AMER INC
Also Called: Intier Sting Systems-Lordstown
3637 Mallard Run (44054-2848)
PHONE..................................330 824-3101
Sean Ewing, *Brnch Mgr*
EMP: 108
SALES (corp-wide): 37.84B **Privately Held**
Web: www.magna.com
SIC: 3714 2531 Motor vehicle parts and accessories; Seats, automobile
HQ: Magna International Of America, Inc.
  750 Tower Dr
  Troy MI 48098

(G-13186)
NORTHFIELD
5190 Oster Rd (44054-1566)
PHONE..................................440 949-1815
EMP: 7 **EST:** 2015
SALES (est): 475.88K **Privately Held**
Web: www.northfieldblock.com
SIC: 3272 Concrete products, nec

(G-13187)
OLDCASTLE APG MIDWEST INC
Also Called: Sheffield Oldcastle
5190 Oster Rd (44054-1566)
PHONE..................................440 949-1815
Jim Jergins, *Mgr*
EMP: 25
SALES (corp-wide): 32.72B **Privately Held**
Web: www.northfieldblock.com
SIC: 3272 Concrete products, precast, nec
HQ: Oldcastle Apg Midwest, Inc.
  400 Prmter Ctr Terr Ste 1
  Atlanta GA 30346
  770 804-3363

(G-13188)
SHEFFIELD METALS CLEVELAND LLC (PA)
Also Called: Sheffield Metals International
5467 Evergreen Pkwy (44054-2400)
PHONE..................................800 283-5262
Michael Blake, *Pr*
▼ **EMP:** 10 **EST:** 2004
SALES (est): 11.1MM **Privately Held**
Web: www.sheffieldmetals.com
SIC: 3444 Sheet metalwork

(G-13189)
SHEFFIELD METALS INTL INC
5467 Evergreen Pkwy (44054-2400)
PHONE..................................440 934-8500
Mike Blake, *Pr*
David Mielcusny, *Genl Mgr*
Jill Wilson, *Pr*
▼ **EMP:** 23 **EST:** 1998
SALES (est): 8.15MM **Privately Held**
Web: www.mazzellacompanies.com
SIC: 3444 Sheet metalwork
PA: Sheffield Metals Cleveland Llc
  5467 Evergreen Pkwy
  Sheffield Village OH 44054

Shelby
Richland County

(G-13190)
AMTO ACQUISITION CORP
Also Called: American Tower

5085 State Route 39 W (44875)
P.O. Box 29 (44875)
PHONE..................................419 347-1185
Doug Schmidt, *Pr*
Dave Wagner, *VP*
EMP: 11 **EST:** 1951
SALES (est): 2.46MM **Privately Held**
Web: www.amertower.com
SIC: 3441 3448 Tower sections, radio and television transmission; Docks, prefabricated metal

(G-13191)
ARCELRMTTAL TBLAR PDTS SHLBY L
Also Called: Arcelormittal Tubular Pdts USA
132 W Main St (44875-1471)
PHONE..................................419 347-2424
Edward Vore, *CEO*
EMP: 631 **EST:** 2005
SALES (est): 131.08MM
SALES (corp-wide): 2.74B **Privately Held**
SIC: 3317 3321 Steel pipe and tubes; Gray and ductile iron foundries
HQ: Arcelormittal Tubular Products Usa Llc
  4 Gateway Ctr
  Pittsburgh PA 15222
  419 342-1200

(G-13192)
ARCELRMTTAL TBLAR PDTS USA LLC
132 W Main St (44875-1471)
PHONE..................................419 347-2424
EMP: 2255
SALES (corp-wide): 2.74B **Privately Held**
Web: tubular.arcelormittal.com
SIC: 3317 Steel pipe and tubes
HQ: Arcelormittal Tubular Products Usa Llc
  4 Gateway Ctr
  Pittsburgh PA 15222
  419 342-1200

(G-13193)
COOPER ENTERPRISES INC
89 Curtis Dr (44875-8400)
P.O. Box 50 (44875-0050)
PHONE..................................419 347-5232
EMP: 70 **EST:** 1965
SALES (est): 23.45MM **Privately Held**
Web: www.cooperenterprises.com
SIC: 5087 2452 Service establishment equipment; Prefabricated wood buildings

(G-13194)
DOFASCO TUBULAR PRODUCTS
132 W Main St (44875-1471)
PHONE..................................419 342-1371
EMP: 6 **EST:** 2019
SALES (est): 229.82K **Privately Held**
SIC: 3317 Steel pipe and tubes

(G-13195)
GB FABRICATION COMPANY
2510 Taylortown Rd (44875-8836)
PHONE..................................419 347-1835
Dave Groff, *Brnch Mgr*
EMP: 34
SALES (corp-wide): 43.56MM **Privately Held**
Web: www.gbmfg.com
SIC: 3469 3441 Metal stampings, nec; Fabricated structural metal
HQ: Gb Fabrication Company
  60 Scott St
  Shiloh OH 44878
  419 896-3191

Shelby - Richland County (G-13196)

(G-13196)
MTD PRODUCTS INC
Also Called: M T D Service Division
305 Mansfield Ave (44875-1884)
PHONE..............................419 342-6455
Jayson Goth, Mgr
EMP: 250
SALES (corp-wide): 15.78B Publicly Held
Web: www.mtdparts.com
SIC: 3524 Lawn and garden equipment
HQ: Mtd Products Inc
5965 Grafton Rd
Valley City OH 44280
330 225-2600

(G-13197)
PHILLIPS MFG AND TOWER CO (PA)
Also Called: Shelby Welded Tube Div
5578 State Route 61 N (44875)
P.O. Box 125 (44875)
PHONE..............................419 347-1720
Angela Phillip, CEO
Theresa Wallace, *
EMP: 85 EST: 1970
SQ FT: 90,000
SALES (est): 37.42MM
SALES (corp-wide): 37.42MM Privately Held
Web: www.phillipstube.com
SIC: 3312 3498 3317 7692 Tubes, steel and iron; Fabricated pipe and fittings; Steel pipe and tubes; Welding repair

(G-13198)
PREMIER TANNING & NUTRITION
35 Mansfield Ave (44875-1322)
PHONE..............................419 342-6259
Jeff Tronewett, Owner
EMP: 6 EST: 2001
SALES (est): 179.93K Privately Held
SIC: 7299 3111 5499 Tanning salon; Leather tanning and finishing; Health and dietetic food stores

(G-13199)
R S HANLINE AND CO INC (PA)
Also Called: Hanline Fresh
17 Republic Ave (44875-2142)
P.O. Box 494 (44875-0494)
PHONE..............................419 347-8077
▲ EMP: 115 EST: 1986
SALES (est): 41.64MM
SALES (corp-wide): 41.64MM Privately Held
Web: www.rshanline.com
SIC: 5141 2099 Groceries, general line; Food preparations, nec

(G-13200)
SHELBY DAILY GLOBE INC
Also Called: Daily Globe
37 W Main St (44875-1238)
P.O. Box 647 (44875-0647)
PHONE..............................419 342-4276
Scott Gove, Pr
EMP: 13 EST: 1900
SQ FT: 6,000
SALES (est): 430.79K Privately Held
Web: www.sdgnewsgroup.com
SIC: 2711 Newspapers, publishing and printing

(G-13201)
SHELBY PRINTING PARTNERS LLC
325 S Martin Dr (44875-1761)
P.O. Box 72 (44875-0072)
PHONE..............................419 342-3171
Edward I Miller, Pr
Raymond Lynch, Treas
Waye Gurney, VP
Art Cooper, Sec

EMP: 10 EST: 1954
SQ FT: 8,000
SALES (est): 452.24K Privately Held
Web: www.shelbyprintinginc.com
SIC: 2752 Offset printing

Sherwood
Defiance County

(G-13202)
QUALITY MACHINING AND MFG INC
14168 State Route 18 (43556-9774)
PHONE..............................419 899-2543
Amber C Yochum, Pr
▲ EMP: 17 EST: 1993
SQ FT: 25,000
SALES (est): 1.55MM Privately Held
Web: www.qmfittings.com
SIC: 3492 3451 3599 Fluid power valves and hose fittings; Screw machine products; Machine and other job shop work

Shiloh
Richland County

(G-13203)
GB FABRICATION COMPANY (HQ)
60 Scott St (44878-8712)
P.O. Box 8 (43515-0008)
PHONE..............................419 896-3191
EMP: 66 EST: 2014
SALES (est): 20.17MM
SALES (corp-wide): 43.56MM Privately Held
Web: www.gbmfg.com
SIC: 3469 Metal stampings, nec
PA: Gb Manufacturing Company
1120 E Main St
Delta OH 43515
419 822-5323

(G-13204)
LEON NEWSWANGER
Also Called: Newswanger Machine
7828 Planktown North Rd (44878-8906)
PHONE..............................419 896-3336
Leon Newswanger, Owner
EMP: 20 EST: 1989
SQ FT: 3,500
SALES (est): 563.9K Privately Held
SIC: 3599 1799 Machine shop, jobbing and repair; Welding on site

(G-13205)
PLYMOUTH LOCOMOTIVE SVC LLC
48 E Main St (44875-8898)
PHONE..............................419 896-2854
David A Shepherd, Prin
EMP: 7 EST: 2002
SALES (est): 990.99K Privately Held
Web: www.plymouthlocomotiveservice.com
SIC: 3312 Wheels, locomotive and car; iron and steel

(G-13206)
PROLINE TRUSS
29 Free Rd (44878-8939)
PHONE..............................419 895-9980
Paul M Reiff, Owner
EMP: 8 EST: 2003
SALES (est): 203.27K Privately Held
SIC: 2439 Trusses, wooden roof

(G-13207)
VOISARD MANUFACTURING INC
60 Scott St (44878-8712)
P.O. Box 296 (44878-0296)

PHONE..............................419 896-3191
EMP: 100
Web: m.gbfab.com
SIC: 3469 Metal stampings, nec

Shreve
Wayne County

(G-13208)
GROWERS CHOICE LTD
5505 S Elyria Rd (44676-9567)
PHONE..............................330 262-8754
Charles R Wood, Pt
EMP: 6 EST: 2007
SALES (est): 492.7K Privately Held
Web: www.growersc.com
SIC: 2499 Wood products, nec

(G-13209)
HYPONEX CORPORATION
Also Called: Scotts- Hyponex
3875 S Elyria Rd (44676-9529)
PHONE..............................330 262-1300
Dennis Tafoya, Brnch Mgr
EMP: 209
SALES (corp-wide): 3.55B Publicly Held
Web: www.suntreksolar.com
SIC: 2873 2875 Fertilizers: natural (organic), except compost; Compost
HQ: Hyponex Corporation
14111 Scottslawn Rd
Marysville OH 43040
937 644-0011

(G-13210)
I CERCO INC (PA)
Also Called: Diamonite Plant
453 W Mcconkey St (44676-9741)
PHONE..............................330 567-2145
Byron Anderson, Pr
◆ EMP: 157 EST: 2003
SQ FT: 160,000
SALES (est): 32.17MM
SALES (corp-wide): 32.17MM Privately Held
Web: www.cercocorp.com
SIC: 3567 Ceramic kilns and furnaces

(G-13211)
J & J PERFORMANCE INC
Also Called: J & J Performance Paintball
410 E Wood St (44676-9325)
PHONE..............................330 567-2455
Joseph West, Pr
EMP: 11 EST: 1988
SALES (est): 439.67K Privately Held
Web: www.jjperformance.com
SIC: 3499 7699 Nozzles, spray: aerosol, paint, or insecticide; Gun services

(G-13212)
L N BRUT MANUFACTURING CO
7300 State Route 754 (44676-9450)
PHONE..............................330 833-9045
Lynn Neiss, Pr
Dolores J Schmidt, Sec
EMP: 8 EST: 1975
SALES (est): 625.44K Privately Held
Web: www.brutmfg.com
SIC: 3589 Sandblasting equipment

(G-13213)
RED HEAD BRASS INC
643 Legion Dr (44676-9271)
PHONE..............................330 567-2903
EMP: 19 EST: 1972
SALES (est): 1.53MM Privately Held
Web: www.redheadbrass.com

SIC: 3545 3569 Tools and accessories for machine tools; Firefighting and related equipment

(G-13214)
RHBA ACQUISITIONS LLC
Also Called: Red Head Brass
643 Legion Dr (44676-9271)
P.O. Box 566 (44676-0566)
PHONE..............................330 567-2903
Edwin Dumire, *
▲ EMP: 60 EST: 2002
SQ FT: 80,000
SALES (est): 9.93MM Privately Held
Web: www.redheadbrass.com
SIC: 3569 Firefighting and related equipment

(G-13215)
SHREVE PRINTING LLC
390 E Wood St (44676-9743)
P.O. Box 605 (44676-0605)
PHONE..............................330 567-2341
EMP: 10 EST: 1958
SQ FT: 10,000
SALES (est): 443.21K Privately Held
SIC: 2752 2759 Offset printing; Letterpress printing

Sidney
Shelby County

(G-13216)
1157 DESIGNCONCEPTS LLC
210 S Lester Ave (45365-7057)
PHONE..............................937 497-1157
Evelyn Flock, Managing Member
EMP: 21 EST: 2007
SALES (est): 4.5MM Privately Held
Web: www.11fiftyseven.com
SIC: 3993 Advertising artwork

(G-13217)
A & B MACHINE INC
2040 Commerce Dr (45365-9393)
P.O. Box 540 (45365-0540)
PHONE..............................937 492-8662
Marc Gilardi, Pr
Robert L Alexander, *
Jimmy Alexander, *
EMP: 32 EST: 1988
SQ FT: 22,500
SALES (est): 4.91MM Privately Held
Web: www.aandbmachine.com
SIC: 3599 Machine shop, jobbing and repair

(G-13218)
ADVANCED COMPOSITES INC (DH)
Also Called: Sidney Plant
1062 S 4th Ave (45365-8977)
PHONE..............................937 575-9800
Seiji Oshima, Pr
Yoichi Kawai, *
Richard Lake, *
Robert Brown, *
▲ EMP: 220 EST: 1986
SQ FT: 128,000
SALES (est): 113.12MM Privately Held
Web: www.advcmp.com
SIC: 3082 3087 Unsupported plastics profile shapes; Custom compound purchased resins
HQ: Mitsui Chemicals America, Inc.
800 Westchester Ave S30
Rye Brook NY 10573

(G-13219)
ALCOA INC
2900 Campbell Rd (45365-8865)
PHONE..............................937 492-8915

GEOGRAPHIC SECTION
Sidney - Shelby County (G-13240)

EMP: 6 EST: 2019
SALES (est): 420.59K Privately Held
Web: www.alcoa.com
SIC: 3599 Industrial machinery, nec

(G-13220)
AMERICAN TRIM LLC
1501 Michigan St Ste 1 (45365-3500)
PHONE..............................419 228-1145
Mike Caughell, Mgr
EMP: 600
SALES (corp-wide): 445.1MM Privately Held
Web: www.amtrim.com
SIC: 3469 3465 Metal stampings, nec; Moldings or trim, automobile: stamped metal
HQ: American Trim, L.L.C.
1005 W Grand Ave
Lima OH 45801

(G-13221)
AMOS MEDIA COMPANY (PA)
Also Called: Coin World
1660 Campbell Rd Ste A (45365)
P.O. Box 4129 (45365)
PHONE..............................937 638-0967
Bruce Boyd, Pr
John O Amos, *
▲ EMP: 200 EST: 1876
SQ FT: 90,000
SALES (est): 37.68MM
SALES (corp-wide): 37.68MM Privately Held
Web: www.coinworld.com
SIC: 2721 2711 2796 7389 Magazines: publishing only, not printed on site; Newspapers, publishing and printing; Platemaking services; Appraisers, except real estate

(G-13222)
ANKIM ENTERPRISES INCORPORATED
2005 Campbell Rd (45365-2474)
P.O. Box 569 (43311-0569)
PHONE..............................937 599-1121
Stan Wright, Pr
Clara Wright, VP
EMP: 18 EST: 1985
SQ FT: 24,000
SALES (est): 1.18MM Privately Held
Web: www.everydaytech.com
SIC: 3678 3679 Electronic connectors; Harness assemblies, for electronic use: wire or cable

(G-13223)
AUGUSTA SPORTSWEAR INC
600 N Stolle Ave (45365-7810)
PHONE..............................937 497-7575
EMP: 7 EST: 2004
SALES (est): 118.07K Privately Held
SIC: 2329 Men's and boys' sportswear and athletic clothing

(G-13224)
AURIA SIDNEY LLC
2000 Schlater Dr (45365-8904)
PHONE..............................937 492-1225
EMP: 262 EST: 2007
SALES (est): 54.06MM Privately Held
SIC: 3714 Motor vehicle parts and accessories
HQ: Auria Solutions Usa Inc.
26999 Centrl Pk Blvd # 30
Southfield MI 48076
248 728-8000

(G-13225)
BAMAL CORP
2580 Ross St (45365-8848)
PHONE..............................937 492-9484
EMP: 8 EST: 2019
SALES (est): 446.3K Privately Held
Web: www.bamal.com
SIC: 3965 Fasteners

(G-13226)
BAUMFOLDER CORPORATION (DH)
1660 Campbell Rd (45365-2480)
PHONE..............................937 492-1281
Janice Benanzer, Pr
◆ EMP: 44 EST: 1917
SQ FT: 125,000
SALES (est): 10MM
SALES (corp-wide): 2.58B Privately Held
Web: www.baumfolder.com
SIC: 3579 7389 3554 Binding machines, plastic and adhesive; Packaging and labeling services; Folding machines, paper
HQ: Heidelberg Americas Inc
1000 Gutenberg Dr Nw
Kennesaw GA 30144

(G-13227)
BELL INDUSTRIAL SERVICES LLC
1553 Target Dr (45365-7330)
PHONE..............................937 507-9193
Larry Bell, Pr
EMP: 15 EST: 2014
SALES (est): 339.75K Privately Held
Web: www.bellindustrialservice.com
SIC: 7623 3589 Refrigeration service and repair; Service industry machinery, nec

(G-13228)
BLUE SKIES OPERATING CORP
1661 Saint Marys Rd (45365-9395)
PHONE..............................877 330-2354
Kristin Hicks, Mgr
EMP: 19
SALES (est): 1.91MM Privately Held
SIC: 3441 Fabricated structural metal
PA: Blue Skies Operating Corporation
2375 Kensington Dr
Columbus OH 43221
877 330-2354

(G-13229)
BRIGHT-ON POLISHING & MFG LLC
10160 Lochard Rd (45365-9230)
PHONE..............................937 489-3985
Joan R Roberts, Prin
EMP: 6 EST: 2012
SALES (est): 79.1K Privately Held
SIC: 3471 Polishing, metals or formed products

(G-13230)
CARGILL INCORPORATED
Cargill
701 S Vandemark Rd (45365-8959)
PHONE..............................937 497-4848
Jason Brewer, Mgr
EMP: 10
SALES (corp-wide): 176.74B Privately Held
Web: www.cargill.com
SIC: 2048 Prepared feeds, nec
PA: Cargill, Incorporated
15407 Mcginty Rd W
Wayzata MN 55391
800 227-4455

(G-13231)
CARGILL INCORPORATED
Cargill
2400 Industrial Dr (45365-8952)
PHONE..............................937 498-4555
Shane Soloman, Mgr
EMP: 60
SALES (corp-wide): 176.74B Privately Held
Web: www.cargill.com
SIC: 2075 2077 Soybean oil mills; Animal and marine fats and oils
PA: Cargill, Incorporated
15407 Mcginty Rd W
Wayzata MN 55391
800 227-4455

(G-13232)
CARS AND PARTS MAGAZINE
911 S Vandemark Rd (45365-8974)
P.O. Box 4129 (45365-4129)
PHONE..............................937 498-0803
Bruce Boyd, Pr
EMP: 98 EST: 1978
SALES (est): 377.09K
SALES (corp-wide): 37.68MM Privately Held
Web: www.carsandparts.com
SIC: 2721 5521 Magazines: publishing and printing; Used car dealers
PA: Amos Media Company
1660 Campbell Rd Ste A
Sidney OH 45365
937 638-0967

(G-13233)
CONFORM AUTOMOTIVE LLC
1630 Ferguson Ct (45365-9398)
PHONE..............................937 492-2708
Danielle Boisbert, Contrlr
EMP: 259
Web: www.conformgroup.com
SIC: 2396 3429 2221 Automotive trimmings, fabric; Hardware, nec; Broadwoven fabric mills, manmade
PA: Conform Automotive, Llc
32500 Telg Rd Ste 207
Bingham Farms MI 48025

(G-13234)
COPELAND ACCESS + INC
1675 Campbell Rd (45365-2479)
P.O. Box 669 (45365-0669)
PHONE..............................937 498-3802
Clinton Clay, Prin
Jan Burns, Asst VP
◆ EMP: 158 EST: 1986
SALES (est): 15.91MM
SALES (corp-wide): 8.02B Publicly Held
Web: www.copeland.com
SIC: 3823 Process control instruments
HQ: Copeland Lp
1675 Campbell Rd
Sidney OH 45365
937 498-3011

(G-13235)
COPELAND LP (HQ)
Also Called: Copeland
1675 W Campbell Rd (45365-2479)
P.O. Box 4309 (45365-4309)
PHONE..............................937 498-3011
Ross B Shuster, CEO
Richard Denuzzo, *
Marjorie Wallman, *
Art Gabbard, *
Tom Croone, *
◆ EMP: 1500 EST: 2006
SQ FT: 807,000
SALES (est): 7.13B
SALES (corp-wide): 8.02B Publicly Held
Web: www.copeland.com
SIC: 3585 Compressors for refrigeration and air conditioning equipment
PA: Blackstone Inc.
345 Park Ave
New York NY 10154
212 583-5000

(G-13236)
COPELAND LP
Condensing Unit Division
756 Brooklyn Ave (45365-9401)
P.O. Box 669 (45365-0669)
PHONE..............................937 498-3011
Tom Croone, VP
EMP: 213
SALES (corp-wide): 8.02B Publicly Held
Web: www.copeland.com
SIC: 3585 Condensers, refrigeration
HQ: Copeland Lp
1675 Campbell Rd
Sidney OH 45365
937 498-3011

(G-13237)
COPELAND LP
Design Services Network
1351 N Vandemark Rd (45365-3501)
P.O. Box 669 (45365-0669)
PHONE..............................937 498-3587
Thomas Crone, Genl Mgr
EMP: 220
SALES (corp-wide): 8.02B Publicly Held
Web: www.copeland.com
SIC: 3585 Condensers, refrigeration
HQ: Copeland Lp
1675 Campbell Rd
Sidney OH 45365
937 498-3011

(G-13238)
COPELAND SCROLL COMPRESSORS LP (DH)
Also Called: Scroll Compressors LLC
1675 Campbell Rd (45365-2479)
P.O. Box 669 (45365-0669)
PHONE..............................937 498-3066
Michael Zwayer, Pt
▲ EMP: 96 EST: 2010
SALES (est): 10.05MM
SALES (corp-wide): 8.02B Publicly Held
Web: www.copeland.com
SIC: 3823 Process control instruments
HQ: Copeland Lp
1675 Campbell Rd
Sidney OH 45365
937 498-3011

(G-13239)
COPERION FOOD EQUIPMENT LLC (DH) ✪
Also Called: Peerless Food Equipment LLC
500 S Vandemark Rd (45365-8991)
PHONE..............................937 492-4158
Ron Howard, Managing Member
Nicholas Farrell, Asst VP
EMP: 35 EST: 2022
SALES (est): 10.18MM Publicly Held
SIC: 3556 Bakery machinery
HQ: K-Tron Investment Co.
300 Delaware Ave Ste 900
Wilmington DE

(G-13240)
DAMAR PRODUCTS INC
516 Park St (45365-1346)
PHONE..............................937 492-9023
EMP: 13
SALES (corp-wide): 1.67MM Privately Held
SIC: 2448 2441 Pallets, wood; Boxes, wood
PA: Damar Products, Inc.
17222 State Route 47 E
Sidney OH 45365

Sidney - Shelby County (G-13241)

937 492-9023

(G-13241)
DETAILED MACHINING INC
2490 Ross St (45365)
PHONE.................................937 492-1264
John Bertsch, *CEO*
EMP: 42 **EST:** 1997
SQ FT: 42,000
SALES (est): 4.38MM **Privately Held**
Web: www.detailedmachining.com
SIC: 3599 Machine shop, jobbing and repair

(G-13242)
DRT AEROSPACE LLC (HQ)
1950 Campbell Rd (45365-2413)
PHONE.................................937 492-6121
EMP: 25 **EST:** 2013
SQ FT: 36,000
SALES (est): 20.72MM **Privately Held**
Web: www.drtholdingsllc.com
SIC: 3728 3724 R and D by manuf., aircraft parts and auxiliary equipment; Aircraft engines and engine parts
PA: Drt Holdings, Inc.
618 Greenmount Blvd
Dayton OH 45419

(G-13243)
DRT PRECISION MFG LLC (HQ)
1985 Campbell Rd (45365-2412)
PHONE.................................937 507-4308
EMP: 36 **EST:** 2016
SALES (est): 23.48MM **Privately Held**
Web: pm.drtholdingsllc.com
SIC: 3599 Machine shop, jobbing and repair
PA: Drt Holdings, Inc.
618 Greenmount Blvd
Dayton OH 45419

(G-13244)
EDGEWELL PERSONAL CARE LLC
1810 Progress Way (45365-8961)
PHONE.................................937 492-1057
EMP: 179
SALES (corp-wide): 2.25B **Publicly Held**
Web: www.edgewell.com
SIC: 2844 Shaving preparations
HQ: Edgewell Personal Care, Llc
1350 Tmbrlake Mnor Pkwy S
Chesterfield MO 63017
314 594-1900

(G-13245)
ELECTRO CONTROLS INC
1625 Ferguson Ct (45365-9398)
P.O. Box 539 (45365-0539)
PHONE.................................866 497-1717
Tim Geise, *Pr*
EMP: 40 **EST:** 2000
SALES (est): 10.31MM **Privately Held**
Web: www.electro-controls.com
SIC: 3613 Control panels, electric

(G-13246)
EMERSON COMMERCIAL RESIDE
1675 Campbell Rd (45365-2479)
PHONE.................................937 493-2828
EMP: 17 **EST:** 2018
SALES (est): 901.63M **Privately Held**
Web: www.copeland.com
SIC: 3823 Process control instruments

(G-13247)
EVERYDAY TECHNOLOGIES INC
324 Adams St Bldg 1 (45365-2328)
PHONE.................................937 497-7774
EMP: 11
SALES (corp-wide): 10.96MM **Privately Held**

Web: www.everydaytech.com
SIC: 3444 1761 Sheet metalwork; Sheet metal work, nec
PA: Everyday Technologies, Inc.
2005 Campbell Rd
Sidney OH 45365
937 492-4171

(G-13248)
EVERYDAY TECHNOLOGIES INC (PA)
2005 Campbell Rd (45365-2474)
PHONE.................................937 492-4171
EMP: 48 **EST:** 1929
SALES (est): 10.96MM
SALES (corp-wide): 10.96MM **Privately Held**
Web: www.everydaytech.com
SIC: 3444 Sheet metalwork

(G-13249)
FRESHWAY FOODS COMPANY INC (DH)
Also Called: Fresh and Limited
601 Stolle Ave (45365-8895)
PHONE.................................937 498-4664
Frank Gilardi Junior, *Ch Bd*
Phil Gilardi, *Pr*
Devon Beer, *CFO*
EMP: 100 **EST:** 1988
SQ FT: 90,000
SALES (est): 81.59MM **Publicly Held**
Web: www.freshwayfoods.com
SIC: 5148 2099 Vegetables, fresh; Food preparations, nec
HQ: Us Foods, Inc.
9399 W Higgins Rd Ste 500
Rosemont IL 60018

(G-13250)
G DENVER AND CO LLC
Also Called: Leroi Compressors
211 E Russell Rd (45365-1732)
PHONE.................................937 498-2555
Richard Wall, *Mgr*
EMP: 25
SALES (corp-wide): 6.88B **Publicly Held**
Web: www.gardnerdenver.com
SIC: 3563 Air and gas compressors
HQ: G. Denver And Co., Llc
800 Beaty St
Davidson NC 28036

(G-13251)
GOLDEN EAGLE AVIATION LLC
14833 Sidney Plattsville Rd (45365-8772)
PHONE.................................937 308-4709
EMP: 7 **EST:** 2008
SALES (est): 116.31K **Privately Held**
Web: we2fly.weebly.com
SIC: 3724 Aircraft engines and engine parts

(G-13252)
HEXA AMERICAS INC
1150 S Vandemark Rd (45365-3571)
PHONE.................................937 497-7900
Hideaki Tanaka, *Pr*
Takuro Miyamoto, *
John Marcum, *
▲ **EMP:** 40 **EST:** 2005
SALES (est): 8.46MM **Privately Held**
Web: www.hexa-chem.co.jp
SIC: 2821 Protein plastics

(G-13253)
HOLLOWAY SPORTSWEAR INC (DH)
2633 Campbell Rd (45365-8837)
PHONE.................................937 497-7575
◆ **EMP:** 100 **EST:** 1946
SALES (est): 71.38MM **Privately Held**

SIC: 2329 2339 2392 Men's and boys' leather, wool and down-filled outerwear; Women's and misses' outerwear, nec; Blankets: made from purchased materials
HQ: Augusta Sportswear, Inc.
425 Park W Dr
Grovetown GA 30813
706 860-4633

(G-13254)
HYDRO ALUMINUM FAYETTEVILLE
401 N Stolle Ave (45365-7806)
PHONE.................................937 492-9194
Eddie Smith, *Prin*
EMP: 10 **EST:** 2007
SALES (est): 349.28K **Privately Held**
SIC: 3354 Aluminum extruded products

(G-13255)
HYDRO EXTRUSION USA LLC
401 N Stolle Ave (45365-7806)
PHONE.................................888 935-5759
Brent Taylor, *Brnch Mgr*
EMP: 175
SIC: 3465 3479 Automotive stampings; Painting of metal products
HQ: Hydro Extrusion Usa, Llc
6250 N River Rd Ste 5000
Rosemont IL 60018

(G-13256)
IVEX PROTECTIVE PACKAGING LLC (PA)
2600 Campbell Rd (45365-8836)
P.O. Box 4699 (45365-4699)
PHONE.................................937 498-9298
Paul Gaulin, *Pr*
Tom Trauscht, *
▼ **EMP:** 25 **EST:** 2005
SALES (est): 15MM
SALES (corp-wide): 15MM **Privately Held**
Web: www.ivexpackaging.com
SIC: 3086 2429 Plastics foam products; Wrappers, excelsior

(G-13257)
KSE MANUFACTURING
175 S Lester Ave (45365-7044)
PHONE.................................937 409-9831
EMP: 11 **EST:** 2012
SALES (est): 968.66K **Privately Held**
SIC: 3369 Nonferrous foundries, nec

(G-13258)
L & F PRODUCTS
1810 Progress Way (45365-8961)
PHONE.................................937 498-4710
Charles Jacoby, *Prin*
EMP: 7 **EST:** 2010
SALES (est): 142.12K **Privately Held**
SIC: 2679 Paper products, converted, nec

(G-13259)
L & W INVESTMENTS INC
2005 Campbell Rd (45365-2474)
PHONE.................................937 492-4171
Cody Lee, *CEO*
EMP: 85 **EST:** 2020
SALES (est): 5.42MM **Privately Held**
SIC: 3444 Sheet metalwork

(G-13260)
LASERFAB TECHNOLOGIES INC
2339 Industrial Dr (45365-8100)
P.O. Box 4812 (45365-4812)
PHONE.................................937 493-0800
Jamie Ellis, *Pr*
Jeff Beigel, *Treas*
EMP: 12 **EST:** 2004
SQ FT: 22,000

SALES (est): 2.74MM **Privately Held**
Web: www.laserfabtech.com
SIC: 3441 Fabricated structural metal

(G-13261)
LOCHARD INC
Also Called: Do It Best
903 Wapakoneta Ave (45365-1409)
P.O. Box 260 (45365-0260)
PHONE.................................937 492-8811
Michael Lochard, *Pr*
Donald W Lochard, *
EMP: 75 **EST:** 1945
SQ FT: 44,500
SALES (est): 8.72MM **Privately Held**
Web: www.lochardplumbingheatingandcooling.com
SIC: 1711 5251 3599 Mechanical contractor; Hardware stores; Machine and other job shop work

(G-13262)
MASTELLER ELECTRIC MOTOR SVC
122 Lane St (45365-2323)
PHONE.................................937 492-8500
Fred Masteller, *Owner*
EMP: 6 **EST:** 1960
SQ FT: 5,000
SALES (est): 459.58K **Privately Held**
Web: www.mastellerelectric.com
SIC: 7694 5063 Electric motor repair; Motors, electric

(G-13263)
MECHANICAL GALV-PLATING CORP
933 Oak Ave (45365-1374)
P.O. Box 56 (45365-0056)
PHONE.................................937 492-3143
Tim Baker, *Pr*
John Garmhausen, *
Susan A Baker, *
▲ **EMP:** 45 **EST:** 1981
SQ FT: 40,000
SALES (est): 4.78MM **Privately Held**
Web: www.mgpcorp.com
SIC: 3471 Electroplating of metals or formed products

(G-13264)
METAL FINISHERS INC
2600 Fair Rd (45365-7532)
P.O. Box 963 (45365-0963)
PHONE.................................937 492-9175
Donald Stephens, *Pr*
Vicki Stephens, *VP*
EMP: 14 **EST:** 1975
SQ FT: 9,600
SALES (est): 508.98K **Privately Held**
Web: www.metalfinishers.com
SIC: 3471 Finishing, metals or formed products

(G-13265)
MIAMI VALLEY POLISHING LL
1317 Pinetree Ct (45365-3431)
PHONE.................................937 498-1634
EMP: 6 **EST:** 2014
SALES (est): 148.15K **Privately Held**
SIC: 3471 Polishing, metals or formed products

(G-13266)
MIAMI VALLEY POLISHING LLC
211 S Lester Ave (45365-7058)
PHONE.................................937 615-9353
Matthew Powers, *Prin*
EMP: 10 **EST:** 2008
SALES (est): 1.69MM **Privately Held**
Web: www.mvpolishing.net
SIC: 3471 Electroplating of metals or formed products

GEOGRAPHIC SECTION

Sidney - Shelby County (G-13288)

(G-13267)
MK TREMPE CORPORATION
Also Called: Elite Enclosure Company
2349 Industrial Dr (45365-8100)
P.O. Box 916 (45365-0916)
   PHONE.................................937 492-3548
Michael C Trempe, *CEO*
Michael Trempe, *Pr*
Karen Trempe, *Sec*
EMP: 43 **EST:** 2015
SQ FT: 63,000
SALES (est): 4.68MM **Privately Held**
Web: www.eliteenclosure.com
SIC: 3441 Fabricated structural metal

(G-13268)
NORCOLD LLC (HQ)
1440 N Vandemark Rd (45365-3548)
P.O. Box 180 (45365-0180)
   PHONE.................................800 543-1219
◆ **EMP:** 8 **EST:** 1960
SQ FT: 150,000
SALES (est): 5.61MM
SALES (corp-wide): 167.51MM **Privately Held**
Web: www.norcold.com
SIC: 3632 Refrigerators, mechanical and absorption: household
PA: Thetford Llc
   7101 Jackson Rd
   Ann Arbor MI 48103
   734 769-6000

(G-13269)
P&THE MFG ACQUISITION LLC ✪
Also Called: Ross Aluminum
815 Oak Ave (45365-1339)
P.O. Box 4487 (45365-4487)
   PHONE.................................937 492-4134
Pancho Hall, *CEO*
Raybon White, *CFO*
Jason Pawel, *Pr*
EMP: 57 **EST:** 2022
SALES (est): 4MM **Privately Held**
SIC: 3334 Primary aluminum

(G-13270)
PEERLESS FOODS INC
Also Called: Peerless Foods Equipment
500 S Vandemark Rd (45365-8991)
   PHONE.................................937 492-4158
Robert L Zielsdorf, *CEO*
Dane A Belden, *
Matthew J Zielsdorf, *
Robert F Zielsdorf, *Parts Vice President*
Thomas Seving, *
◆ **EMP:** 62 **EST:** 1913
SQ FT: 130,000
SALES (est): 25.93MM **Publicly Held**
Web: www.peerlessfood.com
SIC: 3556 Bakery machinery
PA: Hillenbrand, Inc.
   1 Batesville Blvd
   Batesville IN 47006

(G-13271)
PLAYTEX MANUFACTURING INC
1905 Progress Way (45365-8114)
   PHONE.................................937 498-4710
EMP: 34
SALES (corp-wide): 2.25B **Publicly Held**
SIC: 2676 Sanitary paper products
HQ: Playtex Manufacturing, Inc.
   50 N Dupont Hwy
   Dover DE 19901
   302 678-6000

(G-13272)
POLYFILL LLC
960 N Vandemark Rd (45365-3508)
   PHONE.................................937 493-0041
Dan T Moore, *Managing Member*
Richard Sczerowski, *Contrlr*
Ralph Fearnley, *Genl Mgr*
▲ **EMP:** 40 **EST:** 2009
SQ FT: 50,000
SALES (est): 8.81MM **Privately Held**
Web: www.polyfillproducts.com
SIC: 3089 Automotive parts, plastic

(G-13273)
PREFERRED PRINTING (PA)
3700 Michigan St (45365-7018)
   PHONE.................................937 492-6961
Gil Bornhorst, *Owner*
EMP: 6 **EST:** 1983
SQ FT: 2,800
SALES (est): 471.27K
SALES (corp-wide): 471.27K **Privately Held**
Web: www.printingisus.com
SIC: 2752 Offset printing

(G-13274)
QUALITY STEEL FABRICATION
2500 Fair Rd (45365-7523)
P.O. Box 905 (45365-0905)
   PHONE.................................937 492-9503
Robert P Brunswick, *Pr*
Ted Daniel, *VP Opers*
EMP: 15 **EST:** 2002
SQ FT: 25,000
SALES (est): 2.29MM **Privately Held**
Web: www.qsfab.com
SIC: 3441 3444 Fabricated structural metal; Sheet metalwork

(G-13275)
RELIABLE CASTINGS CORPORATION
1521 W Michigan St (45365)
P.O. Box 829 (45365-0829)
   PHONE.................................937 497-5217
Tom Abney, *Mgr*
EMP: 75
SQ FT: 40,000
SALES (corp-wide): 34MM **Privately Held**
Web: www.reliablecastings.com
SIC: 3363 3369 3365 Aluminum die-castings; Nonferrous foundries, nec; Aluminum foundries
PA: Reliable Castings Corporation
   3530 Spring Grove Ave
   Cincinnati OH 45223

(G-13276)
RICHARD KLINGER INC
2350 Campbell Rd (45365-9501)
P.O. Box 725 (45365-0725)
   PHONE.................................937 498-2222
Derek Leighty, *Prin*
EMP: 7 **EST:** 2012
SALES (est): 212.07K **Privately Held**
Web: www.klinger-thermoseal.com
SIC: 2295 Sealing or insulating tape for pipe: coated fiberglass

(G-13277)
RING CONTAINER TECH LLC
603 Oak Ave (45365-1335)
   PHONE.................................937 492-0961
Dennis W Koerner, *VP*
EMP: 78
SALES (corp-wide): 1.37B **Privately Held**
Web: www.ringcontainer.com
SIC: 3085 Plastics bottles
HQ: Ring Container Technologies, Llc.
   1 Industrial Park
   Oakland TN 38060
   800 280-7464

(G-13278)
ROE TRANSPORTATION ENTPS INC
3680 Michigan St (45365-9086)
   PHONE.................................937 497-7161
Chad Roe, *Prin*
EMP: 7 **EST:** 2009
SQ FT: 7,400
SALES (est): 917.16K **Privately Held**
Web: www.roeenterprisesinc.com
SIC: 2875 2499 4212 4953 Potting soil, mixed; Mulch or sawdust products, wood; Dump truck haulage; Recycling, waste materials

(G-13279)
ROSS ALUMINUM CASTINGS LLC
815 Oak Ave (45365-1317)
P.O. Box 4489 (45365-4489)
   PHONE.................................937 492-4134
Mike Francis, *Managing Member*
Robert Wyehl, *
Bob Clements, *
▲ **EMP:** 165 **EST:** 2006
SQ FT: 250,000
SALES (est): 36MM
SALES (corp-wide): 36MM **Privately Held**
Web: www.rossal.com
SIC: 3365 3543 3369 Aluminum and aluminum-based alloy castings; Industrial patterns; Nonferrous foundries, nec
PA: Advanced Metals Group, L.L.C.
   114 S Valley Rd
   Paoli PA 19301
   610 408-8006

(G-13280)
ROSS CASTING & INNOVATION LLC
Also Called: Rci
402 S Kuther Rd (45365-8870)
P.O. Box 89 (45365-0089)
   PHONE.................................937 497-4500
Sampath Ramesh, *Pr*
Wayne Thompson, *
Robert Zangri, *
Brad Hohenstein, *
▲ **EMP:** 350 **EST:** 1999
SQ FT: 120,000
SALES (est): 54.08MM **Privately Held**
Web: www.rciwheels.com
SIC: 3363 Aluminum die-castings
HQ: Abi-Showatech (India) Private Limited
   Stoneacre, No 67,
   Chennai TN 60002

(G-13281)
SCHINDLER ELEVATOR CORPORATION
Also Called: Schindler
920 S Vandemark Rd (45365-8140)
   PHONE.................................937 492-3186
Philip L Warnecke, *Mgr*
EMP: 150
SQ FT: 35,000
SALES (est): **Privately Held**
Web: www.schindler.com
SIC: 3534 Elevators and equipment
HQ: Schindler Elevator Corporation
   20 Whippany Rd
   Morristown NJ 07960
   973 397-6500

(G-13282)
SCHWANS MAMA ROSASS LLC (DH)
Also Called: Mama Rosas's
1910 Fair Rd (45365-8906)
   PHONE.................................937 498-4511
Dimitrios Smyrnios, *CEO*
EMP: 249 **EST:** 2006
SQ FT: 160,000
SALES (est): 39.69MM **Privately Held**
SIC: 2038 Pizza, frozen
HQ: Schwan's Company
   115 W College Dr
   Marshall MN 56258
   507 532-3274

(G-13283)
SCHWARZ PARTNERS PACKAGING LLC
Royal Group, The
2450 Campbell Rd (45365-7533)
   PHONE.................................317 290-1140
Jim Freisthler, *Brnch Mgr*
EMP: 15
SALES (corp-wide): 573.33MM **Privately Held**
Web: theroyalgroup.wpengine.com
SIC: 2653 3412 2671 Boxes, corrugated: made from purchased materials; Metal barrels, drums, and pails; Paper; coated and laminated packaging
HQ: Schwarz Partners Packaging, Llc
   10 W Carmel Dr Ste 300
   Carmel IN 46032
   317 290-1140

(G-13284)
SCSRM CONCRETE COMPANY LTD
4723 Hardin Wapakoneta Rd (45365-8056)
   PHONE.................................937 533-1001
Gerald Bushelman, *Pt*
EMP: 10 **EST:** 1996
SALES (est): 137.58K **Privately Held**
SIC: 3273 Ready-mixed concrete

(G-13285)
SELMCO METAL FABRICATORS INC
1615 Ferguson Ct (45365-9398)
P.O. Box 4368 (45365-4368)
   PHONE.................................937 498-1331
Tim Cotterman, *Pr*
Ron Jones, *Sec*
EMP: 18 **EST:** 1997
SQ FT: 25,000
SALES (est): 2.39MM **Privately Held**
Web: www.selmcometalfabricators.com
SIC: 3444 Sheet metal specialties, not stamped

(G-13286)
SHAFFER METAL FAB INC
2031 Commerce Dr (45365-9393)
P.O. Box 523 (45365-0523)
   PHONE.................................937 492-1384
Michael R Shaffer, *Prin*
Steve Shaffer, *Prin*
EMP: 34 **EST:** 1992
SQ FT: 45,000
SALES (est): 8.7MM **Privately Held**
Web: www.shaffermetalfab.com
SIC: 3441 3444 Fabricated structural metal; Sheet metalwork

(G-13287)
SIDNEY ALIVE
101 S Ohio Ave (45365-2716)
   PHONE.................................937 210-2539
Amy Breinich, *Admn*
EMP: 8 **EST:** 2016
SALES (est): 138.45K **Privately Held**
Web: sidneyalive.wpcomstaging.com
SIC: 2711 Newspapers: publishing only, not printed on site

(G-13288)
SIDNEY MANUFACTURING COMPANY
405 N Main Ave (45365-2345)
P.O. Box 380 (45365-0380)
   PHONE.................................937 492-4154
Jon F Baker, *Pr*
Steven Baker, *

Sidney - Shelby County (G-13289)

▼ EMP: 30 EST: 1966
SQ FT: 125,000
SALES (est): 4.55MM Privately Held
Web: www.sidneymfg.com
SIC: 3556 3444 Food products machinery; Sheet metalwork

(G-13289)
SPONSELLER GROUP INC
1516 Target Dr (45365-7332)
PHONE.................937 492-9949
Ken Hensworth, Mgr
EMP: 6
SALES (corp-wide): 11.2MM Privately Held
Web: www.sponsellergroup.com
SIC: 8711 3599 Consulting engineer; Machine shop, jobbing and repair
PA: Sponseller Group, Inc.
1600 Timber Wolf Dr
Holland OH 43528
110 061 0000

(G-13290)
STD LIQUIDATION INC
1950 Campbell Rd (45365-2413)
P.O. Box 849 (45365-0849)
PHONE.................937 492-6121
EMP: 104
SIC: 3599 3544 Machine and other job shop work; Special dies, tools, jigs, and fixtures

(G-13291)
STOLLE MACHINERY COMPANY LLC
Also Called: Stolle Machinery-Sidney
2900 Campbell Rd (45365-8864)
PHONE.................937 497-5400
Greg Butcher, Mgr
EMP: 125
SALES (corp-wide): 492.99MM Privately Held
Web: www.stollemachinery.com
SIC: 3469 2759 3542 Stamping metal for the trade; Commercial printing, nec; Machine tools, metal forming type
PA: Stolle Machinery Company, Llc
6949 S Potomac St
Centennial CO 80112
303 708-9044

(G-13292)
THERMOSEAL INC (PA)
2350 Campbell Rd (45365-9573)
PHONE.................937 498-2222
◆ EMP: 7 EST: 1994
SALES (est): 2.42MM
SALES (corp-wide): 2.42MM Privately Held
Web: www.klinger-thermoseal.com
SIC: 3053 Gasket materials

(G-13293)
VMI LIQUIDATING INC
2309 Industrial Dr (45365-8100)
P.O. Box 4129 (45365-4129)
PHONE.................937 492-3100
▲ EMP: 40
SIC: 3993 Name plates: except engraved, etched, etc.: metal

(G-13294)
WAPPOO WOOD PRODUCTS INC
Also Called: Interntnal Pckg Pallets Crates
12877 Kirkwood Rd (45365-8102)
PHONE.................937 492-1166
Thomas G Baker, Ch Bd
T Adam Baker, *
Gary O'connor, Prin
Matthew Baker, *
EMP: 40 EST: 1980

SQ FT: 21,800
SALES (est): 12.6MM Privately Held
Web: www.wappoowood.com
SIC: 5031 2435 2436 2421 Lumber: rough, dressed, and finished; Hardwood veneer and plywood; Softwood veneer and plywood; Sawmills and planing mills, general

(G-13295)
WESTERN OHIO CUT STONE LTD
1130 Dingman Slagle Rd (45365-9102)
P.O. Box 419 (45365-0419)
PHONE.................937 492-4722
Thomas Milligan, Managing Member
EMP: 12 EST: 1995
SALES (est): 1.5MM Privately Held
Web: www.westernohiocutstone.com
SIC: 3281 Cut stone and stone products

(G-13296)
WIPE OUT ENTERPRISES INC
6523 Dawson Rd (45365-8672)
PHONE.................937 497-9473
Dave Waesch, Owner
EMP: 7 EST: 2002
SALES (est): 686.98K Privately Held
Web: www.wipeoutenterprises.com
SIC: 3599 Machine shop, jobbing and repair

Silver Lake
Summit County

(G-13297)
GENESIS ONE INDUSTRIES LLC
2976 Millboro Rd (44224-2946)
PHONE.................330 842-9428
Brian Robert Mccort, Owner
EMP: 6 EST: 2018
SALES (est): 239.49K Privately Held
SIC: 3999 Manufacturing industries, nec

Smithville
Wayne County

(G-13298)
BOVILLE INDUS COATINGS INC
7459 Leichty Rd (44677-9708)
P.O. Box 487 (44677-0487)
PHONE.................330 669-8558
EMP: 25 EST: 1996
SQ FT: 30,000
SALES (est): 2.25MM Privately Held
Web: www.boville.com
SIC: 3471 3479 Sand blasting of metal parts; Coating of metals and formed products

(G-13299)
FLYING DUTCHMAN INC
6631 Egypt Rd (44677-9774)
PHONE.................330 669-2297
James Lepley, CEO
Gary Lepley, Pr
Esther Lepley, Assistant Chief Executive Officer
Kevin Lepley, VP
John Waltman, Sec
EMP: 7 EST: 1970
SQ FT: 3,600
SALES (est): 875.47K Privately Held
Web: www.flyingd.com
SIC: 3523 Silo fillers and unloaders

(G-13300)
MK METAL PRODUCTS INC
Maverick Stainless Fabrication
301 W Prospect St (44677-9516)
PHONE.................330 669-2631
Richard L Kemp, CEO

EMP: 15
SALES (corp-wide): 4.61MM Privately Held
Web: www.mkmetalproducts.com
SIC: 3441 Fabricated structural metal
PA: Mk Metal Products Enterprises, Inc.
90 Sawyer Pkwy
Mansfield OH 44903
419 756-3644

(G-13301)
RAY C SPROSTY BAG CO INC
Also Called: Sprosty
5857 Applecreek Rd (44677-9715)
P.O. Box 186 (44677-0186)
PHONE.................330 669-0045
EMP: 10 EST: 1941
SALES (est): 2.42MM Privately Held
Web: www.sprostybag.com
SIC: 5113 2759 Bags, paper and disposable plastic; Bags, plastic: printing, nsk

(G-13302)
RIVERVIEW INDUS WD PDTS INC (PA)
179 S Gilbert Dr (44677)
P.O. Box 408 (44677-0408)
PHONE.................330 669-8509
Michael Meenan, Pr
EMP: 9 EST: 1988
SQ FT: 17,000
SALES (est): 3.17MM Privately Held
Web: www.riverviewpallet.com
SIC: 2448 Pallets, wood

(G-13303)
RIVERVIEW TRANSPORT LLC
Also Called: Riverview Transport, Inc.
179 Gilbert Dr (44677)
P.O. Box 408 (44677-0408)
PHONE.................330 669-8509
EMP: 131 EST: 2012
SALES (est): 270.16K Privately Held
Web: www.riverviewpallet.com
SIC: 2448 Pallets, wood
PA: Riverview Industrial Wood Products, Inc.
179 S Gilbert Dr
Smithville OH 44677

Solon
Cuyahoga County

(G-13304)
911CELLULAR LLC
6001 Cochran Rd Ste 200 (44139-3325)
PHONE.................216 283-6100
Chad Salahshour, Managing Member
EMP: 15 EST: 2013
SALES (est): 1.56MM Privately Held
Web: www.911cellular.com
SIC: 4812 7372 Cellular telephone services; Application computer software

(G-13305)
ACLARA TECHNOLOGIES LLC
30400 Solon Rd (44139-3416)
PHONE.................440 528-7200
Gary Moore, Brnch Mgr
EMP: 104
SALES (corp-wide): 5.37B Publicly Held
Web: www.hubbell.com
SIC: 3824 3825 3829 7371 Mechanical and electromechanical counters and devices; Instruments to measure electricity; Measuring and controlling devices, nec; Custom computer programming services
HQ: Aclara Technologies Llc
77 W Port Plz Dr Ste 500
Saint Louis MO 63146
314 895-6400

(G-13306)
ADVANCED LIGHTING TECH LLC (PA)
6675 Parkland Blvd (44139)
PHONE.................888 440-2358
◆ EMP: 74 EST: 1995
SALES (est): 96.72MM Privately Held
Web: www.adlt.com
SIC: 3645 3641 3646 3648 Residential lighting fixtures; Electric lamps and parts for generalized applications; Commercial lighting fixtures; Lighting equipment, nec

(G-13307)
AEROSPACE MAINT SOLUTIONS LLC
29401 Ambina Dr (44139-3953)
PHONE.................440 729-7703
John P Dooley, Pr
John P Dooley, Managing Member
Thomas Dooley, *
Andrea Rillahan, *
Denette Ditmer, *
▲ EMP: 27 EST: 2005
SQ FT: 7,500
SALES (est): 4.82MM Privately Held
Web: www.aerospacellc.com
SIC: 3728 Aircraft parts and equipment, nec

(G-13308)
ALLEN GRAPHICS INC
Also Called: Printing Partners
27100 Richmond Rd Ste 6 (44139-1030)
PHONE.................440 349-4100
Donald J Allen, Pr
EMP: 9 EST: 1976
SQ FT: 5,000
SALES (est): 814.64K Privately Held
Web: www.allengraphics.com
SIC: 2752 2789 Offset printing; Bookbinding and related work

(G-13309)
ALLOY WELDING & FABRICATING
30340 Solon Industrial Pkwy Ste B (44139-4358)
PHONE.................440 914-0650
William Kelly, Pr
EMP: 10 EST: 1979
SQ FT: 12,000
SALES (est): 951.83K Privately Held
SIC: 3441 Fabricated structural metal

(G-13310)
ALLTECH MED SYSTEMS AMER INC
28900 Fountain Pkwy (44139-4383)
PHONE.................440 424-2240
Mark Zou, Pr
William Joliat, *
Don Russell, *
Sandra Ritchie, Finance*
▼ EMP: 39 EST: 2004
SALES (est): 6.44MM Privately Held
Web: www.alltechmedusa.com
SIC: 3845 Magnetic resonance imaging device, nuclear

(G-13311)
AMALTECH INC
30670 Bainbridge Rd (44139-2267)
PHONE.................440 248-7500
Farouk Altahawi, Pr
EMP: 6 EST: 2009
SALES (est): 395.6K Privately Held
Web: www.amaltech.com
SIC: 3494 Pipe fittings

GEOGRAPHIC SECTION
Solon - Cuyahoga County (G-13335)

(G-13312)
AMERICAN PLATINUM DOOR LLC
Also Called: Construction
30335 Solon Industrial Pkwy (44139-4325)
PHONE..............................440 497-6213
Anthony Lorello, *Managing Member*
EMP: 6 **EST:** 2019
SALES (est): 1.05MM **Privately Held**
Web: www.apdoorandgate.com
SIC: 5021 5211 3088 1751 Lockers; Home centers; Bathroom fixtures, plastics; Garage door, installation or erection

(G-13313)
AMERICAN RUBBER PDTS CO INC
30775 Solon Industrial Pkwy (44139-4338)
PHONE..............................440 461-0900
Doug Kaufman, *Pr*
EMP: 8 **EST:** 1999
SALES (est): 666.48K **Privately Held**
SIC: 3069 Molded rubber products

(G-13314)
ASPHALT FABRICS & SPECIALTIES
7710 Bond St (44139-5312)
PHONE..............................440 786-1077
Brian Reed, *Pr*
EMP: 20 **EST:** 2002
SALES (est): 1.98MM **Privately Held**
Web: www.asphaltfabrics.com
SIC: 2951 Asphalt paving mixtures and blocks

(G-13315)
B D G WRAP-TITE INC (PA)
Also Called: Wrap-Tite
6200 Cochran Rd (44139-3308)
PHONE..............................440 349-5400
Suresh Bafna, *CEO*
Sunil Daga, *
◆ **EMP:** 40 **EST:** 2004
SQ FT: 89,000
SALES (est): 23.04MM
SALES (corp-wide): 23.04MM **Privately Held**
Web: www.wraptite.com
SIC: 3069 5199 Film, rubber; Leather goods, except footwear, gloves, luggage, belting

(G-13316)
BARDONS & OLIVER INC (PA)
5800 Harper Rd (44139-1833)
PHONE..............................440 498-5800
William Beattie, *Pr*
Heath Oliver, *
James S Dalton, *
Richard Moscarino, *
Brett Baldi, *
▲ **EMP:** 120 **EST:** 1891
SQ FT: 94,000
SALES (est): 17.61MM
SALES (corp-wide): 17.61MM **Privately Held**
Web: www.bardonsoliver.com
SIC: 3549 3541 3547 3599 Metalworking machinery, nec; Lathes, metal cutting and polishing; Finishing equipment, rolling mill; Machine and other job shop work

(G-13317)
BARUDAN AMERICA INC (HQ)
Also Called: Barudan
30901 Carter St Frnt A (44139-4384)
PHONE..............................440 248-8770
Ted Yamaue, *Ch Bd*
Shin Hasegawa, *Pr*
Robert Stone, *VP*
Kevin H Hrabak, *Treas*
◆ **EMP:** 12 **EST:** 1985
SQ FT: 34,970
SALES (est): 9.07MM **Privately Held**
Web: www.barudanamerica.com
SIC: 3552 Embroidery machines
PA: Barudan Co., Ltd.
20, Azatsukakoshi, Josuiji Ichinomiya AIC 491-0

(G-13318)
BIRD ELECTRONIC CORPORATION
30303 Aurora Rd (44139-2743)
PHONE..............................440 248-1200
Terrence Grant, *Pr*
Dennis Morgan, *
Thomas L Kuklo, *General Vice President*
▲ **EMP:** 235 **EST:** 1942
SQ FT: 80,000
SALES (est): 51.98MM **Privately Held**
Web: www.birdrf.com
SIC: 3825 Test equipment for electronic and electric measurement
PA: Bird Technologies Group Inc.
30303 Aurora Rd
Solon OH 44139

(G-13319)
BIRD TECHNOLOGIES GROUP INC (PA)
30303 Aurora Rd (44139-2743)
PHONE..............................440 248-1200
EMP: 8 **EST:** 1995
SQ FT: 12,000
SALES (est): 92.97MM **Privately Held**
Web: www.birdrf.com
SIC: 3825 3669 Test equipment for electronic and electric measurement; Intercommunication systems, electric

(G-13320)
BLUE COLLAR M LLC
Also Called: Colbleu Vodka
31005 Bainbridge Rd Ste 2 (44139)
PHONE..............................216 209-5666
Ralph Faulkner, *Managing Member*
EMP: 12 **EST:** 2017
SALES (est): 750K **Privately Held**
SIC: 2085 5182 Vodka (alcoholic beverage); Liquor

(G-13321)
BOWES MANUFACTURING INC
Also Called: Tungsten and Capital
30340 Solon Industrial Pkwy Ste B (44139-4343)
PHONE..............................216 378-2110
Zelda Stutz, *Pr*
EMP: 22 **EST:** 1974
SQ FT: 30,000
SALES (est): 2.43MM **Privately Held**
Web: www.bowesmfg.com
SIC: 3568 3452 3494 3429 Couplings, shaft: rigid, flexible, universal joint, etc.; Bolts, metal; Valves and pipe fittings, nec; Clamps and couplings, hose

(G-13322)
BPI ENERGY HOLDINGS INC
30775 Bainbridge Rd Ste 280 (44139)
PHONE..............................281 556-6200
James G Azlein, *Pr*
EMP: 11 **EST:** 2005
SALES (est): 317.08K **Privately Held**
Web: www.bpi-energy.com
SIC: 1311 Crude petroleum and natural gas

(G-13323)
BRADLEY STONE INDUSTRIES LLC
30801 Carter St (44139-3517)
PHONE..............................440 519-3277
EMP: 18 **EST:** 1991
SALES (est): 4.52MM **Privately Held**
Web: www.bradley-stone.com
SIC: 1423 Crushed and broken granite

(G-13324)
BREAKER TECHNOLOGY INC
30625 Solon Industrial Pkwy (44139-4389)
PHONE..............................440 248-7168
EMP: 19
SALES (corp-wide): 4.16MM **Privately Held**
Web: www.astecindustries.com
SIC: 3532 5084 1629 Mining machinery; Hydraulic systems equipment and supplies; Trenching contractor
PA: Breaker Technology, Inc.
86470 Franklin Blvd
Eugene OR 97405
951 369-0878

(G-13325)
CALIFORNIA CREAMERY OPERATORS
30003 Bainbridge Rd (44139-2205)
PHONE..............................440 264-5351
Tim Shirley, *Ofcr*
EMP: 7 **EST:** 2014
SALES (est): 132.32K **Privately Held**
SIC: 2021 Creamery butter

(G-13326)
CARDPAK INCORPORATED
29601 Solon Rd (44139-3451)
PHONE..............................440 542-3100
EMP: 130
SIC: 2657 2752 Folding paperboard boxes; Commercial printing, lithographic

(G-13327)
CEQUENT CONSUMER PRODUCTS INC
Also Called: Cequent Consumer Products
29000 Aurora Rd Ste 2 (44139-7202)
P.O. Box 673071 (48267-3071)
PHONE..............................440 498-0001
◆ **EMP:** 85
SIC: 5531 3714 Automotive accessories; Motor vehicle parts and accessories

(G-13328)
CHANNEL PRODUCTS INC (PA)
30700 Solon Industrial Pkwy (44139-4333)
PHONE..............................440 423-0113
Teresa Hack, *Pr*
Wayne Monaco, *
James Becker, *Prin*
Suzanne French, *Prin*
Steve Marrero, *Prin*
▲ **EMP:** 70 **EST:** 1972
SQ FT: 50,000
SALES (est): 11.37MM
SALES (corp-wide): 11.37MM **Privately Held**
Web: www.channelproducts.com
SIC: 7363 3679 3643 3625 Manpower pools; Electronic circuits; Current-carrying wiring services; Relays and industrial controls

(G-13329)
CHRISTOPHER TOOL & MFG CO
30500 Carter St Frnt (44139-3580)
PHONE..............................440 248-8080
Patrick Christopher, *CEO*
Steve Fonash, *Pr*
Larry Walker, *VP*
Craig Peck, *VP Opers*
Karen Christopher, *Sec*
EMP: 102 **EST:** 1953
SQ FT: 48,500
SALES (est): 23.54MM **Privately Held**
Web: www.christophertool.com
SIC: 3599 Machine shop, jobbing and repair

(G-13330)
CMBF PRODUCTS INC
Also Called: Carbon Group, The
29001 Solon Rd (44139-3468)
PHONE..............................440 528-4000
Karl Messmer, *Pr*
EMP: 375
SALES (corp-wide): 669.66MM **Privately Held**
Web: www.carlislecbf.com
SIC: 3714 Motor vehicle brake systems and parts
HQ: Cmbf Products, Inc.
920 Lake Rd
Medina OH 44256

(G-13331)
CMC PHARMACEUTICALS INC (PA)
Also Called: CMC Consulting
30625 Solon Rd Ste G (44139-3473)
PHONE..............................216 600-9430
Mike Radomsky, *Pr*
EMP: 6 **EST:** 2014
SQ FT: 1,000
SALES (est): 1.56MM
SALES (corp-wide): 1.56MM **Privately Held**
Web: www.cmcpharm.com
SIC: 2834 Druggists' preparations (pharmaceuticals)

(G-13332)
CO-AX TECHNOLOGY INC
30301 Emerald Valley Pkwy (44139-4394)
PHONE..............................440 914-9200
Gholam Hosein Varghai, *Pr*
Hassan Varghai, *
EMP: 250 **EST:** 1993
SQ FT: 22,000
SALES (est): 45.93MM **Privately Held**
Web: www.coaxinc.com
SIC: 3672 3679 Printed circuit boards; Harness assemblies, for electronic use: wire or cable

(G-13333)
COCHRAN 6573 LLC
6573 Cochran Rd Ste I (44139)
PHONE..............................440 349-4900
Carr F Briggs, *Managing Member*
▲ **EMP:** 15 **EST:** 2006
SALES (est): 985.34K **Privately Held**
Web: www.cadaudio.com
SIC: 3651 Microphones

(G-13334)
CUSTOM PRODUCTS CORPORATION (PA)
7100 Cochran Rd (44139-4306)
PHONE..............................440 528-7100
Timothy Stepanek, *Pr*
John Stepanek, *
William Stepanek Junior, *VP*
▲ **EMP:** 77 **EST:** 1974
SQ FT: 82,000
SALES (est): 11.43MM
SALES (corp-wide): 11.43MM **Privately Held**
Web: www.customproducts.net
SIC: 7389 5131 5199 2761 Packaging and labeling services; Labels; Packaging materials; Manifold business forms

(G-13335)
D D D HAMS INC
34234 Aurora Rd (44139)
PHONE..............................440 487-9572
Dennis D Demshar, *Admn*
EMP: 8 **EST:** 2010

Solon - Cuyahoga County (G-13336)

SALES (est): 122.71K **Privately Held**
SIC: 2013 Prepared pork products, from purchased pork

(G-13336)
DANDI ENTERPRISES INC
Also Called: Dunkin' Donuts
6353 Som Center Rd (44139-2914)
PHONE..................................419 516-9070
EMP: 18 EST: 1996
SALES (est): 244.74K **Privately Held**
Web: www.dunkindonuts.com
SIC: 5461 2051 Doughnuts; Doughnuts, except frozen

(G-13337)
DEMAG CRANES & COMPONENTS CORP (DH)
Also Called: Terex USA
6675 Parkland Blvd Ste 200 (44139-4345)
P.O. Box 39245 (44139-0245)
PHONE..................................440 248-2400
Martin Marincic, Pr
Steve Mayes, *
Todd Robenson, *
Bernard D'ambrosi, Dir
◆ EMP: 200 EST: 1965
SQ FT: 87,000
SALES (est): 62.6MM **Privately Held**
Web: www.demagcranes.com
SIC: 3536 Cranes, industrial plant
HQ: Konecranes, Inc.
   4401 Gateway Blvd
   Springfield OH 45502

(G-13338)
DOCMANN PRINTING & ASSOC INC
5275 Naiman Pkwy Ste E (44139-1033)
PHONE..................................440 975-1775
Todd Brichmann, Pr
James E Docherty, VP
EMP: 7 EST: 1992
SQ FT: 14,000
SALES (est): 684.04K **Privately Held**
Web: www.docmann.com
SIC: 2752 Offset printing

(G-13339)
E B P INC
Also Called: Epic Steel
29125 Hall St (44139-3909)
PHONE..................................216 241-2550
Dan Fremont, Pr
Neff Fremont, *
Mark Fremont, *
Arthur M Hemlock, *
Robert M Lustig, *
EMP: 29 EST: 1963
SALES (est): 4.65MM **Privately Held**
Web: www.epicsteel.com
SIC: 3441 3446 3444 Fabricated structural metal; Architectural metalwork; Sheet metalwork

(G-13340)
EDWARDS VACUUM LLC
7905 Cochran Rd Ste 100 (44139-5470)
PHONE..................................440 248-4453
EMP: 8
SALES (corp-wide): 13.47B **Privately Held**
Web: www.edwardsvacuum.com
SIC: 3563 Air and gas compressors
HQ: Edwards Vacuum Llc
   6416 Inducon Dr W
   Sanborn NY 14132
   800 848-9800

(G-13341)
ELECTROVATIONS INC
30333 Emerald Valley Pkwy (44139-4394)
PHONE..................................330 274-3558
R Charles Vermerris, Pr
EMP: 7 EST: 1987
SALES (est): 337.01K **Privately Held**
SIC: 8711 7389 3357 Electrical or electronic engineering; Design, commercial and industrial; Nonferrous wiredrawing and insulating

(G-13342)
EMBEDDED PLANET INC
31225 Bainbridge Rd Ste N (44139-2293)
PHONE..................................216 245-4180
Mark Leopold, CEO
Mark Lowdermilk, CEO
Timothy J Callahan, Ch Bd
EMP: 15 EST: 1997
SALES (est): 2.69MM **Privately Held**
Web: www.embeddedplanet.com
SIC: 7371 3577 Computer software development; Computer peripheral equipment, nec

(G-13343)
ENERGY FOCUS INC (PA)
Also Called: Energy Focus
32000 Aurora Rd Ste B (44139-2849)
PHONE..................................440 715-1300
Jay Huang, CEO
James Warren, Corporate Secretary
Kin-fu Chen, Ch Bd
▲ EMP: 11 EST: 1985
SQ FT: 62,000
SALES (est): 5.97MM
SALES (corp-wide): 5.97MM **Publicly Held**
Web: www.energyfocus.com
SIC: 3641 3648 3674 Lamps, fluorescent, electric; Lighting equipment, nec; Light emitting diodes

(G-13344)
ERICO GLOBAL COMPANY
31700 Solon Rd (44139-3532)
PHONE..................................440 248-0100
EMP: 50 EST: 2006
SALES (est): 1.57MM **Privately Held**
Web: www.nvent.com
SIC: 3699 Electrical equipment and supplies, nec
PA: Nvent Electric Public Limited Company
   10 Earlsfort Terrace
   Dublin D02T3

(G-13345)
ERICO INTERNATIONAL CORP
34600 Solon Rd (44139-2631)
PHONE..................................440 248-0100
Steve Rohacz, Brnch Mgr
EMP: 400
Web: www.nvent.com
SIC: 3441 3965 Fabricated structural metal; Fasteners
HQ: Erico International Corporation
   1665 Utica Ave S Ste 700
   Saint Louis Park MN 55416
   440 349-2630

(G-13346)
ET&F FASTENING SYSTEMS INC
29019 Solon Rd (44139-3440)
PHONE..................................800 248-2376
John C Tillman, Pr
John C Tillman, Pr
Dave Nolan, VP
▲ EMP: 11 EST: 1984
SQ FT: 15,000
SALES (est): 438.11K **Privately Held**
Web: www.etf-fastening.com
SIC: 3965 3546 5085 Fasteners; Power-driven handtools; Fasteners, industrial: nuts, bolts, screws, etc.

(G-13347)
ETCHED METAL COMPANY
30200 Solon Industrial Pkwy (44139-4311)
PHONE..................................440 248-0240
Scott Nameth, Prin
Mike Mcdivitt, Prin
▲ EMP: 45 EST: 1928
SQ FT: 27,500
SALES (est): 8.37MM **Privately Held**
Web: www.etched-metal.com
SIC: 3479 3613 3596 3993 Name plates: engraved, etched, etc.; Control panels, electric; Scales and balances, except laboratory; Signs and advertising specialties

(G-13348)
FD ROLLS CORP
Also Called: Fd Machinery
30400 Solon Industrial Pkwy (44139-4328)
PHONE..................................216 916-1922
EMP: 25 EST: 2015
SALES (est): 2.48MM **Privately Held**
Web: www.fdmachinery.com
SIC: 3317 Steel pipe and tubes
PA: Dalian Field Heavy Machinery Manufacturing Co., Ltd.
   No.1, Jinma Road, Technology & Economy Development Zone, Tiexi D
   Dalian LN 11620

(G-13349)
FINDAWAY WORLD LLC (PA)
31999 Aurora Rd (44139)
PHONE..................................440 893-0808
Mitch Kroll, CEO
▲ EMP: 50 EST: 2004
SALES (est): 23.3MM **Privately Held**
Web: www.playaway.com
SIC: 5999 8331 3669 5192 Audio-visual equipment and supplies; Job training and related services; Visual communication systems; Periodicals

(G-13350)
FIRE FROM ICE VENTURES LLC
30333 Emerald Valley Pkwy (44139-4394)
PHONE..................................419 944-6705
▲ EMP: 29 EST: 1998
SQ FT: 13,500
SALES (est): 1.47MM **Privately Held**
SIC: 3585 Refrigeration and heating equipment
PA: The Providence Group Inc
   9290 Metcalf Rd
   Willoughby OH

(G-13351)
FLUKE BIOMEDICAL LLC (DH)
28775 Aurora Rd (44139-1837)
PHONE..................................440 248-9300
James Lico, Pr
▲ EMP: 120 EST: 1999
SALES (est): 42.5MM
SALES (corp-wide): 6.07B **Publicly Held**
Web: www.flukebiomedical.com
SIC: 3829 Nuclear radiation and testing apparatus
HQ: Fluke Electronics Corporation
   6920 Seaway Blvd
   Everett WA 98203
   425 347-6100

(G-13352)
FOLIO PHOTONICS INC
6864 Cochran Rd (44139-4336)
PHONE..................................440 420-4500
Kenneth Singer, Ex Dir
EMP: 10 EST: 2012
SQ FT: 9,500
SALES (est): 1.5MM **Privately Held**
Web: www.foliophotonics.com

SIC: 3695 Optical disks and tape, blank

(G-13353)
GLAVIN INDUSTRIES INC
Also Called: Glavin Specialty Co
6835 Cochran Rd Ste A (44139-3927)
P.O. Box 391316 (44139-8316)
PHONE..................................440 349-0049
Daniel Glavin, CEO
David H Glavin, *
Julia S Glavin, *
EMP: 25 EST: 1986
SQ FT: 23,000
SALES (est): 9.49MM **Privately Held**
Web: www.glavinid.com
SIC: 5084 3993 2759 Industrial machinery and equipment; Signs and advertising specialties; Screen printing

(G-13354)
GLENRIDGE MACHINE CO
37435 Fawn Path Dr (44139-2507)
PHONE..................................440 975-1055
▲ EMP: 33
Web: www.glenridgemachine.com
SIC: 3599 7692 Machine shop, jobbing and repair; Welding repair

(G-13355)
GLOBAL TBM COMPANY (HQ)
Also Called: Robbins Company, The
29100 Hall St (44139-3932)
PHONE..................................440 248-3303
Lok Home, Pr
Clark Lubaski, *
◆ EMP: 150 EST: 1985
SQ FT: 79,000
SALES (est): 99.28MM **Privately Held**
Web: www.robbinstbm.com
SIC: 3535 3541 3531 Conveyors and conveying equipment; Machine tools, metal cutting type; Tunneling machinery
PA: Northern Heavy Industries Group Co., Ltd.
   No.16, Kaifa Higway, Economic Tehnology Development Zone
   Shenyang LN 11002

(G-13356)
GRANEX INDUSTRIES INC (PA)
32400 Aurora Rd Ste 4 (44139-2800)
P.O. Box 391720 (44139-8720)
PHONE..................................440 248-4915
M Corey Obrien, Pr
G Scott Obrien, VP
▲ EMP: 10 EST: 2006
SALES (est): 2.56MM **Privately Held**
Web: www.granexindustries.com
SIC: 3281 Curbing, granite or stone

(G-13357)
GRAPHIC PACKAGING INTL LLC
Also Called: Altivity Packaging
6385 Cochran Rd (44139-3961)
PHONE..................................440 248-4370
Mary Turk, Brnch Mgr
EMP: 213
Web: www.graphicpkg.com
SIC: 2631 2657 Folding boxboard; Folding paperboard boxes
HQ: Graphic Packaging International, Llc
   1500 Riveredge Pkwy # 100
   Atlanta GA 30328

(G-13358)
HAB INC
Also Called: Hab Computer Services
28925 Fountain Pkwy (44139-4356)
P.O. Box 1 (54602-0001)
PHONE..................................608 785-7650
Michael Juran, Pr

GEOGRAPHIC SECTION
Solon - Cuyahoga County (G-13380)

EMP: 21 **EST:** 1985
SALES (est): 2.47MM
SALES (corp-wide): 20.23K **Privately Held**
Web: www.mrisoftware.com
SIC: 7371 7372 Computer software development and applications; Prepackaged software
PA: Mri Software Llc
28925 Fountain Pkwy
Solon OH 44139
800 321-8770

(G-13359)
HDT EP INC
30500 Aurora Rd Ste 100 (44139-2776)
PHONE.................................216 438-6111
EMP: 200
SIC: 3585 3564 3433 Air conditioning units, complete: domestic or industrial; Filters, air: furnaces, air conditioning equipment, etc.; Heating equipment, except electric

(G-13360)
HDT EXPEDITIONARY SYSTEMS INC
30500 Aurora Rd Ste 100 (44139-2776)
PHONE.................................216 438-6111
James Maurer, *Pr*
EMP: 14
Web: www.hdtglobal.com
SIC: 3714 3569 Heaters, motor vehicle; Filters
HQ: Hdt Expeditionary Systems, Inc.
30500 Aurora Rd Ste 100
Solon OH 44139
216 438-6111

(G-13361)
HDT TACTICAL SYSTEMS INC
30525 Aurora Rd (44139-2739)
PHONE.................................216 438-6111
▲ **EMP:** 200
SIC: 3569 3714 Filters; Heaters, motor vehicle

(G-13362)
HOSTAR INTERNATIONAL INC (PA)
31005 Solon Rd (44139-3436)
PHONE.................................440 564-5362
Claudia Berg, *Pr*
Todd Bush, *Pr*
Adam Wodka, *VP*
Ron Vitale, *Ex VP*
Dolores Lapalio, *VP*
EMP: 11 **EST:** 1988
SALES (est): 5.39MM
SALES (corp-wide): 5.39MM **Privately Held**
Web: www.hostar.com
SIC: 3535 Unit handling conveying systems

(G-13363)
HUNTER DEFENSE TECH INC (PA)
Also Called: Hdt Global
30500 Aurora Rd Ste 100 (44139-2776)
PHONE.................................216 438-6111
Vincent Buffa, *Pr*
Greg Miller, *
Carl Pates, *
Barry Sullivan, *
▼ **EMP:** 50 **EST:** 2000
SQ FT: 26,000
SALES (est): 416.26MM **Privately Held**
Web: www.hdtglobal.com
SIC: 3433 3569 3822 8331 Room and wall heaters, including radiators; Filters; Environmental controls; Sheltered workshop

(G-13364)
HUNTER ENVIRONMENTAL CORP
Also Called: Hunter Manufacturing Company
30525 Aurora Rd (44139-2739)
PHONE.................................440 248-6111
Eugene Strine, *CEO*
EMP: 16 **EST:** 2016
SALES (est): 1.79MM **Privately Held**
Web: www.hdtglobal.com
SIC: 3564 Filters, air: furnaces, air conditioning equipment, etc.

(G-13365)
HYDRALYTE LLC
27070 Miles Rd Ste A (44139-1162)
PHONE.................................844 301-2109
Oliver Baker, *CEO*
EMP: 6 **EST:** 2015
SALES (est): 73.71K **Privately Held**
SIC: 2087 Flavoring extracts and syrups, nec

(G-13366)
ILLINOIS TOOL WORKS INC
Also Called: Permatex
6875 Parkland Blvd (44139-4377)
PHONE.................................440 914-3100
Krista Bursott, *Contrlr*
EMP: 75
SQ FT: 2,500
SALES (corp-wide): 16.11B **Publicly Held**
Web: www.itw.com
SIC: 2819 2992 2899 2891 Industrial inorganic chemicals, nec; Lubricating oils and greases; Chemical preparations, nec; Adhesives and sealants
PA: Illinois Tool Works Inc.
155 Harlem Ave
Glenview IL 60025
847 724-7500

(G-13367)
IMPACTION CO
6100 Cochran Rd (44139-3311)
PHONE.................................440 349-5652
Joseph Sarakaitis, *Prin*
EMP: 6 **EST:** 2011
SALES (est): 160.51K **Privately Held**
SIC: 3494 Valves and pipe fittings, nec

(G-13368)
INNOCOMP
33195 Wagon Wheel Dr (44139-2368)
PHONE.................................440 248-5104
Jeri Lynn Hoffman, *Pt*
Robert Cecil, *Pt*
Craig Gruber, *Pt*
EMP: 7 **EST:** 1983
SQ FT: 3,500
SALES (est): 590K **Privately Held**
Web: www.innocomp.com
SIC: 3679 Voice controls

(G-13369)
JEFFERSON SMURFIT CORPORATION
6385 Cochran Rd (44139-3961)
PHONE.................................440 248-4370
Lisa Porter, *Genl Mgr*
EMP: 7 **EST:** 2010
SALES (est): 147.6K **Privately Held**
SIC: 2657 Folding paperboard boxes

(G-13370)
JOHNSONITE INC
Also Called: Tarkett USA
30000 Aurora Rd (44139-2728)
PHONE.................................440 543-8916
▲ **EMP:** 450
SIC: 3069 3089 Floor coverings, rubber; Floor coverings, plastics

(G-13371)
JOY GLOBAL UNDERGROUND MIN LLC
Also Called: Bedford Gear
6160 Cochran Rd (44139-3306)
PHONE.................................440 248-7970
Ed Doheny, *Brnch Mgr*
▲ **EMP:** 140
SIC: 3532 Mining machinery
HQ: Joy Global Underground Mining Llc
40 Pennwood Pl Ste 100
Warrendale PA 15086
724 779-4500

(G-13372)
JTM PRODUCTS INC
Also Called: J T M
31025 Carter St (44139-3521)
PHONE.................................440 287-2302
Daniel Schodowski, *Pr*
Greg Myers, *VP*
Brian F Murphy, *Prin*
EMP: 22 **EST:** 1991
SQ FT: 75,000
SALES (est): 6.81MM **Privately Held**
Web: www.jtmproducts.com
SIC: 2992 2841 3053 Oils and greases, blending and compounding; Soap: granulated, liquid, cake, flaked, or chip; Packing: steam engines, pipe joints, air compressors, etc.

(G-13373)
JULIUS PATRICK INDUSTRIES LLC
5845 Elm Hill Dr (44139-1947)
PHONE.................................440 600-7369
Daniel Cusick, *Prin*
EMP: 7 **EST:** 2017
SALES (est): 481.1K **Privately Held**
SIC: 3999 Manufacturing industries, nec

(G-13374)
KANAN ENTERPRISES INC (PA)
Also Called: King Nut Companies
31900 Solon Rd (44139-3536)
PHONE.................................440 248-8484
Martin Kanan, *Pr*
Michael Kanan, *
Matthew Kanan, *
◆ **EMP:** 198 **EST:** 1927
SQ FT: 250,000
SALES (est): 90.76MM
SALES (corp-wide): 90.76MM **Privately Held**
Web: www.kingnut.com
SIC: 2068 2034 Nuts: dried, dehydrated, salted or roasted; Fruits, dried or dehydrated, except freeze-dried

(G-13375)
KANAN ENTERPRISES INC
Also Called: King Nut Companies
30600 Carter St (44139-3503)
PHONE.................................440 248-8484
EMP: 82
SALES (corp-wide): 90.76MM **Privately Held**
Web: www.kingnut.com
SIC: 2068 2034 Nuts: dried, dehydrated, salted or roasted; Fruits, dried or dehydrated, except freeze-dried
PA: Kanan Enterprises, Inc.
31900 Solon Rd
Solon OH 44139
440 248-8484

(G-13376)
KANAN ENTERPRISES INC
Also Called: King Nut Companies, Plant 2
6401 Davis Industrial Pkwy (44139-3566)
PHONE.................................440 349-0719
EMP: 10
SQ FT: 84,130
SALES (corp-wide): 90.76MM **Privately Held**
Web: www.kingnut.com
SIC: 2068 2034 Nuts: dried, dehydrated, salted or roasted; Fruits, dried or dehydrated, except freeze-dried
PA: Kanan Enterprises, Inc.
31900 Solon Rd
Solon OH 44139
440 248-8484

(G-13377)
KEITHLEY INSTRUMENTS LLC (DH)
28775 Aurora Rd (44139-1891)
PHONE.................................440 248-0400
Joseph P Keithley, *Pr*
Linda C Rae, *
Mark J Plush, *
Daniel A Faia, *SUPPORT**
Larry L Pendergrass, *New Product Development Vice President**
▲ **EMP:** 102 **EST:** 1946
SQ FT: 125,000
SALES (est): 94.04MM
SALES (corp-wide): 6.07B **Publicly Held**
Web: www.tek.com
SIC: 3823 7371 3825 Computer interface equipment, for industrial process control; Computer software development; Test equipment for electronic and electric measurement
HQ: Tektronix, Inc.
14150 Sw Karl Braun Dr
Beaverton OR 97077
800 833-9200

(G-13378)
KENNAMETAL INC
6865 Cochran Rd (44139-4398)
PHONE.................................440 349-5151
Brian Maglosky, *Mgr*
EMP: 110
SQ FT: 1,500
SALES (corp-wide): 2.08B **Publicly Held**
Web: www.kennametal.com
SIC: 3545 3532 Tool holders; Mining machinery
PA: Kennametal Inc.
525 William Penn Pl # 3300
Pittsburgh PA 15219
412 248-8000

(G-13379)
KICHLER LIGHTING LLC (HQ)
Also Called: Kichler Lighting
30455 Solon Rd (44139-3415)
P.O. Box 318010 (44131-8010)
PHONE.................................216 573-1000
Vijay Shankar, *Pr*
◆ **EMP:** 500 **EST:** 1938
SQ FT: 630,000
SALES (est): 282.07MM
SALES (corp-wide): 7.97B **Publicly Held**
Web: www.kichler.com
SIC: 3645 3648 3641 Residential lighting fixtures; Lighting equipment, nec; Electric lamps
PA: Masco Corporation
17450 College Pkwy
Livonia MI 48152
313 274-7400

(G-13380)
KYNTRONICS INC (PA)
6565 Davis Industrial Pkwy Ste R (44139-3560)
PHONE.................................440 220-5990
Wayne Foley, *Pr*
EMP: 16 **EST:** 2013
SALES (est): 5.07MM
SALES (corp-wide): 5.07MM **Privately Held**
Web: www.kyntronics.com

Solon - Cuyahoga County (G-13381)

SIC: **3593** Fluid power actuators, hydraulic or pneumatic

(G-13381)
LINK SYSTEMS INC
Also Called: Prolease
28925 Fountain Pkwy (44139-4356)
PHONE.....................800 321-8770
Patrick Ghilani, *Pr*
John Ensign, *Sec*
Roman Telerman, *Treas*
EMP: 15 **EST:** 1992
SALES (est): 2.96MM
SALES (corp-wide): 20.23K **Privately Held**
Web: www.mrisoftware.com
SIC: **7371** 7372 7379 7389 Computer software development; Business oriented computer software; Computer related consulting services
PA: Mri Software Llc
28925 Fountain Pkwy
Solon OH 44139
800 321-8770

(G-13382)
MADISON ELECTRIC PRODUCTS INC (HQ)
30575 Bainbridge Rd Ste 130 (44139)
PHONE.....................216 391-7776
Brad Wiandt, *Pr*
Rob Fisher, *
▲ **EMP:** 37 **EST:** 1988
SALES (est): 10.02MM
SALES (corp-wide): 1.7B **Privately Held**
Web: www.southwire.com
SIC: **3644** Electric conduits and fittings
PA: Southwire Company, Llc
1 Southwire Dr
Carrollton GA 30119
770 832-4529

(G-13383)
MAJESTIC TOOL AND MACHINE INC
30700 Carter St Ste C (44139-3585)
PHONE.....................440 248-5058
Walter Krueger, *Pr*
Todd Krueger, *
Kurt Krueger, *
EMP: 13 **EST:** 1973
SQ FT: 30,000
SALES (est): 976.94K **Privately Held**
Web: www.majestictool.com
SIC: **3599** 7692 3544 Machine shop, jobbing and repair; Welding repair; Special dies, tools, jigs, and fixtures

(G-13384)
MEDICAL QUANT USA INC
Also Called: Multi Radiance Medical
6521 Davis Industrial Pkwy (44139-3549)
PHONE.....................440 542-0761
Max Kanarsky, *Pr*
Galina Marqova, *CFO*
EMP: 14 **EST:** 2004
SALES (est): 3.88MM **Privately Held**
Web: www.multiradiance.com
SIC: **3841** Surgical and medical instruments

(G-13385)
MERCURY IRON AND STEEL CO
Also Called: Misco Refractometer
6275 Cochran Rd (44139-3316)
PHONE.....................440 349-1500
Michael Rainer, *Pr*
EMP: 14 **EST:** 1949
SQ FT: 6,000
SALES (est): 4.94MM **Privately Held**
Web: www.misco.com

SIC: **8711** 3827 3443 3441 Industrial engineers; Optical instruments and lenses; Plate work for the metalworking trade; Fabricated structural metal

(G-13386)
MERCURY MACHINE CO
30250 Carter St (44139-3500)
PHONE.....................440 349-3222
Jonathon Petrenchik, *Pr*
EMP: 67 **EST:** 1954
SQ FT: 10,000
SALES (est): 8.73MM **Privately Held**
Web: www.mercurymachine.com
SIC: **3324** 3544 Steel investment foundries; Industrial molds

(G-13387)
METAULLICS SYSTEMS LP
Also Called: Metaullics Systems
31935 Aurora Rd (44139-2717)
PHONE.....................509 926-6212
▲ **EMP:** 133
SIC: **3569** 3624 3295 3561 Filters, general line: industrial; Carbon and graphite products; Graphite, natural: ground, pulverized, refined, or blended; Pumps and pumping equipment

(G-13388)
MFS SUPPLY LLC (PA)
31100 Solon Rd Ste 16 (44139-3463)
PHONE.....................800 607-0541
Jeff Muencz, *CFO*
Michael Halpern, *Managing Member*
◆ **EMP:** 62 **EST:** 2006
SALES (est): 26.76MM **Privately Held**
Web: www.mfssupply.com
SIC: **2542** Postal lock boxes, mail racks, and related products

(G-13389)
MICHAEL W HYES DESGR GOLDSMITH
Also Called: Hayes, Michael Designer
28200 Miles Rd Unit F (44139-6915)
PHONE.....................440 519-0889
Michael Hayes, *CEO*
Marcy Hayes, *VP*
EMP: 7 **EST:** 1978
SQ FT: 1,250
SALES (est): 357.52K **Privately Held**
Web: www.michaelwhayes.com
SIC: **3911** 5944 7631 Jewelry, precious metal ; Jewelry stores; Jewelry repair services

(G-13390)
MICROPLEX PRINTWARE CORP
30300 Solon Industrial Pkwy Ste E (44139-4382)
PHONE.....................440 374-2424
Andre Fedak, *Pr*
▲ **EMP:** 11 **EST:** 1998
SALES (est): 2.08MM **Privately Held**
Web: www.microplex-usa.com
SIC: **2759** Laser printing

(G-13391)
MILLWOOD INC
30311 Emerald Valley Pkwy Ste 300 (44139)
PHONE.....................440 914-0540
Vern Walker, *Brnch Mgr*
EMP: 56
Web: www.millwoodinc.com
SIC: **2448** Pallets, wood
PA: Millwood, Inc.
3708 International Blvd
Vienna OH 44473

(G-13392)
MOTIONSOURCE INTERNATIONAL LLC
31200 Solon Rd Ste 7 (44139-3583)
PHONE.....................440 287-7037
Charles Hautala, *Prin*
Doug Karpowicz, *Prin*
EMP: 10 **EST:** 2012
SQ FT: 4,000
SALES (est): 2.03MM **Privately Held**
Web: www.motionsource1.com
SIC: **3569** 5084 5013 Lubrication equipment, industrial; Pumps and pumping equipment, nec; Pumps, oil and gas

(G-13393)
MP BIOMEDICALS LLC
29525 Fountain Pkwy (44139-4351)
PHONE.....................440 337-1200
Dragon Kraojovic, *Brnch Mgr*
EMP: 130
SALES (corp-wide): 601.99MM **Privately Held**
Web: www.mpbio.com
SIC: **8731** 2869 2834 8071 Biological research; Enzymes; Pharmaceutical preparations; Medical laboratories
HQ: Mp Biomedicals, Llc
6 Thomas
Irvine CA 92618
949 833-2500

(G-13394)
MUSTARD SEED HEALTH FD MKT INC
6025 Kruse Dr Ste 100 (44139-2378)
PHONE.....................440 519-3663
Margaret Kanfer-nabors, *Ch Bd*
EMP: 35
SALES (corp-wide): 27.81MM **Privately Held**
Web: www.mustardseedmarket.com
SIC: **5499** 7299 5812 2051 Gourmet food stores; Banquet hall facilities; Caterers; Bread, cake, and related products
PA: Mustard Seed Health Food Market, Inc.
3885 Medina Rd
Akron OH 44333
330 666-7333

(G-13395)
NESTLE PREPARED FOODS COMPANY
5750 Harper Rd (44139-1831)
PHONE.....................440 349-5757
EMP: 417
Web: www.nestle.com
SIC: **2038** 5411 2037 Frozen specialties, nec ; Grocery stores; Frozen fruits and vegetables
HQ: Nestle Prepared Foods Company
30003 Bainbridge Rd
Solon OH 44139
440 248-3600

(G-13396)
NESTLE PREPARED FOODS COMPANY (DH)
Also Called: Nestle
30003 Bainbridge Rd (44139-2205)
P.O. Box 2178 (18703-2178)
PHONE.....................440 248-3600
Laurent Freixe, *CEO*
David H Jennings, *
James M Biggar, *
Charles Werner, *
James H Ball, *
▲ **EMP:** 1910 **EST:** 1969
SQ FT: 250,000
SALES (est): 1.53B **Privately Held**

Web: www.nestle.com
SIC: **2038** 5411 2037 Dinners, frozen and packaged; Grocery stores; Vegetables, quick frozen & cold pack, excl. potato products
HQ: The Stouffer Corporation
30003 Bainbridge Rd
Solon OH 44139
440 349-5757

(G-13397)
NESTLE USA INC
Nestle Business Services
30003 Bainbridge Rd (44139-2290)
PHONE.....................440 349-5757
Jim Triskett, *Mgr*
EMP: 525
Web: www.nestleusa.com
SIC: **2023** Evaporated milk
HQ: Nestle Usa, Inc.
1812 N Moore St
Arlington VA 22209
703 682-4600

(G-13398)
NESTLE USA INC
Also Called: Nestle Brands Company
30000 Bainbridge Rd (44139-2206)
PHONE.....................440 264-6600
EMP: 472
Web: www.nestleusa.com
SIC: **2023** Evaporated milk
HQ: Nestle Usa, Inc.
1812 N Moore St
Arlington VA 22209
703 682-4600

(G-13399)
NOCO COMPANY (PA)
Also Called: Noco
30339 Diamond Pkwy Ste 102 (44139-5473)
PHONE.....................216 464-8131
William Nook Senior, *CEO*
◆ **EMP:** 100 **EST:** 1914
SQ FT: 100,000
SALES (est): 31.92MM
SALES (corp-wide): 31.92MM **Privately Held**
Web: www.no.co
SIC: **2899** 5063 5072 3714 Chemical preparations, nec; Wire and cable; Power tools and accessories; Booster (jump-start) cables, automotive

(G-13400)
OAKWOOD LABORATORIES LLC
27070 Miles Rd (44139-1162)
PHONE.....................440 505-2011
Shritin Shah, *Brnch Mgr*
EMP: 18
SALES (corp-wide): 13.9MM **Privately Held**
Web: www.oakwoodlabs.com
SIC: **2834** Vitamin, nutrient, and hematinic preparations for human use
PA: Oakwood Laboratories, L.L.C.
7670 First Pl Ste A
Oakwood Village OH 44146
440 359-0000

(G-13401)
OSB SOFTWARE INC
6240 Som Center Rd Ste 230 (44139-2950)
PHONE.....................440 542-9145
Steven Wiser, *Pr*
EMP: 10 **EST:** 2003
SALES (est): 420.52K **Privately Held**
Web: www.specializedbusinesssoftware.com

▲ = Import ▼ = Export
◆ = Import/Export

GEOGRAPHIC SECTION
Solon - Cuyahoga County (G-13425)

SIC: 7372 Business oriented computer software

(G-13402)
PAUS NORTH AMERICA INC
29001 Solon Rd Unit L (44139)
PHONE..................775 778-5980
EMP: 6 EST: 2021
SALES (est): 75.09K Privately Held
SIC: 3531 Construction machinery

(G-13403)
PDI GROUND SUPPORT SYSTEMS INC
Also Called: Pdi Group, The
6225 Cochran Rd (44139-3315)
PHONE..................216 271-7344
Irwin G Haber, Ch
Ida S Haber, *
▲ EMP: 60 EST: 1992
SQ FT: 110,000
SALES (est): 15.85MM Privately Held
Web: www.thepdigroup.com
SIC: 3714 3715 Axle housings and shafts, motor vehicle; Semitrailers for missile transportation

(G-13404)
PENTAIR
34600 Solon Rd (44139-2631)
PHONE..................440 248-0100
EMP: 49 EST: 2017
SALES (est): 2.74MM Privately Held
Web: www.pentair.com
SIC: 3561 Pumps and pumping equipment

(G-13405)
PLAS-MAC CORP
30250 Carter St (44139-3506)
PHONE..................440 349-3222
Jonathon Petrenchik, Pr
EMP: 100 EST: 1980
SQ FT: 33,000
SALES (est): 7.74MM Privately Held
Web: www.plasmaccorp.com
SIC: 3543 3599 Foundry patternmaking; Air intake filters, internal combustion engine, except auto

(G-13406)
PRECIOUS METAL PLATING CO
33125 Cannon Rd (44139-1657)
PHONE..................440 585-7117
Thomas Talty Junior, Pr
Steve Kubofcik, VP
EMP: 10 EST: 1965
SALES (est): 372.73K Privately Held
Web: www.preciousmetalplatingco.com
SIC: 3471 Electroplating of metals or formed products

(G-13407)
PRECISION BRUSH CO
6700 Parkland Blvd (44139-4341)
PHONE..................440 542-9600
James C Benjamin, Pr
EMP: 14 EST: 1950
SQ FT: 11,000
SALES (est): 2.42MM Privately Held
Web: www.precisionbrush.com
SIC: 3991 Brushes, household or industrial

(G-13408)
PTMJ ENTERPRISES INC
32000 Aurora Rd (44139-2875)
P.O. Box 391437 (44139-8437)
PHONE..................440 543-8000
Peter Joyce, Pr
▲ EMP: 64 EST: 1980
SALES (est): 3.95MM Privately Held

Web: www.signumdisplays.com
SIC: 2541 1799 Display fixtures, wood; Closet organizers, installation and design

(G-13409)
R & D NESTLE CENTER INC
5750 Harper Rd (44139-1831)
PHONE..................440 349-5757
EMP: 89
Web: www.nestle.com
SIC: 2038 Frozen specialties, nec
HQ: R & D Nestle Center Inc
809 Collins Ave
Marysville OH 43040
937 642-7015

(G-13410)
RADIX WIRE & CABLE LLC
Also Called: Radix Wire
30333 Emerald Valley Pkwy (44139-4394)
PHONE..................216 731-9191
Steve Demko, VP Fin
EMP: 70 EST: 2013
SALES (est): 6.02MM Privately Held
Web: www.radix-wire.com
SIC: 2298 3312 3315 Ropes and fiber cables; Wire products, steel or iron; Wire and fabricated wire products

(G-13411)
RADIX WIRE CO (PA)
Also Called: Radix Wire Company, The
30333 Emerald Valley Pkwy (44139-4394)
PHONE..................216 731-9191
Keith D Nootbaar, Pr
Marylou Vermerris, *
Jim Schaefer, *
Brain Bukovec, *
EMP: 60 EST: 1944
SALES (est): 20.56MM
SALES (corp-wide): 20.56MM Privately Held
Web: www.radix-wire.com
SIC: 3357 5051 Nonferrous wiredrawing and insulating; Cable, wire

(G-13412)
RADIX WIRE CO
30333 Emerald Valley Pkwy (44139-4394)
PHONE..................216 731-9191
Bill Toll, Mgr
EMP: 17
SALES (corp-wide): 20.56MM Privately Held
Web: www.radix-wire.com
SIC: 3357 Nonferrous wiredrawing and insulating
PA: Radix Wire Co
30333 Emerald Valley Pkwy
Solon OH 44139
216 731-9191

(G-13413)
RENEGADE BRANDS LLC
5351 Naiman Pkwy Ste A (44139-1014)
PHONE..................216 789-0535
EMP: 48 EST: 2019
SALES (est): 1.65MM Privately Held
Web: www.renegadebrands.com
SIC: 2841 Soap and other detergents

(G-13414)
REPUBLIC STEEL WIRE PROC LLC
31000 Solon Rd (44139-3467)
PHONE..................440 996-0740
Larry Braun, Genl Mgr
Jim Phillips, Genl Mgr
▲ EMP: 32 EST: 2010
SALES (est): 26.43MM Privately Held
Web: www.republicsteel.com

SIC: 3315 Steel wire and related products
HQ: Republic Steel
2633 8th St Ne
Canton OH 44704
330 438-5435

(G-13415)
RIZE HOME LLC (PA)
Also Called: Mantua Bed Frames
31050 Diamond Pkwy (44139-5478)
PHONE..................800 333-8333
David Jaffe, CEO
Edward Weintraub, *
Jeff Weekly, CFO
Marc Spector, *
◆ EMP: 75 EST: 1954
SQ FT: 67,500
SALES (est): 38.73MM
SALES (corp-wide): 38.73MM Privately Held
Web: www.rizehome.com
SIC: 5021 2514 Bedsprings; Frames for box springs or bedsprings: metal

(G-13416)
RTSI LLC
6161 Cochran Rd Ste G (44139-3324)
PHONE..................440 542-3066
Vikki Velimesis, Genl Mgr
EMP: 7 EST: 2013
SALES (est): 894.41K Privately Held
Web: www.rtsillc.com
SIC: 3451 Screw machine products
PA: Kirkwood Holding Inc.
1239 Rockside Rd
Cleveland OH 44134

(G-13417)
SAGEQUEST LLC
31500 Bainbridge Rd Ste 1 (44139-2289)
PHONE..................216 896-7243
EMP: 86
Web: www.sage-quest.com
SIC: 3663 Mobile communication equipment

(G-13418)
SAINT-GOBAIN PRFMCE PLAS CORP
31500 Solon Rd (44139-3528)
PHONE..................440 836-6900
EMP: 66
SALES (corp-wide): 397.78MM Privately Held
Web: www.saint-gobain.com
SIC: 3089 3053 Thermoformed finished plastics products, nec; Gaskets; packing and sealing devices
HQ: Saint-Gobain Performance Plastics Corporation
20 Moores Rd
Malvern PA 19355
440 836-6900

(G-13419)
SCHENCK PROCESS LLC
30825 Aurora Rd # 150 (44139-2733)
PHONE..................513 576-9200
Graham Cooper, Brnch Mgr
EMP: 10
SALES (corp-wide): 2.67MM Privately Held
Web: www.schenckprocessfpm.com
SIC: 3535 3564 5084 Pneumatic tube conveyor systems; Dust or fume collecting equipment, industrial; Pneumatic tools and equipment
HQ: Schenck Process Llc
7901 Nw 107th Ter
Kansas City MO 64153
816 891-9300

(G-13420)
SENSICAL INC
Also Called: Unitus
31115 Aurora Rd (44139-2701)
PHONE..................216 641-1141
John F Haas, Pr
James Haas, *
▲ EMP: 55 EST: 1978
SQ FT: 45,000
SALES (est): 14.56MM Privately Held
Web: www.sensical.com
SIC: 3993 2752 2672 2759 Signs and advertising specialties; Commercial printing, lithographic; Paper; coated and laminated, nec; Promotional printing

(G-13421)
SK WELLMAN CORP
Also Called: Wellman Friction Products
6180 Cochran Rd (44139-3314)
PHONE..................440 528-4000
▲ EMP: 250
SIC: 3499 Friction material, made from powdered metal

(G-13422)
SKIDMORE-WILHELM MFG COMPANY
Also Called: Columbia Industries
30340 Solon Industrial Pkwy Ste B (44139-4343)
PHONE..................216 481-4774
John Obrayan, Pr
Kathleen Wilhelm, Stockholder*
John Wilhelm, Stockholder*
Joanne Hoffman, Corporate Secretary*
▲ EMP: 18 EST: 1944
SQ FT: 15,000
SALES (est): 2.46MM Privately Held
Web: www.skidmore-wilhelm.com
SIC: 3728 3829 3825 3593 Aircraft parts and equipment, nec; Torsion testing equipment; Instruments to measure electricity; Fluid power cylinders and actuators

(G-13423)
SOLON
38235 Mcdowell Dr (44139-4684)
PHONE..................440 498-1798
Susan A Drucker, Mayor
EMP: 10 EST: 2011
SALES (est): 149.3K Privately Held
Web: www.solonohio.org
SIC: 3089 Plastics products, nec

(G-13424)
SOLON SPECIALTY WIRE CO
30000 Solon Rd (44139-3408)
PHONE..................440 248-7600
Dave Haffenr, CEO
▲ EMP: 25 EST: 2002
SQ FT: 180,000
SALES (est): 11.34MM Privately Held
SIC: 3315 Wire, ferrous/iron

(G-13425)
STOCK FAIRFIELD CORPORATION
Also Called: Stock Equipment Company
30825 Aurora Rd # 150 (44139-2733)
PHONE..................440 543-6000
Robert Ciavarella, Pr
EMP: 170 EST: 2007
SALES (est): 34.35MM
SALES (corp-wide): 2.67MM Privately Held
Web: www.schenckprocess.com

Solon - Cuyahoga County (G-13426) — GEOGRAPHIC SECTION

SIC: 5063 8711 3535 3823 Power transmission equipment, electric; Electrical or electronic engineering; Conveyors and conveying equipment; Process control instruments
HQ: Schenck Process Llc
7901 Nw 107th Ter
Kansas City MO 64153
816 891-9300

(G-13426)
SURTECO NORTH AMERICA INC (DH)
Also Called: Omnova North America, Inc.
32125 Solon Rd Ste 15 (44139-3535)
PHONE..............................843 848-3000
Wolfgang Moyses, Ch
Michael C Phillips, CEO
Bernhard Dupmeier, CFO
EMP: 34 EST: 2013
SQ FT: 14,000
SALES (est): 84.50MM
SALES (corp-wide): 246.55MM Privately Held
Web: www.surteco.com
SIC: 3083 Laminated plastics sheets
HQ: Surteco Group Se
Johan-Viktor-Bausch-Str. 2
Buttenwiesen BY 86647
827499880

(G-13427)
SWAGELOK COMPANY
Also Called: Corporate Raw Materials
31400 Aurora Rd (44139-2708)
PHONE..............................440 248-4600
EMP: 12
SALES (corp-wide): 881.02MM Privately Held
SIC: 3491 Pressure valves and regulators, industrial
PA: Swagelok Company
29500 Solon Rd
Solon OH 44139
440 248-4600

(G-13428)
SWAGELOK COMPANY (PA)
29500 Solon Rd (44139-3474)
PHONE..............................440 248-4600
Thomas F Lozick, Ch
James Cavoli, *
Chris Miklich, *
◆ EMP: 900 EST: 1947
SALES (est): 881.02MM
SALES (corp-wide): 881.02MM Privately Held
Web: www.aldvalve.com
SIC: 3494 3491 3599 Pipe fittings; Pressure valves and regulators, industrial; Machine shop, jobbing and repair

(G-13429)
SWAGELOK COMPANY
6100 Cochran Rd (44139-3311)
PHONE..............................440 349-5652
Nancy Brown, Brnch Mgr
EMP: 25
SALES (corp-wide): 881.02MM Privately Held
Web: www.aldvalve.com
SIC: 3494 3491 3599 3498 Pipe fittings; Pressure valves and regulators, industrial; Machine shop, jobbing and repair; Fabricated pipe and fittings
PA: Swagelok Company
29500 Solon Rd
Solon OH 44139
440 248-4600

(G-13430)
SWAGELOK COMPANY
Also Called: Crawford Computer Center
29495 F A Lennon Dr (44139-2764)
PHONE..............................440 349-5836
Arthur Anton, Prin
EMP: 25
SALES (corp-wide): 881.02MM Privately Held
Web: www.aldvalve.com
SIC: 3494 3491 3599 3594 Pipe fittings; Pressure valves and regulators, industrial; Machine shop, jobbing and repair; Fluid power pumps and motors
PA: Swagelok Company
29500 Solon Rd
Solon OH 44139
440 248-4600

(G-13431)
SWAGELOK COMPANY
29495 F A Lennon Dr (44139-2764)
PHONE..............................440 349-5934
Nick Lubar, Mgr
EMP: 100
SALES (corp-wide): 881.02MM Privately Held
Web: www.aldvalve.com
SIC: 5051 3593 3498 3494 Tubing, metal; Fluid power cylinders and actuators; Fabricated pipe and fittings; Valves and pipe fittings, nec
PA: Swagelok Company
29500 Solon Rd
Solon OH 44139
440 248-4600

(G-13432)
SWAGELOK ZALO
6090 Cochran Rd (44139)
PHONE..............................216 524-8950
F J Callahan, Pr
E P Mansour, *
N J Tobbe, *
EMP: 11 EST: 1947
SQ FT: 75,000
SALES (est): 123.08K Privately Held
Web: cleveland.swagelok.com
SIC: 3451 Screw machine products

(G-13433)
TARKETT INC (DH)
Also Called: Tarkett North America
30000 Aurora Rd (44139-2728)
PHONE..............................800 899-8916
Jeff Fenwick, CEO
Jack Lee, *
Peter De Bonis, *
Christer Hiller, *
▲ EMP: 99 EST: 1981
SQ FT: 5,000
SALES (est): 550.72MM Privately Held
Web: www.tarkettna.com
SIC: 3069 Flooring, rubber: tile or sheet
HQ: Tarkett Inc
1001 Rue Yamaska E
Farnham QC J2N 1
450 293-3173

(G-13434)
TARKETT USA INC (DH)
Also Called: Johnsonite
30000 Aurora Rd (44139)
PHONE..............................877 827-5388
Jeff Fenwick, Pr
Nicolas Carre, CFO
EMP: 250 EST: 1996
SALES (est): 566.04MM Privately Held
Web: www.tarkett-group.com
SIC: 3253 Ceramic wall and floor tile
HQ: Tarkett
Tour Initiale
Puteaux

(G-13435)
TECHNOLOGY HOUSE LTD
30700 Carter St (44139-3568)
PHONE..............................440 248-3025
EMP: 91
Web: www.tth.com
SIC: 3599 Machine shop, jobbing and repair
PA: The Technology House Ltd
10036 Aurora Hudson Rd
Streetsboro OH 44241

(G-13436)
TECHTRON SYSTEMS INC
29500 Fountain Pkwy (44139-4350)
PHONE..............................440 505-2990
Paul Teel Junior, Pr
John Teel, Stockholder*
Tina Sudlow, Stockholder*
Pam Teel, *
▲ EMP: 50 EST: 1971
SQ FT: 38,000
SALES (est): 14.08MM Privately Held
Web: www.techtronsys.com
SIC: 3672 Printed circuit boards

(G-13437)
TEXAS TILE MANUFACTURING LLC
30000 Aurora Rd (44139-2728)
PHONE..............................713 869-5811
Gilles De Beaumont, Pr
Lee James, VP
Tom Dowling, Treas
Anthony Matti, Dir
▲ EMP: 41 EST: 2005
SALES (est): 705.88K Privately Held
SIC: 3292 Tile, vinyl asbestos

(G-13438)
THE STOUFFER CORPORATION (DH)
30003 Bainbridge Rd (44139-2205)
PHONE..............................440 349-5757
Peter Knox, Prin
▲ EMP: 8 EST: 1912
SQ FT: 124,000
SALES (est): 1.53B Privately Held
Web: www.goodnes.com
SIC: 2038 Dinners, frozen and packaged
HQ: Tsc Holdings, Inc.
800 N Brand Blvd
Glendale CA 91203
818 549-6000

(G-13439)
TIMEKEEPING SYSTEMS INC
30700 Bainbridge Rd Ste H (44139-6403)
PHONE..............................216 595-0890
George Markwitz, Pr
Barry Markwitz, VP
▲ EMP: 11 EST: 1986
SALES (est): 3.03MM Privately Held
Web: www.guard1.com
SIC: 7371 8711 7372 3577 Custom computer programming services; Engineering services; Prepackaged software; Computer peripheral equipment, nec

(G-13440)
TWINSOURCE LLC
32333 Aurora Rd Ste 50 (44139-2851)
PHONE..............................440 248-6800
Fred Tamjidi, Managing Member
EMP: 10 EST: 1999
SQ FT: 1,500
SALES (est): 1.97MM Privately Held
Web: www.twinsource.net
SIC: 3625 Switches, electronic applications

(G-13441)
VALTRONIC TECHNOLOGY INC
29200 Fountain Pkwy (44139-4347)
PHONE..............................440 349-1239
Martin Zimmermann, CEO
Jay Wimer, *
Donald Styblo, *
Sbastien Robert, *
EMP: 68 EST: 1986
SQ FT: 26,000
SALES (est): 46.64MM Privately Held
Web: www.valtronic.com
SIC: 3672 Printed circuit boards
PA: Valtronic Technologies (Holding) Sa
Route De Bonport 2
Les CharbonniCres VD 1343

(G-13442)
VERSATILE AUTOMATION TECH LTD
Also Called: VA Technology
30355 Solon Industrial Pkwy (44139-1926)
PHONE..............................440 589-6700
James Byrne, Pr
▲ EMP: 6 EST: 1993
SQ FT: 1,300
SALES (est): 2.72MM Privately Held
SIC: 3569 5084 Robots, assembly line: industrial and commercial; Robots, industrial
PA: V A Technology Limited
Halesfield 9
Telford TF7 4

(G-13443)
VR ASSETS LLC
5265 Naiman Pkwy Ste J (44139-1013)
PHONE..............................440 600-2963
Valeri Sakhanevitch, Pr
EMP: 8 EST: 2015
SALES (est): 807.92K Privately Held
Web: www.vrassets.us
SIC: 5045 7379 7378 3571 Computers, peripherals, and software; Computer related services, nec; Computer maintenance and repair; Electronic computers

(G-13444)
VWR CHEMICALS LLC (DH)
28600 Fountain Pkwy (44139-4314)
PHONE..............................800 448-4442
Michael Stubblefield, CEO
▲ EMP: 30 EST: 1967
SALES (est): 23.31MM
SALES (corp-wide): 6.97B Publicly Held
SIC: 2819 Industrial inorganic chemicals, nec
HQ: Vwr Funding, Inc.
100 W Matsonford Rd Ste 1
Radnor PA 19087

(G-13445)
VWR PART OF AVANTOR (DH)
Also Called: Amresco, LLC
28600 Fountain Pkwy (44139-4314)
PHONE..............................440 349-1199
▲ EMP: 39 EST: 1976
SALES (est): 33.48MM
SALES (corp-wide): 6.97B Publicly Held
SIC: 2833 Medicinals and botanicals
HQ: Vwr International, Llc
100 W Matsonford Rd Ste 1
Radnor PA 19087
610 386-1700

(G-13446)
WALLEYE INVESTMENTS LTD
6750 Arnold Miller Pkwy (44139-4363)
PHONE..............................440 564-7210
Willard E Frissell, Managing Member
EMP: 8 EST: 2004
SALES (est): 226.26K Privately Held

SIC: 3089 Injection molding of plastics

(G-13447)
WATER & WASTE WATER EQP CO
32100 Solon Rd Ste 101a (44139-3584)
PHONE..................................440 542-0972
Walter Senney, Pr
EMP: 7 EST: 1978
SALES (est): 692.4K Privately Held
Web: www.wwe-co.com
SIC: 3589 Water treatment equipment, industrial

(G-13448)
WILLIAM J BERGEN & CO
Also Called: Bergen, W J & Co
32520 Arthur Rd (44139-4503)
PHONE..................................440 248-6132
William J Bergen, Owner
EMP: 9 EST: 1979
SQ FT: 3,500
SALES (est): 954.16K Privately Held
SIC: 5112 2752 2759 Business forms; Offset printing; Letterpress printing

Somerset
Perry County

(G-13449)
RHODES MANUFACTURING CO INC
7045 Buckeye Valley Rd Ne (43783-9709)
PHONE..................................740 743-2614
Douglas L Rhodes, Pr
Brian Rhodes, VP
EMP: 20 EST: 1977
SQ FT: 6,000
SALES (est): 2.5MM Privately Held
Web: www.rhodestanksrus.com
SIC: 3443 Industrial vessels, tanks, and containers

(G-13450)
SCHMELZER INDUSTRIES INC
7970 Wesley Chapel Rd Ne (43783-9737)
P.O. Box 249 (43783-0249)
PHONE..................................740 743-2866
Jean Schmelzer, Pr
Monica Schmelzer, *
Timothy Schmelzer, VP
EMP: 25 EST: 1984
SQ FT: 23,700
SALES (est): 3.96MM Privately Held
Web: www.siveils.com
SIC: 2221 5999 Fiberglass fabrics; Fiberglass materials, except insulation

Somerton
Belmont County

(G-13451)
STUMPTOWN LBR PALLET MILLS LTD
55613 Washington St (43713-9794)
PHONE..................................740 757-2275
EMP: 8 EST: 1995
SQ FT: 1,300
SALES (est): 761.31K Privately Held
Web: www.dixxeephoto.com
SIC: 2448 Pallets, wood

Somerville
Butler County

(G-13452)
DUNKELBERGER FUEL LLC
2304 Somerville Rd (45064-9580)
P.O. Box 211 (45064-0211)
PHONE..................................513 726-1999
Janice M Wyatt, Prin
EMP: 6 EST: 2012
SALES (est): 472.69K Privately Held
Web: somerville-oh.auto-usa.org
SIC: 2869 Fuels

(G-13453)
WATSON WOOD WORKS
2765 Frazee Rd (45064-9715)
PHONE..................................513 233-5321
EMP: 6 EST: 2015
SALES (est): 165.39K Privately Held
Web: www.watsonwood.com
SIC: 2431 Millwork

South Charleston
Clark County

(G-13454)
BUCKEYE DIAMOND LOGISTICS INC (PA)
Also Called: Bdl Supply
15 Sprague Rd (45368-9644)
PHONE..................................937 462-8361
Samuel J Mc Adow Junior, Pr
John Mcadow, VP
Marianne Hinson, *
EMP: 120 EST: 1969
SALES (est): 32.81MM
SALES (corp-wide): 32.81MM Privately Held
Web: www.bdlsupply.com
SIC: 2448 2441 Pallets, wood; Boxes, wood

(G-13455)
WOODFORD LOGISTICS
15 Sprague Rd (45368-9644)
PHONE..................................513 417-8453
Steven L Means, Prin
EMP: 16 EST: 2010
SQ FT: 60,000
SALES (est): 450.71K Privately Held
Web: www.bdlsupply.com
SIC: 2448 Pallets, wood

(G-13456)
YAMADA NORTH AMERICA INC
Also Called: Yotec
9000 Columbus Cincinnati Rd (45368-9406)
P.O. Box Y (45368-0825)
PHONE..................................937 462-7111
Kiyoshi Osawa, Pr
William Mallory, *
John C Beeler, *
▲ EMP: 350 EST: 1946
SQ FT: 110,000
SALES (est): 93.49MM Privately Held
Web: www.yamadanorthamerica.com
SIC: 3714 3621 Motor vehicle steering systems and parts; Rotors, for motors
PA: Yamada Manufacturing Co., Ltd.
2-1296, Kobayashicho
Isesaki GNM 379-2

South Euclid
Cuyahoga County

(G-13457)
AEROCONTROLEX GROUP INC
Also Called: Aerocontrolex
4223 Monticello Blvd (44121-2814)
PHONE..................................216 291-6025
Chris Swartz, Pr
EMP: 99 EST: 1954
SQ FT: 55,000
SALES (est): 40.89MM
SALES (corp-wide): 6.58B Publicly Held
Web: www.aerocontrolex.com
SIC: 3492 5084 3594 Valves, hydraulic, aircraft; Industrial machinery and equipment ; Fluid power pumps and motors
HQ: Transdigm, Inc.
1350 Euclid Ave
Cleveland OH 44115

(G-13458)
AGRICOOL VEG & FRUITS LLC
310 S Green Rd (44121-2323)
PHONE..................................310 625-0024
EMP: 8 EST: 2020
SALES (est): 418.48K Privately Held
SIC: 2033 Vegetables and vegetable products, in cans, jars, etc.

(G-13459)
AS CLEAN AS IT GETS OFF BRKROO
4099 Lowden Rd (44121-2314)
PHONE..................................216 256-1143
EMP: 26 EST: 2020
SALES (est): 1.05MM Privately Held
SIC: 3589 7389 Commercial cleaning equipment; Business Activities at Non-Commercial Site

(G-13460)
EJ USA INC
4160 Glenridge Rd (44121-2802)
PHONE..................................216 692-3001
Richard Humkes Junior, Brnch Mgr
EMP: 19
SQ FT: 11,397
Web: www.ejco.com
SIC: 3321 3322 Gray iron castings, nec; Malleable iron foundries
HQ: Ej Usa, Inc.
301 Spring St
East Jordan MI 49727
800 874-4100

South Lebanon
Warren County

(G-13461)
GDW WOODWORKING LLC
120 Vista Ridge Dr (45065-8761)
PHONE..................................513 494-3041
EMP: 7 EST: 2007
SALES (est): 226K Privately Held
SIC: 2431 7389 Millwork; Business services, nec

(G-13462)
OHIO FLEXIBLE PACKAGING CO
512 S Main St (45065-1441)
PHONE..................................513 494-1800
Larry Lehman, Pr
Juith Lehman, Sec
Frank Remmey, VP
EMP: 11 EST: 1984
SQ FT: 10,000
SALES (est): 983.89K Privately Held
Web: www.ohioflex.com
SIC: 2759 Flexographic printing

South Point
Lawrence County

(G-13463)
ALPHA CONTROL LLC
Also Called: Alpha Control Fabg & Mfg
1042 County Road 60 (45680)
P.O. Box 1036 (45680)
PHONE..................................740 377-3400
Greg Joseph, Pr
EMP: 35 EST: 2010
SQ FT: 60,000
SALES (est): 4.55MM Privately Held
Web: www.alphacontrolfab.com
SIC: 3441 Fabricated structural metal

(G-13464)
ALPHA CTRL FABRICATION & MFG
1042 County Road 60 (45680-7465)
P.O. Box 1036 (45680-1036)
PHONE..................................740 377-3400
Gregory T Joseph, Pr
EMP: 12 EST: 2010
SALES (est): 851.47K Privately Held
Web: www.alphacontrolfab.com
SIC: 3441 Fabricated structural metal

(G-13465)
AMERICAN BOTTLING COMPANY
2531 County Road 1 (45680-7879)
PHONE..................................740 377-4371
Rick Hannon, Mgr
EMP: 83
Web: www.keurigdrpepper.com
SIC: 2086 Soft drinks: packaged in cans, bottles, etc.
HQ: The American Bottling Company
6425 Hall Of Fame Ln
Frisco TX 75034

(G-13466)
ENGINES INC OF OHIO
101 Commerce Dr (45680-8457)
P.O. Box 428 (45680-0428)
PHONE..................................740 377-9874
Carl C Grover, Pr
David W Sanders, *
Daniel T Yon, *
EMP: 48 EST: 2005
SQ FT: 100,000
SALES (est): 5.14MM Privately Held
Web: www.engines-inc.com
SIC: 3321 3325 3743 3532 Railroad car wheels and brake shoes, cast iron; Railroad car wheels, cast steel; Interurban cars and car equipment; Mining machinery

(G-13467)
JENNMAR MCSWEENEY LLC
235 Commerce Dr (45680)
PHONE..................................740 377-3354
Joe Mcsweeney, CEO
Frank Calandra, Pr
Sandra Blackburn, VP
▲ EMP: 140 EST: 2013
SQ FT: 30,900
SALES (est): 22.31MM
SALES (corp-wide): 361.92MM Privately Held
SIC: 3532 3531 Bits, except oil and gas field tools, rock; Blades for graders, scrapers, dozers, and snow plows
PA: Jennmar Holdings, Llc
258 Kappa Dr
Pittsburgh PA 15238
412 963-9071

(G-13468)
KINLY SIGNS CORPORATION
Also Called: River Cities Signarama
2485 County Road 1 (45680-7879)
PHONE..................................740 451-7446
Bernard Kincaid, Prin
Heather Kincaid, Prin
EMP: 14 EST: 2018
SALES (est): 428.08K Privately Held
SIC: 3993 Signs and advertising specialties

(G-13469)
KINOLY SIGNS
Also Called: Sign-A-Rama
2485 County Road 1 (45680-7879)
PHONE..................740 451-7446
EMP: 7 **EST:** 2017
SALES (est): 240.64K Privately Held
Web: www.signarama.com
SIC: 3993 Signs and advertising specialties

(G-13470)
MCGINNIS INC (HQ)
502 2nd St E (45680-9446)
P.O. Box 534 (45680-0534)
PHONE..................740 377-4391
Rickey Lee Griffith, Pr
Bruce D Mcginnis, CEO
Bill Jessie, *
D Dwaine Stephens, *
EMP: 193 **EST:** 1971
SQ FT: 5,000
SALES (est): 22.72MM Privately Held
Web: www.mcnational.com
SIC: 4491 3731 Marine cargo handling; Barges, building and repairing
PA: Mcnational, Inc.
502 2nd St E
South Point OH 45680

(G-13471)
MCNATIONAL INC (PA)
502 2nd St E (45680-9446)
P.O. Box 534 (45680-0534)
PHONE..................740 377-4391
Rick Griffith, Pr
C Clayton Johnson, *
C Barry Gipson, *
Bruce D Mcginnis, CEO
EMP: 97 **EST:** 1988
SQ FT: 5,000
SALES (est): 130.89MM Privately Held
Web: www.mcnational.com
SIC: 3731 7699 4491 Barges, building and repairing; Aircraft and heavy equipment repair services; Marine cargo handling

(G-13472)
MCSWEENEYS INC
235 Commerce Dr (45680-8465)
PHONE..................740 894-3353
▲ **EMP:** 140
SIC: 3532 3531 Bits, except oil and gas field tools, rock; Blades for graders, scrapers, dozers, and snow plows

(G-13473)
PRECISIONS PAINT SYSTEMS LLC
5852 County Road 1 (45680-7420)
PHONE..................740 894-6224
Michael Manns, CEO
EMP: 10 **EST:** 2015
SALES (est): 1MM Privately Held
SIC: 2851 Marine paints

(G-13474)
PYRO-CHEM CORPORATION
Also Called: Better Foam Insulation
2491 County Road 1 (45680-7879)
P.O. Box 884 (45680-0884)
PHONE..................740 377-2244
Joseph P Smith, Pr
Gailene M Smith, Sec
EMP: 14 **EST:** 1978
SQ FT: 12,000
SALES (est): 2.17MM Privately Held
SIC: 2899 Fire retardant chemicals

South Salem
Ross County

(G-13475)
JOEY ELLIOTT LOGGING LLC
8040 Upper Twin Rd (45681-9732)
PHONE..................740 626-0061
Joseph L Elliott, Owner
EMP: 6 **EST:** 2017
SALES (est): 119.88K Privately Held
SIC: 2411 Logging camps and contractors

South Webster
Scioto County

(G-13476)
MAE MATERIALS LLC
8336 Bennett School House Rd (45682-9029)
PHONE..................740 778-2242
Mark Allard, Managing Member
EMP: 23 **EST:** 2012
SQ FT: 108,900
SALES (est): 1.73MM Privately Held
SIC: 2951 Asphalt paving mixtures and blocks

South Zanesville
Muskingum County

(G-13477)
COCONIS FURNITURE INC (PA)
4 S Maysville Ave (43701-7401)
PHONE..................740 452-1231
▲ **EMP:** 44 **EST:** 1927
SALES (est): 18.6MM
SALES (corp-wide): 18.6MM Privately Held
Web: www.coconisfurniture.com
SIC: 5712 2515 Furniture stores; Mattresses and bedsprings

Southington
Trumbull County

(G-13478)
QUALITY MATCH PLATE CO INC
4211 State Route 534 (44470-9705)
PHONE..................330 889-2462
James W Dittrich, Pr
Genevieve Dittrich, Sec
Alexis Dittrich, Asst Tr
EMP: 20 **EST:** 1969
SQ FT: 6,200
SALES (est): 505.05K Privately Held
Web: www.qualitymatchplate.com
SIC: 3365 Utensils, cast aluminum

Spencer
Medina County

(G-13479)
ALTA MIRA CORPORATION
Also Called: Spencer Forge & Manufacturing
225 N Main St (44275-9759)
PHONE..................330 648-2461
Laurence E Rich, Pr
Deborah Rich, *
EMP: 65 **EST:** 1986
SQ FT: 83,000
SALES (est): 9.99MM Privately Held
Web: www.spencerforge.com
SIC: 3714 3462 Axles, motor vehicle; Iron and steel forgings

(G-13480)
CRUMLEY RACING STABLE LLC
9675 Chatham Rd (44275-9757)
PHONE..................216 513-0334
Jevon Crumley, Prin
EMP: 6 **EST:** 2005
SALES (est): 90.63K Privately Held
SIC: 2399 Horse harnesses and riding crops, etc.: non-leather

(G-13481)
GILES LOGGING LLC
7340 Richman Rd (44275-9736)
PHONE..................406 855-5284
Wade Giles, Prin
EMP: 6 **EST:** 2016
SALES (est): 96.41K Privately Held
SIC: 2411 Logging

(G-13482)
NICK KOSTECKI EXCAVATING INC
10644 Chatham Rd (44275-9333)
PHONE..................330 242-0706
Leah A Kostecki, Pr
EMP: 12 **EST:** 2007
SALES (est): 587.17K Privately Held
SIC: 3531 Plows: construction, excavating, and grading

(G-13483)
SPENCER FEED & SUPPLY LLC
227 N Main St (44275-9759)
PHONE..................330 648-2111
EMP: 11 **EST:** 2016
SALES (est): 2.1MM Privately Held
Web: www.spencerfeed.com
SIC: 5251 2048 0782 Hardware stores; Livestock feeds; Garden services

(G-13484)
SPENCER MANUFACTURING COMPANY INC
Also Called: Spencer Forge & Manufacturing
225 N Main St (44275-9759)
P.O. Box 68 (44275-0068)
PHONE..................330 648-2461
EMP: 70
Web: www.spencerforge.com
SIC: 3714 3542 Axles, motor vehicle; Machine tools, metal forming type

Spencerville
Allen County

(G-13485)
BLACKFISH SEALCOATING LLC
404 N Elizabeth St (45887-1236)
PHONE..................419 647-4010
Tom Farley, Admn
EMP: 6 **EST:** 2014
SALES (est): 73.77K Privately Held
Web: www.blackfishsealcoating.com
SIC: 2952 Asphalt felts and coatings

(G-13486)
D&D INGREDIENT DISTRS INC
Also Called: D&D Ingredients LLC
1610 S Acadia Rd (45887-9517)
PHONE..................419 692-2667
Arnold Miller, Pr
Ted Williams, COO
EMP: 78 **EST:** 1988
SALES (est): 2.96MM Privately Held
SIC: 2048 Cereal-, grain-, and seed-based feeds

(G-13487)
OHIO DECORATIVE PRODUCTS LLC (PA)
220 S Elizabeth St (45887-1315)
P.O. Box 126 (45887-0126)
PHONE..................419 647-9033
Charles D Moeller, Pr
Rick Moeller, *
Candace Moeller, *
Donald L Jerwers, *
George J Bowers, *
◆ **EMP:** 135 **EST:** 1970
SQ FT: 5,000
SALES (est): 48.87MM
SALES (corp-wide): 48.87MM Privately Held
SIC: 3086 3369 3471 3363 Plastics foam products; Zinc and zinc-base alloy castings, except die-castings; Plating and polishing; Aluminum die-castings

(G-13488)
PFP HOLDINGS LLC
220 S Elizabeth St (45887-1315)
P.O. Box 126 (45887-0126)
PHONE..................419 647-4191
◆ **EMP:** 750
SIC: 3069 5199 Foam rubber; Foam rubber

(G-13489)
S I DISTRIBUTING INC
Also Called: Holland Grills Distributing
13540 Spencerville Rd (45887-9525)
PHONE..................419 647-4909
Dave Durgei, Pr
Todd Keysor, Prin
▲ **EMP:** 13 **EST:** 1993
SQ FT: 22,000
SALES (est): 2.03MM Privately Held
Web: www.sidist.com
SIC: 3523 5083 5023 Cabs, tractors, and agricultural machinery; Agricultural machinery and equipment; Grills, barbecue

Spring Valley
Greene County

(G-13490)
ADVANCED TELEMETRICS INTL
Also Called: A T I
2361 Darnell Dr (45370-8708)
PHONE..................937 862-6948
Phillip Merrill, Pr
EMP: 11 **EST:** 1987
SQ FT: 3,000
SALES (est): 1.33MM Privately Held
Web: www.atitelemetry.com
SIC: 3829 Measuring and controlling devices, nec

(G-13491)
SAILORS TAILOR INC
Also Called: Bean Bag City
1480 Spring Valley Painters Rd (45370-9701)
PHONE..................937 862-7781
Robert Rowland, Pr
Sandra Rowland, Mgr
EMP: 10 **EST:** 1972
SQ FT: 2,400
SALES (est): 483.17K Privately Held
Web: www.sailorstailor.com
SIC: 2394 2519 5712 5551 Liners and covers, fabric: made from purchased materials; Household furniture, except wood or metal: upholstered; Furniture stores ; Marine supplies and equipment

(G-13492)
WORTHINGTON SERVICES LLC
3157 Sears Rd (45370-7723)
PHONE.................................937 848-2164
EMP: 9 **EST:** 2018
SALES (est): 1.21MM
SALES (corp-wide): 4.92B **Publicly Held**
Web: www.worthington.org
SIC: 3316 Strip, steel, cold-rolled, nec: from purchased hot-rolled,
PA: Worthington Enterprises, Inc.
200 W Old Wlson Bridge Rd
Worthington OH 43085
614 438-3210

Springboro
Warren County

(G-13493)
ADVANCED ENGRG SOLUTIONS INC
Also Called: Aesi
250 Advanced Dr (45066-1802)
PHONE.................................937 743-6900
Khang D.o.s., *Pr*
Thomas J Harrington, *
▲ **EMP:** 70 **EST:** 1995
SQ FT: 44,000
SALES (est): 9.83MM **Privately Held**
Web: www.advancedinternational.com
SIC: 8711 3544 Consulting engineer; Special dies, tools, jigs, and fixtures

(G-13494)
ADVANCED INTR SOLUTIONS INC
250 Advanced Dr (45066-1802)
PHONE.................................937 550-0065
Jeffrey S Senney, *Prin*
Khang D.o.s., *VP*
▲ **EMP:** 48 **EST:** 2005
SALES (est): 6.08MM **Privately Held**
Web: www.advancedinternational.com
SIC: 3544 Special dies, tools, jigs, and fixtures

(G-13495)
ALFONS HAAR INC
150 Advanced Dr (45066)
PHONE.................................937 560-2031
◆ **EMP:** 31 **EST:** 1993
SQ FT: 5,000
SALES (est): 8.91MM
SALES (corp-wide): 63.34MM **Privately Held**
Web: www.alfons-haar.us
SIC: 5084 3599 8711 Packaging machinery and equipment; Custom machinery; Engineering services
PA: Alfons Haar Maschinenbau Gmbh & Co. Kg
Fangdieckstr. 67
Hamburg HH 22547
40833910

(G-13496)
BORO DRIVE-THRU LLC
115 S Pioneer Blvd (45066-1178)
PHONE.................................937 743-1700
Bradley Hausfeld, *Prin*
EMP: 7 **EST:** 2010
SALES (est): 180K **Privately Held**
SIC: 3421 Table and food cutlery, including butchers'

(G-13497)
BUCKEYE FABRICATING COMPANY
245 S Pioneer Blvd (45066-1180)
PHONE.................................937 746-9822
Richard K Macaulay, *Pr*
Teri Macaulay, *

▼ **EMP:** 35 **EST:** 1963
SQ FT: 20,000
SALES (est): 7.29MM
SALES (corp-wide): 54.32MM **Privately Held**
Web: www.buckeyefabricating.com
SIC: 3443 Tanks, standard or custom fabricated: metal plate
PA: Lt Corporation, Inc.
2914 Hwy 61 S
Cleveland MS 38732
662 843-4046

(G-13498)
COACH TOOL & DIE LLC
235 S Pioneer Blvd (45066-1180)
PHONE.................................937 890-4716
Dave Hollon, *Pr*
Gregg Kopp, *VP*
EMP: 6 **EST:** 1998
SALES (est): 899.59K **Privately Held**
Web: www.coachtoolinc.com
SIC: 3544 Special dies and tools

(G-13499)
DIGILUBE SYSTEMS INC
216 E Mill St (45066-1614)
PHONE.................................937 748-2209
David Hamilton, *Pr*
EMP: 10 **EST:** 1981
SQ FT: 5,000
SALES (est): 2.78MM **Privately Held**
Web: www.digilube.com
SIC: 3569 2992 5084 5172 Lubricating equipment; Oils and greases, blending and compounding; Conveyor systems; Lubricating oils and greases

(G-13500)
EPLUNO LLC
420 Heatherwoode Cir (45066-1528)
PHONE.................................800 249-5275
EMP: 17 **EST:** 2012
SALES (est): 1.83MM **Privately Held**
Web: www.epluno.com
SIC: 2326 Men's and boy's work clothing

(G-13501)
FEATHER LITE INNOVATIONS INC (PA)
Also Called: Tuf-N-Lite
650 Pleasant Valley Dr (45066-3026)
PHONE.................................937 743-9008
▲ **EMP:** 20 **EST:** 1995
SALES (est): 4.38MM **Privately Held**
Web: s532643390.onlinehome.us
SIC: 3444 5211 Concrete products, sheet metal; Masonry materials and supplies

(G-13502)
GENERAL DYNAMICS-OTS INC
Also Called: General Dynamics
200 S Pioneer Blvd (45066-1179)
PHONE.................................937 746-8500
Anne-marie Stanley, *Dir*
EMP: 178
SQ FT: 220,000
SALES (corp-wide): 42.27B **Publicly Held**
Web: www.gd-ots.com
SIC: 3728 Aircraft parts and equipment, nec
HQ: General Dynamics-Ots, Inc.
100 Carillon Pkwy Ste 100 # 100
Saint Petersburg FL 33716
727 578-8100

(G-13503)
GRAPHIC SYSTEMS SERVICES INC
Also Called: G S S
400 S Pioneer Blvd (45066-3001)
PHONE.................................937 746-0708
EMP: 41 **EST:** 1995

SQ FT: 100,000
SALES (est): 7.63MM
SALES (corp-wide): 573MM **Publicly Held**
Web: www.didde.com
SIC: 7699 3555 Industrial equipment services; Printing presses
PA: Eastman Kodak Company
343 State St
Rochester NY 14650
585 724-4000

(G-13504)
HIGH CONCRETE GROUP LLC
95 Mound Park Dr (45066-2402)
PHONE.................................937 748-2412
Dennis Nemenz, *Bmch Mgr*
EMP: 286
SALES (corp-wide): 694.31MM **Privately Held**
Web: www.highconcrete.com
SIC: 3272 Concrete structural support and building material
HQ: High Concrete Group Llc
125 Denver Rd
Denver PA 17517
717 735-1060

(G-13505)
INTERNATIONAL JUMP ROPE UNION
1103 Lakemont Dr (45066-8185)
PHONE.................................937 409-1006
EMP: 6 **EST:** 2012
SALES (est): 169.54K **Privately Held**
Web: www.worldjumprope.org
SIC: 2298 Cordage and twine

(G-13506)
JK DIGITAL PUBLISHING LLC
Also Called: Greyden Press
20 Heatherwoode Cir (45066-1500)
P.O. Box 224 (44652-0224)
PHONE.................................937 299-0185
EMP: 10 **EST:** 1991
SQ FT: 7,500
SALES (est): 411.07K **Privately Held**
SIC: 2752 3652 Commercial printing, lithographic; Compact laser discs, prerecorded

(G-13507)
KASKELL MANUFACTURING INC
Also Called: Kaskell
240 Hiawatha Trl (45066-3010)
P.O. Box 83 (45305-0083)
PHONE.................................937 704-9700
Diane W Harris, *Pr*
Brian Harris, *VP*
EMP: 10 **EST:** 1996
SQ FT: 4,500
SALES (est): 990.55K **Privately Held**
Web: www.kaskellmfg.com
SIC: 3599 Machine shop, jobbing and repair

(G-13508)
KELCHNER INC (DH)
50 Advanced Dr (45066-1805)
PHONE.................................937 704-9890
Todd Kelchner, *CEO*
Troy Norvell, *
EMP: 114 **EST:** 1948
SQ FT: 8,600
SALES (est): 75.76MM
SALES (corp-wide): 5.9B **Privately Held**
Web: www.kelchner.com
SIC: 1794 1389 Excavation work; Mud service, oil field drilling
HQ: Wood Group Uk Limited
Sir Ian Wood House
Aberdeen AB12
122 450-0400

(G-13509)
MACHINED GLASS SPECIALIST INC
245 Hiawatha Trl (45066-3011)
PHONE.................................937 743-6166
David Behm, *Pr*
Melanie Behm, *Sec*
Maurice Vines, *Genl Mgr*
EMP: 11 **EST:** 1989
SQ FT: 9,000
SALES (est): 2.28MM **Privately Held**
Web: www.mgsfusedquartz.com
SIC: 5039 3211 Glass construction materials; Tempered glass

(G-13510)
MOUND STEEL CORP
25 Mound Park Dr (45066-2410)
PHONE.................................937 748-2937
Thomas C Miller, *CEO*
Thomas C Miller, *Pr*
EMP: 17 **EST:** 1963
SALES (est): 476.66K **Privately Held**
Web: www.moundtechnologies.com
SIC: 3449 Bars, concrete reinforcing: fabricated steel

(G-13511)
MOUND TECHNOLOGIES INC
25 Mound Park Dr (45066-2402)
PHONE.................................937 748-2937
Thomas Miller, *Pr*
John Barger, *
Shelia A Campbell, *
EMP: 45 **EST:** 2003
SQ FT: 40,000
SALES (est): 17.81MM
SALES (corp-wide): 48.46MM **Privately Held**
Web: www.moundtechnologies.com
SIC: 3441 1791 3446 Building components, structural steel; Structural steel erection; Gates, ornamental metal
PA: Heartland, Inc.
1005 N 19th St
Middlesboro KY 40965
606 248-7323

(G-13512)
NO RINSE LABORATORIES LLC
Also Called: Cleanlife Products
868 Pleasant Valley Dr (45066-1159)
PHONE.................................937 746-7357
EMP: 7 **EST:** 1948
SQ FT: 6,000
SALES (est): 1.25MM **Privately Held**
Web: www.cleanlifeproducts.com
SIC: 2836 Veterinary biological products

(G-13513)
NYLE LLC
Also Called: Lynn Electronics
283 Sharts Dr (45066-3030)
PHONE.................................888 235-2097
Charles Hoskins, *Mgr*
EMP: 13
SALES (corp-wide): 31.1MM **Privately Held**
Web: www.thinklynn.com
SIC: 3679 3643 Harness assemblies, for electronic use: wire or cable; Connectors and terminals for electrical devices
PA: Nyle, Llc
555 E Lancaster Ave Fl 3
Radnor PA 19087

(G-13514)
OHIO TOOL & JIG GRIND INC
6948 Clearview Ct (45066-7000)
PHONE.................................937 415-0692
David A Brinker, *Pr*
EMP: 19 **EST:** 1999

Springboro - Warren County (G-13515)

SALES (est): 886.95K **Privately Held**
Web: www.otjg.org
SIC: **3544** Special dies, tools, jigs, and fixtures

(G-13515)
PHYMET INC
75 N Pioneer Blvd (45066-3055)
PHONE.............................937 743-8061
Amy Minck Lachman, *Pr*
EMP: **17** EST: **1986**
SQ FT: 12,500
SALES (est): 2.44MM **Privately Held**
Web: www.micropoly.com
SIC: **2992** 8734 Oils and greases, blending and compounding; Metallurgical testing laboratory

(G-13516)
PSIX LLC
Also Called: Paper Systems Incorporated
185 S Pioneer Blvd (45066-3045)
P.O. Box 150 (45066-0150)
PHONE.............................937 746-6841
Bryan Eovaldi, *Pr*
EMP: **100** EST: **2018**
SALES (est): 12.4MM **Privately Held**
Web: www.papersystems.com
SIC: **2679** Paper products, converted, nec

(G-13517)
QUICK TECH BUSINESS FORMS INC
408 Sharts Dr (45066-3000)
P.O. Box 607 (45066-0607)
PHONE.............................937 743-5952
Kevin Gilliam, *Mgr*
Chris Felker, *
Linda Felker, *
EMP: **10** EST: **1990**
SALES (est): 493.21K **Privately Held**
SIC: **2759** 3999 Financial note and certificate printing and engraving; Barber and beauty shop equipment

(G-13518)
QUICK TECH GRAPHICS INC
408 Sharts Dr Frnt (45066-3021)
P.O. Box 607 (45066-0607)
PHONE.............................937 743-5952
Christopher H Felker, *Pr*
Linda Felker, *
EMP: **25** EST: **1990**
SQ FT: 15,000
SALES (est): 1.33MM **Privately Held**
Web: www.quicktechgraphics.com
SIC: **2761** 5943 2791 2782 Manifold business forms; Office forms and supplies; Typesetting; Blankbooks and looseleaf binders

(G-13519)
SAFE HAVEN BRANDS LLC
Also Called: DK Bicycles
217 S Pioneer Blvd (45066-1183)
PHONE.............................937 550-9407
EMP: **12** EST: **2015**
SALES (est): 669.25K **Privately Held**
SIC: **3751** Bicycles and related parts

(G-13520)
SUNSTAR ENGRG AMERICAS INC (HQ)
Also Called: Sunstar
85 S Pioneer Blvd (45066-3039)
PHONE.............................937 746-8575
▲ EMP: **32** EST: **1993**
SQ FT: 28,000
SALES (est): 41.38MM **Privately Held**
Web: www.sunstar-braking.com
SIC: **3751** 2891 Motorcycles and related parts; Adhesives
PA: Starlecs Inc.
3-1, Asahimachi
Takatsuki OSK 569-1

(G-13521)
THALER MACHINE COMPANY LLC
216 Tahlequah Trl (45066-3052)
P.O. Box 430 (45066-0430)
PHONE.............................937 550-2400
▲ EMP: **135** EST: **1952**
SALES (est): 30MM
SALES (corp-wide): 41.84MM **Privately Held**
Web: www.thalermachine.com
SIC: **3545** Precision measuring tools
PA: Thaler Machine Holdings, Llc
216 Tahlequah Trl
Springboro OH 45066
937 550-2400

(G-13522)
THALER MACHINE HOLDINGS LLC (PA)
216 Tahlequah Trl (45066-3052)
P.O. Box 430 (45066-0430)
PHONE.............................937 550-2400
Greg Donson, *CEO*
EMP: **28** EST: **2019**
SQ FT: 22,000
SALES (est): 41.84MM
SALES (corp-wide): 41.84MM **Privately Held**
Web: www.thalermachine.com
SIC: **3545** Precision measuring tools

(G-13523)
TOOLING ZONE INC
285 S Pioneer Blvd (45066-1180)
PHONE.............................937 550-4180
EMP: **30** EST: **1995**
SQ FT: 9,000
SALES (est): 5.11MM **Privately Held**
Web: www.toolingzone.com
SIC: **3544** Special dies and tools

(G-13524)
TREBNICK SYSTEMS INC
Also Called: Trebnick Tags and Labels
215 S Pioneer Blvd (45066-1180)
PHONE.............................937 743-1550
Gregg Trebnick, *CEO*
Linda Trebnick, *
Aaron Trebnick, *
◆ EMP: **29** EST: **1986**
SQ FT: 24,480
SALES (est): 5.86MM **Privately Held**
Web: www.trebnick.com
SIC: **2752** 2759 Tags, lithographed; Bags, plastic: printing, nsk

Springdale
Hamilton County

(G-13525)
GE AVIATION SYSTEMS LLC
Also Called: GE Aviation
183 Progress Pl (45246-1717)
PHONE.............................620 218-5237
David Joyce, *CEO*
EMP: **20**
SALES (corp-wide): 67.95B **Publicly Held**
Web: www.geaerospace.com
SIC: **3313** Alloys, additive, except copper: not made in blast furnaces
HQ: Ge Aviation Systems Llc
1 Neumann Way
Cincinnati OH 45215
937 898-9600

Springfield
Clark County

(G-13526)
A & E POWDER COATING LTD
1511 Sheridan Ave (45505-2257)
P.O. Box 1226 (45501-1226)
PHONE.............................937 525-3750
Edward Leventhal, *Pr*
EMP: **7** EST: **2000**
SALES (est): 906.93K **Privately Held**
Web: www.aepowdercoating.com
SIC: **3479** Coating of metals and formed products

(G-13527)
ACCURIDE CORPORATION
4800 Gateway Blvd (45502-8818)
PHONE.............................812 962-5000
EMP: **32**
Web: www.accuridecorp.com
SIC: **3714** Wheels, motor vehicle
HQ: Accuride Corporation
38777 6 Mile Rd Ste 410
Livonia MI 48152
812 962-5000

(G-13528)
ACE TRANSFER COMPANY
1020 Hometown St (45504-2055)
PHONE.............................937 398-1103
David J Shaw, *Pr*
EMP: **6** EST: **1994**
SALES (est): 709.08K **Privately Held**
Web: www.acetransco.com
SIC: **2759** Screen printing

(G-13529)
AKZO NOBEL COATINGS INC
1550 Progress Rd (45505-4456)
PHONE.............................937 322-2671
Ron Cecil, *Mgr*
EMP: **31**
SALES (corp-wide): 11.26B **Privately Held**
SIC: **2851** Paints: oil or alkyd vehicle or water thinned
HQ: Akzo Nobel Coatings Inc.
535 Marriott Dr Ste 500
Nashville TN 37214
440 297-5100

(G-13530)
ALL-IN NUTRITIONALS LLC
5060 S Charleston Pike (45502-6315)
PHONE.............................888 400-0333
Lindsey Duncan, *CEO*
EMP: **6** EST: **2018**
SALES (est): 39.59K **Privately Held**
Web: www.allinnutritionals.com
SIC: **2023** Dietary supplements, dairy and non-dairy based

(G-13531)
ALMANDREY FABRICATING TECH
107 Tremont City Rd (45502-9506)
PHONE.............................937 408-0054
Edgardo Delacruz, *Prin*
EMP: **6** EST: **2011**
SALES (est): 244.82K **Privately Held**
SIC: **7692** Welding repair

(G-13532)
AMCAN STAIR & RAIL LLC
20 Zischler St (45504-2853)
PHONE.............................937 781-3084
Mike Edmondson, *Prin*
EMP: **13** EST: **2001**
SALES (est): 502.26K **Privately Held**
Web: www.amcanstairandrail.com
SIC: **2431** Staircases and stairs, wood

(G-13533)
AOT INC
4800 Gateway Blvd (45502-8818)
PHONE.............................937 323-9669
Richard F Dauch, *CEO*
EMP: **52** EST: **1991**
SQ FT: 136,000
SALES (est): 1.07MM **Privately Held**
Web: www.accuridecorp.com
SIC: **3559** Pack-up assemblies, wheel overhaul
HQ: Accuride Corporation
38777 6 Mile Rd Ste 410
Livonia MI 48152
812 962-5000

(G-13534)
APPETZERS R US ST EATS 2 GO LL
2010 Ontario Ave (45505-1733)
PHONE.............................937 460-1470
EMP: **6** EST: **2021**
SALES (est): 236.34K **Privately Held**
SIC: **2599** 7389 Food wagons, restaurant; Business services, nec

(G-13535)
ARCTECH FABRICATING INC (PA)
1317 Lagonda Ave (45503-4001)
P.O. Box 1447 (45501-1447)
PHONE.............................937 525-9353
James C Roberts Ii, *Pr*
Tina Roberts, *
Leonard Mcconnaghey, *CEO*
EMP: **29** EST: **1992**
SQ FT: 13,200
SALES (est): 6.23MM **Privately Held**
Web: www.arctechfabricating.com
SIC: **7692** 3441 Welding repair; Fabricated structural metal

(G-13536)
ARMOLOY OF OHIO INC
1950 E Leffel Ln (45505)
P.O. Box 996 (45501)
PHONE.............................937 323-8702
Steven Neely, *Pr*
EMP: **23** EST: **1976**
SQ FT: 10,000
SALES (est): 1.58MM **Privately Held**
Web: www.armoloyofohio.com
SIC: **3479** Coating of metals and formed products

(G-13537)
B O K INC
508 W Main St (45504-2662)
PHONE.............................937 322-9588
Kenneth Klosterman, *CEO*
Chip Klosterman, *
EMP: **69** EST: **1983**
SALES (est): 244.68K
SALES (corp-wide): 190.57MM **Privately Held**
SIC: **2045** Bread and bread type roll mixes: from purchased flour
PA: Klosterman Baking Co., Llc
4760 Paddock Rd
Cincinnati OH 45229
513 242-1004

(G-13538)
BAN INC
Also Called: Harwood Screw Products
619 S Belmont Ave (45505-2325)
P.O. Box 194 (45501-0194)
PHONE.............................937 325-5539
Bruce Lloyd, *Pr*
Douglas R Lloyd, *
Neita Lloyd, *

GEOGRAPHIC SECTION
Springfield - Clark County (G-13562)

EMP: 25 EST: 1947
SQ FT: 9,000
SALES (est): 1.78MM **Privately Held**
SIC: **3451** Screw machine products

(G-13539)
BAY BUSINESS FORMS INC
1803 W Columbia St (45504-2903)
PHONE.....................937 322-3000
Paulette Bay, *Pr*
Robert E Troop, *CEO*
EMP: 24 EST: 1974
SQ FT: 22,000
SALES (est): 896.4K **Privately Held**
SIC: **5112** 2752 Business forms; Offset printing
PA: The Shamrock Companies Inc
24090 Detroit Rd
Westlake OH 44145

(G-13540)
BRIDGESTONE RET OPERATIONS LLC
Also Called: Firestone
1475 Upper Valley Pike (45504-4023)
PHONE.....................937 325-4638
David Weeks, *Mgr*
EMP: 7
Web: www.bridgestoneamericas.com
SIC: **5531** 7534 Automotive tires; Tire retreading and repair shops
HQ: Bridgestone Retail Operations, Llc
333 E Lake St Ste 300
Bloomingdale IL 60108
630 259-9000

(G-13541)
CASCADE CORPORATION
2501 Sheridan Ave (45505-2519)
P.O. Box 20187 (97294-0187)
PHONE.....................937 327-0300
Rodney Hitman, *Brnch Mgr*
EMP: 92
Web: www.cascorp.com
SIC: **3537** 3713 3593 Trucks, tractors, loaders, carriers, and similar equipment; Truck and bus bodies; Fluid power cylinders and actuators
HQ: Cascade Corporation
2201 Ne 201st Ave
Fairview OR 97024
503 669-6300

(G-13542)
CAVE TOOL & MFG INC
20 Walnut St (45505-1145)
PHONE.....................937 324-0662
Gilbert R Cave, *Pr*
Carrie Cave, *VP*
EMP: 10 EST: 1967
SQ FT: 26,000
SALES (est): 926.38K **Privately Held**
SIC: **3599** Machine shop, jobbing and repair

(G-13543)
CES NATIONWIDE
567 E Leffel Ln (45505-4748)
PHONE.....................937 322-0771
EMP: 7 EST: 2009
SALES (est): 529.5K **Privately Held**
SIC: **3699** 3634 5063 Electrical equipment and supplies, nec; Electric housewares and fans; Electrical supplies, nec

(G-13544)
CHAMPION COMPANY
Also Called: Champion
1100 Kenton St (45505-3136)
PHONE.....................937 324-5681
EMP: 8
SALES (corp-wide): 19.8MM **Privately Held**
Web: www.thechampioncompany.com
SIC: **3412** Metal barrels, drums, and pails
PA: The Champion Company
400 Harrison St
Springfield OH 45505
937 324-5681

(G-13545)
COLBY PROPERTIES LLC
2071 N Bechtle Ave (45504-1583)
PHONE.....................937 390-0816
EMP: 6 EST: 2002
SQ FT: 20,000
SALES (est): 565.21K **Privately Held**
Web: www.privatelendingmadeeasy.com
SIC: **3999** Education aids, devices and supplies

(G-13546)
COMPTONS PRECISION MACHINE
Also Called: Eastern Enterprise
224 Dayton Ave (45506-1206)
P.O. Box 2614 (45501-2614)
PHONE.....................937 325-9139
John Compton, *Pr*
Denise Compton, *Sec*
EMP: 12 EST: 1981
SQ FT: 11,000
SALES (est): 1.65MM **Privately Held**
SIC: **3599** 7692 Machine shop, jobbing and repair; Welding repair

(G-13547)
CORROTEC INC
1125 W North St (45504-2713)
PHONE.....................937 325-3585
David A Stratton, *CEO*
Aristides G Gianakopoulos, *
John C Stratton, *
Walter A Wildman, *
EMP: 37 EST: 1981
SQ FT: 28,500
SALES (est): 12.96MM **Privately Held**
Web: www.corrotec.com
SIC: **3559** 7699 3479 3625 Electroplating machinery and equipment; Tank repair; Coating of metals with plastic or resins; Electric controls and control accessories, industrial

(G-13548)
COX OHIO PUBLISHING - DAYTON
202 N Limestone St (45503-4246)
PHONE.....................937 328-0300
Steve Sidlo, *Prin*
EMP: 10 EST: 2012
SALES (est): 165.33K **Privately Held**
Web: www.daytondailynews.com
SIC: **2741** Miscellaneous publishing

(G-13549)
CRANE PRO SERVICES
4401 Gateway Blvd (45502-9339)
PHONE.....................937 525-5555
George Berner, *Engr*
EMP: 9 EST: 2015
SALES (est): 883.55K **Privately Held**
Web: www.konecranes.com
SIC: **3531** Construction machinery

(G-13550)
CUSTOM RECAPPING INC
Also Called: Custom Tire
126 Linden Ave (45505-1015)
PHONE.....................937 324-4331
Brian W House, *Pr*
Carolyn House, *Sec*
EMP: 6 EST: 1954
SQ FT: 10,000
SALES (est): 756.62K **Privately Held**
Web: www.customtire.biz
SIC: **5531** 7534 Automotive tires; Tire recapping

(G-13551)
DEARTH RESOURCES INC (PA)
Also Called: Hill Bryce Concrete
2301 Sheridan Ave (45505-2515)
P.O. Box 1043 (45501-1043)
PHONE.....................937 325-0651
Debra Grimes, *Pr*
EMP: 6 EST: 1934
SQ FT: 20,000
SALES (est): 797.53K
SALES (corp-wide): 797.53K **Privately Held**
Web: www.brycehill.com
SIC: **3273** 3271 5211 Ready-mixed concrete; Blocks, concrete or cinder: standard; Lumber and other building materials

(G-13552)
DEARTH RESOURCES INC
8801 State Route 36 (45501)
P.O. Box 1043 (45501-1043)
PHONE.....................937 663-4171
Debra Grimes, *Pr*
EMP: 8
SALES (corp-wide): 797.53K **Privately Held**
Web: www.brycehill.com
SIC: **3273** 3271 Ready-mixed concrete; Blocks, concrete or cinder: standard
PA: Dearth Resources, Inc.
2301 Sheridan Ave
Springfield OH 45505
937 325-0651

(G-13553)
DELILLE OXYGEN COMPANY
1101 W Columbia St (45504-2846)
PHONE.....................937 325-9595
Mike Lee, *Mgr*
EMP: 8
SALES (corp-wide): 25.92MM **Privately Held**
Web: www.delille.com
SIC: **2813** 5084 Industrial gases; Welding machinery and equipment
PA: Delille Oxygen Company
772 Marion Rd
Columbus OH 43207
614 444-1177

(G-13554)
DEMMY SAND AND GRAVEL LLC
4324 Fairfield Pike (45502-9707)
EMP: 25 EST: 1944
SALES (est): 2.2MM **Privately Held**
SIC: **1442** 0115 0119 0111 Common sand mining; Corn; Bean (dry field and seed) farm; Wheat

(G-13555)
DILLON MANUFACTURING INC
2115 Progress Rd (45505-4470)
PHONE.....................937 325-8482
Joseph Shouvlin, *Pr*
EMP: 19 EST: 1953
SQ FT: 15,000
SALES (est): 2.31MM **Privately Held**
Web: www.dillonmfg.com
SIC: **3599** Machine shop, jobbing and repair

(G-13556)
DOLE FRESH VEGETABLES INC
Also Called: Dole
600 Benjamin Dr (45502-8860)
PHONE.....................937 525-4300
Lenny Pelifian, *Brnch Mgr*
EMP: 190
SALES (corp-wide): 3.64B **Privately Held**
SIC: **5148** 2099 Fruits, fresh; Food preparations, nec
HQ: Dole Fresh Vegetables, Inc.
2959 Salinas Hwy
Monterey CA 93940

(G-13557)
DUPLEX MILL & MANUFACTURING CO
Also Called: Kelly Duplex
415 Sigler St (45506-1144)
P.O. Box 1266 (45501-1266)
PHONE.....................937 325-5555
Eric W Wise, *Pr*
Frederick Wise, *VP*
EMP: 20 EST: 1908
SQ FT: 50,000
SALES (est): 2.48MM **Privately Held**
Web: www.dmmc.com
SIC: **3535** 3531 Conveyors and conveying equipment; Mixers, nec: ore, plaster, slag, sand, mortar, etc.

(G-13558)
ELECTRIC EEL MFG CO INC
501 W Leffel Ln (45506-3529)
P.O. Box 419 (45501-0419)
PHONE.....................937 323-4644
David Hale, *CEO*
Thomas H Hale, *
▲ EMP: 38 EST: 1968
SQ FT: 21,000
SALES (est): 9.69MM **Privately Held**
Web: www.electriceel.com
SIC: **3423** 3589 Hand and edge tools, nec; Sewer cleaning equipment, power

(G-13559)
ERNEST INDUSTRIES INC
Also Called: Kelly-Creswell Company
1221 Groop Rd (45504-3829)
PHONE.....................937 325-9851
EMP: 11 EST: 1995
SALES (est): 2.65MM **Privately Held**
Web: www.ernestindustries.com
SIC: **3563** Air and gas compressors

(G-13560)
ESTERLINE & SONS MFG CO LLC
6508 Old Clifton Rd (45502-8474)
PHONE.....................937 265-5278
John Maurer, *Managing Member*
▲ EMP: 22 EST: 1957
SQ FT: 1,500
SALES (est): 4.21MM **Privately Held**
Web: www.esterlineandsons.com
SIC: **3599** Machine shop, jobbing and repair

(G-13561)
EVER ROLL SPECIALTIES CO
3988 Lawrenceville Dr (45504-4458)
PHONE.....................937 964-1302
John Hadley, *CEO*
Edwin J Kohl, *
I Scott Wallace, *
▲ EMP: 30 EST: 1945
SQ FT: 43,000
SALES (est): 3.97MM **Privately Held**
Web: www.ever-roll.com
SIC: **3498** 3496 Tube fabricating (contract bending and shaping); Miscellaneous fabricated wire products

(G-13562)
F H BONN CO INC
4300 Gateway Blvd (45502-8819)
P.O. Box 12388 (34979-2388)
PHONE.....................937 323-7024
Neal Bonn, *Pr*
Allan Bonn, *
▲ EMP: 22 EST: 1946

Springfield - Clark County (G-13563)

SQ FT: 43,000
SALES (est): 423.5K **Privately Held**
Web: www.fhbonn.com
SIC: 2211 Plushes and piles, broadwoven cotton: including flannels

(G-13563)
FAMILY PACKAGING INC (PA)
504 W Euclid Ave (45506-2010)
PHONE.................................937 325-4106
Janet Kennedy, *Pr*
James Miles, *VP*
EMP: 6 **EST:** 1992
SQ FT: 47,000
SALES (est): 2.06MM **Privately Held**
SIC: 2653 Boxes, corrugated: made from purchased materials

(G-13564)
FINK MEAT COMPANY INC
2475 Troy Rd (45504-4233)
P.O. Box 1281 (45501-1281)
PHONE.................................937 390-2750
William Craig Minter, *Pr*
Douglas Minter, *VP*
EMP: 7 **EST:** 1921
SQ FT: 8,600
SALES (est): 1.73MM **Privately Held**
Web: www.finkmeatco.com
SIC: 5147 2013 Meats, fresh; Luncheon meat, from purchased meat

(G-13565)
FLASHIONS SPORTSWEAR LTD
1002 N Bechtle Ave (45504-2008)
PHONE.................................937 323-5885
Ronald Turner, *Genl Pt*
Bethany Turner, *Pt*
EMP: 9 **EST:** 1987
SQ FT: 4,000
SALES (est): 962.68K **Privately Held**
Web: www.flashions.com
SIC: 5199 2262 Advertising specialties; Screen printing: manmade fiber and silk broadwoven fabrics

(G-13566)
FLUID QUIP CUSTOM MA
20 Walnut St (45505-1145)
PHONE.................................937 324-0662
EMP: 7 **EST:** 2019
SALES (est): 492.73K **Privately Held**
SIC: 3599 Custom machinery

(G-13567)
FLUID QUIP KS LLC
1940 S Yellow Springs St Ste 2 (45506-3048)
PHONE.................................937 324-0352
Danai Brooks, *CEO*
Mark Schneider, *Ex VP*
EMP: 55 **EST:** 2021
SALES (est): 10.17MM
SALES (corp-wide): 110.62MM **Privately Held**
Web: www.fluidquip.com
SIC: 2046 Wet corn milling
PA: Komline-Sanderson Corporation
12 Holland Ave
Peapack NJ 07977
908 234-1000

(G-13568)
FQ SALE INC (PA)
1940 S Yellow Springs St (45506-3000)
◆ **EMP:** 26 **EST:** 1987
SQ FT: 50,000
SALES (est): 8.45MM
SALES (corp-wide): 8.45MM **Privately Held**
Web: www.fluidquip.com

SIC: 3554 Pulp mill machinery

(G-13569)
FRIENDS ROCKING HORSE CENTER
651 S Limestone St (45505-1965)
PHONE.................................937 324-1111
EMP: 6
SALES (est): 220.67K **Privately Held**
Web: www.rockinghorsecenter.org
SIC: 3944 Rocking horses

(G-13570)
GRAPHIC PAPER PRODUCTS CORP (HQ)
Also Called: Miller Printing Co
6069 Yeazell Rd (45502-9216)
P.O. Box 1666 (45501-1666)
PHONE.................................937 325-5503
Jeanne Lampe, *Pr*
EMP: 82 **EST:** 1891
SALES (est): 22.38MM **Privately Held**
SIC: 2754 2752 2652 2653 Job printing: gravure; Commercial printing, lithographic; Setup paperboard boxes; Boxes, corrugated: made from purchased materials
PA: Patented Acquisition Corporation
2490 Cross Pointe Dr
Miamisburg OH 45342

(G-13571)
HALLMARK INDUSTRIES INC (PA)
Also Called: Miller, Jim Furniture
2233 N Limestone St (45503-2635)
PHONE.................................937 864-7378
James Odell Miller, *Pr*
Diane E Miller, *
EMP: 25 **EST:** 1972
SQ FT: 54,000
SALES (est): 1.95MM
SALES (corp-wide): 1.95MM **Privately Held**
Web: www.hallmarkind.com
SIC: 2512 5712 Living room furniture: upholstered on wood frames; Furniture stores

(G-13572)
HDI LANDING GEAR USA INC (HQ)
663 Montgomery Ave (45506-1847)
PHONE.................................937 325-1586
EMP: 100 **EST:** 2008
SALES (est): 104.95MM
SALES (corp-wide): 400.71MM **Privately Held**
Web: www.herouxdevtek.com
SIC: 3728 Alighting (landing gear) assemblies, aircraft
PA: Heroux-Devtek Inc
1111 Rue Saint-Charles O Bureau 600
Longueuil QC J4K 5
450 679-5450

(G-13573)
HEAT TREATING INC (PA)
1762 W Pleasant St (45506-1128)
PHONE.................................937 325-3121
Chester L Walthall, *Pr*
Judith A Walthall, *
Michael Trimble, *
Keith Thue, *Quality Vice President**
EMP: 28 **EST:** 1959
SQ FT: 33,000
SALES (est): 4.62MM
SALES (corp-wide): 4.62MM **Privately Held**
Web: www.heattreating.com
SIC: 3398 Metal heat treating

(G-13574)
HEF USA CORPORATION (PA)
2015 Progress Rd (45505-4472)
PHONE.................................937 323-2556
▲ **EMP:** 8 **EST:** 1993
SALES (est): 4.83MM **Privately Held**
Web: www.hefusa.net
SIC: 3826 Surface area analyzers

(G-13575)
HEROUX-DEVTEK INC
Also Called: Heroux-Devtek Springfield
663 Montgomery Ave (45506-1847)
PHONE.................................937 325-1586
Gilles Labbe, *Pr*
EMP: 19 **EST:** 2010
SALES (est): 5.76MM
SALES (corp-wide): 400.71MM **Privately Held**
Web: www.herouxdevtek.com
SIC: 3728 Aircraft parts and equipment, nec
PA: Heroux-Devtek Inc
1111 Rue Saint-Charles O Bureau 600
Longueuil QC J4K 5
450 679-5450

(G-13576)
HILLTOP BASIC RESOURCES INC
Enon Washed Sand & Gravel Div
1665 Enon Rd (45502-9102)
PHONE.................................937 882-6357
Jack Blair, *Prin*
EMP: 14
SALES (corp-wide): 59.62MM **Privately Held**
Web: www.hilltopcompanies.com
SIC: 1771 1442 Concrete work; Construction sand and gravel
PA: Hilltop Basic Resources, Inc.
50 E Rvrcnter Blvd Ste 10
Covington KY 41011
513 651-5000

(G-13577)
HOLMES W & SONS PRINTING
Also Called: Holmes Printing
401 E Columbia St (45503-4214)
P.O. Box 2300 (45501-2300)
PHONE.................................937 325-1509
William W Holmes, *Pr*
EMP: 18 **EST:** 1974
SQ FT: 2,500
SALES (est): 1.95MM **Privately Held**
Web: www.thinkholmes.com
SIC: 2752 Offset printing

(G-13578)
HORIZON INDUSTRIES CORPORATION
1801 W Columbia St (45504-2903)
PHONE.................................937 323-0801
John Neiswinger, *Pr*
Richard Koehler, *VP*
EMP: 9 **EST:** 1990
SQ FT: 15,000
SALES (est): 986.49K **Privately Held**
Web: www.horizonindustriescorp.com
SIC: 3544 Special dies and tools

(G-13579)
HORNER INDUSTRIAL SERVICES INC
Also Called: Scherer Industrial Group
5330 Prosperity Dr (45502-9074)
PHONE.................................937 390-6667
Michael Harper, *Dir*
EMP: 10
SALES (corp-wide): 55.43MM **Privately Held**
Web: www.hornerindustrial.com

SIC: 5063 7694 Motors, electric; Electric motor repair
PA: Horner Industrial Services, Inc.
1521 E Washington St
Indianapolis IN 46201
317 639-4261

(G-13580)
HOUSTON MACHINE PRODUCTS INC
1065 W Leffel Ln (45506-3555)
PHONE.................................937 322-8022
Sandra White, *Pr*
EMP: 30 **EST:** 1970
SQ FT: 35,000
SALES (est): 2.74MM **Privately Held**
Web: www.houstonmachine.com
SIC: 3599 3541 3451 Machine shop, jobbing and repair; Machine tools, metal cutting type; Screw machine products

(G-13581)
HUGO BOSCA COMPANY INC (PA)
Also Called: Bosca Accesories
1905 W Jefferson St (45506-1117)
P.O. Box 777 (45501-0777)
PHONE.................................937 323-5523
Christopher B Bosca, *Pr*
D'orsi Bosca, *VP Sls*
Dick Rabe, *CFO*
Cathy Gainer, *COO*
Brian Janetski, *Prin*
▲ **EMP:** 19 **EST:** 1911
SQ FT: 48,000
SALES (est): 4.01MM
SALES (corp-wide): 4.01MM **Privately Held**
Web: www.bosca.com
SIC: 3171 3172 Handbags, women's; Wallets

(G-13582)
INTERNATIONAL LEISURE ACTIVITIES INC
107 Tremont City Rd (45502-9506)
EMP: 7 **EST:** 1969
SALES (est): 945K **Privately Held**
SIC: 2064 5145 Candy and other confectionery products; Candy

(G-13583)
INTERTAPE POLYMER CORP
Also Called: Maiweave
1800 E Pleasant St (45505-3316)
PHONE.................................704 279-3011
EMP: 25
SQ FT: 85,000
SALES (corp-wide): 571.43MM **Privately Held**
Web: www.itape.com
SIC: 3081 Unsupported plastics film and sheet
HQ: Intertape Polymer Corp.
100 Paramount Dr Ste 300
Sarasota FL 34232
888 898-7834

(G-13584)
JMS INDUSTRIES INC
Also Called: JMS Composites
3240 E National Rd (45505-1524)
P.O. Box 507 (45501-0507)
PHONE.................................937 325-3502
Manjit Nagra, *CEO*
Jennifer Nagra, *VP*
▲ **EMP:** 19 **EST:** 1967
SQ FT: 27,000
SALES (est): 2.58MM **Privately Held**
Web: www.jmscomposites.com
SIC: 2821 Molding compounds, plastics

GEOGRAPHIC SECTION
Springfield - Clark County (G-13606)

(G-13585)
K K TOOL CO
115 S Center St (45502-1203)
P.O. Box 995 (45501-0995)
PHONE.................................937 325-1373
John Koehler, *Pr*
Donald Koehler, *
Edward Kurt Koehler, *
Teresa Koehler Yancey, *
Kristopher Kent Koehler, *
EMP: 25 **EST:** 1972
SALES (est): 2.89MM **Privately Held**
Web: www.kktool.net
SIC: 3599 3999 Machine shop, jobbing and repair; Barber and beauty shop equipment

(G-13586)
K WM BEACH MFG CO INC
4655 Urbana Rd (45502-9503)
PHONE.................................937 399-3838
William R Beach, *CEO*
Bret L Beach, *
EMP: 200 **EST:** 1945
SQ FT: 125,000
SALES (est): 10.03MM **Privately Held**
Web: www.kwmbeach.com
SIC: 3053 3714 Gaskets, all materials; Motor vehicle parts and accessories

(G-13587)
KCI HOLDING USA INC (DH)
4401 Gateway Blvd (45502-9339)
PHONE.................................937 525-5533
Bernie D'ambrosi, *Sr VP*
Guy Shumaker, *
Amy Corbisier, *
Todd Robenson, *
Steve Mayes, *
◆ **EMP:** 150 **EST:** 1993
SALES (est): 186.42MM **Privately Held**
Web: www.konecranes.com
SIC: 3536 Cranes, industrial plant
HQ: Konecranes Finance Oy
Koneenkatu 8
HyvinkAA 05830

(G-13588)
KEYAH INTERNATIONAL TRDG LLC (PA)
4655 Urbana Rd (45502-9503)
PHONE.................................937 399-3140
Brett L Beach, *Pr*
Jo Anna Kipp-beach, *CEO*
▲ **EMP:** 20 **EST:** 2000
SQ FT: 30,000
SALES (est): 4.87MM
SALES (corp-wide): 4.87MM **Privately Held**
Web: www.keyahint.com
SIC: 2675 Die-cut paper and board

(G-13589)
KONECRANES INC
Also Called: Americas Components
4505 Gateway Blvd (45502-8863)
PHONE.................................937 328-5100
Troy Posts, *Mgr*
EMP: 50
Web: www.konecranes.com
SIC: 3536 Cranes, industrial plant
HQ: Konecranes, Inc.
4401 Gateway Blvd
Springfield OH 45502

(G-13590)
KONECRANES INC (HQ)
4401 Gateway Blvd (45502-9339)
PHONE.................................937 525-5533
Rob Smith, *CEO*
Pekka Lundmark, *
Steve Kosir, *
Bernard D'ambrosi Junior, *VP*
Guy Shumaker, *
◆ **EMP:** 279 **EST:** 1910
SQ FT: 17,000
SALES (est): 578.29MM **Privately Held**
Web: www.konecranes.com
SIC: 3536 Cranes, industrial plant
PA: Konecranes Oyj
Koneenkatu 8
HyvinkAA 05830

(G-13591)
KONTRON AMERICA INCORPORATED
Also Called: Hartmann Electronic
202 N Limestone St (45503)
P.O. Box 1585 (45501)
PHONE.................................937 324-2420
Andreas Ruben, *Admn*
Andreas Ruben, *Pr*
Folker Hemmann, *Treas*
◆ **EMP:** 7 **EST:** 1997
SQ FT: 3,990
SALES (est): 4.63MM **Privately Held**
Web: www.wiener-us.com
SIC: 5065 3679 Electronic parts; Power supplies, all types: static
PA: Phoenix Mecano Ag
Hofwisenstrasse 6
Stein Am Rhein SH 8260

(G-13592)
KRAFFT AND ASSOCIATES INC
991 W Leffel Ln (45506-3537)
P.O. Box 1292 (45501-1292)
PHONE.................................937 325-4671
William F Krafft, *Pr*
Gretchen Krafft, *Sec*
EMP: 8 **EST:** 1966
SQ FT: 20,000
SALES (est): 1.3MM **Privately Held**
Web: www.krafftandassociates.com
SIC: 3599 Machine shop, jobbing and repair

(G-13593)
KREIDER CORP
400 Harrison St (45505-2067)
PHONE.................................937 325-8787
Aristides Gianakopoulas, *Pr*
James Gianakopoulas, *
Walt Wildeman, *
John Patton, *
EMP: 66 **EST:** 1952
SALES (est): 9.5MM **Privately Held**
Web: www.kreidercorp.com
SIC: 3469 3544 Stamping metal for the trade; Special dies, tools, jigs, and fixtures

(G-13594)
LAGONDA INVESTMENTS III INC
2145 Airpark Dr (45502-7931)
P.O. Box 1511 (45501-1511)
PHONE.................................937 325-7305
Greg Gearhart, *Pr*
EMP: 15 **EST:** 1983
SQ FT: 44,000
SALES (est): 3.51MM
SALES (corp-wide): 1.03MM **Privately Held**
Web: www.unitedfiberglass.com
SIC: 3644 Electric conduits and fittings
PA: Hill & Smith Plc
Westhaven House
Solihull W MIDLANDS B90 4
121 704-7430

(G-13595)
M & H FABRICATING CO INC (PA)
717 Mound St (45505-1130)
P.O. Box 1248 (45501-1248)
PHONE.................................937 325-8708
Michael C De Ramus, *Pr*
EMP: 10 **EST:** 1970
SQ FT: 6,000
SALES (est): 1.9MM
SALES (corp-wide): 1.9MM **Privately Held**
SIC: 3441 Fabricated structural metal

(G-13596)
M & H FABRICATING CO INC
823 Mound St (45505-1132)
P.O. Box 1248 (45501-1248)
PHONE.................................937 325-8708
EMP: 6
SALES (corp-wide): 1.9MM **Privately Held**
SIC: 3443 Tanks, standard or custom fabricated: metal plate
PA: M & H Fabricating Co Inc
717 Mound St
Springfield OH 45505
937 325-8708

(G-13597)
M R ECHO-E INC
2755 Columbus Rd (45503-3203)
PHONE.................................937 322-4972
Ronald K Hill, *Pr*
▲ **EMP:** 10 **EST:** 1947
SALES (est): 336.63K **Privately Held**
Web: www.echoinc.to
SIC: 3229 Tubing, glass

(G-13598)
MACRAY CO LLC
100 W North St (45504-2547)
PHONE.................................937 325-1726
Robert Yingst, *Managing Member*
EMP: 6 **EST:** 1986
SQ FT: 17,600
SALES (est): 796.84K **Privately Held**
Web: www.macraycompany.com
SIC: 3993 1799 5099 Signs and advertising specialties; Sign installation and maintenance; Signs, except electric

(G-13599)
MADER ELC MTR PWR TRNSMSSONS L
205 E Main St (45503-4221)
P.O. Box 626 (45501-0626)
PHONE.................................937 325-5576
Bret Eric Mader, *Managing Member*
EMP: 7 **EST:** 1952
SQ FT: 20,000
SALES (est): 6.64MM **Privately Held**
Web: www.maderelectric.com
SIC: 5063 7694 Motors, electric; Electric motor repair

(G-13600)
MAI-WEAVE LLC
1800 E Pleasant St (45505-3316)
PHONE.................................937 322-1698
▲ **EMP:** 75
SIC: 3081 Packing materials, plastics sheet

(G-13601)
MCGREGOR METAL NATIONAL WORKS LLC
5573 W National Rd (45504)
P.O. Box 1343 (45501)
PHONE.................................937 882-6347
EMP: 50 **EST:** 1945
SALES (est): 4.96MM **Privately Held**
Web: www.carmichael-machine.com
SIC: 3451 Screw machine products

(G-13602)
MCGREGOR MTAL INNSFLLEN WRKS L
Also Called: (Mcgregor Metal Yellow Springs Works Llc, Springfield, OH)
1305 Innisfallen Ave (45506-1827)
P.O. Box 1103 (45501-1103)
PHONE.................................937 322-3880
Dan Mcgregor, *Ch*
James Mcgregor, *Pr*
Dwight Kent, *
Seth Powers, *
James Doyle, *
EMP: 120 **EST:** 1999
SQ FT: 140,000
SALES (est): 33.04MM
SALES (corp-wide): 99.39MM **Privately Held**
Web: www.mcgregormetal.com
SIC: 3469 Stamping metal for the trade
PA: Mcgregor Metal Yellow Springs Works Llc
2100 S Yellow Springs St
Springfield OH 45506
937 325-5561

(G-13603)
MCGREGOR MTAL LEFFEL WORKS LLC
900 W Leffel Ln (45506-3538)
P.O. Box 1103 (45501-1103)
PHONE.................................937 325-5561
Daniel Mcgregor, *Pr*
Dane A Belden, *
Hugh Barnett, *
▲ **EMP:** 60 **EST:** 1991
SQ FT: 44,000
SALES (est): 12.16MM
SALES (corp-wide): 105.36MM **Privately Held**
Web: www.rosecitymfg.com
SIC: 7692 Automotive welding
PA: Mcgregor Metal Yellow Springs Works Llc
2100 S Yellow Springs St
Springfield OH 45506
937 325-5561

(G-13604)
MCGREGOR MTAL YLLOW SPRNG WRKS (PA)
Also Called: McGregor Metalworking
2100 S Yellow Springs St (45506-3354)
P.O. Box 1103 (45501-1103)
PHONE.................................937 325-5561
Jamie Mcgregor, *CEO*
Tom Wright, *
Dwight Kent, *
Pete Dane, *
▲ **EMP:** 90 **EST:** 1939
SQ FT: 98,000
SALES (est): 99.39MM
SALES (corp-wide): 99.39MM **Privately Held**
Web: www.mcgregormetal.com
SIC: 3568 3544 3451 3429 Power transmission equipment, nec; Special dies, tools, jigs, and fixtures; Screw machine products; Hardware, nec

(G-13605)
METAL STAMPINGS UNLIMITED INC
552 W Johnny Lytle Ave (45506-2679)
PHONE.................................937 328-0206
EMP: 10 **EST:** 1996
SQ FT: 12,000
SALES (est): 1.01MM **Privately Held**
SIC: 3469 Stamping metal for the trade

(G-13606)
METALTEK INDUSTRIES INC
829 Pauline St (45503-3815)
P.O. Box 479 (45501-0479)
PHONE.................................937 342-1750
Charles J Muscato, *Pr*
Charles K Muscato, *VP*

Springfield - Clark County (G-13607)

EMP: 14 **EST:** 1950
SALES (est): 2.25MM **Privately Held**
SIC: 2842 3479 Rust removers; Bonderizing of metal or metal products

(G-13607)
MULLER ENGINE & MACHINE CO
Also Called: Miller Engine & Machine Co
1414 S Yellow Springs St (45506-2545)
PHONE..................................937 322-1861
Ginnie Mullen, *Owner*
EMP: 7 **EST:** 1952
SQ FT: 10,000
SALES (est): 578.64K **Privately Held**
Web: www.millerengine.com
SIC: 3511 3599 Wheels, water; Machine shop, jobbing and repair

(G-13608)
MUNCY CORPORATION
2020 Progress Rd (45505-4472)
PHONE..................................937 346-0800
Michael A Priest, *Pr*
EMP: 86 **EST:** 2005
SALES (est): 9.58MM
SALES (corp-wide): 94.51MM **Privately Held**
Web: www.muncycorp.com
SIC: 3465 Automotive stampings
PA: Jmac Inc.
  200 W Ntnwide Blvd Unit 1
  Columbus OH 43215
  614 436-2418

(G-13609)
NATIONAL STAIR CORP
20 Zischler St (45504-2853)
P.O. Box 1261 (45501-1261)
PHONE..................................937 325-1347
John Druckenbroad, *Pr*
Mike Earl, *
Larry Houck, *
EMP: 18 **EST:** 1988
SQ FT: 11,000
SALES (est): 821.81K **Privately Held**
Web: www.nationalstair.com
SIC: 3441 Fabricated structural metal

(G-13610)
NAVISTAR INC
Also Called: Navistar
6125 Urbana Rd (45502-9279)
P.O. Box 600 (45501)
PHONE..................................937 390-4776
Barry Laughlin, *Mgr*
EMP: 130
SALES (corp-wide): 350.31B **Privately Held**
Web: www.navistar.com
SIC: 3711 Truck and tractor truck assembly
HQ: Navistar, Inc.
  2701 Navistar Dr
  Lisle IL 60532
  331 332-5000

(G-13611)
NAVISTAR INC
Navistar
811 N Murray St (45503-3733)
PHONE..................................937 561-3315
Tom Tullis, *Genl Mgr*
EMP: 32
SALES (corp-wide): 350.31B **Privately Held**
Web: www.navistar.com
SIC: 3711 Truck and tractor truck assembly
HQ: Navistar, Inc.
  2701 Navistar Dr
  Lisle IL 60532
  331 332-5000

(G-13612)
NEHER BURIAL VAULT COMPANY
Also Called: Burial Vaults By Neher
1903 Saint Paris Pike (45504-1299)
PHONE..................................937 399-4494
Doreen Pinney, *Pr*
Gary W Pinney, *VP*
EMP: 23 **EST:** 1939
SQ FT: 5,500
SALES (est): 845.18K **Privately Held**
SIC: 3272 Burial vaults, concrete or precast terrazzo

(G-13613)
NU RISERS STAIR COMPANY
2748 Columbus Rd (45503-3204)
PHONE..................................937 322-8100
EMP: 11 **EST:** 1998
SALES (est): 1MM **Privately Held**
Web: www.nurisers.com
SIC: 3446 Stairs, staircases, stair treads: prefabricated metal

(G-13614)
OS KELLY CORPORATION
318 E North St (45503)
P.O. Box 1267 (45501)
PHONE..................................937 322-4921
Theodore Golba, *VP*
▲ **EMP:** 42 **EST:** 1890
SQ FT: 110,000
SALES (est): 13.56MM
SALES (corp-wide): 528.25MM **Privately Held**
SIC: 3321 Gray iron castings, nec
HQ: Steinway, Inc.
  1 Steinway Pl
  Long Island City NY 11105
  718 721-2600

(G-13615)
PARKER TRUTEC INCORPORATED (HQ)
Also Called: Parker Trutec
4700 Gateway Blvd (45502-8817)
PHONE..................................937 323-8833
Keiko Satomi, *Ch Bd*
Yutaka Satomi, *
Joseph Gummel, *
▲ **EMP:** 80 **EST:** 1991
SQ FT: 80,000
SALES (est): 74.3MM **Privately Held**
Web: www.parkertrutec.com
SIC: 3398 3479 Metal heat treating; Painting, coating, and hot dipping
PA: Nihon Parkerizing Co., Ltd.
  1-15-1, Nihonbashi
  Chuo-Ku TKY 103-0

(G-13616)
PATTERSON PRCISION FABRICATION
33 Walnut St (45505-1144)
PHONE..................................937 631-8198
Mark Patterson, *Prin*
EMP: 8 **EST:** 2017
SALES (est): 317.86K **Privately Held**
Web: www.pattersonfab.com
SIC: 3599 Machine shop, jobbing and repair

(G-13617)
PENTAFLEX INC
4981 Gateway Blvd (45502-8867)
PHONE..................................937 325-5551
Dave Arndt, *Pr*
Julie Mcgregor, *Treas*
Walter Wildman, *
◆ **EMP:** 110 **EST:** 1972
SQ FT: 146,000
SALES (est): 21.51MM **Privately Held**
Web: www.pentaflex.com
SIC: 3469 7692 Stamping metal for the trade ; Welding repair

(G-13618)
PEPSI-COLA METRO BTLG CO INC
Also Called: Pepsi-Cola
233 Dayton Ave (45506-1205)
PHONE..................................937 328-6750
Phyllis Beach, *Rgnl Mgr*
EMP: 6
SALES (corp-wide): 86.39B **Publicly Held**
Web: www.pepsico.com
SIC: 2086 Carbonated soft drinks, bottled and canned
HQ: Pepsi-Cola Metropolitan Bottling Company, Inc.
  700 Anderson Hill Rd
  Purchase NY 10577
  914 767-6000

(G-13619)
PHOENIX SAFETY OUTFITTERS LLC
110 W Leffel Ln (45506-3522)
P.O. Box 20445 (43220-0445)
PHONE..................................614 361-0544
EMP: 9 **EST:** 2007
SALES (est): 2.27MM **Privately Held**
Web: www.phoenixoutfitters.com
SIC: 3569 Assembly machines, non-metalworking

(G-13620)
PIECO INC
Also Called: Superior Trims Springfield Div
5225 Prosperity Dr (45502-9540)
PHONE..................................937 399-5100
Bob Banghle, *Brnch Mgr*
EMP: 65
SALES (corp-wide): 37.77MM **Privately Held**
Web: www.pieco.com
SIC: 2396 Automotive trimmings, fabric
PA: Pieco, Inc.
  2151 Industrial Dr
  Findlay OH 45840
  419 422-5335

(G-13621)
PRATT (JET CORR) INC
Also Called: Pratt Industries USA
1515 Baker Rd (45504-4501)
PHONE..................................937 390-7100
Michael Day, *Genl Mgr*
EMP: 1511
Web: www.prattindustries.com
SIC: 2653 Boxes, corrugated: made from purchased materials
HQ: Pratt (Jet Corr), Inc.
  1800 Sarasot Bus Pkwy Ne B
  Conyers GA 30013
  770 929-1300

(G-13622)
PRESS TECHNOLOGY & MFG INC
1401 Fotler St (45504-2051)
PHONE..................................937 327-0755
▲ **EMP:** 8 **EST:** 1992
SQ FT: 30,000
SALES (est): 1.65MM **Privately Held**
Web: www.presstechnology.com
SIC: 3554 Paper mill machinery: plating, slitting, waxing, etc.

(G-13623)
RAINBOW INDUSTRIES INC
Also Called: Rainbow Tarp
5975 E National Rd (45505-1854)
P.O. Box 506 (45369-0506)
PHONE..................................937 323-6493
F Vernon Mccoy, *CEO*
Evelyn Mccoy, *Treas*
Joe Schmid, *Pr*
▲ **EMP:** 7 **EST:** 1894
SQ FT: 6,000
SALES (est): 616.85K **Privately Held**
Web: www.rainbowindustries.com
SIC: 2394 5999 7359 Tarpaulins, fabric: made from purchased materials; Tents; Tent and tarpaulin rental

(G-13624)
RAWAC PLATING COMPANY
125 N Bell Ave (45504-2827)
PHONE..................................937 322-7491
Aristides G Gianakopoulos, *Pr*
Alexandra Gianakopoulos, *
EMP: 13 **EST:** 1943
SALES (est): 460.19K **Privately Held**
Web: www.rawac.com
SIC: 3471 Electroplating of metals or formed products

(G-13625)
REBECCA BENSTON
Also Called: Higher Ground Ministries
2130 W Possum Rd (45506-2814)
PHONE..................................937 360-0669
Rebecca Benston, *Owner*
EMP: 15 **EST:** 2013
SALES (est): 514.35K **Privately Held**
Web: www.highergroundbooksandmedia.com
SIC: 2731 Books, publishing only

(G-13626)
REITER DAIRY LLC DEAN FOODS
1941 Commerce Cir (45504-2011)
PHONE..................................937 323-5777
EMP: 7 **EST:** 2017
SALES (est): 310.26K **Privately Held**
Web: www.dfamilk.com
SIC: 2026 Fluid milk

(G-13627)
REITER DAIRY OF AKRON INC
Also Called: Reiter Dairy
1961 Commerce Cir (45504-2081)
PHONE..................................937 323-5777
EMP: 30
SIC: 2026 Milk processing (pasteurizing, homogenizing, bottling)

(G-13628)
REMINGTON STEEL INC
1120 S Burnett Rd (45505-3408)
P.O. Box 1491 (45501-1491)
PHONE..................................937 322-2414
▲ **EMP:** 59
SIC: 5051 3714 Steel; Clutches, motor vehicle

(G-13629)
RIWCO CORP
2330 Columbus Rd (45503-3547)
P.O. Box 1204 (45501-1204)
PHONE..................................937 322-6521
David Nelson Funk, *Pr*
Robert Samosky, *VP*
EMP: 22 **EST:** 1925
SQ FT: 40,000
SALES (est): 798.64K **Privately Held**
SIC: 3441 Fabricated structural metal

(G-13630)
SCHULERS BAKERY INC (PA)
1911 S Limestone St (45505-4045)
PHONE..................................937 323-4154
Theodore Schuler, *Pr*
Larry Schuler, *
Daniel Edward Schuler, *

EMP: 30 EST: 1937
SALES (est): 2.46MM
SALES (corp-wide): 2.46MM **Privately Held**
Web: www.schulersbakery.com
SIC: **5461** 2052 2051 Doughnuts; Cookies and crackers; Bread, cake, and related products

(G-13631)
SHELLY MATERIALS INC
4301 S Charleston Pike (45502-9376)
PHONE..............................937 325-7386
Todd Palmer, *Mgr*
EMP: 9
SALES (corp-wide): 32.72B **Privately Held**
Web: www.shellyco.com
SIC: **3273** Ready-mixed concrete
HQ: Shelly Materials, Inc.
  80 Park Dr
  Thornville OH 43076
  740 246-6315

(G-13632)
SILFEX INC
1000 Titus Rd (45502-9307)
PHONE..............................937 324-2487
Kit Armstrong, *Genl Mgr*
EMP: 431
SALES (corp-wide): 17.43B **Publicly Held**
Web: www.silfex.com
SIC: **3674** Semiconductors and related devices
HQ: Silfex, Inc.
  950 S Franklin St
  Eaton OH 45320

(G-13633)
SKULD LLC
2864 Columbus Rd (45503-3206)
P.O. Box 973 (45501-0973)
PHONE..............................330 423-7339
Sarah Jordan, *CEO*
Sarah Jordan, *Mgr*
EMP: 6 EST: 2015
SALES (est): 686.8K **Privately Held**
Web: www.skuldllc.com
SIC: **3324** 3321 3365 Steel investment foundries; Gray and ductile iron foundries; Aluminum foundries

(G-13634)
SPRADLIN BROS WELDING CO
2131 Quality Ln (45505-3625)
PHONE..............................800 219-2182
Jeffery Spradlin, *Pr*
Mike Spradlin, *VP*
Tammi Spradlin, *Sec*
Rhonda Spradlin, *Treas*
EMP: 17 EST: 1962
SQ FT: 25,500
SALES (est): 3.72MM **Privately Held**
Web: www.weldedparts.com
SIC: **1799** 7692 3444 3443 Ornamental metal work; Welding repair; Sheet metalwork; Fabricated plate work (boiler shop)

(G-13635)
SPRINGFIELD NEWSPAPERS INC
Also Called: Springfield News Sun
137 E Main St (45502-1363)
PHONE..............................937 323-5533
Ben Mclaughlin, *Editor*
EMP: 44 EST: 1904
SQ FT: 76,268
SALES (est): 2.13MM
SALES (corp-wide): 16.61B **Privately Held**
Web: www.springfieldnewssun.com
SIC: **2711** Job printing and newspaper publishing combined

PA: Cox Enterprises, Inc.
  6305 Pachtree Dunwoody Rd
  Atlanta GA 30328
  678 645-0000

(G-13636)
SPRINGFIELD PLASTICS INC
15 N Bechtle Ave (45504-2897)
PHONE..............................937 322-6071
Frederick B Becker, *Pr*
Janet Becker, *Sec*
EMP: 15
SQ FT: 24,000
SALES (est): 2.28MM **Privately Held**
Web: www.spi-oh.com
SIC: **3089** Injection molding of plastics

(G-13637)
STALDER SPRING WORKS INC
2345 Springfield Xenia Rd (45506-3994)
PHONE..............................937 322-6120
Damon D Kaufman, *Pr*
Dana Kaufman, *VP*
Corella Kaufman, *Sec*
Dennis Kaufman, *Stockholder*
▲ EMP: 27 EST: 1945
SQ FT: 18,000
SALES (est): 2.27MM **Privately Held**
Web: www.stalderspring.com
SIC: **3495** Mechanical springs, precision

(G-13638)
STEWART MANUFACTURING CORP
5230 Prosperity Dr (45502-7503)
PHONE..............................937 390-3333
James S Stewart, *Pr*
Suzanne S Collins, *VP*
EMP: 24 EST: 1974
SQ FT: 18,000
SALES (est): 1.3MM **Privately Held**
SIC: **3823** Differential pressure instruments, industrial process type

(G-13639)
STRIDE OUT RNCH N RODEO SP LLC
4122 Laybourne Rd (45505-3616)
PHONE..............................937 539-1537
Michael Hess, *CEO*
EMP: 11 EST: 2017
SALES (est): 750K **Privately Held**
SIC: **3559** Boots, shoes, and leather working machinery

(G-13640)
SUTPHEN CORPORATION
Also Called: Chassis Division
1701 W County Line Rd (45502)
P.O. Box 2610 (45501-2610)
PHONE..............................937 969-8851
Drew Sutphen, *Mgr*
EMP: 30
SQ FT: 31,000
SALES (corp-wide): 173.19MM **Privately Held**
Web: www.sutphen.com
SIC: **3711** 3714 Chassis, motor vehicle; Motor vehicle parts and accessories
PA: The Sutphen Corporation
  6450 Eiterman Rd
  Dublin OH 43016
  800 726-7030

(G-13641)
SWEET MANUFACTURING COMPANY
2000 E Leffel Ln (45505)
P.O. Box 1086 (45501)
PHONE..............................937 325-1511
Alicia Sweet-hupp, *Pr*
Alan D Sweet, *
◆ EMP: 40 EST: 1955
SQ FT: 75,000

SALES (est): 7.96MM **Privately Held**
Web: www.sweetmfg.com
SIC: **3535** 3523 3534 3537 Conveyors and conveying equipment; Elevators, farm; Elevators and equipment; Industrial trucks and tractors

(G-13642)
TAC INDUSTRIES INC (PA)
2160 Old Selma Rd (45505-4600)
PHONE..............................937 328-5200
James Zahora, *CEO*
Michael Ahern, *
EMP: 280 EST: 1960
SQ FT: 52,800
SALES (est): 10.48MM
SALES (corp-wide): 10.48MM **Privately Held**
Web: www.tacind.com
SIC: **8741** 2399 8331 Management services; Nets, launderers and dyers; Work experience center

(G-13643)
TAYLOR MANUFACTURING CO INC
1101 W Main St (45504-2899)
PHONE..............................937 322-8622
Christopher Taylor, *Pr*
Robert B Taylor, *Pr*
Mildred B Taylor, *Sec*
EMP: 15 EST: 1939
SQ FT: 18,000
SALES (est): 2.27MM **Privately Held**
Web: www.taylor-mfg.com
SIC: **3728** Aircraft parts and equipment, nec

(G-13644)
TECHNIQUES SURFACES USA INC
2015 Progress Rd (45505-4472)
PHONE..............................937 323-2556
Alain Charlois, *Pr*
Kenneth Metzgar, *Dir*
EMP: 7 EST: 2008
SALES (est): 1.39MM **Privately Held**
Web: www.hefusa.net
SIC: **3398** Metal heat treating
PA: H.E.F. Usa Corporation
  2015 Progress Rd
  Springfield OH 45505

(G-13645)
TED BOLLE MILLWORK INC
2834 Hustead Rd (45502-7909)
P.O. Box 82 (45387-0082)
PHONE..............................937 325-8779
EMP: 16 EST: 1953
SALES (est): 1.64MM **Privately Held**
Web: www.bollemillwork.com
SIC: **2431** Millwork

(G-13646)
TEIKURO CORPORATION
4500 Gateway Blvd (45502-8815)
PHONE..............................937 327-3955
Mike Houseman, *Mgr*
EMP: 43
Web: www.teikuro.com
SIC: **3471** Electroplating of metals or formed products
HQ: Teikuro Corporation
  101a Clay St Ste 128
  San Francisco CA 94111
  415 273-2650

(G-13647)
THE CHAMPION COMPANY (PA)
Also Called: The Champion Companies
400 Harrison St (45505-2067)
P.O. Box 967 (45501-0967)
PHONE..............................937 324-5681
Aristides Gianakopoulos, *Pr*

Benjamin G Devoe, *
EMP: 60 EST: 1878
SQ FT: 165,000
SALES (est): 19.8MM
SALES (corp-wide): 19.8MM **Privately Held**
Web: www.championgse.com
SIC: **2869** 3412 Embalming fluids; Metal barrels, drums, and pails

(G-13648)
TINKER OMEGA SINTO LLC
2424 Columbus Rd (45503-3549)
P.O. Box 328 (45501-0328)
PHONE..............................937 322-2272
William F Tinker Junior, *Managing Member*
▲ EMP: 29 EST: 2001
SQ FT: 54,000
SALES (est): 6.88MM **Privately Held**
Web: www.tinkeromega.com
SIC: **3555** Type casting, founding, or melting machines

(G-13649)
TOMCO TOOL INC
203 S Wittenberg Ave (45506-1646)
PHONE..............................937 322-5768
Bryan Stewart, *Pr*
Mark Stewart, *Sec*
Richard Wheeler, *VP*
Patfy Stewart, *Mgr*
EMP: 7 EST: 1970
SQ FT: 18,000
SALES (est): 576.17K **Privately Held**
Web: www.tomco-tool.com
SIC: **3545** 3544 Tools and accessories for machine tools; Special dies, tools, jigs, and fixtures

(G-13650)
TOOL TECH LLC
4901 Urbana Rd (45502-9069)
PHONE..............................614 893-5876
Matt Mcgreevy, *Prin*
Kevin Kroos, *
Kevin Seibert, *
Doug Hanaway, *
Don Gamble, *
EMP: 38 EST: 2017
SALES (est): 2.63MM **Privately Held**
Web: www.tooltech.com
SIC: **3544** Special dies, tools, jigs, and fixtures

(G-13651)
TS USA
2015 Progress Rd (45505-4472)
PHONE..............................937 323-2556
EMP: 10 EST: 2019
SALES (est): 1.12MM **Privately Held**
Web: www.hefusa.net
SIC: **3479** Coating of metals and formed products

(G-13652)
TURN-ALL MACHINE & GEAR CO
5499 Tremont Ln (45502-7522)
P.O. Box 448 (45501-0448)
PHONE..............................937 342-8710
Carl Power, *Pr*
Jane Power, *VP*
EMP: 19 EST: 1972
SALES (est): 1.06MM **Privately Held**
Web: www.turn-all.com
SIC: **3599** Machine shop, jobbing and repair

(G-13653)
VALCO INDUSTRIES LLC
625 Burt St (45505-3266)
P.O. Box 1226 (45501-1226)
PHONE..............................937 399-7400

Springfield - Clark County (G-13654)

Edward H Leventhal, *Pr*
EMP: 35 **EST:** 1974
SQ FT: 44,000
SALES (est): 4.98MM **Privately Held**
Web: www.valco-ind.com
SIC: 3713 3441 3465 Truck cabs, for motor vehicles; Fabricated structural metal; Body parts, automobile: stamped metal

(G-13654)
WESTFIELD STEEL INC
Also Called: Remington Steel
1120 S Burnett Rd (45505-3408)
PHONE.................................937 322-2414
Frank Bair, *Brnch Mgr*
EMP: 60
SALES (corp-wide): 86.07MM **Privately Held**
Web: www.westfieldsteel.com
SIC: 5051 3714 Steel; Clutches, motor vehicle
PA: Westfield Steel Inc
530 W State Road 32
Westfield IN 46074
317 896-5587

(G-13655)
WETSU GROUP INC
125 W North St (45504-2546)
P.O. Box 1985 (45501-1985)
PHONE.................................937 324-9353
EMP: 19 **EST:** 1993
SQ FT: 1,200
SALES (est): 2.21MM **Privately Held**
Web: www.wetsumfg.com
SIC: 3679 Harness assemblies, for electronic use: wire or cable

(G-13656)
WOEBER MUSTARD MFG CO
1966 Commerce Cir (45504-2012)
P.O. Box 388 (45501-0388)
PHONE.................................937 323-6281
Ray Woeber, *Pr*
Richard E Woeber, *
Gloria Woeber, *
D I C K Woeber, *
Rick Schmidt, *
◆ **EMP:** 128 **EST:** 1905
SQ FT: 40,000
SALES (est): 40.15MM **Privately Held**
Web: www.woebermustard.com
SIC: 2099 2035 Food preparations, nec; Mustard, prepared (wet)

(G-13657)
WOODROW MANUFACTURING CO
4300 River Rd (45502-7517)
P.O. Box 1567 (45501-1567)
PHONE.................................937 399-9333
John K Woodrow, *Pr*
Patrick T Mcatee, *VP*
EMP: 28 **EST:** 1964
SQ FT: 26,000
SALES (est): 1.13MM **Privately Held**
Web: www.woodrowcorp.com
SIC: 7336 3479 2752 2396 Silk screen design; Etching on metals; Commercial printing, lithographic; Automotive and apparel trimmings

(G-13658)
YOST SUPERIOR CO
300 S Center St Ste 1 (45506-1696)
P.O. Box 1487 (45501-1487)
PHONE.................................937 323-7591
Bert D Barnes, *Ch Bd*
Gary Dickerhoff, *
David Deerwester, *
▼ **EMP:** 50 **EST:** 1924
SQ FT: 47,000
SALES (est): 8.99MM **Privately Held**
Web: www.yostsuperior.com
SIC: 3495 3496 Mechanical springs, precision; Miscellaneous fabricated wire products

Sterling
Wayne County

(G-13659)
MJC ENTERPRISE INC
7820 Blough Rd (44276-9734)
P.O. Box 182 (44677-0182)
PHONE.................................330 669-3744
EMP: 9 **EST:** 1991
SQ FT: 1,352
SALES (est): 748.94K **Privately Held**
Web: www.mjc-enterprises.com
SIC: 2448 Pallets, wood

Steubenville
Jefferson County

(G-13660)
ATV INSIDER
742 Sunshine Park Rd (43953-7134)
PHONE.................................740 282-7102
David Schloss, *Prin*
EMP: 6 **EST:** 2007
SALES (est): 119.28K **Privately Held**
SIC: 2721 Periodicals, publishing only

(G-13661)
BARIUM & CHEMICALS INC
515 Kingsdale Rd (43952-4321)
P.O. Box 218 (43952-5218)
PHONE.................................740 282-9776
▲ **EMP:** 30 **EST:** 1916
SALES (est): 8.22MM **Privately Held**
Web: www.bariumchemicals.com
SIC: 2819 Barium compounds

(G-13662)
BISHOPS DAILY BLESSINGS LLC
5 Maplewood Dr Apt 15 (43952-7074)
PHONE.................................724 624-3779
EMP: 6
SALES (est): 78.58K **Privately Held**
SIC: 2099 Food preparations, nec

(G-13663)
BULLY TOOLS INC
14 Technology Way (43952-7079)
PHONE.................................740 282-5834
Mark Gracy, *Pr*
EMP: 35 **EST:** 2002
SALES (est): 3.89MM **Privately Held**
Web: www.bullytools.com
SIC: 3423 Hand and edge tools, nec

(G-13664)
CAMPION PIPE FITTING
4205 State Route 213 (43952-6979)
PHONE.................................740 627-1125
Thomas A Campion, *Prin*
EMP: 7 **EST:** 2004
SALES (est): 494.15K **Privately Held**
Web: www.thetallgrasstheatrecompany.com
SIC: 3494 Pipe fittings

(G-13665)
CLANCEY PRINTING INC
263 Main St (43953-3735)
PHONE.................................740 275-4070
EMP: 7 **EST:** 2017
SALES (est): 217.65K **Privately Held**
Web: www.rms-stat.com
SIC: 2752 Offset printing

(G-13666)
DIETRICH VON HLDBRAND LGACY PR
1235 University Blvd (43952-1792)
PHONE.................................703 496-7821
John Crosby, *Dir*
EMP: 7 **EST:** 2004
SALES (est): 489.19K **Privately Held**
Web: www.hildebrandproject.org
SIC: 2759 8299 Commercial printing, nec; Educational services

(G-13667)
FLEETPRIDE INC
620 South St (43952-2802)
PHONE.................................740 282-2711
Larry Remp, *Brnch Mgr*
EMP: 34
Web: www.fleetpride.com
SIC: 7538 5511 7692 Truck engine repair, except industrial; Trucks, tractors, and trailers: new and used; Welding repair
HQ: Fleetpride, Inc.
600 Las Colinas Blvd E # 400
Irving TX 75039
469 249-7500

(G-13668)
HESS CORPORATION
4525 Sunset Blvd (43952-3424)
PHONE.................................740 266-7835
EMP: 6 **EST:** 2019
SALES (est): 87.44K **Privately Held**
SIC: 1382 Oil and gas exploration services

(G-13669)
JEFFCO SHELTERED WORKSHOP
256 John Scott Hwy (43952-3001)
PHONE.................................740 264-4608
Mikel Michalik, *Ex Dir*
EMP: 16 **EST:** 1973
SQ FT: 15,000
SALES (est): 14.44K **Privately Held**
SIC: 8331 8322 2511 Vocational training agency; Refugee service; Wood household furniture

(G-13670)
LT WRIGHT HANDCRAFTED KNIFE CO
130 Warren Ln Unit B (43953-3758)
PHONE.................................740 317-1404
Leonard T Wright, *Pr*
EMP: 10 **EST:** 2014
SALES (est): 466.12K **Privately Held**
Web: www.ltwrightknives.com
SIC: 3421 Knives: butchers', hunting, pocket, etc.

(G-13671)
MARTIN M HARDIN
Also Called: Williams Grgory Martin Fnrl HM
411 N 7th St (43952-1756)
PHONE.................................740 282-1234
Hardin M Martin, *Owner*
EMP: 6 **EST:** 2010
SALES (est): 94.16K **Privately Held**
SIC: 2869 7261 Embalming fluids; Crematory

(G-13672)
MEYER PRODUCTS LLC
324 N 7th St (43952-2249)
PHONE.................................216 486-1313
Andrew Outcalt, *Pr*
◆ **EMP:** 86 **EST:** 2004
SALES (est): 24.41MM
SALES (corp-wide): 26.44MM **Privately Held**
Web: www.meyerproducts.com
SIC: 3531 Blades for graders, scrapers, dozers, and snow plows
PA: The Louis Berkman Company
600 Grant St Ste 3230
Pittsburgh PA 15219
740 283-3722

(G-13673)
NATIONAL COLLOID COMPANY
906 Adams St (43952-2709)
P.O. Box 309 (43952-5309)
PHONE.................................740 282-1171
Michael Barber Junior, *Pr*
▲ **EMP:** 25 **EST:** 1938
SQ FT: 45,000
SALES (est): 28.93MM **Privately Held**
Web: www.natcoll.com
SIC: 2869 5169 2899 2842 Industrial organic chemicals, nec; Caustic soda; Chemical preparations, nec; Polishes and sanitation goods

(G-13674)
OGDEN NEWSPAPERS INC
Also Called: Weirton Daily Times, The
401 Herald Sq (43952-2059)
PHONE.................................304 748-0606
Tammie Macintosh, *Mgr*
EMP: 52
Web: www.ogdennews.com
SIC: 2711 Newspapers: publishing only, not printed on site
HQ: The Ogden Newspapers Inc
1500 Main St
Wheeling WV 26003
304 233-0100

(G-13675)
PUBLIC WORKS DEPT STREET DIV
238 S Lake Erie St (43952-2158)
PHONE.................................740 283-6013
Dominic Nucci, *Mgr*
EMP: 6 **EST:** 2001
SALES (est): 74.3K **Privately Held**
SIC: 3991 Street sweeping brooms, hand or machine

(G-13676)
RUSSELL HUNT
Also Called: Russel Hunt Total Land Care
175 Detmar Rd (43953-7170)
P.O. Box 126 (43952-5126)
PHONE.................................740 264-1196
Russell Hunt, *Prin*
Russell Hunt, *Owner*
EMP: 10 **EST:** 2005
SALES (est): 945.56K **Privately Held**
Web: www.totallawncare.net
SIC: 0782 3524 Landscape contractors; Snowblowers and throwers, residential

(G-13677)
SIGNS LIMITED LLC
356 Technology Way (43952-7079)
PHONE.................................740 282-7715
EMP: 7 **EST:** 2009
SALES (est): 495.71K **Privately Held**
Web: www.signsunlimitedusa.com
SIC: 3993 Electric signs

(G-13678)
SUNNEST SERVICE LLC
619 Slack St (43952-2821)
P.O. Box 16484 (92623-6484)
PHONE.................................740 283-2815
▲ **EMP:** 25 **EST:** 2009
SALES (est): 2.17MM **Privately Held**
SIC: 2514 Metal lawn and garden furniture

GEOGRAPHIC SECTION

Stow - Summit County (G-13701)

(G-13679)
TRI-STATE PUBLISHING COMPANY (PA)
Also Called: Tri-State Printing
157 N 3rd St (43952-2118)
P.O. Box 1119 (43952-6119)
PHONE...............................740 283-3686
TOLL FREE: 800
Richard S Pflug, *Pr*
Dawna L Mccabe, *Sec*
EMP: 21 **EST:** 1953
SQ FT: 11,000
SALES (est): 2.22MM
SALES (corp-wide): 2.22MM **Privately Held**
Web: www.mpbonline.com
SIC: 2752 Offset printing

Stow
Summit County

(G-13680)
ACE PLASTICS COMPANY
122 E Tuscarawas Ave (44224)
PHONE...............................330 928-7720
Peggy Lyn Assaly, *Pr*
Joe Vereecken, *Pr*
EMP: 7 **EST:** 1947
SQ FT: 4,000
SALES (est): 640K **Privately Held**
Web: www.aceframes.com
SIC: 3499 5199 Novelties and giftware, including trophies; Advertising specialties

(G-13681)
ACS PUBLICATIONS LLC
3934 Cardinal Cir (44224-2510)
PHONE...............................330 686-3082
Andrew Shahriari, *Owner*
EMP: 7 **EST:** 2017
SALES (est): 84.36K **Privately Held**
Web: www.acs.org
SIC: 2741 Miscellaneous publishing

(G-13682)
ADVANCE TRANS INC ✪
4833 Darrow Rd Ste 105 (44224-1411)
PHONE...............................330 572-0390
Oscar Brown, *Prin*
EMP: 11 **EST:** 2023
SALES (est): 1.13MM **Privately Held**
SIC: 3537 Trucks, tractors, loaders, carriers, and similar equipment

(G-13683)
ALGIX LLC
3916 Clock Pointe Trl Ste 103 (44224)
PHONE...............................706 207-3425
EMP: 9 **EST:** 2011
SALES (est): 438.48K **Privately Held**
SIC: 2836 Biological products, except diagnostic

(G-13684)
ANDERSON INTERNATIONAL CORP
4545 Boyce Pkwy (44224-1770)
PHONE...............................216 641-1112
Len Trocano, *Pr*
Stephen C Ellis, *
Gary Pace, *
Kathleen O'hearn, *Treas*
◆ **EMP:** 90 **EST:** 1888
SQ FT: 100,000
SALES (est): 22.71MM
SALES (corp-wide): 22.71MM **Privately Held**
Web: www.andersonintl.com

SIC: 3559 3556 Rubber working machinery, including tires; Meat, poultry, and seafood processing machinery
PA: Kimbell Inc
420 Throckmorton St # 710
Fort Worth TX 76102
817 332-6104

(G-13685)
AUBURN METAL PROCESSING LLC (PA)
4550 Darrow Rd (44224-1804)
PHONE...............................315 253-2565
▼ **EMP:** 6 **EST:** 2003
SALES (est): 5.38MM
SALES (corp-wide): 5.38MM **Privately Held**
Web: www.reserve-group.com
SIC: 3444 Forming machine work, sheet metal

(G-13686)
AUSTIN TAPE AND LABEL INC
3350 Cavalier Trl (44224-4906)
PHONE...............................330 928-7999
James Burkle Junior, *Pr*
Darrell K Floyd, *
EMP: 54 **EST:** 1976
SQ FT: 11,000
SALES (est): 4.91MM **Privately Held**
Web: www.austintape.com
SIC: 2672 2759 2671 Tape, pressure sensitive: made from purchased materials; Commercial printing, nec; Paper; coated and laminated packaging

(G-13687)
BAKER MCMILLEN CO (PA)
Also Called: Crook Miller Company
3688 Wyoga Lake Rd (44224-4987)
PHONE...............................330 923-8300
William L Kimmerle, *Pr*
◆ **EMP:** 55 **EST:** 1874
SQ FT: 65,000
SALES (est): 9.43MM
SALES (corp-wide): 9.43MM **Privately Held**
Web: www.summit-growth.com
SIC: 2499 Carved and turned wood

(G-13688)
BLAZE TECHNICAL SERVICES INC
1445 Commerce Dr (44224-1709)
PHONE...............................330 923-0409
Ralph Hickman, *Pr*
Brian Hickman, *Pr*
EMP: 24 **EST:** 1996
SQ FT: 5,000
SALES (est): 2.65MM **Privately Held**
Web: www.blazeprobes.com
SIC: 3829 Thermocouples

(G-13689)
CHANDLER MACHINE COMPANY
Also Called: Chandler Mch & Prod Gear & Bro
4960 Hudson Dr (44224-1789)
PHONE...............................330 688-7615
Jeffery H Capple, *Pr*
EMP: 9 **EST:** 1940
SQ FT: 2,400
SALES (est): 1.03MM **Privately Held**
Web: www.chandlermachineco.com
SIC: 3599 Machine shop, jobbing and repair

(G-13690)
CHANDLER MACHINE COMPANY
4960 Hudson Dr (44224-1789)
PHONE...............................330 688-5585
Jeffery Capple, *Pr*
EMP: 15 **EST:** 1962
SQ FT: 2,400

SALES (est): 985.7K **Privately Held**
Web: www.chandlergearmachining.com
SIC: 3599 Machine shop, jobbing and repair

(G-13691)
CONQUEST INDUSTRIES INC
4488 Allen Rd (44224-1051)
PHONE...............................330 926-9236
Tom Fares, *Prin*
Harry Frederick, *
EMP: 24 **EST:** 1994
SALES (est): 529.39K **Privately Held**
Web: www.irbfmanufacturing.com
SIC: 3599 Machine shop, jobbing and repair

(G-13692)
DES MACHINE SERVICES INC
4115 Baird Rd (44224-3603)
PHONE...............................330 633-6897
William M Smith, *Pr*
Debora Smith, *VP*
EMP: 9 **EST:** 2005
SALES (est): 978.57K **Privately Held**
Web: www.desmachine.com
SIC: 3599 Machine shop, jobbing and repair

(G-13693)
ELECTROMOTIVE INC (PA)
4880 Hudson Dr (44224-1708)
PHONE...............................330 688-6494
Michael Piglia, *CEO*
Jeffrey Bissell, *CFO*
EMP: 50 **EST:** 1970
SALES (est): 128.02MM
SALES (corp-wide): 128.02MM **Privately Held**
Web: www.electromotive.com
SIC: 3679 3677 Solenoids for electronic applications; Electronic coils and transformers

(G-13694)
ELECTRONIC PRINTING PDTS INC
Also Called: Laser Label Technologies
4560 Darrow Rd (44224-1888)
PHONE...............................800 882-4050
James Peruzzi, *Pr*
James W Ransom, *
Jerry S Krempa, *
Ted F Unton, *
Sheri H Edison, *
EMP: 32 **EST:** 2014
SQ FT: 30,000
SALES (est): 5.31MM **Privately Held**
Web: www.lltlabels.com
SIC: 2752 Commercial printing, lithographic
HQ: Morgan Adhesives Company, Llc
4560 Darrow Rd
Stow OH 44224
330 688-1111

(G-13695)
ESTERLE MOLD & MACHINE CO INC (PA)
Also Called: Plastics Division
1539 Commerce Dr (44224-1783)
PHONE...............................330 686-1685
Richard Esterle, *Pr*
Adam Esterle, *
Kathleen Sawyer, *
Carol Esterle, *
EMP: 45 **EST:** 1976
SQ FT: 18,100
SALES (est): 9.68MM
SALES (corp-wide): 9.68MM **Privately Held**
Web: www.esterle.com
SIC: 3498 3599 3544 Fabricated pipe and fittings; Machine shop, jobbing and repair; Industrial molds

(G-13696)
FABRIC SQUARE SHOP
2091 Liberty Rd (44224-3427)
PHONE...............................330 752-3044
Laura Sampsel, *Owner*
EMP: 7 **EST:** 2010
SALES (est): 374.72K **Privately Held**
Web: www.fabricsquareshop.com
SIC: 5949 2211 Fabric stores piece goods; Apparel and outerwear fabrics, cotton

(G-13697)
FALLS FILTRATION TECH INC
115 E Steels Corners Rd (44224-4919)
PHONE...............................330 928-4100
Tom Page, *Pr*
Lou Scalise, *
EMP: 35 **EST:** 2004
SALES (est): 9.03MM **Privately Held**
Web: www.fallsfti.com
SIC: 3569 Filters, general line: industrial

(G-13698)
FERRY INDUSTRIES INC (PA)
Also Called: Ferry & Quintax
4445 Allen Rd Ste A (44224-1058)
PHONE...............................330 920-9200
Adam Covington, *Pr*
Courtney Mahan, *
◆ **EMP:** 59 **EST:** 1927
SQ FT: 70,000
SALES (est): 23.29MM
SALES (corp-wide): 23.29MM **Privately Held**
Web: www.ferryindustries.com
SIC: 3599 3829 Custom machinery; Measuring and controlling devices, nec

(G-13699)
FLEXOTECH GRAPHICS INC (PA)
4830 Hudson Dr (44224-1703)
PHONE...............................330 929-4743
Cris Apley, *Pr*
EMP: 10 **EST:** 1997
SQ FT: 6,500
SALES (est): 1.08MM
SALES (corp-wide): 1.08MM **Privately Held**
Web: www.flexotech.com
SIC: 3555 Printing plates

(G-13700)
GLI HOLDINGS INC
GL Direct
4484 Allen Rd (44224-1051)
PHONE...............................440 892-7760
Neal Gallagher, *Mgr*
EMP: 65
SALES (corp-wide): 23.14MM **Privately Held**
Web: www.gll.com
SIC: 2752 2796 Offset printing; Lithographic plates, positives or negatives
PA: Gli Holdings, Inc.
4246 Hudson Dr
Stow OH 44224
216 651-1500

(G-13701)
GLI HOLDINGS INC (PA)
Also Called: Gli
4246 Hudson Dr (44224)
PHONE...............................216 651-1500
James R Schultz, *Ch*
James R Schultz, *Ch*
Scot D Adkins, *
Anthony Sanson, *
Robert J Schultz, *
▲ **EMP:** 90 **EST:** 1931
SALES (est): 23.14MM
SALES (corp-wide): 23.14MM **Privately Held**

(PA)=Parent Co (HQ)=Headquarters
✪ = New Business established in last 2 years

Stow - Summit County (G-13702) — GEOGRAPHIC SECTION

Web: www.gll.com
SIC: 2752 2796 2789 Offset printing; Lithographic plates, positives or negatives; Bookbinding and related work

(G-13702)
HYDRAULIC MANIFOLDS USA LLC
Also Called: Selling Precision
4540 Boyce Pkwy (44224-1769)
PHONE.....................973 728-1214
Nimit Patel, *Managing Member*
EMP: 30 EST: 2017
SALES (est): 5.02MM **Privately Held**
Web: www.hydraulicmanifoldsusa.com
SIC: 5084 5085 3492 Hydraulic systems equipment and supplies; Hydraulic and pneumatic pistons and valves; Valves, hydraulic, aircraft

(G-13703)
KNH INDUSTRIES INC (PA)
3844 Oneida St (44224-4231)
PHONE.....................330 235-1235
Kim Hinton, *CEO*
EMP: 7 EST: 2019
SALES (est): 97.15K
SALES (corp-wide): 97.15K **Privately Held**
SIC: 2339 Women's and misses' accessories

(G-13704)
KNH INDUSTRIES INC
3900 Darrow Rd Unit 2732 (44224-7346)
PHONE.....................330 510-8390
Kim Hinton, *Brnch Mgr*
EMP: 18
SALES (corp-wide): 97.15K **Privately Held**
SIC: 2339 Women's and misses' accessories
PA: Knh Industries, Inc
 3844 Oneida St
 Stow OH 44224
 330 235-1235

(G-13705)
LASPINA TOOL AND DIE INC
4282 Hudson Dr (44224-2251)
PHONE.....................330 923-9996
Timothy P Laspina, *Owner*
EMP: 19 EST: 1996
SQ FT: 8,500
SALES (est): 2.07MM **Privately Held**
Web: www.laspinatd.com
SIC: 3544 3599 Special dies and tools; Machine shop, jobbing and repair

(G-13706)
LEVAN ENTERPRISES INC (PA)
Also Called: R F Cook Manufacturing Co
4585 Allen Rd (44224-1035)
PHONE.....................330 923-9797
Peter H Levan, *Pr*
Carolyn G Levan, *
EMP: 25 EST: 1986
SQ FT: 18,000
SALES (est): 5.72MM
SALES (corp-wide): 5.72MM **Privately Held**
Web: www.rfcook.com
SIC: 3541 3542 3545 3544 Machine tools, metal cutting type; Machine tools, metal forming type; Precision tools, machinists'; Special dies, tools, jigs, and fixtures

(G-13707)
MACTAC AMERICAS LLC (DH)
Also Called: Mactac
4560 Darrow Rd (44224-1898)
PHONE.....................800 762-2822
Ed Laforge, *Pr*
EMP: 20 EST: 2015
SQ FT: 559,400
SALES (est): 530.11MM **Privately Held**
Web: www.mactac.com
SIC: 2891 Adhesives and sealants
HQ: Lintec Usa Holding, Inc.
 4560 Darrow Rd
 Stow OH 44224

(G-13708)
MATCO TOOLS CORPORATION (HQ)
Also Called: Matco Tools
4403 Allen Rd (44224)
P.O. Box 1429 (44224)
PHONE.....................330 929-4949
Mike Dwyer, *Pr*
Raymond Michaud, *Finance Treasurer**
▲ EMP: 400 EST: 1953
SALES (est): 134.73MM
SALES (corp-wide): 3.1B **Publicly Held**
Web: www.matcotools.com
SIC: 5013 5072 3469 3423 Tools and equipment, automotive; Hardware; Metal stampings, nec; Hand and edge tools, nec
PA: Vontier Corporation
 5438 Wade Park Blvd # 601
 Raleigh NC 27607
 984 275-6000

(G-13709)
MORGAN ADHESIVES COMPANY LLC (DH)
Also Called: Mactac
4560 Darrow Rd (44224-1898)
PHONE.....................330 688-1111
◆ EMP: 500 EST: 1959
SQ FT: 559,400
SALES (est): 473.98MM **Privately Held**
Web: www.mactac.com
SIC: 2891 3565 2672 2823 Adhesives; Labeling machines, industrial; Adhesive papers, labels, or tapes: from purchased material; Cellulosic manmade fibers
HQ: Mactac Americas, Llc
 4560 Darrow Rd
 Stow OH 44224
 800 762-2822

(G-13710)
MOS INTERNATIONAL INC
3213 Peterboro Dr (44224-5913)
PHONE.....................330 329-0905
Jenna Myong Ok Song, *Pr*
EMP: 10 EST: 2008
SQ FT: 3,000
SALES (est): 233.68K **Privately Held**
SIC: 3089 Automotive parts, plastic

(G-13711)
MURRUBBER TECHNOLOGIES INC
1350 Commerce Dr (44224-1737)
PHONE.....................330 688-4881
Anthony J Murru, *CEO*
Anthony J Murru, *Pr*
Tom Rownd, *
Lisa A Kuhen, *
EMP: 40 EST: 1986
SQ FT: 50,000
SALES (est): 8.57MM **Privately Held**
Web: www.murrubber.com
SIC: 3069 2241 Reclaimed rubber and specialty rubber compounds; Rubber and elastic yarns and fabrics

(G-13712)
NATIONAL AEROSPACE PROC LLC
1330 Commerce Dr (44224-1737)
PHONE.....................234 900-6497
Mike Piglia, *Prin*
Michael Fabrizio, *Prin*
EMP: 8 EST: 2020
SALES (est): 525.82K **Privately Held**
Web: www.naprocessing.com

SIC: 3471 Electroplating of metals or formed products

(G-13713)
NATIONAL AVIATION PRODUCTS INC (DH)
4880 Hudson Dr (44224-1708)
PHONE.....................330 688-6494
Peter Piglia, *Ch Bd*
Thomas G Knoll, *Prin*
EMP: 9 EST: 1999
SALES (est): 11.5MM
SALES (corp-wide): 128.02MM **Privately Held**
Web: www.nmgaerospace.com
SIC: 3599 3492 Machine shop, jobbing and repair; Control valves, fluid power: hydraulic and pneumatic
HQ: National Machine Company
 4880 Hudson Dr
 Stow OH 44224
 330 688-6494

(G-13714)
NATIONAL MACHINE COMPANY (HQ)
Also Called: Nmg Aerospace
4880 Hudson Dr (44224-1799)
PHONE.....................330 688-6494
Darryl Piglia, *CEO*
Bill Anop, *
Jeffrey Bissell, *
▲ EMP: 250 EST: 1967
SQ FT: 80,000
SALES (est): 128.02MM
SALES (corp-wide): 128.02MM **Privately Held**
Web: www.nmgaerospace.com
SIC: 3599 3492 Machine shop, jobbing and repair; Control valves, fluid power: hydraulic and pneumatic
PA: Electromotive, Inc.
 4880 Hudson Dr
 Stow OH 44224
 330 688-6494

(G-13715)
NORDEC INC
900 Hampshire Rd (44224-1113)
PHONE.....................330 940-3700
Christine A Snyder, *Pr*
Jason D Sudbrink, *
Jeffrey L Smith, *Product Vice President**
William L Snyder, *Stockholder**
EMP: 60 EST: 1962
SQ FT: 50,000
SALES (est): 7.91MM **Privately Held**
Web: www.nordecinc.com
SIC: 2759 2675 Screen printing; Die-cut paper and board

(G-13716)
OSMANS PIES INC
3678 Elm Rd (44224-3954)
PHONE.....................330 607-9083
Ethel Osman, *Pr*
Terry Osman, *
Cheryl Osman Crowe, *
EMP: 30 EST: 1949
SQ FT: 3,500
SALES (est): 600K **Privately Held**
SIC: 5461 5149 2052 2051 Retail bakeries; Bakery products; Cookies and crackers; Bread, cake, and related products

(G-13717)
POLYSTAR INC
1676 Commerce Dr (44224-1731)
PHONE.....................330 963-5100
David Huston, *CEO*
EMP: 14 EST: 1992
SQ FT: 1,785

SALES (est): 4.47MM **Privately Held**
Web: www.polystarcontainment.com
SIC: 2655 Containers, laminated phenolic and vulcanized fiber

(G-13718)
PRINT-DIGITAL INCORPORATED
Also Called: Print Digital
4688 Darrow Rd (44224-1819)
PHONE.....................330 686-5945
Marvin Weber, *Pr*
Eric Weber, *VP*
EMP: 9 EST: 1984
SQ FT: 4,500
SALES (est): 908.24K **Privately Held**
Web: www.printdigitalinc.com
SIC: 2752 7334 2789 2761 Offset printing; Photocopying and duplicating services; Bookbinding and related work; Manifold business forms

(G-13719)
R & J PRINTING ENTERPRISES INC
Also Called: Newhouse Printing Company
4246 Hudson Rd (44224-2251)
PHONE.....................330 343-1242
John S Carpenter, *Pr*
EMP: 12 EST: 1917
SALES (est): 842.14K **Privately Held**
Web: www.newhouseprinting.com
SIC: 2752 Offset printing

(G-13720)
RAY COMMUNICATIONS INC
Also Called: Raytec Systems
1337 Commerce Dr Ste 11 (44224-1758)
PHONE.....................330 686-0226
Richard A Yarnell, *Pr*
EMP: 9 EST: 1986
SQ FT: 2,400
SALES (est): 2.02MM **Privately Held**
Web: www.raytecsystems.com
SIC: 5065 2542 5999 Communication equipment; Telephone booths: except wood; Telephone equipment and systems

(G-13721)
SAINT-GOBAIN CERAMICS PLAS INC
Also Called: Saint-Gobain Norpro
3840 Fishcreek Rd (44224-4306)
PHONE.....................330 673-5860
EMP: 127
SALES (corp-wide): 397.78MM **Privately Held**
Web: www.saint-gobain.com
SIC: 2819 3679 3544 3297 Industrial inorganic chemicals, nec; Electronic crystals; Special dies and tools; Nonclay refractories
HQ: Saint-Gobain Ceramics & Plastics, Inc.
 20 Moores Rd
 Malvern PA 19355

(G-13722)
SAINT-GOBAIN NORPRO CORP (HQ)
3840 Fishcreek Rd (44224-4306)
PHONE.....................330 673-5860
Antonio Vilela, *Pr*
Joseph H Menendez, *
◆ EMP: 126 EST: 1991
SALES (est): 48.65MM
SALES (corp-wide): 397.78MM **Privately Held**
Web: norpro.saint-gobain.com
SIC: 3533 5211 Oil and gas field machinery; Tile, ceramic
PA: Compagnie De Saint-Gobain
 Tour Saint Gobain
 Courbevoie 92400

(G-13723)
SCOTT BADER INC
4280 Hudson Dr (44224-2251)
P.O. Box 115 (27028-0115)
PHONE..................................330 920-4410
Nick Padfield, *Pr*
▲ **EMP:** 8 **EST:** 1992
SQ FT: 5,500
SALES (est): 5.1MM
SALES (corp-wide): 367.07MM **Privately Held**
Web: www.scottbader.com
SIC: 2821 Plastics materials and resins
HQ: Scott Bader Company Limited
   Wollaston Hall
   Wellingborough NORTHANTS NN29
   193 366-3100

(G-13724)
SELLING PRECISION INC
4540 Boyce Pkwy (44224-1769)
PHONE..................................973 728-1214
William Calcagno Junior, *Pr*
Kenneth Calcagno, *
EMP: 35 **EST:** 1971
SALES (est): 2.59MM **Privately Held**
Web: www.hydraulicmanifoldsusa.com
SIC: 3498 Manifolds, pipe: fabricated from purchased pipe

(G-13725)
SPIRAL BRUSHES INC
1355 Commerce Dr (44224-1751)
PHONE..................................330 686-2861
Ernest R Preston Iii, *Pr*
Laura B Preston, *
◆ **EMP:** 30 **EST:** 1939
SQ FT: 25,000
SALES (est): 4.73MM **Privately Held**
Web: www.spiralbrushes.com
SIC: 3991 Brushes, household or industrial

(G-13726)
SPIROL SHIM CORPORATION (DH)
321 Remington Rd (44224-4915)
PHONE..................................330 920-3655
Jeffrey Koehl, *CEO*
Ken Hagen, *
EMP: 96 **EST:** 2018
SALES (est): 70.93M
SALES (corp-wide): 65.55MM **Privately Held**
Web: www.spirol.com
SIC: 3469 Stamping metal for the trade
HQ: Spirol International Corporation
   30 Rock Ave
   Danielson CT 06239
   860 774-8571

(G-13727)
STEEL PRODUCTS CORP AKRON
2288 Samira Rd (44224-3404)
PHONE..................................330 688-6633
William E Welsh, *Pr*
William Mac Cracken, *Ch Bd*
Lou Nelson, *VP*
EMP: 22 **EST:** 1950
SQ FT: 100,000
SALES (est): 2.21MM **Privately Held**
SIC: 3599 Machine shop, jobbing and repair

(G-13728)
STERIS INSTRUMENT MGT SVCS INC
Also Called: Spectrum Surgical Instruments
4575 Hudson Dr (44224-1725)
PHONE..................................800 783-9251
Rick Costello, *Brnch Mgr*
EMP: 165
Web: www.imsready.com
SIC: 3841 Surgical and medical instruments
HQ: Steris Instrument Management Services, Inc.
   3316 2nd Ave N
   Birmingham AL 35222

(G-13729)
STERIS-IMS
4575 Hudson Dr (44224-1725)
PHONE..................................330 686-4557
EMP: 13 **EST:** 2019
SALES (est): 467.69K **Privately Held**
Web: www.steris-ims.com
SIC: 3842 Surgical appliances and supplies

(G-13730)
SUMMIT RESEARCH GROUP
4466 Darrow Rd Ste 15 (44224-1891)
PHONE..................................330 689-1778
Ron Antal, *Prin*
EMP: 7 **EST:** 2011
SALES (est): 203.22K **Privately Held**
SIC: 2834 Pharmaceutical preparations

(G-13731)
TOTAL REPAIR EXPRESS MICH LLC
Also Called: Dedtru
4575 Hudson Dr (44224-1725)
PHONE..................................248 690-9410
EMP: 11 **EST:** 2011
SALES (est): 434.98K **Privately Held**
SIC: 3599 Machine shop, jobbing and repair

(G-13732)
TRAXIUM LLC
Also Called: Printing Concepts
4246 Hudson Dr (44224-2251)
PHONE..................................330 572-8200
Frank Tuzzio, *
Devin Gilespie, *
Tiffani Gerber, *
EMP: 49 **EST:** 1977
SQ FT: 45,000
SALES (est): 9.88MM **Privately Held**
Web: www.printingconcepts.com
SIC: 7331 2789 2752 2759 Direct mail advertising services; Bookbinding and related work; Offset printing; Letterpress printing

(G-13733)
TUFFY PAD COMPANY
454 Seasons Rd (44224-1020)
P.O. Box 1302 (44224-0302)
PHONE..................................330 688-0043
Joseph M Burks, *Pr*
Margaret Burks, *Sec*
Debbie Burks, *Treas*
EMP: 10 **EST:** 1958
SQ FT: 15,000
SALES (est): 798.53K **Privately Held**
Web: www.tuffypad.com
SIC: 3949 Pads: football, basketball, soccer, lacrosse, etc.

(G-13734)
TURFWARE MANUFACTURING INC
1337 Commerce Dr Ste 4 (44224-1758)
PHONE..................................330 688-8500
John Prusa, *Prin*
EMP: 6 **EST:** 2010
SALES (est): 93K **Privately Held**
Web: www.turfware.com
SIC: 3999 Manufacturing industries, nec

(G-13735)
TWIN SISTERS PRODUCTIONS LLC
4710 Hudson Dr (44224-1706)
PHONE..................................330 631-0361
▲ **EMP:** 40
Web: www.twinsisters.com

(G-13736)
VALV-TROL LLC
1340 Commerce Dr (44224-1737)
P.O. Box 2259 (44224-1000)
PHONE..................................330 686-2800
Kevin Gray, *Pr*
Kenneth R Ingram, *Pr*
Richard Houck, *VP*
Marjorie Ingram, *Ch Bd*
EMP: 10 **EST:** 1947
SQ FT: 10,000
SALES (est): 2.34MM **Privately Held**
Web: www.valv-trol.com
SIC: 3492 3592 3491 5084 Control valves, fluid power: hydraulic and pneumatic; Valves; Industrial valves; Industrial machinery and equipment

(G-13737)
VEOLIA WTS SYSTEMS USA INC
Also Called: General Ionics
887 Hampshire Rd Ste I (44224-1122)
PHONE..................................330 929-1639
Ron Mettler, *Mgr*
EMP: 10
Web: www.suezwatertechnologies.com
SIC: 3589 Water treatment equipment, industrial
HQ: Veolia Wts Systems Usa, Inc.
   3600 Horizon Blvd Ste 100
   Trevose PA 19053
   866 439-2837

(G-13738)
VMI AMERICAS INC (HQ)
4670 Allen Rd (44224-1042)
PHONE..................................330 929-6800
Auke Diaster, *Pr*
▲ **EMP:** 25 **EST:** 1983
SQ FT: 65,000
SALES (est): 20.2MM
SALES (corp-wide): 1.89B **Privately Held**
Web: www.vmi-group.com
SIC: 3565 3544 Packaging machinery; Special dies, tools, jigs, and fixtures
PA: Tkh Group N.V.
   Spinnerstraat 15
   Haaksbergen OV 7481
   535732900

(G-13739)
WOLFE GRINDING INC
4582 Allen Rd (44224-1091)
PHONE..................................330 929-6677
Larry W Wolfe, *Pr*
Phyllis Wolfe, *VP*
EMP: 6 **EST:** 1971
SQ FT: 48,750
SALES (est): 685.66K **Privately Held**
SIC: 3599 Machine shop, jobbing and repair

(G-13740)
WRAYCO INDUSTRIES INC
858 Seasons Rd (44224-1071)
PHONE..................................330 688-5617
▲ **EMP:** 106
Web: www.wrayco.com
SIC: 3441 Fabricated structural metal

(G-13741)
WRAYCO MANUFACTURING IN
5010 Hudson Dr (44224-1797)
PHONE..................................330 688-5617
EMP: 14 **EST:** 2019
SALES (est): 376.45K **Privately Held**
SIC: 3999 Manufacturing industries, nec

Strasburg
Tuscarawas County

(G-13742)
ALRON
805 Margo Dr Sw (44680-9792)
PHONE..................................330 477-3405
Ron Gritzam, *Pt*
Allen Knotz, *Pt*
EMP: 8 **EST:** 2004
SALES (est): 355.13K **Privately Held**
Web: www.alroncustomfabrication.com
SIC: 2295 Metallizing of fabrics

(G-13743)
B A MALCUIT RACING INC
Also Called: Malcuit Racing Engines
707 S Wooster Ave (44680-9702)
P.O. Box 166 (44680-0166)
PHONE..................................330 878-7111
Mark Malcuit, *Pr*
Brad Malcuit, *VP*
EMP: 8 **EST:** 1984
SQ FT: 30,000
SALES (est): 580K **Privately Held**
SIC: 3519 3714 Internal combustion engines, nec; Motor vehicle parts and accessories

(G-13744)
BEACH CITY LUMBER LLC
5177 Austin Ln Nw (44680-9109)
PHONE..................................330 878-4097
Paul Weaver, *Owner*
EMP: 7 **EST:** 1986
SQ FT: 5,000
SALES (est): 503.73K **Privately Held**
SIC: 2421 Lumber: rough, sawed, or planed

(G-13745)
CASE FARMS OF OHIO INC
Also Called: Hatchery
1225 Hensel Ave Ne (44680-9779)
PHONE..................................330 878-7118
EMP: 74
SALES (corp-wide): 490.71MM **Privately Held**
Web: www.casefarms.com
SIC: 2015 Poultry slaughtering and processing
HQ: Case Farms Of Ohio, Inc.
   1818 County Rd 160
   Winesburg OH 44690
   330 359-7141

(G-13746)
GREEN RDCED EMSSONS NETWRK LLC
Also Called: Gre'n Disc
5029 Hilltop Dr Nw (44680-9069)
PHONE..................................330 340-0941
EMP: 8 **EST:** 2010
SALES (est): 425.19K **Privately Held**
SIC: 3714 Motor vehicle parts and accessories

(G-13747)
KLEEN TEST PRODUCTS CORP
216 12th St Ne (44680-9752)
PHONE..................................330 878-5586
Bill Ahlborn, *Brnch Mgr*
EMP: 255
SALES (corp-wide): 331.16MM **Privately Held**
Web: www.kleentest.com
SIC: 2842 Cleaning or polishing preparations, nec

Strasburg - Tuscarawas County (G-13748)

HQ: Kleen Test Products Corporation
1611 S Sunset Rd
Port Washington WI 53074
262 284-6600

(G-13748)
LEIDEN CABINET COMPANY LLC
1230 Hensel Ave Ne (44680-9779)
PHONE..................330 425-8555
Dave Marusa, *Mgr*
EMP: 7
SALES (corp-wide): 17.63MM Privately Held
Web: www.leidencompany.com
SIC: 5046 2541 Store fixtures; Wood partitions and fixtures
PA: Leiden Cabinet Company, Llc
2385 Edison Blvd
Twinsburg OH 44087
330 425-8555

(G-13749)
LINCOLN MANUFACTURING INC
Also Called: LINCOLN MANUFACTURING, INC.
310 Railroad Ave Se (44680-1235)
PHONE..................330 878-7772
Eric Ward, *Pr*
EMP: 17
SALES (corp-wide): 91.09MM Privately Held
Web: www.lincolnmanufacturing.com
SIC: 3999 Barber and beauty shop equipment
PA: Lincoln Manufacturing, Llc
31209 Fm 2978 Rd
Magnolia TX 77354
281 252-9494

(G-13750)
TREMCAR USA INC
436 12th St Ne (44680-9760)
PHONE..................330 878-7708
Daniel Tremblay, *Pr*
Marie Marquis, *
▲ EMP: 57 EST: 1998
SQ FT: 35,000
SALES (est): 11.47MM
SALES (corp-wide): 2.1MM Privately Held
Web: www.tremcar.com
SIC: 3711 Motor vehicles and car bodies
HQ: Tremcar Inc
790 Av Montrichard
Saint-Jean-Sur-Richelieu QC J2X 5
450 347-7822

(G-13751)
UNITED HARDWOODS LTD
5508 Hilltop Dr Nw (44680-9117)
PHONE..................330 878-9510
Norm Shetler, *Prin*
EMP: 9 EST: 2006
SALES (est): 926.64K Privately Held
Web: www.unitedhardwoodsltd.com
SIC: 2421 Custom sawmill

Streetsboro
Portage County

(G-13752)
ACCURATE FAB LLC
1400 Miller Pkwy (44241-4640)
EMP: 6 EST: 2005
SALES (est): 834.07K Privately Held
Web: www.acsteel.net
SIC: 3441 Ship sections, prefabricated metal

(G-13753)
AGRATRONIX LLC
1790 Miller Pkwy (44241-4633)
PHONE..................330 562-2222
Gerald Stephens, *Managing Member*
▲ EMP: 30 EST: 2007
SALES (est): 10.95MM Privately Held
Web: www.agratronix.com
SIC: 5039 3699 3446 Wire fence, gates, and accessories; Electric fence chargers; Fences, gates, posts, and flagpoles

(G-13754)
ALACRIANT INC (PA)
1760 Miller Pkwy (44241-4611)
PHONE..................330 562-7191
Jeff Berkes, *Pr*
James Berkes, *
Ken Quinn, *
EMP: 55 EST: 1997
SQ FT: 72,000
SALES (est): 39.47MM
SALES (corp-wide): 39.47MM Privately Held
Web: www.alacriant.com
SIC: 3499 Strapping, metal

(G-13755)
ALACRIANT INC
2500 Crane Centre Dr (44241-5072)
PHONE..................330 562-7191
Andrew Stanford, *Mgr*
EMP: 30
SALES (corp-wide): 39.47MM Privately Held
Web: www.alacriant.com
SIC: 3499 Strapping, metal
PA: Alacriant Inc.
1760 Miller Pkwy
Streetsboro OH 44241
330 562-7191

(G-13756)
ALLIED CORP INC
8505 State Route 14 (44241-5878)
PHONE..................330 626-3401
Bob Mcgarvey, *Prin*
EMP: 8 EST: 2010
SALES (est): 157.21K Privately Held
SIC: 2911 Asphalt or asphaltic materials, made in refineries

(G-13757)
AURORA PLASTICS LLC (HQ)
Also Called: Aurora Material Solutions
9280 Jefferson St (44241)
PHONE..................330 422-0700
Darrell Hughes, *Pr*
Mike Klein, *
Matthew Kuwatch, *Development*
Steve Harrigan, *
Melissa Neiberlein, *
▲ EMP: 23 EST: 1997
SALES (est): 106.83MM Privately Held
Web: www.auroramaterialsolutions.com
SIC: 2821 3087 Polyvinyl chloride resins, PVC; Custom compound purchased resins
PA: Nautic Partners, Llc
100 Westminster St # 1220
Providence RI 02903

(G-13758)
AUTOMATED LASER FABRICATION CO
1 Singer Dr (44241)
PHONE..................330 562-7200
Paul Y Shapiro, *Pr*
EMP: 11 EST: 2003
SALES (est): 231.52K Privately Held

SIC: 3441 Fabricated structural metal

(G-13759)
AUTOMATED PACKAGING SYSTEMS LLC (HQ)
Also Called: Automated Packg Systems Inc
10175 Philipp Pkwy (44241-4041)
PHONE..................330 528-2000
▲ EMP: 250 EST: 1963
SALES (est): 209.05MM
SALES (corp-wide): 5.49B Publicly Held
Web: www.autobag.com
SIC: 3081 3565 Packing materials, plastics sheet; Packaging machinery
PA: Sealed Air Corporation
2415 Cascade Pointe Blvd
Charlotte NC 28208
980 221-3235

(G-13760)
AUTOMATED PACKG SYSTEMS INC
Also Called: AUTOMATED PACKAGING SYSTEMS, INC.
600 Mondial Pkwy (44241-5211)
PHONE..................330 626-2313
Bernard Lerner, *CEO*
EMP: 6
SQ FT: 173,000
SALES (corp-wide): 5.49B Publicly Held
Web: www.autobag.com
SIC: 3081 3565 Packing materials, plastics sheet; Packaging machinery
HQ: Automated Packaging Systems, Llc
10175 Philipp Pkwy
Streetsboro OH 44241
330 528-2000

(G-13761)
BERRY GLOBAL INC
1275 Ethan Ave (44241-4977)
PHONE..................330 896-6700
Robert Maltarich, *Mgr*
EMP: 10
Web: www.berryglobal.com
SIC: 3089 Bottle caps, molded plastics
HQ: Berry Global, Inc.
101 Oakley St
Evansville IN 47710

(G-13762)
CLEVELAND STEEL CONTAINER CORP
10048 Aurora Hudson Rd (44241-1636)
PHONE..................330 656-5600
Roger Mayle, *Genl Mgr*
EMP: 38
SALES (corp-wide): 138.41MM Privately Held
Web: www.cscpails.com
SIC: 3412 3411 Pails, shipping: metal; Metal cans
PA: Cleveland Steel Container Corporation
100 Executive Pkwy
Hudson OH 44236
440 349-8000

(G-13763)
COMMERCIAL TURF PRODUCTS LTD
1777 Miller Pkwy (44241-4634)
PHONE..................330 995-7000
Mike Sobera, *Genl Mgr*
EMP: 87 EST: 1997
SQ FT: 177,000
SALES (est): 14.03MM
SALES (corp-wide): 15.78B Publicly Held
SIC: 3524 Lawn and garden equipment
HQ: Mtd Products Inc
5965 Grafton Rd
Valley City OH 44280
330 225-2600

(G-13764)
DAVIS MACHINE PRODUCTS INC
74 Sapphire Ln (44241-4128)
PHONE..................440 474-0247
William G Davis, *Pr*
EMP: 6 EST: 1972
SQ FT: 7,200
SALES (est): 444.85K Privately Held
SIC: 3599 Machine shop, jobbing and repair

(G-13765)
DELTA SYSTEMS INC
1734 Frost Rd (44241-5008)
P.O. Box 2459 (44241-0459)
PHONE..................330 626-2811
Joey Arnold, *Pr*
Michael R Jeziorski, *
Mark J Fechtel, *
Dean Barry, *
◆ EMP: 252 EST: 1971
SQ FT: 137,000
SALES (est): 60.93MM Privately Held
Web: www.deltasystemsinc.com
SIC: 3613 3625 Switchgear and switchboard apparatus; Relays and industrial controls

(G-13766)
DELUXE CORPORATION
Also Called: Deluxe Business Systems
10030 Philipp Pkwy (44241-4708)
PHONE..................330 342-1500
Robin Lebine, *Prin*
EMP: 54
SALES (corp-wide): 2.19B Publicly Held
Web: www.deluxe.com
SIC: 2782 Blankbooks and looseleaf binders
PA: Deluxe Corporation
801 Marquette Ave
Minneapolis MN 55402
651 483-7111

(G-13767)
DRC ACQUISITION INC
Also Called: David Round Company, The
10200 Wellman Rd (44241-1615)
PHONE..................330 656-1600
Bradley R Young, *Pr*
▲ EMP: 27 EST: 1869
SQ FT: 30,000
SALES (est): 7.73MM Privately Held
Web: www.davidround.com
SIC: 3536 3531 Hoists; Winches

(G-13768)
DUDICK INC
1818 Miller Pkwy (44241-5067)
PHONE..................330 562-1970
EMP: 24 EST: 2007
SALES (est): 2.65MM Privately Held
Web: www.dudick.com
SIC: 3429 Furniture, builders' and other household hardware

(G-13769)
EBCO INC
Also Called: Protectoplas Div
3500 Crane Centre Dr (44241-5074)
PHONE..................330 562-8265
EMP: 20 EST: 1972
SALES (est): 2.35MM Privately Held
Web: www.protectoplas.com
SIC: 3089 3714 Plastics containers, except foam; Motor vehicle parts and accessories

(G-13770)
EPG INC (DH)
1780 Miller Pkwy (44241-4633)
PHONE..................330 995-9725
Michael Orazen Junior, *Pr*
Michael Scanlon, *VP*

▲ = Import ▼ = Export
◆ = Import/Export

GEOGRAPHIC SECTION
Streetsboro - Portage County (G-13792)

Smith Mckee, *VP Opers*
Gabriel Orazen, *VP*
EMP: 13 **EST:** 1983
SQ FT: 46,000
SALES (est): 24.3MM
SALES (corp-wide): 4.26B **Privately Held**
SIC: 3053 3061 Gaskets, all materials; Mechanical rubber goods
HQ: Trelleborg Corporation
200 Veterans Blvd Ste 3
South Haven MI 49090
269 639-9891

(G-13771)
FORTEC MEDICAL LITHOTRIPSY LLC
10125 Wellman Rd (44241-1614)
PHONE.................................330 656-4301
Drew Forhan, *Managing Member*
EMP: 17 **EST:** 1995
SQ FT: 1,000
SALES (est): 556.17K **Privately Held**
SIC: 3699 Laser systems and equipment

(G-13772)
GORELL ENTERPRISES INC (DH)
Also Called: Gorell Windows & Doors
10250 Philipp Pkwy (44241-4765)
PHONE.................................724 465-1800
Wayne C Gorell, *Ch Bd*
Brian Zimmerman, *
Michael A Rempel, *
Arnold S Levitt, *
EMP: 360 **EST:** 1993
SQ FT: 240,000
SALES (est): 83.37MM
SALES (corp-wide): 1.2B **Privately Held**
SIC: 3089 5031 Plastics hardware and building products; Doors and windows
HQ: Soft-Lite L.L.C.
10250 Philipp Pkwy
Streetsboro OH 44241
330 528-3400

(G-13773)
HP ENTERPRISE INC
Also Called: Jolly Pats
10008 State Route 43 (44241-4940)
PHONE.................................800 232-7950
Rob Miavitz, *Pr*
Brenda Miavitz, *Sec*
◆ **EMP:** 22 **EST:** 1976
SQ FT: 20,000
SALES (est): 5.16MM **Privately Held**
Web: www.jollypets.com
SIC: 3089 Extruded finished plastics products, nec

(G-13774)
HUDSON HINES HILL COMPANY
1818 Millers Pkwy (44241-5067)
PHONE.................................330 562-1970
Tom Dudick, *Pr*
EMP: 55 **EST:** 1982
SALES (est): 9.97MM **Privately Held**
Web: www.dudick.com
SIC: 2851 Lacquers, varnishes, enamels, and other coatings

(G-13775)
INTERNATIONAL PAPER COMPANY
Also Called: International Paper
700 Mondial Pkwy (44241-4511)
PHONE.................................330 626-7300
Chuck Bakaitis, *Brnch Mgr*
EMP: 23
SALES (corp-wide): 18.92B **Publicly Held**
Web: www.internationalpaper.com
SIC: 2653 Boxes, corrugated: made from purchased materials
PA: International Paper Company

6400 Poplar Ave
Memphis TN 38197
901 419-7000

(G-13776)
JOSEPH INDUSTRIES INC
Also Called: BUCKEYE FASTENERS COMPANY
10039 Aurora Hudson Rd (44241-1600)
PHONE.................................330 528-0091
Clyde Faust, *Pr*
Linda Kerekes, *
▲ **EMP:** 52 **EST:** 1969
SQ FT: 76,260
SALES (est): 7.05MM
SALES (corp-wide): 46.16MM **Privately Held**
Web: www.joseph.com
SIC: 3714 5084 3713 3566 Motor vehicle parts and accessories; Lift trucks and parts; Truck and bus bodies; Speed changers, drives, and gears
PA: Fastener Industries, Inc.
1 Berea Cmns Ste 209
Berea OH 44017
440 243-0034

(G-13777)
LANGE GRINDING & MACHINING INC
10165 Philipp Pkwy (44241-4706)
PHONE.................................330 463-3500
Richard C Lange, *Pr*
EMP: 23 **EST:** 1989
SQ FT: 30,000
SALES (est): 2.52MM **Privately Held**
Web: www.langegrinding.com
SIC: 3599 Machine shop, jobbing and repair

(G-13778)
METALFAB GROUP
10145 Philipp Pkwy (44241-5099)
PHONE.................................440 543-6234
EMP: 8 **EST:** 2016
SALES (est): 624.22K **Privately Held**
Web: www.metalfabgroup.com
SIC: 3441 3443 3444 3449 Fabricated structural metal; Fabricated plate work (boiler shop); Sheet metalwork; Miscellaneous metalwork

(G-13779)
MICRO-PISE MSRMENT SYSTEMS LLC
Also Called: Ametek Micro-Poise Measurement
555 Mondial Pkwy (44241-4510)
P.O. Box 1869 (44309-1869)
PHONE.................................330 541-9100
Steve Harris, *Managing Member*
Kenneth Garvey, *Managing Member*
◆ **EMP:** 250 **EST:** 2007
SALES (est): 55.21MM
SALES (corp-wide): 6.6B **Publicly Held**
Web: www.micropoise.com
SIC: 3559 Automotive maintenance equipment
PA: Ametek, Inc.
1100 Cassatt Rd
Berwyn PA 19312
610 647-2121

(G-13780)
MOJONNIER USA LLC
10325 State Route 43 Ste N (44241-4945)
PHONE.................................844 665-6664
Matt Brinn, *Mgr*
EMP: 12 **EST:** 2015
SALES (est): 2.83MM **Privately Held**
Web: www.mojonnier.com
SIC: 3556 Beverage machinery

(G-13781)
NATURAL ESSENTIALS INC (PA)
Also Called: Bulk Apothecary
1830 Miller Pkwy (44241-5067)
PHONE.................................330 562-8022
◆ **EMP:** 158 **EST:** 1992
SQ FT: 17,000
SALES (est): 47.25MM **Privately Held**
Web: www.naturalessentialsinc.com
SIC: 2844 2899 Cosmetic preparations; Oils and essential oils

(G-13782)
NORTHCOAST ENVIRONMENTAL LABS
10100 Wellman Rd (44241-1613)
PHONE.................................330 342-3377
EMP: 8 **EST:** 1994
SQ FT: 3,000
SALES (est): 1.01MM **Privately Held**
SIC: 3826 8731 Environmental testing equipment; Commercial physical research

(G-13783)
PERMCO INC
1500 Frost Rd (44241-5004)
P.O. Box 2068 (44241-0068)
PHONE.................................330 626-2801
Robert L Shell Junior, *Ch*
Bernard Shell, *
Robert L Shell Iii, *COO*
Phillip Todd Shell, *
Lena Shell, *
▲ **EMP:** 110 **EST:** 1964
SALES (est): 42.82MM
SALES (corp-wide): 42.82MM **Privately Held**
Web: www.permco.com
SIC: 3594 Fluid power pumps and motors
PA: Guyan International, Inc.
5 Nichols Dr
Barboursville WV 25504
304 733-1029

(G-13784)
PETROX INC
10005 Ellsworth Rd (44241-1608)
PHONE.................................330 653-5526
Benjamin Cart, *Pr*
Mark Depew, *VP*
EMP: 10 **EST:** 1986
SALES (est): 1MM **Privately Held**
SIC: 1389 5082 Oil field services, nec; Oil field equipment

(G-13785)
PM GRAPHICS INC
10170 Philipp Pkwy (44241-4705)
PHONE.................................330 650-0861
Paul W Mc Ghee Ii, *Pr*
Christine Mcghee, *Sec*
Robert Davis, *
EMP: 50 **EST:** 1959
SQ FT: 35,000
SALES (est): 5.03MM **Privately Held**
Web: www.pmgraphics.com
SIC: 2752 Offset printing

(G-13786)
R R DONNELLEY & SONS COMPANY
Also Called: R R Donnelley
10400 Danner Dr (44241-5070)
PHONE.................................330 562-5250
John Augustiniak, *Mgr*
EMP: 58
SALES (corp-wide): 4.99B **Privately Held**
Web: www.rrd.com
SIC: 2752 Commercial printing, lithographic
HQ: R. R. Donnelley & Sons Company
35 W Wacker Dr
Chicago IL 60601
312 326-8000

(G-13787)
RB&W MANUFACTURING LLC (HQ)
10080 Wellman Rd (44241-1611)
PHONE.................................234 380-8540
Craig Cowan, *Pr*
▲ **EMP:** 9 **EST:** 1998
SALES (est): 4.87MM
SALES (corp-wide): 1.66B **Publicly Held**
Web: www.rbwmfg.com
SIC: 5085 3452 3469 Fasteners, industrial: nuts, bolts, screws, etc.; Bolts, nuts, rivets, and washers; Stamping metal for the trade
PA: Park-Ohio Holdings Corp.
6065 Parkland Blvd Ste 1
Cleveland OH 44124
440 947-2000

(G-13788)
READY FIELD SOLUTIONS LLC
1240 Ethan Ave (44241-4976)
PHONE.................................330 562-0550
EMP: 13 **EST:** 2016
SALES (est): 5.27MM **Privately Held**
Web: www.readyfieldsolutions.com
SIC: 3271 Blocks, concrete: landscape or retaining wall

(G-13789)
S TOYS HOLDINGS LLC
10010 Aurora Hudson Rd (44241-1621)
PHONE.................................330 656-0440
Jack Bresics, *CEO*
Jim Smith, *CFO*
James Schaefer, *COO*
◆ **EMP:** 900 **EST:** 2006
SALES (est): 37.68MM **Privately Held**
Web: www.step2.com
SIC: 3944 3089 Games, toys, and children's vehicles; Plastics containers, except foam

(G-13790)
SAFEGUARD TECHNOLOGY INC
Also Called: Safeguard
1460 Miller Pkwy (44241-4640)
PHONE.................................330 995-5200
William Kosinski, *Pr*
▲ **EMP:** 33 **EST:** 1992
SQ FT: 20,510
SALES (est): 5.31MM **Privately Held**
Web: www.safeguard-technology.com
SIC: 3069 Stair treads, rubber

(G-13791)
SEA AIR SPACE MCHNING MLDING L
10036 Aurora Hudson Rd (44241-1640)
PHONE.................................440 248-3025
EMP: 15 **EST:** 2008
SALES (est): 2.47MM **Privately Held**
Web: www.tth.com
SIC: 3721 3559 Aircraft; Robots, molding and forming plastics

(G-13792)
SELAS HEAT TECHNOLOGY CO LLC (HQ)
11012 Aurora Hudson Rd (44241-1629)
PHONE.................................800 523-6500
David S Bovenizer, *CEO*
▲ **EMP:** 28 **EST:** 2005
SALES (est): 28.97MM
SALES (corp-wide): 41.96MM **Privately Held**
Web: www.selas.com
SIC: 3433 3255 3823 3564 Heating equipment, except electric; Clay refractories; Process control instruments; Blowers and fans
PA: Lionheart Holdings Llc
54 Friends Ln Ste 125
Newtown PA 18940
215 283-8400

Streetsboro - Portage County (G-13793)

(G-13793)
SPECTRUM MACHINE INC (PA)
1668 Frost Rd (44241-5006)
PHONE.................................330 626-3666
Kevin Lamb, *Pr*
Timothy Lamb, *VP*
Todd Lamb, *Sec*
EMP: 15 **EST:** 1987
SQ FT: 31,000
SALES (est): 4.25MM
SALES (corp-wide): 4.25MM **Privately Held**
Web: www.spectrummachine.com
SIC: 3545 3469 3599 Machine tool accessories; Machine parts, stamped or pressed metal; Machine shop, jobbing and repair

(G-13794)
STEP2 COMPANY LLC (HQ)
Also Called: Step 2
10010 Aurora Hudson Rd (44241-1619)
PHONE.................................866 429-5200
Christopher P Quinn, *CEO*
◆ **EMP:** 500 **EST:** 2006
SQ FT: 400,000
SALES (est): 252.12MM **Privately Held**
Web: www.step2.com
SIC: 3089 3944 3423 Molding primary plastics; Games, toys, and children's vehicles; Hand and edge tools, nec
PA: Step2 Discovery, Llc
  3001 N Rouse St
  Pittsburg KS 66762

(G-13795)
TECHNOLOGY HOUSE LTD (PA)
Also Called: North Cape Manufacturing
10036 Aurora Hudson Rd (44241-1640)
PHONE.................................440 248-3025
▲ **EMP:** 8 **EST:** 1996
SQ FT: 14,000
SALES (est): 16.26MM **Privately Held**
Web: www.tth.com
SIC: 8711 3544 3369 Industrial engineers; Special dies, tools, jigs, and fixtures; Nonferrous foundries, nec

(G-13796)
TELCON LLC
1677 Miller Pkwy (44241-4635)
PHONE.................................330 562-5566
EMP: 75 **EST:** 1987
SQ FT: 56,000
SALES (est): 10.42MM **Privately Held**
Web: www.telcon.us
SIC: 3599 3369 Machine shop, jobbing and repair; Nonferrous foundries, nec

(G-13797)
VIKING FORGE LLC
4500 Crane Centre Dr (44241-5080)
PHONE.................................330 562-3366
EMP: 131 **EST:** 2018
SALES (est): 37.5MM
SALES (corp-wide): 42.19MM **Privately Held**
Web: www.viking-forge.com
SIC: 3462 Iron and steel forgings
PA: Forge Holding, Llc
  4500 Crane Centre Dr
  Streetsboro OH 44241
  330 562-3366

(G-13798)
WALTCO LIFT CORP (DH)
1777 Miller Pkwy (44241-4634)
P.O. Box 354 (44278-0354)
PHONE.................................330 633-9191
◆ **EMP:** 120 **EST:** 1960
SQ FT: 70,000
SALES (est): 43.97MM **Privately Held**
Web: www.hiab.com
SIC: 3537 3593 Industrial trucks and tractors; Fluid power cylinders, hydraulic or pneumatic
HQ: Cargotec Holding, Inc.
  415 E Dundee St
  Ottawa KS 66067

(G-13799)
WYATT INDUSTRIES LLC
1790 Miller Pkwy (44241-4633)
PHONE.................................330 954-1790
Beverly Clemens, *CEO*
EMP: 6 **EST:** 2011
SQ FT: 10,000
SALES (est): 331.48K **Privately Held**
SIC: 3089 Plastics processing

Strongsville
Cuyahoga County

(G-13800)
ACROMET METAL FABRICATORS
21693 Drake Rd (44149-6614)
PHONE.................................440 237-8745
EMP: 13 **EST:** 2017
SALES (est): 1.25MM **Privately Held**
Web: www.acromet.com
SIC: 3499 Fabricated metal products, nec

(G-13801)
ACTION INDUSTRIES LTD (PA)
Also Called: Action
13325 Darice Pkwy (44149-3819)
PHONE.................................216 252-7800
John E Marron, *Pr*
Guenter Plamper, *Sec*
▲ **EMP:** 7 **EST:** 1980
SQ FT: 25,000
SALES (est): 3.94MM
SALES (corp-wide): 3.94MM **Privately Held**
Web: www.action-ind.com
SIC: 3699 2431 Door opening and closing devices, electrical; Weather strip, wood

(G-13802)
ADVANCED TECH UTILIZATION CO
Also Called: Advanced Technology
12005 Prospect Rd Unit 1 (44149-2935)
P.O. Box 360461 (44136-0008)
PHONE.................................440 238-3770
Terry Yamrick, *Owner*
EMP: 10 **EST:** 1967
SQ FT: 2,500
SALES (est): 696.4K **Privately Held**
Web: www.newandusedmachines.com
SIC: 3542 5084 Rebuilt machine tools, metal forming types; Metalworking machinery

(G-13803)
AKZO NOBEL PAINTS LLC
Also Called: Glidden Professional Paint Ctr
8381 Pearl Rd (44136-1637)
P.O. Box 3200 (15230-3200)
PHONE.................................440 297-8000
◆ **EMP:** 5000
SIC: 2851 2891 Paints and paint additives; Adhesives

(G-13804)
ALBION INDUSTRIES INC
20246 Progress Dr (44149-3296)
PHONE.................................440 238-1955
Ralph Holstein, *Pr*
Caroline Holstein, *
Roman T Keenen, *
◆ **EMP:** 30 **EST:** 1971
SQ FT: 21,000
SALES (est): 2.31MM **Privately Held**
Web: www.albioncasters.com
SIC: 2514 Frames for box springs or bedsprings: metal

(G-13805)
ALPHAGRAPHICS 507 INC
Also Called: AlphaGraphics
14765 Pearl Rd (44136-5003)
PHONE.................................440 878-9700
Rob Kammer, *Pr*
EMP: 6 **EST:** 1999
SQ FT: 3,000
SALES (est): 786.12K **Privately Held**
Web: www.alphagraphics.com
SIC: 2752 Commercial printing, lithographic

(G-13806)
AMERICAN WATER SERVICES INC
17449 W Sprague Rd (44136-1666)
PHONE.................................440 243-9840
Rick Meloy, *Proj Mgr*
EMP: 7
SALES (est): 558.6K **Privately Held**
SIC: 3823 4941 Water quality monitoring and control systems; Water supply

(G-13807)
AMTANK ARMOR
22555 Ascoa Ct (44149-4700)
PHONE.................................440 268-7735
John Mayles, *Pr*
EMP: 6 **EST:** 2018
SALES (est): 142.9K **Privately Held**
Web: www.atfco.com
SIC: 3441 Fabricated structural metal

(G-13808)
APPH WICHITA INC
Also Called: Apph
15900 Foltz Pkwy (44149-5531)
PHONE.................................316 943-5752
Mike Meshey, *Pr*
Jon Sharrock, *
▲ **EMP:** 50 **EST:** 1959
SALES (est): 3.72MM
SALES (corp-wide): 400.71MM **Privately Held**
SIC: 7699 3594 3728 Aircraft and heavy equipment repair services; Fluid power pumps and motors; Aircraft parts and equipment, nec
PA: Heroux-Devtek Inc
  1111 Rue Saint-Charles O Bureau 600
  Longueuil QC J4K 5
  450 679-5450

(G-13809)
ARMATURE COIL EQUIPMENT INC
Also Called: Ace Equipment Company
22269 Horseshoe Ln (44149-9256)
PHONE.................................216 267-6366
Robert F Heran, *Pr*
Jean Heran, *Sec*
EMP: 12 **EST:** 1919
SALES (est): 2.18MM **Privately Held**
Web: www.armaturecoil.com
SIC: 3549 3567 Coil winding machines for springs; Industrial furnaces and ovens

(G-13810)
ATLANTIC TOOL & DIE COMPANY (PA)
19963 Progress Dr (44149-3211)
PHONE.................................440 238-6931
Frank Mehwald, *Pr*
Mike Mehwald, *
◆ **EMP:** 240 **EST:** 1947
SQ FT: 110,000
SALES (est): 96.49MM
SALES (corp-wide): 96.49MM **Privately Held**
Web: www.atlantictool.com
SIC: 3469 3544 Stamping metal for the trade; Special dies, tools, jigs, and fixtures

(G-13811)
AUTO TECHNOLOGY COMPANY
20026 Progress Dr (44149-3214)
PHONE.................................440 572-7800
Kevin A Smith, *Pr*
Walter Senney, *VP*
EMP: 15 **EST:** 1999
SQ FT: 50,000
SALES (est): 4.45MM **Privately Held**
Web: www.autotechnology.com
SIC: 3826 Environmental testing equipment

(G-13812)
AUTOMATED MFG SOLUTIONS INC
Also Called: AMS
19706 Progress Dr (44149-3208)
PHONE.................................440 878-3711
David Minney, *Pr*
Thomas P Setele, *Pr*
Mark Ogorzaly, *OF OPTN*
EMP: 18 **EST:** 2002
SQ FT: 8,000
SALES (est): 5.12MM **Privately Held**
Web: www.automfgsolutions.com
SIC: 3599 Machine shop, jobbing and repair

(G-13813)
AUTOWAX INC
15015 Foltz Pkwy (44149-4728)
PHONE.................................440 334-4417
Alina Baron, *CEO*
James Baron, *VP*
EMP: 6 **EST:** 2012
SALES (est): 992.72K **Privately Held**
Web: www.autowaxinc.com
SIC: 3711 Motor vehicles and car bodies

(G-13814)
AVERY DENNISON CORPORATION
17700 Foltz Pkwy (44149-5536)
PHONE.................................440 878-7000
Gary Murphy, *Mgr*
EMP: 400
SALES (corp-wide): 8.36B **Publicly Held**
Web: www.averydennison.com
SIC: 2672 Adhesive papers, labels, or tapes: from purchased material
PA: Avery Dennison Corporation
  8080 Norton Pkwy
  Mentor OH 44060
  440 534-6000

(G-13815)
BEARINGS MANUFACTURING COMPANY (PA)
Also Called: BMC
15157 Foltz Pkwy (44149-4730)
PHONE.................................440 846-5517
Steve Sivo, *Pr*
Jeff Walls, *
EMP: 14 **EST:** 2001
SALES (est): 9.55MM
SALES (corp-wide): 9.55MM **Privately Held**
Web: www.bmcbearing.com
SIC: 3562 5085 Ball bearings and parts; Bearings, bushings, wheels, and gears

(G-13816)
BLUE CRESCENT ENTERPRISES INC
Also Called: AlphaGraphics Strongsville
17295 Foltz Pkwy Ste B (44149-5568)
P.O. Box 360379 (44136-0036)
PHONE.................................440 878-9700
Saleh Afif Alafifi, *Pr*

EMP: 7 EST: 2016
SQ FT: 3,800
SALES (est): 550K **Privately Held**
Web: www.alphagraphics.com
SIC: 2752 Commercial printing, lithographic

(G-13817)
BREW KETTLE INC
Also Called: Ringneck Brewing Company
8377 Pearl Rd (44136-1637)
PHONE................................440 234-8788
Chris J Mckim, *Pr*
EMP: 11 EST: 1995
SQ FT: 3,500
SALES (est): 1.14MM **Privately Held**
Web: www.thebrewkettle.com
SIC: 2082 5149 Beer (alcoholic beverage); Groceries and related products, nec

(G-13818)
CARDINAL MACHINE COMPANY
14459 Foltz Pkwy (44149-4797)
PHONE................................440 238-7050
Richard Z Kaszei, *CEO*
Greg Kaszei, *Pr*
EMP: 19 EST: 1974
SQ FT: 10,000
SALES (est): 488.91K **Privately Held**
Web: www.cardinalmachine.net
SIC: 3599 Machine shop, jobbing and repair

(G-13819)
CCL LABEL INC
Also Called: CCL Design
17890 Foltz Pkwy (44149)
PHONE................................440 878-7000
John Walsh, *Brnch Mgr*
EMP: 99
SALES (corp-wide): 4.75B **Privately Held**
Web: www.cclind.com
SIC: 2672 3081 3497 2678 Adhesive papers, labels, or tapes: from purchased material; Unsupported plastics film and sheet; Metal foil and leaf; Notebooks: made from purchased paper
HQ: Ccl Label, Inc.
    161 Worcester Rd Ste 403
    Framingham MA 01701
    508 872-4511

(G-13820)
CCL LABEL INC
Also Called: CCL Design Electronics
17700 Foltz Pkwy (44149-5536) ●
PHONE................................440 878-7277
EMP: 350
SALES (corp-wide): 4.75B **Privately Held**
Web: www.cclind.com
SIC: 2759 Labels and seals: printing, nsk
HQ: Ccl Label, Inc.
    161 Worcester Rd Ste 403
    Framingham MA 01701
    508 872-4511

(G-13821)
CLARK-RELIANCE LLC (PA)
Also Called: Jerguson
16633 Foltz Pkwy (44149-5513)
PHONE................................440 572-1500
Matthew P Figgie Junior, *Ch Bd*
Rick Solon, *Pr*
Mike Pressnell, *VP*
◆ EMP: 155 EST: 1884
SQ FT: 93,000
SALES (est): 54.41MM
SALES (corp-wide): 54.41MM **Privately Held**
Web: www.clarkreliance.com
SIC: 3823 3491 Industrial process control instruments; Process control regulator valves

(G-13822)
CLEVELAND JSM INC
Also Called: Tenk Machine
11792 Alameda Dr (44149-3011)
PHONE................................440 876-3050
Ray Knapp, *Prin*
EMP: 25 EST: 1942
SALES (est): 1.67MM **Privately Held**
SIC: 3599 7699 7692 Custom machinery; Industrial machinery and equipment repair; Welding repair

(G-13823)
COLOR PROCESS INC
13900 Prospect Rd (44149-3834)
PHONE................................440 268-7100
Mark Ingham, *Pr*
Jim Greiner, *
EMP: 25 EST: 1959
SQ FT: 65,000
SALES (est): 5.54MM **Privately Held**
Web: www.colorprocess.info
SIC: 2752 Offset printing

(G-13824)
COMPOSITE PANEL TECH CO
21944 Drake Rd (44149-6609)
PHONE................................704 310-5838
Kim Lanter, *Prin*
EMP: 9 EST: 2014
SALES (est): 224.82K
SALES (corp-wide): 273.45MM **Publicly Held**
SIC: 3713 Truck bodies and parts
PA: The Eastern Co
    3 Enterprise Dr Ste 408
    Shelton CT 06484
    203 729-2255

(G-13825)
CUSTOM IMPRINT
19573 Progress Dr (44149-3203)
PHONE................................440 238-4488
Ed Rebish, *Owner*
EMP: 10 EST: 1999
SALES (est): 418.65K **Privately Held**
Web: www.customimprint.com
SIC: 2752 Commercial printing, lithographic

(G-13826)
CYLINDERS AND VALVES INC
20811 Westwood Dr (44149-3999)
P.O. Box 360555 (44136-0010)
PHONE................................440 238-7343
James P Gardner Iii, *Pr*
Katherine Frederick, *Mgr*
EMP: 8 EST: 1958
SQ FT: 7,500
SALES (est): 1.1MM **Privately Held**
Web: www.cylval.com
SIC: 3594 3593 3494 Motors: hydraulic, fluid power, or air; Fluid power cylinders and actuators; Valves and pipe fittings, nec

(G-13827)
DALTON US INC
15830 Foltz Pkwy (44149-4745)
PHONE................................440 878-7661
EMP: 7 EST: 2020
SALES (est): 388.34K **Privately Held**
SIC: 3089 Injection molding of plastics

(G-13828)
DONPRINT INC
Also Called: Worldmark
17700 Foltz Pkwy (44149-5536)
PHONE................................847 573-7777
▲ EMP: 36
SIC: 2759 Labels and seals: printing, nsk

(G-13829)
DRIVE COMPONENTS LLC
19668 Progress Dr (44149-3206)
PHONE................................440 234-6200
EMP: 7 EST: 2019
SALES (est): 634.1K **Privately Held**
Web: www.drivecomponentsllc.com
SIC: 3568 Power transmission equipment, nec

(G-13830)
DUPLI-SYSTEMS INC
Also Called: Ohio Cut Sheet
8260 Dow Cir (44136-1762)
PHONE................................440 234-9415
Bud Eldridge, *CEO*
Randy Eldridge, *
Todd Eldridge, *
Dave Griffith, *
EMP: 125 EST: 1955
SALES (est): 9.4MM **Privately Held**
Web: www.dupli-systems.com
SIC: 2759 2754 2782 2761 Commercial printing, nec; Forms, business: gravure printing; Blankbooks and looseleaf binders; Manifold business forms

(G-13831)
DUROX COMPANY
12312 Alameda Dr (44149-3023)
PHONE................................440 238-5350
Richard A Mathes, *Sec*
▲ EMP: 70 EST: 1953
SQ FT: 50,000
SALES (est): 20.56MM **Publicly Held**
Web: www.wabteccorp.com
SIC: 3053 Gaskets, all materials
HQ: Wabtec Components Llc
    30 Isabella St
    Pittsburgh PA 15212
    412 825-1000

(G-13832)
EFFICIENT MACHINE PDTS CORP
12133 Alameda Dr (44149-3018)
PHONE................................440 268-0205
Ted Imbrogno, *Pr*
EMP: 40 EST: 1962
SQ FT: 31,000
SALES (est): 6.07MM **Privately Held**
Web: www.efficientm.com
SIC: 3599 Machine shop, jobbing and repair

(G-13833)
ERNST FLOW INDUSTRIES LLC
16633 Foltz Pkwy (44149-5513)
PHONE................................732 938-5641
Roger Ernst, *Pr*
Eugene Ernst Junior, *Treas*
John Ernst, *VP*
EMP: 14 EST: 1962
SQ FT: 9,000
SALES (est): 2.43MM
SALES (corp-wide): 54.41MM **Privately Held**
Web: www.ernstflow.com
SIC: 3823 3824 Flow instruments, industrial process type; Water meters
PA: Clark-Reliance Llc
    16633 Foltz Pkwy
    Strongsville OH 44149
    440 572-1500

(G-13834)
FOUNDATION SOFTWARE LLC (PA)
17999 Foltz Pkwy (44149-5565)
PHONE................................330 220-8383
Fred Ode, *CEO*
Kathleen Ode, *Sec*
Paul Noonan, *CGO*
EMP: 479 EST: 1985
SQ FT: 16,000
SALES (est): 147.47MM
SALES (corp-wide): 147.47MM **Privately Held**
Web: www.foundationsoft.com
SIC: 7372 7371 Prepackaged software; Software programming applications

(G-13835)
GARETH STEVENS PUBLISHING LP
Also Called: Gareth Stevens Publishing
23221 Morgan Ct (44149-5100)
PHONE................................800 542-2595
Roger Rosen, *Pt*
Gary Spears, *Pt*
EMP: 12 EST: 2009
SALES (est): 333.76K **Privately Held**
SIC: 2731 Books, publishing only

(G-13836)
GREAT LAKES BREWING CO
13675 Darice Pkwy (44149-3823)
PHONE................................216 771-4404
EMP: 24
SALES (corp-wide): 37.83MM **Privately Held**
SIC: 2082 Malt beverages
PA: The Great Lakes Brewing Co
    2516 Market Ave
    Cleveland OH 44113
    216 771-4404

(G-13837)
GSH INDUSTRIES INC
15242 Foltz Pkwy (44149-4733)
PHONE................................440 238-3009
EMP: 30 EST: 1986
SALES (est): 6MM **Privately Held**
Web: www.gshindustries.com
SIC: 2821 Plastics materials and resins

(G-13838)
GUARANTEE SPECIALTIES INC
Also Called: Garvin Industries Div
21693 Drake Rd (44149-6614)
P.O. Box 360247 (44136-0005)
PHONE................................216 451-9744
Armando E Pages, *Pr*
Carol Braunschweig, *
▲ EMP: 65 EST: 1916
SQ FT: 75,000
SALES (est): 1.81MM **Privately Held**
SIC: 3463 3465 3469 Plumbing fixture forgings, nonferrous; Automotive stampings ; Stamping metal for the trade

(G-13839)
HAYBNER SHEET METAL INC
18819 Hearthstone Dr (44136-8449)
PHONE................................440 623-0194
Amy Huebner, *Prin*
EMP: 7 EST: 2013
SALES (est): 183.57K **Privately Held**
SIC: 3444 Sheet metalwork

(G-13840)
HDI LANDING GEAR USA INC
Also Called: Heroux Devtek Landing Gear Div
663 Montgomery Ave (44149-5531)
PHONE................................937 325-1586
EMP: 50
SQ FT: 115,000
SALES (corp-wide): 400.71MM **Privately Held**
Web: www.herouxdevtek.com
SIC: 3728 Alighting (landing gear) assemblies, aircraft
HQ: Hdi Landing Gear Usa Inc.
    663 Montgomery Ave
    Springfield OH 45506

Strongsville - Cuyahoga County (G-13841) GEOGRAPHIC SECTION

(G-13841)
HINCHCLIFF LUMBER COMPANY (PA)
Also Called: Hinchcliff Products
13550 Falling Water Rd Ste 105 (44136-4360)
P.O. Box 386 (26287-0386)
PHONE..................440 238-5200
Jay D Phillips, *Pr*
EMP: 76 **EST:** 1923
SQ FT: 100,000
SALES (est): 5.62MM **Privately Held**
Web: www.hinchcliffproducts.com
SIC: 2448 2449 Pallets, wood; Wood containers, nec

(G-13842)
HUGHES CORPORATION (PA)
Also Called: Weschler Instruments
16900 Foltz Pkwy (44149)
PHONE..................440 238-2550
Paul Layne, *CEO*
David E Hughes, *
Douglas Hughes, *
Michael F Dorman, *
Esther Carpenter, *
EMP: 30 **EST:** 1941
SQ FT: 11,500
SALES (est): 26.85MM
SALES (corp-wide): 26.85MM **Privately Held**
Web: www.weschler.com
SIC: 5063 3825 Electrical apparatus and equipment; Instruments to measure electricity

(G-13843)
HUMPHREY POPCORN COMPANY (PA)
11606 Pearl Rd (44136-3320)
P.O. Box 23003 (44123-0003)
PHONE..................216 662-6629
Micheal Prokop, *Pr*
Dudley Humphrey, *
Elizabeth Humphrey, *VP*
EMP: 10 **EST:** 1897
SQ FT: 11,000
SALES (est): 872.4K
SALES (corp-wide): 872.4K **Privately Held**
Web: www.humphreycompany.com
SIC: 0191 2064 5145 General farms, primarily crop; Popcorn balls or other treated popcorn products; Popcorn and supplies

(G-13844)
IMPERIAL DIE & MFG CO
22930 Royalton Rd (44149-3842)
PHONE..................440 268-9080
Ronald Lapossy, *Pr*
Kenneth Lapossy, *Treas*
EMP: 17 **EST:** 1959
SQ FT: 20,000
SALES (est): 2.15MM **Privately Held**
Web: www.imperialdiemfg.com
SIC: 3469 3544 Stamping metal for the trade ; Special dies and tools

(G-13845)
INFINIUM WALL SYSTEMS INC
21000 Infinium Way (44149-5000)
PHONE..................440 572-5000
Shawn Gaffney, *Pr*
Caryn Gaffney, *Stockholder*
▼ **EMP:** 30 **EST:** 2003
SALES (est): 8.81MM **Privately Held**
Web: www.infiniumwalls.com
SIC: 2522 Office furniture, except wood

(G-13846)
INSTRUMENTORS INC
22077 Drake Rd (44149-6606)
PHONE..................440 238-3430
Robert A Heinrich, *Pr*
James R Heinrich, *VP*
Elvera Heinrich, *Sec*
EMP: 6 **EST:** 1973
SQ FT: 10,000
SALES (est): 745.12K **Privately Held**
Web: www.instrumentorsinc.com
SIC: 3829 7699 5084 Measuring and controlling devices, nec; Scientific equipment repair service; Instruments and control equipment

(G-13847)
J & J BECHKE INC (PA)
Also Called: C Q Printing
12931 Pearl Rd (44136-3425)
PHONE..................440 238-1441
John Bechke, *Pr*
Joy Bechke, *VP*
EMP: 6 **EST:** 1978
SQ FT: 2,200
SALES (est): 928.29K
SALES (corp-wide): 928.29K **Privately Held**
Web: www.cqprinting.com
SIC: 2752 Offset printing

(G-13848)
KALINICH FENCE COMPANY INC
12223 Prospect Rd (44149-2994)
PHONE..................440 238-6127
Mike Kalinich Senior, *Pr*
Mike Kalinich Junior, *VP*
Erma Kalinich, *Sec*
EMP: 18 **EST:** 1918
SQ FT: 33,000
SALES (est): 2.42MM **Privately Held**
Web: www.kalinichfenceco.com
SIC: 2499 Fencing, wood

(G-13849)
LANDOLL PUBLISHING SJS LLC
Also Called: Landoll Publishing
14800 Foltz Pkwy (44149-4725)
PHONE..................330 353-2688
John D Helline, *CFO*
EMP: 7 **EST:** 2014
SALES (est): 320.53K **Privately Held**
Web: www.landollpub.com
SIC: 2741 Miscellaneous publishing

(G-13850)
LEES GRINDING INC
15620 Foltz Pkwy (44149-4741)
P.O. Box 360169 (44136-0003)
PHONE..................440 572-4610
Nick D Papanikolaou, *Pr*
EMP: 30 **EST:** 1961
SQ FT: 20,000
SALES (est): 4.88MM **Privately Held**
Web: www.leesgrinding.com
SIC: 3599 Machine shop, jobbing and repair

(G-13851)
LITEHOUSE PRODUCTS LLC (PA)
Also Called: Litehouse Pools & Spas
10883 Pearl Rd Ste 301 (44136-3359)
PHONE..................440 638-2350
▲ **EMP:** 50 **EST:** 2004
SALES (est): 38.85MM
SALES (corp-wide): 38.85MM **Privately Held**
Web: www.litehouse.com
SIC: 5091 3949 5999 5712 Swimming pools, equipment and supplies; Water sports equipment; Swimming pools, above ground ; Outdoor and garden furniture

(G-13852)
LUMITEX INC (PA)
Also Called: Lumitex
8443 Dow Cir (44136-1796)
PHONE..................440 243-8401
Peter W Broer, *Pr*
Thomas E Walden, *
Richard D Gridley, *
Maynard H Murch V, *Dir*
▲ **EMP:** 90 **EST:** 1985
SQ FT: 19,000
SALES (est): 24.74MM
SALES (corp-wide): 24.74MM **Privately Held**
Web: www.lumitex.com
SIC: 3646 3641 3648 3845 Commercial lighting fixtures; Electric lamps; Lighting equipment, nec; Electromedical equipment

(G-13853)
MECHANICAL RUBBER OHIO LLC
12312 Alameda Dr (44149-3023)
PHONE..................845 986-2271
Cedric Glasper, *Pr*
EMP: 22 **EST:** 2020
SALES (est): 3.17MM **Privately Held**
Web: www.mechanicalrubber.com
SIC: 3053 Gaskets, all materials
PA: Mechanical Rubber Products Company, Inc.
77 Forester Ave Ste 1
Warwick NY 10990

(G-13854)
MOMENTIVE PERF MTRLS QUARTZ
22557 Lunn Rd (44149-4871)
PHONE..................408 436-6221
▲ **EMP:** 11 **EST:** 2008
SALES (est): 3.12MM **Privately Held**
Web: www.momentivetech.com
SIC: 2869 Industrial organic chemicals, nec

(G-13855)
MOMENTIVE PRFMCE MTLS QRTZ INC (HQ)
Also Called: Momentive Technologies
22557 Lunn Rd (44149-4871)
PHONE..................440 878-5700
Philip Rose, *Pr*
Ryan Croskey, *
◆ **EMP:** 51 **EST:** 1996
SALES (est): 365MM
SALES (corp-wide): 365MM **Privately Held**
Web: www.momentivetech.com
SIC: 2869 3479 3446 3297 Silicones; Coating of metals with silicon; Architectural metalwork; Nonclay refractories
PA: Momq Holding Company
22557 Lunn Rd
Strongsville OH 44149
440 878-5700

(G-13856)
MOMQ HOLDING COMPANY (PA)
22557 Lunn Rd (44149-4871)
PHONE..................440 878-5700
Philip Rose, *Pr*
Jp Park, *VP*
Ryan Croskey, *CFO*
Daniel Fashimpaur, *Treas*
Dale Brosky, *Tax Director*
EMP: 950 **EST:** 2019
SALES (est): 365MM
SALES (corp-wide): 365MM **Privately Held**
SIC: 3299 Tubing for electrical purposes, quartz

(G-13857)
MONARCH ENGRAVING INC
8293 Dow Cir (44136-1761)
PHONE..................440 638-1500
William Pfeil Junior, *Pr*
Brian Pfeil, *VP*
David Pfeil, *Sec*
EMP: 15 **EST:** 1953
SQ FT: 20,000
SALES (est): 440.34K **Privately Held**
SIC: 3083 2899 Laminated plastics plate and sheet; Chemical preparations, nec

(G-13858)
MUELLER ART COVER & BINDING CO
12005 Alameda Dr (44149-3016)
PHONE..................440 238-3303
TOLL FREE: 888
Edmond Mueller, *Pr*
EMP: 45 **EST:** 1932
SQ FT: 38,000
SALES (est): 2.7MM **Privately Held**
Web: www.muellerartcover.com
SIC: 2782 7336 Looseleaf binders and devices; Graphic arts and related design

(G-13859)
NEWBERRY WOOD ENTERPRISES INC (PA)
12223 Prospect Rd (44149-2939)
PHONE..................440 238-6127
Mike Kalinich, *Pr*
EMP: 9 **EST:** 1983
SQ FT: 25,000
SALES (est): 1.89MM
SALES (corp-wide): 1.89MM **Privately Held**
SIC: 2421 Custom sawmill

(G-13860)
NUTRO CORPORATION
Also Called: Nutro Machinery
11515 Alameda Dr (44149-3006)
PHONE..................440 572-3800
Mark Rooney, *Pr*
George Wharton, *
Lisa Stanton, *
EMP: 55 **EST:** 1951
SQ FT: 65,000
SALES (est): 7.1MM **Privately Held**
Web: www.nutroinc.com
SIC: 3569 3559 Liquid automation machinery and equipment; Paint making machinery

(G-13861)
NUTRO INC
11515 Alameda Dr (44149-3006)
PHONE..................440 572-3800
Mark Rooney, *Prin*
Christian Nuesser, *
EMP: 31 **EST:** 2008
SALES (est): 7.26MM
SALES (corp-wide): 62.94MM **Privately Held**
Web: www.nutro.com
SIC: 3559 3251 Paint making machinery; Ceramic glazed brick, clay
PA: Venjakob Maschinenbau Gmbh & Co. Kg
Augsburger Str. 2-6
Rheda-Wiedenbruck NW 33378
524296030

(G-13862)
OHIO CLLBRTIVE LRNG SLTONS INC (PA)
Also Called: Smart Solutions
17171 Golden Star Dr (44136)

GEOGRAPHIC SECTION

Strongsville - Cuyahoga County (G-13885)

PHONE..................................216 595-5289
Anand Julka, *Pr*
▲ **EMP:** 50 **EST:** 1983
SALES (est): 9.5MM
SALES (corp-wide): 9.5MM **Privately Held**
SIC: 7372 8741 Business oriented computer software; Business management

(G-13863)
OUTOTEC OYJ
Also Called: Outotec North America
11288 Alameda Dr (44149-3037)
PHONE..................................440 783-3336
Tim Robinson, *Brnch Mgr*
EMP: 15
Web: www.metso.com
SIC: 3441 Fabricated structural metal
PA: Metso Oyj
Rauhalanpuisto 9
Espoo 02230

(G-13864)
PA MA INC
Also Called: Pama Tool & Die
11288 Alameda Dr (44149-3037)
P.O. Box 361459 (44136-0025)
PHONE..................................440 846-3799
Ron Pansil, *Pr*
Donna Pansil, *VP*
Danuta Pansil, *Treas*
EMP: 7 **EST:** 1985
SQ FT: 8,000
SALES (est): 723.85K **Privately Held**
SIC: 3544 Special dies and tools

(G-13865)
PIPE LINE DEVELOPMENT COMPANY
Also Called: Plidco Ppline Repr Ppline Mint
11792 Alameda Dr (44149-3011)
PHONE..................................440 871-5700
Kimberly Smith, *Pr*
Dave Pincura, *
◆ **EMP:** 96 **EST:** 1949
SQ FT: 70,000
SALES (est): 20.69MM **Privately Held**
Web: www.plidco.com
SIC: 3498 Pipe fittings, fabricated from purchased pipe

(G-13866)
PPG ARCHITECTURAL COATINGS LLC
Also Called: Synteko
15485 W Sprague Rd (44136-1772)
PHONE..................................440 297-8000
▼ **EMP:** 92
SIC: 2851 2899 2891 2861 Paints and paint additives; Chemical preparations, nec; Adhesives and sealants; Gum and wood chemicals

(G-13867)
PPG INDUSTRIES INC
Also Called: Powder Coatings
19699 Progress Dr (44149-3298)
PHONE..................................440 572-2800
William Shaw, *Brnch Mgr*
EMP: 100
SALES (corp-wide): 17.65B **Publicly Held**
Web: www.ppg.com
SIC: 2851 Paints and allied products
PA: Ppg Industries, Inc.
1 Ppg Pl
Pittsburgh PA 15272
412 434-3131

(G-13868)
PPG INDUSTRIES OHIO INC
Also Called: PPG AF US
9699 Progress Dr (44149)
PHONE..................................440 572-6777
EMP: 136
SALES (corp-wide): 17.65B **Publicly Held**
Web: www.ppg.com
SIC: 2851 Paints and paint additives
HQ: Ppg Industries Ohio, Inc.
3800 W 143rd St
Cleveland OH 44111
216 671-0050

(G-13869)
PRECISION PRODUCTION LLC
Also Called: Precision Production
8250 Dow Cir (44136-1762)
PHONE..................................216 252-0372
Craig Cook, *Pr*
Mathew A Carson, *
Bryon N Shafer, *
▲ **EMP:** 40 **EST:** 1978
SQ FT: 38,000
SALES (est): 6.41MM **Privately Held**
Web: www.precisionproduction.com
SIC: 3599 Machine shop, jobbing and repair

(G-13870)
R M TOOL & DIE INC
19768 Progress Dr (44149-3208)
PHONE..................................440 238-6459
Mike Regian, *CEO*
EMP: 12 **EST:** 1991
SQ FT: 25,000
SALES (est): 1.42MM **Privately Held**
Web: www.rmtoolinc.com
SIC: 3544 Special dies and tools

(G-13871)
RAFTER EQUIPMENT CORPORATION
12430 Alameda Dr (44149-3025)
PHONE..................................440 572-3700
Walter Krenz, *Pr*
Paul Rohde, *
▲ **EMP:** 30 **EST:** 1917
SQ FT: 22,500
SALES (est): 5.86MM **Privately Held**
Web: www.rafterequipment.com
SIC: 3542 3549 3547 3541 Machine tools, metal forming type; Metalworking machinery, nec; Rolling mill machinery; Machine tools, metal cutting type

(G-13872)
ROBERT E MCGRATH INC
Also Called: Olympia Candies
11606 Pearl Rd (44136-3320)
PHONE..................................440 572-7747
EMP: 19 **EST:** 1911
SQ FT: 15,000
SALES (est): 3.78MM **Privately Held**
Web: www.olympiasweettreats.com
SIC: 5145 5441 2096 2066 Candy; Candy; Potato chips and similar snacks; Chocolate and cocoa products

(G-13873)
ROMAN TOOL & DIE
P.O. Box 360258 (44136-0005)
PHONE..................................440 503-5271
Roman Grabowski, *Prin*
EMP: 7 **EST:** 2007
SALES (est): 71.13K **Privately Held**
SIC: 3544 Special dies and tools

(G-13874)
SCEPTER PUBLISHERS
21510 Drake Rd (44149-6617)
P.O. Box 360694 (44136-0012)
PHONE..................................212 354-0670
Robert Singerline, *Pr*
John Powers, *Sls Mgr*
EMP: 7 **EST:** 1952
SQ FT: 700
SALES (est): 1.46MM **Privately Held**
Web: www.scepterpublishers.org
SIC: 2731 Books, publishing only

(G-13875)
SCHWEBEL BAKING COMPANY
22626 Royalton Rd (44149-3838)
PHONE..................................440 846-1921
Steve Leach, *Mgr*
EMP: 7
SALES (corp-wide): 403.34MM **Privately Held**
Web: www.myschwebels.com
SIC: 2051 Bakery: wholesale or wholesale/retail combined
PA: Schwebel Baking Company
965 E Midlothian Blvd
Youngstown OH 44502
330 783-2860

(G-13876)
SENTRO TECH CORPORATION
21294 Drake Rd (44149-6623)
PHONE..................................440 260-0364
Neil Zhu, *Mgr*
▲ **EMP:** 7 **EST:** 1997
SALES (est): 1.13MM **Privately Held**
Web: www.sentrotech.com
SIC: 3567 Industrial furnaces and ovens

(G-13877)
SEVILLE SAND & GRAVEL INC
12663 Bristol Ln (44149-9240)
P.O. Box 360 (44254-0360)
PHONE..................................330 948-0168
FAX: 330 948-4186
EMP: 22 **EST:** 1958
SQ FT: 600
SALES (est): 2MM **Privately Held**
Web: www.sevsg.com
SIC: 1442 Construction sand mining

(G-13878)
SGL CARBON TECHNIC LLC
21945 Drake Rd (44149-6608)
PHONE..................................440 572-3600
Ken Manning, *Pr*
▼ **EMP:** 36 **EST:** 2004
SQ FT: 46,004
SALES (est): 11.07MM
SALES (corp-wide): 1.18B **Privately Held**
Web: www.sglcarbon.com
SIC: 3443 Fabricated plate work (boiler shop)
PA: Sgl Carbon Se
Sohnleinstr. 8
Wiesbaden HE 65201
61160290

(G-13879)
SHEIBAN JEWELRY INC
16938 Pearl Rd (44136-6053)
PHONE..................................440 238-0616
Tony Sheiban, *Pr*
EMP: 10 **EST:** 1976
SQ FT: 3,300
SALES (est): 1.9MM **Privately Held**
Web: www.sheibanjewelers.com
SIC: 5094 5944 7631 3911 Jewelry; Jewelry, precious stones and precious metals; Watch, clock, and jewelry repair; Jewelry, precious metal

(G-13880)
SHERWIN-WILLIAMS COMPANY
Also Called: Sherwin-Williams
11410 Alameda Dr (44149-3005)
PHONE..................................440 846-4328
Blair Lacour, *Pr*
EMP: 17
SQ FT: 24,150
SALES (corp-wide): 22.15B **Publicly Held**
Web: www.sherwin-williams.com
SIC: 5231 2851 Paint; Paints and allied products
PA: The Sherwin-Williams Company
101 W Prospect Ave
Cleveland OH 44115
216 566-2000

(G-13881)
SLY INC (PA)
8300 Dow Cir Ste 600 (44136-6607)
PHONE..................................800 334-2957
E D Davis, *Prin*
Sidney C Vessy, *Prin*
W C Bruce, *Prin*
W C Sly, *Prin*
W W Sly, *Prin*
EMP: 50 **EST:** 1874
SQ FT: 36,000
SALES (est): 21.62MM
SALES (corp-wide): 21.62MM **Privately Held**
Web: www.slyinc.com
SIC: 3564 Dust or fume collecting equipment, industrial

(G-13882)
SOLUTION INDUSTRIES LLC
21555 Drake Rd (44149-6616)
PHONE..................................440 816-9500
John Radel, *Pr*
▲ **EMP:** 18 **EST:** 2014
SALES (est): 492.26K **Privately Held**
Web: www.solutionind.com
SIC: 3965 Fasteners, buttons, needles, and pins

(G-13883)
SPARTRONICS STRONGSVILLE INC
22740 Lunn Rd (44149-4899)
PHONE..................................440 878-4630
EMP: 59 **EST:** 2006
SALES (est): 10.23MM
SALES (corp-wide): 810.86MM **Privately Held**
Web: www.spartronics.com
SIC: 3841 Surgical and medical instruments
HQ: Spartronics Watertown, Llc
2920 Kelly Ave
Watertown SD 57201

(G-13884)
SPIEGELBERG MANUFACTURING INC (HQ)
Also Called: Stud Welding Associates
12200 Alameda Dr (44149-3050)
PHONE..................................440 324-3042
▲ **EMP:** 51 **EST:** 1984
SALES (est): 17.64MM
SALES (corp-wide): 15.62B **Publicly Held**
Web: www.proweldinternational.com
SIC: 3548 Welding apparatus
PA: Stanley Black & Decker, Inc.
1000 Stanley Dr
New Britain CT 06053
860 225-5111

(G-13885)
STEFRA INC
Also Called: E & E Parts Machining
18021 Cliffside Dr (44136-4256)
PHONE..................................440 846-8240
Frank Ungerer, *Pr*
Steve Pucha, *VP*
Colleen Ungerer, *CEO*
EMP: 7 **EST:** 1966
SQ FT: 2,900
SALES (est): 445.2K **Privately Held**
SIC: 3599 Machine shop, jobbing and repair

(PA)=Parent Co (HQ)=Headquarters
✪ = New Business established in last 2 years

Strongsville - Cuyahoga County (G-13886)

(G-13886)
STELFAST LLC (HQ)
22979 Stelfast Pkwy (44149-5561)
PHONE..................440 879-0077
Bill Nikitis, *CEO*
Simmi Sakhuja, *
◆ **EMP:** 32 **EST:** 1972
SQ FT: 85,000
SALES (est): 30.38MM
SALES (corp-wide): 105.65MM **Privately Held**
Web: www.stelfast.com
SIC: 3452 3965 Bolts, metal; Fasteners
PA: Lindstrom, Llc
    2950 100th Ct Ne
    Blaine MN 55449
    763 780-4200

(G-13887)
STUD WELDING ASSOCIATES INC
Also Called: Stud Welding
12200 Alameda Dr (44149-3021)
PHONE..................440 783-3160
▼ **EMP:** 70
SIC: 5085 3496 1799 Fasteners, industrial: nuts, bolts, screws, etc.; Clips and fasteners, made from purchased wire; Welding on site

(G-13888)
SWEETIES OLYMPIA TREATS LLC ○
11606 Pearl Rd (44136-3320)
PHONE..................440 572-7747
Robert Mcgrath, *Pr*
EMP: 18 **EST:** 2022
SALES (est): 3.08MM
SALES (corp-wide): 12.78MM **Privately Held**
SIC: 5145 5441 2096 2066 Candy; Candy; Potato chips and similar snacks; Chocolate and cocoa products
PA: Brookpark Holdings Llc
    6770 Brookpark Rd
    Cleveland OH 44129
    216 739-2244

(G-13889)
TADD SPRING CO INC
15060 Foltz Pkwy (44149-4729)
PHONE..................440 572-1313
Mark Anguilano, *Pr*
EMP: 17 **EST:** 1962
SQ FT: 5,000
SALES (est): 2.42MM **Privately Held**
Web: www.taddspring.com
SIC: 3495 3493 Precision springs; Steel springs, except wire

(G-13890)
TMW ENGINEERING SERVICES LLC
Also Called: Tmw Racks
8536 W 130th St (44136-1907)
PHONE..................440 582-4700
Todd Weeden, *Managing Member*
EMP: 6 **EST:** 2013
SALES (est): 195.58K **Privately Held**
Web: www.tmwracks.com
SIC: 2542 Racks, merchandise display or storage: except wood

(G-13891)
TRANSCENDIA INC
22889 Lunn Rd (44149-4800)
P.O. Box 368003 (44136-9703)
PHONE..................440 638-2000
James Carlin, *Brnch Mgr*
EMP: 80
SQ FT: 25,000
SALES (corp-wide): 290.26MM **Privately Held**
Web: www.transcendia.com

SIC: 3081 Unsupported plastics film and sheet
PA: Transcendia, Inc.
    9201 Belmont Ave
    Franklin Park IL 60131
    847 678-1800

(G-13892)
TSW INDUSTRIES INC
14960 Foltz Pkwy (44149-4727)
PHONE..................440 572-7200
Tich Wan, *Pr*
Lee Wan, *
▲ **EMP:** 30 **EST:** 1981
SQ FT: 41,000
SALES (est): 2.45MM **Privately Held**
Web: www.tswindustries.com
SIC: 3599 Machine shop, jobbing and repair

(G-13893)
WALLOVER ENTERPRISES INC (DH)
21845 Drake Rd (44149-6610)
PHONE..................440 238-9250
George M Marquis, *Pr*
William C Cutri, *
EMP: 30 **EST:** 1863
SQ FT: 28,000
SALES (est): 39.25MM
SALES (corp-wide): 1.95B **Publicly Held**
SIC: 2992 8734 Oils and greases, blending and compounding; Product testing laboratories
HQ: Quaker Houghton Pa, Inc.
    901 E Hector St
    Conshohocken PA 19428
    610 832-4000

(G-13894)
WALLOVER OIL COMPANY INC (DH)
Also Called: Woco
21845 Drake Rd (44149-6610)
PHONE..................440 238-9250
Michael F Barry, *Ch Bd*
Mary Dean Hall, *VP*
◆ **EMP:** 33 **EST:** 1835
SQ FT: 28,000
SALES (est): 33.12MM
SALES (corp-wide): 1.95B **Publicly Held**
Web: www.walloveroil.com
SIC: 2992 2841 Oils and greases, blending and compounding; Soap and other detergents
HQ: Wallover Enterprises Inc.
    21845 Drake Rd
    Strongsville OH 44149
    440 238-9250

(G-13895)
WESTERN RESERVE SLEEVE INC
22360 Royalton Rd (44149-3826)
P.O. Box 361310 (44136-0022)
PHONE..................440 238-8850
Scott Gilbert, *Pr*
Sharon Gilbert, *Sec*
EMP: 12 **EST:** 1993
SALES (est): 3.05MM **Privately Held**
Web: www.a-roo.com
SIC: 3081 Packing materials, plastics sheet

(G-13896)
WILLOW TOOL & MACHINING LTD
15110 Foltz Pkwy Ste 1 (44149-4765)
PHONE..................440 572-2288
Samuel Thomas, *Mng Pt*
Teresa Thomas, *Pt*
William A Thomas, *Pt*
EMP: 14 **EST:** 1972
SQ FT: 7,350
SALES (est): 1.01MM **Privately Held**
Web: www.willowtool.com

SIC: 3541 3599 Machine tools, metal cutting type; Machine shop, jobbing and repair

(G-13897)
WINDSOR WIRE
8300 Dow Cir Ste 600 (44136-6607)
PHONE..................662 634-5908
EMP: 7 **EST:** 2018
SALES (est): 220.8K **Privately Held**
Web: www.windsorwire.com
SIC: 3564 Blowers and fans

Struthers
Mahoning County

(G-13898)
ADD-A-TRAP LLC
488 Como St (44471-1237)
PHONE..................330 750-0417
Robert N Davenport, *CEO*
Ray Hassay, *Pr*
Allan Stratron, *COO*
EMP: 6 **EST:** 2001
SALES (est): 669.63K **Privately Held**
Web: www.addatrap.com
SIC: 3088 Plastics plumbing fixtures

(G-13899)
AMERICAN WIRE SHAPES LLC
81 S Bridge St (44471-1949)
PHONE..................330 744-2905
EMP: 6 **EST:** 2019
SALES (est): 186.95K **Privately Held**
SIC: 3312 Blast furnaces and steel mills

(G-13900)
ASTRO ALUMINUM ENTERPRISES INC
65 Main St (44471-1942)
P.O. Box 208 (44471-0208)
PHONE..................330 755-1414
Paul Cene, *Pr*
James Dibacco, *
EMP: 37 **EST:** 1994
SALES (est): 252K **Privately Held**
Web: www.astroshapes.com
SIC: 3354 Aluminum extruded products

(G-13901)
ASTRO SHAPES LLC
65 Main St (44471-1942)
PHONE..................330 755-1414
Paul Cene, *Pr*
James Dibacco, *
Robert Cene Junior, *VP*
EMP: 325 **EST:** 1971
SQ FT: 300,000
SALES (est): 96.57MM **Privately Held**
Web: www.astroshapes.com
SIC: 3354 3086 Aluminum extruded products ; Insulation or cushioning material, foamed plastics

(G-13902)
ASTRO-COATINGS INC
65 Main St (44471-1942)
P.O. Box 208 (44471-0208)
PHONE..................330 755-1414
Paul Cene, *Pr*
Jim Di Bacco, *
Robert Cene Junior, *VP*
EMP: 26 **EST:** 1986
SQ FT: 25,000
SALES (est): 485.95K **Privately Held**
Web: www.astroshapes.com
SIC: 3354 Aluminum extruded products

(G-13903)
DATCO MANUFACTURING LLC
65 Main St (44471-1942)
PHONE..................330 755-1414
Rick Pursifull, *Ofcr*
EMP: 7 **EST:** 2017
SALES (est): 356.39K **Privately Held**
SIC: 3999 Manufacturing industries, nec

(G-13904)
GIANNIOS CANDY CO INC (PA)
430 Youngstown Poland Rd (44471-1058)
PHONE..................330 755-7000
John G Giannios, *Pr*
EMP: 49 **EST:** 1910
SQ FT: 28,000
SALES (est): 9.57MM
SALES (corp-wide): 9.57MM **Privately Held**
Web: www.giannioscandy.com
SIC: 2066 2064 Chocolate candy, solid; Candy and other confectionery products

(G-13905)
KURTZ TOOL & DIE CO INC
164 State St (44471-1956)
P.O. Box 116 (44471-0116)
PHONE..................330 755-7723
Robert Kurtz Junior, *Pr*
Robert Kurtz Senior, *Stockholder*
EMP: 6 **EST:** 1960
SALES (est): 822.46K **Privately Held**
SIC: 3544 Die sets for metal stamping (presses)

(G-13906)
QUALITY BAR INC
17 Union St Ste 7 (44471-1964)
PHONE..................330 755-0000
Donald A Casey, *Ch Bd*
Carrie Casey, *Pr*
EMP: 33 **EST:** 1995
SALES (est): 844.76K
SALES (corp-wide): 9.93MM **Privately Held**
SIC: 3312 Stainless steel
PA: Casey Equipment Corporation
    275 Kappa Dr
    Pittsburgh PA 15238
    412 963-1111

Stryker
Williams County

(G-13907)
DALTON CORPORATION
310 Ellis St (43557-9329)
P.O. Box 2600 (43557-2600)
PHONE..................419 682-6328
Alan Sheets, *Mgr*
EMP: 9
SALES (corp-wide): 122.27MM **Privately Held**
Web: www.daltoncorporation.com
SIC: 3625 Industrial controls: push button, selector switches, pilot
HQ: The Dalton Corporation
    1900 E Jefferson St
    Warsaw IN 46580
    574 267-8111

(G-13908)
DALTON STRYKER MCHINING FCILTY
310 Ellis St (43557)
PHONE..................419 682-6328
Joe Derita, *Pr*
Ron Schmucker, *
EMP: 48 **EST:** 1988

SALES (est): 1.17MM
SALES (corp-wide): 841.88MM Privately Held
Web: www.daltoncorporation.com
SIC: 3599 Machine shop, jobbing and repair
HQ: Neenah Foundry Company
2121 Brooks Ave
Neenah WI 54956
920 725-7000

(G-13909)
FRANKS SAWMILL INC
Rd 1950 (43557)
P.O. Box 4600 (43557-4600)
PHONE.................................419 682-3831
Dave Frank, *Pr*
Mike Meyer, *Sec*
EMP: 10 **EST:** 1958
SQ FT: 8,000
SALES (est): 678.94K Privately Held
SIC: 2448 Pallets, wood

(G-13910)
LYONDLLBSELL ADVNCED PLYMERS I
103 Railroad Ave (43557-9492)
PHONE.................................419 682-3311
Jeff Miccichi, *Mgr*
EMP: 45
SQ FT: 54,000
Web: www.lyondellbasell.com
SIC: 2865 2851 2821 2816 Color pigments, organic; Lacquers, varnishes, enamels, and other coatings; Plastics materials and resins; Inorganic pigments
HQ: Lyondellbasell Advanced Polymers Inc
1221 Mckinney St Ste 300
Houston TX 77010
713 309-7200

(G-13911)
OHIO TIMBERLAND PRODUCTS INC
102 Railroad Ave (43557-9533)
P.O. Box 330 (43557-0330)
PHONE.................................419 682-6322
Mike Burkholder, *Pr*
Harley Burkholder, *VP*
Donna Burkholder, *Sec*
EMP: 10 **EST:** 1996
SQ FT: 15,000
SALES (est): 2.19MM Privately Held
Web: www.ohiotimberland.com
SIC: 2411 Poles, posts, and pilings: untreated wood

(G-13912)
QUADCO REHABILITATION CTR INC (PA)
Also Called: NORTHWEST PRODUCTS
427 N Defiance St (43557-9472)
PHONE.................................419 682-1011
Bruce Abell, *Ex Dir*
EMP: 287 **EST:** 1967
SQ FT: 24,000
SALES (est): 1.38MM
SALES (corp-wide): 1.38MM Privately Held
Web: www.quadcorehab.org
SIC: 8331 2448 2441 Vocational rehabilitation agency; Wood pallets and skids; Nailed wood boxes and shook

(G-13913)
SAUDER MANUFACTURING CO
Also Called: Stryker Plant
201 Horton St (43557-9310)
P.O. Box 110 (43557-0110)
PHONE.................................419 682-3061
Luther Gautsche, *VP*
EMP: 83
SQ FT: 46,000

SALES (corp-wide): 543.69MM Privately Held
Web: www.saudermfg.com
SIC: 2531 2521 Chairs, portable folding; Wood office furniture
HQ: Sauder Manufacturing Co
930 W Barre Rd
Archbold OH 43502
419 445-7670

(G-13914)
WILLIAMS PORK CO OP
18487 County Road F (43557-9306)
PHONE.................................419 682-9022
Paul Kalmbach, *Pr*
EMP: 9 **EST:** 1997
SALES (est): 677.99K Privately Held
SIC: 2013 Pork, cured: from purchased meat

Sugar Grove
Fairfield County

(G-13915)
COMMERCIAL MUSIC SERVICE CO
Also Called: Chime Master Systems
6312 Goss Rd (43155-9610)
PHONE.................................740 746-8500
Jeffrey A Crook, *Pr*
▼ **EMP:** 8 **EST:** 1959
SALES (est): 993.07K Privately Held
Web: www.chimemaster.com
SIC: 3931 Bells (musical instruments)

(G-13916)
HANDLEBAR & GRILL ON MAIN LLC
201 S Main St (43155)
PHONE.................................740 746-2077
George K Mcgill, *Prin*
EMP: 6 **EST:** 2006
SALES (est): 130K Privately Held
Web: handlebar-grill.business.site
SIC: 2499 Handles, wood

(G-13917)
WARTHMAN DRILLING INC
7525 Lancaster Logan Rd (43155)
P.O. Box 360 (43155-0360)
PHONE.................................740 746-9950
Steven Warthman, *Pr*
EMP: 6 **EST:** 1965
SALES (est): 653.47K Privately Held
Web: www.warthmandrillinginc.com
SIC: 1781 1381 Servicing, water wells; Drilling oil and gas wells

Sugarcreek
Tuscarawas County

(G-13918)
ARCHER-DANIELS-MIDLAND COMPANY
Also Called: ADM
554 Pleasant Valley Rd Nw (44681-7800)
P.O. Box 486 (44681-0486)
PHONE.................................330 852-3025
EMP: 7
SQ FT: 12,000
SALES (corp-wide): 93.94B Publicly Held
Web: www.adm.com
SIC: 2048 Prepared feeds, nec
PA: Archer-Daniels-Midland Company
77 W Wacker Dr Ste 4600
Chicago IL 60601
312 634-8100

(G-13919)
BELDEN BRICK COMPANY LLC
Also Called: Plant 8
700 Edelweiss Dr (44681-9501)
P.O. Box 430 (44681-0430)
PHONE.................................330 456-0031
Doug Mutchelknaus, *Prin*
EMP: 46
SALES (corp-wide): 140.04MM Privately Held
Web: www.beldenbrick.com
SIC: 3251 3271 Structural brick and blocks; Brick, concrete
HQ: The Belden Brick Company Llc
700 Tuscarawas St W Uppr
Canton OH 44702
330 456-0031

(G-13920)
BELDEN BRICK COMPANY LLC
Also Called: Belden Brick Plant 3
690 Dover Rd Ne (44681-7683)
P.O. Box 20910 (44701-0910)
PHONE.................................330 265-2030
EMP: 46
SALES (corp-wide): 140.04MM Privately Held
Web: www.beldenbrick.com
SIC: 3251 3271 Structural brick and blocks; Brick, concrete
HQ: The Belden Brick Company Llc
700 Tuscarawas St W Uppr
Canton OH 44702
330 456-0031

(G-13921)
CARLISLE OAK
3872 Township Road 162 (44681-9621)
PHONE.................................330 852-8734
David Miller, *Owner*
EMP: 7 **EST:** 1991
SALES (est): 359.4K Privately Held
SIC: 2511 Wood household furniture

(G-13922)
CARLISLE PRTG WALNUT CREEK LTD
2673 Township Road 421 (44681-9486)
PHONE.................................330 852-9922
Marcus Wengerd, *Pr*
EMP: 35 **EST:** 1992
SALES (est): 7.82MM Privately Held
Web: www.carlisleprinting.com
SIC: 2621 2791 Catalog, magazine, and newsprint papers; Typesetting

(G-13923)
DUTCH VALLEY WOODWORKING INC
State Rte 39 (44681)
P.O. Box 416 (44681-0416)
PHONE.................................330 852-4319
Dale P Mullet, *Pr*
Ruth Mullet, *Sec*
EMP: 11 **EST:** 1976
SQ FT: 3,200
SALES (est): 494.27K Privately Held
Web: www.dutchvalleywoodworking.com
SIC: 2434 Wood kitchen cabinets

(G-13924)
EAGLE MACHINERY & SUPPLY INC
422 Dutch Vly Dr Ne (44681-7517)
PHONE.................................330 852-1300
Kirk Spillman, *Pr*
Lori Spillman, *Sec*
▲ **EMP:** 21 **EST:** 2003
SQ FT: 20,000
SALES (est): 8.65MM Privately Held
Web: www.eaglemachines.com

SIC: 3541 Machine tool replacement & repair parts, metal cutting types

(G-13925)
FARMERSTOWN MEATS
2933 Township Road 163 (44681-9635)
PHONE.................................330 897-7972
Lucille Gingerich, *Owner*
Raymond Gingerich, *Owner*
EMP: 6 **EST:** 1982
SALES (est): 361.8K Privately Held
SIC: 2011 Meat packing plants

(G-13926)
JACOB & LEVIS LTD
1689 State Route 39 (44681-9666)
PHONE.................................330 852-7600
EMP: 6 **EST:** 2015
SALES (est): 371.21K Privately Held
Web: www.jacobandlevis.com
SIC: 2434 Wood kitchen cabinets

(G-13927)
L & M MINERAL CO
2010 County Road 144 (44681-9439)
PHONE.................................330 852-3696
John E Ling Junior, *Pr*
Merle Mullet, *Treas*
EMP: 8 **EST:** 1954
SALES (est): 634.48K Privately Held
Web: www.andrew-wright.net
SIC: 1459 1221 Clays (common) quarrying; Bituminous coal and lignite-surface mining

(G-13928)
LUXCRAFT LLC
1221 County Road 144 (44681-9425)
PHONE.................................330 852-1036
EMP: 7 **EST:** 1999
SALES (est): 478.63K Privately Held
Web: www.luxcraft.com
SIC: 2421 Outdoor wood structural products

(G-13929)
METAL MNKEY WLDG FBRCATION LLC
806 W Main St (44681-9313)
PHONE.................................330 231-1490
EMP: 6 **EST:** 2012
SALES (est): 54.36K Privately Held
SIC: 3448 Prefabricated metal components

(G-13930)
MIDDAUGH ENTERPRISES INC
Also Called: Idea Works
211 Yoder Ave Ne (44681)
P.O. Box 400 (44681-0400)
PHONE.................................330 852-2471
Steven Middaugh, *Pr*
L Wade Middaugh, *VP*
Jeri Middaugh, *Sec*
EMP: 8 **EST:** 1956
SQ FT: 8,500
SALES (est): 846.04K Privately Held
Web: www.middaughprinters.com
SIC: 2752 2759 Offset printing; Imprinting

(G-13931)
MILLER MANUFACTURING INC
Also Called: Miller Wood Design
2705 Shetler Rd Nw (44681-7604)
P.O. Box 425 (44681-0425)
PHONE.................................330 852-0689
Raymond Miller, *Pr*
▼ **EMP:** 25 **EST:** 1993
SALES (est): 1.12MM Privately Held
SIC: 2493 2499 2435 2431 Particleboard, plastic laminated; Decorative wood and woodwork; Hardwood veneer and plywood; Millwork

Sugarcreek - Tuscarawas County (G-13932)

(G-13932)
MULLET ENTERPRISES INC (PA)
Also Called: Tmk Farm Service
138 2nd St Nw (44681-7824)
P.O. Box 278 (44681-0278)
PHONE.....................330 852-4681
Larry Tietje, Pr
Raymond Mullet, VP
▼ EMP: 8 EST: 2008
SQ FT: 34,000
SALES (est): 6.9MM
SALES (corp-wide): 6.9MM **Privately Held**
SIC: 5153 2041 Grain elevators; Flour and other grain mill products

(G-13933)
PALLET DISTRIBUTORS INC
Also Called: Scenic Wood Products
10343 Copperhead Rd Nw (44681-7768)
PHONE.....................330 852-3531
Martin Troyer, Genl Mgr
EMP: 28
Web: www.epalletinc.com
SIC: 2448 Pallets, wood
PA: Pallet Distributors, Inc.
14701 Detroit Ave Ste 750
Lakewood OH 44107

(G-13934)
PLEASANT VALLEY READY MIX INC
559 Pleasant Valley Rd Nw (44681-7800)
P.O. Box 436 (44681-0436)
PHONE.....................330 852-2613
Daniel O Miller, Pr
EMP: 10 EST: 1989
SQ FT: 3,000
SALES (est): 1.26MM **Privately Held**
SIC: 3273 5211 Ready-mixed concrete; Masonry materials and supplies

(G-13935)
PROVIA HOLDINGS INC (PA)
Also Called: Provia - Heritage Stone
2150 State Route 39 (44681-9201)
PHONE.....................330 852-4711
Bill Mullet, Prin
Brian Miller, *
Larry Troyer, *
Willis Schlabach, *
Phil Wengerd, *
EMP: 180 EST: 1972
SQ FT: 280,000
SALES (est): 140.5MM
SALES (corp-wide): 140.5MM **Privately Held**
Web: www.provia.com
SIC: 3442 5031 Metal doors; Door frames, all materials

(G-13936)
RNR ENTERPRISES LLC
1361 County Road 108 (44681-9631)
PHONE.....................330 852-3022
EMP: 10 EST: 1998
SALES (est): 952.01K **Privately Held**
Web: www.rnrenterprisesltd.com
SIC: 2511 Wood household furniture

(G-13937)
SCHLABACH PRINTERS LLC
Also Called: Schlabach Printers
798 State Route 93 Nw (44681-7726)
PHONE.....................330 852-4687
Dan Miller, Pt
EMP: 20 EST: 1979
SQ FT: 3,500
SALES (est): 2.33MM **Privately Held**
Web: www.schlabachprinters.com
SIC: 2759 2752 Screen printing; Commercial printing, lithographic

(G-13938)
SKYLINE CORPORATION
Also Called: SKYLINE CORPORATION
580 Mill St Nw (44681-9561)
PHONE.....................330 852-2483
Bruce Monteith, Mgr
EMP: 136
SQ FT: 100,000
SALES (corp-wide): 2.61B **Publicly Held**
Web: www.skylinehomes.com
SIC: 2451 3448 2452 Mobile homes; Prefabricated metal buildings and components; Prefabricated wood buildings
PA: Skyline Champion Corporation
755 W Big Beavr Rd # 100
Troy MI 48084
248 614-8211

(G-13939)
STONY POINT HARDWOODS LLC
Also Called: Pro Hardware 13074
7842 Stony Point Rd Nw (44681-7642)
PHONE.....................330 852-4512
Mark Shrock, Owner
EMP: 7 EST: 1976
SALES (est): 310.13K **Privately Held**
SIC: 2448 2435 2431 2426 Pallets, wood; Hardwood veneer and plywood; Millwork; Hardwood dimension and flooring mills

(G-13940)
SUGARCREEK BUDGET PUBLISHERS
Also Called: Budget Newspaper, The
134 Factory St Ne (44681-9301)
P.O. Box 249 (44681-0249)
PHONE.....................330 852-4634
Keith Rathbun, Pr
David Spector, VP
Sonia Cohen, Stockholder
Debbie Kloosterman, Stockholder
EMP: 10 EST: 1890
SQ FT: 4,800
SALES (est): 387.58K **Privately Held**
Web: www.thebudgetnewspaper.com
SIC: 2711 Newspapers: publishing only, not printed on site

(G-13941)
SUGARCREEK PALLET LTD
681 Belden Pkwy Ne (44681-7699)
PHONE.....................330 852-9812
Jonas Borntrager, Prin
EMP: 6 EST: 2002
SALES (est): 114.2K **Privately Held**
SIC: 2448 Pallets, wood

(G-13942)
SUGARCREEK SHAVINGS LLC
3121 Winklepleck Rd Nw (44681-7656)
PHONE.....................330 763-4239
Ruth Troyer, Prin
EMP: 9 EST: 2012
SALES (est): 926.64K **Privately Held**
Web: www.sugarcreekshavings.com
SIC: 2421 Sawdust and shavings

(G-13943)
SUPERB INDUSTRIES INC
330 3rd St Nw (44681-9310)
P.O. Box 708 (44681-0708)
PHONE.....................330 852-0500
John Miller, Pr
Susan Miller, *
▲ EMP: 75 EST: 1986
SQ FT: 50,000
SALES (est): 15.85MM **Privately Held**
Web: www.superbindustries.com
SIC: 3625 3491 Control equipment, electric; Valves, automatic control

(G-13944)
SWP LEGACY LTD
10143 Copperhead Rd Nw (44681-7770)
P.O. Box 396 (44681-0396)
PHONE.....................330 340-9663
Paul Monaco, *
EMP: 55 EST: 1996
SALES (est): 6.95MM **Privately Held**
SIC: 2448 Pallets, wood

(G-13945)
TRUPOINT PRODUCTS LLC
Uknown (44681)
P.O. Box 72 (44687-0072)
PHONE.....................330 204-3302
Myron Miller, Owner
EMP: 10 EST: 2015
SALES (est): 613.11K **Privately Held**
SIC: 3312 3495 Wire products, steel or iron; Wire springs

(G-13946)
TUSCO HARDWOODS LLC
Also Called: M & M Hardwoods
10887 Gerber Valley Rd Nw (44681-7932)
PHONE.....................330 852-4281
EMP: 18 EST: 1966
SQ FT: 10,000
SALES (est): 492.32K **Privately Held**
SIC: 2448 2421 Wood pallets and skids; Sawmills and planing mills, general

(G-13947)
WEAVER BARNS LTD
1696 State Route 39 (44681-9666)
PHONE.....................330 852-2103
EMP: 10 EST: 1993
SALES (est): 1.35MM **Privately Held**
Web: www.weaverbarns.com
SIC: 2452 Prefabricated buildings, wood

(G-13948)
WEAVERS FURNITURE LTD
Also Called: Weaver Craft of Sugarcreek
7011 Old Route 39 Nw (44681-7968)
PHONE.....................330 852-2701
Wayne Weaver, Owner
▲ EMP: 13 EST: 1992
SQ FT: 42,000
SALES (est): 4.56MM **Privately Held**
Web: www.weaverfurniturestore.com
SIC: 2512 5023 Upholstered household furniture; Homefurnishings

(G-13949)
YODER LUMBER CO INC
3799 County Road 70 (44681-9426)
PHONE.....................330 893-3131
Paul Dow, Brnch Mgr
EMP: 51
SALES (corp-wide): 24.4MM **Privately Held**
Web: www.yoderlumber.com
SIC: 5211 2435 2426 2421 Planing mill products and lumber; Hardwood veneer and plywood; Hardwood dimension and flooring mills; Sawmills and planing mills, general
PA: Yoder Lumber Co., Inc.
4515 Township Road 367
Millersburg OH 44654
330 893-3121

Summitville
Columbiana County

(G-13950)
SUMMITVILLE TILES INC (PA)
Also Called: Summitville Laboratories
15364 State Rte 644 (43962)
P.O. Box 73 (43962-0073)
PHONE.....................330 223-1511
▲ EMP: 30 EST: 1995
SALES (est): 24.79MM
SALES (corp-wide): 24.79MM **Privately Held**
Web: www.summitville.com
SIC: 3253 Mosaic tile, glazed and unglazed: ceramic

Sunbury
Delaware County

(G-13951)
BRY-AIR INC
10793 E State Route 37 (43074-9311)
PHONE.....................740 965-2974
Mel Meyers, Pr
Doug Flowery, *
◆ EMP: 43 EST: 1964
SQ FT: 40,000
SALES (est): 8.52MM **Privately Held**
Web: www.bry-air.com
SIC: 3585 3826 3535 3823 Dehumidifiers electric, except portable; Environmental testing equipment; Conveyors and conveying equipment; Process control instruments

(G-13952)
DUFFEE FINISHING INC
4860 N County Line Rd (43074-8305)
PHONE.....................740 965-4848
Nancy Duffee, VP
EMP: 8 EST: 1967
SQ FT: 20,000
SALES (est): 573.93K **Privately Held**
Web: www.duffeefinishing.com
SIC: 3479 3399 Painting of metal products; Powder, metal

(G-13953)
EN-HANCED PRODUCTS INC
14111 Chambers Rd (43074-8361)
PHONE.....................614 882-7400
James M Hance, Pr
EMP: 7 EST: 2001
SALES (est): 685.2K **Privately Held**
Web: www.en-hancedproducts.com
SIC: 3443 Fabricated plate work (boiler shop)

(G-13954)
GERLING AND ASSOCIATES INC
200 Kintner Pkwy (43074-9320)
PHONE.....................740 965-6200
Fred Gerling, Pr
◆ EMP: 80 EST: 1988
SALES (est): 9.34MM **Privately Held**
Web: www.gerlinggroup.com
SIC: 3711 Mobile lounges (motor vehicle), assembly of

(G-13955)
HITACHI ASTEMO AMERICAS INC
707 W Cherry St (43074-9595)
PHONE.....................740 965-1133
EMP: 346
Web: www.hitachi-automotive.us
SIC: 3694 Alternators, automotive
HQ: Hitachi Astemo Americas, Inc.
955 Warwick Rd
Harrodsburg KY 40330
859 734-9451

(G-13956)
ICC SYSTEMS INC
5665 Blue Church Rd Ste 202 (43074-9695)

GEOGRAPHIC SECTION

Swanton - Fulton County (G-13978)

PHONE..................................614 524-0299
EMP: 6 **EST:** 1992
SALES (est): 486.3K **Privately Held**
SIC: 7372 Prepackaged software

(G-13957)
KRISTA MESSER
15301 E State Route 37 (43074-9634)
PHONE..................................734 459-1952
Krista Messer, *Prin*
EMP: 6 **EST:** 2010
SALES (est): 97.15K **Privately Held**
SIC: 3443 Fabricated plate work (boiler shop)

(G-13958)
NELSON TOOL CORPORATION
388 N County Line Rd (43074-9004)
PHONE..................................740 965-1894
Michael Nelson, *Pr*
EMP: 14 **EST:** 1979
SQ FT: 18,200
SALES (est): 2.34MM **Privately Held**
SIC: 3544 Special dies and tools

(G-13959)
OBERFIELDS LLC
471 Kintner Pkwy (43074-8978)
PHONE..................................740 369-7644
Bruce Loris, *Pr*
EMP: 21
SQ FT: 833
SALES (corp-wide): 21.04MM **Privately Held**
Web: www.oberfields.com
SIC: 3272 Concrete products, precast, nec
HQ: Oberfield's, Llc
  528 London Rd
  Delaware OH 43015
  740 369-7644

(G-13960)
OHASHI TECHNICA USA INC (HQ)
111 Burrer Dr (43074-9323)
PHONE..................................740 965-5115
Mamoru Shibasaki, *Prin*
Hikaru Tateiwa, *
▲ **EMP:** 50 **EST:** 1987
SQ FT: 110,000
SALES (est): 26.4MM **Privately Held**
Web: www.ohashiusa.com
SIC: 5013 5072 3452 Automotive supplies and parts; Hardware; Bolts, nuts, rivets, and washers
PA: Ohashi Technica Inc.
  4-3-13, Toranomon
  Minato-Ku TKY 105-0

(G-13961)
OHASHI TECHNICA USA MFG INC
99 Burrer Dr (43074-9319)
PHONE..................................740 965-9002
▲ **EMP:** 19 **EST:** 1994
SQ FT: 60,000
SALES (est): 2.86MM **Privately Held**
SIC: 3965 Fasteners
HQ: Ohashi Technica U.S.A. Inc.
  111 Burrer Dr
  Sunbury OH 43074
  740 965-5115

(G-13962)
OMEGA ENGINEERING INC
Also Called: Omegadyne
149 Stelzer Ct (43074-8528)
PHONE..................................740 965-9340
Dennis Guy, *Brnch Mgr*
EMP: 50
SALES (corp-wide): 653.43MM **Privately Held**
Web: www.omega.com
SIC: 3829 3679 3825 Pressure transducers; Loads, electronic; Instruments to measure electricity
HQ: Omega Engineering, Inc.
  800 Connecticut Ave 5n01
  Norwalk CT 06854
  203 359-1660

(G-13963)
OMEGADYNE INC
Also Called: Omegadyne
149 Stelzer Ct (43074-8528)
PHONE..................................740 965-9340
EMP: 65
SIC: 3829 3679 3825 Pressure transducers; Loads, electronic; Instruments to measure electricity

(G-13964)
RUSSELL T BUNDY ASSOCIATES INC
Also Called: American Pan Company
601 W Cherry St (43074-9803)
PHONE..................................740 965-3008
Brad Moore, *Mgr*
EMP: 9
SALES (corp-wide): 50.03MM **Privately Held**
Web: www.bundybakingsolutions.com
SIC: 3479 Coating of metals and formed products
PA: Russell T. Bundy Associates, Inc.
  417 E Water St Ste 1
  Urbana OH 43078
  937 652-2151

(G-13965)
UNIVERSAL COMPOSITE LLC
Also Called: Uc Trailer Co.
200 Kintner Pkwy (43074-9320)
PHONE..................................614 507-1646
EMP: 11 **EST:** 2008
SALES (est): 444.23K **Privately Held**
SIC: 3711 Automobile assembly, including specialty automobiles

(G-13966)
WHITS FROZEN CUSTARD
101 W Cherry St Unit A (43074-8029)
PHONE..................................740 965-1427
Rick J Dague, *Prin*
EMP: 7 **EST:** 2010
SALES (est): 207.33K **Privately Held**
Web: www.whitscustard.com
SIC: 2024 Ice cream, bulk

Swanton
Fulton County

(G-13967)
AMBROSIA INC
Also Called: Swan Creek Candle Co.
395 W Airport Hwy (43558-1445)
P.O. Box 239 (43558-0239)
PHONE..................................419 825-3896
Ann Albright, *Pr*
EMP: 7
SALES (corp-wide): 4.86MM **Privately Held**
Web: www.swancreekcandle.com
SIC: 3999 Candles
PA: Ambrosia, Inc.
  395 W Airport Hwy
  Swanton OH 43558
  419 825-1151

(G-13968)
AQUABLOK LTD
230 W Airport Hwy (43558-1471)
PHONE..................................419 402-4170
John Collins, *COO*
EMP: 9
SALES (corp-wide): 3.06MM **Privately Held**
Web: www.aquablok.com
SIC: 3299 Nonmetallic mineral statuary and other decorative products
PA: Aquablok, Ltd.
  175 Woodland Ave
  Swanton OH 43558
  419 825-1325

(G-13969)
AQUABLOK LTD (PA)
175 Woodland Ave (43558-1026)
PHONE..................................419 825-1325
John Hall, *Pr*
EMP: 9 **EST:** 1999
SALES (est): 3.06MM
SALES (corp-wide): 3.06MM **Privately Held**
Web: www.aquablok.com
SIC: 3299 3295 Nonmetallic mineral statuary and other decorative products; Minerals, ground or treated

(G-13970)
BROKEN SPINNING WHEEL
14230 Monclova Rd (43558-8711)
PHONE..................................419 825-1609
John Kaczor, *Prin*
EMP: 6 **EST:** 1971
SALES (est): 99.7K **Privately Held**
Web: www.thebrokenspinningwheel.com
SIC: 2252 Socks

(G-13971)
COLUMBUS JACK CORPORATION
Also Called: Columbus Jack Regent
1 Air Cargo Pkwy E (43558-9490)
PHONE..................................614 443-7492
Paul Schwarzbaum, *CEO*
John Cattell, *
▲ **EMP:** 25 **EST:** 1992
SQ FT: 50,000
SALES (est): 6.16MM
SALES (corp-wide): 2.41B **Privately Held**
Web: www.columbusjack.com
SIC: 3542 3728 Presses: hydraulic and pneumatic, mechanical and manual; Aircraft body and wing assemblies and parts
HQ: Tronair, Inc.
  1 Air Cargo Pkwy E
  Swanton OH 43558
  419 866-6301

(G-13972)
DATCOMEDIA LLC
1 Air Cargo Pkwy E (43558-9490)
PHONE..................................419 866-6301
Paul Schwarzbaum, *CEO*
John Cattell, *CFO*
EMP: 6 **EST:** 2008
SALES (est): 1.28MM
SALES (corp-wide): 2.41B **Privately Held**
Web: www.datcomedia.com
SIC: 7372 7371 Prepackaged software; Custom computer programming services
HQ: Tronair, Inc.
  1 Air Cargo Pkwy E
  Swanton OH 43558
  419 866-6301

(G-13973)
EAGLE INDUSTRIAL TRUCK MFG LLC
Also Called: Eagle Tugs
1 Air Cargo Pkwy E (43558-9490)
PHONE..................................419 866-6301
Paul Schwarzbaum, *CEO*
John Cattell, *CFO*
◆ **EMP:** 20 **EST:** 2000
SQ FT: 70,000
SALES (est): 20.94MM
SALES (corp-wide): 2.41B **Privately Held**
Web: www.eagletugs.com
SIC: 5085 3537 Industrial supplies; Industrial trucks and tractors
HQ: Tronair, Inc.
  1 Air Cargo Pkwy E
  Swanton OH 43558
  419 866-6301

(G-13974)
GRAND AIRE INC (PA)
11777 W Airport Service Rd (43558-9387)
PHONE..................................419 861-6700
Zachary Cheema, *CEO*
EMP: 20 **EST:** 1998
SQ FT: 57,000
SALES (est): 9.32MM
SALES (corp-wide): 9.32MM **Privately Held**
Web: www.grandaire.com
SIC: 4522 5172 4512 4581 Air cargo carriers, nonscheduled; Petroleum products, nec; Air transportation, scheduled ; Airports, flying fields, and services

(G-13975)
GSE PRODUCTION AND SUPPORT LLC (DH)
Also Called: GSE Spares
1 Air Cargo Pkwy E (43558-9490)
PHONE..................................419 866-6301
Paul Schwarzbaum, *Managing Member*
John Cattell, *CFO*
▲ **EMP:** 13 **EST:** 1994
SQ FT: 5,000
SALES (est): 4.29MM
SALES (corp-wide): 2.41B **Privately Held**
Web: www.tronair.com
SIC: 3728 3542 Aircraft body and wing assemblies and parts; Presses: hydraulic and pneumatic, mechanical and manual
HQ: Tronair, Inc.
  1 Air Cargo Pkwy E
  Swanton OH 43558
  419 866-6301

(G-13976)
M L B MOLDED URETHANE PDTS LLC
1680 Us Highway 20a (43558-8663)
P.O. Box 464 (43552-0464)
PHONE..................................419 825-9140
EMP: 9 **EST:** 2004
SQ FT: 15,000
SALES (est): 967.9K **Privately Held**
Web: www.mlbproducts.net
SIC: 3086 Plastics foam products

(G-13977)
MAGNA INTERNATIONAL AMER INC
Also Called: Chemical Technologies
428 Church St (43558-1113)
PHONE..................................419 410-4780
EMP: 54
SALES (corp-wide): 37.84B **Privately Held**
Web: www.magna.com
SIC: 3714 Motor vehicle parts and accessories
HQ: Magna International Of America, Inc.
  750 Tower Dr
  Troy MI 48098

(G-13978)
MALABAR
Also Called: Malabar International
1 Air Cargo Pkwy E (43558-9490)
PHONE..................................419 866-6301

Swanton - Fulton County (G-13979)

EMP: 25 EST: 1937
SALES (est): 10.39MM
SALES (corp-wide): 2.41B **Privately Held**
Web: www.malabar.com
SIC: **3728** 3829 3492 3799 Aircraft parts and equipment, nec; Testers for checking hydraulic controls on aircraft; Fluid power valves for aircraft; Trailers and trailer equipment
HQ: Tronair, Inc.
1 Air Cargo Pkwy E
Swanton OH 43558
419 866-6301

(G-13979)
OWENS CORNING SALES LLC
Also Called: Owens Corning
11451 W Airport Service Rd (43558-9389)
PHONE..................419 248-5751
Roger G Waddill, *Brnch Mgr*
EMP: 9
SIC: **3296** Fiberglass Insulation
HQ: Owens Corning Sales, Llc
1 Owens Corning Pkwy
Toledo OH 43659
419 248-8000

(G-13980)
PJS CORRUGATED INC
2330 Us Highway 20 (43558-8649)
PHONE..................419 644-3383
Michael Iozzo, *Pr*
Joseph Iozzo, *VP*
Priscilla Iozzo, *Sec*
EMP: 10 EST: 1992
SQ FT: 10,000
SALES (est): 2.29MM **Privately Held**
SIC: **2653** Boxes, corrugated: made from purchased materials

(G-13981)
SCOTTDEL CUSHION INC
400 Church St (43558-1199)
PHONE..................419 825-0432
Kevin Thornton, *CEO*
Scott Carson, *
▲ EMP: 45 EST: 1943
SQ FT: 185,000
SALES (est): 8.86MM **Privately Held**
Web: www.scottdel.com
SIC: **3086** Carpet and rug cushions, foamed plastics

(G-13982)
SOARING SOFTWARE SOLUTIONS INC
110 W Airport Hwy Ste 1 (43558-1446)
PHONE..................419 442-7676
Richard Lederman, *Pr*
EMP: 13 EST: 1998
SALES (est): 1.99MM **Privately Held**
Web: www.soaringsoftware.com
SIC: **7371** 7372 Computer software systems analysis and design, custom; Prepackaged software

(G-13983)
SPINAL BALANCE INC
11360 S Airfield Rd (43558-7900)
PHONE..................419 530-5935
Anand Agarwal, *CEO*
Arthur Karas, *Sec*
EMP: 8 EST: 2013
SALES (est): 1.23MM **Privately Held**
Web: www.confelicityspine.com
SIC: **3842** Implants, surgical

(G-13984)
SWANTON WLDG MACHINING CO INC (PA)
407 Bdwy Ave (43558-1341)
PHONE..................419 826-4816
Norm D Zeiter, *CEO*
Chuck Morgan, *
Kevin Thornton, *
Jeff Gyurasics, *
Constance Zeiter, *
EMP: 80 EST: 1956
SQ FT: 314,000
SALES (est): 23.66MM
SALES (corp-wide): 23.66MM **Privately Held**
Web: www.swantonweld.com
SIC: **3446** 3444 3443 3599 Architectural metalwork; Sheet metalwork; Fabricated plate work (boiler shop); Machine and other job shop work

(G-13985)
TOLEDO JET CENTER LLC (PA)
Also Called: Toledo Express
11591 W Airport Service Rd (43558-9618)
PHONE..................419 866-9050
Alan R Carsten, *Managing Member*
Bill Pribe, *Genl Mgr*
Mindy Leppala, *Genl Mgr*
William Pribe, *Genl Mgr*
EMP: 9 EST: 2009
SALES (est): 2.97MM **Privately Held**
Web: www.toledojet.com
SIC: **3721** 4581 Aircraft; Aircraft maintenance and repair services

(G-13986)
TRI-COUNTY BLOCK AND BRICK INC
1628 Us Highway 20a (43558)
PHONE..................419 826-7060
TOLL FREE: 800
Roger L Cooley, *Pr*
Karen Cooley, *
Carl Kuhlman, *
Roberta E Cooley, *
EMP: 35 EST: 1953
SQ FT: 4,160
SALES (est): 4.81MM **Privately Held**
Web: www.tricountyblock.com
SIC: **5211** 3271 Lumber and other building materials; Blocks, concrete or cinder: standard

(G-13987)
TRONAIR INC (DH)
1 Air Cargo Pkwy E (43558-9490)
PHONE..................419 866-6301
Howard Jones, *CEO*
John Cattell, *
◆ EMP: 200 EST: 1972
SQ FT: 80,000
SALES (est): 90MM
SALES (corp-wide): 2.41B **Privately Held**
Web: www.tronair.com
SIC: **3728** Aircraft parts and equipment, nec
HQ: Tronair Parent, Inc.
1 Air Cargo Pkwy E
Swanton OH 43558
419 866-6301

Sycamore
Wyandot County

(G-13988)
CREATIVE PLASTIC CONCEPTS LLC (HQ)
206 S Griffith St (44882-9694)
PHONE..................419 927-9588
Nick Reinhart, *Pr*
▲ EMP: 17 EST: 2013
SALES (est): 23.65MM
SALES (corp-wide): 494.03MM **Privately Held**
Web: www.americanplasticsllc.com
SIC: **2499** 5085 Clothes drying frames, racks and reels, wood; Bins and containers, storage
PA: Jansan Acquisition, Llc
11840 Wstline Indus Dr St
Saint Louis MO 63146
314 656-4321

Sylvania
Lucas County

(G-13989)
AD-SENSATIONS INC
3315 Centennial Rd Ste A (43560-9397)
P.O. Box 411 (43560-0411)
PHONE..................419 841-5395
Gary Sears, *Pr*
EMP: 14 EST: 1989
SQ FT: 5,000
SALES (est): 2.26MM **Privately Held**
Web: www.wavehunter.com
SIC: **2759** 5199 Promotional printing; Calendars

(G-13990)
ADVANCE PRODUCTS
6041 Angleview Dr (43560-1209)
PHONE..................419 882-8117
David Frantz, *Owner*
James Frantz, *Owner*
EMP: 10 EST: 1947
SALES (est): 490.2K **Privately Held**
SIC: **3571** 3999 Computers, digital, analog or hybrid; Models, except toy

(G-13991)
BOBBART INDUSTRIES INC
Also Called: American Custom Industries
5035 Alexis Rd Ste 1 (43560-1637)
PHONE..................419 350-5477
Bart Lea, *Pr*
Laura Lea, *Sec*
EMP: 23 EST: 1968
SQ FT: 45,000
SALES (est): 846.57K **Privately Held**
SIC: **3711** 3082 7532 3714 Motor vehicles and car bodies; Unsupported plastics profile shapes; Top and body repair and paint shops; Motor vehicle parts and accessories

(G-13992)
CSW INC
3545 Silica Rd Unit E (43560-9889)
PHONE..................413 589-1311
EMP: 29
SALES (corp-wide): 17.01MM **Privately Held**
Web: www.cswgraphics.com
SIC: **2796** 3544 Platemaking services; Dies, steel rule
PA: Csw, Inc.
45 Tyburski Rd
Ludlow MA 01056
413 589-1311

(G-13993)
DON-ELL CORPORATION (PA)
Also Called: X M C Division
8450 Central Ave (43560-9747)
P.O. Box 351480 (43635-1480)
PHONE..................419 841-7114
Donald R Sell, *Ch Bd*
Robert N Sell, *
EMP: 25 EST: 1956
SQ FT: 12,000
SALES (est): 3.15MM
SALES (corp-wide): 3.15MM **Privately Held**
SIC: **3679** 3089 Electronic switches; Molding primary plastics

(G-13994)
DON-ELL CORPORATION
Also Called: X M C
8456 Central Ave (43560-9747)
PHONE..................419 841-7114
Jim Krumm, *Mgr*
EMP: 8
SALES (corp-wide): 3.15MM **Privately Held**
SIC: **3089** Injection molding of plastics
PA: Don-Ell Corporation
8450 Central Ave
Sylvania OH 43560
419 841-7114

(G-13995)
DURA MAGNETICS INC
5500 Schultz Dr (43560-2304)
PHONE..................419 882-0591
Donald C Kuchers, *CEO*
Robert M Csortos, *Pr*
Catherine A Kuchers, *Sec*
▲ EMP: 17 EST: 1961
SQ FT: 15,000
SALES (est): 3.64MM **Privately Held**
Web: www.duramag.com
SIC: **5084** 3499 Industrial machinery and equipment; Magnets, permanent: metallic

(G-13996)
GRENADA STAMPING ASSEMBLY INC (HQ)
Also Called: Ice Industries Grenada
3810 Herr Rd (43560-8925)
PHONE..................419 842-3600
Jeffrey Snavely, *Prin*
EMP: 35 EST: 2006
SALES (est): 31.48MM **Privately Held**
Web: www.iceindustries.com
SIC: **3469** Stamping metal for the trade
PA: Ice Industries, Inc.
3810 Herr Rd
Sylvania OH 43560

(G-13997)
HEIDELBERG MTLS MDWEST AGG INC
8130 Brint Rd (43560-9719)
PHONE..................419 882-0123
Ron Tipton, *Brnch Mgr*
EMP: 10
SALES (corp-wide): 23.02B **Privately Held**
SIC: **1422** Crushed and broken limestone
HQ: Heidelberg Materials Midwest Agg, Inc.
300 E John Carpenter Fwy
Irving TX

(G-13998)
HEIDELBERG MTLS US CEM LLC
8130 Brint Rd (43560-9719)
PHONE..................972 653-5500
EMP: 10
SALES (corp-wide): 23.02B **Privately Held**
Web: www.heidelbergmaterials.us
SIC: **3273** Ready-mixed concrete
HQ: Heidelberg Materials Us Cement Llc
300 E John Carpenter Fwy
Irving TX 75062
877 534-4442

(G-13999)
HELIOS QUARTZ AMERICA INC
Also Called: Helios Quartz
7345 Sylvania Ave (43560-3534)
PHONE..................419 882-3377
Ivery D Foreman, *Prin*
EMP: 6 EST: 2012

GEOGRAPHIC SECTION

Tallmadge - Summit County (G-14024)

SALES (est): 107.11K **Privately Held**
Web: www.heliosquartz.com
SIC: **1731** 3679 5231 General electrical contractor; Quartz crystals, for electronic application; Glass

(G-14000)
ICE INDUSTRIES INC (PA)
3810 Herr Rd (43560-8925)
PHONE..............................419 842-3600
Howard Ice, *Ch*
Paul Bishop, *
Jeff Boger, *
Bennett Bishop, *
Steve Doseck, *
▲ **EMP:** 26 **EST:** 2002
SQ FT: 10,000
SALES (est): 121MM **Privately Held**
Web: www.iceindustries.com
SIC: **3469** Stamping metal for the trade

(G-14001)
ICE INDUSTRIES COLUMBUS INC
3810 Herr Rd (43560-8925)
PHONE..............................614 475-3853
EMP: 30
SIC: **3441** Fabricated structural metal

(G-14002)
INTEGRATED RESOURCES INC
7901 Sylvania Ave (43560-9732)
PHONE..............................419 885-7122
Scott Stansley, *Pr*
Richard Stansley Junior, *Sec*
EMP: 40 **EST:** 1989
SQ FT: 10,000
SALES (est): 3.25MM **Privately Held**
SIC: **3273** 8741 Ready-mixed concrete; Management services

(G-14003)
KEVIN K TIDD
Also Called: Arrow Print & Copy
5505 Roan Rd (43560-2306)
PHONE..............................419 885-5603
Kevin K Tidd, *Owner*
EMP: 6 **EST:** 1985
SQ FT: 3,500
SALES (est): 509.1K **Privately Held**
Web: www.arrowprint.com
SIC: **2752** 2791 2789 Offset printing; Typesetting; Bookbinding and related work

(G-14004)
MICHIGAN SILKSCREEN INC
5354 Whiteford Rd (43560-2520)
PHONE..............................419 885-1163
Michael Schnaidt, *Pr*
Brenda Schnaidt, *VP*
EMP: 8 **EST:** 1977
SQ FT: 2,500
SALES (est): 440K **Privately Held**
SIC: **2396** Screen printing on fabric articles

(G-14005)
MOLD SHOP INC
8520 Central Ave (43560-9748)
PHONE..............................419 829-2041
Lan Wagner, *Pr*
Donna Wagner, *VP*
EMP: 10 **EST:** 1965
SQ FT: 12,000
SALES (est): 928.15K **Privately Held**
Web: www.usmolds.com
SIC: **3544** Special dies and tools

(G-14006)
MOORE CHROME PRODUCTS COMPANY
Also Called: Moore Metal Finishing
3525 Silica Rd (43560-9814)
PHONE..............................419 843-3510
Scott W Backus, *Pr*
Scott Backus, *Pr*
Mary Huth, *VP*
Larry Huth, *VP*
EMP: 24 **EST:** 1930
SQ FT: 24,000
SALES (est): 862.79K **Privately Held**
SIC: **3471** Electroplating of metals or formed products

(G-14007)
MUIR GRAPHICS INC
5454 Alger Dr Ste A (43560-2348)
PHONE..............................419 882-7993
Linda Rider, *Pr*
Karen Garner, *VP*
Suzanne Emerine, *Sec*
EMP: 9 **EST:** 1974
SQ FT: 10,000
SALES (est): 476.33K **Privately Held**
Web: www.muir-graphics.com
SIC: **2752** Offset printing

(G-14008)
NABCO ENTRANCES INC
Also Called: Nabco Entrances
3407 Silica Rd (43560-9539)
PHONE..............................419 842-0484
EMP: 14
Web: www.nabcoentrances.com
SIC: **3699** Electrical equipment and supplies, nec
HQ: Nabco Entrances, Inc.
S82w18717 Gemini Dr
Muskego WI 53150
262 679-7532

(G-14009)
NEXT SPECIALTY RESINS INC (PA)
Also Called: Next Resins
3315 Centennial Rd Ste J (43560-9419)
P.O. Box 365 (49220-0365)
PHONE..............................419 843-4600
◆ **EMP:** 30 **EST:** 1996
SALES (est): 4.36MM **Privately Held**
Web: www.nextresins.com
SIC: **2821** Melamine resins, melamine-formaldehyde

(G-14010)
NIGHT LIGHTSCAPES LLC
3303 Herr Rd (43560-9780)
PHONE..............................419 304-2486
Tom Walter, *Prin*
EMP: 6 **EST:** 2007
SALES (est): 215.29K **Privately Held**
SIC: **3645** Garden, patio, walkway and yard lighting fixtures: electric

(G-14011)
NORTHERN CONCRETE PIPE INC
3756 Centennial Rd (43560-9734)
PHONE..............................419 841-3361
Jeff Levon, *Prin*
EMP: 10
SALES (corp-wide): 23.97MM **Privately Held**
Web: www.ncp-inc.com
SIC: **3272** Pipe, concrete or lined with concrete
PA: Northern Concrete Pipe, Inc.
401 Kelton St
Bay City MI 48706
989 892-3545

(G-14012)
RONFELDT MANUFACTURING
3810 Herr Rd (43560-8925)
PHONE..............................419 382-5641
EMP: 12 **EST:** 2019
SALES (est): 929.65K **Privately Held**
Web: www.iceindustries.com
SIC: **3999** Manufacturing industries, nec

(G-14013)
SENTAGE CORPORATION
Also Called: Dental Services Group
8730 Resource Park Dr (43560-8939)
PHONE..............................419 842-6730
Lou Azzara, *Pr*
Vicky Rice, *Prin*
EMP: 9 **EST:** 1989
SALES (est): 381.88K **Privately Held**
Web: www.nationaldentex.com
SIC: **8072** 3843 Crown and bridge production; Dental equipment and supplies

(G-14014)
SHARONCO INC
Also Called: Sylvan Studio
5651 Main St (43560-1929)
PHONE..............................419 882-3443
Scott Stampflmeier, *Pr*
Scott Stampfomeier, *Prin*
EMP: 8 **EST:** 2013
SALES (est): 760.97K **Privately Held**
Web: www.sylvanstudio.com
SIC: **3499** 5094 Novelties and giftware, including trophies; Trophies

(G-14015)
STANSLEY MINERAL RESOURCES INC (PA)
3793 Silica Rd # B (43560-9814)
PHONE..............................419 843-2813
Rick Stansley, *CEO*
Jeff Stansley, *
Richard Stansley Junior, *Sec*
Mandy Billau, *
EMP: 35 **EST:** 1978
SQ FT: 10,000
SALES (est): 4.76MM
SALES (corp-wide): 4.76MM **Privately Held**
SIC: **1442** Gravel mining

(G-14016)
SYLVAN STUDIOS INC
5651 Main St (43560-1929)
P.O. Box 59 (43560-0059)
PHONE..............................419 882-3423
Terry E Crandell, *Pr*
EMP: 7 **EST:** 1959
SQ FT: 5,000
SALES (est): 569.81K **Privately Held**
Web: www.sylvanstudio.com
SIC: **2396** 7336 Ribbons and bows, cut and sewed; Commercial art and graphic design

(G-14017)
SYLVANIA MOSE LDGE NO 1579 LYA
Also Called: SYLVANIA MOOSE LODGE 1579
6072 Main St (43560-1266)
PHONE..............................419 885-4953
Gary Muter, *Admn*
EMP: 13 **EST:** 1977
SALES (est): 1.61MM **Privately Held**
Web: www.sylvaniamoose.org
SIC: **8641** 7372 Fraternal associations; Application computer software

(G-14018)
TGM HOLDINGS COMPANY
Also Called: Toledo Grmtor Blffton Mtr Wrks
5439 Roan Rd (43560-2304)
PHONE..............................419 885-3769
John Toth, *Pr*
EMP: 23 **EST:** 1948
SQ FT: 35,000
SALES (est): 1.97MM **Privately Held**
Web: www.toledogear.com
SIC: **3566** Gears, power transmission, except auto

(G-14019)
TOTAL MOLDING SOLUTIONS INC
3315 Centennial Rd Ste J (43560-9419)
PHONE..............................517 424-5900
Rajiv Naik, *Pr*
EMP: 8 **EST:** 2001
SALES (est): 473.78K **Privately Held**
Web: www.totalmoldsolutions.com
SIC: **3089** Injection molding of plastics

(G-14020)
UNIQATIVE LLC
5834 Monroe St Ste A-18 (43560-2267)
PHONE..............................800 337-2870
Dave Krueger, *Prin*
EMP: 6 **EST:** 2017
SALES (est): 137.53K **Privately Held**
Web: www.uniqative.com
SIC: **3442** Metal doors, sash, and trim

Tallmadge
Summit County

(G-14021)
AKRON GASKET & PACKG ENTPS INC
445 Northeast Ave (44278-1444)
PHONE..............................330 633-3742
Carter Ray, *CEO*
Craig Ray, *Pr*
Matthew Ray, *VP*
▲ **EMP:** 19 **EST:** 1974
SQ FT: 40,000
SALES (est): 1.53MM **Privately Held**
Web: www.akron-gasket.com
SIC: **3053** Gaskets, all materials

(G-14022)
AMERICANA DEVELOPMENT INC
Also Called: Martin Wheel
342 West Ave (44278-2113)
PHONE..............................330 633-3278
Jimmy Yang, *Pr*
EMP: 100
SIC: **3714** 3011 Motor vehicle wheels and parts; Pneumatic tires, all types
PA: Americana Development, Inc.
7095 Americana Pkwy
Reynoldsburg OH 43068

(G-14023)
AVTEK INTERNATIONAL INC
382 Commerce St (44278-2135)
PHONE..............................330 633-7500
Thomas Milan, *Pr*
▲ **EMP:** 6 **EST:** 2001
SQ FT: 6,000
SALES (est): 575.72K **Privately Held**
Web: www.avtekintl.net
SIC: **3651** Household audio equipment

(G-14024)
CHEMIONICS CORPORATION
390 Munroe Falls Rd (44278-3399)
PHONE..............................330 733-8834
John Blackfan, *Genl Mgr*
Jim Ferguson, *
Mike Schmidt, *
▲ **EMP:** 32 **EST:** 1978
SQ FT: 80,000
SALES (est): 11.58MM
SALES (corp-wide): 202.63K **Privately Held**
Web: www.chemionics.com

Tallmadge - Summit County (G-14025)

SIC: 2869 3069 3087 2821 Plasticizers, organic: cyclic and acyclic; Reclaimed rubber and specialty rubber compounds; Custom compound purchased resins; Plastics materials and resins
HQ: Protech Powder Coatings, Inc.
21 Audrey Pl
Fairfield NJ 07004

(G-14025)
CIRCLE MOLD INCORPORATED
Also Called: Circle Mold & Machine Co
85 S Thomas Rd (44278-2107)
P.O. Box 513 (44278-0513)
PHONE................................330 633-7017
Edward A Siciliano, CEO
Edward T Siciliano, Pr
Agnes Siciliano, Sec
EMP: 18 EST: 1966
SQ FT: 12,000
SALES (est): 1.63MM Privately Held
Web: www.circlemold.com
SIC: 3599 Machine shop, jobbing and repair

(G-14026)
CLS FINISHING INC
409 Munroe Falls Rd (44278-3339)
P.O. Box 239 (44278-0239)
PHONE................................330 784-4134
Steven Kenneth Geer, Pr
EMP: 10 EST: 1990
SALES (est): 986.28K Privately Held
Web: www.clsfinishing.com
SIC: 3479 Coating of metals and formed products

(G-14027)
DIAMOND MOLD & DIE INC
109 E Garwood Dr (44278-1402)
PHONE................................330 633-5682
Joseph Speer, Pr
Helene Speer, VP
Silvia Schaefer, VP
Corinna Phillips, Sec
EMP: 10 EST: 1968
SQ FT: 5,000
SALES (est): 123.79K Privately Held
SIC: 3544 Forms (molds), for foundry and plastics working machinery

(G-14028)
DIVERSIFIED READY MIX LTD
1680 Southeast Ave (44278-3466)
PHONE................................330 628-3355
Todd Steinel, Prin
EMP: 8 EST: 2010
SALES (est): 150.04K Privately Held
SIC: 3273 Ready-mixed concrete

(G-14029)
E Z MACHINE INC
298 Northeast Ave (44278-1428)
PHONE................................330 784-3363
Eugene Zemlanfky, Pr
EMP: 8 EST: 1988
SALES (est): 763.18K Privately Held
SIC: 3599 Machine shop, jobbing and repair

(G-14030)
EMPIRE TIRE INC
445 Munroe Falls Rd (44278-3339)
PHONE................................330 983-4176
Mohammed Eid, Pr
Samir Abdallah, Pr
EMP: 8 EST: 2014
SALES (est): 301.84K Privately Held
SIC: 3011 Tires and inner tubes

(G-14031)
GREEN TECHNOLOGIES OHIO LLC
460 Tacoma Ave Ste B (44278-2756)
PHONE................................330 630-3350
EMP: 8 EST: 2013
SALES (est): 495.86K Privately Held
Web: www.greentechofohio.com
SIC: 3053 Gaskets, all materials

(G-14032)
HERMAN MACHINE INC
298 Northeast Ave (44278-1494)
PHONE................................330 633-3261
Suzanne E Rickards, Pr
EMP: 10 EST: 1919
SALES (est): 1.81MM Privately Held
Web: www.hermanmachine.net
SIC: 3599 7389 3429 Machine shop, jobbing and repair; Grinding, precision: commercial or industrial; Clamps, metal

(G-14033)
INDUSTRIAL CTRL DSIGN MINT INC
Also Called: Industrial Ctrl Design & Maint
311 Geneva Ave (44278-2702)
PHONE................................330 785-9840
David M Brown Junior, Pr
Jon Coles, VP
EMP: 10 EST: 1999
SQ FT: 14,000
SALES (est): 2.27MM Privately Held
Web: www.icdminc.com
SIC: 3613 7699 5063 Control panels, electric ; Engine repair and replacement, non-automotive; Switchboards

(G-14034)
KARG CORPORATION
241 Southwest Ave (44278-2239)
P.O. Box 197 (44278-0197)
PHONE................................330 633-4916
Michael Karg, Pr
EMP: 23 EST: 1947
SQ FT: 40,000
SALES (est): 2.88MM Privately Held
Web: www.kargcorp.com
SIC: 3552 Braiding machines, textile

(G-14035)
KELLERS FINE LINE WELDING LLC
440 Southeast Ave (44278-2855)
PHONE................................903 348-8304
Kevin Keller, Admn
EMP: 8 EST: 2012
SALES (est): 25.09K Privately Held
Web: www.kellersfinelinewelding.com
SIC: 7692 Welding repair

(G-14036)
MANUFACTURING CONCEPTS
409 Munroe Falls Rd (44278-3339)
P.O. Box 493 (44278-0493)
PHONE................................330 784-9054
Nancy Minne, Pt
Sue Brown, CFO
Mike Cast, Mgr
EMP: 17 EST: 2001
SQ FT: 14,500
SALES (est): 410.5K Privately Held
SIC: 3599 Machine shop, jobbing and repair

(G-14037)
MARIK SPRING INC
121 Northeast Ave (44278-1947)
PHONE................................330 564-0617
Greg A Bedrick, Pr
EMP: 36 EST: 1954
SQ FT: 35,000
SALES (est): 4.45MM Privately Held
Web: www.marikteam.com

SIC: 3493 3496 Flat springs, sheet or strip stock; Miscellaneous fabricated wire products

(G-14038)
MIDWEST FABRICATIONS INC
516 Commerce St (44278-2132)
P.O. Box 399 (44278-0399)
PHONE................................330 633-0191
Robert E Parsons, Pr
Timothy Parsons, *
Barbara Parsons, *
EMP: 21 EST: 1979
SQ FT: 9,000
SALES (est): 691.91K Privately Held
SIC: 3444 Sheet metal specialties, not stamped

(G-14039)
NORTHCOAST WOODCRAFT INC
939 Treat Blvd (44278-2637)
PHONE................................330 677-1189
Sandra Whited, Pr
EMP: 8 EST: 2011
SALES (est): 795.22K Privately Held
Web: www.northcoastwoodcraft.com
SIC: 3553 Cabinet makers' machinery

(G-14040)
NORTHEAST COATINGS INC
415 Munroe Falls Rd (44278-3339)
PHONE................................330 784-7773
Rod Fisher, Pr
Chad Fisher, Mng Pt
EMP: 18 EST: 1991
SQ FT: 12,000
SALES (est): 473.31K Privately Held
Web: www.necoatings.com
SIC: 3479 Coating of metals and formed products

(G-14041)
OWENS CORNING SALES LLC
Owens Corning
170 South Ave (44278-2813)
PHONE................................330 634-0460
Richard W Hooper, Manager
EMP: 102
SIC: 3275 3086 Gypsum products; Plastics foam products
HQ: Owens Corning Sales, Llc
1 Owens Corning Pkwy
Toledo OH 43659
419 248-8000

(G-14042)
OWENS CORNING SALES LLC
Also Called: Owens Corning
275 Southwest Ave (44278-2232)
PHONE................................330 633-6735
Joe Brackman, Brnch Mgr
EMP: 10
SQ FT: 300
SIC: 8711 8731 2821 Building construction consultant; Commercial physical research; Plastics materials and resins
HQ: Owens Corning Sales, Llc
1 Owens Corning Pkwy
Toledo OH 43659
419 248-8000

(G-14043)
P & P MOLD & DIE INC
1034 S Munroe Rd (44278-3336)
PHONE................................330 784-8333
Mary Jean Putra, Pr
William Putra, Treas
Emil Putra, Sec
EMP: 17 EST: 1985
SQ FT: 6,000
SALES (est): 2.47MM Privately Held

SIC: 3599 Machine shop, jobbing and repair

(G-14044)
PROMOLD INC
Also Called: Promold Gauer
487 Commerce St (44278-2134)
PHONE................................330 633-3532
Stefan K Schler, Pr
Mary Ann Schler, VP
EMP: 10 EST: 1977
SQ FT: 9,000
SALES (est): 1.64MM Privately Held
Web: www.gauermold.com
SIC: 3089 Injection molding of plastics

(G-14045)
RHOADS PRINT CENTER INC
Also Called: Copy Print
564 Washburn Rd (44278-2620)
PHONE................................330 678-2042
Richard M Rhoads, Pr
Jill Rhoads, Sec
EMP: 8 EST: 1971
SALES (est): 951.67K Privately Held
Web: www.copyprinttoday.com
SIC: 2752 7334 Offset printing; Photocopying and duplicating services

(G-14046)
SGB USA INC (DH)
180 South Ave (44278)
P.O. Box 188 (80403)
PHONE................................330 472-1187
Robert Ganser Junior, Pr
Asad Jawaid, VP
Denise Morgan, Sec
♦ EMP: 8 EST: 2009
SQ FT: 12,500
SALES (est): 9.97MM Privately Held
Web: www.sgbusa.com
SIC: 3612 Autotransformers, electric (power transformers)
HQ: Starkstrom - Geratebau Gesellschaft Mit Beschrankter Haftung
Ohmstr. 10
Regensburg BY 93055
94178410

(G-14047)
SOLUTION VENTURES INC
368 Vinewood Ave (44278-1351)
PHONE................................330 858-1111
Gary Alshouse, Prin
EMP: 6 EST: 2010
SALES (est): 103.23K Privately Held
SIC: 2759 Commercial printing, nec

(G-14048)
STEERE ENTERPRISES INC
303 Tacoma Ave (44278-2716)
PHONE................................330 633-4926
Mark Stahl, Brnch Mgr
EMP: 102
SALES (corp-wide): 44.42MM Privately Held
Web: www.steere.com
SIC: 3089 Injection molding of plastics
PA: Steere Enterprises, Inc.
285 Commerce St
Tallmadge OH 44278
330 633-4926

(G-14049)
STEERE ENTERPRISES INC (PA)
285 Commerce St (44278-2140)
PHONE................................330 633-4926
▲ EMP: 98 EST: 1949
SALES (est): 44.42MM
SALES (corp-wide): 44.42MM Privately Held
Web: www.steere.com

GEOGRAPHIC SECTION

SIC: 3089 3714 Plastics processing; Motor vehicle parts and accessories

(G-14050)
STORETEK ENGINEERING INC
399 Commerce St (44278-2134)
PHONE.................................330 294-0678
Jim Crews, *Pr*
EMP: 22 **EST:** 2008
SALES (est): 4.96MM **Privately Held**
Web: www.storetekeng.com
SIC: 8711 3559 Consulting engineer; Electronic component making machinery

(G-14051)
SUNSET GOLF LLC
71 West Ave Ste 6 (44278-2236)
P.O. Box 89 (44842-0089)
PHONE.................................419 994-5563
Dan Dieghan, *
▲ **EMP:** 7 **EST:** 1987
SQ FT: 40,000
SALES (est): 411.79K **Privately Held**
SIC: 3949 5941 Golf equipment; Sporting goods and bicycle shops

(G-14052)
TOTAL ENGINE AIRFLOW
285 West Ave (44278-2118)
PHONE.................................330 634-2155
Brian Tooley, *Owner*
Brian Tooley, *Prin*
EMP: 6 **EST:** 2008
SALES (est): 556.37K **Privately Held**
Web: www.totalengineairflow.com
SIC: 3714 Motor vehicle parts and accessories

(G-14053)
TRANS-FOAM INC
Also Called: Cutting Edge Roofing Products
281 Southwest Ave (44278-2232)
PHONE.................................330 630-9444
Todd Jordan, *Pr*
EMP: 9 **EST:** 2000
SALES (est): 1.08MM **Privately Held**
Web: www.jordanpower.com
SIC: 3086 Insulation or cushioning material, foamed plastics

(G-14054)
UNITED DENTAL LABORATORIES (PA)
261 South Ave (44278-2819)
P.O. Box 418 (44278-0418)
PHONE.................................330 253-1810
Richard Delapa Junior, *Pr*
EMP: 35 **EST:** 1923
SQ FT: 15,000
SALES (est): 2.54MM
SALES (corp-wide): 2.54MM **Privately Held**
Web: www.uniteddentallabs.com
SIC: 8072 3843 Denture production; Dental equipment and supplies

(G-14055)
UNIVERSAL POLYMER & RUBBER LTD
Also Called: Universal Rubber & Plastics
165 Northeast Ave (44278-1450)
PHONE.................................330 633-1666
EMP: 14
SALES (corp-wide): 25.23MM **Privately Held**
Web: www.universalpolymer.com
SIC: 3069 Molded rubber products
PA: Universal Polymer & Rubber, Ltd.
  15730 Madison Rd
  Middlefield OH 44062
  440 632-1691

(G-14056)
VERSATILE MACHINE
402 Commerce St (44278-2135)
PHONE.................................330 618-9895
Darren George, *Owner*
EMP: 8 **EST:** 2011
SALES (est): 624.45K **Privately Held**
SIC: 3599 Machine shop, jobbing and repair

(G-14057)
WHOLE SHOP INC
181 S Thomas Rd (44278-2752)
PHONE.................................330 630-5305
Nancie Scott, *Pr*
◆ **EMP:** 19 **EST:** 1974
SQ FT: 27,000
SALES (est): 5MM **Privately Held**
Web: www.wholeshopinc.com
SIC: 3441 7389 Fabricated structural metal; Metal cutting services

(G-14058)
XPANSION INSTRUMENT LLC
1425 Glenoak Dr (44278-2696)
PHONE.................................330 618-0062
EMP: 6 **EST:** 2006
SALES (est): 139.88K **Privately Held**
Web: www.xpansioninstruments.com
SIC: 3829 Measuring and controlling devices, nec

The Plains
Athens County

(G-14059)
TYJEN INC
Also Called: Slater Builders Supply
8 Slater Dr (45780-1321)
PHONE.................................740 797-4064
EMP: 9
SALES (corp-wide): 3.11MM **Privately Held**
Web: www.hockingvalleyconcrete.com
SIC: 3271 Blocks, concrete or cinder: standard
PA: Tyjen, Inc.
  35255 Hocking Dr
  Logan OH 43138
  740 380-3215

(G-14060)
WATTS ANTENNA COMPANY
70 N Plains Rd Ste H (45780-1156)
PHONE.................................740 797-9380
John Johnson, *Pr*
EMP: 7 **EST:** 1978
SALES (est): 589.93K **Privately Held**
Web: www.wattsantenna.com
SIC: 3812 3663 Search and navigation equipment; Antennas, transmitting and communications

Thompson
Geauga County

(G-14061)
PAINE FALLS CENTERPIN LLC
6342 Ledge Rd (44086-9732)
PHONE.................................440 867-4954
Adam N Demarco, *Prin*
EMP: 8 **EST:** 2010
SALES (est): 249.3K **Privately Held**
SIC: 3452 Pins

(G-14062)
R W SIDLEY INCORPORATED
Sidley Contracting
6900 Madison Rd (44086-9774)
P.O. Box 70 (44086-0070)
PHONE.................................440 298-3232
Ray Kennedy, *Mgr*
EMP: 104
SQ FT: 3,000
SALES (corp-wide): 83.57MM **Privately Held**
Web: www.rwsidley.com
SIC: 1799 5032 3272 Erection and dismantling of forms for poured concrete; Limestone; Concrete products, nec
PA: R. W. Sidley Incorporated
  436 Casement Ave
  Painesville OH 44077
  440 352-9343

(G-14063)
R W SIDLEY INCORPORATED
Also Called: Sidley Truck & Equipment
7123 Madison Rd (44086-9775)
P.O. Box 10 (44086-0010)
PHONE.................................440 298-3232
Rob Sidley, *Mgr*
EMP: 20
SALES (corp-wide): 83.57MM **Privately Held**
Web: www.rwsidley.com
SIC: 3273 Ready-mixed concrete
PA: R. W. Sidley Incorporated
  436 Casement Ave
  Painesville OH 44077
  440 352-9343

(G-14064)
SLABE
8000 Plank Rd (44086-9537)
PHONE.................................440 298-3693
David Slabe, *Prin*
EMP: 6 **EST:** 2007
SALES (est): 135.25K **Privately Held**
Web: www.slabemachine.com
SIC: 3599 Machine shop, jobbing and repair

Thornville
Perry County

(G-14065)
BUCKEYE LAKE WINERY
13750 Rosewood Dr Ne (43076-8117)
PHONE.................................614 439-7576
Tracy Higginbotham, *Prin*
EMP: 30 **EST:** 2013
SALES (est): 1.5MM **Privately Held**
Web: www.buckeyelakewinery.com
SIC: 2084 Wines

(G-14066)
JAY TEES LLC
8941 Somerset Rd (43076-9654)
PHONE.................................740 405-1579
Jay Tees, *Prin*
EMP: 37
SIC: 2752 Commercial printing, lithographic
PA: Jay Tees L.L.C.
  5227 National Rd Se
  Hebron OH 43025

(G-14067)
MOREHOUSE LOGGING LLC
13494 Sand Hollow Rd (43076-9377)
PHONE.................................740 501-0256
EMP: 6 **EST:** 2020
SALES (est): 641.63K **Privately Held**
Web: www.morehouselogging.com
SIC: 2411 Logging

(G-14068)
RE CONNORS CONSTRUCTION LTD
13352 Forrest Rd Ne (43076-9164)
PHONE.................................740 644-0261
EMP: 9 **EST:** 2014
SALES (est): 518.14K **Privately Held**
SIC: 1771 1761 3271 7389 Concrete work; Roofing, siding, and sheetmetal work; Concrete block and brick; Business Activities at Non-Commercial Site

(G-14069)
RECOVERY RM CANVAS & UPHL LLC
14935 Rustic Ln (43076-8970)
PHONE.................................740 246-6086
Clark Cook, *Prin*
EMP: 7 **EST:** 2008
SALES (est): 179.87K **Privately Held**
Web: www.wmblake.com
SIC: 2211 Canvas

(G-14070)
ROCKS GENERAL MAINTENANCE LLC
10019 Jacksontown Rd (43076-8802)
PHONE.................................740 323-4711
EMP: 7 **EST:** 2005
SALES (est): 510.74K **Privately Held**
SIC: 3498 Piping systems for pulp, paper, and chemical industries

(G-14071)
SHELLY MATERIALS INC
8775 Blackbird Ln (43076-9515)
PHONE.................................740 246-5009
Larry Shively, *VP*
EMP: 34
SALES (corp-wide): 32.72B **Privately Held**
Web: www.shellyco.com
SIC: 2951 Asphalt paving mixtures and blocks
HQ: Shelly Materials, Inc.
  80 Park Dr
  Thornville OH 43076
  740 246-6315

(G-14072)
SHELLY MATERIALS INC (DH)
Also Called: Shelly Company, The
80 Park Dr (43076-9397)
P.O. Box 266 (43076-0266)
PHONE.................................740 246-6315
John Power, *Pr*
Ted Lemon, *
Doug Radabaugh N, *Sec*
EMP: 100 **EST:** 1938
SALES (est): 461.47MM
SALES (corp-wide): 32.72B **Privately Held**
Web: www.shellyco.com
SIC: 1422 1442 2951 4492 Crushed and broken limestone; Construction sand and gravel; Concrete, asphaltic (not from refineries); Tugboat service
HQ: Shelly Company
  80 Park Dr
  Thornville OH 43076
  740 246-6315

Thurman
Gallia County

(G-14073)
S & J LUMBER COMPANY LLC
Also Called: S & J Lumber
3667 Garners Ford Rd (45685-9301)
PHONE.................................740 245-5804
John Smith, *Owner*
EMP: 18 **EST:** 1980

Tiffin - Seneca County (G-14074) — GEOGRAPHIC SECTION

SQ FT: 3,000
SALES (est): 2.03MM **Privately Held**
SIC: **2421** Sawmills and planing mills, general

Tiffin
Seneca County

(G-14074)
AGRATI - TIFFIN LLC
1988 S County Road 593 (44883-9275)
PHONE..............................419 447-2221
Philip Johnson, *CEO*
EMP: 54 EST: 2007
SALES (est): 21.77MM
SALES (corp-wide): 706.55MM **Privately Held**
Web: www.agrati.com
SIC: **3452** Screws, metal
HQ: Agrati - Park Forest, Llc
   24000 S Western Ave
   Park Forest IL 60466
   708 228-5193

(G-14075)
AMERICAN FINE SINTER CO LTD
957 N County Road 11 (44883-9415)
PHONE..............................419 443-8880
Toshihiro Nakashima, *Pr*
Jeremy A Gibson, *
▲ EMP: 125 EST: 2001
SQ FT: 80,000
SALES (est): 34.06MM **Privately Held**
Web: www.afsus.com
SIC: **3519** Parts and accessories, internal combustion engines
PA: Fine Sinter Co., Ltd.
   1189-11, Nishinohora, Akechicho
   Kasugai AIC 480-0

(G-14076)
ARNOLD MACHINE INC
Also Called: Arnold Machine
19 Heritage Dr (44883-9503)
PHONE..............................419 443-1818
Zachary W Arnold, *Pr*
EMP: 13 EST: 1994
SQ FT: 22,000
SALES (est): 4.78MM **Privately Held**
Web: www.arnoldmachine.com
SIC: **3599** Machine shop, jobbing and repair

(G-14077)
B J PALLETT
324 4th Ave (44883-1227)
PHONE..............................419 447-9665
Bernard Breidenbach Junior, *Owner*
EMP: 9 EST: 1986
SQ FT: 27,500
SALES (est): 880.11K **Privately Held**
SIC: **2448** Pallets, wood

(G-14078)
BALLREICH BROS INC
Also Called: Ballreichs Potato Chips Snacks
186 Ohio Ave (44883-1746)
PHONE..............................419 447-1814
EMP: 105
Web: www.ballreich.com
SIC: **2096** **2099** **4226** Potato chips and other potato-based snacks; Food preparations, nec; Special warehousing and storage, nec

(G-14079)
BSFC LLC (HQ)
186 Ohio Ave (44883-1746)
PHONE..............................419 447-1814
Thomas Miller, *Pr*
EMP: 55 EST: 2019
SALES (est): 10.57MM
SALES (corp-wide): 12.01MM **Privately Held**
Web: www.ballreich.com
SIC: **2096** Potato chips and similar snacks
PA: Grippo Foods, Inc.
   6750 Colerain Ave
   Cincinnati OH 45239
   513 923-1900

(G-14080)
CARMEUSE LIME INC
1967 W County Rd 42 (44883)
PHONE..............................419 986-2000
Amy Kuhn, *Brnch Mgr*
EMP: 13
SALES (corp-wide): 2.67MM **Privately Held**
Web: www.carmeuse.com
SIC: **1422** Agricultural limestone, ground
HQ: Carmeuse Lime, Inc.
   11 Stanwix St Fl 21
   Pittsburgh PA 15222
   412 995-5500

(G-14081)
CCP NEWCO LLC
1780 S County Road 1 (44883-8800)
PHONE..............................419 448-1700
Robert Guerra, *CEO*
EMP: 478
SALES (corp-wide): 494.03MM **Privately Held**
SIC: **3089** Injection molding of plastics
HQ: Ccp Newco Llc
   11840 Wstline Indus Dr St
   Saint Louis MO 63146
   314 656-4301

(G-14082)
CUSTOM MACHINE INC
3315 W Township Road 158 (44883-9453)
PHONE..............................419 986-5122
David Hammer, *Pr*
Jeffery Hammer, *
Phyllis Hammer, *
EMP: 24 EST: 1979
SQ FT: 19,200
SALES (est): 1.86MM **Privately Held**
Web: www.custom-machine-inc.com
SIC: **3544** **3599** **7692** Special dies and tools; Machine shop, jobbing and repair; Welding repair

(G-14083)
DOREL HOME FURNISHINGS INC
Also Called: Ameriwood Industries
458 2nd Ave (44883-9358)
PHONE..............................419 447-7448
Rick Jackson, *Pr*
EMP: 67
SALES (corp-wide): 1.57B **Privately Held**
Web: www.dorel.com
SIC: **2511** Console tables: wood
HQ: Dorel Home Furnishings, Inc.
   410 E 1st St S
   Wright City MO 63390
   636 745-3351

(G-14084)
E SYSTEMS DESIGN & AUTOMTN INC
226 Heritage Dr (44883-9504)
P.O. Box 158 (44883-0158)
PHONE..............................419 443-0220
Don Bagent, *Pr*
Brenda Bagent, *Treas*
EMP: 8 EST: 1994
SQ FT: 9,000
SALES (est): 835.59K **Privately Held**
Web: www.esystems-usa.com
SIC: **3599** Machine shop, jobbing and repair

(G-14085)
F & F SHTMTL & FABRICATION LLC
4720 W Us Highway 224 (44883-8887)
PHONE..............................567 938-8788
EMP: 11 EST: 2018
SALES (est): 1.13MM **Privately Held**
Web: www.ffsheetmetal.com
SIC: **3444** **3441** Sheet metalwork; Fabricated structural metal

(G-14086)
FRANTZ WELL SERVICING INC
7227 N County Road 33 (44883-9611)
PHONE..............................419 992-4564
Roger Frantz, *Prin*
EMP: 8 EST: 1997
SALES (est): 412.56K **Privately Held**
SIC: **1389** Oil field services, nec

(G-14087)
FRY FOODS INC
99 Maule Rd (44883-9400)
P.O. Box 837 (44883-0837)
PHONE..............................419 448-0831
Norman Fry, *Pr*
Beverly Fry, *
Philip Fry, *
Jerry Kaufman, *
David Fry, *
▼ EMP: 50 EST: 1961
SQ FT: 40,000
SALES (est): 22.37MM **Privately Held**
Web: www.fryfoods.com
SIC: **2038** **2033** Snacks, incl. onion rings, cheese sticks, etc.; Canned fruits and specialties

(G-14088)
J H PLASTICS INC
4720 W Us Highway 224 (44883-8887)
PHONE..............................419 937-2035
EMP: 6 EST: 2010
SALES (est): 246.76K **Privately Held**
SIC: **3089** Injection molding of plastics

(G-14089)
JOHNS WELDING & TOWING INC
850 N County Road 11 (44883-9415)
PHONE..............................419 447-8937
Joseph Keller, *Pr*
James Keller, *VP*
EMP: 19 EST: 1956
SQ FT: 20,000
SALES (est): 448.77K **Privately Held**
Web: www.johnsweldingandtowing.com
SIC: **7549** **7692** Towing services; Welding repair

(G-14090)
LAMINATE TECHNOLOGIES INC (PA)
Also Called: Lam Tech
161 Maule Rd (44883-9400)
PHONE..............................800 231-2523
Frederick E Zoeller, *Pr*
A Louise Zoeller, *
Allan Funkhouser, *
▲ EMP: 55 EST: 1985
SQ FT: 80,000
SALES (est): 44.44MM
SALES (corp-wide): 44.44MM **Privately Held**
Web: www.lamtech.net
SIC: **2439** **2891** **2672** Structural wood members, nec; Adhesives and sealants; Paper; coated and laminated, nec

(G-14091)
M & B ASPHALT COMPANY INC (PA)
1525 W County Road 42 (44883)
P.O. Box 130 (44861-0130)
PHONE..............................419 992-4235
EMP: 15 EST: 1946
SALES (est): 7.66MM
SALES (corp-wide): 7.66MM **Privately Held**
Web: www.mgqinc.com
SIC: **1429** **2951** **1611** **2952** Grits mining (crushed stone); Asphalt and asphaltic paving mixtures (not from refineries); Highway and street paving contractor; Asphalt felts and coatings

(G-14092)
M G Q INC
Also Called: Maple Grove Companies
1525 W County Road 42 (44883-8457)
P.O. Box 130 (44861-0130)
PHONE..............................419 992-4236
Lynn Radabaugh, *Pr*
Tim Bell, *
Lynn Radabaugh, *VP*
Bob Chesebro, *
Bruce Chubb, *
▲ EMP: 42 EST: 1999
SALES (est): 8.94MM **Privately Held**
Web: www.mgqinc.com
SIC: **4214** **1481** Local trucking with storage; Mine and quarry services, nonmetallic minerals

(G-14093)
MAPLE GROVE MATERIALS INC
1525 W City Rd Ste 42 (44883)
P.O. Box 136 (44861-0136)
PHONE..............................419 992-4235
Tim Bell, *Pr*
Lynn O Radabaugh, *VP*
Robert Chesebro, *Sec*
EMP: 9 EST: 1984
SQ FT: 2,000
SALES (est): 1.85MM
SALES (corp-wide): 7.66MM **Privately Held**
Web: www.mgqinc.com
SIC: **3281** Limestone, cut and shaped
PA: M. & B. Asphalt Company, Inc.
   1525 W Seneca Cnty Rd 42
   Tiffin OH 44883
   419 992-4235

(G-14094)
ML ADVERTISING & DESIGN LLC
Also Called: Mlad Graphic Design Services
185 Jefferson St (44883-2865)
PHONE..............................419 447-6523
Mark A Levans, *Managing Member*
EMP: 6 EST: 1999
SQ FT: 3,000
SALES (est): 577.29K **Privately Held**
Web: www.mlad.com
SIC: **7336** **2759** Graphic arts and related design; Commercial printing, nec

(G-14095)
NATIONAL MACHINERY LLC (HQ)
161 Greenfield St (44883-2471)
PHONE..............................419 447-5211
◆ EMP: 310 EST: 2002
SQ FT: 650,000
SALES (est): 95.99MM
SALES (corp-wide): 174.06MM **Privately Held**
Web: www.nationalmachinery.com
SIC: **3599** Machine shop, jobbing and repair
PA: Nm Group Global, Llc
   161 Greenfield St
   Tiffin OH 44883

419 447-5211

(G-14096)
NMGG CTG LLC (HQ)
Also Called: Cleaning Technologies Grp
161 Greenfield St (44883-2499)
PHONE..............................419 447-5211
Andrew H Kalnow, *CEO*
Robert J Foster, *CFO*
EMP: 75 **EST:** 2006
SALES (est): 53.03MM
SALES (corp-wide): 174.06MM **Privately Held**
Web: www.nationalmachinery.com
SIC: 3569 3541 Blast cleaning equipment, dustless; Ultrasonic metal cutting machine tools
PA: Nm Group Global, Llc
161 Greenfield St
Tiffin OH 44883
419 447-5211

(G-14097)
OGDEN NEWSPAPERS OHIO INC
Also Called: Advertiser-Tribune, The
320 Nelson St (44883-8956)
P.O. Box 778 (44883-0778)
PHONE..............................419 448-3200
EMP: 12 **EST:** 1991
SALES (est): 837.83K **Privately Held**
Web: www.advertiser-tribune.com
SIC: 2711 Newspapers, publishing and printing

(G-14098)
OHIO INDUSTRIAL COATING CORP
880 S Bon Aire Ave (44883-2581)
PHONE..............................567 230-6719
Zech Cunningham, *Prin*
EMP: 6 **EST:** 2015
SALES (est): 135.84K **Privately Held**
SIC: 3479 Metal coating and allied services

(G-14099)
PALMER BROS TRANSIT MIX CON
1900 S County Road 1 (44883-8826)
PHONE..............................419 447-2018
Rick Corbeck, *Mgr*
EMP: 8
SALES (corp-wide): 5.86MM **Privately Held**
SIC: 3273 Ready-mixed concrete
PA: Palmer Bros Transit Mix Concrete Inc
12205 E Gypsy Lane Rd
Bowling Green OH 43402
419 352-4681

(G-14100)
QUALITY WLDG & FABRICATION LLC
82 N Washington St (44883-2325)
PHONE..............................567 220-6639
EMP: 7 **EST:** 2015
SALES (est): 249.01K **Privately Held**
Web: www.qualityweldingandfab.com
SIC: 7692 Welding repair

(G-14101)
QUICK TAB II INC (PA)
241 Heritage Dr (44883-9504)
P.O. Box 723 (44883-0723)
PHONE..............................419 448-6622
Chuck Daughenbaugn, *CEO*
Charles Eingle, *
Mike Daughenbaugh, *
▼ **EMP:** 64 **EST:** 1992
SQ FT: 30,000
SALES (est): 11.59MM **Privately Held**
Web: www.qt2.com

SIC: 2752 5112 2791 2789 Forms, business: lithographed; Stationery and office supplies; Typesetting; Bookbinding and related work

(G-14102)
SARKA SHTMTL & FABRICATION INC
Also Called: Sarka Conveyor
70 Clinton Ave (44883-1620)
PHONE..............................419 447-4377
Kendall T Parker, *Pr*
Larry D Sarka, *Stockholder*
EMP: 22 **EST:** 1985
SQ FT: 11,000
SALES (est): 5.85MM **Privately Held**
Web: www.sarkaconveyors.com
SIC: 3444 Sheet metalwork

(G-14103)
SEISLOVE VAULT & SEPTIC TANKS
Also Called: Seislove Brial Vlts Sptic Tnks
2168 S State Route 100 (44883-3699)
PHONE..............................419 447-5473
P David Seislove, *Pr*
EMP: 7 **EST:** 1946
SQ FT: 13,000
SALES (est): 481.13K **Privately Held**
Web: www.seislovesinc.com
SIC: 3272 Burial vaults, concrete or precast terrazzo

(G-14104)
SENECA ENVIRONMENTAL PRODUCTS INC
1685 S County Road 1 (44883-9746)
PHONE..............................419 447-1282
EMP: 40
SIC: 3443 3625 3564 Tanks, standard or custom fabricated: metal plate; Noise control equipment; Purification and dust collection equipment

(G-14105)
SENECA SHEET METAL COMPANY
Also Called: Sheet Metal Fabricator
277 Water Street (44883-1698)
PHONE..............................419 447-8434
Robert J Fulton, *Pr*
George H Wells, *VP*
EMP: 10 **EST:** 1966
SQ FT: 55,000
SALES (est): 1.42MM **Privately Held**
Web: www.senecasheetmetal.com
SIC: 3444 1761 Sheet metal specialties, not stamped; Sheet metal work, nec

(G-14106)
STACY EQUIPMENT CO
325 Hall St (44883-1419)
PHONE..............................419 447-6903
Ben Chaffee, *Prin*
EMP: 9 **EST:** 2016
SALES (est): 152.41K **Privately Held**
SIC: 3535 Conveyors and conveying equipment

(G-14107)
TAIHO CORPORATION OF AMERICA
Also Called: Taiho
194 Heritage Dr (44883-9503)
PHONE..............................419 443-1645
Shigeki Awazu, *Pr*
Karl Kortlandt, *VP*
Mike Shannaberger, *VP*
◆ **EMP:** 120 **EST:** 1981
SQ FT: 140
SALES (est): 24.87MM **Privately Held**
Web: www.taihousa.com

SIC: 3714 3585 3568 Air conditioner parts, motor vehicle; Refrigeration and heating equipment; Power transmission equipment, nec
PA: Taiho Kogyo Co., Ltd.
3-65, Midorigaoka
Toyota AIC 471-0

(G-14108)
TIFFIN CANDLE CO LTD
17 Lelar St (44883-3422)
PHONE..............................567 268-9015
Brian Bilger, *Prin*
EMP: 7 **EST:** 2017
SALES (est): 39.69K **Privately Held**
SIC: 3999 Candles

(G-14109)
TIFFIN FOUNDRY & MACHINE INC
423 W Adams St (44883-9284)
P.O. Box 37 (44883-0037)
PHONE..............................419 447-3991
Steven Sobol, *Pr*
Melvin A Jones, *
EMP: 35 **EST:** 2004
SQ FT: 45,000
SALES (est): 4.49MM **Privately Held**
Web: www.tiffinfoundry.com
SIC: 3592 3599 3322 3325 Carburetors, pistons, piston rings and valves; Machine shop, jobbing and repair; Malleable iron foundries; Steel foundries, nec

(G-14110)
TIFFIN METAL PRODUCTS CO (PA)
450 Wall St (44883-1366)
PHONE..............................419 447-8414
Richard S Harrison, *Pr*
Richard M Wyka, *
Ron Myers, *
Michael R Reser, *
Timothy Demith, *
▼ **EMP:** 108 **EST:** 1903
SQ FT: 120,000
SALES (est): 55.27MM
SALES (corp-wide): 55.27MM **Privately Held**
Web: www.steelesolutions.com
SIC: 2599 2542 2531 2522 Boards: planning, display, notice; Lockers (not refrigerated): except wood; Public building and related furniture; Office furniture, except wood

(G-14111)
TIFFIN PAPER COMPANY (PA)
Also Called: TPC Food Service
401 Wall St (44883-1351)
P.O. Box 129 (44883-0129)
PHONE..............................419 447-2121
Thomas M Maiberger, *Pr*
Tony Paulus, *
Kevin Maiberger, *
EMP: 40 **EST:** 1963
SQ FT: 40,000
SALES (est): 29.72MM
SALES (corp-wide): 29.72MM **Privately Held**
Web: www.tpcfoodservice.com
SIC: 5149 2064 Groceries and related products, nec; Candy and other confectionery products

(G-14112)
TIFFIN SCENIC STUDIOS INC (PA)
Also Called: Atlantic and Prfmce Rigging
146 Riverside Dr (44883-1644)
P.O. Box 39 (44883-0039)
PHONE..............................800 445-1546
Brad Hossler, *Pr*
Steve Maiberger, *

Steve Everhart, *
EMP: 33 **EST:** 1901
SQ FT: 24,000
SALES (est): 6.63MM
SALES (corp-wide): 6.63MM **Privately Held**
Web: www.tiffinscenic.com
SIC: 2391 3999 Draperies, plastic and textile: from purchased materials; Stage hardware and equipment, except lighting

(G-14113)
TOLEDO MOLDING & DIE LLC
1441 Maule Rd (44883-9130)
PHONE..............................419 443-9031
Dave Spott, *Mgr*
EMP: 263
Web: www.tmdinc.com
SIC: 3089 Automotive parts, plastic
HQ: Toledo Molding & Die, Llc
1429 Coining Dr
Toledo OH 43612

(G-14114)
VIEWPOINT GRAPHIC DESIGN
132 S Washington St (44883-2840)
PHONE..............................419 447-6073
Pete Krupp, *Owner*
EMP: 6 **EST:** 1985
SQ FT: 5,000
SALES (est): 484.59K **Privately Held**
Web: www.viewpointtiffin.com
SIC: 2759 Screen printing

(G-14115)
WEBSTER INDUSTRIES INC (PA)
Also Called: Webster Manufacturing Company
325 Hall St (44883-1419)
PHONE..............................419 447-8232
Andrew J Felter, *Pr*
Fredric C Spurck, *
Nicholas D Spurck, *
Dean Bogner, *
Steven Hickey, *
◆ **EMP:** 295 **EST:** 1876
SQ FT: 250,000
SALES (est): 76.75MM
SALES (corp-wide): 76.75MM **Privately Held**
Web: www.websterchain.com
SIC: 3535 Bulk handling conveyor systems

Tiltonsville
Jefferson County

(G-14116)
CROFT & SON MFG INC
509 Highland Ave (43963-1110)
P.O. Box 66 (43963-0066)
PHONE..............................740 859-2200
Samuel E Croft, *Pr*
Shirley Pielech, *Sec*
Kathy Lester, *Sec*
EMP: 6 **EST:** 1977
SQ FT: 3,600
SALES (est): 470.63K **Privately Held**
SIC: 3599 Machine shop, jobbing and repair

(G-14117)
WALDEN INDUSTRIES INC
Also Called: Belot Concrete Block
101 Walden Ave (43963-1130)
P.O. Box 68 (43963-0068)
PHONE..............................740 633-5971
TOLL FREE: 800
EMP: 20 **EST:** 1995
SALES (est): 2.02MM **Privately Held**
Web: www.waldenindustries.com

Tipp City
Miami County

(G-14118)
A & B FOUNDRY LLC
Also Called: A&B Fndry McHning Fabrications
4754 Us Route 40 (45371-9481)
PHONE..................................937 412-1900
EMP: 11
SALES (corp-wide): 2.63MM **Privately Held**
Web: www.abfoundry.com
SIC: 3559 Foundry machinery and equipment
PA: A & B Foundry Llc
 835 N Main St
 Franklin OH 45005
 937 369-3007

(G-14119)
ABBOTT LABORATORIES
1 Abbott Park Way (45371-1285)
PHONE..................................937 503-3405
▲ **EMP:** 15
SALES (corp-wide): 40.11B **Publicly Held**
Web: www.abbottnutrition.com
SIC: 2834 Pharmaceutical preparations
PA: Abbott Laboratories
 100 Abbott Park Rd
 Abbott Park IL 60064
 224 667-6100

(G-14120)
ACCU-TOOL INC
9765 Julie Ct (45371-9000)
P.O. Box 440 (45371-0440)
PHONE..................................937 667-5878
EMP: 8 **EST:** 1983
SQ FT: 7,500
SALES (est): 907.08K **Privately Held**
Web: www.accu-tool.com
SIC: 3544 3599 Special dies and tools; Machine shop, jobbing and repair

(G-14121)
ACON INC
11408 Dogleg Rd (45371-9516)
PHONE..................................513 276-2111
Thomas Mescher, Pr
EMP: 7 **EST:** 1970
SQ FT: 12,000
SALES (est): 580.09K **Privately Held**
Web: www.aconinc.net
SIC: 3625 Noise control equipment

(G-14122)
ALPINE GAGE INC
4325 Lisa Dr (45371-9463)
PHONE..................................937 669-8665
Dennis Tresslar, Pr
EMP: 6 **EST:** 2002
SQ FT: 4,400
SALES (est): 478.86K **Privately Held**
Web: www.alpinegage.com
SIC: 3544 Special dies and tools

(G-14123)
B S F INC
320b S 5th St (45371-1625)
PHONE..................................937 890-6121
Tim Boocher, Mgr
EMP: 10
SALES (corp-wide): 2.47MM **Privately Held**
Web: www.bsfinc.net
SIC: 3498 3568 3599 Couplings, pipe: fabricated from purchased pipe; Couplings, shaft: rigid, flexible, universal joint, etc.; Machine shop, jobbing and repair
PA: B S F, Inc.
 8895 N Dixie Dr
 Dayton OH 45414
 937 890-6121

(G-14124)
C IMPERIAL INC
Also Called: Imperial Castings
1322 Commerce Park Dr (45371-3323)
PHONE..................................937 669-5620
Larry Haney, Pr
EMP: 6 **EST:** 1978
SQ FT: 9,000
SALES (est): 628.25K **Privately Held**
Web: www.spcastings.com
SIC: 3443 Fabricated plate work (boiler shop)

(G-14125)
CANINE CREATIONS INC
120b W Broadway St # A (45371-1638)
PHONE..................................937 667-8576
Robin Riedel, Prin
Robert Reidel, Owner
EMP: 7 **EST:** 2004
SALES (est): 343.56K **Privately Held**
Web: www.canine-creations.net
SIC: 0752 3999 Grooming services, pet and animal specialties; Pet supplies

(G-14126)
CAPTOR CORPORATION
5040 S County Road 25a (45371-2899)
PHONE..................................937 667-8484
Donald Cooper, Ch
D Scott Timms, *
Carolyn Kiser, *
Tom Dysinger, Corporate Secretary*
EMP: 85 **EST:** 1965
SQ FT: 35,000
SALES (est): 18.44MM **Privately Held**
Web: www.captorcorp.com
SIC: 3679 Electronic circuits

(G-14127)
CASE CRAFTERS INC
211 S 1st St (45371-1705)
PHONE..................................937 667-9473
Dan Paugh, Pr
Steven Paugh, VP
EMP: 8 **EST:** 1992
SQ FT: 9,200
SALES (est): 955.8K **Privately Held**
Web: www.casecraftersinc.com
SIC: 2541 1751 Cabinets, except refrigerated: show, display, etc.: wood; Cabinet and finish carpentry

(G-14128)
CCR FABRICATIONS LLC
40 Ginghamsburg Rd (45371-9179)
PHONE..................................937 667-6632
Scott Walker, Prin
EMP: 7 **EST:** 2005
SALES (est): 190K **Privately Held**
SIC: 3499 7692 Fabricated metal products, nec; Welding repair

(G-14129)
CHART-TECH TOOL INC
4060 Lisa Dr (45371)
P.O. Box 477 (45371)
PHONE..................................937 667-3543
Eugene Crompton, Pr
Lee Scheidweiler, VP
EMP: 31 **EST:** 1965
SQ FT: 30,000
SALES (est): 1.67MM **Privately Held**
Web: www.ctti-inc.com
SIC: 3541 3545 3544 Machine tools, metal cutting type; Gauges (machine tool accessories); Special dies, tools, jigs, and fixtures

(G-14130)
CONCRETE SEALANTS INC
Also Called: Conseal
9325 State Route 201 (45371)
PHONE..................................937 845-8776
Howard E Wingert, Pr
Cynthia Wingert, *
◆ **EMP:** 50 **EST:** 1970
SQ FT: 100,000
SALES (est): 12.53MM **Privately Held**
Web: www.conseal.com
SIC: 3053 2891 2821 2822 Gaskets; packing and sealing devices; Sealants; Plastics materials and resins; Synthetic rubber

(G-14131)
DAP PRODUCTS INC
Also Called: Darusta Woodlife Division
875 N 3rd St (45371-3053)
PHONE..................................937 667-4461
Gary Williams, Brnch Mgr
EMP: 72
SALES (corp-wide): 7.26B **Publicly Held**
Web: www.dap.com
SIC: 2891 2851 Caulking compounds; Paints and paint additives
HQ: Dap Products Inc.
 2400 Boston St Ste 200
 Baltimore MD 21224
 800 543-3840

(G-14132)
DUNCAN TOOL INC
9790 Julie Ct (45371-9000)
PHONE..................................937 667-9364
Sandra L Duncan, Pr
Dave Duncan, VP
▲ **EMP:** 10 **EST:** 1992
SQ FT: 5,500
SALES (est): 1.64MM **Privately Held**
Web: www.duncantool.com
SIC: 3544 3599 Special dies and tools; Machine shop, jobbing and repair

(G-14133)
EMPIRE MACHINE LLC
222 N 6th St (45371-1830)
PHONE..................................937 506-7793
EMP: 7 **EST:** 2019
SALES (est): 383.31K **Privately Held**
Web: empire-machine-llc.business.site
SIC: 3599 Machine shop, jobbing and repair

(G-14134)
ENVIRNMENT CTRL STHWEST OHIO I
7939 S County Road 25a (45371-9107)
PHONE..................................937 669-9900
EMP: 22 **EST:** 2012
SALES (est): 2.13MM **Privately Held**
Web: www.environmentcontrol.com
SIC: 3822 Environmental controls

(G-14135)
FIELD STONE INC
2750 Us Route 40 (45371-9230)
PHONE..................................937 898-3236
Paul Carmack, Pr
◆ **EMP:** 22 **EST:** 1973
SQ FT: 18,000
SALES (est): 626.08K **Privately Held**
SIC: 3586 3432 Gasoline pumps, measuring or dispensing; Plumbing fixture fittings and trim

(G-14136)
HEIRLOOM WOODWORKS LLC
5930 Rudy Rd (45371-8421)
PHONE..................................937 430-0394
EMP: 6 **EST:** 2010
SALES (est): 254.4K **Privately Held**
SIC: 2431 Millwork

(G-14137)
HIGH-TEC INDUSTRIAL SERVICES ✪
15 Industry Park Ct (45371-3060)
PHONE..................................937 667-1772
Christopher Griffin, Pr
Daniel Whitlock, VP
Kyle Packer, Sec
EMP: 60 **EST:** 2023
SQ FT: 11,000
SALES (est): 2.6MM **Privately Held**
SIC: 1799 7349 3589 Construction site cleanup; Building and office cleaning services; Commercial cleaning equipment

(G-14138)
INDIAN CREEK FABRICATORS INC
1350 Commerce Park Dr (45371-3323)
PHONE..................................937 667-7214
Andrea Dakin, Pr
Michael Dakin, *
EMP: 50 **EST:** 1986
SQ FT: 65,000
SALES (est): 9.66MM **Privately Held**
Web: www.indiancreekfab.com
SIC: 3446 3444 3443 3441 Architectural metalwork; Sheet metalwork; Fabricated plate work (boiler shop); Fabricated structural metal

(G-14139)
J & L WOOD PRODUCTS INC (PA)
155 Lightner Rd (45371-9296)
P.O. Box 69 (45371-0069)
PHONE..................................937 667-4064
Jeffrey Herzog, Pr
Kevin Mcclurg, VP
▲ **EMP:** 32 **EST:** 1968
SQ FT: 30,000
SALES (est): 4.54MM
SALES (corp-wide): 4.54MM **Privately Held**
Web: www.jlwoodproducts.com
SIC: 2448 2441 2449 Pallets, wood; Nailed wood boxes and shook; Rectangular boxes and crates, wood

(G-14140)
LAWN AID INC
480 Hathaway Trl (45371-1105)
PHONE..................................417 533-5555
Robert A Pratt, Prin
EMP: 7 **EST:** 1979
SALES (est): 88.38K **Privately Held**
SIC: 3699 Electrical equipment and supplies, nec

(G-14141)
METEOR CREATIVE INC (DH)
1414 Commerce Park Dr (45371-2845)
PHONE..................................800 273-1535
Thorsten Conrad, VP
EMP: 20 **EST:** 2021
SALES (est): 58.25MM
SALES (corp-wide): 355.83K **Privately Held**
Web: www.meteor-creative.com
SIC: 3089 Extruded finished plastics products, nec
HQ: Meteor Group Gmbh
 Gabrielenstr. 9
 Munchen BY 80636
 89262048400

GEOGRAPHIC SECTION — Tipp City - Miami County (G-14166)

(G-14142)
MORE MANUFACTURING LLC
4025 Lisa Dr Ste A (45371-9462)
PHONE..............................937 233-3898
Matt Lovelace, *Managing Member*
EMP: 12 **EST:** 2007
SQ FT: 6,000
SALES (est): 2.02MM **Privately Held**
Web: www.moremfg.com
SIC: 3541 Machine tool replacement & repair parts, metal cutting types

(G-14143)
MUTUAL TOOL LLC
1350 Commerce Park Dr (45371-3323)
PHONE..............................937 667-5818
EMP: 35 **EST:** 2004
SQ FT: 31,200
SALES (est): 894.09K **Privately Held**
Web: www.indiancreekfab.com
SIC: 3599 3544 Machine shop, jobbing and repair; Special dies, tools, jigs, and fixtures

(G-14144)
N & G TAKHAR OIL LLC
4365 Lisa Dr (45371-9263)
PHONE..............................937 604-0012
Amarjit Signh, *Prin*
EMP: 8 **EST:** 2011
SALES (est): 628.05K **Privately Held**
SIC: 1382 Oil and gas exploration services

(G-14145)
ODAWARA AUTOMATION INC
4805 S County Road 25a (45371-2900)
PHONE..............................937 667-8433
Takayuki Tsugawa, *CEO*
Christopher Spejna, *Pr*
▲ **EMP:** 37 **EST:** 1971
SQ FT: 51,000
SALES (est): 8.99MM **Privately Held**
Web: www.odawara.com
SIC: 3599 Custom machinery
PA: Odawara Engineering Co.,Ltd.
　1577, Matsudasoryo, Matsudamachi
　Ashigara Kami-Gun KNG 258-0

(G-14146)
PDQ TECHNOLOGIES INC
2500 Us Route 40 (45371-9131)
PHONE..............................937 274-4958
Robert Adams, *Admn*
EMP: 20 **EST:** 1989
SALES (est): 484.71K **Privately Held**
SIC: 3599 Machine shop, jobbing and repair

(G-14147)
PECO HOLDINGS CORP (PA)
6555 S State Route 202 (45371-9094)
PHONE..............................937 667-5705
Michael Van Haaren, *Pr*
James Zahora, *VP*
William Rosenberg, *CFO*
EMP: 56 **EST:** 2005
SALES (est): 15.63MM **Privately Held**
SIC: 3599 3548 3549 Machine shop, jobbing and repair; Welding apparatus; Assembly machines, including robotic

(G-14148)
PRECISION STRIP INC
315 Park Ave (45371-1887)
PHONE..............................937 667-6255
Jerry Huber, *Mgr*
EMP: 74
SQ FT: 3,080
SALES (corp-wide): 14.81B **Publicly Held**
Web: www.precision-strip.com
SIC: 4225 3312 General warehousing and storage; Blast furnaces and steel mills
HQ: Precision Strip Inc.
　86 S Ohio St
　Minster OH 45865
　419 628-2343

(G-14149)
PROCESS EQP CO WLDG SVCS LLC
Also Called: Peco Welding Services LLC
319 S 1st St (45371-1707)
PHONE..............................937 667-4451
Michael Loughman, *Managing Member*
EMP: 6 **EST:** 2018
SALES (est): 218.92K **Privately Held**
SIC: 7692 Automotive welding

(G-14150)
PROTO PLASTICS INC
316 Park Ave (45371)
PHONE..............................937 667-8416
Thomas A Gagnon, *Pr*
Thomas Gagnon, *
Sue Gagnon, *
▲ **EMP:** 42 **EST:** 1969
SQ FT: 62,000
SALES (est): 9.23MM **Privately Held**
Web: www.protoplastics.com
SIC: 3089 3544 Injection molding of plastics; Special dies, tools, jigs, and fixtures

(G-14151)
REGAL BELOIT AMERICA INC
Also Called: Regal
531 N 4th St (45371-1857)
PHONE..............................937 667-2431
EMP: 231
SALES (corp-wide): 6.25B **Publicly Held**
SIC: 3621 Motors, electric
HQ: Regal Beloit America, Inc.
　111 W Michigan St
　Milwaukee WI 53203
　608 364-8800

(G-14152)
REPACORP INC (PA)
Also Called: Presto Labels
31 Industry Park Ct (45371-3060)
PHONE..............................937 667-8496
EMP: 71 **EST:** 1974
SALES (est): 23.21MM
SALES (corp-wide): 23.21MM **Privately Held**
Web: www.repacorp.com
SIC: 2759 Commercial printing, nec

(G-14153)
RPG INDUSTRIES INC
3571 Ginghamsburg Frederick Rd (45371-9652)
P.O. Box 233 (45383-0233)
PHONE..............................937 698-9801
EMP: 6 **EST:** 1995
SQ FT: 3,600
SALES (est): 500K **Privately Held**
Web: www.rpgindustries.com
SIC: 3599 Machine shop, jobbing and repair

(G-14154)
SINBON USA LLC
4265 Gibson Dr (45371-9452)
PHONE..............................937 667-8999
Chun-yu Chen, *CEO*
EMP: 20 **EST:** 2017
SALES (est): 5.19MM **Privately Held**
SIC: 3679 Antennas, receiving

(G-14155)
SK MOLD & TOOL INC (PA)
955 N 3rd St (45371)
PHONE..............................937 339-0299
Samuel K Kingrey, *Pr*
Keith Kingrey, *
Vince Hinde, *
EMP: 45 **EST:** 1983
SQ FT: 76,500
SALES (est): 7.12MM
SALES (corp-wide): 7.12MM **Privately Held**
Web: www.skmold.com
SIC: 3544 3599 Special dies and tools; Machine shop, jobbing and repair

(G-14156)
SLONE GEAR INTERNATIONAL INC
207 S 1st St (45371-1705)
P.O. Box 292528 (45429-0528)
PHONE..............................507 401-4327
Brian Slone, *VP Opers*
EMP: 7
SALES (corp-wide): 945.4K **Privately Held**
Web: www.slonegear.com
SIC: 3823 Industrial process measurement equipment
PA: Slone Gear International, Inc
　2154 Liberty Rd
　New Carlisle OH 45344
　937 478-1595

(G-14157)
SP3 WINCO LLC
Also Called: Winco Industries, Inc.
835 N Hyatt St (45371-1558)
P.O. Box 70 (45371-0070)
PHONE..............................937 667-4476
EMP: 20 **EST:** 1961
SALES (est): 5.67MM **Privately Held**
SIC: 3545 Drills (machine tool accessories)
PA: Sp3 Cutting Tools, Inc.
　835 N Hyatt St
　Tipp City OH 45371

(G-14158)
TEAM AMITY MLDS PLSTIC INJCTIO
1435 Commerce Park Dr (45371-2846)
P.O. Box 309 (45371-0309)
PHONE..............................937 667-7856
Leonard L Dickess, *Pr*
Leonord Dickess, *Owner*
EMP: 9 **EST:** 1967
SALES (est): 290.4K **Privately Held**
Web: www.amitymold.com
SIC: 3089 Molding primary plastics

(G-14159)
TECH MOLD AND TOOL CO
4333 Lisa Dr (45371-9463)
PHONE..............................937 667-8851
Dan Isenbarger, *Pr*
Arlene Isenbarger, *Sec*
EMP: 7 **EST:** 1975
SQ FT: 5,100
SALES (est): 650.16K **Privately Held**
SIC: 3544 Special dies and tools

(G-14160)
TRIMBLE INC
Also Called: Trimble Engineering & Cnstr
4450 Gibson Dr (45371-9461)
PHONE..............................937 233-8921
EMP: 17
SALES (corp-wide): 3.8B **Publicly Held**
Web: www.trimble.com
SIC: 3812 Navigational systems and instruments
PA: Trimble Inc.
　10368 Westmoor Dr
　Westminster CO 80021
　720 887-6100

(G-14161)
TROPHY NUT CO (PA)
320 N 2nd St (45371-1960)
P.O. Box 199 (45371-0199)
PHONE..............................937 667-8478
Gerald J Allen, *CEO*
Robert J Bollinger, *
Robert N Wilke, *
David Henning, *
◆ **EMP:** 49 **EST:** 1968
SQ FT: 85,000
SALES: 22.61MM
SALES (corp-wide): 22.61MM **Privately Held**
Web: www.trophynut.com
SIC: 2068 5441 Nuts: dried, dehydrated, salted or roasted; Nuts

(G-14162)
TROPHY NUT CO
1567 Harmony Dr (45371-3319)
P.O. Box 199 (45371-0199)
PHONE..............................937 669-5513
Bob Loy, *Mgr*
EMP: 6
SALES (corp-wide): 22.61MM **Privately Held**
Web: www.trophynut.com
SIC: 2068 Nuts: dried, dehydrated, salted or roasted
PA: Trophy Nut Co.
　320 N 2nd St
　Tipp City OH 45371
　937 667-8478

(G-14163)
UDECX LLC
320 N 4th St (45371-1803)
PHONE..............................877 698-3329
John Van Leeuwen, *CEO*
Patrick Bertke, *Dir*
EMP: 6 **EST:** 2010
SQ FT: 2,200
SALES (est): 549.92K **Privately Held**
Web: www.udecx.com
SIC: 3089 Floor coverings, plastics

(G-14164)
VISION PROJECTS INC
1350 Commerce Park Dr. (45371-3323)
PHONE..............................937 667-8648
George J Minarcek, *CEO*
Chris Dakin, *Treas*
EMP: 6 **EST:** 2003
SQ FT: 20,000
SALES (est): 379.11K **Privately Held**
Web: www.indiancreekfab.com
SIC: 3599 Machine shop, jobbing and repair

(G-14165)
VSCORP LLC
4754 Us Route 40 (45371-9481)
PHONE..............................937 305-3562
EMP: 15 **EST:** 2017
SALES (est): 1MM **Privately Held**
SIC: 3441 Fabricated structural metal

(G-14166)
WENRICK MACHINE AND TOOL CORP
Also Called: Wenrick Machine
4685 Us Route 40 (45371-8339)
PHONE..............................937 667-7307
Tom Wenrick, *Pr*
Betty Wenrick, *Sec*
EMP: 10 **EST:** 1987
SQ FT: 8,000
SALES (est): 779.12K **Privately Held**
Web: www.wenrickmachine.com

Tipp City - Miami County (G-14167)

SIC: 3599 7692 Machine shop, jobbing and repair; Welding repair

(G-14167)
WPC SUCCESSOR INC
Also Called: Weldcraft Products Co
6555 Oh 202 (45371)
P.O. Box 122 (45404-0122)
PHONE.................................937 233-6141
Nancy Massey, *Pr*
EMP: 12 **EST:** 1953
SALES (est): 1.27MM **Privately Held**
SIC: 3499 7692 Machine bases, metal; Welding repair

(G-14168)
WRENA LLC
265 Lightner Rd (45371-9228)
PHONE.................................937 667-4403
Nagesh Palakurthi, *CEO*
Michael R Tanner, *
George J Den, *
Tom Derr, *
David Whitehead, *General Vice President*
EMP: 50 **EST:** 1977
SQ FT: 123,000
SALES (est): 13.8MM **Privately Held**
Web: www.wrenallc.com
SIC: 3465 3544 Body parts, automobile: stamped metal; Special dies and tools
HQ: Angstrom Usa Llc
26980 Trolley Indus Dr
Taylor MI 48180
313 295-0100

Tippecanoe
Harrison County

(G-14169)
EXCO RESOURCES LLC
3618 Fallen Timber Rd Se (44699-9650)
PHONE.................................740 254-4061
EMP: 16
SALES (corp-wide): 394.03MM **Privately Held**
SIC: 1311 Crude petroleum and natural gas production
HQ: Exco Resources, Llc
12377 Merit Dr Ste 1700
Montoursville PA 17754

(G-14170)
GARDNER LUMBER COMPANY INC
5805 Laurel Creek Rd Se (44699-9661)
PHONE.................................740 254-4664
Richard Gardner, *Pr*
Harvey Gardner, *VP*
EMP: 10 **EST:** 1938
SALES (est): 819.01K **Privately Held**
SIC: 2421 2448 5154 Sawmills and planing mills, general; Pallets, wood; Cattle

(G-14171)
GRAY-EERING LTD
3158 Sandy Ridge Rd Se (44699-9657)
PHONE.................................740 498-8816
Glenn Gray, *Pt*
Jay Gray, *Pt*
Lainard Gray, *Pt*
Sandra K Gray, *Sec*
EMP: 7 **EST:** 1978
SALES (est): 469.84K **Privately Held**
Web: www.grayeering.com
SIC: 3535 3536 3534 Conveyors and conveying equipment; Mine hoists; Elevators and equipment

Toledo
Lucas County

(G-14172)
A & B TOOL & MANUFACTURING
2921 South Ave (43609-1327)
PHONE.................................419 382-0215
Timothy J Adams, *Pr*
EMP: 7 **EST:** 1966
SQ FT: 8,000
SALES (est): 734.53K **Privately Held**
SIC: 3544 Special dies and tools

(G-14173)
A&M CHEESE CO
253 Waggoner Blvd (43612-1952)
PHONE.................................419 476-8369
Michael J Sofo, *Pr*
Antonio Sofo, *
Joseph J Sofo Junior, *VP*
EMP: 53 **EST:** 1981
SQ FT: 190,000
SALES (est): 5.18MM **Privately Held**
Web: www.amcheese.com
SIC: 2022 Natural cheese

(G-14174)
ABBOTT TOOL INC
Also Called: ATI
405 Dura Ave (43612-2619)
PHONE.................................419 476-6742
Arthur Stange, *VP*
Leonard Livecchi, *
Karle Stange, *
EMP: 33 **EST:** 1973
SQ FT: 12,000
SALES (est): 3.06MM **Privately Held**
Web: www.abbotttool.com
SIC: 3469 7692 Machine parts, stamped or pressed metal; Welding repair

(G-14175)
ABUTILON COMPANY INC
Also Called: Abco Services
701 N Westwood Ave (43607)
PHONE.................................419 536-6123
Steven Zimmerman, *CEO*
Steve Zimmerman, *CEO*
EMP: 18 **EST:** 1991
SQ FT: 13,000
SALES (est): 4.98MM **Privately Held**
Web: www.abcotruckequipment.com
SIC: 5531 7538 3713 Auto and truck equipment and parts; General automotive repair shops; Truck and bus bodies

(G-14176)
ACCUSHRED LLC
1114 W Central Ave (43610-1061)
PHONE.................................419 244-7473
Nate Segall, *Pr*
Barry Gudelman, *VP*
EMP: 15 **EST:** 2002
SALES (est): 1.56MM **Privately Held**
Web: www.accushred.net
SIC: 3589 Shredders, industrial and commercial

(G-14177)
ADAMS STREET PUBLISHING CO INC
Also Called: Toledo City Paper
1120 Adams St (43604-5509)
PHONE.................................419 244-9859
Collette Jacobs, *Pr*
Marck Jacobs, *CEO*
EMP: 22 **EST:** 1992
SQ FT: 4,268
SALES (est): 2.9MM **Privately Held**
Web: www.adamsstreetpublishing.com
SIC: 2721 Magazines: publishing only, not printed on site

(G-14178)
ADVANCED INCENTIVES INC
1732 W Alexis Rd (43613-2349)
PHONE.................................419 471-9088
EMP: 6 **EST:** 1993
SQ FT: 1,800
SALES (est): 585.65K **Privately Held**
Web: www.advancedincentives.com
SIC: 2759 Screen printing

(G-14179)
ADVANTAGE MOLD INC
525 N Wheeling St (43605-1337)
PHONE.................................419 691-5676
Larry J Bolander, *Pr*
EMP: 8 **EST:** 1999
SQ FT: 13,000
SALES (est): 1.05MM **Privately Held**
Web: www.advantage-mold.com
SIC: 3089 Injection molding of plastics

(G-14180)
AIR-TECH MECHANICAL INC
4444 Monroe St (43613-4732)
PHONE.................................419 292-0074
EMP: 10 **EST:** 2014
SALES (est): 450.63K **Privately Held**
Web: www.airtechtoledo.com
SIC: 3443 1711 Cooling towers, metal plate; Heating and air conditioning contractors

(G-14181)
AIRTEX INDUSTRIES LLC
Also Called: Pumps Group
6056 Deer Park Ct (43614-6000)
PHONE.................................330 899-0340
David Peace, *CEO*
EMP: 476 **EST:** 2005
SALES (est): 3.59MM
SALES (corp-wide): 8.03B **Privately Held**
SIC: 3714 Motor vehicle parts and accessories
HQ: Uci-Airtex Holdings, Inc.
6056 Deer Park Ct
Toledo OH 43614
330 899-0340

(G-14182)
ALLEN INDUSTRIES INC
7844 W Central Ave (43617-1530)
PHONE.................................567 408-7538
EMP: 100
SALES (corp-wide): 76.87MM **Privately Held**
Web: www.allenindustries.com
SIC: 3993 Electric signs
PA: Allen Industries, Inc.
6434 Burnt Poplar Rd
Greensboro NC 27409
336 668-2791

(G-14183)
ALLIED MASK AND TOOLING INC
6051 Telegraph Rd Ste 6 (43612-4573)
P.O. Box 639 (48182-0639)
PHONE.................................419 470-2555
Mike Murray, *Pr*
EMP: 9 **EST:** 1998
SQ FT: 3,600
SALES (est): 680.09K **Privately Held**
Web: www.alliedmask.com
SIC: 3599 3356 3444 3542 Machine shop, jobbing and repair; Nickel; Sheet metalwork; Electroforming machines

(G-14184)
ALRO STEEL CORPORATION
3003 Airport Hwy (43609-1405)
P.O. Box 964 (43697-0964)
PHONE.................................419 720-5300
Keith Daly, *Mgr*
EMP: 57
SALES (corp-wide): 3.43B **Privately Held**
Web: www.alro.com
SIC: 5051 5085 5162 3444 Steel; Industrial supplies; Plastics materials, nec; Sheet metalwork
PA: Alro Steel Corporation
3100 E High St
Jackson MI 49203
517 787-5500

(G-14185)
AMCRAFT INC
Also Called: Amcraft Manufacturing
5144 Enterprise Blvd (43612-3807)
PHONE.................................419 729-7900
David R Frank, *Pr*
▼ **EMP:** 8 **EST:** 1966
SQ FT: 6,000
SALES (est): 914.75K **Privately Held**
Web: www.amcraftinc.com
SIC: 3423 3544 3469 Hand and edge tools, nec; Special dies and tools; Metal stampings, nec

(G-14186)
AMERICAN BOTTLING COMPANY
7 Up Bottling Co of Toledo
224 N Byrne Rd (43607-2605)
PHONE.................................419 535-0777
Jeff Lark, *Mgr*
EMP: 87
Web: www.keurigdrpepper.com
SIC: 2086 Soft drinks: packaged in cans, bottles, etc.
HQ: The American Bottling Company
6425 Hall Of Fame Ln
Frisco TX 75034

(G-14187)
AMERICAN CANVAS PRODUCTS INC
2925 South Ave (43609-1327)
PHONE.................................419 382-8450
EMP: 12 **EST:** 1994
SQ FT: 6,000
SALES (est): 490.47K **Privately Held**
Web: www.americancanvasproductsinc.com
SIC: 2394 Convertible tops, canvas or boat: from purchased materials

(G-14188)
AMERICAN LASER & MACHINE LLC
362 N Westwood Ave (43607-3343)
PHONE.................................419 930-9303
EMP: 6 **EST:** 2019
SALES (est): 342.19K **Privately Held**
Web: www.americanlasermachinc.com
SIC: 3599 Machine shop, jobbing and repair

(G-14189)
AMERICAN MANUFACTURING INC (PA)
2375 Dorr St Ste F (43607-3407)
PHONE.................................419 531-9471
Charles P Gotberg, *Pr*
▲ **EMP:** 10 **EST:** 1971
SALES (est): 18.63MM
SALES (corp-wide): 18.63MM **Privately Held**
Web: www.buyamericanmanufacturing.com
SIC: 3441 Fabricated structural metal

(G-14190)
AMERICAN MNFCTRING OPRTONS INC
1931 E Manhattan Blvd (43608-1534)
PHONE.................................419 269-1560
Jonathan R Saul, *Pr*
EMP: 8 **EST:** 2004
SALES (est): 699.03K **Privately Held**
SIC: 3715 Truck trailers

(G-14191)
AMERICAN POSTS LLC (PA)
810 Chicago St (43611-3609)
PHONE.................................419 720-0652
David Feniger, *Managing Member*
EMP: 30 **EST:** 2005
SALES (est): 10.73MM
SALES (corp-wide): 10.73MM **Privately Held**
Web: www.americanposts.com
SIC: 3312 5051 Rods, iron and steel: made in steel mills; Steel

(G-14192)
AMERICAN STEEL ASSOD PDTS INC
2375 Dorr St Ste F (43607-3407)
PHONE.................................419 531-9471
Charles P Gotberg, *Pr*
EMP: 90 **EST:** 1995
SALES (est): 4.86MM
SALES (corp-wide): 18.63MM **Privately Held**
Web: www.buyamericanmanufacturing.com
SIC: 3441 Fabricated structural metal
PA: American Manufacturing, Inc.
2375 Dorr St Ste F
Toledo OH 43607
419 531-9471

(G-14193)
AMERICAN TOOL AND DIE INC
2024 Champlain St (43611-3700)
PHONE.................................419 726-5394
Richard J Russell Junior, *Pr*
Gerald Russell, *VP*
Paul Philabaum, *VP*
EMP: 15 **EST:** 1963
SQ FT: 20,000
SALES (est): 2.48MM **Privately Held**
Web: www.americantoolanddieinc.com
SIC: 3469 3544 Stamping metal for the trade ; Special dies, tools, jigs, and fixtures

(G-14194)
ANDERSONS INC
801 S Reynolds Rd (43615-6309)
PHONE.................................419 536-0460
Bill Kale, *Mgr*
EMP: 7
SALES (corp-wide): 14.75B **Publicly Held**
Web: www.andersonsinc.com
SIC: 0723 5191 2874 4789 Crop preparation services for market; Farm supplies; Phosphatic fertilizers; Railroad car repair
PA: The Andersons Inc
1947 Briarfield Blvd
Maumee OH 43537
419 893-5050

(G-14195)
APEX BOLT & MACHINE COMPANY
Also Called: Apex Metal Fabricating & Mch
5324 Enterprise Blvd (43612-3870)
PHONE.................................419 729-3741
William G Foradas, *Ch Bd*
Michael S Petree, *
Luanna M Foradas, *
EMP: 39 **EST:** 1973
SQ FT: 51,000
SALES (est): 8.58MM **Privately Held**
Web: www.apexfab.net
SIC: 3441 Fabricated structural metal

(G-14196)
ARBOR FOODS INC
3332 Saint Lawrence Dr Bldg C (43605-1046)
PHONE.................................419 698-4442
Mark S Flegenheimer, *Pr*
Sheila Severn, *Contrlr*
EMP: 50 **EST:** 2016
SALES (est): 2.23MM **Privately Held**
Web: www.streamlinefoods.com
SIC: 3556 Mixers, commercial, food

(G-14197)
ARCHER-DANIELS-MIDLAND COMPANY
Also Called: ADM
1308 Miami St (43605-3354)
PHONE.................................419 705-3292
Dan Hines, *Prin*
EMP: 9
SALES (corp-wide): 93.94B **Publicly Held**
Web: www.adm.com
SIC: 2041 2048 Flour and other grain mill products; Prepared feeds, nec
PA: Archer-Daniels-Midland Company
77 W Wacker Dr Ste 4600
Chicago IL 60601
312 634-8100

(G-14198)
ARCLIN USA LLC
6175 American Rd (43612-3901)
PHONE.................................419 726-5013
Warren Shunk, *Manager*
EMP: 7
SALES (corp-wide): 150.33MM **Privately Held**
Web: www.arclin.com
SIC: 2891 2821 Adhesives and sealants; Plastics materials and resins
HQ: Arclin Usa Llc
1150 Sanctuary Pkwy # 100
Alpharetta GA 30009
678 999-2100

(G-14199)
ARLINGTON RACK & PACKAGING CO
6120 N Detroit Ave (43612-4810)
P.O. Box 12207 (43612-0207)
PHONE.................................419 476-7700
Michael A Flaum, *Pr*
Harley Kripke, *Ch*
Mark Hahm, *VP*
EMP: 8 **EST:** 1990
SQ FT: 110,000
SALES (est): 999.07K **Privately Held**
Web: www.racksandpackaging.com
SIC: 3714 3086 Motor vehicle parts and accessories; Packaging and shipping materials, foamed plastics

(G-14200)
ART IRON INC
860 Curtis St (43609)
P.O. Box 964 (43697)
PHONE.................................419 241-1261
TOLL FREE: 800
▲ **EMP:** 70 **EST:** 1927
SALES (est): 5.05MM **Privately Held**
Web: www.artiron.com
SIC: 3441 3446 Fabricated structural metal; Architectural metalwork

(G-14201)
AUTOTEC CORPORATION
Also Called: Autotec Systems
6155 Brent Dr (43611-1083)
PHONE.................................419 885-2529
Thomas P Ballay, *Pr*
Thomas P Ballay, *Pr*
Jim Proffitt, *VP*
James Mihaly, *CFO*
EMP: 20 **EST:** 1979
SQ FT: 23,000
SALES (est): 4.48MM **Privately Held**
Web: www.autotecinc.com
SIC: 3544 3599 8711 Special dies, tools, jigs, and fixtures; Custom machinery; Designing: ship, boat, machine, and product

(G-14202)
AXIOM ENGINEERED SYSTEMS LLC (PA)
1 Seagate Fl 27 (43604-1558)
PHONE.................................416 435-7313
EMP: 12 **EST:** 2019
SALES (est): 3.48MM
SALES (corp-wide): 3.48MM **Privately Held**
Web: www.axiomgroup.ca
SIC: 3089 Injection molding of plastics

(G-14203)
B & R CUSTOM CHROME
469 Dearborn Ave (43605-1709)
PHONE.................................419 536-7215
Ary Smith, *Prin*
EMP: 6 **EST:** 2007
SALES (est): 146.89K **Privately Held**
Web: www.brchrome.com
SIC: 3471 Chromium plating of metals or formed products

(G-14204)
BAINBRIDGE419 INC
6142 American Rd (43612-3902)
PHONE.................................937 228-2181
Robert Flaute Junior, *Pr*
EMP: 10 **EST:** 1916
SQ FT: 12,000
SALES (est): 399.69K **Privately Held**
Web: www.printprodinc.com
SIC: 2752 Tags, lithographed

(G-14205)
BAJIO BREWING COMPANY LLC ✪
2959 Nebraska Ave (43607-3124)
PHONE.................................419 410-8275
Mark Connor, *Prin*
EMP: 7 **EST:** 2022
SALES (est): 55.21K **Privately Held**
SIC: 5813 2082 Bar (drinking places); Malt beverages

(G-14206)
BANNER MATTRESS CO INC
Also Called: Banner Mattress & Furniture Co
2544 N Reynolds Rd (43615-2820)
PHONE.................................419 324-7181
▲ **EMP:** 85
Web: www.perfectdomain.com
SIC: 5712 2515 Mattresses; Mattresses and bedsprings

(G-14207)
BASILIUS INC
4338 South Ave (43615-6236)
PHONE.................................419 536-5810
Scott Basilius, *Pr*
Dave Keiser, *
▲ **EMP:** 33 **EST:** 1940
SQ FT: 52,000
SALES (est): 4.45MM **Privately Held**
Web: www.basilius.com
SIC: 3544 Forms (molds), for foundry and plastics working machinery

(G-14208)
BCP IMPORTS LLC
146 Main St (43605-2067)
PHONE.................................419 467-0291
Robert Croak, *Prin*
EMP: 6 **EST:** 2013
SALES (est): 118.25K **Privately Held**
SIC: 3961 Keychains, except precious metal

(G-14209)
BEAUTE ASYLUM LLC
2011 Glendale Ave (43614-2802)
PHONE.................................419 377-9933
EMP: 10 **EST:** 2013
SALES (est): 80K **Privately Held**
Web: www.beauteasylum.com
SIC: 7231 3999 5087 Hairdressers; Fingernails, artificial; Beauty salon and barber shop equipment and supplies

(G-14210)
BELL BINDERS LLC
320 21st St (43604-5037)
P.O. Box 313 (43697-0313)
PHONE.................................419 242-3201
EMP: 15 **EST:** 1954
SALES (est): 2.14MM **Privately Held**
Web: www.bellbinders.com
SIC: 2782 3089 Looseleaf binders and devices; Laminating of plastics

(G-14211)
BELOW ZERO INC
3324 Secor Rd Ste 23 (43606-1540)
PHONE.................................419 973-2366
Jian Ping Ou, *Prin*
EMP: 8 **EST:** 2019
SALES (est): 68.34K **Privately Held**
Web: belowzero-icecreamshop.business.site
SIC: 2024 Ice cream and frozen deserts

(G-14212)
BERNARD ENGRAVING CORP
414 N Erie St Ste 100 (43604-5625)
P.O. Box 320034 (06825-0034)
PHONE.................................419 478-5610
EMP: 11 **EST:** 1992
SQ FT: 10,000
SALES (est): 499.2K **Privately Held**
Web: www.bernardengraving.com
SIC: 3111 3089 Die-cutting of leather; Injection molding of plastics

(G-14213)
BISON LEATHER CO
7409 W Central Ave (43617-1122)
PHONE.................................419 517-1737
Barry Cody, *CEO*
EMP: 6 **EST:** 2004
SALES (est): 253.33K **Privately Held**
Web: www.b-bsales.com
SIC: 3172 Personal leather goods, nec

(G-14214)
BLOCK COMMUNICATIONS INC (PA)
Also Called: BCI
405 Madison Ave Ste 2100 (43604)
PHONE.................................419 724-6212
Walter H Carstensen, *Pr*
Allan J Block, *Ch Bd*
Jodi Miehls, *VP*
John R Block, *V Ch Bd*
Sara Labudda, *Treas*
EMP: 14 **EST:** 1965
SQ FT: 64,100
SALES (est): 910.95MM
SALES (corp-wide): 910.95MM **Privately Held**
Web: www.blockcommunications.com

Toledo - Lucas County (G-14215) — GEOGRAPHIC SECTION

SIC: 4841 4833 2711 Cable television services; Television broadcasting stations; Newspapers, publishing and printing

(G-14215)
BOBCO ENTERPRISES INC
Also Called: Taylor Mtl Hdlg & Conveyor
2910 Glanzman Rd (43614-3955)
P.O. Box 39 (43560-0039)
PHONE.................419 867-3560
TOLL FREE: 888
Robert Cordrey, Pr
EMP: 12 EST: 2002
SQ FT: 40,000
SALES (est): 2.4MM Privately Held
Web: www.taylormhc.com
SIC: 5084 3536 3535 Materials handling machinery; Hoists, cranes, and monorails; Conveyors and conveying equipment

(G-14216)
BOLLIN & SONS INC
Also Called: Bollin Label Systems
6001 Brent Dr (43611-1090)
PHONE.................419 693-6573
Mark D Bollin, Pr
Chris Younkman, *
EMP: 40 EST: 1969
SQ FT: 21,000
SALES (est): 14.54MM Privately Held
Web: www.bollin.com
SIC: 5084 7389 2851 2759 Packaging machinery and equipment; Design services; Paints and allied products; Commercial printing, nec

(G-14217)
BP PRODUCTS NORTH AMERICA INC
B P Exploration
2450 Hill Ave (43607-3609)
P.O. Box 932 (43697-0932)
PHONE.................419 537-9540
Jim Brahier, Brnch Mgr
EMP: 48
SQ FT: 11,485
SALES (corp-wide): 171.22B Privately Held
Web: www.bp.com
SIC: 2911 Petroleum refining
HQ: Bp Products North America Inc.
501 Westlake Park Blvd
Houston TX 77079
281 366-2000

(G-14218)
BPREX PLASTIC PACKAGING INC
(DH)
Also Called: Rexam Plastic Packaging
1 Seagate (43604-1558)
PHONE.................419 247-5000
EMP: 10 EST: 1987
SALES (est): 122.21MM Publicly Held
SIC: 3089 3221 Plastics containers, except foam; Food containers, glass
HQ: Berry Global, Inc.
101 Oakley St
Evansville IN 47710

(G-14219)
BPREX PLASTIC SERVICES CO INC
Also Called: Specialty Packg Licensing Ltd
1 Seagate (43604-1563)
PHONE.................419 247-5000
EMP: 38 EST: 1985
SALES (est): 4.47MM Publicly Held
SIC: 3081 Unsupported plastics film and sheet
HQ: Berry Global, Inc.
101 Oakley St
Evansville IN 47710

(G-14220)
BRAIN CHILD PRODUCTS LLC
146 Main St (43605-2067)
PHONE.................419 698-4020
EMP: 12 EST: 2005
SALES (est): 425.87K Privately Held
SIC: 2822 Silicone rubbers

(G-14221)
BROOKS MANUFACTURING
1102 N Summit St (43604-1816)
PHONE.................419 244-1777
Michael Brooks, Owner
EMP: 9 EST: 1968
SQ FT: 5,000
SALES (est): 363.57K Privately Held
SIC: 3931 3592 3824 Brass instruments and parts; Valves; Water meters

(G-14222)
BRYAN DIE CAST PRODUCTS LTD
4 Seagate Ste 803 (43604-2608)
PHONE.................419 252-6208
EMP: 6 EST: 2012
SALES (est): 126.53K Privately Held
Web: www.bryandiecast.com
SIC: 3544 Special dies and tools

(G-14223)
BTW LLC
2226 Greenlawn Dr (43614-5120)
PHONE.................419 382-4443
Paul Long, Pr
EMP: 8 EST: 1998
SALES (est): 823.03K Privately Held
Web: www.btw.com
SIC: 2679 5012 Wrappers, paper (unprinted): made from purchased material; Automobiles and other motor vehicles

(G-14224)
BUILDER TECH WHOLESALE LLC
Also Called: Builder Tech Windows
2931 South Ave (43609-1327)
PHONE.................419 535-7606
EMP: 8 EST: 2000
SQ FT: 6,000
SALES (est): 806.3K Privately Held
SIC: 3089 Windows, plastics

(G-14225)
CABINET CREAT BY LILLIBRIDGE
5344 Jackman Rd Ste A (43613-2987)
PHONE.................419 476-6838
EMP: 12 EST: 1994
SQ FT: 16,000
SALES (est): 460.09K Privately Held
Web: www.cabinetcreationsonline.com
SIC: 2434 Wood kitchen cabinets

(G-14226)
CANBERRA CORPORATION
3610 N Holland Sylvania Rd (43615)
PHONE.................419 724-4300
R Bruce Yacko, Pr
James C Lower, *
William Schneck, *
◆ EMP: 205 EST: 1964
SQ FT: 220,000
SALES (est): 48.89MM Privately Held
Web: www.canberracorp.com
SIC: 2842 Cleaning or polishing preparations, nec

(G-14227)
CAPITAL TIRE INC
Also Called: Beitner Tire
516 E Hudson St (43608-1229)
PHONE.................330 364-4731
Marshall Ferrick, Mgr
EMP: 21
SALES (corp-wide): 79.32MM Privately Held
Web: www.capitaltire.net
SIC: 7534 5531 Tire retreading and repair shops; Automotive tires
PA: Capital Tire, Inc.
7001 Integrity Dr
Rossford OH 43460
419 241-5111

(G-14228)
CBD 4 REAL LLC
1026 N Holland Sylvania Rd (43615)
PHONE.................419 480-9800
EMP: 6 EST: 2018
SALES (est): 39.69K Privately Held
Web: www.hemp4real.com
SIC: 3999

(G-14229)
CDH LIQUIDATION INC
Also Called: Custom Deco
1343 Miami St (43605-3313)
PHONE.................419 720-4096
EMP: 33
SIC: 3231 Products of purchased glass

(G-14230)
CENTRAL COCA-COLA BTLG CO INC
Also Called: Coca-Cola
3970 Catawba St (43612-1404)
PHONE.................419 476-6622
Paul Kenny, Mgr
EMP: 140
SALES (corp-wide): 45.75B Publicly Held
Web: www.coca-cola.com
SIC: 2086 2087 5149 Bottled and canned soft drinks; Syrups, drink; Groceries and related products, nec
HQ: Central Coca-Cola Bottling Company, Inc.
555 Taxter Rd Ste 550
Elmsford NY 10523
914 789-1100

(G-14231)
CHAMPION LABORATORIES INC
6056 Deer Park Ct (43614-6000)
PHONE.................330 899-0340
EMP: 17
SALES (corp-wide): 8.03B Privately Held
Web: www.champlabs.com
SIC: 3714 Filters: oil, fuel, and air, motor vehicle
HQ: Champion Laboratories, Inc.
200 S 4th St
Albion IL 62806
618 445-6011

(G-14232)
CHAMPION SPARK PLUG COMPANY
900 Upton Ave (43607)
PHONE.................419 535-2567
Richard Keller, Pr
▲ EMP: 72 EST: 1907
SQ FT: 15,000
SALES (est): 22.62MM
SALES (corp-wide): 18.04B Privately Held
Web: www.championautoparts.com
SIC: 3714 Motor vehicle parts and accessories
HQ: Tenneco Inc.
7450 Mccormick Blvd
Skokie IL 60076
847 482-5000

(G-14233)
CHANTILLY DEVELOPMENT CORP
Acme Specialty Mfg Co
3101 Monroe St (43606-4605)
P.O. Box 2510 (43606-0510)
PHONE.................419 243-8109
Robert T Skilliter Junior, Prin
EMP: 20
SQ FT: 70,000
SALES (corp-wide): 2.78MM Privately Held
Web: www.acmespecialty.com
SIC: 3714 3231 3429 3221 Frames, motor vehicle; Mirrored glass; Hardware, nec; Glass containers
PA: Chantilly Development Corp
Wollaston Rd
Unionville PA
419 243-8109

(G-14234)
CHASE SIGN & LIGHTING SVC INC
5924 American Rd E (43612-3950)
PHONE.................567 128-3444
EMP: 8 EST: 2015
SALES (est): 354.76K Privately Held
Web: www.chasesign.net
SIC: 3993 Signs and advertising specialties

(G-14235)
CHEM-SALES INC
Also Called: C S I
3860 Dorr St (43607-1003)
P.O. Box 351684 (43635-1684)
EMP: 12 EST: 1980
SALES (est): 2.4MM Privately Held
Web: www.chemsalesinc.com
SIC: 2869 5087 5169 Industrial organic chemicals, nec; Janitors' supplies; Chemicals and allied products, nec

(G-14236)
CHEMPACE CORPORATION
339 Arco Dr (43607-2908)
PHONE.................419 535-0101
Richard Shall, Pr
Ralph E Wooddell, Sec
Terry W O'neill, VP
Sue Klotz, Contrlr
▲ EMP: 18 EST: 1968
SQ FT: 12,500
SALES (est): 3.19MM Privately Held
Web: www.chempace.com
SIC: 2842 Cleaning or polishing preparations, nec

(G-14237)
CHEMTRADE CHEMICALS US LLC
1661 Campbell St (43607-4322)
PHONE.................419 255-0193
J Poure, Brnch Mgr
EMP: 6
SQ FT: 20,000
SALES (corp-wide): 1.34B Privately Held
SIC: 2819 Aluminum sulfate
HQ: Chemtrade Chemicals Us Llc
90 E Halsey Rd
Parsippany NJ 07054

(G-14238)
CHINA ENTERPRISES INC
Also Called: Chang Audio
5151 Monroe St (43623-3462)
PHONE.................419 885-1485
Stella Lee, Pr
Michael Chang, Ex VP
EMP: 7 EST: 1991
SALES (est): 527.3K Privately Held
SIC: 3651 Household audio equipment

(G-14239)
CINDEE SHIVERS LLC
2603 Airport Hwy (43609-1501)
PHONE.................419 385-0503
Janice Shivers, Prin

GEOGRAPHIC SECTION

Toledo - Lucas County (G-14263)

EMP: 7 **EST:** 2010
SALES (est): 125.69K **Privately Held**
SIC: 2024 Ice cream and frozen deserts

(G-14240)
CLAYCOR INC
Also Called: Denbro Plastics Company
5924 American Rd E (43612-3950)
PHONE..............................419 318-7290
Jack Mckisson, *Pr*
EMP: 10 **EST:** 1964
SQ FT: 10,000
SALES (est): 976.74K **Privately Held**
Web: www.denbroplastics.com
SIC: 3089 Injection molding of plastics

(G-14241)
CLEAR IMAGES LLC
121 11th St (43604-5829)
PHONE..............................419 241-9347
EMP: 13 **EST:** 2003
SALES (est): 676.77K **Privately Held**
Web: www.designgraphics.net
SIC: 2759 Screen printing

(G-14242)
CLEVELAND-CLIFFS INC
811 Madison Ave Fl 7 (43604-5626)
P.O. Box 166870 (43616-6870)
PHONE..............................419 243-8198
Lourenco Goncalves, *CEO*
EMP: 25
SALES (corp-wide): 22B **Publicly Held**
Web: www.clevelandcliffs.com
SIC: 1011 Iron ore mining
PA: Cleveland-Cliffs Inc.
200 Public Sq Ste 3300
Cleveland OH 44114
216 694-5700

(G-14243)
CLEVELAND-CLIFFS INC
330 Millard Ave (43605-1028)
PHONE..............................216 694-5700
EMP: 44
SALES (corp-wide): 22B **Publicly Held**
Web: www.clevelandcliffs.com
SIC: 3339 Primary nonferrous metals, nec
PA: Cleveland-Cliffs Inc.
200 Public Sq Ste 3300
Cleveland OH 44114
216 694-5700

(G-14244)
CLINTON FOUNDRY LTD
1202 W Bancroft St (43606-4631)
PHONE..............................419 243-6885
James D Heninger, *Prin*
EMP: 10 **EST:** 1997
SQ FT: 4,500
SALES (est): 731.06K **Privately Held**
Web: www.clinton-patternandfoundry.com
SIC: 3543 Industrial patterns

(G-14245)
CLINTON PATTERN WORKS INC
1215 W Bancroft St (43606-4632)
PHONE..............................419 243-0855
James D Heninger, *Pr*
Timothy Heninger, *VP*
EMP: 17 **EST:** 1941
SQ FT: 25,000
SALES (est): 471.99K **Privately Held**
Web: www.clinton-patternandfoundry.com
SIC: 3543 Industrial patterns

(G-14246)
CM SLICECHIEF CO
Also Called: Slicechief
3333 Maple St (43608-1147)
PHONE..............................419 241-7647
Susan L Brown, *Pr*
Barbara Cairl, *Sec*
EMP: 9 **EST:** 1946
SQ FT: 18,000
SALES (est): 830.81K **Privately Held**
SIC: 3556 Slicers, commercial, food

(G-14247)
COLE ORTHOTICS PROSTHETIC CTR
723 Phillips Ave Bldg F (43612-1351)
PHONE..............................419 476-4248
Daniel P Cole, *Owner*
EMP: 6 **EST:** 1920
SQ FT: 8,000
SALES (est): 528.94K **Privately Held**
Web: www.coleleimop.com
SIC: 3842 Braces, orthopedic

(G-14248)
COMFORT LINE LTD
Also Called: Fiber Frame
5500 Enterprise Blvd (43612-3815)
PHONE..............................419 729-8520
Daniel J La Valley, *Pr*
Richard G La Valley, *
Dianne Tankoos, *
◆ **EMP:** 100 **EST:** 1959
SQ FT: 200,000
SALES (est): 22.34MM **Privately Held**
Web: www.fiberframe.com
SIC: 3089 Windows, plastics

(G-14249)
CONFORMING MATRIX CORPORATION
6255 Suder Ave (43611-1022)
PHONE..............................419 729-3777
Albert J Spelker, *Pr*
Ella Mae Macarthur, *
H E Macarthur, *
Chad Mccomas, *CFO*
EMP: 40 **EST:** 1939
SQ FT: 38,000
SALES (est): 7.02MM **Privately Held**
SIC: 3559 3544 Metal finishing equipment for plating, etc.; Special dies, tools, jigs, and fixtures

(G-14250)
CONNECTRONICS CORP (DH)
Also Called: Wiremax A Heico Company
2745 Avondale Ave (43607-3232)
P.O. Box 3355 (43607-0355)
PHONE..............................419 537-0020
Thomas Ricketts, *CEO*
Thomas L Ricketts, *
Lex Potter, *
Al Mocek, *
Judith W Vetter, *
EMP: 64 **EST:** 1988
SQ FT: 25,000
SALES (est): 11.85MM **Publicly Held**
Web: www.connectronicscorp.com
SIC: 3678 3643 Electronic connectors; Connectors and terminals for electrical devices
HQ: Heico Electronic Technologies Corp.
3000 Taft St
Hollywood FL 33021
954 987-6101

(G-14251)
CONSUMER GUILD FOODS INC
5035 Enterprise Blvd (43612-3839)
PHONE..............................419 726-3406
Wilbur R Ascham, *Pr*
Robert J Petrick, *VP*
Ann Ascham, *Sec*
EMP: 11 **EST:** 1966
SQ FT: 14,500
SALES (est): 381.92K **Privately Held**
SIC: 2035 Dressings, salad: raw and cooked (except dry mixes)

(G-14252)
CONTAINER GRAPHICS CORP
305 Ryder Rd (43607-3105)
PHONE..............................419 531-5133
Bill Beaker, *Brnch Mgr*
EMP: 31
SQ FT: 24,200
SALES (corp-wide): 4MM **Privately Held**
Web: www.containergraphics.com
SIC: 7336 3545 3944 Graphic arts and related design; Cutting tools for machine tools; Dice and dice cups
PA: Container Graphics Corp.
114 Ednbrgh S Dr Ste 104
Cary NC 27511
919 481-4200

(G-14253)
CROWN CORK & SEAL USA INC
5201 Enterprise Blvd (43612-3808)
PHONE..............................419 727-8201
Willaim Lahner, *Mgr*
EMP: 143
SALES (corp-wide): 12.01B **Publicly Held**
Web: www.crowncork.com
SIC: 3411 Metal cans
HQ: Crown Cork & Seal Usa, Inc.
770 Township Line Rd
Yardley PA 19067
215 698-5100

(G-14254)
CULAINE INC
Also Called: Cpg Printing & Graphics
1036 W Laskey Rd (43612-3030)
PHONE..............................419 345-4984
EMP: 6 **EST:** 1970
SQ FT: 4,000
SALES (est): 450.5K **Privately Held**
SIC: 2759 2752 Commercial printing, nec; Commercial printing, lithographic

(G-14255)
CUSTOM DECO LLC
1345 Miami St (43605-3313)
PHONE..............................419 698-2900
Michelle Schkeryantz, *Managing Member*
EMP: 56 **EST:** 2018
SALES (est): 1.07MM **Privately Held**
SIC: 2759 Screen printing

(G-14256)
CYBER SHED INC
5221 Tractor Rd (43612-3439)
PHONE..............................419 724-5855
EMP: 7 **EST:** 2014
SALES (est): 245.87K **Privately Held**
Web: www.cybershed.com
SIC: 2899 3545 3634 3999 Incense; Scales, measuring (machinists' precision tools); Vaporizers, electric: household; Tobacco pipes, pipestems, and bits

(G-14257)
D A L E S CORPORATION
1402 Jackson St (43604-5212)
PHONE..............................419 255-5335
Dale Frantz, *Pr*
Buzz Kutz, *VP*
Lisa Frantz, *Sec*
EMP: 9 **EST:** 1986

SQ FT: 10,000
SALES (est): 233.2K **Privately Held**
Web: www.dalescorp.com
SIC: 3991 Paint and varnish brushes

(G-14258)
DAKKOTA INTEGRATED SYSTEMS LLC
315 Matzinger Rd Unit G (43612-2626)
PHONE..............................517 694-6500
James Horwath, *Contrlr*
EMP: 27
SQ FT: 65,000
SALES (corp-wide): 242.26MM **Privately Held**
Web: www.dakkota.com
SIC: 3711 Automobile assembly, including specialty automobiles
PA: Dakkota Integrated Systems, Llc
123 Brighton Lake Rd # 202
Brighton MI 48116
517 694-6500

(G-14259)
DANA
3044 Jeep Pkwy (43610-1072)
PHONE..............................419 887-3000
EMP: 32 **EST:** 2019
SALES (est): 4.95MM **Privately Held**
Web: www.dana.com
SIC: 3714 Motor vehicle parts and accessories

(G-14260)
DANA LIGHT AXLE MFG LLC
Also Called: Toledo Driveline
3044 Jeep Pkwy (43610-1072)
PHONE..............................419 887-3000
EMP: 300
SQ FT: 100,000
Web: www.dana.com
SIC: 3714 Motor vehicle parts and accessories
HQ: Dana Light Axle Manufacturing, Llc
3939 Technology Dr
Maumee OH 43537

(G-14261)
DARLENES KITCHEN LLC
2629 Greenway St (43607-1349)
PHONE..............................910 633-9744
EMP: 6
SALES (est): 78.58K **Privately Held**
SIC: 2099 7389 Food preparations, nec; Business services, nec

(G-14262)
DECO TOOLS INC
1541 Coining Dr (43612-2978)
PHONE..............................419 476-9321
Mike Bollenbacher, *Pr*
EMP: 25 **EST:** 1955
SQ FT: 30,000
SALES (est): 4.65MM **Privately Held**
Web: www.decotools.com
SIC: 3563 3991 3842 2672 Spraying outfits: metals, paints, and chemicals (compressor); Brooms and brushes; Surgical appliances and supplies; Paper; coated and laminated, nec

(G-14263)
DECOMA SYSTEMS INTEGRATION GRO
Also Called: Team Systems
1800 Nathan Dr (43611-1091)
PHONE..............................419 324-3387
Belinda Stronach, *CEO*
EMP: 100 **EST:** 2005
SALES (est): 28.65MM

Toledo - Lucas County (G-14264) — GEOGRAPHIC SECTION

SALES (corp-wide): 37.84B **Privately Held**
SIC: **3465** Body parts, automobile: stamped metal
PA: Magna International Inc
337 Magna Dr
Aurora ON L4G 7
905 726-2462

(G-14264)
DECORATIVE PANELS INTL INC (DH)
Also Called: D P I
2900 Hill Ave (43607-2929)
PHONE..................................419 535-5921
Tim Clark, *Pr*
Allen Steiber, *Contrlr*
▼ EMP: 75 EST: 2004
SQ FT: 225,000
SALES (est): 89.11MM **Privately Held**
Web: www.decpanels.com
SIC: **2421** Sawmills and planing mills, general
HQ: As America, Inc.
30 Knightsbridge Rd # 301
Piscataway NJ 08854

(G-14265)
DETROIT TOLEDO FIBER LLC
1245 E Manhattan Blvd (43608-1549)
PHONE..................................248 647-0400
Steven Philips, *Pr*
Gary Stanis, *CFO*
EMP: 10 EST: 2012
SALES (est): 1.1MM **Privately Held**
SIC: **3714** Motor vehicle engines and parts
PA: Conform Automotive, Llc
32500 Telg Rd Ste 207
Bingham Farms MI 48025

(G-14266)
DEVILBISS RANSBURG
320 Phillips Ave (43612-1467)
PHONE..................................419 470-2000
Rolan D Kjosen, *Prin*
EMP: 16 EST: 2010
SALES (est): 406.46K **Privately Held**
Web: www.carlisleft.com
SIC: **3559** Special industry machinery, nec

(G-14267)
DFA DAIRY BRANDS ICE CREAM LLC
4117 Fitch Rd (43613-4007)
PHONE..................................419 473-9621
Randy Bevier, *Mgr*
EMP: 331
SALES (corp-wide): 24.52B **Privately Held**
Web: www.dfamilk.com
SIC: **2026** Fluid milk
HQ: Dfa Dairy Brands Ice Cream, Llc
1405 N 98th St
Kansas City KS 66111
816 801-6455

(G-14268)
DISMAT CORPORATION
336 N Westwood Ave (43607-3343)
PHONE..................................419 531-8963
John A Donofrio, *Pr*
EMP: 6 EST: 1945
SQ FT: 12,000
SALES (est): 508.9K **Privately Held**
Web: www.mckays-seasoning.com
SIC: **2099** Food preparations, nec

(G-14269)
DIVERSEY TASKI INC (PA) ○
3115 Frenchmens Rd (43607-2918)
PHONE..................................419 531-2121
Tracy Long, *Pr*
EMP: 50 EST: 2023
SALES (est): 28.07MM
SALES (corp-wide): 28.07MM **Privately Held**

SIC: **3589** Floor washing and polishing machines, commercial

(G-14270)
E-Z SHADE LLC
2720 Centennial Rd (43617-1829)
PHONE..................................419 340-2185
EMP: 6 EST: 2018
SALES (est): 254.86K **Privately Held**
Web: www.ezshadecover.com
SIC: **3999** Manufacturing industries, nec

(G-14271)
ELAIRE CORPORATION
7944 W Central Ave Ste 10 (43617-1550)
PHONE..................................419 843-2192
Mark Neeley, *Pr*
EMP: 8 EST: 2011
SALES (est): 878.51K **Privately Held**
Web: www.elairecorp.com
SIC: **3999** Manufacturing industries, nec

(G-14272)
ELDEN DRAPERIES OF TOLEDO INC
1845 N Reynolds Rd (43615-3531)
PHONE..................................419 535-1909
Betsy Grubb, *Pr*
Gary Grubb, *VP*
EMP: 10
SQ FT: 6,000
SALES (est): 885.45K **Privately Held**
Web: www.eldenblinds.com
SIC: **2391** 5714 Draperies, plastic and textile: from purchased materials; Draperies

(G-14273)
ELECTRO PRIME GROUP LLC (PA)
Also Called: Electro Prime
4510 Lint Ave Ste B (43612-2658)
PHONE..................................419 476-0100
John L Lauffer, *Managing Member*
Kevin Meade, *
▲ EMP: 70 EST: 2005
SQ FT: 20,100
SALES (est): 75.67MM **Privately Held**
Web: www.electroprime.com
SIC: **3471** 5169 Plating and polishing; Anti-corrosion products

(G-14274)
ELEMENT MACHINERY LLC
4801 Bennett Rd (43612-2531)
PHONE..................................855 447-7648
Benjamin Mcgilvery, *CEO*
Samuel Mcgilvery 40, *Pr*
Joseph Box, *VP*
EMP: 6 EST: 2015
SQ FT: 20,000
SALES (est): 1.16MM **Privately Held**
Web: www.elementmachinery.com
SIC: **3547** Rolling mill machinery

(G-14275)
ELEVATOR CNCEPTS BY WURTEC LLC
6200 Brent Dr (43611-1081)
PHONE..................................734 246-4700
Douglas Scott, *Pr*
Leigh Gaither, *VP*
▲ EMP: 10 EST: 1985
SQ FT: 10,000
SALES (est): 1.63MM
SALES (corp-wide): 27.61MM **Privately Held**
Web: www.wurtec.com
SIC: **3534** Elevators and equipment
PA: Wurtec, Incorporated
6200 Brent Dr
Toledo OH 43611
419 726-1066

(G-14276)
EMSSONS FAURECIA CTRL SYSTEMS (DH)
543 Matzinger Rd (43612-2638)
PHONE..................................812 341-2000
David Degraaf, *Pr*
Mark Stidham, *
Christophe Schmidt, *
▲ EMP: 130 EST: 1988
SQ FT: 40,000
SALES (est): 1.39B
SALES (corp-wide): 100.93MM **Privately Held**
SIC: **3714** 5013 Mufflers (exhaust), motor vehicle; Motor vehicle supplies and new parts
HQ: Faurecia Emissions Control Technologies Usa, Llc
2800 High Meadow Cir
Auburn Hills MI 48326

(G-14277)
ENGINEERED IMAGING LLC
110 E Woodruff Ave (43604-5226)
PHONE..................................419 255-1283
EMP: 13 EST: 2021
SALES (est): 3MM **Privately Held**
Web: www.engineeredimaging.com
SIC: **2759** Commercial printing, nec

(G-14278)
ENNIS INC
Tennessee Business Forms
4444 N Detroit Ave (43612-1978)
PHONE..................................800 537-8648
Tina Furgason, *Brnch Mgr*
EMP: 33
SALES (corp-wide): 420.11MM **Publicly Held**
Web: www.enniss.com
SIC: **2752** Commercial printing, lithographic
PA: Ennis, Inc.
2441 Presidential Pkwy
Midlothian TX 76065
972 775-9801

(G-14279)
ERIE STEEL LTD
5540 Jackman Rd (43613-2330)
PHONE..................................419 478-3743
Pat Flynn, *Pr*
EMP: 50 EST: 2004
SALES (est): 5.16MM **Privately Held**
Web: www.erie.com
SIC: **3398** Metal heat treating

(G-14280)
ESTONE GROUP LLC
Also Called: Wholesale and Manufacturer
2900 Carskaddon Ave # 200 (43606-1601)
PHONE..................................888 653-2246
Bing Li, *CEO*
EMP: 20 EST: 2011
SALES (est): 1.17MM **Privately Held**
Web: www.estonetech.com
SIC: **8748** 3663 Business consulting, nec; Mobile communication equipment

(G-14281)
EXCO ENGINEERING USA INC (HQ)
Also Called: Edco Tool & Die
5244 Enterprise Blvd (43612-3874)
PHONE..................................419 726-1595
Jai Singh, *Pr*
Paul Riganelli, *
◆ EMP: 45 EST: 1955
SQ FT: 50,000
SALES (est): 24.62MM
SALES (corp-wide): 375.75MM **Privately Held**
Web: www.excoengusa.com

SIC: **3544** Special dies and tools
PA: Exco Technologies Limited
130 Spy Crt Fl 2
Markham ON L3R 5
905 477-3065

(G-14282)
EXOTHERMICS
5040 Enterprise Blvd (43612-3840)
▲ EMP: 25 EST: 1976
SQ FT: 38,000
SALES (est): 11.55MM
SALES (corp-wide): 36.66B **Publicly Held**
SIC: **3443** Heat exchangers, condensers, and components
HQ: Eclipse, Inc.
201 E 18th St
Muncie IN 47302

(G-14283)
EXP FUELS INC
3070 Airport Hwy (43609-1406)
PHONE..................................419 382-7713
Victor Safadi, *Prin*
EMP: 8 EST: 2012
SALES (est): 178.31K **Privately Held**
SIC: **2869** Fuels

(G-14284)
FASTSIGNS
Also Called: Fastsigns
1100 N Mccord Rd Ste A (43615-8335)
PHONE..................................419 843-1073
Karrie Brock, *Mgr*
EMP: 11 EST: 2011
SALES (est): 292.24K **Privately Held**
Web: www.fastsigns.com
SIC: **3993** Signs and advertising specialties

(G-14285)
FENNER DUNLOP (TOLEDO) LLC
146 S Westwood Ave (43607-2948)
P.O. Box 441 (43697-0441)
PHONE..................................419 531-5300
Cassandra Pan, *
Bill Mooney, *
Ben Ficklen, *
▲ EMP: 54 EST: 2001
SQ FT: 100,000
SALES (est): 5.73MM
SALES (corp-wide): 1.05B **Privately Held**
SIC: **3052** Rubber belting
HQ: Fenner Dunlop Americas, Llc
200 Crprate Ctr Dr Ste 22
Coraopolis PA 15108

(G-14286)
FENWICK GALLERY OF FINE ARTS (PA)
Also Called: Fenwick Frame Shppe Art Gllery
3433 W Alexis Rd Frnt (43623-1400)
PHONE..................................419 475-1651
Beverly A Freshour, *Pr*
EMP: 6
SQ FT: 3,000
SALES (est): 512.56K
SALES (corp-wide): 512.56K **Privately Held**
SIC: **5999** 2499 Art dealers; Picture and mirror frames, wood

(G-14287)
FIBREBOARD CORPORATION (DH)
1 Owens Corning Pkwy (43659-1000)
PHONE..................................419 248-8000
David T Brown, *Pr*
Michael Thaman, *
▲ EMP: 200 EST: 1917
SALES (est): 105.41MM **Publicly Held**

▲ = Import ▼ = Export ◆ = Import/Export

SIC: **3089** 3272 3296 Siding, plastics; Cast stone, concrete; Mineral wool insulation products
HQ: Owens Corning Sales, Llc
1 Owens Corning Pkwy
Toledo OH 43659
419 248-8000

(G-14288)
FINISHING BRANDS HOLDINGS INC
Also Called: Finishing Brands
320 Phillips Ave (43612-1467)
PHONE.................................260 665-8800
▼ **EMP**: 190
SIC: **3563** Spraying outfits: metals, paints, and chemicals (compressor)

(G-14289)
FISKE BROTHERS REFINING CO
1500 Oakdale Ave (43605-3843)
P.O. Box 8038 (43605-0038)
PHONE.................................419 691-2491
William Kuhlman, *Mgr*
EMP: 60
SQ FT: 30,000
SALES (corp-wide): 105.58MM **Privately Held**
Web: www.lubriplate.com
SIC: **2992** 2077 Re-refining lubricating oils and greases, nec; Animal and marine fats and oils
PA: Fiske Brothers Refining Co Inc
129 Lockwood St
Newark NJ 07105
973 589-9150

(G-14290)
FLOWERS BAKING CO OHIO LLC (HQ)
325 W Alexis Rd Ste 1 (43612-3684)
PHONE.................................419 269-9202
Benjamin Barkley, *Prin*
EMP: 27 **EST**: 2017
SALES (est): 3.02MM
SALES (corp-wide): 5.09B **Publicly Held**
SIC: **2051** Bread, cake, and related products
PA: Flowers Foods, Inc.
1919 Flowers Cir
Thomasville GA 31757
229 226-9110

(G-14291)
FLYNN INC
5540 Jackman Rd (43613-2330)
PHONE.................................419 478-3743
Patrick Flynn, *Pr*
Mary Schira, *
EMP: 40 **EST**: 1961
SALES (est): 3.07MM **Privately Held**
Web: www.erie.com
SIC: **3398** Metal heat treating

(G-14292)
FORKLIFT TIRE EAST MICH INC
4934 Lewis Ave (43612-2825)
P.O. Box 235 (48066-0235)
PHONE.................................586 771-1330
Michael Fogel Iii, *Pr*
EMP: 10 **EST**: 1992
SALES (est): 1.32MM **Privately Held**
Web: www.fltbestone.com
SIC: **5014** 7534 Tires and tubes; Tire repair shop

(G-14293)
FOSTER CANNING INC
6725 W Central Ave Ste T (43617-1154)
P.O. Box 30 (43545-0230)
PHONE.................................419 841-6755
Martin Davidson, *Pr*
Martin Davidson, *Sls Dir*
EMP: 40 **EST**: 1939
SQ FT: 100,000
SALES (est): 1.93MM **Privately Held**
SIC: **2033** 2047 Tomato products, packaged in cans, jars, etc.; Dog food

(G-14294)
FRITZIE FREEZE INC
5137 N Summit St Unit 1 (43611-2754)
PHONE.................................419 727-0818
EMP: 8 **EST**: 2007
SALES (est): 251.08K **Privately Held**
Web: fritzie-freeze-inc.edan.io
SIC: **2024** Ice cream, bulk

(G-14295)
FULTON EQUIPMENT CO (PA)
823 Hamilton St (43607-4477)
PHONE.................................419 290-5393
Richard G Paul Junior, *Pr*
EMP: 8 **EST**: 1989
SQ FT: 8,000
SALES (est): 3MM **Privately Held**
SIC: **3441** 3444 3443 Fabricated structural metal; Sheet metalwork; Fabricated plate work (boiler shop)

(G-14296)
G H CUTTER SERVICES INC
6203 N Detroit Ave (43614-4818)
PHONE.................................419 476-0476
Gene Hodapp, *Pr*
Mary Hodapp, *Sec*
EMP: 9 **EST**: 1988
SALES (est): 886.41K **Privately Held**
Web: www.ghcutters.com
SIC: **3599** 7389 Machine shop, jobbing and repair; Grinding, precision: commercial or industrial

(G-14297)
GARDNER SIGNS INC (PA)
3800 Airport Hwy (43615-7106)
PHONE.................................419 385-6669
Weston L Gardner Junior, *CEO*
Scott Gardner, *Pr*
EMP: 17 **EST**: 1945
SQ FT: 13,000
SALES (est): 2.61MM
SALES (corp-wide): 2.61MM **Privately Held**
Web: www.gardnersigns.com
SIC: **3993** Electric signs

(G-14298)
GDY INSTALLATIONS INC
302 Arco Dr (43607-2907)
PHONE.................................419 467-0036
Gary Young, *Brnch Mgr*
EMP: 10
SQ FT: 8,430
Web: www.gdyinstallations.com
SIC: **3272** Furniture, church: concrete
PA: Gdy Installations Inc
2226 Linden Ct
Maumee OH 43537

(G-14299)
GENERAL MILLS INC
Also Called: General Mills
1250 W Laskey Rd (43612-2935)
PHONE.................................419 269-3100
Ann Bombrys, *Brnch Mgr*
EMP: 10
SALES (corp-wide): 20.09B **Publicly Held**
Web: www.generalmills.com
SIC: **2043** Wheat flakes: prepared as cereal breakfast food
PA: General Mills, Inc.
1 General Mills Blvd
Minneapolis MN 55426
763 764-7600

(G-14300)
GIANT INDUSTRIES INC
900 N Westwood Ave (43607-3261)
PHONE.................................419 531-4600
Raymond Simon, *CEO*
Edward Simon, *
Wolfgang Drescher, *
▲ **EMP**: 40 **EST**: 1990
SQ FT: 83,000
SALES (est): 13.28MM **Publicly Held**
Web: www.giantpumps.com
SIC: **3581** 3589 5084 3594 Automatic vending machines; Car washing machinery; Pumps and pumping equipment, nec; Fluid power pumps and motors
PA: Marathon Petroleum Corporation
539 S Main St
Findlay OH 45840

(G-14301)
GOTTFRIED MEDICAL INC
2920 Centennial Rd (43617-1833)
P.O. Box 8966 (43623-0966)
PHONE.................................419 474-2973
Brent Gottfried, *Pr*
Pauline Gottfried, *VP*
Lisa King, *Sec*
EMP: 18 **EST**: 1980
SALES (est): 3.34MM **Privately Held**
Web: www.gottfriedmedical.com
SIC: **3842** Orthopedic appliances

(G-14302)
GREAT AMERICAN COOKIE COMPANY
Also Called: Great American Cookie Co
5001 Monroe St Ste Fc13 (43623-7017)
PHONE.................................419 474-9417
Jack Scott, *Owner*
EMP: 10 **EST**: 1989
SQ FT: 400
SALES (est): 91.02K **Privately Held**
Web: www.greatamericancookies.com
SIC: **5461** 2052 Cookies; Cookies

(G-14303)
GREENWOOD PRTG & GRAPHICS INC
Also Called: Greenwood Printing
3615 Stickney Ave (43608-1307)
P.O. Box 496 (43697-0496)
PHONE.................................419 727-3275
David Stickley, *Owner*
EMP: 8 **EST**: 1981
SQ FT: 5,700
SALES (est): 381.71K **Privately Held**
Web: www.greenwoodprintingandgraphics.com
SIC: **2752** Offset printing

(G-14304)
GT TECHNOLOGIES INC
Also Called: Gt Technlgies Tledo Operations
99 N Fearing Blvd (43607-3602)
PHONE.................................419 324-7300
EMP: 100
SALES (corp-wide): 283.29MM **Privately Held**
Web: www.gttechnologies.com
SIC: **3714** 3469 3465 Motor vehicle engines and parts; Metal stampings, nec; Automotive stampings
PA: Gt Technologies, Inc.
5859 E Executive Dr
Westland MI 48185
734 467-8371

(G-14305)
GWS LEVI UP HOME SOLUTIONS LLC
6020 W Bancroft St Unit 350061 (43615-3200)
PHONE.................................419 667-6041
EMP: 25 **EST**: 1985
SALES (est): 1.3MM **Privately Held**
Web: www.toledogeneralcontractor.com
SIC: **1521** 1389 General remodeling, single-family houses; Construction, repair, and dismantling services

(G-14306)
H&M MACHINE & TOOL LLC
3823 Seiss Ave (43612-1316)
PHONE.................................419 776-9220
John Miller, *Managing Member*
Mike Whatley, *VP*
EMP: 22 **EST**: 2008
SALES (est): 2.46MM **Privately Held**
Web: www.handmmachine.com
SIC: **3544** 3543 Industrial molds; Industrial patterns

(G-14307)
H2FLOW CONTROLS INC
7629 New West Rd (43617-4201)
PHONE.................................419 841-7774
Paul Hackett, *CEO*
David Atkins, *VP*
Russel Weiss, *VP*
EMP: 6 **EST**: 1998
SALES (est): 2.65MM **Privately Held**
Web: www.h2flow.net
SIC: **5065** 3823 Security control equipment and systems; Process control instruments

(G-14308)
HA-INTERNATIONAL LLC
4243 South Ave (43615-6233)
PHONE.................................419 537-0096
Michael Hohol, *Brnch Mgr*
EMP: 30
SQ FT: 62,680
SALES (corp-wide): 250.72K **Privately Held**
Web: www.ha-international.com
SIC: **2869** 3582 2992 Industrial organic chemicals, nec; Commercial laundry equipment; Lubricating oils and greases
HQ: Ha-International, Llc
630 Oakmont Ln
Westmont IL 60559
630 575-5700

(G-14309)
HAFNERS HRDWOOD CONNECTION LLC
Also Called: Hardwood Connection, The
2845 111th St (43611-2826)
PHONE.................................419 726-4828
EMP: 6 **EST**: 1993
SQ FT: 5,600
SALES (est): 386.89K **Privately Held**
SIC: **3999** 7389 Plaques, picture, laminated; Engraving service

(G-14310)
HALE PERFORMANCE COATINGS INC
2282 Albion St (43606-4523)
PHONE.................................419 244-6451
Frederick M Deye, *Pr*
Carol Lambrecht, *
G C Scharfy, *
J C Straub, *
R A Jefferies Junior, *Prin*
EMP: 42 **EST**: 1966
SQ FT: 14,700

SALES (est): 5MM **Privately Held**
Web:
www.haleperformancecoatings.com
SIC: **3471** 3544 Chromium plating of metals or formed products; Special dies, tools, jigs, and fixtures

(G-14311)
HAMMILL MANUFACTURING CO
Co-Op Tool
1517 Coining Dr (43612-2930)
PHONE.............................419 476-9125
Jeff Mack, *Div Mgr*
EMP: 50
SALES (corp-wide): 25.62MM **Privately Held**
Web: www.hammillmedical.com
SIC: **3841** Surgical and medical instruments
PA: Hammill Manufacturing Co.
360 Tomahawk Dr
Maumee OH 43537
419 476-0789

(G-14312)
HAYES BROS ORNAMENTAL IR WORKS
1830 N Reynolds Rd (43615-3530)
PHONE.............................419 531-1491
Gary M Hayes, *Pr*
Patrick Hayes, *VP*
Douglas C Hayes, *Treas*
Gregory M Hayes, *Sec*
EMP: 10 **EST:** 1946
SQ FT: 10,000
SALES (est): 946.92K **Privately Held**
Web: www.hayesbrosiron.com
SIC: **3446** Railings, prefabricated metal

(G-14313)
HEARN PLATING CO LTD
3184 Bellevue Rd (43606-1801)
PHONE.............................419 473-9773
John D Drumheller, *Managing Member*
EMP: 12 **EST:** 1902
SQ FT: 6,400
SALES (est): 2.08MM **Privately Held**
Web: www.hearnplatingcompany.com
SIC: **3471** 3599 Electroplating of metals or formed products; Amusement park equipment

(G-14314)
HECKS DIRECT MAIL & PRTG SVC
Also Called: Heck's Diamond Printing
202 W Florence Ave (43605-3304)
P.O. Box 543 (43697-0543)
PHONE.............................419 661-6028
Cosino Trina, *VP*
EMP: 22
SALES (corp-wide): 2.28MM **Privately Held**
Web: www.hecksprinting.com
SIC: **2752** 7331 5192 Offset and photolithographic printing; Direct mail advertising services; Books, periodicals, and newspapers
PA: Hecks Direct Mail And Printing Service, Inc.
417 Main St
Toledo OH 43605
419 697-3505

(G-14315)
HECKS DIRECT MAIL PRTG SVC INC (PA)
417 Main St (43605-2057)
P.O. Box 543 (43697-0543)
PHONE.............................419 697-3505
Edward Heck, *CEO*
▲ **EMP:** 18 **EST:** 1943
SQ FT: 30,000

SALES (est): 2.28MM
SALES (corp-wide): 2.28MM **Privately Held**
Web: www.hecksprinting.com
SIC: **7331** 2752 2791 2789 Addressing service; Offset printing; Typesetting; Bookbinding and related work

(G-14316)
HEDGES SELECTIVE TL & PROD INC
Also Called: Select Tool & Production
702 W Laskey Rd (43612-3209)
PHONE.............................419 478-8670
Jeffrey Lachapelle, *Pr*
Jeff Lachatelle, *Pr*
Kathy Lachatelle, *VP*
EMP: 16 **EST:** 1972
SQ FT: 15,048
SALES (est): 947.67K **Privately Held**
Web: www.selecttoolanddie.com
SIC: **3544** Special dies and tools

(G-14317)
HEIDTMAN STEEL PRODUCTS INC (HQ)
Also Called: Heidtman Steel
2401 Front St (43605)
PHONE.............................419 691-4646
John C Bates Senior, *Ch*
Tim Berra, *Pr*
Mark Ridenour, *CFO*
Mike Kruse, *VP*
John Bates Junior, *Ex VP*
▲ **EMP:** 45 **EST:** 1954
SQ FT: 15,000
SALES (est): 218.59MM
SALES (corp-wide): 230.06MM **Privately Held**
Web: www.heidtman.com
SIC: **3316** 3312 Strip, steel, cold-rolled, nec: from purchased hot-rolled,; Sheet or strip, steel, hot-rolled
PA: Centaur, Inc.
2401 Front St
Toledo OH 43605
419 469-8000

(G-14318)
HOLLAND ENGRAVING COMPANY
Also Called: Holland Engineering Co
7340 Dorr St (43615-4112)
PHONE.............................419 865-2765
Martin Hartkopf, *Pr*
EMP: 25 **EST:** 1939
SQ FT: 15,600
SALES (est): 2.23MM **Privately Held**
Web: www.holland-eng.com
SIC: **3544** Special dies and tools

(G-14319)
HOOVER & WELLS INC
Also Called: Rez Stone
2011 Seaman St (43605-1908)
PHONE.............................419 691-9220
Margaret Hoover, *Ch Bd*
John Corsini, *
James Mc Collum, *
Barbara Corsini, *
Lisa Pudlicki, *
EMP: 120 **EST:** 1978
SQ FT: 23,448
SALES (est): 32.54MM **Privately Held**
Web: www.hooverwells.com
SIC: **1752** 2891 2851 Wood floor installation and refinishing; Adhesives and sealants; Paints and allied products

(G-14320)
HORWITZ & PINTIS CO
1604 Tracy St (43605-3426)
P.O. Box 60257 (43460-0257)

PHONE.............................419 666-2220
Steve Horwitz, *Pr*
Phyllis Horwitz, *Sec*
EMP: 15 **EST:** 1904
SQ FT: 20,000
SALES (est): 2.42MM **Privately Held**
SIC: **5085** 3412 2655 Drums, new or reconditioned; Metal barrels, drums, and pails; Fiber cans, drums, and similar products

(G-14321)
HOT MAMA FOODS INC
5839 Secor Rd (43623-1421)
PHONE.............................419 474-3402
◆ **EMP:** 15 **EST:** 1988
SQ FT: 5,118
SALES (est): 485.74K **Privately Held**
SIC: **2051** Bread, cake, and related products

(G-14322)
HP INDUSTRIES INC
400 E State Line Rd (43612-4779)
PHONE.............................419 478-0695
Scott Dubuc, *Pr*
Mark Dubuc, *
EMP: 30 **EST:** 1922
SQ FT: 11,000
SALES (est): 4.69MM **Privately Held**
Web: www.hotgraphics.us
SIC: **2752** 2791 2789 2759 Offset printing; Typesetting; Bookbinding and related work; Commercial printing, nec

(G-14323)
HYGGELIGHT LLC
902 N Superior St # A (43604-1741)
PHONE.............................419 309-6321
Christopher Hileman, *Owner*
EMP: 7 **EST:** 2017
SALES (est): 261.4K **Privately Held**
Web: www.thegrowingcandle.com
SIC: **3999** Candles

(G-14324)
I T W AUTOMOTIVE FINISHING
320 Phillips Ave (43612-1467)
PHONE.............................419 470-2000
EMP: 6 **EST:** 2010
SALES (est): 179.11K **Privately Held**
SIC: **3559** Automotive maintenance equipment

(G-14325)
IBIDLTD-BLUE GREEN ENERGY
1456 N Summit St (43604)
PHONE.............................909 547-5160
Garry Inwood, *Brnch Mgr*
EMP: 10
SALES (corp-wide): 118.44K **Privately Held**
Web: www.internationalbrandidltd.com
SIC: **2869** Industrial organic chemicals, nec
PA: Ibidltd-Blue Green Energy
6659 Schaefer Rd Ste 110
Dearborn MI 48126
909 547-5160

(G-14326)
IGNIO SYSTEMS LLC
444 W Laskey Rd Ste V (43612-3460)
PHONE.............................419 708-0503
EMP: 7 **EST:** 2013
SALES (est): 514.22K **Privately Held**
Web: www.igniosystems.com
SIC: **3821** 3625 3822 5063 Ovens, laboratory ; Motor controls, electric; Temperature controls, automatic; Boxes and fittings, electrical

(G-14327)
IMPAC HI-PERFORMANCE MACHINING
5515 Enterprise Blvd (43612-3814)
PHONE.............................419 726-7100
Gerald R Nastachowski, *Owner*
Chris Nastachowski, *Mgr*
EMP: 6 **EST:** 1971
SQ FT: 6,000
SALES (est): 300K **Privately Held**
SIC: **3599** Machine shop, jobbing and repair

(G-14328)
IMPACT PRODUCTS LLC (HQ)
2840 Centennial Rd (43617-1898)
PHONE.............................419 841-2891
Laura Marcero, *
Terry Neal, *Pr*
◆ **EMP:** 76 **EST:** 2001
SQ FT: 155,000
SALES (est): 70.26MM
SALES (corp-wide): 104.62MM **Privately Held**
Web: www.impact-products.com
SIC: **5087** 5084 2392 3089 Janitors' supplies ; Safety equipment; Mops, floor and dust; Buckets, plastics
PA: Supply Source Enterprises, Inc.
150 4th Ave N Ste 1810
Nashville TN 37219
919 387-1059

(G-14329)
INDEPENDENT POWER CONS INC
6051 Telegraph Rd Ste 19 (43612-4560)
PHONE.............................419 476-8383
David Denner, *Pr*
Michael W Denner, *VP*
Patricia M Denner, *Sec*
EMP: 7 **EST:** 1982
SALES (est): 709.66K **Privately Held**
Web: www.ipctoledo.com
SIC: **3469** Machine parts, stamped or pressed metal

(G-14330)
INDUSTRIAL SCREEN PRCESS SVC I (PA)
Also Called: Isps
17 17th St (43604-6708)
P.O. Box 593 (43697-0593)
PHONE.............................419 255-4900
Thomas V Cutcher Senior, *Pr*
Thomas V Cutcher Ii, *VP*
Sharon Cutcher, *Sec*
EMP: 15 **EST:** 1979
SQ FT: 53,000
SALES (est): 2.35MM **Privately Held**
Web: www.ispsinc.com
SIC: **2759** 7373 Screen printing; Computer-aided design (CAD) systems service

(G-14331)
INITIAL DESIGNS INC
Also Called: Seaway Enterprises
2453 Tremainsville Rd Unit 2 (43613-3438)
PHONE.............................419 475-3900
Robert W Stauffer, *Pr*
Carole S Stauffer, *Sec*
EMP: 6 **EST:** 1986
SQ FT: 13,000
SALES (est): 427.27K **Privately Held**
Web: www.initial-design.com
SIC: **2395** Embroidery products, except Schiffli machine

(G-14332)
INNOMARK GROUP LLC
1218 Madison Ave (43604-5540)
PHONE.............................419 720-8102

Mohamad Awad, *Managing Member*
EMP: 8
SALES (est): 358.83K **Privately Held**
SIC: 3993 Signs and advertising specialties

(G-14333)
INNOVATIVE CONTROLS CORP
1354 E Bdwy St (43605-3667)
PHONE...............................419 691-6684
Louis M Soltis, *Pr*
Anson F Schultz, *
EMP: 37 **EST:** 1974
SQ FT: 20,000
SALES (est): 8.69MM **Privately Held**
Web: www.innovativecontrolscorp.com
SIC: 3613 3535 8711 3823 Control panels, electric; Conveyors and conveying equipment; Engineering services; Process control instruments

(G-14334)
INSTA PLAK INC (PA)
Also Called: Insta-Plak
5025 Dorr St (43615-3855)
PHONE...............................419 537-1555
Rexford E Hardin D.d.s., *CEO*
Stephen R Hardin, *Pr*
James Byrd, *VP*
Betty Hardin, *Sec*
EMP: 10 **EST:** 1985
SQ FT: 7,800
SALES (est): 1.38MM
SALES (corp-wide): 1.38MM **Privately Held**
Web: www.instaplak.com
SIC: 2499 3993 Decorative wood and woodwork; Signs, not made in custom sign painting shops

(G-14335)
INTERTEC CORPORATION (PA)
3400 Exec Pkwy (43606-1396)
PHONE...............................419 537-9711
George B Seifried, *Pr*
Darrel G Howard, *Sec*
Scott A Slater, *VP Fin*
◆ **EMP:** 10 **EST:** 1978
SQ FT: 1,000
SALES (est): 28.3MM
SALES (corp-wide): 28.3MM **Privately Held**
Web: www.intertecsystems.com
SIC: 3559 1796 3523 Glass making machinery: blowing, molding, forming, etc.; Machinery installation; Farm machinery and equipment

(G-14336)
INVESTORS UNITED INC (PA)
Also Called: Tiger Lebanese Bakery
4215 Monroe St (43606-1975)
PHONE...............................419 473-8942
Abdul Hammuda, *Pr*
Abdul Shamamit, *Sec*
EMP: 11 **EST:** 1973
SQ FT: 4,500
SALES (est): 1.21MM
SALES (corp-wide): 1.21MM **Privately Held**
Web: www.tigerbakery.com
SIC: 5461 5411 2051 Bread; Delicatessen stores; Bakery, for home service delivery

(G-14337)
IPS TREATMENTS INC
3254 Hill Ave (43607-2911)
PHONE...............................419 241-5955
Fred Pinto, *Pr*
Manit Vichitchot, *VP*
EMP: 9 **EST:** 1994
SQ FT: 16,000

SALES (est): 879.86K **Privately Held**
SIC: 3471 Cleaning, polishing, and finishing

(G-14338)
IRONHEAD FABG & CONTG INC
2245 Front St (43605-1231)
PHONE...............................419 690-0000
Anthony Lamantia, *Pr*
Kathy Lamantia, *
EMP: 23 **EST:** 2002
SQ FT: 33,500
SALES (est): 937.64K **Privately Held**
Web: www.ironheadfab.com
SIC: 3441 Fabricated structural metal

(G-14339)
IRONHEAD MARINE INC
2245 Front St (43605-1231)
PHONE...............................419 690-0000
Kathy Lamantia, *CFO*
EMP: 20 **EST:** 2008
SALES (est): 1.33MM **Privately Held**
Web: www.ironheadmarine.com
SIC: 3731 Shipbuilding and repairing

(G-14340)
ISHOS BROS FUEL VENTURES
2446 W Alexis Rd (43613-2139)
PHONE...............................419 913-5718
EMP: 101
SALES (corp-wide): 646.67K **Privately Held**
SIC: 2869 Fuels
PA: Isho's Bros Fuel Ventures, Inc
1289 Conant St
Maumee OH 43537
586 634-0187

(G-14341)
J & S INDUSTRIAL MCH PDTS INC
123 Oakdale Ave (43605-3322)
PHONE...............................419 691-1380
Nancy Colyer, *Prin*
Donald R Colyer, *
Elton E Bowland, *
John Sehr, *
George Bowland, *
EMP: 85 **EST:** 1946
SQ FT: 32,000
SALES (est): 3.82MM **Privately Held**
Web: www.jsindustrialmachine.com
SIC: 3559 7692 Glass making machinery: blowing, molding, forming, etc.; Welding repair

(G-14342)
JUPMODE
2022 Adams St (43604-4432)
PHONE...............................419 318-2029
EMP: 21 **EST:** 2017
SALES (est): 2.08MM **Privately Held**
Web: www.jupmode.com
SIC: 2759 Screen printing

(G-14343)
JUSTINS DELIGHT LLC
101 W Park St (43608-1727)
PHONE...............................567 234-3575
Danielle Bryant, *Managing Member*
EMP: 6
SALES (est): 246.61K **Privately Held**
SIC: 2599 Food wagons, restaurant

(G-14344)
KAPIOS LLC
Also Called: Kapios Health
2865 N Reynolds Rd Ste 220d (43615-2100)
PHONE...............................567 661-0772
Justin Hammerling, *CEO*

EMP: 6 **EST:** 2017
SALES (est): 345.64K **Privately Held**
Web: www.kapioshealth.com
SIC: 7372 8099 Business oriented computer software; Health and allied services, nec

(G-14345)
KASPER ENTERPRISES INC
Also Called: Harmon Sign Company
7844 W Central Ave (43617-1530)
PHONE...............................419 841-6656
Daniel C Kasper, *Ch Bd*
Jeff Kasper, *Pr*
John E Wagoner, *Prin*
EMP: 7 **EST:** 1937
SQ FT: 55,430
SALES (est): 2.86MM
SALES (corp-wide): 76.87MM **Privately Held**
Web: www.harmonsign.com
SIC: 3993 Neon signs
PA: Allen Industries, Inc.
6434 Burnt Poplar Rd
Greensboro NC 27409
336 668-2791

(G-14346)
KAY TOLEDO TAG INC
6050 Benore Rd (43612-3906)
P.O. Box 5038 (43611-0038)
PHONE...............................419 729-5479
Dan Kay, *Pr*
EMP: 96 **EST:** 1973
SQ FT: 87,000
SALES (est): 19.49MM
SALES (corp-wide): 420.11MM **Publicly Held**
Web: www.kaytag.com
SIC: 2752 2679 2759 2671 Offset printing; Tags and labels, paper; Commercial printing, nec; Paper; coated and laminated packaging
PA: Ennis, Inc.
2441 Presidential Pkwy
Midlothian TX 76065
972 775-9801

(G-14347)
KEYSTONE PRESS INC
1801 Broadway St (43609-3290)
P.O. Box 9183 (43697-9183)
PHONE...............................419 243-7326
Paul A Schultz, *CEO*
David P Schultz, *Pr*
Andrew C Schultz, *VP*
Elizabeth Schultz, *Sec*
EMP: 8 **EST:** 1921
SQ FT: 9,000
SALES (est): 984.57K **Privately Held**
Web: www.keystonepresstoledo.com
SIC: 2752 2759 2796 2791 Offset printing; Letterpress printing; Platemaking services; Typesetting

(G-14348)
KITCHEN DESIGNS PLUS INC
2725 N Reynolds Rd (43615-2031)
PHONE...............................419 536-6605
Pat Mckimmy, *Pr*
EMP: 24 **EST:** 1962
SQ FT: 6,000
SALES (est): 2.47MM **Privately Held**
Web: www.kitchendesignplus.com
SIC: 5031 2434 Kitchen cabinets; Wood kitchen cabinets

(G-14349)
KNIGHT INDUSTRIES CORP
5949 Telegraph Rd (43612-4548)
PHONE...............................419 478-8550
Kevin Ebeid, *VP*

Carrie Ebeid, *
EMP: 14 **EST:** 1986
SQ FT: 104,000
SALES (est): 996.9K **Privately Held**
Web: www.artist-choice.com
SIC: 3211 Picture glass

(G-14350)
KONECRANES INC
Also Called: Crane Pro Services
2221 Tedrow Rd (43614-3860)
PHONE...............................419 382-7575
Terri Dietrich, *Mgr*
EMP: 10
Web: www.konecranes.com
SIC: 3536 Hoists, cranes, and monorails
HQ: Konecranes, Inc.
4401 Gateway Blvd
Springfield OH 45502

(G-14351)
KUHLMAN CORPORATION
444 Kuhlman Dr (43609-2629)
PHONE...............................419 321-1670
Dwayne Palmer, *Brnch Mgr*
EMP: 10
SALES (corp-wide): 42.49MM **Privately Held**
Web: www.gerkencompanies.com
SIC: 3273 Ready-mixed concrete
PA: Kuhlman Corporation
1845 Indian Wood Cir
Maumee OH 43537
419 897-6000

(G-14352)
KUHLMAN ENGINEERING CO
840 Champlain St (43604-3643)
PHONE...............................419 243-2196
Phil Kolling, *Pr*
Norman Kuhlman, *VP*
EMP: 10 **EST:** 1916
SQ FT: 7,500
SALES (est): 883.4K **Privately Held**
SIC: 3444 Sheet metal specialties, not stamped

(G-14353)
KUKA TLEDO PRDCTION OPRTONS LL
3770 Stickney Ave (43608-1310)
PHONE...............................419 727-5500
Lawrence A Drake, *CEO*
Paul Ambros, *
Larry Drake, *
Jake Ladouceur, *
EMP: 247 **EST:** 2004
SALES (est): 37.45MM **Privately Held**
Web: www.kuka.com
SIC: 3713 Truck and bus bodies
HQ: Kuka Systems Gmbh
Blucherstr. 144
Augsburg BY 86165
8217970

(G-14354)
KYLE MEDIA INC
2611 Montebello Rd (43607-1366)
P.O. Box 6469 (43612-0469)
PHONE...............................419 754-4234
Erik R Kyle, *Pr*
EMP: 6 **EST:** 2001
SALES (est): 222.47K **Privately Held**
SIC: 2721 Magazines: publishing only, not printed on site

(G-14355)
KYLE MEDIA INC
Also Called: Great Lakes Scuttlebutt
7862 W Central Ave Ste F (43617-1549)
P.O. Box 351417 (43635-1417)

Toledo - Lucas County (G-14356) — GEOGRAPHIC SECTION

PHONE..............................877 775-2538
Erik Kyle, *CEO*
Erik R Kyle, *CEO*
EMP: 6 **EST:** 1992
SALES (est): 490.33K **Privately Held**
Web: www.greatlakesscuttlebutt.com
SIC: 8999 2721 7311 7313 Writing for publication; Periodicals, publishing and printing; Advertising consultant; Magazine advertising representative

(G-14356)
LA PERLA INC (PA)
Also Called: Tortilla Factory
2742 Hill Ave (43607-2926)
PHONE..............................419 534-2074
TOLL FREE: 800
Santiago Martinez, *Pr*
EMP: 8 **EST:** 1963
SQ FT: 8,000
SALES (est): 952.4K
SALES (corp-wide): 952.1K **Privately Held**
SIC: 2099 5141 Tortillas, fresh or refrigerated; Groceries, general line

(G-14357)
LA PRENSA PUBLICATIONS INC
Also Called: Aztlan Communications
616 Adams St (43604-1420)
PHONE..............................419 870-6565
Becky Mc Queen, *Prin*
EMP: 6 **EST:** 1989
SALES (est): 641.23K **Privately Held**
Web: www.laprensatoledo.com
SIC: 2711 Newspapers: publishing only, not printed on site

(G-14358)
LAKE ERIE WATERKEEPER INC
3900 N Summit St (43611-3042)
PHONE..............................419 691-3788
Sandra Bihn, *Prin*
EMP: 8 **EST:** 2011
SALES (est): 78.93K **Privately Held**
Web: www.lakeeriewaterkeeper.org
SIC: 3949 Water skis

(G-14359)
LBA CUSTOM PRINTING
207 Arco Dr (43607-2906)
P.O. Box 352679 (43635-2679)
PHONE..............................419 535-3151
Brett Bullock, *Prin*
EMP: 6 **EST:** 2008
SALES (est): 120.4K **Privately Held**
Web: www.metzgers.com
SIC: 2752 Offset printing

(G-14360)
LED LIGHTING CENTER INC (PA)
Also Called: Optimal Led
5500 Enterprise Blvd (43612-3815)
PHONE..............................714 271-2633
Steven James, *CEO*
▲ **EMP:** 9 **EST:** 2013
SALES (est): 2.09MM
SALES (corp-wide): 2.09MM **Privately Held**
Web: www.optimalled.com
SIC: 3646 3645 Commercial lighting fixtures; Residential lighting fixtures

(G-14361)
LED LIGHTING CENTER LLC
Also Called: Optimalled
5500 Enterprise Blvd (43612-3815)
PHONE..............................888 988-6353
EMP: 11 **EST:** 2015
SALES (est): 786.25K
SALES (corp-wide): 2.09MM **Privately Held**

SIC: 3646 3645 Commercial lighting fixtures; Residential lighting fixtures
PA: Led Lighting Center Inc.
5500 Enterprise Blvd
Toledo OH 43612
714 271-2633

(G-14362)
LEE WILLIAMS MEATS INC (PA)
3002 131st St (43611-2329)
PHONE..............................419 729-3893
Barry L Williams, *Pr*
Richard W Boldt, *
Mary Jo Cramer, *
Margaret Williams, *
EMP: 25 **EST:** 1955
SQ FT: 3,096
SALES (est): 2.43MM
SALES (corp-wide): 2.43MM **Privately Held**
Web: www.houseofmeats.com
SIC: 5421 2013 Meat markets, including freezer provisioners; Sausages and other prepared meats

(G-14363)
LEMSCO INC
Also Called: Lemsco-Girkins
2056 Canton Ave (43620-1945)
PHONE..............................419 242-4005
Richard J Baldwin, *Pr*
Richard Baldwin, *Pr*
Barbara Baldwin, *Sec*
EMP: 8 **EST:** 1947
SQ FT: 11,000
SALES (est): 544.41K **Privately Held**
Web: www.lemsco.com
SIC: 7694 5999 Electric motor repair; Motors, electric

(G-14364)
LIBBEY GLASS LLC (HQ)
Also Called: Libbey
300 Madison Ave (43604-2634)
P.O. Box 919 (43699-0919)
PHONE..............................419 325-2100
Michael P Bauer, *CEO*
Richard Reynolds, *
Ken Boerger, *
Daniel P Ibele, *
Susan A Kovach, *
◆ **EMP:** 200 **EST:** 1987
SALES (est): 586.22MM **Privately Held**
Web: www.libbey.com
SIC: 3229 3231 Tableware, glass or glass ceramic; Products of purchased glass
PA: Libbey Inc.
300 Madison Ave
Toledo OH 43604

(G-14365)
LIBBEY GLASS LLC
Also Called: Libbey America
940 Ash St (43611-3846)
PHONE..............................419 727-2211
Steve Felix, *Brnch Mgr*
EMP: 125
Web: www.libbey.com
SIC: 3229 3421 3262 Tableware, glass or glass ceramic; Cutlery; Vitreous china table and kitchenware
HQ: Libbey Glass Llc
300 Madison Ave Fl 4
Toledo OH 43604
419 325-2100

(G-14366)
LIBBEY INC (PA)
Also Called: Libbey
300 Madison Ave (43604)
P.O. Box 919 (43699)

PHONE..............................419 325-2100
Michael P Bauer, *CEO*
William A Foley, *Non-Executive Chairman of the Board**
Juan Amezquita, *
James C Burmeister, *
Jennifer Molnar, *Chief Human Resources Officer**
▼ **EMP:** 200 **EST:** 1818
SALES (est): 785.6MM **Privately Held**
Web: www.libbey.com
SIC: 3229 3262 Glass furnishings and accessories; Tableware, vitreous china

(G-14367)
LILY ANN CABINETS
2939 Douglas Rd (43606-3502)
PHONE..............................419 360-2455
Chuck Bennett, *Pr*
EMP: 9 **EST:** 2018
SALES (est): 103.10K **Privately Held**
Web: www.lilyanncabinets.com
SIC: 2434 Wood kitchen cabinets

(G-14368)
LINDE GAS & EQUIPMENT INC
Also Called: Praxair
6055 Brent Dr (43611-1084)
PHONE..............................419 729-7732
EMP: 22
Web: www.lindeus.com
SIC: 2813 Industrial gases
HQ: Linde Gas & Equipment Inc.
10 Riverview Dr
Danbury CT 06810
844 445-4633

(G-14369)
LITHIUM INNOVATIONS CO LLC
3171 N Republic Blvd Ste 101 (43615)
PHONE..............................419 725-3525
Ford B Cauffiel, *Managing Member*
◆ **EMP:** 6 **EST:** 2010
SALES (est): 473.24K **Privately Held**
Web: www.liinnovations.com
SIC: 2819 Lithium compounds, inorganic

(G-14370)
LOVE LAUGH & LAUNDRY
Also Called: Love. Laugh. Laundry.
5333 Secor Rd (43623-2407)
PHONE..............................567 377-1951
Brandi Hopson, *CEO*
EMP: 6 **EST:** 2018
SALES (est): 252.74K **Privately Held**
SIC: 5999 5641 2331 5169 Miscellaneous retail stores, nec; Children's wear; Women's and misses' blouses and shirts; Detergents and soaps, except specialty cleaning

(G-14371)
LRBG CHEMICALS USA INC
2112 Sylvan Ave (43606-4767)
P.O. Box 2570 (43606-0570)
PHONE..............................419 244-5856
James Bennett, *Managing Member*
James Bennett, *VP*
EMP: 30 **EST:** 2018
SQ FT: 70,000
SALES (est): 4.89MM **Privately Held**
Web: www.lrbgchemicals.com
SIC: 2821 Plastics materials and resins

(G-14372)
LUBRIPLATE LUBRICANTS COMPANY
1500 Oakdale Ave (43605-3843)
PHONE..............................419 691-2491
EMP: 8 **EST:** 2017
SALES (est): 3.78MM **Privately Held**

Web: www.lubriplate.com
SIC: 5172 2992 Lubricating oils and greases; Lubricating oils and greases

(G-14373)
LUCAS SPECIALTY PRODUCTS LLC
1101 Pelee St (43607-3434)
PHONE..............................419 290-6168
Robert Urfer, *Prin*
EMP: 8 **EST:** 2010
SALES (est): 206.88K **Privately Held**
SIC: 2842 Sanitation preparations, disinfectants and deodorants

(G-14374)
M&D MACHINE LLC
Also Called: Machine Shop
42 W Sylvania Ave (43612-1445)
PHONE..............................419 214-0201
EMP: 6 **EST:** 2013
SALES (est): 494.9K **Privately Held**
Web: www.mdmachineusa.com
SIC: 3599 Machine shop, jobbing and repair

(G-14375)
MAGIC WOK INC (PA)
Also Called: Magic Wok Enterprises
3352 W Laskey Rd (43623-4030)
PHONE..............................419 531-1818
Sutas Pipatjarasgit, *Pr*
Nucharee Pipatjarasgit, *Sec*
EMP: 7 **EST:** 1983
SQ FT: 580
SALES (est): 875.13K
SALES (corp-wide): 875.13K **Privately Held**
Web: www.magicwok.com
SIC: 5812 2032 Chinese restaurant; Ethnic foods, canned, jarred, etc.

(G-14376)
MAGNA MODULAR SYSTEMS LLC (DH)
Also Called: T.E.A.M. Systems
1800 Jason St (43611)
PHONE..............................419 324-3387
Grahhame Burrow, *CEO*
Keith Mcmahon, *Genl Mgr*
Michael Hanson, *Contrlr*
▲ **EMP:** 70 **EST:** 2005
SQ FT: 140,000
SALES: 98.44MM
SALES (corp-wide): 37.84B **Privately Held**
Web: www.magna.com
SIC: 3714 Motor vehicle body components and frame
HQ: Magna Exteriors Of America, Inc.
750 Tower Dr
Troy MI 48098
248 631-1100

(G-14377)
MALLORY PATTERN WORKS INC
5340 Enterprise Blvd (43612-3811)
PHONE..............................419 726-8001
Al Antoine, *Pr*
Janice Mallory, *Treas*
Shirley Peschel, *Sec*
EMP: 6 **EST:** 1960
SQ FT: 6,000
SALES (est): 726.63K **Privately Held**
Web: www.mallorypatternworks.com
SIC: 3544 3469 Industrial molds; Patterns on metal

(G-14378)
MARTINEZ FOOD PRODUCTS LLC
1220 Belmont Ave (43607-4105)
PHONE..............................419 720-6973
EMP: 6 **EST:** 2005
SALES (est): 435.96K **Privately Held**

GEOGRAPHIC SECTION

Toledo - Lucas County (G-14403)

SIC: 2035 Pickles, sauces, and salad dressings

(G-14379)
MAUMEE MACHINE & TOOL CORP
2960 South Ave (43609-1328)
PHONE.................................419 385-2501
Bruce M Denman, *Pr*
Bruce M Denman, *Pr*
Patrick T Denman, *VP*
John S Buescher, *General Vice President*
EMP: 20 EST: 1966
SALES (est): 1.45MM Privately Held
SIC: 3451 5072 Screw machine products; Screws

(G-14380)
MAUMEE VALLEY FABRICATORS INC
Also Called: Escher Division
4801 Bennett Rd (43612-2531)
PHONE.................................419 476-1411
Patrick Copeland, *Pr*
EMP: 25 EST: 1978
SQ FT: 54,000
SALES (est): 4.69MM Privately Held
Web: www.maumeevalleyfab.com
SIC: 3441 Fabricated structural metal

(G-14381)
MELDRUM MECHANICAL SERVICES
4455 South Ave (43615-6416)
PHONE.................................419 535-3500
Brent R Meldrum Junior, *Pr*
EMP: 10 EST: 2001
SALES (est): 1.88MM Privately Held
Web: www.meldrum-mechanical.com
SIC: 3599 Machine shop, jobbing and repair

(G-14382)
MELNOR GRAPHICS LLC
5225 Telegraph Rd (43612-3570)
PHONE.................................419 476-8808
EMP: 11 EST: 2016
SALES (est): 548.89K Privately Held
SIC: 2759 Circulars: printing, nsk

(G-14383)
METZGERS
150 Arco Dr (43607-2903)
PHONE.................................419 861-8611
John Luscombe, *VP*
Todd Beringer, *S&M/VP*
Andrea Ohrt, *CFO*
Tom Metzger, *CEO*
EMP: 60 EST: 2014
SALES (est): 1.6MM Privately Held
Web: www.metzgers.com
SIC: 2752 Offset printing

(G-14384)
MIDTOWN PALLET & RECYCLING INC
1987 Hawthorne St (43606)
P.O. Box 95 (43542-0095)
PHONE.................................419 241-1311
Rita Stang, *Pr*
EMP: 13 EST: 1993
SQ FT: 10,000
SALES (est): 434.22K Privately Held
Web: www.midtownpallet.com
SIC: 2448 Pallets, wood

(G-14385)
MIDWEST DIE SUPPLY COMPANY
6240 American Rd Ste A (43612-3925)
PHONE.................................419 729-7141
David Brezinski, *Pr*
EMP: 9 EST: 1948
SQ FT: 5,000
SALES (est): 773.7K Privately Held
Web: www.midwestdie.com
SIC: 3599 Machine shop, jobbing and repair

(G-14386)
MIDWESTERN BAG CO INC
3230 Monroe St (43606-4519)
PHONE.................................419 241-3112
Toney Oneal, *Pr*
Paulette Lalor, *VP*
Brian Hoch, *Sec*
EMP: 8 EST: 1985
SQ FT: 43,000
SALES (est): 325.71K Privately Held
SIC: 5199 3069 Bags, baskets, and cases; Bags, rubber or rubberized fabric

(G-14387)
MJB TOLEDO INC (HQ)
Also Called: National Super Service Co
3115 Frenchmens Rd (43607-2918)
PHONE.................................419 531-2121
Mark Bevington, *Pr*
◆ EMP: 100 EST: 1911
SQ FT: 160,000
SALES (est): 28.07MM
SALES (corp-wide): 28.07MM Privately Held
Web: www.nss.com
SIC: 3589 Floor washing and polishing machines, commercial
PA: Diversey Taski, Inc.
   3115 Frenchmens Rd
   Toledo OH 43607
   419 531-2121

(G-14388)
MMP TOLEDO
5847 Secor Rd (43623-1421)
PHONE.................................419 472-0505
Steven Heaney, *Pr*
Teresa Heaney, *Prin*
EMP: 15 EST: 1980
SQ FT: 1,500
SALES (est): 323.75K Privately Held
Web: www.mmptoledo.com
SIC: 2752 Offset printing

(G-14389)
MODERN BUILDERS SUPPLY INC (PA)
Also Called: Polaris Technologies
3500 Phillips Ave (43608-1070)
P.O. Box 80025 (43608-0025)
PHONE.................................419 241-3961
Kevin Leggett, *CEO*
Larry Leggett, *
G Taylor Evans Iii, *Treas*
Eric Leggett, *
Jack Marstellar, *
EMP: 200 EST: 1944
SQ FT: 40,000
SALES (est): 346.23MM
SALES (corp-wide): 346.23MM Privately Held
Web: www.modernbuilderssupply.com
SIC: 3089 5032 3446 3442 Windows, plastics ; Brick, stone, and related material; Architectural metalwork; Metal doors, sash, and trim

(G-14390)
MON-SAY CORP
Also Called: Ergocan
2735 Dorr St (43607-3240)
P.O. Box 8487 (43623-0487)
PHONE.................................419 720-0163
Terry Netterfield, *Pr*
▲ EMP: 7 EST: 1987
SQ FT: 22,000
SALES (est): 965.74K Privately Held
Web: www.ergocan.com

SIC: 3089 Bowl covers, plastics

(G-14391)
MOSSING MACHINE AND TOOL INC
5225 Telegraph Rd (43612-3570)
PHONE.................................419 476-5657
Dave S Mossing, *Pr*
EMP: 8 EST: 1981
SQ FT: 8,000
SALES (est): 942.94K Privately Held
Web: www.hvacwichitaks.com
SIC: 3599 Machine shop, jobbing and repair

(G-14392)
MY WAY HOME FINDER MAGAZINE
5215 Monroe St Ste 14 (43623-3190)
PHONE.................................419 841-6201
James Moody, *Pt*
EMP: 6 EST: 1985
SQ FT: 2,000
SALES (est): 289.69K Privately Held
SIC: 2711 Newspapers

(G-14393)
MYERS
1500 E Alexis Rd (43612-3952)
PHONE.................................419 727-2010
Nick Marsico, *Prin*
EMP: 8 EST: 2002
SALES (est): 159.03K Privately Held
Web: www.myersconc.com
SIC: 2834 Pharmaceutical preparations

(G-14394)
N-VIRO INTERNATIONAL CORP
Also Called: N-Viro
2254 Centennial Rd (43617-1870)
P.O. Box 8770 (43623-0770)
PHONE.................................419 535-6374
Timothy R Kasmoch, *Ch Bd*
Robert W Bohmer, *Ex VP*
James K Mchugh, *CFO*
EMP: 10 EST: 1979
SALES (est): 1.28MM Privately Held
Web: www.nviro.com
SIC: 3589 4959 Water treatment equipment, industrial; Sanitary services, nec

(G-14395)
NATIONAL STAFFING SERVICES LLC
5151 Monroe St Ste 101 (43623-3456)
PHONE.................................785 731-2540
EMP: 7 EST: 2019
SALES (est): 185.12K Privately Held
SIC: 2911 Petroleum refining

(G-14396)
NEW DIE INC
2828 E Manhattan Blvd (43611-1710)
PHONE.................................419 726-7581
EMP: 22 EST: 1996
SQ FT: 7,500
SALES (est): 1.99MM Privately Held
SIC: 3544 Special dies and tools

(G-14397)
NO BURN NORTH AMERICA INC
2930 Centennial Rd (43617-1833)
PHONE.................................419 841-6055
William Kish, *CEO*
Kenneth Rusk, *CFO*
EMP: 10 EST: 2002
SQ FT: 9,000
SALES (est): 182.75K Privately Held
SIC: 2899 Fire retardant chemicals

(G-14398)
NORTH TOLEDO GRAPHICS LLC
Also Called: Nt
5225 Telegraph Rd (43612-3570)

PHONE.................................419 476-8808
Shirleen Kistner, *Managing Member*
Melanie Tremonti, *
EMP: 95 EST: 2004
SQ FT: 210,000
SALES (est): 9.97MM Privately Held
Web: www.northtoledographics.com
SIC: 2752 Offset printing

(G-14399)
NORTHCOAST PMM LLC
Also Called: Blink Print & Mail
4725 Southbridge Rd (43623-3123)
PHONE.................................419 540-8667
Thomas J Pruss, *Managing Member*
EMP: 10 EST: 2017
SALES (est): 454.65K Privately Held
SIC: 7331 2752 Mailing service; Commercial printing, lithographic

(G-14400)
NSG GLASS NORTH AMERICA INC (PA)
811 Madison Ave (43604-5684)
PHONE.................................419 247-4800
Richard A Altman, *Pr*
Gary J Roser, *Sec*
EMP: 32 EST: 2018
SQ FT: 4,000
SALES (est): 10.44MM
SALES (corp-wide): 10.44MM Privately Held
SIC: 3211 Flat glass

(G-14401)
NTA GRAPHICS INC
5225 Telegraph Rd (43612-3547)
PHONE.................................419 476-8808
Gregory Tremonti, *Pr*
David Tremonti, *
Gail Shaffer, *
EMP: 22 EST: 1984
SQ FT: 163,000
SALES (est): 772.11K Privately Held
Web: www.ntagraphics.com
SIC: 2752 Offset printing

(G-14402)
OASIS MDITERRANEAN CUISINE INC
1520 W Laskey Rd (43612-2914)
P.O. Box 8881 (43623-0881)
PHONE.................................419 269-1459
Francois Hashem, *Pr*
▲ EMP: 32 EST: 1985
SQ FT: 30,000
SALES (est): 4MM Privately Held
Web: www.omcfood.com
SIC: 2099 2032 Dips, except cheese and sour cream based; Canned specialties

(G-14403)
OBARS MACHINE AND TOOL COMPANY (PA)
Also Called: Obars Welding & Fabg Div
115 N Westwood Ave # 125 (43607-3341)
PHONE.................................419 535-6307
Greg Obarski, *Pr*
Alvin R Obarski, *
Jeffrey R Obarski, *
Michael Webber, *
EMP: 41 EST: 1946
SQ FT: 30,000
SALES (est): 3.89MM
SALES (corp-wide): 3.89MM Privately Held
Web: www.obarsmachine.com
SIC: 3451 3541 3545 Screw machine products; Machine tools, metal cutting type; Machine tool accessories

Toledo - Lucas County (G-14404) — GEOGRAPHIC SECTION

(G-14404)
OCCV1 INC
1 Owens Corning Pkwy (43659-1000)
PHONE.................................419 248-8000
EMP: 9 **EST:** 2017
SALES (est): 1.35MM **Publicly Held**
SIC: 3272 Concrete products, nec
PA: Owens Corning
  1 Owens Corning Pkwy
  Toledo OH 43659

(G-14405)
OCCV2 LLC
1 Owens Corning Prkwy (43659-1000)
PHONE.................................419 248-8000
EMP: 11 **EST:** 2017
SALES (est): 868.42K **Publicly Held**
SIC: 3299 Nonmetallic mineral products,
PA: Owens Corning
  1 Owens Corning Pkwy
  Toledo OH 43659

(G-14406)
OFF CONTACT INC
Also Called: Off Contact Productions
4756 W Bancroft St (43615-3902)
PHONE.................................419 255-5546
Allen Schall, Pr
▲ **EMP:** 18 **EST:** 1988
SQ FT: 9,600
SALES (est): 675.65K **Privately Held**
Web: www.offcontact.com
SIC: 2759 5084 Screen printing; Industrial machinery and equipment

(G-14407)
OHIO BLENDERS INC (PA)
Also Called: Alfagreen Supreme
2404 N Summit St (43611-3599)
PHONE.................................419 726-2655
Ken Vaupel, CEO
Donald Verhoff, Pr
Ronald Yarnell, VP
Becky Lumbrezer-box, Sec
EMP: 10 **EST:** 1960
SQ FT: 6,000
SALES (est): 4.82MM
SALES (corp-wide): 4.82MM **Privately Held**
Web: ohioblenders.tripod.com
SIC: 2048 2047 Prepared feeds, nec; Dog and cat food

(G-14408)
OHIO BUILDING RESTORATION INC (PA)
830 Mill St (43609-2448)
PHONE.................................419 244-7372
Duane Haas, Pr
Duane W Haas, Pr
John Hall, VP
Debra Haas, Sec
EMP: 21 **EST:** 1949
SQ FT: 6,500
SALES (est): 2.42MM
SALES (corp-wide): 2.42MM **Privately Held**
Web: www.ohiobr.com
SIC: 1741 1721 1799 1389 Tuckpointing or restoration; Exterior commercial painting contractor; Waterproofing; Construction, repair, and dismantling services

(G-14409)
OHIO MODULE MANUFACTURING COMPANY LLC
Also Called: M N A
3900 Stickney Ave (43608-1314)
PHONE.................................419 729-6700
◆ **EMP:** 706

SIC: 3711 Chassis, motor vehicle

(G-14410)
OHIO STEEL PROCESSING LLC
Also Called: Ohio Pickling & Processing
1149 Campbell St (43607-4467)
PHONE.................................419 241-9601
Sergei Kuznetsov, Managing Member
EMP: 90 **EST:** 2020
SALES (est): 5.43MM **Privately Held**
SIC: 3312 Blast furnaces and steel mills

(G-14411)
OHIO TRANSITIONAL MACHINE & TL
3940 Castener St (43612-1402)
PHONE.................................419 476-0820
Marten Whalen, Pr
EMP: 7 **EST:** 1984
SQ FT: 5,000
SALES (est): 712.63K **Privately Held**
Web: ohiotransitional.wixsite.com
SIC: 3599 Machine shop, jobbing and repair

(G-14412)
OI CASTALIA STS INC
1 Seagate (43604-1558)
PHONE.................................419 247-5000
EMP: 30 **EST:** 1987
SALES (est): 3.77MM
SALES (corp-wide): 7.11B **Publicly Held**
SIC: 3221 Glass containers
PA: O-I Glass, Inc.
  1 Michael Owens Way
  Perrysburg OH 43551
  567 336-5000

(G-14413)
OKULEY HVAC & MET FABRICATION
50 W Sylvania Ave (43612-1445)
PHONE.................................419 478-4699
Robert Okuley, Mgr
EMP: 7 **EST:** 2017
SALES (est): 142.71K **Privately Held**
Web: www.okuleyhvac.com
SIC: 3444 Sheet metalwork

(G-14414)
ONESOURCE WATER LLC
Also Called: Pure Water Technology NW Ohio
812 Warehouse Rd Ste F (43615-6476)
PHONE.................................866 917-7873
EMP: 13
SALES (corp-wide): 6.4MM **Privately Held**
SIC: 3589 Swimming pool filter and water conditioning systems
PA: Onesource Water, Llc
  3175 Bass Pro Dr
  Grapevine TX 76051
  866 917-7873

(G-14415)
ONLINE MEGA SELLERS CORP (PA)
Also Called: Distinct Advantage Cabinetry
4236 W Alexis Rd (43623-1255)
PHONE.................................888 384-6468
Timothy Baker, Pr
Craig Poupard, VP
EMP: 8 **EST:** 2013
SQ FT: 250,000
SALES (est): 4.07MM
SALES (corp-wide): 4.07MM **Privately Held**
Web: www.kitchenandbathroomcabinets.com
SIC: 2434 7371 7373 Wood kitchen cabinets ; Computer software systems analysis and design, custom; Systems software development services

(G-14416)
OPC INC
419 N Reynolds Rd (43615-5221)
PHONE.................................419 531-2222
Anne M Cole, Prin
EMP: 8 **EST:** 1992
SALES (est): 331.37K **Privately Held**
SIC: 3842 Braces, orthopedic

(G-14417)
OPP DISSOLUTION LLC
Also Called: Opp
1149 Campbell St (43607-4467)
PHONE.................................419 241-9601
Sergei Kuznetsov, Managing Member
Mike Balk, *
▲ **EMP:** 70 **EST:** 1999
SALES (est): 14.91MM
SALES (corp-wide): 221.96MM **Privately Held**
Web: www.ohiopickling.com
SIC: 3312 Blast furnaces and steel mills
PA: Mnp Corporation
  44225 Utica Rd
  Utica MI 48317
  586 254-1320

(G-14418)
OSTEONOVUS INC
1510 N Westwood Ave Ste 1080 (43606-8202)
PHONE.................................419 530-5940
Anand Agarwal, Pr
EMP: 8 **EST:** 2013
SALES (est): 1.1MM **Privately Held**
Web: www.osteonovus.com
SIC: 3842 Grafts, artificial: for surgery

(G-14419)
OSTEONOVUS INC
1510 N Westwood Ave # 2040 (43606-8202)
PHONE.................................419 530-5940
EMP: 7
SALES (est): 283.16K **Privately Held**
Web: www.osteonovus.com
SIC: 3842 Grafts, artificial: for surgery

(G-14420)
OVERHEAD INC
Also Called: Overhead Door Company
340 New Towne Square Dr (43612-4606)
PHONE.................................419 476-0300
EMP: 7
SQ FT: 11,470
SALES (corp-wide): 9.59MM **Privately Held**
Web: www.overheadinc.com
SIC: 3442 5719 5211 Metal doors, sash, and trim; Fireplace equipment and accessories; Garage doors, sale and installation
PA: Overhead Inc.
  340 New Towne Square Dr
  Toledo OH 43612
  419 476-7811

(G-14421)
OWENS CORNING (PA)
Also Called: Owens Corning
1 Owens Corning Pkwy (43659)
PHONE.................................419 248-8000
Brian D Chambers, Ch Bd
Todd W Fister, Ex VP
Paula Russell, Chief Human Resources Officer
Jose L Mendez-andino, Research & Development
Gina A Beredo, Corporate Secretary
◆ **EMP:** 1000 **EST:** 1938
SQ FT: 400,000
SALES (est): 9.68B **Publicly Held**

Web: www.owenscorning.com
SIC: 3292 2519 Asbestos products; Fiberglass and plastic furniture

(G-14422)
OWENS CORNING HT INC
Owens Corning World Headquar (43659-0001)
PHONE.................................419 248-8000
EMP: 28 **EST:** 2016
SALES (est): 365.38K **Publicly Held**
Web: careers.owenscorning.com
SIC: 3229 Glass fibers, textile
HQ: Owens Corning Sales, Llc
  1 Owens Corning Pkwy
  Toledo OH 43659
  419 248-8000

(G-14423)
OWENS CORNING ROOFG & ASP LLC (HQ)
Also Called: Trumbull Asphalt
1 Owens Corning Pkwy (43659-0001)
PHONE.................................877 858-3855
EMP: 30 **EST:** 2019
SALES (est): 11.63MM **Publicly Held**
SIC: 3296 Fiberglass insulation
PA: Owens Corning
  1 Owens Corning Pkwy
  Toledo OH 43659

(G-14424)
OWENS CORNING SALES LLC (HQ)
1 Owens Corning Pkwy (43659-0001)
P.O. Box 13950 (27709-3950)
PHONE.................................419 248-8000
Brian Chambers, Pr
Stephen K Krull, VP
David L Johns, VP
◆ **EMP:** 1000 **EST:** 2006
SQ FT: 400,000
SALES (est): 1.9B **Publicly Held**
SIC: 3296 2952 3229 3089 Fiberglass insulation; Asphalt felts and coatings; Glass fibers, textile; Windows, plastics
PA: Owens Corning
  1 Owens Corning Pkwy
  Toledo OH 43659

(G-14425)
OWENS CRNING TCHNCAL FBRICS LL
1 Owens Corning Pkwy (43659-1000)
PHONE.................................419 248-5535
EMP: 32 **EST:** 2012
SALES (est): 6.98MM **Publicly Held**
SIC: 3292 Asbestos products
PA: Owens Corning
  1 Owens Corning Pkwy
  Toledo OH 43659

(G-14426)
P & J INDUSTRIES INC (PA)
4934 Lewis Ave (43612-2825)
P.O. Box 6918 (43612-0918)
PHONE.................................419 726-2675
James E Powers Junior, Pr
Marguerite M Powers, *
▼ **EMP:** 120 **EST:** 1980
SALES (est): 8.83MM
SALES (corp-wide): 8.83MM **Privately Held**
Web: www.pjind.com
SIC: 3471 Electroplating of metals or formed products

(G-14427)
P212121 LLC
2027 Bretton Pl (43606-3318)
PHONE.................................253 229-9327

▲ = Import ▼ = Export
◆ = Import/Export

GEOGRAPHIC SECTION

Toledo - Lucas County (G-14451)

Sean Seaver, *Prin*
EMP: 6 **EST:** 2010
SALES (est): 124.14K **Privately Held**
Web: store.p212121.com
SIC: 3821 Chemical laboratory apparatus, nec

(G-14428)
PAGE SLOTTING SAW CO INC
3820 Lagrange St (43612-1425)
PHONE.................................419 476-7475
James Bouldin, *Pr*
EMP: 19 **EST:** 1960
SQ FT: 3,500
SALES (est): 702.75K **Privately Held**
Web: www.legendaryroofinginc.com
SIC: 3541 Machine tools, metal cutting type

(G-14429)
PB FBRCTION MECH CONTRS CORP
750 W Laskey Rd (43607-3209)
PHONE.................................419 478-4869
Charles W Bailey, *Pr*
Hubert Backes, *VP*
EMP: 25 **EST:** 1986
SQ FT: 6,000
SALES (est): 1.16MM **Privately Held**
SIC: 3535 3444 3443 3441 Conveyors and conveying equipment; Sheet metalwork; Fabricated plate work (boiler shop); Fabricated structural metal

(G-14430)
PEAK ELECTRIC INC
Also Called: Peak Electric
320 N Byrne Rd (43607-2607)
PHONE.................................419 726-4848
Milton Mcintyre, *Pr*
Lenora Mcintyre, *VP*
Rhys Petee, *Prin*
EMP: 10 **EST:** 2000
SALES (est): 5.08MM **Privately Held**
Web: www.peakelectrictoledo.com
SIC: 3612 5063 Transformers, except electric ; Electrical apparatus and equipment

(G-14431)
PEDESTRIAN PRESS
2233 Robinwood Ave (43620-1020)
PHONE.................................419 244-6488
Jeffrey Kent Nelson, *Prin*
EMP: 8 **EST:** 2004
SALES (est): 245.55K **Privately Held**
Web: www.pedestrianpress.com
SIC: 2741 Miscellaneous publishing

(G-14432)
PEPSI-COLA METRO BTLG CO INC
Also Called: Pepsico
3245 Hill Ave (43607-2936)
PHONE.................................419 534-2186
Michael Hill, *Brnch Mgr*
EMP: 55
SALES (corp-wide): 86.39B **Publicly Held**
Web: www.pepsico.com
SIC: 2086 Carbonated soft drinks, bottled and canned
HQ: Pepsi-Cola Metropolitan Bottling
  Company, Inc.
  700 Anderson Hill Rd
  Purchase NY 10577
  914 767-6000

(G-14433)
PERFORMANCE PACKAGING INC
5219 Telegraph Rd (43612-3570)
PHONE.................................419 478-8805
Frank Duval, *Pr*
Scott Ruetz, *VP*
▲ **EMP:** 10 **EST:** 2006
SALES (est): 1.01MM **Privately Held**
Web: www.perfpack.com
SIC: 7389 7319 4225 2759 Labeling bottles, cans, cartons, etc.; Display advertising service; General warehousing and storage; Labels and seals: printing, nsk

(G-14434)
PERSTORP POLYOLS INC
600 Matzinger Rd (43612-2695)
PHONE.................................419 729-5448
David Wolf, *Pr*
Larry Fioritto, *
◆ **EMP:** 109 **EST:** 1983
SQ FT: 3,000
SALES (est): 41.75MM **Privately Held**
Web: www.perstorp.com
SIC: 2819 2851 2821 Elements; Paints and allied products; Plastics materials and resins
HQ: Perstorp Ab
  Perstorp Industripark
  Perstorp 284 8
  43538000

(G-14435)
PILKINGTON HOLDINGS INC (DH)
Also Called: P H I
811 Madison Ave Fl 1 (43604)
P.O. Box 799 (43697)
◆ **EMP:** 300 **EST:** 1982
SQ FT: 217,000
SALES (est): 1.32B **Privately Held**
Web: www.pilkington.com
SIC: 3211 Flat glass
HQ: Pilkington Group Limited
  Group Taxation Department European
  Technical Centre
  Ormskirk LANCS L40 5
  169550000

(G-14436)
PILKINGTON NORTH AMERICA INC (DH)
811 Madison Ave Fl 3 (43604-5688)
P.O. Box 799 (43697-0799)
PHONE.................................419 247-3731
Richard Altman, *Pr*
◆ **EMP:** 119 **EST:** 1986
SALES (est): 1.32B **Privately Held**
Web: www.pilkington.com
SIC: 3211 Construction glass
HQ: Pilkington Holdings Inc.
  811 Madison Ave Fl 1
  Toledo OH 43604

(G-14437)
PISTON AUTOMOTIVE LLC
Also Called: Piston Group
1212 E Alexis Rd (43612-3974)
PHONE.................................419 464-0250
Vincent Johnson, *Brnch Mgr*
EMP: 1234
SALES (corp-wide): 2.3B **Privately Held**
Web: www.pistonautomotive.com
SIC: 3714 Motor vehicle parts and accessories
HQ: Piston Automotive, L.L.C.
  12723 Telegraph Rd Ste 1
  Redford MI 48239
  313 541-8674

(G-14438)
PITTSBURG CORNING CORP DI
1 Owens Corning Pkwy (43659-1000)
PHONE.................................724 327-6100
EMP: 7 **EST:** 2017
SALES (est): 224K **Privately Held**
SIC: 3229 Pressed and blown glass, nec

(G-14439)
PITTSBURGH CORNING LLC (HQ)
1 Owens Corning Pkwy (43659-1000)
PHONE.................................724 327-6100
James R Kane, *Pr*
◆ **EMP:** 490 **EST:** 1937
SALES (est): 47.64MM **Publicly Held**
Web: www.owenscorning.com
SIC: 3229 Pressed and blown glass, nec
PA: Owens Corning
  1 Owens Corning Pkwy
  Toledo OH 43659

(G-14440)
PLABELL RUBBER PRODUCTS CORP (PA)
300 S Saint Clair St # 324 (43604-8846)
PHONE.................................419 691-5878
John Jaksetic, *Pr*
Jim Farkas, *VP*
Randy Reif, *Sec*
EMP: 22 **EST:** 1993
SQ FT: 40,000
SALES (est): 2.72MM **Privately Held**
SIC: 3069 3061 Molded rubber products; Mechanical rubber goods

(G-14441)
POWERBUFF INC
1001 Brown Ave (43607-3942)
PHONE.................................419 241-2156
Walter C Anderson, *Pr*
EMP: 11 **EST:** 1994
SQ FT: 50,000
SALES (est): 508.98K **Privately Held**
SIC: 3589 Floor washing and polishing machines, commercial

(G-14442)
PRECISION GRAPHIC SERVICES INC
4612 Corey Rd (43623-2610)
PHONE.................................419 241-5189
Kenneth P Breier, *Pr*
EMP: 10 **EST:** 1976
SALES (est): 429.27K **Privately Held**
Web: www.pgstoledo.com
SIC: 2759 2789 Embossing on paper; Binding only: books, pamphlets, magazines, etc.

(G-14443)
PROJECTS DESIGNED & BUILT
Also Called: PD&b
5949 American Rd E (43612-3950)
PHONE.................................419 726-7400
Ken Martin, *Pr*
▼ **EMP:** 21 **EST:** 1998
SQ FT: 16,000
SALES (est): 5.95MM **Privately Held**
Web: www.pdbinc.com
SIC: 8742 3599 8711 3499 Automation and robotics consultant; Custom machinery; Mechanical engineering; Machine bases, metal

(G-14444)
QUALITY TOOL COMPANY
Also Called: Quality Stamping
577 Mel Simon Dr (43612-4729)
PHONE.................................419 476-8228
James G Pasch, *Pr*
Michael Pasch, *VP*
EMP: 20 **EST:** 1954
SQ FT: 48,000
SALES (est): 4.58MM **Privately Held**
Web: www.qualitytool.com
SIC: 3469 3312 Stamping metal for the trade ; Tool and die steel

(G-14445)
QUIKRETE COMPANIES LLC
873 Western Ave (43609-2774)
PHONE.................................419 241-1148
Becky Garner, *Mgr*
EMP: 19
SQ FT: 10,700
Web: www.quikrete.com
SIC: 3272 3241 Dry mixture concrete; Cement, hydraulic
HQ: The Quikrete Companies Llc
  5 Concourse Pkwy Ste 1900
  Atlanta GA 30328
  404 634-9100

(G-14446)
R & D CUSTOM MACHINE & TL INC
5961 American Rd E (43612-3950)
PHONE.................................419 727-1700
David Skomer, *Pr*
EMP: 25 **EST:** 1982
SQ FT: 16,800
SALES (est): 2.62MM **Privately Held**
Web: www.rdcustommachine.com
SIC: 3599 Machine shop, jobbing and repair

(G-14447)
RADCO FIRE PROTECTION INC
444 W Laskey Rd Ste S (43612-3460)
PHONE.................................419 476-0102
Douglas W Ward, *Pr*
EMP: 7 **EST:** 1985
SQ FT: 1,800
SALES (est): 524.1K **Privately Held**
SIC: 3569 Sprinkler systems, fire: automatic

(G-14448)
RADCO INDUSTRIES INC
3226 Frenchmens Rd (43607-2996)
PHONE.................................419 531-4731
Richard Anderson, *Pr*
Mary Anderson, *VP*
◆ **EMP:** 11 **EST:** 1962
SQ FT: 28,000
SALES (est): 1.94MM **Privately Held**
Web: www.radcoindustries.com
SIC: 3599 Machine shop, jobbing and repair

(G-14449)
RAKA CORPORATION
Also Called: Lockrey Manufacturing
203 Matzinger Rd (43612-2624)
PHONE.................................419 476-6572
Don Vollmar, *CEO*
Mark A Makulinski, *
EMP: 78 **EST:** 1953
SQ FT: 75,000
SALES (est): 11.71MM **Privately Held**
Web: www.lockreymanufacturing.com
SIC: 3451 3444 Screw machine products; Sheet metalwork

(G-14450)
REA POLISHING INC
1606 W Laskey Rd (43612-2916)
PHONE.................................419 470-0216
EMP: 61 **EST:** 1995
SQ FT: 19,600
SALES (est): 5.49MM **Privately Held**
SIC: 3471 Finishing, metals or formed products

(G-14451)
RIKER PRODUCTS INC
4901 Stickney Ave (43612-3716)
P.O. Box 6976 (43612-0976)
PHONE.................................419 729-1626
Mark Foster, *CEO*
Gary Frye, *
Rollie Bauer, *

Toledo - Lucas County (G-14452)

Michael Jaeck, *
▼ EMP: 88 EST: 1932
SQ FT: 250,000
SALES (est): 23.18MM Privately Held
Web: www.rikerprod.com
SIC: 3714 3498 Mufflers (exhaust), motor vehicle; Fabricated pipe and fittings

(G-14452)
RIVER EAST CUSTOM CABINETS
221 S Saint Clair St (43604-8739)
PHONE..............................419 244-3226
Joe Weiser, Pr
John Weiser, VP
EMP: 22 EST: 1984
SQ FT: 15,000
SALES (est): 719.65K Privately Held
Web: www.rivereastcabinets.com
SIC: 5712 2434 Cabinet work, custom; Wood kitchen cabinets

(G-14453)
RIVERSIDE MARINE INDS INC
Also Called: H Hansen Industries
2824 N Summit St (43611-3425)
PHONE..............................419 729-1621
Tony La Mantia, Pr
Larry Ansler, *
Jerry Norton, *
EMP: 60 EST: 1924
SQ FT: 30,000
SALES (est): 8.33MM Privately Held
Web: www.hansenind.com
SIC: 3599 Machine shop, jobbing and repair

(G-14454)
RLM FABRICATING INC
4801 Bennett Rd (43612-2531)
PHONE..............................419 729-6130
Michael Reser, Pr
Patrick Copeland, *
EMP: 30 EST: 2006
SALES (est): 4.01MM Privately Held
Web: www.maumeevalleyfab.com
SIC: 3441 Fabricated structural metal

(G-14455)
RLM FABRICATING INC
5425 Enterprise Blvd (43612-3812)
PHONE..............................419 476-1411
Michael Reser, Pr
EMP: 9 EST: 2006
SALES (est): 198.03K Privately Held
Web: www.maumeevalleyfab.com
SIC: 3441 Fabricated structural metal

(G-14456)
ROBERT BECKER IMPRESSIONS INC
4646 Angola Rd (43615-6407)
PHONE..............................419 385-5303
Robert O Becker, Pr
Jennie Becker, VP
EMP: 12 EST: 1976
SQ FT: 9,000
SALES (est): 943.7K Privately Held
Web: www.beckerimpressions.com
SIC: 7334 5044 2752 Blueprinting service; Blueprinting equipment; Offset printing

(G-14457)
ROCKET VENTURES LLC
300 Madison Ave Ste 270 (43604-1568)
PHONE..............................419 530-6083
EMP: 7 EST: 2017
SALES (est): 162.28K Privately Held
Web: www.rocketventures.org
SIC: 3229 Pressed and blown glass, nec

(G-14458)
ROGAR INTERNATIONAL INC
Also Called: N M Hansen Machine and Tool
4015 Dewey St (43612-1415)
P.O. Box 6938 (43612-0938)
PHONE..............................419 476-5500
Ronnie W Clark, CEO
Roger Burditt, VP
James V Schindler, Sec
R Ken Clark, Treas
EMP: 15 EST: 1909
SQ FT: 30,000
SALES (est): 2.47MM Privately Held
Web: www.nmhansen.com
SIC: 3599 Machine shop, jobbing and repair

(G-14459)
RONFELDT ASSOCIATES INC
2345 S Byrne Rd (43614-5107)
PHONE..............................419 382-5641
Theodore A Markwood, Pr
Howard Ronfeldt, *
Theodore Ronfeld, *
EMP: 59 EST: 1946
SQ FT: 57,000
SALES (est): 2.73MM Privately Held
Web: www.ronfeldt.com
SIC: 3469 3544 Stamping metal for the trade; Special dies, tools, jigs, and fixtures
PA: Ice Industries, Inc.
    3810 Herr Rd
    Sylvania OH 43560

(G-14460)
RONFELDT MANUFACTURING LLC (HQ)
Also Called: Ice Industries Ronfeldt
2345 S Byrne Rd (43614-5107)
PHONE..............................419 382-5641
Howard Ice, Managing Member
Paul Bishop, Pr
Jeff Boger, CFO
EMP: 21 EST: 2007
SALES (est): 22.28MM Privately Held
Web: www.iceindustries.com
SIC: 3469 Stamping metal for the trade
PA: Ice Industries, Inc.
    3810 Herr Rd
    Sylvania OH 43560

(G-14461)
SABCO INDUSTRIES INC
5242 Angola Rd Ste 150 (43615-6334)
PHONE..............................419 531-5347
Robert Sulier, Pr
John Pershing, *
▲ EMP: 28 EST: 1961
SALES (est): 893.85K Privately Held
SIC: 7699 5085 3993 3412 Tank repair and cleaning services; Barrels, new or reconditioned; Signs and advertising specialties; Metal barrels, drums, and pails

(G-14462)
SANDWISCH ENTERPRISES INC (PA)
1644 Campbell St (43607-4381)
PHONE..............................419 944-6446
Daniel Sandwisch, CEO
Peter James Harvey, Pr
William Harvey, VP
Elizabeth Harvey, Sec
EMP: 8 EST: 1978
SQ FT: 14,000
SALES (est): 1.02MM
SALES (corp-wide): 1.02MM Privately Held
Web: www.pandjmfginc.com

SIC: 3471 7389 4213 Finishing, metals or formed products; Grinding, precision: commercial or industrial; Trucking, except local

(G-14463)
SAXON PRODUCTS INC
2283 Fulton St (43620-1272)
PHONE..............................419 241-6771
Edward L Poling, Pr
Tony Berezowski, VP
Mary Mazziotti, Sec
▲ EMP: 9 EST: 1961
SQ FT: 20,000
SALES (est): 878.85K Privately Held
Web: www.saxonproducts.com
SIC: 3496 Miscellaneous fabricated wire products

(G-14464)
SEAPORT MOLD & CASTING COMPANY
1309 W Bancroft St (43606-4634)
PHONE..............................419 243-1422
Michael A Kumor, Pr
Fred Kumor, VP
EMP: 25 EST: 1946
SQ FT: 15,000
SALES (est): 765.78K Privately Held
SIC: 3369 3543 Nonferrous foundries, nec; Industrial patterns

(G-14465)
SEAWAY PATTERN MFG INC
5749 Angola Rd (43615-6319)
PHONE..............................419 865-5724
Richard Johnston, Pr
EMP: 26 EST: 1962
SQ FT: 30,000
SALES (est): 4.08MM Privately Held
Web: www.seawaypatterninc.com
SIC: 3543 3544 Industrial patterns; Industrial molds

(G-14466)
SEM-COM COMPANY INC (PA)
1040 N Westwood Ave (43607-3263)
P.O. Box 8428 (43623-0428)
PHONE..............................419 537-8813
Lawrence V Pfaender, Ch
Michael V Pfaender, Pr
Johann Manning, Sec
James Pfaender, VP
William Garrett, VP
EMP: 9 EST: 1984
SQ FT: 22,500
SALES (est): 1.17MM
SALES (corp-wide): 1.17MM Privately Held
Web: www.sem-com.com
SIC: 3231 2891 3229 Products of purchased glass; Adhesives and sealants; Fiber optics strands

(G-14467)
SENECA PETROLEUM CO INC
2563 Front St (43605-1153)
PHONE..............................419 691-3581
Dean Friend, Brnch Mgr
EMP: 12
SALES (corp-wide): 23.06MM Privately Held
SIC: 2911 1611 Asphalt or asphaltic materials, made in refineries; Highway and street construction
PA: Seneca Petroleum Co., Inc.
    13301 Cicero Ave
    Midlothian IL 60418
    708 396-1100

(G-14468)
SENECA PETROLEUM CO INC
1441 Woodville Rd (43605-3233)
PHONE..............................419 691-3581
Dean Friend, Mgr
EMP: 15
SALES (corp-wide): 23.06MM Privately Held
SIC: 2951 2911 Asphalt and asphaltic paving mixtures (not from refineries); Petroleum refining
PA: Seneca Petroleum Co., Inc.
    13301 Cicero Ave
    Midlothian IL 60418
    708 396-1100

(G-14469)
SFC GRAPHICS CLEVELAND LTD
Also Called: Sfc Graphic Arts Div
110 E Woodruff Ave (43604-5226)
P.O. Box 877 (43697-0877)
PHONE..............................419 255-1283
Tom Clark, CEO
Paul Clark, *
EMP: 34 EST: 1982
SQ FT: 15,000
SALES (est): 957.37K Privately Held
Web: www.engineeredimaging.com
SIC: 2752 Offset printing

(G-14470)
SHELAR INC
5335 Enterprise Blvd (43612-3810)
PHONE..............................419 729-9756
Fred Shelar, Pr
Dennis Krout, VP
▲ EMP: 140 EST: 1987
SQ FT: 70,000
SALES (est): 24.7MM Privately Held
Web: www.sterlingpipeandtube.com
SIC: 3317 Steel pipe and tubes

(G-14471)
SHELLY MATERIALS INC
Also Called: Shelly Liquid Division
352 George Hardy Dr (43605-1063)
PHONE..............................740 246-6315
John Power, Pr
EMP: 26
SALES (corp-wide): 32.72B Privately Held
Web: www.shellyco.com
SIC: 1422 Crushed and broken limestone
HQ: Shelly Materials, Inc.
    80 Park Dr
    Thornville OH 43076
    740 246-6315

(G-14472)
SIGMA TUBE COMPANY
Also Called: Sterling Pipe & Tube
1050 Progress Ave (43612-9800)
PHONE..............................419 729-9756
EMP: 8 EST: 2000
SALES (est): 113.24K Privately Held
SIC: 3312 Pipes and tubes

(G-14473)
SILLY BRANDZ GLOBAL LLC
148 Main St (43605-2067)
PHONE..............................419 697-8324
EMP: 52 EST: 2009
SQ FT: 10,000
SALES (est): 3.26MM Privately Held
SIC: 3961 3085 2396 3999 Keychains, except precious metal; Plastics bottles; Sweat bands, hat and cap: made from purchased materials; Identification tags, except paper

GEOGRAPHIC SECTION

Toledo - Lucas County (G-14497)

(G-14474)
SOJOURNERS TRUTH INC
7 E Bancroft St (43620-1916)
PHONE.................................419 243-0007
Fletcher Word, *Pr*
EMP: 10 **EST:** 2013
SALES (est): 852.33K **Privately Held**
Web: wordpress.thetruthtoledo.com
SIC: 2711 Newspapers, publishing and printing

(G-14475)
STONECO INC
352 George Hardy Dr (43605-1063)
PHONE.................................419 693-3933
William Hodges, *Mgr*
EMP: 9
SALES (corp-wide): 32.72B **Privately Held**
Web: www.shellyco.com
SIC: 2951 Paving mixtures
HQ: Stoneco, Inc.
     1700 Fostoria Ave Ste 200
     Findlay OH 45840
     419 422-8854

(G-14476)
SUNSHINE PRODUCTS
760 Warehouse Rd Ste O (43615-6455)
P.O. Box 350786 (43635-0786)
PHONE.................................303 478-4913
Del Short, *Prin*
EMP: 7 **EST:** 2006
SALES (est): 228.12K **Privately Held**
Web: www.sunshine.org
SIC: 3915 Jewelers' materials and lapidary work

(G-14477)
SUPERIOR IMPRESSIONS INC
327 12th St (43604-7531)
PHONE.................................419 244-8676
Douglas A Shelton, *Pr*
EMP: 8 **EST:** 1967
SQ FT: 6,000
SALES (est): 984.57K **Privately Held**
Web: www.superiorimpressions.com
SIC: 2752 Offset printing

(G-14478)
SUPERIOR PACKAGING
2930 Airport Hwy (43609-1404)
PHONE.................................419 380-3335
Steve Davis, *Owner*
EMP: 10 **EST:** 2007
SALES (est): 1.44MM **Privately Held**
Web: www.dunnagebags.com
SIC: 3629 Electronic generation equipment

(G-14479)
SURFACE ENTERPRISES INC
1465 W Alexis Rd (43612-4044)
PHONE.................................419 476-5670
Susan Kroma, *Pr*
EMP: 6 **EST:** 1995
SQ FT: 9,000
SALES (est): 477.68K **Privately Held**
Web: www.surfaceenterprises.com
SIC: 2434 Wood kitchen cabinets

(G-14480)
SYRACUSE CHINA LLC (DH)
Also Called: Syracuse China Company
300 Madison Ave (43604-1561)
P.O. Box 10060 (43699-0060)
PHONE.................................419 325-2100
◆ **EMP:** 225 **EST:** 1995
SQ FT: 50,000
SALES (est): 52.34MM **Privately Held**
SIC: 2711 Newspapers, publishing and printing
HQ: Libbey Glass Llc
     300 Madison Ave Fl 4
     Toledo OH 43604
     419 325-2100

(G-14481)
TAFT TOOL & PRODUCTION CO
756 S Byrne Rd Ste 1 (43609-1088)
PHONE.................................419 385-2576
Rose Tavtigian, *VP*
Paul Sneider, *Genl Mgr*
EMP: 10 **EST:** 1948
SQ FT: 13,000
SALES (est): 712.96K **Privately Held**
SIC: 3544 3545 7699 Special dies and tools; Gauges (machine tool accessories); Industrial machinery and equipment repair

(G-14482)
TELEX COMMUNICATIONS INC
Also Called: Toledo Business Journals
5660 Southwyck Blvd Ste 150 (43614)
P.O. Box 1206 (43537)
PHONE.................................419 865-0972
Sanford Lubin, *Pr*
EMP: 9 **EST:** 1986
SALES (est): 306.98K **Privately Held**
Web: www.toledobiz.com
SIC: 8742 2721 8748 Industry specialist consultants; Periodicals; Communications consulting

(G-14483)
TEMBEC BTLSR INC
2112 Sylvan Ave (43606-4767)
P.O. Box 2570 (43606-0570)
PHONE.................................419 244-5856
James M Lopez, *Pr*
Lawrence Rowley, *
Dan Wozniak, *
◆ **EMP:** 32 **EST:** 1902
SQ FT: 84,000
SALES (est): 9.65MM
SALES (corp-wide): 1.64B **Publicly Held**
Web: www.lrbgchemicals.com
SIC: 2821 5169 Plastics materials and resins ; Industrial chemicals
HQ: Tembec Inc.
     100-4 Place Ville-Marie
     Montreal QC H3B 2
     514 871-0137

(G-14484)
TEX-TYLER CORPORATION
Also Called: Viking Paper
5148 Stickney Ave (43612-3721)
PHONE.................................419 729-4951
J Anthony Mooter, *Pr*
Robert L Walker, *
EMP: 10 **EST:** 1981
SQ FT: 60,000
SALES (est): 329.69K **Privately Held**
Web: www.packpros.net
SIC: 3444 Sheet metalwork

(G-14485)
THERMAFIBER INC (HQ)
1 Owens Corning Pkwy (43659-1000)
PHONE.................................260 563-2111
◆ **EMP:** 93 **EST:** 1997
SQ FT: 3,000
SALES (est): 75.27K **Publicly Held**
Web: www.curtainwallinsulation.com
SIC: 3296 Fiberglass insulation
PA: Owens Corning
     1 Owens Corning Pkwy
     Toledo OH 43659

(G-14486)
TIMMYS SANDWICH SHOP
5426 Cresthaven Ln (43614-1218)
PHONE.................................419 350-8267
Timothy Foster, *Owner*
EMP: 6 **EST:** 2014
SALES (est): 171.91K **Privately Held**
SIC: 2099 7389 Ready-to-eat meals, salads, and sandwiches; Business services, nec

(G-14487)
TJ METZGERS INC
Also Called: Metzgers
207 Arco Dr (43607-2906)
PHONE.................................419 861-8611
EMP: 72 **EST:** 1976
SQ FT: 63,146
SALES (est): 13.39MM **Privately Held**
Web: www.metzgers.com
SIC: 2789 2791 7335 2752 Bookbinding and related work; Photocomposition, for the printing trade; Color separation, photographic and movie film; Offset printing

(G-14488)
TM MACHINE & TOOL INC
521 Mel Simon Dr (43612-4726)
PHONE.................................419 478-0310
Karyn Weeks, *Pr*
EMP: 8 **EST:** 1984
SQ FT: 20,000
SALES (est): 919.32K **Privately Held**
Web: www.tmmachineandtool.com
SIC: 3544 3599 Special dies and tools; Machine shop, jobbing and repair

(G-14489)
TMD INC
4 E Laskey Rd (43612-3517)
PHONE.................................419 476-4581
Joe Pirrone, *Brnch Mgr*
EMP: 233
SALES (corp-wide): 1.78MM **Privately Held**
Web: www.tmdinc.com
SIC: 3544 Special dies, tools, jigs, and fixtures
PA: Tmd, Inc.
     1429 Coining Dr
     Toledo OH 43612
     419 470-3950

(G-14490)
TNT SOLID SOLUTIONS LLC
6120 N Detroit Ave (43612-4810)
PHONE.................................419 262-6228
Beth Godfrey, *Prin*
EMP: 11 **EST:** 2017
SALES (est): 1.02MM **Privately Held**
Web: www.tntsolidsolutions.com
SIC: 3444 Sheet metalwork

(G-14491)
TOLCO CORPORATION (PA)
Also Called: Tolco
1920 Linwood Ave (43604-5293)
PHONE.................................419 241-1113
George L Notarianni, *Pr*
◆ **EMP:** 72 **EST:** 1961
SQ FT: 30,000
SALES (est): 21.61MM
SALES (corp-wide): 21.61MM **Privately Held**
Web: www.tolcocorp.com
SIC: 5085 3563 3586 3561 Bottler supplies; Spraying outfits: metals, paints, and chemicals (compressor); Measuring and dispensing pumps; Pumps and pumping equipment

(G-14492)
TOLEDO BLADE COMPANY
541 N Superior St (43660-0002)
P.O. Box 921 (43697-0921)
PHONE.................................419 724-6000
Joseph H Zerbey Iv, *Pr*
EMP: 423 **EST:** 1985
SALES (est): 121.52MM
SALES (corp-wide): 910.95MM **Privately Held**
Web: www.toledoblade.com
SIC: 2711 Commercial printing and newspaper publishing combined
PA: Block Communications, Inc.
     405 Madison Ave Ste 2100
     Toledo OH 43604
     419 724-6212

(G-14493)
TOLEDO CONTROLS
3550 Maxwell Rd (43606-1921)
PHONE.................................419 474-2537
EMP: 7 **EST:** 2012
SALES (est): 45.59K **Privately Held**
Web: www.ttoledo.com
SIC: 3823 Process control instruments

(G-14494)
TOLEDO CUT STONE INC
Also Called: Tri-State Archtctural Panl Sls
4011 South Ave (43615-6229)
PHONE.................................419 531-1623
Ted Piel, *Pr*
Kendal Piel, *VP*
Richard Szczepaniak, *Sec*
EMP: 11 **EST:** 1906
SQ FT: 16,400
SALES (est): 866.66K **Privately Held**
SIC: 3281 5032 Building stone products; Building stone

(G-14495)
TOLEDO ENGINEERING CO INC (PA)
Also Called: Teco
3400 Executive Pkwy (43606-1364)
P.O. Box 2927 (43606-0927)
PHONE.................................419 537-9711
Scott A Slater, *Ch*
Todd Seifried, *Pr*
Christopher J Hoyle, *VP*
▲ **EMP:** 75 **EST:** 1929
SQ FT: 50,000
SALES (est): 43.55MM
SALES (corp-wide): 43.55MM **Privately Held**
Web: www.teco.com
SIC: 3559 Glass making machinery: blowing, molding, forming, etc.

(G-14496)
TOLEDO FIBER PRODUCTS CORP
1245 E Manhattan Blvd (43608-1549)
PHONE.................................419 720-0303
Mark Connor, *Prin*
EMP: 9 **EST:** 2010
SALES (est): 321.26K **Privately Held**
SIC: 2221 Textile mills, broadwoven: silk and manmade, also glass

(G-14497)
TOLEDO MACHINING INC
8261 W Bancroft St (43617-1804)
PHONE.................................419 343-7738
Daniel N Young, *Pr*
EMP: 6 **EST:** 2020
SALES (est): 242.25K **Privately Held**
Web: www.toledoprecision.com
SIC: 3599 Machine shop, jobbing and repair

Toledo - Lucas County (G-14498)

(G-14498)
TOLEDO METAL SPINNING COMPANY
1819 Clinton St (43607-1600)
PHONE.............................419 535-5931
Kenneth F Fankhauser, *Pr*
Eric S Fankhauser, *
Craig B Fankhauser, *
▼ **EMP:** 35 **EST:** 1929
SQ FT: 100,000
SALES (est): 9.97MM **Privately Held**
Web: www.toledometalspinning.com
SIC: 3469 3443 Spinning metal for the trade; Cylinders, pressure: metal plate

(G-14499)
TOLEDO MOLDING & DIE LLC (DH)
Also Called: Tmd
1429 Coining Dr (43612-2932)
PHONE.............................419 470-3950
Nilesh Soni, *Managing Member*
Robert Briggs, *Managing Member*
Justin Cousino, *Sec*
◆ **EMP:** 60 **EST:** 1989
SQ FT: 35,000
SALES (est): 389.13MM **Privately Held**
Web: www.tmdinc.com
SIC: 3544 3089 Special dies, tools, jigs, and fixtures; Injection molded finished plastics products, nec
HQ: Grammer Ag
   Grammer Allee 2
   Ursensollen BY 92289
   9621660

(G-14500)
TOLEDO MOLDING & DIE LLC
4 E Laskey Rd (43612-3517)
PHONE.............................419 476-0581
Joe Pirrone, *Mgr*
EMP: 110
Web: www.tmdinc.com
SIC: 3089 3544 Injection molded finished plastics products, nec; Special dies, tools, jigs, and fixtures
HQ: Toledo Molding & Die, Llc
   1429 Coining Dr
   Toledo OH 43612

(G-14501)
TOLEDO OPTICAL LABORATORY INC
Also Called: Toledo Optical
1201 Jefferson Ave (43604-5836)
P.O. Box 2028 (43603-2028)
PHONE.............................419 248-3384
Irland Tashima, *Pr*
Jeffrey Seymenski, *
Toshi Kadowaki, *
EMP: 20 **EST:** 1947
SQ FT: 10,000
SALES (est): 424.11K **Privately Held**
Web: www.walmanoptical.com
SIC: 3851 5048 Eyeglasses, lenses and frames; Lenses, ophthalmic

(G-14502)
TOLEDO PRECISION MACHINING LLC
5222 Tractor Rd Ste H (43612-3458)
PHONE.............................419 724-3010
EMP: 6 **EST:** 2016
SALES (est): 223.73K **Privately Held**
Web: www.toledoprecision.com
SIC: 3599 Machine shop, jobbing and repair

(G-14503)
TOLEDO PRO FIBERGLASS INC
210 Wade St (43604-8852)
PHONE.............................419 241-9390
Don Jardine, *VP*
EMP: 8 **EST:** 1989
SQ FT: 24,000
SALES (est): 808.84K **Privately Held**
Web: www.toledopro.com
SIC: 5999 3714 3711 3089 Fiberglass materials, except insulation; Motor vehicle parts and accessories; Motor vehicles and car bodies; Fiberglass doors

(G-14504)
TOLEDO SIGN COMPANY INC (PA)
2021 Adams St (43604-5431)
PHONE.............................419 244-4444
Brad Heil, *Pr*
Brian Heil Junior, *VP*
EMP: 22 **EST:** 1914
SQ FT: 34,000
SALES (est): 3.46MM
SALES (corp-wide): 3.46MM **Privately Held**
Web: www.toledosign.com
SIC: 3993 Signs and advertising specialties

(G-14505)
TOLEDO SPIRITS COMPANY LLC
1301 N Summit St (43604-1819)
PHONE.............................419 704-3705
Andrew Newby, *Admn*
EMP: 10 **EST:** 2014
SALES (est): 2.19MM **Privately Held**
Web: www.toledospirits.com
SIC: 5921 2085 Wine; Applejack (alcoholic beverage)

(G-14506)
TOLEDO TICKET COMPANY
3963 Catawba St (43612-1492)
P.O. Box 6876 (43612-0876)
PHONE.............................419 476-5424
Roy L Carter, *Ch*
Roy L Carter, *Pr*
Robin G Carter, *
EMP: 50 **EST:** 1910
SQ FT: 50,000
SALES (est): 9.14MM **Privately Held**
Web: www.toledoticket.com
SIC: 2752 2759 Tickets, lithographed; Commercial printing, nec

(G-14507)
TOLEDO TOOL AND DIE CO INC (PA)
Also Called: Toledo Tool & Die
105 W Alexis Rd (43612-3603)
PHONE.............................419 476-4422
Anthony Kujawa Iii, *CEO*
John Hrovatich, *
▲ **EMP:** 252 **EST:** 1940
SQ FT: 60,000
SALES (est): 93.57MM
SALES (corp-wide): 93.57MM **Privately Held**
Web: www.toledotool.com
SIC: 3469 3544 Stamping metal for the trade ; Special dies, tools, jigs, and fixtures

(G-14508)
TOLEDO TOOL AND DIE CO INC
4100 Bennett Rd (43612-1991)
PHONE.............................419 266-8458
EMP: 16 **EST:** 1957
SALES (est): 518.15K **Privately Held**
Web: www.toledotool.com
SIC: 3469 Stamping metal for the trade

(G-14509)
TOLEDO WINDOW & AWNING INC
3035 W Sylvania Ave (43613-4135)
PHONE.............................419 474-3396
Dennis Whitaker, *Pr*
Dawn Whitaker, *VP*
EMP: 11 **EST:** 1950
SQ FT: 2,600
SALES (est): 1.1MM **Privately Held**
Web: www.toledowindow.com
SIC: 3444 5031 5211 Awnings, sheet metal; Doors and windows; Doors, storm: wood or metal

(G-14510)
TOOLING & COMPONENTS CORP
Also Called: Toolcomp
5261 Tractor Rd (43612-3439)
PHONE.............................419 478-9122
EMP: 12 **EST:** 1993
SQ FT: 5,900
SALES (est): 1.06MM **Privately Held**
Web: www.toolcomp.com
SIC: 3599 3544 Machine shop, jobbing and repair; Special dies, tools, jigs, and fixtures

(G-14511)
TRAM INC
5915 Jason St (43611-1088)
PHONE.............................567 315-8694
Tomohisa Sugiura, *Pr*
Doryo Iwanaga, *
EMP: 25 **EST:** 2015
SALES (est): 10.03MM **Privately Held**
SIC: 5012 3711 Automobiles; Motor vehicles and car bodies
PA: Topia Co.,Ltd.
   1477-1, Ichinomiyacho
   Suzuka MIE 513-0

(G-14512)
TRU-FORM STEEL & WIRE INC
5509 Telegraph Rd (43612-2662)
PHONE.............................765 348-5001
Jeffrey Tuttle, *Brnch Mgr*
EMP: 17
SALES (corp-wide): 9.71MM **Privately Held**
Web: www.tru-formsteel.com
SIC: 3315 3441 Steel wire and related products; Fabricated structural metal
PA: Tru-Form Steel & Wire, Inc.
   1204 Gilkey Ave
   Hartford City IN 47348
   765 348-5001

(G-14513)
UNITED COMPONENTS LLC (DH)
Also Called: UCI
6056 Deer Park Ct (43614-6000)
PHONE.............................330 899-0340
David Peace, *CEO*
Mark P Blaufuss, *
Michael G Malady, *
Keith A Zar, *
David L Squier, *
◆ **EMP:** 50 **EST:** 2003
SALES (est): 1.48B
SALES (corp-wide): 8.03B **Privately Held**
SIC: 3714 Motor vehicle parts and accessories
HQ: Uci International, Llc
   2100 International Pkwy
   North Canton OH 44720

(G-14514)
UNIVERSAL URETHANE PDTS INC
410 1st St (43605-2002)
P.O. Box 50617 (43605-0617)
PHONE.............................419 693-7400
Harry G Conrad, *CEO*
Jeffrey A Conrad, *
Scott Conrad, *
EMP: 55 **EST:** 1973
SQ FT: 32,000
SALES (est): 9.11MM **Privately Held**
Web: www.universalurethane.com
SIC: 3069 3312 3061 2851 Molded rubber products; Blast furnaces and steel mills; Mechanical rubber goods; Paints and allied products

(G-14515)
UNIVERSITY OF TOLEDO
University of Toledo Press
2801 W Bancroft St (43606-3390)
PHONE.............................419 530-2311
EMP: 11
SALES (corp-wide): 864.43MM **Privately Held**
Web: www.utoledo.edu
SIC: 2731 Books, publishing only
PA: The University Of Toledo
   2801 W Bancroft St
   Toledo OH 43606
   419 530-4636

(G-14516)
UNLIMITED MACHINE AND TOOL LLC
5139 Tractor Rd Ste C (43612-3432)
PHONE.............................419 269-1730
Tom Mccloskey, *Managing Member*
EMP: 16 **EST:** 2004
SQ FT: 6,000
SALES (est): 1.67MM **Privately Held**
Web: www.unlimmachtool.com
SIC: 3544 3312 Special dies and tools; Tool and die steel and alloys

(G-14517)
UPPER STATE FUEL INC
2433 Wimbledon Park Blvd (43617-2237)
PHONE.............................419 843-5931
Mike Jarouche, *Prin*
▼ **EMP:** 6 **EST:** 2008
SALES (est): 94.78K **Privately Held**
SIC: 2869 Fuels

(G-14518)
VALLEY PLASTICS COMPANY INC
399 Phillips Ave (43612-1349)
PHONE.............................419 666-2349
Walter Norris, *CEO*
EMP: 40 **EST:** 1975
SALES (est): 4.27MM **Privately Held**
Web: www.valleyplasticsinc.com
SIC: 3089 2542 Injection molding of plastics; Partitions and fixtures, except wood

(G-14519)
VIKING PAPER COMPANY (PA)
5148 Stickney Ave (43612-3721)
PHONE.............................419 729-4951
J Anthony Mooter, *Pr*
Robert Walker, *
EMP: 46 **EST:** 1986
SQ FT: 60,000
SALES (est): 26.16MM
SALES (corp-wide): 26.16MM **Privately Held**
Web: www.packpros.net
SIC: 2653 Boxes, corrugated: made from purchased materials

(G-14520)
VINTAGE AUTOMOTIVE ELC INC
Also Called: Vintage Heating and Air
3335 Mcgregor Ln (43623-1917)
PHONE.............................419 472-9349
Jacquelyn Crozier, *Pr*
John Crozier, *VP*
EMP: 10 **EST:** 1974
SQ FT: 4,000
SALES (est): 1.02MM **Privately Held**
Web: www.heatingandairtoledo.com

GEOGRAPHIC SECTION

Trenton - Butler County (G-14542)

SIC: **1711** 7539 5013 5531 Plumbing, heating, air-conditioning; Electrical services; Automotive supplies and parts; Auto and home supply stores

(G-14521)
WALL TECHNOLOGY INC
1 Owens Corning Pkwy (43659-1000)
PHONE..............................715 532-5548
Johna Ryan, *Sec*
EMP: 12 EST: 2001
SALES (est): 262.49K **Privately Held**
SIC: **3446** 3275 Acoustical suspension systems, metal; Gypsum products

(G-14522)
WEST EQUIPMENT COMPANY INC (PA)
1545 E Broadway St (43605-3852)
PHONE..............................419 698-1601
TOLL FREE: 800
Paul Erdmann, *Pr*
Bernard Erdmann, *CEO*
Paul Erdmann, *Pr*
Chad Erdmann, *VP*
Kristi Erdmann, *Prin*
EMP: 6 EST: 1952
SQ FT: 7,200
SALES (est): 6.78MM
SALES (corp-wide): 6.78MM **Privately Held**
Web: www.toledosafetyequipment.com
SIC: **5082** 7699 7359 3496 General construction machinery and equipment; Construction equipment repair; Equipment rental and leasing, nec; Slings, lifting: made from purchased wire

(G-14523)
WESTROCK COMMERCIAL LLC
1635 Coining Dr (43612-2906)
PHONE..............................419 476-9101
EMP: 53
SALES (corp-wide): 20.31B **Publicly Held**
SIC: **5112** 2752 Stationery and office supplies; Commercial printing, lithographic
HQ: Westrock Commercial, Llc
501 S 5th St
Richmond VA 23219
804 444-1000

(G-14524)
WHITEFORD INDUSTRIES INC
Also Called: Rehn Co
3323 South Ave (43609-1105)
PHONE..............................419 381-1155
Andy Klumb, *Pr*
EMP: 12 EST: 1929
SQ FT: 9,000
SALES (est): 418.83K **Privately Held**
Web: www.rehncompany.com
SIC: **3842** 3451 Atomizers, medical; Screw machine products

(G-14525)
WIREMAX LTD
705 Wamba Ave (43607-3252)
P.O. Box 3336 (43607-0336)
PHONE..............................419 531-9500
EMP: 6 EST: 1995
SQ FT: 8,000
SALES (est): 848.31K **Privately Held**
Web: www.wiremax.com
SIC: **3357** Nonferrous wiredrawing and insulating

(G-14526)
WOODCRAFT
5311 Airport Hwy (43615-6801)
PHONE..............................419 389-0560
EMP: 9 EST: 2019
SALES (est): 237.87K **Privately Held**
Web: www.woodcraft.com
SIC: **2511** Wood household furniture

(G-14527)
WURTEC INCORPORATED
800 Seneca St (43608-2952)
PHONE..............................419 726-1066
Nate Dussel, *Mgr*
EMP: 11
SALES (corp-wide): 27.61MM **Privately Held**
Web: www.wurtec.com
SIC: **3534** Elevators and moving stairways
PA: Wurtec, Incorporated
6200 Brent Dr
Toledo OH 43611
419 726-1066

(G-14528)
WURTEC MANUFACTURING SERVICE
6200 Brent Dr (43611-1081)
PHONE..............................419 726-1066
Steven P Wurth, *Pr*
Jane A Wurth, *Sec*
▲ EMP: 20 EST: 1995
SQ FT: 26,000
SALES (est): 2.32MM **Privately Held**
Web: www.wurtec.com
SIC: **3544** 3993 Special dies, tools, jigs, and fixtures; Signs, not made in custom sign painting shops

(G-14529)
XUNLIGHT CORPORATION
3145 Nebraska Ave (43607-3102)
PHONE..............................419 469-8600
▲ EMP: 60
Web: www.xunlight.com
SIC: **3433** Solar heaters and collectors

(G-14530)
YARDER MANUFACTURING COMPANY (PA)
722 Phillips Ave (43612-1333)
P.O. Box 6886 (43612-0886)
PHONE..............................419 476-3933
Richard W Yarder, *Pr*
Matt Yarder, *
Maryann Bailey, *
Amy Conlan, *
EMP: 49 EST: 1930
SQ FT: 55,000
SALES (est): 7.86MM
SALES (corp-wide): 7.86MM **Privately Held**
Web: www.yardermfg.com
SIC: **3499** Boxes for packing and shipping, metal

(G-14531)
YESCO SIGN & LIGHTING SERVICE
5924 American Rd E (43612-3950)
PHONE..............................419 407-6581
Bryan Chase, *Owner*
EMP: 7 EST: 2017
SALES (est): 213.2K **Privately Held**
Web: www.yesco.com
SIC: **3993** Signs and advertising specialties

(G-14532)
ZF ACTIVE SAFETY & ELEC US LLC
5915 Jason St (43611-1088)
PHONE..............................419 726-5599
Dennis Burke, *Brnch Mgr*
EMP: 25
SALES (corp-wide): 144.19K **Privately Held**
SIC: **3714** Motor vehicle parts and accessories
HQ: Zf Active Safety & Electronics Us Llc
34605 W 12 Mile Rd
Farmington Hills MI 48331
765 429-1936

(G-14533)
ZIE BART RHINO LININGS TOLEDO
Also Called: Rhino Linings
3343 N Holland Sylvania Rd (43615)
PHONE..............................419 841-2886
Keith Tucker, *Owner*
EMP: 6 EST: 1991
SALES (est): 452.83K **Privately Held**
SIC: **3713** Truck beds

Toronto
Jefferson County

(G-14534)
RIDGE MACHINE & WELDING CO
1015 Railroad St (43964-1115)
P.O. Box 190 (43964-0190)
PHONE..............................740 537-2821
David Artman, *Pr*
J Curtis Artman, *VP*
Debbie Artman, *Sec*
EMP: 6 EST: 1950
SQ FT: 27,000
SALES (est): 647.2K **Privately Held**
Web: www.ridgemachineandwelding.com
SIC: **3599** 7692 3398 Machine shop, jobbing and repair; Welding repair; Metal heat treating

(G-14535)
TITANIUM METALS CORPORATION
Also Called: Timet Toronto
100 Titanium Way (43964-1990)
P.O. Box 309 (43964-0309)
PHONE..............................740 537-1571
Steve Wright, *Brnch Mgr*
EMP: 527
SALES (corp-wide): 364.48B **Publicly Held**
Web: www.timet.com
SIC: **3566** 3356 Speed changers, drives, and gears; Nonferrous rolling and drawing, nec
HQ: Titanium Metals Corporation
4832 Richmond Rd Ste 100
Warrensville Heights OH 44128
740 537-5600

(G-14536)
U S ARMY CORPS OF ENGINEERS
Also Called: New Cumberland Lock & Dam
29501 State Rte 7 (43964)
PHONE..............................740 537-2571
Matt Dillon, *Mgr*
EMP: 6
Web: usace.army.mil
SIC: **3812** 8711 Navigational systems and instruments; Engineering services
HQ: U S Army Corps Of Engineers
441 G St Nw
Washington DC 20314
202 761-0001

(G-14537)
VALLEY CONVERTING CO INC (PA)
Also Called: Valley
405 Daniels St (43964-1343)
P.O. Box 279 (43964-0279)
PHONE..............................740 537-2152
Gino Biasi, *Ch Bd*
Michael D Biasi, *
▼ EMP: 50 EST: 1973
SQ FT: 107,500
SALES (est): 5.26MM
SALES (corp-wide): 5.26MM **Privately Held**
Web: www.valleyconverting.com
SIC: **2631** Cardboard

Tremont City
Clark County

(G-14538)
MIKE LOPPE
Also Called: Kutrite Manufacturing
2 W Main St (45372)
P.O. Box 186 (45372-0186)
PHONE..............................937 969-8102
Mike Loppe, *Owner*
EMP: 10 EST: 1983
SQ FT: 5,500
SALES (est): 995.27K **Privately Held**
SIC: **3599** 7692 3444 Machine shop, jobbing and repair; Welding repair; Sheet metalwork

Trenton
Butler County

(G-14539)
BC MACHINE SERVICES CORP
3104 Wayne Madison Rd (45067-9746)
PHONE..............................513 428-0327
Ryan Curry, *Pr*
EMP: 13 EST: 2015
SALES (est): 488.75K **Privately Held**
Web: www.bc-machine.com
SIC: **3599** Machine shop, jobbing and repair

(G-14540)
BIDWELL FAMILY CORPORATION (HQ)
400 E State St (45067-1549)
PHONE..............................513 988-6351
Arthur W Bidwell, *CEO*
Martin J Bidwell, *
Johnie Adams, *
Ann F Bidwell, *
Douglas J Howell, *
EMP: 125 EST: 1974
SQ FT: 100,000
SALES (est): 43.8MM
SALES (corp-wide): 520.54MM **Privately Held**
Web: www.shapecorp.com
SIC: **3354** Aluminum extruded products
PA: Shape Corp.
1900 Hayes St
Grand Haven MI 49417
616 846-8700

(G-14541)
MIILER BREWING COMPANY
2525 Wayne Madison Rd (45067-9799)
PHONE..............................513 896-9200
Wayne Mccauley, *Prin*
EMP: 23 EST: 2010
SALES (est): 2.08MM **Privately Held**
SIC: **2082** Beer (alcoholic beverage)

(G-14542)
MOLSON COORS BEV CO USA LLC
2525 Wayne Madison Rd (45067-9768)
P.O. Box 168 (45067-0168)
PHONE..............................513 896-9200
Dennis Puffer, *Brnch Mgr*
EMP: 98
SALES (corp-wide): 11.7B **Publicly Held**
Web: www.molsoncoors.com
SIC: **2082** Beer (alcoholic beverage)

HQ: Molson Coors Beverage Company
Usa Llc
250 S Wacker Dr Ste 800
Chicago IL 60606
312 496-2700

Trotwood
Montgomery County

(G-14543)
CROWNME COIL CARE LLC
Also Called: Arcani Coil Care
4910 Denlinger Rd (45426-2014)
PHONE..................937 797-2070
Jerricha Richardson, *Managing Member*
EMP: 18 **EST:** 2017
SALES (est): 6MM **Privately Held**
Web: arcani.square.site
SIC: 3999 Hair and hair-based products

(G-14544)
J W DEVERS & SON INC
5 N Broadway St (45426-3555)
P.O. Box 26460 (45426-0460)
PHONE..................937 854-3040
Jerry Haupt, *Pr*
Steve Wolf, *VP*
David Henderson, *Sec*
EMP: 10 **EST:** 1948
SALES (est): 919.51K **Privately Held**
Web: www.jwdevers.com
SIC: 5012 3715 Truck bodies; Trailer bodies

(G-14545)
KASEL ENGINEERING LLC
5911 Wolf Creek Pike (45426-2439)
PHONE..................937 854-8875
EMP: 8 **EST:** 2001
SQ FT: 8,000
SALES (est): 785.41K **Privately Held**
Web: www.kaselengineering.com
SIC: 3556 Slicers, commercial, food

(G-14546)
STRYVER MFG INC
15 N Broadway St (45426-3555)
PHONE..................937 854-3048
EMP: 30 **EST:** 1994
SQ FT: 30,000
SALES (est): 4.32MM **Privately Held**
Web: www.stryver.com
SIC: 3599 3548 Machine shop, jobbing and repair; Welding apparatus

(G-14547)
TROTWOOD CORPORATION
11 N Broadway St (45426-3594)
PHONE..................937 854-3047
Bruce J Flora, *Pr*
Lucille Flora, *
Thomas E Flora, *
EMP: 15 **EST:** 1932
SQ FT: 30,000
SALES (est): 427.64K **Privately Held**
Web: www.stryver.com
SIC: 3599 Machine shop, jobbing and repair

Troy
Miami County

(G-14548)
3 SIGMA LLC
1985 W Stanfield Rd (45373-2330)
PHONE..................937 440-3400
Tony Rowley, *Pr*
EMP: 82 **EST:** 1980
SALES (est): 20.38MM
SALES (corp-wide): 76.86MM **Privately Held**
Web: www.3sigma.cc
SIC: 2672 Paper; coated and laminated, nec
PA: Duraco Specialty Tapes Llc
7400 Industrial Dr
Forest Park IL 60130
866 800-0775

(G-14549)
AMERICAN ADVNCED ASSMBLIES LLC
37 Harolds Way (45373-4098)
PHONE..................937 339-6267
Thomas B Fay, *Pr*
EMP: 28 **EST:** 2011
SALES (est): 3.66MM **Privately Held**
Web: www.aaassemblies.com
SIC: 3679 Harness assemblies, for electronic use: wire or cable

(G-14550)
AMETEK INC
Also Called: Ametek Presto Light Power
66 Industry Ct Ste F (45373-2560)
PHONE..................937 440-0800
Patrick Williams, *Prin*
EMP: 10
SALES (corp-wide): 6.6B **Publicly Held**
Web: www.ametek.com
SIC: 5063 3699 Batteries; Electrical equipment and supplies, nec
PA: Ametek, Inc.
1100 Cassatt Rd
Berwyn PA 19312
610 647-2121

(G-14551)
AZTECH PRINTING & PROMOTIONS
402 E Main St (45373-3413)
PHONE..................937 339-0100
Charles Lobaugh, *Prin*
EMP: 6 **EST:** 2007
SALES (est): 90.78K **Privately Held**
Web: www.aztechprinting.com
SIC: 2759 5734 7319 7334 Screen printing; Printers and plotters: computers; Sample distribution; Photocopying and duplicating services

(G-14552)
BRASSGATE INDUSTRIES INC
650 Olympic Dr (45373-2306)
PHONE..................937 339-2192
Douglas W Tyger, *Prin*
EMP: 10 **EST:** 2016
SALES (est): 396.35K **Privately Held**
SIC: 3544 Die sets for metal stamping (presses)

(G-14553)
CHARACTERS INC
190 Peters Ave Ste A (45373-3995)
PHONE..................937 335-1976
Esther Marko, *Pr*
Jason Marko, *VP*
EMP: 9 **EST:** 1961
SQ FT: 8,000
SALES (est): 964.85K **Privately Held**
SIC: 2791 Typesetting

(G-14554)
CHRISTOPHER SWEENEY
Also Called: Cincinnati Phone
924 E Main St (45373-3423)
PHONE..................513 276-4350
Christopher Sweeney, *Owner*
EMP: 6 **EST:** 2007
SALES (est): 130.88K **Privately Held**

SIC: 3661 4813 5812 Telephone station equipment and parts, wire; Telephone communication, except radio; Eating places

(G-14555)
CITY OF TROY
Also Called: Troy Water Treatment Plant
300 E Staunton Rd (45373-2105)
PHONE..................937 339-4826
Tim Ray, *Superintnt*
EMP: 10
SALES (corp-wide): 36.64MM **Privately Held**
Web: www.troyohio.gov
SIC: 3589 4941 Sewage and water treatment equipment; Water supply
PA: City Of Troy
100 S Market St Ste 1
Troy OH 45373
937 335-2224

(G-14556)
CONAGRA FODS PCKAGED FOODS LLC
801 Dye Mill Rd (45373-4223)
PHONE..................937 440-2800
Scott Adkins, *Brnch Mgr*
EMP: 35
SALES (corp-wide): 12.28B **Publicly Held**
SIC: 2099 Food preparations, nec
HQ: Conagra Foods Packaged Foods, Llc
1 Conagra Dr
Omaha NE 68102

(G-14557)
CREATIVE EXTRUDED PRODUCTS
101 Dye Mill Rd (45373-4285)
PHONE..................937 335-3336
EMP: 6
SALES (est): 397.74K **Privately Held**
Web: www.meteor-creative.com
SIC: 3089 Extruded finished plastics products, nec

(G-14558)
CROWE MANUFACTURING SERVICES
Also Called: King of The Road
2731 Walnut Ridge Dr (45373-4562)
PHONE..................800 831-1893
Jamie King, *CEO*
Rob Haviland, *
Robert King, *
EMP: 31 **EST:** 1967
SQ FT: 140,000
SALES (est): 629.24K **Privately Held**
SIC: 3599 3544 Machine and other job shop work; Special dies, tools, jigs, and fixtures

(G-14559)
DARE ELECTRONICS INC
3245 S County Road 25a (45373-9384)
P.O. Box 419 (45373-0419)
PHONE..................937 335-0031
Karen Beagle, *Pr*
EMP: 50 **EST:** 1976
SQ FT: 28,750
SALES (est): 8.33MM **Privately Held**
Web: www.dareelectronics.com
SIC: 3679 3651 Power supplies, all types: static; Amplifiers: radio, public address, or musical instrument

(G-14560)
DAYTON SUPERIOR PDTS CO INC
1370 Lytle Rd (45373-9401)
PHONE..................937 332-1930
Daniel P Gleason, *Pr*
Frank Gleason Junior, *Ch Bd*
▲ **EMP:** 8 **EST:** 1959

SQ FT: 15,000
SALES (est): 1.1MM **Privately Held**
Web: www.daytonsuperiorproducts.com
SIC: 3568 Power transmission equipment, nec

(G-14561)
DELTECH POLYMERS LLC
1250 Union St (45373-4118)
PHONE..................937 339-3150
Robert Elefante, *Ch Bd*
EMP: 8 **EST:** 1990
SQ FT: 435,600
SALES (est): 10.06MM
SALES (corp-wide): 107.44MM **Privately Held**
Web: www.deltech.com
SIC: 3087 2821 Custom compound purchased resins; Polystyrene resins
PA: Deltech Llc
11911 Scenic Hwy
Baton Rouge LA 70807
225 775-0150

(G-14562)
DELTECH POLYMERS OPCO LLC
1250 Union St (45373-4118)
PHONE..................225 358-3306
Rebecca Henry, *Managing Member*
EMP: 6 **EST:** 2021
SALES (est): 180.13K **Privately Held**
SIC: 3087 Custom compound purchased resins

(G-14563)
DESIGN TECHNOLOGIES & MFG CO
Also Called: Des Tech
2000 Corporate Dr (45373-1069)
PHONE..................937 335-0757
D Jeffrey Meredith, *Pr*
William Leffel, *VP*
Debbie Meredith, *Sec*
Marilyn J Freeman, *Prin*
John E Fulker, *Prin*
EMP: 18 **EST:** 1984
SQ FT: 32,000
SALES (est): 5.1MM **Privately Held**
Web: www.destechmfg.com
SIC: 3599 Machine shop, jobbing and repair

(G-14564)
DETRICK DESIGN FABRICATION LLC
425 Wisteria Dr (45373-8850)
PHONE..................937 620-6736
EMP: 6 **EST:** 2014
SALES (est): 247.83K **Privately Held**
Web: www.detrickdesign.com
SIC: 3599 Machine shop, jobbing and repair

(G-14565)
ERNST ENTERPRISES INC
Troy Ready Mix
805 Union St (45373-4109)
PHONE..................937 339-6249
Dwayne Littlejohn, *Mgr*
EMP: 13
SQ FT: 7,446
SALES (corp-wide): 240.08MM **Privately Held**
Web: www.ernstconcrete.com
SIC: 3273 Ready-mixed concrete
PA: Ernst Enterprises, Inc.
3361 Successful Way
Dayton OH 45414
937 233-5555

(G-14566)
EVENFLO COMPANY INC
1801 W Main St (45373-2303)
PHONE..................937 773-3971
Rick Frank, *Brnch Mgr*

GEOGRAPHIC SECTION
Troy - Miami County (G-14588)

EMP: 100
Web: www.evenflo.com
SIC: **2519** 3944 Fiberglass and plastic furniture; Child restraint seats, automotive
HQ: Evenflo Company, Inc.
3131 Newmark Dr Ste 300
Miamisburg OH 45342

(G-14567)
F&P AMERICA MFG INC (HQ)
2101 Corporate Dr (45373-1076)
PHONE..................................937 339-0212
Masafumi Yamano, *Pr*
Akihide Fukuda, *
Hirp Enomoto, *
▲ **EMP: 27 EST:** 1993
SQ FT: 400,000
SALES (est): 163.74MM **Privately Held**
Web: www.fandp.com
SIC: **3714** Motor vehicle steering systems and parts
PA: F-Tech Inc.
19, Shobuchoshowanuma
Kuki STM 346-0

(G-14568)
FAURECIA EXHAUST SYSTEMS INC
Also Called: FAURECIA EXHAUST SYSTEMS, INC.
1255 Archer Dr (45373-3841)
PHONE..................................937 339-0551
Bryan Imhoff, *Mgr*
EMP: 300
SALES (corp-wide): 100.93MM **Privately Held**
SIC: **3714** Exhaust systems and parts, motor vehicle
HQ: Faurecia Emissions Control Systems Na, Llc
543 Matzinger Rd
Toledo OH 43612
812 341-2000

(G-14569)
FLAWLESS SIGNS & WRAPS LLC
66 Industry Ct Ste C (45373-2560)
PHONE..................................937 559-0672
EMP: 6 EST: 2017
SALES (est): 203.06K **Privately Held**
Web: www.flawlesssigns.com
SIC: **3993** Signs and advertising specialties

(G-14570)
FREDS SIGN SERVICE INC
3055 S County Road 25a (45373-9330)
PHONE..................................937 335-1901
Bruce Haas, *Pr*
Kathy Hutson, *Sec*
Eloise Haas, *Treas*
EMP: 8 EST: 1960
SQ FT: 4,000
SALES (est): 720K **Privately Held**
SIC: **7389** 3993 Sign painting and lettering shop; Signs, not made in custom sign painting shops

(G-14571)
FREUDENBERG-NOK GENERAL PARTNR
Also Called: Freudenberg-Nok Sealing Tech
1275 Archer Dr (45373-3841)
P.O. Box 844 (51301-0244)
PHONE..................................937 335-3306
Larry Heimilghton, *Mgr*
EMP: 30
SALES (corp-wide): 12.23B **Privately Held**
Web: www.freudenberg.com
SIC: **2821** Plastics materials and resins
HQ: Freudenberg-Nok General Partnership
47774 W Anchor Ct
Plymouth MI 48170
734 451-0020

(G-14572)
FTECH R&D NORTH AMERICA INC (HQ)
1191 Horizon West Ct (45373-7560)
PHONE..................................937 339-2777
Bing Liu, *COO*
Eldon H Kakuda, *
▲ **EMP: 26 EST:** 2003
SQ FT: 50,000
SALES (est): 18.86MM **Privately Held**
Web: www.fandp.com
SIC: **8731** 3714 Commercial physical research; Motor vehicle parts and accessories
PA: F-Tech Inc.
19, Shobuchoshowanuma
Kuki STM 346-0

(G-14573)
GOKOH CORPORATION (HQ)
1280 Archer Dr (45373-3842)
PHONE..................................937 339-4977
Shuji Hioki, *Pr*
Parker Bailey, *VP*
T Hioki Stkldr, *Prin*
M Fujita Stkldr, *Prin*
Heiju Hashimoto, *Prin*
▲ **EMP: 13 EST:** 1987
SQ FT: 16,000
SALES (est): 9.54MM **Privately Held**
Web: www.gokoh.us
SIC: **5085** 5084 3544 3559 Industrial supplies; Industrial machinery and equipment; Special dies and tools; Foundry machinery and equipment
PA: Goko Sangyo Co., Ltd.
1-2-2, Higashiryoke
Kawaguchi STM 332-0

(G-14574)
GOODRICH CORPORATION
Also Called: Collins Aerospace
101 Waco St (45373-3872)
P.O. Box 340 (45373-0340)
PHONE..................................937 339-3811
EMP: 750
SALES (corp-wide): 68.92B **Publicly Held**
Web: www.collinsaerospace.com
SIC: **3721** 3714 3728 Aircraft; Wheels, motor vehicle; Aircraft landing assemblies and brakes
HQ: Goodrich Corporation
2730 W Tyvola Rd
Charlotte NC 28217
704 423-7000

(G-14575)
GOODRICH CORPORATION
101 Walton St (45373)
P.O. Box 304 (45373-0304)
PHONE..................................216 429-4378
EMP: 11
SALES (corp-wide): 68.92B **Publicly Held**
Web: www.collinsaerospace.com
SIC: **3728** Aircraft parts and equipment, nec
HQ: Goodrich Corporation
2730 W Tyvola Rd
Charlotte NC 28217
704 423-7000

(G-14576)
HAWKINS MACHINE SHOP INC
1112 Race Dr (45373-4228)
PHONE..................................937 335-8737
Dorothy Haulmanmiller, *Pr*
Jeff Haulman, *Sec*
EMP: 8 EST: 1988
SQ FT: 11,000
SALES (est): 758.11K **Privately Held**
SIC: **3599** Machine shop, jobbing and repair

(G-14577)
HINES BUILDERS INC
1587 Lytle Rd (45373-9488)
PHONE..................................937 335-4586
Harold A Hines, *Pr*
Scherre Mumpower, *Sec*
EMP: 10 EST: 1951
SQ FT: 25,000
SALES (est): 270.31K **Privately Held**
SIC: **2448** 1541 2441 Pallets, wood; Industrial buildings, new construction, nec; Nailed wood boxes and shook

(G-14578)
HOBART BROS STICK ELECTRODE
101 Trade Sq E (45373-2476)
PHONE..................................937 332-5375
Steve Knostman, *Owner*
EMP: 15 EST: 2006
SALES (est): 256.05K **Privately Held**
Web: www.hobartbrothers.com
SIC: **7692** Welding repair

(G-14579)
HOBART BROTHERS LLC (HQ)
Also Called: ITW Hobart Brothers
101 Trade Sq E (45373)
PHONE..................................937 332-5439
Sundaram Nagarajan, *VP*
Grant Harvey, *General Vice President**
S E Hobart, *
◆ **EMP: 600 EST:** 1917
SQ FT: 1,000,000
SALES (est): 333.81MM
SALES (corp-wide): 16.11B **Publicly Held**
Web: www.hobartbrothers.com
SIC: **3548** 3537 Welding apparatus; Industrial trucks and tractors
PA: Illinois Tool Works Inc.
155 Harlem Ave
Glenview IL 60025
847 724-7500

(G-14580)
HOBART CABINET COMPANY
1100 Wayne St Ste 1 (45373-3074)
PHONE..................................937 335-4666
Martin E Hobart, *Pr*
EMP: 9 EST: 1907
SALES (est): 883.92K **Privately Held**
Web: www.hobartcabinet.com
SIC: **2522** Office bookcases, wallcases and partitions, except wood

(G-14581)
HOBART LLC
Also Called: Engineering Dept
401 S Market St (45373-3330)
PHONE..................................937 332-3000
Gary Banks, *Mgr*
EMP: 31
SALES (corp-wide): 16.11B **Publicly Held**
Web: www.hobartcorp.com
SIC: **3589** 3556 3596 3585 Dishwashing machines, commercial; Food products machinery; Weighing machines and apparatus; Refrigeration equipment, complete
HQ: Hobart Llc
701 S Ridge Ave
Troy OH 45373

(G-14582)
HOBART LLC (DH)
Also Called: Hobart
701 S Ridge Ave (45373)
P.O. Box 3001 (45374)
PHONE..................................937 332-3000
▲ **EMP: 100 EST:** 1897
SALES (est): 466.47MM
SALES (corp-wide): 16.11B **Publicly Held**
Web: www.hobartcorp.com
SIC: **3589** 3556 3596 3585 Dishwashing machines, commercial; Food products machinery; Weighing machines and apparatus; Refrigeration equipment, complete
HQ: Itw Food Equipment Group Llc
701 S Ridge Ave
Troy OH 45374

(G-14583)
HONDA
1501 Michael Dr (45373-6602)
PHONE..................................937 524-5177
EMP: 11 EST: 2018
SALES (est): 559.53K **Privately Held**
Web: ohio.honda.com
SIC: **3544** Special dies, tools, jigs, and fixtures

(G-14584)
ILLINOIS TOOL WORKS INC
Also Called: ITW Hobart
750 Lincoln Ave (45373-3137)
PHONE..................................937 332-2839
Bob Freef, *Genl Mgr*
EMP: 20
SALES (corp-wide): 16.11B **Publicly Held**
Web: www.itw.com
SIC: **3089** Injection molded finished plastics products, nec
PA: Illinois Tool Works Inc.
155 Harlem Ave
Glenview IL 60025
847 724-7500

(G-14585)
ILLINOIS TOOL WORKS INC
Itwfeg
701 S Ridge Ave (45374-0001)
PHONE..................................937 335-7171
Elaine Everman, *Brnch Mgr*
EMP: 48
SALES (corp-wide): 16.11B **Publicly Held**
Web: www.itw.com
SIC: **3589** Dishwashing machines, commercial
PA: Illinois Tool Works Inc.
155 Harlem Ave
Glenview IL 60025
847 724-7500

(G-14586)
INDEPENDENT MACHINE & WLDG INC
710 Boone Dr (45373-9343)
PHONE..................................937 339-7330
Glenn Reed, *Pr*
Dale F Deaton, *VP*
Carol Owens, *Treas*
EMP: 6 EST: 2000
SALES (est): 453.62K **Privately Held**
SIC: **3599** 7692 Machine shop, jobbing and repair; Welding repair

(G-14587)
INTEGRITY INDUSTRIAL EQUIPMENT
18 E Water St (45373-3435)
P.O. Box 1040 (45373-8040)
PHONE..................................937 335-5658
Jose Lopez, *Prin*
EMP: 7 EST: 2014
SALES (est): 482.15K **Privately Held**
SIC: **3599** Industrial machinery, nec

(G-14588)
ISHMAEL PRECISION TOOL CORP
Also Called: Iptc
55 Industry Ct (45373-2368)
PHONE..................................937 335-8070
Larry R Ishmael, *Pr*

Troy - Miami County (G-14589) — GEOGRAPHIC SECTION

Larry Ishmael, *Pr*
Robert Ishmael, *VP*
Isaiah Wilmoth, *Prin*
Jackie Mathes, *Prin*
▲ **EMP:** 20 **EST:** 1978
SQ FT: 32,000
SALES (est): 2.33MM **Privately Held**
Web: www.ishmaelcorp.com
SIC: 3544 Special dies and tools

(G-14589)
ITW FOOD EQUIPMENT GROUP LLC (HQ)
Also Called: Hobart
701 S Ridge Ave (45374-0001)
PHONE......................937 332-2396
Harold B Smith, *CEO*
Tom Szafranski, *
Chris O Herlihy, *
Axel Beck, *
◆ **EMP:** 1100 **EST:** 2002
SALES (est): 1.38B
SALES (corp-wide): 16.11B **Publicly Held**
Web: www.itwfoodequipment.com
SIC: 5046 3556 Restaurant equipment and supplies, nec; Food products machinery
PA: Illinois Tool Works Inc.
  155 Harlem Ave
  Glenview IL 60025
  847 724-7500

(G-14590)
JAYNA INC (PA)
15 Marybill Dr S (45373-1033)
PHONE......................937 335-8922
Damaroo Shah, *Pr*
Mayank Shah, *
EMP: 47 **EST:** 1988
SQ FT: 40,000
SALES (est): 9.76MM
SALES (corp-wide): 9.76MM **Privately Held**
Web: www.jaynainc.com
SIC: 3599 Machine shop, jobbing and repair

(G-14591)
KERBER SHEETMETAL WORKS INC
Also Called: Ksm Metal Fabrications
104 Foss Way (45373-1430)
PHONE......................937 339-6366
Kathleen Kerber, *Pr*
EMP: 18 **EST:** 1979
SQ FT: 27,000
SALES (est): 4.96MM **Privately Held**
Web: www.ksmmetalfabrication.com
SIC: 3444 Ducts, sheet metal

(G-14592)
KNAPKE CABINETS INC
2 E Main St (45373-3202)
PHONE......................937 335-8383
Bernie Knapke, *Pr*
EMP: 35 **EST:** 2001
SALES (est): 1.62MM **Privately Held**
Web: www.knapkecabinets.com
SIC: 2434 1521 Wood kitchen cabinets; General remodeling, single-family houses

(G-14593)
KSM METAL FABRICATION
104 Foss Way (45373-1430)
PHONE......................937 339-6366
Kathy Kerber, *Pr*
EMP: 10 **EST:** 2014
SALES (est): 659.92K **Privately Held**
Web: www.ksmmetalfabrication.com
SIC: 3499 Fabricated metal products, nec

(G-14594)
LUKENS INC
1040 S Dorset Rd (45373-4708)
PHONE......................937 440-2500
Bill Diederich, *Prin*
Bill Diederich, *CEO*
Michael Van Haaren, *
EMP: 90 **EST:** 1958
SQ FT: 70,000
SALES (est): 9.81MM **Privately Held**
SIC: 3544 Special dies and tools

(G-14595)
MADER AUTOMOTIVE CENTER INC (PA)
Also Called: Bushong Auto Service
225 S Walnut St (45373-3532)
PHONE......................937 339-2681
Dan Mader, *Pr*
EMP: 15 **EST:** 1966
SQ FT: 18,000
SALES (est): 2.22MM
SALES (corp-wide): 2.22MM **Privately Held**
SIC: 5013 5531 3599 Automotive supplies and parts; Automotive parts; Machine shop, jobbing and repair

(G-14596)
MARIETTA MARTIN MATERIALS INC
Also Called: Troy Sand and Gravel
250 Dye Mill Rd (45373-4280)
PHONE......................937 335-8313
Darrell Sparks, *Mgr*
EMP: 7
Web: www.martinmarietta.com
SIC: 1422 Crushed and broken limestone
PA: Martin Marietta Materials Inc
  4123 Parklake Ave
  Raleigh NC 27612

(G-14597)
MEDWAY TOOL CORP
2100 Corporate Dr (45373-1085)
PHONE......................937 335-7717
Tom Drake, *Pr*
EMP: 21 **EST:** 1974
SQ FT: 15,000
SALES (est): 466.38K **Privately Held**
SIC: 3599 3545 3544 3444 Machine shop, jobbing and repair; Machine tool accessories; Special dies, tools, jigs, and fixtures; Sheet metalwork

(G-14598)
NOVACEL INC
421 Union St (45373-4151)
PHONE......................937 335-5611
Tim Shank, *Brnch Mgr*
EMP: 160
Web: www.novacelinc.com
SIC: 2671 Paper; coated and laminated packaging
HQ: Novacel, Inc.
  21 3rd St
  Palmer MA 01069
  413 283-3468

(G-14599)
NOVACEL PRFMCE COATINGS INC
421 Union St (45373-4151)
PHONE......................937 552-4932
David Bullard, *Pr*
◆ **EMP:** 100 **EST:** 2000
SALES (est): 25.52MM **Privately Held**
Web: www.novacel-solutions.com
SIC: 2672 Coated paper, except photographic, carbon, or abrasive
HQ: Novacel
  27 Rue Du Docteur Emile Bataille
  Deville Les Rouen 76250
  323839898

(G-14600)
PAINTED HILL INV GROUP INC
Also Called: Western Ohio Graphics
402 E Main St (45373-3413)
PHONE......................937 339-1756
Anthony W Cockerham, *Pr*
EMP: 10 **EST:** 1977
SQ FT: 13,000
SALES (est): 1.01MM **Privately Held**
SIC: 2752 2396 3993 2759 Offset printing; Screen printing on fabric articles; Signs and advertising specialties; Screen printing

(G-14601)
PEAK FOODS LLC
1903 W Main St (45373-1165)
PHONE......................937 440-0707
Jeff White, *Branch*
EMP: 65 **EST:** 2000
SQ FT: 5,500
SALES (est): 20.08MM
SALES (corp-wide): 51.52MM **Privately Held**
Web: www.peakfoods.com
SIC: 2026 Whipped topping, except frozen or dry mix
PA: Oppenheimer Companies, Inc.
  877 W Main St Ste 700
  Boise ID 83702
  208 342-7771

(G-14602)
POLYMER STAMPING TECH LLC (PA)
1860 State Route 718 (45373-8725)
PHONE......................616 371-4004
Richard D Sofia, *Managing Member*
EMP: 7 **EST:** 2019
SALES (est): 129.91K
SALES (corp-wide): 129.91K **Privately Held**
SIC: 2821 Molding compounds, plastics

(G-14603)
R & D MACHINE INC
1204 S Crawford St (45373-4134)
PHONE......................937 339-2545
Daniel Daffner, *Pr*
Pam Daffner, *Owner*
EMP: 15 **EST:** 1994
SALES (est): 2.37MM **Privately Held**
Web: www.randdmachine.com
SIC: 3312 Tool and die steel

(G-14604)
RAYMATH COMPANY
Also Called: Raymath
2323 W State Route 55 (45373-9234)
PHONE......................937 335-1860
Greg Lefevre, *Pr*
James M Ruef, *
William Moore, *
▲ **EMP:** 140 **EST:** 1982
SQ FT: 50,000
SALES (est): 23.55MM **Privately Held**
Web: www.raymath.com
SIC: 3541 3544 Machine tools, metal cutting type; Special dies and tools

(G-14605)
ROSS SPECIAL PRODUCTS INC
2500 W State Route 55 (45373-9511)
PHONE......................937 335-8406
Dave Pollard, *Pr*
EMP: 17 **EST:** 1984
SQ FT: 13,000
SALES (est): 1.72MM **Privately Held**
SIC: 3089 3544 Injection molding of plastics; Forms (molds), for foundry and plastics working machinery

(G-14606)
RT INDUSTRIES INC (PA)
Also Called: CHAMPION INDUSTRIES DIV
110 Foss Way (45373-1430)
PHONE......................937 335-5784
Ann Hinkle, *Superintnt*
Karen Mayer, *Superintnt*
EMP: 6 **EST:** 1974
SQ FT: 18,000
SALES (est): 3.05MM
SALES (corp-wide): 3.05MM **Privately Held**
Web: www.rtindustries.org
SIC: 3579 8331 7349 2789 Paper cutters, trimmers, and punches; Sheltered workshop; Janitorial service, contract basis; Bookbinding and related work

(G-14607)
SC LIQUIDATION COMPANY LLC (DH)
Also Called: Spinnaker Coating
550 Summit Ave (45373-3047)
PHONE......................937 332-6500
Louis Guzzetti Junior, *CEO*
George Fuehrer, *
Stuart Postle, *
Perry Schiller, *
Kevin Ahlfeld, *
▲ **EMP:** 100 **EST:** 2002
SALES (est): 56.14MM **Privately Held**
Web: www.spinps.com
SIC: 2621 Paper mills
HQ: Mactac Americas, Llc
  4560 Darrow Rd
  Stow OH 44224
  800 762-2822

(G-14608)
SEGNA INC
1316 Barnhart Rd Ste 1316 (45373)
PHONE......................937 335-6700
Junichi Yakahi, *Pr*
◆ **EMP:** 15 **EST:** 2001
SQ FT: 2,100
SALES (est): 1.67MM **Privately Held**
Web: segna.segglobal.com
SIC: 3559 Automotive maintenance equipment

(G-14609)
SEW-EURODRIVE INC
2001 W Main St (45373-1018)
PHONE......................937 335-0036
Gene Hart, *Mgr*
EMP: 100
SQ FT: 32,400
SALES (corp-wide): 4.27B **Privately Held**
Web: www.seweurodrive.com
SIC: 3566 3714 3699 Gears, power transmission, except auto; Motor vehicle parts and accessories; Electrical equipment and supplies, nec
HQ: Sew-Eurodrive, Inc.
  220 Finch Rd
  Wellford SC 29385
  864 423-1154

(G-14610)
SK MOLD & TOOL INC
2120 Corporate Dr (45373-1085)
P.O. Box 495 (45373-0495)
PHONE......................937 339-0299
Vince Hinde, *Brnch Mgr*
EMP: 20
SALES (corp-wide): 7.12MM **Privately Held**
Web: www.skmold.com
SIC: 3544 3599 Special dies and tools; Machine shop, jobbing and repair
PA: Sk Mold & Tool Inc.

955 N 3rd St
Tipp City OH 45371
937 339-0299

(G-14611)
SLIMLINE SURGICAL DEVICES LLC
Also Called: Canyon Run Engineering
1990 W Stanfield Rd (45373-2329)
PHONE..................937 335-0496
Gary Ward, *Pr*
Amy Ward, *Prin*
Carly Witmer, *Prin*
EMP: 7 EST: 2015
SALES (est): 786.59K **Privately Held**
Web: www.crengtech.com
SIC: 3599 Machine shop, jobbing and repair

(G-14612)
SPINNKER PRSSURE SNSTIVE PDTS
550 Summit Ave (45373-3075)
PHONE..................800 543-9452
EMP: 6 EST: 2021
SALES (est): 401.71K **Privately Held**
SIC: 2621 Paper mills

(G-14613)
STRATA-TAC INC
1985 W Stanfield Rd (45373-2330)
PHONE..................630 879-9338
Charles L Casagrande, *Pr*
Andrew Schwarzbauer, *VP*
Thomas Yeager, *VP*
▲ **EMP: 17 EST:** 1995
SALES (est): 6.58MM
SALES (corp-wide): 76.86MM **Privately Held**
Web: www.stratatac.com
SIC: 2672 5085 5113 5131 Labels (unprinted), gummed: made from purchased materials; Adhesives, tape and plasters; Pressure sensitive tape; Synthetic fabrics, nec
PA: Duraco Specialty Tapes Llc
7400 Industrial Dr
Forest Park IL 60130
866 800-0775

(G-14614)
STULL WOODWORKS INC
Also Called: Wood Working
155 Marybill Dr S (45373-1054)
PHONE..................937 698-8181
Brian Stull, *Pr*
Sandy Stull, *VP*
EMP: 6 EST: 1992
SALES (est): 900K **Privately Held**
Web: www.stullwoodworks.com
SIC: 2431 Woodwork, interior and ornamental, nec

(G-14615)
VISION MANUFACTURING INC
513 Garfield Ave (45373-3113)
P.O. Box 267 (45373-0267)
PHONE..................937 332-1801
Jerry Hicks, *Owner*
EMP: 10 EST: 1993
SALES (est): 438.63K **Privately Held**
SIC: 3599 Machine shop, jobbing and repair

(G-14616)
WESTERN OHIO GRAPHICS
Also Called: Quality Quick Print
402 E Main St (45373-3413)
PHONE..................937 335-8769
Bob Hephner, *Owner*
EMP: 12 EST: 1991
SQ FT: 13,000
SALES (est): 485.81K **Privately Held**
Web: www.westernohiographics.com
SIC: 2759 2752 5999 7336 Commercial printing, nec; Offset printing; Banners; Commercial art and graphic design

(G-14617)
YASKAWA AMERICA INC
1050 S Dorset Rd (45373-4708)
PHONE..................937 440-2600
EMP: 130
Web: www.yaskawa.com
SIC: 3569 Robots, assembly line: industrial and commercial
HQ: Yaskawa America, Inc.
2121 S Norman Dr
Waukegan IL 60085
847 887-7000

Tuppers Plains
Meigs County

(G-14618)
REMRAM RECOVERY LLC (PA)
49705 East Park Dr (45783)
P.O. Box 189 (45783-0189)
PHONE..................740 667-0092
Ray Maxson, *Managing Member*
EMP: 10 EST: 2005
SQ FT: 36,000
SALES (est): 1.39MM **Privately Held**
Web: www.remramrecovery.com
SIC: 3089 Panels, building: plastics, nec

(G-14619)
WECAN FABRICATORS LLC
49425 E Park Dr (45783-9000)
P.O. Box 159 (45783-0159)
PHONE..................740 667-0731
Jeffrey Cox, *Managing Member*
EMP: 8 EST: 2002
SQ FT: 4,000
SALES (est): 893.08K **Privately Held**
SIC: 3441 Fabricated structural metal

Twinsburg
Summit County

(G-14620)
48 HR BOOKS INC
1909 Summit Commerce Park (44087-2371)
PHONE..................330 374-6917
James Fulton, *Pr*
▼ **EMP: 16 EST:** 2007
SALES (est): 4.9MM **Privately Held**
Web: www.48hrbooks.com
SIC: 2741 Miscellaneous publishing

(G-14621)
A E WILSON HOLDINGS INC
Also Called: Quest Service Labs
2307 E Aurora Rd (44087-1958)
PHONE..................330 405-0316
Al Wilson, *Pr*
EMP: 8 EST: 2001
SALES (est): 661.04K **Privately Held**
Web: www.questservicelabs.com
SIC: 2759 Commercial printing, nec

(G-14622)
ACE AMERICAN WIRE DIE CO
9041 Dutton Dr (44087-1930)
PHONE..................330 425-7269
Linda Hohl, *Pr*
EMP: 10 EST: 1998
SQ FT: 10,000
SALES (est): 974.27K **Privately Held**
SIC: 3544 Special dies and tools

(G-14623)
ACHILLES AEROSPACE PDTS INC
Also Called: Achilles Aerospace Products
2100 Enterprise Pkwy (44087-2212)
PHONE..................330 425-8444
David L Hoyack, *Pr*
J Michael Corfias, *Contrlr*
EMP: 22 EST: 1989
SQ FT: 20,000
SALES (est): 4.1MM **Privately Held**
Web: www.achillesaerospace.com
SIC: 3728 Aircraft body and wing assemblies and parts

(G-14624)
ADAPTALL AMERICA INC
9047 Dutton Dr (44087-1930)
PHONE..................330 425-4114
C Lane Wood, *Pr*
EMP: 16 EST: 2002
SALES (est): 2.45MM **Privately Held**
Web: www.adaptall.com
SIC: 3494 Pipe fittings

(G-14625)
AIRGAS USA LLC
9155 Dutton Dr (44087-1956)
PHONE..................440 232-6397
Todd Testa, *Brnch Mgr*
EMP: 6
SALES (corp-wide): 101.26MM **Privately Held**
Web: www.airgas.com
SIC: 5169 5084 5085 2813 Industrial gases; Welding machinery and equipment; Welding supplies; Industrial gases
HQ: Airgas Usa, Llc
259 N Radnor Chester Rd
Radnor PA 19087
216 642-6600

(G-14626)
AJD HOLDING CO (PA)
2181 Enterprise Pkwy (44087-2211)
PHONE..................330 405-4477
EMP: 60 EST: 1994
SQ FT: 55,000
SALES (est): 52.8MM **Privately Held**
Web: www.ajdholding.com
SIC: 3469 3544 3315 3537 Stamping metal for the trade; Special dies, tools, jigs, and fixtures; Wire and fabricated wire products; Tractors, used in plants, docks, terminals, etc.: industrial

(G-14627)
ALBEMARLE AMENDMENTS LLC (HQ) ✪
1664 Highland Rd Ste 3 (44087-2249)
PHONE..................330 425-2354
J Kent Masters Junior, *Pr*
EMP: 31 EST: 2022
SALES (est): 8.99MM **Publicly Held**
SIC: 2819 2899 2812 2869 Bromine, elemental; Chemical preparations, nec; Alkalies and chlorine; Industrial organic chemicals, nec
PA: Albemarle Corporation
4250 Congress St Ste 900
Charlotte NC 28209

(G-14628)
ALLIED SEPARATION TECH INC (PA)
Also Called: Air Supply Co
2300 E Enterprise Pkwy (44087-2349)
PHONE..................704 732-8034
Michael E Williams, *Pr*
Lorrie Williams, *VP*
▲ **EMP: 33 EST:** 2009
SALES (est): 2.56MM
SALES (corp-wide): 2.56MM **Privately Held**
SIC: 3569 Filters

(G-14629)
ALLIED SEPARATION TECH INC
Also Called: Allied Supplied Company
2300 E Enterprise Pkwy (44087-2349)
PHONE..................704 736-0420
Mike Williams, *Pr*
Lori Williams, *
EMP: 14 EST: 2002
SALES (est): 399.36K **Privately Held**
SIC: 3714 3564 Oil strainers, motor vehicle; Air purification equipment

(G-14630)
AMERICAN AXLE & MFG INC
8001 Bavaria Rd (44087-2261)
PHONE..................330 486-3200
EMP: 87
SALES (corp-wide): 6.08B **Publicly Held**
Web: www.aam.com
SIC: 3714 Motor vehicle parts and accessories
HQ: American Axle & Manufacturing, Inc.
One Dauch Dr
Detroit MI 48211

(G-14631)
ARGO TOOL CORPORATION
9138 Jody Lynn Ln (44087-4801)
PHONE..................330 425-2407
Laszlo Repay, *Pr*
Linda Repay, *VP*
EMP: 11 EST: 1978
SALES (est): 355.42K **Privately Held**
Web: www.argotool.com
SIC: 3599 Machine shop, jobbing and repair

(G-14632)
AUTOMATION SOFTWARE & ENGRG (PA)
9321 Ravenna Rd Ste A (44087-2461)
PHONE..................330 405-2990
Kenneth Hutchison, *Pr*
EMP: 15 EST: 1990
SQ FT: 6,000
SALES (est): 2.5MM **Privately Held**
SIC: 7372 Prepackaged software

(G-14633)
BADLIME PROMO AND APPAREL LLC
2146 E Aurora Rd (44087-1924)
PHONE..................330 425-7100
EMP: 6 EST: 2018
SALES (est): 52.94K **Privately Held**
Web: www.badlime.com
SIC: 2759 Screen printing

(G-14634)
BAUTEC N TECHNOFORM AMER INC
1755 Enterprise Pkwy Ste 300 (44087)
PHONE..................330 487-6600
Albert Stankus, *Genl Mgr*
▲ **EMP: 30 EST:** 2006
SALES (est): 6.53MM **Privately Held**
Web: www.technoform.com
SIC: 2431 Windows and window parts and trim, wood

(G-14635)
BESSAMAIRE SALES INC
1869 E Aurora Rd Ste 700 (44087-2500)
PHONE..................440 439-1200
EMP: 23 EST: 1953
SQ FT: 50,000
SALES (est): 2.26MM **Privately Held**

Twinsburg - Summit County (G-14636)

Web: www.bessamaire.com
SIC: 3585 Refrigeration and heating equipment

(G-14636)
BESSAMAIRE SALES INTL LLC
1869 E Aurora Rd (44087-1998)
PHONE.................................800 321-5992
EMP: 15
SALES (est): 591.4K Privately Held
SIC: 3433 Heating equipment, except electric

(G-14637)
BIRD CONTROL INTERNATIONAL
1393 Highland Rd (44087-2213)
PHONE.................................330 425-2377
Jack Polnick, Dir
Stanley Baker, Pr
Benjamin Baker, VP
EMP: 10 EST: 1982
SALES (est): 239.5K Privately Held
SIC: 2879 2899 Pesticides, agricultural or household; Chemical preparations, nec

(G-14638)
C C M WIRE INC
Also Called: Wrwp
1920 Case Pkwy S (44087-2358)
PHONE.................................330 425-3421
▲ EMP: 37 EST: 1988
SALES (est): 2.48MM Privately Held
SIC: 3496 3679 3694 3678 Miscellaneous fabricated wire products; Harness assemblies, for electronic use: wire or cable; Engine electrical equipment; Electronic connectors

(G-14639)
CANADUS POWER SYSTEMS LLC
9347 Ravenna Rd Ste A (44087-2463)
PHONE.................................216 831-6600
EMP: 10 EST: 2000
SQ FT: 1,000
SALES (est): 1.71MM Privately Held
Web: www.canadus.com
SIC: 3678 Electronic connectors

(G-14640)
CENTERLESS GRINDING SOLUTIONS
8440 Tower Dr (44087-2000)
PHONE.................................216 520-4612
Rick Keller, Owner
EMP: 7 EST: 2011
SALES (est): 365.31K Privately Held
Web: www.centerlessgrinders.com
SIC: 3599 Machine shop, jobbing and repair

(G-14641)
CENTRAL COCA-COLA BTLG CO INC
Also Called: Coca-Cola
1882 Highland Rd (44087-2223)
PHONE.................................330 425-4401
Rick Bodzenski, Mgr
EMP: 281
SALES (corp-wide): 45.75B Publicly Held
Web: www.coca-cola.com
SIC: 2086 Bottled and canned soft drinks
HQ: Central Coca-Cola Bottling Company, Inc.
555 Taxter Rd Ste 550
Elmsford NY 10523
914 789-1100

(G-14642)
CHURCHILL STEEL PLATE LTD
7851 Bavaria Rd (44087-2263)
PHONE.................................330 425-9000
Jim Stevenson, Pr
James M Fleming V Pes, Treas

Kirk Mooney, *
EMP: 48 EST: 2013
SQ FT: 120,000
SALES (est): 6.98MM Privately Held
Web: www.churchillsteelplate.com
SIC: 3312 Plate, steel

(G-14643)
CLEVELAND ELECTRIC LABS CO (PA)
Also Called: Cleveland Electric Labs
1776 Enterprise Pkwy (44087-2246)
PHONE.................................800 447-2207
Jack Allan Lieske, Pr
Val Jean Lieske, *
Rebecca Lieske, *
C M Lemmon, *
EMP: 42 EST: 1920
SQ FT: 30,000
SALES (est): 10.84MM
SALES (corp-wide): 10.84MM Privately Held
Web: www.clevelandelectriclabs.com
SIC: 3823 7699 Thermocouples, industrial process type; Professional instrument repair services

(G-14644)
COMTEC INCORPORATED
1800 Enterprise Pkwy (44087-2269)
PHONE.................................330 425-8102
Kenneth Drummond, Pr
EMP: 12 EST: 1973
SQ FT: 10,200
SALES (est): 2.12MM Privately Held
Web: www.comtecinc.com
SIC: 3823 3625 8711 Computer interface equipment, for industrial process control; Relays and industrial controls; Engineering services

(G-14645)
CONTRACTORS STEEL COMPANY
8383 Boyle Pkwy (44087-2236)
PHONE.................................330 425-3050
Mitch Kubasek, Mgr
EMP: 59
SQ FT: 58,000
SALES (corp-wide): 582.71MM Privately Held
Web: www.upgllc.com
SIC: 5051 3498 3312 Steel; Fabricated pipe and fittings; Blast furnaces and steel mills
HQ: Contractors Steel Company
48649 Schooner St
Van Buren Twp MI 48111
734 464-4000

(G-14646)
CROWN BATTERY MANUFACTURING CO
1750 Highland Rd Ste 3 (44087-2244)
PHONE.................................330 425-3308
Jeff Wharton, Brnch Mgr
EMP: 8
SALES (corp-wide): 95.41MM Privately Held
Web: www.crownbattery.com
SIC: 3691 Storage batteries
PA: Crown Battery Manufacturing Company
1445 Majestic Dr
Fremont OH 43420
419 334-7181

(G-14647)
DAY-GLO COLOR CORP
1570 Highland Rd (44087-2217)
PHONE.................................216 391-7070
Joe Shaw, Mgr
EMP: 19
SQ FT: 33,500

SALES (corp-wide): 7.26B Publicly Held
Web: www.dayglo.com
SIC: 2816 Inorganic pigments
HQ: Day-Glo Color Corp.
4515 Saint Clair Ave
Cleveland OH 44103
216 391-7070

(G-14648)
DESCO EQUIPMENT CORP
1903 Case Pkwy (44087-2343)
PHONE.................................330 405-1581
Leo E Henry, Pr
Barbara Krane, VP
Gene A Gilbert, Sec
▲ EMP: 21 EST: 1985
SQ FT: 50,000
SALES (est): 1.86MM
SALES (corp-wide): 24.38MM Privately Held
Web: www.descomachine.com
SIC: 3555 Printing presses
PA: Apex Machine Company
3000 Ne 12th Ter
Oakland Park FL 33334
954 563-0209

(G-14649)
DESCO MACHINE COMPANY LLC
1903 Case Pkwy (44087-2343)
PHONE.................................330 405-1581
EMP: 10 EST: 2016
SALES (est): 993.72K Privately Held
Web: www.descomachine.com
SIC: 3999 Manufacturing industries, nec

(G-14650)
DF SUPPLY INC
Also Called: Df Supply
8500 Hadden Rd (44087-2114)
PHONE.................................330 650-9226
◆ EMP: 38 EST: 1982
SQ FT: 10,000
SALES (est): 32MM Privately Held
Web: www.dfsupplyinc.com
SIC: 5031 5211 3499 1731 Fencing, wood; Fencing; Barricades, metal; Access control systems specialization

(G-14651)
DIRECT DIGITAL GRAPHICS INC
1716 Enterprise Pkwy (44087-2204)
PHONE.................................330 405-3770
Mike Boswell, Pr
Kimberly Boswell, Off Mgr
EMP: 8 EST: 1996
SQ FT: 14,000
SALES (est): 778.66K Privately Held
SIC: 2752 Offset printing

(G-14652)
DIXON VALVE & COUPLING CO LLC
1900 Enterprise Pkwy (44087-2296)
PHONE.................................330 425-3000
Louis Young, Mgr
EMP: 10
SALES (corp-wide): 439.82MM Privately Held
Web: www.dixonvalve.com
SIC: 3492 5085 Fluid power valves and hose fittings; Hose, belting, and packing
HQ: Dixon Valve & Coupling Company, Llc
1 Dixon Sq
Chestertown MD 21620

(G-14653)
DOLANA GROUP LLC
8870 Darrow Rd Ste F104 (44087-2178)
PHONE.................................440 622-8615
EMP: 6 EST: 2011
SALES (est): 85K Privately Held

SIC: 3421 Table and food cutlery, including butchers'

(G-14654)
DRIBBLE CREEK INC
Also Called: Kadee Industries
8333 Boyle Pkwy (44087-2236)
PHONE.................................440 439-8650
EMP: 10 EST: 1980
SALES (est): 1.71MM Privately Held
SIC: 3496 2273 Mats and matting; Carpets and rugs

(G-14655)
ENTERPRISEID INC
9321 Ravenna Rd Ste C (44087-2461)
PHONE.................................330 963-0064
Jim Butkovic, Prin
EMP: 6 EST: 2009
SALES (est): 67.82K Privately Held
SIC: 3699 Security control equipment and systems

(G-14656)
EPI OF CLEVELAND INC
Also Called: Engineered Products
2224 E Enterprise Pkwy (44087-2393)
PHONE.................................330 468-2872
Robert Knazek, VP
EMP: 8
SALES (corp-wide): 20.35MM Privately Held
Web: www.epimetal.com
SIC: 3441 5051 Fabricated structural metal; Metals service centers and offices
HQ: E.P.I. Of Cleveland, Inc.
2224 E Enterprise Pkwy
Twinsburg OH 44087
330 468-2872

(G-14657)
ESSILOR LABORATORIES AMER INC
Also Called: Bell Optical
9221 Ravenna Rd # 3 (44087-2472)
P.O. Box 620 (44087-0620)
PHONE.................................330 425-3003
EMP: 8
SALES (corp-wide): 1.42MM Privately Held
SIC: 3851 Eyeglasses, lenses and frames
HQ: Essilor Laboratories Of America, Inc.
13515 N Stemmons Fwy
Dallas TX 75234
972 241-4141

(G-14658)
FABRICATING SOLUTIONS INC
7920 Bavaria Rd (44087-2252)
PHONE.................................330 486-0998
Dewey Lockwood, Pr
EMP: 14 EST: 2003
SALES (est): 2.4MM Privately Held
Web: www.fab-solution.com
SIC: 3499 3444 Fire- or burglary-resistive products; Sheet metalwork

(G-14659)
FACIL NORTH AMERICA INC (HQ)
Also Called: Streetsboro Operations
2242 Pinnacle Pkwy Ste 100 (44087-5301)
PHONE.................................330 487-2500
Rene Achten, CEO
Daniel Michiels, CFO
◆ EMP: 210 EST: 1967
SQ FT: 150,000
SALES (est): 162.26MM
SALES (corp-wide): 8.12MM Privately Held
Web: www.facil.be

▲ = Import ▼ = Export
◆ = Import/Export

GEOGRAPHIC SECTION
Twinsburg - Summit County (G-14680)

SIC: 5072 3452 5085 Nuts (hardware); Nuts, metal; Fasteners, industrial: nuts, bolts, screws, etc.
PA: Facil Corporate
Geleenlaan 20
Genk 3600
89410450

(G-14660)
FERRUM INDUSTRIES INC (HQ)
1831 Highland Rd (44087-2222)
P.O. Box 360230 (44136-0004)
PHONE..................................440 519-1768
Steve Joseph, Pr
Don Moreno, VP
▲ EMP: 6 EST: 2001
SALES (est): 1.01MM
SALES (corp-wide): 5.38MM Privately Held
Web: www.ferrum.net
SIC: 2899 Metal treating compounds
PA: Auburn Metal Processing, Llc
4550 Darrow Rd
Stow OH 44224
315 253-2565

(G-14661)
FONTAINE PIECIAK ENGRG INC
2300 E Enterprise Pkwy (44087-2349)
PHONE..................................413 592-2273
David Pieciak, Pr
Roger Fontaine, VP
EMP: 25 EST: 1942
SQ FT: 20,000
SALES (est): 990.82K Privately Held
SIC: 3677 Filtration devices, electronic

(G-14662)
FREEDOM USA INC
Also Called: Avadirect.com
2045 Midway Dr (44087-1933)
PHONE..................................216 503-6374
Alex Sonis, CEO
EMP: 35 EST: 2000
SQ FT: 8,000
SALES (est): 9.39MM Privately Held
Web: www.avadirect.com
SIC: 3572 7373 7379 3575 Computer storage devices; Systems engineering, computer related; Computer related maintenance services; Computer terminals

(G-14663)
FUCHS LUBRICANTS CO
Also Called: Fuchs Franklin Div
8036 Bavaria Rd (44087-2262)
PHONE..................................330 963-0400
Kipp Kofsky, Brnch Mgr
EMP: 12
SALES (corp-wide): 3.85B Privately Held
Web: www.fuchs.com
SIC: 4225 2992 2899 2851 General warehousing and storage; Lubricating oils and greases; Chemical preparations, nec; Paints and allied products
HQ: Fuchs Lubricants Co.
17050 Lathrop Ave
Harvey IL 60426
708 333-8900

(G-14664)
GANZCORP INVESTMENTS INC
Also Called: Mustang Dynamometer
2300 Pinnacle Pkwy (44087-2368)
PHONE..................................330 963-5400
Dean Ganzhorn, Prin
Dean K Ganzhorn, *
Donald W Ganzhorn Junior, Ex VP
◆ EMP: 60 EST: 1986
SQ FT: 82,000
SALES (est): 14.57MM Privately Held

Web: www.mustangdyne.com
SIC: 3559 Automotive related machinery

(G-14665)
GE VERNOVA INTERNATIONAL LLC
Also Called: GE
8941 Dutton Dr (44087-1939)
PHONE..................................330 963-2066
EMP: 7
SALES (corp-wide): 2.6B Publicly Held
Web: www.ge.com
SIC: 3561 Compressors, except air conditioning; Pumps, oil well and field
HQ: Ge Vernova International Llc
58 Charles St
Cambridge MA 02141
617 443-3000

(G-14666)
GED HOLDINGS INC
9280 Dutton Dr (44087-1967)
PHONE..................................330 963-5401
William Weaver, Pr
EMP: 17 EST: 2000
SALES (est): 354.64K Privately Held
Web: www.gedusa.com
SIC: 3559 3549 5084 Glass making machinery: blowing, molding, forming, etc.; Cutting and slitting machinery; Industrial machinery and equipment

(G-14667)
GENERAL DIE CASTERS INC (HQ)
2150 Highland Rd (44087-2229)
PHONE..................................330 678-2528
Brian Lennon, CEO
Tim Foley, *
▲ EMP: 40 EST: 1957
SQ FT: 31,000
SALES (est): 26.52MM
SALES (corp-wide): 26.52MM Privately Held
Web: www.generaldie.com
SIC: 3364 3363 3544 3369 Zinc and zinc-base alloy die-castings; Aluminum die-castings; Special dies, tools, jigs, and fixtures; Nonferrous foundries, nec
PA: Wolny Enterprises Inc.
12400 S Lombard Ln
Alsip IL 60803
708 388-4914

(G-14668)
GENERAL ELECTRIC COMPANY
Also Called: GE
8499 Darrow Rd (44087-2309)
PHONE..................................330 425-3755
J E Breen, Prin
EMP: 16
SALES (corp-wide): 67.95B Publicly Held
Web: www.ge.com
SIC: 1311 Crude petroleum and natural gas
PA: General Electric Company
1 Aviation Way
Cincinnati OH 45215
617 443-3000

(G-14669)
GOLF MARKETING GROUP INC
Also Called: Shot Selector
9221 Ravenna Rd Ste 7 (44087-2454)
PHONE..................................330 963-5155
Dave Zabell, Pr
Marc Mascarillo, VP
▲ EMP: 8 EST: 1987
SQ FT: 2,000
SALES (est): 1.03MM Privately Held
Web: www.shotselector.com
SIC: 2752 2732 3993 Cards, lithographed; Book printing; Signs and advertising specialties

(G-14670)
GREAT LAKES FASTENERS INC (PA)
Also Called: Great Lakes Fasteners & Sup Co
2204 E Enterprise Pkwy (44087)
PHONE..................................330 425-4488
Kevin Weidinger, Pr
Kevin Weidinger, Pr
Tim Umberger, VP
▲ EMP: 65 EST: 2010
SALES (est): 12.54MM
SALES (corp-wide): 12.54MM Privately Held
Web: www.glfus.com
SIC: 5085 3452 Fasteners, industrial: nuts, bolts, screws, etc.; Bolts, nuts, rivets, and washers

(G-14671)
HANA TECHNOLOGIES INC
2061 Case Pkwy S (44087-2361)
PHONE..................................330 405-4600
John Erdmann, Pr
David Tsing, *
Edward M Stiles Iii, VP
D Scott Worthington, *
Paul R Brown Junior, VP
▲ EMP: 60 EST: 1999
SQ FT: 24,000
SALES (est): 15.43MM Privately Held
Web: www.hana.family
SIC: 3825 Instruments to measure electricity
PA: Hana Microelectronics Group
65/98 Soi Vibhavadi-Rangsit 64 Yaek 2
Lak Si 10210

(G-14672)
HGI HOLDINGS INC
Also Called: Edgepark Medical Supplies
1810 Summit Commerce Park (44087-2300)
PHONE..................................330 963-6996
◆ EMP: 950
SIC: 3841 Hypodermic needles and syringes

(G-14673)
HYDROMOTIVE ENGINEERING CO
9261 Ravenna Rd Bldg B1 (44087-2470)
PHONE..................................330 425-4266
Tom Bucknell, Owner
EMP: 6 EST: 1979
SQ FT: 8,000
SALES (est): 477.56K Privately Held
Web: www.hydromotive.com
SIC: 3429 5088 5551 Marine hardware; Marine supplies; Marine supplies and equipment

(G-14674)
IBYCORP
Also Called: Ibycorp Tool & Die
8968 Dutton Dr (44087-1929)
PHONE..................................330 425-8226
Steven Hamori, Pr
Violet Hamori, Sec
EMP: 6 EST: 1975
SQ FT: 10,000
SALES (est): 531.57K Privately Held
SIC: 3544 Special dies and tools

(G-14675)
ICM DISTRIBUTING COMPANY INC
Also Called: Inventory Controlled Mdsg
1755 Enterprise Pkwy Ste 200 (44087)
PHONE..................................234 212-3030
Harry Singer, Pr
Phillip B Singer, *
▼ EMP: 35 EST: 2006
SQ FT: 80,000
SALES (est): 21.99MM
SALES (corp-wide): 24.01MM Privately Held

Web: www.icmint.com
SIC: 5049 5092 5199 5122 School supplies; Toys, nec; General merchandise, non-durable; Hair preparations
PA: Sandusco, Inc.
1755 Entp Pkwy Ste 200
Twinsburg OH 44087
440 357-5964

(G-14676)
INDUSTRIAL MOLD INC
Also Called: Industrial Prfctn Mold & Mch
2057 E Aurora Rd (44087-1938)
PHONE..................................330 425-7374
David Kuhary, Pr
EMP: 24 EST: 1988
SQ FT: 8,600
SALES (est): 4.67MM Privately Held
Web: www.industrialmold.com
SIC: 3544 5085 3354 Forms (molds), for foundry and plastics working machinery; Industrial supplies; Aluminum extruded products

(G-14677)
JH INDUSTRIES INC
Also Called: Copperloy
1981 E Aurora Rd (44087-1919)
PHONE..................................330 963-4105
John J Hallack, Pr
Jacqueline Hallack, *
Dale Doherty, *
EMP: 30 EST: 1952
SQ FT: 70,000
SALES (est): 4.7MM Privately Held
Web: www.copperloy.com
SIC: 3599 3448 3537 3444 Machine shop, jobbing and repair; Ramps, prefabricated metal; Industrial trucks and tractors; Sheet metalwork

(G-14678)
KELTEC INC (PA)
Also Called: Keltec-Technolab
2300 E Enterprise Pkwy (44087-2349)
PHONE..................................330 425-3100
Edward Kaiser, Pr
Dolores Kaiser, *
◆ EMP: 74 EST: 1982
SQ FT: 100,000
SALES (est): 15.26MM
SALES (corp-wide): 15.26MM Privately Held
Web: www.keltecinc.com
SIC: 3569 Separators for steam, gas, vapor, or air (machinery)

(G-14679)
KING FORGE AND MACHINE COMPANY
Also Called: King Force & Machine
8250 Boyle Pkwy (44087-2234)
PHONE..................................330 963-0600
Raymond W King Junior, Pr
EMP: 10 EST: 1992
SQ FT: 10,000
SALES (est): 752.11K Privately Held
SIC: 3462 Flange, valve, and pipe fitting forgings, ferrous

(G-14680)
KING-INDIANA FORGE INC
8250 Boyle Pkwy (44087-2234)
PHONE..................................330 425-4250
Raymond W King Junior, Pr
EMP: 13 EST: 1993
SQ FT: 250,000
SALES (est): 1.57MM
SALES (corp-wide): 30.98MM Privately Held

Twinsburg - Summit County (G-14681) — GEOGRAPHIC SECTION

SIC: **3462** Iron and steel forgings
PA: Ssp Fittings Corp.
  8250 Boyle Pkwy
  Twinsburg OH 44087
  330 425-4250

(G-14681)
KIWI PROMOTIONAL AP & PRTG CO
Also Called: Inc., K.I.W.I.
2170 E Aurora Rd (44087-1924)
PHONE.................................330 487-5115
Mark Candle, *Pr*
Paul Steels, *
EMP: 37 **EST:** 1987
SQ FT: 28,000
SALES (est): 2.34MM **Privately Held**
Web: www.kiwipromotional.com
SIC: **2396** 2395 Screen printing on fabric articles; Embroidery products, except Schiffli machine

(G-14682)
KRISS KREATIONS
Also Called: Edible Arrangement
9224 Darrow Rd (44087-1897)
PHONE.................................330 405-6102
Kristine Brownfield, *Owner*
EMP: 6 **EST:** 2003
SALES (est): 585.75K **Privately Held**
Web: www.ediblearrangements.com
SIC: **3523** 5999 Shakers, tree: nuts, fruits, etc.; Alarm and safety equipment stores

(G-14683)
L & M PROCESSING LLC
1900 Case Pkwy S (44087-2358)
PHONE.................................330 405-0615
Mike Palumbo, *CEO*
EMP: 6 **EST:** 2016
SALES (est): 440.86K **Privately Held**
Web: www.lmmetalprocessing.com
SIC: **3599** Industrial machinery, nec

(G-14684)
L J STAR INCORPORATED
2396 Edison Blvd (44087-2376)
P.O. Box 1116 (44087-9116)
PHONE.................................330 405-3040
David Star, *Pr*
Leonard J Star, *Ch*
▲ **EMP:** 20 **EST:** 1991
SQ FT: 10,000
SALES (est): 4.9MM **Privately Held**
Web: www.ljstar.com
SIC: **3823** Flow instruments, industrial process type

(G-14685)
LEGACY SUPPLIES INC
8252 Darrow Rd Ste E (44087-2392)
P.O. Box 1173 (44087-9173)
PHONE.................................330 405-4565
Mike Corcelli, *Pr*
Frank Corcelli, *VP*
EMP: 10 **EST:** 1998
SALES (est): 911.96K **Privately Held**
SIC: **3694** 5013 Distributors, motor vehicle engine; Motor vehicle supplies and new parts

(G-14686)
LEIDEN CABINET CO
1842 Enterprise Pkwy (44087-2289)
PHONE.................................330 425-8555
EMP: 6 **EST:** 2017
SALES (est): 53.79K **Privately Held**
Web: www.leidencompany.com
SIC: **2434** Wood kitchen cabinets

(G-14687)
LEIDEN CABINET COMPANY LLC (PA)
Also Called: Leiden Company
2385 Edison Blvd (44087-2376)
PHONE.................................330 425-8555
Melissa Hale, *Pr*
Michael Hopp, *
Michael Schmidt, *Head OF Accounting**
EMP: 83 **EST:** 1940
SQ FT: 210,000
SALES (est): 17.63MM
SALES (corp-wide): 17.63MM **Privately Held**
Web: www.leidencompany.com
SIC: **2541** Store fixtures, wood

(G-14688)
LEXINGTON RUBBER GROUP INC (PA)
Also Called: Qsr
1700 Highland Rd (44087-2221)
P.O. Box 1030 (44087-9030)
PHONE.................................330 425-8472
Randy Ross, *CEO*
Dennis Welhouse, *
▲ **EMP:** 29 **EST:** 1988
SQ FT: 110,000
SALES (est): 119.37MM **Privately Held**
SIC: **3069** Hard rubber and molded rubber products

(G-14689)
LINDE GAS USA LLC
2045 E Aurora Rd (44087-2280)
PHONE.................................330 425-3989
Jim Lawrence, *Prin*
EMP: 15 **EST:** 2006
SALES (est): 3.15MM **Privately Held**
SIC: **2813** Industrial gases

(G-14690)
LINEAR ASICS INC
2061 Case Pkwy S (44087-2361)
PHONE.................................330 474-3920
Mike Ward, *CEO*
EMP: 8 **EST:** 2016
SQ FT: 2,000
SALES (est): 1.13MM **Privately Held**
Web: www.linearasics.com
SIC: **3674** Semiconductors and related devices

(G-14691)
MARSAM METALFAB INC
1870 Enterprise Pkwy (44087-2206)
PHONE.................................330 405-1520
EMP: 25 **EST:** 1990
SQ FT: 30,000
SALES (est): 5.44MM **Privately Held**
Web: www.marsamfab.com
SIC: **1799** 3441 7692 3444 Welding on site; Fabricated structural metal; Welding repair; Sheet metalwork

(G-14692)
MAVAL INDUSTRIES LLC (PA)
Also Called: Maval Manufacturing
1555 Enterprise Pkwy (44087-2239)
PHONE.................................330 405-1600
John Dougherty, *Pr*
Dale Lumby, *
◆ **EMP:** 137 **EST:** 1986
SQ FT: 88,000
SALES (est): 24.57MM
SALES (corp-wide): 24.57MM **Privately Held**
Web: www.mavalgear.com

SIC: **3714** 8711 Power steering equipment, motor vehicle; Consulting engineer

(G-14693)
MCFLUSION INC
2112 Case Pkwy Ste 8 (44087-2378)
PHONE.................................800 341-8616
Ole Madsen, *Pr*
▲ **EMP:** 8 **EST:** 2010
SALES (est): 961.86K **Privately Held**
Web: www.mcflusion.com
SIC: **3559** Pharmaceutical machinery

(G-14694)
MEDINA SUPPLY COMPANY
Also Called: Medina Supply Co
1516 Highland Rd (44087-2217)
PHONE.................................330 425-0752
EMP: 37
SQ FT: 18,612
SALES (corp-wide): 32.72B **Privately Held**
Web: www.shellyco.com
SIC: **3273** Ready-mixed concrete
HQ: Medina Supply Company
  230 E Smith Rd
  Medina OH 44256
  330 723-3681

(G-14695)
METAL IMPROVEMENT COMPANY LLC
1652 Highland Rd (44087-2219)
PHONE.................................330 425-1490
Matt Heschel, *Mgr*
EMP: 28
SALES (corp-wide): 2.85B **Publicly Held**
Web: www.curtisswright.com
SIC: **3398** Shot peening (treating steel to reduce fatigue)
HQ: Metal Improvement Company, Llc
  80 E Rte 4 Ste 310
  Paramus NJ 07652
  201 843-7800

(G-14696)
METALLIC RESOURCES INC
2368 E Enterprise Pkwy (44087)
P.O. Box 368 (44087)
PHONE.................................330 425-3155
Stan Rothschild, *Pr*
William Griffith, *
▲ **EMP:** 32 **EST:** 1979
SQ FT: 26,000
SALES (est): 10.27MM **Privately Held**
Web: www.metallicresources.com
SIC: **3356** 3339 Solder: wire, bar, acid core, and rosin core; Precious metals
PA: Metallic Solders De Mexico, S. De R.L. De C.V.
  Norte 7 No. 35-A
  Matamoros TAM

(G-14697)
MILES RUBBER & PACKING COMPANY (PA)
9020 Dutton Dr (44087-1994)
PHONE.................................330 425-3888
James M Smith, *Pr*
Larry Lempke, *
Janet Schickler, *
K J Ertle, *
EMP: 25 **EST:** 1952
SQ FT: 27,800
SALES (est): 5.41MM
SALES (corp-wide): 5.41MM **Privately Held**
Web: www.milesrubber.com
SIC: **3053** 3069 Gaskets, all materials; Sponge rubber and sponge rubber products

(G-14698)
MOLD-RITE PLASTICS LLC
2222 Highland Rd (44087-2231)
PHONE.................................330 405-7739
EMP: 147
SALES (corp-wide): 114.95MM **Privately Held**
Web: www.mrpcap.com
SIC: **3089** Closures, plastics
PA: Mold-Rite Plastics, Llc
  100 N Field Dr Ste 100 # 100
  Lake Forest IL 60045
  518 849-8431

(G-14699)
MOLD-RITE PLASTICS LLC
2300 Highland Rd (44087-2232)
PHONE.................................330 405-7739
EMP: 147
SALES (corp-wide): 114.95MM **Privately Held**
Web: www.mrpcap.com
SIC: **3089** Injection molding of plastics
PA: Mold-Rite Plastics, Llc
  100 N Field Dr Ste 100 # 100
  Lake Forest IL 60045
  518 849-8431

(G-14700)
MORGAN ADVANCED CERAMICS INC
Also Called: Morgan Advanced Materials
2181 Pinnacle Pkwy (44087-2365)
PHONE.................................330 405-1033
EMP: 31
SALES (corp-wide): 1.39B **Privately Held**
Web: www.morgantechnicalceramics.com
SIC: **2899** Chemical preparations, nec
HQ: Morgan Advanced Ceramics, Inc.
  2425 Whipple Rd
  Hayward CA 94544

(G-14701)
NATIONAL POWER COATING OHIO
2020 Case Pkwy (44087-2344)
PHONE.................................330 405-5587
William D Amato, *Pr*
EMP: 6 **EST:** 1972
SALES (est): 495.38K **Privately Held**
Web: www.nationalpowdercoating.com
SIC: **3479** Coating of metals and formed products

(G-14702)
NATIONAL PWDR COATING OHIO LLC
2060 Case Pkwy (44087-2344)
PHONE.................................330 405-5587
William D Amato, *Prin*
EMP: 11 **EST:** 2007
SALES (est): 407.65K **Privately Held**
Web: www.nationalpowdercoating.com
SIC: **3479** Coating of metals and formed products

(G-14703)
OLIVER PRINTING & PACKG CO LLC (PA)
1760 Enterprise Pkwy (44087-2291)
PHONE.................................330 425-7890
Dan Rodenbush, *Pr*
Stephen Ernst, *
EMP: 60 **EST:** 1952
SQ FT: 21,000
SALES (est): 95.47MM
SALES (corp-wide): 95.47MM **Privately Held**
Web: www.oliverinc.com
SIC: **2752** Offset printing

▲ = Import ▼ = Export ◆ = Import/Export

GEOGRAPHIC SECTION

Twinsburg - Summit County (G-14726)

(G-14704)
OLIVER STEEL PLATE CO
7851 Bavaria Rd (44087-2263)
PHONE.................................330 425-7000
▲ **EMP:** 65
SIC: 5051 3444 3443 3398 Metals service centers and offices; Sheet metalwork; Fabricated plate work (boiler shop); Metal heat treating

(G-14705)
P3 INFRASTRUCTURE INC
2146 Entp Pkwy Ste C (44087)
PHONE.................................330 408-9504
EMP: 12 **EST:** 2017
SALES (est): 424.48K **Privately Held**
Web: www.p3-i.com
SIC: 2851 Paints, asphalt or bituminous

(G-14706)
PARAGON ROBOTICS LLC
2234 E Enterprise Pkwy (44087-2393)
PHONE.................................216 313-9299
EMP: 25 **EST:** 2006
SALES (est): 1.45MM **Privately Held**
Web: www.paragonrobotics.com
SIC: 3695 Computer software tape and disks: blank, rigid, and floppy

(G-14707)
PARO SERVICES CO (PA)
1755 Enterprise Pkwy Ste 100 (44087)
PHONE.................................330 467-1300
Daniel N Zelman, *Pr*
Edward J Kubek Junior, *VP*
Nick La Magna, *VP*
Brian Mccue, *COO*
▲ **EMP:** 10 **EST:** 1998
SQ FT: 60,000
SALES (est): 10.75MM
SALES (corp-wide): 10.75MM **Privately Held**
SIC: 7349 2842 Cleaning service, industrial or commercial; Cleaning or polishing preparations, nec

(G-14708)
PENN MACHINE COMPANY LLC
2182 E Aurora Rd (44087-1924)
PHONE.................................814 288-1547
EMP: 56
SQ FT: 27,000
SALES (corp-wide): 364.48B **Publicly Held**
Web: www.pennmach.com
SIC: 3568 3532 3462 Power transmission equipment, nec; Mining machinery; Iron and steel forgings
HQ: Penn Machine Company Llc
   106 Station St
   Johnstown PA 15905

(G-14709)
PEPPERL + FUCHS INC (DH)
1600 Enterprise Pkwy (44087-2245)
PHONE.................................330 425-3555
Wolfgang Mueller, *Pr*
▲ **EMP:** 130 **EST:** 1983
SQ FT: 55,050
SALES (est): 99.67MM
SALES (corp-wide): 1.05B **Privately Held**
Web: www.pepperl-fuchs.com
SIC: 5065 3625 3822 3674 Electronic parts and equipment, nec; Relays and industrial controls; Environmental controls; Semiconductors and related devices
HQ: Pepperl + Fuchs Enterprises, Inc.
   1600 Enterprise Pkwy
   Twinsburg OH 44087
   330 425-3555

(G-14710)
PEPPERL + FUCHS ENTPS INC (HQ)
1600 Enterprise Pkwy (44087-2245)
PHONE.................................330 425-3555
Doctor Gunther Kegel, *Pr*
James P Bolin Junior, *VP*
Robert Charles Smith, *VP*
Alexander Gress, *Sec*
EMP: 10 **EST:** 1988
SALES (est): 183.78MM
SALES (corp-wide): 1.05B **Privately Held**
Web: www.pepperl-fuchs.com
SIC: 5065 3625 3822 3674 Electronic parts and equipment, nec; Relays and industrial controls; Environmental controls; Semiconductors and related devices
PA: Pepperl+Fuchs Se
   Lilienthalstr. 200
   Mannheim BW 68307
   6217760

(G-14711)
PEPSI-COLA METRO BTLG CO INC
Also Called: Pepsi-Cola
1999 Enterprise Pkwy (44087-2253)
PHONE.................................330 425-8236
Charlie Powers, *Mgr*
EMP: 107
SALES (corp-wide): 86.39B **Publicly Held**
Web: www.pepsico.com
SIC: 2086 5149 Bottled and canned soft drinks; Groceries and related products, nec
HQ: Pepsi-Cola Metropolitan Bottling Company, Inc.
   700 Anderson Hill Rd
   Purchase NY 10577
   914 767-6000

(G-14712)
PEPSI-COLA METRO BTLG CO INC
Also Called: Pepsico
1999 Enterprise Pkwy (44087-2253)
PHONE.................................330 963-5300
Charlie Powers, *Brnch Mgr*
EMP: 10
SALES (corp-wide): 86.39B **Publicly Held**
Web: www.pepsico.com
SIC: 2086 Carbonated soft drinks, bottled and canned
HQ: Pepsi-Cola Metropolitan Bottling Company, Inc.
   700 Anderson Hill Rd
   Purchase NY 10577
   914 767-6000

(G-14713)
PERFECTION MOLD & MACHINE CO
2057 E Aurora Rd Ste Hi (44087-1938)
PHONE.................................330 784-5435
Jack Bailey, *Pr*
EMP: 10 **EST:** 1952
SQ FT: 11,000
SALES (est): 310.64K **Privately Held**
SIC: 3544 Industrial molds

(G-14714)
PERRY WELDING SERVICE INC
2075 Case Pkwy S (44087-2361)
PHONE.................................330 425-2211
Jerry Perry, *Pr*
Margo Perry, *VP*
EMP: 14 **EST:** 1974
SQ FT: 12,000
SALES (est): 2.24MM **Privately Held**
Web: www.perrywelding.com
SIC: 3599 3469 7692 3544 Custom machinery; Machine parts, stamped or pressed metal; Welding repair; Special dies, tools, jigs, and fixtures

(G-14715)
PHOENIX MTAL SLS FBRCATION LLC
Also Called: Manufacturing
2201 Pinnacle Pkwy Ste A (44087-2479)
P.O. Box 476 (44202-0476)
PHONE.................................330 562-0585
Scott Holman, *Pr*
Scott Holman, *Managing Member*
EMP: 10 **EST:** 2010
SALES (est): 2.38MM **Privately Held**
Web: www.pmsaf.com
SIC: 3441 Fabricated structural metal

(G-14716)
PRECISION GEAR LLC
1900 Midway Dr (44087-1957)
PHONE.................................330 487-0888
EMP: 76 **EST:** 1970
SALES (est): 23.17MM
SALES (corp-wide): 6.25B **Publicly Held**
SIC: 3566 Speed changers, drives, and gears
HQ: Rexnord Industries, Llc
   111 W Michigan St
   Milwaukee WI 53203
   414 643-3000

(G-14717)
PREMIER SHOT COMPANY
1666 Enterprise Pkwy (44087-2202)
PHONE.................................330 405-0583
Bob Gillespie, *Pr*
▲ **EMP:** 6 **EST:** 1987
SQ FT: 10,000
SALES (est): 938.73K **Privately Held**
Web: www.premiershot.com
SIC: 3482 Shot, steel (ammunition)

(G-14718)
PRINTING SYSTEM INC
Also Called: 48hr Books
1909 Summit Commerce Park (44087-2371)
PHONE.................................330 375-9128
James Fulton, *Pr*
James T Pachell, *Prin*
EMP: 19 **EST:** 2000
SALES (est): 952.52K **Privately Held**
Web: www.48hrbooks.com
SIC: 2752 Offset printing

(G-14719)
PRODUCTION TL CO CLEVELAND INC
Also Called: Assembly Tool Specialists
9002 Dutton Dr (44087-1931)
PHONE.................................330 425-4466
Jackie Ahrens, *CEO*
Ronald T Carpenter, *Pr*
EMP: 18 **EST:** 1940
SQ FT: 3,800
SALES (est): 2.47MM **Privately Held**
Web: www.assytool.com
SIC: 3999 Barber and beauty shop equipment

(G-14720)
Q HOLDING COMPANY (HQ)
Also Called: Q Holding Mexico
1700 Highland Rd (44087-2221)
PHONE.................................440 903-1827
Mauricio Arellano, *CEO*
Roy Showman, *
▲ **EMP:** 385 **EST:** 1966
SQ FT: 41,000
SALES (est): 402.51MM
SALES (corp-wide): 5.69B **Privately Held**
Web: www.qco.net
SIC: 3061 Mechanical rubber goods
PA: 3i Group Plc
   16 Palace Street
   London SW1E

(G-14721)
QUEST SERVICE LABS INC
2307 E Aurora Rd Unit B10 (44087-1958)
PHONE.................................330 405-0316
EMP: 10 **EST:** 2009
SALES (est): 908.31K **Privately Held**
Web: www.questservicelabs.com
SIC: 2759 Commercial printing, nec

(G-14722)
R A HAMED INTERNATIONAL INC
Also Called: Scott Thomas Furniture
8400 Darrow Rd (44087-2375)
PHONE.................................330 247-0190
Rosemary Hamed, *Pr*
Scott Hamed, *VP*
◆ **EMP:** 16 **EST:** 1977
SQ FT: 19,000
SALES (est): 649.8K **Privately Held**
SIC: 2511 Wood household furniture

(G-14723)
RAVAGO CHEMICAL DIST INC
Also Called: H B Chemical
1665 Enterprise Pkwy (44087-2243)
PHONE.................................330 920-8023
James Duffy, *Pr*
EMP: 38
Web: www.hbchemical.com
SIC: 2899 Chemical preparations, nec
HQ: Ravago Chemical Distribution, Inc.
   1900 Smmit Twr Blvd Ste 9
   Orlando FL 32810
   630 665-3085

(G-14724)
REUTER-STOKES LLC
8499 Darrow Rd Ste 1 (44087-2398)
PHONE.................................330 425-3755
Leo Zanderschur, *Pr*
◆ **EMP:** 260 **EST:** 1956
SQ FT: 110,000
SALES (est): 75.52MM
SALES (corp-wide): 67.95B **Publicly Held**
SIC: 3829 3826 3823 3812 Nuclear radiation and testing apparatus; Environmental testing equipment; Process control instruments; Search and navigation equipment
PA: General Electric Company
   1 Aviation Way
   Cincinnati OH 45215
   617 443-3000

(G-14725)
RHEACO BUILDERS INC
1941 E Aurora Rd (44087-1919)
PHONE.................................330 425-3090
George Rheaco, *Pr*
EMP: 6 **EST:** 1989
SALES (est): 502.61K **Privately Held**
Web: www.rheacoinc.com
SIC: 2434 Wood kitchen cabinets

(G-14726)
RO-MAI INDUSTRIES INC
1605 Enterprise Pkwy (44087-2201)
P.O. Box 366 (44087-0366)
PHONE.................................330 425-9090
Robert Maier, *Pr*
Robert Maier, *Pr*
▲ **EMP:** 30 **EST:** 1984
SQ FT: 26,000
SALES (est): 1.99MM **Privately Held**
Web: www.rmihardware.com

Twinsburg - Summit County (G-14727)

SIC: 3089 Injection molding of plastics

(G-14727)
ROCKWELL AUTOMATION INC
8440 Darrow Rd (44087-2310)
P.O. Box 2167 (53201-2167)
PHONE...............................330 425-3211
Mark Todd, *Brnch Mgr*
EMP: 400
Web: www.rockwellautomation.com
SIC: 3625 Control equipment, electric
PA: Rockwell Automation, Inc.
 1201 S 2nd St
 Milwaukee WI 53204

(G-14728)
ROYAL CHEMICAL COMPANY LTD
1755 Enterprise Pkwy Ste 100 (44087)
PHONE...............................330 467-1300
Eric Cubec, *CFO*
EMP: 15
SALES (corp-wide): 236MM **Privately Held**
Web: www.royalchemical.com
SIC: 2841 Soap: granulated, liquid, cake, flaked, or chip
HQ: Royal Chemical Company, Ltd.
 8679 Freeway Dr
 Macedonia OH 44056
 330 467-1300

(G-14729)
RTD ELECTRONICS INC
1632 Enterprise Pkwy Ste D (44087)
P.O. Box 560192 (44056-0192)
PHONE...............................330 487-0716
Terry L Kellhofer, *Pr*
EMP: 16 **EST:** 2008
SQ FT: 4,000
SALES (est): 972.66K **Privately Held**
Web: www.rtdelectronicsinc.com
SIC: 3679 Harness assemblies, for electronic use: wire or cable

(G-14730)
S A OMA-U INC
9329 Ravenna Rd Ste A (44087-2457)
PHONE...............................330 487-0602
Mauro Nava, *Pr*
Maria Pia Nava, *VP*
Clara Maria Nava, *Treas*
Antonio Villa, *Genl Mgr*
▲ **EMP:** 6 **EST:** 1996
SQ FT: 2,860
SALES (est): 800.45K **Privately Held**
Web: www.omabraid.it
SIC: 3549 3552 Wiredrawing and fabricating machinery and equipment, ex. die; Braiding machines, textile

(G-14731)
S&B METAL PDTS TWINSBURG LLC (PA)
2060 Case Pkwy (44087-2344)
PHONE...............................330 487-5790
Paul Balliette, *Ch*
Cindy Balliette, *
Stephen Campbell, *
▼ **EMP:** 49 **EST:** 1974
SQ FT: 25,000
SALES (est): 9.23MM
SALES (corp-wide): 9.23MM **Privately Held**
Web: www.sbmetal.com
SIC: 3444 Sheet metal specialties, not stamped

(G-14732)
S-TEK INC (PA)
2095 Midway Dr (44087-1933)
P.O. Box 27 (45371-0027)
PHONE...............................440 439-8232
David Lepore, *Pr*
Bob Smith, *Sec*
Fred B Holzworth, *Ex VP*
▲ **EMP:** 7 **EST:** 1988
SALES (est): 1.1MM **Privately Held**
Web: www.stek-inc.com
SIC: 3679 3826 5065 Liquid crystal displays (LCD); Magnetic resonance imaging apparatus; Radio and television equipment and parts

(G-14733)
SCHAFFER GRINDING CO INC
8470 Chamberlin Rd (44087-2085)
PHONE...............................323 724-4476
Chet Schaffer, *Brnch Mgr*
EMP: 15
SQ FT: 10,000
SALES (corp-wide): 5.14MM **Privately Held**
Web: www.schaffergrinding.com
SIC: 3599 Machine shop, jobbing and repair
PA: Schaffer Grinding Co., Inc.
 848 S Maple Ave
 Montebello CA
 323 724-4476

(G-14734)
SEMTORQ INC
Also Called: Nucam
1780 Enterprise Pkwy (44087-2255)
P.O. Box 895 (44087-0895)
PHONE...............................330 487-0600
Greg Lanham, *Dir Opers*
Joseph Seme Junior, *Pr*
Christina Seme, *Sec*
▲ **EMP:** 12 **EST:** 1956
SQ FT: 40,000
SALES (est): 2.55MM **Privately Held**
Web: www.semtorq.com
SIC: 3549 7692 3594 3548 Assembly machines, including robotic; Welding repair; Fluid power pumps and motors; Welding apparatus

(G-14735)
SHELLY MATERIALS INC
1749 Highland Rd (44087-2220)
PHONE...............................330 963-5180
EMP: 17
SALES (corp-wide): 32.72B **Privately Held**
Web: www.shellyco.com
SIC: 3273 Ready-mixed concrete
HQ: Shelly Materials, Inc.
 80 Park Dr
 Thornville OH 43076
 740 246-6315

(G-14736)
SSP FITTINGS CORP (PA)
Also Called: SSP
8250 Boyle Pkwy (44087-2200)
PHONE...............................330 425-4250
Jeffrey E King, *CEO*
Betsy S King, *
David B King, *
O F Douglas, *
F B Douglas, *
▲ **EMP:** 100 **EST:** 1926
SQ FT: 165,000
SALES (est): 30.98MM
SALES (corp-wide): 30.98MM **Privately Held**
Web: www.myssp.com
SIC: 3494 5085 3498 3492 Pipe fittings; Industrial supplies; Fabricated pipe and fittings; Fluid power valves and hose fittings

(G-14737)
STELLAR PROCESS INC
Also Called: Phoenix
3238 Darien Ln (44087-3252)
PHONE...............................866 777-4725
Mona Elzarka, *Prin*
EMP: 12 **EST:** 2016
SALES (est): 1.6MM **Privately Held**
SIC: 3589 Commercial cooking and foodwarming equipment

(G-14738)
STEWART ACQUISITION LLC (PA)
Also Called: Cima Plastics Group
2146 Enterprise Pkwy (44087-2272)
PHONE...............................330 963-0322
▲ **EMP:** 50 **EST:** 1975
SQ FT: 44,000
SALES (est): 8.74MM
SALES (corp-wide): 8.74MM **Privately Held**
Web: www.cimaplastics.com
SIC: 3089 Injection molding of plastics

(G-14739)
SUMMIT AVIONICS INC
2225 E Enterprise Pkwy # 1a (44087)
PHONE...............................330 425-1440
Michael Tartarnella, *Pr*
EMP: 14 **EST:** 2001
SQ FT: 14,000
SALES (est): 519.14K **Privately Held**
Web: www.summitavionics.com
SIC: 3728 Aircraft parts and equipment, nec

(G-14740)
TAC MATERIALS INC
Also Called: Quality Synthetic Rubber Co
1700 Highland Rd (44087)
P.O. Box 1030 (44087)
PHONE...............................330 425-8472
▲ **EMP:** 250 **EST:** 1966
SALES (est): 27.68MM **Privately Held**
SIC: 3061 Mechanical rubber goods
HQ: Datwyler Schweiz Ag
 Militarstrasse 7
 Schattdorf UR 6467

(G-14741)
TCH INDUSTRIES INCORPORATED
2307 E Aurora Rd (44087-1952)
PHONE...............................330 487-5155
Ted Hoaglin, *Pr*
Bill Harr, *VP*
Kathy Hoaglin, *CFO*
Bryan Hoaglin, *VP*
▲ **EMP:** 18 **EST:** 1983
SQ FT: 20,000
SALES (est): 8.56MM **Privately Held**
Web: www.tchindustries.com
SIC: 5085 3494 Industrial tools; Pipe fittings

(G-14742)
TECHNOFORM GL INSUL N AMER INC
1755 Enterprise Pkwy Ste 300 (44087)
PHONE...............................330 487-6600
Albert Stankus, *Pr*
▲ **EMP:** 30 **EST:** 2003
SQ FT: 50,000
SALES (est): 8.25MM
SALES (corp-wide): 444.04MM **Privately Held**
Web: www.technoform.com
SIC: 3429 Hardware, nec
HQ: Technoform Bautec Holding Gmbh
 Max-Planck-Str. 6
 Lohfelden HE 34253
 561 958-3300

(G-14743)
THE HC COMPANIES INC (DH)
Also Called: Pro Cal
2450 Edison Blvd Ste 3 (44087-4335)
P.O. Box 738 (44062-0738)
PHONE...............................440 632-3333
Chris Koscho, *Pr*
John Landefeld, *
▲ **EMP:** 40 **EST:** 2015
SQ FT: 11,000
SALES (est): 180.53MM
SALES (corp-wide): 447.38MM **Privately Held**
Web: www.hc-companies.com
SIC: 3089 5261 Planters, plastics; Lawn and garden supplies
HQ: Wingate Partners V, L.P.
 750 N Saint Paul St # 1000
 Dallas TX 75201

(G-14744)
TLG COCHRAN INC (PA)
2026 Summit Commerce Park (44087-2374)
PHONE...............................440 914-1122
Steven Wake, *Pr*
Joel Hammer, *
Marinko Milos, *
▲ **EMP:** 21 **EST:** 1956
SALES (est): 20.11MM
SALES (corp-wide): 20.11MM **Privately Held**
Web: www.gltproducts.com
SIC: 2821 5033 5131 5085 Polyvinylidene chloride resins; Insulation materials; Tape, textile; Industrial supplies

(G-14745)
TLG LAPORTE INC (PA)
2026 Summit Commerce Park (44087-2374)
PHONE...............................440 914-1122
Timothy Scott, *CEO*
EMP: 8 **EST:** 2014
SALES (est): 2.21MM
SALES (corp-wide): 2.21MM **Privately Held**
Web: www.gltfabricators.com
SIC: 3644 Insulators and insulation materials, electrical

(G-14746)
TRANSTECHBIO INC
2071 Midway Dr (44087-1933)
PHONE...............................734 994-4728
Jian Zong, *Pr*
Jian Zong, *Owner*
EMP: 8 **EST:** 1990
SALES (est): 654.95K **Privately Held**
SIC: 2836 Blood derivatives

(G-14747)
TRI COUNTY CONCRETE INC (PA)
9423 Darrow Rd (44087-1415)
P.O. Box 665 (44087-0665)
PHONE...............................330 425-4464
Tony Farenacci, *Pr*
Fred Farenacci, *VP*
EMP: 19 **EST:** 1964
SQ FT: 62,000
SALES (est): 3.06MM
SALES (corp-wide): 3.06MM **Privately Held**
Web: www.tricountyconcrete.com
SIC: 3273 3272 1442 Ready-mixed concrete; Concrete products, nec; Construction sand and gravel

GEOGRAPHIC SECTION

Uhrichsville - Tuscarawas County (G-14770)

(G-14748)
TRIONIX RESEARCH LAB INC
8037 Bavaria Rd (44087-2261)
PHONE..............................330 425-9055
Doctor Chun Bin Lim, *Pr*
EMP: 6 **EST:** 1986
SQ FT: 150,000
SALES (est): 757.16K **Privately Held**
SIC: 3844 Nuclear irradiation equipment

(G-14749)
TWIN VENTURES INC
2457 Edison Blvd (44087-2340)
PHONE..............................330 405-3838
EMP: 15 **EST:** 1996
SALES (est): 951.46K **Privately Held**
SIC: 3452 5072 Bolts, nuts, rivets, and washers; Hardware

(G-14750)
UNIVERSAL ELECTRONICS INC
1864 Enterprise Pkwy Ste B (44087)
PHONE..............................330 487-1110
Brian Dean, *Mgr*
EMP: 6
Web: www.uei.com
SIC: 3651 Video triggers (remote control TV devices)
PA: Universal Electronics Inc.
15147 N Scottsdale Rd
Scottsdale AZ 85254

(G-14751)
UNIVERSAL RACK & EQP CO INC
Also Called: Universal Coatings Division
8511 Tower Dr (44087-2088)
PHONE..............................330 963-6776
Ken Palik, *Pr*
John Palik, *
▲ **EMP:** 76 **EST:** 1961
SQ FT: 40,000
SALES (est): 824.86K **Privately Held**
SIC: 3479 3559 3443 Coating of metals with plastic or resins; Electroplating machinery and equipment; Fabricated plate work (boiler shop)

(G-14752)
US FITTINGS INC
2182 E Aurora Rd (44087-1924)
P.O. Box 746 (44087-0746)
PHONE..............................234 212-9420
Richard K Raymond, *Pr*
EMP: 15 **EST:** 2013
SQ FT: 1,500
SALES (est): 1.86MM **Privately Held**
SIC: 3494 Pipe fittings

(G-14753)
VISUAL MARKING SYSTEMS INC (PA)
2097 E Aurora Rd (44087-1979)
PHONE..............................330 425-7100
EMP: 97 **EST:** 1963
SALES (est): 18.52MM
SALES (corp-wide): 18.52MM **Privately Held**
Web: www.vmsinc.com
SIC: 2752 3993 3953 2759 Decals, lithographed; Signs and advertising specialties; Marking devices; Commercial printing, nec

(G-14754)
WEATHERCHEM CORPORATION
2222 Highland Rd (44087-2295)
P.O. Box 1150 (44087-9150)
PHONE..............................330 425-4206
◆ **EMP:** 90 **EST:** 1944
SALES (est): 24.25MM
SALES (corp-wide): 24.25MM **Privately Held**
Web: www.weatherchem.com
SIC: 3089 Injection molding of plastics
PA: Weatherhead Industries, Inc.
25825 Science Park Dr # 255
Cleveland OH
330 425-4206

(G-14755)
WEDGE PRODUCTS INC
2181 Enterprise Pkwy (44087-2211)
PHONE..............................330 405-4477
Anthony J Defino, *Pr*
Frank Defino, *
Leonard Defino, *
Mary Defino, *
▲ **EMP:** 300 **EST:** 1925
SQ FT: 55,000
SALES (est): 25.81MM **Privately Held**
Web: www.wedgeproducts.com
SIC: 3469 3643 Stamping metal for the trade ; Current-carrying wiring services
PA: A.J.D. Holding Co.
2181 Enterprise Pkwy
Twinsburg OH 44087

(G-14756)
WITTUR USA INC
Also Called: Tyler Elevator Products
7852 Bavaria Rd (44087-2260)
PHONE..............................216 524-0100
Roberto Zappa, *Pr*
Stefano Girardi, *
Giorgio Scarabello, *
◆ **EMP:** 35 **EST:** 1959
SQ FT: 35,000
SALES (est): 12.05MM **Privately Held**
Web: www.wittur.com
SIC: 3534 Elevators and equipment
HQ: Sematic Spa
Via Pastrengo 9
Seriate BG 24068

(G-14757)
WORLDCLASS PROCESSING CORP
1400 Enterprise Pkwy (44087-2242)
EMP: 39 **EST:** 2000
SQ FT: 250,000
SALES (est): 12.73MM
SALES (corp-wide): 1.54B **Privately Held**
SIC: 3479 Etching and engraving
PA: Samuel, Son & Co., Limited
1900 Ironoak Way
Oakville ON L6H 0
905 279-5460

(G-14758)
WORTHNGTON SMUEL COIL PROC LLC (HQ)
Also Called: Samuel Steel Pickling Company
1400 Enterprise Pkwy (44087-2242)
PHONE..............................330 963-3777
Rick Snyder, *Prin*
EMP: 45 **EST:** 1989
SQ FT: 115,000
SALES (est): 20.65MM
SALES (corp-wide): 4.92B **Publicly Held**
Web: www.samuelsteelpickling.com
SIC: 7389 5051 3471 3398 Metal slitting and shearing; Metals service centers and offices ; Plating and polishing; Metal heat treating
PA: Worthington Enterprises, Inc.
200 W Old Wlson Bridge Rd
Worthington OH 43085
614 438-3210

(G-14759)
WRWP LLC
Also Called: Western Reserve Wire Products
1920 Case Pkwy S (44087-2358)
PHONE..............................330 425-3421
EMP: 18 **EST:** 2014
SALES (est): 9.57MM **Privately Held**
Web: www.wrwp.com
SIC: 3496 Miscellaneous fabricated wire products

(G-14760)
ZINKAN ENTERPRISES INC (PA)
1919 Case Pkwy (44087-2343)
PHONE..............................330 487-1500
Thomas W Mccrystal, *Prin*
Mister Lou Koenig, *Prin*
◆ **EMP:** 10 **EST:** 1982
SQ FT: 15,000
SALES (est): 5.83MM
SALES (corp-wide): 5.83MM **Privately Held**
Web: www.getchemready.com
SIC: 2899 Chemical preparations, nec

Uhrichsville
Tuscarawas County

(G-14761)
ARMSTRONG CUSTOM MOULDING INC
6408 State Route 800 Se (44683-6302)
PHONE..............................740 922-5931
Todd Armstrong, *Pr*
James B Armstrong Junior, *Treas*
James B Armstrong Senior, *Sec*
EMP: 6 **EST:** 1996
SALES (est): 467.54K **Privately Held**
SIC: 2431 2426 Moldings and baseboards, ornamental and trim; Hardwood dimension and flooring mills

(G-14762)
BROOKVILLE GLOVE MANUFACTURING
1020 W 1st St (44683-2210)
PHONE..............................812 673-4893
EMP: 7 **EST:** 2019
SALES (est): 102.82K **Privately Held**
Web: www.brookvilleglove.com
SIC: 3999 Manufacturing industries, nec

(G-14763)
CAROLINA STAIR SUPPLY INC (PA)
316 Herrick St (44683-2123)
PHONE..............................740 922-3333
Clair Edwards, *Pr*
▲ **EMP:** 20 **EST:** 1979
SQ FT: 2,000
SALES (est): 4.5MM **Privately Held**
Web: www.carolinastair.com
SIC: 2431 Staircases and stairs, wood

(G-14764)
DJ S WELD
424 N Main St (44683-1837)
PHONE..............................330 432-2206
Dwight Jones, *Owner*
EMP: 6 **EST:** 2014
SALES (est): 358.56K **Privately Held**
SIC: 3443 Weldments

(G-14765)
FABOHIO INC
521 E 7th St (44683-1613)
P.O. Box 434 (44683-0434)
PHONE..............................740 922-4233
Kurt Shelley, *CEO*
EMP: 20 **EST:** 1963
SQ FT: 22,500
SALES (est): 4.49MM
SALES (corp-wide): 23.2MM **Privately Held**
Web: www.fabohio.com
SIC: 3089 Injection molding of plastics
PA: Bowerston Shale Company (Inc)
515 Main St
Bowerston OH 44695
740 269-2921

(G-14766)
GRADALL INDUSTRIES INC
6307 Barkley Rd Se (44683-7502)
PHONE..............................540 819-6638
Mark Allison, *Ofcr*
EMP: 6 **EST:** 2019
SALES (est): 186.53K **Privately Held**
Web: www.gradall.com
SIC: 3531 Construction machinery

(G-14767)
NOVELIS ALR RECYCLING OHIO LLC
Also Called: Imco Recycling
7335 Newport Rd Se (44683-6368)
PHONE..............................740 922-2373
Sean M Stack, *CEO*
Robert R Holian, *
▲ **EMP:** 164 **EST:** 1992
SALES (est): 47.61MM **Privately Held**
Web: www.novelis.com
SIC: 3341 4953 Aluminum smelting and refining (secondary); Recycling, waste materials
PA: Hindalco Industries Limited
Plot-612/613, Tower 4,
Mumbai MH 40001

(G-14768)
SEALCO INC
Also Called: Sealco
6566 Superior Rd Se (44683-7487)
P.O. Box 307 (44683-0307)
PHONE..............................740 922-4122
Elmer Mcclave, *Pr*
Todd Mcclave, *VP*
▲ **EMP:** 6 **EST:** 1974
SALES (est): 480.2K **Privately Held**
Web: www.sealco.net
SIC: 2499 2448 Plugs, wood; Pallets, wood

(G-14769)
SEYEKCUB INC
615 W 4th St (44683-2007)
PHONE..............................330 324-1394
Robert L Drummond Junior, *Pr*
EMP: 8 **EST:** 2006
SQ FT: 10,000
SALES (est): 990.23K **Privately Held**
Web: www.seyekcubaluminum.com
SIC: 3363 Aluminum die-castings

(G-14770)
STEBBINS ENGINEERING & MFG CO
Also Called: Semco Ceramics
4778 Belden Dr Se (44683-1078)
P.O. Box 90 (44683-0090)
PHONE..............................740 922-3012
Cliff Mcpherson, *Genl Mgr*
EMP: 13
SALES (corp-wide): 47.03MM **Privately Held**
Web: www.stebbinseng.com
SIC: 3253 3255 3251 Ceramic wall and floor tile; Clay refractories; Brick and structural clay tile
PA: The Stebbins Engineering And Manufacturing Company
363 Eastern Blvd
Watertown NY 13601
315 782-3000

Uhrichsville - Tuscarawas County (G-14771)

(G-14771)
TRADING POST
202 N Water St (44683-1845)
PHONE.................................740 922-1199
Richard Sommers, Owner
EMP: 6 EST: 2010
SALES (est): 207.61K Privately Held
SIC: 2711 Newspapers, publishing and printing

(G-14772)
UHRICHSVILLE CARBIDE INC
410 N Water St (44683-1849)
PHONE.................................740 922-9197
Bob Septer, Pr
Karen Septer, Sec
EMP: 17 EST: 1983
SALES (est): 2.4MM Privately Held
Web: www.uhrichsvillecarbide.com
SIC: 3545 5072 7699 3546 Cutting tools for machine tools; Saw blades; Knife, saw and tool sharpening and repair; Power-driven handtools

Union
Montgomery County

(G-14773)
NEW DAWN LABS LLC
102 S Main St (45322-3343)
PHONE.................................203 675-5644
EMP: 10 EST: 2019
SQ FT: 6,000
SALES (est): 906.84K Privately Held
Web: www.newdawnlabs.io
SIC: 3577 8711 Input/output equipment, computer; Electrical or electronic engineering

(G-14774)
PROCTER & GAMBLE DISTRG LLC
Also Called: Procter & Gamble
1800 Union Airpark Blvd (45377)
P.O. Box 2628 (27216-2628)
PHONE.................................937 387-5189
Robert Fix, Genl Mgr
EMP: 127
SALES (corp-wide): 82.01B Publicly Held
SIC: 2841 Soap and other detergents
HQ: Procter & Gamble Distributing Llc
    1 Procter And Gamble Plz
    Cincinnati OH 45202
    513 983-1100

(G-14775)
TE-CO INC
100 Quinter Farm Rd (45322-9705)
PHONE.................................937 836-0961
EMP: 17 EST: 2018
SALES (est): 3.6MM Privately Held
Web: www.te-co.com
SIC: 3545 Machine tool attachments and accessories

Union City
Darke County

(G-14776)
CAL-MAINE FOODS INC
1039 Zumbrum Rd (45390-8646)
PHONE.................................937 968-4874
EMP: 9
SALES (corp-wide): 3.15B Publicly Held
Web: www.calmainefoods.com
SIC: 0252 2015 Chicken eggs; Eggs, processed; frozen
PA: Cal-Maine Foods, Inc.
    1052 Hghland Clny Pkwy St
    Ridgeland MS 39157
    601 948-6813

(G-14777)
CAST METALS TECHNOLOGY INC
305 Se Deerfield Rd (45390-9072)
PHONE.................................937 968-5460
Ryan Olney, Mgr
EMP: 47
Web: www.cm-tec.com
SIC: 3365 Aluminum and aluminum-based alloy castings
PA: Cast Metals Technology, Inc.
    550 Liberty Rd
    Delaware OH 43015

(G-14778)
HA-STE MANUFACTURING CO INC
Also Called: Kangaroo Brand Mops
119 E Elm St (45390-1711)
P.O. Box 168 (47390-0168)
PHONE.................................937 968-4858
John W Stewart, Ch
Robin Stewart, *
EMP: 9 EST: 1959
SQ FT: 5,500
SALES (est): 488.56K Privately Held
Web: www.hastemops.com
SIC: 2392 Mops, floor and dust

(G-14779)
HOG SLAT INCORPORATED
200 N Grandview St (45390-9069)
PHONE.................................937 968-3890
EMP: 21
SALES (corp-wide): 538.94MM Privately Held
Web: www.hogslat.com
SIC: 3523 Farm machinery and equipment
PA: Hog Slat, Incorporated
    206 Fayetteville St
    Newton Grove NC 28366
    800 949-4647

Uniontown
Stark County

(G-14780)
AMERITECH PUBLISHING INC
Also Called: SBC
1530 Corporate Woods Pkwy Ste 100 (44685-6707)
PHONE.................................330 896-6037
Kim Gergel, Mgr
EMP: 1328
SALES (corp-wide): 122.43B Publicly Held
SIC: 2741 Miscellaneous publishing
HQ: Ameritech Publishing, Inc.
    23500 Northwestern Hwy
    Southfield MI

(G-14781)
BBM FAIRWAY INC
Also Called: Modern Time Dealer
3515 Massillon Rd Ste 200 (44685-6113)
PHONE.................................330 899-2200
Greg Smith, Brnch Mgr
EMP: 9
SALES (corp-wide): 10.07MM Privately Held
Web: www.bobit.com
SIC: 2721 Magazines: publishing only, not printed on site
PA: Bbm Fairway, Inc.
    3520 Challenger St
    Torrance CA 90503

(G-14782)
ENVIRONMENTAL CHEMICAL CORP
2167 Prestwick Dr (44685-8840)
P.O. Box 20110 (44701-0110)
PHONE.................................330 453-5200
Richard Morena, Pr
Thomas Wucinich, VP
EMP: 12 EST: 1973
SQ FT: 4,830
SALES (est): 1.9MM Privately Held
Web: www.environmentalchemical.com
SIC: 5169 2842 2899 Chemicals, industrial and heavy; Polishes and sanitation goods; Chemical preparations, nec

(G-14783)
GAYDASH ENTERPRISES INC
Also Called: Gaydash Industries
3640 Tabs Dr (44685-9560)
PHONE.................................330 896-4811
Gerald Gaydash, Pr
Joan Gaydash, Sec
Joel Gaydash, VP
EMP: 13 EST: 1973
SQ FT: 15,000
SALES (est): 254.91K Privately Held
SIC: 3599 Machine shop, jobbing and repair

(G-14784)
GOODRICH AEROSPACE
1555 Corporate Woods Pkwy (44685-7820)
PHONE.................................704 423-7000
Jack Rubino, Mgr
EMP: 9 EST: 2017
SALES (est): 190.67K Privately Held
Web: www.goodrichdeicing.com
SIC: 3728 Aircraft parts and equipment, nec

(G-14785)
HIGH-TECH MOLD & MACHINE INC
3771 Tabs Dr (44685-9563)
PHONE.................................330 896-4466
Anthony Klisan Junior, Pr
Connie Klisan, VP Fin
Stephanie Klisan, VP
EMP: 15 EST: 1984
SQ FT: 15,000
SALES (est): 1.99MM Privately Held
Web: www.hightechmold.com
SIC: 3544 3599 Industrial molds; Machine shop, jobbing and repair

(G-14786)
KOHLER COATING INC
10995 Wright Rd Nw (44685-9809)
PHONE.................................330 499-1407
EMP: 22 EST: 2001
SALES (est): 5MM Privately Held
Web: www.kohlercoating.com
SIC: 3554 Paper industries machinery

(G-14787)
MCAFEE TOOL & DIE INC
1717 Boettler Rd (44685-9588)
PHONE.................................330 896-9555
Gary Mc Afee, Pr
Michael J Francek Junior, VP
Tracee Gates, Stockholder*
Wendy Mcafee, Stockholder
EMP: 41 EST: 1977
SQ FT: 40,000
SALES (est): 4.96MM Privately Held
Web: www.mcafeetool.com
SIC: 3544 3469 Die sets for metal stamping (presses); Metal stampings, nec

(G-14788)
MESSER LLC
4179 Meadow Wood Ln (44685-7716)
PHONE.................................330 608-3008
EMP: 13
SALES (corp-wide): 1.63B Privately Held
Web: www.messeramericas.com
SIC: 2813 Industrial gases
HQ: Messer Llc
    200 Smrst Corp Blvd # 7000
    Bridgewater NJ 08807
    800 755-9277

(G-14789)
NORTH COATINGS INC
4782 Mars Rd (44685-9669)
PHONE.................................330 896-7126
Steve Montgomery, Prin
EMP: 7 EST: 2008
SALES (est): 245.14K Privately Held
Web: www.northcoatings.com
SIC: 2952 Roofing felts, cements, or coatings, nec

(G-14790)
PLASTIC CARD INC (PA)
Also Called: Rainbow Printing
3711 Boettler Oaks Dr (44685-7733)
PHONE.................................330 896-5555
Kenneth Thompson, Pr
Thomas Thompson, *
Rich Krauth, *
▲ EMP: 60 EST: 1978
SQ FT: 24,000
SALES (est): 2.83MM
SALES (corp-wide): 2.83MM Privately Held
Web: www.rainbow-printing.com
SIC: 2396 Printing and embossing on plastics fabric articles

(G-14791)
PLASTICARDS INC (PA)
Also Called: Rainbow Printing
3711 Boettler Oaks Dr (44685-7733)
PHONE.................................330 896-5555
Kenneth Thompson, Pr
Patty Lou Thompson, *
Rich Crowft, *
EMP: 46 EST: 1976
SQ FT: 20,000
SALES (est): 4.88MM
SALES (corp-wide): 4.88MM Privately Held
Web: www.rainbow-printing.com
SIC: 3089 Identification cards, plastics

(G-14792)
RESOURCE AMERICA INC
3500 Massillon Rd Ste 100 (44685-9575)
PHONE.................................330 896-8510
Nancy Mcgurk, Mgr
EMP: 9 EST: 2011
SALES (est): 445.03K Privately Held
SIC: 1382 Oil and gas exploration services

(G-14793)
SHORE PRECISION LLC
3043 Rockingham St Nw (44685-6897)
PHONE.................................330 704-0552
EMP: 7 EST: 2016
SALES (est): 49.25K Privately Held
SIC: 3599 Machine shop, jobbing and repair

(G-14794)
STEERAMERICA INC
Also Called: Steer America
1525 Corporate Woods Pkwy Ste 500 (44685-7883)
PHONE.................................330 563-4407
R Padmanabhan, Ch
Satish Padmanabhan, Pr
Babu Padmanabhan, Dir
Uttam Kumar Bhageria, CFO
Dipak Chattara, Ch

▲ EMP: 13 EST: 2008
SQ FT: 10,000
SALES (est): 4.5MM **Privately Held**
Web: www.steerworld.com
SIC: 3452 Bolts, nuts, rivets, and washers
PA: Steer Engineering Private Limited
No.290, 4th Main, 4th Phase
Bengaluru KA 56005

(G-14795)
TKM PRINT SOLUTIONS INC
3455 Forest Lake Dr (44685-8131)
PHONE..................330 237-4029
Dalton Wayne, *Pr*
EMP: 18 EST: 2008
SALES (est): 3.31MM **Privately Held**
Web: www.discovertkm.com
SIC: 2752 Offset printing

(G-14796)
UNIONTOWN SEPTIC TANKS INC
2781 Raber Rd (44685-8125)
PHONE..................330 699-3386
James N Kungle, *Pr*
Jeff Kungle, *VP*
EMP: 10 EST: 1965
SALES (est): 963.14K **Privately Held**
Web: www.uniontownseptictank.com
SIC: 3272 Concrete products, precast, nec

(G-14797)
XTREME OUTDOORS LLC
1519 Boettler Rd Ste A (44685-8391)
PHONE..................330 731-4137
EMP: 40 EST: 2019
SQ FT: 2,400
SALES (est): 3.78MM **Privately Held**
Web: www.goxtoutdoors.com
SIC: 3792 Travel trailers and campers

University Heights
Cuyahoga County

(G-14798)
NOI ENHANCEMENTS LLC
2554 Claver Rd (44118-4645)
PHONE..................216 218-4136
Joel Fleisher, *Prin*
EMP: 6 EST: 2016
SALES (est): 284.1K **Privately Held**
Web: www.noienhancements.com
SIC: 2844 Toilet preparations

Upper Arlington
Franklin County

(G-14799)
BIO ELCTRCTCAL SCENCE TECH INC
2025 Riverside Dr (43221-4012)
PHONE..................888 614-1227
Carmella Angus, *CEO*
EMP: 8 EST: 2018
SALES (est): 412.53K **Privately Held**
SIC: 3829 Medical diagnostic systems, nuclear

(G-14800)
DAILY GROWLER INC
2812 Fishinger Rd (43221-1129)
P.O. Box 218455 (43221-8455)
PHONE..................614 656-2337
EMP: 7 EST: 2012
SALES (est): 113.66K **Privately Held**
Web: www.thedailygrowler.com
SIC: 2711 Newspapers, publishing and printing

(G-14801)
INDUSTRIAL MFG CO INTL LLC
3366 Riverside Dr Ste 103 (43221-1734)
PHONE..................440 838-4555
EMP: 22 EST: 2005
SALES (est): 1.08MM
SALES (corp-wide): 541.5MM **Privately Held**
Web: www.mfgco.com
SIC: 2542 Lockers (not refrigerated): except wood
PA: Summa Holdings, Inc.
8223 Brecksville Rd # 100
Cleveland OH 44141
440 838-4700

(G-14802)
REMINGTON PRODUCTS COMPANY (PA)
Also Called: Foundation Wellness
3366 Riverside Dr Ste 103 (43221)
P.O. Box 506 (44282)
PHONE..................330 335-1571
Rhonda Newman, *CEO*
Jeff Wert, *
C Kevin Mccomas, *CFO*
▲ EMP: 91 EST: 1930
SQ FT: 102,000
SALES (est): 27.95MM
SALES (corp-wide): 27.95MM **Privately Held**
Web: www.remprod.com
SIC: 3069 3131 Boot or shoe products, rubber; Footwear cut stock

Upper Sandusky
Wyandot County

(G-14803)
ARCHEM AMERICA INC (DH) ✪
245 Commerce Way (43351)
PHONE..................419 294-6304
Paul Kozai, *CEO*
EMP: 19 EST: 2022
SALES (est): 135.2MM **Privately Held**
SIC: 3069 Foam rubber
HQ: Archem Inc.
1-2-70, Konan
Minato-Ku TKY 108-0

(G-14804)
BECA HOUSE COFFEE LLC
965 E Wyandot Ave (43351-9638)
PHONE..................419 731-4961
Heather Jackson, *Owner*
Heather Jackson, *Pr*
Steve Jackson, *Prin*
EMP: 6 EST: 2011
SALES (est): 245.04K **Privately Held**
Web: www.becahouse.com
SIC: 5812 2095 Coffee shop; Coffee roasting (except by wholesale grocers)

(G-14805)
CUSTOM GLASS SOLUTIONS UPPER S
12688 State Highway 67 (43351-9411)
PHONE..................419 294-4921
EMP: 500 EST: 2013
SALES (est): 128.93MM
SALES (corp-wide): 164.32MM **Privately Held**
Web: www.customglasssolutions.com
SIC: 3231 Laminated glass: made from purchased glass
PA: Custom Glass Solutions, Llc
600 Lkview Plz Blvd Ste A
Worthington OH 43085
248 340-1800

(G-14806)
DAILY CHIEF UNION
111 W Wyandot Ave (43351-1367)
P.O. Box 180 (43351-0180)
PHONE..................419 294-2331
Jack L Barnes, *Pr*
Charles G Barnes, *Sec*
Tom Martin, *Mgr*
EMP: 14 EST: 1879
SQ FT: 3,000
SALES (est): 1.1MM
SALES (corp-wide): 9.48MM **Privately Held**
Web: www.dailychiefunion.com
SIC: 2711 Commercial printing and newspaper publishing combined
HQ: Hardin County Publishing Co.
201 E Columbus St
Kenton OH 43326
419 674-4066

(G-14807)
DESIGN AND FABRICATION INC
400 Malabar Dr (43351-9747)
P.O. Box 218 (43351-0218)
PHONE..................419 294-2414
Mike Reamer, *Pr*
Cathy Reamer, *Sec*
EMP: 7 EST: 1994
SQ FT: 7,200
SALES (est): 747.6K **Privately Held**
Web: www.designandfab.com
SIC: 3599 Machine shop, jobbing and repair

(G-14808)
ENGINEERED WIRE PRODUCTS INC (DH)
1200 N Warpole St (43351)
P.O. Box 313 (43351)
PHONE..................419 294-3817
Grafton Redfren, *VP Sls*
Bradley W Evers, *
▲ EMP: 101 EST: 1994
SALES (est): 25.96MM **Privately Held**
Web: www.kci-corp.com
SIC: 3496 3315 Miscellaneous fabricated wire products; Steel wire and related products
HQ: Keystone Consolidated Industries, Inc.
5430 Lyndon B Johnson Fwy
Dallas TX 75240
800 441-0308

(G-14809)
FAIRBORN USA INC (PA)
205 Broadview St (43351-9628)
P.O. Box 151 (43351-0151)
PHONE..................419 294-4987
EMP: 65 EST: 1976
SALES (est): 11.88MM
SALES (corp-wide): 11.88MM **Privately Held**
Web: www.fairbornusa.com
SIC: 3448 Docks, prefabricated metal

(G-14810)
HANDY TWINE KNIFE CO
5676 County Highway 330 (43351-9772)
P.O. Box 146 (43351-0146)
PHONE..................419 294-3424
Lynn L Getz, *Pr*
John Tschantz, *VP*
Brian Caldwell, *Sec*
EMP: 9 EST: 1912
SQ FT: 1,000
SALES (est): 798.17K **Privately Held**
Web: www.handysafetyknife.com
SIC: 3423 5719 Knives, agricultural or industrial; Cutlery

(G-14811)
KALMBACH FEEDS INC (PA)
Also Called: Kalmbach
7148 State Highway 199 (43351-9359)
PHONE..................419 294-3838
Paul Kalmbach, *CEO*
Paul Kalmbach Junior, *Pr*
Jeff Neal, *Marketing**
Andy Bishop, *EXCELLENCE**
Eric Bernstein, *
▲ EMP: 200 EST: 1963
SALES (est): 241.82MM
SALES (corp-wide): 241.82MM **Privately Held**
Web: www.kalmbachfeeds.com
SIC: 2048 Livestock feeds

(G-14812)
KASAI NORTH AMERICA INC
1111 N Warpole St (43351-9094)
PHONE..................419 209-0399
Sam Kennedy, *VP*
EMP: 183
Web: www.kasai-na.com
SIC: 3465 3714 Moldings or trim, automobile: stamped metal; Motor vehicle parts and accessories
HQ: Kasai North America, Inc.
1225 Garrison Dr
Murfreesboro TN 37129
615 546-6040

(G-14813)
KIRBY AND SONS INC
Also Called: Kirby Sand & Gravel
4876 County Highway 43 (43351-9155)
PHONE..................419 927-2260
Gene Kirby, *Pr*
Franklin Kirby, *VP*
Judi Kirby, *Sec*
EMP: 19 EST: 1973
SALES (est): 2.34MM **Privately Held**
Web: www.kirbysand.com
SIC: 1442 4212 Common sand mining; Dump truck haulage

(G-14814)
LIQUI-BOX CORPORATION
519 Raybestos Dr (43351-9666)
PHONE..................419 294-3884
Roger Schultz, *Brnch Mgr*
EMP: 42
SQ FT: 42,000
SALES (corp-wide): 5.49B **Publicly Held**
Web: www.liquibox.com
SIC: 3089 3544 Molding primary plastics; Forms (molds), for foundry and plastics working machinery
HQ: Liqui-Box Corporation
2415 Cascade Pointe Blvd
Charlotte NC 28208
804 325-1400

(G-14815)
MAR-METAL MFG INC
Also Called: Fanci Forms
420 N Warpole St (43351-9301)
P.O. Box 37 (43351-0037)
PHONE..................419 447-1102
Floyd Marshall, *Pr*
Craig Marshall, *
EMP: 25 EST: 1969
SQ FT: 28,000
SALES (est): 624.82K **Privately Held**
SIC: 3544 Special dies and tools

(G-14816)
MENNEL MILLING COMPANY
Also Called: Farm Elevator
7097 County Highway 47 (43351-9190)
PHONE..................419 294-2337

Upper Sandusky - Wyandot County (G-14817)

EMP: 8
SALES (corp-wide): 211.12MM **Privately Held**
Web: www.mennel.com
SIC: 2041 Flour
PA: The Mennel Milling Company
319 S Vine St
Fostoria OH 44830
419 435-8151

(G-14817)
NEW EEZY-GRO INC
Also Called: Golden Eagle
9841 County Highway 49 (43351-9662)
PHONE.................................419 927-6110
EMP: 17
SALES (corp-wide): 14.75B **Publicly Held**
Web: www.eezygro.com
SIC: 2819 5261 Calcium compounds and salts, inorganic, nec; Fertilizer
HQ: New Eezy-Gro Inc.
1947 Briarfield Blvd
Maumee OH
419 893-5050

(G-14818)
NJF MANUFACTURING LLC
7387 Township Highway 104 (43351-9353)
PHONE.................................419 294-0400
Nathan Frey, *Managing Member*
EMP: 9 **EST:** 2017
SALES (est): 602.71K **Privately Held**
SIC: 3999 Manufacturing industries, nec

(G-14819)
OLEN CORPORATION
6326 County Highway 61 (43351-9749)
PHONE.................................419 294-2611
John Miller, *Brnch Mgr*
EMP: 10
SALES (corp-wide): 26.19MM **Privately Held**
Web: www.kokosing.biz
SIC: 3273 5032 Ready-mixed concrete; Stone, crushed or broken
PA: The Olen Corporation
4755 S High St
Columbus OH 43207
614 491-1515

(G-14820)
OVERHEAD DOOR CORPORATION
Also Called: Todco
781 Rt 30w (43351)
PHONE.................................419 294-3874
Mike Traxler, *Mgr*
EMP: 10
Web: www.overheaddoor.com
SIC: 3442 3448 2431 Garage doors, overhead: metal; Ramps, prefabricated metal; Doors, wood
HQ: Overhead Door Corporation
2501 S State Hwy 121 Ste
Lewisville TX 75067
469 549-7100

(G-14821)
PROSPIRA AMERICA CORPORATION
235 Commerce Way (43351-9079)
P.O. Box 450 (43351-0450)
PHONE.................................419 294-6989
Greg Ickes, *Brnch Mgr*
EMP: 100
Web: www.prospira.us
SIC: 3061 Automotive rubber goods (mechanical)
HQ: Prospira America Corporation
2030 Production Dr
Findlay OH 45839
419 423-9552

(G-14822)
REK ASSOCIATES LLC
11218 County Highway 44 (43351-9056)
PHONE.................................419 294-3838
EMP: 15 **EST:** 2017
SALES (est): 581.45K **Privately Held**
SIC: 2048 Prepared feeds, nec

(G-14823)
SCHMIDT MACHINE COMPANY
Also Called: S M C
7013 State Highway 199 (43351-9347)
PHONE.................................419 294-3814
TOLL FREE: 800
Bill Junior, *Pr*
Randy F Schmidt, *
Kevin Schmidt, *
Darlene Mooney, *
Dorothy M Schmidt, *
EMP: 50 **EST:** 1935
SQ FT: 2,500
SALES (est): 9.62MM **Privately Held**
Web: www.schmidtmachine.com
SIC: 3599 7692 5083 Machine shop, jobbing and repair; Welding repair; Farm equipment parts and supplies

(G-14824)
WANNEMACHER ENTERPRISES INC
Also Called: Wannemacher Packaging
422 W Guthrie Dr (43351-1154)
PHONE.................................419 771-1101
Jerry Jackson, *Dir*
Sally Buchholz, *Dir*
EMP: 10 **EST:** 2012
SALES (est): 418.08K **Privately Held**
SIC: 2099 Food preparations, nec

Urbana
Champaign County

(G-14825)
AMERICAN PAN COMPANY (PA)
Also Called: Durashield
417 E Water St (43078-2178)
P.O. Box 628 (43078-0628)
PHONE.................................937 652-3232
Gilbert Bundy, *Pr*
Jason Tingley, *
Michael Cornelis, *
Curt Marino, *
◆ **EMP:** 120 **EST:** 1985
SQ FT: 55,800
SALES (est): 42.9MM
SALES (corp-wide): 42.9MM **Privately Held**
Web: www.americanpan.com
SIC: 3556 Food products machinery

(G-14826)
CHRIS HAUGHEY
Also Called: Cupboard Distributing
1463 S Us Highway 68 (43078-8478)
PHONE.................................937 652-3338
Chris Haughey, *Owner*
EMP: 9 **EST:** 1987
SALES (est): 530.53K **Privately Held**
Web: www.cdwood.com
SIC: 2511 Unassembled or unfinished furniture, household: wood

(G-14827)
CMT MACHINING & FABG LLC
1411 Kennard Kingscreek Rd (43078-9505)
P.O. Box 28 (43078-0028)
PHONE.................................937 652-3740
EMP: 14 **EST:** 1958
SQ FT: 22,000
SALES (est): 1.05MM **Privately Held**
Web: www.cmt-usa.com
SIC: 1761 7692 3599 3544 Sheet metal work, nec; Welding repair; Machine shop, jobbing and repair; Jigs and fixtures

(G-14828)
COLEPAK LLC
1030 S Edgewood Ave (43078-9694)
P.O. Box 650 (43078-0650)
PHONE.................................937 652-3910
Ole Rosgaard, *Pr*
EMP: 58 **EST:** 1987
SQ FT: 113,000
SALES (est): 12.62MM
SALES (corp-wide): 5.22B **Publicly Held**
Web: www.colepak.com
SIC: 2653 2671 Partitions, solid fiber: made from purchased materials; Paper; coated and laminated packaging
PA: Greif, Inc.
425 Winter Rd
Delaware OH 43015
740 549-6000

(G-14829)
DESMOND-STEPHAN MFG COMPANY
121 W Water St (43078-2048)
P.O. Box 30 (43078-0030)
PHONE.................................937 653-7181
Robert B Mcconnell, *Pr*
EMP: 24 **EST:** 1898
SQ FT: 30,000
SALES (est): 2.45MM **Privately Held**
Web: www.desmond-stephan.com
SIC: 3541 Machine tools, metal cutting type

(G-14830)
GRIMES AEROSPACE COMPANY (HQ)
Also Called: Honeywell
550 State Route 55 (43078-9482)
P.O. Box 247 (43078-0247)
PHONE.................................937 484-2000
▲ **EMP:** 800 **EST:** 1986
SALES (est): 103.05MM
SALES (corp-wide): 36.66B **Publicly Held**
SIC: 3728 3647 3646 3645 Aircraft parts and equipment, nec; Vehicular lighting equipment; Commercial lighting fixtures; Residential lighting fixtures
PA: Honeywell International Inc.
855 S Mint St
Charlotte NC 28202
704 627-6200

(G-14831)
GRIMES AEROSPACE COMPANY
Also Called: Honeywell Lightning & Elec
515 N Russell St (43078-1330)
P.O. Box 247 (43078-0247)
PHONE.................................937 484-2000
Ron King, *Mgr*
EMP: 66
SALES (corp-wide): 36.66B **Publicly Held**
SIC: 3728 Aircraft parts and equipment, nec
HQ: Grimes Aerospace Company
550 State Route 55
Urbana OH 43078
937 484-2000

(G-14832)
GRIMES AEROSPACE COMPANY
Also Called: Honeywell
550 State Route 55 (43078-9482)
PHONE.................................937 484-2001
Bruce Blagg, *Brnch Mgr*
EMP: 66
SALES (corp-wide): 36.66B **Publicly Held**
SIC: 5088 7699 3812 3769 Aircraft and parts, nec; Aircraft and heavy equipment repair services; Search and navigation equipment; Space vehicle equipment, nec
HQ: Grimes Aerospace Company
550 State Route 55
Urbana OH 43078
937 484-2000

(G-14833)
HALL COMPANY
420 E Water St (43078)
P.O. Box 727 (43078)
PHONE.................................937 652-1376
Kyle J Hall, *Pr*
James A Hall, *
Carol A Hall, *
Richard J Walser, *
William D Hall Junior, *Asst Tr*
EMP: 47 **EST:** 1954
SQ FT: 38,500
SALES (est): 8.59MM **Privately Held**
Web: www.hallco.com
SIC: 3679 3993 3471 3444 Electronic switches; Signs and advertising specialties; Plating and polishing; Sheet metalwork

(G-14834)
HEARTH AND HOME AT URBANA
1579 E State Route 29 (43078-7501)
PHONE.................................937 653-5263
EMP: 6 **EST:** 2015
SALES (est): 189.99K **Privately Held**
Web: www.hearthandhomeurbana.com
SIC: 2711 Newspapers, publishing and printing

(G-14835)
HONEYWELL INTERNATIONAL INC
Honeywell
550 State Route 55 (43078-9482)
P.O. Box 247 (43078-0247)
PHONE.................................937 484-2000
Randy Marker, *Mgr*
EMP: 800
SALES (corp-wide): 36.66B **Publicly Held**
Web: www.honeywell.com
SIC: 3812 3669 3491 3699 Aircraft control systems, electronic; Fire alarm apparatus, electric; Gas valves and parts, industrial; Security control equipment and systems
PA: Honeywell International Inc.
855 S Mint St
Charlotte NC 28202
704 627-6200

(G-14836)
HUGHEY & PHILLIPS LLC
240 W Twain Ave (43078-1059)
PHONE.................................937 652-3500
Jeff Jacobs, *VP*
Steve Schneider, *
EMP: 50 **EST:** 2009
SALES (est): 9.01MM **Privately Held**
Web: www.hugheyandphillips.com
SIC: 3648 Lighting equipment, nec

(G-14837)
IMELDAS BAKING COMPANY LLC
964 N Main St (43078-1070)
PHONE.................................937 484-5405
Mark Mitchell, *Admn*
EMP: 6 **EST:** 2008
SALES (est): 88.86K **Privately Held**
SIC: 2051 Bakery: wholesale or wholesale/retail combined

(G-14838)
IPL DAYTON INC
1765 W County Line Rd (43078-8476)
P.O. Box 1468 (45501-1468)

GEOGRAPHIC SECTION

Utica - Licking County (G-14859)

◆ EMP: 190 EST: 1969
SALES (est): 43.89MM
SALES (corp-wide): 816.52K Privately Held
Web: www.techii.com
SIC: 3089 Injection molding of plastics
HQ: Plastiques Ipl Inc
1155 Boul Rene-Levesque O Bureau 4100
Montreal QC H3B 3
418 789-2880

(G-14839)
J RETTENMAIER USA LP
1228 Muzzy Rd (43078-9685)
PHONE.................937 652-2101
Dave Mcgill, *Brnch Mgr*
EMP: 91
SALES (corp-wide): 355.83K Privately Held
Web: www.jrsusa.com
SIC: 2823 2299 Cellulosic manmade fibers; Flock (recovered textile fibers)
HQ: J. Rettenmaier Usa Lp
16369 Us Highway 131 S
Schoolcraft MI 49087
269 679-2340

(G-14840)
JACK WALTERS & SONS CORP
Also Called: Walters Buildings
5045 N Us Highway 68 (43078-9315)
PHONE.................937 653-8986
Jerry Kauffman, *Mgr*
EMP: 31
SALES (corp-wide): 23.33MM Privately Held
Web: www.waltersbuildings.com
SIC: 3448 Buildings, portable: prefabricated metal
PA: Jack Walters & Sons, Corp.
6600 Midland Ct
Allenton WI 53002
262 629-5521

(G-14841)
JOE REES WELDING
326 W Twain Ave (43078-1061)
PHONE.................937 652-4067
Joe Rees, *Owner*
Joe Rees, *Prin*
EMP: 6 EST: 1991
SALES (est): 671.7K Privately Held
Web: www.joereeswelding.com
SIC: 3441 Fabricated structural metal

(G-14842)
KOENIG EQUIPMENT INC
Also Called: John Deere Authorized Dealer
3130 E Us Highway 36 (43078-9736)
PHONE.................937 653-5281
Dale Griest, *Mgr*
EMP: 11
SALES (corp-wide): 47.28MM Privately Held
Web: www.koenigequipment.com
SIC: 3524 5082 Lawn and garden equipment; Construction and mining machinery
PA: Koenig Equipment, Inc.
15213 State Route 274
Botkins OH 45306
937 693-5000

(G-14843)
MARSHALL PLASTICS INC
590 S Edgewood Ave (43078-2603)
P.O. Box 38126 (43078-8126)
PHONE.................937 653-4740
Henry Taylor, *Pr*
Richard T Ricketts, *Prin*
EMP: 9 EST: 2002

SALES (est): 991.38K Privately Held
SIC: 3089 Injection molding of plastics

(G-14844)
MUMFORDS POTATO CHIPS & DELI
Also Called: Mumford's Potato Chip
325 N Main St (43078-1605)
PHONE.................937 653-3491
Randy Leopard, *Pt*
Marilyn Leopard, *Pt*
EMP: 9 EST: 1932
SQ FT: 12,000
SALES (est): 613.37K Privately Held
Web: www.mumfordspotatochipsanddeli.com
SIC: 2096 5411 Potato chips and other potato-based snacks; Delicatessen stores

(G-14845)
ORBIS CORPORATION
200 Elm St (43078-1975)
PHONE.................937 652-1361
EMP: 280
SALES (corp-wide): 1.94B Privately Held
Web: www.orbiscorporation.com
SIC: 3089 Synthetic resin finished products, nec
HQ: Orbis Corporation
1055 Corporate Center Dr
Oconomowoc WI 53066
262 560-5000

(G-14846)
PARKER TRUTEC INCORPORATED
Also Called: Nihon Company
4795 Upper Valley Pike (43078-9295)
PHONE.................937 653-8500
Michael Kleiber, *Genl Mgr*
EMP: 90
Web: www.parkertrutec.com
SIC: 3479 3471 2899 2851 Painting of metal products; Plating and polishing; Chemical preparations, nec; Paints and allied products
HQ: Parker Trutec Incorporated
4700 Gateway Blvd
Springfield OH 45502
937 323-8833

(G-14847)
SARICA MANUFACTURING COMPANY
Also Called: Sarica
240 W Twain Ave (43078-1059)
PHONE.................937 484-4030
Steven M Schneider, *Managing Member*
Amy Wolf, *
Constance Schneider, *
EMP: 40 EST: 2005
SQ FT: 30,000
SALES (est): 9.91MM Privately Held
Web: www.saricamfg.com
SIC: 3629 Electronic generation equipment

(G-14848)
TRIAGE ORTHO GROUP
Also Called: Imperial Orthodontics
132 Lafayette Ave (43078-1420)
P.O. Box 549 (43078-0549)
PHONE.................937 653-6431
Vincent Gonzalez, *Owner*
Sandra Gonzalez, *Mgr*
EMP: 7 EST: 1982
SQ FT: 8,900
SALES (est): 732.58K Privately Held
Web: www.honeysucklecreations.com
SIC: 5047 2396 Dentists' professional supplies; Screen printing on fabric articles

(G-14849)
TRULIL INC
Also Called: J W P
625 S Edgewood Ave (43078-8600)
PHONE.................937 652-1242
Clayton W Rose Junior, *Prin*
Lilli A Johnson, *
▼ EMP: 210 EST: 1970
SQ FT: 133,000
SALES (est): 37.73MM Privately Held
Web: www.jwp-inc.com
SIC: 3714 Air brakes, motor vehicle

(G-14850)
ULTRA-MET COMPANY
Also Called: Ultra-Met
720 N Main St (43078-1102)
PHONE.................937 653-7133
Brent Sheerer, *Pr*
Bill Glaser, *
Jeff Hartshorn, *
Jeff Fox, *
◆ EMP: 95 EST: 1964
SQ FT: 50,000
SALES (est): 18.55MM Privately Held
Web: www.ultra-met.com
SIC: 3599 Machine shop, jobbing and repair

(G-14851)
ULTRA-MET COMPANY
120 Fyffe St (43078-1106)
PHONE.................937 653-7133
Brent Sheerer, *Pr*
EMP: 11 EST: 2015
SALES (est): 2.39MM Privately Held
Web: www.ultra-met.com
SIC: 1311 5013 5047 8711 Crude petroleum and natural gas; Automotive engines and engine parts; Instruments, surgical and medical; Aviation and/or aeronautical engineering

Urbancrest
Franklin County

(G-14852)
AMSOIL INC
3389 Urbancrest Industrial Dr (43123-1783)
PHONE.................614 274-9851
Scott Davis, *Mgr*
EMP: 8
SALES (corp-wide): 225MM Privately Held
Web: kadanoil.shopamsoil.com
SIC: 2992 3589 2873 3714 Lubricating oils and greases; Water filters and softeners, household type; Fertilizers: natural (organic), except compost; Motor vehicle parts and accessories
PA: Amsoil Inc.
925 Tower Ave
Superior WI 54880
715 392-7101

(G-14853)
HAYDEN VALLEY FOODS INC (PA)
Also Called: Tropical Nut & Fruit
3150 Urbancrest Industrial Dr (43123-1767)
PHONE.................614 539-7233
▲ EMP: 72 EST: 1984
SALES (est): 32.98MM Privately Held
Web: www.haydenvalleyfoods.com
SIC: 5149 2068 2064 2034 Fruits, dried; Salted and roasted nuts and seeds; Candy and other confectionery products; Dried and dehydrated fruits, vegetables and soup mixes

(G-14854)
PILKINGTON NORTH AMERICA INC
3440 Centerpoint Dr (43123-1794)
PHONE.................419 247-3731
Richard Frampton, *Brnch Mgr*
EMP: 223
Web: www.pilkington.com
SIC: 3211 Construction glass
HQ: Pilkington North America, Inc.
811 Madison Ave Fl 3
Toledo OH 43604
419 247-3731

(G-14855)
TAYLOR COMMUNICATIONS INC
3125 Lewis Centre Way (43123-1784)
PHONE.................614 277-7500
Jeff Wise, *Brnch Mgr*
EMP: 46
SALES (corp-wide): 3.81B Privately Held
Web: www.taylor.com
SIC: 2759 Commercial printing, nec
HQ: Taylor Communications, Inc.
1725 Roe Crest Dr
North Mankato MN 56003
866 541-0937

Utica
Licking County

(G-14856)
ACUITY BRANDS LIGHTING INC
Holophane
140 Carey St (43080-9004)
P.O. Box 535 (43080-0535)
PHONE.................740 892-2011
Kim Lombardi, *Brnch Mgr*
EMP: 120
SALES (corp-wide): 3.95B Publicly Held
Web: lithonia.acuitybrands.com
SIC: 3646 Commercial lighting fixtures
HQ: Acuity Brands Lighting, Inc.
1170 Peachtree St Ne # 23
Atlanta GA 30309

(G-14857)
CARDINAL CT COMPANY
140 Carey St (43080-9004)
PHONE.................740 892-2324
EMP: 30
SALES (corp-wide): 1B Privately Held
Web: www.cardinalcorp.com
SIC: 3211 Tempered glass
HQ: Cardinal Ct Company
775 Prierie Ctr Dr Ste 200
Eden Prairie MN 55344

(G-14858)
CARDINAL GLASS INDUSTRIES INC
140 Carey St (43080-9004)
PHONE.................740 892-2324
Roger D O'Shaughnessy, *Brnch Mgr*
EMP: 30
SALES (corp-wide): 1B Privately Held
Web: www.cardinalcorp.com
SIC: 3211 Tempered glass
PA: Cardinal Glass Industries Inc
775 Prierie Ctr Dr Ste 200
Eden Prairie MN 55344
952 229-2600

(G-14859)
VELVET ICE CREAM COMPANY (PA)
Also Called: Ye Olde Mille Shoppe
11324 Mount Vernon Rd (43080-7703)
P.O. Box 588 (43080-0588)
PHONE.................740 892-3921
EMP: 60 EST: 1960
SALES (est): 21.87MM

Valley City - Medina County (G-14860)

SALES (corp-wide): 21.87MM **Privately Held**
Web: www.velveticecream.com
SIC: **2024** 8412 5812 5947 Ice cream, bulk; Museum; American restaurant; Gift shop

Valley City
Medina County

(G-14860)
A TECH WELDING PRODUCTS INC
5977 Boston Rd (44280-9340)
PHONE..............................614 296-1573
Ronald Williams, *Prin*
EMP: 6 **EST:** 2006
SALES (est): 184.26K **Privately Held**
SIC: 7692 Welding repair

(G-14861)
ARNOLD CORPORATION
Also Called: Arnold Company
5965 Grafton Rd (44280-9329)
P.O. Box 368022 (44136-9722)
PHONE..............................330 225-2600
◆ **EMP:** 107
SIC: 5083 3524 Lawn and garden machinery and equipment; Lawn and garden mowers and accessories

(G-14862)
AUTOMATION TOOL & DIE INC
5576 Innovation Dr (44280-9368)
PHONE..............................330 225-8336
William E Bennett, *Pr*
James R Bennett, *
EMP: 70 **EST:** 1974
SQ FT: 32,000
SALES (est): 12.43MM **Privately Held**
Web: www.automationtd.com
SIC: 3544 Special dies and tools

(G-14863)
BOEHM PRESSED STEEL COMPANY
5440 Wegman Dr (44280-9707)
PHONE..............................330 220-8000
Ted Mcquade, *Pr*
William Reis, *
EMP: 50 **EST:** 1977
SQ FT: 41,000
SALES (est): 8.18MM **Privately Held**
Web: www.boehmstampings.com
SIC: 3469 Stamping metal for the trade

(G-14864)
BOSS INDUSTRIES INC
5478 Grafton Rd (44280-9719)
P.O. Box H (43452-8008)
PHONE..............................330 273-2266
Herb Albrecht, *Pr*
Selma Albrecht, *Sec*
EMP: 13 **EST:** 1985
SQ FT: 12,000
SALES (est): 436.85K **Privately Held**
SIC: 3599 Custom machinery

(G-14865)
CON-BELT INC
5656 Innovation Dr (44280-9370)
PHONE..............................330 273-2003
Marc Zeitler, *Pr*
EMP: 13 **EST:** 1991
SALES (est): 2.48MM **Privately Held**
Web: www.conbelt.com
SIC: 3535 Conveyors and conveying equipment

(G-14866)
CSM CONCEPTS LLC
6450 Grafton Rd (44280-9762)
PHONE..............................330 483-1320
Gordon J Petkosh, *Managing Member*
EMP: 12 **EST:** 2010
SALES (est): 1.84MM **Privately Held**
Web: www.csmconceptsllc.com
SIC: 2542 Office and store showcases and display fixtures

(G-14867)
CUB CADET CORPORATION SALES
614 Liverpool Dr (44280-9717)
P.O. Box 368023 (44280)
PHONE..............................330 273-4550
Curtis E Moll, *Ch Bd*
David Hessler, *
James M Milinski, *
▲ **EMP:** 53 **EST:** 1981
SQ FT: 185,000
SALES (est): 17.84MM
SALES (corp-wide): 15.78B **Publicly Held**
Web: www.cubcadet.com
SIC: 3524 Grass catchers, lawn mower
HQ: Mtd Products Inc
  5965 Grafton Rd
  Valley City OH 44280
  330 225-2600

(G-14868)
CUSTOM SURROUNDINGS INC
6450 Grafton Rd (44280-9762)
PHONE..............................913 839-0100
Christopher Scherry, *Pr*
EMP: 15 **EST:** 1987
SQ FT: 25,000
SALES (est): 422.98K **Privately Held**
Web: www.customsurroundings.com
SIC: 2541 2599 Store fixtures, wood; Cabinets, factory

(G-14869)
EMH INC (PA)
Also Called: Engineered Material Handling
550 Crane Dr (44280-9361)
PHONE..............................330 220-8600
Edis Hazne, *Pr*
Dave Comiono, *
◆ **EMP:** 60 **EST:** 1988
SQ FT: 65,000
SALES (est): 15.56MM
SALES (corp-wide): 15.56MM **Privately Held**
Web: www.emhcranes.com
SIC: 3441 3536 Fabricated structural metal; Cranes and monorail systems

(G-14870)
FUSERASHI INTL TECH INC
Also Called: F I T
5401 Innovation Dr (44280-9353)
PHONE..............................330 273-0140
Mamoru Shimada, *Prin*
◆ **EMP:** 22 **EST:** 1996
SQ FT: 200,000
SALES (est): 9.82MM **Privately Held**
Web: www.fitinc.net
SIC: 3714 Motor vehicle parts and accessories
PA: Fuserashi Co., Ltd.
  11-74, Takaida
  Higashi-Osaka OSK 577-0

(G-14871)
GREENFIELD DIE & MFG CORP (HQ)
Also Called: Canton Manufacturing
880 Steel Dr (44280)
PHONE..............................734 454-4000
James Fanello, *Pr*
Lillian Etzkorn, *VP*

EMP: 61 **EST:** 1955
SALES (est): 5.71MM **Privately Held**
SIC: 3544 3469 Special dies and tools; Metal stampings, nec
PA: Shl Liquidation Industries Inc.
  880 Steel Dr
  Valley City OH 44280

(G-14872)
GROUPER ACQUISITION CO LLC
Also Called: Shiloh Industries, LLC
880 Steel Dr (44280-9736)
PHONE..............................248 299-7500
EMP: 491
SALES (corp-wide): 1.97B **Privately Held**
SIC: 3469 Metal stampings, nec
HQ: Grouper Acquisition Company, Llc
  1780 Pond Run
  Auburn Hills MI 48326
  248 299-7500

(G-14873)
HY-PRODUCTION INC
6000 Grafton Rd (44280-9330)
PHONE..............................330 273-2400
William Kneebusch, *Ch Bd*
Mathew Roach, *
Keith Koprowski, *
▲ **EMP:** 124 **EST:** 1966
SQ FT: 60,000
SALES (est): 23.64MM **Privately Held**
Web: www.hy-production.com
SIC: 3519 3492 3451 3594 Engines, diesel and semi-diesel or dual-fuel; Control valves, fluid power: hydraulic and pneumatic ; Screw machine products; Fluid power pumps and motors

(G-14874)
JOSEPH ADAMS CORP
5740 Grafton Rd (44280)
P.O. Box 583 (44280)
PHONE..............................330 225-9125
Patrick Adams, *Pr*
▲ **EMP:** 10 **EST:** 1948
SQ FT: 100,000
SALES (est): 990.88K **Privately Held**
Web: www.josephadamscorp.com
SIC: 2087 2833 Flavoring extracts and syrups, nec; Botanical products, medicinal: ground, graded, or milled

(G-14875)
KRISDALE INC
Also Called: Krisdale
649 Marks Rd (44280-9774)
PHONE..............................330 225-2392
Glenn D Phelan, *Pr*
EMP: 6 **EST:** 1965
SALES (est): 573.44K **Privately Held**
SIC: 3544 Jigs and fixtures

(G-14876)
LIVERPOOL TOWNSHIP
6700 Center Rd (44280-9435)
P.O. Box 381 (44280-0381)
PHONE..............................330 483-4747
EMP: 9
SIC: 3531 9111 Road construction and maintenance machinery; Mayors' office
PA: Liverpool Township
  6801 School St
  Valley City OH 44280
  330 483-3102

(G-14877)
MACK CONCRETE INDUSTRIES INC (HQ)
201 Columbia Rd (44280-9706)
P.O. Box 335 (44280-0335)
PHONE..............................330 483-3111

Richard W Mack, *Pr*
Betsy Mack, *Pr*
Jim Thompson, *VP*
Barbara Mack, *Sec*
EMP: 12 **EST:** 1932
SQ FT: 20,000
SALES (est): 24.43MM
SALES (corp-wide): 134.58MM **Privately Held**
Web: www.mackconcrete.com
SIC: 3272 Concrete products, precast, nec
PA: Mack Industries, Inc.
  1321 Industrial Pkwy N # 500
  Brunswick OH 44212
  330 460-7005

(G-14878)
MACK INDUSTRIES PA INC (HQ)
201 Columbia Rd (44280-9706)
P.O. Box 335 (44280-0335)
PHONE..............................330 483-3111
Betsy Mack, *Pr*
Barbara Mack, *
EMP: 100 **EST:** 1952
SQ FT: 7,000
SALES (est): 22.5MM
SALES (corp-wide): 134.58MM **Privately Held**
Web: www.mackconcrete.com
SIC: 3272 Concrete products, precast, nec
PA: Mack Industries, Inc.
  1321 Industrial Pkwy N # 500
  Brunswick OH 44212
  330 460-7005

(G-14879)
MIXED LOGIC LLC
5907 E Law Rd (44280-9770)
PHONE..............................440 826-1676
Kevin Borrowman, *Managing Member*
EMP: 7 **EST:** 2000
SALES (est): 354.76K **Privately Held**
SIC: 3699 5999 Electric sound equipment; Electronic parts and equipment

(G-14880)
MODERN TRANSMISSION DEV CO
5903 Grafton Rd (44280-9329)
▲ **EMP:** 250 **EST:** 1994
SALES (est): 99.91MM
SALES (corp-wide): 15.78B **Publicly Held**
SIC: 3714 Motor vehicle transmissions, drive assemblies, and parts
HQ: Mtd Products Inc
  5965 Grafton Rd
  Valley City OH 44280
  330 225-2600

(G-14881)
MTD CONSUMER GROUP INC (DH)
5965 Grafton Rd (44280-9329)
PHONE..............................330 225-2600
Steven E Pryatel, *Prin*
▼ **EMP:** 139 **EST:** 1999
SALES (est): 101.04MM
SALES (corp-wide): 15.78B **Publicly Held**
SIC: 3524 Lawn and garden tractors and equipment
HQ: Mtd Products Inc
  5965 Grafton Rd
  Valley City OH 44280
  330 225-2600

(G-14882)
MTD HOLDINGS INC (HQ)
5965 Grafton Rd (44280)
P.O. Box 368022 (44136)
PHONE..............................330 225-2600
Curtis E Moll, *CEO*
Jeff Deuch, *
◆ **EMP:** 500 **EST:** 1946

SALES (est): 1.84B
SALES (corp-wide): 15.78B **Publicly Held**
Web: www.mtdparts.com
SIC: **3544** 6141 3469 3524 Special dies and tools; Financing: automobiles, furniture, etc., not a deposit bank; Metal stampings, nec; Lawn and garden equipment
PA: Stanley Black & Decker, Inc.
1000 Stanley Dr
New Britain CT 06053
860 225-5111

(G-14883)
MTD INTERNATIONAL OPERATIONS (DH)
5965 Grafton Rd (44280-9329)
PHONE................................330 225-2600
Robert T Moll, *Pr*
EMP: 160 **EST:** 2003
SALES (est): 3.19MM
SALES (corp-wide): 15.78B **Publicly Held**
SIC: 3524 Lawn and garden equipment
HQ: Mtd Holdings Inc
5965 Grafton Rd
Valley City OH 44280
330 225-2600

(G-14884)
MTD PRODUCTS INC (DH)
5965 Grafton Rd (44280)
P.O. Box 368022 (44136)
PHONE................................330 225-2600
Robert T Moll, *Ch*
Jeffery Deuch, *
Michael Griffith, *
◆ **EMP:** 500 **EST:** 1932
SQ FT: 180,000
SALES (est): 1.84B
SALES (corp-wide): 15.78B **Publicly Held**
Web: www.mtdparts.com
SIC: 3524 Lawn and garden equipment
HQ: Mtd Holdings Inc
5965 Grafton Rd
Valley City OH 44280
330 225-2600

(G-14885)
MTD PRODUCTS INC
Also Called: Mtd Consumer Products Supply
5903 Grafton Rd (44280-9329)
P.O. Box 368022 (44136-9722)
PHONE................................330 225-1940
EMP: 269
SALES (corp-wide): 15.78B **Publicly Held**
Web: www.mtdparts.com
SIC: 3524 Lawn and garden equipment
HQ: Mtd Products Inc
5965 Grafton Rd
Valley City OH 44280
330 225-2600

(G-14886)
MTD PRODUCTS INC
Industrial Plastics Co Div
680 Liverpool Dr (44280-9717)
P.O. Box 360585 (44136-0045)
PHONE................................330 225-9127
Mark Tyson, *Prin*
EMP: 101
SQ FT: 90,000
SALES (corp-wide): 15.78B **Publicly Held**
Web: www.mtdparts.com
SIC: 3524 Lawnmowers, residential: hand or power
HQ: Mtd Products Inc
5965 Grafton Rd
Valley City OH 44280
330 225-2600

(G-14887)
NORTHLAKE STEEL CORPORATION
5455 Wegman Dr (44280-9707)
PHONE................................330 220-7717
William K Bissett, *CEO*
Craig O Curie, *
◆ **EMP:** 80 **EST:** 1977
SQ FT: 82,000
SALES (est): 24.21MM **Privately Held**
Web: www.northlakesteel.com
SIC: 3398 3312 Annealing of metal; Bar, rod, and wire products

(G-14888)
RAF ACQUISITION CO
Also Called: Republic Anode Fabricators
5478 Grafton Rd (44280-9719)
PHONE................................440 572-5999
Mike Horonzy, *Pr*
EMP: 30 **EST:** 1932
SQ FT: 20,000
SALES (est): 1.98MM **Privately Held**
Web: www.republicanode.com
SIC: 3471 3479 Chromium plating of metals or formed products; Coating of metals and formed products

(G-14889)
SCHAEFFLER GROUP USA INC
5370 Wegman Dr (44280-9700)
PHONE................................800 274-5001
EMP: 36
SALES (corp-wide): 66.25B **Privately Held**
Web: www.schaeffler.com
SIC: 3562 Ball and roller bearings
HQ: Schaeffler Group Usa Inc.
308 Springhill Farm Rd
Fort Mill SC 29715
803 548-8500

(G-14890)
SHILOH INDUSTRIES INC
Ohio Welded Blank
5569 Innovation Dr (44280-9369)
PHONE................................330 558-2000
Daniel Brown, *Brnch Mgr*
EMP: 600
Web: www.durashiloh.com
SIC: 3465 Automotive stampings
PA: Shl Liquidation Industries Inc.
880 Steel Dr
Valley City OH 44280

(G-14891)
SHL LIQUIDATION AUTOMOTIVE INC
Also Called: Liverpool Manufacturing
880 Steel Dr (44280)
PHONE................................330 558-2600
Lillian Etzkorn, *Pr*
EMP: 52 **EST:** 1999
SALES (est): 4.97MM **Privately Held**
Web: www.durashiloh.com
SIC: 3544 3469 Special dies, tools, jigs, and fixtures; Metal stampings, nec
PA: Shl Liquidation Industries Inc.
880 Steel Dr
Valley City OH 44280

(G-14892)
SHL LIQUIDATION INC DICKSON (HQ)
880 Steel Dr (44280)
PHONE................................615 446-7725
Theodore Zampetis, *CEO*
EMP: 45 **EST:** 2000
SALES (est): 3.22MM **Privately Held**
Web: www.durashiloh.com
SIC: 3465 Automotive stampings
PA: Shl Liquidation Industries Inc.
880 Steel Dr
Valley City OH 44280

(G-14893)
SHL LIQUIDATION INDUSTRIES INC (PA)
Also Called: Shiloh Industries
880 Steel Dr (44280)
PHONE................................248 299-7500
Mike Putz, *CEO*
◆ **EMP:** 271 **EST:** 1950
SALES (est): 1.05B **Privately Held**
Web: www.durashiloh.com
SIC: 3465 3469 3544 Automotive stampings; Metal stampings, nec; Special dies and tools

(G-14894)
SHL LIQUIDATION JEFFERSON INC (HQ)
Also Called: Jefferson Manufacturing Div
880 Steel Dr (44280)
EMP: 72 **EST:** 1998
SQ FT: 18,000
SALES (est): 6.3MM **Privately Held**
Web: www.durashiloh.com
SIC: 3469 3465 Metal stampings, nec; Automotive stampings
PA: Shl Liquidation Industries Inc.
880 Steel Dr
Valley City OH 44280

(G-14895)
SHL LIQUIDATION MEDINA INC (PA)
Also Called: Shiloh Inds Inc Mdina Blnking
5580 Wegman Dr (44280)
EMP: 150 **EST:** 1986
SQ FT: 200,000
SALES (est): 20.43MM
SALES (corp-wide): 20.43MM **Privately Held**
SIC: 3325 3469 3545 Steel foundries, nec; Metal stampings, nec; Machine tool accessories

(G-14896)
SHL LIQUIDATION MFG LLC (HQ)
880 Steel Dr (44280)
PHONE................................330 558-2600
Thomas Dugan, *Managing Member*
Lillian Etzkorn, *
EMP: 50 **EST:** 2014
SALES (est): 498.46MM **Privately Held**
Web: www.durashiloh.com
SIC: 3465 Automotive stampings
PA: Shl Liquidation Industries Inc.
880 Steel Dr
Valley City OH 44280

(G-14897)
SHL LIQUIDATION SECTIONAL CO
Also Called: Wellington Die Division
880 Steel Dr (44280)
PHONE................................330 558-2600
Jack Falcon, *Pr*
James Fanello, *
EMP: 325 **EST:** 1946
SQ FT: 80,000
SALES (est): 26.97MM **Privately Held**
SIC: 3544 Special dies and tools

(G-14898)
SHL LIQUIDATION STAMPING INC (HQ)
Also Called: Wellington Stamping
880 Steel Dr (44280)
PHONE................................330 558-2600
Jack Falcon, *Pr*
James Fanello, *VP*
David J Hessler, *Sec*
EMP: 64 **EST:** 1987
SQ FT: 200,000
SALES (est): 105.01MM **Privately Held**

Web: www.durashiloh.com
SIC: 3465 Automotive stampings
PA: Shl Liquidation Industries Inc.
880 Steel Dr
Valley City OH 44280

(G-14899)
TWB COMPANY LLC
5569 Innovation Dr (44280-9369)
PHONE................................330 558-2026
Jeff Malik, *Brnch Mgr*
EMP: 26
SALES (corp-wide): 4.92B **Publicly Held**
Web: www.twbcompany.com
SIC: 3465 Automotive stampings
HQ: Twb Company, L.L.C.
1600 Nadeau Rd
Monroe MI 48162

(G-14900)
WELSER PROFILE NORTH AMER LLC (DH)
615 Liverpool Dr (44280-9717)
PHONE................................330 225-2500
William Johnson Iii, *Managing Member*
EMP: 32 **EST:** 2020
SALES (est): 8.26MM
SALES (corp-wide): 242.12K **Privately Held**
Web: www.welser.com
SIC: 3449 Custom roll formed products
HQ: Welser Profile Beteiligungs Gmbh
Prochenberg 24a
Ybbsitz 3341
74438000

(G-14901)
WOGEN RESOURCES AMERICA LLC
6980 Country View Dr (44280-9451)
PHONE................................216 272-0062
EMP: 7 **EST:** 2017
SALES (est): 201.06K **Privately Held**
Web: www.wogen.com
SIC: 2816 Metallic and mineral pigments, nec

(G-14902)
ZION INDUSTRIES INC (PA)
6229 Grafton Rd (44280-9312)
PHONE................................330 225-3246
Bob Puls, *Pr*
Micheal Laheta, *
Randy Lane, *
Dorothy Puls, *
EMP: 54 **EST:** 1977
SQ FT: 16,600
SALES (est): 11.08MM
SALES (corp-wide): 11.08MM **Privately Held**
Web: www.zioninduction.com
SIC: 3398 Brazing (hardening) of metal

Van Buren
Hancock County

(G-14903)
NOSTER RUBBER COMPANY
1481 Township Road 229 (45889-9603)
P.O. Box 227 (45889-0227)
PHONE................................419 299-3387
Jeff Wills, *Pr*
EMP: 9 **EST:** 1950
SQ FT: 20,000
SALES (est): 486.21K **Privately Held**
Web: www.nosterrubber.com
SIC: 3069 Molded rubber products

Van Wert
Van Wert County

(G-14904)
ADVANCED BIOLOGICAL MKTG INC
Also Called: Agrauxine By Lesaffre
375 Bonnewitz Ave (45891-1101)
P.O. Box 222 (45891-0222)
PHONE..................................419 232-2461
Hugo Bony, *CEO*
▲ **EMP:** 25 **EST:** 2000
SQ FT: 3,500
SALES (est): 4.83MM **Privately Held**
Web: www.agrauxine.us
SIC: 2879 0116 Insecticides and pesticides; Soybeans

(G-14905)
AEROQUIP CORP
1225 W Main St (45891-9362)
PHONE..................................419 238-1190
Don Waggener, *Prin*
EMP: 8 **EST:** 2008
SALES (est): 121.3K **Privately Held**
SIC: 3052 Rubber and plastics hose and beltings

(G-14906)
ALLIANCE AUTOMATION LLC
1100 John Brown Rd (45891-9184)
PHONE..................................419 238-2520
▲ **EMP:** 80 **EST:** 2004
SALES (est): 27MM **Privately Held**
Web: www.allianceautomation.com
SIC: 3599 Custom machinery

(G-14907)
BRAUN INDUSTRIES INC
1170 Production Dr (45891-9391)
PHONE..................................419 232-7020
TOLL FREE: 800
Kim Braun, *Pr*
Scott Braun, *
Dale A Schroeder, *
Gary Kohls, *
Jill Cilmi, *
EMP: 270 **EST:** 1959
SQ FT: 160,000
SALES (est): 47.52MM **Privately Held**
Web: www.braunambulances.com
SIC: 3711 Ambulances (motor vehicles), assembly of

(G-14908)
BUDD CO PLASTICS DIV
1276 Industrial Dr (45891-2466)
PHONE..................................419 238-4332
Frank Macher, *Prin*
EMP: 7 **EST:** 2010
SALES (est): 152.51K **Privately Held**
SIC: 3089 Injection molding of plastics

(G-14909)
COOL MACHINES INC
740 Fox Rd (45891-2441)
PHONE..................................419 232-4871
David Krendl, *Pr*
Carlos Usuda, *VP*
Andrew Schulte, *Sec*
EMP: 14 **EST:** 2006
SQ FT: 40,000
SALES (est): 3MM **Privately Held**
Web: www.coolmachines.com
SIC: 3532 Mining machinery

(G-14910)
COOPER FOODS
Also Called: Cooper Farms Cooked Meat
6893 Us Route 127 (45891-9601)
PHONE..................................419 232-2440
Paula Fleming, *Prin*
EMP: 27 **EST:** 2009
SALES (est): 3.59MM **Privately Held**
Web: www.cooperfarms.com
SIC: 2015 Poultry slaughtering and processing

(G-14911)
COOPER HATCHERY INC
Also Called: Cooper Farms Cooked Meats
6793 Us Route 127 (45891-9601)
PHONE..................................419 238-4869
Eric Ludwig, *Brnch Mgr*
EMP: 130
SALES (corp-wide): 93.22MM **Privately Held**
Web: www.cooperfarms.com
SIC: 2015 Poultry slaughtering and processing
PA: Cooper Hatchery, Inc.
22348 Road 140
Oakwood OH 45873
419 594-3325

(G-14912)
CQT KENNEDY LLC
Also Called: CORNWELL QUALITY TOOLS
1260 Industrial Dr (45891-2433)
PHONE..................................419 238-2442
Raymond Moeller, *Pr*
Robert Studenic, *Sec*
David Nist, *Treas*
EMP: 95 **EST:** 2016
SQ FT: 190,000
SALES (est): 15.16MM
SALES (corp-wide): 55.65MM **Privately Held**
Web: www.buykennedymfg.com
SIC: 3469 3841 Boxes: tool, lunch, mail, etc.: stamped metal; Surgical and medical instruments
PA: The Cornwell Quality Tools Company
667 Seville Rd
Wadsworth OH 44281
330 336-3506

(G-14913)
DANFOSS POWER SOLUTIONS II LLC
Also Called: Danfoss
1225 W Main St (45891-9362)
PHONE..................................419 238-1190
Joshua Wood, *Brnch Mgr*
EMP: 8
SALES (corp-wide): 11.6B **Privately Held**
SIC: 3542 3594 3052 3492 Crimping machinery, metal; Fluid power pumps; Rubber hose; Hose and tube fittings and assemblies, hydraulic/pneumatic
HQ: Danfoss Power Solutions Ii, Llc
2800 E 13th St
Ames IA 50010
515 239-6000

(G-14914)
EATON CORPORATION
Also Called: Mobile Operations
1225 W Main St (45891-9362)
PHONE..................................419 238-1190
Carey Welker, *Brnch Mgr*
EMP: 900
Web: www.dix-eaton.com
SIC: 3052 3429 Rubber hose; Clamps and couplings, hose
HQ: Eaton Corporation
1000 Eaton Blvd
Cleveland OH 44122
440 523-5000

(G-14915)
EISENHAUER MFG CO LLC
409 Center St (45891)
P.O. Box 390 (45891)
PHONE..................................419 238-0081
EMP: 73 **EST:** 1944
SQ FT: 50,000
SALES (est): 4.37MM **Privately Held**
Web: www.eisenhauermfg.com
SIC: 3469 3412 3411 2396 Stamping metal for the trade; Metal barrels, drums, and pails ; Metal cans; Automotive trimmings, fabric

(G-14916)
GLOBAL PRECISION PARTS INC
7600 Us Route 127 (45891-9363)
PHONE..................................260 563-9030
James A Butz, *Prin*
EMP: 18 **EST:** 2006
SALES (est): 872.24K **Privately Held**
Web: www.globalprecisionpartsinc.com
SIC: 3451 Screw machine products

(G-14917)
GREIF INC
975 Glenn St (45891-2331)
PHONE..................................419 238-0565
Doug Benner, *Mgr*
EMP: 48
SALES (corp-wide): 5.22B **Publicly Held**
Web: www.greif.com
SIC: 2655 Drums, fiber: made from purchased material
PA: Greif, Inc.
425 Winter Rd
Delaware OH 43015
740 549-6000

(G-14918)
HOLLYWOOD DANCE JAMS
8402 Hoaglin Center Rd (45891-9672)
PHONE..................................419 234-0746
Kim Hohman, *Prin*
EMP: 6 **EST:** 2015
SALES (est): 50.24K **Privately Held**
SIC: 2499 Wood products, nec

(G-14919)
KAM MANUFACTURING INC
1197 Grill Rd (45891-9387)
P.O. Box 407 (45891-0407)
PHONE..................................419 238-6037
Kim Adams, *Owner*
▲ **EMP:** 150 **EST:** 1985
SQ FT: 5,500
SALES (est): 8.23MM **Privately Held**
Web: www.kammfg.com
SIC: 2331 2329 3161 Women's and misses' blouses and shirts; Men's and boys' sportswear and athletic clothing; Luggage

(G-14920)
KMC HOLDINGS LLC
Also Called: Kennedy Manufacturing
1260 Industrial Dr (45891-2433)
PHONE..................................419 238-2442
▲ **EMP:** 130
Web: www.buykennedy.com
SIC: 3841 3469 5021 Surgical and medical instruments; Boxes: tool, lunch, mail, etc.: stamped metal; Racks

(G-14921)
LEESBURG LOOMS INCORPORATED
Also Called: Leesburg Loom & Supply
201 N Cherry St (45891-1210)
PHONE..................................419 238-2738
Jim Myers, *Pr*
EMP: 7 **EST:** 1988
SQ FT: 90,000
SALES (est): 692.8K **Privately Held**
Web: www.totalrug.com
SIC: 3552 Fabric forming machinery and equipment

(G-14922)
LEY INDUSTRIES INC
121 S Walnut St (45891-1720)
P.O. Box 191 (45891-0191)
PHONE..................................419 238-6742
Watson N Ley, *Pr*
Esther Ley, *VP*
Watson N Ley Prestreas, *Prin*
EMP: 7 **EST:** 1948
SQ FT: 32,000
SALES (est): 206.27K **Privately Held**
SIC: 3523 Farm machinery and equipment

(G-14923)
MEK VAN WERT INC
595 Fox Rd (45891-2437)
PHONE..................................419 203-4902
Javier Alcaba Berastegui, *CEO*
▼ **EMP:** 8 **EST:** 2017
SALES (est): 800.59K **Privately Held**
SIC: 3341 Secondary precious metals

(G-14924)
NATIONAL DOOR AND TRIM INC
1189 Grill Rd (45891-9386)
PHONE..................................419 238-9345
Thomas Turnwald, *Pr*
Rick Anderson, *
T Turnwald, *
Cory Michaud, *
▲ **EMP:** 48 **EST:** 1978
SQ FT: 50,000
SALES (est): 9.81MM **Privately Held**
Web: www.national-door.com
SIC: 2431 Millwork

(G-14925)
RIDGE TOWNSHIP STONE QUARRY
16905 Middle Point Rd (45891-9771)
PHONE..................................419 968-2222
Roger Davis, *Pr*
EMP: 7 **EST:** 1914
SALES (est): 642.12K **Privately Held**
Web: www.ridgetownshipquarry.com
SIC: 1422 5032 Crushed and broken limestone; Stone, crushed or broken

(G-14926)
SEAL DIV NATL
150 Fisher Ave (45891-1409)
PHONE..................................419 238-0030
EMP: 6 **EST:** 1988
SALES (est): 140.65K **Privately Held**
SIC: 3069 Rubber automotive products

(G-14927)
TECUMSEH PACKG SOLUTIONS INC
Also Called: Van Wert Division
1275 Industrial Dr (45891-2432)
PHONE..................................419 238-1122
James Robideau, *Brnch Mgr*
EMP: 15
SALES (corp-wide): 10.23MM **Privately Held**
Web: www.akers-pkg.com
SIC: 2653 Boxes, corrugated: made from purchased materials
PA: Tecumseh Packaging Solutions, Inc.
707 S Evans St
Tecumseh MI 49286
517 423-2126

(G-14928)
TEIJIN AUTOMOTIVE TECH INC
Also Called: CSP Van Wert

1276 Industrial Dr (45891-2433)
PHONE..............................419 238-4628
Tom Harth, *Brnch Mgr*
EMP: 285
Web: www.teijinautomotive.com
SIC: 3089 3714 Injection molding of plastics; Motor vehicle parts and accessories
HQ: Teijin Automotive Technologies, Inc.
255 Rex Blvd
Auburn Hills MI 48326
248 237-7800

(G-14929)
UNIVERSAL LETTERING INC
Also Called: Universal Lettering Company
1197 Grill Rd # B (45891-9387)
P.O. Box 1055 (45891-6055)
PHONE..............................419 238-9320
Mark Hoops, *Pr*
▲ **EMP:** 11 **EST:** 1990
SQ FT: 20,400
SALES (est): 746.3K **Privately Held**
Web: www.universallettering.com
SIC: 2339 2329 Women's and misses' jackets and coats, except sportswear; Men's and boys' leather, wool and down-filled outerwear

(G-14930)
VAN WERT PALLETS LLC
9042 John Brown Rd (45891-8420)
PHONE..............................419 203-1823
Spencer Wise, *Prin*
EMP: 9 **EST:** 2010
SALES (est): 318.21K **Privately Held**
Web: www.vanwert.org
SIC: 2448 Pallets, wood and wood with metal

Vandalia
Montgomery County

(G-14931)
ADARE PHARMACEUTICALS INC (DH)
845 Center Dr (45377-3129)
PHONE..............................937 898-9669
John Fraher, *CEO*
▲ **EMP:** 167 **EST:** 1980
SQ FT: 870,000
SALES (est): 52.84MM
SALES (corp-wide): 3.2B **Publicly Held**
Web: www.adarepharmasolutions.com
SIC: 2834 Pharmaceutical preparations
HQ: Tpg Capital Management, L.P.
301 Commerce St Ste 3300
Fort Worth TX 76102

(G-14932)
ALL SRVICE PLASTIC MOLDING INC (PA)
850 Falls Creek Dr (45377-8600)
PHONE..............................937 890-0322
Joseph Minneman, *CEO*
Joseph Kavalauskas, *
Joe Kavalauskas, *
Gary Deaton, *
Frank Maus, *
▲ **EMP:** 80 **EST:** 1984
SALES (est): 27.09MM
SALES (corp-wide): 27.09MM **Privately Held**
Web: www.mincogroup.com
SIC: 3089 Injection molding of plastics

(G-14933)
BALANCING COMPANY INC (PA)
898 Center Dr (45377-3130)
P.O. Box 490 (45377-0490)
PHONE..............................937 898-9111
Michael Belcher, *CEO*
Michael W Belcher, *
Jack Boeke, *
EMP: 28 **EST:** 1967
SQ FT: 53,000
SALES (est): 4.76MM
SALES (corp-wide): 4.76MM **Privately Held**
Web: www.balco.com
SIC: 3599 8734 3544 Machine shop, jobbing and repair; Testing laboratories; Special dies, tools, jigs, and fixtures

(G-14934)
BOSTON STOKER INC (PA)
Also Called: Boston Stoker
10855 Engle Rd (45377-9439)
P.O. Box 548 (45377-0548)
PHONE..............................937 890-6401
Henry Dean, *Pr*
Donald M Dean, *Pr*
Sally Dean, *Sec*
EMP: 11 **EST:** 1973
SALES (est): 5.02MM
SALES (corp-wide): 5.02MM **Privately Held**
Web: www.bostonstoker.com
SIC: 2095 5499 5993 Coffee roasting (except by wholesale grocers); Coffee; Tobacco stores and stands

(G-14935)
CROWN EQUIPMENT CORPORATION
Also Called: Crown Lift Trucks
750 Center Dr (45377-3128)
P.O. Box 400 (45377-0400)
PHONE..............................937 454-7545
Lauren Robins, *Brnch Mgr*
EMP: 58
SALES (corp-wide): 7.12B **Privately Held**
Web: www.crown.com
SIC: 3537 Lift trucks, industrial: fork, platform, straddle, etc.
PA: Crown Equipment Corporation
44 S Washington St
New Bremen OH 45869
419 629-2311

(G-14936)
CROWN SOLUTIONS CO LLC
Also Called: Crown Solutions
913 Industrial Park Dr (45377-3115)
PHONE..............................937 890-4075
EMP: 200
SIC: 8711 3589 Consulting engineer; Water treatment equipment, industrial

(G-14937)
DATWYLER SLING SLTIONS USA INC
Also Called: Columbia
875 Center Dr (45377-3129)
PHONE..............................937 387-2800
Brian Bueltel, *Sls Dir*
Mark Bueltel, *Site Accounts Manager*
◆ **EMP:** 67 **EST:** 1985
SQ FT: 100,000
SALES (est): 21.46MM **Privately Held**
Web: usa.datwyler.com
SIC: 5085 3069 3061 Seals, industrial; Molded rubber products; Mechanical rubber goods
HQ: Keystone Holdings, Inc.
875 Center Dr
Vandalia OH 45377

(G-14938)
DOOR FABRICATION SERVICES INC
3250 Old Springfield Rd Ste 1 (45377)
PHONE..............................937 454-9207
Brian Hakers, *Mgr*
▲ **EMP:** 15 **EST:** 2000
SALES (est): 3.29MM
SALES (corp-wide): 2.83B **Privately Held**
SIC: 5046 2431 Partitions; Millwork
PA: Masonite International Corporation
1242 E 5th Ave
Tampa FL 33605
813 877-2726

(G-14939)
EXHIBIT CONCEPTS INC (PA)
700 Crossroads Ct (45377-9675)
PHONE..............................937 890-7000
▼ **EMP:** 90 **EST:** 1978
SALES (est): 10.31MM
SALES (corp-wide): 10.31MM **Privately Held**
Web: www.exhibitconcepts.com
SIC: 7389 5032 2435 Exhibit construction by industrial contractors; Brick, stone, and related material; Hardwood veneer and plywood

(G-14940)
GE AVIATION SYSTEMS LLC
GE Aviation
740 E National Rd (45377-3062)
PHONE..............................937 898-5881
Victor Bonneau, *Brnch Mgr*
EMP: 300
SALES (corp-wide): 67.95B **Publicly Held**
Web: www.geaerospace.com
SIC: 3728 Aircraft parts and equipment, nec
HQ: Ge Aviation Systems Llc
1 Neumann Way
Cincinnati OH 45215
937 898-9600

(G-14941)
GE AVIATION SYSTEMS LLC
GE Aviation
740 E National Rd (45377-3062)
PHONE..............................937 898-5881
Victor Bonneau, *Brnch Mgr*
EMP: 300
SALES (corp-wide): 67.95B **Publicly Held**
Web: www.geaerospace.com
SIC: 3812 3643 3625 3624 Aircraft control systems, electronic; Current-carrying wiring services; Relays and industrial controls; Carbon and graphite products
HQ: Ge Aviation Systems Llc
1 Neumann Way
Cincinnati OH 45215
937 898-9600

(G-14942)
HERAEUS EPURIO LLC
Also Called: Heraeus Prcous Mtls N Amer Dyc
970 Industrial Park Dr (45377-3116)
PHONE..............................937 264-1000
Jrgen Heraeus, *Ch*
Robert Housman, *
Ram B Sharma, *
Santosh K Gupta, *
▲ **EMP:** 31 **EST:** 2012
SQ FT: 28,000
SALES (est): 23.63MM
SALES (corp-wide): 2.67MM **Privately Held**
Web: www.heraeus-group.com
SIC: 2869 2819 8731 Industrial organic chemicals, nec; Chemicals, high purity: refined from technical grade; Chemical laboratory, except testing
HQ: Heraeus Holding Gesellschaft Mit Beschrankter Haftung
Heraeusstr. 12-14
Hanau HE 63450
6181350

(G-14943)
HIGH TECH ELASTOMERS INC (PA)
885 Scholz Dr (45377-3121)
PHONE..............................937 236-6575
▲ **EMP:** 21 **EST:** 1996
SQ FT: 5,000
SALES (est): 2.25MM **Privately Held**
Web: www.htei.com
SIC: 3479 2822 Bonderizing of metal or metal products; Synthetic rubber

(G-14944)
INNOVATIVE PLASTIC MOLDERS LLC
10451 Dog Leg Rd Ste 200 (45377-7502)
PHONE..............................937 898-3775
Brian O' Leary, *Managing Member*
EMP: 50 **EST:** 2003
SQ FT: 12,800
SALES (est): 8.45MM **Privately Held**
Web: www.ipmolders.com
SIC: 3544 3089 Special dies, tools, jigs, and fixtures; Injection molding of plastics

(G-14945)
INTEVA PRODUCTS LLC
Inteva - Vandalia Engrg Ctr
707 Crossroads Ct (45377-9675)
P.O. Box 5051 (45377-5051)
PHONE..............................937 280-8500
EMP: 115
SALES (corp-wide): 3.26B **Privately Held**
Web: www.intevaproducts.com
SIC: 3714 Motor vehicle parts and accessories
HQ: Inteva Products, Llc
1401 Crooks Rd Ste 100
Troy MI 48084

(G-14946)
JB PAVERS AND HARDSCAPES LLC
812 E National Rd (45377-3016)
PHONE..............................937 454-1145
Jim Bliss, *Prin*
EMP: 8 **EST:** 2012
SALES (est): 494.36K **Privately Held**
Web: www.jbmulchco.com
SIC: 3531 Pavers

(G-14947)
MAC ITS LLC (PA)
Also Called: Compass Electronics Solutions
1625 Fieldstone Way (45377-9317)
PHONE..............................937 454-0722
EMP: 8 **EST:** 2017
SALES (est): 8.63MM
SALES (corp-wide): 8.63MM **Privately Held**
Web: www.mac-cable.com
SIC: 3355 Aluminum wire and cable

(G-14948)
MAHLE BEHR DAYTON LLC
250 Northwoods Blvd Bldg 47 (45377-9694)
PHONE..............................937 356-2001
Clayton Brown, *Manager*
EMP: 676
SALES (corp-wide): 3.75MM **Privately Held**
SIC: 3714 Motor vehicle parts and accessories
HQ: Mahle Behr Dayton L.L.C.
1600 Webster St
Dayton OH 45404
937 369-2900

(G-14949)
MAHLE BEHR USA INC
Also Called: Delphi

Vandalia - Montgomery County (G-14950)

250 Northwoods Blvd Bldg 47
(45377-9694)
PHONE..............................937 356-2001
Clayton Brown, *Brnch Mgr*
EMP: 176
SALES (corp-wide): 3.75MM **Privately Held**
SIC: 3714 Motor vehicle parts and accessories
HQ: Mahle Behr Usa Inc.
2700 Daley Dr
Troy MI 48083
248 743-3700

(G-14950)
MANUFCTRED ASSEMBLIES CORP LLC
1625 Fieldstone Way (45377-9317)
PHONE..............................937 454-0722
EMP: 47 **EST:** 2021
SALES (est): 1.82MM **Privately Held**
Web: www.mac-cable.com
SIC: 3999 Manufacturing industries, nec

(G-14951)
MASONITE CORPORATION
3250 Old Springfield Rd Ste 1 (45377)
PHONE..............................937 454-9207
EMP: 368
Web: www.masonite.com
SIC: 2431 Doors, wood
HQ: Masonite Corporation
1242 E 5th Ave
Tampa FL 33605
813 877-2726

(G-14952)
MASONITE INTERNATIONAL CORP
875 Center Dr (45377-3129)
PHONE..............................937 454-9308
Geroge Henderson, *Pr*
EMP: 7
SALES (corp-wide): 2.83B **Privately Held**
Web: www.masonite.com
SIC: 3441 3442 Fabricated structural metal; Metal doors, sash, and trim
PA: Masonite International Corporation
1242 E 5th Ave
Tampa FL 33605
813 877-2726

(G-14953)
MICROFINISH LLC
Also Called: Microfinish
865 Scholz Dr (45377-3121)
PHONE..............................937 264-1598
Dan O'connor, *Pr*
Bill J Jernigan, *
EMP: 60 **EST:** 1984
SQ FT: 8,000
SALES (est): 11.36MM
SALES (corp-wide): 158.19MM **Privately Held**
Web: www.microfinishusa.com
SIC: 3471 Electroplating of metals or formed products
HQ: Gnap, Llc
9000 Byron Commrce Dr Sw S
Byron Center MI 49315
616 583-5000

(G-14954)
MURPHY TRACTOR & EQP CO INC
Also Called: John Deere Authorized Dealer
1015 Industrial Park Dr (45377-3117)
PHONE..............................937 898-4198
EMP: 8
Web: www.murphytractor.com
SIC: 3531 5082 Construction machinery; Construction and mining machinery
HQ: Murphy Tractor & Equipment Co., Inc.
5375 N Deere Rd
Park City KS 67219
855 246-9124

(G-14955)
NIMERS & WOODY II INC (PA)
Also Called: M A C
1625 Fieldstone Way (45377-9317)
PHONE..............................937 454-0722
▲ **EMP:** 173 **EST:** 1976
SALES (est): 24.85MM
SALES (corp-wide): 24.85MM **Privately Held**
Web: www.mac-cable.com
SIC: 3699 5051 3679 Electrical equipment and supplies, nec; Cable, wire; Harness assemblies, for electronic use: wire or cable

(G-14956)
PARLEX USA LLC (DH)
801 Scholz Dr (45377-3121)
P.O. Box 427 (45377-0427)
PHONE..............................937 898-3621
Gary Wright, *Pr*
▲ **EMP:** 26 **EST:** 1970
SQ FT: 130,000
SALES (est): 19.18MM **Privately Held**
SIC: 3672 Wiring boards
HQ: Johnson Electric North America, Inc.
47660 Halyard Dr
Plymouth MI 48170
734 392-5300

(G-14957)
PERMA EDGE INDUSTRIES LLC
800 Scholz Dr (45377-3122)
PHONE..............................937 623-7819
EMP: 8 **EST:** 2016
SALES (est): 455.89K **Privately Held**
Web: www.permapaveredging.com
SIC: 3999 Manufacturing industries, nec

(G-14958)
SAIA-BURGESS LCC
Also Called: Ledex & Dormeyer Products
801 Scholz Dr (45377-3121)
PHONE..............................937 898-3621
Christopher Hasson, *Pr*
Gavin Fielden, *
Gordon Penman, *
Joel Philhours, *
▲ **EMP:** 100 **EST:** 2000
SQ FT: 105,000
SALES (est): 25.33MM **Privately Held**
SIC: 3714 3643 Motor vehicle parts and accessories; Electric switches
HQ: Johnson Electric North America, Inc.
47660 Halyard Dr
Plymouth MI 48170
734 392-5300

(G-14959)
SINBON OHIO LLC
Also Called: C & C Industries
815 S Brown School Rd (45377-9632)
PHONE..............................937 415-2070
Michael Seibert, *Prin*
Michael Seibert, *Managing Member*
Cindy Seibert, *
EMP: 135 **EST:** 1986
SQ FT: 40,000
SALES (est): 25.03MM **Privately Held**
SIC: 3672 Printed circuit boards

(G-14960)
SMYRNA READY MIX CONCRETE LLC
555 Old Springfield Rd (45377-9359)
PHONE..............................937 698-7229
EMP: 77
SALES (corp-wide): 1.05B **Privately Held**
Web: www.smyrnareadymix.com
SIC: 3273 Ready-mixed concrete
PA: Smyrna Ready Mix Concrete, Llc
1000 Hollingshead Cir
Murfreesboro TN 37129
615 355-1028

(G-14961)
SPECTRUM BRANDS INC
Also Called: Spectrum Brnds Globl Auto Care
2800 Concorde Dr (45377-3300)
PHONE..............................567 998-7930
EMP: 9
SALES (corp-wide): 2.92B **Publicly Held**
Web: www.spectrumbrands.com
SIC: 3691 Storage batteries
HQ: Spectrum Brands, Inc.
3001 Deming Way
Middleton WI 53562
608 275-3340

(G-14962)
TRIBORO QUILT MFG CORP
Also Called: TRIBORO QUILT MANUFACTURING CORPORATION
303 Corporate Center Dr Ste 108 (45377-1171)
PHONE..............................937 222-2132
EMP: 10
SALES (corp-wide): 23.16MM **Privately Held**
SIC: 3999 Atomizers, toiletry
PA: Cuddletime, Inc.
172 S Broadway
White Plains NY 10605
914 428-7551

(G-14963)
UNIBILT INDUSTRIES INC
8005 Johnson Station Rd (45377-8617)
P.O. Box 373 (45377-0373)
PHONE..............................937 890-7570
Douglas Scholz, *Pr*
Sharon Scholz, *
EMP: 50 **EST:** 1969
SQ FT: 80,000
SALES (est): 9.69MM **Privately Held**
Web: www.unibiltcustomhomes.com
SIC: 2452 Modular homes, prefabricated, wood

(G-14964)
VALMAC INDUSTRIES INC
825 Scholz Dr (45377-3121)
PHONE..............................937 890-5558
EMP: 21 **EST:** 1985
SALES (est): 1.73MM **Privately Held**
Web: www.valmacind.com
SIC: 3599 Machine and other job shop work

(G-14965)
VANDALIA MASSAGE THERAPY
147 W National Rd (45377-1934)
PHONE..............................937 890-8660
Rick Phillips, *Pt*
EMP: 7 **EST:** 1998
SALES (est): 634.82K **Privately Held**
Web: www.miamivalleymassage.com
SIC: 3999 7299 Massage machines, electric; barber and beauty shops; Massage parlor

(G-14966)
VANDALIA SPORTSWEAR LLC
515 S Dixie Dr (45377-2543)
PHONE..............................937 264-3204
EMP: 6 **EST:** 2013
SALES (est): 97.16K **Privately Held**
Web: www.fourinfinity.com
SIC: 5699 2759 T-shirts, custom printed; Screen printing

(G-14967)
WENTWORTH MOLD INC ELECTRA
Also Called: Electraform Industries Div
852 Scholz Dr (45377-3122)
PHONE..............................937 898-8460
Walter T Kuskowski, *CEO*
Tim Bright, *
Brian Karns, *
Ted W Kuskowski, *
Jeffrey D Barclay, *
▲ **EMP:** 60 **EST:** 1999
SQ FT: 65,000
SALES (est): 14.63MM
SALES (corp-wide): 2.62MM **Privately Held**
Web: www.electraform.com
SIC: 3544 3559 Forms (molds), for foundry and plastics working machinery; Plastics working machinery
PA: Wentworth Technologies Company Limited
156 Adams Blvd
Brantford ON
519 754-5400

(G-14968)
ZED INDUSTRIES INC
3580 Lightner Rd (45377)
P.O. Box 458 (45377)
PHONE..............................937 667-8407
Dave Zelnick, *Ch*
Peter Zelnick, *
Mark Zelnick, *
Helen Zelnick, *
EMP: 70 **EST:** 1969
SQ FT: 30,000
SALES (est): 9.64MM **Privately Held**
Web: www.zedindustries.com
SIC: 3559 Plastics working machinery

Vanlue
Hancock County

(G-14969)
D & H MEATS INC
400 Blanchard St (45890-8702)
P.O. Box 213 (45890-0213)
PHONE..............................419 387-7767
Jared Fry, *Pr*
EMP: 7 **EST:** 1976
SALES (est): 473.93K **Privately Held**
SIC: 2011 5421 Meat packing plants; Meat and fish markets

Venedocia
Van Wert County

(G-14970)
KRENDL RACK CO INC
18413 Haver Rd (45894-9420)
PHONE..............................419 667-4800
Tony Laman, *Pr*
Chris Koverman, *VP*
Jeff Koverman, *Treas*
Robin Laman, *Sec*
EMP: 8 **EST:** 1953
SQ FT: 12,000
SALES (est): 800K **Privately Held**
Web: www.krendlrack.com
SIC: 3471 5051 Electroplating and plating; Plates, metal

GEOGRAPHIC SECTION

Vermilion
Erie County

(G-14971)
ARCHITCTRAL INDUS MET FNSHG LL
Also Called: A & I Metal Finishing
1091 Sunnyside Rd (44089-2759)
PHONE..............................440 963-0410
EMP: 15 **EST:** 2004
SALES (est): 2.33MM **Privately Held**
Web: www.aimetalfinishing.com
SIC: 3479 Coating of metals and formed products

(G-14972)
IRG OPERATING LLC
Also Called: Cleveland Quarries
850 W River Rd (44089-1530)
PHONE..............................440 963-4008
EMP: 36 **EST:** 2007
SALES (est): 4.92MM **Privately Held**
Web: www.clevelandquarries.com
SIC: 1411 Sandstone, dimension-quarrying

(G-14973)
SOLO VINO IMPORTS LTD
450 Nicholson Rd (44089-2537)
PHONE..............................440 714-9591
Gerolama Bonderer, Prin
▲ **EMP:** 6 **EST:** 2013
SALES (est): 223.31K **Privately Held**
Web: www.solovinoimports.com
SIC: 5199 5812 2084 Advertising specialties; Italian restaurant; Wines

(G-14974)
VERMILION CUSTOM CANVAS INC
4523 Liberty Ave (44089-1909)
PHONE..............................440 963-5483
Leonard Davidson, Prin
EMP: 6 **EST:** 2014
SALES (est): 46.58K **Privately Held**
SIC: 2211 Canvas

Verona
Preble County

(G-14975)
KEYSTONE COOPERATIVE INC
Also Called: Verona Agriculture Center
141 S Commerce St (45378-5014)
P.O. Box 682 (45378-0682)
PHONE..............................937 884-5526
Rick Clark, Mgr
EMP: 8
SALES (corp-wide): 557.44MM **Privately Held**
Web: www.keystonecoop.com
SIC: 2873 2879 5261 5153 Nitrogenous fertilizers; Agricultural chemicals, nec; Fertilizer; Grain elevators
PA: Keystone Cooperative, Inc.
770 N High School Rd
Indianapolis IN 46214
800 525-0272

Versailles
Darke County

(G-14976)
ASPEN MACHINE AND PLASTICS
257 Baker Rd (45380-9317)
PHONE..............................937 526-4644
John Moran, Pr
Mary Moran, Sec
EMP: 7 **EST:** 2004
SALES (est): 645.8K **Privately Held**
SIC: 3599 Machine shop, jobbing and repair

(G-14977)
BEST BITE GRILL LLC
22 N Center St (45380-1201)
PHONE..............................419 344-7462
EMP: 10 **EST:** 2013
SALES (est): 143.59K **Privately Held**
Web: www.bestbitegrill.com
SIC: 5812 2099 Grills (eating places); Noodles, fried (Chinese)

(G-14978)
COTA INTERNATIONAL INC
67 Industrial Pkwy (45380-9759)
PHONE..............................937 526-5520
Linda Cota, Pr
Sandra Cota, VP
Phillip Cota, Sec
Craig Cota, Treas
▲ **EMP:** 10 **EST:** 2003
SQ FT: 5,000
SALES (est): 1.05MM **Privately Held**
Web: www.cotainternational.com
SIC: 3713 5065 Truck bodies and parts; Communication equipment

(G-14979)
DIRECT WIRE SERVICE LLP
100 Subler Dr (45380-9788)
PHONE..............................937 526-4447
Eric Barloge, Mng Pt
Dave Berger, Mng Pt
EMP: 8 **EST:** 2004
SQ FT: 6,000
SALES (est): 962.32K **Privately Held**
Web: www.directtoolingconcepts.com
SIC: 3544 Special dies and tools

(G-14980)
G & C RAW LLC
Also Called: G & C Raw Dog Food
225 N West St (45380-1359)
PHONE..............................937 827-0010
Cathy Manning, Managing Member
EMP: 9 **EST:** 2012
SQ FT: 1,800
SALES (est): 970.39K **Privately Held**
Web: www.gandcrawdogfood.com
SIC: 2047 Dog food

(G-14981)
INSPIRTEC LLC
10203 Christian Rd (45380-9580)
P.O. Box 215 (45322-0215)
PHONE..............................614 571-7130
EMP: 6 **EST:** 2019
SALES (est): 917.15K **Privately Held**
SIC: 2873 Fertilizers: natural (organic), except compost

(G-14982)
J & K PALLET INC
30 Subler Dr (45380-9782)
PHONE..............................937 526-5117
John Shardo, Pr
Jerry Shardo, VP
EMP: 6 **EST:** 1989
SQ FT: 24,000
SALES (est): 704.08K **Privately Held**
SIC: 2448 Pallets, wood

(G-14983)
KAMPS INC
Also Called: Pallets-Fam-In-place-packaging
10709 Reed Rd (45380-9701)
PHONE..............................937 526-9333
Nick Schaller, Brnch Mgr
EMP: 6
SALES (corp-wide): 1.74B **Privately Held**
Web: www.kampspallets.com
SIC: 2448 Pallets, wood
HQ: Kamps, Inc.
665 Seward Ave Nw Ste 301
Grand Rapids MI 49504
616 453-9676

(G-14984)
KINGS COMMAND FOODS 2022 LLC ✪
770 N Center St (45380-9610)
PHONE..............................937 827-7131
Steve Wright, Pr
EMP: 29 **EST:** 2022
SALES (est): 10.99MM
SALES (corp-wide): 4.49B **Privately Held**
SIC: 2011 Meat packing plants
PA: Premium Brands Holdings Corporation
100-10991 Shellbridge Way
Richmond BC V6X 3
604 465-3100

(G-14985)
KNAPKE CUSTOM CABINETRY LTD
Also Called: Knapke Custom Cabinetry
9306 Kelch Rd (45380-9679)
PHONE..............................937 459-8866
EMP: 7 **EST:** 1992
SQ FT: 8,800
SALES (est): 467.59K **Privately Held**
Web: www.knapkekitchensandbaths.com
SIC: 2434 Wood kitchen cabinets

(G-14986)
MIDMARK CORPORATION
60 Vista Dr (45380-9310)
PHONE..............................937 526-3662
EMP: 9
SALES (corp-wide): 187.17K **Privately Held**
Web: www.midmark.com
SIC: 3648 3842 3843 2542 Lighting equipment, nec; Stretchers; Dental equipment and supplies; Partitions and fixtures, except wood
PA: Midmark Corporation
10170 Penny Ln Ste 300
Miamisburg OH 45342
937 528-7500

(G-14987)
MIDMARK CORPORATION
160 Industrial Parkway (45380-9757)
PHONE..............................937 526-8387
EMP: 33
SALES (corp-wide): 187.17K **Privately Held**
Web: www.midmark.com
SIC: 3648 Lighting equipment, nec
PA: Midmark Corporation
10170 Penny Ln Ste 300
Miamisburg OH 45342
937 528-7500

(G-14988)
PRECISION FAB PRODUCTS INC
10061 Old State Route 121 (45380-9586)
P.O. Box 256 (45380-0256)
PHONE..............................937 526-5681
Eric D Miller, CEO
Cindy Miller, Pr
David Miller, Treas
EMP: 6 **EST:** 1985
SQ FT: 40,000
SALES (est): 822.46K **Privately Held**
Web: www.pfpfoam.com
SIC: 3069 5712 Foam rubber; Furniture stores

(G-14989)
SMITH PALLET LLC
9855 State Route 121 (45380-9512)
PHONE..............................937 564-6492
Joan M Smith, Prin
EMP: 7 **EST:** 2009
SALES (est): 114.69K **Privately Held**
SIC: 2448 Pallets, wood and wood with metal

(G-14990)
VERSAILLES BUILDING SUPPLY
741 N Center St (45380-1512)
P.O. Box 236 (45380-0236)
PHONE..............................937 526-3238
Richard P Huelsman, Pr
EMP: 7 **EST:** 1948
SQ FT: 14,000
SALES (est): 489.72K **Privately Held**
Web: www.versaillesohio.cc
SIC: 2431 Doors, wood

(G-14991)
VPP INDUSTRIES INC
960 E Main St (45380-1555)
P.O. Box 53 (45380-0053)
PHONE..............................937 526-3775
Vernon Monnin, Pr
Jane Monnin, VP
EMP: 10 **EST:** 1925
SQ FT: 9,600
SALES (est): 1.24MM **Privately Held**
Web: www.vppind.com
SIC: 2752 Offset printing

(G-14992)
WEAVER BROS INC (PA)
Also Called: Tri County Eggs
895 E Main St (45380-1533)
P.O. Box 333 (45380-0333)
PHONE..............................937 526-3907
Timothy John Weaver, Pr
Kreg Kohli, *
Audrey Weaver, *
Geo L Weaver, *
John D Weaver, *
▲ **EMP:** 60 **EST:** 1931
SQ FT: 20,000
SALES (est): 24.19MM
SALES (corp-wide): 24.19MM **Privately Held**
Web: www.weavereggs.com
SIC: 0252 5143 2015 Chicken eggs; Dairy products, except dried or canned; Poultry slaughtering and processing

(G-14993)
WINERY AT WILCOX INC
6572 State Route 47 (45380-9551)
PHONE..............................937 526-3232
Ralph M Williams, Admn
EMP: 7
Web: www.wineryatwilcox.com
SIC: 2084 Wines
PA: The Winery At Wilcox Inc
1867 Mefferts Run Rd
Wilcox PA 15870

Vienna
Trumbull County

(G-14994)
APTIV SERVICES US LLC
Also Called: Delphi
3400 Aero Park Dr (44473-8704)
P.O. Box 431 (44486-0001)
PHONE..............................330 367-6000
Ken Ellsworth, Brnch Mgr
EMP: 120
SALES (corp-wide): 20.05B **Privately Held**

Vienna - Trumbull County (G-14995)

Web: www.aptiv.com
SIC: 3714 Motor vehicle parts and accessories
HQ: Aptiv Services Us, Llc
5725 Innovation Dr
Troy MI 48098

(G-14995)
CLARKWSTERN DTRICH BLDG SYSTEM
1455 Ridge Rd (44473-9702)
PHONE..................330 372-4014
Terry Westerman, *Brnch Mgr*
EMP: 25
SALES (corp-wide): 4.92B **Publicly Held**
Web: www.clarkdietrich.com
SIC: 3441 Fabricated structural metal
HQ: Clarkwestern Dietrich Building Systems Llc
9050 Cntre Pnte Dr Ste 40
West Chester OH 45069

(G-14996)
KUNDEL INDUSTRIES INC (PA)
Also Called: Kundel
1510 Ridge Rd (44473-9704)
P.O. Box 4686 (44515-0686)
PHONE..................330 469-6147
▲ EMP: 44 EST: 1987
SALES (est): 7.01MM
SALES (corp-wide): 7.01MM **Privately Held**
Web: www.kundel.com
SIC: 3531 3536 3444 Construction machinery; Hoists, cranes, and monorails; Sheet metalwork

(G-14997)
LATROBE SPCIALTY MTLS DIST INC (HQ)
1551 Vienna Pkwy (44473-8703)
PHONE..................330 609-5137
Gregory A Pratt, *Ch Bd*
Timothy R Armstrong, *
Thomas F Cramsey, *
James D Dee, *
Matthew S Enoch, *
◆ EMP: 80 EST: 1996
SQ FT: 189,000
SALES (est): 22.1MM
SALES (corp-wide): 2.55B **Publicly Held**
SIC: 3312 5051 Stainless steel; Steel
PA: Carpenter Technology Corporation
1735 Market St Fl 15
Philadelphia PA 19103
610 208-2000

(G-14998)
LITCO CORNER PROTECTION LLC
Also Called: Litco Cornerguard, LLC
1000 Tuscarawas St E (44473)
PHONE..................330 539-5433
Lionel Trebilcock, *Managing Member*
EMP: 15 EST: 2021
SALES (est): 1.51MM
SALES (corp-wide): 22.35MM **Privately Held**
Web: www.litcomfg.com
SIC: 2653 Corrugated and solid fiber boxes
PA: Litco International, Inc.
1 Litco Dr
Vienna OH 44473
330 539-5433

(G-14999)
LITCO INTERNATIONAL INC (PA)
1 Litco Dr (44473-9600)
P.O. Box 150 (44473-0150)
PHONE..................330 539-5433
Lionel Trebilcock, *CEO*
Gary Trebilcock, *

Gary Sharon, *
◆ EMP: 88 EST: 1962
SQ FT: 13,000
SALES (est): 22.35MM
SALES (corp-wide): 22.35MM **Privately Held**
Web: www.litco.com
SIC: 2448 5031 Pallets, wood; Particleboard

(G-15000)
MACK INDUSTRIES PA INC
2207 Sodom Hutchings Rd Ne (44473)
PHONE..................330 638-7680
Ron Hoover, *Mgr*
EMP: 73
SALES (corp-wide): 134.58MM **Privately Held**
Web: www.mackconcrete.com
SIC: 3589 3272 Sewage treatment equipment; Concrete products, nec
HQ: Mack Industries Of Pennsylvania, Inc.
201 Columbia Rd
Valley City OH 44280
330 483-3111

(G-15001)
MILLWOOD INC
Liberty Industries
1328 Ridge Rd (44473-9702)
PHONE..................330 609-0220
Ronald C Ringness, *Sr VP*
EMP: 54
Web: www.millwoodinc.com
SIC: 2448 Pallets, wood
PA: Millwood, Inc.
3708 International Blvd
Vienna OH 44473

(G-15002)
MILLWOOD NATURAL LLC
3708 International Blvd (44473-9796)
PHONE..................330 393-4400
Lionel Trebilcock, *Pt*
EMP: 30 EST: 2013
SALES (est): 2.2MM **Privately Held**
Web: www.millwoodinc.com
SIC: 3565 4731 Packaging machinery; Freight transportation arrangement
PA: Millwood, Inc.
3708 International Blvd
Vienna OH 44473

(G-15003)
RIVERSIDE STEEL INC
3102 Warren Sharon Rd (44473-9521)
PHONE..................330 856-5299
John Radu Junior, *Pr*
John Radu Senior, *Ch*
Catherine Radu, *Sec*
▼ EMP: 11 EST: 1966
SQ FT: 38,000
SALES (est): 1.8MM **Privately Held**
Web: www.riverside-steel.com
SIC: 3441 Fabricated structural metal

(G-15004)
STARR FABRICATING INC
4175 Warren Sharon Rd (44473-9524)
PHONE..................330 394-9891
Thomas B Smith, *Pr*
EMP: 77 EST: 1965
SALES (est): 6.82MM **Privately Held**
Web: www.starrmfg.com
SIC: 3441 3564 3496 3444 Fabricated structural metal; Blowers and fans; Miscellaneous fabricated wire products; Sheet metalwork

(G-15005)
WATER DROP MEDIA INC
289 Youngstown Kingsville Rd Se (44473-9656)
PHONE..................234 600-5817
Dustin Ghizzoni, *Prin*
EMP: 7 EST: 2012
SALES (est): 237.41K **Privately Held**
Web: www.waterdropmedia.com
SIC: 4899 5999 5099 2759 Data communication services; Banners, flags, decals, and posters; Signs, except electric; Screen printing

Vincent
Washington County

(G-15006)
BLANEY HARDWOODS OHIO INC
425 Timberline Dr (45784-5615)
PHONE..................740 678-8288
Randal Blaney, *Pr*
James Blaney, *
EMP: 100 EST: 1978
SQ FT: 3,000
SALES (est): 7.66MM **Privately Held**
SIC: 2421 Kiln drying of lumber

(G-15007)
DECKER DRILLING INC
11565 State Route 676 (45784-5636)
PHONE..................740 749-3939
Dean Decker, *Pr*
Pat Decker, *
EMP: 14 EST: 1999
SALES (est): 2.14MM **Privately Held**
Web: www.deckerdrilling.com
SIC: 1381 Redrilling oil and gas wells

(G-15008)
HENDRICKSON
1051 Windy Ridge Rd (45784-5226)
PHONE..................740 678-8033
Clyde Hendrickson, *Prin*
EMP: 11 EST: 2010
SALES (est): 61.69K **Privately Held**
Web: www.hendrickson-intl.com
SIC: 3714 Motor vehicle parts and accessories

(G-15009)
MICRO MACHINE WORKS INC
8900 State Route 339 (45784-5411)
P.O. Box 70 (45712-0070)
PHONE..................740 678-8471
Linn Yost, *Pr*
Dan Anstatt, *Mgr*
David Yost, *Mgr*
EMP: 17 EST: 1992
SQ FT: 6,592
SALES (est): 1.7MM **Privately Held**
SIC: 3599 Machine shop, jobbing and repair

(G-15010)
VINCENT RX LLC ✪
Also Called: White Oak Pharmacy
8465 State Route 339 (45784-5647)
PHONE..................740 678-2384
Heli Chaudhari, *Prin*
EMP: 6 EST: 2022
SALES (est): 352.05K **Privately Held**
SIC: 2834 Pharmaceutical preparations

Vinton
Gallia County

(G-15011)
IVI MINING GROUP LTD
72116 Grey Rd (45686-8410)
P.O. Box 1101 (45640-7101)
PHONE..................740 418-7745
Jesse Sizemore, *Ch Bd*
EMP: 7 EST: 2014
SQ FT: 5,000
SALES (est): 176K **Privately Held**
SIC: 1041 1221 1222 Placer gold mining; Bituminous coal surface mining; Bituminous coal-underground mining

(G-15012)
STEELIAL WLDG MET FBRCTION INC
Also Called: Steelial Cnctr Mot Fabrication
70764 State Route 124 (45686-8545)
PHONE..................740 669-5300
Larry Allen Hedrick Junior, *Pr*
Krista Lynnete Hedrick, *
EMP: 32 EST: 1998
SQ FT: 40,000
SALES (est): 7.66MM **Privately Held**
Web: www.steelial.com
SIC: 1623 3441 3444 Pipe laying construction; Fabricated structural metal; Sheet metalwork

W Carrollton
Montgomery County

(G-15013)
FIRE & IRON
538 Maple Hill Dr (45449-1766)
PHONE..................937 470-8536
Russell Fortner, *Prin*
EMP: 6 EST: 2017
SALES (est): 55.59K **Privately Held**
Web: www.fireandiron.co.uk
SIC: 2711 Newspapers, publishing and printing

Wadsworth
Medina County

(G-15014)
ACCEL GROUP INC (PA)
325 Quadral Dr (44281-9571)
PHONE..................330 336-0317
James Terranova, *Pr*
▲ EMP: 84 EST: 1980
SQ FT: 191,000
SALES (est): 14.63MM
SALES (corp-wide): 14.63MM **Privately Held**
Web: www.accelgrp.com
SIC: 2542 Partitions and fixtures, except wood

(G-15015)
ADVANCED PLASTICS INC
590 Corporate Pkwy (44281-8398)
PHONE..................330 336-6681
Phil Nye, *Pr*
John Davis, *VP*
EMP: 21 EST: 1999
SQ FT: 12,000
SALES (est): 1.9MM **Privately Held**
Web: www.advancedplastics.net
SIC: 3089 Injection molding of plastics

GEOGRAPHIC SECTION

Wadsworth - Medina County (G-15041)

(G-15016)
AKRON PRODUCTS COMPANY
6600 Ridge Rd (44281-9743)
PHONE..................................330 576-1750
Chester Marshall Junior, *CEO*
EMP: 75 **EST:** 1945
SQ FT: 45,000
SALES (est): 6.33MM **Privately Held**
Web: www.akronproducts.com
SIC: 3446 Fences or posts, ornamental iron or steel

(G-15017)
AL FE HEAT TREATING-OHIO INC
979 Seville Rd (44281-8316)
PHONE..................................330 336-0211
Steve Turner, *Mgr*
EMP: 20
Web: www.aalberts-ht.us
SIC: 3398 Metal heat treating
PA: Al Fe Heat Treating-Ohio, Inc
209 W Mount Hope Ave # 1
Lansing MI 48910

(G-15018)
ALTERNATIVE FLASH INC
1734 Wall Rd Ste B (44281-8354)
PHONE..................................330 334-6111
Daniel Broadbent, *Pr*
Angelo Savakis, *Sec*
EMP: 10 **EST:** 1989
SQ FT: 20,000
SALES (est): 386.26K **Privately Held**
Web: www.alternativeflash.com
SIC: 3061 3544 3398 Mechanical rubber goods; Special dies, tools, jigs, and fixtures; Metal heat treating

(G-15019)
AMERICAN PRO-MOLD INC
350 State St # 7 (44281-1093)
P.O. Box 325 (44282-0325)
PHONE..................................330 336-4111
Edward F Steinkerchner, *Pr*
Mark E Steinkerchner, *VP*
Roberta Steinkerchner, *Sec*
EMP: 17 **EST:** 1978
SQ FT: 10,000
SALES (est): 171.66K **Privately Held**
SIC: 3069 3061 Molded rubber products; Mechanical rubber goods

(G-15020)
BMCA INSULATION PRODUCTS INC
270 Main St (44281-1446)
PHONE..................................330 335-2501
Harley Cummings, *Mgr*
EMP: 12
SALES (corp-wide): 6.27B **Privately Held**
SIC: 2493 Insulation and roofing material, reconstituted wood
HQ: Bmca Insulation Products Inc.
1361 Alps Rd
Wayne NJ

(G-15021)
C J WOODWORKING INC
8676 Markley Dr (44281-8338)
PHONE..................................330 607-4221
Curt Lauer, *Prin*
EMP: 6 **EST:** 2019
SALES (est): 54.13K **Privately Held**
SIC: 2431 Millwork

(G-15022)
CELL-O-CORE CO
276 College St (44281-1575)
PHONE..................................800 239-4370
Craig Cook, *Pr*
EMP: 13 **EST:** 1962
SALES (est): 161.88K **Privately Held**
Web: www.cellocore.com
SIC: 3089 Plastics containers, except foam

(G-15023)
CLAMPCO PRODUCTS INC (PA)
Also Called: Clampco
1743 Wall Rd (44281-9558)
PHONE..................................330 336-8857
James R Venner, *Pr*
Linda Venner, *
◆ **EMP:** 182 **EST:** 1971
SQ FT: 54,000
SALES (est): 35.34MM
SALES (corp-wide): 35.34MM **Privately Held**
Web: www.clampco.com
SIC: 3429 Clamps, metal

(G-15024)
CUSTOM SPORTSWEAR IMPRINTS LLC
238 High St (44281-1861)
PHONE..................................330 335-8326
EMP: 9 **EST:** 1981
SQ FT: 3,000
SALES (est): 1.07MM **Privately Held**
SIC: 5199 2759 7389 Advertising specialties; Screen printing; Embroidery advertising

(G-15025)
D & J ELECTRIC MOTOR REPAIR CO
Also Called: Ohio Belt Control Supply Co
1734 Wall Rd Office (44281-8356)
PHONE..................................330 336-4343
David Zuchniak, *Pr*
John Zuchniak, *VP*
EMP: 10 **EST:** 1973
SQ FT: 20,000
SALES (est): 905.9K **Privately Held**
SIC: 5013 7694 7629 1731 Automotive servicing equipment; Electric motor repair; Electrical equipment repair services; General electrical contractor

(G-15026)
DESHEA PRINTING COMPANY
Also Called: Aldridge Folders
924 Seville Rd (44281-8316)
PHONE..................................330 336-7601
Sherri Gasser, *Pr*
EMP: 6 **EST:** 2015
SALES (est): 474.8K **Privately Held**
Web: www.aldridgefolders.com
SIC: 2752 Photo-offset printing

(G-15027)
E D M STAR-ONE INC
6831 Ridge Rd (44281-8590)
PHONE..................................440 647-0600
Howard White, *Pr*
Samuel White, *VP*
Michael White, *Treas*
Timothy White, *Sec*
EMP: 10 **EST:** 1989
SALES (est): 1.03MM **Privately Held**
Web: www.advancedresources.us
SIC: 3599 Machine shop, jobbing and repair

(G-15028)
EBNER FURNACES INC
Also Called: Ebnerfab
224 Quadral Dr (44281-8327)
PHONE..................................330 335-2311
Robert Ebner, *Pr*
Ralph Myers, *
◆ **EMP:** 80 **EST:** 1986
SQ FT: 150,000
SALES (est): 23MM
SALES (corp-wide): 171.36MM **Privately Held**
Web: www.ebnerfab.com
SIC: 3567 3444 3433 3441 Industrial furnaces and ovens; Sheet metalwork; Heating equipment, except electric; Fabricated structural metal
HQ: Ebner Verwaltung Gmbh
Ebner-Platz 1
Leonding 4060
73268680

(G-15029)
FIVES ST CORP
1 Park Centre Dr Ste 210 (44281-9482)
PHONE..................................234 217-9070
Daniel Balcer, *Pr*
▲ **EMP:** 21 **EST:** 2010
SQ FT: 7,000
SALES (est): 5.01MM
SALES (corp-wide): 409.51MM **Privately Held**
Web: www.fivesgroup.com
SIC: 3531 Construction machinery
HQ: Fives Stein
108 A 112
Maisons Alfort 94700

(G-15030)
FOUNDATION WELLNESS
961 Seville Rd (44281-8316)
PHONE..................................330 335-1571
EMP: 8 **EST:** 2020
SALES (est): 293.12K **Privately Held**
Web: www.foundationwellness.com
SIC: 3069 Boot or shoe products, rubber

(G-15031)
FRONT POCKET INNOVATIONS LLC
471 E Bergey St Ste C (44281-2097)
PHONE..................................330 441-2365
Graig Davis, *CEO*
EMP: 7 **EST:** 2015
SALES (est): 545.78K **Privately Held**
Web: www.theneomag.com
SIC: 5531 3949 3999 Automotive accessories; Sporting and athletic goods, nec; Manufacturing industries, nec

(G-15032)
GOLDSMITH & EGGLETON INC
300 1st St (44281-2084)
PHONE..................................330 336-6616
▲ **EMP:** 18
SIC: 2821 3069 5169 Plastics materials and resins; Reclaimed rubber (reworked by manufacturing processes); Synthetic rubber

(G-15033)
GOLDSMITH & EGGLETON LLC
300 1st St (44281-2084)
PHONE..................................203 855-6000
David Derhagopian, *Managing Member*
▲ **EMP:** 18 **EST:** 2012
SALES (est): 5.8MM **Privately Held**
Web: www.goldsmith-eggleton.com
SIC: 2821 3069 5169 Plastics materials and resins; Reclaimed rubber (reworked by manufacturing processes); Synthetic rubber
PA: Ravago Holdings America, Inc.
1900 Smmit Twr Blvd Ste 9
Orlando FL 32810

(G-15034)
H & S TOOL INC
715 Weber Dr (44281-9550)
P.O. Box 393 (44282-0393)
PHONE..................................330 335-1536
Mark W Hillestad, *Pr*
EMP: 19 **EST:** 1972
SQ FT: 12,500
SALES (est): 4.93MM **Privately Held**
Web: www.climaxportable.com

SIC: 3545 Tools and accessories for machine tools

(G-15035)
HUTNIK COMPANY
Also Called: Ohio Engineering and Mfg Co
350 State St Ste 5 (44281-2417)
PHONE..................................330 336-9700
EMP: 6 **EST:** 1994
SQ FT: 5,000
SALES (est): 485.74K **Privately Held**
Web: www.ohioengr.com
SIC: 3599 3443 7389 Machine shop, jobbing and repair; Cylinders, pressure: metal plate; Design, commercial and industrial

(G-15036)
ICECAP LLC
514 Arcadia Rd (44281-8895)
PHONE..................................216 548-4145
EMP: 8 **EST:** 2012
SALES (est): 78.11K **Privately Held**
SIC: 2431 Millwork

(G-15037)
J C WHITLAM MANUFACTURING CO
200 W Walnut St (44281-1379)
P.O. Box 380 (44282-0380)
PHONE..................................330 334-2524
◆ **EMP:** 22 **EST:** 1900
SALES (est): 6.23MM **Privately Held**
Web: www.jcwhitlam.com
SIC: 2891 2899 2851 2992 Adhesives and sealants; Chemical preparations, nec; Enamels, nec; Lubricating oils and greases

(G-15038)
JERICO PLASTIC INDUSTRIES INC (PA)
Also Called: Jerico Industries
7970 Boneta Rd (44281-8406)
PHONE..................................330 868-4600
EMP: 20 **EST:** 1996
SQ FT: 53,000
SALES (est): 8.52MM **Privately Held**
Web: www.jericoplastic.com
SIC: 2821 Plastics materials and resins

(G-15039)
KEELER ENTERPRISES INC
Also Called: Aldridge Folders
924 Seville Rd (44281-8316)
PHONE..................................330 336-7601
Fred Keeler, *Pr*
Daniel Mills, *VP*
Sheri Gasser, *Treas*
EMP: 8 **EST:** 1974
SQ FT: 10,000
SALES (est): 688.07K **Privately Held**
Web: www.aldridgefolders.com
SIC: 2675 2678 Folders, filing, die-cut: made from purchased materials; Stationery products

(G-15040)
KLEEN POLYMERS INC
145 Rainbow St (44281-1478)
EMP: 13 **EST:** 1991
SQ FT: 8,000
SALES (est): 974.03K **Privately Held**
Web: www.kleenpolymers.com
SIC: 3061 Mechanical rubber goods

(G-15041)
KRAMER & KIEFER INC
Also Called: Medina Tool & Die
2662 Valley Side Ave (44281-9233)
P.O. Box 24 (44258-0024)
PHONE..................................330 336-8742
Clayton Kramer, *Pr*

Wadsworth - Medina County (G-15042)

Robert Kiefer, *VP*
EMP: 6 **EST:** 1950
SQ FT: 6,500
SALES (est): 490.79K **Privately Held**
SIC: 3544 Special dies and tools

(G-15042)
LABELTEK INC
985 Seville Rd (44281-8316)
PHONE..................................330 335-3110
EMP: 58
SIC: 2759 Labels and seals: printing, nsk

(G-15043)
LUKE ENGINEERING & MFG CORP (PA)
Also Called: Luke Engineering & Mfg
456 South Blvd (44281-2032)
P.O. Box 478 (44282-0478)
PHONE..................................330 335-1501
Fred P Hayduk, *Pr*
Chris Jurey, *
◆ **EMP:** 40 **EST:** 1946
SQ FT: 37,000
SALES (est): 8.71MM
SALES (corp-wide): 8.71MM **Privately Held**
Web: www.lukeeng.com
SIC: 3471 3559 Anodizing (plating) of metals or formed products; Metal finishing equipment for plating, etc.

(G-15044)
MICHAEL DAY ENTERPRISES LLC
9774 Trease Rd (44281-9557)
P.O. Box 151 (44282-0151)
PHONE..................................330 335-5100
Michael F Day, *Pr*
EMP: 20 **EST:** 2010
SALES (est): 4.74MM **Privately Held**
Web: www.mdayinc.com
SIC: 2821 Molding compounds, plastics

(G-15045)
MILLER PRODUCTS INC
Mpi Label Systems Div
985 Seville Rd (44281-8316)
PHONE..................................330 335-3110
Randy L Kocher, *Pr*
EMP: 14
SALES (corp-wide): 70.41MM **Privately Held**
Web: www.mpilabels.com
SIC: 2759 Labels and seals: printing, nsk
PA: Miller Products, Inc.
450 Courtney Rd
Sebring OH 44672
330 938-2134

(G-15046)
MILLER PRODUCTS INC
Also Called: M P I Labeltek
985 Seville Rd (44281-8316)
PHONE..................................330 335-3110
Ronald Nagy, *Brnch Mgr*
EMP: 58
SALES (corp-wide): 70.41MM **Privately Held**
Web: www.mpilabels.com
SIC: 2759 Labels and seals: printing, nsk
PA: Miller Products, Inc.
450 Courtney Rd
Sebring OH 44672
330 938-2134

(G-15047)
MYERS INDUSTRIES INC
Akro-Mils
250 Seville Rd (44281-1020)
P.O. Box 989 (44309-0989)
PHONE..................................330 336-6621

Gary Taylor, *Mgr*
EMP: 96
SQ FT: 10,000
SALES (corp-wide): 813.07MM **Publicly Held**
Web: www.myersindustries.com
SIC: 3052 3069 3443 2542 Automobile hose, rubber; Rubber automotive products; Fabricated plate work (boiler shop); Partitions and fixtures, except wood
PA: Myers Industries, Inc.
1293 S Main St
Akron OH 44301
330 253-5592

(G-15048)
NO BURN INC
1392 High St Ste 211 (44281-8262)
PHONE..................................330 336-1500
William Kish, *Pr*
EMP: 8 **EST:** 1998
SQ FT: 4,000
SALES (est): 2.41MM **Privately Held**
Web: www.noburn.com
SIC: 2899 Fire retardant chemicals

(G-15049)
NOVEX OPERATING COMPANY LLC ✪
258 Main St (44281-1446)
PHONE..................................330 335-2371
EMP: 14 **EST:** 2022
SALES (est): 575.35K **Privately Held**
SIC: 3052 3069 Rubber belting; Sheets, hard rubber

(G-15050)
P C M CO (PA)
291 W Bergey St (44281-1334)
P.O. Box 479 (44282-0479)
PHONE..................................330 336-8040
Duane Coffman, *Pr*
Brannon Riley, *
Paul Bebout, *
Seng Sisouphanah, *
Emma Momchilov, *Stockholder**
EMP: 37 **EST:** 1965
SALES (est): 4.5MM
SALES (corp-wide): 4.5MM **Privately Held**
SIC: 3365 Aluminum and aluminum-based alloy castings

(G-15051)
PARKER-HANNIFIN CORPORATION
Pneumatic North America
135 Quadral Dr (44281-8326)
PHONE..................................330 336-3511
Bill Treacy, *Brnch Mgr*
EMP: 42
SALES (corp-wide): 19.07B **Publicly Held**
Web: www.parker.com
SIC: 3621 3643 3593 Electric motor and generator parts; Current-carrying wiring services; Fluid power cylinders and actuators
PA: Parker-Hannifin Corporation
6035 Parkland Blvd
Cleveland OH 44124
216 896-3000

(G-15052)
PARKER-HANNIFIN CORPORATION
Also Called: Ips
135 Quadral Dr (44281-8326)
PHONE..................................330 335-6740
Barbara Mccall, *Brnch Mgr*
EMP: 6
SALES (corp-wide): 19.07B **Publicly Held**
Web: www.parker.com
SIC: 3569 Lubricating systems, centralized
PA: Parker-Hannifin Corporation

6035 Parkland Blvd
Cleveland OH 44124
216 896-3000

(G-15053)
PLASTICS R UNIQUE INC
330 Grandview Ave (44281-1161)
PHONE..................................330 334-4820
Kenneth R Boersma, *Pr*
EMP: 30 **EST:** 1988
SQ FT: 12,300
SALES (est): 5MM **Privately Held**
Web: www.plasticsrunique.com
SIC: 3089 5162 Plastics containers, except foam; Plastics materials, nec

(G-15054)
PREMIUM BALLOON ACC INC
Also Called: Premium Balloon Accessories
6935 Ridge Rd (44281-9706)
P.O. Box 352 (44274-0352)
PHONE..................................330 239-4547
◆ **EMP:** 27 **EST:** 1945
SALES (est): 2.29MM **Privately Held**
Web: www.premiumballoon.com
SIC: 3089 Plastics containers, except foam

(G-15055)
PROFILE RUBBER CORPORATION
6784 Ridge Rd (44281-9743)
P.O. Box 299 (44274-0299)
PHONE..................................330 239-1703
Lewis Winland, *CEO*
John Winland, *Pr*
Jeff Winland, *VP*
EMP: 14 **EST:** 1961
SQ FT: 12,000
SALES (est): 197.24K **Privately Held**
Web: www.profilerubber.com
SIC: 3069 Molded rubber products

(G-15056)
PT TECH LLC (HQ)
1441 Wolf Creek Trl (44281-9742)
P.O. Box 305 (44282-0305)
PHONE..................................330 239-4933
Richard Kyle, *Pr*
EMP: 98 **EST:** 1978
SQ FT: 45,000
SALES (est): 20.9MM
SALES (corp-wide): 4.77B **Publicly Held**
Web: www.pttech.com
SIC: 3714 Clutches, motor vehicle
PA: The Timken Company
4500 Mount Pleasant St Nw
North Canton OH 44720
234 262-3000

(G-15057)
QUALIFORM INC
689 Weber Dr (44281-9550)
PHONE..................................330 336-6777
Andy Antonino, *Pr*
EMP: 40 **EST:** 1976
SQ FT: 17,000
SALES (est): 4.8MM **Privately Held**
Web: www.qualiformrubbermolding.com
SIC: 3069 3544 3061 Molded rubber products; Special dies, tools, jigs, and fixtures; Mechanical rubber goods

(G-15058)
QUALITY REPRODUCTIONS INC
Also Called: Fine Lines
127 Hartman Rd (44281-9402)
PHONE..................................330 335-5000
Bob Grosser, *Pr*
EMP: 9 **EST:** 1985
SQ FT: 7,000
SALES (est): 1.55MM **Privately Held**
Web: www.sstubes.com

SIC: 3714 Motor vehicle parts and accessories

(G-15059)
RADICI PLASTICS USA INC (DH)
960 Seville Rd (44281-8316)
PHONE..................................330 336-7611
Michael Cain, *CEO*
Danilo Micheletti, *
Mattia Imberti, *
◆ **EMP:** 29 **EST:** 1989
SQ FT: 235,000
SALES (est): 52.18MM
SALES (corp-wide): 1.6B **Privately Held**
Web: www.radicigroup.com
SIC: 3087 3089 Custom compound purchased resins; Plastics processing
HQ: Radici Novacips Spa
Via Bedeschi 20
Chignolo D'Isola BG 24040
035 499-7689

(G-15060)
RAINS PLASTICS INC
873 Kings Cross Dr (44281-8902)
PHONE..................................330 283-3768
Todd Rains, *Prin*
EMP: 8 **EST:** 2012
SALES (est): 239.52K **Privately Held**
SIC: 3089 Injection molding of plastics

(G-15061)
RAYDAR INC OF OHIO
1734 Wall Rd Ste B (44281-8354)
PHONE..................................330 334-6111
EMP: 8 **EST:** 1995
SALES (est): 783.38K **Privately Held**
SIC: 3069 Molded rubber products

(G-15062)
RBA INC
487 College St (44281-1105)
PHONE..................................330 336-6700
Robert Bault, *Pr*
Jane Haugh, *Sec*
EMP: 8 **EST:** 1974
SQ FT: 7,000
SALES (est): 800K **Privately Held**
SIC: 2752 7336 Offset printing; Graphic arts and related design

(G-15063)
ROHRER CORPORATION (HQ)
Also Called: Gateway Printing
717 Seville Rd (44281-1091)
P.O. Box 1009 (44282-1009)
PHONE..................................330 335-1541
Tim Swanson, *CEO*
Robert Stopar, *
Chris Rautner, *Chief Human Resource Officer**
Martin Layding, *
▲ **EMP:** 170 **EST:** 1953
SQ FT: 169,000
SALES (est): 142.92MM **Privately Held**
Web: www.rohrer.com
SIC: 3089 2675 Blister or bubble formed packaging, plastics; Die-cut paper and board
PA: Wellspring Capital Management Llc
605 3rd Ave Fl 44
New York NY 10158

(G-15064)
RUBBER CITY INDUSTRIES INC
471 E Bergey St (44281-2097)
PHONE..................................330 990-9641
Robert Price, *Prin*
EMP: 9 **EST:** 2011
SALES (est): 494.91K **Privately Held**
Web: www.rubbercityindustries.com

GEOGRAPHIC SECTION

Walbridge - Wood County (G-15086)

SIC: **3999** Manufacturing industries, nec

(G-15065)
SATTLER COMPANIES INC
Also Called: Sattler Machine Products
1455 Wolf Creek Trl (44281-9742)
P.O. Box 306 (44274-0306)
PHONE.................................330 239-2552
David Sattler, *Pr*
David F Raynor, *Prin*
▲ **EMP:** 24 **EST:** 1972
SQ FT: 22,600
SALES (est): 2.96MM **Privately Held**
Web: www.sattlermachine.com
SIC: **3599** Machine shop, jobbing and repair

(G-15066)
SOPREMA USA INC (HQ)
310 Quadral Dr (44281-9571)
PHONE.................................330 334-0066
Pierre Bindschedler, *Pr*
Gilbert Lorenzo, *
Steven P Goetz, *
J Bret Treier, *
EMP: 30 **EST:** 1991
SALES (est): 50.18MM
SALES (corp-wide): 4.23B **Privately Held**
Web: www.soprema.us
SIC: **3069** Roofing, membrane rubber
PA: Holding Soprema
15 Rue De Saint Nazaire
Strasbourg 67100

(G-15067)
SROUFE HEALTHCARE PRODUCTS LLC
961 Seville Rd (44281-8316)
P.O. Box 347 (46767-0347)
PHONE.................................260 894-4171
▲ **EMP:** 21 **EST:** 1974
SQ FT: 76,800
SALES (est): 750.94K **Privately Held**
SIC: **3842** 2396 Orthopedic appliances; Screen printing on fabric articles

(G-15068)
STABLE STEP LLC
Also Called: Powersteps
961 Seville Rd (44281-8316)
PHONE.................................800 491-1571
EMP: 150 **EST:** 2015
SALES (est): 5.06MM **Privately Held**
SIC: **3842** 5047 5999 Foot appliances, orthopedic; Orthopedic equipment and supplies; Orthopedic and prosthesis applications

(G-15069)
THE CORNWELL QUALITY TOOLS COMPANY (PA)
Also Called: Cornwell Quality Tools
667 Seville Rd (44281-1077)
PHONE.................................330 336-3506
▲ **EMP:** 80 **EST:** 1919
SALES (est): 55.65MM
SALES (corp-wide): 55.65MM **Privately Held**
Web: www.cornwelltools.com
SIC: **5085** 3423 6794 Industrial supplies; Mechanics' hand tools; Franchises, selling or licensing

(G-15070)
TORSION CONTROL PRODUCTS INC
1441 Wolf Creek Trl (44281-9742)
PHONE.................................248 537-1900
Timothy A Thane, *Pr*
EMP: 19 **EST:** 1987
SALES (est): 5.82MM
SALES (corp-wide): 4.77B **Publicly Held**

Web: www.torsioncontrol.com
SIC: **3714** 8711 Transmission housings or parts, motor vehicle; Engineering services
PA: The Timken Company
4500 Mount Pleasant St Nw
North Canton OH 44720
234 262-3000

(G-15071)
WARNER FABRICATING INC
7812 Hartman Rd (44281-8744)
PHONE.................................330 848-3191
James Warner, *CEO*
Mark Warner, *Pr*
EMP: 10 **EST:** 1977
SQ FT: 12,000
SALES (est): 872.31K **Privately Held**
SIC: **3444** Sheet metalwork

(G-15072)
WESTERN ROTO ENGRAVERS INC
Also Called: Wre Color Tech
668 Seville Rd (44281-1080)
PHONE.................................330 336-7636
Dean Ellebruch, *Mgr*
EMP: 37
SQ FT: 11,000
SALES (corp-wide): 12.93MM **Privately Held**
Web: www.wrecolor.com
SIC: **2754** 2791 2759 Rotogravure printing; Typesetting; Commercial printing, nec
PA: Western Roto Engravers, Incorporated
533 Banner Ave
Greensboro NC 27401
336 275-9821

Wakeman
Huron County

(G-15073)
CUSTOM CHASSIS INC
52826 State Route 303 (44889-9537)
PHONE.................................440 839-5574
Matthew Tipple, *Pr*
Jack Schartman, *Sec*
Michael Huhn, *VP*
▲ **EMP:** 9 **EST:** 1990
SQ FT: 13,000
SALES (est): 822.77K **Privately Held**
Web: www.customchassisinc.com
SIC: **3711** Chassis, motor vehicle

(G-15074)
DURAFLOW INDUSTRIES INC
15706 Garfield Rd (44889-8439)
PHONE.................................440 965-5047
Mark Sliman, *Prin*
EMP: 8 **EST:** 2009
SALES (est): 989.15K **Privately Held**
Web: www.duraflowindustries.com
SIC: **3999** Barber and beauty shop equipment

(G-15075)
KRAUSHER MACHINING INC
4267 Butler Rd (44889-8212)
PHONE.................................440 839-2828
Dale K Krausher, *Pr*
Barbara Krausher, *VP*
EMP: 8 **EST:** 1970
SQ FT: 10,000
SALES (est): 718.62K **Privately Held**
Web: www.krausher.com
SIC: **3451** Screw machine products

(G-15076)
M A HARRISON MFG CO INC
14307 State Route 113 (44889-8320)

PHONE.................................440 965-4306
Chad A Harrison, *Pr*
Walter Denham, *CFO*
James Harrison, *Ch*
Keith Harris, *VP*
EMP: 20 **EST:** 1938
SQ FT: 1,544
SALES (est): 1.57MM **Privately Held**
Web: www.maharrisonmfg.com
SIC: **3545** 3366 Precision tools, machinists'; Castings (except die), nec, copper and copper-base alloy

(G-15077)
MATUS WINERY INC
15674 Gore Orphanage Rd (44889-9522)
PHONE.................................440 774-9463
Robert F Matus, *Prin*
EMP: 8 **EST:** 2019
SALES (est): 245.47K **Privately Held**
Web: www.matuswinery.us
SIC: **2084** Wines

Walbridge
Wood County

(G-15078)
AIRTECH
6898 Commodore Dr (43465-9763)
PHONE.................................419 269-1000
Kurt Lang, *Prin*
EMP: 8 **EST:** 2014
SALES (est): 586.8K **Privately Held**
Web: www.airtechmx.com
SIC: **3563** Air and gas compressors

(G-15079)
BLACKHAWK MACHINE LLC
300 Warner St (43465-1142)
PHONE.................................419 779-3958
EMP: 8 **EST:** 2018
SALES (est): 23.7K **Privately Held**
SIC: **3599** Machine shop, jobbing and repair

(G-15080)
CLEVELND-CLFFS TBLAR CMPNNTS L (DH)
30400 E Broadway St (43465-9568)
PHONE.................................419 661-4150
Clifford Smith, *Pr*
Angela Stojkov, *
Brian Bishop, *
Erik Anderson, *
Denise Caruso, *
◆ **EMP:** 105 **EST:** 2001
SQ FT: 330,000
SALES (est): 76.22MM
SALES (corp-wide): 22B **Publicly Held**
Web: www.clevelandcliffs.com
SIC: **3317** Steel pipe and tubes
HQ: Cleveland-Cliffs Steel Corporation
200 Public Sq Ste 3300
Cleveland OH 44114

(G-15081)
FISHER METAL FABRICATING LLC
27953 E Broadway St (43465-9408)
PHONE.................................419 838-7200
EMP: 16 **EST:** 2007
SALES (est): 946.92K **Privately Held**
Web: www.fishermetalfabricating.com
SIC: **3441** Fabricated structural metal

(G-15082)
GREAT LAKES WINDOW INC
30499 Tracy Rd (43465-9794)
P.O. Box 1896 (43603-1896)
PHONE.................................419 666-5555
Lynn Morstadt, *Pr*

EMP: 600 **EST:** 1981
SQ FT: 170,000
SALES (est): 50.41MM
SALES (corp-wide): 5.58B **Privately Held**
Web: www.greatlakeswindow.com
SIC: **3089** 5211 Windows, plastics; Lumber and other building materials
HQ: Ply Gem Industries, Inc.
5020 Weston Pkwy Ste 400
Cary NC 27513
919 677-3900

(G-15083)
JONES-HAMILTON CO (PA)
Also Called: Jones-Hamilton Co.
30354 Tracy Rd (43465)
PHONE.................................419 666-9838
Bernard D Murphy, *Pr*
Brian Brooks C.p.a., *CFO*
Charlie Wheeler, *
Kimberly Sosko C.p.a., *CAO*
◆ **EMP:** 96 **EST:** 1949
SALES (est): 128.65MM
SALES (corp-wide): 128.65MM **Privately Held**
Web: www.jones-hamilton.com
SIC: **2819** Hydrochloric acid

(G-15084)
MATERIAL SCIENCES CORPORATION
Also Called: Walbridge Coatings
30610 E Broadway St (43465-9561)
PHONE.................................419 661-5905
Jeff Ramsay, *Manager*
EMP: 100
SQ FT: 266,000
SALES (corp-wide): 120.84MM **Privately Held**
Web: www.materialsciencescorp.com
SIC: **3479** Coating of metals and formed products
PA: Material Sciences Corporation
6855 Commerce Blvd
Canton MI 48187
734 207-4444

(G-15085)
MSC WALBRIDGE COATINGS INC
Also Called: Walbridge Coatings
30610 E Broadway St (43465)
PHONE.................................419 666-6130
Patrick Murley, *CEO*
EMP: 120 **EST:** 1971
SQ FT: 400,000
SALES (est): 25.66MM
SALES (corp-wide): 120.84MM **Privately Held**
Web: www.materialsciencescorp.com
SIC: **3316** 3479 Cold finishing of steel shapes; Galvanizing of iron, steel, or end-formed products
PA: Material Sciences Corporation
6855 Commerce Blvd
Canton MI 48187
734 207-4444

(G-15086)
RIVERSIDE MCH & AUTOMTN INC
Also Called: Assembly Division
28701 E Broadway St (43465-9625)
PHONE.................................419 855-8308
EMP: 7
Web: www.riverside-machine.com
SIC: **3549** Assembly machines, including robotic
PA: Riverside Machine & Automation, Inc.
1240 N Genoa Clay Ctr Rd
Genoa OH 43430

Walbridge - Wood County (G-15087) — GEOGRAPHIC SECTION

(G-15087)
ROCK EM SOCK EM RETRO LLC (PA)
5902 Moline Martin Rd (43465-9421)
PHONE.....................419 575-9309
Kayla Minniear, *Prin*
EMP: 6 **EST:** 2016
SALES (est): 105.16K
SALES (corp-wide): 105.16K **Privately Held**
Web: www.rockemsockemretro.com
SIC: 2252 Socks

(G-15088)
WESTERN STATES ENVELOPE CO
Also Called: Western States Envelope Label
6859 Commodore Dr (43465-9765)
PHONE.....................419 666-7480
Shelly Hinkle, *Mgr*
EMP: 41
SALES (corp-wide): 106.57MM **Privately Held**
Web: www.wsel.com
SIC: 5112 2677 Envelopes; Envelopes
PA: Western States Envelope Company
4480 N 132nd St
Butler WI 53007
262 781-5540

Waldo
Marion County

(G-15089)
NWP MANUFACTURING INC
Also Called: N W P Manufacturing
2862 County Road 146 (43356-9122)
PHONE.....................419 894-6871
John E Werner Iii, *Pr*
John Werner, *Pr*
Jerry Keiesel, *VP*
EMP: 10 **EST:** 1989
SQ FT: 36,000
SALES (est): 785.16K **Privately Held**
SIC: 2842 2448 Sweeping compounds, oil or water absorbent, clay or sawdust; Pallets, wood

(G-15090)
OHIGRO INC (PA)
6720 Gillette Rd (43356-9105)
P.O. Box 196 (43356-0196)
PHONE.....................740 726-2429
Jerry Ward, *Pr*
Jerry A Ward, *Pr*
James H Ward, *VP*
Jeffrey Ward, *Treas*
EMP: 20 **EST:** 1965
SQ FT: 9,600
SALES (est): 9.87MM
SALES (corp-wide): 9.87MM **Privately Held**
Web: www.ohigro.com
SIC: 5191 5261 2875 0723 Fertilizer and fertilizer materials; Fertilizer; Fertilizers, mixing only; Crop preparation services for market

Walhonding
Coshocton County

(G-15091)
COUNTRY MILE WOODWORKING
6345 Woods Church Rd (43843-9615)
PHONE.....................740 668-2452
Joyce Apelton, *Prin*
EMP: 6 **EST:** 2011
SALES (est): 195.25K **Privately Held**
SIC: 2431 Millwork

(G-15092)
DUGAN DRILLING INC
27238 New Guilford Rd (43005-9612)
P.O. Box 91 (43005-0091)
PHONE.....................740 668-3811
Guy E Dugan, *Pr*
Linda Dugan, *Sec*
EMP: 9 **EST:** 1980
SALES (est): 488.77K **Privately Held**
SIC: 1381 Drilling oil and gas wells

(G-15093)
INDIAN BEAR WINERY LTD
3483 Mccament Rd (43843-9667)
PHONE.....................740 507-3322
EMP: 8 **EST:** 2013
SALES (est): 122.18K **Privately Held**
Web: camp.becauseisaidiwould.org
SIC: 2084 Wines

Walnut Creek
Holmes County

(G-15094)
MAST FARM SERVICE LTD
3585 State Rte 39 (44687)
P.O. Box 142 (44687-0142)
PHONE.....................330 893-2972
Eli Mast Junior, *Owner*
Joy Yutzy, *Prin*
EMP: 12 **EST:** 1986
SALES (est): 2.07MM **Privately Held**
Web: www.mastfarmservice.com
SIC: 3499 Fire- or burglary-resistive products

(G-15095)
STITCHES USA LLC
3149 State Rte 39 (44687)
P.O. Box 724 (44681-0724)
PHONE.....................330 852-0500
EMP: 15 **EST:** 2002
SALES (est): 1.08MM **Privately Held**
Web: www.stitchesusa.com
SIC: 2211 Decorative trim and specialty fabrics, including twist weave

(G-15096)
WALNUT CREEK CHOCOLATE CO INC (PA)
Also Called: Coblentz Chocolate Co
4917 State Rte 515 (44687)
P.O. Box 86 (44687)
PHONE.....................330 893-2995
Jason Coblentz, *Pr*
EMP: 25 **EST:** 1987
SQ FT: 2,000
SALES (est): 2.63MM **Privately Held**
Web: www.coblentzchocolates.com
SIC: 2064 2066 5149 5441 Chocolate covered dates; Chocolate candy, solid; Chocolate; Candy

Walton Hills
Cuyahoga County

(G-15097)
CONTROLLIX CORPORATION
Also Called: Walton Hills
21415 Alexander Rd (44146-5512)
PHONE.....................440 232-8757
John Kelly, *CEO*
EMP: 15 **EST:** 1985
SQ FT: 18,000
SALES (est): 5.39MM **Privately Held**
Web: www.controllix.com
SIC: 3625 5063 Industrial electrical relays and switches; Electrical apparatus and equipment

(G-15098)
DUNHAM PRODUCTS INC
7400 Northfield Rd (44146-6108)
PHONE.....................440 232-0885
Joseph F Klukan, *CEO*
Rosemary Klukan, *Sec*
Jay Maslanka, *Mgr*
Sarah Johnson, *Mgr*
EMP: 15 **EST:** 1946
SQ FT: 7,700
SALES (est): 3.33MM **Privately Held**
Web: www.dunhamproducts.com
SIC: 3451 Screw machine products

(G-15099)
INTIGRAL INC (PA)
Also Called: Est
7850 Northfield Rd (44146-5523)
PHONE.....................440 439-0980
Jason Thomas, *Pr*
Richard Dietrich, *
Edmond Leopold, *
Dick Dietrich, *
Jim Prete, *
▲ **EMP:** 200 **EST:** 1987
SQ FT: 158,000
SALES (est): 51.33MM
SALES (corp-wide): 51.33MM **Privately Held**
Web: www.intigral.com
SIC: 3231 Insulating glass: made from purchased glass

(G-15100)
MASON STRUCTURAL STEEL LLC
7500 Northfield Rd (44146-6187)
PHONE.....................440 439-1040
Scott Berlin, *Pr*
Scott Polster, *VP*
Doug Shymske, *COO*
EMP: 28 **EST:** 2017
SALES (est): 2.83MM **Privately Held**
Web: www.masonsteel.com
SIC: 3441 5031 5074 Fabricated structural metal; Doors and windows; Fireplaces, prefabricated

(G-15101)
MEADOR SUPPLY COMPANY INC
20437 Hannan Pkwy Ste 5 (44146-5384)
P.O. Box 668 (44087-0668)
PHONE.....................330 405-4403
Audrey Kadusky, *Pr*
Don Kadusky, *VP*
EMP: 10 **EST:** 1998
SALES (est): 1.34MM **Privately Held**
Web: www.meadorsupply.co
SIC: 3491 Industrial valves

(G-15102)
MSSI GROUP INC
Also Called: Mason Steel
7500 Northfield Rd (44146-6110)
PHONE.....................440 439-1040
Leonard N Polster, *CEO*
Keith Polster, *
J Moldaver, *
Joseph Patchan, *
Sol W Wyman, *
EMP: 100 **EST:** 1958
SQ FT: 75,000
SALES (est): 17.39MM **Privately Held**
Web: www.masonsteel.com
SIC: 3441 5031 5074 Fabricated structural metal; Doors and windows; Fireplaces, prefabricated

(G-15103)
TRANSTAR HOLDING COMPANY (PA)
7350 Young Dr (44146-5357)
PHONE.....................800 359-3339
Monte Ahuja, *Ch*
Jeffrey R Marshall, *VP*
Ronald H Neill, *Sec*
Stephen B Perry, *VP*
Mark A Kirk, *VP*
EMP: 6 **EST:** 2005
SALES (est): 719.56MM **Privately Held**
Web: www.transtarholding.com
SIC: 3444 3281 2952 Metal roofing and roof drainage equipment; Cut stone and stone products; Asphalt felts and coatings

(G-15104)
VALTRIS SPECIALTY CHEMICALS ◆
7050 Krick Rd (44146-4416)
PHONE.....................216 875-7200
EMP: 11 **EST:** 2022
SALES (est): 1.01MM **Privately Held**
Web: www.valtris.com
SIC: 2899 Chemical preparations, nec

Wapakoneta
Auglaize County

(G-15105)
AMERICAN TRIM LLC
217 Krein Ave (45895)
PHONE.....................419 739-4349
Randy Fosnaugh, *Brnch Mgr*
EMP: 110
SALES (corp-wide): 445.1MM **Privately Held**
Web: www.amtrim.com
SIC: 3469 Porcelain enameled products and utensils
HQ: American Trim, L.L.C.
1005 W Grand Ave
Lima OH 45801

(G-15106)
BECKERMILLS INC
15286 State Route 67 (45895-9121)
PHONE.....................419 738-3450
Jim L Becker, *Prin*
EMP: 7 **EST:** 2008
SALES (est): 125.17K **Privately Held**
SIC: 3565 Aerating machines, for beverages

(G-15107)
BORNHORST PRINTING COMPANY INC
10139 County Road 25a (45895-8360)
PHONE.....................419 738-5901
EMP: 7 **EST:** 1957
SQ FT: 5,200
SALES (est): 760.51K **Privately Held**
Web: www.bornhorstprinting.com
SIC: 2752 Offset printing

(G-15108)
BRADY RUCK COMPANY
Also Called: Apex Bag Company
253 Indl Dr (45895)
PHONE.....................419 738-5126
▲ **EMP:** 20
Web: www.apexbag.com
SIC: 2674 Bags: uncoated paper and multiwall

(G-15109)
EVERYDAY TECHNOLOGIES INC
751 Industrial Dr (45895-9200)
PHONE.....................419 739-6104
Michael Toal, *Brnch Mgr*
EMP: 11

GEOGRAPHIC SECTION

Wapakoneta - Auglaize County (G-15130)

SALES (corp-wide): 10.96MM **Privately Held**
Web: www.everydaytech.com
SIC: 3444 Sheet metalwork
PA: Everyday Technologies, Inc.
2005 Campbell Rd
Sidney OH 45365
937 492-4171

(G-15110)
FENIX LLC (HQ)
820 Willipie St (45895-9201)
PHONE...........................419 739-3400
Steven Wray, *Pr*
Kevin G Shumaker, *VP*
Douglas Stearns, *VP Sls*
▲ **EMP:** 13 **EST:** 2004
SQ FT: 141,000
SALES (est): 16.17MM **Privately Held**
Web: www.fenixllc.com
SIC: 3315 Wire products, ferrous/iron; made in wiredrawing plants
PA: The Seneca Wire Group Inc
820 Willipie St
Wapakoneta OH 45895

(G-15111)
FIVE VINES WINERY LLC
12179 Buckland Holden Rd (45895-9316)
PHONE...........................419 657-2675
Dorotha L Krieg, *Owner*
EMP: 6 **EST:** 2017
SALES (est): 224.97K **Privately Held**
Web: www.fivevineswinerywapak.com
SIC: 2084 Wines

(G-15112)
G A WINTZER AND SON COMPANY (PA)
204 W Auglaize St (45895-1402)
P.O. Box 406 (45895-0406)
PHONE...........................419 739-4900
EMP: 15 **EST:** 1848
SALES (est): 17.95MM
SALES (corp-wide): 17.95MM **Privately Held**
Web: www.gawintzer.com
SIC: 2048 5159 Feeds from meat and from meat and vegetable meals; Hides

(G-15113)
G A WINTZER AND SON COMPANY
12279 S Dixey Hwy (45895)
P.O. Box 406 (45895-0406)
PHONE...........................419 739-4913
EMP: 70
SALES (corp-wide): 17.95MM **Privately Held**
Web: www.gawintzer.com
SIC: 2048 Feeds from meat and from meat and vegetable meals
PA: G. A. Wintzer And Son Company
204 W Auglaize St
Wapakoneta OH 45895
419 739-4900

(G-15114)
GATEWAY PACKAGING COMPANY LLC
Also Called: Apex Bag Company
253 Indl Dr (45895)
PHONE...........................419 738-5126
EMP: 20
SALES (corp-wide): 1.58B **Privately Held**
Web: www.proampac.com
SIC: 2674 Bags: uncoated paper and multiwall
HQ: Gateway Packaging Company Llc
605 Tn 76
White House TN 37188

(G-15115)
GENERAL ALUMINUM MFG COMPANY
Also Called: Wapakoneta Plant
13663 Short Rd (45895-8362)
PHONE...........................419 739-9300
EMP: 113
Web: www.generalaluminum.com
SIC: 3363 3494 3322 3321 Aluminum die-castings; Valves and pipe fittings, nec; Malleable iron foundries; Cast iron pipe and fittings
HQ: General Aluminum Mfg. Llc
5159 S Prospect St
Ravenna OH 44266
330 297-1225

(G-15116)
GRAYS ORANGE BARN INC
14286 State Rte 196 (45895-8630)
PHONE...........................419 568-2718
Timothy Gray, *Pr*
Glen Wagner, *Sec*
EMP: 7 **EST:** 1965
SALES (est): 420K **Privately Held**
SIC: 5431 5451 2099 5148 Fruit stands or markets; Cheese; Spices, including grinding; Fruits, fresh

(G-15117)
HORIZON OHIO PUBLICATIONS INC
Also Called: Shelby County Review
520 Industrial Dr (45895-9200)
P.O. Box 389 (45895-0389)
PHONE...........................419 738-2128
EMP: 51
SALES (corp-wide): 47.1MM **Privately Held**
Web: www.theeveningleader.com
SIC: 2711 2759 2752 Commercial printing and newspaper publishing combined; Commercial printing, nec; Commercial printing, lithographic
HQ: Horizon Ohio Publications Inc
102 E Spring St
Saint Marys OH 45885
419 394-7414

(G-15118)
INGREDIA INC
Also Called: I D I
625 Commerce Rd (45895)
P.O. Box 144 (45822)
PHONE...........................419 738-4060
Gilles Desgrousilliers, *CEO*
Sandrine Delory, *Treas*
◆ **EMP:** 23 **EST:** 2006
SQ FT: 39,000
SALES (est): 9.83MM
SALES (corp-wide): 199.89MM **Privately Held**
Web: www.ingredia.com
SIC: 2023 Dry, condensed and evaporated dairy products
HQ: Ingredia
51 Avenue Fernand Lobbedez
Arras 62000
321238000

(G-15119)
JEWETT SUPPLY
Also Called: Barlamy Supply
607 N Water St (45895-9379)
PHONE...........................419 738-9882
Rife Jewett, *Pt*
Lori Jewett, *Pt*
Lynn Jewett, *Pt*
Lisa Hardeman, *Pt*
Barbara Young, *Pt*
EMP: 10 **EST:** 1968
SQ FT: 768

SALES (est): 106.36K **Privately Held**
SIC: 2499 Handles, poles, dowels and stakes: wood

(G-15120)
KINSTLE TRUCK & AUTO SVC INC
Also Called: Kinstle String/Wstern Star Trc
1770 Wapakoneta Fisher Rd (45895-9799)
P.O. Box 1986 (45895-0986)
PHONE...........................419 738-7493
TOLL FREE: 888
J Michael Kinstle, *Pr*
Barbara Kinstle, *Sec*
EMP: 16 **EST:** 1981
SQ FT: 10,500
SALES (est): 880.39K **Privately Held**
SIC: 5012 5511 7538 3519 Truck tractors; Trucks, tractors, and trailers: new and used; Truck engine repair, except industrial; Engines, diesel and semi-diesel or dual-fuel

(G-15121)
KN RUBBER LLC (HQ)
Also Called: Koneta Rubber
1400 Lunar Dr (45895-9796)
P.O. Box 150 (45895-0150)
PHONE...........................419 739-4200
Rex Mouland, *Contrlr*
◆ **EMP:** 155 **EST:** 1986
SQ FT: 165,000
SALES (est): 40.04MM
SALES (corp-wide): 542.8MM **Privately Held**
Web: www.knrubber.com
SIC: 3069 Rubber automotive products
PA: Kinderhook Industries, Llc
505 5th Ave Fl 25
New York NY 10017
212 201-6780

(G-15122)
KONETA INC
1400 Lunar Dr (45895-9796)
P.O. Box 150 (45895-0150)
PHONE...........................419 739-4200
◆ **EMP:** 90 **EST:** 2007
SALES (est): 6.74MM **Privately Held**
Web: www.konetainc.com
SIC: 3061 Automotive rubber goods (mechanical)

(G-15123)
MIDWEST COMPOSITES LLC
302 Krein Ave (45895-2375)
PHONE...........................419 738-2431
EMP: 13 **EST:** 2011
SALES (est): 561.87K **Privately Held**
SIC: 2231 3229 Upholstery fabrics, wool; Glass fiber products

(G-15124)
MIDWEST ELASTOMERS INC
Also Called: MEI
700 Industrial Dr (45895-9200)
P.O. Box 412 (45895-0412)
PHONE...........................419 738-8844
George Wight, *Pr*
Ron Clark, *
Barbara Link, *
Sue Hunsacker, *
Evan Piland, *
◆ **EMP:** 65 **EST:** 1986
SQ FT: 56,000
SALES (est): 16.15MM **Privately Held**
Web: www.midwestelastomers.com
SIC: 2822 3069 Synthetic rubber; Reclaimed rubber (reworked by manufacturing processes)

(G-15125)
MIDWEST METAL FABRICATORS
712 Maple St (45895-2324)
PHONE...........................419 739-7077
EMP: 11 **EST:** 2005
SALES (est): 1.29MM **Privately Held**
Web: www.mw-metal.com
SIC: 3444 Sheet metalwork

(G-15126)
MIDWEST METAL FABRICATORS LTD
712 Maple St (45895-2324)
PHONE...........................419 739-7077
Verne E Peake, *Pt*
John Neumann, *Pt*
Jason Neumann, *Pt*
EMP: 10 **EST:** 2001
SQ FT: 15,500
SALES (est): 1.5MM **Privately Held**
Web: www.midwestmetalfab.com
SIC: 3444 Sheet metal specialties, not stamped

(G-15127)
MIDWEST SPECIALTIES INC
Also Called: Flexarm
705 Commerce Rd (45895)
PHONE...........................800 837-2503
Nicholas I Kennedy, *CEO*
Penny Kentosh, *Sec*
EMP: 13 **EST:** 1967
SALES (est): 3.16MM **Privately Held**
Web: www.flexmachinetools.com
SIC: 3541 3271 3599 Tapping machines; Concrete block and brick; Machine shop, jobbing and repair

(G-15128)
NATIONAL LIME AND STONE CO
18430 Main Street Rd (45895-9400)
PHONE...........................419 657-6745
Shaun Place, *Mgr*
EMP: 9
SALES (corp-wide): 167.89MM **Privately Held**
Web: www.natlime.com
SIC: 1422 3281 Crushed and broken limestone; Limestone, cut and shaped
PA: The National Lime And Stone Company
551 Lake Cascade Pkwy
Findlay OH 45840
419 422-4341

(G-15129)
PRATT PAPER (OH) LLC
602 Leon Pratt Dr (45895-9548)
PHONE...........................567 320-3353
Anthony Pratt, *Ch*
Brian Mcpheely, *CEO*
EMP: 32 **EST:** 2018
SALES (est): 97.48MM **Privately Held**
SIC: 2621 4953 Paper mills; Recycling, waste materials

(G-15130)
T & S MACHINE INC
712 Maple St (45895-2324)
P.O. Box 579 (45876-0579)
PHONE...........................419 453-2101
David Kriegel, *Pr*
William G Petty, *Pr*
Todd Kriegel, *VP*
EMP: 18 **EST:** 1984
SQ FT: 2,129
SALES (est): 441.19K **Privately Held**
SIC: 3599 Machine shop, jobbing and repair

(PA)=Parent Co (HQ)=Headquarters
✪ = New Business established in last 2 years

Wapakoneta - Auglaize County (G-15131)

(G-15131)
UNITED BUFF AND SUPPLY CO INC
2 E Harrison St (45895-1551)
P.O. Box 373 (45895-0373)
PHONE..................................419 738-2417
Cora F Slife, Pr
EMP: 8 **EST:** 1958
SQ FT: 17,000
SALES (est): 710.15K **Privately Held**
SIC: 3291 Buffing or polishing wheels, abrasive or nonabrasive

(G-15132)
VMAXX INC
323 Commerce Rd (45895-8373)
P.O. Box 36 (44622-0036)
PHONE..................................419 738-4044
Mark Meyer, *
Darren Meyer, Pr
Scott Stiles, Treas
EMP: 10 **EST:** 2001
SQ FT: 20,000
SALES (est): 778.57K **Privately Held**
Web: www.vmaxx.biz
SIC: 3542 Extruding machines (machine tools), metal

(G-15133)
WHITE FEATHER FOODS INC
Also Called: Whitefeather Foods
13845 Cemetery Rd (45895-8479)
P.O. Box 365 (45895-0365)
PHONE..................................419 738-8975
Stephen L Hengstler, Pr
Dave Jeannreret, Contrlr
EMP: 11 **EST:** 1983
SQ FT: 5,000
SALES (est): 436.92K **Privately Held**
Web: www.whitefeatherfoods.com
SIC: 2096 2099 Pork rinds; Food preparations, nec

Warren
Trumbull County

(G-15134)
ADS MACHINERY CORP
1201 Vine Ave Ne Ste 1 (44483-3834)
P.O. Box 1027 (44482-1027)
PHONE..................................330 399-3601
Dale Minton, Pr
K Ramalingham, *
Patricia S Beil, *
EMP: 75 **EST:** 1956
SQ FT: 57,000
SALES (est): 9.86MM **Privately Held**
Web: www.adsmachinery.com
SIC: 3549 3547 Metalworking machinery, nec ; Rolling mill machinery

(G-15135)
AJAX TOCCO MAGNETHERMIC CORP (HQ)
1745 Overland Ave Ne (44483)
PHONE..................................800 547-1527
Thomas Illencik, Pr
Steven White, *
◆ **EMP:** 200 **EST:** 2002
SQ FT: 200,000
SALES (est): 13.99MM
SALES (corp-wide): 1.66B **Publicly Held**
Web: www.ajaxtocco.com
SIC: 3567 7699 3612 Metal melting furnaces, industrial: electric; Industrial machinery and equipment repair; Electric furnace transformers
PA: Park-Ohio Holdings Corp.
    6065 Parkland Blvd Ste 1
    Cleveland OH 44124
    440 947-2000

(G-15136)
ALPHABET INC (HQ)
8640 E Market St (44484-2346)
PHONE..................................330 856-3366
Mark Tervalon, Pr
Michael Jocola, *
Cloyd Abruzzo, *
EMP: 100 **EST:** 1977
SALES (est): 103.54MM **Publicly Held**
SIC: 3679 Electronic circuits
PA: Stoneridge, Inc.
    39675 Mackenzie Dr # 400
    Novi MI 48377

(G-15137)
AM WARREN LLC
Also Called: Arcelormittal Warren
2234 Main Ave. S.W. (44481)
PHONE..................................330 841-2800
Lou Schorsch, CEO
Jeff Foster, Genl Mgr
EMP: 9 **EST:** 2010
SALES (est): 203.77K **Privately Held**
SIC: 3312 Blast furnaces and steel mills

(G-15138)
AMERICAN STEEL & ALLOYS LLC
4000 Mahoning Ave Nw (44483-1924)
PHONE..................................330 847-0487
Mordechai Korf, Prin
EMP: 16 **EST:** 2005
SALES (est): 406.49K **Privately Held**
SIC: 3312 Tool and die steel and alloys

(G-15139)
AMERICAN WAY MANUFACTURING INC
1871 Henn Pkwy Sw (44481-8659)
PHONE..................................330 824-2353
▼ **EMP:** 27 **EST:** 1995
SALES (est): 3.33MM **Privately Held**
SIC: 3089 Fences, gates, and accessories: plastics

(G-15140)
AML INDUSTRIES INC
520 Pine Ave Se Ste 1 (44483-5763)
P.O. Box 4110 (44482-4110)
PHONE..................................330 399-5000
David Gurska, CEO
▲ **EMP:** 26 **EST:** 1989
SQ FT: 30,000
SALES (est): 6.75MM **Privately Held**
Web: www.amlube.com
SIC: 2992 Lubricating oils

(G-15141)
APTIV SERVICES US LLC
Also Called: Delphi Pckard Eea - Wrren Plan
1265 N River Rd Ne (44483-2352)
PHONE..................................330 373-7614
Robert Douce, Brnch Mgr
EMP: 74
SQ FT: 189,000
SALES (corp-wide): 20.05B **Privately Held**
Web: www.aptiv.com
SIC: 2821 Plastics materials and resins
HQ: Aptiv Services Us, Llc
    5725 Innovation Dr
    Troy MI 48098

(G-15142)
APTIV SERVICES US LLC
Also Called: Delphi
4551 Research Pkwy Nw (44483)
PHONE..................................330 306-1000
Robert Seidler, Dir
EMP: 400
SALES (corp-wide): 20.05B **Privately Held**
Web: www.aptiv.com
SIC: 3714 Air conditioner parts, motor vehicle
HQ: Aptiv Services Us, Llc
    5725 Innovation Dr
    Troy MI 48098

(G-15143)
APTIV SERVICES US LLC
Also Called: Delphi
1265 N River Rd Ne (44483)
PHONE..................................330 505-3150
Bill Coates, Brnch Mgr
EMP: 495
SALES (corp-wide): 20.05B **Privately Held**
Web: www.aptiv.com
SIC: 3714 Motor vehicle parts and accessories
HQ: Aptiv Services Us, Llc
    5725 Innovation Dr
    Troy MI 48098

(G-15144)
APTIV SERVICES US LLC
Also Called: S&Ps
1265 N River Rd Ne # Fr11 (44483-2352)
PHONE..................................330 373-3568
Stephanie Pennel, Brnch Mgr
EMP: 1117
SALES (corp-wide): 20.05B **Privately Held**
Web: www.aptiv.com
SIC: 3465 Body parts, automobile: stamped metal
HQ: Aptiv Services Us, Llc
    5725 Innovation Dr
    Troy MI 48098

(G-15145)
ASTRO TECHNICAL SERVICES INC
2401 Parkman Rd Nw (44485-1758)
EMP: 23 **EST:** 1990
SALES (est): 4.37MM
SALES (corp-wide): 24.29MM **Privately Held**
Web: www.warrendb.com
SIC: 3599 Custom machinery
PA: Astro Manufacturing & Design, Inc.
    34459 Curtis Blvd
    Eastlake OH 44095
    888 215-1746

(G-15146)
BLOOM INDUSTRIES INC
Also Called: Incredible Plastics
1052 Mahoney Ave Nw (44483)
PHONE..................................330 898-3878
Ted E Bloom, Pr
EMP: 18 **EST:** 1957
SQ FT: 95,000
SALES (est): 1.07MM **Privately Held**
Web: www.bloomindustries.com
SIC: 3089 3544 Injection molding of plastics; Special dies, tools, jigs, and fixtures

(G-15147)
BOSTON SCNTFIC NRMDLATION CORP
2174 Sarkies Dr Ne (44483-4262)
PHONE..................................330 372-2652
P A Martof, Prin
EMP: 14
SALES (corp-wide): 12.68B **Publicly Held**
SIC: 3841 Surgical and medical instruments
HQ: Boston Scientific Neuromodulation Corporation
    25155 Rye Canyon Loop
    Valencia CA 91355

(G-15148)
BROWNS HANDYMAN REMODELING
2721 Montclair St Ne (44483-5545)
P.O. Box 4113 (44482-4113)
PHONE..................................330 766-0925
Jarome Brown, Mgr
EMP: 6 **EST:** 2016
SALES (est): 80.44K **Privately Held**
SIC: 2951 Asphalt paving mixtures and blocks

(G-15149)
BUCKEYE MEDICAL TECH LLC
405 Niles Cortland Rd Se Ste 202 (44484-2460)
PHONE..................................330 719-9868
EMP: 7 **EST:** 2009
SALES (est): 456.57K **Privately Held**
SIC: 3841 Surgical and medical instruments

(G-15150)
CATTRON HOLDINGS INC (HQ)
655 N River Rd Nw Ste A (44483)
PHONE..................................234 806-0018
Ryan Wooten, CEO
Martin Rapp, *
Michael Pearson, *
EMP: 24 **EST:** 1959
SALES (est): 37.57MM
SALES (corp-wide): 1.26B **Privately Held**
Web: www.cattron.com
SIC: 3625 7622 5065 5063 Relays and industrial controls; Communication equipment repair; Communication equipment; Electric alarms and signaling equipment
PA: Harbour Group Ltd.
    7733 Forsyth Blvd Fl 23
    Saint Louis MO 63105
    314 727-5550

(G-15151)
CATTRON NORTH AMERICA INC (DH)
Also Called: Remtron
655 N River Rd Nw Ste A (44483-2254)
PHONE..................................234 806-0018
Ryan Wooten, Pr
Brian D'angelo, CFO
Mike Santoni, Treas
◆ **EMP:** 19 **EST:** 1973
SQ FT: 25,000
SALES (est): 24.96MM
SALES (corp-wide): 1.26B **Privately Held**
Web: www.cattron.com
SIC: 3625 Relays and industrial controls
HQ: Cattron Holdings, Inc.
    655 N River Rd Nw Ste A
    Warren OH 44483
    234 806-0018

(G-15152)
CDH CUSTOM ROLL FORM LLC
1300 Phoenix Rd Ne (44483-2851)
PHONE..................................330 984-0555
EMP: 10 **EST:** 2019
SALES (est): 555.16K **Privately Held**
Web: www.cdhrollform.com
SIC: 3449 Custom roll formed products

(G-15153)
CHARLES MFG CO
3021 Sferra Ave Nw (44483-2268)
PHONE..................................330 395-3490
David Frazier, Pr
Christine M Frazier, Sec
EMP: 13 **EST:** 1982
SQ FT: 10,000
SALES (est): 2.12MM **Privately Held**
Web: www.charlesmfg.com

GEOGRAPHIC SECTION

Warren - Trumbull County (G-15178)

SIC: **3441** 5039 Fabricated structural metal; Architectural metalwork

(G-15154)
CLARKWESTERN DIETRICH BUILDING
Also Called: Clark Dietrich Building
1985 N River Rd Ne (44483-2527)
PHONE.................................330 372-5564
Bill Courtney, *Managing Member*
EMP: 25
SALES (corp-wide): 4.92B **Publicly Held**
Web: www.clarkdietrich.com
SIC: **3444** 8711 3081 Studs and joists, sheet metal; Engineering services; Vinyl film and sheet
HQ: Clarkwestern Dietrich Building
   Systems Llc
   9050 Cntre Pnte Dr Ste 40
   West Chester OH 45069

(G-15155)
COLOR 3 EMBROIDERY INC
2927 Mahoning Ave Nw (44483-2027)
P.O. Box 870 (44482-0870)
PHONE.................................330 652-9495
Traci Miller, *Pr*
Don Wiley, *VP*
EMP: 8 **EST:** 1995
SALES (est): 900.13K **Privately Held**
Web: www.color3.com
SIC: **2395** Embroidery products, except Schiffli machine

(G-15156)
COMPUTER STITCH DESIGNS INC
1414 Henn Hyde Rd Ne (44484-1227)
PHONE.................................330 856-7826
Sam Argeras, *Pr*
Donna Mc Guire, *Sec*
Darlene Argeras, *Treas*
EMP: 6 **EST:** 1986
SALES (est): 566.44K **Privately Held**
Web: www.computerstitch.com
SIC: **2395** Embroidery products, except Schiffli machine

(G-15157)
CONDO INCORPORATED
3869 Niles Rd Se (44484-3548)
PHONE.................................330 609-6021
John Condoleon, *CEO*
EMP: 55 **EST:** 1989
SQ FT: 40,000
SALES (est): 4.37MM **Privately Held**
Web: www.warrenprecision.net
SIC: **3451** Screw machine products

(G-15158)
CONLEY GROUP INC
Also Called: Concord Steel of Ohio
197 W Market St Ste 202 (44481-1024)
PHONE.................................330 372-2030
Paul Vessey, *Brnch Mgr*
EMP: 30
Web: www.conplastics.com
SIC: **5051** 3471 Steel; Plating and polishing
PA: Conley Group, Inc.
   21 Powder Hill Rd
   Lincoln RI 02865

(G-15159)
CURRENT INC
455 N River Rd Nw (44483-2250)
PHONE.................................330 392-5151
EMP: 8
SALES (corp-wide): 11.74MM **Privately Held**
Web: www.currentcomposites.com

SIC: **2821** Thermosetting materials
PA: Current, Inc.
   30 Tyler Street Ext
   East Haven CT 06512
   203 469-1337

(G-15160)
DIAMOND OILFIELD TECH LLC
106 E Market St Fl 2 (44481-1151)
P.O. Box 328 (44482-0328)
PHONE.................................234 806-4185
Matthew Kleese, *Managing Member*
Peter Karousis, *Managing Member*
EMP: 13 **EST:** 2012
SALES (est): 2.36MM **Privately Held**
SIC: **1389** Oil consultants

(G-15161)
DIETRICH INDUSTRIES INC
Also Called: Dietrich Metal Framing
1300 Phoenix Rd Ne (44483-2851)
PHONE.................................330 372-4014
Greg Samsa, *Brnch Mgr*
EMP: 130
SALES (corp-wide): 4.92B **Publicly Held**
SIC: **3441** Building components, structural steel
HQ: Dietrich Industries, Inc.
   200 W Old Wlson Bridge Rd
   Worthington OH 43085
   800 873-2604

(G-15162)
DIETRICH INDUSTRIES INC
1985 N River Rd Ne (44483-2527)
PHONE.................................330 372-2868
Joe Labus, *Mgr*
EMP: 124
SALES (corp-wide): 4.92B **Publicly Held**
SIC: **3312** Primary finished or semifinished shapes
HQ: Dietrich Industries, Inc.
   200 W Old Wlson Bridge Rd
   Worthington OH 43085
   800 873-2604

(G-15163)
DRAKE MANUFACTURING LLC
Also Called: Drake Manufacturing
4371 N Leavitt Rd Nw (44485-1199)
PHONE.................................330 847-7291
John Lirong Hu, *Pr*
David Tang, *
EMP: 55 **EST:** 2017
SALES (est): 8.28MM **Privately Held**
Web: www.drakemfg.com
SIC: **3599** Machine shop, jobbing and repair

(G-15164)
DRAKE MANUFACTURING SERVICES CO
4371 N Leavitt Rd Nw (44485-1199)
PHONE.................................330 847-7291
◆ **EMP:** 90
SIC: **3541** Machine tool replacement & repair parts, metal cutting types

(G-15165)
DYBROOK PRODUCTS INC
5232 Tod Ave Sw Ste 23 (44481-8728)
P.O. Box 1050 (44062-1050)
PHONE.................................330 392-7665
EMP: 35
Web: www.dybrook.com
SIC: **3061** Mechanical rubber goods

(G-15166)
ELITE CERAMICS AND METALS LLC
5390 Copeland Ave Nw (44483-1232)
PHONE.................................330 787-2777

EMP: 6 **EST:** 2021
SALES (est): 287.47K **Privately Held**
SIC: **3479** 5945 Coating of metals and formed products; Ceramics supplies

(G-15167)
ENGINEERED WIRE PRODUCTS INC
3121 W Market St (44485-3070)
PHONE.................................330 469-6958
John Bankol, *Mgr*
EMP: 48
Web: www.kci-corp.com
SIC: **3496** Miscellaneous fabricated wire products
HQ: Engineered Wire Products, Inc.
   1200 N Warpole St
   Upper Sandusky OH 43351

(G-15168)
ENVIRI CORPORATION
Enviri
101 Tidewater St Ne (44483-2434)
PHONE.................................330 372-1781
EMP: 10
SALES (corp-wide): 2.07B **Publicly Held**
Web: www.enviri.com
SIC: **2816** 2899 Metallic and mineral pigments, nec; Chemical preparations, nec
PA: Enviri Corporation
   100-120 N 18th St # 17
   Philadelphia PA 19103
   267 857-8715

(G-15169)
EVERETT INDUSTRIES LLC
3601 Larchmont Ave Ne (44483-2447)
PHONE.................................330 372-3700
James Vosmik, *Managing Member*
EMP: 24 **EST:** 2017
SQ FT: 25,000
SALES (est): 3.28MM **Privately Held**
Web: www.everettindustries.com
SIC: **3291** Abrasive wheels and grindstones, not artificial

(G-15170)
FLEX-STRUT INC
2900 Commonwealth Ave Ne (44483-2831)
PHONE.................................330 372-9999
EMP: 75 **EST:** 1994
SQ FT: 52,000
SALES (est): 16.47MM **Privately Held**
Web: www.flexstrut.com
SIC: **3441** 3429 Fabricated structural metal; Hardware, nec

(G-15171)
FOXCONN EV SYSTEM LLC
2300 Hallock Young Rd Sw (44481)
PHONE.................................234 285-4001
Young Liu, *CEO*
EMP: 400 **EST:** 2021
SALES (est): 43.13MM **Privately Held**
Web: www.fevsys.com
SIC: **3711** Motor vehicles and car bodies
PA: Hon Hai Precision Industry Co., Ltd.
   No. 2, Ziyou St.
   New Taipei City TAP 23640

(G-15172)
GENERAL ELECTRIC COMPANY
Also Called: GE
1210 Park (44483)
PHONE.................................330 373-1400
David Martin, *Brnch Mgr*
EMP: 21
SALES (corp-wide): 67.95B **Publicly Held**
Web: www.ge.com
SIC: **3641** 3648 3229 Lamps, sealed beam; Lighting equipment, nec; Pressed and blown glass, nec

PA: General Electric Company
   1 Aviation Way
   Cincinnati OH 45215
   617 443-3000

(G-15173)
GENERAL MOTORS LLC
Also Called: General Motors
2369 Ellsworth Bailey Rd Sw (44481-9235)
PHONE.................................330 824-5840
John Donahoe, *Mgr*
EMP: 237
Web: www.gm.com
SIC: **5511** 3714 Automobiles, new and used; Motor vehicle parts and accessories
HQ: General Motors Llc
   300 Rnaissance Ctr Ste L1
   Detroit MI 48243

(G-15174)
GLENWOOD ERECTORS INC
251 Durst Dr Nw (44483-1164)
PHONE.................................330 652-9616
Linda L Trunick, *Pr*
Michael E Trunick, *VP*
EMP: 7 **EST:** 1980
SALES (est): 502.38K **Privately Held**
SIC: **3441** Fabricated structural metal

(G-15175)
GLUNT INDUSTRIES INC
319 N River Rd Nw (44483-2248)
PHONE.................................330 399-7585
Asaf Salama, *CEO*
Dennis Glunt, *
Harold Glunt, *
Stuart Gladstone, *
Gary Shells, *
▲ **EMP:** 125 **EST:** 1971
SQ FT: 150,000
SALES (est): 27.68MM **Privately Held**
Web: www.glunt.com
SIC: **3599** 3549 3444 Machine shop, jobbing and repair; Metalworking machinery, nec; Sheet metalwork

(G-15176)
HKM DRECT MKT CMMNICATIONS INC
387 Chestnut Ave Ne (44483-5856)
PHONE.................................330 395-9538
James Jastatt, *Prin*
EMP: 20
SALES (corp-wide): 23.74MM **Privately Held**
Web: www.hkmdirectmarket.com
SIC: **2759** Commercial printing, nec
PA: Hkm Direct Market Communications, Inc.
   5501 Cass Ave
   Cleveland OH 44102
   800 860-4456

(G-15177)
INCREDIBLE SOLUTIONS INC
1052 Mahoning Ave Nw (44483-4622)
PHONE.................................330 898-3878
Ted Bloom, *CEO*
▲ **EMP:** 16 **EST:** 2005
SALES (est): 5.35MM **Privately Held**
Web: www.incrediblesolutionsinc.com
SIC: **2821** Molding compounds, plastics

(G-15178)
INDUCTION MANAGEMENT SVCS LLC
1745 Overland Ave Ne (44483-2860)
PHONE.................................440 947-2000
EMP: 6 **EST:** 2015
SALES (est): 120.3K **Privately Held**

Warren - Trumbull County (G-15179) GEOGRAPHIC SECTION

Web: www.commercial-heat-treating.com
SIC: 3398 Metal heat treating

(G-15179)
J W GOSS COMPANY (PA)
Also Called: Reds Auto Glass Shop
410 South St Sw (44483-5737)
P.O. Box 1066 (44482-1066)
PHONE..............................330 395-0739
George W Goss, Pr
Judith L Goss, VP
EMP: 14 EST: 1941
SQ FT: 20,000
SALES (est): 1.19MM
SALES (corp-wide): 1.19MM Privately Held
Web: www.mirraclips.com
SIC: 7536 3429 Automotive glass replacement shops; Hangers, wall hardware

(G-15180)
J-WELL SERVICE INC
6345 Tod Ave Sw (44481-9738)
PHONE..............................330 824-2718
James T Adams, Pr
Gerald Bowser, VP
Maxine Adams, Sec
EMP: 9 EST: 1987
SALES (est): 463.83K Privately Held
SIC: 1389 Oil and gas wells: building, repairing and dismantling

(G-15181)
JB INDUSTRIES LTD (PA)
160 Clifton Dr Ne Ste 4 (44484-1820)
PHONE..............................330 856-4587
EMP: 14 EST: 1989
SQ FT: 1,800
SALES (est): 2.08MM Privately Held
Web: www.jb-industries.com
SIC: 8711 3599 Industrial engineers; Machine shop, jobbing and repair

(G-15182)
KELLOGG CO
655 N River Rd Nw (44483-2254)
PHONE..............................330 306-1500
EMP: 6 EST: 2019
SALES (est): 142.21K Privately Held
SIC: 2043 Cereal breakfast foods

(G-15183)
LAIRD TECHNOLOGIES INC
655 N River Rd Nw (44483-2254)
PHONE..............................234 806-0105
EMP: 21
SALES (corp-wide): 2.93B Publicly Held
Web: www.lairdtech.com
SIC: 3443 Nuclear shielding, metal plate
HQ: Laird Technologies, Inc.
    16401 Swingley Ridge Rd
    Chesterfield MO 63017
    636 898-6000

(G-15184)
LITCO MANUFACTURING LLC
1512 Phoenix Rd Ne (44483-2855)
P.O. Box 150 (44473-0150)
PHONE..............................330 539-5433
Lionel F Trebilcock, CEO
Gary Tredilcock, COO
Raymond W Snider, Prin
▲ EMP: 17 EST: 2005
SALES (est): 5.05MM
SALES (corp-wide): 22.35MM Privately Held
Web: www.litcomfg.com
SIC: 2448 Pallets, wood
PA: Litco International, Inc.
    1 Litco Dr
    Vienna OH 44473
    330 539-5433

(G-15185)
LORDSTOWN EV CORPORATION (PA)
2300 Hallock Young Rd Sw (44481-9238)
PHONE..............................678 428-6558
Edward T Hightower, CEO
Julio Rodriguez, CFO
John Lafleur, COO
Rich Schmidt, CPO
EMP: 12 EST: 2019
SALES (est): 11.39MM
SALES (corp-wide): 11.39MM Privately Held
Web: www.lordstownmotors.com
SIC: 3711 3621 Motor vehicles and car bodies; Motors and generators

(G-15186)
LRB TOOL & DIE LTD
3303 Parkman Rd Nw (44481-9142)
PHONE..............................330 898-5783
George Pearce, Managing Member
Lee Ann Westenselder, Sec
EMP: 10 EST: 2001
SALES (est): 996.26K Privately Held
Web: www.lrbtool.com
SIC: 3544 Special dies and tools

(G-15187)
MACPHERSON ENGINEERING INC
Also Called: Macpherson & Company
2809 Mahoning Ave Nw (44483-2025)
P.O. Box 92 (44017-0092)
PHONE..............................440 243-6565
Bruce Mcpherson, Pr
EMP: 16 EST: 1965
SALES (est): 428.9K Privately Held
Web: www.macphersonglass.com
SIC: 3231 Reflecting glass

(G-15188)
MAGNEFORCE INC
155 Shaffer Dr Ne (44484)
P.O. Box 8508 (44484)
PHONE..............................330 856-9300
Richard Miller, Pr
David Miller, VP
EMP: 10 EST: 1988
SQ FT: 5,900
SALES (est): 1.7MM Privately Held
Web: www.magneforce.com
SIC: 3567 Induction heating equipment

(G-15189)
MATALCO (US) INC
5120 Tod Ave Sw (44481-9748)
PHONE..............................234 806-0600
EMP: 23
SALES (corp-wide): 6.29MM Privately Held
Web: www.matalco.com
SIC: 3363 Aluminum die-castings
HQ: Matalco (U.S.), Inc.
    4420 Louisville St Ne
    Canton OH 44705

(G-15190)
MESSER LLC
2000 Pine Ave Se (44483-6550)
PHONE..............................330 394-4541
EMP: 6
SALES (corp-wide): 1.45B Privately Held
SIC: 2813 Nitrogen
HQ: Messer Llc
    200 Somerset Corp Blvd # 7000
    Bridgewater NJ 08807
    908 464-8100

(G-15191)
MODERN METHODS BREWING CO LLC
197 Washington St Nw (44483-4732)
PHONE..............................330 506-4613
Adam M Keck, Managing Member
EMP: 7 EST: 2016
SALES (est): 248.41K Privately Held
Web: www.modernmethodsbrew.com
SIC: 2082 Beer (alcoholic beverage)

(G-15192)
MSSK MANUFACTURING INC
400 Dietz Rd Ne (44483-2708)
P.O. Box 30 (44482-0030)
PHONE..............................330 393-6624
Murray Miller, Pr
Julian Lehman, *
Ken Miller, *
▲ EMP: 21 EST: 1994
SQ FT: 16,000
SALES (est): 2.32MM Privately Held
SIC: 3432 3433 5074 Plumbing fixture fittings and trim; Heating equipment, except electric; Plumbing and hydronic heating supplies

(G-15193)
NOVELIS CORPORATION
390 Griswold St Ne (44483-2738)
P.O. Box 1151 (44482-1151)
PHONE..............................330 841-3456
Mervyn W Bell, Brnch Mgr
EMP: 93
Web: www.novelis.com
SIC: 3355 3353 Aluminum rolling and drawing, nec; Aluminum sheet, plate, and foil
HQ: Novelis Corporation
    One Phpps Plz 3550 Pchtre
    Atlanta GA 30326
    404 760-4000

(G-15194)
OAKES FOUNDRY INC
700 Bronze Rd Ne (44483-2720)
PHONE..............................330 372-4010
Grant Oakes, Pr
EMP: 21 EST: 1929
SQ FT: 2,000
SALES (est): 2.68MM Privately Held
Web: www.oakesfoundry.com
SIC: 3366 Castings (except die), nec, bronze

(G-15195)
OHIO STAR FORGE CO (HQ)
3991 Mahoning Ave Nw (44483)
P.O. Box 430 (44482-0430)
PHONE..............................330 847-6360
William J Orbach, CEO
Ken Saito, *
▲ EMP: 21 EST: 1988
SQ FT: 150,000
SALES (est): 48.17MM Privately Held
Web: www.ohiostarforge.com
SIC: 3462 Iron and steel forgings
PA: Daido Steel Co., Ltd.
    1-1-10, Higashisakura, Higashi-Ku
    Nagoya AIC 461-0

(G-15196)
OHIO TRAILER INC
1899 Tod Ave Sw (44485-4221)
PHONE..............................330 392-4444
John Miller, Pr
EMP: 11 EST: 1996
SQ FT: 20,000
SALES (est): 840.5K Privately Held
Web: www.ohiotrailercompany.com

SIC: 5231 7692 7538 3444 Paint, glass, and wallpaper stores; Welding repair; General automotive repair shops; Sheet metalwork

(G-15197)
ORTHOTICS PRSTHTICS RHBLTTION
Also Called: Billock, John N Cpo
700 Howland Wilson Rd Se (44484-2512)
PHONE..............................330 856-2553
John N Billock, Executive Clinical Director
John N Billock, Executive Clinical Director
EMP: 17 EST: 1975
SQ FT: 9,000
SALES (est): 445.99K Privately Held
Web: www.oandpcentre.com
SIC: 3842 8011 Braces, orthopedic; Offices and clinics of medical doctors

(G-15198)
PHOENIX TOOL COMPANY
1351 Phoenix Rd Ne (44483-2899)
PHONE..............................330 372-4627
Eric Fredenburg, Pr
Jeff Copeland, VP
Joel Fredenburg, Treas
EMP: 8 EST: 1949
SQ FT: 5,000
SALES (est): 993.52K Privately Held
Web: www.phoenixtoolcompany.com
SIC: 3544 Special dies and tools

(G-15199)
PILLAR INDUCTION
1745 Overland Ave Ne (44483-2860)
PHONE..............................262 317-5300
EMP: 11 EST: 2013
SALES (est): 1.14MM Privately Held
SIC: 3567 Industrial furnaces and ovens

(G-15200)
PRINTERS EDGE INC
4965 Mahoning Ave Nw (44483-1405)
PHONE..............................330 372-2232
▲ EMP: 18 EST: 1992
SQ FT: 11,000
SALES (est): 481.35K Privately Held
Web: www.printersedge.com
SIC: 2752 Commercial printing, lithographic

(G-15201)
R W SIDLEY INCORPORATED
425 N River Rd Nw (44483-2250)
PHONE..............................330 392-2721
Rich Kaye, Mgr
EMP: 8
SALES (corp-wide): 83.57MM Privately Held
Web: www.rwsidley.com
SIC: 3273 Ready-mixed concrete
PA: R. W. Sidley Incorporated
    436 Casement Ave
    Painesville OH 44077
    440 352-9343

(G-15202)
REINFORCEMENT SYSTEMS OF OHIO LLC
Also Called: Merksteijn
3121 W Market St (44485-3070)
PHONE..............................330 469-6958
▲ EMP: 8
SIC: 3315 Wire and fabricated wire products

(G-15203)
RSL LLC
1160 Paige Ave Ne (44483-3838)
PHONE..............................330 392-8900
Bo Campbell, Mgr
EMP: 23
SALES (corp-wide): 27.42MM Privately Held

▲ = Import ▼ = Export
◆ = Import/Export

GEOGRAPHIC SECTION

Warrensville Heights - Cuyahoga County (G-15227)

Web: www.rslinc.com
SIC: 2431 3089 3211 3442 Door frames, wood; Composition stone, plastics; Flat glass; Sash, door or window: metal
HQ: Rsl Llc
  3092 English Creek Ave
  Egg Harbor Township NJ 08234
  609 484-1600

(G-15204)
RULTRACT INC
8598 Kimblewick Ln Ne (44484-2066)
PHONE.................330 856-9808
EMP: 8 EST: 1994
SALES (est): 410.25K Privately Held
Web: www.rultract.com
SIC: 3841 Surgical and medical instruments

(G-15205)
SCHAEFER EQUIPMENT INC
1590 Phoenix Rd Ne (44483-2896)
PHONE.................330 372-4006
Rich Barnhart, CEO
Barry Anderson, VP
▲ EMP: 80 EST: 1914
SQ FT: 101,000
SALES (est): 23.29MM Publicly Held
SIC: 3462 Railroad wheels, axles, frogs, or other equipment: forged
HQ: Wabtec Corporation
  30 Isabella St Ste 300
  Pittsburgh PA 15212

(G-15206)
STARR WHEEL GROUP INC
2887 N Salem Warren Rd (44481-9508)
PHONE.................954 935-5536
Ray A Starr Junior, Pr
◆ EMP: 12 EST: 2005
SALES (est): 498.98K Privately Held
Web: www.swg1.com
SIC: 3312 Wheels

(G-15207)
SUMMIT STREET NEWS INC
645 Summit St Nw (44485-2811)
P.O. Box 1270 (44482-1270)
PHONE.................330 609-5600
Kenneth Heyman, Prin
EMP: 6 EST: 2009
SALES (est): 95.15K Privately Held
SIC: 2711 Newspapers, publishing and printing

(G-15208)
TECNOCAP LLC
Also Called: Warren Metal Lithography
2100 Griswold Street Ext Ne (44483-2750)
PHONE.................330 392-7222
Brian Bates, Mgr
EMP: 155
Web: www.tecnocapclosures.com
SIC: 3354 2752 Aluminum extruded products; Lithographing on metal
HQ: Tecnocap Llc
  1701 Wheeling Ave
  Glen Dale WV 26038
  304 845-3402

(G-15209)
THERM-O-LINK INC
Also Called: Vulkor
621 Dana St Ne Ste 5 (44483-3976)
PHONE.................330 393-7600
John Mullen, Mgr
EMP: 7
SQ FT: 18,000
SALES (corp-wide): 23.71MM Privately Held
Web: www.tolwire.com

SIC: 3357 Nonferrous wiredrawing and insulating
PA: Therm-O-Link, Inc.
  10513 Freedom St
  Garrettsville OH 44231
  330 527-2124

(G-15210)
THOMAS STEEL STRIP CORPORATION (HQ)
Also Called: Thomas Processing Company
2518 W Market St (44485-2623)
PHONE.................330 841-6429
Michael Morris, CEO
Anmdries Foerster, COO
Ludgar Kramer, VP Fin
EMP: 40 EST: 1974
SQ FT: 58,000
SALES (est): 103.48MM Privately Held
Web: www.tatasteeleurope.com
SIC: 3471 Plating and polishing
PA: Tata Steel Limited
  Bombay House, 24,
  Mumbai MH 40000

(G-15211)
TRUMBULL CEMENT PRODUCTS CO
2185 Larchmont Ave Ne (44483-2894)
PHONE.................330 372-4342
Jeffrey Carbone, Pr
Darla Carbone, Sec
Julie Carbone, Treas
EMP: 6 EST: 1922
SQ FT: 5,000
SALES (est): 504.63K Privately Held
Web: www.trumbullcementproductscompanyinc.com
SIC: 3271 5211 5032 Blocks, concrete or cinder: standard; Lumber and other building materials; Brick, stone, and related material

(G-15212)
TRUMBULL MOBILE MEALS
323 E Market St (44481-1207)
PHONE.................330 394-2538
Sandra Mathews, Ex Dir
EMP: 10 EST: 1999
SQ FT: 3,567
SALES (est): 518.46K Privately Held
Web: www.trumbullmobilemeals.org
SIC: 8322 2051 Meal delivery program; Bakery, for home service delivery

(G-15213)
ULTIMATE PRINTING CO INC
6090 Mahoning Ave Nw Ste C (44481-9495)
PHONE.................330 847-2941
Richard Wilms, Pr
William Pugh, VP
EMP: 6 EST: 1991
SQ FT: 3,000
SALES (est): 415.06K Privately Held
SIC: 2752 Offset printing

(G-15214)
ULTIUM CELLS LLC (PA)
7400 Tod Ave Sw (44481-9627)
PHONE.................586 295-5429
Kee Eun, Pr
Lincoln Shomer, CFO
EMP: 33 EST: 2020
SALES (est): 73.51MM
SALES (corp-wide): 73.51MM Privately Held
Web: www.ultiumcell.com
SIC: 3692 Dry cell batteries, single or multiple cell

(G-15215)
UNITED REFRACTORIES INC
1929 Larchmont Ave Ne (44483-3507)
PHONE.................330 372-3716
◆ EMP: 30
SIC: 3255 3272 Clay refractories; Concrete products, precast, nec

(G-15216)
VINDICATOR
240 Franklin St Se (44483-5711)
PHONE.................330 841-1600
EMP: 26 EST: 2019
SALES (est): 154.19K Privately Held
Web: www.vindy.com
SIC: 2711 Newspapers, publishing and printing

(G-15217)
VULKOR INCORPORATED (PA)
621 Dana St Ne Ste V (44483-3976)
P.O. Box 6 (44482-0006)
PHONE.................330 393-7600
David J Campbell, Pr
Ronald M Krisher, Stockholder*
Richard Thompson, Stockholder*
EMP: 24 EST: 1992
SQ FT: 780
SALES (est): 4.8MM Privately Held
SIC: 3357 Nonferrous wiredrawing and insulating

(G-15218)
WARREN CONCRETE AND SUPPLY CO
1113 Parkman Rd Nw (44485-2497)
P.O. Box 1408 (44482-1408)
PHONE.................330 393-1581
Harry N Hamilton, Pr
David H Hamilton, Pr
Harry N Hamilton, Sec
Richard Hamilton, VP
James Hamilton, VP
EMP: 24 EST: 1921
SQ FT: 2,000
SALES (est): 744.21K Privately Held
Web: www.warrenconcrete.com
SIC: 3273 5211 5032 Ready-mixed concrete; Lumber and other building materials; Brick, stone, and related material

(G-15219)
WARREN SCREW MACHINE INC
3869 Niles Rd Se (44484-3548)
PHONE.................330 609-6020
John Condoleon, Pr
EMP: 16 EST: 1983
SALES (est): 917.55K Privately Held
Web: www.warrenprecision.net
SIC: 3451 Screw machine products

(G-15220)
WARREN STEEL HOLDINGS LLC
4000 Mahoning Ave Nw (44483-1924)
PHONE.................330 847-0487
◆ EMP: 290
Web: www.warrensteelholdings.com
SIC: 3567 Electrical furnaces, ovens, & heating devices, exc. induction

(G-15221)
WARREN STEEL SPECIALTIES CORP
1309 Niles Rd Se (44484-5106)
P.O. Box 1391 (44482-1391)
PHONE.................330 399-8360
Christopher Shape, Pr
Frederick Shape, VP
Barbara Shape, Sec
EMP: 27 EST: 1931
SQ FT: 21,000

SALES (est): 1.19MM Privately Held
Web: www.warrensteel.com
SIC: 2542 3499 Stands, merchandise display: except wood; Strapping, metal

(G-15222)
WATERPRO
2926 Commonwealth Ave Ne (44483-2831)
PHONE.................330 372-3565
Vern Parker, S
EMP: 6 EST: 2002
SALES (est): 100.48K Privately Held
SIC: 3561 Pumps and pumping equipment

(G-15223)
WELD-ACTION COMPANY INC
2100 N River Rd Ne (44483-2598)
PHONE.................330 372-1063
Todd Huna, Pr
EMP: 6 EST: 1960
SQ FT: 7,158
SALES (est): 1.65MM Privately Held
Web: www.weldaction.com
SIC: 5084 3548 Welding machinery and equipment; Welding and cutting apparatus and accessories, nec

(G-15224)
WHEATLAND TUBE LLC
Also Called: Wheatland Tube Company
901 Dietz Rd Ne (44483-2700)
PHONE.................330 372-6611
Teri Aljoe, Brnch Mgr
EMP: 193
Web: www.wheatland.com
SIC: 3312 3317 Blast furnaces and steel mills; Steel pipe and tubes
HQ: Wheatland Tube, Llc
  1 Council Ave
  Wheatland PA 16161
  800 257-8182

(G-15225)
YOUNGSTOWN BENDING ROLLING INC
1052 Mahoning Ave Nw (44483-4622)
PHONE.................330 898-3878
EMP: 11 EST: 2006
SALES (est): 226.32K Privately Held
Web: www.youngstownbending.com
SIC: 3312 Pipes, iron and steel

Warrensville Heights
Cuyahoga County

(G-15226)
B & F MANUFACTURING CO
19050 Cranwood Pkwy (44128-4047)
PHONE.................216 518-0333
Marsha Kutsikovich, Pr
EMP: 10 EST: 1989
SQ FT: 10,000
SALES (est): 1.77MM Privately Held
SIC: 3599 Machine shop, jobbing and repair

(G-15227)
CHAGRIN VALLEY CUSTOM FURN LLC
26309 Miles Rd Ste 6 (44128-5945)
PHONE.................440 591-5511
EMP: 7
SALES (corp-wide): 877.77K Privately Held
Web: www.chagrinvalleycustomfurniture.com
SIC: 2521 5712 Desks, office: wood; Furniture stores
PA: Chagrin Valley Custom Furniture Llc
  7425 Edwards Lndg

Chagrin Falls OH 44023
216 591-5511

(G-15228)
CHARLES HUFFMAN & ASSOCIATES
Also Called: HUFFMAN, CHARLES & ASSOCIATES
19214 Gladstone Rd (44122-6626)
PHONE..................................216 295-0850
Charles Huffman, *Mgr*
EMP: 6
SALES (corp-wide): 444.15K **Privately Held**
Web: www.mediafundsuperpac.com
SIC: 2759 Commercial printing, nec
PA: Charles Huffman & Associates
17325 Euclid Ave Ste 4002
Cleveland OH 44112
216 295-0850

(G-15229)
GINOS AWARDS INC
Also Called: Gino's Jewelers & Trophy Mfrs
4701 Richmond Rd Ste 200 (44128-5994)
PHONE..................................216 831-6565
Gino Zavarella, *Pr*
▲ **EMP:** 50 **EST:** 1950
SQ FT: 30,000
SALES (est): 8.05MM **Privately Held**
Web: www.ginosonline.com
SIC: 3911 3993 3914 Jewelry, precious metal ; Signs and advertising specialties; Trophies, nsk

(G-15230)
POLIMEROS USA LLC
Also Called: Rotopolymers
26210 Emery Rd Ste 202 (44128-5770)
PHONE..................................216 591-0175
Ron Davis, *Contrlr*
Jose Antonio Gomez Godoy, *Genl Mgr*
EMP: 8 **EST:** 2012
SALES (est): 15.15MM **Privately Held**
Web: www.polimerosusa.com
SIC: 2821 Plastics materials and resins

(G-15231)
WHITMORE PRODUCTIONS INC
Also Called: Whitmore's Bbq
20209 Harvard Ave (44122-6808)
PHONE..................................216 752-3960
Virgil Whitmore, *Pr*
Vance Whitmore, *VP*
Kim Whitmore, *Sec*
Esther Whitmore, *Treas*
EMP: 13 **EST:** 1987
SQ FT: 1,500
SALES (est): 386.79K **Privately Held**
Web: www.whitmoreproductions.com
SIC: 2099 Sauces: dry mixes

Washington Court Hou
Fayette County

(G-15232)
COURTHOUSE MANUFACTURING LLC
Also Called: Chappell Door Company
1730 Washington Avenue, Solar Lane (43160)
PHONE..................................740 335-2727
Wayne Gooley, *Managing Member*
EMP: 38 **EST:** 1955
SQ FT: 84,000
SALES (est): 4.91MM **Privately Held**
Web: www.chappelldoor.net
SIC: 2431 Doors, wood

(G-15233)
STARK TRUSS COMPANY INC
2000 Landmark Blvd (43160)
P.O. Box 8 (43160-0008)
PHONE..................................740 335-4156
Jeff Coulter, *Brnch Mgr*
EMP: 41
SQ FT: 12,000
SALES (corp-wide): 99.05MM **Privately Held**
Web: www.starktruss.com
SIC: 2439 Trusses, wooden roof
PA: Stark Truss Company, Inc.
109 Miles Ave Sw
Canton OH 44710
330 478-2100

(G-15234)
YUSA CORPORATION (HQ)
151 Jamison Rd. Sw (43160)
PHONE..................................740 335-0335
Takeyoshi Usui, *Pr*
Nobuyuki Tateno, *
Yoshiji Iwamoto, *
▲ **EMP:** 37 **EST:** 1987
SQ FT: 250,000
SALES (est): 228.87MM **Privately Held**
Web: www.yusa-oh.com
SIC: 3069 Rubber covered motor mounting rings (rubber bonded)
PA: Yamashita Rubber Co., Ltd.
1239, Kamekubo
Fujimino STM 356-0

Waterford
Washington County

(G-15235)
AIR HEATER SEAL COMPANY INC
15710 Waterford Rd (45786-5001)
P.O. Box 8 (45786-0008)
PHONE..................................740 984-2146
Randy Townsend, *Owner*
Mable Townsend, *Sec*
EMP: 23 **EST:** 1989
SQ FT: 4,500
SALES (est): 1.91MM **Privately Held**
Web: www.airheaterseal.com
SIC: 3053 3441 Gaskets; packing and sealing devices; Fabricated structural metal

(G-15236)
FERROGLOBE USA MTLLURGICAL INC (DH)
Also Called: Globe Metallurgical Inc.
1595 Sparling Rd (45786-6104)
P.O. Box 157 (45715-0157)
PHONE..................................740 984-2361
Alan Kestenbaum, *Ch*
Jeff Bradley, *
Marlin Perkins, *
Stuart Eizenstat, *
Franklin Lavin, *
◆ **EMP:** 141 **EST:** 1871
SALES (est): 180.88MM
SALES (corp-wide): 2.6B **Privately Held**
Web: www.globemetallurgical.com
SIC: 3339 3313 2819 Silicon refining (primary, over 99% pure); Ferrosilicon, not made in blast furnaces; Industrial inorganic chemicals, nec
HQ: Globe Specialty Metals, Inc.
600 Brickell Ave Ste 310
Miami FL 33131

(G-15237)
LAMINATE SHOP
1145 Klinger Rd (45786-5347)
P.O. Box 1218 (45750-6218)
PHONE..................................740 749-3536
Tim Strahler, *Pr*
EMP: 10 **EST:** 1986
SQ FT: 25,000
SALES (est): 760.62K **Privately Held**
Web: www.thelaminateshopinc.com
SIC: 3083 5211 1799 Laminated plastics plate and sheet; Cabinets, kitchen; Counter top installation

(G-15238)
MALTA DYNAMICS LLC (PA)
405 Watertown Rd (45786-5248)
PHONE..................................740 749-3512
Damian Lang, *CEO*
Douglas Taylor, *CFO*
Ken Hebert, *Stockholder*
EMP: 19 **EST:** 2015
SALES (est): 2.58MM
SALES (corp-wide): 2.58MM **Privately Held**
Web: www.maltadynamics.com
SIC: 3531 3821 3851 4581 Winches; Incubators, laboratory; Ophthalmic goods; Aircraft maintenance and repair services

Waterville
Lucas County

(G-15239)
AQUILA PHARMATECH LLC
8225 Farnsworth Rd Ste A7 (43566-9781)
PHONE..................................419 386-2527
EMP: 6 **EST:** 2009
SALES (est): 227.21K **Privately Held**
Web: aquila-pharmatech.lookchem.com
SIC: 3559 Chemical machinery and equipment

(G-15240)
CARRUTH STUDIO INC (PA)
1178 Farnsworth Rd (43566-1074)
PHONE..................................419 878-3060
George Carruth, *Pr*
Debbie Carruth, *Sec*
EMP: 13 **EST:** 1983
SQ FT: 13,600
SALES (est): 2.33MM
SALES (corp-wide): 2.33MM **Privately Held**
Web: www.carruthstudio.com
SIC: 3269 3272 Art and ornamental ware, pottery; Concrete products, nec

(G-15241)
CRUM MANUFACTURING INC
1265 Waterville Monclova Rd (43566-1067)
PHONE..................................419 878-9779
Ernest Crum Junior, *Pr*
EMP: 25 **EST:** 1984
SQ FT: 23,000
SALES (est): 4.55MM **Privately Held**
Web: www.crummfg.com
SIC: 3544 3599 3462 Special dies, tools, jigs, and fixtures; Machine and other job shop work; Automotive forgings, ferrous: crankshaft, engine, axle, etc.

(G-15242)
DUVALL WOODWORKING INC
Also Called: American Products
7551 Dutch Rd (43566-9732)
PHONE..................................419 878-9581
Thomas Duvall, *Pr*
EMP: 7 **EST:** 1992
SQ FT: 12,000
SALES (est): 435.82K **Privately Held**
Web: www.duvallwoodworking.com
SIC: 2431 Millwork

(G-15243)
FRANKLIN
Also Called: Rrysburg Sunoco
747 Michigan Ave (43566-1052)
PHONE..................................419 699-5757
EMP: 6 **EST:** 2010
SALES (est): 189.81K **Privately Held**
SIC: 2869 Fuels

(G-15244)
FURNACE TECHNOLOGIES INC
Also Called: Furn Tech
1070 Disher Dr (43566-1079)
PHONE..................................419 878-2100
Tim Fisher, *Pr*
EMP: 17 **EST:** 1985
SALES (est): 776.29K **Privately Held**
Web: www.thermeq.com
SIC: 3567 Heating units and devices, industrial: electric

(G-15245)
HEIDELBERG MTLS MDWEST AGG INC
600 S River Rd (43566-9754)
P.O. Box 49 (43566-0049)
PHONE..................................419 878-2006
Paul Carbaugh, *Brnch Mgr*
EMP: 9
SALES (corp-wide): 23.02B **Privately Held**
SIC: 2951 Asphalt and asphaltic paving mixtures (not from refineries)
HQ: Heidelberg Materials Midwest Agg, Inc.
300 E John Carpenter Fwy
Irving TX

(G-15246)
JOHNS MANVILLE CORPORATION
7500 Dutch Rd (43566-9731)
PHONE..................................419 878-8111
Rhonda Francis, *Prin*
EMP: 94
SALES (corp-wide): 364.48B **Publicly Held**
Web: www.jm.com
SIC: 3296 3297 3229 2273 Fiberglass insulation; Nonclay refractories; Pressed and blown glass, nec; Carpets and rugs
HQ: Johns Manville Corporation
717 17th St
Denver CO 80202
303 978-2000

(G-15247)
JOHNS MANVILLE CORPORATION
6050 N River Rd (43566-9611)
PHONE..................................419 878-8112
Mary Rhinehart, *Brnch Mgr*
EMP: 54
SALES (corp-wide): 364.48B **Publicly Held**
Web: www.jm.com
SIC: 3296 Fiberglass insulation
HQ: Johns Manville Corporation
717 17th St
Denver CO 80202
303 978-2000

(G-15248)
KAUFMAN ENGINEERED SYSTEMS INC
1260 Waterville Monclova Rd (43566-1066)
PHONE..................................419 878-9727
Andrew J Quinn, *Pr*
Charles R Kaufman, *
Robert J Kaufman, *
EMP: 72 **EST:** 1957
SQ FT: 66,250
SALES (est): 19.54MM **Privately Held**
Web: www.kaufmanengsys.com

SIC: 3567 3565 Industrial furnaces and ovens; Packaging machinery

(G-15249)
LABCRAFT INC
Also Called: Furntech
1070 Disher Dr (43566-1079)
PHONE.............................419 878-4400
Ernest Seeman, *Pr*
EMP: 25 **EST:** 1997
SALES (est): 1.95MM **Privately Held**
Web: www.thermeq.com
SIC: 3499 Machine bases, metal

(G-15250)
MAUMEE VALLEY MEMORIALS INC (DH)
Also Called: Americraft Bronze Co
111 Anthony Wayne Trl (43566-1373)
P.O. Box 289 (43566-0289)
PHONE.............................419 878-9030
Richard Kimball, *Pr*
EMP: 12
SQ FT: 2,500
SALES (est): 5.61MM
SALES (corp-wide): 2.1MM **Privately Held**
Web: www.ohiomonuments.com
SIC: 5999 3281 Monuments, finished to custom order; Cut stone and stone products
HQ: Swenson Granite Company Llc
369 N State St
Concord NH 03301
603 225-4322

(G-15251)
RIMER ENTERPRISES INC
Also Called: Kelic
916 Rimer Dr (43566-1019)
P.O. Box 27 (43566-0027)
PHONE.............................419 878-8156
Chuck Meyers, *Pr*
Eric Nathe, *
▲ **EMP:** 30 **EST:** 1967
SQ FT: 25,000
SALES (est): 4.74MM **Privately Held**
Web: www.rimerinc.com
SIC: 3324 Commercial investment castings, ferrous

(G-15252)
SEAGATE PLASTICS COMPANY LLC (PA)
Also Called: Seagate Plastics
1110 Disher Dr (43566-1256)
PHONE.............................419 878-5010
Kevin Fink, *Pr*
▲ **EMP:** 39 **EST:** 1987
SQ FT: 50,000
SALES (est): 9.4MM
SALES (corp-wide): 9.4MM **Privately Held**
Web: www.seagateplastics.com
SIC: 3089 Injection molding of plastics

(G-15253)
T J F INC
Also Called: Thermeq Co
1070 Disher Dr (43566-1079)
PHONE.............................419 878-4400
Ernest Seeman, *Dir*
EMP: 16 **EST:** 1988
SALES (est): 3.97MM **Privately Held**
Web: www.thermeq.com
SIC: 3585 3433 3449 3567 Refrigeration and heating equipment; Heating equipment, except electric; Miscellaneous metalwork; Industrial furnaces and ovens

(G-15254)
TECH SYSTEMS INC
1070 Disher Dr (43566-1079)
PHONE.............................419 878-2100
Tim Fisher, *Pr*
EMP: 10 **EST:** 1992
SALES (est): 205.13K **Privately Held**
Web: www.techsystemsinc.com
SIC: 3441 Fabricated structural metal

(G-15255)
WATERVILLE SHEET METAL COMPANY
1210 Waterville Monclova Rd (43566-1000)
PHONE.............................419 878-5050
Ron Kelso, *Pr*
EMP: 6 **EST:** 1981
SQ FT: 12,000
SALES (est): 979.2K **Privately Held**
Web: www.waterville.org
SIC: 3444 Sheet metal specialties, not stamped

Wauseon
Fulton County

(G-15256)
ARC METAL STAMPING LLC
Also Called: Kecy Metal Technologies
447 E Walnut St (43567-1278)
PHONE.............................517 448-8954
EMP: 90 **EST:** 2014
SALES (est): 8.24MM **Privately Held**
SIC: 3469 Stamping metal for the trade

(G-15257)
BARN SMALL ENGINE REPA
10295 State Route 108 (43567-9525)
PHONE.............................419 583-6595
Mark Seiler, *Prin*
EMP: 7 **EST:** 2008
SALES (est): 233.82K **Privately Held**
SIC: 3523 Barn cleaners

(G-15258)
BUSSE KNIFE CO
Also Called: Busse Combat Knives
11651 County Road 12 (43567-9622)
PHONE.............................419 923-6471
Jerry Busse, *Pr*
EMP: 15 **EST:** 1984
SQ FT: 37,000
SALES (est): 503.11K **Privately Held**
Web: www.bussecombat.com
SIC: 3421 Knife blades and blanks

(G-15259)
CORNERSTONE WAUSEON INC
Also Called: Wauseon Machine & Mfg Inc
995 Enterprise Ave (43567-9333)
PHONE.............................419 337-0940
Ryan Anair, *CEO*
Peter Paras Junior, *VP*
Matthew Bombick, *
Ellen Hadymon, *
EMP: 190 **EST:** 2013
SALES (est): 20.24MM **Privately Held**
SIC: 3441 3559 7629 3547 Fabricated structural metal; Automotive related machinery; Electrical repair shops; Rolling mill machinery

(G-15260)
E & J DEMARK INC
Also Called: Demark
1115 N Ottokee St (43567-1911)
P.O. Box 416 (43567-0416)
PHONE.............................419 337-5866
J Edwin Hecock, *Pr*
Boonie L Hecock, *
EMP: 33 **EST:** 1984
SQ FT: 29,000
SALES (est): 3.89MM **Privately Held**
Web: www.ejdemark.com
SIC: 3545 3599 Machine tool accessories; Machine shop, jobbing and repair

(G-15261)
FULTON INDUSTRIES INC (PA)
Also Called: Fulton
135 E Linfoot St (43567-1000)
P.O. Box 377 (43567-0377)
PHONE.............................419 335-3015
John Razzano, *Pr*
Glenn Badenhop, *
Kim Griggs, *
Ned Griggs, *
Robert E Swanson, *
EMP: 69 **EST:** 1979
SQ FT: 170,000
SALES (est): 10.38MM
SALES (corp-wide): 10.38MM **Privately Held**
Web: www.fultonindoh.com
SIC: 3469 3648 Stamping metal for the trade ; Flashlights

(G-15262)
HAAS DOOR COMPANY
320 Sycamore St (43567-1100)
PHONE.............................419 337-9900
EMP: 200 **EST:** 1971
SQ FT: 150,000
SALES (est): 26.83MM **Privately Held**
Web: www.haasdoor.com
SIC: 3442 Garage doors, overhead: metal

(G-15263)
HILL MANUFACTURING INC
318 W Chestnut St (43567-1369)
P.O. Box 241 (43567-0241)
PHONE.............................419 335-5006
Marion Hill, *Pr*
Carl T Hill, *
▲ **EMP:** 50 **EST:** 1948
SQ FT: 55,000
SALES (est): 7.61MM **Privately Held**
Web: www.hillmfginc.com
SIC: 3469 Stamping metal for the trade

(G-15264)
INTERNTNAL AUTO CMPNNTS GROUP
555 W Linfoot St (43567-9558)
PHONE.............................419 335-1000
EMP: 46
Web: www.iacgroup.com
SIC: 3714 Motor vehicle parts and accessories
PA: International Automotive Components Group North America, Inc.
27777 Franklin Rd # 2000
Southfield MI 48034

(G-15265)
INTERNTNAL AUTO CMPNNTS GROUP
Also Called: Automotive Industries Division
555 W Linfoot St (43567-9558)
PHONE.............................419 433-5653
EMP: 700
Web: www.iacgroup.com
SIC: 3089 3714 3429 3229 Injection molded finished plastics products, nec; Motor vehicle parts and accessories; Hardware, nec; Pressed and blown glass, nec
PA: International Automotive Components Group North America, Inc.
27777 Franklin Rd # 2000
Southfield MI 48034

(G-15266)
LATROBE SPECIALTY MTLS CO LLC
14614 County Road H (43567-9796)
PHONE.............................419 335-8010
Cheryl Bookheimer, *Brnch Mgr*
EMP: 25
SALES (corp-wide): 2.55B **Publicly Held**
Web: www.latrobefoundry.com
SIC: 3312 Tool and die steel
HQ: Latrobe Specialty Metals Company, Llc
2626 Ligonier St
Latrobe PA 15650
724 537-7711

(G-15267)
LEAR CORPORATION
Also Called: Sheridan Mfg
447 E Walnut St (43567-1278)
PHONE.............................419 335-6010
Cary Wood, *Brnch Mgr*
EMP: 29
SQ FT: 80,000
SALES (corp-wide): 23.47B **Publicly Held**
Web: www.lear.com
SIC: 3714 Motor vehicle parts and accessories
PA: Lear Corporation
21557 Telegraph Rd
Southfield MI 48033
248 447-1500

(G-15268)
MACHINING SOLUTIONS LLC
425 Enterprise Ave (43567-9320)
PHONE.............................419 593-0038
Allen R Smith, *Managing Member*
Matthew Makulinski, *Managing Member*
EMP: 14 **EST:** 2007
SALES (est): 1.01MM **Privately Held**
Web: www.machiningsolutions.us
SIC: 3599 Machine shop, jobbing and repair

(G-15269)
MULTI CAST LLC
225 E Linfoot St (43567-1007)
PHONE.............................419 335-0010
Mike Schnipke, *Managing Member*
EMP: 37 **EST:** 1930
SQ FT: 42,500
SALES (est): 4.39MM **Privately Held**
Web: www.aluminumsandcastingsfoundry.com
SIC: 3365 Aluminum and aluminum-based alloy castings

(G-15270)
NEBRASKA INDUSTRIES CORP
447 E Walnut St (43567-1278)
PHONE.............................419 335-6010
Michael Hemphill, *Pr*
Ray Cox, *
Nicholas Cox, *Stockholder*
EMP: 17 **EST:** 1999
SQ FT: 95,000
SALES (est): 671.2K **Privately Held**
Web: www.nebraskaindustries.com
SIC: 3469 3089 3714 3465 Stamping metal for the trade; Injection molding of plastics; Motor vehicle parts and accessories; Automotive stampings

(G-15271)
NOFZIGER DOOR SALES INC (PA)
Also Called: Haas Doors
320 Sycamore St (43567-1100)
PHONE.............................419 337-9900
Edward L Nofziger, *Pr*
Carol Nofziger, *
▼ **EMP:** 173 **EST:** 1938
SQ FT: 200,000
SALES (est): 39.6MM

Wauseon - Fulton County (G-15272)

SALES (corp-wide): 39.6MM **Privately Held**
Web: www.archboldohiogaragedoors.com
SIC: 3442 1751 5211 Metal doors; Garage door, installation or erection; Doors, wood or metal, except storm

(G-15272)
PERFECTION FINISHERS INC
1151 N Ottokee St (43567-1911)
PHONE...................................419 337-8015
Gerald Haack, *CEO*
EMP: 25 **EST:** 1986
SQ FT: 80,000
SALES (est): 2.44MM **Privately Held**
Web: www.perfectionfinishers.com
SIC: 3479 Coating of metals with plastic or resins

(G-15273)
PUEHLER AGCO INC
3304 State Route 108 (43567-9410)
PHONE...................................419 388-6614
Ben Puehler, *CEO*
EMP: 7 **EST:** 2021
SALES (est): 226.01K **Privately Held**
Web: www.pagco.us
SIC: 3523 Farm machinery and equipment

(G-15274)
TOMAHAWK PRINTING INC
229 N Fulton St (43567-1171)
P.O. Box 413 (43567-0413)
PHONE...................................419 335-3161
Jerry Dehnbostel, *Pr*
Lolita Dehnbostel, *VP*
EMP: 10 **EST:** 1938
SQ FT: 3,000
SALES (est): 500.82K **Privately Held**
Web: www.tomahawkprinting.com
SIC: 2752 2789 Offset printing; Binding only: books, pamphlets, magazines, etc.

(G-15275)
TULUA NUTRITION
11580 County Road L (43567-9252)
PHONE...................................419 764-0664
Logan Baker, *CEO*
EMP: 6 **EST:** 2019
SALES (est): 74.42K **Privately Held**
SIC: 2834 Vitamin, nutrient, and hematinic preparations for human use

(G-15276)
UNLIMTED RCOVERY SOLUTIONS LLC
2701 S Eberd Rd Ste B (43567)
PHONE...................................419 868-4888
EMP: 45 **EST:** 2010
SALES (est): 2.5MM **Privately Held**
SIC: 3713 Dump truck bodies

(G-15277)
WYSE INDUSTRIAL CARTS INC
10510 County Road 12 (43567-9237)
PHONE...................................419 923-7353
Gene Wyse, *Pr*
Randy Wyse, *VP*
EMP: 12 **EST:** 1996
SQ FT: 20,000
SALES (est): 2.44MM **Privately Held**
Web: www.wysecarts.com
SIC: 3448 Ramps, prefabricated metal

Waverly
Pike County

(G-15278)
BEAZER EAST INC
9978 State Route 220 (45690-9012)
PHONE...................................740 947-4677
William H Chattin, *Brnch Mgr*
EMP: 11
SALES (corp-wide): 23.02B **Privately Held**
SIC: 3273 Ready-mixed concrete
HQ: Beazer East, Inc.
600 River Ave Ste 200
Pittsburgh PA 15212
412 428-9407

(G-15279)
CLARKSVILLE STAVE & VENEER CO
Also Called: Wooden US
9329 State Route 220 Ste A (45690-9189)
PHONE...................................740 947-4159
Ben Nathan, *Pr*
Todd Nathan, *VP*
Glenda Nathan, *Sec*
◆ **EMP:** 10 **EST:** 1978
SALES (est): 1.01MM **Privately Held**
SIC: 2421 Sawmills and planing mills, general

(G-15280)
ECHO ENVIRONMENTAL WAVERLY LLC
479 Industrial Park Dr (45690)
PHONE...................................740 710-7901
Alan Stockmeister, *CEO*
EMP: 9 **EST:** 2013
SALES (est): 245.28K **Privately Held**
SIC: 3341 Copper smelting and refining (secondary)

(G-15281)
GEO-TECH POLYMERS LLC
479 Industrial Park Dr (45690-1199)
P.O. Box 61 (48347-0061)
PHONE...................................614 797-2300
▼ **EMP:** 17 **EST:** 2000
SALES (est): 5.05MM **Privately Held**
SIC: 2821 Plastics materials and resins
PA: Vns Federal Services, Llc
1571 Shyville Rd
Piketon OH 45661

(G-15282)
GRAPHIX NETWORK
122 N High St (45690-1342)
PHONE...................................740 941-3771
Johanna Pixley, *Prin*
EMP: 7 **EST:** 2010
SALES (est): 240.79K **Privately Held**
SIC: 2752 Offset printing

(G-15283)
J & R PALLET LTD
1100 Travis Rd (45690-9086)
PHONE...................................740 226-1112
Ramona Southworth, *Prin*
EMP: 6 **EST:** 2005
SALES (est): 225K **Privately Held**
SIC: 2448 Pallets, wood and wood with metal

(G-15284)
KIRCHHOFF AUTO WAVERLY INC (DH)
611 W 2nd St (45690-9701)
PHONE...................................740 947-7763
Dennis Berry, *CEO*
▲ **EMP:** 15 **EST:** 2009
SALES (est): 93.2MM
SALES (corp-wide): 1.69B **Privately Held**
SIC: 3465 Automotive stampings
HQ: Kirchhoff Automotive Ag
Stefanstr. 2
Iserlohn NW 58638
237182000

(G-15285)
MILLS PRIDE PREMIER INC
423 Hopewell Rd (45690-9801)
PHONE...................................740 941-1300
EMP: 8 **EST:** 2014
SALES (est): 165.62K **Privately Held**
SIC: 2434 Wood kitchen cabinets

(G-15286)
MILLTREE LUMBER HOLDINGS
535 Coal Dock Rd (45690-9799)
PHONE...................................740 226-2090
Terry Marr, *Prin*
EMP: 11 **EST:** 2014
SALES (est): 975.64K **Privately Held**
Web: www.millwoodinc.com
SIC: 2448 Pallets, wood

(G-15287)
MILLWOOD INC
535 Coal Dock Rd (45690-9799)
PHONE...................................740 226-2090
Terry Robbins, *Pr*
EMP: 31
Web: www.millwoodinc.com
SIC: 2448 Pallets, wood
PA: Millwood, Inc.
3708 International Blvd
Vienna OH 44473

(G-15288)
NEWS WATCHMAN & PAPER
Also Called: Acm Ohio
860 W Emmitt Ave Ste 5 (45690-1080)
P.O. Box 151 (45690-0151)
PHONE...................................740 947-2149
Norman Guilliland, *Prin*
Carrie Humble, *Prin*
EMP: 10 **EST:** 2005
SALES (est): 649.38K **Privately Held**
Web: www.newswatchman.com
SIC: 2711 7313 Newspapers, publishing and printing; Newspaper advertising representative

(G-15289)
OAK CHIPS INC
Also Called: O C I
9329 State Route 220 Ste A (45690-9189)
PHONE...................................740 947-4159
Edward Todd Nathan, *Pr*
◆ **EMP:** 49 **EST:** 2014
SALES (est): 2.99MM **Privately Held**
Web: www.oakchipsinc.com
SIC: 2448 2861 Pallets, wood; Wood extract products

(G-15290)
PERFORMANX SPECIALTY CHEM LLC
479 Industrial Park Dr (45690-1199)
PHONE...................................614 300-7001
Kim Pellock, *Brnch Mgr*
EMP: 6
SALES (corp-wide): 517.18K **Privately Held**
Web: www.stepan.com
SIC: 2834 Pharmaceutical preparations
PA: Performanx Specialty Chemicals, Llc
300 Westdale Ave
Westerville OH 43082
614 300-7001

(G-15291)
THIRD MILLENNIUM MATERIALS LLC
Also Called: Tmm
974 Prosperity Rd (45690-8938)
PHONE...................................740 947-1023
EMP: 6 **EST:** 2009
SALES (est): 458.05K **Privately Held**
SIC: 3399 Primary metal products

Waynesburg
Stark County

(G-15292)
ACE ASSEMBLY & PACKAGING INC
133 N Mill St (44688-9124)
P.O. Box 55 (44688-0055)
PHONE...................................330 866-9117
Dency S Cilona, *D*
EMP: 8 **EST:** 1999
SALES (est): 259.92K **Privately Held**
SIC: 7389 3999 Packaging and labeling services; Manufacturing industries, nec

(G-15293)
BAUGHMAN MACHINE & WELD SP INC
6498 June Rd Nw (44688-9433)
PHONE...................................330 866-9243
Paul Baughman, *Pr*
John Baughaman, *VP*
Kathy Miller, *Treas*
EMP: 8 **EST:** 1977
SQ FT: 960
SALES (est): 308.87K **Privately Held**
SIC: 7692 Welding repair

(G-15294)
E & M LIBERTY WELDING INC
141 James St (44688-9313)
PHONE...................................330 866-2338
Mark Crowe, *Pr*
Earl Ecenbarger, *VP*
EMP: 8 **EST:** 2004
SALES (est): 50K **Privately Held**
SIC: 7692 1711 Welding repair; Boiler and furnace contractors

Waynesfield
Auglaize County

(G-15295)
ACA MILLWORKS INC
Also Called: Old West Woods
16330 Waynesfield Rd (45896-9618)
P.O. Box 367 (45896-0367)
PHONE...................................419 339-7600
Holly Bowersock, *Prin*
EMP: 15 **EST:** 2002
SALES (est): 505.34K **Privately Held**
Web: www.oldwestwoods.com
SIC: 2431 Millwork

(G-15296)
INDUSTRIAL PAINT & STRIP INC
1000 Commerce Ct (45896-8415)
P.O. Box 967 (43138-0967)
PHONE...................................419 568-2222
EMP: 35 **EST:** 2000
SQ FT: 13,500
SALES (est): 2.98MM **Privately Held**
Web: www.ipswest.com
SIC: 3471 Plating and polishing

GEOGRAPHIC SECTION

Wellington - Lorain County (G-15320)

Waynesville
Warren County

(G-15297)
JAKES WOODSHOP
2734 E State Route 73 (45068-8750)
PHONE.................................937 672-4964
EMP: 6 **EST:** 2018
SALES (est): 212.8K **Privately Held**
SIC: 2499 Decorative wood and woodwork

(G-15298)
JOHN PURDUM
Also Called: Brass Lantern Antiques
100 S Main St (45068-8954)
P.O. Box 597 (45068-0597)
PHONE.................................513 897-9686
John Purdum, *Owner*
EMP: 6 **EST:** 1970
SQ FT: 3,720
SALES (est): 307.39K **Privately Held**
Web: www.waynesvilleshops.com
SIC: 5932 5399 2519 7011 Antiques; Country general stores; Household furniture, except wood or metal: upholstered; Hotels and motels

(G-15299)
MK WELDING & FABRICATION INC
1824 E Lower Springboro Rd (45068)
PHONE.................................937 603-4430
C Alan Edinger, *Pr*
EMP: 7 **EST:** 1989
SALES (est): 526.63K **Privately Held**
Web: www.mkweld.com
SIC: 7692 Welding repair

(G-15300)
OREGONIA VALLEY METALWORKS LLC
184 N Main St (45068-9765)
PHONE.................................513 967-5190
EMP: 7 **EST:** 2018
SALES (est): 236.16K **Privately Held**
Web: www.ovmetalworks.com
SIC: 3441 Fabricated structural metal

(G-15301)
OUTHOUSE PAPER ETC INC
319 Collett Rd (45068-9306)
P.O. Box 101 (45177-0101)
PHONE.................................937 382-2800
Shelley Taylor, *Pr*
EMP: 6 **EST:** 2004
SQ FT: 3,250
SALES (est): 630.84K **Privately Held**
SIC: 2679 Paperboard products, converted, nec

(G-15302)
PATRICK M DAVIDSON
Also Called: Davidson Meat Processing Plant
6490 Corwin Ave (45068-9722)
PHONE.................................513 897-2971
Patrick M Davidson, *Owner*
EMP: 6 **EST:** 1961
SQ FT: 3,000
SALES (est): 422K **Privately Held**
Web: www.davidsonmeatprocessing.com
SIC: 0751 2013 2011 Slaughtering: custom livestock services; Sausages and other prepared meats; Meat packing plants

Wellington
Lorain County

(G-15303)
ARC ELEC
18637 State Route 511 (44090-9700)
PHONE.................................440 774-2800
EMP: 6 **EST:** 2014
SALES (est): 243.88K **Privately Held**
SIC: 3699 1731 Electrical equipment and supplies, nec; Electrical work

(G-15304)
BILLINGTON COMPANY INC
143 Erie St (44090-1206)
P.O. Box 156 (44090-0156)
PHONE.................................440 647-3039
Mark Lupico, *Pr*
EMP: 20 **EST:** 1945
SQ FT: 8,500
SALES (est): 1.62MM **Privately Held**
SIC: 3444 Sheet metalwork

(G-15305)
CLEVELAND CITY FORGE INC
46950 State Route 18 (44090-9791)
PHONE.................................440 647-5400
Richard Kovach, *Pr*
Kenneth Kovach, *
Drew Maddock, *
EMP: 40 **EST:** 1887
SQ FT: 200,000
SALES (est): 5.47MM **Privately Held**
Web: www.clevelandcityforge.com
SIC: 3441 Fabricated structural metal

(G-15306)
EDWARD W DANIEL LLC
46950 State Route 18 Ste B (44090-9791)
PHONE.................................440 647-1960
Ken Wrona, *
Stuart W Cordell, *
EMP: 21 **EST:** 1922
SQ FT: 75,000
SALES (est): 1.84MM **Privately Held**
Web: www.ewdaniel.com
SIC: 3429 5085 3494 3463 Hardware, nec; Industrial supplies; Valves and pipe fittings, nec; Nonferrous forgings

(G-15307)
EXPERT CRANE INC
Also Called: Expert Crane
720 Shiloh Ave (44090-1190)
PHONE.................................216 451-9900
James C Doty, *Pr*
Rebecca Doty, *
EMP: 47 **EST:** 1977
SALES (est): 11MM **Privately Held**
Web: www.expertcrane.com
SIC: 3536 7699 1796 5084 Hoists, cranes, and monorails; Industrial machinery and equipment repair; Machinery installation; Cranes, industrial

(G-15308)
FIVE STAR FABRICATION LLC
18308 Quarry Rd (44090-9460)
PHONE.................................440 666-0427
Matthew Kennedy, *CEO*
EMP: 11 **EST:** 2018
SALES (est): 406.65K **Privately Held**
Web: www.weldandfabnow.com
SIC: 3999 Manufacturing industries, nec

(G-15309)
FOREST CITY TECHNOLOGIES INC
Also Called: Forest City Technologies
232 Maple St (44090-1164)
P.O. Box 86 (44090-0086)
PHONE.................................440 647-2115
Chuck Shilleg, *Mgr*
EMP: 232
SALES (corp-wide): 90.48MM **Privately Held**
Web: www.forestcitytech.com
SIC: 3053 Gaskets and sealing devices
PA: Forest City Technologies, Inc.
299 Clay St
Wellington OH 44090
440 647-2115

(G-15310)
FOREST CITY TECHNOLOGIES INC
Also Called: Forest City Tech Plant 4
401 Magyar St (44090-1278)
P.O. Box 86 (44090-0086)
PHONE.................................440 647-2115
Bob Nelson, *Genl Mgr*
EMP: 139
SALES (corp-wide): 90.48MM **Privately Held**
Web: www.forestcitytech.com
SIC: 3053 Gasket materials
PA: Forest City Technologies, Inc.
299 Clay St
Wellington OH 44090
440 647-2115

(G-15311)
FOREST CITY TECHNOLOGIES INC
Also Called: Adelphia
299 Clay St (44090-1128)
P.O. Box 86 (44090-0086)
PHONE.................................440 647-2115
Buzz Bernning, *Mgr*
EMP: 93
SALES (corp-wide): 90.48MM **Privately Held**
Web: www.forestcitytech.com
SIC: 3053 Gasket materials
PA: Forest City Technologies, Inc.
299 Clay St
Wellington OH 44090
440 647-2115

(G-15312)
FOREST CITY TECHNOLOGIES INC (PA)
299 Clay St (44090-1128)
P.O. Box 86 (44090-0086)
PHONE.................................440 647-2115
John D Cloud, *Pr*
John D Cloud Senior, *Pr*
David Snowball, *VP*
▲ **EMP:** 430 **EST:** 1955
SQ FT: 50,000
SALES (est): 90.48MM
SALES (corp-wide): 90.48MM **Privately Held**
Web: www.forestcitytech.com
SIC: 3053 Gaskets, all materials

(G-15313)
GROUPER ACQUISITION CO LLC
Also Called: Shiloh Industries, LLC
350 Maple St (44090-1171)
PHONE.................................330 558-2600
EMP: 280
SALES (corp-wide): 1.97B **Privately Held**
SIC: 3465 Automotive stampings
HQ: Grouper Acquisition Company, Llc
1780 Pond Run
Auburn Hills MI 48326
248 299-7500

(G-15314)
KALRON LLC
143 Erie St (44090-1206)
P.O. Box 156 (44090-0156)
PHONE.................................440 647-3039
Todd Markus, *Pr*
EMP: 20 **EST:** 2008
SALES (est): 2.96MM
SALES (corp-wide): 24.93MM **Privately Held**
Web: www.kalronllc.com
SIC: 3444 Sheet metalwork
PA: Norlake Manufacturing Company
39301 Taylor Pkwy
North Ridgeville OH 44035
440 353-3200

(G-15315)
KALRON LLC
775 Shiloh Ave (44090-1190)
PHONE.................................440 647-3039
EMP: 13 **EST:** 2019
SALES (est): 866.23K **Privately Held**
Web: www.kalronllc.com
SIC: 3444 Sheet metalwork

(G-15316)
KTS EQUIPMENT INC
Also Called: Ford
47117 State Route 18 (44090-9264)
PHONE.................................440 647-2015
Jill Sheparovich, *Pr*
Lawrence Krystowski, *
Ronald Krystowski, *
Richard Krystowski, *
Jim Mclaughlin, *VP*
EMP: 24 **EST:** 1945
SQ FT: 15,000
SALES (est): 6MM **Privately Held**
Web: www.ktsequipment.com
SIC: 3523 Farm machinery and equipment

(G-15317)
MOHR STAMPING INC
22038 Fairgrounds Rd (44090-9266)
P.O. Box 87 (44090-0087)
PHONE.................................440 647-4316
▼ **EMP:** 25 **EST:** 1967
SALES (est): 4.08MM **Privately Held**
Web: www.mohrstamping.com
SIC: 3469 3544 Metal stampings, nec; Special dies, tools, jigs, and fixtures

(G-15318)
NN INC
125 Bennett St (44090-1202)
PHONE.................................440 647-4711
EMP: 27
SALES (corp-wide): 489.27MM **Publicly Held**
Web: www.nninc.com
SIC: 3562 Ball bearings and parts
PA: Nn, Inc.
6210 Ardrey Kell Rd # 600
Charlotte NC 28277
980 264-4300

(G-15319)
NN AUTOCAM PRECISION COMPONENT
125 Bennett St (44090-1202)
PHONE.................................440 647-4711
EMP: 12 **EST:** 2016
SALES (est): 857.79K **Privately Held**
Web: www.nninc.com
SIC: 3599 Machine shop, jobbing and repair

(G-15320)
PRECISION FITTINGS LLC
709 N Main St (44090-1089)
PHONE.................................440 647-4143
Christopher H Lake, *Pr*
▲ **EMP:** 49 **EST:** 1947
SQ FT: 65,000
SALES (est): 9.36MM **Privately Held**

Wellington - Lorain County (G-15321)

(G-15321)
ROCHESTER MANUFACTURING INC
Also Called: Electroburr
24765 Quarry Rd (44090-9293)
PHONE..................................440 647-2463
Scott Frombaugh, Pr
David Younglas, CEO
EMP: 16 EST: 1978
SQ FT: 14,000
SALES (est): 2.44MM **Privately Held**
Web: www.rochestermfg.com
SIC: 3599 Machine shop, jobbing and repair

(G-15322)
SHL LIQUIDATION INDUSTRIES INC
Also Called: Shiloh Inds Wellington Mfg Div
350 Maple St (44090-1171)
PHONE..................................440 647-2100
Sri Perumal, Brnch Mgr
EMP: 96
Web: www.durashiloh.com
SIC: 3469 Stamping metal for the trade
PA: Shl Liquidation Industries Inc.
880 Steel Dr
Valley City OH 44280

(G-15323)
WHIRLAWAY CORPORATION
125 Bennett St (44090-1202)
PHONE..................................440 647-4711
Thomas G Zupan, Prin
EMP: 88
SALES (corp-wide): 489.27MM **Publicly Held**
Web: www.nninc.com
SIC: 3714 3451 Motor vehicle parts and accessories; Screw machine products
HQ: Whirlaway Corporation
720 Shiloh Ave
Wellington OH 44090
440 647-4711

(G-15324)
WHIRLAWAY CORPORATION
Whirlaway Cincinnatti, A Div Nn
125 Bennett St (44090-1202)
PHONE..................................440 647-4711
Richard Eichmann, Brnch Mgr
EMP: 88
SALES (corp-wide): 489.27MM **Publicly Held**
Web: www.nninc.com
SIC: 3714 3451 Motor vehicle parts and accessories; Screw machine products
HQ: Whirlaway Corporation
720 Shiloh Ave
Wellington OH 44090
440 647-4711

(G-15325)
WHIRLAWAY CORPORATION (HQ)
720 Shiloh Ave (44090-1190)
PHONE..................................440 647-4711
James R Widders, VP
Roderick R Baty, *
▲ EMP: 175 EST: 1973
SALES (est): 52.41MM
SALES (corp-wide): 489.27MM **Publicly Held**
Web: www.nninc.com
SIC: 3714 3451 3469 Motor vehicle brake systems and parts; Screw machine products; Appliance parts, porcelain enameled
PA: Nn, Inc.
6210 Ardrey Kell Rd # 600
Charlotte NC 28277
980 264-4300

Wellston
Jackson County

(G-15326)
BROWN-FORMAN CORPORATION
Also Called: Blue Grass Cooperage - Jackson
468 Salem Church Rd (45692)
P.O. Box 528 (45640-0528)
PHONE..................................740 384-3027
James Gulley, Brnch Mgr
EMP: 14
SALES (corp-wide): 4.23B **Publicly Held**
Web: www.brown-forman.com
SIC: 2429 2449 Cooperage stock products: staves, headings, hoops, etc.; Wood containers, nec
PA: Brown-Forman Corporation
850 Dixie Hwy
Louisville KY 40210
502 585-1100

(G-15327)
GEM BEVERAGES INC
106 E 11th St (45692-1713)
PHONE..................................740 384-2411
Rex Holzapfel, Pr
EMP: 11 EST: 1995
SALES (est): 943.84K **Privately Held**
Web: www.gembeverages.com
SIC: 2086 Soft drinks: packaged in cans, bottles, etc.

(G-15328)
GENERAL MILLS INC
Also Called: General Mills
2403 S Pennsylvania Ave (45692-9503)
P.O. Box 151 (45692-0151)
PHONE..................................740 286-2170
EMP: 39
SALES (corp-wide): 20.09B **Publicly Held**
Web: www.generalmills.com
SIC: 2043 Cereal breakfast foods
PA: General Mills, Inc.
1 General Mills Blvd
Minneapolis MN 55426
763 764-7600

(G-15329)
JACK HUFFMAN
1210 Hiram West Rd (45692-9536)
PHONE..................................740 384-5178
Admiral Jack Huffman, Owner
Jack Huffman, Owner
EMP: 7 EST: 2001
SALES (est): 113.79K **Privately Held**
SIC: 3281 Cut stone and stone products

(G-15330)
JOHNSONS FIRE EQUIPMENT CO
Also Called: Johnsons Emrgncy Vhcl Slutions
20213 State Route 93 (45692-9739)
P.O. Box 339 (26164-0339)
PHONE..................................740 357-4916
Tony Johnson, Pr
Steven Dill, Pr
Ernie O Dill Junior, VP
Marjorie Dill, Sec
EMP: 14 EST: 1966
SQ FT: 15,000
SALES (est): 1.51MM **Privately Held**
Web: www.johnsonsfire.com
SIC: 5999 5087 3569 Fire extinguishers; Firefighting equipment; Firefighting apparatus

(G-15331)
PILLSBURY COMPANY LLC
Also Called: Pillsbury
2403 S Pennsylvania Ave (45692-9503)
P.O. Box 151 (45692-0151)
PHONE..................................740 286-2170
Tim Dill, Mgr
EMP: 83
SALES (corp-wide): 20.09B **Publicly Held**
Web: www.pillsbury.com
SIC: 2041 2033 Flour and other grain mill products; Canned fruits and specialties
HQ: The Pillsbury Company Llc
1 General Mills Blvd
Minneapolis MN 55426

(G-15332)
SUPERIOR HARDWOODS OHIO INC (PA)
134 Wellston Industrial Park Rd (45692)
P.O. Box 606 (45692-0606)
PHONE..................................740 384-5677
Emmett Conway Junior, Pr
EMP: 60 EST: 1983
SALES (est): 8.88MM
SALES (corp-wide): 8.88MM **Privately Held**
Web: www.shlumber.com
SIC: 2421 2426 Sawmills and planing mills, general; Hardwood dimension and flooring mills

(G-15333)
WELLSTON AEROSOL MFG CO
105 W A St (45692-1113)
P.O. Box 326 (45692-0326)
PHONE..................................740 384-2320
Norma Lockard, Pr
Dan Lockard Junior, VP
EMP: 17 EST: 1957
SALES (est): 2.35MM **Privately Held**
SIC: 2813 Aerosols

Wellsville
Columbiana County

(G-15334)
CIMBAR PERFORMANCE MNRL WV LLC
2400 Clark Ave (43968-1070)
PHONE..................................330 532-2034
EMP: 24 EST: 2011
SALES (est): 6.95MM
SALES (corp-wide): 86.16MM **Privately Held**
Web: www.cimbar.com
SIC: 3295 Minerals, ground or otherwise treated
PA: United Minerals And Properties, Inc.
49 Jackson Lake Rd Ste O
Chatsworth GA 30705
770 387-0319

(G-15335)
HILCORP ENERGY CO
2406 Clark Ave (43968-1070)
PHONE..................................330 532-9300
EMP: 6 EST: 2014
SALES (est): 111.45K **Privately Held**
Web: www.hilcorp.com
SIC: 1382 Oil and gas exploration services

(G-15336)
QUALITY LIQUID FEEDS INC
2402 Clark Ave (43968-1070)
P.O. Box 402 (43968-0402)
PHONE..................................330 532-4635
EMP: 10
SALES (corp-wide): 150.71MM **Privately Held**
Web: www.qlf.com
SIC: 2048 Prepared feeds, nec
PA: Quality Liquid Feeds, Inc.
3586 Hwy 23 N
Dodgeville WI 53533
608 935-2345

(G-15337)
STEVENSON MFG CO
Also Called: Stevco
1 1st St (43968-1781)
P.O. Box 135 (43968-0135)
PHONE..................................330 532-1581
Timothy Lynch, Pr
Todd Lynch, VP
EMP: 8 EST: 1800
SQ FT: 115,000
SALES (est): 781.98K **Privately Held**
SIC: 3541 3599 Grinding machines, metalworking; Machine shop, jobbing and repair

(G-15338)
YELLOW CREEK CASTING CO INC
18141 Fife Coal Rd (43968-9760)
PHONE..................................330 532-4608
Ron Kelly, Pr
Lois Kelly, Treas
Gerald Kelly, Sales Process Controller
Sandra Brown, Sec
Jeanne Kelly, Treas
EMP: 11 EST: 1985
SQ FT: 4,500
SALES (est): 1.05MM **Privately Held**
Web: www.yellowcreekcasting.com
SIC: 3321 3322 Gray iron castings, nec; Malleable iron foundries

West Alexandria
Preble County

(G-15339)
AMS GLOBAL LTD
119 E Dayton St (45381-1209)
P.O. Box 746 (45378-0746)
PHONE..................................937 620-1036
Terrence Brennan, Pt
Anna Matthews, Pt
EMP: 11 EST: 2012
SQ FT: 10,000
SALES (est): 211.94K **Privately Held**
SIC: 3089 Plastics processing

(G-15340)
CLEARY MACHINE COMPANY INC
4858 Us Route 35 E (45381-8316)
PHONE..................................937 839-4278
Paul Kasperski, Pr
EMP: 21 EST: 1997
SQ FT: 24,000
SALES (est): 3.95MM **Privately Held**
Web: www.clearymachine.com
SIC: 3599 Machine shop, jobbing and repair

(G-15341)
DDP SPECIALTY ELECTRONIC MA
10 Electric St (45381-1212)
PHONE..................................937 839-4612
EMP: 170
SALES (corp-wide): 2.93B **Publicly Held**
SIC: 2821 2869 2891 3569 Plastics materials and resins; Industrial organic chemicals, nec; Adhesives and sealants; Filters
HQ: Ddp Specialty Electronic Materials Us 5, Llc
400 Arcola Rd
Collegeville PA

GEOGRAPHIC SECTION

West Chester - Butler County (G-15366)

(G-15342)
KIMMATT CORP
Also Called: Best Glass
4459 Preble County Line Rd S (45381-9567)
PHONE.................................937 228-3811
Susan Ballweg, *Pr*
Larry Ballweg, *Treas*
Matthew Ballweg, *VP*
EMP: 8 **EST:** 1975
SALES (est): 988.2K **Privately Held**
SIC: 1793 3496 3231 Glass and glazing work ; Screening, woven wire: made from purchased wire; Strengthened or reinforced glass

(G-15343)
PROMISE MACHINING LLC
24 Rebecca Dr (45381-9366)
PHONE.................................937 305-8011
Tim Lovely, *Prin*
EMP: 6 **EST:** 2008
SALES (est): 103.04K **Privately Held**
SIC: 3599 Machine shop, jobbing and repair

(G-15344)
REXARC INTERNATIONAL INC
35 E 3rd St (45381-1231)
P.O. Box 7 (45381-0007)
PHONE.................................937 839-4604
Robert Moyer, *CEO*
Joseph R Smith, *
James P Bowman, *
Galen Woodhouse, *
Ann C Smith, *
◆ **EMP:** 25 **EST:** 1916
SQ FT: 96,000
SALES (est): 5.04MM **Privately Held**
Web: www.rexarc.com
SIC: 3498 3548 3569 Manifolds, pipe: fabricated from purchased pipe; Gas welding equipment; Gas generators

(G-15345)
TWIN VALLEY METALCRAFT ASM LLC
Also Called: Twin Valley Metalcraft
4739 Enterprise Rd (45381-9518)
PHONE.................................937 787-4634
EMP: 6 **EST:** 2004
SQ FT: 7,000
SALES (est): 517.25K **Privately Held**
Web: www.twinvalleymetalcraft.com
SIC: 3451 3429 3599 Screw machine products; Aircraft hardware; Machine shop, jobbing and repair

(G-15346)
WEBERS BODY & FRAME INC
2017 State Route 503 N (45381-9701)
PHONE.................................937 839-5946
David P Weber, *Pr*
EMP: 9 **EST:** 1982
SALES (est): 950.67K **Privately Held**
Web: www.webersbf.com
SIC: 7532 7536 7692 Body shop, automotive ; Automotive glass replacement shops; Welding repair

(G-15347)
WYSONG GRAVEL CO INC (PA)
Also Called: Camden Ready Mix
2332 State Route 503 N (45381)
P.O. Box 5 (45381-0005)
PHONE.................................937 456-4539
John D Wysong, *Pr*
Carroll Wysong, *VP*
EMP: 10 **EST:** 1922
SQ FT: 1,500
SALES (est): 2.59MM
SALES (corp-wide): 2.59MM **Privately Held**
Web: www.preblecountystorage.com
SIC: 1442 Gravel mining

(G-15348)
WYSONG GRAVEL CO INC
2032 State Route 503 N (45381-9701)
PHONE.................................937 839-5497
Carroll Wysong, *VP*
EMP: 9
SALES (corp-wide): 2.59MM **Privately Held**
Web: www.preblecountystorage.com
SIC: 1442 Gravel mining
PA: Wysong Gravel Co Inc
2332 State Route 503 N
West Alexandria OH 45381
937 456-4539

West Carrollton
Montgomery County

(G-15349)
APPVION INC (PA)
1030 W Alex Bell Rd (45449-1923)
PHONE.................................937 859-8262
EMP: 6 **EST:** 1982
SALES (est): 3MM
SALES (corp-wide): 3MM **Privately Held**
SIC: 2621 Paper mills

(G-15350)
BLUE ENGINEERED PRODUCTS LLC
47 Pierce St (45449-1753)
PHONE.................................937 247-5537
EMP: 6 **EST:** 2019
SALES (est): 325.05K **Privately Held**
Web: www.blueengproducts.net
SIC: 3599 Machine shop, jobbing and repair

(G-15351)
BOUNDLESS CMNTY PATHWAYS INC (PA)
700 Liberty Ln (45449-2135)
PHONE.................................937 461-0034
Phil Hartje, *Genl Mgr*
Elvia Thomas, *Adult Service Director*
EMP: 700 **EST:** 1970
SQ FT: 50,000
SALES (est): 2.9MM
SALES (corp-wide): 2.9MM **Privately Held**
Web: www.moncoent.org
SIC: 8331 2789 Sheltered workshop; Bookbinding and related work

(G-15352)
DOMTAR CORPORATION
Also Called: West Carrollton Mfg Fcilty
820 S Alex Rd (45449-2106)
PHONE.................................937 859-8262
EMP: 37
Web: www.domtar.com
SIC: 2621 Paper mills
HQ: Domtar Corporation
234 Kingsley Park Dr
Fort Mill SC 29715
803 802-7500

(G-15353)
DOMTAR CORPORATION
1030 W Alex Bell Rd (45449-1923)
PHONE.................................937 859-8261
Mark Ferguson, *Mgr*
EMP: 400
Web: www.domtar.com
SIC: 2672 2621 Coated paper, except photographic, carbon, or abrasive; Paper mills
HQ: Domtar Corporation
234 Kingsley Park Dr
Fort Mill SC 29715
803 802-7500

(G-15354)
FOURTEEN VENTURES GROUP LLC
3131 W Alex Bell Rd (45449-2832)
PHONE.................................937 866-2341
Richard Dobson, *Managing Member*
EMP: 8 **EST:** 2014
SALES (est): 497.13K **Privately Held**
SIC: 3993 Signs and advertising specialties

(G-15355)
N2 PUBLISHING
3634 Watertower Ln Ste 4 (45449-4050)
PHONE.................................937 641-8277
Clint Hardman, *VP*
EMP: 10 **EST:** 2017
SALES (est): 91.24K **Privately Held**
Web: www.strollmag.com
SIC: 2741 Miscellaneous publishing

(G-15356)
PLUG POWER INC
219 S Alex Rd (45449-1910)
PHONE.................................518 605-5703
EMP: 9
SALES (corp-wide): 891.34MM **Publicly Held**
SIC: 3629 3674 5541 Electrochemical generators (fuel cells); Fuel cells, solid state ; Gasoline service stations
PA: Plug Power Inc.
968 Albany Shaker Rd
Latham NY 12110
518 782-7700

(G-15357)
WEST CARROLLTON CONVERTING INC
400 E Dixie Dr (45449-1827)
PHONE.................................937 859-3621
Pierce J Lonergan, *Pr*
Alan P Berens, *
◆ **EMP:** 23 **EST:** 1989
SALES (est): 1.57MM **Privately Held**
Web: www.westcarrollton.org
SIC: 2621 Paper mills

(G-15358)
WEST CRRLLTON PRCHMENT CNVRTIN
400 E Dixie Dr (45449-1827)
PHONE.................................513 594-3341
Cameron Lonergan, *Pr*
EMP: 33 **EST:** 2013
SALES (est): 17.75MM **Privately Held**
Web: www.wcpconv.com
SIC: 2759 Flexographic printing

West Chester
Butler County

(G-15359)
ABRA AUTO BODY & GLASS LP
Also Called: ABRA Autobody & Glass
8445 Cincinnati Columbus Rd (45069-3523)
PHONE.................................513 755-7709
John Webb, *Brnch Mgr*
EMP: 10
Web: www.abraauto.com
SIC: 7532 2851 Body shop, automotive; Paint removers
HQ: Abra Auto Body & Glass Lp
7225 Northland Dr N # 110
Brooklyn Park MN 55428
888 872-2272

(G-15360)
ACE MANUFACTURING COMPANY
Also Called: Ace Sanitary
5219 Muhlhauser Rd (45011-9327)
PHONE.................................513 541-2490
Charles H Tobias Junior, *Prin*
Donald A Schenck, *
M R Fredwest, *
▲ **EMP:** 32 **EST:** 1944
SALES (est): 5.13MM **Privately Held**
Web: www.acesanitary.com
SIC: 3599 3492 Hose, flexible metallic; Hose and tube fittings and assemblies, hydraulic/ pneumatic

(G-15361)
ADVANCED OEM SOLUTIONS LLC
9472 Meridian Way (45069-6527)
PHONE.................................513 407-0140
Gavin Dao, *Prin*
EMP: 7 **EST:** 2019
SALES (est): 1.06MM **Privately Held**
Web: www.aos-ndt.com
SIC: 3829 Measuring and controlling devices, nec

(G-15362)
ADVANCED TECHNICAL PDTS SUP CO
6186 Centre Park Dr (45069-3868)
PHONE.................................513 851-6858
Ben Conner, *Pr*
Timothy Conner, *VP*
EMP: 10 **EST:** 1986
SQ FT: 15,000
SALES (est): 1.84MM **Privately Held**
Web: www.advancedtechnicalprod.com
SIC: 3479 Coating of metals and formed products

(G-15363)
ALLGAIER PROCESS TECHNOLOGY
Also Called: Almo Process Technology
9780 Windisch Rd (45069-3808)
PHONE.................................513 402-2566
Tom Schroeder, *Pr*
Dixon F Miller, *Prin*
▲ **EMP:** 6 **EST:** 2010
SALES (est): 1.4MM **Privately Held**
Web: www.allgaierprocess.com
SIC: 3443 3535 Separators, industrial process: metal plate; Belt conveyor systems, general industrial use

(G-15364)
AMYLIN OHIO
8814 Trade Port Dr (45011-8661)
PHONE.................................512 592-8710
EMP: 24 **EST:** 2015
SALES (est): 1.78MM **Privately Held**
SIC: 2834 Pharmaceutical preparations

(G-15365)
ANEST IWATA AMERICAS INC
9525 Glades Dr (45011)
PHONE.................................513 755-3100
Atsuo Shiria, *Pr*
Erin Polley, *Acctg Mgr*
▲ **EMP:** 10 **EST:** 2011
SALES (est): 2.37MM **Privately Held**
Web: www.anestiwata-corp.com
SIC: 3563 Spraying and dusting equipment

(G-15366)
AP TECH GROUP INC
5130 Rialto Rd (45069-2923)
PHONE.................................513 761-8111
James Heimert, *Pr*
Albert C Heimert, *VP*
▼ **EMP:** 15 **EST:** 2004

(PA)=Parent Co (HQ)=Headquarters
✪ = New Business established in last 2 years

West Chester - Butler County (G-15367) — GEOGRAPHIC SECTION

SALES (est): 3.43MM **Privately Held**
Web: www.aptechgroup.com
SIC: 2899 Water treating compounds

(G-15367)
AQUA TECHNOLOGY GROUP LLC
8104 Beckett Center Dr (45069-5015)
PHONE...................513 298-1183
EMP: 8 **EST:** 2010
SQ FT: 15,428
SALES (est): 1.04MM **Privately Held**
Web: www.aquatechnologygroup.com
SIC: 7363 5085 3823 3824 Industrial help service; Industrial supplies; Industrial process control instruments; Fluid meters and counting devices

(G-15368)
ARNOLD GAUGE CO INC (PA)
9823 Harwood Ct (45014-7588)
PHONE...................877 942-4243
Michael Bruns, *Pr*
EMP: 10 **EST:** 1918
SQ FT: 10,000
SALES (est): 1.31MM
SALES (corp-wide): 1.31MM **Privately Held**
Web: www.arnoldgauge.com
SIC: 3545 Gauges (machine tool accessories)

(G-15369)
ARRAY TELEPRESENCE INC
9480 Meridian Way (45069-6527)
PHONE...................800 779-7480
Harold Williams, *CEO*
EMP: 6 **EST:** 2013
SALES (est): 86.36K **Privately Held**
Web: www.aurapresence.com
SIC: 3651 Video camera-audio recorders, household use

(G-15370)
ASLAN WORLDWIDE
8583 Rupp Farm Dr (45069-4526)
PHONE...................513 671-0671
Josh Stebbins, *Prin*
EMP: 10 **EST:** 2008
SALES (est): 622.77K **Privately Held**
Web: www.aslanworldwide.com
SIC: 2441 Boxes, wood

(G-15371)
ASTRAZENECA PHARMACEUTICALS LP
8814 Trade Port Dr (45011-8661)
PHONE...................513 645-2600
Alejandra Sargent, *Brnch Mgr*
EMP: 64
SALES (corp-wide): 45.81B **Privately Held**
Web: www.astrazeneca.com
SIC: 2834 Pharmaceutical preparations
HQ: Astrazeneca Pharmaceuticals Lp
1800 Concord Pike
Wilmington DE 19850

(G-15372)
BAE SYSTEMS SURVIVABILITY SYSTEMS LLC
9113 Le Saint Dr (45014-5453)
PHONE...................513 881-9800
◆ **EMP:** 589
SIC: 3711 Motor vehicles and car bodies

(G-15373)
BARNES GROUP INC
Mro Division
9826 Crescent Park Dr (45069-3800)
PHONE...................513 779-6888
EMP: 48

SALES (corp-wide): 1.26B **Publicly Held**
Web: www.barnesaero.com
SIC: 3728 Aircraft parts and equipment, nec
PA: Barnes Group Inc.
123 Main St
Bristol CT 06010
860 583-7070

(G-15374)
BARNES GROUP INC
Also Called: Windsor Airmotive
9826 Crescent Park Dr (45069-3800)
PHONE...................513 779-6888
Jerry Bach, *Brnch Mgr*
EMP: 15
SALES (corp-wide): 1.26B **Publicly Held**
Web: www.onebarnes.com
SIC: 3724 Aircraft engines and engine parts
PA: Barnes Group Inc.
123 Main St
Bristol CT 06010
860 583-7070

(G-15375)
BELANGER INC (DH)
9393 Princeton Glendale Rd (45011-9707)
PHONE...................517 870-3206
Kevin Long, *Pr*
Peter Bellin, *VP*
EMP: 76 **EST:** 2018
SALES (est): 49.91MM
SALES (corp-wide): 8.44B **Publicly Held**
Web: www.opwglobal.com
SIC: 3291 3589 Abrasive products; Commercial cooking and foodwarming equipment
HQ: Revod Corporation
1403 Foulk Rd
Wilmington DE 19803

(G-15376)
BENCHMARK LAND MANAGEMENT LLC
9431 Butler Warren Rd (45069)
PHONE...................513 310-7850
Diana E Honerlaw, *Prin*
EMP: 8 **EST:** 2012
SALES (est): 410.3K **Privately Held**
Web: www.benchmarklm.com
SIC: 0781 3271 0782 Landscape planning services; Blocks, concrete: landscape or retaining wall; Landscape contractors

(G-15377)
BESI MANUFACTURING INC
9445 Sutton Pl (45011-9705)
PHONE...................513 874-1460
EMP: 6
SALES (corp-wide): 10.29MM **Privately Held**
Web: www.besi-inc.com
SIC: 2399 Seat covers, automobile
PA: Besi Manufacturing Inc
9087 Sutton Pl
West Chester OH 45011
513 874-0232

(G-15378)
BESI MANUFACTURING INC (PA)
9087 Sutton Pl (45011-9316)
PHONE...................513 874-0232
William Moore, *Pr*
Sue Weaver, *
Tom Moore, *
Dave Moore, *
▲ **EMP:** 24 **EST:** 1974
SQ FT: 17,500
SALES (est): 10.29MM
SALES (corp-wide): 10.29MM **Privately Held**
Web: www.besi-inc.com

SIC: 2399 Seat covers, automobile

(G-15379)
BILLERUD AMERICAS CORPORATION
Also Called: Verso Paper
9025 Centre Pointe Dr (45069-4984)
PHONE...................901 369-4105
Tom Huber, *Mgr*
EMP: 58
SALES (corp-wide): 4.06B **Privately Held**
Web: www.billerud.com
SIC: 2653 2656 2631 2611 Boxes, corrugated: made from purchased materials; Food containers (liquid tight), including milk cartons; Container, packaging, and boxboard; Pulp mills
HQ: Billerud Americas Corporation
8540 Gander Creek Dr
Miamisburg OH 45342

(G-15380)
BLACKMER PUMP
9393 Princeton Glendale Rd (45011-9707)
PHONE...................616 240-9239
EMP: 10 **EST:** 2018
SALES (est): 1.06MM **Privately Held**
Web: www.blackmerpumps.com
SIC: 3494 Valves and pipe fittings, nec

(G-15381)
BORKE MOLD SPECIALIST INC
9541 Glades Dr (45011-9410)
PHONE...................513 870-8000
Fritz Borke, *Pr*
Patty Borke, *Sec*
EMP: 20 **EST:** 1990
SQ FT: 14,000
SALES (est): 2.49MM **Privately Held**
Web: www.borkemold.com
SIC: 3089 Injection molding of plastics

(G-15382)
BP 10 INC
Also Called: Bagpack
9486 Sutton Pl (45011-9698)
PHONE...................513 346-3900
Steven Dreyer, *Pr*
Ronald C Dreyer, *
EMP: 30 **EST:** 1988
SQ FT: 40,000
SALES (est): 9.93MM **Privately Held**
Web: www.flex-pack.com
SIC: 5199 2752 Packaging materials; Commercial printing, lithographic

(G-15383)
CABINET AND GRANITE DEPOT LLC
8730 N Pavillion (45069-4894)
PHONE...................513 874-2100
EMP: 10 **EST:** 2012
SALES (est): 721.29K **Privately Held**
Web: www.granitecincinnati.com
SIC: 2434 Wood kitchen cabinets

(G-15384)
CARDINAL HEALTH 414 LLC
9866 Windisch Rd Bldg 3 (45069-3806)
PHONE...................513 759-1900
EMP: 9
SALES (corp-wide): 205.01B **Publicly Held**
SIC: 2834 2835 Pharmaceutical preparations; Radioactive diagnostic substances
HQ: Cardinal Health 414, Llc
7000 Cardinal Pl
Dublin OH 43017
614 757-5000

(G-15385)
CATEXEL NEASE LLC (DH)
Also Called: Nease Co. LLC
9774 Windisch Rd (45069-3808)
PHONE...................513 587-2800
◆ **EMP:** 10 **EST:** 2005
SALES (est): 86.51MM
SALES (corp-wide): 355.83K **Privately Held**
Web: www.neaseco.com
SIC: 2869 Industrial organic chemicals, nec
HQ: Wp Mannheim Gmbh
Sandhofer Str. 96
Mannheim BW 68305

(G-15386)
CBN WESTSIDE HOLDINGS INC
Also Called: TSS Technologies
8800 Global Way (45069-7070)
PHONE...................513 772-7000
D Brock Denton, *Prin*
Brent Nichols, *Prin*
EMP: 23 **EST:** 2001
SALES (est): 774.17K **Privately Held**
SIC: 3599 Machine shop, jobbing and repair

(G-15387)
CBN WESTSIDE TECHNOLOGIES INC
Also Called: TSS Technologies
8800 Global Way (45069-7070)
PHONE...................513 772-7000
Brent Nichols, *Pr*
Charles B Nichols Junior, *VP*
Mark Nichols, *
Scott Nichols, *
Leila B Nichols, *
▲ **EMP:** 400 **EST:** 1948
SQ FT: 75,000
SALES (est): 25.68MM **Privately Held**
SIC: 3599 8711 Machine shop, jobbing and repair; Mechanical engineering

(G-15388)
CEDAR ELEC HOLDINGS CORP
5440 W Chester Rd (45069-2950)
PHONE...................773 804-6288
Dave Smidebush, *Brnch Mgr*
EMP: 70
SALES (corp-wide): 142.84MM **Privately Held**
Web: www.cedarelectronics.com
SIC: 3812 5013 5015 Navigational systems and instruments; Tools and equipment, automotive; Automotive supplies, used: wholesale and retail
PA: Cedar Electronics Holdings Corp.
1701 Golf Rd Ste 3-900
Rolling Meadows IL 60008
800 964-3138

(G-15389)
CFM INTERNATIONAL INC (PA)
6440 Aviation Way (45069-4546)
P.O. Box 15514 (45215-0514)
PHONE...................513 552-2787
Gael Meheust, *Pr*
Cedric Goubet, *Ex VP*
Kevin Fewell, *CFO*
Raymond Scodellaro, *VP*
Maria Deacon, *VP*
EMP: 42 **EST:** 1975
SALES (est): 15.7MM
SALES (corp-wide): 15.7MM **Privately Held**
Web: www.cfmaeroengines.com
SIC: 3724 Aircraft engines and engine parts

(G-15390)
CHEMINSTRUMENTS INC
Also Called: Chemical Instruments
510 Commercial Dr (45014-7593)

▲ = Import ▼ = Export
◆ = Import/Export

GEOGRAPHIC SECTION
West Chester - Butler County (G-15410)

PHONE..................513 860-1598
Keith Muny, *Mgr*
EMP: 7
Web: www.cheminstruments.com
SIC: 3821 Chemical laboratory apparatus, nec
PA: Cheminstruments, Inc.
510 Commercial Dr
West Chester OH 45014

(G-15391)
CHEMINSTRUMENTS INC (PA)
510 Commercial Dr (45014-7593)
PHONE..................513 860-1598
Richard Muny, *Pr*
Keith Muny, *VP*
▲ **EMP:** 8 **EST:** 1992
SQ FT: 15,000
SALES (est): 1.72MM **Privately Held**
Web: www.cheminstruments.com
SIC: 3829 Measuring and controlling devices, nec

(G-15392)
CHEMSULTANTS INTERNATIONAL INC
Also Called: Chem Instruments
510 Commercial Dr (45014-7593)
PHONE..................513 860-1598
Keith Muny, *Mgr*
EMP: 7
SALES (corp-wide): 4.82MM **Privately Held**
Web: www.chemsultants.com
SIC: 3821 Laboratory apparatus and furniture
PA: Chemsultants International, Inc.
9079 Tyler Blvd
Mentor OH 44060
440 974-3080

(G-15393)
CINCINNATI PRECISION MCHY INC
9083 Sutton Pl (45011-9316)
PHONE..................513 860-4133
Pam Ison, *Pr*
Dina Schnitzer, *Sec*
EMP: 9 **EST:** 1992
SQ FT: 4,800
SALES (est): 914.4K **Privately Held**
Web: www.cpmfab.com
SIC: 3599 Machine shop, jobbing and repair

(G-15394)
CIP INTERNATIONAL INC
Also Called: Commercial Interior Products
9575 Le Saint Dr (45014-5447)
PHONE..................513 874-9925
Thomas Huff, *CEO*
Thomas Huff, *Ch Bd*
Kathleen Huff, *
Mark Elminger, *
Jay Voss, *
◆ **EMP:** 83 **EST:** 1975
SQ FT: 140,000
SALES (est): 17.37MM **Privately Held**
Web: www.cipretail.com
SIC: 7389 2541 Interior designer; Store fixtures, wood

(G-15395)
CLARITY RETAIL SERVICES LLC
Also Called: Jkrg Construction Services
5115 Excello Ct (45069-3091)
PHONE..................513 800-9369
James R Gavigan, *Pr*
Lance H Madden, *
EMP: 75 **EST:** 2015
SQ FT: 3,100
SALES (est): 5.31MM **Privately Held**
Web: www.clarity-retail.com

SIC: 7389 8742 3999 3577 Interior designer; Sales (including sales management) consultant; Barber and beauty shop equipment; Graphic displays, except graphic terminals

(G-15396)
CLARKWSTERN DTRICH BLDG SYSTEM (HQ)
Also Called: Clarkdietrich
9050 Centre Pointe Dr Ste 400 (45069)
PHONE..................513 870-1100
▼ **EMP:** 110 **EST:** 2011
SQ FT: 80,000
SALES (est): 282.46MM
SALES (corp-wide): 4.92B **Publicly Held**
Web: www.clarkdietrich.com
SIC: 3444 8711 3081 Studs and joists, sheet metal; Engineering services; Vinyl film and sheet
PA: Worthington Enterprises, Inc.
200 W Wlson Bridge Rd
Worthington OH 43085
614 438-3210

(G-15397)
CLEVELND-CLFFS TLING STMPING H (DH)
9227 Centre Pointe Dr (45069)
PHONE..................519 969-4632
Brian Bishop, *CEO*
EMP: 16 **EST:** 2013
SALES (est): 191.88MM
SALES (corp-wide): 22B **Publicly Held**
Web: www.clevelandcliffs.com
SIC: 3465 Body parts, automobile: stamped metal
HQ: Cleveland-Cliffs Investments Inc.
9227 Centre Pointe Dr
West Chester OH 45069
513 425-5163

(G-15398)
CLEVELND-CLFFS TOLING STAMPING (DH)
9227 Centre Pointe Dr (45069-4822)
PHONE..................216 694-5700
Brian Bishop, *CEO*
EMP: 238 **EST:** 1999
SALES (est): 102.55MM
SALES (corp-wide): 22B **Publicly Held**
Web: www.clevelandcliffs.com
SIC: 3465 Body parts, automobile: stamped metal
HQ: Cleveland-Cliffs Tooling And Stamping Holdings Llc
9227 Centere Pointe Dr
West Chester OH 45069
519 969-4532

(G-15399)
COCA COLA
Also Called: Coca-Cola
6560 Meadowbrook Ct (45069-1485)
PHONE..................513 898-7709
Bill Souders Senior, *Dir*
EMP: 7 **EST:** 2018
SALES (est): 169.96K **Privately Held**
Web: www.coca-cola.com
SIC: 2086 Bottled and canned soft drinks

(G-15400)
CONTECH BRIDGE SOLUTIONS LLC (DH)
Also Called: Bridgetek
9025 Centre Pointe Dr Ste 400 (45069)
PHONE..................513 645-7000
EMP: 15 **EST:** 1994
SQ FT: 1,440
SALES (est): 26.78MM **Privately Held**

Web: www.conteches.com
SIC: 3443 Fabricated plate work (boiler shop)
HQ: Contech Engineered Solutions Llc
9025 Centre Pointe Dr # 400
West Chester OH 45069
513 645-7000

(G-15401)
CONTECH CNSTR PDTS HLDINGS INC
9025 Centre Pointe Dr Ste 400 (45069-9700)
PHONE..................513 645-7000
Ronald Keating, *Prin*
EMP: 1706 **EST:** 2012
SALES (est): 20.9MM **Privately Held**
SIC: 3443 Fabricated plate work (boiler shop)
HQ: Apax Partners Us, Llc
601 Lexington Ave Fl 53
New York NY 10022

(G-15402)
CONTECH ENGNERED SOLUTIONS INC (HQ)
9025 Centre Pointe Dr Ste 400 (45069)
PHONE..................513 645-7000
Michael Rafi, *Pr*
Jim Waters, *CFO*
J Paul Allen, *VP*
EMP: 50 **EST:** 2012
SALES (est): 119.26MM **Privately Held**
Web: www.conteches.com
SIC: 3084 3317 3441 3443 Plastics pipe; Steel pipe and tubes; Fabricated structural metal; Fabricated plate work (boiler shop)
PA: Quikrete Holdings, Inc.
5 Concourse Pkwy Ste 1900
Atlanta GA 30328

(G-15403)
CONTECH ENGNERED SOLUTIONS LLC (HQ)
9025 Centre Pointe Dr Ste 400 (45069-9700)
PHONE..................513 645-7000
Mike Rafi, *Pr*
Jeffrey S Lee, *Sr VP*
Mo Heshmati, *SUPPLY CHAIN*
Steve R Spanagel, *Sls Dir*
Vernon B Cameron, *DRAINAGE Technology*
◆ **EMP:** 150 **EST:** 1986
SQ FT: 75,000
SALES (est): 480.41MM **Privately Held**
Web: www.conteches.com
SIC: 3444 3084 3317 3441 Sheet metalwork; Plastics pipe; Steel pipe and tubes; Fabricated structural metal
PA: Quikrete Holdings, Inc.
5 Concourse Pkwy Ste 1900
Atlanta GA 30328

(G-15404)
CONTECH STRMWTER SOLUTIONS LLC
9025 Centre Pointe Dr Ste 400 (45069)
PHONE..................513 645-7000
Rick Stepien, *Pr*
Rebecca H Appenzeller, *Sec*
EMP: 8 **EST:** 2005
SALES (est): 4.88MM **Privately Held**
Web: www.conteches.com
SIC: 3677 Filtration devices, electronic
HQ: Contech Engineered Solutions Llc
9025 Centre Pointe Dr # 400
West Chester OH 45069
513 645-7000

(G-15405)
CONTROL INTERFACE INC
517 Commercial Dr (45014-7594)

PHONE..................513 874-2062
Tom Osborn, *Pr*
▲ **EMP:** 8 **EST:** 1986
SQ FT: 5,000
SALES (est): 1.5MM **Privately Held**
Web: www.controlinterface.com
SIC: 3613 Control panels, electric

(G-15406)
CORNERSTONE BRANDS INC
Also Called: Grandinroad Catalog
5568 W Chester Rd (45069-2914)
PHONE..................866 668-5962
David Cleavinger, *Brnch Mgr*
EMP: 7
Web: www.grandinroad.com
SIC: 3199 Dog furnishings: collars, leashes, muzzles, etc.: leather
HQ: Cornerstone Brands, Inc.
5568 W Chester Rd
West Chester OH 45069
513 603-1000

(G-15407)
CR HOLDING INC
9100 Centre Pointe Dr Ste 200 (45069)
PHONE..................513 860-5039
Richard Owen, *CEO*
John Samoya, *VP Fin*
EMP: 82 **EST:** 2006
SQ FT: 5,000
SALES (est): 9.34MM **Publicly Held**
SIC: 2841 Soap: granulated, liquid, cake, flaked, or chip
PA: Ares Capital Corporation
245 Park Ave Fl 44
New York NY 10167

(G-15408)
CRANE 1 SERVICES INC (HQ)
9075 Centre Pointe Dr (45069-4890)
PHONE..................937 704-9900
Thomas Boscher, *CEO*
Joseph Schivone, *CFO*
EMP: 21 **EST:** 2007
SALES (est): 103.06MM
SALES (corp-wide): 333.76MM **Privately Held**
Web: www.crane1.com
SIC: 3536 Cranes and monorail systems
PA: L Squared Capital Partners Llc
3434 Via Lido Ste 300
Newport Beach CA 92663
949 398-0168

(G-15409)
CRYOVAC LLC
7410 Union Centre Blvd (45014-2286)
PHONE..................513 771-7770
Sharon Drysdale, *Mgr*
EMP: 10
SALES (corp-wide): 5.49B **Publicly Held**
Web: www.sealedair.com
SIC: 3086 Packaging and shipping materials, foamed plastics
HQ: Cryovac, Llc
2415 Cascade Pointe Blvd
Charlotte NC 28208
980 430-7000

(G-15410)
CUSTOM MILLCRAFT CORP
9092 Le Saint Dr (45014-2241)
PHONE..................513 874-7080
Jody Corbett, *Pr*
EMP: 25 **EST:** 1983
SQ FT: 56,000
SALES (est): 4.79MM **Privately Held**
Web: www.custommillcraft.com

West Chester - Butler County (G-15411)

SIC: **2521** 2522 2542 Cabinets, office: wood; Office furniture, except wood; Partitions and fixtures, except wood

(G-15411)
DA PRECISION PRODUCTS INC
Also Called: Manufacturing
9052 Goldpark Dr (45011-9764)
PHONE.................513 459-1113
Daniel Adams, *CEO*
EMP: 10 **EST:** 2018
SALES (est): 964.85K **Privately Held**
Web: www.daprecision.com
SIC: **8711** 3531 3545 3499 Engineering services; Construction machinery; Precision tools, machinists'; Machine bases, metal

(G-15412)
DEE SIGN CO (PA)
Also Called: Diversified Sign
6163 Allen Rd (45069-3855)
PHONE.................513 779-3333
Braden R Huenefeld, *Ch Bd*
Craig Dixon, *
Joe Kolks, *
◆ **EMP:** 23 **EST:** 1967
SQ FT: 125,000
SALES (est): 6.1MM
SALES (corp-wide): 6.1MM **Privately Held**
Web: www.deesign.com
SIC: **3993** Signs, not made in custom sign painting shops

(G-15413)
DEE SIGN USA LLC
6163 Allen Rd (45069-3855)
PHONE.................513 779-3333
EMP: 11 **EST:** 2009
SALES (est): 858.04K **Privately Held**
Web: www.deesign.com
SIC: **3993** Signs and advertising specialties

(G-15414)
DMG MORI USA INC
9415 Meridian Way (45069-6525)
PHONE.................440 546-7088
EMP: 10
Web: en.dmgmori.com
SIC: **3541** Machine tools, metal cutting type
HQ: Dmg Mori Usa, Inc.
2400 Huntington Blvd
Hoffman Estates IL 60192
847 593-5400

(G-15415)
DOVER CORPORATION
9393 Princeton Glendale Rd (45011-9707)
PHONE.................513 870-3206
EMP: 51
SALES (corp-wide): 8.44B **Publicly Held**
Web: www.dovercorporation.com
SIC: **3632** Household refrigerators and freezers
PA: Dover Corporation
3005 Hghland Pkwy Ste 200
Downers Grove IL 60515
630 541-1540

(G-15416)
DREDGER LLC
5698 Sage Meadow Ct (45069-5547)
PHONE.................513 507-8774
William Mahlock, *Prin*
EMP: 6 **EST:** 2016
SALES (est): 58.77K **Privately Held**
Web: www.dredge.com
SIC: **3731** Shipbuilding and repairing

(G-15417)
DRT HOLDINGS LLC
9025 Centre Pointe Dr Ste 120 (45069)
PHONE.................937 297-6676
EMP: 11 **EST:** 2008
SALES (est): 268.03K **Privately Held**
SIC: **3411** Metal cans

(G-15418)
DS WORLD LLC
4652 Lakes Edge Apt 5 (45069-8588)
PHONE.................925 200-4985
EMP: 6 **EST:** 2018
SALES (est): 63.71K **Privately Held**
Web: www.dentsplysirona.com
SIC: **3577** Computer peripheral equipment, nec

(G-15419)
DWYER COMPANIES INC (PA)
Also Called: Dwyer Concrete Lifting
6083 Schumacher Park Dr (45069)
PHONE.................513 777-0998
EMP: 60 **EST:** 1984
SALES (est): 15.39MM
SALES (corp-wide): 15.39MM **Privately Held**
Web: www.thedwyercompany.com
SIC: **3441** Fabricated structural metal

(G-15420)
EAGLE COMPOSITES LLC
8494 Firebird Dr (45014-2273)
PHONE.................513 330-6108
EMP: 6 **EST:** 2018
SALES (est): 1.03MM **Privately Held**
Web: www.eagle-composites.com
SIC: **3829** Fuel totalizers, aircraft engine

(G-15421)
EATON CORPORATION
9902 Windisch Rd (45069-3804)
PHONE.................513 387-2000
Chris Kuzak, *Admn*
EMP: 35
Web: www.dix-eaton.com
SIC: **3613** Power circuit breakers
HQ: Eaton Corporation
1000 Eaton Blvd
Cleveland OH 44122
440 523-5000

(G-15422)
EAZYTRADE INC (PA)
Also Called: Eazytrade
9743 Crescent Park Dr (45069-3893)
PHONE.................513 257-9189
Toan Phu, *Pr*
EMP: 9 **EST:** 2014
SALES (est): 10MM
SALES (corp-wide): 10MM **Privately Held**
SIC: **3825** Internal combustion engine analyzers, to test electronics

(G-15423)
EAZYTRADE INC
7503 Overglen Dr (45069-9383)
PHONE.................513 257-9189
Toan Phu, *Pr*
EMP: 7
SALES (corp-wide): 10MM **Privately Held**
SIC: **3825** Internal combustion engine analyzers, to test electronics
PA: Eazytrade Inc
9743 Crescent Park Dr
West Chester OH 45069
513 257-9189

(G-15424)
EJ WEBER LTD
7331 Charter Cup Ln (45069-4676)
PHONE.................513 759-0103
Ingrid Weber, *Prin*
EMP: 7 **EST:** 2001
SALES (est): 165.36K **Privately Held**
Web: www.ejweber.com
SIC: **3949** Golf equipment

(G-15425)
ENVIRONMENTAL SAMPLE TECHNOLOGY INC
503 Commercial Dr (45014-7594)
PHONE.................513 642-0100
EMP: 49
SIC: **3826** Analytical instruments

(G-15426)
EROSION CONTROL PRODUCTS CORP
9281 Le Saint Dr (45014-5464)
PHONE.................302 815-6500
Kirc Horne, *Genl Mgr*
EMP: 12 **EST:** 2019
SALES (est): 2.35MM **Privately Held**
SIC: **3524** 5999 Lawn and garden equipment; Farm equipment and supplies
PA: Dhg Inc.
9281 Le Saint Dr
Fairfield OH

(G-15427)
ESCORT INC
5440 W Chester Rd (45069-9004)
PHONE.................513 870-8500
Chris Cowger, *CEO*
Mark Carrm, *
Gail Babirr, *
▲ **EMP:** 250 **EST:** 1997
SQ FT: 32,000
SALES (est): 57.5MM
SALES (corp-wide): 142.84MM **Privately Held**
Web: www.escortradar.com
SIC: **3812** Radar systems and equipment
PA: Cedar Electronics Holdings Corp.
1701 Golf Rd Ste 3-900
Rolling Meadows IL 60008
800 964-3138

(G-15428)
F A TECH CORP
9065 Sutton Pl (45011-9316)
PHONE.................513 942-1920
EMP: 20 **EST:** 1994
SALES (est): 541.12K **Privately Held**
Web: www.brazer.com
SIC: **3599** Machine shop, jobbing and repair

(G-15429)
FINN CORPORATION (HQ)
9281 Le Saint Dr (45014-5464)
PHONE.................513 874-2818
◆ **EMP:** 47 **EST:** 1936
SALES (est): 34.5MM **Privately Held**
Web: www.finncorp.com
SIC: **3524** 3523 Lawn and garden equipment; Farm machinery and equipment
PA: Dhg Inc.
9281 Le Saint Dr
Fairfield OH

(G-15430)
FISHER CONTROLS INTL LLC
5453 W Chester Rd (45069-2963)
PHONE.................513 285-6000
EMP: 12
SALES (corp-wide): 15.16B **Publicly Held**

SIC: **3823** Process control instruments
HQ: Fisher Controls International Llc
205 S Center St
Marshalltown IA 50158
641 754-3011

(G-15431)
FOAM CONCEPTS & DESIGN INC
4602 Mulhauser Rd W Chester Township (45011-9708)
PHONE.................513 860-5589
Jeff Labermeier, *Pr*
EMP: 19 **EST:** 1989
SQ FT: 40,500
SALES (est): 2.4MM **Privately Held**
SIC: **3086** Packaging and shipping materials, foamed plastics

(G-15432)
FRECON TECHNOLOGIES INC
9319 Princeton Glendale Rd (45011-9707)
PHONE.................513 874-8981
Fred J Pfirrmann, *CEO*
▲ **EMP:** 12 **EST:** 1983
SQ FT: 6,000
SALES (est): 2.16MM **Privately Held**
Web: www.frecontechnologies.com
SIC: **3545** Machine tool attachments and accessories

(G-15433)
G F FRANK AND SONS INC
9075 Le Saint Dr (45014-2242)
PHONE.................513 870-9075
George P Frank, *Pr*
John Frank, *VP*
Mark Frank, *VP*
EMP: 15 **EST:** 1948
SQ FT: 40,000
SALES (est): 1.75MM **Privately Held**
Web: www.gffrankandsons.com
SIC: **3556** 3599 Food products machinery; Machine shop, jobbing and repair

(G-15434)
GE ADDITIVE LLC
5115 Excello Ct (45069-3091)
PHONE.................513 341-0597
EMP: 27 **EST:** 2018
SALES (est): 2.7MM
SALES (corp-wide): 67.95B **Publicly Held**
Web: www.ge.com
SIC: **3825** Instruments to measure electricity
HQ: Ge Aviation Systems Llc
1 Neumann Way
Cincinnati OH 45215
937 898-9600

(G-15435)
GE AVIATION SYSTEMS LLC
Also Called: GE Aviation
9647 Roundhouse Dr (45069-4388)
PHONE.................513 779-1910
EMP: 10
SALES (corp-wide): 67.95B **Publicly Held**
Web: www.geaerospace.com
SIC: **3812** Aircraft control systems, electronic
HQ: Ge Aviation Systems Llc
1 Neumann Way
Cincinnati OH 45215
937 898-9600

(G-15436)
GE AVIATION SYSTEMS LLC
Also Called: GE Aviation
7831 Ashford Glen Ct (45069-1614)
PHONE.................513 786-4555
EMP: 11
SALES (corp-wide): 67.95B **Publicly Held**
Web: www.geaerospace.com

SIC: 3812 Aircraft control systems, electronic
HQ: Ge Aviation Systems Llc
1 Neumann Way
Cincinnati OH 45215
937 898-9600

(G-15437)
GE AVIATION SYSTEMS LLC
Also Called: Rapid Quality Manufacturing
5223 Muhlhauser Rd (45011-9327)
PHONE..................................513 889-5150
James C Taylor, *Brnch Mgr*
EMP: 10
SALES (corp-wide): 67.95B **Publicly Held**
Web: www.geaerospace.com
SIC: 3313 Alloys, additive, except copper: not made in blast furnaces
HQ: Ge Aviation Systems Llc
1 Neumann Way
Cincinnati OH 45215
937 898-9600

(G-15438)
GE HONDA AERO ENGINES LLC
9050 Centre Pointe Dr Ste 200 (45069)
PHONE..................................513 552-4322
Bill Dwyer, *CEO*
Steven J Shaknaitis, *Pr*
Jun Yanada, *Ex VP*
Adam Endress, *CFO*
Menelik Mel Solomon, *Dir*
EMP: 11 EST: 2005
SALES (est): 1.31MM **Privately Held**
Web: www.gehonda.com
SIC: 3519 Parts and accessories, internal combustion engines

(G-15439)
GENERAL ELECTRIC COMPANY
Also Called: GE Additive
8556 Trade Center Dr Ste 100 (45011-9354)
PHONE..................................513 341-0214
David Handler, *Brnch Mgr*
EMP: 200
SALES (corp-wide): 67.95B **Publicly Held**
Web: www.ge.com
SIC: 3541 Machine tools, metal cutting type
PA: General Electric Company
1 Aviation Way
Cincinnati OH 45215
617 443-3000

(G-15440)
GENERAL ELECTRIC COMPANY
Also Called: GE
9701 Windisch Rd (45069-3827)
PHONE..................................714 668-0951
EMP: 29
SALES (corp-wide): 67.95B **Publicly Held**
Web: www.ge.com
SIC: 3699 Electrical equipment and supplies, nec
PA: General Electric Company
1 Aviation Way
Cincinnati OH 45215
617 443-3000

(G-15441)
GEORGIA-PACIFIC LLC
Also Called: Georgia-Pacific
9048 Port Union Rialto Rd (45069-3254)
PHONE..................................513 942-4800
EMP: 34
SALES (corp-wide): 36.93B **Privately Held**
Web: www.gp.com
SIC: 2621 Paper mills
HQ: Georgia-Pacific Llc
133 Peachtree St Nw
Atlanta GA 30303
404 652-4000

(G-15442)
GLOBAL PACKAGING & EXPORTS INC (PA)
9166 Sutton Pl (45011-9317)
P.O. Box 62687 (45262-0687)
PHONE..................................513 454-2020
Lori Jordan, *Pr*
EMP: 6 EST: 1980
SQ FT: 19,000
SALES (est): 1.84MM
SALES (corp-wide): 1.84MM **Privately Held**
Web: www.globalpkg.com
SIC: 4783 2448 2441 Packing goods for shipping; Skids, wood; Cases, wood

(G-15443)
GOD SPEED TURBO INNOVATIONS
9862 Crescent Park Dr (45069-3800)
PHONE..................................513 307-5584
Austin Tschanz, *Pr*
EMP: 6 EST: 2017
SALES (est): 78.14K **Privately Held**
Web: www.steedspeed.com
SIC: 3714 Motor vehicle parts and accessories

(G-15444)
GRAPHEL CORPORATION
Also Called: Carbon Products
6115 Centre Park Dr (45069-3869)
PHONE..................................513 779-6166
David Trinkley, *Pr*
Mark Grammer, *
EMP: 140 EST: 1965
SQ FT: 35,000
SALES (est): 23.29MM **Privately Held**
Web: www.graphel.com
SIC: 5052 3599 3624 Coal and other minerals and ores; Machine shop, jobbing and repair; Electrodes, thermal and electrolytic uses: carbon, graphite

(G-15445)
HATFIELD INDUSTRIES LLC
9717 Flagstone Way (45069-7042)
PHONE..................................513 225-0456
Raymond Carl Hatfield, *Prin*
EMP: 6 EST: 2012
SALES (est): 162.58K **Privately Held**
SIC: 3585 Heating equipment, complete

(G-15446)
HONEYWELL INTERNATIONAL INC
Also Called: Honeywell
9290 Le Saint Dr (45014-5454)
PHONE..................................513 874-5882
Robert Young, *Brnch Mgr*
EMP: 25
SALES (corp-wide): 36.66B **Publicly Held**
Web: www.honeywell.com
SIC: 3577 Computer peripheral equipment, nec
PA: Honeywell International Inc.
855 S Mint St
Charlotte NC 28202
704 627-6200

(G-15447)
HYDRO SYSTEMS COMPANY
9393 Princeton Glendale Rd (45011-9707)
PHONE..................................513 271-8800
EMP: 28 EST: 1998
SALES (est): 1.28MM **Privately Held**
Web: www.hydrosystemsco.com
SIC: 3559 Chemical machinery and equipment

(G-15448)
INTELLIGRATED SYSTEMS INC
Also Called: Honeywell Intelligrated
4436 Muhlhauser Rd Ste 300 (45011-9771)
PHONE..................................513 881-5136
EMP: 243
SALES (corp-wide): 36.66B **Publicly Held**
Web: sps.honeywell.com
SIC: 3535 Conveyors and conveying equipment
HQ: Intelligrated Systems, Inc.
7901 Innovation Way
Mason OH 45040
866 936-7300

(G-15449)
IOT DIAGNOSTICS LLC
9361 Allen Rd (45069-3846)
P.O. Box 42414 (45242-0414)
PHONE..................................844 786-7631
Jeremy Drury, *Pr*
EMP: 7 EST: 2017
SALES (est): 414.83K **Privately Held**
Web: www.iotdiag.com
SIC: 7372 Application computer software

(G-15450)
J & K CABINETRY INC
8800 Global Way # 200 (45069-7070)
PHONE..................................513 860-3461
Zhi Wei Huang, *Admn*
EMP: 10 EST: 2014
SALES (est): 217.41K **Privately Held**
Web: www.jkcabinetohio.com
SIC: 2434 Wood kitchen cabinets

(G-15451)
K A VENTURES INC
9418 Sutton Pl (45011-9698)
PHONE..................................513 860-3340
Kevin Addis, *Pr*
Kevin J Addis, *Prin*
Penni Addis, *Sec*
▲ EMP: 13 EST: 1992
SQ FT: 39,000
SALES (est): 323.25K **Privately Held**
Web: www.bascoep.com
SIC: 3211 3231 Flat glass; Products of purchased glass

(G-15452)
KC ROBOTICS INC
9000 Le Saint Dr (45014-2241)
PHONE..................................513 860-4442
Paul Carrier, *Pr*
Kenneth P Carrier Junior, *Pr*
Constance M Carrier, *
◆ EMP: 43 EST: 1989
SQ FT: 18,000
SALES (est): 10.18MM **Privately Held**
Web: www.kcrobotics.com
SIC: 3569 7373 Robots, assembly line: industrial and commercial; Systems integration services

(G-15453)
KCOX ENTERPRISES LLC
7353 Preserve Pl (45069-6579)
PHONE..................................574 952-5084
EMP: 19
SALES (corp-wide): 249.32K **Privately Held**
SIC: 2411 Logging
PA: Kcox Enterprises, Llc
20 N Saint Clair St
Toledo OH 43604
419 241-5175

(G-15454)
KEYS CHEESECAKES AND PIES LLC
9519 Triangle Dr (45011-8950)
PHONE..................................513 356-1221
Keantha Brandy, *Prin*
EMP: 6 EST: 2019
SALES (est): 282.77K **Privately Held**
SIC: 2591 Window blinds

(G-15455)
KNAPPCO CORPORATION
Also Called: Civacon
9393 Princeton Glendale Rd (45011-9707)
PHONE..................................513 870-3100
John F Anderson, *CEO*
Pat Gerard, *
Dan Taylor, *
▲ EMP: 140 EST: 1975
SQ FT: 110,000
SALES (est): 35.97MM
SALES (corp-wide): 8.44B **Publicly Held**
Web: www.opwglobal.com
SIC: 3321 3643 3494 Manhole covers, metal ; Caps and plugs, electric: attachment; Valves and pipe fittings, nec
PA: Dover Corporation
3005 Hghland Pkwy Ste 200
Downers Grove IL 60515
630 541-1540

(G-15456)
KOPCO GRAPHICS INC (PA)
9750 Crescent Prk Dr (45069-3894)
PHONE..................................513 874-7230
EMP: 30 EST: 1989
SALES (est): 24.44MM **Privately Held**
Web: www.fortissolutionsgroup.com
SIC: 5199 2759 Packaging materials; Flexographic printing

(G-15457)
LEM PRODUCTS HOLDING LLC (PA)
Also Called: L.E.M. Products
4440 Muhlhauser Rd Ste 300 (45011-9767)
PHONE..................................513 202-1188
Hill Kohnen, *CEO*
▲ EMP: 20 EST: 1991
SALES (est): 8.78MM **Privately Held**
Web: www.lemproducts.com
SIC: 3556 3949 Cutting, chopping, grinding, mixing, and similar machinery; Hunting equipment

(G-15458)
LONG-STANTON MFG COMPANY
9388 Sutton Pl (45011-9702)
PHONE..................................513 874-8020
Daniel B Cunningham, *Pr*
Tom Kachovec, *
Tim Hershey, *
▲ EMP: 50 EST: 1862
SQ FT: 66,000
SALES (est): 9.5MM **Privately Held**
Web: www.longstanton.com
SIC: 3444 7692 3469 3544 Sheet metalwork ; Welding repair; Metal stampings, nec; Special dies, tools, jigs, and fixtures

(G-15459)
LOST TECHNOLOGY LLP
Also Called: Lost Tech
9501 Woodland Hills Dr (45011-9300)
P.O. Box 8257 (45069-8257)
PHONE..................................513 685-0054
Larry Hansonsmith Parnter, *Prin*
EMP: 7 EST: 2002
SALES (est): 363.14K **Privately Held**
SIC: 7372 Educational computer software

West Chester - Butler County (G-15460) GEOGRAPHIC SECTION

(G-15460)
M S INTERNATIONAL INC
Also Called: MSI Surfaces
8556 Trade Center Dr Ste 300 (45011-9354)
PHONE.................513 712-5300
Max O Schweizer, *Prin*
EMP: 6 **EST:** 1996
SALES (est): 39.74K **Privately Held**
Web: www.msisurfaces.com
SIC: 3253 Ceramic wall and floor tile

(G-15461)
MARTIN MARIETTA MATERIALS INC
Also Called: Martin Marietta Aggregate
9277 Centre Pointe Dr Ste 250 (45069)
P.O. Box 30013 (27622-0013)
PHONE.................513 701-1140
Harry Charles, *Mgr*
EMP: 6
Web: www.martinmarietta.com
SIC: 1423 1422 3295 3297 Crushed and broken granite; Crushed and broken limestone; Magnesite, crude: ground, calcined, or dead-burned; Nonclay refractories
PA: Martin Marietta Materials Inc
4123 Parklake Ave
Raleigh NC 27612

(G-15462)
MARTIN-BROWER COMPANY LLC
Also Called: Distribution Center
4260 Port Union Rd (45011-9768)
PHONE.................513 773-2301
Ryan Rozen, *Genl Mgr*
EMP: 163
Web: www.martinbrower.com
SIC: 2013 2015 5087 Frozen meats, from purchased meat; Poultry, processed: frozen ; Restaurant supplies
HQ: The Martin-Brower Company L L C
6250 N River Rd Ste 9000
Rosemont IL 60018
847 227-6500

(G-15463)
MERCHANTS METALS LLC
Also Called: Meadow Burke Products
8760 Global Way Bldg 1 (45069-7066)
PHONE.................513 942-0268
Debbie Humbert, *Genl Mgr*
EMP: 37
SALES (corp-wide): 1.06B **Privately Held**
Web: www.merchantsmetals.com
SIC: 3496 Miscellaneous fabricated wire products
HQ: Merchants Metals Llc
3 Ravinia Dr Ste 1750
Atlanta GA 30346
770 741-0200

(G-15464)
MILLWOOD INC
4438 Muhlhauser Rd Ste 100 (45011-9776)
PHONE.................513 860-4567
Antonio Delgado, *Brnch Mgr*
EMP: 39
Web: www.millwoodinc.com
SIC: 3565 5084 Packaging machinery; Packaging machinery and equipment
PA: Millwood, Inc.
3708 International Blvd
Vienna OH 44473

(G-15465)
MODEL GRAPHICS& MEDIA INC
Also Called: Model Graphics
2614 Crescentville Rd (45069-3819)
PHONE.................513 541-2355
Steve Fleissner, *Pr*
Barb Fleissner, *
EMP: 48 **EST:** 1984
SQ FT: 38,000
SALES (est): 9.72MM **Privately Held**
Web: www.modelgraphicsinc.com
SIC: 2759 Labels and seals: printing, nsk

(G-15466)
MP ACQUISITION GROUP LLC
Also Called: Metal Panel Systems
9283 Sutton Pl (45011-9705)
PHONE.................513 554-6120
Ben Mackie, *Managing Member*
EMP: 15 **EST:** 2020
SALES (est): 1.12MM **Privately Held**
SIC: 3444 Metal roofing and roof drainage equipment

(G-15467)
NUTRITIONAL MEDICINALS LLC
Also Called: Functional Formularies
9277 Centre Pointe Dr Ste 220 (45069)
PHONE.................937 433-4673
Marc Gibeley, *CEO*
Namrata Maquire, *CFO*
Brian Mcgee, *COO*
EMP: 12 **EST:** 2006
SALES (est): 2.9MM
SALES (corp-wide): 725.97MM **Privately Held**
Web: www.functionalformularies.com
SIC: 2833 8011 Organic medicinal chemicals: bulk, uncompounded; Offices and clinics of medical doctors
PA: Danone
17 Boulevard Haussmann
Paris 75009
149485000

(G-15468)
OHIO ALUMINUM CHEMICALS LLC
4544 Mulhauser Rd (45011-9708)
PHONE.................513 860-3842
EMP: 6 **EST:** 2006
SALES (est): 516.16K **Privately Held**
SIC: 2899 Chemical preparations, nec

(G-15469)
OHIO EAGLE DISTRIBUTING LLC
9300 Allen Rd (45069-3847)
PHONE.................513 539-8483
John W Saputo, *Prin*
EMP: 28 **EST:** 2015
SALES (est): 9.73MM **Privately Held**
Web: www.ohioeagle.com
SIC: 2086 5921 Tea, iced: packaged in cans, bottles, etc.; Wine and beer

(G-15470)
OMER J SMITH INC
Also Called: Paper Products Company
9112 Le Saint Dr (45014-5452)
PHONE.................513 921-4717
Dennis J Smith, *Pr*
Denny J Smith Ii, *VP*
Mary C Smith, *
▲ **EMP:** 30 **EST:** 1932
SQ FT: 80,000
SALES (est): 4.96MM **Privately Held**
Web: www.paperproductscompany.com
SIC: 2653 Boxes, corrugated: made from purchased materials

(G-15471)
OPW ENGINEERED SYSTEMS INC (DH)
9393 Princeton Glendale Rd (45011-9707)
PHONE.................888 771-9438
Robert B Nicholson Iii, *CEO*
Tim Warning, *
Mike Krauser, *
▲ **EMP:** 29 **EST:** 2007
SALES (est): 24.24MM
SALES (corp-wide): 8.44B **Publicly Held**
Web: www.opwglobal.com
SIC: 3494 3825 3625 3568 Valves and pipe fittings, nec; Instruments to measure electricity; Relays and industrial controls; Power transmission equipment, nec
HQ: Opw Fluid Transfer Group
4304 Nw Mattox Rd
Kansas City MO 64150

(G-15472)
OPW FUELING COMPONENTS INC (HQ)
Also Called: Opw Engineered Systems
9393 Princeton Glendale Rd (45011-9707)
PHONE.................800 422-2525
David Crouse, *Pr*
◆ **EMP:** 97 **EST:** 2001
SALES (est): 109.13MM
SALES (corp-wide): 8.44B **Publicly Held**
Web: www.opwglobal.com
SIC: 2899 Fuel treating compounds
PA: Dover Corporation
3005 Highland Pkwy Ste 200
Downers Grove IL 60515
630 541-1540

(G-15473)
ORGANALYTIX LLC
4695 Guildford Ln (45069-9259)
PHONE.................908 938-6711
Shwetha Pai, *CEO*
EMP: 6 **EST:** 2017
SALES (est): 120.7K **Privately Held**
Web: www.organalytix.com
SIC: 7372 8741 8742 Business oriented computer software; Personnel management ; Human resource consulting services

(G-15474)
PATRIOT ARMORED SYSTEMS LLC
Also Called: Patriot Armor
9113 Le Saint Dr (45014-5453)
PHONE.................413 637-1060
EMP: 19
Web: www.pasarmor.com
SIC: 3231 Products of purchased glass
PA: Patriot Armored Systems, Llc
140 Crystal St
Lenox Dale MA 01242

(G-15475)
PHASE ARRAY COMPANY LLC
9472 Meridian Way (45069-6527)
PHONE.................513 785-0801
Dominique Braconnier, *Managing Member*
◆ **EMP:** 7 **EST:** 2017
SALES (est): 951.11K **Privately Held**
Web: www.thephasedarraycompany.com
SIC: 3577 7379 Computer peripheral equipment, nec; Computer related consulting services

(G-15476)
PILOT CHEMICAL COMPANY OHIO (PA)
Also Called: Pilot Chemical Company
9075 Centre Pointe Dr Ste 400 (45069)
PHONE.................513 326-0600
Mike Clark, *CEO*
Glynn E Goertzen, *
Susan K Leslie, *
Christian MacIver, *
Derek Houck, *
◆ **EMP:** 30 **EST:** 1952
SALES (est): 175.88MM
SALES (corp-wide): 175.88MM **Privately Held**
Web: www.pilotchemical.com
SIC: 2843 2841 Finishing agents; Detergents, synthetic organic or inorganic alkaline

(G-15477)
PILOT CHEMICAL CORP (HQ)
9075 Centre Pointe Dr Ste 400 (45069)
PHONE.................513 326-0600
Pamela R Butcher, *Pr*
Susan K Leslie, *
Mike Clark, *
◆ **EMP:** 108 **EST:** 1961
SALES (est): 127.13MM
SALES (corp-wide): 175.88MM **Privately Held**
Web: www.pilotchemical.com
SIC: 2841 2843 Detergents, synthetic organic or inorganic alkaline; Surface active agents
PA: Pilot Chemical Company Of Ohio
9075 Cntre Pnte Dr Ste 40
West Chester OH 45069
513 326-0600

(G-15478)
PILOT POLYMER TECHNOLOGIES
9075 Centre Pointe Dr Ste 400 (45069-4891)
PHONE.................412 735-4799
Patrick Mccarthy, *CEO*
EMP: 8 **EST:** 2006
SALES (est): 2.36MM
SALES (corp-wide): 175.88MM **Privately Held**
Web: www.pilotchemical.com
SIC: 2821 Plastics materials and resins
PA: Pilot Chemical Company Of Ohio
9075 Cntre Pnte Dr Ste 40
West Chester OH 45069
513 326-0600

(G-15479)
PIONEER LABELS INC
Also Called: Datamax Oneil Printer Supplies
9290 Le Saint Dr (45014-5454)
PHONE.................618 546-5418
Paul Sindoni, *Pr*
Christian Lefort, *
Carter Williams, *
John Yuncza, *
▼ **EMP:** 105 **EST:** 1984
SALES (est): 51.29MM
SALES (corp-wide): 36.66B **Publicly Held**
SIC: 2754 2672 2671 Labels: gravure printing ; Paper; coated and laminated, nec; Paper; coated and laminated packaging
HQ: Datamax-O'neil Corporation
4501 Pkwy Commerce Blvd
Orlando FL 32808

(G-15480)
PIPE PRODUCTS INC
5122 Rialto Rd (45069-2923)
P.O. Box 2778 (23609-0778)
PHONE.................513 587-7532
▲ **EMP:** 150
SIC: 5051 3498 5085 Pipe and tubing, steel; Pipe fittings, fabricated from purchased pipe ; Valves and fittings

(G-15481)
POLE/ZERO LLC
Also Called: Pole/Zero Acquisition, Inc.
5558 Union Centre Dr (45069-4821)
PHONE.................513 870-9060
Ronald Ruppersburg, *Pr*
EMP: 180 **EST:** 1990
SQ FT: 50,000
SALES (est): 48.84MM
SALES (corp-wide): 8.44B **Publicly Held**
Web: www.mpgdover.com

GEOGRAPHIC SECTION
West Chester - Butler County (G-15504)

SIC: 3663 Radio and television switching equipment
PA: Dover Corporation
3005 Hghland Pkwy Ste 200
Downers Grove IL 60515
630 541-1540

(G-15482)
POLYMET CORPORATION
7397 Union Centre Blvd (45014-2288)
PHONE.................................513 874-3586
Bill Mosier, *Pr*
Thomas J Dagenback, *
▲ EMP: 45 EST: 1967
SQ FT: 47,000
SALES (est): 10.49MM **Privately Held**
Web: www.polymet.us
SIC: 3496 3548 3341 3315 Miscellaneous fabricated wire products; Welding apparatus; Secondary nonferrous metals; Steel wire and related products

(G-15483)
PRECISION DIE & STAMPING INC
9800 Harwood Ct (45014-7589)
PHONE.................................513 942-8220
Greg Johnson, *Pr*
Mike Stephens, *Prin*
EMP: 8 EST: 1999
SQ FT: 6,500
SALES (est): 732.97K **Privately Held**
Web: www.precisiondieandstamping.com
SIC: 3544 Special dies and tools

(G-15484)
PREMIER COATINGS LTD
9390 Le Saint Dr (45014-5446)
PHONE.................................513 942-1070
Brandon Stock, *Genl Mgr*
EMP: 11 EST: 1999
SQ FT: 20,000
SALES (est): 191.17K **Privately Held**
Web: www.stockmfg.com
SIC: 3291 1721 Coated abrasive products; Painting and paper hanging

(G-15485)
PRETZELHAUS BAKERY LLC
8800 Global Way # 31 (45069-7070)
PHONE.................................513 906-2017
Joe Lang, *Prin*
EMP: 8 EST: 2007
SALES (est): 214.53K **Privately Held**
Web: www.pretzelhausbakery.com
SIC: 2051 Bread, cake, and related products

(G-15486)
PROCTER & GAMBLE COMPANY
Also Called: Procter & Gamble
8256 Union Centre Blvd (45069-7056)
PHONE.................................513 634-9600
Pam Dunnon, *Brnch Mgr*
EMP: 205
SALES (corp-wide): 82.01B **Publicly Held**
Web: us.pg.com
SIC: 2844 2676 3421 2842 Deodorants, personal; Towels, napkins, and tissue paper products; Razor blades and razors; Specialty cleaning
PA: The Procter & Gamble Company
1 Procter & Gamble Plz
Cincinnati OH 45202
513 983-1100

(G-15487)
PROCTER & GAMBLE COMPANY
Also Called: Procter & Gamble
8611 Beckett Rd (45069-4868)
PHONE.................................513 634-9110
Ken Litteken, *Mgr*
EMP: 205
SALES (corp-wide): 82.01B **Publicly Held**
Web: us.pg.com
SIC: 2844 2676 3421 2842 Deodorants, personal; Towels, napkins, and tissue paper products; Razor blades and razors; Specialty cleaning
PA: The Procter & Gamble Company
1 Procter & Gamble Plz
Cincinnati OH 45202
513 983-1100

(G-15488)
PTS PRFSSNAL TECHNICAL SVC INC (PA)
Also Called: Est Analytical
503 Commercial Dr (45014-7594)
PHONE.................................513 642-0111
EMP: 47 EST: 1995
SQ FT: 12,000
SALES (est): 11.58MM **Privately Held**
Web: www.estanalytical.com
SIC: 3826 Analytical instruments

(G-15489)
QUALITURN INC
9081 Le Saint Dr (45014-2242)
PHONE.................................513 868-3333
Mike Barber, *Pr*
EMP: 24 EST: 1988
SQ FT: 1,500
SALES (est): 4.98MM **Privately Held**
Web: www.qualiturn-cnc.com
SIC: 3599 Machine shop, jobbing and repair

(G-15490)
QUANTUM COMMERCE LLC
6748 Dimmick Rd (45069-3931)
P.O. Box 1640 (45071-1640)
PHONE.................................513 777-0737
Gregory Workman Ii, *Prin*
EMP: 7 EST: 2010
SALES (est): 228.2K **Privately Held**
SIC: 3572 Computer storage devices

(G-15491)
QUASONIX INC (PA)
Also Called: Quasonix
6025 Schumacher Park Dr (45069-4812)
PHONE.................................513 942-1287
Terrance Hill, *Pr*
Pamela S Hill, *
EMP: 37 EST: 2002
SQ FT: 15,000
SALES (est): 24.46MM
SALES (corp-wide): 24.46MM **Privately Held**
Web: www.quasonix.com
SIC: 5065 3663 3812 3669 Communication equipment; Airborne radio communications equipment; Antennas, radar or communications; Intercommunication systems, electric

(G-15492)
QUEEN CITY POLYMERS INC (PA)
6101 Schumacher Park Dr (45069-3818)
PHONE.................................513 779-0990
James M Powers, *Pr*
James L Powers, *
EMP: 40 EST: 1982
SQ FT: 33,000
SALES (est): 8.75MM
SALES (corp-wide): 8.75MM **Privately Held**
Web: www.qcpinc.net
SIC: 3089 5162 Injection molding of plastics; Plastics products, nec

(G-15493)
R L INDUSTRIES INC
9355 Le Saint Dr (45014-5458)
PHONE.................................513 874-2800
John R Gierl, *Prin*
EMP: 75 EST: 1962
SALES (est): 536.56K
SALES (corp-wide): 24.36MM **Privately Held**
Web: www.rl-industries.com
SIC: 3089 Plastics and fiberglass tanks
PA: R L Holdings, Inc.
9355 Le Saint Dr
West Chester OH 45014
513 874-2800

(G-15494)
R R DONNELLEY & SONS COMPANY
Also Called: RR Donnelley
8720 Global Way (45069-7066)
PHONE.................................513 552-1512
Brad Hull, *Mgr*
EMP: 7
SALES (corp-wide): 4.99B **Privately Held**
Web: www.rrd.com
SIC: 2759 Commercial printing, nec
HQ: R. R. Donnelley & Sons Company
35 W Wacker Dr
Chicago IL 60601
312 326-8000

(G-15495)
R R DONNELLEY & SONS COMPANY
8740 Global Way (45069-7066)
PHONE.................................513 870-4040
EMP: 20
SALES (corp-wide): 4.99B **Privately Held**
Web: www.rrd.com
SIC: 2657 Folding paperboard boxes
HQ: R. R. Donnelley & Sons Company
35 W Wacker Dr
Chicago IL 60601
312 326-8000

(G-15496)
REPUBLIC WIRE INC
5525 Union Centre Dr (45069-4820)
PHONE.................................513 860-1800
Ron Rosenbeck, *CEO*
Mark Huelsebusch, *
◆ EMP: 75 EST: 1981
SQ FT: 175,000
SALES (est): 46.47MM **Privately Held**
Web: www.republicwire.com
SIC: 3351 3315 Wire, copper and copper alloy; Steel wire and related products

(G-15497)
RESILIENCE US INC
8814 Trade Port Dr (45011-8661)
PHONE.................................513 645-2600
Joshua Matson, *Brnch Mgr*
EMP: 470
SALES (corp-wide): 174.83MM **Privately Held**
SIC: 2834 Pharmaceutical preparations
HQ: Resilience Us, Inc.
3115 Mrryfeld Row Ste 200
San Diego CA 92121
984 202-0854

(G-15498)
RETTERBUSH GRAPHICS PACKG CORP
6392 Gano Rd (45069-4809)
PHONE.................................513 779-4466
Joseph Retterbush, *Pr*
Denny Meador, *VP*
EMP: 14 EST: 1995
SALES (est): 724.62K **Privately Held**
Web: www.retterbushcorp.com
SIC: 2671 2754 Paper, coated or laminated for packaging; Labels: gravure printing

(G-15499)
REV38 LLC
8888 Beckett Ridge (45069-2902)
PHONE.................................937 572-4000
Erick Carlson, *Brnch Mgr*
EMP: 6
SALES (corp-wide): 905.96K **Privately Held**
SIC: 3663 Radio and t.v. communications equipment
PA: Rev38 Llc
131 Waterstone Dr
Franklin OH 45005
937 269-9641

(G-15500)
RITE TRACK EQUIPMENT SERVICES LLC (PA)
Also Called: Rite Track
8655 Rite Track Way (45069-7064)
PHONE.................................513 881-7820
EMP: 56 EST: 1993
SALES (est): 23.37MM **Privately Held**
Web: www.ritetrack.com
SIC: 3559 Semiconductor manufacturing machinery

(G-15501)
ROBERT ROTHSCHILD FARM LLC
Also Called: Robert Rothschild Market Cafe
9958 Crescent Park Dr (45069-3895)
P.O. Box 767 (43078-0767)
PHONE.................................855 969-8050
◆ EMP: 18 EST: 2005
SQ FT: 45,000
SALES (est): 4.38MM **Privately Held**
Web: www.robertrothschild.com
SIC: 0171 2035 2033 2032 Raspberry farm; Pickles, sauces, and salad dressings; Canned fruits and specialties; Canned specialties

(G-15502)
ROCKWELL AUTOMATION INC
9355 Allen Rd (45069-3846)
PHONE.................................513 942-9828
Jim Sell, *Mgr*
EMP: 33
SQ FT: 16,000
Web: www.rockwellautomation.com
SIC: 3625 Relays and industrial controls
PA: Rockwell Automation, Inc.
1201 S 2nd St
Milwaukee WI 53204

(G-15503)
ROTO-DIE COMPANY INC
Also Called: Roto Met Rice
4430 Mulhauser Rd (45011-9708)
PHONE.................................513 942-3500
Mike Frazer, *Mgr*
EMP: 6
SALES (corp-wide): 99.99MM **Privately Held**
Web: www.maxcessintl.com
SIC: 3544 Special dies and tools
PA: Roto-Die Company, Inc.
800 Howerton Ln
Eureka MO 63025
636 587-3600

(G-15504)
RSA CONTROLS INC
6422 Fountains Blvd (45069-2101)
PHONE.................................513 476-6277
Ruth Mcwilliams, *Prin*
EMP: 6 EST: 2010
SALES (est): 92.46K **Privately Held**

(PA)=Parent Co (HQ)=Headquarters
✪ = New Business established in last 2 years

West Chester - Butler County (G-15505)

Web: www.rsacontrols.com
SIC: 3823 Thermal conductivity instruments, industrial process type

(G-15505)
SAFEWAY SAFETY STEP LLC
Also Called: Cleancut
5242 Rialto Rd (45069-2921)
PHONE...................513 942-7837
EMP: 10 **EST:** 2000
SALES (est): 1.75MM Privately Held
Web: www.safewaystep.com
SIC: 3088 Tubs (bath, shower, and laundry), plastics

(G-15506)
SCHNEIDER ELECTRIC USA INC
Also Called: Schneider Electric
9870 Crescent Park Dr (45069-3800)
PHONE...................513 777-4445
Jim Newcomb, *Mgr*
EMP: 75
SALES (corp-wide): 82.05K Privately Held
Web: www.se.com
SIC: 3613 3643 3612 3823 Switchgear and switchboard apparatus; Bus bars (electrical conductors); Power transformers, electric; Controllers, for process variables, all types
HQ: Schneider Electric Usa, Inc.
One Boston Pl Ste 2700
Boston MA 02108
978 975-9600

(G-15507)
SENTRILOCK LLC
7701 Service Center Dr (45069-2440)
PHONE...................513 618-5800
Scott R Fisher, *Managing Member*
John G Wenker, *
EMP: 185 **EST:** 2003
SQ FT: 7,000
SALES (est): 48.7MM Privately Held
Web: www.sentrilock.com
SIC: 3679 Electronic circuits

(G-15508)
SEPPI M SPA
8880 Beckett Rd (45069-2902)
PHONE...................513 443-6339
Pierluigi Defant, *CEO*
EMP: 6
SALES (corp-wide): 36.49MM Privately Held
Web: www.seppi.com
SIC: 3523 Cabs, tractors, and agricultural machinery
PA: Seppi M. Spa
Via Trento 111
Mezzolombardo TN 38017
04611787500

(G-15509)
SPICY OLIVE LLC (PA)
7671 Cox Ln (45069-6546)
PHONE...................513 847-4397
Theresa A Banks, *Prin*
EMP: 6 **EST:** 2012
SALES (est): 949.38K
SALES (corp-wide): 949.38K Privately Held
Web: www.thespicyolive.com
SIC: 2079 Olive oil

(G-15510)
STERLING COATING
9048 Port Union Rialto Rd (45069-3254)
PHONE...................513 942-4900
Craig Lowe, *Genl Mgr*
EMP: 9 **EST:** 2014
SALES (est): 104.83K Privately Held

SIC: 3479 Etching and engraving

(G-15511)
SUMMIT CONTAINER CORPORATION (PA)
8080 Beckett Center Dr Ste 203 (45069-5026)
PHONE...................719 481-8400
Adam C Walker, *CEO*
Dave Johnson, *
EMP: 13 **EST:** 1984
SALES (est): 3.24MM
SALES (corp-wide): 3.24MM Privately Held
Web: www.1teamsummit.com
SIC: 2653 Boxes, corrugated: made from purchased materials

(G-15512)
SUMMIT PACKAGING SOLUTIONS LLC (PA)
8080 Beckett Center Dr Ste 203 (45069-5026)
PHONE...................719 481-8400
Adam Walker, *CEO*
EMP: 12 **EST:** 2015
SALES (est): 9.55MM
SALES (corp-wide): 9.55MM Privately Held
Web: www.1teamsummit.com
SIC: 2631 Container, packaging, and boxboard

(G-15513)
SYSTECON LLC
6121 Schumacher Park Dr (45069-3818)
PHONE...................513 777-7722
Martin P Tierney, *Pr*
Alice Edwards, *Contrlr*
EMP: 85 **EST:** 1949
SQ FT: 60,000
SALES (est): 42.77MM
SALES (corp-wide): 58.86B Privately Held
Web: www.systecon.com
SIC: 3561 Pumps and pumping equipment
HQ: Engie North America Inc.
1360 Post Oak Blvd # 400
Houston TX 77056
713 636-1900

(G-15514)
TENACITY MANUFACTURING COMPANY
4455 Mulhauser Rd (45011-9788)
P.O. Box 15006 (45215-0006)
PHONE...................513 821-0201
Layne Meader, *Pr*
Tim Baumgardner, *Treas*
Jerry Crowder, *Product Vice President*
EMP: 13 **EST:** 1905
SQ FT: 36,500
SALES (est): 1.11MM
SALES (corp-wide): 11.14MM Privately Held
Web: www.tenacitymfg.com
SIC: 3469 2782 Machine parts, stamped or pressed metal; Looseleaf binders and devices
PA: Kofile Products, Inc.
6480 Enduro Dr
Washington MO 63090
636 239-0140

(G-15515)
THREE BOND INTERNATIONAL INC (DH)
6184 Schumacher Park Dr (45069-4802)
PHONE...................513 779-7300
Kazunori Shibayama, *Pr*
▲ **EMP:** 60 **EST:** 1987

SALES (est): 42MM Privately Held
Web: www.threebond.com
SIC: 2891 Adhesives
HQ: Threebond Co., Ltd.
4-3-3, Minamiosawa
Hachioji TKY 192-0

(G-15516)
TOTAL LIFE SAFETY LLC
Also Called: Atech Fire Services
6228 Centre Park Dr Ste C (45069-4825)
PHONE...................866 955-2318
Douglas Patterson, *Managing Member*
EMP: 12 **EST:** 2020
SALES (est): 2MM Privately Held
SIC: 2899 3669 5063 Fire extinguisher charges; Fire detection systems, electric; Fire alarm systems

(G-15517)
TOYOBO KUREHA AMERICA CO LTD
Also Called: Tk America
4591 Brate Dr (45011-3577)
PHONE...................513 771-6788
▲ **EMP:** 9 **EST:** 1994
SALES (est): 2.97MM Privately Held
Web: www.tkamerica.com
SIC: 2297 Nonwoven fabrics
HQ: Kureha Ltd.
255, Oka
Ritto SGA 520-3

(G-15518)
TREY CORRUGATED INC
9048 Port Union Rialto Rd (45069-3254)
PHONE...................513 942-4800
Tim Cossey, *Pr*
EMP: 146 **EST:** 1984
SALES (est): 5.09MM
SALES (corp-wide): 36.93B Privately Held
SIC: 2653 Boxes, corrugated: made from purchased materials
HQ: Georgia-Pacific Corrugated Iii Llc
5645 W 82nd St
Indianapolis IN 46278

(G-15519)
TRUECHOICEPACK CORP
9565 Cincinnati Columbus Rd (45069-4242)
PHONE...................937 630-3832
Heena Rathore, *Pr*
Rakesh Rathore, *CSO*
EMP: 15 **EST:** 2013
SALES (est): 3.44MM
SALES (corp-wide): 14.58MM Privately Held
Web: www.truechoicepack.com
SIC: 3089 3086 5113 Blister or bubble formed packaging, plastics; Packaging and shipping materials, foamed plastics; Disposable plates, cups, napkins, and eating utensils
PA: Che International Group, Llc
255 E 5th St Ste 1900
Cincinnati OH 45202
513 229-7595

(G-15520)
TUCKER PRINTERS INC
8740 Global Way (45069-7066)
PHONE...................585 359-3030
Joe R Davis, *CEO*
Daniel A Tucker, *
EMP: 82 **EST:** 1997
SALES (est): 25.61MM
SALES (corp-wide): 4.99B Privately Held
SIC: 2752 Offset printing
HQ: Consolidated Graphics, Inc.
5858 Westheimer Rd # 200
Houston TX 77057

(G-15521)
TVH PARTS CO
Also Called: C-Tech Industries
8756 Global Way (45069-7066)
PHONE...................877 755-7311
EMP: 18
SALES (corp-wide): 2.67MM Privately Held
Web: www.tvh.com
SIC: 3625 Relays and industrial controls
HQ: Tvh Parts Co.
16355 S Lone Elm Rd
Olathe KS 66062
913 829-1000

(G-15522)
UPA TECHNOLOGY INC
8963 Cincinnati Columbus Rd (45069-3513)
P.O. Box 1755 (45071-1755)
PHONE...................513 755-1380
Michael Justice, *Pr*
Susan Justice, *VP*
◆ **EMP:** 11 **EST:** 1987
SQ FT: 4,500
SALES (est): 2.18MM Privately Held
Web: www.upa.com
SIC: 3829 7699 Measuring and controlling devices, nec; Professional instrument repair services

(G-15523)
USUI INTERNATIONAL CORPORATION
Also Called: UIC West Chester Plant
8748 Jacquemin Dr Ste 100 (45069-4999)
PHONE...................734 354-3626
Devon Thompson, *Opers*
EMP: 100
Web: www.usuiusa.com
SIC: 3714 Motor vehicle parts and accessories
HQ: Usui International Corporation
44780 Helm St
Plymouth MI 48170
734 354-3626

(G-15524)
VALEN FOUNDRY INC ✪
7259 Leemel Dr (45069-3692)
PHONE...................724 712-3500
Scott Wohlstein, *Prin*
EMP: 13 **EST:** 2022
SALES (est): 519.63K Privately Held
SIC: 3399 Metal fasteners

(G-15525)
VINTAGE WINE DISTRIBUTOR INC
9422 Meridian Way (45069-6527)
PHONE...................513 443-4300
EMP: 10
SALES (corp-wide): 9.67MM Privately Held
Web: www.vintwine.com
SIC: 2084 Wines
PA: Vintage Wine Distributor, Inc.
6555 Davis Indus Pkwy
Solon OH 44139
440 248-1750

(G-15526)
WARFIGHTER FCSED LOGISTICS INC
8800 Global Way Ste 100a (45069-7070)
PHONE...................740 513-4692
Darrell Kem, *Pr*
EMP: 20
SALES (corp-wide): 2.6MM Privately Held
Web: www.warfighterfocusedlogistics.com

GEOGRAPHIC SECTION

West Chester - Hamilton County (G-15547)

SIC: **3711** 3724 Military motor vehicle assembly; Lubricating systems, aircraft
PA: Warfighter Focused Logistics Inc.
936 Nw 1st St
Fort Lauderdale FL 33311
740 513-4692

(G-15527)
WESTROCK RKT LLC
Also Called: Rocktenn Merchandising Display
9245 Meridian Way (45069-6523)
PHONE..............................513 860-5546
Bob Akers, *Ltd Pt*
EMP: 78
SALES (corp-wide): 20.31B **Publicly Held**
Web: www.westrock.com
SIC: **2653** Boxes, corrugated: made from purchased materials
HQ: Westrock Rkt, Llc
1000 Abernathy Rd Ste 125
Atlanta GA 30328
770 448-2193

(G-15528)
YKK AP AMERICA INC
Also Called: YKK USA
8748 Jacquemin Dr Ste 400 (45069-4999)
PHONE..............................513 942-7200
Phil Blizzard, *Mgr*
EMP: 25
Web: www.ykkap.com
SIC: **3442** 3449 Sash, door or window: metal ; Curtain wall, metal
HQ: Ykk Ap America Inc.
101 Mretta St Nw Ste 2100
Atlanta GA 30303

(G-15529)
YOCKEY GROUP INC
9053 Le Saint Dr (45014-2242)
PHONE..............................513 860-9053
A James Yockey, *Pr*
EMP: 13 EST: 1998
SALES (est): 577.17K **Privately Held**
SIC: **2759** Commercial printing, nec

West Chester
Hamilton County

(G-15530)
ACTION SPECIALTY PACKAGING LLC (DH)
4758 Devitt Dr (45246-1106)
◆ EMP: 8 EST: 2004
SQ FT: 30,000
SALES (est): 4.27MM
SALES (corp-wide): 635.28MM **Privately Held**
SIC: **2621** 2631 2653 Kraft wrapping paper; Container, packaging, and boxboard; Boxes, corrugated: made from purchased materials
HQ: Storopack, Inc.
4758 Devitt Dr
West Chester OH 45246
513 874-0314

(G-15531)
ADVANCEPIERRE FOODS INC (DH)
Also Called: Tyson
9990 Princeton Glendale Rd (45246-1116)
PHONE..............................513 874-8741
Tom Hayes, *Pr*
John Tyson, *
Dennis Leatherby, *
▲ EMP: 300 EST: 2008
SALES (est): 820.25MM
SALES (corp-wide): 52.88B **Publicly Held**
Web: www.advancepierre.com

SIC: **2013** 2015 Prepared beef products, from purchased beef; Chicken, processed, nsk
HQ: Advancepierre Foods Holdings, Inc.
9990 Prnceton Glendale Rd
West Chester OH 45246

(G-15532)
ADVANCPERRE FOODS HOLDINGS INC (HQ)
Also Called: Advancepierre
9990 Princeton Glendale Rd (45246-1116)
PHONE..............................513 428-5699
EMP: 68 EST: 2008
SALES (est): 933.68MM
SALES (corp-wide): 52.88B **Publicly Held**
Web: investors.advancepierre.com
SIC: **2099** 2013 Sandwiches, assembled and packaged: for wholesale market; Sausages and other prepared meats
PA: Tyson Foods, Inc.
2200 W Don Tyson Pkwy
Springdale AR 72762
479 290-4000

(G-15533)
AGEAN MARBLE MANUFACTURING
9756 Princeton Glendale Rd (45246-1015)
PHONE..............................513 874-1475
Gary Bolte, *Ch*
Lois Bolte, *Sec*
Chris Bolte, *VP*
EMP: 17 EST: 1946
SQ FT: 26,000
SALES (est): 1.73MM **Privately Held**
Web: www.agean.com
SIC: **3272** 5211 5091 3431 Art marble, concrete; Bathroom fixtures, equipment and supplies; Spa equipment and supplies; Metal sanitary ware

(G-15534)
AJJ ENTERPRISES LLC
10073 Commerce Park Dr (45246-1333)
PHONE..............................513 755-9562
Jason Wahl, *Managing Member*
▲ EMP: 10 EST: 2007
SALES (est): 1MM **Privately Held**
Web: www.ajjcornhole.com
SIC: **3944** Games, toys, and children's vehicles

(G-15535)
AMERICAN BUSINESS FORMS INC
Also Called: American Solutions For Bus
10000 International Blvd (45246-4839)
PHONE..............................513 312-2522
EMP: 30
SALES (corp-wide): 380.8MM **Privately Held**
Web: home.americanbus.com
SIC: **5112** 5199 2759 Business forms; Advertising specialties; Promotional printing
PA: American Business Forms, Inc.
31 E Minnesota Ave
Glenwood MN 56334
320 634-5471

(G-15536)
ANEST IWATA USA INC
10148 Commerce Park Dr (45246-1336)
PHONE..............................513 755-3100
Hiroki Nishida, *Pr*
▲ EMP: 10 EST: 1994
SQ FT: 4,800
SALES (est): 5.03MM **Privately Held**
Web: www.anestiwata.com
SIC: **3479** 5013 Painting, coating, and hot dipping; Motor vehicle supplies and new parts
PA: Anest Iwata Corporation

3176, Shinyoshidacho, Kohoku-Ku
Yokohama KNG 223-0

(G-15537)
APF LEGACY SUBS LLC (DH)
9990 Princeton Glendale Rd (45246-1116)
PHONE..............................513 682-7173
EMP: 7 EST: 1993
SALES (est): 17.04MM
SALES (corp-wide): 52.88B **Publicly Held**
SIC: **2099** Food preparations, nec
HQ: Advancepierre Foods, Inc.
9990 Prnceton Glendale Rd
West Chester OH 45246
513 874-8741

(G-15538)
ARCH CUTNG TLS CINCINNATI LLC ✪
133 Circle Freeway Dr (45246-1203)
PHONE..............................513 851-6363
Steven Long, *Pr*
EMP: 15 EST: 2022
SALES (est): 1.13MM **Privately Held**
SIC: **3545** Drill bits, metalworking

(G-15539)
ATMOS360 INC
Also Called: Atmos 360 A Systems Solutions
4690 Interstate Dr Ste A (45246-1142)
PHONE..............................513 772-4777
EMP: 45 EST: 1989
SALES (est): 9MM **Privately Held**
Web: www.atmos360.com
SIC: **8711** 3565 3564 Consulting engineer; Packaging machinery; Blowers and fans

(G-15540)
BAXTERS NORTH AMERICA INC
Also Called: Wornick Company, The
9756 International Blvd (45246-4854)
PHONE..............................513 552-7718
◆ EMP: 48
SALES (corp-wide): 559.89MM **Privately Held**
Web: www.baxtersna.com
SIC: **2032** Baby foods, including meats: packaged in cans, jars, etc.
HQ: Baxters North America, Inc.
4700 Creek Rd
Cincinnati OH 45242
513 552-7485

(G-15541)
BEIERSDORF INC
5232 E Provident Dr (45246-1040)
PHONE..............................513 682-7300
Jim Kenton, *Brnch Mgr*
EMP: 168
SALES (corp-wide): 12.51B **Privately Held**
Web: www.beiersdorfusa.com
SIC: **2844** 5122 3842 2841 Face creams or lotions; Antiseptics; Bandages and dressings; Soap: granulated, liquid, cake, flaked, or chip
HQ: Beiersdorf, Inc.
301 Tresser Blvd Ste 1500
Stamford CT 06901
203 563-5800

(G-15542)
BUILDING CTRL INTEGRATORS LLC
10174 International Blvd (45246-4846)
PHONE..............................513 860-9600
EMP: 7
SALES (corp-wide): 11.3MM **Privately Held**
Web: www.bcicontrols.com
SIC: **3822** Temperature controls, automatic
PA: Building Control Integrators, Llc
383 N Liberty St

Powell OH 43065
614 334-3300

(G-15543)
BUZZ SEATING INC (PA)
4774 Interstate Dr (45246-1112)
P.O. Box 31379 (45231-0379)
PHONE..............................877 263-5737
Dan Ohara, *Pr*
▲ EMP: 7 EST: 2003
SQ FT: 12,982
SALES (est): 2.19MM
SALES (corp-wide): 2.19MM **Privately Held**
Web: www.buzzseating.com
SIC: **2521** Chairs, office: padded, upholstered, or plain: wood

(G-15544)
CECO ENVIRONMENTAL CORP
Effox-Flextor
9759 Inter Ocean Dr (45246-1027)
PHONE..............................513 874-8915
Jack Neiser, *Mgr*
EMP: 47
Web: www.cecoenviro.com
SIC: **3443** 3441 Fabricated plate work (boiler shop); Fabricated structural metal
PA: Ceco Environmental Corp.
14651 Dallas Pkwy Ste 500
Dallas TX 75254

(G-15545)
CLARKE FIRE PRTECTION PDTS INC
133 Circle Freeway Dr (45246-1203)
PHONE..............................513 771-2200
EMP: 27
SALES (corp-wide): 225.9MM **Privately Held**
Web: www.clarkepowerservices.com
SIC: **3519** Diesel, semi-diesel, or duel-fuel engines, including marine
HQ: Clarke Fire Protection Products, Inc.
3133 E Kemper Rd
Cincinnati OH 45241

(G-15546)
CTL-AEROSPACE INC
9970 International Blvd (45246-4852)
PHONE..............................513 874-7900
Jc Owen, *Pr*
EMP: 20
SALES (corp-wide): 61.27MM **Privately Held**
Web: www.ctlaerospace.com
SIC: **3728** Aircraft parts and equipment, nec
PA: Ctl-Aerospace, Inc.
5616 Spellmire Dr
West Chester OH 45246
513 874-7900

(G-15547)
CTL-AEROSPACE INC (PA)
Also Called: OEM
5616 Spellmire Dr (45246-4898)
PHONE..............................513 874-7900
James T Irwin, *Pr*
Robert W Buechner, *
Vicki Osborne, *
John Irwin, *
John Macleod, *
EMP: 205 EST: 1946
SQ FT: 100,000
SALES (est): 61.27MM
SALES (corp-wide): 61.27MM **Privately Held**
Web: www.ctlaerospace.com
SIC: **3728** Aircraft assemblies, subassemblies, and parts, nec

---

(PA)=Parent Co (HQ)=Headquarters
✪ = New Business established in last 2 years

West Chester - Hamilton County (G-15548) GEOGRAPHIC SECTION

(G-15548)
D C CONTROLS LLC
Also Called: Coffey and Associates
4836 Duff Dr Ste E (45246-1194)
PHONE.................................513 225-0813
David A Coffey, *Managing Member*
EMP: 7 **EST:** 2007
SALES (est): 975.9K **Privately Held**
Web: www.dccontrols.net
SIC: 3315 Wire and fabricated wire products

(G-15549)
EFFOX-FLEXTOR-MADER INC (HQ)
9759 Inter Ocean Dr (45246-1027)
PHONE.................................513 874-8915
L James Zeager, *CEO*
EMP: 11 **EST:** 2020
SALES (est): 22.32MM **Publicly Held**
Web: www.efmequipment.com
SIC: 3564 Purification and dust collection equipment
PA: Ceco Environmental Corp.
  14651 Dallas Pkwy Ste 500
  Dallas TX 75254

(G-15550)
ELIASON CORPORATION
10021 Commerce Park Dr (45246-1333)
PHONE.................................800 828-3655
EMP: 33
SALES (corp-wide): 448.01MM **Privately Held**
Web: www.eliasoncorp.com
SIC: 3442 3089 Metal doors; Plastics containers, except foam
HQ: Eliason Corporation
  9229 Shaver Rd
  Portage MI 49024
  269 327-7003

(G-15551)
EMPIRE PACKING COMPANY LP
Also Called: Cincinnatti Processing
113 Circle Freeway Dr (45246-1203)
PHONE.................................513 942-5400
Dennis Hioghmas, *Genl Mgr*
EMP: 60
SALES (corp-wide): 138.53MM **Privately Held**
Web: www.ledbetterfoods.com
SIC: 5147 2013 2011 Meats, fresh; Sausages and other prepared meats; Meat packing plants
PA: Empire Packing Company, L.P.
  1837 Harbor Ave
  Memphis TN 38115
  901 948-4788

(G-15552)
FEDERALEAGLE LLC
Also Called: Eagle Coach Company
64 Circle Freeway Dr (45246)
PHONE.................................513 797-4100
Steven Bentley, *Pr*
Daan Kore, *
EMP: 80 **EST:** 1985
SALES (est): 10.61MM
SALES (corp-wide): 1.62B **Privately Held**
Web: www.federaleaglecoach.com
SIC: 3711 Hearses (motor vehicles), assembly of
PA: J. B. Poindexter & Co., Inc.
  600 Travis St Ste 400
  Houston TX 77002
  713 655-9800

(G-15553)
FIRE-END & CROKER CORP
Also Called: FIRE-END & CROKER CORP.
4690 Interstate Dr Ste P (45246-1142)
PHONE.................................513 870-0517
Bob Orth, *Genl Mgr*
EMP: 37
SALES (corp-wide): 23.71MM **Privately Held**
Web: www.croker.com
SIC: 3699 Fire control or bombing equipment, electronic
HQ: Fire End & Croker Corp.
  7 Westchester Plz Ste 267
  Elmsford NY 10523
  914 592-3640

(G-15554)
FKI LOGISTEX AUTOMATION INC
10045 International Blvd (45246-4845)
PHONE.................................513 881-5251
▲ **EMP:** 700
SIC: 3535 Conveyors and conveying equipment

(G-15555)
FRUTAROM USA HOLDING INC (DH)
5404 Duff Dr (45246-1323)
PHONE.................................201 861-9500
Ori Yehudai, *CEO*
Alon Granot, *CFO*
Amos Anatot, *Ex VP*
EMP: 6 **EST:** 2002
SALES (est): 8.17MM
SALES (corp-wide): 11.48B **Publicly Held**
SIC: 2869 Flavors or flavoring materials, synthetic
HQ: Frutarom Usa Inc.
  5404 Duff Dr
  West Chester OH 45246
  513 870-4900

(G-15556)
FRUTAROM USA INC (HQ)
Also Called: Frutarom
5404 Duff Dr (45246-1323)
PHONE.................................513 870-4900
Ori Yehudai, *Pr*
Luis Gayo, *
Alon Granot, *
Michael J Gill, *
Kevin Woten, *
◆ **EMP:** 120 **EST:** 1933
SQ FT: 360,000
SALES (est): 32.67MM
SALES (corp-wide): 11.48B **Publicly Held**
SIC: 2099 2833 2087 Spices, including grinding; Botanical products, medicinal: ground, graded, or milled; Extracts, flavoring
PA: International Flavors & Fragrances Inc.
  521 W 57th St
  New York NY 10019
  212 765-5500

(G-15557)
GOYAL ENTERPRISES INC
Also Called: Bharat Trading
4836 Business Center Way (45246-1318)
P.O. Box 1728 (45071-1728)
PHONE.................................513 874-9303
Arun Goyal, *Genl Mgr*
Kavita Goyal, *Pr*
EMP: 10 **EST:** 1991
SQ FT: 4,500
SALES (est): 881.45K **Privately Held**
Web: www.gemini-jewelers.com
SIC: 5094 5944 3911 Jewelry; Jewelry, precious stones and precious metals; Bracelets, precious metal

(G-15558)
GRAPHIX ONE CORPORATION
4690 Interstate Dr Ste F (45246-1101)
PHONE.................................513 870-0512
EMP: 8 **EST:** 1997
SQ FT: 10,000
SALES (est): 273.7K **Privately Held**
SIC: 2759 Screen printing

(G-15559)
GREENWORLD ENTERPRISES INC
Also Called: Focal Point Communications
61 Circle Freeway Dr (45246-1201)
PHONE.................................800 525-6999
Joe Shooner, *CEO*
EMP: 6 **EST:** 1982
SQ FT: 3,600
SALES (est): 515.99K **Privately Held**
Web: www.winnipegfreepress.com
SIC: 2711 Newspapers, publishing and printing

(G-15560)
HANDS ON INTERNATIONAL LLC
Also Called: Hands On
9776 Inter Ocean Dr (45216)
PHONE.................................513 502-9000
▲ **EMP:** 7 **EST:** 2010
SALES (est): 865.63K **Privately Held**
Web: www.gohands-on.com
SIC: 5136 2326 7389 Work clothing, men's and boys'; Work apparel, except uniforms; Business Activities at Non-Commercial Site

(G-15561)
HANSEN SCAFFOLDING LLC (PA)
193 Circle Freeway Dr (45246-1203)
PHONE.................................513 574-9000
Aaron Hansen, *Pr*
Jennifer Mcdonald, *Off Mgr*
EMP: 14 **EST:** 1986
SQ FT: 22,000
SALES (est): 2.26MM
SALES (corp-wide): 2.26MM **Privately Held**
Web: www.hansenscaffolding.com
SIC: 7359 3446 Equipment rental and leasing, nec; Scaffolds, mobile or stationary: metal

(G-15562)
HORNER INDUSTRIAL SERVICES INC
4721 Interstate Dr (45246-1111)
PHONE.................................513 874-8722
TOLL FREE: 800
Mark Wolma, *VP*
EMP: 7
SALES (corp-wide): 55.43MM **Privately Held**
Web: www.hornerindustrial.com
SIC: 7694 Armature rewinding shops
PA: Horner Industrial Services, Inc.
  1521 E Washington St
  Indianapolis IN 46201
  317 639-4261

(G-15563)
HYDROTECH INC (PA)
Also Called: Enpro
10052 Commerce Park Dr (45246-1338)
PHONE.................................888 651-5712
◆ **EMP:** 51 **EST:** 1967
SALES (est): 25.63MM
SALES (corp-wide): 25.63MM **Privately Held**
Web: www.hydrotech.com
SIC: 5084 3492 Industrial machinery and equipment; Control valves, fluid power: hydraulic and pneumatic

(G-15564)
ICEE USA
44 Carnegie Way (45246-1224)
PHONE.................................513 771-0630
Bob Keegan, *Prin*
EMP: 8 **EST:** 2010
SALES (est): 228.78K **Privately Held**
Web: www.icee.com
SIC: 2024 Ice cream and frozen deserts

(G-15565)
INTELLIGRATED INC
10045 International Blvd (45246-4845)
PHONE.................................513 874-0788
EMP: 2457
SALES (corp-wide): 36.66B **Publicly Held**
Web: sps.honeywell.com
SIC: 3535 5084 7371 Conveyors and conveying equipment; Industrial machinery and equipment; Custom computer programming services
HQ: Intelligrated, Inc.
  7901 Innovation Way
  Mason OH 45040
  866 936-7300

(G-15566)
INTELLIGRATED SYSTEMS OHIO LLC
Also Called: Fki Logistex
10045 International Blvd (45246-4845)
PHONE.................................513 682-6600
Doug Westman, *Dir*
EMP: 8
SALES (corp-wide): 36.66B **Publicly Held**
SIC: 3535 Conveyors and conveying equipment
HQ: Intelligrated Systems Of Ohio, Llc
  7901 Innovation Way
  Mason OH 45040
  513 701-7300

(G-15567)
KONECRANES INC
Also Called: Crane Pro Services
4866 Duff Dr (45246-1150)
PHONE.................................513 755-2800
Barb Rothert, *Admn*
EMP: 41
Web: www.konecranes.com
SIC: 3536 Hoists, cranes, and monorails
HQ: Konecranes, Inc.
  4401 Gateway Blvd
  Springfield OH 45502

(G-15568)
MAGNUM PIERING INC
156 Circle Freeway Dr (45246-1204)
PHONE.................................513 759-3348
Brian Dwyer, *Pr*
Bill Bonekemper, *
Sharon Appelman, *
EMP: 30 **EST:** 2000
SALES (est): 9.14MM
SALES (corp-wide): 15.39MM **Privately Held**
Web: www.magnumpiering.com
SIC: 3441 3561 Fabricated structural metal; Pumps and pumping equipment
PA: Dwyer Companies, Inc.
  6083 Schumacher Park Dr
  West Chester OH 45069
  513 777-0998

(G-15569)
MCCC SPORTSWEAR INC (PA)
9944 Princeton Glendale Rd (45246-1116)
PHONE.................................513 583-9210
Marta Callahan, *Pr*
▲ **EMP:** 7 **EST:** 1994
SQ FT: 45,000
SALES (est): 3.93MM **Privately Held**
Web: www.mccc-sportswear.com
SIC: 5137 2395 5136 Women's and children's clothing; Embroidery and art needlework; Men's and boy's clothing

GEOGRAPHIC SECTION
West Chester - Hamilton County (G-15592)

(G-15570)
MCNERNEY & ASSOCIATES LLC
Also Called: P J McNerney & Associates
5443 Duff Dr (45246-1323)
PHONE.................................513 241-9951
Patrick Mcnerney, *Mgr*
Patrick J Mcnerney, *Pr*
Jan Mcnerney, *VP*
◆ **EMP:** 42 **EST:** 1983
SALES (est): 4.5MM **Privately Held**
Web: www.pjmcnerney.com
SIC: 2752 4783 Offset printing; Packing goods for shipping

(G-15571)
MICROTEK FINISHING LLC
5579 Spellmire Dr (45246-4841)
PHONE.................................513 766-5600
▲ **EMP:** 22 **EST:** 2009
SQ FT: 5,000
SALES (est): 7.53MM **Privately Held**
Web: www.mmptechnology.com
SIC: 3471 Polishing, metals or formed products
PA: Binc Industries Sa
Route De Geneve 7
Commugny VD

(G-15572)
MIDWEST FILTRATION LLC
9775 International Blvd (45246-4855)
PHONE.................................513 874-6510
Steven Vollmer, *Managing Member*
Frank Strittmatter, *
▲ **EMP:** 79 **EST:** 1985
SQ FT: 110,000
SALES (est): 35.83MM **Privately Held**
Web: www.midwestfiltration.com
SIC: 3569 2653 Filters, general line: industrial; Corrugated and solid fiber boxes

(G-15573)
NORTHROP GRUMMAN SYSTEMS CORP
460 W Crescentville Rd (45246-1221)
PHONE.................................513 881-3296
Patricia A Newby, *Brnch Mgr*
EMP: 270
Web: www.northropgrumman.com
SIC: 3812 Search and navigation equipment
HQ: Northrop Grumman Systems Corporation
2980 Fairview Park Dr
Falls Church VA 22042
703 280-2900

(G-15574)
OCTAL EXTRUSION CORP
5399 E Provident Dr (45246-1044)
PHONE.................................513 881-6100
Joe Barenberg, *CEO*
Cameron Warren, *
EMP: 60 **EST:** 2014
SQ FT: 130,000
SALES (est): 46.69MM **Privately Held**
Web: www.alpekpolyester.com
SIC: 2671 Paper, coated or laminated for packaging
PA: Octal Holding
Al Rawaq Building Salalah Free Zone
Muscat 112

(G-15575)
PF MANAGEMENT INC
Also Called: Pfmi
9990 Princeton Glendale Rd (45246-1116)
PHONE.................................513 874-8741
Norbert E Woodhams, *Pr*
EMP: 7 **EST:** 1970
SQ FT: 220,000
SALES (est): 1.17MM **Privately Held**

SIC: 8741 2015 2051 Management services; Chicken slaughtering and processing; Bread, cake, and related products
HQ: Pierre Holding Corp
9990 Prnceton Glendale Rd
West Chester OH 45246

(G-15576)
PIERRE HOLDING CORP (HQ)
9990 Princeton Glendale Rd (45246-1116)
PHONE.................................513 874-8741
Norbert E Wooadhams, *Pr*
Robert C Naylor, *Marketing*
Joseph W Meyers, *CFO*
EMP: 7 **EST:** 2004
SQ FT: 220,000
SALES (est): 85.26MM **Privately Held**
SIC: 2013 2015 2051 Prepared beef products, from purchased beef; Chicken slaughtering and processing; Bread, cake, and related products
PA: Madison Dearborn Partners Iv Lp
70 W Madison St Ste 3800
Chicago IL 60602

(G-15577)
POWERSONIC INDUSTRIES LLC
5406 Spellmire Dr (45246-4842)
P.O. Box 6506 (45206-0506)
PHONE.................................513 429-2329
Jason Rampersand, *Pr*
▲ **EMP:** 25 **EST:** 2014
SALES (est): 3.03MM **Privately Held**
Web: www.powersonic.net
SIC: 3571 Electronic computers

(G-15578)
PROFESSIONAL CASE INC
Also Called: PCI
4954 Provident Dr (45246-1021)
PHONE.................................513 682-2520
Thomas Brown, *Pr*
Erin Biel, *VP*
EMP: 10 **EST:** 1978
SQ FT: 7,000
SALES (est): 723.52K **Privately Held**
Web: www.professionalcase.com
SIC: 3161 Cases, carrying, nec

(G-15579)
QUALITY ENVELOPE INC
9792 Inter Ocean Dr (45246-1028)
P.O. Box 40862 (45240-0862)
PHONE.................................513 942-7578
Robert Lester, *Pr*
Rick Doxtator, *VP*
Jeffery Leatherwood Senior, *Sec*
EMP: 6 **EST:** 2002
SALES (est): 649.78K **Privately Held**
SIC: 2677 Envelopes

(G-15580)
READING ROCK INCORPORATED (PA)
4600 Devitt Dr (45246-1104)
P.O. Box 46387 (45246-0387)
PHONE.................................513 874-2345
Gordon Rich, *Pr*
Mark Swortwood, *VP*
▲ **EMP:** 136 **EST:** 1946
SQ FT: 64,000
SALES (est): 61.15MM
SALES (corp-wide): 61.15MM **Privately Held**
Web: www.readingrock.com
SIC: 3271 2951 Blocks, concrete or cinder: standard; Asphalt paving mixtures and blocks

(G-15581)
ROOFING ANNEX LLC
4866 Duff Dr Ste E (45246-1151)
PHONE.................................513 942-0555
Chad Janisch, *CEO*
Joey Michels, *VP*
Stephen Michels, *Sec*
EMP: 7 **EST:** 2010
SQ FT: 4,000
SALES (est): 2.37MM **Privately Held**
Web: www.roofingannex.com
SIC: 5031 1761 3444 Windows; Roofing, siding, and sheetmetal work; Gutters, sheet metal

(G-15582)
RUSSELL CAST STONE INC
Also Called: Continental Cast Stone East
4600 Devitt Dr (45246-1104)
PHONE.................................856 753-4000
William Russell Iii, *CEO*
EMP: 58 **EST:** 1999
SALES (est): 5.38MM **Privately Held**
Web: www.russellstone.com
SIC: 3272 Concrete products, nec

(G-15583)
SERVICE EXPRESS LLC
10004 International Blvd (45246-4839)
PHONE.................................513 942-6170
EMP: 11
SIC: 2741 Miscellaneous publishing
PA: Service Express, Llc
3854 Broadmoor Ave Se # 101
Grand Rapids MI 49546

(G-15584)
SEXTON INDUSTRIAL INC
366 Circle Freeway Dr (45246-1208)
PHONE.................................513 530-5555
Abbe Sexton, *Pr*
Ron Sexton, *
Dan Towne, *
EMP: 150 **EST:** 1998
SQ FT: 85,000
SALES (est): 20.08MM **Privately Held**
Web: www.artisanmechanical.com
SIC: 1711 3443 Mechanical contractor; Industrial vessels, tanks, and containers

(G-15585)
SIEB & MEYER AMERICA INC
Also Called: Sieb & Meyer America USA
4884 Duff Dr Ste D (45246-1195)
PHONE.................................513 563-0860
John Endras, *Genl Mgr*
EMP: 10 **EST:** 1996
SALES (est): 2.19MM
SALES (corp-wide): 9.65MM **Privately Held**
Web: www.sieb-meyerusa.com
SIC: 3625 5063 Relays and industrial controls; Electrical apparatus and equipment
PA: First Tool Corp.
612 Linden Ave
Dayton OH 45403
937 254-6197

(G-15586)
SL ENDMILLS INC
133 Circle Freeway Dr (45246-1203)
PHONE.................................513 851-6363
Steven Long, *Pr*
Nancy Long, *Sec*
EMP: 15 **EST:** 1982
SQ FT: 5,000
SALES (est): 2.95MM **Privately Held**
Web: www.customcarbide.com
SIC: 3545 Machine tool accessories

(G-15587)
SLUSH PUPPIE
44 Carnegie Way (45246-1224)
PHONE.................................513 771-0940
Will Radcliff, *Ch Bd*
Dan Keating, *
Robert Schwartz, *
▲ **EMP:** 11 **EST:** 1970
SQ FT: 40,000
SALES (est): 282.44K **Privately Held**
Web: www.slushpuppie.com
SIC: 2087 5078 Syrups, drink; Soda fountain equipment, refrigerated

(G-15588)
SONOCO PRODUCTS COMPANY
Sonoco Consumer Products
4633 Dues Dr (45246-1008)
PHONE.................................513 870-3985
Lowern Laster, *Mgr*
EMP: 29
SALES (corp-wide): 6.78B **Publicly Held**
Web: www.sonoco.com
SIC: 2655 2656 Cans, composite: foil-fiber and other: from purchased fiber; Sanitary food containers
PA: Sonoco Products Company
1 N 2nd St
Hartsville SC 29550
843 383-7000

(G-15589)
SSI MANUFACTURING INC
9615 Inter Ocean Dr (45246-1029)
PHONE.................................513 761-7757
John R Monday, *Pr*
Carl Thiem, *VP*
EMP: 16 **EST:** 1990
SQ FT: 13,500
SALES (est): 522.07K **Privately Held**
Web: www.ssioem.com
SIC: 1751 2522 Cabinet building and installation; Filing boxes, cabinets, and cases: except wood

(G-15590)
STAR DISTRIBUTION AND MFG LLC
Also Called: Star Manufacturring
10179 Commerce Park Dr (45246-1335)
PHONE.................................513 860-3573
Mario Listo, *Pr*
Bob Hinkle, *
EMP: 48 **EST:** 2009
SALES (est): 8.33MM **Privately Held**
Web: www.starmanufacture.com
SIC: 3613 8711 8742 Control panels, electric ; Engineering services; Management engineering

(G-15591)
STOLLE MILK BIOLOGICS INC
4735 Devitt Dr (45246-1105)
PHONE.................................513 489-7997
Con F Sterling Junior, *CEO*
Doctor Robert Stohrer, *Research Vice President*
▲ **EMP:** 17 **EST:** 1986
SQ FT: 1,000
SALES (est): 1MM **Privately Held**
Web: www.smbiologics.com
SIC: 2023 Powdered milk

(G-15592)
STOROPACK INC (DH)
Also Called: Foam Pac Materials Company
4758 Devitt Dr (45246-1106)
PHONE.................................513 874-0314
Hans Reichenecker, *Ch Bd*
Daniel Wachter, *
Gregg Battaglia, *
Joe Lagrasta, *

West Chester - Hamilton County (G-15593)

Lester Whisnant, *
▲ **EMP:** 50 **EST:** 1978
SQ FT: 35,000
SALES (est): 152.02MM
SALES (corp-wide): 635.28MM **Privately Held**
Web: www.storopack.us
SIC: 5199 3086 2671 Packaging materials; Packaging and shipping materials, foamed plastics; Paper; coated and laminated packaging
HQ: Storopack Hans Reichenecker Gmbh
Untere Rietstr. 30
Metzingen BW 72555
71231640

(G-15593)
SUPERIOR IMAGE EMBROIDERY LLC
10152 International Blvd (45246-4846)
PHONE..................513 991-7543
EMP: 8
SALES (est): 348.11K **Privately Held**
SIC: 2395 Embroidery and art needlework

(G-15594)
TEKTRONIX INC
Also Called: Tektronix
9639 Inter Ocean Dr (45246-1029)
PHONE..................248 305-5200
Mike Kitchen, *Mgr*
EMP: 16
SALES (corp-wide): 6.07B **Publicly Held**
Web: www.tek.com
SIC: 3825 7699 Instruments to measure electricity; Laboratory instrument repair
HQ: Tektronix, Inc.
14150 Sw Karl Braun Dr
Beaverton OR 97077
800 833-9200

(G-15595)
THE RANSOHOFF COMPANY
4933 Provident Dr (45246-1020)
PHONE..................513 870-0100
EMP: 120
Web: www.ctgclean.com
SIC: 3569 3541 Blast cleaning equipment, dustless; Deburring machines

(G-15596)
THE SHEPHERD COLOR COMPANY (PA)
4539 Dues Dr (45246-1098)
P.O. Box 465627 (45246-5627)
PHONE..................513 874-0714
◆ **EMP:** 175 **EST:** 1920
SALES (est): 149.59MM
SALES (corp-wide): 149.59MM **Privately Held**
Web: www.shepherdcolor.com
SIC: 2816 Inorganic pigments

(G-15597)
TITANS PACKAGING LLC
33 Circle Freeway Dr (45246-1201)
PHONE..................513 449-0014
Kody Shumate, *Managing Member*
EMP: 11 **EST:** 2020
SALES (est): 592.97K **Privately Held**
SIC: 3565 Packaging machinery

(G-15598)
TOTES ISOTONER CORPORATION (HQ)
Also Called: Isotoner
9655 International Blvd (45246-4861)
PHONE..................513 682-8200
Daniel Rajczak, *Pr*
Chris Lutz, *

▲ **EMP:** 80 **EST:** 1924
SQ FT: 450,000
SALES (est): 98.57MM
SALES (corp-wide): 98.57MM **Privately Held**
Web: www.totes.com
SIC: 2385 5699 Waterproof outerwear; Umbrellas
PA: Indra Holdings Corp.
9655 International Blvd
West Chester OH 45246
513 682-8200

(G-15599)
TOTES ISOTONER HOLDINGS CORP (PA)
9655 International Blvd (45246-4861)
PHONE..................513 682-8200
Daniel S Rajczak, *CEO*
Daniel S Rajczak, *Pr*
Joshua Beckenstein, *
Donna Deye, *
Doug Baker, *
▲ **EMP:** 200 **EST:** 1994
SALES (est): 34.81MM
SALES (corp-wide): 34.81MM **Privately Held**
Web: www.totes.com
SIC: 2381 3151 2211 3021 Gloves, woven or knit: made from purchased materials; Leather gloves and mittens; Umbrella cloth, cotton; Rubber and plastics footwear

(G-15600)
TSK AMERICA CO LTD
9668 Inter Ocean Dr (45246-1030)
PHONE..................513 942-4002
▲ **EMP:** 10 **EST:** 1995
SALES (est): 773.91K **Privately Held**
Web: www.tsklmb.com
SIC: 3568 5051 3562 Bearings, bushings, and blocks; Metals service centers and offices; Ball bearings and parts

(G-15601)
UNITED GROUP SERVICES INC (PA)
9740 Near Dr (45246-1013)
PHONE..................800 633-9690
Mark Mosley, *Stockholder*
Daniel Freese, *
Kevin Sell, *
Don Mattingly, *
EMP: 200 **EST:** 1982
SQ FT: 45,500
SALES (est): 39.18MM
SALES (corp-wide): 39.18MM **Privately Held**
Web: www.united-gs.com
SIC: 3498 1711 Fabricated pipe and fittings; Process piping contractor

(G-15602)
UNIVAR SOLUTIONS USA LLC
4600 Dues Dr (45246-1009)
PHONE..................513 714-5264
Gary Southern, *Brnch Mgr*
EMP: 13
SQ FT: 129,100
SALES (corp-wide): 11.48B **Privately Held**
Web: www.univarsolutions.com
SIC: 5169 2819 2869 2899 Industrial chemicals; Industrial inorganic chemicals, nec; Industrial organic chemicals, nec; Chemical preparations, nec
HQ: Univar Solutions Usa Llc
3075 Hghland Pkwy Ste 200
Downers Grove IL 60515
331 777-6000

(G-15603)
VALCO CINCINNATI INC (PA)
Also Called: Valco Melton
411 Circle Freeway Dr (45246-1284)
P.O. Box 465619 (45246-5619)
PHONE..................513 874-6550
Richard Santefort, *Pr*
Gregory T Amend, *
▲ **EMP:** 180 **EST:** 1952
SQ FT: 43,000
SALES (est): 52.05MM
SALES (corp-wide): 52.05MM **Privately Held**
Web: www.valco-cp.com
SIC: 3586 2891 3561 Measuring and dispensing pumps; Adhesives and sealants ; Industrial pumps and parts

(G-15604)
VALCO MELTON INC
497 Circle Freeway Dr Ste 490 (45246-1257)
PHONE..................513 874-6550
Austin Koehler, *Prin*
▲ **EMP:** 26 **EST:** 2012
SALES (est): 436.9K
SALES (corp-wide): 52.05MM **Privately Held**
Web: www.valcomelton.com
SIC: 3663 Radio and t.v. communications equipment
PA: Valco Cincinnati, Inc.
411 Circle Freeway Dr
West Chester OH 45246
513 874-6550

West Farmington
Trumbull County

(G-15605)
MB WOODWORKING LLC
5175 Stroups Hickox Rd (44491-8710)
PHONE..................330 808-5122
Urie Byler, *Prin*
EMP: 8 **EST:** 2018
SALES (est): 483.3K **Privately Held**
SIC: 2431 Millwork

(G-15606)
MILLERTECH ENERGY SOLUTIONS
Also Called: Lester Miller, Owner
17795 Farmington Rd (44491-9625)
PHONE..................855 629-5484
Lester Miller, *Pr*
EMP: 15 **EST:** 2016
SALES (est): 1.01MM **Privately Held**
SIC: 3691 Batteries, rechargeable

(G-15607)
REYNOLDS INDUSTRIES INC
380 W Main St (44491-9712)
P.O. Box 6 (44491-0006)
PHONE..................330 889-9466
Gregory A Reynolds, *Pr*
EMP: 9 **EST:** 1991
SQ FT: 3,500
SALES (est): 396.57K **Privately Held**
SIC: 3069 4783 Rubber hardware; Packing goods for shipping

West Jefferson
Madison County

(G-15608)
BUCKEYE READY-MIX LLC
6600 State Route 29 (43162-8700)
PHONE..................614 879-6316
Don Harsh, *Brnch Mgr*

EMP: 7
SALES (corp-wide): 48.26MM **Privately Held**
Web: www.buckeyereadymix.com
SIC: 3273 Ready-mixed concrete
PA: Buckeye Ready-Mix, Llc
7657 Taylor Rd Sw
Reynoldsburg OH 43068
614 575-2132

(G-15609)
CONDUIT PIPE PRODUCTS COMPANY
1501 W Main St (43162-9627)
PHONE..................614 879-9114
John Rodgers, *Pr*
Tim Mcghee, *Prin*
EMP: 60 **EST:** 2002
SALES (est): 15.86MM
SALES (corp-wide): 46.15MM **Privately Held**
Web: www.conduitpipe.com
SIC: 3317 Steel pipe and tubes
PA: The Phoenix Forge Group Llc
1020 Macarthur Rd
Reading PA 19605
800 234-8665

(G-15610)
JEFFERSON INDUSTRIES CORP (HQ)
Also Called: J I C
6670 State Route 29 (43162-9677)
PHONE..................614 879-5300
Shiro Shimokagi, *Pr*
Kazuhiko Hara, *VP*
Steve Yoder, *Sr VP*
Hassan Saadat, *VP*
Curtis A Loveland, *Prin*
▲ **EMP:** 194 **EST:** 1988
SQ FT: 370,000
SALES (est): 95.87MM **Privately Held**
Web: www.jic-ohio.com
SIC: 3711 Chassis, motor vehicle
PA: G-Tekt Corporation
1-11-20, Sakuragicho, Omiya-Ku
Saitama STM 330-0

(G-15611)
KELLANOVA
Also Called: Kellog
125 Enterprise Pkwy (43162-9414)
PHONE..................614 879-9659
Richard Emerson, *Prin*
EMP: 7
SALES (corp-wide): 15.31B **Publicly Held**
Web: www.kellanova.com
SIC: 2043 Cereal breakfast foods
PA: Kellanova
412 N Wells St
Chicago IL 60654
269 961-2000

(G-15612)
MEDLINE INDUSTRIES LP
1040 Enterprise Pkwy (43162-9424)
PHONE..................614 879-9728
EMP: 25
SALES (corp-wide): 7.75B **Privately Held**
Web: www.medline.com
SIC: 3842 Surgical appliances and supplies
PA: Medline Industries, Lp
3 Lakes Dr
Northfield IL 60093
800 633-5463

(G-15613)
MENASHA PACKAGING COMPANY LLC
Also Called: Menasha
131 Enterprise Pkwy (43162-9414)
PHONE..................614 202-4084

Ken Pauly, *Brnch Mgr*
EMP: 28
SALES (corp-wide): 1.94B **Privately Held**
Web: www.menasha.com
SIC: 2653 Boxes, corrugated: made from purchased materials
HQ: Menasha Packaging Company, Llc
1645 Bergstrom Rd
Neenah WI 54956
920 751-1000

(G-15614)
PHOENIX FORGE GROUP LLC
Capitol Manufacturing Division
1501 W Main St (43162-9627)
PHONE..............................800 848-6125
David R Halman, *Brnch Mgr*
EMP: 216
SALES (corp-wide): 46.15MM **Privately Held**
Web: www.phoenixforge.com
SIC: 3498 Pipe fittings, fabricated from purchased pipe
PA: The Phoenix Forge Group Llc
1020 Macarthur Rd
Reading PA 19605
800 234-8665

(G-15615)
TOAGOSEI AMERICA INC
Also Called: Krazy Glue
1450 W Main St (43162-9730)
PHONE..............................614 718-3855
Tatsuo Mishio, *Pr*
Toshio Nakao, *
▲ **EMP:** 100 **EST:** 1989
SQ FT: 64,000
SALES (est): 37.06MM **Privately Held**
Web: www.aronalpha.net
SIC: 5169 2891 Chemicals and allied products, nec; Adhesives
PA: Toagosei Co., Ltd.
1-14-1, Nishishimbashi
Minato-Ku TKY 105-0

West Lafayette
Coshocton County

(G-15616)
CABOT LUMBER INC
304 E Union Ave (43845-1250)
P.O. Box 101 (43845-0101)
PHONE..............................740 545-7109
Donald Cabot, *Pr*
Dennis E Cabot, *Treas*
Kenneth Cabot, *Sec*
EMP: 9 **EST:** 1970
SQ FT: 14,000
SALES (est): 947.67K **Privately Held**
SIC: 5031 2448 Lumber: rough, dressed, and finished; Pallets, wood

(G-15617)
GLENN RAVENS WINERY
56183 County Road 143 (43845-3502)
PHONE..............................740 545-1000
Bob Guilliams, *Prin*
EMP: 10 **EST:** 2003
SALES (est): 825.07K **Privately Held**
Web: www.ravensglenn.com
SIC: 2084 5812 Wines; Italian restaurant

(G-15618)
JONES METAL PRODUCTS CO LLC (PA)
200 N Center St (43845-1270)
P.O. Box 179 (43845-0179)
PHONE..............................740 545-6381
Daniel P Erb Iii, *Pr*

Marion M Sutton, *
Michael G Baker, *
Carole M Loos, *
EMP: 48 **EST:** 1923
SQ FT: 140,000
SALES (est): 9.84MM
SALES (corp-wide): 9.84MM **Privately Held**
Web: www.jmpforming.com
SIC: 3842 3444 3469 Surgical appliances and supplies; Forming machine work, sheet metal; Metal stampings, nec

(G-15619)
JONES METAL PRODUCTS COMPANY
Jones-Zylon Company
305 N Center St (43845-1001)
PHONE..............................740 545-6341
EMP: 40
SALES (corp-wide): 11MM **Privately Held**
SIC: 5047 3842 Hospital equipment and supplies, nec; Surgical appliances and supplies
PA: Jones Metal Products Company Llc
200 N Center St
West Lafayette OH 43845
740 545-6381

(G-15620)
JONESZYLON COMPANY LLC
300 N Center St (43845-1002)
P.O. Box 149 (43845-0149)
PHONE..............................740 545-6341
Robert Zachrich, *Pr*
Tracey Zachrich, *Prin*
EMP: 9 **EST:** 2014
SQ FT: 20,000
SALES (est): 1.65MM **Privately Held**
Web: www.joneszylon.com
SIC: 3089 5046 Plastics kitchenware, tableware, and houseware; Food warming equipment

(G-15621)
YANKEE WIRE CLOTH PRODUCTS INC
221 W Main St (43845)
P.O. Box 58 (43845)
PHONE..............................740 545-9129
William D Timmons, *Pr*
Mary Timmons, *
EMP: 16 **EST:** 1963
SQ FT: 35,000
SALES (est): 4.13MM **Privately Held**
Web: www.yankeewire.com
SIC: 3496 Screening, woven wire: made from purchased wire

West Liberty
Logan County

(G-15622)
HOLDREN BROTHERS INC
301 Runkle St (43357-9476)
P.O. Box 459 (43357-0459)
PHONE..............................937 465-7050
Shirley Holdren, *Pr*
EMP: 10 **EST:** 1939
SQ FT: 4,800
SALES (est): 966.66K **Privately Held**
Web: www.holdrenbrothers.com
SIC: 3599 3589 7692 3549 Machine shop, jobbing and repair; Commercial cleaning equipment; Welding repair; Metalworking machinery, nec

(G-15623)
MARIES CANDIES LLC
Also Called: Marie's Candies
311 Zanesfield Rd (43357-9563)
P.O. Box 766 (43357-0766)
PHONE..............................937 465-3061
EMP: 15 **EST:** 1956
SQ FT: 4,100
SALES (est): 477.57K **Privately Held**
Web: www.mariescandies.com
SIC: 2064 5441 Candy bars, including chocolate covered bars; Candy

West Manchester
Preble County

(G-15624)
ROWE PREMIX INC
10107 Us Rr 127 N (45382)
P.O. Box 205 (45382-0205)
PHONE..............................937 678-9015
Gene Rowe, *Pr*
Sharon Rowe, *VP*
EMP: 22 **EST:** 1979
SQ FT: 5,000
SALES (est): 467.67K **Privately Held**
SIC: 2048 Feed premixes

West Mansfield
Logan County

(G-15625)
DAYLAY EGG FARM INC
11177 Township Road 133 (43358-9709)
PHONE..............................937 355-6531
Kurt Lausecker, *Pr*
▲ **EMP:** 135 **EST:** 1978
SQ FT: 3,200
SALES (est): 4.93MM **Privately Held**
SIC: 0252 2015 Chicken eggs; Poultry slaughtering and processing

(G-15626)
M & M CONCEPTS INC
Also Called: Cmg Company Plant 2
2633 State Route 292 (43358-9523)
PHONE..............................937 355-1115
Thomas P Mcgrady, *Pr*
Alexa Mcgrady, *Sec*
Kris Carpenter, *Treas*
Larry Vermillion, *VP*
EMP: 8 **EST:** 2001
SQ FT: 14,000
SALES (est): 858.86K **Privately Held**
Web: www.cmgcompany.net
SIC: 7692 Welding repair

(G-15627)
NATURE PURE LLC
26560 Storms Rd (43358-9662)
P.O. Box 127 (43067-0127)
PHONE..............................937 358-2364
Kurt Lausecker, *CEO*
EMP: 23
Web: www.naturepure.us
SIC: 0252 2015 Chicken eggs; Egg processing
PA: Nature Pure Llc
26586 State Route 739
Raymond OH 43067

(G-15628)
SHELLY MATERIALS INC
20620 Spangler Rd (43358-9653)
PHONE..............................937 358-2224
EMP: 7 **EST:** 2019
SALES (est): 136.95K **Privately Held**

SIC: 3281 Cut stone and stone products

West Milton
Miami County

(G-15629)
BOYDS MCH & MET FINSHG INC
7650 S Kessler Frederick Rd (45383-8790)
PHONE..............................937 698-5623
Larry E Boyd, *Pr*
Stephen Boyd, *VP*
EMP: 16 **EST:** 1974
SQ FT: 1,800
SALES (est): 438.94K **Privately Held**
Web: www.boydsmachine.com
SIC: 3599 Machine shop, jobbing and repair

(G-15630)
OLD MASON WINERY INC
4199 S Iddings Rd (45383-8741)
PHONE..............................937 698-1122
Jeff Clark, *Pr*
Donna Clarke, *VP*
EMP: 9 **EST:** 2013
SALES (est): 457.58K **Privately Held**
Web: www.oldmason.com
SIC: 2084 Wines

(G-15631)
ROBERTSON CABINETS INC
1090 S Main St (45383-1365)
PHONE..............................937 698-3755
William Robertson Senior, *Ch Bd*
Jeff Yantis, *Pr*
Judith Robertson, *VP*
EMP: 13 **EST:** 1979
SQ FT: 22,000
SALES (est): 513.48K **Privately Held**
Web: www.robertsoncabinets.com
SIC: 2541 2431 Cabinets, except refrigerated: show, display, etc.: wood; Millwork

West Salem
Wayne County

(G-15632)
CENSTAR COATINGS INC
11829 Jeffrey Rd (44287-9219)
PHONE..............................330 723-8000
Jim Feterle, *Pr*
EMP: 6 **EST:** 2012
SQ FT: 6,000
SALES (est): 678.67K **Privately Held**
SIC: 3069 Sheeting, rubber or rubberized fabric

(G-15633)
CHARLES MACHINE WORKS INC
Also Called: American Augers
135 State Route 42 (44287-9130)
PHONE..............................800 324-4930
EMP: 50
SALES (corp-wide): 4.55B **Publicly Held**
Web: www.ditchwitch.com
SIC: 3532 Auger mining equipment
HQ: The Charles Machine Works Inc
1959 W Fir St
Perry OK 73077
580 572-2693

(G-15634)
JOHNSON BROS RUBBER CO (PA)
42 W Buckeye St (44287-9747)
P.O. Box 812 (44287-0812)
PHONE..............................419 853-4122
Lawrence G Cooke, *Pr*
Eric Vail, *

West Salem - Wayne County (G-15635)

◆ EMP: 100 EST: 1947
SQ FT: 70,000
SALES (est): 21.76MM
SALES (corp-wide): 21.76MM Privately Held
Web: www.johnsonbrosrubbercompany.com
SIC: 5199 3061 Foams and rubber; Mechanical rubber goods

(G-15635)
PAROBEK TRUCKING CO
192 State Route 42 (44287-9130)
PHONE................................419 869-7500
Keigm Parobek, Owner
EMP: 6 EST: 1984
SALES (est): 412.87K Privately Held
SIC: 3537 4213 4212 Industrial trucks and tractors; Trucking, except local; Local trucking, without storage

West Unity
Williams County

(G-15636)
AGB LLC
15188 Us Highway 127 (43570-9502)
PHONE................................419 924-5216
EMP: 7 EST: 2000
SALES (est): 941.28K Privately Held
SIC: 3469 Stamping metal for the trade

(G-15637)
BENVIC TRINITY LLC
Also Called: Chemres Trinity
600 Oak St (43570)
PHONE................................609 520-0000
EMP: 25 EST: 2021
SALES (est): 2.53MM Privately Held
SIC: 2821 Plastics materials and resins

(G-15638)
CONVERSION TECH INTL INC
700 Oak St (43570-9457)
PHONE................................419 924-5566
Chester Cromwell, Pr
Jason Cromwell, *
▲ EMP: 33 EST: 1999
SQ FT: 130,000
SALES (est): 5.3MM Privately Held
Web: www.conversiontechnologies.com
SIC: 2891 7389 Adhesives; Laminating service

(G-15639)
H K K MACHINING CO
1201 Oak St (43570-9435)
PHONE................................419 924-5116
Duane E King, Pr
Sharon King, VP
EMP: 20 EST: 1966
SQ FT: 23,500
SALES (est): 2.53MM Privately Held
Web: www.hkkmach.com
SIC: 3599 Machine shop, jobbing and repair

(G-15640)
HARDLINE INTERNATIONAL INC
Also Called: Rimm Kleen Systems
1107 Oak St (43570-9429)
PHONE................................419 924-9556
Robert Warmingham, Pr
EMP: 10 EST: 1980
SQ FT: 12,000
SALES (est): 920.7K Privately Held
Web: www.rimmkleensystems.com
SIC: 3479 Aluminum coating of metal products

(G-15641)
KAMCO INDUSTRIES INC (HQ)
1001 E Jackson St (43570-9414)
PHONE................................419 924-5511
Joe Tubbs, VP
Bryan Barshel, *
◆ EMP: 370 EST: 1987
SQ FT: 160,000
SALES (est): 117.33MM Privately Held
Web: www.kumi-na.com
SIC: 3089 Injection molded finished plastics products, nec
PA: Kumi Kasei Co., Ltd.
6-13-10, Sotokanda
Chiyoda-Ku TKY 101-0

(G-15642)
PR-WELD & MANUFACTURING LTD
18258 County Road H50 (43570-9750)
PHONE................................419 633-9204
Rny Rigg, Pt
Paul Rigg, Pt
EMP: 7 EST: 2003
SALES (est): 506.95K Privately Held
Web: pr-weld.webnode.page
SIC: 7692 Welding repair

(G-15643)
RAVAGO AMERICAS LLC
Trinity Specialty Compounding
600 Oak St (43570-9545)
PHONE................................419 924-9090
Timothy L Walkowski, Genl Mgr
EMP: 58
Web: www.amcopolymers.com
SIC: 2821 Plastics materials and resins
HQ: Ravago Americas Llc
1900 Smmit Twr Blvd Ste 9
Orlando FL 32810
800 262-6685

(G-15644)
TRINITY SPECIALTY COMPOUNDING INC
600 Oak St (43570-9545)
P.O. Box 247 (43570-0247)
PHONE................................419 924-9090
EMP: 19
SIC: 3089 Plastics processing

(G-15645)
VISION COLOR LLC
214 S Defiance St (43570-9620)
P.O. Box 264 (43570-0264)
PHONE................................419 924-9450
EMP: 8 EST: 2002
SALES (est): 6.17MM Privately Held
Web: www.visioncolorllc.com
SIC: 3089 Injection molding of plastics
HQ: Tosaf, Inc.
330 Southridge Pkwy
Bessemer City NC 28016
980 533-3000

Westerville
Delaware County

(G-15646)
ABB INC
Also Called: A B B Electric Systems
579 Executive Campus Dr Frnt (43082-9801)
PHONE................................614 818-6300
John Strachan, Brnch Mgr
EMP: 10
Web: www.abb.com
SIC: 3612 3613 Transformers, except electric; Switchgear and switchboard apparatus
HQ: Abb Inc.
305 Gregson Dr
Cary NC 27511

(G-15647)
AMERICAN CERAMIC SOCIETY (PA)
550 Polaris Pkwy Ste 510 (43082-7132)
PHONE................................614 890-4700
Mark Mecklenborg, Ex Dir
Michael Johnson, *
EMP: 35 EST: 1900
SQ FT: 10,126
SALES (est): 9.32MM
SALES (corp-wide): 9.32MM Privately Held
Web: www.ceramics.org
SIC: 2721 8621 Periodicals, publishing and printing; Scientific membership association

(G-15648)
BRIGHTSTAR PROPANE & FUELS
Also Called: Outman Oil
6190 Frost Rd (43082-9027)
PHONE................................614 891-8395
Richard Guttman, Pr
EMP: 14 EST: 2014
SALES (est): 461.77K Privately Held
Web: www.brightstarpropane.com
SIC: 5984 1389 2869 Propane gas, bottled; Construction, repair, and dismantling services; Fuels

(G-15649)
BUCKEYE BUSINESS FORMS INC
Also Called: Proforma Buckeye
7307 Red Bank Rd (43082-8241)
PHONE................................614 882-1890
Ann Kaylor Patton, Pr
James Patton, Sec
EMP: 6 EST: 1966
SQ FT: 13,500
SALES (est): 657.58K Privately Held
Web: www.bbf.cc
SIC: 7311 2752 7331 Advertising agencies; Offset printing; Mailing service

(G-15650)
CAYOSOFT INC (PA)
470 Olde Worthington Rd Ste 200 (43082-8985)
P.O. Box 711 (43216-0711)
PHONE................................614 423-6718
Robert J Bobel, CEO
EMP: 20 EST: 2013
SALES (est): 2.06MM
SALES (corp-wide): 2.06MM Privately Held
Web: www.cayosoft.com
SIC: 7372 Business oriented computer software

(G-15651)
CENTURY GRAPHICS INC
9101 Hawthorne Pt (43082-9231)
PHONE................................614 895-7698
Richard Bonham, Pr
EMP: 12 EST: 1968
SQ FT: 26,000
SALES (est): 415.13K Privately Held
Web: www.centurygraphics.com
SIC: 2796 2789 2759 2752 Platemaking services; Bookbinding and related work; Commercial printing, nec; Offset printing

(G-15652)
CRITICALAIRE LLC
350 Worthington Rd Ste G (43082-6099)
PHONE................................513 475-3800
EMP: 23
Web: www.criticalaire.com
SIC: 3564 Exhaust fans: industrial or commercial
PA: Criticalaire, Llc
4280 Glendale Milford Rd
Blue Ash OH 45242

(G-15653)
DERN TROPHIES CORP
Also Called: Dern Trophy Mfg
6225 Frost Rd (43082-9027)
PHONE................................614 895-3260
Ronald M Spohn, Pr
B Thomas Dern, VP
▲ EMP: 17 EST: 1963
SQ FT: 20,000
SALES (est): 577.88K Privately Held
Web: www.marcoawardsgroup.com
SIC: 3499 5094 3993 Trophies, metal, except silver; Trophies; Signs and advertising specialties

(G-15654)
E - I CORP
214 Hoff Rd Unit M (43082-7157)
PHONE................................614 899-2282
Glenn Meek, Prin
▲ EMP: 10 EST: 2008
SALES (est): 388.29K Privately Held
Web: www.eandicorp.com
SIC: 3589 Sewage treatment equipment

(G-15655)
EWEBSCHEDULE
180 Commerce Park Dr (43082-6067)
PHONE................................614 882-0726
EMP: 7 EST: 2012
SALES (est): 93.13K Privately Held
Web: www.abcsrcm.com
SIC: 7372 Prepackaged software

(G-15656)
FARAH JEWELERS INC
5965 Medallion Dr E (43082-9059)
PHONE................................614 438-6140
EMP: 13 EST: 1996
SALES (est): 827.76K Privately Held
Web: www.farahjewelers.net
SIC: 3911 5944 Jewelry mountings and trimmings; Jewelry stores

(G-15657)
GARAGE SCENES LTD
Also Called: Ready For Flight
7385 State Route 3 Unit 112 (43082-8654)
PHONE................................614 407-6094
Greg Rogers, Managing Member
EMP: 19 EST: 2005
SALES (est): 1.07MM Privately Held
Web: www.garagescenes.com
SIC: 3663 Digital encoders

(G-15658)
IDENTITY GROUP LLC
6111c Maxtown Rd (43082-9051)
PHONE................................614 337-6167
EMP: 7 EST: 2002
SALES (est): 975.1K Privately Held
Web: www.identitygroupllc.com
SIC: 5112 5136 5199 2741 Pens and/or pencils; Uniforms, men's and boys'; Advertising specialties; Catalogs: publishing and printing

(G-15659)
IMT DEFENSE CORP
Also Called: IMT Defense
5386 Club Dr (43082-8312)
PHONE................................614 891-8812
Remo Assini, Pr
James Hacking, Ch Bd
EMP: 7 EST: 2004
SALES (est): 490.89K Privately Held

Web: www.imtdefence.com
SIC: 3812 Defense systems and equipment

(G-15660)
INTEK INC
751 Intek Way (43082-9057)
PHONE..................................614 895-0301
Timothy Harpster, *CEO*
▼ EMP: 16 EST: 1976
SQ FT: 12,800
SALES (est): 2.7MM **Privately Held**
Web: www.intekflow.com
SIC: 3823 8732 Industrial flow and liquid measuring instruments; Commercial nonphysical research

(G-15661)
JST LLC
6240 Frost Rd Ste C (43082-9027)
PHONE..................................614 423-7815
Susan Testaguzza, *Managing Member*
James Testaguzza, *Managing Member*
EMP: 7 EST: 2011
SALES (est): 447.88K **Privately Held**
SIC: 7372 Educational computer software

(G-15662)
LAKE SHORE CRYOTRONICS INC (PA)
575 Mccorkle Blvd (43082-8888)
PHONE..................................614 891-2243
Michael S Swartz, *Pr*
John M Swartz, *
Philip R Swinehart, *
Karen Lint, *
Ed Maloof, *
EMP: 93 EST: 1968
SQ FT: 60,000
SALES (est): 30.84MM
SALES (corp-wide): 30.84MM **Privately Held**
Web: www.lakeshore.com
SIC: 3679 3823 3825 3812 Cryogenic cooling devices for infrared detectors, masers; Process control instruments; Measuring instruments and meters, electric; Search and navigation equipment

(G-15663)
LANCASTER COLONY CORPORATION (PA)
380 Polaris Pkwy Ste 400 (43082)
PHONE..................................614 224-7141
David A Ciesinski, *Pr*
Alan F Harris, *
Thomas K Pigott, *VP*
◆ EMP: 25 EST: 1961
SALES (est): 1.82B
SALES (corp-wide): 1.82B **Publicly Held**
Web: www.lancastercolony.com
SIC: 2035 2038 Dressings, salad: raw and cooked (except dry mixes); Frozen specialties, nec

(G-15664)
LANCASTER GLASS CORPORATION
380 Polaris Pkwy Ste 400 (43082-8069)
PHONE..................................614 224-7141
EMP: 47 EST: 2019
SALES (est): 2.13MM
SALES (corp-wide): 1.82B **Publicly Held**
Web: www.lancasterglasscorp.com
SIC: 2035 Dressings, salad: raw and cooked (except dry mixes)
PA: Lancaster Colony Corporation
380 Polaris Pkwy Ste 400
Westerville OH 43082
614 224-7141

(G-15665)
LIEBERT FIELD SERVICES INC
Also Called: Emerson Network Power System
610 Executive Campus Dr (43082-8870)
P.O. Box 29186 (43229-0186)
PHONE..................................614 841-5763
Lisa Hunt, *Mgr*
EMP: 121 EST: 2001
SALES (est): 18.49MM
SALES (corp-wide): 6.86B **Publicly Held**
Web: www.vertiv.com
SIC: 3823 Process control instruments
HQ: Vertiv Corporation
505 N Cleveland Ave
Westerville OH 43082
614 888-0246

(G-15666)
MAC TOOLS INC
505 N Cleveland Ave Ste 200 (43082-7130)
P.O. Box 50400 (46250-0400)
PHONE..................................614 755-7039
EMP: 20
SIC: 3699 Door opening and closing devices, electrical

(G-15667)
MCNISH CORPORATION
Also Called: E & I
214 Hoff Rd Unit M (43082-7157)
PHONE..................................614 899-2282
Glenn E Meek, *Brnch Mgr*
EMP: 7
SALES (corp-wide): 21.29MM **Privately Held**
Web: www.walker-process.com
SIC: 3589 Water treatment equipment, industrial
PA: Mcnish Corporation
840 N Russell Ave
Aurora IL 60506
630 892-7921

(G-15668)
NEW WORLD SOLUTIONS INC
6444 S Old 3c Hwy (43082-6046)
PHONE..................................614 271-6233
Doug Bardwell, *Prin*
EMP: 6 EST: 2015
SALES (est): 123.49K **Privately Held**
Web: www.newworldsolutionsinc.com
SIC: 3599 Machine shop, jobbing and repair

(G-15669)
NEW YORK FROZEN FOODS INC
380 Polaris Pkwy Ste 400 (43082-8069)
P.O. Box 297737 (43229-7737)
PHONE..................................614 846-2232
Thomas E Moloney, *Brnch Mgr*
EMP: 10
SALES (corp-wide): 1.82B **Publicly Held**
SIC: 3421 Table and food cutlery, including butchers'
HQ: New York Frozen Foods, Inc.
25900 Fargo Ave
Bedford OH 44146
216 292-5655

(G-15670)
NEW YORK FROZEN FOODS INC
Mamma Bella Foods
380 Polaris Pkwy Ste 400 (43082-8069)
PHONE..................................626 338-3000
Bob Willist, *Brnch Mgr*
EMP: 50
SALES (corp-wide): 1.82B **Publicly Held**
SIC: 2051 Buns, bread type: fresh or frozen
HQ: New York Frozen Foods, Inc.
25900 Fargo Ave
Bedford OH 44146
216 292-5655

(G-15671)
OCTOPUS EXPRESS INC
470 Olde Worthington Rd (43082-8985)
PHONE..................................614 412-1222
Matluba Ibragimova, *Prin*
EMP: 20 EST: 2020
SALES (est): 800K **Privately Held**
SIC: 3537 Trucks, tractors, loaders, carriers, and similar equipment

(G-15672)
ORTON EDWARD JR CRMIC FNDATION
6991 S Old 3c Hwy (43082-9026)
P.O. Box 2760 (43086-2760)
PHONE..................................614 895-2663
Jonathan Hinton, *Ch Bd*
Richard R Stedman Attorney, *Prin*
J Gary Childress, *Secretary General**
Doctor James Williams, *Trst*
Doctor Stephen Freiman, *Trst*
▼ EMP: 31 EST: 1896
SQ FT: 34,260
SALES (est): 7.13MM **Privately Held**
Web: www.ortonceramic.com
SIC: 3269 3826 3825 8748 Cones, pyrometric: earthenware; Analytical instruments; Instruments to measure electricity; Testing services

(G-15673)
PYROS PHARMACEUTICALS INC
470 Olde Worthington Rd (43082-8985)
PHONE..................................201 743-9468
Michael Smith, *CEO*
Edwin Urrutia, *
EMP: 35 EST: 2017
SALES (est): 1.39MM **Privately Held**
SIC: 2834 Pharmaceutical preparations

(G-15674)
QUADRIGA AMERICAS LLC (PA)
480 Olde Worthington Rd Ste 350 (43082-8954)
PHONE..................................614 890-6090
Roger Taylor, *CEO*
▼ EMP: 7 EST: 2009
SQ FT: 5,000
SALES (est): 1.66MM
SALES (corp-wide): 1.66MM **Privately Held**
SIC: 2741 Internet publishing and broadcasting

(G-15675)
REVOLUTION GROUP INC
670 Meridian Way (43082-7648)
PHONE..................................614 212-1111
EMP: 80 EST: 1995
SALES (est): 23.8MM **Privately Held**
Web: www.revolutiongroup.com
SIC: 7379 7372 4813 8741 Computer related consulting services; Prepackaged software; Internet connectivity services; Management services

(G-15676)
ROOF MAXX TECHNOLOGIES LLC
Also Called: Roof Maxx
7385 State Route 3 (43082-8654)
PHONE..................................855 766-3629
Michael Feazel, *CEO*
Michael Feazel, *Managing Member*
Todd Feazel, *
Amy Koch, *
EMP: 40 EST: 2017
SALES (est): 4.04MM **Privately Held**
Web: www.roofmaxx.com
SIC: 2952 Asphalt felts and coatings

(G-15677)
S&L FLEET SERVICES INC
670 Meridian Way Ste 252 (43082-2306)
PHONE..................................740 549-2722
Sheldon Lambert, *CEO*
EMP: 20 EST: 2017
SALES (est): 1.19MM **Privately Held**
SIC: 3812 Search and navigation equipment

(G-15678)
SISTER SCHBRTS HMMADE RLLS INC (DH)
Also Called: Sister Schubert's
380 Polaris Pkwy Ste 400 (43082-8069)
P.O. Box 112 (36049-0112)
PHONE..................................334 335-2232
Patricia W Schubert, *Pr*
George Barns, *
▲ EMP: 250 EST: 1993
SQ FT: 55,000
SALES (est): 50.76MM
SALES (corp-wide): 1.82B **Publicly Held**
Web: www.sisterschuberts.com
SIC: 2051 Breads, rolls, and buns
HQ: T.Marzetti Company
380 Polaris Pkwy Ste 400
Westerville OH 43082
614 846-2232

(G-15679)
SKLADANY ENTERPRISES INC
Also Called: Skladany Printing Center
695 Mccorkle Blvd (43082-8790)
PHONE..................................614 823-6882
Thomas Skladany, *Pr*
Debbie Skladany, *VP*
Michael Niezgoda, *VP Sls*
EMP: 8 EST: 1982
SALES (est): 1.05MM **Privately Held**
Web: www.skladany.com
SIC: 2752 Offset printing

(G-15680)
STATUS SOLUTIONS LLC
Also Called: Status Solutions
999 County Line Rd W # A (43082-7237)
PHONE..................................434 296-1789
EMP: 80 EST: 2001
SALES (est): 14.37MM **Privately Held**
Web: www.statussolutions.com
SIC: 3669 5063 Emergency alarms; Alarm systems, nec

(G-15681)
THERM-O-DISC INCORPORATED (HQ)
Also Called: Sensience
570 Polaris Pkwy Ste 500 (43082)
PHONE..................................419 525-8500
Kay Ellen Thurman, *CEO*
Loretta M Tanner, *
William M Van Cleve, *
▲ EMP: 900 EST: 1968
SALES (est): 600.91MM
SALES (corp-wide): 617.26MM **Privately Held**
Web: www.sensience.com
SIC: 3822 3823 Built-in thermostats, filled system and bimetal types; Process control instruments
PA: Sensience, Inc.
30 Rockefeller Plz 54th
New York NY 10112
419 525-8500

(G-15682)
THREAT EXTINGUISHER LLC
8100 Maxtown Rd (43082-9099)
PHONE..................................614 882-2959
Sam Fasone, *Prin*

Westerville - Delaware County (G-15683)

EMP: 6 **EST:** 2018
SALES (est): 232.78K **Privately Held**
Web: www.threatextinguisher.com
SIC: 3999 Fire extinguishers, portable

(G-15683)
TMARZETTI COMPANY (HQ)
Also Called: Inn Maid Products
380 Polaris Pkwy Ste 400 (43082-8069)
P.O. Box 297737 (43229-7737)
PHONE...............................614 846-2232
David Ciesinski, *Pr*
Luis Viso Csco, *Prin*
◆ **EMP:** 147 **EST:** 1927
SQ FT: 28,000
SALES (est): 927.01MM
SALES (corp-wide): 1.82B **Publicly Held**
Web: www.tmarzetticompany.com
SIC: 2035 2098 Dressings, salad: raw and cooked (except dry mixes); Noodles (e.g. egg, plain, and water), dry
PA: Lancaster Colony Corporation
380 Polaris Pkwy Ste 400
Westerville OH 43082
614 224-7141

(G-15684)
TRIMCO
7265 Park Bend Dr (43082-8659)
PHONE...............................614 679-3931
EMP: 7 **EST:** 2010
SALES (est): 100K **Privately Held**
Web: www.trimcohardware.com
SIC: 2431 Millwork

(G-15685)
TURN & EARN CORPORATION
445 Havendale Dr (43082-7412)
PHONE...............................516 761-0236
Michael Grella, *Admn*
EMP: 6 **EST:** 2018
SALES (est): 239.95K **Privately Held**
Web: www.turnandearn.net
SIC: 3599 Machine shop, jobbing and repair

(G-15686)
VERTIV CORPORATION (DH)
Also Called: Geist
505 N Cleveland Ave (43082-7130)
P.O. Box 29186 (43229-0186)
PHONE...............................614 888-0246
Giordano Albertazzi, *CEO*
David Fallon, *CFO*
Jason Forcier, *Ex VP*
◆ **EMP:** 1300 **EST:** 1965
SQ FT: 330,000
SALES (est): 1.3B
SALES (corp-wide): 6.86B **Publicly Held**
Web: www.vertiv.com
SIC: 3585 3613 7629 Air conditioning equipment, complete; Regulators, power; Electronic equipment repair
HQ: Vertiv Group Corporation
505 N Cleveland Ave
Westerville OH 43082
614 888-0246

(G-15687)
VERTIV GROUP CORPORATION (DH)
Also Called: Vertiv Co.
505 N Cleveland Ave (43082-7130)
PHONE...............................614 888-0246
Frank P Simpkins, *VP*
Matthew S Dean, *
Stephen H Liang, *GLOBAL TELECOM AND ASIA PACIFIC**
Michael Neeley, *
Eva M Kalawski, *
EMP: 1000 **EST:** 2016
SALES (est): 2.02B
SALES (corp-wide): 6.86B **Publicly Held**

Web: www.vertiv.com
SIC: 3679 3585 Power supplies, all types: static; Air conditioning units, complete: domestic or industrial
HQ: Vertiv Holdings, Llc
1050 Dearborn Dr
Columbus OH 43085
614 888-0246

(G-15688)
VERTIV HOLDINGS CO (PA)
505 N Cleveland Ave (43082)
PHONE...............................614 888-0246
Giordano Albertazzi, *CEO*
David M Cote, *Ex Ch Bd*
David J Fallon, *CFO*
Erin Dowd, *Chief Human Resources Officer*
Stephanie Gill, *Chief Legal Counsel*
EMP: 56 **EST:** 2016
SALES (est): 6.86B
SALES (corp-wide): 6.86B **Publicly Held**
Web: www.vertiv.com
SIC: 3679 Electronic loads and power supplies

(G-15689)
WESTERVILLE ENDOSCOPY CTR LLC
300 Polaris Pkwy Ste 1500 (43082-7990)
PHONE...............................614 568-1666
Tammy Blankenship, *Prin*
EMP: 7 **EST:** 2012
SALES (est): 560.51K **Privately Held**
Web: www.westervilleendo.com
SIC: 3845 8011 Gastroscopes, electromedical; Internal medicine, physician/surgeon

(G-15690)
WORTHINGTON CYLINDER CORP
333 Maxtown Rd (43082-8757)
PHONE...............................614 840-3800
EMP: 141
SQ FT: 12,880
SALES (corp-wide): 4.92B **Publicly Held**
Web: www.worthingtonenterprises.com
SIC: 3443 Cylinders, pressure: metal plate
HQ: Worthington Cylinder Corporation
200 W Old Wlson Bridge Rd
Worthington OH 43085
614 840-3210

Westerville
Franklin County

(G-15691)
ASSETWATCH INC
Also Called: Nikola Labs
60 Collegeview Rd (43081-1429)
PHONE...............................844 464-5652
Will Zell, *Pr*
EMP: 102 **EST:** 2015
SALES (est): 9.29MM **Privately Held**
Web: www.nikola.tech
SIC: 3823 Process control instruments

(G-15692)
AVCOM SMT INC
213 E Broadway Ave (43081-1656)
P.O. Box 1516 (43086-1516)
PHONE...............................614 882-8176
Paul Wiese, *Pr*
Barbara Wiese, *VP*
EMP: 12 **EST:** 1970
SQ FT: 10,000
SALES (est): 2.87MM **Privately Held**
Web: www.avcomsmt.com
SIC: 3672 Printed circuit boards

(G-15693)
AXIOM TOOL GROUP INC
270 Broad St (43081-1604)
PHONE...............................844 642-4902
Scott Leichtling, *CEO*
EMP: 7 **EST:** 2014
SALES (est): 2.22MM
SALES (corp-wide): 107.37MM **Privately Held**
Web: www.axiomprecision.com
SIC: 3553 Woodworking machinery
PA: Jpw Industries Inc.
427 New Sanford Rd
La Vergne TN 37086
615 793-8900

(G-15694)
BLF ENTERPRISES INC
Also Called: Great Harvest Bread
445 S State St (43081-2956)
PHONE...............................937 642-6425
Bruce Fowler, *Pr*
Linda Fowler, *Sec*
EMP: 10 **EST:** 1993
SQ FT: 2,000
SALES (est): 715.15K **Privately Held**
Web: www.greatharvestwesterville.com
SIC: 5461 2052 2051 Bread; Cookies and crackers; Bread, cake, and related products

(G-15695)
BUFFALO ABRASIVES INC
1093 Smoke Burr Dr (43081-4542)
PHONE...............................614 891-6450
Timothy J Wagner, *Prin*
EMP: 45
SALES (corp-wide): 11.94MM **Privately Held**
Web: www.buffaloabrasives.com
SIC: 3291 Abrasive products
HQ: Buffalo Abrasives, Inc.
960 Erie Ave
North Tonawanda NY 14120
716 693-3856

(G-15696)
COLUMBUS PRESCR REHABILITATION
Also Called: The Mobility Store
975 Eastwind Dr Ste 155 (43081-3344)
PHONE...............................614 294-1600
Mark A Witchey, *Sec*
Jack A Witchey, *Sec*
EMP: 6 **EST:** 1990
SQ FT: 50,000
SALES (est): 668.78K **Privately Held**
SIC: 3842 7352 Wheelchairs; Medical equipment rental

(G-15697)
DAIKIN APPLIED AMERICAS INC
192 Heatherdown Dr (43081-2868)
PHONE...............................614 351-9862
Dale Matheny, *Brnch Mgr*
EMP: 9
Web: www.daikinapplied.com
SIC: 3585 5075 Refrigeration and heating equipment; Warm air heating and air conditioning
HQ: Daikin Applied Americas Inc.
13600 Industrial Pk Blvd
Minneapolis MN 55441
763 553-5330

(G-15698)
DARIFILL INC
750 Green Crest Dr (43081-2837)
PHONE...............................614 890-3274
Steve Aspery, *Pr*
Eric Rousculp, *VP*
Jack Spencer, *VP*

▲ **EMP:** 18 **EST:** 2003
SALES (est): 5.94MM **Privately Held**
Web: www.darifill.com
SIC: 3565 Packaging machinery

(G-15699)
DAVID CHOJNACKI
Also Called: Mandrax Technologies
5471 Camlin Pl E (43081-8527)
PHONE...............................303 905-1918
David Chojnacki, *Owner*
EMP: 22 **EST:** 2014
SQ FT: 3,800
SALES (est): 515.48K **Privately Held**
SIC: 7379 7373 8711 3663 Computer related consulting services; Computer systems analysis and design; Consulting engineer; Space satellite communications equipment

(G-15700)
DEDRONE DEFENSE INC
735 Ceramic Pl Ste 110 (43081-7145)
PHONE...............................614 948-2002
Phillip Pitsky, *Pr*
Alex Morrow, *VP*
EMP: 11 **EST:** 2019
SALES (est): 575.18K **Privately Held**
SIC: 3812 Radar systems and equipment

(G-15701)
DEVRIES & ASSOCIATES INC
654 Brooksedge Blvd Ste A (43081-2962)
PHONE...............................614 890-3821
Mary Devries, *Pr*
EMP: 7 **EST:** 2008
SALES (est): 244.77K **Privately Held**
SIC: 3993 Signs and advertising specialties

(G-15702)
DJMC PARTNERS INC
Also Called: Fastsigns
654 Brooksedge Blvd Ste A (43081-2962)
PHONE...............................614 890-3821
Danell Mcginley, *Prin*
EMP: 10 **EST:** 2016
SALES (est): 506.38K **Privately Held**
Web: www.fastsigns.com
SIC: 3993 Signs and advertising specialties

(G-15703)
DSC SUPPLY COMPANY LLC
237 E Broadway Ave Ste A (43081-1646)
P.O. Box 2125 (43086-2125)
PHONE...............................614 891-1100
Nikki Anderson, *Pr*
EMP: 7 **EST:** 2003
SALES (est): 472.82K **Privately Held**
SIC: 2759 Commercial printing, nec

(G-15704)
ELAN DESIGNS INC
10 E Schrock Rd # 110 (43081-2915)
PHONE...............................614 985-5600
Nelia Anderson, *Pr*
Neilia Anderson, *Pr*
▲ **EMP:** 6 **EST:** 1997
SALES (est): 472.51K **Privately Held**
SIC: 3524 Lawn and garden equipment

(G-15705)
EMROID ME
6065 Shreven Dr (43081-8261)
PHONE...............................614 789-1898
Joe Vulpio, *Owner*
EMP: 6 **EST:** 2005
SALES (est): 269.71K **Privately Held**
SIC: 2395 Embroidery products, except Schiffli machine

GEOGRAPHIC SECTION

Westlake - Cuyahoga County (G-15729)

(G-15706)
GLOBAL SECURITY TECH INC
132 Dorchester Sq S Ste 200 (43081-7310)
PHONE..............................614 890-6400
Greg Kyle, *Prin*
EMP: 9 **EST:** 2000
SALES (est): 651.38K **Privately Held**
Web: www.gstisecurity.com
SIC: 3699 Security control equipment and systems

(G-15707)
GRACE JUICE COMPANY LLC
6318 E Dublin Granville Rd (43081-8705)
PHONE..............................614 398-6879
Leslie Burgie, *Prin*
EMP: 14 **EST:** 2017
SALES (est): 1.47MM **Privately Held**
SIC: 5149 2599 5812 Juices; Food wagons, restaurant; Eating places

(G-15708)
HIGHRISE CREATIVE LLC ✪
Also Called: Fastsigns
654 Brooksedge Blvd Ste A (43081-2962)
PHONE..............................614 890-3821
Jacob Ellzey, *Managing Member*
EMP: 11 **EST:** 2023
SALES (est): 452.49K **Privately Held**
SIC: 3993 Signs and advertising specialties

(G-15709)
IMAGE PRINT INC
6019 Jamesport Dr (43081-7925)
PHONE..............................614 776-3985
Alan Lang, *Genl Mgr*
EMP: 6 **EST:** 2009
SALES (est): 502.25K **Privately Held**
Web: www.imageprintweb.com
SIC: 2752 Offset printing

(G-15710)
INDUSTRIAL FABRICATORS INC
265 E Broadway Ave (43081-1646)
PHONE..............................614 882-7423
Frederick R Landig Junior, *Pr*
Frederick Landig Senior, *Pr*
EMP: 38 **EST:** 1964
SQ FT: 98,000
SALES (est): 8.11MM **Privately Held**
Web: www.ifab.com
SIC: 3444 Sheet metalwork

(G-15711)
JEG ASSOCIATES INC
Also Called: Jeg Associates
509 S Otterbein Ave Ste 7 (43081-2951)
P.O. Box 277 (43086-0277)
PHONE..............................614 882-1295
John Gibson Senior, *Pr*
EMP: 11 **EST:** 1985
SALES (est): 892.83K **Privately Held**
Web: www.jegplastics.com
SIC: 2821 Plastics materials and resins

(G-15712)
JOHNSON CONTROLS INC
Also Called: Johnson Controls
835 Green Crest Dr (43081-2838)
PHONE..............................614 895-6600
Stephen Carter, *Brnch Mgr*
EMP: 72
Web: www.johnsoncontrols.com
SIC: 2531 Seats, automobile
HQ: Johnson Controls, Inc.
 5757 N Green Bay Ave
 Milwaukee WI 53209
 920 245-6409

(G-15713)
LESCO INC
Also Called: Lesco Service Center
7917 Schoolside Dr (43081-4654)
PHONE..............................614 848-3712
EMP: 21
SALES (corp-wide): 4.3B **Publicly Held**
Web: www.lesco.com
SIC: 2875 Fertilizers, mixing only
HQ: Lesco, Inc.
 1385 E 36th St
 Cleveland OH 44114
 216 706-9250

(G-15714)
MES PAINTING AND GRAPHICS
8298 Harlem Rd (43081-9565)
PHONE..............................614 496-1696
EMP: 7 **EST:** 1994
SALES (est): 100.94K **Privately Held**
Web: www.mespaintingandgraphics.com
SIC: 1721 3993 1799 Painting and paper hanging; Signs and advertising specialties; Epoxy application

(G-15715)
MES PAINTING AND GRAPHICS LTD
8298 Harlem Rd (43081-9565)
PHONE..............................614 496-1696
Michael Scherl, *CEO*
EMP: 42 **EST:** 1994
SALES (est): 2.56MM **Privately Held**
Web: www.mespaintingandgraphics.com
SIC: 1721 3993 Commercial painting; Signs and advertising specialties

(G-15716)
MICRO INDUSTRIES CORPORATION (PA)
8399 Green Meadows Dr N (43081)
PHONE..............................740 548-7878
Michael Curran, *Pr*
John Curran, *
William Jackson, *
Amanda Curran, *
EMP: 67 **EST:** 1979
SQ FT: 52,000
SALES (est): 9.8MM
SALES (corp-wide): 9.8MM **Privately Held**
Web: www.microindustries.com
SIC: 8711 3674 Engineering services; Semiconductor circuit networks

(G-15717)
OHIO SHELTERALL INC
Also Called: Moore Outdoor Sign Craftsman
6060 Westerville Rd (43081-4048)
PHONE..............................614 882-1110
Steve P Moore, *Pr*
Tom Moore, *VP*
Dave Moore, *Sec*
Ellen Moore, *Treas*
EMP: 10 **EST:** 1962
SALES (est): 1.13MM **Privately Held**
Web: www.mooresigns.biz
SIC: 7312 7389 7338 3993 Outdoor advertising services; Sign painting and lettering shop; Secretarial and typing service; Signs and advertising specialties

(G-15718)
OPTIMUM SYSTEM PRODUCTS INC (PA)
Also Called: Optimum Graphics
921 Eastwind Dr Ste 133 (43081-3363)
PHONE..............................614 885-4464
John Martin, *CEO*
Dorothy Martin, *
EMP: 40 **EST:** 1985
SQ FT: 75,000
SALES (est): 3.75MM
SALES (corp-wide): 3.75MM **Privately Held**
Web: www.optimumcompanies.com
SIC: 2752 5112 Business form and card printing, lithographic; Business forms

(G-15719)
ROBIN ENTERPRISES COMPANY
111 N Otterbein Ave (43081-5703)
P.O. Box 6180 (43086-6180)
PHONE..............................614 891-0250
Brad Hance, *Pr*
EMP: 120 **EST:** 1966
SQ FT: 90,000
SALES (est): 21.3MM **Privately Held**
Web: www.robinent.com
SIC: 2752 2789 2791 Offset printing; Bookbinding and related work; Typesetting

(G-15720)
SHAWADI LLC
20 S State St Ste B (43081-2105)
PHONE..............................614 839-0698
Andrew Piper, *Managing Member*
Milton A Puckett, *
EMP: 23 **EST:** 2007
SALES (est): 744.01K **Privately Held**
Web: www.javacentral.coffee
SIC: 5812 2095 Cafe; Coffee roasting (except by wholesale grocers)

(G-15721)
TACOMA ENERGY LLC
697 Green Crest Dr (43081-2848)
P.O. Box 1528 (43086-1528)
PHONE..............................614 410-9000
EMP: 25 **EST:** 2011
SALES (est): 8.72MM **Privately Held**
Web: www.tacomaenergy.org
SIC: 8731 3825 Energy research; Electrical energy measuring equipment

(G-15722)
THOMAS TOOL & MOLD COMPANY
271 Broad St (43081-1603)
PHONE..............................614 890-4978
James W Thomas, *Pr*
James P Thomas, *VP*
▲ **EMP:** 11 **EST:** 1989
SQ FT: 7,500
SALES (est): 1.83MM **Privately Held**
Web: www.ttmco.com
SIC: 3089 Injection molding of plastics

(G-15723)
VESCO MEDICAL LLC
60 Collegeview Rd Ste 144 (43081-1429)
PHONE..............................614 914-5991
Thomas Hancock, *Brnch Mgr*
EMP: 6
SALES (corp-wide): 1.27MM **Privately Held**
Web: www.vescomedical.com
SIC: 3841 Surgical and medical instruments
PA: Vesco Medical, Llc
 4400 Chavenelle Rd
 Dubuque IA 52002
 614 914-5991

(G-15724)
WES-GARDE COMPONENTS GROUP INC
300 Enterprise Dr (43081)
PHONE..............................614 885-0319
Joe Jeenan, *Genl Mgr*
EMP: 6
SALES (corp-wide): 82.99MM **Privately Held**
Web: www.wesgarde.com
SIC: 5065 3625 5063 Electronic parts; Switches, electric power; Switches, except electronic, nec
PA: Wes-Garde Components Group, Inc.
 2820 Drane Field Rd
 Lakeland FL 33811
 863 644-7564

(G-15725)
WEST-CAMP PRESS INC (PA)
39 Collegeview Rd (43081-1463)
PHONE..............................614 882-2378
Ed Evina, *Prin*
Dave Mars, *
▲ **EMP:** 75 **EST:** 1961
SQ FT: 55,000
SALES (est): 20.26MM
SALES (corp-wide): 20.26MM **Privately Held**
Web: www.westcamppress.com
SIC: 2752 2796 2791 2789 Offset printing; Platemaking services; Typesetting; Bookbinding and related work

(G-15726)
YESPRESS GRAPHICS LLC
515 S State St (43081-2921)
PHONE..............................614 899-1403
Sunir Patel, *Prin*
EMP: 7 **EST:** 2010
SALES (est): 938.34K **Privately Held**
Web: www.yespress.com
SIC: 2752 Offset printing

Westlake
Cuyahoga County

(G-15727)
ACME DUPLICATING CO INC
Also Called: Acme Printing
1565 Greenleaf Cir (44145-2609)
PHONE..............................216 241-1241
Donald Sebold, *Owner*
EMP: 7 **EST:** 1934
SQ FT: 3,300
SALES (est): 435.59K **Privately Held**
Web: www.namepads.com
SIC: 2752 Offset printing

(G-15728)
AEROCASE INCORPORATED
Also Called: Odell Electronic Cleaning Stns
1061 Bradley Rd (44145-1044)
PHONE..............................440 617-9294
John Koniarczyk, *Pr*
Deborah Koniarczyk, *VP*
EMP: 10 **EST:** 1997
SALES (est): 999.26K **Privately Held**
Web: www.aerocaseinc.com
SIC: 3089 2441 Cases, plastics; Cases, wood

(G-15729)
ALUMINUM LINE PRODUCTS COMPANY (PA)
Also Called: Alpco
24460 Sperry Cir (44145-1591)
PHONE..............................440 835-8880
Richard A Daniel, *Pr*
James E Guerin, *
Gregory P Thompson, *
Ray Avramovich, *
David Lyster, *
◆ **EMP:** 100 **EST:** 1960
SQ FT: 100,000
SALES (est): 36.55MM
SALES (corp-wide): 36.55MM **Privately Held**
Web: www.aluminumline.com

Westlake - Cuyahoga County (G-15730) GEOGRAPHIC SECTION

SIC: **5051** 3365 3999 Steel; Aluminum foundries; Barber and beauty shop equipment

(G-15730)
AMERICAN LAWYERS CO INC (PA)
Also Called: American Lawyers Quarterly
853 Westpoint Pkwy Ste 710 (44145-1546)
PHONE..............................440 333-5190
Thomas W Hamilton, *Ex VP*
Edward D Familo, *Pr*
EMP: 11 EST: 1899
SQ FT: 4,000
SALES (est): 994.02K
SALES (corp-wide): 994.02K **Privately Held**
Web: www.alqlist.com
SIC: **2721** Periodicals, publishing only

(G-15731)
AMERICAN OFFICE SERVICES INC
30257 Clemens Rd Ste C (44145-1004)
PHONE..............................440 899-6888
Scott C Ashbrook, *Pr*
Margo L Ashbrook, *VP*
EMP: 6 **EST:** 1993
SQ FT: 8,000
SALES (est): 1.97MM **Privately Held**
Web: www.americanofficeservices.com
SIC: **7641** 2531 Office furniture repair and maintenance; Stadium seating

(G-15732)
AMERICAN TCHNICAL COATINGS INC
Also Called: A T C
28045 Ranney Pkwy Ste H (44145-1144)
PHONE..............................440 401-2270
Charles Inglefield, *Pr*
EMP: 6 **EST:** 2003
SALES (est): 966.61K **Privately Held**
Web: www.atcmaterials.com
SIC: **3479** Coating of metals and formed products

(G-15733)
APPLIED MARKETING SERVICES INC (HQ)
Also Called: Medical & Home Health
28825 Ranney Pkwy (44145-1173)
PHONE..............................440 716-9962
David J Marquard, *Pr*
David J Marquard Ii, *Pr*
C V Guggenviller, *
▲ **EMP:** 24 **EST:** 1993
SQ FT: 20,000
SALES (est): 8.93MM
SALES (corp-wide): 10.05MM **Privately Held**
Web: www.applied-inc.com
SIC: **3569** 8742 Gas producers, generators, and other gas related equipment; Marketing consulting services
PA: Oxygo Hq Florida Llc
    2200 Principal Row
    Orlando FL 32837
    440 716-9962

(G-15734)
ARCHER CUSTOM CHROME LLC
25703 Rustic Ln (44145-5476)
PHONE..............................216 441-2795
Roy Ansen, *Prin*
EMP: 6 **EST:** 2008
SALES (est): 122.78K **Privately Held**
SIC: **3471** Chromium plating of metals or formed products

(G-15735)
BAY CORPORATION
867 Canterbury Rd (44145-1486)
PHONE..............................440 835-2212
EMP: 24 **EST:** 1979
SALES (est): 3.99MM **Privately Held**
Web: www.baycorporation.com
SIC: **3089** 3494 Fittings for pipe, plastics; Valves and pipe fittings, nec

(G-15736)
BAY STATE POLYMER DISTRIBUTION INC
Also Called: Bay State Polymer
27540 Detroit Rd Ste 102 (44145-2299)
P.O. Box 40055 (44140-0055)
PHONE..............................440 892-8500
◆ **EMP:** 15
SIC: **5162** 3087 Resins, synthetic; Custom compound purchased resins

(G-15737)
BEST PROCESS SOLUTIONS INC
26780 Gershwin Dr (44145-2332)
PHONE..............................330 220 1440
Mike Desalvo, *Pr*
EMP: 30 **EST:** 2012
SALES (est): 3.75MM **Privately Held**
Web: www.bpsvibes.com
SIC: **3441** Fabricated structural metal

(G-15738)
BLACK BOX CORPORATION
Also Called: Black Box Network Services
26100 1st St (44145-1478)
PHONE..............................855 324-9909
EMP: 6
Web: www.blackbox.com
SIC: **3577** 3679 3661 5045 Computer peripheral equipment, nec; Electronic switches; Modems; Computer peripheral equipment
HQ: Black Box Corporation
    1000 Park Dr
    Lawrence PA 15055
    724 746-5500

(G-15739)
BONNE BELL INC
Also Called: Bonne Bell Company, The
1006 Crocker Rd (44145-1031)
PHONE..............................440 835-2440
EMP: 203
SIC: **2844** Cosmetic preparations

(G-15740)
BONNE BELL LLC (PA)
1006 Crocker Rd (44145)
PHONE..............................440 835-2440
Jess A Bell Junior, *Managing Member*
◆ **EMP:** 8 **EST:** 1927
SQ FT: 40,000
SALES (est): 5.35MM
SALES (corp-wide): 5.35MM **Privately Held**
Web: www.aspirebrands.com
SIC: **2844** Cosmetic preparations

(G-15741)
BORCHERS AMERICAS INC (HQ)
Also Called: Om Group
811 Sharon Dr (44145-1522)
PHONE..............................440 899-2950
Devlin Riley, *CEO*
◆ **EMP:** 60 **EST:** 1946
SQ FT: 30,000
SALES (est): 45.3MM
SALES (corp-wide): 1.69B **Privately Held**
Web: www.borchers.com

SIC: **8731** 2819 2899 2992 Commercial physical research; Industrial inorganic chemicals, nec; Chemical preparations, nec ; Lubricating oils and greases
PA: Milliken & Company
    920 Milliken Rd
    Spartanburg SC 29303
    864 503-2020

(G-15742)
CENTURY TOOL & STAMPING CO
24600 Center Ridge Rd Ste 140 (44145-5679)
PHONE..............................216 241-2032
Todd Guist, *Pr*
William Guist Junior, *Pr*
William Guist Lll, *Treas*
James Vespoli, *Treas*
Cathy Hoy, *Sec*
EMP: 10 **EST:** 1950
SALES (est): 232.03K **Privately Held**
SIC: **3599** Machine shop, jobbing and repair

(G-15743)
CHEM-MATERIALS INC
Also Called: Chem-Materials Co
24700 Center Ridge Rd Ste 280 (44145-5606)
PHONE..............................440 455-9465
Philip J Haagensen, *Pr*
▲ **EMP:** 15 **EST:** 1987
SQ FT: 2,000
SALES (est): 4.25MM **Privately Held**
Web: www.chem-materials.com
SIC: **2821** Plastics materials and resins

(G-15744)
CLEVELAND ROLL FORMING ENVIRONMENTAL DIVISION INC
Also Called: Peco
27881 Clemens Rd (44145-1167)
PHONE..............................440 899-3888
EMP: 16 **EST:** 1989
SALES (est): 1.36MM
SALES (corp-wide): 27.08MM **Publicly Held**
SIC: **1796** 8711 3564 Pollution control equipment installation; Engineering services ; Precipitators, electrostatic
PA: Fuel Tech, Inc.
    27601 Bella Vista Pkwy
    Warrenville IL 60555
    630 845-4500

(G-15745)
DIAMOND RESERVE INC
Also Called: National Diamond Tl & Coating
801 Sharon Dr (44145-1522)
PHONE..............................440 892-7877
EMP: 10 **EST:** 1980
SQ FT: 2,000
SALES (est): 1.77MM **Privately Held**
Web: www.nationaldiamondtool.com
SIC: **3545** Diamond cutting tools for turning, boring, burnishing, etc.

(G-15746)
DOME DRILLING COMPANY (PA)
Also Called: Dome Resources
2001 Crocker Rd Ste 420 (44145-6967)
PHONE..............................440 892-9434
Jon O Newton, *Pr*
James E Gessel, *VP*
Noreen C Mc Kinney, *VP Opers*
John James Carney, *Sec*
James A Carney, *Treas*
EMP: 6 **EST:** 1981
SQ FT: 1,200
SALES (est): 1.83MM
SALES (corp-wide): 1.83MM **Privately Held**

Web: www.sinetek.com
SIC: **1311** 1382 Crude petroleum production; Oil and gas exploration services

(G-15747)
ELEVEN 10 LLC
975 Bassett Rd Ste B (44145-1171)
PHONE..............................888 216-4049
EMP: 15 **EST:** 2010
SALES (est): 1.18MM **Privately Held**
Web: www.1110gear.com
SIC: **3842** 5199 First aid, snake bite, and burn kits; First aid supplies

(G-15748)
ENERGIZER BATTERY INC (HQ)
25225 Detroit Rd (44145-2536)
P.O. Box 30382 (44130-0382)
PHONE..............................440 835-7500
Mark S Lavigne, *CEO*
EMP: 42 **EST:** 2012
SALES (est): 34.23MM
SALES (corp-wide): 2.96B **Publicly Held**
Web: www.energizer.com
SIC: **3691** Storage batteries
PA: Energizer Holdings, Inc.
    533 Maryville Univ Dr
    Saint Louis MO 63141
    314 985-2000

(G-15749)
ENERGIZER MANUFACTURING INC
25225 Detroit Rd (44145-2536)
EMP: 9
SALES (corp-wide): 2.96B **Publicly Held**
Web: www.energizerholdings.com
SIC: **3691** Alkaline cell storage batteries
HQ: Energizer Manufacturing, Inc.
    533 Maryville Univ Dr
    Saint Louis MO 63141
    314 985-2000

(G-15750)
ERICHSEN INC
815 Crocker Rd Ste 9 (44145-1072)
PHONE..............................734 474-1471
Patrick Burns, *Pr*
EMP: 9 **EST:** 2017
SALES (est): 207.91K **Privately Held**
Web: www.us-erichsen.de
SIC: **3549** Marking machines, metalworking

(G-15751)
G I PLASTEK INC
24700 Center Ridge Rd Ste 8 (44145-5636)
PHONE..............................440 230-1942
EMP: 7 **EST:** 1995
SQ FT: 3,000
SALES (est): 756.86K **Privately Held**
SIC: **3089** Plastics processing

(G-15752)
GC CONTROLS INC
Also Called: Eurotherm
30311 Clemens Rd (44145-1023)
P.O. Box 450799 (44145-0617)
PHONE..............................440 779-4777
Bob Roberts, *Pr*
Joanne Albers, *Treas*
Gary Albers, *Dir*
EMP: 7 **EST:** 1987
SALES (est): 590.7K **Privately Held**
Web: www.gccontrols.net
SIC: **3625** Industrial controls: push button, selector switches, pilot

(G-15753)
GENERAL BAR INC
25000 Center Ridge Rd Ste 3 (44145-4108)
PHONE..............................440 835-2000

GEOGRAPHIC SECTION

Westlake - Cuyahoga County (G-15775)

Charles Sonnhalter, *Pr*
Michael Sonnhalter, *VP*
EMP: 12 **EST:** 1941
SQ FT: 1,500
SALES (est): 479.77K **Privately Held**
Web: www.generalbar.com
SIC: 2741 8111 Directories, nec: publishing only, not printed on site; Legal services

(G-15754)
GEON PERFORMANCE SOLUTIONS LLC (DH)
25777 Detroit Rd Ste 200 (44145-2484)
P.O. Box 90 (44012-0090)
PHONE................................800 438-4366
Tracy Garrison, *Managing Member*
EMP: 10 **EST:** 2019
SALES (est): 475.64MM
SALES (corp-wide): 2.67MM **Privately Held**
Web: www.geon.com
SIC: 2822 3084 Ethylene-propylene rubbers, EPDM polymers; Plastics pipe
HQ: Sk Echo Group S.a R.L.
  Boulevard Royal 53
  Luxembourg

(G-15755)
HENKEL US OPERATIONS CORP
Also Called: Loctite
26235 1st St (44145-1439)
PHONE................................440 250-7700
EMP: 78
SALES (corp-wide): 23.39B **Privately Held**
Web: www.henkel.com
SIC: 2891 Adhesives and sealants
HQ: Henkel Us Operations Corporation
  1 Henkel Way
  Rocky Hill CT 06067
  860 571-5100

(G-15756)
HMS INDUSTRIES LLC
Also Called: HMS Industries
27995 Ranney Pkwy (44145-1178)
PHONE................................440 899-0001
Biri Saluja, *Managing Member*
▲ **EMP:** 17 **EST:** 2001
SQ FT: 10,000
SALES (est): 2.41MM **Privately Held**
Web: www.hms-ind.com
SIC: 3562 5085 Roller bearings and parts; Industrial supplies

(G-15757)
HYLAND SOFTWARE INC (HQ)
Also Called: Onbase
28105 Clemens Rd (44145-1100)
PHONE................................440 788-5000
Bill Priemer, *CEO*
Nancy Person, *
Ed Mcquiston, *CCO*
John Phelan, *CPO*
Noreen Kilbane, *CAO*
EMP: 1800 **EST:** 1991
SQ FT: 150,000
SALES (est): 827.71MM
SALES (corp-wide): 1.2B **Privately Held**
Web: www.hyland.com
SIC: 7372 Application computer software
PA: Thoma Cressey Bravo, Inc.
  300 N La Slle Dr Ste 4350
  Chicago IL 60654
  312 254-3100

(G-15758)
ICONIC LABS LLC
Also Called: Ic Scientific Solutions
909 Canterbury Rd Ste G (44145-7212)
PHONE................................216 759-4040
Travis Bennett Mng Mbtr, *Prin*
EMP: 14 **EST:** 2016
SQ FT: 3,000
SALES (est): 601.76K **Privately Held**
Web: www.icscientificsolutions.com
SIC: 8731 3565 3479 Engineering laboratory, except testing; Bottling and canning machinery; Coating of metals with silicon

(G-15759)
IIOT WORLD LLC
25985 Rustic Ln (44145-5480)
PHONE................................440 715-0564
EMP: 20 **EST:** 2017
SALES (est): 553.61K **Privately Held**
Web: www.iiot-world.com
SIC: 2711 Newspapers: publishing only, not printed on site

(G-15760)
IMCD US LLC (HQ)
Also Called: Hs Services
2 Equity Way Ste 210 (44145-1050)
PHONE................................216 228-8900
Jean-paul Scheepens, *Pr*
John L Mastrantoni, *
Thomas V Valkenburg, *
Bruce D Jarosz, *
Vlad Miller, *
▲ **EMP:** 46 **EST:** 1978
SALES (est): 227.45MM **Privately Held**
Web: www.imcdus.com
SIC: 2834 5169 5191 Pharmaceutical preparations; Chemicals and allied products, nec; Chemicals, agricultural
PA: Imcd N.V.
  Wilhelminaplein 32
  Rotterdam ZH

(G-15761)
INNOVTIVE CNFCTION SLTIONS LLC
Also Called: Phillips Syrup
28025 Ranney Pkwy (44145-1159)
PHONE................................440 835-8001
EMP: 14 **EST:** 2014
SALES (est): 985.47K **Privately Held**
SIC: 2087 Syrups, drink

(G-15762)
KAEDEN PUBLISHING
Also Called: Kaeden Books
24700 Center Ridge Rd Ste 170 (44145-5668)
P.O. Box 16190 (44116-0190)
PHONE................................440 617-1400
Craig Urmston, *Pr*
Kathleen Urmston, *VP*
▲ **EMP:** 6 **EST:** 1991
SQ FT: 7,500
SALES (est): 998.75K **Privately Held**
Web: www.kaeden.com
SIC: 2741 Miscellaneous publishing

(G-15763)
LS STARRETT COMPANY
Webber Gage Div
24500 Detroit Rd (44145-2580)
PHONE................................440 835-0005
EMP: 80
SQ FT: 35,000
SALES (corp-wide): 256.18MM **Privately Held**
Web: www.starrett.com
SIC: 3545 3829 3823 Gauge blocks; Measuring and controlling devices, nec; Process control instruments
PA: The L S Starrett Company
  121 Crescent St
  Athol MA 01331
  978 249-3551

(G-15764)
MARLIN THERMOCOUPLE WIRE INC
847 Canterbury Rd (44145-1420)
PHONE................................440 835-1950
Allen Tymkewicz, *CEO*
Vivian Coticchia, *
Andy Gehrisch, *
▲ **EMP:** 24 **EST:** 1952
SQ FT: 46,000
SALES (est): 4.73MM **Privately Held**
Web: www.marlintcwire.com
SIC: 3315 Wire, steel: insulated or armored

(G-15765)
MOMENTUM FLEET MGT GROUP INC
24481 Detroit Rd (44145-1580)
PHONE................................440 759-2219
Jack Pyros, *Pr*
EMP: 56 **EST:** 2005
SALES (est): 2.11MM **Privately Held**
Web: www.momentumgroups.com
SIC: 8741 6159 3699 Management services; Automobile finance leasing; Electrical equipment and supplies, nec

(G-15766)
MYERS AND LASCH INC
2530 Wyndgate Ct (44145-2994)
PHONE................................440 235-2050
Phil Puhala, *Owner*
Mike Marhefka, *VP*
EMP: 6 **EST:** 1962
SALES (est): 463.08K **Privately Held**
Web: www.myers-lasch.com
SIC: 3993 Displays and cutouts, window and lobby

(G-15767)
NICKELS MARKETING GROUP INC
4016 Brewster Dr (44145-5301)
PHONE................................440 835-1532
Kay Nickels, *Prin*
EMP: 6 **EST:** 2009
SALES (est): 79.45K **Privately Held**
SIC: 3356 Nickel

(G-15768)
NORDSON CORPORATION (PA)
Also Called: Nordson
28601 Clemens Rd (44145)
PHONE................................440 892-1580
Sundaram Nagarajan, *Pr*
Michael J Merriman Junior, *Ch Bd*
Sarah Siddiqui, *Chief Human Resources Officer*
Jennifer L Mcdonough, *Ex VP*
Stephen Shamrock, *Interim Vice President*
EMP: 1331 **EST:** 1909
SQ FT: 28,000
SALES (est): 2.63B
SALES (corp-wide): 2.63B **Publicly Held**
Web: www.nordson.com
SIC: 3563 Spraying outfits: metals, paints, and chemicals (compressor)

(G-15769)
NORDSON MEDICAL CORPORATION
28601 Clemens Rd (44145-1148)
PHONE................................440 892-1580
Michael F Hilton, *Pr*
EMP: 75 **EST:** 2010
SALES (est): 25.6MM
SALES (corp-wide): 2.63B **Publicly Held**
Web: www.nordson.com
SIC: 3563 Air and gas compressors
PA: Nordson Corporation
  28601 Clemens Rd
  Westlake OH 44145
  440 892-1580

(G-15770)
PAPYRUS-RECYCLED GREETINGS INC
1 American Blvd (44145)
PHONE................................773 348-6410
Leonard Levine, *CFO*
Philip Friedmann, *VP*
Michael Keiser, *VP*
▲ **EMP:** 100 **EST:** 1972
SALES (est): 11.2MM
SALES (corp-wide): 14.52B **Privately Held**
Web: aggreetingsgateway.amgreetings.com
SIC: 2771 5199 Greeting cards; Gifts and novelties
HQ: American Greetings Corporation
  1 American Blvd
  Cleveland OH 44145
  216 252-7300

(G-15771)
PARTY ANIMAL INC
909 Crocker Rd (44145)
PHONE................................440 471-1030
Bryan Cantrall, *Pr*
Bryan Cantrall, *CEO*
Phyllis Cantrall, *VP*
▲ **EMP:** 15 **EST:** 1989
SQ FT: 3,800
SALES (est): 11.03MM **Privately Held**
Web: www.partyanimalinc.com
SIC: 2399 5092 Banners, made from fabric; Toys and games

(G-15772)
PDQ PRINTING SERVICE
29003 Brockway Dr (44145-5212)
PHONE................................216 241-5443
Dorry Smotzer, *Owner*
EMP: 10 **EST:** 1963
SALES (est): 738.01K **Privately Held**
Web: www.pdqprintingandlabel.com
SIC: 2752 Offset printing

(G-15773)
PENGUIN ENTERPRISES INC
Also Called: PS Copy
869 Canterbury Rd Ste 2 (44145-1492)
PHONE................................440 899-5112
Jim Seman, *Pr*
EMP: 35 **EST:** 1984
SALES (est): 2.15MM **Privately Held**
SIC: 2796 2791 2789 2759 Platemaking services; Typesetting; Bookbinding and related work; Commercial printing, nec

(G-15774)
PHILLIPS SYRUP LLC
28025 Ranney Pkwy (44145-1159)
PHONE................................440 835-8001
Jim Kanner, *Managing Member*
EMP: 17 **EST:** 2003
SALES (est): 2.43MM **Privately Held**
Web: www.phillipssyrup.com
SIC: 2087 Flavoring extracts and syrups, nec

(G-15775)
PINES MANUFACTURING INC (PA)
Also Called: Pines Technology
29100 Lakeland Blvd (44145)
PHONE................................440 835-5553
Ian Williamson, *Pr*
Donald Rebar, *Ch Bd*
▲ **EMP:** 45 **EST:** 1993
SQ FT: 48,000
SALES (est): 9.54MM **Privately Held**
Web: www.pines-eng.com
SIC: 5084 3542 3549 3547 Industrial machinery and equipment; Bending machines; Metalworking machinery, nec; Rolling mill machinery

Westlake - Cuyahoga County (G-15776)

GEOGRAPHIC SECTION

(G-15776)
Q-LAB CORPORATION (PA)
Also Called: Q-Lab
800 Canterbury Rd (44145)
PHONE..............................440 835-8700
Douglas M Grossman, *Pr*
Gary Simecek, *
Ron Roberts, *
Brad Reis, *
Kirk Wilhelm, *
▲ **EMP:** 53 **EST:** 1964
SQ FT: 150,000
SALES (est): 59.9MM
SALES (corp-wide): 59.9MM **Privately Held**
Web: www.q-lab.com
SIC: 3823 3829 3826 Process control instruments; Measuring and controlling devices, nec; Analytical instruments

(G-15777)
R AND J CORPORATION
Also Called: Haynes Manufacturing Company
24142 Detroit Rd (44145-1515)
PHONE..............................440 871-6009
Beth Kloos, *Pr*
Timothy Kloos, *VP*
EMP: 42 **EST:** 1902
SQ FT: 23,000
SALES (est): 9.04MM **Privately Held**
Web: www.haynesmfg.com
SIC: 3556 5084 7389 3053 Food products machinery; Food industry machinery; Design, commercial and industrial; Gaskets; packing and sealing devices

(G-15778)
RECTOR INC
Also Called: Profiles In Diversity Journal
1991 Crocker Rd Ste 320 (44145-6971)
P.O. Box 45605 (44145-0605)
PHONE..............................440 892-0444
EMP: 7 **EST:** 1991
SQ FT: 1,000
SALES (est): 816.05K **Privately Held**
Web: www.diversityjournal.com
SIC: 2721 Magazines: publishing only, not printed on site

(G-15779)
RISK INDUSTRIES LLC
Also Called: Pines Technology
30505 Clemens Rd (44145-1000)
PHONE..............................440 835-5553
EMP: 70
Web: www.pines-eng.com
SIC: 3542 Machine tools, metal forming type

(G-15780)
S J T ENTERPRISES INC
28045 Ranney Pkwy Ste B (44145-1144)
PHONE..............................440 617-1100
Timothy J Smith, *Pr*
▲ **EMP:** 22 **EST:** 1985
SQ FT: 17,000
SALES (est): 2.43MM **Privately Held**
Web: www.sjtent.com
SIC: 2741 Miscellaneous publishing

(G-15781)
SAND PROPERTIES&LANDSCAPING
933 Dover Center Rd (44145-1310)
PHONE..............................440 360-7386
Sue A Webb, *Owner*
EMP: 6 **EST:** 2013
SALES (est): 103.92K **Privately Held**
SIC: 7349 8741 0781 1389 Building maintenance services, nec; Management services; Landscape services; Construction, repair, and dismantling services

(G-15782)
SANGRAF INTERNATIONAL INC
159 Crocker Park Blvd Ste 100 (44145)
PHONE..............................216 543-3288
Xiu Qin Hou, *Prin*
▲ **EMP:** 21 **EST:** 2012
SALES (est): 3.57MM **Privately Held**
Web: www.sangrafintl.com
SIC: 3624 Electrodes, thermal and electrolytic uses: carbon, graphite
HQ: Henan Sanli Carbon Products Co., Ltd.
North Side Of Xiaotun Village, Baiquan Town, Xijiao Development
Xinxiang HA 45363

(G-15783)
SARASOTA QUALITY PRODUCTS
27330 Center Ridge Rd (44145-3957)
PHONE..............................440 899-9820
James Schilens, *Pr*
▲ **EMP:** 8 **EST:** 1991
SALES (est): 772.48K **Privately Held**
Web: www.sarasotaqp.com
SIC: 3429 Hardware, nec

(G-15784)
SCOTT FETZER COMPANY
28800 Clemens Rd (44145-1197)
PHONE..............................440 892-3000
Robert Mcbride, *CEO*
William Stephans, *
Trish Scanlon, *
John Gretta, *
EMP: 4904 **EST:** 1985
SQ FT: 2,000
SALES (est): 2.46MM
SALES (corp-wide): 364.48B **Publicly Held**
Web: www.scottfetzer.com
SIC: 2731 2741 5961 Textbooks: publishing only, not printed on site; Atlases: publishing only, not printed on site; Books, mail order (except book clubs)
HQ: Bhsf Inc.
1440 Kiewit Plz
Omaha NE 68131

(G-15785)
SEST INC
24509 Annie Ln (44145-4144)
PHONE..............................440 777-9777
Ashwin Shah, *Pr*
EMP: 10 **EST:** 1997
SQ FT: 1,000
SALES (est): 996.35K **Privately Held**
Web: www.sestinc.com
SIC: 8711 7373 7372 7371 Consulting engineer; Computer-aided engineering (CAE) systems service; Application computer software; Computer software development and applications

(G-15786)
SHAMROCK COMPANIES INC (PA)
Also Called: Shamrock Acquisition Company
24090 Detroit Rd (44145-1513)
P.O. Box 450980 (44145-0623)
PHONE..............................440 899-9510
Tim Connor, *CEO*
Gary A Lesjak, *CFO*
Dave Fechter, *COO*
▲ **EMP:** 65 **EST:** 1982
SQ FT: 42,500
SALES (est): 87.67MM **Privately Held**
Web: www.shamrockcompanies.net
SIC: 5112 5199 7336 7389 Business forms; Advertising specialties; Art design services; Brokers' services

(G-15787)
SHELBY COMPANY
865 Canterbury Rd (44145-1420)
PHONE..............................440 871-9901
Richard J Rapacz, *Pr*
EMP: 33 **EST:** 1923
SQ FT: 50,000
SALES (est): 8.18MM **Privately Held**
Web: www.shelbycompany.com
SIC: 2657 2653 Folding paperboard boxes; Display items, corrugated: made from purchased materials

(G-15788)
SIGNATURE STITCH LLC
27519 Detroit Rd (44145-2243)
PHONE..............................440 382-1388
Patricia Mcfadden, *Prin*
EMP: 6 **EST:** 2013
SALES (est): 185.1K **Privately Held**
SIC: 2395 Embroidery products, except Schiffli machine

(G-15789)
SOUTHPAW INDUSTRIES LLC
1304 Cedarwood Dr Apt C1 (44145-1831)
PHONE..............................714 215-8592
Paul Nget, *Prin*
EMP: 6 **EST:** 2017
SALES (est): 66.56K **Privately Held**
SIC: 3999 Manufacturing industries, nec

(G-15790)
SPECTRE SENSORS INC
2392 Georgia Dr (44145-5806)
PHONE..............................440 250-0372
Glen Keller, *Ch Bd*
John Keller, *Pr*
EMP: 9 **EST:** 2002
SALES (est): 752.15K **Privately Held**
Web: www.spectresensors.com
SIC: 3612 Electronic meter transformers

(G-15791)
STAR METAL PRODUCTS CO INC
30405 Clemens Rd (44145-1018)
PHONE..............................440 899-7000
John C Murray, *CEO*
Eleanor V Murray, *
Arthur Stenzel, *
Mary C Reidy, *
Rita A Dunham, *
EMP: 110 **EST:** 1958
SQ FT: 24,000
SALES (est): 8.33MM **Privately Held**
Web: www.starmetalproducts.com
SIC: 3599 Machine shop, jobbing and repair

(G-15792)
STRUERS INC (DH)
24766 Detroit Rd (44145-2525)
PHONE..............................440 871-0071
Bente Freiberg, *Pr*
Christopher Sopko, *
Steen Jensen, *
◆ **EMP:** 58 **EST:** 1875
SALES (est): 25.7MM **Privately Held**
Web: www.struers.com
SIC: 3829 Measuring and controlling devices, nec
HQ: Struers Aps
Pederstrupvej 84
Ballerup 2750
44600800

(G-15793)
SUPERIOR PNEUMATIC & MFG INC
871 Canterbury Rd Ste E (44145-1482)
P.O. Box 40420 (44140-0420)
PHONE..............................440 871-8780
Bradley Krewson, *Pr*
Walter I Krewson Junior, *CEO*
Robert Janusky, *Ex VP*
EMP: 12 **EST:** 1945
SALES (est): 460.28K **Privately Held**
Web: www.superiorpneumatic.com
SIC: 3546 Power-driven handtools

(G-15794)
SURILI COUTURE LLC
29961 Persimmon Dr (44145-5103)
PHONE..............................440 600-1456
EMP: 14 **EST:** 2016
SALES (est): 977.9K **Privately Held**
Web: www.surilicouture.com
SIC: 2335 Bridal and formal gowns

(G-15795)
TECHNIPLATE INC
796 Carnage Park Oval (44145-1402)
PHONE..............................216 486-8825
Don Perry, *Pr*
Allan Stickler, *CEO*
EMP: 9 **EST:** 1977
SALES (est): 434.53K **Privately Held**
Web: www.techniplate.com
SIC: 3471 Electroplating of metals or formed products

(G-15796)
THERM-ALL INC (PA)
Also Called: Therm-All
830 Canterbury Rd Ste A (44145-1403)
PHONE..............................440 779-9494
Robert Smigel, *Pr*
Ann Sliwa, *Prin*
Dennis Kaczmarek, *VP*
Linda Smigel, *Sec*
Richard Sobiech, *CFO*
EMP: 20 **EST:** 1981
SQ FT: 56,000
SALES (est): 30.11MM
SALES (corp-wide): 30.11MM **Privately Held**
Web: www.therm-all.com
SIC: 3211 Building glass, flat

(G-15797)
TLC PRODUCTS INC
Also Called: TLC Products
26100 1st St (44145-1478)
P.O. Box 45301 (44145-0301)
PHONE..............................216 472-3030
▲ **EMP:** 10 **EST:** 1996
SALES (est): 2.48MM **Privately Held**
Web: www.tlc-products.com
SIC: 3999 2879 Barber and beauty shop equipment; Agricultural chemicals, nec

(G-15798)
TOLI VAULT
2035 Crocker Rd Ste 103 (44145-1996)
PHONE..............................866 998-8654
EMP: 7 **EST:** 2012
SALES (est): 138.99K **Privately Held**
SIC: 3272 Burial vaults, concrete or precast terrazzo

(G-15799)
VERMILION VALLEY VINEYARDS LLC
29457 Hummingbird Cir (44145-5288)
PHONE..............................440 935-1363
Lawrence E Gibson, *Prin*
EMP: 6 **EST:** 2008
SALES (est): 88.07K **Privately Held**
Web: www.vermilion-valleyvineyards.com
SIC: 2084 Wines

(G-15800)
VISION GRAPHIX INC
Also Called: AlphaGraphics Westlake
29275 Clemens Rd (44145-1002)
PHONE..............................440 835-6540
EMP: 6 **EST:** 1992
SQ FT: 4,000
SALES (est): 726K **Privately Held**
Web: www.alphagraphics.com
SIC: 2752 3993 Commercial printing, lithographic; Advertising artwork

(G-15801)
WESTERN/SCOTT FETZER COMPANY (HQ)
28800 Clemens Rd (44145-1134)
PHONE..............................440 892-3000
Kenneth Semelsberger, *Ch Bd*
Robert D Mcbride, *CEO*
John Gretta, *Treas*
◆ **EMP:** 45 **EST:** 1985
SALES (est): 50.12MM
SALES (corp-wide): 226 **Privately Held**
Web: www.westernenterprises.com
SIC: 2813 Oxygen, compressed or liquefied
PA: The Scott Fetzer Company
    28800 Clemens Rd
    Westlake OH 44145
    440 892-3000

(G-15802)
WESTERN/SCOTT FETZER COMPANY
Also Called: Western Enterprises
875 Bassett Rd (44145-1142)
PHONE..............................440 871-2160
Gary Heeman, *Brnch Mgr*
EMP: 250
SALES (corp-wide): 226 **Privately Held**
Web: www.westernenterprises.com
SIC: 3635 Household vacuum cleaners
HQ: Western/Scott Fetzer Company
    28800 Clemens Rd
    Westlake OH 44145

(G-15803)
WESTSHORE METAL FINISHING LLC
26891 Kenley Ct (44145-1456)
PHONE..............................440 892-0774
Richard J Holton, *Prin*
EMP: 6 **EST:** 2010
SALES (est): 112.26K **Privately Held**
SIC: 3471 Cleaning, polishing, and finishing

Weston
Wood County

(G-15804)
CRESSET CHEMICAL CO INC (PA)
13255 Main St (43569-9544)
P.O. Box 367 (43569-0367)
PHONE..............................419 669-2041
George F Baty, *Ch Bd*
Mike Baty, *Pr*
▼ **EMP:** 10 **EST:** 1946
SQ FT: 2,000
SALES (est): 3.93MM
SALES (corp-wide): 3.93MM **Privately Held**
Web: www.cresset.com
SIC: 2899 2841 Chemical preparations, nec; Soap and other detergents

(G-15805)
CRESSET CHEMICAL CO INC
13490 Silver St (43569-9522)
PHONE..............................419 669-2041
George Baty, *Mgr*
EMP: 10
SALES (corp-wide): 3.93MM **Privately Held**
Web: www.cresset.com
SIC: 2899 Chemical preparations, nec
PA: Cresset Chemical Co Inc
    13255 Main St
    Weston OH 43569
    419 669-2041

(G-15806)
MCM PRECISION CASTINGS INC
13133 Beech St (43569-9516)
PHONE..............................419 669-3226
Donald Marion, *Pr*
EMP: 20 **EST:** 1992
SQ FT: 7,896
SALES (est): 2.69MM **Privately Held**
Web: www.mcmprecision.com
SIC: 3369 Castings, except die-castings, precision

(G-15807)
VITAKRAFT SUN SEED INC
20584 Long Judson Rd (43569-9639)
P.O. Box 33 (43402-0033)
PHONE..............................419 832-1641
Brent Weinmann, *Pr*
▲ **EMP:** 60 **EST:** 2001
SQ FT: 50,000
SALES (est): 14.33MM **Privately Held**
Web: www.vitakraftsunseed.com
SIC: 2048 2047 Bird food, prepared; Dog and cat food

Wheelersburg
Scioto County

(G-15808)
CONNIES CANDLES
9103 Ohio River Rd (45694-1927)
P.O. Box 97 (45694-0097)
PHONE..............................740 574-1224
Connie Potters, *Owner*
EMP: 6 **EST:** 1997
SALES (est): 382.25K **Privately Held**
Web: www.conniescandles.com
SIC: 3999 Candles

(G-15809)
GREG BLUME
Also Called: Trophy's Unlimited
7459 Ohio River Rd (45694)
P.O. Box 388 (45694-0388)
PHONE..............................740 574-2308
Greg Blume, *Owner*
EMP: 6 **EST:** 1987
SALES (est): 383.13K **Privately Held**
SIC: 5999 2791 2789 2752 Trophies and plaques; Typesetting; Bookbinding and related work; Offset printing

(G-15810)
TRI-AMERICA CONTRACTORS INC (PA)
1664 State Route 522 (45694-7828)
PHONE..............................740 574-0148
Scott Taylor, *Pr*
Teresa Smith, *
EMP: 37 **EST:** 1997
SQ FT: 34,000
SALES (est): 9.42MM
SALES (corp-wide): 9.42MM **Privately Held**
Web: www.triaminc.com
SIC: 3498 3441 1629 Fabricated pipe and fittings; Fabricated structural metal; Industrial plant construction

(G-15811)
TRI-AMERICA CONTRACTORS INC
Also Called: Tri-America Contractors
1664 State Route 522 (45694-7828)
PHONE..............................740 574-0148
EMP: 14
SALES (corp-wide): 9.42MM **Privately Held**
Web: www.triaminc.com
SIC: 3498 Fabricated pipe and fittings
PA: Tri-America Contractors, Inc.
    1664 State Route 522
    Wheelersburg OH 45694
    740 574-0148

(G-15812)
TRI-STATE KITCHENS LLC
663 Kittle Rd (45694-9267)
PHONE..............................740 574-6727
Rick Moore, *Owner*
EMP: 8 **EST:** 2017
SALES (est): 406.55K **Privately Held**
Web: www.tri-state-kitchens.com
SIC: 2434 Wood kitchen cabinets

Whipple
Washington County

(G-15813)
BRAD GRIZER ON SPOT WELDING
1532 Nichols Rd (45788-5148)
PHONE..............................740 516-3436
Brad Grizer, *Admn*
EMP: 7 **EST:** 2014
SALES (est): 125.17K **Privately Held**
Web: www.grizercastle.com
SIC: 7692 Welding repair

(G-15814)
FULL CIRCLE OIL FIELD SVCS INC
7585 State Route 821 (45788-5164)
PHONE..............................740 371-5422
Mitch Fouss, *Prin*
Danny Warren, *Prin*
Renee Warren, *Prin*
EMP: 10 **EST:** 2011
SALES (est): 770.46K **Privately Held**
Web: www.fcofs.com
SIC: 1389 Oil field services, nec

Whitehouse
Lucas County

(G-15815)
BASF CORPORATION
Coatings & Colorants Division
6125 Industrial Pkwy (43571-9595)
P.O. Box 2757 (43571-0757)
PHONE..............................419 877-5308
Kenneth Terry, *Dir*
EMP: 136
SQ FT: 20,000
SALES (corp-wide): 74.89B **Privately Held**
Web: www.basf.com
SIC: 2869 Industrial organic chemicals, nec
HQ: Basf Corporation
    100 Park Ave
    Florham Park NJ 07932
    800 962-7831

(G-15816)
BITTERSWEET INC (PA)
Also Called: BITTERSWEET FARMS
12660 Archbold Whitehouse Rd (43571-9566)
PHONE..............................419 875-6986
Vicki Obee-hilty, *Ex Dir*
EMP: 70 **EST:** 1977
SQ FT: 20,000
SALES (est): 7.08MM
SALES (corp-wide): 7.08MM **Privately Held**
Web: www.bittersweetfarms.org
SIC: 8361 2032 8052 Mentally handicapped home; Canned specialties; Intermediate care facilities

(G-15817)
DEWESOFT LLC
Also Called: Dewesoft
10730 Logan St (43571-9697)
PHONE..............................855 339-3669
Andrew Nowicki, *CEO*
EMP: 60 **EST:** 2012
SALES (est): 5.08MM **Privately Held**
Web: www.dewesoft.com
SIC: 7373 3825 Systems software development services; Instruments to measure electricity
HQ: Dewesoft D.O.O.
    Gabrsko 11a
    Trbovlje 1420

(G-15818)
GENERAL INTL PWR PDTS LLC
6243 Industrial Pkwy (43571-9594)
PHONE..............................419 877-5234
Craig Valentine, *Pr*
EMP: 26 **EST:** 2014
SALES (est): 2.56MM
SALES (corp-wide): 5.78MM **Privately Held**
Web: www.gipowerproducts.com
SIC: 3553 Woodworking machinery
PA: Dmt Holdings, Inc.
    1201 Pacific Ave Ste 600
    Tacoma WA 98402
    253 545-0015

(G-15819)
GL HELLER CO INC
6246 Industrial Pkwy (43571-9594)
PHONE..............................419 877-5122
Gary Lee Heller, *Pr*
M Jean Heller, *Sec*
EMP: 14 **EST:** 1972
SQ FT: 17,000
SALES (est): 1.02MM **Privately Held**
Web: www.glheller.com
SIC: 3599 Machine shop, jobbing and repair

(G-15820)
KWD AUTOMOTIVE INC
Also Called: Catstrap
6700 Cemetery Rd (43571-9014)
PHONE..............................419 344-8232
Thomas J Birsen, *Pr*
EMP: 6 **EST:** 2015
SALES (est): 597.74K **Privately Held**
Web: www.catstrap.net
SIC: 3714 Motor vehicle parts and accessories

(G-15821)
PROHOS INC
10755 Logan St (43571-9698)
PHONE..............................419 877-0153
William A Green, *Pr*
Joan Green, *Sec*
Kevin Green, *VP*
EMP: 9 **EST:** 1983
SQ FT: 18,000
SALES (est): 1.32MM **Privately Held**
Web: www.prohos-inc.com
SIC: 3599 Machine shop, jobbing and repair

Whitehouse - Lucas County (G-15822)　　GEOGRAPHIC SECTION

(G-15822)
PROHOS MANUFACTURING CO INC
10755 Logan St (43571-9698)
PHONE..............................419 877-0153
William Green, *Pr*
Joan Green, *Sec*
EMP: 8 **EST:** 1983
SQ FT: 18,000
SALES (est): 600K **Privately Held**
Web: www.prohos-inc.com
SIC: 3599 Machine shop, jobbing and repair

Wickliffe
Lake County

(G-15823)
ALL POINTS PRINTING INC
1330 Lloyd Rd (44092-2318)
PHONE..............................440 585-1125
Allen R Paden, *Pr*
Alan J Weber, *VP*
Catherine Weber, *Sec*
Louise Paden, *Treas*
EMP: 6 **EST:** 1954
SQ FT: 3,500
SALES (est): 454.19K **Privately Held**
SIC: 2759 2752 Letterpress printing; Offset printing

(G-15824)
AMERICAN CONTROLS INC
1340 Lloyd Rd (44092-2381)
PHONE..............................440 944-9735
▲ **EMP:** 20
SIC: 3613 8711 Control panels, electric; Electrical or electronic engineering

(G-15825)
BAR PROCESSING CORPORATION
1271 E 289th St (44092-2358)
PHONE..............................440 943-0094
Fritz Michalk, *Mgr*
EMP: 10
SALES (corp-wide): 39.93MM **Privately Held**
Web: www.barprocessingcorp.com
SIC: 3443 Process vessels, industrial: metal plate
HQ: Bar Processing Corporation
26601 W Huron River Dr
Flat Rock MI 48134
734 782-4454

(G-15826)
CASA DI VINO WINERY AND
28932 Euclid Ave (44092-2542)
PHONE..............................440 494-7878
EMP: 7 **EST:** 2017
SALES (est): 474.66K **Privately Held**
SIC: 2084 Wines

(G-15827)
CJ SALT WORLD
29149 Euclid Ave (44092-2467)
PHONE..............................440 343-5661
Clayton Williams, *Prin*
EMP: 8 **EST:** 2013
SALES (est): 132.94K **Privately Held**
SIC: 2899 Salt

(G-15828)
CLEVELAND SPECIAL TOOL INC
1351 E 286th St (44092-2505)
PHONE..............................440 944-1600
Jim Treblas, *Pr*
EMP: 21 **EST:** 1966
SQ FT: 6,000
SALES (est): 485.85K **Privately Held**
SIC: 3599 Machine shop, jobbing and repair

(G-15829)
CP CHEMICALS GROUP LP
Also Called: CP Trading Group
28960 Lakeland Blvd (44092-2370)
PHONE..............................440 833-3000
Joseph Patrick Iii, *Pr*
EMP: 14 **EST:** 2009
SALES (est): 1.21MM **Privately Held**
Web: www.cpchemicalsgroup.com
SIC: 2899 Chemical preparations, nec

(G-15830)
CUSTOM CYCLE ACC MFG DSTRG INC
29110 Anderson Rd (44092-2395)
PHONE..............................440 585-2200
Elizabeth Huntington, *Pr*
Rose Marie Parker, *VP*
EMP: 15 **EST:** 1954
SQ FT: 22,000
SALES (est): 903.86K **Privately Held**
SIC: 3751 Motorcycle accessories

(G-15831)
DSM INDUSTRIES INC
1340 E 289th St (44092-2304)
PHONE..............................440 585-1100
Scott Soble, *Pr*
▲ **EMP:** 16 **EST:** 1944
SQ FT: 106,000
SALES (est): 2.84MM **Privately Held**
Web: www.diamondshine.com
SIC: 2841 Soap: granulated, liquid, cake, flaked, or chip

(G-15832)
EUCLID SPRING CO
30006 Lakeland Blvd (44092-1745)
PHONE..............................440 943-3213
James L Marsey, *Pr*
James L Marsey, *Prin*
William J Marsey, *VP*
EMP: 22 **EST:** 1950
SQ FT: 7,000
SALES (est): 2.34MM **Privately Held**
Web: www.euclidspring.com
SIC: 3495 Wire springs

(G-15833)
GREAT LAKES CRUSHING LTD
30831 Euclid Ave (44092-1042)
PHONE..............................440 944-5500
Mark M Belich, *Managing Member*
Mark M Belich, *Genl Pt*
EMP: 60 **EST:** 1996
SQ FT: 10,000
SALES (est): 8.85MM **Privately Held**
Web: www.glcrushing.com
SIC: 7359 1623 1629 1611 Equipment rental and leasing, nec; Underground utilities contractor; Land clearing contractor; Grading

(G-15834)
HAWTHORNE TOOL LLC
1340 Lloyd Rd Ste C (44092-2381)
PHONE..............................440 516-1891
Dominic Rega, *Pr*
EMP: 10 **EST:** 2004
SALES (est): 589.75K **Privately Held**
SIC: 3544 Dies and die holders for metal cutting, forming, die casting

(G-15835)
HI TECMETAL GROUP INC (PA)
Also Called: Hydro-Vac
28910 Lakeland Blvd (44092-2321)
PHONE..............................216 881-8100
Terence Profughi, *Pr*
Cole Coe, *VP*
Gregory Hercil, *VP*
Harold Baron, *Prin*
Mary Finley, *Prin*
EMP: 20 **EST:** 1943
SALES (est): 9.44MM
SALES (corp-wide): 9.44MM **Privately Held**
Web: www.htgmetals.com
SIC: 3398 7692 Brazing (hardening) of metal ; Welding repair

(G-15836)
KERRY INC
29136 Norman Ave (44092-2341)
PHONE..............................440 229-5200
EMP: 21
Web: www.kerry.com
SIC: 2099 Food preparations, nec
HQ: Kerry Inc.
3400 Millington Rd
Beloit WI 53511
608 363-1200

(G-15837)
LINDE GAS & EQUIPMENT INC
Also Called: Praxair
1140 Lloyd Rd (44092-2314)
PHONE..............................440 944-8844
Don Mocarski, *Mgr*
EMP: 6
Web: www.lindeus.com
SIC: 2813 Industrial gases
HQ: Linde Gas & Equipment Inc.
10 Riverview Dr
Danbury CT 06810
844 445-4633

(G-15838)
LUBRIZOL HOLDINGS LLC
29400 Lakeland Blvd (44092-2201)
PHONE..............................440 943-4200
EMP: 16 **EST:** 2015
SALES (est): 3.24MM
SALES (corp-wide): 364.48B **Publicly Held**
Web: www.lubrizol.com
SIC: 2899 Chemical preparations, nec
HQ: The Lubrizol Corporation
29400 Lakeland Blvd
Wickliffe OH 44092
440 943-4200

(G-15839)
MATTEO ALUMINUM INC
1261 E 289th St (44092-2367)
PHONE..............................440 585-5213
Steve Matteo, *Pr*
EMP: 20 **EST:** 1984
SQ FT: 25,444
SALES (est): 2.22MM **Privately Held**
Web: www.matteoaluminum.com
SIC: 3444 3449 Gutters, sheet metal; Miscellaneous metalwork

(G-15840)
MULTI LAPPING SERVICE INC
30032 Lakeland Blvd (44092)
PHONE..............................440 944-7592
Donna Wohr, *Pr*
Michael Adkins, *VP*
Enos Adkins Iii, *VP*
EMP: 12 **EST:** 1972
SQ FT: 72,000
SALES (est): 439.15K **Privately Held**
SIC: 3829 Whole body counters, nuclear

(G-15841)
NOVEON FCC INC
29400 Lakeland Blvd (44092-2201)
PHONE..............................440 943-4200
▼ **EMP:** 48 **EST:** 1992
SALES (est): 5.37MM
SALES (corp-wide): 364.48B **Publicly Held**
SIC: 2869 2899 Industrial organic chemicals, nec; Chemical preparations, nec
HQ: The Lubrizol Corporation
29400 Lakeland Blvd
Wickliffe OH 44092
440 943-4200

(G-15842)
OHIO MOULDING CORPORATION (HQ)
30396 Lakeland Blvd (44092-1798)
PHONE..............................440 944-2100
▲ **EMP:** 20 **EST:** 1946
SALES (est): 42.47MM **Privately Held**
Web: www.omcoform.com
SIC: 3449 Miscellaneous metalwork
PA: Omco Holdings, Inc.
30396 Lakeland Blvd
Wickliffe OH 44092

(G-15843)
OMCO HOLDINGS INC (PA)
30396 Lakeland Blvd (44092-1748)
PHONE..............................440 944-2100
EMP: 38 **EST:** 2000
SALES (est): 55.43MM **Privately Held**
Web: www.omcoform.com
SIC: 3449 Miscellaneous metalwork

(G-15844)
P O MCINTIRE COMPANY (PA)
29191 Anderson Rd (44092-2357)
PHONE..............................440 269-1848
James Goglin, *Pr*
Scott Goglin, *
EMP: 27 **EST:** 1938
SQ FT: 12,000
SALES (est): 2.04MM
SALES (corp-wide): 2.04MM **Privately Held**
Web: www.pomcintire.com
SIC: 3545 3544 Cutting tools for machine tools; Jigs and fixtures

(G-15845)
PARKER-HANNIFIN CORPORATION
IHP Division
30240 Lakeland Blvd (44092-1797)
PHONE..............................704 637-1190
Terry Mcgee, *Brnch Mgr*
EMP: 6
SALES (corp-wide): 19.07B **Publicly Held**
Web: www.parker.com
SIC: 3052 3429 Rubber hose; Hardware, nec
PA: Parker-Hannifin Corporation
6035 Parkland Blvd
Cleveland OH 44124
216 896-3000

(G-15846)
PARKER-HANNIFIN CORPORATION
Hose Products Div
30240 Lakeland Blvd (44092-1797)
PHONE..............................440 943-5700
Lonnie Gallup, *Brnch Mgr*
EMP: 271
SQ FT: 145,000
SALES (corp-wide): 19.07B **Publicly Held**
Web: www.parker.com
SIC: 3714 3492 Motor vehicle parts and accessories; Fluid power valves and hose fittings
PA: Parker-Hannifin Corporation

6035 Parkland Blvd
Cleveland OH 44124
216 896-3000

(G-15847)
PCC CERAMIC GROUP 1
1470 E 289th St (44092-2306)
PHONE..............................440 516-3672
Daren Kennedy, *VP*
EMP: 9 **EST:** 2007
SALES (est): 511.65K **Privately Held**
Web: www.pccairfoils.com
SIC: 3253   Floor tile, ceramic

(G-15848)
PMC INDUSTRIES CORP
Also Called: A Park Ohio Company
29100 Lakeland Blvd (44092-2323)
PHONE..............................440 943-3300
Edward K Novak, *VP*
▲ **EMP:** 85 **EST:** 1912
SQ FT: 125,000
SALES (est): 28.85MM
SALES (corp-wide): 1.66B **Publicly Held**
Web: www.pmc-colinet.com
SIC: 3317   Steel pipe and tubes
HQ: Park-Ohio Industries, Inc.
   6065 Parkland Blvd
   Cleveland OH 44124
   440 947-2000

(G-15849)
PRECISION MCHNING CNNCTION LLC
Also Called: P M C
29100 Lakeland Blvd (44092-2323)
PHONE..............................440 943-3300
EMP: 10 **EST:** 1999
SALES (est): 4.54MM
SALES (corp-wide): 1.66B **Publicly Held**
SIC: 3494   Valves and pipe fittings, nec
PA: Park-Ohio Holdings Corp.
   6065 Parkland Blvd Ste 1
   Cleveland OH 44124
   440 947-2000

(G-15850)
PROFORMA PRANA
1400 Lloyd Rd Unit 472 (44092-8620)
PHONE..............................440 345-6466
David Roose, *Owner*
EMP: 7 **EST:** 2013
SALES (est): 235.92K **Privately Held**
Web: prana.proforma.com
SIC: 2752   Commercial printing, lithographic

(G-15851)
REGAL DIAMOND PRODUCTS CORP
1405 E 286th St (44092-2506)
P.O. Box 198 (44092-0198)
PHONE..............................440 944-7700
Steve Brewer, *Pr*
▼ **EMP:** 25 **EST:** 1958
SQ FT: 16,500
SALES (est): 2.57MM **Privately Held**
Web: www.regaldiamond.com
SIC: 3291 3545 3425   Abrasive wheels and grindstones, not artificial; Cutting tools for machine tools; Saw blades and handsaws

(G-15852)
RESEARCH ABRASIVE PRODUCTS INC
1400 E 286th St (44092-2507)
PHONE..............................440 944-3200
Ken Dixon Senior, *Pr*
Ken Dixon Junior, *VP*
Margaret Tripp, *
EMP: 40 **EST:** 1971
SQ FT: 32,000
SALES (est): 2.7MM **Privately Held**
Web: www.researchabrasive.com
SIC: 3291   Wheels, abrasive

(G-15853)
THE LUBRIZOL CORPORATION (HQ)
Also Called: Lubricant Additives
29400 Lakeland Blvd (44092)
PHONE..............................440 943-4200
Rebecca Liebert, *Pr*
Deb Langer, *
Jason Sussman, *CLO**
◆ **EMP:** 1300 **EST:** 1928
SALES (est): 1.02B
SALES (corp-wide): 364.48B **Publicly Held**
Web: www.lubrizol.com
SIC: 2899 2869   Oil treating compounds; Industrial organic chemicals, nec
PA: Berkshire Hathaway Inc.
   3555 Farnam St Ste 1440
   Omaha NE 68131
   402 346-1400

(G-15854)
THERMAL TREATMENT CENTER INC (HQ)
Also Called: Nettleton Steel Treating Div
28910 Lakeland Blvd (44092-2321)
PHONE..............................216 881-8100
Carmen Paponitti, *Pr*
Jack Luck, *
Louise Profughi, *
EMP: 35 **EST:** 1945
SALES (est): 7.97MM
SALES (corp-wide): 9.44MM **Privately Held**
Web: www.htgmetals.com
SIC: 3398 8711   Metal heat treating; Engineering services
PA: Hi Tecmetal Group, Inc.
   28910 Lakeland Blvd
   Wickliffe OH 44092
   216 881-8100

(G-15855)
TRULINE INDUSTRIES INC
1400 Silver St (44092-1944)
P.O. Box 227 (44092-0227)
PHONE..............................440 729-0140
Court Durkalski, *CEO*
Frank Durkalski, *
Stuart Watson, *
Joan Durkalski, *
EMP: 52 **EST:** 1939
SQ FT: 24,000
SALES (est): 9.55MM **Privately Held**
Web: www.trulineind.com
SIC: 3728   Aircraft parts and equipment, nec

(G-15856)
UNITED HYDRAULICS
29627 Lakeland Blvd (44092-2203)
P.O. Box 17 (44092-0017)
PHONE..............................440 585-0906
John Birkic, *Pr*
EMP: 8 **EST:** 2002
SALES (est): 247.81K **Privately Held**
Web: www.unitedhyd.com
SIC: 3593 5084   Fluid power cylinders, hydraulic or pneumatic; Industrial machinery and equipment

(G-15857)
UNIVERSAL METAL PRODUCTS INC (PA)
Also Called: Hercules
29980 Lakeland Blvd (44092-1744)
P.O. Box 130 (44092-0130)
PHONE..............................440 943-3040
Hugh S Seaholm, *CEO*
▲ **EMP:** 140 **EST:** 1946
SQ FT: 15,000
SALES (est): 47.27MM
SALES (corp-wide): 47.27MM **Privately Held**
Web: www.universalmetalproducts.com
SIC: 3469   Stamping metal for the trade

(G-15858)
USM PRECISION PRODUCTS INC
Also Called: U S M
1340 Lloyd Rd Ste D (44092-2381)
PHONE..............................440 975-8600
EMP: 100
SIC: 3451   Screw machine products

Willard
Huron County

(G-15859)
GUARDIAN MANUFACTURING CO LLC
Also Called: Guardian Gloves
302 S Conwell Ave (44890-9525)
PHONE..............................419 933-2711
Gene Lamoreaux, *Pr*
Ron Vanderpool, *
▲ **EMP:** 25 **EST:** 1993
SQ FT: 100,000
SALES (est): 4.9MM **Privately Held**
Web: www.guardian-mfg.com
SIC: 3069 3842   Medical and laboratory rubber sundries and related products; Surgical appliances and supplies

(G-15860)
LSC COMMUNICATIONS INC
Also Called: Manufacturing Division
1145 S Conwell Ave (44890-9392)
PHONE..............................419 935-0111
Robert Gospodarek, *Mgr*
EMP: 980
SALES (corp-wide): 8.23B **Privately Held**
Web: www.lsccom.com
SIC: 2741 2732 2759 2752   Directories, nec: publishing and printing; Books, printing only ; Commercial printing, nec; Commercial printing, lithographic
HQ: Lsc Communications, Inc.
   4101 Winfield Rd
   Warrenville IL 60555
   844 572-5720

(G-15861)
MTD PRODUCTS INC
810 Theo Moll Dr (44890-9293)
PHONE..............................419 951-9779
EMP: 9
SALES (corp-wide): 15.78B **Publicly Held**
Web: www.mtdparts.com
SIC: 3524   Lawn and garden equipment
HQ: Mtd Products Inc
   5965 Grafton Rd
   Valley City OH 44280
   330 225-2600

(G-15862)
MTD PRODUCTS INC
Midwest Industries
979 S Conwell Ave (44890-9301)
PHONE..............................419 935-6611
Rob Fox, *Genl Mgr*
EMP: 800
SQ FT: 480,000
SALES (corp-wide): 15.78B **Publicly Held**
Web: www.mtdparts.com
SIC: 3524   Lawn and garden mowers and accessories
HQ: Mtd Products Inc
   5965 Grafton Rd
   Valley City OH 44280
   330 225-2600

(G-15863)
PEPPERIDGE FARM INCORPORATED
3320 State Route 103 E (44890-9777)
PHONE..............................419 933-2611
George Litvak, *Brnch Mgr*
EMP: 9
SALES (corp-wide): 9.36B **Publicly Held**
Web: www.pepperidgefarm.com
SIC: 5461 2052 2099 2053   Retail bakeries; Cookies; Bread crumbs, except made in bakeries; Frozen bakery products, except bread
HQ: Pepperidge Farm, Incorporated
   1 Campbell Pl
   Camden NJ 08103
   800 257-8443

Williamsburg
Clermont County

(G-15864)
DUALITE INC (PA)
1 Dualite Ln (45176-1121)
PHONE..............................513 724-7100
▲ **EMP:** 230 **EST:** 1947
SALES (est): 27.92MM
SALES (corp-wide): 27.92MM **Privately Held**
Web: www.dualite.com
SIC: 3993   Signs and advertising specialties

(G-15865)
G & L MACHINING INC
299 N 3rd St (45176-8101)
PHONE..............................513 724-2600
Gary Abrams, *Pr*
Leslie Abrams, *VP*
EMP: 8 **EST:** 1997
SQ FT: 4,000
SALES (est): 658.65K **Privately Held**
Web: www.glmachining.com
SIC: 3599   Machine shop, jobbing and repair

(G-15866)
NEWBERRY SHEET METAL LLC
5405 State Route 133 (45176-9006)
PHONE..............................513 807-7385
Douglas Newberry, *Prin*
EMP: 6 **EST:** 2019
SALES (est): 158.75K **Privately Held**
SIC: 3444   Sheet metalwork

(G-15867)
W&W ROCK SAND AND GRAVEL
1451 Maple Grove Rd (45176-9636)
P.O. Box 640 (45176-0640)
PHONE..............................513 266-3708
Rick A Wuebold, *Prin*
EMP: 6 **EST:** 2009
SALES (est): 222.64K **Privately Held**
SIC: 1442   Construction sand and gravel

Williamsfield
Ashtabula County

(G-15868)
CBR EXPRESS LLC
7737 Shady Ln (44093-9605)
PHONE..............................440 293-4744
EMP: 6 **EST:** 2004
SALES (est): 24.7K **Privately Held**
SIC: 2741   Miscellaneous publishing

Williamsport - Pickaway County (G-15869)   GEOGRAPHIC SECTION

Williamsport
Pickaway County

(G-15869)
ROOF TO ROAD LLC
27910 Chillicothe Pike (43164-9654)
PHONE...............................740 986-6923
Stephen Johnson, *Managing Member*
Slyvia Johnson, *Asst Sec*
EMP: 7 **EST:** 2002
SALES (est): 863.82K **Privately Held**
SIC: 2951 Road materials, bituminous (not from refineries)

Williston
Ottawa County

(G-15870)
DURIVAGE PATTERN AND MFG INC
20522 State Route 579 W (43468)
P.O. Box 337 (43468-0337)
PHONE...............................419 836-8655
Gary Durivage, *Pr*
Larry Durivage, *
Ron Miller, *
Gretchen Durivage, *
EMP: 21 **EST:** 1969
SQ FT: 24,000
SALES (est): 369.58K **Privately Held**
Web: www.durivagepattern.com
SIC: 3469 3544 3369 3365 Patterns on metal ; Industrial molds; Nonferrous foundries, nec ; Aluminum foundries

Willoughby
Lake County

(G-15871)
2E ASSOCIATES INC
38363 Airport Pkwy (44094-7562)
PHONE...............................440 975-9955
Kevin Ensinger, *Pr*
James L Ensinger, *
Donnell Ensinger, *
Harry Cook, *
Lewis E Janek, *
EMP: 25 **EST:** 1929
SQ FT: 48,000
SALES (est): 9.75MM **Privately Held**
Web: www.power-packconveyor.com
SIC: 5084 3531 3535 Industrial machinery and equipment; Road construction and maintenance machinery; Unit handling conveying systems

(G-15872)
A M D
4580 Beidler Rd (44094-4602)
PHONE...............................440 918-8930
Mike Bollas, *Mgr*
EMP: 6 **EST:** 2009
SALES (est): 118.12K **Privately Held**
SIC: 3674 Integrated circuits, semiconductor networks, etc.

(G-15873)
ACE GRINDING CO INC
37518 N Industrial Pkwy (44094-6279)
PHONE...............................440 951-6760
Brian Danolfo, *Pr*
EMP: 6 **EST:** 1956
SQ FT: 12,000
SALES (est): 529.14K **Privately Held**
Web: www.acegrinding.com
SIC: 3599 Machine shop, jobbing and repair

(G-15874)
ADVANCED RV LLC
4590 Hamann Pkwy (44094-5630)
PHONE...............................440 283-0405
Mike Neundorfer, *Pr*
EMP: 25 **EST:** 2012
SALES (est): 2.85MM **Privately Held**
Web: www.advanced-rv.com
SIC: 3716 7519 7532 Motor homes; Motor home rental; Mobile home and trailer repair

(G-15875)
AMD FABRICATORS INC
4580 Beidler Rd (44094-4602)
PHONE...............................440 946-8855
Michael Watts, *Pr*
EMP: 36 **EST:** 1986
SQ FT: 50,000
SALES (est): 2.41MM **Privately Held**
SIC: 3444 Sheet metalwork

(G-15876)
AMETCO MANUFACTURING CORP
4326 Hamann Pkwy (44094-5626)
P.O. Box 1210 (44096-1210)
PHONE...............................440 951-4300
Steve G Mitrovich, *Pr*
Greg Mitrovich, *
Rona Mitrovich, *
▲ **EMP:** 38 **EST:** 1966
SQ FT: 85,000
SALES (est): 8.72MM **Privately Held**
Web: www.ametco.com
SIC: 3441 3496 Fabricated structural metal; Miscellaneous fabricated wire products

(G-15877)
AMFM INC
Also Called: Omegaone
38373 Pelton Rd (44094-7719)
PHONE...............................440 953-4545
John Ducharme, *Pr*
▲ **EMP:** 18 **EST:** 1987
SALES (est): 3.91MM
SALES (corp-wide): 1.26B **Privately Held**
Web: www.omega1.com
SIC: 3492 Fluid power valves and hose fittings
HQ: Shf, Inc.
  4861 S Sam Houston Pkwy E
  Houston TX 77048
  832 456-2000

(G-15878)
ANDERSON BROTHERS ENTPS INC
38180 Airport Pkwy (44094-8021)
PHONE...............................440 269-3920
H W Domeck, *Pr*
Tenneth Anderson, *Pr*
Theresa Inman, *Contrlr*
EMP: 20 **EST:** 1945
SQ FT: 52,000
SALES (est): 3.17MM
SALES (corp-wide): 51.18MM **Privately Held**
Web: www.paisleyfarmfoods.com
SIC: 2035 Pickles, sauces, and salad dressings
PA: The Fremont Company
  802 N Front St
  Fremont OH 43420
  419 334-8995

(G-15879)
API PATTERN WORKS INC
4456 Hamann Pkwy (44094-5628)
PHONE...............................440 269-1766
Jesse Baden, *Pr*
Michael Scanlon, *
EMP: 31 **EST:** 1997
SQ FT: 20,000
SALES (est): 3.63MM **Privately Held**
Web: www.olympusaero.com
SIC: 3543 Industrial patterns

(G-15880)
APOLLO PRODUCTS INC
4456 Hamann Pkwy (44094-5628)
PHONE...............................440 269-8551
EMP: 15 **EST:** 1994
SQ FT: 5,000
SALES (est): 2.48MM **Privately Held**
Web: www.olympusaero.com
SIC: 3544 3545 Special dies and tools; Machine tool accessories

(G-15881)
APOLLO WELDING & FABG INC (PA)
35600 Curtis Blvd (44095-4109)
PHONE...............................440 942-0227
John Ivan Turkalj, *Pr*
Doug Barth, *VP*
Mary Turkalj, *Sec*
EMP: 20 **EST:** 1987
SQ FT: 25,000
SALES (est): 2.29MM
SALES (corp-wide): 2.29MM **Privately Held**
Web: www.apollowelding.com
SIC: 7692 Welding repair

(G-15882)
APPLIED CONCEPTS INC
Also Called: Applied Bingo Mate
36445 Biltmore Pl Ste E (44094-8228)
PHONE...............................440 229-5033
John Adams, *Pr*
Tom Marzella, *VP*
John Q Adams, *Sec*
EMP: 11 **EST:** 1978
SQ FT: 3,000
SALES (est): 482.63K **Privately Held**
Web: www.electronicbingo.com
SIC: 3944 Electronic game machines, except coin-operated

(G-15883)
APR TOOL INC
4712 Beidler Rd Ste A (44094-4604)
PHONE...............................440 946-0393
Robert Zietz, *Pr*
John Zeitz, *VP*
EMP: 9 **EST:** 1974
SQ FT: 3,200
SALES (est): 977.52K **Privately Held**
Web: www.aprtool.com
SIC: 3599 3544 Machine shop, jobbing and repair; Dies and die holders for metal cutting, forming, die casting

(G-15884)
AQUA LILY PRODUCTS LLC
4505 Beidler Rd (44094-4646)
PHONE...............................951 322-0981
EMP: 8
SALES (corp-wide): 4.62MM **Privately Held**
Web: www.aqualilypad.com
SIC: 3086 Padding, foamed plastics
PA: Aqua Lily Products, Llc
  1806 Conant St
  Elkhart IN 46516
  951 246-9610

(G-15885)
AQUENT STUDIOS
33433 Curtis Blvd (44095-4457)
PHONE...............................216 266-7551
Dave Puette, *Mgr*
EMP: 13 **EST:** 2016
SALES (est): 124.35K **Privately Held**
Web: www.aquent.com

SIC: 2741 Miscellaneous publishing

(G-15886)
ARTISTIC FINISHES INC
38357 Apollo Pkwy (44094)
PHONE...............................440 951-7850
Michael Credico, *Pr*
Robert Fine, *VP*
Bonnie Credico, *Sec*
EMP: 14 **EST:** 1977
SALES (est): 627.65K **Privately Held**
Web: www.artisticfinishes.com
SIC: 2541 2511 Store fixtures, wood; Wood household furniture

(G-15887)
ASKAR PRODUCTIVE RESOURCES LLC
Also Called: Apr Tool
4712a Beidler Rd (44094-4604)
PHONE...............................440 946-0393
Anees Alnaseri, *Managing Member*
EMP: 6 **EST:** 2012
SALES (est): 337.87K **Privately Held**
Web: www.aprtool.com
SIC: 3714 3312 Motor vehicle transmissions, drive assemblies, and parts; Tool and die steel

(G-15888)
B V GRINDING MACHINING INC
1438 E 363rd St (44095-4136)
PHONE...............................440 918-1884
Ivica Ivan Begovic, *Pr*
EMP: 8 **EST:** 1999
SALES (est): 587.14K **Privately Held**
SIC: 3541 Grinding machines, metalworking

(G-15889)
BESCAST INC
4600 E 355th St (44094-4699)
PHONE...............................440 946-5300
Russ Gallagher, *VP*
John W Gallagher, *
Tim Brown, *
David M Brown, *
▲ **EMP:** 170 **EST:** 1945
SQ FT: 85,000
SALES (est): 24.72MM **Privately Held**
Web: www.bescast.com
SIC: 3324 Aerospace investment castings, ferrous

(G-15890)
BIS PRINTING
35401 Euclid Ave (44094-4557)
PHONE...............................440 951-2606
Tom Sturnilo, *Owner*
EMP: 6 **EST:** 2013
SALES (est): 102.5K **Privately Held**
SIC: 2752 Offset printing

(G-15891)
BOWDEN MANUFACTURING CORP
4590 Beidler Rd (44094-4682)
PHONE...............................440 946-1770
EMP: 45 **EST:** 1952
SALES (est): 9.31MM **Privately Held**
Web: www.bowdenmfg.com
SIC: 3599 3841 3714 3561 Machine shop, jobbing and repair; Surgical and medical instruments; Motor vehicle parts and accessories; Pumps and pumping equipment

(G-15892)
BRANDTS CANDIES INC
1238 Lost Nation Rd (44094-7325)
PHONE...............................440 942-1016
Theodore Prindle, *Pr*

GEOGRAPHIC SECTION

Willoughby - Lake County (G-15916)

EMP: 7 **EST:** 1948
SQ FT: 3,000
SALES (est): 448.13K **Privately Held**
Web: www.brandtschocolates.com
SIC: 5441 2066 Candy; Chocolate and cocoa products

(G-15893)
BRIGHTGUY INC
38205b Stevens Blvd (44094-6239)
PHONE................................440 942-8318
Gregory Atwell, *Pr*
Tina Fram, *S&M/VP*
EMP: 6 **EST:** 1998
SALES (est): 945.25K **Privately Held**
Web: www.brightguy.com
SIC: 3648 Lighting equipment, nec

(G-15894)
BRONCO MACHINE INC
38411 Apollo Pkwy (44094-7725)
PHONE................................440 951-5015
Michael Bronaka, *Pr*
Ann Turpin, *VP*
Diana Bronaka, *Treas*
EMP: 10 **EST:** 1962
SQ FT: 6,000
SALES (est): 1.02MM **Privately Held**
Web: www.broncomachine.com
SIC: 3599 Machine shop, jobbing and repair

(G-15895)
BULLSEYE DART SHOPPE INC
Also Called: Bullseye
950c Erie Rd (44095-1811)
PHONE................................440 951-9277
Thomas Nazarak, *Pr*
▲ **EMP:** 8 **EST:** 1983
SQ FT: 14,000
SALES (est): 471.09K **Privately Held**
SIC: 3949 Billiard and pool equipment and supplies, general

(G-15896)
CARBIDE SPECIALIST INC
36430 Reading Ave Ste 10 (44094-8220)
PHONE................................440 951-4027
Ray Northern, *Pr*
Naomi Northern, *Sec*
EMP: 10 **EST:** 1985
SALES (est): 503.05K **Privately Held**
Web: www.carbidespecialists.com
SIC: 3544 Wire drawing and straightening dies

(G-15897)
CAST NYLONS CO LTD (PA)
Also Called: Cast Nylons
4300 Hamann Pkwy (44094-5626)
P.O. Box 901507 (44094)
PHONE................................440 269-2300
EMP: 70 **EST:** 1979
SALES (est): 14.49MM
SALES (corp-wide): 14.49MM **Privately Held**
Web: www.castnylon.com
SIC: 2824 Nylon fibers

(G-15898)
CENTRAL COCA-COLA BTLG CO INC
Also Called: Coca-Cola
4800 E 355th St (44094-4634)
PHONE................................440 269-1433
EMP: 34
SALES (corp-wide): 45.75B **Publicly Held**
Web: www.coca-cola.com
SIC: 2086 Bottled and canned soft drinks
HQ: Central Coca-Cola Bottling Company, Inc.
555 Taxter Rd Ste 550
Elmsford NY 10523
914 789-1100

(G-15899)
CHIPS MANUFACTURING INC
35720 Lakeland Blvd (44095-5307)
PHONE................................440 946-3666
Frank Cipriano, *Pr*
EMP: 9 **EST:** 1991
SQ FT: 7,200
SALES (est): 722.3K **Privately Held**
SIC: 3599 Machine shop, jobbing and repair

(G-15900)
COMMERCIAL ANODIZING CO
38387 Apollo Pkwy (44094-7791)
PHONE................................440 942-8384
Mark S Swetel, *Pr*
Shirley Swetel, *Sec*
EMP: 24 **EST:** 1963
SQ FT: 20,000
SALES (est): 990.24K **Privately Held**
SIC: 3471 Anodizing (plating) of metals or formed products

(G-15901)
CONN-SELMER INC
Also Called: Eastlake Mfg Facility
34199 Curtis Blvd (44095-4008)
PHONE................................440 946-6100
Robert Stone, *Mgr*
EMP: 100
SQ FT: 140,000
SALES (corp-wide): 528.25MM **Privately Held**
Web: www.connselmer.com
SIC: 3931 Guitars and parts, electric and nonelectric
HQ: Conn-Selmer, Inc.
600 Industrial Pkwy
Elkhart IN 46516
574 522-1675

(G-15902)
CONTECH MANUFACTURIG INC
38134 Western Pkwy (44094-8094)
PHONE................................440 946-3322
Edsel Lauer, *Brnch Mgr*
EMP: 7 **EST:** 2016
SALES (est): 420.86K **Privately Held**
Web: www.ctmmixers.com
SIC: 3713 Truck bodies and parts

(G-15903)
CORTEST INC (PA)
Also Called: Cortest
38322 Apollo Pkwy (44094-7724)
PHONE................................440 942-1235
Allen F Denzine, *Pr*
Marsha Denzine, *Sec*
EMP: 10 **EST:** 1977
SQ FT: 10,000
SALES (est): 2.36MM
SALES (corp-wide): 2.36MM **Privately Held**
Web: www.cortest.com
SIC: 3821 5084 Laboratory apparatus and furniture; Industrial machinery and equipment

(G-15904)
COUNTY OF LAKE
Also Called: Lake Cnty Dprtmntal Rtrdtion D
2100 Joseph Lloyd Pkwy (44094-8032)
PHONE................................440 269-2193
Gary Metelko, *Dir*
EMP: 12
SALES (corp-wide): 219.71MM **Privately Held**
Web: www.lakecountyohio.gov
SIC: 8322 8331 3441 Individual and family services; Job training and related services; Fabricated structural metal
PA: County Of Lake

8 N State St Ste 215
Painesville OH 44077
440 350-2500

(G-15905)
D&D QUALITY MACHINING CO INC
36495 Reading Ave Ste 1 (44094-8243)
PHONE................................440 942-2772
EMP: 11 **EST:** 1993
SALES (est): 447.33K **Privately Held**
Web: www.ddqualitymachining.com
SIC: 3599 Machine shop, jobbing and repair

(G-15906)
DAI CERAMICS LLC
38240 Airport Pkwy (44094-8023)
PHONE................................440 946-6964
Richard Ruggerio, *Pr*
EMP: 65 **EST:** 1986
SQ FT: 40,000
SALES (est): 12.28MM
SALES (corp-wide): 2.67MM **Privately Held**
Web: www.daiceramics.com
SIC: 3253 Ceramic wall and floor tile
HQ: Ceramtec North America Llc
1 Technology Pl
Laurens SC 29360
864 682-3215

(G-15907)
DEMILTA SAND AND GRAVEL INC
921 Erie Rd (44095-1812)
PHONE................................440 942-2015
Nick De Milta, *Pr*
Joe De Milta, *VP*
EMP: 20 **EST:** 1979
SQ FT: 1,800
SALES (est): 539.3K **Privately Held**
Web: www.demiltasand.com
SIC: 1442 4212 Common sand mining; Local trucking, without storage

(G-15908)
DM MACHINE CO
38338 Apollo Pkwy Ste 1a (44094-7770)
PHONE................................440 946-0771
Duane Mcintire, *Pr*
Michael Mcintire, *VP*
Dennis Mcintire, *Sec*
EMP: 8 **EST:** 1973
SQ FT: 9,200
SALES (est): 585.74K **Privately Held**
SIC: 3599 Machine shop, jobbing and repair

(G-15909)
DMI MANUFACTURING INC
4780 Beidler Rd (44094-4604)
PHONE................................440 975-8645
EMP: 10 **EST:** 2019
SALES (est): 716K **Privately Held**
Web: www.dmiparts.com
SIC: 3433 Heating equipment, except electric

(G-15910)
DMS INC
37121 Euclid Ave Ste 1 (44094-5671)
PHONE................................440 951-9838
Ben Ulrich, *Pr*
Al Pasquale, *VP*
◆ **EMP:** 105 **EST:** 1976
SQ FT: 1,800
SALES (est): 4.21MM **Privately Held**
SIC: 8742 8711 3316 Management consulting services; Engineering services; Cold finishing of steel shapes

(G-15911)
DUKE GRAPHICS INC
Also Called: Duke Printing

33212 Lakeland Blvd (44095-5205)
PHONE................................440 946-0606
Blake A Leduc, *Pr*
Thomas Chubb, *
EMP: 33 **EST:** 1974
SQ FT: 24,000
SALES (est): 4.67MM **Privately Held**
Web: www.dukeprint.com
SIC: 2752 Offset printing

(G-15912)
DUKE MANUFACTURING INC
38205 Western Pkwy (44094-7591)
PHONE................................440 942-6537
Jeff Newmark, *Pr*
Robert Zaucha, *
▲ **EMP:** 46 **EST:** 1967
SQ FT: 18,000
SALES (est): 5.14MM **Privately Held**
Web: www.duke-mfg.com
SIC: 3599 Machine shop, jobbing and repair

(G-15913)
DYOUNG ENTERPRISE INC
Also Called: Budzar Industries
38241 Willoughby Pkwy (44094-7582)
PHONE................................440 918-0505
Charles Kenyon, *Pr*
Joel Maganza, *
▲ **EMP:** 110 **EST:** 1976
SQ FT: 50,000
SALES (est): 26.31MM **Privately Held**
SIC: 3585 3822 3823 3634 Refrigeration and heating equipment; Environmental controls; Temperature instruments: industrial process type; Electric housewares and fans

(G-15914)
EAGLE WELDING & FABG INC
Also Called: Eagle Welding
1766 Joseph Lloyd Pkwy (44094-8028)
PHONE................................440 946-0692
Mareo Paulic, *Pr*
Nick Paulic, *VP*
Milan Paulic, *Treas*
William Schwenner, *Sec*
EMP: 20 **EST:** 1988
SQ FT: 15,500
SALES (est): 2.29MM **Privately Held**
Web: www.eagle-welding.com
SIC: 3443 3699 7692 3444 Fabricated plate work (boiler shop); Laser systems and equipment; Welding repair; Sheet metalwork

(G-15915)
EASTLAKE MACHINE PRODUCTS LLC
1956 Joseph Lloyd Pkwy (44094-8030)
PHONE................................440 953-1014
Ivan Saric, *Pr*
Richard Moroscak, *
Sandra Saric, *
EMP: 16 **EST:** 1980
SQ FT: 14,000
SALES (est): 988.92K **Privately Held**
SIC: 3599 3451 Machine shop, jobbing and repair; Screw machine products

(G-15916)
EATON CORPORATION
Eastlake Office
34899 Curtis Blvd (44095-4002)
PHONE................................216 523-5000
Doug Koch, *Mgr*
EMP: 13
Web: www.dix-eaton.com
SIC: 3714 5084 Hydraulic fluid power pumps, for auto steering mechanism; Hydraulic systems equipment and supplies
HQ: Eaton Corporation
1000 Eaton Blvd

Willoughby - Lake County (G-15917)

Cleveland OH 44122
440 523-5000

(G-15917)
ERICSON MANUFACTURING CO
4323 Hamann Pkwy (44094-5625)
PHONE..................................440 951-8000
John Ericson Iii, *Pr*
◆ **EMP:** 94 **EST:** 1918
SQ FT: 25,000
SALES (est): 39.39MM **Privately Held**
Web: www.ericson.com
SIC: 3643 3648 Electric connectors; Lighting equipment, nec

(G-15918)
EUCLID DESIGN AND MFG INC
38333 Willoughby Pkwy (44094-7585)
PHONE..................................440 942-0066
Don Nemeth, *Pr*
EMP: 10 **EST:** 1972
SQ FT: 8,000
SALES (est): 902.3K **Privately Held**
SIC: 3544 Special dies and tools

(G-15919)
FAITH TOOL & MANUFACTURING
36575 Reading Ave (44094-8210)
PHONE..................................440 951-5934
Robert Levak, *Prin*
Donna Levak, *VP*
EMP: 8 **EST:** 1976
SALES (est): 820.91K **Privately Held**
Web: www.ftmeng.com
SIC: 3544 Special dies and tools

(G-15920)
FEEDALL INC
38379 Pelton Rd (44094-7719)
PHONE..................................440 942-8100
Roger W Winslow Junior, *Pr*
Michael J O'brien, *Sec*
EMP: 12 **EST:** 1946
SQ FT: 15,300
SALES (est): 2.73MM **Privately Held**
Web: www.feedall.com
SIC: 3535 3545 Conveyors and conveying equipment; Hopper feed devices

(G-15921)
FIRST MACHINE & TOOL CORP
38181 Airport Pkwy (44094-8038)
PHONE..................................440 269-8644
Mladen Laush, *Pr*
Herman Lackner, *VP*
EMP: 14 **EST:** 1982
SQ FT: 5,600
SALES (est): 993.1K **Privately Held**
Web: www.firstmachinegages.com
SIC: 3544 Special dies and tools

(G-15922)
FUSION INCORPORATED (PA)
4658 E 355th St (44094-4630)
PHONE..................................440 946-3300
▲ **EMP:** 85 **EST:** 1932
SALES (est): 9.29MM
SALES (corp-wide): 9.29MM **Privately Held**
Web: www.fusion-inc.com
SIC: 3548 3356 3398 3341 Soldering equipment, except hand soldering irons; Solder: wire, bar, acid core, and rosin core; Metal heat treating; Secondary nonferrous metals

(G-15923)
G-M-I INC
4822 E 355th St (44094-4634)
PHONE..................................440 953-8811
Donald J Restly, *Pr*
Carol L Restly, *Sec*
EMP: 9 **EST:** 1979
SQ FT: 9,200
SALES (est): 816.03K **Privately Held**
Web: www.gmigaskets.com
SIC: 3053 Gaskets, all materials

(G-15924)
GEARTEC INC
4245 Hamann Pkwy (44094-5623)
PHONE..................................440 953-3900
▲ **EMP:** 26 **EST:** 2011
SQ FT: 35,000
SALES (est): 5.74MM
SALES (corp-wide): 334.72MM **Privately Held**
Web: www.geartec.com
SIC: 3566 Gears, power transmission, except auto
HQ: The Electric Materials Company
50 S Washington St
North East PA 16428
814 725-9621

(G-15925)
GENERAL PRECISION CORPORATION
4553 Beidler Rd (44094-4646)
PHONE..................................440 951-9380
Allen Ernst, *Pr*
EMP: 7 **EST:** 1972
SALES (est): 628.46K **Privately Held**
Web: www.generalprecisioncorp.com
SIC: 8711 3365 Engineering services; Machinery castings, aluminum

(G-15926)
GOOD FORTUNES INC
1486 E 361st St (44095-3174)
P.O. Box 43419 (44143-0419)
PHONE..................................440 942-2888
Gene Yee, *Pr*
Yuet Yee, *Prin*
EMP: 9 **EST:** 1981
SQ FT: 5,000
SALES (est): 292.39K **Privately Held**
Web: www.goodfortunecookies.com
SIC: 2052 Bakery products, dry

(G-15927)
HEISLER TOOL COMPANY
38228 Western Pkwy (44094-7590)
PHONE..................................440 951-2424
Timothy M Mccord, *Pr*
Susan Mccord, *VP*
EMP: 15 **EST:** 1986
SQ FT: 22,000
SALES (est): 2.15MM **Privately Held**
Web: www.heislertool.com
SIC: 3599 3549 Custom machinery; Metalworking machinery, nec

(G-15928)
HEY 9 INC
7794 Eagle Creek Ct (44094-9783)
PHONE..................................919 259-2884
EMP: 8 **EST:** 2017
SALES (est): 72K **Privately Held**
SIC: 3429 Hardware, nec

(G-15929)
HUDCO MANUFACTURING INC
38250 Western Pkwy (44094-7590)
PHONE..................................440 951-4040
Donald M Hudak, *Pr*
Joan L Hudak, *Sec*
▲ **EMP:** 8 **EST:** 1981
SQ FT: 6,000
SALES (est): 746.68K **Privately Held**
Web: www.hudcomfg.com
SIC: 3531 Rock crushing machinery, portable

(G-15930)
IDENTIPHOTO CO LTD
1810 Joseph Lloyd Pkwy (44094-8042)
PHONE..................................440 306-9000
▲ **EMP:** 17 **EST:** 1971
SALES (est): 4.13MM **Privately Held**
Web: www.identiphoto.com
SIC: 5043 5045 3999 Photographic equipment and supplies; Computers, peripherals, and software; Identification badges and insignia

(G-15931)
IMAGING SCIENCES LLC
38174 Willoughby Pkwy (44094-7580)
PHONE..................................440 975-9640
Geoffrey R Brown, *Pr*
Geoffrey Brown, *Pr*
EMP: 9 **EST:** 2003
SQ FT: 18,000
SALES (est): 908.49K **Privately Held**
Web: www.imaging-sciences.com
SIC: 3211 Construction glass

(G-15932)
INTEGRA ENCLOSURES INC (PA)
Also Called: Integra
7750 Pyler Blvd (44094)
P.O. Box 1870 (44061-1870)
PHONE..................................440 269-4966
Jim Mcwilliams, *Pr*
EMP: 8 **EST:** 2000
SQ FT: 30,000
SALES (est): 1.86MM
SALES (corp-wide): 1.86MM **Privately Held**
Web: www.integraenclosures.com
SIC: 3089 Injection molding of plastics

(G-15933)
INTELITOOL MFG SVCS INC
36335 Reading Ave Ste 4 (44094-8200)
PHONE..................................440 953-1071
Gary Struna, *Pr*
William Tulloch, *Sr VP*
EMP: 6 **EST:** 1994
SQ FT: 10,500
SALES (est): 506.62K **Privately Held**
Web: www.intelitoolinc.com
SIC: 3544 Special dies and tools

(G-15934)
INTERLAKE STAMPING OHIO INC
4732 E 355th St (44094-4632)
PHONE..................................440 942-0800
Lisa M Habe, *Pr*
Dan Valentino, *
Mark Groenstein, *
Liz Tolbert, *
EMP: 40 **EST:** 1957
SQ FT: 36,000
SALES (est): 8.79MM
SALES (corp-wide): 24.2MM **Privately Held**
Web: www.interlakestamping.com
SIC: 3469 Stamping metal for the trade
PA: Interlake Industries, Inc.
4732 E 355th St
Willoughby OH 44094
440 942-0800

(G-15935)
JOURNAL REGISTER COMPANY
Journal, The
36625 Vine St (44094-6367)
PHONE..................................440 951-0000
Stephen Roszczyk, *Prin*
EMP: 208
SALES (corp-wide): 293.08MM **Privately Held**
Web: www.journalregisteroffset.com
SIC: 2711 Newspapers, publishing and printing
PA: Journal Register Company
5 Hanover Sq Fl 25
New York NY 10004
212 257-7212

(G-15936)
KALCOR COATINGS COMPANY
37721 Stevens Blvd (44094-6231)
PHONE..................................440 946-4700
Cori Zucker, *Pr*
Don Mihalik, *
Kal Zucker, *CIO**
▲ **EMP:** 25 **EST:** 1961
SQ FT: 55,000
SALES (est): 6.54MM **Privately Held**
Web: www.kalcor.com
SIC: 2851 Paints and paint additives

(G-15937)
KEB INDUSTRIES INC
2166 Joseph Lloyd Pkwy (44094-8032)
PHONE..................................440 953-4623
Brad Butler, *Pr*
EMP: 8 **EST:** 2003
SQ FT: 6,500
SALES (est): 917.72K **Privately Held**
Web: www.kebkollets.com
SIC: 3545 Precision tools, machinists'

(G-15938)
KELLY ARSPC THRMAL SYSTEMS LLC
Also Called: Kaps
1625 Lost Nation Rd (44094-8189)
PHONE..................................440 951-4744
Kent Kelly, *
EMP: 28 **EST:** 2005
SALES (est): 2.61MM **Privately Held**
Web: www.kellyaero.com
SIC: 3728 Aircraft parts and equipment, nec
PA: Tailwind Technologies Inc.
1 Propeller Pl
Piqua OH 45356

(G-15939)
KENNEDY GROUP INCORPORATED (PA)
38601 Kennedy Pkwy (44094-7395)
PHONE..................................440 951-7660
Bertram Kennedy, *CEO*
Michael R Kennedy, *
Mary Lou Kennedy, *
Patrick Kennedy, *
Todd Kennedy, *
▲ **EMP:** 83 **EST:** 1974
SQ FT: 80,000
SALES (est): 27.48MM
SALES (corp-wide): 27.48MM **Privately Held**
Web: www.kennedygrp.com
SIC: 2679 2673 3089 3565 Tags and labels, paper; Bags: plastic, laminated, and coated ; Plastics containers, except foam; Packaging machinery

(G-15940)
KOTTLER METAL PRODUCTS CO INC
1595 Lost Nation Rd (44094-7329)
PHONE..................................440 946-7473
Barry Feldman, *Pr*
Harold Feldman, *
Jeff Gray, *
▲ **EMP:** 25 **EST:** 1914
SALES (est): 6.57MM **Privately Held**
Web: www.kottlermetal.com

GEOGRAPHIC SECTION
Willoughby - Lake County (G-15963)

SIC: **3498** 3441 7692 3547 Pipe sections, fabricated from purchased pipe; Fabricated structural metal; Welding repair; Rolling mill machinery

(G-15941)
LABEL TECHNIQUE SOUTHEAST LLC
38601 Kennedy Pkwy (44094-7395)
PHONE................................440 951-7660
EMP: 22 **EST:** 1979
SQ FT: 12,000
SALES (est): 2.23MM
SALES (corp-wide): 27.48MM **Privately Held**
SIC: 2759 2672 2679 Labels and seals: printing, nsk; Paper; coated and laminated, nec; Labels, paper: made from purchased material
PA: The Kennedy Group Incorporated
  38601 Kennedy Pkwy
  Willoughby OH 44094
  440 951-7660

(G-15942)
LAKE COMMUNITY NEWS
Also Called: Painesville Pride
36081 Lake Shore Blvd Ste 5 (44095-1578)
P.O. Box 814 (44255-0814)
PHONE................................440 946-2577
Deanne Nelisse, *Pr*
EMP: 7 **EST:** 1987
SALES (est): 355K **Privately Held**
Web: www.lakecommunitynewsohio.com
SIC: 2711 Newspapers, publishing and printing

(G-15943)
LAKE ERIE INTERLOCK INC
2132 Lost Nation Rd Unit 3 (44094-7178)
PHONE................................440 918-9898
Brian Compton, *Prin*
EMP: 6 **EST:** 2004
SALES (est): 190K **Privately Held**
SIC: 3694 Ignition apparatus and distributors

(G-15944)
LANDERWOOD INDUSTRIES INC
4245 Hamann Pkwy (44094-5623)
PHONE................................440 233-4234
James H Weaver Iii, *Pr*
EMP: 23 **EST:** 1997
SQ FT: 30,000
SALES (est): 704.99K **Privately Held**
SIC: 3462 Gears, forged steel

(G-15945)
LANGA TOOL & MACHINE INC
36430 Reading Ave Ste 1 (44094-8220)
PHONE................................440 953-1138
William Langa, *Pr*
EMP: 14 **EST:** 1979
SQ FT: 7,000
SALES (est): 444.83K **Privately Held**
Web: www.langatool.com
SIC: 3599 Machine shop, jobbing and repair

(G-15946)
LOKRING TECHNOLOGY LLC
38376 Apollo Pkwy (44094-7724)
PHONE................................440 942-0880
Bill Lennon, *Pr*
▲ **EMP:** 82 **EST:** 2003
SALES (est): 25.36MM **Privately Held**
Web: www.lokring.com
SIC: 3312 Pipes and tubes

(G-15947)
LOST NATION FUEL
3525 Lost Nation Rd (44094-7753)
PHONE................................440 951-9088
EMP: 6 **EST:** 2012
SALES (est): 129.31K **Privately Held**
SIC: 2869 Fuels

(G-15948)
MAGNUS ENGINEERED EQP LLC
4500 Beidler Rd (44094-4602)
PHONE................................440 942-8488
William Martin, *Pr*
Jeffrey Mendrala, *CFO*
EMP: 25 **EST:** 2016
SQ FT: 38,000
SALES (est): 4.54MM **Privately Held**
Web: www.magnusequipment.com
SIC: 3452 Bolts, nuts, rivets, and washers

(G-15949)
MAR-BAL PULTRUSION INC
38310 Apollo Pkwy (44094-7724)
PHONE................................440 953-0456
Allen J Goryance, *Pr*
James Gortance, *VP*
EMP: 10 **EST:** 1974
SQ FT: 10,000
SALES (est): 1.02MM **Privately Held**
Web: www.marbalpultrusion.com
SIC: 2519 Furniture, household: glass, fiberglass, and plastic

(G-15950)
MEISTER MEDIA WORLDWIDE INC (PA)
Also Called: Meister Media Worldwide
37733 Euclid Ave (44094-5992)
PHONE................................440 942-2000
Gary T Fitzgerald, *Ch Bd*
Steven L Siemborski, *Vice Chairman*
William J Miller Ii *Prinpl*,
K Elliott Nowels, *
Cynthia Gorman, *
EMP: 100 **EST:** 1932
SQ FT: 29,000
SALES (est): 20.39MM
SALES (corp-wide): 20.39MM **Privately Held**
Web: www.meistermedia.com
SIC: 2721 Magazines: publishing only, not printed on site

(G-15951)
MELINZ INDUSTRIES INC (PA)
Also Called: Riverview Raquetball Club
34099 Melinz Pkwy Unit D (44095-4001)
PHONE................................440 946-3512
Adolph Melinz, *Pr*
Nancy Sloat, *Sec*
Jeff Sloat, *Treas*
EMP: 10 **EST:** 1974
SQ FT: 11,000
SALES (est): 923.47K
SALES (corp-wide): 923.47K **Privately Held**
SIC: 7999 3599 Racquetball club, non-membership; Machine and other job shop work

(G-15952)
METAL SEAL PRECISION LTD
4369 Hamann Pkwy (44094-5625)
PHONE................................440 255-8888
John L Habe, *Brnch Mgr*
EMP: 128
SALES (corp-wide): 27.49MM **Privately Held**
Web: www.metalseal.com
SIC: 3444 Sheet metalwork
PA: Metal Seal Precision, Ltd.
  8687 Tyler Blvd
  Mentor OH 44060
  440 255-8888

(G-15953)
MID-WEST FORGE CORPORATION (PA)
2778 Som Center Rd Ste 200 (44094)
PHONE................................216 481-3030
Robert I Gale Iii, *Ch Bd*
Michael Sherwin, *V Ch Bd*
Paul C Gum, *Pr*
Robert W Dems, *VP*
John T Webster, *CUST SERV*
EMP: 150 **EST:** 1925
SQ FT: 165,000
SALES (est): 46.21MM
SALES (corp-wide): 46.21MM **Privately Held**
Web: www.mid-westforge.com
SIC: 3462 Iron and steel forgings

(G-15954)
MILLENNIUM MACHINE TECH LLC
38323 Apollo Pkwy Ste 7 (44094-7761)
PHONE................................440 269-8080
Jeffrey J Downs, *Managing Member*
EMP: 11 **EST:** 2004
SALES (est): 479.65K **Privately Held**
SIC: 3599 Machine shop, jobbing and repair

(G-15955)
MOMENTIVE PERFORMANCE MTLS INC
4901 Campbell Rd (44094-3366)
PHONE................................740 929-8732
EMP: 166
Web: www.momentive.com
SIC: 2869 Industrial organic chemicals, nec
HQ: Momentive Performance Materials Inc.
  2750 Balltown Rd
  Niskayuna NY 12309

(G-15956)
NATIONAL ROLLER DIE INC
4750 Beidler Rd Unit 4 (44094-4663)
PHONE................................440 951-3850
Will Corral, *Pr*
Jeff Watt, *Superintnt*
Kelly Johnson, *CEO*
EMP: 10 **EST:** 2002
SALES (est): 750.92K **Privately Held**
Web: www.nrdi.net
SIC: 3544 Special dies and tools

(G-15957)
NEUNDORFER INC
Also Called: Neundorfer Engineering Service
4590 Hamann Pkwy (44094-5691)
PHONE................................440 942-8990
Michael Neundorfer, *CEO*
EMP: 50 **EST:** 1958
SQ FT: 38,000
SALES (est): 8.16MM **Privately Held**
Web: www.neundorfer.com
SIC: 8711 3564 Pollution control engineering ; Precipitators, electrostatic

(G-15958)
NEWAY STAMPING & MFG INC
4820 E 345th St (44094-4607)
P.O. Box 1023 (44096-1023)
PHONE................................440 951-8500
Adam Bowden, *Pr*
Jason H Bowden, *
Matthew J Bowden, *
EMP: 85 **EST:** 1970
SQ FT: 15,000
SALES (est): 10.49MM **Privately Held**
Web: www.newaystamping.com
SIC: 3469 3544 Stamping metal for the trade ; Special dies, tools, jigs, and fixtures

(G-15959)
NORBAR TORQUE TOOLS INC
36400 Biltmore Pl (44094-8221)
PHONE................................440 953-1175
Keith Daiber, *Pr*
Bernice Daiber, *Sec*
Terry Daiber, *VP*
▲ **EMP:** 12 **EST:** 1962
SQ FT: 5,000
SALES (est): 4.65MM
SALES (corp-wide): 4.73B **Publicly Held**
Web: www.norbar.com
SIC: 5072 3423 Hand tools; Wrenches, hand tools
PA: Snap-On Incorporated
  2801 80th St
  Kenosha WI 53143
  262 656-5200

(G-15960)
NORTHEASTERN RFRGN CORP
38274 Western Pkwy (44094)
PHONE................................440 942-7676
Carol A Primozic, *Pr*
James A Primozic, *VP*
EMP: 20 **EST:** 1976
SQ FT: 11,000
SALES (est): 3.29MM **Privately Held**
SIC: 3585 1711 7623 Refrigeration equipment, complete; Heating and air conditioning contractors; Refrigeration repair service

(G-15961)
NRC INC
Also Called: Northeastern Process Cooling
38160 Western Pkwy (44094-7588)
PHONE................................440 975-9449
Randolph J Primozic, *Pr*
Patricia A Primozic, *
EMP: 30 **EST:** 1998
SALES (est): 3.79MM **Privately Held**
Web: www.nrcinc.net
SIC: 3585 Refrigeration equipment, complete

(G-15962)
NUPRO COMPANY
4800 E 345th St (44094-4607)
PHONE................................440 951-9729
F J Callahan Junior, *Ch Bd*
William Cosgrove, *
EMP: 79 **EST:** 1956
SQ FT: 60,000
SALES (est): 1.92MM
SALES (corp-wide): 881.02MM **Privately Held**
Web: www.swagelok.com
SIC: 3494 3569 3564 3491 Valves and pipe fittings, nec; Filters, general line: industrial; Blowers and fans; Industrial valves
PA: Swagelok Company
  29500 Solon Rd
  Solon OH 44139
  440 248-4600

(G-15963)
OHIO BROACH & MACHINE COMPANY
35264 Topps Industrial Pkwy (44094-4684)
PHONE................................440 946-1040
Charles P Van De, *Mother*
Christopher C Van De, *Mother*
Richard Van De, *Mother*
Neil Van De, *Mother*
James L Lutz, *
▼ **EMP:** 34 **EST:** 1956
SQ FT: 52,000
SALES (est): 4.35MM **Privately Held**
Web: www.ohiobroach.com

Willoughby - Lake County (G-15964)

SIC: **3541** 7699 3545 3599 Broaching machines; Knife, saw and tool sharpening and repair; Machine tool accessories; Machine shop, jobbing and repair

(G-15964)
OHIO CARBON BLANK INC
38403 Pelton Rd (44094-7721)
PHONE..................440 953-9302
Scott Boncha, *Pr*
EMP: 20 **EST:** 1980
SQ FT: 2,000
SALES (est): 2.43MM **Privately Held**
Web: www.ohiocarbonblank.com
SIC: **3624** Carbon and graphite products

(G-15965)
OMEGA 1 INC
38373 Pelton Rd (44094-7719)
PHONE..................216 663-8424
Richard Profant, *Pr*
EMP: 10 **EST:** 1989
SALES (est): 963.33K **Privately Held**
Web: www.omega1.com
SIC: **3492** 5051 Hose and tube fittings and assemblies, hydraulic/pneumatic; Metals service centers and offices

(G-15966)
ORANGE BLOSSOM PRESS INC
38005 Brown Ave (44094-5836)
P.O. Box 93417 (44101-5417)
PHONE..................216 781-8655
Greg Patt, *Pr*
John O'hara, *VP*
Donna Lirrivee-cohen, *Sec*
EMP: 8 **EST:** 1976
SQ FT: 6,000
SALES (est): 532.28K **Privately Held**
Web: www.orangeblossompress.com
SIC: **2752** 2791 2789 Offset printing; Typesetting; Bookbinding and related work

(G-15967)
PACE CONSOLIDATED INC (PA)
Also Called: Pace Engineering
4800 Beidler Rd (44094-4605)
PHONE..................440 942-1234
Craig Wallace, *CEO*
Randy Murphy, *
◆ **EMP:** 95 **EST:** 1976
SQ FT: 120,000
SALES (est): 23.66MM
SALES (corp-wide): 23.66MM **Privately Held**
Web: www.paceparts.net
SIC: **3531** Construction machinery

(G-15968)
PACE ENGINEERING INC
4800 Beidler Rd (44094-4605)
PHONE..................440 942-1234
Craig R Wallace, *CEO*
EMP: 105 **EST:** 1963
SQ FT: 120,000
SALES (est): 23.66MM
SALES (corp-wide): 23.66MM **Privately Held**
Web: www.paceparts.net
SIC: **3531** Construction machinery
PA: Pace Consolidated, Inc.
   4800 Beidler Rd
   Willoughby OH 44094
   440 942-1234

(G-15969)
PAULO PRODUCTS COMPANY
Also Called: American Brzing Div Paulo Pdts
4428 Hamann Pkwy (44094-5628)
PHONE..................440 942-0153
Bob Muto, *Brnch Mgr*

EMP: 38
SALES (corp-wide): 98.96MM **Privately Held**
Web: www.paulo.com
SIC: **7692** 1799 Brazing; Coating of concrete structures with plastic
PA: Paulo Products Company
   5711 W Park Ave
   Saint Louis MO 63110
   314 647-7500

(G-15970)
PHIL-MATIC SCREW PRODUCTS INC
1457 E 357th St (44095-4127)
P.O. Box 1178 (44096-1178)
PHONE..................440 942-7290
Larry E Phillis, *Pr*
Fraser Young, *VP*
Richard Phillis, *VP*
EMP: 20 **EST:** 1962
SQ FT: 11,300
SALES (est): 418.2K **Privately Held**
Web: www.philmatic.com
SIC: **3599** Machine shop, jobbing and repair

(G-15971)
PM COAL COMPANY LLC
9717 Chillicothe Rd (44094-9200)
PHONE..................440 256-7624
Scott Brown, *Pr*
Jack M Grinwis, *Pt*
EMP: 6 **EST:** 2010
SALES (est): 500.97K **Privately Held**
Web: www.pickandsmather.com
SIC: **1221** Bituminous coal surface mining

(G-15972)
PM MACHINE INC
38205 Western Pkwy (44094-7591)
PHONE..................440 942-6537
Tom Decumbe, *Pr*
EMP: 9 **EST:** 1993
SQ FT: 10,000
SALES (est): 399.19K **Privately Held**
Web: www.pm-mach.com
SIC: **3089** Injection molding of plastics

(G-15973)
PMC GAGE INC (PA)
Also Called: PMC Lonestar
38383 Willoughby Pkwy (44094)
PHONE..................440 953-1672
Nicholas Bosworth, *CEO*
Ann Gross, *
EMP: 43 **EST:** 1999
SALES (est): 9.71MM
SALES (corp-wide): 9.71MM **Privately Held**
Web: www.pmcgagecompanies.com
SIC: **3545** 3826 3829 Measuring tools and machines, machinists' metalworking type; Analytical instruments; Measuring and controlling devices, nec

(G-15974)
PMC MERCURY
38383 Willoughby Pkwy (44094-7585)
PHONE..................440 953-3300
Nick Boxworth, *Pr*
EMP: 16 **EST:** 1951
SQ FT: 38,000
SALES (est): 206.66K **Privately Held**
Web: www.pmcgagecompanies.com
SIC: **3545** Gauges (machine tool accessories)

(G-15975)
POLYFLEX LLC
Also Called: Polyflex
4803 E 345th St (44094-4606)
PHONE..................440 946-0758

EMP: 10 **EST:** 2005
SALES (est): 929.55K **Privately Held**
Web: www.polyflexonline.com
SIC: **3089** Plastics containers, except foam

(G-15976)
PRECISE TOOL & DIE COMPANY INC
38128 Willoughby Pkwy (44094-7580)
PHONE..................440 951-9173
Steve Hunyadi, *CEO*
Eva Pinkerton, *
Elizabeth Hunyadi, *
▲ **EMP:** 35 **EST:** 1969
SQ FT: 22,000
SALES (est): 5.22MM **Privately Held**
Web: www.ptd-inc.com
SIC: **3599** Machine shop, jobbing and repair

(G-15977)
PROGRESSIVE SUPPLY LLC
38601 Kennedy Pkwy (44094-7395)
PHONE..................570 688-9636
EMP: 19 **EST:** 1981
SQ FT: 10,000
SALES (est): 828.06K **Privately Held**
SIC: **2672** Tape, pressure sensitive: made from purchased materials

(G-15978)
QUALITY CNC MACHINING INC
38195 Airport Pkwy (44094-8038)
PHONE..................440 953-0723
Joseph Katic, *Pr*
EMP: 25 **EST:** 1988
SQ FT: 8,000
SALES (est): 3.22MM **Privately Held**
Web: www.qualitycnc.com
SIC: **3599** Machine shop, jobbing and repair

(G-15979)
QUALITY SPECIALISTS INC
Also Called: Www.slidepartsexpress.com
1428 E 363rd St (44095-4136)
PHONE..................440 946-9129
Kenneth Bateman, *Pr*
Rosemary Bateman, *VP*
EMP: 8 **EST:** 1979
SQ FT: 6,000
SALES (est): 811.83K **Privately Held**
SIC: **3544** 3599 Special dies and tools; Custom machinery

(G-15980)
QUALTECH TECHNOLOGIES INC
1685b Joseph Lloyd Pkwy (44094-8044)
PHONE..................440 946-8081
Dave Vance, *Pr*
▲ **EMP:** 50 **EST:** 2002
SQ FT: 18,000
SALES (est): 10.42MM **Privately Held**
Web: www.qualtechinc.com
SIC: **3699** 3672 Electrical equipment and supplies, nec; Printed circuit boards

(G-15981)
R & F FRANCHISE GROUP LLC
37333 Euclid Ave (44094-5617)
PHONE..................440 942-7140
John Frech, *Prin*
EMP: 14 **EST:** 2010
SALES (est): 478.99K **Privately Held**
Web: www.paninisgrill.com
SIC: **3421** Table and food cutlery, including butchers'

(G-15982)
REID ASSET MANAGEMENT COMPANY
Also Called: Magnus Equipment
4500 Beidler Rd (44094-4602)

PHONE..................440 942-8488
Scott Miller, *Brnch Mgr*
EMP: 25
SALES (corp-wide): 5.1MM **Privately Held**
Web: www.magnusequipment.com
SIC: **2842** Polishes and sanitation goods
PA: Reid Asset Management Company
   9555 Rockside Rd Ste 350
   Cleveland OH 44125
   216 642-3223

(G-15983)
RIMECO PRODUCTS INC
2002 Joseph Lloyd Pkwy (44094-8032)
PHONE..................440 918-1220
Valentine Ribic, *Pr*
John Ribic, *VP*
EMP: 20 **EST:** 1992
SQ FT: 12,000
SALES (est): 4.58MM **Privately Held**
Web: www.rimecoproducts.com
SIC: **3599** Machine shop, jobbing and repair

(G-15984)
RINOS WOODWORKING SHOP INC
36475 Biltmore Pl (44094-8222)
PHONE..................440 946-1718
Rino Ritosa, *Pr*
▲ **EMP:** 19 **EST:** 1982
SQ FT: 15,000
SALES (est): 2.4MM **Privately Held**
Web: www.rinoswoodworking.com
SIC: **2541** 2431 Cabinets, except refrigerated: show, display, etc.: wood; Millwork

(G-15985)
SAWYER TECHNICAL MATERIALS LLC (HQ)
Also Called: Sawyer Crystal Systems
35400 Lakeland Blvd (44095-5304)
PHONE..................440 951-8770
Kelly Scott, *Managing Member*
Fred Taylor, *Managing Member*
▲ **EMP:** 35 **EST:** 1957
SQ FT: 100,000
SALES (est): 10.51MM **Privately Held**
Web: www.sawyerllc.com
SIC: **3679** 3471 Quartz crystals, for electronic application; Plating and polishing
PA: Foreasia Corporation
   Taipei City TAP

(G-15986)
SCHEEL PUBLISHING LLC
5900 Som Center Rd (44094-3086)
PHONE..................216 731-8616
J Scheel, *Prin*
EMP: 8 **EST:** 2008
SALES (est): 909.79K **Privately Held**
Web: www.commercialacademy.com
SIC: **2741** Miscellaneous publishing

(G-15987)
SERVICE STAMPINGS INC
4700 Hamann Pkwy (44094-5616)
PHONE..................440 946-2330
Christopher T Reid, *Pr*
Thurston Reid, *
Jefferey J Campbell, *Treasurer Finance*
Robert A Stohlman, *
Donald Bowen, *
EMP: 31 **EST:** 1956
SQ FT: 28,000
SALES (est): 6.09MM **Privately Held**
Web: www.servicestampings.com
SIC: **3469** Stamping metal for the trade

(G-15988)
SFM CORP
4530 Hamann Pkwy (44094-5630)
PHONE.................................440 951-5500
Fred J G Mika, *Pr*
Scott M Mika, *
Fred G Mika, *
EMP: 45 **EST:** 1939
SQ FT: 78,000
SALES (est): 8.24MM **Privately Held**
Web: www.mikafab.com
SIC: 3444 Sheet metal specialties, not stamped

(G-15989)
SHAFTS MFG
1585 E 361st St Unit G1 (44095-5329)
PHONE.................................440 942-6012
Berndy Heckelmann, *Prin*
EMP: 8 **EST:** 2007
SALES (est): 400.03K **Privately Held**
Web: www.tylertreeservicecompany.net
SIC: 3999 Manufacturing industries, nec

(G-15990)
SHERBROOKE CORPORATION
36490 Reading Ave (44094-8207)
P.O. Box 689 (44096-0689)
PHONE.................................440 942-3520
Randy Spoth, *Pr*
Laura Krus, *Sec*
Nancy Spoth, *Treas*
EMP: 22 **EST:** 1993
SQ FT: 9,000
SALES (est): 3.55MM **Privately Held**
Web: www.sherbrookemetals.com
SIC: 3624 3823 3548 Electrodes, thermal and electrolytic uses: carbon, graphite; Process control instruments; Welding apparatus

(G-15991)
SHERBROOKE METALS
37552 N Industrial Pkwy (44094-6214)
PHONE.................................440 542-3066
Nancy Spoth, *Treas*
EMP: 6 **EST:** 2018
SALES (est): 242.68K **Privately Held**
Web: www.sherbrookemetals.com
SIC: 3548 Welding apparatus

(G-15992)
SKINNER MACHINING CO
38127 Willoughby Pkwy (44094-7581)
PHONE.................................216 486-6636
Walter B Harwood, *Pr*
EMP: 8 **EST:** 1962
SALES (est): 1.02MM
SALES (corp-wide): 2.32MM **Privately Held**
SIC: 3599 Electrical discharge machining (EDM)
PA: J W Harwood Co
    18001 Roseland Rd
    Cleveland OH 44112
    216 531-6230

(G-15993)
SKRL DIE CASTING INC
34580 Lakeland Blvd (44095-5221)
PHONE.................................440 946-7200
Sandra Szuch, *Pr*
EMP: 23 **EST:** 1967
SQ FT: 30,000
SALES (est): 824.15K **Privately Held**
Web: www.skrltool.com
SIC: 3544 Special dies and tools

(G-15994)
SLABE MACHINE PRODUCTS LLC
4659 Hamann Pkwy (44094-5631)
PHONE.................................440 946-6555
Edward Slabe Junior, *Pr*
Brendan Slabe, *
Christopher Slabe, *
Judith Slabe, *
▲ **EMP:** 100 **EST:** 1942
SQ FT: 58,000
SALES (est): 24.15MM **Privately Held**
Web: www.slabemachine.com
SIC: 3599 Machine shop, jobbing and repair

(G-15995)
SLOAT INC
34099 Melinz Pkwy Unit A (44095-4001)
PHONE.................................440 951-9554
EMP: 6 **EST:** 1993
SALES (est): 450.56K **Privately Held**
SIC: 2892 Primary explosives, fuses and detonators

(G-15996)
SPENCE TECHNOLOGIES INC
Also Called: R.W.
4752 Topps Industrial Pkwy (44094-4636)
PHONE.................................440 946-3035
William Spence, *Pr*
EMP: 18 **EST:** 1976
SQ FT: 10,320
SALES (est): 2.9MM **Privately Held**
Web: www.spencetechnologies.com
SIC: 3599 Machine shop, jobbing and repair

(G-15997)
STEEL TECHNOLOGIES LLC
Steel Technologies Ohio
2220 Joseph Lloyd Pkwy (44094)
PHONE.................................440 946-8666
Rick Furber, *VP*
EMP: 41
Web: www.steeltechnologies.com
SIC: 3312 Blast furnaces and steel mills
HQ: Steel Technologies Llc
    700 N Hurstbourne Pkwy # 400
    Louisville KY 40222
    502 245-2110

(G-15998)
STICKER CORPORATION (PA)
Also Called: Reighart Steel Products
37877 Elm St (44094-6243)
PHONE.................................440 946-2100
Douglas Reighart, *Pr*
EMP: 11 **EST:** 1947
SQ FT: 18,000
SALES (est): 2.2MM
SALES (corp-wide): 2.2MM **Privately Held**
Web: www.stickercorp.com
SIC: 3585 3549 3547 3443 Heating equipment, complete; Metalworking machinery, nec; Rolling mill machinery; Fabricated plate work (boiler shop)

(G-15999)
STICKER CORPORATION
37941 Elm St (44094-6207)
PHONE.................................440 942-4700
Douglas Reighart, *Brnch Mgr*
EMP: 7
SALES (corp-wide): 2.2MM **Privately Held**
Web: www.stickercorp.com
SIC: 3441 Fabricated structural metal
PA: Sticker Corporation
    37877 Elm St
    Willoughby OH 44094
    440 946-2100

(G-16000)
STRONG-COAT LLC
4420 Sherwin Rd (44094-7994)
PHONE.................................440 299-2068
James Small, *Prin*
EMP: 6 **EST:** 2015
SALES (est): 65.61K **Privately Held**
SIC: 2851 Paints and allied products

(G-16001)
T C SERVICE CO
Also Called: Top Cat Air Tools
38285 Pelton Rd (44094-7740)
PHONE.................................440 954-7500
Edgar G Henry, *Pr*
M Anne Henry, *
Valeria S Henry, *
Gerald J Henry, *
EMP: 40 **EST:** 1962
SQ FT: 60,000
SALES (est): 4.58MM **Privately Held**
Web: www.tcservice.com
SIC: 3546 Power-driven handtools

(G-16002)
TABLOX INC
4821 E 345th St (44094-4606)
PHONE.................................440 953-1951
Dana Talcott, *Pr*
Pam Cleverly, *VP*
EMP: 9 **EST:** 1968
SQ FT: 16,000
SALES (est): 756.2K **Privately Held**
Web: www.tablox.com
SIC: 3471 Electroplating of metals or formed products

(G-16003)
TED J & JANICE HLAVATY
8814 Foxhill Dr (44094-5148)
PHONE.................................440 256-8524
Ted J Hlavaty, *Prin*
EMP: 6 **EST:** 2010
SALES (est): 76.08K **Privately Held**
SIC: 3469 Metal stampings, nec

(G-16004)
TELLING INDUSTRIES LLC (PA)
4420 Sherwin Rd (44094-7995)
PHONE.................................440 974-3370
Edward Slish, *Managing Member*
◆ **EMP:** 10 **EST:** 2004
SQ FT: 400,000
SALES (est): 31.59MM
SALES (corp-wide): 31.59MM **Privately Held**
Web: www.tellingindustries.com
SIC: 3316 Bars, steel, cold finished, from purchased hot-rolled

(G-16005)
TETRAD ELECTRONICS INC (PA)
2048 Joseph Lloyd Pkwy (44094-8032)
PHONE.................................440 946-6443
Ronald K Brehm, *Pr*
Jeffrey Waterman, *
Bruce Vanek, *
Richard Scebbi, *
EMP: 61 **EST:** 1983
SQ FT: 14,000
SALES (est): 6.59MM
SALES (corp-wide): 6.59MM **Privately Held**
Web: www.tetradelectronics.com
SIC: 3672 Printed circuit boards

(G-16006)
TOKU AMERICA INC
Also Called: Striker Hydraulic Breakers
3900 Ben Hur Ave Ste 3 (44094-6398)
PHONE.................................440 954-9923
David Nakamura, *Pr*
Akinori Kihara, *Sec*
▲ **EMP:** 13 **EST:** 2010
SQ FT: 15,000
SALES (est): 10.24MM **Privately Held**
Web: www.toku-america.com
SIC: 3531 Crushers, portable
PA: Toku Pneumatic Co.,Ltd.
    4-3-4, Katakasu, Hakata-Ku
    Fukuoka FUK 812-0

(G-16007)
TOM RICHARDS INC (PA)
Also Called: Process Technology
38809 Mentor Ave (44094-7932)
PHONE.................................440 974-1300
Jody Richards, *Pr*
Leslie N Thomas, *
▲ **EMP:** 107 **EST:** 1978
SQ FT: 72,000
SALES (est): 56.37MM
SALES (corp-wide): 56.37MM **Privately Held**
Web: www.processtechnology.com
SIC: 3559 Metal finishing equipment for plating, etc.

(G-16008)
TOM THUMB CLIP CO INC
36300 Lakeland Blvd Unit 2 (44095)
P.O. Box 709 (44096-0709)
PHONE.................................440 953-9606
Jennifer Baxter, *Pr*
June Baxter, *VP*
EMP: 10 **EST:** 1947
SALES (est): 700.78K **Privately Held**
SIC: 3496 Clips and fasteners, made from purchased wire

(G-16009)
TRU-FAB TECHNOLOGY INC
34820 Lakeland Blvd (44095-5224)
PHONE.................................440 954-9760
EMP: 10 **EST:** 1995
SQ FT: 15,000
SALES (est): 1.73MM **Privately Held**
Web: www.trufab.com
SIC: 3599 7692 Custom machinery; Welding repair

(G-16010)
TRUCAST INC
4382 Hamann Pkwy (44094-5683)
PHONE.................................440 942-4923
EMP: 60 **EST:** 1996
SQ FT: 20,000
SALES (est): 5.82MM **Privately Held**
Web: www.olympusaero.com
SIC: 3599 Machine shop, jobbing and repair

(G-16011)
TRV INCORPORATED
4860 E 345th St (44094-4607)
PHONE.................................440 951-7722
Peter Kolaric, *Pr*
Tom Kolaric, *
Victoria Kolaric, *
EMP: 30 **EST:** 1985
SALES (est): 4.33MM **Privately Held**
SIC: 3599 Machine shop, jobbing and repair

(G-16012)
U S MOLDING MACHINERY CO INC
38294 Pelton Rd (44094-7765)
PHONE.................................440 918-1701
Zac Cohen, *Pr*
Jerry Harper, *
Robert Luck, *
Bill Sprowls, *
EMP: 28 **EST:** 1980

Willoughby - Lake County (G-16013)

SQ FT: 12,500
SALES (est): 4.92MM **Privately Held**
Web: www.usmolding.com
SIC: **3089** 7699 Injection molding of plastics; Industrial equipment services

(G-16013)
UNIVERSAL J&Z MACHINE LLC
4781 E 355th St (44094-4631)
PHONE................................216 486-2220
EMP: 24 EST: 1994
SQ FT: 5,000
SALES (est): 450K **Privately Held**
Web: www.universaljzmachine.com
SIC: **3599** Machine shop, jobbing and repair

(G-16014)
WEAVER SCREEN PRINT LLC
9450 Metcalf Rd (44094-9716)
PHONE................................440 725-0116
Timothy M Weaver, *Prin*
EMP: 6 EST: 2009
SALES (est): 110K **Privately Held**
SIC: **2759** Screen printing

(G-16015)
WEYBRIDGE LLC
Also Called: Mika Metal Fabricating
4530 Hamann Pkwy (44094-5630)
PHONE................................440 951-5500
Benjamin Scott Shelfer, *Ch*
Ryan Thomas, *Pr*
EMP: 6 EST: 2020
SALES (est): 1.03MM **Privately Held**
Web: www.mikafab.com
SIC: **3444** Sheet metal specialties, not stamped

(G-16016)
WILLOUGHBY BREWING COMPANY LLC
4057 Erie St (44094-7804)
P.O. Box 946 (44096-0946)
PHONE................................440 975-0202
Jeremy Banhoron, *Managing Member*
EMP: 18 EST: 1996
SQ FT: 1,200
SALES (est): 895.69K **Privately Held**
Web: www.willoughbybrewing.com
SIC: **2082** 5812 Beer (alcoholic beverage); Eating places

(G-16017)
WILLOUGHBY PRINTING CO INC
37946 Elm St (44094-6287)
PHONE................................440 946-0800
Michael Yutzy, *Pr*
Randi Yutzy, *Mgr*
EMP: 8 EST: 1950
SQ FT: 4,800
SALES (est): 670.19K **Privately Held**
Web: www.willoughbyprinting.com
SIC: **2752** Offset printing

(G-16018)
WILLOW HILL INDUSTRIES LLC
37611 Euclid Ave (44094-5923)
PHONE................................440 942-3003
EMP: 8 EST: 1998
SALES (est): 173.99K **Privately Held**
Web: www.whindustries.com
SIC: **3469** Stamping metal for the trade

(G-16019)
WINTER EQUIPMENT COMPANY INCORPORATED
1900 Joseph Lloyd Pkwy (44094-8030)
PHONE................................440 946-8377
◆ EMP: 25 EST: 1983
SALES (est): 7.07MM **Privately Held**
Web: www.winterequipment.com
SIC: **3531** 5082 Snow plow attachments; Road construction equipment

(G-16020)
ZERO-D PRODUCTS INC
Also Called: Akron Jewelry Rubber
37939 Stevens Blvd (44094-6235)
PHONE................................440 942-5005
William W Mull, *Pr*
Robert J Beausoleil, *VP*
James R Dillhoefer, *Sec*
EMP: 6 EST: 1984
SALES (est): 494.38K **Privately Held**
Web: www.zerodproducts.com
SIC: **3915** Jewelers' findings and materials

Willoughby Hills
Lake County

(G-16021)
ATLANTIC CO
26651 Curtiss Wright Pkwy (44092-2832)
PHONE................................440 944-8988
F Joseph Callahan, *Ch Bd*
William Cosgrove, *
Thomas Janock, *
EMP: 30 EST: 1959
SQ FT: 30,000
SALES (est): 496.79K
SALES (corp-wide): 881.02MM **Privately Held**
SIC: **3432** Plumbing fixture fittings and trim
PA: Swagelok Company
    29500 Solon Rd
    Solon OH 44139
    440 248-4600

(G-16022)
CARBON WEB PRINT LLC
38033 Dodds Hill Dr (44094-9660)
PHONE................................216 402-3504
Mitchell Mclaughlin, *Prin*
EMP: 19 EST: 2017
SALES (est): 79.12K **Privately Held**
Web: www.carbonweb.co
SIC: **2752** Offset printing

(G-16023)
CHAGRIN VLY STL ERECTORS INC
Also Called: Ruple Trucking
2278 River Rd (44094-9685)
PHONE................................440 975-1556
Victoria Ruple, *Pr*
John Ruple, *Pr*
EMP: 13 EST: 1993
SQ FT: 10,040
SALES (est): 2.04MM **Privately Held**
SIC: **3441** 1791 4213 1796 Fabricated structural metal; Structural steel erection; Trucking, except local; Machine moving and rigging

(G-16024)
EUCLID WELDING COMPANY INC
29956 White Rd (44092-1373)
P.O. Box 202 (44092-0202)
PHONE................................216 289-0714
John Varljen, *Pr*
EMP: 10 EST: 1972
SQ FT: 26,000
SALES (est): 706.71K **Privately Held**
SIC: **1799** 3441 3599 Welding on site; Fabricated structural metal; Machine shop, jobbing and repair

(G-16025)
MICRO PRODUCTS CO INC
26653 Curtiss Wright Pkwy (44092-2832)
PHONE................................440 943-0258
Arthur Anton, *Pr*
Frank Roddy, *
Ernie Mansour, *
EMP: 48 EST: 1981
SQ FT: 10,000
SALES (est): 814.99K
SALES (corp-wide): 881.02MM **Privately Held**
SIC: **3471** 7389 Plating of metals or formed products; Grinding, precision: commercial or industrial
PA: Swagelok Company
    29500 Solon Rd
    Solon OH 44139
    440 248-4600

(G-16026)
NEUROS MEDICAL INC
35010 Chardon Rd Ste 210 (44094-9011)
PHONE................................440 951-2505
David Veino, *Pr*
Alan Kaganov, *Ch Bd*
Mark Teague, *CFO*
EMP: 8 EST: 2008
SQ FT: 4,275
SALES (est): 1.55MM **Privately Held**
Web: www.neurosmedical.com
SIC: **3845** Electromedical equipment

(G-16027)
PRODUCE PACKAGING INC
27853 Chardon Rd (44092-2703)
PHONE................................216 391-6129
EMP: 150 EST: 1994
SALES (est): 43.25MM
SALES (corp-wide): 43.25MM **Privately Held**
Web: www.ppifresh.net
SIC: **2099** 5148 4222 Food preparations, nec ; Fresh fruits and vegetables; Refrigerated warehousing and storage
PA: Great Lakes Packers, Inc.
    400 Great Lakes Pkwy
    Bellevue OH 44811
    419 483-2956

(G-16028)
SUPERIOR ENERGY GROUP LTD
34469 Scotch Ln Apt 4 (44094-2987)
PHONE................................216 282-4440
EMP: 25 EST: 2020
SALES (est): 600K **Privately Held**
Web: www.superiorenergy.com
SIC: **1389** Oil field services, nec

(G-16029)
SWAGELOK COMPANY
Also Called: Swagelok Co
26653 Curtiss Wright Pkwy (44092-2832)
P.O. Box 31300 (44131-0300)
PHONE................................440 248-4600
EMP: 56
SALES (corp-wide): 881.02MM **Privately Held**
Web: www.aldvalve.com
SIC: **3491** 3599 Pressure valves and regulators, industrial; Machine shop, jobbing and repair
PA: Swagelok Company
    29500 Solon Rd
    Solon OH 44139
    440 248-4600

Willowick
Lake County

(G-16030)
BEST PLATING RACK CORP
428 E 314th St (44095-3769)
PHONE................................440 944-3270
Robert Evatz, *Owner*
EMP: 15 EST: 2002
SALES (est): 668.83K **Privately Held**
SIC: **3471** Plating of metals or formed products

(G-16031)
EMES SUPPLY LLC
35622 Vine St (44095-3150)
PHONE................................216 400-8025
EMP: 7 EST: 2015
SALES (est): 030.79K **Privately Held**
Web: www.emessupply.com
SIC: **2842** Cleaning or polishing preparations, nec

(G-16032)
JAKPRINTS INC
34440 Vine St (44095-5114)
PHONE................................216 246-3132
EMP: 6 EST: 2019
SALES (est): 345.24K **Privately Held**
SIC: **2752** Offset printing

(G-16033)
OHIO DEPARTMENT PUBLIC SAFETY
Also Called: Ross County License Bureau
31517 Vine St (44095-3561)
PHONE................................440 943-5545
EMP: 6
Web: publicsafety.ohio.gov
SIC: **3469** 9221 Automobile license tags, stamped metal; Police protection
HQ: Ohio Department Of Public Safety
    1970 W Broad St Fl 5
    Columbus OH 43223

(G-16034)
SKYRIDGE ROOFING & MASNRY LLC
34880 Vine St (44095-5141)
PHONE................................440 628-1983
Tiffany Lynn Hyatt, *Owner*
EMP: 7 EST: 2018
SALES (est): 171.56K **Privately Held**
Web: www.skyridgeroof.com
SIC: **2951** Asphalt paving mixtures and blocks

(G-16035)
STAKES MANUFACTURING LLC
Also Called: Stakes Mfg
34440 Vine St (44095-5114)
PHONE................................216 245-4752
Vincent Bartozzi, *CEO*
Vince Bartozzi, *
Jed Seifert, *
Abhinav Somani, *
EMP: 99 EST: 2019
SQ FT: 40,000
SALES (est): 9.41MM **Privately Held**
Web: www.stakesmfg.com
SIC: **3953** 2396 Screens, textile printing; Screen printing on fabric articles

(G-16036)
SUELOS SWEETZ LLC
35560 Vine St (44095-3148)
PHONE................................440 478-1301
Jordan Anderson, *Managing Member*
EMP: 7 EST: 2020
SALES (est): 32K **Privately Held**

SIC: 2051 Bakery products, partially cooked (except frozen)

Wilmington
Clinton County

(G-16037)
ABBOTT IMAGE SOLUTIONS LLC
185 Park Dr Ste A (45177-2890)
PHONE.................................937 382-6677
Greg Abbott, *Owner*
EMP: 13 **EST:** 2012
SALES (est): 1.29MM **Privately Held**
Web: www.abbottis.com
SIC: 3993 Signs and advertising specialties

(G-16038)
AHRESTY WILMINGTON CORPORATION
2627 S South St (45177-2926)
PHONE.................................937 382-6112
Kenichi Nonaka, *Pr*
Justin Rummer, *
▲ **EMP:** 378 **EST:** 1988
SQ FT: 334,000
SALES (est): 96.62MM **Privately Held**
Web: www.ahresty.com
SIC: 3363 Aluminum die-castings
PA: Ahresty Corporation
1-2, Nakahara, Mitsuyacho
Toyohashi AIC 441-3

(G-16039)
ALKERMES INC
265 Olinger Cir (45177-2484)
PHONE.................................937 382-5642
Barry Thrift, *Brnch Mgr*
EMP: 40
SQ FT: 12,000
Web: www.alkermes.com
SIC: 2834 Pharmaceutical preparations
HQ: Alkermes, Inc.
900 Winter St
Waltham MA 02451
781 609-6000

(G-16040)
B&M UNDERGROUND LLC
1403 Gurneyville Rd (45177-8300)
PHONE.................................740 505-3096
Kevin Peelle, *Prin*
EMP: 12 **EST:** 2018
SALES (est): 488.39K **Privately Held**
SIC: 3999 Manufacturing industries, nec

(G-16041)
BARBARA A LIEURANCE
180 E Sugartree St (45177-2333)
PHONE.................................937 382-2864
Barbara Lieurance, *Prin*
EMP: 6 **EST:** 2010
SALES (est): 88.62K **Privately Held**
SIC: 3469 Automobile license tags, stamped metal

(G-16042)
BUSH SPECIALTY VEHICLES INC
80 Park Dr (45177-2038)
PHONE.................................937 382-5502
Larry Vanover, *VP*
EMP: 15 **EST:** 1971
SALES (est): 3.89MM **Privately Held**
Web: www.bushspecialtyvehicles.com
SIC: 3713 Specialty motor vehicle bodies

(G-16043)
CHAMPION BRIDGE COMPANY
261 E Sugartree St (45177-2316)
PHONE.................................937 382-2521
Randy Dell, *Pr*
Gale Gerard, *VP*
EMP: 20 **EST:** 1934
SQ FT: 30,000
SALES (est): 2.44MM **Privately Held**
Web: www.championbridgecompany.com
SIC: 3441 Fabricated structural metal

(G-16044)
CHERRYBEND CUSTOM APLICAT LLC
2326 Cherrybend Rd (45177-9312)
PHONE.................................937 584-4269
EMP: 6 **EST:** 2015
SALES (est): 68.1K **Privately Held**
Web: www.cherrybendhunting.com
SIC: 7372 Application computer software

(G-16045)
COMPTON METAL PRODUCTS INC
416 Steele Rd (45177-9332)
PHONE.................................937 382-2403
James Compton, *Pr*
EMP: 10 **EST:** 1929
SQ FT: 2,000
SALES (est): 308.14K **Privately Held**
SIC: 7699 3599 7692 Engine repair and replacement, non-automotive; Machine shop, jobbing and repair; Welding repair

(G-16046)
COX PRINTING COMPANY
Also Called: Cox Painting
1087 Wayne Rd (45177-2024)
P.O. Box 263 (45039-0263)
PHONE.................................937 382-2312
Pamela Olds, *Pr*
Ramona Cox, *Sec*
Frank A Cox, *Cnslt*
EMP: 7 **EST:** 1949
SQ FT: 2,600
SALES (est): 455.33K **Privately Held**
SIC: 2752 2759 2789 Offset printing; Letterpress printing; Bookbinding and related work

(G-16047)
CPG INTERNATIONAL LLC
Also Called: Timbertech
894 Prairie Rd (45177-8847)
PHONE.................................937 655-8766
EMP: 260
SALES (corp-wide): 1.37B **Publicly Held**
Web: www.azekco.com
SIC: 3089 Plastics hardware and building products
HQ: The Azek Group Llc
1330 W Fulton St Ste 350
Chicago IL 60607
570 558-8000

(G-16048)
CUSTOM MOLDED PRODUCTS LLC
92 Grant St (45177-2324)
PHONE.................................937 382-1070
▲ **EMP:** 84 **EST:** 1999
SQ FT: 11,000
SALES (est): 11.46MM **Privately Held**
Web: www.custommolded.com
SIC: 3089 Injection molding of plastics

(G-16049)
ESSENTIAL PROVISIONS LLC
292 Inwood Rd (45177-8355)
PHONE.................................937 271-0381
Robin Mcgee, *Managing Member*
Namrata Maguire, *CFO*
EMP: 8
SALES (est): 348.11K **Privately Held**

SIC: 2099 7389 Food preparations, nec; Business services, nec

(G-16050)
FERNO-WASHINGTON INC (PA)
Also Called: Ferno
70 Weil Way (45177-9300)
PHONE.................................877 733-0911
Joseph Bourgraf, *Pr*
Elroy Bourgraf, *
◆ **EMP:** 243 **EST:** 1955
SQ FT: 212,000
SALES (est): 90.87MM
SALES (corp-wide): 90.87MM **Privately Held**
Web: www.ferno.com
SIC: 5047 3842 Medical equipment and supplies; Splints, pneumatic and wood

(G-16051)
FORTIS PLASTICS LLC
185 Park Dr (45177-2891)
PHONE.................................937 382-0966
Bob Sheriean, *Prin*
EMP: 12 **EST:** 2010
SALES (est): 155.36K **Privately Held**
SIC: 3089 Molding primary plastics

(G-16052)
HALE MANUFACTURING LLC
1065 Wayne Rd (45177-2024)
PHONE.................................937 382-2127
David Hale, *Pr*
David Hale, *Pt*
EMP: 10 **EST:** 1947
SQ FT: 10,000
SALES (est): 826.87K **Privately Held**
Web: www.halemfg.com
SIC: 3599 Machine shop, jobbing and repair

(G-16053)
HOOD PACKAGING CORPORATION
Also Called: Southern Bag
1961 Rombach Ave (45177-1997)
P.O. Box 745 (45177-0745)
PHONE.................................937 382-6681
Bill Terrill, *Brnch Mgr*
EMP: 200
SQ FT: 150,000
Web: www.hoodpkg.com
SIC: 2674 2673 Shipping bags or sacks, including multiwall and heavy duty; Bags: plastic, laminated, and coated
HQ: Hood Packaging Corporation
25 Woodgreen Pl
Madison MS 39110
601 853-7260

(G-16054)
INNOVTIVE ENGNRED SLUTIONS INC
2695 Progress Way (45177-7702)
PHONE.................................937 382-6710
Randy Workman, *Pr*
Betty Workman, *Pr*
Randy Workman, *VP*
Joseph Eramo, *Prin*
Doug Pierson, *Genl Mgr*
EMP: 35 **EST:** 1985
SQ FT: 4,000
SALES (est): 5.39MM **Privately Held**
Web: www.ies-engineering.com
SIC: 3599 Machine shop, jobbing and repair

(G-16055)
ISOMET LLC
2149 S Us Highway 68 (45177-8629)
PHONE.................................937 382-3867
Robert A Raizk, *Prin*
EMP: 7 **EST:** 2013
SALES (est): 55.22K **Privately Held**

Web: www.isomet.com
SIC: 3827 Optical instruments and lenses

(G-16056)
NEW BURLINGTON WOODWORKS
2581 New Burlington Rd (45177-9032)
PHONE.................................937 488-3503
Ivan Bashaw, *Prin*
EMP: 6 **EST:** 2009
SALES (est): 91.72K **Privately Held**
SIC: 2431 Millwork

(G-16057)
ORANGE FRAZER PRESS INC
37 1/2 W Main St (45177-2236)
P.O. Box 214 (45177-0214)
PHONE.................................937 382-3196
Marcy Hawley, *Pr*
John Baskin, *VP*
EMP: 7 **EST:** 1987
SQ FT: 2,000
SALES (est): 860.93K **Privately Held**
Web: www.orangefrazer.com
SIC: 2741 Miscellaneous publishing

(G-16058)
RELIABLE PRINTING SOLUTIONS
8177 N State Route 134 (45177-8888)
PHONE.................................937 486-5031
Charity C Smith, *Prin*
EMP: 6 **EST:** 2003
SALES (est): 177.25K **Privately Held**
SIC: 2752 Commercial printing, lithographic

(G-16059)
TIMBERTECH LIMITED
Also Called: Timbertech
894 Prairie Rd (45177-8847)
PHONE.................................937 655-8766
◆ **EMP:** 260
SIC: 3089 Plastics hardware and building products

(G-16060)
TOTAL BAKING SOLUTIONS LLC
474 S Nelson Ave (45177-2037)
EMP: 20 **EST:** 2010
SQ FT: 120,000
SALES (est): 2.29MM **Privately Held**
Web: www.allfoodequip.com
SIC: 3556 Ovens, bakery

(G-16061)
TRI STATE MEDIA LLC
325 Davids Dr (45177-2431)
PHONE.................................513 933-0101
John Clary, *Pr*
EMP: 15 **EST:** 2001
SQ FT: 10,500
SALES (est): 3.91MM **Privately Held**
Web: www.tri-statemedia.com
SIC: 2679 Labels, paper: made from purchased material

(G-16062)
VECTOR ELECTROMAGNETICS LLC
1245 Airport Rd (45177-9389)
PHONE.................................937 478-5904
Errol English, *Prin*
EMP: 10 **EST:** 2013
SALES (est): 926.62K **Privately Held**
SIC: 8711 3812 Electrical or electronic engineering; Defense systems and equipment

(G-16063)
WILMINGTON FOREST PRODUCTS
5562 S Us Highway 68 (45177-7112)
PHONE.................................937 382-7813
Thomas D Driscoll, *Pr*

Wilmington - Clinton County (G-16064)

Mary B Driscoll, *VP*
EMP: 6 **EST:** 1979
SQ FT: 7,500
SALES (est): 506.32K **Privately Held**
SIC: 2421 Sawmills and planing mills, general

(G-16064)
WILMINGTON PRCSION MCHNING INC
Also Called: Wilmington Precision Machining
397 Starbuck Rd (45177-8875)
PHONE...................................937 382-3700
Steve Garrison, *Pr*
David D Clay, *
Clifton Hamilton, *
EMP: 24 **EST:** 1996
SQ FT: 9,000
SALES (est): 4.49MM **Privately Held**
Web: www.wpm-inc.net
SIC: 3544 Special dies and tools

Wilmot
Stark County

(G-16065)
AMISH DOOR INC (PA)
Also Called: Amish Door Restaurant
1210 Winesburg St (44689)
P.O. Box 215 (44689-0215)
PHONE...................................330 359-5464
Milo Miller, *Pr*
Yvonne Torrence, *
Katherine Miller, *Stockholder*
Eric Gerber, *
EMP: 155 **EST:** 1957
SQ FT: 7,500
SALES (est): 9.67MM
SALES (corp-wide): 9.67MM **Privately Held**
Web: www.amishdoor.com
SIC: 5947 5812 7011 2051 Gift shop; Restaurant, family: independent; Hotels and motels; Bread, cake, and related products

(G-16066)
COSMO PLASTICS COMPANY
Also Called: Cosmo Plastics Co
211 Winesburg St (44689-9616)
P.O. Box 157 (44689-0157)
PHONE...................................330 359-5429
Vicky Wartcentruber, *Mgr*
EMP: 56
SQ FT: 12,000
SALES (corp-wide): 37.71K **Privately Held**
Web: www.cosmocorp.com
SIC: 3089 Injection molding of plastics
HQ: Cosmo Plastics Company
30201 Aurora Rd
Cleveland OH 44139
440 498-7500

(G-16067)
DAVID E EASTERDAY AND CO INC
Also Called: Easterday & Co
1225 Us Route 62 Unit C (44689-9628)
PHONE...................................330 359-0700
David E Easterday, *Pr*
Valeria Easterday, *Sec*
EMP: 12 **EST:** 1972
SQ FT: 40,000
SALES (est): 2.49MM **Privately Held**
Web: www.woodwrightfinish.com
SIC: 2851 Varnishes, nec

(G-16068)
HARDWOOD SOLUTIONS
112 E Main St (44689-9704)
P.O. Box 191 (44689-0191)
PHONE...................................330 359-5755
Brian Kyle, *Prin*
EMP: 6 **EST:** 2010
SALES (est): 219.42K **Privately Held**
SIC: 2499 Decorative wood and woodwork

(G-16069)
SWISS VALLEY TIRE LLC ◊
1900 Us Route 62 (44689-9604)
PHONE...................................330 231-6187
Robert Ringler, *Pr*
EMP: 6 **EST:** 2022
SALES (est): 64.13K **Privately Held**
SIC: 7534 3011 Tire repair shop; Tire sundries or tire repair materials, rubber

(G-16070)
TREVOR CLATTERBUCK
Also Called: Wholesome Valley Farm
927 Us Route 62 (44689-9610)
PHONE...................................330 359-2129
Trevor Clatterbuck, *Owner*
Derek Suhoski, *Owner*
EMP: 6 **EST:** 2017
SALES (est): 392.31K **Privately Held**
Web: www.wholesomevalleyfarm.com
SIC: 0191 2032 2033 General farms, primarily crop; Canned specialties; Canned fruits and specialties

(G-16071)
WEAVER LUMBER CO
1925 Us Route 62 (44689-9604)
PHONE...................................330 359-5091
Robert Weaver, *Owner*
EMP: 6 **EST:** 1981
SALES (est): 362.18K **Privately Held**
Web: www.weaver-lumber.com
SIC: 2421 Custom sawmill

Winchester
Adams County

(G-16072)
CANTRELL RFINERY SLS TRNSP INC
18856 State Route 136 (45697-9793)
P.O. Box 175 (45697-0175)
PHONE...................................937 695-0318
Robert Cantrell, *Pr*
EMP: 12 **EST:** 2008
SALES (est): 902.55K **Privately Held**
SIC: 3559 Petroleum refinery equipment

(G-16073)
HEIDELBERG MATERIALS US INC
Also Called: Hanson Aggregates Eagle Quarry
13526 Overstake Rd (45697-9644)
PHONE...................................937 442-6009
EMP: 21
SALES (corp-wide): 23.02B **Privately Held**
Web: www.heidelbergmaterials.us
SIC: 3273 Ready-mixed concrete
HQ: Heidelberg Materials Us, Inc.
300 E John Carpenter Fwy
Irving TX 75062

(G-16074)
N & W MACHINING & FABG INC
8 Mathias Rd (45697-9727)
PHONE...................................937 695-5582
Junior Nesbitt, *Pr*
Julene Nesbitt, *Sec*
EMP: 9 **EST:** 1996
SQ FT: 10,000
SALES (est): 870.03K **Privately Held**
Web: www.go-to-low-cost-insurance.com

SIC: 3599 Machine shop, jobbing and repair

Windsor
Ashtabula County

(G-16075)
HERSHBERGER MANUFACTURING
Also Called: Eagle Hardwoods
7584 Rockwood Rd (44099-9741)
P.O. Box 336 (44099-0336)
PHONE...................................440 272-5555
John Hershberger, *Owner*
EMP: 20 **EST:** 1989
SQ FT: 6,500
SALES (est): 1.32MM **Privately Held**
Web: www.hershbergermfg.com
SIC: 2448 4212 Pallets, wood; Local trucking, without storage

(G-16076)
S HOLLEY LUMBER LLC
7143 Noble Rd (44099-9750)
PHONE...................................440 272-5315
EMP: 6 **EST:** 2008
SALES (est): 160.36K **Privately Held**
Web: www.sholleylumber.com
SIC: 2431 2421 Millwork; Lumber stacking or sticking

Winesburg
Holmes County

(G-16077)
9444 OHIO HOLDING CO
1658 Us Route 62 E (44690)
P.O. Box 181 (44690)
PHONE...................................330 359-6291
Robert Ramseyer, *Pr*
▲ **EMP:** 45 **EST:** 1997
SQ FT: 5,500
SALES (est): 9.93MM **Privately Held**
SIC: 2022 Natural cheese

(G-16078)
CASE FARMS OF OHIO INC (HQ)
Also Called: Case Farms Chicken
1818 County Rd 160 (44690)
P.O. Box 185 (44690-0185)
PHONE...................................330 359-7141
Thomas Shelton, *Pr*
Mike Popowycz, *
EMP: 200 **EST:** 1947
SQ FT: 8,000
SALES (est): 28.02MM
SALES (corp-wide): 490.71MM **Privately Held**
Web: www.casefarms.com
SIC: 2015 2011 Poultry slaughtering and processing; Meat packing plants
PA: Case Foods, Inc.
385 Pilch Rd
Troutman NC 28166
704 528-4501

(G-16079)
H & S OPERATING COMPANY INC
2581 County Rd 160 (44690)
P.O. Box 82 (44690-0082)
PHONE...................................330 830-8178
Eric Smith, *Pr*
Ervin Hostetler, *Sec*
EMP: 7 **EST:** 1974
SALES (est): 236.42K **Privately Held**
SIC: 1321 Natural gas liquids

(G-16080)
MARIC DRILLING CO
2581 County Rd 160 (44690)
P.O. Box 82 (44690-0082)
PHONE...................................330 830-8178
EMP: 8 **EST:** 1995
SALES (est): 451.85K **Privately Held**
SIC: 1381 Drilling oil and gas wells

(G-16081)
MERIDIAN INDUSTRIES INC
Also Called: Kent Elastomer Products
7369 Peabody Kent Rd (44690)
P.O. Box 186 (44690-0186)
PHONE...................................330 359-5447
Robert Oborn, *Brnch Mgr*
EMP: 73
SALES (corp-wide): 331.16MM **Privately Held**
Web: www.meridiancompanies.com
SIC: 3069 3949 Tubing, rubber; Sporting and athletic goods, nec
PA: Meridian Industries, Inc.
735 N Water St Ste 630
Milwaukee WI 53202
414 224-0610

(G-16082)
ROBIN INDUSTRIES INC
Also Called: Holmco Division
7227 State Route 515 (44690)
P.O. Box 188 (44690-0188)
PHONE...................................330 359-5418
Paul Rogers, *Prin*
EMP: 23
SALES (corp-wide): 74.78MM **Privately Held**
Web: www.robin-industries.com
SIC: 3069 3061 Molded rubber products; Mechanical rubber goods
PA: Robin Industries, Inc.
6500 Rockside Rd Ste 230
Independence OH 44131
216 631-7000

(G-16083)
WINESBURG MEATS INC
2181 Us Rte 62 (44690-9001)
P.O. Box 202 (44690-0202)
PHONE...................................330 359-5092
Marion Pacula, *Pr*
EMP: 8 **EST:** 1959
SQ FT: 5,500
SALES (est): 963.93K **Privately Held**
Web: www.winesburg-meats.com
SIC: 2011 5421 Meat packing plants; Meat markets, including freezer provisioners

Wintersville
Jefferson County

(G-16084)
ANTHONY MINING CO INC
72 Airport Rd (43953-9204)
P.O. Box 1298 (43952-6298)
PHONE...................................740 282-5301
Albert Carapellotti, *Pr*
Michael Carapellotti, *Sec*
EMP: 6 **EST:** 1957
SQ FT: 1,000
SALES (est): 620.14K **Privately Held**
SIC: 6512 1221 Nonresidential building operators; Bituminous coal and lignite-surface mining

(G-16085)
ARM (USA) INC
1506 Fernwood Rd (43953-7640)
PHONE...................................740 264-6599

◆ **EMP:** 50 **EST:** 1996
SALES (est): 8.95MM **Privately Held**
Web: www.armrides.com
SIC: 3599 Amusement park equipment

Woodsfield
Monroe County

(G-16086)
COUNTRY CLIPPINS LLC
114 S Main St (43793-1023)
PHONE..............................740 472-5228
Leslie Cisler, *Prin*
EMP: 6 **EST:** 2007
SALES (est): 218.43K **Privately Held**
SIC: 3999 Barber and beauty shop equipment

(G-16087)
HEARTLAND RETREADERS INC
103 N Sycamore St (43793-1031)
P.O. Box 386 (43793-0386)
PHONE..............................740 472-0558
Craig Freeman, *Pr*
EMP: 11 **EST:** 1975
SQ FT: 7,500
SALES (est): 477.83K **Privately Held**
SIC: 7534 Rebuilding and retreading tires

(G-16088)
J C L S ENTERPRISES LLC
Also Called: Sew It Seams
742 Lewisville Rd (43793-9061)
P.O. Box 150 (43793-0150)
PHONE..............................740 472-0314
EMP: 7 **EST:** 1986
SALES (est): 702.46K **Privately Held**
SIC: 2331 2321 Blouses, women's and juniors': made from purchased material; Sport shirts, men's and boys': from purchased materials

(G-16089)
OHIO MADE TIRES LLC
47063 Black Walnut Pkwy (43793-9521)
PHONE..............................740 421-4934
EMP: 8 **EST:** 2010
SALES (est): 251.02K **Privately Held**
SIC: 7534 Tire retreading and repair shops

(G-16090)
WOODSFELD TRUE VLUE HM CTR INC
Also Called: True Value
218 State Rte 78 (43793)
P.O. Box 30 (43793-0030)
PHONE..............................740 472-1651
Walter L Kemp, *Pr*
Sally Kemp, *VP*
Charles Orum, *Sec*
EMP: 21 **EST:** 1974
SQ FT: 12,000
SALES (est): 2.45MM **Privately Held**
Web: www.truevalue.com
SIC: 5251 2421 Hardware stores; Lumber: rough, sawed, or planed

Woodville
Sandusky County

(G-16091)
CHIPPEWA TOOL AND MFG CO
1101 Oak St (43469-9792)
P.O. Box 158 (43469-0158)
PHONE..............................419 849-2790
Jim Kusian, *Pr*
EMP: 10 **EST:** 1965

SQ FT: 8,600
SALES (est): 641.65K **Privately Held**
Web: www.chippewatool.com
SIC: 3545 3544 Precision tools, machinists'; Special dies and tools

(G-16092)
CONCRETE MATERIAL SUPPLY LLC
875 E Main St (43469-9814)
PHONE..............................419 261-6404
Tom Bischoff Junior, *Prin*
EMP: 16 **EST:** 2009
SALES (est): 464.32K **Privately Held**
Web: www.concretematerialsupply.com
SIC: 1771 3272 Concrete work; Concrete products, nec

Wooster
Wayne County

(G-16093)
1010 MAGAPP LLC
242 E Liberty St (44691-4348)
PHONE..............................210 701-1754
Jeffrey Kinsey Mg, *Pt*
EMP: 6 **EST:** 2012
SALES (est): 97.17K **Privately Held**
Web: www.golivemagazine.com
SIC: 2721 Periodicals

(G-16094)
ABS MATERIALS INC
Also Called: AMC
1909 Old Mansfield Rd Ste C (44691-9474)
PHONE..............................330 234-7999
J Gary Mcdaniel, *CEO*
Stephen Spoonamore, *
Graham Evans, *
Glenn Johnso, *
Marcene Tesmer, *
EMP: 69 **EST:** 2008
SALES (est): 11.3MM **Privately Held**
Web: www.absmaterials.com
SIC: 2869 Industrial organic chemicals, nec

(G-16095)
ADVANCED DRAINAGE SYSTEMS INC
3113 W Old Lincoln Way (44691-3262)
PHONE..............................330 264-4949
Barry Girvin, *Mgr*
EMP: 24
SALES (corp-wide): 3.07B **Publicly Held**
Web: www.adspipe.com
SIC: 3084 3083 Plastics pipe; Laminated plastics plate and sheet
PA: Advanced Drainage Systems, Inc.
4640 Trueman Blvd
Hilliard OH 43026
614 658-0050

(G-16096)
AKRON BRASS COMPANY
1615 Old Mansfield Rd (44691-7211)
PHONE..............................800 228-1161
EMP: 23
SALES (corp-wide): 3.27B **Publicly Held**
Web: www.akronbrass.com
SIC: 3647 Vehicular lighting equipment
HQ: Akron Brass Company
343 Venture Blvd
Wooster OH 44691

(G-16097)
AKRON BRASS COMPANY (DH)
343 Venture Blvd (44691-7564)
P.O. Box 86 (44691-0086)
PHONE..............................330 264-5678
◆ **EMP:** 325 **EST:** 1988

SQ FT: 20,000
SALES (est): 89.76MM
SALES (corp-wide): 3.27B **Publicly Held**
Web: www.akronbrass.com
SIC: 3647 3699 Vehicular lighting equipment; Electrical equipment and supplies, nec
HQ: Akron Brass Holding Corp.
343 Venture Blvd
Wooster OH 44691
330 264-5678

(G-16098)
AKRON BRASS HOLDING CORP (HQ)
343 Venture Blvd (44691-7564)
PHONE..............................330 264-5678
Sean Tillinghast, *Pr*
EMP: 39 **EST:** 2009
SALES (est): 89.76MM
SALES (corp-wide): 3.27B **Publicly Held**
Web: www.akronbrass.com
SIC: 3647 3699 6719 Vehicular lighting equipment; Electrical equipment and supplies, nec; Investment holding companies, except banks
PA: Idex Corporation
3100 Sanders Rd Ste 301
Northbrook IL 60062
847 498-7070

(G-16099)
ALAN MANUFACTURING INC
3927 E Lincoln Way (44691-8997)
P.O. Box 24875 (44124-0875)
PHONE..............................330 262-1555
Richard Bluestone, *Pr*
▲ **EMP:** 36 **EST:** 1993
SQ FT: 110,000
SALES (est): 2.49MM **Privately Held**
Web: www.alanmfg.com
SIC: 3444 3822 1711 1761 Sheet metalwork; Environmental controls; Plumbing, heating, air-conditioning; Roofing, siding, and sheetmetal work

(G-16100)
ALBRIGHT RADIATOR INC
Also Called: Albright Radiator
331 N Hillcrest Dr (44691-3722)
P.O. Box 214 (44691-0214)
PHONE..............................330 264-8886
TOLL FREE: 800
Dave Albright, *Pr*
Scott Albright, *Sec*
EMP: 6 **EST:** 1928
SQ FT: 4,000
SALES (est): 885.14K **Privately Held**
Web: www.albrightwelding.com
SIC: 7539 7692 3714 Radiator repair shop, automotive; Welding repair; Radiators and radiator shells and cores, motor vehicle

(G-16101)
ARTIFLEX MANUFACTURING INC (HQ)
Also Called: Artiflex Manufacturing, LLC
1425 E Bowman St (44691-3185)
PHONE..............................330 262-2015
Erin Hoffmann, *CEO*
Erik Egerer, *
Greg Wolf, *
◆ **EMP:** 428 **EST:** 2011
SQ FT: 1,200,000
SALES (est): 177.37MM
SALES (corp-wide): 177.37MM **Privately Held**
Web: www.artiflexmfg.com
SIC: 3465 3469 Body parts, automobile: stamped metal; Metal stampings, nec
PA: Its-H Holdings, Llc
731 Broadway Ave Nw
Grand Rapids MI 49504

616 459-8285

(G-16102)
BAUER CORPORATION (PA)
Also Called: Bauer Ladder
2540 Progress Dr (44691-7970)
PHONE..............................800 321-4760
Mark Mcconnell, *Pr*
Ward Mcconnel, *Ch*
Norman Miller Stkldr, *Prin*
John Vasichko, *
EMP: 30 **EST:** 1916
SQ FT: 71,500
SALES (est): 5.15MM **Privately Held**
Web: www.bauerladder.com
SIC: 5082 3499 3446 3441 Ladders; Metal ladders; Architectural metalwork; Fabricated structural metal

(G-16103)
BC INVESTMENT CORPORATION (PA)
1505 E Bowman St (44691-3128)
P.O. Box 165 (44691-0165)
PHONE..............................330 262-3070
Norman L Miller Junior, *Pr*
EMP: 6 **EST:** 1990
SQ FT: 72,500
SALES (est): 6.32MM **Privately Held**
SIC: 2499 3499 4213 3089 Ladders and stepladders, wood; Metal ladders; Trucking, except local; Plastics processing

(G-16104)
BISHOP WELL SERVICES CORP
416 N Bauer Rd (44691-8626)
P.O. Box 511 (44691-0511)
PHONE..............................330 264-2023
EMP: 9 **EST:** 1992
SQ FT: 6,000
SALES (est): 541.35K **Privately Held**
SIC: 1389 Oil field services, nec

(G-16105)
BOB SUMEREL TIRE COMPANY
519 Madison Ave (44691-4705)
PHONE..............................330 262-1220
EMP: 6 **EST:** 2014
SALES (est): 232.84K **Privately Held**
Web: www.bobsumereltire.com
SIC: 7539 7537 7534 5531 Automotive air conditioning repair; Automotive transmission repair shops; Tire retreading and repair shops; Automotive tires

(G-16106)
BOSCH REXROTH CORPORATION
Mannesmann Rexroth
290 E Milltown Rd (44691-6113)
P.O. Box 394 (44691-0394)
PHONE..............................330 263-3300
Mike Bickel, *Brnch Mgr*
EMP: 150
SALES (corp-wide): 230.19MM **Privately Held**
Web: www.boschrexroth-us.com
SIC: 3594 3494 3491 Pumps, hydraulic power transfer; Expansion joints, pipe; Industrial valves
HQ: Bosch Rexroth Corporation
14001 S Lkes Dr S Pt Bus
Charlotte NC 28273
704 583-4338

(G-16107)
BUCKEYE CORRUGATED INC
Also Called: Buckeye Container Division
3350 Long Rd (44691-7953)
PHONE..............................330 264-6336
Jack Nebesky, *Brnch Mgr*
EMP: 68

Wooster - Wayne County (G-16108)

(G-16108)
BUCKEYE OIL PRODUCING CO
544 E Liberty St (44691-3602)
P.O. Box 129 (44691-0129)
PHONE...................330 264-8847
Adam Briggs, *CEO*
Mark Lytle, *Pr*
Steve Sigler, *VP*
EMP: 15 **EST:** 1961
SQ FT: 10,000
SALES (est): 2.09MM **Privately Held**
Web: www.buckeyeoilinc.com
SIC: 1311 1381 Crude petroleum production; Drilling oil and gas wells

(G-16109)
BUILT-RITE BOX & CRATE INC
608 Freedlander Rd (44691-4704)
P.O. Box 1051 (44691-7051)
PHONE...................330 263-0936
John C Meenan, *Pr*
Dave Schaeufele, *VP*
Jodie L Meenan, *Sec*
EMP: 31 **EST:** 1986
SQ FT: 10,000
SALES (est): 1.88MM **Privately Held**
Web: www.builtritebox.com
SIC: 2441 2448 Boxes, wood; Skids, wood

(G-16110)
CLARK-FOWLER ENTERPRISES INC
Also Called: Clark-Fowler Elc Mtr & Sups
510 W Henry St (44691-4773)
PHONE...................330 262-0906
Don Clark, *Pr*
Douglas Fowler, *
Jerry L Clark, *
EMP: 24 **EST:** 1995
SQ FT: 5,000
SALES (est): 5.11MM **Privately Held**
Web: www.clarkfowlerelectric.com
SIC: 7694 5063 Electric motor repair; Motors, electric

(G-16111)
CROWN DIV OF ALLEN GR
1654 Old Mansfield Rd (44691-7211)
PHONE...................330 263-4919
Michael Hooper, *Prin*
EMP: 7 **EST:** 2007
SALES (est): 100.33K **Privately Held**
SIC: 3714 Motor vehicle parts and accessories

(G-16112)
DAISY BRAND LLC
3049 Daisy Way (44691-9819)
PHONE...................330 202-4410
David M Sokolsky, *Managing Member*
EMP: 18
SALES (corp-wide): 211.05MM **Privately Held**
Web: www.daisybrand.com
SIC: 2026 Milk processing (pasteurizing, homogenizing, bottling)
PA: Daisy Brand, Llc
   12750 Merit Dr, Ste 600
   Dallas TX 75251
   972 726-0800

SALES (corp-wide): 196.62MM **Privately Held**
Web: www.bcipkg.com
SIC: 2653 Boxes, corrugated: made from purchased materials
PA: Buckeye Corrugated, Inc.
   822 Kumho Dr Ste 400
   Fairlawn OH 44333
   330 576-0590

(G-16113)
DBW FIBER CORPORATION
1720 Enterprise Corporation (44691)
P.O. Box 61108 (29419)
◆ **EMP:** 73 **EST:** 2006
SQ FT: 37,500
SALES (est): 5.24MM **Privately Held**
Web: www.dbw.de
SIC: 3714 Exhaust systems and parts, motor vehicle

(G-16114)
DRAGON PRODUCTS LLC
3310 Columbus Rd (44691-9134)
PHONE...................330 345-3968
Charles Baker, *Brnch Mgr*
EMP: 40
Web: www.dragonproducts.com
SIC: 3531 3537 Construction machinery; Industrial trucks and tractors
HQ: Dragon Products, Llc
   1655 Louisiana St
   Beaumont TX 77701
   409 833-2665

(G-16115)
E-PAK MANUFACTURING LLC
1109 Pittsburgh Ave (44691-3805)
P.O. Box 269 (44691-0269)
PHONE...................330 264-0825
Bryan Mullet, *Managing Member*
▼ **EMP:** 75 **EST:** 1975
SQ FT: 12,000
SALES (est): 19.15MM **Privately Held**
Web: www.epakmanufacturing.com
SIC: 3443 3441 Dumpsters, garbage; Fabricated structural metal

(G-16116)
ESSC GROUP INC
3340 Burbank Rd (44691-9007)
PHONE...................330 317-3566
Yichun Zhang, *Prin*
▲ **EMP:** 7 **EST:** 2012
SALES (est): 60.36K **Privately Held**
Web: www.esscgroup.com
SIC: 3599 Machine shop, jobbing and repair

(G-16117)
F J DESIGNS INC
Also Called: Cat's Meow Village, The
2163 Great Trails Dr (44691-3738)
PHONE...................330 264-1377
Faline Jones, *CEO*
Emily Pajak-stenger, *Prin*
EMP: 10 **EST:** 1982
SQ FT: 7,000
SALES (est): 417.72K **Privately Held**
Web: www.catsmeow.com
SIC: 2499 2759 3993 Novelties, wood fiber; Commercial printing, nec; Signs and advertising specialties

(G-16118)
FEW ATMTIVE GL APPLCATIONS INC
1720 Enterprise Pkwy (44691-7946)
PHONE...................234 249-1880
▲ **EMP:** 100 **EST:** 2011
SQ FT: 12,000
SALES (est): 9.19MM **Privately Held**
Web: www.few-group.com
SIC: 3089 Windshields, plastics

(G-16119)
FIORITTO OF WOOSTER LLC
2500 Carrie Ln (44691-8485)
PHONE...................330 466-3776
Vicky Fioritto, *Prin*
EMP: 6 **EST:** 2009
SALES (est): 136.4K **Privately Held**

SIC: 1382 Oil and gas exploration services

(G-16120)
FRANKLIN GAS & OIL COMPANY LLC
1615 W Old Lincoln Way (44691-3329)
P.O. Box 1005 (44691-7005)
PHONE...................330 264-8739
James C Morgan, *Managing Member*
EMP: 7 **EST:** 1957
SQ FT: 4,000
SALES (est): 904.38K **Privately Held**
SIC: 1311 Crude petroleum production

(G-16121)
FRITO-LAY NORTH AMERICA INC
Also Called: Frito-Lay
1626 Old Mansfield Rd (44691-9056)
PHONE...................972 334-7000
Mark Vantrease, *Brnch Mgr*
EMP: 127
SALES (corp-wide): 86.39B **Publicly Held**
Web: www.fritolay.com
SIC: 2099 2096 Food preparations, nec; Potato chips and similar snacks
HQ: Frito-Lay North America, Inc.
   7701 Legacy Dr
   Plano TX 75024

(G-16122)
G & S TITANIUM INC
4000 E Lincoln Way (44691-8600)
P.O. Box 1107 (44691-7081)
PHONE...................330 263-0564
◆ **EMP:** 50 **EST:** 1979
SALES (est): 5.02MM **Privately Held**
Web: www.barandwire.com
SIC: 3441 3496 3444 3356 Fabricated structural metal; Miscellaneous fabricated wire products; Sheet metalwork; Nonferrous rolling and drawing, nec

(G-16123)
GDC INC
1700 Old Mansfield Rd (44691-7212)
PHONE...................574 533-3128
Lonnie Abney, *COO*
EMP: 10
SALES (corp-wide): 73.86MM **Privately Held**
Web: www.gdc-corp.com
SIC: 2822 2869 2891 3069 Synthetic rubber; Perfumes, flavorings, and food additives; Adhesives and sealants; Medical and laboratory rubber sundries and related products
PA: Gdc, Inc.
   815 Logan St
   Goshen IN 46528
   574 533-3128

(G-16124)
GLOBAL BODY & EQUIPMENT CO
Also Called: C & C Metal Products
2061 Sylvan Rd (44691-3849)
P.O. Box 857 (44691-0857)
PHONE...................330 264-6640
Robert Lapsley, *Pr*
Bob Lapsley, *
EMP: 100 **EST:** 2002
SALES (est): 14.3MM **Privately Held**
Web: www.globalbodyusa.com
SIC: 3441 Fabricated structural metal

(G-16125)
GREEN ENERGY INC
4489 E Lincoln Way (44691-8602)
PHONE...................330 262-5112
Stephen R Gessel, *Pr*
James E Gessel, *VP*
Debra J Falde, *Sec*

Carl Robert Gessel, *Asst Tr*
EMP: 7 **EST:** 1983
SQ FT: 3,700
SALES (est): 1.01MM **Privately Held**
Web: www.paradiseadventures-kansas.com
SIC: 1311 Crude petroleum production

(G-16126)
GREEN FIELD FARMS CO-OP (PA)
6464 Fredericksburg Rd (44691-9422)
PHONE...................330 263-0246
Leon Wengerd, *CEO*
James Swartzentruber, *CFO*
EMP: 7 **EST:** 2003
SALES (est): 2.07MM **Privately Held**
Web: www.gffarms.com
SIC: 0191 2026 5191 General farms, primarily crop; Fluid milk; Farm supplies

(G-16127)
H & H EQUIPMENT INC
Also Called: Snyder Hot Shot
6247 Ashland Rd (44691-9233)
PHONE...................330 264-5400
Gerald Snyder, *Pr*
EMP: 6 **EST:** 1971
SQ FT: 8,400
SALES (est): 610K **Privately Held**
SIC: 3715 Truck trailers

(G-16128)
HACKWORTH ELECTRIC MOTORS INC
500 E Henry St (44691-1195)
PHONE...................330 345-6049
TOLL FREE: 800
Jeffery Hackworth, *Pr*
Jeffery Hackworth, *Pr*
Brenda Hackworth, *VP*
EMP: 9 **EST:** 1977
SALES (est): 1.75MM **Privately Held**
Web: www.hackworthelectricmotors.com
SIC: 5063 7694 Motors, electric; Electric motor repair

(G-16129)
HAGEN WELL SERVICE LLC
474 Industrial Blvd (44691-8926)
PHONE...................330 264-7500
James R Small, *Pr*
EMP: 9 **EST:** 2008
SALES (est): 704.18K **Privately Held**
Web: www.hagenwellservice.com
SIC: 1389 Oil field services, nec

(G-16130)
HENTHORNE JR JAY MARY BETH
3927 Cleveland Rd (44691-1223)
PHONE...................330 264-1049
Jay Henthorne Junior, *Prin*
EMP: 6 **EST:** 2012
SALES (est): 250.67K **Privately Held**
SIC: 1311 Crude petroleum production

(G-16131)
HYDAC TECHNOLOGY CORP
4265 E Lincoln Way Unit C (44691-8666)
PHONE...................610 266-0100
Matthias Mueller, *Pr*
▲ **EMP:** 12 **EST:** 2010
SALES (est): 1.89MM **Privately Held**
Web: www.hydac.com
SIC: 3492 Fluid power valves and hose fittings

(G-16132)
INGREDIENT INNOVATIONS INTL CO
Also Called: 3i Solutions
146 S Bever St (44691-4326)

GEOGRAPHIC SECTION
Wooster - Wayne County (G-16157)

PHONE.................330 262-4440
Charles Brain, *Pr*
EMP: 7 **EST:** 1997
SQ FT: 12,000
SALES (est): 2.61MM **Publicly Held**
Web: www.3isolutions.com
SIC: 2099 Food preparations, nec
PA: Nu Skin Enterprises, Inc.
75 W Center St
Provo UT 84601

(G-16133)
INTERNATIONAL PAPER COMPANY
International Paper
689 Palmer St (44691-3197)
P.O. Box 1047 (44691-7045)
PHONE.................330 264-1322
Jim Gracey, *Genl Mgr*
EMP: 75
SALES (corp-wide): 18.92B **Publicly Held**
Web: www.internationalpaper.com
SIC: 2653 Boxes, corrugated: made from purchased materials
PA: International Paper Company
6400 Poplar Ave
Memphis TN 38197
901 419-7000

(G-16134)
IRON GATE INDUSTRIES LLC
Also Called: Morrison Custom Welding
1435 S Honeytown Rd (44691-8914)
PHONE.................330 264-0626
EMP: 24 **EST:** 1996
SQ FT: 37,000
SALES (est): 3.87MM **Privately Held**
Web: www.morrisonwelding.com
SIC: 3441 Fabricated structural metal for bridges

(G-16135)
IVIES WHOLISTIC DYNAMICS
2390 Cardinal Court Apt D (44691-2060)
PHONE.................216 469-3103
Ivie Sorkin, *Prin*
EMP: 8 **EST:** 2016
SALES (est): 44.62K **Privately Held**
Web: www.metal-dynamics.com
SIC: 3441 Fabricated structural metal

(G-16136)
JAMES R SMAIL INC
2285 Eagle Pass Ste B (44691-5349)
P.O. Box 1157 (44691-7082)
PHONE.................330 264-7500
James R Smail, *Pr*
Mark A Sparr, *VP*
EMP: 7 **EST:** 1972
SALES (est): 910.6K **Privately Held**
SIC: 1381 Drilling oil and gas wells

(G-16137)
JNP GROUP LLC
449 Freedlander Rd (44691-4734)
P.O. Box 1022 (44691-7022)
PHONE.................800 735-9645
James Pooler, *Pr*
EMP: 12 **EST:** 2010
SALES (est): 720.9K **Privately Held**
SIC: 3585 7389 Refrigeration and heating equipment; Business Activities at Non-Commercial Site

(G-16138)
JRB FAMILY HOLDINGS INC
4255 E Lincoln Way (44691-8601)
◆ **EMP:** 169
Web: www.morbark.com
SIC: 3531 Forestry related equipment

(G-16139)
K S BANDAG INC
737 Industrial Blvd (44691-8999)
PHONE.................330 264-9237
John Kauffman, *Pr*
Mark Hershberger, *VP*
Earl Shaw, *Sec*
EMP: 20 **EST:** 1970
SQ FT: 15,500
SALES (est): 139.21K **Privately Held**
SIC: 7534 Rebuilding and retreading tires

(G-16140)
KEN BEAVERSON INC
3501 W Old Lincoln Way (44691-3253)
PHONE.................330 264-0378
EMP: 8 **EST:** 2005
SALES (est): 171.49K **Privately Held**
Web: www.woostermotorways.com
SIC: 3537 Trucks: freight, baggage, etc.: industrial, except mining

(G-16141)
KENOIL INC
1537 Blachleyville Rd (44691-9752)
P.O. Box 1085 (44691-7081)
PHONE.................330 262-1144
Steve Fleisher, *VP*
EMP: 9 **EST:** 1982
SALES (est): 250.5K **Privately Held**
Web: www.kenoil.net
SIC: 1311 Crude petroleum and natural gas production

(G-16142)
KETMAN CORPORATION
Also Called: Wooster Book Company, The
205 W Liberty St (44691-4831)
PHONE.................330 262-1688
David Wiesenberg, *Pr*
Carol A Rueger, *Sec*
EMP: 8 **EST:** 1991
SQ FT: 7,500
SALES (est): 709.67K **Privately Held**
Web: www.woosterbook.com
SIC: 5942 2731 8742 Comic books; Books, publishing only; Industry specialist consultants

(G-16143)
KILLBUCK CREEK OIL CO LLC
2098 Portage Rd Ste 250 (44691-5707)
PHONE.................330 601-0921
Jim Shoots, *Owner*
EMP: 6 **EST:** 2010
SALES (est): 280.5K **Privately Held**
SIC: 1311 Crude petroleum and natural gas

(G-16144)
KORDA MANUFACTURING INC
3927 E Lincoln Way (44691-8997)
PHONE.................330 262-1555
EMP: 24 **EST:** 1994
SALES (est): 2.15MM **Privately Held**
Web: www.alanmfg.com
SIC: 3444 Sheet metalwork

(G-16145)
LETTERMANS LLC
Also Called: Lettermans
344 Beall Ave (44691-3520)
PHONE.................330 345-2628
Jodi Kennedy, *Prin*
EMP: 6 **EST:** 2014
SALES (est): 121.56K **Privately Held**
Web: www.lettermanswooster.com
SIC: 2329 2339 Men's and boys' sportswear and athletic clothing; Women's and misses' accessories

(G-16146)
LINCOLN WAY VINEYARDS INC
9050 W Old Lincoln Way (44691-7504)
PHONE.................330 804-9463
James Borton, *Pr*
EMP: 10 **EST:** 2008
SALES (est): 250K **Privately Held**
Web: www.lincolnwayvineyards.com
SIC: 2084 Wine cellars, bonded: engaged in blending wines

(G-16147)
LUK CLUTCH SYSTEMS LLC (DH)
Also Called: Luk Clutch Systems
3401 Old Airport Rd (44691-9544)
PHONE.................330 264-4383
◆ **EMP:** 44 **EST:** 1977
SQ FT: 400,000
SALES (est): 100.1MM
SALES (corp-wide): 66.25B **Privately Held**
Web: www.schaeffler.de
SIC: 3568 3566 3714 Power transmission equipment, nec; Speed changers, drives, and gears; Clutches, motor vehicle
HQ: Schaeffler Transmission, Llc.
3401 Old Airport Rd
Wooster OH 44691
330 264-4383

(G-16148)
MAGNI-POWER COMPANY (PA)
Also Called: Magni Fab & Magnetic
5511 E Lincoln Way (44691-8607)
P.O. Box 122 (44691-0122)
PHONE.................330 264-3637
EMP: 90 **EST:** 1948
SALES (est): 24.62MM
SALES (corp-wide): 24.62MM **Privately Held**
Web: www.magnipower.com
SIC: 3441 Fabricated structural metal

(G-16149)
MAINTENANCE + INC
1051 W Liberty St (44691-3307)
P.O. Box 408 (44691-0408)
PHONE.................330 264-6262
William Neckermann, *Pr*
Robert Huebner, *Dir Opers*
◆ **EMP:** 12 **EST:** 1977
SQ FT: 10,000
SALES (est): 1.95MM **Privately Held**
Web: www.maintinc.com
SIC: 2951 Asphalt and asphaltic paving mixtures (not from refineries)

(G-16150)
MCCANN TOOL & DIE INC
Also Called: J R Tool & Die
3230 Columbus Rd (44691-8430)
PHONE.................330 264-8820
Jess R Mccann Senior, *Pr*
J R Mccann Junior, *VP*
Nellie Mccann, *Sec*
EMP: 14 **EST:** 1982
SQ FT: 6,500
SALES (est): 384.37K **Privately Held**
SIC: 3599 3089 Machine shop, jobbing and repair; Injection molding of plastics

(G-16151)
METROMEDIA TECHNOLOGIES INC
1061 Venture Blvd (44691-9358)
PHONE.................330 264-2501
EMP: 80
SALES (corp-wide): 20.45MM **Privately Held**
Web: www.mmt.com
SIC: 3993 Signs, not made in custom sign painting shops
PA: Metromedia Technologies, Inc.
810 7th Ave Fl 29
New York NY 10019
212 273-2100

(G-16152)
MORBARK LLC
4255 E Lincoln Way (44691-8669)
PHONE.................330 264-8699
Dave Herr, *CEO*
EMP: 175
SALES (corp-wide): 1.69B **Publicly Held**
Web: www.morbark.com
SIC: 3531 Forestry related equipment
HQ: Morbark, Llc
8507 S Winn Rd
Winn MI 48896
989 866-2381

(G-16153)
MORTON BUILDINGS INC
1055 Columbus Avenue Ext (44691-9701)
PHONE.................330 345-6188
Gary Schodorf, *Mgr*
EMP: 23
SALES (corp-wide): 213.04MM **Privately Held**
Web: www.mortonbuildings.com
SIC: 3448 5039 Buildings, portable: prefabricated metal; Prefabricated structures
PA: Morton Buildings, Inc.
252 W Adams St
Morton IL 61550
800 447-7436

(G-16154)
MURR CORPORATION
Also Called: Murr Printing and Graphics
201 N Buckeye St (44691-3501)
PHONE.................330 264-2223
TOLL FREE: 800
Joseph F Murr, *Pr*
EMP: 15 **EST:** 1980
SQ FT: 5,800
SALES (est): 687.18K **Privately Held**
Web: www.murrprinting.com
SIC: 2752 5943 Offset printing; Office forms and supplies

(G-16155)
NORTH CENTRAL CON DESIGNS INC
Also Called: Nccd
3331 E Lincoln Way (44691-3762)
PHONE.................419 606-1908
Daniel Zawacki, *Pr*
Mike Wiseman, *VP Opers*
Lori Crum, *Sec*
EMP: 7 **EST:** 2005
SALES (est): 107.69K **Privately Held**
SIC: 3271 1741 Blocks, concrete: insulating; Concrete block masonry laying

(G-16156)
NORTH EAST FUEL INC
3927 Cleveland Rd (44691-1223)
PHONE.................330 264-4454
Timothy E Miller, *Prin*
EMP: 6 **EST:** 2013
SALES (est): 219.48K **Privately Held**
SIC: 2869 Fuels

(G-16157)
NORTHEAST TUBULAR INC
426 S Grant St (44691-4712)
P.O. Box 114 (44676-0114)
PHONE.................330 567-2690
Jeffery W Edington, *Prin*
Paul W Wright, *Prin*
EMP: 9 **EST:** 1989
SALES (est): 359.46K **Privately Held**

Wooster - Wayne County (G-16158)

SIC: 2241 Hose fabric, tubular

(G-16158)
OHIO GRATINGS INC
6355 Lattasburg Rd (44691-9282)
PHONE.................................330 479-4292
Jeremy Chupp, *Prin*
EMP: 7 **EST:** 2017
SALES (est): 76.6K **Privately Held**
Web: www.ohiogratings.com
SIC: 3446 Architectural metalwork

(G-16159)
PRAIRIE LANE CORPORATION
Also Called: Prairie Lane Gravel Co
4489 Prairie Ln (44691-9442)
P.O. Box 233 (44691-0233)
PHONE.................................330 262-3322
Ralph Miller, *Pr*
James Lanham, *Sec*
EMP: 7 **EST:** 1954
SQ FT: 2,400
SALES (est): 713.27K **Privately Held**
Web: www.prairielanelakepark.com
SIC: 1442 7032 6519 Construction sand and gravel; Sporting and recreational camps; Farm land leasing

(G-16160)
PRENTKE ROMICH COMPANY (PA)
Also Called: Prc-Saltillo
1022 Heyl Rd (44691-9744)
PHONE.................................330 262-1984
Dave Hershberger, *CEO*
Barry Romich, *
Jan Hughes, *
Lee Miller, *
EMP: 130 **EST:** 1966
SQ FT: 8,000
SALES (est): 108.45MM
SALES (corp-wide): 108.45MM **Privately Held**
Web: www.prentrom.com
SIC: 3442 Metal doors, sash, and trim

(G-16161)
RBB SYSTEMS INC
1909 Old Mansfield Rd (44691-9474)
PHONE.................................330 263-4502
Bruce Hendrick, *Pr*
Michele Hendrick, *
Richard L Beery, *
EMP: 135 **EST:** 1973
SQ FT: 20,000
SALES (est): 7.05MM **Privately Held**
Web: www.rbbsystems.com
SIC: 3625 Relays and industrial controls

(G-16162)
REILLOC MACHINE CO INC
1457 Fox Lake Rd (44691-9616)
PHONE.................................330 601-0379
Joshua J Collier, *Prin*
EMP: 6 **EST:** 2008
SALES (est): 120K **Privately Held**
SIC: 3599 Machine and other job shop work

(G-16163)
RICELAND CABINET INC
326 N Hillcrest Dr (44691-3745)
PHONE.................................330 601-1071
Leroy Miller, *Pr*
Myron Miller, *
David A Miller, *
Paul A Miller, *
Wanda Mullet, *
EMP: 92 **EST:** 1979
SQ FT: 24,220
SALES (est): 6.94MM **Privately Held**
Web: www.ricelandcabinet.com

SIC: 2434 3281 2541 Wood kitchen cabinets; Cut stone and stone products; Wood partitions and fixtures

(G-16164)
RICELAND CABINET CORPORATION
326 N Hillcrest Dr Ste A (44691-3745)
PHONE.................................330 601-1071
Kit Carin, *Prin*
EMP: 15 **EST:** 2006
SALES (est): 624.33K **Privately Held**
Web: www.ricelandcabinet.com
SIC: 2434 Wood kitchen cabinets

(G-16165)
RS&B INDUSTRIES LLC
1147 Akron Rd (44691-2501)
PHONE.................................330 255-6000
EMP: 16 **EST:** 2015
SALES (est): 975.37K **Privately Held**
SIC: 3000 Manufacturing industries, nec

(G-16166)
SCHAEFFLER TRANSM SYSTEMS LLC
3177 Old Airport Rd (44691-9520)
PHONE.................................330 202-6212
EMP: 895
SALES (corp-wide): 66.25B **Privately Held**
Web: www.schaeffler.us
SIC: 3714 3566 Motor vehicle parts and accessories; Speed changers, drives, and gears
HQ: Schaeffler Transmission Systems, Llc
3401 Old Airport Rd
Wooster OH 44691
330 264-4383

(G-16167)
SCHAEFFLER TRANSM SYSTEMS LLC (DH)
3401 Old Airport Rd (44691-9581)
PHONE.................................330 264-4383
Marc Mcgrath, *Regional Chief Executive Officer*
◆ **EMP:** 30 **EST:** 2004
SALES (est): 113.12MM
SALES (corp-wide): 66.25B **Privately Held**
Web: www.schaeffler.us
SIC: 3714 3566 Motor vehicle parts and accessories; Speed changers, drives, and gears
HQ: Schaeffler Transmission, Llc.
3401 Old Airport Rd
Wooster OH 44691
330 264-4383

(G-16168)
SCHAEFFLER TRANSMISSION LLC (DH)
3401 Old Airport Rd (44691-9581)
PHONE.................................330 264-4383
Klaus Rosenfeld, *CEO*
Marc Mcgrath, *Pr*
Ashi Uppal, *
▲ **EMP:** 299 **EST:** 2004
SALES (est): 447.99MM
SALES (corp-wide): 66.25B **Privately Held**
Web: www.schaeffler.us
SIC: 3714 Motor vehicle engines and parts
HQ: Schaeffler Group Usa Inc.
308 Springhill Farm Rd
Fort Mill SC 29715
803 548-8500

(G-16169)
SCOT INDUSTRIES INC
6578 Ashland Rd (44691-9233)
P.O. Box 1106 (44691-7081)
PHONE.................................330 262-7585

Robert G Gralinski, *Mgr*
EMP: 99
SQ FT: 2,018
SALES (corp-wide): 98.03MM **Privately Held**
Web: www.scotindustries.com
SIC: 5051 7389 3498 3471 Steel; Metal cutting services; Fabricated pipe and fittings; Plating and polishing
PA: Scot Industries, Inc.
3756 F M 250 N
Lone Star TX 75668
903 639-2551

(G-16170)
SEAMAN CORPORATION (PA)
1000 Venture Blvd (44691-9358)
PHONE.................................330 262-1111
Richard N Seaman, *Ch Bd*
John Crum, *
Terrance Link, *
◆ **EMP:** 130 **EST:** 1951
SQ FT: 90,000
SALES (est): 128.86MM
SALES (corp-wide): 128.86MM **Privately Held**
Web: www.seamancorp.com
SIC: 2221 Nylon broadwoven fabrics

(G-16171)
SHEARER FARM INC
Also Called: John Deere Authorized Dealer
7762 Cleveland Rd (44691-7700)
PHONE.................................330 345-9023
EMP: 140
Web: www.agprocompanies.com
SIC: 3523 5082 Fertilizing machinery, farm; Construction and mining machinery

(G-16172)
SIGN DESIGN WOOSTER INC
Also Called: Sign Design
1537 W Old Lincoln Way (44691-3327)
PHONE.................................330 262-8838
Ken Stiffler, *Pr*
Stephanie Stiffler, *Sec*
EMP: 8 **EST:** 1981
SQ FT: 2,000
SALES (est): 946.31K **Privately Held**
Web: www.signdesignwooster.com
SIC: 3993 Signs, not made in custom sign painting shops

(G-16173)
SMITHVILLE MFG CO
6563 Cleveland Rd (44691-9690)
P.O. Box 258 (44677-0258)
PHONE.................................330 345-5818
Allen Nayman, *Pr*
EMP: 14 **EST:** 1972
SQ FT: 624
SALES (est): 1.28MM **Privately Held**
Web: www.smithvillemfg.com
SIC: 3469 3544 Stamping metal for the trade; Special dies and tools

(G-16174)
SPEED NORTH AMERICA INC
1700a Old Mansfield Rd (44691-7212)
P.O. Box 79 (44691-0079)
PHONE.................................330 202-7775
Emmanuel Legrand, *Pr*
◆ **EMP:** 38 **EST:** 2007
SALES (est): 9.37MM
SALES (corp-wide): 660MM **Privately Held**
Web: www.speedgroupe.com
SIC: 3524 Hedge trimmers, electric
HQ: Tecomec Srl
Strada Della Mirandola 11
Reggio Nell'emilia RE 42124
052 295-9001

(G-16175)
STAHL/SCOTT FETZER COMPANY (HQ)
Also Called: Arbortech
3201 W Old Lincoln Way (44691-3298)
PHONE.................................800 277-8245
Craig Aszkler, *Pr*
Bob Businger, *
Patricia Scanoln, *
W W T Stephens, *
EMP: 105 **EST:** 1955
SQ FT: 70,000
SALES (est): 24.76MM
SALES (corp-wide): 226 **Privately Held**
Web: www.stahltruckbodies.com
SIC: 3715 Trailer bodies
PA: The Scott Fetzer Company
28800 Clemens Rd
Westlake OH 44145
440 892-3000

(G-16176)
TEKFOR INC
Also Called: Tekfor USA
3690 Long Rd (44691-7962)
PHONE.................................330 202-7420
Kevin Weldi, *Pr*
▲ **EMP:** 265 **EST:** 2001
SQ FT: 100,000
SALES (est): 96.34MM
SALES (corp-wide): 355.83K **Privately Held**
Web: www.aam.com
SIC: 3462 Automotive forgings, ferrous: crankshaft, engine, axle, etc.
HQ: Neumayer Tekfor Holding Gmbh
Hauptstr. 115
Offenburg BW 77652

(G-16177)
THE WOOSTER BRUSH COMPANY (PA)
604 Madison Ave (44691-4796)
P.O. Box 6010 (44691-6010)
PHONE.................................330 264-4440
◆ **EMP:** 238 **EST:** 1851
SALES (est): 51.67MM
SALES (corp-wide): 51.67MM **Privately Held**
Web: www.woosterbrush.com
SIC: 3991 Paint and varnish brushes

(G-16178)
TRICOR INDUSTRIAL INC (PA)
Also Called: Tricor Metals
3225 W Old Lincoln Way (44691-3258)
P.O. Box 752 (44691-0752)
PHONE.................................330 264-3299
Nancy A Stitzlein, *CEO*
Michael D Stitzlein, *
◆ **EMP:** 77 **EST:** 1977
SQ FT: 140,000
SALES (est): 90.27MM
SALES (corp-wide): 90.27MM **Privately Held**
Web: www.tricormetals.com
SIC: 5085 5169 3444 5051 Fasteners, industrial: nuts, bolts, screws, etc.; Chemicals and allied products, nec; Sheet metalwork; Metals service centers and offices

(G-16179)
UNITED TITANIUM INC (PA)
Also Called: United Titanium
3450 Old Airport Rd (44691-9581)
PHONE.................................330 264-2111
C Michael Reardon, *Pr*
Charlie Gray, *General Vice President*
▲ **EMP:** 117 **EST:** 1962
SQ FT: 150,000

GEOGRAPHIC SECTION

Worthington - Franklin County (G-16202)

SALES (est): 25.75MM
SALES (corp-wide): 25.75MM **Privately Held**
Web: www.unitedtitanium.com
SIC: 3452 Bolts, nuts, rivets, and washers

(G-16180)
VIB-ISO LLC
Also Called: Vib-ISO
449 Freedlander Rd (44691-4734)
P.O. Box 1022 (44691-7022)
PHONE..............................800 735-9645
James Pooler, *Managing Member*
EMP: 12 **EST:** 2012
SALES (est): 1.08MM **Privately Held**
SIC: 3822 Environmental controls

(G-16181)
WAYNE COUNTY RUBBER INC
1205 E Bowman St (44691-3182)
PHONE..............................330 264-5553
Laurie Schang, *Pr*
Arnie Berkowitz, *
EMP: 30 **EST:** 1991
SQ FT: 170,000
SALES (est): 3.96MM **Privately Held**
Web: www.waynecountyrubber.com
SIC: 2822 3069 Synthetic rubber; Custom compounding of rubber materials

(G-16182)
WHITE JEWELERS INC
516 N Bever St Apt 1 (44691-6201)
PHONE..............................330 264-3324
Heather Maxwell, *Owner*
EMP: 6 **EST:** 1928
SALES (est): 590.91K **Privately Held**
Web: www.whitejewelers.net
SIC: 5944 7631 3911 Jewelry, precious stones and precious metals; Watch repair; Jewelry, precious metal

(G-16183)
WOOSTER ABRUZZI COMPANY (PA)
3310 Columbus Rd (44691-9134)
PHONE..............................330 345-3968
Doug Drughal, *Pr*
Bill Stanton, *Stockholder*
EMP: 21 **EST:** 2010
SQ FT: 14,000
SALES (est): 5MM **Privately Held**
SIC: 1389 3444 4212 Construction, repair, and dismantling services; Sheet metalwork; Local trucking, without storage

(G-16184)
WOOSTER DAILY RECORD INC LLC (HQ)
Also Called: Farmer Hub
212 E Liberty St (44691-4348)
P.O. Box 918 (44691-0918)
PHONE..............................330 264-1125
TOLL FREE: 800
EMP: 120 **EST:** 1890
SQ FT: 25,000
SALES (est): 49.08MM
SALES (corp-wide): 467.21MM **Privately Held**
Web: www.the-daily-record.com
SIC: 2711 Commercial printing and newspaper publishing combined
PA: Dix 1898, Inc.
212 E Liberty St
Wooster OH
330 264-3511

(G-16185)
WOOSTER PRINTING & LITHO INC
1345 W Old Lincoln Way (44691-3323)
EMP: 22 **EST:** 1947
SQ FT: 8,400

SALES (est): 328.1K **Privately Held**
Web: www.wooster.edu
SIC: 2752 Offset printing

(G-16186)
WOOSTER PRODUCTS INC (PA)
1000 Spruce St (44691-4682)
P.O. Box 6005 (44691-6005)
PHONE..............................330 264-2844
G K Jim Arora, *Pr*
Doctor Urmil Arora, *VP*
▼ **EMP:** 70 **EST:** 1921
SQ FT: 100,000
SALES (est): 10.93MM
SALES (corp-wide): 10.93MM **Privately Held**
Web: www.woosterproducts.com
SIC: 3446 2851 Stairs, staircases, stair treads: prefabricated metal; Paints and allied products

(G-16187)
WOOSTER PRODUCTS INC
Also Called: Plant 2
1000 Spruce St (44691-4682)
P.O. Box 6005 (44691-6005)
PHONE..............................330 264-2854
Adrienne Rodgers, *Brnch Mgr*
EMP: 10
SALES (corp-wide): 10.93MM **Privately Held**
Web: www.woosterproducts.com
SIC: 3446 Stairs, staircases, stair treads: prefabricated metal
PA: Wooster Products Inc
1000 Spruce St
Wooster OH 44691
330 264-2844

(G-16188)
WORTHINGTON CYLINDER CORP
899 Venture Blvd (44691-7521)
PHONE..............................330 262-1762
EMP: 20
SALES (corp-wide): 4.92B **Publicly Held**
Web: www.worthingtonenterprises.com
SIC: 3443 Cylinders, pressure: metal plate
HQ: Worthington Cylinder Corporation
200 W Old Wlson Bridge Rd
Worthington OH 43085
614 840-3210

Worthington
Franklin County

(G-16189)
ALBRIGHT ALBRIGHT & SCHN
89 E Wilson Bridge Rd Ste D (43085-2379)
PHONE..............................614 825-4829
James B Albright, *Pr*
EMP: 11 **EST:** 2001
SALES (est): 308.67K **Privately Held**
SIC: 3851 Contact lenses

(G-16190)
CGAS EXPLORATION INC (HQ)
110 E Wilson Bridge Rd Ste 250 (43085-2317)
PHONE..............................614 436-4631
Kenneth Kirk, *Pr*
John Erwin, *CFO*
William Grubaugh, *Ex VP*
EMP: 7 **EST:** 1946
SQ FT: 27,500
SALES (est): 2.1MM
SALES (corp-wide): 4.85MM **Privately Held**

SIC: 1311 1382 Crude petroleum production; Oil and gas exploration services
PA: Cgas Inc
110 E Wilson Bridge Rd # 250
Worthington OH 43085
614 975-4697

(G-16191)
CGAS INC (PA)
110 E Wilson Bridge Rd Ste 250 (43085-2317)
PHONE..............................614 975-4697
Kenneth Kirk, *Pr*
William Grubaugh, *Ex VP*
John O Erwin, *CFO*
EMP: 12 **EST:** 1972
SQ FT: 36,000
SALES (est): 4.85MM
SALES (corp-wide): 4.85MM **Privately Held**
SIC: 1311 Crude petroleum production

(G-16192)
CUSTOM GLASS SOLUTIONS LLC (PA)
600 Lakeview Plaza Blvd Ste A (43085)
PHONE..............................248 340-1800
Matthew J Dietrich, *CEO*
David B Jaffe, *Sec*
Gary Greene, *Treas*
EMP: 29 **EST:** 2006
SALES (est): 164.32MM
SALES (corp-wide): 164.32MM **Privately Held**
Web: www.customglasssolutions.com
SIC: 3211 Flat glass

(G-16193)
DIETRICH INDUSTRIES INC (HQ)
200 W Old Wilson Bridge Rd (43085-2247)
PHONE..............................800 873-2604
John E Roberts, *Pr*
Samuel Depasquale, *
Dale T Brinkman, *
Richard F Berdik, *
Andy Rose, *
▼ **EMP:** 107 **EST:** 1959
SALES (est): 48.97MM
SALES (corp-wide): 4.92B **Publicly Held**
SIC: 3441 Fabricated structural metal
PA: Worthington Enterprises, Inc.
200 W Old Wlson Bridge Rd
Worthington OH 43085
614 438-3210

(G-16194)
FIBERTECH NETWORKS
720 Lakeview Plaza Blvd (43085-4733)
PHONE..............................614 436-3565
David Burch, *Prin*
EMP: 11 **EST:** 2010
SALES (est): 223.44K **Privately Held**
SIC: 3089 Plastics products, nec

(G-16195)
HANNIBAL COMPANY INC
Also Called: Heartland Bread & Roll
6536 Proprietors Rd (43085-3233)
PHONE..............................614 846-5060
Rebecca Henderson, *Pr*
EMP: 10 **EST:** 1991
SALES (est): 888.38K **Privately Held**
Web: www.hannibal.de
SIC: 2051 Breads, rolls, and buns

(G-16196)
HDR POWER SYSTEMS LLC
Also Called: Ametek HDR Power Systems
530 Lakeview Plaza Blvd Ste C (43085)
PHONE..............................614 308-5500
▲ **EMP:** 50 **EST:** 1981

SALES (est): 4.52MM
SALES (corp-wide): 6.6B **Publicly Held**
Web: www.hdrpower.com
SIC: 3629 Power conversion units, a.c. to d.c.: static-electric
HQ: Solidstate Controls, Llc
875 Dearborn Dr
Columbus OH 43085
614 846-7500

(G-16197)
IDEAL INTEGRATIONS LLC
Also Called: Thinkcsc
7420 Worthington Galena Rd (43085-1528)
PHONE..............................614 786-7100
Kurt Camealy, *Technical Vice President*
EMP: 22
SALES (corp-wide): 24.68MM **Privately Held**
Web: www.idealintegrations.net
SIC: 7372 Business oriented computer software
PA: Ideal Integrations, Llc
800 Regis Ave
Pittsburgh PA 15236
412 349-6680

(G-16198)
IGLOO PRESS LLC
39 W New England Ave (43085-3535)
PHONE..............................614 787-5528
Ian Brown, *Prin*
EMP: 7 **EST:** 2012
SALES (est): 413.86K **Privately Held**
SIC: 2741 Miscellaneous publishing

(G-16199)
INTRISM INC
6969 Worthington Galena Rd Ste J (43085-2322)
PHONE..............................614 733-9304
Kyle Vandeveer, *Pr*
EMP: 10 **EST:** 2015
SALES (est): 972.62K **Privately Held**
Web: www.intrism.com
SIC: 2499 5945 Engraved wood products; Toys and games

(G-16200)
KNAPE INDUSTRIES INC
6592 Proprietors Rd (43085-3233)
PHONE..............................614 885-3016
John Knape, *Pr*
Joyce Knape, *VP*
EMP: 22 **EST:** 1970
SQ FT: 14,000
SALES (est): 4.39MM **Privately Held**
Web: www.knapeindustries.com
SIC: 3599 Machine shop, jobbing and repair

(G-16201)
MAXX IRON LLC
287 E North St (43085-3207)
PHONE..............................614 753-9697
Mary Johnson, *Prin*
EMP: 7 **EST:** 2015
SALES (est): 729.12K **Privately Held**
SIC: 3462 Iron and steel forgings

(G-16202)
METTLER-TOLEDO LLC
Also Called: Toledo Scales & Systems
720 Dearborn Park Ln (43085-5703)
P.O. Box 999 (43085-0999)
PHONE..............................614 438-4511
Gary Wilkins, *Mgr*
EMP: 38
SALES (corp-wide): 3.79B **Publicly Held**
Web: www.mt.com
SIC: 3596 Industrial scales
HQ: Mettler-Toledo, Llc

Worthington - Franklin County (G-16203)

1900 Polaris Pkwy Fl 6
Columbus OH 43240
614 438-4511

(G-16203)
METTLER-TOLEDO LLC
Toledo Scales & Systems
1150 Dearborn Dr (43085-4766)
PHONE...............................614 438-4390
Todd Manifold, *Genl Mgr*
EMP: 200
SALES (corp-wide): 3.79B **Publicly Held**
Web: www.mt.com
SIC: 3596 Industrial scales
HQ: Mettler-Toledo, Llc
1900 Polaris Pkwy Fl 6
Columbus OH 43240
614 438-4511

(G-16204)
MICROWELD ENGINEERING INC
7451 Oakmeadows Dr (43085-1713)
PHONE...............................614 847-9410
Robert Lloyd, *Pr*
Daniel Mitchell, *PRODUCTION*
EMP: 9 **EST:** 1987
SALES (est): 581.74K **Privately Held**
Web: www.microweldengineering.com
SIC: 3369 8731 7692 3728 Aerospace castings, nonferrous: except aluminum; Commercial physical research; Welding repair; Aircraft parts and equipment, nec

(G-16205)
MIDDLETON ENTERPRISES INC
7100 N High St (43085-2316)
PHONE...............................614 885-2514
Richard O Chakroff, *Pr*
Barbara M Chakroff, *Sec*
Christopher Norman, *VP*
EMP: 7 **EST:** 1954
SQ FT: 4,000
SALES (est): 664.89K **Privately Held**
SIC: 3728 Aircraft parts and equipment, nec

(G-16206)
NOXGEAR LLC
966 Proprietors Rd (43085-3152)
PHONE...............................937 317-0199
Simon Curran, *CEO*
EMP: 10 **EST:** 2012
SALES (est): 821.73K **Privately Held**
Web: www.noxgear.com
SIC: 5999 3999 Miscellaneous retail stores, nec; Manufacturing industries, nec

(G-16207)
PRECISION ENGNEERED COMPONENTS
Also Called: Precision Engrg Components
7030 Wrthington Galena Rd (43085-2376)
PHONE...............................614 436-0392
Michael Ward, *Prin*
EMP: 14 **EST:** 1999
SQ FT: 6,500
SALES (est): 173.49K **Privately Held**
SIC: 3519 3451 3492 3599 Internal combustion engines, nec; Screw machine products; Fluid power valves and hose fittings; Machine shop, jobbing and repair

(G-16208)
PURE SAFETY GROUP INC
7007 N High St (43085-2329)
PHONE...............................614 436-0700
EMP: 19
SALES (corp-wide): 11.87MM **Privately Held**
Web: www.puresafetygroup.com
SIC: 3429 Hardware, nec
HQ: Pure Safety Group, Inc.

9201 Winkler Dr
Houston TX 77017
713 928-3936

(G-16209)
QUALITY CUSTOM SIGNS LLC
651 Lakeview Plaza Blvd Ste F (43085)
PHONE...............................614 580-7233
EMP: 8 **EST:** 2019
SALES (est): 559.25K **Privately Held**
Web: www.qcsigns.net
SIC: 3993 Signs and advertising specialties

(G-16210)
RECYCLED SYSTEMS FURNITURE INC
Also Called: Rsfi Office Furniture
401 E Wilson Bridge Rd (43085)
PHONE...............................614 880-9110
Ron Morris, *Pr*
Jim Ellison, *
EMP: 25 **EST:** 1992
SQ FT: 100,000
SALES (est): 2.63MM **Privately Held**
Web: www.officefurniturecolumbusohio.com
SIC: 7641 5712 2522 Office furniture repair and maintenance; Office furniture; Office furniture, except wood

(G-16211)
ROD OR TAMMY WHITLATCH
Also Called: Melaluca
1411 Abbeyhill Dr (43085-1728)
PHONE...............................614 848-5198
Rod Whitlatch, *Prin*
EMP: 6 **EST:** 2001
SALES (est): 88.13K **Privately Held**
SIC: 3639 Household appliances, nec

(G-16212)
SPORTS IMPORTS INCORPORATED
6950 Worthington Galena Rd (43085-2360)
P.O. Box 21040 (43221-0040)
PHONE...............................614 771-0246
Brad Underwood, *Pr*
Susan K Dunlap, *Ch*
Cyndie Dunlap, *Ch Bd*
◆ **EMP:** 19 **EST:** 1976
SALES (est): 3.05MM **Privately Held**
Web: www.sportsimports.com
SIC: 3949 Sporting and athletic goods, nec

(G-16213)
SWAGG PRODUCTIONS2015LLC
Also Called: Gmerecords
628 Arborway Ct (43085-4801)
P.O. Box 47 (43109-0047)
PHONE...............................614 601-7414
Travis Mcdaniels, *Managing Member*
EMP: 12 **EST:** 2015
SALES (est): 444.84K **Privately Held**
SIC: 2731 7819 7929 7389 Book music: publishing and printing; Sound effects and music production, motion picture; Entertainers and entertainment groups; Business services, nec

(G-16214)
TATUM PETROLEUM CORPORATION
667 Lkview Plz Blvd Ste E (43085)
P.O. Box 2607 (43702-2607)
PHONE...............................740 819-6810
Zachary Thomas Tatum, *Pr*
EMP: 15 **EST:** 1976
SQ FT: 2,400
SALES (est): 205.25K **Privately Held**
SIC: 1311 Crude petroleum production

(G-16215)
TEE HEE CO INC
740 Lakeview Plaza Blvd Ste 125 (43085)
PHONE...............................614 515-5581
Tobias H Elsass, *Prin*
EMP: 6 **EST:** 2015
SALES (est): 152.35K **Privately Held**
SIC: 2759 Screen printing

(G-16216)
THE SHARON COMPANIES LTD
200 W Old Wilson Bridge Rd (43085-2247)
P.O. Box 2168 (97208-2168)
PHONE...............................614 438-3210
EMP: 140
SIC: 3446 Stairs, staircases, stair treads: prefabricated metal

(G-16217)
WELLPOINT
6740 N High St (43085-2512)
PHONE...............................614 771-9600
EMP: 7 **EST:** 2019
SALES (est): 303.53K **Privately Held**
SIC: 3531 Wellpoint systems

(G-16218)
WHEMPYS CORP
6969 Worthington Galena Rd Ste P (43085-2322)
PHONE...............................614 888-6670
David Reed, *Pr*
Kathy Reed, *Sec*
Eugene Reed, *Mgr*
EMP: 9 **EST:** 1980
SQ FT: 2,000
SALES (est): 1.02MM **Privately Held**
Web: www.whempys.com
SIC: 5719 1711 7349 1741 Fireplace equipment and accessories; Heating systems repair and maintenance; Chimney cleaning; Chimney construction and maintenance

(G-16219)
WORTHINGTON CYLINDER CORP (HQ)
Also Called: Worthington Cylinder
200 W Old Wilson Bridge Rd (43085-2247)
PHONE...............................614 840-3210
Carol L Barnum, *Prin*
Jim Knox, *
◆ **EMP:** 185 **EST:** 1982
SQ FT: 125,000
SALES (est): 598MM
SALES (corp-wide): 4.92B **Publicly Held**
Web: www.worthingtonindustries.com
SIC: 3443 Cylinders, pressure: metal plate
PA: Worthington Industries, Inc.
200 W Old Wlson Bridge Rd
Worthington OH 43085
614 438-3210

(G-16220)
WORTHINGTON ENTERPRISES INC (PA)
Also Called: Worthington
200 W Old Wilson Bridge Rd (43085-2247)
PHONE...............................614 438-3210
B Andrew Rose, *Pr*
John Blystone, *
Geoffrey G Gilmore, *Ex VP*
Joseph B Hayek, *VP*
Patrick J Kennedy, *VP*
◆ **EMP:** 250 **EST:** 1955
SALES (est): 4.92B
SALES (corp-wide): 4.92B **Publicly Held**
Web: www.worthingtonenterprises.com

SIC: 3449 3325 Fabricated bar joists and concrete reinforcing bars; Alloy steel castings, except investment

(G-16221)
WORTHINGTON INDUSTRIES LSG LLC
200 W Old Wilson Bridge Rd (43085-2247)
PHONE...............................614 438-3210
EMP: 33 **EST:** 2014
SALES (est): 10.6MM
SALES (corp-wide): 4.92B **Publicly Held**
Web: www.worthingtonenterprises.com
SIC: 3316 Cold finishing of steel shapes
PA: Worthington Enterprises, Inc.
200 W Old Wlson Bridge Rd
Worthington OH 43085
614 438-3210

(G-16222)
WORTHINGTON MILITARY CNSTR INC
200 W Old Wilson Bridge Rd (43085-2247)
PHONE...............................615 599-6446
EMP: 13 **EST:** 2019
SALES (est): 1.39MM
SALES (corp-wide): 4.92B **Publicly Held**
Web: www.worthingtonenterprises.com
SIC: 3316 Strip, steel, cold-rolled, nec: from purchased hot-rolled,
PA: Worthington Enterprises, Inc.
200 W Old Wlson Bridge Rd
Worthington OH 43085
614 438-3210

(G-16223)
WORTHINGTON STEEL COMPANY (PA)
Also Called: Worthington Steel
100 W Old Wilson Bridge Rd (43085)
PHONE...............................800 944-2255
John H Mc Connell, *Ch Bd*
Dale T Brinkman, *Sec*
Mark A Russell, *Pr*
Andy Rose, *CFO*
◆ **EMP:** 309 **EST:** 1992
SALES (est): 425MM
SALES (corp-wide): 425MM **Privately Held**
Web: www.worthingtonsteel.com
SIC: 3316 3471 3312 Cold-rolled strip or wire ; Electroplating and plating; Chemicals and other products derived from coking

(G-16224)
WORTHNGTON STL MEXICO SA DE CV
200 W Old Wlson Bridge Rd (43085-2247)
PHONE...............................800 944-2255
EMP: 6
SALES (est): 95.29K **Privately Held**
SIC: 3316 Strip, steel, cold-rolled, nec: from purchased hot-rolled,

Wshngtn Ct Hs
Fayette County

(G-16225)
ALL-AMERICAN FIRE EQP INC
Also Called: All American Fire Equiptment
5101 Us Highway 22 Sw (43160-9695)
PHONE...............................800 972-6035
EMP: 10
Web: www.allamericanfire.us
SIC: 5099 3569 Safety equipment and supplies; Firefighting and related equipment
PA: All-American Fire Equipment, Inc.
85 Kiwanavista Ln
Ona WV 25545

GEOGRAPHIC SECTION

Xenia - Greene County (G-16249)

(G-16226)
BRASS BULL 1 LLC
Also Called: Print Shop, The
1020 Leesburg Ave (43160-1272)
PHONE.................................740 335-8030
EMP: 6 **EST:** 1974
SQ FT: 6,500
SALES (est): 493.19K **Privately Held**
Web: www.theprintshopwch.com
SIC: 2752 2791 2759 2396 Offset printing; Typesetting; Commercial printing, nec; Automotive and apparel trimmings

(G-16227)
C H WASHINGTON WATER PLAN
220 Park Ave (43160-1181)
PHONE.................................740 636-2382
Joe Burbage, *Dir*
EMP: 6 **EST:** 2002
SALES (est): 176.99K **Privately Held**
SIC: 3823 Water quality monitoring and control systems

(G-16228)
CRESTAR CRUSTS INC
Also Called: Crestar Foods
1104 Clinton Ave (43160-1215)
PHONE.................................740 335-4813
Richard Hayward, *Pr*
Dan Walsh, *
EMP: 29 **EST:** 1998
SQ FT: 120,000
SALES (est): 1.34MM
SALES (corp-wide): 2.04MM **Privately Held**
SIC: 2041 Pizza dough, prepared
HQ: Richelieu Foods, Inc.
222 Forbes Rd Ste 401
Braintree MA 02184
781 786-6800

(G-16229)
DOMTAR PAPER COMPANY LLC
1803 Lowes Blvd (43160-8611)
PHONE.................................740 333-0003
EMP: 261
Web: www.domtar.com
SIC: 2621 Paper mills
HQ: Domtar Paper Company, Llc
234 Kingsley Park Dr
Fort Mill SC 29715

(G-16230)
DOUG MARINE MOTORS INC
1120 Clinton Ave (43160-1215)
P.O. Box 1042 (43160-8042)
PHONE.................................740 335-3700
Doug Marine, *Pr*
Bill D Marine, *
EMP: 22 **EST:** 1984
SQ FT: 8,000
SALES (est): 6.92MM **Privately Held**
Web: www.dougmarinemotors.net
SIC: 5511 7538 5531 5012 Automobiles, new and used; General automotive repair shops; Auto and home supply stores; Automobiles and other motor vehicles

(G-16231)
FIBER -TECH INDUSTRIES INC
2000 Kenskill Ave (43160-9311)
PHONE.................................740 335-9400
Harris Armstrong, *CEO*
Jerry Kroll, *
Wayne Durnin, *
Robert Pfeifer, *
EMP: 75 **EST:** 1983
SQ FT: 180,000
SALES (est): 431.79K
SALES (corp-wide): 1.04MM **Privately Held**
Web: www.fiber-tech.net
SIC: 3089 Air mattresses, plastics
PA: Celstar Group, Inc.
40 N Main St Ste 1730
Dayton OH 45423
740 335-9400

(G-16232)
FIBERGLASS TECHNOLOGY INDS INC
2000 Kenskill Ave (43160-9311)
PHONE.................................740 335-9400
EMP: 30
SALES (corp-wide): 1.04MM **Privately Held**
Web: www.fiber-tech.net
SIC: 3089 Panels, building: plastics, nec
HQ: Fiberglass Technology Industries, Inc.
3808 N Sullivan Rd # 31
Spokane Valley WA 99216
509 928-8880

(G-16233)
HALLIDAY HOLDINGS INC
1544 Old Us 35 Se (43160-8624)
P.O. Box 700 (43160-0700)
PHONE.................................740 335-1430
John Halliday, *Pr*
William Halliday Ii, *VP*
EMP: 40 **EST:** 1947
SQ FT: 50,000
SALES (est): 4.42MM **Privately Held**
Web: www.hallidaylumber.com
SIC: 2448 2426 Pallets, wood; Dimension, hardwood

(G-16234)
J K PRECAST LLC
1001 Armbrust Ave (43160-2457)
PHONE.................................740 335-2188
James E Kimmey, *Owner*
EMP: 8 **EST:** 2000
SQ FT: 20,500
SALES (est): 900K **Privately Held**
Web: www.jkprecast.com
SIC: 3272 3089 Septic tanks, concrete; Septic tanks, plastics

(G-16235)
JAMES KIMMEY
Also Called: J K Precast
1000 Armbrust Ave (43160-1392)
PHONE.................................740 335-5746
James Kimmey, *Owner*
EMP: 11 **EST:** 1999
SALES (est): 669.54K **Privately Held**
Web: www.jkprecast.com
SIC: 3272 Septic tanks, concrete

(G-16236)
PLASTILENE INC
1010 Mead St (43160-9310)
PHONE.................................614 592-8699
Guillermo Umana, *CEO*
Stefano Pacini, *Pr*
Gian Luca Fiori, *Treas*
Gabriel Jaramillo, *Sec*
EMP: 28 **EST:** 2021
SALES (est): 2.61MM **Privately Held**
SIC: 2761 Manifold business forms
PA: Plastilene Sas
Carrera 4 58 66 Zona Industrial Cazuca Entrada 1
Soacha CUN

(G-16237)
QUALITEE DESIGN SPORTSWEAR CO (PA)
1270 Us Highway 22 Nw Ste 9 (43160-9187)
PHONE.................................740 333-8337
EMP: 10 **EST:** 1992
SQ FT: 6,500
SALES (est): 990.82K **Privately Held**
Web: www.qualiteedesign.com
SIC: 7336 2395 5999 2759 Silk screen design; Embroidery and art needlework; Trophies and plaques; Screen printing

(G-16238)
RAM MACHINING INC
806 Delaware St (43160-1552)
PHONE.................................740 333-5522
EMP: 6 **EST:** 1992
SALES (est): 492.45K **Privately Held**
SIC: 3599 Machine shop, jobbing and repair

(G-16239)
RICHELIEU FOODS INC
1104 Clinton Ave (43160-1278)
PHONE.................................740 335-4813
Richard Hayward, *Prin*
EMP: 25 **EST:** 2012
SALES (est): 2.61MM **Privately Held**
Web: www.richelieufoods.com
SIC: 2099 Food preparations, nec

(G-16240)
RITEN INDUSTRIES INCORPORATED
1100 Lakeview Ave (43160-1037)
P.O. Box 340 (43160-0340)
PHONE.................................740 335-5353
Andrew Lachelt, *Pr*
John E Lachat, *Stockholder**
EMP: 40 **EST:** 1933
SQ FT: 28,500
SALES (est): 6.71MM **Privately Held**
Web: www.riten.com
SIC: 3545 Machine tool attachments and accessories

(G-16241)
SOUTH CENTRAL INDUSTRIAL LLC
1825 Old Us 35 Se (43160-3500)
PHONE.................................740 333-5401
EMP: 17 **EST:** 2011
SQ FT: 60,000
SALES (est): 3.66MM
SALES (corp-wide): 48.46MM **Privately Held**
Web: www.sciohio.com
SIC: 3441 Fabricated structural metal
PA: Heartland, Inc.
1005 N 19th St
Middlesboro KY 40965
606 248-7323

(G-16242)
TONYS WLDG & FABRICATION LLC
2305 Robinson Rd Se (43160-8675)
PHONE.................................740 333-4000
Linda Borland, *Prin*
EMP: 20 **EST:** 2015
SALES (est): 7.91MM **Privately Held**
Web: www.twfabrication.com
SIC: 7692 Welding repair

(G-16243)
VALUTEX REINFORCEMENTS INC
2302 Kenskill Ave (43160-9309)
PHONE.................................800 251-2507
Dan Brames, *Genl Mgr*
EMP: 20 **EST:** 2011
SALES (est): 747.5K **Privately Held**
Web: www.valutex.net
SIC: 2221 3299 Glass and fiberglass broadwoven fabrics; Nonmetallic mineral statuary and other decorative products

(G-16244)
WCH MOLDING LLC
1850 Lowes Blvd (43160-8611)
PHONE.................................740 335-6320
Gene J Kuzma, *Pr*
Jeff Kuzma, *VP*
EMP: 20 **EST:** 2004
SALES (est): 3.43MM
SALES (corp-wide): 23.81MM **Privately Held**
SIC: 3089 Molding primary plastics
PA: Gk Packaging, Inc.
7680 Commerce Pl
Plain City OH 43064
614 873-3900

(G-16245)
WCR INCORPORATED
809 Delaware St (43160-1551)
PHONE.................................740 333-3448
EMP: 9
SALES (corp-wide): 43.23MM **Privately Held**
Web: www.wcrhx.com
SIC: 3443 Heat exchangers, plate type
PA: Wcr Incorporated
2377 Commerce Center Blvd B
Fairborn OH 45324
937 223-0703

(G-16246)
WEYERHAEUSER COMPANY
Also Called: Washington Crt Hse Converting
1803 Lowes Blvd (43160-8611)
PHONE.................................740 335-4480
Jim Fink, *Mgr*
EMP: 6
SALES (corp-wide): 7.67B **Publicly Held**
Web: www.weyerhaeuser.com
SIC: 2653 Boxes, corrugated: made from purchased materials
PA: Weyerhaeuser Company
220 Occidental Ave S
Seattle WA 98104
206 539-3000

Xenia
Greene County

(G-16247)
ACTION AIR & HYDRAULICS INC
1087 Bellbrook Ave (45385-4011)
P.O. Box 655 (45385-0655)
PHONE.................................937 372-8614
Peter J Pacier, *CEO*
Pat Minnela, *Sec*
EMP: 6 **EST:** 1983
SQ FT: 2,500
SALES (est): 498.61K **Privately Held**
SIC: 3822 Energy cutoff controls, residential or commercial types

(G-16248)
ALPHABET EMBROIDERY STUDIOS
Also Called: Americas Best Cstm Digitizing
1291 Bellbrook Ave (45385-4015)
PHONE.................................937 372-6557
Dee Thompson, *Pr*
Mark Thompson, *VP*
EMP: 8 **EST:** 1984
SQ FT: 10,000
SALES (est): 239.06K **Privately Held**
Web: www.alphabetembroidery.com
SIC: 2395 Embroidery products, except Schiffli machine

(G-16249)
B5 SYSTEMS INC
1463 Bellbrook Ave (45385-4019)

Xenia - Greene County (G-16250)

PHONE.................937 372-4768
Philip Burke, *Pr*
Judd Burke, *VP*
Mark Keller, *VP*
EMP: 8 **EST:** 2008
SALES (est): 2.52MM **Privately Held**
Web: www.b5systems.com
SIC: 3679 Electronic circuits

(G-16250)
BARCO INC
Presentation & Simulation Div
600 Bellbrook Ave (45385-4053)
PHONE.................937 372-7579
Al Herman, *Brnch Mgr*
EMP: 21
SALES (corp-wide): 878.69MM **Privately Held**
Web: www.barco.com
SIC: 3663 8731 Radio and t.v. communications equipment; Electronic research
HQ: Barco, Inc.
 3059 Premiere Pkwy # 400
 Duluth GA 30097

(G-16251)
BEF FOODS INC
Also Called: Bob Evans
640 Birch Rd (45385-7600)
P.O. Box 44 (45385-0044)
PHONE.................937 372-4493
Tom Sefton, *Mgr*
EMP: 197
SQ FT: 3,000
Web: www.bobevansgrocery.com
SIC: 2011 Sausages, from meat slaughtered on site
HQ: Bef Foods, Inc.
 8200 Walton Pkwy
 New Albany OH 43054
 614 492-7700

(G-16252)
BESTWOOD CABINETRY LLC
117 W Main St (45385-2914)
PHONE.................937 661-9621
Anthony Hinzman, *Prin*
EMP: 6 **EST:** 2017
SALES (est): 58.05K **Privately Held**
SIC: 2434 Wood kitchen cabinets

(G-16253)
BURKE PRODUCTS INC
1355 Enterprise Ln (45385-6504)
PHONE.................937 372-3516
Shiv Bakhshi, *Pr*
Aaron Bakshi, *VP*
▲ **EMP:** 20 **EST:** 1966
SQ FT: 10,000
SALES (est): 4.94MM **Privately Held**
Web: www.burkeproducts.com
SIC: 3674 3599 Solid state electronic devices, nec; Machine shop, jobbing and repair

(G-16254)
C&C INDY CYLINDER HEAD LLC
1031 Cincinnati Ave (45385-9353)
PHONE.................937 708-8563
EMP: 6 **EST:** 2019
SALES (est): 1.1MM **Privately Held**
SIC: 3714 Motor vehicle parts and accessories

(G-16255)
CIL ISOTOPE SEPARATIONS LLC
1689 Burnett Dr (45385-5691)
PHONE.................937 376-5413
Joel Bradley, *CEO*
Peter Dodwell, *Pr*
Maureen Duffy, *VP*
Steve Igo, *VP*
▲ **EMP:** 10 **EST:** 2006
SQ FT: 8,000
SALES (est): 13.78MM **Privately Held**
Web: www.isotope.com
SIC: 2819 Industrial inorganic chemicals, nec
HQ: Otsuka Pharmaceutical Co., Ltd.
 2-16-4, Konan
 Minato-Ku TKY 108-0

(G-16256)
CITY OF XENIA
Also Called: Xenia City Water Treatment Div
1831 Us Route 68 N (45385-9547)
PHONE.................937 376-7269
Roger Beehler, *Brnch Mgr*
EMP: 36
SALES (corp-wide): 9.23MM **Privately Held**
Web: ci.xenia.oh.us
SIC: 3589 Water treatment equipment, industrial
PA: City Of Xenia
 107 E Main St
 Xenia OH 45385
 937 376-7232

(G-16257)
CUSTOM MANUFACTURING SOLUTIONS (PA)
479 Bellbrook Ave (45385-3639)
P.O. Box 840 (45385-0840)
PHONE.................937 372-0777
Mike Collinsworth, *Pr*
Raj Soin, *
EMP: 51 **EST:** 1989
SQ FT: 82,000
SALES (est): 8.84MM
SALES (corp-wide): 8.84MM **Privately Held**
Web: www.cusmfgsol.com
SIC: 3599 Machine shop, jobbing and repair

(G-16258)
D & J MACHINE SHOP
1296 S Patton St (45385-5672)
PHONE.................937 256-2730
Chuck Lehman, *Owner*
EMP: 6 **EST:** 1966
SALES (est): 435.8K **Privately Held**
SIC: 3599 Machine shop, jobbing and repair

(G-16259)
DESTIN DIE CASTING LLC
851 Bellbrook Ave (45385-4057)
PHONE.................937 347-1111
EMP: 45 **EST:** 2014
SALES (est): 10.62MM **Privately Held**
Web: www.krdiecasting.com
SIC: 3363 Aluminum die-castings
PA: American Metal Technologies Llc
 8213 Durand Ave
 Sturtevant WI 53177

(G-16260)
DISCOUNT SMOKES & GIFTS XENIA
37 E Main St (45385-3201)
PHONE.................937 372-0259
William Lampiasi, *Pr*
EMP: 6 **EST:** 2008
SALES (est): 1.4MM **Privately Held**
Web: www.xeniasmokeshop.com
SIC: 2111 Cigarettes

(G-16261)
FAIRBORN CEMENT COMPANY LLC
3250 Linebaugh Rd (45385-8567)
PHONE.................937 879-8393
Gerald Essl, *Pr*
Ray Meier, *
EMP: 110 **EST:** 2016
SALES: 26.51MM
SALES (corp-wide): 2.15B **Publicly Held**
Web: www.fairborncement.com
SIC: 3241 Natural cement
PA: Eagle Materials Inc.
 5960 Berkshire Ln Ste 900
 Dallas TX 75225
 214 432-2000

(G-16262)
FIVEPOINT LLC
825 Bellbrook Ave Unit B (45385-4076)
PHONE.................937 374-3193
EMP: 10 **EST:** 2001
SQ FT: 70,000
SALES (est): 314.77K **Privately Held**
Web: www.fivepoint.com
SIC: 3575 Computer terminals

(G-16263)
H & K PALLET SERVICES
1039 Jasper Ave (45385-3303)
PHONE.................937 608-1140
Jonathon Holley, *Admn*
EMP: 6 **EST:** 2013
SALES (est): 191.91K **Privately Held**
SIC: 2448 Pallets, wood

(G-16264)
IDIALOGS LLC
121 Pawleys Plantation Ct (45385-9120)
PHONE.................937 372-2890
EMP: 8 **EST:** 2012
SALES (est): 531.75K **Privately Held**
Web: www.idialogs.com
SIC: 7372 Application computer software

(G-16265)
JADE TOOL COMPANY
1280 Burnett Dr (45385-5687)
PHONE.................937 376-4740
Jeff Sakalaskas, *Pr*
Dan Baker, *Sec*
EMP: 9 **EST:** 1969
SQ FT: 3,600
SALES (est): 982.69K **Privately Held**
Web: www.jadetoolco.com
SIC: 3599 Machine shop, jobbing and repair

(G-16266)
JAMIES TIRE & SERVICE
213 W Main St (45385-2916)
PHONE.................937 372-9254
EMP: 6 **EST:** 2021
SALES (est): 212.26K **Privately Held**
Web: www.jamiestire.com
SIC: 3011 Tires and inner tubes

(G-16267)
KOTOBUKI-RELIABLE DIE CASTING INC
851 Bellbrook Ave (45385-4057)
PHONE.................937 347-1111
EMP: 23
SIC: 3542 Die casting machines

(G-16268)
MAHLE BEHR USA INC
1003 Bellbrook Ave (45385-4011)
PHONE.................937 369-2610
EMP: 12 **EST:** 1993
SALES (est): 351.25K **Privately Held**
SIC: 3585 3443 Refrigeration and heating equipment; Fabricated plate work (boiler shop)

(G-16269)
MRL MATERIALS RESOURCES LLC
Also Called: Mrl
123 Fairground Rd (45385-9543)
P.O. Box 341091 (45434-1091)
PHONE.................937 531-6657
EMP: 40 **EST:** 2009
SALES (est): 4.12MM **Privately Held**
Web: www.icmrl.net
SIC: 8999 8734 3812 8711 Scientific consulting; Metallurgical testing laboratory; Defense systems and equipment; Engineering services

(G-16270)
NATIONAL CARTON & COATING COMPANY
1439 Lavelle Dr (45385-5679)
PHONE.................937 347-1042
EMP: 80
Web: www.nationalcarton.com
SIC: 2631 Packaging board

(G-16271)
OHTA PRESS US INC
1125 S Patton St (45385-5671)
PHONE.................937 374-3382
Shigeki Ikuta, *Pr*
▲ **EMP:** 15 **EST:** 1996
SQ FT: 12,000
SALES (est): 1.64MM **Privately Held**
Web: www.xegc.org
SIC: 3714 Motor vehicle parts and accessories

(G-16272)
SAVE EDGE INC
Also Called: Save Edge USA
360 W Church St (45385-2948)
PHONE.................937 376-8268
George Whyde, *Pr*
▲ **EMP:** 25 **EST:** 1975
SALES (est): 2.64MM **Privately Held**
Web: www.saveedge.com
SIC: 5085 7699 3423 3315 Industrial tools; Knife, saw and tool sharpening and repair; Hand and edge tools, nec; Steel wire and related products

(G-16273)
STEINBARGER PRECISION CNC INC
634 Cincinnati Ave (45385-5013)
PHONE.................937 376-0322
Steve Steinbarger, *Pr*
EMP: 6 **EST:** 2006
SQ FT: 1,000
SALES (est): 563K **Privately Held**
Web: www.spcncinc.com
SIC: 3599 Machine shop, jobbing and repair

(G-16274)
SUPERION INC
1285 S Patton St (45385-5673)
PHONE.................937 374-0033
Alton Choiniere, *Pr*
Masaru Yokokawa, *
▲ **EMP:** 40 **EST:** 1990
SQ FT: 12,000
SALES (est): 7.97MM **Privately Held**
Web: www.alliedmachine.com
SIC: 3423 3541 3545 3425 Knives, agricultural or industrial; Machine tools, metal cutting type; Machine tool accessories ; Saw blades and handsaws
PA: Sanyo Tool Mfg,Co, Ltd.
 3-6-21, Osaki
 Shinagawa-Ku TKY 141-0

(G-16275)
TIMAC MANUFACTURING COMPANY
825 Bellbrook Ave (45385-4076)
P.O. Box 329 (45385-0329)
PHONE..................................937 372-3305
Tim Mcintire, *Pr*
EMP: 17 EST: 1978
SQ FT: 5,000
SALES (est): 628.76K **Privately Held**
Web: www.timacspring.com
SIC: 3495 Wire springs

(G-16276)
TJAR INNOVATIONS LLC
1004 Cincinnati Ave (45385-9353)
P.O. Box 357 (45385-0357)
PHONE..................................937 347-1999
Tony Arsenault, *VP*
EMP: 12 EST: 2001
SALES (est): 2.56MM **Privately Held**
Web: www.tjarinnovations.com
SIC: 3089 Injection molding of plastics

(G-16277)
TREALITY SVS LLC (PA)
600 Bellbrook Ave (45385-4053)
PHONE..................................937 372-7579
Mark Saturno, *VP*
EMP: 45 EST: 2014
SQ FT: 200,000
SALES (est): 7.02MM
SALES (corp-wide): 7.02MM **Privately Held**
Web: www.trealitysvs.com
SIC: 3577 Computer peripheral equipment, nec

(G-16278)
TRIAD GOVERNMENTAL SYSTEMS
358 S Monroe St (45385-3442)
PHONE..................................937 376-5446
Tod A Rapp, *Pr*
EMP: 20 EST: 1983
SALES (est): 934.01K **Privately Held**
Web: www.triadgsi.com
SIC: 7371 7372 Computer software development; Prepackaged software

(G-16279)
TROPHY SPORTS CENTER LLC
26 Kinsey Rd (45385-1520)
PHONE..................................937 376-2311
Edwin Colon Junior, *Managing Member*
EMP: 12 EST: 1984
SQ FT: 3,000
SALES (est): 411.5K **Privately Held**
Web: www.trophysportscenter.com
SIC: 5699 5999 2211 5632 Sports apparel; Trophies and plaques; Apparel and outerwear fabrics, cotton; Apparel accessories

(G-16280)
WA HAMMOND DRIERITE CO LTD
138 Dayton Ave (45385)
P.O. Box 460 (45385)
PHONE..................................937 376-2927
Joan L Hammond, *Pt*
James F Hammond, *Pt*
EMP: 21 EST: 1932
SQ FT: 80,000
SALES (est): 6.76MM **Privately Held**
Web: secure.drierite.com
SIC: 2819 Industrial inorganic chemicals, nec

(G-16281)
XENIA DAILY GAZETTE
1836 W Park Sq (45385-2668)
PHONE..................................937 372-4444
Barbara Vandeventer, *Genl Mgr*
EMP: 30 EST: 1883
SALES (est): 473.72K
SALES (corp-wide): 3.39MM **Privately Held**
Web: www.xeniagazette.com
SIC: 2711 2791 2752 Newspapers, publishing and printing; Typesetting; Commercial printing, lithographic
PA: Aim Media Midwest Operating, Llc
   1001 N County Road 25a
   Troy OH 45373
   937 247-2700

Yellow Springs
Greene County

(G-16282)
BENNETT & BENNETT INC (PA)
888 Dayton St (45387-1777)
PHONE..................................937 324-1100
Bill Bennett, *Pr*
Michelle Bennett, *Treas*
EMP: 6 EST: 1991
SALES (est): 1.61MM **Privately Held**
Web: www.4bennett.com
SIC: 3679 Static power supply converters for electronic applications

(G-16283)
BUSHWORKS INCORPORATED
1280 Grinnell Dr Unit 1 (45387-2099)
PHONE..................................937 767-1713
John Bush, *Pr*
EMP: 8 EST: 1975
SALES (est): 627.51K **Privately Held**
Web: www.bushworks.net
SIC: 2499 Woodenware, kitchen and household

(G-16284)
MIAMI VALLEY EDUCTL CMPT ASSN
Also Called: Mveca
888 Dayton St Unit 102 (45387-1778)
PHONE..................................937 767-1468
Thor Sage, *Dir*
Sue Welsh, *Sec*
Gary Bosserman, *Dir*
EMP: 13 EST: 1980
SALES (est): 6.85MM **Privately Held**
Web: www.mveca.org
SIC: 7372 7374 Prepackaged software; Computer time-sharing

(G-16285)
MORRIS BEAN & COMPANY
777 E Hyde Rd (45387-9726)
PHONE..................................937 767-7301
Edward Myers, *Pr*
William Magro, *
Lawrence E Kleinschnitz, *
EMP: 175 EST: 1932
SQ FT: 185,000
SALES (est): 24.74MM **Privately Held**
Web: www.morrisbean.com
SIC: 3365 3769 3369 Aluminum and aluminum-based alloy castings; Space vehicle equipment, nec; Nonferrous foundries, nec

(G-16286)
VERNAY MANUFACTURING INC (HQ)
120 E South College St (45387-1623)
PHONE..................................937 767-7261
Thomas Allen, *Pr*
Hugh Barnett, *Sec*
▲ **EMP: 22 EST:** 1979
SQ FT: 40,000
SALES (est): 13.93MM
SALES (corp-wide): 84.72MM **Privately Held**
Web: www.vernay.com
SIC: 3069 Molded rubber products
PA: Vernay Laboratories, Inc.
   1005 Virginia Ave Ste 320
   Atlanta GA 30354
   404 994-2000

(G-16287)
XYLEM INC
Also Called: Ysi
1700 Brannum Ln Ste 1725 (45387-1106)
PHONE..................................937 767-7241
Russel Meinka, *Brnch Mgr*
EMP: 49
Web: www.xylem.com
SIC: 3823 Process control instruments
PA: Xylem Inc.
   301 Water St Se Ste 200
   Washington DC 20003

(G-16288)
YELLOW SPRINGS NEWS INC
253 And A Half Xenia Ave (45387)
P.O. Box 187 (45387-0187)
PHONE..................................937 767-7373
Diane Chiddister, *Off Mgr*
Robert Hasek, *Advt Mgr*
EMP: 19 EST: 1880
SQ FT: 4,000
SALES (est): 855.82K **Privately Held**
Web: www.ysnews.com
SIC: 2711 Job printing and newspaper publishing combined

(G-16289)
YELLOW SPRINGS POTTERY LLC
222 Xenia Ave Ste 1 (45387-1866)
PHONE..................................937 767-1666
Janet Murie, *Prin*
Marcia Cochran, *Prin*
Jerry Davis, *Prin*
Kim Kramer, *Prin*
Eliza Bush, *Prin*
EMP: 10 EST: 2003
SALES (est): 604.73K **Privately Held**
Web: www.yellowspringspottery.com
SIC: 5023 3269 Pottery; Pottery products, nec

(G-16290)
YOUNGS JERSEY DAIRY INC
Also Called: Golden Jersey Inn
6880 Springfield Xenia Rd (45387-9610)
PHONE..................................937 325-0629
C Daniel Young, *CEO*
C Robert Young, *
William H Young, *
Debra Whittaker, *
EMP: 300 EST: 1964
SQ FT: 35,000
SALES (est): 10.58MM **Privately Held**
Web: www.youngsdairy.com
SIC: 5812 5451 5947 7999 Ice cream stands or dairy bars; Dairy products stores; Gift shop; Golf driving range

(G-16291)
YSI ENVIRONMENTAL INC
Also Called: Xylem Ysi, A Xylem Brand
1725 Brannum Ln (45387-1107)
PHONE..................................937 767-7241
Richard Omlor, *Pr*
EMP: 55 EST: 2000
SALES (est): 1.99MM **Privately Held**
Web: www.ysi.com
SIC: 3826 Analytical instruments

(G-16292)
YSI INCORPORATED (HQ)
Also Called: Yellow Springs International
1700 Brannum Ln # 1725 (45387-1106)
PHONE..................................937 767-7241
Richard J Omlor, *Pr*
Leon Erdman, *
Gayle Rominger, *
◆ **EMP: 100 EST:** 1948
SQ FT: 120,000
SALES (est): 38.97MM **Publicly Held**
Web: www.ysi.com
SIC: 3826 3823 3841 Water testing apparatus; Process control instruments; Diagnostic apparatus, medical
PA: Xylem Inc.
   301 Water St Se Ste 200
   Washington DC 20003

Yorkshire
Darke County

(G-16293)
WINNER CORPORATION (PA)
Also Called: Winner's Meat Service
8544 State Route 705 (45388-9784)
P.O. Box 39 (45351-0039)
PHONE..................................419 582-4321
Brian K Winner, *Pr*
Alan Winner, *
Terrance Winner, *
Ted Winner, *
Jay Winner, *
EMP: 40 EST: 1928
SQ FT: 6,500
SALES (est): 33.94MM
SALES (corp-wide): 33.94MM **Privately Held**
Web: www.winnersmeats.com
SIC: 0213 0751 5154 5147 Hog feedlot; Slaughtering: custom livestock services; Hogs; Meats and meat products

Yorkville
Jefferson County

(G-16294)
OHIO COATINGS COMPANY
2100 Tin Plate Pl (43971-1053)
PHONE..................................740 859-5500
EMP: 73 EST: 1993
SQ FT: 134,000
SALES (est): 11.05MM **Privately Held**
Web: www.ohiocoatingscompany.com
SIC: 3479 2819 3312 3398 Coating of metals and formed products; Tin (stannic/stannous) compounds or salts, inorganic; Coated or plated products; Annealing of metal

Youngstown
Mahoning County

(G-16295)
1062 TECHNOLOGIES INC
Also Called: Center Street Technologies
1062 Ohio Works Dr (44510-1077)
PHONE..................................303 453-9251
Michael Garvey, *CEO*
Charles George, *CFO*
EMP: 6 EST: 2016
SALES (est): 778.21K **Privately Held**
Web: www.centerstreettech.com
SIC: 3531 Construction machinery

(G-16296)
4S COMPANY
3730 Mahoning Ave (44515-3020)
PHONE..................................330 792-5518
Debra Woodford, *Pr*
EMP: 10 EST: 2006

Youngstown - Mahoning County (G-16297)

SALES (est): 693.46K **Privately Held**
Web: www.foursco.com
SIC: 3999 Manufacturing industries, nec

(G-16297)
A A S AMELS SHEET METAL INC
222 Steel St (44509-2547)
P.O. Box 2407 (44509-0407)
PHONE.................................330 793-9326
Andrew A Samuels Junior, *Pr*
George Timar, *
EMP: 18 EST: 1930
SQ FT: 12,000
SALES (est): 435.49K **Privately Held**
Web: www.aasamuels.net
SIC: 1711 3585 3564 3444 Ventilation and duct work contractor; Refrigeration and heating equipment; Blowers and fans; Sheet metalwork

(G-16298)
A1 INDUSTRIAL PAINTING INC
894 Coitsville Hubbard Rd (44505)
P.O. Box 509 (44405)
PHONE.................................330 750-9441
EMP: 50 EST: 2008
SALES (est): 5.62MM **Privately Held**
Web: www.a1industrialpainting.com
SIC: 1721 1389 Industrial painting; Construction, repair, and dismantling services

(G-16299)
ABI ORTHTC/PROSTHETIC LABS LTD
930 Trailwood Dr (44512-5007)
PHONE.................................330 758-1143
EMP: 23 EST: 1978
SALES (est): 3.9MM
SALES (corp-wide): 1.12B **Privately Held**
SIC: 3842 Braces, orthopedic
PA: Hanger, Inc.
10910 Domain Dr Ste 300
Austin TX 78758
512 777-3800

(G-16300)
ACCUFORM MANUFACTURING INC
2750 Intertech Dr (44509-4023)
PHONE.................................330 797-9291
Bob Hockenberry, *Pr*
Thomas Manos, *
EMP: 32 EST: 1989
SQ FT: 1,056
SALES (est): 2.37MM **Privately Held**
Web: www.accuformprecision.com
SIC: 3599 3543 3544 Machine shop, jobbing and repair; Foundry patternmaking; Special dies, tools, jigs, and fixtures

(G-16301)
ACE LUMBER COMPANY
1039 Poland Ave (44502-2138)
P.O. Box 508 (44501-0508)
PHONE.................................330 744-3167
Herbert Soss, *Pr*
Diann Zenda, *Stockholder*
Susan Soss, *Stockholder*
Julie Soss, *Stockholder*
EMP: 13 EST: 1941
SQ FT: 300,000
SALES (est): 40.08M **Privately Held**
Web: www.acelumberco.com
SIC: 2431 5211 Millwork; Lumber products

(G-16302)
ACID DEVELOPMENT LLC
5700 Patriot Blvd (44515-1170)
PHONE.................................330 502-4164
EMP: 6 EST: 2011
SALES (est): 102.2K **Privately Held**
SIC: 1389 Acidizing wells

(G-16303)
ACME STEAK & SEAFOOD INC
31 Bissell Ave (44505-2707)
P.O. Box 688 (44501-0688)
PHONE.................................330 270-8000
Michael A Mike Iii, *Pr*
EMP: 10 EST: 1947
SALES (est): 3.69MM **Privately Held**
Web: www.acmesteak.com
SIC: 5146 5113 5149 5147 Seafoods; Disposable plates, cups, napkins, and eating utensils; Canned goods: fruit, vegetables, seafood, meats, etc.; Meats, fresh

(G-16304)
ACMI LLC
229 N Four Mile Run Rd Ste A (44515-3064)
PHONE.................................330 501-0728
Josh Hillard, *Managing Member*
EMP: 9 EST: 2012
SALES (est): 713.77K **Privately Held**
SIC: 3441 Fabricated structural metal

(G-16305)
AESTHETIC POWDER COATING LLC
281 Ohltown Rd (44515-1929)
PHONE.................................330 360-2422
Dennis Gagne, *Admn*
EMP: 8 EST: 2012
SALES (est): 56.02K **Privately Held**
SIC: 3479 Coating of metals and formed products

(G-16306)
ALIQUIPPA & OHIO RIVER RR CO
123 Division Street Ext (44510-1070)
PHONE.................................740 622-8092
EMP: 7 EST: 2019
SALES (est): 278.39K **Privately Held**
SIC: 3743 Railroad equipment

(G-16307)
ALLIED CONSOLIDATED INDS INC (PA)
2100 Poland Ave (44502-2751)
PHONE.................................330 744-0808
John Ramun, *Pr*
Louise Ramun, *
EMP: 104 EST: 1985
SQ FT: 24,000
SALES (est): 29.53MM **Privately Held**
Web: www.alliedgator.com
SIC: 3535 3531 Conveyors and conveying equipment; Construction machinery

(G-16308)
ALUMO EXTRUSIONS AND MFG CO
3749 Mahoning Ave Ste 2 (44515-3052)
PHONE.................................330 779-3333
Frank Moulin, *Pr*
John Moulin, *VP*
Rose Palermo, *Sec*
EMP: 20 EST: 1975
SQ FT: 66,000
SALES (est): 2.78MM **Privately Held**
Web: www.brucewardlaw.com
SIC: 5039 5031 3089 Doors, sliding; Doors, garage; Doors, folding: plastics or plastics coated fabric

(G-16309)
AMERICAN PAPER GROUP INC
Also Called: American Paper Products Co Div
8401 Southern Blvd (44512-6709)
P.O. Box 3120 (44513-3120)
PHONE.................................330 758-4545
Thomas W Pietrocini, *Ch Bd*
Don Allevach, *
EMP: 400 EST: 1915
SQ FT: 95,000
SALES (est): 27.71MM **Privately Held**
SIC: 2677 7331 Envelopes; Mailing service

(G-16310)
AMERICAN ROLL FORMED PDTS CORP (DH)
Also Called: Arf
3805 Hendricks Rd Ste A (44515-1536)
PHONE.................................440 352-0753
Rob Touzalin, *Pr*
Jeff Laturell, *
▼ EMP: 102 EST: 1960
SQ FT: 70,000
SALES (est): 17.78MM **Privately Held**
Web: www.arfpcorp.com
SIC: 3498 3449 Fabricated pipe and fittings; Custom roll formed products
HQ: Hynes Holding Company
3805 Henricks Rd
Youngstown OH 44515
330 799-3221

(G-16311)
AMTHOR STEEL INC
5019 Belmont Ave (44505-1019)
PHONE.................................330 759-0200
George Ohlin, *Mgr*
EMP: 7
SALES (corp-wide): 4.43MM **Privately Held**
Web: www.amthorsteel.com
SIC: 3312 Blast furnaces and steel mills
PA: Amthor Steel, Inc.
1717 Gaskell Ave
Erie PA 16503
814 452-4700

(G-16312)
ANATOMICAL CONCEPTS INC
1399 E Western Reserve Rd (44514-5224)
PHONE.................................330 757-3569
William W De Toro, *Pr*
Richard A Riffle, *VP*
William W Detoro, *Pr*
EMP: 15 EST: 1990
SQ FT: 1,600
SALES (est): 1.99MM **Privately Held**
Web: www.anatomicalconceptsinc.com
SIC: 3842 Braces, orthopedic

(G-16313)
ANGELS UNIFORM & PRINT SP LLC ◆
840 Woodford Ave (44511-2361)
PHONE.................................330 707-6506
EMP: 6 EST: 2023
SALES (est): 78.58K **Privately Held**
SIC: 2326 Medical and hospital uniforms, men's

(G-16314)
ASTRO SHAPES
4605 Lake Park Rd (44512-1814)
PHONE.................................330 755-1414
EMP: 6 EST: 2020
SALES (est): 2.5MM **Privately Held**
Web: www.astroshapes.com
SIC: 3354 Aluminum extruded products

(G-16315)
AUSTINTOWN METAL WORKS INC
45 Victoria Rd (44515-2023)
PHONE.................................330 259-4673
Jim Myers, *Pr*
EMP: 10 EST: 2002
SALES (est): 605.26K **Privately Held**
Web: www.worldwideagrotech.com
SIC: 3444 3449 Sheet metalwork; Bars, concrete reinforcing: fabricated steel

(G-16316)
AZTEC MANUFACTURING INC
4325 Simon Rd (44512-1327)
PHONE.................................330 783-9747
James J Rutana, *Dir*
Damian P Degenova, *Dir*
Maria E Rutana, *Dir*
EMP: 20 EST: 1992
SQ FT: 6,000
SALES (est): 2.12MM **Privately Held**
Web: www.aztecmetalfab.com
SIC: 3365 3444 Aluminum foundries; Sheet metalwork

(G-16317)
BAKER PLASTICS INC
900 Mahoning Ave (44502-1488)
PHONE.................................330 743-3142
Bonnie Baker, *Pr*
Robert E Baker, *Ch*
Ruth Luarde, *Sec*
EMP: 7 EST: 1946
SQ FT: 15,000
SALES (est): 884.27K **Privately Held**
Web: www.bakerplastics.com
SIC: 3089 3993 5099 5046 Novelties, plastics; Signs and advertising specialties; Novelties, durable; Store fixtures and display equipment

(G-16318)
BARFECTIONS LLC
4718 Belmont Ave (44505)
PHONE.................................330 759-3100
Mike Handel, *Contrlr*
EMP: 8
SALES (corp-wide): 2.67MM **Privately Held**
SIC: 2064 Candy and other confectionery products
PA: Barfections Llc
1598 Motor Inn Dr
Girard OH 44420
330 759-3100

(G-16319)
BERLIN INDUSTRIES INC
Also Called: Berlin Inds Protector Pdts
1275 Boardman Poland Rd Ste 1 (44514-3911)
PHONE.................................330 549-2100
Scott Gorley, *Pr*
EMP: 19 EST: 1985
SQ FT: 35,000
SALES (est): 5.07MM **Privately Held**
SIC: 2834 5047 Veterinary pharmaceutical preparations; Veterinarians' equipment and supplies
PA: Kobayashi Pharmaceutical Co.,Ltd.
4-4-10, Doshomachi, Chuo-Ku
Osaka OSK 541-0

(G-16320)
BLACK LION PRODUCTS LLC
3710 Hendricks Rd (44515-1537)
PHONE.................................234 232-3680
Antonio Campana, *Managing Member*
Mia Richardson, *
EMP: 25 EST: 2009
SQ FT: 250,000
SALES (est): 3.39MM **Privately Held**
Web: www.blpmfg.com
SIC: 3441 Fabricated structural metal

(G-16321)
BOARDMAN MOLDED INTL LLC
1110 Thalia Ave (44512-1825)
PHONE.................................800 233-4575

GEOGRAPHIC SECTION

Youngstown - Mahoning County (G-16344)

Ron Kessler, *Managing Member*
EMP: 113 **EST:** 2007
SALES (est): 4.7MM
SALES (corp-wide): 25.21MM **Privately Held**
Web: www.boardmanmolded.com
SIC: 3089 Injection molding of plastics
PA: Boardman Molded Products, Inc.
   1110 Thalia Ave
   Youngstown OH 44512
   330 788-2400

(G-16322)
BOARDMAN MOLDED PRODUCTS INC (PA)
1110 Thalia Ave (44512-1825)
P.O. Box 1858 (44501-1858)
PHONE....................330 788-2400
Ken Palmman, *CEO*
Daniel A Kessler, *
◆ **EMP:** 87 **EST:** 1978
SQ FT: 85,000
SALES (est): 25.21MM
SALES (corp-wide): 25.21MM **Privately Held**
Web: www.boardmanmolded.com
SIC: 3089 3466 3429 2273 Injection molding of plastics; Crowns and closures; Hardware, nec; Carpets and rugs

(G-16323)
BOLTECH INCORPORATED
1201 Crescent St (44502-1303)
P.O. Box 749 (44501-0749)
PHONE....................330 746-6881
Alex Benyo, *Pr*
Brian Benyo, *VP*
C R Pallante, *Prin*
EMP: 9 **EST:** 1998
SQ FT: 6,500
SALES (est): 1.58MM **Privately Held**
Web: www.brilex.com
SIC: 3537 Trucks, tractors, loaders, carriers, and similar equipment

(G-16324)
BRENTWOOD ORIGINALS INC
1309 N Meridian Rd (44509-1099)
PHONE....................330 793-2255
Tim Domer, *Brnch Mgr*
EMP: 147
SQ FT: 130,000
SALES (corp-wide): 103.82MM **Privately Held**
Web: www.brentwoodoriginals.com
SIC: 2392 Pillows, bed: made from purchased materials
PA: Brentwood Originals, Inc.
   3780 Kilroy Arprt Way # 540
   Long Beach CA 90806
   310 637-6804

(G-16325)
BRIDGESTONE RET OPERATIONS LLC
Also Called: Firestone
7401 Market St Rear (44512-5624)
PHONE....................330 758-0921
Anthony Sangialosi, *Mgr*
EMP: 7
Web: www.bridgestoneamericas.com
SIC: 5531 7534 Automotive tires; Rebuilding and retreading tires
HQ: Bridgestone Retail Operations, Llc
   333 E Lake St Ste 300
   Bloomingdale IL 60108
   630 259-9000

(G-16326)
BRIDGESTONE RET OPERATIONS LLC
Also Called: Firestone
3335 Belmont Ave (44505-1805)
PHONE....................330 759-3697
Robert Kephart, *Mgr*
EMP: 7
SQ FT: 4,600
Web: www.bridgestoneamericas.com
SIC: 5531 7534 Automotive tires; Rebuilding and retreading tires
HQ: Bridgestone Retail Operations, Llc
   333 E Lake St Ste 300
   Bloomingdale IL 60108
   630 259-9000

(G-16327)
BRILEX INDUSTRIES INC
101 Andrews Ave (44503-1607)
PHONE....................330 744-1114
Jessica Llyod, *Brnch Mgr*
EMP: 53
Web: www.brilex.com
SIC: 3542 3549 3441 Machine tools, metal forming type; Metalworking machinery, nec; Fabricated structural metal
PA: Brilex Industries, Inc.
   1201 Crescent St
   Youngstown OH 44502

(G-16328)
BRILEX INDUSTRIES INC (PA)
Also Called: Brilex Tech Services
1201 Crescent St (44502-1303)
P.O. Box 749 (44501-0749)
PHONE....................330 744-1114
▲ **EMP:** 57 **EST:** 1996
SQ FT: 54,000
SALES (est): 64.77MM **Privately Held**
Web: www.brilex.com
SIC: 3441 3542 3549 Fabricated structural metal; Machine tools, metal forming type; Metalworking machinery, nec

(G-16329)
BROCKER MACHINE INC
1530 Poland Ave (44502-2147)
PHONE....................330 744-5858
EMP: 18 **EST:** 1994
SQ FT: 10,000
SALES (est): 565.4K **Privately Held**
Web: www.brockermachine.com
SIC: 3599 Machine shop, jobbing and repair

(G-16330)
BUSINESS JOURNAL
25 E Boardman St Ste 306 (44503-1803)
P.O. Box 714 (44501-0714)
PHONE....................330 744-5023
Jeff Leo Herrmann, *CEO*
Andrea Wood, *Ch Bd*
EMP: 42 **EST:** 1984
SQ FT: 2,700
SALES (est): 2.38MM **Privately Held**
Web: www.businessjournaldaily.com
SIC: 2711 Newspapers, publishing and printing

(G-16331)
CARNEY PLASTICS INC
1010 W Rayen Ave (44502-1317)
PHONE....................330 746-8273
Sean Carney, *Pr*
▲ **EMP:** 9 **EST:** 1986
SALES (est): 946.91K **Privately Held**
Web: www.carneyplastics.com
SIC: 3089 5162 Injection molding of plastics; Plastics products, nec

(G-16332)
CCA YOUNGSTOWN
2240 Hubbard Rd (44505-3157)
PHONE....................615 263-3000
EMP: 8 **EST:** 2011
SALES (est): 218.76K **Privately Held**
SIC: 7372 Business oriented computer software

(G-16333)
CENTRAL COCA-COLA BTLG CO INC
Also Called: Coca-Cola
531 E Indianola Ave (44502-2319)
PHONE....................330 783-1982
John Flynt, *Brnch Mgr*
EMP: 46
SALES (corp-wide): 45.75B **Publicly Held**
Web: www.coca-cola.com
SIC: 2086 Bottled and canned soft drinks
HQ: Central Coca-Cola Bottling Company, Inc.
   555 Taxter Rd Ste 550
   Elmsford NY 10523
   914 789-1100

(G-16334)
CENTRAL-1-OPTICAL LLC
6981 Southern Blvd Ste B (44512-4657)
PHONE....................330 783-9660
Lloyd Yazbek, *Pr*
Linda B Yazbek, *
Richard J Thomas, *
Pamela A Thomas, *
Joyce Fiersdorf, *
▲ **EMP:** 80 **EST:** 1996
SQ FT: 10,000
SALES (est): 4.45MM **Privately Held**
Web: www.centraloneoptical.com
SIC: 3851 5995 Eyeglasses, lenses and frames; Optical goods stores

(G-16335)
CITY CONCRETE LLC
151 Old Division St (44510)
PHONE....................330 743-2825
Gary Carrocce, *Brnch Mgr*
EMP: 19
SALES (corp-wide): 2.19MM **Privately Held**
SIC: 3273 Ready-mixed concrete
PA: City Concrete, L.L.C
   4075 Shallow Creek Dr
   Struthers OH

(G-16336)
CITY MACHINE TECHNOLOGIES INC (PA)
773 W Rayen Ave (44502-1112)
P.O. Box 1466 (44501-1466)
PHONE....................330 747-2639
Michael J Kovach, *Pr*
Claudia Kovach, *Sec*
EMP: 18 **EST:** 1986
SQ FT: 17,000
SALES (est): 8.05MM
SALES (corp-wide): 8.05MM **Privately Held**
Web: www.cmtcompanies.com
SIC: 3621 7694 3599 7692 Motors and generators; Armature rewinding shops; Machine shop, jobbing and repair; Welding repair

(G-16337)
CITY PRINTING CO INC
122 Oak Hill Ave (44502-1428)
PHONE....................330 747-5691
Joseph A Valentini, *Pr*
EMP: 26 **EST:** 1920
SQ FT: 11,000
SALES (est): 1.15MM **Privately Held**
Web: www.cityprinting.com
SIC: 2752 Offset printing

(G-16338)
CLASSIC FUEL INJECTION LLC
2750 Intertech Dr (44509-4023)
PHONE....................330 757-7171
Robert Hockienberry, *Prin*
EMP: 6 **EST:** 2011
SALES (est): 126.97K **Privately Held**
SIC: 2869 Fuels

(G-16339)
CLASSIC OPTICAL LABS INC
3710 Belmont Ave (44505-1406)
P.O. Box 1341 (44501-1341)
PHONE....................330 759-8245
Dawn Friedkin, *Pr*
▲ **EMP:** 195 **EST:** 1987
SQ FT: 30,000
SALES (est): 12.54MM **Privately Held**
Web: www.classicoptical.com
SIC: 3851 Ophthalmic goods

(G-16340)
CLIMATE PROS LLC
52 E Myrtle Ave (44507-1268)
PHONE....................330 744-2732
Roy Guerrieri, *Brnch Mgr*
EMP: 88
Web: www.hattenbach.com
SIC: 5078 1711 2434 2541 Commercial refrigeration equipment; Refrigeration contractor; Wood kitchen cabinets; Cabinets, except refrigerated: show, display, etc.: wood
PA: Climate Pros, Llc
   2190 Gladstone Ct Ste E
   Glendale Heights IL 60139

(G-16341)
CORONADO STEEL CO
2360 Funston Dr (44510-1399)
PHONE....................330 744-1143
EMP: 44 **EST:** 1958
SALES (est): 5.3MM **Privately Held**
Web: www.coronadosteel.com
SIC: 3325 Alloy steel castings, except investment

(G-16342)
CRAFCO INC
912 Salt Springs Rd (44509-1171)
PHONE....................330 270-3034
John Perry, *Brnch Mgr*
EMP: 17
SALES (corp-wide): 1.44B **Privately Held**
Web: www.crafco.com
SIC: 2951 Asphalt paving mixtures and blocks
HQ: Crafco, Inc.
   6165 W Detroit St
   Chandler AZ 85226
   602 276-0406

(G-16343)
CROWES CABINETS INC
590 E Western Reserve Rd Bldg 8 (44514)
PHONE....................330 729-9911
Diane Crowe, *Pr*
EMP: 20 **EST:** 1978
SQ FT: 6,000
SALES (est): 2.37MM **Privately Held**
Web: www.crowescabinets.com
SIC: 2434 Wood kitchen cabinets

(G-16344)
CUBBISON COMPANY (PA)
380 Victoria Rd (44515-2054)
PHONE....................330 793-2481

Youngstown - Mahoning County (G-16345)   GEOGRAPHIC SECTION

Timothy Merrifield, *Pr*
EMP: 54 **EST:** 1971
SQ FT: 27,000
SALES (est): 14.97MM
SALES (corp-wide): 14.97MM **Privately Held**
Web: www.cubbison.com
SIC: 3469 3993 3479 Metal stampings, nec; Name plates: except engraved, etched, etc.: metal; Etching and engraving

(G-16345)
CUSTOM TARPAULIN PRODUCTS INC
8095 Southern Blvd (44512-6336)
PHONE..............................330 758-1801
Brian Robinson, *VP*
Beth Robinson, *Sec*
EMP: 15 **EST:** 1990
SALES (est): 487.13K **Privately Held**
Web: www.customtarpaulin.com
SIC: 2394 Tarpaulins, fabric: made from purchased materials

(G-16346)
DA INVESTMENTS INC
4605 Lake Park Rd (44512-1814)
PHONE..............................330 781-6100
Thomas E Hutch Junior, *Pr*
EMP: 90 **EST:** 1986
SQ FT: 32,000
SALES (est): 9.77MM **Privately Held**
SIC: 3354 3444 Aluminum extruded products; Sheet metalwork

(G-16347)
DE KAY FABRICATORS INC
295 S Meridian Rd (44509-2924)
PHONE..............................330 793-0826
Bryan Kennedy, *Pr*
EMP: 8 **EST:** 1975
SQ FT: 10,000
SALES (est): 739.16K **Privately Held**
SIC: 3498 Tube fabricating (contract bending and shaping)

(G-16348)
DEARING COMPRESSOR AND PUMP COMPANY (PA)
3974 Simon Rd (44512-1318)
P.O. Box 6044 (44501-6044)
PHONE..............................330 783-2258
EMP: 32 **EST:** 1945
SALES (est): 19.44MM
SALES (corp-wide): 19.44MM **Privately Held**
Web: www.dearingcomp.com
SIC: 7699 7359 5084 5085 Compressor repair; Equipment rental and leasing, nec; Compressors, except air conditioning; Industrial supplies

(G-16349)
DILETTO WINERY LLC
8578 Market St (44512-6726)
P.O. Box 3505 (44513-3505)
PHONE..............................440 991-6217
EMP: 19
SALES (corp-wide): 192.94K **Privately Held**
Web: www.queenofspadesbar.com
SIC: 2084 Wines
PA: Diletto Winery, Llc
813 N Market St
Lisbon OH 44432
330 286-3925

(G-16350)
DINESOL BUILDING PRODUCTS LTD
168 N Meridian Rd (44509-2036)
PHONE..............................330 270-0212
Michael Janak, *Sec*
Kenneth Leonard, *VP*
C Kenneth Fibus, *Ch*
EMP: 20 **EST:** 2002
SALES (est): 2MM **Privately Held**
SIC: 3089 Shutters, plastics

(G-16351)
DR PEPPER BOTTLERS ASSOCIATES
Also Called: Dr Pepper
500 Pepsi Pl (44502-1432)
PHONE..............................330 746-7651
Danny Rittenberry, *Prin*
EMP: 9 **EST:** 2010
SALES (est): 141.55K **Privately Held**
Web: www.drpepper.com
SIC: 2086 Soft drinks: packaged in cans, bottles, etc.

(G-16352)
DUCA MANUFACTURING & CONSULTING INC (PA)
761 Mcclurg Rd (44512-6428)
PHONE..............................330 758-0828
▲ **EMP:** 28 **EST:** 1978
SALES (est): 4.09MM
SALES (corp-wide): 4.09MM **Privately Held**
Web: www.ducamfg.com
SIC: 3567 3677 3498 Metal melting furnaces, industrial: electric; Electronic coils and transformers; Fabricated pipe and fittings

(G-16353)
DUCA MFG & CONSULTING INC
697 Mcclurg Rd (44512-6408)
PHONE..............................330 726-7175
EMP: 7
SALES (corp-wide): 4.09MM **Privately Held**
Web: www.ducamfg.com
SIC: 3567 Industrial furnaces and ovens
PA: Duca Manufacturing & Consulting, Inc.
761 Mcclurg Rd
Youngstown OH 44512
330 758-0828

(G-16354)
EJ USA INC
4150 Simon Rd (44512-1322)
PHONE..............................330 782-3900
Bill Denidovich, *Mgr*
EMP: 19
Web: www.ejco.com
SIC: 3449 3321 Custom roll formed products; Manhole covers, metal
HQ: Ej Usa, Inc.
301 Spring St
East Jordan MI 49727
800 874-4100

(G-16355)
EPCO EXTRUSION PAINTING CO
4605 Lake Park Rd (44512-1814)
PHONE..............................330 781-6100
Thomas E Hutch Junior, *Pr*
EMP: 32 **EST:** 1989
SALES (est): 991.18K **Privately Held**
SIC: 3479 Aluminum coating of metal products

(G-16356)
FIRELINE INC (PA)
Also Called: Fireline Tcon
300 Andrews Ave (44505-3061)
PHONE..............................330 743-1164
Barbara Burley, *Pr*
Ed Ress, *
David Holmquist, *
Gloria Jones, *
◆ **EMP:** 119 **EST:** 1967
SQ FT: 85,000
SALES (est): 23.23MM
SALES (corp-wide): 23.23MM **Privately Held**
Web: www.firelineinc.com
SIC: 3299 Nonmetallic mineral statuary and other decorative products

(G-16357)
FITHIAN-WILBERT BURIAL VLT CO
6234 Market St (44512-3329)
PHONE..............................330 758-2327
Heather Davis, *Pr*
EMP: 13 **EST:** 1924
SALES (est): 473.72K **Privately Held**
Web: www.fithian-wilbert.com
SIC: 3272 Burial vaults, concrete or precast terrazzo

(G-16358)
FOOD 4 YOUR SOUL
3957 S Schenley Ave (44511-3428)
PHONE..............................330 402-4073
Michelle White, *Owner*
EMP: 10 **EST:** 2009
SALES (est): 266.49K **Privately Held**
SIC: 2099 Food preparations, nec

(G-16359)
FORGE INDUSTRIES INC (PA)
4450 Market St (44512-1512)
PHONE..............................330 960-2468
William T James Ii, *Ch Bd*
W Thomas James Iii, *VP*
Carl G James, *
Dan Maisonville, *
Gary Davis, *
▲ **EMP:** 1250 **EST:** 1900
SQ FT: 1,500
SALES (est): 1.51B
SALES (corp-wide): 1.51B **Privately Held**
SIC: 5085 3566 3599 3531 Bearings; Gears, power transmission, except auto; Machine shop, jobbing and repair; Road construction and maintenance machinery

(G-16360)
FSCREATIONS CORPORATION (HQ)
Also Called: Einstruction Corporation
255 W Federal St (44503-1207)
PHONE..............................330 746-3015
Rich Fennessy, *CEO*
Tim Torno, *
▲ **EMP:** 100 **EST:** 1982
SQ FT: 8,000
SALES (est): 35.81MM
SALES (corp-wide): 91.49MM **Privately Held**
Web: www.echo360.com
SIC: 7371 7379 5045 7372 Computer software development; Computer related consulting services; Computers, peripherals, and software; Prepackaged software
PA: Turning Technologies, Llc
6000 Mahoning Ave Ste 254
Youngstown OH 44515
330 746-3015

(G-16361)
GARVEY CORPORATION
Also Called: M7 Technologies
1019 Ohio Works Dr (44510-1078)
PHONE..............................330 779-0700
Michael S Garvey, *Pr*
Jeanette Garvey, *
EMP: 35 **EST:** 1979
SQ FT: 20,000
SALES (est): 5.35MM **Privately Held**
Web: www.m7tek.com
SIC: 3599 Machine shop, jobbing and repair

(G-16362)
GASSER CHAIR CO INC (PA)
4136 Logan Way (44505-1797)
PHONE..............................330 534-2234
Gary L Gasser, *CEO*
Mark E Gasser, *
Evelyn Mihin, *COO*
▲ **EMP:** 25 **EST:** 1947
SQ FT: 22,000
SALES (est): 24.66MM
SALES (corp-wide): 24.66MM **Privately Held**
Web: www.gasserchair.com
SIC: 2531 2521 Chairs, table and arm; Chairs, office: padded, upholstered, or plain: wood

(G-16363)
GASSER CHAIR CO INC
Also Called: Production Div
2457 Logan Ave (44505-2550)
PHONE..............................330 759-2234
EMP: 53
SALES (corp-wide): 24.66MM **Privately Held**
Web: www.gasserchair.com
SIC: 2531 2522 2521 2511 Chairs, table and arm; Office furniture, except wood; Wood office furniture; Wood household furniture
PA: Gasser Chair Co., Inc.
4136 Logan Way
Youngstown OH 44505
330 534-2234

(G-16364)
GEI OF COLUMBIANA INC
4040 Lake Park Rd (44512-1801)
PHONE..............................330 783-0270
Michael C Schuler, *Pr*
EMP: 22 **EST:** 2000
SALES (est): 469.11K **Privately Held**
SIC: 3354 3471 Shapes, extruded aluminum, nec; Polishing, metals or formed products

(G-16365)
GENERAL EXTRUSIONS INTL LLC ◆
4040 Lake Park Rd (44512)
PHONE..............................330 783-0270
Gilles Teste, *CEO*
EMP: 170 **EST:** 2023
SALES (est): 5.19MM **Privately Held**
SIC: 3354 3471 Shapes, extruded aluminum, nec; Polishing, metals or formed products

(G-16366)
GENEVA LIBERTY STEEL LTD (PA)
Also Called: Genmak Geneva Liberty
947 Martin Luther King Jr Blvd (44502)
P.O. Box 6124 (44501)
PHONE..............................330 740-0103
EMP: 40 **EST:** 2002
SQ FT: 85,000
SALES (est): 49.39MM
SALES (corp-wide): 49.39MM **Privately Held**
Web: www.genevaliberty.com
SIC: 3316 7389 Strip, steel, flat bright, cold-rolled: purchased hot-rolled; Scrap steel cutting

(G-16367)
GENEX TOOL AND DIE INC
4000 Lake Park Rd (44512-1801)
PHONE..............................330 788-2466

GEOGRAPHIC SECTION

Youngstown - Mahoning County (G-16389)

Herbert F Schuler, *Pr*
Michael Schuler, *Sec*
EMP: 11 **EST**: 1966
SQ FT: 23,000
SALES (est): 106.76K Privately Held
SIC: 3541 Machine tools, metal cutting type

(G-16368)
GEORGE A MITCHELL COMPANY
Also Called: Mitchell
557 Mcclurg Rd (44512-6443)
P.O. Box 3727 (44513-3727)
PHONE..............................330 758-5777
George A Mitchell, *Pr*
Paul F Russo, *VP*
Mark A Mitchell, *VP*
Patricia Jasinski, *Sec*
▼ **EMP**: 20 **EST**: 1963
SQ FT: 22,000
SALES (est): 4.14MM Privately Held
Web: www.mitchellmachinery.com
SIC: 3542 3541 3547 Extruding machines (machine tools), metal; Machine tools, metal cutting type; Rolling mill machinery

(G-16369)
GERM-BUSTERS SOLUTIONS LLC
3649 Northwood Ave (44511-2603)
PHONE..............................330 610-0480
EMP: 7 **EST**: 2020
SALES (est): 150K Privately Held
SIC: 2842 Polishes and sanitation goods

(G-16370)
GL INTERNATIONAL LLC
Also Called: Gli Pool Products
215 Sinter Ct (44510-1076)
PHONE..............................330 744-8812
Gary Crandall, *Managing Member*
Larry Schwimmer, *
▲ **EMP**: 130 **EST**: 2006
SALES (est): 27.42MM Privately Held
Web: www.glipoolproducts.com
SIC: 3949 Swimming pools, plastic

(G-16371)
GOODYEAR TIRE & RUBBER COMPANY
Also Called: Goodyear
3651 Belmont Ave (44505-1490)
PHONE..............................330 759-9343
Jim March, *Mgr*
EMP: 8
SALES (corp-wide): 20.07B Publicly Held
Web: www.goodyearautoservice.com
SIC: 5531 7534 Automotive tires; Tire repair shop
PA: The Goodyear Tire & Rubber Company
200 Innovation Way
Akron OH 44316
330 796-2121

(G-16372)
GORILLA JOE PRINTING CO LLC
31 Woodbine Ave E (44505-2939)
PHONE..............................234 719-1861
Joe Sudrovic, *Prin*
EMP: 7 **EST**: 2015
SALES (est): 258.08K Privately Held
Web: www.gorillajoeprinting.com
SIC: 2752 Commercial printing, lithographic

(G-16373)
GREAT LAKES TELCOM LTD (PA)
Also Called: BROADBAND HOSPITALITY
590 E Western Reserve Rd Bldg 9c (44514)
PHONE..............................330 629-8848
Vincent Lucci Junior, *CEO*
EMP: 30 **EST**: 1998
SQ FT: 9,200

SALES (est): 28.97MM Privately Held
SIC: 3663 4813 1623 1731 Satellites, communications; Internet connectivity services; Telephone and communication line construction; Telephone and telephone equipment installation

(G-16374)
GRENGA MACHINE & WELDING
56 Wayne Ave (44502-1938)
PHONE..............................330 743-1113
Joe Grenga, *Owner*
EMP: 10 **EST**: 1963
SQ FT: 30,000
SALES (est): 827K Privately Held
SIC: 5051 5084 3599 3443 Steel; Industrial machinery and equipment; Machine shop, jobbing and repair; Fabricated plate work (boiler shop)

(G-16375)
GRINDING EQUIPMENT & MCHY LLC
15 S Worthington St (44502-1335)
PHONE..............................330 747-2313
James Johnson, *Pr*
Tracy Gross, *Off Mgr*
EMP: 13 **EST**: 1982
SQ FT: 10,000
SALES (est): 1.3MM Privately Held
Web: www.gem-usa.com
SIC: 3599 Machine shop, jobbing and repair

(G-16376)
GUNDERSON RAIL SERVICES LLC
Also Called: Greenbrier Rail Services
3710 Hendricks Rd Bldg 2a (44515-1537)
PHONE..............................330 792-6521
Adam Strysseler, *Mgr*
EMP: 78
SALES (corp-wide): 3.94B Publicly Held
Web: www.gbrx.com
SIC: 3743 3444 3441 Railroad equipment; Sheet metalwork; Fabricated structural metal
HQ: Gunderson Rail Services Llc
1 Centerpointe Dr Ste 200
Lake Oswego OR 97035
503 684-7000

(G-16377)
HYNES HOLDING COMPANY (HQ)
Also Called: Hynes Industries
3805 Hendricks Rd (44515)
P.O. Box 3805 (44513-3805)
PHONE..............................330 799-3221
Rick C Organ, *CEO*
Ryan R Day, *CFO*
Robert T Moe, *COO*
Mike Giabattista, *CPO*
EMP: 16 **EST**: 2014
SALES (est): 18.82MM Privately Held
SIC: 3449 Custom roll formed products
PA: Hynes Industries, Inc.
3805 Hendricks Rd
Youngstown OH 44515
800 321-9257

(G-16378)
HYNES INDUSTRIES INC (PA)
3805 Hendricks Rd (44515)
PHONE..............................800 321-9257
Rick Organ, *CEO*
Robert Moe, *COO*
Ryan Day, *CFO*
Mike Giambattista, *CPO*
George Droder, *CCO*
▲ **EMP**: 101 **EST**: 1965
SQ FT: 154,000
Web: www.hynesindustries.com

SIC: 3441 3316 3449 Fabricated structural metal; Wire, flat, cold-rolled strip: not made in hot-rolled mills; Custom roll formed products

(G-16379)
INDUSTRIAL MILL MAINTENANCE
1609 Wilson Ave Ste 2 (44506-1838)
P.O. Box 1465 (44501-1465)
PHONE..............................330 746-1155
Michael Mccarthy Senior, *Pr*
Kathy Mccarthy, *VP*
EMP: 22 **EST**: 1991
SQ FT: 5,600
SALES (est): 2.85MM Privately Held
SIC: 3471 1721 3444 3441 Sand blasting of metal parts; Industrial painting; Sheet metalwork; Fabricated structural metal

(G-16380)
INTIGRAL INC
45 Karago Ave (44512-5950)
PHONE..............................440 439-0980
Michael Mchugh, *Mgr*
EMP: 9
SALES (corp-wide): 51.33MM Privately Held
Web: www.intigral.com
SIC: 3231 Insulating glass: made from purchased glass
PA: Intigral, Inc.
7850 Northfield Rd
Walton Hills OH 44146
440 439-0980

(G-16381)
JAMEN TOOL & DIE CO (PA)
Also Called: Truex Tool & Die Div
4450 Lake Park Rd (44512-1809)
PHONE..............................330 788-6521
Carmen P Chicone Senior, *Pr*
Antonette Chicone, *VP*
Paul Chicone, *Sec*
Carmen Chicone Junior, *Stockholder*
EMP: 19 **EST**: 1965
SQ FT: 5,000
SALES (est): 4.33MM
SALES (corp-wide): 4.33MM Privately Held
SIC: 3544 Extrusion dies

(G-16382)
JAMEN TOOL & DIE CO
Also Called: Mor-X Plastics
914 E Indianola Ave (44502-2674)
PHONE..............................330 782-6731
Bob Marcum, *Mgr*
EMP: 28
SALES (corp-wide): 4.33MM Privately Held
SIC: 3544 Industrial molds
PA: Jamen Tool & Die Co.
4450 Lake Park Rd
Youngstown OH 44512
330 788-6521

(G-16383)
JAMESTOWN INDUSTRIES INC
650 N Meridian Rd Ste 3 (44509-1245)
PHONE..............................330 779-0670
Clark Babb, *Mgr*
EMP: 60
SQ FT: 32,000
SALES (corp-wide): 5.07MM Privately Held
Web: www.jamestown-inc.com
SIC: 3493 Steel springs, except wire
PA: Jamestown Industries, Inc.
2210 Arbor Blvd Ste 99
Moraine OH 45439
937 643-9401

(G-16384)
JOHN ZIDIAN COMPANY (PA)
Also Called: Zidian Specialty Foods
574 Mcclurg Rd (44512-6405)
PHONE..............................330 743-6050
Tom Zidian, *CEO*
Harry Shood, *CFO*
▲ **EMP**: 26 **EST**: 2011
SALES (est): 4.74MM
SALES (corp-wide): 4.74MM Privately Held
Web: www.giarussa.com
SIC: 2032 Italian foods, nec: packaged in cans, jars, etc.

(G-16385)
JOHNSON CONTROLS INC
Also Called: Johnson Controls
1044 N Meridian Rd Ste A (44509-1070)
PHONE..............................330 270-4385
Edward Dunkerley, *Mgr*
EMP: 21
Web: www.johnsoncontrols.com
SIC: 2531 Seats, automobile
HQ: Johnson Controls, Inc.
5757 N Green Bay Ave
Milwaukee WI 53209
920 245-6409

(G-16386)
KIRALY TOOL AND DIE INC
1250 Crescent St (44502-1303)
PHONE..............................330 744-5773
Steve Kiraly, *Pr*
Shari Kiraly, *VP*
EMP: 10 **EST**: 1999
SQ FT: 9,500
SALES (est): 1.59MM Privately Held
Web: www.kiralytool.com
SIC: 3542 3544 Machine tools, metal forming type; Special dies, tools, jigs, and fixtures

(G-16387)
LAKE PARK TOOL & MACHINE LLC
Also Called: Lake Park Tool & Machine
1221 Velma Ct (44512-1829)
PHONE..............................330 788-2437
Oscar Lund, *Pr*
Susanne Wildner, *Prin*
Dave Cornelius, *Prin*
EMP: 13 **EST**: 2015
SALES (est): 2.34MM Privately Held
Web: www.kind-co.de
SIC: 3599 Machine shop, jobbing and repair

(G-16388)
LARICCIAS ITALIAN FOODS INC
7438 Southern Blvd (44512)
PHONE..............................330 729-0222
Tessa Lariccia, *Pr*
Michael Allegretto, *VP*
EMP: 10 **EST**: 1910
SQ FT: 4,000
SALES (est): 937.28K Privately Held
Web: www.laricciasitalianmarketplace.com
SIC: 5411 2098 2035 Grocery stores, independent; Macaroni and spaghetti; Pickles, sauces, and salad dressings

(G-16389)
LIBERTY PATTERN AND MOLD INC
1131 Meadowbrook Ave (44512-1822)
PHONE..............................330 788-9463
John Plaskett, *Pr*
EMP: 7 **EST**: 1917
SQ FT: 4,800
SALES (est): 491.19K Privately Held
Web: www.libpattern.com

(PA)=Parent Co (HQ)=Headquarters
✲ = New Business established in last 2 years

Youngstown - Mahoning County (G-16390) GEOGRAPHIC SECTION

SIC: 3543 Industrial patterns

(G-16390)
LUMENFORCE LED LLC ◆
5411 Market St (44512-2615)
PHONE....................330 330-8962
James Rosen, *Managing Member*
EMP: 35 **EST:** 2023
SALES (est): 1.91MM **Privately Held**
SIC: 3646 Commercial lighting fixtures

(G-16391)
M F Y INC
Also Called: Youngstown Metal Fabricating
1640 Wilson Ave (44506-1839)
PHONE....................330 747-1334
Andrew Weaver Junior, *Pr*
EMP: 15 **EST:** 1972
SQ FT: 35,000
SALES (est): 1.91MM **Privately Held**
Web: www.youngstownmetalfab.com
SIC: 3446 Stairs, staircases, stair treads: prefabricated metal

(G-16392)
M I P INC
701 Jones St (44502-2160)
P.O. Box 5467 (44514-0467)
PHONE....................330 744-0215
Richard B Weaver Junior, *Pr*
Melvin Weaver Junior, *Pr*
Leigh Marsden, *Pr*
Linda Weaver, *VP*
Russel W Brown, *VP*
EMP: 19 **EST:** 1974
SQ FT: 50,000
SALES (est): 2.01MM **Privately Held**
Web: www.mipplating.com
SIC: 3471 Electroplating of metals or formed products

(G-16393)
MACTON CORPORATION
3200 Innovation Pl (44509-4025)
PHONE....................330 259-8555
Peter Mcgonagle, *Pr*
Thomas E Young Senior, *VP*
Paul Spicer, *VP*
John C Shepherd, *VP*
Steve Schumacher, *VP*
▼ **EMP:** 60 **EST:** 1947
SALES (est): 20MM
SALES (corp-wide): 20MM **Privately Held**
Web: www.macton.com
SIC: 3537 Industrial trucks and tractors
PA: Bbm Railway Equipment, Llc
3200 Innovation Pl
Youngstown OH 44509
330 259-8555

(G-16394)
MAGNETIC ANALYSIS CORPORATION
Also Called: Mac Mfg and Test Facilities
675 Mcclurg Rd (44512-6408)
PHONE....................330 758-1367
Manuel Morales, *Manager*
EMP: 8
SQ FT: 19,000
SALES (corp-wide): 25MM **Privately Held**
Web: www.mac-ndt.com
SIC: 3829 Testing equipment: abrasion, shearing strength, etc.
PA: Magnetic Analysis Corporation
103 Fairview Park Dr
Elmsford NY 10523
914 530-2000

(G-16395)
MAK FABRICATING INC
1609 Wilson Ave (44506-1838)
P.O. Box 212 (44501-0212)
PHONE....................330 747-0040
Dan Maccarthy, *Pr*
EMP: 10 **EST:** 1997
SQ FT: 54,000
SALES (est): 1.09MM **Privately Held**
SIC: 3499 Fire- or burglary-resistive products

(G-16396)
MDE ENERGY TRANSFER
5017 Lynn St (44512-1709)
PHONE....................330 788-5747
Jeff Saluga, *Prin*
EMP: 6 **EST:** 2005
SALES (est): 170.19K **Privately Held**
SIC: 3559 Sewing machines and attachments, industrial, nec

(G-16397)
MEDIAJACKED SOUND STUDIO LLC ◆
2903 Mahoning Ave (44509-2633)
PHONE....................330 391-3123
Emanuel Valentin, *Managing Member*
EMP: 6 **EST:** 2022
SALES (est): 274.95K **Privately Held**
SIC: 3861 Sound recording and reproducing equipment, motion picture

(G-16398)
MERIDIAN ARTS AND GRAPHICS
16 Belgrade St (44505-1818)
PHONE....................330 759-9099
Ted Webb, *Pr*
Robert Millham, *VP*
Cheryl Millham, *Sec*
EMP: 19 **EST:** 1993
SQ FT: 10,000
SALES (est): 471.05K **Privately Held**
Web: www.rsi.biz
SIC: 7336 2752 Art design services; Lithographing on metal

(G-16399)
MICROMD
790 Boardman Canfield Rd (44512-4385)
PHONE....................850 217-7412
Brian Batchler, *Pdt Mgr*
EMP: 9 **EST:** 2017
SALES (est): 205.99K **Privately Held**
Web: www.micromd.com
SIC: 3841 Surgical and medical instruments

(G-16400)
MID-STATE SALES INC
Also Called: Youngstown Rubber Products
519 N Meridian Rd (44509-1227)
P.O. Box 1377 (44501-1377)
PHONE....................330 744-2158
TOLL FREE: 800
James B Tomaino, *Mgr*
EMP: 8
SALES (corp-wide): 13.73MM **Privately Held**
Web: www.midstate-sales.com
SIC: 5085 3492 Rubber goods, mechanical; Hose and tube fittings and assemblies, hydraulic/pneumatic
PA: Mid-State Sales, Inc.
1101 Gahanna Pkwy
Columbus OH 43230
614 864-1811

(G-16401)
MIKES TRANSM & AUTO SVC LLC ◆
202 S Meridian Rd (44509-2923)
PHONE....................330 799-8266
Steve P Decost, *CEO*
Steve P Decost, *Managing Member*
EMP: 10 **EST:** 2023
SALES (est): 345.52K **Privately Held**
Web: www.mikestransmissionauto.com
SIC: 1731 7549 3559 7537 General electrical contractor; High performance auto repair and service; Automotive maintenance equipment; Automotive transmission repair shops

(G-16402)
MORDIES INC
Also Called: Tri-R Dies
556 Bev Rd (44512)
PHONE....................330 758-8050
Benjamin Morucci, *Pr*
Mary Morucci, *Sec*
EMP: 22 **EST:** 1978
SQ FT: 6,000
SALES (est): 1.16MM **Privately Held**
Web: www.trirdies.com
SIC: 3544 Extrusion dies

(G-16403)
NATIONAL TOOL & EQUIPMENT INC
60 Karago Ave (44512-5949)
PHONE....................330 629-8665
James Simon Junior, *CEO*
Alex Simon, *Sec*
Anthony Vross, *Pr*
James Simon Senior Stkldr, *Prin*
EMP: 10 **EST:** 1993
SQ FT: 8,000
SALES (est): 977.89K **Privately Held**
SIC: 7699 5084 5072 5251 Engine repair and replacement, non-automotive; Fans, industrial; Hand tools; Tools

(G-16404)
NORTHEAST FABRICATORS LLC
365 E Boardman St (44503-1829)
P.O. Box 629 (44501-0629)
PHONE....................330 747-3484
EMP: 20
Web: www.northeastfabricators.com
SIC: 3443 Weldments

(G-16405)
OHIO FOAM CORPORATION
1201 Ameritech Blvd (44509-4022)
PHONE....................330 799-4553
Jerry Mouser, *Brnch Mgr*
EMP: 24
SALES (corp-wide): 7.68MM **Privately Held**
Web: www.ohiofoam.com
SIC: 3069 Foam rubber
PA: Ohio Foam Corporation
820 Plymouth St
Bucyrus OH 44820
419 563-0399

(G-16406)
ONEALS TARPAULIN & AWNING CO
Also Called: Air Locke Dock Seal Division
549 W Indianola Ave (44511-2460)
PHONE....................330 788-6504
Greg O'neal, *Pr*
Dan O'neal, *VP*
Larry O'neal, *Sec*
EMP: 18 **EST:** 1935
SQ FT: 32,000
SALES (est): 924.67K **Privately Held**
Web: www.onealawnings.com
SIC: 3448 2394 Prefabricated metal buildings and components; Awnings, fabric: made from purchased materials

(G-16407)
ORACLE LLC
Also Called: Oracle
4144 Helena Ave (44512-1205)
PHONE....................724 979-2269
Philip Chow, *Prin*
Sylvia Siew, *Prin*
EMP: 12 **EST:** 2018
SALES (est): 522.11K **Privately Held**
SIC: 7372 Prepackaged software

(G-16408)
P & L HEAT TRTING GRINDING INC
313 E Wood St (44503-1691)
PHONE....................330 746-1339
William H Pociask, *Pr*
Helen Premec, *
EMP: 26 **EST:** 1978
SQ FT: 16,000
SALES (est): 1.04MM **Privately Held**
Web: www.plheattreating.com
SIC: 3398 3599 3471 Metal heat treating; Grinding castings for the trade; Plating and polishing

(G-16409)
P & L METALCRAFTS LLC
Also Called: Metalcrafts
1050 Ohio Works Dr (44510-1077)
PHONE....................330 793-2178
John Lyras, *Managing Member*
▲ **EMP:** 12 **EST:** 2013
SALES (est): 2.68MM **Privately Held**
Web: www.metalcraftsyng.com
SIC: 3446 3444 3441 Ornamental metalwork; Sheet metalwork; Fabricated structural metal

(G-16410)
P & L PRECISION GRINDING LLC
948 Poland Ave (44502-2137)
PHONE....................330 746-8081
EMP: 11 **EST:** 2009
SQ FT: 15,000
SALES (est): 1MM **Privately Held**
SIC: 7699 7389 3398 Knife, saw and tool sharpening and repair; Grinding, precision: commercial or industrial; Metal heat treating

(G-16411)
PAMTON 3D PRINTING LLC
904 S Hazelwood Ave (44509-2236)
PHONE....................330 792-5503
EMP: 6 **EST:** 2017
SALES (est): 244.94K **Privately Held**
Web: www.pamton3d.com
SIC: 2752 Commercial printing, lithographic

(G-16412)
PANELMATIC INC
Also Called: Panelmatic Youngstown
1125 Meadowbrook Ave (44512-1884)
PHONE....................330 782-8007
Gary M Urso, *Brnch Mgr*
EMP: 29
SALES (corp-wide): 56.9MM **Privately Held**
Web: www.panelmatic.com
SIC: 3613 8711 Control panels, electric; Designing: ship, boat, machine, and product
PA: Panelmatic, Inc.
6806 Willow Brook Park
Houston TX 77066
888 757-1957

(G-16413)
PANELMATIC YOUNGSTOWN INC
1125 Meadowbrook Ave (44512-1884)
PHONE....................330 782-8007
Richard Leach, *Pr*

David D Adamson, *
▼ EMP: 40 EST: 1976
SQ FT: 44,000
SALES (est): 8.04MM
SALES (corp-wide): 42.48MM **Privately Held**
Web: www.panelmatic.com
SIC: 3613 Control panels, electric
PA: Panelmatic, Inc.
  258 Donald Dr
  Fairfield OH 77066
  513 829-3666

(G-16414)
PARK PLC PRNTG CPYG & DGTL IMG
3410 Canfield Rd Ste B (44511-2713)
PHONE...............................330 799-1739
Kay F Probst, Pr
EMP: 6 EST: 2007
SALES (est): 459.68K **Privately Held**
SIC: 2759 Commercial printing, nec

(G-16415)
PATRICIA M BOKESCH
5360 Nashua Dr (44515-5125)
PHONE...............................330 793-4682
Patricia M Bokesch, Prin
EMP: 6 EST: 2010
SALES (est): 63.58K **Privately Held**
SIC: 3479 Metal coating and allied services

(G-16416)
PAUL SHOVLIN
Also Called: Pauls Tire Company
807 Mulberry Ln (44512-2364)
PHONE...............................330 757-0032
Paul Shovlin, Owner
EMP: 6 EST: 1970
SALES (est): 564.13K **Privately Held**
SIC: 5531 7534 7389 Automotive tires; Tire repair shop; Business services, nec

(G-16417)
PESCE BAKERY COMPANY LTD
45 N Hine St (44506-1299)
PHONE...............................330 746-6537
Gary Cellone, Pt
EMP: 7 EST: 1910
SALES (est): 196.26K **Privately Held**
SIC: 2051 Bread, cake, and related products

(G-16418)
PHANTOM FIREWORKS WSTN REG LLC
Also Called: Phantom Fireworks
2445 Belmont Ave (44505-2405)
PHONE...............................330 746-1064
EMP: 11
SALES (est): 1.1MM **Privately Held**
Web: www.fireworks.com
SIC: 2899 Fireworks

(G-16419)
PLY-TRIM INC (PA)
550 N Meridian Rd (44509-1226)
PHONE...............................330 799-7876
Harry Hoffman, Ch Bd
Kathleen Hoffman, Ch Bd
EMP: 21 EST: 1981
SQ FT: 48,000
SALES (est): 7.49MM
SALES (corp-wide): 7.49MM **Privately Held**
Web: www.plytrim.com
SIC: 2431 Millwork

(G-16420)
POLY TEC EAST INC
550 N Meridian Rd (44509-1226)
PHONE...............................330 799-7876
▲ EMP: 8
SALES (est): 531.06K **Privately Held**
SIC: 3083 Laminated plastics sheets

(G-16421)
POLYTECH COMPONENT CORP
8469 Southern Blvd (44512-6709)
PHONE...............................330 726-3235
Paul Colby, Pr
Robert Barber, VP
Michael Durina, VP
William White, Treas
Illene Colby, Sec
EMP: 12 EST: 1990
SQ FT: 6,000
SALES (est): 122.43K **Privately Held**
SIC: 3599 Machine shop, jobbing and repair

(G-16422)
PRECISION OF OHIO INC
3850 Hendricks Rd (44515-1528)
PHONE...............................330 793-0900
Mike Pallotta, Mgr
▲ EMP: 10 EST: 2000
SALES (est): 226.25K **Privately Held**
SIC: 3441 Fabricated structural metal

(G-16423)
PROUT BOILER HTG & WLDG INC
3124 Temple St (44510-1048)
PHONE...............................330 744-0293
Wes Prout, Pr
Richard Dalleske, *
Donald Raybuck, *
Linda Prout, Stockholder*
EMP: 50 EST: 1945
SQ FT: 3,000
SALES (est): 10.17MM **Privately Held**
Web: www.proutboiler.com
SIC: 1711 7692 3443 Boiler maintenance contractor; Welding repair; Fabricated plate work (boiler shop)

(G-16424)
QUICKSILVER DIE CASTING SVC
33 Delaware Ave (44514-1625)
PHONE...............................330 757-1160
Larry Curtis, Owner
EMP: 6 EST: 2002
SALES (est): 145.41K **Privately Held**
SIC: 3544 Special dies and tools

(G-16425)
R & M FLUID POWER INC
7953 Southern Blvd (44512-6091)
PHONE...............................330 758-2766
Robert Gustafson Senior, Ch Bd
Robert Gustafson Ii, VP
Melissa Ricciardi, *
Jennifer Kenetz, *
EMP: 25 EST: 1978
SQ FT: 40,000
SALES (est): 3.4MM **Privately Held**
Web: www.rmfluidpower.com
SIC: 3593 5084 Fluid power cylinders, hydraulic or pneumatic; Hydraulic systems equipment and supplies

(G-16426)
R W SIDLEY INCORPORATED
3424 Oregon Ave (44509-1075)
PHONE...............................330 793-7374
EMP: 8
SALES (corp-wide): 83.57MM **Privately Held**
Web: www.rwsidley.com
SIC: 5032 3273 Brick, stone, and related material; Ready-mixed concrete
PA: R. W. Sidley Incorporated
  436 Casement Ave
  Painesville OH 44077
  440 352-9343

(G-16427)
RAM PLASTICS CO
1837 Celeste Cir (44511-1007)
PHONE...............................330 549-3342
Leonard A Olson, Prin
EMP: 9 EST: 1976
SALES (est): 228.06K **Privately Held**
SIC: 3081 Packing materials, plastics sheet

(G-16428)
RL SMITH GRAPHICS LLC
Also Called: RI Smith Graphics
493 Bev Rd Bldg 7b (44512-6459)
PHONE...............................330 629-8616
Ronald L Smith, Managing Member
EMP: 8 EST: 2010
SALES (est): 935.27K **Privately Held**
Web: www.rlsmithgraphics.com
SIC: 2752 Commercial printing, lithographic

(G-16429)
RNW HOLDINGS INC
200 Division Street Ext (44510-1000)
P.O. Box 478 (44501-0478)
PHONE...............................330 792-0600
Major Hammond, Brnch Mgr
EMP: 42
SIC: 5093 1795 3341 Scrap and waste materials; Wrecking and demolition work; Secondary nonferrous metals
HQ: Rnw Holdings, Inc.
  26949 Chagrin Blvd # 305
  Cleveland OH 44122
  216 831-0510

(G-16430)
ROCKBROOK BUSINESS SVCS LLC
507 Oak Hill Ave (44502-1823)
PHONE...............................234 817-8107
Racole Taltoan, Brnch Mgr
EMP: 29
SALES (corp-wide): 630.26K **Privately Held**
Web: www.rockbrook3.com
SIC: 2711 Newspapers, publishing and printing
PA: Rockbrook Business Services Llc
  775 N Garland Ave
  Youngstown OH 44506
  234 817-8107

(G-16431)
ROMLINE EXPRESS LLC
1572 Brownlee Ave (44514-1010)
PHONE...............................234 855-1905
Stefan Ciuhulescu, Prin
EMP: 6 EST: 2014
SALES (est): 268.94K **Privately Held**
SIC: 2541 Wood partitions and fixtures

(G-16432)
RUSCO PRODUCTS INC
Also Called: Rusco Design Center
423 E Western Reserve Rd (44514-3350)
PHONE...............................330 758-0378
William R Bryson, Pr
Patricia Bryson, Sec
EMP: 6 EST: 1942
SALES (est): 506.19K **Privately Held**
Web: www.rusco.com
SIC: 1799 2541 Kitchen and bathroom remodeling; Table or counter tops, plastic laminated

(G-16433)
SCHWEBEL BAKING COMPANY (PA)
965 E Midlothian Blvd (44502-2869)
P.O. Box 6013 (44501-6013)
PHONE...............................330 783-2860
Paul Schwebel, Pr
Alyson Winick, *
David Alter, *
EMP: 450 EST: 1906
SQ FT: 125,000
SALES (est): 403.34MM
SALES (corp-wide): 403.34MM **Privately Held**
Web: www.schwebels.com
SIC: 2051 Bread, cake, and related products

(G-16434)
SCHWEBEL BAKING COMPANY
920 E Midlothian Blvd (44502-2838)
PHONE...............................330 783-2860
EMP: 6
SALES (corp-wide): 403.34MM **Privately Held**
Web: www.schwebels.com
SIC: 2051 Bread, cake, and related products
PA: Schwebel Baking Company
  965 E Midlothian Blvd
  Youngstown OH 44502
  330 783-2860

(G-16435)
SDMK LLC
Also Called: Fastsigns
7340 Market St (44512-5610)
PHONE...............................330 965-0970
Marc Sikora, Pr
Kevin Sikora, VP
EMP: 6 EST: 2016
SALES (est): 488.71K **Privately Held**
Web: www.fastsigns.com
SIC: 3993 Signs and advertising specialties

(G-16436)
SDS NATIONAL LLC
Also Called: SDS Logistics Services
19 Colonial Dr Ste 27 (44505-2162)
PHONE...............................330 759-8066
Andrew Weiss, Managing Member
EMP: 6 EST: 2001
SALES (est): 1.86MM **Privately Held**
SIC: 3559 4731 Recycling machinery; Freight transportation arrangement

(G-16437)
SID-MAR FOODS INC
1481 South Ave Ste 182 (44522-2239)
PHONE...............................330 743-0112
Charlie Brown, Pr
Richard Seidler, CEO
EMP: 7 EST: 1992
SQ FT: 7,000
SALES (est): 489.12K **Privately Held**
SIC: 2015 Poultry slaughtering and processing

(G-16438)
SIMCO GAS OHIO 2005 PARTNE
200 Victoria Rd Bldg 4 (44515-2047)
PHONE...............................330 799-2268
Charles W Masters, Prin
EMP: 11 EST: 2005
SALES (est): 194.54K **Privately Held**
SIC: 2911 Gases and liquefied petroleum gases

(G-16439)
SIMON ROOFING AND SHTMTL CORP (PA)
Also Called: Simon Roofing
70 Karago Ave (44512-5949)
P.O. Box 951109 (44193-0005)
PHONE...............................330 629-7392
Stephen Manser, Pr
Rocco Augustine, VP

Youngstown - Mahoning County (G-16440)

Alex J Simon Junior, *CFO*
EMP: 105 **EST:** 1900
SQ FT: 30,000
SALES (est): 86.22MM
SALES (corp-wide): 86.22MM **Privately Held**
Web: www.simonroofing.com
SIC: 1761 2952 Roofing contractor; Asphalt felts and coatings

(G-16440)
SIT INC
Also Called: Step In Time
1305 Boardman Canfield Rd (44512-4034)
P.O. Box 3725 (44513-3725)
PHONE..................................330 758-8468
Geri Slavin, *Pr*
EMP: 25 **EST:** 1992
SQ FT: 3,500
SALES (est): 2.02MM **Privately Held**
SIC: 2759 2395 Screen printing; Embroidery products, except Schiffli machine

(G-16441)
SOLAR ARTS GRAPHIC DESIGNS
824 Tod Ave (44502-1326)
PHONE..................................330 744-0535
Daniel Klingensmith, *Pr*
Catherine Klingensmith, *VP*
EMP: 6 **EST:** 1977
SALES (est): 485.36K **Privately Held**
Web: www.solar-arts.com
SIC: 2396 5199 Printing and embossing on plastics fabric articles; Advertising specialties

(G-16442)
SPACE-LINKS INC
1110 Thalia Ave (44512-1825)
P.O. Box 1858 (44501-1858)
PHONE..................................330 788-2401
Ronald N Kessler, *Pr*
EMP: 21 **EST:** 1971
SQ FT: 15,000
SALES (est): 980.51K **Privately Held**
Web: www.spacelinks1.com
SIC: 3069 Mats or matting, rubber, nec

(G-16443)
SPACELINKS ENTERPRISES INC
1110 Thalia Ave (44512-1825)
PHONE..................................330 788-2401
Daniel Kessler, *Pr*
Jamie Bill, *Stockholder*
Samantha Cessker, *Stockholder*
Seth Kessler, *Stockholder*
EMP: 24 **EST:** 1995
SQ FT: 90,000
SALES (est): 791.04K **Privately Held**
Web: www.spacelinks1.com
SIC: 2273 Mats and matting

(G-16444)
SPECIALTY SWITCH COMPANY LLC
Also Called: Specialty Trans Components
525 Mcclurg Rd (44512-6406)
PHONE..................................330 427-3000
Terry Turvey, *Pr*
▲ **EMP:** 15 **EST:** 1986
SQ FT: 7,000
SALES (est): 2.18MM **Privately Held**
Web: www.transformercomponents.com
SIC: 3679 5063 Electronic switches; Electrical apparatus and equipment

(G-16445)
SPECTRUM METAL FINISHING INC
535 Bev Rd (44512-6490)
PHONE..................................330 758-8358
Neil Chrisman, *Pr*
Thomas Hutch, *

▼ **EMP:** 57 **EST:** 1964
SQ FT: 60,000
SALES (est): 9.95MM **Privately Held**
Web: www.spectrummetal.com
SIC: 3471 Finishing, metals or formed products

(G-16446)
SPIREX CORPORATION
375 Victoria Rd Ste 1 (44515-2053)
PHONE..................................330 726-1166
▲ **EMP:** 200
Web: www.valleyextreme.com
SIC: 3599 3535 3494 3443 Machine shop, jobbing and repair; Conveyors and conveying equipment; Valves and pipe fittings, nec; Fabricated plate work (boiler shop)

(G-16447)
STAR MANUFACTURING LLC
Also Called: Commercial Metal Forming
1775 Logan Ave (44505-2622)
PHONE..................................330 740-8300
Bob Messaros, *CEO*
Jim Petrides, *
EMP: 148 **EST:** 2016
SALES (est): 51.97MM
SALES (corp-wide): 51.97MM **Privately Held**
SIC: 3272 Tanks, concrete
PA: Ce Star Holdings, Llc
 1775 Logan Ave
 Youngstown OH 44505
 800 826-5867

(G-16448)
STEEL FORMING INC
Also Called: Commercial Metal Forming
1775 Logan Ave (44505-2622)
P.O. Box 599 (44501-0599)
PHONE..................................714 532-6321
◆ **EMP:** 203
Web: www.cmforming.com
SIC: 3469 Metal stampings, nec

(G-16449)
SUMMIT POLYMERS LLC
1900 Hubbard Rd (44505-3128)
PHONE..................................330 506-7715
EMP: 10 **EST:** 2017
SALES (est): 245.36K **Privately Held**
SIC: 3089 Injection molding of plastics

(G-16450)
T C REDI MIX YOUNGSTOWN INC (PA)
2400 Poland Ave (44502-2782)
PHONE..................................330 755-2143
Sherry Andrews, *Pr*
Sandra Raider, *VP*
Susan Kirkwood, *Sec*
EMP: 20 **EST:** 1974
SQ FT: 3,000
SALES (est): 4.13MM
SALES (corp-wide): 4.13MM **Privately Held**
Web: t-c-redi-mix-inc.hub.biz
SIC: 3273 5211 Ready-mixed concrete; Lumber and other building materials

(G-16451)
TAYLOR-WINFIELD TECH INC
Also Called: Taylor Winfield Indus Wldg Eqp
3200 Innovation Pl (44509-4025)
P.O. Box 779 (44501-0779)
PHONE..................................330 259-8500
EMP: 50 **EST:** 2010
SQ FT: 25,000
SALES (est): 12.4MM **Privately Held**
Web: www.taylor-winfield.com

SIC: 3548 Welding apparatus
PA: Brilex Industries, Inc.
 1201 Crescent St
 Youngstown OH 44502

(G-16452)
TECHNIWELD
1120 Oak Hill Ave (44502-1861)
PHONE..................................412 357-2176
EMP: 6 **EST:** 2016
SALES (est): 150.7K **Privately Held**
Web: www.twusa.com
SIC: 7692 Welding repair

(G-16453)
THE FLORAND COMPANY
4404 Lake Park Rd (44512-1809)
PHONE..................................330 747-8986
Andrew Hirt, *Pr*
Kevin Carney, *VP*
Florence Hirt, *Treas*
EMP: 16 **EST:** 1989
SALES (est): 1.12MM **Privately Held**
Web: www.florand.com
SIC: 3312 Plate, sheet and strip, except coated products

(G-16454)
THE VINDICATOR PRINTING COMPANY (PA)
Also Called: Vindy.com
107 Vindicator Sq (44503)
P.O. Box 780 (44501)
PHONE..................................330 747-1471
EMP: 320 **EST:** 1869
SALES (est): 23.94MM
SALES (corp-wide): 23.94MM **Privately Held**
Web: www.vindy.com
SIC: 2711 Newspapers, publishing and printing

(G-16455)
TIMEKAP INC
Also Called: Timekap Indus Sls Svc & Mch
2315 Belmont Ave (44505-2404)
PHONE..................................330 747-2122
Patrick Chrystal, *Pr*
Scott Lawrence, *VP*
EMP: 6 **EST:** 1994
SQ FT: 15,000
SALES (est): 524.69K **Privately Held**
SIC: 3599 Machine shop, jobbing and repair

(G-16456)
TMI INC
6475 Victoria East Rd (44515-2051)
P.O. Box 4596 (44515-0596)
PHONE..................................330 270-9780
Michael J Myhal Junior, *Pr*
Rebecca Myhal, *
▼ **EMP:** 28 **EST:** 1984
SQ FT: 30,000
SALES (est): 4.24MM **Privately Held**
Web: www.teamtmi.com
SIC: 3069 Molded rubber products

(G-16457)
TRAFFIC DETECTORS & SIGNS INC
Also Called: Traffic Detectors & Signs
7521 Forest Hill Ave (44514-2635)
PHONE..................................330 707-9060
Leila M Meris, *Prin*
EMP: 6 **EST:** 2003
SALES (est): 611.46K **Privately Held**
SIC: 1611 3993 Highway signs and guardrails; Signs and advertising specialties

(G-16458)
TRANSIT FITTINGS N AMER INC
295 S Meridian Rd (44509-2924)
PHONE..................................330 797-2516
Admiral Jeff Fox, *Prin*
EMP: 6 **EST:** 2019
SALES (est): 750K **Privately Held**
SIC: 3711 Bus and other large specialty vehicle assembly

(G-16459)
TRANSIT SITTINGS OF NA
295 S Meridian Rd (44509-2924)
PHONE..................................330 797-2516
Wayne Donitzen, *Off Mgr*
EMP: 6 **EST:** 1999
SALES (est): 391.93K **Privately Held**
SIC: 3498 Fabricated pipe and fittings

(G-16460)
TRIVIUM ALUM PACKG USA CORP (DH)
1 Performance Pl (44502-2082)
PHONE..................................330 744-9505
Michael Mapes, *CEO*
Delfin Gibert, *
Brenda Oman, *
▲ **EMP:** 31 **EST:** 1992
SQ FT: 476,000
SALES (est): 114.98MM
SALES (corp-wide): 1.42B **Privately Held**
Web: www.triviumpackaging.com
SIC: 3411 3354 Aluminum cans; Aluminum extruded products
HQ: Trivium Packaging B.V.
 Schiphol Boulevard 149
 Luchthaven Schiphol NH

(G-16461)
TRUMBULL MANUFACTURING INC
3850 Hendricks Rd (44515-1528)
PHONE..................................330 270-7888
Sam H Miller, *CEO*
Michael W Rosenberg, *Prin*
EMP: 22 **EST:** 1922
SALES (est): 10MM **Privately Held**
Web: www.trumbull-mfg.com
SIC: 3589 Water treatment equipment, industrial

(G-16462)
TURNING TECHNOLOGIES LLC (PA)
6000 Mahoning Ave (44515-2225)
PHONE..................................330 746-3015
Mike Broderick, *Managing Member*
Dave Kauer, *
Doctor Tina Rooks, *Sr VP*
Kevin Owens, *
Sheila Hura, *
◆ **EMP:** 152 **EST:** 2002
SALES (est): 91.49MM
SALES (corp-wide): 91.49MM **Privately Held**
Web: www.echo360.com
SIC: 7372 Business oriented computer software

(G-16463)
U S WEATHERFORD L P
1100 Performance Pl (44502-4001)
PHONE..................................330 746-2502
EMP: 172
Web: www.weatherford.com
SIC: 1389 Oil field services, nec
HQ: U S Weatherford L P
 179 Weatherford Dr
 Schriever LA 70395
 985 493-6100

GEOGRAPHIC SECTION

Youngstown - Mahoning County (G-16488)

(G-16464)
UNITED STATES CONTROLS
8511 Foxwood Ct (44514-4302)
PHONE...................330 758-1147
EMP: 6 **EST:** 2018
SALES (est): 398K **Privately Held**
Web: www.unitedstatescontrols.com
SIC: 3492 Fluid power valves and hose fittings

(G-16465)
V & M STAR LP
2669 Martin Luther King Jr Blvd (44510)
PHONE...................330 742-6300
Brian R Colquhoun, *Prin*
▲ **EMP:** 19 **EST:** 2012
SALES (est): 2.33MM **Privately Held**
Web: www.vmtubes.net
SIC: 3061 Oil and gas field machinery rubber goods (mechanical)

(G-16466)
VALLOUREC STAR LP (HQ)
2669 Martin Luther King Jr Blvd (44510-1062)
PHONE...................330 742-6300
Edouard Guinotte, *Ch Bd*
Olivier Mallet, *CEO*
Pascal Braquehais, *MIDDLE EAST ASIA*
Philippe Carlier, *Senior Vice President Technology*
Franois Curie, *Pers/VP*
▲ **EMP:** 139 **EST:** 2002
SALES (est): 215.37MM
SALES (corp-wide): 2.17MM **Privately Held**
Web: www.vallourec.com
SIC: 3317 Pipes, seamless steel
PA: Vallourec
12 Rue De La Verrerie
Meudon 92190
149093500

(G-16467)
VAM USA LLC
1053 Ohio Works Dr (44510-1078)
PHONE...................330 742-3130
EMP: 24 **EST:** 2012
SALES (est): 3.71MM **Privately Held**
Web: www.vam-usa.com
SIC: 1389 Oil field services, nec

(G-16468)
VARCO LP
Also Called: Tuboscope
2669 Martin Luther King Jr Blvd (44510-1062)
P.O. Box 2185 (44504-0185)
PHONE...................330 746-2922
EMP: 20
SALES (corp-wide): 8.58B **Publicly Held**
Web: www.nov.com
SIC: 1389 Testing, measuring, surveying, and analysis services
HQ: Varco, L.P.
2835 Holmes Rd
Houston TX 77051
713 799-5272

(G-16469)
VETERANS REPRESENTATIVE CO LLC
1584 Tamarisk Trl (44514-3632)
PHONE...................330 779-0768
EMP: 10 **EST:** 2006
SQ FT: 800
SALES (est): 832.19K **Privately Held**
Web: www.veteranrepco.com
SIC: 2522 Chairs, office: padded or plain: except wood

(G-16470)
VICTOR ORGAN COMPANY
5340 Mahoning Ave (44515-2415)
PHONE...................330 792-1321
Victor Marsilo, *Owner*
EMP: 8 **EST:** 1987
SQ FT: 6,500
SALES (est): 496.81K **Privately Held**
SIC: 3931 7699 Organs, all types: pipe, reed, hand, electronic, etc.; Organ tuning and repair

(G-16471)
VINYL TOOL & DIE COMPANY
1144 Meadowbrook Ave (44512-1821)
PHONE...................330 782-0254
Paul Chicone, *Pr*
Carmen Chicone Senior, *VP*
Carmen Chicone Junior, *Sec*
EMP: 10 **EST:** 1988
SALES (est): 232.27K **Privately Held**
Web: www.vinyltoolanddie.com
SIC: 3544 Extrusion dies

(G-16472)
VINYLUME PRODUCTS INC
3745 Hendricks Rd (44515-1500)
PHONE...................330 799-2000
Jack M White, *CEO*
Orlando White, *
Helen White, *
EMP: 26 **EST:** 1964
SQ FT: 200,000
SALES (est): 5.35MM **Privately Held**
Web: www.vinylumewindows.com
SIC: 3089 3442 3211 Window frames and sash, plastics; Metal doors, sash, and trim; Flat glass

(G-16473)
W B BECHERER INC
Also Called: Modernfold
7905 Southern Blvd (44512-6025)
P.O. Box 3186 (44513-3186)
PHONE...................330 758-6616
William B Becherer Senior, *Pr*
William B Becherer Junior, *Treas*
Bruce Becherer, *Sec*
EMP: 9 **EST:** 1950
SQ FT: 4,000
SALES (est): 1.13MM **Privately Held**
Web: www.rmcks.org
SIC: 2542 Partitions and fixtures, except wood

(G-16474)
WARRIOR IMPORTS INC
Also Called: Hardcore Offroad Tires
112 S Meridian Rd (44509-2640)
PHONE...................954 935-5536
Ray Starr, *Pr*
Corey Burt, *Prin*
▲ **EMP:** 20 **EST:** 2001
SQ FT: 100,000
SALES (est): 1.42MM **Privately Held**
Web: www.warriorimport.com
SIC: 3262 Vitreous china table and kitchenware

(G-16475)
YELLOW CREEK INDUSTRIES
64 Poland Mnr (44514-2058)
PHONE...................330 757-1065
Joseph Mazur, *Prin*
EMP: 6 **EST:** 2010
SALES (est): 74.78K **Privately Held**
SIC: 3999 Manufacturing industries, nec

(G-16476)
YOUNGSTOWN ARC ENGRAVING CO
Also Called: Youngstown Lithographing Co
380 Victoria Rd (44515-2011)
PHONE...................330 793-2471
E Craig Olsen, *Pr*
Tim Merrifield, *
George B Snyder, *
EMP: 9 **EST:** 1900
SQ FT: 30,000
SALES (est): 207.51K **Privately Held**
SIC: 2796 7335 2791 2789 Photoengraving plates, linecuts or halftones; Commercial photography; Typesetting; Bookbinding and related work

(G-16477)
YOUNGSTOWN BELT RAILROAD CO
123 Division Street Ext (44510-1070)
PHONE...................740 622-8092
EMP: 7 **EST:** 2019
SALES (est): 325.16K **Privately Held**
SIC: 3743 Railroad equipment

(G-16478)
YOUNGSTOWN BENDING ROLLING
3710 Hendricks Rd Bldg 2b (44515-1537)
PHONE...................330 799-2227
Daniel Kish, *Prin*
EMP: 9 **EST:** 2006
SALES (est): 490.64K **Privately Held**
Web: www.youngstownbending.com
SIC: 3531 Railroad related equipment

(G-16479)
YOUNGSTOWN BOLT & SUPPLY CO
340 N Meridian Rd (44509-1246)
PHONE...................330 799-3201
Al Fedorisin, *Pr*
Lorraine Fedorisin, *VP*
EMP: 6 **EST:** 1981
SQ FT: 20,000
SALES (est): 794.83K **Privately Held**
Web: www.youngstownbolt.com
SIC: 5085 3965 Fasteners, industrial: nuts, bolts, screws, etc.; Fasteners

(G-16480)
YOUNGSTOWN CURVE FORM INC
1102 Rigby St (44506-1500)
PHONE...................330 744-3028
Frank Laskay, *Pr*
EMP: 10 **EST:** 1964
SQ FT: 7,800
SALES (est): 858.16K **Privately Held**
SIC: 5031 2541 Building materials, interior; Table or counter tops, plastic laminated

(G-16481)
YOUNGSTOWN FENCE INCORPORATED
235 E Indianola Ave (44507-1546)
PHONE...................330 788-8110
Frank J Mikitaw, *Pr*
Suzanne Mikitaw, *VP*
EMP: 6 **EST:** 1943
SQ FT: 34,000
SALES (est): 745.67K **Privately Held**
Web: www.youngstownfence.com
SIC: 1799 5211 2499 Fence construction; Fencing; Fencing, wood

(G-16482)
YOUNGSTOWN HARD CHROME PLTG GR
8451 Southern Blvd (44512-6709)
P.O. Box 3508 (44513-3508)
PHONE...................330 758-9721
Richard S Mccarthy, *Pr*
Daniel J Mccarthy, *VP*
EMP: 28 **EST:** 1962
SQ FT: 35,000
SALES (est): 2.73MM **Privately Held**
Web: www.youngstownhardchrome.com
SIC: 3471 3599 Chromium plating of metals or formed products; Grinding castings for the trade

(G-16483)
YOUNGSTOWN HEAT TRTING NTRDING
1118 Meadowbrook Ave (44512)
PHONE...................330 788-3025
Carmen P Chicone Senior, *Pr*
EMP: 6 **EST:** 1973
SQ FT: 5,000
SALES (est): 446.36K **Privately Held**
SIC: 3398 Annealing of metal

(G-16484)
YOUNGSTOWN LETTER SHOP INC
3650 Connecticut Ave (44515-3001)
PHONE...................330 793-4935
Jean Tuscano, *Pr*
EMP: 9 **EST:** 1920
SALES (est): 1.02MM **Privately Held**
Web: www.ylssites.com
SIC: 7331 2752 7521 Mailing service; Offset printing; Parking garage

(G-16485)
YOUNGSTOWN PLASTIC TOOLING (PA)
1209 Velma Ct (44512-1829)
PHONE...................330 782-7222
Donald J Liga, *Pr*
Janet Liga, *
EMP: 15 **EST:** 1984
SQ FT: 20,000
SALES (est): 2.7MM
SALES (corp-wide): 2.7MM **Privately Held**
Web: www.yptm.com
SIC: 3559 8711 Plastics working machinery; Machine tool design

(G-16486)
YOUNGSTOWN PRE-PRESS INC
3691 Leharps Dr (44515)
P.O. Box 2375 (44509)
PHONE...................330 793-3690
EMP: 11 **EST:** 1995
SQ FT: 4,000
SALES (est): 572.36K **Privately Held**
SIC: 7336 2752 Graphic arts and related design; Lithographing on metal

(G-16487)
YOUNGSTOWN SHADE & ALUM LLC
Also Called: Richards Intriors Bldg Cmpnents
3335 South Ave (44502-2407)
P.O. Box 8627 (44484-0627)
PHONE...................330 782-2373
Richard Gula, *Owner*
EMP: 8 **EST:** 1947
SQ FT: 15,000
SALES (est): 1.6MM **Privately Held**
SIC: 1542 2591 3444 3442 Commercial and office buildings, renovation and repair; Venetian blinds; Awnings, sheet metal; Metal doors, sash, and trim

(G-16488)
YOUNGSTOWN SPECIALTY MTLS INC
571 Andrews Ave (44505-3064)
PHONE...................330 259-1110
Frank Wadlinger, *CEO*
Michael Miklus, *VP*
Richard Wadlinger, *CFO*
EMP: 8 **EST:** 2001

Youngstown - Mahoning County (G-16489)

SQ FT: 20,000
SALES (est): 1.81MM Privately Held
Web: www.yngspecmetals.com
SIC: 3053 5051 Gaskets; packing and sealing devices; Steel

(G-16489)
YOUNGSTOWN TOOL & DIE COMPANY
2572 Salt Springs Rd (44509-1030)
PHONE..................330 747-4464
Fred Fisher, *Pr*
EMP: 62 **EST:** 1961
SALES (est): 9.83MM Privately Held
Web: www.youngstowntool.com
SIC: 3544 3354 Special dies and tools; Aluminum extruded products

(G-16490)
YOUNGSTOWN TUBE CO
401 Andrews Ave (44505-3062)
PHONE..................330 743-7414
William Veri, *Pr*
EMP: 30 **EST:** 1991
SQ FT: 93,000
SALES (est): 3.99MM Privately Held
Web: www.youngstowntube.com
SIC: 3312 Pipes, iron and steel

(G-16491)
YSD INDUSTRIES INC
3710 Hendricks Rd (44515)
PHONE..................330 792-6521
Jerome D Hines, *Pr*
Michael Feschak, *
Jeff Span, *
Bruce Wylie, *
Adam Stryffeler, *
▲ **EMP:** 24 **EST:** 2004
SQ FT: 30,000
SALES (est): 2.38MM
SALES (corp-wide): 969.86K Privately Held
SIC: 5088 3444 3441 Railroad equipment and supplies; Sheet metalwork; Fabricated structural metal
PA: Global Railway Industries Ltd
611 10 Ave Sw Suite 12
Calgary AB T2R 0

Zaleski
Vinton County

(G-16492)
LMP MACHINE LLC
115 E Chestnut St (45698)
P.O. Box 255 (45698-0255)
PHONE..................740 596-4559
EMP: 9 **EST:** 1968
SQ FT: 4,800
SALES (est): 720.38K Privately Held
Web: www.sledgehammerpulling.com
SIC: 3599 Machine shop, jobbing and repair

Zanesville
Muskingum County

(G-16493)
5 BS INC (PA)
Also Called: B-Wear Sportswear
1000 5 Bs Dr (43701-7630)
P.O. Box 520 (43702-0520)
PHONE..................740 454-8453
Todd Biles, *Pr*
Paula Moore, *
John Klies, *
Chris Nash, *
Leland Biles, *

▲ **EMP:** 250 **EST:** 1969
SQ FT: 170,000
SALES (est): 50.14MM
SALES (corp-wide): 50.14MM Privately Held
Web: www.5bs.com
SIC: 2339 2395 Athletic clothing: women's, misses', and juniors'; Embroidery products, except Schiffli machine

(G-16494)
ACE TRUCK EQUIPMENT CO
1130 Newark Rd (43701-2619)
P.O. Box 2605 (43702-2605)
PHONE..................740 453-0551
David Beitzel, *Pr*
Robert D Beitzel, *CEO*
Dora Beitzel, *Sec*
EMP: 21 **EST:** 1955
SQ FT: 30,500
SALES (est): 2.78MM Privately Held
Web: www.acetruck.net
SIC: 5531 5012 3713 Truck equipment and parts; Truck bodies; Truck and bus bodies

(G-16495)
ADAMS BROS CONCRETE PDTS LTD
3401 East Pike (43701-8419)
PHONE..................740 452-7566
Scott M Zemba, *Admn*
EMP: 19 **EST:** 2009
SALES (est): 2.95MM Privately Held
Web: www.adamsbrosconcrete.com
SIC: 3273 Ready-mixed concrete

(G-16496)
ADAMS BROTHERS INC
1501 Woodlawn Ave (43701-5955)
P.O. Box 27 (43702-0027)
PHONE..................740 819-0323
William Adams Iv, *Pr*
Nancy Adams, *VP*
Katie Brown, *Treas*
EMP: 16 **EST:** 1908
SALES (est): 822.33K Privately Held
Web: www.adamsbrosconcrete.com
SIC: 3273 5211 Ready-mixed concrete; Lumber and other building materials

(G-16497)
AJ ENTERPRISE LLC
2300 National Rd (43701-9286)
PHONE..................740 231-2205
Cory Mcgilton, *Prin*
EMP: 15 **EST:** 2019
SALES (est): 1.05MM Privately Held
Web: www.ajenterprise.net
SIC: 1389 Oil and gas field services, nec

(G-16498)
ALFRED NICKLES BAKERY INC
Also Called: Nickles Bakery 45
1147 Newark Rd (43701-2618)
PHONE..................740 453-6522
Les Bell, *Genl Mgr*
EMP: 46
SALES (corp-wide): 151.88MM Privately Held
Web: www.nicklesbakery.com
SIC: 2051 5461 Bakery: wholesale or wholesale/retail combined; Retail bakeries
PA: Alfred Nickles Bakery, Inc.
26 Main St N
Navarre OH 44662
330 879-5635

(G-16499)
ALLIED MACHINE WORKS INC
120 Graham St (43701-3100)
PHONE..................740 454-2534
Richard J Straker, *Pr*

Patricia Folden, *Prin*
EMP: 8 **EST:** 1964
SQ FT: 56,058
SALES (est): 772.37K Privately Held
SIC: 3599 7629 3533 Machine shop, jobbing and repair; Electrical repair shops; Oil and gas field machinery

(G-16500)
ANCHOR GLASS CONTAINER CORP
Zanesville Mould Division
1206 Brandywine Blvd Ste C (43701-1731)
PHONE..................740 452-2743
Steve Brock, *Brnch Mgr*
EMP: 65
Web: www.anchorglass.com
SIC: 3321 3221 3544 Gray iron ingot molds, cast; Glass containers; Special dies, tools, jigs, and fixtures
PA: Anchor Glass Container Corporation
3001 N Rocky Point Dr E # 300
Tampa FL 33607

(G-16501)
AXION INTERNATIONAL HOLDINGS INC
4005 All American Way (43701-7251)
PHONE..................740 452-2500
EMP: 120
Web: www.axionsi.com
SIC: 3089 Prefabricated plastics buildings

(G-16502)
AXION INTERNATIONAL INC
4005 All American Way (43701-7306)
PHONE..................740 452-2500
EMP: 6
Web: www.axionsi.com
SIC: 5084 3089 Recycling machinery and equipment; Plastics hardware and building products

(G-16503)
AXION STRL INNOVATIONS LLC (PA)
1100 Brandywine Blvd Ste H (43701)
P.O. Box 3508 (43702)
PHONE..................740 452-2500
Allen Kronstadt, *Managing Member*
Claude Brown, *Managing Member*
Matt Elli, *Managing Member*
Dave Crane, *Managing Member*
EMP: 17 **EST:** 2015
SALES (est): 9.82MM
SALES (corp-wide): 9.82MM Privately Held
Web: www.axionsi.com
SIC: 3089 Extruded finished plastics products, nec

(G-16504)
BALLAS EGG PRODUCTS CORP
40 N 2nd St (43701-3402)
P.O. Box 2217 (43702-2217)
PHONE..................614 453-0386
Leonard Ballas, *Pr*
Joseph G Saliba, *VP*
Craig Ballas, *
▼ **EMP:** 100 **EST:** 1961
SQ FT: 200,000
SALES (est): 8.48MM Privately Held
Web: www.wabashvalleyeggs.com
SIC: 2015 5144 Egg processing; Eggs

(G-16505)
BARNES ADVERTISING CORPORATION
1580 Fairview Rd (43701-0934)
P.O. Box 277 (43702-0277)
PHONE..................740 453-6836
TOLL FREE: 800

Maryjane Shackelford, *Pr*
John Barnes, *VP*
EMP: 22 **EST:** 1916
SALES (est): 768.48K Privately Held
Web: www.barnesadvertisingcorp.com
SIC: 7312 3993 Billboard advertising; Signs and advertising specialties

(G-16506)
BATTERY UNLIMITED
1080 Linden Ave (43701-2952)
PHONE..................740 452-5030
Kent Curry, *Owner*
EMP: 6 **EST:** 1985
SALES (est): 501.3K Privately Held
Web: www.batteriesunlimitedohio.com
SIC: 5063 5531 5999 7699 Batteries; Batteries, automotive and truck; Batteries, non-automotive; Battery service and repair

(G-16507)
BE PRODUCTS INC
Also Called: Ballas Egg Products
40 N 2nd St (43701-3402)
P.O. Box 2217 (43702-2217)
PHONE..................740 453-0386
Criag Ballas, *Pr*
Craig Ballas, *Pr*
Leonard Ballas, *VP*
EMP: 26 **EST:** 1928
SQ FT: 125,000
SALES (est): 991.26K Privately Held
Web: www.zmchamber.com
SIC: 2015 Egg processing

(G-16508)
BILCO COMPANY
3400 Jim Granger Dr (43701-7231)
PHONE..................740 455-9020
Charles Chirdon, *Pr*
EMP: 50
SALES (corp-wide): 819.66MM Privately Held
Web: www.bilco.com
SIC: 3442 3272 Metal doors; Areaways, basement window: concrete
HQ: The Bilco Company
37 Water St
West Haven CT 06516
203 934-6363

(G-16509)
BIMBO QSR US LLC
750 Airport Rd (43701-9694)
P.O. Box 256 (43017-0256)
PHONE..................740 562-4188
David Marion, *Brnch Mgr*
EMP: 8
Web: www.bimboqsr.com
SIC: 2051 Bakery: wholesale or wholesale/retail combined
HQ: Bimbo Qsr Us, Llc
1801 W 31st Pl
Chicago IL 60608
773 376-4444

(G-16510)
BISHOP MACHINE TOOL & DIE
Also Called: Bishop Machine Shop
2304 Hoge Ave (43701-2166)
PHONE..................740 453-8818
Robert L Bishop, *Pt*
John R Bishop, *Pt*
Alva Bishop Junior, *Mgr*
EMP: 10 **EST:** 1964
SQ FT: 2,000
SALES (est): 695.79K Privately Held
Web: www.sprintermarking.com
SIC: 3599 3953 Machine shop, jobbing and repair; Marking devices

GEOGRAPHIC SECTION

Zanesville - Muskingum County (G-16533)

(G-16511)
BLOOMER CANDY CO
3610 National Rd (43701-8812)
P.O. Box 3450 (43702-3450)
PHONE.................................740 452-7501
William S Barry, *Pr*
Teresa Young-barry, *Sec*
Tom Barry, *
Pat Barry, *
Robert Barry, *
EMP: 130 **EST:** 1893
SQ FT: 150,000
SALES (est): 5.47MM **Privately Held**
Web: www.bloomercandy.com
SIC: 5145 2064 Confectionery; Candy and other confectionery products

(G-16512)
BOB SUMEREL TIRE CO INC
1140 Newark Rd (43701-2619)
PHONE.................................740 454-9728
Steve Dickerson, *Brnch Mgr*
EMP: 7
SALES (corp-wide): 97.34MM **Privately Held**
Web: www.bobsumereltire.com
SIC: 7534 5531 Tire retreading and repair shops; Automotive tires
PA: Bob Sumerel Tire Co., Inc.
    1257 Cox Ave
    Erlanger KY 41018
    859 283-2700

(G-16513)
BUCKEYE COMPANIES (PA)
999 Zane St (43701-3863)
P.O. Box 1480 (43702-1480)
PHONE.................................740 452-3641
C E Straker, *Pr*
M Dean Cole, *
Stephen R Straker, *
EMP: 31 **EST:** 1982
SALES (est): 10.11MM
SALES (corp-wide): 10.11MM **Privately Held**
Web: www.thebuckeyecompanies.com
SIC: 3533 5083 Drill rigs; Agricultural machinery and equipment

(G-16514)
BUCKEYE ENERGY RESOURCES INC
Also Called: Seth Enterprises
999 Zane St (43701-3863)
PHONE.................................740 452-9506
C E Staker, *Ch*
Stephen Straker, *Pr*
M Dean Cole, *Sec*
Charles E Straker, *CEO*
EMP: 6 **EST:** 1981
SALES (est): 942.25K
SALES (corp-wide): 10.11MM **Privately Held**
Web: www.sethenterprises.com
SIC: 4213 1311 Trucking, except local; Crude petroleum and natural gas
PA: Buckeye Companies
    999 Zane St
    Zanesville OH 43701
    740 452-3641

(G-16515)
BUCKINGHAM COAL COMPANY LLC
11 N 4th St (43701-3409)
P.O. Box 340 (43702-0340)
EMP: 80 **EST:** 1994
SALES (est): 25MM
SALES (corp-wide): 814.89MM **Privately Held**
SIC: 1221 Bituminous coal and lignite- surface mining

HQ: Wcc Land Holding Company, Inc.
    9540 Maroon Cir Unit 300
    Englewood CO 80112
    855 922-6463

(G-16516)
CAMERON DRILLING CO INC
3636 Adamsville Rd (43701-6954)
PHONE.................................740 453-3300
James H Cameron, *Pr*
Richard M Cameron, *VP*
EMP: 10 **EST:** 1966
SQ FT: 3,000
SALES (est): 475.76K **Privately Held**
SIC: 1311 Crude petroleum production

(G-16517)
CARL RITTBERGER SR INC
1900 Lutz Ln (43701-9260)
PHONE.................................740 452-2767
TOLL FREE: 800
Andrew Rittberger, *Pr*
Pauline Butler, *
EMP: 27 **EST:** 1910
SQ FT: 100,000
SALES (est): 1.76MM **Privately Held**
Web: www.rittbergers.com
SIC: 2013 2011 Sausages and other prepared meats; Meat packing plants

(G-16518)
CASTING SOLUTIONS LLC
2345 Licking Rd (43701-2728)
P.O. Box 3148 (43702-3148)
PHONE.................................740 452-9371
Jeremiah Clegg, *Pr*
EMP: 106 **EST:** 2001
SALES (est): 24.39MM
SALES (corp-wide): 240.55MM **Publicly Held**
Web: www.castingsolutions.com
SIC: 3321 Gray iron castings, nec
PA: Burnham Holdings, Inc.
    1241 Harrisburg Pike
    Lancaster PA 17604
    717 390-7800

(G-16519)
CENTRAL COCA-COLA BTLG CO INC
Also Called: Coca-Cola
154 S 7th St (43701-4332)
PHONE.................................740 452-3608
Dave Llewellen, *Mgr*
EMP: 34
SALES (corp-wide): 45.75B **Publicly Held**
Web: www.coca-cola.com
SIC: 2086 Bottled and canned soft drinks
HQ: Central Coca-Cola Bottling Company, Inc.
    555 Taxter Rd Ste 550
    Elmsford NY 10523
    914 789-1100

(G-16520)
CENTRAL OHIO BANDAG LP
1600 S Point Dr (43701-7366)
PHONE.................................740 454-9728
Steven Dickerson, *Pt*
Wayne Anderson, *
Bob Sumerel, *
EMP: 10 **EST:** 1971
SQ FT: 19,000
SALES (est): 485.7K **Privately Held**
Web: www.bobsumereltire.com
SIC: 7534 5014 Tire recapping; Truck tires and tubes

(G-16521)
CLEARPATH UTLITY SOLUTIONS LLC
8155 Ridge Rd (43701-8283)

PHONE.................................740 661-4240
Maureen E Riley, *Managing Member*
Rodney Riley, *Prin*
EMP: 10 **EST:** 2007
SALES (est): 3.55MM **Privately Held**
Web: www.directionaldrilling.com
SIC: 1381 Directional drilling oil and gas wells

(G-16522)
CLOSETS BY MIKE
517 Winton Ave (43701-1918)
PHONE.................................740 607-2212
Michael Lmills, *Prin*
EMP: 6 **EST:** 2011
SALES (est): 76.44K **Privately Held**
SIC: 3088 Shower stalls, fiberglass and plastics

(G-16523)
CONNS POTATO CHIP CO INC (PA)
1805 Kemper Ct (43701-4634)
PHONE.................................740 452-4615
Monte Hunter, *Pr*
Thomas George Senior, *VP*
EMP: 30 **EST:** 1952
SQ FT: 100,000
SALES (est): 8.79MM
SALES (corp-wide): 8.79MM **Privately Held**
Web: www.connspotatochips.com
SIC: 2096 5963 Potato chips and other potato-based snacks; Snacks, direct sales

(G-16524)
CREATIVE PACKAGING LLC
1781 Kemper Ct (43701-4606)
P.O. Box 305 (43702-0305)
PHONE.................................740 452-8497
Keith Imhoff, *Managing Member*
EMP: 48 **EST:** 1978
SQ FT: 125,000
SALES (est): 10.68MM **Privately Held**
Web: www.creativepkg.com
SIC: 2653 2671 Boxes, corrugated: made from purchased materials; Paper; coated and laminated packaging

(G-16525)
CUSTOM COIL & TRANSFORMER CO
2900 Newark Rd (43701-7759)
P.O. Box 8063 (43702-8063)
PHONE.................................740 452-5211
Marty Lucas, *Pr*
Martin C Marty Lucas, *Pr*
Pam Lucas, *
EMP: 8 **EST:** 1962
SQ FT: 9,000
SALES (est): 328.81K **Privately Held**
Web: www.customcoil.com
SIC: 3621 3677 3612 Coils, for electric motors or generators; Electronic coils and transformers; Transformers, except electric

(G-16526)
DMV CORPORATION
1024 Military Rd (43701-1343)
P.O. Box 878 (43702-0878)
PHONE.................................740 452-4787
Allan Patterson, *Pr*
EMP: 9 **EST:** 1968
SQ FT: 1,500
SALES (est): 995.27K **Privately Held**
Web: www.dmvcorp.com
SIC: 3851 Ophthalmic goods

(G-16527)
DOW CAMERON OIL & GAS LLC
5555 Eden Park Dr (43701-7052)
PHONE.................................740 452-1568
EMP: 8 **EST:** 2003

SALES (est): 953.51K **Privately Held**
Web: www.dowcameronoilgas.com
SIC: 1389 Oil and gas wells: building, repairing and dismantling

(G-16528)
DR PEPPER BOTTLING COMPANY
Also Called: Dr Pepper
335 N 6th St (43701-3636)
PHONE.................................740 452-2721
Rick Stone, *Prin*
EMP: 7 **EST:** 2011
SALES (est): 126.6K **Privately Held**
Web: www.drpepper.com
SIC: 2086 Soft drinks: packaged in cans, bottles, etc.

(G-16529)
ECLIPSE RESOURCES - OHIO LLC
4900 Boggs Rd (43701-9491)
P.O. Box 910 (43702-0910)
PHONE.................................740 452-4503
Benjamin W Hulburt, *Managing Member*
Christopher K Hulburt, *
Thomas S Liberatore, *
Brian Panetta, *
Bryan M Moody, *
EMP: 113 **EST:** 2013
SALES (est): 1.95MM
SALES (corp-wide): 6.52B **Publicly Held**
SIC: 1381 Drilling oil and gas wells
HQ: Eclipse Resources I, Lp
    122 W John Crptr Fwy Ste
    Irving TX 75039
    814 308-9754

(G-16530)
FINELINE IMPRINTS INC
516 State St (43701-3237)
P.O. Box 2688 (43702-2688)
PHONE.................................740 453-1083
TOLL FREE: 800
Robert Kessler, *Pr*
EMP: 19 **EST:** 1982
SQ FT: 12,000
SALES (est): 348.63K **Privately Held**
Web: www.finelineimprints.com
SIC: 5999 2396 3993 2395 Trophies and plaques; Screen printing on fabric articles; Signs and advertising specialties; Pleating and stitching

(G-16531)
FLOW-LINER SYSTEMS LTD
4830 Northpointe Dr (43701-7273)
PHONE.................................800 348-0020
Jeff Tanner, *CEO*
▲ **EMP:** 25 **EST:** 2000
SQ FT: 30,000
SALES (est): 4.86MM **Privately Held**
Web: www.flow-liner.com
SIC: 1799 3443 Protective lining installation, underground (sewage, etc.); Liners/lining

(G-16532)
FORMATION CEMENTING INC
1800 Timber Port Dr (43701)
P.O. Box 2667 (43702-2667)
PHONE.................................740 453-6926
Brian G Jasper, *Pr*
Rae Anne Jasper, *Sec*
EMP: 7 **EST:** 1979
SQ FT: 500
SALES (est): 831.38K **Privately Held**
SIC: 1389 Oil and gas wells: building, repairing and dismantling

(G-16533)
FRANKLIN PRINTING COMPANY
Also Called: Franklin's Printing
984 Beverly Ave (43701-1413)

Zanesville - Muskingum County (G-16534)

PHONE..................................740 452-6375
Everett Jackson Junior, *Pr*
Alice Lucille Jackson, *Sec*
EMP: 10 **EST:** 1949
SQ FT: 7,000
SALES (est): 741.17K **Privately Held**
Web: www.franklinprinting.us
SIC: 2752 7331 2791 2789 Offset printing; Addressing service; Typesetting; Bookbinding and related work

(G-16534)
G & J PEPSI-COLA BOTTLERS INC
Also Called: Pepsico
336 N Sixth St (43701)
PHONE..................................740 354-9191
TOLL FREE: 800
Rick Stone, *Brnch Mgr*
EMP: 35
SALES (corp-wide): 404.54MM **Privately Held**
Web: www.gjpepsi.com
SIC: 2086 5149 Carbonated soft drinks, bottled and canned; Groceries and related products, nec
PA: G & J Pepsi-Cola Bottlers Inc
9435 Waterstone Blvd # 390
Cincinnati OH 45249
513 785-6060

(G-16535)
HALLIBURTON ENERGY SVCS INC
4999 E Pointe Dr (43701-7680)
PHONE..................................740 617-2917
EMP: 13
Web: www.halliburton.com
SIC: 1389 Oil field services, nec
HQ: Halliburton Energy Services, Inc.
3000 N Sam Houston Pkwy E
Houston TX 77032
281 871-4000

(G-16536)
HANNON COMPANY
Electric Motor & Service Co
218 Adams St (43701-4902)
P.O. Box 667 (43702-0667)
PHONE..................................740 453-0527
Michael Arrasmith, *Brnch Mgr*
EMP: 15
SALES (corp-wide): 35.51MM **Privately Held**
Web: www.hanco.com
SIC: 7694 7699 5063 Electric motor repair; Welding equipment repair; Motors, electric
PA: The Hannon Company
1605 Waynesburg Dr Se
Canton OH 44707
330 456-4728

(G-16537)
HYDRO SUPPLY CO
3112 East Pike (43701-8975)
PHONE..................................740 454-3842
Charles William Kimble, *Pr*
Judy K Kimble, *Sec*
EMP: 15 **EST:** 1983
SQ FT: 6,500
SALES (est): 1.61MM **Privately Held**
SIC: 5084 7699 3599 Hydraulic systems equipment and supplies; Industrial machinery and equipment repair; Machine shop, jobbing and repair

(G-16538)
IG WATTEEUW USA LLC
1000 Linden Ave (43701)
PHONE..................................740 588-1722
▲ **EMP:** 11 **EST:** 2013
SQ FT: 51,946
SALES (est): 4.24MM

SALES (corp-wide): 833.11K **Privately Held**
Web: www.igwpower.com
SIC: 3714 5085 Gears, motor vehicle; Gears
HQ: Ig Watteeuw International
Kampveldstraat 51
Oostkamp VWV 8020
50826907

(G-16539)
IGW USA
1000 Linden Ave (43701-3098)
PHONE..................................740 588-1722
EMP: 12 **EST:** 2019
SALES (est): 1.02MM **Privately Held**
Web: www.igwpower.com
SIC: 3714 Motor vehicle parts and accessories

(G-16540)
J A B WELDING SERVICE INC
Also Called: Bakers Welding
2820 S River Rd (43701-7184)
PHONE..................................740 453-5868
Jeffrey A Baker, *Pr*
Cyndy Baker, *VP*
EMP: 18 **EST:** 1984
SQ FT: 20,000
SALES (est): 1.35MM **Privately Held**
Web: www.bakersweldingcrane.com
SIC: 7692 Welding repair

(G-16541)
KELLANOVA
Also Called: Kellog
1675 Fairview Rd (43701-5168)
PHONE..................................740 453-5501
Gary Pilnick, *Owner*
EMP: 103
SALES (corp-wide): 15.31B **Publicly Held**
Web: www.kellanova.com
SIC: 2043 Cereal breakfast foods
PA: Kellanova
412 N Wells St
Chicago IL 60654
269 961-2000

(G-16542)
KESSLER SIGN COMPANY (PA)
Also Called: Kessler Outdoor Advertising
2669 National Rd (43701-8257)
P.O. Box 785 (43702-0785)
PHONE..................................740 453-0668
TOLL FREE: 800
Robert Kessler, *CEO*
Adam Kessler, *
Rodger Kessler, *
David Kessler, *
Elaine Kessler-kuntz, *Treas*
EMP: 50 **EST:** 1971
SQ FT: 25,000
SALES (est): 9.7MM
SALES (corp-wide): 9.7MM **Privately Held**
Web: www.kesslersignco.com
SIC: 3993 7312 Signs, not made in custom sign painting shops; Outdoor advertising services

(G-16543)
MAR-ZANE INC (HQ)
Also Called: Mar-Zane Materials
3570 S River Rd (43701-7731)
P.O. Box 1585 (43702-1585)
PHONE..................................740 453-0721
Gerald N Little, *Pr*
Wade Hamm, *VP*
EMP: 12 **EST:** 1963
SQ FT: 5,000
SALES (est): 23.94MM
SALES (corp-wide): 433.35MM **Privately Held**

Web: www.shellyandsands.com
SIC: 2951 Asphalt paving mixtures and blocks
PA: Shelly And Sands, Inc.
3570 S River Rd
Zanesville OH 43701
740 453-0721

(G-16544)
MCCLELLAND INC (PA)
Also Called: O K Coal & Concrete
98 E La Salle St (43701-6281)
P.O. Box 1815 (43702-1815)
PHONE..................................740 452-3036
Joe Mc Clelland, *Pr*
Jack Mc Clelland, *
Richard Mc Clelland, *
Gala Lemon, *
EMP: 25 **EST:** 1934
SQ FT: 1,500
SALES (est): 6.71MM
SALES (corp-wide): 6.71MM **Privately Held**
Web: www.okcoalandconcrete.com
SIC: 3273 7992 1442 Ready-mixed concrete; Public golf courses; Construction sand and gravel

(G-16545)
MICHAEL ZAKANY LLC
Also Called: Jose Madrid Salsa
601 Putnam Ave (43701-5504)
P.O. Box 1061 (43702-1061)
PHONE..................................740 221-3934
Michael Zakany, *Pr*
EMP: 8 **EST:** 1989
SQ FT: 300
SALES (est): 947.13K **Privately Held**
Web: www.josemadridsalsa.com
SIC: 2035 5149 Pickles, sauces, and salad dressings; Seasonings, sauces, and extracts
PA: Unique Pizza And Subs Corp
302 W Otterman St
Greensburg PA 15601

(G-16546)
MOCK WOODWORKING COMPANY LLC
4400 West Pike (43701-9208)
PHONE..................................740 452-2701
Douglas F Mock, *Managing Member*
EMP: 44 **EST:** 1954
SQ FT: 46,000
SALES (est): 9.53MM **Privately Held**
Web: www.mockwoodworking.com
SIC: 2434 2541 2531 Wood kitchen cabinets; Office fixtures, wood; Public building and related furniture

(G-16547)
NEFF MACHINERY AND SUPPLIES
Also Called: Neff Parts
112 S Shawnee Ave (43701-6221)
P.O. Box 1822 (43702-1822)
PHONE..................................740 454-0128
Robert Neff, *Pr*
EMP: 14 **EST:** 1988
SQ FT: 20,000
SALES (est): 416.79K **Privately Held**
Web: www.neffsince1931.com
SIC: 3599 5084 5013 Machine and other job shop work; Machine tools and accessories; Motor vehicle supplies and new parts

(G-16548)
NESTLE PURINA PETCARE COMPANY
5 N 2nd St (43701-3402)
P.O. Box 38 (43702-0038)
PHONE..................................740 454-8575

EMP: 85
Web: www.purina.com
SIC: 2047 Dog and cat food
HQ: Nestle Purina Petcare Company
800 Chouteau Ave
Saint Louis MO 63102
314 982-1000

(G-16549)
NEW WAYNE INC
Also Called: Wayne Manufacturing
1555 Ritchey Pkwy (43701-7050)
PHONE..................................740 453-3454
Michael Higgins, *Pr*
Kurt Paul, *VP*
Mike Paul, *CFO*
EMP: 8 **EST:** 1953
SQ FT: 40,000
SALES (est): 896.06K **Privately Held**
Web: www.waynemanufacturing.net
SIC: 3441 3443 Fabricated structural metal; Fabricated plate work (boiler shop)

(G-16550)
OMCO USA LLC
1000 Linden Ave (43701-3098)
PHONE..................................740 588-1722
Teresa Reef, *Prin*
▲ **EMP:** 18 **EST:** 2005
SALES (est): 2.38MM **Privately Held**
Web: www.omcomould.com
SIC: 3559 Ammunition and explosives, loading machinery

(G-16551)
OWENS-BROCKWAY GLASS CONT INC
OWENS-BROCKWAY GLASS CONTAINER, INC.
1700 State St (43701-3116)
PHONE..................................740 455-4516
John Elliot, *Brnch Mgr*
EMP: 38
SALES (corp-wide): 7.11B **Publicly Held**
Web: www.o-i.com
SIC: 3221 Glass containers
HQ: Owens-Brockway Glass Container Inc.
1 Michael Owens Way
Perrysburg OH 43551

(G-16552)
OXFORD MINING COMPANY INC
1855 Kemper Ct (43701-4634)
PHONE..................................740 588-0190
Joe Douglas, *Brnch Mgr*
EMP: 121
SALES (corp-wide): 814.89MM **Privately Held**
SIC: 1221 Bituminous coal and lignite-surface mining
HQ: Oxford Mining Company, Inc.
544 Chestnut St
Coshocton OH 43812
740 622-6302

(G-16553)
PATRIOT STAINLESS WELDING
1555 Fairview Rd (43701-8889)
PHONE..................................740 297-6040
EMP: 12 **EST:** 2020
SALES (est): 993.7K **Privately Held**
Web: www.gopatriot.us
SIC: 7692 Welding repair

(G-16554)
PEABODY COAL COMPANY
2810 East Pike Apt 3 (43701-9197)
PHONE..................................740 450-2420
J T Kneen, *Prin*
EMP: 28
SALES (corp-wide): 4.95B **Publicly Held**

SIC: 1241 Coal mining services
HQ: Peabody Coal Company
    701 Market St
    Saint Louis MO 63101
    314 342-3400

(G-16555)
PHILLIPS MEAT PROCESSING LLC
2790 Ridge Rd (43701-7873)
PHONE.................................740 453-3337
Dale Phillips, *Owner*
EMP: 10 **EST:** 1999
SALES (est): 944.28K **Privately Held**
Web: www.phillipsmeats.com
SIC: 2011 Meat packing plants

(G-16556)
PLASKOLITE LLC
1175 5 Bs Dr (43701-7376)
PHONE.................................740 450-1109
Mark Gringley, *Brnch Mgr*
EMP: 143
SALES (corp-wide): 443.48MM **Privately Held**
Web: www.plaskolite.com
SIC: 2821 3083 Acrylic resins; Laminated plastics sheets
PA: Plaskolite, Llc
    400 W Nationwide Blvd # 400
    Columbus OH 43215
    614 294-3281

(G-16557)
PORTERS WELDING INC (PA)
601 Linden Ave (43701-3397)
PHONE.................................740 452-4181
Virginia Porter, *Pr*
Daryl Porter, *VP*
Kimberly Browning, *Sec*
EMP: 9 **EST:** 1944
SQ FT: 70,000
SALES (est): 947.11K
SALES (corp-wide): 947.11K **Privately Held**
SIC: 3441 Fabricated structural metal

(G-16558)
PRECISION FABG & STAMPING INC
1755 Kemper Ct (43701-4606)
P.O. Box 2065 (43702-2065)
PHONE.................................740 453-7310
Charlie Sode, *Pr*
Christine Sode, *Sec*
EMP: 9 **EST:** 1984
SQ FT: 10,000
SALES (est): 989.88K **Privately Held**
Web: www.precisionfabricating.com
SIC: 3441 Fabricated structural metal

(G-16559)
PRODUCERS SERVICE CORPORATION
109 Graham St (43701-3103)
P.O. Box 2277 (43702-2277)
PHONE.................................740 454-6253
EMP: 98 **EST:** 1981
SALES (est): 49.65MM **Privately Held**
SIC: 1389 Hydraulic fracturing wells
PA: Psc Holdings, Inc.
    109 Graham St
    Zanesville OH 43701

(G-16560)
PSC HOLDINGS INC (PA)
109 Graham St (43701-3103)
P.O. Box 2277 (43702-2277)
PHONE.................................740 454-6253
EMP: 6 **EST:** 2008
SALES (est): 55.29MM **Privately Held**
SIC: 1389 Hydraulic fracturing wells

(G-16561)
S & S AGGREGATES INC (HQ)
3570 S River Rd (43701-7731)
P.O. Box 1585 (43702-1585)
PHONE.................................740 453-0721
Gerald Little, *Pr*
Wade Hamm, *Ex VP*
EMP: 13 **EST:** 1923
SQ FT: 15,000
SALES (est): 5.17MM
SALES (corp-wide): 433.35MM **Privately Held**
Web: www.shellyandsands.com
SIC: 1442 3272 3271 Sand mining; Concrete products, nec; Concrete block and brick
PA: Shelly And Sands, Inc.
    3570 S River Rd
    Zanesville OH 43701
    740 453-0721

(G-16562)
SHELLY AND SANDS INC (PA)
3570 S River Rd (43701-9052)
P.O. Box 1585 (43702-1585)
PHONE.................................740 453-0721
Richard H Mcclelland, *Pr*
Larry E Young, *VP*
Gerald N Little, *Pr*
EMP: 12 **EST:** 1942
SQ FT: 5,000
SALES (est): 433.35MM
SALES (corp-wide): 433.35MM **Privately Held**
Web: www.shellyandsands.com
SIC: 5541 1442 2951 Filling stations, gasoline; Construction sand mining; Asphalt and asphaltic paving mixtures (not from refineries)

(G-16563)
SHIRLEY KS LLC
1150 Newark Rd (43701-2619)
PHONE.................................740 331-7934
Robert Zachrich, *CEO*
Renee Coll, *Pr*
EMP: 6 **EST:** 2020
SALES (est): 915.69K **Privately Held**
Web: www.shirleyks.com
SIC: 3089 Plastics products, nec

(G-16564)
SHIRLEY KS STORAGE TRAYS LLC
1150 Newark Rd (43701-2619)
P.O. Box 2519 (43702-2519)
PHONE.................................740 868-8140
EMP: 8 **EST:** 2013
SALES (est): 883.45K **Privately Held**
Web: www.shirleyks.com
SIC: 3089 Plastics containers, except foam

(G-16565)
SPRINTER MARKING INC
1805 Chandlersville Rd (43701-4644)
PHONE.................................740 453-1000
Bob Bishop, *Pr*
Al Bishop, *Sec*
John Bishop, *Treas*
EMP: 9 **EST:** 1989
SQ FT: 6,000
SALES (est): 536.3K **Privately Held**
Web: www.sprintermarking.com
SIC: 3953 Date stamps, hand: rubber or metal

(G-16566)
STEVEN CRUMBAKER JR
Also Called: Precision Wldg & Installation
3445 Church Hill Rd (43701-8479)
PHONE.................................740 995-0613
Steven Crumbaker Junior, *Owner*
EMP: 6 **EST:** 2019
SALES (est): 750K **Privately Held**
Web: www.pwiohio.com
SIC: 7692 Welding repair

(G-16567)
US WATER COMPANY LLC
Also Called: Culligan
1115 Newark Rd (43701-2618)
PHONE.................................740 453-0604
Richard Dovenbarger, *Mgr*
EMP: 9
SALES (corp-wide): 7.56MM **Privately Held**
Web: www.uswatercompany.com
SIC: 5999 7389 2899 5074 Water purification equipment; Water softener service; Water treating compounds; Plumbing and hydronic heating supplies
PA: U.S. Water Company, Llc
    270 W Palatine Rd
    Wheeling IL 60090
    815 526-3375

(G-16568)
VICTOR MCKENZIE DRLG CO INC
3596 Maple Ave Ste A (43701-1686)
P.O. Box 3323 (43702-3323)
PHONE.................................740 453-0834
Victor Mckenzie, *Pr*
Sandy Mckenzie, *Sec*
EMP: 10 **EST:** 1954
SALES (est): 152.75K **Privately Held**
SIC: 1381 Drilling oil and gas wells

(G-16569)
WD PUMPCO LLC
620 Marietta St (43701-3633)
P.O. Box 1003 (43702-1003)
PHONE.................................740 454-2576
EMP: 6 **EST:** 2015
SALES (est): 932.69K **Privately Held**
SIC: 3586 Measuring and dispensing pumps

(G-16570)
WHITE MACHINE & MFG CO (PA)
120 Graham St (43701-3100)
PHONE.................................740 453-5451
Kenneth F Vlah, *Pr*
EMP: 18 **EST:** 1955
SQ FT: 20,000
SALES (est): 1.95MM
SALES (corp-wide): 1.95MM **Privately Held**
SIC: 3599 3441 Machine shop, jobbing and repair; Fabricated structural metal

(G-16571)
WORTHINGTON FOODS INC
1675 Fairview Rd (43701-5168)
PHONE.................................740 453-5501
Jackie Minarik, *Prin*
▲ **EMP:** 87 **EST:** 1967
SALES (est): 11.19MM
SALES (corp-wide): 15.31B **Publicly Held**
SIC: 2038 Frozen specialties, nec
PA: Kellanova
    412 N Wells St
    Chicago IL 60654
    269 961-2000

(G-16572)
Y CITY RECYCLING LLC
4005 All American Way (43701-7306)
PHONE.................................740 452-2500
Brian Coll, *CEO*
Matt Elli, *
EMP: 15 **EST:** 2012
SALES (est): 611.45K **Privately Held**

(G-16573)
ZANESVILLE FABRICATORS INC
2981 E Military Rd (43701-1654)
P.O. Box 1816 (43702-1816)
PHONE.................................740 452-2439
Joseph E Nash, *Pr*
EMP: 7 **EST:** 1978
SALES (est): 514.5K **Privately Held**
Web: www.zanesvillefabricators.com
SIC: 2541 Counter and sink tops

(G-16574)
ZANESVILLE PALLET CO INC
2235 Licking Rd (43701-2728)
P.O. Box 2757 (43702-2757)
PHONE.................................740 454-3700
TOLL FREE: 800
Lee Gunnels, *Pr*
Zane Lambert, *VP*
EMP: 15 **EST:** 1993
SALES (est): 850.95K **Privately Held**
Web: www.zanesvillepallet.com
SIC: 2448 Pallets, wood

Zoarville
Tuscarawas County

(G-16575)
BUCKEYE FRANKLIN CO
3471 New Zoarville Rd Ne (44656-9707)
P.O. Box 117 (44656-0117)
PHONE.................................330 859-2465
R Dean Smith, *Pr*
Hazel Yockey, *Sec*
EMP: 11 **EST:** 1966
SQ FT: 15,000
SALES (est): 142.15K **Privately Held**
Web: www.buckeyeoilinc.com
SIC: 1311 Natural gas production

SIC INDEX

Standard Industrial Classification Alphabetical Index

SIC NO	PRODUCT

A

3291 Abrasive products
8721 Accounting, auditing, and bookkeeping
2891 Adhesives and sealants
7322 Adjustment and collection services
7311 Advertising agencies
7319 Advertising, nec
2879 Agricultural chemicals, nec
3563 Air and gas compressors
4522 Air transportation, nonscheduled
4512 Air transportation, scheduled
3721 Aircraft
3724 Aircraft engines and engine parts
3728 Aircraft parts and equipment, nec
4581 Airports, flying fields, and services
2812 Alkalies and chlorine
3363 Aluminum die-castings
3354 Aluminum extruded products
3365 Aluminum foundries
3355 Aluminum rolling and drawing, nec
3353 Aluminum sheet, plate, and foil
3483 Ammunition, except for small arms, nec
7999 Amusement and recreation, nec
3826 Analytical instruments
2077 Animal and marine fats and oils
0279 Animal specialties, nec
0752 Animal specialty services
1231 Anthracite mining
2389 Apparel and accessories, nec
3446 Architectural metalwork
8712 Architectural services
7694 Armature rewinding shops
3292 Asbestos products
2952 Asphalt felts and coatings
2951 Asphalt paving mixtures and blocks
5531 Auto and home supply stores
7533 Auto exhaust system repair shops
3581 Automatic vending machines
7521 Automobile parking
5012 Automobiles and other motor vehicles
2396 Automotive and apparel trimmings
5599 Automotive dealers, nec
7536 Automotive glass replacement shops
7539 Automotive repair shops, nec
7549 Automotive services, nec
3465 Automotive stampings
7537 Automotive transmission repair shops

B

2673 Bags: plastic, laminated, and coated
2674 Bags: uncoated paper and multiwall
3562 Ball and roller bearings
7241 Barber shops
7231 Beauty shops
0211 Beef cattle feedlots
5181 Beer and ale
2063 Beet sugar
0171 Berry crops
2836 Biological products, except diagnostic
1221 Bituminous coal and lignite-surface mining
1222 Bituminous coal-underground mining
2782 Blankbooks and looseleaf binders
3312 Blast furnaces and steel mills
3564 Blowers and fans
5551 Boat dealers
3732 Boatbuilding and repairing
3452 Bolts, nuts, rivets, and washers
2732 Book printing
2731 Book publishing
5942 Book stores
2789 Bookbinding and related work
5192 Books, periodicals, and newspapers
2086 Bottled and canned soft drinks
7933 Bowling centers
2051 Bread, cake, and related products
3251 Brick and structural clay tile

5032 Brick, stone, and related material
1622 Bridge, tunnel, and elevated highway
2211 Broadwoven fabric mills, cotton
2221 Broadwoven fabric mills, manmade
2231 Broadwoven fabric mills, wool
3991 Brooms and brushes
7349 Building maintenance services, nec
3995 Burial caskets
8611 Business associations
8748 Business consulting, nec
7389 Business services, nec

C

4841 Cable and other pay television services
3578 Calculating and accounting equipment
2064 Candy and other confectionery products
5441 Candy, nut, and confectionery stores
2033 Canned fruits and specialties
2032 Canned specialties
2394 Canvas and related products
3624 Carbon and graphite products
2895 Carbon black
3955 Carbon paper and inked ribbons
3592 Carburetors, pistons, rings, valves
1751 Carpentry work
7217 Carpet and upholstery cleaning
2273 Carpets and rugs
0119 Cash grains, nec
5961 Catalog and mail-order houses
2823 Cellulosic manmade fibers
3241 Cement, hydraulic
3253 Ceramic wall and floor tile
2043 Cereal breakfast foods
2022 Cheese; natural and processed
1479 Chemical and fertilizer mining
2899 Chemical preparations, nec
5169 Chemicals and allied products, nec
2131 Chewing and smoking tobacco
0252 Chicken eggs
8351 Child day care services
5641 Children's and infants' wear stores
2066 Chocolate and cocoa products
2111 Cigarettes
8641 Civic and social associations
1459 Clay and related minerals, nec
3255 Clay refractories
5052 Coal and other minerals and ores
1241 Coal mining services
2295 Coated fabrics, not rubberized
7993 Coin-operated amusement devices
3316 Cold finishing of steel shapes
7336 Commercial art and graphic design
5046 Commercial equipment, nec
3582 Commercial laundry equipment
3646 Commercial lighting fixtures
8732 Commercial nonphysical research
7335 Commercial photography
8731 Commercial physical research
2754 Commercial printing, gravure
2752 Commercial printing, lithographic
2759 Commercial printing, nec
4899 Communication services, nec
3669 Communications equipment, nec
5734 Computer and software stores
7376 Computer facilities management
7373 Computer integrated systems design
7378 Computer maintenance and repair
3577 Computer peripheral equipment, nec
7379 Computer related services, nec
7377 Computer rental and leasing
3572 Computer storage devices
3575 Computer terminals
5045 Computers, peripherals, and software
3271 Concrete block and brick
3272 Concrete products, nec
1771 Concrete work

5145 Confectionery
5082 Construction and mining machinery
3531 Construction machinery
5039 Construction materials, nec
1442 Construction sand and gravel
2679 Converted paper products, nec
3535 Conveyors and conveying equipment
2052 Cookies and crackers
3366 Copper foundries
3351 Copper rolling and drawing
2298 Cordage and twine
0115 Corn
2653 Corrugated and solid fiber boxes
3961 Costume jewelry
0724 Cotton ginning
4215 Courier services, except by air
2021 Creamery butter
0721 Crop planting and protection
0723 Crop preparation services for market
3466 Crowns and closures
1311 Crude petroleum and natural gas
1423 Crushed and broken granite
1422 Crushed and broken limestone
1429 Crushed and broken stone, nec
3643 Current-carrying wiring devices
2391 Curtains and draperies
3087 Custom compound purchased resins
7371 Custom computer programming services
3281 Cut stone and stone products
3421 Cutlery
2865 Cyclic crudes and intermediates

D

0241 Dairy farms
5451 Dairy products stores
5143 Dairy products, except dried or canned
7374 Data processing and preparation
8243 Data processing schools
4424 Deep sea domestic transportation of freight
2034 Dehydrated fruits, vegetables, soups
3843 Dental equipment and supplies
8072 Dental laboratories
5311 Department stores
2835 Diagnostic substances
2675 Die-cut paper and board
1411 Dimension stone
7331 Direct mail advertising services
5963 Direct selling establishments
7342 Disinfecting and pest control services
2085 Distilled and blended liquors
2047 Dog and cat food
3942 Dolls and stuffed toys
5714 Drapery and upholstery stores
2591 Drapery hardware and blinds and shades
1381 Drilling oil and gas wells
5813 Drinking places
5912 Drug stores and proprietary stores
5122 Drugs, proprietaries, and sundries
2023 Dry, condensed, evaporated products
5099 Durable goods, nec

E

5812 Eating places
2079 Edible fats and oils
3634 Electric housewares and fans
3641 Electric lamps
4911 Electric services
5063 Electrical apparatus and equipment
5064 Electrical appliances, television and radio
3699 Electrical equipment and supplies, nec
3629 Electrical industrial apparatus
7629 Electrical repair shops
1731 Electrical work
3845 Electromedical equipment
3313 Electrometallurgical products
3675 Electronic capacitors

SIC INDEX

SIC NO	PRODUCT
3677	Electronic coils and transformers
3679	Electronic components, nec
3571	Electronic computers
3678	Electronic connectors
5065	Electronic parts and equipment, nec
3676	Electronic resistors
8211	Elementary and secondary schools
3534	Elevators and moving stairways
3694	Engine electrical equipment
8711	Engineering services
7929	Entertainers and entertainment groups
2677	Envelopes
3822	Environmental controls
7359	Equipment rental and leasing, nec
1794	Excavation work
9111	Executive offices
2892	Explosives

F

SIC NO	PRODUCT
2381	Fabric dress and work gloves
3499	Fabricated metal products, nec
3498	Fabricated pipe and fittings
3443	Fabricated plate work (boiler shop)
3069	Fabricated rubber products, nec
3441	Fabricated structural metal
2399	Fabricated textile products, nec
8744	Facilities support services
5651	Family clothing stores
5083	Farm and garden machinery
3523	Farm machinery and equipment
4221	Farm product warehousing and storage
5191	Farm supplies
5159	Farm-product raw materials, nec
3965	Fasteners, buttons, needles, and pins
1061	Ferroalloy ores, except vanadium
2875	Fertilizers, mixing only
2655	Fiber cans, drums, and similar products
0139	Field crops, except cash grain
2261	Finishing plants, cotton
2262	Finishing plants, manmade
5146	Fish and seafoods
3211	Flat glass
2087	Flavoring extracts and syrups, nec
5713	Floor covering stores
1752	Floor laying and floor work, nec
5992	Florists
2041	Flour and other grain mill products
5193	Flowers and florists supplies
3824	Fluid meters and counting devices
2026	Fluid milk
3593	Fluid power cylinders and actuators
3594	Fluid power pumps and motors
3492	Fluid power valves and hose fittings
2657	Folding paperboard boxes
2099	Food preparations, nec
3556	Food products machinery
5139	Footwear
3131	Footwear cut stock
4731	Freight transportation arrangement
5148	Fresh fruits and vegetables
2092	Fresh or frozen packaged fish
2053	Frozen bakery products, except bread
2037	Frozen fruits and vegetables
2038	Frozen specialties, nec
5431	Fruit and vegetable markets
5989	Fuel dealers, nec
5983	Fuel oil dealers
7261	Funeral service and crematories
2371	Fur goods
5021	Furniture
2599	Furniture and fixtures, nec
5712	Furniture stores

G

SIC NO	PRODUCT
3944	Games, toys, and children's vehicles
7212	Garment pressing and cleaners' agents
4932	Gas and other services combined
4923	Gas transmission and distribution
3053	Gaskets; packing and sealing devices
5541	Gasoline service stations
7538	General automotive repair shops
0191	General farms, primarily crop
9199	General government, nec
3569	General industrial machinery,
8062	General medical and surgical hospitals
4225	General warehousing and storage
5947	Gift, novelty, and souvenir shop
2369	Girl's and children's outerwear, nec
1793	Glass and glazing work
3221	Glass containers
1041	Gold ores
5153	Grain and field beans
0172	Grapes
3321	Gray and ductile iron foundries
2771	Greeting cards
5149	Groceries and related products, nec
5141	Groceries, general line
5411	Grocery stores
3761	Guided missiles and space vehicles
2861	Gum and wood chemicals
3275	Gypsum products

H

SIC NO	PRODUCT
3423	Hand and edge tools, nec
3996	Hard surface floor coverings, nec
5072	Hardware
5251	Hardware stores
3429	Hardware, nec
2426	Hardwood dimension and flooring mills
2435	Hardwood veneer and plywood
2353	Hats, caps, and millinery
8099	Health and allied services, nec
3433	Heating equipment, except electric
7353	Heavy construction equipment rental
1629	Heavy construction, nec
7363	Help supply services
1611	Highway and street construction
5945	Hobby, toy, and game shops
0213	Hogs
3536	Hoists, cranes, and monorails
6719	Holding companies, nec
5023	Homefurnishings
2252	Hosiery, nec
7011	Hotels and motels
3142	House slippers
5722	Household appliance stores
3639	Household appliances, nec
3651	Household audio and video equipment
3631	Household cooking equipment
2392	Household furnishings, nec
2519	Household furniture, nec
3633	Household laundry equipment
3632	Household refrigerators and freezers
3635	Household vacuum cleaners

I

SIC NO	PRODUCT
2024	Ice cream and frozen deserts
8322	Individual and family services
5113	Industrial and personal service paper
1541	Industrial buildings and warehouses
3567	Industrial furnaces and ovens
2813	Industrial gases
2819	Industrial inorganic chemicals, nec
7218	Industrial launderers
5084	Industrial machinery and equipment
3599	Industrial machinery, nec
2869	Industrial organic chemicals, nec
3543	Industrial patterns
1446	Industrial sand
5085	Industrial supplies
3537	Industrial trucks and tractors
3491	Industrial valves
7375	Information retrieval services
2816	Inorganic pigments
1796	Installing building equipment
3825	Instruments to measure electricity
6411	Insurance agents, brokers, and service
8052	Intermediate care facilities
3519	Internal combustion engines, nec
6282	Investment advice
6726	Investment offices, nec
6799	Investors, nec
3462	Iron and steel forgings
1011	Iron ores

J

SIC NO	PRODUCT
3915	Jewelers' materials and lapidary work
5094	Jewelry and precious stones
5944	Jewelry stores
3911	Jewelry, precious metal
8331	Job training and related services
8222	Junior colleges

K

SIC NO	PRODUCT
2253	Knit outerwear mills
2259	Knitting mills, nec

L

SIC NO	PRODUCT
3821	Laboratory apparatus and furniture
2258	Lace and warp knit fabric mills
3083	Laminated plastics plate and sheet
0781	Landscape counseling and planning
3524	Lawn and garden equipment
0782	Lawn and garden services
1031	Lead and zinc ores
0052	Lead pencils and art goods
3151	Leather gloves and mittens
3199	Leather goods, nec
3111	Leather tanning and finishing
8111	Legal services
6311	Life insurance
3648	Lighting equipment, nec
3274	Lime
7213	Linen supply
5984	Liquefied petroleum gas dealers
5921	Liquor stores
5154	Livestock
0751	Livestock services, except veterinary
4214	Local trucking with storage
4212	Local trucking, without storage
2411	Logging
2992	Lubricating oils and greases
3161	Luggage
5948	Luggage and leather goods stores
5211	Lumber and other building materials
5031	Lumber, plywood, and millwork

M

SIC NO	PRODUCT
2098	Macaroni and spaghetti
3545	Machine tool accessories
3541	Machine tools, metal cutting type
3542	Machine tools, metal forming type
3695	Magnetic and optical recording media
3322	Malleable iron foundries
2083	Malt
2082	Malt beverages
8742	Management consulting services
8741	Management services
2761	Manifold business forms
2097	Manufactured ice
3999	Manufacturing industries, nec
4493	Marinas
4491	Marine cargo handling
3953	Marking devices
1741	Masonry and other stonework
2515	Mattresses and bedsprings
3829	Measuring and controlling devices, nec
3586	Measuring and dispensing pumps
5421	Meat and fish markets
2011	Meat packing plants
5147	Meats and meat products
3061	Mechanical rubber goods
5047	Medical and hospital equipment
7352	Medical equipment rental
8071	Medical laboratories
2833	Medicinals and botanicals
8699	Membership organizations, nec
7997	Membership sports and recreation clubs
7041	Membership-basis organization hotels
5136	Men's and boy's clothing
2329	Men's and boy's clothing, nec
2321	Men's and boy's furnishings
2323	Men's and boy's neckwear
2311	Men's and boy's suits and coats
2322	Men's and boy's underwear and nightwear
2326	Men's and boy's work clothing
5611	Men's and boys' clothing stores

SIC INDEX

SIC NO	PRODUCT
3143	Men's footwear, except athletic
3412	Metal barrels, drums, and pails
3411	Metal cans
3479	Metal coating and allied services
3442	Metal doors, sash, and trim
3497	Metal foil and leaf
3398	Metal heat treating
2514	Metal household furniture
1081	Metal mining services
3431	Metal sanitary ware
3469	Metal stampings, nec
5051	Metals service centers and offices
3549	Metalworking machinery, nec
2431	Millwork
3296	Mineral wool
3295	Minerals, ground or treated
3532	Mining machinery
5699	Miscellaneous apparel and accessories
6159	Miscellaneous business credit
3496	Miscellaneous fabricated wire products
5499	Miscellaneous food stores
5399	Miscellaneous general merchandise
5719	Miscellaneous homefurnishings
3449	Miscellaneous metalwork
1499	Miscellaneous nonmetallic mining
7299	Miscellaneous personal services
2741	Miscellaneous publishing
5999	Miscellaneous retail stores, nec
6515	Mobile home site operators
2451	Mobile homes
7822	Motion picture and tape distribution
7812	Motion picture and video production
3716	Motor homes
3714	Motor vehicle parts and accessories
5015	Motor vehicle parts, used
5013	Motor vehicle supplies and new parts
3711	Motor vehicles and car bodies
5571	Motorcycle dealers
3751	Motorcycles, bicycles, and parts
3621	Motors and generators
8412	Museums and art galleries
5736	Musical instrument stores
3931	Musical instruments

N

SIC NO	PRODUCT
2441	Nailed wood boxes and shook
2241	Narrow fabric mills
9711	National security
4924	Natural gas distribution
1321	Natural gas liquids
4922	Natural gas transmission
5511	New and used car dealers
5994	News dealers and newsstands
7383	News syndicates
2711	Newspapers
2873	Nitrogenous fertilizers
3297	Nonclay refractories
8733	Noncommercial research organizations
3644	Noncurrent-carrying wiring devices
5199	Nondurable goods, nec
3364	Nonferrous die-castings except aluminum
3463	Nonferrous forgings
3369	Nonferrous foundries, nec
3356	Nonferrous rolling and drawing, nec
3357	Nonferrous wiredrawing and insulating
3299	Nonmetallic mineral products,
1481	Nonmetallic mineral services
6512	Nonresidential building operators
1542	Nonresidential construction, nec
2297	Nonwoven fabrics

O

SIC NO	PRODUCT
5044	Office equipment
2522	Office furniture, except wood
3579	Office machines, nec
8041	Offices and clinics of chiropractors
8011	Offices and clinics of medical doctors
8042	Offices and clinics of optometrists
8049	Offices of health practitioner
1382	Oil and gas exploration services
3533	Oil and gas field machinery
1389	Oil and gas field services, nec
1531	Operative builders
3851	Ophthalmic goods
5048	Ophthalmic goods
5995	Optical goods stores
3827	Optical instruments and lenses
3489	Ordnance and accessories, nec
2824	Organic fibers, noncellulosic
0783	Ornamental shrub and tree services
7312	Outdoor advertising services

P

SIC NO	PRODUCT
5142	Packaged frozen goods
3565	Packaging machinery
4783	Packing and crating
5231	Paint, glass, and wallpaper stores
1721	Painting and paper hanging
2851	Paints and allied products
5198	Paints, varnishes, and supplies
3554	Paper industries machinery
2621	Paper mills
2671	Paper; coated and laminated packaging
2672	Paper; coated and laminated, nec
2631	Paperboard mills
2542	Partitions and fixtures, except wood
7514	Passenger car rental
6794	Patent owners and lessors
2721	Periodicals
6141	Personal credit institutions
3172	Personal leather goods, nec
2999	Petroleum and coal products, nec
5171	Petroleum bulk stations and terminals
5172	Petroleum products, nec
2911	Petroleum refining
2834	Pharmaceutical preparations
2874	Phosphatic fertilizers
7334	Photocopying and duplicating services
7384	Photofinish laboratories
3861	Photographic equipment and supplies
5043	Photographic equipment and supplies
2035	Pickles, sauces, and salad dressings
5131	Piece goods and notions
1742	Plastering, drywall, and insulation
3085	Plastics bottles
3086	Plastics foam products
5162	Plastics materials and basic shapes
2821	Plastics materials and resins
3084	Plastics pipe
3088	Plastics plumbing fixtures
3089	Plastics products, nec
2796	Platemaking services
3471	Plating and polishing
2395	Pleating and stitching
5074	Plumbing and hydronic heating supplies
3432	Plumbing fixture fittings and trim
1711	Plumbing, heating, air-conditioning
9221	Police protection
2842	Polishes and sanitation goods
3264	Porcelain electrical supplies
2096	Potato chips and similar snacks
3269	Pottery products, nec
5144	Poultry and poultry products
0254	Poultry hatcheries
2015	Poultry slaughtering and processing
3568	Power transmission equipment, nec
3546	Power-driven handtools
3448	Prefabricated metal buildings
2452	Prefabricated wood buildings
7372	Prepackaged software
2048	Prepared feeds, nec
2045	Prepared flour mixes and doughs
3652	Prerecorded records and tapes
3229	Pressed and blown glass, nec
3334	Primary aluminum
3692	Primary batteries, dry and wet
3331	Primary copper
3399	Primary metal products
3339	Primary nonferrous metals, nec
3672	Printed circuit boards
5111	Printing and writing paper
2893	Printing ink
3555	Printing trades machinery
3823	Process control instruments
3231	Products of purchased glass
5049	Professional equipment, nec
8621	Professional organizations
2531	Public building and related furniture
7992	Public golf courses
8743	Public relations services
2611	Pulp mills
3561	Pumps and pumping equipment

R

SIC NO	PRODUCT
3663	Radio and t.v. communications equipment
7622	Radio and television repair
4832	Radio broadcasting stations
5731	Radio, television, and electronic stores
7313	Radio, television, publisher representatives
4812	Radiotelephone communication
3743	Railroad equipment
2061	Raw cane sugar
3273	Ready-mixed concrete
6531	Real estate agents and managers
6798	Real estate investment trusts
6519	Real property lessors, nec
2493	Reconstituted wood products
5735	Record and prerecorded tape stores
5561	Recreational vehicle dealers
4222	Refrigerated warehousing and storage
3585	Refrigeration and heating equipment
5078	Refrigeration equipment and supplies
7623	Refrigeration service and repair
4953	Refuse systems
9621	Regulation, administration of transportation
3625	Relays and industrial controls
8661	Religious organizations
4741	Rental of railroad cars
7699	Repair services, nec
8361	Residential care
1522	Residential construction, nec
3645	Residential lighting fixtures
5461	Retail bakeries
5261	Retail nurseries and garden stores
7641	Reupholstery and furniture repair
2095	Roasted coffee
2384	Robes and dressing gowns
3547	Rolling mill machinery
5033	Roofing, siding, and insulation
1761	Roofing, siding, and sheetmetal work
3021	Rubber and plastics footwear
3052	Rubber and plastics hose and beltings

S

SIC NO	PRODUCT
2068	Salted and roasted nuts and seeds
2656	Sanitary food containers
2676	Sanitary paper products
4959	Sanitary services, nec
2013	Sausages and other prepared meats
3425	Saw blades and handsaws
2421	Sawmills and planing mills, general
3596	Scales and balances, except laboratory
8299	Schools and educational services
5093	Scrap and waste materials
3451	Screw machine products
3812	Search and navigation equipment
3341	Secondary nonferrous metals
7338	Secretarial and court reporting
6211	Security brokers and dealers
7382	Security systems services
3674	Semiconductors and related devices
3263	Semivitreous table and kitchenware
5087	Service establishment equipment
3589	Service industry machinery, nec
7819	Services allied to motion pictures
8999	Services, nec
2652	Setup paperboard boxes
4952	Sewerage systems
5949	Sewing, needlework, and piece goods
3444	Sheet metalwork
3731	Shipbuilding and repairing
7251	Shoe repair and shoeshine parlors
5661	Shoe stores
6153	Short-term business credit
3993	Signs and advertising specialties
3914	Silverware and plated ware

SIC INDEX

SIC NO	PRODUCT
1521	Single-family housing construction
8051	Skilled nursing care facilities
3484	Small arms
3482	Small arms ammunition
2841	Soap and other detergents
8399	Social services, nec
2436	Softwood veneer and plywood
0711	Soil preparation services
2075	Soybean oil mills
0116	Soybeans
9661	Space research and technology
3769	Space vehicle equipment, nec
3544	Special dies, tools, jigs, and fixtures
3559	Special industry machinery, nec
2429	Special product sawmills, nec
1799	Special trade contractors, nec
4226	Special warehousing and storage, nec
8093	Specialty outpatient clinics, nec
3566	Speed changers, drives, and gears
3949	Sporting and athletic goods, nec
5091	Sporting and recreation goods
7032	Sporting and recreational camps
5941	Sporting goods and bicycle shops
5112	Stationery and office supplies
2678	Stationery products
5943	Stationery stores
3325	Steel foundries, nec
3324	Steel investment foundries
3317	Steel pipe and tubes
3493	Steel springs, except wire
3315	Steel wire and related products
3691	Storage batteries
3259	Structural clay products, nec
1791	Structural steel erection
2439	Structural wood members, nec
6552	Subdividers and developers, nec
2843	Surface active agents
3841	Surgical and medical instruments
3842	Surgical appliances and supplies
8713	Surveying services
3613	Switchgear and switchboard apparatus
2822	Synthetic rubber

T

SIC NO	PRODUCT
3795	Tanks and tank components
7291	Tax return preparation services
3661	Telephone and telegraph apparatus
4813	Telephone communication, except radio
4833	Television broadcasting stations
1743	Terrazzo, tile, marble, mosaic work
8734	Testing laboratories
2393	Textile bags
2299	Textile goods, nec
3552	Textile machinery
7922	Theatrical producers and services
2284	Thread mills
2282	Throwing and winding mills
0811	Timber tracts
2296	Tire cord and fabrics
7534	Tire retreading and repair shops
3011	Tires and inner tubes
5014	Tires and tubes
5194	Tobacco and tobacco products
5993	Tobacco stores and stands
2844	Toilet preparations
7532	Top and body repair and paint shops
4492	Towing and tugboat service
5092	Toys and hobby goods and supplies
3612	Transformers, except electric
5088	Transportation equipment and supplies
3799	Transportation equipment, nec
4789	Transportation services, nec
3792	Travel trailers and campers
3713	Truck and bus bodies
7513	Truck rental and leasing, without drivers
3715	Truck trailers
4231	Trucking terminal facilities
4213	Trucking, except local
3511	Turbines and turbine generator sets
0253	Turkeys and turkey eggs
2791	Typesetting

U

SIC NO	PRODUCT
3081	Unsupported plastics film and sheet
3082	Unsupported plastics profile shapes
2512	Upholstered household furniture
5521	Used car dealers
5932	Used merchandise stores
7519	Utility trailer rental

V

SIC NO	PRODUCT
3494	Valves and pipe fittings, nec
0161	Vegetables and melons
3647	Vehicular lighting equipment
7841	Video tape rental
3262	Vitreous china table and kitchenware
3261	Vitreous plumbing fixtures
8249	Vocational schools, nec

W

SIC NO	PRODUCT
5075	Warm air heating and air conditioning
7631	Watch, clock, and jewelry repair
3873	Watches, clocks, watchcases, and parts
4941	Water supply
1781	Water well drilling
1623	Water, sewer, and utility lines
2385	Waterproof outerwear
3548	Welding apparatus
7692	Welding repair
2046	Wet corn milling
0111	Wheat
5182	Wine and distilled beverages
2084	Wines, brandy, and brandy spirits
3495	Wire springs
5632	Women's accessory and specialty stores
5137	Women's and children's clothing
2341	Women's and children's underwear
2331	Women's and misses' blouses and shirts
2339	Women's and misses' outerwear, nec
2337	Women's and misses' suits and coats
5621	Women's clothing stores
3144	Women's footwear, except athletic
3171	Women's handbags and purses
2335	Women's, junior's, and misses' dresses
2449	Wood containers, nec
2511	Wood household furniture
2434	Wood kitchen cabinets
2521	Wood office furniture
2448	Wood pallets and skids
2541	Wood partitions and fixtures
2491	Wood preserving
2499	Wood products, nec
2517	Wood television and radio cabinets
3553	Woodworking machinery
1795	Wrecking and demolition work

X

SIC NO	PRODUCT
3844	X-ray apparatus and tubes

Y

SIC NO	PRODUCT
2281	Yarn spinning mills

SIC INDEX

Standard Industrial Classification Numerical Index

SIC NO	PRODUCT

01 agricultural production - crops
0111 Wheat
0115 Corn
0116 Soybeans
0119 Cash grains, nec
0139 Field crops, except cash grain
0161 Vegetables and melons
0171 Berry crops
0172 Grapes
0191 General farms, primarily crop

02 agricultural production - livestock and animal specialties
0211 Beef cattle feedlots
0213 Hogs
0241 Dairy farms
0252 Chicken eggs
0253 Turkeys and turkey eggs
0254 Poultry hatcheries
0279 Animal specialties, nec

07 agricultural services
0711 Soil preparation services
0721 Crop planting and protection
0723 Crop preparation services for market
0724 Cotton ginning
0751 Livestock services, except veterinary
0752 Animal specialty services
0781 Landscape counseling and planning
0782 Lawn and garden services
0783 Ornamental shrub and tree services

08 forestry
0811 Timber tracts

10 metal mining
1011 Iron ores
1031 Lead and zinc ores
1041 Gold ores
1061 Ferroalloy ores, except vanadium
1081 Metal mining services

12 coal mining
1221 Bituminous coal and lignite-surface mining
1222 Bituminous coal-underground mining
1231 Anthracite mining
1241 Coal mining services

13 oil and gas extraction
1311 Crude petroleum and natural gas
1321 Natural gas liquids
1381 Drilling oil and gas wells
1382 Oil and gas exploration services
1389 Oil and gas field services, nec

14 mining and quarrying of nonmetallic minerals, except fuels
1411 Dimension stone
1422 Crushed and broken limestone
1423 Crushed and broken granite
1429 Crushed and broken stone, nec
1442 Construction sand and gravel
1446 Industrial sand
1459 Clay and related minerals, nec
1479 Chemical and fertilizer mining
1481 Nonmetallic mineral services
1499 Miscellaneous nonmetallic mining

15 construction - general contractors & operative builders
1521 Single-family housing construction
1522 Residential construction, nec
1531 Operative builders
1541 Industrial buildings and warehouses
1542 Nonresidential construction, nec

16 heavy construction, except building construction, contractor
1611 Highway and street construction
1622 Bridge, tunnel, and elevated highway
1623 Water, sewer, and utility lines
1629 Heavy construction, nec

17 construction - special trade contractors
1711 Plumbing, heating, air-conditioning
1721 Painting and paper hanging
1731 Electrical work
1741 Masonry and other stonework
1742 Plastering, drywall, and insulation
1743 Terrazzo, tile, marble, mosaic work
1751 Carpentry work
1752 Floor laying and floor work, nec
1761 Roofing, siding, and sheetmetal work
1771 Concrete work
1781 Water well drilling
1791 Structural steel erection
1793 Glass and glazing work
1794 Excavation work
1795 Wrecking and demolition work
1796 Installing building equipment
1799 Special trade contractors, nec

20 food and kindred products
2011 Meat packing plants
2013 Sausages and other prepared meats
2015 Poultry slaughtering and processing
2021 Creamery butter
2022 Cheese; natural and processed
2023 Dry, condensed, evaporated products
2024 Ice cream and frozen deserts
2026 Fluid milk
2032 Canned specialties
2033 Canned fruits and specialties
2034 Dehydrated fruits, vegetables, soups
2035 Pickles, sauces, and salad dressings
2037 Frozen fruits and vegetables
2038 Frozen specialties, nec
2041 Flour and other grain mill products
2043 Cereal breakfast foods
2045 Prepared flour mixes and doughs
2046 Wet corn milling
2047 Dog and cat food
2048 Prepared feeds, nec
2051 Bread, cake, and related products
2052 Cookies and crackers
2053 Frozen bakery products, except bread
2061 Raw cane sugar
2063 Beet sugar
2064 Candy and other confectionery products
2066 Chocolate and cocoa products
2068 Salted and roasted nuts and seeds
2075 Soybean oil mills
2077 Animal and marine fats and oils
2079 Edible fats and oils
2082 Malt beverages
2083 Malt
2084 Wines, brandy, and brandy spirits
2085 Distilled and blended liquors
2086 Bottled and canned soft drinks
2087 Flavoring extracts and syrups, nec
2092 Fresh or frozen packaged fish
2095 Roasted coffee
2096 Potato chips and similar snacks
2097 Manufactured ice
2098 Macaroni and spaghetti
2099 Food preparations, nec

21 tobacco products
2111 Cigarettes
2131 Chewing and smoking tobacco

22 textile mill products
2211 Broadwoven fabric mills, cotton
2221 Broadwoven fabric mills, manmade
2231 Broadwoven fabric mills, wool
2241 Narrow fabric mills
2252 Hosiery, nec
2253 Knit outerwear mills
2258 Lace and warp knit fabric mills
2259 Knitting mills, nec
2261 Finishing plants, cotton
2262 Finishing plants, manmade
2273 Carpets and rugs
2281 Yarn spinning mills
2282 Throwing and winding mills
2284 Thread mills
2295 Coated fabrics, not rubberized
2296 Tire cord and fabrics
2297 Nonwoven fabrics
2298 Cordage and twine
2299 Textile goods, nec

23 apparel, finished products from fabrics & similar materials
2311 Men's and boy's suits and coats
2321 Men's and boy's furnishings
2322 Men's and boy's underwear and nightwear
2323 Men's and boy's neckwear
2326 Men's and boy's work clothing
2329 Men's and boy's clothing, nec
2331 Women's and misses' blouses and shirts
2335 Women's, junior's, and misses' dresses
2337 Women's and misses' suits and coats
2339 Women's and misses' outerwear, nec
2341 Women's and children's underwear
2353 Hats, caps, and millinery
2369 Girl's and children's outerwear, nec
2371 Fur goods
2381 Fabric dress and work gloves
2384 Robes and dressing gowns
2385 Waterproof outerwear
2389 Apparel and accessories, nec
2391 Curtains and draperies
2392 Household furnishings, nec
2393 Textile bags
2394 Canvas and related products
2395 Pleating and stitching
2396 Automotive and apparel trimmings
2399 Fabricated textile products, nec

24 lumber and wood products, except furniture
2411 Logging
2421 Sawmills and planing mills, general
2426 Hardwood dimension and flooring mills
2429 Special product sawmills, nec
2431 Millwork
2434 Wood kitchen cabinets
2435 Hardwood veneer and plywood
2436 Softwood veneer and plywood
2439 Structural wood members, nec
2441 Nailed wood boxes and shook
2448 Wood pallets and skids
2449 Wood containers, nec
2451 Mobile homes
2452 Prefabricated wood buildings
2491 Wood preserving
2493 Reconstituted wood products
2499 Wood products, nec

25 furniture and fixtures
2511 Wood household furniture
2512 Upholstered household furniture
2514 Metal household furniture
2515 Mattresses and bedsprings
2517 Wood television and radio cabinets
2519 Household furniture, nec

SIC INDEX

SIC NO	PRODUCT
2521	Wood office furniture
2522	Office furniture, except wood
2531	Public building and related furniture
2541	Wood partitions and fixtures
2542	Partitions and fixtures, except wood
2591	Drapery hardware and blinds and shades
2599	Furniture and fixtures, nec

26 paper and allied products

2611 Pulp mills
2621 Paper mills
2631 Paperboard mills
2652 Setup paperboard boxes
2653 Corrugated and solid fiber boxes
2655 Fiber cans, drums, and similar products
2656 Sanitary food containers
2657 Folding paperboard boxes
2671 Paper; coated and laminated packaging
2672 Paper; coated and laminated, nec
2673 Bags: plastic, laminated, and coated
2674 Bags: uncoated paper and multiwall
2675 Die-cut paper and board
2676 Sanitary paper products
2677 Envelopes
2678 Stationery products
2679 Converted paper products, nec

27 printing, publishing and allied industries

2711 Newspapers
2721 Periodicals
2731 Book publishing
2732 Book printing
2741 Miscellaneous publishing
2752 Commercial printing, lithographic
2754 Commercial printing, gravure
2759 Commercial printing, nec
2761 Manifold business forms
2771 Greeting cards
2782 Blankbooks and looseleaf binders
2789 Bookbinding and related work
2791 Typesetting
2796 Platemaking services

28 chemicals and allied products

2812 Alkalies and chlorine
2813 Industrial gases
2816 Inorganic pigments
2819 Industrial inorganic chemicals, nec
2821 Plastics materials and resins
2822 Synthetic rubber
2823 Cellulosic manmade fibers
2824 Organic fibers, noncellulosic
2833 Medicinals and botanicals
2834 Pharmaceutical preparations
2835 Diagnostic substances
2836 Biological products, except diagnostic
2841 Soap and other detergents
2842 Polishes and sanitation goods
2843 Surface active agents
2844 Toilet preparations
2851 Paints and allied products
2861 Gum and wood chemicals
2865 Cyclic crudes and intermediates
2869 Industrial organic chemicals, nec
2873 Nitrogenous fertilizers
2874 Phosphatic fertilizers
2875 Fertilizers, mixing only
2879 Agricultural chemicals, nec
2891 Adhesives and sealants
2892 Explosives
2893 Printing ink
2895 Carbon black
2899 Chemical preparations, nec

29 petroleum refining and related industries

2911 Petroleum refining
2951 Asphalt paving mixtures and blocks
2952 Asphalt felts and coatings
2992 Lubricating oils and greases
2999 Petroleum and coal products, nec

30 rubber and miscellaneous plastic products

3011 Tires and inner tubes
3021 Rubber and plastics footwear
3052 Rubber and plastics hose and beltings
3053 Gaskets; packing and sealing devices
3061 Mechanical rubber goods
3069 Fabricated rubber products, nec
3081 Unsupported plastics film and sheet
3082 Unsupported plastics profile shapes
3083 Laminated plastics plate and sheet
3084 Plastics pipe
3085 Plastics bottles
3086 Plastics foam products
3087 Custom compound purchased resins
3088 Plastics plumbing fixtures
3089 Plastics products, nec

31 leather and leather products

3111 Leather tanning and finishing
3131 Footwear cut stock
3142 House slippers
3143 Men's footwear, except athletic
3144 Women's footwear, except athletic
3151 Leather gloves and mittens
3161 Luggage
3171 Women's handbags and purses
3172 Personal leather goods, nec
3199 Leather goods, nec

32 stone, clay, glass, and concrete products

3211 Flat glass
3221 Glass containers
3229 Pressed and blown glass, nec
3231 Products of purchased glass
3241 Cement, hydraulic
3251 Brick and structural clay tile
3253 Ceramic wall and floor tile
3255 Clay refractories
3259 Structural clay products, nec
3261 Vitreous plumbing fixtures
3262 Vitreous china table and kitchenware
3263 Semivitreous table and kitchenware
3264 Porcelain electrical supplies
3269 Pottery products, nec
3271 Concrete block and brick
3272 Concrete products, nec
3273 Ready-mixed concrete
3274 Lime
3275 Gypsum products
3281 Cut stone and stone products
3291 Abrasive products
3292 Asbestos products
3295 Minerals, ground or treated
3296 Mineral wool
3297 Nonclay refractories
3299 Nonmetallic mineral products,

33 primary metal industries

3312 Blast furnaces and steel mills
3313 Electrometallurgical products
3315 Steel wire and related products
3316 Cold finishing of steel shapes
3317 Steel pipe and tubes
3321 Gray and ductile iron foundries
3322 Malleable iron foundries
3324 Steel investment foundries
3325 Steel foundries, nec
3331 Primary copper
3334 Primary aluminum
3339 Primary nonferrous metals, nec
3341 Secondary nonferrous metals
3351 Copper rolling and drawing
3353 Aluminum sheet, plate, and foil
3354 Aluminum extruded products
3355 Aluminum rolling and drawing, nec
3356 Nonferrous rolling and drawing, nec
3357 Nonferrous wiredrawing and insulating
3363 Aluminum die-castings
3364 Nonferrous die-castings except aluminum
3365 Aluminum foundries
3366 Copper foundries
3369 Nonferrous foundries, nec
3398 Metal heat treating
3399 Primary metal products

34 fabricated metal products

3411 Metal cans
3412 Metal barrels, drums, and pails
3421 Cutlery
3423 Hand and edge tools, nec
3425 Saw blades and handsaws
3429 Hardware, nec
3431 Metal sanitary ware
3432 Plumbing fixture fittings and trim
3433 Heating equipment, except electric
3441 Fabricated structural metal
3442 Metal doors, sash, and trim
3443 Fabricated plate work (boiler shop)
3444 Sheet metalwork
3446 Architectural metalwork
3448 Prefabricated metal buildings
3449 Miscellaneous metalwork
3451 Screw machine products
3452 Bolts, nuts, rivets, and washers
3462 Iron and steel forgings
3463 Nonferrous forgings
3465 Automotive stampings
3466 Crowns and closures
3469 Metal stampings, nec
3471 Plating and polishing
3479 Metal coating and allied services
3482 Small arms ammunition
3483 Ammunition, except for small arms, nec
3484 Small arms
3489 Ordnance and accessories, nec
3491 Industrial valves
3492 Fluid power valves and hose fittings
3493 Steel springs, except wire
3494 Valves and pipe fittings, nec
3495 Wire springs
3496 Miscellaneous fabricated wire products
3497 Metal foil and leaf
3498 Fabricated pipe and fittings
3499 Fabricated metal products, nec

35 industrial and commercial machinery and computer equipment

3511 Turbines and turbine generator sets
3519 Internal combustion engines, nec
3523 Farm machinery and equipment
3524 Lawn and garden equipment
3531 Construction machinery
3532 Mining machinery
3533 Oil and gas field machinery
3534 Elevators and moving stairways
3535 Conveyors and conveying equipment
3536 Hoists, cranes, and monorails
3537 Industrial trucks and tractors
3541 Machine tools, metal cutting type
3542 Machine tools, metal forming type
3543 Industrial patterns
3544 Special dies, tools, jigs, and fixtures
3545 Machine tool accessories
3546 Power-driven handtools
3547 Rolling mill machinery
3548 Welding apparatus
3549 Metalworking machinery, nec
3552 Textile machinery
3553 Woodworking machinery
3554 Paper industries machinery
3555 Printing trades machinery
3556 Food products machinery
3559 Special industry machinery, nec
3561 Pumps and pumping equipment
3562 Ball and roller bearings
3563 Air and gas compressors
3564 Blowers and fans
3565 Packaging machinery
3566 Speed changers, drives, and gears
3567 Industrial furnaces and ovens
3568 Power transmission equipment, nec
3569 General industrial machinery,
3571 Electronic computers
3572 Computer storage devices
3575 Computer terminals

SIC INDEX

SIC NO	PRODUCT
3577	Computer peripheral equipment, nec
3578	Calculating and accounting equipment
3579	Office machines, nec
3581	Automatic vending machines
3582	Commercial laundry equipment
3585	Refrigeration and heating equipment
3586	Measuring and dispensing pumps
3589	Service industry machinery, nec
3592	Carburetors, pistons, rings, valves
3593	Fluid power cylinders and actuators
3594	Fluid power pumps and motors
3596	Scales and balances, except laboratory
3599	Industrial machinery, nec

36 electronic & other electrical equipment & components

SIC NO	PRODUCT
3612	Transformers, except electric
3613	Switchgear and switchboard apparatus
3621	Motors and generators
3624	Carbon and graphite products
3625	Relays and industrial controls
3629	Electrical industrial apparatus
3631	Household cooking equipment
3632	Household refrigerators and freezers
3633	Household laundry equipment
3634	Electric housewares and fans
3635	Household vacuum cleaners
3639	Household appliances, nec
3641	Electric lamps
3643	Current-carrying wiring devices
3644	Noncurrent-carrying wiring devices
3645	Residential lighting fixtures
3646	Commercial lighting fixtures
3647	Vehicular lighting equipment
3648	Lighting equipment, nec
3651	Household audio and video equipment
3652	Prerecorded records and tapes
3661	Telephone and telegraph apparatus
3663	Radio and t.v. communications equipment
3669	Communications equipment, nec
3672	Printed circuit boards
3674	Semiconductors and related devices
3675	Electronic capacitors
3676	Electronic resistors
3677	Electronic coils and transformers
3678	Electronic connectors
3679	Electronic components, nec
3691	Storage batteries
3692	Primary batteries, dry and wet
3694	Engine electrical equipment
3695	Magnetic and optical recording media
3699	Electrical equipment and supplies, nec

37 transportation equipment

SIC NO	PRODUCT
3711	Motor vehicles and car bodies
3713	Truck and bus bodies
3714	Motor vehicle parts and accessories
3715	Truck trailers
3716	Motor homes
3721	Aircraft
3724	Aircraft engines and engine parts
3728	Aircraft parts and equipment, nec
3731	Shipbuilding and repairing
3732	Boatbuilding and repairing
3743	Railroad equipment
3751	Motorcycles, bicycles, and parts
3761	Guided missiles and space vehicles
3769	Space vehicle equipment, nec
3792	Travel trailers and campers
3795	Tanks and tank components
3799	Transportation equipment, nec

38 measuring, photographic, medical, & optical goods, & clocks

SIC NO	PRODUCT
3812	Search and navigation equipment
3821	Laboratory apparatus and furniture
3822	Environmental controls
3823	Process control instruments
3824	Fluid meters and counting devices
3825	Instruments to measure electricity
3826	Analytical instruments
3827	Optical instruments and lenses
3829	Measuring and controlling devices, nec
3841	Surgical and medical instruments
3842	Surgical appliances and supplies
3843	Dental equipment and supplies
3844	X-ray apparatus and tubes
3845	Electromedical equipment
3851	Ophthalmic goods
3861	Photographic equipment and supplies
3873	Watches, clocks, watchcases, and parts

39 miscellaneous manufacturing industries

SIC NO	PRODUCT
3911	Jewelry, precious metal
3914	Silverware and plated ware
3915	Jewelers' materials and lapidary work
3931	Musical instruments
3942	Dolls and stuffed toys
3944	Games, toys, and children's vehicles
3949	Sporting and athletic goods, nec
3952	Lead pencils and art goods
3953	Marking devices
3955	Carbon paper and inked ribbons
3961	Costume jewelry
3965	Fasteners, buttons, needles, and pins
3991	Brooms and brushes
3993	Signs and advertising specialties
3995	Burial caskets
3996	Hard surface floor coverings, nec
3999	Manufacturing industries, nec

42 motor freight transportation

SIC NO	PRODUCT
4212	Local trucking, without storage
4213	Trucking, except local
4214	Local trucking with storage
4215	Courier services, except by air
4221	Farm product warehousing and storage
4222	Refrigerated warehousing and storage
4225	General warehousing and storage
4226	Special warehousing and storage, nec
4231	Trucking terminal facilities

44 water transportation

SIC NO	PRODUCT
4424	Deep sea domestic transportation of freight
4491	Marine cargo handling
4492	Towing and tugboat service
4493	Marinas

45 transportation by air

SIC NO	PRODUCT
4512	Air transportation, scheduled
4522	Air transportation, nonscheduled
4581	Airports, flying fields, and services

47 transportation services

SIC NO	PRODUCT
4731	Freight transportation arrangement
4741	Rental of railroad cars
4783	Packing and crating
4789	Transportation services, nec

48 communications

SIC NO	PRODUCT
4812	Radiotelephone communication
4813	Telephone communication, except radio
4832	Radio broadcasting stations
4833	Television broadcasting stations
4841	Cable and other pay television services
4899	Communication services, nec

49 electric, gas and sanitary services

SIC NO	PRODUCT
4911	Electric services
4922	Natural gas transmission
4923	Gas transmission and distribution
4924	Natural gas distribution
4932	Gas and other services combined
4941	Water supply
4952	Sewerage systems
4953	Refuse systems
4959	Sanitary services, nec

50 wholesale trade - durable goods

SIC NO	PRODUCT
5012	Automobiles and other motor vehicles
5013	Motor vehicle supplies and new parts
5014	Tires and tubes
5015	Motor vehicle parts, used
5021	Furniture
5023	Homefurnishings
5031	Lumber, plywood, and millwork
5032	Brick, stone, and related material
5033	Roofing, siding, and insulation
5039	Construction materials, nec
5043	Photographic equipment and supplies
5044	Office equipment
5045	Computers, peripherals, and software
5046	Commercial equipment, nec
5047	Medical and hospital equipment
5048	Ophthalmic goods
5049	Professional equipment, nec
5051	Metals service centers and offices
5052	Coal and other minerals and ores
5063	Electrical apparatus and equipment
5064	Electrical appliances, television and radio
5065	Electronic parts and equipment, nec
5072	Hardware
5074	Plumbing and hydronic heating supplies
5075	Warm air heating and air conditioning
5078	Refrigeration equipment and supplies
5082	Construction and mining machinery
5083	Farm and garden machinery
5084	Industrial machinery and equipment
5085	Industrial supplies
5087	Service establishment equipment
5088	Transportation equipment and supplies
5091	Sporting and recreation goods
5092	Toys and hobby goods and supplies
5093	Scrap and waste materials
5094	Jewelry and precious stones
5099	Durable goods, nec

51 wholesale trade - nondurable goods

SIC NO	PRODUCT
5111	Printing and writing paper
5112	Stationery and office supplies
5113	Industrial and personal service paper
5122	Drugs, proprietaries, and sundries
5131	Piece goods and notions
5136	Men's and boy's clothing
5137	Women's and children's clothing
5139	Footwear
5141	Groceries, general line
5142	Packaged frozen goods
5143	Dairy products, except dried or canned
5144	Poultry and poultry products
5145	Confectionery
5146	Fish and seafoods
5147	Meats and meat products
5148	Fresh fruits and vegetables
5149	Groceries and related products, nec
5153	Grain and field beans
5154	Livestock
5159	Farm-product raw materials, nec
5162	Plastics materials and basic shapes
5169	Chemicals and allied products, nec
5171	Petroleum bulk stations and terminals
5172	Petroleum products, nec
5181	Beer and ale
5182	Wine and distilled beverages
5191	Farm supplies
5192	Books, periodicals, and newspapers
5193	Flowers and florists supplies
5194	Tobacco and tobacco products
5198	Paints, varnishes, and supplies
5199	Nondurable goods, nec

52 building materials, hardware, garden supplies & mobile homes

SIC NO	PRODUCT
5211	Lumber and other building materials
5231	Paint, glass, and wallpaper stores
5251	Hardware stores
5261	Retail nurseries and garden stores

53 general merchandise stores

SIC NO	PRODUCT
5311	Department stores
5399	Miscellaneous general merchandise

54 food stores

SIC NO	PRODUCT
5411	Grocery stores
5421	Meat and fish markets
5431	Fruit and vegetable markets
5441	Candy, nut, and confectionery stores

SIC INDEX

SIC NO	PRODUCT
5451	Dairy products stores
5461	Retail bakeries
5499	Miscellaneous food stores

55 automotive dealers and gasoline service stations

5511 New and used car dealers
5521 Used car dealers
5531 Auto and home supply stores
5541 Gasoline service stations
5551 Boat dealers
5561 Recreational vehicle dealers
5571 Motorcycle dealers
5599 Automotive dealers, nec

56 apparel and accessory stores

5611 Men's and boys' clothing stores
5621 Women's clothing stores
5632 Women's accessory and specialty stores
5641 Children's and infants' wear stores
5651 Family clothing stores
5661 Shoe stores
5699 Miscellaneous apparel and accessories

57 home furniture, furnishings and equipment stores

5712 Furniture stores
5713 Floor covering stores
5714 Drapery and upholstery stores
5719 Miscellaneous homefurnishings
5722 Household appliance stores
5731 Radio, television, and electronic stores
5734 Computer and software stores
5735 Record and prerecorded tape stores
5736 Musical instrument stores

58 eating and drinking places

5812 Eating places
5813 Drinking places

59 miscellaneous retail

5912 Drug stores and proprietary stores
5921 Liquor stores
5932 Used merchandise stores
5941 Sporting goods and bicycle shops
5942 Book stores
5943 Stationery stores
5944 Jewelry stores
5945 Hobby, toy, and game shops
5947 Gift, novelty, and souvenir shop
5948 Luggage and leather goods stores
5949 Sewing, needlework, and piece goods
5961 Catalog and mail-order houses
5963 Direct selling establishments
5983 Fuel oil dealers
5984 Liquefied petroleum gas dealers
5989 Fuel dealers, nec
5992 Florists
5993 Tobacco stores and stands
5994 News dealers and newsstands
5995 Optical goods stores
5999 Miscellaneous retail stores, nec

61 nondepository credit institutions

6141 Personal credit institutions
6153 Short-term business credit
6159 Miscellaneous business credit

62 security & commodity brokers, dealers, exchanges & services

6211 Security brokers and dealers
6282 Investment advice

63 insurance carriers

6311 Life insurance

64 insurance agents, brokers and service

6411 Insurance agents, brokers, and service

65 real estate

6512 Nonresidential building operators
6515 Mobile home site operators
6519 Real property lessors, nec
6531 Real estate agents and managers

6552 Subdividers and developers, nec

67 holding and other investment offices

6719 Holding companies, nec
6726 Investment offices, nec
6794 Patent owners and lessors
6798 Real estate investment trusts
6799 Investors, nec

70 hotels, rooming houses, camps, and other lodging places

7011 Hotels and motels
7032 Sporting and recreational camps
7041 Membership-basis organization hotels

72 personal services

7212 Garment pressing and cleaners' agents
7213 Linen supply
7217 Carpet and upholstery cleaning
7218 Industrial launderers
7231 Beauty shops
7241 Barber shops
7251 Shoe repair and shoeshine parlors
7261 Funeral service and crematories
7291 Tax return preparation services
7299 Miscellaneous personal services

73 business services

7311 Advertising agencies
7312 Outdoor advertising services
7313 Radio, television, publisher representatives
7319 Advertising, nec
7322 Adjustment and collection services
7331 Direct mail advertising services
7334 Photocopying and duplicating services
7335 Commercial photography
7336 Commercial art and graphic design
7338 Secretarial and court reporting
7342 Disinfecting and pest control services
7349 Building maintenance services, nec
7352 Medical equipment rental
7353 Heavy construction equipment rental
7359 Equipment rental and leasing, nec
7363 Help supply services
7371 Custom computer programming services
7372 Prepackaged software
7373 Computer integrated systems design
7374 Data processing and preparation
7375 Information retrieval services
7376 Computer facilities management
7377 Computer rental and leasing
7378 Computer maintenance and repair
7379 Computer related services, nec
7382 Security systems services
7383 News syndicates
7384 Photofinish laboratories
7389 Business services, nec

75 automotive repair, services and parking

7513 Truck rental and leasing, without drivers
7514 Passenger car rental
7519 Utility trailer rental
7521 Automobile parking
7532 Top and body repair and paint shops
7533 Auto exhaust system repair shops
7534 Tire retreading and repair shops
7536 Automotive glass replacement shops
7537 Automotive transmission repair shops
7538 General automotive repair shops
7539 Automotive repair shops, nec
7549 Automotive services, nec

76 miscellaneous repair services

7622 Radio and television repair
7623 Refrigeration service and repair
7629 Electrical repair shops
7631 Watch, clock, and jewelry repair
7641 Reupholstery and furniture repair
7692 Welding repair
7694 Armature rewinding shops
7699 Repair services, nec

78 motion pictures

7812 Motion picture and video production
7819 Services allied to motion pictures
7822 Motion picture and tape distribution
7841 Video tape rental

79 amusement and recreation services

7922 Theatrical producers and services
7929 Entertainers and entertainment groups
7933 Bowling centers
7992 Public golf courses
7993 Coin-operated amusement devices
7997 Membership sports and recreation clubs
7999 Amusement and recreation, nec

80 health services

8011 Offices and clinics of medical doctors
8041 Offices and clinics of chiropractors
8042 Offices and clinics of optometrists
8049 Offices of health practitioner
8051 Skilled nursing care facilities
8052 Intermediate care facilities
8062 General medical and surgical hospitals
8071 Medical laboratories
8072 Dental laboratories
8093 Specialty outpatient clinics, nec
8099 Health and allied services, nec

81 legal services

8111 Legal services

82 educational services

8211 Elementary and secondary schools
8222 Junior colleges
8243 Data processing schools
8249 Vocational schools, nec
8299 Schools and educational services

83 social services

8322 Individual and family services
8331 Job training and related services
8351 Child day care services
8361 Residential care
8399 Social services, nec

84 museums, art galleries and botanical and zoological gardens

8412 Museums and art galleries

86 membership organizations

8611 Business associations
8621 Professional organizations
8641 Civic and social associations
8661 Religious organizations
8699 Membership organizations, nec

87 engineering, accounting, research, and management services

8711 Engineering services
8712 Architectural services
8713 Surveying services
8721 Accounting, auditing, and bookkeeping
8731 Commercial physical research
8732 Commercial nonphysical research
8733 Noncommercial research organizations
8734 Testing laboratories
8741 Management services
8742 Management consulting services
8743 Public relations services
8744 Facilities support services
8748 Business consulting, nec

89 services, not elsewhere classified

8999 Services, nec

91 executive, legislative & general government, except finance

9111 Executive offices
9199 General government, nec

92 justice, public order and safety

9221 Police protection

SIC INDEX

SIC NO	PRODUCT
96 administration of economic programs	
9621 Regulation, administration of transportation	
9661 Space research and technology	
97 national security and international affairs	
9711 National security	

SIC SECTION

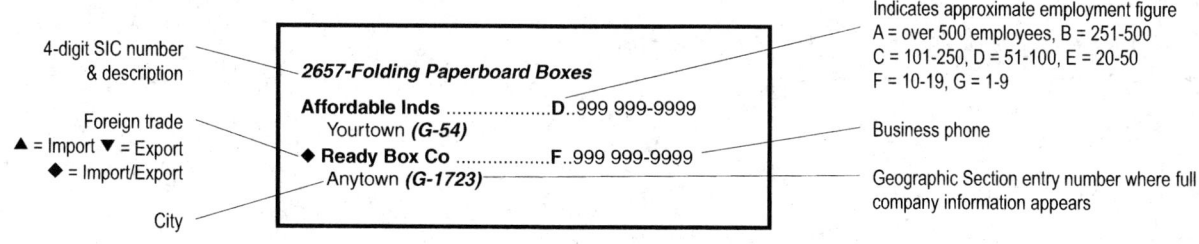

4-digit SIC number & description — *2657-Folding Paperboard Boxes*
Foreign trade ▲ = Import ▼ = Export ◆ = Import/Export
City

Indicates approximate employment figure
A = over 500 employees, B = 251-500
C = 101-250, D = 51-100, E = 20-50
F = 10-19, G = 1-9

Business phone

Geographic Section entry number where full company information appears

See footnotes for symbols and codes identification.
- The SIC codes in this section are from the latest Standard Industrial Classification manual published by the U.S. Government's Office of Management and Budget. For more information regarding SICs, see the Explanatory Notes.
- Companies may be listed under multiple classifications.

---

01 AGRICULTURAL PRODUCTION - CROPS

0111 Wheat
Demmy Sand and Gravel LLC................ E
  Springfield *(G-13554)*
Friesen Transfer Ltd........................... G..... 614 873-5672
  Plain City *(G-12579)*
Schlessman Seed Co........................... E..... 419 499-2572
  Milan *(G-10886)*
Wildcat Creek Farms Inc..................... F..... 419 263-2549
  Payne *(G-12324)*

0115 Corn
Brinkman Turkey Farms Inc................. F..... 419 365-5127
  Findlay *(G-7487)*
Demmy Sand and Gravel LLC................ E
  Springfield *(G-13554)*
Friesen Transfer Ltd........................... G..... 614 873-5672
  Plain City *(G-12579)*
Schlessman Seed Co........................... E..... 419 499-2572
  Milan *(G-10886)*
Wildcat Creek Farms Inc..................... F..... 419 263-2549
  Payne *(G-12324)*

0116 Soybeans
▲ Advanced Biological Mktg Inc............ E..... 419 232-2461
  Van Wert *(G-14904)*
Schlessman Seed Co........................... E..... 419 499-2572
  Milan *(G-10886)*
Wildcat Creek Farms Inc..................... F..... 419 263-2549
  Payne *(G-12324)*

0119 Cash grains, nec
Demmy Sand and Gravel LLC................ E
  Springfield *(G-13554)*
Wildcat Creek Farms Inc..................... F..... 419 263-2549
  Payne *(G-12324)*

0139 Field crops, except cash grain
Cleveland Bean Sprout Inc.................... F..... 216 881-2112
  Cleveland *(G-3832)*
Infinitaire Industries LLC..................... G..... 216 600-2051
  Euclid *(G-7175)*

0161 Vegetables and melons
Chefs Garden Inc............................... C..... 419 433-4947
  Huron *(G-8630)*
Cleveland Bean Sprout Inc.................... F..... 216 881-2112
  Cleveland *(G-3832)*

Russell L Garber................................ G..... 937 548-6224
  Greenville *(G-8058)*

0171 Berry crops
◆ Robert Rothschild Farm LLC............... F..... 855 969-8050
  West Chester *(G-15501)*

0172 Grapes
Ferrante Wine Farm Inc...................... E..... 440 466-8466
  Geneva *(G-7936)*

0191 General farms, primarily crop
Clovervale Farms LLC......................... D..... 440 960-0146
  Amherst *(G-473)*
Green Field Farms Co-Op..................... G..... 330 263-0246
  Wooster *(G-16126)*
Humphrey Popcorn Company................ F..... 216 662-6629
  Strongsville *(G-13843)*
Trevor Clatterbuck.............................. G..... 330 359-2129
  Wilmot *(G-16070)*
Wagner Farms Sawmill Ltd Lblty........... F..... 419 653-4126
  Leipsic *(G-9141)*

02 AGRICULTURAL PRODUCTION - LIVESTOCK AND ANIMAL SPECIALTIES

0211 Beef cattle feedlots
Dairy Farmers America Inc................... E..... 330 670-7800
  Medina *(G-10317)*

0213 Hogs
Winner Corporation............................ E..... 419 582-4321
  Yorkshire *(G-16293)*

0241 Dairy farms
Calvary Christian Ch of Ohio................ F..... 740 828-9000
  Frazeysburg *(G-7714)*
▲ Miceli Dairy Products Co.................. D..... 216 791-6222
  Cleveland *(G-4400)*
Youngs Jersey Dairy Inc...................... B..... 937 325-0629
  Yellow Springs *(G-16290)*

0252 Chicken eggs
Cal-Maine Foods Inc........................... D..... 937 337-9576
  Rossburg *(G-12861)*
Cal-Maine Foods Inc........................... G..... 937 968-4874
  Union City *(G-14776)*
▲ Daylay Egg Farm Inc....................... C..... 937 355-6531
  West Mansfield *(G-15625)*

Nature Pure LLC................................ E..... 937 358-2364
  West Mansfield *(G-15627)*
Nature Pure LLC................................ F..... 937 358-2364
  Raymond *(G-12746)*
▲ Weaver Bros Inc............................. D..... 937 526-3907
  Versailles *(G-14992)*

0253 Turkeys and turkey eggs
Cooper Hatchery Inc........................... C..... 419 594-3325
  Oakwood *(G-12030)*
V H Cooper & Co Inc.......................... C..... 419 375-4116
  Fort Recovery *(G-7626)*

0254 Poultry hatcheries
Cooper Hatchery Inc........................... C..... 419 594-3325
  Oakwood *(G-12030)*

0279 Animal specialties, nec
Deer Creek Honey Farms Ltd................ G..... 740 852-0899
  London *(G-9386)*

07 AGRICULTURAL SERVICES

0711 Soil preparation services
Garick LLC....................................... E..... 216 581-0100
  Cleveland *(G-4102)*
Ream and Haager Laboratory Inc.......... F..... 330 343-3711
  Dover *(G-6840)*

0721 Crop planting and protection
Ruhe Sales Inc................................... F..... 419 943-3357
  Leipsic *(G-9140)*

0723 Crop preparation services for market
Andersons Inc................................... G..... 419 536-0460
  Toledo *(G-14194)*
Andersons Inc................................... C..... 419 893-5050
  Maumee *(G-10165)*
Ohigro Inc.. E..... 740 726-2429
  Waldo *(G-15090)*
Schlessman Seed Co........................... E..... 419 499-2572
  Milan *(G-10886)*
▼ Verhoff Alfalfa Mills Inc................... G..... 419 523-4767
  Ottawa *(G-12195)*

0724 Cotton ginning
▼ Compass Systems & Sales LLC......... D..... 330 733-2111
  Norton *(G-11940)*

0751 Livestock services, except veterinary
Patrick M Davidson............................ G..... 513 897-2971
  Waynesville *(G-15302)*

07 AGRICULTURAL SERVICES

Winner Corporation................................E 419 582-4321
  Yorkshire (G-16293)

0752 Animal specialty services

Canine Creations Inc............................G 937 667-8576
  Tipp City (G-14125)
◆ Heading4ward Investment Co..............D 937 293-9994
  Moraine (G-11185)

0781 Landscape counseling and planning

▲ Acro Tool & Die Company....................E 330 773-5173
  Akron (G-17)
All Ways Green Lawn & Turf LLC............G 937 763-4766
  Seaman (G-13114)
Benchmark Land Management LLC........G 513 310-7850
  West Chester (G-15376)
Evolution Lawn & Landscape LLC..........G 330 268-5306
  Mineral City (G-11017)
Fine Line Excvtq & Ldscpg LLC..............G 330 541-0590
  Ravenna (G-12715)
Green Impressions LLC.........................D 440 240-8508
  Sheffield Village (G-13182)
Hauser Services Llc................................E 440 632-5126
  Middlefield (G-10755)
▲ Meridienne International Inc.................G 330 274-8317
  Aurora (G-725)
Morel Landscaping LLC..........................F 216 551-4395
  Richfield (G-12791)
Sand PROperties&landscaping...............G 440 360-7386
  Westlake (G-15781)

0782 Lawn and garden services

Benchmark Land Management LLC........G 513 310-7850
  West Chester (G-15376)
Bismark Lawncare LLC............................F 440 361-5561
  Austinburg (G-742)
▲ Brewer Company..................................G 800 394-0017
  Milford (G-10896)
Evolution Lawn & Landscape LLC..........G 330 268-5306
  Mineral City (G-11017)
Green Impressions LLC.........................D 440 240-8508
  Sheffield Village (G-13182)
Innovative Sport Surfacing LLC...............F 440 205-0875
  Mentor (G-10473)
Mapledale Farm Inc...............................F 440 286-3489
  Chardon (G-2458)
Mid-Wood Inc...F 419 257-3431
  North Baltimore (G-11696)
Richland Newhope Inds Inc....................C 419 774-4400
  Mansfield (G-9712)
Russell Hunt..F 740 264-1196
  Steubenville (G-13676)
◆ Scotts Company LLC...........................C 937 644-0011
  Marysville (G-9934)
Smith & Thompson Entps LLC................F 330 386-9345
  East Liverpool (G-7000)
Spencer Feed & Supply LLC..................F 330 648-2111
  Spencer (G-13483)
Triple A Builders Inc..............................G 216 249-0327
  Cleveland (G-4832)

0783 Ornamental shrub and tree services

Grand Archt Etrnl Eye 314 LLC...............F 800 377-8147
  Cleveland (G-4138)
Morel Landscaping LLC..........................F 216 551-4395
  Richfield (G-12791)
Smith & Thompson Entps LLC................F 330 386-9345
  East Liverpool (G-7000)

08 FORESTRY

0811 Timber tracts

▲ Acro Tool & Die Company....................E 330 773-5173
  Akron (G-17)

10 METAL MINING

1011 Iron ores

Cleveland-Cliffs Inc.................................E 419 243-8198
  Toledo (G-14242)
Cleveland-Cliffs Intl Holdg Co.................D 216 694-5700
  Cleveland (G-3863)
Cliffs & Associates Ltd............................G 216 694-5700
  Cleveland (G-3869)
Cliffs Empire Inc.....................................G 216 694-5700
  Cleveland (G-3870)
Cliffs Mining Company.............................F 216 694-5700
  Cleveland (G-3872)
Cliffs Mining Holding Sub Co...................F 216 694-5700
  Cleveland (G-3873)
Cliffs Mining Services Company..............C 218 262-5913
  Cleveland (G-3874)
Cliffs Natural Resources Explo................C 216 694-5700
  Cleveland (G-3875)
Ironunits LLC..E 216 694-5303
  Cleveland (G-4237)
The Cleveland-Cliffs Iron Co...................C 216 694-5700
  Cleveland (G-4781)
Tilden Mining Company LC.....................A 216 694-5700
  Cleveland (G-4796)
Wabush Mnes Clffs Min Mnging A..........B 216 694-5700
  Cleveland (G-4888)

1031 Lead and zinc ores

Abatement Lead Tstg Risk Assss............G 330 785-6420
  Akron (G-13)

1041 Gold ores

Fantasia Enterprises LLC.......................F 330 400-8741
  Massillon (G-10095)
Ivi Mining Group Ltd...............................G 740 418-7745
  Vinton (G-15011)

1061 Ferroalloy ores, except vanadium

▲ Rhenium Alloys Inc.............................E 440 365-7388
  North Ridgeville (G-11858)

1081 Metal mining services

Cliffs UTAC Holding LLC.........................D 216 694-5700
  Cleveland (G-3877)
Galt Alloys Enterprise..............................F 330 309-8194
  Canton (G-2108)
Mining and Reclamation Inc..................G 740 327-5555
  Dresden (G-6855)
Omega Cementing Co............................G 330 695-7147
  Apple Creek (G-508)
Western Kentucky Coal Co LLC.............E 740 338-3334
  Saint Clairsville (G-12929)

12 COAL MINING

1221 Bituminous coal and lignite-surface mining

Anthony Mining Co Inc..........................G 740 282-5301
  Wintersville (G-16084)
B&N Coal Inc..E 740 783-3575
  Dexter City (G-6802)
Buckingham Coal Company LLC...........D
  Zanesville (G-16515)
▼ Cliffs Logan County Coal LLC...........C 216 694-5700
  Cleveland (G-3871)
Coal Resources Inc..............................E 216 765-1240
  Saint Clairsville (G-12899)
Coal Services Inc..................................B 740 795-5220
  Powhatan Point (G-12684)
Commercial Minerals Inc......................G 330 549-2165
  North Lima (G-11803)
D & D Mining Co Inc..............................F 330 549-3127
  New Springfield (G-11540)
Franklin County Coal Company..............B 740 338-3100
  Saint Clairsville (G-12905)
Harrison County Coal Company..............F 740 338-3100
  Saint Clairsville (G-12906)
Holmes Limestone Co............................G 330 893-2721
  Berlin (G-1307)
Ivi Mining Group Ltd...............................G 740 418-7745
  Vinton (G-15011)
J & D Mining Inc.....................................E 330 339-4935
  New Philadelphia (G-11506)
Kimble Company....................................C 330 343-1226
  Dover (G-6830)
L & M Mineral Co....................................G 330 852-3696
  Sugarcreek (G-13927)
Marietta Coal Co....................................E 740 695-2197
  Saint Clairsville (G-12908)
McElroy Coal Company..........................F 724 485-4000
  Saint Clairsville (G-12911)
Meigs County Coal Company.................B 740 338-3100
  Saint Clairsville (G-12912)
Muhlenberg County Coal Co LLC...........G 740 338-3100
  Saint Clairsville (G-12914)
Murray American Energy Inc................C 740 338-3100
  Saint Clairsville (G-12915)
Nacco Industries Inc..............................E 440 229-5151
  Cleveland (G-4434)
Oxford Mining Company Inc..................C 740 588-0190
  Zanesville (G-16552)
Oxford Mining Company Inc..................G 740 622-6302
  Coshocton (G-5991)
Oxford Mining Company LLC.................F 740 622-6302
  Coshocton (G-5992)
Oxford Mining Company - KY LLC.........E 740 622-6302
  Coshocton (G-5993)
PM Coal Company LLC.........................G 440 256-7624
  Willoughby (G-15971)
Rayle Coal Co..F 740 695-2197
  Saint Clairsville (G-12920)
Rosebud Mining Company....................D 740 768-2275
  Bergholz (G-1301)
Straight Creek Bushman LLC................G 513 732-1698
  Batavia (G-950)
Subtropolis Mining Co............................E 330 549-2165
  Petersburg (G-12450)
Symmes Creek Mining LLC...................G 740 353-1509
  Portsmouth (G-12658)
Thompson Bros Mining Co....................F 330 549-3979
  New Springfield (G-11542)
Valley Mining Inc....................................C 740 922-3942
  Dennison (G-6797)
Washington County Coal Company........B 740 338-3100
  Saint Clairsville (G-12928)
Waterloo Coal Company Inc..................D 740 286-0004
  Jackson (G-8727)
Westmoreland Resources Gp LLC........D 740 622-6302
  Coshocton (G-5999)

1222 Bituminous coal-underground mining

Coal Services Inc..................................B 740 795-5220
  Powhatan Point (G-12684)
Ivi Mining Group Ltd...............................G 740 418-7745
  Vinton (G-15011)
Kenamerican Resources Inc.................C 740 338-3100
  Saint Clairsville (G-12907)
Rosebud Mining Company....................D 740 768-2275
  Bergholz (G-1301)

SIC SECTION

13 OIL AND GAS EXTRACTION

Sterling Mining Corporation.................. F 330 549-2165
North Lima *(G-11814)*

Utahamerican Energy Inc...................... C 435 888-4000
Powhatan Point *(G-12685)*

Western KY Coal Resources LLC......... E 740 338-3100
Saint Clairsville *(G-12931)*

1231 Anthracite mining

Coal Services Inc............................... B 740 795-5220
Powhatan Point *(G-12684)*

Mill Creek Mining Company.................. G 216 765-1240
Saint Clairsville *(G-12913)*

1241 Coal mining services

American Cnsld Ntral Rsrces In............ E 740 338-3100
Saint Clairsville *(G-12894)*

American Coal Company...................... F 740 338-3334
Saint Clairsville *(G-12895)*

Appalachian Fuels LLC......................... C 606 928-0460
Dublin *(G-6862)*

Coal Services Inc............................... B 740 795-5220
Powhatan Point *(G-12684)*

Crimson Oak Grove Rsources LLC........ F 740 338-3100
Saint Clairsville *(G-12900)*

Emery Cnty Coal Resources Inc........... G 740 338-3100
Saint Clairsville *(G-12902)*

▼ Global Coal Sales Group LLC........... G 614 221-0101
Dublin *(G-6886)*

Ohio Valley Coal Company................... B 740 926-1351
Saint Clairsville *(G-12918)*

Peabody Coal Company....................... E 740 450-2420
Zanesville *(G-16554)*

Rosebud Mining Company................... D 740 658-4217
Freeport *(G-7761)*

Strata Mine Services LLC..................... F 740 695-0488
Saint Clairsville *(G-12927)*

Suncoke Energy Inc............................ E 513 727-5571
Middletown *(G-10860)*

Terradyn Corporation.......................... F 614 805-0897
Dublin *(G-6951)*

Western KY Cnsld Resources LLC........ G 740 338-3100
Saint Clairsville *(G-12930)*

Western KY Resources Fing LLC.......... G 740 338-3100
Saint Clairsville *(G-12932)*

13 OIL AND GAS EXTRACTION

1311 Crude petroleum and natural gas

American Rodpump Ltd...................... G 440 987-9457
Dublin *(G-6860)*

Apache Acquisitions LLC..................... G 419 782-8003
Defiance *(G-6669)*

Bakerwell Inc...................................... E 330 276-2161
Killbuck *(G-8916)*

Bijoe Development Inc........................ E 330 674-5981
Millersburg *(G-10946)*

BP Products North America Inc............ F 419 698-6400
Oregon *(G-12104)*

Bpi Energy Holdings Inc...................... F 281 556-6200
Solon *(G-13322)*

Brendel Producing Company................ G 330 854-4151
Canton *(G-2052)*

Buckeye Energy Resources Inc............ G 740 452-9506
Zanesville *(G-16514)*

Buckeye Franklin Co........................... F 330 859-2465
Zoarville *(G-16575)*

Buckeye Oil Producing Co................... F 330 264-8847
Wooster *(G-16108)*

Cameron Drilling Co Inc...................... F 740 453-3300
Zanesville *(G-16516)*

Cgas Exploration Inc........................... G 614 436-4631
Worthington *(G-16190)*

Cgas Inc.. F 614 975-4697
Worthington *(G-16191)*

City of Lancaster................................ E 740 687-6670
Lancaster *(G-9002)*

D & L Energy Inc................................ E 330 270-1201
Canton *(G-2087)*

Derrick Petroleum Inc......................... G 740 668-5711
Bladensburg *(G-1346)*

Devco Oil Inc..................................... F 740 439-3833
Cambridge *(G-1932)*

Dome Drilling Company...................... G 440 892-9434
Westlake *(G-15746)*

Elkhead Gas & Oil Co......................... G 740 763-3966
Newark *(G-11574)*

Enrevo Pyro LLC................................ G 203 517-5002
Brookfield *(G-1669)*

Everflow Eastern Partners LP.............. G 330 533-2692
Canfield *(G-2006)*

Exco Resources (pa) LLC................... F 740 796-5231
Adamsville *(G-7)*

Exco Resources LLC........................... F 740 254-4061
Tippecanoe *(G-14169)*

Franklin Gas & Oil Company LLC.......... G 330 264-8739
Wooster *(G-16120)*

General Electric Company................... F 330 425-3755
Twinsburg *(G-14668)*

Green Energy Inc............................... G 330 262-5112
Wooster *(G-16125)*

Henthorne Jr Jay Mary Beth................ G 330 264-1049
Wooster *(G-16130)*

Interstate Gas Supply LLC................... B 877 995-4447
Dublin *(G-6900)*

JMB Energy Inc.................................. E 330 505-9610
Mineral Ridge *(G-11021)*

John D Oil and Gas Company............... G 440 255-6325
Mentor *(G-10484)*

Kenoil Inc.. G 330 262-1144
Wooster *(G-16141)*

Killbuck Creek Oil Co LLC................... G 330 601-0921
Wooster *(G-16143)*

◆ Knight Material Tech LLC..................D 330 488-1651
East Canton *(G-6979)*

Marietta Resources Corporation........... F 740 373-6305
Marietta *(G-9806)*

Pin Oak Energy Partners LLC............... F 888 748-0763
Akron *(G-275)*

Purvi Oil Inc...................................... G 419 207-8234
Ashland *(G-606)*

R D Holder Oil Co Inc......................... F 740 522-3136
Heath *(G-8328)*

RCM Engineering Company................. G 330 666-0575
Akron *(G-299)*

Robert Barr....................................... G 740 826-7325
New Concord *(G-11433)*

Sairam Oil Inc.................................... G 440 289-8232
Parma *(G-12294)*

Sheridan One Stop Carryout Inc........... G 740 687-1300
Lancaster *(G-9038)*

Tatum Petroleum Corporation.............. F 740 819-6810
Worthington *(G-16214)*

Temple Oil and Gas LLC...................... G 740 452-7878
Crooksville *(G-6050)*

Triad Hunter LLC................................ F 740 374-2940
Marietta *(G-9839)*

Ultra-Met Company............................ F 937 653-7133
Urbana *(G-14851)*

W H Patten Drilling Co Inc................... G 740 674-3046
Millersburg *(G-11004)*

W P Brown Enterprises Inc.................. G 740 685-2594
Byesville *(G-1902)*

William S Miller Inc............................. G 330 223-1794
Kensington *(G-8791)*

Williams Partners LP........................... F 330 414-6201
North Canton *(G-11775)*

Xto Energy Inc................................... G 740 671-9901
Bellaire *(G-1190)*

1321 Natural gas liquids

Condevco Inc..................................... G 740 373-5302
New Matamoras *(G-11476)*

Consolidated Gas Coop Inc.................. G 419 946-6600
Mount Gilead *(G-11232)*

H & S Operating Company Inc............. G 330 830-8178
Winesburg *(G-16079)*

Husky Marketing and Supply Co........... E 614 210-2300
Dublin *(G-6894)*

Markwest Utica Emg LLC.................... C 740 942-4810
Jewett *(G-8767)*

RCM Engineering Company................. G 330 666-0575
Akron *(G-299)*

1381 Drilling oil and gas wells

Anderson Energy Inc.......................... G 740 678-8608
Fleming *(G-7585)*

Artex Oil Company............................. E 740 373-3313
Marietta *(G-9777)*

Bakerwell Service Rigs Inc.................. F 330 276-2161
Killbuck *(G-8917)*

Brendel Producing Company................ G 330 854-4151
Canton *(G-2052)*

Buckeye Oil Producing Co................... F 330 264-8847
Wooster *(G-16108)*

Clearpath Utlity Solutions LLC.............. F 740 661-4240
Zanesville *(G-16521)*

Decker Drilling Inc.............................. F 740 749-3939
Vincent *(G-15007)*

Directional One Svcs Inc USA............... G 740 371-5031
Marietta *(G-9788)*

Doris Kimble...................................... G 330 343-1226
Dover *(G-6816)*

Dugan Drilling Inc............................... G 740 668-3811
Walhonding *(G-15092)*

Eclipse Resources - Ohio LLC.............. C 740 452-4503
Zanesville *(G-16529)*

Fortis Energy Services Inc................... D 248 283-7100
Saint Clairsville *(G-12904)*

Frank Csapo...................................... G 330 435-4458
Creston *(G-6039)*

Gills Petroleum Llc............................. G 740 702-2600
Chillicothe *(G-2505)*

Groundhogs 2000 LLC........................ G 440 653-1647
Bedford *(G-1122)*

Hocking Hlls Enrgy Well Svcs L........... G 740 385-6690
Logan *(G-9364)*

J D Drilling Company.......................... F 740 949-2512
Racine *(G-12693)*

Jackson Wells Services....................... F 419 886-2017
Bellville *(G-1243)*

James R Smail Inc.............................. G 330 264-7500
Wooster *(G-16136)*

Kilbarger Construction Inc................... C 740 385-6019
Logan *(G-9367)*

Maric Drilling Co................................. G 330 830-8178
Winesburg *(G-16080)*

Mattmark Partners Inc........................ F 740 439-3109
Cambridge *(G-1941)*

Moore Well Services Inc..................... F 330 650-4443
Mogadore *(G-11078)*

▲ Ngo Development Corporation.......... E 740 344-3790
Newark *(G-11598)*

Nomac Drilling LLC............................. C 330 476-7040
Carrollton *(G-2312)*

Nomac Drilling LLC............................. C 724 324-2205
Saint Clairsville *(G-12916)*

Employee Codes: A=Over 500 employees, B=251-500
C=101-250, D=51-100, E=20-50, F=10-19, G=1-9

13 OIL AND GAS EXTRACTION

Osair Inc .... G 440 974-6500
   Mentor (G-10516)
Petro Quest Inc .... G 740 593-3800
   Athens (G-690)
Roughcut LLC .... F 505 686-3615
   Saint Clairsville (G-12922)
Stratagraph Ne Inc .... F 740 373-3091
   Marietta (G-9834)
Temple Oil and Gas LLC .... G 740 452-7878
   Crooksville (G-6050)
Timco Inc .... F 740 685-2594
   Byesville (G-1900)
Victor McKenzie Drlg Co Inc .... F 740 453-0834
   Zanesville (G-16568)
Viking Well Service Inc .... G 681 205-1999
   Lore City (G-9447)
Warren Drilling Co Inc .... C 740 783-2775
   Dexter City (G-6803)
Warthman Drilling Inc .... G 740 746-9950
   Sugar Grove (G-13917)

1382 Oil and gas exploration services

AB Resources LLC .... E 440 922-1098
   Brecksville (G-1604)
Access Midstream .... G 330 679-2019
   Salineville (G-13037)
Antero Resources Corporation .... E 303 357-7310
   Caldwell (G-1906)
Antero Resources Corporation .... D 740 760-1000
   Marietta (G-9775)
Artex Energy Group LLC .... G 740 373-3313
   Marietta (G-9776)
Atlas America Inc .... F 330 339-3155
   New Philadelphia (G-11485)
BD Oil Gathering Corp .... E 740 374-9355
   Marietta (G-9778)
Beck Energy Corporation .... E 330 297-6891
   Ravenna (G-12706)
Blue Racer Midstream LLC .... D 740 630-7556
   Cambridge (G-1923)
Canton Oil Well Service Inc .... E 330 494-1221
   Canton (G-2066)
Cardinal Operating Company .... G 614 846-5757
   Columbus (G-5238)
Cgas Exploration Inc .... G 614 436-4631
   Worthington (G-16190)
David R Hill Inc .... G 740 685-5168
   Byesville (G-1893)
Diversified Production LLC .... C 740 373-8771
   Marietta (G-9789)
Dlz Ohio Inc .... C 614 888-0040
   Columbus (G-5332)
Dome Drilling Company .... G 440 892-9434
   Westlake (G-15746)
Elkhead Gas & Oil Co .... G 740 763-3966
   Newark (G-11574)
Empress Royalty Ltd .... G 614 943-1903
   Columbus (G-5352)
Equitrans Midstream Corpo .... C 304 626-7934
   Saint Clairsville (G-12903)
Everflow Eastern Partners LP .... G 330 533-2692
   Canfield (G-2006)
Fioritto of Wooster LLC .... G 330 466-3776
   Wooster (G-16119)
G&O Resources Ltd .... F 330 253-2525
   Akron (G-159)
Gonzoil Inc .... G 330 497-5888
   Canton (G-2115)
Hess Corporation .... G 740 266-7835
   Steubenville (G-13668)
Hilcorp Energy Co .... G 330 536-6406
   Lowellville (G-9516)

Hilcorp Energy Co .... G 330 532-9300
   Wellsville (G-15335)
Hocking Hlls Enrgy Well Svcs L .... G 740 385-6690
   Logan (G-9364)
Hunter Eureka Pipeline LLC .... E 740 374-2940
   Marietta (G-9800)
Husky Marketing and Supply Co .... E 614 210-2300
   Dublin (G-6894)
John D Oil and Gas Company .... G 440 255-6325
   Mentor (G-10484)
K Petroleum Inc .... F 614 532-5420
   Gahanna (G-7839)
Knox Energy Inc .... F 740 927-6731
   Pataskala (G-12301)
Knox Energy Inc .... G 614 885-4828
   Columbus (G-5512)
Lake Region Oil Inc .... G 330 828-8420
   Dalton (G-6134)
M3 Midstream LLC .... E 330 223-2220
   Kensington (G-8790)
M3 Midstream LLC .... E 330 679-5580
   Salineville (G-13039)
M3 Midstream LLC .... E 740 945-1170
   Scio (G-13111)
Miller Energy LLC .... G 614 367-1812
   Columbus (G-5570)
Mori Shuji .... G 614 459-1296
   Columbus (G-5580)
N & G Takhar Oil LLC .... G 937 604-0012
   Tipp City (G-14144)
New World Energy Resources .... F 740 344-4087
   Newark (G-11597)
Ngo Development Corporation .... B 740 622-9560
   Coshocton (G-5987)
Northwood Energy Corporation .... E 614 457-1024
   Columbus (G-5604)
Precision Geophysical Inc .... E 330 674-2198
   Millersburg (G-10989)
Prominence Energy Corporation .... G 513 818-8329
   Cincinnati (G-3304)
Quantum Energy LLC .... F 440 285-7381
   Chardon (G-2464)
Reserve Energy Exploration Co .... G 440 543-0770
   Chagrin Falls (G-2419)
Resource America Inc .... G 330 896-8510
   Uniontown (G-14792)
Sadaf Oil & Gas Inc .... G 330 448-6631
   Brookfield (G-1673)
Santec Resources Inc .... F 614 664-9540
   Columbus (G-5746)
Second Oil Ltd .... G 419 830-4688
   Mc Clure (G-10267)
Silcor Oilfield Services Inc .... F 330 448-8500
   Brookfield (G-1674)
St Paul Park Refining Co .... G 419 422-2121
   Findlay (G-7568)
Stevens Oil & Gas LLC .... G 740 374-4542
   Marietta (G-9831)
T-N-T Rgulatory Compliance Inc .... G 513 442-2464
   Cincinnati (G-3438)
Tgs Systems LLC .... G 614 431-6927
   Columbus (G-5819)
Triad Energy Corporation .... F 740 374-2940
   Marietta (G-9838)
Unlimited Energy Services LLC .... G 304 517-7097
   Beverly (G-1322)
Utica East Ohio Midstream LLC .... B 740 431-4168
   Dennison (G-6796)
Utica East Ohio Midstream LLC .... G 740 945-2226
   Scio (G-13113)
Whitacre Enterprises Inc .... E 740 934-2331
   Graysville (G-8024)

Zane Petroleum Inc .... F 740 454-8779
   Columbus (G-5891)

1389 Oil and gas field services, nec

A1 Industrial Painting Inc .... E 330 750-9441
   Youngstown (G-16298)
Acid Development LLC .... G 330 502-4164
   Youngstown (G-16302)
Adapt Oil .... G 330 658-1482
   Doylestown (G-6852)
Aim Services Company .... F 800 321-9038
   Girard (G-7959)
Aj Enterprise LLC .... F 740 231-2205
   Zanesville (G-16497)
Akron Bldg Closeout Mtls LLC .... G 234 738-0867
   Barberton (G-853)
All Trades Contractors LLC .... G 440 850-5693
   Cleveland (G-3634)
Altier Brothers Inc .... F 740 347-4329
   Corning (C-6067)
American Egle Prprty Prsrvtion .... G 855 440-6938
   North Ridgeville (G-11828)
Appalachian Oilfield Svcs LLC .... F 337 216-0066
   Sardis (G-13110)
Appalachian Well Surveys Inc .... G 740 255-7652
   Cambridge (G-1922)
Artisan Constructors LLC .... E 216 800-7641
   Cleveland (G-3680)
B&L Services .... G 740 390-4272
   Fredericktown (G-7738)
Bakerwell Inc .... E 330 276-2161
   Killbuck (G-8916)
Barnes Services LLC .... G 440 319-2088
   Maple Heights (G-9747)
Barneys Hot Shot Service LLC .... G 740 517-9593
   Quaker City (G-12692)
Bhl International Inc .... G 216 458-8472
   Cleveland (G-3734)
Bijoe Development Inc .... E 330 674-5981
   Millersburg (G-10946)
Bishop Well Services Corp .... G 330 264-2023
   Wooster (G-16104)
Bismark Lawncare LLC .... F 440 361-5561
   Austinburg (G-742)
Brightstar Propane & Fuels .... F 614 891-8395
   Westerville (G-15648)
Buckeye Pipe Inspection LLC .... G 440 476-8369
   Chardon (G-2441)
Bunnell Hill Construction Inc .... F 513 932-6010
   Lebanon (G-9065)
Care Industries .... G 614 584-6595
   Grove City (G-8082)
Carper Well Service Inc .... F 740 374-2567
   Marietta (G-9782)
CDK Perforating LLC .... D 817 862-9834
   Marietta (G-9783)
Circleville Oil Co .... G 740 477-3341
   Circleville (G-3544)
Cirigliano Enterprises LLC .... G 567 525-4571
   Findlay (G-7492)
Commercial Cnstr Group LLC .... G 513 722-1357
   Milford (G-10902)
Complete Energy Services Inc .... F 440 577-1070
   Pierpont (G-12474)
Concrete One Construction LLC .... F 740 595-9680
   Delaware (G-6711)
Crescent Services LLC .... G 405 603-1200
   Cambridge (G-1930)
Critical Ctrl Enrgy Svcs Inc .... F 330 539-4267
   Girard (G-7966)
Danos and Curole .... G 740 609-3599
   Martins Ferry (G-9897)

Darin Jordan...G.....740 819-3525
 Nashport *(G-11336)*
Diamond Oilfield Tech LLC..........................F.....234 806-4185
 Warren *(G-15160)*
Dollars N Cent Inc..F.....971 381-0406
 Cleveland *(G-3966)*
Dow Cameron Oil & Gas LLC.....................G.....740 452-1568
 Zanesville *(G-16527)*
Elite Property Group LLC............................F.....216 356-7469
 Elyria *(G-7139)*
Endless Home Improvements LLC............G.....614 599-1799
 Columbus *(G-5353)*
EP Ferris & Associates Inc.........................E.....614 299-2999
 Columbus *(G-5357)*
Everflow Eastern Partners LP.....................G.....330 537-3863
 Salem *(G-12993)*
Facility Service Pros LLC............................G.....419 577-6123
 Collins *(G-5004)*
Fishburn Tank Truck Service......................F.....419 253-6031
 Marengo *(G-9767)*
Formation Cementing Inc............................G.....740 453-6926
 Zanesville *(G-16532)*
Frantz Well Servicing Inc............................G.....419 992-4564
 Tiffin *(G-14086)*
Full Circle Oil Field Svcs Inc......................F.....740 371-5422
 Whipple *(G-15814)*
Genco..G.....419 207-7648
 Ashland *(G-576)*
Global Energy Partners LLC.......................E.....419 756-8027
 Mansfield *(G-9660)*
Grand Archt Etrnl Eye 314 LLC..................F.....800 377-8147
 Cleveland *(G-4138)*
Greer & Whitehead Cnstr Inc.....................G.....513 202-1757
 Harrison *(G-8277)*
Gws Levi Up Home Solutions LLC............E.....419 667-6041
 Toledo *(G-14305)*
Hagen Well Service LLC............................G.....330 264-7500
 Wooster *(G-16129)*
Halliburton Energy Svcs Inc.......................F.....740 617-2917
 Zanesville *(G-16535)*
Holly Robakowski...G.....440 854-9317
 Cleveland *(G-4196)*
Ingle-Barr Inc...D.....740 702-6117
 Chillicothe *(G-2513)*
Inland Tarp & Liner LLC..............................E.....419 436-6001
 Fostoria *(G-7638)*
Inline Undgrd Hrzntal Drctnal......................G.....740 808-0316
 Bremen *(G-1638)*
J-Well Service Inc..G.....330 824-2718
 Warren *(G-15180)*
Joseph G Pappas..G.....330 383-2917
 East Liverpool *(G-6995)*
JT Plus Well Service LLC...........................F.....740 347-0070
 Corning *(G-5958)*
Karlco Oilfield Services Inc.........................F.....440 576-3415
 Jefferson *(G-8748)*
Kelchner Inc...C.....937 704-9890
 Springboro *(G-13508)*
Killbuck Oil and Gas LLC............................G.....330 447-8423
 Akron *(G-206)*
Klx Energy Services LLC............................E.....740 922-1155
 Midvale *(G-10880)*
L & S Home Improvement..........................G.....330 906-3199
 Coventry Township *(G-6013)*
Leak Finder Inc..G.....440 735-0130
 Hudson *(G-8602)*
Lindev Investors Group Inc........................G.....440 856-9201
 Montville *(G-11149)*
Lld Gas & Oil Corp......................................G.....330 364-6331
 Dover *(G-6832)*
Lubrisource Inc...F.....937 432-9292
 Middletown *(G-10836)*

Mac Oil Field Service Inc.............................E.....330 674-7371
 Millersburg *(G-10978)*
MB Renovations & Designs LLC................G.....614 772-6139
 Columbus *(G-5548)*
MGM Construction Inc................................F.....440 234-7660
 Berea *(G-1288)*
Nabors & Nabors Ltd...................................G.....440 846-0000
 Brunswick *(G-1775)*
Nine Downhole Technologies LLC.............G.....817 862-9834
 Marietta *(G-9811)*
Northeastern Oilfield Svcs LLC..................G.....330 581-3304
 Canton *(G-2178)*
Northfield Propane LLC...............................G.....330 854-4320
 Orrville *(G-12141)*
Oaktree Wireline LLC..................................G.....330 352-7250
 New Philadelphia *(G-11520)*
Ohio Building Restoration Inc....................E.....419 244-7372
 Toledo *(G-14408)*
Ohio Luxury Builders LLC..........................G.....330 881-0073
 Austintown *(G-753)*
Omega Cementing Co.................................G.....330 695-7147
 Apple Creek *(G-508)*
Omnipresence Cleaning LLC......................F.....937 250-4749
 Dayton *(G-6491)*
Ottawa Oil Co Inc...F.....419 425-3301
 Findlay *(G-7548)*
P & M Enterprises Group Inc......................G.....330 316-0387
 Canton *(G-2190)*
Panhandle Olfld Svc Cmpnies In................E.....330 340-9525
 Cambridge *(G-1947)*
Paragon Intgrted Svcs Group LL................E.....724 639-5126
 Newcomerstown *(G-11650)*
Performance Technologies LLC.................D.....330 875-1216
 Louisville *(G-9468)*
Personnel Selection Services.....................F.....440 835-3255
 Cleveland *(G-4542)*
Petrox Inc..F.....330 653-5526
 Streetsboro *(G-13784)*
Pettigrew Pumping Inc................................F.....330 297-7900
 Ravenna *(G-12728)*
Primo Services LLC.....................................F.....513 725-7888
 Cincinnati *(G-3276)*
Producers Service Corporation..................D.....740 454-6253
 Zanesville *(G-16559)*
Prospect Rock LLC......................................F.....740 512-0542
 Saint Clairsville *(G-12919)*
PSC Holdings Inc...G.....740 454-6253
 Zanesville *(G-16560)*
R Anthony Enterprises LLC.......................F.....419 341-0961
 Marion *(G-9874)*
Radon Eliminator LLC..................................F.....330 844-0703
 North Canton *(G-11755)*
Ralph Robinson Inc.....................................G.....740 385-2747
 Logan *(G-9375)*
Ream and Haager Laboratory Inc..............F.....330 343-3711
 Dover *(G-6840)*
Recon..D.....740 609-3050
 Bridgeport *(G-1648)*
Ruscilli Real Estate Services......................F.....614 923-6400
 Dublin *(G-6932)*
Samb LLC Services.....................................G.....937 660-0115
 Englewood *(G-7241)*
Sand PROperties&landscaping..................G.....440 360-7386
 Westlake *(G-15781)*
Siler Excavation Services...........................E.....513 400-8628
 Milford *(G-10923)*
Stallion Oilfield Cnstr LLC...........................D.....330 868-2083
 Paris *(G-12282)*
▲ Stingray Pressure Pumping LLC.............D.....405 648-4177
 Belmont *(G-1249)*
Stratagraph Ne Inc......................................F.....740 373-3091
 Marietta *(G-9834)*

Superior Energy Group Ltd........................E.....216 282-4440
 Willoughby Hills *(G-16028)*
Superior Property Restoration....................F.....513 509-6849
 Cincinnati *(G-3433)*
T A W Inc..G.....330 339-1212
 New Philadelphia *(G-11527)*
Third Salvo Company..................................G.....740 818-9669
 Amesville *(G-472)*
TJ Oil & Gas Inc...G.....740 623-0190
 Fresno *(G-7826)*
Tk Gas Services Inc....................................E.....740 826-0303
 New Concord *(G-11434)*
Tkn Oilfield Services LLC............................F.....740 516-2583
 Marietta *(G-9837)*
Triple J Oilfield Services LLC.....................G.....740 609-3050
 Bridgeport *(G-1650)*
U S Weatherford L P...................................C.....330 746-2502
 Youngstown *(G-16463)*
United Chart Processors Inc......................G.....740 373-5801
 Marietta *(G-9840)*
Universal Well Services Inc........................D.....814 333-2656
 Millersburg *(G-11002)*
Vam Usa Llc...E.....330 742-3130
 Youngstown *(G-16467)*
Varco LP...E.....330 746-2922
 Youngstown *(G-16468)*
W Pole Contracting Inc................................F.....330 325-7177
 Ravenna *(G-12741)*
Washita Valley Enterprises Inc...................F.....330 510-1568
 Louisville *(G-9473)*
Well Service Group Inc...............................G.....330 308-0880
 New Philadelphia *(G-11532)*
◆ Westerman Inc..C.....800 338-8265
 Bremen *(G-1640)*
Wooster Abruzzi Company..........................E.....330 345-3968
 Wooster *(G-16183)*
Wrights Well Service LLC...........................G.....740 380-9602
 Logan *(G-9378)*
Wyoming Casing Service Inc.....................D.....330 479-8785
 Canton *(G-2270)*

14 MINING AND QUARRYING OF NONMETALLIC MINERALS, EXCEPT FUELS

1411 Dimension stone

▲ Designer Stone Co....................................G.....740 492-1300
 Port Washington *(G-12632)*
Gregory Stone Co Inc.................................G.....937 275-7455
 Dayton *(G-6363)*
Helmart Company Inc.................................G.....513 941-3095
 Cincinnati *(G-2992)*
Heritage Marble of Ohio Inc.......................F.....614 436-1464
 Columbus *(G-5427)*
Irg Operating LLC..E.....440 963-4008
 Vermilion *(G-14972)*
Marble Cliff Limestone Inc..........................G.....614 488-3030
 Hilliard *(G-8419)*
National Lime and Stone Co.......................E.....419 562-0771
 Bucyrus *(G-1863)*
North Hill Marble & Granite Co..................F.....330 253-2179
 Akron *(G-267)*
S E Johnson Companies Inc......................E.....419 893-8731
 Maumee *(G-10228)*
Solid Surface Concepts Inc........................E.....513 948-8677
 Cincinnati *(G-3401)*
▲ Stone Statements Incorporated................G.....513 489-7866
 Cincinnati *(G-3423)*
Stoneco Inc...E.....419 422-8854
 Findlay *(G-7569)*

14 MINING AND QUARRYING OF NONMETALLIC MINERALS, EXCEPT FUELS

Waterloo Coal Company Inc............................ D 740 286-0004
  Jackson *(G-8727)*
Wyandot Dolomite Inc................................... E 419 396-7641
  Carey *(G-2286)*

1422 Crushed and broken limestone

Allgeier & Son Inc.. F 513 574-3735
  Cincinnati *(G-2611)*
Ayers Limestone Quarry Inc........................... F 740 633-2958
  Martins Ferry *(G-9896)*
Beazer East Inc.. E 937 364-2311
  Hillsboro *(G-8455)*
Bluffton Stone Co... E 419 358-6941
  Bluffton *(G-1501)*
Carmeuse Lime Inc....................................... E 419 986-5200
  Bettsville *(G-1319)*
Carmeuse Lime Inc....................................... F 419 638-2511
  Millersville *(G-11016)*
Carmeuse Lime Inc....................................... F 419 986-2000
  Tiffin *(G-14080)*
Conag Inc.. F 419 394-8870
  Saint Marys *(G-12950)*
Crushed Stone Sandusky.............................. G 419 483-4390
  Castalia *(G-2321)*
Cumberland Limestone LLC........................... E 740 638-3942
  Cumberland *(G-6054)*
Custar Stone Co... E 419 669-4327
  Napoleon *(G-11311)*
Drummond Dolomite Inc................................ F 440 942-7000
  Mentor *(G-10449)*
Duff Quarry Inc... F 419 273-2518
  Forest *(G-7591)*
Duff Quarry Inc... F 937 686-2811
  Huntsville *(G-8622)*
Heidelberg Mtls Mdwest Agg Inc..................... G 419 983-2211
  Bloomville *(G-1355)*
Heidelberg Mtls Mdwest Agg Inc..................... F 419 882-0123
  Sylvania *(G-13997)*
Kellstone Inc... E 419 746-2396
  Kelleys Island *(G-8789)*
King Limestone Inc....................................... F 740 638-4500
  Cumberland *(G-6055)*
▲ Lang Stone Company Inc.......................... E 614 235-4099
  Columbus *(G-5520)*
Latham Limestone LLC................................. G 740 493-2677
  Latham *(G-9051)*
Marietta Martin Materials Inc......................... G 740 247-2211
  Racine *(G-12694)*
Marietta Martin Materials Inc......................... G 937 335-8313
  Troy *(G-14596)*
Martin Marietta Materials Inc......................... F 513 701-1120
  Mason *(G-10025)*
Martin Marietta Materials Inc......................... F 513 701-1140
  West Chester *(G-15461)*
Maysville Materials LLC................................ G 740 849-0474
  Mount Perry *(G-11250)*
National Lime and Stone Co.......................... E 419 562-0771
  Bucyrus *(G-1863)*
National Lime and Stone Co.......................... E 419 396-7671
  Carey *(G-2281)*
National Lime and Stone Co.......................... E 740 548-4206
  Delaware *(G-6740)*
National Lime and Stone Co.......................... F 419 423-3400
  Findlay *(G-7541)*
National Lime and Stone Co.......................... E 419 228-3434
  Lima *(G-9273)*
National Lime and Stone Co.......................... E 740 387-3485
  Marion *(G-9865)*
National Lime and Stone Co.......................... G 330 966-4830
  North Canton *(G-11748)*
National Lime and Stone Co.......................... G 419 657-6745
  Wapakoneta *(G-15128)*

Oglebay Norton Mar Svcs Co LLC.................. A 216 861-3300
  Cleveland *(G-4492)*
Ohio Asphaltic Limestone Corp...................... F 937 364-2191
  Hillsboro *(G-8462)*
◆ Omya Industries Inc................................. D 513 387-4600
  Mason *(G-10036)*
Onco Wva Inc... G 216 861-3300
  Cleveland *(G-4505)*
Ontex Inc... F 216 861-3300
  Cleveland *(G-4506)*
Oster Sand and Gravel Inc............................ G 330 833-2649
  Massillon *(G-10133)*
Piqua Materials Inc....................................... D 937 773-4824
  Piqua *(G-12547)*
Piqua Materials Inc....................................... E 513 771-0820
  Cincinnati *(G-3258)*
R W Sidley Incorporated............................... F 440 352-9343
  Painesville *(G-12261)*
Ridge Township Stone Quarry....................... G 419 968-2222
  Van Wert *(G-14925)*
Sergeant Stone Inc....................................... G 740 452-7434
  Corning *(G-5959)*
Sharon Stone Inc.. G 740 732-7100
  Caldwell *(G-1913)*
Shelly Company.. G 216 688-0684
  Cleveland *(G-4691)*
Shelly Materials Inc....................................... E 740 666-5841
  Ostrander *(G-12176)*
Shelly Materials Inc....................................... E 740 246-6315
  Toledo *(G-14471)*
Shelly Materials Inc....................................... D 740 246-6315
  Thornville *(G-14072)*
Stoneco Inc.. E 419 893-7645
  Maumee *(G-10236)*
Stoneco Inc.. E 419 393-2555
  Oakwood *(G-12033)*
Stoneco Inc.. G 419 686-3311
  Portage *(G-12637)*
The National Lime and Stone Company........ E 419 422-4341
  Findlay *(G-7575)*
Uniontown Stone... G 740 968-4313
  Flushing *(G-7588)*
Wagner Quarries Company........................... E 419 625-8141
  Sandusky *(G-13104)*
Wyandot Dolomite Inc.................................. E 419 396-7641
  Carey *(G-2286)*

1423 Crushed and broken granite

Bradley Stone Industries LLC....................... F 440 519-3277
  Solon *(G-13323)*
Martin Marietta Materials Inc......................... G 513 701-1140
  West Chester *(G-15461)*
The National Lime and Stone Company........ E 419 422-4341
  Findlay *(G-7575)*

1429 Crushed and broken stone, nec

Great Lakes Crushing Ltd............................. D 440 944-5500
  Wickliffe *(G-15833)*
M & B Asphalt Company Inc......................... F 419 992-4235
  Tiffin *(G-14091)*
Medina Supply Company............................... E 330 364-4411
  Medina *(G-10351)*
Sands Hill Mining LLC.................................. G 740 384-4211
  Gallipolis *(G-7901)*

1442 Construction sand and gravel

Alden Sand & Gravel Co Inc......................... G 330 928-3249
  Cuyahoga Falls *(G-6061)*
Arden J Neer Sr... F 937 585-6733
  Bellefontaine *(G-1200)*
Beck Sand & Gravel Inc............................... G 330 626-3863
  Ravenna *(G-12707)*

Bonsal American Inc..................................... F 513 398-7300
  Cincinnati *(G-2677)*
Broadway Sand and Gravel LLC.................... G 937 853-5555
  Dayton *(G-6237)*
C F Poeppelman Inc..................................... E 937 448-2191
  Bradford *(G-1600)*
Carl E Oeder Sons Sand & Grav................... F 513 494-1555
  Lebanon *(G-9066)*
Central Allied Enterprises Inc........................ E 330 477-6751
  Canton *(G-2071)*
Central Ready Mix LLC................................. E 513 402-5001
  Cincinnati *(G-2717)*
Constrction Aggrgtes Corp Mich................... E 616 842-7900
  Independence *(G-8659)*
▼ Covia Solutions Inc................................. G 404 214-3200
  Independence *(G-8661)*
D H Bowman & Sons Inc.............................. G 419 886-2711
  Bellville *(G-1241)*
Demilta Sand and Gravel Inc......................... E 440 942-2015
  Willoughby *(G-13907)*
Demmy Sand and Gravel LLC....................... E
  Springfield *(G-13554)*
Enon Sand and Gravel LLC.......................... G 513 771-0820
  Cincinnati *(G-2873)*
Fisher Sand & Gravel Inc.............................. G 330 745-9239
  Norton *(G-11943)*
Fleming Construction Co............................... F 740 494-2177
  Prospect *(G-12689)*
Foundry Sand Service LLC........................... F 330 823-6152
  Sebring *(G-13120)*
Fouremans Sand & Gravel Inc...................... G 937 547-1005
  Greenville *(G-8045)*
Gravel Doctor of Ohio................................... G 844 472-8353
  Millersport *(G-11011)*
Hanson Aggregates East............................... G 513 353-1100
  Cleves *(G-4953)*
Hilltop Basic Resources Inc.......................... D 513 621-1500
  Cincinnati *(G-3000)*
Hilltop Basic Resources Inc.......................... F 937 859-3616
  Miamisburg *(G-10646)*
Hilltop Basic Resources Inc.......................... F 937 882-6357
  Springfield *(G-13576)*
Hocking Valley Concrete Inc......................... F 740 385-2165
  Logan *(G-9365)*
Holmes Redimix Inc...................................... E 330 674-0865
  Holmesville *(G-8545)*
Holmes Supply Corp..................................... G 330 279-2634
  Holmesville *(G-8547)*
Hugo Sand Company.................................... G 216 570-1212
  Kent *(G-8818)*
J P Sand & Gravel Company........................ F 614 497-0083
  Lockbourne *(G-9337)*
James Bunnell Inc... F 513 353-1100
  Cleves *(G-4955)*
John L Garber Materials Corp....................... F 419 884-1567
  Mansfield *(G-9673)*
▲ John R Jurgensen Co............................... B 513 771-0820
  Cincinnati *(G-3044)*
Kenmore Construction Co Inc....................... D 330 832-8888
  Massillon *(G-10116)*
Kipps Gravel Company Inc........................... G 513 732-1024
  Kingston *(G-8931)*
Kirby and Sons Inc....................................... F 419 927-2260
  Upper Sandusky *(G-14813)*
Lake Erie Aggregates Inc.............................. G 419 541-0130
  Huron *(G-8636)*
Lakeside Sand & Gravel Inc......................... E 330 274-2569
  Mantua *(G-9738)*
Martin Marietta Materials Inc......................... G 513 701-1140
  West Chester *(G-15461)*
Masons Sand and Gravel Co........................ G 614 491-3611
  Obetz *(G-12062)*

Massillon Materials Inc .... F 330 837-4767
  Dalton (G-6136)
McClelland Inc .... E 740 452-3036
  Zanesville (G-16544)
Mechanicsburg Sand & Gravel ..... F 937 834-2606
  Mechanicsburg (G-10286)
Medina Supply Company .... E 330 723-3681
  Medina (G-10352)
Morrow Gravel Company Inc .... E 513 771-0820
  Cincinnati (G-3175)
National Lime and Stone Co .... E 419 396-7671
  Carey (G-2281)
National Lime and Stone Co .... F 614 497-0083
  Lockbourne (G-9340)
Nelson Sand & Gravel Inc .... F 440 224-0198
  Kingsville (G-8933)
Ohio Valley Sand LLC .... G 740 661-4240
  New Philadelphia (G-11521)
Ohio Valley Sand LLC .... G 330 440-6495
  Newcomerstown (G-11649)
Oscar Brugmann Sand & Gravel ... E 330 274-8224
  Mantua (G-9742)
Oster Sand and Gravel Inc .... G 330 874-3322
  Bolivar (G-1531)
Oster Sand and Gravel Inc .... G 330 833-2649
  Massillon (G-10133)
Oster Sand and Gravel Inc .... G 330 494-5472
  Canton (G-2189)
Parry Co .... G 740 884-4893
  Chillicothe (G-2523)
Phillips Companies .... E 937 426-5461
  Beavercreek Township (G-1089)
Phillips Ready Mix Co .... E 937 426-5151
  Beavercreek Township (G-1090)
Phoenix Asphalt Company Inc ...... G 330 339-4935
  Magnolia (G-9597)
Portable Crushing LLC .... F 330 618-5251
  New Franklin (G-11442)
Prairie Lane Corporation .... G 330 262-3322
  Wooster (G-16159)
Putnam Aggregates Co .... G 419 523-6004
  Ottawa (G-12189)
R W Sidley Incorporated .... G 440 564-2221
  Newbury (G-11635)
Rjw Trucking Company Ltd .... E 740 363-5343
  Delaware (G-6746)
S & S Aggregates Inc .... B 419 938-5604
  Perrysville (G-12448)
S & S Aggregates Inc .... F 740 453-0721
  Zanesville (G-16561)
Sand Rock Enterprises Inc .... F 740 407-2735
  Glenford (G-7979)
Seville Sand & Gravel Inc .... E 330 948-0168
  Strongsville (G-13877)
Sharps Valet Parking Svc Inc .... G 574 223-5230
  Cincinnati (G-3386)
Shelly and Sands Inc .... F 740 453-0721
  Zanesville (G-16562)
Shelly Materials Inc .... F 740 247-2311
  Racine (G-12695)
Shelly Materials Inc .... D 740 246-6315
  Thornville (G-14072)
Smith Concrete Co .... E 740 373-7441
  Dover (G-6843)
Stafford Gravel Inc .... F 419 298-2440
  Edgerton (G-7081)
Stansley Mineral Resources Inc ... E 419 843-2813
  Sylvania (G-14015)
Stocker Concrete Company .... F 740 254-4626
  Gnadenhutten (G-7989)
Stocker Sand & Gravel Co .... F 740 254-4635
  Gnadenhutten (G-7990)

Streamside Materials Llc .... G 419 423-1290
  Findlay (G-7570)
The National Lime and Stone Company. E 419 422-4341
  Findlay (G-7575)
The Olen Corporation .... D 614 491-1515
  Columbus (G-5823)
Tiger Sand & Gravel LLC .... F 330 833-6325
  Massillon (G-10150)
Tri County Concrete Inc .... F 330 425-4464
  Twinsburg (G-14747)
Tuffco Sand and Gravel Inc .... G 614 873-3977
  Plain City (G-12596)
W&W Rock Sand and Gravel .... G 513 266-3708
  Williamsburg (G-15867)
Ward Construction Co .... F 419 943-2450
  Leipsic (G-9142)
Watson Gravel Inc .... G 513 422-3781
  Middletown (G-10870)
Watson Gravel Inc .... E 513 863-0070
  Hamilton (G-8258)
Wayne Concrete Company LLC ... F 937 545-9919
  Medway (G-10400)
Weber Sand & Gravel Inc .... G 419 636-7920
  Bryan (G-1844)
Weber Sand & Gravel Inc .... G 419 298-2388
  Edgerton (G-7083)
Welch Holdings Inc .... E 513 353-3220
  Cincinnati (G-3512)
Welch Sand & Gravel Inc .... F 513 353-3220
  Cincinnati (G-3513)
White Gravel Mines Productions ... G 740 776-0510
  Portsmouth (G-12660)
Wysong Gravel Co Inc .... F 937 452-1523
  Camden (G-1965)
Wysong Gravel Co Inc .... G 937 839-5497
  West Alexandria (G-15348)
Wysong Gravel Co Inc .... F 937 456-4539
  West Alexandria (G-15347)
X L Sand and Gravel Co .... E 330 426-9876
  Negley (G-11355)
Youngs Sand & Gravel Co Inc ...... F 419 994-3040
  Loudonville (G-9454)

1446 Industrial sand

▼ CED Process Minerals Inc .... F 330 666-5500
  Akron (G-104)
◆ Covia Holdings LLC .... D 800 255-7263
  Independence (G-8660)
Farsight Management Inc .... F 330 602-8338
  Dover (G-6824)
Wedron Silica LLC .... D 815 433-2449
  Independence (G-8690)

1459 Clay and related minerals, nec

Hilltop Glass & Mirror LLC .... G 513 931-3688
  Cincinnati (G-3002)
L & M Mineral Co .... G 330 852-3696
  Sugarcreek (G-13927)
Waterloo Coal Company Inc .... D 740 286-0004
  Jackson (G-8727)

1479 Chemical and fertilizer mining

Glf International Inc .... F 216 621-6901
  Cleveland (G-4127)

1481 Nonmetallic mineral services

Barr Engineering Incorporated ..... E 614 714-0299
  Columbus (G-5175)
▲ M G Q Inc .... E 419 992-4236
  Tiffin (G-14092)
Robin Industries Inc .... F 330 893-3501
  Berlin (G-1308)

Stoepfel Drilling Co .... G 419 532-3307
  Ottawa (G-12194)
Tresslers Plumbing LLC .... G 419 784-2142
  Defiance (G-6697)

1499 Miscellaneous nonmetallic mining

Graftech Holdings Inc .... D 216 676-2000
  Independence (G-8669)
Massillon Metaphysics .... G 330 837-1653
  Massillon (G-10123)
The National Lime and Stone Company. E 419 422-4341
  Findlay (G-7575)

15 CONSTRUCTION - GENERAL CONTRACTORS & OPERATIVE BUILDERS

1521 Single-family housing construction

Acme Home Improvement Co Inc .. F 614 252-2129
  Columbus (G-5098)
Al Yoder Construction Co .... G 330 359-5726
  Millersburg (G-10939)
Artisan Constructors LLC .... E 216 800-7641
  Cleveland (G-3680)
Building Concepts Inc .... F 419 298-2371
  Edgerton (G-7072)
C-Link Enterprises LLC .... F 937 222-2829
  Dayton (G-6244)
Cardinal Builders Inc .... E 614 237-1000
  Columbus (G-5236)
Cirigliano Enterprises LLC .... G 567 525-4571
  Findlay (G-7492)
Custom Blind Corporation .... F 937 643-2907
  Dayton (G-6270)
Fence One Inc .... F 216 441-2600
  Cleveland (G-4056)
Gillard Construction Inc .... F 740 376-9744
  Marietta (G-9795)
Golden Angle Archtctral Group .... G 614 531-7932
  Columbus (G-5406)
Gws Levi Up Home Solutions LLC .. E 419 667-6041
  Toledo (G-14305)
▲ Hoge Lumber Company .... E 419 753-2263
  New Knoxville (G-11447)
Ingle-Barr Inc .... D 740 702-6117
  Chillicothe (G-2513)
JC Electric Llc .... F 330 760-2915
  Garrettsville (G-7917)
Knapke Cabinets Inc .... E 937 335-8383
  Troy (G-14592)
Manufactured Housing Entps Inc .. E 419 636-4511
  Bryan (G-1827)
Ohio Luxury Bulders LLC .... G 330 881-0073
  Austintown (G-753)
Patio Enclosures .... F 513 733-4646
  Cincinnati (G-3236)
Plumb Builders Inc .... F 937 293-1111
  Dayton (G-6508)
R L Waller Construction Inc .... F 740 772-6185
  Chillicothe (G-2531)
RE Connors Construction Ltd ...... G 740 644-0261
  Thornville (G-14068)
Ssr Community Dev Group LLC ... G 216 466-2674
  Cleveland (G-4724)
Superior Property Restoration ..... F 513 509-6849
  Cincinnati (G-3433)
The Galehouse Companies Inc .... E 330 658-2023
  Doylestown (G-6854)
Third Salvo Company .... G 740 818-9669
  Amesville (G-472)

15 CONSTRUCTION - GENERAL CONTRACTORS & OPERATIVE BUILDERS

Thomas J Weaver Inc............................. F 740 622-2040
  Coshocton *(G-5998)*

Van Dyke Custom Iron Inc..................... G 614 860-9300
  Pickerington *(G-12472)*

Volpe Millwork Inc................................ G 216 581-0200
  Cleveland *(G-4882)*

Waxco International Inc......................... F 937 746-4845
  Miamisburg *(G-10701)*

1522 Residential construction, nec

American Egle Prprty Prsrvtion............... G 855 440-6938
  North Ridgeville *(G-11828)*

Artisan Constructors LLC....................... E 216 800-7641
  Cleveland *(G-3680)*

Bison Builders LLC................................ F 614 636-0365
  Columbus *(G-5191)*

Cardinal Builders Inc............................. E 614 237-1000
  Columbus *(G-5236)*

Dunn Industrial Services........................ G 513 738-4999
  Hamilton *(G-8200)*

1531 Operative builders

Artisan Constructors LLC....................... E 216 800-7641
  Cleveland *(G-3680)*

Commercial Cnstr Group LLC................. G 513 722-1357
  Milford *(G-10902)*

▲ P R Machine Works Inc...................... D 419 529-5748
  Ontario *(G-12094)*

Superior Structures Inc.......................... F 513 942-5954
  Harrison *(G-8295)*

The Galehouse Companies Inc................ E 330 658-2023
  Doylestown *(G-6854)*

Universal Dsign Fbrication LLC............... F 419 202-5269
  Sandusky *(G-13101)*

▲ Urban Industries of Ohio Inc................ E 419 468-3578
  Galion *(G-7886)*

1541 Industrial buildings and warehouses

Agridry LLC.. F 419 459-4399
  Edon *(G-7085)*

Atlantic Welding LLC............................. F 937 570-5094
  Piqua *(G-12505)*

Baker-Shindler Contracting Co................ E 419 782-5080
  Defiance *(G-6671)*

◆ Enerfab LLC...................................... B 513 641-0500
  Cincinnati *(G-2872)*

Falls Mtal Fbrctors Indus Svcs................. F 330 253-7181
  Akron *(G-148)*

Fleming Construction Co........................ F 740 494-2177
  Prospect *(G-12689)*

Halman Inc... F
  Ashtabula *(G-637)*

Hines Builders Inc................................. F 937 335-4586
  Troy *(G-14577)*

Ingle-Barr Inc....................................... D 740 702-6117
  Chillicothe *(G-2513)*

Iron Bean Inc.. F 518 641-9917
  Perrysburg *(G-12393)*

Jim Nier Construction Inc....................... E 740 289-3925
  Piketon *(G-12477)*

Milos Whole World Gourmet LLC............ G 740 589-6456
  Nelsonville *(G-11358)*

Pawnee Maintenance Inc........................ F 740 373-6861
  Marietta *(G-9815)*

R G Smith Company.............................. D 330 456-3415
  Canton *(G-2207)*

Stamm Contracting Company Inc............ E 330 274-8230
  Mantua *(G-9743)*

Thomas J Weaver Inc............................. F 740 622-2040
  Coshocton *(G-5998)*

▲ Universal Fabg Cnstr Svcs Inc.............. E 614 274-1128
  Columbus *(G-5845)*

1542 Nonresidential construction, nec

Aecom Energy & Cnstr Inc..................... G 419 698-6277
  Oregon *(G-12101)*

Baker-Shindler Contracting Co................ E 419 782-5080
  Defiance *(G-6671)*

Beachy Barns Ltd................................. F 614 873-4193
  Plain City *(G-12565)*

Bent Wood Solutions LLC...................... G 330 674-1454
  Millersburg *(G-10943)*

Brenmar Construction Inc...................... D 740 286-2151
  Jackson *(G-8711)*

Bud Corp.. G 740 967-9992
  Johnstown *(G-8771)*

Commercial Cnstr Group LLC................. G 513 722-1357
  Milford *(G-10902)*

Facility Service Pros LLC....................... G 419 577-6123
  Collins *(G-5004)*

Falls Mtal Fbrctors Indus Svcs................. F 330 253-7181
  Akron *(G-148)*

Fleming Construction Co........................ F 740 494-2177
  Prospect *(G-12689)*

Ingle-Barr Inc....................................... D 740 702-6117
  Chillicothe *(G-2513)*

Jim Nier Construction Inc....................... E 740 289-3925
  Piketon *(G-12477)*

Kellys Wldg & Fabrication Ltd................ G 440 593-6040
  Conneaut *(G-5922)*

Ludy Greenhouse Mfg Corp.................... D 800 255-5839
  New Madison *(G-11475)*

MGM Construction Inc........................... F 440 234-7660
  Berea *(G-1288)*

Rebsco Inc... F 937 548-2246
  Greenville *(G-8057)*

◆ Rough Brothers Mfg Inc...................... D 513 242-0310
  Cincinnati *(G-3352)*

Scs Construction Services Inc................. E 513 929-0260
  Cincinnati *(G-3371)*

Shelly and Sands Inc............................. F 740 859-2104
  Rayland *(G-12745)*

Stamm Contracting Company Inc............ E 330 274-8230
  Mantua *(G-9743)*

The Galehouse Companies Inc................ E 330 658-2023
  Doylestown *(G-6854)*

Third Salvo Company............................ G 740 818-9669
  Amesville *(G-472)*

Thomas Cabinet Shop Inc...................... F 937 847-8239
  Dayton *(G-6621)*

Thomas J Weaver Inc............................. F 740 622-2040
  Coshocton *(G-5998)*

Youngstown Shade & Alum LLC............. G 330 782-2373
  Youngstown *(G-16487)*

16 HEAMY CONSTRUCTION, EXCEPT BUILDING CONSTRUCTION, CONTRACTOR

1611 Highway and street construction

A & A Safety Inc.................................. F 937 567-9781
  Beavercreek *(G-1068)*

A & A Safety Inc.................................. E 513 943-6100
  Amelia *(G-447)*

◆ Barrett Paving Materials Inc................ E 973 533-1001
  Hamilton *(G-8183)*

Central Allied Enterprises Inc................. E 330 477-6751
  Canton *(G-2071)*

Gerken Materials Inc............................. E 419 533-2421
  Napoleon *(G-11315)*

Great Lakes Crushing Ltd...................... D 440 944-5500
  Wickliffe *(G-15833)*

Hull Ready Mix Concrete Inc.................. F 419 625-8070
  Sandusky *(G-13064)*

Image Pavement Maintenance................ F 937 833-9200
  Brookville *(G-1739)*

▲ John R Jurgensen Co......................... B 513 771-0820
  Cincinnati *(G-3044)*

Kenmore Construction Co Inc................. D 330 832-8888
  Massillon *(G-10116)*

Koski Construction Co........................... G 440 997-5337
  Ashtabula *(G-644)*

M & B Asphalt Company Inc................... F 419 992-4235
  Tiffin *(G-14091)*

Morlock Asphalt Ltd.............................. F 419 686-4601
  Portage *(G-12635)*

Nes Corp.. E 440 834-0438
  Hiram *(G-8487)*

Paul Peterson Company......................... F 614 486-4375
  Columbus *(G-5660)*

S E Johnson Companies Inc................... E 419 893-8731
  Maumee *(G-10228)*

Security Fence Group Inc...................... E 513 681-3700
  Cincinnati *(G-3374)*

Seneca Petroleum Co Inc....................... F 419 691-3581
  Toledo *(G-14467)*

Shelly Materials Inc............................... E 740 666-5841
  Ostrander *(G-12176)*

Smalls Asphalt Paving Inc..................... F 740 427-4096
  Gambier *(G-7908)*

▲ Terminal Ready-Mix Inc..................... E 440 288-0181
  Lorain *(G-9441)*

Traffic Detectors & Signs Inc.................. G 330 707-9060
  Youngstown *(G-16457)*

Valley Asphalt Corporation.................... E 513 771-0820
  Cincinnati *(G-3486)*

W G Lockhart Construction Co................ E 330 745-6520
  Akron *(G-372)*

Ward Construction Co........................... F 419 943-2450
  Leipsic *(G-9142)*

Wilson Blacktop Corp............................ F 740 635-3566
  Martins Ferry *(G-9901)*

Wyandot Dolomite Inc........................... E 419 396-7641
  Carey *(G-2286)*

1622 Bridge, tunnel, and elevated highway

▼ Ohio Bridge Corporation..................... C 740 432-6334
  Cambridge *(G-1945)*

S E Johnson Companies Inc................... E 419 893-8731
  Maumee *(G-10228)*

1623 Water, sewer, and utility lines

Bi-Con Services Inc............................... B 740 685-2542
  Derwent *(G-6798)*

Bob Lanes Welding Inc.......................... F 740 373-3567
  Marietta *(G-9779)*

Don Wartko Construction Co.................. D 330 673-5252
  Kent *(G-8810)*

▼ Eastern Automated Piping.................. G 740 535-8184
  Mingo Junction *(G-11044)*

Fishel Company.................................... C 614 850-4400
  Columbus *(G-5377)*

Fleming Construction Co........................ F 740 494-2177
  Prospect *(G-12689)*

Global Energy Partners LLC................... E 419 756-8027
  Mansfield *(G-9660)*

Great Lakes Crushing Ltd...................... D 440 944-5500
  Wickliffe *(G-15833)*

Great Lakes Telcom Ltd......................... E 330 629-8848
  Youngstown *(G-16373)*

Groundhogs 2000 LLC........................... G 440 653-1647
  Bedford *(G-1122)*

Mt Pleasant Blacktopping Inc................. G 513 874-3777
  Fairfield *(G-7385)*

SIC SECTION

17 CONSTRUCTION - SPECIAL TRADE CONTRACTORS

Neptune Equipment Company............... E 513 851-8008
  Cincinnati *(G-3186)*
Parallel Technologies Inc...................... D 614 798-9700
  Dublin *(G-6920)*
Steelial Wldg Met Fbrction Inc................ E 740 669-5300
  Vinton *(G-15012)*
Sterling Process Equipmen..................... E 614 868-5151
  Columbus *(G-5794)*

1629 Heavy construction, nec

Advanced Indus Machining Inc............... F 614 596-4183
  Powell *(G-12662)*
Artesian of Pioneer Inc........................... F 419 737-2352
  Pioneer *(G-12490)*
Atlantic Welding LLC.............................. F 937 570-5094
  Piqua *(G-12505)*
◆ Babcock & Wilcox Company................A 330 753-4511
  Akron *(G-73)*
Biedenbach Logging.............................. G 740 732-6477
  Sarahsville *(G-13105)*
Breaker Technology Inc.......................... F 440 248-7168
  Solon *(G-13324)*
C & L Erectors & Riggers Inc................. F 740 332-7185
  Laurelville *(G-9054)*
◆ Enerfab LLC..B 513 641-0500
  Cincinnati *(G-2872)*
Fine Line Excvtg & Ldscpg LLC............. G 330 541-0590
  Ravenna *(G-12715)*
Great Lakes Crushing Ltd....................... D 440 944-5500
  Wickliffe *(G-15833)*
▼ Htec Systems Inc.................................. F 937 438-3010
  Dayton *(G-6376)*
Image Pavement Maintenance................ F 937 833-9200
  Brookville *(G-1739)*
Kars Ohio LLC....................................... G 614 655-1099
  Pataskala *(G-12300)*
Miller Logging Inc................................... F 330 279-4721
  Holmesville *(G-8550)*
Siemens Energy Inc................................ E 740 393-8897
  Mount Vernon *(G-11295)*
Tri-America Contractors Inc................... E 740 574-0148
  Wheelersburg *(G-15810)*
Valley Mining Inc.................................... C 740 922-3942
  Dennison *(G-6797)*

17 CONSTRUCTION - SPECIAL TRADE CONTRACTORS

1711 Plumbing, heating, air-conditioning

A A S Amels Sheet Meta L Inc................ F 330 793-9326
  Youngstown *(G-16297)*
Accurate Mechanical Inc........................ D 740 681-1332
  Lancaster *(G-8985)*
Air-Tech Mechanical Inc......................... F 419 292-0074
  Toledo *(G-14180)*
▲ Alan Manufacturing Inc......................... E 330 262-1555
  Wooster *(G-16099)*
Approved Plumbing Co............................ F 216 663-5063
  Cleveland *(G-3671)*
Asidaco LLC.. G 800 204-1544
  Dayton *(G-6215)*
◆ Babcock & Wilcox Company................A 330 753-4511
  Akron *(G-73)*
Budde Sheet Metal Works Inc................ E 937 224-0868
  Dayton *(G-6241)*
◆ Chick Master Incubator Company.......D 330 722-5591
  Medina *(G-10308)*
Cincinnati Air Conditioning Co................ D 513 721-5422
  Cincinnati *(G-2739)*
Climate Pros LLC................................... D 216 881-5200
  Cleveland *(G-3878)*
Climate Pros LLC................................... D 330 744-2732
  Youngstown *(G-16340)*
Columbus Heating & Vent Co................. C 614 274-1177
  Columbus *(G-5265)*
Complete Mechanical Svcs LLC............. D 513 489-3080
  Blue Ash *(G-1382)*
Debra-Kuempel Inc................................. D 513 271-6500
  Cincinnati *(G-2822)*
E & M Liberty Welding Inc...................... G 330 866-2338
  Waynesburg *(G-15294)*
▼ Eastern Automated Piping..................... G 740 535-8184
  Mingo Junction *(G-11044)*
◆ Enerfab LLC..B 513 641-0500
  Cincinnati *(G-2872)*
Fellhauer Mechanical Systems............... E 419 734-3674
  Port Clinton *(G-12617)*
Franck and Fric Incorporated................. D 216 524-4451
  Cleveland *(G-4090)*
GM Mechanical Inc................................. D 937 473-3006
  Covington *(G-6024)*
Greer & Whitehead Cnstr Inc.................. G 513 202-1757
  Harrison *(G-8277)*
Grid Industrial Heating Inc...................... G 330 332-9931
  Salem *(G-12998)*
Gundlach Sheet Metal Works Inc........... E 419 626-4525
  Sandusky *(G-13062)*
Hess Advanced Solutions Llc................. G 937 829-4794
  Dayton *(G-6368)*
Holgate Metal Fab Inc............................. F 419 599-2000
  Napoleon *(G-11319)*
Hvac Inc.. F 330 343-5511
  Dover *(G-6827)*
Industrial Power Systems Inc................. B 419 531-3121
  Rossford *(G-12867)*
Integrated Development & Mfg............... F 440 247-5100
  Chagrin Falls *(G-2380)*
Ioppolo Concrete Corporation................ E 440 439-6606
  Bedford *(G-1130)*
J D Indoor Comfort Inc........................... F 440 949-8758
  Sheffield Village *(G-13184)*
Jacobs Mechanical Co............................ C 513 681-6800
  Cincinnati *(G-3033)*
Jfdb Ltd.. C 513 870-0601
  Cincinnati *(G-3042)*
Kauffman Lumber & Supply.................... F 330 893-9186
  Millersburg *(G-10971)*
◆ Kinetics Noise Control Inc.....................C 614 889-0480
  Dublin *(G-6905)*
Kirk Williams Company Inc..................... D 614 875-9023
  Grove City *(G-8100)*
▲ Langdon Inc.. E 513 733-5955
  Cincinnati *(G-3095)*
Lochard Inc... D 937 492-8811
  Sidney *(G-13261)*
Lowry Furnace Co Inc............................. G 330 745-4822
  Akron *(G-224)*
Mack Industries...................................... E 419 353-7081
  Bowling Green *(G-1572)*
Nbw Inc... E 216 377-1700
  Cleveland *(G-4442)*
Northeastern Rfrgn Corp........................ E 440 942-7676
  Willoughby *(G-15960)*
PB Fbrction Mech Contrs Corp............... E 419 478-4869
  Toledo *(G-14429)*
Personal Plumber Service Corp.............. F 440 324-4321
  Elyria *(G-7195)*
▲ Pioneer Pipe Inc..................................... A 740 376-2400
  Marietta *(G-9817)*
Professional Supply Inc.......................... F 419 332-7373
  Fremont *(G-7803)*
Prout Boiler Htg & Wldg Inc.................... E 330 744-0293
  Youngstown *(G-16423)*
Schweizer Dipple Inc.............................. D 440 786-8090
  Cleveland *(G-4676)*
Sexton Industrial Inc............................... C 513 530-5555
  West Chester *(G-15584)*
Temperature Controls Co Inc.................. F 330 773-6633
  New Franklin *(G-11444)*
Terrasmart LLC....................................... E 239 362-0211
  Columbus *(G-5818)*
The Hattenbach Company....................... D 216 881-5200
  Cleveland *(G-4785)*
United Group Services Inc...................... C 800 633-9690
  West Chester *(G-15601)*
Vector Mechanical LLC........................... G 216 337-4042
  Cleveland *(G-4863)*
Vintage Automotive Elc Inc..................... F 419 472-9349
  Toledo *(G-14520)*
Weather King Heating & AC.................... G 330 908-0281
  Northfield *(G-11914)*
Whempys Corp.. G 614 888-6670
  Worthington *(G-16218)*
Young Regulator Company Inc............... E 440 232-9452
  Bedford *(G-1161)*

1721 Painting and paper hanging

A & A Safety Inc..................................... F 937 567-9781
  Beavercreek *(G-1068)*
A & A Safety Inc..................................... E 513 943-6100
  Amelia *(G-447)*
A1 Industrial Painting Inc....................... E 330 750-9441
  Youngstown *(G-16298)*
All Ohio Companies Inc.......................... F 216 420-9274
  Cleveland *(G-3631)*
Banks Manufacturing Company.............. F 440 458-8661
  Grafton *(G-7997)*
Industrial Mill Maintenance.................... E 330 746-1155
  Youngstown *(G-16379)*
Js Fabrications Inc................................. G 419 333-0323
  Fremont *(G-7790)*
Kars Ohio LLC.. G 614 655-1099
  Pataskala *(G-12300)*
Mes Painting and Graphics.................... G 614 496-1696
  Westerville *(G-15714)*
Mes Painting and Graphics Ltd.............. E 614 496-1696
  Westerville *(G-15715)*
Napoleon Machine LLC.......................... E 419 591-7010
  Napoleon *(G-11327)*
Ohio Building Restoration Inc................. E 419 244-7372
  Toledo *(G-14408)*
Premier Coatings Ltd.............................. F 513 942-1070
  West Chester *(G-15484)*
Procoat Painting Inc............................... G 513 735-2500
  Batavia *(G-945)*
Semper Quality Industry Inc................... G 440 352-8111
  Mentor *(G-10552)*
Ssr Community Dev Group LLC............. G 216 466-2674
  Cleveland *(G-4724)*

1731 Electrical work

ARC Elec.. G 440 774-2800
  Wellington *(G-15303)*
Asg Division Jergens Inc........................ E 888 486-6163
  Cleveland *(G-3688)*
Asidaco LLC.. G 800 204-1544
  Dayton *(G-6215)*
Atlas Industrial Contrs LLC.................... B 614 841-4500
  Columbus *(G-5163)*
Computer Enterprise Inc......................... G 216 228-7156
  Lakewood *(G-8972)*
Controls Inc.. E 330 239-4345
  Medina *(G-10312)*
Crase Communications Inc.................... F 419 468-1173
  Galion *(G-7869)*

17 CONSTRUCTION - SPECIAL TRADE CONTRACTORS

D & E Electric Inc .... G 513 738-1172
  Okeana (G-12067)
D & J Electric Motor Repair Co .... F 330 336-4343
  Wadsworth (G-15025)
▲ Darana Hybrid Inc .... D 513 860-4490
  Hamilton (G-8199)
◆ Df Supply Inc .... E 330 650-9226
  Twinsburg (G-14650)
Dss Installations Ltd .... F 513 761-7000
  Cincinnati (G-2842)
Fishel Company .... C 614 850-4400
  Columbus (G-5377)
▲ Gatesair Inc .... D 513 459-3400
  Mason (G-9995)
Graham Electric .... F 614 231-8500
  Columbus (G-5409)
Grand Archt Etrnl Eye 314 LLC .... F 800 377-8147
  Cleveland (G-4138)
Great Lakes Telcom Ltd .... G 330 629-8848
  Youngstown (G-16373)
Helios Quartz America Inc .... G 419 882-3377
  Sylvania (G-13999)
Hess Advanced Solutions Llc .... G 937 829-4794
  Dayton (G-6368)
Importers Direct LLC .... F 330 436-3260
  Akron (G-189)
Industrial Electronic Service .... F 937 746-9750
  Carlisle (G-2288)
Industrial Power Systems Inc .... B 419 531-3121
  Rossford (G-12867)
▲ Instrmntation Ctrl Systems Inc .... E 513 662-2600
  Cincinnati (G-3024)
JC Electric Llc .... F 330 760-2915
  Garrettsville (G-7917)
Jeff Bonham Electric Inc .... F 937 233-7662
  Dayton (G-6388)
▲ Jobap Assembly Inc .... F 440 632-5393
  Middlefield (G-10760)
Legrand North America LLC .... B 937 224-0639
  Dayton (G-6403)
Magnum Computers Inc .... F 216 781-1757
  Cleveland (G-4351)
Mikes Transm & Auto Svc LLC .... F 330 799-8266
  Youngstown (G-16401)
Mirus Adapted Tech LLC .... E 614 402-4585
  Dublin (G-6910)
▲ P S C Inc .... G 216 531-3375
  Cleveland (G-4517)
Radon Eliminator LLC .... F 330 844-0703
  North Canton (G-11755)
Safe-Grain Inc .... G 513 398-2500
  Loveland (G-9503)
Security Fence Group Inc .... E 513 681-3700
  Cincinnati (G-3374)
Siemens Energy Inc .... E 740 393-8897
  Mount Vernon (G-11295)
Tcb Automation LLC .... F 330 556-6444
  Dover (G-6847)
Tekworx LLC .... F 513 533-4711
  Blue Ash (G-1479)
The Wagner-Smith Company .... B 866 338-0398
  Moraine (G-11214)
Town Cntry Technical Svcs Inc .... F 614 866-7700
  Reynoldsburg (G-12775)
Valley Electric Company .... G 419 332-6405
  Fremont (G-7818)
Vertiv Group Corporation .... F 440 460-3600
  Cleveland (G-4864)
Waibel Electric Co Inc .... F 740 964-2956
  Etna (G-7253)
▲ Weidmann Electrical Tech Inc .... G 937 508-2112
  Cleveland (G-4900)

1741 Masonry and other stonework

Albert Freytag Inc .... E 419 628-2018
  Minster (G-11047)
G L Pierce Inc .... G 513 772-7202
  Cincinnati (G-2927)
North Central Con Designs Inc .... G 419 606-1908
  Wooster (G-16155)
▲ North Central Insulation Inc .... F 419 886-2030
  Bellville (G-1246)
North Hill Marble & Granite Co .... F 330 253-2179
  Akron (G-267)
Ohio Building Restoration Inc .... E 419 244-7372
  Toledo (G-14408)
Pioneer Cldding Glzing Systems .... E 216 816-4242
  Cleveland (G-4554)
◆ Rmi Titanium Company LLC .... E 330 652-9952
  Niles (G-11684)
▲ The Schaefer Group Inc .... E 937 253-3342
  Beavercreek (G-1082)
Third Salvo Company .... G 740 818-9669
  Amesville (G-472)
Whempys Corp .... G 614 888-6670
  Worthington (G-16218)

1742 Plastering, drywall, and insulation

Holland Assocts LLC DBA Archou .... F 513 891-0006
  Cincinnati (G-3003)
▲ North Central Insulation Inc .... F 419 886-2030
  Bellville (G-1246)
One Wish LLC .... F 800 505-6883
  Bedford (G-1147)

1743 Terrazzo, tile, marble, mosaic work

◆ Cutting Edge Countertops Inc .... E 419 873-9500
  Perrysburg (G-12372)
▲ Distinctive Marble & Gran Inc .... F 614 760-0003
  Plain City (G-12575)
Prints & Paints Flr Cvg Co Inc .... E 419 462-5663
  Galion (G-7883)
Stuart-Dean Co Inc .... G 412 765-2752
  Cleveland (G-4742)

1751 Carpentry work

A & J Woodworking Inc .... G 419 695-5655
  Delphos (G-6759)
Accent Manufacturing Inc .... F 330 724-7704
  Norton (G-11936)
Acme Home Improvement Co Inc .... F 614 252-2129
  Columbus (G-5098)
AK Fabrication Inc .... F 330 458-1037
  Canton (G-2032)
Alside Inc .... D 419 865-0934
  Maumee (G-10161)
American Platinum Door LLC .... G 440 497-6213
  Solon (G-13312)
Architctral Mllwk Cbinetry Inc .... G 440 708-0086
  Chagrin Falls (G-2389)
Artisan Constructors LLC .... E 216 800-7641
  Cleveland (G-3680)
Cabinet Restylers Inc .... D 419 281-8449
  Ashland (G-561)
Case Crafters Inc .... G 937 667-9473
  Tipp City (G-14127)
Couch Business Development Inc .... F 937 253-1099
  Dayton (G-6264)
Dgl Woodworking Inc .... F 937 837-7091
  Dayton (G-6298)
Display Dynamics Inc .... F 937 832-2830
  Englewood (G-7229)
Division Overhead Door Inc .... F 513 872-0888
  Cincinnati (G-2834)

East Woodworking Company .... G 216 791-5950
  Cleveland (G-3990)
Finelli Ornamental Iron Co .... E 440 248-0050
  Cleveland (G-4061)
General Awning Company Inc .... F 216 749-0110
  Cleveland (G-4111)
Golden Angle Archtctral Group .... G 614 531-7932
  Columbus (G-5406)
Hardwood Lumber Company Inc .... F 440 834-1891
  Middlefield (G-10754)
Joseph Sabatino .... G 330 332-5879
  Salem (G-13007)
Midwest Curtainwalls Inc .... D 216 641-7900
  Cleveland (G-4410)
Millwood Wholesale Inc .... F 330 359-6109
  Dundee (G-6968)
Murray Display Fixtures Ltd .... F 614 875-1594
  Grove City (G-8109)
▼ Nofziger Door Sales Inc .... C 419 337-9900
  Wauseon (G-15271)
Overhead Door Corporation .... F 440 593-5226
  Conneaut (G-5929)
Overhead Door of Pike County .... G 740 289-3925
  Piketon (G-12481)
Premier Construction Company .... F 513 874-2611
  Fairfield (G-7395)
Riverside Cnstr Svcs Inc .... E 513 723-0900
  Cincinnati (G-3344)
Seemray LLC .... E 440 536-8705
  Cleveland (G-4685)
Sheridan Woodworks Inc .... F 216 663-9333
  Cleveland (G-4692)
Snows Wood Shop Inc .... E 419 836-3805
  Oregon (G-12111)
Ssi Manufacturing Inc .... F 513 761-7757
  West Chester (G-15589)
Thomas Cabinet Shop Inc .... F 937 847-8239
  Dayton (G-6621)
Traichal Construction Company .... E 800 255-3667
  Niles (G-11689)
Tri County Door Service Inc .... F 216 531-2245
  Euclid (G-7303)
Triple A Builders Inc .... G 216 249-0327
  Cleveland (G-4832)
Yoder Window & Siding Ltd .... F 330 695-6960
  Fredericksburg (G-7735)

1752 Floor laying and floor work, nec

▲ Done-Rite Bowling Service Co .... E 440 232-3280
  Bedford (G-1118)
Hoover & Wells Inc .... C 419 691-9220
  Toledo (G-14319)
◆ Tremco Incorporated .... B
  Beachwood (G-1031)
Triple A Builders Inc .... G 216 249-0327
  Cleveland (G-4832)
X-Treme Finishes Inc .... F 330 474-0614
  North Royalton (G-11903)

1761 Roofing, siding, and sheetmetal work

Acme Home Improvement Co Inc .... F 614 252-2129
  Columbus (G-5098)
▲ Alan Manufacturing Inc .... E 330 262-1555
  Wooster (G-16099)
All-Type Welding & Fabrication .... E 440 439-3990
  Cleveland (G-3635)
American Way Exteriors LLC .... G 937 221-8860
  Dayton (G-6204)
Anchor Metal Processing Inc .... F 216 362-6463
  Cleveland (G-3662)
Anchor Metal Processing Inc .... E 216 362-1850
  Cleveland (G-3663)

SIC SECTION

17 CONSTRUCTION - SPECIAL TRADE CONTRACTORS

Avon Lake Sheet Metal Co .... E 440 933-3505
   Avon Lake *(G-800)*

Budde Sheet Metal Works Inc .... E 937 224-0868
   Dayton *(G-6241)*

Cabinet Restylers Inc .... D 419 281-8449
   Ashland *(G-561)*

Cardinal Builders Inc .... E 614 237-1000
   Columbus *(G-5236)*

▲ Champion Opco LLC .... B 513 327-7338
   Cincinnati *(G-2725)*

Cmt Machining & Fabg LLC .... F 937 652-3740
   Urbana *(G-14827)*

Defabco Inc .... D 614 231-2700
   Columbus *(G-5323)*

Dimensional Metals Inc .... E 740 927-3633
   Reynoldsburg *(G-12761)*

Ducts Inc .... F 216 391-2400
   Cleveland *(G-3977)*

Everyday Technologies Inc .... F 937 497-7774
   Sidney *(G-13247)*

Federal Iron Works Company .... E 330 482-5910
   Columbiana *(G-5039)*

Franck and Fric Incorporated .... D 216 524-4451
   Cleveland *(G-4090)*

General Awning Company Inc .... F 216 749-0110
   Cleveland *(G-4111)*

Golden Angle Archtctral Group .... G 614 531-7932
   Columbus *(G-5406)*

Holgate Metal Fab Inc .... F 419 599-2000
   Napoleon *(G-11319)*

Jim Nier Construction Inc .... E 740 289-3925
   Piketon *(G-12477)*

Kettering Roofing & Shtmtl Inc .... F 513 281-6413
   Cincinnati *(G-3075)*

◆ Kirk & Blum Manufacturing Co .... C 513 458-2600
   Cincinnati *(G-3078)*

Martina Metal LLC .... E 614 291-9700
   Columbus *(G-5544)*

MGM Construction Inc .... F 440 234-7660
   Berea *(G-1288)*

Ohio Luxury Builders LLC .... G 330 881-0073
   Austintown *(G-753)*

◆ Owens Corning Sales LLC .... A 419 248-8000
   Toledo *(G-14424)*

Precision Impacts LLC .... D 937 530-8254
   Miamisburg *(G-10671)*

R G Smith Company .... D 330 456-3415
   Canton *(G-2207)*

RE Connors Construction Ltd .... G 740 644-0261
   Thornville *(G-14068)*

Related Metals Inc .... G 330 799-4866
   Canfield *(G-2016)*

Rmt Acquisition Inc .... E 513 241-5566
   Cincinnati *(G-3347)*

Roofing Annex LLC .... G 513 942-0555
   West Chester *(G-15581)*

Scs Construction Services Inc .... E 513 929-0260
   Cincinnati *(G-3371)*

Seneca Sheet Metal Company .... F 419 447-8434
   Tiffin *(G-14105)*

Simon Roofing and Shtmtl Corp .... C 330 629-7392
   Youngstown *(G-16439)*

Ssr Community Dev Group LLC .... G 216 466-2674
   Cleveland *(G-4724)*

◆ Tremco Incorporated .... B
   Beachwood *(G-1031)*

Triple A Builders Inc .... G 216 249-0327
   Cleveland *(G-4832)*

Waxco International Inc .... F 937 746-4845
   Miamisburg *(G-10701)*

Yoder Window & Siding Ltd .... F 330 695-6960
   Fredericksburg *(G-7735)*

1771 Concrete work

Concrete Material Supply LLC .... F 419 261-6404
   Woodville *(G-16092)*

Concrete One Construction LLC .... F 740 595-9680
   Delaware *(G-6711)*

D H Bowman & Sons Inc .... G 419 886-2711
   Bellville *(G-1241)*

Eldorado Stone LLC .... E 330 698-3931
   Apple Creek *(G-498)*

G Big Inc .... E 740 867-5758
   Chesapeake *(G-2473)*

Gateway Con Forming Svcs Inc .... D 513 353-2000
   Miamitown *(G-10708)*

Gerdau Ameristeel US Inc .... G 740 671-9410
   Bellaire *(G-1186)*

Hilltop Basic Resources Inc .... F 937 882-6357
   Springfield *(G-13576)*

Image Pavement Maintenance .... F 937 833-9200
   Brookville *(G-1739)*

Koski Construction Co .... G 440 997-5337
   Ashtabula *(G-644)*

M & B Asphalt Company Inc .... F 419 992-4235
   Tiffin *(G-14091)*

Morel Landscaping LLC .... F 216 551-4395
   Richfield *(G-12791)*

Morrow Gravel Company Inc .... E 513 771-0820
   Cincinnati *(G-3175)*

Mount Hope Planing .... G 330 359-0538
   Millersburg *(G-10984)*

Mt Pleasant Blacktopping Inc .... G 513 874-3777
   Fairfield *(G-7385)*

Phillips Ready Mix Co .... E 937 426-5151
   Beavercreek Township *(G-1090)*

Protective Industrial Polymers .... F 440 327-0015
   North Ridgeville *(G-11854)*

▲ R W Sidley Incorporated .... E 440 352-9343
   Painesville *(G-12260)*

RE Connors Construction Ltd .... G 740 644-0261
   Thornville *(G-14068)*

Sika Mbcc US LLC .... A 216 839-7500
   Beachwood *(G-1024)*

Smalls Asphalt Paving Inc .... F 740 427-4096
   Gambier *(G-7908)*

Stamm Contracting Company Inc .... E 330 274-8230
   Mantua *(G-9743)*

◆ Trewbric III Inc .... E 614 444-2184
   Columbus *(G-5835)*

Triple A Builders Inc .... G 216 249-0327
   Cleveland *(G-4832)*

W M Dauch Concrete Inc .... G 419 562-6917
   Bucyrus *(G-1874)*

Ward Construction Co .... F 419 943-2450
   Leipsic *(G-9142)*

Wilson Blacktop Corp .... F 740 635-3566
   Martins Ferry *(G-9901)*

1781 Water well drilling

Stoepfel Drilling Co .... G 419 532-3307
   Ottawa *(G-12194)*

Warthman Drilling Inc .... G 740 746-9950
   Sugar Grove *(G-13917)*

1791 Structural steel erection

Affiliated Metal Industries Inc .... F 440 235-3345
   Olmsted Falls *(G-12075)*

Atlantic Welding LLC .... F 937 570-5094
   Piqua *(G-12505)*

◆ Cbc Global .... E 330 482-3373
   Columbiana *(G-5030)*

Chagrin Vly Stl Erectors Inc .... F 440 975-1556
   Willoughby Hills *(G-16023)*

Chc Fabricating Corp .... D 513 821-7757
   Cincinnati *(G-2729)*

Concord Fabricators Inc .... E 614 875-2500
   Grove City *(G-8083)*

Evers Welding Co Inc .... F 513 385-7352
   Cincinnati *(G-2887)*

Frederick Steel Company LLC .... D 513 821-6400
   Cincinnati *(G-2922)*

FSRc Tanks Inc .... G 234 221-2015
   Bolivar *(G-1525)*

G & P Construction LLC .... E 855 494-4830
   North Royalton *(G-11875)*

Lake Building Products Inc .... E 216 486-1500
   Cleveland *(G-4306)*

Marysville Steel Inc .... E 937 642-5971
   Marysville *(G-9927)*

Mound Technologies Inc .... E 937 748-2937
   Springboro *(G-13511)*

Pro-Fab Inc .... E 330 644-0044
   Akron *(G-284)*

Rex Welding Inc .... F 740 387-1650
   Marion *(G-9875)*

Rittman Inc .... D 330 927-6855
   Rittman *(G-12827)*

Smith Brothers Erection Inc .... G 740 373-3575
   Marietta *(G-9826)*

Upright Steel LLC .... E 216 923-0852
   Cleveland *(G-4853)*

Wernke Wldg & Stl Erection Co .... F 513 353-4173
   North Bend *(G-11708)*

White Mule Company .... E 740 382-9008
   Ontario *(G-12097)*

1793 Glass and glazing work

A Service Glass Inc .... E 937 426-4920
   Beavercreek *(G-1038)*

▲ Afg Industries Inc .... D 614 322-4580
   Grove City *(G-8074)*

All State GL Block Fctry Inc .... G 440 205-8410
   Mentor *(G-10411)*

Kimmatt Corp .... G 937 228-3811
   West Alexandria *(G-15342)*

Niles Mirror & Glass Inc .... E 330 652-6277
   Niles *(G-11679)*

Pentagon Protection Usa LLC .... F 614 734-7240
   Dublin *(G-6922)*

Pioneer Cldding Glzing Systems .... E 216 816-4242
   Cleveland *(G-4554)*

Solon Glass Center Inc .... F 440 248-5018
   Cleveland *(G-4713)*

1794 Excavation work

16363 Sca Inc .... G 330 448-0000
   Masury *(G-10155)*

Alden Sand & Gravel Co Inc .... G 330 928-3249
   Cuyahoga Falls *(G-6061)*

Allgeier & Son Inc .... F 513 574-3735
   Cincinnati *(G-2611)*

◆ Barrett Paving Materials Inc .... E 973 533-1001
   Hamilton *(G-8183)*

Castalia Trenching & Ready Mix .... F 419 684-5502
   Castalia *(G-2320)*

D H Bowman & Sons Inc .... G 419 886-2711
   Bellville *(G-1241)*

Don Wartko Construction Co .... D 330 673-5252
   Kent *(G-8810)*

Fine Line Excvtg & Ldscpg LLC .... G 330 541-0590
   Ravenna *(G-12715)*

Fleming Construction Co .... F 740 494-2177
   Prospect *(G-12689)*

Foremans Sand & Gravel Inc .... G 937 547-1005
   Greenville *(G-8045)*

17 CONSTRUCTION - SPECIAL TRADE CONTRACTORS

◆ Gayston Corporation............................C 937 743-6050
   Miamisburg *(G-10640)*

GM Mechanical Inc..................................D 937 473-3006
   Covington *(G-6024)*

Kelchner Inc...C 937 704-9890
   Springboro *(G-13508)*

Kipps Gravel Company Inc.....................G 513 732-1024
   Kingston *(G-8931)*

Koski Construction Co...........................G 440 997-5337
   Ashtabula *(G-644)*

Paul R Lipp & Son Inc............................F 330 227-9614
   Rogers *(G-12847)*

Personal Plumber Service Corp..............F 440 324-4321
   Elyria *(G-7195)*

Phillips Companies.................................E 937 426-5461
   Beavercreek Township *(G-1089)*

Phillips Ready Mix Co............................E 937 426-5151
   Beavercreek Township *(G-1090)*

Rbm Environmental & Cnstr Inc..............F 419 693-5840
   Oregon *(G-12110)*

Siler Excavation Services.......................E 513 400-8628
   Milford *(G-10923)*

1795 Wrecking and demolition work

Allgeier & Son Inc..................................F 513 574-3735
   Cincinnati *(G-2611)*

Js Fabrications Inc.................................G 419 333-0323
   Fremont *(G-7790)*

Rnw Holdings Inc...................................E 330 792-0600
   Youngstown *(G-16429)*

1796 Installing building equipment

Atlas Industrial Contrs LLC....................B 614 841-4500
   Columbus *(G-5163)*

Chagrin Vly Stl Erectors Inc...................F 440 975-1556
   Willoughby Hills *(G-16023)*

Cincinnati Crane & Hoist LLC.................F 513 202-1408
   Harrison *(G-8268)*

Cleveland Roll Forming En.....................F 440 899-3888
   Westlake *(G-15744)*

◆ Clopay Corporation................................C 800 282-2260
   Mason *(G-9979)*

Expert Crane Inc....................................E 216 451-9900
   Wellington *(G-15307)*

Industrial Millwright Svcs LLC................E 419 523-9147
   Ottawa *(G-12181)*

Industrial Power Systems Inc.................B 419 531-3121
   Rossford *(G-12867)*

◆ Intertec Corporation...............................F 419 537-9711
   Toledo *(G-14335)*

K F T Inc..D 513 241-5910
   Cincinnati *(G-3055)*

L Haberny Co Inc...................................F 440 543-5999
   Chagrin Falls *(G-2404)*

◆ McGill Airclean LLC................................D 614 829-1200
   Columbus *(G-5550)*

Nbw Inc..E 216 377-1700
   Cleveland *(G-4442)*

Otis Elevator Company...........................E 216 573-2333
   Cleveland *(G-4512)*

▲ Spallinger Millwright Svc Co..................E 419 225-5830
   Lima *(G-9291)*

1799 Special trade contractors, nec

ABC Signs Inc..F 513 241-8884
   Cincinnati *(G-2590)*

Advantic Building Group LLC.................F 513 290-4796
   Miamisburg *(G-10606)*

▲ Afg Industries Inc..................................D 614 322-4580
   Grove City *(G-8074)*

Akay Holdings Inc..................................E 330 753-8458
   Barberton *(G-852)*

Akron Bldg Closeout Mtls LLC................G 234 738-0867
   Barberton *(G-853)*

All Ohio Companies Inc..........................F 216 420-9274
   Cleveland *(G-3631)*

All Ohio Welding Inc...............................G 937 663-7116
   Saint Paris *(G-12970)*

All Signs of Chillicothe Inc......................G 740 773-5016
   Chillicothe *(G-2492)*

American Way Exteriors LLC..................G 937 221-8860
   Dayton *(G-6204)*

Archer Corporation.................................E 330 455-9995
   Canton *(G-2038)*

Banks Manufacturing Company..............F 440 458-8661
   Grafton *(G-7997)*

Barr Engineering Incorporated................E 614 714-0299
   Columbus *(G-5175)*

◆ Barrett Paving Materials Inc...................E 973 533-1001
   Hamilton *(G-8183)*

Beck Studios Inc....................................E 513 831-6650
   Milford *(G-10895)*

Bob Lanes Welding Inc..........................F 740 373-3567
   Marietta *(G-9779)*

Bogie Industries Inc Ltd.........................E 330 745-3105
   Akron *(G-89)*

Boyer Signs & Graphics Inc...................E 216 383-7242
   Columbus *(G-5206)*

Brilliant Electric Sign Co Ltd..................D 216 741-3800
   Brooklyn Heights *(G-1685)*

Burdens Machine & Welding Inc............F 740 345-9246
   Newark *(G-11569)*

Cabinet Restylers Inc.............................D 419 281-8449
   Ashland *(G-561)*

Cardinal Builders Inc.............................E 614 237-1000
   Columbus *(G-5236)*

Carmens Installation Co.........................F 216 321-4040
   Cleveland *(G-3793)*

Carpe Diem Industries LLC....................D 419 358-0129
   Bluffton *(G-1502)*

Carpe Diem Industries LLC....................D 419 659-5639
   Columbus Grove *(G-5897)*

Classic Countertops LLC.......................G 330 882-4220
   Akron *(G-112)*

▲ Cleveland Granite & Marble LLC...........E 216 291-7637
   Cleveland *(G-3841)*

Connaughton Wldg & Fence LLC...........E 513 867-0230
   Hamilton *(G-8195)*

Crafted Surface and Stone LLC.............E 440 658-3799
   Chagrin Falls *(G-2391)*

Custom Way Welding Inc......................F 937 845-9469
   New Carlisle *(G-11414)*

Cuyahoga Fence LLC............................F 216 830-2200
   Cleveland *(G-3930)*

Danite Holdings Ltd...............................E 614 444-3333
   Columbus *(G-5316)*

Double D D Mtls Instlltion Inc................F 937 898-2534
   Dayton *(G-6302)*

Dover Fabrication and Burn Inc.............G 330 339-1057
   Dover *(G-6819)*

Envirnmntal Cmpliance Tech LLC..........F 216 634-0400
   North Royalton *(G-11874)*

Euclid Welding Company Inc.................F 216 289-0714
   Willoughby Hills *(G-16024)*

Extreme Microbial Tech LLC..................E 844 885-0088
   Moraine *(G-11179)*

Fdi Cabinetry LLC..................................G 513 353-4500
   Cleves *(G-4952)*

Fence One Inc.......................................F 216 441-2600
   Cleveland *(G-4056)*

▲ Flow-Liner Systems Ltd........................E 800 348-0020
   Zanesville *(G-16531)*

Gus Holthaus Signs Inc.........................E 513 861-0060
   Cincinnati *(G-2978)*

High-TEC Industrial Services.................D 937 667-1772
   Tipp City *(G-14137)*

Hilltop Glass & Mirror LLC.....................G 513 931-3688
   Cincinnati *(G-3002)*

Holdsworth Industrial Fabg LLC.............G 330 874-3945
   Bolivar *(G-1527)*

Hy-Blast Inc...E 513 424-0704
   Middletown *(G-10829)*

Identitek Systems Inc.............................D 330 832-9844
   Massillon *(G-10111)*

Image Pavement Maintenance................F 937 833-9200
   Brookville *(G-1739)*

Imperial On-Pece Fibrgls Pools.............F 740 747-2971
   Ashley *(G-622)*

Indoor Envmtl Specialists Inc................E 937 433-5202
   Dayton *(G-6381)*

Industrial Fiberglass Spc Inc..................E 937 222-9000
   Dayton *(G-6382)*

Janson Industries..................................D 330 455-7029
   Canton *(G-2133)*

Kcn Technologies LLC..........................G 440 439-4219
   Bedford *(G-1131)*

Kellys Wldg & Fabrication Ltd................G 440 593-6040
   Conneaut *(G-5922)*

Knowlton Machine Inc............................E 419 281-6802
   Ashland *(G-587)*

L B Foster Company.............................F 330 652-1461
   Mineral Ridge *(G-11022)*

Laminate Shop.......................................F 740 749-3536
   Waterford *(G-15237)*

Leak Finder Inc......................................G 440 735-0130
   Hudson *(G-8602)*

▲ Lefeld Welding & Stl Sups Inc...............E 419 678-2397
   Coldwater *(G-4995)*

Leon Newswanger..................................E 419 896-3336
   Shiloh *(G-13204)*

M & M Certified Welding Inc..................F 330 467-1729
   Macedonia *(G-9562)*

Macray Co LLC.....................................G 937 325-1726
   Springfield *(G-13598)*

Marsam Metalfab Inc.............................G 330 405-1520
   Twinsburg *(G-14691)*

Massillon Machine & Die Inc.................G 330 833-8913
   Massillon *(G-10122)*

◆ Master Builders LLC.............................E 800 228-3318
   Beachwood *(G-998)*

Mel Wacker Signs Inc............................G 330 832-1726
   Massillon *(G-10126)*

▲ Meridienne International Inc..................G 330 274-8317
   Aurora *(G-725)*

Mes Painting and Graphics....................G 614 496-1696
   Westerville *(G-15714)*

▲ Mesocoat Inc...F 216 453-0866
   Euclid *(G-7286)*

MGM Construction Inc...........................F 440 234-7660
   Berea *(G-1288)*

Nancys Draperies Inc............................G 330 855-7751
   Marshallville *(G-9894)*

▲ National Electro-Coatings Inc................D 216 898-0080
   Cleveland *(G-4436)*

▲ Nestaway LLC.......................................D 216 587-1500
   Cleveland *(G-4449)*

Ohio Building Restoration Inc................E 419 244-7372
   Toledo *(G-14408)*

Ohio Luxury Builders LLC.....................G 330 881-0073
   Austintown *(G-753)*

◆ Organized Living Inc.............................E 513 489-9300
   Cincinnati *(G-3230)*

Parking & Traffic Control SEC...............F 440 243-7565
   Cleveland *(G-4533)*

Paul Peterson Company........................F 614 486-4375
   Columbus *(G-5660)*

SIC SECTION

20 FOOD AND KINDRED PRODUCTS

Paulo Products Company............................. E 440 942-0153
  Willoughby (G-15969)
Pietra Naturale Inc..................................... F 937 438-8882
  Dayton (G-6506)
▲ Ptmj Enterprises Inc................................ D 440 543-8000
  Solon (G-13408)
Quality Fabricated Metals Inc.................... E 330 332-7008
  Salem (G-13025)
R W Sidley Incorporated............................ C 440 298-3232
  Thompson (G-14062)
Richtech Industries Inc.............................. G 440 937-4401
  Avon (G-787)
Rusco Products Inc................................... G 330 758-0378
  Youngstown (G-16432)
Security Fence Group Inc......................... E 513 681-3700
  Cincinnati (G-3374)
Signature Sign Co Inc................................ F 216 426-1234
  Cleveland (G-4702)
Sika Mbcc US LLC..................................... A 216 839-7500
  Beachwood (G-1024)
South Akron Awning Co............................. F 330 848-7611
  Akron (G-333)
Spradlin Bros Welding Co.......................... F 800 219-2182
  Springfield (G-13634)
Steve Vore Welding and Steel................... F 419 375-4087
  Fort Recovery (G-7624)
▲ Stone Statements Incorporated............. G 513 489-7866
  Cincinnati (G-3423)
Stuart-Dean Co Inc.................................... G 412 765-2752
  Cleveland (G-4742)
▼ Stud Welding Associates Inc................. D 440 783-3160
  Strongsville (G-13887)
Style-Line Incorporated............................. E 614 291-0600
  Columbus (G-5796)
United - Maier Signs Inc............................ D 513 681-6600
  Cincinnati (G-3478)
Universal Dsign Fbrication LLC................. F 419 202-5269
  Sandusky (G-13101)
▲ Universal Fabg Cnstr Svcs Inc.............. E 614 274-1128
  Columbus (G-5845)
Vector Mechanical LLC.............................. G 216 337-4042
  Cleveland (G-4863)
Waco Scaffolding & Equipment Inc........... A 216 749-8900
  Cleveland (G-4889)
Weldments Inc... F 937 235-9261
  Dayton (G-6649)
X-Treme Finishes Inc................................ F 330 474-0614
  North Royalton (G-11903)
Youngstown Fence Incorporated............... G 330 788-8110
  Youngstown (G-16481)

20 FOOD AND KINDRED PRODUCTS

2011 Meat packing plants

Acme Steak & Seafood Inc....................... F 330 270-8000
  Youngstown (G-16303)
Atlantic Veal & Lamb LLC.......................... F 330 435-6400
  Creston (G-6038)
Baltic Country Meats................................. G 330 897-7025
  Baltic (G-834)
Bef Foods Inc.. C 937 372-4493
  Xenia (G-16251)
Bob Evans Farms Inc................................ A 740 245-5305
  Bidwell (G-1324)
C J Kraft Enterprises Inc.......................... G 740 653-9606
  Lancaster (G-8997)
Carl Rittberger Sr Inc................................ E 740 452-2767
  Zanesville (G-16517)
Case Farms of Ohio Inc............................ C 330 359-7141
  Winesburg (G-16078)

Caven and Sons Meat Packing Co............ F 937 368-3841
  Conover (G-5935)
Comber Holdings Inc................................. E 216 961-8600
  Cleveland (G-3886)
D & H Meats Inc.. G 419 387-7767
  Vanlue (G-14969)
Daisyfield Pork LLC................................... G 419 626-2251
  Sandusky (G-13049)
Dee-Jays Cstm Btchring Proc LL.............. F 740 694-7492
  Fredericktown (G-7743)
Dumas Deer Processing LLC.................... G 330 805-3429
  Mogadore (G-11071)
Empire Packing Company LP.................... A 901 948-4788
  Mason (G-9989)
Empire Packing Company LP.................... D 513 942-5400
  West Chester (G-15551)
Farmerstown Meats................................... G 330 897-7972
  Sugarcreek (G-13925)
Food Plant Engineering LLC..................... F 513 618-3165
  Blue Ash (G-1396)
Fresh Mark Inc.. A 330 455-5253
  Canton (G-2105)
Fresh Mark Inc.. A 330 332-8508
  Salem (G-12996)
◆ Fresh Mark Inc...................................... B 330 832-7491
  Massillon (G-10097)
HK Cooperative Inc................................... F 419 626-2551
  Sandusky (G-13063)
Hormel Foods Corp Svcs LLC.................. F 513 563-0211
  Cincinnati (G-3008)
J H Routh Packing Company.................... B 419 626-2251
  Sandusky (G-13068)
John Stehlin & Sons Co............................ F 513 385-6164
  Cincinnati (G-3045)
Karn Meats Inc.. E 614 252-3712
  Columbus (G-5504)
King Kold Inc... E 937 836-2731
  Englewood (G-7235)
Kings Command Foods 2022 LLC............. E 937 827-7131
  Versailles (G-14984)
Mahan Packing Co..................................... F 330 889-2454
  Bristolville (G-1653)
Mannings Packing Co................................ G 937 446-3278
  Sardinia (G-13107)
Marshallville Packing Co Inc..................... F 330 855-2871
  Marshallville (G-9893)
Mc Connells Market.................................. G 740 765-4300
  Richmond (G-12802)
Medina Foods Inc..................................... E 330 725-1390
  Litchfield (G-9328)
National Beef Ohio LLC............................. D 800 449-2333
  North Baltimore (G-11697)
National Beef Packing Co LLC.................. B 419 257-5500
  North Baltimore (G-11698)
North Country Charcuterie LLC................ F 614 670-5726
  Columbus (G-5602)
Ohio Beef USA LLC................................... F 419 257-5536
  North Baltimore (G-11699)
Ohio Packing Company............................. C 614 445-0627
  Columbus (G-5625)
Patrick M Davidson................................... G 513 897-2971
  Waynesville (G-15302)
Phillips Meat Processing LLC.................... F 740 453-3337
  Zanesville (G-16555)
Pioneer Packing Co................................... D 419 352-5283
  Bowling Green (G-1585)
Presslers Meats Inc.................................. F 330 644-5636
  Akron (G-283)
Roots Meat Market LLC............................ E 419 332-0041
  Fremont (G-7804)
Smithfield Direct LLC................................ D 419 422-2233
  Findlay (G-7563)

◆ Smithfield Packaged Meats Corp.......... C 513 782-3800
  Cincinnati (G-3399)
Sugar Creek Packing Co........................... G 937 268-6601
  Dayton (G-6597)
The Ellenbee-Leggett Company Inc.......... C 513 874-3200
  Fairfield (G-7417)
Tr Boes Holdings Inc................................ E 419 595-2255
  New Riegel (G-11538)
Tri-State Beef Co Inc................................ F 513 579-1722
  Cincinnati (G-3464)
Troyers Trail Bologna Inc......................... F 330 893-2414
  Dundee (G-6971)
V H Cooper & Co Inc................................ A 419 678-4853
  Saint Henry (G-12940)
V H Cooper & Co Inc................................ A 419 678-4853
  Saint Henry (G-12941)
V H Cooper & Co Inc................................ C 419 375-4116
  Fort Recovery (G-7626)
Werling and Sons Inc................................ F 937 338-3281
  Burkettsville (G-1879)
Winesburg Meats Inc................................ G 330 359-5092
  Winesburg (G-16083)
Winner Corporation................................... E 419 582-4321
  Yorkshire (G-16293)
Youngs Locker Service Inc....................... F 740 599-6833
  Danville (G-6150)

2013 Sausages and other prepared meats

A To Z Portion Ctrl Meats Inc.................. E 419 358-2926
  Bluffton (G-1498)
▲ Advancepierre Foods Inc..................... B 513 874-8741
  West Chester (G-15531)
Advancperre Foods Holdings Inc.............. D 513 428-5699
  West Chester (G-15532)
Amish Wedding Foods Inc........................ E 330 674-9199
  Millersburg (G-10941)
B&G Foods Inc.. E 513 482-8226
  Cincinnati (G-2653)
Brinkman Turkey Farms Inc...................... F 419 365-5127
  Findlay (G-7487)
Carl Rittberger Sr Inc............................... E 740 452-2767
  Zanesville (G-16517)
Caven and Sons Meat Packing Co............ F 937 368-3841
  Conover (G-5935)
Charqui Jerky Co...................................... G 614 286-2938
  Powell (G-12668)
D D D Hams Inc.. G 440 487-9572
  Solon (G-13335)
Duma Meats Inc.. G 330 628-3438
  Mogadore (G-11070)
Empire Packing Company LP.................... D 513 942-5400
  West Chester (G-15551)
Fink Meat Company Inc............................ G 937 390-2750
  Springfield (G-13564)
Frank Brunckhorst Company LLC............. G 614 662-5300
  Groveport (G-8142)
Fresh Mark Inc.. A 330 455-5253
  Canton (G-2105)
Fresh Mark Inc.. A 330 332-8508
  Salem (G-12996)
◆ Fresh Mark Inc...................................... B 330 832-7491
  Massillon (G-10097)
Hoffman Meat Processing......................... G 419 864-3994
  Cardington (G-2275)
Honeybaked Foods Inc............................. A 567 703-0002
  Holland (G-8512)
Honeybaked Ham Company..................... E 513 583-9700
  Cincinnati (G-3006)
Iowa Quality Meats Ltd............................. C 515 225-6868
  Cincinnati (G-3030)
John Krusinski.. F 216 441-0100
  Cleveland (G-4258)

20 FOOD AND KINDRED PRODUCTS

John Stehlin & Sons Co .... F 513 385-6164
  Cincinnati (G-3045)
Karn Meats Inc .... E 614 252-3712
  Columbus (G-5504)
Keystone Foods LLC .... C 419 257-2341
  North Baltimore (G-11695)
King Kold Inc .... E 937 836-2731
  Englewood (G-7235)
Kraft Heinz Foods Company .... D 740 622-0523
  Coshocton (G-5982)
Lee Williams Meats Inc .... E 419 729-3893
  Toledo (G-14362)
Lipari Foods Operating Co LLC .... E 330 893-2479
  Millersburg (G-10973)
Lipari Foods Operating Co LLC .... E 330 674-9199
  Millersburg (G-10974)
Lous Sausage Ltd .... E 216 752-5060
  Cleveland (G-4336)
Marshallville Packing Co Inc .... F 330 855-2871
  Marshallville (G-9893)
Martin-Brower Company LLC .... C 513 773-2301
  West Chester (G-15462)
North Country Charcuterie LLC .... F 614 670-5726
  Columbus (G-5602)
Owens Foods Inc .... B
  New Albany (G-11388)
Patrick M Davidson .... G 513 897-2971
  Waynesville (G-15302)
Pettisville Meats Incorporated .... F 419 445-0921
  Pettisville (G-12453)
Pierre Holding Corp .... G 513 874-8741
  West Chester (G-15576)
Raneys Beef Jerky LLC .... G 606 694-1054
  Ironton (G-8702)
Rays Sausage Inc .... G 216 921-8782
  Cleveland (G-4617)
Simply Unique Snacks LLC .... G 513 223-7736
  Cincinnati (G-3394)
Sugar Creek Packing Co .... G 937 268-6601
  Dayton (G-6597)
◆ Sugar Creek Packing Co .... B 740 335-3586
  Blue Ash (G-1472)
Sunrise Foods Inc .... E 614 276-2880
  Columbus (G-5798)
Susan Hill Hams .... G 440 543-5967
  Chagrin Falls (G-2426)
The Ellenbee-Leggett Company Inc ...... C 513 874-3200
  Fairfield (G-7417)
Tri-State Beef Co Inc .... F 513 579-1722
  Cincinnati (G-3464)
◆ White Castle System Inc .... B 614 228-5781
  Columbus (G-5876)
Williams Pork Co Op .... G 419 682-9022
  Stryker (G-13914)
Winner Corporation .... E 419 582-4321
  Yorkshire (G-16293)
Youngs Locker Service Inc .... F 740 599-6833
  Danville (G-6150)

2015 Poultry slaughtering and processing

▲ Advancepierre Foods Inc .... B 513 874-8741
  West Chester (G-15531)
▼ Ballas Egg Products Corp .... D 614 453-0386
  Zanesville (G-16504)
BE Products Inc .... E 740 453-0386
  Zanesville (G-16507)
Brinkman Turkey Farms Inc .... F 419 365-5127
  Findlay (G-7487)
Cal-Maine Foods Inc .... D 937 337-9576
  Rossburg (G-12861)
Cal-Maine Foods Inc .... G 937 968-4874
  Union City (G-14776)

Case Farms .... G 330 452-0230
  Canton (G-2070)
Case Farms LLC .... E 330 832-0030
  Massillon (G-10083)
Case Farms of Ohio Inc .... D 330 878-7118
  Strasburg (G-13745)
Case Farms of Ohio Inc .... C 330 359-7141
  Winesburg (G-16078)
Cooper Foods .... E 419 232-2440
  Van Wert (G-14910)
Cooper Hatchery Inc .... C 419 238-4869
  Van Wert (G-14911)
Cooper Hatchery Inc .... C 419 594-3325
  Oakwood (G-12030)
▲ Daylay Egg Farm Inc .... C 937 355-6531
  West Mansfield (G-15625)
Fort Recovery Equity Inc .... E 419 375-4119
  Fort Recovery (G-7616)
Fort Recovery Equity Exchange .... G 937 338-8901
  Rossburg (G-12862)
Gerber Farm Division Inc .... F 800 362-7381
  Orrville (G-12126)
Just Natural Provision Company .... G 216 431-7922
  Cleveland (G-4267)
Martin-Brower Company LLC .... C 513 773-2301
  West Chester (G-15462)
Nature Pure LLC .... E 937 358-2364
  West Mansfield (G-15627)
▲ Ohio Fresh Eggs LLC .... G 740 893-7200
  Croton (G-6052)
Pf Management Inc .... G 513 874-8741
  West Chester (G-15575)
Pierre Holding Corp .... G 513 874-8741
  West Chester (G-15576)
Rcf Kitchens Indiana LLC .... G 765 478-6600
  Beavercreek (G-1079)
Roots Poultry Inc .... F 419 332-0041
  Fremont (G-7805)
Sid-Mar Foods Inc .... G 330 743-0112
  Youngstown (G-16437)
The Ellenbee-Leggett Company Inc ...... C 513 874-3200
  Fairfield (G-7417)
V H Cooper & Co Inc .... A 419 678-4853
  Saint Henry (G-12941)
V H Cooper & Co Inc .... C 419 375-4116
  Fort Recovery (G-7626)
▲ Weaver Bros Inc .... D 937 526-3907
  Versailles (G-14992)
Whitewater Processing LLC .... D 513 367-4133
  Harrison (G-8297)

2021 Creamery butter

Black Radish Creamery Ltd .... G 614 517-9520
  Columbus (G-5197)
Butt Kickn Creamery Inc .... G 419 482-6610
  Perrysburg (G-12366)
California Creamery Operators .... G 440 264-5351
  Solon (G-13325)
Dairy Farmers America Inc .... E 330 670-7800
  Medina (G-10317)
Heavenly Creamery Inc .... G 440 593-6080
  Conneaut (G-5920)
Minerva Dairy Inc .... D 330 868-4196
  Minerva (G-11035)
New Dairy Cincinnati LLC .... D 214 258-1200
  Cincinnati (G-3188)
New Dairy Ohio LLC .... D 214 258-1200
  Cleveland (G-4453)

2022 Cheese; natural and processed

▲ 9444 Ohio Holding Co .... E 330 359-6291
  Winesburg (G-16077)

A&M Cheese Co .... D 419 476-8369
  Toledo (G-14173)
Alpine Dairy LLC .... E 330 359-6291
  Dundee (G-6963)
Amish Wedding Foods Inc .... E 330 674-9199
  Millersburg (G-10941)
▼ Brewster Cheese Company .... C 330 767-3492
  Brewster (G-1642)
Bunker Hill Cheese Co Inc .... D 330 893-2131
  Millersburg (G-10949)
Dairy Farmers America Inc .... E 330 670-7800
  Medina (G-10317)
◆ Great Lakes Cheese Co Inc .... B 440 834-2500
  Hiram (G-8485)
Guggisberg Cheese Inc .... E 330 893-2550
  Millersburg (G-10956)
▲ Hans Rothenbuhler & Son Inc .... E 440 632-6000
  Middlefield (G-10753)
▲ Holmes Cheese Co .... E 330 674-6451
  Millersburg (G-10904)
Inter American Products Inc .... D 800 645-2233
  Cincinnati (G-3025)
Kathys Krafts and Kollectibles .... G 423 787-3709
  Medina (G-10341)
Krafts Exotika LLC .... G 216 563-1178
  Cleveland (G-4298)
▲ Lake Erie Frozen Foods Mfg Co .... D 419 289-9204
  Ashland (G-588)
Lakeview Farms LLC .... C 419 695-9925
  Delphos (G-6769)
Land OLakes Inc .... D 330 678-1578
  Kent (G-8827)
Lipari Foods Operating Co LLC .... E 330 893-2479
  Millersburg (G-10973)
Lipari Foods Operating Co LLC .... E 330 674-9199
  Millersburg (G-10974)
▲ Miceli Dairy Products Co .... D 216 791-6222
  Cleveland (G-4400)
Middlebury Cheese Company LLC .... F 330 893-2500
  Millersburg (G-10980)
Middlfield Original Cheese Coop .... F 440 632-5567
  Middlefield (G-10768)
Minerva Dairy Inc .... D 330 868-4196
  Minerva (G-11035)
Pearl Valley Cheese Inc .... E 740 545-6002
  Fresno (G-7823)
Rothenbhler Whey Ingrdents Inc .... F 440 632-0157
  Middlefield (G-10785)
Rothenbuhler Cheese Chalet LLC .... F 800 327-9477
  Middlefield (G-10786)
Rothenbuhler Holding Company .... E 440 632-6000
  Middlefield (G-10787)
Tri State Dairy LLC .... G 419 542-8788
  Hicksville (G-8381)
Tri State Dairy LLC .... G 330 897-5555
  Baltic (G-842)

2023 Dry, condensed, evaporated products

Ai Life LLC .... F 513 605-1079
  Mason (G-9947)
All-In Nutritionals LLC .... G 888 400-0333
  Springfield (G-13530)
Cbd Relieve ME Inc .... G 216 544-1696
  Euclid (G-7265)
Eagle Family Foods Group LLC .... E 330 382-3725
  Cleveland (G-3987)
▲ Freedom Health LLC .... E 330 562-0888
  Aurora (G-715)
▲ Hans Rothenbuhler & Son Inc .... E 440 632-6000
  Middlefield (G-10753)
Heart Healthy Homes Corp .... G 216 521-6029
  Lakewood (G-8976)

SIC SECTION

20 FOOD AND KINDRED PRODUCTS

▲ Infinit Nutrition LLC .... F 513 791-3500
Blue Ash *(G-1409)*

◆ Ingredia Inc .... E 419 738-4060
Wapakoneta *(G-15118)*

Innovated Health LLC .... G 330 858-0651
Cuyahoga Falls *(G-6091)*

Instantwhip-Columbus Inc .... E 614 871-9447
Grove City *(G-8098)*

Instantwhip-Dayton Inc .... G 937 435-4371
Dayton *(G-6385)*

▲ Instantwhip-Dayton Inc .... G 937 235-5930
Dayton *(G-6384)*

◆ J M Smucker Company .... A 330 682-3000
Orrville *(G-12129)*

Lifestyle Nutraceuticals Ltd .... G 513 376-7218
Cincinnati *(G-3105)*

Minerva Dairy Inc .... D 330 868-4196
Minerva *(G-11035)*

▲ Muscle Feast LLC .... F 740 877-8808
Nashport *(G-11339)*

Nestle Usa Inc .... D 216 861-8350
Cleveland *(G-4450)*

Nestle Usa Inc .... A 440 349-5757
Solon *(G-13397)*

Nestle Usa Inc .... B 440 264-6600
Solon *(G-13398)*

New Dairy Ohio Transport LLC .... D 214 258-1200
Cleveland *(G-4454)*

New Diry Cincinnati Trnspt LLC .... D 214 258-1200
Cincinnati *(G-3189)*

Nu Pet Company .... F 330 682-3000
Orrville *(G-12142)*

Rich Products Corporation .... C 614 771-1117
Hilliard *(G-8436)*

▲ Stolle Milk Biologics Inc .... F 513 489-7997
West Chester *(G-15591)*

Wileys Finest LLC .... C 740 622-1072
Coshocton *(G-6002)*

▲ Yoders Fine Foods LLC .... F 740 668-4961
Gambier *(G-7910)*

2024 Ice cream and frozen deserts

Archies Too .... G 419 427-2663
Findlay *(G-7477)*

Below Zero Inc .... G 419 973-2366
Toledo *(G-14211)*

Cfgsc LLC .... G 513 772-5920
Cincinnati *(G-2720)*

Cindee Shivers LLC .... G 419 385-0503
Toledo *(G-14239)*

Country Parlour Ice Cream Co .... F 440 237-4040
Cleveland *(G-3908)*

Crmd LLC .... G 440 225-7179
Columbus *(G-5308)*

Cygnus Home Service LLC .... E 419 222-9977
Lima *(G-9234)*

Dairy Shed .... G 937 848-3504
Bellbrook *(G-1191)*

Danone Us LLC .... E 513 229-0092
Mason *(G-9982)*

Danone Us LLC .... B 419 628-1295
Minster *(G-11049)*

Dietsch Brothers Incorporated .... E 419 422-4474
Findlay *(G-7501)*

Double Dippin Inc .... G 937 847-2572
Miamisburg *(G-10636)*

Fritzie Freeze Inc .... G 419 727-0818
Toledo *(G-14294)*

Gibson Bros Inc .... F 440 774-2401
Oberlin *(G-12051)*

Graeters Ice Cream Company .... D 513 721-3323
Cincinnati *(G-2968)*

Home City Ice Company .... F 419 562-4953
Delaware *(G-6731)*

Honeybaked Ham Company .... E 513 583-9700
Cincinnati *(G-3006)*

ICEE USA .... G 513 771-0630
West Chester *(G-15564)*

International Brand Services .... G 513 376-8209
Cincinnati *(G-3028)*

Jenis Splendid Ice Creams LLC .... E 614 488-3224
Columbus *(G-5492)*

Johnsons Real Ice Cream LLC .... C 614 231-0014
Columbus *(G-5500)*

Lombardo Gelato Company .... G 480 274-1018
Bedford *(G-1134)*

▲ Malleys Candies Inc .... D 216 362-8700
Cleveland *(G-4353)*

Moundbuilders Babe Ruth Basbal .... G 740 345-6830
Newark *(G-11594)*

New Bltmore Ice Cream Pdts Inc .... E 330 904-6687
Canton *(G-2171)*

Pierres Ice Cream Company Inc .... D 216 432-1144
Cleveland *(G-4552)*

Rita of Miamisburg LLC .... E 937 247-5244
Miamisburg *(G-10677)*

Rita of Miamisburg LLC .... G 937 247-5244
Franklin *(G-7697)*

Robert E McGrath Inc .... C 440 572-7747
Strongsville *(G-13872)*

Salted Dough .... G 216 288-2124
Broadview Heights *(G-1666)*

Smithfoods Inc .... E 330 683-8710
Orrville *(G-12151)*

St Clairsville Dairy Queen .... G 740 635-1800
Saint Clairsville *(G-12924)*

Stella Lou Llc .... E 937 935-9536
Powell *(G-12681)*

Streetpops Inc .... G 513 446-7505
Cincinnati *(G-3424)*

Superior Dairy Inc .... C 330 477-4515
Canton *(G-2239)*

Sweeties Olympia Treats LLC .... F 440 572-7747
Strongsville *(G-13888)*

Toft Dairy Inc .... D 419 625-4376
Sandusky *(G-13097)*

Twisty Treat LLC .... G 419 873-8033
Perrysburg *(G-12441)*

United Dairy Inc .... B 740 373-4121
Marietta *(G-9841)*

United Dairy Inc .... C 740 633-1451
Martins Ferry *(G-9900)*

United Dairy Farmers Inc .... C 513 396-8700
Cincinnati *(G-3479)*

Velvet Ice Cream Company .... D 740 892-3921
Utica *(G-14859)*

Weldon Ice Cream Company .... G 740 467-2400
Millersport *(G-11015)*

Whits Frozen Custard .... G 740 965-1427
Sunbury *(G-13966)*

Wil-Mark Froyo LLC .... F 330 421-6043
Rittman *(G-12829)*

Youngs Jersey Dairy Inc .... B 937 325-0629
Yellow Springs *(G-16290)*

ZS Cream & Bean LLC .... G 440 652-6369
Hinckley *(G-8480)*

2026 Fluid milk

American Confections Co LLC .... G 614 888-8838
Coventry Township *(G-6006)*

Borden Dairy Co Cincinnati LLC .... E 513 948-8811
Cleveland *(G-3748)*

Consun Food Industries Inc .... F 440 322-6301
Elyria *(G-7128)*

Dairy Farmers America Inc .... E 330 670-7800
Medina *(G-10317)*

Daisy Brand LLC .... F 330 202-4410
Wooster *(G-16112)*

Dfa Dairy Brands Ice Cream LLC .... B 419 473-9621
Toledo *(G-14267)*

Green Field Farms Co-Op .... G 330 263-0246
Wooster *(G-16126)*

Instantwhip Connecticut Inc .... F 614 488-2536
Columbus *(G-5463)*

Instantwhip Foods Inc .... F 614 488-2536
Columbus *(G-5464)*

Instantwhip Products Co PA .... F 614 488-2536
Columbus *(G-5465)*

Instantwhip-Buffalo Inc .... F 614 488-2536
Columbus *(G-5466)*

Instantwhip-Chicago Inc .... E 614 488-2536
Columbus *(G-5467)*

Instantwhip-Columbus Inc .... E 614 871-9447
Grove City *(G-8098)*

Instantwhip-Dayton Inc .... G 937 435-4371
Dayton *(G-6385)*

▲ Instantwhip-Dayton Inc .... G 937 235-5930
Dayton *(G-6384)*

Instantwhip-Syracuse Inc .... F 614 488-2536
Columbus *(G-5468)*

Lakeview Farms LLC .... C 419 695-9925
Delphos *(G-6769)*

Louis Instantwhip-St Inc .... F 614 488-2536
Columbus *(G-5535)*

Peak Foods Llc .... D 937 440-0707
Troy *(G-14601)*

Philadelphia Instantwhip Inc .... F 614 488-2536
Columbus *(G-5672)*

Reiter Dairy LLC Dean Foods .... G 937 323-5777
Springfield *(G-13626)*

Reiter Dairy of Akron Inc .... E 937 323-5777
Springfield *(G-13627)*

Smithfoods Inc .... E 330 683-8710
Orrville *(G-12151)*

Snowville Creamery LLC .... E 740 698-2301
Pomeroy *(G-12614)*

Superior Dairy Inc .... C 330 477-4515
Canton *(G-2239)*

Toft Dairy Inc .... D 419 625-4376
Sandusky *(G-13097)*

United Dairy Inc .... B 740 373-4121
Marietta *(G-9841)*

United Dairy Inc .... C 740 633-1451
Martins Ferry *(G-9900)*

United Dairy Farmers Inc .... C 513 396-8700
Cincinnati *(G-3479)*

2032 Canned specialties

Abbott Laboratories .... A 614 624-3191
Columbus *(G-5085)*

Ajinomoto Hlth Ntrtn N Amer In .... D 330 762-6652
Akron *(G-25)*

B&G Foods Inc .... E 513 482-8226
Cincinnati *(G-2653)*

Baxters North America Inc .... E 513 552-7463
Blue Ash *(G-1364)*

Baxters North America Inc .... C 513 552-7400
Blue Ash *(G-1365)*

Baxters North America Inc .... E 513 552-7728
Blue Ash *(G-1366)*

◆ Baxters North America Inc .... E 513 552-7718
West Chester *(G-15540)*

▼ Baxters North America Inc .... E 513 552-7485
Cincinnati *(G-2661)*

Beckman & Gast Company .... F 419 678-4195
Saint Henry *(G-12934)*

20 FOOD AND KINDRED PRODUCTS

Bittersweet Inc .... D 419 875-6986
   Whitehouse *(G-15816)*
Calm Distributors LLC .... G 614 678-5554
   Columbus *(G-5228)*
Cheese Holdings Inc .... E 330 893-2479
   Millersburg *(G-10951)*
Clovervale Farms LLC .... D 440 960-0146
   Amherst *(G-473)*
Conagra Brands Inc .... D 419 445-8015
   Archbold *(G-527)*
Food Designs Inc .... F 216 651-9221
   Cleveland *(G-4078)*
▲ Hayden Valley Foods Inc .... D 614 539-7233
   Urbancrest *(G-14853)*
Heritage Cooperative Inc .... F 740 828-2215
   Nashport *(G-11338)*
JES Foods/Celina Inc .... F 419 586-7446
   Celina *(G-2339)*
John Zidian Company .... F 330 965-8455
   North Jackson *(G-11785)*
▲ John Zidian Company .... E 330 743-6050
   Youngstown *(G-16384)*
L J Minor Corp .... F 216 861-8350
   Cleveland *(G-4302)*
Lonolife Inc .... G 614 296-2250
   Columbus *(G-5533)*
Magic Wok Inc .... G 419 531-1818
   Toledo *(G-14375)*
▲ More Than Gourmet Holdings Inc ..... E 330 762-6652
   Akron *(G-253)*
▲ Oasis Mditerranean Cuisine Inc .... E 419 269-1459
   Toledo *(G-14402)*
◆ Robert Rothschild Farm LLC .... F 855 969-8050
   West Chester *(G-15501)*
▲ Skyline Cem Holdings LLC .... C 513 874-1188
   Fairfield *(G-7408)*
Trevor Clatterbuck .... G 330 359-2129
   Wilmot *(G-16070)*
Wornick Holding Company Inc .... E 513 794-9800
   Blue Ash *(G-1495)*

2033 Canned fruits and specialties

Agricool Veg & Fruits LLC .... G 310 625-0024
   South Euclid *(G-13458)*
Annarino Foods Ltd .... F 937 274-3663
   Dayton *(G-6207)*
B&G Foods Inc .... E 513 482-8226
   Cincinnati *(G-2653)*
Beckman & Gast Company .... F 419 678-4195
   Saint Henry *(G-12934)*
Bellisio Foods Inc .... C 740 286-5505
   Jackson *(G-8710)*
Clovervale Farms LLC .... D 440 960-0146
   Amherst *(G-473)*
Coopers Mill Inc .... F 419 562-4215
   Bucyrus *(G-1854)*
◆ Country Pure Foods Inc .... C 330 753-2293
   Akron *(G-116)*
Dominion Liquid Tech LLC .... E 513 272-2824
   Cincinnati *(G-2836)*
Dutch Country Kettles Ltd .... G 937 780-6718
   Leesburg *(G-9124)*
Foster Canning Inc .... E 419 841-6755
   Toledo *(G-14293)*
Fremont Company .... E 419 363-2924
   Rockford *(G-12833)*
▼ Fremont Company .... D 419 334-8995
   Fremont *(G-7780)*
▼ Fry Foods Inc .... E 419 448-0731
   Tiffin *(G-14087)*
Gwj Liquidation Inc .... F 216 475-5770
   Cleveland *(G-4158)*

Hirzel Canning Company .... G 419 523-3225
   Ottawa *(G-12180)*
▲ Hirzel Canning Company .... E 419 693-0531
   Northwood *(G-11919)*
Inter American Products Inc .... D 800 645-2233
   Cincinnati *(G-3025)*
◆ J M Smucker Company .... A 330 682-3000
   Orrville *(G-12129)*
J M Smucker Flight Dept .... G 330 497-0073
   North Canton *(G-11739)*
JES Foods Inc .... F 216 883-8987
   Medina *(G-10339)*
JES Foods/Celina Inc .... F 419 586-7446
   Celina *(G-2339)*
Knudsen & Sons Inc .... G 330 682-3000
   Orrville *(G-12133)*
Kraft Heinz Company .... A 330 837-8331
   Massillon *(G-10118)*
Kraft Heinz Foods Company .... G 419 334-5724
   Fremont *(G-7792)*
◆ Meiers Wine Cellars Inc .... E 513 891-2900
   Cincinnati *(G-3146)*
Milos Whole World Gourmet LLC .... G 740 589-6456
   Nelsonville *(G-11358)*
Nu Pet Company .... F 330 682-3000
   Orrville *(G-12142)*
▲ Ohio Pure Foods Inc .... D 330 753-2293
   Akron *(G-271)*
Pillsbury Company LLC .... E 419 845-3751
   Caledonia *(G-1917)*
Pillsbury Company LLC .... D 740 286-2170
   Wellston *(G-15331)*
▼ Portion Pac Inc .... B 513 398-0400
   Mason *(G-10039)*
RC Industries Inc .... E 330 879-5486
   Navarre *(G-11352)*
Refresco Us Inc .... C 937 790-1400
   Carlisle *(G-2293)*
◆ Robert Rothschild Farm LLC .... F 855 969-8050
   West Chester *(G-15501)*
Rosebuds Ranch and Garden LLC ...... F 937 214-1801
   Covington *(G-6031)*
Smucker Foodservice Inc .... F 877 858-3855
   Orrville *(G-12153)*
▼ Smucker International Inc .... E 330 682-3000
   Orrville *(G-12154)*
Smucker Manufacturing Inc .... F 888 550-9555
   Orrville *(G-12155)*
Smucker Retail Foods Inc .... E 330 682-3000
   Orrville *(G-12157)*
The Fremont Kraut Company .... E 419 332-6481
   Fremont *(G-7812)*
Trevor Clatterbuck .... G 330 359-2129
   Wilmot *(G-16070)*
Two Grndmthers Gourmet Kit LLC .... G 614 746-0888
   Reynoldsburg *(G-12778)*
Welch Foods Inc A Cooperative .... D 513 632-5610
   Cincinnati *(G-3511)*
▲ Yoders Fine Foods LLC .... F 740 668-4961
   Gambier *(G-7910)*

2034 Dehydrated fruits, vegetables, soups

Appalachia Freeze Dry Co LLC .... F 740 412-0169
   Richmond Dale *(G-12804)*
Frezerve Inc .... G 440 661-4037
   Ashtabula *(G-633)*
Green Gourmet Foods LLC .... F 740 400-4212
   Baltimore *(G-845)*
▲ Hayden Valley Foods Inc .... D 614 539-7233
   Urbancrest *(G-14853)*
▲ Hirzel Canning Company .... E 419 693-0531
   Northwood *(G-11919)*

Kanan Enterprises Inc .... D 440 248-8484
   Solon *(G-13375)*
Kanan Enterprises Inc .... F 440 349-0719
   Solon *(G-13376)*
◆ Kanan Enterprises Inc .... C 440 248-8484
   Solon *(G-13374)*
Kettle Creations LLC .... E 567 940-9401
   Lima *(G-9260)*

2035 Pickles, sauces, and salad dressings

Anderson Brothers Entps Inc .... E 440 269-3920
   Willoughby *(G-15878)*
Annarino Foods Ltd .... F 937 274-3663
   Dayton *(G-6207)*
B&G Foods Inc .... E 513 482-8226
   Cincinnati *(G-2653)*
Belton Foods LLC .... E 937 890-7768
   Dayton *(G-6226)*
Cle Pickles Inc .... G 440 473-3740
   Cleveland *(G-3826)*
Consumer Guild Foods Inc .... F 419 726-3406
   Toledo *(G-14251)*
Dave Krissinger .... G 440 669-9957
   Chardon *(G-2447)*
Fremont Company .... E 419 363-2924
   Rockford *(G-12833)*
Hinkle Fine Foods Inc .... F 937 836-3665
   Dayton *(G-6369)*
◆ J M Smucker Company .... A 330 682-3000
   Orrville *(G-12129)*
JES Foods/Celina Inc .... F 419 586-7446
   Celina *(G-2339)*
▲ Kaiser Foods Inc .... E 513 621-2053
   Cincinnati *(G-3058)*
Kaiser Pickles LLC .... F 513 621-2053
   Cincinnati *(G-3060)*
Kaiser Pickles LLC .... G 513 621-2053
   Cincinnati *(G-3059)*
Lancaster Colony Corporation .... F 614 792-9774
   Dublin *(G-6906)*
◆ Lancaster Colony Corporation .... E 614 224-7141
   Westerville *(G-15663)*
Lancaster Glass Corporation .... E 614 224-7141
   Westerville *(G-15664)*
Lariccias Italian Foods Inc .... F 330 729-0222
   Youngstown *(G-16388)*
Lbzb Restaurants Inc .... F 567 413-4700
   Bowling Green *(G-1570)*
Lhpc Inc .... E 330 527-2696
   Garrettsville *(G-7920)*
Mark Grzianis St Treats Ex Inc .... F 330 414-6266
   Kent *(G-8832)*
Martinez Food Products LLC .... G 419 720-6973
   Toledo *(G-14378)*
Michael Zakany LLC .... G 740 221-3934
   Zanesville *(G-16545)*
▲ National Foods Packaging Inc .... E 216 622-2740
   Cleveland *(G-4437)*
Nu Pet Company .... F 330 682-3000
   Orrville *(G-12142)*
▼ Portion Pac Inc .... B 513 398-0400
   Mason *(G-10039)*
Randys Pickles LLC .... G 440 864-6611
   Cleveland *(G-4614)*
RC Industries Inc .... E 330 879-5486
   Navarre *(G-11352)*
Ribs King Inc .... G 513 791-1942
   Cincinnati *(G-3337)*
◆ Robert Rothschild Farm LLC .... F 855 969-8050
   West Chester *(G-15501)*
Sunrise Foods Inc .... E 614 276-2880
   Columbus *(G-5798)*

20 FOOD AND KINDRED PRODUCTS

◆ Tmarzetti Company .... C 614 846-2232
Westerville (G-15683)

Tulkoff Food Products Ohio LLC .... G 410 864-0523
Cincinnati (G-3474)

◆ Woeber Mustard Mfg Co .... C 937 323-6281
Springfield (G-13656)

2037 Frozen fruits and vegetables

Beverages Holdings LLC .... A 513 483-3300
Blue Ash (G-1369)

Big Gus Onion Rings Inc .... F 216 883-9045
Cleveland (G-3735)

Buckeye Smoothies LLC .... G 740 589-2900
Athens (G-678)

◆ Country Pure Foods Inc .... C 330 753-2293
Akron (G-116)

Creek Smoothies LLC .... G 937 429-1519
Beavercreek (G-1044)

Cygnus Home Service LLC .... E 419 222-9977
Lima (G-9234)

Heinz Foreign Investment Co .... F 330 837-8331
Massillon (G-10105)

▲ HJ Heinz Company LP .... D 330 837-8331
Massillon (G-10107)

▲ Lake Erie Frozen Foods Mfg Co .... D 419 289-9204
Ashland (G-588)

National Frt Vgtable Tech Corp .... E 740 400-4055
Columbus (G-5590)

Nestle Prepared Foods Company .... B 440 349-5757
Solon (G-13395)

▲ Nestle Prepared Foods Company .... A 440 248-3600
Solon (G-13396)

Ohios Best Juice Company LLC .... F 440 258-0834
Reynoldsburg (G-12771)

Simply Unique Snacks LLC .... G 513 223-7736
Cincinnati (G-3394)

2038 Frozen specialties, nec

Athens Foods Inc .... C 216 676-8500
Cleveland (G-3697)

◆ Bellisio .... F 740 286-5505
Jackson (G-8709)

Bellisio Foods Inc .... C 740 286-5505
Jackson (G-8710)

Brilista Foods Company Inc .... G 614 299-4132
Columbus (G-5217)

Chef 2 Chef Foods LLC .... G 216 696-0080
Cleveland (G-3815)

Clovervale Farms LLC .... D 440 960-0146
Amherst (G-473)

Dioguardis Italian Foods Inc .... F 330 492-3777
Canton (G-2093)

▼ Frozen Specialties Inc .... C 419 445-9015
Archbold (G-528)

▼ Fry Foods Inc .... E 419 448-0831
Tiffin (G-14087)

Jtm Provisions Company Inc .... B 513 367-4900
Harrison (G-8281)

Jtm Provisions Company Inc .... B 513 367-4900
Harrison (G-8280)

▲ Kahiki Foods Inc .... C 614 322-3180
Gahanna (G-7840)

King Kold Inc .... E 937 836-2731
Englewood (G-7235)

▲ Lake Erie Frozen Foods Mfg Co .... D 419 289-9204
Ashland (G-588)

◆ Lancaster Colony Corporation .... E 614 224-7141
Westerville (G-15663)

Lopaus Point LLC .... F 614 302-7242
Groveport (G-8152)

McDonalds .... F 513 336-0820
Mason (G-10028)

Nestle Prepared Foods Company .... B 440 349-5757
Solon (G-13395)

▲ Nestle Prepared Foods Company .... A 440 248-3600
Solon (G-13396)

Paleomd LLC .... G 248 854-0031
Bedford (G-1149)

R & D Nestle Center Inc .... D 440 349-5757
Solon (G-13409)

Rsw Distributors LLC .... E 502 587-8877
Blue Ash (G-1462)

Schwans Mama Rosass LLC .... C 937 498-4511
Sidney (G-13282)

▲ Skyline Cem Holdings LLC .... C 513 874-1188
Fairfield (G-7408)

Sunrise Foods Inc .... E 614 276-2880
Columbus (G-5798)

▲ The Stouffer Corporation .... G 440 349-5757
Solon (G-13438)

▲ Worthington Foods Inc .... D 740 453-5501
Zanesville (G-16571)

2041 Flour and other grain mill products

1-2-3 Gluten Free Inc .... G 216 378-9233
Chagrin Falls (G-2365)

Archer-Daniels-Midland Company .... E 419 435-6633
Fostoria (G-7628)

Archer-Daniels-Midland Company .... G 419 705-3292
Toledo (G-14197)

Bunge North America East LLC .... G 419 483-5340
Bellevue (G-1224)

Cargill Incorporated .... E 937 236-1971
Dayton (G-6246)

Countyline Co-Op Inc .... F 419 287-3241
Pemberville (G-12334)

Crestar Crusts Inc .... E 740 335-4813
Wshngtn Ct Hs (G-16228)

H Nagel & Son Co .... F 513 665-4550
Cincinnati (G-2981)

I Dream of Cakes .... G 937 533-6024
Eaton (G-7061)

Keynes Bros Inc .... D 740 385-6824
Logan (G-9366)

Legacy Farmers Cooperative .... F 419-423-2611
Findlay (G-7528)

Mennel Milling Company .... D 419 436-5130
Fostoria (G-7644)

Mennel Milling Company .... E 740 385-6824
Logan (G-9371)

Mennel Milling Company .... G 419 294-2337
Upper Sandusky (G-14816)

Minster Farmers Coop Exch .... D 419 628-4705
Minster (G-11056)

▼ Mullet Enterprises Inc .... G 330 852-4681
Sugarcreek (G-13932)

Pettisville Grain Co .... E 419 446-2547
Pettisville (G-12452)

Pillsbury Company LLC .... E 419 845-3751
Caledonia (G-1917)

Pillsbury Company LLC .... D 740 286-2170
Wellston (G-15331)

Premier Feeds LLC .... G 937 584-2411
Sabina (G-12891)

Sunrise Cooperative Inc .... G 419 628-4705
Minster (G-11062)

▲ The Mennel Milling Company .... E 419 435-8151
Fostoria (G-7656)

2043 Cereal breakfast foods

General Mills Inc .... D 513 771-8200
Cincinnati (G-2944)

General Mills Inc .... F 419 269-3100
Toledo (G-14299)

General Mills Inc .... E 740 286-2170
Wellston (G-15328)

Kellanova .... G 614 879-9659
West Jefferson (G-15611)

Kellanova .... C 740 453-5501
Zanesville (G-16541)

Kellogg Co .... G 330 306-1500
Warren (G-15182)

Kween and Co .... F 440 724-4342
Brooklyn Heights (G-1694)

Niese Farms .... G 419 347-1204
Crestline (G-6035)

Olde Man Granola LLC .... F 419 819-9576
Findlay (G-7545)

Treehouse Private Brands Inc .... B 740 654-8880
Lancaster (G-9046)

Treehouse Private Brands Inc .... E 740 654-8880
Lancaster (G-9047)

2045 Prepared flour mixes and doughs

◆ Abitec Corporation .... E 614 429-6464
Columbus (G-5090)

Athens Foods Inc .... C 216 676-8500
Cleveland (G-3697)

B & D Commissarys LLC .... G 740 743-3890
Mount Perry (G-11249)

B O K Inc .... D 937 322-9588
Springfield (G-13537)

Bakemark USA LLC .... F 440 323-5100
Elyria (G-7114)

Busken Bakery Inc .... D 513 871-2114
Cincinnati (G-2695)

Cassanos Inc .... E 937 294-8400
Dayton (G-6248)

Fleetchem LLC .... E 513 539-1111
Monroe (G-11106)

Kween and Co .... F 440 724-4342
Brooklyn Heights (G-1694)

Mid American Ventures Inc .... F 216 524-0974
Cleveland (G-4405)

Minus G LLC .... G 440 817-0338
Newbury (G-11630)

▲ National Foods Packaging Inc .... E 216 622-2740
Cleveland (G-4437)

◆ Procter & Gamble Mfg Co .... F 513 983-1100
Cincinnati (G-3298)

Rich Products Corporation .... C 614 771-1117
Hilliard (G-8436)

2046 Wet corn milling

Cargill Incorporated .... E 937 236-1971
Dayton (G-6246)

Fluid Quip Ks LLC .... D 937 324-0352
Springfield (G-13567)

Poet Biorefining Marion LLC .... E 740 383-4400
Marion (G-9873)

Primary Pdts Ingrdnts Amrcas L .... G 937 235-4074
Dayton (G-6521)

2047 Dog and cat food

Bil-Jac Foods Inc .... E 330 722-7888
Medina (G-10301)

Bravo LLC .... F 866 922-9222
Moraine (G-11163)

Cargill Incorporated .... E 419 394-3374
Saint Marys (G-12949)

Foster Canning Inc .... E 419 841-6755
Toledo (G-14293)

G & C Raw LLC .... G 937 827-0010
Versailles (G-14980)

Hartz Mountain Corporation .... D 513 877-2131
Pleasant Plain (G-12607)

20 FOOD AND KINDRED PRODUCTS

JM Smucker LLC .... D 330 682-3000
  Orrville *(G-12132)*
▼ Kelly Foods Corporation .... E 330 722-8855
  Medina *(G-10342)*
Land OLakes Inc .... E 330 879-2158
  Massillon *(G-10119)*
Mars Petcare Us Inc .... F 419 943-4280
  Leipsic *(G-9133)*
Milos Kitchen LLC .... G 330 682-3000
  Orrville *(G-12136)*
Nestle Purina Petcare Company .... D 740 454-8575
  Zanesville *(G-16548)*
Ohio Blenders Inc .... F 419 726-2655
  Toledo *(G-14407)*
♦ Ohio Pet Foods Inc .... E 330 424-1431
  Lisbon *(G-9323)*
Petrition LLC .... G 717 572-5665
  Lodi *(G-9354)*
♦ Pro-Pet LLC .... D 419 394-3374
  Saint Marys *(G-12964)*
▲ Vitakraft Sun Seed Inc .... D 419 832-1641
  Weston *(G-15807)*

2048 Prepared feeds, nec

Alsatian Llc .... G 330 661-0600
  Medina *(G-10293)*
Archer-Daniels-Midland Company .... G 330 852-3025
  Sugarcreek *(G-13918)*
Archer-Daniels-Midland Company .... G 419 705-3292
  Toledo *(G-14197)*
Brightpet Nutrition Group LLC .... E 330 424-1431
  Lisbon *(G-9308)*
Cargill Incorporated .... C 330 745-0031
  Akron *(G-100)*
Cargill Incorporated .... C 216 651-7200
  Cleveland *(G-3792)*
Cargill Incorporated .... E 419 394-3374
  Saint Marys *(G-12949)*
Cargill Incorporated .... F 937 497-4848
  Sidney *(G-13230)*
Centerra Co-Op .... E 419 281-2153
  Ashland *(G-562)*
Cooper Farms Inc .... D 419 375-4116
  Fort Recovery *(G-7614)*
Cooper Hatchery Inc .... C 419 594-3325
  Oakwood *(G-12030)*
Csa Nutrition Services Inc .... E 800 257-3788
  Brookville *(G-1731)*
D&D Ingredient Distrs Inc .... D 419 692-2667
  Spencerville *(G-13486)*
Direct Action Co Inc .... F 330 364-3219
  Dover *(G-6815)*
Four Natures Keepers Inc .... F 740 363-8007
  Delaware *(G-6722)*
G A Wintzer and Son Company .... D 419 739-4913
  Wapakoneta *(G-15113)*
G A Wintzer and Son Company .... F 419 739-4900
  Wapakoneta *(G-15112)*
Gerber & Sons Inc .... E 330 897-6201
  Baltic *(G-837)*
Granville Milling Co .... G 740 345-1305
  Newark *(G-11578)*
▼ Hamlet Protein Inc .... E 567 525-5627
  Findlay *(G-7518)*
Hanby Farms Inc .... E 740 763-3554
  Nashport *(G-11337)*
Hartz Mountain Corporation .... D 513 877-2131
  Pleasant Plain *(G-12607)*
▲ Kalmbach Feeds Inc .... C 419 294-3838
  Upper Sandusky *(G-14811)*
▼ Kelly Foods Corporation .... E 330 722-8855
  Medina *(G-10342)*

L E Sommer Kidron Inc .... G 330 857-2031
  Apple Creek *(G-503)*
Land OLakes Inc .... E 330 879-2158
  Massillon *(G-10119)*
Legacy Farmers Cooperative .... F 419 423-2611
  Findlay *(G-7528)*
▲ Magnus International Group Inc .... G 216 592-8355
  Painesville *(G-12248)*
Mars Horsecare Us Inc .... E 330 828-2251
  Dalton *(G-6135)*
Medinutra LLC .... G 614 292-6848
  Dublin *(G-6909)*
Mid-Wood Inc .... F 419 257-3331
  North Baltimore *(G-11696)*
Nature Pure LLC .... F 937 358-2364
  Raymond *(G-12746)*
Natures Way Bird Products LLC .... E 440 554-6166
  Chagrin Falls *(G-2410)*
Occidental Chemical Corp .... E 513 242-2900
  Cincinnati *(G-3211)*
Ohio Blenders Inc .... F 419 726-2655
  Toledo *(G-14407)*
♦ Ohio Pet Foods Inc .... E 330 424-1431
  Lisbon *(G-9323)*
Pettisville Grain Co .... E 419 446-2547
  Pettisville *(G-12452)*
Premier Feeds LLC .... G 937 584-2411
  Sabina *(G-12891)*
Premier Grain LLC .... G 937 584-6552
  Sabina *(G-12892)*
♦ Pro-Pet LLC .... D 419 394-3374
  Saint Marys *(G-12964)*
Provimi North America Inc .... E 937 770-2400
  Lewisburg *(G-9191)*
Provimi North America Inc .... F 937 770-2400
  Lewisburg *(G-9192)*
▲ Provimi North America Inc .... B 937 770-2400
  Lewisburg *(G-9190)*
Purina Mills LLC .... G 330 682-1951
  Orrville *(G-12146)*
Quality Liquid Feeds Inc .... F 330 532-4635
  Wellsville *(G-15336)*
Rek Associates LLC .... F 419 294-3838
  Upper Sandusky *(G-14822)*
▼ Republic Mills Inc .... E 419 758-3511
  Okolona *(G-12071)*
Ridley USA Inc .... F 800 837-8222
  Botkins *(G-1543)*
Rowe Premix Inc .... E 937 678-9015
  West Manchester *(G-15624)*
Spencer Feed & Supply LLC .... F 330 648-2111
  Spencer *(G-13483)*
Stony Hill Mixing Ltd .... G 330 674-0814
  Millersburg *(G-10995)*
The F L Emmert Co Inc .... F 513 721-5808
  Cincinnati *(G-3448)*
▲ The Mennel Milling Company .... E 419 435-8151
  Fostoria *(G-7656)*
Toledo Alfalfa Mills Inc .... E 419 836-3705
  Oregon *(G-12112)*
▼ Verhoff Alfalfa Mills Inc .... F 419 523-4767
  Ottawa *(G-12195)*
▲ Vitakraft Sun Seed Inc .... D 419 832-1641
  Weston *(G-15807)*
Woodstock Products Inc .... G 216 641-3811
  Cleveland *(G-4921)*

2051 Bread, cake, and related products

614 Cupcakes LLC .... G 614 245-8800
  New Albany *(G-11363)*
Alfred Nickles Bakery Inc .... E 740 453-6522
  Zanesville *(G-16498)*

Amish Door Inc .... C 330 359-5464
  Wilmot *(G-16065)*
Arlington Valley Farms LLC .... E 216 426-5000
  Hudson *(G-8586)*
B & J Baking Company .... F 513 541-2386
  Cincinnati *(G-2649)*
Beckers Bake Shop Inc .... G 216 752-4161
  Broadview Heights *(G-1655)*
Bimbo Bkries USA Clvland Hts D .... G 216 641-5700
  Cleveland *(G-3737)*
Bimbo Qsr Us LLC .... G 740 562-4188
  Zanesville *(G-16509)*
Blf Enterprises Inc .... F 937 642-6425
  Westerville *(G-15694)*
Bread Kneads Inc .... G 419 422-3863
  Findlay *(G-7486)*
Breaking Bread Pizza Company .... G 614 754-4777
  Columbus *(G-5059)*
Brooks Pastries Inc .... G 614 274-4880
  Plain City *(C-12667)*
Buns of Delaware Inc .... F 740 363-2867
  Delaware *(G-6706)*
Cake House Cleveland LLC .... F 216 870-4659
  Cleveland *(G-3782)*
Calvary Christian Ch of Ohio .... F 740 828-9000
  Frazeysburg *(G-7714)*
Chestnut Land Company .... G 330 652-1939
  Niles *(G-11663)*
Cincy Cupcakes LLC .... G 513 985-4440
  Cincinnati *(G-2764)*
Country Crust Bakery .... G 888 860-2940
  Bainbridge *(G-830)*
Crispie Creme Chillicothe Inc .... G 740 774-3770
  Chillicothe *(G-2500)*
Crumbs Inc .... F 740 592-3803
  Athens *(G-680)*
Dandi Enterprises Inc .... F 419 516-9070
  Solon *(G-13336)*
DC Orrville Inc .... F 330 683-0646
  Orrville *(G-12123)*
Donut Place Kings Inc .... G 937 829-9725
  Dayton *(G-6301)*
DUrso Bakery Inc .... F 330 652-4741
  Niles *(G-11667)*
Evans Bakery Inc .... G 937 228-4151
  Dayton *(G-6326)*
Flowers Baking Co Ohio LLC .... E 937 260-4412
  Dayton *(G-6336)*
Flowers Baking Co Ohio LLC .... E 419 269-9202
  Toledo *(G-14290)*
Fragapane Bakeries Inc .... F 440 779-6050
  North Olmsted *(G-11823)*
Gardner Pie Company .... C 330 245-2030
  Coventry Township *(G-6010)*
Garys Chesecakes Fine Desserts .... G 513 574-1700
  Cincinnati *(G-2932)*
Gawa Traders Wholesale & Dist .... E 614 697-1440
  Columbus *(G-5396)*
Gibson Bros Inc .... F 440 774-2401
  Oberlin *(G-12051)*
Giminetti Baking Company .... F 513 751-7655
  Cincinnati *(G-2951)*
Graeters Ice Cream Company .... D 513 721-3323
  Cincinnati *(G-2968)*
Hannibal Company Inc .... F 614 846-5060
  Worthington *(G-16195)*
Harvest Commissary LLC .... E 513 706-1951
  Granville *(G-8017)*
Heinens Inc .... C 330 562-5297
  Aurora *(G-718)*
Home Bakery .... F 419 678-3018
  Coldwater *(G-4993)*

SIC SECTION   20 FOOD AND KINDRED PRODUCTS

◆ Hot Mama Foods Inc .... F 419 474-3402
  Toledo (G-14321)

Imeldas Baking Company LLC .... G 937 484-5405
  Urbana (G-14837)

◆ Interbake Foods LLC .... D 614 294-4931
  Columbus (G-5471)

Investors United Inc .... F 419 473-8942
  Toledo (G-14336)

▲ Jasmine Distributing Ltd .... E 216 251-9420
  Cleveland (G-4251)

K & B Acquisitions Inc .... F 937 253-1163
  Dayton (G-6396)

Kellanova .... B 513 271-3500
  Cincinnati (G-3072)

Kennedys Bakery Inc .... F 740 432-2301
  Cambridge (G-1938)

Killer Brownie Ltd .... D 937 535-5690
  Miamisburg (G-10651)

Klosterman Baking Co .... F 513 398-2707
  Mason (G-10017)

Klosterman Baking Co LLC .... D 513 242-5667
  Cincinnati (G-3081)

Klosterman Baking Co LLC .... E 513 242-1004
  Cincinnati (G-3082)

Krispy Kreme Doughnut Corp .... E 614 798-0812
  Columbus (G-5515)

Krispy Kreme Doughnut Corp .... D 614 876-0058
  Columbus (G-5516)

Main Street Gourmet LLC .... C 330 929-0000
  Cuyahoga Falls (G-6101)

Mary Ann Donut Shoppe Inc .... G 330 478-1655
  Canton (G-2152)

McHappys Donuts of Parkersburg .... D 740 593-8744
  Athens (G-687)

McL Inc .... E 614 861-6259
  Columbus (G-5554)

Meeks Pastry Shop .... G 419 782-4871
  Defiance (G-6692)

Morgan4140 LLC .... F 513 873-1426
  Cincinnati (G-3173)

Mustard Seed Health Fd Mkt Inc .... E 440 519-3663
  Solon (G-13394)

New Horizons Baking Co LLC .... C 419 668-8226
  Norwalk (G-11980)

New York Frozen Foods Inc .... E 626 338-3000
  Westerville (G-15670)

New York Frozen Foods Inc .... B 216 292-5655
  Bedford (G-1144)

Norcia Bakery .... F 330 454-1077
  Canton (G-2174)

▲ Orlando Baking Company .... B 216 361-1872
  Cleveland (G-4509)

Osmans Pies Inc .... E 330 607-9083
  Stow (G-13716)

Papa Joes Pies Inc .... F 440 960-7437
  Amherst (G-481)

Pesce Bakery Company Ltd .... G 330 746-6537
  Youngstown (G-16417)

Pf Management Inc .... G 513 874-8741
  West Chester (G-15575)

Pierre Holding Corp .... G 513 874-8741
  West Chester (G-15576)

Pretzelhaus Bakery LLC .... G 513 906-2017
  West Chester (G-15485)

Quality Bakery Company Inc .... C 614 224-1424
  Columbus (G-5702)

Rich Products Corporation .... C 614 771-1117
  Hilliard (G-8436)

Riesbeck Food Markets Inc .... C 740 695-3401
  Saint Clairsville (G-12921)

Rudys Strudel Shop .... G 440 886-4430
  Cleveland (G-4662)

Scheiders Foods LLC .... F 740 404-6641
  Mount Perry (G-11252)

Schulers Bakery Inc .... E 937 323-4154
  Springfield (G-13630)

Schwebel Baking Company .... G 330 783-2860
  Hebron (G-8361)

Schwebel Baking Company .... G 330 926-9410
  North Canton (G-11758)

Schwebel Baking Company .... G 440 846-1921
  Strongsville (G-13875)

Schwebel Baking Company .... G 330 783-2860
  Youngstown (G-16434)

Schwebel Baking Company .... B 330 783-2860
  Youngstown (G-16433)

Servatii Inc .... G 513 271-5040
  Cincinnati (G-3383)

▲ Sister Schbrts Hmmade Rlls Inc .... C 334 335-2232
  Westerville (G-15678)

Skyliner .... G 740 738-0874
  Bridgeport (G-1649)

Studgionsgroup LLC .... E 216 804-1561
  Cleveland (G-4743)

Suelos Sweetz LLC .... G 440 478-1301
  Willowick (G-16036)

Sweet Persuasions LLC .... G 614 216-9052
  Pickerington (G-12471)

Thurns Bakery & Deli .... G 614 221-9246
  Columbus (G-5825)

Toast With Cake LLC .... G 937 554-5900
  Miamisburg (G-10695)

Trumbull Mobile Meals .... F 330 394-2538
  Warren (G-15212)

Uncle Jays Cakes LLC .... G 513 882-3433
  Cincinnati (G-3476)

Unger Kosher Bakery Inc .... F 216 321-7176
  Cleveland Heights (G-4944)

Uprising Food Inc .... G 513 313-1087
  Cincinnati (G-3484)

Wal-Bon of Ohio Inc .... F 740 423-8178
  Belpre (G-1262)

Wal-Bon of Ohio Inc .... F 740 423-6351
  Belpre (G-1261)

◆ White Castle System Inc .... B 614 228-5781
  Columbus (G-5876)

2052 Cookies and crackers

Basic Grain Products Inc .... D 419 678-2304
  Coldwater (G-4982)

Beckers Bake Shop Inc .... G 216 752-4161
  Broadview Heights (G-1655)

Blf Enterprises Inc .... F 937 642-6425
  Westerville (G-15694)

Cerelia USA Corp .... E 614 471-9994
  Columbus (G-5243)

Cheryl & Co .... F 614 776-1500
  Obetz (G-12058)

Cleveland Bean Sprout Inc .... F 216 881-2112
  Cleveland (G-3832)

Consolidated Biscuit Company .... F 419 293-2911
  Mc Comb (G-10268)

Cookie Bouquets Inc .... G 614 888-2171
  Columbus (G-5293)

Ditsch Usa LLC .... E 513 782-8888
  Cincinnati (G-2830)

Frischco Inc .... F 740 363-7537
  Delaware (G-6723)

Good Fortunes Inc .... G 440 942-2888
  Willoughby (G-15926)

Great American Cookie Company .... F 419 474-9417
  Toledo (G-14302)

Hearthside Food Solutions LLC .... A 419 293-2911
  Mc Comb (G-10270)

◆ Interbake Foods LLC .... D 614 294-4931
  Columbus (G-5471)

Keebler Company .... D 513 271-3500
  Cincinnati (G-3071)

Kellanova .... B 513 271-3500
  Cincinnati (G-3072)

Kennedys Bakery Inc .... F 740 432-2301
  Cambridge (G-1938)

Main Street Gourmet LLC .... C 330 929-0000
  Cuyahoga Falls (G-6101)

Norcia Bakery .... F 330 454-1077
  Canton (G-2174)

◆ Norse Dairy Systems LP .... B 614 294-4931
  Columbus (G-5601)

Osmans Pies Inc .... E 330 607-9083
  Stow (G-13716)

Pepperidge Farm Incorporated .... G 419 933-2611
  Willard (G-15863)

Rudys Strudel Shop .... G 440 886-4430
  Cleveland (G-4662)

Schulers Bakery Inc .... E 937 323-4154
  Springfield (G-13630)

Yz Enterprises Inc .... E 419 893-8777
  Maumee (G-10246)

2053 Frozen bakery products, except bread

Big Mouth Egg Rolls LLC .... F 614 404-3607
  Columbus (G-5186)

Gardner Pie Company .... C 330 245-2030
  Coventry Township (G-6010)

Kissicakes-N-Sweets LLC .... G 614 940-2779
  Columbus (G-5511)

Main Street Gourmet LLC .... C 330 929-0000
  Cuyahoga Falls (G-6101)

Pepperidge Farm Incorporated .... G 419 933-2611
  Willard (G-15863)

2061 Raw cane sugar

Derma Glow Med Spa Corp .... G 440 641-1406
  Cleveland (G-3953)

2063 Beet sugar

Michigan Sugar Company .... F 419 332-9931
  Fremont (G-7797)

2064 Candy and other confectionery products

Albanese Concessions LLC .... G 614 402-4937
  Canal Winchester (G-1978)

▲ Amerisource Health Svcs LLC .... D 614 492-8177
  Columbus (G-5131)

▲ Anthony-Thomas Candy Company .... C 614 274-8405
  Columbus (G-5147)

Appalachia Freeze Dry Co LLC .... F 740 412-0169
  Richmond Dale (G-12804)

Barfections LLC .... G 330 759-3100
  Hubbard (G-8562)

Barfections LLC .... G 330 759-3100
  Youngstown (G-16318)

Barfections LLC .... F 330 759-3100
  Girard (G-7962)

Bloomer Candy Co .... C 740 452-7501
  Zanesville (G-16511)

Chocolate Pig Inc .... G 440 461-4511
  Cleveland (G-3820)

Cincinnati Premier Candy Llc .... G 513 253-0079
  Cincinnati (G-2758)

Crawford Acquisition Corp .... G 216 486-0702
  Cleveland (G-3915)

▲ Crazy Monkey Baking Inc .... G 419 903-0403
  Ashland (G-569)

20 FOOD AND KINDRED PRODUCTS

Dauphin Holdings Inc .... F 330 733-4022
  Akron (G-124)
▲ Decko Products Inc .... D 419 626-5757
  Sandusky (G-13050)
Esther Price Candies Corporation .... E 937 253-2121
  Dayton (G-6324)
Executive Sweets East Inc .... G 440 359-9866
  Oakwood Village (G-12038)
Fawn Confectionery Inc .... F 513 574-9612
  Cincinnati (G-2897)
Flossys Sweet Tooth LLC .... G 614 425-7939
  Chillicothe (G-2503)
Giannios Candy Co Inc .... E 330 755-7000
  Struthers (G-13904)
Gibson Bros Inc .... F 440 774-2401
  Oberlin (G-12051)
Good Nutrition LLC .... F 216 534-6617
  Oakwood Village (G-12039)
Graeters Ice Cream Company .... D 513 721-3323
  Cincinnati (G-2968)
Great Lakes Popcorn Company .... F 419 732-3080
  Port Clinton (G-12620)
▲ Hake Head LLC .... F 614 291-2244
  Columbus (G-5416)
▲ Hayden Valley Foods Inc .... D 614 539-7233
  Urbancrest (G-14853)
Humphrey Popcorn Company .... F 216 662-6629
  Strongsville (G-13843)
▼ International Confections .... C 800 288-8002
  Columbus (G-5474)
International Leisure Activities Inc .... G
  Springfield (G-13582)
Island Delights Inc .... G 866 887-4100
  Seville (G-13143)
◆ Jml Holdings Inc .... E 419 866-7500
  Holland (G-8515)
Life Is Sweet LLC .... F 330 342-0172
  Cincinnati (G-3104)
Light Vision .... F 513 351-9444
  Cincinnati (G-3106)
▲ Malleys Candies Inc .... D 216 362-8700
  Cleveland (G-4353)
Maries Candies LLC .... F 937 465-3061
  West Liberty (G-15623)
Marshas Buckeyes LLC .... E 419 872-7666
  Perrysburg (G-12398)
Milk Hney Cndy Soda Shoppe LLC .... F 330 492-5884
  Canton (G-2165)
Moundbuilders Babe Ruth Basbal .... G 740 345-6830
  Newark (G-11594)
Piqua Chocolate Company Inc .... E 937 773-1981
  Piqua (G-12544)
Richards Maple Products Inc .... G 440 286-4160
  Chardon (G-2466)
▲ Spangler Candy Company .... C 419 636-4221
  Bryan (G-1838)
Suzin L Chocolatiers .... G 440 323-3372
  Elyria (G-7208)
Tiffin Paper Company .... E 419 447-2121
  Tiffin (G-14111)
Walnut Creek Chocolate Co Inc .... E 330 893-2995
  Walnut Creek (G-15096)

2066 Chocolate and cocoa products

72 Chocolate LLC .... G 216 672-6040
  Cleveland (G-3573)
American Confections Co LLC .... G 614 888-8838
  Coventry Township (G-6006)
▲ Anthony-Thomas Candy Company ...... C 614 274-8405
  Columbus (G-5147)
▲ Benjamin P Forbes Company .... F 440 838-4400
  Broadview Heights (G-1656)
Brandts Candies Inc .... G 440 942-1016
  Willoughby (G-15892)
Brantley Partners IV LP .... G 216 464-8400
  Cleveland (G-3754)
Cheryl & Co .... F 614 776-1500
  Obetz (G-12058)
Chocolate Ecstasy Inc .... G 330 434-4199
  Akron (G-108)
Chocolate Pig Inc .... G 440 461-4511
  Cleveland (G-3820)
Dietsch Brothers Incorporated .... E 419 422-4474
  Findlay (G-7501)
Executive Sweets East Inc .... G 440 359-9866
  Oakwood Village (G-12038)
Fannie May Confections Inc .... A 330 494-0833
  North Canton (G-11726)
Fawn Confectionery Inc .... F 513 574-9612
  Cincinnati (G-2897)
Giannios Candy Co Inc .... E 330 755-7000
  Struthers (G-13904)
Golden Turtle Chocolate Fctry .... G 513 932-1990
  Lebanon (G-9085)
Gorant Chocolatier LLC .... C 330 726-8821
  Boardman (G-1513)
Graeters Ice Cream Company .... D 513 721-3323
  Cincinnati (G-2968)
▲ Harry London Candies Inc .... E 330 494-0833
  North Canton (G-11736)
Hartville Chocolates Inc .... F 330 877-1999
  Hartville (G-8300)
▼ L C F Inc .... G 330 877-3322
  Hartville (G-8302)
Lil Turtles .... G 330 897-6400
  Baltic (G-839)
Linneas Candy Supplies Inc .... E 330 678-7112
  Kent (G-8828)
▲ Malleys Candies Inc .... D 216 362-8700
  Cleveland (G-4353)
Milk Hney Cndy Soda Shoppe LLC .... F 330 492-5884
  Canton (G-2165)
Robert E McGrath Inc .... F 440 572-7747
  Strongsville (G-13872)
Sweeties Olympia Treats LLC .... F 440 572-7747
  Strongsville (G-13888)
Walnut Creek Chocolate Co Inc .... E 330 893-2995
  Walnut Creek (G-15096)

2068 Salted and roasted nuts and seeds

▲ Anthony-Thomas Candy Company ...... C 614 274-8405
  Columbus (G-5147)
CJ Dannemiller Co .... E 330 825-7808
  Norton (G-11939)
▲ Hayden Valley Foods Inc .... D 614 539-7233
  Urbancrest (G-14853)
Kanan Enterprises Inc .... D 440 248-8484
  Solon (G-13375)
Kanan Enterprises Inc .... F 440 349-0719
  Solon (G-13376)
◆ Kanan Enterprises Inc .... C 440 248-8484
  Solon (G-13374)
▲ Malleys Candies Inc .... D 216 362-8700
  Cleveland (G-4353)
Nosh Butters LLC .... G 773 710-0668
  Cleveland (G-4482)
Nuts Are Good Inc .... F 586 619-2400
  Columbus (G-5608)
Simply Unique Snacks LLC .... G 513 223-7736
  Cincinnati (G-3394)
Southside Wolfies .... G 419 422-5450
  Findlay (G-7566)
Trophy Nut Co .... G 937 669-5513
  Tipp City (G-14162)
◆ Trophy Nut Co .... E 937 667-8478
  Tipp City (G-14161)

2075 Soybean oil mills

Archer-Daniels-Midland Company .... E 419 435-6633
  Fostoria (G-7628)
Bunge North America East LLC .... G 419 483-5340
  Bellevue (G-1224)
Cargill Incorporated .... D 937 498-4555
  Sidney (G-13231)
Schlessman Seed Co .... E 419 499-2572
  Milan (G-10886)
Solae LLC .... C 419 483-0400
  Bellevue (G-1235)

2077 Animal and marine fats and oils

Archer-Daniels-Midland Company .... E 419 435-6633
  Fostoria (G-7628)
Cargill Incorporated .... D 937 498-4555
  Sidney (G-13231)
Darling Ingredients Inc .... G 972 717-0300
  Cincinnati (G-2819)
Darling Ingredients Inc .... G 216 651-9300
  Cleveland (G-3940)
Darling Ingredients Inc .... G 216 351-3440
  Cleveland (G-3941)
Fiske Brothers Refining Co .... D 419 691-2491
  Toledo (G-14289)
Griffin Industries LLC .... F 513 549-0041
  Blue Ash (G-1400)
▲ Holmes By-Products Co Inc .... E 330 893-2322
  Millersburg (G-10963)
Inland Products Inc .... F 740 245-5514
  Rio Grande (G-12818)
Inland Products Inc .... E 614 443-3425
  Columbus (G-5460)
◆ The Dupps Company .... E 937 855-6555
  Germantown (G-7953)
▼ Werner G Smith Inc .... F 216 861-3676
  Cleveland (G-4904)
Wileys Finest LLC .... C 740 622-1072
  Coshocton (G-6002)

2079 Edible fats and oils

Cincinnati Biorefining Corp .... F 513 482-8800
  Cincinnati (G-2743)
◆ Cincinnati Renewable Fuels LLC .... D 513 482-8800
  Cincinnati (G-2759)
Inter American Products Inc .... D 800 645-2233
  Cincinnati (G-3025)
◆ Liquid Manufacturing Solutions .... E 937 401-0821
  Franklin (G-7684)
Olive Romanum Oil Inc .... G 330 554-4102
  Kent (G-8840)
◆ Procter & Gamble Mfg Co .... F 513 983-1100
  Cincinnati (G-3298)
Spicy Olive LLC .... F 513 376-9061
  Montgomery (G-11131)
Spicy Olive LLC .... G 513 847-4397
  West Chester (G-15509)
Wileys Finest LLC .... C 740 622-1072
  Coshocton (G-6002)

2082 Malt beverages

2 Tones Brewing Co .... G 740 412-0845
  Columbus (G-5075)
Anheuser-Busch LLC .... D 330 438-2036
  Canton (G-2037)
Anheuser-Busch LLC .... B 614 847-6213
  Columbus (G-5146)
Artisan Ales LLC .... E 216 544-8703
  Cleveland (G-3679)

SIC SECTION

20 FOOD AND KINDRED PRODUCTS

Bajio Brewing Company LLC...............G..... 419 410-8275
  Toledo (G-14205)
Branch & Bone Artisan Ales LLC...........F..... 937 723-7608
  Dayton (G-6235)
Brew Cleveland LLC..............................G..... 440 455-9218
  North Olmsted (G-11820)
Brew Kettle Inc...................................F..... 440 234-8788
  Strongsville (G-13817)
Brew Kettle Strongsville LLC...............F..... 440 915-7074
  Medina (G-10307)
Brewdog Brewing Company LLC...........F..... 614 908-3051
  Canal Winchester (G-1981)
Brewery Real Estate Partnr..................G..... 614 224-9023
  Columbus (G-5210)
Brewpub Restaurant Corporation..........E..... 614 228-2537
  Columbus (G-5211)
BT 4 LLC...G..... 513 771-2739
  Cincinnati (G-2692)
Bummin Beaver Brewery LLC...............G..... 440 543-9900
  Chagrin Falls (G-2390)
Cincinnati Beverage Company..............E..... 513 904-8910
  Cincinnati (G-2741)
Cineen Inc..G..... 440 236-3658
  Columbia Station (G-5009)
Columbus Kombucha Company LLC....G..... 614 262-0000
  Columbus (G-5270)
Dayton Heidelberg Distrg Co................C..... 440 989-1027
  Lorain (G-9410)
▲ District Brewing Company Inc.........E..... 614 224-3626
  Columbus (G-5331)
Dswdwk LLC.......................................G..... 513 853-5021
  Cincinnati (G-2843)
Fifty West Brewing Company LLC........E..... 740 775-2337
  Chillicothe (G-2502)
Frontwaters Rest & Brewing Co...........G..... 419 798-8058
  Marblehead (G-9765)
Georgetown Vineyards Inc..................E..... 740 435-3222
  Cambridge (G-1936)
Great Lakes Brewing Co....................E..... 216 771-4404
  Cleveland (G-4141)
◆ Great Lakes Brewing Co.................C..... 216 771-4404
  Cleveland (G-4142)
Great Lakes Brewing Co....................E..... 216 771-4404
  Strongsville (G-13836)
Green Room Brewing LLC..................G..... 614 421-2337
  Columbus (G-5412)
Hansa Brewery LLC............................G..... 216 631-6585
  Cleveland (G-4169)
Lock 15 Brewing Company LLC..........E..... 234 900-8277
  Akron (G-221)
Lock 27 Brewing LLC.........................F..... 937 433-2739
  Dayton (G-6414)
Mansfield Brew Works LLC.................F..... 419 631-3153
  Mansfield (G-9684)
Miiler Brewing Company....................E..... 513 896-9200
  Trenton (G-14541)
Modern Methods Brewing Co LLC.......G..... 330 506-4613
  Warren (G-15191)
Moeller Brew Barn LLC......................G..... 937 400-8628
  Dayton (G-6455)
Moeller Brew Barn LLC......................G..... 937 400-8626
  Monroe (G-11116)
Moeller Brew Barn LLC......................G..... 419 925-3005
  Maria Stein (G-9772)
Molson Coors Bev Co USA LLC..........D..... 513 896-9200
  Trenton (G-14542)
Municipal Brew Works LLC.................G..... 513 889-8369
  Hamilton (G-8230)
Nine Giant Brewing LLC.....................G..... 510 220-5104
  Cincinnati (G-3199)
Noble Beast Brewing LLC...................G..... 570 809-6405
  Cleveland (G-4461)

Phunkenship - Platform Beer Co.........F..... 216 417-7743
  Cleveland (G-4549)
Platform Beers LLC.............................F..... 440 539-3245
  Cleveland (G-4561)
Rhinegeist Holding Company Inc........F..... 513 381-1367
  Cincinnati (G-3336)
Rocky River Brewing Co....................F..... 440 895-2739
  Rocky River (G-12842)
Royal Docks Brewing Co LLC..............D..... 330 353-9103
  Massillon (G-10140)
◆ Samuel Adams Brewery Company Ltd.D..... 513 412-3200
  Cincinnati (G-3361)
Snyder Intl Brewing Group LLC..........E..... 216 619-7424
  Cleveland (G-4711)
South Side Drive Thru........................G..... 937 295-2927
  Fort Loramie (G-7610)
TS Oak Inc...G..... 513 252-7241
  Cincinnati (G-3472)
Wedco LLC..G..... 513 309-0781
  Mount Orab (G-11247)
Wild Ohio Brewing Company...............G..... 614 262-0000
  Columbus (G-5877)
Willoughby Brewing Company LLC....F..... 440 975-0202
  Willoughby (G-16016)

2083 Malt

Ohio Crafted Malt House LLC.............F..... 614 961-7805
  New Albany (G-11386)

2084 Wines, brandy, and brandy spirits

Amani Vines LLC................................F..... 440 335-5432
  Cleveland (G-3646)
Barrel Run Crssing Wnery Vnyrd........G..... 330 325-1075
  Rootstown (G-12851)
Biscotti Winery LLC...........................F..... 440 466-1248
  Geneva (G-7933)
Breitenbach Wine Cellars Inc.............G..... 330 343-3603
  Dover (G-6810)
Buckeye Lake Winery........................E..... 614 439-7576
  Thornville (G-14065)
Camelot Cellars Winery......................F..... 614 441-8860
  Plain City (G-12570)
Casa Di Vino Winery and....................G..... 440 494-7878
  Wickliffe (G-15826)
Chad M Marsh....................................G..... 419 994-0587
  Loudonville (G-9448)
Chalet Debonne Vineyards Inc...........F..... 440 466-3485
  Madison (G-9588)
Cyrpress Wine Cellars........................G..... 419 295-2124
  Mansfield (G-9644)
Delaware City Vineyard......................G..... 740 362-6383
  Delaware (G-6712)
Diletto Winery LLC............................F..... 440 991-6217
  Youngstown (G-16349)
Drake Brothers Ltd.............................G..... 415 819-4941
  Columbus (G-5335)
E & J Gallo Winery.............................E..... 513 381-4050
  Cincinnati (G-2847)
Ferrante Wine Farm Inc.....................E..... 440 466-8466
  Geneva (G-7936)
Five Vines Winery LLC......................G..... 419 657-2675
  Wapakoneta (G-15111)
Georgetown Vineyards Inc.................E..... 740 435-3222
  Cambridge (G-1936)
Gillig Custom Winery Inc...................G..... 419 202-6057
  Findlay (G-7513)
Glenn Ravens Winery........................F..... 740 545-1000
  West Lafayette (G-15617)
Happy Grape LLC..............................G..... 419 884-9463
  Mansfield (G-9666)
High Low Winery................................G..... 844 466-4456
  Akron (G-184)

Hillside Winery...................................G..... 419 456-3108
  Gilboa (G-7957)
Indian Bear Winery Ltd......................G..... 740 507-3322
  Walhonding (G-15093)
J E Nicolozakes Co...........................G..... 740 310-1606
  Cambridge (G-1937)
John Christ Winery Inc......................G..... 440 933-9672
  Avon Lake (G-813)
Kelleys Island Winery Inc...................G..... 419 746-2678
  Kelleys Island (G-8788)
Klingshirn Winery Inc.........................G..... 440 933-6666
  Avon Lake (G-814)
Laurentia Winery................................F..... 440 296-9170
  Madison (G-9593)
Lincoln Way Vineyards Inc.................F..... 330 804-9463
  Wooster (G-16146)
▲ Lonz Winery LLC..........................F..... 419 625-5474
  Sandusky (G-13075)
Losantiville Winery LLC.....................G..... 513 918-3015
  Cincinnati (G-3114)
Marie Noble Wine Company...............E..... 216 633-0025
  Euclid (G-7282)
Mastropietro Winery Inc....................G..... 330 547-2151
  Berlin Center (G-1309)
Matus Winery Inc...............................G..... 440 774-9463
  Wakeman (G-15077)
McAlear Winery LLC..........................G..... 567 703-1281
  Maumee (G-10219)
◆ Meiers Wine Cellars Inc................E..... 513 891-2900
  Cincinnati (G-3146)
Milo Family Vineyards Ltd..................G..... 440 922-0190
  Brecksville (G-1627)
Moyer Vineyards Inc..........................F..... 937 549-2957
  Mount Orab (G-11243)
Old Firehouse Winery Inc..................E..... 440 466-9300
  Geneva (G-7943)
Old Mason Winery Inc........................G..... 937 698-1122
  West Milton (G-15630)
Old Mill Winery Inc.............................G..... 440 466-5560
  Geneva (G-7944)
▲ Paramount Distillers Inc................B..... 216 671-6300
  Cleveland (G-4522)
Perennial Vineyards LLC....................F..... 330 832-3677
  Navarre (G-11349)
Pleasant Hill Vineyards LLC...............G..... 740 502-3567
  Athens (G-691)
Quinami LLC......................................G..... 419 797-4445
  Port Clinton (G-12626)
R & T Estate LLC...............................F..... 216 862-0822
  Cleveland (G-4611)
Revel Otr Urban Winery.....................G..... 513 929-4263
  Cincinnati (G-3333)
Sandra Weddington............................F..... 740 417-4286
  Delaware (G-6749)
Sapphire Creek Wnery Grdns LLC.....F..... 440 543-7777
  Chagrin Falls (G-2422)
Sarahs Vineyard Inc...........................G..... 330 929-8057
  Cuyahoga Falls (G-6116)
Shawne Springs Winery.....................G..... 740 623-0744
  Coshocton (G-5996)
▲ Solo Vino Imports Ltd...................G..... 440 714-9591
  Vermilion (G-14973)
Swiss Heritage Winery......................G..... 330 343-4108
  Dover (G-6846)
Tramonte & Sons LLC.......................F..... 513 770-5501
  Lebanon (G-9114)
Twenty One Barrels Ltd....................G..... 937 467-4498
  Bradford (G-1602)
Ugly Bunny Winery LLC.....................F..... 330 988-9057
  Loudonville (G-9453)
Vermilion Valley Vineyards LLC..........G..... 440 935-1363
  Westlake (G-15799)

20 FOOD AND KINDRED PRODUCTS

Vino Bellissimo .... G 419 296-4267
  Lima *(G-9300)*
Vino Di Piccin LLC .... F 740 738-0261
  Lansing *(G-9050)*
Vinoklet Winery Inc .... E 513 385-9309
  Cincinnati *(G-3500)*
Vintage Wine Distributor Inc .... F 513 443-4300
  West Chester *(G-15525)*
Vpl LLC .... F 330 549-0195
  Columbiana *(G-5055)*
Wine Mill .... G 234 571-2594
  Peninsula *(G-12346)*
Winery At Spring Hill Inc .... G 440 466-0626
  Geneva *(G-7946)*
Winery At Wilcox Inc .... G 937 526-3232
  Versailles *(G-14993)*
Winery At Wolf Creek .... F 330 666-9285
  Barberton *(G-900)*
Woodland Cellars LLC .... G 330 240-4883
  Hubbard *(G-8573)*
Wyandotte Winery LLC .... G 614 357-7522
  Columbus *(G-5887)*

2085 Distilled and blended liquors

Blue Collar M LLC .... F 216 209-5666
  Solon *(G-13320)*
Brain Brew Ventures 30 Inc .... F 513 310-6374
  Newtown *(G-11661)*
Five Points Distillery LLC .... F 937 776-4634
  Dayton *(G-6334)*
Karrikin Spirits Company LLC .... F 513 561-5000
  Cincinnati *(G-3064)*
▲ Kdc US Holdings Inc .... F 434 845-7073
  Groveport *(G-8148)*
Luxco Inc .... G 216 671-6300
  Cleveland *(G-4341)*
March First Manufacturing LLC .... G 513 266-3076
  Cincinnati *(G-3130)*
▲ Paramount Distillers Inc .... B 216 671-6300
  Cleveland *(G-4522)*
Simple Times LLC .... G 614 504-3551
  Columbus *(G-5772)*
Toledo Spirits Company LLC .... F 419 704-3705
  Toledo *(G-14505)*
Tri-Tech Laboratories LLC .... G 434 845-7073
  Groveport *(G-8164)*
Veriano Fine Foods Spirits Ltd .... F 614 745-7705
  New Albany *(G-11394)*
Watershed Distillery LLC .... E 614 357-1936
  Columbus *(G-5866)*
Western Reserve Distillers LLC .... G 330 780-9599
  Lakewood *(G-8984)*

2086 Bottled and canned soft drinks

Abbott Laboratories .... A 614 624-3191
  Columbus *(G-5085)*
▲ Akron Coca-Cola Bottling Co .... A 330 784-2653
  Akron *(G-31)*
American Bottling Company .... E 330 733-3830
  Akron *(G-58)*
American Bottling Company .... D 513 381-4891
  Cincinnati *(G-2615)*
American Bottling Company .... D 513 242-5151
  Cincinnati *(G-2616)*
American Bottling Company .... D 614 237-4201
  Columbus *(G-5120)*
American Bottling Company .... C 614 237-4201
  Columbus *(G-5121)*
American Bottling Company .... D 937 236-0333
  Dayton *(G-6198)*
American Bottling Company .... D 419 229-7777
  Lima *(G-9220)*

American Bottling Company .... D 740 423-9230
  Little Hocking *(G-9333)*
American Bottling Company .... E 740 922-5253
  Midvale *(G-10874)*
American Bottling Company .... D 740 377-4371
  South Point *(G-13465)*
American Bottling Company .... D 419 535-0777
  Toledo *(G-14186)*
Belton Foods LLC .... E 937 890-7768
  Dayton *(G-6226)*
Beverages Holdings LLC .... A 513 483-3300
  Blue Ash *(G-1369)*
Borden Dairy Co Cincinnati LLC .... E 513 948-8811
  Cleveland *(G-3748)*
Cadbury Schweppes Bottling .... G 614 238-0469
  Columbus *(G-5225)*
Central Coca-Cola Btlg Co Inc .... E 330 875-1487
  Akron *(G-105)*
Central Coca-Cola Btlg Co Inc .... E 740 474-2180
  Circleville *(G-3543)*
Central Coca-Cola Btlg Co Inc .... C 614 863-7200
  Columbus *(G-5241)*
Central Coca-Cola Btlg Co Inc .... E 440 324-3335
  Elyria *(G-7125)*
Central Coca-Cola Btlg Co Inc .... D 419 522-2653
  Mansfield *(G-9637)*
Central Coca-Cola Btlg Co Inc .... C 419 476-6622
  Toledo *(G-14230)*
Central Coca-Cola Btlg Co Inc .... B 330 425-4401
  Twinsburg *(G-14641)*
Central Coca-Cola Btlg Co Inc .... E 440 269-1433
  Willoughby *(G-15898)*
Central Coca-Cola Btlg Co Inc .... E 330 783-1982
  Youngstown *(G-16333)*
Central Coca-Cola Btlg Co Inc .... E 740 452-3608
  Zanesville *(G-16519)*
Central Investment LLC .... F 513 563-4700
  Cincinnati *(G-2716)*
Cleveland Coca-Cola Btlg Inc .... C 216 690-2653
  Bedford Heights *(G-1167)*
Coca Cola .... G 513 898-7709
  West Chester *(G-15399)*
Coca Cola Offices .... G 678 327-8959
  Cincinnati *(G-2779)*
Coca-Cola .... G 937 446-4644
  Sardinia *(G-13106)*
Coca-Cola Company .... E 614 491-6305
  Columbus *(G-5259)*
Coca-Cola Consolidated Inc .... A 513 527-6600
  Cincinnati *(G-2780)*
Coca-Cola Consolidated Inc .... B 937 878-5000
  Dayton *(G-6257)*
Coca-Cola Consolidated Inc .... G 419 422-3743
  Lima *(G-9228)*
Coca-Cola Consolidated Inc .... C 740 353-3133
  Portsmouth *(G-12642)*
Consolidated Bottling Company .... C 419 227-3541
  Lima *(G-9229)*
♦ Country Pure Foods Inc .... C 330 753-2293
  Akron *(G-116)*
Currier Richard & James .... G 440 988-4132
  Amherst *(G-474)*
Dr Pepper Bottlers Associates .... G 330 746-7651
  Youngstown *(G-16351)*
Dr Pepper Bottling Company .... G 740 452-2721
  Zanesville *(G-16528)*
Dr Pepper Snapple Group .... F 419 223-0072
  Lima *(G-9237)*
Dr Pepper/Seven Up Inc .... F 513 875-2466
  Fayetteville *(G-7465)*
Dr Pepper/Seven Up Inc .... F 419 229-7777
  Lima *(G-9238)*

Fbg Bottling Group LLC .... F 614 580-7063
  Columbus *(G-5371)*
G & J Pepsi-Cola Bottlers Inc .... E 740 593-3366
  Athens *(G-683)*
G & J Pepsi-Cola Bottlers Inc .... E 740 774-2148
  Chillicothe *(G-2504)*
G & J Pepsi-Cola Bottlers Inc .... E 866 647-2734
  Columbus *(G-5393)*
G & J Pepsi-Cola Bottlers Inc .... A 614 253-8771
  Columbus *(G-5394)*
G & J Pepsi-Cola Bottlers Inc .... B 740 354-9191
  Franklin Furnace *(G-7712)*
G & J Pepsi-Cola Bottlers Inc .... D 513 896-3700
  Hamilton *(G-8210)*
G & J Pepsi-Cola Bottlers Inc .... E 740 354-9191
  Zanesville *(G-16534)*
G & J Pepsi-Cola Bottlers Inc .... F 513 785-6060
  Cincinnati *(G-2924)*
Gehm & Sons Limited .... G 330 724-8423
  Akron *(G-164)*
Gem Beverages Inc .... F 740 384-2411
  Wellston *(G-15327)*
Gordon Brothers Btlg Group Inc .... G 330 337-8754
  Salem *(G-12997)*
Hornell Brewing Co Inc .... G 516 812-0384
  Cincinnati *(G-3009)*
Keurig Dr Pepper Inc .... D 614 237-4201
  Columbus *(G-5509)*
L & J Drive Thru LLC .... G 330 767-2185
  Brewster *(G-1644)*
Life Support Development Ltd .... G 614 221-1765
  Columbus *(G-5525)*
♦ Meiers Wine Cellars Inc .... E 513 891-2900
  Cincinnati *(G-3146)*
National Beverage Corp .... G 614 491-5415
  Obetz *(G-12063)*
▲ Niagara Bottling LLC .... G 614 751-7420
  Gahanna *(G-7846)*
Ohio Beverage Systems Inc .... F 216 475-3900
  Cleveland *(G-4495)*
Ohio Eagle Distributing LLC .... E 513 539-8483
  West Chester *(G-15469)*
▲ Ohio Pure Foods Inc .... D 330 753-2293
  Akron *(G-271)*
On US LLC .... E 330 286-3436
  Kent *(G-8841)*
P-Americas LLC .... B 513 948-5100
  Cincinnati *(G-3233)*
Pepsi-Cola Metro Btlg Co Inc .... F 614 261-8193
  Columbus *(G-5668)*
Pepsi-Cola Metro Btlg Co Inc .... E 937 461-4664
  Dayton *(G-6501)*
Pepsi-Cola Metro Btlg Co Inc .... F 440 323-5524
  Elyria *(G-7193)*
Pepsi-Cola Metro Btlg Co Inc .... G 937 328-6750
  Springfield *(G-13618)*
Pepsi-Cola Metro Btlg Co Inc .... D 419 534-2186
  Toledo *(G-14432)*
Pepsi-Cola Metro Btlg Co Inc .... C 330 425-8236
  Twinsburg *(G-14711)*
Pepsi-Cola Metro Btlg Co Inc .... F 330 963-5300
  Twinsburg *(G-14712)*
Pepsico .... G 513 229-3046
  Mason *(G-10037)*
Shasta Beverages .... G 614 409-2965
  Groveport *(G-8159)*
Shasta Beverages Inc .... D 614 491-5415
  Obetz *(G-12064)*
♦ Smithfoods Orrville Inc .... C 330 683-8710
  Orrville *(G-12152)*
▼ Smucker International Inc .... E 330 682-3000
  Orrville *(G-12154)*

20 FOOD AND KINDRED PRODUCTS

Smucker Natural Foods Inc.................... A 330 682-3000
　Orrville *(G-12156)*

2087 Flavoring extracts and syrups, nec

Abbott Laboratories............................... A 614 624-3191
　Columbus *(G-5085)*

Agrana Fruit Us Inc................................ C 937 693-3821
　Anna *(G-488)*

◆ Agrana Fruit Us Inc............................. E 440 546-1199
　Brecksville *(G-1605)*

Belton Foods LLC................................. E 937 890-7768
　Dayton *(G-6226)*

◆ Berghausen Corporation..................... E 513 591-4491
　Cincinnati *(G-2665)*

Cargill Incorporated.............................. E 937 236-1971
　Dayton *(G-6246)*

Central Coca-Cola Btlg Co Inc................ C 419 476-6622
　Toledo *(G-14230)*

Dominion Liquid Tech LLC...................... E 513 272-2824
　Cincinnati *(G-2836)*

Flavor Producers LLC........................... E 513 771-0777
　Cincinnati *(G-2906)*

▲ Flavor Systems Intl Inc...................... E 513 870-4900
　Cincinnati *(G-2907)*

◆ Frutarom USA Inc.............................. C 513 870-4900
　West Chester *(G-15556)*

Givaudan Flavors Corporation................ G 513 786-0124
　Cincinnati *(G-2954)*

Givaudan Flavors Corporation................ G 513 948-8000
　Cincinnati *(G-2956)*

◆ Givaudan Flavors Corporation............ C 513 948-8000
　Cincinnati *(G-2955)*

Givaudan Fragrances Corp..................... E 513 948-3428
　Cincinnati *(G-2957)*

Gwj Liquidation Inc................................ F 216 475-5770
　Cleveland *(G-4158)*

Hen of Woods LLC................................ G 513 954-8871
　Cincinnati *(G-2993)*

Hydralyte LLC....................................... G 844 301-2109
　Solon *(G-13365)*

Innovtive Cnfction Sltions LLC................. F 440 835-8001
　Westlake *(G-15761)*

Inter American Products Inc................... D 800 645-2233
　Cincinnati *(G-3025)*

◆ J M Smucker Company..................... A 330 682-3000
　Orrville *(G-12129)*

▲ Joseph Adams Corp......................... F 330 225-9125
　Valley City *(G-14874)*

Mane Inc.. C 513 248-9876
　Cincinnati *(G-3128)*

◆ Mane Inc... D 513 248-9876
　Lebanon *(G-9096)*

Mapledale Farm Inc............................... F 440 286-3389
　Chardon *(G-2458)*

Nu Pet Company................................... F 330 682-3000
　Orrville *(G-12142)*

Phillips Syrup LLC................................. F 440 835-8001
　Westlake *(G-15774)*

Primary Pdts Ingrdnts Amrcas L............. D 937 236-5906
　Dayton *(G-6520)*

▲ Sensus LLC..................................... F 513 892-7100
　Fairfield Township *(G-7432)*

▲ Slush Puppie................................... F 513 771-0940
　West Chester *(G-15587)*

▲ Wiley Companies............................. C 740 622-0755
　Coshocton *(G-6000)*

Wiley Organics Inc................................ C 740 622-0755
　Coshocton *(G-6001)*

2092 Fresh or frozen packaged fish

Pacific Atlantic Provs Inc........................ G 330 467-0150
　Northfield *(G-11909)*

2095 Roasted coffee

Altraserv LLC....................................... G 614 889-2500
　Plain City *(G-12561)*

Beca House Coffee LLC......................... G 419 731-4961
　Upper Sandusky *(G-14804)*

Boston Stoker Inc.................................. F 937 890-6401
　Vandalia *(G-14934)*

Euclid Coffee Co Inc.............................. G 216 481-3330
　Cleveland *(G-4033)*

▲ Folger Coffee Company..................... F 800 937-9745
　Orrville *(G-12125)*

Frezerve Inc... G 440 661-4037
　Ashtabula *(G-633)*

Hinterland Cof Strategies LLC................. G 440 829-5604
　Cleveland *(G-4190)*

Inter American Products Inc................... D 800 645-2233
　Cincinnati *(G-3025)*

Iron Bean Inc.. F 518 641-9917
　Perrysburg *(G-12393)*

Mc Concepts Llc.................................... G 330 933-6402
　Canton *(G-2155)*

▲ Millstone Coffee Inc.......................... D 513 983-1100
　Cincinnati *(G-3165)*

Nutz4coffee Ltd..................................... G 216 236-5292
　Cleveland *(G-4488)*

Ohio Coffee Collaborative Ltd................. F 614 564-9852
　Columbus *(G-5613)*

Queen Beanery Coffeehouse LLC........... G 937 798-4023
　Peebles *(G-12330)*

Rosebuds Ranch and Garden LLC.......... F 937 214-1801
　Covington *(G-6031)*

Shawadi LLC.. E 614 839-0698
　Westerville *(G-15720)*

Spot On Main LLC................................ F 740 285-0441
　Jackson *(G-8723)*

Staufs Coffee Roasters Limited.............. G 614 486-4479
　Columbus *(G-5792)*

Wheeling Coffee & Spice Co.................. F 304 232-0141
　Saint Clairsville *(G-12933)*

2096 Potato chips and similar snacks

Advanced Green Tech Inc...................... G 614 397-8130
　Plain City *(G-12560)*

Backattack Snacks................................ G 216 236-4580
　Brookpark *(G-1706)*

Ballreich Bros Inc.................................. C 419 447-1814
　Tiffin *(G-14078)*

Basic Grain Products Inc........................ D 419 678-2304
　Coldwater *(G-4982)*

Birds Eye Foods Inc.............................. D 330 854-0818
　Canal Fulton *(G-1968)*

Bsfc LLC... C 419 447-1814
　Tiffin *(G-14079)*

CJ Dannemiller Co................................. E 330 825-7808
　Norton *(G-11939)*

Conns Potato Chip Co Inc...................... E 614 252-2150
　Columbus *(G-5287)*

Conns Potato Chip Co Inc...................... E 740 452-4615
　Zanesville *(G-16523)*

Crack Corn Ltd..................................... F 440 467-0108
　Massillon *(G-10087)*

Evans Food Group Ltd........................... F 626 636-8110
　Portsmouth *(G-12643)*

Evans Food Group Ltd........................... G 740 285-3078
　Portsmouth *(G-12644)*

Frito-Lay North America Inc.................... D 330 477-7009
　Canton *(G-2106)*

Frito-Lay North America Inc.................... C 972 334-7000
　Wooster *(G-16121)*

Grippo Foods Inc................................... D 513 923-1900
　Cincinnati *(G-2974)*

Grippo Potato Chip Co Inc...................... E 513 923-1900
　Cincinnati *(G-2975)*

Herr Foods Incorporated........................ E 740 773-8282
　Chillicothe *(G-2509)*

Herr Foods Incorporated........................ F 800 344-3777
　Chillicothe *(G-2510)*

Jones Potato Chip Co............................ E 419 529-9424
　Mansfield *(G-9674)*

Mike-Sells Potato Chip Co...................... D 937 228-9400
　Dayton *(G-6446)*

Mike-Sells Potato Chip Co...................... D 937 228-9400
　Sabina *(G-12887)*

Mike-Sells Potato Chip Co...................... E 937 228-9400
　Dayton *(G-6447)*

Mike-Sells West Virginia Inc................... D 937 228-9400
　Dayton *(G-6448)*

Mumfords Potato Chips & Deli................ G 937 653-3491
　Urbana *(G-14844)*

Robert E McGrath Inc............................ F 440 572-7747
　Strongsville *(G-13872)*

◆ Rudolph Foods Company Inc............ C 909 383-7463
　Lima *(G-9287)*

Shearers Foods LLC............................. G 330 767-3426
　Brewster *(G-1646)*

Shearers Foods LLC............................. F 330 767-7969
　Massillon *(G-10143)*

◆ Shearers Foods LLC........................ A 800 428-6843
　Massillon *(G-10142)*

◆ Snack Alliance Inc............................ B 330 767-3426
　Massillon *(G-10146)*

Sweeties Olympia Treats LLC................ F 440 572-7747
　Strongsville *(G-13888)*

White Feather Foods Inc........................ F 419 738-8975
　Wapakoneta *(G-15133)*

2097 Manufactured ice

Donohues Hilltop Ice Co Ltd................... E 740 432-3348
　Cambridge *(G-1933)*

Haller Enterprises Inc............................ F 330 733-9693
　Akron *(G-177)*

Home City Ice Company......................... G 513 851-4040
　Cincinnati *(G-3005)*

Home City Ice Company......................... G 937 461-6028
　Dayton *(G-6371)*

Home City Ice Company......................... F 419 562-4953
　Delaware *(G-6731)*

Home City Ice Company......................... F 614 836-2877
　Groveport *(G-8146)*

Home City Ice Company......................... F 513 353-9346
　Harrison *(G-8279)*

Home City Ice Company......................... G 513 598-3000
　Olmsted Twp *(G-12087)*

Lori Holding Co..................................... E 740 342-3230
　New Lexington *(G-11453)*

Luc Ice Inc.. G 419 734-2201
　Huron *(G-8639)*

Millersburg Ice Company........................ E 330 674-3016
　Millersburg *(G-10983)*

Velvet Ice Cream Company.................... E 419 562-2009
　Bucyrus *(G-1872)*

Zygo Inc... G 513 281-0888
　Cincinnati *(G-3539)*

2098 Macaroni and spaghetti

Big Noodle LLC..................................... G 614 558-7170
　Columbus *(G-5187)*

Flour Management LLC.......................... F 216 910-9019
　Bedford Heights *(G-1171)*

Flour Management LLC.......................... G 216 910-9019
　Moreland Hills *(G-11219)*

Fusion Noodle Company Inc................... G 740 589-5511
　Athens *(G-682)*

20 FOOD AND KINDRED PRODUCTS

▲ International Noodle Company........ F 614 888-0665
  Lewis Center *(G-9166)*
Laricccias Italian Foods Inc............ F 330 729-0222
  Youngstown *(G-16388)*
Pho & Rice LLC............................. G 216 563-1122
  Cleveland Heights *(G-4942)*
◆ Tmarzetti Company........................ C 614 846-2232
  Westerville *(G-15683)*
YAR Corporation............................. G 330 652-1222
  Niles *(G-11693)*

2099 Food preparations, nec

Advancperre Foods Holdings Inc......... D 513 428-5699
  West Chester *(G-15532)*
Agrana Fruit Us Inc......................... C 937 693-3821
  Anna *(G-488)*
Alimento Ventures Inc..................... E 855 510-2866
  Blue Ash *(G-1361)*
Amir Foods Inc.............................. F 440 646-9388
  Cleveland *(G-3658)*
Amir International Foods Inc............. G 614 332-1742
  Grove City *(G-8079)*
Amish Wedding Foods Inc................ E 330 674-9199
  Millersburg *(G-10941)*
▲ Andys Mdterranean Fd Pdts LLC..... G 513 281-9791
  Cincinnati *(G-2627)*
Apf Legacy Subs LLC..................... G 513 682-7173
  West Chester *(G-15537)*
Ascot Valley Foods Ltd................... E 330 376-9411
  Cuyahoga Falls *(G-6068)*
B&G Foods Inc.............................. E 513 482-8226
  Cincinnati *(G-2653)*
Ballreich Bros Inc........................... C 419 447-1814
  Tiffin *(G-14078)*
Basic Grain Products Inc.................. D 419 678-2304
  Coldwater *(G-4982)*
Beehex LLC.................................. F 512 633-5304
  Columbus *(G-5180)*
Best Bite Grill LLC......................... F 419 344-7462
  Versailles *(G-14977)*
Bfc Inc.. E 330 364-6645
  Dover *(G-6809)*
Big Gus Onion Rings Inc.................. F 216 883-9045
  Cleveland *(G-3735)*
Bishops Daily Blessings LLC............ G 724 624-3779
  Steubenville *(G-13662)*
Brantley Partners IV LP................... G 216 464-8400
  Cleveland *(G-3754)*
Bread Kneads Inc........................... G 419 422-3863
  Findlay *(G-7486)*
Buckeye Valley Pizza Hut Ltd........... E 419 586-5900
  Celina *(G-2324)*
Caruso Foods LLC.......................... D 513 860-9200
  Cincinnati *(G-2705)*
Chefs Garden Inc........................... C 419 433-4947
  Huron *(G-8630)*
Chieffos Frozen Foods Inc................ G 330 652-1222
  Niles *(G-11664)*
Cincinnati Premier Candy Llc............ G 513 253-0079
  Cincinnati *(G-2758)*
CJ Dannemiller Co.......................... E 330 825-7808
  Norton *(G-11939)*
Clcb LLC...................................... G 316 284-0401
  Saint Clairsville *(G-12898)*
Conagra Brands Inc........................ D 419 445-8015
  Archbold *(G-527)*
Conagra Fods Pckaged Foods LLC...... E 937 440-2800
  Troy *(G-14556)*
Country Parlour Ice Cream Co........... F 440 237-4040
  Cleveland *(G-3908)*
Cuyahoga Vending Co Inc................ C 440 353-9495
  North Ridgeville *(G-11837)*

Darlenes Kitchen LLC..................... G 910 633-9744
  Toledo *(G-14261)*
Deer Creek Honey Farms Ltd........... G 740 852-0899
  London *(G-9386)*
Dismat Corporation........................ G 419 531-8963
  Toledo *(G-14268)*
Dno Inc....................................... D 614 231-3601
  Columbus *(G-5334)*
Dole Fresh Vegetables Inc............... C 937 525-4300
  Springfield *(G-13556)*
Domino Foods Inc.......................... C 216 432-3222
  Cleveland *(G-3968)*
Dure Foods Us LLC........................ F 614 409-9030
  Columbus *(G-5337)*
Empanadas Aqui LLC...................... E 513 312-9566
  Maineville *(G-9599)*
Essential Provisions LLC.................. G 937 271-0381
  Wilmington *(G-16049)*
Firehouse Foods............................ G 614 592-8115
  Columbus *(G-5376)*
Food 4 Your Soul........................... F 330 402-4073
  Youngstown *(G-16358)*
Food Designs Inc........................... F 216 651-9221
  Cleveland *(G-4078)*
Foodies Vegan Ltd......................... F 513 487-3037
  Cincinnati *(G-2913)*
Frank L Harter & Son Inc................. G 513 574-1330
  Cincinnati *(G-2920)*
Fremont Company........................... E 419 363-2924
  Rockford *(G-12833)*
Freshway Foods Company Inc.......... D 937 498-4664
  Sidney *(G-13249)*
Frito-Lay North America Inc............ D 330 477-7009
  Canton *(G-2106)*
Frito-Lay North America Inc............ C 972 334-7000
  Wooster *(G-16121)*
Frog Ranch Foods Ltd.................... F 740 767-3705
  Glouster *(G-7983)*
◆ Frutarom USA Inc........................ C 513 870-4900
  West Chester *(G-15556)*
General Mills Inc........................... D 513 771-8200
  Cincinnati *(G-2944)*
Generations Ace Inc....................... G 440 835-4872
  Bay Village *(G-965)*
Gold Star Chili Inc......................... E 513 631-1990
  Cincinnati *(G-2964)*
Gold Star Chili Inc......................... E 513 231-4541
  Cincinnati *(G-2963)*
Gomez Salsa LLC........................... E 513 314-1978
  Cincinnati *(G-2965)*
Graffiti Foods Limited..................... F 614 759-1921
  Columbus *(G-5408)*
Grays Orange Barn Inc................... G 419 568-2718
  Wapakoneta *(G-15116)*
Great Lakes Popcorn Company........... G 419 732-3080
  Port Clinton *(G-12620)*
Grippo Potato Chip Co Inc............... E 513 923-1900
  Cincinnati *(G-2975)*
▲ Gsi of Ohio LLC.......................... F 216 431-3344
  Cleveland *(G-4154)*
Harvest Commissary LLC................. E 513 706-1951
  Granville *(G-8017)*
Hen of Woods LLC........................ G 513 954-8871
  Cincinnati *(G-2993)*
Heritage Cooperative Inc................. F 740 828-2215
  Nashport *(G-11338)*
Herold Salads Inc.......................... E 216 991-7500
  Cleveland *(G-4186)*
Hilltop Recreation Inc..................... F 937 549-2904
  Manchester *(G-9619)*
Holmes Made Foods LLC................. G 216 618-5043
  Cleveland *(G-4197)*

Honeybaked Ham Company............... E 513 583-9700
  Cincinnati *(G-3006)*
Hydrofresh Ltd.............................. G 567 765-1010
  Delphos *(G-6765)*
Ingredient Innovations Intl Co........... G 330 262-4440
  Wooster *(G-16132)*
Inter American Products Inc............. D 800 645-2233
  Cincinnati *(G-3025)*
◆ J M Smucker Company................. A 330 682-3000
  Orrville *(G-12129)*
John Krusinski.............................. F 216 441-0100
  Cleveland *(G-4258)*
◆ Kantner Ingredients Inc................ G 614 766-3638
  Columbus *(G-5503)*
Kerry Inc..................................... E 440 229-5200
  Wickliffe *(G-15836)*
Kraft Heinz Company...................... A 330 837-8331
  Massillon *(G-10118)*
Kraft Heinz Foods Company............. D 419 332-7357
  Fremont *(G-7793)*
Krema Group Inc........................... F 614 889-4824
  Plain City *(G-12584)*
La Perla Inc................................. G 419 534-2074
  Toledo *(G-14356)*
Lakeview Farms LLC...................... C 419 695-9925
  Delphos *(G-6769)*
Las Americas Inc........................... G 440 459-2030
  Cleveland *(G-4314)*
Lasenor Usa LLC........................... F 800 754-1228
  Salem *(G-13010)*
Lbzb Restaurants Inc...................... F 567 413-4700
  Bowling Green *(G-1570)*
Lipari Foods Operating Co LLC.......... E 330 893-2479
  Millersburg *(G-10973)*
Lipari Foods Operating Co LLC.......... E 330 674-9199
  Millersburg *(G-10974)*
Lyle Tate.................................... G 937 698-6526
  Ludlow Falls *(G-9528)*
Main Street Gourmet LLC................ C 330 929-0000
  Cuyahoga Falls *(G-6101)*
◆ Mane Inc.................................. D 513 248-9876
  Lebanon *(G-9096)*
Miami Valley Meals Inc................... G 937 938-7141
  Dayton *(G-6439)*
Mid American Ventures Inc.............. F 216 524-0974
  Cleveland *(G-4405)*
Momma Js Blazing Kitchen LLC......... G 216 551-8791
  Cleveland Heights *(G-4941)*
▲ Mrs Mllers Hmmade Noodles Ltd.... F 330 694-5814
  Fredericksburg *(G-7728)*
Nat2 Inc...................................... E 614 270-2507
  Heath *(G-8325)*
Nat2 Inc...................................... G 614 270-2507
  Lewis Center *(G-9173)*
Nates Nectar LLC.......................... G 937 935-3289
  De Graff *(G-6665)*
▲ National Foods Packaging Inc........ E 216 622-2740
  Cleveland *(G-4437)*
Natures Health Food LLC................ F 419 260-9265
  Mount Victory *(G-11301)*
New Horizons Fd Solutions LLC......... E 614 861-3639
  Columbus *(G-5595)*
North Country Charcuterie LLC......... F 614 670-5726
  Columbus *(G-5602)*
Nu Pet Company............................ F 330 682-3000
  Orrville *(G-12142)*
▲ Oasis Mdterranean Cuisine Inc....... E 419 269-1459
  Toledo *(G-14402)*
Ohio Hckry Hrvest Brnd Pdts In........ E 330 644-6266
  Coventry Township *(G-6014)*
Old Classic Delight Inc................... D 419 394-7955
  Saint Marys *(G-12959)*

One Tortilla Co. .... G 614 570-9312
  Columbus (G-5640)
Orval Kent Food Company LLC .... E 419 695-5015
  Delphos (G-6770)
Pepperidge Farm Incorporated .... G 419 933-2611
  Willard (G-15863)
Pfizer Inc. .... F 937 746-3603
  Franklin (G-7691)
Pita Wrap LLC .... G 330 886-8091
  Boardman (G-1516)
Plant Plant Co. .... E 303 809-9588
  Heath (G-8326)
◆ Procter & Gamble Mfg Co .... F 513 983-1100
  Cincinnati (G-3298)
Produce Packaging Inc. .... C 216 391-6129
  Willoughby Hills (G-16027)
Pure Foods LLC .... G 303 358-8375
  Highland Heights (G-8391)
Purushealth LLC .... F 800 601-0580
  Shaker Heights (G-13158)
▲ R S Hanline and Co Inc .... C 419 347-8077
  Shelby (G-13199)
Rich Products Corporation .... C 614 771-1117
  Hilliard (G-8436)
Richelieu Foods Inc. .... E 740 335-4813
  Wshngtn Ct Hs (G-16239)
Rosebuds Ranch and Garden LLC .... F 937 214-1801
  Covington (G-6031)
Roy Retrac Incorporated .... G 740 564-5552
  Columbus (G-5732)
◆ Rudolph Foods Company Inc .... C 909 383-7463
  Lima (G-9287)
Russos Ravioli LLC .... F 513 833-7700
  Cincinnati (G-3357)
Salsa Rica II LLC .... G 740 616-9918
  Hilliard (G-8438)
Savor Seasonings LLC .... F 513 732-2333
  Batavia (G-947)
Savory Foods Inc. .... D 740 354-6655
  Portsmouth (G-12655)
◆ Sensoryffcts Powdr Systems Inc .... D 419 783-5518
  Defiance (G-6694)
Smartsoda Holdings Inc. .... E 888 998-9668
  Cleveland (G-4708)
▼ Smucker International Inc .... G 330 682-3000
  Orrville (G-12154)
Solae LLC .... F 419 483-5340
  Bellevue (G-1236)
Sunrise Foods Inc. .... E 614 276-2880
  Columbus (G-5798)
Tarrier Foods Corp. .... E 614 876-8594
  Columbus (G-5810)
Timmys Sandwich Shop .... G 419 350-8267
  Toledo (G-14486)
Tortillas La Reyna LLC .... G 630 247-9453
  Columbus (G-5828)
▼ Tortilleria La Bamba LLC .... G 216 515-1600
  Cleveland (G-4809)
Unger Kosher Bakery Inc. .... F 216 321-7476
  Cleveland Heights (G-4944)
Wal-Bon of Ohio Inc. .... F 740 423-8178
  Belpre (G-1262)
Wannemacher Enterprises Inc .... F 419 771-1101
  Upper Sandusky (G-14824)
Weston Brands Inc. .... G 800 814-4895
  Independence (G-8691)
White Castle System Inc. .... E 513 563-2290
  Cincinnati (G-3518)
White Feather Foods Inc. .... F 419 738-8975
  Wapakoneta (G-15133)
Whitmore Productions Inc. .... F 216 752-3960
  Warrensville Heights (G-15231)

Wildcat Creek Farms Inc. .... F 419 263-2549
  Payne (G-12324)
◆ Woeber Mustard Mfg Co .... C 937 323-6281
  Springfield (G-13656)
▲ Wyandot Usa LLC .... C 740 383-4031
  Marion (G-9892)
Zidian Management Corp .... E 330 743-6050
  Boardman (G-1520)
▲ Zidian Manufacturing Inc .... D 330 965-8455
  Boardman (G-1521)

21 TOBACCO PRODUCTS

2111 Cigarettes

Discount Smokes & Gifts Xenia .... G 937 372-0259
  Xenia (G-16260)
Memphis Smokehouse Inc. .... G 216 351-5321
  Cleveland (G-4393)

2131 Chewing and smoking tobacco

◆ Scandinavian Tob Group Ln Ltd .... C 770 934-4594
  Akron (G-325)
Smoke Rings Inc. .... G 419 420-9966
  Findlay (G-7564)

22 TEXTILE MILL PRODUCTS

2211 Broadwoven fabric mills, cotton

Akron Cotton Products Inc. .... G 330 434-7171
  Akron (G-32)
Canton Sterilized Wiping Cloth .... G 330 455-5179
  Canton (G-2068)
Carmens Installation Co. .... F 216 321-4040
  Cleveland (G-3793)
▼ Ccp Industries Inc .... B 216 535-4227
  Richmond Heights (G-12807)
Cleveland Drapery Stitch Inc. .... F 216 252-3857
  Cleveland (G-3838)
Compass Energy LLC .... F 866 665-2225
  Cleveland (G-3891)
Creative Canvas LLC .... G 740 359-3173
  Flushing (G-7586)
Denim6729 Inc. .... G 216 854-3634
  Cleveland (G-3951)
▲ F H Bonn Co Inc .... E 937 323-7024
  Springfield (G-13562)
Fabric Square Shop .... G 330 752-3044
  Stow (G-13696)
Heritage Hill LLC .... G 513 237-0240
  Blue Ash (G-1407)
▲ Inside Outfitters Inc .... E 614 798-3500
  Lewis Center (G-9165)
Kdae Inc. .... G 844 543-8339
  Lewis Center (G-9167)
Linsalata Cpitl Prtners Fund I .... G 440 684-1400
  Cleveland (G-4330)
Lumenomics Inc. .... E 614 798-3500
  Lewis Center (G-9170)
▲ MGF Sourcing US LLC .... D 614 904-3300
  Columbus (G-5561)
▲ Mmi Textiles Inc .... G 440 899-8050
  Brooklyn (G-1679)
Nancys Draperies Inc. .... G 330 855-7751
  Marshallville (G-9894)
Noble Denim Workshop .... G 513 560-5640
  Cincinnati (G-3202)
R J Manray Inc. .... G 330 559-6716
  Canfield (G-2015)
Recovery Rm Canvas & Uphl LLC .... G 740 246-6086
  Thornville (G-14069)
Rj Canvas Works Inc. .... G 216 337-6099
  Cleveland (G-4640)

Roach Studios LLC .... F 614 725-1405
  Columbus (G-5727)
▲ Sk Textile Inc .... C 800 888-9112
  Cincinnati (G-3396)
STI Liquidation Inc. .... E 614 733-0099
  Plain City (G-12592)
Stitches Usa LLC .... F 330 852-0500
  Walnut Creek (G-15095)
Struggle Grind Success LLC .... G 330 834-6738
  Boardman (G-1518)
◆ Synthomer Inc .... C 216 682-7000
  Beachwood (G-1025)
▲ Totes Isotoner Holdings Corp .... C 513 682-8200
  West Chester (G-15599)
Tranzonic Companies .... C 440 446-0643
  Cleveland (G-4818)
Trophy Sports Center LLC .... F 937 376-2311
  Xenia (G-16279)
◆ Tz Acquisition Corp .... E 216 535-4300
  Richmond Heights (G-12812)
Vermilion Custom Canvas Inc. .... G 440 963-5483
  Vermilion (G-14974)
Weiskopf Industries Corp. .... F 440 442-4400
  Cleveland (G-4901)
Wonder-Shirts Inc. .... G 917 679-2336
  Dublin (G-6959)

2221 Broadwoven fabric mills, manmade

▲ Architectural Fiberglass Inc .... E 216 641-8300
  Cleveland (G-3673)
Cleveland Drapery Stitch Inc. .... F 216 252-3857
  Cleveland (G-3838)
Conform Automotive LLC .... B 937 492-2708
  Sidney (G-13233)
▲ Inside Outfitters Inc .... E 614 798-3500
  Lewis Center (G-9165)
◆ King Bag and Manufacturing Co .... E 513 541-5440
  Cincinnati (G-3076)
Lumenomics Inc. .... E 614 798-3500
  Lewis Center (G-9170)
Marsh Composites LLC .... G 937 350-1214
  Dayton (G-6169)
▲ Mmi Textiles Inc .... G 440 899-8050
  Brooklyn (G-1679)
PCR Restorations Inc. .... F 419 747-7957
  Mansfield (G-9709)
Schmelzer Industries Inc. .... E 740 743-2866
  Somerset (G-13450)
◆ Seaman Corporation .... C 330 262-1111
  Wooster (G-16170)
Toledo Fiber Products Corp. .... G 419 720-0303
  Toledo (G-14496)
Valutex Reinforcements Inc. .... E 800 251-2507
  Wshngtn Ct Hs (G-16243)
▲ Weaver Leather LLC .... D 330 674-7548
  Millersburg (G-11007)

2231 Broadwoven fabric mills, wool

Midwest Composites LLC .... F 419 738-2431
  Wapakoneta (G-15123)
R J Manray Inc. .... G 330 559-6716
  Canfield (G-2015)

2241 Narrow fabric mills

A & P Technology Inc. .... E 513 688-3200
  Cincinnati (G-2545)
A & P Technology Inc. .... E 513 688-3200
  Cincinnati (G-2546)
A & P Technology Inc. .... E 513 688-3200
  Cincinnati (G-2547)
A & P Technology Inc. .... E 513 688-3200
  Cincinnati (G-2548)

22 TEXTILE MILL PRODUCTS

◆ A & P Technology Inc............................E 513 688-3200
  Cincinnati *(G-2549)*
Community Action Program Corp...........F 740 374-8501
  Marietta *(G-9786)*
Crane Consumables Inc..........................E 513 539-9980
  Middletown *(G-10814)*
CT Specialty Polymers Ltd....................G 440 632-9311
  Middlefield *(G-10744)*
◆ Denizen Inc...F 937 615-9561
  Piqua *(G-12513)*
▲ Grove Engineered Products...................G 419 659-5939
  Columbus Grove *(G-5898)*
◆ Keuchel & Associates Inc.....................E 330 945-9455
  Cuyahoga Falls *(G-6095)*
◆ Mitchellace Inc.......................................D 740 354-2813
  Portsmouth *(G-12650)*
Murrubber Technologies Inc...................E 330 688-4881
  Stow *(G-13711)*
Northeast Tubular Inc.............................E 330 567-2690
  Wooster *(G-16157)*
▲ Samsel Rope & Marine Supply Co......E 216 241-0333
  Cleveland *(G-4670)*
◆ Shore To Shore Inc................................D 937 866-1908
  Dayton *(G-6570)*
▲ Sole Choice Inc......................................E 740 354-2813
  Portsmouth *(G-12656)*
US Cotton LLC..D 216 676-6400
  Cleveland *(G-4856)*

2252 Hosiery, nec

Broken Spinning Wheel...........................G 419 825-1609
  Swanton *(G-13970)*
Forepleasure..G 330 821-1293
  Alliance *(G-404)*
Hype Socks LLC......................................F 855 497-3769
  Columbus *(G-5448)*
Rock Em Sock Em Retro LLC...............G 419 575-9309
  Walbridge *(G-15087)*

2253 Knit outerwear mills

Digitek Corp...F 513 794-3190
  Mason *(G-9984)*
E Retailing Associates LLC....................D 614 300-5785
  Columbus *(G-5339)*
Fine Points Inc...F 216 229-6644
  Cleveland *(G-4060)*
▲ Pjs Wholesale Inc..................................G 614 402-9363
  Columbus *(G-5676)*
Spalding..F 440 286-5717
  Chardon *(G-2469)*
Tha Presidential Suite LLC....................G 216 338-7287
  Dublin *(G-6952)*
Wonder-Shirts Inc....................................G 917 679-2336
  Dublin *(G-6959)*

2258 Lace and warp knit fabric mills

Murray Fabrics Inc..................................F 216 881-4041
  Cleveland *(G-4430)*

2259 Knitting mills, nec

Ansell Healthcare Products LLC............C 740 622-4369
  Coshocton *(G-5969)*

2261 Finishing plants, cotton

▲ Atlantis Sportswear Inc........................E 937 773-0680
  Piqua *(G-12506)*
▼ Duracote Corporation............................E 330 296-9600
  Ravenna *(G-12712)*
◆ Image Group Inc....................................E 419 866-3300
  Holland *(G-8514)*
Phantasm Dsgns Sprtsn More Ltd..........G 419 538-6737
  Ottawa *(G-12188)*

Precision Imprint.....................................G 740 592-5916
  Athens *(G-692)*
West-Camp Press Inc..............................D 216 426-2660
  Cleveland *(G-4905)*

2262 Finishing plants, manmade

717 Inc..G 440 925-0402
  Lakewood *(G-8965)*
B Richardson Inc.....................................G 330 724-2122
  Akron *(G-72)*
Flashions Sportswear Ltd.......................G 937 323-5885
  Springfield *(G-13565)*
Kaylo Enterprises LLC............................G 330 535-1860
  Akron *(G-202)*
▲ Mmi Textiles Inc....................................G 440 899-8050
  Brooklyn *(G-1679)*
Phantasm Dsgns Sprtsn More Ltd..........G 419 538-6737
  Ottawa *(G-12188)*
Sportsco Imprinting.................................G 513 641-5111
  Cincinnati *(G-3409)*
Tranzonic Companies..............................C 440 446-0643
  Cleveland *(G-4818)*
◆ Tz Acquisition Corp................................E 216 535-4300
  Richmond Heights *(G-12812)*

2273 Carpets and rugs

3359 Kingston LLC.................................G 614 871-8989
  Grove City *(G-8071)*
4blar LLC...G 513 576-0441
  Milford *(G-10889)*
Alliance Carpet Cushion Co...................E 740 966-5001
  Johnstown *(G-8768)*
Angstrom Fiber Englewood LLC...........E 734 756-1164
  Englewood *(G-7223)*
◆ Boardman Molded Products Inc............D 330 788-2400
  Youngstown *(G-16322)*
▼ Ccp Industries Inc..................................B 216 535-4227
  Richmond Heights *(G-12807)*
Columbus Public School Dst..................F 614 365-6517
  Columbus *(G-5275)*
David Moore...G 614 836-9331
  Groveport *(G-8137)*
Dribble Creek Inc....................................F 440 439-8650
  Twinsburg *(G-14654)*
▲ Durable Corporation...............................D 800 537-1603
  Norwalk *(G-11962)*
Johns Manville Corporation...................D 419 878-8111
  Waterville *(G-15246)*
Jpc Llc...G 513 310-1608
  Akron *(G-10015)*
Mat Basics Incorporated.........................G 513 793-0313
  Blue Ash *(G-1428)*
Mohawk 11 Inc..G 614 771-0327
  Hilliard *(G-8420)*
Mohawk Industries Inc............................F 800 837-3812
  Grove City *(G-8108)*
Shaw Industries Inc.................................A 513 942-3692
  Fairfield *(G-7407)*
Spacelinks Enterprises Inc.....................E 330 788-2401
  Youngstown *(G-16443)*
Tranzonic Companies..............................C 440 446-0643
  Cleveland *(G-4818)*
Xt Innovations Ltd...................................G 419 562-1989
  Bucyrus *(G-1876)*

2281 Yarn spinning mills

Unifi LLC..G 614 288-9217
  Reynoldsburg *(G-12779)*

2282 Throwing and winding mills

Alliance Carpet Cushion Co...................E 740 966-5001
  Johnstown *(G-8768)*

2284 Thread mills

Alvin L Roepke..G 419 862-3891
  Elmore *(G-7099)*

2295 Coated fabrics, not rubberized

Alron...G 330 477-3405
  Strasburg *(G-13742)*
Bexley Fabrics Inc..................................G 614 231-7272
  Columbus *(G-5184)*
▲ Biothane Coated Webbing Corp.............E 440 327-0485
  North Ridgeville *(G-11832)*
▲ Buckeye Fabric Finishers Inc...............F 740 622-3251
  Coshocton *(G-5975)*
▲ Buschman Corporation...........................F 216 431-6633
  Cleveland *(G-3774)*
Complex Group NC LLC........................F 513 671-3300
  Fairfield *(G-7344)*
◆ Diamond Polymers Incorporated..........D 330 773-2700
  Akron *(G-128)*
▼ Duracote Corporation.............................E 330 296-9600
  Ravenna *(G-12712)*
Durez Corporation...................................E 567 295-6400
  Kenton *(G-8882)*
Excello Fabric Finishers Inc..................G 740 622-7444
  Coshocton *(G-5977)*
Form Manufacturing Llc........................F 419 678-1400
  Coldwater *(G-4988)*
Laserflex Corporation.............................D 614 850-9600
  Hilliard *(G-8418)*
▲ Laurenco Systems of Ohio LLC............G
  Leavittsburg *(G-9058)*
Prints & Paints Flr Cvg Co Inc..............E 419 462-5663
  Galion *(G-7883)*
Richard Klinger Inc.................................G 937 498-2222
  Sidney *(G-13276)*
◆ Schneller LLC..C 330 676-7183
  Kent *(G-8858)*
Shaheen Oriental Rug Co Inc.................F 330 493-9000
  Canton *(G-2222)*

2296 Tire cord and fabrics

Cleveland Canvas Goods Mfg Co..........E 216 361-4567
  Cleveland *(G-3835)*
Mfh Partners Inc......................................B 440 461-4100
  Cleveland *(G-4398)*

2297 Nonwoven fabrics

▲ Amantea Nonwovens LLC......................F 513 842-6600
  Cincinnati *(G-2614)*
Autoneum North America Inc................B 419 693-0511
  Oregon *(G-12103)*
▼ Ccp Industries Inc..................................B 216 535-4227
  Richmond Heights *(G-12807)*
▲ Toyobo Kureha America Co Ltd............G 513 771-6788
  West Chester *(G-15517)*

2298 Cordage and twine

▲ Atwood Rope Manufacturing Inc...........E 614 920-0534
  Canal Winchester *(G-1979)*
Atwood Rope Manufacturing Inc...........G 614 920-0534
  Millersport *(G-11010)*
Automted Cmpnent Spcalists LLC........E 513 335-4285
  Cincinnati *(G-2645)*
Connect Television..................................G 614 876-4402
  Hilliard *(G-8409)*
◆ Core Optix Inc..F 855 267-3678
  Cincinnati *(G-2796)*
Infinitaire Industries LLC.......................G 216 600-2051
  Euclid *(G-7275)*
International Jump Rope Union..............G 937 409-1006
  Springboro *(G-13505)*

23 APPAREL, FINISHED PRODUCTS FROM FABRICS & SIMILAR MATERIALS

Katimex USA Inc .... G 440 338-3500
  Chagrin Falls *(G-2381)*
Radix Wire & Cable LLC .... D 216 731-9191
  Solon *(G-13410)*

2299 Textile goods, nec

Big Productions Inc .... G 440 775-0015
  Oberlin *(G-12049)*
Construction Techniques Inc .... F 216 267-7310
  Cleveland *(G-3900)*
Dayton Bag & Burlap Co .... F 937 253-1722
  Dayton *(G-6273)*
J Rettenmaier USA LP .... D 937 652-2101
  Urbana *(G-14839)*
Meridian Industries Inc .... E 330 359-5809
  Beach City *(G-968)*
▲ NC Works Inc .... E 937 514-7781
  Franklin *(G-7688)*
▲ Ohio Table Pad Company .... F 419 872-6400
  Perrysburg *(G-12407)*
▲ Ohio Table Pad of Indiana .... D 419 872-6400
  Perrysburg *(G-12409)*
Rose Remington .... G 513 755-1695
  Liberty Township *(G-9210)*
◆ Standard Textile Co Inc .... B 513 761-9255
  Cincinnati *(G-3415)*

23 APPAREL, FINISHED PRODUCTS FROM FABRICS & SIMILAR MATERIALS

2311 Men's and boy's suits and coats

Bea-Ecc Apparels Inc .... G 216 650-6336
  Cleveland *(G-3726)*
Empirical Manufacturing Co Inc .... E 513 948-1616
  Cincinnati *(G-2867)*
J & G Goecke Clothing LLC .... G 419 692-9981
  Delphos *(G-6766)*
◆ Lion Apparel Inc .... C 937 898-1949
  Dayton *(G-6408)*
Lion Apparel Inc .... D 937 898-1949
  Dayton *(G-6409)*
Lion First Responder Ppe Inc .... D 937 898-1949
  Dayton *(G-6410)*
Lion Group Inc .... D 937 898-1949
  Dayton *(G-6411)*
◆ The Fechheimer Brothers Co .... C 513 793-5400
  Blue Ash *(G-1480)*
Vgs Inc .... C 216 431-7800
  Cleveland *(G-4866)*

2321 Men's and boy's furnishings

Columbus Apparel Studio LLC .... F 614 706-7292
  Columbus *(G-5261)*
J C L S Enterprises LLC .... G 740 472-0314
  Woodsfield *(G-16088)*

2322 Men's and boy's underwear and nightwear

Tranzonic Companies .... D 216 535-4300
  Richmond Heights *(G-12811)*

2323 Men's and boy's neckwear

Outfit Good LLC .... G 419 565-3770
  Columbus *(G-5647)*

2326 Men's and boy's work clothing

Angels Uniform & Print Sp LLC .... G 330 707-6506
  Youngstown *(G-16313)*

Barton-Carey Medical Pdts Inc .... E 419 887-1285
  Maumee *(G-10169)*
Cintas Corporation .... D 513 631-5750
  Cincinnati *(G-2770)*
◆ Cintas Corporation .... A 513 459-1200
  Cincinnati *(G-2769)*
Cintas Corporation No 2 .... D 330 966-7800
  Canton *(G-2074)*
Cintas Sales Corporation .... B 513 459-1200
  Cincinnati *(G-2771)*
Cleveland Canvas Goods Mfg Co .... E 216 361-4567
  Cleveland *(G-3835)*
DCW Acquisition Inc .... E 216 451-0666
  Cleveland *(G-3949)*
Epluno LLC .... F 800 249-5275
  Springboro *(G-13500)*
Geauga Group LLC .... G 440 543-8797
  Chagrin Falls *(G-2397)*
▲ Hands On International LLC .... G 513 502-9000
  West Chester *(G-15560)*
Honeywell First Responder Pdts .... G 937 264-1726
  Dayton *(G-6372)*
Kip-Craft Incorporated .... D 216 898-5500
  Cleveland *(G-4293)*
Leisure Time Pdts Design Corp .... G 440 934-1032
  Avon *(G-779)*
Linsalata Cpitl Prtners Fund I .... G 440 684-1400
  Cleveland *(G-4330)*
Model Medical LLC .... F 216 972-0573
  Shaker Heights *(G-13156)*
▲ Morning Pride Mfg LLC .... A 937 264-2662
  Dayton *(G-6457)*
▲ Rich Industries Inc .... E 330 339-4113
  New Philadelphia *(G-11526)*
Samson .... G 614 504-8038
  Columbus *(G-5744)*
School Uniforms and More Inc .... G 216 365-1957
  Cleveland *(G-4674)*
Seven Mile Creek Corporation .... G 937 456-3320
  Eaton *(G-7069)*
Tranzonic Companies .... C 440 446-0643
  Cleveland *(G-4818)*
◆ Tz Acquisition Corp .... E 216 535-4300
  Richmond Heights *(G-12812)*
Vgs Inc .... C 216 431-7800
  Cleveland *(G-4866)*

2329 Men's and boy's clothing, nec

Adidas North America Inc .... F 330 562-4689
  Aurora *(G-704)*
Augusta Sportswear Inc .... G 937 497-7575
  Sidney *(G-13223)*
Carrera Holdings Inc .... E 216 687-1311
  Cleveland *(G-3795)*
Columbus Apparel Studio LLC .... F 614 706-7292
  Columbus *(G-5261)*
Fallon Pharaohs .... G 216 990-2746
  Cleveland *(G-4048)*
◆ Holloway Sportswear Inc .... D 937 497-7575
  Sidney *(G-13253)*
▲ Kam Manufacturing Inc .... C 419 238-6037
  Van Wert *(G-14919)*
Lettermans LLC .... G 330 345-2628
  Wooster *(G-16145)*
◆ Neff Motivation Inc .... C 937 548-3194
  Greenville *(G-8053)*
Noxgear LLC .... G 937 248-1860
  Columbus *(G-5605)*
Rocky Brands Inc .... B 740 753-9100
  Nelsonville *(G-11359)*
▲ Universal Lettering Inc .... F 419 238-9320
  Van Wert *(G-14929)*

▲ Vesi Incorporated .... E 513 563-6002
  Cincinnati *(G-3497)*

2331 Women's and misses' blouses and shirts

Columbus Apparel Studio LLC .... F 614 706-7292
  Columbus *(G-5261)*
J C L S Enterprises LLC .... G 740 472-0314
  Woodsfield *(G-16088)*
▲ Kam Manufacturing Inc .... C 419 238-6037
  Van Wert *(G-14919)*
Love Laugh & Laundry .... G 567 377-1951
  Toledo *(G-14370)*
Rocky Brands Inc .... B 740 753-9100
  Nelsonville *(G-11359)*

2335 Women's, junior's, and misses' dresses

Centennial Barn .... G 513 761-1697
  Cincinnati *(G-2715)*
Purple Orchid Boutique LLC .... G 614 554-7686
  Columbus *(G-5698)*
Renee Grace LLC .... G 513 399-5616
  Cincinnati *(G-3332)*
Surili Couture LLC .... F 440 600-1456
  Westlake *(G-15794)*

2337 Women's and misses' suits and coats

Cintas Corporation .... D 513 631-5750
  Cincinnati *(G-2770)*
◆ Cintas Corporation .... A 513 459-1200
  Cincinnati *(G-2769)*
Cintas Corporation No 2 .... D 330 966-7800
  Canton *(G-2074)*
◆ The Fechheimer Brothers Co .... C 513 793-5400
  Blue Ash *(G-1480)*

2339 Women's and misses' outerwear, nec

▲ 5 BS Inc .... C 740 454-8453
  Zanesville *(G-16493)*
Barton-Carey Medical Pdts Inc .... E 419 887-1285
  Maumee *(G-10169)*
Blingflingforever LLC .... G 216 215-6955
  Mentor On The Lake *(G-10601)*
Bodied Beauties LLC .... G 216 971-1155
  Richmond Heights *(G-12806)*
Carrera Holdings Inc .... E 216 687-1311
  Cleveland *(G-3795)*
Columbus Apparel Studio LLC .... F 614 706-7292
  Columbus *(G-5261)*
Fluff Boutique .... G 513 227-6614
  Cincinnati *(G-2911)*
Geauga Group LLC .... G 440 543-8797
  Chagrin Falls *(G-2397)*
Hipsy LLC .... G 513 403-5333
  Fairfield *(G-7367)*
◆ Holloway Sportswear Inc .... D 937 497-7575
  Sidney *(G-13253)*
Kip-Craft Incorporated .... D 216 898-5500
  Cleveland *(G-4293)*
Knh Industries Inc .... F 330 510-8390
  Stow *(G-13704)*
Knh Industries Inc .... G 330 235-1235
  Stow *(G-13703)*
Lettermans LLC .... G 330 345-2628
  Wooster *(G-16145)*
Owl Be Sweatin .... G 513 260-2026
  Cincinnati *(G-3231)*
Rocky Brands Inc .... B 740 753-9100
  Nelsonville *(G-11359)*
◆ The Fechheimer Brothers Co .... C 513 793-5400
  Blue Ash *(G-1480)*

23 APPAREL, FINISHED PRODUCTS FROM FABRICS & SIMILAR MATERIALS

▲ Universal Lettering Inc.................... F 419 238-9320
   Van Wert *(G-14929)*
▲ Vesi Incorporated............................ E 513 563-6002
   Cincinnati *(G-3497)*

2341 Women's and children's underwear

Tranzonic Companies........................ D 216 535-4300
   Richmond Heights *(G-12811)*
Vs Service Company LLC................. A 614 415-2348
   Reynoldsburg *(G-12780)*

2353 Hats, caps, and millinery

▲ Barbs Graffiti Inc............................ E 216 881-5550
   Cleveland *(G-3719)*
Blonde Swan..................................... F 419 307-8591
   Fremont *(G-7768)*
Bows Barrettes & Baubles................ F 440 247-2697
   Moreland Hills *(G-11218)*
◆ Pukka Inc....................................... E 419 429-7808
   Findlay *(G-7554)*
Thomas Creative Apparel Inc........... F 419 929-1506
   New London *(G-11470)*

2369 Girl's and children's outerwear, nec

Emblem Athletic LLC........................ G 614 743-6955
   Powell *(G-12671)*

2371 Fur goods

Ananda Anani LLC............................ G 440 406-6086
   Akron *(G-63)*
Blonde Swan..................................... F 419 307-8591
   Fremont *(G-7768)*

2381 Fabric dress and work gloves

Admj Holdings LLC.......................... E 216 588-0038
   Cleveland *(G-3601)*
▲ Totes Isotoner Holdings Corp......... C 513 682-8200
   West Chester *(G-15599)*
▲ Wcm Holdings Inc........................... C 513 705-2100
   Cincinnati *(G-3509)*
▲ West Chester Holdings LLC........... C 513 705-2100
   Cincinnati *(G-3516)*

2384 Robes and dressing gowns

Thomas Creative Apparel Inc........... F 419 929-1506
   New London *(G-11470)*

2385 Waterproof outerwear

Paradigm International Inc............... G 740 370-2428
   Piketon *(G-12482)*
▲ Totes Isotoner Corporation.............. D 513 682-8200
   West Chester *(G-15598)*

2389 Apparel and accessories, nec

Akron Design & Costume LLC......... G 330 644-0425
   Coventry Township *(G-6004)*
Costume Specialists Inc................... E 614 464-2115
   Columbus *(G-5298)*
Deborah Meredith.............................. G 330 644-0425
   Coventry Township *(G-6008)*
Direct Disposables LLC.................... G 440 717-3335
   Brecksville *(G-1613)*
Fancy ME Boutique LLC................... G 419 357-8927
   Sandusky *(G-13058)*
▲ Fire-Dex LLC................................... D 330 723-0000
   Medina *(G-10324)*
Front and Center MGT Group LLC... G 740 383-5176
   Marion *(G-9853)*
MA Workwear LLC............................ G 800 459-4405
   Akron *(G-233)*
New London Regalia Mfg Co........... G 419 929-1516
   New London *(G-11465)*

Ralphie Gianni Mfg & Co Ltd........... F 216 507-3873
   Euclid *(G-7298)*
▲ Rich Industries Inc........................... E 330 339-4113
   New Philadelphia *(G-11526)*
Rocky Brands Inc............................. B 740 753-9100
   Nelsonville *(G-11359)*
Salindia LLC...................................... G 614 501-4799
   Columbus *(G-5742)*
Schenz Theatrical Supply Inc.......... F 513 542-6100
   Cincinnati *(G-3369)*
Snaps Inc.. G 419 477-5100
   Mount Cory *(G-11228)*
▲ Status Mens Accessories................ G 440 786-9394
   Oakwood Village *(G-12042)*
Thomas Creative Apparel Inc........... F 419 929-1506
   New London *(G-11470)*
Walter F Stephens Jr Inc................. E 937 746-0521
   Franklin *(G-7709)*

2391 Curtains and draperies

Accent Drapery Co Inc..................... E 614 488-0741
   Columbus *(G-5092)*
Drapery Stitch of Delphos................ F 419 692-3921
   Delphos *(G-6763)*
Drapery Sttch - Cincinnati Inc......... F 513 561-2443
   Cincinnati *(G-2841)*
Elden Draperies of Toledo Inc......... F 419 535-1909
   Toledo *(G-14272)*
Electra Tarp Inc................................ F 330 477-7168
   Canton *(G-2095)*
Ikiriska LLC....................................... F 614 389-8994
   Powell *(G-12675)*
Janson Industries.............................. D 330 455-7029
   Canton *(G-2135)*
▲ Sk Textile Inc................................... C 800 888-9112
   Cincinnati *(G-3396)*
STI Liquidation Inc........................... E 614 733-0099
   Plain City *(G-12592)*
Style-Line Incorporated.................... E 614 291-0600
   Columbus *(G-5796)*
Tiffin Scenic Studios Inc.................. E 800 445-1546
   Tiffin *(G-14112)*
Vocational Services Inc.................... E 216 431-8085
   Cleveland *(G-4880)*

2392 Household furnishings, nec

A & W Table Pad Co......................... F 800 541-0271
   Cleveland *(G-3575)*
Brentwood Originals Inc................... C 330 793-2255
   Youngstown *(G-16324)*
▲ Casco Mfg Solutions Inc................. D 513 681-0003
   Cincinnati *(G-2706)*
▼ Ccp Industries Inc........................... B 216 535-4227
   Richmond Heights *(G-12807)*
Columbus Canvas Products Inc....... F 614 375-1397
   Columbus *(G-5263)*
DCW Acquisition Inc......................... E 216 451-0666
   Cleveland *(G-3949)*
Dorex LLC.. E 216 271-7064
   Newburgh Heights *(G-11613)*
▲ Down-Lite International Inc.............. C 513 229-3696
   Mason *(G-9985)*
Downhome Inc................................... E 513 921-3373
   Cincinnati *(G-2839)*
◆ Downhome Inc................................. F 513 921-3373
   Cincinnati *(G-2840)*
◆ Easy Way Leisure Company LLC... E 513 731-5640
   Cincinnati *(G-2855)*
Ekco Cleaning Inc............................. C 513 733-8882
   Cincinnati *(G-2860)*
Fluvitex USA Inc............................... C 614 610-1199
   Groveport *(G-8141)*

▲ Greendale Home Fashions LLC....... D 859 916-5475
   Cincinnati *(G-2971)*
Ha-Ste Manufacturing Co Inc.......... G 937 968-4858
   Union City *(G-14778)*
▲ Henty Usa LLC................................ F 513 984-5590
   Cincinnati *(G-2995)*
◆ Holloway Sportswear Inc................. D 937 497-7575
   Sidney *(G-13253)*
◆ Impact Products LLC....................... D 419 841-2891
   Toledo *(G-14328)*
◆ Master Mfg Co Inc........................... E 216 641-0500
   Cleveland *(G-4367)*
▲ Nestaway LLC.................................. D 216 587-1500
   Cleveland *(G-4449)*
Ohio Table Pad Company................ G 419 872-6400
   Perrysburg *(G-12408)*
▲ Ohio Table Pad Company................ F 419 872-6400
   Perrysburg *(G-12407)*
◆ Saturday Knight Ltd........................ D 513 641-1400
   Cincinnati *(G-3363)*
Seven Mile Creek Corporation......... G 937 456-3320
   Eaton *(G-7069)*
Sewline Products Inc........................ G 419 929-1114
   New London *(G-11469)*
STI Liquidation Inc........................... E 614 733-0099
   Plain City *(G-12592)*
Tally Ho Slipcovers........................... G 614 448-6170
   Columbus *(G-5807)*

2393 Textile bags

American Made Bags LLC................ F 330 475-1385
   Akron *(G-59)*
▼ Baggallini Inc................................... F 800 448-8753
   Pickerington *(G-12456)*
Capital City Awning Company......... E 614 221-5404
   Columbus *(G-5231)*
Cleveland Canvas Goods Mfg Co... E 216 361-4567
   Cleveland *(G-3835)*
Columbus Canvas Products Inc....... F 614 375-1397
   Columbus *(G-5263)*
Dayton Bag & Burlap Co.................. E 419 733-7108
   Kettering *(G-8905)*
DCW Acquisition Inc......................... E 216 451-0666
   Cleveland *(G-3949)*
▲ Global-Pak Inc................................. E 330 482-1993
   Lisbon *(G-9312)*
◆ King Bag and Manufacturing Co..... E 513 541-5440
   Cincinnati *(G-3076)*
Lamports Filter Media Inc............... G 216 881-2050
   Cleveland *(G-4309)*
Luxaire Cushion Co.......................... F 330 872-0995
   Newton Falls *(G-11654)*
Queen City Carpets LLC.................. F 513 823-8238
   Cincinnati *(G-3316)*
R J Manray Inc................................. G 330 559-6716
   Canfield *(G-2015)*
▲ Rich Industries Inc........................... E 330 339-4113
   New Philadelphia *(G-11526)*
Sailors Tailor Inc.............................. F 937 862-7781
   Spring Valley *(G-13491)*
Seven Mile Creek Corporation......... G 937 456-3320
   Eaton *(G-7069)*

2394 Canvas and related products

ABC Signs Inc.................................. F 513 241-8884
   Cincinnati *(G-2590)*
▼ Advantage Tent Fittings Inc............ F 740 773-3015
   Chillicothe *(G-2491)*
American Canvas Products Inc........ F 419 382-8450
   Toledo *(G-14187)*
Awning Fabri Caters Inc.................. G 216 476-4888
   Cleveland *(G-3712)*

23 APPAREL, FINISHED PRODUCTS FROM FABRICS & SIMILAR MATERIALS

Canvas Specialty Mfg Co............................ G...... 216 881-0647
   Cleveland *(G-3785)*

Capital City Awning Company..................... E...... 614 221-5404
   Columbus *(G-5231)*

◆ Celina Tent Inc.. D...... 419 586-3610
   Celina *(G-2327)*

◆ Chalfant Sew Fabricators Inc................... E...... 216 521-7922
   Cleveland *(G-3805)*

Cleveland Canvas Goods Mfg Co................ E...... 216 361-4567
   Cleveland *(G-3835)*

Columbus Canvas Products Inc................... F...... 614 375-1397
   Columbus *(G-5263)*

Custom Canvas & Boat Repr Inc................. G...... 419 732-3314
   Lakeside *(G-8959)*

Custom Tarpaulin Products Inc.................... F...... 330 758-1801
   Youngstown *(G-16345)*

DCW Acquisition Inc................................... E...... 216 451-0666
   Cleveland *(G-3949)*

Delphos Tent and Awning Inc..................... F...... 419 692-5776
   Delphos *(G-6762)*

Electra Tarp Inc.. F...... 330 477-7168
   Canton *(G-2095)*

Fabric Forms Inc.. G...... 513 281-6300
   Cincinnati *(G-2893)*

Forest City Companies Inc.......................... E...... 216 586-5279
   Cleveland *(G-4081)*

Galion Canvas Products.............................. G...... 419 468-5333
   Galion *(G-7876)*

Glawe Manufacturing Co Inc....................... F...... 937 754-0064
   Fairborn *(G-7317)*

Griffin Fisher Co Inc.................................... G...... 513 961-2110
   Cincinnati *(G-2973)*

▲ Inside Outfitters Inc.................................. E...... 614 798-3500
   Lewis Center *(G-9165)*

Lesch Boat Cover Canvas Co LLC............... G...... 419 668-6374
   Norwalk *(G-11977)*

Lumenomics Inc... E...... 614 798-3500
   Lewis Center *(G-9170)*

◆ Main Awning & Tent Inc.......................... G...... 513 621-6947
   Cincinnati *(G-3127)*

National Bias Fabric Co.............................. F...... 216 361-0530
   Cleveland *(G-4435)*

▲ Ohio Awning & Manufacturing Co........... E...... 216 861-2400
   Cleveland *(G-4494)*

ONeals Tarpaulin & Awning Co................... F...... 330 788-6504
   Youngstown *(G-16406)*

PCR Restorations Inc................................. F...... 419 747-7957
   Mansfield *(G-9709)*

Queen City Awning & Tent Co..................... E...... 513 530-9660
   Cincinnati *(G-3315)*

▲ Rainbow Industries Inc........................... G...... 937 323-6493
   Springfield *(G-13623)*

RFW Holdings Inc....................................... G...... 440 331-8300
   Cleveland *(G-4631)*

Sailors Tailor Inc.. F...... 937 862-7781
   Spring Valley *(G-13491)*

▲ Samsel Rope & Marine Supply Co......... E...... 216 241-0333
   Cleveland *(G-4670)*

Schaaf Co Inc.. G...... 513 241-7044
   Cincinnati *(G-3367)*

▲ Scherba Industries Inc........................... D...... 330 273-3200
   Brunswick *(G-1790)*

South Akron Awning Co.............................. F...... 330 848-7611
   Akron *(G-333)*

Tarpco Inc.. F...... 330 677-8277
   Kent *(G-8871)*

Tarped Out Inc.. E...... 330 325-7722
   Ravenna *(G-12738)*

Toledo Tarp Service Inc.............................. E...... 419 837-5098
   Perrysburg *(G-12440)*

Tri County Tarp LLC................................... E...... 419 288-3350
   Gibsonburg *(G-7956)*

Wolf G T Awning & Tent Co........................ F...... 937 548-4161
   Greenville *(G-8065)*

Youngstown Shade & Alum LLC.................. G...... 330 782-2373
   Youngstown *(G-16487)*

2395 Pleating and stitching

▲ 5 BS Inc.. C...... 740 454-8453
   Zanesville *(G-16493)*

Albany Screen Printing LLC........................ F...... 614 585-3279
   Reynoldsburg *(G-12750)*

Alley Cat Designs Inc.................................. G...... 937 291-8803
   Dayton *(G-6193)*

Alphabet Embroidery Studios...................... G...... 937 372-6557
   Xenia *(G-16248)*

Appleheart Inc... G...... 937 384-0430
   Miamisburg *(G-10612)*

▲ Atlantis Sportswear Inc........................... E...... 937 773-0680
   Piqua *(G-12506)*

Aubrey Rose Apparel LLC........................... G...... 513 728-2681
   Cincinnati *(G-2644)*

▲ Barbs Graffiti Inc..................................... E...... 216 881-5550
   Cleveland *(G-3719)*

Bdp Services Inc.. G...... 740 828-9685
   Nashport *(G-11335)*

Big Kahuna Graphics LLC........................... G...... 330 455-2625
   Canton *(G-2048)*

Cal Sales Embroidery.................................. G...... 440 236-3820
   Columbia Station *(G-5007)*

Campbell Signs & Apparel LLC................... F...... 330 386-4768
   East Liverpool *(G-6989)*

▲ Catania Medallic Specialty Inc................ E...... 440 933-9595
   Avon Lake *(G-801)*

Cdss Inc... G...... 614 626-8747
   Gahanna *(G-7832)*

Charles Wisvari.. G...... 740 671-9960
   Bellaire *(G-1184)*

Chris Stepp... G...... 513 248-0822
   Milford *(G-10898)*

Color 3 Embroidery Inc............................... G...... 330 652-9495
   Warren *(G-15155)*

Computer Stitch Designs Inc....................... G...... 330 856-7826
   Warren *(G-15156)*

Craco Embroidery Inc................................. G...... 513 563-6999
   Cincinnati *(G-2801)*

Design Original Inc..................................... F...... 937 596-5121
   Jackson Center *(G-8731)*

Dublin Embroiderer Inc............................... G...... 614 789-1898
   Dublin *(G-6881)*

Eastgate Custom Graphics Ltd.................... G...... 513 528-7922
   Cincinnati *(G-2854)*

Embroidery Design Group LLC.................... F...... 614 798-8152
   Columbus *(G-5351)*

Embroidery Network Inc.............................. G...... 330 678-4887
   Kent *(G-8813)*

Embroidme... G...... 330 484-8484
   Canton *(G-2097)*

Emroid ME.. G...... 614 789-1898
   Westerville *(G-15705)*

Fineline Imprints Inc................................... F...... 740 453-1083
   Zanesville *(G-16530)*

Finn Graphics Inc....................................... E...... 513 941-6161
   Cincinnati *(G-2905)*

Fully Promoted of Canton........................... G...... 330 484-8484
   Canton *(G-2107)*

Got Graphix Llc.. F...... 330 703-9047
   Fairlawn *(G-7440)*

Graphic Stitch Inc....................................... G...... 937 642-6707
   Marysville *(G-9911)*

Ideal Drapery Company Inc........................ F...... 330 745-9873
   Barberton *(G-874)*

Initial Designs Inc....................................... G...... 419 475-3900
   Toledo *(G-14331)*

K Ventures Inc.. F...... 419 678-2308
   Coldwater *(G-4994)*

Kiwi Promotional AP & Prtg Co................... E...... 330 487-5115
   Twinsburg *(G-14681)*

Kts Cstm Lgs/Xclsvely You Inc.................... G...... 440 285-9803
   Chardon *(G-2456)*

Kts Custom Logos....................................... G...... 440 285-9803
   Chardon *(G-2457)*

Kuhls Hot Sportspot.................................... F...... 513 474-2282
   Cincinnati *(G-3091)*

Logo This.. G...... 419 445-1355
   Archbold *(G-535)*

Markt LLC.. G...... 740 397-5900
   Mount Vernon *(G-11278)*

▲ McCc Sportswear Inc............................. G...... 513 583-9210
   West Chester *(G-15569)*

Miswest Ambrodery.................................... F...... 513 661-2770
   Cincinnati *(G-3167)*

Mr Emblem Inc... F...... 419 697-1888
   Oregon *(G-12108)*

◆ Neff Motivation Inc.................................. C...... 937 548-3194
   Greenville *(G-8053)*

Novak J F Manufacturing Co LLC................ G...... 216 741-5112
   Cleveland *(G-4484)*

Ohio Embroidery LLC................................. G...... 330 479-0029
   Canton *(G-2183)*

Part 2 Screen Prtg Design Inc..................... G...... 614 294-4429
   Columbus *(G-5657)*

Phantasm Dsgns Sprtsn More Ltd............... G...... 419 538-6737
   Ottawa *(G-12188)*

Precision Imprint.. G...... 740 592-5916
   Athens *(G-692)*

Qualitee Design Sportswear Co.................. F...... 740 333-8337
   Wshngtn Ct Hs *(G-16237)*

Quality Rubber Stamp Inc........................... G...... 614 235-2700
   Lancaster *(G-9034)*

Queen City Spirit LLC................................. F...... 513 533-2662
   Cincinnati *(G-3320)*

R J Manray Inc.. G...... 330 559-6716
   Canfield *(G-2015)*

Randy Gray... G...... 513 533-3200
   Cincinnati *(G-3324)*

Red Barn Screen Printing & EMB................ G...... 740 474-6657
   Circleville *(G-3555)*

Rnp Inc... G
   Dellroy *(G-6758)*

Sew & Sew Embroidery Inc........................ F...... 330 676-1600
   Kent *(G-8863)*

▲ Shamrock Companies Inc....................... D...... 440 899-9510
   Westlake *(G-15786)*

Signature Stitch LLC.................................. G...... 440 382-1388
   Westlake *(G-15788)*

Sit Inc... E...... 330 758-8468
   Youngstown *(G-16440)*

Sportsco Imprinting.................................... G...... 513 641-5111
   Cincinnati *(G-3409)*

Stitchgrrl LLC... G...... 216 269-4398
   Cleveland *(G-4736)*

Sun Shine Awards...................................... F...... 740 425-2504
   Barnesville *(G-905)*

Superior Image Embroidery LLC................. G...... 513 991-7543
   West Chester *(G-15593)*

T & L Custom Screening Inc........................ G...... 937 237-3121
   Dayton *(G-6605)*

▲ Thread Works Custom Embroidery........ G...... 937 478-5231
   Beavercreek *(G-1066)*

Top Shelf Embroidery LLC.......................... G...... 440 209-8566
   Mentor *(G-10577)*

Truck Stop Embroidery............................... F...... 419 257-2860
   North Baltimore *(G-11702)*

Unisport Inc.. F...... 419 529-4727
   Ontario *(G-12096)*

Employee Codes: A=Over 500 employees, B=251-500
C=101-250, D=51-100, E=20-50, F=10-19, G=1-9

23 APPAREL, FINISHED PRODUCTS FROM FABRICS & SIMILAR MATERIALS

United Sport Apparel............................F 330 722-0818
  Medina (G-10391)

Vector International Corp...................G 440 942-2002
  Mentor (G-10591)

Wholesale Imprints Inc........................E 440 224-3527
  North Kingsville (G-11797)

▲ Zimmer Enterprises Inc..................E 937 428-1057
  Dayton (G-6663)

2396 Automotive and apparel trimmings

A C Hadley - Printing Inc...................G 937 426-0952
  Beavercreek (G-1037)

Adcraft Decals Incorporated..............E 216 524-2934
  Cleveland (G-3598)

All Streets Auto LLC.............................F 330 714-7717
  Cleveland (G-3633)

American Imprssions Sportswear.....G 614 848-6677
  Columbus (G-5125)

◆ Anomatic Corporation....................E 740 522-2203
  New Albany (G-11366)

▲ Associated Premium Corporation...E 513 679-4444
  Cincinnati (G-2637)

▲ Atlantis Sportswear Inc..................E 937 773-0680
  Piqua (G-12506)

Bates Metal Products Inc...................D 740 498-8371
  Port Washington (G-12631)

Bdp Services Inc...................................G 740 828-9685
  Nashport (G-11335)

Big Kahuna Graphics LLC..................G 330 455-2625
  Canton (G-2048)

Brandon Screen Printing......................F 419 229-9837
  Lima (G-9224)

Brass Bull 1 LLC..................................G 740 335-8030
  Wshngtn Ct Hs (G-16226)

Brown Cnty Bd Mntl Rtardation.........E 937 378-4891
  Georgetown (G-7950)

Cal Sales Embroidery..........................G 440 236-3820
  Columbia Station (G-5007)

Charizma Corp......................................G 216 621-2220
  Cleveland (G-3807)

Charles Wisvari....................................G 740 671-9960
  Bellaire (G-1184)

▲ City Apparel Inc..............................F 419 434-1155
  Findlay (G-7493)

Conform Automotive LLC....................B 937 492-2708
  Sidney (G-13233)

Design Original Inc..............................F 937 596-5121
  Jackson Center (G-8731)

Dupli-Systems Inc...............................C 440 234-9415
  Strongsville (G-13830)

Eisenhauer Mfg Co LLC.......................D 419 238-0081
  Van Wert (G-14915)

Fineline Imprints Inc............................F 740 453-1083
  Zanesville (G-16530)

▲ Fortner Upholstering Inc................F 614 475-8282
  Columbus (G-5384)

▲ General Theming Contrs LLC.......C 614 252-6342
  Columbus (G-5397)

▼ Greenfield Research Inc................C 937 981-7763
  Greenfield (G-8032)

Griffin Fisher Co Inc.............................G 513 961-2110
  Cincinnati (G-2973)

Hall Company..E 937 652-1376
  Urbana (G-14833)

◆ Hfi LLC..B 614 491-0700
  Canal Winchester (G-1987)

Hollywood Imprints LLC.......................F 614 501-6040
  Gahanna (G-7838)

Hunt Products Inc................................G 440 667-2457
  Newburgh Heights (G-11617)

Jls Funeral Home..................................F 614 625-1220
  Columbus (G-5497)

Kent Stow Screen Printing Inc...........G 330 923-5118
  Akron (G-205)

Kiwi Promotional AP & Prtg Co.........E 330 487-5115
  Twinsburg (G-14681)

Lesch Boat Cover Canvas Co LLC....G 419 668-6374
  Norwalk (G-11977)

Lockfast LLC...G 800 543-7157
  Loveland (G-9491)

M&Ms Autosales LLC...........................F 234 334-7022
  Akron (G-231)

Michigan Silkscreen Inc......................G 419 885-1163
  Sylvania (G-14004)

Mr Emblem Inc.....................................G 419 697-1888
  Oregon (G-12108)

National Bias Fabric Co.......................F 216 361-0530
  Cleveland (G-4435)

Northeastern Plastics Inc...................G 330 453-5925
  Canton (G-2179)

Ohio State Institute Fin Inc................G 614 861-8811
  Reynoldsburg (G-12770)

Painted Hill Inv Group Inc..................F 937 339-1756
  Troy (G-14600)

Peska Inc..F 440 998-4664
  Ashtabula (G-654)

Pieco Inc..D 937 399-5100
  Springfield (G-13620)

Pieco Inc..E 419 422-5335
  Findlay (G-7551)

▲ Plastic Card Inc..............................D 330 896-5555
  Uniontown (G-14790)

◆ Plus Mark LLC................................D 216 252-6770
  Cleveland (G-4562)

Promospark Inc....................................F 513 844-2211
  Fairfield (G-7399)

Quality Rubber Stamp Inc..................G 614 235-2700
  Lancaster (G-9034)

R & A Sports Inc..................................E 216 289-2254
  Euclid (G-7297)

Randy Gray...G 513 533-3200
  Cincinnati (G-3324)

Roach Studios LLC..............................F 614 725-1405
  Columbus (G-5727)

Schilling Graphics Inc.........................E 419 468-1037
  Galion (G-7884)

Screen Works Inc................................E 937 264-9111
  Dayton (G-6564)

Silly Brandz Global LLC.....................D 419 697-8324
  Toledo (G-14473)

Solar Arts Graphic Designs................G 330 744-0535
  Youngstown (G-16441)

Spirit Avionics Ltd................................G 614 237-4271
  Columbus (G-5786)

▲ Sroufe Healthcare Products LLC...E 260 894-4171
  Wadsworth (G-15067)

Stakes Manufacturing LLC..................D 216 245-4752
  Willowick (G-16035)

Sylvan Studios Inc..............................G 419 882-3423
  Sylvania (G-14016)

T & L Custom Screening Inc.............G 937 237-3121
  Dayton (G-6605)

Tee Creations.......................................G 937 878-2822
  Fairborn (G-7325)

Telempu N Hayashi Amer Corp........G 513 932-9319
  Lebanon (G-9113)

Tim L Humbert.....................................G 330 497-4944
  Canton (G-2245)

Triage Ortho Group.............................G 937 653-6431
  Urbana (G-14848)

Trim Systems Operating Corp...........B 740 772-5998
  Chillicothe (G-2539)

▲ TS Tech Americas Inc...................B 614 575-4100
  Reynoldsburg (G-12776)

▲ Universal Drect Flfilment Corp....C 330 650-5000
  Hudson (G-8617)

◆ Universal Screen Arts Inc.............E 330 650-5000
  Hudson (G-8618)

Vandava Inc..G 614 277-8003
  Grove City (G-8128)

Vector International Corp...................G 440 942-2002
  Mentor (G-10591)

▲ Vgu Industries Inc.........................E 216 676-9093
  Cleveland (G-4867)

Visual Marking Systems Inc..............D 330 425-7100
  Twinsburg (G-14753)

▼ W J Egli Company Inc...................F 330 823-3666
  Alliance (G-435)

West & Barker Inc...............................E 330 652-9923
  Niles (G-11691)

Wholesale Imprints Inc.......................E 440 224-3527
  North Kingsville (G-11797)

Woodrow Manufacturing Co..............E 937 399-9333
  Springfield (G-13057)

Zide Sport Shop of Ohio Inc.............F 740 373-8199
  Marietta (G-9846)

2399 Fabricated textile products, nec

Annin & Co...E 740 498-5008
  Newcomerstown (G-11642)

Annin & Co Inc.....................................C 740 622-4447
  Coshocton (G-5968)

Besi Manufacturing Inc......................G 513 874-1460
  West Chester (G-15377)

▲ Besi Manufacturing Inc................E 513 874-0232
  West Chester (G-15378)

Crumley Racing Stable LLC..............G 216 513-0334
  Spencer (G-13480)

▲ Drifter Marine Inc..........................G 419 666-8144
  Perrysburg (G-12377)

Flag Lady Inc.......................................G 614 263-1776
  Columbus (G-5378)

Griffin Fisher Co Inc...........................G 513 961-2110
  Cincinnati (G-2973)

Markers Inc..G 440 933-5927
  Avon Lake (G-816)

◆ Neff Motivation Inc........................C 937 548-3194
  Greenville (G-8053)

▲ Party Animal Inc.............................F 440 471-1030
  Westlake (G-15771)

Rockhead Group Usa LLC.................G 216 310-1569
  Beachwood (G-1019)

School Pride Limited..........................E 614 568-0697
  Columbus (G-5753)

Seven Mile Creek Corporation.........G 937 456-3320
  Eaton (G-7069)

Sewline Products Inc.........................G 419 929-1114
  New London (G-11469)

Signme LLC...G 614 221-7803
  Columbus (G-5771)

TAC Industries Inc..............................B 937 328-5200
  Springfield (G-13642)

Ver Mich Ltd..G 330 493-7330
  Canton (G-2261)

Watershed Mangement LLC..............F 740 852-5607
  Mount Sterling (G-11258)

24 LUMBER AND WOOD PRODUCTS, EXCEPT FURNITURE

2411 Logging

A and R Logging LLC..........................G 740 352-6182
  Mc Dermott (G-10273)

Alfman Logging LLC...........................F 740 982-6227
  Crooksville (G-6043)

SIC SECTION
24 LUMBER AND WOOD PRODUCTS, EXCEPT FURNITURE

Anthony W Hilderbrant .... G 740 682-1035
    Oak Hill *(G-12016)*

Bailee Logging LLC .... G 330 881-4688
    Salineville *(G-13038)*

Beachs Trees Slctive Hrvstg LL .... G 513 289-5976
    Cincinnati *(G-2553)*

Biedenbach Logging .... G 740 732-6477
    Sarahsville *(G-13105)*

Blair Logging .... G 740 934-2730
    Lower Salem *(G-9519)*

Blankenship Logging LLC .... G 740 372-3833
    Otway *(G-12205)*

Border Lumber & Logging Ltd .... G 330 897-0177
    Fresno *(G-7821)*

C & L Erectors & Riggers Inc .... F 740 332-7185
    Laurelville *(G-9054)*

Craig Saylor .... G 740 352-8363
    Portland *(G-12638)*

Custom Material Hdlg Eqp LLC .... G 513 235-5336
    Cincinnati *(G-2808)*

Dale R Adkins .... G 740 682-7312
    Oak Hill *(G-12017)*

David Adkins Logging .... G 740 533-0297
    Kitts Hill *(G-8943)*

Denver Adkins .... G 740 682-3123
    Oak Hill *(G-12018)*

▼ Facemyer Lumber Co Inc .... F 740 992-5965
    Pomeroy *(G-12613)*

Geauga Counting Logging LLC .... G 440 478-7896
    Garrettsville *(G-7915)*

Gerald D Damron .... G 740 894-3680
    Chesapeake *(G-2474)*

Ghost Logging LLC .... G 740 504-1819
    Gambier *(G-7906)*

Giles Logging LLC .... G 406 855-5284
    Spencer *(G-13481)*

Haessly Lumber Sales Co .... D 740 373-6681
    Marietta *(G-9798)*

HK Logging & Lumber Ltd .... G 440 632-1997
    Middlefield *(G-10757)*

Jason C Gibson .... F 740 663-4520
    Chillicothe *(G-2514)*

Jefferson Logging Company LLC .... G 304 634-9203
    Crown City *(G-6053)*

JM Logging Inc .... G 740 441-0941
    Gallipolis *(G-7895)*

Joey Elliott Logging LLC .... G 740 626-0061
    South Salem *(G-13475)*

Kcox Enterprises LLC .... F 574 952-5084
    West Chester *(G-15453)*

Lee Saylor Logging LLC .... G 740 682-0479
    Oak Hill *(G-12021)*

Miller Logging .... G 440 693-4001
    Middlefield *(G-10769)*

Miller Logging Inc .... F 330 279-4721
    Holmesville *(G-8550)*

Morehouse Logging LLC .... G 740 501-0256
    Thornville *(G-14067)*

Northeast Logging & Lumber LLC .... G 440 272-5100
    Middlefield *(G-10778)*

Oakbridge Timber Framing .... G 419 994-1052
    Loudonville *(G-9450)*

Ohio Timberland Products Inc .... F 419 682-6322
    Stryker *(G-13911)*

Powell Logging .... G 740 372-6131
    Otway *(G-12207)*

R & D Logging LLC .... G 740 259-6127
    Lucasville *(G-9526)*

Randy Carter Logging Inc .... G 740 634-2604
    Bainbridge *(G-832)*

Ray H Miller Logging Lumb .... G 330 683-2055
    Apple Creek *(G-509)*

Raymond Robinson .... G 937 890-1886
    Dayton *(G-6542)*

Rocky Mountain Logging Co LLC .... G 440 313-8574
    Hiram *(G-8488)*

Sean Ison Logging LLC .... G 740 835-7222
    Sardinia *(G-13109)*

Select Logging .... G 419 564-0361
    Marengo *(G-9770)*

Stark Truss Company Inc .... D 419 298-3777
    Edgerton *(G-7082)*

Superior Hardwoods of Ohio .... E 740 384-6862
    Jackson *(G-8726)*

Sy Logging Llc .... G 440 437-5744
    Orwell *(G-12170)*

Terry G Sickles .... G 740 286-8880
    Ray *(G-12744)*

Travis Cochran .... G 740 294-2368
    Frazeysburg *(G-7716)*

Whites Logging & Land Clearin .... G 419 921-9878
    Fredericktown *(G-7760)*

Y&B Logging .... G 440 437-1053
    Orwell *(G-12172)*

2421 Sawmills and planing mills, general

Automated Bldg Components Inc .... E 419 257-2152
    North Baltimore *(G-11694)*

Baillie Lumber Co LP .... E 419 462-2000
    Galion *(G-7861)*

Beach City Lumber Llc .... G 330 878-4097
    Strasburg *(G-13744)*

Beaver Wood Products .... F 740 226-6211
    Beaver *(G-1035)*

Blaney Hardwoods Ohio Inc .... D 740 678-8288
    Vincent *(G-15006)*

▲ Bruewer Woodwork Mfg Co .... D 513 353-3505
    Cleves *(G-4946)*

Calvin W Lafferty .... G 740 498-6566
    Kimbolton *(G-8927)*

Cherokee Hardwoods Inc .... G 440 632-0322
    Middlefield *(G-10741)*

◆ Clarksville Stave & Veneer Co .... F 740 947-4159
    Waverly *(G-15279)*

Coblentz Brothers Inc .... E 330 857-7211
    Apple Creek *(G-496)*

▲ Combs Manufacturing Inc .... D 330 784-3151
    Akron *(G-114)*

Conover Lumber Company Inc .... F 937 368-3010
    Conover *(G-5936)*

Contract Lumber Inc .... F 614 751-1109
    Columbus *(G-5289)*

Crownover Lumber Company Inc .... D 740 596-5229
    Mc Arthur *(G-10263)*

▼ Decorative Panels Intl Inc .... D 419 535-5921
    Toledo *(G-14264)*

Denoon Lumber Company LLC .... D 740 768-2220
    Bergholz *(G-1300)*

Don Puckett Lumber Inc .... F 740 887-4191
    Londonderry *(G-9398)*

▼ Facemyer Lumber Co Inc .... F 740 992-5965
    Pomeroy *(G-12613)*

Gardner Lumber Company Inc .... F 740 254-4664
    Tippecanoe *(G-14170)*

Gross Lumber Inc .... F 330 683-2055
    Apple Creek *(G-501)*

Haessly Lumber Sales Co .... D 740 373-6681
    Marietta *(G-9798)*

▼ Hartzell Hardwoods Inc .... D 937 773-7054
    Piqua *(G-12521)*

Industrial Timber & Land Co .... G 740 596-5294
    Hamden *(G-8173)*

◆ Itl Corp .... E 216 831-3140
    Cleveland *(G-4240)*

Kauffman Lumber & Supply .... F 330 893-9186
    Millersburg *(G-10971)*

Knisley Lumber .... F 740 634-2935
    Bainbridge *(G-831)*

Lansing Bros Sawmill .... G 937 588-4291
    Piketon *(G-12478)*

Luxcraft LLC .... G 330 852-1036
    Sugarcreek *(G-13928)*

Mac Lean J S Co .... E 614 878-5454
    Columbus *(G-5538)*

Marathon At Sawmill .... F 614 734-0836
    Columbus *(G-5540)*

MB Manufacturing Corp .... G 513 682-1461
    Fairfield *(G-7381)*

Miller Logging Inc .... F 330 279-4721
    Holmesville *(G-8550)*

Miller Lumber Co Inc .... E 330 674-0273
    Millersburg *(G-10981)*

Millwood Lumber Inc .... E 740 254-4681
    Gnadenhutten *(G-7985)*

Mohler Lumber Company .... E 330 499-5461
    North Canton *(G-11744)*

Mowhawk Lumber Ltd .... E 330 698-5333
    Apple Creek *(G-507)*

Newberry Wood Enterprises Inc .... G 440 238-6127
    Strongsville *(G-13859)*

No Name Lumber LLC .... G 740 289-3722
    Piketon *(G-12479)*

Ohio Valley Stave Inc .... G 740 259-6222
    Mc Dermott *(G-10274)*

▼ Ohio Valley Veneer Inc .... E 740 493-2901
    Piketon *(G-12480)*

R & D Hilltop Lumber Inc .... E 740 342-3051
    New Lexington *(G-11456)*

Raber Lumber Co .... G 330 893-2797
    Charm *(G-2471)*

Runkles Sawmill LLC .... G 937 663-0115
    Saint Paris *(G-12974)*

S & J Lumber Company LLC .... F 740 245-5804
    Thurman *(G-14073)*

S Holley Lumber LLC .... G 440 272-5315
    Windsor *(G-16076)*

S&R Lumber LLC .... F 740 352-6135
    Piketon *(G-12484)*

Salt Creek Lumber Company Inc .... G 330 695-3500
    Fredericksburg *(G-7733)*

Sawmill 9721 LLC .... G 614 937-4400
    Powell *(G-12680)*

Sawmill Commons 4420 .... E 614 764-7878
    Columbus *(G-5748)*

Sawmill Road Management Co LLC .... E 937 342-9071
    Columbus *(G-5749)*

Stark Truss Company Inc .... D 330 756-3050
    Beach City *(G-971)*

▲ Stephen M Trudick .... E 440 834-1891
    Burton *(G-1886)*

Stony Point Hardwoods LLC .... G 330 852-4512
    Sugarcreek *(G-13939)*

Sugarcreek Shavings LLC .... G 330 763-4239
    Sugarcreek *(G-13942)*

Superior Hardwoods of Ohio .... E 740 384-6862
    Jackson *(G-8726)*

Superior Hardwoods of Ohio .... F 740 596-2561
    Mc Arthur *(G-10264)*

Superior Hardwoods Ohio Inc .... E 740 439-2727
    Cambridge *(G-1956)*

Superior Hardwoods Ohio Inc .... D 740 384-5677
    Wellston *(G-15332)*

T & D Thompson Inc .... E 740 332-8515
    Laurelville *(G-9056)*

▼ Taylor Lumber Worldwide Inc .... C 740 259-6222
    Piketon *(G-12486)*

24 LUMBER AND WOOD PRODUCTS, EXCEPT FURNITURE

The F A Requarth Company .... E 937 224-1141
  Dayton *(G-6618)*

▲ The Mead Corporation .... B 937 495-6323
  Dayton *(G-6619)*

Tiger Wood Co Ltd .... G 330 893-2744
  Millersburg *(G-10999)*

▼ Trumbull County Hardwoods .... E 440 632-0555
  Middlefield *(G-10794)*

Tusco Hardwoods LLC .... F 330 852-4281
  Sugarcreek *(G-13946)*

United Hardwoods Ltd .... G 330 878-9510
  Strasburg *(G-13751)*

▲ Urban Industries of Ohio Inc .... E 419 468-3578
  Galion *(G-7886)*

Wagner Farms Sawmill Ltd Lblty .... F 419 653-4126
  Leipsic *(G-9141)*

Walnut Creek Lumber Co Ltd .... F 330 852-4559
  Dundee *(G-6972)*

◆ Walnut Creek Planing Ltd .... D 330 893-3244
  Millersburg *(G-11005)*

Wappoo Wood Products Inc .... E 937 492-1166
  Sidney *(G-13294)*

Weaver Lumber Co .... G 330 359-5091
  Wilmot *(G-16071)*

Whitewater Forest Products LLC .... F 513 724-0157
  Batavia *(G-960)*

Wilmington Forest Products .... G 937 382-7813
  Wilmington *(G-16063)*

Windsor Mill Lumber LLC .... G 440 272-5930
  Middlefield *(G-10797)*

Woodsfeld True Vlue HM Ctr Inc .... E 740 472-1651
  Woodsfield *(G-16090)*

Wooldridge Lumber Co .... E 740 289-4912
  Piketon *(G-12487)*

Yoder Lumber Co Inc .... D 330 674-1435
  Millersburg *(G-11009)*

Yoder Lumber Co Inc .... D 330 893-3131
  Sugarcreek *(G-13949)*

▼ Yoder Lumber Co Inc .... D 330 893-3121
  Millersburg *(G-11008)*

2426 Hardwood dimension and flooring mills

Armstrong Custom Moulding Inc .... G 740 922-5931
  Uhrichsville *(G-14761)*

Baillie Lumber Co LP .... E 419 462-2000
  Galion *(G-7861)*

Beaver Wood Products .... F 740 226-6211
  Beaver *(G-1035)*

Canfield Manufacturing Co Inc .... G 330 533-3333
  North Jackson *(G-11780)*

Cardinal Building Supply LLC .... G 614 706-4499
  Columbus *(G-5237)*

Carter-Jones Lumber Company .... F 330 674-9060
  Millersburg *(G-10950)*

Cherokee Hardwoods Inc .... G 440 632-0322
  Middlefield *(G-10741)*

Crafted Elements LLC .... G 816 739-1307
  New Philadelphia *(G-11494)*

Created Hardwood Ltd .... G 330 556-1825
  Dundee *(G-6964)*

Crownover Lumber Company Inc .... D 740 596-5229
  Mc Arthur *(G-10263)*

Denoon Lumber Company LLC .... D 740 768-2220
  Bergholz *(G-1300)*

Dutch Heritage Woodcraft .... F 330 893-2211
  Berlin *(G-1306)*

Gross Lumber Inc .... F 330 683-2055
  Apple Creek *(G-501)*

Haessly Lumber Sales Co .... D 740 373-6681
  Marietta *(G-9798)*

Halliday Holdings Inc .... E 740 335-1430
  Wshngtn Ct Hs *(G-16233)*

▼ Hartzell Hardwoods Inc .... D 937 773-7054
  Piqua *(G-12521)*

Hillside Wood Ltd .... G 330 359-5991
  Millersburg *(G-10959)*

Hochstetler Wood .... G 330 893-2384
  Millersburg *(G-10961)*

Holmes Lumber & Bldg Ctr Inc .... E 330 479-8314
  Canton *(G-2125)*

Holmes Lumber & Bldg Ctr Inc .... C 330 674-9060
  Millersburg *(G-10967)*

Itl LLC .... E 216 831-3140
  Beachwood *(G-992)*

◆ Itl Corp .... E 216 831-3140
  Cleveland *(G-4240)*

J McCoy Lumber Co Ltd .... F 937 587-3423
  Peebles *(G-12328)*

Knisley Lumber .... F 740 634-2935
  Bainbridge *(G-831)*

McKay-Gross Division .... F 330 683-2055
  Apple Creek *(G-504)*

Mid Ohio Wood Products Inc .... E 740 323-0427
  Newark *(G-11591)*

Mohler Lumber Company .... E 330 499-5461
  North Canton *(G-11744)*

Ogonek Custom Hardwood Inc .... G 833 718-2531
  Barberton *(G-885)*

▼ Ohio Valley Veneer Inc .... E 740 493-2901
  Piketon *(G-12480)*

◆ Prestige Enterprise Intl Inc .... D 513 469-6044
  Blue Ash *(G-1456)*

◆ Regency Seating Inc .... E 330 848-3700
  Akron *(G-300)*

◆ Robbins Inc .... E 513 871-8988
  Cincinnati *(G-3348)*

▲ Roppe Holding Company .... B 419 435-8546
  Fostoria *(G-7653)*

Sportsmans Haven Inc .... G 740 432-7243
  Cambridge *(G-1955)*

▲ Stephen M Trudick .... E 440 834-1891
  Burton *(G-1886)*

Stony Point Hardwoods LLC .... G 330 852-4512
  Sugarcreek *(G-13939)*

Superior Hardwoods of Ohio .... F 740 596-2561
  Mc Arthur *(G-10264)*

Superior Hardwoods Ohio Inc .... E 740 439-2727
  Cambridge *(G-1956)*

Superior Hardwoods Ohio Inc .... D 740 384-5677
  Wellston *(G-15332)*

T & D Thompson Inc .... E 740 332-8515
  Laurelville *(G-9056)*

Timothy Whatman .... E 419 883-2443
  Bellville *(G-1248)*

▼ Trumbull County Hardwoods .... E 440 632-0555
  Middlefield *(G-10794)*

Urban Hershberger .... G 330 763-0407
  Millersburg *(G-11003)*

Urbn Timber LLC .... G 614 981-3043
  Columbus *(G-5850)*

Wagner Farms Sawmill Ltd Lblty .... F 419 653-4126
  Leipsic *(G-9141)*

◆ Walnut Creek Planing Ltd .... D 330 893-3244
  Millersburg *(G-11005)*

Wappoo Wood Products Inc .... E 937 492-1166
  Sidney *(G-13294)*

Woodcraft Industries Inc .... D 440 632-9655
  Middlefield *(G-10798)*

Woodcraft Industries Inc .... C 440 437-7811
  Orwell *(G-12171)*

Wooden Horse .... G 740 503-5243
  Baltimore *(G-849)*

Yoder Lumber Co Inc .... D 330 893-3131
  Sugarcreek *(G-13949)*

▼ Yoder Lumber Co Inc .... D 330 893-3121
  Millersburg *(G-11008)*

2429 Special product sawmills, nec

Brown-Forman Corporation .... F 740 384-3027
  Wellston *(G-15326)*

▼ IVEX Protective Packaging LLC .... E 937 498-9298
  Sidney *(G-13256)*

2431 Millwork

A & J Woodworking Inc .... G 419 695-5655
  Delphos *(G-6759)*

Aca Millworks Inc .... F 419 339-7600
  Waynesfield *(G-15295)*

Ace Lumber Company .... F 330 744-3167
  Youngstown *(G-16301)*

▲ Action Industries Ltd .... G 216 252-7800
  Strongsville *(G-13801)*

▼ Advantage Tent Fittings Inc .... F 740 773-3015
  Chillicothe *(G-2491)*

Ailes Millwork Inc .... E 330 678-4300
  Kent *(G-8796)*

All Pro Ovrhd Door Systems LLC .... G 614 444-3667
  Columbus *(G-5111)*

Amcan Stair & Rail LLC .... F 937 781-3084
  Springfield *(G-13532)*

American Plastech LLC .... G 330 538-0576
  North Jackson *(G-11777)*

American Stirways Cstm Railing .... G 513 367-6700
  North Bend *(G-11703)*

Anderson Door Co .... F 216 475-5700
  Cleveland *(G-3666)*

Anthony Flottemesch & Son Inc .... F 513 561-1212
  Cincinnati *(G-2628)*

Armstrong Custom Moulding Inc .... G 740 922-5931
  Uhrichsville *(G-14761)*

Art Woodworking & Mfg Co .... E 513 681-2986
  Cincinnati *(G-2635)*

Automated Bldg Components Inc ...... E 419 257-2152
  North Baltimore *(G-11694)*

Baird Brothers Sawmill Inc .... C 330 533-3122
  Canfield *(G-2000)*

▲ Bautec N Technoform Amer Inc .... E 330 487-6600
  Twinsburg *(G-14634)*

Bench Made Woodworking LLC .... G 513 702-2698
  Cincinnati *(G-2664)*

Berlin Woodworking LLC .... G 330 893-3234
  Millersburg *(G-10945)*

▲ Bruewer Woodwork Mfg Co .... D 513 353-3505
  Cleves *(G-4946)*

Buckeye Woodworking .... G 330 698-1070
  Apple Creek *(G-495)*

Burkholder Woodworking Llc .... G 440 313-8203
  Middlefield *(G-10735)*

C & W Custom Wdwkg Co Inc .... F 513 891-6340
  Cincinnati *(G-2697)*

C J Woodworking Inc .... G 330 607-4221
  Wadsworth *(G-15021)*

C L Woodworking LLC .... G 440 487-7940
  Middlefield *(G-10736)*

Carden Door Company LLC .... G 513 459-2233
  Mason *(G-9967)*

▲ Carolina Stair Supply Inc .... E 740 922-3333
  Uhrichsville *(G-14763)*

Carter-Jones Lumber Company .... F 330 674-9060
  Millersburg *(G-10950)*

▲ Cascade Ohio Inc .... B 440 593-5800
  Conneaut *(G-5916)*

Cassady Woodworks Inc .... E 937 256-7948
  Dayton *(G-6155)*

Cincinnati Stair & Handrail .... F 513 722-3947
  Cincinnati *(G-2761)*

SIC SECTION
24 LUMBER AND WOOD PRODUCTS, EXCEPT FURNITURE

Cindoco Wood Products Co .... F 937 444-2504
  Mount Orab *(G-11240)*
◆ Clopay Building Pdts Co Inc .... E 513 770-4800
  Mason *(G-9978)*
◆ Clopay Corporation .... C 800 282-2260
  Mason *(G-9979)*
Country Comfort Wdwkg LLC .... G 330 695-4408
  Fredericksburg *(G-7720)*
Country Mile Woodworking .... G 740 668-2452
  Walhonding *(G-15091)*
Courthouse Manufacturing LLC .... E 740 335-2727
  Washington Court Hou *(G-15232)*
Cox Interior Inc .... G 614 473-9169
  Columbus *(G-5302)*
Cox Interior Inc .... F 270 789-3129
  Norwood *(G-11994)*
Curves and More Woodworking .... G 614 239-7837
  Columbus *(G-5310)*
Custom Carving Source LLC .... G 513 407-1008
  Cincinnati *(G-2807)*
Custom Kerf Woodworking LLC .... G 330 745-7651
  Barberton *(G-865)*
Darby Creek Millwork LLC .... G 614 873-3267
  Plain City *(G-12573)*
Decker Custom Wood Llc .... G 419 332-3464
  Fremont *(G-7775)*
Dendratec Ltd .... G 330 473-4878
  Dalton *(G-6130)*
Dennelli Custom Wdwkg Inc .... G 740 927-1900
  Pataskala *(G-12296)*
Denoon Lumber Company LLC .... D 740 768-2220
  Bergholz *(G-1300)*
◆ Designer Doors Inc .... F 330 772-6391
  Burghill *(G-1878)*
Display Dynamics Inc .... E 937 832-2830
  Englewood *(G-7229)*
Division Overhead Door Inc .... F 513 872-0888
  Cincinnati *(G-2834)*
Dlg Woodworks & Finishing Inc .... G 513 649-1245
  Franklin *(G-7670)*
▲ Door Fabrication Services Inc .... F 937 454-9207
  Vandalia *(G-14938)*
Dowel Yoder & Molding .... G 330 231-2962
  Fredericksburg *(G-7723)*
Dublin Millwork Co Inc .... G 614 889-7776
  Dublin *(G-6882)*
Dutch Heritage Woodcraft .... F 330 893-2211
  Berlin *(G-1306)*
Duvall Woodworking Inc .... G 419 878-9581
  Waterville *(G-15242)*
Encompass Woodworking LLC .... G 513 569-2841
  Cincinnati *(G-2869)*
Fairfield Wood Works Ltd .... G 740 689-1953
  Lancaster *(G-9015)*
Fdi Cabinetry LLC .... G 513 353-4500
  Cleves *(G-4952)*
Fifth Avenue Lumber Co .... E 614 833-6655
  Canal Winchester *(G-1986)*
▼ Fixture Dimensions Inc .... E 513 360-7512
  Liberty Twp *(G-9216)*
Forum III Inc .... G 513 961-5123
  Cincinnati *(G-2917)*
Forum Works LLC .... E 937 349-8685
  Milford Center *(G-10928)*
Framework Industries LLC .... G 234 759-2080
  North Lima *(G-11805)*
Freds Woodworking & Remodelin .... G 330 802-8646
  Barberton *(G-868)*
Fryburg Door Inc .... G 330 674-5252
  Millersburg *(G-10955)*
▼ Gateway Industrial Pdts Inc .... E 440 324-4112
  Elyria *(G-7154)*

Gdw Woodworking LLC .... G 513 494-3041
  South Lebanon *(G-13461)*
Gerstenslager Construction .... G 330 832-3604
  Massillon *(G-10100)*
Gracie International Corp .... G 717 725-9138
  Dublin *(G-6887)*
Great Lakes Stair & Mllwk Co .... G 330 225-2005
  Hinckley *(G-8473)*
Greenhart Rstoration Mllwk LLC .... G 330 502-6050
  Boardman *(G-1514)*
Gross & Sons Custom Millwork .... G 419 227-0214
  Lima *(G-9246)*
Heartland Stairways Inc .... G 330 279-2554
  Holmesville *(G-8543)*
Heirloom Woodworks LLC .... G 937 430-0394
  Tipp City *(G-14136)*
Hinckley Wood Products Ltd .... F 330 220-9999
  Hinckley *(G-8474)*
Hj Systems Inc .... F 614 351-9777
  Columbus *(G-5443)*
Hobby Hill Wood Working .... G 330 893-4518
  Millersburg *(G-10960)*
Holes Custom Woodworking .... G 419 586-8171
  Celina *(G-2337)*
▲ Holmes Custom Moulding Ltd .... E 330 893-3598
  Millersburg *(G-10966)*
Holmes Lumber & Bldg Ctr Inc .... E 330 479-8314
  Canton *(G-2125)*
Holmes Lumber & Bldg Ctr Inc .... C 330 674-9060
  Millersburg *(G-10967)*
Hrh Door Corp .... E 513 674-9300
  Cincinnati *(G-3011)*
◆ Hrh Door Corp .... A 850 208-3400
  Mount Hope *(G-11238)*
Hyde Park Lumber Company .... E 513 271-1500
  Cincinnati *(G-3013)*
Icecap LLC .... G 216 548-4145
  Wadsworth *(G-15036)*
Idx Corporation .... C 937 401-3225
  Dayton *(G-6378)*
J McCoy Lumber Co Ltd .... F 937 587-3423
  Peebles *(G-12328)*
Jeffrey D Layton .... G 513 706-4352
  Cincinnati *(G-3039)*
Jeld-Wen Inc .... C 740 964-1431
  Etna *(G-7255)*
Jeld-Wen Inc .... C 740 397-1144
  Mount Vernon *(G-11274)*
Jeld-Wen Inc .... G 740 397-3403
  Mount Vernon *(G-11275)*
Jh Woodworking LLC .... G 330 276-7600
  Killbuck *(G-8920)*
Judy Mills Company Inc .... E 513 271-4241
  Cincinnati *(G-3053)*
Khempco Bldg Sup Co Ltd Partnr .... D 740 549-0465
  Delaware *(G-6733)*
L & L Ornamental Iron Co .... E 513 353-1930
  Cleves *(G-4958)*
L and J Woodworking .... F 330 359-3216
  Dundee *(G-6966)*
▲ L E Smith Company .... D 419 636-4555
  Bryan *(G-1825)*
Laborie Enterprises LLC .... G 419 686-6245
  Portage *(G-12634)*
Liechty Specialties Inc .... G 419 445-6696
  Archbold *(G-534)*
Lima Millwork Inc .... F 419 331-3303
  Elida *(G-7094)*
Logan Glass Technologies LLC .... G 740 385-2114
  Logan *(G-9369)*
M H Woodworking LLC .... G 330 893-3929
  Millersburg *(G-10977)*

M21 Industries LLC .... E 937 781-1377
  Dayton *(G-6419)*
Mac Lean J S Co .... E 614 878-5454
  Columbus *(G-5538)*
▲ Mag Resources LLC .... F 330 294-0494
  Barberton *(G-878)*
Maple Hill Woodworking LLC .... G 330 674-2500
  Millersburg *(G-10979)*
Marsh Industries Inc .... E 330 308-8667
  New Philadelphia *(G-11515)*
▲ Marsh Industries Inc .... D 800 426-4244
  New Philadelphia *(G-11516)*
Masonite Corporation .... B 937 454-9207
  Vandalia *(G-14951)*
MB Woodworking Llc .... G 330 808-5122
  West Farmington *(G-15605)*
Mc Alister Woodworking .... G 614 989-6264
  Columbus *(G-5549)*
McCoy Group Inc .... G 330 753-1041
  Barberton *(G-881)*
Menard Inc .... F 513 250-4566
  Cincinnati *(G-3148)*
Menard Inc .... C 419 998-4348
  Lima *(G-9267)*
Menard Inc .... C 513 583-1444
  Loveland *(G-9496)*
Midwest Commercial Mllwk Inc .... F 419 224-5001
  Lima *(G-9271)*
Midwest Wood Trim Inc .... E 419 592-3389
  Napoleon *(G-11324)*
Midwest Woodworking Co Inc .... F 513 631-6684
  Cincinnati *(G-3164)*
Miller and Slay Wdwkg LLC .... G 513 265-3816
  Morrow *(G-11224)*
▼ Miller Manufacturing Inc .... E 330 852-0689
  Sugarcreek *(G-13931)*
Mills Customs Woodworks .... G 216 407-3600
  Cleveland *(G-4415)*
Millwood Wholesale Inc .... F 330 359-6109
  Dundee *(G-6968)*
Millwork Elements LLC .... G 614 905-8163
  Columbus *(G-5571)*
Millwork Enterprises LLC .... G 216 644-1481
  Olmsted Falls *(G-12081)*
Moonlight Woodworks LLC .... G 440 836-3738
  Bedford *(G-1139)*
Morningstar Cstm Woodworks LLC .... G 740 508-7178
  Portland *(G-12639)*
Mount Hope Planing .... G 330 359-0538
  Millersburg *(G-10984)*
▲ National Door and Trim Inc .... E 419 238-9345
  Van Wert *(G-14924)*
New Burlington Woodworks .... G 937 488-3503
  Wilmington *(G-16056)*
▲ Novo Manufacturing LLC .... D 740 269-2221
  Bowerston *(G-1546)*
Oak Pointe LLC .... E 740 498-9820
  Newcomerstown *(G-11648)*
Ogonek Custom Hardwood Inc .... G 833 718-2531
  Barberton *(G-885)*
Ohio Custom Door LLC .... E 330 695-6301
  Fredericksburg *(G-7730)*
Ohio Wood Connection LLC .... G 513 581-0361
  Cincinnati *(G-3218)*
Ohio Woodworking Co Inc .... G 513 631-0870
  Cincinnati *(G-3219)*
Overhead Door Corporation .... D 740 383-6376
  Marion *(G-9870)*
Overhead Door Corporation .... F 419 294-3874
  Upper Sandusky *(G-14820)*
P & T Millwork Inc .... F 440 543-2151
  Chagrin Falls *(G-2412)*

Employee Codes: A=Over 500 employees, B=251-500
C=101-250, D=51-100, E=20-50, F=10-19, G=1-9

24 LUMBER AND WOOD PRODUCTS, EXCEPT FURNITURE

Pease Industies Inc .... D 513 870-3600
  Fairfield *(G-7393)*

Pickens Window Service Inc .... F 513 931-4432
  Cincinnati *(G-3255)*

Ply-Trim Inc .... E 330 799-7876
  Youngstown *(G-16419)*

Precise Custom Millwork Inc .... G 614 539-7855
  Grove City *(G-8115)*

Precision Wood Products Inc .... F 937 787-3523
  Camden *(G-1963)*

Prigge Woodworking .... G 419 274-1005
  Hamler *(G-8260)*

Profac Inc .... D 440 942-0205
  Mentor *(G-10533)*

▲ Profac Inc .... C 440 942-0205
  Mentor *(G-10532)*

Quality Woodproducts LLC .... G 330 279-2217
  Fredericksburg *(G-7731)*

R C Moore Lumber Co .... F 740 732-4950
  Caldwell *(G-1912)*

Ramsey Stairs & Wdwkg LLC .... G 614 694-2101
  Columbus *(G-5710)*

Raymond J Detweiler .... G 440 632-1255
  Middlefield *(G-10783)*

Rebsco Inc .... F 937 548-2246
  Greenville *(G-8057)*

Renewal By Andersen LLC .... G 614 781-9600
  Columbus *(G-5070)*

Reserve Millwork LLC .... E 216 531-6982
  Bedford *(G-1153)*

Richardson Woodworking .... G 614 893-8850
  Blacklick *(G-1343)*

Rick Alan Custom Woodworks Inc .... G 513 394-6957
  Mason *(G-10050)*

▲ Rinos Woodworking Shop Inc .... F 440 946-1718
  Willoughby *(G-15984)*

Ripper Woodwork Inc .... G 513 922-1944
  Cincinnati *(G-3342)*

Riverside Cnstr Svcs Inc .... E 513 723-0900
  Cincinnati *(G-3344)*

Robertson Cabinets Inc .... F 937 698-3755
  West Milton *(G-15631)*

Robura Inc .... G 330 857-7404
  Orrville *(G-12148)*

Rockwood Products Ltd .... E 330 893-2392
  Millersburg *(G-10991)*

Roettger Hardwood Inc .... F 937 693-6811
  Kettlersville *(G-8912)*

Round Mate Systems .... G 419 675-3334
  Kenton *(G-8899)*

Rsl LLC .... E 330 392-8900
  Warren *(G-15203)*

Rush Fixture & Millwork Co .... F 216 241-9100
  Cleveland *(G-4663)*

Rush Woodworks .... G 419 569-2370
  Mansfield *(G-9715)*

S Holley Lumber LLC .... G 440 272-5315
  Windsor *(G-16076)*

S R Door Inc .... D 740 927-3558
  Hebron *(G-8360)*

Salem Mill & Cabinet Co .... G 330 337-9568
  Salem *(G-13028)*

Saw Dust Ltd .... G 740 862-0612
  Baltimore *(G-847)*

Seemray Inc .... E 440 536-8705
  Cleveland *(G-4685)*

▲ Seneca Millwork Inc .... G 419 435-6671
  Fostoria *(G-7654)*

Sheridan Woodworks Inc .... F 216 663-9333
  Cleveland *(G-4692)*

Solid Surface Concepts Inc .... E 513 948-8677
  Cincinnati *(G-3401)*

Stein Inc .... G 419 747-2611
  Mansfield *(G-9721)*

▲ Stephen M Trudick .... E 440 834-1891
  Burton *(G-1886)*

Stony Point Hardwoods LLC .... G 330 852-4512
  Sugarcreek *(G-13939)*

Stratton Creek Wood Works LLC .... F 330 876-0005
  Kinsman *(G-8938)*

Stull Woodworks Inc .... G 937 698-8181
  Troy *(G-14614)*

Summit Millwork LLC .... G 330 920-4000
  Cuyahoga Falls *(G-6120)*

Swiss Woodcraft Inc .... E 330 925-1807
  Rittman *(G-12828)*

T & D Thompson Inc .... E 740 332-8515
  Laurelville *(G-9056)*

Ted Bolle Millwork Inc .... F 937 325-8779
  Springfield *(G-13645)*

Teledoor LLC .... G 419 227-3000
  Lima *(G-9293)*

The F A Requarth Company .... E 937 224-1141
  Dayton *(G-6618)*

The Galehouse Companies Inc .... E 330 658-2023
  Doylestown *(G-6854)*

Timber Framing LLC .... G 330 749-7837
  Orrville *(G-12159)*

Todco .... F 740 223-2542
  Marion *(G-9886)*

Todd Peak Woodwork LLC .... G 513 560-6760
  Maineville *(G-9602)*

Trimco .... G 614 679-3931
  Westerville *(G-15684)*

Trimtec Systems Ltd .... F 614 820-0340
  Grove City *(G-8126)*

▲ Turnwood Industry Inc .... G 330 278-2421
  Hinckley *(G-8478)*

Tuscarora Wood Midwest LLC .... G 937 603-8882
  Covington *(G-6032)*

Versailles Building Supply .... G 937 526-3238
  Versailles *(G-14990)*

Village Woodworking .... G 740 326-4461
  Fredericktown *(G-7758)*

Volpe Millwork Inc .... G 216 581-0200
  Cleveland *(G-4882)*

Watson Wood Works .... G 513 233-5321
  Somerville *(G-13453)*

Wengerd Wood Inc .... F 330 359-4300
  Dundee *(G-6973)*

Whitmer Woodworks Inc .... G 614 873-1196
  Plain City *(G-12602)*

Wilson Custom Woodworking Inc .... G 513 233-5613
  Kings Mills *(G-8930)*

Windy Hills Woodworking .... G 419 892-3389
  Lucas *(G-9520)*

Windy Knoll Woodworking LLC .... G 440 636-5092
  Huntsburg *(G-8621)*

▲ Wittrock Wdwkg & Mfg Co Inc .... D 513 891-5800
  Blue Ash *(G-1492)*

Woodcraft Industries Inc .... D 440 632-9655
  Middlefield *(G-10798)*

Woodcraft Industries Inc .... C 440 437-7811
  Orwell *(G-12171)*

Woodgrain Enterprises LLC .... G 216 854-8151
  Cleveland *(G-4919)*

Woodworks Design .... G 440 693-4414
  Middlefield *(G-10799)*

Woodworks Unlimited .... G 740 574-0500
  Franklin Furnace *(G-7713)*

Woodworks Zanesville .... G 740 624-3396
  Mount Gilead *(G-11236)*

Wyman Woodworking .... G 614 338-0615
  Columbus *(G-5888)*

▼ Yoder Lumber Co Inc .... D 330 893-3121
  Millersburg *(G-11008)*

Yoder Window & Siding Ltd .... F 330 695-6960
  Fredericksburg *(G-7735)*

Yoder Woodworking .... G 740 399-9400
  Butler *(G-1892)*

Youngstown Shade & Alum LLC .... G 330 782-2373
  Youngstown *(G-16487)*

▲ Yutzy Woodworking Ltd .... E 330 359-6166
  Dundee *(G-6975)*

2434 Wood kitchen cabinets

4-B Wood Specialties Inc .... F 330 769-2188
  Seville *(G-13133)*

A & J Woodworking Inc .... G 419 695-5655
  Delphos *(G-6759)*

A-Display Service Corp .... F 614 469-1230
  Columbus *(G-5082)*

▲ Affordable Cabinet Doors .... G 513 734-9663
  Bethel *(G-1318)*

Agean Marble Manufacturing .... F 513 874-1475
  West Chester *(G-15533)*

Ailes Millwork Inc .... E 330 678-4300
  Kent *(G-8796)*

Al-Co Products Inc .... G 419 399-3867
  Latty *(G-9053)*

Alpine Cabinets .... G 330 359-5724
  Dundee *(G-6962)*

American Wood Reface Inc .... G 440 944-3750
  Medina *(G-10294)*

Anthony Flottemesch & Son Inc .... F 513 561-1212
  Cincinnati *(G-2628)*

Approved Plumbing Co .... F 216 663-5063
  Cleveland *(G-3671)*

As America Inc .... E 419 522-4211
  Mansfield *(G-9626)*

Benchmark-Cabinets LLC .... G 740 694-1144
  Fredericktown *(G-7739)*

Bestwood Cabinetry LLC .... G 937 661-9621
  Xenia *(G-16252)*

Bison Builders LLC .... F 614 636-0365
  Columbus *(G-5191)*

▲ Bruewer Woodwork Mfg Co .... D 513 353-3505
  Cleves *(G-4946)*

Cabinet and Granite Depot LLC .... F 513 874-2100
  West Chester *(G-15383)*

Cabinet Concepts Inc .... G 440 232-4644
  Oakwood Village *(G-12036)*

Cabinet Creat By Lillibridge .... F 419 476-6838
  Toledo *(G-14225)*

Cabinet Shop .... G 614 885-9676
  Columbus *(G-5061)*

Cabinet Specialties Inc .... G 330 695-3463
  Fredericksburg *(G-7718)*

Cabinetworks Group Mich LLC .... E 440 247-3091
  Chagrin Falls *(G-2368)*

Cabinetworks Group Mich LLC .... C 440 632-2547
  Middlefield *(G-10737)*

◆ Cabintwrks Group Mddlfield LLC .... A 888 562-7744
  Middlefield *(G-10738)*

Carter-Jones Lumber Company .... F 330 674-9060
  Millersburg *(G-10950)*

Cass Woodworking Inc .... F 800 589-8841
  Galion *(G-7864)*

Cedee Cedar Inc .... F 740 363-3148
  Delaware *(G-6707)*

Clancys Cabinets LLC .... G 419 445-4455
  Archbold *(G-526)*

▲ Clark Son Actn Liquidation Inc .... G 330 866-9330
  East Sparta *(G-7013)*

Cleveland Cabinets LLC .... G 216 459-7676
  Cleveland *(G-3834)*

SIC SECTION
24 LUMBER AND WOOD PRODUCTS, EXCEPT FURNITURE

Climate Pros LLC.................................D..... 216 881-5200
  Cleveland *(G-3878)*

Climate Pros LLC.................................D..... 330 744-2732
  Youngstown *(G-16340)*

Colby Woodworking Inc.......................E..... 937 224-7676
  Dayton *(G-6258)*

Colonial Cabinets Inc..........................G..... 440 355-9663
  Lagrange *(G-8946)*

Counter-Advice Inc..............................F..... 937 291-1600
  Franklin *(G-7668)*

Countryside Cabinets..........................G..... 740 397-6488
  Fredericktown *(G-7742)*

Creative Cabinets Ltd..........................F..... 740 689-0603
  Lancaster *(G-9004)*

Creative Edge Cbnets Wdwkg LLC.......G..... 419 453-3416
  Ottoville *(G-12198)*

Crowes Cabinets Inc...........................E..... 330 729-9911
  Youngstown *(G-16343)*

Custom Woodworking Inc.....................G..... 419 456-3330
  Ottawa *(G-12177)*

D Lewis Inc...G..... 740 695-2615
  Saint Clairsville *(G-12901)*

Dgl Woodworking Inc...........................F..... 937 837-7091
  Dayton *(G-6298)*

Distinctive Surfaces LLC....................F..... 614 431-0898
  Columbus *(G-5330)*

Dover Cabinet Industries Inc...............F..... 330 343-9074
  Dover *(G-6817)*

Dutch Valley Woodworking Inc............F..... 330 852-4319
  Sugarcreek *(G-13923)*

E J Skok Industries.............................E..... 216 292-7533
  Bedford *(G-1119)*

East Oberlin Cabinets LLC..................G..... 440 775-1166
  Oberlin *(G-12050)*

Fairfield Wood Works Ltd....................G..... 740 689-1953
  Lancaster *(G-9015)*

Fdi Cabinetry LLC...............................G..... 513 353-4500
  Cleves *(G-4952)*

Forum III Inc......................................G..... 513 961-5123
  Cincinnati *(G-2917)*

Franklin Cabinet Company Inc............E..... 937 743-9606
  Franklin *(G-7676)*

Gillard Construction Inc......................F..... 740 376-9744
  Marietta *(G-9795)*

Gross & Sons Custom Millwork...........G..... 419 227-0214
  Lima *(G-9246)*

Hampshire Co.....................................F..... 937 773-3493
  Piqua *(G-12518)*

Holmes Lumber & Bldg Ctr Inc............E..... 330 479-8314
  Canton *(G-2125)*

Holmes Lumber & Bldg Ctr Inc............C..... 330 674-9060
  Millersburg *(G-10967)*

Idx Corporation...................................C..... 937 401-3225
  Dayton *(G-6378)*

J & K Cabinetry Inc.............................F..... 513 860-3461
  West Chester *(G-15450)*

Jacob & Levis Ltd...............................G..... 330 852-7600
  Sugarcreek *(G-13926)*

Johannings Inc....................................G..... 330 875-1706
  Louisville *(G-9463)*

JP Cabinets LLC.................................G..... 440 232-9780
  Cleveland *(G-4264)*

◆ Kellogg Cabinets Inc.......................G..... 614 833-9596
  Canal Winchester *(G-1988)*

Kinnemyers Cornerstone Cab Inc........G..... 513 353-3030
  Cleves *(G-4957)*

Kinsella Manufacturing Co Inc............F..... 513 561-5285
  Cincinnati *(G-3077)*

Kitchen Designs Plus Inc....................E..... 419 536-6605
  Toledo *(G-14348)*

Kitchens By Java................................G..... 419 621-7677
  Sandusky *(G-13071)*

▲ Kitchens By Rutenschroer Inc.........G..... 513 251-8333
  Cincinnati *(G-3080)*

Knapke Cabinets Inc...........................E..... 937 335-8383
  Troy *(G-14592)*

Knapke Custom Cabinetry Ltd............G..... 937 459-8866
  Versailles *(G-14985)*

Kreager Co LLC..................................G..... 740 345-1605
  Newark *(G-11585)*

Laminated Concepts Inc.....................F..... 216 475-4141
  Maple Heights *(G-9753)*

Larsen Cusotm Cabinetry....................G..... 614 282-3929
  Columbus *(G-5522)*

Leiden Cabinet Co..............................G..... 330 425-8555
  Twinsburg *(G-14686)*

Lily Ann Cabinets................................G..... 419 360-2455
  Toledo *(G-14367)*

Lima Millwork Inc................................F..... 419 331-3303
  Elida *(G-7094)*

Mac Lean J S Co.................................E..... 614 878-5454
  Columbus *(G-5538)*

Mammana Custom Woodworking Inc....E..... 216 581-9059
  Maple Heights *(G-9754)*

Marsh Industries Inc...........................E..... 330 308-8667
  New Philadelphia *(G-11515)*

Marzano Inc..G..... 216 459-2051
  Cleveland *(G-4364)*

▲ Masterbrand Cabinets LLC..............B..... 812 482-2527
  Beachwood *(G-999)*

Miami Vly Counters & Spc Inc............G..... 937 865-0562
  Miamisburg *(G-10658)*

Midwest Woodworking Co Inc............F..... 513 631-6684
  Cincinnati *(G-3164)*

Miller Cabinet Ltd...............................F..... 614 873-4221
  Plain City *(G-12586)*

Mills Pride Premier Inc........................G..... 740 941-1300
  Waverly *(G-15285)*

Mock Woodworking Company LLC.....E..... 740 452-2701
  Zanesville *(G-16546)*

Modern Designs Inc............................G..... 330 644-1771
  Green *(G-8025)*

Mro Built LLC.....................................D..... 330 526-0555
  North Canton *(G-11746)*

Nicklaus Group LLC............................F..... 740 277-5700
  Lancaster *(G-9029)*

Northeast Cabinet Co LLC..................G..... 614 759-0800
  Columbus *(G-5603)*

Ohio River Valley Cabinet...................G..... 740 975-8846
  Newark *(G-11599)*

Online Mega Sellers Corp...................G..... 888 384-6468
  Toledo *(G-14415)*

Phelps Creek Wood Works Llc..........G..... 440 693-4314
  Middlefield *(G-10780)*

Pro Choice Cabinetry LLC..................G..... 937 313-9297
  Dayton *(G-6525)*

Profiles In Design Inc.........................F..... 513 751-2212
  Cincinnati *(G-3302)*

Red Barn Cabinet Co..........................G..... 937 884-9800
  Arcanum *(G-519)*

Reserve Millwork LLC.........................E..... 216 531-6982
  Bedford *(G-1153)*

Rheaco Builders Inc...........................G..... 330 425-3090
  Twinsburg *(G-14725)*

Riceland Cabinet Inc..........................D..... 330 601-1071
  Wooster *(G-16163)*

Riceland Cabinet Corporation.............F..... 330 601-1071
  Wooster *(G-16164)*

Richard Benhase & Assoc Inc............G..... 513 772-1896
  Cincinnati *(G-3338)*

River East Custom Cabinets...............E..... 419 244-3226
  Toledo *(G-14452)*

Riverside Cnstr Svcs Inc....................E..... 513 723-0900
  Cincinnati *(G-3344)*

Roettger Hardwood Inc......................F..... 937 693-6811
  Kettlersville *(G-8912)*

Royal Cabinet Design Co Inc..............F..... 216 267-5330
  Cleveland *(G-4656)*

S & G Manufacturing Group LLC........C..... 614 529-0100
  Hilliard *(G-8437)*

Salem Mill & Cabinet Co.....................G..... 330 337-9568
  Salem *(G-13028)*

Signature Cabinetry Inc.....................F..... 614 252-2227
  Columbus *(G-5768)*

Snows Wood Shop Inc.......................E..... 419 836-3805
  Oregon *(G-12111)*

Springhill Dimensions........................E..... 330 317-1926
  Dalton *(G-6143)*

▲ Supply One Corporation..................F..... 937 297-1111
  Bellbrook *(G-1194)*

Surface Enterprises Inc.....................G..... 419 476-5670
  Toledo *(G-14479)*

TDS Custom Cabinets LLC.................G..... 614 517-2220
  Columbus *(G-5814)*

The Hattenbach Company...................D..... 216 881-5200
  Cleveland *(G-4785)*

Thomas Cabinet Shop Inc..................F..... 937 847-8239
  Dayton *(G-6621)*

▼ Tiffin Metal Products Co.................C..... 419 447-8414
  Tiffin *(G-14110)*

Trail Cabinet......................................G..... 330 893-3791
  Dundee *(G-6969)*

Tri-State Kitchens LLC.......................G..... 740 574-6727
  Wheelersburg *(G-15812)*

Troyers Cabinet Shop Ltd..................F..... 937 464-7702
  Belle Center *(G-1198)*

Trutech Cabinetry LLC........................G..... 614 338-0680
  Columbus *(G-5840)*

▲ Turnwood Industry Inc....................G..... 330 278-2421
  Hinckley *(G-8478)*

Wilson Cabinet Co..............................G..... 330 276-8711
  Killbuck *(G-8925)*

Woodcraft Industries Inc....................D..... 440 632-9655
  Middlefield *(G-10798)*

Woodcraft Industries Inc....................C..... 440 437-7811
  Orwell *(G-12171)*

Wurms Woodworking Company..........E..... 419 492-2184
  New Washington *(G-11552)*

X44 Corp..F..... 330 657-2335
  Peninsula *(G-12347)*

2435 Hardwood veneer and plywood

▲ American Veneer Edgebanding Co....G..... 740 928-2700
  Heath *(G-8316)*

▲ Arkansas Face Veneer Co Inc..........F..... 937 773-6295
  Piqua *(G-12504)*

Automated Bldg Components Inc........E..... 419 257-2152
  North Baltimore *(G-11694)*

Beaver Wood Products.......................F..... 740 226-6211
  Beaver *(G-1035)*

▲ Bruewer Woodwork Mfg Co.............D..... 513 353-3505
  Cleves *(G-4946)*

▲ Dimension Hardwood Veneers Inc...E..... 419 272-2245
  Edon *(G-7086)*

◆ Erath Veneer Corp Virginia..............E..... 540 483-5223
  Granville *(G-8016)*

▼ Exhibit Concepts Inc......................D..... 937 890-7000
  Vandalia *(G-14939)*

Fifth Avenue Lumber Co.....................E..... 614 833-6655
  Canal Winchester *(G-1986)*

Fryburg Door Inc................................D..... 330 674-5252
  Millersburg *(G-10955)*

Haessly Lumber Sales Co...................D..... 740 373-6681
  Marietta *(G-9798)*

Hartzell Industries Inc........................F..... 937 773-6295
  Piqua *(G-12522)*

24 LUMBER AND WOOD PRODUCTS, EXCEPT FURNITURE

Knisley Lumber .... F 740 634-2935
  Bainbridge *(G-831)*

Mac Lean J S Co .... E 614 878-5454
  Columbus *(G-5538)*

Miller Crist .... G 330 359-7877
  Fredericksburg *(G-7726)*

▼ Miller Manufacturing Inc .... E 330 852-0689
  Sugarcreek *(G-13931)*

Mohler Lumber Company .... E 330 499-5461
  North Canton *(G-11744)*

▼ Ohio Valley Veneer Inc .... E 740 493-2901
  Piketon *(G-12480)*

S & G Manufacturing Group LLC .... C 614 529-0100
  Hilliard *(G-8437)*

▲ Sims-Lohman Inc .... E 513 651-3510
  Cincinnati *(G-3395)*

Starecasing Systems Inc .... G 312 203-5632
  Columbus *(G-5790)*

Stony Point Hardwoods LLC .... G 330 852-4512
  Sugarcreek *(G-13939)*

Universal Veneer Mill Corp .... C 740 522-1147
  Newark *(G-11611)*

◆ Universal Veneer Sales Corp .... C 740 522-1147
  Newark *(G-11612)*

Wappoo Wood Products Inc .... E 937 492-1166
  Sidney *(G-13294)*

Yoder Lumber Co Inc .... D 330 893-3131
  Sugarcreek *(G-13949)*

2436 Softwood veneer and plywood

▲ American Veneer Edgebanding Co .... G 740 928-2700
  Heath *(G-8316)*

Beaver Wood Products .... F 740 226-6211
  Beaver *(G-1035)*

◆ Clopay Building Pdts Co Inc .... E 513 770-4800
  Mason *(G-9978)*

S & G Manufacturing Group LLC .... C 614 529-0100
  Hilliard *(G-8437)*

◆ Universal Production Corp .... E 740 522-1147
  Newark *(G-11610)*

Wappoo Wood Products Inc .... E 937 492-1166
  Sidney *(G-13294)*

2439 Structural wood members, nec

Automated Bldg Components Inc .... E 419 257-2152
  North Baltimore *(G-11694)*

Buckeye Components LLC .... E 330 482-5163
  Columbiana *(G-5029)*

Building Concepts Inc .... F 419 298-2371
  Edgerton *(G-7072)*

Byler Truss .... G 330 465-5412
  Ashland *(G-560)*

Carter-Jones Lumber Company .... F 330 674-9060
  Millersburg *(G-10950)*

Columbus Roof Trusses Inc .... F 740 763-3000
  Newark *(G-11571)*

Columbus Roof Trusses Inc .... E 614 272-6464
  Columbus *(G-5276)*

Dutchcraft Truss Component Inc .... F 330 862-2220
  Minerva *(G-11030)*

Fifth Avenue Lumber Co .... E 614 833-6655
  Canal Winchester *(G-1986)*

Holmes Lumber & Bldg Ctr Inc .... E 330 479-8314
  Canton *(G-2125)*

Holmes Lumber & Bldg Ctr Inc .... C 330 674-9060
  Millersburg *(G-10967)*

Khempco Bldg Sup Co Ltd Partnr .... D 740 549-0465
  Delaware *(G-6733)*

▲ Laminate Technologies Inc .... D 800 231-2523
  Tiffin *(G-14090)*

Ohio Valley Truss Company .... E 937 393-3995
  Hillsboro *(G-8463)*

Proline Truss .... G 419 895-9980
  Shiloh *(G-13206)*

R & L Truss Inc .... F 419 587-3440
  Grover Hill *(G-8170)*

Richland Laminated Columns LLC .... F 419 895-0036
  Greenwich *(G-8070)*

Schilling Truss Inc .... F 740 984-2396
  Beverly *(G-1320)*

Socar of Ohio Inc .... D 419 596-3100
  Continental *(G-5938)*

Stark Truss Company Inc .... D 330 756-3050
  Beach City *(G-971)*

Stark Truss Company Inc .... E 330 478-2100
  Canton *(G-2233)*

Stark Truss Company Inc .... E 330 478-6063
  Canton *(G-2234)*

Stark Truss Company Inc .... D 419 298-3777
  Edgerton *(G-7082)*

Stark Truss Company Inc .... E 740 335-4156
  Washington Court Hou *(G-15003)*

Stark Truss Company Inc .... F 330 478-2100
  Canton *(G-2235)*

▲ Thomas Do-It Center Inc .... E 740 446-2002
  Gallipolis *(G-7903)*

Truss Worx LLC .... G 419 363-2100
  Rockford *(G-12834)*

Waynedale Truss and Panel Co .... E 330 698-7373
  Apple Creek *(G-513)*

Waynedale Truss and Panel Co .... G 330 683-4471
  Dalton *(G-6144)*

2441 Nailed wood boxes and shook

Aerocase Incorporated .... F 440 617-9294
  Westlake *(G-15728)*

Aslan Worldwide .... F 513 671-0671
  West Chester *(G-15370)*

Buckeye Diamond Logistics Inc .... C 937 462-8361
  South Charleston *(G-13454)*

Built-Rite Box & Crate Inc .... E 330 263-0936
  Wooster *(G-16109)*

▲ Caravan Packaging Inc .... G 440 243-4100
  Cleveland *(G-3790)*

Cassady Woodworks Inc .... E 937 256-7948
  Dayton *(G-6155)*

Cedar Craft Products Inc .... F 614 759-1600
  Blacklick *(G-1333)*

Clark Rm Inc .... F 419 425-9889
  Findlay *(G-7494)*

Damar Products Inc .... F 937 492-9023
  Sidney *(G-13240)*

Forest City Companies Inc .... E 216 586-5279
  Cleveland *(G-4081)*

Global Packaging & Exports Inc .... G 513 454-2020
  West Chester *(G-15442)*

▲ H Gerstner & Sons Inc .... E 937 228-1662
  Dayton *(G-6364)*

Hann Manufacturing Inc .... E 740 962-3752
  Mcconnelsville *(G-10281)*

Hines Builders Inc .... F 937 335-4586
  Troy *(G-14577)*

▲ J & L Wood Products Inc .... E 937 667-4064
  Tipp City *(G-14139)*

▲ Kennedy Group Incorporated .... D 440 951-7660
  Willoughby *(G-15939)*

Lalac One LLC .... E 216 432-4422
  Cleveland *(G-4307)*

Lima Pallet Company Inc .... E 419 229-5736
  Lima *(G-9262)*

Ohio Box & Crate Inc .... F 440 526-3133
  Burton *(G-1885)*

Quadco Rehabilitation Ctr Inc .... B 419 682-1011
  Stryker *(G-13912)*

Schaefer Box & Pallet Co .... E 513 738-2500
  Hamilton *(G-8241)*

Sterling Industries Inc .... F 419 523-3788
  Ottawa *(G-12193)*

Thomas J Weaver Inc .... F 740 622-2040
  Coshocton *(G-5998)*

Traveling Recycle WD Pdts Inc .... F 419 968-2649
  Middle Point *(G-10713)*

Van Orders Pallet Company Inc .... F 419 875-6932
  Liberty Center *(G-9205)*

2448 Wood pallets and skids

A & D Wood Products Inc .... G 419 331-8859
  Elida *(G-7093)*

A & M Pallet .... G 937 295-3093
  Russia *(G-12881)*

A & M Pallet Shop Inc .... G 440 632-1941
  Middlefield *(G-10729)*

A W Taylor Lumber Incorporated .... F 440 577-1889
  Pierpont *(G-12473)*

AA Pallets LLC .... G 216 856-2614
  Cleveland *(G-3582)*

AAA Plastics & Pallets Inc .... G 330 844-2556
  Mogadore *(G-11065)*

Able Pallet Mfg & Repr .... G 614 444-2115
  Columbus *(G-5091)*

Aero Pallets Inc .... G 330 260-7107
  Carrollton *(G-2303)*

Anderson Pallet & Packg Inc .... F 937 962-2614
  Lewisburg *(G-9185)*

Arrowhead Pallet LLC .... G 440 693-4241
  Middlefield *(G-10732)*

B J Pallett .... G 419 447-9665
  Tiffin *(G-14077)*

Belco Works Inc .... D 740 695-0500
  Saint Clairsville *(G-12897)*

Boscowood Ventures Inc .... F 440 429-5669
  Lorain *(G-9404)*

BR Pallet Inc .... E 419 427-2200
  Alvada *(G-441)*

Buckeye Diamond Logistics Inc .... C 937 462-8361
  South Charleston *(G-13454)*

Built-Rite Box & Crate Inc .... E 330 263-0936
  Wooster *(G-16109)*

Cabot Lumber Inc .... G 740 545-7109
  West Lafayette *(G-15616)*

Caesarcreek Pallets Ltd .... F 937 416-4447
  Jamestown *(G-8741)*

Carrillo Pallets LLC .... G 513 942-2210
  Cincinnati *(G-2704)*

Chep (usa) Inc .... G 614 497-9448
  Columbus *(G-5248)*

Cima Inc .... E 513 382-8976
  Hamilton *(G-8191)*

Clark Rm Inc .... F 419 425-9889
  Findlay *(G-7494)*

Coblentz Brothers Inc .... E 330 857-7211
  Apple Creek *(G-496)*

Cox Wood Product Inc .... F 740 372-4735
  Otway *(G-12206)*

Crosscreek Pallet Co .... G 440 632-1940
  Middlefield *(G-10743)*

Custom Palet Manufacturing .... G 440 693-4603
  Middlefield *(G-10745)*

D P Products Inc .... G 440 834-9663
  Middlefield *(G-10747)*

Damar Products Inc .... F 937 492-9023
  Sidney *(G-13240)*

DM Pallet Service Inc .... F 614 491-0881
  Columbus *(G-5333)*

▲ Emergency Products & RES Inc .... G 330 673-5003
  Kent *(G-8814)*

SIC SECTION
24 LUMBER AND WOOD PRODUCTS, EXCEPT FURNITURE

Findlay Pallet Inc.................................. G 419 423-0511
  Findlay *(G-7507)*
Findlay Pallet Inc.................................. G 419 423-0511
  Findlay *(G-7508)*
Frankes Wood Products LLC........... E 937 642-0706
  Marysville *(G-9910)*
Franks Sawmill Inc............................. F 419 682-3831
  Stryker *(G-13909)*
Gardner Lumber Company Inc......... F 740 254-4664
  Tippecanoe *(G-14170)*
Global Packaging & Exports Inc....... G 513 454-2020
  West Chester *(G-15442)*
GM Pallets Company........................ F 859 408-1781
  Cincinnati *(G-2960)*
Grant Street Pallet Inc....................... G 330 424-0355
  Lisbon *(G-9313)*
Gross Lumber Inc.............................. F 330 683-2055
  Apple Creek *(G-501)*
H & K Pallet Services........................ G 937 608-1140
  Xenia *(G-16263)*
Hacker Wood Products Inc............... G 513 737-4462
  Hamilton *(G-8215)*
Haessly Lumber Sales Co................. D 740 373-6681
  Marietta *(G-9798)*
Halliday Holdings Inc........................ E 740 335-1430
  Wshngtn Ct Hs *(G-16233)*
Hann Manufacturing Inc.................... E 740 962-3752
  Mcconnelsville *(G-10281)*
Hershberger Manufacturing............... E 440 272-5455
  Windsor *(G-16075)*
Hinchcliff Lumber Company.............. D 440 238-5200
  Strongsville *(G-13841)*
Hines Builders Inc.............................. F 937 335-4586
  Troy *(G-14577)*
Hope Timber & Marketing Group...... F 740 344-1788
  Newark *(G-11580)*
▼ Hope Timber Pallet Recycl LLC..... F 740 344-1788
  Newark *(G-11582)*
▲ Inca Presswood-Pallets Ltd........... E 330 343-3361
  Dover *(G-6828)*
Industrial Hardwood Inc.................... G 419 666-2503
  Perrysburg *(G-12391)*
Inland Hardwood Corporation........... F 740 373-7187
  Marietta *(G-9802)*
J & K Pallet Inc................................. G 937 526-5117
  Versailles *(G-14982)*
▲ J & L Wood Products Inc.............. E 937 667-4064
  Tipp City *(G-14139)*
J & R Pallet Inc................................. G 740 226-1112
  Waverly *(G-15283)*
J I T Pallets Inc................................. G 330 424-0355
  Lisbon *(G-9317)*
Joe Gonda Company Incorporated.... G 440 458-6000
  Grafton *(G-8003)*
Kamps Inc.. G 937 526-9333
  Versailles *(G-14983)*
Kamps Pallets.................................... G 616 818-4323
  Columbus *(G-5502)*
Kauffman Lumber & Supply.............. F 330 893-9186
  Millersburg *(G-10971)*
Kmak Group LLC................................ F 937 308-1023
  London *(G-9390)*
Lima Pallet Company Inc.................. E 419 229-5736
  Lima *(G-9262)*
◆ Litco International Inc................... D..... 330 539-5433
  Vienna *(G-14999)*
▲ Litco Manufacturing LLC............... F 330 539-5433
  Warren *(G-15184)*
Lynk Packaging Inc............................ E 330 562-8080
  Aurora *(G-723)*
Makers Supply LLC............................ G 937 203-8245
  Piqua *(G-12534)*

Mid Ohio Wood Products Inc........... E 740 323-0427
  Newark *(G-11591)*
Mid Ohio Wood Recycling Inc.......... G 419 673-8470
  Kenton *(G-8891)*
Middlefield Pallet Inc........................ F 440 632-0553
  Middlefield *(G-10766)*
Midtown Pallet & Recycling Inc........ F 419 241-1311
  Toledo *(G-14384)*
Milltree Lumber Holdings.................. F 740 226-2090
  Waverly *(G-15286)*
Millwood Inc...................................... D 330 857-3075
  Apple Creek *(G-505)*
Millwood Inc...................................... E 216 881-1414
  Cleveland *(G-4416)*
Millwood Inc...................................... D 330 359-5220
  Dundee *(G-6967)*
Millwood Inc...................................... D 440 914-0540
  Solon *(G-13391)*
Millwood Inc...................................... D 330 609-0220
  Vienna *(G-15001)*
Millwood Inc...................................... E 740 226-2090
  Waverly *(G-15287)*
Millwood Incorporated...................... F 330 704-6707
  Apple Creek *(G-506)*
Mjc Enterprise Inc............................. G 330 669-3744
  Sterling *(G-13659)*
Montgomerys Pallet Service Inc....... G 330 297-6677
  Ravenna *(G-12725)*
◆ Morgan Wood Products Inc..........F 614 336-4000
  Powell *(G-12678)*
Mpi Logistics and Service Inc.......... E 330 832-5309
  Massillon *(G-10130)*
Msf Acres LLC................................... F 330 857-0257
  Orrville *(G-12139)*
Mt Eaton Pallet Ltd.......................... F 330 893-2986
  Millersburg *(G-10985)*
National Pallet & Mulch LLC............ F 937 237-1643
  Dayton *(G-6465)*
Nelson Company............................... G 614 444-1164
  Columbus *(G-5592)*
Nwp Manufacturing Inc..................... F 419 894-6871
  Waldo *(G-15089)*
◆ Oak Chips Inc...............................E 740 947-4159
  Waverly *(G-15289)*
Ohio Box & Crate Inc........................ F 440 526-3133
  Burton *(G-1885)*
Ohio State Pallet Corp..................... G 614 332-3961
  Homer *(G-8552)*
Ohio Wood Recycling Inc................. G 614 491-0881
  Columbus *(G-5631)*
Olympic Forest Products Co............ E 216 421-2775
  Cleveland *(G-4500)*
Pallet Distributors Inc....................... E 330 852-3531
  Sugarcreek *(G-13933)*
Pallet Source Inc.............................. F 419 660-8882
  Norwalk *(G-11985)*
Pallet Specs Plus LLC...................... F 513 351-3200
  Norwood *(G-11997)*
Pallet World Inc................................. E 419 874-9333
  Perrysburg *(G-12419)*
Pallets & Crates Inc.......................... F 330 527-4534
  Garrettsville *(G-7924)*
Pettits Pallets Inc.............................. G 614 351-4920
  Galloway *(G-7905)*
Plastic Pallet and Container.............. G 330 631-4664
  Cuyahoga Falls *(G-6108)*
Premier Pallet and Recycl Inc........... F 330 767-2221
  Navarre *(G-11350)*
PRU Industries Inc............................ F 937 746-8702
  Franklin *(G-7694)*
Quadco Rehabilitation Ctr Inc........... E 419 445-1950
  Archbold *(G-543)*

Quadco Rehabilitation Ctr Inc........... B 419 682-1011
  Stryker *(G-13912)*
Quality Pllets Recyclables LLC.......... G 419 396-3244
  Carey *(G-2284)*
Queen City Pallets Inc...................... E 513 821-6700
  Cincinnati *(G-3318)*
R W Long Lumber & Box Co Inc....... F 513 932-5124
  Lebanon *(G-9106)*
Raber Lumber Co............................. G 330 893-2797
  Charm *(G-2471)*
Richland Newhope Inds Inc.............. C 419 774-4400
  Mansfield *(G-9712)*
Ridgco Pallet LLC............................. F 330 340-0048
  Gnadenhutten *(G-7988)*
Riverview Indus WD Pdts Inc........... G 330 669-8509
  Smithville *(G-13302)*
Riverview Transport LLC.................. C 330 669-8509
  Smithville *(G-13303)*
Russell L Garber................................ G 937 548-6224
  Greenville *(G-8058)*
S & W Express Inc........................... G 330 683-2747
  Orrville *(G-12149)*
Satco Inc... D 513 707-6150
  Loveland *(G-9504)*
Savvy Mtngs Special Events Ltd...... G 916 774-3838
  Berea *(G-1293)*
Schaefer Box & Pallet Co.................. E 513 738-2500
  Hamilton *(G-8241)*
Schnider Pallet LLC.......................... G 440 632-5346
  Middlefield *(G-10788)*
Schrock John..................................... G 937 544-8457
  Peebles *(G-12332)*
Schutz Container Systems Inc......... D 419 872-2477
  Perrysburg *(G-12425)*
▲ Sealco Inc...................................... G 740 922-4122
  Uhrichsville *(G-14768)*
Silvesco Inc....................................... F 740 373-6661
  Marietta *(G-9824)*
Smith Pallet LLC................................ G 937 564-6492
  Versailles *(G-14989)*
Southern Ohio Lumber LLC............. G 614 436-4472
  Peebles *(G-12333)*
Southwood Pallet LLC....................... D 330 682-3747
  Orrville *(G-12158)*
Sterling Industries Inc....................... F 419 523-3788
  Ottawa *(G-12193)*
Stony Point Hardwoods LLC............. G 330 852-4512
  Sugarcreek *(G-13939)*
Stumptown Lbr Pallet Mills Ltd........ G 740 757-2275
  Somerton *(G-13451)*
Sugarcreek Pallet Ltd....................... G 330 852-9812
  Sugarcreek *(G-13941)*
Swp Legacy Ltd................................ D 330 340-9663
  Sugarcreek *(G-13944)*
T & D Thompson Inc......................... E 740 332-8515
  Laurelville *(G-9056)*
T&A Pallets Inc................................. G 330 968-4743
  Ravenna *(G-12737)*
Terry Lumber and Supply Co............ F 330 659-6800
  Peninsula *(G-12342)*
Thomas J Weaver Inc....................... F 740 622-2040
  Coshocton *(G-5998)*
Tolson Pallet Mfg Inc....................... F 937 787-3511
  Gratis *(G-8023)*
Traveling Recycle WD Pdts Inc........ F 419 968-2649
  Middle Point *(G-10713)*
Tri State Pallet Inc........................... E 937 746-8702
  Franklin *(G-7707)*
Troyers Pallet Shop.......................... G 330 897-1038
  Fresno *(G-7827)*
Troymill Lumber Company................ G 440 632-6353
  Independence *(G-8688)*

Employee Codes: A=Over 500 employees, B=251-500
C=101-250, D=51-100, E=20-50, F=10-19, G=1-9

24 LUMBER AND WOOD PRODUCTS, EXCEPT FURNITURE

Troymill Manufacturing Inc...............F 440 632-5580
　Middlefield *(G-10793)*
Tusco Hardwoods LLC..................F 330 852-4281
　Sugarcreek *(G-13946)*
Universal Pallets Inc...........................E 614 444-1095
　Columbus *(G-5846)*
Valley View Pallets LLC..................G 740 599-0010
　Danville *(G-6149)*
Van Orders Pallet Company Inc...........F 419 875-6932
　Liberty Center *(G-9205)*
Van Wert Pallets LLC........................G 419 203-1823
　Van Wert *(G-14930)*
Wellman Container Corporation.........E 513 860-3040
　Cincinnati *(G-3515)*
Winesburg Hardwood Lbr Co LLC......F 330 893-2705
　Dundee *(G-6974)*
Wjf Enterprises LLC..........................G 513 871-7320
　Cincinnati *(G-3523)*
Woodford Logistics............................F 513 417-8453
　South Charleston *(G-13455)*
Yoder Lumber Co Inc.......................D 330 674-1435
　Millersburg *(G-11009)*
▼ Yoder Lumber Co Inc...................D 330 893-3121
　Millersburg *(G-11008)*
Zanesville Pallet Co Inc...................F 740 454-3700
　Zanesville *(G-16574)*

2449 Wood containers, nec

Brimar Packaging Inc.......................E 440 934-3080
　Avon *(G-764)*
Brown-Forman Corporation...............F 740 384-3027
　Wellston *(G-15326)*
Cassis Packaging Co.......................F 937 223-8868
　Dayton *(G-6249)*
Cima Inc..E 513 382-8976
　Hamilton *(G-8191)*
▲ Cima Inc....................................G 513 382-8976
　Hamilton *(G-8192)*
Clark Rm Inc...................................F 419 425-9889
　Findlay *(G-7494)*
Custom Built Crates Inc...................E
　Milford *(G-10904)*
Denoon Lumber Company LLC.......D 740 768-2220
　Bergholz *(G-1300)*
Frankes Wood Products LLC...........E 937 642-0706
　Marysville *(G-9910)*
Greif Inc...E 740 657-6500
　Delaware *(G-6725)*
◆ Greif Inc....................................E 740 549-6000
　Delaware *(G-6724)*
Haessly Lumber Sales Co................D 740 373-6681
　Marietta *(G-9798)*
Hinchcliff Lumber Company.............D 440 238-5200
　Strongsville *(G-13841)*
▲ J & L Wood Products Inc...........E 937 667-4064
　Tipp City *(G-14139)*
Joe Gonda Company Incorporated...G 440 458-6000
　Grafton *(G-8003)*
Overseas Packing LLC....................E 440 232-2917
　Bedford *(G-1148)*
Schaefer Box & Pallet Co................E 513 738-2500
　Hamilton *(G-8241)*
Silvesco Inc....................................F 740 373-6661
　Marietta *(G-9824)*
T & D Thompson Inc........................E 740 332-8515
　Laurelville *(G-9056)*
Terry Lumber and Supply Co............F 330 659-6800
　Peninsula *(G-12342)*
Traveling Recycle WD Pdts Inc........F 419 968-2649
　Middle Point *(G-10713)*
Wellman Container Corporation.......E 513 860-3040
　Cincinnati *(G-3515)*

2451 Mobile homes

Clayton Homes................................F 937 592-3039
　Bellefontaine *(G-1202)*
Freedom Homes..............................G 740 446-3093
　Gallipolis *(G-7892)*
Manufactured Housing Entps Inc......E 419 636-4511
　Bryan *(G-1827)*
Mobile Conversions Inc...................F 513 797-1991
　Amelia *(G-460)*
Muster Rdu Inc...............................G 614 537-5440
　Lancaster *(G-9026)*
Palm Harbor Homes Inc..................G 937 725-9465
　New Vienna *(G-11543)*
Skyline Corporation.........................C 330 852-2483
　Sugarcreek *(G-13938)*

2452 Prefabricated wood buildings

Al Yoder Construction Co................G 330 359-5726
　Millersburg *(G-10939)*
Beachy Barns Ltd...........................F 614 873-4193
　Plain City *(G-12565)*
Carter-Jones Lumber Company.......E 440 834-8164
　Middlefield *(G-10739)*
Consoldted Anlytcal Systems In.......F 513 542-1200
　Cincinnati *(G-2787)*
Cooper Enterprises Inc....................D 419 347-5232
　Shelby *(G-13193)*
Everything In America.....................G 347 871-6872
　Cleveland *(G-4039)*
Fifth Avenue Lumber Co..................E 614 833-6655
　Canal Winchester *(G-1986)*
Gillard Construction Inc...................F 740 376-9744
　Marietta *(G-9795)*
Hochstetler Milling LLC....................E 419 368-0004
　Loudonville *(G-9449)*
J Aaron Weaver..............................G 440 474-9185
　Rome *(G-12848)*
J L Wannemacher Sls Svc Inc.........F 419 453-3445
　Ottoville *(G-12200)*
Millers Storage Barns LLC..............F 330 893-3293
　Millersburg *(G-10982)*
Morton Buildings Inc.......................E 419 675-2311
　Kenton *(G-8894)*
Nef Ltd...G 419 445-6696
　Archbold *(G-538)*
Patio Enclosures............................F 513 733-4646
　Cincinnati *(G-3236)*
Premier Construction Company.......F 513 874-2611
　Fairfield *(G-7395)*
Rona Enterprises Inc.......................G 740 927-9971
　Pataskala *(G-12306)*
Skyline Corporation.........................C 330 852-2483
　Sugarcreek *(G-13938)*
Unibilt Industries Inc.......................E 937 890-7570
　Vandalia *(G-14963)*
Vinyl Design Corporation.................E 419 283-4009
　Holland *(G-8536)*
Weaver Barns Ltd..........................F 330 852-2103
　Sugarcreek *(G-13947)*

2491 Wood preserving

Clark Rm Inc...................................F 419 425-9889
　Findlay *(G-7494)*
Couch Business Development Inc...F 937 253-1099
　Dayton *(G-6264)*
Flagship Trading Corporation..........E
　Cleveland *(G-4066)*
ISK Americas Incorporated..............F 440 357-4600
　Concord Township *(G-5908)*
Joseph Sabatino.............................G 330 332-5879
　Salem *(G-13007)*

Luxus Products LLC........................G 937 444-6500
　Mount Orab *(G-11242)*
The F A Requarth Company............E 937 224-1141
　Dayton *(G-6618)*
Urbn Timber LLC............................G 614 981-3043
　Columbus *(G-5850)*
Wood Duck Enterprises Ltd............G 937 776-0606
　Beavercreek *(G-1067)*

2493 Reconstituted wood products

Bmca Insulation Products Inc..........F 330 335-2501
　Wadsworth *(G-15020)*
Frankes Wood Products LLC...........E 937 642-0706
　Marysville *(G-9910)*
GMI Companies Inc........................G 937 981-0244
　Greenfield *(G-8029)*
GMI Companies Inc........................E 513 932-3445
　Lebanon *(G-9084)*
◆ GMI Companies Inc...................C 513 932-3445
　Lebanon *(C 0083)*
▲ Marsh Industries Inc..................D 800 426-4244
　New Philadelphia *(G-11516)*
◆ Michael Kaufman Companies Inc...F 330 673-4881
　Kent *(G-8836)*
▼ Miller Manufacturing Inc.............E 330 852-0689
　Sugarcreek *(G-13931)*
Mpc Inc..E 440 835-1405
　Cleveland *(G-4424)*
Rsp Industries Inc...........................F 440 823-4502
　Chagrin Falls *(G-2384)*
Solas Ltd.......................................E 650 501-0889
　Avon *(G-788)*
◆ Tectum Inc.................................C 740 345-9691
　Newark *(G-11608)*
Tri-State Supply Co Inc...................F 614 272-6767
　Columbus *(G-5836)*

2499 Wood products, nec

77 Coach Supply Ltd......................G 330 674-1454
　Millersburg *(G-10937)*
Adroit Thinking Inc..........................F 419 542-9363
　Hicksville *(G-8370)*
Akron Centl Engrv Mold Mch Inc.....G 330 475-1388
　Akron *(G-28)*
Alfrebro LLC..................................F 513 539-7373
　Monroe *(G-11093)*
American Wood Fibers Inc..............E 740 420-3233
　Circleville *(G-3541)*
Atkins Custom Framing Ltd.............F 740 816-1501
　Delaware *(G-6702)*
◆ Baker McMillen Co....................D 330 923-8300
　Stow *(G-13687)*
Barkman Products LLC..................G 330 893-2520
　Millersburg *(G-10942)*
Bc Investment Corporation..............G 330 262-3070
　Wooster *(G-16103)*
Berlin Wood Products Inc...............G 330 893-3281
　Berlin *(G-1304)*
◆ Black Squirrel Holdings Inc........E 513 577-7107
　Cincinnati *(G-2671)*
Blang Acquisition LLC....................F 937 223-2155
　Dayton *(G-6231)*
Bonfoey Co....................................F 216 621-0178
　Cleveland *(G-3747)*
Brown Wood Products Company.....G 330 339-8000
　New Philadelphia *(G-11488)*
Bushworks Incorporated..................G 937 767-1713
　Yellow Springs *(G-16283)*
Canfield Manufacturing Co Inc........G 330 533-3333
　North Jackson *(G-11780)*
Cass Frames Inc............................G 419 468-2863
　Galion *(G-7863)*

25 FURNITURE AND FIXTURES

◆ Cincinnati Dowel & WD Pdts Co............E 937 444-2502
    Mount Orab *(G-11239)*

▲ CM Paula Company............................. E 513 759-7473
    Mason *(G-9980)*

▲ Columbus Washboard Compan.......... G 740 380-3828
    Logan *(G-9362)*

Country Outdoor WD Stoves Cows........ G 740 967-0315
    Alexandria *(G-383)*

County Line Wood Working LLC............ G 330 316-3057
    Baltic *(G-835)*

▲ Creative Plastic Concepts LLC............ F 419 927-9588
    Sycamore *(G-13988)*

Ely Road Reel Company Ltd.................. E 330 683-1818
    Apple Creek *(G-499)*

Engraved In Usa LLC............................ G 513 301-7760
    Fairfield *(G-7357)*

F J Designs Inc.................................... F 330 264-1477
    Wooster *(G-16117)*

Fenwick Gallery of Fine Arts................. G 419 475-1651
    Toledo *(G-14286)*

Frame Warehouse................................. G 614 861-4582
    Reynoldsburg *(G-12765)*

Garick LLC... E 216 581-0100
    Cleveland *(G-4102)*

◆ Gayston Corporation............................C 937 743-6050
    Miamisburg *(G-10640)*

Growers Choice Ltd............................. G 330 262-8754
    Shreve *(G-13208)*

H Hafner & Sons Inc............................. E 513 321-1895
    Cincinnati *(G-2979)*

Hackman Frames LLC.......................... F 614 841-0007
    Columbus *(G-5415)*

Handlebar & Grill On Main LLC............. G 740 746-2077
    Sugar Grove *(G-13916)*

Hardwood Solutions............................ G 330 359-5755
    Wilmot *(G-16068)*

Hardwood Store Inc............................. G 937 864-2899
    Enon *(G-7250)*

Hauser Services Llc............................. E 440 632-5126
    Middlefield *(G-10755)*

Hit Trophy Inc...................................... G 419 445-5356
    Archbold *(G-532)*

Hollywood Dance Jams........................ G 419 234-0746
    Van Wert *(G-14918)*

▲ Holmes Wheel Shop Inc....................... E 330 279-2891
    Holmesville *(G-8548)*

Hope Timber & Marketing Group.......... F 740 344-1788
    Newark *(G-11580)*

Hope Timber Mulch LLC....................... G 740 344-1788
    Newark *(G-11581)*

House of 10000 Picture Frames........... G 937 254-5541
    Dayton *(G-6373)*

Insta Plak Inc....................................... F 419 537-1555
    Toledo *(G-14334)*

Intrism Inc.. F 614 733-9304
    Worthington *(G-16199)*

Irvine Wood Recovery Inc..................... E 513 831-0060
    Miamiville *(G-10711)*

J & D Wood Ltd..................................... G 937 778-9663
    Piqua *(G-12528)*

J R Custom Unlimited Inc..................... F 513 894-9800
    Hamilton *(G-8223)*

Jaf Usa LLC.. G 919 935-2726
    Granville *(G-8019)*

Jakes Woodshop.................................. G 937 672-4964
    Waynesville *(G-15297)*

Jewett Supply....................................... F 419 738-9882
    Wapakoneta *(G-15119)*

Juno Enterprises LLC........................... G 419 448-9350
    New Riegel *(G-11536)*

Kalinich Fence Company Inc................. F 440 238-6127
    Strongsville *(G-13848)*

Katch Kitchen LLC................................. E 513 537-8056
    Cincinnati *(G-3065)*

Latham Lumber & Pallet Co.................. G 740 493-2707
    Latham *(G-9052)*

Lazars Art Gllery Crtive Frmng.............. G 330 477-8351
    Canton *(G-2144)*

Mark Andronis...................................... G 740 259-5613
    Lucasville *(G-9524)*

Miami Valley Spray Foam LLC.............. G 419 295-6536
    Lewisburg *(G-9188)*

▼ Miller Manufacturing Inc....................... E 330 852-0689
    Sugarcreek *(G-13931)*

Mt Perry Foods Inc............................... D 740 743-3890
    Mount Perry *(G-11251)*

▲ Mulch Manufacturing Inc....................... E 614 864-4004
    Reynoldsburg *(G-12769)*

Nalk Woods LLC.................................. G 216 548-0994
    Macedonia *(G-9563)*

Newbury Woodworks............................ G 440 564-5273
    Newbury *(G-11632)*

▲ P & R Specialty Inc.............................. E 937 773-0263
    Piqua *(G-12541)*

P & T Millwork Inc................................. F 440 543-2151
    Chagrin Falls *(G-2412)*

▲ P Graham Dunn Inc.............................. B 330 828-2105
    Dalton *(G-6138)*

Peters Family Enterprises Inc.............. G 419 339-0555
    Elida *(G-7096)*

▲ Puttmann Industries Inc....................... F 513 202-9444
    Harrison *(G-8287)*

Randy Lewis Inc................................... F 330 784-0456
    Akron *(G-296)*

Rcs Cross Woods Maple LLC................ E 614 825-0670
    Columbus *(G-5713)*

Rhk Hardwoods LLC............................. G 740 835-1097
    Piketon *(G-12483)*

Roe Transportation Entps Inc............... G 937 497-7161
    Sidney *(G-13278)*

Ryanworks Inc...................................... F 937 438-1282
    Dayton *(G-6555)*

◆ Scotts Company LLC............................C 937 644-0011
    Marysville *(G-9934)*

▲ Sealco Inc... G 740 922-4122
    Uhrichsville *(G-14768)*

Signature Sign Co Inc........................... F 216 426-1234
    Cleveland *(G-4702)*

Singleton Reels Inc............................... E 330 274-2961
    Rootstown *(G-12857)*

Solas Ltd.. E 650 501-0889
    Avon *(G-788)*

▲ Solid Dimensions Inc........................... G 419 663-1134
    Norwalk *(G-11989)*

Sonoco Products Company................... E 614 759-8470
    Columbus *(G-5778)*

Steeles 5 Acre Mill Inc.......................... G 419 542-9363
    Hicksville *(G-8380)*

Tok Dawgs Chicken LLC....................... G 614 813-2698
    Columbus *(G-5827)*

◆ Walnut Creek Planing Ltd....................D 330 893-3244
    Millersburg *(G-11005)*

Westcott Woodworks HM Svcs LLC...... G 419 706-2250
    Norwalk *(G-11990)*

Wmg Wood More................................... G 440 350-3970
    Painesville *(G-12278)*

Wurms Woodworking Company............ E 419 492-2184
    New Washington *(G-11552)*

▼ Yoder Lumber Co Inc........................... D 330 893-3121
    Millersburg *(G-11008)*

Youngstown Fence Incorporated.......... G 330 788-8110
    Youngstown *(G-16481)*

Zaenkert Surveying Essentials............. G 513 738-2917
    Okeana *(G-12070)*

25 FURNITURE AND FIXTURES

2511 Wood household furniture

Andal Woodworking............................. F 330 897-8059
    Baltic *(G-833)*

Anthony Flottemesch & Son Inc........... F 513 561-1212
    Cincinnati *(G-2628)*

◆ Archbold Furniture Co.........................E 567 444-4666
    Archbold *(G-523)*

Artistic Finishes Inc............................. F 440 951-7850
    Willoughby *(G-15886)*

Basic Cases Inc................................... G 216 662-3900
    Cleveland *(G-3724)*

Berlin Gardens Gazebos Ltd................. F 330 893-3411
    Berlin *(G-1303)*

◆ Cabintwrks Group Mddlfield LLC........A 888 562-7744
    Middlefield *(G-10738)*

Carlisle Oak... G 330 852-8734
    Sugarcreek *(G-13921)*

Chris Haughey..................................... G 937 652-3338
    Urbana *(G-14826)*

Criswell Furniture LLC......................... F 330 695-2082
    Fredericksburg *(G-7722)*

Custom Surfaces Inc........................... G 440 439-2310
    Bedford *(G-1114)*

Diversified Products & Svcs................ F 740 393-6202
    Mount Vernon *(G-11270)*

Dorel Home Furnishings Inc................ D 419 447-7448
    Tiffin *(G-14083)*

Dutch Heritage Woodcraft.................... F 330 893-2211
    Berlin *(G-1306)*

East Oberlin Cabinets LLC................... G 440 775-1166
    Oberlin *(G-12050)*

◆ Foundations Worldwide Inc.................E 330 722-5033
    Medina *(G-10326)*

Fountain Nook Woodcraft..................... G 330 473-2162
    Apple Creek *(G-500)*

▲ Furniture By Otmar Inc........................ F 937 435-2039
    Dayton *(G-6342)*

Gasser Chair Co Inc............................. D 330 759-2234
    Youngstown *(G-16363)*

Gencraft Designs LLC.......................... E 330 359-6251
    Navarre *(G-11342)*

Grabo Interiors Inc.............................. G 216 391-6677
    Cleveland *(G-4134)*

◆ Greenway Home Products Inc.............F
    Perrysburg *(G-12387)*

Hardwood Lumber Company Inc.......... F 440 834-1891
    Middlefield *(G-10754)*

◆ Hen House Inc.....................................F 419 663-3377
    Norwalk *(G-11973)*

Hochstetler Wood................................ F 330 893-2384
    Millersburg *(G-10961)*

Hochstetler Wood Ltd.......................... G 330 893-1601
    Millersburg *(G-10962)*

Holmes Panel LLC................................ G 330 897-5040
    Baltic *(G-838)*

Hopewood Inc...................................... G 330 359-5656
    Millersburg *(G-10969)*

Idx Corporation....................................C 937 401-3225
    Dayton *(G-6378)*

Integral Design Inc.............................. F 216 524-0555
    Cleveland *(G-4230)*

James L Deckebach LLC...................... G 513 321-3733
    Cincinnati *(G-3037)*

Jeffco Sheltered Workshop.................. F 740 264-4608
    Steubenville *(G-13669)*

▲ Kitchens By Rutenschroer Inc............. G 513 251-8333
    Cincinnati *(G-3080)*

Lauber Manufacturing Co..................... G 419 446-2450
    Archbold *(G-533)*

25 FURNITURE AND FIXTURES

Lima Millwork Inc .... F 419 331-3303
Elida *(G-7094)*

Mamabees HM Gds Lifestyle LLC .... G 419 277-2914
Fostoria *(G-7642)*

Michaels Pre-Cast Con Pdts .... F 513 683-1292
Loveland *(G-9497)*

Mielke Furniture Repair Inc .... G 419 625-4572
Sandusky *(G-13082)*

Miller Cabinet Ltd .... F 614 873-4221
Plain City *(G-12586)*

Millwood Wholesale Inc .... F 330 359-6109
Dundee *(G-6968)*

▲ Morris Furniture Co Inc .... C 937 874-7100
Fairborn *(G-7320)*

N Wasserstrom & Sons Inc .... G 614 737-5410
Columbus *(G-5587)*

North Amercn Kit Solutions Inc .... E 800 854-3267
Elyria *(G-7186)*

Pedagogy Furniture .... G 888 394-8484
Chardon *(G-2463)*

Penwood Mfg .... G 330 359-5600
Fresno *(G-7824)*

◆ Progressive Furniture Inc .... E 419 446-4500
Archbold *(G-542)*

◆ R A Hamed International Inc .... F 330 247-0190
Twinsburg *(G-14722)*

Richard Benhase & Assoc Inc .... G 513 772-1896
Cincinnati *(G-3338)*

Rnr Enterprises LLC .... F 330 852-3022
Sugarcreek *(G-13936)*

Specialty Svcs Cabinetry Inc .... G 614 421-1599
Columbus *(G-5784)*

Stark Truss Company Inc .... E 330 478-2100
Canton *(G-2233)*

Stark Truss Company Inc .... D 419 298-3777
Edgerton *(G-7082)*

Tappan Chairs LLC .... G 800 840-9121
Blue Ash *(G-1477)*

Textiles Inc .... G 614 529-8642
Hilliard *(G-8446)*

▲ Textiles Inc .... G 740 852-0782
London *(G-9195)*

Vocational Services Inc .... E 216 431-8085
Cleveland *(G-4880)*

Waller Brothers Stone Company .... E 740 858-1948
Mc Dermott *(G-10275)*

Weaver Woodcraft L L C .... G 330 695-2150
Apple Creek *(G-514)*

Western & Southern Lf Insur Co .... A 513 629-1800
Cincinnati *(G-3517)*

▼ Wine Cellar Innovations LLC .... C 513 321-3733
Cincinnati *(G-3522)*

Woodcraft .... G 419 389-0560
Toledo *(G-14526)*

Woodworking Shop LLC .... F 513 330-9663
Miamisburg *(G-10702)*

2512 Upholstered household furniture

Buckeye Seating LLC .... F 330 893-7700
Millersburg *(G-10947)*

Custom Craft Collection Inc .... F 440 998-3000
Ashtabula *(G-630)*

▲ Fortner Upholstering Inc .... F 614 475-8282
Columbus *(G-5384)*

Franklin Cabinet Company Inc .... E 937 743-9606
Franklin *(G-7676)*

Hallmark Industries Inc .... E 937 864-7378
Springfield *(G-13571)*

Hopewood Inc .... G 330 359-5656
Millersburg *(G-10969)*

▲ Morris Furniture Co Inc .... C 937 874-7100
Fairborn *(G-7320)*

Njm Furniture Outlet Inc .... F 330 893-3514
Millersburg *(G-10987)*

Robert Mayo Industries .... G 330 426-2587
East Palestine *(G-7008)*

◆ Sauder Woodworking Co .... A 419 446-2711
Archbold *(G-546)*

▲ Weavers Furniture Ltd .... F 330 852-2701
Sugarcreek *(G-13948)*

Y & T Woodcraft Inc .... G 330 464-3432
Apple Creek *(G-515)*

2514 Metal household furniture

◆ Albion Industries Inc .... E 440 238-1955
Strongsville *(G-13804)*

▲ Angels Landing Inc .... G 513 687-3681
Moraine *(G-11158)*

Bailey & Jensen Inc .... G 937 272-1784
Centerville *(G-2360)*

C-Link Enterprises LLC .... F 937 222-2829
Dayton *(G-0244)*

Invacare Corporation .... G 800 333-6900
Elyria *(G-7166)*

◆ Invacare Corporation .... A 440 329-6000
Elyria *(G-7164)*

▲ Invacare Holdings Corporation .... C 440 329-6000
Elyria *(G-7169)*

Metal Fabricating Corporation .... D 216 631-8121
Cleveland *(G-4396)*

◆ Rize Home LLC .... D 800 333-8333
Solon *(G-13415)*

▲ Sunnest Service LLC .... E 740 283-2815
Steubenville *(G-13678)*

2515 Mattresses and bedsprings

Ahmf Inc .... E 614 921-1223
Columbus *(G-5107)*

▲ Banner Mattress Co Inc .... D 419 324-7181
Toledo *(G-14206)*

▲ Casco Mfg Solutions Inc .... D 513 681-0003
Cincinnati *(G-2706)*

▲ Coconis Furniture Inc .... E 740 452-1231
South Zanesville *(G-13477)*

Homecare Mattress Inc .... F 937 746-2556
Franklin *(G-7680)*

HSP Bedding Solutions LLC .... E 440 437-4425
Orwell *(G-12165)*

Midwest Quality Bedding Inc .... E 614 504-5971
Columbus *(G-5566)*

Protective Industrial Polymers .... F 440 327-0015
North Ridgeville *(G-11854)*

▲ Quilting Inc .... D 614 504-5971
Plain City *(G-12591)*

Sealy Mattress Mfg Co LLC .... F 800 697-3259
Medina *(G-10374)*

◆ Solstice Sleep Products Inc .... E 614 279-8850
Columbus *(G-5777)*

Tru Comfort Mattress .... G 614 595-8600
Dublin *(G-6954)*

V-I-S-c-e-r-o-t-o-n-i-c Inc .... D 330 690-3355
Akron *(G-368)*

Walter F Stephens Jr Inc .... E 937 746-0521
Franklin *(G-7709)*

2517 Wood television and radio cabinets

Innerwood & Company .... F 513 677-2229
Loveland *(G-9486)*

Kraftmaid Trucking Inc .... D 440 632-2531
Middlefield *(G-10762)*

◆ Progressive Furniture Inc .... E 419 446-4500
Archbold *(G-542)*

2519 Household furniture, nec

Bulk Carrier Trnsp Eqp Co .... E 330 339-3333
New Philadelphia *(G-11489)*

Daniels Amish Collection LLC .... C 330 276-0110
Killbuck *(G-8919)*

Entertrainment Junction .... E 513 326-1100
Cincinnati *(G-2876)*

Evenflo Company Inc .... D 937 773-3971
Troy *(G-14566)*

Hershy Way Ltd .... G 330 893-2809
Millersburg *(G-10958)*

Jan S Kleinman .... G 440 473-9776
Mayfield Hts *(G-10257)*

John Purdum .... E 513 897-9686
Waynesville *(G-15298)*

▲ Kitchens By Rutenschroer Inc .... E 513 251-8333
Cincinnati *(G-3080)*

Mar-Bal Pultrusion Inc .... F 440 953-0456
Willoughby *(G-15949)*

Office Magic Inc .... F 510 782-6100
Medina *(G-10357)*

◆ Owens Corning .... A 419 248-8000
Toledo *(G-14421)*

Sailors Tailor Inc .... F 937 862-7781
Spring Valley *(G-13491)*

Sauder Woodworking Co .... F 419 446-2711
Archbold *(G-545)*

◆ The Little Tikes Company .... A 330 650-3000
Hudson *(G-8616)*

2521 Wood office furniture

Basic Cases Inc .... G 216 662-3900
Cleveland *(G-3724)*

Buckeye Seating LLC .... F 330 893-7700
Millersburg *(G-10947)*

▲ Buzz Seating Inc .... G 877 263-5737
West Chester *(G-15543)*

Chagrin Valley Custom Furn LLC .... G 440 591-5511
Warrensville Heights *(G-15227)*

Crow Works LLC .... E 888 811-2769
Killbuck *(G-8918)*

Custom Millcraft Corp .... E 513 874-7080
West Chester *(G-15410)*

▼ Dvuv LLC .... E 216 741-5511
Cleveland *(G-3981)*

East Woodworking Company .... G 216 791-5950
Cleveland *(G-3990)*

Frontier Signs & Displays Inc .... E 513 367-0813
Harrison *(G-8275)*

Gasser Chair Co Inc .... D 330 759-2234
Youngstown *(G-16363)*

▲ Gasser Chair Co Inc .... E 330 534-2234
Youngstown *(G-16362)*

Geograph Industries Inc .... E 513 202-9200
Harrison *(G-8276)*

GMI Companies Inc .... G 937 981-0244
Greenfield *(G-8029)*

GMI Companies Inc .... G 513 932-3445
Lebanon *(G-9084)*

◆ GMI Companies Inc .... C 513 932-3445
Lebanon *(G-9083)*

▲ Hoge Lumber Company .... E 419 753-2263
New Knoxville *(G-11447)*

Idx Corporation .... C 937 401-3225
Dayton *(G-6378)*

Innerwood & Company .... F 513 677-2229
Loveland *(G-9486)*

Innovative Woodworking Inc .... G 513 531-1940
Cincinnati *(G-3023)*

Interior Products Co Inc .... E 216 641-1919
Cleveland *(G-4232)*

Lima Millwork Inc .... F 419 331-3303
Elida *(G-7094)*

SIC SECTION
25 FURNITURE AND FIXTURES

Mel Heitkamp Builders Ltd................... G 419 375-0405
  Fort Recovery (G-7623)
Miller Cabinet Ltd................................. F 614 873-4221
  Plain City (G-12586)
Richard Benhase & Assoc Inc............. G 513 772-1896
  Cincinnati (G-3338)
Sauder Manufacturing Co..................... D 419 682-3061
  Stryker (G-13913)
▲ Senator International Inc.................. E 419 887-5806
  Maumee (G-10229)
Specialty Svcs Cabinetry Inc................ G 614 421-1599
  Columbus (G-5784)
Symatic Inc... F 330 225-1510
  Medina (G-10381)
▼ Tiffin Metal Products Co................... C 419 447-8414
  Tiffin (G-14110)
▼ Workstream Inc................................. D 513 870-4400
  Fairfield (G-7428)

2522 Office furniture, except wood

Americas Mdular Off Specialist............. G 614 277-0216
  Grove City (G-8078)
Axess International LLC....................... G 330 460-4840
  Brunswick (G-1750)
▲ Biofit Engineered Product................. E 419 823-1089
  Bowling Green (G-1556)
▲ Casco Mfg Solutions Inc................... D 513 681-0003
  Cincinnati (G-2706)
Custom Craft Collection Inc.................. F 440 998-3000
  Ashtabula (G-630)
Custom Millcraft Corp........................... E 513 874-7080
  West Chester (G-15410)
Dgl Woodworking Inc........................... F 937 837-7091
  Dayton (G-6298)
East Woodworking Company............... G 216 791-5950
  Cleveland (G-3990)
Edsal Sandusky Corporation................ E 419 626-5465
  Sandusky (G-13052)
▲ Ergo Desktop LLC............................ E 567 890-3746
  Celina (G-2331)
Frontier Signs & Displays Inc............... G 513 367-0813
  Harrison (G-8275)
Furniture Concepts Inc......................... F 216 292-9100
  Cleveland (G-4093)
Gasser Chair Co Inc............................ D 330 759-2234
  Youngstown (G-16363)
Geograph Industries Inc....................... E 513 202-9200
  Harrison (G-8276)
GMI Companies Inc.............................. G 937 981-0244
  Greenfield (G-8029)
GMI Companies Inc.............................. G 513 932-3445
  Lebanon (G-9084)
◆ GMI Companies Inc........................... C 513 932-3445
  Lebanon (G-9083)
Hobart Cabinet Company..................... G 937 335-4666
  Troy (G-14580)
▼ Infinium Wall Systems Inc................. E 440 572-5000
  Strongsville (G-13845)
Innovative Woodworking Inc................ G 513 531-1940
  Cincinnati (G-3023)
Jsc Employee Leasing Corp................. D 330 773-8971
  Akron (G-199)
◆ M/W International Inc........................ F 440 526-6900
  Lorain (G-9423)
Marsh Industries Inc............................. E 330 308-8667
  New Philadelphia (G-11515)
Metal Fabricating Corporation.............. D 216 631-8121
  Cleveland (G-4396)
▲ National Electro-Coatings Inc........... D 216 898-0080
  Cleveland (G-4436)
Office Magic Inc................................... F 510 782-6100
  Medina (G-10357)

Pucel Enterprises Inc........................... D 216 881-4604
  Cleveland (G-4598)
Recycled Systems Furniture Inc........... E 614 880-9110
  Worthington (G-16210)
▲ Senator International Inc.................. E 419 887-5806
  Maumee (G-10229)
Ssi Manufacturing Inc........................... F 513 761-7757
  West Chester (G-15589)
Starr Fabricating Inc............................. D 330 394-9891
  Vienna (G-15004)
▲ The Columbus Show Case Co........... C
  Columbus (G-5820)
▼ Tiffin Metal Products Co................... C 419 447-8414
  Tiffin (G-14110)
Veterans Representative Co LLC........ F 330 779-0768
  Youngstown (G-16469)
▼ Workstream Inc................................. D 513 870-4400
  Fairfield (G-7428)

2531 Public building and related furniture

American Office Services Inc............... G 440 899-6888
  Westlake (G-15731)
Bell Vault and Monu Works Inc............ E 937 866-2444
  Miamisburg (G-10615)
Bill Davis Stadium................................ F 614 292-2624
  Columbus (G-5188)
▲ Biofit Engineered Product................. E 419 823-1089
  Bowling Green (G-1556)
Brocar Products Inc............................. E 513 922-2888
  Cincinnati (G-2688)
▲ C E White Co..................................... D 419 492-2157
  New Washington (G-11545)
Clarios LLC... D 419 636-4211
  Bryan (G-1814)
Clarios LLC... E 440 205-7221
  Mentor (G-10438)
Commercial Vehicle Group Inc............. B 614 289-5360
  New Albany (G-11374)
◆ Evenflo Company Inc......................... E 937 415-3300
  Miamisburg (G-10638)
Franklin Cabinet Company Inc............. E 937 743-9606
  Franklin (G-7676)
Gasser Chair Co Inc............................ D 330 759-2234
  Youngstown (G-16363)
▲ Gasser Chair Co Inc......................... E 330 534-2234
  Youngstown (G-16362)
General Motors LLC............................. A 216 265-5000
  Cleveland (G-4116)
GMI Companies Inc.............................. G 937 981-0244
  Greenfield (G-8029)
GMI Companies Inc.............................. G 513 932-3445
  Lebanon (G-9084)
◆ GMI Companies Inc........................... C 513 932-3445
  Lebanon (G-9083)
▲ Grand-Rock Company Inc................. E 440 639-2000
  Painesville (G-12240)
Group Endeavor LLC........................... D 234 571-5096
  Akron (G-174)
Hann Manufacturing Inc....................... E 740 962-3752
  Mcconnelsville (G-10281)
▲ Jay Industries Inc.............................. A 419 747-4161
  Mansfield (G-9671)
Johnson Controls Inc........................... E 216 587-0100
  Brecksville (G-1624)
Johnson Controls Inc........................... D 513 489-0950
  Cincinnati (G-3048)
Johnson Controls Inc........................... F 513 671-6338
  Cincinnati (G-3049)
Johnson Controls Inc........................... D 614 895-6600
  Westerville (G-15712)
Johnson Controls Inc........................... E 330 270-4385
  Youngstown (G-16385)

Magna International Amer Inc.............. C 330 824-3101
  Sheffield Village (G-13185)
▲ Marsh Industries Inc......................... D 800 426-4244
  New Philadelphia (G-11516)
McGill Septic Tank Co.......................... E 330 876-2171
  Kinsman (G-8936)
Michaels Pre-Cast Con Pdts................ F 513 683-1292
  Loveland (G-9497)
Mock Woodworking Company LLC..... E 740 452-2701
  Zanesville (G-16546)
Modern Manufacturing Inc.................... G 513 251-3600
  Cincinnati (G-3171)
N Wasserstrom & Sons Inc................. G 614 737-5410
  Columbus (G-5587)
Oberfields LLC..................................... E 614 252-0955
  Columbus (G-5610)
Sauder Manufacturing Co..................... D 419 682-3061
  Stryker (G-13913)
◆ Sauder Manufacturing Co.................. C 419 445-7670
  Archbold (G-544)
▲ Setex Inc... B 419 394-7800
  Saint Marys (G-12967)
▲ Shiffler Equipment Sales Inc............. E 440 285-9175
  Chardon (G-2467)
Soft Touch Wood LLC......................... E 330 545-4204
  Girard (G-7975)
▼ Tiffin Metal Products Co................... C 419 447-8414
  Tiffin (G-14110)
Trailway II... G 330 893-9195
  Dundee (G-6970)
Tri-State Supply Co Inc....................... F 614 272-6767
  Columbus (G-5836)
W C Heller & Co Inc............................. F 419 485-3176
  Montpelier (G-11145)
Wurms Woodworking Company........... E 419 492-2184
  New Washington (G-11552)
Yanfeng US Auto Intr Systems I.......... E 419 662-4905
  Northwood (G-11935)

2541 Wood partitions and fixtures

▲ 3jd Inc.. F 513 324-9655
  Moraine (G-11151)
A & J Woodworking Inc........................ G 419 695-5655
  Delphos (G-6759)
A G Industries Inc................................ D 216 252-7300
  Cleveland (G-3580)
A J Construction Co............................. G 330 539-9544
  Girard (G-7958)
Accent Manufacturing Inc..................... F 330 724-7704
  Norton (G-11936)
Action Group Inc.................................. D 614 868-8868
  Blacklick (G-1330)
Amtekco Industries LLC....................... D 614 228-6590
  Columbus (G-5136)
Amtekco Industries Inc........................ E 614 228-6525
  Columbus (G-5137)
▲ Archer Counter Design Inc................ G 513 396-7526
  Cincinnati (G-2631)
Artistic Finishes Inc............................. F 440 951-7850
  Willoughby (G-15886)
As America Inc..................................... E 419 522-4211
  Mansfield (G-9626)
Automated Bldg Components Inc......... E 419 257-2152
  North Baltimore (G-11694)
Baker Store Equipment Company......... F
  Shaker Heights (G-13150)
Benchmark-Cabinets LLC.................... G 740 694-1144
  Fredericktown (G-7739)
▲ Bruewer Woodwork Mfg Co............... D 513 353-3505
  Cleves (G-4946)
Cabinet Restylers Inc........................... D 419 281-8449
  Ashland (G-561)

Employee Codes: A=Over 500 employees, B=251-500
C=101-250, D=51-100, E=20-50, F=10-19, G=1-9

25 FURNITURE AND FIXTURES

Cameo Countertops Inc .... E 419 865-6371
  Holland (G-8496)
◆ Cap & Associates Inc .... C 614 863-3363
  Columbus (G-5229)
Case Crafters Inc .... G 937 667-9473
  Tipp City (G-14127)
Cassady Woodworks Inc .... E 937 256-7948
  Dayton (G-6155)
◆ CIP International Inc .... D 513 874-9925
  West Chester (G-15394)
Climate Pros LLC .... D 216 881-5200
  Cleveland (G-3878)
Climate Pros LLC .... D 330 744-2732
  Youngstown (G-16340)
Couch Business Development Inc .... F 937 253-1099
  Dayton (G-6264)
Counter Concepts Inc .... F 330 848-4848
  Doylestown (G-6853)
Countertop Sales .... F 614 626-4476
  Columbus (G-5300)
Crafted Surface and Stone LLC .... E 440 658-3799
  Chagrin Falls (G-2391)
Creative Products Inc .... G 419 866-5501
  Holland (G-8500)
Custom Design Cabinets & Tops .... G 440 639-9900
  Painesville (G-12225)
Custom Surroundings Inc .... F 913 839-0100
  Valley City (G-14868)
Customworks Inc .... G 614 262-1002
  Columbus (G-5312)
D Lewis Inc .... G 740 695-2615
  Saint Clairsville (G-12901)
Designer Cntemporary Laminates .... G 440 946-8207
  Painesville (G-12228)
Display Dynamics Inc .... E 937 832-2830
  Englewood (G-7229)
Diversified Products & Svcs .... F 740 393-6202
  Mount Vernon (G-11270)
E J Skok Industries .... E 216 292-7533
  Bedford (G-1119)
▼ Fixture Dimensions Inc .... E 513 360-7512
  Liberty Twp (G-9216)
▲ Formatech Inc .... E 330 273-2800
  Brunswick (G-1760)
◆ Formica Corporation .... E 513 786-3400
  Cincinnati (G-2916)
Forum III Inc .... G 513 961-5123
  Cincinnati (G-2917)
Franklin Cabinet Company Inc .... E 937 743-9606
  Franklin (G-7676)
◆ Gabriel Logan LLC .... D 740 380-6809
  Groveport (G-8144)
Gary L Gast .... G 419 626-5915
  Sandusky (G-13059)
Geograph Industries Inc .... E 513 202-9200
  Harrison (G-8276)
GMI Companies Inc .... G 937 981-0244
  Greenfield (G-8029)
GMI Companies Inc .... G 937 981-7724
  Greenfield (G-8030)
GMI Companies Inc .... G 513 932-3445
  Lebanon (G-9084)
◆ GMI Companies Inc .... C 513 932-3445
  Lebanon (G-9083)
Gross & Sons Custom Millwork .... G 419 227-0214
  Lima (G-9246)
Helmart Company Inc .... G 513 941-3095
  Cincinnati (G-2992)
Home Stor & Off Solutions Inc .... E 216 362-4660
  Cleveland (G-4199)
▲ Idx Dayton LLC .... C 937 401-3460
  Dayton (G-6379)

Ingle-Barr Inc .... D 740 702-6117
  Chillicothe (G-2513)
Kdm Signs Inc .... F 513 769-3900
  Cincinnati (G-3070)
◆ Kellogg Cabinets Inc .... G 614 833-9596
  Canal Winchester (G-1988)
Kinsella Manufacturing Co Inc .... F 513 561-5285
  Cincinnati (G-3077)
▲ Kitchens By Rutenschroer Inc .... G 513 251-8333
  Cincinnati (G-3080)
▲ L E Smith Company .... D 419 636-4555
  Bryan (G-1825)
Laminated Concepts Inc .... F 216 475-4141
  Maple Heights (G-9753)
Leiden Cabinet Company LLC .... G 330 425-8555
  Strasburg (G-13748)
Leiden Cabinet Company LLC .... D 330 425-8555
  Twinsburg (G-14687)
Lemon Group LLC .... G 614 409-9850
  Blue Ash (G-15600)
Lima Millwork Inc .... F 419 331-3303
  Elida (G-7094)
M21 Industries LLC .... E 937 781-1377
  Dayton (G-6419)
Mac Lean J S Co .... E 614 878-5454
  Columbus (G-5538)
◆ Michael Kaufman Companies Inc .... F 330 673-4881
  Kent (G-8836)
Midwest Woodworking Co Inc .... F 513 631-6684
  Cincinnati (G-3164)
Miller Cabinet Ltd .... F 614 873-4221
  Plain City (G-12586)
Mock Woodworking Company LLC .... E 740 452-2701
  Zanesville (G-16546)
Murray Display Fixtures Ltd .... F 614 875-1594
  Grove City (G-8109)
Norton Industries Inc .... E 888 357-2345
  Lakewood (G-8980)
Ohio Woodworking Co Inc .... G 513 631-0870
  Cincinnati (G-3219)
Partitions Plus Incorporated .... E 419 422-2600
  Findlay (G-7550)
Pfi Displays Inc .... E 330 925-9015
  Rittman (G-12826)
▲ Ptmj Enterprises Inc .... D 440 543-8000
  Solon (G-13408)
R & R Fabrications Inc .... E 419 678-4831
  Saint Henry (G-12937)
Regalia Products Inc .... F 614 579-8399
  Columbus (G-5716)
Reserve Millwork LLC .... E 216 531-6982
  Bedford (G-1153)
Riceland Cabinet Inc .... D 330 601-1071
  Wooster (G-16163)
▲ Rinos Woodworking Shop Inc .... F 440 946-1718
  Willoughby (G-15984)
Robertson Cabinets Inc .... F 937 698-3755
  West Milton (G-15631)
Romline Express LLC .... G 234 855-1905
  Youngstown (G-16431)
Rusco Products Inc .... G 330 758-0378
  Youngstown (G-16432)
▲ Scenic Solutions Ltd Lblty Co .... G 937 866-5062
  Dayton (G-6560)
Scio Laminated Products Inc .... F 740 945-1321
  Scio (G-13112)
Shur-Fit Distributors Inc .... F 937 746-0567
  Franklin (G-7702)
Solid Surface Concepts Inc .... E 513 948-8677
  Cincinnati (G-3401)
Symatic Inc .... F 330 225-1510
  Medina (G-10381)

▲ The Columbus Show Case Co C
  Columbus (G-5820)
The Hattenbach Company .... D 216 881-5200
  Cleveland (G-4785)
Thomas Cabinet Shop Inc .... F 937 847-8239
  Dayton (G-6621)
Tusco Limited Partnership .... C 740 254-4343
  Gnadenhutten (G-7991)
Ultrabuilt Play Systems Inc .... F 419 652-2294
  Nova (G-12005)
Village Cabinet Shop Inc .... G 704 966-0801
  Cincinnati (G-3499)
▼ W J Egli Company Inc .... F 330 823-3666
  Alliance (G-435)
Wdi Group Inc .... D 216 251-5509
  Cleveland (G-4898)
▼ Wine Cellar Innovations LLC .... C 513 321-3733
  Cincinnati (G-3522)
Youngstown Curve Form Inc .... F 330 744-3028
  Youngstown (G-16480)
Zanesville Fabricators Inc .... G 740 452-2439
  Zanesville (G-16573)

2542 Partitions and fixtures, except wood

3-D Technical Services Company .... E 937 746-2901
  Franklin (G-7659)
▲ Accel Group Inc .... D 330 336-0317
  Wadsworth (G-15014)
▲ B-R-O-T Incorporated .... E 216 267-5335
  Cleveland (G-3717)
Bates Metal Products Inc .... D 740 498-8371
  Port Washington (G-12631)
▼ Benko Products Inc .... E 440 934-2180
  Sheffield Village (G-13181)
Busch & Thiem Inc .... E 419 625-7515
  Sandusky (G-13047)
◆ Cap & Associates Inc .... C 614 863-3363
  Columbus (G-5229)
▲ Cdc Corporation .... E 715 532-5548
  Maumee (G-10173)
Communication Exhibits Inc .... D 330 854-4040
  Canal Fulton (G-1970)
Component Systems Inc .... E 216 252-9292
  Cleveland (G-3893)
Control Electric Co .... E 216 671-8010
  Columbia Station (G-5011)
▲ Crescent Metal Products Inc .... C 440 350-1100
  Mentor (G-10445)
CSM Concepts LLC .... F 330 483-1320
  Valley City (G-14866)
Custom Millcraft Corp .... E 513 874-7080
  West Chester (G-15410)
D Lewis Inc .... G 740 695-2615
  Saint Clairsville (G-12901)
Danco Metal Products LLC .... D 440 871-2300
  Avon Lake (G-803)
Display Dynamics Inc .... E 937 832-2830
  Englewood (G-7229)
Dwayne Bennett Industries .... G 440 466-5724
  Geneva (G-7934)
▲ E-B Display Company Inc .... C 330 833-4101
  Massillon (G-10092)
◆ Esmet Inc .... E 330 452-9132
  Canton (G-2098)
▲ Formatech Inc .... E 330 273-2800
  Brunswick (G-1760)
G & P Construction LLC .... E 855 494-4830
  North Royalton (G-11875)
GMR Furniture Services Ltd .... G 216 244-5072
  Cleveland (G-4130)
▲ Gwp Holdings Inc .... E 513 860-4050
  Fairfield (G-7364)

SIC SECTION

26 PAPER AND ALLIED PRODUCTS

HP Manufacturing Company Inc............ D 216 361-6500
   Cleveland *(G-4204)*

▲ Idx Dayton LLC............................. C 937 401-3460
   Dayton *(G-6379)*

Industrial Mfg Co Intl LLC.................... E 440 838-4555
   Upper Arlington *(G-14801)*

◆ Industrial Mfg Co LLC......................F 440 838-4700
   Brecksville *(G-1621)*

Integral Design Inc.............................. F 216 524-0555
   Cleveland *(G-4230)*

◆ Kellogg Cabinets Inc........................G 614 833-9596
   Canal Winchester *(G-1988)*

Mac Lean J S Co................................ E 614 878-5454
   Columbus *(G-5538)*

◆ Marlite Inc.....................................C 330 343-6621
   Dover *(G-6833)*

Metal Fabricating Corporation............... D 216 631-8121
   Cleveland *(G-4396)*

◆ Mfs Supply LLC...............................D 800 607-0541
   Solon *(G-13388)*

Midmark Corporation.......................... G 937 526-3662
   Versailles *(G-14986)*

◆ Midmark Corporation....................... A 937 528-7500
   Miamisburg *(G-10661)*

▲ Mills Partition Company LLC............ D 740 375-0770
   Marion *(G-9863)*

▼ Modern Retail Solutions LLC........... E 330 527-4308
   Garrettsville *(G-7923)*

Mro Built LLC.................................... D 330 526-0555
   North Canton *(G-11746)*

Myers Industries Inc........................... D 330 336-6621
   Wadsworth *(G-15047)*

Nor-Fab Inc....................................... G 330 467-6580
   Northfield *(G-11908)*

Ohio Displays Inc............................... F 216 961-5600
   Elyria *(G-7189)*

Onq Solutions Inc............................... G 234 542-0289
   Akron *(G-272)*

◆ Organized Living Inc........................E 513 489-9300
   Cincinnati *(G-3230)*

Panacea Products Corporation............. E 614 429-6320
   Columbus *(G-5653)*

◆ Panacea Products Corporation..........E 614 850-7000
   Columbus *(G-5652)*

Paul Yoder.. G 740 439-5811
   Senecaville *(G-13130)*

▲ Pete Gaietto & Associates Inc........... D 513 771-0903
   Cincinnati *(G-3249)*

Pfi Displays Inc.................................. E 330 925-9015
   Rittman *(G-12826)*

Prestige Store Interiors Inc.................. F 419 476-2106
   Maumee *(G-10224)*

Pucel Enterprises Inc.......................... D 216 881-4604
   Cleveland *(G-4598)*

Rack Processing Company Inc............. E 937 294-1911
   Moraine *(G-11207)*

Rack Processing Company Inc............. E 937 294-1911
   Moraine *(G-11206)*

Ray Communications Inc..................... G 330 686-0226
   Stow *(G-13720)*

Republic Storage Systems LLC............. B 330 438-5800
   Canton *(G-2215)*

Rogers Display Inc.............................. E 440 951-9200
   Mentor *(G-10547)*

Stanley Industrial & Auto LLC.............. C 614 755-7089
   Dublin *(G-6943)*

Stein Holdings Inc.............................. E 440 526-9301
   Independence *(G-8686)*

Stiber Fabricating Inc.......................... F 216 771-7210
   Cleveland *(G-4735)*

◆ Ternion Inc.....................................E 216 642-6180
   Cleveland *(G-4777)*

▼ Tiffin Metal Products Co................... C 419 447-8414
   Tiffin *(G-14110)*

Tmw Engineering Services LLC............ G 440 582-4700
   Strongsville *(G-13890)*

Tri County Tarp LLC........................... E 419 288-3350
   Gibsonburg *(G-7956)*

Tusco Limited Partnership................... C 740 254-4343
   Gnadenhutten *(G-7991)*

Valley Plastics Company Inc................ E 419 666-2349
   Toledo *(G-14518)*

W B Becherer Inc............................... G 330 758-6616
   Youngstown *(G-16473)*

▼ W J Egli Company Inc..................... F 330 823-3666
   Alliance *(G-435)*

Warren Steel Specialties Corp............... E 330 399-8360
   Warren *(G-15221)*

2591 Drapery hardware and blinds and shades

11 92 Holdings LLC............................ F 216 920-7790
   Chagrin Falls *(G-2366)*

Black Gate Blinds LLC........................ G 937 402-6158
   Peebles *(G-12325)*

Blind Factory Showroom...................... F 614 771-6549
   Hilliard *(G-8405)*

Cincinnati Window Shade Inc.............. F 513 631-7200
   Cincinnati *(G-2763)*

Custom Blind Corporation.................... F 937 643-2907
   Dayton *(G-6270)*

Designer Window Treatments Inc.......... G 419 822-4967
   Delta *(G-6782)*

Electra Tarp Inc................................. F 330 477-7168
   Canton *(G-2095)*

Golden Drapery Supply Inc.................. E 216 351-3283
   Cleveland *(G-4133)*

▲ Inside Outfitters Inc......................... E 614 798-3500
   Lewis Center *(G-9165)*

Keys Cheesecakes and Pies LLC.......... G 513 356-1221
   West Chester *(G-15454)*

Lumenomics Inc................................. E 614 798-3500
   Lewis Center *(G-9170)*

▲ Mag Resources LLC........................ F 330 294-0494
   Barberton *(G-878)*

Rustic Cheesecake LLC....................... G 419 680-6156
   Fremont *(G-7807)*

Youngstown Shade & Alum LLC............ G 330 782-2373
   Youngstown *(G-16487)*

2599 Furniture and fixtures, nec

Appetzers R US St Eats 2 Go LL........... G 937 460-1470
   Springfield *(G-13534)*

Aster Industries Inc............................ E 330 762-7965
   Akron *(G-66)*

Belmont Community Hospital............... E 740 671-1216
   Bellaire *(G-1183)*

▲ Biofit Engineered Product................ E 419 823-1089
   Bowling Green *(G-1556)*

Bolons Custom Kitchens Inc................ G 330 499-0092
   Canton *(G-2050)*

Brodwill LLC...................................... G 513 258-2716
   Cincinnati *(G-2689)*

Cateringstone.................................... G 513 410-1064
   Cincinnati *(G-2709)*

Crow Works LLC................................ E 888 811-2769
   Killbuck *(G-8918)*

Custom Surroundings Inc.................... F 913 839-0100
   Valley City *(G-14868)*

Darpro Storage Solutions LLC.............. E 567 233-3190
   Marengo *(G-9766)*

Epix Tube Co Inc............................... F 937 529-4858
   Dayton *(G-6321)*

Franklin Cabinet Company Inc.............. E 937 743-9606
   Franklin *(G-7676)*

GMI Companies Inc............................ G 937 981-0244
   Greenfield *(G-8029)*

GMI Companies Inc............................ G 513 932-3445
   Lebanon *(G-9084)*

◆ GMI Companies Inc.........................C 513 932-3445
   Lebanon *(G-9083)*

Grace Juice Company LLC.................. F 614 398-6879
   Westerville *(G-15707)*

Home Idea Center Inc......................... F 419 375-4951
   Fort Recovery *(G-7619)*

Howard B Claflin Co............................ G 330 928-1704
   Hudson *(G-8596)*

I 5S of Huron Inc................................ G 419 433-9075
   Huron *(G-8634)*

Justins Delight LLC............................. G 567 234-3575
   Toledo *(G-14343)*

Kinnemyers Cornerstone Cab Inc.......... G 513 353-3030
   Cleves *(G-4957)*

◆ Master Mfg Co Inc..........................E 216 641-0500
   Cleveland *(G-4367)*

McLeod Bar Group LLC....................... F 614 299-2099
   Columbus *(G-5555)*

Meccas Lounge LLC........................... G 419 239-6918
   Sandusky *(G-13080)*

◆ Michael Kaufman Companies Inc.......F 330 673-4881
   Kent *(G-8836)*

Modroto.. G 440 998-1202
   Ashtabula *(G-649)*

Moorchild LLC.................................... F 513 649-8867
   Middletown *(G-10845)*

Mro Built LLC.................................... D 330 526-0555
   North Canton *(G-11746)*

Pride 821 LLC................................... G 330 754-6320
   Canton *(G-2200)*

Sweets and Meats LLC........................ F 513 888-4227
   Cincinnati *(G-3437)*

Textiles Inc....................................... G 614 529-8642
   Hilliard *(G-8446)*

▼ Tiffin Metal Products Co................... C 419 447-8414
   Tiffin *(G-14110)*

Venu On 3rd...................................... G 937 222-2891
   Dayton *(G-6643)*

Vivo Brothers LLC............................... F 330 629-8686
   Columbiana *(G-5054)*

Woodworking Shop LLC....................... F 513 330-9663
   Miamisburg *(G-10702)*

26 PAPER AND ALLIED PRODUCTS

2611 Pulp mills

Advanced Green Tech Inc..................... G 614 397-8130
   Plain City *(G-12560)*

Billerud Americas Corporation.............. D 901 369-4105
   West Chester *(G-15379)*

◆ Billerud US Prod Holdg LLC.............B 877 855-7243
   Miamisburg *(G-10619)*

Caraustar Industries Inc...................... D 740 862-4167
   Baltimore *(G-843)*

Caraustar Industries Inc...................... F 216 961-5060
   Cleveland *(G-3788)*

Flegal Brothers Inc............................. E 419 298-3539
   Edgerton *(G-7075)*

Mondi Pakaging.................................. G 541 686-2665
   Lancaster *(G-9025)*

ND Paper Inc..................................... B 937 528-3822
   Dayton *(G-6467)*

Polymer Tech & Svcs Inc..................... F 740 929-5500
   Heath *(G-8327)*

26 PAPER AND ALLIED PRODUCTS

River Valley Paper Company LLC............ E 330 535-1001
   Akron *(G-305)*

Riverview Productions Inc......................... G 740 441-1950
   Gallipolis *(G-7900)*

Rumpke Transportation Co LLC................. B 513 242-4600
   Cincinnati *(G-3356)*

▲ The Mead Corporation................................ B 937 495-6323
   Dayton *(G-6619)*

Waste Parchment Inc..................................... F 330 674-6868
   Millersburg *(G-11006)*

World Wide Recyclers Inc............................. G 614 554-3296
   Columbus *(G-5881)*

2621 Paper mills

◆ Action Specialty Packaging LLC........... G
   West Chester *(G-15530)*

▲ Ampac Plastics LLC.................................... B 513 671-1777
   Cincinnati *(G-2624)*

Appvion Inc... G 717 731-7522
   Monroe *(G-11094)*

Appvion Inc... E 937 859-8262
   West Carrollton *(G-15349)*

Associated Hygienic Pdts LLC.................... A 770 497-9800
   Delaware *(G-6701)*

B & B Paper Converters Inc........................ F 216 941-8100
   Cleveland *(G-3713)*

Billerud Americas Corporation.................. D 901 369-4105
   West Chester *(G-15379)*

Billerud Americas Corporation.................. B 877 855-7243
   Miamisburg *(G-10616)*

Billerud Commercial LLC.............................. F 877 855-7243
   Miamisburg *(G-10617)*

Billerud Escanaba LLC.................................. F 877 855-7243
   Miamisburg *(G-10618)*

◆ Billerud US Prod Holdg LLC.................... B 877 855-7243
   Miamisburg *(G-10619)*

Blue Ridge Paper Products LLC............... D 440 235-7200
   Olmsted Falls *(G-12077)*

Carlisle Prtg Walnut Creek Ltd................. E 330 852-9922
   Sugarcreek *(G-13922)*

◆ Cheney Pulp and Paper Company........ E 937 746-9991
   Franklin *(G-7666)*

Corrchoice Cincinnati..................................... G 330 833-2884
   Massillon *(G-10086)*

Domtar Corporation... E 937 859-8262
   West Carrollton *(G-15352)*

Domtar Corporation... B 937 859-8261
   West Carrollton *(G-15353)*

Domtar Paper Company LLC...................... B 740 333-0003
   Wshngtn Ct Hs *(G-16229)*

▼ Duracorp LLC.. D 740 549-3336
   Lewis Center *(G-9158)*

Eclipse 3d/Pi LLC.. E 614 626-8536
   Columbus *(G-5343)*

English Oak LLC... G 614 600-8038
   Powell *(G-12672)*

Essity Operations Wausau LLC................. E 513 217-3644
   Middletown *(G-10822)*

Essity Prof Hygiene N Amer LLC............. F 513 217-3644
   Middletown *(G-10823)*

Fuzzy Ten LLC.. G 614 276-4738
   Columbus *(G-5392)*

Georgia-Pacific LLC.. E 614 491-9100
   Columbus *(G-5400)*

Georgia-Pacific LLC.. D 330 794-4444
   Mogadore *(G-11074)*

Georgia-Pacific LLC.. E 513 942-4800
   West Chester *(G-15441)*

Glatfelter Corporation..................................... G 740 772-3893
   Chillicothe *(G-2506)*

Glatfelter Corporation..................................... F 740 775-6119
   Chillicothe *(G-2507)*

Glatfelter Corporation..................................... D 740 772-3111
   Chillicothe *(G-2508)*

Glatfelter Corporation..................................... G 740 289-5100
   Piketon *(G-12476)*

Gr8 News Packaging LLC............................ F 314 739-1202
   Lockbourne *(G-9335)*

Graphic Packaging Intl LLC......................... B 419 673-0711
   Kenton *(G-8884)*

Graphic Paper Products Corp.................... D 937 325-5503
   Springfield *(G-13570)*

Gvr Warehouse and Packg LLC................ G 440 272-1005
   Orwell *(G-12164)*

Gvs Industries Inc.. G 513 851-3606
   Hamilton *(G-8214)*

Hanchett Paper Company............................ D 513 782-4440
   Cincinnati *(G-2984)*

Honey Cell Inc Mid West............................. E 513 360-0280
   Monroe *(G-11109)*

Honeycomb Midwest...................................... E 513 360-0280
   Monroe *(G-11110)*

International Paper Company.................... D 937 456-4131
   Eaton *(G-7062)*

International Paper Company.................... E 513 248-6319
   Loveland *(G-9488)*

International Paper Company.................... E 740 383-4061
   Marion *(G-9857)*

International Paper Company.................... F 937 578-7718
   Marysville *(G-9922)*

International Paper Company.................... E 800 473-0830
   Middletown *(G-10831)*

International Paper Company.................... D 740 397-5215
   Mount Vernon *(G-11273)*

John Adams.. G 614 564-9307
   Columbus *(G-5499)*

Kaylo Enterprises LLC................................... G 330 535-1860
   Akron *(G-202)*

▲ Kenag Inc... E 419 281-1204
   Ashland *(G-586)*

Kn8designs LLC.. G 859 380-5926
   Cincinnati *(G-3083)*

New Page Corporation................................... E 877 855-7243
   Miamisburg *(G-10665)*

Newpage Group Inc.. A 937 242-9500
   Miamisburg *(G-10666)*

Novolex Holdings Inc..................................... B 937 746-1933
   Franklin *(G-7690)*

▲ Novolyte Technologies Inc........................ B 216 867-1040
   Cleveland *(G-4485)*

Ohio Pulp Mills Inc.. E 513 631-7400
   Cincinnati *(G-3216)*

Owens Corning Sales LLC.......................... F 614 399-3915
   Mount Vernon *(G-11284)*

Paper Service Inc.. E 330 227-3546
   Lisbon *(G-9324)*

Pixelle Spcialty Solutions LLC................... A 740 772-3111
   Chillicothe *(G-2525)*

Pixelle Spcialty Solutions LLC................... C 419 333-6700
   Fremont *(G-7801)*

◆ Plus Mark LLC.. D 216 252-6770
   Cleveland *(G-4562)*

◆ Polymer Packaging Inc............................. D 330 832-2000
   North Canton *(G-11751)*

Pratt Industries Inc... F 937 583-4990
   Lewisburg *(G-9189)*

Pratt Paper (oh) LLC..................................... E 567 320-3353
   Wapakoneta *(G-15129)*

Rumford Paper Company............................ G 937 242-9230
   Miamisburg *(G-10680)*

▲ SC Liquidation Company LLC................ D 937 332-6500
   Troy *(G-14607)*

◆ Special Pack Inc.. E 330 458-3204
   Canton *(G-2229)*

Specialty America Inc................................... F 516 252-2438
   Columbus *(G-5781)*

Spinnker Prssure Snstive Pdts................. G 800 543-9452
   Troy *(G-14612)*

▲ The Mead Corporation................................ B 937 495-6323
   Dayton *(G-6619)*

Veritiv... F 614 323-3335
   Columbus *(G-5858)*

Verso Paper Inc.. E 901 369-4100
   Miamisburg *(G-10698)*

Verso Quinnesec Rep LLC.......................... C 901 369-4100
   Miamisburg *(G-10699)*

Wausau Paper Corp.. B 513 217-3623
   Middletown *(G-10871)*

Welch Packaging Group Inc....................... C 614 870-2000
   Columbus *(G-5869)*

◆ West Carrollton Converting Inc............. E 937 859-3621
   West Carrollton *(G-15357)*

2631 Paperboard mills

◆ Action Specialty Packaging LLC........... G
   West Chester *(G-15530)*

Ball Corporation... E 234 360-2141
   Canton *(G-2043)*

Billerud Americas Corporation.................. D 901 369-4105
   West Chester *(G-15379)*

▲ Buckeye Boxes Inc..................................... D 614 274-8484
   Columbus *(G-5219)*

Caraustar Industries Inc.............................. D 740 862-4167
   Baltimore *(G-843)*

Caraustar Industries Inc.............................. E 513 871-7112
   Cincinnati *(G-2701)*

Caraustar Industries Inc.............................. F 216 939-3001
   Cleveland *(G-3789)*

Caraustar Industries Inc.............................. E 330 665-7700
   Copley *(G-5946)*

Centor Inc... C 800 321-3391
   Berlin *(G-1305)*

Centor Inc... F 567 336-8094
   Perrysburg *(G-12369)*

Churmac Industries Inc................................ F 740 773-5800
   Chillicothe *(G-2498)*

Coburn Inc.. D 419 368-4051
   Hayesville *(G-8315)*

English Oak LLC.. G 614 600-8038
   Powell *(G-12672)*

▲ Fibercorr Mills LLC..................................... D 330 837-5151
   Massillon *(G-10096)*

G S K Inc.. G 937 547-1611
   Greenville *(G-8046)*

Georgia-Pacific LLC.. C 740 477-3347
   Circleville *(G-3553)*

Graphic Packaging Intl LLC......................... C 513 424-4200
   Middletown *(G-10828)*

Graphic Packaging Intl LLC......................... C 440 248-4370
   Solon *(G-13357)*

Inland Paperboard Pkg................................. G 562 946-6127
   Milford *(G-10911)*

▼ Loroco Industries Inc................................. D 513 891-9544
   Cincinnati *(G-3113)*

Martin Paper Products Inc.......................... F 740 756-9271
   Carroll *(G-2300)*

Millcraft Purchasing Corp............................ E 216 441-5505
   Cleveland *(G-4414)*

National Bias Fabric Co................................ F 216 361-0530
   Cleveland *(G-4435)*

National Carton & Coating Company...... D 937 347-1042
   Xenia *(G-16270)*

Norse Dairy Systems Inc............................. C 614 294-4931
   Columbus *(G-5600)*

▲ P & R Specialty Inc................................... E 937 773-0263
   Piqua *(G-12541)*

SIC SECTION
26 PAPER AND ALLIED PRODUCTS

Pactiv LLC... D 614 771-5400
   Columbus *(G-5650)*

Premier Packaging Systems LLC........... G 419 439-1900
   Defiance *(G-6693)*

Quilting Creations Intl.............................. G 330 874-4741
   Bolivar *(G-1535)*

Safeway Packaging Inc........................... E 419 629-3200
   New Bremen *(G-11408)*

Saica Pack US LLC................................. E 513 399-5602
   Hamilton *(G-8240)*

▲ Smith-Lustig Paper Box Mfg Co........ F 216 621-0453
   Bedford *(G-1155)*

Sonoco Products Company..................... E 614 759-8470
   Columbus *(G-5778)*

Sonoco Products Company..................... E 330 688-8247
   Munroe Falls *(G-11305)*

Soterra LLC... G 740 549-6072
   Delaware *(G-6752)*

Summit Packaging Solutions LLC........... F 719 481-8400
   West Chester *(G-15512)*

▲ The Mead Corporation........................ B 937 495-6323
   Dayton *(G-6619)*

Thorwald Holdings Inc............................. F 740 756-9271
   Lancaster *(G-9044)*

▼ Valley Converting Co Inc................... E 740 537-2152
   Toronto *(G-14537)*

Wellman Container Corporation.............. E 513 860-3040
   Cincinnati *(G-3515)*

2652 Setup paperboard boxes

A To Z Paper Box Company.................... G 330 325-8722
   Rootstown *(G-12850)*

Boxit Corporation.................................... D 216 416-9475
   Cleveland *(G-3751)*

Boxit Corporation.................................... F 216 631-6900
   Cleveland *(G-3750)*

Brimar Packaging Inc............................. E 440 934-3080
   Avon *(G-764)*

◆ Chilcote Company................................C 216 781-6000
   Cleveland *(G-3819)*

Clarke-Boxit Corporation........................ E 716 487-1950
   Cleveland *(G-3825)*

Graphic Paper Products Corp................. D 937 325-5503
   Springfield *(G-13570)*

Sandusky Packaging Corporation........... E 419 626-8520
   Sandusky *(G-13092)*

▼ The Apex Paper Box Company.......... G 216 631-4000
   Cleveland *(G-4778)*

2653 Corrugated and solid fiber boxes

1923 W 25th St Inc................................. G 216 696-7529
   Cleveland *(G-3570)*

A-Kobak Container Company Inc........... F 330 225-7791
   Hinckley *(G-8471)*

◆ Action Specialty Packaging LLC.........G
   West Chester *(G-15530)*

Adapt-A-Pak Inc...................................... E 937 845-0386
   Fairborn *(G-7307)*

▲ Akers Packaging Service Inc............. C 513 422-6312
   Middletown *(G-10802)*

Akers Packaging Solutions Inc................ D 513 422-6312
   Middletown *(G-10803)*

American Corrugated Products Inc......... C 614 870-2000
   Columbus *(G-5124)*

American Made Corrugated Packg......... F 937 981-2111
   Greenfield *(G-8027)*

Archbold Container Corp........................ C 800 446-2520
   Archbold *(G-522)*

Argrov Box Co... F 937 898-1700
   Dayton *(G-6212)*

B & B Box Company Inc......................... F 419 872-5600
   Perrysburg *(G-12363)*

▲ BDS Packaging Inc............................ F 937 643-0530
   Moraine *(G-11161)*

Billerud Americas Corporation................. D 901 369-4105
   West Chester *(G-15379)*

Brimar Packaging Inc............................. E 440 934-3080
   Avon *(G-764)*

▲ Buckeye Boxes Inc............................ D 614 274-8484
   Columbus *(G-5219)*

Buckeye Corrugated Inc......................... D 330 264-6336
   Wooster *(G-16107)*

Buckeye Corrugated Inc......................... G 330 576-0590
   Fairlawn *(G-7434)*

Cambridge Packaging Inc....................... E 740 432-3351
   Cambridge *(G-1925)*

▲ Cameron Packaging Inc..................... G 419 222-9404
   Lima *(G-9227)*

Charles Messina..................................... F 216 663-3344
   Cleveland *(G-3809)*

Chillicothe Packaging Corp..................... E 740 773-5800
   Chillicothe *(G-2497)*

Clecorr Inc.. E 216 961-5500
   Cleveland *(G-3829)*

◆ Cleveland Supplyone Inc....................E 216 514-7000
   Cleveland *(G-3857)*

Colepak LLC... D 937 652-3910
   Urbana *(G-14828)*

Combined Containerboard Inc................ D 513 530-5700
   Cincinnati *(G-2782)*

Corpad Company Inc.............................. D 419 522-7818
   Mansfield *(G-9641)*

Creative Packaging LLC......................... E 740 452-8497
   Zanesville *(G-16524)*

Digital Color Intl LLC.............................. F
   Akron *(G-130)*

Dixie Container Corporation.................... D 513 860-1145
   Fairfield *(G-7353)*

Family Packaging Inc............................. G 937 325-4106
   Springfield *(G-13563)*

Folding Carton Service Inc..................... F 419 281-4099
   Ashland *(G-573)*

Gatton Packaging Inc............................. G 419 886-2577
   Bellville *(G-1242)*

Gbc International LLC............................. G 513 943-7283
   Cincinnati *(G-2560)*

Georgia-Pacific LLC................................ C 740 477-3347
   Circleville *(G-3553)*

Georgia-Pacific Pcpi Inc......................... D 513 932-9855
   Lebanon *(G-9081)*

Graphic Paper Products Corp................. D 937 325-5503
   Springfield *(G-13570)*

Green Bay Packaging Inc....................... C 419 332-5593
   Fremont *(G-7789)*

Green Bay Packaging Inc....................... D 513 489-8700
   Lebanon *(G-9087)*

Greif Inc.. E 740 657-6500
   Delaware *(G-6725)*

◆ Greif Inc..E 740 549-6000
   Delaware *(G-6724)*

Hinkle Manufacturing Inc........................ D 419 666-5550
   Perrysburg *(G-12389)*

Honeymoon Paper Products Inc............. D 513 755-7200
   Fairfield *(G-7368)*

International Paper Company.................. C 740 369-7691
   Delaware *(G-6732)*

International Paper Company.................. E 330 626-7300
   Streetsboro *(G-13775)*

International Paper Company.................. D 330 264-1322
   Wooster *(G-16133)*

Jamestown Cont Cleveland Inc............... B 216 831-3700
   Cleveland *(G-4250)*

Jeff Lori Jed Holdings Inc....................... E 513 423-0319
   Middletown *(G-10833)*

Jet Container Company........................... D 614 444-2133
   Columbus *(G-5494)*

Jordon Auto Service & Tire Inc............... G 216 214-6528
   Cleveland *(G-4259)*

Joseph T Snyder Industries Inc.............. G 216 883-6900
   Cleveland *(G-4260)*

Larsen Packaging Products Inc.............. F 937 644-5511
   Marysville *(G-9923)*

▲ Lewisburg Container Company.......... C 937 962-2681
   Lewisburg *(G-9187)*

Litco Corner Protection LLC................... F 330 539-5433
   Vienna *(G-14998)*

Lynk Packaging Inc................................. E 330 562-8080
   Aurora *(G-723)*

▲ Marshalltown Packaging Inc.............. G 641 753-5272
   Columbus *(G-5543)*

Martin Paper Products Inc...................... F 740 756-9271
   Carroll *(G-2300)*

Massillon Container Co........................... E 330 879-5653
   Navarre *(G-11345)*

McKinley Packaging Company................ F 216 663-3344
   Maple Heights *(G-9755)*

Menasha Packaging Company LLC........ E 614 202-4084
   West Jefferson *(G-15613)*

Metro Containers Inc.............................. D 513 351-6800
   Cincinnati *(G-3158)*

▲ Miami Vly Packg Solutions Inc.......... F 937 224-1800
   Dayton *(G-6441)*

Midwest Box Company........................... E 216 281-9021
   Cleveland *(G-4409)*

Midwest Container Corporation.............. E 513 870-3000
   Lebanon *(G-9097)*

▲ Midwest Filtration LLC....................... D 513 874-6510
   West Chester *(G-15572)*

Mount Vernon Packaging Inc.................. F 740 397-3221
   Mount Vernon *(G-11280)*

Northeast Box Company......................... D 440 992-5500
   Ashtabula *(G-653)*

Novolex Holdings Inc.............................. B 937 746-1933
   Franklin *(G-7690)*

▲ Omer J Smith Inc............................... E 513 921-4717
   West Chester *(G-15470)*

Orbis Corporation.................................... D 262 560-5000
   Perrysburg *(G-12413)*

Packaging Corporation America.............. C 419 282-5809
   Ashland *(G-597)*

Packaging Corporation America.............. D 330 644-9542
   Coventry Township *(G-6015)*

Packaging Corporation America.............. E 513 424-3542
   Middletown *(G-10848)*

Packaging Corporation America.............. C 740 344-1126
   Newark *(G-11601)*

▲ Piqua Paper Box Company................ E 937 773-0313
   Piqua *(G-12548)*

Pjs Corrugated Inc.................................. F 419 644-3383
   Swanton *(G-13980)*

Pratt (jet Corr) Inc................................... A 937 390-7100
   Springfield *(G-13621)*

Pratt (target Container) Inc..................... D 513 770-0851
   Mason *(G-10041)*

Pratt Industries Inc.................................. F 513 262-6253
   Dayton *(G-6509)*

Pratt Industries Inc.................................. F 937 583-4990
   Lewisburg *(G-9189)*

▲ Prestige Display and Packaging LLC F 513 285-1040
   Fairfield *(G-7396)*

Pro-Pak Industries Inc............................ C 419 729-0751
   Maumee *(G-10225)*

Protective Packg Solutions LLC.............. E 513 769-5777
   Cincinnati *(G-3306)*

Raymar Holdings Corporation................. E 614 497-3033
   Columbus *(G-5712)*

Employee Codes: A=Over 500 employees, B=251-500
C=101-250, D=51-100, E=20-50, F=10-19, G=1-9

26 PAPER AND ALLIED PRODUCTS

Riverview Packaging Inc .... E 937 743-9530
  Franklin *(G-7698)*
Safeway Packaging Inc .... E 419 629-3200
  New Bremen *(G-11408)*
Schwarz Partners Packaging LLC .... D 740 387-3700
  Marion *(G-9879)*
Schwarz Partners Packaging LLC .... F 317 290-1140
  Sidney *(G-13283)*
Shelby Company .... E 440 871-9901
  Westlake *(G-15787)*
Skybox Packaging LLC .... C 419 525-7209
  Mansfield *(G-9719)*
▲ Smith-Lustig Paper Box Mfg Co .... F 216 621-0453
  Bedford *(G-1155)*
Sobel Corrugated Containers Inc .... C 216 475-2100
  Cleveland *(G-4712)*
▼ Softbox Systems Inc .... D 864 630-7860
  Monroe *(G-11120)*
Solas Ltd .... E 650 501-0889
  Avon *(G-788)*
Sonoco Products Company .... E 614 759-8470
  Columbus *(G-5778)*
Southern Champion Tray LP .... D 513 755-7200
  Fairfield *(G-7410)*
Square One Solutions LLC .... F 419 425-5445
  Findlay *(G-7567)*
Summit Container Corporation .... F 719 481-8400
  West Chester *(G-15511)*
Systems Pack Inc .... E 330 467-5729
  Macedonia *(G-9583)*
Tavens Container Inc .... D 216 883-3333
  Bedford *(G-1156)*
Tecumseh Packg Solutions Inc .... F 419 238-1122
  Van Wert *(G-14927)*
Temple Inland .... G 513 425-0830
  Middletown *(G-10862)*
▲ The Mead Corporation .... B 937 495-6323
  Dayton *(G-6619)*
Trey Corrugated Inc .... C 513 942-4800
  West Chester *(G-15518)*
Tri-State Paper Inc .... F 937 885-3365
  Dayton *(G-6631)*
Unipac Inc .... E 740 929-2000
  Hebron *(G-8369)*
Valley Containers Inc .... F 330 544-2244
  Mineral Ridge *(G-11024)*
▲ Value Added Packaging Inc .... F 937 832-9595
  Englewood *(G-7247)*
Viking Paper Company .... E 419 729-4951
  Toledo *(G-14519)*
Wellman Container Corporation .... E 513 860-3040
  Cincinnati *(G-3515)*
Westrock Rkt LLC .... D 513 860-5546
  West Chester *(G-15527)*
Weyerhaeuser Co Containeerboar .... F 740 397-5215
  Mount Vernon *(G-11300)*
Weyerhaeuser Company .... G 740 335-4480
  Wshngtn Ct Hs *(G-16246)*
Wolford Industrial Park .... G 216 281-3980
  Cleveland *(G-4917)*

2655 Fiber cans, drums, and similar products

Acme Spirally Wound Paper Pdts .... F 216 267-2950
  Cleveland *(G-3592)*
Advanced Paper Tube Inc .... F 216 281-5691
  Cleveland *(G-3608)*
Caraustar Indus Cnsmr Pdts Gro .... D 330 868-4111
  Minerva *(G-11028)*
Caraustar Industries Inc .... E 330 665-7700
  Copley *(G-5946)*
Caraustar Industries Inc .... E 937 298-9969
  Moraine *(G-11165)*

Custom Paper Tubes Inc .... E 216 362-2964
  Cleveland *(G-3925)*
Erdie Industries Inc .... E 440 288-0166
  Lorain *(G-9411)*
Greif Inc .... E 740 657-6500
  Delaware *(G-6725)*
Greif Inc .... D 330 879-2936
  Massillon *(G-10102)*
Greif Inc .... E 419 238-0565
  Van Wert *(G-14917)*
◆ Greif Inc .... E 740 549-6000
  Delaware *(G-6724)*
Greif USA LLC .... D 740 549-6000
  Delaware *(G-6727)*
Horwitz & Pintis Co .... F 419 666-2220
  Toledo *(G-14320)*
Howard B Claflin Co .... G 330 928-1704
  Hudson *(G-8596)*
Hpc Holdings LLC .... F 330 666-3751
  Fairlawn *(G-7442)*
▲ Midwest Specialty Pdts Co Inc .... F 513 874-7070
  Fairfield *(G-7384)*
Modroto .... G 440 998-1202
  Ashtabula *(G-649)*
▲ North Coast Composites Inc .... F 216 398-8550
  Cleveland *(G-4465)*
Ohio Paper Tube Co .... E 330 478-5171
  Canton *(G-2185)*
Operational Support Svcs LLC .... F 419 425-0889
  Findlay *(G-7547)*
Polystar Inc .... F 330 963-5100
  Stow *(G-13717)*
Sonoco Products Company .... D 937 429-0040
  Beavercreek Township *(G-1094)*
Sonoco Products Company .... E 614 759-8470
  Columbus *(G-5778)*
Sonoco Products Company .... E 330 688-8247
  Munroe Falls *(G-11305)*
Sonoco Products Company .... E 513 870-3985
  West Chester *(G-15588)*

2656 Sanitary food containers

◆ American Greetings Corporation .... A 216 252-7300
  Cleveland *(G-3652)*
Billerud Americas Corporation .... D 901 369-4105
  West Chester *(G-15379)*
Champion International .... G 440 235-7200
  Olmsted Falls *(G-12079)*
Clovernook Ctr For Blind Vslly .... C 513 522-3860
  Cincinnati *(G-2775)*
▼ Duracorp LLC .... D 740 549-3336
  Lewis Center *(G-9158)*
Graphic Packaging Intl LLC .... B 419 673-0711
  Kenton *(G-8884)*
Huhtamaki Inc .... C 513 201-1525
  Batavia *(G-925)*
Huhtamaki Inc .... D 937 746-9700
  Franklin *(G-7681)*
▲ Island Aseptics LLC .... C 740 685-2548
  Byesville *(G-1898)*
Kerry Inc .... E 760 685-2548
  Byesville *(G-1899)*
◆ Norse Dairy Systems LP .... B 614 294-4931
  Columbus *(G-5601)*
Novolex Holdings Inc .... B 937 746-1933
  Franklin *(G-7690)*
Ohio State Plastics .... D 614 299-5618
  Columbus *(G-5627)*
Premier Industries Inc .... E 513 271-2550
  Cincinnati *(G-3272)*
Ricking Holding Co .... E 513 825-3551
  Cleveland *(G-4633)*

Solas Ltd .... E 650 501-0889
  Avon *(G-788)*
Sonoco Products Company .... E 513 870-3985
  West Chester *(G-15588)*
▲ Sunamericaconverting LLC .... D 330 821-6300
  Alliance *(G-430)*
▲ The Mead Corporation .... B 937 495-6323
  Dayton *(G-6619)*
Washington Products Inc .... F 330 837-5101
  Massillon *(G-10154)*

2657 Folding paperboard boxes

American Corrugated Products Inc .... C 614 870-2000
  Columbus *(G-5124)*
Americraft Carton Inc .... G 419 668-1006
  Norwalk *(G-11954)*
Boxit Corporation .... D 216 416-9475
  Cleveland *(G-3751)*
Boxit Corporation .... F 216 631-6900
  Cleveland *(G-3750)*
Brimar Packaging Inc .... E 440 934-3080
  Avon *(G-764)*
Cardpak Incorporated .... C 440 542-3100
  Solon *(G-13326)*
◆ Chilcote Company .... C 216 781-6000
  Cleveland *(G-3819)*
Gpi Ohio LLC .... F 605 332-6721
  Groveport *(G-8145)*
Graphic Packaging Intl LLC .... C 513 424-4200
  Middletown *(G-10828)*
Graphic Packaging Intl LLC .... E 419 668-1006
  Norwalk *(G-11970)*
Graphic Packaging Intl LLC .... C 440 248-4370
  Solon *(G-13357)*
Jefferson Smurfit Corporation .... G 440 248-4370
  Solon *(G-13369)*
Oak Hills Carton Co .... E 513 948-4200
  Cincinnati *(G-3210)*
R R Donnelley & Sons Company .... E 513 870-4040
  West Chester *(G-15495)*
Ranpak Holdings Corp .... F 440 354-4445
  Concord Township *(G-5911)*
Saica Pack US LLC .... E 513 399-5602
  Hamilton *(G-8240)*
Sandusky Packaging Corporation .... E 419 626-8520
  Sandusky *(G-13092)*
Shelby Company .... E 440 871-9901
  Westlake *(G-15787)*
▼ The Apex Paper Box Company .... G 216 631-4000
  Cleveland *(G-4778)*
Unipac Inc .... E 740 929-2000
  Hebron *(G-8369)*

2671 Paper; coated and laminated packaging

Amatech Inc .... E 614 252-2506
  Columbus *(G-5119)*
American Corrugated Products Inc .... C 614 870-2000
  Columbus *(G-5124)*
▲ Ampac Plastics LLC .... B 513 671-1777
  Cincinnati *(G-2624)*
Austin Tape and Label Inc .... D 330 928-7999
  Stow *(G-13686)*
Bollin & Sons Inc .... E 419 693-6573
  Toledo *(G-14216)*
▲ Central Coated Products Inc .... D 330 821-9830
  Alliance *(G-398)*
Central Ohio Paper & Packg Inc .... F 419 621-9239
  Huron *(G-8629)*
Charter Next Generation Inc .... C 740 369-2770
  Delaware *(G-6709)*
Charter Next Generation Inc .... C 419 884-8150
  Lexington *(G-9195)*

26 PAPER AND ALLIED PRODUCTS

Charter Next Generation Inc .... C 419 884-8150
  Lexington *(G-9196)*
Charter Next Generation Inc .... C 419 884-8150
  Lexington *(G-9197)*
Charter Next Generation Inc .... C 419 884-8150
  Lexington *(G-9198)*
Charter Next Generation Inc .... C 419 884-8150
  Lexington *(G-9199)*
Charter Next Generation Inc .... C 330 830-6030
  Massillon *(G-10084)*
Colepak LLC .... D 937 652-3910
  Urbana *(G-14828)*
▲ Command Plastic Corporation .... F 800 321-8001
  Bedford *(G-1112)*
Cpg - Ohio LLC .... D 513 825-4800
  Cincinnati *(G-2800)*
▼ Crayex Corporation .... D 937 773-7000
  Piqua *(G-12511)*
Creative Packaging LLC .... E 740 452-8497
  Zanesville *(G-16524)*
▲ Custom Products Corporation .... D 440 528-7100
  Solon *(G-13334)*
Diversipak Inc .... E 513 321-7884
  Cincinnati *(G-2833)*
Dubose Strapping Inc .... E 419 221-0626
  Lima *(G-9239)*
E-Z Stop Service Center .... G 330 448-2236
  Brookfield *(G-1668)*
▲ Engineered Films Division Inc .... D 419 884-8150
  Lexington *(G-9201)*
Future Polytech Inc .... E 614 942-1209
  Columbus *(G-5391)*
Georgia-Pacific LLC .... C 740 477-3347
  Circleville *(G-3553)*
Gt Industrial Supply Inc .... F 513 771-7000
  Cincinnati *(G-2976)*
Hunt Products Inc .... G 440 667-2457
  Newburgh Heights *(G-11617)*
Joseph T Snyder Industries Inc .... G 216 883-6900
  Cleveland *(G-4260)*
Kay Toledo Tag Inc .... C 419 729-5479
  Toledo *(G-14346)*
▲ Kroy LLC .... C 216 426-5600
  Cleveland *(G-4299)*
Linneas Candy Supplies Inc .... E 330 678-7112
  Kent *(G-8828)*
Liqui-Box Corporation .... E 419 289-9696
  Ashland *(G-589)*
▼ Loroco Industries Inc .... D 513 891-9544
  Cincinnati *(G-3113)*
National Glass Svc Group LLC .... F 614 652-3699
  Dublin *(G-6914)*
◆ Nilpeter Usa Inc .... C 513 489-4400
  Cincinnati *(G-3198)*
Norse Dairy Systems Inc .... C 614 294-4931
  Columbus *(G-5600)*
North American Plas Chem Inc .... E 216 531-3400
  Euclid *(G-7290)*
Novacel Inc .... C 937 335-5611
  Troy *(G-14598)*
Octal Extrusion Corp .... D 513 881-6100
  West Chester *(G-15574)*
Orflex Inc .... B
  Cincinnati *(G-3228)*
▼ Pioneer Labels Inc .... C 618 546-5418
  West Chester *(G-15479)*
Plastic Works Inc .... F 440 331-5575
  Cleveland *(G-4560)*
Plastipak Packaging Inc .... B 937 596-6142
  Jackson Center *(G-8736)*
◆ Polychem LLC .... C 440 357-1500
  Mentor *(G-10526)*

Prime Industries Inc .... E
  Lorain *(G-9431)*
Retterbush Graphics Packg Corp .... F 513 779-4466
  West Chester *(G-15498)*
Safeway Packaging Inc .... E 419 629-3200
  New Bremen *(G-11408)*
Schilling Graphics Inc .... E 419 468-1037
  Galion *(G-7884)*
Schwarz Partners Packaging LLC .... F 317 290-1140
  Sidney *(G-13283)*
Signode Industrial Group LLC .... D 513 248-2990
  Loveland *(G-9505)*
Sonoco Products Company .... E 614 759-8470
  Columbus *(G-5778)*
Springdot Inc .... D 513 542-4000
  Cincinnati *(G-3411)*
▲ Storopack Inc .... E 513 874-0314
  West Chester *(G-15592)*
▲ Stretchtape Inc .... E 216 486-9400
  Cleveland *(G-4737)*
Sun America LLC .... C 330 821-6300
  Alliance *(G-429)*
Superior Label Systems Inc .... B 513 336-0825
  Mason *(G-10061)*
Tech/III Inc .... E 513 482-7500
  Fairfield *(G-7415)*
▲ The Hooven - Dayton Corp .... C 937 233-4473
  Miamisburg *(G-10694)*
Thomas Products Co Inc .... E 513 756-9009
  Cincinnati *(G-3453)*
Universal Packg Systems Inc .... C 513 732-2000
  Batavia *(G-957)*
Universal Packg Systems Inc .... C 513 735-4777
  Batavia *(G-958)*
Universal Packg Systems Inc .... C 513 674-9400
  Cincinnati *(G-3483)*
Valgroup North America Inc .... C 419 423-6500
  Findlay *(G-7577)*
Versa-Pak Ltd .... E 419 586-5466
  Celina *(G-2355)*
Visual Marking Systems Inc .... D 330 425-7100
  Twinsburg *(G-14753)*
Zebco Industries Inc .... F 740 654-4510
  Lancaster *(G-9049)*

2672 Paper; coated and laminated, nec

3 Sigma LLC .... D 937 440-3400
  Troy *(G-14548)*
3M Company .... E 330 725-1444
  Medina *(G-10288)*
▲ Acpo Ltd .... D 419 898-8273
  Oak Harbor *(G-12009)*
Adcraft Decals Incorporated .... E 216 524-2934
  Cleveland *(G-3598)*
Austin Tape and Label Inc .... D 330 928-7999
  Stow *(G-13686)*
Avery Dennison Corporation .... E 513 682-7500
  Cincinnati *(G-2648)*
Avery Dennison Corporation .... G 216 267-8700
  Cleveland *(G-3707)*
Avery Dennison Corporation .... C 440 358-4691
  Concord Township *(G-5901)*
Avery Dennison Corporation .... F 440 534-6527
  Mentor *(G-10425)*
Avery Dennison Corporation .... D 440 639-3900
  Mentor *(G-10427)*
Avery Dennison Corporation .... C 440 358-2828
  Mentor *(G-10428)*
Avery Dennison Corporation .... F 937 865-2439
  Miamisburg *(G-10613)*
Avery Dennison Corporation .... F 419 898-8273
  Oak Harbor *(G-12010)*

Avery Dennison Corporation .... C 440 358-3466
  Painesville *(G-12217)*
Avery Dennison Corporation .... B 440 358-2564
  Painesville *(G-12218)*
Avery Dennison Corporation .... B 440 878-7000
  Strongsville *(G-13814)*
Avery Dennison Corporation .... B 440 534-6000
  Mentor *(G-10426)*
Avery Dnnison G Holdings I LLC .... E 440 534-6000
  Mentor *(G-10429)*
Beiersdorf Inc .... C 513 682-7300
  West Chester *(G-15541)*
BMC Growth Fund LLC .... C 937 291-4110
  Miamisburg *(G-10620)*
Boehm Inc .... E 614 875-9010
  Grove City *(G-8080)*
Bollin & Sons Inc .... E 419 693-6573
  Toledo *(G-14216)*
Bucher Printing .... G 937 228-2022
  Dayton *(G-6238)*
CCL Label Inc .... D 216 676-2703
  Cleveland *(G-3801)*
CCL Label Inc .... D 440 878-7000
  Strongsville *(G-13819)*
▲ Central Coated Products Inc .... D 330 821-9830
  Alliance *(G-398)*
◆ Cortape Inc .... F 330 929-6700
  Cuyahoga Falls *(G-6076)*
Deco Tools Inc .... E 419 476-9321
  Toledo *(G-14262)*
▲ Dermamed Coatin .... F 330 474-3786
  Kent *(G-8809)*
Domtar Corporation .... B 937 859-8261
  West Carrollton *(G-15353)*
Gary I Teach Jr .... G 614 582-7483
  London *(G-9387)*
GBS Corp .... C 330 863-1828
  Malvern *(G-9612)*
▲ GBS Corp .... C 330 494-5330
  North Canton *(G-11729)*
Glatfelter Corporation .... G 419 333-6700
  Fremont *(G-7787)*
Hall Company .... E 937 652-1376
  Urbana *(G-14833)*
▲ ID Images LLC .... D 330 220-7300
  Brunswick *(G-1770)*
◆ Kardol Quality Products LLC .... G 513 933-8206
  Blue Ash *(G-1416)*
◆ Kent Adhesive Products Co .... D 330 678-1626
  Kent *(G-8821)*
Label Technique Southeast LLC .... E 440 951-7660
  Willoughby *(G-15941)*
Lam Pro Inc .... F 216 426-0661
  Cleveland *(G-4308)*
▲ Laminate Technologies Inc .... D 800 231-2523
  Tiffin *(G-14090)*
Linneas Candy Supplies Inc .... E 330 678-7112
  Kent *(G-8828)*
Lockfast LLC .... G 800 543-7157
  Loveland *(G-9491)*
▼ Loroco Industries Inc .... D 513 891-9544
  Cincinnati *(G-3113)*
Magnum Tapes Films .... G 877 460-8402
  Caldwell *(G-1911)*
Miller Products Inc .... C 330 938-2134
  Sebring *(G-13122)*
▲ Miller Studio Inc .... E 330 339-1100
  New Philadelphia *(G-11519)*
◆ Morgan Adhesives Company LLC ..... B 330 688-1111
  Stow *(G-13709)*
▼ Mr Label Inc .... E 513 681-2088
  Cincinnati *(G-3177)*

26 PAPER AND ALLIED PRODUCTS

Multi-Color Corporation............................G..... 513 459-3283
  Mason (G-10032)
▲ Multi-Color Corporation............................F..... 513 381-1480
  Batavia (G-939)
◆ Nilpeter Usa Inc......................................C..... 513 489-4400
  Cincinnati (G-3198)
◆ Novacel Prfmce Coatings Inc...................D..... 937 552-4932
  Troy (G-14599)
Novagard Solutions Inc.............................C..... 216 881-8111
  Cleveland (G-4483)
▲ Ohio Laminating & Binding Inc................F..... 614 771-4868
  Hilliard (G-8426)
Oliver Healthcare Packaging Co................C..... 513 860-6880
  Hamilton (G-8234)
▼ Pioneer Labels Inc.................................C..... 618 546-5418
  West Chester (G-15479)
Progressive Supply LLC............................F..... 570 688-9636
  Willoughby (G-15977)
R R Donnelley & Sons Company...............D..... 440 774-2101
  Oberlin (G-12055)
Roemer Industries Inc..............................D..... 330 448-2000
  Masury (G-10158)
▲ Sensical Inc...D..... 216 641-1141
  Solon (G-13420)
◆ SRC Liquidation LLC..............................A..... 937 221-1000
  Dayton (G-6586)
▲ Strata-Tac Inc..F..... 630 879-9388
  Troy (G-14613)
▲ Stretchtape Inc......................................E..... 216 486-9400
  Cleveland (G-4737)
Superior Label Systems Inc......................B..... 513 336-0825
  Mason (G-10061)
◆ Technicote Inc..E..... 800 358-4448
  Miamisburg (G-10691)
Technicote Westfield Inc...........................E..... 937 859-4448
  Miamisburg (G-10692)
Tekni-Plex Inc...E..... 419 491-2399
  Holland (G-8532)
▲ The Hooven - Dayton Corp....................C..... 937 233-4473
  Miamisburg (G-10694)
Thomas Products Co Inc..........................E..... 513 756-9009
  Cincinnati (G-3453)
▲ Waytek Corporation...............................E..... 937 743-6142
  Franklin (G-7711)

2673 Bags: plastic, laminated, and coated

American Plastics LLC..............................C..... 419 423-1213
  Findlay (G-7476)
◆ Ampac Holdings LLC.............................A..... 513 671-1777
  Cincinnati (G-2622)
Automated Packg Systems Inc..................E..... 330 342-2000
  Bedford (G-1103)
Automated Packg Systems Inc..................C..... 216 663-2000
  Cleveland (G-3702)
B K Plastics Inc......................................G..... 937 473-2087
  Covington (G-6019)
▲ Buckeye Boxes Inc................................D..... 614 274-8484
  Columbus (G-5219)
Buckeye Packaging Co Inc.......................D..... 330 935-0301
  Alliance (G-396)
Charter Nex Films - Delaware Oh Inc..........E..... 740 369-2770
  Delaware (G-6708)
▲ Command Plastic Corporation................F..... 800 321-8001
  Bedford (G-1112)
Cpg - Ohio LLC.......................................D..... 513 825-4800
  Cincinnati (G-2800)
▼ Crayex Corporation...............................D..... 937 773-7000
  Piqua (G-12511)
Custom Poly Bag LLC..............................D..... 330 935-2408
  Alliance (G-399)
▲ Dazpak Flexible Packaging Corp............C..... 614 252-2121
  Columbus (G-5318)

▲ Engineered Films Division Inc.................D..... 419 884-8150
  Lexington (G-9201)
◆ Flavorseal LLC......................................D..... 440 937-3900
  Avon (G-774)
General Films Inc....................................D..... 888 436-3456
  Covington (G-6023)
Global Plastic Tech Inc.............................G..... 440 879-6045
  Lorain (G-9412)
Hood Packaging Corporation.....................C..... 937 382-6681
  Wilmington (G-16053)
▲ Kennedy Group Incorporated.................D..... 440 951-7660
  Willoughby (G-15939)
Liqui-Box Corporation...............................E..... 419 289-9696
  Ashland (G-589)
Noramco Inc...D..... 216 531-3400
  Euclid (G-7288)
North American Plas Chem Inc.................E..... 216 531-3400
  Euclid (G-7290)
▼ Packaging Materials Inc........................E..... 740 432-6337
  Cambridge (G-1940)
Pitt Plastics Inc.......................................D..... 614 868-8660
  Columbus (G-5675)
Safeway Packaging Inc............................E..... 419 629-3200
  New Bremen (G-11408)
Signature Flexible Packg LLC...................F..... 614 252-2121
  Columbus (G-5769)

2674 Bags: uncoated paper and multiwall

◆ Ampac Holdings LLC.............................A..... 513 671-1777
  Cincinnati (G-2622)
▲ Brady Ruck Company...........................E..... 419 738-5126
  Wapakoneta (G-15108)
Cleveland Canvas Goods Mfg Co..............E..... 216 361-4567
  Cleveland (G-3835)
Ecopac LLC..G..... 732 715-0236
  Cincinnati (G-2858)
Gateway Packaging Company LLC............E..... 419 738-5126
  Wapakoneta (G-15114)
Greif Inc...E..... 740 657-6500
  Delaware (G-6725)
◆ Greif Inc...E..... 740 549-6000
  Delaware (G-6724)
Hood Packaging Corporation.....................C..... 937 382-6681
  Wilmington (G-16053)
▲ Mid-America Packaging LLC..................A..... 330 963-4199
  New Philadelphia (G-11517)
Pantrybag..F..... 614 927-8744
  Columbus (G-5654)

2675 Die-cut paper and board

▲ Art Guild Binders Inc.............................E..... 513 242-3000
  Cincinnati (G-2634)
▲ Buckeye Boxes Inc...............................D..... 614 274-8484
  Columbus (G-5219)
◆ Chilcote Company.................................C..... 216 781-6000
  Cleveland (G-3819)
Foldedpak Inc...E..... 740 527-1090
  Hebron (G-8341)
Forest Converting Co Inc.........................E..... 513 631-4190
  Cincinnati (G-2915)
GBS Corp...C..... 330 863-1828
  Malvern (G-9612)
▲ GBS Corp...C..... 330 494-5330
  North Canton (G-11729)
Georgia-Pacific LLC.................................C..... 740 477-3347
  Circleville (G-3553)
Harris Paper Crafts Inc............................F..... 614 299-2141
  Columbus (G-5421)
Honeymoon Paper Products Inc................D..... 513 755-7200
  Fairfield (G-7368)
Hunt Products Inc....................................G..... 440 667-2457
  Newburgh Heights (G-11617)

Keeler Enterprises Inc..............................G..... 330 336-7601
  Wadsworth (G-15039)
◆ Kent Adhesive Products Co...................D..... 330 678-1626
  Kent (G-8821)
▲ Keyah International Trdg LLC................E..... 937 399-3140
  Springfield (G-13588)
Lam Pro Inc..F..... 216 426-0661
  Cleveland (G-4308)
▼ Loroco Industries Inc............................D..... 513 891-9544
  Cincinnati (G-3113)
Multi-Craft Litho Inc.................................E..... 859 581-2754
  Blue Ash (G-1442)
Nordec Inc..D..... 330 940-3700
  Stow (G-13715)
▲ P & R Specialty Inc..............................E..... 937 773-0263
  Piqua (G-12541)
▲ Printers Bindery Services Inc................D..... 513 821-8039
  Batavia (G-944)
◆ Rohrer Corporation................................C..... 330 335-1541
  Wadsworth (G-15063)
◆ Smead Manufacturing Company.............C..... 740 385-5601
  Logan (G-9377)
Southern Champion Tray LP.....................D..... 513 755-7200
  Fairfield (G-7410)
Springdot Inc..D..... 513 542-4000
  Cincinnati (G-3411)
Stat Industries Inc...................................G..... 740 779-6561
  Chillicothe (G-2537)
Stat Industries Inc...................................G..... 513 860-4482
  Hamilton (G-8245)
Stat Industries Inc...................................G..... 740 779-6561
  Chillicothe (G-2536)
Stuart Company......................................E..... 513 621-9462
  Cincinnati (G-3425)
Vya Inc..E..... 513 772-5400
  Cincinnati (G-3506)
Williams Steel Rule Die Co.......................F..... 216 431-3232
  Cleveland (G-4910)

2676 Sanitary paper products

◆ Absorbent Products Company Inc...........E..... 419 352-5353
  Bowling Green (G-1549)
◆ Aci Industries Converting Ltd..................F..... 740 368-4160
  Delaware (G-6700)
Attends Healthcare Pdts Inc.....................G..... 740 368-7880
  Delaware (G-6703)
▲ Eleeo Brands LLC................................G
  Cincinnati (G-2863)
Eleeo Brands LLC..................................E..... 513 572-8100
  Cincinnati (G-2864)
▲ Giant Industries Inc..............................E..... 419 531-4600
  Toledo (G-14300)
▲ Health Care Products Inc......................E..... 419 678-9620
  Coldwater (G-4992)
Linsalata Cpitl Prtners Fund I....................G..... 440 684-1400
  Cleveland (G-4330)
▲ Novex Products Inc..............................E..... 440 244-3330
  Lorain (G-9427)
PGT Healthcare LLP................................E..... 513 983-1100
  Cincinnati (G-3254)
Playtex Manufacturing Inc........................E..... 937 498-4710
  Sidney (G-13271)
▲ Principle Business Entps Inc.................C..... 419 352-1551
  Bowling Green (G-1586)
Procter & Gamble Company.....................D..... 513 983-1100
  Cincinnati (G-3281)
Procter & Gamble Company.....................F..... 513 266-4375
  Cincinnati (G-3282)
Procter & Gamble Company.....................G..... 513 871-7557
  Cincinnati (G-3283)
Procter & Gamble Company.....................F..... 513 482-6789
  Cincinnati (G-3286)

SIC SECTION — 27 PRINTING, PUBLISHING AND ALLIED INDUSTRIES

Procter & Gamble Company .... C 513 983-3000
   Cincinnati *(G-3288)*

Procter & Gamble Company .... E 513 627-7115
   Cincinnati *(G-3289)*

Procter & Gamble Company .... F 513 945-0340
   Cincinnati *(G-3292)*

Procter & Gamble Company .... D 513 622-1000
   Mason *(G-10043)*

Procter & Gamble Company .... C 513 634-9600
   West Chester *(G-15486)*

Procter & Gamble Company .... C 513 634-9110
   West Chester *(G-15487)*

◆ Procter & Gamble Company .... A 513 983-1100
   Cincinnati *(G-3280)*

Procter & Gamble Far East Inc .... C 513 983-1100
   Cincinnati *(G-3295)*

Procter & Gamble Mexico Inc .... G 513 983-1100
   Cincinnati *(G-3297)*

Procter & Gamble Paper Pdts Co .... E 513 983-2222
   Cincinnati *(G-3300)*

◆ Procter & Gamble Paper Pdts Co .... F 513 983-1100
   Cincinnati *(G-3299)*

Sposie LLC .... F 888 977-2229
   Maumee *(G-10234)*

▲ Tambrands Sales Corp .... C 513 983-1100
   Cincinnati *(G-3441)*

This Is L Inc .... G 415 630-5172
   Cincinnati *(G-3452)*

Tranzonic Companies .... C 440 446-0643
   Cleveland *(G-4818)*

Tranzonic Companies .... D 216 535-4300
   Richmond Heights *(G-12811)*

◆ Tz Acquisition Corp .... E 216 535-4300
   Richmond Heights *(G-12812)*

2677 Envelopes

Access Envelope Inc .... F 513 889-0888
   Middletown *(G-10801)*

American Paper Group Inc .... B 330 758-4545
   Youngstown *(G-16309)*

◆ Ampac Holdings LLC .... A 513 671-1777
   Cincinnati *(G-2622)*

Church Budget Monthly Inc .... G 330 337-1122
   Salem *(G-12983)*

Church-Budget Envelope Company .... E 800 446-9780
   Salem *(G-12984)*

▲ E-1 (2012) Holdings Inc .... C 330 482-3900
   Columbiana *(G-5037)*

▲ Envelope 1 Inc .... D 330 482-3900
   Columbiana *(G-5038)*

Envelope Mart of Ohio Inc .... F 440 365-8177
   Elyria *(G-7150)*

▲ Jbm Packaging Company .... C 513 933-8333
   Lebanon *(G-9090)*

▲ Keene Building Products Co .... D 440 605-1020
   Cleveland *(G-4279)*

Ohio Envelope Manufacturing Co .... E 216 267-2920
   Cleveland *(G-4497)*

Pac Worldwide Corporation .... E 800 535-0039
   Monroe *(G-11117)*

Quality Envelope Inc .... G 513 942-7578
   West Chester *(G-15579)*

◆ SRC Liquidation LLC .... A 937 221-1000
   Dayton *(G-6586)*

United Envelope LLC .... B 513 542-4700
   Cincinnati *(G-3480)*

Western States Envelope Co .... E 419 666-7480
   Walbridge *(G-15088)*

2678 Stationery products

◆ American Greetings Corporation .... A 216 252-7300
   Cleveland *(G-3652)*

Atelierkopii LLC .... G 216 559-0815
   Cleveland *(G-3696)*

Avery Dennison Corporation .... B 440 534-6000
   Mentor *(G-10426)*

▼ Bookfactory LLC .... E 937 226-7100
   Dayton *(G-6234)*

CCL Label Inc .... D 216 676-2703
   Cleveland *(G-3801)*

CCL Label Inc .... D 440 878-7000
   Strongsville *(G-13819)*

▲ CM Paula Company .... E 513 759-7473
   Mason *(G-9980)*

Keeler Enterprises Inc .... G 330 336-7601
   Wadsworth *(G-15039)*

Selco Industries Inc .... E 419 861-0336
   Holland *(G-8530)*

◆ Steel City Corporation .... E 330 792-7663
   Ashland *(G-615)*

Westrock Mwv LLC .... D 937 495-6323
   Dayton *(G-6651)*

2679 Converted paper products, nec

4wallscom LLC .... F 216 432-1400
   Cleveland *(G-3572)*

◆ American Greetings Corporation .... A 216 252-7300
   Loveland *(G-3652)*

Avery Dennison Corporation .... C 440 358-4691
   Concord Township *(G-5901)*

Avery Dennison Corporation .... D 440 639-3900
   Mentor *(G-10427)*

Btw LLC .... G 419 382-4443
   Toledo *(G-14223)*

▼ Buckeye Paper Co Inc .... E 330 477-5925
   Canton *(G-2054)*

▲ Buschman Corporation .... F 216 431-6633
   Cleveland *(G-3774)*

Caraustar Industries Inc .... F 216 961-5060
   Cleveland *(G-3788)*

Caraustar Industries Inc .... E 330 665-7700
   Copley *(G-5946)*

CCL Label Inc .... D 216 676-2703
   Cleveland *(G-3801)*

▲ Cindus Corporation .... D 513 948-9951
   Cincinnati *(G-2766)*

E-Z Grader Company .... G 440 247-7511
   Chagrin Falls *(G-2375)*

Eagles Nest Holdings LLC .... E 419 526-4123
   Mansfield *(G-9649)*

▲ Fibercorr Mills LLC .... D 330 837-5151
   Massillon *(G-10096)*

◆ Formica Corporation .... E 513 786-3400
   Cincinnati *(G-2916)*

Fremont Printing Inc .... F 480 272-3443
   Fremont *(G-7784)*

▲ Gemini Fiber Corporation .... F 330 874-4131
   Bolivar *(G-1526)*

◆ General Data Company Inc .... B 513 752-7978
   Cincinnati *(G-2561)*

Green Meadows Paper Company .... D 330 837-5151
   Massillon *(G-10101)*

H Lee Philippi Co .... F 513 321-5330
   Cincinnati *(G-2980)*

Harris Paper Crafts Inc .... F 614 299-2141
   Columbus *(G-5421)*

J and N Incorporated .... F 234 759-3741
   North Lima *(G-11807)*

Kay Toledo Tag Inc .... D 419 729-5479
   Toledo *(G-14346)*

▲ Kennedy Group Incorporated .... D 440 951-7660
   Willoughby *(G-15939)*

◆ Kent Adhesive Products Co .... D 330 678-1626
   Kent *(G-8821)*

L & F Products .... G 937 498-4710
   Sidney *(G-13258)*

▲ Label Aid Inc .... E 419 433-2888
   Huron *(G-8635)*

Label Technique Southeast LLC .... E 440 951-7660
   Willoughby *(G-15941)*

Markham Converting Limited .... F 419 353-2458
   Bowling Green *(G-1574)*

▲ Millcraft Group LLC .... D 216 441-5500
   Independence *(G-8675)*

Multi-Color Corporation .... G 513 459-3283
   Mason *(G-10032)*

▲ Multi-Color Corporation .... F 513 381-1480
   Batavia *(G-939)*

Oak Hills Carton Co .... E 513 948-4200
   Cincinnati *(G-3210)*

Orbytel Print and Packg Inc .... G 216 267-8734
   Cleveland *(G-4508)*

Outhouse Paper Etc Inc .... G 937 382-2800
   Waynesville *(G-15301)*

Pressed Paperboard Tech LLC .... C 419 423-4030
   Findlay *(G-7552)*

Psix LLC .... D 937 746-6841
   Springboro *(G-13516)*

Roberds Converting Co Inc .... E 513 683-6667
   Loveland *(G-9501)*

◆ Shore To Shore Inc .... D 937 866-1908
   Dayton *(G-6570)*

Signode Industrial Group LLC .... D 513 248-2990
   Loveland *(G-9505)*

Stumps Converting Inc .... F 419 492-2542
   New Washington *(G-11551)*

T&T Graphics Inc .... D 937 847-6000
   Miamisburg *(G-10688)*

Tekni-Plex Inc .... E 419 491-2399
   Holland *(G-8532)*

◆ The Blonder Company .... C 216 431-3560
   Cleveland *(G-4780)*

▲ The Hooven - Dayton Corp .... C 937 233-4473
   Miamisburg *(G-10694)*

Tri State Media LLC .... F 513 933-0101
   Wilmington *(G-16061)*

Verstrete In Mold Lbels USA In .... F 513 943-0080
   Batavia *(G-959)*

Warren Printing & Off Pdts Inc .... F 419 523-3635
   Ottawa *(G-12196)*

27 PRINTING, PUBLISHING AND ALLIED INDUSTRIES

2711 Newspapers

A Gatehouse Media Company .... F 330 580-8579
   Canton *(G-2024)*

Active Daily Living LLC .... G 513 607-6769
   Cincinnati *(G-2596)*

Adams Publishing Group LLC .... E 740 592-6612
   Athens *(G-673)*

Aim Media Midwest Oper LLC .... G 740 354-6621
   Portsmouth *(G-12640)*

Akron Legal News Inc .... F 330 296-7578
   Akron *(G-35)*

Alderwoods (oklahoma) Inc .... G 903 597-6611
   Cincinnati *(G-2606)*

Alliance Publishing Co Inc .... C 330 453-1304
   Alliance *(G-393)*

American City Bus Journals Inc .... C 513 337-9450
   Cincinnati *(G-2617)*

American City Bus Journals Inc .... B 937 528-4400
   Dayton *(G-6199)*

American Community Newspapers .... G 614 888-4567
   Columbus *(G-5123)*

27 PRINTING, PUBLISHING AND ALLIED INDUSTRIES — SIC SECTION

▲ Amos Media Company .... C 937 638-0967
  Sidney *(G-13221)*
Archbold Buckeye Inc .... F 419 445-4466
  Archbold *(G-521)*
Arens Corporation .... G 937 473-2028
  Covington *(G-6018)*
Arens Corporation .... F 937 473-2028
  Covington *(G-6017)*
Ashland Publishing Co .... B 419 281-0581
  Ashland *(G-552)*
At Your Service .... G 513 498-9392
  Hamilton *(G-8181)*
Atrium At Anna Maria Inc .... F 330 562-7777
  Aurora *(G-706)*
Belem Group LLC .... G 614 604-6870
  Columbus *(G-5181)*
Block Communications Inc .... F 419 724-6212
  Toledo *(G-14214)*
Boardman News .... G 330 758-6397
  Boardman *(G-1510)*
Brecksvll-Brdview Hts Gztte In .... G 440 526-7977
  Brecksville *(G-1610)*
Brekkie Shack Grandview LLC .... G 614 306-5618
  Columbus *(G-5208)*
Brothers Publishing Co LLC .... E 937 548-3330
  Greenville *(G-8040)*
Brown Publishing Co Inc .... F 740 286-2187
  Jackson *(G-8712)*
Brown Publishing Inc LLC .... G 513 794-5040
  Blue Ash *(G-1374)*
Bryan Publishing Company .... D 419 636-1111
  Bryan *(G-1811)*
Bryan West Main Stop .... G 419 636-1616
  Bryan *(G-1812)*
Business Journal .... E 330 744-5023
  Youngstown *(G-16330)*
Carrollton Publishing Company .... F 330 627-5591
  Carrollton *(G-2305)*
Catholic Diocese of Columbus .... G 614 224-5195
  Columbus *(G-5240)*
Chagrin Valley Publishing Co .... E 440 247-5335
  Chagrin Falls *(G-2370)*
Chesterland News Inc .... G 440 729-7667
  Chesterland *(G-2480)*
Choice Marketing .... G 614 638-8404
  Columbus *(G-5249)*
Chronicle Telegram .... G 330 725-4166
  Medina *(G-10309)*
Cincinnati Enquirer .... D 513 721-2700
  Cincinnati *(G-2748)*
Cincinnati Ftn Sq News Inc .... F 513 421-4049
  Mason *(G-9975)*
Cincinnati Site Solutions LLC .... G 513 373-5001
  Cincinnati *(G-2760)*
Cleveland Activist .... G 888 817-3777
  Cleveland *(G-3830)*
Cleveland Jewish Publ Co .... E 216 454-8300
  Cleveland *(G-3844)*
Cleveland Jewish Publ Co Fdn .... F 216 454-8300
  Beachwood *(G-977)*
Clevelandcom .... D 216 862-7159
  Cleveland *(G-3865)*
Coffee News .... G 614 679-2967
  Hilliard *(G-8407)*
Columbus Jewish News .... G 216 342-5184
  Beachwood *(G-979)*
Columbus Messenger Company .... E 614 272-5422
  Columbus *(G-5272)*
Columbus Podcast Company LLC .... G 614 405-8298
  Columbus *(G-5274)*
Columbus-Sports Publications .... F 614 486-2202
  Columbus *(G-5282)*

Comcorp Inc .... C 718 981-1234
  Cleveland *(G-3887)*
Communicator Needs .... G 614 781-1160
  Columbus *(G-5283)*
Copley Ohio Newspapers Inc .... C 330 364-5577
  New Philadelphia *(G-11493)*
Copley Ohio Newspapers Inc .... D 585 598-0030
  Canton *(G-2081)*
County Classifieds .... G 937 592-8847
  Bellefontaine *(G-1203)*
Cox Newspapers LLC .... F 937 866-3331
  Miamisburg *(G-10629)*
Crain Communications Inc .... E 216 522-1383
  Cleveland *(G-3914)*
Crain Communications Inc .... E 330 836-9180
  Cuyahoga Falls *(G-6077)*
Daily Chief Union .... F 419 294-2331
  Upper Sandusky *(G-14806)*
Daily Fantasy Circuit Inc .... G 614 989-8689
  Columbus *(G-5314)*
Daily Growler Inc .... G 614 656-2337
  Upper Arlington *(G-14800)*
Daily Needs Assistance Inc .... G 614 824-8340
  Plain City *(G-12572)*
Daily Reporter .... E 614 224-4835
  Columbus *(G-5315)*
Dayton City Paper Group Llc .... F 937 222-8855
  Dayton *(G-6275)*
Defiance Publishing Co Ltd .... A 419 784-5441
  Defiance *(G-6677)*
Delaware Gazette Company .... E 740 363-1161
  Delaware *(G-6714)*
Delphos Herald Inc .... G 419 399-4015
  Paulding *(G-12312)*
Delphos Herald Inc .... D 419 695-0015
  Delphos *(G-6760)*
Digicom Inc .... F 216 642-3838
  Brooklyn Heights *(G-1690)*
Dispatch Consumer Services .... C 740 687-1893
  Lancaster *(G-9013)*
Dispatch Printing Company .... A
  Columbus *(G-5329)*
Douthit Communications Inc .... D 419 855-7465
  Millbury *(G-10930)*
Douthit Communications Inc .... D 419 625-5825
  Sandusky *(G-13051)*
Dow Jones & Company Inc .... E 419 352-4696
  Bowling Green *(G-1563)*
Eastern Ohio Newspapers Inc .... G 740 633-1131
  Martins Ferry *(G-9898)*
Euclid Media Group LLC .... F 216 241-7550
  Cleveland *(G-4035)*
Fire & Iron .... G 937 470-8536
  W Carrollton *(G-15013)*
Fostoria Focus Inc .... G 419 435-6397
  Fostoria *(G-7635)*
Franklin Communications Inc .... E 614 459-9769
  Columbus *(G-5386)*
Funny Times Inc .... G 216 371-8600
  Cleveland *(G-4092)*
Gannett Stllite Info Ntwrk LLC .... E 419 334-1012
  Fremont *(G-7785)*
Gannett Stllite Info Ntwrk LLC .... E 304 485-1891
  Marietta *(G-9794)*
Gate West Coast Ventures LLC .... F 513 891-1000
  Blue Ash *(G-1397)*
Gazette Publishing Company .... D 419 335-2010
  Napoleon *(G-11314)*
Geauga Publishing Company Ltd .... G 419 625-5825
  Sandusky *(G-13060)*
Graphic Publications Inc .... G 330 343-4917
  Dover *(G-6825)*

Greater Cleveland FCC .... G 440 333-5984
  Cleveland *(G-4149)*
Greenworld Enterprises Inc .... G 800 525-6999
  West Chester *(G-15559)*
Hamilton Journal News Inc .... E 513 863-8200
  Liberty Township *(G-9208)*
Hardin County Publishing Co .... E 419 674-4066
  Kenton *(G-8885)*
Harrison News Herald Inc .... G 740 942-2118
  Cadiz *(G-1903)*
Health Sense Inc .... G 440 354-8057
  Painesville *(G-12244)*
Hearth and Home At Urbana .... G 937 653-5263
  Urbana *(G-14834)*
Heartland Education Cmnty Inc .... G 330 684-3034
  Orrville *(G-12127)*
Herald Reflector Inc .... E 419 668-3771
  Norwalk *(G-11974)*
Hirt Publishing Co Inc .... E 419 946-3010
  Mount Gilead *(G-11204)*
Holmes County Hub Inc .... G 330 674-1811
  Millersburg *(G-10965)*
Horizon Ohio Publications Inc .... D 419 738-2128
  Wapakoneta *(G-15117)*
Horizon Ohio Publications Inc .... F 419 394-7414
  Saint Marys *(G-12953)*
Hubbard Publishing Co .... E 937 592-3060
  Bellefontaine *(G-1212)*
Iheartcommunications Inc .... G 419 223-2060
  Lima *(G-9254)*
Iiot World LLC .... E 440 715-0564
  Westlake *(G-15759)*
Indian Lake Shoppers Edge .... G 937 843-6600
  Russells Point *(G-12878)*
Irok Inc .... G 330 819-3612
  Akron *(G-193)*
Isaac Foster Mack Co .... C 419 625-5500
  Sandusky *(G-13067)*
Journal News .... G 513 829-7900
  Fairfield *(G-7376)*
Journal Register Company .... D 440 245-6901
  Lorain *(G-9416)*
Journal Register Company .... G 440 951-0000
  Willoughby *(G-15935)*
Keith O King .... G 419 339-5028
  Lima *(G-9259)*
King Media Enterprises Inc .... E 216 588-6700
  Cleveland *(G-4290)*
Kml Acquisitions Ltd .... G 614 732-9777
  Plain City *(G-12582)*
Kroner Publications Inc .... E 330 544-5500
  Niles *(G-11675)*
La Prensa Publications Inc .... G 419 870-6565
  Toledo *(G-14357)*
Lake Community News .... G 440 946-2577
  Willoughby *(G-15942)*
Lakewood Observer Inc .... G 216 712-7070
  Lakewood *(G-8978)*
Leader Publications Inc .... F 330 665-9595
  Fairlawn *(G-7443)*
Mansfield Journal Co .... C 330 364-8641
  New Philadelphia *(G-11513)*
Marion Star .... G 740 328-8542
  Newark *(G-11589)*
Marketing Essentials LLC .... E 419 629-0080
  New Bremen *(G-11404)*
Marysville Newspaper Inc .... E 937 644-9111
  Marysville *(G-9926)*
Medina Hntngton RE Group II LL .... E 330 591-2777
  Medina *(G-10348)*
Messenger Publishing Company .... C 740 592-6612
  Athens *(G-688)*

SIC SECTION

27 PRINTING, PUBLISHING AND ALLIED INDUSTRIES

Mirror .... G 419 893-8135
   Maumee *(G-10221)*

Mirror Publishing Co Inc .... F 419 893-8135
   Maumee *(G-10222)*

Morgan County Publishing Co .... G 740 962-3377
   Mcconnelsville *(G-10284)*

My Way Home Finder Magazine .... G 419 841-6201
   Toledo *(G-14392)*

Napoleon Inc .... F 419 592-5055
   Napoleon *(G-11326)*

News Watchman & Paper .... F 740 947-2149
   Waverly *(G-15288)*

Newspaper Network Central OH .... G 419 524-3545
   Mansfield *(G-9705)*

Ocm LLC .... B 937 247-2700
   Miamisburg *(G-10667)*

Ogden News Publishing Ohio Inc .... D 419 422-5151
   Findlay *(G-7544)*

Ogden News Publishing Ohio Inc .... E 567 743-9843
   Norwalk *(G-11984)*

Ogden News Publishing Ohio Inc .... E 419 625-5500
   Sandusky *(G-13083)*

Ogden Newspapers Inc .... D 304 748-0606
   Steubenville *(G-13674)*

Ogden Newspapers Ohio Inc .... F 419 448-3200
   Tiffin *(G-14097)*

Ogden Newspapers Ohio Inc .... E 330 424-9541
   Lisbon *(G-9322)*

Ohio Irish American News .... G 216 647-1144
   Cleveland *(G-4498)*

Ohio News Network .... E 614 460-3700
   Columbus *(G-5622)*

Ohio Newspaper Services Inc .... G 614 486-6677
   Columbus *(G-5623)*

Ohio Newspapers Inc .... A 937 225-2000
   Dayton *(G-6490)*

Ohio Newspapers Foundation .... G 614 486-6677
   Columbus *(G-5624)*

Ohio Rights Group .... G 614 300-0529
   Columbus *(G-5626)*

Pataskala Post .... F 740 964-6226
   Pataskala *(G-12303)*

Peebles Messenger Newspaper .... G 937 587-1451
   Peebles *(G-12329)*

Perry County Tribune .... F 740 342-4121
   New Lexington *(G-11455)*

Plain Dealer Publishing Co .... G 216 999-5000
   Cleveland *(G-4557)*

PMG Cincinnati Inc .... F 513 421-7275
   Columbus *(G-5681)*

Post .... F 513 768-8000
   Reading *(G-12747)*

Premier Prtg Centl Ohio Ltd .... E 937 642-0988
   Marysville *(G-9932)*

Primrose School of Marysville .... G 937 642-2125
   Marysville *(G-9933)*

Progressor Times .... G 419 396-7567
   Carey *(G-2283)*

Progrssive Communications Corp .... D 740 397-5333
   Mount Vernon *(G-11290)*

Pulse Journal .... G 513 829-7900
   Liberty Township *(G-9209)*

Record Herald Publishing Co .... E 717 762-2151
   Cincinnati *(G-3327)*

Register Herald Office .... F 937 456-5553
   Eaton *(G-7068)*

Reporter Newspaper Inc .... F 330 535-7061
   Akron *(G-301)*

Richardson Publishing Company .... F 330 753-1068
   Barberton *(G-894)*

Ringer LLC .... G 216 228-1442
   Lakewood *(G-8982)*

Robert Turner .... G 937 434-1346
   Centerville *(G-2364)*

Rockbrook Business Svcs LLC .... E 234 817-8107
   Youngstown *(G-16430)*

Samuel L Peters LLC .... G 513 745-1500
   Blue Ash *(G-1463)*

Sdg News Group Inc .... F 419 929-3411
   New London *(G-11468)*

Sentinel Daily .... F 740 992-2155
   Gallipolis *(G-7902)*

Sesh Communications .... F 513 851-1693
   Cincinnati *(G-3384)*

Shelby Daily Globe Inc .... F 419 342-4276
   Shelby *(G-13200)*

Sidney Alive .... G 937 210-2539
   Sidney *(G-13287)*

Smart Business Network Inc .... E 440 250-7000
   Cleveland *(G-4705)*

Sojourners Truth Inc .... F 419 243-0007
   Toledo *(G-14474)*

Spectrum News Ohio .... E 614 384-2640
   Columbus *(G-5785)*

Spectrum Publications .... G 740 439-3531
   Cambridge *(G-1954)*

Springfield Newspapers Inc .... E 937 323-5533
   Springfield *(G-13635)*

Standard Printing Co Inc .... E 419 586-2371
   Celina *(G-2350)*

Stark Cnty Fdrtion Cnsrvtion C .... E 330 268-1652
   Canton *(G-2231)*

Streamline Media & Pubg LLC .... G 614 822-1817
   Reynoldsburg *(G-12774)*

Sugarcreek Budget Publishers .... F 330 852-4634
   Sugarcreek *(G-13940)*

Summit Street News Inc .... G 330 609-5600
   Warren *(G-15207)*

◆ Syracuse China LLC .... C 419 325-2100
   Toledo *(G-14480)*

The Cleveland Jewish Publ Co .... E 216 454-8300
   Beachwood *(G-1027)*

The Gazette Printing Co Inc .... G 440 593-6030
   Conneaut *(G-5934)*

The Gazette Printing Co Inc .... D 440 576-9125
   Jefferson *(G-8760)*

The Vindicator Printing Company .... B 330 747-1471
   Youngstown *(G-16454)*

Toledo Blade Company .... B 419 724-6000
   Toledo *(G-14492)*

Trading Post .... G 740 922-1199
   Uhrichsville *(G-14771)*

Travelers Vacation Guide .... G 440 582-4949
   North Royalton *(G-11898)*

Tribune Printing Inc .... G 419 542-7764
   Hicksville *(G-8382)*

Trogdon Publishing Inc .... E 330 721-7678
   Medina *(G-10389)*

University Sports Publications .... G 614 291-6416
   Columbus *(G-5847)*

Upper Arlington Crew Inc .... F 614 485-0089
   Columbus *(G-5848)*

Village Reporter .... G 419 485-4851
   Montpelier *(G-11144)*

Vindicator .... E 330 841-1600
   Warren *(G-15216)*

Welch Publishing Co .... G 419 666-5344
   Rossford *(G-12873)*

Welch Publishing Co .... E 419 874-2528
   Perrysburg *(G-12444)*

Winkler Co Inc .... G 937 294-2662
   Dayton *(G-6655)*

Wooster Daily Record Inc LLC .... C 330 264-1125
   Wooster *(G-16184)*

World Journal .... G 216 458-0988
   Cleveland *(G-4922)*

Xenia Daily Gazette .... E 937 372-4444
   Xenia *(G-16281)*

Yellow Springs News Inc .... F 937 767-7373
   Yellow Springs *(G-16288)*

Ylt Red Cleveland LLC .... G 216 664-0941
   Cleveland *(G-4928)*

2721 Periodicals

1010 Magapp LLC .... G 210 701-1754
   Wooster *(G-16093)*

400 SW 7th Street Partners Ltd .... E 440 826-4700
   Cincinnati *(G-2580)*

400 SW 7th Street Partners Ltd .... E 772 781-2144
   Cincinnati *(G-2581)*

614 Media Group LLC .... E 614 488-4400
   Columbus *(G-5079)*

Adams Street Publishing Co Inc .... E 419 244-9859
   Toledo *(G-14177)*

Agri Communicators Inc .... E 614 273-0465
   Columbus *(G-5105)*

AGS Custom Graphics Inc .... D 330 963-7770
   Macedonia *(G-9534)*

Alcohol & Drug Addiction Svcs .... F 216 348-4830
   Cleveland *(G-3624)*

▲ Alonovus Corp .... E 330 674-2300
   Millersburg *(G-10940)*

American Ceramic Society .... E 614 890-4700
   Westerville *(G-15647)*

American Lawyers Co Inc .... F 440 333-5190
   Westlake *(G-15730)*

▲ Amos Media Company .... C 937 638-0967
   Sidney *(G-13221)*

◆ Angstrom Graphics Inc .... C 216 271-5300
   Cleveland *(G-3668)*

Arens Corporation .... G 937 473-2028
   Covington *(G-6018)*

Arens Corporation .... F 937 473-2028
   Covington *(G-6017)*

▲ Asm International .... D 440 338-5151
   Novelty *(G-12007)*

Atv Insider .... G 740 282-7102
   Steubenville *(G-13660)*

Babcox Media Inc .... D 330 670-1234
   Akron *(G-76)*

Baker Media Group LLC .... F 330 253-0056
   Akron *(G-77)*

Bbm Fairway Inc .... G 330 899-2200
   Uniontown *(G-14781)*

▲ Benjamin Media Inc .... E 330 467-7588
   Brecksville *(G-1608)*

Breakwall Publishing LLC .... G 813 575-2570
   Medina *(G-10306)*

C & S Associates Inc .... E 440 461-9661
   Highland Heights *(G-8383)*

Carmel Publishing Inc .... F 330 478-9200
   Canton *(G-2069)*

Cars and Parts Magazine .... D 937 498-0803
   Sidney *(G-13232)*

Center For Inquiry Inc .... G 330 671-7192
   Peninsula *(G-12339)*

CFM Religion Pubg Group LLC .... D 513 931-4050
   Cincinnati *(G-2723)*

Cincinnati Family Magazine .... G 513 842-0077
   Blue Ash *(G-1379)*

Cincinnati Media LLC .... E 513 562-2755
   Cincinnati *(G-2754)*

Clutch Mov .... G 740 525-5510
   Marietta *(G-9784)*

Collective Arts Network .... G 216 235-3564
   Lakewood *(G-8971)*

Employee Codes: A=Over 500 employees, B=251-500
C=101-250, D=51-100, E=20-50, F=10-19, G=1-9

27 PRINTING, PUBLISHING AND ALLIED INDUSTRIES

SIC SECTION

Communication Resources Inc............G..... 800 992-2144
  Canton *(G-2079)*
Crain Communications Inc................E..... 216 522-1383
  Cleveland *(G-3914)*
Crain Communications Inc................E..... 330 836-9180
  Cuyahoga Falls *(G-6077)*
▲ Creative Ip LLC..................................G..... 234 571-2466
  Akron *(G-118)*
Cruisin Times Holdings LLC................G..... 234 646-2095
  Ashtabula *(G-629)*
Cruisin Times Magazine......................G..... 440 331-4615
  Rocky River *(G-12837)*
Dominion Enterprises..........................G..... 216 472-1870
  Cleveland *(G-3967)*
▲ F+w Media Inc...................................A..... 513 531-2690
  Blue Ash *(G-1393)*
Family Motor Coach Assn Inc............E..... 513 474-3622
  Cincinnati *(G-2894)*
Family Motor Coaching Inc.................D..... 513 474-3622
  Cincinnati *(G-2895)*
Firelands Media Group LLC................G..... 440 543-8566
  Chagrin Falls *(G-2396)*
Gardner Business Media Inc..............F..... 513 527-8800
  Cincinnati *(G-2929)*
Gardner Business Media Inc..............C..... 513 527-8800
  Cincinnati *(G-2930)*
Generals Books....................................G..... 614 870-1861
  Columbus *(G-5398)*
Gie Media Inc......................................E..... 800 456-0707
  Cleveland *(G-4125)*
Gongwer News Service Inc................F..... 614 221-1992
  Columbus *(G-5407)*
Great Lakes Publishing Company......D..... 216 771-2833
  Cleveland *(G-4146)*
Greater Cincinnati Bowl Assn............E..... 513 761-7387
  Cincinnati *(G-2970)*
▲ Highlights For Children Inc..............C..... 614 486-0631
  Columbus *(G-5436)*
Incorprted Trstees of The Gspl...........D..... 216 749-2100
  Middleburg Heights *(G-10721)*
Informa Media Inc...............................A..... 216 696-7000
  Cleveland *(G-4225)*
Insights Sccess Media Tech LLC.......E..... 614 602-1754
  Dublin *(G-6899)*
Kent Information Services Inc...........G..... 330 672-2110
  Kent *(G-8824)*
Kyle Media Inc.....................................G..... 419 754-4234
  Toledo *(G-14354)*
Kyle Media Inc.....................................G..... 877 775-2538
  Toledo *(G-14355)*
Lippincott and Peto Inc......................F..... 330 864-2122
  Akron *(G-220)*
Liturgical Publications Inc.................D..... 216 325-6825
  Cleveland *(G-4332)*
▲ Lorenz Corporation..........................D..... 937 228-6118
  Dayton *(G-6416)*
Lyle Printing & Publishing Co.............E..... 330 337-3419
  Salem *(G-13013)*
Marketing Essentials LLC..................E..... 419 629-0080
  New Bremen *(G-11404)*
Matthew Bender & Company Inc.....C..... 518 487-3000
  Miamisburg *(G-10655)*
Meister Media Worldwide Inc............D..... 440 942-2000
  Willoughby *(G-15950)*
New Publishing Holdings LLC...........A..... 513 531-2690
  Blue Ash *(G-1443)*
North Coast Minority Media LLC.......G..... 216 407-4327
  Cleveland *(G-4472)*
Ohio Designer Craftsmen Entps........F..... 614 486-7119
  Columbus *(G-5615)*
Ohio Guitar Shows Inc........................G..... 740 592-4614
  Athens *(G-689)*

Pardson Inc..F..... 740 373-5285
  Marietta *(G-9814)*
Pearson Education Inc........................G..... 614 876-0371
  Columbus *(G-5663)*
Pearson Education Inc........................E..... 614 841-3700
  Columbus *(G-5664)*
Peninsula Publishing LLC...................G..... 330 524-3359
  Independence *(G-8679)*
Pjl Enterprise Inc.................................F..... 937 293-1415
  Moraine *(G-11198)*
Publishing Group Ltd..........................F..... 614 572-1240
  Columbus *(G-5697)*
Rector Inc...G..... 440 892-0444
  Westlake *(G-15778)*
Relx Inc..G..... 937 865-6800
  Miamisburg *(G-10673)*
Rubber World Magazine Inc...............G..... 330 864-2122
  Akron *(G-313)*
Schaeffers Investment Research Inc......D..... 513 589-3800
  Blue Ash *(G-1465)*
Sesh Communications.........................F..... 513 851-1693
  Cincinnati *(G-3384)*
▲ St Media Group Intl Inc....................D..... 513 421-2050
  Blue Ash *(G-1467)*
▲ Standard Publishing LLC.................C..... 513 931-4050
  Cincinnati *(G-3414)*
Status Entertainment Group LLC.......G..... 216 252-2243
  Cleveland *(G-4732)*
Sterling Associates Inc........................G..... 330 630-3500
  Akron *(G-338)*
Suburban Communications Inc..........F..... 440 632-0130
  Middlefield *(G-10791)*
Telex Communications Inc.................G..... 419 865-0972
  Toledo *(G-14482)*
Toastmasters International.................F..... 937 429-2680
  Dayton *(G-6174)*
University Sports Publications............G..... 614 291-6416
  Columbus *(G-5847)*
Venue Lifestyle & Event Guide............F..... 513 405-6822
  Cincinnati *(G-3493)*
Virtus Stunts LLC................................G..... 440 543-0472
  Chagrin Falls *(G-2433)*
Welch Publishing Co...........................E..... 419 874-2528
  Perrysburg *(G-12444)*
Youngs Publishing Inc........................G..... 937 259-6575
  Dayton *(G-6176)*

2731 Book publishing

American Legal Publishing Corp........E..... 513 421-4248
  Cincinnati *(G-2619)*
▲ Asm International............................D..... 440 338-5151
  Novelty *(G-12007)*
Auguste Moone Enterprises Ltd........E..... 216 333-9248
  Cleveland Heights *(G-4937)*
B & S Transport Inc............................G..... 330 767-4319
  Navarre *(G-11340)*
▼ Bearing Precious Seed Intl Inc.......E..... 513 575-1706
  Milford *(G-10894)*
Benchmark Education Co LLC..........C..... 845 215-9808
  Groveport *(G-8132)*
▲ Bendon Inc.......................................D..... 419 207-3600
  Ashland *(G-556)*
▼ Bookfactory LLC..............................E..... 937 226-7100
  Dayton *(G-6234)*
◆ Bookmasters Inc..............................C..... 419 281-1802
  Ashland *(G-557)*
Bright Star Books Inc..........................G..... 330 888-2156
  Akron *(G-93)*
Carmel Publishing Inc........................F..... 330 478-9200
  Canton *(G-2069)*
Cengage Learning Inc........................C..... 513 234-9567
  Mason *(G-9970)*

Cengage Learning Inc........................B..... 415 839-2300
  Mason *(G-9972)*
◆ Cengage Learning Inc....................D..... 617 289-7700
  Mason *(G-9971)*
Cengage Lrng Holdings II Inc.............E..... 617 289-7700
  Mason *(G-9973)*
Christian Missionary Alliance............C..... 380 208-6200
  Reynoldsburg *(G-12758)*
Communication Resources Inc..........G..... 800 992-2144
  Canton *(G-2079)*
Conway Greene Co Inc......................G..... 440 230-2627
  North Royalton *(G-11872)*
Cox Ohio Publishing...........................E..... 937 743-6700
  Franklin *(G-7669)*
CSS Publishing Company..................E..... 419 227-1818
  Lima *(G-9232)*
Decent Hill Publishers LLC................G..... 216 548-1255
  Hilliard *(G-8410)*
Dreamscape Media LLC....................G..... 877 983-7326
  Holland *(G-8508)*
Elloras Cave Publishing Inc...............E..... 330 253-3521
  Akron *(G-138)*
Equipping Ministries Intl Inc...............G..... 513 742-1100
  Cincinnati *(G-2882)*
▲ F+w Media Inc.................................A..... 513 531-2690
  Blue Ash *(G-1393)*
Follett Hgher Edcatn Group Inc........C..... 419 281-5100
  Ashland *(G-574)*
Gardner Business Media Inc..............F..... 513 527-8800
  Cincinnati *(G-2929)*
Gardner Business Media Inc..............C..... 513 527-8800
  Cincinnati *(G-2930)*
Gareth Stevens Publishing LP...........F..... 800 542-2595
  Strongsville *(G-13835)*
Gie Media Inc......................................E..... 800 456-0707
  Cleveland *(G-4125)*
▲ Golf Galaxy Golfworks Inc..............C..... 740 328-4193
  Newark *(G-11577)*
Highlights Consumer Svcs Inc..........F..... 570 253-1164
  Columbus *(G-5435)*
Horrorhound Ltd..................................F..... 513 239-7263
  Cincinnati *(G-3010)*
Hubbard Company.............................E..... 419 784-4455
  Defiance *(G-6682)*
J S C Publishing.................................G..... 614 424-6911
  Columbus *(G-5483)*
Just Business Inc...............................F..... 866 577-3303
  Dayton *(G-6395)*
Kelley Communication Dev................G..... 937 298-6132
  Dayton *(G-6398)*
Kendall/Hunt Publishing Co...............C..... 877 275-4725
  Cincinnati *(G-3073)*
Ketman Corporation...........................G..... 330 262-1688
  Wooster *(G-16142)*
Lachina Creative Inc..........................E..... 216 292-7959
  Cleveland *(G-4304)*
Liturgical Publications Inc.................D..... 216 325-6825
  Cleveland *(G-4332)*
Marysville Newspaper Inc..................E..... 937 644-9111
  Marysville *(G-9926)*
▲ Master Communications Inc..........G..... 208 821-3473
  Cincinnati *(G-3133)*
Matthew Bender & Company Inc.....C..... 518 487-3000
  Miamisburg *(G-10655)*
McGraw-Hill Global Educatn LLC......B..... 614 755-4151
  Blacklick *(G-1340)*
McGraw-Hill Global Educatn LLC......D..... 800 338-3987
  Columbus *(G-5553)*
McGraw-Hill Schl Edcatn Hldngs......A..... 419 207-7400
  Ashland *(G-591)*
McGraw-Hill Schl Edcatn Hldngs......A..... 614 430-4000
  Columbus *(G-5064)*

27 PRINTING, PUBLISHING AND ALLIED INDUSTRIES

New Publishing Holdings LLC............... A 513 531-2690
   Blue Ash *(G-1443)*

North Coast Media LLC........................ D 216 706-3700
   Cleveland *(G-4471)*

Oxford Resources Inc........................... G 614 873-7955
   Plain City *(G-12589)*

Pardson Inc... F 740 373-5285
   Marietta *(G-9814)*

▲ Precision Metalforming Assn............. E 216 901-8800
   Independence *(G-8681)*

Rebecca Benston................................. F 937 360-0669
   Springfield *(G-13625)*

Relx Inc... C 937 865-6800
   Miamisburg *(G-10674)*

Reynolds Industries Group LLC........... E 614 363-9149
   Blacklick *(G-1342)*

Scepter Publishers............................... G 212 354-0670
   Strongsville *(G-13874)*

Scott Fetzer Company.......................... A 440 892-3000
   Westlake *(G-15784)*

▲ St Media Group Intl Inc.................... D 513 421-2050
   Blue Ash *(G-1467)*

Swagg Productions2015llc................... F 614 601-7414
   Worthington *(G-16213)*

▲ Teachers Publishing Group.............. F 614 486-0631
   Hilliard *(G-8445)*

Tgs International Inc............................ E 330 893-4828
   Millersburg *(G-10997)*

Tomahawk Entrmt Group LLC.............. F 216 505-0548
   Euclid *(G-7302)*

University of Toledo.............................. F 419 530-2311
   Toledo *(G-14515)*

Wolters Kluwer Clinical D..................... D 330 650-6506
   Hudson *(G-8619)*

Woodburn Press Ltd............................. G 937 293-9245
   Dayton *(G-6659)*

World Harvest Church Inc.................... C 614 837-1990
   Canal Winchester *(G-1994)*

▲ Zaner-Bloser Inc.............................. C 614 486-0221
   Columbus *(G-5892)*

2732 Book printing

1st Impressions Plus LLC.................... G 330 696-7605
   Akron *(G-9)*

American Printing & Lithog Co............. F 513 867-0602
   Hamilton *(G-8177)*

Bip Printing Solutions LLC................... F 216 832-5673
   Beachwood *(G-974)*

Digicom Inc.. F 216 642-3838
   Brooklyn Heights *(G-1690)*

▲ Golf Marketing Group Inc................ G 330 963-5155
   Twinsburg *(G-14669)*

Hf Group LLC....................................... C 440 729-9411
   Chesterland *(G-2481)*

Hf Group LLC....................................... F 440 729-2445
   Aurora *(G-719)*

Hubbard Company............................... E 419 784-4455
   Defiance *(G-6682)*

J & L Management Corporation........... G 440 205-1199
   Mentor *(G-10478)*

Lsc Communications Inc..................... A 419 935-0111
   Willard *(G-15860)*

Morse Enterprises Inc.......................... G 513 229-3600
   Mason *(G-10031)*

Multi-Craft Litho Inc.............................. E 859 581-2754
   Blue Ash *(G-1442)*

Quebecor World Johnson Hardin......... E 614 326-0299
   Cincinnati *(G-3314)*

Society of The Precious Blood............. E 419 925-4516
   Celina *(G-2349)*

Star City Press LLC............................. G 740 500-0320
   Chillicothe *(G-2535)*

The Press of Ohio Inc.......................... B 330 678-5868
   Kent *(G-8875)*

2741 Miscellaneous publishing

▼ 48 Hr Books Inc................................ F 330 374-6917
   Twinsburg *(G-14620)*

ACS Publications LLC......................... G 330 686-3082
   Stow *(G-13681)*

Action Express Inc............................... G 929 351-3620
   Columbus *(G-5100)*

Ahalogy.. E 314 974-5599
   Cincinnati *(G-2603)*

American City Bus Journals Inc.......... C 513 337-9450
   Cincinnati *(G-2617)*

American Gild of English Hndbe.......... G 937 438-0085
   Cincinnati *(G-2618)*

American Legal Publishing Corp......... E 513 421-4248
   Cincinnati *(G-2619)*

American Publishers LLC.................... D 419 626-0623
   Huron *(G-8626)*

Ameritech Publishing Inc..................... A 614 895-6123
   Columbus *(G-5132)*

Ameritech Publishing Inc..................... A 330 896-6037
   Uniontown *(G-14780)*

▲ Amos Media Company...................... C 937 638-0967
   Sidney *(G-13221)*

Anadem Inc.. G 614 262-2539
   Columbus *(G-5138)*

Aquent Studios..................................... F 216 266-7551
   Willoughby *(G-15885)*

Archer Publishing LLC......................... G 440 338-5233
   Bay Village *(G-963)*

AT&T Corp.. E 614 223-8236
   Columbus *(G-5161)*

Bandages & Boo-Boos Press LLC....... G 614 271-6193
   Medina *(G-10300)*

Bcmr Publications LLC........................ G 740 441-7778
   Gallipolis *(G-7888)*

Beaver Productions............................. G 330 352-4603
   Akron *(G-81)*

Becker Gllagher Legal Pubg Inc.......... F 513 677-5044
   Cincinnati *(G-2662)*

Berry Company.................................... G 513 768-7800
   Cincinnati *(G-2667)*

Bluffton News Pubg & Prtg Co............ G 419 358-4610
   Bluffton *(G-1499)*

Cbr Express LLC.................................. G 440 293-4744
   Williamsfield *(G-15868)*

Cbus Inc... F 614 327-6971
   Pickerington *(G-12458)*

Cdc Publishing..................................... G 772 770-6003
   Cincinnati *(G-2712)*

Cerkl Incorporated............................... D 513 813-8425
   Blue Ash *(G-1378)*

Chatterbox Sports LLC........................ F 513 545-4754
   Hamilton *(G-8190)*

Checkered Express Inc........................ F 330 530-8169
   Girard *(G-7965)*

Christian Blue Pages........................... G 937 847-2583
   Miamisburg *(G-10627)*

Cincinnati Crt Index Press Inc.............. G 513 241-1450
   Cincinnati *(G-2745)*

Clark Optimization LLC........................ E 330 417-2164
   Canton *(G-2076)*

Cleveland Press.................................... G 440 289-3227
   Cleveland *(G-3850)*

Cleveland Press.................................... G 440 442-5101
   Cleveland *(G-3851)*

Computer Workshop Inc...................... E 614 798-9505
   Dublin *(G-6877)*

Conquest Maps LLC............................ F 614 654-1627
   Columbus *(G-5288)*

County Classifieds................................ G 937 592-8847
   Bellefontaine *(G-1203)*

Cox Ohio Publishing - Dayton.............. F 937 328-0300
   Springfield *(G-13548)*

Cox Publishing Hq................................ G 937 225-2000
   Dayton *(G-6265)*

Creative Nest LLC................................ G 614 216-8102
   Columbus *(G-5307)*

Deemsys Inc... D 614 322-9928
   Gahanna *(G-7833)*

▲ Depot Direct Inc............................... E 419 661-1233
   Perrysburg *(G-12375)*

Diocesan Publications Inc................... E 614 718-9500
   Dublin *(G-6879)*

Dips Publishing Inc.............................. G 216 801-7886
   Cleveland *(G-3959)*

Discover Publications........................... G 877 872-3080
   Columbus *(G-5328)*

Dotcentral LLC..................................... F 330 809-0112
   Massillon *(G-10090)*

Douthit Communications Inc............... D 419 625-5825
   Sandusky *(G-13051)*

Ebsco Industries Inc............................ F 513 398-3695
   Mason *(G-9987)*

Echopress Ltd...................................... G 216 373-7560
   Avon Lake *(G-804)*

▼ Educational Direction Inc................. G 330 836-8439
   Fairlawn *(G-7437)*

Elloras Cave Publishing Inc................. E 330 253-3521
   Akron *(G-138)*

Evans Creative Group LLC.................. G 614 657-9439
   Columbus *(G-5364)*

Fleetmaster Express Inc....................... D 866 425-0666
   Findlay *(G-7510)*

Forest Hill Publishing LLC................... G 216 761-8316
   Cleveland *(G-4082)*

Franklin Covey Co................................ G 513 680-0975
   Cincinnati *(G-2921)*

Fullgospel Publishing........................... F 216 339-1973
   Shaker Heights *(G-13154)*

Gardner Business Media Inc................ C 513 527-8800
   Cincinnati *(G-2930)*

Gatekeeper Press LLC......................... E 866 535-0913
   Grove City *(G-8095)*

Gb Liquidating Company Inc............... E 513 248-7600
   Milford *(G-10907)*

General Bar Inc..................................... F 440 835-2000
   Westlake *(G-15753)*

Golias Publishing Company Inc........... G 330 425-4744
   Medina *(G-10331)*

Graphic Paper Products Corp.............. D 937 325-5503
   Springfield *(G-13570)*

Guardian Publications Inc.................... G 216 621-5005
   Cleveland *(G-4156)*

Haines Criss Cross............................... G 330 494-9111
   North Canton *(G-11735)*

Haines Publishing Inc.......................... E 330 494-9111
   Canton *(G-2120)*

Harmon Homes..................................... G 513 602-6896
   Fairfield *(G-7365)*

Identity Group LLC.............................. G 614 337-6167
   Westerville *(G-15658)*

Igloo Press LLC.................................... G 614 787-5528
   Worthington *(G-16198)*

Incorprted Trstees of The Gspl............ F 216 749-1428
   Cleveland *(G-4222)*

Intelacomm Inc..................................... G 888 610-9250
   Newbury *(G-11627)*

Interweave Press LLC.......................... G 513 531-2690
   Blue Ash *(G-1410)*

IPA Ltd.. F 614 523-3974
   Columbus *(G-5479)*

27 PRINTING, PUBLISHING AND ALLIED INDUSTRIES

ITM Marketing Inc................................ C 740 295-3575
  Coshocton *(G-5981)*
J & E Publications LLC....................... G 614 457-7989
  Columbus *(G-5482)*
Jewish Federation of Cinti................... G 513 487-4900
  Blue Ash *(G-1413)*
K-Sha Press Inc.................................... G 216 252-0037
  Cleveland *(G-4271)*
▲ Kaeden Publishing............................ G 440 617-1400
  Westlake *(G-15762)*
L J Publishing LLC............................... G 888 749-5994
  Hinckley *(G-8476)*
Lake Publishing Inc............................. G 440 299-8500
  Mentor *(G-10490)*
Landoll Publishing Sjs LLC.................. G 330 353-2688
  Strongsville *(G-13849)*
Lanier & Associates Inc....................... G 216 391-7735
  Cleveland *(G-4311)*
Legatum Project Inc............................. G 216 533-8843
  Shaker Heights *(G-13155)*
▲ Lexisnexis Group............................... C 937 865-6800
  Miamisburg *(G-10654)*
Lidsen Publishing Inc.......................... G 216 378-7542
  Beachwood *(G-995)*
Liette L & S Express LLC..................... G 419 394-7077
  Saint Marys *(G-12956)*
▲ Lorenz Corporation............................ D 937 228-6118
  Dayton *(G-6416)*
Lsc Communications Inc..................... A 419 935-0111
  Willard *(G-15860)*
M R I Education Foundation................. E 513 281-3400
  Cincinnati *(G-3119)*
Marketing Essentials LLC..................... E 419 629-0080
  New Bremen *(G-11404)*
Midwest Menu Mate Inc...................... F 740 323-2599
  Newark *(G-11592)*
Miller Express Inc................................ G 330 714-6751
  Copley *(G-5951)*
N2 Publishing...................................... F 937 641-8277
  West Carrollton *(G-15355)*
Northstar Publishing Inc...................... G 330 721-9126
  Medina *(G-10356)*
Ogr Publishing Inc............................... G 330 757-3020
  Hilliard *(G-8425)*
Ohlinger Dev & Editorial Co................ D 614 261-5360
  Columbus *(G-5633)*
Ohlinger Publishing Svcs Inc................ E 614 261-5360
  Columbus *(G-5634)*
Omnipresence Cleaning LLC................ F 937 250-4749
  Dayton *(G-6491)*
ONeil & Associates Inc........................ C 937 865-0800
  Miamisburg *(G-10669)*
Orange Frazer Press Inc....................... G 937 382-3196
  Wilmington *(G-16057)*
Organized Lightning LLC..................... G 407 965-2730
  Blue Ash *(G-1447)*
Patrigraphica Ltd................................. G 513 460-5380
  Cincinnati *(G-3238)*
Pedestrian Press.................................. G 419 244-6488
  Toledo *(G-14431)*
Pflaum Publishing Group..................... F 937 293-1415
  Moraine *(G-11197)*
Pjl Enterprise Inc................................. D 937 293-1415
  Moraine *(G-11199)*
▲ Posterservice Incorporated................. G 513 577-7100
  Cincinnati *(G-3268)*
Printery Inc... G 513 574-1099
  Cincinnati *(G-3277)*
Promatch Solutions LLC...................... F 877 299-0185
  Moraine *(G-11205)*
Propress Inc.. F 216 631-8200
  Cleveland *(G-4593)*

PS Pinchot-Swogger Pubg LLC.............. G 330 448-1742
  Masury *(G-10157)*
Publishing Group Ltd........................... F 614 572-1240
  Columbus *(G-5697)*
▼ Quadriga Americas LLC...................... G 614 890-6090
  Westerville *(G-15674)*
Quality Solutions Inc............................ E 440 933-9946
  Cleveland *(G-4608)*
Questline Inc....................................... E 614 255-3166
  Dublin *(G-6930)*
▼ Rcl Publishing Group LLC................... F 972 390-6400
  Cincinnati *(G-3325)*
Recob Great Lakes Express Inc............ G 216 265-7940
  Cleveland *(G-4619)*
Richard Wright................................... G 740 829-2127
  Coshocton *(G-5994)*
Richland Source.................................. E 419 610-2100
  Mansfield *(G-9714)*
Road Apple Music............................... G 513 217-4444
  Middletown *(G-10836)*
▲ S J T Enterprises Inc........................... E 440 617-1100
  Westlake *(G-15780)*
Samhain Publishing Ltd (llc)................. G 513 453-4688
  Cincinnati *(G-3360)*
Schaeffers Investment Research Inc...... D 513 589-3800
  Blue Ash *(G-1465)*
Scheel Publishing LLC......................... G 216 731-8616
  Willoughby *(G-15986)*
Scott Fetzer Company......................... A 440 892-3000
  Westlake *(G-15784)*
Scrambl-Gram Inc................................ G 419 635-2321
  Port Clinton *(G-12628)*
Scriptype Publishing Inc...................... E 330 659-0303
  Richfield *(G-12796)*
Sea Bird Publications Inc..................... G 513 869-2200
  Fairfield *(G-7406)*
See Ya There Inc................................. G 614 856-9037
  Millersport *(G-11014)*
Senior Impact Publications LLC............ F 513 791-8800
  Cincinnati *(G-3379)*
Service Express LLC............................ F 513 942-6170
  West Chester *(G-15583)*
Severn River Publishing LLC................ G 703 819-4686
  Kings Mills *(G-8929)*
Spear Stone Press............................... G 513 899-7337
  Morrow *(G-11225)*
Spiral Publishing LLC.......................... G 614 876-4347
  Hilliard *(G-8441)*
Star Brite Express Car WA................... G 330 674-0062
  Millersburg *(G-10994)*
Star City Press LLC.............................. G 740 500-0320
  Chillicothe *(G-2535)*
State Printing..................................... G 614 995-1740
  Columbus *(G-5791)*
Suburban Communications Inc............. F 440 632-0130
  Middlefield *(G-10791)*
The419... G 855 451-1018
  Lima *(G-9298)*
Tiny Lion Music Groups...................... G 419 874-7353
  Perrysburg *(G-12435)*
Tower Press Development................... G 216 241-4069
  Cleveland *(G-4812)*
Trogdan Publishing............................. G 614 880-0178
  Powell *(G-12683)*
Trogdon Publishing Inc....................... E 330 721-7678
  Medina *(G-10389)*
▲ Universal Drect Flfllment Corp............ C 330 650-5000
  Hudson *(G-8617)*
◆ Universal Screen Arts Inc................... E 330 650-5000
  Hudson *(G-8618)*
Upright Press LLC............................... G 614 619-7337
  Columbus *(G-5849)*

User Friendly Phone Book LLC............. E 216 674-6500
  Independence *(G-8689)*
Van-Griner LLC................................... G 419 733-7951
  Cincinnati *(G-3487)*
Van-Griner LLC................................... G 419 733-7951
  Minster *(G-11064)*
Vengeance Is Mine LLC....................... G 614 670-4745
  Columbus *(G-5856)*
Walter H Drane Co Inc........................ G 216 514-1022
  Beachwood *(G-1032)*
▲ Weekend Learning Publs LLC.............. G 614 336-7711
  Columbus *(G-5868)*
Willis Music Company......................... F 513 671-3288
  Cincinnati *(G-3520)*
Woodburn Press Ltd........................... G 937 293-9245
  Dayton *(G-6659)*
Works In Progress Inc......................... F 802 658-3797
  Cincinnati *(G-3526)*
Xcellence Publications Inc................... G 216 326-1891
  Cleveland *(C-1037)*

2752 Commercial printing, lithographic

1one Stop Printing Inc......................... F 614 216-1438
  Columbus *(G-5074)*
3d Printing... G 501 248-0468
  Lewis Center *(G-9143)*
7 7 Print Solutions LLC........................ F 513 600-4597
  Fairfield *(G-7328)*
A F Krainz Co..................................... G 216 431-4341
  Cleveland *(G-3579)*
A Grade Notes Inc............................... G 614 299-9999
  Dublin *(G-6856)*
A Z Printing Inc.................................. G 513 733-3900
  Cincinnati *(G-2585)*
A-A Blueprint Co Inc........................... E 330 794-8803
  Akron *(G-11)*
Academy Graphic Comm Inc................ E 216 661-2550
  Cleveland *(G-3589)*
Acme Duplicating Co Inc..................... G 216 241-1241
  Westlake *(G-15727)*
Acme Printing Co Inc.......................... G 419 626-4426
  Sandusky *(G-13041)*
▲ Activities Press Inc............................. E 440 953-1200
  Mentor *(G-10404)*
Ad Choice Inc..................................... G 419 697-8889
  Oregon *(G-12100)*
Adcraft Decals Incorporated................. E 216 524-2934
  Cleveland *(G-3598)*
Admark Printing Inc............................ G 937 833-5111
  Brookville *(G-1728)*
Advantage Print Solutions LLC.............. G 614 519-2392
  Columbus *(G-5104)*
AGS Custom Graphics Inc.................... D 330 963-7770
  Macedonia *(G-9534)*
Akron Litho-Print Company Inc............ F 330 434-3145
  Akron *(G-36)*
Akron Thermography Inc..................... F 330 896-9712
  Akron *(G-46)*
Akron Thermography Inc..................... F 330 896-9712
  Akron *(G-47)*
▲ Alberts Screen Print Inc...................... C 330 753-7559
  Norton *(G-11938)*
All Points Printing Inc......................... G 440 585-1125
  Wickliffe *(G-15823)*
Allegra Print & Imaging....................... G 419 427-8095
  Findlay *(G-7475)*
Allen Graphics Inc............................... G 440 349-4100
  Solon *(G-13308)*
Alliance Publishing Co Inc................... C 330 453-1304
  Alliance *(G-393)*
AlphaGraphics..................................... G 513 204-6070
  Mason *(G-9948)*

SIC SECTION
27 PRINTING, PUBLISHING AND ALLIED INDUSTRIES

AlphaGraphics 507 Inc ..... G 440 878-9700
Strongsville *(G-13805)*

Alvito Custom Imprints LLC ..... G 614 207-1004
Columbus *(G-5118)*

American Colorscans Inc ..... E 614 895-0233
Columbus *(G-5122)*

American Printing Inc ..... F 330 630-1121
Akron *(G-62)*

American Printing & Lithog Co ..... F 513 867-0602
Hamilton *(G-8177)*

Amsive OH LLC ..... D 937 885-8000
Miamisburg *(G-10611)*

Anderson Graphics Inc ..... E 330 745-2165
Barberton *(G-855)*

Andrin Enterprises Inc ..... F 937 276-7794
Moraine *(G-11157)*

◆ **Angstrom Graphics Inc** ..... C 216 271-5300
Cleveland *(G-3668)*

Angstrom Graphics Inc Midwest ..... C 216 271-5300
Cleveland *(G-3669)*

Anthony Business Forms Inc ..... G 937 253-0072
Dayton *(G-6153)*

Arens Corporation ..... G 937 473-2028
Covington *(G-6018)*

Arens Corporation ..... F 937 473-2028
Covington *(G-6017)*

Artco LLC ..... G 740 493-2901
Piketon *(G-12475)*

Artistic Photography Prtg Inc ..... G 813 310-6965
Bedford *(G-1102)*

Auld Corporation ..... G 614 454-1010
Columbus *(G-5165)*

Avon Lake Printing ..... G 440 933-2078
Avon Lake *(G-799)*

B & B Printing Graphics Inc ..... F 419 893-7068
Maumee *(G-10167)*

B R Printers Inc ..... D 513 271-6035
Cincinnati *(G-2652)*

Baesman Group Inc ..... D 614 771-2300
Hilliard *(G-8402)*

Bainbridge419 Inc ..... F 937 228-2181
Toledo *(G-14204)*

Banbury Investments Inc ..... G 513 677-4500
Cincinnati *(G-2655)*

Barnhart Printing Corp ..... F 330 456-2279
Canton *(G-2044)*

Bates Printing Inc ..... F 330 833-5830
Massillon *(G-10078)*

Bay Business Forms Inc ..... E 937 322-3000
Springfield *(G-13539)*

BCT Alarm Services Inc ..... G 440 669-8153
Lorain *(G-9402)*

Beach Company ..... E 740 622-0905
Coshocton *(G-5973)*

Beckman Xmo ..... F 614 864-2232
Columbus *(G-5178)*

Berea Printing Company ..... G 440 243-1080
Berea *(G-1268)*

Best Graphics & Printing Inc ..... G 513 535-3529
Cincinnati *(G-2668)*

Bethart Enterprises Inc ..... F 513 863-6161
Hamilton *(G-8185)*

Bindery & Spc Pressworks Inc ..... D 614 873-4623
Plain City *(G-12566)*

Bis Printing ..... G 440 951-2606
Willoughby *(G-15890)*

Bizzy Bee Printing Inc ..... G 614 771-1222
Columbus *(G-5192)*

Black River Group Inc ..... E 419 524-6699
Mansfield *(G-9628)*

Bloch Printing Company ..... G 330 576-6760
Copley *(G-5945)*

Blooms Printing Inc ..... F 740 922-1765
Dennison *(G-6793)*

Blue Crescent Enterprises Inc ..... G 440 878-9700
Strongsville *(G-13816)*

Bodnar Printing Co Inc ..... F 440 277-8295
Lorain *(G-9403)*

Bohlender Engraving Company ..... G 513 621-4095
Cincinnati *(G-2676)*

Bolger ..... G 440 979-9577
Cleveland *(G-3745)*

◆ **Bookmasters Inc** ..... C 419 281-1802
Ashland *(G-557)*

Bornhorst Printing Company Inc ..... G 419 738-5901
Wapakoneta *(G-15107)*

BP 10 Inc ..... E 513 346-3900
West Chester *(G-15382)*

Bramkamp Printing Company Inc ..... E 513 241-1865
Blue Ash *(G-1373)*

Brand Printer LLC ..... G 614 404-2615
Powell *(G-12664)*

Brandon Screen Printing ..... F 419 229-9837
Lima *(G-9224)*

Brass Bull 1 LLC ..... G 740 335-8030
Wshngtn Ct Hs *(G-16226)*

Brentwood Printing & Sty ..... G 513 522-2679
Cincinnati *(G-2680)*

Brothers Printing Co Inc ..... F 216 621-6050
Cleveland *(G-3764)*

Buckeye Business Forms Inc ..... G 614 882-1890
Westerville *(G-15649)*

Bucyrus Graphics Inc ..... F 419 562-2906
Bucyrus *(G-1851)*

Bush Inc ..... F 216 362-6700
Cleveland *(G-3775)*

C Massouh Printing Co Inc ..... F 330 408-7330
Canal Fulton *(G-1969)*

Capehart Enterprises LLC ..... F 614 769-7746
Columbus *(G-5230)*

Capitol Citicom Inc ..... E 614 472-2679
Columbus *(G-5234)*

Capitol Square Printing Inc ..... G 614 221-2850
Columbus *(G-5235)*

Carbon Web Print LLC ..... F 216 402-3504
Willoughby Hills *(G-16022)*

Carbonless On Demandcom LLC ..... F 330 837-8611
Massillon *(G-10082)*

Cardinal Printing Inc ..... G 330 773-7300
Akron *(G-99)*

Cardpak Incorporated ..... C 440 542-3100
Solon *(G-13326)*

Castle Printing Inc ..... G 740 439-2208
Cambridge *(G-1926)*

Cbp Co Inc ..... F 513 860-9053
Cincinnati *(G-2710)*

Century Graphics Inc ..... F 614 895-7698
Westerville *(G-15651)*

Charger Press Inc ..... G 513 542-3113
Miamitown *(G-10707)*

Cincinnati Convertors Inc ..... F 513 731-6600
Cincinnati *(G-2744)*

Cincinnati Print Solutions LLC ..... G 513 943-9500
Milford *(G-10900)*

City of Cleveland ..... E 216 664-3013
Cleveland *(G-3822)*

City Printing Co Inc ..... E 330 747-5691
Youngstown *(G-16337)*

Clancey Printing Inc ..... G 740 275-4070
Steubenville *(G-13665)*

Cleveland Letter Service Inc ..... G 216 781-8300
Chagrin Falls *(G-2371)*

Coachella Trotting & Prtg Ltd ..... G 614 326-1009
Columbus *(G-5258)*

Color Bar Printing Centers Inc ..... G 216 595-3939
Cleveland *(G-3883)*

Color Process Inc ..... E 440 268-7100
Strongsville *(G-13823)*

Coloramic Process Inc ..... F 440 275-1199
Austinburg *(G-743)*

Commercial Prtg Greenville Inc ..... G 937 548-3835
Greenville *(G-8043)*

▲ **Consoldated Graphics Group Inc** ..... C 216 881-9191
Cleveland *(G-3896)*

Consolidated Graphics Inc ..... C 740 654-2112
Lancaster *(G-9003)*

Copley Ohio Newspapers Inc ..... C 330 364-5577
New Philadelphia *(G-11493)*

Copy King Inc ..... E 216 861-3377
Cleveland *(G-3905)*

Corporate Dcment Solutions Inc ..... G 513 595-8200
Cincinnati *(G-2797)*

COS Blueprint Inc ..... E 330 376-0022
Akron *(G-115)*

County Classifieds ..... G 937 592-8847
Bellefontaine *(G-1203)*

Cox Printing Company ..... G 937 382-2312
Wilmington *(G-16046)*

Coyne Graphic Finishing Inc ..... E 740 397-6232
Mount Vernon *(G-11269)*

Cpmm Services Group Inc ..... E 614 447-0165
Columbus *(G-5304)*

Culaine Inc ..... G 419 345-4984
Toledo *(G-14254)*

Custom Graphics Inc ..... C 330 963-7770
Macedonia *(G-9543)*

Custom Imprint ..... F 440 238-4488
Strongsville *(G-13825)*

Custom Needle-Print LLC ..... G 330 432-5506
New Philadelphia *(G-11497)*

Cwh Graphics LLC ..... G 866 241-8515
Bedford Heights *(G-1169)*

D & J Printing Inc ..... B 330 678-5868
Kent *(G-8806)*

Daubenmires Printing Co LLC ..... G 513 425-7223
Middletown *(G-10817)*

David A and Mary A Mathis ..... G 330 837-8611
Massillon *(G-10089)*

◆ **Davis Printing Company** ..... E 330 745-3113
Barberton *(G-866)*

Dayton Legal Blank Inc ..... F 937 435-4405
Dayton *(G-6281)*

DC Printing LLC ..... G 937 640-1957
Dayton *(G-6294)*

DC Reprographics Co ..... F 614 297-1200
Columbus *(G-5319)*

Deerfield Ventures Inc ..... G 614 875-0688
Grove City *(G-8087)*

Delphos Herald Inc ..... D 419 695-0015
Delphos *(G-6760)*

Denny Printing LLC ..... G 417 825-4936
Grove City *(G-8088)*

Deshea Printing Company ..... G 330 336-7601
Wadsworth *(G-15026)*

Digital Color Intl LLC ..... F
Akron *(G-130)*

Direct Digital Graphics Inc ..... G 330 405-3770
Twinsburg *(G-14651)*

Directconnectgroup Ltd ..... F 216 281-2866
Cleveland *(G-3960)*

Distributor Graphics Inc ..... G 440 260-0024
Cleveland *(G-3963)*

Ditty Printing LLC ..... G 614 893-7439
Galena *(G-7853)*

Djsc Inc ..... E 740 928-2697
Hebron *(G-8340)*

S I C

Employee Codes: A=Over 500 employees, B=251-500
C=101-250, D=51-100, E=20-50, F=10-19, G=1-9

2024 Harris Ohio
Industrial Directory

789

27 PRINTING, PUBLISHING AND ALLIED INDUSTRIES

Dla Document Services.................. F 937 257-6014
Dayton (G-6159)

Docmann Printing & Assoc Inc........... G 440 975-1775
Solon (G-13338)

Document Concepts Inc................. E 330 575-5685
North Canton (G-11723)

Doll Inc............................... G 419 586-7880
Celina (G-2329)

▲ Dorn Color LLC....................... C 216 634-2252
Cleveland (G-3969)

Dr JS Print Shop Ltd.................. G 513 571-6553
Monroe (G-11105)

Dsk Imaging LLC....................... F 513 554-1797
Blue Ash (G-1386)

Duke Graphics Inc..................... E 440 946-0606
Willoughby (G-15911)

Duncan Press Corporation.............. F 330 477-4529
North Canton (G-11724)

Dupli-Systems Inc..................... C 440 234-9415
Strongsville (G-13830)

◆ Dynamic Design & Systems Inc.......... G 440 708-1010
Chagrin Falls (G-2393)

E Bee Printing Inc.................... G 614 224-0416
Columbus (G-5338)

E&O Fbn Inc........................... F 513 241-5150
Cincinnati (G-2851)

Eg Enterprise Services Inc............ F 216 431-3300
Cleveland (G-4001)

Electronic Printing Pdts Inc.......... E 800 882-4050
Stow (G-13694)

Empire Printing Inc................... G 513 242-3900
Fairfield (G-7356)

Engler Printing Co.................... G 419 332-2181
Fremont (G-7777)

Enlarging Arts Inc.................... G 330 434-3433
Akron (G-142)

Ennis Inc............................. E 800 537-8648
Toledo (G-14278)

Enquirer Printing Co Inc.............. F 513 241-1956
Cincinnati (G-2874)

Enquirer Printing Company............. G 513 241-1956
Cincinnati (G-2875)

Envoi Design Inc...................... G 513 651-4229
Cincinnati (G-2877)

▲ Etched Metal Company................. E 440 248-0240
Solon (G-13347)

Eugene Stewart........................ G 937 898-1117
Dayton (G-6325)

▲ Eurostampa North America Inc......... C 513 821-2275
Cincinnati (G-2885)

Eveready Printing Inc................. E 216 587-2389
Cleveland (G-4038)

Evolution Crtive Solutions Inc........ E 513 681-4450
Cincinnati (G-2888)

Excelsior Printing Co................. G 740 927-2934
Pataskala (G-12297)

Express Grphics Prtg Dsign Inc........ G 513 728-3344
Cincinnati (G-2892)

Fair Publishing House Inc............. E 419 668-3746
Norwalk (G-11967)

Far Corner............................ G 330 767-3734
Navarre (G-11341)

Fgs-Wi LLC............................ E 630 375-8597
Newark (G-11576)

▲ Fine Line Graphics Corp.............. C 614 486-0276
Columbus (G-5375)

Finn Graphics Inc..................... E 513 941-6161
Cincinnati (G-2905)

Fleet Graphics Inc.................... G 937 252-2552
Dayton (G-6335)

Folks Creative Printers Inc........... F 740 383-6465
Marion (G-9852)

Follow Print Club On Facebook......... G 216 707-2579
Cleveland (G-4077)

Foote Printing Company Inc............ F 216 431-1757
Cleveland (G-4079)

Frame Warehouse....................... G 614 861-4582
Reynoldsburg (G-12765)

Franklin Printing Company............. F 740 452-6375
Zanesville (G-16533)

Freeport Press Inc.................... C 330 308-3300
New Philadelphia (G-11503)

Fremont Printing Inc.................. F 480 272-3443
Fremont (G-7784)

Friends Service Co Inc................ F 800 427-1704
Dayton (G-6339)

Friends Service Co Inc................ D 419 427-1704
Findlay (G-7512)

Frisby Printing Company............... F 330 665-4565
Fairlawn (G-7439)

Fully Involved Printing Co LLC........ G 440 635-6858
Mentor (G-10460)

Fx Digital Media Inc.................. G 216 241-4040
Cleveland (G-4094)

Galley Printing Inc................... E 330 220-5577
Brunswick (G-1763)

Gannett Stllite Info Ntwrk LLC........ E 419 334-1012
Fremont (G-7785)

Gaspar Services LLC................... G 330 467-8292
Macedonia (G-9554)

Gb Liquidating Company Inc............ E 513 248-7600
Milford (G-10907)

GBS Corp.............................. C 330 863-1828
Malvern (G-9612)

Genie Repros Inc...................... F 216 696-6677
Cleveland (G-4119)

Gerald L Herrmann Company Inc......... F 513 661-1818
Cincinnati (G-2949)

Gergel-Kellem Company Inc............. D 216 398-2000
Olmsted Falls (G-12080)

Geygan Enterprises Inc................ F 513 932-4222
Lebanon (G-9082)

Gli Holdings Inc...................... D 440 892-7760
Stow (G-13700)

▲ Gli Holdings Inc..................... D 216 651-1500
Stow (G-13701)

Globus Printing & Packg Co Inc........ D 419 628-2381
Minster (G-11053)

▲ Golf Marketing Group Inc............. G 330 963-5155
Twinsburg (G-14669)

Gordons Graphics Inc.................. G 330 863-2322
Malvern (G-9613)

Gorilla Joe Printing Co LLC........... G 234 719-1861
Youngstown (G-16372)

Graphic Info Systems Inc.............. F 513 948-1300
Mason (G-9999)

Graphic Paper Products Corp........... D 937 325-5503
Springfield (G-13570)

Graphic Print Solutions Inc........... G 513 948-3344
Cincinnati (G-2969)

Graphic Village LLC................... C 513 241-1865
Blue Ash (G-1399)

Graphix Network....................... G 740 941-3771
Waverly (G-15282)

Graphtech Communications Inc.......... F 216 676-1020
Brunswick (G-1766)

Great Lakes Printing Inc.............. F 440 993-8781
Ashtabula (G-636)

Greenwood Prtg & Graphics Inc......... G 419 727-3275
Toledo (G-14303)

Greg Blume............................ G 740 574-2308
Wheelersburg (G-15809)

Gtlp Holdings LLC..................... E 513 489-6700
Cincinnati (G-2977)

▲ Haman Enterprises Inc................ F 614 888-7574
Columbus (G-5417)

Harper Engraving & Printing Co........ D 614 276-0700
Columbus (G-5420)

Hartco Printing Company............... G 614 761-1292
Dublin (G-6890)

Hartmann Inc.......................... G 513 276-7318
Blue Ash (G-1403)

Hawks & Associates Inc................ E 513 752-4311
Cincinnati (G-2563)

Headlee Enterprises Ltd............... G 614 785-1476
Columbus (G-5063)

Hecks Direct Mail & Prtg Svc.......... E 419 661-6028
Toledo (G-14314)

▲ Hecks Direct Mail Prtg Svc Inc....... F 419 697-3505
Toledo (G-14315)

Heeter Printing Company Inc........... E 440 946-0606
Eastlake (G-7034)

Herald Inc............................ E 419 492-2133
New Washington (G-11547)

Heskamp Printing Co Inc............... E 513 871-6770
Cincinnati (G-2997)

Hi-Point Graphics LLC................. G 937 407-6524
Bellefontaine (G-1211)

Highland Computer Forms Inc........... D 937 393-4215
Hillsboro (G-8459)

Hilltop Printing...................... G 419 782-9898
Defiance (G-6681)

Hkm Drect Mkt Cmmnications Inc........ C 800 860-4456
Cleveland (G-4193)

Holmes Printing Solutions LLC......... F 330 234-9699
Fredericksburg (G-7724)

Holmes W & Sons Printing.............. F 937 325-1509
Springfield (G-13577)

Horizon Ohio Publications Inc......... D 419 738-2128
Wapakoneta (G-15117)

Hoster Graphics Company Inc........... F 614 299-9770
Columbus (G-5446)

HOT Graphic Services Inc.............. E 419 242-7000
Northwood (G-11920)

Howland Printing Inc.................. G 330 637-8255
Cortland (G-5964)

Howling Print and Promo Inc........... G 440 363-4999
Chardon (G-2452)

HP Acquisition II LLC................. F 216 241-4040
Chagrin Falls (G-2379)

HP Industries Inc..................... E 419 478-0695
Toledo (G-14322)

Hubbard Company....................... E 419 784-4455
Defiance (G-6682)

Hubbard Publishing Co................. E 937 592-3060
Bellefontaine (G-1212)

Hyde Brothers Prtg & Mktg LLC......... G 740 373-2054
Marietta (G-9801)

▼ ICM Distributing Company Inc......... E 234 212-3030
Twinsburg (G-14675)

Identity Group LLC.................... G 614 337-6167
Westerville (G-15658)

Image Concepts Inc.................... F 216 524-9000
Cleveland (G-4215)

Image Print Inc....................... G 614 776-3985
Westerville (G-15709)

Imprint LLC........................... G 216 233-0066
Cleveland (G-4221)

Inkscape Print and Promos LLC......... F 330 893-0160
Millersburg (G-10970)

Innmark Communications LLC............ C 937 454-5555
Miamisburg (G-10648)

Innovative Graphics Ltd............... F 877 406-3636
Columbus (G-5461)

Inskeep Brothers Inc.................. F 614 898-6620
Columbus (G-5462)

27 PRINTING, PUBLISHING AND ALLIED INDUSTRIES

Instant Graphications Inc .... G 330 819-5267
   Akron *(G-191)*

Instant Replay Ltd .... G 937 592-0534
   Bellefontaine *(G-1214)*

Instant Surface Solutions Inc .... G 513 266-1667
   Cincinnati *(G-2566)*

Irwin Engraving & Printing Co .... G 216 391-7300
   Cleveland *(G-4238)*

Isaac Foster Mack Co .... C 419 625-5500
   Sandusky *(G-13067)*

J & J Bechke Inc .... G 440 238-1441
   Strongsville *(G-13847)*

J & L Management Corporation .... G 440 205-1199
   Mentor *(G-10478)*

J Solutions LLC .... G 614 732-4857
   Columbus *(G-5484)*

▲ Jack Walker Printing Co .... F 440 352-4222
   Mentor *(G-10481)*

Jakprints Inc .... C 877 246-3132
   Cleveland *(G-4249)*

Jakprints Inc .... G 216 246-3132
   Willowick *(G-16032)*

Jay Tees LLC .... E 740 405-1579
   Thornville *(G-14066)*

Jbnovember LLC .... E 513 272-7000
   Cincinnati *(G-3038)*

Jk Digital Publishing LLC .... F 937 299-0185
   Springboro *(G-13506)*

Joe The Printer Guy LLC .... G 216 651-3880
   Lakewood *(G-8977)*

Jos Berning Printing Co .... F 513 721-0781
   Cincinnati *(G-3051)*

Jt Premier Printing Corp .... F 216 831-8785
   Cleveland *(G-4266)*

Kahny Printing Inc .... E 513 251-2911
   Cincinnati *(G-3057)*

Kay Toledo Tag Inc .... D 419 729-5479
   Toledo *(G-14346)*

Keener Printing Inc .... F 216 531-7595
   Cleveland *(G-4280)*

▲ Kehl-Kolor Inc .... E 419 281-3107
   Ashland *(G-585)*

Kem Advertising and Prtg LLC .... G 330 818-5061
   Barberton *(G-876)*

Kenwel Printers Inc .... E 614 261-1011
   Columbus *(G-5508)*

Kevin K Tidd .... G 419 885-5603
   Sylvania *(G-14003)*

Key Maneuvers Inc .... G 440 285-0774
   Chardon *(G-2454)*

Keystone Press Inc .... G 419 243-7326
   Toledo *(G-14347)*

Kimpton Printing & Spc Co .... F 330 467-1640
   Macedonia *(G-9561)*

Kinkos Inc .... F 216 661-9950
   Cleveland *(G-4291)*

Klingstedt Brothers Company .... F 330 456-8319
   Canton *(G-2140)*

KMS 2000 Inc .... F 330 454-9444
   Canton *(G-2141)*

▲ Kramer Graphics Inc .... E 937 296-9600
   Moraine *(G-11188)*

▼ Krehbiel Holdings Inc .... D
   Cincinnati *(G-3089)*

Krieg Rev 2 Inc .... E 513 542-1522
   Cincinnati *(G-3090)*

L & T Collins Inc .... G 740 345-4494
   Newark *(G-11586)*

Lahlouh Inc .... G 650 692-6600
   Monroe *(G-11115)*

Lake Shore Graphic Inds Inc .... F 419 626-8631
   Sandusky *(G-13073)*

Larmax Inc .... G 513 984-0783
   Blue Ash *(G-1419)*

Laurenee Ltd .... G 513 662-2225
   Cincinnati *(G-3097)*

Lba Custom Printing .... G 419 535-3151
   Toledo *(G-14359)*

LBL Lithographers Inc .... G 440 350-0106
   Painesville *(G-12247)*

Lee Corporation .... G 513 771-3602
   Cincinnati *(G-3099)*

Legalcraft Inc .... F 330 494-1261
   Canton *(G-2145)*

Lesher Printers Inc .... F 419 332-8253
   Fremont *(G-7794)*

Letterman Printing Inc .... G 513 523-1111
   Oxford *(G-12210)*

Lilienthal/Southeastern Inc .... G 740 439-1640
   Cambridge *(G-1940)*

Litho-Print Ltd .... F 937 222-4351
   Dayton *(G-6413)*

Little Printing Company .... F 937 773-4595
   Piqua *(G-12532)*

Liturgical Publications Inc .... D 216 325-6825
   Cleveland *(G-4332)*

Loving Choice Adoption-Prntng .... G 330 994-1451
   Canton *(G-2146)*

Lsc Communications Inc .... A 419 935-0111
   Willard *(G-15860)*

LSc Service Corp .... G 440 331-1359
   Cleveland *(G-4337)*

Lyle Printing & Publishing Co .... E 330 337-3419
   Salem *(G-13013)*

M Rosenthal Company .... F 513 563-0081
   Cincinnati *(G-3120)*

Malik Media LLC .... F 614 933-0328
   New Albany *(G-11383)*

Mansfield Journal Co .... C 330 364-8641
   New Philadelphia *(G-11513)*

Marbee Inc .... G 419 422-9441
   Findlay *(G-7535)*

Marco Printed Products Co .... G 937 433-7030
   Dayton *(G-6430)*

Mariotti Printing Co LLC .... G 440 245-4120
   Lorain *(G-9424)*

Mark Advertising Agency Inc .... F 419 626-9000
   Sandusky *(G-13079)*

Master Printing Group Inc .... F 216 351-2246
   Berea *(G-1287)*

Mathews Printing Company .... F 614 444-1010
   Columbus *(G-5546)*

Mbas Printing Inc .... G 513 489-3000
   Blue Ash *(G-1432)*

◆ McNerney & Associates LLC .... E 513 241-9951
   West Chester *(G-15570)*

Mercer Color Corporation .... G 419 678-8273
   Coldwater *(G-4998)*

Meridian Arts and Graphics .... F 330 759-9099
   Youngstown *(G-16398)*

Messenger Publishing Company .... C 740 592-6612
   Athens *(G-688)*

Metzgers .... D 419 861-8611
   Toledo *(G-14383)*

Meyers Printing & Design Inc .... F 937 461-6000
   Dayton *(G-6437)*

Miami Valley Publishing LLC .... C 937 879-5678
   Fairborn *(G-7319)*

Middaugh Enterprises Inc .... G 330 852-2471
   Sugarcreek *(G-13930)*

Middleton Printing Co Inc .... G 614 294-7277
   Gahanna *(G-7845)*

Milford Printers .... E 513 831-6630
   Milford *(G-10914)*

Millennium Printing LLC .... G 513 489-3000
   Blue Ash *(G-1440)*

Minuteman Press .... G 937 701-7100
   Dayton *(G-6452)*

Minuteman Press .... G 513 454-7318
   Hamilton *(G-8229)*

Minuteman Press .... F 937 451-8222
   Piqua *(G-12537)*

Minuteman Press Inc .... F 513 741-9056
   Cincinnati *(G-3166)*

Mj Bornhorst Enterprises LLC .... F 937 295-3469
   Fort Loramie *(G-7604)*

Mmp Printing Inc .... E 513 381-0990
   Cincinnati *(G-3168)*

Mmp Toledo .... F 419 472-0505
   Toledo *(G-14388)*

Monks Copy Shop Inc .... F 614 461-6438
   Columbus *(G-5579)*

Morse Enterprises Inc .... G 513 229-3600
   Mason *(G-10031)*

Mound Printing Company Inc .... E 937 866-2872
   Miamisburg *(G-10664)*

Muir Graphics Inc .... G 419 882-7993
   Sylvania *(G-14007)*

Multi-Color Australia LLC .... D 513 381-1480
   Batavia *(G-938)*

Multi-Craft Litho Inc .... E 859 581-2754
   Blue Ash *(G-1442)*

Murr Corporation .... F 330 264-2223
   Wooster *(G-16154)*

Network Printing & Graphics .... F 614 230-2084
   Columbus *(G-5593)*

Newmast Mktg & Communications .... G 614 837-1200
   Columbus *(G-5597)*

News Gazette Printing Company .... F 419 227-2527
   Lima *(G-9274)*

North Coast Litho Inc .... E 216 881-1952
   Cleveland *(G-4470)*

North Shore Printing LLC .... G 740 876-9066
   Portsmouth *(G-12651)*

North Toledo Graphics LLC .... D 419 476-8808
   Toledo *(G-14398)*

Northcoast Pmm LLC .... F 419 540-8667
   Toledo *(G-14399)*

Northeast Blueprint and Sup Co .... G 216 261-7500
   Cleveland *(G-4475)*

◆ Novelty Advertising Co Inc .... E 740 622-3113
   Coshocton *(G-5988)*

Nta Graphics Inc .... E 419 476-8808
   Toledo *(G-14401)*

O Connor Office Pdts & Prtg .... G 740 852-2209
   London *(G-9392)*

Odyssey Press Inc .... F 614 410-0356
   Huron *(G-8642)*

▲ Ohio Art Company .... D 419 636-3141
   Bryan *(G-1833)*

Ohio Esc Print Shop .... G 419 774-2512
   Ontario *(G-12092)*

Old Trail Printing Company .... C 614 443-4852
   Columbus *(G-5636)*

Oliver Printing & Packg Co LLC .... D 330 425-7890
   Twinsburg *(G-14703)*

Onetouchpoint East Corp .... D 513 421-1600
   Cincinnati *(G-3225)*

Optimum System Products Inc .... E 614 885-4464
   Westerville *(G-15718)*

Orange Blossom Press Inc .... G 216 781-8655
   Willoughby *(G-15966)*

Oregon Vlg Print Shoppe Inc .... F 937 222-9418
   Dayton *(G-6494)*

Orwell Printing .... G 440 285-2233
   Chardon *(G-2462)*

Employee Codes: A=Over 500 employees, B=251-500
C=101-250, D=51-100, E=20-50, F=10-19, G=1-9

27 PRINTING, PUBLISHING AND ALLIED INDUSTRIES

Ovp Inc .... G 740 423-5171
  Belpre *(G-1259)*
Page One Group .... G 740 397-4240
  Mount Vernon *(G-11286)*
Painesville Publishing Inc .... G 440 354-4142
  Austinburg *(G-748)*
Painted Hill Inv Group Inc .... F 937 339-1756
  Troy *(G-14600)*
Pamton 3d Printing LLC .... G 330 792-5503
  Youngstown *(G-16411)*
▲ Paragraphics Inc .... E 330 493-1074
  Canton *(G-2191)*
Park Press Direct .... G 419 626-4426
  Sandusky *(G-13086)*
Payday 124 Inc .... D 614 509-1080
  Columbus *(G-5662)*
PDQ Printing Service .... F 216 241-5443
  Westlake *(G-15772)*
Peerless Printing Company .... F 513 721-4657
  Cincinnati *(G-3245)*
Pen-Ann Corporation .... G 740 373-2054
  Marietta *(G-9816)*
Penguin Enterprises Inc .... E 440 899-5112
  Westlake *(G-15773)*
Perfection Printing .... F 513 874-2173
  Fairfield *(G-7394)*
Perrons Printing Company .... F 440 236-8870
  Columbia Station *(G-5016)*
Persistence of Vision Inc .... G 440 591-5443
  Chagrin Falls *(G-2415)*
Phil Vedda & Sons Inc .... G 216 671-2222
  Cleveland *(G-4546)*
Phoenix Grphics Communications .... G 330 697-4171
  Munroe Falls *(G-11304)*
Pinnacle Press Inc .... F 330 453-7060
  Canton *(G-2197)*
PIP Printing .... G 513 245-0590
  Cincinnati *(G-3257)*
PM Graphics Inc .... E 330 650-0861
  Streetsboro *(G-13785)*
Porath Business Services Inc .... F 216 626-0060
  Cleveland *(G-4564)*
Post Printing Co .... D 859 254-7714
  Minster *(G-11058)*
Precious Mmories Cstm Prtg Inc .... F 216 721-3909
  Cleveland *(G-4571)*
Preferred Printing .... G 937 492-6961
  Sidney *(G-13273)*
Preisser Inc .... E 614 345-0199
  Columbus *(G-5688)*
Premier Printing Corporation .... F 216 478-9720
  Cleveland *(G-4582)*
Premier Prtg Centl Ohio Ltd .... E 937 642-0988
  Marysville *(G-9932)*
Prime Printing Inc .... E 937 438-3707
  Dayton *(G-6522)*
Print Centers of Ohio Inc .... F 419 526-4139
  Mansfield *(G-9711)*
▼ Print Direct For Less 2 Inc .... F 440 236-8870
  Columbia Station *(G-5018)*
Print Factory PII .... G 330 549-9640
  North Lima *(G-11810)*
▲ Print Marketing Inc .... G 330 625-1500
  Homerville *(G-8553)*
Print Shop of Canton Inc .... F 330 497-3212
  Canton *(G-2202)*
Print Syndicate Inc .... E 617 290-9550
  Columbus *(G-5691)*
Print Syndicate LLC .... F 614 519-0341
  Columbus *(G-5692)*
Print-Digital Incorporated .... G 330 686-5945
  Stow *(G-13718)*

Printers Devil Inc .... E 330 650-1218
  Hudson *(G-8608)*
▲ Printers Edge Inc .... F 330 372-2232
  Warren *(G-15200)*
Printex Incorporated .... F 740 773-0088
  Chillicothe *(G-2529)*
Printing Arts Press Inc .... F 740 397-6106
  Mount Vernon *(G-11289)*
Printing Connection Inc .... G 216 898-4878
  Brookpark *(G-1723)*
Printing Dimensions Inc .... F 937 256-0044
  Dayton *(G-6523)*
Printing Express .... G 937 276-7794
  Moraine *(G-11203)*
Printing Express Inc .... G 740 533-9217
  Ironton *(G-8701)*
Printing Resources Inc .... G 216 881-7660
  Cleveland *(G-4588)*
Printing Service Company .... D 937 425-6100
  Miamisburg *(G-10872)*
Printing Services .... F 440 708-1999
  Chagrin Falls *(G-2417)*
Printing System Inc .... F 330 375-9128
  Twinsburg *(G-14718)*
Printpoint Inc .... G 937 223-9041
  Dayton *(G-6524)*
Pro-Decal Inc .... G 330 484-0089
  Canton *(G-2203)*
Professional Screen Printing .... G 740 687-0760
  Lancaster *(G-9033)*
Proforma Prana .... G 440 345-6466
  Wickliffe *(G-15850)*
Program Managers Inc .... G 937 431-1982
  Beavercreek *(G-1078)*
Progressive Printers Inc .... D 937 222-1267
  Dayton *(G-6533)*
Progrssive Communications Corp .... D 740 397-5333
  Mount Vernon *(G-11290)*
Promatch Solutions LLC .... F 877 299-0185
  Moraine *(G-11205)*
Quebecor World Johnson Hardin .... E 614 326-0299
  Cincinnati *(G-3314)*
Queen City Reprographics .... C 513 326-2300
  Cincinnati *(G-3319)*
Quez Media Marketing Inc .... F 216 910-0202
  Independence *(G-8683)*
Quick As A Wink Printing Co .... G 419 224-9786
  Lima *(G-9281)*
▼ Quick Tab II Inc .... D 419 448-6622
  Tiffin *(G-14101)*
Quick Tech Graphics Inc .... F 937 743-5952
  Springboro *(G-13518)*
R & J Bardon Inc .... G 614 457-5500
  Columbus *(G-5705)*
R & J Printing Enterprises Inc .... F 330 343-1242
  Stow *(G-13719)*
R R Donnelley & Sons Company .... D 440 774-2101
  Oberlin *(G-12055)*
R R Donnelley & Sons Company .... D 330 562-5250
  Streetsboro *(G-13786)*
R&D Marketing Group Inc .... G 216 398-9100
  Brooklyn Heights *(G-1697)*
Randd Assoc Prtg & Promotions .... G 937 294-1874
  Dayton *(G-6541)*
Rba Inc .... G 330 336-6700
  Wadsworth *(G-15062)*
Record Herald Publishing Co .... E 717 762-2151
  Cincinnati *(G-3327)*
Reliable Printing Solutions .... G 937 486-5031
  Wilmington *(G-16058)*
▲ Repro Acquisition Company LLC .... F 216 738-3800
  Cleveland *(G-4626)*

Resilient Holdings Inc .... F 614 847-5600
  Columbus *(G-5718)*
Reynolds and Reynolds Company .... F 419 584-7000
  Celina *(G-2346)*
Rhoads Print Center Inc .... G 330 678-2042
  Tallmadge *(G-14045)*
▲ Richardson Printing Corp .... D 800 848-9752
  Marietta *(G-9820)*
RI Smith Graphics LLC .... G 330 629-8616
  Youngstown *(G-16428)*
Robert Becker Impressions Inc .... F 419 385-5303
  Toledo *(G-14456)*
Robin Enterprises Company .... C 614 891-0250
  Westerville *(G-15719)*
Ron Toelke .... G 513 598-1881
  Cincinnati *(G-3350)*
Rotary Forms Press Inc .... E 937 393-3426
  Hillsboro *(G-8465)*
RPI Color Service Inc .... D 513 471-4040
  Cincinnati *(G-3353)*
RS Imprints LLC .... G 330 872-5905
  Newton Falls *(G-11656)*
S Beckman Print Grphic Sltons .... E 614 864-2232
  Columbus *(G-5736)*
Schilling Graphics Inc .... E 419 468-1037
  Galion *(G-7884)*
Schlabach Printers LLC .... E 330 852-4687
  Sugarcreek *(G-13937)*
Schuerholz Inc .... G 937 294-5218
  Dayton *(G-6561)*
Scorecards Unlimited LLC .... G 614 885-0796
  Columbus *(G-5755)*
Scott Francis Antique Prints .... G 216 737-0873
  Cleveland *(G-4679)*
Scratch Off Works LLC .... G 440 333-4302
  Rocky River *(G-12843)*
Sdg News Group Inc .... F 419 929-3411
  New London *(G-11468)*
Sdo Sports Ltd .... G 440 546-9998
  Cleveland *(G-4683)*
Seemless Printing LLC .... G 513 871-2366
  Cincinnati *(G-3375)*
Sekuworks LLC .... E 513 202-1210
  Harrison *(G-8290)*
Selby Service/Roxy Press Inc .... G 513 241-3445
  Cincinnati *(G-3378)*
Seneca Enterprises Inc .... F 814 432-7890
  Batavia *(G-948)*
▲ Sensical Inc .... D 216 641-1141
  Solon *(G-13420)*
Sfc Graphics Cleveland Ltd .... E 419 255-1283
  Toledo *(G-14469)*
Shamrock Printing LLC .... G 740 349-2244
  Newark *(G-11605)*
Sharp Enterprises Inc .... F 937 295-2965
  Fort Loramie *(G-7609)*
▲ Shawnee Systems Inc .... D 513 561-9932
  Cincinnati *(G-3387)*
Shelby Printing Partners LLC .... F 419 342-3171
  Shelby *(G-13201)*
Shout Out Loud Prints .... G 614 432-8990
  Columbus *(G-5765)*
Shreve Printing LLC .... F 330 567-2341
  Shreve *(G-13215)*
Skladany Enterprises Inc .... G 614 823-6882
  Westerville *(G-15679)*
Slimans Printery Inc .... F 330 454-9141
  Canton *(G-2226)*
◆ SMI Holdings Inc .... D 740 927-3464
  Pataskala *(G-12309)*
Snow Printing Co Inc .... F 419 229-7669
  Lima *(G-9290)*

Company	Code	Phone
Soondook LLC	E	614 389-5757
Columbus (G-5779)		
◆ Source3media Inc	E	330 467-9003
Macedonia (G-9575)		
Southern Ohio Printing	G	513 241-5150
Cincinnati (G-3404)		
SP Mount Printing Company	E	216 881-3316
Cleveland (G-4718)		
SPAOS Inc	G	937 890-0783
Dayton (G-6580)		
Specialty Lithographing Co	F	513 621-0222
Cincinnati (G-3405)		
Springdot Inc	D	513 542-4000
Cincinnati (G-3411)		
Sprint Print Inc	G	740 622-4429
Coshocton (G-5997)		
Standard Printing Co of Canton	D	330 453-8247
Canton (G-2230)		
Star Printing Company Inc	E	330 376-0514
Akron (G-336)		
Starr Services Inc	G	513 241-7708
Cincinnati (G-3417)		
Start Printing Co LLC	G	513 424-2121
Middletown (G-10859)		
Stein-Palmer Printing Co	G	740 633-3894
Saint Clairsville (G-12925)		
Stephen Andrews Inc	G	330 725-2672
Lodi (G-9357)		
Stepping Stone Enterprises Inc	F	419 472-0505
Maumee (G-10235)		
Stevenson Color Inc	C	513 321-7500
Cincinnati (G-3422)		
Suburban Press Incorporated	E	216 961-0766
Cleveland (G-4744)		
Superior Impressions Inc	G	419 244-8676
Toledo (G-14477)		
Swimmer Printing Inc	G	216 623-1005
Cleveland (G-4761)		
T D Dynamics Inc	F	216 881-0800
Cleveland (G-4765)		
Taylor Communications Inc	F	614 351-6868
Columbus (G-5812)		
Taylor Communications Inc	E	937 221-1000
Dayton (G-6609)		
Taylor Quick Print	G	740 439-2208
Cambridge (G-1957)		
Tecnocap LLC	C	330 392-7222
Warren (G-15208)		
The Gazette Printing Co Inc	G	440 593-6030
Conneaut (G-5934)		
Theb Inc	G	216 391-4800
Cleveland (G-4790)		
Tiny Footprints Daycare LLC	G	216 938-7306
Cleveland (G-4797)		
Tj Metzgers Inc	D	419 861-8611
Toledo (G-14487)		
Tkm Print Solutions Inc	F	330 237-4029
Uniontown (G-14795)		
Toledo Ticket Company	E	419 476-5424
Toledo (G-14506)		
Tomahawk Printing Inc	F	419 335-3161
Wauseon (G-15274)		
Tope Printing Inc	G	330 674-4993
Millersburg (G-11000)		
▲ Tpl Holdings LLC	E	800 475-4030
Mogadore (G-11088)		
Tradewinds Prin Twear	G	740 214-5005
Roseville (G-12860)		
◆ Transfer Express Inc	D	440 918-1900
Mentor (G-10581)		
Traxium LLC	E	330 572-8200
Stow (G-13732)		
Traxler Printing	G	614 593-1270
Columbus (G-5833)		
◆ Trebnick Systems Inc	E	937 743-1550
Springboro (G-13524)		
Tri-State Publishing Company	E	740 283-3686
Steubenville (G-13679)		
Tribune Printing Inc	G	419 542-7764
Hicksville (G-8382)		
Truax Printing Inc	E	419 994-4166
Loudonville (G-9452)		
True Dinero Records & Tech LLC	G	513 428-4610
Cincinnati (G-3470)		
Tucker Printers Inc	D	585 359-3030
West Chester (G-15520)		
Ultimate Printing Co Inc	G	330 847-2941
Warren (G-15213)		
▼ United Trade Printers LLC	E	614 326-4829
Dublin (G-6955)		
UPS Store	G	419 289-6688
Ashland (G-619)		
USA Quickprint Inc	F	330 455-5119
Canton (G-2259)		
V & C Enterprises Co	G	614 221-1412
Columbus (G-5853)		
◆ Vectra Inc	C	614 351-6868
Columbus (G-5855)		
Victory Direct LLC	G	614 626-0000
Gahanna (G-7852)		
Vision Graphix Inc	G	440 835-6540
Westlake (G-15800)		
Vision Press Inc	G	440 357-6362
Painesville (G-12275)		
Visual Art Graphic Services	G	330 274-2775
Mantua (G-9745)		
Visual Marking Systems Inc	D	330 425-7100
Twinsburg (G-14753)		
Vpp Industries Inc	F	937 526-3775
Versailles (G-14991)		
Vya Inc	E	513 772-5400
Cincinnati (G-3506)		
Warren Printing & Off Pdts Inc	F	419 523-3635
Ottawa (G-12196)		
Watkins Printing Company	G	614 297-8270
Columbus (G-5867)		
Welch Publishing Co	E	419 874-2528
Perrysburg (G-12444)		
Wernet Inc	G	330 452-2200
Canton (G-2266)		
West Bend Printing & Pubg Inc	G	419 258-2000
Antwerp (G-494)		
West-Camp Press Inc	E	614 895-0233
Columbus (G-5872)		
▲ West-Camp Press Inc	D	614 882-2378
Westerville (G-15725)		
Western Ohio Graphics	F	937 335-8769
Troy (G-14616)		
Westrock Commercial LLC	D	419 476-9101
Toledo (G-14523)		
▲ Wfsr Holdings LLC	A	877 735-4966
Dayton (G-6654)		
White Tiger Inc	F	740 852-4873
London (G-9397)		
Wicked Premiums LLC	G	216 364-0322
Brecksville (G-1637)		
William J Bergen & Co	G	440 248-6132
Solon (G-13448)		
Willoughby Printing Co Inc	G	440 946-0800
Willoughby (G-16017)		
▲ Wis 1985 Inc	F	423 581-4916
Dayton (G-6657)		
Woodrow Manufacturing Co	E	937 399-9333
Springfield (G-13657)		
Wooster Printing & Litho Inc	E	
Wooster (G-16185)		
◆ Workflowone LLC	A	877 735-4966
Dayton (G-6661)		
Xenia Daily Gazette	E	937 372-4444
Xenia (G-16281)		
Yespress Graphics LLC	G	614 899-1403
Westerville (G-15726)		
Youngstown ARC Engraving Co	G	330 793-2471
Youngstown (G-16476)		
Youngstown Letter Shop Inc	G	330 793-4935
Youngstown (G-16484)		
Youngstown Pre-Press Inc	F	330 793-3690
Youngstown (G-16486)		
Zip Publishing	G	614 485-0721
Columbus (G-5893)		
Zippitycom Print LLC	F	216 438-0001
Cleveland (G-4935)		

2754 Commercial printing, gravure

Company	Code	Phone
◆ Angstrom Graphics Inc	C	216 271-5300
Cleveland (G-3668)		
Anthony Business Forms Inc	G	937 253-0072
Dayton (G-6153)		
Brook & Whittle Limited	E	513 860-2457
Hamilton (G-8187)		
Cham Cor Industries Inc	G	740 967-9015
Johnstown (G-8772)		
Dupli-Systems Inc	C	440 234-9415
Strongsville (G-13830)		
E-Z Stop Service Center	G	330 448-2236
Brookfield (G-1668)		
Fx Digital Media Inc	F	216 241-4040
Cleveland (G-4095)		
Graphic Paper Products Corp	D	937 325-5503
Springfield (G-13570)		
Kenyetta Bagby Enterprise LLC	F	614 584-3426
Reynoldsburg (G-12768)		
Klingstedt Brothers Company	F	330 456-8319
Canton (G-2140)		
Lloyd F Helber	G	740 756-9607
Carroll (G-2299)		
M PI Label Systems	G	330 938-2134
Sebring (G-13121)		
Mpi Labels of Baltimore Inc	E	330 938-2134
Sebring (G-13124)		
Multi-Color Australia LLC	D	513 381-1480
Batavia (G-938)		
Ohio Envelope Manufacturing Co	E	216 267-2920
Cleveland (G-4497)		
▲ Ohio Gravure Technologies Inc	F	937 439-1582
Miamisburg (G-10668)		
▼ Pioneer Labels Inc	C	618 546-5418
West Chester (G-15479)		
Retterbush Graphics Packg Corp	F	513 779-4466
West Chester (G-15498)		
Sekuworks LLC	E	513 202-1210
Harrison (G-8290)		
▲ Shamrock Companies Inc	D	440 899-9510
Westlake (G-15786)		
The Photo-Type Engraving Company	D	513 281-0999
Cincinnati (G-3450)		
Western Roto Engravers Inc	E	330 336-7636
Wadsworth (G-15072)		
▲ Wfsr Holdings LLC	A	877 735-4966
Dayton (G-6654)		
◆ Workflowone LLC	A	877 735-4966
Dayton (G-6661)		

2759 Commercial printing, nec

Company	Code	Phone
1st Impressions Plus LLC	G	330 696-7605
Akron (G-9)		

Employee Codes: A=Over 500 employees, B=251-500
C=101-250, D=51-100, E=20-50, F=10-19, G=1-9

27 PRINTING, PUBLISHING AND ALLIED INDUSTRIES

4 Over LLC .... E 937 610-0629
  Dayton (G-6177)
44stronger LLC .... G 440 371-6455
  Grafton (G-7996)
4d Screenprinting Ltd .... G 513 353-1070
  Cleves (G-4945)
A C Hadley - Printing Inc .... G 937 426-0952
  Beavercreek (G-1037)
A E Wilson Holdings Inc .... G 330 405-0316
  Twinsburg (G-14621)
A To Z Paper Box Company .... G 330 325-8722
  Rootstown (G-12850)
A-A Blueprint Co Inc .... E 330 794-8803
  Akron (G-11)
Aardvark Screen Prtg & EMB LLC .... F 419 354-6686
  Bowling Green (G-1548)
Ableprint / Toucan Inc .... F 419 522-9742
  Mansfield (G-9621)
Absolute Impressions Inc .... F 614 840-0599
  Lewis Center (G-9146)
Ace Transfer Company .... G 937 398-1103
  Springfield (G-13528)
Acme Printing Co Inc .... G 419 626-4426
  Sandusky (G-13041)
Ad-Sensations Inc .... F 419 841-5395
  Sylvania (G-13989)
Adcraft Decals Incorporated .... E 216 524-2934
  Cleveland (G-3598)
Advanced Incentives Inc .... G 419 471-9088
  Toledo (G-14178)
◆ Advanced Specialty Products .... G 419 882-6528
  Bowling Green (G-1550)
Advertising Joe LLC Mean .... G 440 247-8200
  Chagrin Falls (G-2367)
▲ Aero Fulfillment Services Corp .... D 800 225-7145
  Mason (G-9945)
Agnone-Kelly Enterprises Inc .... G 800 634-6503
  Cincinnati (G-2602)
AGS Custom Graphics Inc .... D 330 963-7770
  Macedonia (G-9534)
◆ Airwaves LLC .... C 740 548-1200
  Lewis Center (G-9147)
Akron Litho-Print Company Inc .... F 330 434-3145
  Akron (G-36)
Albany Screen Printing LLC .... F 614 585-3279
  Reynoldsburg (G-12750)
▲ Alberts Screen Print Inc .... C 330 753-7559
  Norton (G-11938)
All Points Printing Inc .... G 440 585-1125
  Wickliffe (G-15823)
Allied Silk Screen Inc .... G 937 223-4921
  Dayton (G-6195)
Alvin L Roepke .... G 419 862-3891
  Elmore (G-7099)
American Business Forms Inc .... E 513 312-2522
  West Chester (G-15535)
American Imprssions Sportswear .... G 614 848-6677
  Columbus (G-5125)
American Printing & Lithog Co .... F 513 867-0602
  Hamilton (G-8177)
Anderson Graphics Inc .... E 330 745-2165
  Barberton (G-855)
Anthony Business Forms Inc .... G 937 253-0072
  Dayton (G-6153)
Appleheart Inc .... G 937 384-0430
  Miamisburg (G-10612)
▲ Ares Sportswear Ltd .... D 614 767-1950
  Hilliard (G-8398)
Ashton LLC .... F 614 833-4165
  Pickerington (G-12455)
Assocted Vsual Cmmncations Inc .... E 330 452-4449
  Canton (G-2040)

Austin Tape and Label Inc .... D 330 928-7999
  Stow (G-13686)
Aztech Printing & Promotions .... G 937 339-0100
  Troy (G-14551)
Badlime Promo and Apparel LLC .... G 330 425-7100
  Twinsburg (G-14633)
Ball Jackets LLC .... E 937 572-1114
  Jamestown (G-8740)
Barnhart Printing Corp .... F 330 456-2279
  Canton (G-2044)
Bates Printing Inc .... F 330 833-5830
  Massillon (G-10078)
Bayard Inc .... D 937 293-1415
  Moraine (G-11160)
Benchmark Prints .... F 419 332-7640
  Fremont (G-7766)
Berea Printing Company .... G 440 243-1080
  Berea (G-1268)
Better Living Concepts Inc .... F 330 494-2213
  Canton (G-2047)
Big Kahuna Graphics LLC .... G 330 455-2625
  Canton (G-2048)
Bindery & Spc Pressworks Inc .... D 614 873-4623
  Plain City (G-12566)
Bizall Inc .... G 216 939-9580
  Cleveland (G-3738)
Boehm Inc .... E 614 875-9010
  Grove City (G-8080)
Bohlender Engraving Company .... G 513 621-4095
  Cincinnati (G-2676)
Bollin & Sons Inc .... E 419 693-6573
  Toledo (G-14216)
▲ Bottomline Ink Corporation .... E 419 897-8000
  Perrysburg (G-12364)
Bramkamp Printing Company Inc .... F 513 241-1865
  Blue Ash (G-1373)
Brass Bull 1 LLC .... G 740 335-8030
  Wshngtn Ct Hs (G-16226)
Broadway Printing LLC .... G 513 621-3429
  Cincinnati (G-2687)
Brook & Whittle Limited .... E 513 860-2457
  Hamilton (G-8187)
Brothers Printing Co Inc .... F 216 621-6050
  Cleveland (G-3764)
Buckeye Packaging Co Inc .... D 330 935-0301
  Alliance (G-396)
C P S Enterprises Inc .... G 216 441-7969
  Cleveland (G-3779)
Campbell Signs & Apparel LLC .... F 330 386-4768
  East Liverpool (G-6989)
Carbonless Cut Sheet Forms Inc .... F 740 826-1700
  New Concord (G-11431)
Carey Color Inc .... D 330 239-1835
  Sharon Center (G-13164)
▲ Casad Company Inc .... F 419 586-9457
  Coldwater (G-4984)
CCL Label Inc .... D 856 273-0700
  New Albany (G-11372)
CCL Label Inc .... B 440 878-7277
  Strongsville (G-13820)
Century Graphics Inc .... F 614 895-7698
  Westerville (G-15651)
Century Marketing Corporation .... C 419 354-2591
  Bowling Green (G-1558)
Charles Huffman & Associates .... G 216 295-0850
  Warrensville Heights (G-15228)
Cincinnati Print Solutions LLC .... G 513 943-9500
  Milford (G-10900)
Clear Images LLC .... G 419 241-9347
  Toledo (G-14241)
▼ Cleveland Menu Printing Inc .... E 216 241-5266
  Cleveland (G-3847)

Club 513 LLC .... G 800 530-2574
  Cincinnati (G-2776)
▲ CMC Group Inc .... D 419 354-2591
  Bowling Green (G-1561)
Collotype Labels Usa Inc .... D 513 381-1480
  Batavia (G-917)
▲ Coloring Book Solutions LLC .... G 419 281-9641
  Ashland (G-566)
Commercial Decal Ohio Inc .... F 330 385-7178
  East Liverpool (G-6991)
Concept 9 Inc .... G 614 294-3743
  Columbus (G-5285)
▲ Consolodated Graphics Group Inc .... G 216 881-9191
  Cleveland (G-3896)
Contemprary Image Labeling Inc .... G 513 583-5699
  Lebanon (G-9068)
Corporate Dcment Solutions Inc .... G 513 595-8200
  Cincinnati (G-2797)
Cox Printing Company .... G 937 382-2312
  Wilmington (G-16046)
Culaine Inc .... G 419 345-4984
  Toledo (G-14254)
Custom Deco LLC .... D 419 698-2900
  Toledo (G-14255)
Custom Poly Bag LLC .... D 330 935-2408
  Alliance (G-399)
▲ Custom Products Corporation .... D 440 528-7100
  Solon (G-13334)
Custom Sportswear Imprints LLC .... G 330 335-8326
  Wadsworth (G-15024)
D&D Design Concepts Inc .... F 513 752-2191
  Batavia (G-919)
Data Image .... G 740 763-7008
  Heath (G-8319)
Dayton Legal Blank Inc .... F 937 435-4405
  Dayton (G-6281)
Dbh Asscates - Ohio Ltd Partnr .... G 330 676-2006
  Kent (G-8808)
Dee Printing Inc .... F 614 777-8700
  Columbus (G-5322)
Delaware Data Products .... G 740 369-5449
  Delaware (G-6713)
Dietrich Von Hldbrand Lgacy PR .... G 703 496-7821
  Steubenville (G-13666)
Diocesan Publications Inc .... E 614 718-9500
  Dublin (G-6879)
Djsc Inc .... E 740 928-2697
  Hebron (G-8340)
Dlh Enterprises LLC .... G 330 253-6960
  Akron (G-132)
▲ Donprint Inc .... E 847 573-7777
  Strongsville (G-13828)
Drycal Inc .... G 440 974-1999
  Mentor (G-10450)
DSC Supply Company LLC .... G 614 891-1100
  Westerville (G-15703)
Dupli-Systems Inc .... C 440 234-9415
  Strongsville (G-13830)
Dyenamo Distributing LLC .... G 419 462-9474
  Galion (G-7870)
◆ Dynamic Design & Systems Inc .... G 440 708-1010
  Chagrin Falls (G-2393)
E & E Nameplates Inc .... G 419 468-3617
  Galion (G-7871)
E&O Fbn Inc .... F 513 241-5150
  Cincinnati (G-2851)
Ebel-Binder Printing Co Inc .... G 513 471-1067
  Cincinnati (G-2856)
Eci Macola/Max LLC .... C 978 539-6186
  Dublin (G-6883)
Edge 247 Corp .... G 216 771-7000
  Cleveland (G-4000)

SIC SECTION
27 PRINTING, PUBLISHING AND ALLIED INDUSTRIES

Electronic Imaging Svcs Inc .... F 740 549-2487
  Lewis Center *(G-9159)*
Empire Printing Inc .... G 513 242-3900
  Fairfield *(G-7356)*
Engineered Imaging LLC .... F 419 255-1283
  Toledo *(G-14277)*
Equip Business Solutions Co .... G 614 854-9755
  Jackson *(G-8715)*
Everythings Image Inc .... F 513 469-6727
  Blue Ash *(G-1392)*
F J Designs Inc .... F 330 264-1377
  Wooster *(G-16117)*
Fair Publishing House Inc .... E 419 668-3746
  Norwalk *(G-11967)*
First Impression Wear LLC .... G 937 456-3900
  Eaton *(G-7059)*
Flexoparts Com .... G 513 932-2060
  Lebanon *(G-9077)*
Foghorn Designs .... G 419 706-3861
  Norwalk *(G-11968)*
Folks Creative Printers Inc .... F 740 383-6326
  Marion *(G-9852)*
Foote Printing Company Inc .... F 216 431-1757
  Cleveland *(G-4079)*
▲ Forward Movement Publications ...... E 513 721-6659
  Cincinnati *(G-2918)*
Fulton Sign & Decal Inc .... G 440 951-1515
  Mentor *(G-10461)*
Funky Ink Prints LLC .... G 330 241-7291
  Brunswick *(G-1762)*
Gb Liquidating Company Inc .... E 513 248-7600
  Milford *(G-10907)*
▲ GBS Corp .... C 330 494-5330
  North Canton *(G-11729)*
◆ General Data Company Inc .... B 513 752-7978
  Cincinnati *(G-2561)*
▲ General Theming Contrs LLC .... C 614 252-6342
  Columbus *(G-5397)*
Geygan Enterprises Inc .... F 513 932-4222
  Lebanon *(G-9082)*
Glavin Industries Inc .... E 440 349-0049
  Solon *(G-13353)*
Glen D Lala .... G 937 274-7770
  Dayton *(G-6354)*
Gordons Graphics Inc .... G 330 863-2322
  Malvern *(G-9613)*
Got Graphix Llc .... F 330 703-9047
  Fairlawn *(G-7440)*
Gq Business Products Inc .... G 513 792-4750
  Loveland *(G-9482)*
Grady McCauley Inc .... D 330 494-9444
  Akron *(G-172)*
▲ Grafisk Maskinfabrik Amer LLC .... F 630 432-4370
  Lebanon *(G-9086)*
Graphic Stitch Inc .... G 937 642-6767
  Marysville *(G-9911)*
Graphix One Corporation .... G 513 870-0512
  West Chester *(G-15558)*
Grassroots Strategies LLC .... G 614 783-6515
  Columbus *(G-5411)*
Great Lakes Printing Inc .... F 440 993-8781
  Ashtabula *(G-636)*
Green Leaf Printing and Design .... G 937 222-3634
  Dayton *(G-6361)*
▲ Haman Enterprises Inc .... F 614 888-7574
  Columbus *(G-5417)*
Handcrafted Jewelry Inc .... G 330 650-9011
  Hudson *(G-8595)*
Harper Engraving & Printing Co .... D 614 276-0700
  Columbus *(G-5420)*
Hartman Distributing LLC .... G 740 616-7764
  Heath *(G-8321)*

Hawks & Associates Inc .... E 513 752-4311
  Cincinnati *(G-2563)*
Heartland Publications LLC .... C 860 664-1075
  Miamisburg *(G-10645)*
▲ Hecks Direct Mail Prtg Svc Inc .... F 419 697-3505
  Toledo *(G-14315)*
Heskamp Printing Co Inc .... G 513 871-6770
  Cincinnati *(G-2997)*
HI Tech Printing Co Inc .... E 513 874-5325
  Fairfield *(G-7366)*
Hkm Drect Mkt Cmmnications Inc ...... E 440 934-3060
  Sheffield Village *(G-13183)*
Hkm Drect Mkt Cmmnications Inc ...... E 330 395-9538
  Warren *(G-15176)*
Hkm Drect Mkt Cmmnications Inc ...... C 800 860-4456
  Cleveland *(G-4193)*
Homestretch Sportswear Inc .... G 419 678-4282
  Saint Henry *(G-12936)*
Horizon Ohio Publications Inc .... D 419 738-2128
  Wapakoneta *(G-15117)*
HP Industries Inc .... E 419 478-0695
  Toledo *(G-14322)*
Hr Graphics .... G 216 455-0534
  Cleveland *(G-4205)*
Humtown Pattern Company .... D 330 482-5555
  Columbiana *(G-5041)*
Imagine This Renovations .... G 330 833-6739
  Navarre *(G-11344)*
Impact Printing and Design LLC .... F 833 522-6200
  Columbus *(G-5456)*
Industrial Screen Prcess Svc I .... F 419 255-4900
  Toledo *(G-14330)*
Ink Slingers LLC .... G 740 867-3528
  Chesapeake *(G-2475)*
Innomark Communications LLC .... D 513 285-1040
  Fairfield *(G-7372)*
▲ Innovtive Lbling Solutions Inc .... D
  Hamilton *(G-8220)*
Irwin Engraving & Printing Co .... G 216 391-7300
  Cleveland *(G-4238)*
▲ Jack Walker Printing Co .... F 440 352-4222
  Mentor *(G-10481)*
▼ Jamac Inc .... E 419 625-9790
  Sandusky *(G-13069)*
Jupmode .... E 419 318-2029
  Toledo *(G-14342)*
Just Name It Inc .... G 614 626-8662
  Ashland *(G-582)*
◆ Kaufman Container Company .... C 216 898-2000
  Cleveland *(G-4276)*
Kay Toledo Tag Inc .... D 419 729-5479
  Toledo *(G-14346)*
Kdm Signs Inc .... G 513 554-1393
  Cincinnati *(G-3068)*
▲ Kdm Signs Inc .... C 513 769-1932
  Cincinnati *(G-3069)*
Kenwel Printers Inc .... E 614 261-1011
  Columbus *(G-5508)*
Keystone Press Inc .... G 419 243-7326
  Toledo *(G-14347)*
KMS 2000 Inc .... F 330 454-9444
  Canton *(G-2141)*
Knight Line Signature AP Corp .... G 330 545-8108
  Girard *(G-7970)*
Kopco Graphics Inc .... E 513 874-7230
  West Chester *(G-15456)*
▲ Label Aid Inc .... E 419 433-2888
  Huron *(G-8635)*
Label Technique Southeast LLC .... E 440 951-7660
  Willoughby *(G-15941)*
Labeltek Inc .... D 330 335-3110
  Wadsworth *(G-15042)*

Lake Screen Printing Inc .... G 440 244-5707
  Lorain *(G-9419)*
Laser Graphics .... G 419 433-2509
  Berlin Heights *(G-1316)*
Laser Printing Solutions Inc .... F 216 351-4444
  Cleveland *(G-4315)*
Lee Corporation .... G 513 771-3602
  Cincinnati *(G-3099)*
Letterman Printing Inc .... G 513 523-1111
  Oxford *(G-12210)*
Liberty Sportswear LLC .... G 513 755-8740
  Hamilton *(G-8227)*
License Ad Plate Company .... F 216 265-4200
  Cleveland *(G-4323)*
Lilienthal/Southeastern Inc .... G 740 439-1640
  Cambridge *(G-1940)*
Lima Sporting Goods Inc .... E 419 222-1036
  Lima *(G-9265)*
▲ Lorenz Corporation .... D 937 228-6118
  Dayton *(G-6416)*
Lsc Communications Inc .... A 419 935-0111
  Willard *(G-15860)*
Lyle Printing & Publishing Co .... E 330 337-3419
  Salem *(G-13013)*
M & H Screen Printing .... G 740 522-1957
  Newark *(G-11587)*
M PI Label Systems .... G 330 938-2134
  Sebring *(G-13121)*
M Rosenthal Company .... F 513 563-0081
  Cincinnati *(G-3120)*
Marbee Inc .... G 419 422-9441
  Findlay *(G-7535)*
Marcus Uppe Inc .... E 216 263-4000
  Cleveland *(G-4357)*
Mariotti Printing Co LLC .... G 440 245-4120
  Lorain *(G-9424)*
Markham Converting Limited .... F 419 353-2458
  Bowling Green *(G-1574)*
Markt LLC .... G 740 397-5900
  Mount Vernon *(G-11278)*
▲ McC - Mason W&S .... C 513 459-1100
  Mason *(G-10027)*
McC-Norway LLC .... F 513 381-1480
  Batavia *(G-932)*
McDaniel Envelope Company Inc .... G 330 868-5929
  Minerva *(G-11034)*
Meder Special-Tees Ltd .... G 513 921-3800
  Cincinnati *(G-3140)*
Melnor Graphics LLC .... F 419 476-8808
  Toledo *(G-14382)*
Metro Flex Inc .... G 937 299-5360
  Moraine *(G-11194)*
▲ Microplex Printware Corp .... F 440 374-2424
  Solon *(G-13390)*
Mid-Ohio Screen Print Inc .... G 614 875-1774
  Grove City *(G-8106)*
Middaugh Enterprises Inc .... G 330 852-2471
  Sugarcreek *(G-13930)*
Middleton Printing Co Inc .... G 614 294-7277
  Gahanna *(G-7845)*
Miller Products Inc .... F 330 335-3110
  Wadsworth *(G-15045)*
Miller Products Inc .... D 330 335-3110
  Wadsworth *(G-15046)*
ML Advertising & Design LLC .... G 419 447-6523
  Tiffin *(G-14094)*
ML Erectors LLC .... G 440 328-3227
  Elyria *(G-7182)*
Mmp Printing Inc .... E 513 381-0990
  Cincinnati *(G-3168)*
Model GRAphics& Media Inc .... E 513 541-2355
  West Chester *(G-15465)*

Employee Codes: A=Over 500 employees, B=251-500
C=101-250, D=51-100, E=20-50, F=10-19, G=1-9

27 PRINTING, PUBLISHING AND ALLIED INDUSTRIES

Moonshine Screen Printing Inc..................G..... 513 523-7775
Oxford (G-12211)

Morrison Sign Company Inc.....................E..... 614 276-1181
Columbus (G-5582)

Mpi Labels of Baltimore Inc.....................E..... 330 938-2134
Sebring (G-13124)

▼ Mr Label Inc...E..... 513 681-2088
Cincinnati (G-3177)

Mr O Fficials LLC....................................G..... 216 240-2534
Cleveland (G-4428)

Multi-Color Australia LLC........................D..... 513 381-1480
Batavia (G-938)

Multi-Color Corporation..........................G..... 513 459-3283
Mason (G-10032)

▲ Multi-Color Corporation.....................F..... 513 381-1480
Batavia (G-939)

Multi-Craft Litho Inc................................E..... 859 581-2754
Blue Ash (G-1442)

◆ Murphy Dog LLC................................E..... 614 755-4278
Blacklick (G-1341)

Mustang Printing....................................F..... 419 592-2746
Napoleon (G-11325)

Ncrformscom...G..... 800 709-1938
Hudson (G-8606)

◆ Neff Motivation Inc.............................C..... 937 548-3194
Greenville (G-8053)

Network Printing & Graphics..................F..... 614 230-2084
Columbus (G-5593)

◆ Nilpeter Usa Inc.................................C..... 513 489-4400
Cincinnati (G-3198)

Nordec Inc...D..... 330 940-3700
Stow (G-13715)

Northeastern Plastics Inc.......................G..... 330 453-5925
Canton (G-2179)

▲ Novavision LLC.................................D..... 419 354-1427
Bowling Green (G-1577)

Odyssey Press Inc.................................F..... 614 410-0356
Huron (G-8642)

▲ Off Contact Inc..................................F..... 419 255-5546
Toledo (G-14406)

OH Road LLC..G..... 614 582-4765
Columbus (G-5612)

Ohio Envelope Manufacturing Co...........E..... 216 267-2920
Cleveland (G-4497)

Ohio Flexible Packaging Co...................F..... 513 494-1800
South Lebanon (G-13462)

Ohio Label Inc.......................................F..... 614 777-0180
Columbus (G-5620)

Old Trail Printing Company....................C..... 614 443-4852
Columbus (G-5636)

Omni Systems Inc..................................D..... 216 377-5160
Mayfield Village (G-10259)

Onetouchpoint East Corp.......................D..... 513 421-1600
Cincinnati (G-3225)

P S Graphics Inc....................................G..... 440 356-9656
Rocky River (G-12840)

▼ Packaging Materials Inc.....................E..... 740 432-6337
Cambridge (G-1946)

Painted Hill Inv Group Inc......................F..... 937 339-1756
Troy (G-14600)

Papel Couture..G..... 614 848-5700
Columbus (G-5655)

Park PLC Prntng Cpyg & Dgtl IMG.........G..... 330 799-1739
Youngstown (G-16414)

Part 2 Screen Prtg Design Inc................G..... 614 294-4429
Columbus (G-5657)

Penguin Enterprises Inc.........................E..... 440 899-5112
Westlake (G-15773)

▲ Performance Packaging Inc................F..... 419 478-8505
Toledo (G-14433)

PJ Bush Associates Inc.........................E..... 216 362-6700
Cleveland (G-4556)

Pops Printed Apparel LLC......................G..... 614 372-5651
Columbus (G-5682)

Post Printing Co.....................................D..... 859 254-7714
Minster (G-11058)

Pounce Signs & Print Wear....................G..... 408 377-4680
London (G-9393)

Precision Business Solutions..................F..... 419 661-8700
Perrysburg (G-12420)

Precision Graphic Services Inc...............F..... 419 241-5189
Toledo (G-14442)

Precision Imprint...................................G..... 740 592-5916
Athens (G-692)

◆ Premier Southern Ticket Co Inc..........E..... 513 489-6700
Cincinnati (G-3273)

Press of Ohio Inc...................................E..... 330 678-5868
Kent (G-8847)

Primal Screen Inc..................................F..... 330 677-1766
Kent (G-8848)

Printeesweet...G..... 888 410-2160
Hopedale (G-8557)

Printex Incorporated..............................F..... 740 773-0088
Chillicothe (G-2529)

Printing Dimensions Inc.........................F..... 937 256-0044
Dayton (G-6523)

Printing Unlimited Inc............................G..... 419 874-9828
Perrysburg (G-12421)

▲ Prodigy Print Inc................................F
Dayton (G-6528)

Proforma Systems Advantage................G..... 419 224-8747
Lima (G-9279)

Progressive Printers Inc.........................D..... 937 222-1267
Dayton (G-6533)

Promospark Inc.....................................G..... 513 844-2211
Fairfield (G-7398)

Qualitee Design Sportswear Co.............F..... 740 333-8337
Wshngtn Ct Hs (G-16237)

Quebecor World Johnson Hardin...........E..... 614 326-0299
Cincinnati (G-3314)

Queen City Office Machine....................F..... 513 251-7200
Cincinnati (G-3317)

Queen City Spirit LLC............................F..... 513 533-2662
Cincinnati (G-3320)

Quest Service Labs Inc.........................F..... 330 405-0316
Twinsburg (G-14721)

Quick As A Wink Printing Co.................G..... 419 224-9786
Lima (G-9281)

Quick Tech Business Forms Inc............F..... 937 743-5952
Springboro (G-13517)

R R Donnelley & Sons Company............B..... 740 928-6110
Hebron (G-8358)

R R Donnelley & Sons Company............D..... 440 774-2101
Oberlin (G-12055)

R R Donnelley & Sons Company............G..... 513 552-1512
West Chester (G-15494)

R&D Marketing Group Inc......................G..... 216 398-9100
Brooklyn Heights (G-1697)

Ray C Sprosty Bag Co Inc.....................F..... 330 669-0045
Smithville (G-13301)

Reece Brothers Inc................................G..... 419 212-9226
Bryan (G-1837)

Repacorp Inc..D..... 937 667-8496
Tipp City (G-14152)

Reynolds and Reynolds Company..........F..... 419 584-7000
Celina (G-2346)

S F Mock & Associates LLC..................F..... 937 438-0196
Dayton (G-6556)

Sams Graphic Industries........................F..... 330 821-4710
Alliance (G-422)

Samuels Products Inc............................E..... 513 891-4456
Blue Ash (G-1464)

Schilling Graphics Inc............................E..... 419 468-1031
Galion (G-7884)

Schlabach Printers LLC.........................E..... 330 852-4687
Sugarcreek (G-13937)

Sekuworks LLC......................................E..... 513 202-1210
Harrison (G-8290)

Selby Service/Roxy Press Inc................G..... 513 241-3445
Cincinnati (G-3378)

Seneca Label Inc...................................E..... 440 237-1600
Brunswick (G-1791)

▲ Sensical Inc.......................................D..... 216 641-1141
Solon (G-13420)

Shops By Todd Inc.................................G..... 937 458-3192
Beavercreek (G-1061)

Shreve Printing LLC...............................G..... 330 567-2341
Shreve (G-13215)

Sit Inc..E..... 330 758-8468
Youngstown (G-16440)

Sk Screen Printing Inc...........................E..... 330 475-0286
Akron (G-332)

Slimans Printery Inc..............................F..... 330 454-9141
Canton (G-2226)

Smartbill Ltd..F..... 740 928-6909
Hebron (G-8362)

Snow Printing Co Inc.............................F..... 419 229-7669
Lima (G-9290)

Solution Ventures Inc............................G..... 330 858-1111
Tallmadge (G-14047)

▲ Spear Inc...D..... 513 459-1100
Mason (G-10058)

Specialty Printing and Proc....................F..... 614 322-9035
Columbus (G-5783)

Springdot Inc...D..... 513 542-4000
Cincinnati (G-3411)

◆ SRC Liquidation LLC..........................A..... 937 221-1000
Dayton (G-6586)

▲ SRI Ohio Inc......................................E..... 740 653-5800
Lancaster (G-9041)

Standard Register Technologies.............G..... 937 443-1000
Dayton (G-6590)

Standout Stickers Inc............................G..... 877 449-7703
Brunswick (G-1792)

Star Printing Company Inc....................E..... 330 376-0514
Akron (G-336)

Starr Services Inc..................................G..... 513 241-7708
Cincinnati (G-3417)

Stephen Andrews Inc.............................G..... 330 725-2672
Lodi (G-9357)

Steves Sports Inc..................................G..... 440 735-0044
Northfield (G-11911)

Stolle Machinery Company LLC.............C..... 937 497-5400
Sidney (G-13291)

Storad Label Co.....................................F..... 740 382-6440
Marion (G-9885)

▲ Studio Eleven Inc...............................F..... 937 295-2225
Fort Loramie (G-7611)

Suburban Press Incorporated................E..... 216 961-0766
Cleveland (G-4744)

Superior Label Systems Inc...................B..... 513 336-0825
Mason (G-10061)

T & L Custom Screening Inc.................G..... 937 237-3121
Dayton (G-6605)

T-Shirt Co..E..... 513 821-7100
Cincinnati (G-3439)

T&T Graphics Inc...................................D..... 937 847-6000
Miamisburg (G-10688)

Taylor Communications Inc...................E..... 419 678-6000
Coldwater (G-5002)

Taylor Communications Inc...................G..... 937 221-1000
Dayton (G-6609)

Taylor Communications Inc...................E..... 614 277-7500
Urbancrest (G-14855)

Tech/III Inc..E..... 513 482-7500
Fairfield (G-7415)

SIC SECTION
27 PRINTING, PUBLISHING AND ALLIED INDUSTRIES

Tee Hee Co Inc .... G 614 515-5581
  Worthington *(G-16215)*
▲ The Cyril-Scott Company .... C 740 654-2112
  Lancaster *(G-9043)*
▲ The D B Hess Company .... E 330 678-5868
  Kent *(G-8874)*
▲ The Hooven - Dayton Corp .... C 937 233-4473
  Miamisburg *(G-10694)*
The Label Team Inc .... F 330 332-1067
  Salem *(G-13033)*
Thomas Products Co Inc .... E 513 756-9009
  Cincinnati *(G-3453)*
Tj Metzgers Inc .... D 419 861-8611
  Toledo *(G-14487)*
Toledo Ticket Company .... E 419 476-5424
  Toledo *(G-14506)*
Tope Printing Inc .... G 330 674-4993
  Millersburg *(G-11000)*
Tpo Hess Holdings Inc .... E 815 334-6140
  Kent *(G-8876)*
◆ Transfer Express Inc .... D 440 918-1900
  Mentor *(G-10581)*
Traxium LLC .... E 330 572-8200
  Stow *(G-13732)*
Traxler Tees LLC .... F 614 593-1270
  Columbus *(G-5834)*
◆ Trebnick Systems Inc .... E 937 743-1550
  Springboro *(G-13524)*
Tree Free Resources LLC .... G 740 751-4844
  Marion *(G-9887)*
▲ Treefrogg Specialties Inc .... G 513 212-3581
  Batavia *(G-954)*
True Dinero Records & Tech LLC .... G 513 428-4610
  Cincinnati *(G-3470)*
▲ Underground Sports Shop Inc .... F 513 751-1662
  Cincinnati *(G-3477)*
Unisport Inc .... F 419 529-4727
  Ontario *(G-12096)*
United Sport Apparel .... F 330 722-0818
  Medina *(G-10391)*
Universal Ch Directories LLC .... G 419 522-5011
  Mansfield *(G-9729)*
Universal North Inc .... F 440 230-1366
  North Royalton *(G-11899)*
Vandalia Sportswear LLC .... G 937 264-3204
  Vandalia *(G-14966)*
Verstrete In Mold Lbels USA In .... F 513 943-0080
  Batavia *(G-959)*
▲ Vgu Industries Inc .... E 216 676-9093
  Cleveland *(G-4867)*
Victory Postcards Inc .... G 614 764-8975
  Dublin *(G-6957)*
Viewpoint Graphic Design .... G 419 447-6073
  Tiffin *(G-14114)*
Visual Marking Systems Inc .... D 330 425-7100
  Twinsburg *(G-14753)*
Vya Inc .... E 513 772-5400
  Cincinnati *(G-3506)*
W/S Packaging Group Inc .... D 513 459-8800
  Mason *(G-10069)*
Ward/Kraft Forms of Ohio Inc .... E 740 694-0015
  Fredericktown *(G-7759)*
Warren Printing & Off Pdts Inc .... F 419 523-3635
  Ottawa *(G-12196)*
Water Drop Media Inc .... G 234 600-5817
  Vienna *(G-15005)*
Watson Haran & Company Inc .... G 937 436-1414
  Dayton *(G-6648)*
Weaver Screen Print LLC .... G 440 725-0116
  Willoughby *(G-16014)*
West Crrllton Prchment Cnvrtin .... E 513 594-3341
  West Carrollton *(G-15358)*

◆ West-Camp Press Inc .... D 614 882-2378
  Westerville *(G-15725)*
Western Ohio Graphics .... F 937 335-8769
  Troy *(G-14616)*
Western Roto Engravers Inc .... E 330 336-7636
  Wadsworth *(G-15072)*
◆ Wfsr Holdings LLC .... A 877 735-4966
  Dayton *(G-6654)*
William J Bergen & Co .... G 440 248-6132
  Solon *(G-13448)*
Williams Steel Rule Die Co .... F 216 431-3232
  Cleveland *(G-4910)*
◆ Workflowone LLC .... A 877 735-4966
  Dayton *(G-6661)*
Yockey Group Inc .... F 513 860-9053
  West Chester *(G-15529)*
Youngstown ARC Engraving Co .... G 330 793-2471
  Youngstown *(G-16476)*

2761 Manifold business forms

Anderson Graphics Inc .... E 330 745-2165
  Barberton *(G-855)*
Anthony Business Forms Inc .... G 937 253-0072
  Dayton *(G-6153)*
▲ Custom Products Corporation .... D 440 528-7100
  Solon *(G-13334)*
Dupli-Systems Inc .... C 440 234-9415
  Strongsville *(G-13830)*
▲ Eleet Cryogenics Inc .... E 330 874-4009
  Bolivar *(G-1524)*
GBS Corp .... C 330 863-1828
  Malvern *(G-9612)*
▲ GBS Corp .... C 330 494-5330
  North Canton *(G-11729)*
Geygan Enterprises Inc .... F 513 932-4222
  Lebanon *(G-9082)*
Glatfelter Corporation .... G 419 333-6700
  Fremont *(G-7787)*
▲ Kroy LLC .... C 216 426-5600
  Cleveland *(G-4299)*
Plastilene Inc .... E 614 592-8699
  Wshngtn Ct Hs *(G-16236)*
Print-Digital Incorporated .... G 330 686-5945
  Stow *(G-13718)*
Quick Tech Graphics Inc .... E 937 743-5952
  Springboro *(G-13518)*
R R Donnelley & Sons Company .... D 440 774-2101
  Oberlin *(G-12055)*
Reynolds and Reynolds Company .... F 419 584-7000
  Celina *(G-2346)*
Rotary Forms Press Inc .... E 937 393-3426
  Hillsboro *(G-8465)*
S F Mock & Associates LLC .... F 937 438-0196
  Dayton *(G-6556)*
▲ Shawnee Systems Inc .... D 513 561-9932
  Cincinnati *(G-3387)*
◆ SRC Liquidation LLC .... A 937 221-1000
  Dayton *(G-6586)*
Taylor Communications Inc .... E 937 221-1000
  Dayton *(G-6609)*
Taylor Communications Inc .... F 732 356-0081
  Dayton *(G-6610)*
Taylor Communications Inc .... F 937 221-3347
  Grove City *(G-8121)*
Taylor Communications Inc .... F 216 265-1800
  Richfield *(G-12800)*
Thomas Products Co Inc .... E 513 756-9009
  Cincinnati *(G-3453)*
Unit Sets Inc .... G 937 840-6123
  Hillsboro *(G-8468)*
▲ Wfsr Holdings LLC .... A 877 735-4966
  Dayton *(G-6654)*

2771 Greeting cards

◆ American Greetings Corporation .... A 216 252-7300
  Cleveland *(G-3652)*
Naptime Productions LLC .... G 419 662-9521
  Rossford *(G-12868)*
▲ Papyrus-Recycled Greetings Inc .... D 773 348-6410
  Westlake *(G-15770)*
◆ Plus Mark LLC .... D 216 252-6770
  Cleveland *(G-4562)*
Those Chrcters From Clvland LL .... F 216 252-7300
  Cleveland *(G-4795)*

2782 Blankbooks and looseleaf binders

▲ Art Guild Binders Inc .... E 513 242-3000
  Cincinnati *(G-2634)*
Bell Binders LLC .... F 419 242-3201
  Toledo *(G-14210)*
Deluxe Corporation .... D 330 342-1500
  Streetsboro *(G-13766)*
Dupli-Systems Inc .... C 440 234-9415
  Strongsville *(G-13830)*
Lilienthal/Southeastern Inc .... G 740 439-1640
  Cambridge *(G-1940)*
Live Off Loyalty Inc .... G 513 413-2401
  Cincinnati *(G-3109)*
M & R Phillips Enterprises .... F 740 323-0580
  Newark *(G-11588)*
Mueller Art Cover & Binding Co .... E 440 238-3303
  Strongsville *(G-13858)*
Quick Tech Graphics Inc .... E 937 743-5952
  Springboro *(G-13518)*
Tenacity Manufacturing Company .... F 513 821-0201
  West Chester *(G-15514)*
William Exline Inc .... E 216 941-0800
  Cleveland *(G-4909)*

2789 Bookbinding and related work

A-A Blueprint Co Inc .... E 330 794-8803
  Akron *(G-11)*
AAA Laminating and Bindery Inc .... G 513 860-2680
  Fairfield *(G-7329)*
▲ Activities Press Inc .... E 440 953-1200
  Mentor *(G-10404)*
AGS Custom Graphics Inc .... D 330 963-7770
  Macedonia *(G-9534)*
Allen Graphics Inc .... G 440 349-4100
  Solon *(G-13308)*
American Printing & Lithog Co .... F 513 867-0602
  Hamilton *(G-8177)*
Anderson Graphics Inc .... E 330 745-2165
  Barberton *(G-855)*
Andrin Enterprises Inc .... F 937 276-7794
  Moraine *(G-11157)*
▲ Art Guild Binders Inc .... E 513 242-3000
  Cincinnati *(G-2634)*
Baesman Group Inc .... D 614 771-2300
  Hilliard *(G-8402)*
Barnhart Printing Corp .... F 330 456-2279
  Canton *(G-2044)*
Bindery & Spc Presworks Inc .... D 614 873-4623
  Plain City *(G-12566)*
Bindery Tech Inc .... G 440 934-3247
  North Ridgeville *(G-11831)*
Bindtech LLC .... D 615 834-0404
  Macedonia *(G-9539)*
Bindusa .... F 513 247-3000
  Blue Ash *(G-1370)*
Bip Printing Solutions LLC .... F 216 832-5673
  Beachwood *(G-974)*
Black River Group Inc .... E 419 524-6699
  Mansfield *(G-9628)*

Employee Codes: A=Over 500 employees, B=251-500
C=101-250, D=51-100, E=20-50, F=10-19, G=1-9

27 PRINTING, PUBLISHING AND ALLIED INDUSTRIES

Blains Folding Service Inc .... G 216 631-4700
  Cleveland (G-3740)
▼ Bookfactory LLC .... E 937 226-7100
  Dayton (G-6234)
Boundless Cmnty Pathways Inc .... A 937 461-0034
  West Carrollton (G-15351)
Century Graphics Inc .... F 614 895-7698
  Westerville (G-15651)
Cincinnati Bindery & Packg Inc .... G 859 816-0282
  Cincinnati (G-2742)
Classic Laminations Inc .... E 440 735-1333
  Oakwood Village (G-12037)
Cleveland Letter Service Inc .... G 216 781-8300
  Chagrin Falls (G-2371)
▲ Consolidated Graphics Group Inc ..... C 216 881-9191
  Cleveland (G-3896)
Copley Ohio Newspapers Inc .... C 330 364-5577
  New Philadelphia (G-11493)
COS Blueprint Inc .... E 330 376-0022
  Akron (G-115)
Cott Systems Inc .... D 614 847-4405
  Columbus (G-5299)
Cox Printing Company .... G 937 382-2312
  Wilmington (G-16046)
▲ Creative Ip LLC .... G 234 571-2466
  Akron (G-118)
Customformed Products Inc .... F 937 388-0480
  Miamisburg (G-10631)
◆ Davis Printing Company .... E 330 745-3113
  Barberton (G-866)
Dayton Bindery Service Inc .... E 937 235-3111
  Dayton (G-6274)
Dayton Legal Blank Inc .... F 937 435-4405
  Dayton (G-6281)
Eugene Stewart .... G 937 898-1117
  Dayton (G-6325)
Folks Creative Printers Inc .... F 740 383-6326
  Marion (G-9852)
Franklin Printing Company .... F 740 452-6375
  Zanesville (G-16533)
G W Steffen Bookbinders Inc .... E 330 963-0300
  Macedonia (G-9553)
▲ Gli Holdings Inc .... D 216 651-1500
  Stow (G-13701)
Greg Blume .... G 740 574-2308
  Wheelersburg (G-15809)
Harris Paper Crafts Inc .... F 614 299-2141
  Columbus (G-5421)
▲ Hecks Direct Mail Prtg Svc Inc .... F 419 697-3505
  Toledo (G-14315)
Hf Group LLC .... C 440 729-9411
  Chesterland (G-2482)
HP Industries Inc .... E 419 478-0695
  Toledo (G-14322)
Innomark Communications LLC .... C 937 454-5555
  Miamisburg (G-10648)
▲ Jack Walker Printing Co .... F 440 352-4222
  Mentor (G-10481)
▲ Kehl-Kolor Inc .... E 419 281-3107
  Ashland (G-585)
Kenwel Printers Inc .... E 614 261-1011
  Columbus (G-5508)
Kevin K Tidd .... G 419 885-5603
  Sylvania (G-14003)
Keystone Press Inc .... G 419 243-7326
  Toledo (G-14347)
Krieg Rev 2 Inc .... E 513 542-1522
  Cincinnati (G-3090)
Laipplys Prtg Mktg Sltions Inc .... G 740 387-9282
  Marion (G-9859)
Lam Pro Inc .... F 216 426-0661
  Cleveland (G-4308)

Lee Corporation .... G 513 771-3602
  Cincinnati (G-3099)
Lilienthal/Southeastern Inc .... G 740 439-1640
  Cambridge (G-1940)
Liturgical Publications Inc .... D 216 325-6825
  Cleveland (G-4332)
Macke Brothers Inc .... E 513 771-7500
  Cincinnati (G-3123)
Mmp Printing Inc .... E 513 381-0990
  Cincinnati (G-3168)
Multi-Craft Litho Inc .... E 859 581-2754
  Blue Ash (G-1442)
Network Printing & Graphics .... F 614 230-2084
  Columbus (G-5593)
North End Press Incorporated .... F 740 653-6514
  Lancaster (G-9030)
▲ Ohio Laminating & Binding Inc .... F 614 771-4868
  Hilliard (G-8426)
Old Trail Printing Company .... C 614 443-4852
  Columbus (G-5636)
Onetouchpoint East Corp .... D 513 421-1600
  Cincinnati (G-3225)
Orange Blossom Press Inc .... G 216 781-8655
  Willoughby (G-15966)
Painesville Publishing Inc .... G 440 354-4142
  Austinburg (G-748)
Penguin Enterprises Inc .... E 440 899-5112
  Westlake (G-15773)
Precision Graphic Services Inc .... F 419 241-5189
  Toledo (G-14442)
Prime Printing Inc .... E 937 438-3707
  Dayton (G-6522)
Print-Digital Incorporated .... G 330 686-5945
  Stow (G-13718)
▲ Printers Bindery Services Inc .... D 513 821-8039
  Batavia (G-944)
▲ Prodigy Print Inc .... F
  Dayton (G-6528)
Promatch Solutions LLC .... F 877 299-0185
  Moraine (G-11205)
▼ Quick Tab II Inc .... D 419 448-6622
  Tiffin (G-14101)
▲ Repro Acquisition Company LLC ..... F 216 738-3800
  Cleveland (G-4626)
Riverside Mfg Acquisition LLC .... F 585 458-2090
  Cleveland (G-4638)
Rmt Holdings Inc .... F 419 221-1168
  Lima (G-9286)
Robin Enterprises Company .... C 614 891-0250
  Westerville (G-15719)
RT Industries Inc .... G 937 335-5784
  Troy (G-14606)
Spring Grove Manufacturing Inc .... F 513 542-6900
  Cincinnati (G-3410)
Standard Printing Co of Canton .... D 330 453-8247
  Canton (G-2230)
Star Printing Company Inc .... E 330 376-0514
  Akron (G-336)
Strong Bindery Inc .... G 216 231-0001
  Cleveland (G-4741)
Suburban Press Incorporated .... E 216 961-0766
  Cleveland (G-4744)
▲ The D B Hess Company .... E 330 678-5868
  Kent (G-8874)
Tj Metzgers Inc .... D 419 861-8611
  Toledo (G-14487)
Tomahawk Printing Inc .... F 419 335-3161
  Wauseon (G-15274)
Traxium LLC .... E 330 572-8200
  Stow (G-13732)
Watkins Printing Company .... E 614 297-8270
  Columbus (G-5867)

▲ West-Camp Press Inc .... D 614 882-2378
  Westerville (G-15725)
▲ Wfsr Holdings LLC .... A 877 735-4966
  Dayton (G-6654)
Youngstown ARC Engraving Co .... G 330 793-2471
  Youngstown (G-16476)

2791 Typesetting

A-A Blueprint Co Inc .... E 330 794-8803
  Akron (G-11)
▲ Activities Press Inc .... E 440 953-1200
  Mentor (G-10404)
AGS Custom Graphics Inc .... D 330 963-7770
  Macedonia (G-9534)
American Printing & Lithog Co .... F 513 867-0602
  Hamilton (G-8177)
Anderson Graphics Inc .... E 330 745-2165
  Barberton (G-855)
Andrin Enterprises Inc .... F 937 276-7794
  Moraine (G-11157)
Anthony Business Forms Inc .... G 937 253-0072
  Dayton (G-6153)
Asist Translation Services .... F 614 451-6744
  Columbus (G-5158)
Baesman Group Inc .... D 614 771-2300
  Hilliard (G-8402)
Bindery & Spc Pressworks Inc .... D 614 873-4623
  Plain City (G-12566)
Black River Group Inc .... E 419 524-6699
  Mansfield (G-9628)
◆ Bookmasters Inc .... C 419 281-1802
  Ashland (G-557)
Brass Bull 1 LLC .... G 740 335-8030
  Wshngtn Ct Hs (G-16226)
Brothers Publishing Co LLC .... E 937 548-3330
  Greenville (G-8040)
Carlisle Prtg Walnut Creek Ltd .... E 330 852-9922
  Sugarcreek (G-13922)
Characters Inc .... G 937 335-1976
  Troy (G-14553)
Colortech Graphics & Printing .... F 614 766-2400
  Columbus (G-5260)
▲ Consoldated Graphics Group Inc ..... C 216 881-9191
  Cleveland (G-3896)
Copley Ohio Newspapers Inc .... C 330 364-5577
  New Philadelphia (G-11493)
COS Blueprint Inc .... E 330 376-0022
  Akron (G-115)
Daubenmires Printing Co LLC .... G 513 425-7223
  Middletown (G-10817)
◆ Davis Printing Company .... E 330 745-3113
  Barberton (G-866)
Dayton Legal Blank Inc .... F 937 435-4405
  Dayton (G-6281)
E&O Fbn Inc .... F 513 241-5150
  Cincinnati (G-2851)
Eugene Stewart .... G 937 898-1117
  Dayton (G-6325)
Flexoplate Inc .... F 513 489-0433
  Blue Ash (G-1395)
Franklin Printing Company .... F 740 452-6375
  Zanesville (G-16533)
Geygan Enterprises Inc .... F 513 932-4222
  Lebanon (G-9082)
Greg Blume .... G 740 574-2308
  Wheelersburg (G-15809)
Harlan Graphic Arts Svcs Inc .... E 513 251-5700
  Cincinnati (G-2985)
▲ Hecks Direct Mail Prtg Svc Inc .... F 419 697-3505
  Toledo (G-14315)
Hkm Drect Mkt Cmmnications Inc ..... C 800 860-4456
  Cleveland (G-4193)

28 CHEMICALS AND ALLIED PRODUCTS

HOT Graphic Services Inc .... E 419 242-7000
   Northwood *(G-11920)*

HP Industries Inc .... E 419 478-0695
   Toledo *(G-14322)*

Hubbard Publishing Co .... E 937 592-3060
   Bellefontaine *(G-1212)*

Imprints .... F 330 650-0467
   Hudson *(G-8599)*

▲ Jack Walker Printing Co .... F 440 352-4222
   Mentor *(G-10481)*

Keener Printing Inc .... F 216 531-7595
   Cleveland *(G-4280)*

▲ Kehl-Kolor Inc .... E 419 281-3107
   Ashland *(G-585)*

Kevin K Tidd .... G 419 885-5603
   Sylvania *(G-14003)*

Keystone Press Inc .... G 419 243-7326
   Toledo *(G-14347)*

Laurenee Ltd .... G 513 662-2225
   Cincinnati *(G-3097)*

Lee Corporation .... G 513 771-3602
   Cincinnati *(G-3099)*

Middleton Printing Co Inc .... G 614 294-7277
   Gahanna *(G-7845)*

Mmp Printing Inc .... E 513 381-0990
   Cincinnati *(G-3168)*

Multi-Craft Litho Inc .... E 859 581-2754
   Blue Ash *(G-1442)*

Network Printing & Graphics .... F 614 230-2084
   Columbus *(G-5593)*

Old Trail Printing Company .... C 614 443-4852
   Columbus *(G-5636)*

Onetouchpoint East Corp .... D 513 421-1600
   Cincinnati *(G-3225)*

Orange Blossom Press Inc .... G 216 781-8655
   Willoughby *(G-15966)*

Painesville Publishing Inc .... G 440 354-4142
   Austinburg *(G-748)*

Penguin Enterprises Inc .... E 440 899-5112
   Westlake *(G-15773)*

Photo-Type Engraving Company .... E 614 308-1900
   Columbus *(G-5674)*

Preisser Inc .... E 614 345-0199
   Columbus *(G-5688)*

Prime Printing Inc .... E 937 438-3707
   Dayton *(G-6522)*

Printery Inc .... G 513 574-1099
   Cincinnati *(G-3277)*

Printing Arts Press Inc .... F 740 397-6106
   Mount Vernon *(G-11289)*

Progrssive Communications Corp .... D 740 397-5333
   Mount Vernon *(G-11290)*

Quick As A Wink Printing Co .... G 419 224-9786
   Lima *(G-9281)*

▼ Quick Tab II Inc .... D 419 448-6622
   Tiffin *(G-14101)*

Quick Tech Graphics Inc .... E 937 743-5952
   Springboro *(G-13518)*

Robin Enterprises Company .... C 614 891-0250
   Westerville *(G-15719)*

▲ Royal Acme Corporation .... E 216 241-1477
   Cleveland *(G-4654)*

RR Donnelley & Sons Company .... G 614 221-8385
   Columbus *(G-5733)*

▲ St Media Group Intl Inc .... D 513 421-2050
   Blue Ash *(G-1467)*

Standard Printing Co of Canton .... D 330 453-8247
   Canton *(G-2230)*

Suburban Press Incorporated .... E 216 961-0766
   Cleveland *(G-4744)*

The Photo-Type Engraving Company ..... D 513 281-0999
   Cincinnati *(G-3450)*

Tim L Humbert .... G 330 497-4944
   Canton *(G-2245)*

Tj Metzgers Inc .... D 419 861-8611
   Toledo *(G-14487)*

Watkins Printing Company .... E 614 297-8270
   Columbus *(G-5867)*

▲ West-Camp Press Inc .... D 614 882-2378
   Westerville *(G-15725)*

Western Roto Engravers Inc .... E 330 336-7636
   Wadsworth *(G-15072)*

▲ Wfsr Holdings LLC .... A 877 735-4966
   Dayton *(G-6654)*

Winkler Co Inc .... G 937 294-2662
   Dayton *(G-6655)*

Wolters Kluwer Clinical D .... D 330 650-6506
   Hudson *(G-8619)*

◆ Workflowone LLC .... A 877 735-4966
   Dayton *(G-6661)*

Xenia Daily Gazette .... E 937 372-4444
   Xenia *(G-16281)*

Youngstown ARC Engraving Co .... G 330 793-2471
   Youngstown *(G-16476)*

2796 Platemaking services

Acme Printing Co Inc .... G 419 626-4426
   Sandusky *(G-13041)*

▲ Amos Media Company .... C 937 638-0967
   Sidney *(G-13221)*

Anderson & Vreeland Inc .... D 419 636-5002
   Bryan *(G-1807)*

Art-American Printing Plates .... F 216 241-4420
   Cleveland *(G-3678)*

Buckler Industries Inc .... E 419 589-6134
   Mansfield *(G-9633)*

Century Graphics Inc .... F 614 895-7698
   Westerville *(G-15651)*

Converters/Prepress Inc .... F 937 743-0935
   Carlisle *(G-2287)*

Csw Inc .... E 413 589-1311
   Sylvania *(G-13992)*

Dynamic Dies Inc .... E 419 865-0249
   Holland *(G-8507)*

E C Shaw Company of Ohio .... E 513 721-6334
   Cincinnati *(G-2848)*

Flexoplate Inc .... F 513 489-0433
   Blue Ash *(G-1395)*

Gli Holdings Inc .... D 440 892-7760
   Stow *(G-13700)*

▲ Gli Holdings Inc .... D 216 651-1500
   Stow *(G-13701)*

Hadronics Inc .... D 513 321-9350
   Cincinnati *(G-2983)*

Harris Paper Crafts Inc .... F 614 299-2141
   Columbus *(G-5421)*

▲ Kehl-Kolor Inc .... E 419 281-3107
   Ashland *(G-585)*

Keystone Press Inc .... G 419 243-7326
   Toledo *(G-14347)*

▲ Mark-All Enterprises LLC .... E 800 433-3615
   Akron *(G-235)*

Master Marking Company Inc .... F 330 688-6797
   Cuyahoga Falls *(G-6102)*

Penguin Enterprises Inc .... E 440 899-5112
   Westlake *(G-15773)*

Pinnacle Graphics Imaging Inc .... G 216 781-1800
   Cleveland *(G-4553)*

Plate Engraving Corporation .... G 330 239-2155
   Medina *(G-10365)*

Precision Reflex Inc .... F 419 629-2603
   New Bremen *(G-11407)*

Prime Printing Inc .... E 937 438-3707
   Dayton *(G-6522)*

Quality Rubber Stamp Inc .... G 614 235-2700
   Lancaster *(G-9034)*

R E May Inc .... E 216 771-6332
   Cleveland *(G-4612)*

Roban Inc .... G 330 794-1059
   Lakemore *(G-8958)*

Sams Graphic Industries .... F 330 821-4710
   Alliance *(G-422)*

Southern Graphic Systems LLC .... E 513 648-4641
   Cincinnati *(G-3403)*

Stevenson Color Inc .... C 513 321-7500
   Cincinnati *(G-3422)*

The Photo-Type Engraving Company ..... D 513 281-0999
   Cincinnati *(G-3450)*

Universal Urethane Pdts Inc .... D 419 693-7400
   Toledo *(G-14514)*

▲ West-Camp Press Inc .... D 614 882-2378
   Westerville *(G-15725)*

Williams Steel Rule Die Co .... F 216 431-3232
   Cleveland *(G-4910)*

◆ Wood Graphics Inc .... E 513 771-6300
   Cincinnati *(G-3525)*

Youngstown ARC Engraving Co .... G 330 793-2471
   Youngstown *(G-16476)*

28 CHEMICALS AND ALLIED PRODUCTS

2812 Alkalies and chlorine

Albemarle Amendments LLC .... E 330 425-2354
   Twinsburg *(G-14627)*

Church & Dwight Co Inc .... F 740 852-3621
   London *(G-9384)*

Church & Dwight Co Inc .... F 419 992-4244
   Old Fort *(G-12072)*

Eltech Systems Corporation .... G 440 285-0380
   Concord Township *(G-5906)*

Geon Company .... A 216 447-6000
   Cleveland *(G-4121)*

◆ GFS Chemicals Inc .... E 740 881-5501
   Powell *(G-12674)*

▲ INEOS KOH INC .... C 440 997-5221
   Ashtabula *(G-639)*

Jci Jones Chemicals Inc .... F 330 825-2531
   New Franklin *(G-11438)*

▲ National Colloid Company .... E 740 282-1171
   Steubenville *(G-13673)*

National Lime and Stone Co .... E 419 396-7671
   Carey *(G-2281)*

Occidental Chemical Corp .... E 513 242-2900
   Cincinnati *(G-3211)*

▲ Valvsys LLC .... G 513 870-1234
   Hamilton *(G-8256)*

2813 Industrial gases

Airgas Usa LLC .... E 330 454-1330
   Canton *(G-2031)*

Airgas Usa LLC .... G 937 222-8312
   Moraine *(G-11154)*

Airgas Usa LLC .... G 440 232-6397
   Twinsburg *(G-14625)*

Atlantic Welding LLC .... F 937 570-5094
   Piqua *(G-12505)*

Cold Jet International LLC .... D 513 831-3211
   Loveland *(G-9478)*

Delille Oxygen Company .... G 937 325-9595
   Springfield *(G-13553)*

Delille Oxygen Company .... E 614 444-1177
   Columbus *(G-5324)*

Eco Energy International LLC .... E 419 544-5000
   Mansfield *(G-9650)*

28 CHEMICALS AND ALLIED PRODUCTS

Endurance Manufacturing Inc................F..... 330 628-2600
   Akron *(G-139)*
Helium Seo...D..... 513 563-3065
   Blue Ash *(G-1406)*
Invacare Corporation...............................G..... 800 333-6900
   Elyria *(G-7166)*
◆ Invacare Corporation..............................A..... 440 329-6000
   Elyria *(G-7164)*
Linde Gas & Equipment Inc....................G..... 513 821-2192
   Cincinnati *(G-3107)*
Linde Gas & Equipment Inc....................G..... 614 846-7048
   Columbus *(G-5528)*
Linde Gas & Equipment Inc....................E..... 614 443-7687
   Columbus *(G-5529)*
Linde Gas & Equipment Inc....................E..... 419 729-7732
   Toledo *(G-14368)*
Linde Gas & Equipment Inc....................G..... 440 944-8844
   Wickliffe *(G-15837)*
Linde Gas USA LLC................................F..... 330 425-3989
   Twinsburg *(G-14689)*
Linde Inc..F..... 440 994-1000
   Ashtabula *(G-646)*
Linde Inc..G..... 330 825-4449
   Barberton *(G-877)*
Linde Inc..F..... 440 237-8690
   Cleveland *(G-4327)*
Linde Inc..G..... 419 698-8005
   Oregon *(G-12106)*
Matheson Tri-Gas Inc..............................G..... 419 865-8881
   Holland *(G-8518)*
Matheson Tri-Gas Inc..............................G..... 513 727-9638
   Middletown *(G-10842)*
Messer LLC..E..... 216 533-7256
   Cleveland *(G-4395)*
Messer LLC..G..... 419 822-3909
   Delta *(G-6788)*
Messer LLC..G..... 614 539-2259
   Grove City *(G-8105)*
Messer LLC..F..... 419 227-9585
   Lima *(G-9268)*
Messer LLC..G..... 419 221-5043
   Lima *(G-9269)*
Messer LLC..F..... 513 831-4742
   Miamiville *(G-10712)*
Messer LLC..F..... 330 608-3008
   Uniontown *(G-14788)*
Messer LLC..G..... 330 394-4541
   Warren *(G-15190)*
National Gas & Oil Corporation...............E..... 740 344-2102
   Newark *(G-11596)*
Neon...G..... 216 541-5600
   Cleveland *(G-4444)*
Neon City...G..... 440 301-2000
   Cleveland *(G-4445)*
Neon Health Services Inc........................E..... 216 231-7700
   Cleveland *(G-4446)*
Northast Ohio Nghbrhood Hlth S............E..... 216 751-3100
   Cleveland *(G-4474)*
Ohio Nitrogen LLC...................................G..... 216 839-5485
   Beachwood *(G-1006)*
Osair Inc..G..... 440 974-6500
   Mentor *(G-10516)*
◆ Plasti-Kote Co Inc...................................C..... 330 725-4511
   Medina *(G-10363)*
Reliable Mfg Co LLC................................G..... 740 756-9373
   Carroll *(G-2302)*
Welders Supply Inc.................................F..... 216 241-1696
   Cleveland *(G-4903)*
Wellston Aerosol Mfg Co........................F..... 740 384-2320
   Wellston *(G-15333)*
◆ Western/Scott Fetzer Company..............E..... 440 892-3000
   Westlake *(G-15801)*

Wright Brothers Inc.................................F..... 513 731-2222
   Cincinnati *(G-3527)*
▲ Zenex International.................................F..... 440 232-4155
   Bedford *(G-1162)*
Zephyr Solutions LLC..............................F..... 440 937-9993
   Avon *(G-795)*

2816 Inorganic pigments

◆ American Colors Inc................................E..... 419 621-4000
   Sandusky *(G-13043)*
Americhem Inc..E..... 330 926-3185
   Cuyahoga Falls *(G-6065)*
◆ Americhem Inc..D..... 330 929-4213
   Cuyahoga Falls *(G-6064)*
Ampacet Corporation..............................D..... 740 929-5521
   Newark *(G-11561)*
Arconic..E..... 330 471-1844
   Canton *(G-2039)*
Avient Corporation..................................E..... 419 668-4844
   Norwalk *(G-11933)*
◆ Chromascape LLC...................................E..... 330 998-7574
   Independence *(G-8658)*
◆ Colormatrix Corporation..........................C..... 216 622-0100
   Berea *(G-1272)*
Day-Glo Color Corp.................................F..... 216 391-7070
   Cleveland *(G-3945)*
Day-Glo Color Corp.................................F..... 216 391-7070
   Twinsburg *(G-14647)*
▲ Day-Glo Color Corp.................................C..... 216 391-7070
   Cleveland *(G-3944)*
▲ Degussa Incorporated.............................G..... 513 733-5111
   Cincinnati *(G-2823)*
◆ Eckart America Corporation....................D..... 440 954-7600
   Painesville *(G-12231)*
Enviri Corporation...................................F..... 330 372-1781
   Warren *(G-15168)*
Ferro International Svcs Inc...................G..... 216 875-5600
   Mayfield Heights *(G-10248)*
General Color Investments Inc...............D..... 330 868-4161
   Minerva *(G-11031)*
▲ Gsdi Specialty Dispersions Inc...............E..... 330 848-9200
   Massillon *(G-10103)*
Ironics Inc...G..... 330 652-0583
   Niles *(G-11673)*
ISK Americas Incorporated.....................F..... 440 357-4600
   Concord Township *(G-5908)*
◆ Kish Company Inc..................................F..... 440 205-9970
   Mentor *(G-10487)*
Lancer Dispersions Inc...........................D
   Akron *(G-216)*
Leonhardt Plating Company...................F..... 513 242-1410
   Cincinnati *(G-3102)*
Lyondllbsell Advnced Plymers I..............E..... 419 682-3311
   Stryker *(G-13910)*
▲ Mason Color Works Inc..........................F..... 330 385-4400
   East Liverpool *(G-6998)*
McCann Color Inc....................................E..... 330 498-4840
   Canton *(G-2156)*
Obron Atlantic Corporation.....................D..... 440 954-7600
   Painesville *(G-12252)*
PMC Specialties Group Inc.....................F..... 513 242-3300
   Cincinnati *(G-3263)*
PMC Specialties Group Inc.....................E..... 513 242-3300
   Cincinnati *(G-3262)*
Revlis Corporation..................................F..... 330 535-2108
   Barberton *(G-893)*
Sun Chemical Corporation......................C..... 513 681-5950
   Cincinnati *(G-3431)*
◆ The Shepherd Color Company................C..... 513 874-0714
   West Chester *(G-15596)*
◆ Thorworks Industries Inc.......................C..... 419 626-4375
   Sandusky *(G-13096)*

◆ Vibrantz Color Solutions Inc...................C..... 440 997-5137
   Ashtabula *(G-664)*
Vibrantz Corporation..............................E..... 724 207-2152
   Cleveland *(G-4869)*
◆ Vibrantz Corporation..............................D..... 216 875-5600
   Mayfield Heights *(G-10256)*
Vwm-Republic Inc...................................F..... 216 641-2575
   Cleveland *(G-4886)*
Whiterock Pigments Inc.........................F..... 216 391-7765
   Cleveland *(G-4906)*
Wogen Resources America LLC..............G..... 216 272-0062
   Valley City *(G-14901)*

2819 Industrial inorganic chemicals, nec

5th Element Fitness LLC........................G..... 614 537-6038
   Columbus *(G-5078)*
Airgas Usa LLC......................................G..... 937 222-8312
   Moraine *(G-11154)*
Airgas Usa LLC......................................G..... 440 232-6397
   Twinsburg *(G-14025)*
▲ Akron Dispersions Inc............................G..... 330 666-0045
   Copley *(G-5942)*
Albemarle Amendments LLC..................E..... 330 425-2354
   Twinsburg *(G-14627)*
▲ Alchem Corporation................................G..... 330 725-2436
   Medina *(G-10292)*
Aldrich Chemical....................................D..... 937 859-1808
   Miamisburg *(G-10608)*
Alfrebro LLC..F..... 513 539-7373
   Monroe *(G-11093)*
Alpha Zeta Holdings Inc........................G..... 216 271-1601
   Cleveland *(G-3640)*
◆ Aluchem Inc..E..... 513 733-8519
   Cincinnati *(G-2612)*
Aluchem of Jackson Inc........................G..... 740 286-2455
   Jackson *(G-8708)*
◆ Americhem Inc..D..... 330 929-4213
   Cuyahoga Falls *(G-6064)*
Arboris LLC..E..... 740 522-9350
   Newark *(G-11565)*
▲ Baerlocher Production Usa LLC..............E..... 513 482-6300
   Cincinnati *(G-2654)*
▲ Baerlocher Usa LLC...............................F..... 330 364-6000
   Dover *(G-6808)*
▲ Barium & Chemicals Inc........................E..... 740 282-9776
   Steubenville *(G-13661)*
BASF Catalysts LLC................................C..... 216 360-5005
   Cleveland *(G-3723)*
BASF Catalysts LLC................................C..... 440 322-3741
   Elyria *(G-7115)*
BASF Corporation...................................D..... 614 662-5682
   Columbus *(G-5176)*
Bio-Systems Corporation.......................E..... 608 365-9550
   Bowling Green *(G-1555)*
BLaster Holdings LLC.............................G..... 216 901-5800
   Cleveland *(G-3741)*
BLaster LLC..E..... 216 901-5800
   Cleveland *(G-3742)*
Bleachtech LLC......................................E..... 216 921-1980
   Seville *(G-13139)*
Bond Chemicals Inc...............................F..... 330 725-5935
   Medina *(G-10303)*
◆ Borchers Americas Inc...........................D..... 440 899-2950
   Westlake *(G-15741)*
Calgon Carbon Corporation....................G..... 614 258-9501
   Columbus *(G-5226)*
▲ Calvary Industries Inc...........................E..... 513 874-1113
   Fairfield *(G-7342)*
▲ Capital Resin Corporation......................D..... 614 445-7177
   Columbus *(G-5233)*
Chem Technologies Ltd.........................D..... 440 632-9311
   Middlefield *(G-10740)*

SIC SECTION
28 CHEMICALS AND ALLIED PRODUCTS

▲ Chemspec Usa Inc .... D 330 669-8512
   Orrville *(G-12121)*

Chemtrade Chemicals US LLC .... G 419 255-0193
   Toledo *(G-14237)*

Chemtrade Logistics Inc .... E 216 566-8070
   Cleveland *(G-3817)*

Chemtrade Refinery Svcs Inc .... F 419 641-4151
   Cairo *(G-1905)*

Christy Catalytics LLC .... G 740 982-1302
   Crooksville *(G-6045)*

▲ Cil Isotope Separations LLC .... F 937 376-5413
   Xenia *(G-16255)*

▲ Cirba Solutions Us Inc .... E 740 653-6290
   Lancaster *(G-9000)*

◆ Columbia Chemical Corporation .... E 330 225-3200
   Brunswick *(G-1753)*

▲ Coolant Control Inc .... E 513 471-8770
   Cincinnati *(G-2795)*

◆ Current Lighting Solutions LLC .... B 216 462-4700
   Beachwood *(G-982)*

Db Parent Inc .... G 513 475-3265
   Cincinnati *(G-2821)*

◆ Detrex Corporation .... F 216 749-2605
   Cleveland *(G-3954)*

Diverseylever Inc .... G 513 554-4200
   Cincinnati *(G-2831)*

Diversified Brands .... G 216 595-8777
   Bedford *(G-1117)*

◆ Dover Chemical Corporation .... C 330 343-7711
   Dover *(G-6818)*

Dupont Electronic Polymers LP .... D 937 268-3411
   Dayton *(G-6308)*

Eagle Chemicals Inc .... F 513 868-9662
   Hamilton *(G-8204)*

Elco Corporation .... E 440 997-6131
   Ashtabula *(G-631)*

Element 41 Inc .... F 440 579-5531
   Painesville *(G-12232)*

Element 41 Inc .... G 216 410-5646
   Chardon *(G-2450)*

Elements Hr Inc .... G 614 488-6944
   Columbus *(G-5348)*

◆ Eliokem Inc .... D 330 734-1100
   Fairlawn *(G-7438)*

▲ Engelhard Corp .... G 440 322-3741
   Elyria *(G-7149)*

Essential Elements Usa LLC .... E 513 482-5700
   Cincinnati *(G-2884)*

Evonik Corporation .... D 513 554-8969
   Cincinnati *(G-2889)*

Ferro Corporation .... D 216 577-7144
   Bedford *(G-1121)*

◆ Ferroglobe USA Mtllurgical Inc .... C 740 984-2361
   Waterford *(G-15236)*

Flexsys Inc .... B 212 605-6000
   Akron *(G-156)*

Four Elements Inc .... G 330 591-4505
   Medina *(G-10327)*

◆ Gayston Corporation .... C 937 743-6050
   Miamisburg *(G-10640)*

General Electric Company .... E 216 268-3846
   Cleveland *(G-4114)*

GFS Chemicals Inc .... E 614 351-5347
   Columbus *(G-5402)*

GFS Chemicals Inc .... D 614 224-5345
   Columbus *(G-5403)*

◆ GFS Chemicals Inc .... E 740 881-5501
   Powell *(G-12674)*

Helena Agri-Enterprises LLC .... G 614 275-4200
   Columbus *(G-5426)*

Helena Agri-Enterprises LLC .... G 419 596-3806
   Continental *(G-5937)*

▲ Heraeus Epurio LLC .... E 937 264-1000
   Vandalia *(G-14942)*

Hilltop Energy Inc .... F 330 859-2108
   Mineral City *(G-11018)*

Illinois Tool Works Inc .... D 440 914-3100
   Solon *(G-13366)*

Ineos Pigments Asu LLC .... E 440 994-1999
   Ashtabula *(G-640)*

Ineos Pigments USA Inc .... C 440 994-1400
   Ashtabula *(G-641)*

Intrepid Co .... G 440 355-6089
   Lagrange *(G-8949)*

▲ J R M Chemical Inc .... F 216 475-8488
   Cleveland *(G-4245)*

Jmp Industries .... G 216 749-6030
   Cleveland *(G-4257)*

◆ Jones-Hamilton Co .... D 419 666-9838
   Walbridge *(G-15083)*

Kc Marketing LLC .... E 513 471-8770
   Cincinnati *(G-3067)*

Kerry Flavor Systems Us LLC .... F 513 539-7373
   Monroe *(G-11113)*

Kingscote Chemicals Inc .... G 330 523-5300
   Richfield *(G-12790)*

◆ Lithium Innovations Co LLC .... G 419 725-3525
   Toledo *(G-14369)*

Littlern Corporation .... G 330 848-8847
   Fairlawn *(G-7444)*

◆ Malco Products Inc .... C 330 753-0361
   Barberton *(G-879)*

Marsulex Inc .... E 419 698-8181
   Oregon *(G-12107)*

McGean-Rohco Inc .... F 216 441-4900
   Newburgh Heights *(G-11618)*

◆ McGean-Rohco Inc .... D 216 441-4900
   Newburgh Heights *(G-11619)*

▲ Nachurs Alpine Solutions LLC .... E 740 382-5701
   Marion *(G-9864)*

▲ National Colloid Company .... E 740 282-1171
   Steubenville *(G-13673)*

New Eezy-Gro Inc .... F 419 927-6110
   Upper Sandusky *(G-14817)*

Norlab Inc .... F 440 282-5265
   Lorain *(G-9426)*

Nutrien AG Solutions Inc .... G 513 941-4100
   North Bend *(G-11705)*

Occidental Chemical Corp .... E 513 242-2900
   Cincinnati *(G-3211)*

▲ Occidental Chemical Durez .... F 419 675-1310
   Kenton *(G-8895)*

Ohio Coatings Company .... D 740 859-5500
   Yorkville *(G-16294)*

Om Group Inc .... F 216 781-0083
   Cleveland *(G-4501)*

Omnova Wallcovering USA Inc .... D 216 682-7000
   Beachwood *(G-1008)*

Omya Distribution LLC .... F 513 387-4600
   Mason *(G-10035)*

◆ Omya Inc .... C 513 387-4600
   Blue Ash *(G-1446)*

P Q Corp .... G 216 621-0840
   Cleveland *(G-4516)*

Pcs Phosphate Company Inc .... C 513 738-1261
   Harrison *(G-8283)*

◆ Perstorp Polyols Inc .... C 419 729-5448
   Toledo *(G-14434)*

PMC Specialties Group Inc .... F 513 242-3300
   Cincinnati *(G-3263)*

◆ PMC Specialties Group Inc .... E 513 242-3300
   Cincinnati *(G-3262)*

▲ Polymerics Inc .... E 330 928-2210
   Cuyahoga Falls *(G-6110)*

Primary Pdts Ingrdnts Amrcas L .... D 937 236-5906
   Dayton *(G-6520)*

Pureti Group LLC .... F 513 708-3631
   Blue Ash *(G-1458)*

PVS Chemical Solutions Inc .... F 330 666-0888
   Copley *(G-5955)*

Qc LLC .... E 847 682-9072
   North Lima *(G-11811)*

Quanta International LLC .... F 513 354-3639
   Cincinnati *(G-3313)*

Saint-Gobain Ceramics Plas Inc .... C 330 673-5860
   Stow *(G-13721)*

Shepherd Material Science Co .... F 513 731-1110
   Norwood *(G-11998)*

▲ Shepherd Widnes Ltd .... D 513 731-1110
   Norwood *(G-11999)*

Solvay Advanced Polymers LLC .... D 740 373-9242
   Marietta *(G-9827)*

Synthomer Inc .... F 330 734-1237
   Akron *(G-342)*

◆ Synthomer Inc .... C 216 682-7000
   Beachwood *(G-1025)*

◆ The Shepherd Chemical Company .... C 513 731-1110
   Norwood *(G-12001)*

▲ Union Camp Corp .... G 330 343-7701
   Dover *(G-6849)*

◆ United Initiators Inc .... D 440 323-3112
   Elyria *(G-7215)*

Univar Solutions USA LLC .... F 513 714-5264
   West Chester *(G-15602)*

Usalco Michigan City Plant LLC .... F 513 737-7100
   Fairfield *(G-7422)*

Vibrantz Corporation .... F 442 224-6100
   Cleveland *(G-4870)*

▲ VWR Chemicals LLC .... E 800 448-4442
   Solon *(G-13444)*

WA Hammond Drierite Co Ltd .... E 937 376-2927
   Xenia *(G-16280)*

Wisconsin Indus Sand Co LLC .... E 715 235-0942
   Independence *(G-8692)*

◆ Zaclon LLC .... E 216 271-1601
   Cleveland *(G-4930)*

2821 Plastics materials and resins

A R E Logistics LLC .... G 330 327-7315
   Massillon *(G-10074)*

A Westlake Axiall Co .... G 614 754-3677
   Columbus *(G-5081)*

Accurate Plastics LLC .... F 330 701-0019
   Kent *(G-8793)*

▼ Ada Solutions Inc .... G 440 576-0423
   Jefferson *(G-8744)*

Advanced Fiber LLC .... E 419 562-1337
   Bucyrus *(G-1849)*

Al-Co Products Inc .... G 419 399-3867
   Latty *(G-9053)*

Altera Polymers LLC .... F 864 973-7000
   Jefferson *(G-8745)*

American Polymers Corporation .... G 330 666-6048
   Akron *(G-61)*

American Turf Recycling LLC .... G 440 323-0306
   Elyria *(G-7109)*

Americas Styrenics LLC .... D 740 302-8667
   Ironton *(G-8696)*

Amros Industries Inc .... E 216 433-0010
   Cleveland *(G-3659)*

Anchor Hocking Glass Company .... G 740 681-6025
   Lancaster *(G-8988)*

Aptiv Services Us LLC .... D 330 373-7614
   Warren *(G-15141)*

Arclin USA LLC .... G 419 726-5013
   Toledo *(G-14198)*

Employee Codes: A=Over 500 employees, B=251-500
C=101-250, D=51-100, E=20-50, F=10-19, G=1-9

28 CHEMICALS AND ALLIED PRODUCTS

▲ Aurora Plastics LLC .... E 330 422-0700
　Streetsboro *(G-13757)*
Avient Corporation .... F 440 930-3727
　Avon Lake *(G-798)*
Avient Corporation .... F 800 727-4338
　Greenville *(G-8037)*
Avient Corporation .... F 330 834-3812
　Massillon *(G-10077)*
◆ Avient Corporation .... D 440 930-1000
　Avon Lake *(G-797)*
Aviles Construction Co Inc .... F 216 939-1084
　Cleveland *(G-3708)*
Axiom International Inc .... G 330 396-5942
　Akron *(G-71)*
Bakelite Chemicals LLC .... D 404 652-4000
　Columbus *(G-5172)*
Bamberger Polymers Inc .... F 614 718-9104
　Dublin *(G-6866)*
BCi and V Investments Inc .... F 330 538-0660
　North Jackson *(G-11770)*
Benvic Trinity LLC .... E 609 520-0000
　West Unity *(G-15637)*
Biobent Holdings LLC .... G 513 658-5560
　Columbus *(G-5190)*
Biothane Coated Webbing Corp ... G 440 327-0485
　North Olmsted *(G-11819)*
▲ Biothane Coated Webbing Corp ... E 440 327-0485
　North Ridgeville *(G-11832)*
Cameo Countertops Inc .... E 419 865-6371
　Holland *(G-8496)*
▲ Capital Resin Corporation .... D 614 445-7177
　Columbus *(G-5233)*
Carlisle Plastics Company .... G 937 845-9411
　New Carlisle *(G-11412)*
▲ Chem-Materials Inc .... F 440 455-9465
　Westlake *(G-15743)*
▲ Chemionics Corporation .... E 330 733-8834
　Tallmadge *(G-14024)*
Chroma Color Corporation .... E 740 363-6622
　Delaware *(G-6710)*
Clyde Tool & Die Inc .... F 419 547-9574
　Clyde *(G-4971)*
◆ Concrete Sealants Inc .... E 937 845-8776
　Tipp City *(G-14130)*
Covestro LLC .... C 740 929-2015
　Hebron *(G-8337)*
Crane Blending Center .... E 614 542-1199
　Columbus *(G-5305)*
▲ Crg Plastics Inc .... F 937 298-2025
　Dayton *(G-6267)*
▲ Crown Plastics Co LLC .... D 513 367-0238
　Harrison *(G-8272)*
Current Inc .... G 330 392-5151
　Warren *(G-15159)*
Cuyahoga Molded Plastics Co (inc) .. E 216 261-2744
　Euclid *(G-7266)*
Ddp Specialty Electronic MA .... C 937 839-4612
　West Alexandria *(G-15341)*
Deltech Polymers LLC .... E 937 339-3150
　Troy *(G-14561)*
Dentsply Sirona Inc .... E 419 865-9497
　Maumee *(G-10200)*
Diamant Polymers Inc .... G 513 979-4011
　Cincinnati *(G-2828)*
◆ Diamond Polymers Incorporated ... D 330 773-2700
　Akron *(G-128)*
Dupont Specialty Pdts USA LLC ... D 740 474-0635
　Circleville *(G-3547)*
Dupont Specialty Pdts USA LLC ... E 740 474-0220
　Circleville *(G-3548)*
Durez Corporation .... E 567 295-6400
　Kenton *(G-8882)*

E C Shaw Company of Ohio .... E 513 721-6334
　Cincinnati *(G-2848)*
E P S Specialists Ltd Inc .... G 513 489-3676
　Cincinnati *(G-2850)*
Eagle Elastomer Inc .... E 330 923-7070
　Peninsula *(G-12340)*
Elyria Foundry Company LLC ...... D 440 322-4657
　Elyria *(G-7141)*
Engineered Polymer Systems LLC .. G 216 255-2116
　Medina *(G-10319)*
Ep Bollinger LLC .... A 513 941-1101
　Cincinnati *(G-2878)*
Epsilyte Holdings LLC .... D 937 778-9500
　Piqua *(G-12515)*
◆ Etna Products Incorporated ...... E 440 543-9845
　Chagrin Falls *(G-2395)*
◆ Evans Adhesive Corporation Ltd ... E 614 451-2665
　Columbus *(G-5363)*
Evergreen Recycling LLC .... E 419 547-1400
　Clyde *(G-4972)*
Fibre Glast Dvlpments Corp LLC ... F 937 833-5200
　Brookville *(G-1735)*
Flex Technologies Inc .... D 330 897-6311
　Baltic *(G-836)*
◆ Flexsys America LP .... D 330 666-4111
　Akron *(G-155)*
◆ Franklin International Inc .... B 614 443-0241
　Columbus *(G-5387)*
Freeman Manufacturing & Sup Co ... E 440 934-1902
　Avon *(G-775)*
Freudenberg-Nok General Partnr ... E 937 335-3306
　Troy *(G-14571)*
◆ Gabriel Phenoxies Inc .... E 704 499-9801
　Akron *(G-160)*
Gayson Silicon Dispersions Inc ..... G 330 848-8422
　Avon Lake *(G-808)*
General Polymers .... F 330 896-7126
　Akron *(G-167)*
Genius Solutions Engrg Co .... E 419 794-9914
　Maumee *(G-10202)*
▼ Geo-Tech Polymers LLC .... F 614 797-2300
　Waverly *(G-15281)*
Geon Company .... A 216 447-6000
　Cleveland *(G-4121)*
Geon Performance Solutions LLC ... E 440 930-1000
　Avon Lake *(G-809)*
Geon Performance Solutions LLC ... D 440 987-4553
　Elyria *(G-7155)*
▲ Goldsmith & Eggleton Inc .... F 330 336-6616
　Wadsworth *(G-15032)*
◆ Goldsmith & Eggleton LLC .... F 203 855-6000
　Wadsworth *(G-15033)*
Gsh Industries Inc .... E 440 238-3009
　Strongsville *(G-13837)*
Hancor Inc .... E 419 424-8225
　Findlay *(G-7521)*
▲ Hexa Americas Inc .... E 937 497-7900
　Sidney *(G-13252)*
Hexion Inc .... C 888 443-9466
　Columbus *(G-5428)*
◆ Hexion LLC .... D 614 225-4000
　Columbus *(G-5429)*
▼ Hexion Topco LLC .... D 614 225-4000
　Columbus *(G-5430)*
▼ Hexion US Finance Corp .... E 614 225-4000
　Columbus *(G-5431)*
▲ Hexpol Compounding LLC .... E 440 834-4644
　Burton *(G-1881)*
Hexpol Holding Inc .... F 440 834-4644
　Burton *(G-1882)*
◆ Hfi LLC .... B 614 491-0700
　Canal Winchester *(G-1987)*

Hggc Citadel Plas Holdings Inc ..... E 330 666-3751
　Fairlawn *(G-7441)*
Hpc Holdings LLC .... A 440 224-7204
　North Kingsville *(G-11796)*
Hpc Holdings LLC .... F 330 666-3751
　Fairlawn *(G-7442)*
Huntsman Advnced Mtls Amrcas L ... E 330 374-2424
　Akron *(G-185)*
Huntsman Advnced Mtls Amrcas L ... E 866 800-2436
　Akron *(G-186)*
Huntsman Corporation .... D 330 374-2418
　Akron *(G-187)*
▲ ICP Adhesives and Sealants Inc .... E 330 753-4585
　Norton *(G-11944)*
▲ Ier Fujikura Inc .... C 330 425-7121
　Macedonia *(G-9556)*
Illinois Tool Works Inc .... C 513 489-7600
　Blue Ash *(G-1408)*
▲ Incredible Solutions Inc .... F 330 898-3878
　Warren *(G-13177)*
Industrial Thermoset Plas Inc ...... F 440 975-0411
　Mentor *(G-10472)*
▲ Ineos LLC .... D 419 226-1200
　Lima *(G-9255)*
◆ Ineos ABS (usa) LLC .... C 513 467-2400
　Addyston *(G-8)*
Ineos Composites Us LLC .... E 614 790-9299
　Columbus *(G-5458)*
Ineos Neal LLC .... E 610 790-3333
　Dublin *(G-6896)*
▲ Ineos Nitriles USA LLC .... F 281 535-6600
　Lima *(G-9256)*
Ineos Solvents Sales US Corp ..... B 614 790-3333
　Dublin *(G-6897)*
Integra Enclosures Limited .... D 440 269-4966
　Mentor *(G-10474)*
Integrated Chem Concepts Inc ..... G 440 838-5666
　Brecksville *(G-1622)*
▲ Interntnal Tchncal Plymr Syste ... E 330 505-1218
　Niles *(G-11672)*
▲ Isochem Incorporated .... F 614 775-9328
　New Albany *(G-11380)*
J P Industrial Products Inc .... F 330 627-1377
　Carrollton *(G-2310)*
▲ J P Industrial Products Inc ...... G 330 424-1110
　Lisbon *(G-9319)*
Jaco Products LLC .... G 614 219-1670
　Hilliard *(G-8415)*
◆ Jain America Foods Inc .... E 614 850-9400
　Columbus *(G-5486)*
JB Polymers Inc .... G 216 941-7041
　Oberlin *(G-12053)*
Jeg Associates Inc .... F 614 882-1295
　Westerville *(G-15711)*
Jerico Plastic Industries Inc .... E 330 868-4600
　Wadsworth *(G-15038)*
▲ JMS Industries Inc .... F 937 325-3502
　Springfield *(G-13584)*
◆ Kardol Quality Products LLC .... G 513 933-8206
　Blue Ash *(G-1416)*
Kathom Manufacturing Co Inc ..... E 513 868-8890
　Middletown *(G-10835)*
◆ Key Resin Company .... F 513 943-4225
　Batavia *(G-927)*
Kirtley Mold Inc .... G 330 472-2427
　Akron *(G-211)*
Kraton Corporation .... D 740 423-7571
　Belpre *(G-1255)*
Kraton Polymers US LLC .... B 740 423-7571
　Belpre *(G-1257)*
Lattice Composites LLC .... B 440 543-7526
　Chagrin Falls *(G-2406)*

28 CHEMICALS AND ALLIED PRODUCTS

Lrbg Chemicals USA Inc .... E 419 244-5856
 Toledo *(G-14371)*

Lubrizol Global Management Inc .... E 440 933-0400
 Avon Lake *(G-815)*

Lyondell Chemical Company .... C 440 352-9393
 Fairport Harbor *(G-7455)*

Lyondllbsell Advnced Plymers I .... C 330 773-2700
 Akron *(G-226)*

Lyondllbsell Advnced Plymers I .... C 330 630-0308
 Akron *(G-227)*

Lyondllbsell Advnced Plymers I .... D 330 630-3315
 Akron *(G-228)*

Lyondllbsell Advnced Plymers I .... E 330 498-4840
 Akron *(G-229)*

Lyondllbsell Advnced Plymers I .... E 440 224-7544
 Geneva *(G-7942)*

Lyondllbsell Advnced Plymers I .... D 419 872-1408
 Perrysburg *(G-12397)*

Lyondllbsell Advnced Plymers I .... E 419 682-3311
 Stryker *(G-13910)*

▲ Maintenance Repair Supply Inc .... F 740 922-3006
 Midvale *(G-10881)*

◆ Mar-Bal Inc .... D 440 543-7526
 Chagrin Falls *(G-2407)*

Material Processing & Hdlg Co .... F 419 436-9562
 Fostoria *(G-7643)*

Meggitt (erlanger) LLC .... D 513 851-5550
 Cincinnati *(G-3143)*

◆ Mexichem Specialty Resins Inc .... E 440 930-1435
 Avon Lake *(G-817)*

Michael Day Enterprises LLC .... E 330 335-5100
 Wadsworth *(G-15044)*

Mitsubishi Chemical Amer Inc .... C 586 755-1660
 Bellevue *(G-1229)*

Modern Plastics Recovery Inc .... F 419 622-4611
 Haviland *(G-8314)*

◆ Multi-Plastics Inc .... D 740 548-4894
 Lewis Center *(G-9172)*

▲ Multibase Inc .... D 330 666-0505
 Copley *(G-5952)*

▲ Mum Industries Inc .... D 440 269-4966
 Mentor *(G-10508)*

Nanofiber Solutions LLC .... F 614 319-3075
 Dublin *(G-6913)*

▼ Nanosperse LLC .... G 937 296-5030
 Kettering *(G-8908)*

National Polymer Dev Co Inc .... G 440 708-1245
 Chagrin Falls *(G-2408)*

◆ Network Polymers Inc .... E 330 773-2700
 Akron *(G-261)*

Next Generation Plastics LLC .... F 330 668-1200
 Fairlawn *(G-7445)*

◆ Next Specialty Resins Inc .... E 419 843-4600
 Sylvania *(G-14009)*

North American Composites .... G 440 930-0602
 Avon Lake *(G-819)*

Nu-Tech Polymers Co Inc .... G 513 942-6003
 Cincinnati *(G-3207)*

Oak View Enterprises Inc .... E 513 860-4446
 Bucyrus *(G-1864)*

Occidental Chemical Corp .... E 513 242-2900
 Cincinnati *(G-3211)*

Ohio Foam Corporation .... F 419 492-2151
 New Washington *(G-11550)*

Ohio Plastics & Belting Co LLC .... G 330 882-6764
 New Franklin *(G-11440)*

Ohio Rotational Molding LLC .... F 419 608-5040
 Holgate *(G-8490)*

OK Industries Inc .... E 419 435-2361
 Fostoria *(G-7649)*

OPC Polymers LLC .... C 614 253-8511
 Columbus *(G-5642)*

▲ OSI Global Sourcing LLC .... F 614 471-4800
 Columbus *(G-5645)*

▲ Ovation Plymr Tech Engnred Mtl ...... E 330 723-5686
 Medina *(G-10359)*

Owens Corning Sales LLC .... F 330 633-6735
 Tallmadge *(G-14042)*

▲ Performnce Plymr Solutions Inc .... F 937 298-3713
 Moraine *(G-11196)*

◆ Perstorp Polyols Inc .... C 419 729-5448
 Toledo *(G-14434)*

▲ Pet Processors LLc .... D 440 354-4321
 Painesville *(G-12257)*

Pilot Polymer Technologies .... G 412 735-4799
 West Chester *(G-15478)*

Pitt Plastics Inc .... D 614 868-8660
 Columbus *(G-5675)*

Plaskolite LLC .... E 614 294-3281
 Columbus *(G-5677)*

Plaskolite LLC .... C 740 450-1109
 Zanesville *(G-16556)*

◆ Plaskolite LLC .... C 614 294-3281
 Columbus *(G-5678)*

Plastic Compounders Inc .... E 740 432-7371
 Cambridge *(G-1948)*

Plastic Materials Inc .... E 330 468-5706
 Macedonia *(G-9565)*

◆ Plastic Suppliers Inc .... E 614 471-9100
 Columbus *(G-5679)*

Polimeros Usa LLC .... G 216 591-0175
 Warrensville Heights *(G-15230)*

▲ Poly-Carb Inc .... D 440 248-1223
 Macedonia *(G-9567)*

▼ Polymer Concepts Inc .... G 440 953-9605
 Mentor *(G-10527)*

◆ Polymer Packaging Inc .... D 330 832-2000
 North Canton *(G-11751)*

Polymer Stamping Tech LLC .... G 616 371-4004
 Troy *(G-14602)*

Polymer Tech & Svcs Inc .... F 740 929-5500
 Heath *(G-8327)*

Polymerics Inc .... E 330 677-1131
 Kent *(G-8845)*

▲ Polymerics Inc .... E 330 928-2210
 Cuyahoga Falls *(G-6110)*

Polynew Inc .... G 330 897-3202
 Baltic *(G-840)*

Polynt Composites USA Inc .... E 816 391-6000
 Sandusky *(G-13088)*

Polyone Corporation .... D 330 467-8108
 Macedonia *(G-9568)*

Polyone Funding Corporation .... E 440 930-1000
 Avon Lake *(G-822)*

Polyone LLC .... E 440 930-1000
 Avon Lake *(G-823)*

Ppl Holding Company .... G 216 514-1840
 Cleveland *(G-4570)*

◆ Prime Conduit Inc .... F 216 464-3400
 Beachwood *(G-1012)*

Prime Industries Inc .... E
 Lorain *(G-9431)*

▲ Progressive Foam Tech Inc .... C 330 756-3200
 Beach City *(G-970)*

Protech Pet LLC .... F 419 552-4617
 Gibsonburg *(G-7955)*

Pyrograf Products Inc .... F 937 766-2020
 Cedarville *(G-2323)*

▲ Rauh Polymers Inc .... F 330 376-1120
 Akron *(G-298)*

Ravago Americas LLC .... E 330 825-2505
 Medina *(G-10368)*

Ravago Americas LLC .... D 419 924-9090
 West Unity *(G-15643)*

Ray Fogg Construction Inc .... E 216 351-7976
 Cleveland *(G-4616)*

Renegade Materials Corp .... G 513 469-9919
 Blue Ash *(G-1460)*

▲ Renegade Materials Corporation .... D 937 350-5274
 Miamisburg *(G-10675)*

◆ Resinoid Engineering Corp .... D 740 928-6115
 Hebron *(G-8359)*

Return Polymers Inc .... D 419 289-1998
 Ashland *(G-610)*

◆ Roechling Indus Cleveland LP .... C 216 486-0100
 Cleveland *(G-4645)*

Rotopolymers .... F 216 645-0333
 Cleveland *(G-4653)*

Saco Aei Polymers Inc .... F 330 995-1600
 Aurora *(G-735)*

Saint-Gobain Prfmce Plas Corp .... D 614 889-2220
 Dublin *(G-6933)*

Saint-Gobain Prfmce Plas Corp .... C 330 296-9948
 Ravenna *(G-12731)*

▲ Scott Bader Inc .... G 330 920-4410
 Stow *(G-13723)*

Scott Molders Incorporated .... D 330 673-5777
 Kent *(G-8859)*

Sherwood Rtm Corp .... G 330 875-7151
 Louisville *(G-9471)*

▼ Soelter Corporation .... F 800 838-8984
 Brookville *(G-1744)*

Solvay Spclty Polymers USA LLC .... F 740 373-9242
 Marietta *(G-9828)*

Sonoco Prtective Solutions Inc .... E 419 420-0029
 Findlay *(G-7565)*

Sorbothane Inc .... E 330 678-9444
 Kent *(G-8866)*

Spartech Mexico Holding Co Two .... E 440 930-3619
 Avon Lake *(G-824)*

Specialty Polymer Product .... G 216 281-8300
 Rocky River *(G-12844)*

STC International Co Ltd .... G 561 308-6002
 Lebanon *(G-9112)*

◆ Tembec Btlsr Inc .... E 419 244-5856
 Toledo *(G-14483)*

Thermocolor LLC .... E 419 626-5677
 Sandusky *(G-13095)*

▲ Tlg Cochran Inc .... E 440 914-1122
 Twinsburg *(G-14744)*

Transdigm Inc .... F 330 676-7147
 Kent *(G-8878)*

◆ Tribotech Composites Inc .... G 216 901-1300
 Cleveland *(G-4826)*

◆ Triple Arrow Industries Inc .... G 614 437-5588
 Marysville *(G-9943)*

Uniloy Century LLC .... D 419 332-2693
 Fremont *(G-7816)*

◆ Uniloy Milacron Inc .... D 513 487-5000
 Batavia *(G-956)*

Univar Solutions USA LLC .... F 800 531-7106
 Dublin *(G-6956)*

Urethane Polymers Intl .... F 216 430-3655
 Cleveland *(G-4855)*

V & A Process Inc .... F 440 288-8137
 Lorain *(G-9442)*

Vinyl Mng Llc DBA Vinylone .... E 440 261-5799
 Cleveland *(G-4876)*

Westlake Corporation .... E 614 986-2497
 Columbus *(G-5874)*

Win Cd Inc .... F 330 929-1999
 Cuyahoga Falls *(G-6129)*

Win Plastic Extrusions LLC .... E 330 929-1999
 Cincinnati *(G-3521)*

Yoders Produce Inc .... E 330 695-5900
 Fredericksburg *(G-7736)*

28 CHEMICALS AND ALLIED PRODUCTS

2822 Synthetic rubber

Allied Polymers .... G 330 975-4200
  Seville *(G-13134)*
Ansell Healthcare Products LLC .... C 740 622-4369
  Coshocton *(G-5969)*
Blair Sales Inc .... D 330 769-5586
  Seville *(G-13138)*
Brain Child Products LLC .... F 419 698-4020
  Toledo *(G-14220)*
◆ Brp Manufacturing Company .... E 800 858-0482
  Lima *(G-9226)*
Canton OH Rubber Specity Prods .... G 330 454-3847
  Canton *(G-2065)*
▲ Cardinal Rubber Company .... E 330 745-2191
  Barberton *(G-864)*
◆ Concrete Sealants Inc .... E 937 845-8776
  Tipp City *(G-14130)*
Covestro LLC .... C 740 929-2015
  Hebron *(G-8337)*
Crushproof Tubing Co .... E 419 293-2111
  Mc Comb *(G-10269)*
◆ East West Copolymer LLC .... D 225 267-3400
  Cleveland *(G-3989)*
◆ Flexsys America LP .... D 330 666-4111
  Akron *(G-155)*
Gdc Inc .... F 574 533-3128
  Wooster *(G-16123)*
Geon Performance Solutions LLC .... F 800 438-4366
  Westlake *(G-15754)*
Great Lakes Polymer Proc Inc .... F 313 655-4024
  Akron *(G-173)*
▲ High Tech Elastomers Inc .... E 937 236-6575
  Vandalia *(G-14943)*
Index Inc .... G 440 632-5400
  Middlefield *(G-10758)*
◆ Innoplast Inc .... F 440 543-8660
  Cleveland *(G-4227)*
◆ Key Resin Company .... F 513 943-4225
  Batavia *(G-927)*
Kraton Employees Recreation CLB ..... F 740 423-7571
  Belpre *(G-1256)*
Kraton Polymers US LLC .... B 740 423-7571
  Belpre *(G-1257)*
Lyondell Chemical Company .... C 513 530-4000
  Cincinnati *(G-3118)*
Mantaline Corporation .... C 330 274-2264
  Mantua *(G-9740)*
McHale Group Ltd .... G 330 923-7070
  Cuyahoga Falls *(G-6103)*
Meggitt (erlanger) LLC .... D 513 851-5550
  Cincinnati *(G-3143)*
◆ Mexichem Specialty Resins Inc .... E 440 930-1435
  Avon Lake *(G-817)*
◆ Midwest Elastomers Inc .... D 419 738-8844
  Wapakoneta *(G-15124)*
Mitsubishi Chemical Amer Inc .... C 586 755-1660
  Bellevue *(G-1229)*
Mohican Industries Inc .... G 330 869-0500
  Akron *(G-251)*
Mondo Polymer Technologies Inc .... E 740 376-9396
  Marietta *(G-9810)*
▲ North Coast Seal Incorporated .... F 216 898-5000
  Brookpark *(G-1722)*
Novagard Solutions Inc .... C 216 881-8111
  Cleveland *(G-4483)*
Polyshield Corporation .... F 614 755-7674
  Pickerington *(G-12466)*
Protective Industrial Polymers .... F 440 327-0015
  North Ridgeville *(G-11854)*
Recycled Polymer Solutions LLC .... G 937 821-4020
  Lima *(G-9283)*

S P E Inc .... E 330 733-0101
  Mogadore *(G-11082)*
◆ Shin-Etsu Silicones of America Inc ... C 330 630-9460
  Akron *(G-328)*
▲ Shincor Silicones Inc .... E 330 630-9460
  Akron *(G-329)*
T L Squire and Company Inc .... G 330 668-2604
  Akron *(G-345)*
Toyo Seiki Usa Inc .... F 513 546-9657
  Blue Ash *(G-1483)*
Universal Urethane Pdts Inc .... D 419 693-7400
  Toledo *(G-14514)*
Vibronic .... G 937 274-1114
  Dayton *(G-6644)*
Wayne County Rubber Inc .... E 330 264-5553
  Wooster *(G-16181)*

2823 Cellulosic manmade fibers

Advanced Fiber LLC .... E 419 562-1337
  Bucyrus *(G-1849)*
◆ Flexsys America LP .... D 330 666-4111
  Akron *(G-155)*
J Rettenmaier USA LP .... D 937 652-2101
  Urbana *(G-14839)*
◆ Mfg Composite Systems Company ... B 440 997-5851
  Ashtabula *(G-648)*
Morgan Adhesives Company LLC ...... B 330 688-1111
  Stow *(G-13709)*

2824 Organic fibers, noncellulosic

Bridge Components Incorporated .... G 614 873-0777
  Columbus *(G-5212)*
Cast Nylons Co Ltd .... D 440 269-2300
  Willoughby *(G-15897)*
▲ Dowco LLC .... E 330 773-6654
  Akron *(G-133)*
Matrix Meats Inc .... F 614 602-1846
  Dublin *(G-6908)*

2833 Medicinals and botanicals

B & A Holistic Fd & Herbs LLC .... F 614 747-2200
  Columbus *(G-5169)*
Clean Remedies LLC .... F 440 670-2112
  Avon *(G-766)*
Earthley Wellness .... F 614 625-1064
  Columbus *(G-5342)*
◆ Frutarom USA Inc .... C 513 870-4900
  West Chester *(G-15556)*
Galapagos Inc .... E 937 890-3068
  Dayton *(G-6344)*
Graminex LLC .... F 419 278-1023
  Deshler *(G-6800)*
▲ Joseph Adams Corp .... F 330 225-9125
  Valley City *(G-14874)*
Natural Optons Armatherapy LLC .... F 419 886-3736
  Bellville *(G-1245)*
Neuronoff Inc .... F 216 505-1818
  Cleveland *(G-4452)*
Nomah Naturals Inc .... G 330 212-8785
  Cleveland *(G-4462)*
Nufacturing Inc .... E 330 814-5259
  Brunswick *(G-1776)*
Nutritional Medicinals LLC .... F 937 433-4673
  West Chester *(G-15467)*
One Orijin LLC .... G 630 362-5291
  Columbus *(G-5639)*
Pfizer Inc .... F 937 746-3603
  Franklin *(G-7691)*
Pharmacia Hepar LLC .... E 937 746-3603
  Franklin *(G-7692)*
Range Impact Inc .... G 216 304-6556
  Cleveland *(G-4615)*

Reiki Ladi .... G 513 235-7515
  Cincinnati *(G-3329)*
USB Corporation .... D 216 765-5000
  Cleveland *(G-4857)*
Valley Vitamins II Inc .... F 330 533-0051
  Columbus *(G-5854)*
▲ VWR Part of Avantor .... E 440 349-1199
  Solon *(G-13445)*

2834 Pharmaceutical preparations

2 Retrievers LLC .... G 216 200-9040
  Cleveland *(G-3571)*
Abbott .... F 608 931-1057
  Columbus *(G-5084)*
Abbott Laboratories .... A 614 624-3191
  Columbus *(G-5085)*
Abbott Laboratories .... F 614 624-3192
  Columbus *(G-5086)*
Abbott Laboratories .... D 847 937-6100
  Columbus *(G-5087)*
Abbott Laboratories 800 551-5838
  Columbus *(G-5088)*
Abbott Laboratories .... A 614 624-7677
  Columbus *(G-5089)*
▲ Abbott Laboratories .... F 937 503-3405
  Tipp City *(G-14119)*
Abeona Therapeutics Inc .... E 646 813-4701
  Cleveland *(G-3586)*
◆ Abitec Corporation .... E 614 429-6464
  Columbus *(G-5090)*
▲ Adare Pharmaceuticals Inc .... C 937 898-9669
  Vandalia *(G-14931)*
Aerpio Therapeutics LLC .... E 513 985-1920
  Blue Ash *(G-1360)*
Alkermes Inc .... E 937 382-5642
  Wilmington *(G-16039)*
Allergan Sales LLC .... C 513 271-6800
  Cincinnati *(G-2609)*
Allergan Sales LLC .... E 513 271-6800
  Cincinnati *(G-2610)*
American Regent Inc .... D 614 436-2222
  Columbus *(G-5129)*
American Regent Inc .... D 614 436-2222
  Hilliard *(G-8397)*
American Regent Inc .... D 614 436-2222
  New Albany *(G-11365)*
Amerix Ntra-Pharmaceutical Inc .... G 567 204-7756
  Lima *(G-9222)*
Amylin Ohio .... E 512 592-8710
  West Chester *(G-15364)*
Analiza Inc .... E 216 432-9050
  Cleveland *(G-3660)*
Andelyn Biosciences Inc .... G 614 332-0554
  Dublin *(G-6861)*
Andelyn Biosciences Inc .... C 844 228-2366
  Columbus *(G-5143)*
Andrew M Farnham .... F 419 298-4300
  Edgerton *(G-7071)*
Aprecia Pharmaceuticals LLC .... F 513 984-5000
  Blue Ash *(G-1362)*
Astrazeneca Pharmaceuticals LP .... D 513 645-2600
  West Chester *(G-15371)*
Barr Laboratories Inc .... A 513 731-9900
  Cincinnati *(G-2657)*
BASF Corporation .... D 614 662-5682
  Columbus *(G-5176)*
Baxters LLC .... G 234 678-5484
  Akron *(G-79)*
Bayer .... E 513 336-6600
  Fairfield *(G-7336)*
▲ Ben Venue Laboratories Inc .... A 800 989-3320
  Bedford *(G-1105)*

28 CHEMICALS AND ALLIED PRODUCTS

Berlin Industries Inc .... F 330 549-2100
   Youngstown *(G-16319)*

Biosortia Pharmaceuticals Inc .... F 614 636-4850
   Dublin *(G-6867)*

Bld Pharmatech Co Limited .... G 330 333-6550
   Blue Ash *(G-1371)*

Bnoat Oncology .... G 330 285-2537
   Akron *(G-88)*

Boehrnger Inglheim Phrmcctcals .... E 440 286-5667
   Chardon *(G-2440)*

Buderer Drug Company Inc .... E 419 627-2800
   Sandusky *(G-13046)*

Camargo Phrm Svcs LLC .... F 513 561-3329
   Cincinnati *(G-2698)*

Cardinal Health 414 LLC .... G 513 759-1900
   West Chester *(G-15384)*

▲ Cardinal Health 414 LLC .... C 614 757-5000
   Dublin *(G-6873)*

Ceutix Pharma Inc .... G 614 388-8800
   Columbus *(G-5245)*

Chester Labs Inc .... F 513 458-3871
   Cincinnati *(G-2731)*

Clear Skies Ahead LLC .... G 440 632-3157
   Middlefield *(G-10742)*

Clinical Specialties Inc .... D 888 873-7888
   Hudson *(G-8591)*

CMC Pharmaceuticals Inc .... G 216 600-9430
   Solon *(G-13331)*

Dayton Laser & Aesthetic Medic .... G 937 208-8282
   Dayton *(G-6280)*

Diasome Pharmaceuticals Inc .... F 216 444-7110
   Cleveland *(G-3957)*

Encapsulation Technologies LLC .... G 419 819-6319
   Austinburg *(G-744)*

Eyescience Labs LLC .... G 614 885-7100
   Powell *(G-12673)*

▲ Flow Dry Technology Inc .... C 937 833-2161
   Brookville *(G-1736)*

Ftd Investments LLC .... A 937 833-2161
   Brookville *(G-1737)*

Galenas LLC .... F 330 208-9423
   Akron *(G-161)*

Ganeden Biotech Inc .... E 440 229-5200
   Mayfield Heights *(G-10249)*

▲ Gebauer Company .... E 216 581-3030
   Cleveland *(G-4108)*

Genoa Healthcare LLC .... G 513 727-0471
   Middletown *(G-10826)*

Girindus America Inc .... E 513 679-3000
   Cincinnati *(G-2952)*

Glaxosmithkline LLC .... G 330 608-2365
   Copley *(G-5949)*

Graminex LLC .... F 419 278-1023
   Deshler *(G-6800)*

Hikma Labs Inc .... G 614 276-4000
   Columbus *(G-5437)*

▲ Hikma Labs Inc .... C 614 276-4000
   Columbus *(G-5438)*

Hikma Pharmaceuticals USA Inc .... F 732 542-1191
   Bedford *(G-1124)*

Hikma Pharmaceuticals USA Inc .... E 614 276-4000
   Columbus *(G-5439)*

Hikma Pharmaceuticals USA Inc .... F 732 542-1191
   Lockbourne *(G-9336)*

Hikma Specialty USA Inc .... E 856 489-2110
   Columbus *(G-5440)*

▲ Imcd Us LLC .... E 216 228-8900
   Westlake *(G-15760)*

Invirsa Inc .... G 614 344-1765
   Columbus *(G-5478)*

Isp Chemicals LLC .... D 614 876-3637
   Columbus *(G-5481)*

Kurome Therapeutics Inc .... G 513 445-3852
   Cincinnati *(G-3092)*

Lib Therapeutics Inc .... F 859 240-7764
   Cincinnati *(G-3103)*

◆ Lubrizol Global Management Inc ...... F 216 447-5000
   Cleveland *(G-4339)*

Masters Pharmaceutical Inc .... G 513 290-2969
   Fairfield *(G-7380)*

Medpace Core Laboratories LLC .... F 513 579-9911
   Cincinnati *(G-3141)*

Medpace Holdings Inc .... C 513 579-9911
   Cincinnati *(G-3142)*

Meridian Bioscience Inc .... C 513 271-3700
   Cincinnati *(G-3149)*

Millers Liniments Llc .... G 440 548-5800
   Middlefield *(G-10770)*

Molorokalin Inc .... E 330 629-1332
   Canfield *(G-2012)*

Mp Biomedicals LLC .... C 440 337-1200
   Solon *(G-13393)*

Mvp Pharmacy .... G 614 449-8000
   Columbus *(G-5586)*

Myers .... G 419 727-2010
   Toledo *(G-14393)*

N-Molecular Inc .... F 440 439-5356
   Oakwood Village *(G-12040)*

Nanofiber Solutions LLC .... F 614 319-3075
   Dublin *(G-6913)*

Navidea Biopharmaceuticals Inc .... G 614 793-7500
   Dublin *(G-6915)*

Next Generation Hearing Case .... G 513 451-0360
   Cincinnati *(G-3193)*

Nigerian Assn Pharmacists & PH .... G 513 861-2329
   Cincinnati *(G-3197)*

Nnodum Pharmaceuticals Corp .... F 513 861-2329
   Cincinnati *(G-3201)*

Nostrum Laboratories Inc .... E 419 636-1168
   Bryan *(G-1831)*

Novartis Corporation .... G 919 577-5000
   Cincinnati *(G-3206)*

Oak Tree Intl Holdings Inc .... E 702 462-7295
   Elyria *(G-7188)*

Oakwood Laboratories LLC .... F 440 505-2011
   Solon *(G-13400)*

Oakwood Laboratories LLC .... E 440 359-0000
   Oakwood Village *(G-12041)*

Ohio Dermatological Assn .... G 330 465-8281
   Dalton *(G-6137)*

Omnicare Phrm of Midwest LLC .... D 513 719-2600
   Cincinnati *(G-3222)*

Optum Infusion Svcs 550 LLC .... D 866 442-4679
   Cincinnati *(G-3227)*

Organon Inc .... F 440 729-2290
   Chesterland *(G-2487)*

Patheon Pharmaceuticals Inc .... A 513 948-9111
   Blue Ash *(G-1450)*

Patheon Pharmaceuticals Inc .... A 513 948-9111
   Cincinnati *(G-3235)*

PBM Covington LLC .... F 937 473-2050
   Covington *(G-6029)*

Performanx Specialty Chem LLC .... G 614 300-7001
   Waverly *(G-15290)*

Perrigo .... F 937 473-2050
   Covington *(G-6030)*

Pfizer Inc .... F 937 746-3603
   Franklin *(G-7691)*

Pharmacia Hepar LLC .... E 937 746-3603
   Franklin *(G-7692)*

Pharmaforce Inc C
   Columbus *(G-5671)*

Piedmont Water Services LLC .... F 216 554-4747
   Cleveland *(G-4550)*

Polynt Composites USA Inc .... E 816 391-6000
   Sandusky *(G-13088)*

▲ Prasco LLC .... E 513 204-1100
   Mason *(G-10040)*

Principled Dynamics Inc .... F 419 351-6303
   Holland *(G-8525)*

Pyros Pharmaceuticals Inc .... E 201 743-9468
   Westerville *(G-15673)*

Quality Care Products LLC .... E 734 847-2704
   Holland *(G-8526)*

Resilience Us Inc .... B 513 645-2600
   West Chester *(G-15497)*

River City Pharma .... F 513 870-1680
   Fairfield *(G-7403)*

Safecor Health LLC .... G 614 351-6117
   Columbus *(G-5738)*

Safecor Health LLC .... F 781 933-8780
   Columbus *(G-5739)*

Sara Wood Pharmaceuticals LLC .... G 513 833-5502
   Mason *(G-10054)*

Sarepta Therapeutics .... F 614 766-3296
   Dublin *(G-6935)*

Sermonix Pharmaceuticals Inc .... F 614 864-4919
   Columbus *(G-5760)*

Soleo Health Inc .... E 844 467-8200
   Dublin *(G-6941)*

Sollis Therapeutics Inc .... E 614 701-9894
   Columbus *(G-5776)*

Standard Wellness Company LLC .... C 330 931-1037
   Cleveland *(G-4729)*

Summit Research Group .... G 330 689-1778
   Stow *(G-13730)*

Teva Womens Health LLC .... C 513 731-9900
   Cincinnati *(G-3446)*

Tri-Tech Laboratories Inc .... C 740 927-2817
   Johnstown *(G-8780)*

Tri-Tech Laboratories LLC .... C 434 845-7073
   Johnstown *(G-8781)*

Tulua Nutrition .... G 419 764-0664
   Wauseon *(G-15275)*

USB Corporation .... D 216 765-5000
   Cleveland *(G-4857)*

Vincent Rx LLC .... G 740 678-2384
   Vincent *(G-15010)*

Wedgewood Connect Ohio LLC .... G 800 331-8272
   Albany *(G-382)*

◆ West-Ward Columbus Inc .... A 614 276-4000
   Columbus *(G-5873)*

Wright Enrichment Incorporated .... F 337 783-3096
   Plain City *(G-12604)*

WV CHS Pharmacy Services LLC .... G 844 595-4652
   Blue Ash *(G-1496)*

Z M O Company .... G 614 875-0230
   Columbus *(G-5890)*

2835 Diagnostic substances

Cardinal Health 414 LLC .... G 513 759-1900
   West Chester *(G-15384)*

▲ Cardinal Health 414 LLC .... C 614 757-5000
   Dublin *(G-6873)*

Cleveland AEC West LLC .... G 216 362-6000
   Cleveland *(G-3831)*

Diagnostic Hybrids Inc .... C 740 593-1784
   Athens *(G-681)*

GE Healthcare Inc .... F 513 241-5955
   Cincinnati *(G-2937)*

Meridian Bioscience Inc .... C 513 271-3700
   Cincinnati *(G-3149)*

Meridian Life Science Inc .... F 513 271-3700
   Cincinnati *(G-3150)*

Nanofiber Solutions LLC .... F 614 319-3075
   Dublin *(G-6913)*

28 CHEMICALS AND ALLIED PRODUCTS

Navidea Biopharmaceuticals Inc............ G 614 793-7500
  Dublin *(G-6915)*
Petnet Solutions Inc..................... G 865 218-2000
  Cincinnati *(G-3252)*
Petnet Solutions Cleveland LLC........... F 865 218-2000
  Cleveland *(G-4543)*
Quest Diagnostics Incorporated........... G 513 229-5500
  Mason *(G-10045)*
Quidel Corporation....................... D 858 552-1100
  Athens *(G-694)*
Quidel Corporation....................... E 740 589-3300
  Athens *(G-695)*
Revvity Health Sciences Inc.............. E 330 825-4525
  Akron *(G-303)*
Thermo Fisher Scientific Inc............. E 800 871-8909
  Oakwood Village *(G-12044)*
USB Corporation.......................... D 216 765-5000
  Cleveland *(G-4857)*
Vetgraft LLC............................. G 614 203-0603
  New Albany *(G-11393)*

2836 Biological products, except diagnostic

ABI Inc.................................. F 800 847-8950
  Cleveland *(G-3587)*
Algix LLC................................ G 706 207-3425
  Stow *(G-13683)*
Bio-Blood Components Inc................. C 614 294-3183
  Columbus *(G-5189)*
Copernicus Therapeutics Inc.............. F 216 231-0227
  Cleveland *(G-3904)*
Decaria Brothers Inc..................... G 330 385-0825
  East Liverpool *(G-6993)*
EMD Millipore Corporation................ C 513 631-0445
  Norwood *(G-11995)*
Envirozyme LLC........................... E 800 232-2847
  Bowling Green *(G-1565)*
Ferro Corporation........................ D 216 577-7144
  Bedford *(G-1121)*
Forge Biologics Inc...................... G 216 401-7611
  Grove City *(G-8094)*
General Envmtl Science Corp.............. G 216 464-0680
  Beachwood *(G-988)*
Jsh International LLC.................... G 330 734-0251
  Akron *(G-200)*
No Rinse Laboratories LLC................ G 937 746-7357
  Springboro *(G-13512)*
PEC Biofuels LLC......................... G 419 542-8210
  Hicksville *(G-8378)*
Protein Technologies Ltd................. G 513 769-0840
  Cincinnati *(G-3307)*
Revvity Health Sciences Inc.............. E 330 825-4525
  Akron *(G-303)*
Transtechbio Inc......................... G 734 994-4728
  Twinsburg *(G-14746)*

2841 Soap and other detergents

AIN Industries Inc....................... G 440 781-0950
  Cleveland *(G-3616)*
Amish Country Soap Co.................... E 866 687-1724
  Berlin *(G-1302)*
Beiersdorf Inc........................... C 513 682-7300
  West Chester *(G-15541)*
Chemstation International Inc............ E 937 294-8265
  Moraine *(G-11166)*
Cincinnati - Vulcan Company.............. D 513 242-5300
  Cincinnati *(G-2736)*
Cleaning Lady Inc........................ G 419 589-5566
  Mansfield *(G-9638)*
Cr Holding Inc........................... D 513 860-5039
  West Chester *(G-15407)*
▼ Cresset Chemical Co Inc................ F 419 669-2041
  Weston *(G-15804)*
♦ Damon Industries Inc................... D 330 821-5310
  Alliance *(G-400)*
▲ DSM Industries Inc.................... F 440 585-1100
  Wickliffe *(G-15831)*
Edmar Chemical Company................... G 440 247-9560
  Chagrin Falls *(G-2376)*
▲ Foam-Tex Solutions Corp............... G 216 889-2702
  Cleveland *(G-4075)*
Henkel US Operations Corp................ C 740 363-1351
  Delaware *(G-6730)*
Jtm Products Inc......................... E 440 287-2302
  Solon *(G-13372)*
♦ KAO USA Inc........................... B 513 421-1400
  Cincinnati *(G-3062)*
♦ Kardol Quality Products LLC........... G 513 933-8206
  Blue Ash *(G-1416)*
Kutol Products Company Inc............... E 513 527-5500
  Sharonville *(G-13172)*
▲ Kutol Products Company Inc............ D 513 527-5500
  Sharonville *(G-13171)*
♦ Malco Products Inc.................... C 330 753-0361
  Barberton *(G-879)*
Mentorbio LLC............................ G 440 796-2995
  Mentor *(G-10501)*
Natreeola Soap Company LLC............... G 513 390-2247
  Middletown *(G-10846)*
♦ Pilot Chemical Company Ohio........... E 513 326-0600
  West Chester *(G-15476)*
Pilot Chemical Corp...................... C 513 424-9700
  Middletown *(G-10851)*
♦ Pilot Chemical Corp................... C 513 326-0600
  West Chester *(G-15477)*
▲ Pioneer Manufacturing Inc............. D 216 671-5500
  Cleveland *(G-4555)*
Pneumatic Specialties Inc................ G 440 729-4400
  Chesterland *(G-2488)*
▼ Polar Inc............................. F 937 297-0911
  Moraine *(G-11201)*
Procter & Gamble Company................. D 513 983-1100
  Cincinnati *(G-3281)*
Procter & Gamble Company................. F 513 266-4375
  Cincinnati *(G-3282)*
Procter & Gamble Company................. G 513 871-7557
  Cincinnati *(G-3283)*
Procter & Gamble Company................. F 513 482-6789
  Cincinnati *(G-3286)*
Procter & Gamble Company................. C 513 983-3000
  Cincinnati *(G-3288)*
Procter & Gamble Company................. E 513 627-7115
  Cincinnati *(G-3289)*
Procter & Gamble Company................. F 513 945-0340
  Cincinnati *(G-3292)*
Procter & Gamble Company................. D 513 622-1000
  Mason *(G-10043)*
Procter & Gamble Company................. C 513 634-9600
  West Chester *(G-15486)*
Procter & Gamble Company................. C 513 634-9110
  West Chester *(G-15487)*
Procter & Gamble Distrg LLC.............. C 937 387-5189
  Union *(G-14774)*
Procter & Gamble Mexico Inc.............. G 513 983-1100
  Cincinnati *(G-3297)*
♦ Procter & Gamble Mfg Co............... F 513 983-1100
  Cincinnati *(G-3298)*
Renegade Brands LLC...................... G 216 342-4347
  Cleveland *(G-4624)*
Renegade Brands LLC...................... E 216 789-0535
  Solon *(G-13413)*
Royal Chemical Company Ltd............... F 330 467-1300
  Twinsburg *(G-14728)*
Royal Chemical Company Ltd............... D 330 467-1300
  Macedonia *(G-9571)*
Soapyfluffs LLC.......................... G 937 823-0015
  Hamilton *(G-8243)*
State Industrial Products Corp........... D 740 929-6370
  Hebron *(G-8363)*
♦ State Industrial Products Corp........ B 877 747-6986
  Cleveland *(G-4731)*
Trillium Health Care Products............ F 513 242-2227
  Cincinnati *(G-3465)*
♦ Wallover Oil Company Inc.............. E 440 238-9250
  Strongsville *(G-13894)*
▼ Washing Systems LLC................... C 800 272-1974
  Loveland *(G-9509)*

2842 Polishes and sanitation goods

▲ Alco-Chem Inc......................... E 330 253-3535
  Akron *(G-49)*
Aromair Fine Fragrance Company........... B 614 984-2900
  New Albany *(G-11368)*
B&D Water Inc............................ F 330 771-3318
  Quaker City *(G-12691)*
♦ Betco Corporation Ltd................. C 419 241-2156
  Bowling Green *(G-1554)*
BLaster Holdings LLC..................... G 216 901-5800
  Cleveland *(G-3741)*
BLaster LLC.............................. E 216 901-5800
  Cleveland *(G-3742)*
♦ Canberra Corporation.................. G 419 724-4300
  Toledo *(G-14226)*
Carbonklean Llc.......................... G 614 980-9515
  Powell *(G-12666)*
Chemical Methods Incorporated............ E 216 476-8400
  Brunswick *(G-1751)*
▲ Chempace Corporation.................. F 419 535-0101
  Toledo *(G-14236)*
Chemstation International Inc............ E 937 294-8265
  Moraine *(G-11166)*
Cincinnati - Vulcan Company.............. D 513 242-5300
  Cincinnati *(G-2736)*
Consolidated Coatings Corp............... A 216 514-7596
  Cleveland *(G-3898)*
Custom Chemical Packaging LLC............ G 330 331-7416
  Medina *(G-10316)*
♦ D & J Distributing & Mfg.............. E 419 865-2552
  Holland *(G-8501)*
♦ Damon Industries Inc.................. D 330 821-5310
  Alliance *(G-400)*
Ddp Specialty Electronic MA.............. C 937 839-4612
  West Alexandria *(G-15341)*
Ecolab Inc............................... E 513 932-0830
  Lebanon *(G-9072)*
Edmar Chemical Company................... G 440 247-9560
  Chagrin Falls *(G-2376)*
EMD Millipore Corporation................ C 513 631-0445
  Norwood *(G-11995)*
Emes Supply LLC.......................... G 216 400-8025
  Willowick *(G-16031)*
Environmental Chemical Corp.............. F 330 453-5200
  Uniontown *(G-14782)*
EZ Brite Brands Inc...................... F 440 871-7817
  Cleveland *(G-4045)*
Ferro Corporation........................ D 216 577-7144
  Bedford *(G-1121)*
Finale Products Inc...................... G 419 874-2662
  Perrysburg *(G-12381)*
♦ Fresh Products LLC.................... D 419 531-9741
  Perrysburg *(G-12384)*
Fuchs Lubricants Co...................... F 330 963-0400
  Twinsburg *(G-14663)*
Germ-Busters Solutions LLC............... G 330 610-0480
  Youngstown *(G-16369)*
Glister Inc.............................. E 614 252-6400
  Columbus *(G-5404)*

SIC SECTION
28 CHEMICALS AND ALLIED PRODUCTS

Gojo Canada Inc .... F 330 255-6000
  Akron (G-169)
Gojo Industries Inc .... G 330 255-6000
  Cuyahoga Falls (G-6087)
▼ Gojo Industries Inc .... F 330 255-6527
  Cuyahoga Falls (G-6088)
Gojo Industries Inc .... G 330 255-6000
  Navarre (G-11343)
◆ Gojo Industries Inc .... C 330 255-6000
  Akron (G-170)
Henkel US Operations Corp .... C 216 475-3600
  Cleveland (G-4180)
Henkel US Operations Corp .... C 740 363-1351
  Delaware (G-6730)
James C Robinson .... G 513 969-7482
  Cincinnati (G-3036)
Jason Incorporated .... C 513 860-3400
  Hamilton (G-8224)
Jax Wax Inc .... F 614 476-6769
  Columbus (G-5489)
K-O-K Products Inc .... F 740 548-0526
  Galena (G-7855)
◆ Kardol Quality Products LLC .... G 513 933-8206
  Blue Ash (G-1416)
Kcs Cleaning Service .... F 740 418-5479
  Oak Hill (G-12020)
Kinzua Environmental Inc .... E 216 881-4040
  Cleveland (G-4292)
Kleen Test Products Corp .... B 330 878-5586
  Strasburg (G-13747)
▲ Kona Blackbird Inc .... E 440 285-3189
  Chardon (G-2455)
Leonhardt Plating Company .... F 513 242-1410
  Cincinnati (G-3102)
Lucas Specialty Products LLC .... G 419 290-6168
  Toledo (G-14373)
◆ Malco Products Inc .... C 330 753-0361
  Barberton (G-879)
▲ McCrary Metal Polishing Co Inc .... F 937 492-1979
  Port Jefferson (G-12630)
McGean-Rohco Inc .... F 216 441-4900
  Newburgh Heights (G-11618)
Metal Polishing Spc L L C .... G 513 321-0363
  Cincinnati (G-3154)
Metaltek Industries Inc .... F 937 342-1750
  Springfield (G-13606)
Milsek Furniture Polish Inc .... G 330 542-2700
  Salem (G-13018)
Mold Masters Intl LLC .... C 440 953-0220
  Eastlake (G-7042)
▲ National Colloid Company .... E 740 282-1171
  Steubenville (G-13673)
New Waste Concepts Inc .... F 877 736-6924
  Perrysburg (G-12402)
◆ Nilodor Inc .... E 800 443-4321
  Bolivar (G-1530)
Nwp Manufacturing Inc .... F 419 894-6871
  Waldo (G-15089)
Ohio Auto Supply Company .... F 330 454-5105
  Canton (G-2182)
Ohio Mills Corporation .... G 216 431-3979
  Cleveland (G-4499)
Orchem Corporation .... E 513 874-9700
  Dayton (G-6493)
▲ Paro Services Co .... F 330 467-1300
  Twinsburg (G-14707)
Personal Plumber Service Corp .... F 440 324-4321
  Elyria (G-7195)
Pilot Chemical Corp .... C 513 424-9700
  Middletown (G-10851)
▲ Pioneer Manufacturing Inc .... D 216 671-5500
  Cleveland (G-4555)

Pneumatic Specialties Inc .... G 440 729-4400
  Chesterland (G-2488)
Polynt Composites USA Inc .... E 816 391-6000
  Sandusky (G-13088)
Procter & Gamble Company .... D 513 983-1100
  Cincinnati (G-3281)
Procter & Gamble Company .... F 513 266-4375
  Cincinnati (G-3282)
Procter & Gamble Company .... G 513 871-7557
  Cincinnati (G-3283)
Procter & Gamble Company .... F 513 482-6789
  Cincinnati (G-3286)
Procter & Gamble Company .... C 513 983-3000
  Cincinnati (G-3288)
Procter & Gamble Company .... E 513 627-7115
  Cincinnati (G-3289)
Procter & Gamble Company .... F 513 945-0340
  Cincinnati (G-3292)
Procter & Gamble Company .... D 513 622-1000
  Mason (G-10043)
Procter & Gamble Company .... C 513 634-9600
  West Chester (G-15486)
Procter & Gamble Company .... C 513 634-9110
  West Chester (G-15487)
◆ Procter & Gamble Company .... A 513 983-1100
  Cincinnati (G-3280)
Procter & Gamble Far East Inc .... C 513 983-1100
  Cincinnati (G-3295)
Procter & Gamble Mexico Inc .... G 513 983-1100
  Cincinnati (G-3297)
Products Chemical Company LLC .... F 216 218-1155
  Cleveland (G-4589)
R&R Sanitation .... F 419 561-8090
  Crestline (G-6036)
Reid Asset Management Company .... E 440 942-8488
  Willoughby (G-15982)
◆ Republic Powdered Metals Inc .... D 330 225-3192
  Medina (G-10370)
Rose Products and Services Inc .... F 614 443-7647
  Columbus (G-5731)
◆ RPM International Inc .... D 330 273-5090
  Medina (G-10372)
Saint Ctherines Metalworks Inc .... G 216 409-0576
  Cleveland (G-4668)
Sherwin-Williams Company .... C 330 830-6000
  Massillon (G-10144)
Smart Sonic Corporation .... G 818 610-7900
  Cleveland (G-4707)
◆ State Industrial Products Corp .... B 877 747-6986
  Cleveland (G-4731)
Tolco Corporation .... D 419 241-1113
  Toledo (G-14491)
Tranzonic Companies .... C 440 446-0643
  Cleveland (G-4818)
◆ Tremco Incorporated .... B
  Beachwood (G-1031)
▲ Troy Chemical Industries Inc .... F 440 834-4408
  Burton (G-1887)
◆ Tz Acquisition Corp .... E 216 535-4300
  Richmond Heights (G-12812)
Univar Solutions USA LLC .... F 513 714-5264
  West Chester (G-15602)
▼ Ventco Inc .... F 440 834-8888
  Chagrin Falls (G-2432)
Vitex Corporation .... F 216 883-0920
  Cleveland (G-4879)
▲ Woodbine Products Company .... F 330 725-0165
  Medina (G-10395)

2843 Surface active agents

BASF Corporation .... D 614 662-5682
  Columbus (G-5176)

◆ Berghausen Corporation .... E 513 591-4891
  Cincinnati (G-2665)
Chemron Corp .... G 419 352-5565
  Bowling Green (G-1559)
Howard Industries Inc .... F 614 444-9900
  Columbus (G-5447)
Peter Cremer N Amer Enrgy Inc .... E 513 557-3943
  Cincinnati (G-3250)
◆ Pilot Chemical Company Ohio .... E 513 326-0600
  West Chester (G-15476)
◆ Pilot Chemical Corp .... C 513 326-0600
  West Chester (G-15477)

2844 Toilet preparations

AA Hand Sanitizer .... G 513 506-7575
  Cincinnati (G-2587)
◆ Abitec Corporation .... E 614 429-6464
  Columbus (G-5090)
Aeroscena LLC .... F 800 671-1890
  Cleveland (G-3611)
B & P Company Inc .... G 937 298-0265
  Dayton (G-6221)
▲ Barbasol LLC .... E 419 903-0738
  Ashland (G-555)
◆ Bath & Body Works LLC .... B 614 856-6000
  Reynoldsburg (G-12753)
◆ Beautyavenues LLC .... B 614 856-6000
  Reynoldsburg (G-12754)
Beiersdorf Inc .... C 513 682-7300
  West Chester (G-15541)
Bocchi Laboratories Ohio LLC .... B 614 741-7458
  New Albany (G-11370)
Bonne Bell Inc .... G 440 835-2440
  Westlake (G-15739)
◆ Bonne Bell LLC .... G 440 835-2440
  Westlake (G-15740)
Brand5 LLC .... F 614 920-9254
  Pickerington (G-12457)
Bright Holdco LLC .... E 614 741-7458
  New Albany (G-11371)
◆ Cameo Inc .... E 419 661-9611
  Perrysburg (G-12367)
Colgate-Palmolive Company .... C 212 310-2000
  Cambridge (G-1929)
Cosmetic Technologies LLC .... G 614 656-1130
  New Albany (G-11375)
Dover Wipes Company .... D 513 983-1100
  Cincinnati (G-2838)
Edgewell Personal Care LLC .... C 937 492-1057
  Sidney (G-13244)
French Transit LLC .... G 650 431-3959
  Mason (G-9994)
◆ Gojo Industries Inc .... C 330 255-6000
  Akron (G-170)
High Ridge Brands Co .... G 614 497-1660
  Columbus (G-5433)
IMH LLC .... F 513 800-9830
  Columbus (G-5454)
IMH LLC .... G 614 436-0991
  Columbus (G-5455)
Interco Division 10 Ohio Inc .... G 614 875-2959
  Grove City (G-8099)
John Frieda Prof Hair Care Inc .... E 800 521-3189
  Cincinnati (G-3043)
KAO Brands Company .... G 513 977-2931
  Cincinnati (G-3061)
KAO USA Inc .... F 513 629-5210
  Cincinnati (G-3063)
◆ KAO USA Inc .... B 513 421-1400
  Cincinnati (G-3062)
Kathleen Williams .... G 740 360-3515
  Marion (G-9858)

Employee Codes: A=Over 500 employees, B=251-500
C=101-250, D=51-100, E=20-50, F=10-19, G=1-9

28 CHEMICALS AND ALLIED PRODUCTS

Kdc One .... G 614 984-2871
   New Albany *(G-11382)*

▲ Kdc US Holdings Inc .... F 434 845-7073
   Groveport *(G-8148)*

Luminex HM Dcor Frgrnce Hldg C .... B 513 563-1113
   Blue Ash *(G-1427)*

Mantra Haircare LLC .... F 440 526-3304
   Broadview Heights *(G-1661)*

Meridian Industries Inc .... E 330 359-5809
   Beach City *(G-968)*

Merle Norman Cosmetics Inc .... E 419 282-0630
   Mansfield *(G-9690)*

Midwest Bath Salt Company LLC .... G 513 770-9177
   Mason *(G-10029)*

Monique Bath and Body Ltd .... G 513 440-7370
   Canton *(G-2166)*

My Soaps LLC .... G 614 832-4634
   Johnstown *(G-8775)*

Natural Beauty Products Inc .... F 513 420-9400
   Middletown *(G-10847)*

Natural Essentials Inc .... F 330 562-8022
   Aurora *(G-726)*

◆ Natural Essentials Inc .... C 330 562-8022
   Streetsboro *(G-13781)*

▲ Nehemiah Manufacturing Co LLC ..... D 513 351-5700
   Cincinnati *(G-3185)*

Noi Enhancements LLC .... G 216 218-4136
   University Heights *(G-14798)*

Oasis Consumer Healthcare LLC .... G 216 394-0544
   Cleveland *(G-4489)*

Olay LLC .... F 787 535-2191
   Blue Ash *(G-1445)*

Pfizer Inc .... F 937 746-3603
   Franklin *(G-7691)*

Primal Life Organics LLC .... E 800 260-4946
   Copley *(G-5954)*

Procter & Gamble Company .... E 513 626-2500
   Blue Ash *(G-1457)*

Procter & Gamble Company .... D 513 983-1100
   Cincinnati *(G-3281)*

Procter & Gamble Company .... F 513 266-4375
   Cincinnati *(G-3282)*

Procter & Gamble Company .... G 513 871-7557
   Cincinnati *(G-3283)*

Procter & Gamble Company .... E 513 983-1100
   Cincinnati *(G-3284)*

Procter & Gamble Company .... F 513 634-2070
   Cincinnati *(G-3285)*

Procter & Gamble Company .... F 513 482-6789
   Cincinnati *(G-3286)*

Procter & Gamble Company .... F 513 634-5069
   Cincinnati *(G-3287)*

Procter & Gamble Company .... C 513 983-3000
   Cincinnati *(G-3288)*

Procter & Gamble Company .... E 513 627-7115
   Cincinnati *(G-3289)*

Procter & Gamble Company .... G 513 658-9853
   Cincinnati *(G-3290)*

Procter & Gamble Company .... B 513 983-1100
   Cincinnati *(G-3291)*

Procter & Gamble Company .... F 513 945-0340
   Cincinnati *(G-3292)*

Procter & Gamble Company .... E 513 242-5752
   Cincinnati *(G-3293)*

Procter & Gamble Company .... D 513 622-1000
   Mason *(G-10043)*

Procter & Gamble Company .... C 513 634-9600
   West Chester *(G-15486)*

Procter & Gamble Company .... C 513 634-9110
   West Chester *(G-15487)*

◆ Procter & Gamble Company .... A 513 983-1100
   Cincinnati *(G-3280)*

Procter & Gamble Distrg Co .... G 513 983-1100
   Cincinnati *(G-3294)*

Procter & Gamble Far East Inc .... C 513 983-1100
   Cincinnati *(G-3295)*

Procter & Gamble Hair Care LLC .... C 513 983-4502
   Cincinnati *(G-3296)*

Procter & Gamble Mexico Inc .... G 513 983-1100
   Cincinnati *(G-3297)*

Procter & Gamble Mfg Co .... C 419 226-5500
   Lima *(G-9278)*

◆ Procter & Gamble Mfg Co .... F 513 983-1100
   Cincinnati *(G-3298)*

▲ Proft & Gamble .... G 513 945-0340
   Cincinnati *(G-3303)*

Redex Industries Inc .... F 800 345-7339
   Salem *(G-13026)*

Scarlett Kitty LLC .... F 678 438-3796
   Dayton *(G-6559)*

Sysco Guest Supply LLC .... E 440 960-2515
   Lorain *(G-9440)*

Tri-Tech Laboratories LLC .... C 614 656-1130
   New Albany *(G-11391)*

Tri-Tech Laboratories LLC .... G 434 845-7073
   Groveport *(G-8164)*

Universal Packg Systems Inc .... C 513 732-2000
   Batavia *(G-957)*

Universal Packg Systems Inc .... C 513 735-4777
   Batavia *(G-958)*

Universal Packg Systems Inc .... C 513 674-9400
   Cincinnati *(G-3483)*

US Cotton LLC .... D 216 676-6400
   Cleveland *(G-4856)*

Veepak OH LLC .... F 740 927-9002
   New Albany *(G-11393)*

▲ Woodbine Products Company .... F 330 725-0165
   Medina *(G-10395)*

Zena Baby Soap Company .... G 216 317-6433
   Bedford Heights *(G-1182)*

2851 Paints and allied products

ABRA Auto Body & Glass LP .... G 513 247-3400
   Cincinnati *(G-2592)*

ABRA Auto Body & Glass LP .... G 513 367-9200
   Harrison *(G-8263)*

ABRA Auto Body & Glass LP .... F 513 755-7709
   West Chester *(G-15359)*

◆ Aexcel Corporation .... E 440 974-3800
   Mentor *(G-10407)*

◆ Akrochem Corporation .... D 330 535-2100
   Akron *(G-26)*

◆ Akron Paint & Varnish Inc .... D 330 773-8911
   Akron *(G-38)*

Akzo Nobel Coatings Inc .... C 614 294-3361
   Columbus *(G-5110)*

Akzo Nobel Coatings Inc .... E 419 433-9143
   Huron *(G-8625)*

Akzo Nobel Coatings Inc .... E 937 322-2671
   Springfield *(G-13529)*

◆ Akzo Nobel Paints LLC .... A 440 297-8000
   Strongsville *(G-13803)*

All Coatings Co Inc .... G 330 821-3806
   Alliance *(G-389)*

Aluminum Coating Manufacturers .... F 216 341-2000
   Cleveland *(G-3644)*

◆ Americhem Inc .... D 330 929-4213
   Cuyahoga Falls *(G-6064)*

▲ Aps-Materials Inc .... D 937 278-6547
   Dayton *(G-6210)*

Avient Corporation .... E 419 668-4844
   Norwalk *(G-11955)*

Axalt Powde Coati Syste Usa I .... G 614 921-8000
   Hilliard *(G-8400)*

Axalt Powde Coati Syste Usa I .... G 614 600-4104
   Hilliard *(G-8401)*

Basic Coatings LLC .... F 419 241-2156
   Bowling Green *(G-1553)*

Bollin & Sons Inc .... E 419 693-6573
   Toledo *(G-14216)*

Brinkman LLC .... F 419 204-5934
   Lima *(G-9225)*

▲ Buckeye Fabric Finishers Inc .... F 740 622-3251
   Coshocton *(G-5975)*

Cahill Services Inc .... G 216 410-5595
   Lakewood *(G-8968)*

Certon Technologies Inc .... F 440 786-7185
   Bedford *(G-1111)*

◆ Chemmasters Inc .... E 440 428-2105
   Madison *(G-9589)*

▼ Chemspec Usa LLC .... D 330 669-8512
   Orrville *(G-12120)*

▲ Chemspec Usa Inc .... D 330 669-8512
   Orrville *(G-12121)*

◆ Coloramics LLC .... E 614 876-1171
   Hilliard *(G-8408)*

◆ Comex North America Inc .... D 303 307-2100
   Cleveland *(G-3888)*

Consolidated Coatings Corp .... A 216 514-7596
   Cleveland *(G-3898)*

CPC Holding Inc .... E 216 383-3932
   Cleveland *(G-3910)*

CPI Industrial Co .... E 614 445-0800
   Mount Sterling *(G-11255)*

CTS National Corporation .... E 216 566-2000
   Cleveland *(G-3918)*

Dap Products Inc .... D 937 667-4461
   Tipp City *(G-14131)*

David E Easterday and Co Inc .... F 330 359-0700
   Wilmot *(G-16067)*

Day-Glo Color Corp .... F 216 391-7070
   Cleveland *(G-3945)*

▲ Day-Glo Color Corp .... C 216 391-7070
   Cleveland *(G-3944)*

Deco Plas Properties LLC .... F 419 485-0632
   Montpelier *(G-11136)*

Dip Coat Customs LLC .... E 513 503-1243
   Cincinnati *(G-2829)*

Epoxy Systems Blstg Cating Inc .... F 513 924-1800
   Cleves *(G-4950)*

◆ Epsilon Management Corporation ..... C 216 634-2500
   Cleveland *(G-4025)*

Ferro Corporation .... D 216 577-7144
   Bedford *(G-1121)*

Fuchs Lubricants Co .... F 330 963-0400
   Twinsburg *(G-14663)*

General Electric Company .... E 216 268-3846
   Cleveland *(G-4114)*

Grand Archt Etrnl Eye 314 LLC .... F 800 377-8147
   Cleveland *(G-4138)*

◆ Harrison Paint Company .... E 330 455-5120
   Canton *(G-2122)*

Henkel US Operations Corp .... C 216 475-3600
   Cleveland *(G-4180)*

Hexpol Compounding LLC .... C 440 834-4644
   Burton *(G-1880)*

High Life .... G 330 978-4124
   Cortland *(G-5963)*

Hoover & Wells Inc .... E 419 691-9220
   Toledo *(G-14319)*

Hudson Hines Hill Company .... D 330 562-1970
   Streetsboro *(G-13774)*

Ineos Neal LLC .... E 610 790-3333
   Dublin *(G-6896)*

Ineos Solvents Sales US Corp .... B 614 790-3333
   Dublin *(G-6897)*

SIC SECTION

28 CHEMICALS AND ALLIED PRODUCTS

◆ J C Whitlam Manufacturing Co............E 330 334-2524
  Wadsworth *(G-15037)*

▲ Kalcor Coatings Company...................E 440 946-4700
  Willoughby *(G-15936)*

◆ Kardol Quality Products LLC..............G 513 933-8206
  Blue Ash *(G-1416)*

Kars Ohio LLC..G 614 655-1099
  Pataskala *(G-12300)*

Karyall-Telday Inc..................................F 216 281-4063
  Cleveland *(G-4274)*

Leonhardt Plating Company...................F 513 242-1410
  Cincinnati *(G-3102)*

Lyondllbsell Advnced Plymers I............E 419 682-3311
  Stryker *(G-13910)*

Mameco International Inc......................D 216 752-4400
  Cleveland *(G-4354)*

Mansfield Paint Co Inc...........................G 330 725-2436
  Medina *(G-10346)*

◆ Master Builders LLC...........................E 800 228-3318
  Beachwood *(G-998)*

Matrix Sys Auto Finishes LLC...............B 248 668-8135
  Massillon *(G-10125)*

McBmrdd..G 937 910-7301
  Dayton *(G-6431)*

McCann Color Inc..................................E 330 498-4840
  Canton *(G-2156)*

Meggitt (erlanger) LLC..........................D 513 851-5550
  Cincinnati *(G-3143)*

Mid-America Chemical Corp.................G 216 749-0100
  Cleveland *(G-4406)*

▼ Nanosperse LLC.................................G 937 296-5030
  Kettering *(G-8908)*

▲ Nippon Paint Auto Americas Inc........F 201 692-1111
  Cleveland *(G-4460)*

▲ North Shore Strapping Company......E 216 661-5200
  Brooklyn Heights *(G-1696)*

▲ Npa Coatings Inc...............................C 216 651-5900
  Cleveland *(G-4486)*

OPC Polymers LLC................................C 614 253-8511
  Columbus *(G-5642)*

P3 Infrastructure Inc.............................F 330 408-9504
  Twinsburg *(G-14705)*

Parker Trutec Incorporated..................D 937 653-8500
  Urbana *(G-14846)*

◆ Perstorp Polyols Inc..........................C 419 729-5448
  Toledo *(G-14434)*

◆ Plasti-Kote Co Inc..............................C 330 725-4511
  Medina *(G-10363)*

Pmbp Legacy Co Inc..............................E 330 253-8148
  Akron *(G-278)*

▲ Polymerics Inc...................................E 330 928-2210
  Cuyahoga Falls *(G-6110)*

Polynt Composites USA Inc..................E 816 391-6000
  Sandusky *(G-13088)*

▲ Postle Industries Inc.........................E 216 265-9000
  Cleveland *(G-4565)*

▼ PPG Architectural Coatings LLC......D 440 297-8000
  Strongsville *(G-13866)*

PPG Architectural Finishes Inc............F 513 242-3050
  Cincinnati *(G-3269)*

PPG Architectural Finishes Inc............F 513 563-0220
  Cincinnati *(G-3270)*

PPG Industries Inc................................E 330 825-0831
  Barberton *(G-891)*

PPG Industries Inc................................E 740 774-8734
  Chillicothe *(G-2526)*

PPG Industries Inc................................E 740 774-7600
  Chillicothe *(G-2527)*

PPG Industries Inc................................E 740 774-7600
  Chillicothe *(G-2528)*

PPG Industries Inc................................C 740 474-3161
  Circleville *(G-3554)*

PPG Industries Inc................................E 216 671-7793
  Cleveland *(G-4567)*

PPG Industries Inc................................G 740 363-9610
  Delaware *(G-6743)*

PPG Industries Inc................................F 419 331-2011
  Lima *(G-9277)*

PPG Industries Inc................................E 513 576-0360
  Milford *(G-10917)*

PPG Industries Inc................................D 440 572-2800
  Strongsville *(G-13867)*

PPG Industries Ohio Inc.......................C 412 434-3888
  Cleveland *(G-4569)*

PPG Industries Ohio Inc.......................B 740 363-9610
  Delaware *(G-6744)*

PPG Industries Ohio Inc.......................D 412 434-1542
  Euclid *(G-7295)*

PPG Industries Ohio Inc.......................C 440 572-6777
  Strongsville *(G-13868)*

◆ PPG Industries Ohio Inc...................A 216 671-0050
  Cleveland *(G-4568)*

Precisions Paint Systems LLC.............F 740 894-6224
  South Point *(G-13473)*

Premier Ink Systems Inc.......................F 513 367-2300
  Harrison *(G-8286)*

Priest Services Inc................................G 440 333-1123
  Mayfield Heights *(G-10254)*

Quality Durable Indus Floors...............F 937 696-2833
  Farmersville *(G-7460)*

◆ Republic Powdered Metals Inc........D 330 225-3192
  Medina *(G-10370)*

RPM Consumer Holding Company.......E 330 273-5090
  Medina *(G-10371)*

◆ RPM International Inc.......................D 330 273-5090
  Medina *(G-10372)*

Sheffield Bronze Paint Corp.................E 216 481-8330
  Cleveland *(G-4690)*

Sherwin-Williams Company..................G 216 566-2000
  Cleveland *(G-4694)*

Sherwin-Williams Company..................G 330 528-0124
  Hudson *(G-8611)*

Sherwin-Williams Company..................C 330 830-6000
  Massillon *(G-10144)*

Sherwin-Williams Company..................F 440 846-4328
  Strongsville *(G-13880)*

Sherwin-Williams Company..................A 216 566-2000
  Cleveland *(G-4693)*

Sherwin-Williams Mfg Co......................F 216 566-2000
  Cleveland *(G-4695)*

◆ Sherwn-Wllams Auto Fnshes Corp..E 216 332-8330
  Cleveland *(G-4696)*

Strong-Coat LLC....................................G 440 299-2068
  Willoughby *(G-16000)*

Superior Printing Ink Co Inc.................G 216 328-1720
  Cleveland *(G-4750)*

▲ Teknol Inc...D 937 264-0190
  Dayton *(G-6613)*

The Garland Company Inc.....................E 216 641-7500
  Cleveland *(G-4783)*

Tnemec Co Inc.......................................G 614 850-8160
  Hilliard *(G-8449)*

◆ Tremco Incorporated........................B
  Beachwood *(G-1031)*

Treved Exteriors....................................G 513 771-3888
  Cincinnati *(G-3463)*

Trexler Rubber Co Inc...........................E 330 296-9677
  Ravenna *(G-12739)*

Universal Urethane Pdts Inc................D 419 693-7400
  Toledo *(G-14514)*

Urethane Polymers Intl.........................F 216 430-3655
  Cleveland *(G-4855)*

Vanguard Paints and Finishes Inc.......E 740 373-5261
  Marietta *(G-9842)*

Vibrantz Corporation.............................C 216 875-6213
  Cleveland *(G-4868)*

◆ Vibrantz Corporation........................D 216 875-5600
  Mayfield Heights *(G-10256)*

▼ Waterlox Coatings Corporation.......F 216 641-4877
  Cleveland *(G-4896)*

▼ Wooster Products Inc.......................D 330 264-2844
  Wooster *(G-16186)*

X-Treme Finishes Inc............................F 330 474-0614
  North Royalton *(G-11903)*

▲ Zircoa Inc...C 440 248-0500
  Cleveland *(G-4936)*

2861 Gum and wood chemicals

◆ Damon Industries Inc........................D 330 821-5310
  Alliance *(G-400)*

◆ Oak Chips Inc.....................................E 740 947-4159
  Waverly *(G-15289)*

▼ PPG Architectural Coatings LLC......D 440 297-8000
  Strongsville *(G-13866)*

2865 Cyclic crudes and intermediates

Accel Corporation..................................G 440 327-7418
  Avon *(G-760)*

Altivia Petrochemicals LLC..................E 740 532-3420
  Haverhill *(G-8308)*

Americhem Inc.......................................E 330 926-3185
  Cuyahoga Falls *(G-6065)*

◆ Americhem Inc...................................D 330 929-4213
  Cuyahoga Falls *(G-6064)*

Avient Corporation................................E 419 668-4844
  Norwalk *(G-11955)*

◆ Berghausen Corporation...................E 513 591-4491
  Cincinnati *(G-2665)*

Color Products Inc................................G 513 860-2749
  Hamilton *(G-8194)*

◆ Colormatrix Corporation...................C 216 622-0100
  Berea *(G-1272)*

Ferro Corporation..................................E 330 682-8015
  Orrville *(G-12124)*

Flint CPS Inks North Amer LLC............E 513 619-2089
  Cincinnati *(G-2909)*

Flint Group US LLC...............................C 513 552-7232
  Fairfield *(G-7360)*

Hexpol Compounding LLC....................C 440 834-4644
  Burton *(G-1880)*

Lyondllbsell Advnced Plymers I............E 419 682-3311
  Stryker *(G-13910)*

◆ Marathon Petroleum Company LP...F 419 422-2121
  Findlay *(G-7532)*

Marion County Coal Company..............D 740 338-3100
  Saint Clairsville *(G-12910)*

Neyra Interstate Inc..............................E 513 733-1000
  Cincinnati *(G-3196)*

Pmbp Legacy Co Inc..............................F 330 253-8148
  Akron *(G-279)*

▲ Polymerics Inc...................................E 330 928-2210
  Cuyahoga Falls *(G-6110)*

◆ Republic Powdered Metals Inc........D 330 225-3192
  Medina *(G-10370)*

▲ Revlis Corporation............................E 330 535-2100
  Akron *(G-302)*

◆ RPM International Inc.......................D 330 273-5090
  Medina *(G-10372)*

Standridge Color Corporation..............F 770 464-3362
  Defiance *(G-6695)*

Sun Chemical Corporation....................D 513 753-9550
  Amelia *(G-467)*

Sun Chemical Corporation....................E 513 830-8667
  Cincinnati *(G-3430)*

Sun Chemical Corporation....................C 513 681-5950
  Cincinnati *(G-3431)*

Employee Codes: A=Over 500 employees, B=251-500
C=101-250, D=51-100, E=20-50, F=10-19, G=1-9

28 CHEMICALS AND ALLIED PRODUCTS

◆ Vibrantz Color Solutions Inc............C 440 997-5137
Ashtabula *(G-664)*

Vibrantz Corporation....................C 216 875-6213
Cleveland *(G-4868)*

2869 Industrial organic chemicals, nec

A-Gas US Holdings Inc....................F 419 867-8990
Bowling Green *(G-1547)*

◆ Abitec Corporation.......................E 614 429-6464
Columbus *(G-5090)*

ABS Materials Inc.........................D 330 234-7999
Wooster *(G-16094)*

Adr Fuel Inc...............................G 419 872-2178
Perrysburg *(G-12359)*

Albemarle Amendments LLC...........E 330 425-2354
Twinsburg *(G-14627)*

▲ Alco-Chem Inc..........................E 330 253-3535
Akron *(G-49)*

Aldrich Chemical..........................D 937 859-1808
Miamisburg *(G-10608)*

Alpha Zeta Holdings Inc..................E 216 271-1601
Cleveland *(G-3640)*

American Made Fuels Inc................G 330 417-7663
Canton *(G-2036)*

Ampacet Corporation....................D 740 929-5521
Newark *(G-11561)*

Andersons Mrathon Holdings LLC......E 937 316-3700
Greenville *(G-8036)*

B P Oil Company..........................G 513 671-4107
Cincinnati *(G-2651)*

Bam Fuel Inc..............................G 740 397-6674
Howard *(G-8558)*

BASF......................................E 419 408-5398
Arlington *(G-548)*

BASF Corp................................G 513 681-9100
Cincinnati *(G-2658)*

BASF Corporation........................C 513 482-3000
Cincinnati *(G-2659)*

BASF Corporation........................D 614 662-5682
Columbus *(G-5176)*

BASF Corporation........................E 440 329-2525
Elyria *(G-7116)*

BASF Corporation........................G 937 547-6700
Greenville *(G-8038)*

BASF Corporation........................C 419 877-5308
Whitehouse *(G-15815)*

Beloit Fuel LLC...........................G 330 584-1915
North Benton *(G-11709)*

▲ Biowish Technologies Inc..............G 312 572-6700
Cincinnati *(G-2669)*

Biowish Technologies Inc................G 312 572-6700
Cincinnati *(G-2670)*

Blinged & Bronzed........................F 330 631-1255
Akron *(G-87)*

◆ Borchers Americas Inc.................D 440 899-2950
Westlake *(G-15741)*

Brightstar Propane & Fuels..............F 614 891-8395
Westerville *(G-15648)*

Buckman Ltd.............................G 419 420-1687
Findlay *(G-7489)*

Canton OH Rubber Specialty Prods.....G 330 454-3847
Canton *(G-2065)*

Cargill Incorporated.....................F 513 941-7400
Cincinnati *(G-2702)*

◆ Carson-Saeks Inc......................E 937 278-5311
Dayton *(G-6247)*

Catexel Nease LLC......................D 513 738-1255
Harrison *(G-8267)*

◆ Catexel Nease LLC....................F 513 587-2800
West Chester *(G-15385)*

Chem-Sales Inc..........................F
Toledo *(G-14235)*

Chemcore Inc............................F 937 228-6118
Dayton *(G-6253)*

▲ Chemionics Corporation..............E 330 733-8834
Tallmadge *(G-14024)*

Classic Fuel Injection LLC...............G 330 757-7171
Youngstown *(G-16338)*

Coil Specialty Chemicals LLC...........G 740 236-2407
Marietta *(G-9785)*

Controlled Release Society Inc.........G 513 948-8000
Cincinnati *(G-2792)*

Corrugated Chemicals Inc..............G 513 561-7773
Cincinnati *(G-2798)*

Coshocton Ethanol LLC.................F 740 623-3046
Coshocton *(G-5976)*

Ddp Specialty Electronic MA...........C 937 839-4612
West Alexandria *(G-15341)*

Dnd Emulsions Inc......................F 419 525-4988
Mansfield *(G-9646)*

◆ Dover Chemical Corporation.........C 330 343-7711
Dover *(G-6818)*

Dunkelberger Fuel LLC..................G 513 726-1999
Somerville *(G-13452)*

East Side Fuel Plus Operations.........G 419 563-0777
Bucyrus *(G-1859)*

Eco Fuel Solution LLC..................G 440 282-8592
Amherst *(G-476)*

Ecochem Alternative Fuels LLC........E 614 764-3835
Plain City *(G-12577)*

Elco Corporation.........................E 440 997-6131
Ashtabula *(G-631)*

◆ Elco Corporation......................E 800 321-0467
Cleveland *(G-4002)*

Eqm Technologies & Energy Inc.......E 513 825-7500
Cincinnati *(G-2881)*

Equistar Chemicals LP..................D 513 530-4000
Cincinnati *(G-2883)*

Evonik Corporation......................E 330 668-2235
Akron *(G-145)*

Exp Fuels Inc............................G 419 382-7713
Toledo *(G-14283)*

Ferro Corporation.......................D 216 577-7144
Bedford *(G-1121)*

Fly Race Fuels LLC.....................G 419 744-9402
North Fairfield *(G-11776)*

Franklin.................................G 419 699-5757
Waterville *(G-15243)*

Frutarom USA Holding Inc..............G 201 861-9500
West Chester *(G-15555)*

Fuel America............................G 419 586-5609
Celina *(G-2333)*

Gdc Inc..................................F 574 533-3128
Wooster *(G-16123)*

Geon Company..........................A 216 447-6000
Cleveland *(G-4121)*

GFS Chemicals Inc......................D 614 224-5345
Columbus *(G-5403)*

◆ GFS Chemicals Inc....................E 740 881-5501
Powell *(G-12674)*

Givaudan Flavors Corporation..........F 513 948-3428
Cincinnati *(G-2953)*

Givaudan Flavors Corporation..........G 513 786-0124
Cincinnati *(G-2954)*

◆ Givaudan Flavors Corporation.......C 513 948-8000
Cincinnati *(G-2955)*

Givaudan Fragrances Corp............E 513 948-3428
Cincinnati *(G-2957)*

◆ Givaudan Fragrances Corp..........B 513 948-8000
Cincinnati *(G-2958)*

Green Harvest Energy LLC............G 330 716-3068
Columbiana *(G-5040)*

Guardian Energy Holdings LLC........C 567 940-9500
Lima *(G-9247)*

Guardian Lima LLC.....................E 567 940-9500
Lima *(G-9248)*

Gushen America Inc....................G 708 664-2852
Heath *(G-8320)*

H&G Legacy Co..........................F 513 921-1075
Cincinnati *(G-2982)*

Ha-International LLC....................E 419 537-0096
Toledo *(G-14308)*

▲ Hardy Industrial Tech LLC............D 440 350-6300
Painesville *(G-12243)*

▲ Heraeus Epurio LLC..................E 937 264-1000
Vandalia *(G-14942)*

▼ Hexion Topco LLC....................D 614 225-4000
Columbus *(G-5430)*

◆ Hunt Imaging LLC....................E 440 826-0433
Berea *(G-1283)*

Ibidltd-Blue Green Energy..............F 909 547-5160
Toledo *(G-14325)*

Ishos Bros Fuel Ventures...............C 419 913-5718
Toledo *(G-14340)*

◆ Jatrodiesel Inc........................F
Miamisburg *(G-10649)*

Kc Marketing LLC.......................E 513 471-8770
Cincinnati *(G-3067)*

Kerry Flavor Systems Us LLC..........F 513 539-7373
Monroe *(G-11113)*

▲ Lipo Technologies Inc................E 937 264-1222
Englewood *(G-7236)*

Littlern Corporation.....................G 330 848-8847
Fairlawn *(G-7444)*

Lost Nation Fuel........................G 440 951-9088
Willoughby *(G-15947)*

Lyondell Chemical Company...........C 513 530-4000
Cincinnati *(G-3118)*

Lyondllbsell Advncd Plymers I........D 440 224-7291
Conneaut *(G-5927)*

Maroon Intrmdiate Holdings LLC......C 440 937-1000
Avon *(G-781)*

Mart Plus Fuel..........................G 216 261-0420
Euclid *(G-7283)*

Martin M Hardin........................G 740 282-1234
Steubenville *(G-13671)*

◆ Michelman Inc.......................C 513 793-7766
Blue Ash *(G-1438)*

Mid-America Chemical Corp..........G 216 749-0100
Cleveland *(G-4406)*

Midwest Fuel LLC.....................G 740 753-5960
Nelsonville *(G-11357)*

▲ Momentive Perf Mtrls Quartz.......F 408 436-6221
Strongsville *(G-13854)*

Momentive Performance Mtls Inc....A 614 986-2495
Columbus *(G-5578)*

Momentive Performance Mtls Inc....A 740 928-7010
Hebron *(G-8349)*

Momentive Performance Mtls Inc....C 440 878-5705
Richmond Heights *(G-12809)*

Momentive Performance Mtls Inc....C 740 929-8732
Willoughby *(G-15955)*

◆ Momentive Prfmce Mtls Qrtz Inc...D 440 878-5700
Strongsville *(G-13855)*

Mp Biomedicals LLC..................C 440 337-1200
Solon *(G-13393)*

▲ Nachurs Alpine Solutions LLC......E 740 382-5701
Marion *(G-9864)*

▲ National Colloid Company..........E 740 282-1171
Steubenville *(G-13673)*

Nationwide Chemical Products.......G 419 714-7075
Perrysburg *(G-12401)*

North East Fuel Inc....................G 330 264-4454
Wooster *(G-16156)*

Novagard Solutions Inc................C 216 881-8111
Cleveland *(G-4483)*

SIC SECTION

28 CHEMICALS AND ALLIED PRODUCTS

Novation Solutions LLC............................F 330 620-6721
   Barberton *(G-884)*

▼ Noveon Fcc Inc..E 440 943-4200
   Wickliffe *(G-15841)*

Occidental Chemical Corp..........................E 513 242-2900
   Cincinnati *(G-3211)*

Ohio Biosystems Coop Inc.........................G 419 980-7663
   Loudonville *(G-9451)*

OPC Polymers LLC.....................................C 614 253-8511
   Columbus *(G-5642)*

Orion Engineered Carbons LLC..................E 740 423-9571
   Belpre *(G-1258)*

Oxyrase Inc...F 419 589-8800
   Ontario *(G-12093)*

P S P Inc...F 330 283-5635
   Kent *(G-8842)*

Poet Biorefining - Leipsic LLC....................E 419 943-7447
   Leipsic *(G-9135)*

Poet Biorefining Marion LLC......................E 740 383-4400
   Marion *(G-9873)*

Poet Borefining - Fostoria LLC...................E 419 436-0954
   Fostoria *(G-7650)*

Polychem Dispersions Inc.........................E 800 545-3530
   Middlefield *(G-10782)*

Polymer Diagnostics Inc............................E 440 930-1361
   Avon Lake *(G-821)*

Quality Extractions Group LLC..................G 567 698-9802
   Northwood *(G-11928)*

◆ Reclamation Technologies Inc...............E 800 372-1301
   Bowling Green *(G-1587)*

▲ Research Organics LLC.........................D 216 883-8025
   Cleveland *(G-4628)*

▲ Revlis Corporation..................................E 330 535-2100
   Akron *(G-302)*

Rex American Resources Corp..................C 937 276-3931
   Dayton *(G-6547)*

▲ Rezkem Chemicals LLC........................F 330 653-9104
   Hudson *(G-8610)*

Ronald T Dodge Co....................................F 937 439-4497
   Dayton *(G-6552)*

Sdg Inc..F 440 893-0771
   Cleveland *(G-4682)*

Shepherd Material Science Co...................F 513 731-1110
   Norwood *(G-11998)*

Shin-Etsu Silicones Amer Inc.....................F 330 630-9860
   Akron *(G-327)*

◆ Shin-Etsu Silicones of America Inc......C 330 630-9460
   Akron *(G-328)*

▲ Shincor Silicones Inc.............................E 330 630-9460
   Akron *(G-329)*

Silicone Solutions Inc.................................F 330 920-3125
   Cuyahoga Falls *(G-6117)*

Symrise Inc...C 440 324-6060
   Elyria *(G-7209)*

◆ Tedia Company LLC..............................C 513 874-5340
   Fairfield *(G-7416)*

The Andersons Clymers Ethanol LLC........E 574 722-2627
   Maumee *(G-10239)*

The Champion Company............................D 937 324-5681
   Springfield *(G-13647)*

◆ The Lubrizol Corporation.......................A 440 943-4200
   Wickliffe *(G-15853)*

◆ The Shepherd Chemical Company.......C 513 731-1110
   Norwood *(G-12001)*

Twin Rvers Tech - Pnsville LLC.................E 440 350-6300
   Painesville *(G-12273)*

Ultimate Chem Solutions Inc......................F 440 998-6751
   Ashtabula *(G-662)*

Union Carbide Corporation........................F 216 529-3784
   Cleveland *(G-4844)*

◆ United Initiators Inc................................D 440 323-3112
   Elyria *(G-7215)*

Univar Solutions USA LLC..........................F 513 714-5264
   West Chester *(G-15602)*

▼ Upper State Fuel Inc..............................G 419 843-5931
   Toledo *(G-14517)*

Vadose Syn Fuels Inc.................................G 330 564-0545
   Munroe Falls *(G-11307)*

Vantage Spclty Ingredients Inc..................E 937 264-1222
   Englewood *(G-7248)*

Vibrantz Technologies Inc..........................G 330 765-4378
   Orrville *(G-12161)*

Wacker Chemical Corporation...................C 330 899-0847
   Canton *(G-2264)*

▼ Werner G Smith Inc...............................F 216 861-3676
   Cleveland *(G-4904)*

▲ Wiley Companies....................................C 740 622-0755
   Coshocton *(G-6000)*

2873 Nitrogenous fertilizers

Agrium Advanced Tech US Inc...................G 614 276-5103
   Columbus *(G-5106)*

Amsoil Inc..G 614 274-9851
   Urbancrest *(G-14852)*

CF Industries Inc..C 330 385-5424
   East Liverpool *(G-6990)*

Envirokure Incorporated............................F 215 289-9800
   Hicksville *(G-8374)*

Hawthorne Collective Inc...........................E 937 644-0011
   Columbus *(G-5423)*

Hyponex Corporation.................................C 330 262-1300
   Shreve *(G-13209)*

Hyponex Corporation.................................D 937 644-0011
   Marysville *(G-9920)*

Inspirtec LLC..G 614 571-7130
   Versailles *(G-14981)*

Keystone Cooperative Inc..........................G 937 884-5526
   Verona *(G-14975)*

Nutrien AG Solutions Inc............................G 513 941-4100
   North Bend *(G-11705)*

Pcs Nitrogen Inc..F 419 226-1200
   Lima *(G-9275)*

Pcs Nitrogen Ohio LP.................................D 419 879-8989
   Lima *(G-9276)*

R & J AG Manufacturing Inc......................F 419 962-4707
   Ashland *(G-608)*

Royster-Clark Inc..G 513 941-4100
   North Bend *(G-11706)*

Scotts Company LLC.................................F 937 454-2782
   Dayton *(G-6563)*

◆ Scotts Company LLC............................C 937 644-0011
   Marysville *(G-9934)*

Scotts Miracle-Gro Company.....................E 937 578-5065
   Marysville *(G-9936)*

▲ Scotts Miracle-Gro Company................B 937 644-0011
   Marysville *(G-9935)*

Smgm LLC...E 937 644-0011
   Marysville *(G-9939)*

Summers Organization LLC.......................E 740 286-1322
   Jackson *(G-8725)*

Synagro Midwest Inc..................................F 937 384-0669
   Miamisburg *(G-10687)*

Talus Renewables Inc................................E 650 248-5374
   Cleveland Heights *(G-4943)*

▼ Turf Care Supply LLC............................D 877 220-1014
   Brunswick *(G-1796)*

2874 Phosphatic fertilizers

Andersons Inc...G 419 536-0460
   Toledo *(G-14194)*

Andersons Inc...C 419 893-5050
   Maumee *(G-10165)*

Occidental Chemical Corp..........................E 513 242-2900
   Cincinnati *(G-3211)*

◆ Scotts Company LLC............................C 937 644-0011
   Marysville *(G-9934)*

2875 Fertilizers, mixing only

All Ways Green Lawn & Turf LLC..............G 937 763-4766
   Seaman *(G-13114)*

Countyline Co-Op Inc.................................F 419 287-3241
   Pemberville *(G-12334)*

Garick LLC..E 216 581-0100
   Cleveland *(G-4102)*

Hyponex Corporation.................................C 330 262-1300
   Shreve *(G-13209)*

Hyponex Corporation.................................D 937 644-0011
   Marysville *(G-9920)*

Insta-Gro Manufacturing Inc......................G 419 845-3046
   Caledonia *(G-1916)*

▲ Kurtz Bros Compost Services..............F 330 864-2621
   Akron *(G-213)*

Legacy Farmers Cooperative.....................F 419 423-2611
   Findlay *(G-7528)*

Lesco Inc...F 740 633-6366
   Martins Ferry *(G-9899)*

Lesco Inc...E 614 848-3712
   Westerville *(G-15713)*

Midwest Compost Inc.................................F 419 547-7979
   Clyde *(G-4974)*

▲ Nachurs Alpine Solutions LLC............E 740 382-5701
   Marion *(G-9864)*

Nutrien AG Solutions Inc............................G 614 873-4253
   Milford Center *(G-10929)*

Nutrien AG Solutions Inc............................G 513 941-4100
   North Bend *(G-11705)*

Ohigro Inc..E 740 726-2429
   Waldo *(G-15090)*

Opal Diamond LLC.....................................G 330 653-5876
   Rocky River *(G-12839)*

Ottokee Group Inc......................................G 419 636-1932
   Bryan *(G-1834)*

Price Farms Organics Ltd.........................F 740 369-1000
   Delaware *(G-6745)*

Roe Transportation Entps Inc....................G 937 497-7161
   Sidney *(G-13278)*

Van Tilburg Farms Inc................................F 419 586-3077
   Celina *(G-2354)*

Werlor Inc..E 419 784-4285
   Defiance *(G-6698)*

2879 Agricultural chemicals, nec

A Best Trmt & Pest Ctrl Sups.....................G 330 434-5555
   Akron *(G-10)*

Abbott Laboratories....................................D 847 937-6100
   Columbus *(G-5087)*

▲ Advanced Biological Mktg Inc.............E 419 232-2461
   Van Wert *(G-14904)*

BASF Corporation.......................................D 614 662-5682
   Columbus *(G-5176)*

Bird Control International..........................F 330 425-2377
   Twinsburg *(G-14637)*

◆ Damon Industries Inc............................D 330 821-5310
   Alliance *(G-400)*

Dupont...G 740 412-9752
   Orient *(G-12114)*

▲ Hawthorne Hydroponics LLC..............F 888 478-6544
   Marysville *(G-9914)*

Keystone Cooperative Inc..........................G 937 884-5526
   Verona *(G-14975)*

Monsanto Company....................................F 937 548-7858
   Greenville *(G-8052)*

Mystic Chemical Products Co....................F 216 251-4416
   Cleveland *(G-4433)*

▲ Quality Borate Co LLC..........................F 216 896-1949
   Cleveland *(G-4604)*

28 CHEMICALS AND ALLIED PRODUCTS

- ◆ Scotts Company LLC .... C 937 644-0011
  Marysville (G-9934)
- Scotts Miracle-Gro Company .... E 937 578-5065
  Marysville (G-9936)
- ▲ Scotts Miracle-Gro Company .... B 937 644-0011
  Marysville (G-9935)
- ▲ TLC Products Inc .... F 216 472-3030
  Westlake (G-15797)

2891 Adhesives and sealants

- ▲ Adchem Adhesives Inc .... F 440 526-1976
  Cleveland (G-3597)
- Adherex Group .... F 201 440-3806
  Cleveland (G-3600)
- Adhesives Lab USA North LLC .... F 567 825-2004
  Lima (G-9217)
- Akron Coating Adhesives Co Inc .... F 330 724-4716
  Akron (G-30)
- ◆ Akron Paint & Varnish Inc .... D 330 773-8911
  Akron (G-38)
- ◆ Akzo Nobel Paints LLC .... A 440 297-8000
  Strongsville (G-13803)
- Alpha Coatings Inc .... C 419 435-5111
  Fostoria (G-7627)
- Aluminum Coating Manufacturers .... F 216 341-2000
  Cleveland (G-3644)
- Arclin USA Inc .... G 419 726-5013
  Toledo (G-14198)
- Avery Dennison Corporation .... B 440 358-2564
  Painesville (G-12218)
- Besten Equipment Inc .... E 216 581-1166
  Akron (G-85)
- Bostik Inc .... E 419 289-9588
  Ashland (G-559)
- Bostik Inc .... E 614 232-8510
  Columbus (G-5205)
- Brewer Company .... G 513 576-6300
  Cincinnati (G-2681)
- ▲ Cardinal Rubber Company .... E 330 745-2191
  Barberton (G-864)
- Century Industries Corporation .... E 330 457-2367
  New Waterford (G-11556)
- Certon Technologies Inc .... F 440 786-7185
  Bedford (G-1111)
- ◆ Chemmasters Inc .... E 440 428-2105
  Madison (G-9589)
- Chemspec Ltd .... F 330 364-4422
  New Philadelphia (G-11492)
- ◆ Chemspec Ltd .... E 330 896-0355
  Canton (G-2073)
- ▲ Chemspec Usa Inc .... D 330 669-8512
  Orrville (G-12121)
- Choice Brands Adhesives Ltd .... E 800 330-5566
  Cincinnati (G-2733)
- ▲ Cincinnati Assn For The Blind .... C 513 221-8558
  Cincinnati (G-2740)
- ◆ Concrete Sealants Inc .... E 937 845-8776
  Tipp City (G-14130)
- Consolidated Coatings Corp .... A 216 514-7596
  Cleveland (G-3898)
- ▲ Conversion Tech Intl Inc .... E 419 924-5566
  West Unity (G-15638)
- ▲ CP Industries Inc .... F 740 763-2886
  Newark (G-11573)
- Dap Products Inc .... D 937 667-4461
  Tipp City (G-14131)
- Ddp Specialty Electronic MA .... C 937 839-4612
  West Alexandria (G-15341)
- Durez Corporation .... E 567 295-6400
  Kenton (G-8882)
- ▲ Edge Adhesives Inc .... E 614 875-6343
  Grove City (G-8090)

- Egc Operating Company LLC .... D 440 285-5835
  Chardon (G-2449)
- Elmers Products Inc .... D 614 225-4000
  Columbus (G-5349)
- Engineered Conductive Mtl LLC .... G 740 362-4444
  Delaware (G-6720)
- Entrochem Inc .... F 614 946-7602
  Columbus (G-5356)
- Evans Adhesive Corporation .... E 614 451-2665
  Columbus (G-5362)
- ◆ Evans Adhesive Corporation Ltd .... E 614 451-2665
  Columbus (G-5363)
- ▲ FedPro Inc .... E 216 464-6440
  Cleveland (G-4055)
- Foam Seal Inc .... C 216 881-8111
  Cleveland (G-4074)
- ◆ Franklin International Inc .... B 614 443-0241
  Columbus (G-5387)
- Gdc Inc .... F 574 533-3128
  Wooster (G-16123)
- Glenrock Company .... E 513 489-6710
  Blue Ash (G-1398)
- ▼ Gold Key Processing Inc .... C 440 632-0901
  Middlefield (G-10752)
- Har Equipment Sales Inc .... F 440 786-7189
  Bedford (G-1123)
- Hartline Products Coinc .... E 216 851-7189
  Cleveland (G-4171)
- HB Fuller Company .... G 833 672-1482
  Bellevue (G-1227)
- HB Fuller Company .... E 513 719-3600
  Blue Ash (G-1404)
- HB Fuller Company .... F 513 719-3600
  Blue Ash (G-1405)
- HB Fuller Company .... G 440 708-1212
  Chagrin Falls (G-2399)
- Henkel US Operations Corp .... E 513 830-0260
  Cincinnati (G-2994)
- Henkel US Operations Corp .... C 216 475-3600
  Cleveland (G-4180)
- Henkel US Operations Corp .... C 440 255-8900
  Mentor (G-10469)
- Henkel US Operations Corp .... D 440 250-7700
  Westlake (G-15755)
- Hexpol Compounding LLC .... C 440 834-4644
  Burton (G-1880)
- Hoover & Wells Inc .... C 419 691-9220
  Toledo (G-14319)
- ▲ ICP Adhesives and Sealants Inc .... E 330 753-4585
  Norton (G-11944)
- Illinois Tool Works Inc .... C 513 489-7600
  Blue Ash (G-1408)
- Illinois Tool Works Inc .... D 440 914-3100
  Solon (G-13366)
- ◆ J C Whitlam Manufacturing Co .... E 330 334-2524
  Wadsworth (G-15037)
- Jetcoat LLC .... E 800 394-0047
  Columbus (G-5496)
- Laird Technologies Inc .... D 216 939-2300
  Cleveland (G-4305)
- ▲ Laminate Technologies Inc .... D 800 231-2523
  Tiffin (G-14090)
- ▲ Laurenco Systems of Ohio LLC .... G
  Leavittsburg (G-9058)
- ◆ Lubrizol Global Management Inc .... F 216 447-5000
  Cleveland (G-4339)
- M Argueso & Co Inc .... C 216 252-4122
  Cleveland (G-4344)
- Mactac Americas LLC .... E 800 762-2822
  Stow (G-13707)
- Mameco International Inc .... D 216 752-4400
  Cleveland (G-4354)

- ▲ Merryweather Foam Inc .... E 330 753-0353
  Barberton (G-882)
- Millennium Adhesive Pdts LLC .... F 440 708-1212
  Chagrin Falls (G-2383)
- Mitsubishi Chemical Amer Inc .... D 419 483-2931
  Bellevue (G-1230)
- ◆ Morgan Adhesives Company LLC .... B 330 688-1111
  Stow (G-13709)
- ▲ Nagase Chemtex America LLC .... E 740 362-4444
  Delaware (G-6739)
- ▼ Nanosperse LLC .... G 937 296-5030
  Kettering (G-8908)
- National Polymer Inc .... F 440 708-1245
  Chagrin Falls (G-2409)
- Neyra Interstate Inc .... E 513 733-1000
  Cincinnati (G-3196)
- P & T Products Inc .... E 419 621-1966
  Sandusky (G-13085)
- ▲ Paramelt Argueso Kindt Inc .... G 216 252-4122
  Cleveland (G-4521)
- Pmbp Legacy Co Inc .... E 330 253-8148
  Akron (G-278)
- ▲ Polymerics Inc .... E 330 928-2210
  Cuyahoga Falls (G-6110)
- ▼ PPG Architectural Coatings LLC .... D 440 297-8000
  Strongsville (G-13866)
- ▲ Premier Building Solutions LLC .... E 330 244-2907
  Massillon (G-10136)
- Priest Services Inc .... G 440 333-1123
  Mayfield Heights (G-10254)
- Quanex Ig Systems Inc .... D 740 435-0444
  Cambridge (G-1949)
- ▲ Renegade Materials Corporation .... D 937 350-5274
  Miamisburg (G-10675)
- ◆ Republic Powdered Metals Inc .... D 330 225-3192
  Medina (G-10370)
- Royal Adhesives .... G 440 708-1212
  Chagrin Falls (G-2420)
- Royal Adhesives & Sealants LLC .... F 440 708-1212
  Chagrin Falls (G-2421)
- RPM Consumer Holding Company .... E 330 273-5090
  Medina (G-10371)
- ◆ RPM International Inc .... D 330 273-5090
  Medina (G-10372)
- ▼ Rubex Inc .... G 614 875-6343
  Grove City (G-8118)
- Ruscoe Company .... E 330 253-8148
  Akron (G-314)
- Sem-Com Company Inc .... G 419 537-8813
  Toledo (G-14466)
- Shelli R McMurray .... G 614 275-4381
  Columbus (G-5761)
- Sherwin-Williams Company .... C 330 830-6000
  Massillon (G-10144)
- ▲ Shincor Silicones Inc .... E 330 630-9460
  Akron (G-329)
- Signature Flexible Packg LLC .... F 614 252-2121
  Columbus (G-5769)
- Sika Mbcc US LLC .... A 216 839-7500
  Beachwood (G-1024)
- Silicone Solutions Inc .... F 330 920-3125
  Cuyahoga Falls (G-6117)
- ◆ Simona Boltaron Inc .... D 740 498-5900
  Newcomerstown (G-11651)
- ▲ Sirrus Inc .... E 513 448-0308
  Loveland (G-9506)
- Sonoco Products Company .... D 937 429-0040
  Beavercreek Township (G-1094)
- Spectra Group Limited Inc .... G 419 837-9783
  Millbury (G-10936)
- Spectrum Adhesives Inc .... G 740 763-2886
  Newark (G-11606)

SIC SECTION
28 CHEMICALS AND ALLIED PRODUCTS

Sportsmaster .... G 440 257-3900
  Mentor *(G-10559)*

Summitville Tiles Inc .... E 330 868-6463
  Minerva *(G-11040)*

▲ Sunstar Engrg Americas Inc ...... E 937 746-8575
  Springboro *(G-13520)*

◆ Synthomer USA LLC .... E 678 400-6655
  Beachwood *(G-1026)*

◆ Technical Rubber Company Inc ... C 740 967-9015
  Johnstown *(G-8779)*

Technicote Inc .... E 330 928-1476
  Cuyahoga Falls *(G-6121)*

Techno Adhesives Co .... G 513 771-1584
  Cincinnati *(G-3443)*

▲ Teknol Inc .... D 937 264-0190
  Dayton *(G-6613)*

▲ Thermagon Inc .... D 216 939-2300
  Cleveland *(G-4791)*

◆ Thorworks Industries Inc .... C 419 626-4375
  Sandusky *(G-13096)*

Three Bond International Inc .... E 937 610-3000
  Dayton *(G-6622)*

▲ Three Bond International Inc ..... D 513 779-7300
  West Chester *(G-15515)*

▲ Toagosei America Inc .... D 614 718-3855
  West Jefferson *(G-15615)*

Tremco Cpg Inc .... E 419 289-2050
  Ashland *(G-618)*

Tremco Cpg Inc .... F 216 514-7783
  Beachwood *(G-1030)*

◆ Tremco Incorporated .... B
  Beachwood *(G-1031)*

◆ Truseal Technologies Inc .... E 216 910-1500
  Akron *(G-364)*

▲ United McGill Corporation .... E 614 829-1200
  Groveport *(G-8165)*

▲ Valco Cincinnati Inc .... C 513 874-6550
  West Chester *(G-15603)*

▲ Waytek Corporation .... E 937 743-6142
  Franklin *(G-7711)*

2892 Explosives

Austin Powder Company .... G 419 299-3347
  Findlay *(G-7478)*

Austin Powder Company .... C 740 596-5286
  Mc Arthur *(G-10262)*

Austin Powder Company .... G 740 968-1555
  Saint Clairsville *(G-12896)*

▲ Austin Powder Company .... D 216 464-2400
  Cleveland *(G-3698)*

◆ Austin Powder Holdings Company ... D 216 464-2400
  Cleveland *(G-3699)*

Hilltop Energy Inc .... F 330 859-2108
  Mineral City *(G-11018)*

Sloat Inc .... G 440 951-9554
  Willoughby *(G-15995)*

2893 Printing ink

American Inks and Coatings Co .... G 513 552-7200
  Fairfield *(G-7334)*

Chef Ink LLC .... G 937 474-2032
  Dayton *(G-6252)*

◆ Eckart America Corporation .... D 440 954-7600
  Painesville *(G-12231)*

Flint CPS Inks North Amer LLC .... E 513 619-2089
  Cincinnati *(G-2909)*

▲ Glass Coatings & Concepts LLC .. E 513 539-5300
  Monroe *(G-11108)*

◆ Ink Technology Corporation .... E 216 486-6720
  Cleveland *(G-4226)*

INX International Ink Co .... F 707 693-2990
  Lebanon *(G-9089)*

Joules Angstrom Uv Prtg Inks C ... E 740 964-9113
  Pataskala *(G-12299)*

Kennedy Ink Company Inc .... F 513 871-2515
  Cincinnati *(G-3074)*

Kohl & Madden Inc .... F 513 326-6900
  Cincinnati *(G-3086)*

Magnum Magnetics Corporation ... E 740 516-6237
  Caldwell *(G-1910)*

Magnum Magnetics Corporation ... E 513 360-0790
  Middletown *(G-10840)*

Phoenix Inkjet Clour Sltons LL ..... G 937 602-8486
  Dayton *(G-6504)*

Premier Ink Systems Inc .... F 513 367-2300
  Harrison *(G-8286)*

Printink Inc .... G 513 943-0599
  Amelia *(G-461)*

▲ Red Tie Group Inc .... E
  Cleveland *(G-4621)*

Retail Project Management Inc .... G 614 299-9880
  Columbus *(G-5721)*

Sun Chemical Corporation .... D 513 753-9550
  Amelia *(G-467)*

Sun Chemical Corporation .... E 513 671-0407
  Cincinnati *(G-3427)*

Sun Chemical Corporation .... E 513 681-5950
  Cincinnati *(G-3428)*

Sun Chemical Corporation .... E 513 681-5950
  Cincinnati *(G-3429)*

Sun Chemical Corporation .... E 513 830-8667
  Cincinnati *(G-3430)*

Sun Chemical Corporation .... D 419 891-3514
  Maumee *(G-10237)*

Superior Printing Ink Co Inc .... G 216 328-1720
  Cleveland *(G-4750)*

Vibrantz Corporation .... C 216 875-6213
  Cleveland *(G-4868)*

Wikoff Color Corporation .... G 513 423-0727
  Middletown *(G-10873)*

Zeres Inc .... E 419 354-5555
  Bowling Green *(G-1598)*

2895 Carbon black

◆ Chromascape LLC .... E 330 998-7574
  Independence *(G-8658)*

◆ Jacobi Carbons Inc .... D 215 546-3900
  Columbus *(G-5485)*

2899 Chemical preparations, nec

Addivant .... G 440 352-1719
  Concord Township *(G-5900)*

▲ Akron Dispersions Inc .... E 330 666-0045
  Copley *(G-5942)*

Albemarle Amendments LLC .... E 330 425-2354
  Twinsburg *(G-14627)*

Aldrich Chemical .... D 937 859-1808
  Miamisburg *(G-10608)*

Alterra Energy LLC .... G 800 569-6061
  Akron *(G-56)*

▼ AP Tech Group Inc .... F 513 761-8111
  West Chester *(G-15366)*

▲ Apex Advanced Technologies LLC .. G 216 898-1595
  Cleveland *(G-3670)*

◆ Applied Specialties Inc .... E 440 933-9442
  Avon Lake *(G-796)*

▲ Aps-Materials Inc .... D 937 278-6547
  Dayton *(G-6210)*

Aqua Science Inc .... E 614 252-5000
  Columbus *(G-5151)*

Aquablue Incorporated .... G 330 343-0220
  New Philadelphia *(G-11484)*

Ashland Chemco Inc .... F 216 961-4690
  Cleveland *(G-3689)*

Ashland Chemco Inc .... C 614 790-3333
  Columbus *(G-5156)*

Ashland Spcalty Ingredients GP ... C 614 529-3311
  Columbus *(G-5157)*

◆ ASK Chemicals LLC .... B 800 848-7485
  Dublin *(G-6863)*

Ask Chemicals LP .... G 614 763-0248
  Columbus *(G-5159)*

Attia Applied Sciences Inc .... G 740 369-1891
  Delaware *(G-6704)*

BASF Corporation .... D 614 662-5682
  Columbus *(G-5176)*

▲ Bernard Laboratories Inc .... E 513 681-7373
  Cincinnati *(G-2666)*

Bird Control International .... F 330 425-2377
  Twinsburg *(G-14637)*

Blackthorn LLC .... F 937 836-9296
  Clayton *(G-3564)*

BLaster LLC .... E 216 901-5800
  Cleveland *(G-3742)*

Bomat Inc .... G 216 692-8382
  Cleveland *(G-3746)*

Bond Chemicals Inc .... F 330 725-5935
  Medina *(G-10303)*

Bond Distributing LLC .... G 440 461-7920
  Eastlake *(G-7022)*

◆ Borchers Americas Inc .... D 440 899-2950
  Westlake *(G-15741)*

Broco Products Inc .... G 216 531-0880
  Cleveland *(G-3761)*

▲ Buckeye Fabric Finishers Inc .... F 740 622-3251
  Coshocton *(G-5975)*

◆ Buckingham Src Inc .... F 216 941-6115
  Cleveland *(G-3768)*

Cargill Incorporated .... F 513 941-7400
  Cincinnati *(G-2702)*

Cargill Incorporated .... C 216 651-7200
  Cleveland *(G-3792)*

Cfo Ntic .... G 216 450-5700
  Beachwood *(G-976)*

Chem Technologies Ltd .... D 440 632-9311
  Middlefield *(G-10740)*

Chemical Methods Incorporated ... E 216 476-8400
  Brunswick *(G-1751)*

◆ Chemmasters Inc .... E 440 428-2105
  Madison *(G-9589)*

Chemstation International Inc ...... E 937 294-8265
  Moraine *(G-11166)*

Cinchempro Inc .... C 513 724-6111
  Batavia *(G-914)*

Cincinnati - Vulcan Company .... D 513 242-5300
  Cincinnati *(G-2736)*

City of Mount Vernon .... G 740 393-9508
  Mount Vernon *(G-11268)*

CJ Salt World .... G 440 343-5661
  Wickliffe *(G-15827)*

Color Resolutions International LLC ... C 513 552-7200
  Fairfield *(G-7349)*

▲ Coolant Control Inc .... E 513 471-8770
  Cincinnati *(G-2795)*

Coventya Inc .... F 315 768-6635
  Brooklyn Heights *(G-1688)*

CP Chemicals Group LP .... F 440 833-3000
  Wickliffe *(G-15829)*

Cresset Chemical Co Inc .... F 419 669-2041
  Weston *(G-15805)*

▼ Cresset Chemical Co Inc .... F 419 669-2041
  Weston *(G-15804)*

Cyber Shed Inc .... G 419 724-5855
  Toledo *(G-14256)*

◆ Damon Industries Inc .... D 330 821-5310
  Alliance *(G-400)*

28 CHEMICALS AND ALLIED PRODUCTS

- Dayton Superior Corporation............C 937 866-0711
  Miamisburg (G-10633)
- Dinol US Inc................................E 740 548-1656
  Lewis Center (G-9157)
- Distillata Company.........................D 216 771-2900
  Cleveland (G-3962)
- Dover Chemical Corporation............C 330 343-7711
  Dover (G-6818)
- Edgewater Capital Partners LP........G 216 292-3838
  Independence (G-8666)
- Elco Corporation............................E 440 997-6131
  Ashtabula (G-631)
- EMD Millipore Corporation..............C 513 631-0445
  Norwood (G-11995)
- Emery Oleochemicals LLC...............E 513 762-2500
  Cincinnati (G-2866)
- Ensign Product Company Inc..........G 216 341-5911
  Cleveland (G-4020)
- Enviri Corporation..........................F 330 372-1781
  Warren (G-15168)
- Environmental Chemical Corp.........F 330 453-5200
  Uniontown (G-14782)
- ESP Akron Sub LLC.......................D 330 374-2242
  Akron (G-144)
- Essential Elements Usa LLC............E 513 482-5700
  Cincinnati (G-2884)
- Etna Products Incorporated............E 440 543-9845
  Chagrin Falls (G-2395)
- Euclid Chemical Company...............E 800 321-7628
  Cleveland (G-4032)
- Ferrum Industries Inc....................G 440 519-1768
  Twinsburg (G-14660)
- Flexsys America LP........................D 330 666-4111
  Akron (G-155)
- Formlabs Ohio Inc..........................E 419 837-9783
  Millbury (G-10932)
- Fuchs Lubricants Co......................F 330 963-0400
  Twinsburg (G-14663)
- Fusion Ceramics Inc......................E 330 627-5821
  Carrollton (G-2307)
- Fusion Incorporated.......................D 440 946-3300
  Willoughby (G-15922)
- Galapagos Inc...............................E 937 890-3068
  Dayton (G-6344)
- Gasflux Company...........................G 440 365-1941
  Elyria (G-7153)
- General Electric Company...............E 216 268-3846
  Cleveland (G-4114)
- GFS Chemicals Inc........................D 614 224-5345
  Columbus (G-5403)
- GFS Chemicals Inc........................E 740 881-5501
  Powell (G-12674)
- H&G Legacy Co.............................F 513 921-1075
  Cincinnati (G-2982)
- Hexion LLC...................................D 614 225-4000
  Columbus (G-5429)
- Hexpol Compounding LLC...............C 440 834-4644
  Burton (G-1880)
- Howard Industries Inc....................F 614 444-9900
  Columbus (G-5447)
- Hunt Imaging LLC..........................E 440 826-0433
  Berea (G-1283)
- Huntsman Corporation....................D 330 374-2418
  Akron (G-187)
- Illinois Tool Works Inc....................D 440 914-3100
  Solon (G-13366)
- Innovative Food Processors Inc......G 507 334-2730
  Defiance (G-6683)
- Intercontinental Chemical Corp.......E 513 541-7100
  Cincinnati (G-3026)
- Italmatch Sc LLC...........................F 216 749-2605
  Cleveland (G-4239)

- J C Whitlam Manufacturing Co........E 330 334-2524
  Wadsworth (G-15037)
- J W Harris Co Inc..........................B 513 754-2000
  Mason (G-10014)
- Kona Blackbird Inc.........................E 440 285-3189
  Chardon (G-2455)
- Kost Usa Inc.................................E 513 583-7070
  Cincinnati (G-3088)
- Leonhardt Plating Company............F 513 242-1410
  Cincinnati (G-3102)
- Lfg Specialties LLC........................E 419 424-4999
  Findlay (G-7529)
- Lg Chem Ohio Petrochemical Inc....G 470 792-5127
  Ravenna (G-12723)
- Link To Success Inc......................G 888 959-4203
  Norwalk (G-11978)
- Liquid Development Company.........G 216 641-9366
  Independence (G-8671)
- Lubrizol Advanced Mtls Inc.............F 216 447-5000
  Brecksville (G-1625)
- Lubrizol Corporation.......................E 216 447-5447
  Brecksville (G-1626)
- Lubrizol Global Management Inc.....E 440 933-0400
  Avon Lake (G-815)
- Lubrizol Global Management Inc.....F 216 447-5000
  Cleveland (G-4339)
- Lubrizol Holdings LLC....................E 440 943-4200
  Wickliffe (G-15838)
- Luxfer Magtech Inc........................E 513 772-3066
  Cincinnati (G-3116)
- Malco Products Inc........................C 330 753-0361
  Barberton (G-879)
- Master Bldrs Sltons Admxtres U.....E 216 839-7500
  Beachwood (G-997)
- Master Builders LLC......................E 800 228-3318
  Beachwood (G-998)
- Master Chemical Corporation..........D 419 874-7902
  Perrysburg (G-12399)
- McGean-Rohco Inc........................F 216 441-4900
  Newburgh Heights (G-11618)
- McGean-Rohco Inc........................D 216 441-4900
  Newburgh Heights (G-11619)
- Midwest Glycol Services LLC..........E 419 946-3326
  Marion (G-9862)
- Milacron LLC.................................E 513 487-5000
  Blue Ash (G-1439)
- Monarch Engraving Inc..................F 440 638-1500
  Strongsville (G-13857)
- Morgan Advanced Ceramics Inc......E 330 405-1033
  Twinsburg (G-14700)
- Morton Salt Inc.............................E 513 941-1578
  Cincinnati (G-3176)
- Morton Salt Inc.............................D 216 664-0728
  Cleveland (G-4423)
- Morton Salt Inc.............................C 330 925-3015
  Rittman (G-12825)
- Mxr Imaging Inc............................G 614 219-2011
  Hilliard (G-8423)
- National Colloid Company...............E 740 282-1171
  Steubenville (G-13673)
- Natural Essentials Inc....................C 330 562-8022
  Streetsboro (G-13781)
- Natures Own Source LLC...............G 440 838-5135
  Brecksville (G-1628)
- Net Braze LLC..............................F 937 444-1444
  Mount Orab (G-11244)
- No Burn Inc..................................G 330 336-1500
  Wadsworth (G-15048)
- No Burn North America Inc............F 419 841-6055
  Toledo (G-14397)
- Noco Company..............................D 216 464-8131
  Solon (G-13399)

- Nof Metal Coatings N Amer Inc.......E 440 285-2231
  Chardon (G-2459)
- Northern Chem Blnding Corp Inc.....G 216 781-7799
  Cleveland (G-4476)
- Noveon Fcc Inc.............................E 440 943-4200
  Wickliffe (G-15841)
- Ohio Aluminum Chemicals LLC.......G 513 860-3842
  West Chester (G-15468)
- Opw Fueling Components Inc........D 800 422-2525
  West Chester (G-15472)
- Parker Trutec Incorporated............D 937 653-8500
  Urbana (G-14846)
- Pchem LLC...................................G 419 699-1582
  Northwood (G-11926)
- Pemro Corporation.........................F 800 440-5441
  Cleveland (G-4540)
- Peter Cremer North America LP.....D 513 471-7200
  Cincinnati (G-3251)
- Phantom Fireworks Wstn Reg LLC..F 330 746-1064
  Youngstown (G-16418)
- Plating Process Systems Inc..........G
  Mentor (G-10525)
- Polymer Additives Holdings Inc......C 216 875-7200
  Independence (G-8680)
- Polymerics Inc...............................E 330 677-1131
  Kent (G-8845)
- PPG Architectural Coatings LLC......D 440 297-8000
  Strongsville (G-13866)
- Premier Chemicals.........................G 440 234-4600
  Cleveland (G-4579)
- Premier Ink Systems Inc................F 513 367-2300
  Harrison (G-8286)
- Primary Pdts Ingrdnts Amrcas L.....D 937 236-5906
  Dayton (G-6520)
- Proklean Services LLC...................E 330 273-0122
  Brunswick (G-1783)
- Pyro-Chem Corporation..................F 740 377-2244
  South Point (G-13474)
- Quaker Chemical Corporation.........E 513 422-9600
  Middletown (G-10853)
- Ques Industries Inc.......................F 216 267-8989
  Cleveland (G-4610)
- Quikrete Companies LLC................G 614 885-4406
  Columbus (G-5704)
- Railtech Matweld Inc.....................E 419 592-5050
  Napoleon (G-11332)
- Rambasek Realty Inc....................F 937 228-1189
  Dayton (G-6540)
- Ravago Chemical Dist Inc..............E 330 920-8023
  Twinsburg (G-14723)
- Republic Powdered Metals Inc........D 330 225-3192
  Medina (G-10370)
- Research Organics LLC..................D 216 883-8025
  Cleveland (G-4628)
- Rhenium Alloys Inc.......................E 440 365-7388
  North Ridgeville (G-11858)
- Rossborough Automotive Corp........F 216 941-6115
  Cleveland (G-4651)
- Rozzi Company Inc........................E 513 683-0620
  Martinsville (G-9902)
- Rozzi Company Inc........................E 513 683-0620
  Loveland (G-9502)
- RP Hoskins Inc..............................E 216 631-1000
  Cleveland (G-4658)
- RPM International Inc....................D 330 273-5090
  Medina (G-10372)
- SC Fire Protection Ltd..................G 330 468-3300
  Macedonia (G-9572)
- Sigma-Aldrich Corporation..............D 216 206-5424
  Cleveland (G-4701)
- Signet Enterprises LLC..................E 330 762-9102
  Akron (G-331)

29 PETROLEUM REFINING AND RELATED INDUSTRIES

▲ SRC Worldwide Inc .... F 216 941-6115
   Cleveland *(G-4723)*

◆ State Industrial Products Corp .... B 877 747-6986
   Cleveland *(G-4731)*

Stellar Group Inc .... F 330 769-8484
   Seville *(G-13145)*

Summitville Tiles Inc .... E 330 868-6463
   Minerva *(G-11040)*

Sun Chemical Corporation .... E 513 671-0407
   Cincinnati *(G-3427)*

◆ Superior Flux & Mfg Co .... F 440 349-3000
   Cleveland *(G-4747)*

▲ Teknol Inc .... D 937 264-0190
   Dayton *(G-6613)*

The Lubrizol Corporation .... C 440 357-7064
   Painesville *(G-12270)*

◆ The Lubrizol Corporation .... A 440 943-4200
   Wickliffe *(G-15853)*

Total Life Safety LLC .... F 866 955-2318
   West Chester *(G-15516)*

Tuf-N-Lite LLC .... F 513 472-8400
   Middletown *(G-10868)*

◆ U S Chemical & Plastics .... G 330 830-6000
   Massillon *(G-10152)*

▲ Unitrex Ltd .... D 216 831-1900
   Bedford Heights *(G-1180)*

Univar Solutions USA LLC .... F 513 714-5264
   West Chester *(G-15602)*

Urethane Polymers Intl .... F 216 430-3655
   Cleveland *(G-4855)*

US Water Company LLC .... G 740 453-0604
   Zanesville *(G-16567)*

Usalco Fairfield Plant LLC .... E 513 737-7100
   Fairfield *(G-7421)*

Valtris Specialty Chemicals .... F 216 875-7200
   Walton Hills *(G-15104)*

Vibrantz Corporation .... C 216 875-6213
   Cleveland *(G-4868)*

Vibrantz Corporation .... E 216 875-5600
   Cleveland *(G-4871)*

▲ Wild Berry Incense Inc .... F 513 523-8583
   Oxford *(G-12214)*

◆ Zinkan Enterprises Inc .... F 330 487-1500
   Twinsburg *(G-14760)*

29 PETROLEUM REFINING AND RELATED INDUSTRIES

2911 Petroleum refining

Aecom Energy & Cnstr Inc .... G 419 698-6277
   Oregon *(G-12101)*

Allied Corp Inc .... G 330 626-3401
   Streetsboro *(G-13756)*

Appalachian Solvents LLC .... G 740 680-3649
   Cambridge *(G-1921)*

Blaster Corporation .... F 216 901-5800
   Medina *(G-10302)*

BLaster Holdings LLC .... G 216 901-5800
   Cleveland *(G-3741)*

BLaster LLC .... E 216 901-5800
   Cleveland *(G-3742)*

BP Products North America Inc .... E 419 537-9540
   Toledo *(G-14217)*

Capital City Oil Inc .... G 740 397-4483
   Mount Vernon *(G-11266)*

Crowley Blue Wtr Partners LLC .... F 419 422-2121
   Findlay *(G-7499)*

Cyberutility LLC .... G 216 291-8723
   Cleveland *(G-3934)*

Eidp Inc .... F 440 934-6444
   Avon *(G-772)*

Enrevo Pyro LLC .... G 203 517-5002
   Brookfield *(G-1669)*

Federal Parkway Diesel Co LLC .... G 614 571-0388
   Columbus *(G-5374)*

Foam Seal Inc .... C 216 881-8111
   Cleveland *(G-4074)*

▼ Functional Products Inc .... F 330 963-3060
   Macedonia *(G-9552)*

Gfl Environmental Svcs USA Inc .... E 614 441-4001
   Columbus *(G-5401)*

Gfl Environmental Svcs USA Inc .... E 281 486-4182
   Norwalk *(G-11969)*

Gress Oil & Gas Inc .... F 740 622-8356
   Coshocton *(G-5980)*

Husky Lima Refinery .... D 419 226-2300
   Lima *(G-9253)*

Hydrodec Inc .... G 330 454-8202
   Canton *(G-2127)*

▼ Hydrodec of North America LLC .... E 330 454-8202
   Canton *(G-2128)*

Ineos Neal LLC .... E 610 790-3333
   Dublin *(G-6896)*

▲ Isp Lima LLC .... E 419 998-8700
   Lima *(G-9257)*

Jet Fuel Strategies LLC .... G 440 323-4220
   Elyria *(G-7172)*

Jet Fuel Tech Inc .... G 614 463-1986
   Columbus *(G-5495)*

◆ Knight Material Tech LLC .... D 330 488-1651
   East Canton *(G-6979)*

◆ Lima Refining Company .... E 419 226-2300
   Lima *(G-9263)*

Marathon Oil Company .... E 419 422-2121
   Findlay *(G-7531)*

▲ Marathon Petroleum Corporation .... A 419 422-2121
   Findlay *(G-7533)*

Marathon Ptro Cnada Trdg Sup U .... F 419 422-2121
   Findlay *(G-7534)*

Mkfour Inc .... G 620 629-1120
   Granville *(G-8021)*

Mplx GP LLC .... F 419 422-2121
   Findlay *(G-7540)*

National Staffing Services LLC .... G 785 731-2540
   Toledo *(G-14395)*

Ohio Refining Company LLC .... A 614 210-2300
   Dublin *(G-6917)*

Oil Works LLC .... G 614 245-3090
   Columbus *(G-5635)*

PEC Biofuels LLC .... G 419 542-8210
   Hicksville *(G-8378)*

Petroleum Holdings LLC .... G 443 676-0150
   Salem *(G-13021)*

PSC 272 TRC Pbf .... E 419 466-7129
   Oregon *(G-12109)*

Rd Holder Oil Co .... G 740 653-4031
   Lancaster *(G-9037)*

Seneca Petroleum Co Inc .... F 419 691-3581
   Toledo *(G-14467)*

Seneca Petroleum Co Inc .... F 419 691-3581
   Toledo *(G-14468)*

Shacks Stop N Go LLC .... G 614 296-9292
   Pickerington *(G-12470)*

Simco Gas Ohio 2005 Partne .... F 330 799-2268
   Youngstown *(G-16438)*

Solvent Solutions LLC .... G 937 648-4962
   Dayton *(G-6579)*

Stark Materials Inc .... F 330 497-1648
   Canton *(G-2232)*

Troy Valley Petroleum .... G 937 604-0012
   Dayton *(G-6636)*

2951 Asphalt paving mixtures and blocks

Advanced Fiber LLC .... E 419 562-1337
   Bucyrus *(G-1849)*

All Coatings Co Inc .... G 330 821-3806
   Alliance *(G-389)*

Aluminum Coating Manufacturers .... F 216 341-2000
   Cleveland *(G-3644)*

Asphalt Fabrics & Specialties .... E 440 786-1077
   Solon *(G-13314)*

Atlas Roofing Corporation .... C 937 746-9941
   Franklin *(G-7663)*

◆ Barrett Paving Materials Inc .... E 973 533-1001
   Hamilton *(G-8183)*

Bluffton Stone Co .... E 419 358-6941
   Bluffton *(G-1501)*

Bowerston Shale Company .... E 740 269-2921
   Bowerston *(G-1544)*

▲ Brewer Company .... G 800 394-0017
   Milford *(G-10896)*

Browns Handyman Remodeling .... G 330 766-0925
   Warren *(G-15148)*

Central Allied Enterprises Inc .... E 330 477-6751
   Canton *(G-2071)*

Central Oil Asphalt Corp .... G 614 224-8111
   Columbus *(G-5242)*

Crafco Inc .... F 330 270-3034
   Youngstown *(G-16342)*

Extendit Company .... G 330 743-4343
   New Springfield *(G-11541)*

Gbr Property Maintenance LLC .... F 937 879-0200
   Fairborn *(G-7316)*

Gerken Materials Inc .... E 419 533-2421
   Napoleon *(G-11315)*

Heidelberg Mtls Mdwest Agg Inc .... G 419 983-2211
   Bloomville *(G-1355)*

Heidelberg Mtls Mdwest Agg Inc .... G 419 878-2006
   Waterville *(G-15245)*

Heritage Group Inc .... A 330 875-5566
   Louisville *(G-9460)*

Holmes Supply Corp .... G 330 279-2634
   Holmesville *(G-8547)*

Hy-Grade Corporation .... E 216 341-7711
   Cleveland *(G-4210)*

Image Pavement Maintenance .... F 937 833-9200
   Brookville *(G-1739)*

Kokosing Materials Inc .... F 740 694-5872
   Fredericktown *(G-7750)*

Kokosing Materials Inc .... F 419 522-2715
   Mansfield *(G-9677)*

Kokosing Materials Inc .... F 740 745-3341
   Saint Louisville *(G-12943)*

Kokosing Materials Inc .... E 614 491-1199
   Columbus *(G-5513)*

Kokosing Materials Inc .... F 740 694-9585
   Fredericktown *(G-7751)*

Koski Construction Co .... G 440 997-5337
   Ashtabula *(G-644)*

LA Rose Paving Co .... G 440 632-0330
   Middlefield *(G-10763)*

M & B Asphalt Company Inc .... F 419 992-4235
   Tiffin *(G-14091)*

Mae Materials LLC .... E 740 778-2242
   South Webster *(G-13476)*

◆ Maintenance + Inc .... F 330 264-6262
   Wooster *(G-16149)*

Mar-Zane Inc .... F 740 453-0721
   Zanesville *(G-16543)*

◆ Marathon Petroleum Company LP ...... F 419 422-2121
   Findlay *(G-7532)*

Miller Bros Paving Inc .... F 419 445-1015
   Archbold *(G-536)*

Morrow Gravel Company Inc .... E 513 771-0820
   Cincinnati *(G-3175)*

Employee Codes: A=Over 500 employees, B=251-500
C=101-250, D=51-100, E=20-50, F=10-19, G=1-9

29 PETROLEUM REFINING AND RELATED INDUSTRIES

Mplx Terminals LLC .... D 330 479-5539
　Canton (G-2167)
Mt Pleasant Blacktopping Inc .... G 513 874-3777
　Fairfield (G-7385)
Nes Corp .... E 440 834-0438
　Hiram (G-8487)
Perma Edge Paver Edging .... G 844 334-4464
　Dayton (G-6502)
▲ Reading Rock Incorporated .... C 513 874-2345
　West Chester (G-15580)
Roof To Road LLC .... G 740 986-6923
　Williamsport (G-15869)
Russell Standard Corporation .... G 330 733-9400
　Akron (G-318)
Rutland Township .... G 740 742-2805
　Bidwell (G-1326)
S E Johnson Companies Inc .... E 419 893-8731
　Maumee (G-10228)
Seal Master Corporation .... E 330 673-8410
　Kent (G-8860)
Seal Masters LLC .... G 216 860-7710
　Parma (G-12295)
Seneca Petroleum Co Inc .... F 419 691-3581
　Toledo (G-14468)
Shelly and Sands Inc .... G 740 859-2104
　Rayland (G-12745)
Shelly and Sands Inc .... F 740 453-0721
　Zanesville (G-16562)
Shelly Materials Inc .... F 419 622-2101
　Convoy (G-5940)
Shelly Materials Inc .... E 740 666-5841
　Ostrander (G-12176)
Shelly Materials Inc .... E 740 246-5009
　Thornville (G-14071)
Shelly Materials Inc .... G 419 273-2510
　Forest (G-7592)
Shelly Materials Inc .... F 740 246-6315
　Thornville (G-14072)
Skyridge Roofing & Masnry LLC .... G 440 628-1983
　Willowick (G-16034)
Smalls Asphalt Paving Inc .... F 740 427-4096
　Gambier (G-7908)
Smith & Thompson Entps LLC .... F 330 386-9345
　East Liverpool (G-7000)
Stark Materials Inc .... F 330 497-1648
　Canton (G-2232)
Stoneco Inc .... E 419 393-2555
　Oakwood (G-12033)
Stoneco Inc .... G 419 693-3933
　Toledo (G-14475)
Stoneco Inc .... E 419 422-8854
　Findlay (G-7569)
◆ Thorworks Industries Inc .... C 419 626-4375
　Sandusky (G-13096)
Valley Asphalt Corporation .... G 513 381-0652
　Morrow (G-11226)
Valley Asphalt Corporation .... E 513 771-0820
　Cincinnati (G-3486)
Wilson Blacktop Corp .... F 740 635-3566
　Martins Ferry (G-9901)
Wyandot Dolomite Inc .... E 419 396-7641
　Carey (G-2286)

2952 Asphalt felts and coatings

All Seal .... G 740 852-2628
　London (G-9380)
Aluminum Coating Manufacturers .... F 216 341-2000
　Cleveland (G-3644)
American Orginal Bldg Pdts LLC .... G 330 786-3000
　Akron (G-60)
Atlas Roofing Corporation .... C 937 746-9941
　Franklin (G-7663)

Blackfish Sealcoating LLC .... G 419 647-4010
　Spencerville (G-13485)
Brewer Company .... G 513 576-6300
　Cincinnati (G-2681)
▲ Brewer Company .... G 800 394-0017
　Milford (G-10896)
Broke Boys Sealcoating LLC .... G 614 477-0322
　Mount Sterling (G-11254)
C Green & Sons Incorporated .... F 740 745-2998
　Saint Louisville (G-12942)
Century Industries Corporation .... E 330 457-2367
　New Waterford (G-11556)
Certainteed LLC .... C 419 499-2581
　Milan (G-10882)
◆ Chemspec Ltd .... E 330 896-0355
　Canton (G-2073)
Consolidated Coatings Corp .... A 216 514-7596
　Cleveland (G-3898)
Dnd Emulsions Inc .... F 419 525-4988
　Mansfield (G-9646)
Fluid Applied Roofing LLC .... F 855 860-2300
　Beavercreek Township (G-1084)
Garland Industries Inc .... G 216 641-7500
　Cleveland (G-4104)
Garland/Dbs Inc .... C 216 641-7500
　Cleveland (G-4105)
Hy-Grade Corporation .... E 216 341-7711
　Cleveland (G-4210)
▼ Hyload Inc .... G 330 336-6604
　Seville (G-13142)
Iko Production Inc .... E 937 746-4561
　Franklin (G-7682)
◆ Isaiah Industries Inc .... D 937 773-9840
　Piqua (G-12527)
Johns Manville Corporation .... E 419 499-1400
　Milan (G-10884)
Kettering Roofing & Shtmtl Inc .... F 513 281-6413
　Cincinnati (G-3075)
M & B Asphalt Company Inc .... F 419 992-4235
　Tiffin (G-14091)
Metal Sales Manufacturing Corp .... F 440 319-3779
　Jefferson (G-8753)
Mfm Building Products Corp .... E 740 622-2645
　Coshocton (G-5984)
◆ Mfm Building Products Corp .... F 740 622-2645
　Coshocton (G-5985)
National Tool & Equipment Inc .... F 330 629-8665
　Youngstown (G-16403)
Neyra Interstate Inc .... E 513 733-1000
　Cincinnati (G-3196)
North Coatings Inc .... G 330 896-7126
　Uniontown (G-14789)
◆ Owens Corning Sales LLC .... A 419 248-8000
　Toledo (G-14424)
▲ Pioneer Manufacturing Inc .... D 216 671-5500
　Cleveland (G-4555)
Roof Maxx Technologies LLC .... E 855 766-3629
　Westerville (G-15676)
RP Hoskins Inc .... E 216 631-1000
　Cleveland (G-4658)
Simon Roofing and Shtmtl Corp .... C 330 629-7392
　Youngstown (G-16439)
Sr Products .... F 330 998-6500
　Macedonia (G-9576)
◆ State Industrial Products Corp .... B 877 747-6986
　Cleveland (G-4731)
Terry Asphalt Materials Inc .... E 513 874-6192
　Hamilton (G-8247)
The Garland Company Inc .... D 216 641-7500
　Cleveland (G-4783)
◆ Thorworks Industries Inc .... C 419 626-4375
　Sandusky (G-13096)

Transtar Holding Company .... G 800 359-3339
　Walton Hills (G-15103)
◆ Tremco Incorporated .... B
　Beachwood (G-1031)
Youngs Sealcoating LLC .... G 330 591-5446
　Medina (G-10396)

2992 Lubricating oils and greases

American Ultra Specialties Inc .... F 330 656-5000
　Hudson (G-8584)
▲ Aml Industries Inc .... E 330 399-5000
　Warren (G-15140)
Amsoil Inc .... G 614 274-9851
　Urbancrest (G-14852)
BLaster LLC .... E 216 901-5800
　Cleveland (G-3742)
◆ Borchers Americas Inc .... D 440 899-2950
　Westlake (G-15741)
Cambridge Mill Products Inc .... G 330 863-1121
　Malvern (G-9609)
Chemical Methods Incorporated .... E 216 476-8400
　Brunswick (G-1751)
▲ Chemical Solvents Inc .... E 216 741-9310
　Cleveland (G-3816)
Cincinnati - Vulcan Company .... D 513 242-5300
　Cincinnati (G-2736)
Cochem Inc .... E 216 341-8914
　Cleveland (G-3880)
Digilube Systems Inc .... F 937 748-2209
　Springboro (G-13499)
Dnd Emulsions Inc .... F 419 525-4988
　Mansfield (G-9646)
Douglas W & B C Richardson .... G 440 247-5262
　Chagrin Falls (G-2373)
Emaxx Northeast Ohio LLC .... G 844 645-6299
　Canton (G-2096)
Eni USA R&M Co Inc .... F 330 723-6457
　Medina (G-10320)
Ensign Product Company Inc .... G 216 341-5911
　Cleveland (G-4020)
◆ Etna Products Incorporated .... E 440 543-9845
　Chagrin Falls (G-2395)
Fiske Brothers Refining Co .... D 419 691-2491
　Toledo (G-14289)
Fuchs Lubricants Co .... F 330 963-0400
　Twinsburg (G-14663)
Ha-International LLC .... E 419 537-0096
　Toledo (G-14308)
Illinois Tool Works Inc .... D 440 914-3100
　Solon (G-13366)
Interlube Corporation .... F 513 531-1777
　Cincinnati (G-3027)
◆ J C Whitlam Manufacturing Co .... E 330 334-2524
　Wadsworth (G-15037)
Jtm Products Inc .... E 440 287-2302
　Solon (G-13372)
Kc Marketing LLC .... E 513 471-8770
　Cincinnati (G-3067)
Kkr LLC .... G 440 564-7168
　Newbury (G-11629)
Kost Usa Inc .... E 513 583-7070
　Cincinnati (G-3088)
Lubriplate Lubricants Company .... G 419 691-2491
　Toledo (G-14372)
▲ Magnus International Group Inc .... G 216 592-8355
　Painesville (G-12248)
McO Inc .... G 216 341-8914
　Cleveland (G-4384)
▲ North Shore Strapping Company .... E 216 661-5200
　Brooklyn Heights (G-1696)
Perma-Fix of Dayton Inc .... F 937 268-6501
　Dayton (G-6503)

Phymet Inc .... F 937 743-8061
  Springboro (G-13515)
◆ Plasti-Kote Co Inc .... C 330 725-4511
  Medina (G-10363)
▲ Quaker Chemical Corporation .... E 513 422-9600
  Middletown (G-10853)
R and J Corporation .... E 440 871-6009
  Westlake (G-15777)
R Holdings 2500 Co .... E 800 883-7876
  Columbus (G-5707)
◆ State Industrial Products Corp .... B 877 747-6986
  Cleveland (G-4731)
The Lubrizol Corporation .... C 440 357-7064
  Painesville (G-12270)
Triad Energy Corporation .... F 740 374-2940
  Marietta (G-9838)
Universal Oil Inc .... E 216 771-4300
  Cleveland (G-4851)
▼ Ventco Inc .... F 440 834-8888
  Chagrin Falls (G-2432)
Wallover Enterprises Inc .... E 440 238-9250
  Strongsville (G-13893)
◆ Wallover Oil Company Inc .... E 440 238-9250
  Strongsville (G-13894)
Wallover Oil Hamilton Inc .... E 513 896-6692
  Hamilton (G-8257)
Western Reserve Lubricants .... G 440 951-5700
  Painesville (G-12277)

2999 Petroleum and coal products, nec

Buckeye Terminals .... G 330 453-4170
  Canton (G-2055)
Citi 2 Citi Logistics .... G 614 306-4109
  Columbus (G-5250)
◆ The Kindt-Collins Company LLC .... D 216 252-4122
  Cleveland (G-4788)

30 RUBBER AND MISCELLANEOUS PLASTIC PRODUCTS

3011 Tires and inner tubes

◆ 31 Inc .... D 740 498-8324
  Newcomerstown (G-11640)
American Airless Inc .... F 614 552-0146
  Reynoldsburg (G-12751)
Americana Development Inc .... D 330 633-3278
  Tallmadge (G-14022)
B & S Transport Inc .... G 330 767-4319
  Navarre (G-11340)
BF & CD Roberts RE Imprv .... G 937 277-2632
  Dayton (G-6228)
▲ Bkt USA Inc .... F 330 836-1090
  Copley (G-5944)
Bridgstone Amrcas Tire Oprtons .... D 330 379-3714
  Akron (G-92)
◆ Chemspec Ltd .... E 330 896-0355
  Canton (G-2073)
◆ Cooper Tire & Rubber Co LLC .... A 419 423-1321
  Findlay (G-7497)
▲ Cooper Tire Vhcl Test Ctr Inc .... F 419 423-1321
  Findlay (G-7498)
▲ Denman Tire Corporation .... C 330 675-4242
  Leavittsburg (G-9057)
Empire Tire Inc .... G 330 983-4176
  Tallmadge (G-14030)
◆ Goodyear Tire & Rubber Company ...... A 330 796-2121
  Akron (G-171)
▲ Grove Engineered Products .... G 419 659-5939
  Columbus Grove (G-5898)
H & H Industries Inc .... D 740 682-7721
  Oak Hill (G-12019)

Jamies Tire & Service .... G 937 372-9254
  Xenia (G-16266)
Nice Body Automotive LLC .... G 440 752-5568
  Elyria (G-7185)
North American Assemblies LLC .... E 843 420-5354
  Dublin (G-6916)
Oliver Rubber Co .... G 419 420-6235
  Findlay (G-7546)
Swiss Valley Tire LLC .... G 330 231-6187
  Wilmot (G-16069)
◆ Technical Rubber Company Inc .... C 740 967-9015
  Johnstown (G-8779)
Titan Tire Corporation .... B 419 633-4221
  Bryan (G-1840)
Titan Tire Corporation Bryan .... E 419 633-4224
  Bryan (G-1841)
Troy Engnred Cmpnnts Assmblies .... G 937 335-8070
  Dayton (G-6635)
Truflex Rubber Products Co .... C 740 967-9015
  Johnstown (G-8782)
Umd Contractors Inc .... F 740 694-8614
  Fredericktown (G-7757)
◆ Yokohama Tws North America Inc .... E 866 633-8473
  Akron (G-379)

3021 Rubber and plastics footwear

Advantage Products Corporation .... G 513 489-2283
  Blue Ash (G-1359)
Calzurocom .... G 800 257-9472
  Plain City (G-12569)
Cobblers Corner LLC .... F 330 482-4005
  Columbiana (G-5032)
Georgia-Boot Inc .... D 740 753-1951
  Nelsonville (G-11356)
Mettler Footwear Inc .... G 330 703-0079
  Hudson (G-8605)
Mulhern Belting Inc .... E 201 337-5700
  Fairfield (G-7386)
▲ Totes Isotoner Holdings Corp .... C 513 682-8200
  West Chester (G-15599)
US Footwear Holdings LLC .... C 740 753-9100
  Nelsonville (G-11360)

3052 Rubber and plastics hose and beltings

◆ Advanced Technology Products Inc .... D 937 349-4055
  Milford Center (G-10927)
Aeroquip Corp .... G 419 238-1190
  Van Wert (G-14905)
Allied Fabricating & Wldg Co .... E 614 751-6664
  Columbus (G-5113)
Cmt Machining & Fabg LLC .... F 937 652-3740
  Urbana (G-14827)
Cooper-Standard Automotive Inc .... D 419 352-3533
  Bowling Green (G-1562)
Crushproof Tubing Co .... E 419 293-2111
  Mc Comb (G-10269)
Danfoss Power Solutions II LLC .... G 419 238-1190
  Van Wert (G-14913)
Eaton Aeroquip LLC .... A 419 891-7775
  Maumee (G-10201)
◆ Eaton Aeroquip LLC .... C 440 523-5000
  Cleveland (G-3991)
Eaton Corporation .... E 330 274-0743
  Aurora (G-712)
Eaton Corporation .... A 419 238-1190
  Van Wert (G-14914)
▲ Engineered Plastics Corp .... E 330 376-7700
  Akron (G-141)
▲ Fenner Dunlop (toledo) LLC .... D 419 531-5300
  Toledo (G-14285)
◆ HBD Industries Inc .... E 614 526-7000
  Dublin (G-6891)

Hbd/Thermoid Inc .... C 937 593-5010
  Bellefontaine (G-1210)
▼ Hbd/Thermoid Inc .... D 614 526-7000
  Dublin (G-6892)
Kent Elastomer Products Inc .... F 800 331-4762
  Mogadore (G-11077)
Kentak Products Company .... D 330 386-3700
  East Liverpool (G-6996)
▲ Kentak Products Company .... E 330 382-2000
  East Liverpool (G-6997)
Mm Outsourcing LLC .... F 937 661-4300
  Leesburg (G-9126)
Myers Industries Inc .... D 330 336-6621
  Wadsworth (G-15047)
Myers Industries Inc .... E 330 253-5592
  Akron (G-260)
Novex Operating Company LLC .... F 330 335-2371
  Wadsworth (G-15049)
Parker-Hannifin Corporation .... G 704 637-1190
  Wickliffe (G-15845)
Polychem LLC .... D 419 547-1400
  Clyde (G-4975)
Rust Belt Broncos LLC .... E 330 533-0048
  Canfield (G-2017)
◆ Sumiriko Ohio Inc .... E 419 358-2121
  Bluffton (G-1507)
Vulcan Corporation .... D 513 621-2850
  Cincinnati (G-3502)
◆ Watteredge LLC .... D 440 933-6110
  Avon Lake (G-828)

3053 Gaskets; packing and sealing devices

◆ Accel Performance Group LLC .... C 216 658-6413
  Independence (G-8651)
Air Heater Seal Company Inc .... E 740 984-2146
  Waterford (G-15235)
▲ Akalina Associates Inc .... C 440 992-2195
  Ashtabula (G-626)
▲ Akron Gasket & Packg Entps Inc .... F 330 633-3742
  Tallmadge (G-14021)
AMG Products LLC .... F 614 507-7749
  Mount Vernon (G-11262)
AP Services LLC .... D 216 267-3200
  Middleburg Heights (G-10715)
Blackthorn LLC .... F 937 836-9296
  Clayton (G-3564)
Cgs Liquidation Company LLC .... F 614 878-6041
  Columbus (G-5246)
◆ Cincinnati Gasket Pkg Mfg Inc .... E 513 761-3458
  Cincinnati (G-2749)
◆ Concrete Sealants Inc .... E 937 845-8776
  Tipp City (G-14130)
▲ Dana Limited .... B 419 887-3000
  Maumee (G-10186)
Die-Cut Products Co .... F 216 771-6994
  Cleveland (G-3958)
▲ Durox Company .... D 440 238-5350
  Strongsville (G-13831)
Eagleburgmann Industries LP .... F 513 563-7325
  Cincinnati (G-2853)
Egc Operating Company LLC .... D 440 285-5835
  Chardon (G-2449)
Emssons Faurecia Ctrl Systems .... B 937 743-0551
  Franklin (G-7672)
Epg Inc .... D 330 995-5125
  Aurora (G-714)
Epg Inc .... F 330 995-9725
  Streetsboro (G-13770)
Espi Enterprises Inc .... G 440 543-8108
  Chagrin Falls (G-2394)
▲ Ferrotherm Corporation .... C 216 883-9350
  Cleveland (G-4058)

30 RUBBER AND MISCELLANEOUS PLASTIC PRODUCTS

▲ Flow Dry Technology Inc................... C 937 833-2161
   Brookville *(G-1736)*

Forest City Technologies Inc.............. C 440 647-2115
   Wellington *(G-15309)*

Forest City Technologies Inc.............. C 440 647-2115
   Wellington *(G-15310)*

Forest City Technologies Inc.............. D 440 647-2115
   Wellington *(G-15311)*

▲ Forest City Technologies Inc.............. B 440 647-2115
   Wellington *(G-15312)*

▲ Fouty & Company Inc..................... E 419 693-0017
   Oregon *(G-12105)*

Freudenberg-Nok General Partnr......... C 419 427-5221
   Findlay *(G-7511)*

G-M-I Inc................................ G 440 953-8811
   Willoughby *(G-15923)*

Gasko Fabricated Products LLC............ E 330 239-1781
   Medina *(G-10330)*

◆ Grand River Rubber & Plas................ C 440 998-2900
   Ashtabula *(G-635)*

Green Technologies Ohio LLC............. G 330 630-3350
   Tallmadge *(G-14031)*

High Quality Plastics Inc................ G 419 422-8290
   Findlay *(G-7522)*

Hunt Products Inc........................ G 440 667-2457
   Newburgh Heights *(G-11617)*

▲ Ier Fujikura Inc......................... C 330 425-7121
   Macedonia *(G-9556)*

▲ Industry Products Co..................... B 937 778-0585
   Piqua *(G-12526)*

▲ Ishikawa Gasket America Inc............. F 419 353-7300
   Maumee *(G-10208)*

▲ James K Green Enterprises Inc........... G 614 878-6041
   Columbus *(G-5487)*

▲ Jbc Technologies Inc..................... D 440 327-4522
   North Ridgeville *(G-11847)*

Jet Rubber Company...................... E 330 325-1821
   Rootstown *(G-12853)*

Johnson Bros Rubber Co Inc.............. E 419 752-4814
   Greenwich *(G-8067)*

Jtm Products Inc......................... E 440 287-2302
   Solon *(G-13372)*

K Wm Beach Mfg Co Inc.................. C 937 399-3838
   Springfield *(G-13586)*

Klinger Agency Inc....................... G 419 893-9759
   Maumee *(G-10212)*

May Lin Silicone Products Inc............ G 330 825-9019
   Barberton *(G-880)*

Mechanical Dynamics Analis LLC......... E 440 946-0082
   Euclid *(G-7285)*

Mechanical Rubber Ohio LLC............. E 845 986-2271
   Strongsville *(G-13853)*

Middlefield Plastics Inc................... E 440 834-4638
   Middlefield *(G-10767)*

Miles Rubber & Packing Company......... E 330 425-3888
   Twinsburg *(G-14697)*

Netherland Rubber Company.............. F 513 733-0883
   Cincinnati *(G-3187)*

Newman Diaphragms LLC................ E 513 932-7379
   Lebanon *(G-9098)*

▲ Newman International Inc................ F 513 932-7379
   Lebanon *(G-9099)*

Newman Sanitary Gasket Company....... E 513 932-7379
   Lebanon *(G-9100)*

▲ North Coast Seal Incorporated........... F 216 898-5000
   Brookpark *(G-1722)*

◆ Ohio Gasket and Shim Co Inc............ E 330 630-0626
   Akron *(G-270)*

▲ P & R Specialty Inc...................... E 937 773-0263
   Piqua *(G-12541)*

Paramont Machine Company LLC........ F 330 339-3489
   New Philadelphia *(G-11522)*

Paul J Tatulinski Ltd...................... F 330 584-8251
   North Benton *(G-11710)*

Phoenix Associates....................... E 440 543-9701
   Chagrin Falls *(G-2416)*

Quanex Ig Systems Inc.................... E 740 439-2338
   Cambridge *(G-1950)*

◆ Quanex Ig Systems Inc.................... D 216 910-1500
   Akron *(G-291)*

R and J Corporation...................... E 440 871-6009
   Westlake *(G-15777)*

▲ Royal Acme Corporation................. E 216 241-1477
   Cleveland *(G-4654)*

Rubbertec Industrial Pdts Co.............. F 740 657-3345
   Lewis Center *(G-9179)*

Saint-Gobain Prfmce Plas Corp............ D 440 836-6900
   Solon *(G-13418)*

Seal Master Corporation.................. E 330 673-8410
   Kent *(G-8861)*

SKF USA Inc............................. E 440 720-0275
   Cleveland *(G-4704)*

▲ Soffseal Inc............................. E 513 934-0815
   Cincinnati *(G-3400)*

Superior Plastics Intl Inc.................. G 419 424-3113
   Findlay *(G-7571)*

◆ Sur-Seal LLC............................ C 513 574-8500
   Cincinnati *(G-3434)*

◆ Thermoseal Inc.......................... F 937 498-2222
   Sidney *(G-13292)*

◆ Vertex Inc............................... E 330 628-6230
   Mogadore *(G-11090)*

Youngstown Specialty Mtls Inc............ G 330 259-1110
   Youngstown *(G-16488)*

3061 Mechanical rubber goods

▲ Akalina Associates Inc................... C 440 992-2195
   Ashtabula *(G-626)*

Alloy Extrusion Company.................. E 330 677-4946
   Kent *(G-8798)*

Alternative Flash Inc..................... F 330 334-6111
   Wadsworth *(G-15018)*

American Pro-Mold Inc................... F 330 336-4111
   Wadsworth *(G-15019)*

ARC Rubber Inc.......................... F 440 466-4555
   Geneva *(G-7931)*

◆ Brp Manufacturing Company.............. E 800 858-0482
   Lima *(G-9226)*

C & M Rubber Co Inc.................... F 937 299-2782
   Dayton *(G-6242)*

Canton OH Rubber Speclty Prods......... G 330 454-3847
   Canton *(G-2065)*

▲ Cardinal Rubber Company................ E 330 745-2191
   Barberton *(G-864)*

Chardon Custom Polymers LLC.......... F 440 285-2161
   Chardon *(G-2442)*

Clark Rubber & Plastic Company......... C 440 255-9793
   Mentor *(G-10439)*

Colonial Rubber Company................ E 330 296-2831
   Ravenna *(G-12711)*

▲ Contitech North America Inc............. F 330 664-7180
   Fairlawn *(G-7435)*

◆ Datwyler Sling Sltions USA Inc............ D 937 387-2800
   Vandalia *(G-14937)*

Dayton Molded Urethanes LLC........... E 937 279-1910
   Dayton *(G-6284)*

Duramax Global Corp.................... F 440 834-5400
   Hiram *(G-8482)*

Dybrook Products Inc.................... E 330 392-7665
   Warren *(G-15165)*

Epg Inc.................................. D 330 995-5125
   Aurora *(G-714)*

Epg Inc.................................. F 330 995-9725
   Streetsboro *(G-13770)*

Extruded Slcone Pdts Gskets In........... E 330 733-0101
   Mogadore *(G-11072)*

Frankes Wood Products LLC............. E 937 642-0706
   Marysville *(G-9910)*

Harwood Entp Holdings Inc............... F 330 923-3256
   Cuyahoga Falls *(G-6090)*

◆ Hygenic Company LLC................... B 330 633-8460
   Akron *(G-188)*

▲ Ier Fujikura Inc......................... C 330 425-7121
   Macedonia *(G-9556)*

Jakmar Incorporated..................... F 513 631-4303
   Cincinnati *(G-3034)*

◆ Johnson Bros Rubber Co................. D 419 853-4122
   West Salem *(G-15634)*

Karman Rubber Company................. D 330 864-2161
   Akron *(G-201)*

Kleen Polymers Inc....................... F
   Wadsworth *(G-15040)*

◆ Koneta Inc.............................. D 419 739-4200
   Wapakoneta *(G-15122)*

Macdivitt Rubber Company LLC.......... E 440 259-5937
   Perry *(G-12354)*

Mantaline Corporation.................... G 330 569-3147
   Hiram *(G-8486)*

Mantaline Corporation.................... G 330 274-2264
   Mantua *(G-9739)*

Mantaline Corporation.................... G 330 274-2264
   Mantua *(G-9740)*

Martin Industries Inc..................... F 419 862-2694
   Elmore *(G-7102)*

Meridian Industries Inc................... D 330 673-1011
   Kent *(G-8834)*

Mm Outsourcing LLC..................... F 937 661-4300
   Leesburg *(G-9126)*

◆ Namoh Ohio Holdings Inc................ E
   Norwood *(G-11996)*

Performance Elastomers Corporation...... D 330 297-2255
   Ravenna *(G-12727)*

Plabell Rubber Products Corp............. E 419 691-5878
   Toledo *(G-14440)*

Prospira America Corporation............. D 419 294-6989
   Upper Sandusky *(G-14821)*

▲ Q Holding Company..................... B 440 903-1827
   Twinsburg *(G-14720)*

Qualiform Inc............................ E 330 336-6777
   Wadsworth *(G-15057)*

Quanex Ig Systems Inc.................... E 740 439-2338
   Cambridge *(G-1950)*

◆ Quanex Ig Systems Inc.................... D 216 910-1500
   Akron *(G-291)*

Robin Industries Inc...................... F 330 893-3501
   Berlin *(G-1308)*

Robin Industries Inc...................... E 330 695-9300
   Fredericksburg *(G-7732)*

Robin Industries Inc...................... E 330 359-5418
   Winesburg *(G-16082)*

▲ Robin Industries Inc...................... F 216 631-7000
   Independence *(G-8684)*

Rubber-Tech Inc.......................... E 937 274-1114
   Dayton *(G-6554)*

Saint-Gobain Prfmce Plas Corp............ C 330 798-6981
   Akron *(G-324)*

▲ Shreiner Sole Company Inc.............. F 330 276-6135
   Killbuck *(G-8922)*

▲ Soffseal Inc............................. E 513 934-0815
   Cincinnati *(G-3400)*

Sperry & Rice LLC....................... F 330 276-2801
   Killbuck *(G-8923)*

Sperry & Rice LLC....................... G 765 647-4141
   Killbuck *(G-8924)*

▲ TAC Materials Inc....................... C 330 425-8472
   Twinsburg *(G-14740)*

SIC SECTION
30 RUBBER AND MISCELLANEOUS PLASTIC PRODUCTS

◆ The D S Brown Company.................C..... 419 257-3561
  North Baltimore (G-11701)

▲ Tigerpoly Manufacturing Inc............ B..... 614 871-0045
  Grove City (G-8122)

▲ United Feed Screws Ltd.................... F..... 330 798-5532
  Akron (G-367)

Universal Urethane Pdts Inc................. D..... 419 693-7400
  Toledo (G-14514)

▲ V & M Star LP................................... F..... 330 742-6300
  Youngstown (G-16465)

◆ Vertex Inc... E..... 330 628-6230
  Mogadore (G-11090)

Woodlawn Rubber Co........................... F..... 513 489-1718
  Blue Ash (G-1494)

Yokohama Tire Corporation.................. D..... 440 352-3321
  Painesville (G-12281)

◆ Yokohama Tws North America Inc..... E..... 866 633-8473
  Akron (G-379)

3069 Fabricated rubber products, nec

Ace Products & Consulting LLC........... F..... 330 577-4088
  Ravenna (G-12700)

Action Rubber Co Inc........................... F..... 937 866-5975
  Dayton (G-6182)

▲ Akalina Associates Inc.................... C..... 440 992-2195
  Ashtabula (G-626)

American Pro-Mold Inc........................ F..... 330 336-4111
  Wadsworth (G-15019)

American Rubber Pdts Co Inc.............. G..... 440 461-0900
  Solon (G-13313)

Ansell Healthcare Products LLC........... E..... 740 622-4311
  Coshocton (G-5970)

ARC Rubber Inc.................................. F..... 440 466-4555
  Geneva (G-7931)

Archem America Inc............................. F..... 419 294-6304
  Upper Sandusky (G-14803)

◆ B D G Wrap-Tite Inc......................... E..... 440 349-5400
  Solon (G-13315)

Bdu Holdings Inc................................ F..... 330 374-1810
  Akron (G-80)

◆ Blair Rubber Company..................... D..... 330 769-5583
  Seville (G-13137)

Boomerang Rubber Inc........................ E..... 937 693-4611
  Botkins (G-1541)

◆ Brp Manufacturing Company............ E..... 800 858-0482
  Lima (G-9226)

Canton OH Rubber Specity Prods........ G..... 330 454-3847
  Canton (G-2065)

▲ Cardinal Rubber Company............... E..... 330 745-2191
  Barberton (G-864)

Censtar Coatings Inc........................... G..... 330 723-8000
  West Salem (G-15632)

Cent-Roll Products Inc......................... E..... 513 829-5201
  Fairfield (G-7345)

◆ Chalfant Sew Fabricators Inc........... E..... 216 521-7922
  Cleveland (G-3805)

Chardon Custom Polymers LLC........... F..... 440 285-2161
  Chardon (G-2442)

▲ Chemionics Corporation................... E..... 330 733-8834
  Tallmadge (G-14024)

Clark Rubber & Plastic Company......... C..... 440 255-9793
  Mentor (G-10439)

Colonial Rubber Company.................... E..... 330 296-2831
  Ravenna (G-12711)

◆ Contitech Usa Inc........................... F..... 330 664-7000
  Fairlawn (G-7436)

Curtis Hilbruner................................... G..... 330 947-3527
  Atwater (G-702)

◆ Custom Rubber Corporation............ D..... 216 391-2928
  Cleveland (G-3926)

Dandy Products Inc............................. G..... 513 625-3000
  Goshen (G-7992)

◆ Datwyler Sling Sltions USA Inc........ D..... 937 387-2800
  Vandalia (G-14937)

Delphos Rubber Company.................... E..... 419 692-3000
  Delphos (G-6761)

◆ Deruijter Intl USA Inc...................... F..... 419 678-3909
  Coldwater (G-4986)

Die-Cut Products Co............................. F..... 216 771-6994
  Cleveland (G-3958)

◆ Dnh Mixing Inc................................ E..... 330 296-6327
  Mogadore (G-11069)

▲ DTR Equipment Inc......................... F..... 419 692-3000
  Delphos (G-6764)

▲ Durable Corporation........................ D..... 800 537-1603
  Norwalk (G-11962)

◆ Duramax Marine LLC...................... D..... 440 834-5400
  Hiram (G-8483)

Eagle Elastomer Inc............................. E..... 330 923-7070
  Peninsula (G-12340)

◆ Eaton Aeroquip LLC........................ C..... 440 523-5000
  Cleveland (G-3991)

Elastostar Rubber Corp........................ E..... 614 841-4400
  Plain City (G-12578)

Elbex Corporation................................ D..... 330 673-3233
  Kent (G-8812)

Enduro Rubber Company...................... G..... 330 296-9603
  Ravenna (G-12713)

Express Pharmacy & Dme LLC............. G..... 210 981-9690
  Columbus (G-5366)

◆ Firestone Polymers LLC.................. D..... 330 379-7000
  Akron (G-153)

First Brnds Group Holdings LLC........... E..... 216 589-0198
  Cleveland (G-4063)

First Brnds Group Intrmdate LL........... F..... 216 589-0198
  Cleveland (G-4064)

Flexsys America LP............................. F..... 618 482-6371
  Columbus (G-5379)

◆ Flexsys America LP......................... D..... 330 666-4111
  Akron (G-155)

Foundation Wellness............................ G..... 330 335-1571
  Wadsworth (G-15030)

G Grafton Machine & Rubber................. F..... 330 297-1062
  Ravenna (G-12716)

Garro Tread Corporation...................... G..... 330 376-3125
  Akron (G-162)

Gdc Inc.. F..... 574 533-3128
  Wooster (G-16123)

Gen-Rubber LLC.................................. G..... 440 655-3643
  Galion (G-7877)

▼ Gold Key Processing Inc................. C..... 440 632-0901
  Middlefield (G-10752)

▲ Goldsmith & Eggleton Inc................ F..... 330 336-6616
  Wadsworth (G-15032)

▲ Goldsmith & Eggleton LLC............... F..... 203 855-6000
  Wadsworth (G-15033)

◆ Grand River Rubber & Plas.............. C..... 440 998-2900
  Ashtabula (G-635)

◆ Green Tokai Co Ltd......................... A..... 937 833-5444
  Brookville (G-1738)

Grypmat Inc.. G..... 419 953-7607
  Celina (G-2334)

▲ Guardian Manufacturing Co LLC....... E..... 419 933-2711
  Willard (G-15859)

Hannecard Roller Coatings Inc............. E..... 330 753-8458
  Barberton (G-871)

Hexpol Compounding LLC..................... C..... 440 682-4038
  Akron (G-183)

Hsm Solutions Inc............................... G..... 513 898-9586
  Mason (G-10003)

◆ Hygenic Company LLC.................... B..... 330 633-8460
  Akron (G-188)

▼ Hyload Inc...................................... G..... 330 336-6604
  Seville (G-13142)

Hytech Silicone Products Inc............... G..... 330 297-1888
  Ravenna (G-12720)

▲ Ier Fujikura Inc............................... C..... 330 425-7121
  Macedonia (G-9556)

Innovative Sport Surfacing LLC............ F..... 440 205-0875
  Mentor (G-10473)

International Automotive Compo........... F..... 330 279-6557
  Holmesville (G-8549)

▲ International Sources Inc................ G..... 440 735-9890
  Bedford (G-1129)

ISO Technologies Inc........................... F..... 740 928-0084
  Hebron (G-8346)

▲ James K Green Enterprises Inc....... G..... 614 878-6041
  Columbus (G-5487)

Jet Rubber Company............................ E..... 330 325-1821
  Rootstown (G-12853)

▲ Johnsonite Inc................................. B..... 440 543-8916
  Solon (G-13370)

Karman Rubber Company..................... D..... 330 864-2161
  Akron (G-201)

Keener Rubber Company...................... F..... 330 821-1880
  Alliance (G-407)

▲ Kent Elastomer Products Inc........... C..... 330 673-1011
  Kent (G-8823)

Killian Latex Inc................................... F..... 330 644-6746
  Akron (G-207)

Kiltex Corporation................................ F..... 330 644-6746
  Akron (G-208)

◆ Kn Rubber LLC................................ C..... 419 739-4200
  Wapakoneta (G-15121)

Krupp Rubber Machinery..................... G..... 330 864-0800
  Akron (G-212)

◆ Lauren International Ltd.................. C..... 234 303-2400
  New Philadelphia (G-11510)

Leisure Time Pdts Design Corp............ G..... 440 934-1032
  Avon (G-779)

▲ Lexington Rubber Group Inc............ E..... 330 425-8472
  Twinsburg (G-14688)

Lockfast LLC....................................... G..... 800 543-7157
  Loveland (G-9491)

Lrp Solutions Inc................................. G..... 419 678-3909
  Coldwater (G-4997)

◆ Ludlow Composites Corporation....... C..... 419 332-5531
  Fremont (G-7796)

M7 Hrp LLC.. F..... 330 923-3256
  Akron (G-232)

Macdivitt Rubber Company LLC........... E..... 440 259-5937
  Perry (G-12354)

Magnum Tapes Films........................... G..... 877 460-8402
  Caldwell (G-1911)

Maine Rubber Preforms LLC................ G..... 216 387-1268
  Burton (G-1884)

Mameco International Inc..................... D..... 216 752-4400
  Cleveland (G-4354)

Mantaline Corporation.......................... C..... 330 274-2264
  Mantua (G-9740)

Martin Industries Inc............................ F..... 419 862-2694
  Elmore (G-7102)

◆ Master Mfg Co Inc.......................... E..... 216 641-0500
  Cleveland (G-4367)

May Lin Silicone Products Inc.............. G..... 330 825-9019
  Barberton (G-880)

▲ MCR of Norwalk Inc........................ E..... 419 668-8261
  Norwalk (G-11979)

Meridian Industries Inc........................ D..... 330 673-1011
  Kent (G-8834)

Meridian Industries Inc........................ D..... 330 359-5447
  Winesburg (G-16081)

▲ Merryweather Foam Inc................... E..... 330 753-0353
  Barberton (G-882)

▲ Meteor Sealing Systems LLC........... C..... 330 343-9595
  Dover (G-6835)

30 RUBBER AND MISCELLANEOUS PLASTIC PRODUCTS

◆ Midwest Elastomers Inc .... D 419 738-8844
  Wapakoneta (G-15124)
Midwestern Bag Co Inc .... G 419 241-3112
  Toledo (G-14386)
Miles Rubber & Packing Company ...... E 330 425-3888
  Twinsburg (G-14697)
Mitchell Plastics Inc .... E 330 825-2461
  Barberton (G-883)
Mullins Rubber Products Inc .... D 937 233-4211
  Dayton (G-6461)
Murrubber Technologies Inc .... E 330 688-4881
  Stow (G-13711)
Myers Industries Inc .... D 330 336-6621
  Wadsworth (G-15047)
Myers Industries Inc .... E 330 253-5592
  Akron (G-260)
▲ Neff-Perkins Company .... D 440 632-1658
  Middlefield (G-10776)
Newact Inc .... F 513 321-5177
  Batavia (G-940)
Newell Brands Inc .... F 330 733-1184
  Kent (G-8839)
Niles Roll Service Inc .... F 330 544-0026
  Niles (G-11680)
▲ North Coast Seal Incorporated .... F 216 898-5000
  Brookpark (G-1722)
Noster Rubber Company .... G 419 299-3387
  Van Buren (G-14903)
▲ Novatex North America Inc .... D 419 282-4264
  Ashland (G-595)
Novex Operating Company LLC .... F 330 335-2371
  Wadsworth (G-15049)
Ohio Foam Corporation .... G 614 252-4877
  Columbus (G-5619)
Ohio Foam Corporation .... F 419 492-2151
  New Washington (G-11550)
Ohio Foam Corporation .... E 330 799-4553
  Youngstown (G-16405)
▲ Okamoto Sandusky Mfg LLC .... D 419 626-1633
  Sandusky (G-13084)
Ottawa Rubber Company .... F 419 865-1378
  Holland (G-8521)
◆ Park-Ohio Holdings Corp .... F 440 947-2000
  Cleveland (G-4524)
Park-Ohio Industries Inc .... C 440 947-2000
  Cleveland (G-4525)
▲ Park-Ohio Products Inc .... D 216 961-7200
  Cleveland (G-4526)
Parkohio Worldwide LLC .... E 440 947-2000
  Cleveland (G-4534)
Perfect Products Company .... E
  Malvern (G-9614)
◆ Pfp Holdings LLC .... A 419 647-4191
  Spencerville (G-13488)
Philpott Rubber LLC .... G 330 225-3344
  Aurora (G-732)
▲ Philpott Rubber LLC .... E 330 225-3344
  Brunswick (G-1780)
Pinnacle Roller Co .... F 513 369-4830
  Cincinnati (G-3256)
Pioneer National Latex Inc .... D 419 289-3300
  Ashland (G-601)
Pioneer National Latex Inc .... E 419 289-3300
  Ashland (G-602)
Plabell Rubber Products Corp .... E 419 691-5878
  Toledo (G-14440)
Plymouth Foam LLC .... D 740 254-1188
  Gnadenhutten (G-7987)
▲ Polymerics Inc .... E 330 928-2210
  Cuyahoga Falls (G-6110)
Ppafco Inc .... E 614 488-7259
  Columbus (G-5685)

Prcc Holdings Inc .... C 330 798-4790
  Copley (G-5953)
Precision Fab Products Inc .... G 937 526-5681
  Versailles (G-14988)
▲ Preferred Compounding Corp .... C 330 798-4790
  Barberton (G-892)
Profile Rubber Corporation .... F 330 239-1703
  Wadsworth (G-15055)
Q Model Inc .... F 330 733-6545
  Akron (G-288)
Qualiform Inc .... E 330 336-6777
  Wadsworth (G-15057)
R C Musson Rubber Co .... D 330 773-7651
  Akron (G-294)
Rainbow Master Mixing Inc .... F 330 374-1810
  Akron (G-295)
Raydar Inc of Ohio .... G 330 334-6111
  Wadsworth (G-15061)
▲ Remington Products Company .... D 330 335-1571
  Upper Arlington (G-14802)
▲ Republic Powdered Metals Inc .... D 330 225-3192
  Medina (G-10370)
Reynolds Industries Inc .... G 330 889-9466
  West Farmington (G-15607)
◆ Rhein Chemie Corporation .... C 440 279-2367
  Chardon (G-2465)
Right Restoration LLC .... G 440 614-0480
  Blacklick (G-1344)
◆ Rjf International Corporation .... A 330 668-2069
  Fairlawn (G-7447)
Robin Industries Inc .... F 330 893-3501
  Berlin (G-1308)
Robin Industries Inc .... E 330 695-9300
  Fredericksburg (G-7732)
Robin Industries Inc .... E 330 359-5418
  Winesburg (G-16082)
▲ Robin Industries Inc .... F 216 631-7000
  Independence (G-8684)
Roller Source Inc .... F 440 748-4033
  Columbia Station (G-5019)
◆ Roppe Corporation .... B 419 435-8546
  Fostoria (G-7651)
Roppe Holding Company .... G 419 435-6601
  Fostoria (G-7652)
▲ Roppe Holding Company .... B 419 435-8546
  Fostoria (G-7653)
◆ RPM International Inc .... D 330 273-5090
  Medina (G-10372)
◆ Rubber Associates Inc .... D 330 745-2186
  New Franklin (G-11443)
◆ Rubber Grinding Inc .... D 419 692-3000
  Delphos (G-6771)
Rubber-Tech Inc .... E 937 274-1114
  Dayton (G-6554)
S P E Inc .... E 330 733-0101
  Mogadore (G-11082)
▲ Safeguard Technology Inc .... E 330 995-5200
  Streetsboro (G-13790)
▲ Scherba Industries Inc .... D 330 273-3200
  Brunswick (G-1790)
Seal Div Natl .... G 419 238-0030
  Van Wert (G-14926)
Shields Wright Rubber Co .... G 216 741-8200
  Brooklyn Heights (G-1700)
Shreiner Company .... G 800 722-9915
  Killbuck (G-8921)
▲ Shreiner Sole Company Inc .... F 330 276-6135
  Killbuck (G-8922)
▲ Soffseal Inc .... E 513 934-0815
  Cincinnati (G-3400)
Soprema USA Inc .... E 330 334-0066
  Wadsworth (G-15066)

Sorbothane Inc .... E 330 678-9444
  Kent (G-8866)
Space-Links Inc .... E 330 788-2401
  Youngstown (G-16442)
▲ Sparton Enterprises LLC .... E 877 772-7866
  Barberton (G-896)
Spiralcool Company .... G 419 483-2510
  Bellevue (G-1237)
▲ Starpoint 20 LLC .... G 330 825-2373
  Norton (G-11950)
◆ Sumiriko Ohio Inc .... E 419 358-2121
  Bluffton (G-1507)
Sur-Seal LLC .... C 513 574-8500
  Cincinnati (G-3434)
▼ Survitec Group (usa) Inc .... G 330 239-4331
  Sharon Center (G-13168)
◆ Synthomer Inc .... C 216 682-7000
  Beachwood (G-1025)
T-Mac Machine Inc .... G 330 673-0621
  Kent (G-8870)
Tahoma Enterprises Inc .... D 330 745-9016
  Barberton (G-897)
▼ Tahoma Rubber & Plastics Inc .... D 330 745-9016
  Barberton (G-898)
Tallmadge Finishing Co Inc .... F 330 633-7466
  Akron (G-347)
Tarkett Inc .... E 440 543-8916
  Chagrin Falls (G-2428)
▲ Tarkett Inc .... D 800 899-8916
  Solon (G-13433)
Tb Backstop Inc .... F 330 434-4442
  Akron (G-349)
◆ The R C A Rubber Company .... D 330 784-1291
  Akron (G-352)
Timco Rubber Products Inc .... E 216 267-6242
  Berea (G-1296)
▼ Tmi Inc .... E 330 270-9780
  Youngstown (G-16456)
▼ Topps Products Inc .... F 913 685-2500
  Cleveland (G-4806)
Trexler Rubber Co Inc .... E 330 296-9677
  Ravenna (G-12739)
◆ Trico Products Corporation .... C 248 371-1700
  Cleveland (G-4829)
Tristan Rubber Molding Inc .... F 330 499-4055
  North Canton (G-11771)
Truflex Rubber Products Co .... C 740 967-9015
  Johnstown (G-8782)
Ultimate Rb Inc .... F 419 692-3000
  Delphos (G-6774)
◆ Ultimate Systems Ltd .... E 419 692-3005
  Delphos (G-6775)
United Roller Co LLC .... F 440 564-9698
  Newbury (G-11638)
Universal Polymer & Rubber Ltd .... F 330 633-1666
  Tallmadge (G-14055)
▲ Universal Polymer & Rubber Ltd .... C 440 632-1691
  Middlefield (G-10795)
Universal Urethane Pdts Inc .... D 419 693-7400
  Toledo (G-14514)
▲ Vernay Manufacturing Inc .... E 937 767-7261
  Yellow Springs (G-16286)
◆ Vertex Inc .... E 330 628-6230
  Mogadore (G-11090)
Vulcan International Corp .... G 513 621-2850
  Cincinnati (G-3503)
Wayne County Rubber Inc .... E 330 264-5553
  Wooster (G-16181)
West & Barker Inc .... E 330 652-9923
  Niles (G-11691)
▲ Westlake Dimex LLC .... C 740 374-3100
  Marietta (G-9844)

30 RUBBER AND MISCELLANEOUS PLASTIC PRODUCTS

Woodbridge Group .... C 419 334-3666
  Fremont *(G-7820)*
Woodlawn Rubber Co .... F 513 489-1718
  Blue Ash *(G-1494)*
▲ Yokohama Inds Amricas Ohio Inc .... D 440 352-3321
  Painesville *(G-12280)*
▲ Yusa Corporation .... E 740 335-0335
  Washington Court Hou *(G-15234)*

3081 Unsupported plastics film and sheet

▲ Advanced Polymer Coatings Ltd .... E 440 937-6218
  Avon *(G-761)*
American Insulation Tech LLC .... F 513 733-4248
  Milford *(G-10892)*
◆ Ampac Holdings LLC .... A 513 671-1777
  Cincinnati *(G-2622)*
▲ Automated Packaging Systems LLC ...... C 330 528-2000
  Streetsboro *(G-13759)*
Automated Packg Systems Inc .... C 216 663-2000
  Cleveland *(G-3702)*
Automated Packg Systems Inc .... G 330 626-2313
  Streetsboro *(G-13760)*
Avery Dennison Corporation .... D 440 639-3900
  Mentor *(G-10427)*
Avery Dennison Corporation .... B 440 534-6000
  Mentor *(G-10426)*
◆ Avient Corporation .... D 440 930-1000
  Avon Lake *(G-797)*
◆ Berry Film Products Co Inc .... D 800 225-6729
  Mason *(G-9960)*
Berry Global Inc .... G 419 887-1602
  Maumee *(G-10171)*
Berry Global Inc .... D 419 465-2291
  Monroeville *(G-11122)*
▲ Berry Plastics Filmco Inc .... D 330 562-6111
  Aurora *(G-709)*
Blako Industries Inc .... E 419 246-6172
  Dunbridge *(G-6961)*
Bprex Plastic Services Co Inc .... E 419 247-5000
  Toledo *(G-14219)*
Buckeye Packaging Co Inc .... D 330 935-0301
  Alliance *(G-396)*
CCL Label Inc .... D 216 676-2703
  Cleveland *(G-3801)*
CCL Label Inc .... D 440 878-7000
  Strongsville *(G-13819)*
Charter Nex Films - Delaware Oh Inc ..... E 740 369-2770
  Delaware *(G-6708)*
Clarkwestern Dietrich Building .... E 330 372-5564
  Warren *(G-15154)*
▼ Clarkwestrn Drtich Bldg System .... C 513 870-1100
  West Chester *(G-15396)*
◆ Clopay Corporation .... C 800 282-2260
  Mason *(G-9979)*
▲ Command Plastic Corporation .... F 800 321-8001
  Bedford *(G-1112)*
Cool Seal Usa LLC .... F 419 666-1111
  Perrysburg *(G-12371)*
▼ Crayex Corporation .... D 937 773-7000
  Piqua *(G-12511)*
▲ Crown Plastics Co LLC .... D 513 367-0238
  Harrison *(G-8272)*
◆ DJM Plastics Ltd .... F 419 424-5250
  Findlay *(G-7502)*
Dupont Specialty Pdts USA LLC .... E 740 474-0220
  Circleville *(G-3548)*
◆ General Data Company Inc .... B 513 752-7978
  Cincinnati *(G-2561)*
General Films Inc .... D 888 436-3456
  Covington *(G-6023)*
▲ Industry Products Co .... B 937 778-0585
  Piqua *(G-12526)*

Intertape Polymer Corp .... E 704 279-3011
  Springfield *(G-13583)*
◆ Jain America Foods Inc .... G 614 850-9400
  Columbus *(G-5486)*
◆ Liqui-Box Corporation .... E 419 289-9696
  Ashland *(G-589)*
◆ Ludlow Composites Corporation .... C 419 332-5531
  Fremont *(G-7796)*
Magnum Tapes Films .... G 877 460-8402
  Caldwell *(G-1911)*
◆ MAI-Weave LLC .... D 937 322-1698
  Springfield *(G-13600)*
◆ Mar-Bal Inc .... D 440 543-7526
  Chagrin Falls *(G-2407)*
Mikron Industries Inc .... D 713 961-4600
  Akron *(G-248)*
New Tech Plastics Inc .... D 937 473-3011
  Covington *(G-6028)*
◆ North Shore Strapping Company .... E 216 661-5200
  Brooklyn Heights *(G-1696)*
Orbis Rpm LLC .... G 419 307-8511
  Columbus *(G-5644)*
Orbis Rpm LLC .... F 419 355-8310
  Fremont *(G-7799)*
▼ Packaging Materials Inc .... E 740 432-6337
  Cambridge *(G-1946)*
◆ Priority Custom Molding Inc .... F 937 431-8770
  Beavercreek *(G-1058)*
Profusion Industries LLC .... D 740 374-6400
  Marietta *(G-9818)*
Profusion Industries LLC .... G 800 938-2858
  Fairlawn *(G-7446)*
Putnam Plastics Inc .... G 937 866-6261
  Dayton *(G-6535)*
Ram Plastics Co .... G 330 549-3342
  Youngstown *(G-16427)*
▲ Renegade Materials Corporation .... D 937 350-5274
  Miamisburg *(G-10675)*
◆ Rjf International Corporation .... A 330 668-2069
  Fairlawn *(G-7447)*
Rotary Products Inc .... F 740 747-2623
  Ashley *(G-623)*
Rotary Products Inc .... F 740 747-2623
  Ashley *(G-624)*
Sancap Liner Technology Inc .... D 330 821-1166
  Alliance *(G-423)*
▲ Scherba Industries Inc .... D 330 273-3200
  Brunswick *(G-1790)*
◆ Simona Boltaron Inc .... D 740 498-5900
  Newcomerstown *(G-11651)*
Simona PMC LLC .... D 419 429-0042
  Findlay *(G-7561)*
Spartech LLC .... C 937 548-1395
  Greenville *(G-8059)*
Spartech LLC .... D 419 399-4050
  Paulding *(G-12320)*
Specialty Films Inc .... D 614 471-9100
  Columbus *(G-5782)*
▲ Summit Plastic Company .... D 330 633-3668
  Mogadore *(G-11087)*
◆ Synthomer Inc .... C 216 682-7000
  Beachwood *(G-1025)*
Toga-Pak Inc .... E 937 294-7311
  Dayton *(G-6626)*
Transcendia Inc .... C 740 929-5100
  Hebron *(G-8367)*
Transcendia Inc .... D 440 638-2000
  Strongsville *(G-13891)*
Tsp Inc .... E 513 732-8900
  Batavia *(G-955)*
Valgroup LLC .... E 419 423-6500
  Findlay *(G-7576)*

▲ Walton Plastics Inc .... E 440 786-7711
  Bedford *(G-1160)*
Western Reserve Sleeve Inc .... F 440 238-8850
  Strongsville *(G-13895)*
World Connections Corps .... F 419 363-2681
  Rockford *(G-12835)*

3082 Unsupported plastics profile shapes

ABC Technologies Dlhb Inc .... E 330 488-0716
  East Canton *(G-6977)*
▲ Advanced Composites Inc .... C 937 575-9800
  Sidney *(G-13218)*
▲ Akron Polymer Products Inc .... D 330 628-5551
  Akron *(G-40)*
Alkon Corporation .... E 614 799-6650
  Dublin *(G-6858)*
▲ Alkon Corporation .... D 419 355-9111
  Fremont *(G-7762)*
Bobbart Industries Inc .... E 419 350-5477
  Sylvania *(G-13991)*
▲ Cosmo Plastics Company .... C 440 498-7500
  Cleveland *(G-3907)*
Dayton Technologies .... F 513 539-5474
  Monroe *(G-11100)*
▲ Deceuninck North America LLC .... E 513 539-4444
  Monroe *(G-11101)*
▼ Duracote Corporation .... E 330 296-9600
  Ravenna *(G-12712)*
Global Manufacturing Solutions .... F 937 236-8315
  Dayton *(G-6355)*
HP Manufacturing Company Inc .... D 216 361-6500
  Cleveland *(G-4204)*
Inventive Extrusions Corp .... F 330 874-3000
  Bolivar *(G-1528)*
Kentak Products Company .... D 330 386-3700
  East Liverpool *(G-6996)*
▲ Kentak Products Company .... E 330 382-2000
  East Liverpool *(G-6997)*
▲ Machining Technologies Inc .... E 419 862-3110
  Elmore *(G-7101)*
Meridian Industries Inc .... D 330 673-1011
  Kent *(G-8834)*
Normandy Products Co .... D 440 632-5050
  Middlefield *(G-10777)*
Roach Wood Products & Plas Inc .... G 740 532-4855
  Ironton *(G-8703)*
◆ Trico Products Corporation .... C 248 371-1700
  Cleveland *(G-4829)*
Wurms Woodworking Company .... E 419 492-2184
  New Washington *(G-11552)*

3083 Laminated plastics plate and sheet

Advanced Drainage Systems Inc .... E 419 424-8324
  Findlay *(G-7474)*
Advanced Drainage Systems Inc .... E 419 599-9565
  Napoleon *(G-11308)*
Advanced Drainage Systems Inc .... E 330 264-4949
  Wooster *(G-16095)*
Applied Medical Technology Inc .... E 440 717-4000
  Brecksville *(G-1606)*
Arthur Corporation .... D 419 433-7202
  Huron *(G-8627)*
▲ Biothane Coated Webbing Corp .... E 440 327-0485
  North Ridgeville *(G-11832)*
▲ Bruewer Woodwork Mfg Co .... D 513 353-3505
  Cleves *(G-4946)*
Cool Seal Usa LLC .... F 419 666-1111
  Perrysburg *(G-12371)*
Counter Concepts Inc .... F 330 848-4848
  Doylestown *(G-6853)*
Designed Images Inc .... G 440 708-2526
  Chagrin Falls *(G-2392)*

Employee Codes: A=Over 500 employees, B=251-500
C=101-250, D=51-100, E=20-50, F=10-19, G=1-9

30 RUBBER AND MISCELLANEOUS PLASTIC PRODUCTS

Designer Cntemporary Laminates....... G 440 946-8207
Painesville (G-12228)

▼ Duracote Corporation........................ E 330 296-9600
Ravenna (G-12712)

Durivage Pattern and Mfg Inc............. E 419 836-8655
Williston (G-15870)

◆ Elster Perfection Corporation............ D 440 428-1171
Geneva (G-7935)

Fdi Cabinetry LLC............................... G 513 353-4500
Cleves (G-4952)

▼ Flex Technologies Inc........................ E 740 922-5992
Midvale (G-10878)

▲ Fowler Products Inc........................... F 419 683-4057
Crestline (G-6033)

Franklin Cabinet Company Inc............ E 937 743-9606
Franklin (G-7676)

General Electric Company................... F 740 623-5379
Coshocton (G-5979)

◆ Hancor Inc... B 614 658-0050
Hilliard (G-8413)

Idx Corporation.................................... C 937 401-3225
Dayton (G-6378)

Iko Production Inc............................... E 937 746-4561
Franklin (G-7682)

Industrial Molded Plastics................... F 330 673-1464
Kent (G-8819)

◆ Interntnal Cnvrter Cldwell Inc............. C 740 732-5665
Caldwell (G-1909)

Laminate Shop..................................... F 740 749-3536
Waterford (G-15237)

Meridian Industries Inc........................ D 330 673-1011
Kent (G-8834)

▲ Meridienne International Inc............... G 330 274-8317
Aurora (G-725)

Mkgs Corp... F 937 254-8181
Dayton (G-6453)

Monarch Engraving Inc........................ F 440 638-1500
Strongsville (G-13857)

◆ Organized Living Inc........................... E 513 489-9300
Cincinnati (G-3230)

Overhead Door Corporation................. F 440 593-5226
Conneaut (G-5929)

Plaskolite LLC....................................... E 614 294-3281
Columbus (G-5677)

Plaskolite LLC....................................... C 740 450-1109
Zanesville (G-16556)

Plextrusions Inc.................................... F 330 668-2587
North Ridgeville (G-11853)

▲ Poly TEC East Inc................................ G 330 799-7876
Youngstown (G-16420)

◆ Production Tube Cutting Inc.............. E 937 254-6138
Dayton (G-6530)

Quality Rubber Stamp Inc................... G 614 235-2700
Lancaster (G-9034)

Recto Molded Products Inc................. D 513 871-5544
Cincinnati (G-3328)

◆ Resinoid Engineering Corp.................. D 740 928-6115
Hebron (G-8359)

◆ Roechling Indus Cleveland LP........... C 216 486-0100
Cleveland (G-4645)

◆ Rowmark LLC....................................... D 419 425-8974
Findlay (G-7557)

Saint-Gobain Prfmce Plas Corp......... C 330 798-6981
Akron (G-324)

▲ Snyder Manufacturing Inc.................. G 330 343-4456
Dover (G-6844)

Southern Cabinetry Inc....................... E 740 245-5992
Bidwell (G-1327)

Spartech LLC.. D 419 399-4050
Paulding (G-12320)

Surteco North America Inc................. E 843 848-3000
Solon (G-13426)

Ti Inc... E 419 332-8484
Fremont (G-7815)

▲ TS Trim Industries Inc........................ B 614 837-4114
Canal Winchester (G-1993)

Wurms Woodworking Company......... E 419 492-2184
New Washington (G-11552)

3084 Plastics pipe

ADS.. G 419 422-6521
Findlay (G-7471)

ADS International.................................. G 513 896-2094
Hamilton (G-8174)

ADS International.................................. G 614 658-0050
Hilliard (G-8392)

ADS Ventures Inc.................................. G 614 658-0050
Hilliard (G-8393)

Advanced Drainage of Ohio Inc........... D 614 658-0050
Hilliard (G-8395)

Advanced Drainage Systems Inc........ G 419 424-8222
Findlay (G-7473)

Advanced Drainage Systems Inc........ E 419 424-8324
Findlay (G-7474)

Advanced Drainage Systems Inc........ D 513 863-1384
Hamilton (G-8175)

Advanced Drainage Systems Inc........ C 740 852-2980
London (G-9379)

Advanced Drainage Systems Inc........ E 419 599-9565
Napoleon (G-11308)

Advanced Drainage Systems Inc........ E 330 264-4949
Wooster (G-16095)

▼ Advanced Drainage Systems Inc........ D 614 658-0050
Hilliard (G-8396)

Baughman Tile Company.................... D 800 837-3160
Paulding (G-12311)

Cantex Inc... D 330 995-3665
Aurora (G-710)

Contech Engnered Solutions Inc........ E 513 645-7000
West Chester (G-15402)

◆ Contech Engnered Solutions LLC...... C 513 645-7000
West Chester (G-15403)

Drainage Products Inc......................... F 419 622-6951
Haviland (G-8310)

Dura-Line Corporation......................... D 440 322-1000
Elyria (G-7133)

Dura-Line Services LLC...................... E 440 322-1000
Elyria (G-7134)

◆ Elster Perfection Corporation............ D 440 428-1171
Geneva (G-7935)

▼ Flex Technologies Inc........................ E 740 922-5992
Midvale (G-10878)

▲ Fowler Products Inc........................... F 419 683-4057
Crestline (G-6033)

Geon Performance Solutions LLC...... F 800 438-4366
Westlake (G-15754)

Hancor Inc... E 419 424-8222
Findlay (G-7520)

Hancor Inc... E 419 424-8225
Findlay (G-7521)

◆ Hancor Inc.. B 614 658-0050
Hilliard (G-8413)

Harrison Mch & Plastic Corp.............. E 330 527-5641
Garrettsville (G-7916)

▼ Heritage Plastics Liquidation Inc....... D 330 627-8002
Carrollton (G-2309)

Nupco Inc.. G 419 629-2259
New Bremen (G-11406)

Plas-Tanks Industries Inc................... E 513 942-3800
Hamilton (G-8235)

Ray Lewis Enterprises LLC................. G 330 424-9585
Lisbon (G-9325)

Tolloti Pipe LLC.................................... F 330 364-6627
New Philadelphia (G-11529)

Tolloti Plastic Pipe Inc......................... E 330 364-6627
New Philadelphia (G-11530)

3085 Plastics bottles

Al Root Company.................................. G 330 725-6677
Medina (G-10290)

▲ Al Root Company.................................. C 330 723-4359
Medina (G-10291)

Alpha Packaging Holdings Inc............ B 216 252-5595
Cleveland (G-3638)

Ark Operations Inc............................... G 419 871-1186
Dayton (G-6213)

Eco-Groupe Inc..................................... F 937 898-2603
Dayton (G-6312)

◆ Encon Inc.. C 937 898-2603
Dayton (G-6320)

Graham Packaging Pet Tech Inc........ E 419 334-4197
Fremont (G-7788)

Graham Packg Plastic Pdts Inc.......... C 419 421-8037
Findlay (G-7515)

▲ Novatex North America Inc................. D 419 282-4264
Ashland (G-595)

PC Molding LLC.................................... G 614 873-7712
Plain City (G-12590)

▲ Phoenix Technologies Intl LLC........... E 419 353-7738
Bowling Green (G-1583)

Plastipak Packaging Inc...................... C 740 928-4435
Hebron (G-8356)

Plastipak Packaging Inc...................... B 937 596-6142
Jackson Center (G-8736)

Rexam PLC.. F 330 893-2451
Millersburg (G-10990)

Ring Container Tech LLC..................... D 937 492-0961
Sidney (G-13277)

Silly Brandz Global LLC...................... D 419 697-8324
Toledo (G-14473)

Southeastern Container Inc................ D 419 352-6300
Bowling Green (G-1589)

3086 Plastics foam products

▲ Acor Orthopaedic LLC......................... E 216 662-4500
Cleveland (G-3594)

ADS Ventures Inc.................................. G 614 658-0050
Hilliard (G-8393)

ADS Worldwide Inc............................... G 614 658-0050
Hilliard (G-8394)

▼ Advanced Drainage Systems Inc........ D 614 658-0050
Hilliard (G-8396)

All Foam Products Co.......................... G 330 849-3636
Middlefield (G-10730)

Allied Shipping and Packa.................. F 937 222-7422
Moraine (G-11155)

Amatech Inc.. E 614 252-2506
Columbus (G-5119)

American Corrugated Products Inc.... C 614 870-2000
Columbus (G-5124)

◆ Ampac Packaging LLC....................... C 513 671-1777
Cincinnati (G-2623)

Aqua Lily Products LLC...................... G 951 322-0981
Willoughby (G-15884)

Archbold Container Corp.................... C 800 446-2520
Archbold (G-522)

Arkay Industries Inc............................. E 513 360-0390
Monroe (G-11095)

Arlington Rack & Packaging Co......... G 419 476-7700
Toledo (G-14199)

▼ Armaly LLC... E 740 852-3621
London (G-9381)

Astro Shapes LLC................................ B 330 755-1414
Struthers (G-13901)

Atlas Roofing Corporation................... C 937 746-9941
Franklin (G-7663)

SIC SECTION

30 RUBBER AND MISCELLANEOUS PLASTIC PRODUCTS

B B Bradley Company Inc .... G 614 777-5600
  Columbus *(G-5171)*

B B Bradley Company Inc .... E 440 354-2005
  Concord Township *(G-5902)*

Creative Foam Dayton Mold .... F 937 279-9987
  Dayton *(G-6266)*

Cryovac LLC .... F 513 771-7770
  West Chester *(G-15409)*

Custom Foam Products Inc .... F 937 295-2700
  Fort Loramie *(G-7597)*

Dayton Polymeric Products Inc .... D 937 279-9987
  Dayton *(G-6287)*

Ddp Specialty Electronic MA .... C 937 839-4612
  West Alexandria *(G-15341)*

Deufol Worldwide Packaging LLC .... E 440 232-1100
  Bedford *(G-1116)*

▲ Eps Specialties Ltd Inc .... F 513 489-3676
  Cincinnati *(G-2880)*

Extol of Ohio Inc .... F 419 668-2072
  Norwalk *(G-11964)*

Foam Concepts & Design Inc .... F 513 860-5589
  West Chester *(G-15431)*

Gdc Inc .... F 574 533-3128
  Wooster *(G-16123)*

▲ Greif Packaging LLC .... E 740 549-6000
  Delaware *(G-6726)*

Hedstrom Plastics LLC .... D 419 289-9310
  Ashland *(G-578)*

◆ Hfi LLC .... B 614 491-0700
  Canal Winchester *(G-1987)*

Hinkle Manufacturing Inc .... D 419 666-5550
  Perrysburg *(G-12389)*

Hitti Enterprises Inc .... F 440 243-4100
  Cleveland *(G-4191)*

▲ ICP Adhesives and Sealants Inc ...... E 330 753-4585
  Norton *(G-11944)*

Interior Dnnage Spcialites Inc .... E 614 291-0900
  Columbus *(G-5473)*

ISO Technologies Inc .... E 740 928-0084
  Heath *(G-8322)*

▼ IVEX Protective Packaging LLC .... E 937 498-9298
  Sidney *(G-13256)*

J P Industrial Products Inc .... E 330 424-3388
  Lisbon *(G-9318)*

◆ Jain America Foods Inc .... G 614 850-9400
  Columbus *(G-5486)*

▲ Johnsonite Inc .... B 440 632-3441
  Middlefield *(G-10761)*

M L B Molded Urethane Pdts LLC .... G 419 825-9140
  Swanton *(G-13976)*

▲ Merryweather Foam Inc .... E 330 753-0353
  Barberton *(G-882)*

Myers Industries Inc .... E 330 253-5592
  Akron *(G-260)*

◆ Ohio Decorative Products LLC .... C 419 647-9033
  Spencerville *(G-13487)*

Ohio Foam Corporation .... G 614 252-4877
  Columbus *(G-5619)*

Orbis Corporation .... D 262 560-5000
  Perrysburg *(G-12413)*

Owens Corning Sales LLC .... C 330 634-0460
  Tallmadge *(G-14041)*

Palpac Industries Inc .... F 419 523-3230
  Ottawa *(G-12187)*

Paratus Supply Inc .... F 330 745-3600
  Barberton *(G-888)*

Plastic Forming Company Inc .... E 330 830-5167
  Massillon *(G-10134)*

Plastic Works Inc .... F 440 331-5575
  Cleveland *(G-4560)*

Prime Industries Inc .... E
  Lorain *(G-9431)*

Proampac Orlando Inc .... F 513 671-1777
  Cincinnati *(G-3279)*

S & A Industries Corporation .... E 330 733-6040
  Akron *(G-319)*

▲ S & A Industries Corporation .... D 330 733-6040
  Akron *(G-320)*

▲ Scott Port-A-Fold Inc .... F 419 748-8880
  Napoleon *(G-11334)*

▲ Scottdel Cushion Inc .... E 419 825-0432
  Swanton *(G-13981)*

Skybox Packaging LLC .... C 419 525-7209
  Mansfield *(G-9719)*

Smithers-Oasis Company .... F 330 673-5831
  Kent *(G-8864)*

◆ Smithers-Oasis Company .... F 330 945-5100
  Kent *(G-8865)*

Solo Products Inc .... F 513 321-7884
  Cincinnati *(G-3402)*

Sonoco Prtective Solutions Inc .... E 419 420-0029
  Findlay *(G-7565)*

Special Design Products Inc .... E 614 272-6700
  Columbus *(G-5780)*

▲ Storopack Inc .... E 513 874-0314
  West Chester *(G-15592)*

▲ Team Wendy LLC .... D 216 738-2518
  Cleveland *(G-4770)*

◆ Technifab Inc .... E 440 934-8324
  Avon *(G-789)*

Teprecision Intl Corp .... G 855 891-7732
  Kent *(G-8873)*

Trans-Foam Inc .... G 330 630-9444
  Tallmadge *(G-14053)*

Truechoicepack Corp .... F 937 630-3832
  West Chester *(G-15519)*

Wellman Container Corporation .... E 513 860-3040
  Cincinnati *(G-3515)*

Zebco Industries Inc .... F 740 654-4510
  Lancaster *(G-9049)*

Zing Pac Inc .... G 440 248-7997
  Cleveland *(G-4934)*

3087 Custom compound purchased resins

▲ Accel Corporation .... D 440 934-7711
  Avon *(G-759)*

▲ Advanced Composites Inc .... C 937 575-9800
  Sidney *(G-13218)*

▲ Aurora Plastics LLC .... E 330 422-0700
  Streetsboro *(G-13757)*

Avient Corporation .... E 419 668-4844
  Norwalk *(G-11955)*

◆ Avient Corporation .... D 440 930-1000
  Avon Lake *(G-797)*

◆ Bay State Polymer Distribution Inc ... F 440 892-8500
  Westlake *(G-15736)*

▲ Chemionics Corporation .... E 330 733-8834
  Tallmadge *(G-14024)*

Deltech Polymers LLC .... G 937 339-3150
  Troy *(G-14561)*

Deltech Polymers Opco LLC .... G 225 358-3306
  Troy *(G-14562)*

Dyneon LLC .... B 859 334-4500
  Cincinnati *(G-2846)*

Flex Technologies Inc .... D 330 897-6311
  Baltic *(G-836)*

▼ Flex Technologies Inc .... E 740 922-5992
  Midvale *(G-10878)*

Freeman Manufacturing & Sup Co ...... E 440 934-1902
  Avon *(G-775)*

General Color Investments Inc .... D 330 868-4161
  Minerva *(G-11031)*

Hexpol Compounding LLC .... C 440 834-4644
  Burton *(G-1880)*

Hexpol Compounding LLC .... C 440 632-1962
  Middlefield *(G-10756)*

▲ Hexpol Compounding LLC .... E 440 834-4644
  Burton *(G-1881)*

Hexpol Holding Inc .... F 440 834-4644
  Burton *(G-1882)*

Howard Industries Inc .... F 614 444-9900
  Columbus *(G-5447)*

Jpi Coastal LLC .... G 330 424-1110
  Lisbon *(G-9320)*

Killian Latex Inc .... F 330 644-6746
  Akron *(G-207)*

Lancer Dispersions Inc .... D
  Akron *(G-216)*

McCann Plastics LLC .... D 330 499-1515
  Canton *(G-2157)*

▼ Nanosperse LLC .... G 937 296-5030
  Kettering *(G-8908)*

Polymera Inc .... G 740 527-2069
  Hebron *(G-8357)*

Polyone Corporation .... D 330 467-8108
  Macedonia *(G-9568)*

◆ Radici Plastics Usa Inc .... E 330 336-7611
  Wadsworth *(G-15059)*

Sherwin-Williams Company .... C 330 830-6000
  Massillon *(G-10144)*

Thermafab Alloy Inc .... F 216 861-0540
  Olmsted Falls *(G-12082)*

Tymex Plastics Inc .... E 216 429-8950
  Cleveland *(G-4841)*

◆ Vibrantz Color Solutions Inc .... C 440 997-5137
  Ashtabula *(G-664)*

3088 Plastics plumbing fixtures

◆ Ad Industries Inc .... A 303 744-1911
  Dayton *(G-6183)*

Add-A-Trap LLC .... G 330 750-0417
  Struthers *(G-13898)*

American Platinum Door LLC .... G 440 497-6213
  Solon *(G-13312)*

Bobbart Industries Inc .... E 419 350-5477
  Sylvania *(G-13991)*

Certified Walk In Tubs .... G 614 436-4848
  Columbus *(G-5244)*

▲ Cincinnati Machines Inc .... E 513 536-2432
  Batavia *(G-915)*

Closets By Mike .... G 740 607-2212
  Zanesville *(G-16522)*

◆ Crane Plumbing LLC .... A 419 522-4211
  Mansfield *(G-9642)*

Cultured Marble Inc .... G 330 549-2282
  Poland *(G-12610)*

▲ Dbhl Inc .... D 216 267-7100
  Cleveland *(G-3946)*

◆ E L Mustee & Sons Inc .... D 216 267-3100
  Brookpark *(G-1713)*

◆ Hancor Inc .... B 614 658-0050
  Hilliard *(G-8413)*

◆ Lubrizol Global Management Inc ..... F 216 447-5000
  Cleveland *(G-4339)*

◆ Mansfield Plumbing Pdts LLC .... A 419 938-5211
  Perrysville *(G-12447)*

Marble Arch Products Inc .... G 937 746-8388
  Franklin *(G-7685)*

Meese Inc .... F 440 998-1202
  Ashtabula *(G-647)*

Safeway Safety Step LLC .... F 513 942-7837
  West Chester *(G-15505)*

Tower Industries Ltd .... E 330 837-2216
  Massillon *(G-10151)*

3089 Plastics products, nec

Employee Codes: A=Over 500 employees, B=251-500
C=101-250, D=51-100, E=20-50, F=10-19, G=1-9

30 RUBBER AND MISCELLANEOUS PLASTIC PRODUCTS

1 888 U Pitch It .... G 440 796-9028
   Mentor *(G-10401)*

20/20 Custom Molded Plas LLC .... D 419 485-2020
   Montpelier *(G-11133)*

A Aabaco Plastics Inc .... E 216 663-9494
   Cleveland *(G-3577)*

AB Plastics Inc .... G 513 576-6333
   Milford *(G-10891)*

ABC Plastics Inc .... E 330 948-3322
   Lodi *(G-9344)*

ABC Technologies Dlhb Inc .... E 330 479-7595
   Canton *(G-2025)*

ABC Technologies Dlhb Inc .... E 330 488-0716
   East Canton *(G-6977)*

Accutech Plastic Molding Inc .... G 937 233-0017
   Dayton *(G-6181)*

◆ Aco Inc .... E 440 639-7230
   Mentor *(G-10403)*

◆ Ad Industries Inc .... A 303 744-1911
   Dayton *(G-6183)*

Ada Extrusions Inc .... G 440 285-7653
   Akron *(G-20)*

Advanced Plastic Systems Inc .... F 614 759-6550
   Gahanna *(G-7829)*

Advanced Plastics Inc .... E 330 336-6681
   Wadsworth *(G-15015)*

Advantage Mold Inc .... G 419 691-5676
   Toledo *(G-14179)*

Aerocase Incorporated .... F 440 617-9294
   Westlake *(G-15728)*

▲ Akron Polymer Products Inc .... D 330 628-5551
   Akron *(G-40)*

▲ Akron Porcelain & Plastics Co .... C 330 745-2159
   Akron *(G-41)*

Al-Cast Mold & Pattern .... G 330 968-4490
   Kent *(G-8797)*

All About Plastics LLC .... G 937 547-0098
   Greenville *(G-8035)*

All Srvice Plastic Molding Inc .... C 937 415-3674
   Fairborn *(G-7309)*

▲ All Srvice Plastic Molding Inc .... D 937 890-0322
   Vandalia *(G-14932)*

▲ Alliance Equipment Company Inc .... F 330 821-2291
   Alliance *(G-392)*

◆ Allied Moulded Products Inc .... C 419 636-4217
   Bryan *(G-1804)*

Alpha Inc .... G 419 996-7355
   Lima *(G-9303)*

Alpha Omega Import Export LLC .... G 740 885-9155
   Marietta *(G-9774)*

Alpha Packaging Holdings Inc .... B 216 252-5595
   Cleveland *(G-3638)*

▲ Alpla Inc .... F 419 991-9484
   Lima *(G-9304)*

Alside Inc .... D 419 865-0934
   Maumee *(G-10161)*

Alumo Extrusions and Mfg Co .... E 330 779-3333
   Youngstown *(G-16308)*

Amclo Group Inc .... E 216 791-8400
   North Royalton *(G-11867)*

Amcor Rigid Packaging Usa LLC .... G 419 483-4343
   Bellevue *(G-1221)*

▲ AMD Plastics Inc .... F 216 289-4862
   Euclid *(G-7260)*

Amelia Plastics .... G 513 386-4926
   Amelia *(G-451)*

Ameri-Kart Corp .... D 800 232-0847
   Akron *(G-57)*

American Molded Plastics Inc .... F 330 872-3838
   Newton Falls *(G-11652)*

American Molding Company Inc .... G 330 620-6799
   Barberton *(G-854)*

▲ American Plastic Tech Inc .... C 440 632-5203
   Middlefield *(G-10731)*

American Plastics LLC .... C 419 423-1213
   Findlay *(G-7476)*

▼ American Way Manufacturing Inc .... E 330 824-2353
   Warren *(G-15139)*

AMP Plastics of Ohio LLC .... E
   Montpelier *(G-11134)*

Ampacet Corp .... G 513 247-5403
   Mason *(G-9949)*

Ampacet Corporation .... F 513 247-5400
   Cincinnati *(G-2625)*

AMS Global Ltd .... F 937 620-1036
   West Alexandria *(G-15339)*

◆ Anchor Hocking LLC .... A 740 687-2500
   Columbus *(G-5139)*

Anchor Hocking Holdings Inc .... A 740 687-2500
   Columbus *(G-5141)*

Apogee Plastics Corp .... F 937 864-1966
   Fairborn *(G-7310)*

Apollo Plastics Inc .... F 440 951-7774
   Mentor *(G-10420)*

Apsx LLC .... F 513 716-5992
   Blue Ash *(G-1363)*

Arkay Industries Inc .... E 513 360-0390
   Monroe *(G-11095)*

Arkay Plastics Alabama Inc .... F 513 360-0390
   Monroe *(G-11096)*

▼ Armaly LLC .... E 740 852-3621
   London *(G-9381)*

Arthur Corporation .... D 419 433-7202
   Huron *(G-8627)*

Aspec Inc .... G 513 561-9922
   Cincinnati *(G-2636)*

▲ Associated Materials LLC .... A 330 929-1811
   Cuyahoga Falls *(G-6069)*

Associated Materials Group Inc .... C 330 929-1811
   Cuyahoga Falls *(G-6070)*

▲ Associated Plastics Corp .... D 419 634-3910
   Ada *(G-3)*

▲ Astro Manufacturing & Design Inc .. C 888 215-1746
   Eastlake *(G-7019)*

Astro Model Development Corp .... G 440 946-8855
   Eastlake *(G-7020)*

▲ Atc Group Inc .... D 440 293-4064
   Andover *(G-484)*

Atlanta Rotomolding Inc .... G 404 328-1004
   Kent *(G-8800)*

Automation Plastics Corp .... D 330 562-5148
   Aurora *(G-707)*

Axiom Engineered Systems LLC .... F 416 435-7313
   Toledo *(G-14202)*

Axion International Holdings Inc .... C 740 452-2500
   Zanesville *(G-16501)*

Axion International Inc .... G 740 452-2500
   Zanesville *(G-16502)*

Axion Strl Innovations LLC .... F 740 452-2500
   Zanesville *(G-16503)*

Axium Packaging LLC .... A 614 706-5955
   New Albany *(G-11369)*

▲ B & B Molded Products Inc .... E 419 592-8700
   Defiance *(G-6670)*

Bakelite N Sumitomo Amer Inc .... E 419 675-1282
   Kenton *(G-8881)*

Baker Plastics Inc .... G 330 743-3142
   Youngstown *(G-16317)*

Bay Corporation .... E 440 835-2212
   Westlake *(G-15735)*

Bc Investment Corporation .... G 330 262-3070
   Wooster *(G-16103)*

Beach Mfg Plastic Molding Div .... G 937 882-6400
   New Carlisle *(G-11411)*

Bell Binders LLC .... F 419 242-3201
   Toledo *(G-14210)*

Berlekamp Plastics Inc .... F 419 334-4481
   Fremont *(G-7767)*

Bernard Engraving Corp .... F 419 478-5610
   Toledo *(G-14212)*

Berry Global Inc .... G 419 887-1602
   Maumee *(G-10171)*

Berry Global Inc .... D 419 465-2291
   Monroeville *(G-11122)*

Berry Global Inc .... F 330 896-6700
   Streetsboro *(G-13761)*

Blackthorn LLC .... F 937 836-9296
   Clayton *(G-3564)*

Bloom Industries Inc .... F 330 898-3878
   Warren *(G-15146)*

▲ Bmf Devices Inc .... F 937 866-3451
   Miamisburg *(G-10621)*

Boardman Molded Intl LLC .... C 800 233-4575
   Youngstown *(G-16321)*

◆ Boardman Molded Products Inc ..... D 330 788-2400
   Youngstown *(G-16322)*

Boat Decor LLC .... G 216 831-1889
   Beachwood *(G-975)*

Borke Mold Specialist Inc .... E 513 870-8000
   West Chester *(G-15381)*

Bourbon Plastics Inc .... E 574 342-0893
   Cuyahoga Falls *(G-6073)*

◆ Bprex Healthcare Brookville Inc ..... C 847 541-9700
   Perrysburg *(G-12365)*

Bprex Plastic Packaging Inc .... F 419 247-5000
   Toledo *(G-14218)*

Brittany Stamping LLC .... A 216 267-0850
   Cleveland *(G-3760)*

Brown Company of Findlay Ltd .... F 419 425-3002
   Findlay *(G-7488)*

Buckeye Design & Engr Svc LLC .... G 419 375-4241
   Fort Recovery *(G-7613)*

Budd Co Plastics Div .... G 419 238-4332
   Van Wert *(G-14908)*

Buecomp Inc .... G 419 284-3840
   Bloomville *(G-1354)*

Builder Tech Wholesale LLC .... G 419 535-7606
   Toledo *(G-14224)*

▲ C A Joseph Co .... G 330 385-6869
   East Liverpool *(G-6988)*

C-Mold Inc .... E
   Shaker Heights *(G-13151)*

Calorplast USA LLC .... G 513 576-6333
   Milford *(G-10897)*

Cantex Inc .... D 330 995-3665
   Aurora *(G-710)*

Caps Inc .... G 513 377-0800
   Cincinnati *(G-2700)*

Caraustar Industries Inc .... E 330 665-7700
   Copley *(G-5946)*

Carbon Polymers Company .... D 330 948-3007
   Lodi *(G-9348)*

Cardinal Products Inc .... G 440 237-8280
   North Royalton *(G-11870)*

Carlisle Plastics Company .... G 937 845-9411
   New Carlisle *(G-11412)*

▲ Carney Plastics Inc .... G 330 746-8273
   Youngstown *(G-16331)*

Carson Industries LLC .... G 419 592-2309
   Napoleon *(G-11310)*

Ccp Newco LLC .... B 419 448-1700
   Tiffin *(G-14081)*

▲ Cell-O-Core Co .... E 330 239-4370
   Sharon Center *(G-13165)*

Cell-O-Core Co .... F 800 239-4370
   Wadsworth *(G-15022)*

SIC SECTION
30 RUBBER AND MISCELLANEOUS PLASTIC PRODUCTS

Century Container LLC............................. E 330 457-2367
   Columbiana *(G-5031)*

Century Container LLC............................. F 330 457-2367
   New Waterford *(G-11554)*

▼ Century Container Corporation................ C 330 457-2367
   New Waterford *(G-11555)*

Century Mold Company Inc........................ D 513 539-9283
   Middletown *(G-10806)*

▲ Champion Opco LLC................................. B 513 327-7338
   Cincinnati *(G-2725)*

Chapin Customer Molding Inc..................... F 440 458-6550
   Elyria *(G-7126)*

Chica Bands LLC....................................... G 513 871-4300
   Cincinnati *(G-2732)*

Chuck Meadors Plastics Co......................... F 440 813-4466
   Jefferson *(G-8746)*

Claflin Co... G 330 650-0582
   Hudson *(G-8589)*

Clark Rubber & Plastic Company................. C 440 255-9793
   Mentor *(G-10439)*

Classic Laminations Inc............................. E 440 735-1333
   Oakwood Village *(G-12037)*

Claycor Inc.. F 419 318-7290
   Toledo *(G-14240)*

Cleveland Reclaim Inds Inc........................ G 440 282-4917
   Lorain *(G-9407)*

Cleveland Specialty Pdts Inc...................... E 216 281-8300
   Cleveland *(G-3855)*

▲ CM Paula Company................................ E 513 759-7473
   Mason *(G-9980)*

▲ Comdess Company Inc............................. E 330 769-2094
   Seville *(G-13141)*

◆ Comfort Line Ltd....................................D 419 729-8520
   Toledo *(G-14248)*

Composite Technologies Co LLC.................. D 937 228-2880
   Dayton *(G-6262)*

Consolidated Metco Inc............................. E 740 772-6758
   Chillicothe *(G-2499)*

Converge Group Inc.................................. G 419 281-0000
   Ashland *(G-568)*

Core Composites Cincinnati LLC................. D 513 724-6111
   Batavia *(G-918)*

▲ Core Molding Technologies Inc................. A 614 870-5000
   Columbus *(G-5296)*

Corvac Composites LLC............................. D 248 807-0969
   Greenfield *(G-8028)*

Cosmo Plastics Company............................ D 330 359-5429
   Wilmot *(G-16066)*

▲ Cosmo Plastics Company.......................... C 440 498-7500
   Cleveland *(G-3907)*

Cpg International LLC............................... B 937 655-8766
   Wilmington *(G-16047)*

Cpp Group Holdings LLC............................ E 216 453-4800
   Cleveland *(G-3912)*

Creative Extruded Products........................ G 937 335-3336
   Troy *(G-14557)*

Creative Liquid Coatings Inc....................... C 419 485-1110
   Montpelier *(G-11135)*

Creative Millwork Ohio Inc......................... D 440 992-3566
   Ashtabula *(G-628)*

Creative Plastics Intl................................ F 937 596-6769
   Jackson Center *(G-8730)*

▲ Crg Plastics Inc..................................... F 937 298-2025
   Dayton *(G-6267)*

Crown Cork & Seal Usa Inc........................ D 740 681-3000
   Lancaster *(G-9006)*

Ctc Plastics... C 937 281-4002
   Dayton *(G-6268)*

Ctc Plastics... E 937 228-9184
   Dayton *(G-6269)*

▲ Custom Molded Products LLC................... D 937 382-1070
   Wilmington *(G-16048)*

Custom Poly Bag LLC................................. D 330 935-2408
   Alliance *(G-399)*

Custom Pultrusions Inc.............................. D 330 562-5201
   Aurora *(G-711)*

Cuyahoga Molded Plastics Co..................... G 216 261-2744
   Mentor *(G-10447)*

Cuyahoga Molded Plastics Co (inc).............. E 216 261-2744
   Euclid *(G-7266)*

D and D Plastics Inc.................................. F 330 376-0668
   Akron *(G-122)*

D K Manufacturing..................................... E 740 654-5566
   Lancaster *(G-9008)*

D M Tool & Plastics Inc............................. F 937 962-4140
   Brookville *(G-1733)*

D M Tool & Plastics Inc............................. F 937 962-4140
   Lewisburg *(G-9186)*

D Martone Industries Inc........................... E 440 632-5800
   Middlefield *(G-10746)*

Dadco Inc.. F 513 489-2244
   Cincinnati *(G-2816)*

Daddy Katz LLC....................................... G 937 296-0347
   Moraine *(G-11168)*

Dak Enterprises Inc.................................. F 740 828-3291
   Marysville *(G-9907)*

Dalton US Inc.. G 440 878-7661
   Strongsville *(G-13827)*

▲ Dawn Enterprises Inc............................. E 216 642-5506
   Cleveland *(G-3943)*

Dayton Molded Urethanes LLC................... D 937 279-9987
   Dayton *(G-6283)*

◆ Dayton Superior Corporation....................C 937 866-0711
   Miamisburg *(G-10633)*

Deflecto LLC... C 330 602-0840
   Dover *(G-6814)*

▲ Deimling/Jeliho Plastics Inc.................... E 513 752-6653
   Amelia *(G-454)*

Denney Plastics Machining LLC.................. F 330 308-5300
   New Philadelphia *(G-11498)*

Design Molded Products LLC..................... E 330 963-4400
   Macedonia *(G-9545)*

Design Molded Products LLC..................... F 330 963-4400
   Macedonia *(G-9544)*

Dester Corporation................................... F 419 362-8020
   Lima *(G-9236)*

◆ Dester Corporation................................F 419 362-8020
   Lima *(G-9235)*

Die-Gem Co Inc.. F 330 784-7400
   Akron *(G-129)*

Diemaster Tool & Mold Inc........................ F 330 467-4281
   Macedonia *(G-9546)*

Dimco Gray... G 937 291-4720
   Dayton *(G-6299)*

▲ Dimcogray Corporation........................... D 937 433-7600
   Centerville *(G-2361)*

Dinesol Building Products Ltd.................... E 330 270-0212
   Youngstown *(G-16350)*

▲ Dinesol Plastics Inc............................... C 330 544-7171
   Niles *(G-11666)*

Diskin Enterprises LLC.............................. E 330 527-4308
   Garrettsville *(G-7913)*

Diversity-Vuteq LLC.................................. G 614 490-5034
   Gahanna *(G-7834)*

◆ DJM Plastics Ltd...................................F 419 424-5250
   Findlay *(G-7502)*

DK Manfcturing Frazeysburg Inc................. F 740 828-3291
   Frazeysburg *(G-7715)*

DK Manufacturing Lancaster Inc................. D 740 654-5566
   Lancaster *(G-9014)*

▲ Dometic Sanitation Corporation............... E 330 439-5550
   Big Prairie *(G-1328)*

Don-Ell Corporation.................................. G 419 841-7114
   Sylvania *(G-13994)*

Don-Ell Corporation.................................. E 419 841-7114
   Sylvania *(G-13993)*

Dover High Prfmce Plas Inc........................ E 330 343-3477
   Dover *(G-6820)*

Doyle Manufacturing Inc............................ D 419 865-2548
   Holland *(G-8505)*

▲ Dreco Inc.. C 440 327-6021
   North Ridgeville *(G-11838)*

Drummond Corporation.............................. F 440 834-9660
   Middlefield *(G-10748)*

Dublin Plastics Inc................................... G 216 641-5904
   Cleveland *(G-3975)*

Dunstone Company Inc.............................. F 704 841-1380
   Hiram *(G-8481)*

Duo-Corp.. F 330 549-2149
   North Lima *(G-11804)*

Dyna-Vac Plastics Inc............................... G 937 773-0092
   Piqua *(G-12514)*

Dynamic Plastics Inc................................. G 937 437-7261
   New Paris *(G-11481)*

▲ E P P Inc.. D 440 322-8577
   Elyria *(G-7138)*

Eaton Corporation.................................... E 330 274-0743
   Aurora *(G-712)*

Ebco Inc... E 330 562-8265
   Streetsboro *(G-13769)*

▲ Edge Plastics Inc................................... C 419 522-6696
   Mansfield *(G-9651)*

Electr-Gnral Plas Corp Clumbus.................. G 614 871-2915
   Grove City *(G-8092)*

Electro-Cap International Inc...................... F 937 456-6099
   Eaton *(G-7058)*

Eliason Corporation.................................. E 800 828-3655
   West Chester *(G-15550)*

Elra Industries Inc.................................... G 513 868-6228
   Hamilton *(G-8206)*

◆ Elster Perfection Corporation..................D 440 428-1171
   Geneva *(G-7935)*

◆ Encon Inc...C 937 898-2603
   Dayton *(G-6320)*

Encore Industries Inc................................ C 419 626-8000
   Sandusky *(G-13053)*

▲ Encore Industries Inc............................. C 419 626-8000
   Cambridge *(G-1935)*

Encore Plastics Southeast LLC................... F 419 626-8000
   Sandusky *(G-13054)*

Engineered Profiles LLC............................ B 614 754-3700
   Columbus *(G-5355)*

▼ Enpac LLC... D 440 975-0070
   Eastlake *(G-7028)*

▼ Enpress LLC.. E 440 510-0108
   Eastlake *(G-7029)*

▲ Environmental Sampling Sup Inc.............. D 330 497-9396
   North Canton *(G-11725)*

Epc-Columbia Inc..................................... D 740 420-5252
   Circleville *(G-3549)*

Evans Industries Inc................................. E 330 453-1122
   Canton *(G-2099)*

Exterior Portfolio LLC............................... C 614 754-3400
   Columbus *(G-5367)*

Extrudex Limited Partnership..................... E 440 352-7101
   Painesville *(G-12235)*

Fabohio Inc... E 740 922-4233
   Uhrichsville *(G-14765)*

Fastformingcom LLC................................. F 330 927-3277
   Rittman *(G-12821)*

Fci Inc... D 216 251-5200
   Cleveland *(G-4052)*

Fdi Enterprises.. G 440 269-8282
   Cleveland *(G-4053)*

Felicity Plastics Machinery........................ F 513 876-7003
   Felicity *(G-7467)*

30 RUBBER AND MISCELLANEOUS PLASTIC PRODUCTS

▲ Ferriot Inc .... C 330 786-3000
  Akron *(G-152)*
▲ Few Atmtve GL Applcations Inc .... D 234 249-1880
  Wooster *(G-16118)*
Fiber -Tech Industries Inc .... D 740 335-9400
  Wshngtn Ct Hs *(G-16231)*
Fiberglass Technology Inds Inc .... E 740 335-9400
  Wshngtn Ct Hs *(G-16232)*
Fibertech Networks .... F 614 436-3565
  Worthington *(G-16194)*
▲ Fibreboard Corporation .... C 419 248-8000
  Toledo *(G-14287)*
Fields Process Technology Inc .... G 216 781-4787
  Cleveland *(G-4059)*
▲ Findlay Machine & Tool LLC .... E 419 434-3100
  Findlay *(G-7506)*
▲ First Choice Packaging Inc .... C 419 333-4100
  Fremont *(G-7778)*
Flambeau Inc .... D 440 632-6131
  Middlefield *(G-10750)*
Flex Technologies Inc .... D 330 359-5415
  Mount Eaton *(G-11230)*
▼ Flex Technologies Inc .... E 740 922-5992
  Midvale *(G-10878)*
Florida Production Engrg Inc .... C 740 420-5252
  Circleville *(G-3551)*
Formco Inc .... G 330 966-2111
  Canton *(G-2103)*
▲ Forrest Enterprises Inc .... F 937 773-1714
  Piqua *(G-12516)*
Fortis Plastics LLC .... F 937 382-0966
  Wilmington *(G-16051)*
Fountain Specialists Inc .... G 513 831-5717
  Milford *(G-10906)*
▲ Fowler Products Inc .... F 419 683-4057
  Crestline *(G-6033)*
▼ Fox Lite Inc .... E 937 864-1966
  Fairborn *(G-7315)*
Fpe Inc .... C 740 420-5252
  Circleville *(G-3552)*
Frantz Medical Development Ltd .... G 440 255-1455
  Mentor *(G-10457)*
Fremont Plastic Products Inc .... C 419 332-6407
  Fremont *(G-7783)*
▲ Fukuvi Usa Inc .... D 937 236-7288
  Dayton *(G-6341)*
Future Molding Inc .... F 419 281-0000
  Ashland *(G-575)*
G & J Extrusions Inc .... G 330 753-0162
  New Franklin *(G-11436)*
G I Plastek Inc .... G 440 230-1942
  Westlake *(G-15751)*
◆ G M R Technology Inc .... E 440 992-6003
  Ashtabula *(G-634)*
G S K Inc .... G 937 547-1611
  Greenville *(G-8046)*
G3 Packaging LLC .... G 334 799-0015
  Monroe *(G-11107)*
Gas Assist Injction Mlding Exp .... G 440 632-5203
  Middlefield *(G-10751)*
▼ Gateway Industrial Pdts Inc .... E 440 324-4112
  Elyria *(G-7154)*
Genpak LLC .... E 614 276-5156
  Columbus *(G-5399)*
▲ Gentek Building Products Inc .... F 800 548-4542
  Cuyahoga Falls *(G-6086)*
◆ Ghp II LLC .... C 740 687-2500
  Lancaster *(G-9017)*
Global Plastic Tech Inc .... E 330 963-6830
  Brecksville *(G-1619)*
Gorell Enterprises Inc .... B 724 465-1800
  Streetsboro *(G-13772)*

Graham Packaging Pet Tech Inc .... E 419 334-4197
  Fremont *(G-7788)*
Graham Packaging Pet Tech Inc .... E 513 398-5000
  Mason *(G-9998)*
GRANGER PLASTICS CO THE .... E 513 424-1955
  Middletown *(G-10827)*
◆ Graphic Art Systems Inc .... E 216 581-9050
  Cleveland *(G-4140)*
Great Lakes Window Inc .... A 419 666-5555
  Walbridge *(G-15082)*
Greenfield Precision Plas LLC .... F 937 803-0328
  Greenfield *(G-8031)*
Greenlight Optics LLC .... E 513 247-9777
  Loveland *(G-9483)*
Greenville Techniology Inc .... G 937 642-6744
  Marysville *(G-9912)*
Greif Inc .... E 740 657-6500
  Delaware *(G-6725)*
◆ Greif Inc .... E 740 549-6000
  Delaware *(G-8724)*
Griffin Technology Inc .... C 585 924-7121
  Hudson *(G-8594)*
H & H Engineered Molded Pdts .... C 440 415-1814
  Geneva *(G-7937)*
H P Manufacturing Co .... G 216 361-6500
  Cleveland *(G-4161)*
Hamilton Custom Molding Inc .... E 513 844-6643
  Hamilton *(G-8217)*
Hancor Inc .... E 419 424-8225
  Findlay *(G-7521)*
◆ Hancor Inc .... B 614 658-0050
  Hilliard *(G-8413)*
Hanlon Composites LLC .... E 216 261-7056
  Euclid *(G-7272)*
Hanlon Industries Inc .... E 216 261-7056
  Cleveland *(G-4168)*
Harbor Industrial Corp .... F 440 599-8366
  Conneaut *(G-5919)*
▲ Harmony Systems and Svc Inc .... D 937 778-1082
  Piqua *(G-12519)*
Harrison Mch & Plastic Corp .... E 330 527-5641
  Garrettsville *(G-7916)*
Hathaway Stamp Co .... E 513 621-1052
  Cincinnati *(G-2989)*
▼ Haviland Plastic Products Co .... E 419 622-3110
  Haviland *(G-8313)*
Hendrickson International Corp .... D 740 929-5600
  Hebron *(G-8343)*
HI Lite Plastic Products .... G 614 235-9050
  Columbus *(G-5432)*
◆ HP Enterprise Inc .... E 800 232-7950
  Streetsboro *(G-13773)*
HP Liquidating Inc .... D 614 861-1791
  Blacklick *(G-1337)*
HP Manufacturing Company Inc .... D 216 361-6500
  Cleveland *(G-4204)*
Hudson Extrusions Inc .... E 330 653-6015
  Hudson *(G-8597)*
I-Plus Inc .... G 216 432-9200
  Cleveland *(G-4213)*
ICO Products LLC .... G 419 867-3900
  Holland *(G-8513)*
Ieg Plastics LLC .... F 937 565-4211
  Bellefontaine *(G-1213)*
Illinois Tool Works Inc .... D 419 633-3236
  Bryan *(G-1822)*
Illinois Tool Works Inc .... G 419 636-3161
  Bryan *(G-1823)*
Illinois Tool Works Inc .... E 937 332-2839
  Troy *(G-14584)*
Iml Containers Ohio Inc .... F 330 754-1066
  Canton *(G-2129)*

◆ Impact Products LLC .... D 419 841-2891
  Toledo *(G-14328)*
Imperial Family Inc .... D 330 927-5065
  Rittman *(G-12822)*
Indelco Custom Products Inc .... E 216 797-7300
  Euclid *(G-7274)*
Industrial Container Svcs LLC .... E 513 921-2056
  Cincinnati *(G-3020)*
Industrial Farm Tank Inc .... E 937 843-2972
  Lewistown *(G-9194)*
Inhance Technologies LLC .... E 614 846-6400
  Columbus *(G-5459)*
Innovation Plastics LLC .... E 513 818-1771
  Fostoria *(G-7639)*
Innovations In Plastic Inc .... G 216 541-6060
  Cleveland *(G-4228)*
Innovative Plastic Molders LLC .... E 937 898-3775
  Vandalia *(G-14944)*
Integra Enclosures Inc .... G 440 269-4966
  Willoughby *(G-15932)*
Integral Design Inc .... F 216 524-0555
  Cleveland *(G-4230)*
Interntnal Auto Cmpnnts Group .... A 419 433-5653
  Wauseon *(G-15265)*
◆ Interntnal Cnvrter Cldwell Inc .... C 740 732-5665
  Caldwell *(G-1909)*
▼ Interpak Inc .... E 440 974-8999
  Mentor *(G-10476)*
Inventive Extrusions Corp .... F 330 874-3000
  Bolivar *(G-1528)*
◆ IPL Dayton Inc C
  Urbana *(G-14838)*
Iten Industries Inc .... F 440 997-6134
  Ashtabula *(G-643)*
◆ Iten Industries Inc .... C 440 997-6134
  Ashtabula *(G-642)*
J & O Plastics Inc .... E 330 927-3169
  Rittman *(G-12823)*
J H Plastics Inc .... G 419 937-2035
  Tiffin *(G-14088)*
J K Plastics Co .... E 440 632-1482
  Middlefield *(G-10759)*
J K Precast LLC .... G 740 335-2188
  Wshngtn Ct Hs *(G-16234)*
Jaco Manufacturing Company .... E 440 234-4000
  Berea *(G-1284)*
Jaco Manufacturing Company .... D 440 234-4000
  Berea *(G-1285)*
Jaco Products LLC .... G 614 219-1670
  Hilliard *(G-8415)*
▲ Janorpot LLC .... E 330 564-0232
  Mogadore *(G-11076)*
▼ Japo Inc .... E 614 263-2850
  Columbus *(G-5488)*
▲ Jay Industries Inc .... A 419 747-4161
  Mansfield *(G-9671)*
Jdh Holdings Inc .... C 330 963-4400
  Macedonia *(G-9559)*
▲ Johnsonite Inc .... B 440 543-8916
  Solon *(G-13370)*
Joneszylon Company LLC .... G 740 545-6341
  West Lafayette *(G-15620)*
▲ Joslyn Manufacturing Company .... E 330 467-8111
  Macedonia *(G-9560)*
JPS Technologies Inc .... F 513 984-6400
  Blue Ash *(G-1415)*
JPS Technologies Inc .... F 513 984-6400
  Blue Ash *(G-1414)*
Just Plastics Inc .... F 419 468-5506
  Galion *(G-7881)*
◆ Kamco Industries Inc .... B 419 924-5511
  West Unity *(G-15641)*

SIC SECTION

30 RUBBER AND MISCELLANEOUS PLASTIC PRODUCTS

Kar-Del Plastics Inc............................ G 419 289-9739
  Ashland *(G-583)*

Kasai North America Inc.................... E 614 356-1494
  Dublin *(G-6903)*

Kathom Manufacturing Co Inc............ E 513 868-8890
  Middletown *(G-10835)*

Keene Village Plastics Ltd................. G 330 753-0100
  Euclid *(G-7279)*

▲ Kennedy Group Incorporated.......... D 440 951-7660
  Willoughby *(G-15939)*

Kirtland Plastics Inc........................... D 440 951-4466
  Kirtland *(G-8941)*

Kittyhawk Molding Company Inc........ E 937 746-3663
  Carlisle *(G-2289)*

▲ Klw Plastics Inc............................... G 513 539-2673
  Monroe *(G-11114)*

Kmak Group LLC................................ F 937 308-1023
  London *(G-9390)*

Koebbe Products Inc.......................... D 513 735-1400
  Batavia *(G-928)*

Kolhfab Cstm Plstic Fbrication........... G 937 237-2098
  Dayton *(G-6399)*

Kreate Extrusion LLC......................... G 419 683-4057
  Findlay *(G-7527)*

Kuhns Mold & Tool Co Inc.................. D 937 833-2178
  Brookville *(G-1740)*

▲ Kurz-Kasch Inc................................ E 740 498-8343
  Newcomerstown *(G-11647)*

L C Liming & Sons Inc....................... G 513 876-2555
  Felicity *(G-7468)*

Lam Pro Inc....................................... F 216 426-0661
  Cleveland *(G-4308)*

Lancer Dispersions Inc...................... D
  Akron *(G-216)*

◆ Landmark Plastic Corporation........ C 330 785-2200
  Akron *(G-217)*

Larmco Windows Inc......................... E 216 502-2832
  Cleveland *(G-4313)*

▲ Laszeray Technology LLC................ D 440 582-8430
  North Royalton *(G-11883)*

Lee Plastic Company LLC.................. G 937 456-5720
  Eaton *(G-7065)*

▲ Lenz Inc... E 937 277-9364
  Dayton *(G-6405)*

Lerner Assoc..................................... G 330 348-0360
  Aurora *(G-722)*

Lewart Plastics LLC........................... F 216 281-2333
  Cleveland *(G-4321)*

Linneas Candy Supplies Inc............... E 330 678-7112
  Kent *(G-8828)*

Liqui-Box Corporation........................ E 419 289-9696
  Ashland *(G-589)*

Liqui-Box Corporation........................ E 419 294-3884
  Upper Sandusky *(G-14814)*

Lotus Pipes & Rockdrills USA............. F 516 209-6995
  Cleveland *(G-4335)*

Louis G Freeman Co.......................... G 513 263-1720
  Batavia *(G-929)*

Luckys Bottles Inc............................. F 614 447-9522
  Columbus *(G-5536)*

◆ M T M Molded Products Company.... E 937 890-7461
  Dayton *(G-6418)*

M W Solutions Inc............................. F 419 782-1611
  Defiance *(G-6689)*

▲ Mag-Nif Inc.................................... D 440 255-9366
  Mentor *(G-10498)*

Magic Molding Inc............................. G 937 778-0836
  Covington *(G-6027)*

Majestic Plastics Inc.......................... D 937 593-9500
  Bellefontaine *(G-1215)*

◆ Malish Corporation......................... D 440 951-5356
  Mentor *(G-10499)*

◆ Mar-Bal Inc..................................... D 440 543-7526
  Chagrin Falls *(G-2407)*

Marne Plastics LLC............................ G 614 732-4666
  Grove City *(G-8104)*

Marsh Composites LLC...................... G 937 350-1214
  Dayton *(G-6169)*

Marshall Plastics Inc.......................... G 937 653-4740
  Urbana *(G-14843)*

Materials Processing Inc.................... G 330 730-5959
  Dover *(G-6834)*

Maverick Corporation........................ F 513 469-9919
  Blue Ash *(G-1430)*

McCann Tool & Die Inc...................... F 330 264-8820
  Wooster *(G-16150)*

McNeal Enterprises LLC..................... G 740 703-7108
  Chillicothe *(G-2516)*

MCS Midwest LLC.............................. G 513 217-0805
  Franklin *(G-7686)*

Mdi of Ohio Inc.................................. E 937 866-2345
  Canton *(G-2158)*

Medal Components LLC..................... G 864 561-9464
  Holgate *(G-8489)*

Meese Inc.. F 440 998-1202
  Ashtabula *(G-647)*

Mega Plastics Co............................... E 330 527-2211
  Garrettsville *(G-7922)*

Meggitt (erlanger) LLC....................... D 513 851-5550
  Cincinnati *(G-3143)*

Mercury Plastics LLC......................... C 440 632-5281
  Middlefield *(G-10764)*

▲ Merryweather Foam Inc................... E 330 753-0353
  Barberton *(G-882)*

Meteor Creative Inc........................... E 800 273-1535
  Tipp City *(G-14141)*

Miami Specialties Inc......................... G 937 778-1850
  Piqua *(G-12536)*

▲ Miami Valley Plastics Inc................. E 937 273-3200
  Eldorado *(G-7092)*

Middlefield Plastics Inc...................... E 440 834-4638
  Middlefield *(G-10767)*

Mikron Industries Inc......................... D 713 961-4600
  Akron *(G-248)*

Modern Builders Supply Inc............... E 419 526-0002
  Mansfield *(G-9698)*

Modern Builders Supply Inc............... C 419 241-3961
  Toledo *(G-14389)*

Modern Mold Corporation.................. G 440 236-9600
  Columbia Station *(G-5014)*

Mold-Rite Plastics LLC....................... C 330 405-7739
  Twinsburg *(G-14698)*

Mold-Rite Plastics LLC....................... C 330 405-7739
  Twinsburg *(G-14699)*

Molded Extruded................................ G 216 475-5491
  Bedford Heights *(G-1177)*

Molded Fiber Glass Companies.......... D 440 997-5851
  Ashtabula *(G-651)*

Molded Fiber Glass Companies.......... E 440 994-5100
  Ashtabula *(G-652)*

◆ Molded Fiber Glass Companies....... A 440 997-5851
  Ashtabula *(G-650)*

Molders World Inc............................. F 513 469-6653
  Blue Ash *(G-1441)*

Molding Dynamics Inc....................... F 440 786-8100
  Bedford *(G-1138)*

Molding Technologies Ltd.................. F 740 929-2065
  Hebron *(G-8348)*

Moldmakers Inc................................. F 419 673-0902
  Kenton *(G-8892)*

▲ Molten North America Corp............. C 419 425-2700
  Findlay *(G-7539)*

▲ Mon-Say Corp.................................. G 419 720-0163
  Toledo *(G-14390)*

Montville Plastics & Rbr LLC.............. D 440 548-2005
  Parkman *(G-12284)*

Montville Plastics & Rubber Inc.......... E 440 548-3211
  Parkman *(G-12285)*

▲ Moore Industries Inc....................... D 419 485-5572
  Montpelier *(G-11139)*

◆ Moriroku Technology N Amer Inc..... A 937 548-3217
  Marysville *(G-9928)*

Mos International Inc........................ F 330 329-0905
  Stow *(G-13710)*

MTI Acquisition LLC........................... F 740 929-2065
  Hebron *(G-8351)*

Mvp Plastics Inc................................ F 440 834-1790
  Middlefield *(G-10773)*

Mye Automotive Inc........................... D 330 253-5592
  Akron *(G-258)*

Myers Industries Inc......................... D 330 253-5592
  Akron *(G-259)*

Myers Industries Inc......................... C 330 821-4700
  Alliance *(G-417)*

Myers Industries Inc......................... E 440 632-1006
  Middlefield *(G-10774)*

Myers Industries Inc......................... E 330 253-5592
  Akron *(G-260)*

National Access Design LLC.............. F 513 351-3400
  Cincinnati *(G-3179)*

National Fleet Svcs Ohio LLC............. F 440 930-5177
  Avon Lake *(G-818)*

Nebraska Industries Corp.................. F 419 335-6010
  Wauseon *(G-15270)*

▲ Neff-Perkins Company.................... D 440 632-1658
  Middlefield *(G-10776)*

Newell Brands Inc............................. E 330 733-7771
  Mogadore *(G-11079)*

◆ Nickolas Plastics LLC..................... C 419 423-1213
  Findlay *(G-7543)*

Nifco America Corporation................. C 614 836-3808
  Canal Winchester *(G-1990)*

Nifco America Corporation................. C 614 836-8691
  Groveport *(G-8155)*

▲ Nifco America Corporation............. B 614 920-6800
  Canal Winchester *(G-1989)*

▲ Nissen Chemitec America Inc......... B 740 852-3200
  London *(G-9391)*

Nitrojection...................................... G 440 729-2711
  Chesterland *(G-2486)*

North Canton Plastics Inc.................. E 330 497-0071
  Canton *(G-2176)*

North Coast Custom Molding Inc........ F 419 905-6447
  Dunkirk *(G-6976)*

▲ North Coast Seal Incorporated....... F 216 898-5000
  Brookpark *(G-1722)*

Northshore Mold Inc......................... G 440 838-8212
  Cleveland *(G-4480)*

Northwest Molded Plastics................ G 419 459-4414
  Edon *(G-7090)*

Norwesco Inc.................................... F 740 654-6402
  Lancaster *(G-9031)*

▲ Novatex North America Inc............. D 419 282-4264
  Ashland *(G-595)*

Octsys Security Corp........................ G 614 470-4510
  Columbus *(G-5611)*

▲ Ohio Precision Molding Inc............. E 330 745-9393
  Barberton *(G-886)*

Omega Polymer Technologies Inc....... G 330 562-5201
  Aurora *(G-730)*

Omega Pultrusions Incorporated........ C 330 562-5201
  Aurora *(G-731)*

Oneida Consumer LLC....................... F 740 687-2500
  Columbus *(G-5641)*

Orbis Corporation.............................. B 937 652-1361
  Urbana *(G-14845)*

Employee Codes: A=Over 500 employees, B=251-500
C=101-250, D=51-100, E=20-50, F=10-19, G=1-9

30 RUBBER AND MISCELLANEOUS PLASTIC PRODUCTS

Orbit Manufacturing Inc .... F 513 732-6097
   Batavia (G-942)
▲ Osburn Associates Inc .... F 740 385-5732
   Logan (G-9372)
Overhead Door Corporation .... F 440 593-5226
   Conneaut (G-5929)
◆ Owens Corning Sales LLC .... A 419 248-8000
   Toledo (G-14424)
P S Plastics Inc .... F 614 262-7070
   Columbus (G-5649)
▲ P T I Inc .... E 419 445-2800
   Archbold (G-540)
▲ Paarlo Plastics Inc .... D 330 494-3798
   North Canton (G-11749)
Palpac Industries Inc .... F 419 523-3230
   Ottawa (G-12187)
Paragon Plastics .... G 330 542-9825
   New Middletown (G-11479)
▲ Patrick Products Inc .... C 419 943-4137
   Leipsic (O-9104)
Pave Technology Co .... F 937 890-1100
   Dayton (G-6499)
PCR Restorations Inc .... F 419 747-7957
   Mansfield (G-9709)
Pease Industies Inc .... D 513 870-3600
   Fairfield (G-7393)
Performance Plastics Ltd .... D 513 321-8404
   Cincinnati (G-3248)
Pickens Plastics Inc .... G 440 576-4001
   Jefferson (G-8755)
▲ Pinnacle Industrial Entps Inc .... C 419 352-8688
   Bowling Green (G-1584)
Pioneer Custom Molding Inc .... E 419 737-3252
   Pioneer (G-12495)
Pioneer Plastics Corporation .... C 330 896-2356
   Akron (G-276)
Plas-Tanks Industries Inc .... E 513 942-3800
   Hamilton (G-8235)
Plas-TEC Corp .... D 419 272-2731
   Edon (G-7091)
Plastic Enterprises Inc .... G 440 366-0220
   Elyria (G-7196)
▲ Plastic Enterprises Inc .... E 440 324-3240
   Elyria (G-7197)
▼ Plastic Extrusion Tech Ltd .... E 440 632-5611
   Middlefield (G-10781)
Plastic Forming Company Inc .... E 330 830-5167
   Massillon (G-10134)
▲ Plastic Moldings Company Llc .... D 513 921-5040
   Blue Ash (G-1451)
Plasticards Inc .... E 330 896-5555
   Uniontown (G-14791)
Plasticraft Usa LLC .... G 513 761-2999
   Cincinnati (G-3260)
Plastics Cnvrting Slutions Ltd .... G 330 722-2537
   Medina (G-10364)
Plastics Family Holdings Inc .... F 614 272-0777
   Columbus (G-5680)
Plastics Mentor LLC .... G 440 352-1357
   Mentor (G-10524)
Plastics R Unique Inc .... E 330 334-4820
   Wadsworth (G-15053)
Plastikos Corporation .... E 513 732-0961
   Batavia (G-943)
Plastipak Packaging Inc .... C 740 928-4435
   Hebron (G-8356)
Plate Engraving Corporation .... G 330 239-2155
   Medina (G-10365)
Pleasant Precision Inc .... E 419 675-0556
   Kenton (G-8896)
PM Machine Inc .... G 440 942-6537
   Willoughby (G-15972)

PMC Smart Solutions LLC .... D 513 921-5040
   Blue Ash (G-1452)
Podnar Plastics Inc .... G 330 673-2255
   Kent (G-8843)
Podnar Plastics Inc .... E 330 673-2255
   Kent (G-8844)
▲ Polyfill LLC .... E 937 493-0041
   Sidney (G-13272)
Polyflex LLC .... F 440 946-0758
   Willoughby (G-15975)
▼ Polymer & Steel Tech Inc .... E 440 510-0108
   Eastlake (G-7045)
Polyquest Inc .... F 330 888-9448
   Sagamore Hills (G-12893)
Polysource LLC .... E 937 778-9500
   Piqua (G-12549)
Ppafco Inc .... E 614 488-7259
   Columbus (G-5685)
Precision Engineered Plas Inc .... E 216 334-1105
   Cleveland (G-4574)
Precision Foam Fabrication Inc .... F 330 270-2440
   Austintown (G-754)
Precision Mfg & Assembly LLC .... D 937 252-3507
   Dayton (G-6515)
▼ Precision Polymer Casting .... F 440 205-1900
   Perry (G-12356)
Precision Polymers Inc .... E 614 322-9951
   Reynoldsburg (G-12772)
◆ Precison Thrmplstic Cmpnnts In .... D 419 227-4500
   Lima (G-9305)
Preferred Solutions Inc .... F 216 642-1200
   Independence (G-8682)
Preformed Line Products Co .... F 330 920-1718
   Peninsula (G-12341)
Premiere Mold and Machine Co .... G 330 874-3000
   Bolivar (G-1533)
◆ Premium Balloon ACC Inc .... E 330 239-4547
   Wadsworth (G-15054)
▲ Premix-Hadlock Composites LLC .... C 440 335-4301
   Conneaut (G-5930)
Prime Engineered Plastics Corp .... F 330 452-5110
   Canton (G-2201)
▲ Priority Custom Molding Inc .... F 937 431-8770
   Beavercreek (G-1058)
Pro-TEC Industries Inc .... G 440 937-4142
   Avon (G-783)
Professional Plastics Corp .... G 614 336-2498
   Dublin (G-6928)
Proficient Plastics Inc .... F 440 205-9700
   Mentor (G-10535)
Profile Plastics Inc .... G 330 452-7000
   Canton (G-2204)
Profusion Industries LLC .... G 800 938-2858
   Fairlawn (G-7446)
Progressive Molding Tech .... G 330 220-7030
   Medina (G-10366)
Progrssive Molding Bolivar Inc .... E 330 874-3000
   Bolivar (G-1534)
Promold Inc .... F 330 633-3532
   Tallmadge (G-14044)
▲ Proto Plastics Inc .... E 937 667-8416
   Tipp City (G-14150)
Proto-Mold Products Co Inc .... E 937 778-1959
   Piqua (G-12550)
Pvc Industries Inc .... E 518 877-8670
   Hamilton (G-8237)
▲ PVS Plastics Technology Corp .... E 937 233-4376
   Huber Heights (G-8579)
Pyramid Plastics Inc .... E 216 641-5904
   Cleveland (G-4601)
Quality Blow Molding Inc .... D 440 458-6550
   Elyria (G-7198)

Qube Corporation .... F 440 543-2393
   Chagrin Falls (G-2418)
Queen City Polymers Inc .... E 513 779-0990
   West Chester (G-15492)
R A M Plastics Co Inc .... E 330 549-3107
   North Lima (G-11812)
R and S Technologies Inc .... F 419 483-3691
   Bellevue (G-1232)
R L Industries Inc .... D 513 874-2800
   West Chester (G-15493)
Radar Love Co .... F 419 951-4750
   Findlay (G-7555)
◆ Radici Plastics Usa Inc .... E 330 336-7611
   Wadsworth (G-15059)
▲ Rage Corporation .... D 614 771-4771
   Hilliard (G-8435)
Rains Plastics Inc .... G 330 283-3768
   Wadsworth (G-15060)
Randy Lewis Inc .... F 330 784-0456
   Akron (G-296)
Raven Concealment Systems LLC .... E 440 508-9000
   North Ridgeville (G-11856)
▲ Reactive Resin Products Co .... E 419 666-6119
   Perrysburg (G-12423)
Recto Molded Products Inc .... D 513 871-5544
   Cincinnati (G-3328)
Reinalt-Thomas Corporation .... G 330 863-1936
   Carrollton (G-2314)
Remram Recovery LLC .... F 740 667-0092
   Tuppers Plains (G-14618)
◆ Replex Mirror Company .... E 740 397-5535
   Mount Vernon (G-11291)
Reserve Industries Inc .... G 440 871-2796
   Bay Village (G-966)
◆ Resinoid Engineering Corp .... D 740 928-6115
   Hebron (G-8359)
▼ Resource Mtl Hdlg & Recycl Inc .... E 440 834-0727
   Middlefield (G-10784)
Retterbush Fiberglass Corp .... E 937 778-1936
   Piqua (G-12552)
Revere Plas Systems Group LLC .... B 419 547-6918
   Clyde (G-4976)
Revere Plastics Systems LLC .... C 573 785-0871
   Clyde (G-4977)
Rexles Inc .... G 419 732-8188
   Port Clinton (G-12627)
◆ Rez-Tech Corporation .... E 330 673-4009
   Kent (G-8853)
◆ Rjf International Corporation .... A 330 668-2069
   Fairlawn (G-7447)
RMC USA Incorporation .... D 440 992-4906
   Jefferson (G-8758)
▲ Ro-MAI Industries Inc .... E 330 425-9090
   Twinsburg (G-14726)
◆ Roechling Indus Cleveland LP .... C 216 486-0100
   Cleveland (G-4645)
▲ Rohrer Corporation .... C 330 335-1541
   Wadsworth (G-15063)
Roppe Holding Company .... G 419 435-6601
   Fostoria (G-7652)
Ross Special Products Inc .... F 937 335-8406
   Troy (G-14605)
Roto Solutions Inc .... E 330 279-2424
   Holmesville (G-8551)
Rotosolutions Inc .... F 419 903-0800
   Ashland (G-611)
◆ Rowmark LLC .... D 419 425-8974
   Findlay (G-7557)
▲ Royal Plastics Inc .... C 440 352-1357
   Mentor (G-10548)
RPM Consumer Holding Company .... E 330 273-5090
   Medina (G-10371)

30 RUBBER AND MISCELLANEOUS PLASTIC PRODUCTS

Rsl LLC .... E 330 392-8900
  Warren (G-15203)
◆ RTS Companies (us) Inc .... E 440 275-3077
  Austinburg (G-749)
Rubbermaid Home Products .... D 330 733-7771
  Mogadore (G-11080)
Rubbermaid Incorporated .... A 330 733-7771
  Mogadore (G-11081)
Ryan Development Corporation .... F 937 587-2266
  Peebles (G-12331)
◆ S Toys Holdings LLC .... A 330 656-0440
  Streetsboro (G-13789)
▲ S&V Industries Inc .... E 330 666-1986
  Medina (G-10373)
Saint-Gobain Hycomp LLC .... C 440 234-2002
  Cleveland (G-4669)
Saint-Gobain Prfmce Plas Corp .... D 440 836-6900
  Solon (G-13418)
Samuel Son & Co (usa) Inc .... D 740 522-2500
  Heath (G-8331)
Sandusky Technologies LLC .... G 419 332-8484
  Fremont (G-7808)
Schmidt Progressive LLC .... E 513 934-2600
  Lebanon (G-9110)
Schnipke Engraving Co Inc .... C 419 453-3376
  Ottoville (G-12204)
◆ Scientific Plastics Ltd .... F 305 557-3737
  Ravenna (G-12733)
Scott Molders Incorporated .... D 330 673-5777
  Kent (G-8859)
▲ Seagate Plastics Company LLC .... E 419 878-5010
  Waterville (G-15252)
Shelly Fisher .... G 419 522-6696
  Mansfield (G-9717)
Shelves West LLC .... G 928 692-1449
  Findlay (G-7560)
Shiloh Industries Inc .... F 937 236-5100
  Dayton (G-6569)
Shirley KS LLC .... G 740 331-7934
  Zanesville (G-16563)
Shirley KS Storage Trays LLC .... G 740 868-8140
  Zanesville (G-16564)
Siebtechnik Tema Inc .... F 513 489-7811
  Cincinnati (G-3389)
◆ Silgan Dispensing Systems Corp .... D 330 425-4260
  Macedonia (G-9574)
Silgan Plastics LLC .... C 419 523-3737
  Ottawa (G-12191)
Silmarillion Partners Inc .... C 419 821-4700
  Alliance (G-424)
Silver Line Building Pdts LLC .... A 740 382-5595
  Marion (G-9881)
Skribs Tool and Die Inc .... E 440 951-7774
  Mentor (G-10555)
Slm LLC .... G 330 874-7131
  Bolivar (G-1537)
Solon .... F 440 498-1798
  Solon (G-13423)
Solutions In Polycarbonate LLC .... F 330 572-2860
  Medina (G-10378)
Sonoco Products Company .... E 614 759-8470
  Columbus (G-5778)
Sonoco Prtective Solutions Inc .... E 419 420-0029
  Findlay (G-7565)
Soterra LLC .... G 740 549-6072
  Delaware (G-6752)
Southeastern Container Inc .... D 419 352-6300
  Bowling Green (G-1589)
Spartech LLC .... C 937 548-1395
  Greenville (G-8059)
Spartech LLC .... D 419 399-4050
  Paulding (G-12320)

▲ Spectrum Plastics Corporation .... G 330 926-9766
  Cuyahoga Falls (G-6118)
SPI Liquidation Inc .... D
  Middlefield (G-10790)
Springfield Plastics Inc .... F 937 322-6071
  Springfield (G-13636)
Springseal Inc .... F 330 626-0673
  Ravenna (G-12735)
Stanek E F and Assoc Inc .... C 216 341-7700
  Macedonia (G-9580)
▲ Stanley Electric US Co Inc .... D 740 852-5200
  London (G-9394)
Starks Plastics LLC .... F 513 541-4591
  Cincinnati (G-3416)
Steere Enterprises Inc .... C 330 633-4926
  Tallmadge (G-14048)
▲ Steere Enterprises Inc .... D 330 633-4926
  Tallmadge (G-14049)
Step2 Company LLC .... B 419 938-6343
  Perrysville (G-12449)
◆ Step2 Company LLC .... B 866 429-5200
  Streetsboro (G-13794)
Sterilite Corporation .... B 330 830-2204
  Massillon (G-10148)
▲ Stewart Acquisition LLC .... E 330 963-0322
  Twinsburg (G-14738)
Stonyridge Inc .... F 937 845-9482
  New Carlisle (G-11426)
Stuchell Products LLC .... E 330 821-4299
  Alliance (G-428)
Style Crest Enterprises Inc .... D 419 355-8586
  Fremont (G-7811)
◆ Suburban Plastics Co .... B 847 741-4900
  Bolivar (G-1538)
Summit Polymers LLC .... F 330 506-7715
  Youngstown (G-16449)
Sun State Plastics Inc .... E 330 494-5220
  Canton (G-2238)
Superior Fibers Inc .... B 740 394-2491
  Shawnee (G-13177)
Superior Plastics Inc .... F 614 733-0307
  Plain City (G-12593)
◆ Superior Plastics Inc .... E 614 733-0307
  Plain City (G-12594)
▼ Swapil Inc .... D
  Columbus (G-5804)
Synergy Manufacturing LLC .... E 740 352-5933
  Piketon (G-12485)
Tahoma Enterprises Inc .... D 330 745-9016
  Barberton (G-897)
▼ Tahoma Rubber & Plastics Inc .... D 330 745-9016
  Barberton (G-898)
Tbk Holdings LLC .... G 313 584-0400
  Perrysburg (G-12429)
Team Amity Mlds Plstic Injctio .... G 937 667-7856
  Tipp City (G-14158)
Team Plastics Inc .... F 216 251-8270
  Cleveland (G-4769)
Tech-Way Industries Inc .... D 937 746-1004
  Franklin (G-7705)
Teijin Automotive Tech Inc .... B 419 396-1980
  Carey (G-2285)
Teijin Automotive Tech Inc .... C 440 945-4800
  Conneaut (G-5933)
Teijin Automotive Tech Inc .... B 419 257-2231
  North Baltimore (G-11700)
Teijin Automotive Tech Inc .... B 419 238-4628
  Van Wert (G-14928)
Tetra Mold & Tool Inc .... E 937 845-1651
  New Carlisle (G-11428)
Tez Tool & Fabrication Inc .... G 440 323-2300
  Elyria (G-7210)

Th Plastics Inc .... D 419 352-2770
  Bowling Green (G-1591)
Th Plastics Inc .... D 419 425-5825
  Findlay (G-7574)
The Crane Group Companies Limited ... E 614 754-3000
  Columbus (G-5821)
▲ The Hc Companies Inc .... E 440 632-3333
  Twinsburg (G-14743)
Thermoplastic Accessories Corp .... F 614 771-4777
  Hilliard (G-8448)
▲ Thermoprene Inc .... F 440 543-8660
  Cleveland (G-4793)
◆ Thogus Products Company .... D 440 933-8850
  Avon Lake (G-825)
▲ Thomas Tool & Mold Company .... F 614 890-4978
  Westerville (G-15722)
▲ Tigerpoly Manufacturing Inc .... B 614 871-0045
  Grove City (G-8122)
◆ Timbertech Limited .... B 937 655-8766
  Wilmington (G-16059)
Tjar Innovations LLC .... F 937 347-1999
  Xenia (G-16276)
Tmd Wek North LLC .... C 440 576-6940
  Jefferson (G-8761)
Toledo Molding & Die LLC .... C 419 354-6050
  Bowling Green (G-1592)
Toledo Molding & Die LLC .... C 419 692-6022
  Delphos (G-6772)
Toledo Molding & Die LLC .... B 419 443-9031
  Tiffin (G-14113)
Toledo Molding & Die LLC .... C 419 476-0581
  Toledo (G-14500)
◆ Toledo Molding & Die LLC .... D 419 470-3950
  Toledo (G-14499)
Toledo Pro Fiberglass Inc .... G 419 241-9390
  Toledo (G-14503)
▲ Tom Smith Industries Inc .... D 937 832-1555
  Englewood (G-7245)
Tooling Tech Holdings LLC .... F 937 295-3672
  Fort Loramie (G-7612)
Total Molding Solutions Inc .... G 517 424-5900
  Sylvania (G-14019)
Total Plastics Resources LLC .... G 440 891-1140
  Cleveland (G-4810)
Toth Mold & Die Inc .... F 440 232-8530
  Bedford (G-1158)
Treemen Industries Inc .... E 330 965-3777
  Boardman (G-1519)
Trellborg Sling Prfiles US Inc .... C 330 995-9725
  Aurora (G-737)
Tri-Craft Inc .... E 440 826-1050
  Cleveland (G-4822)
▲ Trifecta Tool and Engrg LLC .... G 937 291-0933
  Dayton (G-6633)
Trilogy Plastics Alliance Inc .... E 330 821-4700
  Alliance (G-434)
Trimold LLC .... B 740 474-7591
  Circleville (G-3559)
Trinity Specialty Compounding Inc ..... F 419 924-9090
  West Unity (G-15644)
Triple Diamond Plastics LLC .... D 419 533-0085
  Liberty Center (G-9204)
Truechoicepack Corp .... F 937 630-3832
  West Chester (G-15519)
Trusscore USA Inc .... E 888 418-4679
  Dayton (G-6637)
TS Tech Co Ltd .... G 740 420-5617
  Circleville (G-3560)
Tsp Inc .... E 513 732-8900
  Batavia (G-955)
U S Development Corp .... D 330 673-6900
  Kent (G-8879)

Employee Codes: A=Over 500 employees, B=251-500
C=101-250, D=51-100, E=20-50, F=10-19, G=1-9

30 RUBBER AND MISCELLANEOUS PLASTIC PRODUCTS

U S Molding Machinery Co Inc............ E 440 918-1701
  Willoughby *(G-16012)*
Udecx LLC... G 877 698-3329
  Tipp City *(G-14163)*
Ultra Tech International Inc.................. G 440 974-8999
  Mentor *(G-10587)*
Ultratech Polymers Inc......................... F 330 945-9410
  Cuyahoga Falls *(G-6127)*
▲ United Security Seals Inc.................. E 614 443-7633
  Columbus *(G-5843)*
United States Plastic Corp.................... D 419 228-2242
  Lima *(G-9299)*
▲ Universal Polymer & Rubber Ltd...... C 440 632-1691
  Middlefield *(G-10795)*
UPL International Inc............................. E 330 433-2860
  North Canton *(G-11773)*
▲ US Coexcell Inc................................. E 419 897-9110
  Maumee *(G-10243)*
Valley Plastics Company Inc................. E 419 666-2349
  Toledo *(G-14518)*
Venture Packaging Inc........................... D 419 465-2534
  Monroeville *(G-11127)*
Venture Packaging Midwest Inc............ E 419 465-2534
  Monroeville *(G-11128)*
◆ Venture Plastics Inc........................... C 330 872-5774
  Newton Falls *(G-11660)*
Vicas Manufacturing Co Inc.................. E 513 791-7741
  Cincinnati *(G-3498)*
Vinyl Design Corporation....................... E 419 283-4009
  Holland *(G-8536)*
Vinyl Profiles Acquisition LLC............... E 330 538-0660
  North Jackson *(G-11794)*
Vinylume Products Inc........................... E 330 799-2000
  Youngstown *(G-16472)*
Vision Color LLC.................................. G 419 924-9450
  West Unity *(G-15645)*
Vnl Molding Ltd.................................... G 330 220-5951
  Brunswick *(G-1799)*
Vts Co Ltd.. G 419 273-4010
  Forest *(G-7594)*
Walleye Investments Ltd...................... G 440 564-7210
  Solon *(G-13446)*
▼ Warwick Products Company............. E 216 334-1200
  Cleveland *(G-4894)*
Wasca LLC... E 937 723-9031
  Dayton *(G-6647)*
Waugs Inc.. G 440 315-4851
  Ashland *(G-620)*
Wch Molding LLC................................. E 740 335-6320
  Wshngtn Ct Hs *(G-16244)*
◆ Weatherchem Corporation................ D 330 425-4206
  Twinsburg *(G-14754)*
West & Barker Inc............................... E 330 652-9923
  Niles *(G-11691)*
Westar Plastics Llc............................... G 419 636-1333
  Bryan *(G-1845)*
▲ Westlake Dimex LLC........................ C 740 374-3100
  Marietta *(G-9844)*
WI Inc.. C 440 576-6940
  Akron *(G-375)*
▲ Windsor Mold USA Inc..................... F 419 483-0653
  Bellevue *(G-1240)*
Wisco Products Incorporated................ E 937 228-2101
  Dayton *(G-6658)*
Woodbridge Englewood Inc.................. E 937 540-9889
  Englewood *(G-7249)*
▲ World Class Plastics Inc.................... D 937 843-3003
  Russells Point *(G-12880)*
▲ World Resource Solutons Corp......... G 614 733-3737
  Plain City *(G-12603)*
▲ Worthignton Products Inc.................. G 330 452-7400
  East Canton *(G-6982)*

Wyatt Industries LLC............................. G 330 954-1790
  Streetsboro *(G-13799)*
◆ Xaloy LLC... C 330 726-4000
  Austintown *(G-757)*
Y City Recycling LLC............................ F 740 452-2500
  Zanesville *(G-16572)*
▲ Yachiyo of America Inc..................... C 614 876-3220
  Columbus *(G-5889)*
Yanfeng US Auto Intr Systems I........... G 419 636-4211
  Bryan *(G-1846)*
Yanfeng US Auto Intr Systems I........... D 419 633-1873
  Bryan *(G-1847)*
▼ Zehrco-Giancola Composites Inc...... C 440 994-6317
  Ashtabula *(G-666)*

31 LEATHER AND LEATHER PRODUCTS

3111 Leather tanning and finishing

Bernard Engraving Corp....................... F 419 478-5610
  Toledo *(G-14212)*
Fount LLC.. G 216 855-8751
  Cleveland *(G-4087)*
▲ Leather Resource of America Inc..... E 440 262-5761
  Conneaut *(G-5923)*
Premier Tanning & Nutrition................. G 419 342-6259
  Shelby *(G-13198)*

3131 Footwear cut stock

Classic Countertops LLC...................... G 330 882-4220
  Akron *(G-112)*
▲ Remington Products Company......... D 330 335-1571
  Upper Arlington *(G-14802)*

3142 House slippers

▲ Principle Business Entps Inc............. C 419 352-1551
  Bowling Green *(G-1586)*
R G Barry Corporation.......................... F 212 244-3145
  Pickerington *(G-12468)*

3143 Men's footwear, except athletic

▲ Acor Orthopaedic LLC...................... E 216 662-4500
  Cleveland *(G-3594)*
Careismatic Brands LLC....................... G 561 843-8727
  Groveport *(G-8135)*
Georgia-Boot Inc.................................. D 740 753-1951
  Nelsonville *(G-11356)*
Rbr Enterprises LLC............................. F 866 437-9327
  Brecksville *(G-1630)*
Rocky Brands Inc................................. B 740 753-9100
  Nelsonville *(G-11359)*

3144 Women's footwear, except athletic

▲ Acor Orthopaedic LLC...................... E 216 662-4500
  Cleveland *(G-3594)*
Careismatic Brands LLC....................... G 561 843-8727
  Groveport *(G-8135)*
FP Holdco Inc....................................... G 614 729-7205
  Pickerington *(G-12462)*
Georgia-Boot Inc.................................. D 740 753-1951
  Nelsonville *(G-11356)*
Rocky Brands Inc................................. B 740 753-9100
  Nelsonville *(G-11359)*

3151 Leather gloves and mittens

▲ Totes Isotoner Holdings Corp........... C 513 682-8200
  West Chester *(G-15599)*

3161 Luggage

Cleveland Canvas Goods Mfg Co........ E 216 361-4567
  Cleveland *(G-3835)*

▲ Clipper Products Inc......................... G 513 688-7300
  Cincinnati *(G-2555)*
Eagle Creek Inc................................... D 513 385-4442
  Cincinnati *(G-2852)*
▲ Kam Manufacturing Inc.................... C 419 238-6037
  Van Wert *(G-14919)*
L M Engineering Inc............................. E 330 270-2400
  Austintown *(G-752)*
Made Men Circle LLC.......................... G 216 501-0414
  Cleveland Heights *(G-4940)*
Northhill T-Shirt Print Dsign.................. G 330 208-0338
  Akron *(G-268)*
Plastic Forming Company Inc.............. E 330 830-5167
  Massillon *(G-10134)*
Professional Case Inc.......................... F 513 682-2520
  West Chester *(G-15578)*
T & CS Repairs & Retail LLC............... E 704 964-7325
  Akron *(G-344)*
Travelers Custom Case Inc.................. F 216 621-8447
  Mentor *(G-10382)*
▲ Weaver Leather LLC........................ D 330 674-7548
  Millersburg *(G-11007)*
Whitman Corporation........................... G 513 541-3223
  Okeana *(G-12069)*

3171 Women's handbags and purses

▲ Hugo Bosca Company Inc............... F 937 323-5523
  Springfield *(G-13581)*
Judith Leiber LLC................................ E 614 449-4217
  Columbus *(G-5501)*
Ravenworks Deer Skin......................... G 937 354-5151
  Mount Victory *(G-11302)*

3172 Personal leather goods, nec

Bison Leather Co................................. G 419 517-1737
  Toledo *(G-14213)*
Down Home... G 740 393-1186
  Mount Vernon *(G-11271)*
▲ Hamilton Manufacturing Corp.......... E 419 867-4858
  Holland *(G-8511)*
▲ Hugo Bosca Company Inc............... F 937 323-5523
  Springfield *(G-13581)*
Ravenworks Deer Skin......................... G 937 354-5151
  Mount Victory *(G-11302)*
Total Education Solutions Inc.............. D 330 668-4041
  Fairlawn *(G-7453)*
▲ Weaver Leather LLC........................ D 330 674-7548
  Millersburg *(G-11007)*
Williams Leather Products Inc............. G 740 223-1604
  Marion *(G-9890)*

3199 Leather goods, nec

Cornerstone Brands Inc....................... G 866 668-5962
  West Chester *(G-15406)*
Diy Holster LLC.................................... G 419 921-2168
  Elyria *(G-7132)*
▲ Holmes Wheel Shop Inc.................. E 330 279-2891
  Holmesville *(G-8548)*
▲ Leather Resource of America Inc..... E 440 262-5761
  Conneaut *(G-5923)*
LLC Bowman Leather........................... G 330 893-1954
  Millersburg *(G-10976)*
Rantek Products LLC........................... G 419 485-2421
  Montpelier *(G-11141)*
River City Leather Inc.......................... G 740 645-5044
  Gallipolis *(G-7899)*
Sustainment Actions LLC.................... F 330 805-3468
  Columbus *(G-5803)*
◆ Tarahill Inc.. F 706 864-0808
  Columbus *(G-5808)*
▲ Weaver Leather LLC........................ D 330 674-7548
  Millersburg *(G-11007)*

SIC SECTION

32 STONE, CLAY, GLASS, AND CONCRETE PRODUCTS

Whitman Corporation............................ G 513 541-3223
   Okeana *(G-12069)*

32 STONE, CLAY, GLASS, AND CONCRETE PRODUCTS

3211 Flat glass

Cardinal CT Company............................ E 740 892-2324
   Utica *(G-14857)*

Cardinal Glass Industries Inc................ E 740 892-2324
   Utica *(G-14858)*

Clearvue Insulating Glass Co.............. F 216 651-1140
   Cleveland *(G-3828)*

▲ Continental GL Sls & Inv Group........ E 614 679-1201
   Powell *(G-12669)*

Custom Glass Solutions LLC............... E 248 340-1800
   Worthington *(G-16192)*

◆ Glasstech Inc....................................... C 419 661-9500
   Perrysburg *(G-12386)*

Guardian Fabrication LLC..................... C 419 855-7706
   Millbury *(G-10933)*

Imaging Sciences LLC.......................... G 440 975-9640
   Willoughby *(G-15931)*

▲ K A Ventures Inc................................ F 513 860-3340
   West Chester *(G-15451)*

Kaaa/Hamilton Enterprises Inc............. E 513 874-5874
   Fairfield *(G-7377)*

Knight Industries Corp........................... E 419 478-8550
   Toledo *(G-14349)*

Machined Glass Specialist Inc............. F 937 743-6166
   Springboro *(G-13509)*

◆ Newell Holdings Delaware Inc........... D 740 681-6461
   Lancaster *(G-9028)*

Niles Mirror & Glass Inc........................ E 330 652-6277
   Niles *(G-11679)*

Nsg Glass North America Inc.............. C 734 755-5816
   Luckey *(G-9527)*

Nsg Glass North America Inc.............. E 419 247-4800
   Toledo *(G-14400)*

◆ Pilkington Holdings Inc...................... B
   Toledo *(G-14435)*

Pilkington North America Inc............... C 800 547-9280
   Northwood *(G-11927)*

Pilkington North America Inc............... B 419 247-3211
   Rossford *(G-12869)*

Pilkington North America Inc............... C 419 247-3731
   Urbancrest *(G-14854)*

◆ Pilkington North America Inc............ C 419 247-3731
   Toledo *(G-14436)*

Rsl LLC... E 330 392-8900
   Warren *(G-15203)*

S R Door Inc.. D 740 927-3558
   Hebron *(G-8360)*

Schodorf Truck Body & Eqp Co........... E 614 228-6793
   Columbus *(G-5751)*

Sonalysts Inc... E 937 429-9711
   Beavercreek *(G-1064)*

Taylor Products Inc............................... E 419 263-2313
   Payne *(G-12323)*

Therm-All Inc... E 440 779-9494
   Westlake *(G-15796)*

Trulite GL Alum Solutions LLC.............. D 740 929-2443
   Hebron *(G-8368)*

Vinylume Products Inc.......................... E 330 799-2000
   Youngstown *(G-16472)*

Wt Acquisition Company Ltd................ E 513 577-7980
   Cincinnati *(G-3528)*

3221 Glass containers

Anchor Glass Container Corp............... D 740 452-2743
   Zanesville *(G-16500)*

◆ Anchor Hocking LLC.......................... A 740 687-2500
   Columbus *(G-5139)*

Bprex Plastic Packaging Inc................. F 419 247-5000
   Toledo *(G-14218)*

Chantilly Development Corp................. E 419 243-8109
   Toledo *(G-14233)*

▲ Envases Media Inc............................. E 419 636-5461
   Bryan *(G-1817)*

◆ Ghp II LLC... C 740 687-2500
   Lancaster *(G-9017)*

O-I Glass Inc.. C 567 336-5000
   Perrysburg *(G-12405)*

Oi California Containers Inc................. F 567 336-5000
   Perrysburg *(G-12410)*

Oi Castalia STS Inc............................... E 419 247-5000
   Toledo *(G-14412)*

Owens-Brockway Glass Cont Inc......... E 740 455-4516
   Zanesville *(G-16551)*

◆ Owens-Brockway Glass Cont Inc..... C 567 336-8449
   Perrysburg *(G-12414)*

▲ Owens-Illinois General Inc................ A 567 336-5000
   Perrysburg *(G-12415)*

◆ Owens-Illinois Group Inc................... D 567 336-5000
   Perrysburg *(G-12416)*

Owens-Illinois Inc.................................. A 567 336-5000
   Perrysburg *(G-12417)*

◆ Paddock Enterprises LLC.................. C 567 336-5000
   Perrysburg *(G-12418)*

Pyromatics Corp.................................... F 440 352-3500
   Mentor *(G-10538)*

Tiama Americas Inc............................... E 269 274-3107
   Maumee *(G-10240)*

Waterco of The Central States............. E 937 294-0375
   Fairfield *(G-7426)*

3229 Pressed and blown glass, nec

All State GL Block Fctry Inc.................. G 440 205-8410
   Mentor *(G-10411)*

◆ American De Rosa Lamparts LLC.... D
   Cuyahoga Falls *(G-6063)*

◆ Anchor Hocking LLC.......................... A 740 687-2500
   Columbus *(G-5139)*

▼ Anchor Hocking Consmr GL Corp.... G 740 653-2527
   Lancaster *(G-8987)*

Anchor Hocking Corporation................ F 614 633-4247
   Columbus *(G-5140)*

Anchor Hocking Glass Corp PA........... G 740 681-6275
   Lancaster *(G-8989)*

Anderson Glass Co Inc......................... E 614 476-4877
   Columbus *(G-5145)*

Blockamerica Corporation.................... G 614 274-0700
   Columbus *(G-5201)*

Brubaker Metalcrafts Inc....................... G 937 456-5834
   Eaton *(G-7055)*

◆ Cincinnati Gasket Pkg Mfg Inc......... E 513 761-3458
   Cincinnati *(G-2749)*

Current Elec & Enrgy Solutions........... G 513 575-4600
   Loveland *(G-9479)*

Dal-Little Fabricating Inc...................... G 216 883-3323
   Cleveland *(G-3938)*

G L Pierce Inc.. G 513 772-7202
   Cincinnati *(G-2927)*

General Electric Company..................... E 740 385-2114
   Logan *(G-9363)*

General Electric Company..................... E 330 373-1400
   Warren *(G-15172)*

◆ Ghp II LLC... C 740 687-2500
   Lancaster *(G-9017)*

Glass Block Headquarters Inc.............. G 216 941-5470
   Cleveland *(G-4126)*

◆ Glasstech Inc..................................... C 419 661-9500
   Perrysburg *(G-12386)*

Hilltop Glass & Mirror LLC.................... G 513 931-3688
   Cincinnati *(G-3002)*

Industrial Fiberglass Spc Inc................ E 937 222-9000
   Dayton *(G-6382)*

Integris Composites Inc........................ D 740 928-0326
   Hebron *(G-8345)*

Interntnal Auto Cmpnnts Group........... A 419 433-5653
   Wauseon *(G-15265)*

Jack Pine Studio LLC........................... G 740 332-2223
   Laurelville *(G-9055)*

▲ John Krizay Inc.................................. E 330 332-5607
   Salem *(G-13006)*

Johns Manville Corporation.................. D 419 878-8111
   Waterville *(G-15246)*

Katies Light House LLC....................... F 419 645-5451
   Cridersville *(G-6042)*

Knoble Glass & Metal Inc..................... G 513 753-1246
   Cincinnati *(G-3084)*

Libbey Glass LLC.................................. C 419 727-2211
   Toledo *(G-14365)*

◆ Libbey Glass LLC............................... C 419 325-2100
   Toledo *(G-14364)*

▼ Libbey Inc... C 419 325-2100
   Toledo *(G-14366)*

▲ M R Echo-E Inc................................. F 937 322-4972
   Springfield *(G-13597)*

◆ Mfg Composite Systems Company.. B 440 997-5851
   Ashtabula *(G-648)*

Midwest Composites LLC..................... F 419 738-2431
   Wapakoneta *(G-15123)*

Modern China Company Inc................ E 330 938-6104
   Sebring *(G-13123)*

▲ Mosser Glass Inc.............................. E 740 439-1827
   Cambridge *(G-1944)*

Nextgen Fiber Optics LLC.................... G 513 549-4691
   Cincinnati *(G-3194)*

Owens Corning Ht Inc.......................... E 419 248-8000
   Toledo *(G-14422)*

◆ Owens Corning Sales LLC................ A 419 248-8000
   Toledo *(G-14424)*

Pittsburg Corning Corp Di.................... G 724 327-6100
   Toledo *(G-14438)*

◆ Pittsburgh Corning LLC.................... B 724 327-6100
   Toledo *(G-14439)*

Plasticraft Usa LLC............................... G 513 761-2999
   Cincinnati *(G-3260)*

Rocket Ventures LLC............................ G 419 530-6083
   Toledo *(G-14457)*

Scottrods LLC....................................... G 419 499-2705
   Monroeville *(G-11125)*

Sem-Com Company Inc........................ G 419 537-8813
   Toledo *(G-14466)*

Techneglas Inc...................................... E 419 873-2000
   Perrysburg *(G-12431)*

Technical Glass Products Inc............... F 425 396-8420
   Perrysburg *(G-12433)*

▲ Technical Glass Products Inc.......... F 440 639-6399
   Painesville *(G-12267)*

Variety Glass Inc................................... F 740 432-3643
   Cambridge *(G-1959)*

Wilson Optical Labs Inc........................ E 440 357-7000
   Mentor *(G-10595)*

3231 Products of purchased glass

A & B Iron & Metal Co Inc.................... G 937 228-1561
   Dayton *(G-6178)*

A Service Glass Inc.............................. E 937 426-4920
   Beavercreek *(G-1038)*

Aag Glass LLC...................................... E 513 286-8268
   Batavia *(G-907)*

Adria Scientific GL Works Co............... G 440 474-6691
   Geneva *(G-7929)*

Employee Codes: A=Over 500 employees, B=251-500
C=101-250, D=51-100, E=20-50, F=10-19, G=1-9

32 STONE, CLAY, GLASS, AND CONCRETE PRODUCTS

▲ Afg Industries Inc................................ D 614 322-4580
  Grove City *(G-8074)*

Americana Glass Co Inc........................ F 330 938-6135
  Sebring *(G-13116)*

◆ Amerihua Intl Entps Inc....................... G 740 549-0300
  Lewis Center *(G-9148)*

◆ Anchi Inc.. A 740 653-2527
  Lancaster *(G-8986)*

Anderson Glass Co Inc.......................... E 614 476-4877
  Columbus *(G-5145)*

▲ Atc Lighting & Plastics Inc.................. C 440 466-7670
  Andover *(G-485)*

◆ Auto Temp Inc...................................C 513 732-6969
  Batavia *(G-909)*

◆ Basco Manufacturing Company...........C 513 573-1900
  Mason *(G-9957)*

Beach Manufacturing Co....................... C 937 882-6372
  Donnelsville *(G-6806)*

Bruening Glass Works Inc..................... G 440 333-4768
  Cleveland *(G-3705)*

Cdh Liquidation Inc............................... E 419 720-4096
  Toledo *(G-14229)*

Champion Window Co of Toledo............ E 419 841-0154
  Perrysburg *(G-12370)*

Chantilly Development Corp................... E 419 243-8109
  Toledo *(G-14233)*

Custom Glass Solutions Upper S........... B 419 294-4921
  Upper Sandusky *(G-14805)*

▲ East Palestine China Dctg LLC........... F 330 426-9600
  East Palestine *(G-7005)*

▲ Enclosure Suppliers LLC.................... E 513 782-3900
  Cincinnati *(G-2868)*

▲ Environmental Sampling Sup Inc....... D 330 497-9396
  North Canton *(G-11725)*

▲ Franklin Art Glass Studios................. E 614 221-2972
  Columbus *(G-5385)*

Fuyao Glass America Inc...................... F 937 496-5777
  Dayton *(G-6343)*

General Electric Company..................... E 740 385-2114
  Logan *(G-9363)*

Ghp II LLC.. F 740 681-6825
  Lancaster *(G-9018)*

Glass Surface Systems Inc................... D 330 745-8500
  Barberton *(G-870)*

◆ Glasstech Inc....................................C 419 661-9500
  Perrysburg *(G-12386)*

Great Day Improvements LLC............... B 267 223-1289
  Macedonia *(G-9555)*

Guardian Fabrication LLC..................... C 419 855-7706
  Millbury *(G-10933)*

Intigral Inc... G 440 439-0980
  Youngstown *(G-16380)*

▲ Intigral Inc... C 440 439-0980
  Walton Hills *(G-15099)*

Jafe Decorating Inc............................... C 937 547-1888
  Greenville *(G-8047)*

▲ K A Ventures Inc................................ F 513 860-3340
  West Chester *(G-15451)*

Kimmatt Corp.. G 937 228-3811
  West Alexandria *(G-15342)*

◆ Libbey Glass LLC..............................C 419 325-2100
  Toledo *(G-14364)*

Macpherson Engineering Inc................. F 440 243-6565
  Warren *(G-15187)*

Middlefield Glass Incorporated.............. F 440 632-5699
  Middlefield *(G-10765)*

Miller-Holzwarth Inc............................... D 330 342-7224
  Salem *(G-13017)*

▲ North Central Insulation Inc.............. F 419 886-2030
  Bellville *(G-1246)*

Ohio Mirror Technologies Inc................ F 419 399-5903
  Paulding *(G-12318)*

Oldcastle Buildingenvelope Inc.............. D 800 537-4064
  Perrysburg *(G-12411)*

Patriot Armored Systems LLC............... F 413 637-1060
  West Chester *(G-15474)*

▲ Pei Liquidation Company................... C 330 467-4267
  Macedonia *(G-9564)*

Pilkington North America Inc................ B 419 247-3211
  Rossford *(G-12869)*

Potters Industries LLC.......................... D 216 621-0840
  Cleveland *(G-4566)*

Pyromatics Corp.................................... F 440 352-3500
  Mentor *(G-10538)*

Ransome AC LLC.................................. G 234 205-6907
  Akron *(G-297)*

Rumpke Transportation Co LLC............. B 513 242-4600
  Cincinnati *(G-3356)*

◆ Safelite Group Inc.............................A 614 210-9000
  Columbus *(G-5740)*

Scs Construction Services Inc.............. E 513 929-0260
  Cincinnati *(G-3371)*

Sem-Com Company Inc........................ G 419 537-8813
  Toledo *(G-14466)*

▲ Sims Bros Inc.................................... D 740 387-9041
  Marion *(G-9883)*

Solon Glass Center Inc......................... F 440 248-5018
  Cleveland *(G-4713)*

Stoner Glass Act Studio LLC................. G 330 360-3294
  Newton Falls *(G-11658)*

Strategic Materials Inc.......................... G 740 349-9523
  Newark *(G-11607)*

Studio Arts and Glass Inc..................... F 330 494-9779
  Canton *(G-2237)*

Taylor Products Inc............................... E 419 263-2313
  Payne *(G-12322)*

Taylor Products Inc............................... E 419 263-2313
  Payne *(G-12323)*

Technicolor Usa Inc.............................. A 614 474-8821
  Circleville *(G-3557)*

Trulite GL Alum Solutions LLC.............. D 740 929-2443
  Hebron *(G-8368)*

Whitney Stained GL Studio Inc............. G 216 348-1616
  Cleveland *(G-4907)*

XS Smith Inc.. E 252 940-5060
  Cincinnati *(G-3533)*

Zomir LLC.. G 513 771-1516
  Cincinnati *(G-3537)*

3241 Cement, hydraulic

A & A Quality Paving & Cem LLC.......... G 440 886-9595
  Cleveland *(G-3574)*

Fairborn Cement Company LLC............. C 937 879-8393
  Xenia *(G-16261)*

Hartline Products Coinc........................ G 216 851-7189
  Cleveland *(G-4171)*

Holcim (us) Inc..................................... G 216 781-9330
  Cleveland *(G-4194)*

Holcim (us) Inc..................................... C 419 399-4861
  Paulding *(G-12314)*

Holcim Quarries Ny Inc........................ E 216 566-0545
  Cleveland *(G-4195)*

Huron Cement Products Company........ E 419 433-4161
  Huron *(G-8633)*

▲ Kona Blackbird Inc............................ E 440 285-3189
  Chardon *(G-2455)*

Lafarge Holcim...................................... G 419 798-4866
  Lakeside Marblehead *(G-8960)*

Lehigh Portland Cement....................... G 513 769-3666
  Cincinnati *(G-3100)*

Lone Star Industries Inc....................... F 513 467-0430
  Cincinnati *(G-3110)*

Quikrete Companies LLC...................... E 614 885-4406
  Columbus *(G-5704)*

Quikrete Companies LLC...................... E 330 296-6080
  Ravenna *(G-12729)*

Quikrete Companies LLC...................... F 419 241-1148
  Toledo *(G-14445)*

Skyway Cement Company LLC............. E 513 478-0034
  Fairfield *(G-7409)*

Wallseye Concrete Corp........................ F 440 235-1800
  Cleveland *(G-4892)*

3251 Brick and structural clay tile

Afc Company... F 330 533-5581
  Canfield *(G-1997)*

Armstrong World Industries Inc............. E 614 771-9307
  Hilliard *(G-8399)*

Belden Brick Company LLC.................. E 330 456-0031
  Sugarcreek *(G-13919)*

Belden Brick Company LLC.................. E 330 265-2030
  Sugarcreek *(G-13920)*

Bowerston Shale Company................... C 740 763-3921
  Newark *(G-11567)*

Bowerston Shale Company................... E 740 269-2921
  Bowerston *(G-1544)*

Glen-Gery Corporation.......................... D 419 845-3321
  Caledonia *(G-1915)*

Glen-Gery Corporation.......................... F 419 468-4890
  Galion *(G-7879)*

Glen-Gery Corporation.......................... E 419 468-5002
  Iberia *(G-8648)*

Kepcor Inc.. F 330 868-6434
  Minerva *(G-11032)*

▲ Kona Blackbird Inc............................ E 440 285-3189
  Chardon *(G-2455)*

LBC Clay Co LLC................................. G 330 674-0674
  Millersburg *(G-10972)*

Minteq International Inc....................... E 330 343-8821
  Dover *(G-6836)*

Nutro Inc.. E 440 572-3800
  Strongsville *(G-13861)*

Resco Products Inc.............................. G 740 682-7794
  Oak Hill *(G-12024)*

Stebbins Engineering & Mfg Co............ F 740 922-3012
  Uhrichsville *(G-14770)*

◆ The Belden Brick Company LLC........E 330 456-0031
  Canton *(G-2243)*

Whitacre Greer Company...................... E 330 823-1610
  Alliance *(G-436)*

3253 Ceramic wall and floor tile

Dai Ceramics LLC................................ D 440 946-6964
  Willoughby *(G-15906)*

Kepcor Inc.. F 330 868-6434
  Minerva *(G-11032)*

M S International Inc........................... G 513 712-5300
  West Chester *(G-15460)*

Mohawk Industries Inc......................... F 800 837-3812
  Grove City *(G-8108)*

▲ Ohio Tile & Marble Co....................... E 513 541-4211
  Cincinnati *(G-3217)*

PCC Ceramic Group 1.......................... G 440 516-3672
  Wickliffe *(G-15847)*

Stebbins Engineering & Mfg Co............ F 740 922-3012
  Uhrichsville *(G-14770)*

◆ Studio Vertu Inc................................G 513 241-9038
  Cincinnati *(G-3426)*

Summitville Tiles Inc............................ E 330 868-6771
  Minerva *(G-11041)*

▲ Summitville Tiles Inc......................... E 330 223-1511
  Summitville *(G-13950)*

Tarkett USA Inc.................................... B 440 543-8916
  Chagrin Falls *(G-2429)*

Tarkett USA Inc.................................... C 877 827-5388
  Solon *(G-13434)*

SIC SECTION

32 STONE, CLAY, GLASS, AND CONCRETE PRODUCTS

Wccv Floor Coverings LLC......................F..... 330 688-0114
  Peninsula *(G-12344)*

3255 Clay refractories

Afc Company...F..... 330 533-5581
  Canfield *(G-1997)*
Bowerston Shale Company......................E..... 740 269-2921
  Bowerston *(G-1544)*
Ethima Inc...D..... 419 626-4912
  Sandusky *(G-13057)*
Ferro Corp..G..... 800 245-8225
  Crooksville *(G-6046)*
Glen-Gery Corporation............................D..... 419 845-3321
  Caledonia *(G-1915)*
Glen-Gery Corporation............................E..... 419 468-5002
  Iberia *(G-8648)*
I Cerco Inc...C..... 740 982-2050
  Crooksville *(G-6047)*
◆ Industrial Ceramic Products Inc..........D..... 937 642-3897
  Marysville *(G-9921)*
Lakeway Mfg Inc.......................................E..... 419 433-3030
  Huron *(G-8637)*
Magneco/Metrel Inc.................................D..... 330 426-9468
  Negley *(G-11354)*
Minteq International Inc..........................E..... 330 343-8821
  Dover *(G-6836)*
Nock and Son Company..........................F..... 740 682-7741
  Oak Hill *(G-12022)*
Resco Products Inc..................................G..... 330 488-1226
  East Canton *(G-6981)*
Resco Products Inc..................................G..... 740 682-7794
  Oak Hill *(G-12024)*
▲ Selas Heat Technology Co LLC............E..... 800 523-6500
  Streetsboro *(G-13792)*
Seven Lakeway Refractories LLC.........F..... 419 433-3030
  Huron *(G-8645)*
Specialty Ceramics Inc...........................D..... 330 482-0800
  Columbiana *(G-5051)*
Stebbins Engineering & Mfg Co.............F..... 740 922-3012
  Uhrichsville *(G-14770)*
Summitville Tiles Inc...............................E..... 330 868-6463
  Minerva *(G-11040)*
◆ United Refractories Inc........................E..... 330 372-3716
  Warren *(G-15215)*
Veitsch-Radex America LLC..................D..... 717 793-7122
  Ashtabula *(G-663)*
◆ Wahl Refractory Solutions LLC.........D..... 419 334-2658
  Fremont *(G-7819)*
Whitacre Greer Company........................E..... 330 823-1610
  Alliance *(G-436)*

3259 Structural clay products, nec

Baughman Tile Company........................D..... 800 837-3160
  Paulding *(G-12311)*
Clay Logan Products Company..............D..... 740 385-2184
  Logan *(G-9361)*
Haviland Drainage Products Co.............F..... 800 860-6294
  Haviland *(G-8312)*
Terreal North America LLC....................C..... 888 582-9052
  New Lexington *(G-11459)*

3261 Vitreous plumbing fixtures

Accent Manufacturing Inc......................F..... 330 724-7704
  Norton *(G-11936)*
As America Inc..E..... 419 522-4211
  Mansfield *(G-9626)*
As America Inc..F..... 330 332-9954
  Salem *(G-12977)*
Bridgits Bath LLC....................................G..... 937 259-1960
  Dayton *(G-6236)*
◆ Crane Plumbing LLC...............................A..... 419 522-4211
  Mansfield *(G-9642)*

East Woodworking Company.................G..... 216 791-5950
  Cleveland *(G-3990)*
◆ Mansfield Plumbing Pdts LLC..............A..... 419 938-5211
  Perrysville *(G-12447)*
Watersource LLC.....................................G..... 419 747-9552
  Mansfield *(G-9731)*

3262 Vitreous china table and kitchenware

Americana Glass Co Inc.........................F..... 330 938-6135
  Sebring *(G-13116)*
Libbey Glass LLC....................................C..... 419 727-2211
  Toledo *(G-14365)*
▼ Libbey Inc...C..... 419 325-2100
  Toledo *(G-14366)*
◆ The China Hall Company......................C..... 330 385-2900
  East Liverpool *(G-7001)*
▲ Warrior Imports Inc..............................E..... 954 935-5536
  Youngstown *(G-16474)*

3263 Semivitreous table and kitchenware

Anchor Hocking Glass Company............G..... 740 681-6025
  Lancaster *(G-8988)*
Modern China Company Inc..................E..... 330 938-6104
  Sebring *(G-13123)*

3264 Porcelain electrical supplies

▲ Akron Porcelain & Plastics Co............C..... 330 745-2159
  Akron *(G-41)*
CAM-Lem Inc..G..... 216 391-7750
  Cleveland *(G-3783)*
▲ Channel Products Inc............................D..... 440 423-0113
  Solon *(G-13328)*
▲ Electrodyne Company Inc....................F..... 513 732-2822
  Batavia *(G-921)*
Ethima Inc...D..... 419 626-4912
  Sandusky *(G-13057)*
Fram Group Operations LLC..................E..... 419 436-5827
  Fostoria *(G-7637)*
▲ Materion Brush Inc................................D..... 216 486-4200
  Mayfield Heights *(G-10250)*
▲ Newell - Psn LLC....................................G..... 304 387-2700
  Columbiana *(G-5046)*
Petro Ware Inc...E..... 740 982-1302
  Crooksville *(G-6049)*
Vibrantz Corporation.................................C..... 216 875-6213
  Cleveland *(G-4868)*
Weldco Inc..E..... 513 744-9353
  Cincinnati *(G-3514)*

3269 Pottery products, nec

All Fired Up Pnt Your Own Pot................G..... 330 865-5858
  Copley *(G-5943)*
Beaumont Bros Stoneware Inc..............E..... 740 982-0055
  Crooksville *(G-6044)*
Benzle Porcelain Company.....................G..... 614 876-2159
  Hilliard *(G-8404)*
Bodycote Imt Inc......................................F..... 740 852-5000
  London *(G-9382)*
Brittany Stamping LLC...........................A..... 216 267-0850
  Cleveland *(G-3760)*
Carruth Studio Inc...................................F..... 419 878-3060
  Waterville *(G-15240)*
▲ Clay Burley Products Co.....................E..... 740 452-3633
  Roseville *(G-12859)*
◆ E R Advanced Ceramics Inc...............E..... 330 426-9433
  East Palestine *(G-7004)*
▲ Ei Ceramics..G..... 513 881-2000
  Hamilton *(G-8205)*
Javanation...F..... 419 584-1705
  Celina *(G-2338)*
▼ Orton Edward Jr Crmic Fndation........E..... 614 895-2663
  Westerville *(G-15672)*

Strictly Stitchery Inc................................F..... 440 543-7128
  Cleveland *(G-4739)*
W C Bunting Co Inc..................................F..... 330 385-2050
  East Liverpool *(G-7002)*
Yellow Springs Pottery LLC...................F..... 937 767-1666
  Yellow Springs *(G-16289)*

3271 Concrete block and brick

American Concrete Products Inc..........F..... 937 224-1433
  Dayton *(G-6200)*
Beazer East Inc..F..... 740 474-3169
  Circleville *(G-3542)*
Belden Brick Company LLC...................E..... 330 456-0031
  Sugarcreek *(G-13919)*
Belden Brick Company LLC...................E..... 330 265-2030
  Sugarcreek *(G-13920)*
Benchmark Land Management LLC.....G..... 513 310-7850
  West Chester *(G-15376)*
Cantelli Block and Brick Inc..................E..... 419 433-0102
  Sandusky *(G-13048)*
Cement Products Inc..............................E..... 419 524-4342
  Mansfield *(G-9636)*
Charles Svec Inc......................................E..... 216 662-5200
  Maple Heights *(G-9748)*
Dearth Resources Inc............................G..... 937 663-4171
  Springfield *(G-13552)*
Dearth Resources Inc............................G..... 937 325-0651
  Springfield *(G-13551)*
E C S Corp...G..... 440 323-1707
  Elyria *(G-7136)*
Fine Line Excvtg & Ldscpg LLC............G..... 330 541-0590
  Ravenna *(G-12715)*
Green Impressions LLC..........................D..... 440 240-8508
  Sheffield Village *(G-13182)*
Green Vision Materials Inc....................F..... 440 564-5500
  Newbury *(G-11625)*
Hazelbaker Industries Ltd.....................F
  Columbus *(G-5424)*
ICC Safety Service Inc............................G..... 614 261-4557
  Columbus *(G-5452)*
J P Sand & Gravel Company...................F..... 614 497-0083
  Lockbourne *(G-9337)*
Koltcz Concrete Block Co......................E..... 440 232-3630
  Bedford *(G-1132)*
▲ Meridienne International Inc.............G..... 330 274-8317
  Aurora *(G-725)*
Midwest Specialties Inc.........................F..... 800 837-2503
  Wapakoneta *(G-15127)*
National Lime and Stone Co..................F..... 614 497-0083
  Lockbourne *(G-9340)*
North Central Con Designs Inc.............G..... 419 606-1908
  Wooster *(G-16155)*
Northfield Block Co.................................G..... 513 242-3644
  Cincinnati *(G-3204)*
Oberfields LLC..E..... 614 252-0955
  Columbus *(G-5610)*
▲ Osborne Inc...E..... 440 942-7000
  Mentor *(G-10517)*
Portsmouth Block Inc.............................E..... 740 353-4113
  Portsmouth *(G-12653)*
Prairie Builders Supply Inc....................G..... 419 332-7546
  Fremont *(G-7802)*
Quality Block & Supply Inc....................E..... 330 364-4411
  Mount Eaton *(G-11231)*
R W Sidley Incorporated........................G..... 440 564-2221
  Newbury *(G-11635)*
RE Connors Construction Ltd...............G..... 740 644-0261
  Thornville *(G-14068)*
▲ Reading Rock Incorporated................C..... 513 874-2345
  West Chester *(G-15580)*
Ready Field Solutions LLC....................F..... 330 562-0550
  Streetsboro *(G-13788)*

32 STONE, CLAY, GLASS, AND CONCRETE PRODUCTS

S & S Aggregates Inc .... F 740 453-0721
   Zanesville *(G-16561)*

Snyder Concrete Products Inc .... G 937 224-1433
   Dayton *(G-6577)*

▲ Snyder Concrete Products Inc .... E 937 885-5176
   Moraine *(G-11211)*

Ssr Community Dev Group LLC .... G 216 466-2674
   Cleveland *(G-4724)*

St Henry Tile Co Inc .... G 937 548-1101
   Greenville *(G-8061)*

St Henry Tile Co Inc .... E 419 678-4841
   Saint Henry *(G-12938)*

Stiger Pre Cast Inc .... G 740 482-2313
   Nevada *(G-11362)*

Stocker Concrete Company .... F 740 254-4626
   Gnadenhutten *(G-7989)*

Stocker Sand & Gravel Co .... F 740 254-4635
   Gnadenhutten *(G-7990)*

Sunny Brook Prest Concrete Co .... G 330 673-7667
   Kent *(C 8860)*

The Ideal Builders Supply .... E 216 741-1600
   Cleveland *(G-4787)*

Tri-County Block and Brick Inc .... E 419 826-7060
   Swanton *(G-13986)*

Tri-M Block and Supply Inc .... F 330 264-8771
   Cuyahoga Falls *(G-6122)*

Triple A Builders Inc .... G 216 249-0327
   Cleveland *(G-4832)*

Trumbull Cement Products Co .... G 330 372-4342
   Warren *(G-15211)*

Tyjen Inc .... G 740 797-4064
   The Plains *(G-14059)*

William Dauch Concrete Company .... F 419 668-4458
   Norwalk *(G-11991)*

3272 Concrete products, nec

A L D Precast Corp .... G 614 449-3366
   Columbus *(G-5080)*

◆ Aco Inc .... E 440 639-7230
   Mentor *(G-10403)*

Adler & Company Inc .... G 513 248-1500
   Cincinnati *(G-2597)*

Agean Marble Manufacturing .... F 513 874-1475
   West Chester *(G-15533)*

Akron Vault Company Inc .... E 330 784-5475
   Akron *(G-48)*

Alexander Wilbert Vault Co .... G 419 468-3477
   Galion *(G-7859)*

Allen Enterprises Inc .... E 740 532-5913
   Ironton *(G-8694)*

◆ American Spring Wire Corp .... C 216 292-4620
   Bedford Heights *(G-1163)*

Artistic Rock LLC .... G 216 291-8856
   Cleveland *(G-3683)*

Ash Sewer & Drain Service .... G 330 376-9714
   Akron *(G-65)*

Babbert Real Estate Inv Co Ltd .... D 614 837-8444
   Canal Winchester *(G-1980)*

Baumgardner Products Co .... G 330 376-2466
   Akron *(G-78)*

Baxter Burial Vault Svc Inc .... F 513 641-1010
   Cincinnati *(G-2660)*

Baxter Holdings Inc .... E 513 860-3593
   Hamilton *(G-8184)*

Bell Vault and Monu Works Inc .... E 937 866-2444
   Miamisburg *(G-10615)*

Bilco Company .... E 740 455-9020
   Zanesville *(G-16508)*

Bluffton Precast Concrete Co .... E 419 358-6946
   Bluffton *(G-1500)*

Carey Precast Concrete Company .... G 419 396-7142
   Carey *(G-2278)*

Carruth Studio Inc .... F 419 878-3060
   Waterville *(G-15240)*

Cement Products Inc .... E 419 524-4342
   Mansfield *(G-9636)*

Charles Svc Inc .... E 216 662-5200
   Maple Heights *(G-9748)*

Clark Grave Vault Company .... C 614 294-3761
   Columbus *(G-5251)*

Columbus Art Memorial Inc .... G 614 221-9333
   Columbus *(G-5262)*

Complete Cylinder Service Inc .... G 513 772-1500
   Cincinnati *(G-2784)*

Concrete Material Supply LLC .... F 419 261-6404
   Woodville *(G-16092)*

Contech Bridge Solutions LLC .... G 937 878-2170
   Dayton *(G-6263)*

Cox Inc .... G 740 858-4400
   Lucasville *(G-9521)*

DCA Construction Products LLC .... E 330 527-4308
   Garrettsville *(G-7912)*

Dm2018 LLC .... E 513 893-5483
   Liberty Twp *(G-9214)*

E A Cox Inc .... G 740 858-4400
   Lucasville *(G-9522)*

E C Babbert Inc .... D 614 837-8444
   Canal Winchester *(G-1985)*

E C S Corp .... G 440 323-1707
   Elyria *(G-7136)*

E Pompili Sons Inc .... G 216 581-8080
   Cleveland *(G-3985)*

Eldorado Stone LLC .... E 330 698-3931
   Apple Creek *(G-498)*

Encore Precast LLC .... E 513 726-5678
   Seven Mile *(G-13132)*

◆ Euclid Chemical Company .... E 800 321-7628
   Cleveland *(G-4032)*

Fabcon Companies LLC .... D 614 875-8601
   Grove City *(G-8093)*

▲ Fibreboard Corporation .... C 419 248-8000
   Toledo *(G-14287)*

◆ Fin Pan Inc .... F 513 870-9200
   Hamilton *(G-8208)*

Fithian-Wilbert Burial Vlt Co .... F 330 758-2327
   Youngstown *(G-16357)*

Forterra Pipe & Precast LLC .... F 614 445-3830
   Columbus *(G-5382)*

Forterra Pipe & Precast LLC .... E 330 467-7890
   Macedonia *(G-9551)*

Fountain Specialists Inc .... G 513 831-5717
   Milford *(G-10906)*

Galena Vault Ltd .... G 740 965-2200
   Galena *(G-7854)*

Gdy Installations Inc .... F 419 467-0036
   Toledo *(G-14298)*

Growco Inc .... F 419 886-4628
   Mansfield *(G-9665)*

Haviland Culvert Company .... G 419 622-6951
   Haviland *(G-8311)*

Hazelbaker Industries Ltd .... F
   Columbus *(G-5424)*

Headwaters Incorporated .... F 989 671-1500
   Manchester *(G-9618)*

High Concrete Group LLC .... B 937 748-2412
   Springboro *(G-13504)*

Hilltop Basic Resources Inc .... D 513 621-1500
   Cincinnati *(G-3000)*

Huron Cement Products Company .... E 419 433-4161
   Huron *(G-8633)*

J K Precast LLC .... G 740 335-2188
   Wshngtn Ct Hs *(G-16234)*

Jackson Monument Inc .... G 740 286-1590
   Jackson *(G-8716)*

James Kimmey .... F 740 335-5746
   Wshngtn Ct Hs *(G-16235)*

Jerry Offenberger Cnstr LLC .... G 740 374-2578
   Marietta *(G-9803)*

▲ Jet Stream International Inc .... D 330 505-9988
   Hubbard *(G-8566)*

K M B Inc .... E 330 889-3451
   Bristolville *(G-1652)*

K-Mar Structures LLC .... F 231 924-5777
   Junction City *(G-8783)*

KSA Limited Partnership .... F 740 776-3238
   Portsmouth *(G-12647)*

Landon Vault Company .... E 614 443-5505
   Columbus *(G-5519)*

▲ Lang Stone Company Inc .... E 614 235-4099
   Columbus *(G-5520)*

▼ Lindsay Precast LLC .... E 800 837-7788
   Canal Fulton *(G-1972)*

◆ Ludowici Roof Tile Inc .... D 740 342-1995
   New Lexington *(G-11454)*

Mack Concrete Industries Inc .... G 330 483-3111
   Valley City *(G-14877)*

Mack Industries .... E 419 353-7081
   Bowling Green *(G-1572)*

Mack Industries Inc .... G 740 393-1121
   Mount Vernon *(G-11277)*

Mack Industries PA Inc .... D 330 638-7680
   Vienna *(G-15000)*

Mack Industries PA Inc .... D 330 483-3111
   Valley City *(G-14878)*

McGill Septic Tank Co .... E 330 876-2171
   Kinsman *(G-8936)*

Michaels Pre-Cast Con Pdts .... F 513 683-1292
   Loveland *(G-9497)*

National Con Burial Vlt Assn .... G 407 788-1996
   Dayton *(G-6463)*

Neher Burial Vault Company .... E 937 399-4494
   Springfield *(G-13612)*

Next Surface Inc .... D 440 576-0194
   Jefferson *(G-8754)*

North American Cast Stone Inc .... F 440 286-1999
   Chardon *(G-2460)*

Northern Concrete Pipe Inc .... F 419 841-3361
   Sylvania *(G-14011)*

Northfield .... G 440 949-1815
   Sheffield Village *(G-13186)*

▲ Norwalk Concrete Inds Inc .... E 419 668-8167
   Norwalk *(G-11982)*

Oberfields LLC .... E 614 252-0955
   Columbus *(G-5610)*

Oberfields LLC .... E 740 369-7644
   Sunbury *(G-13959)*

Oberfields LLC .... D 740 369-7644
   Delaware *(G-6742)*

Occv1 Inc .... G 419 248-8000
   Toledo *(G-14404)*

OK Brugmann Jr & Sons Inc .... F 330 274-2106
   Mantua *(G-9741)*

Oldcastle Apg Midwest Inc .... E 440 949-1815
   Sheffield Village *(G-13187)*

Oldcastle Infrastructure Inc .... E 419 592-2309
   Napoleon *(G-11329)*

Olde Wood Ltd .... E 330 866-1441
   Magnolia *(G-9596)*

One Wish LLC .... F 800 505-6883
   Bedford *(G-1147)*

Orrville Trucking & Grading Co .... E 330 682-4010
   Orrville *(G-12144)*

P L M Corporation .... G 216 341-8008
   Cleveland *(G-4515)*

Pavestone LLC .... D 513 474-3783
   Cincinnati *(G-3242)*

32 STONE, CLAY, GLASS, AND CONCRETE PRODUCTS

Pawnee Maintenance Inc .... F 740 373-6861
Marietta *(G-9815)*

Paws & Remember NW Ohio LLC .... G 419 662-9000
Northwood *(G-11925)*

Premere Precast Products .... G 740 533-3333
Ironton *(G-8700)*

Premiere Con Solutions LLC .... F 419 737-9808
Pioneer *(G-12496)*

Prestress Services Inds LLC .... C 859 299-0461
Grove City *(G-8116)*

Quaker City Concrete Pdts LLC .... G 330 427-2239
Leetonia *(G-9130)*

Quanex Building Products Corp .... F 360 345-1241
Akron *(G-290)*

Quikrete Companies LLC .... E 614 885-4406
Columbus *(G-5704)*

Quikrete Companies LLC .... E 513 367-6135
Harrison *(G-8288)*

Quikrete Companies LLC .... E 330 296-6080
Ravenna *(G-12729)*

Quikrete Companies LLC .... F 419 241-1148
Toledo *(G-14445)*

R & C Monument Company LLC .... G 216 297-5444
Maple Heights *(G-9758)*

R W Sidley Incorporated .... G 440 564-2221
Newbury *(G-11635)*

R W Sidley Incorporated .... C 440 298-3232
Thompson *(G-14062)*

Ramp Creek III Ltd .... G 740 522-0660
Heath *(G-8329)*

Rock Decor Company .... E 330 830-9760
Apple Creek *(G-510)*

Rocla Concrete Tie Inc .... E 740 776-3238
Portsmouth *(G-12654)*

Russell Cast Stone Inc .... D 856 753-4000
West Chester *(G-15582)*

S & S Aggregates Inc .... F 740 453-0721
Zanesville *(G-16561)*

Seislove Vault & Septic Tanks .... G 419 447-5473
Tiffin *(G-14103)*

Septic Products Inc .... G 419 282-5933
Ashland *(G-613)*

Smith Concrete Co .... E 740 373-7441
Dover *(G-6843)*

▲ Snyder Concrete Products Inc .... E 937 885-5176
Moraine *(G-11211)*

Southern Ohio Vault Co Inc .... G 740 456-5898
Portsmouth *(G-12657)*

Spoerr Precast Concrete Inc .... F 419 625-9132
Sandusky *(G-13094)*

St Henry Tile Co Inc .... G 937 548-1101
Greenville *(G-8061)*

Star Manufacturing LLC .... C 330 740-8300
Youngstown *(G-16447)*

Stiger Pre Cast Inc .... G 740 482-2313
Nevada *(G-11362)*

Stuart Burial Vault Co Inc .... E 740 569-4158
Bremen *(G-1639)*

Tamarron Technology Inc .... F 800 277-3207
Cincinnati *(G-3440)*

Toli Vault .... G 866 998-8654
Westlake *(G-15798)*

Tri County Concrete Inc .... G 330 425-4464
Twinsburg *(G-14747)*

Turner Vault Co .... E 419 537-1133
Northwood *(G-11932)*

Uniontown Septic Tanks Inc .... G 330 699-3386
Uniontown *(G-14796)*

United Precast Inc .... C 740 393-1121
Mount Vernon *(G-11298)*

◆ United Refractories Inc .... E 330 372-3716
Warren *(G-15215)*

Whempys Corp .... G 614 888-6670
Worthington *(G-16218)*

William Dauch Concrete Company .... F 419 668-4458
Norwalk *(G-11991)*

Wilsons Country Creations Inc .... G 330 377-4190
Killbuck *(G-8926)*

Wyandot Dolomite Inc .... E 419 396-7641
Carey *(G-2286)*

Youngstown Burial Vault Co .... G 330 782-0015
Girard *(G-7977)*

3273 Ready-mixed concrete

Ace Ready Mix Concrete Co Inc .... F 330 745-8125
Norton *(G-11937)*

Adams Bros Concrete Pdts Ltd .... F 740 452-7566
Zanesville *(G-16495)*

Adams Brothers Inc .... F 740 819-0323
Zanesville *(G-16496)*

AK Ready Mix LLC .... G 740 286-8900
Jackson *(G-8707)*

Alexis Concrete Enterprise Inc .... F 440 366-0031
Elyria *(G-7106)*

All Ohio Ready Mix Concrete .... G 419 841-3838
Perrysburg *(G-12360)*

Allega Concrete Corp .... E 216 447-0814
Richfield *(G-12781)*

Alliance Redi-Mix Inc .... F 330 821-9244
Alliance *(G-394)*

Anderson Concrete Corp .... C 614 443-0123
Columbus *(G-5144)*

ASAP Ready Mix Inc .... G 513 797-1774
Amelia *(G-453)*

Associated Associates Inc .... E 330 626-3300
Mantua *(G-9734)*

Baird Concrete Products Inc .... F 740 623-8600
Coshocton *(G-5972)*

Baker-Shindler Contracting Co .... E 419 782-5080
Defiance *(G-6671)*

Barrett Paving Materials Inc .... F 937 293-9033
Moraine *(G-11159)*

Beazer East Inc .... F 740 474-3169
Circleville *(G-3542)*

Beazer East Inc .... E 937 364-2311
Hillsboro *(G-8455)*

Beazer East Inc .... F 740 947-4677
Waverly *(G-15278)*

Bhi Transition Inc .... E 937 663-4152
Saint Paris *(G-12971)*

Brock Corporation .... G 440 235-1806
Olmsted Falls *(G-12078)*

Buckeye Ready Mix Concrete .... G 330 798-5511
Akron *(G-94)*

Buckeye Ready-Mix LLC .... F 740 967-4801
Johnstown *(G-8770)*

Buckeye Ready-Mix LLC .... G 614 879-6316
West Jefferson *(G-15608)*

Buckeye Ready-Mix LLC .... G 740 654-4423
Lancaster *(G-8995)*

Buckeye Ready-Mix LLC .... E 937 642-2951
Marysville *(G-9905)*

Buckeye Ready-Mix LLC .... E 614 575-2132
Reynoldsburg *(G-12757)*

C F Poeppelman Inc .... E 937 448-2191
Bradford *(G-1600)*

Caldwell Lumber & Supply Co .... E 740 732-2306
Caldwell *(G-1908)*

Camden Ready Mix Co .... G 937 456-4539
Camden *(G-1962)*

Car Bros Inc .... F 440 232-1840
Bedford *(G-1109)*

Carr Bros Inc .... F 440 232-3700
Bedford *(G-1110)*

Carr Bros Bldrs Sup & Coal Co .... E 440 232-3700
Cleveland *(G-3794)*

Cashen Ready Mix .... G 440 354-3227
Painesville *(G-12222)*

Castalia Trenching & Rdymx LLC .... F 419 684-5502
Castalia *(G-2319)*

Castalia Trenching & Ready Mix .... F 419 684-5502
Castalia *(G-2320)*

Cemco Construction Corporation .... G 440 567-7708
Concord Township *(G-5903)*

Cement Products Inc .... E 419 524-4342
Mansfield *(G-9636)*

Cemex Cement Inc .... C 937 873-9858
Fairborn *(G-7311)*

Cemex Materials LLC .... C 330 654-2501
Diamond *(G-6804)*

Center Concrete Inc .... G 419 782-2495
Defiance *(G-6673)*

Center Concrete Inc .... G 800 453-4224
Edgerton *(G-7073)*

Central Ready Mix LLC .... E 513 402-5001
Cincinnati *(G-2717)*

Central Ready-Mix of Ohio LLC .... G 614 252-3452
Cincinnati *(G-2718)*

Cioffi Holdings LLC .... F 330 794-9448
Akron *(G-111)*

City Concrete LLc .... G 330 743-2825
Youngstown *(G-16335)*

Citywide Materials Inc .... E 513 533-1111
Cincinnati *(G-2772)*

Collinwood Shale Brick Sup Co .... E 216 587-2700
Cleveland *(G-3882)*

Consumeracq Inc .... E 440 277-9305
Lorain *(G-9408)*

Consumers Builders Supply Co .... G 440 277-9306
Lorain *(G-9409)*

D G M Inc .... F 740 286-2131
Jackson *(G-8713)*

D W Dickey and Son Inc .... C 330 424-1441
Lisbon *(G-9311)*

Dan K Williams Inc .... G 419 893-3251
Maumee *(G-10175)*

Dearth Resources Inc .... G 937 663-4171
Springfield *(G-13552)*

Dearth Resources Inc .... G 937 325-0651
Springfield *(G-13551)*

Deco Crete Supply .... G 614 372-5142
Columbus *(G-5321)*

Diano Construction and Sup Co .... F 330 456-7229
Canton *(G-2091)*

Diversified Ready Mix Ltd .... G 330 628-3355
Tallmadge *(G-14028)*

Eagle Specialty Materials LLC .... G 216 401-6075
Columbus *(G-5341)*

Ellis Brothers Inc Upg .... G 740 397-9191
Mount Vernon *(G-11272)*

Elyria Concrete Inc .... F 440 322-2750
Elyria *(G-7140)*

Ernst Enterprises Inc .... E 937 848-6811
Bellbrook *(G-1192)*

Ernst Enterprises Inc .... F 937 866-9441
Carrollton *(G-2306)*

Ernst Enterprises Inc .... G 513 367-1939
Cleves *(G-4951)*

Ernst Enterprises Inc .... E 614 443-9456
Columbus *(G-5358)*

Ernst Enterprises Inc .... F 614 308-0063
Columbus *(G-5359)*

Ernst Enterprises Inc .... E 937 878-9378
Fairborn *(G-7313)*

Ernst Enterprises Inc .... E 513 874-8300
Lebanon *(G-9073)*

Employee Codes: A=Over 500 employees, B=251-500
C=101-250, D=51-100, E=20-50, F=10-19, G=1-9

32 STONE, CLAY, GLASS, AND CONCRETE PRODUCTS

Ernst Enterprises Inc .... F 513 422-3651
Middletown (G-10821)

Ernst Enterprises Inc .... F 937 339-6249
Troy (G-14565)

Ernst Enterprises Inc .... E 937 233-5555
Dayton (G-6322)

Fairborn Cement Plant .... F 937 879-8466
Fairborn (G-7314)

G Big Inc .... E 740 867-5758
Chesapeake (G-2473)

Geauga Concrete Inc .... F 440 338-4915
Newbury (G-11624)

Grafton Ready Mix Concret Inc .... C 440 926-2911
Grafton (G-8001)

Heidelberg Materials Us Inc .... E 937 587-2671
Peebles (G-12327)

Heidelberg Materials Us Inc .... E 937 442-6009
Winchester (G-16073)

Heidelberg Mtls US Cem LLC .... F 330 499-9100
Middlebranch (G-10714)

Heidelberg Mtls US Cem LLC .... F 972 653-5500
Sylvania (G-13998)

Hilltop Basic Resources Inc .... F 937 795-2020
Aberdeen (G-1)

Hilltop Basic Resources Inc .... F 513 242-8400
Cincinnati (G-2999)

Hilltop Basic Resources Inc .... D 513 621-1500
Cincinnati (G-3000)

Hilltop Big Bend Quarry LLC .... E 513 651-5000
Cincinnati (G-3001)

Hocking Valley Concrete Inc .... G 740 592-5335
Athens (G-686)

Hocking Valley Concrete Inc .... G 740 342-1948
New Lexington (G-11452)

Hocking Valley Concrete Inc .... F 740 385-2165
Logan (G-9365)

Hull Ready Mix Concrete Inc .... F 419 625-8070
Sandusky (G-13064)

Huron Cement Products Company .... E 419 433-4161
Huron (G-8633)

Huth Ready Mix & Supply Co .... E 330 833-4191
Massillon (G-10108)

IMI-Irving Materials Inc .... E 513 844-8444
Hamilton (G-8219)

Integrated Resources Inc .... E 419 885-7122
Sylvania (G-14002)

Ioppolo Concrete Corporation .... E 440 439-6606
Bedford (G-1130)

Irving Materials Inc .... G 513 769-3666
Cincinnati (G-3032)

Irving Materials Inc .... F 513 844-8444
Hamilton (G-8222)

K & L Ready Mix Inc .... F 419 293-2937
Mc Comb (G-10271)

K & L Ready Mix Inc .... F 419 523-4376
Ottawa (G-12183)

K M B Inc .... E 330 889-3451
Bristolville (G-1652)

Kuhlman Corporation .... E 330 724-9900
Coventry Township (G-6012)

Kuhlman Corporation .... F 419 321-1670
Toledo (G-14351)

▲ Kuhlman Corporation .... E 419 897-6000
Maumee (G-10213)

Lancaster W Side Coal Co Inc .... F 740 862-4713
Lancaster (G-9021)

Lexington Concrete & Sup Inc .... G 419 529-3232
Mansfield (G-9679)

M & B Asphalt Company Inc .... G 419 992-4236
Old Fort (G-12073)

M & R Redi Mix Inc .... E 419 445-7771
Pettisville (G-12451)

Mack Concrete Industries Inc .... E 330 784-7008
Akron (G-234)

Market Ready .... G 513 289-9231
Maineville (G-9601)

McClelland .... E 740 452-3036
Zanesville (G-16544)

McConnell Ready Mix .... G 440 458-4325
Elyria (G-7179)

McGovney Ready Mix Inc .... E 740 353-4111
Portsmouth (G-12648)

Medina Supply Company .... E 330 425-0752
Twinsburg (G-14694)

Medina Supply Company .... E 330 723-3681
Medina (G-10352)

▲ Mini Mix Inc .... G 513 353-3811
Cleves (G-4960)

Mix Marketing LLC .... G 614 791-0489
Dublin (G-6911)

Moritz Concrete Inc .... E 419 529-3232
Mansfield (G-9699)

Moritz Materials Inc .... E 419 281-0575
Ashland (G-593)

Moritz Ready Mix Inc .... F 419 253-0001
Marengo (G-9769)

National Lime and Stone Co .... F 419 423-3400
Findlay (G-7541)

OK Brugmann Jr & Sons Inc .... F 330 274-2106
Mantua (G-9741)

Olen Corporation .... F 419 294-2611
Upper Sandusky (G-14819)

Orrville Trucking & Grading Co .... E 330 682-4010
Orrville (G-12144)

Osborne Inc .... F 440 232-1440
Cleveland (G-4510)

▲ Osborne Inc .... E 440 942-7000
Mentor (G-10517)

Osborne Co .... E 440 942-7000
Mentor (G-10518)

Pahl Ready Mix Concrete Inc .... F 419 636-4238
Bryan (G-1835)

Palmer Bros Transit Mix Con .... F 419 332-6363
Fremont (G-7800)

Palmer Bros Transit Mix Con .... F 419 686-2366
Portage (G-12636)

Palmer Bros Transit Mix Con .... G 419 447-2018
Tiffin (G-14099)

Palmer Bros Transit Mix Con .... F 419 352-4681
Bowling Green (G-1582)

Paul H Rohe Company Inc .... G 513 326-6789
Cincinnati (G-3240)

Paul R Lipp & Son Inc .... F 330 227-9614
Rogers (G-12847)

Phillips Ready Mix Co .... E 937 426-5151
Beavercreek Township (G-1090)

Placecrete Inc .... E 937 298-2121
Moraine (G-11200)

Pleasant Valley Ready Mix Inc .... F 330 852-2613
Sugarcreek (G-13934)

Quality Block & Supply Inc .... E 330 364-4411
Mount Eaton (G-11231)

Quality Ready Mix Inc .... F 419 394-8870
Saint Marys (G-12965)

Quikrete Companies LLC .... E 513 367-6135
Harrison (G-8288)

Quikrete Companies LLC .... E 330 296-6080
Ravenna (G-12729)

R W Sidley Inc .... E 440 224-2664
Kingsville (G-8934)

R W Sidley Incorporated .... G 330 499-5616
Canton (G-2209)

R W Sidley Incorporated .... G 440 564-2221
Newbury (G-11635)

R W Sidley Incorporated .... E 440 298-3232
Thompson (G-14063)

R W Sidley Incorporated .... G 330 392-2721
Warren (G-15201)

R W Sidley Incorporated .... G 330 793-7374
Youngstown (G-16426)

Reliable Ready Mix Co .... E 330 453-8266
Canton (G-2212)

Rockport Ready Mix Inc .... E 216 432-9465
Cleveland (G-4642)

Ross-Co Redi-Mix Co Inc .... F 740 775-4466
Chillicothe (G-2533)

S J Roth Enterprises Inc .... D 513 543-1140
Cincinnati (G-3358)

Sakrete Inc .... E 513 242-3644
Cincinnati (G-3359)

Sardinia Concrete Company .... E 513 248-0090
Milford (G-10921)

Sardinia Ready Mix Inc .... E 937 446-2523
Sardinia (G-13108)

Schwab Industries Inc .... F 330 364-4411
Dover (G-6842)

Scioto Ready Mix LLC .... D 740 924-9273
Pataskala (G-12308)

Scsrm Concrete Company Ltd .... F 937 533-1001
Sidney (G-13284)

Shelly Materials Inc .... E 740 775-4567
Chillicothe (G-2534)

Shelly Materials Inc .... E 614 871-6704
Grove City (G-8119)

Shelly Materials Inc .... F 330 723-3681
Medina (G-10377)

Shelly Materials Inc .... G 937 325-7386
Springfield (G-13631)

Shelly Materials Inc .... E 330 963-5180
Twinsburg (G-14735)

Show Ready Professionals .... G 614 817-5849
Columbus (G-5766)

Sidwell Materials Inc .... F 740 968-4313
Saint Clairsville (G-12923)

Small Sand & Gravel Inc .... E 740 427-3130
Gambier (G-7907)

Smalls Inc .... F 740 427-3633
Gambier (G-7909)

Smith Concrete .... F 740 439-7714
Cambridge (G-1952)

Smith Concrete Co .... G 740 593-5633
Athens (G-697)

Smith Concrete Co .... E 740 373-7441
Dover (G-6843)

Smyrna Ready Mix Concrete LLC .... E 937 855-0410
Germantown (G-7952)

Smyrna Ready Mix Concrete LLC .... D 937 773-0841
Piqua (G-12554)

Smyrna Ready Mix Concrete LLC .... D 937 698-7229
Vandalia (G-14960)

Spurlino Materials LLC .... G 513 202-1111
Cleves (G-4964)

Spurlino Materials LLC .... E 513 705-0111
Middletown (G-10858)

St Henry Tile Co Inc .... E 419 678-4841
Saint Henry (G-12938)

Stamm Contracting Company Inc .... E 330 274-8230
Mantua (G-9743)

Stocker Concrete Company .... F 740 254-4626
Gnadenhutten (G-7989)

T C Redi Mix Youngstown Inc .... E 330 755-2143
Youngstown (G-16450)

Tech Ready Mix Inc .... E 216 361-5000
Cleveland (G-4772)

▲ Terminal Ready-Mix Inc .... E 440 288-0181
Lorain (G-9441)

The National Lime and Stone Company. E 419 422-4341
 Findlay (G-7575)
Trail Mix... G 330 657-2277
 Peninsula (G-12343)
Tri County Concrete Inc................................... F 330 425-4464
 Cleveland (G-4821)
Tri County Concrete Inc................................... F 330 425-4464
 Twinsburg (G-14747)
Turner Concrete Products............................... F 419 662-9007
 Northwood (G-11931)
Twin Cities Concrete Co.................................. B 330 627-2158
 Carrollton (G-2316)
Twin Cities Concrete Co.................................. F 330 343-4491
 Dover (G-6848)
W G Lockhart Construction Co....................... E 330 745-6520
 Akron (G-372)
W M Dauch Concrete Inc................................ G 419 562-6917
 Bucyrus (G-1874)
Walden Industries Inc.................................... E 740 633-5971
 Tiltonsville (G-14117)
Warren Concrete and Supply Co..................... E 330 393-1581
 Warren (G-15218)
Weber Ready Mix Inc..................................... E 419 394-9097
 Saint Marys (G-12969)
Wells Group LLC.. F 740 532-9240
 Ironton (G-8706)
Westview Concrete Corp................................ F 440 458-5800
 Elyria (G-7218)
Westview Concrete Corp................................ E 440 235-1800
 Olmsted Falls (G-12084)
William Dauch Concrete Company................. F 419 562-6917
 Bucyrus (G-1875)
William Dauch Concrete Company................. F 419 668-4458
 Norwalk (G-11991)
William Oeder Ready Mix Inc........................ E 513 899-3901
 Martinsville (G-9903)
Williams Concrete Inc.................................... E 419 893-3251
 Maumee (G-10245)
Winters Products Inc..................................... F 740 286-4149
 Jackson (G-8728)

3274 Lime

Ayers Limestone Quarry Inc........................... F 740 633-2958
 Martins Ferry (G-9896)
Bluffton Stone Co... E 419 358-6941
 Bluffton (G-1501)
▼ Graymont Dolime (oh) Inc............................ D 419 855-8682
 Genoa (G-7947)
Mineral Processing Company........................ G 419 396-3501
 Carey (G-2280)
National Lime and Stone Co........................... E 419 396-7671
 Carey (G-2281)
Piqua Materials Inc.. D 937 773-4824
 Piqua (G-12547)
Shelly Materials Inc....................................... E 740 666-5841
 Ostrander (G-12176)
Sugarcreek Lime Service................................ G 330 364-4460
 Dover (G-6845)

3275 Gypsum products

Caraustar Industries Inc................................. E 330 665-7700
 Copley (G-5946)
Ernst Enterprises Inc..................................... E 419 222-2015
 Lima (G-9241)
Mineral Processing Company......................... G 419 396-3501
 Carey (G-2280)
Next Sales LLC.. F 330 704-4126
 Dover (G-6837)
Owens Corning Sales LLC.............................. C 330 634-0460
 Tallmadge (G-14041)
Priest Services Inc... G 440 333-1123
 Mayfield Heights (G-10254)

United States Gypsum Company.................... B 419 734-3161
 Gypsum (G-8171)
Wall Technology Inc.. F 715 532-5548
 Toledo (G-14521)

3281 Cut stone and stone products

9729 Flagstone Way LLC................................ G 513 239-1950
 Milford (G-10890)
Accent Manufacturing Inc.............................. F 330 724-7704
 Akron (G-15)
Accent Manufacturing Inc.............................. F 330 724-7704
 Norton (G-11936)
Agean Marble Manufacturing......................... F 513 874-1475
 West Chester (G-15533)
Al-Co Products Inc... G 419 399-3867
 Latty (G-9053)
As America Inc... E 419 522-4211
 Mansfield (G-9626)
Beazer East Inc... E 937 364-2311
 Hillsboro (G-8455)
Bell Vault and Monu Works Inc....................... E 937 866-2444
 Miamisburg (G-10615)
Blu Bird LLC.. F 513 271-5646
 Cincinnati (G-2672)
Blu Bird LLC.. G 614 276-3585
 Columbus (G-5202)
Briar Hill Stone Co Inc.................................... D 216 377-5100
 Glenmont (G-7980)
Briar Hill Stone Company............................... F 330 377-5100
 Glenmont (G-7981)
Cardinal Aggregate Inc................................... F 419 872-4380
 Perrysburg (G-12368)
▲ Castelli Marble LLC...................................... G 216 361-1222
 Cleveland (G-3799)
Classic Stone Company Inc........................... F 614 833-3946
 Columbus (G-5252)
Creative Countertops Ohio Inc....................... F 937 540-9450
 Englewood (G-7226)
◆ Cutting Edge Countertops Inc......................E 419 873-9500
 Perrysburg (G-12372)
▲ Distinctive Marble & Gran Inc...................... F 614 760-0003
 Plain City (G-12575)
▲ Dutch Quality Stone Inc............................... D 877 359-7866
 Mount Eaton (G-11229)
Engineered Marble Inc................................... G 614 308-0041
 Columbus (G-5354)
▲ Granex Industries Inc................................... F 440 248-4915
 Solon (G-13356)
Heritage Marble of Ohio Inc...........................F 614 436-1464
 Columbus (G-5427)
Jack Huffman... G 740 384-5178
 Wellston (G-15329)
Jalco Industries Inc.. F 740 286-3808
 Jackson (G-8717)
Kellstone Inc... E 419 746-2396
 Kelleys Island (G-8789)
Kipton Properties Inc..................................... F 440 315-3699
 Oberlin (G-12054)
▲ Lang Stone Company Inc............................. E 614 235-4099
 Columbus (G-5520)
Lima Millwork Inc... F 419 331-3303
 Elida (G-7094)
Maggard Mmrals Lser Art Tech L.................... G 513 282-6969
 Lebanon (G-9095)
Maple Grove Materials Inc............................. G 419 992-4235
 Tiffin (G-14093)
Marsh Industries Inc...................................... E 330 308-8667
 New Philadelphia (G-11515)
Maumee Valley Memorials Inc....................... F 419 878-9030
 Waterville (G-15250)
Medina Supply Company................................ E 330 723-3681
 Medina (G-10352)

Melvin Stone Co LLC...................................... F 513 771-0820
 Cincinnati (G-3147)
◆ Michael Kaufman Companies Inc.................F 330 673-4881
 Kent (G-8836)
National Lime and Stone Co........................... E 419 562-0771
 Bucyrus (G-1863)
National Lime and Stone Co........................... E 419 396-7671
 Carey (G-2281)
National Lime and Stone Co........................... G 419 657-6745
 Wapakoneta (G-15128)
North Hill Marble & Granite Co....................... F 330 253-2179
 Akron (G-267)
▲ Ohio Tile & Marble Co................................... E 513 541-4211
 Cincinnati (G-3217)
Pavestone LLC.. D 513 474-3783
 Cincinnati (G-3242)
Pietra Naturale Inc... F 937 438-8882
 Dayton (G-6506)
Piqua Granite & Marble Co Inc....................... G 937 773-2000
 Piqua (G-12546)
▲ Quarrymasters Inc.. G 330 612-0474
 Akron (G-292)
Rainbow Cultured Marble............................... F 330 225-3400
 Brunswick (G-1786)
Riceland Cabinet Inc...................................... D 330 601-1071
 Wooster (G-16163)
Rock Solid Cut Stone & Sup Inc..................... G 330 877-2775
 Hartville (G-8305)
Shelly Materials Inc....................................... G 937 358-2224
 West Mansfield (G-15628)
Sims-Lohman Inc... D 440 799-8285
 Brooklyn Heights (G-1701)
Solid Surface Concepts Inc............................ E 513 948-8677
 Cincinnati (G-3401)
◆ Studio Vertu Inc... G..... 513 241-9038
 Cincinnati (G-3426)
▲ Take It For Granite LLC................................. F 513 735-0555
 Cincinnati (G-2574)
▲ Terra Surfaces LLC....................................... G 937 836-1900
 Dayton (G-6614)
Toledo Cut Stone Inc...................................... F 419 531-1623
 Toledo (G-14494)
Transtar Holding Company............................. G 800 359-3339
 Walton Hills (G-15103)
Waller Brothers Stone Company..................... E 740 858-1948
 Mc Dermott (G-10275)
Western Ohio Cut Stone Ltd........................... F 937 492-4722
 Sidney (G-13295)
Zelaya Stoneworks LLC.................................. F 513 777-8030
 Liberty Township (G-9211)

3291 Abrasive products

Abrasive Products.. G 513 502-9150
 Cincinnati (G-2593)
Abrasive Source Inc....................................... F 937 526-9753
 Russia (G-12882)
▲ Abrasive Supply Company Inc.......... F 330 894-2818
 Minerva (G-11025)
▲ Abrasive Technology LLC.................. C 740 548-4100
 Lewis Center (G-9144)
Abrasive Technology Lapidary....................... E 740 548-4855
 Lewis Center (G-9145)
Action Super Abrasive Pdts Inc..................... E 330 673-7333
 Kent (G-8795)
Alb Tyler Holdings Inc.................................... G 440 946-7171
 Mentor (G-10410)
◆ Ali Industries LLC...B 937 878-3946
 Fairborn (G-7308)
▲ Alliance Abrasives LLC................................. F 330 823-7957
 Alliance (G-390)
▲ B & P Polishing Inc....................................... F 330 753-4202
 Barberton (G-858)

32 STONE, CLAY, GLASS, AND CONCRETE PRODUCTS

Belanger Inc .... D 517 870-3206
  West Chester (G-15375)
Buckeye Abrasive Inc .... F 330 753-1041
  Barberton (G-862)
Buffalo Abrasives Inc .... E 614 891-6450
  Westerville (G-15695)
▲ Carborundum Grinding Whee .... E 740 385-2171
  Logan (G-9360)
▲ Cleveland Granite & Marble LLC .... E 216 291-7637
  Cleveland (G-3841)
◆ Diamond Innovations Inc .... B 614 438-2000
  Columbus (G-5326)
Even Cut Abrasive Company .... F 216 881-9595
  Cleveland (G-4037)
Everett Industries LLC .... E 330 372-3700
  Warren (G-15169)
▲ Hec Investments Inc .... C 937 278-9123
  Dayton (G-6367)
Hones Harbor House Gifts .... G 216 334-9836
  Ashtabula (G-000)
Hoover Fabrication Ltd .... G 330 575-1118
  Salem (G-13001)
Jason Incorporated .... C 513 860-3400
  Hamilton (G-8224)
◆ Lawrence Industries Inc .... E 216 518-7000
  Cleveland (G-4318)
Libra Guaymas LLC .... C 440 974-7770
  Mentor (G-10492)
▲ Mill-Rose Company .... C 440 255-9171
  Mentor (G-10505)
Nanolap Technologies LLC .... F 877 658-4949
  Englewood (G-7237)
National Lime and Stone Co .... E 419 396-7671
  Carey (G-2281)
Noritake Co Inc .... C 513 234-0770
  Mason (G-10033)
Performance Superabrasives LLC .... G 440 946-7171
  Mentor (G-10523)
Premier Coatings Ltd .... F 513 942-1070
  West Chester (G-15484)
▲ Qibco Buffing Pads Inc .... G 937 743-0805
  Carlisle (G-2292)
▼ Regal Diamond Products Corp .... E 440 944-7700
  Wickliffe (G-15851)
Research Abrasive Products Inc .... E 440 944-3200
  Wickliffe (G-15852)
Schumann Enterprises Inc .... E 216 267-6850
  Cleveland (G-4675)
Steel Dynamics LLC .... E
  Marietta (G-9830)
▲ Sure-Foot Industries Corp .... E 440 234-4446
  Cleveland (G-4756)
Tomson Steel Company .... E 513 420-8600
  Middletown (G-10866)
▲ Unisand Incorporated .... E 330 722-0222
  Medina (G-10390)
United Buff and Supply Co Inc .... G 419 738-2417
  Wapakoneta (G-15131)
◆ US Technology Corporation .... E 330 455-1181
  Canton (G-2258)
US Technology Media Inc .... F 330 874-3094
  Bolivar (G-1540)
Vibra Finish Co .... E 513 870-6300
  Fairfield (G-7423)

3292 Asbestos products

American Way Exteriors LLC .... G 937 221-8860
  Dayton (G-6204)
◆ Owens Corning .... A 419 248-8000
  Toledo (G-14421)
Owens Crning Tchncal Fbrics LL .... E 419 248-5535
  Toledo (G-14425)

▲ Texas Tile Manufacturing LLC .... E 713 869-5811
  Solon (G-13437)

3295 Minerals, ground or treated

Aquablok Ltd .... G 419 825-1325
  Swanton (G-13969)
Cimbar Performance Mnrl WV LLC .... E 330 532-2034
  Wellsville (G-15334)
◆ Continental Mineral Proce .... E 513 771-7190
  Cincinnati (G-2790)
Edw C Levy Co .... G 330 484-6328
  Canton (G-2094)
EMD Millipore Corporation .... C 513 631-0445
  Norwood (G-11995)
Enviri Corporation .... G 740 367-7322
  Cheshire (G-2477)
Ethima Inc .... D 419 626-4912
  Sandusky (G-13057)
GRB Holdings Inc .... D 937 236-3250
  Dayton (G-3330)
Howard Industries Inc .... F 614 444-9900
  Columbus (G-5447)
▲ Industrial Quartz Corporation .... E 440 942-0909
  Mentor (G-10471)
Ironics Inc .... G 330 652-0583
  Niles (G-11673)
◆ Kish Company Inc .... F 440 205-9970
  Mentor (G-10487)
Martin Marietta Materials Inc .... G 513 701-1140
  West Chester (G-15461)
▲ Metaullics Systems LP .... C 509 926-6212
  Solon (G-13387)
▲ Seaforth Mineral & Ore Co Inc .... F 216 292-5820
  Beachwood (G-1022)
Trans Ash Inc .... F 859 341-1528
  Cincinnati (G-3461)

3296 Mineral wool

American Insulation Tech LLC .... F 513 733-4248
  Milford (G-10892)
Autoneum North America Inc .... B 419 693-0511
  Oregon (G-12103)
Blackthorn LLC .... F 937 836-9296
  Clayton (G-3564)
Brendons Fiber Works .... G 614 353-6599
  Columbus (G-5209)
Cpic Automotive Inc .... G 740 587-3262
  Granville (G-8015)
Essi Acoustical Products .... F 216 251-7888
  Cleveland (G-4030)
▲ Extol of Ohio Inc .... F 419 668-2072
  Norwalk (G-11963)
▲ Fibreboard Corporation .... C 419 248-8000
  Toledo (G-14287)
▲ ICP Adhesives and Sealants Inc .... E 330 753-4585
  Norton (G-11944)
Johns Manville Corporation .... G 419 782-0180
  Defiance (G-6684)
Johns Manville Corporation .... D 419 784-7000
  Defiance (G-6685)
Johns Manville Corporation .... E 419 784-7000
  Defiance (G-6686)
Johns Manville Corporation .... F 419 878-8111
  Defiance (G-6687)
Johns Manville Corporation .... G 419 467-8189
  Maumee (G-10209)
Johns Manville Corporation .... D 419 878-8111
  Waterville (G-15246)
Johns Manville Corporation .... D 419 878-8112
  Waterville (G-15247)
◆ Kinetics Noise Control Inc .... C 614 889-0480
  Dublin (G-6905)

Metal Building Intr Pdts Co .... F 440 322-6500
  Elyria (G-7180)
◆ Mid-Continent Minerals Corp .... F 216 283-5700
  Cleveland (G-4408)
Midwest Acoust-A-Fiber Inc .... F 740 369-3624
  Delaware (G-6737)
Mpc Inc .... E 440 835-1405
  Cleveland (G-4424)
Owens Corning .... F 614 754-4098
  Columbus (G-5648)
Owens Corning .... G 419 248-8000
  Navarre (G-11348)
Owens Corning Roofg & Asp LLC .... E 330 764-7800
  Medina (G-10360)
Owens Corning Roofg & Asp LLC .... E 877 858-3855
  Toledo (G-14423)
Owens Corning Sales LLC .... F 614 539-0830
  Grove City (G-8114)
Owens Corning Sales LLC .... G 740 928-6620
  Hebron (G-8354)
Owens Corning Sales LLC .... F 614 399-3915
  Mount Vernon (G-11284)
Owens Corning Sales LLC .... G 419 248-5751
  Swanton (G-13979)
◆ Owens Corning Sales LLC .... A 419 248-8000
  Toledo (G-14424)
Owens Crning Inslting Systm .... A 740 328-2300
  Newark (G-11600)
◆ Premier Manufacturing Corp .... C 216 941-9700
  Cleveland (G-4581)
▲ Refractory Specialties Inc .... E 330 938-2101
  Sebring (G-13125)
Sorbothane Inc .... E 330 678-9444
  Kent (G-8866)
◆ Tectum Inc .... C 740 345-9691
  Newark (G-11608)
◆ Thermafiber Inc .... D 260 563-2111
  Toledo (G-14485)

3297 Nonclay refractories

A & M Refractories Inc .... E 740 456-8020
  New Boston (G-11396)
◆ Allied Mineral Products LLC .... B 614 876-0244
  Columbus (G-5114)
Castruction Company Inc .... F 330 332-9622
  Salem (G-12982)
◆ Ccpi Inc .... E 937 783-2476
  Blanchester (G-1349)
▲ E I Ceramics LLC .... D 513 772-7001
  Cincinnati (G-2849)
Ethima Inc .... D 419 626-4912
  Sandusky (G-13057)
Ets Schaefer LLC .... F 330 468-6600
  Macedonia (G-9549)
Ets Schaefer LLC .... E 330 468-6600
  Beachwood (G-987)
I Cerco Inc .... C 740 982-2050
  Crooksville (G-6047)
Impact Armor Technologies LLC .... F 216 706-2024
  Cleveland (G-4218)
◆ Industrial Ceramic Products Inc .... D 937 642-3897
  Marysville (G-9921)
Johns Manville Corporation .... D 419 878-8111
  Waterville (G-15246)
Magneco/Metrel Inc .... D 330 426-9468
  Negley (G-11354)
Martin Marietta Materials Inc .... G 513 701-1140
  West Chester (G-15461)
Minteq International Inc .... F 419 636-4561
  Bryan (G-1828)
Minteq International Inc .... E 330 343-8821
  Dover (G-6836)

SIC SECTION

33 PRIMARY METAL INDUSTRIES

◆ Momentive Prfmce Mtls Qrtz Inc..............D 440 878-5700
   Strongsville *(G-13855)*

Ohio Vly Stmpng-Assemblies Inc............... E 419 522-0983
   Mansfield *(G-9708)*

▲ Ormet Primary Aluminum Corp................ A 740 483-1381
   Hannibal *(G-8262)*

Plibrico Company LLC................................. F 740 682-7755
   Oak Hill *(G-12023)*

Pmbp Legacy Co Inc.................................... E 330 253-8148
   Akron *(G-278)*

Pyromatics Corp... F 440 352-3500
   Mentor *(G-10538)*

▲ Refractory Specialties Inc....................... E 330 938-2101
   Sebring *(G-13125)*

Resco Products Inc..................................... G 740 682-7794
   Oak Hill *(G-12024)*

Saint-Gobain Ceramics Plas Inc................. C 330 673-5860
   Stow *(G-13721)*

◆ US Refractory Products LLC................... E 440 386-4580
   North Ridgeville *(G-11863)*

▲ Vacuform Inc.. E 330 938-9674
   Sebring *(G-13129)*

◆ Wahl Refractory Solutions LLC.............D 419 334-2658
   Fremont *(G-7819)*

▲ Zircoa Inc... C 440 248-0500
   Cleveland *(G-4936)*

3299 Nonmetallic mineral products,

Aquablok Ltd.. G 419 402-4170
   Swanton *(G-13968)*

Aquablok Ltd.. G 419 825-1325
   Swanton *(G-13969)*

Astro Met Inc.. F 513 772-1242
   Cincinnati *(G-2638)*

Cleveland Mica Co....................................... F 216 226-1360
   Lakewood *(G-8970)*

Cultured Marble Inc..................................... G 330 549-2282
   Poland *(G-12610)*

◆ Fireline Inc..C 330 743-1164
   Youngstown *(G-16356)*

Holmes Supply Corp.................................... G 330 279-2634
   Holmesville *(G-8547)*

Imperial Stucco LLC.................................... G 614 787-5888
   Dublin *(G-6895)*

Maverick Corporation................................... F 513 469-9919
   Blue Ash *(G-1430)*

Maxim Integrated Products LLC................. E 216 375-1057
   Cleveland *(G-4370)*

▲ Mazzolini Artcraft Co Inc........................ F 216 431-7529
   Cleveland *(G-4376)*

Momq Holding Company............................. A 440 878-5700
   Strongsville *(G-13856)*

Mtc Electroceramics.................................... G 440 232-8600
   Bedford *(G-1142)*

Occv2 LLC.. F 419 248-8000
   Toledo *(G-14405)*

▲ R W Sidley Incorporated......................... E 440 352-9343
   Painesville *(G-12260)*

Refractory Coating Tech Inc....................... E 800 807-7464
   Lorain *(G-9433)*

Richtech Industries Inc................................ G 440 937-4401
   Avon *(G-787)*

The Fischer & Jirouch Company................. G 216 361-3840
   Cleveland *(G-4782)*

Valutex Reinforcements Inc........................ E 800 251-2507
   Wshngtn Ct Hs *(G-16243)*

33 PRIMARY METAL INDUSTRIES

3312 Blast furnaces and steel mills

A-1 Welding & Fabrication............................ F 440 233-8474
   Lorain *(G-9399)*

Acadia Scientific LLC.................................. G 267 980-1644
   Perrysburg *(G-12358)*

Acme Surface Dynamics Inc....................... F 330 821-3900
   Alliance *(G-388)*

▲ Aco Inc...E 440 639-7230
   Mentor *(G-10403)*

▲ Adams Elevator Equipment Co.............. D 847 581-2900
   Holland *(G-8492)*

Alba Manufacturing Inc............................... D 513 874-0551
   Fairfield *(G-7332)*

▲ All Ohio Threaded Rod Co Inc............... E 216 426-1800
   Cleveland *(G-3632)*

Alro Steel Corporation................................. E 937 253-6121
   Dayton *(G-6196)*

AM Warren LLC... G 330 841-2800
   Warren *(G-15137)*

American Culvert & Fabg Co....................... F 740 432-6334
   Cambridge *(G-1919)*

American Hvy Plate Sltions LLC................. C 740 331-4620
   Clarington *(G-3562)*

American Posts LLC..................................... E 419 720-0652
   Toledo *(G-14191)*

American Steel & Alloys LLC...................... F 330 847-0487
   Warren *(G-15138)*

American Wire Shapes LLC......................... G 330 744-2905
   Struthers *(G-13899)*

Amthor Steel Inc... G 330 759-0200
   Youngstown *(G-16311)*

▼ Arrowstrip Inc... F 740 633-2609
   Martins Ferry *(G-9895)*

Askar Productive Resources LLC............... G 440 946-0393
   Willoughby *(G-15887)*

ATI Flat Rlled Pdts Hldngs LLC.................. F 330 875-2244
   Louisville *(G-9455)*

ATI Solutions Properties LLC..................... G 937 609-7681
   Dayton *(G-6216)*

B & G Tool Company.................................... G 614 451-2538
   Columbus *(G-5170)*

◆ Bd Laplace LLC..B 985 652-4900
   Cleveland *(G-3725)*

Big Wheels Leasing LLC............................. G 330 769-1594
   Seville *(G-13136)*

Brenmar Construction Inc........................... D 740 286-2151
   Jackson *(G-8711)*

Bridge Components Inds Inc...................... F 614 873-0777
   Columbus *(G-5213)*

Buschman Corporation................................ G 216 431-6633
   Cleveland *(G-3773)*

▲ Buschman Corporation........................... F 216 431-6633
   Cleveland *(G-3774)*

C & R Inc... E 614 497-1130
   Groveport *(G-8134)*

Canton Carnival Wheels Inc........................ G 330 837-3878
   Massillon *(G-10081)*

◆ Canton Drop Forge Inc...........................B 330 477-4511
   Canton *(G-2061)*

Carter Scott-Browne.................................... G 513 398-3970
   Mason *(G-9969)*

▲ Challenger Hardware Company............. G 216 591-1141
   Independence *(G-8656)*

Charles C Lewis Company........................... F 440 439-3150
   Cleveland *(G-3808)*

Charter Manufacturing Co Inc.................... D 216 883-3800
   Cleveland *(G-3813)*

Churchill Steel Plate Ltd............................. E 330 425-9000
   Twinsburg *(G-14642)*

Cleveland-Cliffs Columbus LLC................. E 614 492-8287
   Columbus *(G-5254)*

◆ Cleveland-Cliffs Inc................................C 216 694-5700
   Cleveland *(G-3862)*

Cleveland-Cliffs Steel Corp......................... B 419 755-3011
   Mansfield *(G-9639)*

Cleveland-Cliffs Steel Corp......................... F 513 425-3593
   Middletown *(G-10808)*

Cleveland-Cliffs Steel Corp......................... C 513 425-5000
   Middletown *(G-10809)*

Cleveland-Cliffs Steel Corp......................... B 513 425-3694
   Middletown *(G-10810)*

◆ Cleveland-Cliffs Steel Corp...................D 216 694-5700
   Cleveland *(G-3864)*

Clevelnd-Clffs Clvland Wrks LL................. E 216 429-6000
   Cleveland *(G-3867)*

▲ Clevelnd-Clffs Clvland Wrks LL............ C 216 429-6000
   Cleveland *(G-3866)*

◆ Clevelnd-Cliffs Stl Holdg Corp..............B 216 694-5700
   Cleveland *(G-3868)*

Cliffs Steel Inc.. E 216 694-5700
   Cleveland *(G-3876)*

Cohen Brothers Inc...................................... F 513 217-5200
   Middletown *(G-10812)*

Cohen Brothers Inc...................................... E 513 422-3696
   Middletown *(G-10811)*

Columbiana Foundry Company................... C 330 482-3336
   Columbiana *(G-5034)*

Community Care On Wheels........................ G 330 882-5506
   Clinton *(G-4968)*

Contractors Steel Company........................ D 330 425-3050
   Twinsburg *(G-14645)*

CPM Tool Co LLC... G 937 258-1176
   Dayton *(G-6156)*

Crest Bending Inc... E 419 492-2108
   New Washington *(G-11546)*

Custom Blast & Coat Inc.............................. G 419 225-6024
   Lima *(G-9233)*

Dietrich Industries Inc................................. C 330 372-2868
   Warren *(G-15162)*

▼ Eastern Automated Piping...................... G 740 535-8184
   Mingo Junction *(G-11044)*

Egypt Structural Steel Proc......................... F 419 628-2375
   Minster *(G-11051)*

◆ Elster Perfection Corporation...............D 440 428-1171
   Geneva *(G-7935)*

Ernst America Inc... F 937 434-3133
   Moraine *(G-11176)*

▲ Ernst Metal Technologies LLC............... E 937 434-3133
   Moraine *(G-11178)*

Evolve Solutions LLC................................... E 440 357-8964
   Painesville *(G-12233)*

FBC Chemical Corporation.......................... E 216 341-2000
   Cleveland *(G-4051)*

Forge Products Corporation....................... E 216 231-2600
   Cleveland *(G-4083)*

▲ Franklin Iron & Metal Corp..................... C 937 253-8184
   Dayton *(G-6338)*

▲ Fulton County Processing Ltd............... C 419 822-9266
   Delta *(G-6783)*

▲ Garden Street Iron & Metal Inc............. E 513 721-4660
   Cincinnati *(G-2928)*

Geauga Coatings LLC.................................. G 440 221-7286
   Chardon *(G-2451)*

George Manufacturing Inc........................... F 513 932-1067
   Lebanon *(G-9079)*

Gerdau Ameristeel US Inc........................... G 740 671-9410
   Bellaire *(G-1186)*

Gerdau Ameristeel US Inc........................... F 513 869-7660
   Hamilton *(G-8211)*

GKN Sinter Metals LLC................................ C 740 441-3203
   Gallipolis *(G-7894)*

▲ Global Metal Services Ltd...................... G 440 591-1264
   Chagrin Falls *(G-2398)*

◆ Gray America Corp..................................E 937 293-9313
   Moraine *(G-11182)*

Great Lakes Mfg Group Ltd......................... G 440 391-8266
   Rocky River *(G-12838)*

Employee Codes: A=Over 500 employees, B=251-500
C=101-250, D=51-100, E=20-50, F=10-19, G=1-9

33 PRIMARY METAL INDUSTRIES

Gregory Roll Form Inc .... D 330 477-4800
  Canton *(G-2118)*

Grenga Machine & Welding .... F 330 743-1113
  Youngstown *(G-16374)*

Hadronics Inc .... D 513 321-9350
  Cincinnati *(G-2983)*

Harvard Coil Processing Inc .... E 216 883-6366
  Cleveland *(G-4172)*

▲ Heidtman Steel Products Inc .... E 419 691-4646
  Toledo *(G-14317)*

◆ Hickman Williams & Company .... F 513 621-1946
  Cincinnati *(G-2998)*

Holgate Metal Fab Inc .... F 419 599-2000
  Napoleon *(G-11319)*

I Jalcite Inc .... F 216 622-5000
  Cleveland *(G-4212)*

JSW Steel USA Ohio Inc .... B 740 535-8172
  Mingo Junction *(G-11046)*

Kda Manufacturing LLC .... F 330 590-7431
  Norton *(G-11341)*

◆ Kirtland Capital Partners LP .... E 216 593-0100
  Beachwood *(G-993)*

L T V Steel Company Inc .... A 216 622-5000
  Cleveland *(G-4303)*

▲ L&H Threaded Rods Corp .... C 937 294-6666
  Moraine *(G-11189)*

Lapham-Hickey Steel Corp .... E 614 443-4881
  Columbus *(G-5521)*

◆ Latrobe Spcialty Mtls Dist Inc .... D 330 609-5137
  Vienna *(G-14997)*

Latrobe Specialty Mtls Co LLC .... E 419 335-8010
  Wauseon *(G-15266)*

Liberty Iron & Metal Inc .... E 724 347-4534
  Girard *(G-7971)*

▲ Lokring Technology LLC .... D 440 942-0880
  Willoughby *(G-15946)*

Long View Steel Corp .... F 419 747-1108
  Mansfield *(G-9680)*

Lukjan Metal Products Inc .... C 440 599-8127
  Conneaut *(G-5926)*

▲ Lynx Precision Products Corp .... F 866 305-9012
  Mason *(G-10023)*

Major Metals Company .... E 419 886-4600
  Mansfield *(G-9681)*

Marion Cnty Coal Resources Inc .... F 740 338-3100
  Saint Clairsville *(G-12909)*

Marion County Coal Company .... D 740 338-3100
  Saint Clairsville *(G-12910)*

Marion Dofasco Inc .... G 740 382-3979
  Marion *(G-9860)*

◆ McDonald Steel Corporation .... D 330 530-9118
  Mc Donald *(G-10279)*

▼ McIntosh Manufacturing LLC .... D 513 424-5307
  Middletown *(G-10843)*

McWane Inc .... B 740 622-6651
  Coshocton *(G-5983)*

Mercer Tool Corporation .... E 419 394-7277
  Saint Marys *(G-12957)*

Metallus Inc .... G 216 825-2533
  Canton *(G-2160)*

Metallus Inc .... F 800 967-1218
  Canton *(G-2161)*

Metallus Inc .... E 330 471-7000
  Canton *(G-2162)*

◆ Metallus Inc .... A 330 471-7000
  Canton *(G-2159)*

▲ Miba Sinter USA LLC .... F 740 962-4242
  Mcconnelsville *(G-10283)*

Mid-America Steel Corp .... E 800 282-3466
  Cleveland *(G-4407)*

Msls Group LLC .... E 330 723-4431
  Medina *(G-10355)*

Nanogate North America LLC .... B 419 747-1096
  Mansfield *(G-9702)*

New Age Design & Tool Inc .... F 440 355-5400
  Lagrange *(G-8953)*

Nichidai America Corporation .... F 419 423-7511
  Findlay *(G-7542)*

▲ North Shore Strapping Company .... E 216 661-5200
  Brooklyn Heights *(G-1696)*

◆ Northlake Steel Corporation .... D 330 220-7717
  Valley City *(G-14887)*

Nucor Corporation .... G 937 390-2300
  Beavercreek *(G-1057)*

Nucor Corporation .... E 407 855-2990
  Cincinnati *(G-3208)*

Nucor Corporation .... F 901 275-3826
  Cincinnati *(G-3209)*

Nucor Steel Marion Inc .... E 740 383-6068
  Marion *(G-9867)*

◆ Nucor Steel Marion Inc .... B 740 383-4011
  Marion *(G-9868)*

Nuflux LLC .... G 330 399-1122
  Cortland *(G-5966)*

Ohio Coatings Company .... D 740 859-5500
  Yorkville *(G-16294)*

◆ Ohio Gratings Inc .... B 800 321-9800
  Canton *(G-2184)*

Ohio Steel Processing LLC .... E 419 241-9601
  Toledo *(G-14410)*

Ohio Steel Sheet and Plate Inc .... E 800 827-2401
  Hubbard *(G-8569)*

▲ Ohio Valley Alloy Services Inc .... E 740 373-1900
  Marietta *(G-9812)*

▲ Opp Dissolution LLC .... D 419 241-9601
  Toledo *(G-14417)*

OReilly Precision Pdts Inc .... E 937 526-4677
  Russia *(G-12886)*

Phillips Mfg and Tower Co .... D 419 347-1720
  Shelby *(G-13197)*

Phillips Tube Group Inc .... E 205 338-4771
  Middletown *(G-10850)*

▲ Pioneer Pipe Inc .... A 740 376-2400
  Marietta *(G-9817)*

Plymouth Locomotive Svc LLC .... G 419 896-2854
  Shiloh *(G-13205)*

Precision Cut Fabricating Inc .... F 440 877-1260
  North Royalton *(G-11891)*

Precision Strip Inc .... D 937 667-6255
  Tipp City *(G-14148)*

◆ Prime Conduit Inc .... F 216 464-3400
  Beachwood *(G-1012)*

▼ Qual-Fab Inc .... E 440 327-5000
  Avon *(G-784)*

Quality Bar Inc .... E 330 755-0000
  Struthers *(G-13906)*

Quality Tool Company .... E 419 476-8228
  Toledo *(G-14444)*

R & D Machine Inc .... F 937 339-2545
  Troy *(G-14603)*

Racelite Southcoast Inc .... F 216 581-4600
  Maple Heights *(G-9759)*

Radix Wire & Cable LLC .... D 216 731-9191
  Solon *(G-13410)*

Republic Engineered Products .... F 440 277-2000
  Lorain *(G-9434)*

Republic Steel .... F 330 438-5533
  Canton *(G-2213)*

Republic Steel .... E 440 277-2000
  Lorain *(G-9435)*

◆ Republic Steel .... F 330 438-5435
  Canton *(G-2214)*

Republic Technology Corp .... F 216 622-5000
  Cleveland *(G-4627)*

Rmi Titanium Company LLC .... C 330 471-1844
  Canton *(G-2216)*

Rmi Titanium Company LLC .... C 330 453-2118
  Canton *(G-2217)*

Royal Metal Products LLC .... C 740 397-8842
  Mount Vernon *(G-11293)*

▲ Rti Alloys .... G 330 652-9952
  Niles *(G-11686)*

▲ S&V Industries Inc .... E 330 666-1986
  Medina *(G-10373)*

Seilkop Industries Inc .... F 513 353-3090
  Miamitown *(G-10709)*

Seneca Railroad & Mining Co .... F 419 483-7764
  Bellevue *(G-1234)*

Sertek LLC .... D 614 504-5828
  Dublin *(G-6936)*

Shaq Inc .... D 770 427-0402
  Beachwood *(G-1023)*

Shear Service Inc .... G 216 341-2700
  Cleveland *(G-4689)*

Sigma Tube Company .... G 419 729-9756
  Toledo *(G-14472)*

Stainless Specialties Inc .... E 440 942-4242
  Eastlake *(G-7049)*

◆ Starr Wheel Group Inc .... F 954 935-5536
  Warren *(G-15206)*

Steel Technologies LLC .... E 419 523-5199
  Ottawa *(G-12192)*

Steel Technologies LLC .... E 440 946-8666
  Willoughby *(G-15997)*

Steve Vore Welding and Steel .... F 419 375-4087
  Fort Recovery *(G-7624)*

Suburban Steel Supply Co .... D 614 737-5501
  Gahanna *(G-7850)*

▲ Tencom Ltd .... G 419 865-5877
  Holland *(G-8533)*

The Florand Company .... F 330 747-8986
  Youngstown *(G-16453)*

▲ The Hamilton Caster & Mfg .... D 513 863-3300
  Hamilton *(G-8248)*

Thrift Tool Inc .... G 937 275-3600
  Dayton *(G-6623)*

Timken Receivables Corporation .... E 234 262-3000
  North Canton *(G-11768)*

Tms International LLC .... E 216 441-9702
  Cleveland *(G-4798)*

Tms International LLC .... F 513 425-6462
  Middletown *(G-10863)*

Tms International LLC .... E 513 422-4572
  Middletown *(G-10864)*

Tms International Corp .... F 513 422-9497
  Middletown *(G-10865)*

Trenchless Rsrces Globl Hldngs .... F 419 419-6498
  Bowling Green *(G-1593)*

Tru-Cal Inc .... F 419 202-1296
  Milan *(G-10888)*

Trupoint Products LLC .... F 330 204-3302
  Sugarcreek *(G-13945)*

▲ United Security Seals Inc .... E 614 443-7633
  Columbus *(G-5843)*

▲ United Wheel and Hub LLC .... G 419 483-2639
  Sandusky *(G-13100)*

Universal Metals Cutting Inc .... G 330 580-5192
  Canton *(G-2257)*

Universal Urethane Pdts Inc .... D 419 693-7400
  Toledo *(G-14514)*

Unlimited Machine and Tool LLC .... F 419 269-1730
  Toledo *(G-14516)*

Wheatland Tube LLC .... C 724 342-6851
  Niles *(G-11692)*

Wheatland Tube LLC .... C 330 372-6611
  Warren *(G-15224)*

SIC SECTION
33 PRIMARY METAL INDUSTRIES

Wings N Wheels.. G 419 586-6531
   Celina *(G-2356)*

▼ Witt Industries Inc................................... D 513 871-5700
   Mason *(G-10071)*

Wodin Inc... E 440 439-4222
   Cleveland *(G-4916)*

Worthington Enterprises Inc..................... D 513 539-9291
   Monroe *(G-11121)*

◆ Worthington Steel Company................... B 800 944-2255
   Worthington *(G-16223)*

Worthngton Smuel Coil Proc LLC............. E 330 963-3777
   Twinsburg *(G-14758)*

◆ Xtek Inc.. B 513 733-7800
   Cincinnati *(G-3534)*

Youngstown Bending Rolling Inc.............. F 330 898-3878
   Warren *(G-15225)*

Youngstown Tube Co.................................. E 330 743-7414
   Youngstown *(G-16490)*

Zekelman Industries Inc............................. C 740 432-2146
   Cambridge *(G-1961)*

3313 Electrometallurgical products

◆ ERAMET MARIETTA INC......................... C 740 374-1000
   Marietta *(G-9792)*

◆ Ferroglobe USA Mtllurgical Inc............... C 740 984-2361
   Waterford *(G-15236)*

GE Aviation Systems LLC........................... E 620 218-5237
   Springdale *(G-13525)*

GE Aviation Systems LLC........................... F 513 889-5150
   West Chester *(G-15437)*

International Metal Supply LLC................ G 330 764-1004
   Medina *(G-10338)*

Morris Technologies Inc............................. E 513 733-1611
   Cincinnati *(G-3174)*

Newton Materion Inc................................. B 216 692-3990
   Euclid *(G-7287)*

Real Alloy Specialty Pdts LLC................... A 216 755-8836
   Beachwood *(G-1014)*

Real Alloy Specification LLC.................... D 216 755-8900
   Beachwood *(G-1016)*

▲ Rhenium Alloys Inc................................... E 440 365-7388
   North Ridgeville *(G-11858)*

Theken Port Park LLC................................ D 330 733-7600
   Akron *(G-354)*

3315 Steel wire and related products

Advance Industries Group LLC................. E 216 741-1800
   Cleveland *(G-3602)*

AJD Holding Co... D 330 405-4477
   Twinsburg *(G-14626)*

◆ American Spring Wire Corp...................... C 216 292-4620
   Bedford Heights *(G-1163)*

▲ American Wire & Cable Company........... E 440 235-1140
   Olmsted Twp *(G-12085)*

Armco Inc.. G 740 829-3000
   Coshocton *(G-5971)*

Bayloff Stmped Pdts Knsman Inc............. D 330 876-4511
   Kinsman *(G-8935)*

Bekaert Corporation................................... E 330 683-5060
   Orrville *(G-12119)*

◆ Bekaert Corporation................................... E 330 867-3325
   Fairlawn *(G-7433)*

Cherokee Manufacturing LLC................... F 800 777-5030
   Perry *(G-12350)*

Contour Forming Inc.................................. F 740 345-9777
   Newark *(G-11572)*

Custom Cltch Jint Hydrlics Inc.................. F 216 431-1630
   Cleveland *(G-3923)*

D C Controls LLC.. G 513 225-0813
   West Chester *(G-15548)*

D M L Steel Tech... G 513 737-9911
   Liberty Twp *(G-9213)*

◆ Dayton Superior Corporation................... C 937 866-0711
   Miamisburg *(G-10633)*

▲ Engineered Wire Products Inc................. C 419 294-3817
   Upper Sandusky *(G-14808)*

Euclid Steel & Wire Inc.............................. E 216 731-6744
   Lakewood *(G-8974)*

▲ Fenix LLC.. F 419 739-3400
   Wapakoneta *(G-15110)*

Hawthorne Wire Ltd................................... F 216 712-4747
   Lakewood *(G-8975)*

Heilind Electronics Inc............................... E 440 473-9600
   Cleveland *(G-4177)*

▲ Injection Alloys Incorporated................... F 513 422-8819
   Middletown *(G-10830)*

Jae Nail... G 216 225-3743
   Cleveland *(G-4248)*

▲ JR Manufacturing Inc................................ C 419 375-8021
   Fort Recovery *(G-7621)*

▲ Madsen Wire Products Inc....................... G 937 829-6561
   Dayton *(G-6421)*

▲ Marlin Thermocouple Wire Inc............... E 440 835-1950
   Westlake *(G-15764)*

Master-Halco Inc.. F 513 869-7600
   Fairfield *(G-7379)*

Maverick Nail & Staple Ltd....................... G 513 843-5270
   Batavia *(G-931)*

▼ Midwestern Industries Inc........................ D 330 837-4203
   Massillon *(G-10127)*

◆ Pioneer Corp... D 330 857-0267
   Dalton *(G-6140)*

▲ Polymet Corporation................................. E 513 874-3586
   West Chester *(G-15482)*

Radix Wire & Cable LLC............................ D 216 731-9191
   Solon *(G-13410)*

Ram Sensors Inc... E 440 835-3540
   Cleveland *(G-4613)*

Randy Lewis Inc.. F 330 784-0456
   Akron *(G-296)*

Regency Steel Supply Inc LLC.................. G 440 306-0269
   Eastlake *(G-7046)*

▲ Reinforcement Systems of .... G 330 469-6958
   Warren *(G-15202)*

▲ Republic Steel Wire Proc LLC.................. E 440 996-0740
   Solon *(G-13414)*

◆ Republic Wire Inc...................................... D 513 860-1800
   West Chester *(G-15496)*

▲ Richards Whl Fence Co Inc....................... E 330 773-0423
   Akron *(G-304)*

S & S Wldg Fabg Machining Inc............... F 330 392-7878
   Newton Falls *(G-11657)*

▲ Save Edge Inc... E 937 376-8268
   Xenia *(G-16272)*

▲ Scovil Hanna LLC...................................... E 216 581-1500
   Cleveland *(G-4681)*

Seneca Wire & Manufacturing Co Inc..... F 419 435-9261
   Fostoria *(G-7655)*

▲ Solon Specialty Wire Co............................ E 440 248-7600
   Solon *(G-13424)*

▲ Stop Stick Ltd... E 513 202-5500
   Harrison *(G-8294)*

Summit Engineered Products Inc............ F 330 854-5388
   Canal Fulton *(G-1975)*

▲ Torque 2020 CMA Acqisition LLC........... C 330 874-2900
   Bolivar *(G-1539)*

Tru-Form Steel & Wire Inc........................ F 765 348-5001
   Toledo *(G-14512)*

Unison Industries LLC................................ F 937 426-0621
   Alpha *(G-439)*

Wire Products Company Inc..................... G 216 267-0777
   Cleveland *(G-4912)*

3316 Cold finishing of steel shapes

▲ All Ohio Threaded Rod Co Inc................ E 216 426-1800
   Cleveland *(G-3632)*

Alro Steel Corporation............................... E 937 253-6121
   Dayton *(G-6196)*

◆ American Spring Wire Corp...................... C 216 292-4620
   Bedford Heights *(G-1163)*

ATI Flat Rlled Pdts Hldngs LLC................ F 330 875-2244
   Louisville *(G-9455)*

Bar Processing Corporation...................... F 330 872-0914
   Newton Falls *(G-11653)*

Bekaert Corporation................................... E 330 683-5060
   Orrville *(G-12119)*

Clark Grave Vault Company...................... C 614 294-3761
   Columbus *(G-5251)*

▲ Clouth Sprenger LLC................................. F 937 642-8390
   Lebanon *(G-9067)*

Consolidated Metal Pdts Inc.................... D 513 251-2624
   Cincinnati *(G-2788)*

◆ Dms Inc.. C 440 951-9838
   Willoughby *(G-15910)*

Geneva Liberty Steel Ltd.......................... E 330 740-0103
   Youngstown *(G-16366)*

▲ Heidtman Steel Products Inc................... E 419 691-4646
   Toledo *(G-14317)*

▲ Hynes Industries Inc.................................. C 800 321-9257
   Youngstown *(G-16378)*

Lakeway Mfg Inc... E 419 433-3030
   Huron *(G-8637)*

Lapham-Hickey Steel Corp....................... D 419 399-4803
   Paulding *(G-12317)*

LLC Ring Masters.. E 330 832-1511
   Massillon *(G-10120)*

Mid-America Steel Corp............................ E 800 282-3466
   Cleveland *(G-4407)*

MSC Walbridge Coatings Inc.................... C 419 666-6130
   Walbridge *(G-15085)*

◆ Nucor Steel Marion Inc............................. B 740 383-4011
   Marion *(G-9868)*

Sandvik Inc.. C 614 438-6579
   Columbus *(G-5745)*

◆ Superior Forge & Steel Corp.................... C 419 222-4412
   Lima *(G-9293)*

Telling Industries LLC................................ E 740 435-8900
   Cambridge *(G-1958)*

◆ Telling Industries LLC................................ F 440 974-3370
   Willoughby *(G-16004)*

Worthington Cylinder Corp....................... C 440 576-5847
   Jefferson *(G-8763)*

Worthington Industries Inc....................... E 614 438-3190
   Columbus *(G-5884)*

Worthington Industries Inc....................... F 614 438-3113
   Columbus *(G-5885)*

Worthington Industries Lsg LLC.............. E 614 438-3210
   Worthington *(G-16221)*

Worthington Military Cnstr Inc................ F 615 599-6446
   Worthington *(G-16222)*

Worthington Services LLC........................ G 937 848-2164
   Spring Valley *(G-13492)*

◆ Worthington Steel Company................... B 800 944-2255
   Worthington *(G-16223)*

Worthngton Stl Mexico SA De Cv............ G 800 944-2255
   Worthington *(G-16224)*

3317 Steel pipe and tubes

Alro Steel Corporation............................... E 937 253-6121
   Dayton *(G-6196)*

Arcelrmttal Tblar Pdts Shlby L................. A 419 347-2424
   Shelby *(G-13191)*

Arcelrmttal Tblar Pdts USA LLC............... A 419 347-2424
   Shelby *(G-13192)*

Atlantic Welding LLC................................. F 937 570-5094
   Piqua *(G-12505)*

Employee Codes: A=Over 500 employees, B=251-500
C=101-250, D=51-100, E=20-50, F=10-19, G=1-9

33 PRIMARY METAL INDUSTRIES

Busch & Thiem Inc .... E 419 625-7515
Sandusky (G-13047)

Caparo Bull Moose Inc .... G 330 448-4878
Masury (G-10156)

Cgi Group Benefits LLC .... G 440 246-6191
Lorain (G-9406)

Chart International Inc .... D 440 753-1490
Cleveland (G-3812)

◆ Clevelnd-Clffs Tblar Cmpnnts L .... C 419 661-4150
Walbridge (G-15080)

▲ Commercial Honing LLC .... D 330 343-8896
Dover (G-6813)

Conduit Pipe Products Company .... D 614 879-9114
West Jefferson (G-15609)

Contech Engnered Solutions Inc .... E 513 645-7000
West Chester (G-15402)

◆ Contech Engnered Solutions LLC .... C 513 645-7000
West Chester (G-15403)

Crest Bending Inc .... E 419 492-2108
New Washington (G-11948)

Dofasco Tubular Products .... G 419 342-1371
Shelby (G-13194)

◆ Dom Tube Corp .... A 412 299-2616
Alliance (G-402)

Fd Rolls Corp .... E 216 916-1922
Solon (G-13348)

Grae-Con Process Piping LLC .... E 740 282-6830
Marietta (G-9796)

◆ H-P Products Inc .... C 330 875-5556
Louisville (G-9459)

▲ Jackson Tube Service Inc .... C 937 773-8550
Piqua (G-12530)

James O Emert Jr .... G 330 650-6990
Hudson (G-8600)

Kenco Products Co Inc .... G 216 351-7610
Cleveland (G-4282)

◆ Kirtland Capital Partners LP .... E 216 593-0100
Beachwood (G-993)

Lock Joint Tube Ohio LLC .... C 210 278-3757
Orwell (G-12167)

▲ Lsp Tubes Inc .... D 216 378-2092
Orwell (G-12168)

Major Metals Company .... E 419 886-4600
Mansfield (G-9681)

Mattr US Inc .... E 513 683-7800
Loveland (G-9495)

Metallus Inc .... E 330 471-7000
Canton (G-2163)

Phillips Mfg and Tower Co .... D 419 347-1720
Shelby (G-13197)

▲ PMC Industries Corp .... D 440 943-3300
Wickliffe (G-15848)

Ptc Alliance LLC .... E 330 821-5700
Alliance (G-421)

▲ Reliacheck Manufacturing Inc .... E 440 933-6162
Brookpark (G-1724)

▲ Shelar Inc .... C 419 729-9756
Toledo (G-14470)

T & D Fabricating Inc .... E 440 951-5646
Eastlake (G-7051)

Terrasmart LLC .... E 239 362-0211
Columbus (G-5818)

TI Group Auto Systems LLC .... E 740 929-2049
Hebron (G-8366)

Tubetech Inc .... G 330 426-9476
East Palestine (G-7011)

Unison Industries LLC .... B 904 667-9904
Dayton (G-6175)

United Tube Corporation .... D 330 725-4196
Medina (G-10392)

Vallourec Star LP .... C 330 742-6227
Girard (G-7976)

▲ Vallourec Star LP .... C 330 742-6300
Youngstown (G-16466)

Wheatland Tube LLC .... C 724 342-6851
Niles (G-11692)

Wheatland Tube LLC .... C 330 372-6611
Warren (G-15224)

Woodsage LLC .... C 419 866-8000
Holland (G-8539)

Zekelman Industries Inc .... E 216 910-3700
Beachwood (G-1033)

Zekelman Industries Inc .... C 740 432-2146
Cambridge (G-1961)

3321 Gray and ductile iron foundries

A C Williams Co Inc .... E 330 296-6110
Ravenna (G-12699)

Akron Gear & Engineering Inc .... E 330 773-6608
Akron (G-34)

Amsted Industries Incorporated .... D 614 836-2323
Groveport (G-8129)

Anchor Glass Container Corp .... D 740 452-2743
Zanesville (G-16500)

Arcelrmttal Tblar Pdts Shlby L .... A 419 347-2424
Shelby (G-13191)

Barberton Steel Industries Inc .... E 330 745-6837
Barberton (G-861)

Blanchester Foundry Co Inc .... F
Blanchester (G-1348)

Brittany Stamping LLC .... A 216 267-0850
Cleveland (G-3760)

Cast Metals Incorporated .... F 419 278-2010
Deshler (G-6799)

Cast-Fab Technologies Inc .... C 513 758-1000
Cincinnati (G-2707)

Castco Inc .... F 440 365-2333
Elyria (G-7123)

Casting Solutions LLC .... C 740 452-9371
Zanesville (G-16518)

Castings Usa Inc .... G 330 339-3611
New Philadelphia (G-11491)

Chris Erhart Foundry & Mch Co .... E 513 421-6550
Cincinnati (G-2734)

▲ Cmt Imports Inc .... G 513 615-1851
Cincinnati (G-2777)

Col-Pump Company Inc .... D 330 482-1029
Columbiana (G-5033)

Columbiana Foundry Company .... C 330 482-3336
Columbiana (G-5034)

D Picking & Co .... G 419 562-6891
Bucyrus (G-1856)

▲ Dd Foundry Inc .... F 216 362-4100
Brookpark (G-1712)

Domestic Casting Company LLC .... F 717 532-6615
Delaware (G-6718)

Ej Usa Inc .... G 614 871-2436
Grove City (G-8091)

Ej Usa Inc .... F 216 692-3001
South Euclid (G-13460)

Ej Usa Inc .... F 330 782-3900
Youngstown (G-16354)

◆ Ellwood Engineered Castings Co .... C 330 568-3000
Hubbard (G-8563)

Elyria Foundry Company LLC .... D 440 322-4657
Elyria (G-7141)

Engines Inc of Ohio .... E 740 377-9874
South Point (G-13466)

Foote Foundry LLC .... E 740 694-1595
Fredericktown (G-7746)

Ford Motor Company .... D 216 676-7918
Brookpark (G-1715)

General Aluminum Mfg Company .... C 419 739-9300
Wapakoneta (G-15115)

General Motors LLC .... B 419 782-7010
Defiance (G-6678)

Hamilton Brass & Alum Castings .... E
Hamilton (G-8216)

Hobart LLC .... E 937 332-2797
Piqua (G-12525)

Hobart LLC .... E 937 332-3000
Troy (G-14581)

▲ Hobart LLC .... D 937 332-3000
Troy (G-14582)

Howmet Aerospace Inc .... A 216 641-3600
Newburgh Heights (G-11615)

Kenton Iron Products Inc .... E 419 674-4178
Kenton (G-8886)

▲ Knappco Corporation .... C 513 870-3100
West Chester (G-15455)

▲ Korff Holdings LLC .... C 330 332-1566
Salem (G-13008)

▲ Liberty Casting Company LLC .... D 740 363-1941
Delaware (G-6735)

McWane Inc .... B 740 622-6651
Coshocton (G-5983)

Miami-Cast Inc .... F 937 866-2951
Miamisburg (G-10659)

Old Smo Inc .... G 419 394-3346
Saint Marys (G-12960)

Old Smo Inc .... C 419 394-3346
Saint Marys (G-12961)

▲ OS Kelly Corporation .... E 937 322-4921
Springfield (G-13614)

Osco Industries Inc .... D 740 286-5004
Jackson (G-8720)

◆ Osco Industries Inc .... B 740 354-3183
Portsmouth (G-12652)

Pioneer City Casting Company .... E 740 423-7533
Belpre (G-1260)

Piqua Champion Foundry Inc .... D
Piqua (G-12543)

Quality Castings Company .... B 330 682-6010
Orrville (G-12147)

Sancast Inc .... E 740 622-8660
Coshocton (G-5995)

Skuld LLC .... G 330 423-7339
Springfield (G-13633)

T & B Foundry Company .... E 216 391-4200
Cleveland (G-4764)

Tangent Air Inc .... E 740 474-1114
Circleville (G-3556)

▲ Thyssnkrupp Rothe Erde USA Inc .... C 330 562-4000
Aurora (G-362)

Tiffin Foundry & Machine Inc .... E 419 447-3991
Tiffin (G-14109)

Tri Cast Limited Partnership .... E 330 733-8718
Akron (G-362)

Tri-Cast Inc .... E 330 733-8718
Akron (G-363)

Vanex Tube Corporation .... D 330 544-9500
Niles (G-11690)

▲ W E Lott Company .... F 419 563-9400
Bucyrus (G-1873)

▲ Wallace Forge Company .... D 330 488-1203
Canton (G-2265)

Whemco-Ohio Foundry Inc .... C 419 222-2111
Lima (G-9302)

Yellow Creek Casting Co Inc .... C 330 532-4608
Wellsville (G-15338)

3322 Malleable iron foundries

Cast-Fab Technologies Inc .... C 513 758-1000
Cincinnati (G-2707)

Ej Usa Inc .... F 216 692-3001
South Euclid (G-13460)

SIC SECTION   33 PRIMARY METAL INDUSTRIES

◆ Ellwood Engineered Castings Co.......C 330 568-3000
  Hubbard *(G-8563)*
General Aluminum Mfg Company...........C 419 739-9300
  Wapakoneta *(G-15115)*
General Motors LLC.................................B 419 782-7010
  Defiance *(G-6678)*
Kenton Iron Products Inc.........................E 419 674-4178
  Kenton *(G-8886)*
Old Smo Inc..C 419 394-3346
  Saint Marys *(G-12961)*
Osco Industries Inc.................................D 740 286-5004
  Jackson *(G-8720)*
Pioneer City Casting Company..............E 740 423-7533
  Belpre *(G-1260)*
Sancast Inc...E 740 622-8660
  Coshocton *(G-5995)*
T & B Foundry Company..........................E 216 391-4200
  Cleveland *(G-4764)*
Tiffin Foundry & Machine Inc..................E 419 447-3991
  Tiffin *(G-14109)*
▲ W E Lott Company..................................F 419 563-9400
  Bucyrus *(G-1873)*
Whemco-Ohio Foundry Inc.....................C 419 222-2111
  Lima *(G-9302)*
Yellow Creek Casting Co Inc....................F 330 532-4608
  Wellsville *(G-15338)*

3324 Steel investment foundries

Aeropact Manufacturing LLC..................F 419 373-1711
  Bowling Green *(G-1551)*
B W Grinding Co.......................................E 419 923-1376
  Lyons *(G-9531)*
▲ Bescast Inc..C 440 946-5300
  Willoughby *(G-15889)*
Brost Foundry Company.........................E 216 641-1131
  Cleveland *(G-3763)*
▲ Castalloy Inc..D 216 961-7990
  Cleveland *(G-3798)*
▲ Cmt Imports Inc....................................G 513 615-1851
  Cincinnati *(G-2777)*
▲ Consoldted Precision Pdts Corp........C 216 453-4800
  Cleveland *(G-3897)*
▲ Consolidated Foundries Inc...............C 909 595-2252
  Cleveland *(G-3899)*
▲ Dd Foundry Inc.....................................F 216 362-4100
  Brookpark *(G-1712)*
General Aluminum Mfg Company...........C 419 739-9300
  Wapakoneta *(G-15115)*
Harbor Castings Inc................................E 330 499-7178
  Cuyahoga Falls *(G-6089)*
Mercury Machine Co................................D 440 349-3222
  Solon *(G-13386)*
Mold Masters Intl LLC.............................C 440 953-0220
  Eastlake *(G-7042)*
P-Mac Ltd..G 419 235-2245
  Bowling Green *(G-1580)*
PCC Airfoils LLC.......................................C 440 255-9770
  Mentor *(G-10521)*
PCC Airfoils LLC.......................................C 330 868-6441
  Minerva *(G-11038)*
Precision Castparts Corp........................F 440 350-6150
  Painesville *(G-12258)*
▲ Rimer Enterprises Inc..........................E 419 878-8156
  Waterville *(G-15251)*
Skuld LLC..G 330 423-7339
  Springfield *(G-13633)*
▲ Steel Ceilings Inc..................................E 740 967-1063
  Johnstown *(G-8778)*
▲ W E Lott Company................................F 419 563-9400
  Bucyrus *(G-1873)*
▲ Xapc Co..C 216 362-4100
  Cleveland *(G-4926)*

3325 Steel foundries, nec

▲ Alcon Industries Inc.............................D 216 961-1100
  Cleveland *(G-3625)*
Brost Foundry Company.........................E 216 641-1131
  Cleveland *(G-3763)*
Castings Usa Inc.....................................G 330 339-3611
  New Philadelphia *(G-11491)*
Columbiana Foundry Company..............C 330 482-3336
  Columbiana *(G-5034)*
▲ Columbus Steel Castings Co..............A 614 444-2121
  Columbus *(G-5278)*
Coronado Steel Co..................................E 330 744-1143
  Youngstown *(G-16341)*
▲ Dd Foundry Inc......................................F 216 362-4100
  Brookpark *(G-1712)*
Durivage Pattern and Mfg Inc.................E 419 836-8655
  Williston *(G-15870)*
Elyria Foundry Company LLC.................D 440 322-4657
  Elyria *(G-7141)*
Engines Inc of Ohio.................................E 740 377-9874
  South Point *(G-13466)*
▲ Evertz Technology Svc USA Inc..........F 513 422-8400
  Middletown *(G-10824)*
Harbor Castings Inc................................E 330 499-7178
  Cuyahoga Falls *(G-6089)*
▲ Jmac Inc...E 614 436-2418
  Columbus *(G-5498)*
▲ Jrm 2 Company......................................D 513 554-1700
  Cincinnati *(G-3052)*
▲ Korff Holdings LLC................................G 330 332-1566
  Salem *(G-13008)*
Lakeway Mfg Inc......................................E 419 433-3030
  Huron *(G-8637)*
Precision Polymer Casting LLC.............G 440 343-0461
  Moreland Hills *(G-11220)*
Premier Inv Cast Group LLC...................E 937 299-7333
  Moraine *(G-11202)*
Rampp Company......................................E 740 373-7886
  Marietta *(G-9819)*
◆ Sandusky International Inc..................C 419 626-5340
  Sandusky *(G-13090)*
Shl Liquidation Medina Inc.....................C
  Valley City *(G-14895)*
Tiffin Foundry & Machine Inc..................E 419 447-3991
  Tiffin *(G-14109)*
United Engineering & Fndry Co..............E 330 456-2761
  Canton *(G-2253)*
▲ W E Lott Company.................................F 419 563-9400
  Bucyrus *(G-1873)*
Whemco-Ohio Foundry Inc.....................C 419 222-2111
  Lima *(G-9302)*
Worthington Enterprises Inc..................D 513 539-9291
  Monroe *(G-11121)*
◆ Worthington Enterprises Inc..............C 614 438-3210
  Worthington *(G-16220)*
Worthngton Stelpac Systems LLC.........C 614 438-3205
  Columbus *(G-5886)*

3331 Primary copper

Hildreth Mfg LLC......................................E 740 375-5832
  Marion *(G-9856)*
▲ Sam Dong Ohio Inc...............................D 740 363-1985
  Delaware *(G-6748)*

3334 Primary aluminum

◆ Alcan Primary Products Corp..............A
  Independence *(G-8653)*
Homan Metals LLC...................................G 513 721-5010
  Cincinnati *(G-3004)*
Kaiser Aluminum Fab Pdts LLC..............C 740 522-1151
  Heath *(G-8323)*
◆ Ormet Corporation................................A 740 483-1381
  Hannibal *(G-8261)*
▲ Ormet Primary Aluminum Corp..........A 740 483-1381
  Hannibal *(G-8262)*
P&The Mfg Acquisition LLC....................D 937 492-4134
  Sidney *(G-13269)*
Real Alloy Specialty Pdts LLC................A 216 755-8836
  Beachwood *(G-1014)*
Real Alloy Specification LLC..................D 216 755-8900
  Beachwood *(G-1016)*

3339 Primary nonferrous metals, nec

◆ Aci Industries Ltd.................................E 740 368-4160
  Delaware *(G-6699)*
▲ Advance Materials Products Inc........G 330 650-4000
  Hudson *(G-8582)*
◆ American Spring Wire Corp.................C 216 292-4620
  Bedford Heights *(G-1163)*
◆ AMG Aluminum North America LLC...F 659 348-3620
  Cambridge *(G-1920)*
Cleveland-Cliffs Inc................................E 216 694-5700
  Toledo *(G-14243)*
Elemetal Refining LLC............................C 740 286-6457
  Jackson *(G-8714)*
Elmet Euclid LLC.....................................D 216 692-3990
  Euclid *(G-7267)*
Elmet Technologies Inc..........................E 216 692-3990
  Cleveland *(G-4007)*
◆ Ferroglobe USA Mtllurgical Inc..........C 740 984-2361
  Waterford *(G-15236)*
Galt Alloys Inc Main Ofc.........................G 330 453-4678
  Canton *(G-2109)*
Gdc Industries LLC..................................G 937 367-7229
  Dayton *(G-6346)*
▲ Magnesium Refining Techno...............D 419 483-9199
  Cleveland *(G-4350)*
Materion Brush Inc.................................A 419 862-2745
  Elmore *(G-7103)*
▲ Materion Brush Inc...............................D 216 486-4200
  Mayfield Heights *(G-10250)*
◆ Materion Corporation...........................C 216 486-4200
  Mayfield Heights *(G-10251)*
▲ Metallic Resources Inc........................E 330 425-3155
  Twinsburg *(G-14696)*
Newton Materion Inc..............................B 216 692-3990
  Euclid *(G-7287)*
Ohio Valley Specialty Company.............F 740 373-2276
  Marietta *(G-9813)*
◆ Quality Gold Inc....................................B 513 942-7659
  Fairfield *(G-7400)*
▲ Rhenium Alloys Inc...............................E 440 365-7388
  North Ridgeville *(G-11858)*
Silicon Processors Inc...........................G 740 373-2252
  Marietta *(G-9823)*
Swift Manufacturing Co Inc....................G 740 237-4405
  Ironton *(G-8704)*
▲ Zircoa Inc...C 440 248-0500
  Cleveland *(G-4936)*

3341 Secondary nonferrous metals

A & B Iron & Metal Co Inc......................G 937 228-1561
  Dayton *(G-6178)*
◆ Aci Industries Ltd.................................E 740 368-4160
  Delaware *(G-6699)*
Agmet LLC...F 216 663-8200
  Cleveland *(G-3615)*
Applied Materials Finshg Ltd.................E 330 336-5645
  Brooklyn Heights *(G-1682)*
Auris Noble LLC.......................................E 330 321-6649
  Akron *(G-68)*
Beck Aluminum Alloys Ltd.....................D 216 861-4455
  Mayfield Heights *(G-10247)*

Employee Codes: A=Over 500 employees, B=251-500
C=101-250, D=51-100, E=20-50, F=10-19, G=1-9

33 PRIMARY METAL INDUSTRIES

▲ Cirba Solutions Us Inc .... E 740 653-6290
  Lancaster (G-9000)
Circuit Board Mining LLC .... G 419 348-1057
  Alvada (G-442)
Cohen Brothers Inc .... F 513 217-5200
  Middletown (G-10812)
Cohen Brothers Inc .... E 513 422-3696
  Middletown (G-10811)
Continental Metal Proc Co .... E 216 268-0000
  Cleveland (G-3902)
Continental Metal Proc Co .... F 216 268-0000
  Cleveland (G-3901)
Echo Environmental Waverly LLC .... G 740 710-7901
  Waverly (G-15280)
Elemetal Refining LLC .... C 740 286-6457
  Jackson (G-8714)
▼ Fex LLC .... F 412 604-0400
  Mingo Junction (G-11045)
▲ Fpt Cleveland LLC .... C 216 441-3800
  Cleveland (G-4000)
▲ Franklin Iron & Metal Corp .... C 937 253-8184
  Dayton (G-6338)
▲ Fusion Incorporated .... D 440 946-3300
  Willoughby (G-15922)
G A Avril Company .... F 513 641-0566
  Cincinnati (G-2925)
▲ Garden Street Iron & Metal Inc .... E 513 721-4660
  Cincinnati (G-2928)
Gnw Aluminum Inc .... E 330 821-7955
  Alliance (G-405)
◆ I Schumann & Co LLC .... C 440 439-2300
  Bedford (G-1126)
▲ Jrm 2 Company .... D 513 554-1700
  Cincinnati (G-3052)
Materion Brush Inc .... A 419 862-2745
  Elmore (G-7103)
▲ Materion Brush Inc .... D 216 486-4200
  Mayfield Heights (G-10250)
◆ Materion Corporation .... C 216 486-4200
  Mayfield Heights (G-10251)
▼ Mek Van Wert Inc .... G 419 203-4902
  Van Wert (G-14923)
Metal Shredders Inc .... F 937 866-0777
  Miamisburg (G-10656)
Metalico Akron Inc .... F 330 376-1400
  Akron (G-246)
Mw Metals Group LLC .... D 937 222-5992
  Dayton (G-6462)
▲ National Bronze Mtls Ohio Inc .... E 440 277-1226
  Lorain (G-9425)
▲ Novelis Alr Recycling Ohio LLC .... C 740 922-2373
  Uhrichsville (G-14767)
Novelis Corporation .... C 740 983-2571
  Ashville (G-670)
◆ Oakwood Industries Inc .... D 440 232-8700
  Bedford (G-1146)
Ohio Metal Processing LLC .... G 740 912-2057
  Jackson (G-8719)
▲ Ohio Valley Alloy Services Inc .... E 740 373-1900
  Marietta (G-9812)
Old Rar Inc .... A 216 545-7249
  Beachwood (G-1007)
▲ Polymet Corporation .... E 513 874-3586
  West Chester (G-15482)
Precision Strip Inc .... D 419 674-4186
  Kenton (G-8897)
▲ R L S Corporation .... F 740 773-1440
  Chillicothe (G-2530)
▲ Real Alloy Recycling LLC .... D 216 755-8900
  Beachwood (G-1013)
Real Alloy Specialty Pdts LLC .... A 440 563-3487
  Rock Creek (G-12832)

Real Alloy Specialty Pdts LLC .... A 216 755-8836
  Beachwood (G-1014)
Real Alloy Specification LLC .... D 216 755-8900
  Beachwood (G-1016)
Rm Advisory Group Inc .... E 513 242-2100
  Cincinnati (G-3346)
Rmi Titanium Company LLC .... C 330 471-1844
  Canton (G-2216)
Rmi Titanium Company LLC .... C 330 453-2118
  Canton (G-2217)
Rnw Holdings Inc .... E 330 792-0600
  Youngstown (G-16429)
Rumpke Transportation Co LLC .... B 513 242-4600
  Cincinnati (G-3356)
▲ Sims Bros Inc .... D 740 387-9041
  Marion (G-9883)
Thyssenkrupp Materials NA Inc .... D 216 883-8100
  Independence (G-8687)
Victory White Metal Company .... E 216 271-1400
  Cleveland (G-4075)
W R G Inc .... E 216 351-8494
  Avon Lake (G-827)
▲ Wieland Metal Svcs Foils LLC .... D 330 823-1700
  Alliance (G-437)

3351 Copper rolling and drawing

◆ Alcan Corporation .... E 440 460-3307
  Cleveland (G-3622)
▲ American Wire & Cable Company .... E 440 235-1140
  Olmsted Twp (G-12085)
Arem Co .... F 440 974-6740
  Mentor (G-10423)
Avtron Aerospace Inc .... C 216 750-5152
  Cleveland (G-3709)
Commconnect .... F 937 414-0505
  Dayton (G-6259)
◆ Core Optix Inc .... F 855 267-3678
  Cincinnati (G-2796)
Federal Metal Company .... F 440 232-8700
  Bedford (G-1120)
Jj Seville LLC .... F 330 769-2071
  Seville (G-13144)
▲ Materion Brush Inc .... D 216 486-4200
  Mayfield Heights (G-10250)
◆ Materion Corporation .... C 216 486-4200
  Mayfield Heights (G-10251)
◆ Production Tube Cutting Inc .... E 937 254-6138
  Dayton (G-6530)
◆ Republic Wire Inc .... D 513 860-1800
  West Chester (G-15496)
Stoutheart Corporation .... E 800 556-6470
  Chagrin Falls (G-2425)
T & D Fabricating Inc .... E 440 951-5646
  Eastlake (G-7051)

3353 Aluminum sheet, plate, and foil

B&B Distributors LLC .... F 440 324-1293
  Elyria (G-7113)
Holmes Manufacturing .... G 330 231-6327
  Millersburg (G-10968)
Howmet Aerospace Inc .... C 330 848-4000
  Barberton (G-872)
Howmet Aerospace Inc .... E 330 544-7633
  Niles (G-11671)
Howmet Aerospace Inc .... D 330 222-1501
  Salem (G-13002)
◆ Interntnl Cnvrter Cldwell Inc .... C 740 732-5665
  Caldwell (G-1909)
▲ Monarch Steel Company Inc .... E 216 587-8000
  Cleveland (G-4420)
Novelis Alr Almnum-Alabama LLC .... E 256 353-1550
  Beachwood (G-1003)

Novelis Corporation .... D 330 841-3456
  Warren (G-15193)
PB Fbrction Mech Contrs Corp .... E 419 478-4869
  Toledo (G-14429)
▲ Wieland Metal Svcs Foils LLC .... D 330 823-1700
  Alliance (G-437)

3354 Aluminum extruded products

Accu-Tek Tool & Die Inc .... G 330 726-1946
  Salem (G-12975)
◆ Alanod Westlake Metal Ind Inc .... E 440 327-8184
  North Ridgeville (G-11826)
Allite Inc .... G 937 200-0831
  Miamisburg (G-10610)
▲ Alufab Inc .... G 513 528-7281
  Cincinnati (G-2551)
Aluminum Extruded Shapes Inc .... C 513 563-2205
  Cincinnati (G-2613)
▲ American Aluminum Extrusions .... C 330 458-0300
  Canton (G-2033)
◆ AMG Aluminum North America LLC .... F 659 348-3620
  Cambridge (G-1920)
Arem Co .... F 440 974-6740
  Mentor (G-10423)
Astro Aluminum Enterprises Inc .... E 330 755-1414
  Struthers (G-13900)
Astro Shapes .... E 330 755-1414
  Youngstown (G-16314)
Astro Shapes LLC .... B 330 755-1414
  Struthers (G-13901)
Astro-Coatings Inc .... E 330 755-1414
  Struthers (G-13902)
Bidwell Family Corporation .... C 513 988-6351
  Trenton (G-14540)
BRT Extrusions Inc .... C 330 544-0177
  Niles (G-11662)
Central Aluminum Company LLC .... E 614 491-5700
  Obetz (G-12057)
Da Investments Inc .... D 330 781-6100
  Youngstown (G-16346)
▲ Extrudex Aluminum Inc .... C 330 538-4444
  North Jackson (G-11783)
◆ Flexrack By Qcells LLC .... C 216 998-5988
  Cleveland (G-4069)
▲ Fom USA Incorporated .... G 234 248-4400
  Medina (G-10325)
Gei of Columbiana Inc .... E 330 783-0270
  Youngstown (G-16364)
General Extrusions Intl LLC .... C 330 783-0270
  Youngstown (G-16365)
◆ H-P Products Inc .... C 330 875-5556
  Louisville (G-9459)
Hydro Aluminum Fayetteville .... F 937 492-9194
  Sidney (G-13254)
Industrial Mold Inc .... E 330 425-7374
  Twinsburg (G-14676)
◆ Isaiah Industries Inc .... D 937 773-9840
  Piqua (G-12527)
Knoble Glass & Metal Inc .... G 513 753-1246
  Cincinnati (G-3084)
L & L Ornamental Iron Co .... E 513 353-1930
  Cleves (G-4958)
Langstons Ultmate Clg Svcs Inc .... F 330 298-9150
  Ravenna (G-12722)
M-D Building Products Inc .... F 513 539-2255
  Middletown (G-10837)
▲ McKnight Industries Inc .... E 937 592-9010
  Bellefontaine (G-1216)
▲ National Metal Shapes Inc .... E 740 363-9559
  Delaware (G-6741)
Novelis Alr Aluminum LLC .... A 216 910-3400
  Beachwood (G-1004)

▲ Orrvilon Inc .... C 330 684-9400
  Orrville (G-12145)
Owens Corning Sales LLC .... F 740 983-1300
  Ashville (G-671)
Patton Aluminum Products Inc .... F 937 845-9404
  New Carlisle (G-11424)
Pennex Aluminum Company LLC .... D 330 427-6704
  Leetonia (G-9129)
Star Extruded Shapes Inc .... B 330 533-9863
  Canfield (G-2018)
Star Fab Inc .... E 330 482-1601
  Columbiana (G-5052)
▲ Star Fab Inc .... C 330 533-9863
  Canfield (G-2019)
Systems Kit LLC MB .... E 330 945-4500
  Akron (G-343)
T & D Fabricating Inc .... E 440 951-5646
  Eastlake (G-7051)
Tecnocap Inc .... C 330 392-7222
  Warren (G-15208)
Tri County Tarp LLC .... E 419 288-3350
  Gibsonburg (G-7956)
▲ Trivium Alum Packg USA Corp .... E 330 744-9505
  Youngstown (G-16460)
▲ Urban Industries of Ohio Inc .... E 419 468-3578
  Galion (G-7886)
▲ Vari-Wall Tube Specialists Inc .... D 330 482-0000
  Columbiana (G-5053)
Youngstown Tool & Die Company ...... D 330 747-4464
  Youngstown (G-16489)
Zarbana Alum Extrusions LLC .... E 330 482-5092
  Columbiana (G-5056)
Zarbana Industries Inc .... E 330 482-5092
  Columbiana (G-5057)

3355 Aluminum rolling and drawing, nec

◆ Alcan Corporation .... E 440 460-3307
  Cleveland (G-3622)
Aleris Rm Inc .... A 216 910-3400
  Beachwood (G-973)
Aluminum Extrusion Tech LLC .... G 330 533-3994
  Canfield (G-1999)
◆ AMG Aluminum North America LLC .. F 659 348-3620
  Cambridge (G-1920)
Amh Holdings II Inc .... B 330 929-1811
  Cuyahoga Falls (G-6066)
Eastman Kodak Company .... E 937 259-3000
  Dayton (G-6311)
Homan Metals Inc .... G 513 721-5010
  Cincinnati (G-3004)
Howmet Aerospace Inc .... E 330 544-7633
  Niles (G-11671)
Kaiser Aluminum Fab Pdts LLC .... C 740 522-1151
  Heath (G-8323)
Mac Its LLC .... G 937 454-0722
  Vandalia (G-14947)
Novelis Alr Aluminum LLC .... A 216 910-3400
  Beachwood (G-1004)
Novelis Alr Rolled Pdts LLC .... A 740 983-2571
  Ashville (G-669)
▲ Novelis Alr Rolled Pdts LLC .... E 216 910-3400
  Beachwood (G-1005)
Novelis Corporation .... D 330 841-3456
  Warren (G-15193)
◆ Pandrol Inc .... D 419 592-5050
  Napoleon (G-11330)
Powermount Systems Inc .... G 740 499-4330
  La Rue (G-8945)
Real Alloy Specialty Pdts LLC .... E 440 322-0072
  Elyria (G-7199)
Real Alloy Specialty Pdts LLC .... C 216 755-8836
  Beachwood (G-1015)

Waxco International Inc .... F 937 746-4845
  Miamisburg (G-10701)

3356 Nonferrous rolling and drawing, nec

Air Craft Wheels LLC .... G 440 937-7903
  Ravenna (G-12701)
Allied Mask and Tooling Inc .... G 419 470-2555
  Toledo (G-14183)
BCi and V Investments Inc .... F 330 538-0660
  North Jackson (G-11778)
Bunting Bearings LLC .... E 419 522-3323
  Mansfield (G-9634)
◆ Canton Drop Forge Inc .... B 330 477-4511
  Canton (G-2061)
▲ Cleanlife Energy LLC .... F 800 316-2532
  Cleveland (G-3827)
Consolidated Metal Pdts Inc .... D 513 251-2624
  Cincinnati (G-2788)
Contour Forming Inc .... F 740 345-9777
  Newark (G-11572)
Curtiss-Wright Flow Ctrl Corp .... D 216 267-3200
  Cleveland (G-3922)
Economy Flame Hardening Inc .... F 216 431-9333
  Cleveland (G-3999)
Elemetal Refining LLC .... C 740 286-6457
  Jackson (G-8714)
ESAB Group Incorporated .... G 440 813-2506
  Ashtabula (G-632)
▲ Fusion Incorporated .... D 440 946-3300
  Willoughby (G-15922)
◆ G & S Titanium Inc .... E 330 263-0564
  Wooster (G-16122)
G A Avril Company .... F 513 731-5133
  Cincinnati (G-2926)
G A Avril Company .... F 513 641-0566
  Cincinnati (G-2925)
Gem City Metal Tech LLC .... E 937 252-8998
  Dayton (G-6349)
◆ J W Harris Co Inc .... B 513 754-2000
  Mason (G-10014)
Kilroy Company .... D 440 951-8700
  Cleveland (G-4289)
Lite Metals Company .... E 330 296-6110
  Ravenna (G-12724)
▲ Materion Brush Inc .... D 216 486-4200
  Mayfield Heights (G-10250)
◆ Materion Corporation .... C 216 486-4200
  Mayfield Heights (G-10251)
Mestek Inc .... F 419 288-2703
  Bradner (G-1603)
Metal Merchants Usa Inc .... F 330 723-3228
  Medina (G-10353)
▲ Metallic Resources Inc .... E 330 425-3155
  Twinsburg (G-14696)
Newton Materion Inc .... B 216 692-3990
  Euclid (G-7287)
Nickel Plate Railcar LLC .... G 440 382-6580
  Mentor (G-10510)
Nickels Marketing Group Inc .... G 440 835-1532
  Westlake (G-15767)
▲ Nova Machine Products Inc .... C 216 267-3200
  Middleburg Heights (G-10724)
Patriot Special Metals Inc .... D 330 580-9600
  Canton (G-2194)
▲ Rhenium Alloys Inc .... E 440 365-7388
  North Ridgeville (G-11858)
Rmi Titanium Company LLC .... G 330 652-9955
  Niles (G-11685)
◆ Rmi Titanium Company LLC .... E 330 652-9952
  Niles (G-11684)
◆ Rti International Metals Inc .... A
  Niles (G-11687)

Tailwind Technologies Inc .... A 937 778-4200
  Piqua (G-12555)
Th Magnesium Inc .... G 513 285-7568
  Cincinnati (G-3447)
Tin Wizard Heating & Coolg Inc .... G 330 467-9826
  Macedonia (G-9584)
Titanium Contractors Ltd .... G 513 256-2152
  Cincinnati (G-3456)
Titanium Metals Corporation .... A 740 537-1571
  Toronto (G-14535)
Victory White Metal Company .... F 216 641-2575
  Cleveland (G-4873)
▲ Victory White Metal Company .... D 216 271-1400
  Cleveland (G-4874)
▲ Water Star Inc .... F 440 996-0800
  Concord Township (G-5914)

3357 Nonferrous wiredrawing and insulating

◆ Alcan Corporation .... E 440 460-3307
  Cleveland (G-3622)
▲ American Wire & Cable Company ... E 440 235-1140
  Olmsted Twp (G-12085)
◆ Arnco Corporation .... D 800 847-7661
  Elyria (G-7112)
Astro Industries Inc .... E 937 429-5900
  Beavercreek (G-1041)
AT&T Corp .... G 513 792-9300
  Cincinnati (G-2639)
Calvert Wire & Cable Corp .... E 330 494-3248
  North Canton (G-11718)
Cbst Acquisition LLC .... D 513 361-9600
  Cincinnati (G-2711)
▲ Connectors Unlimited Inc .... E 440 357-1161
  Painesville (G-12224)
◆ Core Optix Inc .... F 855 267-3678
  Cincinnati (G-2796)
Electrovations Inc .... G 330 274-3558
  Solon (G-13341)
▼ Flex Technologies Inc .... E 740 922-5992
  Midvale (G-10878)
Legrand North America LLC .... B 937 224-0639
  Dayton (G-6403)
▲ Mueller Electric Company Inc .... E 216 771-5225
  Akron (G-256)
Ohio Associated Entps LLC .... F 440 354-3148
  Painesville (G-12253)
Projects Unlimited Inc .... C 937 918-2200
  Dayton (G-6534)
Radix Wire Co .... F 330 995-3677
  Aurora (G-733)
Radix Wire Co .... F 216 731-9191
  Solon (G-13412)
Radix Wire Co .... D 216 731-9191
  Solon (G-13411)
▲ Rah Investment Holding Inc .... D 330 832-8124
  Massillon (G-10138)
◆ Ribbon Technology Corporation ...... F 614 864-5444
  Gahanna (G-7848)
Sam Dong America Inc .... F 740 363-1985
  Delaware (G-6747)
Schneider Electric Usa Inc .... B 513 523-4171
  Oxford (G-12213)
Scott Fetzer Company .... C 216 267-9000
  Cleveland (G-4678)
Therm-O-Link Inc .... G 330 393-7600
  Warren (G-15209)
▲ Therm-O-Link Inc .... D 330 527-2124
  Garrettsville (G-7926)
Vulkor Incorporated .... E 330 393-7600
  Warren (G-15217)
Wiremax Ltd .... G 419 531-9500
  Toledo (G-14525)

Employee Codes: A=Over 500 employees, B=251-500
C=101-250, D=51-100, E=20-50, F=10-19, G=1-9

33 PRIMARY METAL INDUSTRIES

Xponet Inc .... E 440 354-6617
  Painesville *(G-12279)*

3363 Aluminum die-castings

Accro-Cast Corporation .... E 937 228-0497
  Dayton *(G-6179)*
▲ Ahresty Wilmington Corporation ..... B 937 382-6112
  Wilmington *(G-16038)*
Akron Foundry Co .... C 330 745-3101
  Akron *(G-33)*
American Light Metals LLC .... C 330 908-3065
  Macedonia *(G-9535)*
Apex Aluminum Die Cast Co Inc .... E 937 773-0432
  Piqua *(G-12503)*
▲ Cmt Imports Inc .... G 513 615-1851
  Cincinnati *(G-2777)*
CSM Horvath Ledgebrook Inc .... G 419 522-1133
  Mansfield *(G-9643)*
Destin Die Casting LLC .... E 937 347-1111
  Xenia *(G-10235)*
▼ Edc Liquidating Inc .... C 330 467-0750
  Macedonia *(G-9548)*
◆ Fort Recovery Industries Inc .... C 419 375-4121
  Fort Recovery *(G-7617)*
General Aluminum Mfg Company ...... C 419 739-9300
  Wapakoneta *(G-15115)*
General Die Casters Inc .... D 330 467-6700
  Northfield *(G-11906)*
▲ General Die Casters Inc .... E 330 678-2528
  Twinsburg *(G-14667)*
Krengel Equipment LLC .... C 440 946-3570
  Eastlake *(G-7037)*
Matalco (us) Inc .... E 234 806-0600
  Warren *(G-15189)*
▲ Matalco (us) Inc .... D 330 452-4760
  Canton *(G-2153)*
Model Pattern & Foundry Co .... F 513 542-2322
  Cincinnati *(G-3169)*
▲ Ohio Aluminum Industries Inc .... C 216 641-8865
  Cleveland *(G-4493)*
◆ Ohio Decorative Products LLC .... C 419 647-9033
  Spencerville *(G-13487)*
Omni USA Inc .... E 330 830-5500
  Massillon *(G-10132)*
◆ Park-Ohio Holdings Corp .... F 440 947-2000
  Cleveland *(G-4524)*
Park-Ohio Industries Inc .... C 440 947-2000
  Cleveland *(G-4525)*
Plaster Process Castings Co .... E 216 663-1814
  Cleveland *(G-4559)*
Ramco Electric Motors Inc .... D 937 548-2525
  Greenville *(G-8056)*
Ravana Industries Inc .... G 330 536-4015
  Lowellville *(G-9518)*
Reliable Castings Corporation .... D 937 497-5217
  Sidney *(G-13275)*
▲ Ross Casting & Innovation LLC ..... B 937 497-4500
  Sidney *(G-13280)*
Seilkop Industries Inc .... F 513 679-5680
  Cincinnati *(G-3376)*
Seilkop Industries Inc .... E 513 761-1035
  Cincinnati *(G-3377)*
Seyekcub Inc .... G 330 324-1394
  Uhrichsville *(G-14769)*
SRS Die Casting Holdings LLC .... E 330 467-0750
  Macedonia *(G-9577)*
SRS Light Metals Inc .... F 330 467-0750
  Macedonia *(G-9578)*
The Basic Aluminum Castings Co ..... D 216 481-5606
  Cleveland *(G-4779)*
◆ The Kindt-Collins Company LLC ..... D 216 252-4122
  Cleveland *(G-4788)*
▲ Thompson Aluminum Casting Co ... D 216 206-2781
  Cleveland *(G-4794)*
United States Drill Head Co .... E 513 941-0300
  Cincinnati *(G-3482)*
▲ W E Lott Company .... F 419 563-9400
  Bucyrus *(G-1873)*
Yoder Industries Inc .... C 937 278-5769
  Dayton *(G-6662)*

3364 Nonferrous die-castings except aluminum

◆ American De Rosa Lamparts LLC ..... D
  Cuyahoga Falls *(G-6063)*
American Light Metals LLC .... C 330 908-3065
  Macedonia *(G-9535)*
D Picking & Co .... G 419 562-6891
  Bucyrus *(G-1856)*
▲ Dd Foundry Inc .... F 216 362-4100
  Brookpark *(G-1712)*
▼ Edc Liquidating Inc .... C 330 467-0750
  Macedonia *(G-9548)*
▲ Empire Brass Co .... G 216 431-6565
  Cleveland *(G-4012)*
Federal Metal Company .... F 440 232-8700
  Bedford *(G-1120)*
General Die Casters Inc .... D 330 467-6700
  Northfield *(G-11906)*
▲ General Die Casters Inc .... E 330 678-2528
  Twinsburg *(G-14667)*
Hamilton Brass & Alum Castings .... E
  Hamilton *(G-8216)*
M & M Dies Inc .... G 216 883-6628
  Cleveland *(G-4342)*
Martina Metal LLC .... E 614 291-9700
  Columbus *(G-5544)*
Model Pattern & Foundry Co .... F 513 542-2322
  Cincinnati *(G-3169)*
◆ Oakwood Industries Inc .... D 440 232-8700
  Bedford *(G-1146)*
Plaster Process Castings Co .... E 216 663-1814
  Cleveland *(G-4559)*
SRS Die Casting Holdings LLC .... E 330 467-0750
  Macedonia *(G-9577)*
SRS Light Metals Inc .... F 330 467-0750
  Macedonia *(G-9578)*
Support Svc LLC .... G 419 617-0660
  Lexington *(G-9203)*
◆ The Kindt-Collins Company LLC ..... D 216 252-4122
  Cleveland *(G-4788)*
▲ Thompson Aluminum Casting Co ... D 216 206-2781
  Cleveland *(G-4794)*
Yoder Industries Inc .... C 937 278-5769
  Dayton *(G-6662)*

3365 Aluminum foundries

Acuity Brands Lighting Inc .... D 740 349-4343
  Newark *(G-11560)*
Air Craft Wheels LLC .... G 440 937-7903
  Ravenna *(G-12701)*
Akron Foundry Co .... C 330 745-3101
  Akron *(G-33)*
Albco Foundry Inc .... E 330 424-7716
  Lisbon *(G-9307)*
◆ Aluminum Line Products Company ..... D 440 835-8880
  Westlake *(G-15729)*
◆ AMG Aluminum North America LLC ..... F 659 348-3620
  Cambridge *(G-1920)*
Aztec Manufacturing Inc .... E 330 783-9947
  Youngstown *(G-16316)*
Boscott Metals Inc .... E 937 448-2018
  Bradford *(G-1599)*
Brost Foundry Company .... E 216 641-1131
  Cleveland *(G-3763)*
C M M S - Re LLC .... F 513 489-5111
  Blue Ash *(G-1375)*
Cast Metals Technology Inc .... E 937 968-5460
  Union City *(G-14777)*
Castek Inc .... E 440 365-2333
  Elyria *(G-7124)*
▲ Consoldted Precision Pdts Corp ..... C 216 453-4800
  Cleveland *(G-3897)*
▲ Dd Foundry Inc .... F 216 362-4100
  Brookpark *(G-1712)*
Durivage Pattern and Mfg Inc .... E 419 836-8655
  Williston *(G-15870)*
▲ Enprotech Industrial Tech LLC .... E 216 883-3220
  Cleveland *(G-4019)*
Francis Manufacturing Company ...... C 937 526-4551
  Russia *(G-12883)*
General Aluminum Mfg Company ..... B 440 593-6225
  Conneaut *(G-5918)*
General Aluminum Mfg Company ..... C 330 297-1020
  Ravenna *(G-12717)*
◆ General Aluminum Mfg LLC .... C 330 297-1225
  Ravenna *(G-12718)*
▲ General Die Casters Inc .... E 330 678-2528
  Twinsburg *(G-14667)*
General Motors LLC .... B 419 782-7010
  Defiance *(G-6678)*
General Precision Corporation .... G 440 951-9380
  Willoughby *(G-15925)*
Howmet Aluminum Casting Inc .... E 216 641-4340
  Newburgh Heights *(G-11616)*
Htci Co .... F 937 845-1204
  New Carlisle *(G-11417)*
Iabf Inc .... G 614 279-4498
  Columbus *(G-5451)*
▲ Jrm 2 Company .... D 513 554-1700
  Cincinnati *(G-3052)*
Lite Metals Company .... E 330 296-6110
  Ravenna *(G-12724)*
Mansfield Brass & Aluminu .... D 419 492-2154
  New Washington *(G-11548)*
▲ Miba Bearings US LLC .... B 740 962-4242
  Mcconnelsville *(G-10282)*
Miller Castings Inc .... D 330 482-2923
  Columbiana *(G-5045)*
Model Pattern & Foundry Co .... F 513 542-2322
  Cincinnati *(G-3169)*
Morris Bean & Company .... C 937 767-7301
  Yellow Springs *(G-16285)*
Mpe Aeroengines Inc .... E 937 878-3800
  Huber Heights *(G-8578)*
Multi Cast LLC .... E 419 335-0010
  Wauseon *(G-15269)*
Nelson Aluminum Foundry Inc .... G 440 543-1941
  Chagrin Falls *(G-2411)*
New Mansfield Brass & Alum Co .... F 419 492-2166
  New Washington *(G-11549)*
Non-Ferrous Casting Company .... G 937 228-1162
  Dayton *(G-6473)*
P C M Co .... E 330 336-8040
  Wadsworth *(G-15050)*
Piqua Emery Cutter & Fndry Co .... D 937 773-4134
  Piqua *(G-12545)*
▲ Pride Cast Metals Inc .... D 513 541-1295
  Cincinnati *(G-3274)*
Quality Match Plate Co Inc .... E 330 889-2462
  Southington *(G-13478)*
▲ Range Kleen Mfg Inc .... B 419 331-8000
  Elida *(G-7098)*
Ransom & Randolph LLC .... G 419 865-9497
  Maumee *(G-10227)*

Reliable Castings Corporation................. D 937 497-5217
  Sidney (G-13275)
Reliable Castings Corporation................. D
  Cincinnati (G-3331)
▲ Ross Aluminum Castings LLC.............. C 937 492-4134
  Sidney (G-13279)
Rotocast Technologies Inc....................... E 330 798-9091
  Akron (G-310)
Seilkop Industries Inc............................... F 513 679-5680
  Cincinnati (G-3376)
Skuld LLC... G 330 423-7339
  Springfield (G-13633)
▼ Specialized Castings Ltd....................... F 937 669-5620
  Greenville (G-8060)
▲ Stripmatic Products Inc....................... E 216 241-7143
  Cleveland (G-4740)
T W Corporation....................................... E 440 461-3234
  Akron (G-346)
Tessec LLC... D 937 576-0010
  Dayton (G-6615)
▲ Thompson Aluminum Casting Co....... D 216 206-2781
  Cleveland (G-4794)
Tri - Flex of Ohio Inc............................... G 330 705-7084
  North Canton (G-11770)
◆ US Metalcraft Inc................................. E 419 692-4962
  Delphos (G-6776)
Yoder Industries Inc................................. C 937 278-5769
  Dayton (G-6662)
Zephyr Industries Inc............................... G 419 281-4485
  Ashland (G-621)

3366 Copper foundries

Accurate Products Company.................... G 740 498-7202
  Newcomerstown (G-11641)
▲ Advance Bronze Inc............................. F 330 948-1231
  Lodi (G-9345)
Advance Bronzehubco Div....................... E 304 232-4414
  Lodi (G-9346)
Albco Foundry Inc.................................... E 330 424-7716
  Lisbon (G-9307)
American Bronze Corporation................. E 216 341-7800
  Cleveland (G-3651)
Brost Foundry Company.......................... E 419 522-1133
  Mansfield (G-9632)
Brost Foundry Company.......................... E 216 641-1131
  Cleveland (G-3763)
Buckeye Machining Inc........................... G 216 731-9535
  Euclid (G-7264)
Bunting Bearings LLC.............................. E 419 522-3323
  Mansfield (G-9634)
▲ Bunting Bearings LLC.......................... D 419 866-7000
  Holland (G-8495)
Calmego Specialized Pdts LLC................ F 937 669-5620
  Greenville (G-8041)
▲ Climax Metal Products Company....... D 440 943-8898
  Mentor (G-10440)
D Picking & Co.. G 419 562-6891
  Bucyrus (G-1856)
Dupont Specialty Pdts USA LLC.............. C 216 901-3600
  Cleveland (G-3978)
◆ Falcon Foundry Company..................... D 330 536-6221
  Lowellville (G-9514)
Foundry Artists Inc................................. G 216 391-9030
  Cleveland (G-4086)
Hadronics Inc... D 513 321-9350
  Cincinnati (G-2983)
High Tech Castings.................................. F 937 845-1204
  New Carlisle (G-11416)
Hot Brass Inc... G 440 564-5179
  Newbury (G-11626)
Johnson Metall Inc.................................. D 440 245-6826
  Lorain (G-9415)

M A Harrison Mfg Co Inc......................... E 440 965-4306
  Wakeman (G-15076)
Maass Midwest Mfg Inc........................... G 419 894-6424
  Arcadia (G-516)
McNeil Industries Inc.............................. E 440 951-7756
  Painesville (G-12251)
▲ Meierjohan-Wengler Inc...................... D 513 771-6074
  Cincinnati (G-3145)
Metaltek International Inc....................... D 419 626-5340
  Sandusky (G-13081)
Model Pattern & Foundry Co.................... F 513 542-2322
  Cincinnati (G-3169)
▲ National Bronze Mtls Ohio Inc............ E 440 277-1226
  Lorain (G-9425)
Non-Ferrous Casting Company................ G 937 228-1162
  Dayton (G-6473)
Oakes Foundry Inc.................................. E 330 372-4010
  Warren (G-15194)
Orrville Bronze & Aluminum Co.............. E 330 682-4015
  Orrville (G-12143)
Piqua Emery Cutter & Fndry Co............... D 937 773-4134
  Piqua (G-12545)
▲ Pride Cast Metals Inc.......................... D 513 541-1295
  Cincinnati (G-3274)
Randall Bearings Inc............................... F 419 678-2486
  Coldwater (G-5000)
▲ Randall Bearings Inc........................... D 419 223-1075
  Lima (G-9282)
Ryder-Heil Bronze Inc............................. E 419 562-2841
  Bucyrus (G-1868)
▲ S C Industries Inc................................ E 216 732-9000
  Euclid (G-7300)
▲ Santos Industrial Ltd............................ F 937 299-7333
  Moraine (G-11210)
▲ Semco Inc... D 800 848-5764
  Marion (G-9880)
▲ Stripmatic Products Inc....................... E 216 241-7143
  Cleveland (G-4740)
Whip Guide Co... F 440 543-5151
  Chagrin Falls (G-2434)

3369 Nonferrous foundries, nec

A C Williams Co Inc................................ E 330 296-6110
  Ravenna (G-12699)
Air Craft Wheels LLC............................. G 440 937-7903
  Ravenna (G-12701)
Akron Foundry Co.................................... C 330 745-3101
  Akron (G-33)
Albco Foundry Inc.................................... E 330 424-7716
  Lisbon (G-9307)
▲ Alcon Industries Inc............................. D 216 961-1100
  Cleveland (G-3625)
Apex Aluminum Die Cast Co Inc............. E 937 773-0432
  Piqua (G-12503)
Brost Foundry Company.......................... E 216 641-1131
  Cleveland (G-3763)
Bunting Bearings LLC.............................. E 419 522-3323
  Mansfield (G-9634)
▲ Catania Medallic Specialty Inc............ E 440 933-9595
  Avon Lake (G-801)
Columbiana Foundry Company................ C 330 482-3336
  Columbiana (G-5034)
Consoldted Precision Pdts Corp............... B 440 953-0053
  Eastlake (G-7023)
Cpp-Cleveland Inc................................... C 440 953-0053
  Eastlake (G-7024)
Cpp-Cleveland Inc................................... D 216 453-4800
  Cleveland (G-3913)
Curtiss-Wright Flow Ctrl Corp................. D 216 267-3200
  Cleveland (G-3922)
▲ Dd Foundry Inc..................................... F 216 362-4100
  Brookpark (G-1712)

Dmk Industries Inc.................................. F 513 727-4549
  Middletown (G-10818)
Durivage Pattern and Mfg Inc................. E 419 836-8655
  Williston (G-15870)
Ecm Industries LLC................................. E 513 533-6242
  Cincinnati (G-2857)
◆ Ellwood Engineered Castings Co........ C 330 568-3000
  Hubbard (G-8563)
Elyria Foundry Company LLC.................. D 440 322-4657
  Elyria (G-7141)
Esco Turbine Technologies...................... C 440 953-0053
  Eastlake (G-7031)
Francis Manufacturing Company............. C 937 526-4551
  Russia (G-12883)
◆ Frohn North America Inc..................... G 770 819-0089
  Bedford Heights (G-1173)
◆ Garfield Alloys Inc................................ F 216 587-4843
  Cleveland (G-4101)
General Aluminum Mfg Company............ B 440 593-6225
  Conneaut (G-5918)
General Aluminum Mfg Company............ E 330 297-1020
  Ravenna (G-12717)
◆ General Aluminum Mfg LLC................. C 330 297-1225
  Ravenna (G-12718)
▲ General Die Casters Inc....................... E 330 678-2528
  Twinsburg (G-14667)
General Motors LLC................................. B 419 782-7010
  Defiance (G-6678)
Harbor Castings Inc................................. E 330 499-7178
  Cuyahoga Falls (G-6089)
Hydro-Aire Aerospace Corp..................... C 440 323-3211
  Elyria (G-7159)
Iabf Inc... G 614 279-4498
  Columbus (G-5451)
▲ Ilsco LLC.. C 513 533-6200
  Cincinnati (G-3017)
▲ Jrm 2 Company..................................... D 513 554-1700
  Cincinnati (G-3052)
Kse Manufacturing................................... F 937 409-9831
  Sidney (G-13257)
Lite Metals Company............................... E 330 296-6110
  Ravenna (G-12724)
Materion Brush Inc.................................. A 419 862-2745
  Elmore (G-7103)
McM Precision Castings Inc................... E 419 669-3226
  Weston (G-15806)
Microweld Engineering Inc..................... G 614 847-9410
  Worthington (G-16204)
Morris Bean & Company.......................... C 937 767-7301
  Yellow Springs (G-16285)
Nelson Aluminum Foundry Inc................ G 440 543-1941
  Chagrin Falls (G-2411)
▲ Nova Machine Products Inc................. C 216 267-3200
  Middleburg Heights (G-10724)
◆ Ohio Decorative Products LLC............ C 419 647-9033
  Spencerville (G-13487)
Old Smo Inc... C 419 394-3346
  Saint Marys (G-12961)
◆ PCC Airfoils LLC................................... E 216 831-3590
  Cleveland (G-4536)
PCC Airfoils LLC...................................... F 216 766-6206
  Beachwood (G-1009)
PCC Airfoils LLC...................................... C 216 692-7900
  Cleveland (G-4537)
PCC Airfoils LLC...................................... B 740 982-6025
  Crooksville (G-6048)
PCC Airfoils LLC...................................... B 440 585-8247
  Eastlake (G-7044)
PCC Airfoils LLC...................................... C 440 255-9770
  Mentor (G-10521)
PCC Airfoils LLC...................................... C 330 868-6441
  Minerva (G-11038)

Employee Codes: A=Over 500 employees, B=251-500
C=101-250, D=51-100, E=20-50, F=10-19, G=1-9

33 PRIMARY METAL INDUSTRIES

PCC Airfoils LLC .... D 440 350-6150
   Painesville *(G-12256)*
Piqua Emery Cutter & Fndry Co .... D 937 773-4134
   Piqua *(G-12545)*
Precision Castparts Corp .... F 440 350-6150
   Painesville *(G-12258)*
Reliable Castings Corporation .... D 937 497-5217
   Sidney *(G-13275)*
▲ Ross Aluminum Castings LLC .... C 937 492-4134
   Sidney *(G-13279)*
Rossborough Supply Co .... F 216 941-6115
   Cleveland *(G-4652)*
Sam Americas Inc .... E 330 628-1118
   Mogadore *(G-11083)*
◆ Sandusky International Inc .... C 419 626-5340
   Sandusky *(G-13090)*
Seaport Mold & Casting Company .... E 419 243-1422
   Toledo *(G-14464)*
Seilkop Industries Inc .... F 513 679-5680
   Cincinnati *(G-3376)*
T & B Foundry Company .... E 216 391-4200
   Cleveland *(G-4764)*
▲ Technology House Ltd .... G 440 248-3025
   Streetsboro *(G-13795)*
Telcon LLC .... D 330 562-5566
   Streetsboro *(G-13796)*
▲ Thompson Aluminum Casting Co ...... D 216 206-2781
   Cleveland *(G-4794)*
◆ Voss Industries LLC .... C 216 771-7655
   Cleveland *(G-4884)*
Warren Castings Inc .... E 216 883-2520
   Cleveland *(G-4893)*
Yoder Industries Inc .... C 937 278-5769
   Dayton *(G-6662)*

3398 Metal heat treating

Akron Steel Treating Co .... E 330 773-8211
   Akron *(G-45)*
Al Fe Heat Treating-Ohio Inc .... E 330 336-0211
   Wadsworth *(G-15017)*
Al-Fe Heat Treating LLC .... F 419 782-7200
   Defiance *(G-6668)*
Alternative Flash Inc .... F 330 334-6111
   Wadsworth *(G-15018)*
AM Castle & Co .... F 330 425-7000
   Bedford *(G-1100)*
▲ Amac Enterprises Inc .... C 216 362-1880
   Parma *(G-12286)*
▲ American Metal Treating Co .... E 216 431-4492
   Cleveland *(G-3654)*
American Quality Stripping Inc .... E 419 625-6288
   Sandusky *(G-13044)*
American Steel Treating Inc .... D 419 874-2044
   Perrysburg *(G-12361)*
ATI Flat Rlled Pdts Hldngs LLC .... F 330 875-2244
   Louisville *(G-9455)*
Atmosphere Annealing LLC .... D 330 478-0314
   Kenton *(G-8880)*
B&C Machine Co LLC .... E 330 745-4013
   Barberton *(G-859)*
Bekaert Corporation .... E 330 683-5060
   Orrville *(G-12119)*
Berkshire Road Holdings Inc .... F 216 883-4200
   Cleveland *(G-3731)*
Bob Lanes Welding Inc .... F 740 373-3567
   Marietta *(G-9779)*
Bodycote Imt Inc .... F 740 852-5000
   London *(G-9382)*
Bodycote Srfc Tech Prperty LLC .... C 513 770-4900
   Mason *(G-9961)*
Bodycote Srfc Tech Wrtburg Inc .... E 513 770-4900
   Mason *(G-9962)*

Bodycote Surfc Tech Mexico LLC .... C 513 770-4900
   Mason *(G-9965)*
Bodycote Thermal Proc Inc .... E 513 921-2300
   Cincinnati *(G-2675)*
Bodycote Thermal Proc Inc .... E 440 473-2020
   Cleveland *(G-3744)*
Bodycote Thermal Proc Inc .... G 740 852-4955
   London *(G-9383)*
Bolttech Mannings Inc .... G 614 836-0021
   Groveport *(G-8133)*
Bowdil Company .... F 800 356-8663
   Canton *(G-2051)*
Carpe Diem Industries LLC .... D 419 358-0129
   Bluffton *(G-1502)*
Carpe Diem Industries LLC .... D 419 659-5639
   Columbus Grove *(G-5897)*
Certified Heat Treating Inc .... F 937 866-0245
   Dayton *(G-6250)*
Cincinnati Gearing Systems Inc .... D 513 527-8600
   Cincinnati *(G-2731)*
Cincinnati Stl Treating Co LLC .... E 513 271-3173
   Cincinnati *(G-2762)*
▲ Cleveland-Cliffs Columbus LLC .... D 614 492-6800
   Richfield *(G-12784)*
◆ Clifton Steel Company .... D 216 662-6111
   Maple Heights *(G-9749)*
Dayton Forging Heat Treating .... G 937 253-4126
   Dayton *(G-6278)*
Derrick Company Inc .... E 513 321-8122
   Cincinnati *(G-2825)*
Detroit Flame Hardening Co .... F 513 942-1400
   Fairfield *(G-7352)*
Dewitt Inc .... G 216 662-0800
   Maple Heights *(G-9750)*
▲ Die Co Inc .... E 440 942-8856
   Eastlake *(G-7025)*
▲ Dowa Tht America Inc .... E 419 354-4144
   Bowling Green *(G-1564)*
Erie Steel Ltd .... E 419 478-3743
   Toledo *(G-14279)*
Euclid Heat Treating Co .... D 216 481-8444
   Euclid *(G-7269)*
FB Acquisition LLC .... E 513 459-7782
   Lebanon *(G-9074)*
Fbf Limited .... E 513 541-6300
   Cincinnati *(G-2898)*
Flynn Inc .... E 419 478-3743
   Toledo *(G-14291)*
▲ Fusion Incorporated .... D 440 946-3300
   Willoughby *(G-15922)*
General Steel Corporation .... F 216 883-4200
   Cleveland *(G-4118)*
Gerdau McSteel Atmsphere Annli .... E 330 478-0314
   Canton *(G-2112)*
Gt Technologies Inc .... D 419 782-8955
   Defiance *(G-6680)*
H & M Metal Processing Co .... E 330 745-3075
   Akron *(G-176)*
Heat Treating Inc .... E 937 325-3121
   Springfield *(G-13573)*
Heat Treating Equipment Inc .... E 740 549-3700
   Lewis Center *(G-9162)*
Heat Treating Inc .... F 614 759-9963
   Gahanna *(G-7837)*
Heat Treating Technologies .... F 419 224-8324
   Lima *(G-9249)*
HI Tecmetal Group Inc .... E 216 881-8100
   Wickliffe *(G-15835)*
Induction Management Svcs LLC .... G 440 947-2000
   Warren *(G-15178)*
Kando of Cincinnati Inc .... E 513 459-7782
   Lebanon *(G-9092)*

Kowalski Heat Treating Co .... F 216 631-4411
   Cleveland *(G-4297)*
Lapham-Hickey Steel Corp .... E 614 443-4881
   Columbus *(G-5521)*
Lapham-Hickey Steel Corp .... D 419 399-4803
   Paulding *(G-12317)*
McOn Inds Inc .... E 937 294-2681
   Moraine *(G-11192)*
Metal Improvement Company LLC ...... D 513 489-6484
   Blue Ash *(G-1436)*
Metal Improvement Company LLC ...... E 330 425-1490
   Twinsburg *(G-14695)*
Metallurgical Service Inc .... E 937 294-2681
   Moraine *(G-11193)*
Moore Mc Millen Holdings .... E 330 745-3075
   Cuyahoga Falls *(G-6105)*
National Peening .... F 216 342-9155
   Bedford Heights *(G-1178)*
▲ Neturen America Corporation .... F 513 863-1900
   Hamilton *(G-8231)*
◆ Northlake Steel Corporation .... D 330 220-7717
   Valley City *(G-14887)*
Northwind Industries Inc .... E 216 433-0666
   Cleveland *(G-4481)*
Ohio Coatings Company .... D 740 859-5500
   Yorkville *(G-16294)*
Ohio Flame Hardening Company .... E 513 336-6160
   Cincinnati *(G-3214)*
Ohio Metallurgical Service Inc .... D 440 365-4104
   Elyria *(G-7190)*
Ohio Vertical Heat Treat Inc .... G 330 456-7176
   Canton *(G-2187)*
▲ Oliver Steel Plate Co .... D 330 425-7000
   Twinsburg *(G-14704)*
P & L Heat Trting Grinding Inc .... E 330 746-1339
   Youngstown *(G-16408)*
P & L Precision Grinding Llc .... F 330 746-8081
   Youngstown *(G-16410)*
▲ Parker Trutec Incorporated .... D 937 323-8833
   Springfield *(G-13615)*
Precision Powder Coating Inc .... E 330 478-0741
   Canton *(G-2199)*
Pressure Technology Ohio Inc .... E 215 628-1975
   Concord Township *(G-5910)*
Pride Investments LLC .... F 937 461-1121
   Dayton *(G-6519)*
Pro-TEC Coating Company LLC .... D 419 943-1100
   Leipsic *(G-9139)*
Ridge Machine & Welding Co .... G 740 537-2821
   Toronto *(G-14534)*
Ropama Inc .... F 440 358-1304
   Painesville *(G-12262)*
Surface Enhancement Tech LLC .... F 513 561-1520
   Cincinnati *(G-3435)*
Team Inc .... F 614 263-1808
   Columbus *(G-5815)*
Techniques Surfaces Usa Inc .... G 937 323-2556
   Springfield *(G-13644)*
Thermal Solutions Inc .... G 614 263-1808
   Columbus *(G-5824)*
Thermal Treatment Center Inc .... E 216 881-8100
   Wickliffe *(G-15854)*
Universal Heat Treating Inc .... E 216 641-2000
   Aurora *(G-738)*
Vicon Fabricating Company Ltd .... E 440 205-6700
   Mentor *(G-10592)*
Weiss Industries Inc .... E 419 526-2480
   Mansfield *(G-9732)*
Winston Heat Treating Inc .... E 937 226-0110
   Dayton *(G-6656)*
Worthngton Smuel Coil Proc LLC .... E 330 963-3777
   Twinsburg *(G-14758)*

34 FABRICATED METAL PRODUCTS

◆ Xtek Inc...B 513 733-7800
Cincinnati *(G-3534)*

Youngstown Heat Trting Ntrding............ G 330 788-3025
Youngstown *(G-16483)*

Zion Industries Inc............................ D 330 225-3246
Valley City *(G-14902)*

3399 Primary metal products

A-Gas US Holdings Inc........................... F 419 867-8990
Bowling Green *(G-1547)*

Additive Metal Alloys............................. G 419 215-5800
Maumee *(G-10159)*

Additive Metal Alloys Ltd..................... G 800 687-6110
Holland *(G-8493)*

Bogie Industries Inc Ltd........................ E 330 745-3105
Akron *(G-89)*

Contitech Usa Inc................................... D 937 644-8900
Marysville *(G-9906)*

◆ Destiny Manufacturing Inc.................. E 330 273-9000
Brunswick *(G-1757)*

Duffee Finishing Inc............................... G 740 965-4848
Sunbury *(G-13952)*

▲ E-B Wire Works Inc.............................. D 330 833-4101
Massillon *(G-10093)*

◆ Eckart America Corporation................D 440 954-7600
Painesville *(G-12231)*

F M P Inc... G 330 628-1118
Mogadore *(G-11073)*

J & K Powder Coating............................ G 330 540-6145
Mineral Ridge *(G-11020)*

▲ Key Finishes LLC................................. G 614 351-8393
Columbus *(G-5510)*

Liberty Steel Pressed Pdts LLC............. G 330 538-2236
North Jackson *(G-11786)*

▲ Midwest Motor Supply Co.................... C 800 233-1294
Columbus *(G-5565)*

Nuflux LLC... G 330 399-1122
Cortland *(G-5966)*

Obron Atlantic Corporation.................... D 440 954-7600
Painesville *(G-12252)*

Ohio Valley Manufacturing Inc............... D 419 522-5818
Mansfield *(G-9707)*

Powdermet Inc....................................... E 216 404-0053
Euclid *(G-7293)*

◆ Rmi Titanium Company LLC................E 330 652-9952
Niles *(G-11684)*

Royal Powder Corporation..................... G 216 898-0074
Cleveland *(G-4657)*

Seaway Bolt And Specials Company..... D 440 236-5015
Columbia Station *(G-5021)*

Semtec Inc.. G 330 497-7224
North Canton *(G-11760)*

◆ Shinagawa Inc......................................E 330 628-1118
Mogadore *(G-11084)*

Stein LLC.. D 216 883-7444
Cleveland *(G-4734)*

▲ Stein LLC.. F 440 526-9301
Independence *(G-8685)*

Third Millennium Materials LLC............. G 740 947-1023
Waverly *(G-15291)*

▼ Transmet Corporation......................... G 614 276-5522
Columbus *(G-5832)*

◆ Truck Fax Inc.......................................G 216 921-8866
Cleveland *(G-4835)*

Valen Foundry Inc.................................. F 724 712-3500
West Chester *(G-15524)*

Vital & Fhr North America LLC.............. E 650 405-9975
Bowling Green *(G-1595)*

▲ Waterford Tank Fabrication Ltd........... D 740 984-4100
Beverly *(G-1323)*

34 FABRICATED METAL PRODUCTS

3411 Metal cans

◆ Anchor Hocking LLC..........................A 740 687-2500
Columbus *(G-5139)*

Ball Arosol Specialty Cont Inc................ E 330 534-1903
Hubbard *(G-8561)*

Ball Corporation..................................... D 614 771-9112
Columbus *(G-5173)*

Ball Corporation..................................... E 419 423-3071
Findlay *(G-7480)*

Ball Corporation..................................... F 330 244-2313
North Canton *(G-11716)*

Ball Metal Beverage Cont Corp.............. C 419 423-3071
Findlay *(G-7481)*

Broodle Brands LLC.............................. G 855 276-6353
Cincinnati *(G-2690)*

Bway Corporation................................... E 513 388-2200
Cincinnati *(G-2696)*

Cardinal Welding Inc.............................. G 330 426-2404
East Palestine *(G-7003)*

Cleveland Steel Container Corp............. E 330 656-5600
Streetsboro *(G-13762)*

Crown Cork & Seal Usa Inc.................... D 740 681-3000
Lancaster *(G-9006)*

Crown Cork & Seal Usa Inc.................... D 740 681-6593
Lancaster *(G-9007)*

Crown Cork & Seal Usa Inc.................... B 330 833-1011
Massillon *(G-10088)*

Crown Cork & Seal Usa Inc.................... C 937 299-2027
Moraine *(G-11167)*

Crown Cork & Seal Usa Inc.................... C 419 727-8201
Toledo *(G-14253)*

Drt Holdings LLC................................... F 937 297-6676
West Chester *(G-15417)*

Eisenhauer Mfg Co LLC......................... D 419 238-0081
Van Wert *(G-14915)*

Encore Industries Inc............................. C 419 626-8000
Sandusky *(G-13053)*

▲ Envases Media Inc.............................. E 419 636-5461
Bryan *(G-1817)*

◆ G & S Metal Products Co Inc.............C 216 441-0700
Cleveland *(G-4096)*

G W Cobb Co.. F 216 341-0100
Cleveland *(G-4099)*

◆ Ghp II LLC...C 740 687-2500
Lancaster *(G-9017)*

Independent Can Company.................... F 440 593-5300
Conneaut *(G-5921)*

Industrial Container Svcs LLC............... E 614 864-1900
Blacklick *(G-1338)*

Industrial Container Svcs LLC............... E 513 921-8811
Cincinnati *(G-3021)*

◆ Organized Living Inc..........................E 513 489-9300
Cincinnati *(G-3230)*

◆ Packaging Specialties Inc..................E 330 723-6000
Medina *(G-10361)*

▲ SSP Industrial Group Inc.................... G 330 665-2900
Fairlawn *(G-7452)*

Stolle Machinery Company LLC............. D 330 244-0555
Canton *(G-2236)*

▲ Trivium Alum Packg USA Corp........... E 330 744-9505
Youngstown *(G-16460)*

▲ Winzeler Stamping Co......................... E 419 485-3147
Montpelier *(G-11147)*

▼ Witt Industries Inc.............................. D 513 871-5700
Mason *(G-10071)*

3412 Metal barrels, drums, and pails

Champion Company................................ G 937 324-5681
Springfield *(G-13544)*

Cleveland Steel Container Corp............. E 330 544-2271
Niles *(G-11665)*

Cleveland Steel Container Corp............. E 330 656-5600
Streetsboro *(G-13762)*

◆ Cleveland Steel Container..................E 440 349-8000
Hudson *(G-8590)*

Deufol Worldwide Packaging LLC........... E 440 232-1100
Bedford *(G-1116)*

Drum Parts Inc....................................... F 216 271-0702
Cleveland *(G-3974)*

Eisenhauer Mfg Co LLC......................... D 419 238-0081
Van Wert *(G-14915)*

Georgia-Pacific LLC............................... C 740 477-3347
Circleville *(G-3553)*

Green Bay Packaging Inc....................... C 419 332-5593
Fremont *(G-7789)*

Green Bay Packaging Inc....................... D 513 489-8700
Lebanon *(G-9087)*

Greif Inc... E 740 657-6500
Delaware *(G-6725)*

◆ Greif Inc...E 740 549-6000
Delaware *(G-6724)*

Horwitz & Pintis Co................................ F 419 666-2220
Toledo *(G-14320)*

Industrial Container Svcs LLC............... E 614 864-1900
Blacklick *(G-1338)*

Industrial Container Svcs LLC............... E 513 921-8811
Cincinnati *(G-3021)*

Mauser Usa LLC..................................... D 513 398-1300
Mason *(G-10026)*

North Coast Container LLC................... E 216 441-6214
Cleveland *(G-4466)*

Overseas Packing LLC........................... E 440 232-2917
Bedford *(G-1148)*

◆ Packaging Specialties Inc..................E 330 723-6000
Medina *(G-10361)*

▲ Sabco Industries Inc........................... E 419 531-5347
Toledo *(G-14461)*

Schwarz Partners Packaging LLC.......... F 317 290-1140
Sidney *(G-13283)*

▲ SSP Industrial Group Inc.................... G 330 665-2900
Fairlawn *(G-7452)*

Strawser Steel Drum Ohio Ltd.............. E 614 856-5982
Mount Vernon *(G-11297)*

Syme Inc... E 330 723-6000
Medina *(G-10382)*

Tavens Container Inc............................. D 216 883-3333
Bedford *(G-1156)*

The Champion Company......................... D 937 324-5681
Springfield *(G-13647)*

▲ Werk-Brau Company............................ C 419 422-2912
Findlay *(G-7581)*

Williams Scotsman Inc........................... D 614 449-8675
Columbus *(G-5878)*

▼ Witt Industries Inc.............................. D 513 871-5700
Mason *(G-10071)*

3421 Cutlery

Accu-Grind Inc.. G 330 677-2225
Kent *(G-8792)*

Advetech Inc... E 330 533-2227
Canfield *(G-1995)*

American Punch Co................................ E 216 731-4501
Euclid *(G-7262)*

▲ American Quicksilver Company........... G 513 871-4517
Cincinnati *(G-2620)*

Boro Drive-Thru LLC.............................. G 937 743-1700
Springboro *(G-13496)*

Busse Knife Co....................................... F 419 923-6471
Wauseon *(G-15258)*

34 FABRICATED METAL PRODUCTS

▲ Crescent Manufacturing Company... D 419 332-6484
   Fremont *(G-7772)*
Dolana Group LLC .... G 440 622-8515
   Twinsburg *(G-14653)*
E Warther & Sons Inc .... F 330 343-7513
   Dover *(G-6823)*
Edgewell Per Care Brands LLC .... F 330 527-2191
   Garrettsville *(G-7914)*
Edgewell Personal Care Company .... F 740 374-1905
   Marietta *(G-9791)*
El Nuevo Naranjo .... G 614 863-4212
   Galloway *(G-7904)*
◆ G & S Metal Products Co Inc .... C 216 441-0700
   Cleveland *(G-4096)*
General Cutlery Inc .... F 419 332-2316
   Fremont *(G-7786)*
Gillette Company LLC .... D 513 983-1100
   Cincinnati *(G-2950)*
▲ Heinemann Saw Company .... E 330 456-4721
   Canton *(G-2123)*
Kabab-G Inc .... E 216 476-3335
   Cleveland *(G-4272)*
Klenk Industries Inc .... F 330 453-7857
   Canton *(G-2139)*
Libbey Glass LLC .... C 419 727-2211
   Toledo *(G-14365)*
Lt Wright Handcrafted Knife Co .... F 740 317-1404
   Steubenville *(G-13670)*
Madison Property Holdings Inc .... E 800 215-3210
   Cincinnati *(G-3124)*
New York Frozen Foods Inc .... F 614 846-2232
   Westerville *(G-15669)*
◆ Npk Construction Equipment Inc .... D 440 232-7900
   Bedford *(G-1145)*
Procter & Gamble Company .... D 513 983-1100
   Cincinnati *(G-3281)*
Procter & Gamble Company .... F 513 266-4375
   Cincinnati *(G-3282)*
Procter & Gamble Company .... G 513 871-7557
   Cincinnati *(G-3283)*
Procter & Gamble Company .... F 513 482-6789
   Cincinnati *(G-3286)*
Procter & Gamble Company .... C 513 983-3000
   Cincinnati *(G-3288)*
Procter & Gamble Company .... E 513 627-7115
   Cincinnati *(G-3289)*
Procter & Gamble Company .... F 513 945-0340
   Cincinnati *(G-3292)*
Procter & Gamble Company .... D 513 622-1000
   Mason *(G-10043)*
Procter & Gamble Company .... C 513 634-9600
   West Chester *(G-15486)*
Procter & Gamble Company .... C 513 634-9110
   West Chester *(G-15487)*
◆ Procter & Gamble Company .... A 513 983-1100
   Cincinnati *(G-3280)*
Procter & Gamble Mexico Inc .... C 513 983-1100
   Cincinnati *(G-3297)*
R & F Franchise Group LLC .... F 440 942-7140
   Willoughby *(G-15981)*

3423 Hand and edge tools, nec

▲ A JC Inc .... F 800 428-2438
   Hudson *(G-8581)*
Advetech Inc .... E 330 533-2227
   Canfield *(G-1996)*
Advetech Inc .... E 330 533-2227
   Canfield *(G-1995)*
Allegion Access Tech LLC .... E 440 461-5500
   Cleveland *(G-3636)*
▼ Amcraft Inc .... G 419 729-7900
   Toledo *(G-14185)*

◆ American Agritech LLC .... E 480 777-2000
   Marysville *(G-9904)*
◆ American Power Pull Corp .... G 419 335-7050
   Archbold *(G-520)*
Ames Companies Inc .... E 740 783-2535
   Dexter City *(G-6801)*
ASG .... F 216 486-6163
   Cleveland *(G-3687)*
Asg Division Jergens Inc .... E 888 486-6163
   Cleveland *(G-3688)*
Bully Tools Inc .... E 740 282-5834
   Steubenville *(G-13663)*
C B Mfg & Sls Co Inc .... F 937 866-5986
   Dayton *(G-6243)*
▲ C B Mfg & Sls Co Inc .... D 937 866-5986
   Miamisburg *(G-10624)*
Cannon Salt & Supply Inc .... G 440 232-1700
   Bedford *(G-1108)*
Cornwell Quality Tools Company .... D 330 628-2627
   Mogadore *(G-11088)*
D & M Saw & Tool Inc .... G 513 871-5433
   Cincinnati *(G-2811)*
▲ E Z Grout Corporation .... E 740 749-3512
   Malta *(G-9606)*
▲ Eaton Electric Holdings LLC .... B 440 523-5000
   Cleveland *(G-3995)*
Edgerton Forge Inc .... D 419 298-2333
   Edgerton *(G-7074)*
▲ Electric Eel Mfg Co Inc .... E 937 323-4644
   Springfield *(G-13558)*
▲ Empire Plow Company Inc .... E 216 641-2290
   Berea *(G-1276)*
◆ Everhard Products Inc .... C 330 453-7786
   Canton *(G-2100)*
Falcon Industries Inc .... E 330 723-0099
   Medina *(G-10322)*
◆ Furukawa Rock Drill USA Co Ltd .... F 330 673-5826
   Kent *(G-8816)*
▲ Hamilton Industrial Grinding Inc .... E 513 863-1221
   Hamilton *(G-8218)*
Handy Twine Knife Co .... G 419 294-3424
   Upper Sandusky *(G-14810)*
J & S Tool Corporation .... F 216 676-8330
   Cleveland *(G-4243)*
▲ Matco Tools Corporation .... B 330 929-4949
   Stow *(G-13708)*
Michael Byrne Manufacturing Co Inc .... E 419 525-1214
   Mansfield *(G-9691)*
Midwest Knife Grinding Inc .... F 330 854-1030
   Canal Fulton *(G-1973)*
Myers Industries Inc .... E 440 632-1006
   Middlefield *(G-10774)*
▲ Norbar Torque Tools Inc .... F 440 953-1175
   Willoughby *(G-15959)*
Panacea Products Corporation .... E 614 429-6320
   Columbus *(G-5653)*
Randolph Tool Company Inc .... F 330 877-4923
   Hartville *(G-8304)*
◆ Rex International USA Inc .... E 800 321-7950
   Ashtabula *(G-659)*
▲ Ridge Tool Company .... A 440 323-5581
   Elyria *(G-7202)*
Ridge Tool Manufacturing Co .... E 440 323-5581
   Elyria *(G-7203)*
▲ S & H Industries Inc .... E 216 831-0550
   Cleveland *(G-4664)*
S & H Industries Inc .... F 216 831-0550
   Bedford *(G-1154)*
◆ Save Edge Inc .... E 937 376-8268
   Xenia *(G-16272)*
Sewer Rodding Equipment Co .... C 419 991-2065
   Lima *(G-9288)*

Shinano Pneumatic Inds USA Inc .... G 614 529-6600
   Columbus *(G-5763)*
Simon Ellis Superabrasives Inc .... G 937 226-0683
   Dayton *(G-6575)*
Simonds International LLC .... E 978 424-0100
   Kimbolton *(G-8928)*
Stanley Industrial & Auto LLC .... C 614 755-7089
   Dublin *(G-6943)*
▲ Stanley Industrial & Auto LLC .... D 614 755-7000
   Dublin *(G-6944)*
Step2 Company LLC .... B 419 938-6343
   Perrysville *(G-12449)*
◆ Step2 Company LLC .... B 866 429-5200
   Streetsboro *(G-13794)*
Stride Tool LLC .... C 440 247-4600
   Glenwillow *(G-7982)*
Sumitomo Elc Carbide Mfg Inc .... F 440 354-0600
   Grand River *(G-8013)*
▲ Superion Inc .... E 937 374-0033
   Xenia *(G-16274)*
◆ Superior Tool Corporation .... E 216 398-8600
   Cleveland *(G-4752)*
▲ The Cornwell Quality Tool .... D 330 336-3506
   Wadsworth *(G-15069)*
White Industrial Tool Inc .... F 330 773-6889
   Akron *(G-374)*
Wise Edge LLC .... G 330 208-0889
   Akron *(G-376)*
▲ Wright Tool Company .... C 330 848-0600
   Barberton *(G-901)*
Your Carpenter Inc .... G 216 621-2166
   Cleveland *(G-4929)*

3425 Saw blades and handsaws

◆ Callahan Cutting Tools Inc .... G 614 294-1649
   Columbus *(G-5227)*
Cammel Saw Company .... F 330 477-3764
   Canton *(G-2058)*
▲ Crescent Manufacturing Company ..... D 419 332-6484
   Fremont *(G-7772)*
Dynatech Systems Inc .... F 440 365-1774
   Elyria *(G-7135)*
▲ Heinemann Saw Company .... E 330 456-4721
   Canton *(G-2123)*
J & S Tool Corporation .... F 216 676-8330
   Cleveland *(G-4243)*
◆ M K Morse Company .... B 330 453-8187
   Canton *(G-2149)*
Martindale Electric Company .... E 216 521-8567
   Cleveland *(G-4363)*
▲ Peerless Saw Company .... E 614 836-5790
   Groveport *(G-8157)*
▼ Regal Diamond Products Corp .... E 440 944-7700
   Wickliffe *(G-15851)*
▲ Superion Inc .... E 937 374-0033
   Xenia *(G-16274)*
Uhrichsville Carbide Inc .... F 740 922-9197
   Uhrichsville *(G-14772)*
Woodworking Shop LLC .... F 513 330-9663
   Miamisburg *(G-10702)*

3429 Hardware, nec

▲ A JC Inc .... F 800 428-2438
   Hudson *(G-8581)*
AB Bonded Locksmiths Inc .... G 513 531-7334
   Cincinnati *(G-2589)*
Acorn Technology Corporation .... E 216 663-1244
   Shaker Heights *(G-13149)*
▲ Action Coupling & Eqp Inc .... D 330 279-4242
   Holmesville *(G-8541)*
Aluminum Bearing Co of America .... G 216 267-8560
   Cleveland *(G-3643)*

SIC SECTION

34 FABRICATED METAL PRODUCTS

Ampex Metal Products Company......... D 216 267-9242
  Brookpark *(G-1704)*

Annin & Co Inc.. C 740 622-4447
  Coshocton *(G-5968)*

◆ Arnco Corporation................................... D 800 847-7661
  Elyria *(G-7112)*

Arrow Tru-Line Inc.................................... G 419 636-7013
  Bryan *(G-1808)*

▲ Bianchi Usa Inc...................................... F 440 801-1083
  North Olmsted *(G-11818)*

◆ Boardman Molded Products Inc......... D 330 788-2400
  Youngstown *(G-16322)*

Bowes Manufacturing Inc........................ E 216 378-2110
  Solon *(G-13321)*

▲ Case Maul Clamps Inc......................... F 419 668-6563
  Norwalk *(G-11958)*

Chantilly Development Corp.................... E 419 243-8109
  Toledo *(G-14233)*

◆ Clampco Products Inc........................... C 330 336-8857
  Wadsworth *(G-15023)*

Cleveland Steel Specialty Co................... E 216 464-9400
  Bedford Heights *(G-1168)*

Conform Automotive LLC........................ B 937 492-2708
  Sidney *(G-13233)*

Curtiss-Wright Flow Ctrl Corp................. D 216 267-3200
  Cleveland *(G-3922)*

Custom Metal Works Inc.......................... F 419 668-7831
  Norwalk *(G-11959)*

Dayton Superior Corporation................... F 937 682-4015
  Rushsylvania *(G-12874)*

Deadbolts Plus.. G 614 405-2117
  Columbus *(G-5320)*

Desco Corporation.................................... G 614 888-8855
  New Albany *(G-11378)*

▲ Die Co Inc... E 440 942-8856
  Eastlake *(G-7025)*

Dudick Inc.. E 330 562-1970
  Streetsboro *(G-13768)*

◆ Eaton Aeroquip LLC............................... C 440 523-5000
  Cleveland *(G-3991)*

Eaton Corporation.................................... E 330 274-0743
  Aurora *(G-712)*

Eaton Corporation.................................... A 419 238-1190
  Van Wert *(G-14914)*

Edward W Daniel LLC.............................. E 440 647-1960
  Wellington *(G-15306)*

◆ Elster Perfection Corporation.............. D 440 428-1171
  Geneva *(G-7935)*

◆ Esmet Inc.. E 330 452-9132
  Canton *(G-2098)*

▼ Esterline Technologies Corp.............. E 216 706-2960
  Cleveland *(G-4031)*

Etl Performance Products Inc................. G 234 575-7226
  Salem *(G-12992)*

Faull & Son LLC.. F 330 652-4341
  Niles *(G-11668)*

▲ Federal Equipment Company............. D 513 621-5260
  Cincinnati *(G-2899)*

Feitl Manufacturing Co Inc...................... E 330 405-6600
  Macedonia *(G-9550)*

First Francis Company Inc....................... E 440 352-8927
  Painesville *(G-12237)*

Flex-Strut Inc... D 330 372-9999
  Warren *(G-15170)*

Florida Production Engrg Inc.................. D 937 996-4361
  New Madison *(G-11474)*

◆ Fort Recovery Industries Inc.............. C 419 375-4121
  Fort Recovery *(G-7617)*

▲ Fortner Upholstering Inc..................... F 614 475-8282
  Columbus *(G-5384)*

Gateway Con Forming Svcs Inc.............. D 513 353-2000
  Miamitown *(G-10708)*

◆ Group Industries Inc............................. E 216 271-0702
  Cleveland *(G-4152)*

Hbd/Thermoid Inc..................................... C 937 593-5010
  Bellefontaine *(G-1210)*

▼ Hbd/Thermoid Inc................................. D 614 526-7000
  Dublin *(G-6892)*

Hdt Expeditionary Systems Inc............... F 513 943-1111
  Cincinnati *(G-2564)*

Heller Machine Products Inc................... G 216 281-2951
  Cleveland *(G-4179)*

▲ Hercules Industries Inc....................... E 740 494-2620
  Prospect *(G-12690)*

Herman Machine Inc................................ F 330 633-3261
  Tallmadge *(G-14032)*

Hey 9 Inc... G 919 259-2884
  Willoughby *(G-15928)*

◆ Hfi LLC.. B 614 491-0700
  Canal Winchester *(G-1987)*

Hydromotive Engineering Co.................. G 330 425-4266
  Twinsburg *(G-14673)*

▲ Independence 2 LLC............................ F 800 414-0545
  Hubbard *(G-8564)*

Interntnl Auto Cmpnnts Group............... A 419 433-5653
  Wauseon *(G-15265)*

J L R Products Inc.................................... F 330 832-9557
  Massillon *(G-10112)*

J W Goss Company.................................. F 330 395-0739
  Warren *(G-15179)*

Kasai North America Inc......................... E 614 356-1494
  Dublin *(G-6903)*

▼ Kirk Key Interlock Company LLC....... E 330 833-8223
  North Canton *(G-11740)*

L & W Inc... E 734 397-6300
  Avon *(G-778)*

Langenau Manufacturing Company....... E 216 651-3400
  Cleveland *(G-4310)*

Leetonia Tool Company........................... F 330 427-6944
  Leetonia *(G-9127)*

Linear It Solutions LLC............................ F 614 306-0761
  Marysville *(G-9924)*

▲ Marlboro Manufacturing Inc.............. F 330 935-2221
  Alliance *(G-413)*

Master Mfg Co Inc................................... E 216 641-0500
  Cleveland *(G-4367)*

▲ Matdan Corporation............................. E 513 794-0500
  Blue Ash *(G-1429)*

Maumee Hose & Fitting Inc.................... G 419 893-7252
  Maumee *(G-10218)*

McGregor Mtal Yllow Sprng Wrks......... D 937 325-5561
  Springfield *(G-13604)*

Medallion... G 513 936-0597
  Blue Ash *(G-1433)*

Meese Inc.. F 440 998-1202
  Ashtabula *(G-647)*

Midlake Products & Mfg Co.................... D 330 875-4202
  Louisville *(G-9464)*

▲ Miller Studio Inc................................... E 330 339-1100
  New Philadelphia *(G-11519)*

◆ Napoleon Spring Works Inc................ C 419 445-1010
  Archbold *(G-537)*

Netherland Rubber Company.................. F 513 733-0883
  Cincinnati *(G-3187)*

▲ Nova Machine Products Inc.............. C 216 267-3200
  Middleburg Heights *(G-10724)*

Ohio Hydraulics Inc.................................. E 513 771-2590
  Cincinnati *(G-3215)*

Ottawa Products Co................................ E 419 836-5115
  Curtice *(G-6057)*

Parker-Hannifin Corporation.................... G 704 637-1190
  Wickliffe *(G-15845)*

Peterson American Corporation............. E 419 867-8511
  Holland *(G-8523)*

◆ Premier Farnell Holding Inc................ E 330 523-4273
  Richfield *(G-12794)*

Pure Safety Group Inc............................. F 614 436-0700
  Worthington *(G-16208)*

Qualitor Subsidiary H Inc........................ C 419 562-7987
  Bucyrus *(G-1865)*

▲ R & R Tool Inc....................................... E 937 783-8665
  Blanchester *(G-1352)*

Racelite Southcoast Inc........................... F 216 581-4600
  Maple Heights *(G-9759)*

Restricted Key.. G 614 405-2109
  Columbus *(G-5720)*

S & K Products Company....................... E 419 268-2244
  Celina *(G-2347)*

S Lehman Central Warehouse................ G 330 828-8828
  Dalton *(G-6142)*

▲ Samsel Rope & Marine Supply Co.... E 216 241-0333
  Cleveland *(G-4670)*

▲ Sarasota Quality Products................. G 440 899-9820
  Westlake *(G-15783)*

Sensible Products Inc.............................. G 330 659-4212
  Richfield *(G-12797)*

Sheet Metal Products Co Inc.................. E 440 392-9000
  Mentor *(G-10554)*

◆ Specialty Hardware Inc....................... G 216 291-1160
  Cleveland *(G-2820)*

▲ Summers Acquisition Corp................ E 216 941-7700
  Cleveland *(G-4745)*

◆ Superior Metal Products Inc.............. E 419 228-1145
  Lima *(G-9294)*

▲ Te-Co Manufacturing LLC.................. D 937 836-0961
  Englewood *(G-7244)*

▲ Technoform GL Insul N Amer Inc..... E 330 487-6600
  Twinsburg *(G-14742)*

Tessec LLC... D 937 576-0010
  Dayton *(G-6615)*

▲ Texmaster Tools Inc............................ F 740 965-8778
  Fredericktown *(G-7755)*

Thermo-Rite Mfg Company..................... E 330 633-8680
  Akron *(G-356)*

▲ Trim Parts Inc....................................... F 513 934-0815
  Lebanon *(G-9115)*

Twin Valley Metalcraft Asm LLC............ G 937 787-4634
  West Alexandria *(G-15345)*

United Die & Mfg Sales Co..................... E 330 938-6141
  Sebring *(G-13128)*

▲ Universal Industrial Pdts Inc............. F 419 737-9584
  Pioneer *(G-12500)*

Verhoff Machine & Welding Inc.............. C 419 596-3202
  Continental *(G-5939)*

Voss Industries LLC................................. D 216 771-7655
  Berea *(G-1298)*

◆ Voss Industries LLC............................. C 216 771-7655
  Cleveland *(G-4884)*

Washington Products Inc........................ F 330 837-5101
  Massillon *(G-10154)*

Wecall Inc.. G 440 437-8202
  Chardon *(G-2470)*

▲ Whiteside Manufacturing Co............. E 740 363-1179
  Delaware *(G-6757)*

Wilson Bohannan Company..................... D 740 382-3639
  Marion *(G-9891)*

▲ Winzeler Stamping Co........................ E 419 485-3147
  Montpelier *(G-11147)*

▲ Worthignton Products Inc.................. G 330 452-7400
  East Canton *(G-6982)*

3431 Metal sanitary ware

Accent Manufacturing Inc....................... F 330 724-7704
  Norton *(G-11936)*

Agean Marble Manufacturing................. F 513 874-1475
  West Chester *(G-15533)*

34 FABRICATED METAL PRODUCTS

As America Inc .... E 419 522-4211
  Mansfield *(G-9626)*

BJ Equipment Ltd .... E 614 497-1188
  Columbus *(G-5193)*

◆ Crane Plumbing LLC .... A 419 522-4211
  Mansfield *(G-9642)*

Extrudex Limited Partnership .... E 440 352-7101
  Painesville *(G-12235)*

◆ Lvd Acquisition LLC .... D 614 861-1350
  Columbus *(G-5537)*

◆ Mansfield Plumbing Pdts LLC .... A 419 938-5211
  Perrysville *(G-12447)*

Zurn Industries LLC .... F 814 455-0921
  Hilliard *(G-8454)*

3432 Plumbing fixture fittings and trim

▲ American Brass Mfg Co .... F 216 431-6565
  Cleveland *(G-3650)*

As America Inc .... F 330 332-9954
  Salem *(G-12977)*

Atlantic Co .... E 440 944-8988
  Willoughby Hills *(G-16021)*

▲ Empire Brass Co .... G 216 431-6565
  Cleveland *(G-4012)*

Ferguson Enterprises LLC .... G 216 635-2493
  Parma *(G-12289)*

◆ Field Stone Inc .... E 937 898-3236
  Tipp City *(G-14135)*

Fort Recovery Industries Inc .... D 419 375-3005
  Fort Recovery *(G-7618)*

◆ Fort Recovery Industries Inc .... C 419 375-4121
  Fort Recovery *(G-7617)*

▼ Krendl Machine Company .... D 419 692-3060
  Delphos *(G-6768)*

Langenau Manufacturing Company .... E 216 651-3400
  Cleveland *(G-4310)*

Lsq Manufacturing Inc .... F 330 725-4905
  Medina *(G-10345)*

Maass Midwest Mfg Inc .... G 419 894-6424
  Arcadia *(G-516)*

◆ Mansfield Plumbing Pdts LLC .... A 419 938-5211
  Perrysville *(G-12447)*

▲ Merit Brass Co .... C 216 261-9800
  Cleveland *(G-4394)*

◆ Moen Incorporated .... E 800 289-6636
  North Olmsted *(G-11824)*

▲ Mssk Manufacturing Inc .... E 330 393-6624
  Warren *(G-15192)*

Next Gerenation Crimping .... G 440 237-6300
  North Royalton *(G-11888)*

Toolbold Corporation .... F 440 543-1660
  Cleveland *(G-4802)*

W A S P Inc .... G 740 439-2398
  Cambridge *(G-1960)*

◆ Waxman Industries Inc .... C 440 439-1830
  Bedford Heights *(G-1181)*

◆ Wolff Bros Supply Inc .... F 440 327-1650
  North Ridgeville *(G-11864)*

Zekelman Industries Inc .... C 740 432-2146
  Cambridge *(G-1961)*

3433 Heating equipment, except electric

Accent Manufacturing Inc .... F 330 724-7704
  Norton *(G-11936)*

Aitken Products Inc .... G 440 466-5711
  Geneva *(G-7930)*

▲ Beckett Air Incorporated .... D 440 327-9999
  North Ridgeville *(G-11829)*

▼ Beckett Gas Inc .... D 440 327-3141
  North Ridgeville *(G-11830)*

Bessamaire Sales Intl LLC .... F 800 321-5992
  Twinsburg *(G-14636)*

Data Cooling Technologies LLC .... E 330 954-3800
  Cleveland Heights *(G-4939)*

◆ Dcm Manufacturing Inc .... E 216 265-8006
  Cleveland *(G-3948)*

Dmi Manufacturing Inc .... F 800 238-5384
  Mentor *(G-10448)*

Dmi Manufacturing Inc .... F 440 975-8645
  Willoughby *(G-15909)*

▲ Duro Dyne Midwest Corp .... C 513 870-6000
  Hamilton *(G-8201)*

◆ Ebner Furnaces Inc .... D 330 335-2311
  Wadsworth *(G-15028)*

▲ Enerco Group Inc .... C 216 916-3000
  Cleveland *(G-4015)*

▲ Enerco Technical Products Inc .... D 216 916-3000
  Cleveland *(G-4016)*

Es Thermal Inc .... E 440 323-3291
  Berea *(G-1277)*

Ets Schaefer LLC .... F 330 468-6600
  Macedonia *(G-3543)*

Ets Schaefer LLC .... F 330 468-6600
  Beachwood *(G-987)*

Famous Industries Inc .... F 740 685-2592
  Byesville *(G-1896)*

First Solar Inc .... E 419 661-1478
  Perrysburg *(G-12382)*

◆ Fives N Amercn Combustn Inc .... C 216 271-6000
  Cleveland *(G-4065)*

Glo-Quartz Electric Htr Co Inc .... E 440 255-9701
  Mentor *(G-10464)*

Grid Industrial Heating Inc .... G 330 332-9931
  Salem *(G-12998)*

◆ Hartzell Fan Inc .... C 937 773-7411
  Piqua *(G-12520)*

Hdt Ep Inc .... C 216 438-6111
  Solon *(G-13359)*

Hdt Expeditionary Systems Inc .... F 440 466-6640
  Geneva *(G-7938)*

▼ Hunter Defense Tech Inc .... E 216 438-6111
  Solon *(G-13363)*

Iosil Energy Corporation .... F
  Groveport *(G-8147)*

Lakeway Mfg Inc .... E 419 433-3030
  Huron *(G-8637)*

M & S Equipment Leasing Co .... F 216 662-8800
  Cleveland *(G-4343)*

▲ Mr Heater Inc .... E 216 916-3000
  Cleveland *(G-4427)*

▲ Mssk Manufacturing Inc .... E 330 393-6624
  Warren *(G-15192)*

Nbbi .... G 614 888-8320
  Columbus *(G-5591)*

▲ Onix Corporation .... E 800 844-0076
  Perrysburg *(G-12412)*

▼ Qual-Fab Inc .... E 440 327-5000
  Avon *(G-784)*

▲ RW Beckett Corporation .... C 440 327-1060
  North Ridgeville *(G-11860)*

▲ Selas Heat Technology Co LLC .... E 800 523-6500
  Streetsboro *(G-13792)*

Sgm Co Inc .... E 440 255-1190
  Mentor *(G-10553)*

Specialty Ceramics Inc .... D 330 482-0800
  Columbiana *(G-5051)*

Stelter and Brinck Inc .... E 513 367-9300
  Harrison *(G-8293)*

Sticker Corporation .... F 440 946-2100
  Willoughby *(G-15998)*

Swagelok Company .... E 440 349-5836
  Solon *(G-13430)*

T J F Inc .... F 419 878-4400
  Waterville *(G-15253)*

Thermo Systems Technology Inc .... F 216 292-8250
  Cleveland *(G-4792)*

Weather King Heating & AC .... G 330 908-0281
  Northfield *(G-11914)*

Ws Thermal Process Tech Inc .... G 440 385-6829
  Lorain *(G-9445)*

▲ Xunlight Corporation .... D 419 469-8600
  Toledo *(G-14529)*

3441 Fabricated structural metal

277 Northfield Inc .... F 440 439-1029
  Bedford *(G-1097)*

3d Partners LLC .... G 330 323-6453
  Canton *(G-2023)*

▲ A & G Manufacturing Co Inc .... E 419 468-7433
  Galion *(G-7858)*

A-1 Fabricators Finishers LLC .... D 513 724-0383
  Batavia *(G-906)*

A+ Engineering Fabrication Inc .... F 419 832-0748
  Grand Rapids *(G-0000)*

AC Green LLC .... F 740 292-2604
  Athens *(G-672)*

Accu-Tech Manufacturing Co .... F 330 848-8100
  Coventry Township *(G-6003)*

Accurate Fab LLC .... F 330 562-3140
  Aurora *(G-703)*

Accurate Fab LLC .... G
  Streetsboro *(G-13752)*

Ace Boiler & Welding Co Inc .... G 330 745-4443
  Barberton *(G-851)*

Acme Home Improvement Co Inc .... F 614 252-2129
  Columbus *(G-5098)*

Acmi LLC .... G 330 501-0728
  Youngstown *(G-16304)*

Advance Industrial Mfg Inc .... E 614 871-3333
  Grove City *(G-8073)*

Advance Industries Group LLC .... E 216 741-1800
  Cleveland *(G-3602)*

Advance Metal Products Inc .... F 216 741-1800
  Cleveland *(G-3604)*

Affiliated Metal Industries .... G 216 267-0155
  Cleveland *(G-3613)*

Air Heater Seal Company Inc .... E 740 984-2146
  Waterford *(G-15235)*

▲ Akron Rebar Co .... E
  Akron *(G-42)*

Albert Freytag Inc .... E 419 628-2018
  Minster *(G-11047)*

▲ Alcon Industries Inc .... D 216 961-1100
  Cleveland *(G-3625)*

Allen Industrial Company .... F 440 327-4100
  North Ridgeville *(G-11827)*

Allied Fabricating & Wldg Co .... E 614 751-6664
  Columbus *(G-5113)*

Alloy Fabricators Inc .... E 330 948-3535
  Lodi *(G-9347)*

Alloy Welding & Fabricating .... E 440 914-0650
  Solon *(G-13309)*

Alpha Control LLC .... E 740 377-3400
  South Point *(G-13463)*

Alpha Ctrl Fabrication & Mfg .... F 740 377-3400
  South Point *(G-13464)*

Alro Steel Corporation .... E 937 253-6121
  Dayton *(G-6196)*

Ameco USA Met Fbrction Sltons .... G 440 899-9400
  Cleveland *(G-3648)*

◆ American Ir Met Cleveland LLC .... E 216 266-0509
  Cleveland *(G-3653)*

▲ American Manufacturing Inc .... F 419 531-9471
  Toledo *(G-14189)*

American Metal Stamping Co LLC .... F 216 531-3100
  Euclid *(G-7261)*

SIC SECTION

34 FABRICATED METAL PRODUCTS

American Steel Assod Pdts Inc............... D 419 531-9471
  Toledo (G-14192)
American Steel LLC............................. G 330 482-4299
  Columbiana (G-5027)
▲ Ametco Manufacturing Corp................. E 440 951-4300
  Willoughby (G-15876)
Amrod Bridge & Iron LLC....................... E
  Mc Donald (G-10276)
Amtank Armor..................................... G 440 268-7735
  Strongsville (G-13807)
Amto Acquisition Corp.......................... F 419 347-1185
  Shelby (G-13190)
Apex Bolt & Machine Company................. E 419 729-3741
  Toledo (G-14195)
▲ Appian Manufacturing Corp................. E 614 445-2230
  Columbus (G-5149)
Applied Energy Tech Inc....................... F 419 537-9052
  Maumee (G-10166)
Applied Engneered Surfaces Inc............... E 440 366-0440
  Elyria (G-7111)
Arbenz Inc....................................... E 614 274-6800
  Columbus (G-5152)
Arctech Fabricating Inc........................ E 937 525-9353
  Springfield (G-13535)
Armor Consolidated Inc......................... A 513 923-5260
  Mason (G-9952)
▲ Armor Metal Group Mason Inc.............. C 513 769-0700
  Mason (G-9954)
Arrow Fabricating Co............................ F 216 641-0490
  Novelty (G-12006)
▲ Art Iron Inc.................................. D 419 241-1261
  Toledo (G-14200)
◆ Astro-TEC Mfg Inc............................ E 330 854-2209
  Canal Fulton (G-1967)
Automated Laser Fabrication Co............... F 330 562-7200
  Streetsboro (G-13758)
Avenue Fabricating Inc.......................... E 513 752-1911
  Batavia (G-910)
Axis Corporation................................. F 937 592-1958
  Bellefontaine (G-1201)
Banks Manufacturing Company................... F 440 458-8661
  Grafton (G-7997)
Bauer Corporation............................... E 800 321-4760
  Wooster (G-16102)
Beauty Cft Met Fabricators Inc................. F 440 439-0710
  Bedford (G-1104)
Berkshire Road Holdings Inc.................... F 216 883-4200
  Cleveland (G-3731)
Berran Industrial Group Inc.................... E 330 253-5800
  Akron (G-83)
Best Process Solutions Inc..................... F 330 220-1440
  Westlake (G-15737)
Bethel Engineering and Eqp Inc................ E 419 568-1100
  New Hampshire (G-11445)
Bgh Specialty Steel Inc......................... G 330 467-0324
  Macedonia (G-9535)
Bickers Metal Products Inc..................... E 513 353-4000
  Miamitown (G-10705)
Bird Equipment LLC............................. E 330 549-1004
  North Lima (G-11801)
Black Lion Products LLC........................ E 234 232-3680
  Youngstown (G-16320)
Blackburns Fabrication Inc..................... E 614 875-0784
  Columbus (G-5198)
Blevins Metal Fabrication Inc.................. E 419 522-6082
  Mansfield (G-9629)
Blue Chip Manufacturing & Sales Inc........... E 614 475-3853
  Columbus (G-5203)
Blue Skies Operating Corp...................... F 877 330-2354
  Sidney (G-13228)
Boardman Steel Inc.............................. D 330 758-0951
  Columbiana (G-5028)

Breitinger Company.............................. C 419 526-4255
  Mansfield (G-9631)
Brilex Industries Inc........................... D 330 744-1114
  Youngstown (G-16327)
▲ Brilex Industries Inc....................... D 330 744-1114
  Youngstown (G-16328)
◆ Buck Equipment Inc.......................... E 614 539-3039
  Grove City (G-8081)
Buckeye Custom Fabrication LLC................ G 330 831-5619
  Lisbon (G-9309)
Buckeye Steel Inc............................... F 740 425-2306
  Barnesville (G-902)
Burghardt Manufacturing Inc.................... G 330 253-7590
  Akron (G-95)
Burghardt Metal Fabg Inc....................... F 330 794-1830
  Akron (G-96)
C A Joseph Co................................... F 330 532-4646
  Irondale (G-8693)
C-N-D Industries Inc............................ E 330 478-8811
  Massillon (G-10080)
C&C Fabrication LLC............................ F 419 592-1408
  Napoleon (G-11309)
Camelot Manufacturing Inc...................... F 419 678-2603
  Coldwater (G-4983)
Cast-Fab Technologies Inc...................... C 513 758-1000
  Cincinnati (G-2707)
Ceco Environmental Corp........................ E 513 874-8915
  West Chester (G-15544)
Central Ohio Fabricators LLC................... E 740 393-3892
  Mount Vernon (G-11267)
Chagrin Vly Stl Erectors Inc................... F 440 975-1556
  Willoughby Hills (G-16023)
Champion Bridge Company........................ E 937 382-2521
  Wilmington (G-16043)
Charles Mfg Co.................................. F 330 395-3490
  Warren (G-15153)
Chattanooga Laser Cutting LLC.................. F 513 779-7200
  Cincinnati (G-2728)
Chc Fabricating Corp............................ D 513 821-7757
  Cincinnati (G-2729)
Chc Manufacturing Inc........................... E 513 821-7757
  Cincinnati (G-2730)
▲ Cincinnati Industrial McHy Inc............. C 513 923-5600
  Mason (G-9977)
Cincinnati Laser Cutting LLC................... E 513 779-7200
  Cincinnati (G-2753)
Cincy Glass Inc................................. G 513 241-0455
  Cincinnati (G-2765)
Clarkwstern Dtrich Bldg System................. E 330 372-4014
  Vienna (G-14995)
Clearvue Products LLC........................... F 440 871-4209
  Bay Village (G-964)
◆ Clermont Steel Fabricators LLC............. D 513 732-6033
  Batavia (G-916)
Cleveland City Forge Inc....................... E 440 647-5400
  Wellington (G-15305)
◆ Clifton Steel Company....................... D 216 662-6111
  Maple Heights (G-9749)
Clipsons Metal Working Inc..................... G 513 772-6393
  Cincinnati (G-2774)
Cohen Brothers Inc.............................. E 513 422-3696
  Middletown (G-10811)
Com-Fab Inc..................................... F 740 857-1107
  Plain City (G-12571)
Comm Steel Inc.................................. E 216 881-4600
  North Royalton (G-11871)
Commercial Mtal Fbricators Inc................. E 937 233-4911
  Dayton (G-6260)
Concord Fabricators Inc......................... E 614 875-2500
  Grove City (G-8083)
Contech Engnered Solutions Inc................. E 513 645-7000
  West Chester (G-15402)

◆ Contech Engnered Solutions LLC............. C 513 645-7000
  West Chester (G-15403)
▲ Continental GL Sls & Inv Group............. E 614 679-1201
  Powell (G-12669)
Cornerstone Wauseon Inc........................ C 419 337-0940
  Wauseon (G-15259)
County of Lake.................................. F 440 269-2193
  Willoughby (G-15904)
Coventry Steel Services Inc.................... F 216 883-4477
  Cleveland (G-3909)
Cramers Inc..................................... E 330 477-4571
  Canton (G-2083)
Creative Fab & Welding LLC..................... E 937 780-5000
  Leesburg (G-9123)
Cw Liquidation Inc.............................. D
  Cleveland (G-3932)
Dal-Little Fabricating Inc..................... G 216 883-3323
  Cleveland (G-3938)
Davis Fabricators Inc........................... E 419 898-5297
  Oak Harbor (G-12013)
Dearing Compressor and Pu...................... E 330 783-2258
  Youngstown (G-16348)
Debra-Kuempel Inc............................... D 513 271-6500
  Cincinnati (G-2822)
Defabco Inc..................................... D 614 231-2700
  Columbus (G-5323)
Diamond Mfg Bluffton Ltd....................... D 419 358-0129
  Bluffton (G-1503)
Diamond Wipes Intl Inc......................... G 419 562-3575
  Bucyrus (G-1857)
Dietrich Industries Inc......................... C 330 372-4014
  Warren (G-15161)
▼ Dietrich Industries Inc..................... C 800 873-2604
  Worthington (G-16193)
DL Schwartz Co LLC............................. G 260 692-1464
  Hicksville (G-8373)
Dover Conveyor Inc.............................. E 740 922-9390
  Midvale (G-10876)
Dover Tank and Plate Company................... E 330 343-4443
  Dover (G-6822)
◆ Dracool-Usa Inc.............................. E 937 743-5899
  Franklin (G-7671)
▲ DS Techstar Inc.............................. G 419 424-0888
  Findlay (G-7503)
Dwayne Bennett Industries...................... G 440 466-5724
  Geneva (G-7934)
Dwyer Companies Inc............................ D 513 777-0998
  West Chester (G-15419)
E B P Inc....................................... E 216 241-2550
  Solon (G-13339)
▼ E-Pak Manufacturing LLC..................... D 330 264-0825
  Wooster (G-16115)
◆ Ebner Furnaces Inc........................... D 330 335-2311
  Wadsworth (G-15028)
Egypt Structural Steel Proc.................... F 419 628-2375
  Minster (G-11051)
◆ Emh Inc...................................... D 330 220-8600
  Valley City (G-14869)
Enterprise Welding Fbrctn...................... F 440 354-3868
  Mentor (G-10452)
EPI of Cleveland Inc............................ G 330 468-2872
  Twinsburg (G-14656)
Erico International Corp....................... B 440 248-0100
  Solon (G-13345)
▲ Erico Products Inc........................... B 440 248-0100
  Cleveland (G-4027)
Euclid Welding Company Inc..................... F 216 289-0714
  Willoughby Hills (G-16024)
Evers Welding Co Inc............................ F 513 385-7352
  Cincinnati (G-2887)
F & F Shtmtl & Fabrication LLC................. F 567 938-8788
  Tiffin (G-14085)

Employee Codes: A=Over 500 employees, B=251-500
C=101-250, D=51-100, E=20-50, F=10-19, G=1-9

2024 Harris Ohio
Industrial Directory

853

34 FABRICATED METAL PRODUCTS

F M Machine Co... E 330 773-8237
  Akron *(G-147)*
Fab-Steel Co Inc... F 419 666-5100
  Northwood *(G-11918)*
▲ Fabco Inc.. E 419 422-4533
  Findlay *(G-7504)*
Fabx LLC.. F 614 565-5835
  Columbus *(G-5369)*
Farasey Steel Fabricators Inc................. F 216 641-1853
  Cleveland *(G-4050)*
Fastfeed Corporation................................. G 330 948-7333
  Lodi *(G-9350)*
Fenix Fabrication Inc................................. E 330 745-8731
  Akron *(G-151)*
Fiedeldey Stl Fabricators Inc.................. E 513 353-3300
  Cincinnati *(G-2901)*
Firelands Fabrication................................ F 419 929-0680
  New London *(G-11461)*
Fisher Metal Fabricating LLC................ F 419 838-7200
  Walbridge *(G-15001)*
Flex-Strut Inc.. D 330 372-9999
  Warren *(G-15170)*
Fostoria MT&f Corp.................................. F 419 435-7676
  Fostoria *(G-7636)*
Franck and Fric Incorporated................. D 216 524-4451
  Cleveland *(G-4090)*
Frederick Steel Company LLC............... D 513 821-6400
  Cincinnati *(G-2922)*
Fulton Equipment Co............................... G 419 290-5393
  Toledo *(G-14295)*
◆ G & S Titanium Inc................................ E 330 263-0564
  Wooster *(G-16122)*
▲ Galion-Godwin Truck Bdy Co LLC... F 330 359-5495
  Dundee *(G-6965)*
Garland Welding Co Inc.......................... F 330 536-6506
  Lowellville *(G-9515)*
Gb Fabrication Company......................... E 419 347-1835
  Shelby *(G-13195)*
General Machine & Saw Company....... D 740 382-1104
  Marion *(G-9854)*
General Steel Corporation....................... F 216 883-4200
  Cleveland *(G-4118)*
George Steel Fabricating Inc.................. E 513 932-2887
  Lebanon *(G-9080)*
Gilson Machine & Tool Co Inc............... E 419 592-2911
  Napoleon *(G-11316)*
Glenwood Erectors Inc............................ G 330 652-9616
  Warren *(G-15174)*
Global Body & Equipment Co................ D 330 264-6640
  Wooster *(G-16124)*
▲ Gokoh Corporation................................ F 937 339-4977
  Troy *(G-14573)*
Graber Metal Works Inc.......................... F 440 237-8422
  North Royalton *(G-11877)*
Greenpoint Metals Inc.............................. E 937 743-4075
  Franklin *(G-7678)*
◆ Gregory Industries Inc......................... D 330 477-4800
  Canton *(G-2117)*
Grenga Machine & Welding................... F 330 743-1113
  Youngstown *(G-16374)*
Gunderson Rail Services LLC................ D 330 792-6521
  Youngstown *(G-16376)*
▲ Gwp Holdings Inc................................. E 513 860-4050
  Fairfield *(G-7364)*
Halman Inc... F
  Ashtabula *(G-637)*
◆ Halvorsen Company.............................. E 216 341-7500
  Cleveland *(G-4165)*
Halvorsons LLC... G 440 503-1162
  Cleveland *(G-4166)*
Hancock Structural Steel LLC................ F 419 424-1217
  Findlay *(G-7519)*

Harvey Brothers Inc................................. G 513 541-2622
  Cincinnati *(G-2987)*
Herman Manufacturing LLC................... F 216 251-6400
  Cleveland *(G-4185)*
High Production Technology LLC......... F 419 591-7000
  Napoleon *(G-11318)*
Holgate Metal Fab Inc.............................. F 419 599-2000
  Napoleon *(G-11319)*
Hoppel Fabrication Specialties............... F 330 823-5700
  Louisville *(G-9461)*
▲ Horizon Metals Inc.............................. E 440 235-3338
  Berea *(G-1282)*
Hr Machine llc... G 937 222-7644
  Dayton *(G-6375)*
Hunkar Technologies Inc........................ C 513 272-1010
  Cincinnati *(G-3012)*
▲ Hynes Industries Inc........................... C 800 321-9257
  Youngstown *(G-16378)*
Ice Industries Columbus Inc.................. E 614 475-3853
  Sylvania *(G-14001)*
Indian Creek Fabricators Inc.................. E 937 667-7214
  Tipp City *(G-14138)*
Industrial Mill Maintenance................... E 330 746-1155
  Youngstown *(G-16379)*
Iron Gate Industries LLC........................ E 330 264-0626
  Wooster *(G-16134)*
Ironfab LLC... F 614 443-3900
  Columbus *(G-5480)*
Ironhead Fabg & Contg Inc................... F 419 690-0000
  Toledo *(G-14338)*
Ivies Wholistic Dynamics........................ G 216 469-3103
  Wooster *(G-16135)*
J & L Specialty Steel Inc......................... G 330 875-6200
  Louisville *(G-9462)*
J & M Fabrications LLC........................... G 330 860-4346
  Clinton *(G-4969)*
J A McMahon Incorporated.................... E 330 652-2588
  Niles *(G-11674)*
J Horst Manufacturing Co....................... D 330 828-2216
  Dalton *(G-6133)*
Jh Industries Inc....................................... E 330 963-4105
  Twinsburg *(G-14677)*
JJ&pl Services-Consulting LLC............. E 330 923-5783
  Cuyahoga Falls *(G-6093)*
Joe Rees Welding...................................... G 937 652-4067
  Urbana *(G-14841)*
Johnson-Nash Metal Pdts Inc................ E 513 874-7022
  Fairfield *(G-7375)*
Jomac Ltd.. E 330 627-7727
  Carrollton *(G-2311)*
JP Suggins Mobile Wldg Inc.................. F 216 566-7131
  Cleveland *(G-4265)*
▲ JR Manufacturing Inc......................... C 419 375-8021
  Fort Recovery *(G-7621)*
Js Fabrications Inc................................... G 419 333-0323
  Fremont *(G-7790)*
Judo Steel Company Inc......................... F
  Dayton *(G-6393)*
Kebco Prcision Fabricators Inc.............. F 330 456-0808
  Canton *(G-2137)*
Kecoat LLC.. F 330 527-0215
  Garrettsville *(G-7919)*
Kellys Wldg & Fabrication Ltd.............. G 440 593-6040
  Conneaut *(G-5922)*
Kenton Strl & Orn Ir Works.................. D 419 674-4025
  Kenton *(G-8887)*
Kings Welding and Fabg Inc.................. F 330 738-3592
  Mechanicstown *(G-10287)*
Kirwan Industries Inc.............................. G 513 333-0766
  Cincinnati *(G-3079)*
▲ Kottler Metal Products Co Inc.......... E 440 946-7473
  Willoughby *(G-15940)*

Kramer Power Equipment Co................ F 937 456-2132
  Eaton *(G-7063)*
L & W Inc... E 734 397-6300
  Avon *(G-778)*
Lake Building Products Inc.................... E 216 486-1500
  Cleveland *(G-4306)*
Lake Building Products Ltd.................... F 216 486-1500
  Euclid *(G-7281)*
Lake Erie Ship Repr Fbrction L............. F 440 228-7110
  Jefferson *(G-8752)*
Lake Erie Steel & Fabrication................. G 440 232-6200
  Bedford Heights *(G-1175)*
▲ Langdon Inc.. E 513 733-5955
  Cincinnati *(G-3095)*
Lapham-Hickey Steel Corp..................... E 614 443-4881
  Columbus *(G-5521)*
Laserfab Technologies Inc...................... F 937 493-0800
  Sidney *(G-13260)*
Laserflex Corporation............................... D 614 850-9600
  Hilliard *(G-8410)*
▲ Lefeld Welding & Stl Sups Inc......... E 419 678-2397
  Coldwater *(G-4995)*
Leitner Fabrication LLC........................... E 330 721-7374
  Medina *(G-10344)*
Lilly Industries Inc................................... E 419 946-7908
  Mount Gilead *(G-11235)*
Louis Arthur Steel Company.................. E 440 997-5545
  Geneva *(G-7940)*
Louis Arthur Steel Company.................. G 440 997-5545
  Geneva *(G-7941)*
Lyco Corporation....................................... E 412 973-9176
  Lowellville *(G-9517)*
M & H Fabricating Co Inc....................... F 937 325-8708
  Springfield *(G-13595)*
M & M Fabrication Inc............................. F 740 779-3071
  Chillicothe *(G-2515)*
M K Metals.. G 330 482-3351
  Leetonia *(G-9128)*
M R Trailer Sales Inc............................... G 330 339-7701
  New Philadelphia *(G-11512)*
Machine Tool Design & Fab LLC........... F 419 435-7676
  Fostoria *(G-7641)*
Mad River Steel Ltd................................. F 937 845-4046
  New Carlisle *(G-11420)*
Magnesium Products Group Inc............ G 310 971-5799
  Maumee *(G-10216)*
Magni-Power Company............................. D 330 264-3637
  Wooster *(G-16148)*
Magnum Piering Inc................................. E 513 759-3348
  West Chester *(G-15568)*
Manco Manufacturing Co......................... G 419 925-4152
  Maria Stein *(G-9771)*
Marsam Metalfab Inc................................ E 330 405-1520
  Twinsburg *(G-14691)*
Martina Metal LLC.................................... E 614 291-9700
  Columbus *(G-5544)*
Martins Steel Fabrication Inc................. E 330 882-4311
  New Franklin *(G-11439)*
Marysville Steel Inc.................................. E 937 642-5971
  Marysville *(G-9927)*
Mason Structural Steel LLC.................... E 440 439-1040
  Walton Hills *(G-15100)*
Masonite International Corp................... F 937 454-9308
  Vandalia *(G-14952)*
Maumee Valley Fabricators Inc............. E 419 476-1411
  Toledo *(G-14380)*
Mc Brown Industries Inc......................... F 419 963-2800
  Findlay *(G-7536)*
Mc Elwain Industries Inc........................ F 419 532-3126
  Ottawa *(G-12184)*
McNeil Holdings LLC................................ G 614 298-0300
  Columbus *(G-5557)*

SIC SECTION
34 FABRICATED METAL PRODUCTS

McWane Inc .... B 740 622-6651
   Coshocton *(G-5983)*

Mercury Iron and Steel Co .... F 440 349-1500
   Solon *(G-13385)*

Metal Man Inc .... G 614 830-0968
   Groveport *(G-8154)*

Metal Sales Manufacturing Corp .... F 440 319-3779
   Jefferson *(G-8753)*

Metalfab Group .... G 440 543-6234
   Streetsboro *(G-13778)*

Metlweb Ltd .... F 513 563-8822
   Cincinnati *(G-3157)*

Midwest Steel Fabricators Inc .... G 937 437-0371
   New Paris *(G-11483)*

Miracle Welding Inc .... G 937 746-9977
   Franklin *(G-7687)*

Mk Metal Products Inc .... F 330 669-2631
   Smithville *(G-13300)*

Mk Metal Products Entps Inc .... E 419 756-3644
   Mansfield *(G-9697)*

Mk Trempe Corporation .... E 937 492-3548
   Sidney *(G-13267)*

Mound Technologies Inc .... E 937 748-2937
   Springboro *(G-13511)*

Mssi Group Inc .... D 440 439-1040
   Walton Hills *(G-15102)*

National Stair Corp .... F 937 325-1347
   Springfield *(G-13609)*

Nct Technologies Group Inc .... F 937 882-6800
   New Carlisle *(G-11421)*

New Wayne Inc .... G 740 453-3454
   Zanesville *(G-16549)*

Niles Building Products Company .... F 330 544-0880
   Niles *(G-11677)*

▲ Northern Manufacturing Co Inc .... C 419 898-2821
   Oak Harbor *(G-12014)*

Northwind Industries Inc .... E 216 433-0666
   Cleveland *(G-4481)*

◆ Nucor Steel Marion Inc .... B 740 383-4011
   Marion *(G-9868)*

Ohio Fabricators Company .... F 740 622-5922
   Coshocton *(G-5990)*

◆ Ohio Gratings Inc .... B 800 321-9800
   Canton *(G-2184)*

▲ Ohio Metal Technologies Inc .... D 740 928-8288
   Hebron *(G-8353)*

Ohio Steel Industries Inc .... D 740 927-9500
   Pataskala *(G-12302)*

◆ Ohio Steel Industries Inc .... D 614 471-4800
   Columbus *(G-5628)*

Olson Sheet Metal Cnstr Co .... G 330 745-8225
   Barberton *(G-887)*

Oregonia Valley Metalworks LLC .... G 513 967-5190
   Waynesville *(G-15300)*

Outotec Oyj .... F 440 783-3336
   Strongsville *(G-13863)*

Overhead Door Corporation .... D 740 383-6376
   Marion *(G-9870)*

▲ P & L Metalcrafts LLC .... F 330 793-2178
   Youngstown *(G-16409)*

Pakfab USA Engnred Sltions Inc .... F 937 547-0413
   Greenville *(G-8054)*

PB Fbrction Mech Contrs Corp .... E 419 478-4869
   Toledo *(G-14429)*

▲ PC Campana Inc .... D 800 321-0151
   Lorain *(G-9428)*

▲ PC Campana Inc .... E 800 321-0151
   Lorain *(G-9429)*

Pemjay Inc .... F 740 254-4591
   Gnadenhutten *(G-7986)*

Penny Fab LLC .... F 740 967-3669
   Columbus *(G-5667)*

Perfection Fabricators Inc .... F 440 365-5850
   Elyria *(G-7194)*

Perry Welding Service Inc .... F 330 425-2211
   Twinsburg *(G-14714)*

Phoenix Mtal Sls Fbrcation LLC .... F 330 562-0585
   Twinsburg *(G-14715)*

◆ Pioneer Corp .... D 330 857-0267
   Dalton *(G-6140)*

Pioneer Machine Inc .... G 330 948-6500
   Lodi *(G-9355)*

▲ Pioneer Pipe Inc .... A 740 376-2400
   Marietta *(G-9817)*

Pittman Engineering Inc .... F 330 821-4365
   Alliance *(G-419)*

Porters Welding Inc .... G 740 452-4181
   Zanesville *(G-16557)*

Precise Metal Form Inc .... F 419 636-5221
   Bryan *(G-1836)*

Precision Cutoff LLC .... E 419 866-8000
   Holland *(G-8524)*

Precision Fabg & Stamping Inc .... G 740 453-7310
   Zanesville *(G-16558)*

Precision Laser & Forming Inc .... E 419 943-4350
   Leipsic *(G-9136)*

▲ Precision of Ohio Inc .... F 330 793-0900
   Youngstown *(G-16422)*

Precision Quincy Inds Inc .... B 888 312-5442
   Mason *(G-10042)*

Precision Welding Corporation .... E 216 524-6110
   Cleveland *(G-4577)*

Pro-Fab Inc .... E 330 644-0044
   Akron *(G-284)*

Prototype Fabricators Co .... F 216 252-0080
   Cleveland *(G-4595)*

Pucel Enterprises Inc .... D 216 881-4604
   Cleveland *(G-4598)*

Puritas Metal Products Inc .... G 440 353-1917
   North Ridgeville *(G-11855)*

Q S I Fabrication .... G 419 832-1680
   Grand Rapids *(G-8009)*

Quality Steel Fabrication .... F 937 492-9503
   Sidney *(G-13274)*

R G Smith Company .... D 330 456-3415
   Canton *(G-2207)*

R L Torbeck Industries Inc .... E 513 367-0080
   Harrison *(G-8289)*

R L Waller Construction Inc .... F 740 772-6185
   Chillicothe *(G-2531)*

Rads LLC .... F 330 671-0464
   Berea *(G-1292)*

Rance Industries Inc .... F 330 482-1745
   Columbiana *(G-5049)*

Rankin Mfg Inc .... E 419 929-8338
   New London *(G-11466)*

Rbm Environmental & Cnstr Inc .... F 419 693-5840
   Oregon *(G-12110)*

Republic Storage Systems LLC .... B 330 438-5800
   Canton *(G-2215)*

Response Metal Fabricators .... E 937 222-9000
   Dayton *(G-6546)*

Rex Welding Inc .... F 740 387-1650
   Marion *(G-9875)*

Richard Steel Company Inc .... G 216 520-6390
   Cleveland *(G-4632)*

Ripley Metalworks LLC .... F 937 392-4992
   Ripley *(G-12819)*

Rittman Inc .... D 330 927-6855
   Rittman *(G-12827)*

▼ Riverside Steel Inc .... F 330 856-5299
   Vienna *(G-15003)*

Riwco Corp .... E 937 322-6521
   Springfield *(G-13629)*

RLM Fabricating Inc .... E 419 729-6130
   Toledo *(G-14454)*

RLM Fabricating Inc .... G 419 476-1411
   Toledo *(G-14455)*

Rmi Titanium Company LLC .... D 330 544-9470
   Niles *(G-11683)*

Rmt Acquisition Inc .... E 513 241-5566
   Cincinnati *(G-3347)*

Robinson Inc .... G 614 898-0654
   Columbus *(G-5730)*

Rock Hard Industries LLC .... G 440 327-3077
   North Ridgeville *(G-11859)*

▼ Rol-Fab Inc .... E 216 662-2500
   Cleveland *(G-4646)*

Romar Metal Fabricating Inc .... G 740 682-7731
   Oak Hill *(G-12025)*

Rose Metal Industries LLC .... E 216 426-8615
   Cleveland *(G-4647)*

Rose Metal Industries LLC .... E 216 881-3355
   Cleveland *(G-4648)*

Rose Properties Inc .... F 216 881-6000
   Cleveland *(G-4649)*

Rsv Wlding Fbrction McHning In .... F 419 592-0993
   Napoleon *(G-11333)*

◆ Rti International Metals Inc .... A
   Niles *(G-11687)*

S & G Manufacturing Group LLC .... C 614 529-0100
   Hilliard *(G-8437)*

Sabre Industries Inc .... F 419 542-1420
   Hicksville *(G-8379)*

▲ Sausser Steel Company Inc .... F 419 422-9632
   Findlay *(G-7559)*

Schoonover Industries Inc .... E 419 289-8332
   Ashland *(G-612)*

Schuck Mtal Fbrction Dsign Inc .... F 419 586-1054
   Celina *(G-2348)*

Shaffer Metal Fab Inc .... E 937 492-1384
   Sidney *(G-13286)*

Sharon Manufacturing Inc .... E 330 239-1561
   Sharon Center *(G-13167)*

Sintered Metal Industries Inc .... F 330 650-4000
   Hudson *(G-8612)*

Socar of Ohio Inc .... D 419 596-3100
   Continental *(G-5938)*

Somerville Manufacturing Inc .... E 740 336-7847
   Marietta *(G-9829)*

South Central Industrial LLC .... F 740 333-5401
   Wshngtn Ct Hs *(G-16241)*

Spradlin Bros Welding Co .... F 800 219-2182
   Springfield *(G-13634)*

Srt Sales & Service LLC .... G 330 620-0681
   Copley *(G-5956)*

St Lawrence Holdings LLC .... E 330 562-9000
   Maple Heights *(G-9761)*

◆ St Lawrence Steel Corporation .... E 330 562-9000
   Maple Heights *(G-9762)*

Stainless Specialties Inc .... E 440 942-4242
   Eastlake *(G-7049)*

Standard Wldg & Stl Pdts Inc .... F 330 273-2777
   Medina *(G-10379)*

Starr Fabricating Inc .... D 330 394-9891
   Vienna *(G-15004)*

Stays Lighting Inc .... G 440 328-3254
   Elyria *(G-7206)*

▼ Steel & Alloy Utility Pdts Inc .... E 330 530-2220
   Mc Donald *(G-10280)*

▲ Steel Eqp Specialists Inc .... D 330 823-8260
   Alliance *(G-427)*

Steel It LLC .... E 513 253-3111
   Cincinnati *(G-3418)*

Steel Quest Inc .... G 513 772-5030
   Cincinnati *(G-3419)*

Employee Codes: A=Over 500 employees, B=251-500
C=101-250, D=51-100, E=20-50, F=10-19, G=1-9

34 FABRICATED METAL PRODUCTS

Steelial Wldg Met Fbrction Inc............... E 740 669-5300
  Vinton (G-15012)
Steeltec Products LLC............................ F 216 681-1114
  Cleveland (G-4733)
Steimel Metal Fab LLC............................ G 513 863-5310
  Hamilton (G-8246)
Steve Vore Welding and Steel................. F 419 375-4087
  Fort Recovery (G-7624)
Sticker Corporation................................. G 440 942-4700
  Willoughby (G-15999)
Stock Mfg & Design Co Inc..................... F 513 353-3600
  Cleves (G-4965)
Stover International LLC........................ E 740 363-5251
  Delaware (G-6753)
Straightaway Fabrications Ltd................. F 419 281-9440
  Ashland (G-616)
Suburban Steel Supply Co .... D 614 737-5501
  Gahanna (G-7850)
Suburban Stl Sup Co Ltd Partnr............... G 317 783-6555
  Columbus (G-5707)
Sulecki Precision Products Inc................ F 440 255-5454
  Mentor (G-10569)
Superior Metal Worx LLC....................... F 614 879-9400
  Columbus (G-5799)
Superior Soda Service LLC..................... G 937 657-9700
  Beavercreek (G-1081)
Superior Steel Service LLC.................... F 513 724-7888
  Batavia (G-951)
Surface Recovery Tech LLC.................... F 937 879-5864
  Fairborn (G-7323)
Tarrier Steel Company Inc...................... E 614 444-4000
  Columbus (G-5811)
Tech Dynamics Inc................................. E 419 666-1666
  Perrysburg (G-12430)
Tech Systems Inc.................................... F 419 878-2100
  Waterville (G-15254)
Ted M Figgins... F 740 277-3750
  Lancaster (G-9042)
Terrasmart LLC....................................... E 239 362-0211
  Columbus (G-5818)
▲ The Armor Group Inc......................... C 513 923-5260
  Mason (G-10065)
◆ The D S Brown Company.....................C 419 257-3561
  North Baltimore (G-11701)
The Mansfield Strl & Erct Co.................. F 419 522-5911
  Mansfield (G-9726)
Thieman Quality Metal Fab Inc.............. D 419 629-2612
  New Bremen (G-11409)
Thomas Steel Inc.................................... E 419 483-7540
  Bellevue (G-1238)
TJ Clark International LLC...................... G 614 388-8869
  Delaware (G-6755)
Transco Railway Products Inc................ E 330 872-0934
  Newton Falls (G-11659)
Tri-America Contractors Inc.................... E 740 574-0148
  Wheelersburg (G-15810)
Tri-Fab Inc... E 330 337-3425
  Salem (G-13034)
Tri-State Fabricators Inc........................ E 513 752-5005
  Amelia (G-469)
Triad Capital Group LLC........................ F 440 236-6677
  Columbia Station (G-5023)
Triangle Precision Industries.................. D 937 299-6776
  Dayton (G-6632)
Tristate Steel Contractors LLC................ G 513 648-9000
  Cincinnati (G-3466)
Tru-Fab Inc... E 937 435-1733
  Miamisburg (G-10696)
Tru-Form Steel & Wire Inc..................... F 765 348-5001
  Toledo (G-14512)
▲ Truck Cab Manufacturers Inc............. E 513 922-1300
  Cincinnati (G-3469)

Turn-Key Industrial Svcs LLC................. D 614 274-1128
  Grove City (G-8127)
Umd Automated Systems Inc................. D 740 694-8614
  Fredericktown (G-7756)
Union Fabricating and Mch Co............... G 419 626-5963
  Sandusky (G-13099)
Unique Fabrications Inc.......................... F 419 355-1700
  Fremont (G-7817)
United Metal Fabricators Inc.................. E 216 662-2000
  Maple Heights (G-9763)
Universal Dsign Fbrication LLC............... F 419 202-5269
  Sandusky (G-13101)
▲ Universal Fabg Cnstr Svcs Inc........... E 614 274-1128
  Columbus (G-5845)
Upright Steel LLC................................... E 216 923-0852
  Cleveland (G-4853)
Upright Steel Fabricators LLC................. F 216 923-0852
  Cleveland (G-4854)
V & S Schuler Engineering Inc............... D 330 452-5200
  Middlefield (G-10790)
V & S Schuler Engineering Inc............... E 330 452-5200
  Canton (G-2260)
Valco Industries LLC............................... E 937 399-7400
  Springfield (G-13653)
Vanscoyk Sheet Metal Corp.................... G 937 845-0581
  New Carlisle (G-11429)
Verhoff Machine & Welding Inc............... C 419 596-3202
  Continental (G-5939)
Vicon Fabricating Company Ltd.............. E 440 205-6700
  Mentor (G-10592)
Viking Fabricators Inc............................. E 740 374-5246
  Marietta (G-9843)
Vscorp LLC.. F 937 305-3562
  Tipp City (G-14165)
Wanner Metal Worx Inc.......................... E 740 369-4034
  Delaware (G-6756)
Warmus and Associates Inc................... F 330 659-4440
  Bath (G-962)
◆ Warren Fabricating Corporation..........D 330 534-5017
  Hubbard (G-8572)
▲ Waterford Tank Fabrication Ltd.......... D 740 984-4100
  Beverly (G-1323)
Wecan Fabricators LLC.......................... G 740 667-0731
  Tuppers Plains (G-14619)
Welage Corporation................................ F 513 681-2300
  Cincinnati (G-3510)
Welding Improvement Company............ G 330 424-9666
  Lisbon (G-9327)
Werks Kraft Engineering LLC................. E 330 721-7374
  Medina (G-10394)
Wernke Wldg & Stl Erection Co.............. F 513 353-4173
  North Bend (G-11708)
Wernli Realty Corporation...................... F 937 258-7878
  Beavercreek (G-1083)
Westwood Fbrction Shtmetal Inc............ E 937 837-0494
  Dayton (G-6652)
▲ Whitacre Engineering Company......... E 330 455-8505
  Canton (G-2268)
White Machine & Mfg Co....................... F 740 453-5451
  Zanesville (G-16570)
◆ Whole Shop Inc...................................F 330 630-5305
  Tallmadge (G-14057)
William Niccum...................................... G 330 415-0154
  East Sparta (G-7015)
Williams Scotsman Inc........................... D 614 449-8675
  Columbus (G-5878)
Wiseman Bros Fabg & Stl Ltd................ F 740 988-5121
  Beaver (G-1036)
▼ Witt Industries Inc.............................. D 513 871-5700
  Mason (G-10071)
Wm Lang & Sons Company................... F 513 541-3304
  Cincinnati (G-3524)

Worthington Enterprises Inc................... D 513 539-9291
  Monroe (G-11121)
▲ Wrayco Industries Inc......................... C 330 688-5617
  Stow (G-13740)
▲ Ysd Industries Inc.............................. E 330 792-6521
  Youngstown (G-16491)
Zimmerman Steel & Sup Co LLC............ F 330 828-1010
  Dalton (G-6146)

3442 Metal doors, sash, and trim

All Pro Ovrhd Door Systems LLC........... G 614 444-3667
  Columbus (G-5111)
Aluminum Color Industries Inc............... E 330 536-6295
  Lowellville (G-9510)
Anderson Door Co.................................. F 216 475-5700
  Cleveland (G-3666)
Arch Angle Window and Door LLC......... F 800 548-0214
  Medina (G-10297)
Architctral Mllwk Cbinetry Inc................ G 440 708-0086
  Chagrin Falls (G-2389)
▲ Associated Materials LLC................. A 330 929-1811
  Cuyahoga Falls (G-6069)
Associated Materials Group Inc............. C 330 929-1811
  Cuyahoga Falls (G-6070)
Associated Mtls Holdings LLC................ A 330 929-1811
  Cuyahoga Falls (G-6071)
Atrium Centers Inc................................. E 513 830-5014
  Cincinnati (G-2643)
Automted Cmpnent Spcalists LLC.......... E 513 335-4285
  Cincinnati (G-2645)
Bilco Company....................................... E 740 455-9020
  Zanesville (G-16508)
Brainerd Industries Inc........................... E 937 228-0488
  Miamisburg (G-10622)
Burt Manufacturing Company Inc........... E 330 762-0061
  Akron (G-97)
Capitol Aluminum & Glass Corp............. D 800 331-8268
  Bellevue (G-1225)
▲ Cascade Ohio Inc.............................. B 440 593-5800
  Conneaut (G-5916)
▲ Champion Opco LLC......................... B 513 327-7338
  Cincinnati (G-2725)
◆ Champion Win Co Cleveland LLC......F 440 899-2562
  Macedonia (G-9541)
Champion Window Co of Toledo............ E 419 841-0154
  Perrysburg (G-12370)
Chase Industries Inc............................... E 513 603-2936
  Cincinnati (G-2727)
Cleveland Shutters Inc........................... G 440 234-7600
  Berea (G-1271)
◆ Clopay Corporation..............................C 800 282-2260
  Mason (G-9979)
Creative Millwork Ohio Inc..................... D 440 992-3566
  Ashtabula (G-628)
Custom Quality Products Inc.................. E
  Cincinnati (G-2809)
Dale Kestler... G 513 871-9000
  Cincinnati (G-2817)
Desco Corporation.................................. G 614 888-8855
  New Albany (G-11378)
Division Overhead Door Inc.................... F 513 872-0888
  Cincinnati (G-2834)
Duo-Corp... F 330 549-2149
  North Lima (G-11804)
Eliason Corporation................................ E 800 828-3655
  West Chester (G-15550)
Euclid Jalousies Inc............................... G 440 953-1112
  Cleveland (G-4034)
Fostoria MT&f Corp................................ F 419 435-7676
  Fostoria (G-7636)
Francis-Schulze Co................................ E 937 295-3941
  Russia (G-12884)

SIC SECTION
34 FABRICATED METAL PRODUCTS

Haas Door Company............................ C 419 337-9900
  Wauseon (G-15262)
Hrh Door Corp..................................... E 513 674-9300
  Cincinnati (G-3011)
Hrh Door Corp..................................... E 330 828-2291
  Dalton (G-6132)
◆ Hrh Door Corp.................................. A 850 208-3400
  Mount Hope (G-11238)
Kawneer Company Inc........................ C 216 252-3203
  Cleveland (G-4278)
M-D Building Products Inc................. F 513 539-2255
  Middletown (G-10837)
M-D Building Products Inc................. C 513 539-2255
  Middletown (G-10838)
Masonite International Corp............... G 937 454-9308
  Vandalia (G-14952)
Mestek Inc.. D 419 288-2703
  Bowling Green (G-1576)
Mestek Inc.. F 419 288-2703
  Bradner (G-1603)
Midwest Curtainwalls Inc.................... D 216 641-7900
  Cleveland (G-4410)
Modern Builders Supply Inc.............. C 419 241-3961
  Toledo (G-14389)
National Access Design LLC.............. F 513 351-3400
  Cincinnati (G-3179)
Niles Building Products Company...... F 330 544-0880
  Niles (G-11677)
Nofziger Door Sales Inc..................... F 419 445-2961
  Archbold (G-539)
▼ Nofziger Door Sales Inc................. C 419 337-9900
  Wauseon (G-15271)
▲ Orrvilon Inc..................................... C 330 684-9400
  Orrville (G-12145)
Overhead Door Corporation............... D 740 383-6376
  Marion (G-9870)
Overhead Door Corporation............... F 419 294-3874
  Upper Sandusky (G-14820)
Overhead Door of Pike County.......... G 740 289-3925
  Piketon (G-12481)
Overhead Inc...................................... G 419 476-0300
  Toledo (G-14420)
Pease Industies Inc........................... D 513 870-3600
  Fairfield (G-7393)
Phillips Manufacturing Co................... D 330 652-4335
  Niles (G-11682)
Prentke Romich Company................. C 330 262-1984
  Wooster (G-16160)
Provia Holdings Inc............................ C 330 852-4711
  Sugarcreek (G-13935)
Quanex Screens LLC......................... E 419 662-5001
  Perrysburg (G-12422)
Renewal By Andersen LLC................ G 614 781-9600
  Columbus (G-5070)
Rsl LLC... E 330 392-8900
  Warren (G-15203)
S R Door Inc....................................... D 740 927-3558
  Hebron (G-8360)
Senneca Holdings Inc........................ E 800 543-4455
  Cincinnati (G-3380)
▲ Stephen M Trudick.......................... E 440 834-1891
  Burton (G-1886)
Superior Weld and Fabg Co Inc........ G 216 249-5122
  Cleveland (G-4753)
Thomas J Weaver Inc........................ F 740 622-2040
  Coshocton (G-5998)
Traichal Construction Company......... E 800 255-3667
  Niles (G-11689)
Tri County Door Service Inc.............. F 216 531-2245
  Euclid (G-7303)
Uniqative LLC..................................... G 800 337-2870
  Sylvania (G-14020)

Vinylume Products Inc....................... E 330 799-2000
  Youngstown (G-16472)
YKK AP America Inc........................... E 513 942-7200
  West Chester (G-15528)
Youngstown Shade & Alum LLC........ G 330 782-2373
  Youngstown (G-16487)

3443 Fabricated plate work (boiler shop)

A A S Amels Sheet Meta L Inc........... F 330 793-9326
  Youngstown (G-16297)
▲ A & G Manufacturing Co Inc........... E 419 468-7433
  Galion (G-7858)
A-1 Welding & Fabrication.................. F 440 233-8474
  Lorain (G-9399)
Active Chemical Systems Inc............ F 440 543-7755
  Chagrin Falls (G-2388)
Advance Industrial Mfg Inc................ E 614 871-3333
  Grove City (G-8073)
Advanced Welding Inc....................... E 937 746-6800
  Franklin (G-7662)
Air-Tech Mechanical Inc..................... F 419 292-0074
  Toledo (G-14180)
Allen Industrial Company................... F 440 327-4100
  North Ridgeville (G-11827)
▲ Allgaier Process Technology.......... G 513 402-2566
  West Chester (G-15363)
▼ Alloy Engineering Company........... D 440 243-6800
  Berea (G-1264)
▲ Allpass Corporation........................ F 440 998-6300
  Madison (G-9587)
AM Castle & Co.................................. F 330 425-7000
  Bedford (G-1100)
▲ American Tank & Fabricating Co.... D 216 252-1500
  Cleveland (G-3656)
AMF Burns... G 330 650-6500
  Hudson (G-8585)
▲ Amko Service Company................. E 330 364-8857
  Midvale (G-10875)
Apex Welding Incorporated................ F 440 232-6770
  Bedford (G-1101)
Ares Inc.. D 419 635-2175
  Port Clinton (G-12615)
Armor Consolidated Inc..................... A 513 923-5260
  Mason (G-9952)
▲ Armor Metal Group Mason Inc....... C 513 769-0700
  Mason (G-9954)
▲ AT&f Advanced Metals LLC........... E 330 684-1122
  Cleveland (G-3695)
Ayling and Reichert Co Consent........ E 419 898-2471
  Oak Harbor (G-12011)
Babcock & Wilcox Company.............. E 330 753-4511
  Barberton (G-860)
◆ Babcock & Wilcox Company........... A 330 753-4511
  Akron (G-73)
Bar Processing Corporation............... F 440 943-0094
  Wickliffe (G-15825)
Baxter Holdings Inc............................ E 513 860-3593
  Hamilton (G-8184)
Bi-Con Services Inc............................ B 740 685-2542
  Derwent (G-6798)
▲ Bico Akron Inc................................. D 330 794-1716
  Mogadore (G-11067)
BJ Equipment Ltd............................... E 614 497-1188
  Columbus (G-5193)
Blackwood Sheet Metal Inc............... G 614 291-3115
  Columbus (G-5200)
Blevins Metal Fabrication Inc............. E 419 522-6082
  Mansfield (G-9629)
Breitinger Company............................ C 419 526-4255
  Mansfield (G-9631)
▼ Buckeye Fabricating Company....... E 937 746-9822
  Springboro (G-13497)

Budget Dumpsters............................. G 419 690-9896
  Curtice (G-6056)
Bwxt Nclear Oprtions Group Inc........ A 216 912-3000
  Cleveland (G-3776)
C & R Inc.. E 614 497-1130
  Groveport (G-8134)
C A Joseph Co.................................... F 330 532-4646
  Irondale (G-8693)
▲ C A Litzler Co Inc............................ E 216 267-8020
  Cleveland (G-3778)
C Imperial Inc..................................... E 937 669-5620
  Tipp City (G-14124)
Capital Tool Company........................ E 216 661-5750
  Cleveland (G-3787)
▲ Cardinal Pumps Exchangers Inc.... F 330 332-8558
  Salem (G-12981)
◆ Cbc Global....................................... E 330 482-3373
  Columbiana (G-5030)
Ceco Environmental Corp.................. E 513 874-8915
  West Chester (G-15544)
Chart Asia Inc..................................... C 440 753-1490
  Cleveland (G-3810)
Chart Industries Inc............................ B 440 753-1490
  Cleveland (G-3811)
Chart International Inc........................ A 440 753-1490
  Cleveland (G-3812)
Chromium Corporation....................... E 216 271-4910
  Cleveland (G-3821)
▲ Cincinnati Heat Exchangers Inc..... G 513 770-0777
  Mason (G-9976)
Cleveland Steel Specialty Co............. E 216 464-9400
  Bedford Heights (G-1168)
◆ Clifton Steel Company.................... D 216 662-6111
  Maple Heights (G-9749)
Commercial Mtal Fbricators Inc......... E 937 233-4911
  Dayton (G-6260)
Compco Columbiana Company......... D 330 482-0200
  Columbiana (G-5035)
Compco Youngstown Company......... D 330 482-6488
  Columbiana (G-5036)
Complete Mechanical Svcs LLC........ D 513 489-3080
  Blue Ash (G-1382)
Contech Bridge Solutions LLC.......... F 513 645-7000
  West Chester (G-15400)
Contech Cnstr Pdts Hldings Inc........ A 513 645-7000
  West Chester (G-15401)
Contech Engnered Solutions Inc...... E 513 645-7000
  West Chester (G-15402)
◆ Contech Engnered Solutions LLC...... C 513 645-7000
  West Chester (G-15403)
Convault of Ohio Inc.......................... G 614 252-8422
  Columbus (G-5291)
Cooper-Standard Automotive Inc...... D 740 342-3523
  New Lexington (G-11451)
Cramers Inc.. E 330 477-4571
  Canton (G-2083)
Curtiss-Wright Flow Ctrl Corp........... D 513 528-7900
  Cincinnati (G-2556)
Dabar Industries LLC......................... F 614 873-3949
  Columbus (G-5313)
Danco Metal Products LLC................ D 440 871-2300
  Avon Lake (G-803)
Debra-Kuempel Inc............................ D 513 271-6500
  Cincinnati (G-2822)
Defabco Inc... D 614 231-2700
  Columbus (G-5323)
▲ Defiance Metal Products Co.......... B 419 784-5332
  Defiance (G-6676)
Diller Metals Inc.................................. G 419 943-3364
  Leipsic (G-9132)
Dj S Weld.. G 330 432-2206
  Uhrichsville (G-14764)

Employee Codes: A=Over 500 employees, B=251-500
C=101-250, D=51-100, E=20-50, F=10-19, G=1-9

34 FABRICATED METAL PRODUCTS

Dover Tank and Plate Company .... E 330 343-4443
  Dover (G-6822)
Dynamat Inc .... F 513 860-5094
  Hamilton (G-8202)
▲ Dynamic Control North Amer Inc .... F 513 860-5094
  Hamilton (G-8203)
▼ E-Pak Manufacturing LLC .... D 330 264-0825
  Wooster (G-16115)
Eagle Welding & Fabg Inc .... E 440 946-0692
  Willoughby (G-15914)
▲ Eaton Fabricating Company Inc .... E 440 926-3121
  Grafton (G-7998)
◆ Ebner Furnaces Inc .... D 330 335-2311
  Wadsworth (G-15028)
Efco Corp .... G 614 876-1226
  Columbus (G-5347)
▲ Eleet Cryogenics Inc .... E 330 874-4009
  Bolivar (G-1524)
Elliott Machine Works Inc .... E 419 468-4709
  Galion (G-7074)
En-Hanced Products Inc .... G 614 882-7400
  Sunbury (G-13953)
◆ Enerfab LLC .... B 513 641-0500
  Cincinnati (G-2872)
Energy Hbr Nclear Gnration LLC .... G 888 254-6359
  Akron (G-140)
Enviri Corporation .... G 216 961-1570
  Cleveland (G-4022)
▲ Exothermics .... E
  Toledo (G-14282)
▲ Fabco Inc .... E 419 422-4533
  Findlay (G-7504)
Fabrication Shop Inc .... F 419 435-7934
  Fostoria (G-7631)
Fabstar Tanks Inc .... E 419 587-3639
  Grover Hill (G-8169)
Fiba Technologies Inc .... F 330 602-7300
  Midvale (G-10877)
▲ Flow-Liner Systems Ltd .... E 800 348-0020
  Zanesville (G-16531)
FSRc Tanks Inc .... G 234 221-2015
  Bolivar (G-1525)
Fulton Equipment Co .... G 419 290-5393
  Toledo (G-14295)
Gaspar Inc .... D 330 477-2222
  Canton (G-2110)
◆ Gayston Corporation .... C 937 743-6050
  Miamisburg (G-10640)
▲ General Technologies Inc .... E 419 747-1800
  Mansfield (G-9659)
▲ General Tool Company .... C 513 733-5500
  Cincinnati (G-2946)
▲ Giuseppes Concessions LLC .... F 614 554-2551
  Marengo (G-9768)
Graber Metal Works Inc .... F 440 237-8422
  North Royalton (G-11877)
Grenga Machine & Welding .... F 330 743-1113
  Youngstown (G-16374)
H P E Inc .... G 330 833-3161
  Massillon (G-10104)
◆ Halvorsen Company .... E 216 341-7500
  Cleveland (G-4165)
Hamilton Tanks LLC .... F 614 445-8446
  Columbus (G-5418)
▲ Hammelmann Corporation .... F 937 859-8777
  Miamisburg (G-10642)
Hason USA Corp .... F 513 248-0287
  Cincinnati (G-2988)
Heat Exchange Applied Tech Inc .... F 330 682-4328
  Orrville (G-12128)
Hutnik Company .... G 330 336-9700
  Wadsworth (G-15035)

Hydraulic Specialists Inc .... F 740 922-3343
  Midvale (G-10879)
▼ Hydro-Thrift Corporation .... E 330 837-5141
  Massillon (G-10110)
Indian Creek Fabricators Inc .... E 937 667-7214
  Tipp City (G-14138)
Industrial Container Svcs LLC .... E 614 864-1900
  Blacklick (G-1338)
Industrial Container Svcs LLC .... E 513 921-2056
  Cincinnati (G-3020)
Industrial Container Svcs LLC .... E 513 921-8811
  Cincinnati (G-3021)
Industrial Fabrication and Mch .... G 330 454-7644
  Canton (G-2131)
Industrial Farm Tank Inc .... E 937 843-2972
  Lewistown (G-9194)
Industrial Repair and Mfg .... F 419 822-0314
  Delta (G-6786)
▲ Industrial Repair and Mfg .... E 419 822-4232
  Delta (G-6787)
Industrial Tank & Containment .... F 330 448-4876
  Brookfield (G-1670)
▲ Jergens Inc .... C 216 486-5540
  Cleveland (G-4253)
Jh Industries Inc .... E 330 963-4105
  Twinsburg (G-14677)
Jis Distribution LLC .... F 216 706-6552
  Cleveland (G-4256)
JMw Welding and Mfg Inc .... E 330 484-2428
  Canton (G-2136)
Kard Welding Inc .... E 419 628-2598
  Minster (G-11054)
▲ Kendall Holdings Ltd .... E 614 486-4750
  Columbus (G-5507)
Kenton Strl & Orn Ir Works .... D 419 674-4025
  Kenton (G-8887)
◆ Kirk & Blum Manufacturing Co .... C 513 458-2600
  Cincinnati (G-3078)
Krista Messer .... G 734 459-1952
  Sunbury (G-13957)
Laird Technologies Inc .... E 234 806-0105
  Warren (G-15183)
▲ Langdon Inc .... E 513 733-5955
  Cincinnati (G-3095)
Lapham-Hickey Steel Corp .... E 614 443-4881
  Columbus (G-5521)
Lincoln Electric Automtn Inc .... E 614 471-5926
  Columbus (G-5527)
Lion Industries LLC .... E 740 676-1100
  Bellaire (G-1188)
Liquid Luggers LLC .... E 330 426-2538
  East Palestine (G-7006)
▲ Long-Stanton Mfg Company .... E 513 874-8020
  West Chester (G-15458)
Louis Arthur Steel Company .... G 440 997-5545
  Geneva (G-7941)
◆ Loveman Steel Corporation .... D 440 232-6200
  Bedford (G-1135)
M & H Fabricating Co Inc .... F 937 325-8708
  Springfield (G-13596)
Mack Iron Works Company .... E 419 626-3712
  Sandusky (G-13078)
Mahle Behr Dayton LLC .... A 937 369-2000
  Dayton (G-6425)
Mahle Behr USA Inc .... F 937 369-2610
  Xenia (G-16268)
▼ Marathon Industrial Cntrs Inc .... F 440 324-2748
  Elyria (G-7177)
▲ Mc Machine Llc .... E 216 398-3666
  Cleveland (G-4378)
Mercury Iron and Steel Co .... F 440 349-1500
  Solon (G-13385)

Metal Fabricating Corporation .... D 216 631-8121
  Cleveland (G-4396)
Metalfab Group .... G 440 543-6234
  Streetsboro (G-13778)
Micc Manufacturing Corporation .... G 567 331-0101
  Perrysburg (G-12400)
▼ Midwestern Industries Inc .... D 330 837-4203
  Massillon (G-10127)
Modern Welding Co Ohio Inc .... E 740 344-9425
  Newark (G-11593)
Moore Mr Specialty Company .... G 330 332-1229
  Salem (G-13020)
▼ Morrison Products Inc .... C 216 486-4000
  Cleveland (G-4422)
Myers Industries Inc .... D 330 253-5592
  Akron (G-259)
Myers Industries Inc .... D 330 336-6621
  Wadsworth (G-15047)
Nbw Inc .... E 216 377-1700
  Cleveland (G-4442)
New Wayne Inc .... G 740 453-3454
  Zanesville (G-16549)
North Coast Dumpster Svcs LLC .... G 216 644-5647
  Cleveland (G-4467)
Northeast Fabricators LLC .... E 330 747-3484
  Youngstown (G-16404)
Novoco LLC .... E 330 359-5315
  Fredericksburg (G-7729)
Odom Industries Inc .... E 513 248-0287
  Milford (G-10915)
Ohio Heat Transfer .... G 513 870-5323
  Hamilton (G-8233)
▲ Ohio Heat Transfer Ltd .... F 740 695-0635
  Saint Clairsville (G-12917)
▲ Oliver Steel Plate Co .... D 330 425-7000
  Twinsburg (G-14704)
OSI Environmental LLC .... E 440 237-4600
  North Royalton (G-11890)
PB Fbrction Mech Contrs Corp .... E 419 478-4869
  Toledo (G-14429)
Phe Manufacturing Inc .... G 937 790-1582
  Franklin (G-7693)
▲ Pioneer Pipe Inc .... A 740 376-2400
  Marietta (G-9817)
Precision Fabricators Inc .... G 513 288-3358
  Harrison (G-8285)
Prout Boiler Htg & Wldg Inc .... E 330 744-0293
  Youngstown (G-16423)
Pucel Enterprises Inc .... D 216 881-4604
  Cleveland (G-4598)
Quintus Technologies LLC .... E 614 891-2732
  Lewis Center (G-9176)
R G Smith Company .... D 330 456-3415
  Canton (G-2207)
Rampp Company .... E 740 373-7886
  Marietta (G-9819)
RCE Heat Exchangers LLC .... E 330 627-0300
  Carrollton (G-2313)
Rcr Partnership .... G 419 340-1202
  Genoa (G-7948)
Rebsco Inc .... F 937 548-2246
  Greenville (G-8057)
Rhodes Manufacturing Co Inc .... E 740 743-2614
  Somerset (G-13449)
▲ Ridge Corporation .... D 614 421-7434
  Etna (G-7256)
▲ Rimrock Corporation .... E 614 471-5926
  Columbus (G-5723)
Rimrock Holdings Corporation .... C 614 471-5926
  Columbus (G-5724)
Rmt Acquisition Inc .... E 513 241-5566
  Cincinnati (G-3347)

SIC SECTION

34 FABRICATED METAL PRODUCTS

Roger Schweitzer Sons........................ G 513 241-4423
  Monroe *(G-11119)*
Rose Metal Industries LLC................... F 216 881-3355
  Cleveland *(G-4648)*
Ross Hx LLC.. E 513 217-1565
  Middletown *(G-10857)*
S-P Company Inc................................. D 330 782-5651
  Columbiana *(G-5050)*
▲ Sausser Steel Company Inc............. F 419 422-9632
  Findlay *(G-7559)*
Schaeffer Metal Products Inc............... G 330 296-6226
  Ravenna *(G-12732)*
Schweizer Dipple Inc........................... D 440 786-8090
  Cleveland *(G-4676)*
Seneca Environmental Products Inc..... E 419 447-1282
  Tiffin *(G-14104)*
Sexton Industrial Inc............................ C 513 530-5555
  West Chester *(G-15584)*
▼ Sgl Carbon Technic LLC................... E 440 572-3600
  Strongsville *(G-13878)*
Sharon Manufacturing Inc.................... E 330 239-1561
  Sharon Center *(G-13167)*
▲ Spirex Corporation........................... C 330 726-1166
  Youngstown *(G-16446)*
Spradlin Bros Welding Co..................... F 800 219-2182
  Springfield *(G-13634)*
St Lawrence Holdings LLC................... E 330 562-9000
  Maple Heights *(G-9761)*
◆ St Lawrence Steel Corporation.........E 330 562-9000
  Maple Heights *(G-9762)*
STA-Warm Electric Company................ F 330 296-6461
  Ravenna *(G-12736)*
Stanwade Metal Products Inc............... E 330 772-2421
  Hartford *(G-8298)*
▼ Steel & Alloy Utility Pdts Inc............. E 330 530-2220
  Mc Donald *(G-10280)*
Steel Valley Tank & Welding................ F 740 598-4994
  Brilliant *(G-1651)*
Steve Vore Welding and Steel.............. F 419 375-4087
  Fort Recovery *(G-7624)*
Sticker Corporation.............................. F 440 946-2100
  Willoughby *(G-15998)*
◆ Strohecker Incorporated...................E 330 426-9496
  East Palestine *(G-7009)*
Swagelok Company.............................. D 440 349-5934
  Solon *(G-13431)*
Swanton Wldg Machining Co Inc........... D 419 826-4816
  Swanton *(G-13984)*
▲ The Armor Group Inc....................... C 513 923-5260
  Mason *(G-10065)*
▼ Toledo Metal Spinning Company...... E 419 535-5931
  Toledo *(G-14498)*
Triangle Precision Industries................ D 937 299-6776
  Dayton *(G-6632)*
Triumph Thermal Systems LLC............ D 419 273-2511
  Forest *(G-7593)*
Universal Dsign Fbrication LLC............ F 419 202-5269
  Sandusky *(G-13101)*
Universal Hydraulik USA Corp.............. G 419 873-6340
  Perrysburg *(G-12442)*
▲ Universal Rack & Eqp Co Inc........... D 330 963-6776
  Twinsburg *(G-14751)*
▲ Val-Co Pax Inc................................. D 717 354-4586
  Coldwater *(G-5003)*
Verhoff Machine & Welding Inc............ C 419 596-3202
  Continental *(G-5939)*
Viking Fabricators Inc.......................... E 740 374-5246
  Marietta *(G-9843)*
Vortec Corporation............................... E
  Blue Ash *(G-1489)*
◆ Warren Fabricating Corporation.........D 330 534-5017
  Hubbard *(G-8572)*

Washington Products Inc...................... F 330 837-5101
  Massillon *(G-10154)*
Wcr Incorporated.................................. G 740 333-3448
  Wshngtn Ct Hs *(G-16245)*
◆ Wcr Incorporated..............................E 937 223-0703
  Fairborn *(G-7327)*
Will-Burt Company................................ F 330 682-7015
  Orrville *(G-12162)*
▲ Will-Burt Company............................ C 330 682-7015
  Orrville *(G-12163)*
▲ Worthington Products Inc.................. G 330 452-7400
  East Canton *(G-6982)*
Worthington Cylinder Corp................... D 740 569-4143
  Bremen *(G-1641)*
Worthington Cylinder Corp................... C 614 438-7900
  Columbus *(G-5882)*
Worthington Cylinder Corp................... C 614 840-3800
  Westerville *(G-15690)*
Worthington Cylinder Corp................... E 330 262-1762
  Wooster *(G-16188)*
◆ Worthington Cylinder Corp................C 614 840-3210
  Worthington *(G-16219)*

3444 Sheet metalwork

A A S Amels Sheet Meta L Inc.............. F 330 793-9326
  Youngstown *(G-16297)*
A & C Welding Inc................................ E 330 762-4777
  Peninsula *(G-12337)*
▲ A & G Manufacturing Co Inc............. E 419 468-7433
  Galion *(G-7858)*
▲ Acro Tool & Die Company................ E 330 773-5173
  Akron *(G-17)*
▲ Active Metal and Molds Inc.............. F 419 281-9623
  Ashland *(G-549)*
Advanced Welding Inc.......................... E 937 746-6800
  Franklin *(G-7662)*
Affiliated Metal Industries Inc............... F 440 235-3345
  Olmsted Falls *(G-12075)*
Ahner Fabricating & Shtmtl Inc............. E 419 626-6641
  Sandusky *(G-13042)*
Airsources Inc...................................... G 610 983-0102
  North Canton *(G-11714)*
▲ Alan Manufacturing Inc.................... E 330 262-1555
  Wooster *(G-16099)*
All Metal Fabricators Inc...................... F 216 267-0033
  Cleveland *(G-3630)*
Allen County Fabrication Inc................ E 419 227-7447
  Lima *(G-9219)*
Allfab Inc... E 614 491-4944
  Columbus *(G-5112)*
Allied Fabricating & Wldg Co................ E 614 751-6664
  Columbus *(G-5113)*
Allied Mask and Tooling Inc................. G 419 470-2555
  Toledo *(G-14183)*
Alro Steel Corporation......................... E 614 878-7271
  Columbus *(G-5116)*
Alro Steel Corporation......................... D 419 720-5300
  Toledo *(G-14184)*
Alumetal Manufacturing Company........ E 419 268-2311
  Coldwater *(G-4981)*
Aluminum Color Industries Inc............. E 330 536-6295
  Lowellville *(G-9510)*
Aluminum Extruded Shapes Inc........... C 513 563-2205
  Cincinnati *(G-2613)*
AM Castle & Co................................... F 330 425-7000
  Bedford *(G-1100)*
AMD Fabricators Inc............................ E 440 946-8855
  Willoughby *(G-15875)*
American Culvert & Fabg Co................ F 740 432-6334
  Cambridge *(G-1919)*
▲ American Frame Corporation........... D 419 893-5595
  Maumee *(G-10163)*

▲ Ampp Incorporated........................... C 419 666-4747
  Perrysburg *(G-12362)*
Anchor Metal Processing Inc................ F 216 362-6463
  Cleveland *(G-3662)*
Anchor Metal Processing Inc................ E 216 362-1850
  Cleveland *(G-3663)*
Antique Auto Sheet Metal Inc.............. F 937 833-4422
  Brookville *(G-1729)*
Apex Welding Incorporated.................. F 440 232-6770
  Bedford *(G-1101)*
Arbenz Inc... E 614 274-6800
  Columbus *(G-5152)*
Armor Metal Group Elkhart Inc............. F 800 672-6373
  Mason *(G-9953)*
▲ Armor Metal Group Mason Inc.......... C 513 769-0700
  Mason *(G-9954)*
Arsco Custom Metals LLC.................... D 513 385-0555
  Cincinnati *(G-2633)*
▲ Astro Manufacturing & Design Inc.... C 888 215-1746
  Eastlake *(G-7019)*
▼ Auburn Metal Processing LLC.......... G 315 253-2565
  Stow *(G-13685)*
Austintown Metal Works Inc................. F 330 259-4673
  Youngstown *(G-16315)*
Autoneum North America Inc............... B 419 693-0511
  Oregon *(G-12103)*
Avon Lake Sheet Metal Co................... F 440 933-3505
  Avon Lake *(G-800)*
Aztec Manufacturing Inc...................... E 330 783-9747
  Youngstown *(G-16316)*
▲ B-R-O-T Incorporated....................... E 216 267-5335
  Cleveland *(G-3717)*
Bainter Machining Company................ G 740 653-2422
  Lancaster *(G-8993)*
Bayloff Stmped Pdts Knsman Inc......... D 330 876-4511
  Kinsman *(G-8935)*
Beacon Metal Fabricators Inc............... F 216 391-7444
  Cleveland *(G-3727)*
Berran Industrial Group Inc.................. E 330 253-5800
  Akron *(G-83)*
Bickers Metal Products Inc.................. E 513 353-4000
  Miamitown *(G-10705)*
Billington Company Inc........................ E 440 647-3039
  Wellington *(G-15304)*
▲ Biofit Engineered Product................ E 419 823-1089
  Bowling Green *(G-1556)*
BJ Equipment Ltd................................ E 614 497-1188
  Columbus *(G-5193)*
Blesco Services................................... E 614 871-4900
  Mount Sterling *(G-11253)*
Blevins Metal Fabrication Inc............... E 419 522-6082
  Mansfield *(G-9629)*
Bob Lanes Welding Inc........................ F 740 373-3567
  Marietta *(G-9779)*
Bogie Industries Inc Ltd....................... E 330 745-3105
  Akron *(G-89)*
Breining Mech Systems Inc.................. G 216 391-2400
  Cleveland *(G-3755)*
Breitinger Company............................. C 419 526-4255
  Mansfield *(G-9631)*
Bridges Sheet Metal............................. G 330 339-3185
  New Philadelphia *(G-11487)*
Buckeye Metal Works Inc..................... G 614 239-8000
  Columbus *(G-5220)*
Bud Corp... G 740 967-9992
  Johnstown *(G-8771)*
Budde Sheet Metal Works Inc.............. E 937 224-0868
  Dayton *(G-6241)*
Burt Manufacturing Company Inc......... E 330 762-0061
  Akron *(G-97)*
Busch & Thiem Inc.............................. E 419 625-7515
  Sandusky *(G-13047)*

Employee Codes: A=Over 500 employees, B=251-500
C=101-250, D=51-100, E=20-50, F=10-19, G=1-9

34 FABRICATED METAL PRODUCTS

Byg Industries Inc .... G 216 961-5436
Cleveland (G-3777)

C & R Inc .... E 614 497-1130
Groveport (G-8134)

C A Joseph Co .... F 330 532-4646
Irondale (G-8693)

C L W Inc .... G 740 374-8443
Marietta (G-9780)

C-N-D Industries Inc .... E 330 478-8811
Massillon (G-10080)

Cabletek Wiring Products Inc .... E 800 562-9378
Elyria (G-7121)

Champion Window Co of Toledo .... E 419 841-0154
Perrysburg (G-12370)

Cinfab LLC .... C 513 396-6100
Cincinnati (G-2768)

Clarkwestern Dietrich Building .... E 330 372-5564
Warren (G-15154)

▼ Clarkwstern Dtrich Bldg System .... C 513 870-1100
West Chester (G-15555)

Cleveland Steel Specialty Co .... E 216 464-9400
Bedford Heights (G-1168)

Columbus Steelmasters Inc .... F 614 231-2141
Columbus (G-5279)

Commercial Mtal Fbricators Inc .... E 937 233-4911
Dayton (G-6260)

Compco Youngstown Company .... D 330 482-6488
Columbiana (G-5036)

Contech Engnered Solutions Inc .... E 513 645-7000
West Chester (G-15402)

◆ Contech Engnered Solutions LLC .... C 513 645-7000
West Chester (G-15403)

Contour Forming Inc .... F 740 345-9777
Newark (G-11572)

Controls and Sheet Metal Inc .... E 513 721-3610
Cincinnati (G-2793)

COW Industries Inc .... E 614 443-6537
Columbus (G-5301)

Cramers Inc .... E 330 477-4571
Canton (G-2083)

Crest Products Inc .... F 440 942-5770
Mentor (G-10446)

▲ Crown Electric Engrg & Mfg LLC .... E 513 539-7394
Middletown (G-10816)

Custom Metal Products Inc .... F 614 855-2263
New Albany (G-11376)

▲ D B S Stinless Stl Fabricators .... G 513 856-9600
Hamilton (G-8198)

Da Investments Inc .... D 330 781-6100
Youngstown (G-16346)

Danco Metal Products LLC .... F 440 871-2300
Avon Lake (G-803)

▲ Darana Hybrid Inc .... D 513 860-4490
Hamilton (G-8199)

Defabco Inc .... D 614 231-2700
Columbus (G-5323)

Delafoil Pennsylvania Inc .... E 610 327-9565
Perrysburg (G-12374)

Delma Corp .... D 937 253-2142
Dayton (G-6296)

Di Iorio Sheet Metal Inc .... F 216 961-3703
Cleveland (G-3955)

Die-Cut Products Co .... F 216 771-6994
Cleveland (G-3958)

Dimensional Metals Inc .... E 740 927-3633
Reynoldsburg (G-12761)

Dover Tank and Plate Company .... E 330 343-4443
Dover (G-6822)

Duct Fabricators Inc .... G 216 391-2400
Cleveland (G-3976)

Ducts Inc .... F 216 391-2400
Cleveland (G-3977)

▲ Duro Dyne Midwest Corp .... C 513 870-6000
Hamilton (G-8201)

Dynamic Weld Corporation .... E 419 582-2900
Osgood (G-12173)

E & K Products Co Inc .... G 216 631-2510
Cleveland (G-3983)

E B P Inc .... E 216 241-2550
Solon (G-13339)

Eagle Welding & Fabg Inc .... E 440 946-0692
Willoughby (G-15914)

▲ Eastern Sheet Metal Inc .... D 513 793-3440
Blue Ash (G-1388)

▲ Eaton Fabricating Company Inc .... E 440 926-3121
Grafton (G-7998)

◆ Ebner Furnaces Inc .... D 330 335-2311
Wadsworth (G-15028)

Edwards Sheet Metal Works Inc .... E 740 694-0010
Fredericktown (G-7745)

Efco Corp .... G 614 876-1226
Columbus (G-5547)

Enterprise Welding & Fabg Inc .... C 440 354-4128
Mentor (G-10451)

Ethima Inc .... D 419 626-4912
Sandusky (G-13057)

Everyday Technologies Inc .... F 937 497-7774
Sidney (G-13247)

Everyday Technologies Inc .... F 419 739-6104
Wapakoneta (G-15109)

Everyday Technologies Inc .... E 937 492-4171
Sidney (G-13248)

F & F Shtmtl & Fabrication LLC .... F 567 938-8788
Tiffin (G-14085)

▲ Fabco Inc .... E 419 422-4533
Findlay (G-7504)

Fabcor Inc .... E 419 628-4428
Minster (G-11052)

Fabricating Solutions Inc .... F 330 486-0998
Twinsburg (G-14658)

Fabtech Ohio Inc .... G 308 532-1860
Mentor (G-10453)

Falcon Industries Inc .... E 330 723-0099
Medina (G-10322)

Famous Industries Inc .... E 330 535-1811
Akron (G-150)

Feather Lite Innovations Inc .... F 513 893-5483
Liberty Twp (G-9215)

▲ Feather Lite Innovations Inc .... E 937 743-9008
Springboro (G-13501)

Firestone Laser and Mfg LLC .... E 330 337-9551
Salem (G-12994)

First Francis Company Inc .... E 440 352-8927
Painesville (G-12237)

Flood Heliarc Inc .... F 614 835-3929
Groveport (G-8140)

Franck and Fric Incorporated .... D 216 524-4451
Cleveland (G-4090)

Freeman Enclosure Systems LLC .... C 877 441-8555
Batavia (G-924)

Fulton Equipment Co .... G 419 290-5393
Toledo (G-14295)

◆ G & S Titanium Inc .... E 330 263-0564
Wooster (G-16122)

G T Metal Fabricators Inc .... F 440 237-8745
Cleveland (G-4098)

G2 Materials LLC .... G 216 293-4211
Cleveland (G-4100)

Galion LLC .... C 419 468-5214
Galion (G-7875)

▲ Galion-Godwin Truck Bdy Co LLC .... F 330 359-5495
Dundee (G-6965)

Gaspar Inc .... D 330 477-2222
Canton (G-2110)

Gem City Metal Tech LLC .... E 937 252-8998
Dayton (G-6349)

General Awning Company Inc .... F 216 749-0110
Cleveland (G-4111)

▲ General Technologies Inc .... E 419 747-1800
Mansfield (G-9659)

▲ General Tool Company .... C 513 733-5500
Cincinnati (G-2946)

▲ Gentek Building Products Inc .... F 800 548-4542
Cuyahoga Falls (G-6086)

George Manufacturing Inc .... F 513 932-1067
Lebanon (G-9079)

Gilson Screen Incorporated .... E 419 256-7711
Malinta (G-9604)

▲ Glunt Industries Inc .... C 330 399-7585
Warren (G-15175)

GM Mechanical Inc .... D 937 473-3006
Covington (G-6024)

Golden Angle Archtctral Group .... G 614 531-7932
Columbus (G-5466)

Graber Metal Works Inc .... F 440 237-8422
North Royalton (G-11877)

Great Day Improvements LLC .... B 267 223-1289
Macedonia (G-9555)

Gunderson Rail Services LLC .... D 330 792-6521
Youngstown (G-16376)

Gundlach Sheet Metal Works Inc .... E 419 626-4525
Sandusky (G-13062)

Gutter Logic Charlotte LLC .... G 833 714-5479
North Canton (G-11734)

▲ Gwp Holdings Inc .... E 513 860-4050
Fairfield (G-7364)

Hall Company .... E 937 652-1376
Urbana (G-14833)

◆ Halvorsen Company .... E 216 341-7500
Cleveland (G-4165)

Harray LLC .... G 888 568-8371
Cincinnati (G-2986)

Harrison Mch & Plastic Corp .... E 330 527-5641
Garrettsville (G-7916)

Hartzell Mfg Co LLC .... E 937 859-5955
Miamisburg (G-10643)

Haybner Sheet Metal Inc .... G 440 623-0194
Strongsville (G-13839)

HCC Holdings Inc .... F 800 203-1155
Cleveland (G-4173)

Heim Sheet Metal Inc .... G 330 424-7820
Lisbon (G-9314)

▲ Hidaka Usa Inc .... E 614 889-8611
Dublin (G-6893)

Higgins Construction & Supply Co Inc .... F 937 364-2331
Hillsboro (G-8458)

Highway Safety Corp .... F 740 387-6991
Marion (G-9855)

Holgate Metal Fab Inc .... F 419 599-2000
Napoleon (G-11319)

Hvac Inc .... G 330 343-5511
Dover (G-6827)

I-M-A Enterprises Inc .... F 330 948-3535
Lodi (G-9351)

Indian Creek Fabricators Inc .... E 937 667-7214
Tipp City (G-14138)

Industrial Fabricators Inc .... E 614 882-7423
Westerville (G-15710)

Industrial Mill Maintenance .... G 330 746-1155
Youngstown (G-16379)

Innovative Mech Systems LLC .... G 937 813-8713
Dayton (G-6164)

Interstate Contractors LLC .... E 513 372-5393
Mason (G-10013)

◆ Isaiah Industries Inc .... D 937 773-9840
Piqua (G-12527)

34 FABRICATED METAL PRODUCTS

Jacobs Mechanical Co .... C 513 681-6800
  Cincinnati (G-3033)
Jh Industries Inc .... E 330 963-4105
  Twinsburg (G-14677)
Jim Nier Construction Inc .... E 740 289-3925
  Piketon (G-12477)
Joining Metals Inc .... F 440 259-1790
  Perry (G-12352)
Jones Metal Products Co LLC .... E 740 545-6381
  West Lafayette (G-15618)
Joyce Manufacturing Co .... D 440 239-9100
  Berea (G-1286)
Kalron LLC .... E 440 647-3039
  Wellington (G-15314)
Kalron LLC .... F 440 647-3039
  Wellington (G-15315)
Kenton Strl & Orn Ir Works .... C 419 674-4025
  Kenton (G-8887)
Kerber Sheetmetal Works Inc .... F 937 339-6366
  Troy (G-14591)
Kettering Roofing & Shtmtl Inc .... F 513 281-6413
  Cincinnati (G-3075)
Kidron Inc .... B 330 857-3011
  Kidron (G-8915)
Kilroy Company .... D 440 951-8700
  Cleveland (G-4289)
◆ Kirk & Blum Manufacturing Co .... C 513 458-2600
  Cincinnati (G-3078)
Kirk Williams Company Inc .... D 614 875-9023
  Grove City (G-8100)
Knight Manufacturing Co Inc .... G 740 676-5516
  Shadyside (G-13146)
Korda Manufacturing Inc .... E 330 262-1555
  Wooster (G-16144)
Kramer Power Equipment Co .... F 937 456-2232
  Eaton (G-7063)
Kuhlman Engineering Co .... F 419 243-2196
  Toledo (G-14352)
Kuhn Fabricating Inc .... G 440 277-4182
  Lorain (G-9418)
▲ Kundel Industries Inc .... E 330 469-6147
  Vienna (G-14996)
L & W Investments Inc .... D 937 492-4171
  Sidney (G-13259)
Lambert Sheet Metal Inc .... F 614 237-0384
  Columbus (G-5518)
▲ Langdon Inc .... E 513 733-5955
  Cincinnati (G-3095)
Lima Sheet Metal Machine & Mfg .... E 419 229-1161
  Lima (G-9264)
▲ Long-Stanton Mfg Company .... E 513 874-8020
  West Chester (G-15458)
Louis Arthur Steel Company .... G 440 997-5545
  Geneva (G-7941)
Lowry Furnace Co Inc .... G 330 745-4822
  Akron (G-224)
▲ Lt Enterprises of Ohio LLC .... E 330 526-6908
  North Canton (G-11741)
Lukjan Metal Pdts Holdg Co Inc .... F 440 599-8127
  Conneaut (G-5925)
Lukjan Metal Products Inc .... C 440 599-8127
  Conneaut (G-5926)
Lund Equipment Company .... E 330 659-4800
  Akron (G-225)
M3 Technologies Inc .... F 216 898-9936
  Cleveland (G-4347)
Mack Iron Works Company .... E 419 626-3712
  Sandusky (G-13078)
Mantych Metalworking Inc .... E 937 258-1373
  Dayton (G-6168)
Marsam Metalfab Inc .... E 330 405-1520
  Twinsburg (G-14691)

Martina Metal LLC .... E 614 291-9700
  Columbus (G-5544)
Matern Metal Works Inc .... F 419 529-3100
  Mansfield (G-9687)
Matteo Aluminum Inc .... E 440 585-5213
  Wickliffe (G-15839)
May Industries of Ohio Inc .... E 440 237-8012
  North Royalton (G-11886)
May Tool & Die Co .... G 440 237-8012
  Cleveland (G-4371)
▲ Mc Machine Llc .... E 216 398-3666
  Cleveland (G-4378)
McGill Airflow LLC .... D 614 829-1200
  Columbus (G-5551)
◆ McGill Corporation .... F 614 829-1200
  Groveport (G-8153)
McWane Inc .... B 740 622-6651
  Coshocton (G-5983)
Medway Tool Corp .... E 937 335-7717
  Troy (G-14597)
Meese Inc .... F 440 998-1202
  Ashtabula (G-647)
Mestek Inc .... D 419 288-2703
  Bowling Green (G-1576)
Mestek Inc .... F 419 288-2703
  Bradner (G-1603)
Metal Coaters .... D 740 432-7351
  Cambridge (G-1942)
Metal Fabricating Corporation .... D 216 631-8121
  Cleveland (G-4396)
Metal Sales Manufacturing Corp .... F 440 319-3779
  Jefferson (G-8753)
Metal Seal Precision Ltd .... C 440 255-8888
  Willoughby (G-15952)
▼ Metal Seal Precision Ltd .... D 440 255-8888
  Mentor (G-10503)
Metal-Max Inc .... G 330 673-9926
  Kent (G-8835)
Metalfab Group .... G 440 543-6234
  Streetsboro (G-13778)
Metlweb Ltd .... F 513 563-8822
  Cincinnati (G-3157)
Midwest Fabrications Inc .... E 330 633-0191
  Tallmadge (G-14038)
Midwest Metal Fabricators .... F 419 739-7077
  Wapakoneta (G-15125)
Midwest Metal Fabricators Ltd .... F 419 739-7077
  Wapakoneta (G-15126)
Midwest Metal Products LLC .... E 614 539-7322
  Grove City (G-8107)
Mike Loppe .... F 937 969-8102
  Tremont City (G-14538)
◆ Modern Ice Equipment & Sup Co .... E 513 367-2101
  Cincinnati (G-3170)
Modern Manufacturing Inc .... G 513 251-3600
  Cincinnati (G-3171)
Modern Sheet Metal Works Inc .... E 513 353-3666
  Cleves (G-4961)
Mp Acquisition Group LLC .... F 513 554-6120
  West Chester (G-15466)
▲ MRS Industrial Inc .... E 614 308-1070
  Columbus (G-5584)
Mwgh LLC .... C 513 521-4114
  Cincinnati (G-3178)
◆ N Wasserstrom & Sons Inc .... C 614 228-5550
  Columbus (G-5588)
National Indus Concepts Inc .... C 615 989-9101
  Chillicothe (G-2520)
▼ National Sign Systems Inc .... D 614 850-2540
  Hilliard (G-8424)
Newberry Sheet Metal LLC .... G 513 807-7385
  Williamsburg (G-15866)

Niles Manufacturing & Finshg .... C 330 544-0402
  Niles (G-11678)
▲ Nissin Precision N Amer Inc .... D 937 836-1910
  Englewood (G-7238)
Norrenbrock Company Inc .... G 513 316-1383
  Lebanon (G-9102)
Northwind Industries Inc .... E 216 433-0666
  Cleveland (G-4481)
Novelis Corporation .... C 740 983-2571
  Ashville (G-670)
▲ Oatey Co .... B 800 203-1155
  Cleveland (G-4490)
◆ Oatey Supply Chain Svcs Inc .... C 216 267-7100
  Cleveland (G-4491)
Obr Cooling Towers Inc .... E 419 243-3443
  Northwood (G-11924)
Ohio Blow Pipe Company .... E 216 681-7379
  Cleveland (G-4496)
◆ Ohio Gratings Inc .... B 800 321-9800
  Canton (G-2184)
Ohio Steel Sheet and Plate Inc .... E 800 827-2401
  Hubbard (G-8569)
Ohio Trailer Inc .... F 330 392-4444
  Warren (G-15196)
Okuley Hvac & Met Fabrication .... G 419 478-4699
  Toledo (G-14413)
▲ Oliver Steel Plate Co .... D 330 425-7000
  Twinsburg (G-14704)
Omco Solar Inc .... G 216 621-6633
  Cleveland (G-4502)
◆ Options Plus Incorporated .... F 740 694-9811
  Fredericktown (G-7752)
Owens Corning Sales LLC .... F 740 983-1300
  Ashville (G-671)
▲ P & L Metalcrafts LLC .... F 330 793-2178
  Youngstown (G-16409)
Paul Wilke & Son Inc .... F 513 921-3163
  Cincinnati (G-3241)
PB Fbrction Mech Contrs Corp .... E 419 478-4869
  Toledo (G-14429)
▲ Pei Liquidation Company .... C 330 467-4267
  Macedonia (G-9564)
Pennant Moldings Inc .... C 937 584-5411
  Sabina (G-12890)
Phillips Manufacturing Co .... D 330 652-4335
  Niles (G-11682)
Plas-Tanks Industries Inc .... E 513 942-3800
  Hamilton (G-8235)
▲ Porcelain Steel Buildings Company .... D 614 228-5781
  Columbus (G-5683)
Precision Duct Fabrication LLC .... F 614 580-9385
  Columbus (G-5686)
Precision Metal Products Inc .... C 614 526-7000
  Dublin (G-6926)
Precision Mtal Fabrication Inc .... D 937 235-9261
  Dayton (G-6516)
Precision Welding Corporation .... E 216 524-6110
  Cleveland (G-4577)
Production Manufacturing Inc .... E 513 892-2331
  Hamilton (G-8236)
Quality Steel Fabrication .... F 937 492-9503
  Sidney (G-13274)
Quass Sheet Metal Inc .... G 330 477-4841
  Canton (G-2205)
R G Smith Company .... D 330 456-3415
  Canton (G-2207)
R L Torbeck Industries Inc .... E 513 367-0080
  Harrison (G-8289)
Raka Corporation .... D 419 476-6572
  Toledo (G-14449)
Rapid Machine Inc .... F 419 737-2377
  Pioneer (G-12497)

Employee Codes: A=Over 500 employees, B=251-500
C=101-250, D=51-100, E=20-50, F=10-19, G=1-9

34 FABRICATED METAL PRODUCTS

Reilly-Duerr Tank Co .... G 513 554-1022
  Cincinnati (G-3330)
Related Metals Inc .... G 330 799-4866
  Canfield (G-2016)
Rex Welding Inc .... F 740 387-1650
  Marion (G-9875)
Rmt Acquisition Inc .... E 513 241-5566
  Cincinnati (G-3347)
▲ Robinson Fin Machines Inc .... E 419 674-4152
  Kenton (G-8898)
▲ Rockwell Metals Company LLC .... F 440 242-2420
  Lorain (G-9436)
Roconex Corporation .... F 937 339-2616
  Miamisburg (G-10678)
Romar Metal Fabricating Inc .... G 740 682-7731
  Oak Hill (G-12025)
Roofing Annex LLC .... G 513 942-0555
  West Chester (G-15581)
Royal Metal Products LLC .... C 740 397-8842
  Mount Vernon (G-11200)
Royalton Archtctral Fbrication .... F 440 582-0400
  North Royalton (G-11893)
S & D Architectural Metals .... G 440 582-2560
  North Royalton (G-11896)
S & G Manufacturing Group LLC .... C 614 529-0100
  Hilliard (G-8437)
▼ S&B Metal Pdts Twinsburg LLC .... E 330 487-5790
  Twinsburg (G-14731)
Sarka Shtmtl & Fabrication Inc .... E 419 447-4377
  Tiffin (G-14102)
▲ Sausser Steel Company Inc .... F 419 422-9632
  Findlay (G-7559)
Schoonover Industries Inc .... E 419 289-8332
  Ashland (G-612)
Schweizer Dipple Inc .... D 440 786-8090
  Cleveland (G-4676)
Scott Fetzer Company .... C 216 267-9000
  Cleveland (G-4678)
Selmco Metal Fabricators Inc .... F 937 498-1331
  Sidney (G-13285)
Seneca Sheet Metal Company .... F 419 447-8434
  Tiffin (G-14105)
SFM Corp .... E 440 951-5500
  Willoughby (G-15988)
Shaffer Metal Fab Inc .... F 937 492-1384
  Sidney (G-13286)
Shape Supply Inc .... G 513 863-6695
  Hamilton (G-8242)
Sheet Metal Products Co Inc .... E 440 392-9000
  Mentor (G-10554)
Sheetmetal Crafters .... F 330 452-6700
  Canton (G-2224)
Sheetmetal Crafters Inc .... F 330 452-6700
  Canton (G-2225)
▼ Sheffield Metals Cleveland LLC .... F 800 283-5262
  Sheffield Village (G-13188)
▼ Sheffield Metals Intl Inc .... E 440 934-8500
  Sheffield Village (G-13189)
▼ Sidney Manufacturing Company .... E 937 492-4154
  Sidney (G-13288)
Sigman Cladding Inc .... G 330 497-5200
  North Canton (G-11761)
Skyline Material Sales LLC .... G 937 661-1770
  Greenfield (G-8053)
Smith Rn Sheet Metal Shop Inc .... F 740 653-5011
  Lancaster (G-9039)
Somerville Manufacturing Inc .... E 740 336-7847
  Marietta (G-9829)
Spradlin Bros Welding Co .... F 800 219-2182
  Springfield (G-13634)
▲ Staber Industries Inc .... E 614 836-5995
  Groveport (G-8160)

Standard Technologies LLC .... D 419 332-6434
  Fremont (G-7810)
Starr Fabricating Inc .... D 330 394-9891
  Vienna (G-15004)
▼ Steel & Alloy Utility Pdts Inc .... E 330 530-2220
  Mc Donald (G-10280)
Steelial Wldg Met Fbrction Inc .... E 740 669-5300
  Vinton (G-15012)
Steve Vore Welding and Steel .... F 419 375-4087
  Fort Recovery (G-7624)
Sulecki Precision Products Inc .... F 440 255-5454
  Mentor (G-10569)
Swanton Wldg Machining Co Inc .... D 419 826-4816
  Swanton (G-13984)
Systech Handling Inc .... F 419 445-8226
  Archbold (G-547)
Tallmadge Spinning & Metal Co .... F 330 794-2277
  Akron (G-348)
Tangent Air Inc .... E 740 474-1114
  Circleville (G-3550)
Taylor Metal .... G 614 401-8007
  Columbus (G-5813)
TDS-Bf/Ls Holdings Inc .... E 440 327-5800
  North Ridgeville (G-11862)
▲ Technibus Inc .... D 330 479-4202
  Canton (G-2241)
◆ Tectum Inc .... C 740 345-9691
  Newark (G-11608)
Tex-Tyler Corporation .... F 419 729-4951
  Toledo (G-14484)
▲ The Armor Group Inc .... C 513 923-5260
  Mason (G-10065)
▲ Thermo Vent Manufacturing Inc .... F 330 239-0239
  Medina (G-10386)
TL Industries Inc .... C 419 666-8144
  Perrysburg (G-12436)
TNT Solid Solutions LLC .... F 419 262-6228
  Toledo (G-14490)
Toledo Window & Awning Inc .... F 419 474-3396
  Toledo (G-14509)
Tool and Die Systems .... F 440 327-5800
  Elyria (G-7212)
Transtar Holding Company .... G 800 359-3339
  Walton Hills (G-15103)
Tri-Fab Inc .... E 330 337-3425
  Salem (G-13034)
Tri-Mac Mfg & Svcs Co .... F 513 896-4445
  Hamilton (G-8251)
Tri-State Fabricators Inc .... E 513 752-5005
  Amelia (G-469)
Triangle Precision Industries .... D 937 299-6776
  Dayton (G-6632)
◆ Tricor Industrial Inc .... D 330 264-3299
  Wooster (G-16178)
Tru Form Metal Products Inc .... G 216 252-3700
  Cleveland (G-4834)
▲ United McGill Corporation .... E 614 829-1200
  Groveport (G-8165)
▲ Universal Steel Company .... D 216 883-4972
  Cleveland (G-4852)
V & S Schuler Engineering Inc .... E 330 452-5200
  Canton (G-2260)
Varmland Inc .... F 216 741-1510
  Cleveland (G-4861)
Venti-Now .... G 513 334-3375
  Montgomery (G-11132)
Verhoff Machine & Welding Inc .... C 419 596-3202
  Continental (G-5939)
Vicart Prcsion Fabricators Inc .... E 614 771-0080
  Hilliard (G-8452)
▼ W J Egli Company Inc .... F 330 823-3666
  Alliance (G-435)

SIC SECTION

Warner Fabricating Inc .... F 330 848-3191
  Wadsworth (G-15071)
◆ Warren Fabricating Corporation .... D 330 534-5017
  Hubbard (G-8572)
Waterville Sheet Metal Company .... G 419 878-5050
  Waterville (G-15255)
Weld Tech LLC .... G 419 357-3214
  Berlin Heights (G-1317)
Weybridge LLC .... G 440 951-5500
  Willoughby (G-16015)
▲ Will-Burt Company .... C 330 682-7015
  Orrville (G-12163)
Wolf Metals Inc .... G 614 461-6361
  Columbus (G-5880)
Wooster Abruzzi Company .... E 330 345-3968
  Wooster (G-16183)
Youngstown Shade & Alum LLC .... G 330 782-2373
  Youngstown (G-16487)
▲ Ysd Industries Inc .... E 330 792-6521
  Youngstown (G-10491)
Z Line Kitchen and Bath LLC .... G 614 777-5004
  Marysville (G-9944)
Z-Kan Metal Products LLC .... G 330 695-2397
  Fredericksburg (G-7737)

3446 Architectural metalwork

▲ A & G Manufacturing Co Inc .... E 419 468-7433
  Galion (G-7858)
▲ Agratronix LLC .... E 330 562-2222
  Streetsboro (G-13753)
Akron Products Company .... D 330 576-1750
  Wadsworth (G-15016)
All Ohio Companies Inc .... F 216 420-9274
  Cleveland (G-3631)
Annin & Co Inc .... C 740 622-4447
  Coshocton (G-5968)
Armor Consolidated Inc .... A 513 923-5260
  Mason (G-9952)
▲ Armor Metal Group Mason Inc .... C 513 769-0700
  Mason (G-9954)
▲ Art Iron Inc .... D 419 241-1261
  Toledo (G-14200)
AT&f Advanced Metals LLC .... F 330 684-1122
  Orrville (G-12117)
▲ AT&f Advanced Metals LLC .... E 330 684-1122
  Cleveland (G-3695)
Auld Corporation .... G 614 454-1010
  Columbus (G-5165)
Autogate Inc .... E 419 588-2796
  Berlin Heights (G-1312)
Bauer Corporation .... E 800 321-4760
  Wooster (G-16102)
Beacon Metal Fabricators Inc .... F 216 391-7444
  Cleveland (G-3727)
◆ Bil-Jax Inc .... F 419 445-8915
  Archbold (G-525)
Blevins Metal Fabrication Inc .... E 419 522-6082
  Mansfield (G-9629)
Chc Fabricating Corp .... D 513 821-7757
  Cincinnati (G-2729)
Chc Manufacturing Inc .... E 513 821-7757
  Cincinnati (G-2730)
Cozmyk Enterprises Inc .... F 614 231-1370
  Columbus (G-5303)
Cramers Inc .... E 330 477-4571
  Canton (G-2083)
Cuyahoga Fence LLC .... F 216 830-2200
  Cleveland (G-3930)
Debra-Kuempel Inc .... D 513 271-6500
  Cincinnati (G-2822)
Dover Tank and Plate Company .... E 330 343-4443
  Dover (G-6822)

SIC SECTION

34 FABRICATED METAL PRODUCTS

E B P Inc .... E 216 241-2550
   Solon *(G-13339)*

E C S Corp .... G 440 323-1707
   Elyria *(G-7136)*

Enviri Corporation .... F 740 387-1150
   Marion *(G-9851)*

Federal Iron Works Company .... E 330 482-5910
   Columbiana *(G-5039)*

Finelli Ornamental Iron Co .... E 440 248-0050
   Cleveland *(G-4061)*

Fortin Welding & Mfg Inc .... E 614 291-4342
   Columbus *(G-5383)*

Gem City Metal Tech LLC .... E 937 252-8998
   Dayton *(G-6349)*

Glas Ornamental Metals Inc .... G 330 753-0215
   Barberton *(G-869)*

Graber Metal Works Inc .... F 440 237-8422
   North Royalton *(G-11877)*

▲ Gwp Holdings Inc .... E 513 860-4050
   Fairfield *(G-7364)*

Hansen Scaffolding LLC .... F 513 574-9000
   West Chester *(G-15561)*

Hart & Cooley LLC .... E 937 832-7800
   Englewood *(G-7232)*

Haulotte North America Mfg Inc .... G 567 444-4159
   Archbold *(G-530)*

Hayes Bros Ornamental Ir Works .... F 419 531-1491
   Toledo *(G-14312)*

Hrh Door Corp .... E 330 828-2291
   Dalton *(G-6132)*

Indian Creek Fabricators Inc .... E 937 667-7214
   Tipp City *(G-14138)*

Jason Incorporated .... C 513 860-3400
   Hamilton *(G-8224)*

Jerry Harolds Doors Unlimited .... G 740 635-4949
   Bridgeport *(G-1647)*

Joyce Manufacturing Co .... D 440 239-9100
   Berea *(G-1286)*

Kenton Strl & Orn Ir Works .... D 419 674-4025
   Kenton *(G-8887)*

◆ Kinetics Noise Control Inc .... C 614 889-0480
   Dublin *(G-6905)*

L & L Ornamental Iron Co .... E 513 353-1930
   Cleves *(G-4958)*

Lakeway Mfg Inc .... E 419 433-3030
   Huron *(G-8637)*

▲ Langdon Inc .... E 513 733-5955
   Cincinnati *(G-3095)*

M F Y Inc .... F 330 747-1334
   Youngstown *(G-16391)*

Mack Iron Works Company .... E 419 626-3712
   Sandusky *(G-13078)*

Metal Maintenance Inc .... F 513 661-3300
   Cleves *(G-4959)*

Michaels Pre-Cast Con Pdts .... F 513 683-1292
   Loveland *(G-9497)*

Modern Builders Supply Inc .... C 419 241-3961
   Toledo *(G-14389)*

◆ Momentive Prfmce Mtls Qrtz Inc .... D 440 878-5700
   Strongsville *(G-13855)*

Mound Technologies Inc .... E 937 748-2937
   Springboro *(G-13511)*

Newman Brothers Inc .... E
   Cincinnati *(G-3191)*

Nu Risers Stair Company .... F 937 322-8100
   Springfield *(G-13613)*

Ohio Gratings Inc .... G 330 479-4292
   Wooster *(G-16158)*

◆ Ohio Gratings Inc .... B 800 321-9800
   Canton *(G-2184)*

Okolona Iron & Metal LLC .... F 419 758-3701
   Napoleon *(G-11328)*

One Wish LLC .... F 800 505-6883
   Bedford *(G-1147)*

▲ P & L Metalcrafts LLC .... F 330 793-2178
   Youngstown *(G-16409)*

Phase II Enterprises Inc .... G 330 484-2113
   Canton *(G-2196)*

Quality Architectural and Fabr .... F 937 743-2923
   Franklin *(G-7695)*

Randy Lewis Inc .... F 330 784-0456
   Akron *(G-296)*

Royalton Archtctral Fbrication .... F 440 582-0400
   North Royalton *(G-11893)*

▲ Sausser Steel Company Inc .... F 419 422-9632
   Findlay *(G-7559)*

Sewah Studios Inc .... F 740 373-2087
   Marietta *(G-9822)*

Sky Climber Wind Solutions LLC .... E 740 203-3900
   Delaware *(G-6751)*

▲ Spallinger Millwright Svc Co .... E 419 225-5830
   Lima *(G-9291)*

Stephens Pipe & Steel LLC .... C 740 869-2257
   Mount Sterling *(G-11257)*

Swanton Wldg Machining Co Inc .... D 419 826-4816
   Swanton *(G-13984)*

Tarrier Steel Company Inc .... E 614 444-4000
   Columbus *(G-5811)*

▲ The Armor Group Inc .... C 513 923-5260
   Mason *(G-10065)*

The Sharon Companies Ltd .... C 614 438-3210
   Worthington *(G-16216)*

◆ Trewbric III Inc .... E 614 444-2184
   Columbus *(G-5835)*

Triangle Precision Industries .... D 937 299-6776
   Dayton *(G-6632)*

Upright Steel LLC .... E 216 923-0852
   Cleveland *(G-4853)*

▲ Urban Industries of Ohio Inc .... E 419 468-3578
   Galion *(G-7886)*

Van Dyke Custom Iron Inc .... G 614 860-9300
   Pickerington *(G-12472)*

Viking Fabricators Inc .... E 740 374-5246
   Marietta *(G-9843)*

Waco Scaffolding & Equipment Inc .... A 216 749-8900
   Cleveland *(G-4889)*

Wall Technology Inc .... F 715 532-5548
   Toledo *(G-14521)*

Wooster Products Inc .... F 330 264-2854
   Wooster *(G-16187)*

▼ Wooster Products Inc .... F 330 264-2844
   Wooster *(G-16186)*

Worthington Mid-Rise Cnstr Inc .... E 216 472-1511
   Cleveland *(G-4923)*

Wright Brothers Inc .... F 513 731-2222
   Cincinnati *(G-3527)*

3448 Prefabricated metal buildings

Affordable Barn Co Ltd .... F 330 674-3001
   Millersburg *(G-10938)*

American Ramp Systems .... G 440 336-4988
   North Olmsted *(G-11816)*

Amto Acquisition Corp .... F 419 347-1185
   Shelby *(G-13190)*

▲ Benchmark Archtectural Systems ...... E 614 444-0110
   Columbus *(G-5182)*

▼ Benko Products Inc .... E 440 934-2180
   Sheffield Village *(G-13181)*

C Green & Sons Incorporated .... F 740 745-2998
   Saint Louisville *(G-12942)*

Cdc Fab Co .... F 419 866-7705
   Maumee *(G-10174)*

Commercial Dock & Door Inc .... E 440 951-1210
   Mentor *(G-10441)*

Connect Housing Blocks LLC .... E 614 503-4344
   Columbus *(G-5286)*

Consoldted Anlytcal Systems In .... F 513 542-1200
   Cincinnati *(G-2787)*

Cornerstone Bldg Brands Inc .... C 937 584-3300
   Middletown *(G-10813)*

◆ Cropking Incorporated .... F 330 302-4203
   Lodi *(G-9349)*

▲ Enclosure Suppliers LLC .... E 513 782-3900
   Cincinnati *(G-2868)*

Fairborn USA Inc .... D 419 294-4987
   Upper Sandusky *(G-14809)*

Golden Giant Inc .... E 419 674-4038
   Kenton *(G-8883)*

Great Day Improvements LLC .... B 267 223-1289
   Macedonia *(G-9555)*

▲ Hoge Lumber Company .... E 419 753-2263
   New Knoxville *(G-11447)*

Homecare Mattress Inc .... F 937 746-2556
   Franklin *(G-7680)*

Iron Works Inc .... F 937 420-2100
   Fort Loramie *(G-7601)*

Jack Walters & Sons Corp .... E 937 653-8986
   Urbana *(G-14840)*

Jentgen Steel Services LLC .... F 614 268-6340
   Columbus *(G-5493)*

▼ Jet Dock Systems Inc .... E 216 750-2264
   Cleveland *(G-4254)*

Jh Industries Inc .... E 330 963-4105
   Twinsburg *(G-14677)*

Joyce Manufacturing Co .... D 440 239-9100
   Berea *(G-1286)*

Lab-Pro Inc .... G 937 434-9600
   Miamisburg *(G-10653)*

Ludy Greenhouse Mfg Corp .... D 800 255-5839
   New Madison *(G-11475)*

Metal Mnkey Wldg Fbrcation LLC .... G 330 231-1490
   Sugarcreek *(G-13929)*

Morton Buildings Inc .... G 419 399-4549
   Kenton *(G-8893)*

Morton Buildings Inc .... E 419 675-2311
   Kenton *(G-8894)*

Morton Buildings Inc .... E 330 345-6188
   Wooster *(G-16153)*

ONeals Tarpaulin & Awning Co .... F 330 788-6504
   Youngstown *(G-16406)*

Overhead Door Corporation .... F 419 294-3874
   Upper Sandusky *(G-14820)*

Patton Aluminum Products Inc .... F 937 845-9404
   New Carlisle *(G-11424)*

▲ Pei Liquidation Company .... C 330 467-4267
   Macedonia *(G-9564)*

Pioneer Cldding Glzing Systems .... E 216 816-4242
   Cleveland *(G-4554)*

Prospiant Inc .... E 513 242-0310
   Cincinnati *(G-3305)*

R L Torbeck Industries Inc .... E 513 367-0080
   Harrison *(G-8289)*

Rayhaven Group Inc .... G 330 659-3183
   Richfield *(G-12795)*

Rebsco Inc .... F 937 548-2246
   Greenville *(G-8057)*

Reliable Metal Buildings LLC .... G 419 737-1300
   Pioneer *(G-12499)*

Republic Technology Corp .... E 216 622-5000
   Cleveland *(G-4627)*

◆ Rough Brothers Mfg Inc .... D 513 242-0310
   Cincinnati *(G-3352)*

Sheds Direct Inc .... G 330 674-3001
   Millersburg *(G-10993)*

Sheltervision LLC .... G 419 852-7788
   Minster *(G-11061)*

34 FABRICATED METAL PRODUCTS

Skyline Corporation .... C 330 852-2483
  Sugarcreek (G-13938)
Superior Structures Inc .... F 513 942-5954
  Harrison (G-8295)
Williams Scotsman Inc .... D 614 449-8675
  Columbus (G-5878)
Wyse Industrial Carts Inc .... F 419 923-7353
  Wauseon (G-15277)
XS Smith Inc .... E 252 940-5060
  Cincinnati (G-3533)

3449 Miscellaneous metalwork

Action Group Inc .... D 614 868-8868
  Blacklick (G-1330)
▲ Active Metal and Molds Inc .... F 419 281-9623
  Ashland (G-549)
Advance Industrial Mfg Inc .... E 614 871-3333
  Grove City (G-8073)
▲ Akron Rebar Co .... E
  Akron (G-13)
▼ American Roll Formed Pdts Corp .... C 440 352-0753
  Youngstown (G-16310)
Arrow Tru-Line Inc .... G 419 636-7013
  Bryan (G-1808)
Austintown Metal Works Inc .... F 330 259-4673
  Youngstown (G-16315)
◆ Barsplice Products Inc .... E 937 275-8700
  Dayton (G-6223)
Bridge Components Incorporated .... G 614 873-0777
  Columbus (G-5212)
Burghardt Metal Fabg Inc .... F 330 794-1830
  Akron (G-96)
Cdh Custom Roll Form LLC .... F 330 984-0555
  Warren (G-15152)
Ej Usa Inc .... F 330 782-3900
  Youngstown (G-16354)
Fc Industries Inc .... E 937 275-8700
  Dayton (G-6330)
Formasters Corporation .... F 440 639-9206
  Mentor (G-10456)
Fortin Welding & Mfg Inc .... E 614 291-4342
  Columbus (G-5383)
▲ Foundation Systems Anchors Inc .... F 330 454-1700
  Canton (G-2104)
Gateway Con Forming Svcs Inc .... D 513 353-2000
  Miamitown (G-10708)
Hynes Holding Company .... F 330 799-3221
  Youngstown (G-16377)
▲ Hynes Industries Inc .... C 800 321-9257
  Youngstown (G-16378)
Industrial Millwright Svcs LLC .... E 419 523-9147
  Ottawa (G-12181)
Kenton Strl & Orn Ir Works .... F 419 674-4025
  Kenton (G-8887)
Lion Industries LLC .... E 740 676-1100
  Bellaire (G-1188)
Matteo Aluminum Inc .... E 440 585-5213
  Wickliffe (G-15839)
Metal Sales Manufacturing Corp .... F 440 319-3779
  Jefferson (G-8753)
Metalfab Group .... G 440 543-6234
  Streetsboro (G-13778)
Midwest Curtainwalls Inc .... F 216 641-7900
  Cleveland (G-4410)
Mound Steel Corp .... F 937 748-2937
  Springboro (G-13510)
▲ Nmc Metals Inc .... E 330 652-2501
  Niles (G-11681)
▼ Ohio Bridge Corporation .... C 740 432-6334
  Cambridge (G-1945)
▲ Ohio Moulding Corporation .... F 440 944-2100
  Wickliffe (G-15842)

Omco Holdings Inc .... E 440 944-2100
  Wickliffe (G-15843)
Precision Impacts LLC .... D 937 530-8254
  Miamisburg (G-10671)
Scs Construction Services Inc .... E 513 929-0260
  Cincinnati (G-3371)
Simcote Inc .... F 740 382-5000
  Marion (G-9882)
Sky Climber Fabricating LLC .... F 740 990-9430
  Delaware (G-6750)
Smith Brothers Erection Inc .... G 740 373-3575
  Marietta (G-9826)
Steel Structures of Ohio LLC .... C 330 374-9900
  Akron (G-337)
T J F Inc .... F 419 878-4400
  Waterville (G-15253)
Ventari Corporation .... F 937 278-4269
  Miamisburg (G-10697)
▲ Ver-Mac Industries Inc .... E 740 397-6511
  Mount Vernon (G-11200)
Veterans Steel Inc .... F 216 938-7476
  Cleveland (G-4865)
◆ Watteredge LLC .... D 440 933-6110
  Avon Lake (G-828)
Welser Profile North Amer LLC .... E 330 225-2500
  Valley City (G-14900)
Will-Burt Company .... G 330 682-7015
  Orrville (G-12162)
▲ Will-Burt Company .... C 330 682-7015
  Orrville (G-12163)
◆ Worthington Enterprises Inc .... C 614 438-3210
  Worthington (G-16220)
Wt Acquisition Company Ltd .... E 513 577-7980
  Cincinnati (G-3528)
YKK AP America Inc .... E 513 942-7200
  West Chester (G-15528)

3451 Screw machine products

Abco Bar & Tube Cutng Svc Inc .... E 513 697-9487
  Maineville (G-9598)
Abel Manufacturing Company .... F 513 681-5000
  Cincinnati (G-2591)
▲ Acme Machine Automatics Inc .... F 419 453-0010
  Ottoville (G-12197)
Adams Automatic Inc .... F 440 235-4416
  Olmsted Falls (G-12074)
Alco Manufacturing Corp LLC .... E 440 458-5165
  Elyria (G-7105)
Amco Products Inc .... F 937 433-7982
  Dayton (G-6152)
Amerascrew Inc .... E 419 522-2232
  Mansfield (G-9624)
American Aero Components Llc .... G 937 367-5068
  Dayton (G-6197)
◆ American Micro Products Inc .... C 513 732-2674
  Batavia (G-908)
Amt Machine Systems Limited .... F 740 965-2693
  Columbus (G-5134)
▲ Ashley F Ward Inc .... C 513 398-1414
  Mason (G-9955)
Atlas Machine Products Co .... G 216 228-3688
  Oberlin (G-12048)
Ban Inc .... E 937 325-5539
  Springfield (G-13538)
Bront Machining Inc .... E 937 228-4551
  Moraine (G-11164)
Chardon Metal Products Co .... E 440 285-2147
  Chardon (G-2443)
Clear Creek Screw Machine Co .... G 740 969-2113
  Amanda (G-445)
Condo Incorporated .... D 330 609-6021
  Warren (G-15157)

▲ Day-Hio Products Inc .... F 937 445-0782
  Dayton (G-6272)
Deloscrew Products .... F 740 363-1971
  Delaware (G-6716)
Dunham Products Inc .... F 440 232-0885
  Walton Hills (G-15098)
Eastlake Machine Products LLC .... F 440 953-1014
  Willoughby (G-15915)
Ecm Industries LLC .... E 513 533-6242
  Cincinnati (G-2857)
▲ Elyria Manufacturing Corp .... D 440 365-4171
  Elyria (G-7142)
Engstrom Manufacturing Inc .... E 513 573-0010
  Mason (G-9990)
Eureka Screw Machine Pdts Co .... G 216 883-1715
  Cleveland (G-4036)
Fairfield Machined Pdts Inc .... F 740 756-4409
  Carroll (G-2298)
Fannin Machine Company LLC .... E 419 524-9525
  Mansfield (G-6654)
Forrest Machine Pdts Co Ltd .... E 419 589-3774
  Mansfield (G-9658)
Gent Machine Company .... E 216 481-2334
  Cleveland (G-4120)
Global Precision Parts Inc .... F 260 563-9030
  Van Wert (G-14916)
H & S Precision Screw Pdts Inc .... E 937 437-0316
  New Paris (G-11482)
H & W Screw Products Inc .... F 937 866-2577
  Franklin (G-7679)
Helix Operating Company LLC .... G 855 435-4958
  Beachwood (G-990)
Heller Machine Products Inc .... G 216 281-2951
  Cleveland (G-4179)
Houston Machine Products Inc .... E 937 322-8022
  Springfield (G-13580)
▲ Hy-Production Inc .... C 330 273-2400
  Valley City (G-14873)
▲ Hyland Machine Company .... E 937 233-8600
  Dayton (G-6377)
▲ Ilsco LLC .... C 513 533-6200
  Cincinnati (G-3017)
Integrity Manufacturing Corp .... F 937 233-6792
  Dayton (G-6386)
JAD Machine Company Inc .... F 419 256-6332
  Malinta (G-9605)
Karma Metal Products Inc .... F 419 524-4371
  Mansfield (G-9676)
▲ Kernells Autmtc Machining Inc .... E 419 588-2164
  Berlin Heights (G-1315)
▲ Kerr Lakeside Inc .... D 216 261-2100
  Euclid (G-7280)
Krausher Machining Inc .... G 440 839-2828
  Wakeman (G-15075)
Kts Met-Bar Products Inc .... G 440 288-9308
  Lorain (G-9417)
Lehner Screw Machine LLC .... E 330 688-6616
  Akron (G-218)
Lenco Industries Inc .... F 937 277-9364
  Dayton (G-6404)
Machine Tek Systems Inc .... E 330 527-4450
  Garrettsville (G-7921)
Magnetic Screw Machine Pdts .... G 937 348-2807
  Marysville (G-9925)
Maumee Machine & Tool Corp .... E 419 385-2501
  Toledo (G-14379)
McDaniel Products Inc .... F 419 524-5841
  Mansfield (G-9689)
McDaniel Products Inc .... G 419 524-5841
  Mansfield (G-9688)
McGregor Metal National Works LLC .... E 937 882-6347
  Springfield (G-13601)

SIC SECTION
34 FABRICATED METAL PRODUCTS

▲ McGregor Mtal Yllow Sprng Wrks ..... D 937 325-5561
  Springfield *(G-13604)*
Meistermatic Inc .... E 216 481-7773
  Chesterland *(G-2484)*
Metal Seal & Products Inc .... C 440 946-8500
  Mentor *(G-10502)*
Mettlr-Tledo Globl Hldings LLC .... D 614 438-4511
  Columbus *(G-5068)*
Midwest Precision LLC .... D 440 951-2333
  Eastlake *(G-7041)*
Mosher Machine & Tool Co Inc .... E 937 258-8070
  Beavercreek Township *(G-1085)*
Murray Machine and Tool Inc .... G 216 267-1126
  Cleveland *(G-4431)*
Nolte Precise Manufacturing Inc .... D 513 923-3100
  Cincinnati *(G-3203)*
▲ Nook Industries LLC .... B 216 271-7900
  Cleveland *(G-4463)*
◆ NSK Industries Inc .... D 330 923-4112
  Cuyahoga Falls *(G-6107)*
Obars Machine and Tool Company .... E 419 535-6307
  Toledo *(G-14403)*
▲ Ohio Metal Products Company .... E 937 228-6101
  Dayton *(G-6489)*
Ohio Screw Products Inc .... D 440 322-6341
  Elyria *(G-7191)*
Paramont Machine Company LLC .... F 330 339-3489
  New Philadelphia *(G-11522)*
▲ Pfi Precision Inc .... E 937 845-3563
  New Carlisle *(G-11425)*
Pohlman Precision LLC .... E 636 537-1909
  Massillon *(G-10135)*
Port Clinton Manufacturing LLC .... E 419 734-2141
  Port Clinton *(G-12623)*
Precision Engneered Components .... F 614 436-0392
  Worthington *(G-16207)*
▲ Precision Fittings LLC .... E 440 647-4143
  Wellington *(G-15320)*
◆ Premier Farnell Corp .... D 330 659-0459
  Richfield *(G-12793)*
Profile Grinding Inc .... E 216 351-0600
  Cleveland *(G-4590)*
Qcsm LLC .... G 216 650-8731
  Cleveland *(G-4602)*
Qualitor Subsidiary H Inc .... C 419 562-7987
  Bucyrus *(G-1865)*
▲ Quality Machining and Mfg Inc .... F 419 899-2543
  Sherwood *(G-13202)*
R T & T Machining Co Inc .... F 440 974-8479
  Mentor *(G-10543)*
R W Screw Products Inc .... C 330 837-9211
  Massillon *(G-10137)*
Raka Corporation .... D 419 476-6572
  Toledo *(G-14449)*
Rely-On Manufacturing Inc .... G 937 254-0118
  Dayton *(G-6545)*
Richland Screw Mch Pdts Inc .... E 419 524-1272
  Mansfield *(G-9713)*
Rtsi LLC .... G 440 542-3066
  Solon *(G-13416)*
▲ Semtorq Inc .... F 330 487-0600
  Twinsburg *(G-14734)*
Shanafelt Manufacturing Co .... E 330 455-0315
  Canton *(G-2223)*
Soemhejee Inc .... E 419 298-2306
  Edgerton *(G-7080)*
Stadco Inc .... E 937 878-0911
  Fairborn *(G-7322)*
Superior Bar Products Inc .... G 419 784-2590
  Defiance *(G-6696)*
Supply Technologies LLC .... F 740 363-1971
  Delaware *(G-6754)*

Swagelok Zalo .... F 216 524-8950
  Solon *(G-13432)*
Tri-K Enterprises Inc .... G 330 832-7380
  Canton *(G-2248)*
Triangle Machine Products Co .... E 216 524-5872
  Cleveland *(G-4824)*
Twin Valley Metalcraft Asm LLC .... G 937 787-4634
  West Alexandria *(G-15345)*
Usm Precision Products Inc .... D 440 975-8600
  Wickliffe *(G-15858)*
Valley Tool & Die Inc .... D 440 237-0160
  North Royalton *(G-11900)*
Vanamatic Company .... D 419 692-6085
  Delphos *(G-6778)*
Vulcan Products Co Inc .... F 419 468-1039
  Galion *(G-7887)*
Warren Screw Machine Inc .... F 330 609-6020
  Warren *(G-15219)*
Watters Manufacturing Co Inc .... E 216 281-8600
  Cleveland *(G-4897)*
Whirlaway Corporation .... E 440 647-4711
  Wellington *(G-15323)*
Whirlaway Corporation .... D 440 647-4711
  Wellington *(G-15324)*
▲ Whirlaway Corporation .... C 440 647-4711
  Wellington *(G-15325)*
Whiteford Industries Inc .... F 419 381-1155
  Toledo *(G-14524)*
Wood-Sebring Corporation .... G 216 267-3191
  Cleveland *(G-4918)*

3452 Bolts, nuts, rivets, and washers

Abco Bar & Tube Cutng Svc Inc .... E 513 697-9487
  Maineville *(G-9598)*
◆ Agrati - Medina LLC .... C 330 725-8853
  Medina *(G-10289)*
Agrati - Tiffin LLC .... D 419 447-2221
  Tiffin *(G-14074)*
Airfasco Inc .... E 330 430-6190
  Canton *(G-2029)*
Airfasco Inds Fstner Group LLC .... E 330 430-6190
  Canton *(G-2030)*
▲ Akko Fastener Inc .... F 513 489-8300
  Middletown *(G-10804)*
▲ Altenloh Brinck & Co Inc .... C 419 636-6715
  Bryan *(G-1805)*
Altenloh Brinck & Co US Inc .... E 419 737-2381
  Pioneer *(G-12489)*
▲ Altenloh Brinck & Co US Inc .... F 419 636-6715
  Bryan *(G-1806)*
▲ Amanda Bent Bolt Company .... C 740 385-6893
  Logan *(G-9358)*
◆ American Micro Products Inc .... C 513 732-2674
  Batavia *(G-908)*
Ampex Metal Products Company .... D 216 267-9242
  Brookpark *(G-1704)*
Andre Corporation .... E 574 293-0207
  Mason *(G-9950)*
▲ Atlas Bolt & Screw Company LLC ..... C 419 289-6171
  Ashland *(G-554)*
Auto Bolt Company .... D 216 881-3913
  Cleveland *(G-3700)*
Bowes Manufacturing Inc .... E 216 378-2110
  Solon *(G-13321)*
Brainard Rivet Company .... E 330 545-4931
  Girard *(G-7963)*
▲ Cold Headed Fas Assemblies Inc ..... F 330 833-0800
  Massillon *(G-10085)*
Component Solutions Group Inc .... F 937 434-8100
  Dayton *(G-6261)*
Consolidated Metal Pdts Inc .... D 513 251-2624
  Cincinnati *(G-2788)*

Core Manufacturing LLC .... G 440 946-8002
  Mentor *(G-10443)*
▲ Crawford Products Inc .... E 614 890-1822
  Columbus *(G-5306)*
Curtiss-Wright Flow Ctrl Corp .... D 216 267-3200
  Cleveland *(G-3922)*
◆ Dayton Superior Corporation .... C 937 866-0711
  Miamisburg *(G-10633)*
Die-Cut Products Co .... F 216 771-6994
  Cleveland *(G-3958)*
▲ Dimcogray Corporation .... D 937 433-7600
  Centerville *(G-2361)*
Edward W Daniel LLC .... E 440 647-1960
  Wellington *(G-15306)*
Elgin Fastener Group .... G 440 239-1165
  Brookpark *(G-1714)*
Engstrom Manufacturing Inc .... G 513 573-0010
  Mason *(G-9990)*
Express Trading Pins LLC .... F 419 394-2550
  Saint Marys *(G-12951)*
◆ Facil North America Inc .... C 330 487-2500
  Twinsburg *(G-14659)*
Fastener Industries Inc .... E 440 891-2031
  Berea *(G-1279)*
◆ Fastener Industries Inc .... G 440 243-0034
  Berea *(G-1280)*
◆ Gray America Corp .... E 937 293-9313
  Moraine *(G-11182)*
▲ Great Lakes Fasteners Inc .... D 330 425-4488
  Twinsburg *(G-14670)*
◆ Group Industries Inc .... E 216 271-0702
  Cleveland *(G-4152)*
▲ Hexagon Industries Inc .... E 216 249-0200
  Cleveland *(G-4187)*
▲ Industrial Nut Corp .... D 419 625-8543
  Sandusky *(G-13066)*
Ivostud LLC .... G 440 925-4227
  Brookpark *(G-1719)*
Iwata Bolt USA Inc .... F 513 942-5050
  Fairfield *(G-7374)*
Jacodar Inc .... F 330 832-9557
  Massillon *(G-10113)*
Jacodar Fsa LLC .... E 330 454-1832
  Canton *(G-2134)*
▲ Jergens Inc .... C 216 486-5540
  Cleveland *(G-4253)*
Jerry Tools Inc .... F 513 242-3211
  Cincinnati *(G-3041)*
▲ Kerr Lakeside Inc .... D 216 261-2100
  Euclid *(G-7280)*
▲ Keystone Bolt & Nut Company .... D 216 524-9626
  Cleveland *(G-4285)*
Lapel Pins Unlimited LLC .... G 614 562-3218
  Lewis Center *(G-9169)*
Lear Mfg Co Inc .... F 440 324-1111
  Elyria *(G-7173)*
Long-Lok Fasteners Corporation .... E 513 772-1880
  Cincinnati *(G-3112)*
Magnus Engineered Eqp LLC .... E 440 942-8488
  Willoughby *(G-15948)*
Master Products Company .... D 216 341-1740
  Cleveland *(G-4368)*
▲ Matdan Corporation .... E 513 794-0500
  Blue Ash *(G-1429)*
Mid-West Fabricating Co .... E 740 277-7021
  Lancaster *(G-9024)*
▲ Miller Studio Inc .... E 330 339-1100
  New Philadelphia *(G-11519)*
◆ Namoh Ohio Holdings Inc .... E
  Norwood *(G-11996)*
◆ Nelson Stud Welding Inc .... D 440 329-0400
  Elyria *(G-7184)*

Employee Codes: A=Over 500 employees, B=251-500
C=101-250, D=51-100, E=20-50, F=10-19, G=1-9

2024 Harris Ohio
Industrial Directory

865

34 FABRICATED METAL PRODUCTS

North Coast Rivet Inc .... F 440 366-6829
  Elyria *(G-7187)*
	Advanced FME Products Inc .... F 440 953-0700
	  Mentor *(G-10405)*
		King-Indiana Forge Inc .... F 330 425-4250
		  Twinsburg *(G-14680)*

▲ Nova Machine Products Inc .... C 216 267-3200
  Middleburg Heights *(G-10724)*
	Aero Tech Tool & Mold Inc .... G 440 942-3327
	  Mentor *(G-10406)*
		Landerwood Industries Inc .... E 440 233-4234
		  Willoughby *(G-15944)*

▲ Ohashi Technica USA Inc .... E 740 965-5115
  Sunbury *(G-13960)*
	Akron Gear & Engineering Inc .... E 330 773-6608
	  Akron *(G-34)*
		Lextech Industries Ltd .... G 216 883-7900
		  Cleveland *(G-4322)*

Paine Falls Centerpin LLC .... G 440 867-4954
  Thompson *(G-14061)*
	Alliance Forging Group LLC .... G 330 680-4861
	  Akron *(G-55)*
		Majestic Fireplace Distr .... G 440 439-1040
		  Bedford *(G-1136)*

▲ Paulin Industries Inc .... E 216 433-7633
  Parma *(G-12293)*
	Alta Mira Corporation .... D 330 648-2461
	  Spencer *(G-13479)*
		Maxx Iron LLC .... G 614 753-9697
		  Worthington *(G-16201)*

Peterson American Corporation ...... E 419 867-8711
  Holland *(G-8523)*
	American Cold Forge LLC .... E 419 836-1062
	  Northwood *(G-11917)*
		Metal Forming & Coining LLC .... D 419 893-8748
		  Maumee *(G-10220)*

Pin Oak Development LLC .... G 440 933-9862
  Avon Lake *(G-820)*
	▲ Anchor Flange Company .... D 513 527-3512
	  Cincinnati *(G-2626)*
		Mid-West Forge Corporation .... C 216 481-3030
		  Willoughby *(G-15953)*

▲ Precision Fittings LLC .... E 440 647-4143
  Wellington *(G-15320)*
	▲ Anchor Industries Incorporated ..... E 440 473-1414
	  Cleveland *(G-3661)*
		▲ Ohio Star Forge Co .... E 330 847-6360
		  Warren *(G-15195)*

Pressure Washer Mfrs Assn Inc ..... G 216 241-7333
  Cleveland *(G-4586)*
	Ashta Enterprises Ltd Lblty Co .... G 216 252-7620
	  Cleveland *(G-3690)*
		◆ Park-Ohio Holdings Corp .... F 440 947-2000
		  Cleveland *(G-4524)*

Qrp Inc .... D 910 371-0700
  Doron *(C-1201)*
	Brooker Bros Forging Co Inc .... E 419 668-2535
	  Norwalk *(C-11067)*
		Park-Ohio Industries Inc .... C 440 947-2000
		  Cleveland *(C-1526)*

Quality Concepts Telecom Ltd .... G 740 385-2003
  Logan *(G-9374)*
	Bula Forge & Machine Inc .... E 216 252-7600
	  Cleveland *(G-3771)*
		Penn Machine Company LLC .... D 814 288-1547
		  Twinsburg *(G-14708)*

◆ Ramco Specialties Inc .... D 330 653-5135
  Hudson *(G-8609)*
	Cailin Development LLC .... F 216 408-6261
	  Cleveland *(G-3781)*
		Presrite Corporation .... D 440 576-0015
		  Jefferson *(G-8757)*

▲ RB&w Manufacturing LLC .... G 234 380-8540
  Streetsboro *(G-13787)*
	◆ Canton Drop Forge Inc .... B 330 477-4511
	  Canton *(G-2061)*
		Presrite Corporation .... B 216 441-5990
		  Cleveland *(G-4584)*

Rs Manufacturing Inc .... F 440 946-8002
  Mentor *(G-10549)*
	Carbo Forge Inc .... E 419 334-9788
	  Fremont *(G-7769)*
		Pumpco Concrete Pumping LLC .... F 740 809-1473
		  Johnstown *(G-8776)*

Saf-Holland Inc .... G 513 874-7888
  Fairfield *(G-7404)*
	Cincinnati Gearing Systems Inc .... E 513 527-8634
	  Cincinnati *(G-2750)*
		▲ Queen City Forging Company ...... F 513 321-2003
		  Cincinnati *(G-2573)*

Simpson Strong-Tie Company Inc ... C 614 876-8060
  Columbus *(G-5773)*
	Colfor Manufacturing Inc .... B 330 863-0404
	  Minerva *(G-11029)*
		R E H Inc .... G 330 876-2775
		  Kinsman *(G-8937)*

▲ Solon Manufacturing Company ..... E 440 286-7149
  Chardon *(G-2468)*
	▲ Colfor Manufacturing Inc .... B 330 470-6207
	  Malvern *(G-9610)*
		Rose Metal Industries LLC .... F 216 881-3355
		  Cleveland *(G-4648)*

◆ Stafast Products Inc .... E 440 357-5546
  Painesville *(G-12264)*
	Cordier Group Holdings Inc .... B 330 477-4511
	  Canton *(G-2082)*
		Rudd Equipment Company Inc ...... D 513 321-7833
		  Cincinnati *(G-3354)*

▲ Stanley Industrial & Auto LLC ...... D 614 755-7000
  Dublin *(G-6944)*
	Crum Manufacturing Inc .... E 419 878-9779
	  Waterville *(G-15241)*
		▲ Sakamura USA Inc .... F 740 223-7777
		  Marion *(G-9878)*

▲ Steeramerica Inc .... F 330 563-4407
  Uniontown *(G-14794)*
	Dayton Forging Heat Treating .... D 937 253-4126
	  Dayton *(G-6278)*
		▲ Schaefer Equipment Inc .... D 330 372-4006
		  Warren *(G-15205)*

◆ Stelfast LLC .... E 440 879-0077
  Strongsville *(G-13886)*
	▲ Dayton Superior Corporation .... C 937 866-0711
	  Miamisburg *(G-10633)*
		◆ Sifco Industries Inc .... C 216 881-8600
		  Cleveland *(G-4700)*

Supply Technologies LLC .... E 614 759-9939
  Columbus *(G-5802)*
	Edgerton Forge Inc .... D 419 298-2333
	  Edgerton *(G-7074)*
		Solmet Technologies Inc .... E 330 915-4160
		  Canton *(G-2228)*

Supply Technologies LLC .... G 937 898-5795
  Dayton *(G-6601)*
	Edward W Daniel LLC .... E 440 647-1960
	  Wellington *(G-15306)*
		Stahl Gear & Machine Co .... E 216 431-2820
		  Cleveland *(G-4725)*

◆ Supply Technologies LLC .... C 440 947-2100
  Cleveland *(G-4755)*
	▲ Ferrotherm Corporation .... C 216 883-9350
	  Cleveland *(G-4058)*
		◆ Superior Forge & Steel Corp .... C 419 222-4412
		  Lima *(G-9293)*

Tessec Manufacturing Svcs LLC .... E 937 985-3552
  Dayton *(G-6616)*
	▲ Firth Rixson Inc .... D 860 760-1040
	  Newburgh Heights *(G-11614)*
		T & W Forge Inc .... D
		  Alliance *(G-431)*

◆ Tinnerman Palnut Engineered PR ... E 330 220-5100
  Brunswick *(G-1795)*
	For Call Inc .... E 330 863-0404
	  Malvern *(G-9611)*
		▲ Tekfor Inc .... B 330 202-7420
		  Wooster *(G-16176)*

Twin Ventures Inc .... F 330 405-3838
  Twinsburg *(G-14749)*
	Forge Products Corporation .... E 216 231-2600
	  Cleveland *(G-4083)*
		▲ Tfo Tech Co Ltd .... C 740 426-6381
		  Jeffersonville *(G-8766)*

▲ United Titanium Inc .... C 330 264-2111
  Wooster *(G-16179)*
	Gear Company of America Inc ...... D 216 671-5400
	  Cleveland *(G-4107)*
		▲ Thyssnkrupp Rothe Erde USA Inc .. C 330 562-4000
		  Aurora *(G-736)*

Valley Tool & Die Inc .... D 440 237-0160
  North Royalton *(G-11900)*
	Geneva Gear & Machine Inc .... F 937 866-0318
	  Dayton *(G-6351)*
		TRM Manufacturing Inc .... E 330 769-2600
		  Cuyahoga Falls *(G-6123)*

Vapor Pin Enterprises Inc .... G 614 504-6915
  Plain City *(G-12598)*
	GKN PLC .... G 740 446-9211
	  Gallipolis *(G-7893)*
		Tymoca Partners LLC .... F 440 946-4327
		  Eastlake *(G-7052)*

▲ Wallace Forge Company .... D 330 488-1203
  Canton *(G-2265)*
	GKN Sinter Metals LLC .... C 740 441-3203
	  Gallipolis *(G-7894)*
		US Tsubaki Power Transm LLC ..... C 419 626-4560
		  Sandusky *(G-13102)*

Wecall Inc .... G 440 437-8202
  Chardon *(G-2470)*
	◆ HBD Industries Inc .... E 614 526-7000
	  Dublin *(G-6891)*
		Viking Forge LLC .... C 330 562-3366
		  Streetsboro *(G-13797)*

Wheel Group Holdings LLC .... G 614 253-6247
  Columbus *(G-5875)*
	Horseshoe Express Inc .... G 330 692-1209
	  Canfield *(G-2007)*
		▲ W E Lott Company .... F 419 563-9400
		  Bucyrus *(G-1873)*

Wodin Inc .... E 440 439-4222
  Cleveland *(G-4916)*
	▲ J & H Manufacturing LLC .... F 330 482-2636
	  Columbiana *(G-5042)*
		▲ Wallace Forge Company .... D 330 488-1203
		  Canton *(G-2265)*

### 3462 Iron and steel forgings	Ken Forging Inc .... C 440 993-8901 	
	  Jefferson *(G-8749)*
		Wodin Inc .... E 440 439-4222
		  Cleveland *(G-4916)*

Accurate Gear Manufacturing Co ... G 513 761-3220
  Cincinnati *(G-2595)*
	King Forge and Machine Company .. F 330 963-0600
	  Twinsburg *(G-14679)*
		▲ Wright Tool Company .... C 330 848-0600
		  Barberton *(G-901)*

Wyman-Gordon Company.................... E 216 341-0085
  Cleveland *(G-4925)*

3463 Nonferrous forgings

American Cold Forge LLC.................... E 419 836-1062
  Northwood *(G-11917)*
◆ Canton Drop Forge Inc.................... B 330 477-4511
  Canton *(G-2061)*
Clarke Power Services Inc.................... F 513 771-2200
  Cincinnati *(G-2773)*
▲ Colfor Manufacturing Inc.................... B 330 470-6207
  Malvern *(G-9610)*
Edward W Daniel LLC.................... E 440 647-1960
  Wellington *(G-15306)*
Forge Products Corporation.................... E 216 231-2600
  Cleveland *(G-4083)*
▲ Guarantee Specialties Inc.................... D 216 451-9744
  Strongsville *(G-13838)*
Howmet Aerospace Inc.................... A 216 641-3600
  Newburgh Heights *(G-11615)*
Howmet Aerospace Inc.................... E 330 544-7633
  Niles *(G-11671)*
◆ Mansfield Plumbing Pdts LLC........... A 419 938-5211
  Perrysville *(G-12447)*
Mp Technologies Inc.................... F 440 838-4466
  Ashland *(G-594)*
▲ Thyssnkrupp Rothe Erde USA Inc..... C 330 562-4000
  Aurora *(G-736)*
Turbine Eng Cmpnents Tech Corp........ B 216 692-5200
  Cleveland *(G-4837)*
▲ Wallace Forge Company.................... D 330 488-1203
  Canton *(G-2265)*
Wodin Inc.................... E 440 439-4222
  Cleveland *(G-4916)*

3465 Automotive stampings

American Trim LLC.................... A 419 228-1145
  Sidney *(G-13220)*
▲ Anchor Tool & Die Co.................... B 216 362-1850
  Cleveland *(G-3664)*
Antique Auto Sheet Metal Inc............ F 937 833-4422
  Brookville *(G-1729)*
Aptiv Services Us LLC.................... A 330 373-3568
  Warren *(G-15144)*
◆ Artiflex Manufacturing Inc.................... B 330 262-2015
  Wooster *(G-16101)*
Autotx Inc.................... G 216 510-6666
  Cleveland *(G-3706)*
Buyers Products Company.................... B 440 974-8888
  Mentor *(G-10434)*
Cleveland Metal Processing Inc........... C 440 243-3404
  Cleveland *(G-3848)*
Clevelnd-Clffs Tling Stmping H.............. F 519 969-4632
  West Chester *(G-15397)*
Clevelnd-Clffs Toling Stamping............ C 216 694-5700
  West Chester *(G-15398)*
Cole Tool & Die Company.................... E 419 522-1272
  Ontario *(G-12090)*
Compco Quaker Mfg Inc.................... E 330 482-0200
  Salem *(G-12986)*
Custom Floaters LLC.................... G 216 337-9118
  Brookpark *(G-1709)*
Decoma Systems Integration Gro........ D 419 324-3387
  Toledo *(G-14263)*
Elyria Spring & Specialty Inc.................... F 440 323-5502
  Elyria *(G-7146)*
Exact-Tool & Die Inc.................... E 216 676-9140
  Cleveland *(G-4040)*
Falls Stamping & Welding Co............ F 216 771-9635
  Cleveland *(G-4049)*
Falls Stamping & Welding Co............ C 330 928-1191
  Cuyahoga Falls *(G-6083)*

Falls Tool and Die Inc.................... G 330 633-4884
  Akron *(G-149)*
▲ Feintool Cincinnati Inc.................... C 513 247-0110
  Blue Ash *(G-1394)*
▲ Feintool US Operations Inc.............. C 513 247-0110
  Cincinnati *(G-2900)*
◆ Findlay Products Corporation............ C 419 423-3324
  Findlay *(G-7509)*
Florida Production Engrg Inc.................... D 937 996-4361
  New Madison *(G-11474)*
General Motors LLC.................... A 216 265-5000
  Cleveland *(G-4116)*
Grouper Acquisition Co LLC.................... B 330 558-2600
  Wellington *(G-15313)*
Gt Technologies Inc.................... D 419 324-7300
  Toledo *(G-14304)*
▲ Guarantee Specialties Inc.................... D 216 451-9744
  Strongsville *(G-13838)*
Hayford Technologies Inc.................... D 419 524-7627
  Mansfield *(G-9667)*
Honda Dev & Mfg Amer LLC.............. C 937 644-0724
  Marysville *(G-9915)*
Hydro Extrusion Usa LLC.................... C 888 935-5759
  Sidney *(G-13255)*
JA Acquisition Corp.................... F 419 287-3223
  Pemberville *(G-12335)*
Kasai North America Inc.................... C 419 209-0399
  Upper Sandusky *(G-14812)*
▲ Kirchhoff Auto Waverly Inc.............. F 740 947-7763
  Waverly *(G-15284)*
L & W Inc.................... E 734 397-6300
  Avon *(G-778)*
Lakepark Industries Inc.................... C 419 752-4471
  Greenwich *(G-8068)*
Langenau Manufacturing Company..... E 216 651-3400
  Cleveland *(G-4310)*
◆ Matsu Ohio Inc.................... C 419 298-2394
  Edgerton *(G-7077)*
Milark Industries Inc.................... D 419 524-7627
  Mansfield *(G-9693)*
Milark Industries Inc.................... D 419 524-7627
  Mansfield *(G-9694)*
Muncy Corporation.................... D 937 346-0800
  Springfield *(G-13608)*
▲ Murotech Ohio Corporation............ C 419 394-6529
  Saint Marys *(G-12958)*
◆ Namoh Ohio Holdings Inc.................... E
  Norwood *(G-11996)*
Nebraska Industries Corp.................... F 419 335-6010
  Wauseon *(G-15270)*
Nn Metal Stampings LLC.................... E 419 737-2311
  Pioneer *(G-12493)*
Northern Stamping Co.................... F 216 883-8888
  Cleveland *(G-4477)*
Northern Stamping Co.................... F 216 642-8081
  Cleveland *(G-14479)*
◆ Northern Stamping Co.................... C 216 883-8888
  Cleveland *(G-4478)*
Oerlikon Frction Systems US In........... E 937 233-9191
  Dayton *(G-6484)*
▲ P & A Industries Inc.................... D 419 422-7070
  Findlay *(G-7549)*
Pennant Companies.................... E 614 451-1782
  Sabina *(G-12889)*
▲ Quaker Mfg Corp.................... C 330 332-4631
  Salem *(G-13024)*
▲ R K Industries Inc.................... D 419 523-5001
  Ottawa *(G-12190)*
Regal Metal Products Co.................... E 330 868-6343
  Minerva *(G-11039)*
Shiloh Industries Inc.................... A 330 558-2000
  Valley City *(G-14890)*

Shl Liquidation Inc Dickson.................... E 615 446-7725
  Valley City *(G-14892)*
◆ Shl Liquidation Industries Inc............ B 248 299-7500
  Valley City *(G-14893)*
Shl Liquidation Jefferson Inc................... D
  Valley City *(G-14894)*
Shl Liquidation Mfg LLC.................... E 330 558-2600
  Valley City *(G-14896)*
Shl Liquidation Stamping Inc............. D 330 558-2600
  Valley City *(G-14898)*
▲ SSP Industrial Group Inc.................... G 330 665-2900
  Fairlawn *(G-7452)*
◆ Stamco Industries Inc.................... E 216 731-9333
  Cleveland *(G-4727)*
▲ Stripmatic Products Inc.................... E 216 241-7143
  Cleveland *(G-4740)*
▲ T A Bacon Co.................... E 216 851-1404
  Chesterland *(G-2489)*
▲ Taylor Metal Products Co.................... C 419 522-3471
  Mansfield *(G-9724)*
▲ Tfo Tech Co Ltd.................... C 740 426-6381
  Jeffersonville *(G-8766)*
Tower Atmtve Oprtons USA I LL....... B 419 358-8966
  Bluffton *(G-1508)*
Trellborg Sling Prfiles US Inc.............. C 330 995-9725
  Aurora *(G-737)*
Triton Duro Werks Inc.................... F 216 267-1117
  Cleveland *(G-4833)*
▲ Trucut Incorporated.................... D 330 938-9806
  Sebring *(G-13127)*
▲ TS Trim Industries Inc.................... B 614 837-4114
  Canal Winchester *(G-1993)*
Twb Company LLC.................... E 330 558-2026
  Valley City *(G-14899)*
Valco Industries LLC.................... E 937 399-7400
  Springfield *(G-13653)*
Valley Tool & Die Inc.................... D 440 237-0160
  North Royalton *(G-11900)*
◆ Vehtek Systems Inc.................... A 419 373-8741
  Bowling Green *(G-1594)*
▲ Winzeler Stamping Co.................... E 419 485-3147
  Montpelier *(G-11147)*
Wrena LLC.................... E 937 667-4403
  Tipp City *(G-14168)*
▲ Yachiyo of America Inc.................... C 614 876-3220
  Columbus *(G-5889)*
Yanfeng US Auto Intr Systems I......... D 419 633-1873
  Bryan *(G-1847)*

3466 Crowns and closures

◆ Boardman Molded Products Inc........ D 330 788-2400
  Youngstown *(G-16322)*
Crown Cork & Seal Usa Inc.................... D 740 681-3000
  Lancaster *(G-9006)*
Eisenhauer Mfg Co LLC.................... D 419 238-0081
  Van Wert *(G-14915)*
Winzeler Couplings & Mtls LLC.......... D 419 485-3147
  Montpelier *(G-11146)*

3469 Metal stampings, nec

◆ A J Rose Mfg Co.................... C 216 631-4645
  Avon *(G-758)*
▲ A-1 Resources Ltd.................... F 330 695-9351
  Fredericksburg *(G-7717)*
AAA Stamping Inc.................... E 216 749-4494
  Cleveland *(G-3583)*
Abbott Tool Inc.................... E 419 476-6742
  Toledo *(G-14174)*
Abl Products Inc.................... F 216 281-2400
  Cleveland *(G-3588)*
▲ Acro Tool & Die Company.................... E 330 773-5173
  Akron *(G-17)*

Employee Codes: A=Over 500 employees, B=251-500
C=101-250, D=51-100, E=20-50, F=10-19, G=1-9

34 FABRICATED METAL PRODUCTS

Adh Industries Inc .... G 330 283-5822
   Akron *(G-21)*

◆ **Advanced Technology Corp** .... F 440 293-4064
   Andover *(G-483)*

Afc Stamping & Production Inc .... C 937 275-8700
   Dayton *(G-6188)*

Agb LLC .... G 419 924-5216
   West Unity *(G-15636)*

AJD Holding Co .... D 330 405-4477
   Twinsburg *(G-14626)*

Allied Tool & Die Inc .... F 216 941-6196
   Cleveland *(G-3637)*

Amano USA Holdings Inc .... G 973 403-1900
   Loveland *(G-9475)*

Amaroq Inc .... G 419 747-2110
   Mansfield *(G-9623)*

Amclo Group Inc .... E 216 791-8400
   North Royalton *(G-11867)*

▼ **Amcraft Inc** .... G 419 729-7900
   Toledo *(G-14105)*

American Rugged Enclosures Inc .... F 513 942-3004
   Hamilton *(G-8178)*

American Tool & Mfg Co .... F 419 522-2452
   Mansfield *(G-9625)*

American Tool and Die Inc .... F 419 726-5394
   Toledo *(G-14193)*

American Trim LLC .... A 419 228-1145
   Sidney *(G-13220)*

American Trim LLC .... C 419 739-4349
   Wapakoneta *(G-15105)*

◆ **American Trim LLC** .... E 419 228-1145
   Lima *(G-9221)*

AMG Industries LLC .... D 740 397-4044
   Mount Vernon *(G-11261)*

Ampex Metal Products Company .... D 216 267-9242
   Brookpark *(G-1704)*

Amtekco Industries LLC .... D 614 228-6590
   Columbus *(G-5136)*

Amtekco Industries Inc .... E 614 228-6525
   Columbus *(G-5137)*

Anchor Fabricators Inc .... E 937 836-5117
   Clayton *(G-3563)*

Anchor Hocking Holdings Inc .... A 740 687-2500
   Columbus *(G-5141)*

▲ **Anchor Tool & Die Co** .... B 216 362-1850
   Cleveland *(G-3664)*

Andre Corporation .... E 574 293-0207
   Mason *(G-9950)*

◆ **Anomatic Corporation** .... E 740 522-2203
   New Albany *(G-11366)*

Arbor Industries Inc .... D 440 255-4720
   Mentor *(G-10421)*

ARC Metal Stamping LLC .... D 517 448-8954
   Wauseon *(G-15256)*

▼ **Armorsource LLC** .... E 740 928-0070
   Hebron *(G-8336)*

Arrow Tru-Line Inc .... G 419 636-7013
   Bryan *(G-1808)*

◆ **Arrow Tru-Line Inc** .... C 419 446-2785
   Archbold *(G-524)*

▲ **Art Technologies LLC** .... D 513 942-8800
   Hamilton *(G-8180)*

◆ **Artiflex Manufacturing Inc** .... B 330 262-2015
   Wooster *(G-16101)*

Artisan Equipment Inc .... F 740 756-9135
   Carroll *(G-2294)*

▼ **Artisan Tool & Die Corp** .... D 216 883-2769
   Cleveland *(G-3681)*

Artistic Metal Spinning Inc .... G 216 961-3336
   Cleveland *(G-3682)*

◆ **Atlantic Tool & Die Company** .... C 440 238-6931
   Strongsville *(G-13810)*

Atra Metal Spinning Inc .... F 440 354-9525
   Painesville *(G-12216)*

Automatic Stamp Products Inc .... F 216 781-7933
   Cleveland *(G-3704)*

Ayling and Reichert Co Consent .... E 419 898-2471
   Oak Harbor *(G-12011)*

B&A Ison Steel Inc .... F 216 663-4300
   Cleveland *(G-3716)*

Banner Metals Group Inc .... E 614 291-3105
   Columbus *(G-5174)*

Barbara A Lieurance .... G 937 382-2864
   Wilmington *(G-16041)*

Barnes Group Inc .... G 440 526-5900
   Brecksville *(G-1607)*

Bates Metal Products Inc .... D 740 498-8371
   Port Washington *(G-12631)*

Bayloff Stmped Pdts Knsman Inc .... D 330 876-4511
   Kinsman *(G-8935)*

Bennett Machine & Stamping Co .... E 440 415-0401
   Conova *(G-7002)*

Beverly Dove Inc .... G 740 495-5200
   New Holland *(G-11446)*

Boehm Pressed Steel Company .... E 330 220-8000
   Valley City *(G-14863)*

Brainerd Industries Inc .... E 937 228-0488
   Miamisburg *(G-10622)*

Breitinger Company .... C 419 526-4255
   Mansfield *(G-9631)*

Brittany Stamping LLC .... A 216 267-0850
   Cleveland *(G-3760)*

Brw Tool Inc .... F 419 394-3371
   Saint Marys *(G-12948)*

Buckley Manufacturing Company .... F 513 821-4444
   Cincinnati *(G-2693)*

C & S Industrial Ltd .... G 440 327-2360
   North Ridgeville *(G-11835)*

Camelot Manufacturing Inc .... F 419 678-2603
   Coldwater *(G-4983)*

Carolina Stamping Company .... F 216 271-5100
   Highland Heights *(G-8384)*

▲ **Catania Medallic Specialty Inc** .... E 440 933-9595
   Avon Lake *(G-801)*

Central Ohio Met Stmping Fbrct .... E 614 861-3332
   New Albany *(G-11373)*

Clemens License Agency .... G 614 288-8007
   Pickerington *(G-12459)*

◆ **Cleveland Die & Mfg Co** .... C 440 243-3404
   Middleburg Heights *(G-10716)*

Cleveland Metal Stamping Co .... F 440 234-0010
   Berea *(G-1270)*

Cole Tool & Die Company .... E 419 522-1272
   Ontario *(G-12090)*

◆ **Com-Corp Industries Inc** .... D 216 431-6266
   Cleveland *(G-3885)*

Compco Columbiana Company .... D 330 482-0200
   Columbiana *(G-5035)*

Compco Quaker Mfg Inc .... E 330 482-0200
   Salem *(G-12986)*

Compco Youngstown Company .... D 330 482-6488
   Columbiana *(G-5036)*

Connaughton Wldg & Fence LLC .... G 513 867-0230
   Hamilton *(G-8195)*

Continental Business Entps Inc .... F 440 439-4400
   Bedford *(G-1113)*

Contour Forming Inc .... F 740 345-9777
   Newark *(G-11572)*

◆ **Coreworth Holdings LLC** .... G 419 468-7100
   Iberia *(G-8647)*

Cql Mfg LLC .... D 330 482-5846
   Salem *(G-12987)*

Cqt Kennedy LLC .... D 419 238-2472
   Van Wert *(G-14912)*

Cubbison Company .... D 330 793-2481
   Youngstown *(G-16344)*

Customformed Products Inc .... F 937 388-0480
   Miamisburg *(G-10631)*

D J Klingler Inc .... G 513 891-2284
   Montgomery *(G-11129)*

Danco Metal Products LLC .... D 440 871-2300
   Avon Lake *(G-803)*

Dayton Rogers of Ohio Inc .... D 614 491-1477
   Obetz *(G-12059)*

Deerfield Manufacturing Inc .... E 513 398-2010
   Mason *(G-9983)*

▲ **Defiance Stamping Co** .... D 419 782-5781
   Napoleon *(G-11312)*

Delafoil Pennsylvania Inc .... E 610 327-9565
   Perrysburg *(G-12374)*

Delta Tool & Die Stl Block Inc .... E 419 822-5939
   Delta *(G-6781)*

Dependable Stamping Company .... E 216 486-5522
   Cleveland *(G-3052)*

◆ **Destiny Manufacturing Inc** .... E 330 273-9000
   Brunswick *(G-1757)*

▲ **Diamond America Corporation** .... E 330 762-9269
   Akron *(G-126)*

▲ **Die Co Inc** .... E 440 942-8856
   Eastlake *(G-7025)*

▲ **Die-Matic Corporation** .... D 216 749-4656
   Brooklyn Heights *(G-1689)*

▼ **Die-Mension Corporation** .... F 330 273-5872
   Brunswick *(G-1758)*

Dove Die and Stamping Company .... E 216 267-3720
   Cleveland *(G-3970)*

Durivage Pattern and Mfg Inc .... E 419 836-8655
   Williston *(G-15870)*

▲ **Duro Dyne Midwest Corp** .... C 513 870-6000
   Hamilton *(G-8201)*

Dyco Manufacturing Inc .... F 419 485-5525
   Montpelier *(G-11137)*

E C Shaw Company of Ohio .... E 513 721-6334
   Cincinnati *(G-2848)*

Eagle Precision Products LLC .... G 440 582-9393
   North Royalton *(G-11873)*

Ecm Industries LLC .... E 513 533-6242
   Cincinnati *(G-2857)*

▲ **Ecp Corporation** .... E 440 934-0444
   Avon *(G-771)*

Eisenhauer Mfg Co LLC .... D 419 238-0081
   Van Wert *(G-14915)*

Elyria Metal Spinning Fabg Co .... G 440 323-8068
   Elyria *(G-7143)*

Elyria Spring & Specialty Inc .... F 440 323-5502
   Elyria *(G-7146)*

Elyria Spring Spclty Holdg Inc .... F 440 323-5502
   Elyria *(G-7147)*

Englewood Precision Inc .... G 937 836-1910
   Englewood *(G-7231)*

Ernst America Inc .... F 937 434-3133
   Moraine *(G-11176)*

Ernst Metal Technologies LLC .... D 937 434-3133
   Moraine *(G-11177)*

▲ **Ernst Metal Technologies LLC** .... E 937 434-3133
   Moraine *(G-11178)*

Eurocase Archtctral Cbnets MII .... F 330 674-0681
   Millersburg *(G-10954)*

Exact-Tool & Die Inc .... E 216 676-9140
   Cleveland *(G-4040)*

F & G Tool and Die Co .... F 937 746-3658
   Franklin *(G-7673)*

F C Brengman and Assoc LLC .... E 740 756-4308
   Carroll *(G-2297)*

▲ **Fairfield Manufacturing Inc** .... B 513 642-0081
   Fairfield *(G-7358)*

SIC SECTION

34 FABRICATED METAL PRODUCTS

Falls Stamping & Welding Co................ C 330 928-1191
  Cuyahoga Falls *(G-6083)*
Falls Tool and Die Inc.......................... G 330 633-4884
  Akron *(G-149)*
Famous Industries Inc......................... F 740 685-2592
  Byesville *(G-1896)*
Faull & Son LLC.................................. F 330 652-4341
  Niles *(G-11668)*
Fc Industries Inc................................. E 937 275-8700
  Dayton *(G-6330)*
▲ Feintool US Operations Inc.............. C 513 247-0110
  Cincinnati *(G-2900)*
Feitl Manufacturing Co Inc................... E 330 405-6600
  Macedonia *(G-9550)*
◆ Findlay Products Corporation............ C 419 423-3324
  Findlay *(G-7509)*
Five Handicap Inc................................ F 419 525-2511
  Mansfield *(G-9656)*
Flood Heliarc Inc................................. F 614 835-3929
  Groveport *(G-8140)*
Formasters Corporation....................... F 440 639-9206
  Mentor *(G-10456)*
◆ Freeway Corporation......................... C 216 524-9700
  Cleveland *(G-4091)*
Fremont Plastic Products Inc................ C 419 332-6407
  Fremont *(G-7783)*
Frepeg Industries Inc........................... F 440 255-8595
  Mentor *(G-10459)*
Fulton Industries Inc............................ D 419 335-3015
  Wauseon *(G-15261)*
Fulton Manufacturing Inds LLC............. E
  Brecksville *(G-1617)*
◆ G & S Metal Products Co Inc............. C 216 441-0700
  Cleveland *(G-4096)*
Gb Fabrication Company...................... E 419 347-1835
  Shelby *(G-13195)*
Gb Fabrication Company...................... D 419 896-3191
  Shiloh *(G-13203)*
▲ Gb Manufacturing Company.............. D 419 822-5323
  Delta *(G-6784)*
Gem City Metal Tech LLC...................... E 937 252-8998
  Dayton *(G-6349)*
▲ General Technologies Inc.................. E 419 747-1800
  Mansfield *(G-9659)*
Gentzler Tool & Die Corp...................... E 330 896-1941
  Akron *(G-168)*
Greenfield Die & Mfg Corp................... D 734 454-4000
  Valley City *(G-14871)*
Grenada Stamping Assembly Inc.......... E 419 842-3600
  Sylvania *(G-13996)*
Grouper Acquisition Co LLC.................. B 248 299-7500
  Valley City *(G-14872)*
Gt Technologies Inc............................. D 419 324-7300
  Toledo *(G-14304)*
▲ Guarantee Specialties Inc.................. D 216 451-9744
  Strongsville *(G-13838)*
▲ Gwp Holdings Inc............................. E 513 860-4050
  Fairfield *(G-7364)*
H&M Mtal Stamping Assembly Inc....... F 216 898-9030
  Brookpark *(G-1717)*
▲ Hamlin Newco LLC........................... D 330 753-7791
  Akron *(G-178)*
Hamlin Steel Products LLC................... E 330 753-7791
  Akron *(G-179)*
Hashier & Hashier Mfg......................... G 440 933-4883
  Avon Lake *(G-810)*
Hayford Technologies Inc..................... D 419 524-7627
  Mansfield *(G-9667)*
Herd Manufacturing Inc....................... E 216 651-4221
  Cleveland *(G-4184)*
▲ Hidaka Usa Inc................................. E 614 889-8611
  Dublin *(G-6893)*

▲ Hill Manufacturing Inc....................... E 419 335-5006
  Wauseon *(G-15263)*
Ice Industries Inc................................. E 513 398-2010
  Mason *(G-10005)*
▲ Ice Industries Inc.............................. E 419 842-3600
  Sylvania *(G-14000)*
▲ Ilsco LLC.. C 513 533-6200
  Cincinnati *(G-3017)*
Impact Industries Inc........................... E 440 327-2360
  North Ridgeville *(G-11845)*
Imperial Die & Mfg Co.......................... F 440 268-9080
  Strongsville *(G-13844)*
Imperial Metal Spinning Co.................. G 216 524-5020
  Cleveland *(G-4220)*
Independent Power Cons Inc................ G 419 476-8383
  Toledo *(G-14329)*
Independent Stamping Inc................... E 216 251-3500
  Cleveland *(G-4223)*
Interlake Stamping Ohio Inc................. E 440 942-0800
  Willoughby *(G-15934)*
J B Stamping Inc.................................. E 216 631-0013
  Cleveland *(G-4244)*
J Schrader Company............................. F 216 961-2890
  Cleveland *(G-4246)*
JA Acquisition Corp.............................. F 419 287-3223
  Pemberville *(G-12335)*
▲ Jet Stream International Inc.............. D 330 505-9988
  Hubbard *(G-8566)*
Jones Metal Products Co LLC................ E 740 545-6381
  West Lafayette *(G-15618)*
K & H Industries LLC............................ F 513 921-6770
  Cincinnati *(G-3054)*
Kg63 LLC.. F 216 941-7766
  Cleveland *(G-4286)*
◆ Kg63 LLC.. F 216 941-7766
  Cleveland *(G-4287)*
▲ KMC Holdings LLC........................... C 419 238-2442
  Van Wert *(G-14920)*
Knight Manufacturing Co Inc................ G 740 676-5516
  Shadyside *(G-13146)*
Knight Manufacturing Co Inc................ F 740 676-9532
  Shadyside *(G-13147)*
Knowlton Manufacturing Co Inc........... F 513 631-7353
  Cincinnati *(G-3085)*
Kreider Corp.. D 937 325-8787
  Springfield *(G-13593)*
L & W Inc... E 734 397-6300
  Avon *(G-778)*
La Ganke & Sons Stamping Co.............. F 216 451-0278
  Columbia Station *(G-5013)*
Lakepark Industries Inc........................ C 419 752-4471
  Greenwich *(G-8068)*
Langenau Manufacturing Company....... E 216 651-3400
  Cleveland *(G-4310)*
Lewark Metal Spinning Inc................... E 937 275-3303
  Dayton *(G-6406)*
Lextech Industries Ltd......................... G 216 883-7900
  Cleveland *(G-4322)*
▲ Logan Machine Company.................. D 330 633-6163
  Akron *(G-223)*
▲ Long-Stanton Mfg Company.............. E 513 874-8020
  West Chester *(G-15458)*
Mahoning Valley Manufacturing........... E 330 537-4492
  Beloit *(G-1251)*
Mallory Pattern Works Inc.................... G 419 726-8001
  Toledo *(G-14377)*
Mansfield Industries Inc....................... F 419 524-1300
  Mansfield *(G-9686)*
Manufacturers Service Inc.................... E 216 267-3771
  Cleveland *(G-4355)*
Master Products Company.................... D 216 341-1740
  Cleveland *(G-4368)*

▲ Matco Tools Corporation................... B 330 929-4949
  Stow *(G-13708)*
Maumee Assembly & Stamping LLC..... B 419 304-2887
  Maumee *(G-10217)*
May Industries of Ohio Inc................... E 440 237-8012
  North Royalton *(G-11886)*
McAfee Tool & Die Inc.......................... E 330 896-9555
  Uniontown *(G-14787)*
McGlennon Metal Products Inc............. F 614 252-7114
  Columbus *(G-5552)*
McGregor Mtal Innsfllen Wrks L............ C 937 322-3880
  Springfield *(G-13607)*
▲ McGregor Mtal Yllow Sprng Wrks....... D 937 325-5561
  Springfield *(G-13604)*
Metal & Wire Products Company.......... F 330 332-1015
  Salem *(G-13015)*
Metal & Wire Products Company.......... E 330 332-9448
  Salem *(G-13016)*
Metal Fabricating Corporation.............. D 216 631-8121
  Cleveland *(G-4396)*
Metal Products Company..................... E 330 652-2558
  Powell *(G-12677)*
Metal Stampings Unlimited Inc............. F 937 328-0206
  Springfield *(G-13605)*
Mic-Ray Metal Products Inc.................. F 216 791-2206
  Cleveland *(G-4399)*
Mid-America Steel Corp....................... F 800 282-3466
  Cleveland *(G-4407)*
Middletown License Agency Inc............ G 513 422-7225
  Middletown *(G-10844)*
Midway Products Group Inc................. G 419 422-7070
  Findlay *(G-7537)*
Milark Industries Inc............................ D 419 524-7627
  Mansfield *(G-9693)*
Milark Industries Inc............................ D 419 524-7627
  Mansfield *(G-9694)*
Modern Engineering Inc....................... G 440 593-5414
  Conneaut *(G-5928)*
Modern Pipe Supports Corp................. F 216 361-1666
  Cleveland *(G-4418)*
Mohawk Manufacturing Inc.................. G 860 632-2345
  Mount Vernon *(G-11279)*
▼ Mohr Stamping Inc.......................... E 440 647-4316
  Wellington *(G-15317)*
Monode Steel Stamp Inc...................... F 440 975-8802
  Mentor *(G-10507)*
MSC Industries Inc.............................. G 440 474-8788
  Rome *(G-12849)*
◆ Mtd Holdings Inc.............................. B 330 225-2600
  Valley City *(G-14882)*
Nasg Auto-Seat Tec LLC....................... E 419 359-5954
  Ridgeville Corners *(G-12815)*
Nasg Ohio LLC..................................... F 419 634-3125
  Ada *(G-4)*
▲ Nasg Seating Bryan LLC................... D 419 633-0662
  Bryan *(G-1829)*
Nation Tool & Die Ltd.......................... E 419 822-5939
  Delta *(G-6789)*
Nebraska Industries Corp..................... F 419 335-6010
  Wauseon *(G-15270)*
New Bremen Machine & Tool Co........... E 419 629-3295
  New Bremen *(G-11405)*
Neway Stamping & Mfg Inc.................. D 440 951-8500
  Willoughby *(G-15958)*
Niles Manufacturing & Finshg............... C 330 544-0402
  Niles *(G-11678)*
Nn Metal Stampings LLC...................... E 419 737-2311
  Pioneer *(G-12493)*
Northern Stamping Co.......................... F 216 883-8888
  Cleveland *(G-4477)*
◆ Northern Stamping Co...................... C 216 883-8888
  Cleveland *(G-4478)*

Employee Codes: A=Over 500 employees, B=251-500
C=101-250, D=51-100, E=20-50, F=10-19, G=1-9

34 FABRICATED METAL PRODUCTS

Northwind Industries Inc .... E 216 433-0666
Cleveland (G-4481)

Northwood Industries Inc .... F 419 666-2100
Perrysburg (G-12404)

Norwood Medical LLC .... A 937 228-4101
Dayton (G-6476)

Norwood Tool Company .... G 937 228-4101
Dayton (G-6478)

Ohio Associated Entps LLC .... F 440 354-3148
Painesville (G-12253)

Ohio Department Public Safety .... G 440 943-5545
Willowick (G-16033)

◆ Ohio Gasket and Shim Co Inc .... E 330 630-0626
Akron (G-270)

Ohio Valley Manufacturing Inc .... D 419 522-5818
Mansfield (G-9707)

Omni Manufacturing Inc .... F 419 394-7424
Saint Marys (G-12963)

▲ Omni Manufacturing Inc .... D 419 394-7424
Saint Marys (G-12963)

Oneida Consumer LLC .... F 740 687-2500
Columbus (G-5641)

Orick Stamping Inc .... D 419 331-0600
Elida (G-7095)

Ottawa Products Co .... E 419 836-5115
Curtice (G-6057)

P M Motor Company .... F 440 327-9999
North Ridgeville (G-11852)

▲ Pacific Manufacturing Ohio Inc .... B 513 860-3900
Fairfield (G-7390)

Pacific Manufacturing Tenn Inc .... G 513 900-7862
Jackson (G-8721)

Parma Heights License Bureau .... G 440 888-0388
Cleveland (G-4535)

▼ Pax Machine Works Inc .... D 419 586-2337
Celina (G-2342)

▲ PE Usa LLC .... F 513 771-7374
Cincinnati (G-3244)

Peerless Metal Products Inc .... F 216 431-6905
Cleveland (G-4538)

Pennant Moldings Inc .... C 937 584-5411
Sabina (G-12890)

◆ Pentaflex Inc .... C 937 325-5551
Springfield (G-13617)

Perry Welding Service Inc .... F 330 425-2211
Twinsburg (G-14714)

Phillips Mch & Stamping Corp .... G 330 882-6714
New Franklin (G-11441)

▲ Plating Technology Inc .... D 937 268-6882
Dayton (G-6507)

Precision Metal Products Inc .... E 216 447-1900
Cleveland (G-4575)

Precision Metal Products Inc .... F 216 447-1900
Cleveland (G-4576)

Precision Pressed Powdered Met .... F 937 433-6802
Dayton (G-6517)

◆ Production Products Inc .... D 734 241-7242
Columbus Grove (G-5899)

Progress Tool & Stamping Inc .... E 419 628-2384
Minster (G-11059)

◆ Progressive Stamping Inc .... C 419 453-1111
Ottoville (G-12203)

Q Model Inc .... F 330 733-6545
Akron (G-288)

Qfm Stamping Inc .... F 330 337-3311
Columbiana (G-5048)

▲ Quaker Mfg Corp .... C 330 332-4631
Salem (G-13024)

Quality Fabricated Metals Inc .... E 330 332-7008
Salem (G-13025)

Quality Stamping Products Co .... F 216 441-2700
Cleveland (G-4609)

Quality Tool Company .... E 419 476-8228
Toledo (G-14444)

R K Metals Ltd .... E 513 874-6055
Fairfield (G-7402)

R L Rush Tool & Pattern Inc .... G 419 562-9849
Bucyrus (G-1866)

Racelite Southcoast Inc .... F 216 581-4600
Maple Heights (G-9759)

▲ Range Kleen Mfg Inc .... B 419 331-8000
Elida (G-7098)

Rapid Machine Inc .... F 419 737-2377
Pioneer (G-12497)

Ratliff Metal Spinning Company .... F 937 836-3900
Englewood (G-7240)

▲ RB&w Manufacturing LLC .... G 234 380-8540
Streetsboro (G-13787)

Ridge Tool Manufacturing Co .... E 440 323-5581
Elyria (G-7203)

Rjm Stamping Co .... F 614 443-1191
Columbus (G-5705)

Roemer Industries Inc .... D 330 448-2000
Masury (G-10158)

Ronfeldt Associates Inc .... D 419 382-5641
Toledo (G-14459)

Ronfeldt Manufacturing LLC .... D 419 382-5641
Toledo (G-14460)

Ronlen Industries Inc .... G 330 273-6468
Brunswick (G-1789)

S & K Products Company .... E 419 268-2244
Celina (G-2347)

S-P Company Inc .... D 330 782-5651
Columbiana (G-5050)

Saco Lowell Parts LLC .... E 330 794-1535
Akron (G-322)

Schott Metal Products Company .... E 330 773-7873
Akron (G-326)

Scott Fetzer Company .... C 216 267-9000
Cleveland (G-4678)

Seilkop Industries Inc .... E 513 761-1035
Cincinnati (G-3377)

Service Stampings Inc .... E 440 946-2330
Willoughby (G-15987)

Seven Ranges Mfg Corp .... E 330 627-7155
Carrollton (G-2315)

Shl Liquidation Automotive Inc .... D 330 558-2600
Valley City (G-14891)

Shl Liquidation Industries Inc .... D 440 647-2100
Wellington (G-15322)

◆ Shl Liquidation Industries Inc .... B 248 299-7500
Valley City (G-14893)

Shl Liquidation Jefferson Inc .... D
Valley City (G-14894)

Shl Liquidation Medina Inc C
Valley City (G-14895)

Smithville Mfg Co .... F 330 345-5818
Wooster (G-16173)

Soemhejee Inc .... E 419 298-2306
Edgerton (G-7080)

Spectrum Machine Inc .... F 330 626-3666
Streetsboro (G-13793)

Spirol Shim Corporation .... D 330 920-3655
Stow (G-13726)

Stamped Steel Products Inc .... F 330 538-3951
North Jackson (G-11791)

Stanley Industrial & Auto LLC .... C 614 755-7089
Dublin (G-6943)

◆ Steel Forming Inc .... C 714 532-6321
Youngstown (G-16448)

Stolle Machinery Company LLC .... C 937 497-5400
Sidney (G-13291)

Stolle Properties Inc .... A 513 932-8664
Blue Ash (G-1471)

▲ Stripmatic Products Inc .... E 216 241-7143
Cleveland (G-4740)

Suburban Manufacturing Co .... D 440 953-2024
Eastlake (G-7050)

Suburbanite Inc .... G 419 756-4390
Mansfield (G-9723)

◆ Sunfield Inc .... D 740 928-0405
Hebron (G-8364)

◆ Superior Metal Products Inc .... E 419 228-1145
Lima (G-9294)

▲ Superior Production LLC .... C 614 444-2181
Columbus (G-5800)

Supply Technologies LLC .... G 937 898-5795
Dayton (G-6601)

◆ Supply Technologies LLC .... C 440 947-2100
Cleveland (G-4755)

T & D Fabricating Inc .... E 440 951-5646
Eastlake (G-7051)

T and W Stamping Acquisition .... G 330 821-5777
Alliance (G-123)

T&W Stamping Inc .... G 330 270-0891
Austintown (G-755)

▲ Takk Industries Inc .... F 513 353-4306
Cleves (G-4966)

Takumi Stamping Inc .... C 513 642-0081
Fairfield (G-7413)

▲ Talan Products Inc .... D 216 458-0170
Cleveland (G-4766)

▲ Talent Tool & Die Inc .... E 440 239-8777
Berea (G-1295)

▲ Taylor Metal Products Co .... C 419 522-3471
Mansfield (G-9724)

TDS-Bf/Ls Holdings Inc .... E 440 327-5800
North Ridgeville (G-11862)

TEC Design & Manufacturing Inc .... F 937 435-2147
Dayton (G-6611)

Tech-Med Inc .... F 216 486-0900
Euclid (G-7301)

Ted J & Janice Hlavaty .... G 440 256-8524
Willoughby (G-16003)

Tenacity Manufacturing Company ...... F 513 821-0201
West Chester (G-15514)

Tfi Manufacturing Inc .... G 440 290-9411
Mentor (G-10575)

The Kordenbrock Tool and Die Co ..... F 513 326-4390
Cincinnati (G-3449)

The Reliable Spring Wire Frms .... E 440 365-7400
Elyria (G-7211)

The W L Jenkins Company .... F 330 477-3407
Canton (G-2244)

▲ Thk Manufacturing America Inc ...... C 740 928-1415
Hebron (G-8365)

▼ Toledo Metal Spinning Company ..... E 419 535-5931
Toledo (G-14498)

Toledo Tool and Die Co Inc .... F 419 266-8458
Toledo (G-14508)

▲ Toledo Tool and Die Co Inc .... B 419 476-4422
Toledo (G-14507)

Torrmetal LLC .... E 216 671-1616
Cleveland (G-4807)

Torrmetal Corporation .... E 216 671-1616
Cleveland (G-4808)

▲ Transue & Williams Stampg Corp ... E 330 821-5777
Austintown (G-756)

Tri-Craft Inc .... E 440 826-1050
Cleveland (G-4822)

▲ Triad Metal Products Company .... E 216 676-6505
Chagrin Falls (G-2430)

Triton Duro Werks Inc .... F 216 267-1117
Cleveland (G-4833)

▲ Trucut Incorporated .... D 330 938-9806
Sebring (G-13127)

SIC SECTION

34 FABRICATED METAL PRODUCTS

Twist Inc .... G 937 675-9581
  Jamestown *(G-8743)*

▲ Twist Inc .... C 937 675-9581
  Jamestown *(G-8742)*

United Die & Mfg Sales Co .... E 330 938-6141
  Sebring *(G-13128)*

Universal Metal Products Inc .... E 419 287-3223
  Pemberville *(G-12336)*

▲ Universal Metal Products Inc .... C 440 943-3040
  Wickliffe *(G-15857)*

V K C Inc .... F 440 951-9634
  Mentor *(G-10590)*

Valley Tool & Die Inc .... D 440 237-0160
  North Royalton *(G-11900)*

▼ Varbros LLC .... D 216 267-5200
  Cleveland *(G-4860)*

Verhoff Machine & Welding Inc .... C 419 596-3202
  Continental *(G-5939)*

Voisard Manufacturing Inc .... D 419 896-3191
  Shiloh *(G-13207)*

◆ Voss Industries LLC .... C 216 771-7655
  Cleveland *(G-4884)*

Washington Products Inc .... F 330 837-5101
  Massillon *(G-10154)*

Wasserstrom Co .... G 614 737-8568
  Columbus *(G-5864)*

▲ Wedge Products Inc .... B 330 405-4477
  Twinsburg *(G-14755)*

Weiss Industries Inc .... E 419 526-2480
  Mansfield *(G-9732)*

Welage Corporation .... F 513 681-2300
  Cincinnati *(G-3510)*

Westlake Tool & Die Mfg Co .... D 440 934-5305
  Avon *(G-791)*

▲ Whirlaway Corporation .... C 440 647-4711
  Wellington *(G-15325)*

Willow Hill Industries LLC .... G 440 942-3003
  Willoughby *(G-16018)*

▲ Winzeler Stamping Co .... E 419 485-3147
  Montpelier *(G-11147)*

Wire Products Company Inc .... G 216 267-0777
  Cleveland *(G-4912)*

Wisco Products Incorporated .... E 937 228-2101
  Dayton *(G-6658)*

▼ Witt Industries Inc .... D 513 871-5700
  Mason *(G-10071)*

▲ WLS Stamping Co .... D 216 271-5100
  Cleveland *(G-4914)*

Wtd Real Estate Inc .... D 440 934-5305
  Avon *(G-794)*

Yonghe Precision Castings Ohio .... G 330 447-6685
  Holland *(G-8540)*

▲ Ysk Corporation .... B 740 774-7315
  Chillicothe *(G-2542)*

3471 Plating and polishing

A & B Deburring Company .... F 513 723-0444
  Cincinnati *(G-2582)*

Abel Metal Processing Inc .... E 216 881-4156
  Cleveland *(G-3585)*

Acme Industrial Group Inc .... E 330 821-3900
  Alliance *(G-387)*

Advanced Surface Technology .... G 216 476-8600
  Cleveland *(G-3609)*

Aetna Plating Co .... F 216 341-9111
  Cleveland *(G-3612)*

Ak-Isg Steel Coating Company .... F 216 429-6901
  Cleveland *(G-3619)*

Akron Plating Co Inc .... F 330 773-6878
  Akron *(G-39)*

Allen Aircraft Products Inc .... E 330 296-9621
  Ravenna *(G-12702)*

Allen Aircraft Products Inc .... E 330 296-1531
  Ravenna *(G-12703)*

▲ Allen Aircraft Products Inc .... D 330 296-9621
  Ravenna *(G-12704)*

Aluminum Color Industries Inc .... E 330 536-6295
  Lowellville *(G-9510)*

Aluminum Extruded Shapes Inc .... C 513 563-2205
  Cincinnati *(G-2613)*

Amac Enterprises Inc .... F 216 362-1880
  Cleveland *(G-3645)*

▲ Amac Enterprises Inc .... C 216 362-1880
  Parma *(G-12286)*

American Indus Maintanence .... G 937 254-3400
  Dayton *(G-6201)*

American Quality Stripping Inc .... E 419 625-6288
  Sandusky *(G-13044)*

Anchor Fabricators Inc .... E 937 836-5117
  Clayton *(G-3563)*

Anodizing Specialists Inc .... E 440 951-0257
  Mentor *(G-10418)*

Anomatic Corporation .... B 740 522-2203
  Newark *(G-11564)*

◆ Anomatic Corporation .... E 740 522-2203
  New Albany *(G-11366)*

Applied Metals Tech Ltd .... E 216 741-3236
  Brooklyn Heights *(G-1683)*

Archer Custom Chrome LLC .... G 216 441-2795
  Westlake *(G-15734)*

Arem Co .... F 440 974-6740
  Mentor *(G-10423)*

Areway Acquisition Inc .... D 216 651-9022
  Brooklyn *(G-1675)*

ATI Flat Rlled Pdts Hldngs LLC .... F 330 875-2244
  Louisville *(G-9455)*

▲ Atom Blasting & Finishing Inc .... G 440 235-4765
  Columbia Station *(G-5006)*

◆ Automated Wheel LLC .... F 216 651-9022
  Cleveland *(G-3703)*

Automation Finishing Inc .... F 216 251-8805
  Cleveland *(G-3705)*

B & R Custom Chrome .... G 419 536-7215
  Toledo *(G-14203)*

▲ Badboy Blasters Incorporated .... F 330 454-2699
  Canton *(G-2042)*

Bar Processing Corporation .... F 330 872-0914
  Newton Falls *(G-11653)*

▲ Barker Products Company .... E
  Cleveland *(G-3721)*

Beringer Plating Inc .... G 330 633-8409
  Akron *(G-82)*

Best Plating Rack Corp .... F 440 944-3270
  Willowick *(G-16030)*

Boville Indus Coatings Inc .... E 330 669-8558
  Smithville *(G-13298)*

Bricker Plating Inc .... G 419 636-1990
  Bryan *(G-1810)*

Bright-On Polishing & Mfg LLC .... G 937 489-3985
  Sidney *(G-13229)*

Buffex Metal Finishing Inc .... F 216 631-2202
  Cleveland *(G-3770)*

Burton Metal Finishing Inc .... E 614 252-9523
  Columbus *(G-5222)*

Canton Plating Co Inc .... G 330 452-7808
  Canton *(G-2067)*

Carlisle and Finch Company .... E 513 681-6080
  Cincinnati *(G-2703)*

Carpe Diem Industries LLC .... D 419 358-0129
  Bluffton *(G-1502)*

Carpe Diem Industries LLC .... D 419 659-5639
  Columbus Grove *(G-5897)*

Centria Inc .... G 740 432-7351
  Cambridge *(G-1927)*

Champion Plating Inc .... F 216 881-1050
  Cleveland *(G-3806)*

Charles J Meyers .... G 513 922-2866
  Cincinnati *(G-2726)*

Chemical Methods Incorporated .... E 216 476-8400
  Brunswick *(G-1751)*

▲ Chemical Solvents Inc .... E 216 741-9310
  Cleveland *(G-3816)*

Chrome Deposit Corporation .... E 330 773-7800
  Akron *(G-109)*

Chrome Deposit Corporation .... E 513 539-8486
  Monroe *(G-11097)*

Chromium Corporation .... E 216 271-4910
  Cleveland *(G-3821)*

Cincinnati Abrasive Supply Co .... G 513 941-8866
  Cincinnati *(G-2738)*

Cincinnati Gearing Systems Inc .... D 513 527-8600
  Cincinnati *(G-2751)*

City Plating and Polishing LLC .... E 216 267-8158
  Cleveland *(G-3824)*

Cleveland Black Oxide Inc .... F 216 861-4431
  Cleveland *(G-3833)*

Cleveland LLC .... F 216 249-3098
  Cleveland *(G-3845)*

Cleveland Plating LLC .... G 216 249-0300
  Cleveland *(G-3849)*

▲ Cleveland-Cliffs Columbus LLC .... D 614 492-6800
  Richfield *(G-12784)*

Commercial Anodizing Co .... E 440 942-8384
  Willoughby *(G-15900)*

▲ Commercial Honing LLC .... D 330 343-8896
  Dover *(G-6813)*

Conley Group Inc .... E 330 372-2030
  Warren *(G-15158)*

Custom Nickel LLC .... F 937 222-1995
  Dayton *(G-6271)*

D-G Custom Chrome LLC .... G 513 531-1881
  Cincinnati *(G-2815)*

Derrick Company Inc .... E 513 321-8122
  Cincinnati *(G-2825)*

Diamond Hard Chrome Co Inc .... F 216 391-3618
  Mentor On The Lake *(G-10602)*

▲ Die Co Inc .... F 440 942-8856
  Eastlake *(G-7025)*

Durable Plating Co .... G 216 391-2132
  Cleveland *(G-3979)*

Duray Plating Company Inc .... E 216 941-5540
  Cleveland *(G-3980)*

E L Stone Company .... E 330 825-4565
  Norton *(G-11941)*

Electro Polish Company .... E 937 222-3611
  Dayton *(G-6314)*

Electro Prime Assembly Inc .... F 419 476-0100
  Rossford *(G-12863)*

Electro Prime Group LLC .... D 419 666-5000
  Rossford *(G-12864)*

▲ Electro Prime Group LLC .... D 419 476-0100
  Toledo *(G-14273)*

Electro-Metallics Co .... G 513 423-8091
  Middletown *(G-10820)*

Electrolizing Corp of Ohio .... E 800 451-8655
  Cleveland *(G-4005)*

Electrolizing Corporation Ohio .... F 216 451-8653
  Cleveland *(G-4006)*

Elyria Plating Corporation .... E 440 365-8300
  Elyria *(G-7145)*

◆ Epsilon Management Corporation ...... C 216 634-2500
  Cleveland *(G-4025)*

Equinox Enterprises LLC .... F 419 627-0022
  Sandusky *(G-13056)*

Erieview Metal Treating Co .... D 216 663-1780
  Cleveland *(G-4029)*

Employee Codes: A=Over 500 employees, B=251-500
C=101-250, D=51-100, E=20-50, F=10-19, G=1-9

34 FABRICATED METAL PRODUCTS

▲ Etched Metal Company .... E 440 248-0240
  Solon (G-13347)
Flight Bright Ltd .... F 216 663-6677
  Cleveland (G-4070)
Future Finishes Inc .... F 513 860-0020
  Hamilton (G-8209)
Gei of Columbiana Inc .... E 330 783-0270
  Youngstown (G-16364)
General Extrusions Intl LLC .... C 330 783-0270
  Youngstown (G-16365)
GRB Holdings Inc .... D 937 236-3250
  Dayton (G-6360)
▲ Guaranteed Fnshg Unlimited Inc .. E 216 252-8200
  Cleveland (G-4155)
H & R Metal Finishing Inc .... G 440 942-6656
  Eastlake (G-7033)
Hadronics Inc .... D 513 321-9350
  Cincinnati (G-2983)
Hale Performance Coatings Inc .... E 419 244-6451
  Toledo (G-14310)
Hall Company .... E 937 652-1376
  Urbana (G-14833)
Hartzell Mfg Co LLC .... E 937 859-5955
  Miamisburg (G-10643)
Hearn Plating Co Ltd .... F 419 473-9773
  Toledo (G-14313)
Hy-Blast Inc .... E 513 424-0704
  Middletown (G-10829)
Industrial Mill Maintenance .... E 330 746-1155
  Youngstown (G-16379)
Industrial Paint & Strip Inc .... E 419 568-2222
  Waynesfield (G-15296)
Ips Treatments Inc .... G 419 241-9955
  Toledo (G-14337)
J Horst Manufacturing Co .... D 330 828-2216
  Dalton (G-6133)
Jason Incorporated .... C 513 860-3400
  Hamilton (G-8224)
JM Hamilton Group Inc .... E 419 229-4010
  Lima (G-9258)
Jotco Inc .... G 513 721-4943
  Mansfield (G-9675)
Kel-Mar Inc .... E 419 806-4600
  Bowling Green (G-1569)
Kelly Plating Co .... E 216 961-1080
  Cleveland (G-4281)
Krendl Rack Co Inc .... G 419 667-4800
  Venedocia (G-14970)
Lake City Plating LLC .... E 440 964-3555
  Jefferson (G-8751)
Lake City Plating LLC .... C 440 964-3555
  Ashtabula (G-645)
Lake County Plating Corp .... F 440 255-8835
  Mentor (G-10489)
Ledbetter Partners LLC .... G 937 253-5311
  Dayton (G-6402)
Leonhardt Plating Company .... F 513 242-1410
  Cincinnati (G-3102)
Luke Engineering & Mfg Corp ...... E 330 925-3344
  Rittman (G-12824)
◆ Luke Engineering & Mfg Corp .... E 330 335-1501
  Wadsworth (G-15043)
Lustrous Metal Coatings Inc .... E 330 478-4653
  Canton (G-2147)
M I P Inc .... F 330 744-0215
  Youngstown (G-16392)
Master Chrome Service Inc .... F 216 961-2012
  Cleveland (G-4365)
McGean-Rohco Inc .... F 216 441-4900
  Newburgh Heights (G-11618)
◆ McGean-Rohco Inc .... D 216 441-4900
  Newburgh Heights (G-11619)

Mechanical Finishers Inc LLC .... E 513 641-5419
  Cincinnati (G-3138)
Mechanical Finishing Inc .... E 513 641-5419
  Cincinnati (G-3139)
▲ Mechanical Galv-Plating Corp ..... E 937 492-3143
  Sidney (G-13263)
Metal Finishers Inc .... F 937 492-9175
  Sidney (G-13264)
Metal Finishing Needs Ltd .... G 216 561-6334
  Middleburg Heights (G-10723)
Metal Seal & Products Inc .... C 440 946-8500
  Mentor (G-10502)
Metalbrite Polishing LLC .... F 937 278-9739
  Dayton (G-6435)
Miami Valley Polishing LL .... G 937 498-1634
  Sidney (G-13265)
Miami Valley Polishing LLC .... F 937 615-9353
  Sidney (G-13266)
▲ Miba Bearings US LLC .... B 740 962-4242
  McConnelsville (G-10000)
Micro Lapping & Grinding Co ...... E 216 267-6500
  Cleveland (G-4401)
Micro Metal Finishing LLC .... D 513 541-3095
  Cincinnati (G-3161)
Micro Products Co Inc .... E 440 943-0258
  Willoughby Hills (G-16025)
Microfinish LLC .... D 937 264-1598
  Vandalia (G-14953)
Microsheen Corporation .... F 216 481-5610
  Cleveland (G-4403)
▲ Microtek Finishing LLC .... E 513 766-5600
  West Chester (G-15571)
Mid-Ohio Finishing LLC .... G 330 466-9117
  Lakeville (G-8964)
Milestone Services Corp .... G 330 374-9988
  Akron (G-249)
Miller Plating LLC .... E 330 952-2550
  Medina (G-10354)
Mmf Inc .... G 614 252-2522
  Columbus (G-5573)
Monaco Plating Inc .... F 216 206-2360
  Cleveland (G-4419)
Moore Chrome Products Company . E 419 843-3510
  Sylvania (G-14006)
MPC Plastics Inc .... E 216 881-7220
  Cleveland (G-4425)
▲ MPC Plating LLC .... D 216 881-7220
  Cleveland (G-4426)
Mpc Plating Inc .... G 216 881-7220
  Brooklyn (G-1680)
National Aerospace Proc LLC ...... G 234 900-6497
  Stow (G-13712)
National Plating Corporation .... E 216 341-6707
  Cleveland (G-4438)
National Polishing Systems Inc ... E 330 659-6547
  Broadview Heights (G-1662)
Newbury Sndblst & Pntg Inc .... E 440 564-7204
  Newbury (G-11631)
Newsome & Work Metalizing Co . G 330 376-7144
  Akron (G-263)
Nicks Plating Co .... F 937 773-3175
  Piqua (G-12538)
Niles Manufacturing & Fnshg ...... C 330 544-0402
  Niles (G-11678)
▲ Novavision LLC .... D 419 354-1427
  Bowling Green (G-1577)
◆ Ohio Decorative Products LLC .... C 419 647-9033
  Spencerville (G-13487)
▲ Ohio Metal Products Company .... E 937 228-6101
  Dayton (G-6489)
Ohio Roll Grinding Inc .... E 330 453-1884
  Louisville (G-9466)

P & C Metal Polishing Inc .... F 513 771-9143
  Cincinnati (G-3232)
▼ P & J Industries Inc .... C 419 726-2675
  Toledo (G-14426)
P & L Heat Trting Grinding Inc .... D 330 746-1339
  Youngstown (G-16408)
Parker Rst-Proof Cleveland Inc ... E 216 481-6680
  Cleveland (G-4530)
Parker Trutec Incorporated .... D 937 653-8500
  Urbana (G-14846)
Paxos Plating Inc .... E 330 479-0022
  Canton (G-2195)
Piedmont Chemical Company Inc . G 937 428-6640
  Dayton (G-6505)
Pki Inc .... F 513 832-8749
  Cincinnati (G-3259)
Plasman AB LP .... C 216 252-2995
  Cleveland (G-4558)
Plate-All Metal Company Inc .... G 330 633-6166
  Akron (G-277)
▲ Plating Technology Inc .... F 937 268-6882
  Dayton (G-6507)
Polymet Recovery LLC .... G 330 630-9006
  Akron (G-281)
Porter-Guertin Co Inc .... F 513 241-7663
  Cincinnati (G-3266)
Precious Metal Plating Co .... F 440 585-7117
  Solon (G-13406)
Precision Finishing Systems .... E 937 415-5794
  Dayton (G-6511)
Precision Powder Coating Inc ..... E 330 478-0741
  Canton (G-2199)
Pro Line Collision and Pnt LLC .... G 937 223-7611
  Dayton (G-6526)
▲ Quality Plating Co .... E 216 361-0151
  Cleveland (G-4607)
R A Heller Company .... F 513 771-6100
  Cincinnati (G-3321)
Rack Processing Company Inc .... E 937 294-1911
  Moraine (G-11207)
Rack Processing Company Inc .... E 937 294-1911
  Moraine (G-11206)
Raf Acquisition Co .... E 440 572-5999
  Valley City (G-14888)
Rawac Plating Company .... F 937 322-7491
  Springfield (G-13624)
REA Polishing Inc .... D 419 470-0216
  Toledo (G-14450)
▲ Reifel Industries Inc .... D 419 737-2138
  Pioneer (G-12498)
Roberts Demand No 3 Corp .... E 216 641-0660
  Cleveland (G-4641)
Russell Products Co Inc .... G 330 535-3391
  Akron (G-315)
Russell Products Co Inc .... F 330 535-9246
  Akron (G-316)
◆ Russell Products Co Inc .... F 330 535-9246
  Akron (G-317)
S & K Metal Polsg & Buffing .... E 513 732-6662
  Batavia (G-946)
Sandwisch Enterprises Inc .... G 419 944-6446
  Toledo (G-14462)
▲ Sawyer Technical Materials LLC .. E 440 951-8770
  Willoughby (G-15985)
Scot Industries Inc .... D 330 262-7585
  Wooster (G-16169)
Shalmet Corporation .... E 440 236-8840
  Elyria (G-7204)
Sifco Applied Srfc Cncepts LLC ... E 216 524-0099
  Cleveland (G-4699)
◆ Sifco Industries Inc .... C 216 881-8600
  Cleveland (G-4700)

Smith Electro Chemical Co............................ E 513 351-7227
 Cincinnati *(G-3398)*

South Shore Finishers Inc........................... G 216 664-1792
 Cleveland *(G-4717)*

▼ Spectrum Metal Finishing Inc................... D 330 758-8358
 Youngstown *(G-16445)*

Springco Metal Coatings Inc....................... C 216 941-0020
 Cleveland *(G-4722)*

Stricker Refinishing Inc................................ G 216 696-2906
 Cleveland *(G-4738)*

Stuart-Dean Co Inc.................................... G 412 765-2752
 Cleveland *(G-4742)*

Sun Polishing Corp..................................... G 440 237-5525
 Cleveland *(G-4746)*

Superfinishers Inc...................................... G 330 467-2125
 Macedonia *(G-9582)*

Tablox Inc... G 440 953-1951
 Willoughby *(G-16002)*

Tatham Schulz Incorporated..................... E 216 861-4431
 Cleveland *(G-4767)*

Techmetals Inc... D 937 253-5311
 Dayton *(G-6612)*

Techniplate Inc... G 216 486-8825
 Westlake *(G-15795)*

Teikuro Corporation................................... E 937 327-3955
 Springfield *(G-13646)*

Thomas Steel Strip Corporation................ E 330 841-6429
 Warren *(G-15210)*

Toledo Metal Finishing Inc........................ G 419 661-1422
 Northwood *(G-11929)*

Trans-Acc Inc... E 513 793-6410
 Blue Ash *(G-1484)*

Tri-State Fabricators Inc............................ E 513 752-5005
 Amelia *(G-469)*

Tri-State Plating & Polishing..................... G 304 529-2579
 Proctorville *(G-12688)*

Tubetech Inc.. G 330 426-9476
 East Palestine *(G-7011)*

▲ Twist Inc... C 937 675-9581
 Jamestown *(G-8742)*

Twr Services LLC..................................... G 513 604-4796
 Cincinnati *(G-2575)*

U S Chrome Corporation Ohio.................. F 877 872-7716
 Dayton *(G-6638)*

United Surface Finishing Inc..................... E 330 453-2786
 Canton *(G-2256)*

Varland Metal Service Inc......................... E 513 861-0555
 Cincinnati *(G-3488)*

Vectron Inc... E 440 323-3369
 Elyria *(G-7216)*

Wagner Rustproofing Co Inc..................... E 216 361-4930
 Cleveland *(G-4891)*

Wall Polishing LLC.................................... G 937 698-1330
 Ludlow Falls *(G-9530)*

Westshore Metal Finishing LLC................ G 440 892-0774
 Westlake *(G-15803)*

▲ Whitaker Finishing LLC......................... F 419 666-7746
 Northwood *(G-11934)*

▲ Wieland Metal Svcs Foils LLC.............. D 330 823-1700
 Alliance *(G-437)*

Witt Enterprises Inc................................... E 440 992-8333
 Ashtabula *(G-665)*

Woodhill Plating Works Company............. E 216 883-1344
 Cleveland *(G-4920)*

Worthington Enterprises Inc..................... D 513 539-9291
 Monroe *(G-11121)*

◆ Worthington Steel Company.................. B 800 944-2255
 Worthington *(G-16223)*

Worthngton Smuel Coil Proc LLC............. E 330 963-3777
 Twinsburg *(G-14758)*

Yoder Industries Inc.................................. C 937 278-5769
 Dayton *(G-6662)*

Youngstown Hard Chrome Pltg Gr........... E 330 758-9721
 Youngstown *(G-16482)*

3479 Metal coating and allied services

A & E Powder Coating Ltd......................... G 937 525-3750
 Springfield *(G-13526)*

A Plus Powder Coaters Inc....................... E 330 482-4389
 Columbiana *(G-5025)*

AAA Galvanizing - Joliet Inc..................... F 513 871-5700
 Cincinnati *(G-2588)*

Advanced Technical Pdts Sup Co............. F 513 851-6858
 West Chester *(G-15362)*

Advantage Powder Coating Inc................ D 419 782-2363
 Defiance *(G-6667)*

Aesthetic Finishers Inc.............................. E 937 778-8777
 Piqua *(G-12501)*

Aesthetic Powder Coating LLC................. G 330 360-2422
 Youngstown *(G-16305)*

Ak-Isg Steel Coating Company................. F 216 429-6901
 Cleveland *(G-3619)*

Akron Steel Treating Co............................ E 330 773-8211
 Akron *(G-45)*

Alexander Pierce Corp.............................. F 330 798-9840
 Akron *(G-52)*

Allied Coating Corporation........................ F 937 615-0391
 Piqua *(G-12502)*

Alpha Coatings Inc.................................... C 419 435-5111
 Fostoria *(G-7627)*

Alsher APM.. G 216 496-8288
 Cleveland *(G-3641)*

American Metal Coatings Inc.................... E 216 451-3131
 Mentor *(G-10414)*

American Tchnical Coatings Inc............... G 440 401-2270
 Westlake *(G-15732)*

▲ Anest Iwata Usa Inc.............................. F 513 755-3100
 West Chester *(G-15536)*

▲ Aps-Materials Inc.................................. D 937 278-6547
 Dayton *(G-6210)*

Architctral Indus Met Fnshg LL................. F 440 963-0410
 Vermilion *(G-14971)*

Armoloy of Ohio Inc................................... E 937 323-8702
 Springfield *(G-13536)*

Art Galvanizing Works Inc........................ F 216 749-0020
 Cleveland *(G-3677)*

B Exterior Coatings LLC........................... G 937 561-2654
 Miamisburg *(G-10614)*

Bekaert Corporation.................................. E 330 683-5060
 Orrville *(G-12119)*

Bodycote Surface Tech Inc....................... F 513 770-4922
 Mason *(G-9963)*

Bodycote Surfc Tech Group Inc................ F 513 770-4900
 Mason *(G-9964)*

Boville Indus Coatings Inc........................ E 330 669-8558
 Smithville *(G-13298)*

BTA of Motorcars Inc................................ F 440 716-1000
 North Olmsted *(G-11821)*

Canfield Coating LLC................................ E 330 533-3311
 Canfield *(G-2002)*

Canfield Metal Coating Corp..................... D 330 702-3876
 Canfield *(G-2003)*

Canton Galvanizing................................... G 330 685-7316
 Canton *(G-2062)*

Canton Galvanizing LLC........................... E 330 685-9060
 Canton *(G-2063)*

▲ Cardinal Rubber Company.................... E 330 745-2191
 Barberton *(G-864)*

Carpe Diem Industries LLC...................... D 419 358-0129
 Bluffton *(G-1502)*

Carpe Diem Industries LLC...................... D 419 659-5639
 Columbus Grove *(G-5897)*

Cast Plus Inc... F 937 743-7278
 Franklin *(G-7665)*

◆ Ccpi Inc.. E 937 783-2476
 Blanchester *(G-1349)*

Central Aluminum Company LLC............. E 614 491-5700
 Obetz *(G-12057)*

Centria Inc... G 740 432-7351
 Cambridge *(G-1927)*

▲ Certified Tool & Grinding Inc................. G 937 865-5934
 Miamisburg *(G-10625)*

Cincinnati Thermal Spray Inc.................... E 513 793-1037
 Blue Ash *(G-1380)*

▲ Cincinnati Thermal Spray Inc................ F 513 793-0670
 Blue Ash *(G-1381)*

Classic Coatings....................................... G 330 421-3703
 North Olmsted *(G-11822)*

Cleveland Coatings Inc............................. G 330 467-4326
 Northfield *(G-11905)*

▲ Cleveland-Cliffs Columbus LLC............ D 614 492-6800
 Richfield *(G-12784)*

CLS Finishing Inc...................................... F 330 784-4134
 Tallmadge *(G-14026)*

Coating Systems Inc................................. F 513 367-5600
 Harrison *(G-8271)*

Columbus V&S Galvanizing LLC.............. D 614 449-8281
 Columbus *(G-5280)*

Continental Coatings LLC......................... G 216 429-1843
 Cleveland Heights *(G-4938)*

Corrotec Inc... E 937 325-3585
 Springfield *(G-13547)*

Creative Coatings LLC............................. F 216 226-9058
 Lakewood *(G-8973)*

Crown Group Co....................................... E 586 575-9800
 Lima *(G-9230)*

Cubbison Company................................... D 330 793-2481
 Youngstown *(G-16344)*

Dayton Coating Tech LLC......................... F 937 278-2060
 Dayton *(G-6277)*

De Vore Engraving Co............................... G 330 454-6820
 Canton *(G-2089)*

Doak Laser.. G 740 374-0090
 Marietta *(G-9790)*

Duffee Finishing Inc.................................. F 740 965-4848
 Sunbury *(G-13952)*

Dunn Industrial Services........................... G 513 738-4999
 Hamilton *(G-8200)*

Duracoat Powder Finishing Inc................. F 419 636-3111
 Bryan *(G-1816)*

E L Stone Company.................................. E 330 825-4565
 Norton *(G-11941)*

Elite Ceramics and Metals LLC................ G 330 787-2777
 Warren *(G-15166)*

Ellison Surface Tech - W LLC................... E 513 770-4900
 Mason *(G-9988)*

Enamelac Company.................................. F 216 481-8878
 Cleveland *(G-4014)*

◆ Enerfab LLC...B 513 641-0500
 Cincinnati *(G-2872)*

Epco Extrusion Painting Co...................... E 330 781-6100
 Youngstown *(G-16355)*

▲ Etched Metal Company......................... E 440 248-0240
 Solon *(G-13347)*

Etchworks.. G 330 274-8345
 Mantua *(G-9736)*

Euclid Refinishing Compnay Inc............... F 440 275-3356
 Austinburg *(G-745)*

Finishing Department................................ G 419 737-3334
 Pioneer *(G-12492)*

Gem Coatings Ltd..................................... F 740 589-2998
 Athens *(G-684)*

General Plastics North Corp..................... B 800 542-2466
 Cincinnati *(G-2945)*

George Manufacturing Inc........................ F 513 932-1067
 Lebanon *(G-9079)*

34 FABRICATED METAL PRODUCTS

▲ Glass Coatings & Concepts LLC....... E 513 539-5300
Monroe *(G-11108)*

▲ Godfrey & Wing Inc........................ E 330 562-1440
Aurora *(G-716)*

▲ Gramke Enterprises Ltd.................. G 614 252-8711
Columbus *(G-5410)*

Great Lakes Etching Finshg Co......... F 440 439-3624
Cleveland *(G-4143)*

Greber Machine Tool Inc.................. G 440 322-3685
Elyria *(G-7156)*

▲ Greenkote Usa Inc......................... G 440 243-2865
Brookpark *(G-1716)*

Greens Pure Coatings LLC............... G 513 907-2765
Amelia *(G-455)*

▲ Gwp Holdings Inc.......................... E 513 860-4050
Fairfield *(G-7364)*

Hadronics Inc................................... D 513 321-9350
Cincinnati *(G-2983)*

Hardline International Inc................. F 419 924-9556
West Unity *(G-13040)*

Hartzell Mfg Co LLC....................... F 937 859-5955
Miamisburg *(G-10643)*

Harwood Entp Holdings Inc.............. F 330 923-3256
Cuyahoga Falls *(G-6090)*

Hathaway Stamp Idntfction Cncn....... G 513 621-1052
Cincinnati *(G-2990)*

▲ Hemmelrath Coatings Inc............... F
Lima *(G-9250)*

Herbert E Orr Company Inc............. C 419 399-4866
Paulding *(G-12313)*

▲ Heritage Industrial Finshg Inc......... D 330 798-9840
Akron *(G-182)*

▲ High Tech Elastomers Inc.............. E 937 236-6575
Vandalia *(G-14943)*

Highway Safety Corp........................ F 740 387-6991
Marion *(G-9855)*

Hydro Extrusion Usa LLC................. C 888 935-5759
Sidney *(G-13255)*

▲ I V Miller & Sons........................... F 732 493-4040
Medina *(G-10336)*

Iconic Labs LLC............................... F 216 759-4040
Westlake *(G-15758)*

Imperial Metal Solutions LLC............ F 216 781-4094
Cleveland *(G-4219)*

Industrial and Mar Eng Svc Co......... F 740 694-0791
Fredericktown *(G-7749)*

Industrial Coating Tech Inc............... G 513 376-9945
Cincinnati *(G-3019)*

Ion Vacuum Ivac Tech Corp............. F 216 662-5158
Cleveland *(G-4235)*

Ionbond LLC..................................... F 216 831-0880
Cleveland *(G-4236)*

JM Hamilton Group Inc.................... E 419 229-4010
Lima *(G-9258)*

K-J Kustom Powder Coat.................. G 740 961-5267
Portsmouth *(G-12646)*

Kars Ohio LLC................................. G 614 655-1099
Pataskala *(G-12300)*

Kecamm LLC.................................... G 330 527-2918
Garrettsville *(G-7918)*

Kiss Custom Coatings LLC............... G 440 941-5002
Cleveland *(G-4295)*

Kyocera Hardcoating Tech Ltd.......... F 330 686-2136
Cuyahoga Falls *(G-6097)*

Legacy Finishing Inc......................... G 937 743-7278
Franklin *(G-7683)*

Lighting Systems Inc........................ G 513 372-3332
Blue Ash *(G-1423)*

Lisbon Powder Coating..................... G 234 567-1324
Lisbon *(G-9321)*

Logan Coatings LLC......................... F 740 380-0047
Logan *(G-9368)*

▼ Loroco Industries Inc..................... D 513 891-9544
Cincinnati *(G-3113)*

Master Marking Company Inc............ F 330 688-6797
Cuyahoga Falls *(G-6102)*

Material Sciences Corporation........... C 330 702-3882
Canfield *(G-2011)*

Material Sciences Corporation........... D 419 661-5905
Walbridge *(G-15084)*

Medina Powder Coating Corp............ G 330 952-1977
Medina *(G-10349)*

Medina Powder Group Inc................ G 330 952-2711
Medina *(G-10350)*

▲ Mesocoat Inc................................. F 216 453-0866
Euclid *(G-7286)*

Metaltek Industries Inc..................... F 937 342-1750
Springfield *(G-13606)*

Metokote Corporation....................... G 937 233-1565
Dayton *(G-6436)*

▲ Metokote Corporation.................... B 419 996-7800
Lima *(G-9107)*

Miamisburg Coating........................... F 937 866-1323
Miamisburg *(G-10660)*

Michael W Newton............................ G 740 352-9334
Lucasville *(G-9525)*

Mills Custom Coatings...................... G 330 280-0633
Massillon *(G-10128)*

Mmf Incorporated............................. F 614 252-0078
Columbus *(G-5574)*

Momentive Performance Mtls Inc...... A 740 928-7010
Hebron *(G-8349)*

Momentive Performance Mtls Inc...... C 440 878-5705
Richmond Heights *(G-12809)*

◆ Momentive Prfmce Mtls Qrtz Inc... D 440 878-5700
Strongsville *(G-13855)*

MSC Walbridge Coatings Inc............ F 419 666-6130
Walbridge *(G-15085)*

National Power Coating Ohio............. G 330 405-5587
Twinsburg *(G-14701)*

National Pwdr Coating Ohio LLC...... F 330 405-5587
Twinsburg *(G-14702)*

Niles Manufacturing & Finshg........... C 330 544-0402
Niles *(G-11678)*

Northeast Coatings Inc..................... F 330 784-7773
Tallmadge *(G-14040)*

◆ NSK Industries Inc....................... D 330 923-4112
Cuyahoga Falls *(G-6107)*

Office Magic Inc............................... F 510 782-6100
Medina *(G-10357)*

Ohio Coatings Company.................... D 740 859-5500
Yorkville *(G-16294)*

Ohio Galvanizing LLC....................... E 740 387-6474
Marion *(G-9869)*

Ohio Industrial Coating Corp............. G 567 230-6719
Tiffin *(G-14098)*

▲ Old World Stones........................... G 330 299-1128
Litchfield *(G-9329)*

Omni Manufacturing Inc.................... F 419 394-7424
Saint Marys *(G-12963)*

▲ Omni Manufacturing Inc................. D 419 394-7424
Saint Marys *(G-12962)*

Parker Rst-Proof Cleveland Inc........ E 216 481-6680
Cleveland *(G-4530)*

Parker Trutec Incorporated............... D 937 653-8500
Urbana *(G-14846)*

▲ Parker Trutec Incorporated............ D 937 323-8833
Springfield *(G-13615)*

Patricia M Bokesch.......................... G 330 793-4682
Youngstown *(G-16415)*

Pelletier Brothers Mfg Inc................ F 740 774-4704
Chillicothe *(G-2524)*

Perfection Finishers Inc.................... E 419 337-8015
Wauseon *(G-15272)*

Pioneer Custom Coating LLC............ G 419 737-3152
Pioneer *(G-12494)*

Pki Inc... F 513 832-8749
Cincinnati *(G-3259)*

Poly-Met Inc..................................... F 330 630-9006
Akron *(G-280)*

▲ Porcelain Steel Buildings Company.. D 614 228-5781
Columbus *(G-5683)*

▲ Powder Alloy Corporation............... E 513 984-4016
Loveland *(G-9499)*

Powder Coating Plus LLC................. F 419 446-0089
Archbold *(G-541)*

Precision Coatings Inc...................... F 216 441-0805
Cleveland *(G-4573)*

Precision Coatings Systems.............. E 937 642-4727
Marysville *(G-9931)*

Primax Coating.................................. G 513 455-0629
Cincinnati *(G-3275)*

▲ Pro-TEC Coating Company Inc....... C 419 943-1211
Leipsic *(G-9107)*

Pro-TEC Coating Company LLC........ D 419 943-1100
Leipsic *(G-9138)*

Procoat Painting Inc......................... G 513 735-2500
Batavia *(G-945)*

Production Paint Finishers Inc........... D 937 448-2627
Bradford *(G-1601)*

Progressive Mfg Co Inc.................... G 330 784-4717
Akron *(G-286)*

Progressive Powder Coating Inc....... E 440 974-3478
Mentor *(G-10537)*

Protech Powder Coatings Inc........... F 216 244-2761
Cleveland *(G-4594)*

Protective Coating Tech LLC............ G 419 340-8645
Maumee *(G-10226)*

Rack Coating Service Inc................. G 330 854-2869
Canal Fulton *(G-1974)*

Rack Processing Company Inc......... E 937 294-1911
Moraine *(G-11207)*

Raf Acquisition Co............................ E 440 572-5999
Valley City *(G-14888)*

▲ Reifel Industries Inc....................... D 419 737-2138
Pioneer *(G-12498)*

Reliable Coating Svc Co Inc............. G 513 217-4680
Middletown *(G-10855)*

Roban Inc... G 330 794-1059
Lakemore *(G-8958)*

Roemer Industries Inc....................... D 330 448-2000
Masury *(G-10158)*

Russell Products Co Inc................... F 330 535-9246
Akron *(G-316)*

◆ Russell Products Co Inc................ F 330 535-9246
Akron *(G-317)*

Russell T Bundy Associates Inc....... F 419 526-4454
Mansfield *(G-9716)*

Russell T Bundy Associates Inc....... G 740 965-3008
Sunbury *(G-13964)*

Ryder Engraving Inc......................... G 740 927-7193
Pataskala *(G-12307)*

Schnipke Engraving Co Inc............... C 419 453-3376
Ottoville *(G-12204)*

Scholz & Ey Engravers Inc............... F 614 444-8052
Columbus *(G-5752)*

Scioto Industrial Coatings Inc........... G 740 352-1011
Minford *(G-11043)*

Seacor Painting Corporation.............. G 330 755-6361
Campbell *(G-1966)*

Semper Quality Industry Inc............. G 440 352-8111
Mentor *(G-10552)*

Sermatech International.................... G 513 489-9800
Blue Ash *(G-1466)*

SH Bell Company.............................. E 412 963-9910
East Liverpool *(G-6999)*

SIC SECTION

34 FABRICATED METAL PRODUCTS

▲ Signature Partners Inc .... D 419 678-1400
  Coldwater *(G-5001)*
Simcote Inc .... F 740 382-5000
  Marion *(G-9882)*
Springco Metal Coatings Inc .... C 216 941-0020
  Cleveland *(G-4722)*
▲ Star Fab Inc .... C 330 533-9863
  Canfield *(G-2019)*
Steel Vly Indus Coatings LLC .... G 330 519-4348
  North Lima *(G-11813)*
Sterling Coating .... G 513 942-4900
  West Chester *(G-15510)*
◆ Synthomer USA LLC .... E 678 400-6655
  Beachwood *(G-1026)*
TDS-Bf/Ls Holdings Inc .... E 440 327-5800
  North Ridgeville *(G-11862)*
▲ Techneglas LLC .... F 419 873-2000
  Perrysburg *(G-12432)*
Terra Coat LLC .... F 216 254-8157
  Northfield *(G-11913)*
Thornton Powder Coatings Inc .... G 419 522-7183
  Mansfield *(G-9727)*
Topkote Inc .... G 440 428-0525
  Madison *(G-9594)*
Trans-Acc Inc .... E 513 793-6410
  Blue Ash *(G-1484)*
Treemen Industries Inc .... E 330 965-3777
  Boardman *(G-1519)*
Tri-State Fabricators Inc .... E 513 752-5005
  Amelia *(G-469)*
TS USA .... F 937 323-2556
  Springfield *(G-13651)*
Tsp Inc .... E 513 732-8900
  Batavia *(G-955)*
▲ Universal Rack & Eqp Co Inc .... D 330 963-6776
  Twinsburg *(G-14751)*
▲ Vacono America LLC .... E 216 938-7428
  Cleveland *(G-4859)*
Visionmark Nameplate Co LLC .... E 419 977-3131
  New Bremen *(G-11410)*
▲ Voigt & Schweitzer LLC .... F 614 449-8281
  Columbus *(G-5861)*
▲ Water Star Inc .... F 440 996-0800
  Concord Township *(G-5914)*
Westwood Finishing Company .... F 937 837-1488
  Dayton *(G-6653)*
▼ Witt Industries Inc .... D 513 871-5700
  Mason *(G-10071)*
Woodrow Manufacturing Co .... E 937 399-9333
  Springfield *(G-13657)*
Worldclass Processing Corp .... E
  Twinsburg *(G-14757)*
X-Treme Finishes Inc .... F 330 474-0614
  North Royalton *(G-11903)*
Yanfeng US Auto Intr Systems I .... D 419 633-1873
  Bryan *(G-1847)*

3482 Small arms ammunition

Ares Inc .... D 419 635-2175
  Port Clinton *(G-12615)*
BTR Enterprises LLC .... G 740 975-2526
  Newark *(G-11568)*
Galion LLC .... C 419 468-5214
  Galion *(G-7875)*
▲ Premier Shot Company .... G 330 405-0583
  Twinsburg *(G-14717)*
R & S Monitions Inc .... G 614 846-0597
  Columbus *(G-5706)*

3483 Ammunition, except for small arms, nec

L3harris Fzing Ord Systems Inc .... A 513 943-2000
  Cincinnati *(G-2570)*

▲ Marine Jet Power Inc .... G 614 759-9000
  Blacklick *(G-1339)*

3484 Small arms

▲ Acme Machine Automatics Inc .... E 419 453-0010
  Ottoville *(G-12197)*
Ares Inc .... D 419 635-2175
  Port Clinton *(G-12615)*
Highpoint Firearms .... E 419 747-9444
  Mansfield *(G-9668)*
Kaeper Machine Inc .... E 440 974-1010
  Mentor *(G-10486)*
Kelblys Rifle Range Inc .... G 330 683-4674
  North Lawrence *(G-11798)*
◆ Ohio Ordnance Works Inc .... E 440 285-3481
  Chardon *(G-2461)*
Reloading Supplies Corp .... G 440 228-0367
  Ashtabula *(G-658)*
Stealth Arms LLC .... G 419 925-7005
  Celina *(G-2351)*
TS Sales LLC .... F 727 804-8060
  Akron *(G-365)*
▲ Zshot Inc .... G 800 385-8581
  Columbus *(G-5894)*

3489 Ordnance and accessories, nec

Area 419 Firearms LLC .... F 419 830-8353
  Delta *(G-6779)*
Ares Inc .... D 419 635-2175
  Port Clinton *(G-12615)*
Excelitas Technologies Corp .... C 866 539-5916
  Miamisburg *(G-10639)*

3491 Industrial valves

4matic Valve Automtn Ohio LLC .... F 614 806-1221
  Columbus *(G-5077)*
▼ Akron Steel Fabricators Co .... E 330 644-0616
  Akron *(G-44)*
Alkon Corporation .... E 614 799-6650
  Dublin *(G-6858)*
▲ Alkon Corporation .... D 419 355-9111
  Fremont *(G-7762)*
Bosch Rexroth Corporation .... C 330 263-3300
  Wooster *(G-16106)*
◆ Clark-Reliance LLC .... C 440 572-1500
  Strongsville *(G-13821)*
Curtiss-Wright Flow Control .... E 440 838-7690
  Brecksville *(G-1611)*
Elite Industrial Controls Inc .... G 440 477-6923
  Grafton *(G-7999)*
Flow Technology Inc .... E 513 745-6000
  Cincinnati *(G-2910)*
▲ Hearth Products Controls Co .... F 937 436-9800
  Miamisburg *(G-10644)*
Honeywell International Inc .... A 937 484-2000
  Urbana *(G-14835)*
◆ Kaplan Industries Inc .... D 856 779-8181
  Harrison *(G-8282)*
Maass Midwest Mfg Inc .... G 419 894-6424
  Arcadia *(G-516)*
Meador Supply Company Inc .... F 330 405-4403
  Walton Hills *(G-15101)*
Nupro Company .... D 440 951-9729
  Willoughby *(G-15962)*
Parker-Hannifin Corporation .... E 419 542-6611
  Hicksville *(G-8377)*
Parker-Hannifin Corporation .... F 937 644-3915
  Marysville *(G-9930)*
Pima Valve LLC .... D 330 337-9535
  Salem *(G-13022)*
▲ Richards Industrials Inc .... D 513 533-5600
  Cincinnati *(G-3339)*

◆ Rogers Industrial Products Inc .... E 330 535-3331
  Akron *(G-309)*
S DH Flow Contro Ls LLC .... G 513 834-8432
  Amelia *(G-463)*
Seawin Inc .... E 419 355-9111
  Fremont *(G-7809)*
Sherwood Valve LLC .... E 216 264-5023
  Cleveland *(G-4697)*
▲ Superb Industries Inc .... D 330 852-0500
  Sugarcreek *(G-13943)*
Swagelok Company .... F 440 248-4600
  Solon *(G-13427)*
Swagelok Company .... E 440 349-5652
  Solon *(G-13429)*
Swagelok Company .... E 440 349-5836
  Solon *(G-13430)*
Swagelok Company .... D 440 248-4600
  Willoughby Hills *(G-16029)*
◆ Swagelok Company .... A 440 248-4600
  Solon *(G-13428)*
▲ Tylok International Inc .... D 216 261-7310
  Cleveland *(G-4840)*
Valv-Trol LLC .... F 330 686-2800
  Stow *(G-13736)*
Vickers International Inc .... E 419 867-2200
  Maumee *(G-10244)*
Watts Water .... F 614 491-5143
  Groveport *(G-8167)*
◆ Waxman Industries Inc .... C 440 439-1830
  Bedford Heights *(G-1181)*
◆ William Powell Company .... D 513 852-2000
  Cincinnati *(G-3519)*
Xomox Corporation .... G 513 745-6000
  Blue Ash *(G-1497)*
Xomox Corporation .... E 936 271-6500
  Cincinnati *(G-3531)*
Xomox Pft Corp .... B 936 271-6500
  Cincinnati *(G-3532)*

3492 Fluid power valves and hose fittings

▲ Ace Manufacturing Company .... E 513 541-2490
  West Chester *(G-15360)*
Aerocontrolex Group Inc .... D 216 291-6025
  South Euclid *(G-13457)*
▲ Alkon Corporation .... D 419 355-9111
  Fremont *(G-7762)*
▲ Amfm Inc .... F 440 953-4545
  Willoughby *(G-15877)*
Cho Bedford Inc .... D 330 343-8896
  Dover *(G-6811)*
Custom Cltch Jint Hydrlics Inc .... F 216 431-1630
  Cleveland *(G-3923)*
▲ Dana Limited .... B 419 887-3000
  Maumee *(G-10186)*
Danfoss Power Solutions II LLC .... G 419 238-1190
  Van Wert *(G-14913)*
Dixon Valve & Coupling Co LLC .... F 330 425-3000
  Twinsburg *(G-14652)*
DNC Hydraulics LLC .... F 419 963-2800
  Rawson *(G-12743)*
▲ Dyna-Flex Inc .... F 440 946-9424
  Painesville *(G-12230)*
Eaton Aeroquip LLC .... A 419 891-7775
  Maumee *(G-10201)*
◆ Eaton Aeroquip LLC .... C 440 523-5000
  Cleveland *(G-3991)*
◆ Eaton Corporation .... B 440 523-5000
  Cleveland *(G-3994)*
Freudenberg-Nok General Partnr ...... C 419 427-5221
  Findlay *(G-7511)*
Hombre Capital Inc .... F 440 838-5335
  Brecksville *(G-1620)*

Employee Codes: A=Over 500 employees, B=251-500
C=101-250, D=51-100, E=20-50, F=10-19, G=1-9

34 FABRICATED METAL PRODUCTS

▲ Hunt Valve Company Inc .... D 330 337-9535
Salem (G-13004)

▲ Hy-Production Inc .... C 330 273-2400
Valley City (G-14873)

▲ Hydac Technology Corp .... F 610 266-0100
Wooster (G-16131)

Hydraulic Manifolds USA LLC .... E 973 728-1214
Stow (G-13702)

Hydraulic Parts Store Inc .... E 330 364-6667
New Philadelphia (G-11505)

◆ Hydrotech Inc .... D 888 651-5712
West Chester (G-15563)

▲ Ic-Fluid Power Inc .... F 419 661-8811
Rossford (G-12866)

▼ Industrial Connections Inc .... G 330 274-2155
Mantua (G-9737)

◆ Kirtland Capital Partners LP .... E 216 593-0100
Beachwood (G-993)

Malabar .... E 419 866-6301
Owanton (O-10970)

Mid-State Sales Inc .... G 330 744-2158
Youngstown (G-16400)

▲ Mid-State Sales Inc .... D 614 864-1811
Columbus (G-5564)

National Aviation Products Inc .... G 330 688-6494
Stow (G-13713)

▲ National Machine Company .... C 330 688-6494
Stow (G-13714)

Netherland Rubber Company .... F 513 733-0883
Cincinnati (G-3187)

Ohio Hydraulics Inc .... E 513 771-2590
Cincinnati (G-3215)

Omega 1 Inc .... F 216 663-8424
Willoughby (G-15965)

Parker-Hannifin Corporation .... D 937 456-5571
Eaton (G-7067)

Parker-Hannifin Corporation .... E 419 542-6611
Hicksville (G-8377)

Parker-Hannifin Corporation .... B 440 943-5700
Wickliffe (G-15846)

▲ Parker-Hannifin Corporation .... A 216 896-3000
Cleveland (G-4532)

Pima Valve LLC .... D 330 337-9535
Salem (G-13022)

Pioneer Solutions LLC .... E 216 383-3400
Euclid (G-7292)

Poc Hydraulic Technologies LLC .... G 614 761-8555
Dublin (G-6924)

Precision Engineered Components .. F 614 436-0392
Worthington (G-16207)

◆ Pressure Connections Corp .... D 614 863-6930
Columbus (G-5689)

▲ Quality Machining and Mfg Inc .... F 419 899-2543
Sherwood (G-13202)

SMC Corporation of America .... F 330 659-2006
Richfield (G-12798)

▲ SSP Fittings Corp .... D 330 425-4250
Twinsburg (G-14736)

State Metal Hose Inc .... G 614 527-4700
Hilliard (G-8443)

Superior Holding LLC .... E 216 651-9400
Cleveland (G-4748)

Superior Products LLC .... D 216 651-9400
Cleveland (G-4751)

Swagelok Company .... E 440 349-5836
Solon (G-13430)

▲ Taiyo America Inc .... F 419 300-8811
Saint Marys (G-12968)

▲ The Sheffer Corporation .... D 513 489-9770
Blue Ash (G-1481)

▲ Thogus Products Company .... D 440 933-8450
Avon Lake (G-825)

Transdigm Inc .... F 216 291-6025
Cleveland (G-4815)

▲ Tylok International Inc .... D 216 261-7310
Cleveland (G-4840)

United States Controls .... G 330 758-1147
Youngstown (G-16464)

US Controls Acquisition Ltd .... G 330 758-1147
Poland (G-12612)

Valv-Trol LLC .... F 330 686-2800
Stow (G-13736)

Zaytran Inc .... E 440 324-2814
Elyria (G-7220)

3493 Steel springs, except wire

Betts Co DBA Betts Hd .... G 330 533-0111
Canfield (G-2001)

▲ Dayton Progress Corporation ...... A 937 859-5111
Dayton (G-6288)

Elyria Spring & Specialty Inc .... F 440 323-5502
Elyria (O-7140)

Golden Spring Company Inc .... G 937 848-2513
Bellbrook (G-1193)

Hendrickson International Corp ..... D 740 929-5600
Hebron (G-8343)

Jamestown Industries Inc .... D 330 779-0670
Youngstown (G-16383)

▲ Kern-Liebers Usa Inc .... D 419 865-2437
Holland (G-8517)

▲ Liteflex Disc LLC .... D 937 836-7025
Dayton (G-6412)

Marik Spring Inc .... E 330 564-0617
Tallmadge (G-14037)

Matthew Warren Inc .... E 614 418-0250
Columbus (G-5547)

◆ Napoleon Spring Works Inc .... C 419 445-1010
Archbold (G-537)

Peterson American Corporation .... E 419 867-8711
Holland (G-8523)

Service Spring Corp .... G 419 867-0212
Maumee (G-10230)

▼ Service Spring Corp .... D 419 838-6081
Maumee (G-10231)

▲ Solon Manufacturing Company ... E 440 286-7149
Chardon (G-2468)

Tadd Spring Co Inc .... F 440 572-1313
Strongsville (G-13889)

Zsi Manufacturing Inc .... F 440 266-0701
Concord Township (G-5915)

3494 Valves and pipe fittings, nec

16363 Sca Inc .... G 330 448-0000
Masury (G-10155)

Adaptall America Inc .... F 330 425-4114
Twinsburg (G-14624)

◆ Alloy Precision Tech Inc .... D 440 266-7700
Mentor (G-10412)

Amaltech Inc .... G 440 248-7500
Solon (G-13311)

▲ Anchor Flange Company .... D 513 527-3512
Cincinnati (G-2626)

Bay Corporation .... E 440 835-2212
Westlake (G-15735)

Blackmer Pump .... F 616 248-9239
West Chester (G-15380)

Bosch Rexroth Corporation .... C 330 263-3300
Wooster (G-16106)

Bowden Manufacturing Corp .... E 440 946-1770
Willoughby (G-15891)

Bowes Manufacturing Inc .... E 216 378-2110
Solon (G-13321)

Calvin J Magsig .... G 419 862-3311
Elmore (G-7100)

Campion Pipe Fitting .... G 740 627-1125
Steubenville (G-13664)

Crane Pumps & Systems Inc .... C 937 773-2442
Piqua (G-12508)

Cylinders and Valves Inc .... G 440 238-7343
Strongsville (G-13826)

Drainage Pipe & Fittings LLC .... G 419 538-6337
Ottawa (G-12179)

Eaton Corporation .... E 330 274-0743
Aurora (G-712)

Edward W Daniel LLC .... E 440 647-1960
Wellington (G-15306)

▲ Fcx Performance Inc .... E 614 253-1996
Columbus (G-5373)

General Aluminum Mfg Company .. C 419 739-9300
Wapakoneta (G-15115)

▲ General Plug and Mfg Co .... C 440 926-2411
Grafton (G-8000)

Greater Cleve Pipe Ftting Fund ..... F 216 524-8334
Cleveland (O-4140)

H P E Inc .... G 330 833-3161
Massillon (G-10104)

◆ H-P Products Inc .... C 330 875-5556
Louisville (G-9459)

Impaction Co .... G 440 349-5652
Solon (G-13367)

Insulpro Inc .... E 614 262-3768
Columbus (G-5469)

◆ Kirtland Capital Partners LP .... E 216 593-0100
Beachwood (G-993)

▲ Knappco Corporation .... C 513 870-3100
West Chester (G-15455)

Lsq Manufacturing Inc .... F 330 725-4905
Medina (G-10345)

Mack Iron Works Company .... E 419 626-3712
Sandusky (G-13078)

▲ Mid-State Sales Inc .... D 614 864-1811
Columbus (G-5564)

Northcoast Valve and Gate Inc ...... G 440 392-9910
Mentor (G-10512)

Nupro Company .... D 440 951-9729
Willoughby (G-15962)

▲ Opw Engineered Systems Inc ..... E 888 771-9438
West Chester (G-15471)

Parker-Hannifin Corporation .... C 614 279-7070
Columbus (G-5656)

Parker-Hannifin Corporation .... D 937 456-5571
Eaton (G-7067)

Piersante and Associates Inc .... G 330 533-9904
Canfield (G-2014)

Pima Valve LLC .... D 330 337-9535
Salem (G-13022)

Precision McHning Cnnction LLC ... F 440 943-3300
Wickliffe (G-15849)

◆ Pressure Connections Corp .... D 614 863-6930
Columbus (G-5689)

▲ Richards Industrials Inc .... E 513 533-5600
Cincinnati (G-3339)

▲ Robeck Fluid Power Co .... D 330 562-1140
Aurora (G-734)

▲ Spirex Corporation .... C 330 726-1166
Youngstown (G-16446)

▲ SSP Fittings Corp .... D 330 425-4250
Twinsburg (G-14736)

Stelter and Brinck Inc .... E 513 367-9300
Harrison (G-8293)

Stephens Pipe & Steel LLC .... C 740 869-2257
Mount Sterling (G-11257)

Superior Holding LLC .... E 216 651-9400
Cleveland (G-4748)

Superior Products LLC .... D 216 651-9400
Cleveland (G-4751)

SIC SECTION
34 FABRICATED METAL PRODUCTS

Swagelok Company.............................. F 440 442-6611
  Cleveland *(G-4757)*

Swagelok Company.............................. E 440 473-1050
  Cleveland *(G-4758)*

Swagelok Company.............................. E 440 349-5652
  Solon *(G-13429)*

Swagelok Company.............................. E 440 349-5836
  Solon *(G-13430)*

Swagelok Company.............................. D 440 349-5934
  Solon *(G-13431)*

◆ Swagelok Company.............................. A 440 248-4600
  Solon *(G-13428)*

▲ TCH Industries Incorporated............ F 330 487-5155
  Twinsburg *(G-14741)*

▲ The Sheffer Corporation....................... D 513 489-9770
  Blue Ash *(G-1481)*

◆ Thogus Products Company................... D 440 933-8850
  Avon Lake *(G-825)*

▲ Tylok International Inc............................ D 216 261-7310
  Cleveland *(G-4840)*

US Fittings Inc... F 234 212-9420
  Twinsburg *(G-14752)*

Victaulic... G 513 479-1764
  Loveland *(G-9508)*

◆ Waxman Industries Inc........................... C 440 439-1830
  Bedford Heights *(G-1181)*

Wells Inc.. F 419 457-2611
  Risingsun *(G-12820)*

◆ William Powell Company........................ D 513 852-2000
  Cincinnati *(G-3519)*

Xomox Corporation................................. E 936 271-6500
  Cincinnati *(G-3531)*

Xomox Pft Corp....................................... B 936 271-6500
  Cincinnati *(G-3532)*

3495 Wire springs

Allied Shipping and Packa...................... F 937 222-7422
  Moraine *(G-11155)*

Aswpengg LLC.. E 216 292-4620
  Bedford Heights *(G-1164)*

B & P Spring Production Co.................... E 216 486-4260
  Cleveland *(G-3714)*

Barnes Group Inc.................................... G 440 526-5900
  Brecksville *(G-1607)*

Barnes Group Inc.................................... C 419 891-9292
  Maumee *(G-10168)*

▲ Bloomngburg Spring Wire Form I....... E 740 437-7614
  Bloomingburg *(G-1353)*

▲ Dayton Progress Corporation.............. A 937 859-5111
  Dayton *(G-6288)*

Elyria Spring & Specialty Inc................... F 440 323-5502
  Elyria *(G-7146)*

Elyria Spring Spclty Holdg Inc................. F 440 323-5502
  Elyria *(G-7147)*

Euclid Spring Co..................................... E 440 943-3213
  Wickliffe *(G-15832)*

Kern-Liebers Texas Inc.......................... F 419 865-2437
  Holland *(G-8516)*

▲ Kern-Liebers Usa Inc............................ D 419 865-2437
  Holland *(G-8517)*

Malabar... E 419 866-6301
  Swanton *(G-13978)*

Matthew Warren Inc................................ E 614 418-0250
  Columbus *(G-5547)*

Ohio Wire Form & Spring Co.................. E 614 444-3676
  Columbus *(G-5630)*

Six C Fabrication Inc.............................. B 330 296-5594
  Ravenna *(G-12734)*

▲ Solon Manufacturing Company........... E 440 286-7149
  Chardon *(G-2468)*

▼ Spring Team Inc.................................... D 440 275-5981
  Austinburg *(G-750)*

Spring Works Incorporated..................... E 614 351-9345
  Columbus *(G-5788)*

▲ Stalder Spring Works Inc.................... E 937 322-6120
  Springfield *(G-13637)*

▲ Supro Spring & Wire Forms Inc......... E 330 722-5628
  Medina *(G-10380)*

Tadd Spring Co Inc................................ F 440 572-1313
  Strongsville *(G-13889)*

The Reliable Spring Wire Frms............. E 440 365-7400
  Elyria *(G-7211)*

Timac Manufacturing Company............. F 937 372-3305
  Xenia *(G-16275)*

Trupoint Products LLC.......................... F 330 204-3302
  Sugarcreek *(G-13945)*

Twist Inc... G 937 675-9581
  Jamestown *(G-8743)*

▲ Twist Inc.. C 937 675-9581
  Jamestown *(G-8742)*

Wire Products Company Inc.................. G 216 267-0777
  Cleveland *(G-4912)*

▼ Yost Superior Co................................. E 937 323-7591
  Springfield *(G-13658)*

3496 Miscellaneous fabricated wire products

A K Athletic Equipment Inc.................... E 614 920-3069
  Canal Winchester *(G-1977)*

Adcura Mfg... G 937 222-3800
  Dayton *(G-6184)*

Advance Wire Forming Inc.................... F 216 432-3250
  Cleveland *(G-3605)*

Akron Belting & Supply Company......... G 330 633-8212
  Akron *(G-27)*

Alabama Sling Center Inc...................... E 440 239-7000
  Cleveland *(G-3620)*

◆ Alcan Corporation................................ E 440 460-3307
  Cleveland *(G-3622)*

▲ Amanda Bent Bolt Company.............. C 740 385-6893
  Logan *(G-9358)*

▲ Ametco Manufacturing Corp.............. E 440 951-4300
  Willoughby *(G-15876)*

Assembly Specialty Pdts Inc................. E 216 676-5600
  Cleveland *(G-3693)*

Bekaert Corporation............................... F 330 683-5060
  Orrville *(G-12118)*

▲ Bloomngburg Spring Wire Form I..... E 740 437-7614
  Bloomingburg *(G-1353)*

▲ Brushes Inc.. F 216 267-8084
  Cleveland *(G-3767)*

Busch & Thiem Inc................................. E 419 625-7515
  Sandusky *(G-13047)*

C & F Fabrications Inc........................... E 937 666-3234
  East Liberty *(G-6984)*

▲ C C M Wire Inc.................................. E 330 425-3421
  Twinsburg *(G-14638)*

Canron Manufacturing Inc...................... F 330 497-1131
  Greentown *(G-8034)*

Cleveland Wire Cloth Mfg LLC.............. E 216 341-1832
  Cleveland *(G-3861)*

Contitech Usa Inc................................... D 937 644-8900
  Marysville *(G-9906)*

Conveyor Guard Corp........................... G 614 337-1727
  Columbus *(G-5292)*

Dayton Wire Products Inc...................... E 937 236-8000
  Dayton *(G-6291)*

Diamond Child Clothing Co LLC............ G 614 575-6238
  Blacklick *(G-1335)*

▲ Die Co Inc... E 440 942-8856
  Eastlake *(G-7025)*

Dribble Creek Inc................................... F 440 439-8650
  Twinsburg *(G-14654)*

Dysinger Incorporated............................ E 937 297-7761
  Dayton *(G-6310)*

Efco Corp.. G 614 876-1226
  Columbus *(G-5347)*

Elyria Spring & Specialty Inc................... F 440 323-5502
  Elyria *(G-7146)*

Engineered Wire Products Inc............... E 330 469-6958
  Warren *(G-15167)*

▲ Engineered Wire Products Inc.......... C 419 294-3817
  Upper Sandusky *(G-14808)*

▲ Ever Roll Specialties Co.................... E 937 964-1302
  Springfield *(G-13561)*

Fence One Inc....................................... F 216 441-2600
  Cleveland *(G-4056)*

◆ G & S Titanium Inc.............................. E 330 263-0564
  Wooster *(G-16122)*

Gateway Con Forming Svcs Inc........... D 513 353-2000
  Miamitown *(G-10708)*

General Chain & Mfg Corp.................... E 513 541-6005
  Cincinnati *(G-2940)*

▼ Helical Line Products Co................... E 440 933-9263
  Avon Lake *(G-811)*

Illinois Tool Works Inc............................ E 216 292-7161
  Bedford *(G-1127)*

Interntnal Tchncal Catings Inc............... C 800 567-6592
  Columbus *(G-5476)*

KEffs Inc... A 614 443-0586
  Columbus *(G-5505)*

Kimmatt Corp.. E 937 228-3811
  West Alexandria *(G-15342)*

Malin Wire Co... E 216 267-9080
  Cleveland *(G-4352)*

◆ Manufacturers Equipment Co............ F 513 424-3573
  Middletown *(G-10841)*

Marik Spring Inc..................................... E 330 564-0617
  Tallmadge *(G-14037)*

Mason Company LLC............................ E 937 780-2321
  Leesburg *(G-9125)*

▲ May Conveyor Inc............................. F 440 237-8012
  North Royalton *(G-11885)*

Mazzella Jhh Company Inc................... D 440 239-7000
  Cleveland *(G-4374)*

▲ Mazzella Lifting Tech Inc................... D 440 239-7000
  Cleveland *(G-4375)*

McM Ind Co Inc..................................... F 216 641-6300
  Cleveland *(G-4383)*

◆ McM Ind Co Inc................................. F 216 292-4506
  Cleveland *(G-4382)*

Meese Inc.. F 440 998-1202
  Ashtabula *(G-647)*

Merchants Metals LLC........................... E 513 942-0268
  West Chester *(G-15463)*

Microplex Inc... E 330 498-0600
  North Canton *(G-11743)*

◆ Mid-West Fabricating Co................... C 740 969-4411
  Amanda *(G-446)*

▼ Midwestern Industries Inc.................. D 330 837-4203
  Massillon *(G-10127)*

▲ Mueller Electric Company Inc........... E 216 771-5225
  Akron *(G-256)*

▲ Ofco Inc... D 740 622-5922
  Coshocton *(G-5989)*

Ohio Wire Form & Spring Co................ E 614 444-3676
  Columbus *(G-5630)*

◆ Options Plus Incorporated................. F 740 694-9811
  Fredericktown *(G-7752)*

Panacea Products Corporation............. E 614 429-6320
  Columbus *(G-5653)*

◆ Panacea Products Corporation......... E 614 850-7000
  Columbus *(G-5652)*

Pennant Inc.. E 937 584-5411
  Columbus *(G-5666)*

Peterson American Corporation............ E 419 867-8711
  Holland *(G-8523)*

Employee Codes: A=Over 500 employees, B=251-500
C=101-250, D=51-100, E=20-50, F=10-19, G=1-9

34 FABRICATED METAL PRODUCTS

▲ Polymet Corporation .... E 513 874-3586
West Chester (G-15482)

◆ Premier Manufacturing Corp .... C 216 941-9700
Cleveland (G-4581)

Providence REES Inc .... F 614 833-6231
Columbus (G-5696)

▲ Pwp Inc .... E 216 251-2181
Ashland (G-607)

▲ Qualtek Electronics Corp .... C 440 951-3300
Mentor (G-10541)

R G Smith Company .... D 330 456-3415
Canton (G-2207)

◆ Rjs Corporation .... E 330 896-2387
Akron (G-306)

Roy I Kaufman Inc .... G 740 382-0643
Marion (G-9877)

▲ Royal Wire Products Inc .... D 440 237-8787
North Royalton (G-11892)

Saraga Northern Lights LLC .... F 614 928-3100
Columbus (G-3747)

▲ Saxon Products Inc .... G 419 241-6771
Toledo (G-14463)

Schweizer Dipple Inc .... D 440 786-8090
Cleveland (G-4676)

▼ Spring Team Inc .... D 440 275-5981
Austinburg (G-750)

Starr Fabricating Inc .... D 330 394-9891
Vienna (G-15004)

Stephens Pipe & Steel LLC .... C 740 869-2257
Mount Sterling (G-11257)

Stolle Machinery Company LLC .... C 937 497-5400
Dayton (G-6596)

▼ Stud Welding Associates Inc .... D 440 783-3160
Strongsville (G-13887)

▼ T & R Welding Systems Inc .... F 937 228-7517
Dayton (G-6606)

▲ Therm-O-Link Inc .... D 330 527-2124
Garrettsville (G-7926)

Tom Thumb Clip Co Inc .... F 440 953-9606
Willoughby (G-16008)

Top Knotch Products Inc .... G 419 543-2266
Cleveland (G-4804)

▲ Tyler Haver Inc .... E 440 974-1047
Mentor (G-10585)

Unified Scrning Crshing - OH I ...... G 937 836-3201
Englewood (G-7246)

Utility Wire Products Inc .... F 216 441-2180
Cleveland (G-4858)

▲ Ver-Mac Industries Inc .... E 740 397-6511
Mount Vernon (G-11299)

▼ W J Egli Company Inc .... F 330 823-3666
Alliance (G-435)

West Equipment Company Inc .... G 419 698-1601
Toledo (G-14522)

Willison Wred Den Incorportate ...... G 440 236-9693
Columbia Station (G-5024)

Wire Products Company LLC .... C 216 267-0777
Cleveland (G-4913)

Wrwp LLC .... F 330 425-3421
Twinsburg (G-14759)

WS Tyler Screening Inc .... E 440 974-1047
Mentor (G-10598)

Yankee Wire Cloth Products Inc ...... F 740 545-9129
West Lafayette (G-15621)

▼ Yost Superior Co .... E 937 323-7591
Springfield (G-13658)

3497 Metal foil and leaf

Avery Dennison Corporation .... D 440 639-3900
Mentor (G-10427)

Avery Dennison Corporation .... B 440 534-6000
Mentor (G-10426)

CCL Label Inc .... D 216 676-2703
Cleveland (G-3801)

CCL Label Inc .... D 440 878-7000
Strongsville (G-13819)

Compco Quaker Mfg Inc .... E 330 482-0200
Salem (G-12986)

Foil Tapes LLC .... G 216 255-6655
Cleveland (G-4076)

▲ Quaker Mfg Corp .... C 330 332-4631
Salem (G-13024)

▲ Wieland Metal Svcs Foils LLC .... D 330 823-1700
Alliance (G-437)

3498 Fabricated pipe and fittings

◆ Alloy Precision Tech Inc .... D 440 266-7700
Mentor (G-10412)

▼ American Roll Formed Pdts Corp ..... C 440 352-0753
Youngstown (G-16310)

▲ Appian Manufacturing Corp .... E 614 445-2230
Columbus (G-3143)

Arem Co .... F 440 974-6740
Mentor (G-10423)

Atlas Industrial Contrs LLC .... B 614 841-4500
Columbus (G-5163)

B S F Inc .... F 937 890-6121
Tipp City (G-14123)

B S F Inc .... F 937 890-6121
Dayton (G-6222)

Bi-Con Services Inc .... B 740 685-2542
Derwent (G-6798)

Chardon Metal Products Co .... E 440 285-2147
Chardon (G-2443)

Contractors Steel Company .... D 330 425-3050
Twinsburg (G-14645)

Crest Bending Inc .... F 419 492-2108
New Washington (G-11546)

De Kay Fabricators Inc .... G 330 793-0826
Youngstown (G-16347)

▲ Duca Manufacturing & Cons .... E 330 758-0828
Youngstown (G-16352)

▲ Duro Dyne Midwest Corp .... C 513 870-6000
Hamilton (G-8201)

◆ Ebner Furnaces Inc .... D 330 335-2311
Wadsworth (G-15028)

Elliott Tool Technologies Ltd .... D 937 253-6133
Dayton (G-6318)

◆ Elster Perfection Corporation ...... D 440 428-1171
Geneva (G-7935)

Esterle Mold & Machine Co Inc .... E 330 686-1685
Stow (G-13695)

▲ Ever Roll Specialties Co .... E 937 964-1302
Springfield (G-13561)

Famous Industries Inc .... F 740 685-2592
Byesville (G-1896)

Faull & Son LLC .... F 330 652-4341
Niles (G-11668)

GM Mechanical Inc .... D 937 473-3006
Covington (G-6024)

H-P Products Inc .... C 330 875-7193
Louisville (G-9458)

◆ H-P Products Inc .... C 330 875-5556
Louisville (G-9459)

Honeywell Smart Energy .... D 440 415-1606
Geneva (G-7939)

Hycom Inc .... E 330 753-2330
Barberton (G-873)

▲ Hydro Tube Enterprises Inc .... D 440 774-1022
Oberlin (G-12052)

Indelco Custom Products Inc .... E 216 797-3000
Euclid (G-7274)

Industrial Power Systems Inc .... B 419 531-3121
Rossford (G-12867)

▲ Industrial Quartz Corporation ...... E 440 942-0909
Mentor (G-10471)

Ipsco Tubulars Inc .... D 330 448-6772
Brookfield (G-1671)

John H Hosking Co .... G 513 422-9425
Middletown (G-10834)

Kenley Enterprises LLC .... F 419 630-0921
Bryan (G-1824)

Kings Welding and Fabg Inc .... F 330 738-3592
Mechanicstown (G-10287)

◆ Kirtland Capital Partners LP .... E 216 593-0100
Beachwood (G-993)

▲ Kottler Metal Products Co Inc ...... E 440 946-7473
Willoughby (G-15940)

Mitchell Piping LLC .... E 330 245-0258
Hartville (G-8303)

Ms Murcko & Sons LLC .... G 724 854-4907
Hubbard (G-8568)

Normandy Products Co .... D 440 632-5050
Middlefield (G-10777)

Parker-Hannifin Corporation .... E 937 456-5571
Eaton (G-7067)

Phillips Mfg and Tower Co .... D 419 347-1720
Shelby (G-13197)

Phoenix Forge Group LLC .... C 800 848-6125
West Jefferson (G-15614)

▲ Pioneer Pipe Inc .... A 740 376-2400
Marietta (G-9817)

◆ Pipe Line Development Company ...... D 440 871-5700
Strongsville (G-13865)

▲ Pipe Products Inc .... C 513 587-7532
West Chester (G-15480)

Precision Bending Tech Inc .... F 440 974-2500
Mentor (G-10528)

▲ Precision Fittings LLC .... E 440 647-4143
Wellington (G-15320)

◆ Pressure Connections Corp .... D 614 863-6930
Columbus (G-5689)

◆ Production Tube Cutting Inc .... E 937 254-6138
Dayton (G-6530)

▼ Qual-Fab Inc .... E 440 327-5000
Avon (G-784)

Quality Mechanicals Inc .... E 513 559-0998
Cincinnati (G-3311)

▲ Rafter Equipment Corporation .... E 440 572-3700
Strongsville (G-13871)

Rbm Environmental & Cnstr Inc .... F 419 693-5840
Oregon (G-12110)

◆ Rexarc International Inc .... E 937 839-4604
West Alexandria (G-15344)

▲ Rhenium Alloys Inc .... E 440 365-7388
North Ridgeville (G-11858)

▼ Riker Products Inc .... D 419 729-1626
Toledo (G-14451)

Rocks General Maintenance LLC .... G 740 323-4711
Thornville (G-14070)

S-P Company Inc .... D 330 782-5651
Columbiana (G-5050)

Scot Industries Inc .... D 330 262-7585
Wooster (G-16169)

◆ Scott Process Systems Inc .... C 330 877-2350
Hartville (G-8307)

Seal Tite LLC .... D 937 393-4268
Hillsboro (G-8466)

Selling Precision Inc .... E 973 728-1214
Stow (G-13724)

▲ SSP Fittings Corp .... D 330 425-4250
Twinsburg (G-14736)

▲ Stam Inc .... E 440 974-2500
Mentor (G-10561)

▲ Stripmatic Products Inc .... E 216 241-7143
Cleveland (G-4740)

34 FABRICATED METAL PRODUCTS

Suburban Steel Supply Co .... D 614 737-5501
  Gahanna *(G-7850)*
Swagelok Company .... E 440 349-5652
  Solon *(G-13429)*
Swagelok Company .... D 440 349-5934
  Solon *(G-13431)*
T & D Fabricating Inc .... E 440 951-5646
  Eastlake *(G-7051)*
TI Group Auto Systems LLC .... E 740 929-2049
  Hebron *(G-8366)*
Transit Sittings of NA .... G 330 797-2516
  Youngstown *(G-16459)*
Tri-America Contractors Inc .... F 740 574-0148
  Wheelersburg *(G-15811)*
Tri-America Contractors Inc .... F 740 574-0148
  Wheelersburg *(G-15810)*
Tri-State Fabricators Inc .... E 513 752-5005
  Amelia *(G-469)*
Unison Industries LLC .... B 904 667-9904
  Dayton *(G-6175)*
United Group Services Inc .... C 800 633-9690
  West Chester *(G-15601)*
Unity Tube Inc .... F 330 426-4282
  East Palestine *(G-7012)*
US Tubular Products Inc .... D 330 832-1734
  North Lawrence *(G-11800)*
Vanex Tube Corporation .... D 330 544-9500
  Niles *(G-11690)*
Vortec Corporation .... E
  Blue Ash *(G-1489)*
▼ W J Egli Company Inc .... F 330 823-3666
  Alliance *(G-435)*
Zekelman Industries Inc .... C 740 432-2146
  Cambridge *(G-1961)*

3499 Fabricated metal products, nec

Accurate Mechanical Inc .... D 740 681-1332
  Lancaster *(G-8985)*
Ace Plastics Company .... G 330 928-7720
  Stow *(G-13680)*
Acromet Metal Fabricators .... F 440 237-8745
  Strongsville *(G-13800)*
Addup Inc .... E 513 745-4510
  Blue Ash *(G-1357)*
Alacriant Inc .... E 330 562-7191
  Streetsboro *(G-13755)*
Alacriant Inc .... D 330 562-7191
  Streetsboro *(G-13754)*
Alchemical Transmutation Corp .... G 216 313-8674
  Cleveland *(G-3623)*
All Ohio Welding Inc .... G 937 663-7116
  Saint Paris *(G-12970)*
American Metal Fabricating LLC .... G 440 277-5600
  Elyria *(G-7108)*
B M Machine .... E 419 595-2898
  New Riegel *(G-11534)*
Bauer Corporation .... E 800 321-4760
  Wooster *(G-16102)*
Bc Investment Corporation .... G 330 262-3070
  Wooster *(G-16103)*
◆ Black Squirrel Holdings Inc .... E 513 577-7107
  Cincinnati *(G-2671)*
Camaco LLC .... A 440 288-4444
  Lorain *(G-9405)*
Cast-Fab Technologies Inc .... C 513 758-1000
  Cincinnati *(G-2707)*
Ccr Fabrications LLC .... G 937 667-6632
  Tipp City *(G-14128)*
Central Machinery Company LLC .... F 740 387-1289
  Marion *(G-9849)*
Champion Strapping Pdts Inc .... G 614 527-1454
  Columbus *(G-5247)*

Cincinnati Mtals Fbrcation Inc .... G 513 382-2988
  Cincinnati *(G-2756)*
Cincy Safe Company .... F 513 900-9152
  Milford *(G-10901)*
COW Industries Inc .... E 614 443-6537
  Columbus *(G-5301)*
Crest Craft Co .... F 513 271-4858
  Blue Ash *(G-1383)*
Custom Fabrication By Fisher .... G 513 738-4600
  Okeana *(G-12066)*
DA Precision Products Inc .... F 513 459-1113
  West Chester *(G-15411)*
▲ Dern Trophies Corp .... F 614 895-3260
  Westerville *(G-15653)*
◆ Df Supply Inc .... E 330 650-9226
  Twinsburg *(G-14650)*
Die-Cut Products Co .... F 216 771-6994
  Cleveland *(G-3958)*
Diebold Nixdorf Incorporated .... C 740 928-1010
  Hebron *(G-8339)*
Diebold Nixdorf Incorporated .... A 330 490-4000
  North Canton *(G-11722)*
Donald E Didion II .... E 419 483-2226
  Bellevue *(G-1226)*
Dubose Strapping Inc .... E 419 221-0626
  Lima *(G-9239)*
Dunn Industrial Services .... G 513 738-4999
  Hamilton *(G-8200)*
▲ Dura Magnetics Inc .... F 419 882-0591
  Sylvania *(G-13995)*
▼ Eastern Automated Piping .... G 740 535-8184
  Mingo Junction *(G-11044)*
Exair Corporation .... E 513 671-3322
  Cincinnati *(G-2891)*
EZ Grout Corporation Inc .... E 740 962-2024
  Malta *(G-9607)*
F & F Shtmtl & Fabrication LLC .... G 419 618-3171
  New Riegel *(G-11535)*
Fabricating Solutions Inc .... F 330 486-0998
  Twinsburg *(G-14658)*
◆ Flexmag Industries Inc .... D 740 373-3492
  Marietta *(G-9793)*
Fountain Specialists Inc .... G 513 831-5717
  Milford *(G-10906)*
Frame Warehouse .... G 614 861-4582
  Reynoldsburg *(G-12765)*
Fusion Metal Fabrication LLC .... G 937 753-1090
  Covington *(G-6022)*
GCI Metals Inc .... F 937 835-7123
  Dayton *(G-6345)*
General Metals Powder Co LLC .... E 330 633-1226
  Akron *(G-166)*
Gerdau Ameristeel US Inc .... G 740 671-9410
  Bellaire *(G-1186)*
▲ Hamilton Products Group Inc .... E 800 876-6066
  Milford *(G-10908)*
▲ Hamilton Safe Co .... F 513 874-3733
  Milford *(G-10909)*
▲ Hamilton Security Products Co .... E 513 874-3733
  Milford *(G-10910)*
Hit Trophy Inc .... G 419 445-5356
  Archbold *(G-532)*
IBI Brake Products Inc .... G 440 543-7962
  Chagrin Falls *(G-2402)*
Infinite Energy Mfg LLC .... F 440 759-5920
  Cleveland *(G-4224)*
J & J Performance Inc .... F 330 567-2455
  Shreve *(G-13211)*
◆ Jay Mid-South LLC .... E 256 439-6600
  Mansfield *(G-9672)*
JB Entrprses Prts Dtailing LLC .... G 440 309-4984
  Elyria *(G-7171)*

Jfdb Ltd .... C 513 870-0601
  Cincinnati *(G-3042)*
Johnson Mfg Systems LLC .... F 937 866-4744
  Miamisburg *(G-10650)*
Kard Welding LLC .... E 419 628-2598
  Minster *(G-11054)*
Karyall-Telday Inc .... F 216 281-4063
  Cleveland *(G-4274)*
Ksm Metal Fabrication .... F 937 339-6366
  Troy *(G-14593)*
Labcraft Inc .... E 419 878-4400
  Waterville *(G-15249)*
Lewark Metal Spinning Inc .... E 937 275-3303
  Dayton *(G-6406)*
Linsalata Cpitl Prtners Fund I .... G 440 684-1400
  Cleveland *(G-4330)*
Magnet Engineering Inc .... G 513 248-4578
  Batavia *(G-930)*
▼ Magnum Magnetics Corporation .... D 740 373-7770
  Marietta *(G-9805)*
MAK Fabricating Inc .... F 330 747-0040
  Youngstown *(G-16395)*
Mandrel Group LLC .... F 330 881-1266
  Mc Donald *(G-10278)*
◆ Mansfield Engineered Comp .... C 419 524-1331
  Mansfield *(G-9685)*
Mansfield Welding Service LLC .... G 419 594-2738
  Oakwood *(G-12031)*
Mast Farm Service Ltd .... F 330 893-2972
  Walnut Creek *(G-15094)*
Master Magnetics Inc .... F 740 373-0909
  Marietta *(G-9807)*
McIntosh Safe Corp .... F 937 222-7008
  Dayton *(G-6432)*
McNeil Group Inc .... E 614 298-0300
  Columbus *(G-5556)*
Mdb Fabricating Inc .... G 216 799-7017
  Cleveland *(G-4385)*
Midwest Strapping Products .... G 614 527-1454
  Columbus *(G-5567)*
Miscellnous Mtals Fbrction Inc .... F 740 779-3071
  Chillicothe *(G-2519)*
Natures Mark LLC .... G 513 557-3200
  Cincinnati *(G-3182)*
▲ North Shore Strapping Company .... E 216 661-5200
  Brooklyn Heights *(G-1696)*
◆ Ohio Gasket and Shim Co Inc .... E 330 630-0626
  Akron *(G-270)*
Ohio Laser LLC .... E 614 873-7030
  Plain City *(G-12587)*
▲ Ohio Magnetics Inc .... E 216 662-8484
  Maple Heights *(G-9756)*
Organized Living .... G 513 277-3700
  Cincinnati *(G-3229)*
Penny Fab LLC .... F 740 967-3669
  Columbus *(G-5667)*
◆ Peter Graham Dunn Inc .... E 330 816-0035
  Dalton *(G-6139)*
Pfi USA .... F 937 547-0413
  Greenville *(G-8055)*
▼ Projects Designed & Built .... E 419 726-7400
  Toledo *(G-14443)*
PS Superior Inc .... E 216 587-1000
  Cleveland *(G-4596)*
Pucel Enterprises Inc .... D 216 881-4604
  Cleveland *(G-4598)*
Pucel Enterprises Inc .... G 800 336-4986
  Cleveland *(G-4599)*
Quest Technologies Inc .... F 937 743-1200
  Franklin *(G-7696)*
R L Torbeck Industries Inc .... E 513 367-0080
  Harrison *(G-8289)*

Employee Codes: A=Over 500 employees, B=251-500
C=101-250, D=51-100, E=20-50, F=10-19, G=1-9

34 FABRICATED METAL PRODUCTS

Rmi Titanium Company LLC............................C 330 455-4010
  Canton (G-2218)
Seaway Bolt And Specials Company......D 440 236-5015
  Columbia Station (G-5021)
Sharonco Inc...G 419 882-3443
  Sylvania (G-14014)
Shim Shack..G 877 557-3930
  Harrison (G-8291)
▲ SK Wellman Corp.....................................C 440 528-4000
  Solon (G-13421)
▲ Sulo Enterprises Inc..................................F 440 926-3322
  Grafton (G-8005)
Tribco Incorporated....................................E 216 486-2000
  Cleveland (G-4825)
Vortec Corporation.....................................E
  Blue Ash (G-1489)
◆ Voss Industries LLC.................................C 216 771-7655
  Cleveland (G-4884)
Voyale Minority Enterprise LLC..................E 216 271-3661
  Cleveland (G-1895)
◆ Walker National Inc..................................E 614 492-1614
  Columbus (G-5862)
Warren Steel Specialties Corp....................E 330 399-8360
  Warren (G-15221)
Williamson Safe Inc....................................F 937 393-9919
  Hillsboro (G-8470)
▲ Winkle Industries Inc................................D 330 823-9730
  Alliance (G-438)
Wpc Successor Inc.....................................F 937 233-6141
  Tipp City (G-14167)
Yarder Manufacturing Company................E 419 476-3933
  Toledo (G-14530)
Zeda Inc...F 513 966-4633
  Cincinnati (G-3535)

35 INDUSTRIAL AND COMMERCIAL MACHINERY AND COMPUTER EQUIPMENT

3511 Turbines and turbine generator sets

Alin Machining Company Inc.....................D 740 223-0200
  Marion (G-9847)
Babcock & Wilcox Company......................D 740 687-6500
  Lancaster (G-8991)
Babcock & Wilcox Entps Inc......................F 740 687-4370
  Lancaster (G-8992)
Babcock & Wilcox Holdings Inc.................A 704 625-4900
  Akron (G-75)
Canvus Inc...E 216 340-7500
  Rocky River (G-12836)
◆ Diamond Power Intl Inc............................D 740 687-6500
  Lancaster (G-9012)
Eaton Leasing Corporation.........................B 216 382-2292
  Beachwood (G-986)
Fluid System Service Inc............................G 216 651-2450
  Cleveland (G-4072)
Fluidpower Assembly Inc...........................E 419 394-7486
  Saint Marys (G-12952)
◆ Mendenhall Technical Services Inc..........E 513 860-1280
  Fairfield (G-7383)
◆ Metalex Manufacturing Inc.......................C 513 489-0507
  Blue Ash (G-1437)
▲ Miba Bearings US LLC.............................B 740 962-4242
  Mcconnelsville (G-10282)
Muller Engine & Machine Co.....................G 937 322-1861
  Springfield (G-13607)
Onpower Inc..E 513 228-2100
  Lebanon (G-9103)
Pfpc Enterprises Inc....................................F 513 941-6200
  Cincinnati (G-3253)

Precision Castparts Corp............................F 440 350-6150
  Painesville (G-12258)
◆ Rolls-Royce Energy Systems Inc............A 703 834-1700
  Mount Vernon (G-11292)
Siemens Energy Inc....................................E 740 393-8897
  Mount Vernon (G-11295)
Siemens Energy Inc....................................E 740 504-1947
  Mount Vernon (G-11296)
Steam Trbine Altrntive Rsrces....................E 740 387-5535
  Marion (G-9884)

3519 Internal combustion engines, nec

▲ American Fine Sinter Co Ltd...................C 419 443-8880
  Tiffin (G-14075)
B A Malcuit Racing Inc................................G 330 878-7111
  Strasburg (G-13743)
Bowden Manufacturing Corp......................E 440 946-1770
  Willoughby (G-15891)
Brinkley Technology Group LLC................F 330 830-2498
  Massillon (G-10070)
Chemequip Sales Inc..................................E 330 724-8300
  Coventry Township (G-6007)
Clarke Fire Prtection Pdts Inc.....................E 513 771-2200
  West Chester (G-15545)
Country Sales & Service LLC.....................F 330 683-2500
  Orrville (G-12122)
Cummins - Allison Corp..............................G 513 469-2924
  Blue Ash (G-1384)
Cummins - Allison Corp..............................G 440 824-5050
  Cleveland (G-3919)
Cummins Inc..E 614 604-6004
  Grove City (G-8085)
◆ Detroit Desl Rmnfctrng-Ast Inc...............B 740 439-7701
  Byesville (G-1894)
Detroit Desl Rmnufacturing LLC................C 740 439-7701
  Cambridge (G-1931)
◆ Dmax Ltd..D 937 425-9700
  Moraine (G-11172)
▲ DW Hercules LLC....................................F 330 830-2498
  Massillon (G-10091)
Enjet Aero Dayton Inc.................................E 937 878-3800
  Huber Heights (G-8576)
Ford Motor Company..................................A 419 226-7000
  Lima (G-9243)
GE Honda Aero Engines LLC....................F 513 552-4322
  West Chester (G-15438)
GE Rolls Royce Fighter...............................F 513 243-2787
  Cincinnati (G-2939)
General Electric Company..........................A 617 443-3000
  Cincinnati (G-2942)
▲ General Engine Products LLC.................D 937 704-0160
  Franklin (G-7677)
▲ Hy-Production Inc....................................C 330 273-2400
  Valley City (G-14873)
Industrial Parts Depot LLC..........................G 440 237-9164
  North Royalton (G-11880)
◆ Jatrodiesel Inc..F
  Miamisburg (G-10649)
Kinstle Truck & Auto Svc Inc......................F 419 738-7493
  Wapakoneta (G-15120)
M & S Equipment Leasing Co....................F 216 662-8800
  Cleveland (G-4343)
Maags Automotive & Mch Inc....................G 419 626-1539
  Sandusky (G-13076)
▲ Miba Bearings US LLC............................B 740 962-4242
  Mcconnelsville (G-10282)
▲ Miscor Group Ltd.....................................B 330 830-3500
  Massillon (G-10129)
Performace Diesel Inc.................................F 740 392-3693
  Mount Vernon (G-11287)
Performance Research Inc.........................E 614 475-8300
  Columbus (G-5670)

Precision Castparts Corp............................F 440 350-6150
  Painesville (G-12258)
Precision Engneered Components............F 614 436-0392
  Worthington (G-16207)
Western Branch Diesel LLC.......................F 330 454-8800
  Canton (G-2267)

3523 Farm machinery and equipment

Afs Technology LLC...................................F 937 545-0627
  Dayton (G-6190)
American Baler Co......................................D 419 483-5790
  Bellevue (G-1222)
Barn Small Engine Repa.............................G 419 583-6595
  Wauseon (G-15257)
Birds Eye Foods Inc....................................D 330 854-0818
  Canal Fulton (G-1968)
Brueneman Sales Inc..................................G 513 520-3377
  Harrison (G-8266)
▲ Buckeye Tractor Corporation..................G 419 659-2162
  Columbus Grove (G-5090)
Cailin Development LLC.............................F 216 408-6261
  Cleveland (G-3781)
◆ Chick Master Incubator Company..........D 330 722-5591
  Medina (G-10308)
Country Manufacturing Inc.........................F 740 694-9926
  Fredericktown (G-7741)
Creamer Metal Products Inc......................F 740 852-1752
  London (G-9385)
Empire Plow Company Inc.........................E 216 641-2290
  Berea (G-1276)
Fecon LLC..E 513 696-4430
  Lebanon (G-9075)
▲ Fecon LLC...D 513 696-4430
  Lebanon (G-9076)
Field Gymmy Inc..G 419 538-6511
  Glandorf (G-7978)
◆ Finn Corporation......................................E 513 874-2818
  West Chester (G-15429)
Flying Dutchman Inc...................................G 330 669-2297
  Smithville (G-13299)
◆ Fort Recovery Equipment Inc..................F 419 375-1006
  Fort Recovery (G-7615)
Fremont Plastic Products Inc.....................C 419 332-6407
  Fremont (G-7783)
Gerald Grain Center Inc..............................E 419 445-2451
  Archbold (G-529)
H & S Company Inc....................................E 419 394-4444
  Celina (G-2335)
▲ Hawkline Nevada LLC.............................G 937 444-4295
  Mount Orab (G-11241)
Heintz Farms Enterprise Partnr.................G 937 464-2535
  Belle Center (G-1196)
Hershy Way Ltd...G 330 893-2809
  Millersburg (G-10958)
Hog Slat Incorporated.................................E 937 968-3890
  Union City (G-14779)
Hord Elevator LLC......................................C 419 562-1198
  Edison (G-7084)
◆ Intertec Corporation.................................F 419 537-9711
  Toledo (G-14335)
◆ J & M Manufacturing Co Inc....................C 419 375-2376
  Fort Recovery (G-7620)
Kriss Kreations..G 330 405-6102
  Twinsburg (G-14682)
Kts Equipment Inc......................................E 440 647-2015
  Wellington (G-15316)
Ley Industries Inc..G 419 238-6742
  Van Wert (G-14922)
M & S AG Solutions LLC...........................F 419 598-8675
  Napoleon (G-11323)
Max Roush...G 937 288-2557
  Cincinnati (G-3135)

SIC SECTION
35 INDUSTRIAL AND COMMERCIAL MACHINERY AND COMPUTER EQUIPMENT

Meristem Crop Prfmce Group LLC......... E 833 637-4783
  Columbus *(G-5559)*
Norden Mfg LLC.................................... E 440 693-4630
  North Bloomfield *(G-11712)*
Ntech Industries Inc............................... E 707 467-3747
  Dayton *(G-6481)*
◆ Ohio Machinery Co............................ C 440 526-6200
  Broadview Heights *(G-1665)*
Ohio Windmill & Pump Co Inc................ G 330 547-6300
  Berlin Center *(G-1310)*
Pax Steel Products Inc.......................... G 419 678-1481
  Coldwater *(G-4999)*
Precision Assemblies Inc...................... F 330 549-2630
  North Lima *(G-11809)*
Puehler Agco Inc................................... G 419 388-6614
  Wauseon *(G-15273)*
Randall Richard & Moore LLC............... E 330 455-8873
  Canton *(G-2210)*
Randall Brothers LLC............................ G 419 395-1764
  Holgate *(G-8491)*
Reinke Company Inc............................. G 614 570-2578
  Columbus *(G-5717)*
▲ Rhinestahl Corporation...................... D 513 489-1317
  Mason *(G-10048)*
▲ S I Distributing Inc............................. F 419 647-4909
  Spencerville *(G-13489)*
Safe-Grain Inc....................................... G 513 398-2500
  Dayton *(G-6557)*
Seppi M SPA.. G 513 443-6339
  West Chester *(G-15508)*
Shearer Farm Inc.................................. C 330 345-9023
  Wooster *(G-16171)*
Stein-Way Equipment............................ G 330 857-8700
  Apple Creek *(G-511)*
Stephens Pipe & Steel LLC................... C 740 869-2257
  Mount Sterling *(G-11257)*
◆ Sweet Manufacturing Company.......... E 937 325-1511
  Springfield *(G-13641)*
TD Landscape Inc................................. F 740 694-0244
  Fredericktown *(G-7754)*
Tractor Supply Company....................... G 740 963-8023
  Pataskala *(G-12310)*
◆ Unverferth Mfg Co Inc........................ C 419 532-3121
  Kalida *(G-8787)*
▲ Val-Co Pax Inc.................................. D 717 354-4586
  Coldwater *(G-5003)*

3524 Lawn and garden equipment

◆ Arnold Corporation............................. C 330 225-2600
  Valley City *(G-14861)*
Cannon Salt & Supply Inc..................... G 440 232-1700
  Bedford *(G-1108)*
Commercial Turf Products Ltd.............. D 330 995-7000
  Streetsboro *(G-13763)*
▲ Cub Cadet Corporation Sales............ D 330 273-4550
  Valley City *(G-14867)*
▲ Elan Designs Inc............................... G 614 985-5600
  Westerville *(G-15704)*
Erosion Control Products Corp.............. F 302 815-6500
  West Chester *(G-15426)*
Extrudex Limited Partnership................ E 440 352-7101
  Painesville *(G-12235)*
◆ Finn Corporation................................ E 513 874-2818
  West Chester *(G-15429)*
Franklin Equipment LLC........................ D 614 228-2014
  Groveport *(G-8143)*
◆ Gardner Inc....................................... C 614 456-4000
  Columbus *(G-5395)*
Hawthorne Gardening Company............ E 360 883-8846
  Marysville *(G-9913)*
Johnson & Johnson Services LLC......... F 513 289-4514
  Cincinnati *(G-3047)*

Karl Kuemmerling Inc............................ F
  Massillon *(G-10114)*
Koenig Equipment Inc........................... F 937 653-5281
  Urbana *(G-14842)*
Mo-Trim Inc.. G 740 439-2725
  Cambridge *(G-1943)*
▼ Mtd Consumer Group Inc.................. C 330 225-2600
  Valley City *(G-14881)*
◆ Mtd Holdings Inc................................ B 330 225-2600
  Valley City *(G-14882)*
Mtd International Operations................. C 330 225-2600
  Valley City *(G-14883)*
Mtd Products Inc................................... C 419 342-6455
  Shelby *(G-13196)*
Mtd Products Inc................................... B 330 225-1940
  Valley City *(G-14885)*
Mtd Products Inc................................... C 330 225-9127
  Valley City *(G-14886)*
Mtd Products Inc................................... G 419 951-9779
  Willard *(G-15861)*
Mtd Products Inc................................... A 419 935-6611
  Willard *(G-15862)*
◆ Mtd Products Inc................................ B 330 225-2600
  Valley City *(G-14884)*
◆ Oase North America Inc..................... G 800 365-3880
  Aurora *(G-728)*
◆ Park-Ohio Holdings Corp.................... F 440 947-2000
  Cleveland *(G-4524)*
Park-Ohio Industries Inc........................ C 440 947-2000
  Cleveland *(G-4525)*
▲ Power Distributors LLC...................... D 614 876-3533
  Columbus *(G-5684)*
Rotoline USA LLC................................. G 330 677-3223
  Kent *(G-8856)*
Russell Hunt... F 740 264-1196
  Steubenville *(G-13676)*
◆ Scotts Company LLC......................... C 937 644-0011
  Marysville *(G-9934)*
Scotts Temecula Operations LLC.......... E 800 221-1760
  Marysville *(G-9937)*
Smg Growing Media Inc........................ F 937 644-0011
  Marysville *(G-9938)*
◆ Speed North America Inc................... E 330 202-7775
  Wooster *(G-16174)*
Tierra-Derco International LLC.............. G 419 929-2240
  New London *(G-11471)*
▲ Venture Products Inc......................... D 330 683-0075
  Orrville *(G-12160)*

3531 Construction machinery

1062 Technologies Inc.......................... G 303 453-9251
  Youngstown *(G-16295)*
2e Associates Inc.................................. E 440 975-9955
  Willoughby *(G-15871)*
▲ A JC Inc... F 800 428-2438
  Hudson *(G-8581)*
▲ ACS Industries Inc............................ D 330 678-2511
  Kent *(G-8794)*
▼ Aim Attachments................................ G 614 539-3030
  Grove City *(G-8075)*
Allied Consolidated Inds Inc.................. C 330 744-0808
  Youngstown *(G-16307)*
Altec Industries..................................... G 419 289-6066
  Ashland *(G-550)*
Altec Industries Inc................................ G 614 295-4895
  Columbus *(G-5117)*
Altec Industries Inc................................ F 205 408-2341
  Cuyahoga Falls *(G-6062)*
▲ American Alloy Corporation................ E 216 642-9638
  Cleveland *(G-3649)*
American Highway Products LLC.......... F 330 874-3270
  Bolivar *(G-1522)*

◆ American Power Pull Corp.................. G 419 335-7050
  Archbold *(G-520)*
Ballinger Industries Inc.......................... G 419 421-4704
  Findlay *(G-7483)*
▲ Ballinger Industries Inc...................... F 419 422-4533
  Findlay *(G-7482)*
▲ Barbco Inc... E 330 488-9400
  East Canton *(G-6978)*
Basetek LLC... F 877 712-2273
  Middlefield *(G-10733)*
Brewpro Inc.. G 513 577-7200
  Cincinnati *(G-2682)*
◆ Buck Equipment Inc........................... E 614 539-3039
  Grove City *(G-8081)*
◆ Bucyrus Blades Inc............................ C 419 562-6015
  Bucyrus *(G-1850)*
Caterpillar Industrial Inc........................ E 440 247-8484
  Chagrin Falls *(G-2369)*
◆ Chemineer Inc.................................... C 937 454-3200
  Dayton *(G-6254)*
Cityscapes International Inc.................. C 614 850-2540
  Hilliard *(G-8406)*
Concord Road Equipment Mfg Inc......... E 440 357-5344
  Painesville *(G-12223)*
Concord Road Equipment Mfg LLC....... E 440 357-5344
  Mentor *(G-10442)*
Crane Pro Services................................ G 937 525-5555
  Springfield *(G-13549)*
Crh US.. G 216 642-3920
  Independence *(G-8662)*
Curtis Industires.................................... G 216 430-5759
  Cleveland *(G-3921)*
CW Machine Worx Ltd.......................... F 740 654-5304
  Carroll *(G-2295)*
D & L Excavating Ltd............................ G 419 271-0635
  Port Clinton *(G-12616)*
DA Precision Products Inc.................... F 513 459-1113
  West Chester *(G-15411)*
Desco Corporation................................ G 614 888-8855
  New Albany *(G-11378)*
Dimensional Metals Inc......................... E 740 927-3633
  Reynoldsburg *(G-12761)*
Donald E Dornon................................... G 740 926-9144
  Beallsville *(G-1034)*
Dragon Products LLC........................... E 330 345-3968
  Wooster *(G-16114)*
▲ Drc Acquisition Inc............................. E 330 656-1600
  Streetsboro *(G-13767)*
Duplex Mill & Manufacturing Co............ E 937 325-5555
  Springfield *(G-13557)*
Dynamic Plastics Inc............................. G 937 437-7261
  New Paris *(G-11481)*
◆ E R Advanced Ceramics Inc............... E 330 426-9433
  East Palestine *(G-7004)*
▲ E Z Grout Corporation........................ E 740 749-3512
  Malta *(G-9606)*
Eagle Crusher Co Inc............................ D 419 562-1183
  Bucyrus *(G-1858)*
◆ Eagle Crusher Co Inc......................... D 419 468-2288
  Galion *(G-7872)*
Enviri Corporation................................. F 740 387-1150
  Marion *(G-9851)*
▲ Fabco Inc... E 419 422-4533
  Findlay *(G-7504)*
▲ Fecon LLC... D 513 696-4430
  Lebanon *(G-9076)*
Field Gymmy Inc................................... G 419 538-6511
  Glandorf *(G-7978)*
▲ Fives St Corp..................................... E 234 217-9070
  Wadsworth *(G-15029)*
▲ Forge Industries Inc........................... A 330 960-2468
  Youngstown *(G-16359)*

Employee Codes: A=Over 500 employees, B=251-500
C=101-250, D=51-100, E=20-50, F=10-19, G=1-9

35 INDUSTRIAL AND COMMERCIAL MACHINERY AND COMPUTER EQUIPMENT

G & T Manufacturing Co .... F 440 639-7777
  Mentor *(G-10462)*
Geauga Highway Co .... F 440 834-4580
  Hiram *(G-8484)*
Gledhill Road Machinery Co .... E 419 468-4400
  Galion *(G-7878)*
◆ Global TBM Company .... C 440 248-3303
  Solon *(G-13355)*
Gradall Industries Inc .... G 540 819-6638
  Uhrichsville *(G-14766)*
▲ Gradall Industries LLC .... C 330 339-2211
  New Philadelphia *(G-11504)*
Gradeworks .... G 440 487-4201
  Kirtland *(G-8940)*
Grand Archt Etrnl Eye 314 LLC .... F 800 377-8147
  Cleveland *(G-4138)*
Grand Harbor Yacht Sales & Svc .... G 440 442-2919
  Cleveland *(G-4139)*
H Y O Inc .... E 614 488-2861
  Columbus *(G-3414)*
◆ Haulotte US Inc .... F 419 445-8915
  Archbold *(G-531)*
Hickmans Construction Co LLC .... F 866 271-2565
  Euclid *(G-7273)*
▲ Hudco Manufacturing Inc .... G 440 951-4040
  Willoughby *(G-15929)*
Ironhawk Industrial Dist LLC .... G 216 502-3700
  Euclid *(G-7276)*
JB Pavers and Hardscapes LLC .... G 937 454-1145
  Vandalia *(G-14946)*
▲ Jennmar McSweeney LLC .... C 740 377-3354
  South Point *(G-13467)*
Jlg Industries Inc .... E 330 684-0132
  Orrville *(G-12130)*
Jlg Industries Inc .... D 330 684-0200
  Orrville *(G-12131)*
Jordankelly LLC .... F 216 855-8550
  Akron *(G-197)*
▲ Jrb Attachments LLC .... G 330 734-3000
  Akron *(G-198)*
◆ Jrb Family Holdings Inc C
  Wooster *(G-16138)*
Kaffenbarger Truck Eqp Co .... E 513 772-6800
  Cincinnati *(G-3056)*
Kubota Tractor Corporation .... E 614 835-3800
  Groveport *(G-8150)*
▲ Kundel Industries Inc .... E 330 469-6147
  Vienna *(G-14996)*
Lake Township Trustees .... E 419 836-1143
  Millbury *(G-10934)*
Liverpool Township .... G 330 483-4747
  Valley City *(G-14876)*
Malta Dynamics LLC .... F 740 749-3512
  Waterford *(G-15238)*
McNeilus Truck and Mfg Inc .... E 513 874-2022
  Fairfield *(G-7382)*
▲ McSweeneys Inc .... C 740 894-3353
  South Point *(G-13472)*
Mesa Industries Inc .... F 513 999-9781
  Cincinnati *(G-3152)*
◆ Mesa Industries Inc .... E 513 321-2950
  Cincinnati *(G-3151)*
Meyer Products LLC .... E 216 486-1313
  Cleveland *(G-4397)*
◆ Meyer Products LLC .... D 216 486-1313
  Steubenville *(G-13672)*
Michael Byrne Manufacturing Co Inc .... E 419 525-1214
  Mansfield *(G-9691)*
▲ Minnich Manufacturing Co Inc .... E 419 903-0010
  Mansfield *(G-9696)*
Morbark LLC .... C 330 264-8699
  Wooster *(G-16152)*

Msk Trencher Mfg Inc .... F 419 394-4444
  Celina *(G-2341)*
Murphy Tractor & Eqp Co Inc .... G 330 220-4999
  Brunswick *(G-1774)*
Murphy Tractor & Eqp Co Inc .... G 330 477-9304
  Canton *(G-2169)*
Murphy Tractor & Eqp Co Inc .... G 614 876-1141
  Columbus *(G-5585)*
Murphy Tractor & Eqp Co Inc .... G 419 221-3666
  Lima *(G-9272)*
Murphy Tractor & Eqp Co Inc .... G 937 898-4198
  Vandalia *(G-14954)*
Nick Kostecki Excavating Inc .... F 330 242-0706
  Spencer *(G-13482)*
Norris Manufacturing LLC .... F 330 602-5005
  Dover *(G-6838)*
Nov Inc .... D 937 454-3200
  Dayton *(G-6479)*
◆ Npk Construction Equipment Inc .... D 440 232-7900
  Bedford *(G-1115)*
Otc Industrial Technologies .... F 800 837-6827
  Columbus *(G-5646)*
◆ Pace Consolidated Inc .... D 440 942-1234
  Willoughby *(G-15967)*
Pace Engineering Inc .... C 440 942-1234
  Willoughby *(G-15968)*
Paus North America Inc .... G 775 778-5980
  Solon *(G-13402)*
◆ Pubco Corporation .... D 216 881-5300
  Cleveland *(G-4597)*
Quikstir Inc .... E 419 732-2601
  Port Clinton *(G-12625)*
Richland Township Bd Trustees .... F 419 358-4897
  Bluffton *(G-1506)*
▲ Rnm Holdings Inc .... G 937 704-9900
  Franklin *(G-7699)*
Roadsafe Traffic Systems Inc .... G 614 274-9782
  Columbus *(G-5728)*
Ryman Grinders Inc .... G 330 652-5080
  Niles *(G-11688)*
◆ Sandvik Rock Proc Sltons N AME .... F 216 431-2600
  Cleveland *(G-4671)*
◆ Sandvik Rock Proc Sltons N AME .... E 216 431-2600
  Cleveland *(G-4672)*
▲ Scott Port-A-Fold Inc .... F 419 748-8880
  Napoleon *(G-11334)*
Snow Dragon LLC .... F 440 295-0238
  Cleveland *(G-4710)*
Splendid LLC .... F 614 396-6481
  Columbus *(G-5787)*
Streamline Excavating LLC .... G 330 495-8617
  Malvern *(G-9616)*
Terex Utilities Inc .... F 419 470-8408
  Perrysburg *(G-12434)*
▼ Tgs Industries Inc .... E 330 339-2211
  New Philadelphia *(G-11528)*
The Wagner-Smith Company .... B 866 338-0398
  Moraine *(G-11214)*
◆ Thorworks Industries Inc .... C 419 626-4375
  Sandusky *(G-13096)*
▲ Toku America Inc .... F 440 954-9923
  Willoughby *(G-16006)*
Turn-Key Tunneling Inc .... E 614 275-4832
  Columbus *(G-5841)*
▲ Uhrden Inc .... G 330 456-0031
  Canton *(G-2249)*
Wellpoint .... G 614 771-9600
  Worthington *(G-16217)*
Werk Brau .... G 419 421-4703
  Findlay *(G-7580)*
Werk-Brau Company .... C 419 422-2912
  Findlay *(G-7582)*

▲ Werk-Brau Company .... C 419 422-2912
  Findlay *(G-7581)*
◆ Winter Equipment Company .... E 440 946-8377
  Willoughby *(G-16019)*
Wonderly Trucking & Excvtg LLC .... F 419 837-6294
  Perrysburg *(G-12446)*
Youngstown Bending Rolling .... G 330 799-2227
  Youngstown *(G-16478)*

3532 Mining machinery

▲ Belle Center Air Tool Co Inc .... G 937 464-7474
  Belle Center *(G-1195)*
Bowdil Company .... F 800 356-8663
  Canton *(G-2051)*
Breaker Technology Inc .... F 440 248-7168
  Solon *(G-13324)*
▼ Brydet Development Corporation .... F 740 623-0455
  Coshocton *(G-5974)*
Cailin Development LLC .... E 216 408-6261
  Cleveland *(G-3781)*
Carr Tool Company .... E 513 825-2900
  Fairfield *(G-7343)*
Charles Machine Works Inc .... E 800 324-4930
  West Salem *(G-15633)*
Cleveland Vibrator Company .... F 800 221-3298
  Cleveland *(G-3859)*
Cool Machines Inc .... E 419 232-4871
  Van Wert *(G-14909)*
▲ Davey Kent Inc .... E 330 673-5400
  Kent *(G-8807)*
Dover Conveyor Inc .... E 740 922-9390
  Midvale *(G-10876)*
◆ Eagle Crusher Co Inc .... D 419 468-2288
  Galion *(G-7872)*
Engines Inc of Ohio .... E 740 377-9874
  South Point *(G-13466)*
Epiroc USA LLC .... F 844 437-4762
  Independence *(G-8667)*
▲ Jennmar McSweeney LLC .... C 740 377-3354
  South Point *(G-13467)*
▲ Joy Global Underground Min LLC .... C 440 248-7970
  Solon *(G-13371)*
Kaffenbarger Truck Eqp Co .... E 513 772-6800
  Cincinnati *(G-3056)*
Kennametal Inc .... C 440 349-5151
  Solon *(G-13378)*
Komatsu Mining Corp .... D 216 503-5029
  Independence *(G-8670)*
Maag Automatik Inc .... E 330 677-2225
  Kent *(G-8830)*
▲ McSweeneys Inc .... C 740 894-3353
  South Point *(G-13472)*
Nolan Company .... G 740 269-1512
  Bowerston *(G-1545)*
Nolan Company .... E 330 453-7922
  Canton *(G-2173)*
◆ Npk Construction Equipment Inc .... D 440 232-7900
  Bedford *(G-1145)*
Penn Machine Company LLC .... D 814 288-1547
  Twinsburg *(G-14708)*
◆ Reduction Engineering Inc .... E 330 677-2225
  Kent *(G-8852)*
▲ Siebtechnik Tema Inc .... E 513 489-7811
  Cincinnati *(G-3390)*
Strata Mine Services Inc .... F 740 695-6880
  Saint Clairsville *(G-12926)*
▲ Uhrden Inc .... E 330 456-0031
  Canton *(G-2249)*
◆ Warren Fabricating Corporation .... D 330 534-5017
  Hubbard *(G-8572)*
Zen Industries Inc .... E 216 432-3240
  Cleveland *(G-4932)*

35 INDUSTRIAL AND COMMERCIAL MACHINERY AND COMPUTER EQUIPMENT

3533 Oil and gas field machinery

Allied Machine Works Inc .... G 740 454-2534
   Zanesville *(G-16499)*
Black Gold Capital LLC .... E 614 348-7460
   Columbus *(G-5196)*
Buckeye Companies .... E 740 452-3641
   Zanesville *(G-16513)*
Buckeye Oil Equipment Co .... F 937 387-0671
   Dayton *(G-6239)*
Cameron International Corp .... E 740 654-4260
   Lancaster *(G-8998)*
Electrnic Dsign For Indust Inc .... E 740 401-4000
   Belpre *(G-1252)*
◆ Furukawa Rock Drill Usa Inc .... F 330 673-5826
   Kent *(G-8815)*
H & S Company Inc .... E 419 394-4444
   Celina *(G-2335)*
H P E Inc .... G 330 833-3161
   Massillon *(G-10104)*
Jet Rubber Company .... E 330 325-1821
   Rootstown *(G-12853)*
◆ Multi Products Company .... E 330 674-5981
   Millersburg *(G-10986)*
OSI Environmental LLC .... E 440 237-4600
   North Royalton *(G-11890)*
Pride of The Hills Manufacturing Inc . D 330 567-3108
   Big Prairie *(G-1329)*
Rampp Company .... E 740 373-7886
   Marietta *(G-9819)*
◆ Rmi Titanium Company LLC .... E 330 652-9952
   Niles *(G-11684)*
◆ Saint-Gobain Norpro Corp .... C 330 673-5860
   Stow *(G-13722)*
Stonebridge Oilfield Svcs LLC .... G 740 373-6134
   Marietta *(G-9833)*
Tiger General LLC .... F 330 239-4949
   Medina *(G-10387)*
Timco Inc .... F 740 685-2594
   Byesville *(G-1900)*
Under Hill Water Well .... G 740 852-0858
   London *(G-9396)*

3534 Elevators and moving stairways

▲ Adams Elevator Equipment Co .... D 847 581-2900
   Holland *(G-8492)*
Avt Beckett Elevators USA Inc .... G 844 360-0288
   Logan *(G-9359)*
▼ Benko Products Inc .... E 440 934-2180
   Sheffield Village *(G-13181)*
◆ Canton Elevator Inc .... D 330 833-3600
   North Canton *(G-11719)*
Cleveland Elevator Inc .... G 216 924-0505
   Cuyahoga Falls *(G-6075)*
▲ Elevator Cncepts By Wurtec LLC ... F 734 246-4700
   Toledo *(G-14275)*
▲ Federal Equipment Company .... D 513 621-5260
   Cincinnati *(G-2899)*
Gray-Eering Ltd .... G 740 498-8816
   Tippecanoe *(G-14171)*
Heartland Stairways Inc .... G 330 279-2554
   Holmesville *(G-8544)*
Holmes Stair Parts Ltd .... E 330 279-2797
   Holmesville *(G-8546)*
Otis Elevator Company .... E 216 573-2333
   Cleveland *(G-4512)*
Schindler Elevator Corporation .... F 419 861-5900
   Holland *(G-8529)*
Schindler Elevator Corporation .... C 937 492-3186
   Sidney *(G-13281)*
◆ Sweet Manufacturing Company ...... E 937 325-1511
   Springfield *(G-13641)*

Versalift East Inc .... B 610 866-1400
   Canton *(G-2262)*
◆ Wittur Usa Inc .... E 216 524-0100
   Twinsburg *(G-14756)*
Wurtec Incorporated .... F 419 726-1066
   Toledo *(G-14527)*

3535 Conveyors and conveying equipment

2e Associates Inc .... E 440 975-9955
   Willoughby *(G-15871)*
◆ Ad Industries Inc .... A 303 744-1911
   Dayton *(G-6183)*
Advanced Equipment Systems LLC ... G 216 289-6505
   Euclid *(G-7258)*
◆ Air Technical Industries Inc .... E 440 951-5191
   Mentor *(G-10409)*
Alan Bortree .... G 937 585-6962
   De Graff *(G-6664)*
Alba Manufacturing Inc .... D 513 874-0551
   Fairfield *(G-7332)*
▲ Allgaier Process Technology .... G 513 402-2566
   West Chester *(G-15363)*
Allied Consolidated Inds Inc .... C 330 744-0808
   Youngstown *(G-16307)*
Allied Fabricating & Wldg Co .... E 614 751-6664
   Columbus *(G-5113)*
◆ Ambaflex Inc .... E 330 478-1858
   Canton *(G-2034)*
▲ American Solving Inc .... G 440 234-7373
   Brookpark *(G-1703)*
Automation Systems Design Inc .... E 937 387-0351
   Dayton *(G-6218)*
▲ Barth Industries Co LLC .... E 216 267-1950
   Cleveland *(G-3722)*
◆ Blair Rubber Company .... D 330 769-5583
   Seville *(G-13137)*
Bobco Enterprises Inc .... F 419 867-3560
   Toledo *(G-14215)*
◆ Bry-Air Inc .... E 740 965-2974
   Sunbury *(G-13951)*
Bulk Handling Equipment Co .... G 330 468-5703
   Northfield *(G-11904)*
▲ C A Litzler Co Inc .... E 216 267-8020
   Cleveland *(G-3778)*
▲ Cincinnati Mine Machinery Co .... D 513 522-7777
   Cincinnati *(G-2755)*
Coating Systems Group Inc .... F 440 816-9306
   Middleburg Heights *(G-10717)*
Con-Belt Inc .... F 330 273-2003
   Valley City *(G-14865)*
Conveyor Metal Works Inc .... E 740 477-8700
   Frankfort *(G-7657)*
Conveyor Solutions LLC .... F 513 367-4845
   Cleves *(G-4948)*
Conveyor Technologies Ltd .... G 513 248-0663
   Milford *(G-10903)*
▲ Daifuku America Corporation .... C 614 863-1888
   Reynoldsburg *(G-12760)*
Decision Systems Inc .... F 330 456-7600
   Canton *(G-2090)*
Defabco Inc .... D 614 231-2700
   Columbus *(G-5323)*
Dematic Corp .... D 440 526-2770
   Brecksville *(G-1612)*
Dillin Engineered Systems Corp .... E 419 666-6789
   Perrysburg *(G-12376)*
Dover Conveyor Inc .... E 740 922-9390
   Midvale *(G-10876)*
Duplex Mill & Manufacturing Co .... E 937 325-5555
   Springfield *(G-13557)*
◆ Eagle Crusher Co Inc .... D 419 468-2288
   Galion *(G-7872)*

Enviri Corporation .... F 740 387-1150
   Marion *(G-9851)*
ES Industries Inc .... F 419 643-2625
   Lima *(G-9242)*
Esco Turbine Tech Cleveland .... F 440 953-0053
   Eastlake *(G-7030)*
Fabacraft Inc .... E 513 677-0500
   Maineville *(G-9600)*
▲ Fabco Inc .... E 419 422-4533
   Findlay *(G-7504)*
Falcon Industries Inc .... E 330 723-0099
   Medina *(G-10322)*
▲ Federal Equipment Company .... D 513 621-5260
   Cincinnati *(G-2899)*
Feedall Inc .... F 440 942-8100
   Willoughby *(G-15920)*
▲ Fenner Dunlop Port Clinton LLC ..... C 419 635-2191
   Port Clinton *(G-12618)*
▲ Fki Logistex Automation Inc .... A 513 881-5251
   West Chester *(G-15554)*
▲ Formtek Inc .... D 216 292-4460
   Cleveland *(G-4084)*
Fred D Pfening Company .... E 614 294-5361
   Columbus *(G-5389)*
◆ Glassline Corporation .... E 419 666-9712
   Perrysburg *(G-12385)*
▲ Global TBM Company .... C 440 248-3303
   Solon *(G-13355)*
Gray-Eering Ltd .... G 740 498-8816
   Tippecanoe *(G-14171)*
◆ Grob Systems Inc .... A 419 358-9015
   Bluffton *(G-1504)*
Hawthorne-Seving Inc .... E 419 643-5531
   Cridersville *(G-6041)*
Hoist Equipment Co Inc .... E 440 232-0300
   Bedford Heights *(G-1174)*
Hostar International Inc .... F 440 564-5362
   Solon *(G-13362)*
Ibiza Holdings Inc .... G 513 701-7300
   Mason *(G-10004)*
Imperial Conveying Systems LLC ...... F 330 491-3200
   Canton *(G-2130)*
Innovative Controls Corp .... E 419 691-6684
   Toledo *(G-14333)*
Ins Robotics Inc .... G 888 293-5325
   Hilliard *(G-8414)*
Intelligrated Inc .... A 513 874-0788
   West Chester *(G-15565)*
▲ Intelligrated Inc .... E 866 936-7300
   Mason *(G-10007)*
Intelligrated Headquarters LLC .... E 866 936-7300
   Mason *(G-10008)*
▲ Intelligrated Products LLC .... E 740 490-0300
   London *(G-9389)*
Intelligrated Sub Holdings Inc .... D 513 701-7300
   Mason *(G-10009)*
Intelligrated Systems Inc .... C 513 881-5136
   West Chester *(G-15448)*
▲ Intelligrated Systems Inc .... A 866 936-7300
   Mason *(G-10010)*
Intelligrated Systems LLC .... A 513 701-7300
   Mason *(G-10011)*
Intelligrated Systems Ohio LLC .... G 513 682-6600
   West Chester *(G-15566)*
◆ Intelligrated Systems Ohio LLC ...... A 513 701-7300
   Mason *(G-10012)*
Joy Global Underground Min LLC ..... E 440 248-7970
   Cleveland *(G-4262)*
K F T Inc .... D 513 241-5910
   Cincinnati *(G-3055)*
Kleenline LLC .... F 800 259-5973
   Loveland *(G-9489)*

Employee Codes: A=Over 500 employees, B=251-500
C=101-250, D=51-100, E=20-50, F=10-19, G=1-9

35 INDUSTRIAL AND COMMERCIAL MACHINERY AND COMPUTER EQUIPMENT

Kolinahr Systems Inc .... F 513 745-9401
   Blue Ash *(G-1417)*
Laser Automation Inc .... F 440 543-9291
   Chagrin Falls *(G-2405)*
◆ Lewco Inc .... C 419 625-4014
   Sandusky *(G-13074)*
▲ Logitech Inc .... E 614 871-2822
   Grove City *(G-8102)*
◆ Manufacturers Equipment Co .... F 513 424-3573
   Middletown *(G-10841)*
▲ Material Holdings Inc .... E 513 583-5500
   Loveland *(G-9494)*
▲ Mayfran International Inc .... C 440 461-4100
   Cleveland *(G-4373)*
Met Fab Fabrication and Mch .... G 513 724-3715
   Batavia *(G-933)*
Mfh Partners Inc .... B 440 461-4100
   Cleveland *(G-4398)*
Midwest Conveyor Products Inc .... E 419 281-1235
   Ashland *(G-502)*
Miller Products Inc .... E 330 308-5934
   New Philadelphia *(G-11518)*
Mulhern Belting Inc .... E 201 337-5700
   Fairfield *(G-7386)*
◆ Nesco Inc .... E 440 461-6000
   Cleveland *(G-4448)*
▲ Ocs Intellitrak Inc .... F 513 742-5600
   Fairfield *(G-7388)*
▲ Ohio Magnetics Inc .... E 216 662-8484
   Maple Heights *(G-9756)*
▲ Opw Engineered Systems Inc .... E 888 771-9438
   West Chester *(G-15471)*
PB Fbrction Mech Contrs Corp .... E 419 478-4869
   Toledo *(G-14429)*
Pfpc Enterprises Inc .... F 513 941-6200
   Cincinnati *(G-3253)*
◆ Pneumatic Scale Corporation .... C 330 923-0491
   Cuyahoga Falls *(G-6109)*
Pomacon Inc .... F 330 273-1576
   Brunswick *(G-1781)*
Pro Mach Inc .... D 513 771-7374
   Cincinnati *(G-3278)*
Quickdraft Inc .... E 330 477-4574
   Canton *(G-2206)*
Richmond Machine Co .... E 419 485-5740
   Montpelier *(G-11142)*
Rolcon Inc .... F 513 821-7259
   Cincinnati *(G-3349)*
Sandusky Fabricating & Sls Inc .... E 419 626-4465
   Sandusky *(G-13089)*
Schenck Process LLC .... F 513 576-9200
   Solon *(G-13419)*
Sparks Belting Company Inc .... G 216 398-7774
   Cleveland *(G-4719)*
▲ Spirex Corporation .... C 330 726-1166
   Youngstown *(G-16446)*
Stacy Equipment Co .... G 419 447-6903
   Tiffin *(G-14106)*
◆ Stock Equipment Company Inc .... C 440 543-6000
   Chagrin Falls *(G-2424)*
Stock Fairfield Corporation .... C 440 543-6000
   Solon *(G-13425)*
◆ Sweet Manufacturing Company .... E 937 325-1511
   Springfield *(G-13641)*
Tkf Conveyor Systems LLC .... C 513 621-5260
   Cincinnati *(G-3457)*
▲ Uhrden Inc .... E 330 456-0031
   Canton *(G-2249)*
Ulterior Products LLC .... G 614 441-9465
   Radnor *(G-12696)*
◆ Webster Industries Inc .... B 419 447-8232
   Tiffin *(G-14115)*

Werks Kraft Engineering LLC .... E 330 721-7374
   Medina *(G-10394)*

3536 Hoists, cranes, and monorails

ACC Automation Co Inc .... E 330 928-3821
   Akron *(G-14)*
Acme Lifting Products Inc .... G 440 838-4430
   Cleveland *(G-3591)*
◆ Air Technical Industries Inc .... E 440 951-5191
   Mentor *(G-10409)*
Altec Industries Inc .... F 205 408-2341
   Cuyahoga Falls *(G-6062)*
◆ American Power Pull Corp .... G 419 335-7050
   Archbold *(G-520)*
ARI Phoenix Inc .... E 513 229-3750
   Sharonville *(G-13170)*
Bobco Enterprises Inc .... F 419 867-3560
   Toledo *(G-14215)*
Cattron Holdings Inc .... E 234 806-0018
   Warren *(G-16160)*
Cincinnati Crane & Hoist LLC .... F 513 202-1408
   Harrison *(G-8268)*
Crane 1 Services Inc .... E 937 704-9900
   West Chester *(G-15408)*
◆ Demag Cranes & Components Corp ..... C 440 248-2400
   Solon *(G-13337)*
Deshazo .... F 513 402-7466
   Monroe *(G-11102)*
▲ Drc Acquisition Inc .... E 330 656-1600
   Streetsboro *(G-13767)*
▲ Eaton Electric Holdings LLC .... B 440 523-5000
   Cleveland *(G-3995)*
◆ Emh Inc .... D 330 220-8600
   Valley City *(G-14869)*
Enviri Corporation .... F 740 387-1150
   Marion *(G-9851)*
Expert Crane Inc .... E 216 451-9900
   Wellington *(G-15307)*
▲ Federal Equipment Company .... D 513 621-5260
   Cincinnati *(G-2899)*
Flatiron Crane Oper Co LLC .... C 330 332-3300
   Salem *(G-12995)*
Gray-Eering Ltd .... G 740 498-8816
   Tippecanoe *(G-14171)*
◆ Hiab USA Inc .... D 419 482-6000
   Perrysburg *(G-12388)*
Hoist Equipment Co Inc .... E 440 232-0300
   Bedford Heights *(G-1174)*
IBI Brake Products Inc .... G 440 543-7962
   Chagrin Falls *(G-2402)*
◆ Kci Holding USA Inc .... C 937 525-5533
   Springfield *(G-13587)*
Konecranes Inc .... F 440 461-8400
   Broadview Heights *(G-1660)*
Konecranes Inc .... E 614 863-0150
   Gahanna *(G-7842)*
Konecranes Inc .... E 937 328-5100
   Springfield *(G-13589)*
Konecranes Inc .... F 419 382-7575
   Toledo *(G-14350)*
Konecranes Inc .... E 513 755-2800
   West Chester *(G-15567)*
◆ Konecranes Inc .... B 937 525-5933
   Springfield *(G-13590)*
▲ Kundel Industries Inc .... E 330 469-6147
   Vienna *(G-14996)*
▲ Lift-Tech International Inc .... B 330 424-7248
   Salem *(G-13011)*
Morgan Engineering Systems Inc .... E 330 821-4721
   Alliance *(G-414)*
▼ Morgan Engineering Systems Inc .... E 330 823-6930
   Alliance *(G-415)*

Radocy Inc .... F 419 666-4400
   Rossford *(G-12870)*
Rnm Holdings Inc .... F 614 444-5556
   Columbus *(G-5726)*
Rnm Holdings Inc .... F 419 867-8712
   Holland *(G-8528)*
Trane Technologies Company LLC .... E 419 633-6800
   Bryan *(G-1842)*
▲ Uhrden Inc .... E 330 456-0031
   Canton *(G-2249)*

3537 Industrial trucks and tractors

2c Transport LLC .... G 513 799-5278
   Cincinnati *(G-2579)*
ADSr Ent LLC .... F 773 280-2129
   Columbus *(G-5102)*
Advance Trans Inc .... F 330 572-0390
   Stow *(G-13682)*
AJD Holding Co .... D 330 405-4477
   Twinsburg *(G-14626)*
All Around Primo Logistics LLC .... G 513 725-7888
   Cincinnati *(G-2607)*
Back In Black Co .... E 419 425-5555
   Findlay *(G-7479)*
Boltech Incorporated .... G 330 746-6881
   Youngstown *(G-16323)*
Bpr-Rico Equipment Inc .... D 330 723-4050
   Medina *(G-10304)*
▲ Bpr-Rico Manufacturing Inc .... D 330 723-4050
   Medina *(G-10305)*
Brattiegirlz LLC .... G 513 607-4757
   Columbus *(G-5207)*
◆ Canton Elevator Inc .... D 330 833-3600
   North Canton *(G-11719)*
Cascade Corporation .... D 937 327-0300
   Springfield *(G-13541)*
City Machine Technologies Inc .... F 330 747-2639
   Youngstown *(G-16336)*
▲ Crescent Metal Products Inc .... C 440 350-1100
   Mentor *(G-10445)*
Crown Credit Company .... F 419 629-2311
   New Bremen *(G-11399)*
Crown Equipment Corporation .... E 419 586-1100
   Celina *(G-2328)*
Crown Equipment Corporation .... D 513 874-2600
   Cincinnati *(G-2803)*
Crown Equipment Corporation .... E 937 295-4062
   Fort Loramie *(G-7596)*
Crown Equipment Corporation .... D 614 274-7700
   Grove City *(G-8084)*
Crown Equipment Corporation .... E 419 629-2311
   New Bremen *(G-11401)*
Crown Equipment Corporation .... E 419 629-2311
   New Bremen *(G-11402)*
Crown Equipment Corporation .... D 937 454-7545
   Vandalia *(G-14935)*
◆ Crown Equipment Corporation .... A 419 629-2311
   New Bremen *(G-11400)*
Dragon Products LLC .... E 330 345-3968
   Wooster *(G-16114)*
◆ Eagle Industrial Truck Mfg LLC .... E 419 866-6301
   Swanton *(G-13973)*
Elliott Machine Works Inc .... E 419 468-4709
   Galion *(G-7874)*
Enviri Corporation .... F 740 387-1150
   Marion *(G-9851)*
Express Ground Services Inc .... G 216 870-9374
   Cleveland *(G-4044)*
Flawless Logistics LLC .... G 330 201-7070
   Canton *(G-2101)*
Forklift Solutions LLC .... G 419 717-9496
   Napoleon *(G-11313)*

SIC SECTION
35 INDUSTRIAL AND COMMERCIAL MACHINERY AND COMPUTER EQUIPMENT

Forte Industrial Equipmen.................. E 513 398-2800
  Mason *(G-9993)*
Freedom Forklift Sales LLC.................. G 330 289-0879
  Akron *(G-158)*
G & T Manufacturing Co....................... F 440 639-7777
  Mentor *(G-10462)*
G P Manufacturing Inc........................... G 937 544-3190
  Peebles *(G-12326)*
Gconsent LLC.. F 614 886-2416
  Dublin *(G-6885)*
General Electric Company.................... E 513 977-1500
  Cincinnati *(G-2943)*
Global Trucking LLC............................... F 614 598-6264
  Columbus *(G-5405)*
▲ Gradall Industries LLC........................ C 330 339-2211
  New Philadelphia *(G-11504)*
Grand Aire Inc... E 419 861-6700
  Swanton *(G-13974)*
Grand Harbor Yacht Sales & Svc........ G 440 442-2919
  Cleveland *(G-4139)*
Heritage Truck Equipment Inc............ D 330 699-4491
  Hartville *(G-8301)*
◆ Hobart Brothers LLC............................ A 937 332-5439
  Troy *(G-14579)*
Hoist Equipment Co Inc........................ E 440 232-0300
  Bedford Heights *(G-1174)*
Hyster-Yale Materials Hdlg Inc............ C 440 449-9600
  Cleveland *(G-4211)*
◆ Intelligrated Systems Ohio LLC....... A 513 701-7300
  Mason *(G-10012)*
Iron Works Inc.. F 937 420-2100
  Fort Loramie *(G-7601)*
▲ Jet Products Incorporated................. G 937 866-7969
  Dayton *(G-6389)*
Jh Industries Inc...................................... E 330 963-4105
  Twinsburg *(G-14677)*
Ken Beaverson Inc.................................. G 330 264-0378
  Wooster *(G-16140)*
Lane Field Materials Inc........................ G 330 526-8082
  Canton *(G-2143)*
Load32 LLC... F 614 984-6648
  Columbus *(G-5530)*
▼ Macton Corporation........................... D 330 259-8555
  Youngstown *(G-16393)*
Martin Sheet Metal Inc......................... E 216 377-8200
  Cleveland *(G-4362)*
McCullough Industries Inc................... E 419 673-0767
  Kenton *(G-8888)*
Mcl Inc... F 800 245-9490
  Kenton *(G-8889)*
Mcl Inc... F 800 245-9490
  Kenton *(G-8890)*
Medrano Usa Inc..................................... E 614 272-5856
  Columbus *(G-5558)*
Miller Products Inc................................. E 330 308-5934
  New Philadelphia *(G-11518)*
Miners Tractor Sales Inc....................... G 330 325-9914
  Rootstown *(G-12854)*
Mitchs Welding & Hitches.................... G 419 893-3117
  Maumee *(G-10223)*
Newsafe Transport Service Inc........... F 740 387-1679
  Marion *(G-9866)*
Octopus Express Inc.............................. E 614 412-1222
  Westerville *(G-15671)*
Ohio Truck Equipment LLC.................. F 740 830-6488
  Mount Vernon *(G-11283)*
Parobek Trucking Co.............................. G 419 869-7500
  West Salem *(G-15635)*
Perfecto Industries Inc......................... E 937 778-1900
  Piqua *(G-12542)*
Pollock Research & Design Inc........... G 330 332-3300
  Salem *(G-13023)*

Premier Container Inc........................... E 800 230-7132
  Cleveland *(G-4580)*
Pucel Enterprises Inc............................. D 216 881-4604
  Cleveland *(G-4598)*
Ready Rigs LLC.. F 740 963-9203
  Reynoldsburg *(G-12773)*
River City Body Company.................... F 513 772-9317
  Cincinnati *(G-3343)*
S&M Trucking LLC................................... F 661 310-2585
  Mason *(G-10052)*
Saf-Holland Inc.. G 513 874-7888
  Fairfield *(G-7404)*
Sb Trans LLC... F 407 477-2545
  Cincinnati *(G-3365)*
Shanafelt Manufacturing Co................ E 330 455-0315
  Canton *(G-2223)*
Shawn Fleming Ind Trckg LLC............. G 937 707-8539
  Dayton *(G-6568)*
Shousha Trucking LLC.......................... G 937 270-4471
  Dayton *(G-6571)*
Skylift Inc.. D 440 960-2100
  Lorain *(G-9438)*
Stock Fairfield Corporation.................. C 440 543-6000
  Solon *(G-13425)*
Surplus Freight Inc................................. G 614 235-7660
  Gahanna *(G-7851)*
Suspension Technology Inc................. F 330 458-3058
  Canton *(G-2240)*
◆ Sweet Manufacturing Company........ E 937 325-1511
  Springfield *(G-13641)*
Tarpco Inc... F 330 677-8277
  Kent *(G-8871)*
Tbt Hauling LLC....................................... G 904 635-7631
  Bowling Green *(G-1590)*
Tilt-Or-Lift Inc.. G 419 893-6944
  Maumee *(G-10241)*
▲ Trailer Component Mfg Inc............... E 440 255-2888
  Mentor *(G-10580)*
Transco Railway Products.................... G 419 562-1031
  Bucyrus *(G-1869)*
Trip Transport LLC................................. G 773 969-1402
  Columbus *(G-5838)*
Triumphant Enterprises Inc................ F 513 617-1668
  Goshen *(G-7995)*
▲ Uhrden Inc.. E 330 456-0031
  Canton *(G-2249)*
Venturo Manufacturing Inc................. F 513 772-8448
  Cincinnati *(G-3492)*
Volens LLC.. G 216 544-1200
  Macedonia *(G-9585)*
◆ Waltco Lift Corp................................... C 330 633-9191
  Streetsboro *(G-13798)*
▲ Whiteside Manufacturing Co............. E 740 363-1179
  Delaware *(G-6757)*
Youngstown-Kenworth Inc................. G 330 534-9761
  Hubbard *(G-8574)*

3541 Machine tools, metal cutting type

▲ Acro Tool & Die Company.................. E 330 773-5173
  Akron *(G-17)*
Advanced Innovative Mfg Inc............. D 330 562-2468
  Aurora *(G-705)*
Advetech Inc.. E 330 533-2227
  Canfield *(G-1995)*
Alcon Tool Co Ltd................................... G 330 773-9171
  Akron *(G-50)*
▼ Alcon Tool Company............................ E 330 773-9171
  Akron *(G-51)*
Applied Automation Entp Inc.............. E 419 929-2428
  New London *(G-11460)*
Apsx LLC.. F 513 716-5992
  Blue Ash *(G-1363)*

Arch Cutting Tls - Mentor LLC............ G 440 350-9393
  Mentor *(G-10422)*
▲ Areway LLC... D 216 651-9022
  Brooklyn *(G-1676)*
Axxess LLC.. G 330 861-0911
  Barberton *(G-856)*
B V Grinding Machining Inc................. G 440 918-1884
  Willoughby *(G-15888)*
▲ Barbco Inc... E 330 488-9400
  East Canton *(G-6978)*
▲ Bardons & Oliver Inc............................ C 440 498-5800
  Solon *(G-13316)*
▲ Barth Industries Co LLC...................... E 216 267-1950
  Cleveland *(G-3722)*
Beverly Dove Inc..................................... G 740 495-5200
  New Holland *(G-11446)*
▼ Bor-It Mfg Co Inc................................... E 419 289-6639
  Ashland *(G-558)*
Bortnick Tractor Sales Inc.................... G 330 924-2555
  Cortland *(G-5960)*
Bud May Inc... F 216 676-8850
  Cleveland *(G-3769)*
Butech Inc... C 330 337-0000
  Salem *(G-12978)*
▲ Butech Inc... D 330 337-0000
  Salem *(G-12979)*
C M M S - Re LLC.................................... F 513 489-5111
  Blue Ash *(G-1375)*
◆ Callahan Cutting Tools Inc................. G 614 294-1649
  Columbus *(G-5227)*
Cardinal Builders Inc............................. E 614 237-1000
  Columbus *(G-5236)*
Carter Manufacturing Co Inc.............. E 513 398-7303
  Mason *(G-9968)*
▲ Channel Products Inc.......................... D 440 423-0113
  Solon *(G-13328)*
Chart-Tech Tool Inc............................... E 937 667-3543
  Tipp City *(G-14129)*
▲ Cincinnati Gilbert Mch Tl LLC............ F 513 541-4815
  Cincinnati *(G-2752)*
▲ Cincinnati Mine Machinery Co.......... D 513 522-7777
  Cincinnati *(G-2755)*
▲ Cincinnati Radiator Inc...................... F 513 874-5555
  Hamilton *(G-8193)*
Commercial Grinding Svcs Inc........... E 330 273-5040
  Medina *(G-10311)*
▲ Competetive Carbide Inc.................... E 440 350-9393
  Madison *(G-9590)*
Criterion Tool & Die Inc........................ E 216 267-1733
  Brookpark *(G-1708)*
▲ Cutting Systems Inc............................. F 216 928-0500
  Cleveland *(G-3929)*
◆ Damon Industries Inc.......................... D 330 821-5310
  Alliance *(G-400)*
Dayton Machine Tool Company......... E 937 222-6444
  Dayton *(G-6282)*
Dbcr Inc... E 330 920-1900
  Cuyahoga Falls *(G-6078)*
Desmond-Stephan Mfgcompany........ E 937 653-7181
  Urbana *(G-14829)*
Diversified Honing Inc.......................... G 330 874-4663
  Bolivar *(G-1523)*
Dixie Machinery Inc.............................. F 513 360-0091
  Monroe *(G-11103)*
Dmg Mori... G 513 808-4842
  Cincinnati *(G-2835)*
Dmg Mori Usa Inc.................................. F 440 546-7088
  West Chester *(G-15414)*
◆ Drake Manufacturing Services Co....... D 330 847-7291
  Warren *(G-15164)*
▲ Eagle Machinery & Supply Inc.......... E 330 852-1300
  Sugarcreek *(G-13924)*

35 INDUSTRIAL AND COMMERCIAL MACHINERY AND COMPUTER EQUIPMENT

Elliott Tool Technologies Ltd............D 937 253-6133
Dayton *(G-6318)*

Esi-Extrusion Services Inc...............E 330 374-3388
Akron *(G-143)*

Falcon Industries Inc.......................E 330 723-0099
Medina *(G-10322)*

Falcon Tool & Machine Inc..............G 937 534-9999
Dayton *(G-6328)*

Fischer Special Tooling Corp...........E 440 951-8411
Mentor *(G-10455)*

Frazier Machine and Prod Inc..........E 419 874-7321
Perrysburg *(G-12383)*

◆ Fredon Corporation......................D 440 951-5200
Mentor *(G-10458)*

General Electric Company................C 513 341-0214
West Chester *(G-15439)*

Genex Tool and Die Inc...................F 330 788-2466
Youngstown *(G-16367)*

▼ George A Mitchell Company........E 330 758-5777
Youngstown *(G-16360)*

◆ Glassline Corporation...................E 419 666-9712
Perrysburg *(G-12385)*

▲ Global Specialty Machines LLC....F 513 701-0452
Mason *(G-9997)*

◆ Global TBM Company..................C 440 248-3303
Solon *(G-13355)*

◆ Glt Inc...F 937 237-0055
Dayton *(G-6358)*

Grind-All Corporation.......................E 330 220-1600
Brunswick *(G-1767)*

▲ H & D Steel Service Inc..............E 800 666-3390
North Royalton *(G-11878)*

Hammer Jammer LLC......................G 937 549-4062
Manchester *(G-9617)*

Herco Inc..F 740 498-5181
Newcomerstown *(G-11645)*

Houston Machine Products Inc.........E 937 322-8022
Springfield *(G-13580)*

Hyper Tool Company........................E 440 543-5151
Chagrin Falls *(G-2401)*

Industrial Paper Shredders Inc..........F 888 637-4733
North Lima *(G-11806)*

Interstate Tool Corporation..............E 216 671-1077
Cleveland *(G-4234)*

J & S Tool Corporation.....................F 216 676-8330
Cleveland *(G-4243)*

▲ J-C-R Tech Inc.............................F 937 783-2296
Blanchester *(G-1351)*

Jrp Solutions Llc..............................G 330 825-5989
Norton *(G-11946)*

K L M Manufacturing Company.........G 740 666-5171
Ostrander *(G-12174)*

Ken Emerick Machine Products........G 440 834-4501
Burton *(G-1883)*

Kilroy Company...............................D 440 951-8700
Cleveland *(G-4289)*

Kmi Processing LLC..........................E 330 862-2185
Minerva *(G-11033)*

L M Equipment & Design Inc............E 330 332-9951
Salem *(G-13009)*

Lahm-Trosper Inc.............................E 937 252-8791
Dayton *(G-6401)*

Lawrence Industries Inc...................C 216 518-1400
Cleveland *(G-4317)*

◆ Lawrence Industries Inc...............E 216 518-7000
Cleveland *(G-4318)*

Leland-Gifford Inc............................G 330 785-9730
Akron *(G-219)*

Levan Enterprises Inc......................E 330 923-9797
Stow *(G-13706)*

Lincoln Electric Automtn Inc.............E 614 471-5926
Columbus *(G-5527)*

Lower Investments LLC....................G 765 825-4151
Mason *(G-10022)*

◆ Makino Inc....................................B 513 573-7200
Mason *(G-10024)*

Martindale Electric Company............E 216 521-8567
Cleveland *(G-4363)*

Masheen Specialties........................G 330 652-7535
Mineral Ridge *(G-11023)*

Masters Prcision Machining Inc........F 330 419-1933
Kent *(G-8833)*

Max - Pro Tools Inc..........................F 800 456-0931
Cleveland *(G-4369)*

Melin Tool Company Inc...................D 216 362-4200
Cleveland *(G-4392)*

Miami Ice Machine Inc.....................G 513 863-6707
Overpeck *(G-12208)*

Michael Byrne Manufacturing Co Inc...E 419 525-1214
Mansfield *(G-9691)*

Midwest Knife Grinding Inc..............F 330 854-1030
Canal Fulton *(C-1073)*

Midwest Specialties Inc...................F 800 837-2503
Wapakoneta *(G-15127)*

◆ Milacron Marketing Company LLC...D 513 536-2000
Batavia *(G-936)*

Monaghan & Associates Inc.............F 937 253-7706
Dayton *(G-6456)*

More Manufacturing LLC..................F 937 233-3898
Tipp City *(G-14142)*

Morlock Asphalt Ltd........................F 419 686-4601
Portage *(G-12635)*

Mrd Solutions LLC............................F 440 942-6969
Eastlake *(G-7043)*

National Machine Tool Company.......G 513 541-6682
Cincinnati *(G-3180)*

◆ Nesco Inc....................................F 440 461-6000
Cleveland *(G-4448)*

Nmgg Ctg LLC..................................D 419 447-5211
Tiffin *(G-14096)*

Northwood Industries Inc.................F 419 666-2100
Perrysburg *(G-12404)*

Obars Machine and Tool Company.....E 419 535-6307
Toledo *(G-14403)*

▼ Ohio Broach & Machine Company...E 440 946-1040
Willoughby *(G-15963)*

Ohio Screw Products Inc..................D 440 322-6341
Elyria *(G-7191)*

OReilly Precision Pdts Inc................E 937 526-4677
Russia *(G-12886)*

Page Slotting Saw Co Inc.................F 419 476-7475
Toledo *(G-14428)*

◆ Peerless Saw Company................E 614 836-5790
Groveport *(G-8157)*

Phillips Manufacturing Co.................D 330 652-4335
Niles *(G-11682)*

▲ Portage Machine Concepts Inc....F 330 628-2343
Akron *(G-282)*

▲ Rafter Equipment Corporation.....E 440 572-3700
Strongsville *(G-13871)*

Rapid Machine Inc...........................F 419 737-2377
Pioneer *(G-12497)*

Ravana Industries Inc......................G 330 536-4015
Lowellville *(G-9518)*

▲ Raymath Company.......................C 937 335-1860
Troy *(G-14604)*

Reliable Products Co........................F 419 394-5854
Saint Marys *(G-12966)*

◆ Rex International USA Inc............E 800 321-7950
Ashtabula *(G-659)*

Ridge Tool Company.........................D 740 432-8782
Cambridge *(G-1951)*

Ridge Tool Company.........................D 440 329-4737
Elyria *(G-7201)*

◆ Ridge Tool Company....................A 440 323-5581
Elyria *(G-7202)*

Ridge Tool Manufacturing Co............E 440 323-5581
Elyria *(G-7203)*

▲ Rimrock Corporation....................E 614 471-5926
Columbus *(G-5723)*

Rimrock Holdings Corporation...........C 614 471-5926
Columbus *(G-5724)*

▼ Roll-In Saw Inc............................F 216 459-9001
Brookpark *(G-1725)*

Roto Tech Inc..................................F 937 859-8503
Moraine *(G-11209)*

Sinico Mtm US Inc...........................G 216 264-8344
Middleburg Heights *(G-10727)*

Slater Road Mills Inc........................E 330 332-9951
Salem *(G-13032)*

▲ Specialty Metals Proc Inc............E 330 656-2767
Hudson *(G-8614)*

Stadco Inc.......................................E 937 878-0911
Fairborn *(G-7332)*

STC International Co Ltd..................G 561 308-6002
Lebanon *(G-9112)*

Stevenson Mfg Co............................G 330 532-1581
Wellsville *(G-15337)*

Sumitomo Elc Carbide Mfg Inc.........F 440 354-0600
Grand River *(G-8013)*

▲ Superion Inc................................E 937 374-0033
Xenia *(G-16274)*

Superior Machining Inc....................E 937 236-9619
Dayton *(G-6599)*

Tailored Systems Inc.......................G 937 299-3900
Moraine *(G-11213)*

Technidrill Systems Inc....................E 330 678-9980
Kent *(G-8872)*

The Ransohoff Company..................C 513 870-0100
West Chester *(G-15595)*

▲ The Vulcan Tool Company............G 937 253-6194
Dayton *(G-6620)*

Tooling Connection Inc....................G 419 594-3339
Oakwood *(G-12034)*

Tykma Inc.......................................D 877 318-9562
Chillicothe *(G-2540)*

U S Alloy Die Corp...........................F 216 749-9700
Cleveland *(G-4842)*

Updike Supply Company...................E 937 482-4000
Huber Heights *(G-8580)*

Uvonics Co......................................F 614 458-1163
Columbus *(G-5852)*

Walter Grinders Inc.........................F 937 859-1975
Miamisburg *(G-10700)*

West Ohio Tool Co...........................F 937 842-6688
Russells Point *(G-12879)*

Willow Tool & Machining Ltd............F 440 572-2288
Strongsville *(G-13896)*

Wise Edge LLC.................................G 330 208-0889
Akron *(G-376)*

Wonder Machine Services Inc..........E 440 937-7500
Avon *(G-792)*

◆ Zagar Inc....................................E 216 731-0500
Cleveland *(G-4931)*

3542 Machine tools, metal forming type

Accurate Manufacturing Company....E 614 878-6510
Columbus *(G-5096)*

▲ Addition Manufacturing Te...........C 513 228-7000
Lebanon *(G-9059)*

Advanced Tech Utilization Co...........F 440 238-3770
Strongsville *(G-13802)*

◆ Aida-America Corporation............D 937 237-2382
Dayton *(G-6192)*

Airam Press Co Ltd..........................F 937 473-5672
Covington *(G-6016)*

35 INDUSTRIAL AND COMMERCIAL MACHINERY AND COMPUTER EQUIPMENT

Akay Holdings Inc .... E 330 753-8458
  Barberton (G-852)
Allied Mask and Tooling Inc .... G 419 470-2555
  Toledo (G-14183)
American Fluid Power Inc .... G 877 223-8742
  Elyria (G-7107)
Anderson & Vreeland Inc .... D 419 636-5002
  Bryan (G-1807)
Apeks LLC .... E 740 809-1174
  Johnstown (G-8769)
▲ Barth Industries Co LLC .... E 216 267-1950
  Cleveland (G-3722)
Bendco Machine & Tool Inc .... F 419 628-3802
  Minster (G-11048)
Brilex Industries Inc .... D 330 744-1114
  Youngstown (G-16327)
▲ Brilex Industries Inc .... D 330 744-1114
  Youngstown (G-16328)
Carnaudmetalbox Machinery USA .... G 740 681-6788
  Lancaster (G-8999)
Columbia Stamping Inc .... E 440 236-6677
  Columbia Station (G-5010)
▲ Columbus Jack Corporation .... E 614 443-7492
  Swanton (G-13971)
Columbus Water Section Permit .... G 614 645-8039
  Columbus (G-5281)
▼ Compass Systems & Sales LLC .... D 330 733-2111
  Norton (G-11940)
D C Morrison Company Inc .... E 859 581-7511
  Cincinnati (G-2812)
Danfoss Power Solutions II LLC .... G 419 238-1190
  Van Wert (G-14913)
Decked LLC .... F 208 806-0251
  Defiance (G-6675)
Diverse Mfg Solutions LLC .... F 740 363-3600
  Delaware (G-6717)
Eaton Corporation .... C 216 281-2211
  Cleveland (G-3992)
Ebog Legacy Inc .... D 330 239-4933
  Sharon Center (G-13166)
Elliott Tool Technologies Ltd .... D 937 253-6133
  Dayton (G-6318)
Exito Manufacturing LLC .... G 937 291-9871
  Beavercreek (G-1073)
F & G Tool and Die Co .... G 937 746-3658
  Franklin (G-7673)
Falls Mtal Fbrctors Indus Svcs .... F 330 253-7181
  Akron (G-148)
First Tool Corp .... E 937 254-6197
  Dayton (G-6333)
Fluidpower Assembly Inc .... G 419 394-7486
  Saint Marys (G-12952)
▲ French Oil Mill Machinery Co .... D 937 773-3420
  Piqua (G-12517)
Gem City Metal Tech LLC .... E 937 252-8998
  Dayton (G-6349)
▼ George A Mitchell Company .... E 330 758-5777
  Youngstown (G-16368)
▲ Green Corp Magnetic Inc .... F 614 801-4000
  Grove City (G-8096)
▲ GSE Production and Support LLC .... F 419 866-6301
  Swanton (G-13975)
H&G Legacy Co .... F 513 921-1075
  Cincinnati (G-2982)
High Production Technology LLC .... G 419 599-1511
  Napoleon (G-11317)
High Production Technology LLC .... F 419 591-7000
  Napoleon (G-11318)
Hunter Hydraulics Inc .... G 330 455-3983
  Canton (G-2126)
Industrial Rlbility Spclsts Inc .... G 800 800-6345
  Chillicothe (G-2511)

J & S Tool Corporation .... F 216 676-8330
  Cleveland (G-4243)
K & L Tool Inc .... E 419 258-2086
  Antwerp (G-493)
Kiraly Tool and Die Inc .... F 330 744-5773
  Youngstown (G-16386)
Kotobuki-Reliable Die Casting Inc .... E 937 347-1111
  Xenia (G-16267)
Levan Enterprises Inc .... E 330 923-9797
  Stow (G-13706)
Madison Property Holdings Inc .... E 800 215-3210
  Cincinnati (G-3124)
◆ McNeil & Nrm Inc .... D 330 761-1855
  Akron (G-240)
Metal & Wire Products Company .... E 330 332-9448
  Salem (G-13016)
Monode Marking Products Inc .... F 419 929-0346
  New London (G-11464)
Monode Marking Products Inc .... E 440 975-8802
  Mentor (G-10506)
Monode Steel Stamp Inc .... F 440 975-8802
  Mentor (G-10507)
◆ NIDEC MINSTER CORPORATION .... B 419 628-2331
  Minster (G-11057)
Phoenix Hydraulic Presses Inc .... F 614 850-8940
  Hilliard (G-8432)
▲ Pines Manufacturing Inc .... E 440 835-5553
  Westlake (G-15775)
Pioneer Solutions LLC .... E 216 383-3400
  Euclid (G-7292)
▲ Rafter Equipment Corporation .... E 440 572-3700
  Strongsville (G-13871)
Ram Products Inc .... E 614 443-4634
  Columbus (G-5709)
▲ Ready Technology Inc .... F 937 866-7200
  Dayton (G-6544)
▼ Recycling Eqp Solutions Corp .... G 330 920-1500
  Cuyahoga Falls (G-6113)
Risk Industries LLC .... D 440 835-5553
  Westlake (G-15779)
Ritime Incorporated .... G 330 273-3443
  Cleveland (G-4636)
◆ Rogers Industrial Products Inc .... E 330 535-3331
  Akron (G-309)
▲ Semtorq Inc .... F 330 487-0600
  Twinsburg (G-14734)
Spencer Manufacturing Company Inc .. D 330 648-2461
  Spencer (G-13484)
Starkey Machinery Inc .... E 419 468-2560
  Galion (G-7885)
Stolle Machinery Company LLC .... C 937 497-5400
  Sidney (G-13291)
Stover International LLC .... E 740 363-5251
  Delaware (G-6753)
Stutzman Manufacturing Ltd .... G 330 674-4359
  Millersburg (G-10996)
◆ Taylor - Winfield Corporation .... C 330 259-8500
  Hubbard (G-8571)
TEC Design & Manufacturing Inc .... F 937 435-2147
  Dayton (G-6611)
▲ Technical Machine Products Inc .... F
  Cleveland (G-4773)
Terminal Equipment Inds Inc .... G 330 468-0322
  Northfield (G-11912)
Tfi Manufacturing LLC .... G 440 290-9411
  Mentor (G-10575)
The Basic Aluminum Castings Co .... D 216 481-5606
  Cleveland (G-4779)
▲ The Vulcan Tool Company .... G 937 253-6194
  Dayton (G-6620)
▲ THT Presses Inc .... E 937 898-2012
  Dayton (G-6624)

Tri-K Enterprises Inc .... G 330 832-7380
  Canton (G-2248)
▲ Trucut Incorporated .... D 330 938-9806
  Sebring (G-13127)
Turner Machine Co .... F 330 332-5821
  Salem (G-13035)
Twist Inc .... G 937 675-9581
  Jamestown (G-8743)
▲ Twist Inc .... C 937 675-9581
  Jamestown (G-8742)
Uhrichsville Carbide Inc .... F 740 922-9197
  Uhrichsville (G-14772)
Valley Tool & Die Inc .... D 440 237-0160
  North Royalton (G-11900)
Vmaxx Inc .... F 419 738-4044
  Wapakoneta (G-15132)
▲ Yizumi-HPM Corporation .... E 740 382-5600
  Iberia (G-8649)

3543 Industrial patterns

Accuform Manufacturing Inc .... E 330 797-9291
  Youngstown (G-16300)
Advantic Building Group LLC .... F 513 290-4796
  Miamisburg (G-10606)
Air Power Dynamics LLC .... C 440 701-2100
  Mentor (G-10408)
Anchor Pattern Company .... G 614 443-2221
  Columbus (G-5142)
API Pattern Works Inc .... E 440 269-1766
  Willoughby (G-15879)
Cascade Pattern Company Inc .... E 440 323-4300
  Elyria (G-7122)
Cincinnati Pattern Company .... E 513 241-9872
  Cincinnati (G-2757)
Clinton Foundry Ltd .... F 419 243-6885
  Toledo (G-14244)
Clinton Pattern Works Inc .... F 419 243-0855
  Toledo (G-14245)
▲ Colonial Patterns Inc .... F 330 673-6475
  Kent (G-8805)
Dayton Pattern Inc .... G 937 277-0761
  Dayton (G-6286)
Design Pattern Works Inc .... G 937 252-0797
  Dayton (G-6297)
Elyria Pattern Co Inc .... G 440 323-1526
  Elyria (G-7144)
Feiner Pattern Works Inc .... F 513 851-9800
  Fairfield (G-7359)
Founders Service & Mfg Inc .... G 330 584-7759
  Deerfield (G-6666)
Freeman Manufacturing & Sup Co ...... E 440 934-1902
  Avon (G-775)
H&M Machine & Tool LLC .... E 419 776-9220
  Toledo (G-14306)
Humtown Pattern Company .... D 330 482-5555
  Columbiana (G-5041)
Industrial Pattern & Mfg Co .... F 614 252-0934
  Columbus (G-5457)
Industrial Technologies Inc .... G 330 434-2033
  Akron (G-190)
▲ J-Lenco Inc .... E 740 499-2260
  Morral (G-11221)
Ketco Inc .... E 937 426-9331
  Beavercreek (G-1053)
Liberty Pattern and Mold Inc .... G 330 788-9463
  Youngstown (G-16389)
Lorain Modern Pattern Inc .... F 440 365-6780
  Elyria (G-7174)
Mold Masters Inc .... G 216 561-6653
  Shaker Heights (G-13157)
National Pattern Mfgco .... F 330 682-6871
  Orrville (G-12140)

Employee Codes: A=Over 500 employees, B=251-500
C=101-250, D=51-100, E=20-50, F=10-19, G=1-9

35 INDUSTRIAL AND COMMERCIAL MACHINERY AND COMPUTER EQUIPMENT

Past Patterns .... G 937 223-3722
  Dayton (G-6498)
PCC Airfoils LLC .... C 216 692-7900
  Cleveland (G-4537)
Plas-Mac Corp .... D 440 349-3222
  Solon (G-13405)
R L Rush Tool & Pattern Inc .... G 419 562-9849
  Bucyrus (G-1866)
Reliable Castings Corporation .... D
  Cincinnati (G-3331)
Reliable Pattern Works Inc .... G 440 232-8820
  Cleveland (G-4623)
▲ Ross Aluminum Castings LLC .... C 937 492-4134
  Sidney (G-13279)
Seaport Mold & Casting Company .... E 419 243-1422
  Toledo (G-14464)
Seaway Pattern Mfg Inc .... E 419 865-5724
  Toledo (G-14465)
Seilkop Industries Inc .... F 513 679-5680
  Cincinnati (G-3376)
Sherwood Rtm Corp .... G 330 875-7151
  Louisville (G-9471)
Sinel Company Inc .... F 937 433-4772
  Dayton (G-6576)
Spectracam Ltd .... G 937 223-3805
  Dayton (G-6582)
Tempcraft Corporation .... A 216 391-3885
  Cleveland (G-4775)
Th Manufacturing Inc .... G 330 893-3572
  Millersburg (G-10998)
◆ Transducers Direct Llc .... F 513 247-0601
  Cincinnati (G-3462)
TW Manufacturing Co .... E 440 439-3243
  Cleveland (G-4838)
United States Drill Head Co .... G 513 941-0300
  Cincinnati (G-3482)

3544 Special dies, tools, jigs, and fixtures

5me LLC .... E 513 719-1600
  Cincinnati (G-2544)
A & B Tool & Manufacturing .... G 419 382-0215
  Toledo (G-14172)
A G Industries Inc .... E 330 220-0050
  Brunswick (G-1746)
Accu-Rite Tool & Die Co Corp .... G 330 497-9959
  Canton (G-2027)
Accu-Tek Tool & Die Inc .... G 330 726-1946
  Salem (G-12975)
Accu-Tool Inc .... G 937 667-5878
  Tipp City (G-14120)
Accuform Manufacturing Inc .... E 330 797-9291
  Youngstown (G-16300)
Ace American Wire Die Co .... F 330 425-7269
  Twinsburg (G-14622)
▲ Acro Tool & Die Company .... E 330 773-5173
  Akron (G-17)
▲ Addition Manufacturing Te .... C 513 228-7000
  Lebanon (G-9059)
Adept Manufacturing Corp .... F 937 222-7110
  Dayton (G-6185)
▲ Advanced Engrg Solutions Inc .... D 937 743-6900
  Springboro (G-13493)
▲ Advanced Intr Solutions Inc .... E 937 550-0065
  Springboro (G-13494)
Aero Tech Tool & Mold Inc .... G 440 942-3327
  Mentor (G-10406)
Afc Tool Co Inc .... E 937 275-8700
  Dayton (G-6189)
Aims-CMI Technology LLC .... F 937 832-2000
  Englewood (G-7221)
AJD Holding Co .... D 330 405-4477
  Twinsburg (G-14626)

Akron Centl Engrv Mold Mch Inc .... E 330 794-8704
  Akron (G-29)
Allied Tool & Die Inc .... F 216 941-6196
  Cleveland (G-3637)
▲ Alpha Tool & Mold Inc .... F 440 473-2343
  Cleveland (G-3639)
Alpine Gage Inc .... G 937 669-8665
  Tipp City (G-14122)
Alternative Flash Inc .... F 330 334-6111
  Wadsworth (G-15018)
Amaroq Inc .... G 419 747-2110
  Mansfield (G-9623)
▼ Amcraft Inc .... G 419 729-7900
  Toledo (G-14185)
American Cube Mold Inc .... G 330 558-0044
  Brunswick (G-1748)
American Punch Co .... E 216 731-4501
  Euclid (G-7262)
American Tool and Die Inc .... F 419 726-5394
  Toledo (G-11103)
Amerimold Inc .... G 800 950-8020
  Mogadore (G-11066)
Amex Dies Inc .... F 330 545-9766
  Girard (G-7961)
Ampex Metal Products Company .... D 216 267-9242
  Brookpark (G-1704)
Anchor Glass Container Corp .... D 740 452-2743
  Zanesville (G-16500)
▲ Anchor Tool & Die Co .... B 216 362-1850
  Cleveland (G-3664)
Antwerp Tool & Die Inc .... F 419 258-5271
  Antwerp (G-491)
Apollo Plastics Inc .... G 440 951-7774
  Mentor (G-10420)
Apollo Products Inc .... G 440 269-8551
  Willoughby (G-15880)
Apr Tool Inc .... G 440 946-0393
  Willoughby (G-15883)
Arnett Tool Inc .... G 937 437-0361
  New Paris (G-11480)
Artisan Equipment Inc .... F 740 756-9135
  Carroll (G-2294)
▼ Artisan Tool & Die Corp .... D 216 883-2769
  Cleveland (G-3681)
Aspec Inc .... G 513 561-9922
  Cincinnati (G-2636)
Atama Tech LLC .... G 614 763-0399
  Powell (G-12663)
Athens Mold and Machine Inc .... D 740 593-6613
  Athens (G-675)
▲ Atlantic Tool & Die Company .... C 440 238-6931
  Strongsville (G-13810)
Aukerman J F Steel Rule Die .... G 937 456-4498
  Eaton (G-7054)
Automation Plastics Corp .... D 330 562-5148
  Aurora (G-707)
Automation Tool & Die Inc .... G 330 558-8128
  Brunswick (G-1749)
Automation Tool & Die Inc .... D 330 225-8336
  Valley City (G-14862)
Autotec Corporation .... E 419 885-2529
  Toledo (G-14201)
B V Mfg Inc .... F 330 549-5331
  New Springfield (G-11539)
B-K Tool & Design Inc .... D 419 532-3890
  Kalida (G-8784)
Balancing Company Inc .... E 937 898-9111
  Vandalia (G-14933)
Banco Die Inc .... F 330 821-8511
  Alliance (G-395)
Banner Metals Group Inc .... E 614 291-3905
  Columbus (G-5174)

▲ Basilius Inc .... E 419 536-5810
  Toledo (G-14207)
Bk Tool Company Inc .... F 513 870-9622
  Fairfield (G-7339)
Bloom Industries Inc .... F 330 898-3878
  Warren (G-15146)
Blue Ash Tool & Die Co Inc .... F 513 793-4530
  Blue Ash (G-1372)
Bollinger Tool & Die Inc .... G 419 866-5180
  Holland (G-8494)
Brassgate Industries Inc .... F 937 339-2192
  Troy (G-14552)
Brothers Tool and Mfg Ltd .... F 513 353-9700
  Miamitown (G-10706)
Brw Tool Inc .... F 419 394-3371
  Saint Marys (G-12948)
Bryan Die-Cast Products Ltd .... G 419 252-6208
  Toledo (G-14222)
C & S Industrial Ltd .... G 440 327-2360
  North Ridgeville (G-11935)
Caliber Mold and Machine Inc .... E 330 633-8171
  Akron (G-98)
CAM-Lem Inc .... G 216 391-7750
  Cleveland (G-3783)
Capital Precision Machine & Tl .... G 937 258-1176
  Dayton (G-6154)
Capital Tool Company .... E 216 661-5750
  Cleveland (G-3787)
Carbide Specialist Inc .... F 440 951-4027
  Willoughby (G-15896)
Carter Manufacturing Co Inc .... E 513 398-7303
  Mason (G-9968)
CD Company LLC .... D 419 332-2693
  Fremont (G-7770)
Centaur Tool & Die Inc .... E 419 352-7704
  Bowling Green (G-1557)
Chart-Tech Tool Inc .... E 937 667-3543
  Tipp City (G-14129)
Chippewa Tool and Mfg Co .... F 419 849-2790
  Woodville (G-16091)
Clark Fixture Technologies Inc .... E 419 354-1541
  Bowling Green (G-1560)
◆ Cleveland Die & Mfg Co .... C 440 243-3404
  Middleburg Heights (G-10716)
Cleveland Metal Processing Inc .... C 440 243-3404
  Cleveland (G-3848)
Cleveland Roll Forming Co .... G 216 281-0202
  Cleveland (G-3854)
◆ Cleveland Steel Tool Company .... E 216 681-7400
  Cleveland (G-3856)
Clyde Tool & Die Inc .... F 419 547-9574
  Clyde (G-4971)
CMI Technology Inc .... F 937 832-2000
  Englewood (G-7225)
Cmt Machining & Fabg LLC .... F 937 652-3740
  Urbana (G-14827)
Coach Tool & Die LLC .... G 937 890-4716
  Springboro (G-13498)
Coldwater Machine Company LLC .... C 419 678-4877
  Coldwater (G-4985)
Cole Tool & Die Company .... E 419 522-1272
  Ontario (G-12090)
Colonial Machine Company Inc .... D 330 673-5859
  Kent (G-8804)
▲ Colonial Patterns Inc .... F 330 673-6475
  Kent (G-8805)
Columbia Stamping Inc .... E 440 236-6677
  Columbia Station (G-5010)
Compco Quaker Mfg Inc .... E 330 482-0200
  Salem (G-12986)
Condor Tool & Die Inc .... E 216 671-6000
  Cleveland (G-3895)

35 INDUSTRIAL AND COMMERCIAL MACHINERY AND COMPUTER EQUIPMENT

Conforming Matrix Corporation............ E 419 729-3777
  Toledo *(G-14249)*
Continental Business Entps Inc............ F 440 439-4400
  Bedford *(G-1113)*
Contour Forming Inc............................. F 740 345-9777
  Newark *(G-11572)*
Contour Tool Inc................................. E 440 365-7333
  North Ridgeville *(G-11836)*
Cornerstone Manufacturing Inc............ G 937 456-5930
  Eaton *(G-7057)*
Cornerstone Wauseon Inc..................... C 419 337-0940
  Wauseon *(G-15259)*
Criterion Tool & Die Inc....................... E 216 267-1733
  Brookpark *(G-1708)*
Crowe Manufacturing Services.............. E 800 831-1893
  Troy *(G-14558)*
Crum Manufacturing Inc...................... E 419 878-9779
  Waterville *(G-15241)*
Csw Inc... E 413 589-1311
  Sylvania *(G-13992)*
Custom Machine Inc............................ E 419 986-5122
  Tiffin *(G-14082)*
Customformed Products Inc................. F 937 388-0480
  Miamisburg *(G-10631)*
D A Fitzgerald Co Inc.......................... G 937 548-0511
  Greenville *(G-8044)*
Darke Precision Inc............................. F 937 548-2232
  Piqua *(G-12512)*
▲ Dayton Progress Corporation.............. A 937 859-5111
  Dayton *(G-6288)*
Dayton Progress Intl Corp.................... D 937 859-5111
  Dayton *(G-6289)*
Dayton Stencil Works Company............ F 937 223-3233
  Dayton *(G-6290)*
▲ DC Legacy Corp................................. E 330 896-4220
  Akron *(G-125)*
Dcd Technologies Inc........................... E 216 481-0056
  Cleveland *(G-3947)*
Deca Mfg Co.. F 419 884-0071
  Mansfield *(G-9645)*
▲ Defiance Metal Products Co................. B 419 784-5332
  Defiance *(G-6676)*
Delta Tool & Die Stl Block Inc.............. E 419 822-5939
  Delta *(G-6781)*
▲ Diamond America Corporation............. E 330 762-9269
  Akron *(G-126)*
Diamond Mold & Die Inc...................... F 330 633-5682
  Tallmadge *(G-14027)*
Die Guys Inc....................................... F 330 239-3437
  Medina *(G-10318)*
▲ Die-Matic Corporation......................... D 216 749-4656
  Brooklyn Heights *(G-1689)*
▼ Die-Mension Corporation..................... F 330 273-5872
  Brunswick *(G-1758)*
Direct Wire Service LLP...................... G 937 526-4447
  Versailles *(G-14979)*
Diversified Mold Castings LLC............ E 216 663-1814
  Cleveland *(G-3964)*
DMG Tool & Die LLC........................... G 937 407-0810
  Bellefontaine *(G-1207)*
Dove Die and Stamping Company........ E 216 267-3720
  Cleveland *(G-3970)*
Dover Machine Co................................ F 330 343-4123
  Dover *(G-6821)*
Doyle Manufacturing Inc...................... D 419 865-2548
  Holland *(G-8505)*
◆ Drt Mfg Co LLC.................................. D 937 297-6670
  Dayton *(G-6307)*
Duco Tool & Die Inc............................ F 419 628-2031
  Minster *(G-11050)*
▲ Duncan Tool Inc.................................. F 937 667-9364
  Tipp City *(G-14132)*

Durivage Pattern and Mfg Inc............... E 419 836-8655
  Williston *(G-15870)*
Dyco Manufacturing Inc....................... F 419 485-5525
  Montpelier *(G-11137)*
Dynamic Dies Inc................................. E 513 705-9524
  Middletown *(G-10819)*
Dynamic Dies Inc................................. E 419 865-0249
  Holland *(G-8507)*
Dynamic Tool & Mold Inc..................... G 440 237-8665
  Cleveland *(G-3982)*
Dysinger Incorporated.......................... E 937 297-7761
  Dayton *(G-6310)*
E D M Fastar Inc................................. G 216 676-0100
  Cleveland *(G-3984)*
Eagle Precision Products LLC.............. G 440 582-9393
  North Royalton *(G-11873)*
Ecm Industries LLC............................ E 513 533-6242
  Cincinnati *(G-2857)*
Edfa LLC... G 937 222-1415
  Dayton *(G-6313)*
▲ EMI Corp.. D 937 596-5511
  Jackson Center *(G-8733)*
Engineered Mfg & Eqp Co.................... G 937 642-7776
  Marysville *(G-9908)*
Enterprise Tool & Die Company........... F 216 351-1300
  Cleveland *(G-4021)*
Esi-Extrusion Services Inc................... E 330 374-3388
  Akron *(G-143)*
Estee 2 Inc.. E 937 224-7853
  Dayton *(G-6323)*
Esterle Mold & Machine Co Inc............ E 330 686-1685
  Stow *(G-13695)*
Euclid Design and Mfg Inc................... F 440 942-0066
  Willoughby *(G-15918)*
Exact-Tool & Die Inc............................ E 216 676-9140
  Cleveland *(G-4040)*
◆ Exco Engineering USA Inc................... E 419 726-1595
  Toledo *(G-14281)*
Exito Manufacturing LLC..................... G 937 291-9871
  Beavercreek *(G-1073)*
F & G Tool and Die Co......................... E 937 294-1405
  Moraine *(G-11180)*
Fabcor Inc... F 419 628-4428
  Minster *(G-11052)*
Fabrication Shop Inc........................... F 419 435-7934
  Fostoria *(G-7631)*
Faith Tool & Manufacturing.................. G 440 951-5934
  Willoughby *(G-15919)*
Falls Stamping & Welding Co............... G 330 928-1191
  Cuyahoga Falls *(G-6083)*
Falls Tool and Die Inc......................... G 330 633-4884
  Akron *(G-149)*
Faull & Son LLC.................................. F 330 652-4341
  Niles *(G-11668)*
Fc Industries Inc................................. E 937 275-8700
  Dayton *(G-6330)*
Feitl Manufacturing Co Inc................... E 330 405-6600
  Macedonia *(G-9550)*
Feller Tool Co..................................... F 440 324-6277
  Elyria *(G-7151)*
▲ Ferriot Inc.. C 330 786-3000
  Akron *(G-152)*
First Machine & Tool Corp................... F 440 269-8644
  Willoughby *(G-15921)*
First Tool Corp.................................... E 937 254-6197
  Dayton *(G-6333)*
Fischer Special Tooling Corp............... E 440 951-8411
  Mentor *(G-10455)*
Founders Service & Mfg Inc................. G 330 584-7759
  Deerfield *(G-6666)*
▼ Fremar Industries Inc......................... E 330 220-3700
  Brunswick *(G-1761)*

Fremont Cutting Dies Inc..................... G 419 334-5153
  Fremont *(G-7781)*
G & S Custom Tooling LLC.................. G 419 286-2888
  Fort Jennings *(G-7595)*
Gasdorf Tool and Mch Co Inc............... E 419 227-0103
  Lima *(G-9244)*
Gem City Engineering Co..................... C 937 223-5544
  Dayton *(G-6348)*
▲ General Die Casters Inc...................... E 330 678-2528
  Twinsburg *(G-14667)*
▲ General Tool Company......................... E 513 733-5500
  Cincinnati *(G-2946)*
Gentzler Tool & Die Corp..................... E 330 896-1941
  Akron *(G-168)*
Gilson Machine & Tool Co Inc.............. E 419 592-2911
  Napoleon *(G-11316)*
▲ Gokoh Corporation............................... F 937 339-4977
  Troy *(G-14573)*
Gordon Tool Inc................................... F 419 263-3151
  Payne *(G-12321)*
Green Machine Tool Inc....................... F 937 253-0771
  Dayton *(G-6161)*
Greenfield Die & Mfg Corp................... D 734 454-4000
  Valley City *(G-14871)*
H Machining Inc.................................. F 419 636-6890
  Bryan *(G-1820)*
H&M Machine & Tool LLC.................... F 419 776-9220
  Toledo *(G-14306)*
Hale Performance Coatings Inc............ E 419 244-6451
  Toledo *(G-14310)*
Hamilton Custom Molding Inc.............. G 513 844-6643
  Hamilton *(G-8217)*
Hamilton Mold & Machine Co............... E 216 732-8200
  Cleveland *(G-4167)*
Hardin Creek Machine & Tl Inc............ F 419 678-4913
  Coldwater *(G-4991)*
Hawthorne Tool LLC............................ F 440 516-1891
  Wickliffe *(G-15834)*
Hedalloy Die Corporation..................... F 216 341-3768
  Cleveland *(G-4176)*
Hedges Selective Tl & Prod Inc............ F 419 478-8670
  Toledo *(G-14316)*
▲ Herbert Usa Inc.................................. D 330 929-4297
  Akron *(G-181)*
Herd Manufacturing Inc....................... E 216 651-4221
  Cleveland *(G-4184)*
Hi-Tech Wire Inc................................. D 419 678-8376
  Saint Henry *(G-12935)*
▲ Hi-Tek Manufacturing Inc.................... C 513 459-1094
  Mason *(G-10001)*
High-Tech Mold & Machine Inc............ F 330 896-4466
  Uniontown *(G-14785)*
Hocker Tool and Die Inc...................... E 937 274-3443
  Dayton *(G-6370)*
Hofacker Prcsion Machining LLC......... F 937 832-7712
  Clayton *(G-3565)*
Holland Engraving Company................. E 419 865-2765
  Toledo *(G-14318)*
Home Asb & Mold Removal Inc............ G 216 661-6696
  Cleveland *(G-4198)*
Homeworth Fabrication Mch Inc........... F 330 525-5459
  Homeworth *(G-8554)*
Honda... F 937 524-5177
  Troy *(G-14583)*
▲ Honda Engineering North A................. B 937 642-5000
  Marysville *(G-9918)*
Horizon Industries Corporation............. G 937 323-0801
  Springfield *(G-13578)*
Hunt Products Inc............................... G 440 667-2457
  Newburgh Heights *(G-11617)*
I AM King Apparel Llc......................... G 513 284-9195
  Cincinnati *(G-3014)*

Employee Codes: A=Over 500 employees, B=251-500
C=101-250, D=51-100, E=20-50, F=10-19, G=1-9

35 INDUSTRIAL AND COMMERCIAL MACHINERY AND COMPUTER EQUIPMENT — SIC SECTION

Ibycorp .... G 330 425-8226
   Twinsburg (G-14674)
▲ Ilsco LLC .... C 513 533-6200
   Cincinnati (G-3017)
Impact Industries Inc .... E 440 327-2360
   North Ridgeville (G-11845)
Imperial Die & Mfg Co .... F 440 268-9080
   Strongsville (G-13844)
Independent Stamping Inc .... E 216 251-3500
   Cleveland (G-4223)
Industrial Mold Inc .... E 330 425-7374
   Twinsburg (G-14676)
▲ Industry Products Co .... B 937 778-0585
   Piqua (G-12526)
Innovative Plastic Molders LLC .... E 937 898-3775
   Vandalia (G-14944)
Innovative Tool & Die Inc .... G 419 599-0492
   Napoleon (G-11320)
Intelitool Mfg Svcs Inc .... G 440 953-1071
   Willoughby (G-15033)
▲ Ishmael Precision Tool Corp .... E 937 335-8070
   Troy (G-14588)
J & J Tool & Die Inc .... G 330 343-4721
   Dover (G-6829)
J & M Industries Inc .... G 440 951-1985
   Mentor (G-10479)
J & S Tool Corporation .... F 216 676-8330
   Cleveland (G-4243)
J M Mold Inc .... G 937 778-0077
   Piqua (G-12529)
J Tek Tool & Mold Inc .... F 419 547-9476
   Clyde (G-4973)
J W Harwood Co .... F 216 531-6230
   Cleveland (G-4247)
▲ J-C-R Tech Inc .... F 937 783-2296
   Blanchester (G-1351)
Jamen Tool & Die Co .... E 330 782-6731
   Youngstown (G-16382)
Jamen Tool & Die Co .... F 330 788-6521
   Youngstown (G-16381)
Jena Tool Inc .... D 937 296-1122
   Moraine (G-11187)
▲ Jergens Inc .... C 216 486-5540
   Cleveland (G-4253)
Jet Di Inc .... G 330 607-7913
   Brunswick (G-1772)
Johnston Mfg Co Inc .... G 440 269-1420
   Mentor (G-10485)
K & L Tool Inc .... E 419 258-2086
   Antwerp (G-493)
K B Machine & Tool Inc .... G 937 773-1624
   Piqua (G-12531)
▲ Kalt Manufacturing Company .... D 440 327-2102
   North Ridgeville (G-11848)
Ken Forging Inc .... C 440 993-8091
   Jefferson (G-8749)
Kent Mold and Manufacturing Co .... E 330 673-3469
   Kent (G-8825)
Kiffer Industries Inc .... E 216 267-1818
   Cleveland (G-4288)
Kilroy Company .... D 440 951-8700
   Cleveland (G-4289)
Kiraly Tool and Die Inc .... F 330 744-5773
   Youngstown (G-16386)
Kirtland Plastics Inc .... D 440 951-4466
   Kirtland (G-8941)
Knowlton Manufacturing Co Inc .... F 513 631-7353
   Cincinnati (G-3085)
Koebbe Products Inc .... D 513 753-4200
   Amelia (G-458)
Kramer & Kiefer Inc .... G 330 336-8475
   Wadsworth (G-15041)

Kreider Corp .... D 937 325-8787
   Springfield (G-13593)
Krengel Equipment LLC .... C 440 946-3570
   Eastlake (G-7037)
Krisdale Inc .... G 330 225-2392
   Valley City (G-14875)
Kuhns Mold & Tool Co Inc .... D 937 833-2178
   Brookville (G-1740)
Kurtz Tool & Die Co Inc .... G 330 755-7723
   Struthers (G-13905)
La Ganke & Sons Stamping Co .... F 216 451-0278
   Columbia Station (G-5013)
Lahm-Trosper Inc .... E 937 252-8791
   Dayton (G-6401)
▲ Lako Tool & Manufacturing Inc .... F 419 662-5256
   Perrysburg (G-12396)
Langenau Manufacturing Company .... E 216 651-3400
   Cleveland (G-4310)
Lanko Industries Inc .... G 440 269-1641
   Mentor (G-10491)
Laspina Tool and Die Inc .... F 330 923-9996
   Stow (G-13705)
▲ Laszeray Technology LLC .... D 440 582-8430
   North Royalton (G-11883)
Levan Enterprises Inc .... E 330 923-9797
   Stow (G-13706)
Lightning Mold & Machine Inc .... F 440 593-6460
   Conneaut (G-5924)
Lincoln Electric Automtn Inc .... C 419 678-4877
   Coldwater (G-4996)
Lincoln Electric Automtn Inc .... B 937 295-2120
   Fort Loramie (G-7603)
Liqui-Box Corporation .... E 419 294-3884
   Upper Sandusky (G-14814)
▲ Logan Machine Company .... D 330 633-6163
   Akron (G-223)
Lomar Enterprises Inc .... E 614 409-9104
   Groveport (G-8151)
▲ Long-Stanton Mfg Company .... E 513 874-8020
   West Chester (G-15458)
Lorain Rled Die Pdts Indus Sup .... G 440 281-8607
   North Ridgeville (G-11849)
▼ Loroco Industries Inc .... D 513 891-9544
   Cincinnati (G-3113)
Lostcreek Tool & Machine Inc .... F 937 773-6022
   Piqua (G-12533)
Lowry Tool & Die Inc .... F 330 332-1722
   Salem (G-13012)
Lrb Tool & Die Ltd .... F 330 898-5783
   Warren (G-15186)
Lukens Inc .... D 937 440-2500
   Troy (G-14594)
Lunar Tool & Mold Inc .... E 440 237-2141
   North Royalton (G-11884)
M & M Dies Inc .... G 216 883-6628
   Cleveland (G-4342)
Machine Tek Systems Inc .... E 330 527-4450
   Garrettsville (G-7921)
Machine Tool Design & Fab LLC .... F 419 435-7676
   Fostoria (G-7641)
◆ Magnum Tool Corp .... F 937 228-0900
   Dayton (G-6422)
Mahoning Valley Tool & Mch LLC .... F 330 482-0870
   Columbiana (G-5044)
Majestic Tool and Machine Inc .... F 440 248-5058
   Solon (G-13383)
Mallory Pattern Works Inc .... G 419 726-8001
   Toledo (G-14377)
Manufacturers Service Inc .... E 216 267-3771
   Cleveland (G-4355)
Mar-Con Tool Company .... E 937 299-2244
   Moraine (G-11191)

Mar-Metal Mfg Inc .... E 419 447-1102
   Upper Sandusky (G-14815)
Mar-Vel Tool Co .... F 937 223-2137
   Dayton (G-6429)
Marsh Technologies Inc .... F 330 545-0085
   Girard (G-7972)
▼ Martin Pultrusion Group Inc .... G 440 439-9130
   Cleveland (G-4361)
Master Craft Products Inc .... F 216 281-5910
   Cleveland (G-4366)
Master Marking Company Inc .... F 330 688-6797
   Cuyahoga Falls (G-6102)
Match Mold & Machine Inc .... F 330 830-5503
   Massillon (G-10124)
May Industries of Ohio Inc .... E 440 237-8012
   North Royalton (G-11886)
McAfee Tool & Die Inc .... E 330 896-9555
   Uniontown (G-14787)
▲ McGregor Mtal Yllow Sprng Wrks .... D 937 325-5561
   Springfield (G-13604)
McRon Finance Corp .... E 513 487-5000
   Cincinnati (G-3136)
Mdf Tool Corporation .... F 440 237-2277
   North Royalton (G-11887)
Medway Tool Corp .... E 937 335-7717
   Troy (G-14597)
Meese Inc .... F 440 998-1202
   Ashtabula (G-647)
Meggitt (erlanger) LLC .... D 513 851-5550
   Cincinnati (G-3143)
Mercury Machine Co .... D 440 349-3222
   Solon (G-13386)
Metal & Wire Products Company .... E 330 332-9448
   Salem (G-13016)
◆ Metalex Manufacturing Inc .... C 513 489-0507
   Blue Ash (G-1437)
Miami Valley Punch & Mfg .... F 937 237-0533
   Dayton (G-6440)
▲ Midwest Mold & Texture Corp .... E 513 732-1300
   Batavia (G-934)
Midwest Tool & Engineering Co .... E
   Dayton (G-6445)
Milacron Holdings Corp .... C 513 487-5000
   Batavia (G-935)
▲ Milacron Plas Tech Group LLC .... C 513 536-2000
   Batavia (G-937)
Minco Tool and Mold Inc .... D 937 890-7905
   Dayton (G-6451)
Modern Manufacturing Inc .... E 513 251-3600
   Cincinnati (G-3171)
▼ Mohr Stamping Inc .... E 440 647-4316
   Wellington (G-15317)
Mold Shop Inc .... F 419 829-2041
   Sylvania (G-14005)
Mold Surface Textures Inc .... G 330 678-8590
   Kent (G-8838)
Moldmakers Inc .... F 419 673-0902
   Kenton (G-8892)
Monarch Products Co .... F 330 868-7717
   Minerva (G-11037)
Monitor Mold & Machine Co .... F 330 697-7800
   Rootstown (G-12855)
Mordies Inc .... E 330 758-8050
   Youngstown (G-16402)
Mt Vernon Mold Works Inc .... E 618 242-6040
   Akron (G-255)
◆ Mtd Holdings Inc .... B 330 225-2600
   Valley City (G-14882)
Mutual Tool LLC .... E 937 667-5818
   Tipp City (G-14143)
Nation Tool & Die Ltd .... E 419 822-5939
   Delta (G-6789)

35 INDUSTRIAL AND COMMERCIAL MACHINERY AND COMPUTER EQUIPMENT

National Pattern Mfgco .... F 330 682-6871
Orrville *(G-12140)*

National Roller Die Inc .... F 440 951-3850
Willoughby *(G-15956)*

Nelson Tool Corporation .... F 740 965-1894
Sunbury *(G-13958)*

◆ Nesco Inc .... E 440 461-6000
Cleveland *(G-4448)*

New Bremen Machine & Tool Co .... E 419 629-3295
New Bremen *(G-11405)*

New Castings Inc .... C 330 645-6653
Akron *(G-262)*

New Die Inc .... E 419 726-7581
Toledo *(G-14396)*

Neway Stamping & Mfg Inc .... D 440 951-8500
Willoughby *(G-15958)*

Nichols Mold Inc .... G 330 297-9719
Ravenna *(G-12726)*

Nn Metal Stampings LLC .... E 419 737-2311
Pioneer *(G-12493)*

Noble Tool Corp .... E 937 461-4040
Dayton *(G-6472)*

Northwestern Tools Inc .... F 937 298-9994
Dayton *(G-6475)*

Numerics Unlimited Inc .... E 937 849-0100
New Carlisle *(G-11423)*

▲ Oakley Die & Mold Co .... E 513 754-8500
Mason *(G-10034)*

Ohio Associated Entps LLC .... F 440 354-3148
Painesville *(G-12253)*

Ohio Custom Dies LLC .... F 330 538-3396
North Jackson *(G-11787)*

Ohio Specialty Dies LLC .... F 330 538-3396
North Jackson *(G-11788)*

Ohio Tool & Jig Grind Inc .... F 937 415-0692
Springboro *(G-13514)*

Omni Manufacturing Inc .... F 419 394-7424
Saint Marys *(G-12963)*

▲ Omni Manufacturing Inc .... D 419 394-7424
Saint Marys *(G-12962)*

Orick Stamping Inc .... D 419 331-0600
Elida *(G-7095)*

P J Tool Company Inc .... G 937 254-2817
Dayton *(G-6497)*

P O McIntire Company .... E 440 269-1848
Wickliffe *(G-15844)*

PA MA Inc .... G 440 846-3799
Strongsville *(G-13864)*

Pacific Tool & Die Co .... E 330 273-7363
Brunswick *(G-1778)*

Palisin & Associates Inc .... E 216 252-3930
Cleveland *(G-4520)*

Perfection Mold & Machine Co .... F 330 784-5435
Twinsburg *(G-14713)*

Perry Welding Service Inc .... F 330 425-2211
Twinsburg *(G-14714)*

Phillips Mch & Stamping Corp .... G 330 882-6714
New Franklin *(G-11441)*

Phoenix Tool Company .... G 330 372-4627
Warren *(G-15198)*

Pier Tool & Die Inc .... E 440 236-3188
Columbia Station *(G-5017)*

▲ Plastic Enterprises Inc .... F 440 324-3240
Elyria *(G-7197)*

Plastic Mold Technology Inc .... G 330 848-4921
Barberton *(G-890)*

Pleasant Precision Inc .... E 419 675-0556
Kenton *(G-8896)*

Porter Precision Products Co .... D 513 385-1569
Cincinnati *(G-3265)*

Precast Products LLC .... E 419 668-1639
Norwalk *(G-11986)*

Precision Details Inc .... F 937 596-0068
Jackson Center *(G-8737)*

Precision Die & Stamping Inc .... G 513 942-8220
West Chester *(G-15483)*

Precision Die Masters Inc .... F 440 255-1204
Mentor *(G-10529)*

Premere Enterprises Inc .... G 330 874-3000
Bolivar *(G-1532)*

Prime Industries Inc .... E
Lorain *(G-9431)*

Pro-Tech Manufacturing Inc .... F 937 444-6484
Mount Orab *(G-11246)*

Progage Inc .... F 440 951-4477
Mentor *(G-10536)*

Progress Tool & Stamping Inc .... E 419 628-2384
Minster *(G-11059)*

Progrssive Molding Bolivar Inc .... E 330 874-3000
Bolivar *(G-1534)*

Project Engineering Company .... F 937 743-9114
Germantown *(G-7951)*

Promac Inc .... F 937 864-1961
Enon *(G-7251)*

▲ Proto Plastics Inc .... E 937 667-8416
Tipp City *(G-14150)*

▲ PSK Steel Corp .... E 330 759-1251
Hubbard *(G-8570)*

Pyramid Mold & Machine Co Inc .... F 330 673-5200
Kent *(G-8850)*

▲ Quaker Mfg Corp .... C 330 332-4631
Salem *(G-13024)*

Qualiform Inc .... E 330 336-6777
Wadsworth *(G-15057)*

Quality Specialists Inc .... G 440 946-9129
Willoughby *(G-15979)*

Queen City Tool Works Inc .... G 513 874-0111
Fairfield *(G-7401)*

Quicksilver Die Casting Svc .... G 330 757-1160
Youngstown *(G-16424)*

R M Tool & Die Inc .... F 440 238-6459
Strongsville *(G-13870)*

R T & T Machining Co Inc .... F 440 974-8479
Mentor *(G-10543)*

▲ Rage Corporation .... D 614 771-4771
Hilliard *(G-8435)*

Ram Tool Inc .... G 937 277-0717
Dayton *(G-6539)*

Rapid Machine Inc .... F 419 737-2377
Pioneer *(G-12497)*

▲ Raymath Company .... C 937 335-1860
Troy *(G-14604)*

▲ Ready Technology Inc .... F 937 866-7200
Dayton *(G-6544)*

Regal Metal Products Co .... E 330 868-6343
Minerva *(G-11039)*

Reserve Industries Inc .... G 440 871-2796
Bay Village *(G-966)*

Reuther Mold & Mfg Co Inc .... D 330 923-5266
Cuyahoga Falls *(G-6114)*

▲ Reymond Products Intl Inc .... E 330 339-3583
New Philadelphia *(G-11525)*

Rhinestahl Corporation .... E 513 229-5300
Mason *(G-10049)*

Rock Iron Corporation .... F 419 529-9411
Crestline *(G-6037)*

Rockstedt Tool & Die Inc .... F 330 273-9000
Brunswick *(G-1788)*

Roman Tool & Die .... G 440 503-5271
Strongsville *(G-13873)*

Ron-Al Mold & Machine Inc .... F 330 673-7919
Kent *(G-8855)*

Ronfeldt Associates Inc .... D 419 382-5641
Toledo *(G-14459)*

Ronlen Industries Inc .... E 330 273-6468
Brunswick *(G-1789)*

Ross Special Products Inc .... F 937 335-8406
Troy *(G-14605)*

Roto-Die Company Inc .... G 513 942-3500
West Chester *(G-15503)*

Rotocast Technologies Inc .... E 330 798-9091
Akron *(G-310)*

RPM Carbide Die Inc .... E 419 894-6426
Arcadia *(G-517)*

▲ Saehwa IMC Na Inc .... D 330 645-6653
Akron *(G-323)*

Saint-Gobain Ceramics Plas Inc .... C 330 673-5860
Stow *(G-13721)*

Schmitmeyer Inc .... G 937 295-2091
Fort Loramie *(G-7607)*

Schnipke Engraving Co Inc .... C 419 453-3376
Ottoville *(G-12204)*

Seaway Pattern Mfg Inc .... E 419 865-5724
Toledo *(G-14465)*

Seilkop Industries Inc .... F 513 353-3090
Miamitown *(G-10709)*

Seilkop Industries Inc .... E 513 761-1035
Cincinnati *(G-3377)*

◆ Select Industries Corporation .... C 937 233-9191
Dayton *(G-6567)*

Select Machine Inc .... F 330 678-7676
Kent *(G-8862)*

Self Made Holdings LLC .... E 440 477-1052
Canton *(G-2220)*

Shalix Inc .... F 216 941-3546
Cleveland *(G-4687)*

Shl Liquidation Automotive Inc .... D 330 558-2600
Valley City *(G-14891)*

◆ Shl Liquidation Industries Inc .... B 248 299-7500
Valley City *(G-14893)*

Shl Liquidation Sectional Co .... B 330 558-2600
Valley City *(G-14897)*

Short Run Machine Products Inc .... F 440 969-1313
Ashtabula *(G-660)*

Sk Mold & Tool Inc .... E 937 339-0299
Troy *(G-14610)*

Sk Mold & Tool Inc .... E 937 339-0299
Tipp City *(G-14155)*

Skribs Tool and Die Inc .... E 440 951-7774
Mentor *(G-10555)*

Skrl Die Casting Inc .... E 440 946-7200
Willoughby *(G-15993)*

Sluterbeck Tool & Die Co Inc .... F 937 836-5736
Clayton *(G-14604)*

Smithville Mfg Co .... F 330 345-5818
Wooster *(G-16173)*

Spectracam Ltd .... G 937 223-3805
Dayton *(G-6582)*

Spintech Holdings Inc .... E 937 912-3250
Miamisburg *(G-10684)*

Stan-Kell LLC .... E 440 998-1116
Ashtabula *(G-661)*

▲ Stanco Precision Mfg Inc .... G 937 274-1785
Dayton *(G-6589)*

◆ Standard Engineering Group Inc .... G 330 494-4300
North Canton *(G-11762)*

Starkey Machinery Inc .... E 419 468-2560
Galion *(G-7885)*

Std Liquidation Inc .... C 937 492-6121
Sidney *(G-13290)*

Stolle Machinery Company LLC .... C 937 497-5400
Dayton *(G-6596)*

Straight 72 Inc .... D 740 943-5730
Marysville *(G-9940)*

Sulecki Precision Products Inc .... F 440 255-5454
Mentor *(G-10569)*

Employee Codes: A=Over 500 employees, B=251-500
C=101-250, D=51-100, E=20-50, F=10-19, G=1-9

35 INDUSTRIAL AND COMMERCIAL MACHINERY AND COMPUTER EQUIPMENT

Sumitomo Elc Carbide Mfg Inc .... F 440 354-0600
   Grand River *(G-8013)*

▲ Summit Tool Company .... D 330 535-7177
   Akron *(G-341)*

Superior Die .... G 937 225-6369
   Dayton *(G-6598)*

Superior Mold & Die Co .... F 330 688-8251
   Munroe Falls *(G-11306)*

▲ Superior Production LLC .... C 614 444-2181
   Columbus *(G-5800)*

Sure Tool & Manufacturing Co .... E 937 253-9111
   Dayton *(G-6602)*

Sutterlin Machine & Tl Co Inc .... F 440 357-0817
   Mentor *(G-10571)*

Symbol Tool & Die Inc .... G 440 582-5989
   North Royalton *(G-11897)*

Taft Tool & Production Co .... F 419 385-2576
   Toledo *(G-14481)*

▲ Talent Tool & Die Inc .... E 440 239-8777
   Berea *(C-1206)*

Tangible Solutions Inc .... E 937 912-4603
   Fairborn *(G-7324)*

Taylor Tool & Die Inc .... G 937 845-1491
   New Carlisle *(G-11427)*

▲ Te-Co Manufacturing LLC .... D 937 836-0961
   Englewood *(G-7244)*

Tech Industries Inc .... F 216 861-7337
   Cleveland *(G-4771)*

Tech Mold and Tool Co .... G 937 667-8851
   Tipp City *(G-14159)*

Technical Tool & Gauge Inc .... E 330 273-1778
   Brunswick *(G-1793)*

▲ Technology House Ltd .... G 440 248-3025
   Streetsboro *(G-13795)*

Tempcraft Corporation .... A 216 391-3885
   Cleveland *(G-4775)*

Tessec Manufacturing Svcs LLC .... E 937 985-3552
   Dayton *(G-6616)*

Tetra Mold & Tool Inc .... E 937 845-1651
   New Carlisle *(G-11428)*

The Kordenbrock Tool and Die Co .... F 513 326-4390
   Cincinnati *(G-3449)*

▲ The Louis G Freeman Compa .... D 419 334-9709
   Fremont *(G-7813)*

▲ The Vulcan Tool Company .... G 937 253-6194
   Dayton *(G-6620)*

Tipco Punch Inc .... E 513 874-9140
   Hamilton *(G-8250)*

Tipp Machine & Tool Inc .... C 937 890-8428
   Dayton *(G-6625)*

Tm Machine & Tool Inc .... G 419 478-0310
   Toledo *(G-14488)*

Tmd Inc .... C 419 476-4581
   Toledo *(G-14489)*

Toledo Molding & Die LLC .... C 419 476-0581
   Toledo *(G-14500)*

◆ Toledo Molding & Die LLC .... D 419 470-3950
   Toledo *(G-14499)*

▲ Toledo Tool and Die Co Inc .... B 419 476-4422
   Toledo *(G-14507)*

▲ Tom Smith Industries Inc .... D 937 832-1555
   Englewood *(G-7245)*

Tomahawk Tool Supply .... G 419 485-8737
   Montpelier *(G-11143)*

Tomco Tool Inc .... G 937 322-5768
   Springfield *(G-13649)*

Toney Tool Manufacturing Inc .... E 937 890-8535
   Dayton *(G-6627)*

Tool Tech LLC .... E 614 893-5876
   Springfield *(G-13650)*

Tool Technologies Van Dyke .... F 937 349-4900
   Marysville *(G-9942)*

Toolcraft Products Inc .... E 937 223-8271
   Dayton *(G-6628)*

Tooling & Components Corp .... F 419 478-9122
   Toledo *(G-14510)*

Tooling Connection Inc .... G 419 594-3339
   Oakwood *(G-12034)*

Tooling Zone Inc .... E 937 550-4180
   Springboro *(G-13523)*

Toolrite Manufacturing Inc .... F 937 278-1962
   Dayton *(G-6629)*

Top Tool & Die Inc .... F 216 267-5878
   Cleveland *(G-4805)*

Torrmetal LLC .... E 216 671-1616
   Cleveland *(G-4807)*

Torrmetal Corporation .... E 216 671-1616
   Cleveland *(G-4808)*

Tradye Machine & Tool Inc .... G 740 625-7550
   Centerburg *(G-2358)*

Trexler Rubber Co Inc .... E 330 296-9677
   Ravenna *(C-12730)*

Tri-Craft Inc .... E 440 826-1050
   Cleveland *(G-4822)*

▲ Trim Parts Inc .... E 513 934-0815
   Lebanon *(G-9115)*

Trim Tool & Machine Inc .... E 216 889-1916
   Cleveland *(G-4830)*

Trimline Die Corporation .... E 440 355-6900
   Lagrange *(G-8956)*

Troy Precision Carbide Die Inc .... F 440 834-4477
   Burton *(G-1889)*

Tru-Tex International Corp .... E 513 825-8844
   Cincinnati *(G-3468)*

▲ Trucut Incorporated .... D 330 938-9806
   Sebring *(G-13127)*

True Industries Inc .... E 330 296-4342
   Ravenna *(G-12740)*

▲ Tuf-Tug Inc .... F 937 299-1213
   Moraine *(G-11216)*

TW Manufacturing Co .... E 440 439-3243
   Cleveland *(G-4838)*

Twin Valley Mold & Tool LLC .... G 937 962-1403
   Lewisburg *(G-9193)*

U S Alloy Die Corp .... F 216 749-9700
   Cleveland *(G-4842)*

United Extrusion Dies Inc .... F 330 533-2915
   Canfield *(G-2022)*

United Finshg & Die Cutng Inc .... F 216 881-0239
   Cleveland *(G-4846)*

Universal Tool Technology LLC .... F 937 222-4608
   Dayton *(G-6640)*

Unlimited Machine and Tool LLC .... F 419 269-1730
   Toledo *(G-14516)*

Valley Tool & Die Inc .... D 440 237-0160
   North Royalton *(G-11900)*

Van Wert Machine Inc .... F 419 692-6836
   Delphos *(G-6777)*

Velocity Concept Dev Group LLC .... G 740 685-2637
   Byesville *(G-1901)*

Village Plastics Co .... G 330 753-0100
   Euclid *(G-7306)*

Vinyl Tool & Die Company .... F 330 782-0254
   Youngstown *(G-16471)*

Vinyltech Inc .... E 330 538-0369
   North Jackson *(G-11795)*

▲ Vmi Americas Inc .... E 330 929-6800
   Stow *(G-13738)*

Walest Incorporated .... G 216 362-8110
   Brunswick *(G-1800)*

Walker Tool & Machine Company .... F 419 661-8000
   Perrysburg *(G-12443)*

Weiss Industries Inc .... E 419 526-2480
   Mansfield *(G-9732)*

Welage Corporation .... F 513 681-2300
   Cincinnati *(G-3510)*

▲ Wentworth Mold Inc Electra .... D 937 898-8460
   Vandalia *(G-14967)*

White Machine Inc .... G 440 237-3282
   North Royalton *(G-11902)*

Williams Steel Rule Die Co .... F 216 431-3232
   Cleveland *(G-4910)*

Wilmington Prcsion McHning Inc .... E 937 382-3700
   Wilmington *(G-16064)*

Windsor Tool Inc .... F 216 671-1900
   Cleveland *(G-4911)*

Wire Shop Inc .... E 440 354-6842
   Mentor *(G-10596)*

▲ WLS Stamping Co .... D 216 271-5100
   Cleveland *(G-4914)*

Worthington Industries Inc .... E 614 438-3028
   Columbus *(G-5883)*

Wrena LLC .... E 937 667-4403
   Tipp City *(C-11168)*

▲ Wurtec Manufacturing Service .... E 419 726-1066
   Toledo *(G-14528)*

XCEL Mold and Machine Inc .... E 330 499-8450
   Canton *(G-2271)*

Youngstown Tool & Die Company .... D 330 747-4464
   Youngstown *(G-16489)*

Yugo Mold Inc .... F 330 606-0710
   Akron *(G-380)*

3545 Machine tool accessories

▲ Accretech SBS Inc .... G 513 373-4844
   Cincinnati *(G-2594)*

Advanced Holding Designs Inc .... F 330 928-4456
   Cuyahoga Falls *(G-6060)*

Akron Gear & Engineering Inc .... E 330 773-6608
   Akron *(G-34)*

◆ Alliance Knife Inc .... E 513 367-9000
   Harrison *(G-8264)*

▲ Allied Machine & Engrg Corp .... C 330 343-4283
   Dover *(G-6807)*

▲ Angstrom Precision Metals LLC .... F 440 255-6700
   Mentor *(G-10417)*

Anthe Machine Works Inc .... E 859 431-1035
   Cincinnati *(G-2552)*

Antwerp Tool & Die Inc .... F 419 258-5271
   Antwerp *(G-491)*

Apollo Products Inc .... F 440 269-8551
   Willoughby *(G-15880)*

Arch Cutng Tls Cincinnati LLC .... F 513 851-6363
   West Chester *(G-15538)*

Arnold Gauge Co Inc .... F 877 942-4243
   West Chester *(G-15368)*

B & R Machine Co .... F 216 961-7370
   Cleveland *(G-3715)*

BAP Manufacturing Inc .... E 419 332-5041
   Fremont *(G-7765)*

Bender Engineering Company .... G 330 938-2355
   Beloit *(G-1250)*

▲ Big Chief Manufacturing Ltd .... E 513 934-3888
   Lebanon *(G-9064)*

Blue Ash Tool & Die Co Inc .... F 513 793-4530
   Blue Ash *(G-1372)*

Capital Tool Company .... E 216 661-5750
   Cleveland *(G-3787)*

Carbide Probes Inc .... E 937 429-9123
   Beavercreek *(G-1042)*

Certified Comparator Products .... G 937 426-9677
   Beavercreek *(G-1072)*

Chardon Tool & Supply Co Inc .... E 440 286-6440
   Chardon *(G-2445)*

Chart-Tech Tool Inc .... E 937 667-3543
   Tipp City *(G-14129)*

35 INDUSTRIAL AND COMMERCIAL MACHINERY AND COMPUTER EQUIPMENT

Chippewa Tool and Mfg Co............................F 419 849-2790
  Woodville (G-16091)
Clapp & Haney Brazed Tl Co Inc.................F 740 922-3515
  Dennison (G-6794)
Coldwater Machine Company LLC...............C 419 678-4877
  Coldwater (G-4985)
Commercial Grinding Svcs Inc.....................E 330 273-5040
  Medina (G-10311)
Container Graphics Corp.............................E 419 531-5133
  Toledo (G-14252)
Contour Tool Inc..E 440 365-7333
  North Ridgeville (G-11836)
▲ Covert Manufacturing Inc......................B 419 468-1761
  Galion (G-7868)
Cowles Industrial Tool Co LLC...................E 330 799-9100
  Austintown (G-751)
Cutter Solutins Intl LLC..............................G 850 725-5600
  Hudson (G-8592)
Cyber Shed Inc...G 419 724-5855
  Toledo (G-14256)
D C Morrison Company Inc........................E 859 581-7511
  Cincinnati (G-2812)
DA Precision Products Inc.........................F 513 459-1113
  West Chester (G-15411)
▲ Dayton Progress Corporation................A 937 859-5111
  Dayton (G-6288)
Diamond Products Limited.........................G 440 323-4616
  Elyria (G-7129)
◆ Diamond Products Limited....................B 440 323-4616
  Elyria (G-7130)
Diamond Reserve Inc................................F 440 892-7877
  Westlake (G-15745)
▲ Diamonds Products LLC......................G 440 323-4616
  Elyria (G-7131)
◆ Drt Mfg Co LLC....................................D 937 297-6670
  Dayton (G-6307)
Dysinger Incorporated................................E 937 297-7761
  Dayton (G-6310)
E & J Demark Inc......................................E 419 337-5866
  Wauseon (G-15260)
Feedall Inc..F 440 942-8100
  Willoughby (G-15920)
Fischer Special Tooling Corp.....................E 440 951-8411
  Mentor (G-10455)
Flex-E-On Inc...F 330 928-4496
  Cuyahoga Falls (G-6084)
Fox Tool Co Inc..F 330 928-3402
  Cuyahoga Falls (G-6085)
▲ Frecon Technologies Inc.......................F 513 874-8981
  West Chester (G-15432)
◆ Furukawa Rock Drill USA Co Ltd..........F 330 673-5826
  Kent (G-8816)
Gem Tool LLC..G 216 771-8444
  Cleveland (G-4109)
George Whalley Company.........................E 216 453-0099
  Fairport Harbor (G-7454)
◆ Glassline Corporation............................E 419 666-9712
  Perrysburg (G-12385)
◆ Gleason Metrology Systems Corp.........E 937 384-8901
  Dayton (G-6353)
H & S Tool Inc..F 330 335-1536
  Wadsworth (G-15034)
H Duane Leis Acquisitions.........................F 937 835-5621
  New Lebanon (G-11449)
H Machining Inc..F 419 636-6890
  Bryan (G-1820)
H3d Tool Corporation.................................E 740 498-5181
  Newcomerstown (G-11644)
Hammill Manufacturing Co.........................D 419 476-0789
  Maumee (G-10204)
▲ Hapco Inc...F 330 678-9353
  Kent (G-8817)

HI Carb Corp..E 216 486-5000
  Eastlake (G-7035)
▲ High Quality Tools Inc..........................F 440 975-9684
  Eastlake (G-7036)
▲ Hudson Supply Company Inc...............G 216 518-3000
  Cleveland (G-4207)
Hyper Tool Company.................................E 440 543-5151
  Chagrin Falls (G-2401)
Imco Carbide Tool Inc................................D 419 661-6313
  Perrysburg (G-12390)
Interstate Tool Corporation.........................E 216 671-1077
  Cleveland (G-4234)
▲ Jergens Inc...C 216 486-5540
  Cleveland (G-4253)
Jerry Tools Inc..F 513 242-3211
  Cincinnati (G-3041)
Johnson Bros Rubber Co Inc....................E 419 752-4814
  Greenwich (G-8067)
Kaeper Machine Inc..................................E 440 974-1010
  Mentor (G-10486)
▲ Kalt Manufacturing Company...............D 440 327-2102
  North Ridgeville (G-11848)
Karma Metal Products Inc.........................F 419 524-4371
  Mansfield (G-9676)
Keb Industries Inc.....................................G 440 953-4623
  Willoughby (G-15937)
Kennametal Inc...D 440 437-5131
  Orwell (G-12166)
Kennametal Inc...C 440 349-5151
  Solon (G-13378)
Kiffer Industries Inc....................................E 216 267-1818
  Cleveland (G-4288)
Kilroy Company..D 440 951-8700
  Cleveland (G-4289)
▲ Knb Tools of America Inc.....................E 614 733-0400
  Plain City (G-12583)
Kongsberg Prcsion Ctng Systems.............E 937 800-2169
  Miamisburg (G-10652)
Kyocera SGS Precision Tls Inc.................D 330 922-1953
  Cuyahoga Falls (G-6099)
▲ Kyocera SGS Precision Tls Inc............E 330 688-6667
  Cuyahoga Falls (G-6098)
Levan Enterprises Inc...............................E 330 923-9797
  Stow (G-13706)
Lincoln Electric Automtn Inc......................C 419 678-4877
  Coldwater (G-4996)
Lord Corporation.......................................C 937 278-9431
  Dayton (G-6415)
LS Starrett Company.................................D 440 835-0005
  Westlake (G-15763)
Luther Machine Inc....................................G 440 259-5014
  Perry (G-12353)
M & J Tooling Ltd......................................F 937 951-3527
  Dayton (G-6417)
M A Harrison Mfg Co Inc..........................E 440 965-4306
  Wakeman (G-15076)
▲ Machining Technologies Inc.................E 419 862-3110
  Elmore (G-7101)
Master Carbide Tools Company................F 440 352-1112
  Perry (G-12355)
Matrix Tool & Machine Inc........................E 440 255-0300
  Mentor (G-10500)
Mdf Tool Corporation.................................F 440 237-2277
  North Royalton (G-11887)
Medway Tool Corp....................................F 937 335-7717
  Troy (G-14597)
Melin Tool Company Inc............................D 216 362-4200
  Cleveland (G-4392)
◆ Metalex Manufacturing Inc....................C 513 489-0507
  Blue Ash (G-1437)
Midwest Tool & Engineering Co................E
  Dayton (G-6445)

Monaghan & Associates Inc.....................F 937 253-7706
  Dayton (G-6456)
MSC Industries Inc....................................G 440 474-8788
  Rome (G-12849)
National Rolled Thread Die Co..................F 440 232-8101
  Cleveland (G-4439)
▲ Oakley Die & Mold Co.........................E 513 754-8500
  Mason (G-10034)
Obars Machine and Tool Company............E 419 535-6307
  Toledo (G-14403)
▼ Ohio Broach & Machine Company.......E 440 946-1040
  Willoughby (G-15963)
Ohio Drill & Tool Co..................................E 330 525-7717
  Homeworth (G-8555)
Omwp Company.......................................E 330 453-8438
  Canton (G-2188)
▲ Osg-Sterling Die Inc............................D 216 267-1300
  Parma (G-12292)
P O McIntire Company..............................E 440 269-1848
  Wickliffe (G-15844)
Pemco Inc..E 216 524-2990
  Cleveland (G-4539)
Performance Superabrasives LLC............G 440 946-7171
  Mentor (G-10523)
PMC Gage Inc..E 440 953-1672
  Willoughby (G-15973)
PMC Mercury..F 440 953-3300
  Willoughby (G-15974)
Positrol Inc..E 513 272-0500
  Cincinnati (G-3267)
Precise Tool & Mfg Corp...........................F 216 524-1500
  Cleveland (G-4572)
Precision Gage & Tool Company..............F 937 866-9666
  Dayton (G-6512)
Preston...F 740 788-8208
  Newark (G-11602)
Quality Cutter Grinding Co.........................E 216 362-6444
  Cleveland (G-4605)
R A Heller Company..................................F 513 771-6100
  Cincinnati (G-3321)
R T & T Machining Co Inc........................F 440 974-8479
  Mentor (G-10543)
Red Head Brass Inc..................................F 330 567-2903
  Shreve (G-13213)
▼ Regal Diamond Products Corp............E 440 944-7700
  Wickliffe (G-15851)
Retention Knob Supply & Mfg Co..............F 937 686-6405
  Huntsville (G-8624)
◆ Rex International USA Inc....................E 800 321-7950
  Ashtabula (G-659)
Rhgs Company...G 513 721-6299
  Cincinnati (G-3334)
Ridge Tool Manufacturing Co....................E 440 323-5581
  Elyria (G-7203)
Riten Industries Incorporated....................E 740 335-5353
  Wshngtn Ct Hs (G-16240)
▲ Rol - Tech Inc......................................F 214 905-8050
  Fort Loramie (G-7606)
Roto Tech Inc...F 937 859-8503
  Moraine (G-11209)
Schumann Enterprises Inc........................E 216 267-6850
  Cleveland (G-4675)
Self Made Holdings LLC...........................E 330 477-1052
  Canton (G-2220)
Setco Industries Inc..................................E 513 941-5110
  Cincinnati (G-3385)
Sharp Tool Service Inc..............................E 330 273-4144
  Cleveland (G-4688)
Shl Liquidation Medina Inc........................C
  Valley City (G-14895)
Shook Manufactured Pdts Inc...................G 440 247-9130
  Chagrin Falls (G-2385)

Employee Codes: A=Over 500 employees, B=251-500
C=101-250, D=51-100, E=20-50, F=10-19, G=1-9

35 INDUSTRIAL AND COMMERCIAL MACHINERY AND COMPUTER EQUIPMENT — SIC SECTION

▲ Shook Manufactured Pdts Inc............ G 330 848-9780
   Akron *(G-330)*

Sjk Machine LLC.............................. F 330 868-3072
   North Lawrence *(G-11799)*

▲ Skidmore-Wilhelm Mfg Company......... F 216 481-4774
   Solon *(G-13422)*

SL Endmills Inc.............................. F 513 851-6363
   West Chester *(G-15586)*

Sorbothane Inc.............................. E 330 678-9444
   Kent *(G-8866)*

Sp3 Winco LLC............................... E 937 667-4476
   Tipp City *(G-14157)*

Spectrum Machine Inc..................... F 330 626-3666
   Streetsboro *(G-13793)*

Stanley Bittinger............................ G 740 942-4302
   Cadiz *(G-1904)*

Starrett Communications Inc............. G 614 798-0606
   Dublin *(G-6946)*

STC International Co Ltd................... G 561 308-6002
   Lebanon *(G-9112)*

Stitching Gluing Solutions LLC........... G 513 588-3168
   Blue Ash *(G-1470)*

Sumitomo Elc Carbide Mfg Inc............ F 440 354-0600
   Grand River *(G-8013)*

▲ Superion Inc................................ E 937 374-0033
   Xenia *(G-16274)*

Supplier Inspection Svcs Inc.............. F 877 263-7097
   Dayton *(G-6600)*

Taft Tool & Production Co.................. F 419 385-2576
   Toledo *(G-14481)*

Te-Co Inc..................................... F 937 836-0961
   Union *(G-14775)*

▲ Te-Co Manufacturing LLC................. D 937 836-0961
   Englewood *(G-7244)*

Technidrill Systems Inc.................... E 330 678-9980
   Kent *(G-8872)*

Tessa Precision Product Inc.............. E 440 392-3470
   Painesville *(G-12269)*

▲ Thaler Machine Company LLC............ C 937 550-2400
   Springboro *(G-13521)*

Thaler Machine Holdings LLC............. E 937 550-2400
   Springboro *(G-13522)*

Tomco Tool Inc.............................. F 937 322-5768
   Springfield *(G-13649)*

Tool Systems Incorporated................ F 440 461-6363
   Cleveland *(G-4801)*

Troyke Manufacturing Company.......... F 513 769-4242
   Cincinnati *(G-3467)*

Uhrichsville Carbide Inc................... F 740 922-9197
   Uhrichsville *(G-14772)*

United States Drill Head Co............... E 513 941-0300
   Cincinnati *(G-3482)*

Whip Guide Co.............................. F 440 543-5151
   Chagrin Falls *(G-2434)*

Wise Edge LLC.............................. G 330 208-0889
   Akron *(G-376)*

X-Press Tool Inc............................. F 330 225-8748
   Brunswick *(G-1802)*

3546 Power-driven handtools

▲ A JC Inc..................................... F 800 428-2438
   Hudson *(G-8581)*

Allegion Access Tech LLC.................. E 440 461-5500
   Cleveland *(G-3636)*

Apex Tool Group LLC....................... C 937 222-7871
   Dayton *(G-6209)*

Black & Decker (us) Inc.................... G 614 895-3112
   Columbus *(G-5195)*

Black & Decker Corporation............... G 440 842-9100
   Cleveland *(G-3739)*

♦ Ch Transition Company LLC.............. C 800 543-6400
   Cincinnati *(G-2724)*

Chicago Pneumatic Tool Co LLC.......... F 704 883-3500
   Broadview Heights *(G-1657)*

Corbett R Caudill Chipping Inc............ G 740 596-5984
   Hamden *(G-8172)*

▲ ET&f Fastening Systems Inc.............. F 800 248-2376
   Solon *(G-13346)*

♦ F & M Mafco Inc............................ C 513 367-2151
   Harrison *(G-8273)*

♦ Furukawa Rock Drill Usa Inc............. F 330 673-5826
   Kent *(G-8815)*

♦ Furukawa Rock Drill USA Co Ltd......... F 330 673-5826
   Kent *(G-8816)*

Hall-Toledo Inc............................... F 419 893-4334
   Maumee *(G-10203)*

Huron Cement Products Company....... E 419 433-4161
   Huron *(G-8633)*

▲ Kyocera Senco Indus Tls Inc............. D 513 388-2000
   Cincinnati *(G-3093)*

Madison Property Holdings Inc........... G 800 215-3210
   Cincinnati *(G-3124)*

Michael Byrne Manufacturing Co Inc.... E 419 525-1214
   Mansfield *(G-9691)*

♦ Npk Construction Equipment Inc........ D 440 232-7900
   Bedford *(G-1145)*

Ohio Drill & Tool Co......................... E 330 525-7717
   Homeworth *(G-8555)*

♦ Rex International USA Inc................ E 800 321-7950
   Ashtabula *(G-659)*

♦ Ridge Tool Company....................... A 440 323-5581
   Elyria *(G-7202)*

Ridge Tool Manufacturing Co............. E 440 323-5581
   Elyria *(G-7203)*

♦ Rjs Corporation............................. E 330 896-2387
   Akron *(G-306)*

Scepter Supply LLC......................... G 307 634-6074
   Marietta *(G-9821)*

Sewer Rodding Equipment Co............ C 419 991-2065
   Lima *(G-9288)*

Stanley Bittinger............................ G 740 942-4302
   Cadiz *(G-1904)*

▲ Stanley Industrial & Auto LLC............ D 614 755-7000
   Dublin *(G-6944)*

Suburban Manufacturing Co.............. D 440 953-2024
   Eastlake *(G-7050)*

Sumitomo Elc Carbide Mfg Inc............ F 440 354-0600
   Grand River *(G-8013)*

Superior Pneumatic & Mfg Inc............ F 440 871-8780
   Westlake *(G-15793)*

T C Service Co................................ F 440 954-7500
   Willoughby *(G-16001)*

Technidrill Systems Inc.................... E 330 678-9980
   Kent *(G-8872)*

Trane Technologies Company LLC....... E 419 633-6800
   Bryan *(G-1842)*

Uhrichsville Carbide Inc................... F 740 922-9197
   Uhrichsville *(G-14772)*

Wolf Machine Company.................... E 513 791-5194
   Blue Ash *(G-1493)*

X-Press Tool Inc............................. F 330 225-8748
   Brunswick *(G-1802)*

♦ Zagar Inc..................................... E 216 731-0500
   Cleveland *(G-4931)*

3547 Rolling mill machinery

▲ Addition Manufacturing Te................ C 513 228-7000
   Lebanon *(G-9059)*

ADS Machinery Corp........................ D 330 399-3601
   Warren *(G-15134)*

▲ Bardons & Oliver Inc...................... C 440 498-5800
   Solon *(G-13316)*

Bendco Machine & Tool Inc................ F 419 628-3802
   Minster *(G-11048)*

♦ Circle Machine Rolls Inc................... E 330 938-9010
   Sebring *(G-13119)*

Cornerstone Wauseon Inc................. C 419 337-0940
   Wauseon *(G-15259)*

♦ E R Advanced Ceramics Inc.............. E 330 426-9433
   East Palestine *(G-7004)*

Element Machinery LLC.................... G 855 447-7648
   Toledo *(G-14274)*

▲ Enprotech Industrial Tech LLC........... E 216 883-3220
   Cleveland *(G-4019)*

♦ Fives Bronx Inc............................. D 330 244-1960
   North Canton *(G-11727)*

▲ Formtek Inc.................................. D 216 292-4460
   Cleveland *(G-4084)*

Formtek Metal Forming Inc................ D 216 292-4460
   Cleveland *(G-4085)*

▼ George A Mitchell Company.............. E 330 758-5777
   Youngstown *(G-16368)*

H P E Inc....................................... G 330 833-3161
   Massillon *(G-10104)*

Hydranamics Inc............................. D 419 468-3530
   Galion *(G-7880)*

J Horst Manufacturing Co.................. D 330 828-2216
   Dalton *(G-6133)*

▲ Kottler Metal Products Co Inc............ E 440 946-7473
   Willoughby *(G-15940)*

Multi Galvanizing LLC....................... G 330 453-1441
   Canton *(G-2168)*

♦ Park Corporation............................ B 216 267-4870
   Medina *(G-10362)*

Perfecto Industries Inc..................... E 937 778-1900
   Piqua *(G-12542)*

▲ Pines Manufacturing Inc.................. E 440 835-5553
   Westlake *(G-15775)*

♦ Rafter Equipment Corporation........... E 440 572-3700
   Strongsville *(G-13871)*

♦ Ridge Tool Company....................... A 440 323-5581
   Elyria *(G-7202)*

Ridge Tool Manufacturing Co............. E 440 323-5581
   Elyria *(G-7203)*

Rki Inc... C 888 953-9400
   Mentor *(G-10546)*

Sentek Corporation......................... G 614 586-1123
   Columbus *(G-5759)*

▲ Steel Eqp Specialists Inc.................. D 330 823-8260
   Alliance *(G-427)*

Sticker Corporation......................... F 440 946-2100
   Willoughby *(G-15998)*

Turner Machine Co.......................... F 330 332-5821
   Salem *(G-13035)*

♦ United Rolls Inc............................. D 330 456-2761
   Canton *(G-2255)*

♦ Warren Fabricating Corporation......... D 330 534-5017
   Hubbard *(G-8572)*

♦ Xtek Inc....................................... B 513 733-7800
   Cincinnati *(G-3534)*

3548 Welding apparatus

Accurate Manufacturing Company....... E 614 878-6510
   Columbus *(G-5096)*

Aerowave Inc................................. G 440 731-8464
   Elyria *(G-7104)*

AK Fabrication Inc........................... F 330 458-1037
   Canton *(G-2032)*

♦ Ch Transition Company LLC.............. C 800 543-6400
   Cincinnati *(G-2724)*

Firelands Manufacturing LLC.............. G 419 687-8237
   Plymouth *(G-12608)*

▲ Fusion Incorporated....................... D 440 946-3300
   Willoughby *(G-15922)*

Harris Calorific Inc........................... G 216 383-4107
   Cleveland *(G-4170)*

SIC SECTION
35 INDUSTRIAL AND COMMERCIAL MACHINERY AND COMPUTER EQUIPMENT

Hobart Brothers LLC .... G 937 332-5953
  Piqua *(G-12524)*
◆ Hobart Brothers LLC .... A 937 332-5439
  Troy *(G-14579)*
Imax Industries Inc .... F 440 639-0242
  Painesville *(G-12246)*
Ivostud LLC .... G 440 925-4227
  Brookpark *(G-1719)*
◆ J W Harris Co Inc .... B 513 754-2000
  Mason *(G-10014)*
Kaliburn Inc .... E 843 695-4073
  Cleveland *(G-4273)*
◆ Lincoln Electric Company .... A 216 481-8100
  Cleveland *(G-4324)*
Lincoln Electric Holdings Inc .... A 216 481-8100
  Cleveland *(G-4325)*
◆ Luvata Ohio Inc .... D 740 363-1981
  Delaware *(G-6736)*
Mansfield Welding Service LLC .... G 419 594-2738
  Oakwood *(G-12031)*
◆ Miller Weldmaster Corporation .... D 330 833-6739
  Navarre *(G-11346)*
◆ Nelson Stud Welding Inc .... D 440 329-0400
  Elyria *(G-7184)*
O E Meyer Co .... E 614 428-5656
  Columbus *(G-5609)*
O E Meyer Co .... G 419 332-6931
  Fremont *(G-7798)*
Otto Konigslow Mfg Co .... F 216 851-7900
  Cleveland *(G-4513)*
Peco Holdings Corp .... D 937 667-5705
  Tipp City *(G-14147)*
▲ Polymet Corporation .... E 513 874-3586
  West Chester *(G-15482)*
▲ Postle Industries Inc .... E 216 265-9000
  Cleveland *(G-4565)*
Process Development Corp .... E 937 890-3388
  Dayton *(G-6527)*
◆ Production Products Inc .... D 734 241-7242
  Columbus Grove *(G-5899)*
Quality Components Inc .... F 440 255-0606
  Mentor *(G-10540)*
◆ Rexarc International Inc .... E 937 839-4604
  West Alexandria *(G-15344)*
Romans Mobile Welding LLC .... G 513 603-0961
  Amelia *(G-462)*
◆ Select-Arc Inc .... C 937 295-5215
  Fort Loramie *(G-7608)*
▲ Semtorq Inc .... F 330 487-0600
  Twinsburg *(G-14734)*
Sherbrooke Corporation .... E 440 942-3520
  Willoughby *(G-15990)*
Sherbrooke Metals .... G 440 542-3066
  Willoughby *(G-15991)*
Smart Force LLC .... E 216 481-8100
  Cleveland *(G-4706)*
▲ Spiegelberg Manufacturing Inc .... D 440 324-3042
  Strongsville *(G-13884)*
Stryver Mfg Inc .... E 937 854-3048
  Trotwood *(G-14546)*
Summit Machine Solutions LLC .... G 330 785-0781
  Akron *(G-340)*
◆ Taylor - Winfield Corporation .... C 330 259-8500
  Hubbard *(G-8571)*
Taylor-Winfield Tech Inc .... E 330 259-8500
  Youngstown *(G-16451)*
Tech-Sonic Inc .... F 614 792-3117
  Columbus *(G-5816)*
Weld-Action Company Inc .... G 330 372-1063
  Warren *(G-15223)*
Worker Automation Inc .... G 937 473-2111
  Dayton *(G-6660)*

3549 Metalworking machinery, nec

Added Edge Assembly Inc .... F 216 464-4305
  Cleveland *(G-3599)*
▲ Addition Manufacturing Te .... C 513 228-7000
  Lebanon *(G-9059)*
ADS Machinery Corp .... D 330 399-3601
  Warren *(G-15134)*
Advance Manufacturing Corp .... E 216 333-1684
  Cleveland *(G-3603)*
▲ Arku Inc .... E 513 985-0500
  Cincinnati *(G-2632)*
Armature Coil Equipment Inc .... F 216 267-6366
  Strongsville *(G-13809)*
▲ Bardons & Oliver Inc .... C 440 498-5800
  Solon *(G-13316)*
▲ Barth Industries Co LLC .... E 216 267-1950
  Cleveland *(G-3722)*
Berran Industrial Group Inc .... E 330 253-5800
  Akron *(G-83)*
Brilex Industries Inc .... D 330 744-1114
  Youngstown *(G-16327)*
▲ Brilex Industries Inc .... D 330 744-1114
  Youngstown *(G-16328)*
▲ C A Litzler Co Inc .... E 216 267-8020
  Cleveland *(G-3778)*
Cincinnati Incorporated .... C 513 367-7100
  Harrison *(G-8269)*
Cline Machine and Automtn Inc .... E 740 474-4237
  Circleville *(G-3545)*
Ctm Integration Incorporated .... E 330 332-1800
  Salem *(G-12988)*
Dayton Machine Tool Company .... E 937 222-6444
  Dayton *(G-6282)*
Erichsen Inc .... G 734 474-1471
  Westlake *(G-15750)*
Esi-Extrusion Services Inc .... E 330 374-3388
  Akron *(G-143)*
EZ Grout Corporation Inc .... E 740 962-2024
  Malta *(G-9607)*
Flexomation LLC .... G 513 825-0555
  Cincinnati *(G-2908)*
▲ Formtek Inc .... D 216 292-4460
  Cleveland *(G-4084)*
Forrest Machine Pdts Co Ltd .... E 419 589-3774
  Mansfield *(G-9658)*
Ged Holdings Inc .... F 330 963-5401
  Twinsburg *(G-14666)*
Gem City Engineering Co .... C 937 223-5544
  Dayton *(G-6348)*
Generic Systems Inc .... F 419 841-8460
  Holland *(G-8510)*
Gilson Machine & Tool Co Inc .... E 419 592-2911
  Napoleon *(G-11316)*
▲ Glunt Industries Inc .... C 330 399-7585
  Warren *(G-15175)*
Hahn Manufacturing Company .... E 216 391-9300
  Cleveland *(G-4163)*
Heisler Tool Company .... F 440 951-2424
  Willoughby *(G-15927)*
Helix Linear Technologies Inc .... E 216 485-2263
  Beachwood *(G-989)*
Helix Operating Company LLC .... G 855 435-4958
  Beachwood *(G-990)*
Holdren Brothers Inc .... F 937 465-7050
  West Liberty *(G-15622)*
▼ Hunter Defense Tech Inc .... E 216 438-6111
  Solon *(G-13363)*
J Horst Manufacturing Co .... D 330 828-2216
  Dalton *(G-6133)*
▲ Kalt Manufacturing Company .... D 440 327-2102
  North Ridgeville *(G-11848)*

Kenley Enterprises LLC .... F 419 630-0921
  Bryan *(G-1824)*
◆ Kent Corporation .... E 440 582-3400
  North Royalton *(G-11881)*
Kilroy Company .... D 440 951-8700
  Cleveland *(G-4289)*
Master Marking Company Inc .... F 330 688-6797
  Cuyahoga Falls *(G-6102)*
Midwest Laser Systems Inc .... E 419 424-0062
  Alvada *(G-443)*
◆ Milacron LLC .... E 513 487-5000
  Blue Ash *(G-1439)*
Peco Holdings Corp .... D 937 667-5705
  Tipp City *(G-14147)*
Perfecto Industries Inc .... E 937 778-1900
  Piqua *(G-12542)*
▲ Pines Manufacturing Inc .... E 440 835-5553
  Westlake *(G-15775)*
Precision Metal Products Inc .... E 216 447-1900
  Cleveland *(G-4575)*
▲ Rafter Equipment Corporation .... E 440 572-3700
  Strongsville *(G-13871)*
Refurb-World LLC .... E 440 471-9030
  North Ridgeville *(G-11857)*
Riverside Mch & Automtn Inc .... G 419 855-8308
  Walbridge *(G-15086)*
Riverside Mch & Automtn Inc .... G 419 855-8308
  Genoa *(G-7949)*
▲ S A Oma-U Inc .... G 330 487-0602
  Twinsburg *(G-14730)*
▲ Semtorq Inc .... F 330 487-0600
  Twinsburg *(G-14734)*
Simon De Young Corporation .... G 440 834-3000
  Middlefield *(G-10789)*
South Shore Controls Inc .... E 440 259-2500
  Mentor *(G-10557)*
Stainless Automation .... G 216 961-4550
  Cleveland *(G-4726)*
Stein LLC .... D 216 883-7444
  Cleveland *(G-4734)*
Sticker Corporation .... F 440 946-2100
  Willoughby *(G-15998)*
Stover International LLC .... E 740 363-5251
  Delaware *(G-6753)*
Todd Industries Inc .... E 440 439-2900
  Cleveland *(G-4799)*
Tri-Mac Mfg & Svcs Co .... F 513 896-4445
  Hamilton *(G-8251)*

3552 Textile machinery

Alley Cat Designs Inc .... G 937 291-8803
  Dayton *(G-6193)*
American Precision Spindles .... G 267 436-6000
  Cleveland *(G-3655)*
◆ Barudan America Inc .... F 440 248-8770
  Solon *(G-13317)*
▲ C A Litzler Co Inc .... E 216 267-8020
  Cleveland *(G-3778)*
Karg Corporation .... E 330 633-4916
  Tallmadge *(G-14034)*
Knitting Machinery Corp .... F 937 548-2338
  Greenville *(G-8050)*
Leesburg Looms Incorporated .... G 419 238-2738
  Van Wert *(G-14921)*
Open Additive LLC .... G 937 306-6140
  Dayton *(G-6492)*
Painted Hill Inv Group Inc .... F 937 339-1756
  Troy *(G-14600)*
Randy Gray .... G 513 533-3200
  Cincinnati *(G-3324)*
▲ S A Oma-U Inc .... G 330 487-0602
  Twinsburg *(G-14730)*

Employee Codes: A=Over 500 employees, B=251-500
C=101-250, D=51-100, E=20-50, F=10-19, G=1-9

35 INDUSTRIAL AND COMMERCIAL MACHINERY AND COMPUTER EQUIPMENT — SIC SECTION

Schilling Graphics Inc............................. E 419 468-1037
 Galion *(G-7884)*
Simon De Young Corporation..................... G 440 834-3000
 Middlefield *(G-10789)*
Slater Road Mills Inc............................. E 330 332-9951
 Salem *(G-13032)*
Western Ohio Graphics........................... F 937 335-8769
 Troy *(G-14616)*
Wise Edge LLC................................... G 330 208-0889
 Akron *(G-376)*
Wolf Machine Company.......................... E 513 791-5194
 Blue Ash *(G-1493)*

3553 Woodworking machinery

Axiom Tool Group Inc............................ G 844 642-4902
 Westerville *(G-15693)*
Bent Wood Solutions LLC........................ G 330 674-1454
 Millersburg *(G-10943)*
Diamond Machinery LLC......................... G 216 312-1235
 Cleveland *(G-3956)*
General Intl Pwr Pdts LLC........................ G 419 877-5234
 Whitehouse *(G-15818)*
Northcoast Woodcraft Inc........................ G 330 677-1189
 Tallmadge *(G-14039)*
Polychem Oms Systems LLC..................... F 330 427-1230
 North Canton *(G-11750)*
Seilkop Industries Inc............................ E 513 761-1035
 Cincinnati *(G-3377)*
Trico Enterprises LLC............................ F 216 970-9984
 Lakewood *(G-8983)*

3554 Paper industries machinery

Andritz Inc....................................... D 513 677-5620
 Loveland *(G-9476)*
◆ Baumfolder Corporation........................ E 937 492-1281
 Sidney *(G-13226)*
◆ Chemineer Inc................................. C 937 454-3200
 Dayton *(G-6254)*
Custom Threading Systems LLC................. G 937 846-1405
 New Carlisle *(G-11413)*
◆ Fq Sale Inc.................................... E
 Springfield *(G-13568)*
▲ French Oil Mill Machinery Co.................. G 937 773-3420
 Piqua *(G-12517)*
G Fordyce Co.................................... G 937 393-3241
 Hillsboro *(G-8457)*
▲ J E Doyle Company........................... F 330 564-0743
 Norton *(G-11945)*
◆ Jen-Coat Inc.................................. C 513 671-1777
 Cincinnati *(G-3040)*
◆ Kadant Black Clawson Inc..................... D 513 229-8100
 Lebanon *(G-9091)*
▲ Kohler Coating Inc............................ E 330 499-1407
 Canton *(G-2142)*
Kohler Coating Inc............................... E 330 499-1407
 Uniontown *(G-14786)*
▼ Magna Machine Co........................... C 513 851-6900
 Cincinnati *(G-3125)*
▼ McIntosh Manufacturing LLC.................. D 513 424-5307
 Middletown *(G-10843)*
▲ Miami Machine Corporation................... F 513 863-6707
 Overpeck *(G-12209)*
National Oilwell Varco LP........................ D 937 454-4660
 Dayton *(G-6464)*
◆ Nilpeter Usa Inc.............................. C 513 489-4400
 Cincinnati *(G-3198)*
▲ Press Technology & Mfg Inc................... G 937 327-0755
 Springfield *(G-13622)*
Rebiltco Inc...................................... G 513 424-2024
 Middletown *(G-10854)*
Spectex LLC..................................... F 603 330-3334
 Cincinnati *(G-3406)*

Tri-Mac Mfg & Svcs Co........................... F 513 896-4445
 Hamilton *(G-8251)*
Vail Rubber Works Inc........................... F 513 705-2060
 Middletown *(G-10869)*

3555 Printing trades machinery

A/C Laser Technologies Inc...................... F 330 784-3355
 Akron *(G-12)*
Alchem Aluminum Europe Inc................... G 216 910-3400
 Beachwood *(G-972)*
Anderson & Vreeland Inc........................ D 419 636-5002
 Bryan *(G-1807)*
Armor... G 614 459-1414
 Columbus *(G-5155)*
Beehex Inc...................................... G 512 633-5304
 Columbus *(G-5179)*
Carco America LLC.............................. G 216 928-5409
 Cleveland *(G-3791)*
Commonwealth Aluminum Mtls LLC............. F 216 910-3400
 Beachwood *(G-980)*
Container Graphics Corp......................... G 937 746-5666
 Franklin *(G-7667)*
▲ Desco Equipment Corp........................ E 330 405-1581
 Twinsburg *(G-14648)*
Dynamic Dies Inc................................ E 419 865-0249
 Holland *(G-8507)*
E C Shaw Company of Ohio..................... F 513 721-6334
 Cincinnati *(G-2848)*
Finzer Roller Inc................................. F 937 746-4069
 Franklin *(G-7675)*
Flexoplate Inc................................... F 513 489-0433
 Blue Ash *(G-1395)*
Flexotech Graphics Inc.......................... F 330 929-4743
 Stow *(G-13699)*
▲ Gew Inc...................................... G 440 237-4439
 Cleveland *(G-4124)*
Graphic Systems Services Inc.................... E 937 746-0708
 Springboro *(G-13503)*
Great Lakes Graphics Inc........................ F 216 391-0077
 Cleveland *(G-4144)*
Hadronics Inc.................................... D 513 321-9350
 Cincinnati *(G-2983)*
Imco Recycling of Indiana Inc.................... G 216 910-3400
 Beachwood *(G-991)*
Incorprted Trstees of The Gspl................... F 216 749-1428
 Cleveland *(G-4222)*
◆ Kase Equipment Corporation.................. D 216 642-9040
 Cleveland *(G-4275)*
◆ Nilpeter Usa Inc.............................. C 513 489-4400
 Cincinnati *(G-3198)*
▲ R & D Equipment Inc......................... E 419 668-8439
 Norwalk *(G-11987)*
Retain Loyalty LLC.............................. G 330 830-0839
 Massillon *(G-10139)*
Roconex Corporation............................ F 937 339-2616
 Miamisburg *(G-10678)*
Schilling Graphics Inc............................ E 419 468-1037
 Galion *(G-7884)*
Suspension Feeder Corporation.................. F 419 763-1377
 Fort Recovery *(G-7625)*
▲ Tinker Omega Sinto LLC...................... E 937 322-2272
 Springfield *(G-13648)*
Tykma Inc....................................... D 877 318-9562
 Chillicothe *(G-2540)*
Wise Edge LLC.................................. G 330 208-0889
 Akron *(G-376)*
◆ Wood Graphics Inc............................ E 513 771-6300
 Cincinnati *(G-3525)*

3556 Food products machinery

Abj Equipfix LLC................................ E 419 684-6936
 Castalia *(G-2318)*

Acreo Inc.. G 513 734-3327
 Amelia *(G-448)*
◆ American Pan Company....................... C 937 652-3232
 Urbana *(G-14825)*
◆ Anderson International Corp................... D 216 641-1112
 Stow *(G-13684)*
Arbor Foods Inc.................................. E 419 698-4442
 Toledo *(G-14196)*
Binos Inc.. G 330 938-0888
 Sebring *(G-13118)*
Biro Manufacturing Company.................... F 419 798-4451
 North Canton *(G-11717)*
◆ Biro Manufacturing Company.................. D 419 798-4451
 Marblehead *(G-9764)*
◆ Chemineer Inc................................. C 937 454-3200
 Dayton *(G-6254)*
Christy Machine Company....................... F 419 332-6451
 Fremont *(G-7771)*
▲ Cleveland Range LLC......................... C 216 481-4900
 Cleveland *(G-3852)*
CM Sliceчnief Co................................ G 419 241-7647
 Toledo *(G-14246)*
Coperion Food Equipment LLC................... E 937 492-4158
 Sidney *(G-13239)*
▲ Crescent Metal Products Inc.................. C 440 350-1100
 Mentor *(G-10445)*
Drink Modern Technologies LLC................. G 216 577-1536
 Cleveland *(G-3973)*
Edge Exponential LLC........................... F 614 226-4421
 Columbus *(G-5346)*
ES Industries Inc................................. F 419 643-2625
 Lima *(G-9242)*
Fred D Pfening Company......................... G 614 294-5361
 Columbus *(G-5388)*
Fred D Pfening Company......................... G 614 294-5361
 Columbus *(G-5389)*
▲ French Oil Mill Machinery Co.................. D 937 773-3420
 Piqua *(G-12517)*
Frost Engineering Inc............................ E 513 541-6330
 Cincinnati *(G-2923)*
◆ G & S Metal Products Co Inc.................. C 216 441-0700
 Cleveland *(G-4096)*
G F Frank and Sons Inc.......................... F 513 870-9075
 West Chester *(G-15433)*
◆ Garland Commercial Industries LLC........... E 800 338-2204
 Cleveland *(G-4103)*
◆ Gold Medal Products Co....................... B 513 769-7676
 Cincinnati *(G-2962)*
▲ Harry C Lobalzo & Sons Inc................... E 330 666-6758
 Akron *(G-180)*
Hawthorne-Seving Inc........................... E 419 643-5551
 Cridersville *(G-6041)*
Heavenly Creamery Inc.......................... G 440 593-6080
 Conneaut *(G-5920)*
Hobart LLC...................................... E 937 332-2797
 Piqua *(G-12525)*
Hobart LLC...................................... E 937 332-3000
 Troy *(G-14581)*
▲ Hobart LLC................................... D 937 332-3000
 Troy *(G-14582)*
▼ Ingredient Masters Inc........................ G 513 231-7432
 Batavia *(G-926)*
Innovative Controls Corp......................... E 419 691-6684
 Toledo *(G-14333)*
◆ ITW Food Equipment Group LLC.............. A 937 332-2396
 Troy *(G-14589)*
◆ JE Grote Company Inc........................ D 614 868-8414
 Columbus *(G-5491)*
John Bean Technologies Corp.................... B 419 626-0304
 Sandusky *(G-13070)*
Kasel Engineering LLC........................... G 937 854-8875
 Trotwood *(G-14545)*

2024 Harris Ohio Industrial Directory

35 INDUSTRIAL AND COMMERCIAL MACHINERY AND COMPUTER EQUIPMENT

▲ Lem Products Holding LLC............... E 513 202-1188
West Chester *(G-15457)*

Lima Sheet Metal Machine & Mfg............ E 419 229-1161
Lima *(G-9264)*

▲ Lincoln Foodservice Products LLC.. B 260 459-8200
Cleveland *(G-4326)*

Listermann Mfg Co Inc........................... G 513 731-1130
Cincinnati *(G-3108)*

▼ Magna Machine Co............................. C 513 851-6900
Cincinnati *(G-3125)*

Martin Mohr.. F 740 727-2233
New Boston *(G-11397)*

◆ Maverick Innvtive Slutions LLC........... D 419 281-7944
Ashland *(G-590)*

◆ Meyer Company.................................. C 216 587-3400
Chagrin Falls *(G-2382)*

Mojonnier Usa LLC................................. F 844 665-6664
Streetsboro *(G-13780)*

◆ N Wasserstrom & Sons Inc................. C 614 228-5550
Columbus *(G-5588)*

National Oilwell Varco LP....................... D 937 454-4660
Dayton *(G-6464)*

▼ Nemco Food Equipment Ltd................ D 419 542-7751
Hicksville *(G-8376)*

Norse Dairy Systems Inc........................ C 614 294-4931
Columbus *(G-5600)*

◆ Norse Dairy Systems LP...................... B 614 294-4931
Columbus *(G-5601)*

Npk LLC.. G 740 927-2801
New Albany *(G-11385)*

◆ Peerless Foods Inc.............................. D 937 492-4158
Sidney *(G-13270)*

Peerless Stove & Mfg Co........................ F 419 625-4514
Sandusky *(G-13087)*

Premier Industries Inc............................ E 513 271-2550
Cincinnati *(G-3272)*

◆ Prime Equipment Group LLC.............. D 614 253-8590
Columbus *(G-5690)*

R and J Corporation................................ E 440 871-6009
Westlake *(G-15777)*

Railroad Brewing Company.................... G 440 723-8234
Avon *(G-785)*

Royalton Foodservice Eqp Co................. F 440 237-0806
North Royalton *(G-11894)*

RS Industries Inc.................................... G 216 351-8200
Brooklyn Heights *(G-1699)*

Sarka Bros Machining Inc...................... G 419 532-2393
Kalida *(G-8786)*

▼ Sidney Manufacturing Company......... E 937 492-4154
Sidney *(G-13288)*

▲ Siebtechnik Tema Inc......................... E 513 489-7811
Cincinnati *(G-3390)*

▲ Simmons Feed & Supply LLC............. E 800 754-1228
Salem *(G-13031)*

Sir Steak Machinery Inc......................... E 419 526-9181
Mansfield *(G-9718)*

Sterling Process Equipmen..................... E 614 868-5151
Columbus *(G-5794)*

the Perfect Score Company..................... F 440 439-9320
Bedford Heights *(G-1179)*

▲ Tomlinson Industries LLC................... C 216 587-3400
Cleveland *(G-4800)*

Total Baking Solutions LLC..................... E
Wilmington *(G-16060)*

Wolf Machine Company........................... E 513 791-5194
Blue Ash *(G-1493)*

3559 Special industry machinery, nec

A & B Foundry LLC................................. F 937 412-1900
Tipp City *(G-14118)*

Agmet Metals Inc.................................... E 440 439-7400
Oakwood Village *(G-12035)*

Alstart Enterprises LLC........................... F 330 533-3222
Canfield *(G-1998)*

Amano Cincinnati Incorporated............... F 513 697-9000
Loveland *(G-9474)*

American Manufacturing & Eqp............... G 513 829-2248
Fairfield *(G-7335)*

▲ American Plastic Tech Inc.................. C 440 632-5203
Middlefield *(G-10731)*

◆ Anderson International Corp............... D 216 641-1112
Stow *(G-13684)*

Aot Inc... D 937 323-9669
Springfield *(G-13533)*

Aquila Pharmatech LLC.......................... G 419 386-2527
Waterville *(G-15239)*

ARS Recycling Systems LLC.................. F 330 536-8210
Lowellville *(G-9511)*

Auto-Tap Inc.. G 216 671-1043
Cleveland *(G-3701)*

Autotool Inc... E 614 733-0222
Plain City *(G-12563)*

Azsr Technologies Distr LLC................... G 216 315-8285
Brookpark *(G-1705)*

Besten Inc... F 216 910-2880
Cleveland *(G-3732)*

Bethel Engineering and Eqp Inc.............. E 419 568-1100
New Hampshire *(G-11445)*

Broco Products Inc................................. G 216 531-0880
Cleveland *(G-3761)*

Budget Molders Supply Inc..................... F 216 367-7050
Macedonia *(G-9540)*

CAM-Lem Inc... G 216 391-7750
Cleveland *(G-3783)*

Cantrell Rfinery Sls Trnsp Inc................. F 937 695-0318
Winchester *(G-16072)*

Chart International Inc............................ D 440 753-1490
Cleveland *(G-3812)*

◆ Chemineer Inc.................................... C 937 454-3200
Dayton *(G-6254)*

City of Cleveland..................................... B 216 664-2711
Cleveland *(G-3823)*

Cohesant Inc... E 216 910-1700
Beachwood *(G-978)*

Conforming Matrix Corporation............... E 419 729-3777
Toledo *(G-14249)*

Conviber Inc.. F 330 723-6006
Medina *(G-10313)*

Cornerstone Wauseon Inc...................... C 419 337-0940
Wauseon *(G-15259)*

Corrotec Inc.. E 937 325-3585
Springfield *(G-13547)*

Crowne Group LLC................................. F 216 589-0198
Cleveland *(G-3917)*

Decision Systems Inc............................. F 330 456-7600
Canton *(G-2090)*

▲ Dengensha America Corporation........ F 440 439-8081
Bedford *(G-1115)*

Designetics Inc....................................... D 419 866-0700
Holland *(G-8504)*

Devilbiss Ransburg................................. F 419 470-2000
Toledo *(G-14266)*

◆ Eaton Corporation............................... B 440 523-5000
Cleveland *(G-3994)*

▲ Eden Cryogenics LLC......................... E 614 873-3949
Columbus *(G-5345)*

◆ Empire Systems Inc........................... F 440 653-9300
Avon Lake *(G-806)*

Encore Industries Inc.............................. C 419 626-8000
Sandusky *(G-13053)*

Enerfab Inc.. G 513 771-2300
Cincinnati *(G-2871)*

▲ Equipment Mfrs Intl Inc...................... E 216 651-6700
Cleveland *(G-4026)*

Ernest Industries Inc............................... E 937 325-9851
Lowellville *(G-9513)*

Esi-Extrusion Services Inc...................... E 330 374-3388
Akron *(G-143)*

Exomet Inc.. E 440 593-1161
Conneaut *(G-5917)*

Fawcett Co Inc.. G 330 659-4187
Richfield *(G-12787)*

File 13 Inc... F 937 642-4855
Marysville *(G-9909)*

Force Robots LLC................................... G 216 881-8360
Cleveland *(G-4080)*

Fremont Flask Co.................................... F 419 332-2231
Fremont *(G-7782)*

▲ French Oil Mill Machinery Co.............. D 937 773-3420
Piqua *(G-12517)*

◆ Ganzcorp Investments Inc.................. D 330 963-5400
Twinsburg *(G-14664)*

Ged Holdings Inc.................................... F 330 963-5401
Twinsburg *(G-14666)*

General Fabrications Corp...................... E 419 625-6055
Sandusky *(G-13061)*

Girard Machine Company Inc................. E 330 545-9731
Girard *(G-7969)*

▼ Glenn Hunter & Associates Inc.......... D 419 533-0925
Delta *(G-6785)*

▲ Gokoh Corporation............................. F 937 339-4977
Troy *(G-14573)*

Guild Associates Inc............................... G 843 573-0095
Dublin *(G-6889)*

▲ Guild Associates Inc.......................... D 614 798-8215
Dublin *(G-6888)*

▲ Haeco Inc... G 513 722-1030
Loveland *(G-9484)*

Heartland Group Holdings LLC............... D 614 441-4001
Columbus *(G-5425)*

▲ High Temperature Systems Inc.......... F 440 543-8271
Chagrin Falls *(G-2400)*

Hydro Systems Company........................ E 513 271-8800
West Chester *(G-15447)*

I T W Automotive Finishing..................... G 419 470-2000
Toledo *(G-14324)*

◆ Industrial Thermal Systems Inc......... F 513 561-2100
Cincinnati *(G-3022)*

▼ Ingredient Masters Inc....................... G 513 231-7432
Batavia *(G-926)*

◆ Innoplast Inc...................................... F 440 543-8660
Cleveland *(G-4227)*

Inpower LLC.. F 740 548-0965
Lewis Center *(G-9164)*

Integrity Parking LLC.............................. F 440 543-4123
Aurora *(G-720)*

▲ Intelliworks Ht LLC............................ G 419 660-9050
Norwalk *(G-11975)*

◆ Intertec Corporation........................... F 419 537-9711
Toledo *(G-14335)*

J & S Industrial Mch Pdts Inc.................. D 419 691-1380
Toledo *(G-14341)*

J McCaman Enterprises Inc.................... G 330 825-2401
New Franklin *(G-11437)*

Jaco Manufacturing Company................. E 440 234-4000
Berea *(G-1284)*

▲ JC Carter LLC.................................... G 440 569-1818
Richmond Heights *(G-12808)*

JM Hamilton Group Inc........................... E 419 229-4010
Lima *(G-9258)*

◆ Johndow Industries Inc...................... E 330 753-6895
Barberton *(G-875)*

◆ Knight Material Tech LLC................... D 330 488-1651
East Canton *(G-6979)*

▲ Kobelco Stewart Bolling Inc............... D 330 655-3111
Hudson *(G-8601)*

35 INDUSTRIAL AND COMMERCIAL MACHINERY AND COMPUTER EQUIPMENT

Lifeformations Inc................................... E 419 352-2101
  Bowling Green (G-1571)
Linden-Two Inc..................................... E 330 928-4064
  Cuyahoga Falls (G-6100)
▲ Liquid Development Company............. G 216 641-9366
  Independence (G-8671)
◆ Luke Engineering & Mfg Corp............. E 330 335-1501
  Wadsworth (G-15043)
M W Solutions LLC................................ F 419 782-1611
  Defiance (G-6689)
Manufctring Bus Dev Sltons LLC........... D 419 294-1313
  Findlay (G-7530)
▲ McFlusion Inc..................................... G 800 341-8616
  Twinsburg (G-14693)
◆ McNeil & Nrm Inc.............................. D 330 761-1855
  Akron (G-240)
McNeil & Nrm Intl Inc........................... D 330 253-2525
  Akron (G-241)
MDE Energy Transfer............................. G 330 788-5747
  Youngstown (G-16396)
◆ Micro-Pise Msrment Systems LLC...... C 330 541-9100
  Streetsboro (G-13779)
▼ Midwestern Industries Inc.................. D 330 837-4203
  Massillon (G-10127)
Mikes Transm & Auto Svc LLC............... F 330 799-8266
  Youngstown (G-16401)
Mirion Technologies Ist Corp.................. D 614 367-2050
  Pickerington (G-12464)
Mjcj Holdings Inc.................................. G 937 885-0800
  Miamisburg (G-10663)
▲ Mm Industries Inc............................ E 330 332-5947
  Salem (G-13019)
Modular Assmbly Innvations LLC........... E 614 389-4860
  Dublin (G-6912)
Morgan Engineering Systems Inc........... E 330 545-9731
  Girard (G-7973)
Nutro Corporation................................. D 440 572-3800
  Strongsville (G-13860)
Nutro Inc.. E 440 572-3800
  Strongsville (G-13861)
▲ Ohio Magnetics Inc.......................... E 216 662-8484
  Maple Heights (G-9756)
▲ Omco Usa LLC................................ F 740 588-1722
  Zanesville (G-16550)
◆ Plastic Process Equipment Inc............ E 216 367-7000
  Macedonia (G-9566)
Poly Products Inc.................................. G 216 391-7659
  Cleveland (G-4563)
Process Development Corp.................... E 937 890-3388
  Dayton (G-6527)
Prodeva Inc.. F 937 596-6713
  Jackson Center (G-8738)
Production Design Services Inc.............. D 937 866-3377
  Dayton (G-6529)
◆ Production Tube Cutting Inc............... E 937 254-6138
  Dayton (G-6530)
Ray Muro.. G 440 984-8845
  Oberlin (G-12056)
Rda Group LLC..................................... G 440 724-4347
  Avon (G-786)
Rite Track Equipment Services LLC........ D 513 881-7820
  West Chester (G-15500)
◆ Rjs Corporation................................ E 330 896-2387
  Akron (G-306)
▲ RMS Equipment LLC........................ A 330 564-1360
  Cuyahoga Falls (G-6115)
Roberts Machine Products LLC............. F 937 682-4015
  Rushsylvania (G-12875)
▼ RSI Company.................................. F 216 360-9800
  Beachwood (G-1020)
▲ Rubber City Machinery Corp.............. E 330 434-3500
  Akron (G-312)

SDS National LLC.................................. G 330 759-8066
  Youngstown (G-16436)
Sea Air Space McHning Mlding L........... F 440 248-3025
  Streetsboro (G-13791)
◆ Segna Inc.. F 937 335-6700
  Troy (G-14608)
Service Station Equipment Co................ G 216 431-6100
  Cleveland (G-4686)
▼ Singleton Corporation....................... F 216 651-7800
  Cleveland (G-4703)
Stainless Automation............................ G 216 961-4550
  Cleveland (G-4726)
Starkey Machinery Inc........................... E 419 468-2560
  Galion (G-7885)
▲ Steelastic Company LLC................... E 330 633-0505
  Cuyahoga Falls (G-6119)
Steinert Industries Inc........................... F 330 678-0028
  Kent (G-8868)
Storetek Engineering Inc....................... E 330 294-0678
  Tallmadge (G-14050)
Stride Out Rnch N Rodeo Sp LLC.......... F 937 539-1537
  Springfield (G-13639)
Summit Design and Tech Inc................. F 330 733-6662
  Akron (G-339)
Taikisha Usa Inc.................................. D 614 444-5602
  Columbus (G-5806)
▲ Technical Machine Products Inc......... F
  Cleveland (G-4773)
Tiba LLC... E 614 328-2040
  Columbus (G-5826)
▲ Toledo Engineering Co Inc............... D 419 537-9711
  Toledo (G-14495)
▲ Tom Richards Inc........................... C 440 974-1300
  Willoughby (G-16007)
Toney Tool Manufacturing Inc................ E 937 890-8535
  Dayton (G-6627)
Tooltex Inc.. F 614 539-3222
  Grove City (G-8123)
▲ Universal Rack & Eqp Co Inc............ D 330 963-6776
  Twinsburg (G-14751)
Velocys Inc... D 614 733-3300
  Plain City (G-12599)
Vulcan Machinery Corporation.............. E 330 376-6025
  Akron (G-371)
▲ Wentworth Mold Inc Electra............. D 937 898-8460
  Vandalia (G-14967)
Wesco Machine Inc.............................. F 330 688-6973
  Ravenna (G-12742)
◆ Woodman Agitator Inc..................... F 440 937-9865
  Avon (G-793)
Youngstown Plastic Tooling.................. F 330 782-7222
  Youngstown (G-16485)
Zed Industries Inc................................ D 937 667-8407
  Vandalia (G-14968)
▲ Zook Enterprises LLC....................... E 440 543-1010
  Chagrin Falls (G-2438)

3561 Pumps and pumping equipment

A & F Machine Products Co.................. E 440 826-0959
  Berea (G-1263)
▼ Advanced Fuel Systems Inc.............. G 614 252-8422
  Columbus (G-5103)
▲ Ashland Water Group Inc................. G 877 326-3561
  Ashland (G-553)
Ayling and Reichert Co Consent............ E 419 898-2471
  Oak Harbor (G-12011)
Bergstrom Company Ltd Partnr............ E 440 232-2282
  Cleveland (G-3730)
Bowden Manufacturing Corp................ E 440 946-1770
  Willoughby (G-15891)
Certified Labs & Service Inc................. G 419 289-7462
  Ashland (G-563)

Chaos Entertainment............................ G 937 520-5260
  Dayton (G-6251)
▲ Cima Inc.. G 513 382-8976
  Hamilton (G-8192)
City of Newark.................................... E 740 349-6765
  Newark (G-11570)
Columbia Industrial Pdts Inc................ F 216 431-6633
  Cleveland (G-3884)
Crane Pumps & Systems Inc................ C 937 778-8947
  Piqua (G-12510)
◆ Crane Pumps & Systems Inc............ B 937 773-2442
  Piqua (G-12509)
Custom Cltch Jint Hydrlics Inc............. F 216 431-1630
  Cleveland (G-3923)
◆ Dreison International Inc................. C 216 362-0755
  Cleveland (G-3972)
◆ E R Advanced Ceramics Inc............. E 330 426-9433
  East Palestine (G-7004)
Eaton Aeroquip LLC............................. A 419 891-7775
  Maumee (G-10201)
Eric Allshouse LLC............................... G 330 333-4250
  Canfield (G-2005)
Fill-Rite Company................................ E 419 755-1011
  Mansfield (G-9655)
▲ Fischer Global Enterprises LLC......... F 513 583-4900
  Loveland (G-9480)
Flow Control US Holding Corp.............. C 419 289-1144
  Ashland (G-572)
Flowserve Corporation......................... E 937 226-4000
  Dayton (G-6337)
Flowserve Corporation......................... G 513 874-6990
  Loveland (G-9481)
Fluid Automation Inc........................... E 248 912-1970
  North Canton (G-11728)
GE Vernova International LLC............... G 330 963-2066
  Twinsburg (G-14665)
General Electric Company..................... E 216 883-1000
  Cleveland (G-4115)
Gerow Equipment Company Inc............ G 216 383-8800
  Cleveland (G-4122)
▲ Giant Industries Inc........................ E 419 531-4600
  Toledo (G-14300)
Gorman-Rupp Company...................... B 419 755-1011
  Mansfield (G-9661)
Gorman-Rupp Company...................... G 419 755-1245
  Mansfield (G-9662)
Gorman-Rupp Company...................... C 419 755-1011
  Mansfield (G-9663)
▼ Hydromatic Pumps Inc.................... D 419 289-1144
  Ashland (G-580)
Idex Corporation................................. E 419 526-7222
  Mansfield (G-9670)
Indelco Custom Products Inc............... E 216 797-7300
  Euclid (G-7274)
Interstate Pump Company Inc.............. G 330 222-1006
  Salem (G-13005)
▲ Keen Pump Company Inc................ E 419 207-9400
  Ashland (G-584)
Lakecraft Inc....................................... E 419 734-2828
  Port Clinton (G-12621)
Lubrisource Inc................................... F 937 432-9292
  Middletown (G-10836)
M T Systems Inc................................. G 330 453-4646
  Canton (G-2150)
Maag Reduction Inc............................. F 704 716-9000
  Kent (G-8831)
Magnum Piering Inc............................ E 513 759-3348
  West Chester (G-15568)
▲ Metaullics Systems LP..................... C 509 926-6212
  Solon (G-13387)
▲ Molten Mtal Eqp Innvations LLC....... E 440 632-9119
  Middlefield (G-10771)

SIC SECTION
35 INDUSTRIAL AND COMMERCIAL MACHINERY AND COMPUTER EQUIPMENT

▲ Pckd Enterprises Inc............................ F 440 632-9119
  Middlefield (G-10779)
Pentair... E 440 248-0100
  Solon (G-13404)
Pentair Pump Group Inc...................... F 419 281-9918
  Ashland (G-598)
Quikstir Inc.. E 419 732-2601
  Port Clinton (G-12625)
Rolcon Inc... F 513 821-7259
  Cincinnati (G-3349)
Rumpke Transportation Co LLC............ F 513 851-0122
  Cincinnati (G-3355)
◆ Seepex Inc...................................... C 937 864-7150
  Enon (G-7252)
Stahl Gear & Machine Co..................... E 216 431-2820
  Cleveland (G-4725)
Suburban Manufacturing Co................. D 440 953-2024
  Eastlake (G-7050)
Systecon LLC.................................... D 513 777-7722
  West Chester (G-15513)
Tark Inc... E 937 434-6766
  Miamisburg (G-10689)
Teikoku USA Inc................................. F 304 699-1156
  Marietta (G-9835)
Thieman Tailgates Inc......................... D 419 586-7727
  Celina (G-2353)
TJ Clark International LLC................... G 614 388-8869
  Delaware (G-6755)
◆ Tolco Corporation........................... D 419 241-1113
  Toledo (G-14491)
Trane Technologies Company LLC........ E 419 633-6800
  Bryan (G-1842)
Trane Technologies Company LLC........ G 419 636-4242
  Bryan (G-1843)
Trane Technologies Company LLC........ E 513 459-4580
  Cincinnati (G-3459)
Transdigm Inc.................................... F 216 291-6025
  Cleveland (G-4815)
Transdigm Inc.................................... E 440 352-6182
  Painesville (G-12272)
▲ Uhrden Inc..................................... E 330 456-0031
  Canton (G-2249)
▲ Valco Cincinnati Inc....................... C 513 874-6550
  West Chester (G-15603)
Vertiflo Pump Company...................... F 513 530-0888
  Cincinnati (G-3496)
Vickers International Inc..................... E 419 867-2200
  Maumee (G-10244)
◆ Warren Rupp Inc............................ C 419 524-8388
  Mansfield (G-9730)
Waterpro... G 330 372-3565
  Warren (G-15222)
▲ Wayne/Scott Fetzer Company.......... C 800 237-0987
  Harrison (G-8296)

3562 Ball and roller bearings

Bearings Manufacturing Company........ F 440 846-5517
  Strongsville (G-13815)
Extreme Caster Services Inc................ G 330 637-9030
  Cortland (G-5962)
Ggb US Holdco LLC............................ F 234 262-3000
  North Canton (G-11730)
Gt Technologies Inc............................ D 419 782-8955
  Defiance (G-6680)
▲ HMS Industries LLC....................... F 440 899-0001
  Westlake (G-15756)
▲ Jay Dee Service Corporation.......... G 330 425-1546
  Macedonia (G-9558)
◆ Kaydon Corporation....................... D 231 755-3741
  Avon (G-777)
Miller Bearing Company Inc................. E 330 678-8844
  Kent (G-8837)

Nn Inc... E 440 647-4711
  Wellington (G-15318)
Schaeffler Group USA Inc.................... E 800 274-5001
  Valley City (G-14889)
Superior Caster Inc............................ F 513 539-8980
  Middletown (G-10861)
▲ The Hamilton Caster & Mfg............ D 513 863-3300
  Hamilton (G-8248)
▲ Thyssnkrupp Rothe Erde USA Inc... C 330 562-4000
  Aurora (G-736)
Timken Company................................ F 614 836-3337
  Groveport (G-8162)
◆ Timken Company........................... A 234 262-3000
  North Canton (G-11766)
Timken Newco I LLC........................... E 234 262-3000
  North Canton (G-11767)
▲ Tsk America Co Ltd...................... F 513 942-4002
  West Chester (G-15600)

3563 Air and gas compressors

Aci Services Inc................................. E 740 435-0240
  Cambridge (G-1918)
◆ Airbase Industries LLC................... F 937 540-1140
  Englewood (G-7222)
Airtech.. G 419 269-1000
  Walbridge (G-15078)
Airtx International Ltd........................ F 513 631-0660
  Cincinnati (G-2605)
▲ Anest Iwata Americas Inc.............. F 513 755-3100
  West Chester (G-15365)
Ariel Corporation................................ D 330 896-2660
  Akron (G-64)
Ariel Corporation................................ F 740 397-0311
  Mount Vernon (G-11263)
◆ Ariel Corporation........................... C 740 397-0311
  Mount Vernon (G-11264)
▲ Armour Spray Systems Inc............ F 216 398-3838
  Cleveland (G-3675)
▼ Ats Ohio Inc.................................. C 614 888-2344
  Lewis Center (G-9151)
Autobody Supply Company Inc............. D 614 228-4328
  Columbus (G-5166)
◆ Ch Transition Company LLC........... C 800 543-6400
  Cincinnati (G-2724)
Cohesant Inc..................................... E 216 910-1700
  Beachwood (G-978)
Deco Tools Inc................................... E 419 476-9321
  Toledo (G-14262)
◆ Eaton Comprsr Fabrication Inc....... E 877 283-7614
  Englewood (G-7230)
Edwards Vacuum LLC......................... G 440 248-4453
  Solon (G-13340)
Ernest Industries Inc.......................... F 937 325-9851
  Springfield (G-13559)
Field Gymmy Inc................................. G 419 538-6511
  Glandorf (G-7978)
▼ Finishing Brands Holdings Inc........ C 260 665-8800
  Toledo (G-14288)
Finishmaster Inc................................ F 614 228-4328
  Groveport (G-8139)
G Denver and Co LLC.......................... E 937 498-2555
  Sidney (G-13250)
General Fabrications Corp................... E 419 625-6055
  Sandusky (G-13061)
Glascraft Inc...................................... C 330 966-3000
  North Canton (G-11731)
Ingersoll Rand.................................... F 440 277-7100
  Lorain (G-9414)
Kingsly Compression Inc..................... G 740 439-0772
  Cambridge (G-1939)
Lincoln Electric Automtn Inc................ E 614 471-5926
  Columbus (G-5527)

Lsq Manufacturing Inc......................... F 330 725-4905
  Medina (G-10345)
National Compressor Svcs LLC............. E 419 868-4980
  Holland (G-8519)
Nordson Corporation........................... B 440 985-4496
  Amherst (G-478)
Nordson Corporation........................... E 440 985-4458
  Amherst (G-479)
Nordson Corporation........................... B 440 985-4000
  Amherst (G-480)
Nordson Corporation........................... A 440 892-1580
  Westlake (G-15768)
Nordson Medical Corporation............... D 440 892-1580
  Westlake (G-15769)
Paratus Supply Inc............................. F 330 745-3600
  Barberton (G-888)
Potemkin Industries Inc...................... F 740 397-4888
  Mount Vernon (G-11288)
▲ Powerex-Iwata Air Tech Inc........... D 888 769-7979
  Harrison (G-8284)
Quikstir Inc.. E 419 732-2601
  Port Clinton (G-12625)
▲ Rimrock Corporation..................... E 614 471-5926
  Columbus (G-5723)
Rimrock Holdings Corporation............. C 614 471-5926
  Columbus (G-5724)
Rubberset Company........................... G 800 345-4939
  Cleveland (G-4661)
◆ Tolco Corporation........................... D 419 241-1113
  Toledo (G-14491)
Trail Sprayer & Service LLC................ F 330 720-2966
  Kent (G-8877)
Transdigm Inc.................................... F 216 291-6025
  Cleveland (G-4815)
Tri State Equipment Company............. G 513 738-7227
  Shandon (G-13161)
◆ United Air Specialists Inc............... C 513 891-0400
  Blue Ash (G-1486)
▲ Wiwa LLC...................................... F 419 757-0141
  Alger (G-384)
Wiwa LP.. G 419 757-0141
  Alger (G-385)

3564 Blowers and fans

A A S Amels Sheet Meta L Inc............. F 330 793-9326
  Youngstown (G-16297)
◆ Ad Industries Inc........................... A 303 744-1911
  Dayton (G-6183)
Air Enterprises Inc............................. A 330 794-9770
  Akron (G-24)
▼ Air-Rite Inc................................... E 216 228-8200
  Cleveland (G-3617)
▲ Airecon Manufacturing Corp.......... E 513 561-5522
  Cincinnati (G-2604)
Allied Separation Tech Inc................... F 704 736-0420
  Twinsburg (G-14629)
◆ American Fan Company.................. C 513 874-2400
  Fairfield (G-7333)
American Manufacturing & Eqp........... G 513 829-2248
  Fairfield (G-7335)
Americraft Mfg Co Inc......................... F 513 489-1047
  Cincinnati (G-2621)
ARI Phoenix Inc.................................. E 513 229-3750
  Sharonville (G-13170)
Atmos360 Inc..................................... E 513 772-4777
  West Chester (G-15539)
▲ Beckett Air Incorporated............... D 440 327-9999
  North Ridgeville (G-11829)
◆ Bry-Air Inc.................................... E 740 965-2974
  Sunbury (G-13951)
Buckeye BOP LLC................................ G 740 498-9898
  Newcomerstown (G-11643)

Employee Codes: A=Over 500 employees, B=251-500
C=101-250, D=51-100, E=20-50, F=10-19, G=1-9

35 INDUSTRIAL AND COMMERCIAL MACHINERY AND COMPUTER EQUIPMENT

Burt Manufacturing Company Inc......... E 330 762-0061
   Akron *(G-97)*

Cardinal Air Design LLC....................... G 440 638-4717
   North Royalton *(G-11869)*

Ceco Filters Inc................................... G 513 458-2600
   Cincinnati *(G-2713)*

Ceco Group Global Holdings LLC......... G 513 458-2600
   Cincinnati *(G-2714)*

Cincinnati A Flter Sls Svc Inc................ E 513 242-3400
   Cincinnati *(G-2737)*

Cincinnati Fan & Ventilat...................... D 513 573-0600
   Mason *(G-9974)*

Cleveland Roll Forming En................... F 440 899-3888
   Westlake *(G-15744)*

Criticalaire LLC................................... E 513 475-3800
   Westerville *(G-15652)*

◆ Dreison International Inc................... C 216 362-0755
   Cleveland *(G-3972)*

▲ Duro Dyne Midwest Corp................. C 513 870-6000
   Hamilton *(G-8201)*

Effox-Flextor-Mader Inc........................ E 513 874-8915
   West Chester *(G-15549)*

Envirofab Inc....................................... F 216 651-1767
   Cleveland *(G-4023)*

Extreme Microbial Tech LLC................ E 844 885-0088
   Moraine *(G-11179)*

Famous Industries Inc......................... F 740 685-2592
   Byesville *(G-1896)*

Flex Technologies Inc.......................... D 330 359-5415
   Mount Eaton *(G-11230)*

FM AF LLC... C 866 771-6266
   Fairfield *(G-7362)*

◆ Guardian Technologies LLC.............. E 866 603-5900
   Euclid *(G-7270)*

◆ H-P Products Inc.............................. C 330 875-5556
   Louisville *(G-9459)*

◆ Hartzell Fan Inc................................ C 937 773-7411
   Piqua *(G-12520)*

Hdt Ep Inc... C 216 438-6111
   Solon *(G-13359)*

Hdt Expeditionary Systems Inc............. F 440 466-6640
   Geneva *(G-7938)*

Herman Manufacturing LLC................. F 216 251-6400
   Cleveland *(G-4185)*

▲ Howden North America Inc.............. C 513 874-2400
   Fairfield *(G-7369)*

Howden North America Inc.................. F 330 721-7374
   Medina *(G-10334)*

Howden North America Inc.................. E 330 867-8540
   Medina *(G-10335)*

▲ Howden USA Company..................... E 513 874-2400
   Fairfield *(G-7370)*

Humongous Holdings Llc.................... F 216 663-8830
   Cleveland *(G-4208)*

Hunter Environmental Corp.................. F 440 248-6111
   Solon *(G-13364)*

Illinois Tool Works Inc.......................... E 262 248-8277
   Bryan *(G-1821)*

Indoor Envmtl Specialists Inc............... E 937 433-5202
   Dayton *(G-6381)*

Kirk Williams Company Inc.................. D 614 875-9023
   Grove City *(G-8100)*

▲ Langdon Inc..................................... E 513 733-5955
   Cincinnati *(G-3095)*

Lau Holdings LLC................................ G 937 476-6500
   Dayton *(G-6166)*

Lau Holdings LLC................................ D 216 486-4000
   Cleveland *(G-4316)*

▼ Lau Industries Inc............................ A 216 894-3903
   Dayton *(G-6167)*

◆ McGill Airclean LLC.......................... D 614 829-1200
   Columbus *(G-5550)*

◆ McGill Corporation........................... F 614 829-1200
   Groveport *(G-8153)*

Mestek Inc... F 419 288-2703
   Bradner *(G-1603)*

Met-Pro Technologies LLC................... F 513 458-2600
   Cincinnati *(G-3153)*

▼ Midwestern Industries Inc............... D 330 837-4203
   Massillon *(G-10127)*

▲ Multi-Wing America Inc.................... E 440 834-9400
   Middlefield *(G-10772)*

Neundorfer Inc..................................... E 440 942-8990
   Willoughby *(G-15957)*

Nupro Company................................... D 440 951-9729
   Willoughby *(G-15962)*

Ohio Blow Pipe Company..................... E 216 681-7379
   Cleveland *(G-4496)*

OSI Environmental LLC....................... E 440 237-4600
   North Royalton *(G-11890)*

Plas-Tanks Industries Inc..................... E 513 942-3800
   Hamilton *(G-8235)*

▲ Qualtek Electronics Corp.................. C 440 951-3300
   Mentor *(G-10541)*

Quickdraft Inc...................................... E 330 477-4574
   Canton *(G-2206)*

Rmt Acquisition Inc............................. E 513 241-5566
   Cincinnati *(G-3347)*

Schenck Process LLC.......................... F 513 576-9200
   Solon *(G-13419)*

▲ Selas Heat Technology Co LLC......... E 800 523-6500
   Streetsboro *(G-13792)*

Seneca Environmental Products Inc..... E 419 447-1282
   Tiffin *(G-14104)*

▼ Shupert Manufacturing Inc.............. F 937 859-7492
   Miamisburg *(G-10682)*

▲ Skuttle Mfg Co................................. F 740 373-9169
   Marietta *(G-9825)*

Sly Inc... E 800 334-2957
   Strongsville *(G-13881)*

Starr Fabricating Inc............................ D 330 394-9891
   Vienna *(G-15004)*

Stelter and Brinck Inc.......................... E 513 367-9300
   Harrison *(G-8293)*

▲ Thermo Vent Manufacturing Inc....... F 330 239-0239
   Medina *(G-10386)*

▲ Tisch Environmental Inc.................. E 513 467-9000
   Cleves *(G-4967)*

▲ Tlt-Babcock Inc................................ D 330 867-8540
   Akron *(G-359)*

▲ Tlt-Turbo Inc.................................... G 330 776-5115
   Akron *(G-360)*

◆ Tosoh America Inc........................... B 614 539-8622
   Grove City *(G-8124)*

Troy Filters Ltd.................................... E 614 777-8222
   Columbus *(G-5839)*

◆ United Air Specialists Inc................. C 513 891-0400
   Blue Ash *(G-1486)*

▲ United McGill Corporation................ E 614 829-1200
   Groveport *(G-8165)*

Vector Mechanical LLC........................ G 216 337-4042
   Cleveland *(G-4863)*

▼ Verantis Corporation........................ E 440 243-0700
   Middleburg Heights *(G-10728)*

Vortec and Paxton Products................. F 513 891-7474
   Blue Ash *(G-1488)*

Weather King Heating & AC................. G 330 908-0281
   Northfield *(G-11914)*

Windsor Wire....................................... G 662 634-5908
   Strongsville *(G-13897)*

3565 Packaging machinery

▲ Advanced Poly-Packaging Inc........... C 330 785-4000
   Akron *(G-23)*

Atmos360 Inc...................................... E 513 772-4777
   West Chester *(G-15539)*

Audion Automation Ltd........................ E 216 267-1911
   Berea *(G-1265)*

▲ Audion Automation Ltd.................... F 216 267-1911
   Berea *(G-1266)*

▲ Automated Packaging Systems LLC.. C 330 528-2000
   Streetsboro *(G-13759)*

Automated Packg Systems Inc............ E 330 342-2000
   Bedford *(G-1103)*

Automated Packg Systems Inc............ G 330 626-2313
   Streetsboro *(G-13760)*

Barry-Wehmiller Companies Inc........... F 330 923-0491
   Cuyahoga Falls *(G-6072)*

Beckermills Inc.................................... G 419 738-3450
   Wapakoneta *(G-15106)*

◆ Combi Packaging Systems Llc......... D 330 456-9333
   Canton *(G-2078)*

▲ Crown Closures Machinery.............. E 740 681-6593
   Lancaster *(G-9005)*

Ctm Integration Incorporated............... E 330 332-1800
   Salem *(G-12988)*

Ctm Labeling Systems......................... E 330 332-1800
   Salem *(G-12989)*

▲ Darifill Inc....................................... F 614 890-3274
   Westerville *(G-15698)*

Exact Equipment Corporation.............. E 215 295-2000
   Columbus *(G-5062)*

Expo Packaging Inc............................. G 216 267-9700
   Cleveland *(G-4043)*

Food Equipment Mfg Corp................... E 216 672-5859
   Bedford Heights *(G-1172)*

G and J Automatic Systems Inc........... E 216 741-6070
   Cleveland *(G-4097)*

General Data Healthcare Inc................ G 513 752-7978
   Cincinnati *(G-2562)*

GL Industries Inc................................. E 513 874-1233
   Hamilton *(G-8212)*

◆ Glassline Corporation...................... E 419 666-9712
   Perrysburg *(G-12385)*

Gunnison Associates Llc..................... G 330 562-5230
   Aurora *(G-717)*

H & G Equipment Inc........................... F 513 761-2060
   Blue Ash *(G-1401)*

H&G Legacy Co.................................... F 513 921-1075
   Cincinnati *(G-2982)*

Huhtamaki Inc..................................... C 513 201-1525
   Batavia *(G-925)*

Huhtamaki Inc..................................... D 937 746-9700
   Franklin *(G-7681)*

Hunkar Technologies Inc...................... C 513 272-1010
   Cincinnati *(G-3012)*

Iconic Labs LLC................................... F 216 759-4040
   Westlake *(G-15758)*

Kaufman Engineered Systems Inc....... D 419 878-9727
   Waterville *(G-15248)*

▲ Kennedy Group Incorporated........... D 440 951-7660
   Willoughby *(G-15939)*

Kolinahr Systems Inc........................... F 513 745-9401
   Blue Ash *(G-1417)*

M PI Label Systems............................. G 330 938-2134
   Sebring *(G-13121)*

◆ Miconvi Properties Inc..................... E 440 954-3500
   Eastlake *(G-7039)*

Millwood Inc.. E 513 860-4567
   West Chester *(G-15464)*

Millwood Natural LLC.......................... E 330 393-4400
   Vienna *(G-15002)*

◆ Morgan Adhesives Company LLC..... B 330 688-1111
   Stow *(G-13709)*

Mpi Labels of Baltimore Inc.................. E 330 938-2134
   Sebring *(G-13124)*

35 INDUSTRIAL AND COMMERCIAL MACHINERY AND COMPUTER EQUIPMENT

◆ Nilpeter Usa Inc..................................C..... 513 489-4400
Cincinnati (G-3198)

Norse Dairy Systems Inc......................C..... 614 294-4931
Columbus (G-5600)

◆ OKL Can Line Inc.................................E
Cincinnati (G-3220)

Ossid Inc..G..... 724 463-3232
Dublin (G-6919)

▲ Pack Line Corp....................................E..... 212 564-0664
Cleveland (G-4519)

Pak Master LLC.....................................E..... 330 523-5319
Richfield (G-12792)

▲ PE Usa LLC..F..... 513 771-7374
Cincinnati (G-3244)

◆ Pneumatic Scale Corporation............C..... 330 923-0491
Cuyahoga Falls (G-6109)

Precision Replacement LLC................G..... 330 908-0410
Macedonia (G-9569)

◆ Quadrel Inc..E..... 440 602-4700
Mentor (G-10539)

▲ Reactive Resin Products Co...............E..... 419 666-6119
Perrysburg (G-12423)

Recon Systems LLC.............................G..... 330 488-0368
East Canton (G-6980)

Rpmi Packaging Inc..............................F..... 513 398-4040
Lebanon (G-9109)

S A Langmack Company.....................F..... 216 541-0500
Cleveland (G-4666)

▲ Scanacon Incorporated......................G..... 330 877-7600
Hartville (G-8306)

Superior Label Systems Inc................B..... 513 336-0825
Mason (G-10061)

Switchback Group Inc..........................E..... 216 290-6040
Cleveland (G-4762)

System Packaging of Glassline..........D..... 419 666-9712
Perrysburg (G-12427)

Titans Packaging LLC..........................F..... 513 449-0014
West Chester (G-15597)

Unity Enterprises Inc...........................G..... 614 231-1370
Columbus (G-5844)

Universal Packg Systems Inc.............C..... 513 732-2000
Batavia (G-957)

Universal Packg Systems Inc.............C..... 513 735-4777
Batavia (G-958)

Universal Packg Systems Inc.............C..... 513 674-9400
Cincinnati (G-3483)

Vistech Mfg Solutions LLC..................F..... 513 933-9300
Lebanon (G-9120)

▲ Vmi Americas Inc................................E..... 330 929-6800
Stow (G-13738)

3566 Speed changers, drives, and gears

Akron Gear & Engineering Inc............E..... 330 773-6608
Akron (G-34)

Ametek Tchnical Indus Pdts Inc..........D..... 330 673-3451
Kent (G-8799)

Atc Legacy Inc......................................G..... 330 590-8105
Sharon Center (G-13162)

B & B Gear and Machine Co Inc.........E..... 937 687-1771
New Lebanon (G-11448)

▲ Bunting Bearings LLC........................D..... 419 866-7000
Holland (G-8495)

Cage Gear & Machine LLC..................E..... 330 452-1532
Canton (G-2057)

Canton Gear Mfg Designing Inc.........F..... 330 455-2771
Canton (G-2064)

▲ Cleveland Gear Company Inc............D..... 216 641-9000
Cleveland (G-3840)

Dayton Gear and Tool Co....................E..... 937 866-4327
Dayton (G-6279)

Eaton Leasing Corporation.................B..... 216 382-2292
Beachwood (G-986)

Ebog Legacy Inc...................................D..... 330 239-4933
Sharon Center (G-13166)

▲ Force Control Industries Inc..............E..... 513 868-0900
Fairfield (G-7363)

▲ Forge Industries Inc...........................A..... 330 960-2468
Youngstown (G-16359)

Gear Company of America Inc...........D..... 216 671-5400
Cleveland (G-4107)

▲ Geartec Inc...E..... 440 953-3900
Willoughby (G-15924)

Geneva Gear & Machine Inc...............F..... 937 866-0318
Dayton (G-6351)

▲ Great Lakes Power Products Inc.......D..... 440 951-5111
Mentor (G-10465)

◆ HBD Industries Inc..............................E..... 614 526-7000
Dublin (G-6891)

▲ Hefty Hoist Inc....................................E..... 740 467-2515
Millersport (G-11012)

◆ Horsburgh & Scott Co........................C..... 216 431-3900
Cleveland (G-4202)

◆ Industrial Mfg Co LLC........................F..... 440 838-4700
Brecksville (G-1621)

▲ ITT Torque Systems Inc....................C..... 216 524-8800
Cleveland (G-4241)

Jonmar Gear and Machine Inc...........G..... 330 854-6500
Canal Fulton (G-1971)

▲ Joseph Industries Inc........................D..... 330 528-0091
Streetsboro (G-13776)

▲ Julie Maynard Inc...............................F..... 937 443-0408
Dayton (G-6394)

Kenmore Gear & Machine Co Inc.......G..... 330 753-6671
Akron (G-204)

▲ Linde Hydraulics Corporation...........E..... 330 533-6801
Canfield (G-2009)

Little Mountain Precision LLC............F..... 440 290-2903
Mentor (G-10495)

◆ Luk Clutch Systems LLC...................E..... 330 264-4383
Wooster (G-16147)

▼ Matlock Electric Co Inc.....................E..... 513 731-9600
Cincinnati (G-3134)

Pentagear Products LLC.....................F..... 937 660-8182
Dayton (G-6500)

Petro Gear Corporation........................F..... 216 431-2820
Cleveland (G-4544)

Precision Gear LLC..............................D..... 330 487-0888
Twinsburg (G-14716)

Radocy Inc..F..... 419 666-4400
Rossford (G-12870)

Richard A Scott....................................G..... 937 898-1592
Dayton (G-6549)

Robertson Manufacturing Co..............F..... 216 531-8222
Concord Township (G-5912)

RTC Converters Inc..............................F..... 937 743-2300
Franklin (G-7700)

Schaeffler Transm Systems LLC........A..... 330 202-6212
Wooster (G-16166)

◆ Schaeffler Transm Systems LLC......E..... 330 264-4383
Wooster (G-16167)

Sew-Eurodrive Inc................................D..... 937 335-0036
Troy (G-14609)

▲ Skidmore-Wilhelm Mfg Company.....F..... 216 481-4774
Solon (G-13422)

Spang & Company................................E..... 440 350-6108
Mentor (G-10558)

Stahl Gear & Machine Co....................E..... 216 431-2820
Cleveland (G-4725)

Tgm Holdings Company......................E..... 419 885-3769
Sylvania (G-14018)

Timken Newco I LLC............................E..... 234 262-3000
North Canton (G-11767)

Titanium Metals Corporation..............A..... 740 537-1571
Toronto (G-14535)

Tridelta Industries Inc..........................G..... 440 255-1080
Mentor (G-10584)

◆ Wasserstrom Company......................B..... 614 228-6525
Columbus (G-5865)

Werks Kraft Engineering LLC..............E..... 330 721-7374
Medina (G-10394)

3567 Industrial furnaces and ovens

A E F Inc..F..... 216 360-9800
Cleveland (G-3578)

▲ A Jacks Manufacturing Co................E..... 216 531-1010
Cleveland (G-3581)

◆ Abp Induction LLC.............................F..... 262 878-6390
Massillon (G-10075)

Agridry LLC...F..... 419 459-4399
Edon (G-7085)

◆ Ajax Tocco Magnethermic Corp.......C..... 800 547-1527
Warren (G-15135)

Armature Coil Equipment Inc.............F..... 216 267-6366
Strongsville (G-13809)

▼ Benko Products Inc...........................E..... 440 934-2180
Sheffield Village (G-13181)

▲ C A Litzler Co Inc...............................E..... 216 267-8020
Cleveland (G-3778)

▲ CA Litzler Holding Company............D..... 216 267-8020
Cleveland (G-3780)

▲ CMI Industry Americas Inc...............D..... 330 332-4661
Salem (G-12985)

▲ Crescent Metal Products Inc............C..... 440 350-1100
Mentor (G-10445)

Custom Services and Designs............G..... 937 866-7636
Miamisburg (G-10630)

Delta H Technologies LLC...................G..... 740 756-7676
Carroll (G-2296)

▲ Duca Manufacturing & Cons.............E..... 330 758-0828
Youngstown (G-16352)

Duca Mfg & Consulting Inc.................G..... 330 726-7175
Youngstown (G-16353)

◆ Ebner Furnaces Inc............................D..... 330 335-2311
Wadsworth (G-15028)

▲ Facultatieve Tech Americas Inc........E..... 330 723-6339
Medina (G-10321)

Furnace Technologies Inc...................F..... 419 878-2100
Waterville (G-15244)

◆ Garland Commercial Industries LLC..E..... 800 338-2204
Cleveland (G-4103)

Glo-Quartz Electric Htr Co Inc............E..... 440 255-9701
Mentor (G-10464)

Hannon Company.................................D..... 330 456-4728
Canton (G-2121)

◆ Harrop Industries Inc.........................E..... 614 231-3621
Columbus (G-5422)

▲ Heat Sensor Technologie LLC..........D..... 513 228-0481
Lebanon (G-9088)

I Cerco Inc..C..... 740 982-2050
Crooksville (G-6047)

◆ I Cerco Inc...C..... 330 567-2145
Shreve (G-13210)

Induction Tooling Inc...........................F..... 440 237-0711
North Royalton (G-11879)

Kaufman Engineered Systems Inc.....D..... 419 878-9727
Waterville (G-15248)

L Haberny Co Inc..................................F..... 440 543-5999
Chagrin Falls (G-2404)

Lakeway Mfg Inc...................................E..... 419 433-3030
Huron (G-8637)

Lanly Company.....................................E..... 216 731-1115
Cleveland (G-4312)

◆ Lewco Inc...C..... 419 625-4014
Sandusky (G-13074)

Magneforce Inc.....................................F..... 330 856-9300
Warren (G-15188)

Employee Codes: A=Over 500 employees, B=251-500
C=101-250, D=51-100, E=20-50, F=10-19, G=1-9

2024 Harris Ohio Industrial Directory

35 INDUSTRIAL AND COMMERCIAL MACHINERY AND COMPUTER EQUIPMENT

▲ Micropyretics Heaters Intl Inc............E..... 513 772-0404
Cincinnati (G-3162)

Miller Core II Inc...........................G..... 330 359-0500
Beach City (G-969)

Novagard Solutions Inc.....................C..... 216 881-8111
Cleveland (G-4483)

▲ P S C Inc................................G..... 216 531-3375
Cleveland (G-4517)

◆ Park-Ohio Holdings Corp..................F..... 440 947-2000
Cleveland (G-4524)

Park-Ohio Industries Inc...................C..... 440 947-2000
Cleveland (G-4525)

Pillar Induction...........................F..... 262 317-5300
Warren (G-15199)

▲ RAD-Con Inc..............................E..... 440 871-5720
Lakewood (G-8981)

Resilience Fund III LP.....................E..... 216 292-0200
Cleveland (G-4629)

▲ Selas Heat Technology Co LLC.............E..... 800 523-6500
Streetsboro (G-13792)

▲ Sentro Tech Corporation..................G..... 440 260-0364
Strongsville (G-13876)

Star-Tjcm Inc..............................E..... 740 342-3514
New Lexington (G-11458)

Stelter and Brinck Inc.....................E..... 513 367-9300
Harrison (G-8293)

◆ Strohecker Incorporated..................E..... 330 426-9496
East Palestine (G-7009)

▲ Surface Combustion Inc...................D..... 419 891-7150
Maumee (G-10238)

T E Q HI Inc...............................E..... 877 448-3701
Columbus (G-5805)

T J F Inc..................................F..... 419 878-4400
Waterville (G-15253)

◆ Taylor - Winfield Corporation............C..... 330 259-8500
Hubbard (G-8571)

▲ The Schaefer Group Inc...................E..... 937 253-3342
Beavercreek (G-1082)

Thermo Systems Technology Inc..............F..... 216 292-8250
Cleveland (G-4792)

▲ United McGill Corporation................E..... 614 829-1200
Groveport (G-8165)

◆ Warren Steel Holdings LLC................B..... 330 847-0487
Warren (G-15220)

3568 Power transmission equipment, nec

Abl Products Inc...........................F..... 216 281-2400
Cleveland (G-3588)

▲ Advance Bronze Inc.......................F..... 330 948-1231
Lodi (G-9345)

Akron Gear & Engineering Inc...............E..... 330 773-6608
Akron (G-34)

B S F Inc..................................F..... 937 890-6121
Tipp City (G-14123)

B S F Inc..................................F..... 937 890-6121
Dayton (G-6222)

Bdi Inc....................................C..... 330 498-4980
Canton (G-2045)

Bowes Manufacturing Inc....................E..... 216 378-2110
Solon (G-13321)

▲ Bucyrus Precision Tech Inc...............C..... 419 563-9950
Bucyrus (G-1852)

Bunting Bearings LLC.......................E..... 419 522-3323
Mansfield (G-9634)

Cleveland Rebabbitting Svc Inc.............G..... 216 433-0123
Cleveland (G-3853)

▲ Climax Metal Products Company............D..... 440 943-8898
Mentor (G-10440)

Custom Cltch Jint Hydrlics Inc.............F..... 216 431-1630
Cleveland (G-3923)

Danfoss Power Solutions II LLC.............G..... 419 238-1190
Van Wert (G-14913)

Dayton Superior Pdts Co Inc................G..... 937 332-1930
Troy (G-14560)

Drive Components LLC.......................G..... 440 234-6200
Strongsville (G-13829)

Dryden Shafts LLC..........................E..... 937 365-7420
Moraine (G-11173)

Dupont Specialty Pdts USA LLC..............C..... 216 901-3600
Cleveland (G-3978)

Eaton Corporation..........................C..... 216 281-2211
Cleveland (G-3992)

Ebog Legacy Inc............................D..... 330 239-4933
Sharon Center (G-13166)

Excel Loading Systems LLC..................G..... 513 504-1069
Hamilton (G-8207)

▲ Force Control Industries Inc.............E..... 513 868-0900
Fairfield (G-7363)

General Electric Company...................E..... 216 883-1000
Cleveland (G-4115)

General Metals Powder Co LLC...............E..... 330 633-1226
Akron (G-166)

Geneva Gear & Machine Inc..................F..... 937 866-6318
Dayton (G-6351)

GKN Sinter Metals LLC......................C..... 740 441-3203
Gallipolis (G-7894)

Hite Parts Exchange Inc....................F..... 614 272-5115
Columbus (G-5442)

J L R Products Inc.........................F..... 330 832-9557
Massillon (G-10112)

Lextech Industries Ltd.....................G..... 216 883-7900
Cleveland (G-4322)

▲ Logan Clutch Corporation.................E..... 440 808-4258
Cleveland (G-4334)

▲ Luk Clutch Systems LLC...................E..... 330 264-4383
Wooster (G-16147)

Master Products Company....................D..... 216 341-1740
Cleveland (G-4368)

▲ McGregor Mtal Yllow Sprng Wrks...........D..... 937 325-5561
Springfield (G-13604)

Mechanical Dynamics Analis LLC.............E..... 440 946-0082
Euclid (G-7285)

Mfh Partners Inc...........................B..... 440 461-4100
Cleveland (G-4398)

▲ NIDEC MINSTER CORPORATION................B..... 419 628-2331
Minster (G-11057)

▲ Opw Engineered Systems Inc...............E..... 888 771-9438
West Chester (G-15471)

Penn Machine Company LLC...................D..... 814 288-1547
Twinsburg (G-14708)

Poly Products Inc..........................G..... 216 391-7659
Cleveland (G-4563)

Rail Bearing Service LLC...................B..... 234 262-3000
North Canton (G-11756)

Rampe Manufacturing Company................F..... 440 352-8995
Fairport Harbor (G-7458)

Randall Bearings Inc.......................F..... 419 678-2486
Coldwater (G-5000)

▲ Randall Bearings Inc.....................D..... 419 223-1075
Lima (G-9282)

Robertson Manufacturing Co.................E..... 216 531-8222
Concord Township (G-5912)

Saf-Holland Inc............................G..... 513 874-7888
Fairfield (G-7404)

Sintered Metal Industries Inc..............F..... 330 650-4000
Hudson (G-8612)

Southeastern Shafting Mfg Inc..............F..... 740 342-4629
New Lexington (G-11457)

▲ Stripmatic Products Inc..................E..... 216 241-7143
Cleveland (G-4740)

◆ Taiho Corporation of America.............C..... 419 443-1645
Tiffin (G-14107)

Timken Newco I LLC.........................E..... 234 262-3000
North Canton (G-11767)

▲ Torque 2020 CMA Acqisition LLC...........C..... 330 874-2900
Bolivar (G-1539)

▲ Tsk America Co Ltd.......................F..... 513 942-4002
West Chester (G-15600)

US Tsubaki Power Transm LLC................C..... 419 626-4560
Sandusky (G-13102)

Western Branch Diesel LLC..................F..... 330 454-8800
Canton (G-2267)

Wiholi Inc.................................F..... 440 543-8233
Chagrin Falls (G-2435)

◆ Xtek Inc.................................B..... 513 733-7800
Cincinnati (G-3534)

3569 General industrial machinery,

1200 Feet Limited..........................G..... 419 827-6061
Lakeville (G-8962)

A-1 Sprinkler Company Inc..................D..... 937 859-6198
Miamisburg (G-10604)

▲ Abanaki Corporation......................F..... 440 543-7400
Chagrin Falls (G-2387)

Action Coupling & Eqp Inc..................D..... 330 279-4242
Holmesville (G-8541)

▲ Advanced Design Industries Inc...........E..... 440 277-4141
Sheffield Village (G-13180)

◆ Air Technical Industries Inc.............E..... 440 951-5191
Mentor (G-10409)

All-American Fire Eqp Inc..................F..... 800 972-6035
Wshngtn Ct Hs (G-16225)

▲ Allied Separation Tech Inc...............E..... 704 732-8034
Twinsburg (G-14628)

American Baler Co..........................D..... 419 483-5790
Bellevue (G-1222)

◆ American Rescue Technology Inc...........F..... 937 293-6240
Dayton (G-6203)

▲ Applied Marketing Services Inc...........E..... 440 716-9962
Westlake (G-15733)

Aquapro Systems LLC........................F..... 877 278-2797
Oakwood (G-12026)

▲ Astro Manufacturing & Design Inc.........C..... 888 215-1746
Eastlake (G-7019)

▲ Ats Systems Oregon Inc...................C..... 541 738-0932
Lewis Center (G-9152)

Avc Inc....................................F..... 513 458-2600
Cincinnati (G-2647)

Cascade Corporation........................E..... 419 425-3675
Findlay (G-7491)

Central Machinery Company LLC..............G..... 740 387-1289
Marion (G-9850)

Chart International Inc....................D..... 440 753-1490
Cleveland (G-3812)

Chromalloy Corporation.....................F..... 937 890-3775
Dayton (G-6255)

▲ Cleveland Gear Company Inc...............D..... 216 641-9000
Cleveland (G-3840)

Cline Fire LLC.............................G..... 419 571-4119
Mansfield (G-9640)

◆ Columbus Industries Inc..................D..... 740 983-2552
Ashville (G-667)

Columbus Industries One LLC................F..... 740 983-2552
Ashville (G-668)

Computer Allied Technology Co..............G..... 614 457-2292
Columbus (G-5284)

Cummins Filtration Inc.....................C
Findlay (G-7500)

Ddp Specialty Electronic MA................C..... 937 839-4612
West Alexandria (G-15341)

Digilube Systems Inc.......................F..... 937 748-2209
Springboro (G-13499)

▲ Dosmatic USA Inc.........................F..... 972 245-9765
Cincinnati (G-2837)

◆ E R Advanced Ceramics Inc................E..... 330 426-9433
East Palestine (G-7004)

SIC SECTION
35 INDUSTRIAL AND COMMERCIAL MACHINERY AND COMPUTER EQUIPMENT

Evoqua Water Technologies LLC............ G 614 861-5440
  Pickerington *(G-12461)*

Falls Filtration Tech Inc............................ E 330 928-4100
  Stow *(G-13697)*

Filter Technology Inc............................... G 614 921-9801
  Baltimore *(G-844)*

Fire Fab Corp.. G 330 759-9834
  Girard *(G-7967)*

Fire Foe Corp.. E 330 759-9834
  Girard *(G-7968)*

Fluid Automation Inc................................ E 248 912-1970
  North Canton *(G-11728)*

Gem City Engineering Co......................... C 937 223-5544
  Dayton *(G-6348)*

◆ Globe Pipe Hanger Products Inc........... E 216 362-6300
  Cleveland *(G-4129)*

Gould Fire Protection Inc......................... G 419 957-2416
  Findlay *(G-7514)*

▲ Groeneveld Atlantic South..................... G 330 225-4949
  Brunswick *(G-1768)*

▲ Gvs Filtration Inc................................... B 419 423-9040
  Findlay *(G-7517)*

H P E Inc... G 330 833-3161
  Massillon *(G-10104)*

Hdt Expeditionary Systems Inc................ F 216 438-6111
  Solon *(G-13360)*

▲ Hdt Tactical Systems Inc....................... C 216 438-6111
  Solon *(G-13361)*

▲ Hellan Strainer Company...................... G 216 206-4200
  Cleveland *(G-4178)*

Hitachi Automation Ohio Inc..................... F 937 753-1148
  Covington *(G-6025)*

▼ Hunter Defense Tech Inc...................... E 216 438-6111
  Solon *(G-13363)*

▲ Hyradix Inc.. E 847 391-1200
  Plain City *(G-12581)*

Innovative Assembly Svcs LLC................ G 419 399-3886
  Paulding *(G-12315)*

Johnsons Fire Equipment Co.................... F 740 357-4916
  Wellston *(G-15330)*

Joyce Dayton LLC..................................... F 440 449-3333
  Cleveland *(G-4263)*

Joyce/Dayton Corp..................................... E 937 294-6261
  Dayton *(G-6391)*

▲ Joyce/Dayton Corp................................ E 937 294-6261
  Dayton *(G-6390)*

▼ Kavon Filter Products Co....................... F 732 938-3135
  Cleveland *(G-4277)*

◆ Kc Robotics Inc..................................... E 513 860-4442
  West Chester *(G-15452)*

◆ Keltec Inc.. D 330 425-3100
  Twinsburg *(G-14678)*

Koester Corporation................................. E 419 599-0291
  Napoleon *(G-11322)*

La Mfg Inc... G 513 577-7200
  Cincinnati *(G-3094)*

Lincoln Electric Automtn Inc..................... E 614 471-5926
  Columbus *(G-5527)*

▲ Metaullics Systems LP.......................... C 509 926-6212
  Solon *(G-13387)*

▲ Midwest Filtration LLC.......................... D 513 874-6510
  West Chester *(G-15572)*

Motionsource International LLC............... F 440 287-7037
  Solon *(G-13392)*

Newco Industries....................................... F 717 566-9560
  Canton *(G-2172)*

Nmgg Ctg LLC.. D 419 447-5211
  Tiffin *(G-14096)*

Nov Inc.. D 937 454-3200
  Dayton *(G-6479)*

Nupro Company.. G 440 951-9729
  Willoughby *(G-15962)*

Nutro Corporation..................................... D 440 572-3800
  Strongsville *(G-13860)*

Ohlheiser Corp.. G 860 953-7632
  Columbus *(G-5632)*

OSI Environmental LLC............................ E 440 237-4600
  North Royalton *(G-11890)*

Parker-Hannifin Corporation..................... G 330 335-6740
  Wadsworth *(G-15052)*

Pax Products Inc....................................... F 419 586-2337
  Celina *(G-2343)*

Petro Ware Inc.. E 740 982-1302
  Crooksville *(G-6049)*

Phoenix Safety Outfitters LLC.................. G 614 361-0544
  Springfield *(G-13619)*

◆ Pneumatic Scale Corporation............... C 330 923-0491
  Cuyahoga Falls *(G-6109)*

Programmable Control Svc Inc................ G 740 927-0744
  Pataskala *(G-12304)*

R Holdings 2500 Co.................................. E 800 883-7876
  Columbus *(G-5707)*

Radco Fire Protection Inc......................... G 419 476-0102
  Toledo *(G-14447)*

Raymond W Reisiger................................. G 740 400-4090
  Baltimore *(G-846)*

Ready Robotics Corporation..................... E 833 732-3967
  Columbus *(G-5714)*

Recognition Robotics Inc.......................... F 440 590-0499
  Elyria *(G-7200)*

Red Head Brass Inc.................................. F 330 567-2903
  Shreve *(G-13213)*

▲ Reladyne Reliability Svcs Inc................ E 888 478-6996
  Canton *(G-2211)*

Remtec Engineering.................................. E 513 860-4299
  Mason *(G-10047)*

Rennco Automation Systems Inc............. E 419 861-2340
  Holland *(G-8527)*

◆ Rexarc International Inc........................ E 937 839-4604
  West Alexandria *(G-15344)*

▲ Rhba Acquisitions LLC......................... D 330 567-2903
  Shreve *(G-13214)*

▲ Rimrock Corporation............................. E 614 471-5926
  Columbus *(G-5723)*

Rimrock Holdings Corporation................. C 614 471-5926
  Columbus *(G-5724)*

Rixan Associates Inc................................ E 937 438-3005
  Dayton *(G-6550)*

◆ Rotex Global LLC.................................. C 513 541-1236
  Cincinnati *(G-3351)*

Rti Remmele Engineering Inc................... D 651 635-4179
  Cleveland *(G-4660)*

S A Langmack Company........................... F 216 541-0500
  Cleveland *(G-4666)*

Sensory Robotics Inc................................ G 513 545-9501
  Cincinnati *(G-3382)*

Sentient Studios Ltd.................................. E 330 204-8636
  Fairlawn *(G-7449)*

▲ Siebtechnik Tema Inc............................ E 513 489-7811
  Cincinnati *(G-3390)*

Siemens Industry Inc................................ E 513 576-2088
  Milford *(G-10922)*

Stateline Power Corp................................ F 937 547-1006
  Greenville *(G-8062)*

▼ Steel & Alloy Utility Pdts Inc................. E 330 530-2220
  Mc Donald *(G-10280)*

Swift Filters Inc... E 440 735-0995
  Oakwood Village *(G-12043)*

Test Measurement Systems Inc............... G 888 867-4872
  North Canton *(G-11764)*

The Ransohoff Company........................... C 513 870-0100
  West Chester *(G-15595)*

◆ The Western States Machin.................. D 513 863-4758
  Fairfield *(G-7418)*

Tyco Fire Products LP.............................. G 216 265-0505
  Cleveland *(G-4839)*

Versatile Automation Tech Corp.............. G 330 220-2600
  Brunswick *(G-1798)*

▲ Versatile Automation Tech Ltd............. G 440 589-6700
  Solon *(G-13442)*

Wayne Morgan Corp................................. G 419 222-4181
  Lima *(G-9301)*

Winston Oil Co Inc.................................... G 740 373-9664
  Marietta *(G-9845)*

Yaskawa America Inc............................... C 937 440-2600
  Troy *(G-14617)*

Zephyr Industries Inc............................... G 419 281-4485
  Ashland *(G-621)*

3571 Electronic computers

696 Ledgerock Cir..................................... G 330 289-0996
  Brunswick *(G-1745)*

Accurate Insullation LLC.......................... F 302 241-0940
  Columbus *(G-5095)*

Advance Products..................................... F 419 882-8117
  Sylvania *(G-13990)*

Apple & Apple LLC................................... F 740 972-2209
  Lewis Center *(G-9150)*

Apple of His Eye Inc................................. G 513 521-0655
  Cincinnati *(G-2630)*

AT&T Corp... G 513 792-9300
  Cincinnati *(G-2639)*

Cardinal Health Tech LLC........................ E 614 757-5000
  Dublin *(G-6874)*

Coffman Media LLC.................................. F 614 956-7015
  Dublin *(G-6875)*

Dapsco.. F 937 294-5331
  Moraine *(G-11169)*

Dell Inc.. F 614 491-4603
  Lockbourne *(G-9334)*

Delohio Tech... G 740 816-5628
  Delaware *(G-6715)*

Eaj Services LLC...................................... F 513 792-3400
  Blue Ash *(G-1387)*

◆ Eaton Corporation................................. B 440 523-5000
  Cleveland *(G-3994)*

Fleet Graphics Inc.................................... G 937 252-2552
  Dayton *(G-6335)*

General Dynmics Mssion Systems........... G 937 723-2001
  Dayton *(G-6350)*

Global Realms LLC................................... G 614 828-7284
  Gahanna *(G-7836)*

Griffin Technology Inc.............................. C 585 924-7121
  Hudson *(G-8594)*

▲ Grimes Aerospace Company................ A 937 484-2000
  Urbana *(G-14830)*

Inns Holdings Ltd..................................... F 740 345-3700
  Newark *(G-11584)*

Interntnal Pdts Srcing Group I.................. C 614 334-1500
  Columbus *(G-5475)*

Journey Systems LLC.............................. F 513 831-6200
  Milford *(G-10912)*

Lorain Apples.. G 440 282-4471
  Lorain *(G-9420)*

Magnum Computers Inc............................ F 216 781-1757
  Cleveland *(G-4351)*

Park Place Technologies LLC................. C 877 778-8707
  Cleveland *(G-4523)*

▲ Powersonic Industries LLC................... E 513 429-2329
  West Chester *(G-15577)*

Predicor LLC... G 419 460-1831
  Cleveland *(G-4578)*

Smartronix Inc.. F 216 378-3300
  Northfield *(G-11910)*

▲ Systemax Manufacturing Inc................ D 937 368-2300
  Dayton *(G-6604)*

35 INDUSTRIAL AND COMMERCIAL MACHINERY AND COMPUTER EQUIPMENT

Teradata Operations Inc................ B 937 866-0032
  Miamisburg (G-10693)
Town Cntry Technical Svcs Inc........... F 614 866-7700
  Reynoldsburg (G-12775)
Tracewell Systems Inc................... D 614 846-6175
  Lewis Center (G-9182)
Vr Assets LLC............................ G 440 600-2963
  Solon (G-13443)
Walter North............................. F 937 204-6050
  Dayton (G-6646)

3572 Computer storage devices

1 Emc LLC............................... G 216 990-2586
  Findlay (G-7469)
Capsa Solutions LLC..................... D 800 437-6633
  Canal Winchester (G-1983)
CHI Corporation......................... G 440 498-2300
  Cleveland (G-3818)
Freedom Usa Inc......................... E 216 503-6374
  Twinsburg (G-14662)
Gemco Pacific Energy LLC............... F 216 937-1371
  Cleveland (G-4110)
Magnext Ltd............................. F 614 433-0011
  Columbus (G-5539)
Park Place Technologies LLC............ C 877 778-8707
  Cleveland (G-4523)
▲ Pinnacle Data Systems Inc............. C 614 748-1150
  Groveport (G-8158)
Quantum................................. F 740 328-2548
  Newark (G-11604)
Quantum Commerce LLC................... G 513 777-0737
  West Chester (G-15490)
Quantum Integration Llc................ G 330 609-0355
  Cortland (G-5967)
Quantum Solutions Group................ G 614 442-0664
  Columbus (G-5703)
Solsys Inc.............................. G 419 886-4683
  Mansfield (G-9720)
Town Cntry Technical Svcs Inc.......... F 614 866-7700
  Reynoldsburg (G-12775)
Tracewell Systems Inc.................. D 614 846-6175
  Lewis Center (G-9182)

3575 Computer terminals

Copier Resources Inc................... G 614 268-1100
  Columbus (G-5295)
Fivepoint LLC........................... F 937 374-3193
  Xenia (G-16262)
Freedom Usa Inc......................... E 216 503-6374
  Twinsburg (G-14662)
▲ Pinnacle Data Systems Inc............. C 614 748-1150
  Groveport (G-8158)
Td Synnex Corporation.................. E 614 669-6889
  Groveport (G-8161)

3577 Computer peripheral equipment, nec

Abstract Displays Inc.................. F 513 985-9700
  Blue Ash (G-1356)
AGE Graphics LLC....................... G 740 989-0006
  Little Hocking (G-9332)
Airwave Communications Cons............ G 419 331-1526
  Lima (G-9218)
Applied Vision Corporation............. D 330 926-2222
  Cuyahoga Falls (G-6067)
AT&T Corp.............................. G 513 792-9300
  Cincinnati (G-2639)
Black Box Corporation.................. F 800 676-8850
  Brecksville (G-1609)
Black Box Corporation.................. G 800 837-7777
  Dublin (G-6868)
Black Box Corporation.................. G 855 324-9909
  Westlake (G-15738)

Brackish Media LLC..................... F 513 394-2871
  Cincinnati (G-2679)
Cisco Systems Inc...................... G 330 523-2000
  Richfield (G-12783)
Clarity Retail Services LLC............ D 513 800-9369
  West Chester (G-15395)
Contact Control Interfaces LLC......... E 609 333-3264
  Cincinnati (G-2789)
▼ Data Processing Sciences............. D 513 791-7100
  Cincinnati (G-2820)
Dataq Instruments Inc.................. E 330 668-1444
  Akron (G-123)
Ds World LLC............................ G 925 200-4985
  West Chester (G-15418)
Eastman Kodak Company.................. E 937 259-3000
  Dayton (G-6311)
Embedded Planet Inc.................... F 216 245-4180
  Solon (G-13342)
Gameday Vision.......................... F 330 830-4550
  Massillon (G-10098)
◆ Gleason Metrology Systems Corp....... E 937 384-8901
  Dayton (G-6353)
Government Acquisitions Inc............ E 513 721-8700
  Cincinnati (G-2967)
▲ Grimes Aerospace Company.............. A 937 484-2000
  Urbana (G-14830)
Honeywell International Inc............ E 513 874-5882
  West Chester (G-15446)
Hunkar Technologies Inc................ C 513 272-1010
  Cincinnati (G-3012)
ID Images Inc........................... E 330 220-7300
  Brunswick (G-1769)
Interactive Products Corp.............. G 513 313-3397
  Monroe (G-11111)
Kern Inc................................ C 440 930-7315
  Cleveland (G-4284)
L3harris Electrodynamics Inc........... C 847 259-0740
  Cincinnati (G-2569)
▲ Microcom Corporation.................. E 740 548-6262
  Lewis Center (G-9171)
New Dawn Labs LLC...................... F 203 675-5644
  Union (G-14773)
◆ Phase Array Company LLC............... G 513 785-0801
  West Chester (G-15475)
▲ Qualtek Electronics Corp.............. C 440 951-3300
  Mentor (G-10541)
▲ Scriptel Corporation.................. F 877 848-6824
  Columbus (G-5756)
Sierra Nevada Corporation.............. C 937 431-2800
  Beavercreek (G-1062)
Signature Technologies Inc............. F 937 859-6323
  Miamisburg (G-10683)
Small Business Products................ G 800 553-6485
  Cincinnati (G-3397)
Stellar Systems Inc.................... G 513 921-8748
  Cincinnati (G-3421)
Superior Label Systems Inc............. B 513 336-0825
  Mason (G-10061)
Sutter Llc.............................. F 513 891-2261
  Blue Ash (G-1476)
▲ Systemax Manufacturing Inc............ D 937 368-2300
  Dayton (G-6604)
▲ Tech Pro Inc........................... G 330 923-3546
  Akron (G-350)
▲ Timekeeping Systems Inc............... F 216 595-0890
  Solon (G-13439)
Treality Svs LLC........................ E 937 372-7579
  Xenia (G-16277)
Uvonics Co.............................. F 614 458-1163
  Columbus (G-5852)
Video Products Inc..................... D 330 562-2622
  Aurora (G-740)

▲ Vmetro Inc............................. D 281 584-0728
  Fairborn (G-7326)
Vyral LLC............................... F 937 993-7765
  Dayton (G-6645)
Xponet Inc.............................. E 440 354-6617
  Painesville (G-12279)
Yonezawa Usa Inc....................... F 614 799-2210
  Plain City (G-12605)

3578 Calculating and accounting equipment

Atm Nerds LLC........................... F 614 983-3056
  Columbus (G-5164)
Cambrdge Ohio Prod Assmbly Cor......... G 740 432-6383
  Cambridge (G-1924)
Diebold Nixdorf Incorporated........... D 330 490-4000
  Canton (G-2092)
Diebold Nixdorf Incorporated........... D 740 928-0200
  Hebron (G-8338)
Diebold Nixdorf Incorporated........... D 740 928-1010
  Hebron (G-8339)
Diebold Nixdorf Incorporated........... E 336 662-1115
  North Canton (G-11721)
Diebold Nixdorf Incorporated........... A 330 490-4000
  North Canton (G-11722)
Ganymede Technologies Corp............. G 419 562-5522
  Bucyrus (G-1860)
Ginko Voting Systems LLC............... F 937 291-4060
  Dayton (G-6352)
Glenn Michael Brick.................... F 740 391-5735
  Flushing (G-7587)
NCR Technology Center.................. G 937 445-1936
  Dayton (G-6466)
Testlink Usa Inc....................... E 513 272-1081
  Cincinnati (G-3445)
Thyme Inc............................... F 484 872-8430
  Akron (G-357)
Total Touch LLC......................... E 800 726-2117
  Cleveland (G-4811)
Verifone Inc............................ C 800 837-4366
  Columbus (G-5857)

3579 Office machines, nec

◆ Baumfolder Corporation................ E 937 492-1281
  Sidney (G-13226)
Industrial Electronic Service.......... F 937 746-9750
  Carlisle (G-2288)
Kaylo Enterprises LLC.................. G 330 535-1860
  Akron (G-202)
Kern Inc................................ C 440 930-7315
  Cleveland (G-4284)
Ricoh Usa Inc........................... F 412 281-6700
  Cleveland (G-4634)
RT Industries Inc...................... G 937 335-5784
  Troy (G-14606)
Symatic Inc............................. F 330 225-1510
  Medina (G-10381)

3581 Automatic vending machines

Best Result Marketing Inc.............. G 234 212-1194
  Bedford (G-1106)
Five Star Healthy Vending LLC.......... F 330 549-6011
  Akron (G-154)
▲ Giant Industries Inc.................. E 419 531-4600
  Toledo (G-14300)
◆ Gold Medal Products Co................ B 513 769-7676
  Cincinnati (G-2962)
Innovative Vend Solutions LLC.......... F 866 931-9413
  Dayton (G-6383)
Ring Snack LLC.......................... G 216 334-4356
  Cleveland (G-4635)
Securastock LLC......................... F 330 957-5711
  Cleveland (G-4684)

Tranzonic Companies.................................. D 216 535-4300
  Richmond Heights (G-12811)
▲ Ve Global Vending Inc........................... F 216 785-2611
  Cleveland (G-4862)

3582 Commercial laundry equipment

Ellis Laundry and Lin Sup Inc.................. G 330 339-4941
  New Philadelphia (G-11500)
Ha-International LLC................................ E 419 537-0096
  Toledo (G-14308)
▲ Husqvarna US Holding Inc.................. D 216 898-1800
  Cleveland (G-4209)
Process Development Corp...................... E 937 890-3388
  Dayton (G-6527)
Whirlpool Corporation.............................. C 419 547-7711
  Clyde (G-4979)

3585 Refrigeration and heating equipment

A A S Amels Sheet Meta L Inc.................. F 330 793-9326
  Youngstown (G-16297)
Air Enterprises Inc.................................... A 330 794-9770
  Akron (G-24)
▼ Bard Manufacturing Company Inc....... D 419 636-1194
  Bryan (G-1809)
▲ Beckett Air Incorporated...................... D 440 327-9999
  North Ridgeville (G-11829)
Bessamaire Sales Inc............................... E 440 439-1200
  Twinsburg (G-14635)
Beverage Engineering Inc........................ F 216 641-6678
  Brooklyn Heights (G-1684)
Bodor Vents Inc....................................... G 513 348-3853
  Cincinnati (G-2674)
▲ Boston Beer Company.......................... F 267 240-4429
  Cincinnati (G-2678)
▲ Briskheat Corporation........................... C 614 294-3376
  Columbus (G-5218)
Bry Air Inc... G 614 839-0250
  Columbus (G-5060)
◆ Bry-Air Inc... E 740 965-2974
  Sunbury (G-13951)
◆ C Nelson Mfg Co................................... E 419 898-3305
  Oak Harbor (G-12012)
Chilltex LLC.. G 937 710-3308
  Anna (G-489)
Columbus Heating & Vent Co................. C 614 274-1177
  Columbus (G-5265)
Copeland LP... C 937 498-3011
  Sidney (G-13236)
Copeland LP... C 937 498-3587
  Sidney (G-13237)
◆ Copeland LP.. A 937 498-3011
  Sidney (G-13235)
◆ Crawford Ae LLC................................... D 330 794-9770
  Akron (G-117)
◆ Cryogenic Equipment & Svcs Inc......... F 513 761-4200
  Hamilton (G-8196)
◆ Csafe LLC.. G 513 360-7189
  Monroe (G-11099)
Daikin Applied Americas Inc.................... G 614 351-9862
  Westerville (G-15697)
▲ Duro Dyne Midwest Corp..................... C 513 870-6000
  Hamilton (G-8201)
▲ Dyoung Enterprise Inc.......................... C 440 918-0505
  Willoughby (G-15913)
◆ Eaton Aeroquip LLC.............................. C 440 523-5000
  Cleveland (G-3991)
◆ Ecu Corporation.................................... F 513 898-9294
  Cincinnati (G-2859)
Ellis & Watts Global Inds Inc.................... E 513 752-9000
  Batavia (G-922)
Emerson Network Power......................... F 614 841-8054
  Ironton (G-8697)

Famous Industries Inc............................. F 740 685-2592
  Byesville (G-1896)
Famous Realty Cleveland Inc................. F 740 685-2533
  Byesville (G-1897)
▲ Fire From Ice Ventures LLC................ E 419 944-6705
  Solon (G-13350)
Forzza Corporation.................................. E 440 998-6300
  Madison (G-9592)
Fred D Pfening Company........................ E 614 294-5361
  Columbus (G-5389)
◆ Guardian Technologies LLC................ E 866 603-5900
  Euclid (G-7270)
Hanon Systems Usa LLC........................ C 313 920-0583
  Carey (G-2279)
Hatfield Industries LLC............................ G 513 225-0456
  West Chester (G-15445)
Hdt Ep Inc.. C 216 438-6111
  Solon (G-13359)
Hdt Expeditionary Systems Inc............... F 440 466-6640
  Geneva (G-7938)
Hobart LLC... E 937 332-2797
  Piqua (G-12525)
Hobart LLC... E 937 332-3000
  Troy (G-14581)
▲ Hobart LLC... D 937 332-3000
  Troy (G-14582)
▲ Hydro-Dyne Inc.................................... E 330 832-5076
  Massillon (G-10109)
▼ Hydro-Thrift Corporation..................... E 330 837-5141
  Massillon (G-10110)
Insource Tech Inc.................................... F 419 399-3600
  Paulding (G-12316)
J D Indoor Comfort Inc............................ F 440 949-8758
  Sheffield Village (G-13184)
J&I Duct Fab Llc...................................... F 937 473-2121
  Covington (G-6026)
▲ Jbar A/C Inc.. E 216 447-4294
  Cleveland (G-4252)
Jnp Group LLC.. F 800 735-9645
  Wooster (G-16137)
Lennox Industries Inc.............................. G 216 739-1909
  Cleveland (G-4320)
Lfg Specialties LLC................................. E 419 424-4999
  Findlay (G-7529)
◆ Lintern Corporation.............................. E 440 255-9333
  Mentor (G-10494)
◆ Lvd Acquisition LLC............................. D 614 861-1350
  Columbus (G-5537)
Mahle Behr Dayton LLC.......................... A 937 369-2000
  Dayton (G-6425)
Mahle Behr USA Inc................................ F 937 369-2610
  Xenia (G-16268)
◆ Maverick Innvtive Slutions LLC........... D 419 281-7944
  Ashland (G-590)
Northeastern Rfrgn Corp......................... E 440 942-7676
  Willoughby (G-15960)
Nrc Inc... E 440 975-9449
  Willoughby (G-15961)
Obhc Inc... G 440 236-5112
  Columbia Station (G-5015)
Professional Supply Inc.......................... F 419 332-7373
  Fremont (G-7803)
Royal Metal Products LLC...................... C 740 397-8842
  Mount Vernon (G-11293)
▼ RSI Company.. F 216 360-9800
  Beachwood (G-1020)
Rtx Corporation....................................... B 330 784-5477
  North Canton (G-11757)
Snap Rite Manufacturing Inc.................. E 910 897-4080
  Cleveland (G-4709)
Sticker Corporation................................. F 440 946-2100
  Willoughby (G-15998)

T J F Inc.. F 419 878-4400
  Waterville (G-15253)
◆ Taiho Corporation of America.............. C 419 443-1645
  Tiffin (G-14107)
Taylor & Moore Co.................................. E 513 733-5530
  Cincinnati (G-3442)
◆ Tempest Inc.. E 216 883-6500
  Cleveland (G-4776)
Ten Dogs Global Industries LLC............. G 513 752-9000
  Batavia (G-952)
▲ The Columbus Show Case Co............. C
  Columbus (G-5820)
Trane Company....................................... F 419 491-2278
  Holland (G-8534)
Trane Inc.. E 440 946-7823
  Cleveland (G-4814)
Trane US Inc.. D 513 771-8884
  Cincinnati (G-3460)
Trane US Inc.. C 614 473-3131
  Columbus (G-5830)
Trane US Inc.. G 614 473-8701
  Columbus (G-5831)
Trane US Inc.. G 614 497-6300
  Groveport (G-8163)
US Controls Acquisition Ltd................... G 330 758-1147
  Poland (G-12612)
Vertiv Corporation.................................. G 614 491-9286
  Groveport (G-8166)
Vertiv Corporation.................................. G 614 888-0246
  Lockbourne (G-9341)
◆ Vertiv Corporation................................ A 614 888-0246
  Westerville (G-15686)
Vertiv Group Corporation...................... A 614 888-0246
  Westerville (G-15687)
Vertiv JV Holdings LLC.......................... A 614 888-0246
  Columbus (G-5859)
Virginia Air Distributors Inc................... G 614 262-1129
  Columbus (G-5860)
Vortec Corporation................................. E
  Blue Ash (G-1489)
Whirlpool Corporation............................ F 614 409-4340
  Lockbourne (G-9343)
Yukon Industries Inc............................... E 440 478-4174
  Mentor (G-10599)

3586 Measuring and dispensing pumps

Bergstrom Company Ltd Partnr.............. E 440 232-2282
  Cleveland (G-3730)
Cohesant Inc.. E 216 910-1700
  Beachwood (G-978)
Energy Manufacturing Ltd...................... G 419 355-9304
  Fremont (G-7776)
◆ Field Stone Inc..................................... E 937 898-3236
  Tipp City (G-14135)
◆ Gojo Industries Inc............................... C 330 255-6000
  Akron (G-170)
▲ Graco Ohio Inc..................................... D 330 494-1313
  North Canton (G-11733)
Lubrisource Inc....................................... F 937 432-9292
  Middletown (G-10836)
◆ Seepex Inc.. C 937 864-7150
  Enon (G-7252)
◆ Tolco Corporation................................. D 419 241-1113
  Toledo (G-14491)
Tranzonic Companies.............................. D 216 535-4300
  Richmond Heights (G-12811)
▲ Valco Cincinnati Inc............................. C 513 874-6550
  West Chester (G-15603)
WD Pumpco LLC..................................... G 740 454-2576
  Zanesville (G-16569)

3589 Service industry machinery, nec

35 INDUSTRIAL AND COMMERCIAL MACHINERY AND COMPUTER EQUIPMENT

Accushred LLC .... F 419 244-7473
  Toledo (G-14176)
Active Aeration Systems Inc .... G 614 873-3626
  Plain City (G-12559)
Advanced Green Tech Inc .... G 614 397-8130
  Plain City (G-12560)
▲ Ameriwater LLC .... E 937 461-8833
  Dayton (G-6205)
Amsoil Inc .... G 614 274-9851
  Urbancrest (G-14852)
Aqua Ohio Inc .... F 740 867-8700
  Chesapeake (G-2472)
Aqua Pennsylvania Inc .... G 440 257-6190
  Mentor On The Lake (G-10600)
Aquapro Systems LLC .... F 877 278-2797
  Oakwood (G-12026)
Artesian of Pioneer Inc .... F 419 737-2352
  Pioneer (G-12490)
As Clean As It Gets Off Brkroo .... E 216 256-1143
  South Euclid (G-13450)
Beckman Environmental Svcs Inc ..... F 513 752-3570
  Batavia (G-912)
Belanger Inc .... D 517 870-3206
  West Chester (G-15375)
Bell Industrial Services LLC .... F 937 507-9193
  Sidney (G-13227)
Best Equipment Co Inc .... E 440 237-3515
  North Royalton (G-11868)
Chemtreat .... F 937 644-2525
  East Liberty (G-6985)
Choice Ballast Solutions LLC .... G 440 973-9841
  Columbia Station (G-5008)
City of Ashland .... G 419 289-8728
  Ashland (G-565)
City of Athens .... E 740 592-3344
  Athens (G-679)
City of Chardon .... E 440 286-2657
  Chardon (G-2446)
City of Middletown .... D 513 425-7781
  Middletown (G-10807)
City of Ravenna .... G 330 296-5214
  Ravenna (G-12710)
City of Troy .... F 937 339-4826
  Troy (G-14555)
City of Xenia .... E 937 376-7269
  Xenia (G-16256)
▲ Cleveland Range LLC .... C 216 481-4900
  Cleveland (G-3852)
Cold Jet International LLC .... D 513 831-3211
  Loveland (G-9478)
County of Lake .... F 440 428-1794
  Madison (G-9591)
Crown Solutions Co LLC .... C 937 890-4075
  Vandalia (G-14936)
De Nora Holdings Us Inc .... B 440 710-5300
  Concord Township (G-5904)
▲ De Nora North America Inc .... E 440 357-4000
  Painesville (G-12226)
De Nora Tech LLC .... G 440 285-0368
  Painesville (G-12227)
◆ De Nora Tech LLC .... D 440 710-5334
  Concord Township (G-5905)
◆ Detrex Corporation .... F 216 749-2605
  Cleveland (G-3954)
Diversey Taski Inc .... E 419 531-2121
  Toledo (G-14269)
▲ E - I Corp .... F 614 899-2282
  Westerville (G-15654)
◆ Eagle Crusher Co Inc .... D 419 468-2288
  Galion (G-7872)
▲ Electric Eel Mfg Co Inc .... E 937 323-4644
  Springfield (G-13558)

◆ Enting Water Conditioning Inc .... E 937 294-5100
  Moraine (G-11175)
Evers Enterprises Inc .... G 513 541-7200
  Cincinnati (G-2886)
Evoqua Water Technologies LLC ..... G 614 491-5917
  Groveport (G-8138)
◆ Garland Commercial Industries LLC .. E 800 338-2204
  Cleveland (G-4103)
▲ Giant Industries Inc .... E 419 531-4600
  Toledo (G-14300)
◆ Gold Medal Products Co .... B 513 769-7676
  Cincinnati (G-2962)
Greene County .... G 937 429-0127
  Dayton (G-6162)
▲ Hammersmith Bros Invstmnts Inc .. E 513 353-3000
  North Bend (G-11704)
◆ Henny Penny Corporation .... A 937 456-8400
  Eaton (G-7060)
◆ HI-Vac Corporation .... C 740 374-2306
  Marietta (G-9799)
High-TEC Industrial Services .... D 937 667-1772
  Tipp City (G-14137)
Hobart LLC .... E 937 332-2797
  Piqua (G-12525)
Hobart LLC .... E 937 332-3000
  Troy (G-14581)
▲ Hobart LLC .... D 937 332-3000
  Troy (G-14582)
Holdren Brothers Inc .... F 937 465-7050
  West Liberty (G-15622)
Illinois Tool Works Inc .... E 937 335-7171
  Troy (G-14585)
Image By J & K LLC .... F 888 667-6929
  Maumee (G-10207)
Imet Corporation .... G 440 799-3135
  Cleveland (G-4217)
Industrial Fluid MGT Inc .... F 419 748-7460
  Mc Clure (G-10266)
◆ JE Grote Company Inc .... D 614 868-8414
  Columbus (G-5491)
◆ Jet Inc .... E 440 461-2000
  Cleveland (G-4255)
▲ Kaivac Inc .... D 513 887-4600
  Hamilton (G-8225)
Kellermyer Bergensons Svcs LLC .... D 419 867-4300
  Maumee (G-10210)
◆ Kinetico Incorporated .... B 440 564-9111
  Newbury (G-11628)
Knight Manufacturing Co Inc .... G 740 676-5516
  Shadyside (G-13146)
L N Brut Manufacturing Co .... G 330 833-9045
  Shreve (G-13212)
Legends Auto Spa LLC .... G 216 333-8030
  Bedford (G-1133)
Lima Sheet Metal Machine & Mfg ..... E 419 229-1161
  Lima (G-9264)
Mack Industries PA Inc .... D 330 638-7680
  Vienna (G-15000)
McNish Corporation .... G 614 899-2282
  Westerville (G-15667)
◆ MJB Toledo Inc .... D 419 531-2121
  Toledo (G-14387)
Monarch Water Systems Inc .... F 937 426-5773
  Beavercreek (G-1056)
MPW Industrial Svcs Group Inc .... B 740 927-8790
  Hebron (G-8350)
Mt Vernon Cy Wastewater Trtmnt ..... G 740 393-9502
  Mount Vernon (G-11281)
N-Viro International Corp .... F 419 535-6374
  Toledo (G-14394)
National Pride Equipment Inc .... G 419 289-2886
  Mansfield (G-9703)

New Aqua LLC .... F 614 265-9000
  Columbus (G-5594)
◆ Norwalk Wastewater Eqp Co .... D 419 668-4471
  Norwalk (G-11983)
Obic LLC .... G 419 633-3147
  Bryan (G-1832)
Onesource Water LLC .... F 866 917-7873
  Toledo (G-14414)
▲ Or-Tec Inc .... G 216 475-5225
  Maple Heights (G-9757)
Pelton Environmental Pdts Inc .... G 440 838-1221
  Lewis Center (G-9175)
Powerbuff Inc .... F 419 241-2156
  Toledo (G-14441)
R D Baker Enterprises Inc .... G 937 461-5225
  Dayton (G-6537)
Route 62 .... G 740 548-5418
  Johnstown (G-8777)
Russ Jr Enterprises Inc .... F 440 237-4642
  North Royalton (G-11895)
Sammy S Auto Detail .... F 614 263-2728
  Columbus (G-5743)
▲ Siebtechnik Tema Inc .... E 513 489-7811
  Cincinnati (G-3390)
Smart Sonic Corporation .... G 818 610-7900
  Cleveland (G-4707)
Squeaky Clean Cincinnati Inc .... F 513 729-2712
  Cincinnati (G-3412)
Stellar Process Inc .... F 866 777-4725
  Twinsburg (G-14737)
Tangent Company LLC .... G 440 543-2775
  Chagrin Falls (G-2427)
Tipton Environmental Intl Inc .... F 513 735-2777
  Batavia (G-953)
Total Water Solutions LLC .... G 234 567-5912
  Leetonia (G-9131)
Trinity Water Solutions LLC .... E 740 318-0585
  Caldwell (G-1914)
Trumbull Manufacturing Inc .... E 330 270-7888
  Youngstown (G-16461)
Under Pressure Systems Inc .... G 330 602-4466
  New Philadelphia (G-11531)
United McGill Corporation .... F 614 920-1267
  Lithopolis (G-9331)
Veolia Wts Systems Usa Inc .... G 513 794-1010
  Cincinnati (G-3494)
Veolia Wts Systems Usa Inc .... F 330 929-1639
  Stow (G-13737)
Village of Ansonia .... E 937 337-5741
  Greenville (G-8063)
W3 Ultrasonics LLC .... G 330 284-3667
  North Canton (G-11774)
Water & Waste Water Eqp Co .... G 440 542-0972
  Solon (G-13447)
Wateropolis Corp .... G 440 564-5061
  Newbury (G-11639)
Wb Industries Inc .... G 440 708-0309
  Burton (G-1890)
◆ William R Hague Inc .... D 614 836-2115
  Groveport (G-8168)

3592 Carburetors, pistons, rings, valves

Ad Piston Ring LLC .... F 216 781-5200
  Cleveland (G-3595)
Aswpengg LLC .... E 216 292-4620
  Bedford Heights (G-1164)
Brooks Manufacturing .... G 419 244-1777
  Toledo (G-14221)
Buckeye BOP LLC .... G 740 498-9898
  Newcomerstown (G-11643)
▲ Celina Alum Precision Tech Inc .... B 419 586-2278
  Celina (G-2325)

SIC SECTION
35 INDUSTRIAL AND COMMERCIAL MACHINERY AND COMPUTER EQUIPMENT

◆ Group Industries Inc............................E 216 271-0702
  Cleveland (G-4152)
Hite Parts Exchange Inc.........................F 614 272-5115
  Columbus (G-5442)
Peterson American Corporation..............E 419 867-8711
  Holland (G-8523)
Race Winning Brands Inc........................B 440 951-6600
  Mentor (G-10544)
▲ Seabiscuit Motorsports Inc..................B 440 951-6600
  Mentor (G-10551)
Tiffin Foundry & Machine Inc..................E 419 447-3991
  Tiffin (G-14109)
Valv-Trol LLC...F 330 686-2800
  Stow (G-13736)

3593 Fluid power cylinders and actuators

▲ American Hydraulic Svcs Inc................E 606 739-8680
  Ironton (G-8695)
B & H Machine Inc...................................E 330 868-6425
  Minerva (G-11027)
Cascade Corporation..............................D 937 327-0300
  Springfield (G-13541)
Cho Bedford Inc......................................E 330 343-8896
  Dover (G-6812)
▲ Control Line Equipment Inc.................F 216 433-7766
  Cleveland (G-3903)
▲ Custom Hoists Inc...............................C 419 368-4721
  Ashland (G-570)
Cylinders and Valves Inc........................G 440 238-7343
  Strongsville (G-13826)
▲ Dana Limited.......................................B 419 887-3000
  Maumee (G-10186)
Eaton Aeroquip LLC................................A 419 891-7775
  Maumee (G-10201)
Eaton Leasing Corporation.....................B 216 382-2292
  Beachwood (G-986)
Emerson Process Management..............C 419 529-4311
  Ontario (G-12091)
Emmco Inc..G 216 429-2020
  Euclid (G-7268)
▲ Hunger Hydraulics CC Ltd..................F 419 666-4510
  Rossford (G-12865)
Hunt Valve Actuator LLC........................D 330 337-9535
  Salem (G-13003)
Hydranamics Inc.....................................D 419 468-3530
  Galion (G-7880)
Hydraulic Parts Store Inc........................E 330 364-6667
  New Philadelphia (G-11505)
Hydraulic Specialists Inc........................F 740 922-3343
  Midvale (G-10879)
▲ Ic-Fluid Power Inc................................F 419 661-8811
  Rossford (G-12866)
J D Hydraulic Inc.....................................F 419 686-5234
  Portage (G-12633)
Kyntrol Holdings Inc................................D 440 220-5990
  Eastlake (G-7038)
Kyntronics Inc..F 440 220-5990
  Solon (G-13380)
North Coast Instruments Inc..................G 216 251-2353
  Cleveland (G-4469)
Parker-Hannifin Corporation...................E 330 336-3511
  Wadsworth (G-15051)
▲ Parker-Hannifin Corporation...............A 216 896-3000
  Cleveland (G-4532)
Poc Hydraulic Technologies LLC...........G 614 761-8555
  Dublin (G-6924)
Qcsm LLC...G 216 650-8731
  Cleveland (G-4602)
R & J Cylinder & Machine Inc.................D 330 364-8263
  New Philadelphia (G-11524)
R & M Fluid Power Inc............................E 330 758-2766
  Youngstown (G-16425)

◆ Robeck Fluid Power Co........................D 330 562-1140
  Aurora (G-734)
Sebring Fluid Power Corp.......................G 330 938-9984
  Sebring (G-13126)
▲ Skidmore-Wilhelm Mfg Company........F 216 481-4774
  Solon (G-13422)
▲ Steel Eqp Specialists Inc.....................D 330 823-8260
  Alliance (G-427)
Suburban Manufacturing Co...................D 440 953-2024
  Eastlake (G-7050)
Swagelok Company.................................D 440 349-5934
  Solon (G-13431)
▲ The Sheffer Corporation......................D 513 489-9770
  Blue Ash (G-1481)
United Hydraulics....................................G 440 585-0906
  Wickliffe (G-15856)
◆ Waltco Lift Corp....................................C 330 633-9191
  Streetsboro (G-13798)
Worthington Cylinder Corp......................C 614 438-7900
  Columbus (G-5882)
Xomox Corporation..................................E 936 271-6500
  Cincinnati (G-3531)
Xomox Pft Corp..B 936 271-6500
  Cincinnati (G-3532)
Zaytran Inc...E 440 324-2814
  Elyria (G-7220)

3594 Fluid power pumps and motors

Aerocontrolex Group Inc........................D 216 291-6025
  South Euclid (G-13457)
Alkid Corporation....................................E 216 896-3000
  Cleveland (G-3629)
▲ Anchor Flange Company....................D 513 527-3512
  Cincinnati (G-2626)
▲ Apph Wichita Inc.................................E 316 943-5752
  Strongsville (G-13808)
Bergstrom Company Ltd Partnr..............E 440 232-2282
  Cleveland (G-3730)
Bosch Rexroth Corporation....................C 330 263-3300
  Wooster (G-16106)
Custom Cltch Jint Hydrlics Inc................F 216 431-1630
  Cleveland (G-3923)
Cylinders and Valves Inc........................G 440 238-7343
  Strongsville (G-13826)
Danfoss Power Solutions II LLC.............G 419 238-1190
  Van Wert (G-14913)
Eaton Aeroquip LLC................................A 419 891-7775
  Maumee (G-10201)
◆ Eaton Corporation...............................B 440 523-5000
  Cleveland (G-3994)
Eaton Leasing Corporation.....................B 216 382-2292
  Beachwood (G-986)
Emerson Process Management..............C 419 529-4311
  Ontario (G-12091)
Fluid Power Solutions LLC......................G 614 777-8954
  Hilliard (G-8412)
▲ Force Control Industries Inc................E 513 868-0900
  Fairfield (G-7363)
◆ Furukawa Rock Drill USA Co Ltd........F 330 673-5826
  Kent (G-8816)
▲ Giant Industries Inc............................E 419 531-4600
  Toledo (G-14300)
Gorman-Rupp Company.........................C 419 755-1011
  Mansfield (G-9663)
H Y O Inc...E 614 488-2861
  Columbus (G-5414)
Hite Parts Exchange Inc.........................F 614 272-5115
  Columbus (G-5442)
▲ Hy-Production Inc...............................C 330 273-2400
  Valley City (G-14873)
Hydraulic Parts Store Inc........................E 330 364-6667
  New Philadelphia (G-11505)

▲ Linde Hydraulics Corporation.............E 330 533-6801
  Canfield (G-2009)
Midwest Tool & Engineering Co..............E
  Dayton (G-6445)
◆ Oase North America Inc......................G 800 365-3880
  Aurora (G-728)
Parker Hannifin Partner B LLC................E 216 896-3000
  Cleveland (G-4528)
Parker Royalty Partnership.....................E 216 896-3000
  Cleveland (G-4529)
Parker-Hannifin Corporation...................G 330 261-1618
  Berlin Center (G-1311)
Parker-Hannifin Corporation...................F 937 644-3915
  Marysville (G-9930)
Parker-Hannifin Corporation...................E 440 266-2300
  Mentor (G-10520)
Parker-Hannifin Corporation...................C 419 644-4311
  Metamora (G-10603)
▲ Parker-Hannifin Corporation...............A 216 896-3000
  Cleveland (G-4532)
▲ Permco Inc...C 330 626-2801
  Streetsboro (G-13783)
Pfpc Enterprises Inc...............................F 513 941-6200
  Cincinnati (G-3253)
Quad Fluid Dynamics Inc........................F 330 220-3005
  Brunswick (G-1785)
Radocy Inc..F 419 666-4400
  Rossford (G-12870)
▲ Robeck Fluid Power Co......................D 330 562-1140
  Aurora (G-734)
▲ Semtorq Inc...F 330 487-0600
  Twinsburg (G-14734)
Starkey Machinery Inc............................E 419 468-2560
  Galion (G-7885)
Suburban Manufacturing Co...................D 440 953-2024
  Eastlake (G-7050)
Sunset Industries Inc..............................E 440 306-8284
  Mentor (G-10570)
Swagelok Company.................................E 440 349-5836
  Solon (G-13430)
Trane Technologies Company LLC........E 419 633-6800
  Bryan (G-1842)
Vertiflo Pump Company...........................F 513 530-0888
  Cincinnati (G-3496)
Vickers International Inc.........................E 419 867-2200
  Maumee (G-10244)

3596 Scales and balances, except laboratory

▲ Etched Metal Company.......................E 440 248-0240
  Solon (G-13347)
Exact Equipment Corporation.................F 215 295-2000
  Columbus (G-5062)
Hobart LLC..E 937 332-2797
  Piqua (G-12525)
Hobart LLC..E 937 332-3000
  Troy (G-14581)
▲ Hobart LLC...D 937 332-3000
  Troy (G-14582)
▲ Holtgreven Scale & Elec Corp.............F 419 422-4779
  Findlay (G-7524)
Interface Logic Systems Inc...................G 614 236-8388
  Columbus (G-5472)
K Davis Inc..G 419 307-7051
  Fremont (G-7791)
Mettler-Toledo LLC..................................C 614 841-7300
  Columbus (G-5560)
Mettler-Toledo LLC..................................E 614 438-4511
  Worthington (G-16202)
Mettler-Toledo LLC..................................C 614 438-4390
  Worthington (G-16203)
Mettler-Toledo Intl Fin Inc.......................F 614 438-4511
  Columbus (G-5065)

35 INDUSTRIAL AND COMMERCIAL MACHINERY AND COMPUTER EQUIPMENT

◆ Mettler-Toledo Intl Inc .... A 614 438-4511
   Columbus *(G-5066)*

◆ Mettler-Toledo LLC .... A 614 438-4511
   Columbus *(G-5067)*

Rainin Instrument LLC .... E 510 564-1600
   Columbus *(G-5069)*

3599 Industrial machinery, nec

2-M Manufacturing Company Inc .... E 440 269-1270
   Eastlake *(G-7016)*

3249 Inc .... F 937 294-5692
   Moraine *(G-11150)*

3d Sales & Consulting Inc .... E 513 422-1198
   Middletown *(G-10800)*

5 S Inc .... G 440 968-0212
   Montville *(G-11148)*

A - Y Machining LLC .... G 216 404-0400
   Cleveland *(G-3576)*

A & B Foundry LLC .... F 937 369-3007
   Franklin *(G-7660)*

A & B Machine Inc .... E 937 492-8662
   Sidney *(G-13217)*

A & G Manufacturing Co Inc .... F 419 468-7433
   Galion *(G-7857)*

▲ A & G Manufacturing Co Inc .... E 419 468-7433
   Galion *(G-7858)*

A & L Industries .... G 419 698-3733
   Oregon *(G-12098)*

A & R Machine Co Inc .... G 330 832-4631
   Massillon *(G-10073)*

A and V Grinding Inc .... G 937 444-4141
   Cincinnati *(G-2583)*

A&B Foundry & Machining LLC .... E 937 746-3634
   Franklin *(G-7661)*

A&D Machining LLC .... G 330 786-0964
   Barberton *(G-850)*

A+ Engineering Fabrication Inc .... F 419 832-0748
   Grand Rapids *(G-8008)*

AAM Mold and Machine Inc .... F 440 998-2040
   Ashtabula *(G-625)*

Abco Bar & Tube Cutng Svc Inc ...... E 513 697-9487
   Maineville *(G-9598)*

Accu-Grind & Mfg Co Inc .... E 937 224-3303
   Dayton *(G-6180)*

Accu-Tool Inc .... G 937 667-5878
   Tipp City *(G-14120)*

Accuform Manufacturing Inc .... E 330 797-9291
   Youngstown *(G-16300)*

Accurate Manufacturing Company .... E 614 878-6510
   Columbus *(G-5096)*

Accurate Metal Machining Inc .... C 440 350-8225
   Painesville *(G-12215)*

Accurate Tech Inc .... G 440 951-9153
   Mentor *(G-10402)*

Ace Boiler & Welding Co Inc .... G 330 745-4443
   Barberton *(G-851)*

Ace Grinding Co Inc .... G 440 951-6760
   Willoughby *(G-15873)*

▲ Ace Manufacturing Company .... E 513 541-2490
   West Chester *(G-15360)*

▲ Ace Precision Industries Inc .... E 330 633-8523
   Akron *(G-16)*

Action Machine & Mfg Inc .... G 513 899-3889
   Morrow *(G-11223)*

Action Precision Products Inc .... F 419 737-2348
   Pioneer *(G-12488)*

▲ Active Metal and Molds Inc .... F 419 281-9623
   Ashland *(G-549)*

▲ Addition Manufacturing Te .... C 513 228-7000
   Lebanon *(G-9059)*

ADI Machining Inc .... E 440 277-4141
   Sheffield Village *(G-13179)*

▲ Advance Apex Inc .... E 614 539-3000
   Grove City *(G-8072)*

Advance Manufacturing Corp .... E 216 333-1684
   Cleveland *(G-3603)*

▲ Advanced Design Industries Inc ..... E 440 277-4141
   Sheffield Village *(G-13180)*

Advanced Indus Machining Inc .... F 614 596-4183
   Powell *(G-12662)*

Advanced Welding Inc .... E 937 746-6800
   Franklin *(G-7662)*

Advantage Machine Shop .... G 330 337-8377
   Salem *(G-12976)*

Advetech Inc .... E 330 533-2227
   Canfield *(G-1995)*

Aeroserv Inc .... F 513 932-9227
   Mason *(G-9946)*

Aerotech Enterprise .... F 440 729-2616
   Chesterland *(G-2478)*

Aframian Partnership LLC .... G 614 868-8634
   Reynoldsburg *(G-12749)*

AGR Consulting Inc .... F 440 974-4030
   Eastlake *(G-7018)*

Aims-CMI Technology LLC .... F 937 832-2000
   Englewood *(G-7221)*

Aircraft & Auto Fittings Co .... G 216 486-0047
   Cleveland *(G-3618)*

Ajax-Ceco .... F 440 295-0244
   Euclid *(G-7259)*

Akay Holdings Inc .... E 330 753-8458
   Barberton *(G-852)*

Akro Tool Co Inc .... G 513 858-1555
   Fairfield *(G-7331)*

▼ Akron Equipment Company .... D 330 645-3780
   Coventry Township *(G-6005)*

Akron Gear & Engineering Inc .... E 330 773-6608
   Akron *(G-34)*

▼ Akron Special Machinery Inc .... E 330 753-1077
   Akron *(G-43)*

Albion Machine & Tool Co Inc .... G 216 267-9627
   Cleveland *(G-3621)*

Alcoa Inc .... G 937 492-8915
   Sidney *(G-13219)*

◆ Alfons Haar Inc .... E 937 560-2031
   Springboro *(G-13495)*

Alfred Machine Co .... D 440 248-4600
   Cleveland *(G-3628)*

All Craft Manufacturing Co .... F 513 661-3383
   Cincinnati *(G-2608)*

All-Tech Manufacturing Ltd .... E 330 633-1095
   Akron *(G-53)*

All-Type Welding & Fabrication .... E 440 439-3990
   Cleveland *(G-3635)*

Allen Randall Enterprises Inc .... F 330 374-9850
   Akron *(G-54)*

▲ Alliance Automation LLC .... D 419 238-2520
   Van Wert *(G-14906)*

Allied Machine Works Inc .... G 740 454-2534
   Zanesville *(G-16499)*

Allied Mask and Tooling Inc .... G 419 470-2555
   Toledo *(G-14183)*

Allied Pdstal Boom Systems LLC ..... G 419 663-0279
   Norwalk *(G-11952)*

Allied Pedestal Boom Sys LLC .... G 419 663-0279
   Norwalk *(G-11953)*

Alloy Machining and Fabg Inc .... G 330 482-5543
   Columbiana *(G-5026)*

◆ Alloy Precision Tech Inc .... D 440 266-7700
   Mentor *(G-10412)*

Alternative Surface Grinding .... G 330 273-3443
   Brunswick *(G-1747)*

Alton Products Inc .... F 419 893-0201
   Maumee *(G-10162)*

Amarok Industries LLC .... F 216 898-1948
   Cleveland *(G-3647)*

American Aero Components Llc ...... G 937 367-5068
   Dayton *(G-6197)*

American Fluid Power Inc .... G 440 773-7462
   Chesterland *(G-2479)*

American Laser & Machine LLC ...... G 419 930-9303
   Toledo *(G-14188)*

American Punch Co .... E 216 731-4501
   Euclid *(G-7262)*

American Tool Works Inc .... F 513 844-6363
   Hamilton *(G-8179)*

Amerimold Inc .... G 800 950-8020
   Mogadore *(G-11066)*

Amon Inc .... E 513 734-1700
   Amelia *(G-452)*

Ampsco Division .... C 614 444-2181
   Columbus *(G-5133)*

▲ Amt Machine Systems Ltd .... F 614 635-8050
   Columbus *(G-5135)*

Anchor Fabricators Inc .... E 937 836-5117
   Clayton *(G-3563)*

Anchor Metal Processing Inc .... F 216 362-6463
   Cleveland *(G-3662)*

Anchor Metal Processing Inc .... F 216 362-1850
   Cleveland *(G-3663)*

Andersons Inc .... E 419 891-2930
   Maumee *(G-10164)*

Androm Industries Inc .... G 614 408-9067
   Newark *(G-11563)*

▲ Ansco Machine Company .... E 330 929-8181
   Peninsula *(G-12338)*

Apex Specialty Co Inc .... E 330 725-6663
   Medina *(G-10296)*

Apollo Manufacturing Co LLC .... E 440 951-9972
   Mentor *(G-10419)*

Applied Experience LLC .... G 614 943-2970
   Plain City *(G-12562)*

Apr Tool Inc .... G 440 946-0393
   Willoughby *(G-15883)*

Aqua Precision LLC .... F 937 912-9582
   Dayton *(G-6211)*

ARC Drilling Inc .... E 216 525-0920
   Cleveland *(G-3672)*

Argo Tool Corporation .... F 330 425-2407
   Twinsburg *(G-14631)*

◆ ARM (usa) Inc .... E 740 264-6599
   Wintersville *(G-16085)*

Armor Aftermarket Inc .... G 513 923-5600
   Mason *(G-9951)*

Arnold Machine Inc .... F 419 443-1818
   Tiffin *(G-14076)*

Artisan Equipment Inc .... F 740 756-9135
   Carroll *(G-2294)*

Artisan Grinding Service Inc .... F 937 667-7383
   Dayton *(G-6214)*

Ashcraft Machine & Supply Inc ...... F 740 349-8110
   Newark *(G-11566)*

Ashland Precision Tooling LLC .... E 419 289-1736
   Ashland *(G-551)*

Ashta Forge & Machine Inc .... F 216 252-7000
   Cleveland *(G-3691)*

Aspen Machine and Plastics .... G 937 526-4644
   Versailles *(G-14976)*

Assembly Machining Wire Pdts .... G 614 443-1110
   Columbus *(G-5160)*

Associated Press Repair Inc .... G 216 881-2288
   Gates Mills *(G-7927)*

▲ Astro Manufacturing & Design Inc .. C 888 215-1746
   Eastlake *(G-7019)*

Astro Technical Services Inc .... E
   Warren *(G-15145)*

SIC SECTION
35 INDUSTRIAL AND COMMERCIAL MACHINERY AND COMPUTER EQUIPMENT

Athens Mold and Machine Inc .... D 740 593-6613
  Athens *(G-675)*
◆ Atlas Industries Inc .... A 419 355-1000
  Fremont *(G-7763)*
Atlas Machine and Supply Inc .... E 502 584-7262
  Hamilton *(G-8182)*
Ats Machine & Tool Co .... F 440 255-1120
  Eastlake *(G-7021)*
Auglaize Erie Machine Company .... E 419 629-2068
  New Bremen *(G-11398)*
Austinburg Machine Inc .... G 440 275-2001
  Austinburg *(G-741)*
Automated Mfg Solutions Inc .... F 440 878-3711
  Strongsville *(G-13812)*
Automatic Parts .... E 419 524-5841
  Mansfield *(G-9627)*
Automator Marking Systems Inc .... G 740 983-0157
  Chillicothe *(G-2493)*
Autotec Corporation .... E 419 885-2529
  Toledo *(G-14201)*
Awu Corp .... G 740 504-8448
  Macedonia *(G-9536)*
Axle Machine Services Ltd .... G 419 827-2000
  Lakeville *(G-8963)*
B & B Gear and Machine Co Inc .... E 937 687-1771
  New Lebanon *(G-11448)*
▲ B & C Research Inc .... B 330 848-4000
  Barberton *(G-857)*
B & D Machinists Inc .... F 513 831-8588
  Milford *(G-10893)*
B & F Manufacturing Co .... F 216 518-0333
  Warrensville Heights *(G-15226)*
B & G Tool Company .... G 614 451-2538
  Columbus *(G-5170)*
B & H Machine Inc .... E 330 868-6425
  Minerva *(G-11027)*
B & R Machine Co .... F 216 961-7370
  Cleveland *(G-3715)*
B & T Welding and Machine Co .... G 740 687-1908
  Lancaster *(G-8990)*
B B & H Tool Company .... G 614 868-8634
  Reynoldsburg *(G-12752)*
B M Machine .... G 419 595-2898
  Alvada *(G-440)*
B S F Inc .... F 937 890-6121
  Tipp City *(G-14123)*
B&C Machine Co LLC .... E 330 745-4013
  Barberton *(G-859)*
Bainter Machining Company .... F 740 756-4598
  Lancaster *(G-8994)*
Bainter Machining Company .... G 740 653-2422
  Lancaster *(G-8993)*
Balancing Company Inc .... E 937 898-9111
  Vandalia *(G-14933)*
Barcon LLC .... G 866 883-4804
  New Waterford *(G-11553)*
▲ Bardons & Oliver Inc .... C 440 498-5800
  Solon *(G-13316)*
Barile Precision Grinding Inc .... F 216 267-6500
  Cleveland *(G-3720)*
Bc Machine Services Corp .... F 513 428-0327
  Trenton *(G-14539)*
Beacon Metal Fabricators Inc .... F 216 391-7444
  Cleveland *(G-3727)*
Beaumont Machine LLC .... F 513 383-5061
  Batavia *(G-911)*
Beaverson Machine Inc .... G 419 923-8064
  Delta *(G-6780)*
Beckman Machine LLC .... E 513 242-2700
  Cincinnati *(G-2663)*
Beemer Machine Company Inc .... G 330 678-3822
  Kent *(G-8801)*

▲ Berea Manufacturing Inc .... F 440 260-0590
  Berea *(G-1267)*
Berran Industrial Group Inc .... E 330 253-5800
  Akron *(G-83)*
Best Inc .... G 419 394-2745
  Saint Marys *(G-12946)*
Best Mold & Manufacturing Inc .... E 330 896-9988
  Akron *(G-84)*
Best Performance Inc .... G 419 394-2299
  Saint Marys *(G-12947)*
Beta Industries Inc .... F 937 299-7385
  Dayton *(G-6227)*
Beverage Mch & Fabricators Inc .... F 216 252-5100
  Cleveland *(G-3733)*
Bic Manufacturing Inc .... E 216 531-9393
  Euclid *(G-7263)*
Blc Precision Machine Co Inc .... E 937 783-1406
  Blanchester *(G-1347)*
Bickett Machine and Gas Supply .... G 740 353-5710
  Portsmouth *(G-12641)*
Bishop Machine Tool & Die .... F 740 453-8818
  Zanesville *(G-16510)*
Black Machining & Tech Inc .... F 513 752-8625
  Batavia *(G-913)*
Blackhawk Machine LLC .... F 419 779-3958
  Walbridge *(G-15079)*
Blacklick Machine Company .... G 614 866-9300
  Blacklick *(G-1332)*
Blairs Cnc Turning Inc .... G 937 461-1100
  Dayton *(G-6230)*
Blue Chip Tool Inc .... F 513 489-3561
  Cincinnati *(G-2673)*
Blue Engineered Products LLC .... G 937 247-5537
  West Carrollton *(G-15350)*
Boivin Machine .... G 330 928-3942
  Akron *(G-90)*
Bollari/Davis Inc .... F 330 296-4445
  Ravenna *(G-12708)*
Bond Machine Company Inc .... F 937 746-4941
  Franklin *(G-7664)*
▼ Bonnot Company .... E 330 896-6544
  Akron *(G-91)*
Borman Enterprises Inc .... F 216 459-9292
  Cleveland *(G-3749)*
Boss Industries Inc .... F 330 273-2266
  Valley City *(G-14864)*
Bowden Manufacturing Corp .... E 440 946-1770
  Willoughby *(G-15891)*
Bowdil Company .... F 800 356-8663
  Canton *(G-2051)*
Boyce Machine Inc .... G 330 678-3210
  Kent *(G-8802)*
Boyds Mch & Met Finshg Inc .... F 937 698-5623
  West Milton *(G-15629)*
Brandts Custom Machining LLC .... G 419 566-3192
  Mansfield *(G-9630)*
Brinkley Technology Group LLC .... F 330 830-2498
  Massillon *(G-10079)*
Brocker Machine Inc .... F 330 744-5858
  Youngstown *(G-16329)*
Bronco Machine Inc .... F 440 951-5015
  Willoughby *(G-15894)*
Bront Machining Inc .... E 937 228-4551
  Moraine *(G-11164)*
Brooklyn Machine & Mfg Co Inc .... G 216 341-1846
  Cleveland *(G-3762)*
Brown Cnc Machining Inc .... F 937 865-9191
  Miamisburg *(G-10623)*
Buckeye Mch Fabricators Inc .... E 419 273-2521
  Forest *(G-7590)*
Buckeye State Wldg & Fabg Inc .... F 440 322-0319
  Elyria *(G-7120)*

Buckys Machine and Fab Ltd .... G 419 981-5050
  Mc Cutchenville *(G-10272)*
Budde Precision Machining Corp .... F 937 278-1962
  Dayton *(G-6240)*
Bula Forge Machine .... G 216 252-7600
  Cleveland *(G-3772)*
▲ Bullen Ultrasonics Inc .... D 937 456-7133
  Eaton *(G-7056)*
Burdens Machine & Welding Inc .... F 740 345-9246
  Newark *(G-11569)*
▲ Burke Products Inc .... E 937 372-3516
  Xenia *(G-16253)*
Burton Industries Inc .... E 440 974-1700
  Mentor *(G-10433)*
Byg Industries Inc .... G 216 961-5436
  Cleveland *(G-3777)*
C & H Enterprises Ltd .... G 510 226-6083
  Findlay *(G-7490)*
C & K Machine Co Inc .... G 419 237-3203
  Fayette *(G-7461)*
C A Joseph Co .... F 330 532-4646
  Irondale *(G-8693)*
▲ C A Joseph Co .... G 330 385-6869
  East Liverpool *(G-6988)*
C-N-D Industries Inc .... E 330 478-8811
  Massillon *(G-10080)*
C&W Swiss Inc .... F 937 832-2889
  Englewood *(G-7224)*
Cage Gear & Machine LLC .... E 330 452-1532
  Canton *(G-2057)*
Calvin J Magsig .... G 419 862-3311
  Elmore *(G-7100)*
CAM Machine Inc .... F 937 663-5000
  Saint Paris *(G-12972)*
Cardinal Machine Company .... F 440 238-7050
  Strongsville *(G-13818)*
Cascade Unlimited LLC .... G 440 352-7995
  Painesville *(G-12221)*
▲ Case-Maul Manufacturing Co .... F 419 524-1061
  Mansfield *(G-9635)*
Cave Tool & Mfg Inc .... F 937 324-0662
  Springfield *(G-13542)*
Cbn Westside Holdings Inc .... E 513 772-7000
  West Chester *(G-15386)*
▲ Cbn Westside Technologies Inc .... B 513 772-7000
  West Chester *(G-15387)*
CBs Boring and Mch Co Inc .... F 419 784-9500
  Defiance *(G-6672)*
Celina Percision Machine .... F 419 586-9222
  Celina *(G-2326)*
Centerless Grinding Service .... G 216 251-4100
  Cleveland *(G-3803)*
Centerless Grinding Solutions .... G 216 520-4612
  Twinsburg *(G-14640)*
Central Machinery Company LLC .... F 740 387-1289
  Marion *(G-9849)*
Central State Enterprises Inc .... E 419 468-8191
  Galion *(G-7865)*
Century Tool & Stamping Co .... F 216 241-2032
  Westlake *(G-15742)*
Certified Welding Co .... G 216 961-5410
  Cleveland *(G-3804)*
CF Tools LLC .... G 740 294-0419
  Fresno *(G-7822)*
Chandler Machine Company .... G 330 688-7615
  Stow *(G-13689)*
Chandler Machine Company .... F 330 688-5585
  Stow *(G-13690)*
Chardon Metal Products Co .... E 440 285-2147
  Chardon *(G-2443)*
Charles Brent Nichols .... G 513 772-7000
  Cleves *(G-4947)*

Employee Codes: A=Over 500 employees, B=251-500
C=101-250, D=51-100, E=20-50, F=10-19, G=1-9

2024 Harris Ohio
Industrial Directory

35 INDUSTRIAL AND COMMERCIAL MACHINERY AND COMPUTER EQUIPMENT

Charles Costa Inc ..... F 330 376-3636
Akron (G-107)

▼ Chickasaw Machine & Tl Co Inc ..... E 419 925-4325
Chickasaw (G-2490)

Chips Manufacturing Inc ..... G 440 946-3666
Willoughby (G-15899)

Christopher Tool & Mfg Co ..... C 440 248-8080
Solon (G-13329)

Cinci Cnc LLC ..... G 513 722-6756
Milford (G-10899)

▲ Cincinnati Babbitt Inc ..... F 513 942-5088
Fairfield (G-7346)

Cincinnati Grinding Technologies Inc ..... G 866 983-1097
Fairfield (G-7347)

Cincinnati Precision McHy Inc ..... G 513 860-4133
West Chester (G-15393)

▲ Cincinnati Radiator Inc ..... F 513 874-5555
Hamilton (G-8193)

Cinex Inc ..... E 513 921-2825
Cincinnati (C-2767)

▲ Circle Machine Rolls Inc ..... E 330 938-9010
Sebring (G-13119)

Circle Mold Incorporated ..... F 330 633-7017
Tallmadge (G-14025)

City Machine Technologies Inc ..... F 330 747-2639
Youngstown (G-16336)

Clapp & Haney Brazed Tl Co Inc ..... F 740 922-3515
Dennison (G-6794)

Clear Creek Screw Machine Co ..... G 740 969-2113
Amanda (G-445)

Cleary Machine Company Inc ..... E 937 839-4278
West Alexandria (G-15340)

Cleveland Indus Training Ctr ..... G 216 531-3446
Cleveland (G-3843)

Cleveland Jsm Inc ..... E 440 876-3050
Strongsville (G-13822)

Cleveland Special Tool Inc ..... F 440 944-1600
Wickliffe (G-15828)

◆ Cleveland Tool and Machine Inc ..... F 216 267-6010
Cleveland (G-3858)

▲ Clinton Machine Co Inc ..... F 330 882-2060
New Franklin (G-11435)

Clipsons Metal Working Inc ..... G 513 772-6393
Cincinnati (G-2774)

CMI Technology Inc ..... F 937 832-2000
Englewood (G-7225)

Cmt Machining & Fabg LLC ..... F 937 652-3740
Urbana (G-14827)

Cnc Painting Inc ..... F 513 662-1018
Cincinnati (G-2778)

Cnc Precision Machine Inc ..... D 440 548-3880
Parkman (G-12283)

▲ Cold Headed Fas Assemblies Inc ..... F 330 833-0800
Massillon (G-10085)

▲ Colfor Manufacturing Inc ..... B 330 470-6207
Malvern (G-9610)

Columbus Machine Works Inc ..... F 614 409-0244
Columbus (G-5271)

▲ Combs Manufacturing Inc ..... D 330 784-3151
Akron (G-114)

▲ Commercial Honing LLC ..... D 330 343-8896
Dover (G-6813)

Compco Quaker Mfg Inc ..... E 330 482-0200
Salem (G-12986)

Component Mfg & Design ..... F 330 225-8080
Brunswick (G-1754)

Compton Metal Products Inc ..... F 937 382-2403
Wilmington (G-16045)

Comptons Precision Machine ..... F 937 325-9139
Springfield (G-13546)

Comturn Manufacturing LLC ..... G 219 267-6911
Cleveland (G-3894)

Concept Machine & Tool Inc ..... E 937 473-3334
Covington (G-6020)

Conquest Industries Inc ..... E 330 926-9236
Stow (G-13691)

Core-Tech Enterprises LLC ..... G 440 946-8324
Mentor (G-10444)

Cornerstone Wauseon Inc ..... C 419 337-0940
Wauseon (G-15259)

Covert Manufacturing Inc ..... F 419 468-1761
Galion (G-7867)

Creative Mold and Machine Inc ..... E 440 338-5146
Newbury (G-11621)

Creative Processing Inc ..... F 440 834-4070
Mantua (G-9735)

Creative Products Inc ..... G 513 727-9872
Middletown (G-10815)

Creative Tool & Die LLC ..... G 614 836-0080
Groveport (G-8136)

Criterion Tool & Die Inc ..... E 216 267-1733
Brookpark (G-1708)

Croft & Son Mfg Inc ..... G 740 859-2200
Tiltonsville (G-14116)

Crossroads Machine Inc ..... G 937 832-2000
Englewood (G-7228)

Crowe Manufacturing Services ..... E 800 831-1893
Troy (G-14558)

Crum Manufacturing Inc ..... E 419 878-9779
Waterville (G-15241)

Ctek Tool & Machine Company ..... G 513 742-0423
Cincinnati (G-2805)

CTS Waterjet LLC ..... G 513 641-0600
Cincinnati (G-2806)

Curtis Steel & Supply Inc ..... F 330 376-7141
Akron (G-119)

Custom Crankshaft Inc ..... G 330 382-1200
East Liverpool (G-6992)

Custom Fab By Fisher LLC ..... F 513 738-4600
Hamilton (G-8197)

Custom Machine Inc ..... E 419 986-5122
Tiffin (G-14082)

Custom Manufacturing Solutions ..... D 937 372-0777
Xenia (G-16257)

Custom Metal Works Inc ..... F 419 668-7831
Norwalk (G-11959)

Custom Tooling Company ..... F 513 733-5790
Cincinnati (G-2810)

Cutting Dynamics Inc ..... D 440 249-4666
Avon (G-770)

Cutting Dynamics Inc ..... D 440 930-2862
Avon Lake (G-802)

Cutting Edge Manufacturing LLC ..... E 419 355-0921
Fremont (G-7774)

Cuyahoga Machine Company LLC ..... F 216 267-3560
Brookpark (G-1711)

D & B Industries Inc ..... G 937 253-8658
Dayton (G-6157)

D & E Machine Co ..... G 513 932-2184
Lebanon (G-9069)

D & J Machine Shop ..... F 937 256-2730
Xenia (G-16258)

D & L Machine Co Inc ..... E 330 785-0781
Akron (G-121)

D 4 Industries Inc ..... G 419 523-9555
Ottawa (G-12178)

D M Tool & Plastics Inc ..... F 937 962-4140
Brookville (G-1733)

D M Tool & Plastics Inc ..... F 937 962-4140
Lewisburg (G-9186)

D&D Quality Machining Co Inc ..... F 440 942-2772
Willoughby (G-15905)

Dalton Stryker McHining Fcilty ..... E 419 682-3928
Stryker (G-13908)

Dana Off Highway Products LLC ..... D 614 864-1116
Blacklick (G-1334)

David Bixel ..... F 440 474-4410
Rock Creek (G-12831)

Davis Machine Products Inc ..... G 440 474-0247
Streetsboro (G-13764)

Dawsduke Ltd ..... G 614 270-6278
Canal Winchester (G-1984)

Day-TEC Tool & Mfg Inc ..... F 937 847-0022
Miamisburg (G-10632)

Dayton One LLC ..... G 937 265-0227
Dayton (G-6285)

Dayton Systems Group Inc ..... E 937 885-5665
Miamisburg (G-10634)

De Angelo Instrument Inc ..... G 330 929-7266
Cuyahoga Falls (G-6079)

Deangelo Instrument Inc ..... G 330 654-9264
Diamond (G-6805)

Dearborn Inc ..... E 440 234-1353
Berea (G-1273)

Deffren Machine Tool Svc Inc ..... F 610 060 1666
Fairfield (G-7351)

▲ Deimling/Jeliho Plastics Inc ..... D 513 752-6653
Amelia (G-454)

Delta Manufacturing Inc ..... F 330 386-1270
East Liverpool (G-6994)

Deltec Incorporated ..... E 513 732-0800
Batavia (G-920)

DES Machine Services Inc ..... G 330 633-6897
Stow (G-13692)

Design and Fabrication Inc ..... G 419 294-2414
Upper Sandusky (G-14807)

Design Technologies & Mfg Co ..... F 937 335-0757
Troy (G-14563)

Detailed Machining Inc ..... E 937 492-1264
Sidney (G-13241)

Detrick Design Fabrication LLC ..... G 937 620-6736
Troy (G-14564)

▲ Detroit Diesl Specialty Tl Inc ..... C 740 435-4452
Byesville (G-1895)

Deuce Machining LLC ..... G 513 875-2291
Fayetteville (G-7464)

Devault Machine & Mould Co LLC ..... G 740 654-5925
Lancaster (G-9009)

Dilco Industries Inc ..... E 330 337-6732
Salem (G-12991)

Dillon Manufacturing Inc ..... F 937 325-8482
Springfield (G-13555)

Dimension Industries Inc ..... F 440 236-3265
Columbia Station (G-5012)

Direct Tool LLC ..... E 614 687-3111
Mechanicsburg (G-10285)

Diversified Mch Components LLC ..... E 440 942-5701
Eastlake (G-7026)

DM Machine Co ..... G 440 946-0771
Willoughby (G-15908)

Dover Machine Co ..... F 330 343-4123
Dover (G-6821)

Drabik Manufacturing Inc ..... F 216 267-1616
Cleveland (G-3971)

Drake Manufacturing LLC ..... D 330 847-7291
Warren (G-15163)

Drt Holdings Inc ..... D 937 298-7391
Dayton (G-6305)

Drt Mfg Co LLC ..... C 937 298-7391
Dayton (G-6306)

Drt Precision Mfg LLC ..... E 937 507-4308
Sidney (G-13243)

▲ Duke Manufacturing Inc ..... E 440 942-6537
Willoughby (G-15912)

▲ Duncan Tool Inc ..... F 937 667-9364
Tipp City (G-14132)

SIC SECTION
35 INDUSTRIAL AND COMMERCIAL MACHINERY AND COMPUTER EQUIPMENT

Dunham Machine Inc.............................. G 216 398-4500
   Independence *(G-8663)*

Duray Machine Company Inc................. F 440 277-4119
   Amherst *(G-475)*

Dwd2 Inc... F 513 563-0070
   Cincinnati *(G-2844)*

Dynamic Industries Inc........................... E 513 861-6767
   Cincinnati *(G-2845)*

Dynamic Machine Works......................... G 419 564-7925
   Mansfield *(G-9648)*

Dynapoint Technologies Inc.................... G 937 859-5193
   Dayton *(G-6309)*

E & J Demark Inc.................................... G 419 337-5866
   Wauseon *(G-15260)*

E & K Products Co Inc............................ G 216 631-2510
   Cleveland *(G-3983)*

E D M Star-One Inc................................ F 440 647-0600
   Wadsworth *(G-15027)*

E Systems Design & Automtn Inc........... G 419 443-0220
   Tiffin *(G-14084)*

E Z Machine Inc...................................... G 330 784-3363
   Tallmadge *(G-14029)*

Eaglehead Manufacturing Co.................. F 440 951-0400
   Eastlake *(G-7027)*

▲ East End Welding LLC......................... C 330 677-6000
   Kent *(G-8811)*

Eastlake Machine Products LLC............. G 440 953-1014
   Willoughby *(G-15915)*

▲ Eaton Fabricating Company Inc........... E 440 926-3121
   Grafton *(G-7998)*

Edinburg Fixture and Mch Inc................. G 330 947-1700
   Rootstown *(G-12852)*

Edward D Segen & Co LLC.................... G 937 295-3672
   Fort Loramie *(G-7598)*

Edwards Machine Service Inc................ G 937 295-2929
   Fort Loramie *(G-7599)*

Efficient Machine Pdts Corp................... E 440 268-0205
   Strongsville *(G-13832)*

Eitle Machine Tool Inc............................ G 419 935-8753
   Attica *(G-700)*

Electrowind... G 937 229-0101
   Dayton *(G-6316)*

Elk Technologies LLC............................. G 937 902-4165
   Dayton *(G-6317)*

Eltool Corporation................................... G 513 723-1772
   Mansfield *(G-9652)*

Elyria Metal Spinning Fabg Co............... G 440 323-8068
   Elyria *(G-7143)*

EMC Precision Machining II LLC............ F 440 365-4171
   Elyria *(G-7148)*

Empire Machine LLC.............................. G 937 506-7793
   Tipp City *(G-14133)*

▲ Enprotech Industrial Tech LLC............. E 216 883-3220
   Cleveland *(G-4019)*

Eos Technology Inc................................ F 216 281-2999
   Cleveland *(G-4024)*

▲ Essc Group Inc.................................... G 330 317-3566
   Wooster *(G-16116)*

Esterle Mold & Machine Co Inc.............. E 330 686-1685
   Stow *(G-13695)*

▲ Esterline & Sons Mfg Co LLC.............. E 937 265-5278
   Springfield *(G-13560)*

Eti Tech LLC.. F 937 832-4200
   Kettering *(G-8907)*

Etko Machine Inc................................... G 330 745-4033
   Norton *(G-11942)*

Euclid Precision Grinding Co.................. G 440 946-8888
   Eastlake *(G-7032)*

Euclid Welding Company Inc................. F 216 289-0714
   Willoughby Hills *(G-16024)*

▲ Ewart-Ohlson Machine Company......... E 330 928-2171
   Cuyahoga Falls *(G-6081)*

▲ Exact Cutting Service Inc.................... E 440 546-1319
   Brecksville *(G-1616)*

Excel Machine & Tool Inc...................... F 419 678-3318
   Coldwater *(G-4987)*

Excellent Tool & Die Inc........................ G 216 671-9222
   Cleveland *(G-4041)*

F & G Tool and Die Co........................... E 937 294-1405
   Moraine *(G-11180)*

F & S Hydraulics Inc.............................. G 513 575-1600
   Milford *(G-10905)*

F A Tech Corp.. E 513 942-1920
   West Chester *(G-15428)*

F M Machine Co.................................... E 330 773-8237
   Akron *(G-147)*

Fabricating Machine Tools Ltd............... G 440 666-9187
   Cleveland *(G-4046)*

Fabriweld Corporation........................... C 419 663-0279
   Norwalk *(G-11965)*

▲ Fabriweld Corporation......................... E 419 668-3358
   Norwalk *(G-11966)*

Falcon Innovations Inc........................... G 216 252-0676
   Cleveland *(G-4047)*

Falcon Tool & Machine Inc.................... G 937 534-9999
   Dayton *(G-6328)*

Farr Automation Inc............................... F 419 289-1883
   Ashland *(G-571)*

Fate Industries Inc................................. G 440 327-1770
   North Ridgeville *(G-11839)*

Fdc Machine Repair Inc......................... E 216 362-1082
   Parma *(G-12288)*

Federal Hose Manufacturing LLC........... E 800 346-4673
   Cleveland *(G-4054)*

Feilhauers Machine Shop Inc................. F 513 202-0545
   Harrison *(G-8274)*

Feller Tool Co.. F 440 324-6277
   Elyria *(G-7151)*

▲ Ferralloy Inc.. G 440 250-1900
   Cleveland *(G-4057)*

◆ Ferry Industries Inc............................ D 330 920-9200
   Stow *(G-13698)*

Filmtec Fabrications LLC....................... E 419 435-1819
   Fostoria *(G-7632)*

First Francis Company Inc..................... E 440 352-8927
   Painesville *(G-12237)*

▲ Flash Industrial Tech Ltd.................... G 440 786-8979
   Cleveland *(G-4067)*

Flohr Machine Company Inc.................. E 330 745-3030
   Barberton *(G-867)*

◆ Floturn Inc... C 513 860-8040
   Fairfield *(G-7361)*

Fluid Quip Custom MA........................... G 937 324-0662
   Springfield *(G-13566)*

Foltz Machine LLC................................. E 330 453-9235
   Canton *(G-2102)*

▲ Forge Industries Inc............................ A 330 960-2468
   Youngstown *(G-16359)*

Fostoria MT&f Corp................................ F 419 435-7676
   Fostoria *(G-7636)*

Frantz Grinding Co................................. G 330 343-8689
   New Philadelphia *(G-11502)*

Frazier Machine and Prod Inc................. E 419 874-7321
   Perrysburg *(G-12383)*

Fredericktown Tomato Show.................. G 740 694-4816
   Fredericktown *(G-7747)*

▼ Fredon Corporation............................. D 440 951-5200
   Mentor *(G-10458)*

Fredrick Welding & Machining................ F 614 866-9650
   Reynoldsburg *(G-12766)*

Fries Machine & Tool Inc....................... F 937 898-6432
   Dayton *(G-6340)*

◆ Furukawa Rock Drill Usa Inc............... F 330 673-5826
   Kent *(G-8815)*

Fwy Machine Company LLC................. G 216 533-7515
   Hinckley *(G-8472)*

G & L Machining Inc.............................. G 513 724-2600
   Williamsburg *(G-15865)*

G F Frank and Sons Inc........................ F 513 870-9075
   West Chester *(G-15433)*

G Grafton Machine & Rubber................ F 330 297-1062
   Ravenna *(G-12716)*

G H Cutter Services Inc......................... G 419 476-0476
   Toledo *(G-14296)*

Garvey Corporation................................ E 330 779-0700
   Youngstown *(G-16361)*

Gasdorf Tool and Mch Co Inc................ E 419 227-0103
   Lima *(G-9244)*

Gaydash Enterprises Inc........................ F 330 896-4811
   Uniontown *(G-14783)*

▲ General Plug and Mfg Co.................... C 440 926-2411
   Grafton *(G-8000)*

General Sheave Company Inc................ G 216 781-8120
   Cleveland *(G-4117)*

▲ General Tool Company......................... C 513 733-5500
   Cincinnati *(G-2946)*

George Steel Fabricating Inc.................. E 513 932-2887
   Lebanon *(G-9080)*

Gilson Machine & Tool Co Inc................ E 419 592-2911
   Napoleon *(G-11316)*

Girard Machine Company Inc................. E 330 545-9731
   Girard *(G-7969)*

GL Heller Co Inc................................... F 419 877-5122
   Whitehouse *(G-15819)*

▲ Glenridge Machine Co......................... E 440 975-1055
   Solon *(G-13354)*

Global Laser Tek LLC............................ E 513 701-0452
   Mason *(G-9996)*

▲ Global Srcing Support Svcs LLC........ G 800 645-2986
   Cincinnati *(G-2959)*

▲ Globe Products Inc............................. F 937 233-0233
   Dayton *(G-6357)*

▲ Glunt Industries Inc............................. C 330 399-7585
   Warren *(G-15175)*

▼ Gmd Industries LLC............................ D 937 252-3643
   Dayton *(G-6359)*

Going My Way Trnsp Svcs LLC............. G 423 623-3802
   Cleveland *(G-4132)*

Graber Metal Works Inc......................... F 440 237-8422
   North Royalton *(G-11877)*

Grand Harbor Yacht Sales & Svc........... G 440 442-2919
   Cleveland *(G-4139)*

Graphel Corporation............................... C 513 779-6166
   West Chester *(G-15444)*

Green Machine Tool Inc........................ F 937 253-0771
   Dayton *(G-6161)*

Grenga Machine & Welding................... F 330 743-1113
   Youngstown *(G-16374)*

Grinding Equipment & McHy LLC........... F 330 747-2313
   Youngstown *(G-16375)*

Gt Technologies Inc............................... D 419 782-8955
   Defiance *(G-6680)*

Guyer Precision Inc................................ F 440 354-8024
   Painesville *(G-12242)*

H & B Machine & Tool Inc..................... F 216 431-3254
   Cleveland *(G-4159)*

H & H Machine Shop Akron Inc............. E 330 773-3327
   Akron *(G-175)*

H & H Quick Machine Inc...................... F 330 935-0944
   Louisville *(G-9457)*

H & M Machine Shop Inc....................... F 419 453-3414
   Ottoville *(G-12199)*

H & W Tool Co....................................... G 216 795-5520
   Euclid *(G-7271)*

H K K Machining Co.............................. E 419 924-5116
   West Unity *(G-15639)*

35 INDUSTRIAL AND COMMERCIAL MACHINERY AND COMPUTER EQUIPMENT

H&H Machine Shop Ravenna LL............ G 330 296-4445
  Ravenna *(G-12719)*
Habco Tool and Dev Co Inc................... E 440 946-5546
  Mentor *(G-10466)*
Hafco-Case Inc.. G 216 267-4644
  Cleveland *(G-4162)*
Hahn Automation Group Us Inc............. D 937 886-3232
  Miamisburg *(G-10641)*
Hahn Manufacturing Company............... E 216 391-9300
  Cleveland *(G-4163)*
Hale Manufacturing LLC......................... F 937 382-2127
  Wilmington *(G-16052)*
Hall Acquisition LLC............................... E 330 627-2119
  Carrollton *(G-2308)*
Halo Metal Prep Inc............................... G 216 741-0506
  Cleveland *(G-4164)*
Hannon Company.................................... F 330 343-7758
  Dover *(G-6826)*
Hardin Creek Machine & TI Inc.............. F 419 678-4913
  Coldwater *(G-1001)*
Harding Machine Acquisition Co............ D 937 666-3031
  East Liberty *(G-6987)*
Harris Welding and Machine Co.............. F 419 281-8351
  Ashland *(G-577)*
Haulette Manufacturing Inc.................... D 419 586-1717
  Celina *(G-2336)*
Hawkins Machine Shop Inc.................... G 937 335-8737
  Troy *(G-14576)*
▲ Hazenstab Machine Inc...................... F 330 337-1865
  Salem *(G-13000)*
HBE Machine Incorporated.................... G 419 668-9426
  Monroeville *(G-11124)*
Hearn Plating Co Ltd............................. F 419 473-9773
  Toledo *(G-14313)*
Heat Precision Machining Inc................ F 937 233-3140
  Dayton *(G-6366)*
Heisler Tool Company............................. F 440 951-2424
  Willoughby *(G-15927)*
Hephaestus Technologies LLC................ E 216 252-0430
  Cleveland *(G-4183)*
Herd Manufacturing Inc......................... E 216 651-4221
  Cleveland *(G-4184)*
Herman Machine Inc.............................. F 330 633-3261
  Tallmadge *(G-14032)*
Heule Tool Corporation........................... E 513 860-9900
  Loveland *(G-9485)*
▲ Hi-Tek Manufacturing Inc.................. C 513 459-1094
  Mason *(G-10001)*
High Tech Metal Products LLC............. F 419 227-9414
  Lima *(G-9252)*
High-Tech Mold & Machine Inc............ F 330 896-4466
  Uniontown *(G-14785)*
Highland Products Corp........................... F 440 352-4777
  Mentor *(G-10470)*
Hillman Precision Inc............................. F 419 289-1557
  Ashland *(G-579)*
Hofacker Prcsion Machining LLC............ F 937 832-7712
  Clayton *(G-3565)*
Holdren Brothers Inc.............................. F 937 465-7050
  West Liberty *(G-15622)*
◆ Hose Master LLC................................. B 216 481-2020
  Cleveland *(G-4203)*
Houston Machine Products Inc.............. E 937 322-8022
  Springfield *(G-13580)*
Howland Machine Corp............................ E 330 544-4029
  Niles *(G-11670)*
▼ Htec Systems Inc................................ F 937 438-3010
  Dayton *(G-6376)*
Hubbell Machine Tooling Inc................. E 216 524-1797
  Cleveland *(G-4206)*
Hutnik Company...................................... G 330 336-9700
  Wadsworth *(G-15035)*

Hutter Racing Engines Ltd..................... F 440 285-2175
  Chardon *(G-2453)*
▲ Hy-Production Inc.............................. C 330 273-2400
  Valley City *(G-14873)*
Hydro Supply Co..................................... F 740 454-3842
  Zanesville *(G-16537)*
I G Brenner Inc....................................... F 740 345-8845
  Newark *(G-11583)*
Icon Machining LLC............................... G 740 532-6739
  Ironton *(G-8698)*
Impac Hi-Performance Machining........... G 419 726-7100
  Toledo *(G-14327)*
Indelco Custom Products Inc................. E 216 797-7300
  Euclid *(G-7274)*
Independent Machine & Wldg Inc.......... G 937 339-7330
  Troy *(G-14586)*
Industrial Machining Services................. E 937 295-2022
  Fort Loramie *(G-7600)*
Innovative Tool & Die Inc..................... G 419 599-0492
  Napoleon *(G-11320)*
Innovtive Engnred Slutions Inc............... E 937 382-6710
  Wilmington *(G-16054)*
Inovent Engineering Inc......................... G 330 468-0019
  Macedonia *(G-9557)*
Integrity Industrial Equipment................ G 937 335-5658
  Troy *(G-14587)*
Integrity Manufacturing Corp................... F 937 233-6792
  Dayton *(G-6386)*
International Bellows.............................. F 937 294-6261
  Englewood *(G-7234)*
International Machining Inc................... E 330 225-1963
  Brunswick *(G-1771)*
◆ International Metal Hose Co............... D 419 483-7690
  Bellevue *(G-1228)*
◆ Interscope Manufacturing Inc............ E 513 423-8866
  Middletown *(G-10832)*
Intertek LLC.. F 440 323-3325
  Elyria *(G-7160)*
J & C Industries Inc............................... F 216 362-8867
  Cleveland *(G-4242)*
J & D Steel Service Center LLC............ G 330 759-7430
  Hubbard *(G-8565)*
J & P Products Inc................................. E 440 974-2830
  Mentor *(G-10480)*
J B Manufacturing Inc........................... E 330 676-9744
  Kent *(G-8820)*
J Horst Manufacturing Co...................... D 330 828-2216
  Dalton *(G-6133)*
J&J Precision Fabricators Ltd................. D 330 482-4964
  Columbiana *(G-5043)*
J&M Precision Die Casting LLC............. F 440 365-7388
  Elyria *(G-7170)*
Jade Products Inc.................................. F 440 352-1700
  Mentor *(G-10482)*
Jade Tool Company................................. G 937 376-4740
  Xenia *(G-16265)*
Jamar Precision Grinding Co................... G 330 220-0099
  Hinckley *(G-8475)*
Jay-Em Aerospace Corporation............... E 330 923-0333
  Cuyahoga Falls *(G-6092)*
Jayna Inc... E 937 335-8922
  Troy *(G-14590)*
JB Industries Ltd.................................... F 330 856-4587
  Warren *(G-15181)*
Jbj Technologies Inc............................. G 216 469-7297
  Euclid *(G-7277)*
Jed Industries Inc................................... F 440 639-9973
  Grand River *(G-8011)*
Jerl Machine Inc.................................... D 419 873-0270
  Perrysburg *(G-12394)*
Jh Industries Inc................................... E 330 963-4105
  Twinsburg *(G-14677)*

Jilco Precision Mold Mch Inc.................. G 330 633-9645
  Akron *(G-196)*
Jit Company Ohio.................................... G 614 529-8010
  Hilliard *(G-8417)*
Jj Sleeves Inc.. G 440 205-1055
  Mentor *(G-10483)*
Jlc Industrial LLC.................................... G 513 236-0462
  Amelia *(G-457)*
Joe Fuller Inc.. G 740 886-6182
  Proctorville *(G-12686)*
Johnson Mfg Systems LLC...................... F 937 866-4744
  Miamisburg *(G-10650)*
Johnson Prcision Machining Inc............. G 513 353-4252
  Cleves *(G-4956)*
Jonashtons LLC.. G 419 488-2363
  Cloverdale *(G-4970)*
Jordan Valve.. G 513 533-5600
  Cincinnati *(G-3050)*
Jotco Inc... G 513 721-4943
  Mansfield *(G-9675)*
K & G Machine Company......................... F 216 732-7115
  Cleveland *(G-4268)*
K & J Machine Inc................................. F 740 425-3282
  Barnesville *(G-903)*
K & K Precision Inc............................... E 513 336-0032
  Mason *(G-10016)*
K K Tool Co... G 937 325-1373
  Springfield *(G-13585)*
K S Machine Inc...................................... E 216 687-0459
  Cleveland *(G-4269)*
K-M-S Industries Inc.............................. F 440 243-6680
  Brookpark *(G-1720)*
▲ Kalt Manufacturing Company.............. D 440 327-2102
  North Ridgeville *(G-11848)*
Kaskell Manufacturing Inc....................... F 937 704-9700
  Springboro *(G-13507)*
▼ Kavon Filter Products Co.................... F 732 938-3135
  Cleveland *(G-4277)*
Kaws Inc.. E 513 521-8292
  Cincinnati *(G-3066)*
Kda Manufacturing LLC........................... G 330 590-7431
  Norton *(G-11947)*
Keban Industries Inc................................ G 216 446-0159
  Broadview Heights *(G-1659)*
▲ Ken-Dal Corporation............................. F 330 644-7118
  Coventry Township *(G-6011)*
Kenmore Development & Mch Co............ F 330 753-2274
  Akron *(G-203)*
Kent Post Acquisition Inc....................... G 330 678-6343
  Kent *(G-8826)*
Kerek Industries Ltd Lblty Co.................. F
  Cleveland *(G-4283)*
Kiffer Industries Inc................................. E 216 267-1818
  Cleveland *(G-4288)*
Kiley Machine Company........................... G 513 875-3223
  Fayetteville *(G-7466)*
Kimble Machines Inc.............................. F 419 485-8449
  Montpelier *(G-11138)*
▲ King Machine and Tool Co................... F 330 833-7217
  Massillon *(G-10117)*
Kings Welding and Fabg Inc................... F 330 738-3592
  Mechanicstown *(G-10287)*
Knape Industries Inc.............................. E 614 885-3016
  Worthington *(G-16200)*
Knight Manufacturing Co Inc................... F 740 676-9532
  Shadyside *(G-13147)*
Knowlton Machine Inc.............................. G 419 281-6802
  Ashland *(G-587)*
Knox Machine & Tool.............................. G 740 392-3133
  Mount Vernon *(G-11276)*
Knutsen Machine Products Inc................ G 216 751-6500
  Cleveland *(G-4296)*

SIC SECTION
35 INDUSTRIAL AND COMMERCIAL MACHINERY AND COMPUTER EQUIPMENT

Koester Machined Products Co .... F 419 782-0291
Defiance *(G-6688)*

Krafft and Associates Inc .... G 937 325-4671
Springfield *(G-13592)*

▲ **Kram Precision Machining Inc** .... G 937 849-1301
New Carlisle *(G-11419)*

Kramer Power Equipment Co .... F 937 456-2232
Eaton *(G-7063)*

▼ **Krendl Machine Company** .... D 419 692-3060
Delphos *(G-6768)*

Krenz Precision Machining Inc .... D 440 237-1800
North Royalton *(G-11882)*

Kuzma Industries LLC .... G 419 701-7005
Fostoria *(G-7640)*

Kyron Tool & Machine Co Inc .... F 614 231-6000
Columbus *(G-5517)*

L & L Machine Inc .... F 419 272-5000
Edon *(G-7087)*

L & M Processing LLC .... G 330 405-0615
Twinsburg *(G-14683)*

L J Manufacturing Inc .... G 440 352-1979
Mentor *(G-10488)*

Lab Quality Machining Inc .... G 513 625-0219
Goshen *(G-7993)*

Lake Park Tool & Machine LLC .... F 330 788-2437
Youngstown *(G-16387)*

Lakecraft Inc .... G 419 734-2828
Port Clinton *(G-12621)*

Lancaster Metal Products Inc .... F 740 653-3421
Lancaster *(G-9020)*

Land Specialties LLC .... G 330 663-6974
East Sparta *(G-7014)*

Langa Tool & Machine Inc .... F 440 953-1138
Willoughby *(G-15945)*

Lange Grinding & Machining Inc .... E 330 463-3500
Streetsboro *(G-13777)*

Larcom and Mitchell LLC .... G 740 595-3750
Delaware *(G-6734)*

Laserflex Corporation .... D 614 850-9600
Hilliard *(G-8418)*

Laspina Tool and Die Inc .... F 330 923-9996
Stow *(G-13705)*

Last Arrow Manufacturing LLC .... D 330 683-7777
Orrville *(G-12134)*

Latanick Equipment Inc .... E 419 433-2200
Huron *(G-8638)*

Lawrence Industries Inc .... C 216 518-1400
Cleveland *(G-4317)*

◆ **Lawrence Industries Inc** .... E 216 518-7000
Cleveland *(G-4318)*

Leader Engnrng-Fabrication Inc .... G 419 636-1731
Bryan *(G-1826)*

Lees Grinding Inc .... E 440 572-4610
Strongsville *(G-13850)*

Lehner Screw Machine LLC .... G 330 688-6616
Akron *(G-218)*

Lennox Machine Inc .... F 419 525-1020
Mansfield *(G-9678)*

Leon Newswanger .... E 419 896-3336
Shiloh *(G-13204)*

Lewis Unlimited Inc .... G 216 514-8282
Beachwood *(G-994)*

Libra Industries LLC .... C 440 974-7770
Mentor *(G-10493)*

Lightning Mold & Machine Inc .... F 440 593-6460
Conneaut *(G-5924)*

Lima Sheet Metal Machine & Mfg .... E 419 229-1161
Lima *(G-9264)*

Lincoln Electric Automtn Inc .... B 937 295-2120
Fort Loramie *(G-7603)*

Little Mountain Precision LLC .... F 440 290-2903
Mentor *(G-10495)*

Lj Manfcturing Inc Mentor Ohio .... G 440 953-3726
Mentor *(G-10496)*

Lmp Machine LLC .... G 740 596-4559
Zaleski *(G-16492)*

Lochard Inc .... D 937 492-8811
Sidney *(G-13261)*

▲ **Logan Machine Company** .... D 330 633-6163
Akron *(G-223)*

Lostcreek Tool & Machine Inc .... F 937 773-6022
Piqua *(G-12533)*

Lous Machine Company Inc .... F 513 856-9199
Hamilton *(G-8228)*

▲ **Lri Post-Acquisition Inc** .... F 419 227-2200
Lima *(G-9266)*

M & J Machine Company .... F 330 645-0042
Akron *(G-230)*

M A C Machine .... G 410 944-6171
Canton *(G-2148)*

M S B Machine Inc .... G 330 686-7740
Munroe Falls *(G-11303)*

M&D Machine LLC .... G 419 214-0201
Toledo *(G-14374)*

▲ **Machine Concepts Inc** .... E 419 628-3498
Minster *(G-11055)*

Machine Development Corp .... G 513 825-5885
Cincinnati *(G-3121)*

Machine Products Company .... E 937 890-6600
Dayton *(G-6420)*

Machine Tek Systems Inc .... E 330 527-4450
Garrettsville *(G-7921)*

▲ **Machine-Pro Technologies Inc** .... D 419 584-0086
Celina *(G-2340)*

Machining Solutions LLC .... F 419 593-0038
Wauseon *(G-15268)*

▲ **Machintek Co** .... D 513 551-1000
Fairfield *(G-7378)*

Macpro Inc .... F 513 575-3000
Loveland *(G-9492)*

Mader Automotive Center Inc .... F 937 339-2681
Troy *(G-14595)*

▼ **Magna Machine Co** .... C 513 851-6900
Cincinnati *(G-3125)*

Mainstream Waterjet LLC .... E 513 683-5426
Loveland *(G-9493)*

◆ **Majestic Manufacturing Inc** .... E 330 457-2447
New Waterford *(G-11558)*

Majestic Tool and Machine Inc .... F 440 248-5058
Solon *(G-13383)*

Mantych Metalworking Inc .... E 937 258-1373
Dayton *(G-6168)*

Manufacturing Concepts .... F 330 784-9054
Tallmadge *(G-14036)*

Mar-Con Tool Company .... E 937 299-2244
Moraine *(G-11191)*

Margo Tool Technology Inc .... F 740 653-8115
Lancaster *(G-9023)*

Marich Machine and Tool Co .... G 216 391-5502
Cleveland *(G-4358)*

Markham Machine Company Inc .... F 330 762-7676
Akron *(G-237)*

Markwith Tool Company Inc .... F 937 548-6808
Greenville *(G-8051)*

Marmax Machine Co .... G 937 698-9900
Ludlow Falls *(G-9529)*

Massillon Machine & Die Inc .... G 330 833-8913
Massillon *(G-10122)*

Master Swaging Inc .... G 937 596-6171
Jackson Center *(G-8735)*

▲ **Materials Science Intl Inc** .... E 614 870-0400
Columbus *(G-5545)*

Matrix Tool & Machine Inc .... E 440 255-0300
Mentor *(G-10500)*

Mc Brown Industries Inc .... F 419 963-2800
Findlay *(G-7536)*

McCann Tool & Die Inc .... F 330 264-8820
Wooster *(G-16150)*

▲ **McCrary Metal Polishing Co Inc** ...... F 937 492-1979
Port Jefferson *(G-12630)*

McF Industries .... F 330 526-6337
North Canton *(G-11742)*

◆ **McNeil & Nrm Inc** .... D 330 761-1855
Akron *(G-240)*

McNeil & Nrm Intl Inc .... D 330 253-2525
Akron *(G-241)*

◆ **McSwain Manufacturing LLC** .... C 513 619-1222
Cincinnati *(G-3137)*

Medway Tool Corp .... E 937 335-7717
Troy *(G-14597)*

Meldrum Mechanical Services .... F 419 535-3500
Toledo *(G-14381)*

Melinz Industries Inc .... F 440 946-3512
Willoughby *(G-15951)*

Mellott Bronze Inc .... F 330 435-6304
Creston *(G-6040)*

Met Fab Fabrication and Mch .... G 513 724-3715
Batavia *(G-933)*

Meta Manufacturing Corporation .... E 513 793-6382
Blue Ash *(G-1435)*

Metalctting Spclists Group Ltd .... G 330 962-4980
Akron *(G-245)*

◆ **Metalex Manufacturing Inc** .... C 513 489-0507
Blue Ash *(G-1437)*

Metcut Research Associates Inc .... D 513 271-5100
Cincinnati *(G-3156)*

Metro Design Inc .... E 440 458-4200
Elyria *(G-7181)*

Metzger Machine Co .... F 513 241-3360
Cincinnati *(G-3159)*

◆ **Meyer Tool Inc** .... A 513 681-7362
Cincinnati *(G-3160)*

Miami Valley Precision Inc .... F 937 866-1804
Miamisburg *(G-10657)*

Miami Vly Mfg & Assembly Inc .... F 937 254-6665
Dayton *(G-6171)*

Michael Byrne Manufacturing Co Inc .... E 419 525-1214
Mansfield *(G-9691)*

Michalek Manufacturing LLC .... G 740 763-0910
Newark *(G-11590)*

Mickes Quality Machining LLC .... G 614 746-6639
Columbus *(G-5562)*

Micro Lapping & Grinding Co .... F 216 267-6500
Cleveland *(G-4401)*

Micro Machine Ltd .... G 330 438-7078
Brewster *(G-1645)*

Micro Machine Works Inc .... F 740 678-8471
Vincent *(G-15009)*

Micron Manufacturing Inc .... D 440 355-4200
Lagrange *(G-8952)*

Midstate Machine Ohio Facility .... F 513 619-1222
Cincinnati *(G-3163)*

Midway Machining Inc .... F 740 373-8976
Marietta *(G-9809)*

Midwest Die Supply Company .... G 419 729-7141
Toledo *(G-14385)*

Midwest Laser Systems Inc .... E 419 424-0062
Alvada *(G-443)*

Midwest Machine Service Inc .... G 216 631-8151
Cleveland *(G-4411)*

Midwest Precision .... G 216 658-0058
Brooklyn Heights *(G-1695)*

Midwest Specialties Inc .... F 800 837-2503
Wapakoneta *(G-15127)*

Mike Loppe .... F 937 969-8102
Tremont City *(G-14538)*

Employee Codes: A=Over 500 employees, B=251-500
C=101-250, D=51-100, E=20-50, F=10-19, G=1-9

35 INDUSTRIAL AND COMMERCIAL MACHINERY AND COMPUTER EQUIPMENT

▲ Mil-Mar Century Corporation............. F 937 275-4860
  Miamisburg (G-10662)
Mill & Motion Inc................................. F 216 524-4000
  Independence (G-8673)
▲ Millat Industries Corp......................... D 937 434-6666
  Dayton (G-6449)
Millennium Machine Tech LLC............. F 440 269-8080
  Willoughby (G-15954)
Miller Fabrication and Welding............. G 419 884-0459
  Mansfield (G-9695)
Miller Precision Manufact.................... D 419 453-3251
  Ottoville (G-12202)
Minerva Welding and Fabg Inc............ E 330 868-7731
  Minerva (G-11036)
Miracle Welding Inc............................. G 937 746-9977
  Franklin (G-7687)
Modern Engineering Inc....................... G 440 593-5414
  Conneaut (G-5928)
Modern Industries Inc........................... G 216 432-2855
  Cleveland (G-4117)
Modern Machine Development............ F 937 253-4576
  Dayton (G-6454)
Monroe Tool and Mfg Co..................... E 216 883-7360
  Cleveland (G-4421)
Montgomery Mch Fabrication Inc........ E 740 286-2863
  Jackson (G-8718)
▲ Monti Incorporated............................. D 513 761-7775
  Cincinnati (G-3172)
Morgan Engineering Systems Inc......... E 330 545-9731
  Girard (G-7973)
Morris Technologies Inc....................... E 513 733-1611
  Cincinnati (G-3174)
Mosher Machine & Tool Co Inc............ E 937 258-8070
  Beavercreek Township (G-1085)
Mossing Machine and Tool Inc............. G 419 476-5657
  Toledo (G-14391)
Mound Manufacturing Center Inc......... F 937 236-8387
  Dayton (G-6459)
Mountaineer Industries LLC................. F 740 676-1100
  Bellaire (G-1189)
Mrt LLC... G 330 533-0721
  Canfield (G-2013)
Mt Vernon Machine & Tool Inc............. E 740 397-0311
  Mount Vernon (G-11282)
Muller Engine & Machine Co............... G 937 322-1861
  Springfield (G-13607)
Munson Machine Company Inc........... G 740 967-6867
  Johnstown (G-8774)
Murray Machine and Tool Inc............... G 216 267-1126
  Cleveland (G-4431)
Muskingum Grinding and Mch Co........ F 740 622-4741
  Coshocton (G-5986)
Mutual Tool LLC................................. E 937 667-5818
  Tipp City (G-14143)
Myers Machining Inc........................... F 330 874-3005
  Bolivar (G-1529)
Myers Precision Grinding Inc............... E 216 587-3737
  Cleveland (G-4432)
Mysta Equipment Co........................... G 330 879-5353
  Navarre (G-11347)
N & W Machining & Fabg Inc.............. G 937 695-5582
  Winchester (G-16074)
Napoleon Machine LLC....................... E 419 591-7010
  Napoleon (G-11327)
Narrow Way Custom Tech Inc.............. E 937 743-1611
  Carlisle (G-2290)
▲ Nasg Sting Rdgvlle Corners LLC....... B 419 267-5240
  Ridgeville Corners (G-12816)
Nasg Tooling and Automtn LLC........... F 419 359-5954
  Ridgeville Corners (G-12817)
National Aviation Products Inc............. G 330 688-6494
  Stow (G-13713)

▲ National Machine Company.............. C 330 688-6494
  Stow (G-13714)
◆ National Machinery LLC................... B 419 447-5211
  Tiffin (G-14095)
Nauvoo Machine LLC........................... G 440 632-1990
  Middlefield (G-10775)
Neff Machinery and Supplies............... F 740 454-0128
  Zanesville (G-16547)
Neil R Scholl Inc.................................. F 740 653-6593
  Lancaster (G-9027)
New Cut Tool and Mfg Corp................. F 740 676-1666
  Shadyside (G-13148)
New Pme Inc.. E 513 671-1717
  Cincinnati (G-3190)
New World Solutions Inc..................... G 614 271-6233
  Westerville (G-15668)
▲ Next Wave Automation LLC............. E 419 491-4520
  Perrysburg (G-12403)
▲ Nfm/Welding Engineers Inc.............. C 330 837-3868
  Massillon (G-10131)
Nichols Mold Inc................................. G 330 297-9719
  Ravenna (G-12726)
Nippon Stl Intgrted Crnkshaft.............. F 419 435-0411
  Fostoria (G-7647)
Nk Machine Inc................................... G 513 737-8035
  Hamilton (G-8232)
Nn Autocam Precision Component....... F 440 647-4711
  Wellington (G-15319)
No-Bull Tactical & Machine LLC.......... G 937 470-7687
  New Carlisle (G-11422)
Norman Noble Inc............................... D 216 761-5387
  Cleveland (G-4464)
North Amrcn Stamping Group LLC....... G 419 633-0662
  Bryan (G-1830)
North Canton Tool Co.......................... G 330 452-0545
  Canton (G-2177)
North Ridge Enterprises Inc.................. F 440 965-5300
  Norwalk (G-11981)
Northern Precision Inc......................... F 513 860-4701
  Fairfield (G-7387)
Northshore Mold Inc............................ G 440 838-8212
  Cleveland (G-4480)
Northwind Industries Inc..................... E 216 433-0666
  Cleveland (G-4481)
Norvin Hill Machinery LLC.................. F 419 752-0278
  Greenwich (G-8069)
Nova Metal Products Inc..................... E 440 269-1741
  Mentor (G-10513)
◆ Npk Construction Equipment Inc...... D 440 232-7900
  Bedford (G-1145)
Oak Industrial Inc................................ G 440 263-2780
  North Royalton (G-11889)
▲ Oakley Die & Mold Co..................... E 513 754-8500
  Mason (G-10034)
Oaks Welding Inc................................ G 330 482-4216
  Columbiana (G-5047)
▲ Odawara Automation Inc.................. E 937 667-8433
  Tipp City (G-14145)
Odyssey Machine Company Ltd.......... G 419 455-6621
  Perrysburg (G-12406)
▼ Ohio Broach & Machine Company.... E 440 946-1040
  Willoughby (G-15963)
◆ Ohio Gasket and Shim Co Inc.......... E 330 630-0626
  Akron (G-270)
Ohio Hydraulics Inc............................. E 513 771-2590
  Cincinnati (G-3215)
Ohio Metal Fabricating Inc................... F 937 233-2400
  Dayton (G-6488)
Ohio Precision Inc.............................. G 330 453-9710
  Canton (G-2186)
Ohio Roll Grinding Inc......................... E 330 453-1884
  Louisville (G-9466)

Ohio Tool Works LLC........................... D 419 281-3700
  Ashland (G-596)
Ohio Transitional Machine & Tl............ G 419 476-0820
  Toledo (G-14411)
Omega Machine & Tool Inc.................. G 440 946-6846
  Mentor (G-10515)
Ometek Inc.. D 614 861-6729
  Columbus (G-5637)
Omni Technical Products Inc............... F 216 433-1970
  Cleveland (G-4504)
OReilly Precision Pdts Inc.................... E 937 526-4677
  Russia (G-12886)
Outlook Tool Inc.................................. G 937 235-6330
  Dayton (G-6495)
Ovase Manufacturing LLC.................... F 937 275-0617
  Dayton (G-6496)
P & L Heat Trting Grinding Inc............ E 330 746-1339
  Youngstown (G-16408)
P & P Machine Tool Inc....................... G 440 232-7404
  Cleveland (G-4514)
P & P Mold & Die Inc.......................... F 330 784-8333
  Tallmadge (G-14043)
P J Tool Company Inc......................... C 937 254-2817
  Dayton (G-6497)
▲ P R Machine Works Inc................... D 419 529-5748
  Ontario (G-12094)
P2p Mfg LLC....................................... F 216 282-4110
  Cleveland (G-4518)
Palmer Products Inc............................ G 330 630-9397
  Akron (G-273)
Paramont Machine Company LLC........ F 330 339-3489
  New Philadelphia (G-11522)
Parkn Manufacturing LLC.................... F 330 723-8172
  Litchfield (G-9330)
Path Robotics Inc................................ D 614 816-1991
  Columbus (G-5659)
Path Robotics Inc................................ D 330 808-2788
  Columbus (G-5658)
Path Technologies Inc......................... G 440 358-1500
  Painesville (G-12255)
Patriot Mfg Group Inc.......................... D 937 746-2117
  Carlisle (G-2291)
Patriot Precision Products.................... G 330 966-7177
  Canton (G-2192)
Patterson Prcision Fabrication.............. G 937 631-8198
  Springfield (G-13616)
Pattons Trck & Hvy Eqp Svc Inc........... E 740 385-4067
  Logan (G-9373)
Paul Wilke & Son Inc........................... F 513 921-3163
  Cincinnati (G-3241)
PDQ Technologies Inc......................... E 937 274-4958
  Tipp City (G-14146)
Peco Holdings Corp............................. D 937 667-5705
  Tipp City (G-14147)
Pemco Inc... E 216 524-2990
  Cleveland (G-4539)
Perfect Prcision Machining Ltd............ G 330 475-0324
  Akron (G-274)
Perfecto Industries Inc......................... E 937 778-1900
  Piqua (G-12542)
Perry Welding Service Inc.................... F 330 425-2211
  Twinsburg (G-14714)
PHI Werkes LLC.................................. G 419 586-9222
  Celina (G-2344)
Phil-Matic Screw Products Inc............. F 440 942-7290
  Willoughby (G-15970)
Phillips Mfg & Mch Corp...................... G 330 823-9178
  Alliance (G-418)
Pierce-Wright Precision Inc................. G 216 362-2870
  Cleveland (G-4551)
▲ Pioneer Industrial Systems LLC........ G 419 737-9506
  Alvordton (G-444)

SIC SECTION

35 INDUSTRIAL AND COMMERCIAL MACHINERY AND COMPUTER EQUIPMENT

Pioneer Machine Inc .... G 330 948-6500
  Lodi (G-9355)
Pittman Engineering Inc .... F 330 821-4365
  Alliance (G-419)
Plas-Mac Corp .... D 440 349-3222
  Solon (G-13405)
PME of Ohio Inc .... E 513 671-1717
  Cincinnati (G-3264)
Pohl Machining Inc .... E 513 353-2929
  Cleves (G-4962)
Polytech Component Corp .... F 330 726-3235
  Youngstown (G-16421)
▲ Positech Corp .... F 513 942-7411
  Blue Ash (G-1454)
Post Products Inc .... G 330 678-0048
  Kent (G-8846)
▲ Precise Tool & Die Company Inc .... E 440 951-9173
  Willoughby (G-15976)
Precision Aircraft Components .... E 937 278-0265
  Dayton (G-6510)
Precision Assemblies Inc .... F 330 549-2630
  North Lima (G-11809)
Precision Cnc .... G 614 496-1048
  Pickerington (G-12467)
Precision Cnc LLC .... E 740 689-9009
  Lancaster (G-9032)
Precision Component & Mch Inc .... E 740 867-6366
  Chesapeake (G-2476)
Precision Component Inds LLC .... E 330 477-6287
  Canton (G-2198)
Precision Engineered Components .... F 614 436-0392
  Worthington (G-16207)
Precision Hydrlc Cnnctors Inc .... F 440 953-3778
  Euclid (G-7296)
Precision Machi Ne Tool .... G 614 564-9360
  Columbus (G-5687)
Precision Machine & Tool Co .... F 419 334-8405
  Port Clinton (G-12624)
Precision Machining Services .... E 937 222-4608
  Dayton (G-6513)
Precision McHning Srfacing Inc .... G 440 439-9850
  Bedford (G-1150)
Precision Metals Group LLC .... F 440 255-8888
  Mentor (G-10530)
▲ Precision Production LLC .... E 216 252-0372
  Strongsville (G-13869)
Precision Reflex Inc .... F 419 629-2603
  New Bremen (G-11407)
Precision Sheetrock LLC .... G 440 477-7803
  Huntsburg (G-8620)
Precision Tool Grinding Inc .... G 419 339-9959
  Elida (G-7097)
Precision Works Machine LLC .... G 330 863-0871
  Malvern (G-9615)
Premier Aerospace Group LLC .... E 937 233-8300
  Dayton (G-6518)
▲ Pride Cast Metals Inc .... D 513 541-1295
  Cincinnati (G-3274)
▲ Princeton Tool Inc .... C 440 290-8666
  Mentor (G-10531)
Pro-Gram Engineering Corp .... G 330 745-1004
  Akron (G-285)
Process Development Corp .... E 937 890-3388
  Dayton (G-6527)
Prodeva Inc .... F 937 596-6713
  Jackson Center (G-8738)
Production Design Services Inc .... D 937 866-3377
  Dayton (G-6529)
Production Tube Cutting .... G 937 299-7144
  Oakwood (G-12029)
Proficient Machining Co .... E 440 942-4942
  Mentor (G-10534)

Profile Grinding Inc .... E 216 351-0600
  Cleveland (G-4590)
Progressive Mfg Co Inc .... G 330 784-4717
  Akron (G-286)
Prohos Inc .... G 419 877-0153
  Whitehouse (G-15821)
Prohos Manufacturing Co Inc .... G 419 877-0153
  Whitehouse (G-15822)
▼ Projects Designed & Built .... E 419 726-7400
  Toledo (G-14443)
Promac Inc .... F 937 864-1961
  Enon (G-7251)
Promise Machining LLC .... G 937 305-8011
  West Alexandria (G-15343)
Proto Machine & Mfg Inc .... F 330 677-1700
  Kent (G-8849)
Pvm Incorporated .... G 614 871-0302
  Grove City (G-8117)
Qcsm LLC .... G 216 650-8731
  Cleveland (G-4602)
Qqe Summit LLC .... F 937 236-3250
  Beavercreek Township (G-1091)
▲ Quaker Mfg Corp .... C 330 332-4631
  Salem (G-13024)
Qualiturn Inc .... E 513 868-3333
  West Chester (G-15489)
Quality CNC Machining Inc .... G 440 953-0723
  Willoughby (G-15978)
Quality Craft Machine Inc .... G 330 928-4064
  Cuyahoga Falls (G-6112)
Quality Design Machining Inc .... G 440 352-7290
  Orwell (G-12169)
Quality Industries Inc .... G 216 961-5566
  Cleveland (G-4606)
▲ Quality Machining and Mfg Inc .... F 419 899-2543
  Sherwood (G-13202)
Quality Mfg Company Inc .... G 513 921-4500
  Cincinnati (G-3312)
Quality Specialists Inc .... G 440 946-9129
  Willoughby (G-15979)
Queen City Laser .... G 513 696-4444
  Lebanon (G-9105)
Queen City Tool Works Inc .... G 513 874-0111
  Fairfield (G-7401)
Quest Technologies Inc .... F 937 743-1200
  Franklin (G-7696)
Quick Service Welding & Mch Co .... F 330 673-3818
  Kent (G-8851)
R & D Custom Machine & Tl Inc .... E 419 727-1700
  Toledo (G-14446)
R & J Cylinder & Machine Inc .... D 330 364-8263
  New Philadelphia (G-11524)
R & J Tool Inc .... F 937 833-3200
  Brookville (G-1743)
R A Heller Company .... F 513 771-6100
  Cincinnati (G-3321)
R and S Technologies Inc .... F 419 483-3691
  Bellevue (G-1232)
R J K Enterprises Inc .... F 440 257-6018
  Mentor (G-10542)
▲ R R R Development Co .... D 330 966-8855
  North Canton (G-11754)
R T & T Machining Co Inc .... F 440 974-8479
  Mentor (G-10543)
R Vandewalle Inc .... G 513 921-2657
  Cincinnati (G-3322)
▲ R W Machine & Tool Inc .... F 330 296-5211
  Ravenna (G-12730)
◆ Radco Industries Inc .... F 419 531-4731
  Toledo (G-14448)
Ram Innovative Tech LLC .... F 330 956-4056
  Louisville (G-9469)

Ram Machining Inc .... G 740 333-5522
  Wshngtn Ct Hs (G-16238)
▲ Ram Precision Industries Inc .... D 937 885-7700
  Dayton (G-6538)
Randolph Tool Company Inc .... F 330 877-4923
  Hartville (G-8304)
Rankin Mfg Inc .... E 419 929-8338
  New London (G-11466)
Ray-Tech Industries LLC .... G 419 923-0169
  Lyons (G-9533)
Reese Machine Company Inc .... F 440 992-3942
  Ashtabula (G-657)
Reilloc Machine Co Inc .... G 330 601-0379
  Wooster (G-16162)
Remington Engrg Machining Inc .... G 513 965-8999
  Milford (G-10920)
Reno Machine .... G 419 836-3093
  Curtice (G-6058)
Repko Machine Inc .... G 216 267-1144
  Cleveland (G-4625)
Reuther Mold & Mfg Co Inc .... D 330 923-5266
  Cuyahoga Falls (G-6114)
Revolution Machine Works Inc .... G 706 505-6525
  Cleveland (G-4630)
▲ Reymond Products Intl Inc .... E 330 339-3583
  New Philadelphia (G-11525)
Reynolds Machinery Inc .... F 937 847-8121
  Dayton (G-6548)
RI Alto Mfg Inc .... F 740 914-4230
  Marion (G-9876)
Richmond Machine Co .... E 419 485-5740
  Montpelier (G-11142)
Ridge Machine & Welding Co .... G 740 537-2821
  Toronto (G-14534)
Riffle Machine Works Inc .... G 740 775-2838
  Chillicothe (G-2532)
Rimeco Products Inc .... E 440 918-1220
  Willoughby (G-15983)
Risher & Co .... E 216 732-8351
  Euclid (G-7299)
Ritime Incorporated .... G 330 273-3443
  Cleveland (G-4636)
Riverside Marine Inds Inc .... D 419 729-1621
  Toledo (G-14453)
Riverside Mch & Automtn Inc .... D 419 855-8308
  Genoa (G-7949)
Rjs Machine Shop Services LLC .... G 937 927-0137
  Seaman (G-13115)
◆ RL Best Company .... E 330 758-8601
  Boardman (G-1517)
RL Craig Inc .... F 330 424-1525
  Lisbon (G-9326)
Rmt Corporation .... F 937 274-2121
  Dayton (G-6551)
Robert Long Manufacturing Co .... G 330 678-0911
  Kent (G-8854)
Robert Smart Inc .... F 330 454-8881
  Canton (G-2219)
Roberts Machine Products LLC .... F 937 682-4015
  Rushsylvania (G-12875)
▲ Roberts Manufacturing Co Inc .... E 419 594-2712
  Oakwood (G-12032)
Robey Tool Inc .... G 614 251-0412
  Columbus (G-5729)
Rochester Manufacturing Inc .... F 440 647-2463
  Wellington (G-15321)
Roerig Machine .... G 440 647-4718
  New London (G-11467)
Rogar International Inc .... F 419 476-5500
  Toledo (G-14458)
Rolling Enterprises Inc .... E 937 866-4917
  Moraine (G-11208)

Employee Codes: A=Over 500 employees, B=251-500
C=101-250, D=51-100, E=20-50, F=10-19, G=1-9

2024 Harris Ohio
Industrial Directory

915

35 INDUSTRIAL AND COMMERCIAL MACHINERY AND COMPUTER EQUIPMENT

Rotary Smer Spcalist Group LLC............ G 330 299-8210
  Barberton *(G-895)*
Royalton Industries Inc......................... F 440 748-9900
  Columbia Station *(G-5020)*
Royalton Manufacturing Inc.................. E 440 237-2233
  Akron *(G-311)*
Rpg Industries Inc................................. G 937 698-9801
  Tipp City *(G-14153)*
RTZ Manufacturing Co........................... G 614 848-8366
  Heath *(G-8330)*
Rw Screw LLC....................................... E 330 837-9211
  Massillon *(G-10141)*
S and S Tool Inc................................... G 440 593-4000
  Conneaut *(G-5931)*
S R P M Inc.. E 440 248-8440
  Cleveland *(G-4667)*
S T Tool & Design Inc........................... F 440 357-1250
  Mentor *(G-10550)*
S-P Company Inc................................. D 330 782-5651
  Columbiana *(G-5050)*
Salco Machine Inc................................ E 330 456-8281
  Louisville *(G-9470)*
Salem Manufacturing & Sls Inc............. G 614 572-4242
  Columbus *(G-5741)*
Sample Machining Inc........................... E 937 258-3338
  Dayton *(G-6558)*
Sandusky Machine & Tool Inc.............. E 419 626-8359
  Sandusky *(G-13091)*
▲ Sattler Companies Inc....................... E 330 239-2552
  Wadsworth *(G-15065)*
Schaffer Grinding Co Inc...................... F 323 724-4476
  Twinsburg *(G-14733)*
Schmidt Machine Company................... E 419 294-3814
  Upper Sandusky *(G-14823)*
Schmitmeyer Inc................................... G 937 295-2091
  Fort Loramie *(G-7607)*
Schwab Machine Inc............................. G 419 626-0245
  Sandusky *(G-13093)*
Sebring Fluid Power Corp..................... G 330 938-9984
  Sebring *(G-13126)*
Seco Machine Inc................................. E 330 499-2150
  North Canton *(G-11759)*
Secondary Machining Svcs Inc.............. G 440 593-3040
  Conneaut *(G-5932)*
Seebach Inc.. F 937 275-3565
  Dayton *(G-6566)*
Select Machine Inc............................... F 330 678-7676
  Kent *(G-8862)*
Selecteon Corporation........................... E 614 710-1132
  Columbus *(G-5758)*
Self Made Holdings LLC....................... G 330 477-1052
  Canton *(G-2220)*
▲ Semco Inc.. D 800 848-5764
  Marion *(G-9880)*
Sepma Technologies LLC...................... G 937 660-3783
  Kettering *(G-8910)*
Sequa Can Machinery Inc..................... E 330 493-0444
  Canton *(G-2221)*
Shore Precision LLC............................. G 330 704-0552
  Uniontown *(G-14793)*
Shoreline Machine Products Co............. F 216 481-8033
  Cleveland *(G-4698)*
Short Run Machine Products Inc.......... F 440 969-1313
  Ashtabula *(G-660)*
▲ Siebtechnik Tema Inc....................... E 513 489-7811
  Cincinnati *(G-3390)*
Sk Mold & Tool Inc.............................. E 937 339-0299
  Troy *(G-14610)*
Sk Mold & Tool Inc.............................. E 937 339-0299
  Tipp City *(G-14155)*
Skinner Machining Co........................... G 216 486-6630
  Willoughby *(G-15992)*

Slabe... G 440 298-3693
  Thompson *(G-14064)*
▲ Slabe Machine Products LLC............ D 440 946-6555
  Willoughby *(G-15994)*
Slimline Surgical Devices LLC............. G 937 335-0496
  Troy *(G-14611)*
Smith Machine Inc................................ G 330 821-9898
  Alliance *(G-425)*
Solmet Drilling Solutions LLC.............. F 330 455-4328
  Canton *(G-2227)*
Southeastern Shafting Mfg Inc............. F 740 342-4629
  New Lexington *(G-11457)*
Southern Ohio Mfg Inc......................... E 513 943-2555
  Amelia *(G-465)*
Southstern McHning Feld Svc In.......... E 740 689-1147
  Lancaster *(G-9040)*
Special Machined Components.............. G 513 459-1113
  Mason *(G-10059)*
Specialty Machines Inc.......................... E 937 837-8852
  Dayton *(G-6581)*
Spectrum Machine Inc.......................... F 330 626-3666
  Streetsboro *(G-13793)*
Spence Technologies Inc....................... F 440 946-3035
  Willoughby *(G-15996)*
▲ Spirex Corporation............................ C 330 726-1166
  Youngstown *(G-16446)*
Sponseller Group Inc............................ G 937 492-9949
  Sidney *(G-13289)*
Sponseller Group Inc............................ E 419 861-3000
  Holland *(G-8531)*
Spz Machine Company Inc................... G 330 848-3286
  Norton *(G-11949)*
SRS Manufacturing Corp....................... E 937 746-3086
  Franklin *(G-7703)*
Stafford Gage & Tool Inc..................... G 937 277-9944
  Dayton *(G-6588)*
Stan-Kell LLC....................................... E 440 998-1116
  Ashtabula *(G-661)*
▲ Stanco Precision Mfg Inc.................. G 937 274-1785
  Dayton *(G-6589)*
Standard Aero Inc................................ F 937 840-1053
  Hillsboro *(G-8467)*
Standard Jig Boring Svc LLC................ D 330 644-5405
  Akron *(G-335)*
▲ Standard Jig Boring Svc LLC............ E 330 896-9530
  Akron *(G-334)*
Standard Machine Inc........................... E 216 631-4440
  Cleveland *(G-4728)*
◆ Standby Screw Machine Pdts Co....... B 440 243-8200
  Berea *(G-1294)*
▼ Stanley Industries Inc....................... E 216 475-4000
  Cleveland *(G-4730)*
Star Metal Products Co Inc.................. C 440 899-7000
  Westlake *(G-15791)*
▼ Stark Industrial LLC......................... E 330 966-8108
  North Canton *(G-11763)*
Starwin Industries LLC......................... G 937 293-8568
  Dayton *(G-6591)*
Staub Laser Cutting Inc....................... E 937 890-4486
  Dayton *(G-6593)*
Std Liquidation Inc................................ C 937 492-6121
  Sidney *(G-13290)*
▲ Steck Manufacturing Co LLC............. F 937 222-0062
  Dayton *(G-6594)*
▲ Steel Eqp Specialists Inc.................. D 330 823-8260
  Alliance *(G-427)*
Steel Products Corp Akron................... E 330 688-6633
  Stow *(G-13727)*
Stefra Inc.. G 440 846-8240
  Strongsville *(G-13885)*
Stegemeyer Machine Inc....................... G 513 321-5651
  Cincinnati *(G-3420)*

Steinbarger Precision Cnc Inc................ G 937 376-0322
  Xenia *(G-16273)*
Steinert Industries Inc.......................... F 330 678-0028
  Kent *(G-8868)*
Stevenson Mfg Co................................. G 330 532-1581
  Wellsville *(G-15337)*
Strassells Machine Inc.......................... F 419 747-1088
  Mansfield *(G-9722)*
Stryver Mfg Inc..................................... E 937 854-3048
  Trotwood *(G-14546)*
Suburban Manufacturing Co................... D 440 953-2024
  Eastlake *(G-7050)*
Sulecki Precision Products Inc.............. F 440 255-5454
  Mentor *(G-10569)*
▲ Summit Machine Ltd......................... E 330 628-2663
  Mogadore *(G-11085)*
Summit Machining Co Ltd..................... F 330 628-2663
  Mogadore *(G-11086)*
Sunset Industries Inc............................ E 440 306-8284
  Mentor *(G-10570)*
Superalloy Mfg Solutions Corp.............. F 510 000-0000
  Blue Ash *(G-1474)*
Superfine Manufacturing Inc................. F 330 897-9024
  Fresno *(G-7825)*
Superfinishers Inc................................. G 330 467-2125
  Macedonia *(G-9582)*
Superior Machine Tool Inc.................... F 419 675-2363
  Kenton *(G-8901)*
Superior Mold & Die Co........................ F 330 688-8251
  Munroe Falls *(G-11306)*
Superior Precision Products.................. G 216 881-3696
  Cleveland *(G-4749)*
▲ Superior Quality Machine Co............. G 330 527-7146
  Garrettsville *(G-7925)*
Superior Welding Co............................. F 614 252-8539
  Columbus *(G-5801)*
Swagelok Company................................ E 440 461-7714
  Cleveland *(G-4759)*
Swagelok Company................................ E 440 349-5652
  Solon *(G-13429)*
Swagelok Company................................ E 440 349-5836
  Solon *(G-13430)*
Swagelok Company................................ D 440 248-4600
  Willoughby Hills *(G-16029)*
◆ Swagelok Company............................ A 440 248-4600
  Solon *(G-13428)*
Swanton Wldg Machining Co Inc.......... D 419 826-4816
  Swanton *(G-13984)*
Swihart Industries Inc........................... E 937 277-4796
  Dayton *(G-6603)*
Systech Handling Inc............................ F 419 445-8226
  Archbold *(G-547)*
T & S Machine Inc................................ F 419 453-2101
  Wapakoneta *(G-15130)*
T-Mac Machine Inc............................... G 330 673-0621
  Kent *(G-8870)*
T&T Machine Inc................................... F 440 354-0605
  Painesville *(G-12265)*
Tahoma Engineered Solutions Inc......... E 330 345-6169
  Ashland *(G-617)*
Tahoma Machining Ltd.......................... F 330 952-2410
  Medina *(G-10383)*
Tailored Systems Inc............................. G 937 299-3900
  Moraine *(G-11213)*
Tarman Machine Company Inc.............. F 614 834-4010
  Canal Winchester *(G-1992)*
Tat Machine & Tool Ltd........................ G 419 836-7706
  Curtice *(G-6059)*
TDS-Bf/Ls Holdings Inc........................ E 440 327-5800
  North Ridgeville *(G-11862)*
▲ Te-Co Manufacturing LLC.................. D 937 836-0961
  Englewood *(G-7244)*

35 INDUSTRIAL AND COMMERCIAL MACHINERY AND COMPUTER EQUIPMENT

Technology House Ltd .... D 440 248-3025
  Solon (G-13435)
Ted M Figgins .... F 740 277-3750
  Lancaster (G-9042)
Tegr Inc .... E 419 678-4991
  Saint Henry (G-12939)
Tek Gear & Machine Inc .... G 330 455-3331
  Canton (G-2242)
Tek Group International .... E 330 706-0000
  Canal Fulton (G-1976)
Tekraft Industries Inc .... G 440 352-8321
  Painesville (G-12268)
Telcon LLC .... D 330 562-5566
  Streetsboro (G-13796)
Ten Mfg LLC .... F 440 487-1100
  Mentor (G-10574)
Tenney Tool & Supply Co .... G 330 666-2807
  Barberton (G-899)
Terydon Inc .... E 330 879-2448
  Navarre (G-11353)
Tessa Precision Product Inc .... E 440 392-3470
  Painesville (G-12269)
Tessec LLC .... D 937 576-0010
  Dayton (G-6615)
Tgm LLC .... F 419 636-8567
  Bryan (G-1839)
The Kordenbrock Tool and Die Co ..... F 513 326-4390
  Cincinnati (G-3449)
Thees Machine & Tool Company ..... G 419 586-4766
  Celina (G-2352)
Ti Inc .... E 419 332-8484
  Fremont (G-7815)
Tiffin Foundry & Machine Inc ...... E 419 447-3991
  Tiffin (G-14109)
Timekap Inc .... G 330 747-2122
  Youngstown (G-16455)
▼ Timkensteel Material Svcs LLC ...... C 281 449-0319
  Canton (G-2246)
Tipp Machine & Tool Inc .... C 937 890-8428
  Dayton (G-6625)
Tm Machine & Tool Inc .... G 419 478-0310
  Toledo (G-14488)
Todd Industries Inc .... E 440 439-2900
  Cleveland (G-4799)
Toledo Machining Inc .... G 419 343-7738
  Toledo (G-14497)
Toledo Precision Machining LLC .... G 419 724-3010
  Toledo (G-14502)
Tom Barbour Auto Parts Inc .... F 740 354-4654
  Portsmouth (G-12659)
Tool and Die Welding .... G 513 265-3095
  Middletown (G-10867)
Toolbold Corporation .... E 216 676-9840
  Cleveland (G-4803)
Tooling & Components Corp .... F 419 478-9122
  Toledo (G-14510)
Total Manufacturing Co Inc .... E 440 205-9700
  Mentor (G-10578)
Total Quality Machining Inc .... F 937 746-7765
  Franklin (G-7706)
Total Repair Express Mich LLC .... F 248 690-9410
  Stow (G-13731)
Tq Manufacturing Company Inc .... F 440 255-9000
  Mentor (G-10579)
Tracer Specialties Inc .... G 216 696-2363
  Cleveland (G-4813)
Tradye Machine & Tool Inc .... G 740 625-7550
  Centerburg (G-2358)
▲ Trailer Component Mfg Inc .... G 440 255-2888
  Mentor (G-10580)
Treadway Manufacturing LLC ..... G 937 266-3423
  Dayton (G-6630)

Trec Industries Inc .... F 216 741-4114
  Cleveland (G-4819)
Tri-R Tooling Inc .... F 419 522-8665
  Mansfield (G-9728)
Triangle Precision Industries ...... D 937 299-6776
  Dayton (G-6632)
Trico Machine Products Corp ..... F 216 662-4194
  Cleveland (G-4828)
Trinel Inc .... F 216 265-9190
  Cleveland (G-4831)
Trotwood Corporation .... F 937 854-3047
  Trotwood (G-14547)
Troy Manufacturing Co .... E 440 834-8262
  Burton (G-1888)
Tru-Bore Machine Co Inc .... G 330 928-6215
  Cuyahoga Falls (G-6124)
Tru-Fab Technology Inc .... F 440 954-9760
  Willoughby (G-16009)
Trucast Inc .... D 440 942-4923
  Willoughby (G-16010)
True Step LLC .... F 513 933-0933
  Lebanon (G-9116)
Trulou Holdings Inc .... E 513 347-0100
  Cincinnati (G-3471)
Trust Manufacturing LLC .... G 216 531-8787
  Euclid (G-7304)
Trv Incorporated .... E 440 951-7722
  Willoughby (G-16011)
TSR Machinery Services Inc ...... E 513 874-9697
  Fairfield (G-7420)
TSS Acquisition Company .... G 513 772-7000
  Cincinnati (G-3473)
▲ Tsw Industries Inc .... E 440 572-7200
  Strongsville (G-13892)
Tubular Techniques Inc .... G 614 529-4130
  Hilliard (G-8450)
Turn & Earn Corporation .... G 516 761-0236
  Westerville (G-15685)
Turn-All Machine & Gear Co .... F 937 342-8710
  Springfield (G-13652)
Turner Machine Co .... F 330 332-5821
  Salem (G-13035)
Twin Creek Mfg LLC .... G 937 634-3470
  Camden (G-1964)
Twin Valley Metalcraft Asm LLC .... G 937 787-4634
  West Alexandria (G-15345)
U S Alloy Die Corp .... F 216 749-9700
  Cleveland (G-4842)
Ultra Machine Inc .... G 440 323-7632
  Elyria (G-7214)
▲ Ultra Tech Machinery Inc .... E 330 929-5544
  Cuyahoga Falls (G-6126)
◆ Ultra-Met Company .... D 937 653-7133
  Urbana (G-14850)
▲ United Grinding and Machine Co ..... E 330 453-7402
  Canton (G-2254)
United Machine and Tool Inc ...... G 440 946-7677
  Eastlake (G-7053)
▲ United Precision Services Inc ...... G 513 851-6900
  Cincinnati (G-3481)
United Tool and Machine Inc ...... F 937 843-5603
  Lakeview (G-8961)
▲ Universal Fabg Cnstr Svcs Inc .... E 614 274-1128
  Columbus (G-5845)
▼ Universal Grinding Corporation .... E 216 631-9410
  Cleveland (G-4849)
Universal J&Z Machine LLC ...... E 216 486-2220
  Willoughby (G-16013)
Universal Tool Technology LLC .... F 937 222-4608
  Dayton (G-6640)
Valley Machine Tool Inc .... E 513 899-2737
  Morrow (G-11227)

Valmac Industries Inc .... E 937 890-5558
  Vandalia (G-14964)
Vectron Inc .... E 440 323-3369
  Elyria (G-7216)
▲ Ver-Mac Industries Inc .... E 740 397-6511
  Mount Vernon (G-11299)
Verhoff Machine & Welding Inc .... C 419 596-3202
  Continental (G-5939)
Versatile Machine .... G 330 618-9895
  Tallmadge (G-14056)
Versi-Tech Incorporated .... F 586 944-2230
  Apple Creek (G-512)
Vicas Manufacturing Co Inc .... E 513 791-7741
  Cincinnati (G-3498)
Vics Turning Coinc .... G 216 531-5016
  Cleveland (G-4872)
Vision Manufacturing Inc .... F 937 332-1801
  Troy (G-14615)
Vision Projects Inc .... G 937 667-8648
  Tipp City (G-14164)
Vrc Inc .... D 440 243-6666
  Berea (G-1299)
Vtd Systems Inc .... E 440 323-4122
  Elyria (G-7217)
Wade Dynamics Inc .... G 216 431-8484
  Cleveland (G-4890)
▲ Wagner Machine Inc .... E 330 706-0700
  Norton (G-11951)
Walest Incorporated .... G 216 362-8110
  Brunswick (G-1800)
◆ Warren Fabricating Corporation .... D 330 534-5017
  Hubbard (G-8572)
Wavy Ticket LLC .... E 513 827-0886
  Okeana (G-12068)
Wedgeworks Mch TI Boring Inc .... G 216 441-1200
  Cleveland (G-4899)
Wellex AMG .... G 513 734-1700
  Amelia (G-470)
Wellex Manufacturing Inc .... G 513 734-1700
  Amelia (G-471)
Wenrick Machine and Tool Corp .... F 937 667-7307
  Tipp City (G-14166)
Wesco Machine Inc .... F 330 688-6973
  Ravenna (G-12742)
▲ Westbrook Mfg Inc .... B 937 254-2004
  Dayton (G-6650)
Western Cutterheads LLC .... G 270 665-5302
  Fredericksburg (G-7734)
White Machine Inc .... G 440 237-3282
  North Royalton (G-11902)
White Machine & Mfg Co .... F 740 453-5451
  Zanesville (G-16570)
Whitebrook Inc .... G 330 575-7405
  Canton (G-2269)
Whitt Machine Inc .... F 513 423-7624
  Middletown (G-10872)
Will-Burt Company .... F 330 682-7015
  Orrville (G-12162)
▲ Will-Burt Company .... C 330 682-7015
  Orrville (G-12163)
Willis Cnc .... F 440 926-0434
  Grafton (G-8007)
Willow Tool & Machining Ltd ..... F 440 572-2288
  Strongsville (G-13896)
Wipe Out Enterprises Inc .... G 937 497-9473
  Sidney (G-13296)
Wire Shop Inc .... E 440 354-6842
  Mentor (G-10596)
Wise Edge LLC .... G 330 208-0889
  Akron (G-376)
Wismar Prcsion Toling Prod Inc .... F 440 296-0487
  Mentor (G-10597)

Employee Codes: A=Over 500 employees, B=251-500
C=101-250, D=51-100, E=20-50, F=10-19, G=1-9

2024 Harris Ohio
Industrial Directory

35 INDUSTRIAL AND COMMERCIAL MACHINERY AND COMPUTER EQUIPMENT

Wm Plotz Machine and Forge Co............... E 216 861-0441
   Cleveland *(G-4915)*

Wodin Inc.. E 440 439-4222
   Cleveland *(G-4916)*

Wolfe Grinding Inc............................... G 330 929-6677
   Stow *(G-13739)*

Wolff Tool & Mfg Company Inc............. F 440 933-7797
   Avon Lake *(G-829)*

Wonder Machine Services Inc............... E 440 937-7500
   Avon *(G-792)*

Wray Precision Products Inc................ G 513 228-5000
   Lebanon *(G-9121)*

Wrong Turn Fabrication LLC................ G 330 802-8686
   Rootstown *(G-12858)*

Wulco Inc.. D 513 679-2600
   Cincinnati *(G-3530)*

Wulco Inc.. D 513 379-6115
   Hamilton *(G-8259)*

▲ Wulco Inc....................................... D 513 679-2600
   Cincinnati *(G-3529)*

X-Mil Inc... E 937 444-1323
   Mount Orab *(G-11248)*

Xact Spec Industries LLC..................... G 440 543-8157
   Chagrin Falls *(G-2437)*

Xact Spec Industries LLC..................... E 440 543-8157
   Chagrin Falls *(G-2436)*

Youngstown Hard Chrome Pltg Gr........ E 330 758-9721
   Youngstown *(G-16482)*

Zeiger Industries Inc........................... E 330 484-4413
   Canton *(G-2272)*

Zephyr Industries Inc.......................... G 419 281-4485
   Ashland *(G-621)*

36 ELECTRONIC & OTHER ELECTRICAL EQUIPMENT & COMPONENTS

3612 Transformers, except electric

ABB Inc... F 614 818-6300
   Westerville *(G-15646)*

Acuity Brands Lighting Inc................... D 740 349-4343
   Newark *(G-11560)*

▲ AES Beaver Valley LLC.................... D
   Dayton *(G-6151)*

◆ Ajax Tocco Magnethermic Corp........ C 800 547-1527
   Warren *(G-15135)*

Arisdyne Systems Inc.......................... F 216 458-1991
   Cleveland *(G-3674)*

Clark Substations LLC......................... F 330 452-5200
   Canton *(G-2077)*

Contact Industries Inc......................... E 419 884-9788
   Lexington *(G-9200)*

▲ Control Transformer Inc.................. E 330 637-6015
   Cortland *(G-5961)*

Custom Coil & Transformer Co............. G 740 452-5211
   Zanesville *(G-16525)*

Darrah Electric Company...................... F 216 631-0912
   Cleveland *(G-3942)*

Dongan Electric Mfg Co....................... G 419 737-2304
   Pioneer *(G-12491)*

E Technologies Inc.............................. G 440 247-7000
   Chagrin Falls *(G-2374)*

▲ Eaton Electric Holdings LLC............. B 440 523-5000
   Cleveland *(G-3995)*

Eaton Leasing Corporation................... B 216 382-2292
   Beachwood *(G-986)*

Fishel Company................................... C 614 850-4400
   Columbus *(G-5377)*

◆ Foster Transformer Company........... E 513 681-2420
   Cincinnati *(G-2919)*

▲ Fostoria Bshngs Inslators Corp........ G 419 435-7514
   Fostoria *(G-7633)*

▲ Fostoria Bushings Inc..................... G 419 435-7514
   Fostoria *(G-7634)*

General Electric Company.................... E 216 883-1000
   Cleveland *(G-4115)*

Hannon Company................................. D 330 456-4728
   Canton *(G-2121)*

Ignition Systems Inc........................... F 330 653-9674
   Hudson *(G-8598)*

▲ LTI Power Systems Inc.................... E 440 327-5050
   Elyria *(G-7176)*

M & S Equipment Leasing Co................ F 216 662-8800
   Cleveland *(G-4343)*

▼ Matlock Electric Co Inc.................... E 513 731-9600
   Cincinnati *(G-3134)*

Millennium Cell Inc............................. G 614 688-5160
   Columbus *(G-5569)*

Morlan & Associates Inc...................... F 614 889-6152
   Hilliard *(G-8421)*

▼ Morlan & Associates Inc.................. F 614 889-6152
   Hilliard *(G-8422)*

▼ Norlake Manufacturing Company...... D 440 350-0200
   North Ridgeville *(G-11851)*

Npas Inc... F 614 595-6916
   Mansfield *(G-9706)*

◆ Ohio Semitronics Inc...................... D 614 777-1005
   Hilliard *(G-8427)*

▲ Otc Services Inc............................. D 330 871-2444
   Louisville *(G-9467)*

Peak Electric Inc................................. F 419 726-4848
   Toledo *(G-14430)*

Pmp Industries Inc.............................. G 513 563-3028
   Blue Ash *(G-1453)*

▲ Qualtek Electronics Corp................. C 440 951-3300
   Mentor *(G-10541)*

Schneider Electric Usa Inc................... B 513 523-4171
   Oxford *(G-12213)*

Schneider Electric Usa Inc................... D 513 777-4445
   West Chester *(G-15506)*

◆ SGB Usa Inc................................... G 330 472-1187
   Tallmadge *(G-14046)*

Siemens Industry Inc.......................... E 937 593-6010
   Bellefontaine *(G-1219)*

Spectre Sensors Inc............................ G 440 250-0372
   Westlake *(G-15790)*

Staco Energy Products Co................... E 937 253-1191
   Dayton *(G-6587)*

◆ Staco Energy Products Co............... G 937 253-1191
   Miamisburg *(G-10685)*

Tesa Inc... G 614 847-8200
   Lewis Center *(G-9181)*

Transformer Associates Limited........... G 330 430-0750
   Canton *(G-2247)*

3613 Switchgear and switchboard apparatus

ABB Inc... F 614 818-6300
   Westerville *(G-15646)*

Acorn Technology Corporation............. E 216 663-1244
   Shaker Heights *(G-13149)*

Adgo Incorporated.............................. E 513 752-6880
   Cincinnati *(G-2550)*

All Pack Services LLC.......................... G 614 935-0964
   Grove City *(G-8076)*

▲ Altronic LLC.................................. C 330 545-9768
   Girard *(G-7960)*

▲ American Controls Inc.................... E 440 944-9735
   Wickliffe *(G-15824)*

Asco Power Technologies LP............... C 216 573-7600
   Cleveland *(G-3685)*

Assembly Works Inc............................ G 419 433-5010
   Huron *(G-8628)*

Avtron Loadbank Inc........................... C 216 573-7600
   Cleveland *(G-3711)*

Bcs Technologies Ltd.......................... F 513 829-4577
   Fairfield *(G-7337)*

Bentronix Corp.................................... G 440 632-0606
   Middlefield *(G-10734)*

CDI Industries Inc............................... E 440 243-1100
   Cleveland *(G-3802)*

Columbus Controls Inc........................ E 614 882-9029
   Columbus *(G-5264)*

Control Craft LLC................................ F 513 674-0056
   Cincinnati *(G-2791)*

▲ Control Interface Inc...................... G 513 874-2062
   West Chester *(G-15405)*

Custom Craft Controls Inc................... F 330 630-9599
   Akron *(G-120)*

◆ Delta Systems Inc.......................... B 330 626-2811
   Streetsboro *(G-13765)*

Eaton Corporation............................... E 513 387-2000
   West Chester *(G-15421)*

▲ Eaton Electric Holdings LLC............. B 440 523-5000
   Cleveland *(G-3995)*

Electro Controls Inc............................ E 866 497-1717
   Sidney *(G-13245)*

Emerson Network Power...................... F 614 841-8054
   Ironton *(G-8697)*

Epanel Plus Ltd.................................. G 513 772-0888
   Cincinnati *(G-2879)*

▲ Etched Metal Company.................... E 440 248-0240
   Solon *(G-13347)*

Flood Heliarc Inc................................ F 614 835-3929
   Groveport *(G-8140)*

General Electric Company.................... E 216 883-1000
   Cleveland *(G-4115)*

Hy-Tech Controls Inc.......................... E 440 232-4040
   Bedford *(G-1125)*

◆ Ideal Electric Power Co................... E 419 522-3611
   Mansfield *(G-9669)*

Industrial and Mar Eng Svc Co............. F 740 694-0791
   Fredericktown *(G-7749)*

Industrial Ctrl Dsign Mnt Inc............... F 330 785-9840
   Tallmadge *(G-14033)*

Industrial Solutions Inc....................... E 614 431-8118
   Lewis Center *(G-9163)*

◆ Industrial Thermal Systems Inc....... F 513 561-2100
   Cincinnati *(G-3022)*

Innovative Control Systems................. G 513 894-3712
   Fairfield Township *(G-7431)*

Innovative Controls Corp..................... E 419 691-6684
   Toledo *(G-14333)*

▲ Instrmntation Ctrl Systems Inc........ E 513 662-2600
   Cincinnati *(G-3024)*

International Bus Mchs Corp................ S 513 826-1001
   Cincinnati *(G-3029)*

Jeff Bonham Electric Inc...................... E 937 233-7662
   Dayton *(G-6388)*

▲ Joslyn Hi-Voltage Company LLC....... C 216 271-6600
   Cleveland *(G-4261)*

Koester Corporation............................ E 419 599-0291
   Napoleon *(G-11322)*

Layerzero Power Systems Inc.............. E 440 399-9000
   Aurora *(G-721)*

Marathon Special Products Corp.......... C 419 352-8441
   Bowling Green *(G-1573)*

Mercury Iron and Steel Co................... F 440 349-1500
   Solon *(G-13385)*

Milathan Wholesalers.......................... E 614 697-1458
   Columbus *(G-5568)*

◆ Myers Power Products Inc............... C 330 834-3200
   North Canton *(G-11747)*

Npas Inc... F 614 595-6916
   Mansfield *(G-9706)*

▲ Osborne Coinage Company LLC........ D 877 480-0456
   Blue Ash *(G-1448)*

36 ELECTRONIC & OTHER ELECTRICAL EQUIPMENT & COMPONENTS

▲ Pacs Industries Inc .... D 740 397-5021
  Mount Vernon (G-11285)
Panel Master LLC .... E 440 355-4442
  Lagrange (G-8954)
Panel-Fab Inc .... D 513 771-1462
  Cincinnati (G-3234)
Panelmatic Inc .... E 330 782-8007
  Youngstown (G-16412)
Panelmatic Bldg Solutions Inc .... E 330 619-5235
  Brookfield (G-1672)
Panelmatic Cincinnati Inc .... E 513 829-1960
  Fairfield (G-7392)
▼ Panelmatic Youngstown Inc .... E 330 782-8007
  Youngstown (G-16413)
Primex .... E 513 831-9959
  Milford (G-10919)
Regal Beloit America Inc .... C 419 352-8441
  Bowling Green (G-1588)
Roemer Industries Inc .... D 330 448-2000
  Masury (G-10158)
Schneider Automation Inc .... C 612 426-0709
  Fairfield (G-7405)
Schneider Electric Usa Inc .... D 513 777-4445
  West Chester (G-15506)
Scott Fetzer Company .... C 216 267-9000
  Cleveland (G-4678)
Siemens Industry Inc .... E 937 593-6010
  Bellefontaine (G-1219)
▲ Spectra-Tech Manufacturing Inc .... E 513 735-9300
  Batavia (G-949)
Star Distribution and Mfg LLC .... E 513 860-3573
  West Chester (G-15590)
Tcb Automation LLC .... F 330 556-6444
  Dover (G-6847)
Te Connectivity Corporation .... C 419 521-9500
  Mansfield (G-9725)
Toledo Transducers Inc .... E 419 724-4170
  Maumee (G-10242)
▲ Trucut Incorporated .... D 330 938-9806
  Sebring (G-13127)
UCI Controls Inc .... E 216 398-0330
  Cleveland (G-4843)
◆ United Rolls Inc .... D 330 456-2761
  Canton (G-2255)
Vacuum Electric Switch Co Inc .... F 330 374-5156
  Mogadore (G-11089)
Vertiv Corporation .... G 614 888-0246
  Lockbourne (G-9341)
◆ Vertiv Corporation .... A 614 888-0246
  Westerville (G-15686)
▲ Westbrook Mfg Inc .... B 937 254-2004
  Dayton (G-6650)

3621 Motors and generators

Accurate Electronics Inc .... C 330 682-7015
  Orrville (G-12116)
Allied Motion At Dayton .... F 937 228-3171
  Dayton (G-6194)
Ametek Tchnical Indus Pdts Inc .... D 330 673-3451
  Kent (G-8799)
Ares Inc .... D 419 635-2175
  Port Clinton (G-12615)
Babcock & Wilcox Entps Inc .... C 330 753-4511
  Akron (G-74)
Battle Motors Inc .... C 888 328-5443
  New Philadelphia (G-11486)
Brinkley Technology Group LLC .... F 330 830-2498
  Massillon (G-10079)
Bwx Technologies Inc .... D 740 687-4180
  Lancaster (G-8996)
Carter Carburetor LLC .... A 216 314-2711
  Cleveland (G-3796)

Charles Auto Electric Co Inc .... G 330 535-6269
  Akron (G-106)
Chemequip Sales Inc .... E 330 724-8300
  Coventry Township (G-6007)
City Machine Technologies Inc .... F 330 747-2639
  Youngstown (G-16336)
Cleveland Wind Company LLC .... G 216 269-7667
  Cleveland (G-3860)
Crescent & Sprague .... F 740 373-2331
  Marietta (G-9787)
Cummins Inc .... E 614 604-6004
  Grove City (G-8085)
Custom Coil & Transformer Co .... G 740 452-5211
  Zanesville (G-16525)
◆ Dayton-Phoenix Group Inc .... D 937 496-3900
  Dayton (G-6292)
◆ Dcm Manufacturing Inc .... E 216 265-8006
  Cleveland (G-3948)
◆ Dreison International Inc .... C 216 362-0755
  Cleveland (G-3972)
Eagle Machining LLC .... C 419 237-1366
  Fayette (G-7462)
Electric Service Co Inc .... E 513 271-6387
  Cincinnati (G-2861)
▲ Electrocraft Arkansas Inc .... D 501 268-4203
  Gallipolis (G-7890)
Energy Technologies Inc .... D 419 522-4444
  Mansfield (G-9653)
GE Aviation Systems LLC .... B 937 898-5881
  Vandalia (G-14941)
General Electric Company .... E 216 883-1000
  Cleveland (G-4115)
◆ Gleason Metrology Systems Corp .... E 937 384-8901
  Dayton (G-6353)
▲ Globe Motors Inc .... C 334 983-3542
  Dayton (G-6356)
▲ Grand-Rock Company Inc .... E 440 639-2000
  Painesville (G-12240)
H W Fairway International Inc .... F 330 678-2540
  Canton (G-2119)
Hannon Company .... D 330 456-4728
  Canton (G-2121)
◆ HBD Industries Inc .... E 614 526-7000
  Dublin (G-6891)
Hv Coil .... F 330 260-4126
  Newcomerstown (G-11646)
◆ Ideal Electric Power Co .... E 419 522-3611
  Mansfield (G-9669)
◆ Imperial Electric Company .... B 330 734-3600
  North Canton (G-11738)
Industrial and Mar Eng Svc Co .... F 740 694-0791
  Fredericktown (G-7749)
JD Power Systems LLC .... F 614 317-9394
  Hilliard (G-8416)
Kirkwood Holding Inc .... G 216 267-6200
  Cleveland (G-4294)
▲ Linde Hydraulics Corporation .... E 330 533-6801
  Canfield (G-2009)
Lordstown Ev Corporation .... F 678 428-6558
  Warren (G-15185)
Martin Diesel Inc .... E 419 782-9911
  Defiance (G-6691)
Nidec Motor Corporation .... C 575 434-0633
  Akron (G-264)
▲ Ohio Magnetics Inc .... E 216 662-8484
  Maple Heights (G-9756)
◆ Ohio Semitronics Inc .... D 614 777-1005
  Hilliard (G-8427)
One Three Energy Inc .... F 513 996-6973
  Cincinnati (G-3224)
Parker-Hannifin Corporation .... E 330 336-3511
  Wadsworth (G-15051)

Peerless-Winsmith Inc .... B 330 399-3651
  Dublin (G-6921)
Precision Design Inc .... G 419 289-1553
  Ashland (G-605)
Qaf Technologies Inc .... E 440 941-4348
  Columbus (G-5701)
Ramco Electric Motors Inc .... D 937 548-2525
  Greenville (G-8056)
Regal Beloit America Inc .... E 608 364-8800
  Lima (G-9284)
Regal Beloit America Inc .... C 937 667-2431
  Tipp City (G-14151)
Rv Mobile Power LLC .... G 855 427-7978
  Columbus (G-5735)
Safran Usa Inc .... C 513 247-7000
  Sharonville (G-13173)
Siemens Industry Inc .... C 513 841-3100
  Norwood (G-12000)
Stateline Power Corp .... F 937 547-1006
  Greenville (G-8062)
▲ Surenergy LLC .... G 419 626-8000
  Oak Harbor (G-12015)
▲ Swiger Coil Systems Ltd .... C 216 362-7500
  Cleveland (G-4760)
Thermelectricity LLC .... G 330 972-8054
  Akron (G-355)
▲ Tigerpoly Manufacturing Inc .... B 614 871-0045
  Grove City (G-8122)
Tremont Electric Incorporated .... G 888 214-3137
  Cleveland (G-4820)
Tridelta Industries Inc .... G 440 255-1080
  Mentor (G-10584)
Turtlecreek Township .... F 513 932-4080
  Lebanon (G-9117)
◆ Vanner Holdings Inc .... D 614 771-2718
  Hilliard (G-8451)
Wabtec Corporation .... F 216 362-7500
  Cleveland (G-4887)
Waibel Electric Co Inc .... F 740 964-2956
  Etna (G-7253)
▲ Yamada North America Inc .... B 937 462-7111
  South Charleston (G-13456)

3624 Carbon and graphite products

Active Chemical Systems Inc .... F 440 543-7755
  Chagrin Falls (G-2388)
◆ American Spring Wire Corp .... C 216 292-4620
  Bedford Heights (G-1163)
Applied Sciences Inc .... F 937 766-2020
  Cedarville (G-2322)
◆ De Nora Tech LLC .... D 440 710-5334
  Concord Township (G-5905)
GE Aviation Systems LLC .... B 937 898-5881
  Vandalia (G-14941)
Ges AGM .... E 216 658-6528
  Cleveland (G-4123)
◆ Ges Graphite Inc .... E 216 658-6660
  Parma (G-12290)
Graftech Holdings Inc .... D 216 676-2000
  Independence (G-8669)
Graftech International Ltd .... D 216 676-2000
  Brooklyn Heights (G-1691)
◆ Graftech Intl Holdings Inc .... C 216 676-2000
  Brooklyn Heights (G-1692)
Graftech Intl Trdg Inc .... D 216 676-2000
  Cleveland (G-4136)
Graftech NY Inc .... F 216 676-2000
  Cleveland (G-4137)
Graphel Corporation .... C 513 779-6166
  West Chester (G-15444)
◆ Graphite Sales Inc .... F 419 652-3388
  Nova (G-12003)

Employee Codes: A=Over 500 employees, B=251-500
C=101-250, D=51-100, E=20-50, F=10-19, G=1-9

36 ELECTRONIC & OTHER ELECTRICAL EQUIPMENT & COMPONENTS

▲ Metaullics Systems LP .... C 509 926-6212
  Solon *(G-13387)*
▲ Mill-Rose Company .... C 440 255-9171
  Mentor *(G-10505)*
▼ Morgan Advanced Materials .... C 419 435-8182
  Fostoria *(G-7645)*
Morgan AM&t .... G 419 435-8182
  Fostoria *(G-7646)*
Neograf Solutions LLC .... C 216 529-3777
  Lakewood *(G-8979)*
Ocsial LLC .... F 415 906-5271
  Gahanna *(G-7847)*
Ohio Carbon Blank Inc .... E 440 953-9302
  Willoughby *(G-15964)*
Randall Bearings Inc .... F 419 678-2486
  Coldwater *(G-5000)*
▲ Randall Bearings Inc .... D 419 223-1075
  Lima *(G-9282)*
▲ Sangraf International Inc .... E 216 543-3288
  Westlake *(G-15703)*
Sentinel Management Inc .... E 440 821-7372
  Lorain *(G-9437)*
Sherbrooke Corporation .... E 440 942-3520
  Willoughby *(G-15990)*
▼ Wolf Composite Solutions .... F 614 219-6990
  Columbus *(G-5879)*
Xperion E & E USA LLC .... E 740 788-9560
  Heath *(G-8333)*
Zyvex Performance Mtls Inc .... G 614 481-2222
  Columbus *(G-5895)*

3625 Relays and industrial controls

Acon Inc .... G 513 276-2111
  Tipp City *(G-14121)*
▲ Altronic LLC .... C 330 545-9768
  Girard *(G-7960)*
Amano Cincinnati Incorporated .... F 513 697-9000
  Loveland *(G-9474)*
Apex Control Systems Inc .... D 330 938-2588
  Sebring *(G-13117)*
Asco Power Technologies LP .... C 216 573-7600
  Cleveland *(G-3685)*
Automation Technology Inc .... E 937 233-6084
  Dayton *(G-6219)*
Autoneum North America Inc .... B 419 693-0511
  Oregon *(G-12103)*
Avtron Holdings LLC .... E 216 642-1230
  Cleveland *(G-3710)*
Avtron Loadbank Inc .... C 216 573-7600
  Cleveland *(G-3711)*
▼ Bay Controls LLC .... E 419 891-4390
  Maumee *(G-10170)*
Cattron Holdings Inc .... E 234 806-0018
  Warren *(G-15150)*
♦ Cattron North America Inc .... F 234 806-0018
  Warren *(G-15151)*
▲ Chandler Systems Incorporated .. D 888 363-9434
  Ashland *(G-564)*
▲ Channel Products Inc .... E 440 423-0113
  Solon *(G-13328)*
Cincinnati Ctrl Dynamics Inc .... G 513 242-7300
  Cincinnati *(G-2746)*
Clark Substations LLC .... F 330 452-5200
  Canton *(G-2077)*
Command Alkon Incorporated .... E 614 799-0600
  Dublin *(G-6876)*
Comtec Incorporated .... F 330 425-8102
  Twinsburg *(G-14644)*
Contact Industries Inc .... E 419 884-9788
  Lexington *(G-9200)*
Control Electric Co .... E 216 671-8010
  Columbia Station *(G-5011)*

Controllix Corporation .... F 440 232-8757
  Walton Hills *(G-15097)*
Controls Inc .... E 330 239-4345
  Medina *(G-10312)*
Corrotec Inc .... E 937 325-3585
  Springfield *(G-13547)*
Curtiss-Wright Controls .... E 937 252-5601
  Fairborn *(G-7312)*
Dalton Corporation .... G 419 682-6328
  Stryker *(G-13907)*
Davis Technologies Inc .... E 330 823-2544
  Alliance *(G-401)*
♦ Delta Systems Inc .... B 330 626-2811
  Streetsboro *(G-13765)*
▲ Dimcogray Corporation .... D 937 433-7600
  Centerville *(G-2361)*
Divelbiss Corporation .... E 800 245-2327
  Fredericktown *(G-7744)*
Eaton Corporation .... C 216 281-2211
  Cleveland *(G-3992)*
Eaton Corporation .... C 440 826-1115
  Cleveland *(G-3993)*
♦ Eaton Corporation .... B 440 523-5000
  Cleveland *(G-3994)*
Eaton Electrical .... F 787 257-4470
  Cleveland *(G-3996)*
▲ Electrocraft Ohio Inc .... E 740 441-6200
  Gallipolis *(G-7891)*
Elite Industrial Controls Inc .... E 567 234-1057
  Berlin Heights *(G-1314)*
Energy Technologies Inc .... D 419 522-4444
  Mansfield *(G-9653)*
♦ Filnor Inc .... F 330 821-8731
  Alliance *(G-403)*
Future Controls Corporation .... E 440 275-3191
  Austinburg *(G-747)*
Gc Controls Inc .... G 440 779-4777
  Westlake *(G-15752)*
GE Aviation Systems LLC .... B 937 898-5881
  Vandalia *(G-14941)*
Harris Instrument Corporation .... G 740 369-3580
  Delaware *(G-6729)*
Helm Instrument Company Inc .... E 419 893-4356
  Maumee *(G-10205)*
Hite Parts Exchange Inc .... F 614 272-5915
  Columbus *(G-5442)*
♦ Ideal Electric Power Co .... E 419 522-3611
  Mansfield *(G-9669)*
Ignio Systems LLC .... G 419 708-0503
  Toledo *(G-14326)*
Industrial and Mar Eng Svc Co .... F 740 694-0791
  Fredericktown *(G-7749)*
Innovative Controls Corp .... E 419 691-6684
  Toledo *(G-14333)*
▲ ITT Torque Systems Inc .... C 216 524-8800
  Cleveland *(G-4241)*
♦ Keene Building Products Co .... D 440 605-1020
  Cleveland *(G-4279)*
♦ Kinetics Noise Control Inc .... C 614 889-0480
  Dublin *(G-6905)*
L3harris Electrodynamics Inc .... C 847 259-0740
  Cincinnati *(G-2569)*
▲ Logisync Corporation .... F 440 937-0388
  Avon *(G-780)*
M Technologies Inc .... F 330 477-9009
  Canton *(G-2151)*
Maags Automotive & Mch Inc .... G 419 626-1539
  Sandusky *(G-13076)*
Machine Drive Company .... D 513 793-7077
  Cincinnati *(G-3122)*
Miami Control Systems Inc .... G 937 233-8146
  Dayton *(G-6438)*

Moog Inc .... E 330 682-0010
  Orrville *(G-12138)*
Norgren Inc .... C 937 833-4033
  Brookville *(G-1742)*
Npas Inc .... F 614 595-6916
  Mansfield *(G-9706)*
▲ Ohio Magnetics Inc .... E 216 662-8484
  Maple Heights *(G-9756)*
♦ Ohio Semitronics Inc .... D 614 777-1005
  Hilliard *(G-8427)*
▲ Opw Engineered Systems Inc .... E 888 771-9438
  West Chester *(G-15471)*
Otp Holding LLC .... E 614 733-0979
  Plain City *(G-12588)*
Panel Master LLC .... E 440 355-4442
  Lagrange *(G-8954)*
▲ Pepperl + Fuchs Inc .... C 330 425-3555
  Twinsburg *(G-14709)*
Pepperl + Fuchs Entps Inc .... F 330 425-3555
  Twinsburg *(G-14710)*
PMC Systems Limited .... E 330 538-2268
  North Jackson *(G-11789)*
Primex .... E 513 831-9059
  Milford *(G-10919)*
Projects Unlimited Inc .... C 937 918-2200
  Dayton *(G-6534)*
Quality Controls Inc .... F 513 272-3900
  Cincinnati *(G-3310)*
▲ R-K Electronics Inc .... F 513 204-6060
  Mason *(G-10046)*
Ramco Electric Motors Inc .... D 937 548-2525
  Greenville *(G-8056)*
Rbb Systems Inc .... C 330 263-4502
  Wooster *(G-16161)*
Regal Beloit America Inc .... E 608 364-8800
  Lima *(G-9284)*
Rockwell Automation Inc .... F 440 646-7900
  Cleveland *(G-4643)*
Rockwell Automation Inc .... D 440 646-5000
  Cleveland *(G-4644)*
Rockwell Automation Inc .... B 330 425-3211
  Twinsburg *(G-14727)*
Rockwell Automation Inc .... E 513 942-9828
  West Chester *(G-15502)*
♦ Rogers Industrial Products Inc ... E 330 535-3331
  Akron *(G-309)*
Schneider Electric Usa Inc .... D 513 777-4445
  West Chester *(G-15506)*
Sdk Associates Inc .... G 330 745-3648
  Norton *(G-11948)*
Seneca Environmental Products Inc ... E 419 447-1282
  Tiffin *(G-14104)*
Sieb & Meyer America Inc .... F 513 563-0860
  West Chester *(G-15585)*
SMC Corporation of America .... F 330 659-2006
  Richfield *(G-12798)*
Spang & Company .... E 440 350-6108
  Mentor *(G-10558)*
▲ SSC Controls Company .... E 440 205-1600
  Mentor *(G-10560)*
▲ Standex Electronics Inc .... D 513 871-3777
  Fairfield *(G-7411)*
Stock Fairfield Corporation .... C 440 543-6000
  Solon *(G-13425)*
▲ Superb Industries Inc .... D 330 852-0500
  Sugarcreek *(G-13943)*
Te Connectivity Corporation .... C 419 521-9500
  Mansfield *(G-9725)*
Tech Products Corporation .... F 937 438-1100
  Miamisburg *(G-10690)*
Tekworx LLC .... F 513 533-4777
  Blue Ash *(G-1479)*

SIC SECTION
36 ELECTRONIC & OTHER ELECTRICAL EQUIPMENT & COMPONENTS

Temple Israel.................................G.....330 762-8617
  Akron (G-351)

Thermotion Corp.............................F.....440 639-8325
  Mentor (G-10576)

Toledo Electromotive Inc..................G.....419 874-7751
  Perrysburg (G-12438)

Toledo Transducers Inc....................E.....419 724-4170
  Maumee (G-10242)

Transdigm Inc.................................F.....216 291-6025
  Cleveland (G-4815)

Tridelta Industries Inc.....................G.....440 255-1080
  Mentor (G-10584)

◆ TT Electronics Integrated..............B.....440 352-8961
  Perry (G-12357)

Tvh Parts Co...................................F.....877 755-7311
  West Chester (G-15521)

Twinsource LLC..............................F.....440 248-6800
  Solon (G-13440)

US Controls Acquisition Ltd............G.....330 758-1147
  Poland (G-12612)

Utility Relay Co Ltd........................E.....440 708-1000
  Chagrin Falls (G-2431)

Uvonics Co.....................................F.....614 458-1163
  Columbus (G-5852)

▲ Valve Related Controls Inc...........F.....513 677-8724
  Loveland (G-9507)

▲ Venture Mfg Co...........................E.....937 233-8792
  Dayton (G-6642)

Vintage Automotive Elc Inc..............F.....419 472-9349
  Toledo (G-14520)

Wes-Garde Components Group Inc...G.....614 885-0319
  Westerville (G-15724)

◆ Wrc Holdings Inc.........................F.....330 733-6662
  Akron (G-377)

3629 Electrical industrial apparatus

10155 Broadview Business..............G.....440 546-1901
  Broadview Heights (G-1654)

Asg Division Jergens Inc................E.....888 486-6163
  Cleveland (G-3688)

▲ Brookwood Group Inc..................F.....513 791-3030
  Cincinnati (G-2691)

Caudabe LLC.................................G.....513 501-9799
  Blue Ash (G-1376)

▲ Core Technology Inc....................F.....440 934-9935
  Avon (G-769)

D C Systems Inc.............................F.....330 273-3030
  Brunswick (G-1756)

Dan-Mar Company Inc....................E.....419 660-8830
  Norwalk (G-11961)

Energy Technologies Inc.................D.....419 522-4444
  Mansfield (G-9653)

▲ Erico Products Inc.......................B.....440 248-0100
  Cleveland (G-4027)

Eti Tech LLC.................................F.....937 832-4200
  Kettering (G-8907)

Exide Technologies LLC.................G.....614 863-3866
  Gahanna (G-7835)

Graftech Global Entps Inc................F.....216 676-2000
  Cleveland (G-4135)

▲ HDR Power Systems LLC............E.....614 308-5500
  Worthington (G-16196)

◆ Lubrizol Global Management Inc...F.....216 447-5000
  Cleveland (G-4339)

Myers Controlled Power LLC.........E.....909 923-1800
  Canton (G-2170)

◆ Noco Company............................D.....216 464-8131
  Solon (G-13399)

Plug Power Inc...............................G.....518 605-5703
  West Carrollton (G-15356)

Proteus Electronics Inc....................G.....419 886-2296
  Bellville (G-1247)

Sarica Manufacturing Company........E.....937 484-4030
  Urbana (G-14847)

▲ Solidstate Controls LLC................C.....614 846-7500
  Columbus (G-5775)

Spirit Avionics Ltd..........................F.....614 237-4271
  Columbus (G-5786)

Superior Packaging..........................F.....419 380-3335
  Toledo (G-14478)

▲ Takk Industries Inc......................F.....513 353-4306
  Cleves (G-4966)

▲ Tecmark Corporation...................D.....440 205-7600
  Mentor (G-10573)

TL Industries Inc............................C.....419 666-8144
  Perrysburg (G-12436)

◆ Vanner Holdings Inc....................D.....614 771-2718
  Hilliard (G-8451)

3631 Household cooking equipment

◆ Garland Commercial Industries LLC..E.....800 338-2204
  Cleveland (G-4103)

Gosun Inc.......................................F.....888 868-6154
  Cincinnati (G-2966)

Nacco Industries Inc........................E.....440 229-5151
  Cleveland (G-4434)

Royalton Foodservice Eqp Co..........F.....440 237-0806
  North Royalton (G-11894)

3632 Household refrigerators and freezers

Dover Corporation...........................D.....513 870-3206
  West Chester (G-15415)

◆ Norcold LLC................................G.....800 543-1219
  Sidney (G-13268)

Whirlpool Corporation.....................C.....419 547-7711
  Clyde (G-4979)

Whirlpool Corporation.....................D.....419 423-8123
  Findlay (G-7583)

Whirlpool Corporation.....................F.....614 409-4340
  Lockbourne (G-9343)

Whirlpool Corporation.....................E.....740 383-7122
  Marion (G-9889)

3633 Household laundry equipment

Kitchenaid Inc................................G.....937 316-4782
  Greenville (G-8049)

▲ Staber Industries Inc....................E.....614 836-5995
  Groveport (G-8160)

Whirlpool Corporation.....................C.....419 547-7711
  Clyde (G-4979)

Whirlpool Corporation.....................G.....419 547-2610
  Clyde (G-4980)

Whirlpool Corporation.....................F.....614 409-4340
  Lockbourne (G-9343)

Whirlpool Corporation.....................E.....740 383-7122
  Marion (G-9889)

3634 Electric housewares and fans

Acorn Technology Corporation........E.....216 663-1244
  Shaker Heights (G-13149)

◆ Ad Industries Inc.........................A.....303 744-1911
  Dayton (G-6183)

Aitken Products Inc........................G.....440 466-5711
  Geneva (G-7930)

Ces Nationwide..............................G.....937 322-0771
  Springfield (G-13543)

▲ Cleveland Range LLC..................C.....216 481-4900
  Cleveland (G-3852)

Cyber Shed Inc...............................G.....419 724-5855
  Toledo (G-14256)

▲ Dyoung Enterprise Inc.................C.....440 918-0505
  Willoughby (G-15913)

Glo-Quartz Electric Htr Co Inc........E.....440 255-9701
  Mentor (G-10464)

◆ Hinkley Lighting Inc....................E.....440 653-5500
  Avon Lake (G-812)

◆ Hmi Industries Inc.......................E.....440 846-7800
  Brooklyn (G-1678)

Johnson Bros Rubber Co Inc...........E.....419 752-4814
  Greenwich (G-8067)

Nacco Industries Inc........................E.....440 229-5151
  Cleveland (G-4434)

Nutone Inc......................................A.....888 336-3948
  Blue Ash (G-1444)

◆ Procter & Gamble Company..........A.....513 983-1100
  Cincinnati (G-3280)

▲ Qualtek Electronics Corp..............C.....440 951-3300
  Mentor (G-10541)

Revair LLC....................................F.....440 462-6100
  Macedonia (G-9570)

▲ Skuttle Mfg Co............................F.....740 373-9169
  Marietta (G-9825)

▲ The Kitchen Collection LLC.........A.....740 773-9150
  Chillicothe (G-2538)

Ventilation Systems Jsc...................F.....513 348-3853
  Cincinnati (G-3491)

◆ Vita-Mix Manufacturing Corporation..C.....440 235-4840
  Olmsted Falls (G-12083)

Whirlpool Corporation.....................D.....937 548-4126
  Greenville (G-8064)

3635 Household vacuum cleaners

H-P Products Inc............................C.....330 875-7193
  Louisville (G-9458)

J K Plastics Co................................G.....440 632-1482
  Middlefield (G-10759)

Powerclean Equipment Company......F.....513 202-0001
  Cleves (G-4963)

Rent-A-Mom Inc.............................G.....216 901-9599
  Seven Hills (G-13131)

Royal Appliance Intl Co..................F.....440 996-2000
  Cleveland (G-4655)

Scott Fetzer Company.....................E.....216 252-1190
  Cleveland (G-4677)

▲ Stanley Steemer Intl Inc...............C.....614 764-2007
  Dublin (G-6945)

Western/Scott Fetzer Company........C.....440 871-2160
  Westlake (G-15802)

3639 Household appliances, nec

ABC Appliance Inc.........................E.....419 693-4414
  Oregon (G-12099)

▲ Anaheim Manufacturing Company.E.....800 767-6293
  North Olmsted (G-11817)

◆ New Path International LLC.........E.....614 410-3974
  Powell (G-12679)

ORourke Sales Co...........................G.....877 599-6548
  Grove City (G-8113)

▲ RAD Technologies Incorporated...F.....513 641-0523
  Cincinnati (G-3323)

◆ Robura Inc...................................D.....800 438-5346
  Dalton (G-6141)

Rod or Tammy Whitlatch................G.....614 848-5198
  Worthington (G-16211)

Rv Mobile Power LLC....................G.....855 427-7978
  Columbus (G-5735)

Sandco Industries............................E.....419 547-3273
  Clyde (G-4978)

Whirlpool Corporation.....................C.....419 547-7711
  Clyde (G-4979)

Whirlpool Corporation.....................D.....419 423-8123
  Findlay (G-7583)

3641 Electric lamps

◆ Advanced Lighting Tech LLC........D.....888 440-2358
  Solon (G-13306)

36 ELECTRONIC & OTHER ELECTRICAL EQUIPMENT & COMPONENTS

Carlisle and Finch Company.............. E 513 681-6080
  Cincinnati (G-2703)
Current Elec & Enrgy Solutions............ G 513 575-4600
  Loveland (G-9479)
◆ Current Lighting Solutions LLC............ B 216 462-4700
  Beachwood (G-982)
▲ Energy Focus Inc.............. F 440 715-1300
  Solon (G-13343)
General Electric Company.............. B 419 563-1200
  Bucyrus (G-1861)
General Electric Company.............. E 216 391-8741
  Cleveland (G-4112)
General Electric Company.............. E 440 593-1156
  Mc Donald (G-10277)
General Electric Company.............. E 330 373-1400
  Warren (G-15172)
◆ Kichler Lighting LLC.............. B 216 573-1000
  Solon (G-13379)
▲ Lumitex Inc.............. D 440 243-8401
  Strongsville (G-13852)
Osram Sylvania Inc.............. D 800 463-9275
  Independence (G-8670)
Savant Technologies LLC.............. A 800 435-4448
  East Cleveland (G-6983)

3643 Current-carrying wiring devices

Accurate Electronics Inc.............. C 330 682-7015
  Orrville (G-12116)
Alcon Inc.............. E 513 722-1037
  Amelia (G-449)
Alert Safety Lite Products Co.............. F 440 232-5020
  Cleveland (G-3626)
Amidac Wind Corporation.............. G 213 973-4000
  Elyria (G-7110)
Apex Control Systems Inc.............. D 330 938-2588
  Sebring (G-13117)
Astro Industries Inc.............. E 937 429-5900
  Beavercreek (G-1041)
▲ Bardes Corporation.............. B 513 533-6200
  Cincinnati (G-2656)
▲ Brumall Manufacturing Corp.............. E 440 974-2622
  Mentor (G-10432)
▲ C C M Wire Inc.............. E 330 425-3421
  Twinsburg (G-14638)
Cambrdge Ohio Prod Assmbly Cor.............. G 740 432-6383
  Cambridge (G-1924)
▼ Chalfant Manufacturing Company.............. G 330 273-3510
  Avon (G-765)
▲ Channel Products Inc.............. D 440 423-0113
  Solon (G-13328)
Connectronics Corp.............. D 419 537-0020
  Toledo (G-14250)
▲ Crown Electric Engrg & Mfg LLC.............. E 513 539-7394
  Middletown (G-10816)
D & E Electric Inc.............. G 513 738-1172
  Okeana (G-12067)
De Nora Tech Inc.............. C 440 285-0100
  Chardon (G-2448)
Desco Corporation.............. G 614 888-8855
  New Albany (G-11378)
◆ Dreison International Inc.............. C 216 362-0755
  Cleveland (G-3972)
▲ Dynalab Inc.............. D 614 866-9999
  Reynoldsburg (G-12764)
Ecm Industries LLC.............. E 513 533-6242
  Cincinnati (G-2857)
◆ Electric Cord Sets Inc.............. G 216 261-1000
  Cleveland (G-4003)
▲ Erico Products Inc.............. B 440 248-0100
  Cleveland (G-4027)
Ericson Manufacturing Co.............. D 440 951-8000
  Willoughby (G-15917)

GE Aviation Systems LLC.............. B 937 898-5881
  Vandalia (G-14941)
▲ General Plug and Mfg Co.............. C 440 926-2411
  Grafton (G-8000)
Hermetic Seal Technology Inc.............. F 513 851-4899
  Cincinnati (G-2996)
▲ Ilsco LLC.............. C 513 533-6200
  Cincinnati (G-3017)
Innovest Energy Group LLC.............. G 440 644-1027
  Chesterland (G-2483)
▲ International Hydraulics Inc.............. E 440 951-7186
  Mentor (G-10475)
Kathom Manufacturing Co Inc.............. E 513 868-8890
  Middletown (G-10835)
▲ Knappco Corporation.............. C 513 870-3100
  West Chester (G-15455)
Legrand AV Inc.............. E 574 267-8101
  Blue Ash (G-1422)
Legrand North America LLC.............. B 937 224-0639
  Dayton (G-6403)
Marathon Special Products Corp.............. C 419 352-8441
  Bowling Green (G-1573)
▲ Mueller Electric Company Inc.............. E 216 771-5225
  Akron (G-256)
Newact Inc.............. F 513 321-5177
  Batavia (G-940)
Nyle LLC.............. F 888 235-2097
  Springboro (G-13513)
Ohio Associated Entps LLC.............. E 440 354-3148
  Painesville (G-12254)
Parker-Hannifin Corporation.............. E 330 336-3511
  Wadsworth (G-15051)
Pave Technology Co.............. E 937 890-1100
  Dayton (G-6499)
Projects Unlimited Inc.............. C 937 918-2200
  Dayton (G-6534)
▲ Qualtek Electronics Corp.............. C 440 951-3300
  Mentor (G-10541)
Reliable Hermetic Seals LLC.............. F 888 747-3250
  Beavercreek (G-1060)
◆ Rogers Industrial Products Inc.............. E 330 535-3331
  Akron (G-309)
▲ Royal Plastics Inc.............. C 440 352-1357
  Mentor (G-10548)
▲ Saia-Burgess Lcc.............. D 937 898-3621
  Vandalia (G-14958)
Sanreed Management Group LLC.............. A 513 722-1037
  Amelia (G-464)
Schneider Electric Usa Inc.............. D 513 777-4445
  West Chester (G-15506)
Siemens Industry Inc.............. E 937 593-6010
  Bellefontaine (G-1219)
Simpson Strong-Tie Company Inc.............. C 614 876-8060
  Columbus (G-5773)
▲ Solon Manufacturing Company.............. E 440 286-7149
  Chardon (G-2468)
▲ Tecmark Corporation.............. D 440 205-7600
  Mentor (G-10573)
▼ The National Telephone Su.............. E 216 361-0221
  Cleveland (G-4789)
▲ The Vulcan Tool Company.............. G 937 253-6194
  Dayton (G-6620)
Tip Products Inc.............. E 216 252-2535
  New London (G-11472)
Tridelta Industries Inc.............. G 440 255-1080
  Mentor (G-10584)
◆ Watteredge LLC.............. D 440 933-6110
  Avon Lake (G-828)
▲ Wedge Products Inc.............. B 330 405-4477
  Twinsburg (G-14755)
Xponet Inc.............. E 440 354-6917
  Painesville (G-12279)

3644 Noncurrent-carrying wiring devices

Allied Tube & Conduit Corp.............. F 740 928-1018
  Hebron (G-8335)
◆ Arnco Corporation.............. D 800 847-7661
  Elyria (G-7112)
Barracuda Technologies Inc.............. G 216 469-1566
  Aurora (G-708)
Bourbon Plastics Inc.............. E 574 342-0893
  Cuyahoga Falls (G-6073)
Danco Metal Products LLC.............. D 440 871-2300
  Avon Lake (G-803)
Dees Family Raceway LLC.............. G 740 772-5431
  Chillicothe (G-2501)
▲ Eaton Electric Holdings LLC.............. B 440 523-5000
  Cleveland (G-3995)
▲ Erico Products Inc.............. B 440 248-0100
  Cleveland (G-4027)
Indian Lake Raceway LLC.............. G 937 837-7533
  Clayton (G-3566)
Koebbe Products Inc.............. D 513 753-4200
  Amelia (G-458)
Lagonda Investments III Inc.............. F 937 325-7305
  Springfield (G-13594)
▲ Madison Electric Products Inc.............. E 216 391-7776
  Solon (G-13382)
▲ Monti Incorporated.............. D 513 761-7775
  Cincinnati (G-3172)
▲ Mueller Electric Company Inc.............. E 216 771-5225
  Akron (G-256)
▲ Osborne Coinage Company LLC.............. D 877 480-0456
  Blue Ash (G-1448)
Power Shelf LLC.............. G 419 775-6125
  Plymouth (G-12609)
Preformed Line Products Co.............. A 440 461-5200
  Mayfield Village (G-10260)
Raceway Beverage LLC.............. G 513 932-2214
  Lebanon (G-9107)
Raceway Petroleum Inc.............. F 440 989-2660
  Lorain (G-9432)
▲ Red Seal Electric Company.............. E 216 941-3900
  Cleveland (G-4620)
Regal Beloit America Inc.............. C 419 352-8441
  Bowling Green (G-1588)
◆ Roechling Indus Cleveland LP.............. C 216 486-0100
  Cleveland (G-4645)
Saylor Products Corporation.............. F 419 832-2125
  Grand Rapids (G-8010)
Standex International Corp.............. D 513 533-7171
  Fairfield (G-7412)
State of Ohio Dayton Raceway.............. E 937 237-7802
  Dayton (G-6592)
Tlg Laporte Inc.............. G 440 914-1122
  Twinsburg (G-14745)
Tri-Fab Inc.............. E 330 337-3425
  Salem (G-13034)
Tri-State Hobbies Raceway LLC.............. G 513 889-3954
  Hamilton (G-8252)
◆ Vertiv Energy Systems Inc.............. A 440 288-1122
  Lorain (G-9443)
Vertiv Group Corporation.............. G 440 288-1122
  Lorain (G-9444)
Von Roll Usa Inc.............. D 216 433-7474
  Cleveland (G-4883)
Zekelman Industries Inc.............. C 740 432-2146
  Cambridge (G-1961)

3645 Residential lighting fixtures

Acuity Brands Lighting Inc.............. D 740 349-4343
  Newark (G-11560)
◆ Advanced Lighting Tech LLC.............. D 888 440-2358
  Solon (G-13306)

36 ELECTRONIC & OTHER ELECTRICAL EQUIPMENT & COMPONENTS

◆ Besa Lighting Co Inc .... E 614 475-7046
   Blacklick *(G-1331)*

EL Ostendorf Inc .... G 440 247-7631
   Chagrin Falls *(G-2377)*

Evolution Lawn & Landscape LLC .... G 330 268-5306
   Mineral City *(G-11017)*

▲ Grimes Aerospace Company .... A 937 484-2000
   Urbana *(G-14830)*

◆ Hinkley Lighting Inc .... E 440 653-5500
   Avon Lake *(G-812)*

J Schrader Company .... F 216 961-2890
   Cleveland *(G-4246)*

JB Machining Concepts LLC .... G 419 523-0096
   Ottawa *(G-12182)*

◆ Kichler Lighting LLC .... B 216 573-1000
   Solon *(G-13379)*

▲ Led Lighting Center Inc .... G 714 271-2633
   Toledo *(G-14360)*

Led Lighting Center LLC .... F 888 988-6533
   Toledo *(G-14361)*

Lt Moses Willard Inc .... E 513 248-5500
   Amelia *(G-459)*

Manairco Inc .... G 419 524-2121
   Mansfield *(G-9683)*

Mega Bright LLC .... F 330 577-8859
   Cuyahoga Falls *(G-6104)*

▲ Megalight Inc .... E 800 957-1797
   Hudson *(G-8604)*

▲ Microsun Lamps LLC .... G 888 328-8701
   Dayton *(G-6443)*

Morel Landscaping LLC .... F 216 551-4395
   Richfield *(G-12791)*

Night Lightscapes LLC .... G 419 304-2486
   Sylvania *(G-14010)*

3646 Commercial lighting fixtures

Acuity Brands Lighting Inc .... C 800 754-0463
   Granville *(G-8014)*

Acuity Brands Lighting Inc .... D 740 349-4343
   Newark *(G-11560)*

Acuity Brands Lighting Inc .... C 740 892-2011
   Utica *(G-14856)*

◆ Advanced Lighting Tech LLC .... D 888 440-2358
   Solon *(G-13306)*

◆ Besa Lighting Co Inc .... E 614 475-7046
   Blacklick *(G-1331)*

◆ Best Lighting Products Inc .... D 740 964-1198
   Etna *(G-7254)*

Current Lighting Solutions LLC .... B 216 266-4416
   Cleveland *(G-3920)*

◆ Current Lighting Solutions LLC .... B 216 462-4700
   Beachwood *(G-982)*

▲ Damak 1 LLC .... E 513 858-6004
   Fairfield *(G-7350)*

Daycoa Inc .... F 937 849-1315
   Medway *(G-10397)*

▲ Eaton Electric Holdings LLC .... B 440 523-5000
   Cleveland *(G-3995)*

Evp International LLC .... G 513 761-7614
   Cincinnati *(G-2890)*

GE Lighting Inc .... D 216 266-2121
   Cleveland *(G-4106)*

General Electric Company .... E 330 458-3200
   Canton *(G-2111)*

▲ Genesis Lamp Corp .... F 440 354-0095
   Painesville *(G-12239)*

▲ Grimes Aerospace Company .... A 937 484-2000
   Urbana *(G-14830)*

◆ Hinkley Lighting Inc .... E 440 653-5500
   Avon Lake *(G-812)*

Holophane Corporation .... A 330 823-5535
   Alliance *(G-406)*

Holophane Corporation .... F 740 349-4194
   Newark *(G-11579)*

◆ Holophane Corporation .... C 866 759-1577
   Granville *(G-8018)*

Importers Direct LLC .... F 330 436-3260
   Akron *(G-189)*

J Schrader Company .... F 216 961-2890
   Cleveland *(G-4246)*

JB Machining Concepts LLC .... G 419 523-0096
   Ottawa *(G-12182)*

▲ King Luminaire Company Inc .... E 440 576-9073
   Jefferson *(G-8750)*

▲ Led Lighting Center Inc .... G 714 271-2633
   Toledo *(G-14360)*

Led Lighting Center LLC .... F 888 988-6533
   Toledo *(G-14361)*

▲ Light Craft Manufacturing Inc .... F 419 332-0536
   Fremont *(G-7795)*

LSI Industries Inc .... C 913 281-1100
   Blue Ash *(G-1425)*

▲ LSI Lightron Inc .... A 845 562-5500
   Blue Ash *(G-1426)*

Lumenforce Led LLC .... E 330 330-8962
   Youngstown *(G-16390)*

▲ Lumitex Inc .... D 440 243-8401
   Strongsville *(G-13852)*

Magnum Asset Acquisition LLC .... E 330 915-2382
   Hudson *(G-8603)*

Mega Bright LLC .... G 216 712-4689
   Cleveland *(G-4390)*

Mega Bright LLC .... F 330 577-8859
   Cuyahoga Falls *(G-6104)*

▲ Megalight Inc .... E 800 957-1797
   Hudson *(G-8604)*

▲ Nordic Light America Inc .... F 614 981-9497
   Canal Winchester *(G-1991)*

Norton Industries Inc .... E 888 357-2345
   Lakewood *(G-8980)*

NRG Industrial Lighting Mfg Co .... G 419 354-8207
   Bowling Green *(G-1578)*

SMS Technologies Inc .... F 419 465-4175
   Monroeville *(G-11126)*

Stress-Crete Company .... E 440 576-9073
   Jefferson *(G-8759)*

Treemen Industries Inc .... E 330 965-3777
   Boardman *(G-1519)*

3647 Vehicular lighting equipment

◆ Advanced Technology Corp .... F 440 293-4064
   Andover *(G-483)*

Akron Brass Company .... E 614 529-7230
   Columbus *(G-5109)*

Akron Brass Company .... E 800 228-1161
   Wooster *(G-16096)*

◆ Akron Brass Company .... B 330 264-5678
   Wooster *(G-16097)*

Akron Brass Holding Corp .... E 330 264-5678
   Wooster *(G-16098)*

▲ Atc Group Inc .... D 440 293-4064
   Andover *(G-484)*

▲ Atc Lighting & Plastics Inc .... C 440 466-7670
   Andover *(G-485)*

Grimes Aerospace Company .... D 937 484-2001
   Urbana *(G-14832)*

▲ Grimes Aerospace Company .... A 937 484-2000
   Urbana *(G-14830)*

▲ K-D Lamp Company .... E 440 293-4064
   Andover *(G-486)*

▲ Lighting Products Inc .... G 440 293-4064
   Andover *(G-487)*

Rvtronix Corporation .... E 440 359-7200
   Eastlake *(G-7048)*

▲ Stanley Electric US Co Inc .... D 740 852-5200
   London *(G-9394)*

Treemen Industries Inc .... E 330 965-3777
   Boardman *(G-1519)*

Washington Products Inc .... F 330 837-5101
   Massillon *(G-10154)*

3648 Lighting equipment, nec

Aat USA LLC .... E 614 388-8866
   Columbus *(G-5083)*

Acuity Brands Lighting Inc .... D 740 349-4343
   Newark *(G-11560)*

◆ ADB Safegate Americas LLC .... C 614 861-1304
   Gahanna *(G-7828)*

◆ Advanced Lighting Tech LLC .... D 888 440-2358
   Solon *(G-13306)*

Akron Brass Company .... E 614 529-7230
   Columbus *(G-5109)*

Architectural Busstrut Corp .... F 614 933-8695
   New Albany *(G-11367)*

▲ Atc Lighting & Plastics Inc .... C 440 466-7670
   Andover *(G-485)*

B2d Solutions Inc .... G 855 484-1145
   Cleveland *(G-3718)*

Beelighting Inc .... G 937 296-4460
   Dayton *(G-6224)*

Brightguy Inc .... G 440 942-8318
   Willoughby *(G-15893)*

Carlisle and Finch Company .... E 513 681-6080
   Cincinnati *(G-2703)*

Cooper Lighting LLC .... F 800 334-6871
   Columbus *(G-5294)*

▲ Delta Power Supply Inc .... F 513 771-3835
   Cincinnati *(G-2824)*

▲ Energy Focus Inc .... F 440 715-1300
   Solon *(G-13343)*

◆ Ericson Manufacturing Co .... D 440 951-8000
   Willoughby *(G-15917)*

Fulton Industries Inc .... D 419 335-3015
   Wauseon *(G-15261)*

General Electric Company .... E 330 373-1400
   Warren *(G-15172)*

▲ Genesis Lamp Corp .... F 440 354-0095
   Painesville *(G-12239)*

▲ Global Lighting Tech Inc .... E 440 922-4584
   Brecksville *(G-1618)*

◆ Holophane Corporation .... C 866 759-1577
   Granville *(G-8018)*

Hughey & Phillips LLC .... E 937 652-3500
   Urbana *(G-14836)*

Importers Direct LLC .... F 330 436-3260
   Akron *(G-189)*

Jasper Paula .... G 740 559-3983
   Pennsville *(G-12348)*

◆ Kichler Lighting LLC .... B 216 573-1000
   Solon *(G-13379)*

◆ Lintern Corporation .... E 440 255-9333
   Mentor *(G-10494)*

LSI Industries Inc .... B 513 793-3200
   Cincinnati *(G-3115)*

▲ Lumitex Inc .... D 440 243-8401
   Strongsville *(G-13852)*

Manairco Inc .... G 419 524-2121
   Mansfield *(G-9683)*

Miami Valley Lighting LLC .... G 937 224-6000
   Dayton *(G-6170)*

Midmark Corporation .... G 937 526-3662
   Versailles *(G-14986)*

Midmark Corporation .... E 937 526-8387
   Versailles *(G-14987)*

◆ Midmark Corporation .... A 937 528-7500
   Miamisburg *(G-10661)*

36 ELECTRONIC & OTHER ELECTRICAL EQUIPMENT & COMPONENTS — SIC SECTION

▲ National Biological Corp .... E 216 831-0600
   Beachwood *(G-1001)*

Pro Lighting LLC .... G 614 561-0089
   Hilliard *(G-8433)*

Smashray Ltd .... G 989 620-7507
   Maumee *(G-10232)*

Spotlight Writing LLC .... G 216 751-6889
   Cleveland *(G-4721)*

Starbright Lighting USA LLC .... G 330 650-2000
   Hudson *(G-8615)*

▼ Sunless Inc .... D 440 836-0199
   Macedonia *(G-9581)*

◆ Union Metal Corporation .... B 330 456-7653
   Canton *(G-2250)*

◆ Vanner Holdings Inc .... D 614 771-2718
   Hilliard *(G-8451)*

▲ Will-Burt Company .... C 330 682-7015
   Orrville *(G-12163)*

3661 Household audio and video equipment

5 Core Inc .... F 951 386-6372
   Belletontaine *(G-1199)*

Althar LLC .... F 216 408-9860
   Cleveland *(G-3642)*

Andersound PA Service .... G 216 401-4631
   Cleveland *(G-3667)*

Array Telepresence Inc .... G 800 779-7480
   West Chester *(G-15369)*

▲ Avtek International Inc .... G 330 633-7500
   Tallmadge *(G-14023)*

C T I Audio Inc .... G 440 593-1111
   Brooklyn Heights *(G-1686)*

China Enterprises Inc .... G 419 885-1485
   Toledo *(G-14238)*

▲ Cochran 6573 LLC .... F 440 349-4900
   Solon *(G-13333)*

Dare Electronics Inc .... E 937 335-0031
   Troy *(G-14559)*

Db Unlimited LLC .... F 937 401-2602
   Dayton *(G-6293)*

Dr Z Amps Inc .... F 216 475-1444
   Maple Heights *(G-9751)*

Eprad Inc .... G 419 666-3266
   Perrysburg *(G-12379)*

Fellhauer Mechanical Systems .... E 419 734-3674
   Port Clinton *(G-12617)*

▲ Floyd Bell Inc .... D 614 294-4000
   Columbus *(G-5381)*

◆ J & C Group Inc of Ohio .... F 440 205-9658
   Mentor *(G-10477)*

▲ Mitsubishi Elc Auto Amer Inc .... B 513 573-6614
   Mason *(G-10030)*

Ohio Hd Video .... F 614 656-1162
   New Albany *(G-11387)*

◆ Phantom Sound .... G 513 759-4477
   Mason *(G-10038)*

◆ Pioneer Automotive Tech Inc .... C 937 746-2293
   Miamisburg *(G-10670)*

Pro Audio .... G 513 752-7500
   Cincinnati *(G-2572)*

Tech Products Corporation .... F 937 438-1100
   Miamisburg *(G-10690)*

Technicolor Usa Inc .... A 614 474-8821
   Circleville *(G-3557)*

Tune Town Car Audio .... G 419 627-1100
   Sandusky *(G-13098)*

Tvone Ncsa .... F 859 282-7303
   Cincinnati *(G-3475)*

Universal Electronics Inc .... G 330 487-1110
   Twinsburg *(G-14750)*

3652 Prerecorded records and tapes

Cabconnect Inc .... F 773 282-3565
   Dayton *(G-6245)*

Cuttercroix LLC .... F 330 289-6185
   Cleveland *(G-3927)*

Fluid Handling Dynamics Ltd .... F 419 633-0560
   Bryan *(G-1818)*

Jk Digital Publishing LLC .... F 937 299-0185
   Springboro *(G-13506)*

Qca Inc .... F 513 681-8400
   Cincinnati *(G-3309)*

3661 Telephone and telegraph apparatus

7signal Inc .... E 216 777-2900
   Independence *(G-8650)*

◆ Arnco Corporation .... D 800 847-7661
   Elyria *(G-7112)*

AT&T Corp .... G 513 792-9300
   Cincinnati *(G-2639)*

Atx Networks .... G 440 427-9036
   Olmsted Twp *(G-12086)*

Black Box Corporation .... G 855 324-9909
   Westlake *(G-15738)*

C Dcap Modem Line .... G 419 748-7409
   Mc Clure *(G-10265)*

Christopher Sweeney .... G 513 276-4350
   Troy *(G-14554)*

Commercial Electric Pdts Corp .... E 216 241-2886
   Cleveland *(G-3889)*

Concentrix Cvg LLC .... C 972 454-8000
   Cincinnati *(G-2786)*

Cotsworks Inc .... D 440 446-8800
   Highland Heights *(G-8385)*

Crase Communications Inc .... F 419 468-1173
   Galion *(G-7869)*

Cutting Edge Technologies Inc .... F 216 574-4759
   Cleveland *(G-3928)*

DTE Inc .... E 419 522-3428
   Mansfield *(G-9647)*

▲ Dynalab Inc .... D 614 866-9999
   Reynoldsburg *(G-12764)*

Electrodata Inc .... F 216 663-3333
   Bedford Heights *(G-1170)*

Em4 Inc .... E 410 987-5600
   Cleveland *(G-4010)*

▲ Floyd Bell Inc .... D 614 294-4000
   Columbus *(G-5381)*

Fremont Plastic Products Inc .... C 419 332-6407
   Fremont *(G-7783)*

▲ Kentrox Inc .... D 614 798-2000
   Dublin *(G-6904)*

Preformed Line Products Co .... A 440 461-5200
   Mayfield Village *(G-10260)*

Pro Oncall Technologies LLC .... F 614 761-1400
   Dublin *(G-6927)*

Siemens AG .... E 513 576-2451
   Mason *(G-10055)*

Siemens Energy Inc .... E 740 393-8200
   Mount Vernon *(G-11294)*

Total Call Center Solutions .... F 330 869-9844
   Akron *(G-361)*

◆ Vertiv Energy Systems Inc .... A 440 288-1122
   Lorain *(G-9443)*

Vertiv Group Corporation .... G 440 460-3600
   Cleveland *(G-4864)*

Vertiv Group Corporation .... G 440 288-1122
   Lorain *(G-9444)*

Wan Dynamics Inc .... F 877 400-9490
   Medina *(G-10393)*

3663 Radio and t.v. communications equipment

Accurate Electronics Inc .... C 330 682-7015
   Orrville *(G-12116)*

AG Antenna Group LLC .... G 513 289-6521
   Cincinnati *(G-2601)*

Armada Power LLC .... G 614 721-4844
   Columbus *(G-5154)*

Barco Inc .... E 937 372-7579
   Xenia *(G-16250)*

CDI Industries Inc .... E 440 243-1100
   Cleveland *(G-3802)*

Central USA Wireless LLC .... F 513 469-1500
   Cincinnati *(G-2719)*

Circle Prime Manufacturing .... E 330 923-0019
   Cuyahoga Falls *(G-6074)*

Control Industries Inc .... G 937 653-7694
   Findlay *(G-7496)*

David Chojnacki .... E 303 905-1918
   Westerville *(G-15699)*

Diamond Electronics Inc .... D 740 652-9222
   Lancaster *(G-9010)*

Edi Displays Inc .... F 937 429-7423
   Beavercreek *(G-1050)*

Eei Acquisition Corp .... E 440 564 5484
   Middlefield *(G-10749)*

Electro-Magwave Inc .... G 216 453-1160
   Cleveland *(G-4004)*

Engineered Endeavors Inc .... E 440 564-5484
   Newbury *(G-11623)*

Estone Group LLC .... E 888 653-2246
   Toledo *(G-14280)*

Garage Scenes Ltd .... F 614 407-6094
   Westerville *(G-15657)*

▲ Gatesair Inc .... D 513 459-3400
   Mason *(G-9995)*

Great Lakes Telcom Ltd .... E 330 629-8848
   Youngstown *(G-16373)*

Imagine Communications Corp .... G 513 459-3400
   Mason *(G-10006)*

L-3 Cmmncations Nova Engrg Inc .... C 877 282-1168
   Mason *(G-10018)*

L3 Technologies Inc .... G 937 257-8501
   Dayton *(G-6165)*

Linear Acoustic Inc .... G 717 735-3611
   Cleveland *(G-4328)*

Liquid Image Corp America .... G 216 458-9800
   Cleveland *(G-4331)*

LSI Industries Inc .... B 513 793-3200
   Cincinnati *(G-3115)*

Motorola Solutions Inc .... G 330 664-1610
   Akron *(G-254)*

▲ Nissin Precision N Amer Inc .... D 937 836-1910
   Englewood *(G-7238)*

◆ Ohio Semitronics Inc .... D 614 777-1005
   Hilliard *(G-8427)*

Pole/Zero LLC .... C 513 870-9060
   West Chester *(G-15481)*

Punch Components Inc .... E 419 224-1242
   Lima *(G-9280)*

Quasonix Inc .... E 513 942-1287
   West Chester *(G-15491)*

Rev38 LLC .... G 937 572-4000
   West Chester *(G-15499)*

Sagequest LLC .... D 216 896-7243
   Solon *(G-13417)*

Satellite Data Inc .... G 440 926-9300
   Grafton *(G-8004)*

Starwin Industries LLC .... E 937 293-8568
   Dayton *(G-6591)*

▲ Tencom Ltd .... G 419 865-5877
   Holland *(G-8533)*

▲ Valco Melton Inc .... E 513 874-6550
   West Chester *(G-15604)*

36 ELECTRONIC & OTHER ELECTRICAL EQUIPMENT & COMPONENTS

Watts Antenna Company .... G 740 797-9380
  The Plains *(G-14060)*
Wireless Retail LLC .... F 614 657-5182
  Blacklick *(G-1345)*

3669 Communications equipment, nec

A & A Safety Inc .... F 937 567-9781
  Beavercreek *(G-1068)*
Ademco Inc .... G 440 439-7002
  Bedford *(G-1098)*
Ademco Inc .... F 513 772-1851
  Blue Ash *(G-1358)*
▲ Athens Technical Specialists .... F 740 592-2874
  Athens *(G-676)*
Bender Communications Inc .... F 740 382-0000
  Marion *(G-9848)*
Bird Technologies Group Inc .... G 440 248-1200
  Solon *(G-13319)*
▲ Ceia Usa Ltd .... D 330 310-4741
  Hudson *(G-8588)*
City Elyria Communication .... G 440 322-3329
  Elyria *(G-7127)*
City of Canton .... D 330 489-3370
  Canton *(G-2075)*
▼ Data Processing Sciences .... D 513 791-7100
  Cincinnati *(G-2820)*
▲ Findaway World LLC .... E 440 893-0808
  Solon *(G-13349)*
▲ Floyd Bell Inc .... D 614 294-4000
  Columbus *(G-5381)*
General Dynmics Mssion Systems .... F 513 253-4770
  Beavercreek *(G-1051)*
Honeywell International Inc .... A 937 484-2000
  Urbana *(G-14835)*
Intelligent Signal Tech Intl .... G 614 530-4784
  Loveland *(G-9487)*
Ohio Department Transportation .... E 614 351-2898
  Columbus *(G-5614)*
▲ Ohio Magnetics Inc .... E 216 662-8484
  Maple Heights *(G-9756)*
Paul Peterson Company .... F 614 486-4375
  Columbus *(G-5660)*
PM Power Products LLC .... G 614 652-6509
  Dublin *(G-6923)*
Quasonix Inc .... E 513 942-1287
  West Chester *(G-15491)*
Security Fence Group Inc .... E 513 681-3700
  Cincinnati *(G-3374)*
Signature Technologies Inc .... E 937 859-6323
  Miamisburg *(G-10683)*
Sound Communications Inc .... E 614 875-8500
  Grove City *(G-8120)*
Status Solutions LLC .... D 434 296-1789
  Westerville *(G-15680)*
Total Life Safety LLC .... F 866 955-2318
  West Chester *(G-15516)*
Union Metal Industries Corp .... E 330 456-7653
  Canton *(G-2251)*
Voice Products Inc .... F 216 360-0433
  Cleveland *(G-4881)*
Waveflex Inc .... G 740 513-1334
  Galena *(G-7856)*

3672 Printed circuit boards

Accurate Electronics Inc .... C 330 682-7015
  Orrville *(G-12116)*
Alektronics Inc .... F 937 429-2118
  Beavercreek *(G-1069)*
Avcom Smt Inc .... F 614 882-8176
  Westerville *(G-15692)*
Blue Creek Enterprises Inc .... E 937 222-9969
  Dayton *(G-6232)*

C E Electronics Inc .... D 419 636-6705
  Bryan *(G-1813)*
▼ Cartessa Corp .... F 513 738-4477
  Shandon *(G-13159)*
Circle Prime Manufacturing .... E 330 923-0019
  Cuyahoga Falls *(G-6074)*
Circuit Center .... G 513 435-2131
  Dayton *(G-6256)*
Cleveland Circuits Corp .... E 216 267-9020
  Cleveland *(G-3836)*
Cleveland Coretec Inc .... G 314 727-2087
  North Jackson *(G-11781)*
Co-Ax Technology Inc .... C 440 914-9200
  Solon *(G-13332)*
Ddi North Jackson Corp .... G 330 538-3900
  North Jackson *(G-11782)*
Deca Mfg Co .... F 419 884-0071
  Mansfield *(G-9645)*
▲ Dynalab Inc .... D 614 866-9999
  Reynoldsburg *(G-12764)*
Flextronics Intl USA Inc .... E 513 755-2500
  Liberty Township *(G-9207)*
▲ Interactive Engineering Corp .... E 330 239-6888
  Medina *(G-10337)*
Journey Electronics Corp .... G 513 539-9836
  Monroe *(G-11112)*
L3 Technologies Inc .... E 513 943-2000
  Cincinnati *(G-2568)*
Lad Technology Inc .... F 561 543-9858
  Concord Township *(G-5909)*
Levison Enterprises LLC .... E 419 838-7365
  Millbury *(G-10935)*
Libra Industries LLC .... C 440 974-7770
  Mentor *(G-10493)*
▲ Logisync Corporation .... F 440 937-0388
  Avon *(G-780)*
▲ McGregor & Associates Inc .... C 937 833-6768
  Brookville *(G-1741)*
Metzenbaum Sheltered Inds Inc .... D 440 729-1919
  Chesterland *(G-2485)*
Naprotek Holdings LLC .... D 408 830-5000
  Independence *(G-8676)*
Npas Inc .... F 614 595-6916
  Mansfield *(G-9706)*
Ohio Fire Suppression LLC .... G 216 269-6032
  Aurora *(G-729)*
▲ Parlex USA LLC .... E 937 898-3621
  Vandalia *(G-14956)*
Philway Products Inc .... C 419 281-7777
  Ashland *(G-600)*
Projects Unlimited Inc .... C 937 918-2200
  Dayton *(G-6534)*
▲ Qualtech Technologies Inc .... E 440 946-8081
  Willoughby *(G-15980)*
Quarter Century Design LLC .... G 937 434-5127
  Dayton *(G-6536)*
▲ R-K Electronics Inc .... F 513 204-6060
  Mason *(G-10046)*
Sinbon Ohio LLC .... C 937 415-2070
  Vandalia *(G-14959)*
▲ Techtron Systems Inc .... E 440 505-2990
  Solon *(G-13436)*
Tetrad Electronics Inc .... D 440 946-6443
  Willoughby *(G-16005)*
Ttm Technologies Inc .... C 330 538-3900
  North Jackson *(G-11792)*
Ttm Technologies North America LLC .... D 330 572-3400
  North Jackson *(G-11793)*
Uvonics Co .... F 614 458-1163
  Columbus *(G-5852)*
Valtronic Technology Inc .... D 440 349-1239
  Solon *(G-13441)*

Versitec Manufacturing Inc .... E 440 354-4283
  Painesville *(G-12274)*
Vexos Inc .... C 440 284-2500
  Lagrange *(G-8957)*
▲ Vmetro Inc .... D 281 584-0728
  Fairborn *(G-7326)*
Wurth Electronics Ics Inc .... E 937 415-7700
  Miamisburg *(G-10703)*

3674 Semiconductors and related devices

A M D .... G 440 918-8930
  Willoughby *(G-15872)*
AT&T Corp .... G 513 792-9300
  Cincinnati *(G-2639)*
Bestlight Led Corporation .... G 440 205-1552
  Mentor *(G-10430)*
▲ Burke Products Inc .... E 937 372-3516
  Xenia *(G-16253)*
Ceso Inc .... E 937 435-8584
  Miamisburg *(G-10626)*
▲ Cks Solution Incorporated .... E 513 947-1277
  Fairfield *(G-7348)*
Communication Concepts Inc .... G 937 426-8600
  Beavercreek *(G-1043)*
D F Electronics Inc .... D 513 772-7792
  Cincinnati *(G-2813)*
Dan-Mar Company Inc .... E 419 660-8830
  Norwalk *(G-11961)*
Darrah Electric Company .... F 216 631-0912
  Cleveland *(G-3942)*
Em4 Inc .... E 608 240-4800
  Cleveland *(G-4009)*
▲ Energy Focus Inc .... F 440 715-1300
  Solon *(G-13343)*
Ezurio LLC .... D 330 434-7929
  Akron *(G-146)*
First Solar Inc .... E 419 661-1478
  Perrysburg *(G-12382)*
Gen Digital Inc .... G 330 252-1171
  Akron *(G-165)*
Gopowerx Inc .... F 440 707-6029
  Richfield *(G-12789)*
Greenfield Solar Corp .... G 216 535-9200
  North Ridgeville *(G-11842)*
▲ Hawthorne Hydroponics LLC .... F 888 478-6544
  Marysville *(G-9914)*
Heraeus Electro-Nite Co LLC .... G 330 725-1419
  Medina *(G-10333)*
Honeywell International Inc .... D 302 327-8920
  Columbus *(G-5444)*
Hyper Tech Research Inc .... F 614 481-8050
  Columbus *(G-5449)*
Intel Interpeace .... G 330 922-4450
  Akron *(G-192)*
▲ Isofoton North America Inc .... F 419 591-4330
  Napoleon *(G-11321)*
Lam Research Corporation .... G 937 472-3311
  Eaton *(G-7064)*
Leidos Inc .... D 937 656-8433
  Beavercreek *(G-1055)*
Linear Asics Inc .... G 330 474-3920
  Twinsburg *(G-14690)*
▲ Materion Brush Inc .... D 216 486-4200
  Mayfield Heights *(G-10250)*
◆ Materion Corporation .... C 216 486-4200
  Mayfield Heights *(G-10251)*
Measurement Specialties Inc .... E 937 427-1231
  Dayton *(G-6433)*
Micro Industries Corporation .... D 740 548-7878
  Westerville *(G-15716)*
Mok Industries LLC .... F 614 934-1734
  Columbus *(G-5577)*

Employee Codes: A=Over 500 employees, B=251-500
C=101-250, D=51-100, E=20-50, F=10-19, G=1-9

36 ELECTRONIC & OTHER ELECTRICAL EQUIPMENT & COMPONENTS — SIC SECTION

Niobium Microsystems Inc .... C 937 203-8117
 Dayton (G-6471)
◆ Ohio Semitronics Inc .... D 614 777-1005
 Hilliard (G-8427)
▲ Pepperl + Fuchs Inc .... C 330 425-3555
 Twinsburg (G-14709)
Pepperl + Fuchs Entps Inc .... F 330 425-3555
 Twinsburg (G-14710)
Plug Power Inc .... G 518 605-5703
 West Carrollton (G-15356)
◆ Powertech Inc .... G 901 850-9393
 Beachwood (G-1011)
Redhawk Energy Systems LLC .... G 740 927-8244
 Pataskala (G-12305)
Refocus Holdings Inc .... F 216 751-8384
 Cleveland (G-4622)
◆ Rexon Components Inc .... E 216 292-7373
 Beachwood (G-1018)
Rv Mobile Power LLC .... G 855 427-7978
 Columbus (G-3706)
Saint-Gobain Ceramics Plas Inc .... B 440 542-2712
 Newbury (G-11637)
Salient Systems Inc .... E 614 792-5800
 Dublin (G-6934)
SCI Engineered Materials Inc .... E 614 486-0261
 Columbus (G-5754)
Signature Technologies Inc .... E 937 859-6323
 Miamisburg (G-10683)
Silfex Inc .... B 937 324-2487
 Springfield (G-13632)
▲ Silfex Inc .... D 937 472-3311
 Eaton (G-7070)
Spang & Company .... E 440 350-6108
 Mentor (G-10558)
▲ Techneglas LLC .... E 419 873-2000
 Perrysburg (G-12432)
Toledo Solar Inc .... F 567 202-4145
 Perrysburg (G-12439)
▲ Tosoh SMD Inc .... C 614 875-7912
 Grove City (G-8125)
Tri-Tech Led Systems LLC .... G 614 593-2868
 Baltimore (G-848)
▲ Ustek Incorporated .... G 614 538-8000
 Columbus (G-5851)
Uvonics Co .... F 614 458-1163
 Columbus (G-5852)
Viavi Solutions Inc .... G 316 522-4981
 Columbus (G-5073)

3675 Electronic capacitors

CPI Group Limited .... F 216 525-0046
 Cleveland (G-3911)
Oren Elliot Products LLC .... E 419 298-0015
 Edgerton (G-7079)
Soemhejee Inc .... E 419 298-2306
 Edgerton (G-7080)
Standex International Corp .... D 513 533-7171
 Fairfield (G-7412)

3676 Electronic resistors

Apex Control Systems Inc .... D 330 938-2588
 Sebring (G-13117)
Measurement Specialties Inc .... E 937 427-1231
 Dayton (G-6433)

3677 Electronic coils and transformers

Barnes International LLC .... E 419 352-7501
 Bowling Green (G-1552)
Contech Strmwter Solutions LLC .... G 513 645-7000
 West Chester (G-15404)
Custom Coil & Transformer Co .... G 740 452-5211
 Zanesville (G-16525)

▲ Duca Manufacturing & Cons .... E 330 758-0828
 Youngstown (G-16352)
Electric Service Co Inc .... E 513 271-6387
 Cincinnati (G-2861)
Electromotive Inc .... E 330 688-6494
 Stow (G-13693)
Fontaine Pieciak Engrg Inc .... E 413 592-2273
 Twinsburg (G-14661)
◆ Foster Transformer Company .... E 513 681-2420
 Cincinnati (G-2919)
Illinois Tool Works Inc .... E 262 248-8277
 Bryan (G-1821)
▲ Industrial Quartz Corporation .... E 440 942-0909
 Mentor (G-10471)
▲ Kurz-Kasch Inc .... E 740 498-8343
 Newcomerstown (G-11647)
M2m Imaging Corporation .... G 440 684-9690
 Cleveland (G-4346)
◆ Micropure Filtration Inc .... E 952 472-2323
 Cleveland (G-4402)
▼ Norlake Manufacturing Company .... D 110 052 2200
 North Ridgeville (G-11851)
Npas Inc .... F 614 595-0916
 Mansfield (G-9706)
Nu Stream Filtration Inc .... F 937 949-3174
 Dayton (G-6482)
PCC Airfoils LLC .... C 216 692-7900
 Cleveland (G-4537)
Rapid Mr International LLC .... G 614 486-6300
 Columbus (G-5711)
Schneider Electric Usa Inc .... B 513 523-4171
 Oxford (G-12213)
Staco Energy Products Co .... E 937 253-1191
 Dayton (G-6587)
◆ Staco Energy Products Co .... E 937 253-1191
 Miamisburg (G-10685)
▲ Swiger Coil Systems Ltd .... C 216 362-7500
 Cleveland (G-4760)
▲ USA Instruments Inc .... C 330 562-1000
 Aurora (G-739)
Wabtec Corporation .... F 216 362-7500
 Cleveland (G-4887)

3678 Electronic connectors

◆ American Micro Products Inc .... C 513 732-2674
 Batavia (G-908)
Ankim Enterprises Incorporated .... F 937 599-1121
 Sidney (G-13222)
Astro Industries Inc .... E 937 429-5900
 Beavercreek (G-1041)
▲ C C M Wire Inc .... E 330 425-3421
 Twinsburg (G-14638)
Canadus Power Systems LLC .... F 216 831-6600
 Twinsburg (G-14639)
Connective Design Incorporated .... F 937 746-8252
 Miamisburg (G-10628)
▲ Connectors Unlimited Inc .... E 440 357-1161
 Painesville (G-12224)
Connectronics Corp .... D 419 537-0020
 Toledo (G-14250)
▲ Custom Connector Corporation .... E 216 241-1679
 Cleveland (G-3924)
Dcm Soundex Inc .... F 937 522-0371
 Dayton (G-6295)
▲ Dynalab Inc .... D 614 866-9999
 Reynoldsburg (G-12764)
Ecm Industries LLC .... E 513 533-6242
 Cincinnati (G-2857)
HCC/Sealtron .... C 513 733-8400
 Cincinnati (G-2991)
▲ Ilsco LLC .... C 513 533-6200
 Cincinnati (G-3017)

▲ Lastar Inc .... B 937 224-0639
 Moraine (G-11190)
Mueller Electric Company Inc .... F 614 888-8855
 New Albany (G-11384)
◆ Network Technologies Inc .... D 330 562-7070
 Aurora (G-727)
Ohio Associated Entps LLC .... F 440 354-3148
 Painesville (G-12253)
Powell Electrical Systems Inc .... D 330 966-1750
 North Canton (G-11753)
Qnnect LLC .... F 864 275-8970
 Painesville (G-12259)
Standex International Corp .... D 513 533-7171
 Fairfield (G-7412)
Xponet Inc .... E 440 354-6617
 Painesville (G-12279)

3679 Electronic components, nec

Accurate Electronics Inc .... C 330 682-7015
 Orrville (G-12116)
Advanced Cryogenic Entps LLC .... G 330 922-0750
 Akron (G-22)
Aeroseal LLC .... E 937 428-9300
 Dayton (G-6187)
▲ Aeroseal LLC .... E 937 428-9300
 Miamisburg (G-10607)
Alphabet Inc .... D 330 856-3366
 Warren (G-15136)
American Advnced Assmblies LLC .... E 937 339-6267
 Troy (G-14549)
Ankim Enterprises Incorporated .... F 937 599-1121
 Sidney (G-13222)
Astro Industries Inc .... E 937 429-5900
 Beavercreek (G-1041)
B5 Systems Inc .... G 937 372-4768
 Xenia (G-16249)
Bennett & Bennett Inc .... G 937 324-1100
 Yellow Springs (G-16282)
Berry Investments Inc .... G 937 293-0398
 Moraine (G-11162)
Black Box Corporation .... G 855 324-9909
 Westlake (G-15738)
▲ C C M Wire Inc .... E 330 425-3421
 Twinsburg (G-14638)
C DI Services LLC .... G 440 354-1433
 Painesville (G-12220)
C E Electronics Inc .... D 419 636-6705
 Bryan (G-1813)
Captor Corporation .... D 937 667-8484
 Tipp City (G-14126)
CCS International Circuits LLC .... G 440 563-3462
 Roaming Shores (G-12830)
CEC Electronics Corp .... G 330 916-8100
 Akron (G-102)
▲ Channel Products Inc .... D 440 423-0113
 Solon (G-13328)
▲ Cks Solution Incorporated .... E 513 947-1277
 Fairfield (G-7348)
▲ Cleanlife Energy LLC .... F 800 316-2532
 Cleveland (G-3827)
Co-Ax Technology Inc .... C 440 914-9200
 Solon (G-13332)
Connective Design Incorporated .... F 937 746-8252
 Miamisburg (G-10628)
Cutting Edge Technologies Inc .... E 216 574-4759
 Cleveland (G-3928)
D H S LLC .... F 937 599-2485
 Bellefontaine (G-1204)
Dare Electronics Inc .... E 937 335-0031
 Troy (G-14559)
Darrah Electric Company .... F 216 631-0912
 Cleveland (G-3942)

SIC SECTION
36 ELECTRONIC & OTHER ELECTRICAL EQUIPMENT & COMPONENTS

Dcm Soundex Inc .... F 937 522-0371
   Dayton *(G-6295)*

Deca Mfg Co .... F 419 884-0071
   Mansfield *(G-9645)*

Dish One Up Satellite Inc .... D 216 482-3875
   Cleveland *(G-3961)*

Don-Ell Corporation .... E 419 841-7114
   Sylvania *(G-13993)*

Drivetrain USA Inc .... F 614 733-0940
   Plain City *(G-12576)*

▲ Dynalab Ems Inc .... D 614 866-9999
   Reynoldsburg *(G-12762)*

▲ Dynalab Ff Inc .... D 614 866-9999
   Reynoldsburg *(G-12763)*

▲ Dynalab Inc .... D 614 866-9999
   Reynoldsburg *(G-12764)*

Electro-Line Inc .... F 937 461-5683
   Dayton *(G-6315)*

Electromotive Inc .... E 330 688-6494
   Stow *(G-13693)*

◆ Electronauts LLC .... F 859 261-3600
   Cincinnati *(G-2862)*

Eti Tech LLC .... F 937 832-4200
   Kettering *(G-8907)*

Ewh Spectrum LLC .... D 937 593-8010
   Bellefontaine *(G-1208)*

Gem City Engineering Co .... C 937 223-5544
   Dayton *(G-6348)*

Gmelectric Inc .... G 330 477-3392
   Canton *(G-2114)*

▲ Great Lakes Glasswerks Inc .... G 440 358-0460
   Painesville *(G-12241)*

◆ Guitamer Company .... G 614 898-9370
   Columbus *(G-5413)*

Hall Company .... E 937 652-1376
   Urbana *(G-14833)*

Helios Quartz America Inc .... G 419 882-3377
   Sylvania *(G-13999)*

Innocomp .... G 440 248-5104
   Solon *(G-13368)*

▲ Inservco Inc .... D 847 855-9600
   Lagrange *(G-8948)*

▲ Kent Displays Inc .... D 330 673-8784
   Kent *(G-8822)*

◆ Kontron America Incorporated .... G 937 324-2420
   Springfield *(G-13591)*

▲ L & J Cable Inc .... E 937 526-9445
   Russia *(G-12885)*

La Grange Elec Assemblies Co .... E 440 355-5388
   Lagrange *(G-8950)*

Laird Technologies Inc .... F 330 434-7929
   Akron *(G-215)*

Lake Shore Cryotronics Inc .... D 614 891-2243
   Westerville *(G-15662)*

Leidos Inc .... D 937 656-8433
   Beavercreek *(G-1055)*

Lintech Electronics LLC .... F 513 528-6190
   Cincinnati *(G-2571)*

Malabar Properties LLC .... F 419 884-0071
   Mansfield *(G-9682)*

Mega Techway Inc .... C 440 605-0700
   Cleveland *(G-4391)*

Microplex Inc .... E 330 498-0600
   North Canton *(G-11743)*

▲ MJM Industries Inc .... C 440 350-1230
   Fairport Harbor *(G-7456)*

Mjo Industries Inc .... D 800 590-4055
   Huber Heights *(G-8577)*

Mueller Electric Company Inc .... F 614 888-8855
   New Albany *(G-11384)*

◆ Niktec Inc .... G 513 282-3747
   Franklin *(G-7689)*

◆ Nimers & Woody II Inc .... C 937 454-0722
   Vandalia *(G-14955)*

Nyle LLC .... F 888 235-2097
   Springboro *(G-13513)*

Ogc Industries Inc .... F 330 456-1500
   Canton *(G-2181)*

Ohio Power Systems LLC .... F 419 396-4041
   Carey *(G-2282)*

◆ Ohio Semitronics Inc .... D 614 777-1005
   Hilliard *(G-8427)*

Ohio Wire Harness LLC .... F 937 292-7355
   Bellefontaine *(G-1217)*

Omega Engineering Inc .... E 740 965-9340
   Sunbury *(G-13962)*

Omegadyne Inc .... D 740 965-9340
   Sunbury *(G-13963)*

Parker-Hannifin Corporation .... F 937 644-3915
   Marysville *(G-9930)*

Performance Electronics Ltd .... G 513 777-5233
   Cincinnati *(G-3247)*

Precision Manufacturing Co Inc .... D 937 236-2170
   Dayton *(G-6514)*

Projects Unlimited Inc .... C 937 918-2200
   Dayton *(G-6534)*

Qlog Corp .... G 513 874-1211
   Hamilton *(G-8238)*

◆ Quality Quartz Engineering Inc .... D 937 236-3250
   Beavercreek Township *(G-1092)*

▲ Quality Quartz Engineering Inc .... E 510 791-1013
   Beavercreek Township *(G-1093)*

Quality Switch Inc .... E 330 872-5707
   Newton Falls *(G-11655)*

Quartz Scientific Inc .... E 360 574-6254
   Fairport Harbor *(G-7457)*

Ra Consultants LLC .... E 513 469-6600
   Blue Ash *(G-1459)*

Rct Industries Inc .... F 937 602-1100
   Dayton *(G-6543)*

Reliable Hermetic Seals LLC .... F 888 747-3250
   Beavercreek *(G-1060)*

Rpa Electronic Distrs Inc .... G 937 223-7001
   Dayton *(G-6553)*

RTD Electronics Inc .... F 330 487-0716
   Twinsburg *(G-14729)*

Russell Group United LLC .... F 614 353-6853
   Columbus *(G-5734)*

▲ S-Tek Inc .... G 440 439-8232
   Twinsburg *(G-14732)*

Saint-Gobain Ceramics Plas Inc .... C 330 673-5860
   Stow *(G-13721)*

▲ Sawyer Technical Materials LLC ..... E 440 951-8770
   Willoughby *(G-15985)*

Sentrilock LLC .... C 513 618-5800
   West Chester *(G-15507)*

Shiloh Industries Inc .... F 937 236-5100
   Dayton *(G-6569)*

Sinbon Usa LLC .... E 937 667-8999
   Tipp City *(G-14154)*

Sovereign Circuits Inc .... G 330 538-3900
   North Jackson *(G-11790)*

▲ Specialty Switch Company LLC ...... F 330 427-3000
   Youngstown *(G-16444)*

Spectron Inc .... G 937 461-5590
   Dayton *(G-6583)*

Staci Holdings Inc .... G 440 284-2500
   Lagrange *(G-8955)*

The W L Jenkins Company .... F 330 477-3407
   Canton *(G-2244)*

◆ Thermtrol Corporation .... A 330 497-4148
   North Canton *(G-11765)*

Tinycircuits .... G 330 329-5753
   Akron *(G-358)*

TL Industries Inc .... C 419 666-8144
   Perrysburg *(G-12436)*

▲ Twin Point Inc .... G 419 923-7525
   Delta *(G-6791)*

US Lighting Group Inc .... E 216 896-7000
   Euclid *(G-7305)*

Valley Electric Company .... G 419 332-6405
   Fremont *(G-7818)*

Vertiv Group Corporation .... A 614 888-0246
   Westerville *(G-15687)*

Vertiv Holdings Co .... D 614 888-0246
   Westerville *(G-15688)*

Vertiv JV Holdings LLC .... A 614 888-0246
   Columbus *(G-5859)*

▲ Westbrook Mfg Inc .... B 937 254-2004
   Dayton *(G-6650)*

Wetsu Group Inc .... F 937 324-9353
   Springfield *(G-13655)*

▲ Workman Electronic Pdts Inc .... G 419 923-7525
   Delta *(G-6792)*

3691 Storage batteries

Acculon Energy Inc .... F 614 259-7792
   Columbus *(G-5094)*

All Power Battery Inc .... G 330 453-5236
   Canton *(G-2033)*

Cirba Solutions Us Inc .... D 740 653-6290
   Lancaster *(G-9001)*

Clarios LLC .... A 419 865-0542
   Holland *(G-8498)*

Crown Battery Manufacturing Co .... G 330 425-3308
   Twinsburg *(G-14646)*

◆ Crown Battery Manufacturing Co ..... B 419 334-7181
   Fremont *(G-7773)*

Energizer Battery Inc .... E 440 835-7500
   Westlake *(G-15748)*

Energizer Manufacturing Inc .... G
   Westlake *(G-15749)*

Enersys .... C 216 252-4242
   Cleveland *(G-4017)*

Glx Power Systems Inc .... G 440 338-6526
   Chagrin Falls *(G-2378)*

Graywacke Inc .... F 419 884-7014
   Mansfield *(G-9664)*

Lithchem Intl Toxco Inc .... F 740 653-6290
   Lancaster *(G-9022)*

Millertech Energy Solutions .... F 855 629-5484
   West Farmington *(G-15606)*

Reliant Worth Corp .... G 440 232-1422
   Bedford *(G-1152)*

Spectrum Brands Inc .... G 567 998-7930
   Vandalia *(G-14961)*

Toxco Inc .... E 740 653-6290
   Lancaster *(G-9045)*

Transdigm Inc .... F 216 291-6025
   Cleveland *(G-4815)*

Xerion Advanced Battery Corp .... F 720 229-0697
   Kettering *(G-8911)*

3692 Primary batteries, dry and wet

D C Systems Inc .... F 330 273-3030
   Brunswick *(G-1756)*

Glx Power Systems Inc .... G 440 338-6526
   Chagrin Falls *(G-2378)*

▲ Inventus Power (ohio) Inc .... F 614 351-2191
   Dublin *(G-6901)*

Ultium Cells LLC .... E 586 295-5429
   Warren *(G-15214)*

3694 Engine electrical equipment

▲ Altronic LLC .... C 330 545-9768
   Girard *(G-7960)*

Employee Codes: A=Over 500 employees, B=251-500
C=101-250, D=51-100, E=20-50, F=10-19, G=1-9

36 ELECTRONIC & OTHER ELECTRICAL EQUIPMENT & COMPONENTS

Asidaco LLC .... G 800 204-1544
  Dayton *(G-6215)*
Brinkley Technology Group LLC .... F 330 830-2498
  Massillon *(G-10079)*
▲ C C M Wire Inc .... E 330 425-3421
  Twinsburg *(G-14638)*
Charles Auto Electric Co Inc .... G 330 535-6269
  Akron *(G-106)*
Commercial Vehicle Group Inc .... B 614 289-5360
  New Albany *(G-11374)*
Cummins Inc .... E 614 604-6004
  Grove City *(G-8085)*
Cuyahoga Rebuilders Inc .... G 216 635-0659
  Cleveland *(G-3931)*
Cycle Electric Inc .... E 937 884-7300
  Brookville *(G-1732)*
Egr Products Company Inc .... F 330 833-6554
  Dalton *(G-6131)*
Electra Sound Inc .... D 216 433-9600
  Avon Lake *(G-005)*
◆ Electripack Inc .... E 937 433-2602
  Moraine *(G-11174)*
Ewh Spectrum LLC .... D 937 593-8010
  Bellefontaine *(G-1208)*
Exact-Tool & Die Inc .... E 216 676-9140
  Cleveland *(G-4040)*
▲ Ferrotherm Corporation .... C 216 883-9350
  Cleveland *(G-4058)*
Flex Technologies Inc .... D 330 359-5415
  Mount Eaton *(G-11230)*
Gmelectric Inc .... G 330 477-3392
  Canton *(G-2114)*
▲ GSW Manufacturing Inc .... B 419 423-7111
  Findlay *(G-7516)*
Hitachi Astemo Americas Inc .... C 937 783-4961
  Blanchester *(G-1350)*
Hitachi Astemo Americas Inc .... B 740 965-1133
  Sunbury *(G-13955)*
Lake Erie Interlock Inc .... G 440 918-9898
  Willoughby *(G-15943)*
Legacy Supplies Inc .... F 330 405-4565
  Twinsburg *(G-14685)*
M W Solutions LLC .... F 419 782-1611
  Defiance *(G-6689)*
Machine Products Company .... E 937 890-6600
  Dayton *(G-6420)*
▲ Mueller Electric Company Inc .... E 216 771-5225
  Akron *(G-256)*
Power Acquisition LLC .... D 614 228-5000
  Dublin *(G-6925)*
Rv Mobile Power LLC .... G 855 427-7978
  Columbus *(G-5735)*
▲ Sk Tech Inc .... C 937 836-3535
  Englewood *(G-7242)*
▲ Stanley Electric US Co Inc .... D 740 852-5200
  London *(G-9394)*
Sumitomo Elc Wirg Systems Inc .... E 937 642-7579
  Marysville *(G-9941)*
Thirion Brothers Eqp Co LLC .... G 440 357-8004
  Painesville *(G-12271)*
▲ Tri-W Group Inc .... A 614 228-5000
  Columbus *(G-5837)*
▲ United Ignition Wire Corp .... G 216 898-1112
  Cleveland *(G-4847)*
Vintage Automotive Elc Inc .... F 419 472-9349
  Toledo *(G-14520)*
W W Williams Company LLC .... D 614 228-5000
  Dublin *(G-6958)*
Weldon Pump LLC .... E 440 232-2482
  Oakwood Village *(G-12047)*

3695 Magnetic and optical recording media

CD Solutions Inc .... G 937 676-2376
  Pleasant Hill *(G-12606)*
Clockingme LLC .... F 614 400-9727
  Columbus *(G-5255)*
Folio Photonics Inc .... F 440 420-4500
  Solon *(G-13352)*
Ginko Voting Systems LLC .... E 937 291-4060
  Dayton *(G-6352)*
Paragon Robotics LLC .... E 216 313-9299
  Twinsburg *(G-14706)*
Signalysis Inc .... F 513 528-6164
  Cincinnati *(G-3392)*

3699 Electrical equipment and supplies, nec

A L Callahan Door Sales .... G 419 884-3667
  Mansfield *(G-9620)*
Aat USA LLC .... E 614 388-8866
  Columbus *(G-5083)*
▲ Action Industries Ltd .... G 216 252-7800
  Strongsville *(G-13801)*
▲ Agratronix LLC .... E 330 502-2222
  Streetsboro *(G-13753)*
Ahkeo Labs LLC .... G 216 406-1919
  Mayfield Village *(G-10258)*
Akron Brass Company .... E 614 529-7230
  Columbus *(G-5109)*
◆ Akron Brass Company .... B 330 264-5678
  Wooster *(G-16097)*
Akron Brass Holding Corp .... E 330 264-5678
  Wooster *(G-16098)*
Alert Safety Lite Products Co .... F 440 232-5020
  Cleveland *(G-3626)*
Alfalight Inc .... G 608 240-4800
  Cleveland *(G-3627)*
Allen Fields Assoc Inc .... E 513 228-1010
  Lebanon *(G-9061)*
◆ Allied Moulded Products Inc .... C 419 636-4217
  Bryan *(G-1804)*
American Quality Door Co .... G 330 296-0393
  Ravenna *(G-12705)*
Ametek Inc .... F 937 440-0800
  Troy *(G-14550)*
Amy Electric .... G 740 349-9484
  Newark *(G-11562)*
ARC Elec .... G 440 774-2800
  Wellington *(G-15303)*
Azz Inc .... D 330 456-3241
  Canton *(G-2041)*
▲ Barth Industries Co LLC .... E 216 267-1950
  Cleveland *(G-3722)*
Beta Industries Inc .... F 937 299-7385
  Dayton *(G-6227)*
▲ Cecil C Peck Co .... F 330 785-0781
  Akron *(G-103)*
Ces Nationwide .... G 937 322-0771
  Springfield *(G-13543)*
Checkpoint Systems Inc .... D 330 456-7776
  Canton *(G-2072)*
Ci Disposition Co .... D 216 587-5200
  Brooklyn Heights *(G-1687)*
Circle Prime Manufacturing .... E 330 923-0019
  Cuyahoga Falls *(G-6074)*
Clark Substations LLC .... F 330 452-5200
  Canton *(G-2077)*
Commercial Electric Pdts Corp .... E 216 241-2886
  Cleveland *(G-3889)*
Corrpro Companies Inc .... E 330 725-6681
  Medina *(G-10314)*
Corrpro Companies Intl Inc .... E 330 723-5082
  Medina *(G-10315)*
Diebold Nixdorf Incorporated .... A 330 490-4000
  North Canton *(G-11722)*

SIC SECTION

Double D D Mtls Instltion Inc .... G 937 898-2534
  Dayton *(G-6302)*
E-Beam Services Inc .... E 513 933-0031
  Lebanon *(G-9071)*
Eagle Welding & Fabg Inc .... E 440 946-0692
  Willoughby *(G-15914)*
Electro Plasma Incorporated .... C 419 838-7365
  Millbury *(G-10931)*
▲ Emx Industries Inc .... F 216 518-9888
  Cleveland *(G-4013)*
Enespro Ppe .... G 800 553-0672
  Brooklyn *(G-1677)*
Engineered Mfg & Eqp Co .... G 937 642-7776
  Marysville *(G-9908)*
Enterpriseid Inc .... G 330 963-0064
  Twinsburg *(G-14655)*
Erico Global Company .... E 440 248-0100
  Solon *(G-13344)*
Ever Secure SEC Systems Inc .... F 937 369-8294
  Dayton *(G-6327)*
▲ Federal Equipment Company .... D 513 621-5260
  Cincinnati *(G-2899)*
▲ Fernandes Enterprises LLC .... F 937 890-6444
  Dayton *(G-6331)*
Fire-End & Croker Corp .... E 513 870-0517
  West Chester *(G-15553)*
▲ Flightsafety International Inc .... C 614 324-3500
  Columbus *(G-5380)*
FM Systems .... F 330 273-3000
  Brunswick *(G-1759)*
Fortec Medical Lithotripsy LLC .... F 330 656-4301
  Streetsboro *(G-13771)*
General Electric Company .... E 714 668-0951
  West Chester *(G-15440)*
Global Security Tech Inc .... G 614 890-6400
  Westerville *(G-15706)*
◆ GMI Holdings Inc .... B 800 354-3643
  Mount Hope *(G-11237)*
Graham Electric .... F 614 231-8500
  Columbus *(G-5409)*
Great Lakes Power Service Co .... G 440 259-0025
  Perry *(G-12351)*
H W Fairway International Inc .... F 330 678-2540
  Canton *(G-2119)*
◆ Halex/Scott Fetzer Company .... E 800 749-3261
  Harrison *(G-8278)*
Hannon Company .... D 330 456-4728
  Canton *(G-2121)*
Hanon Systems Usa LLC .... C 313 920-0583
  Carey *(G-2279)*
Hess Advanced Solutions Llc .... G 937 829-4794
  Dayton *(G-6368)*
Highcom Global Security Inc .... G 727 592-9400
  Columbus *(G-5434)*
Holland Assocts LLC DBA Archou .... F 513 891-0006
  Cincinnati *(G-3003)*
Honeywell International Inc .... A 937 484-2000
  Urbana *(G-14835)*
◆ I T Verdin Co .... E 513 241-4010
  Cincinnati *(G-3015)*
Innovar Systems Limited .... E 330 538-3942
  North Jackson *(G-11784)*
▼ Invue Security Products Inc .... E 330 456-7776
  Canton *(G-2133)*
JC Electric Llc .... F 330 760-2915
  Garrettsville *(G-7917)*
▲ Jobap Assembly Inc .... F 440 632-5393
  Middlefield *(G-10760)*
Kiemle-Hankins Company .... E 419 661-2430
  Perrysburg *(G-12395)*
Kraft Electrical Contg Inc .... E 614 836-9300
  Groveport *(G-8149)*

SIC SECTION

37 TRANSPORTATION EQUIPMENT

Laser Automation Inc .... F 440 543-9291
   Chagrin Falls *(G-2405)*
Lawn Aid Inc .... G 417 533-5555
   Tipp City *(G-14140)*
▼ Lindsay Precast LLC .... E 800 837-7788
   Canal Fulton *(G-1972)*
Lucky Thirteen Inc .... G 216 631-0013
   Cleveland *(G-4340)*
Mac Tools Inc .... E 614 755-7039
   Westerville *(G-15666)*
◆ Mace Security Intl Inc .... D 440 424-5325
   Cleveland *(G-4349)*
▼ Matlock Electric Co Inc .... E 513 731-9600
   Cincinnati *(G-3134)*
Midwest Security Services .... E 937 853-9000
   Dayton *(G-6444)*
Mixed Logic LLC .... G 440 826-1676
   Valley City *(G-14879)*
Momentum Fleet MGT Group Inc .... D 440 759-2219
   Westlake *(G-15765)*
▲ Mueller Electric Company Inc .... E 216 771-5225
   Akron *(G-256)*
Nabco Entrances Inc .... F 419 842-0484
   Sylvania *(G-14008)*
Niftech Inc .... F 440 257-6018
   Mentor *(G-10511)*
▲ Nimers & Woody II Inc .... C 937 454-0722
   Vandalia *(G-14955)*
Ohio Home & Leisure Products I .... G 614 833-4144
   Pickerington *(G-12465)*
▲ Overly Hautz Motor Base Co .... E 513 932-0025
   Lebanon *(G-9104)*
Pacific Highway Products LLC .... G 740 914-5217
   Marion *(G-9871)*
Peerless Laser Processors Inc .... F 614 836-5790
   Groveport *(G-8156)*
Pentagon Protection Usa LLC .... F 614 734-7240
   Dublin *(G-6922)*
◆ Philips Med Systems Clvland In .... B 440 483-3000
   Cleveland *(G-4547)*
Powell Electrical Systems Inc .... D 330 966-1750
   North Canton *(G-11753)*
Primex .... E 513 831-9959
   Milford *(G-10919)*
Pt Metals LLC .... E 330 767-3003
   Navarre *(G-11351)*
▲ Qualtech Technologies Inc .... E 440 946-8081
   Willoughby *(G-15980)*
R F I .... G 740 654-4502
   Lancaster *(G-9035)*
▲ Rah Investment Holding Inc .... D 330 832-8124
   Massillon *(G-10138)*
Resonetics LLC .... E 937 865-4070
   Kettering *(G-8909)*
▼ Riverside Drives Inc .... E 216 362-1211
   Cleveland *(G-4637)*
Sage Integration Holdings LLC .... E 330 733-8183
   Kent *(G-8857)*
▲ Say Security Group USA LLC .... F 419 634-0004
   Ada *(G-5)*
Schneider Electric Usa Inc .... B 513 523-4171
   Oxford *(G-12213)*
Securcom Inc .... E 419 628-1049
   Minster *(G-11060)*
Securtex International Inc .... F 937 312-1414
   Dayton *(G-6565)*
Sew-Eurodrive Inc .... D 937 335-0036
   Troy *(G-14609)*
Smart Sonic Corporation .... G 818 610-7900
   Cleveland *(G-4707)*
Soundworks Inc .... G 408 219-5737
   Lorain *(G-9439)*

Spang & Company .... E 440 350-6108
   Mentor *(G-10558)*
Spikes Beverage Company Inc .... G 513 429-5134
   Cincinnati *(G-3408)*
Square D Services .... G 440 526-9070
   Broadview Heights *(G-1667)*
Tech-Sonic Inc .... F 614 792-3117
   Columbus *(G-5816)*
Technlogy Install Partners LLC .... E 888 586-7040
   Cleveland *(G-4774)*
The W L Jenkins Company .... F 330 477-3407
   Canton *(G-2244)*
Tip Products Inc .... E 216 252-2535
   New London *(G-11472)*
◆ Vanner Holdings Inc .... D 614 771-2718
   Hilliard *(G-8451)*
Vesco LLC .... E 330 374-5156
   Mogadore *(G-11091)*
Vortec Corporation .... E
   Blue Ash *(G-1489)*
Wesco Distribution Inc .... F 419 666-1670
   Northwood *(G-11933)*

37 TRANSPORTATION EQUIPMENT

3711 Motor vehicles and car bodies

Ackerman .... G 440 246-2034
   Lorain *(G-9401)*
◆ Airstream Inc .... B 937 596-6111
   Jackson Center *(G-8729)*
Antique Auto Sheet Metal Inc .... F 937 833-4422
   Brookville *(G-1729)*
Autowax Inc .... G 440 334-4417
   Strongsville *(G-13813)*
◆ Bae Systems Survivability .... A 513 881-9800
   West Chester *(G-15372)*
Bobbart Industries Inc .... E 419 350-5477
   Sylvania *(G-13991)*
Braun Industries Inc .... B 419 232-7020
   Van Wert *(G-14907)*
Brookville Roadster Inc .... F 937 833-4605
   Brookville *(G-1730)*
Copley Fire & Rescue Assn .... E 330 666-6464
   Copley *(G-5947)*
▲ Custom Chassis Inc .... G 440 839-5574
   Wakeman *(G-15073)*
D&D Clssic Auto Rstoration Inc .... F 937 473-2229
   Covington *(G-6021)*
Dakkota Integrated Systems LLC .... E 517 694-6500
   Toledo *(G-14258)*
Eldorado National Kansas Inc .... C 937 596-6849
   Jackson Center *(G-8732)*
Falls Stamping & Welding Co .... C 330 928-1191
   Cuyahoga Falls *(G-6083)*
Federaleagle LLC .... D 513 797-4100
   West Chester *(G-15552)*
Ford Motor Company .... C 440 933-1215
   Avon Lake *(G-807)*
FOXCONN EV SYSTEM LLC .... B 234 285-4001
   Warren *(G-15171)*
▲ Galion-Godwin Truck Bdy Co LLC ...... F 330 359-5495
   Dundee *(G-6965)*
◆ Gerling and Associates Inc .... D 740 965-6200
   Sunbury *(G-13954)*
Great Lakes Assemblies LLC .... D 937 645-3900
   East Liberty *(G-6986)*
▼ Halcore Group Inc .... C 614 539-8181
   Grove City *(G-8097)*
Honda Dev & Mfg Amer LLC .... C 937 644-0724
   Marysville *(G-9915)*

Honda Dev & Mfg Amer LLC .... B 937 642-5000
   Marysville *(G-9917)*
◆ Honda Dev & Mfg Amer LLC .... A 937 642-5000
   Marysville *(G-9916)*
Horizon Global Corporation .... E 734 656-3000
   Cleveland *(G-4200)*
Hyo Seong America Corporation .... F 513 682-6182
   Fairfield *(G-7371)*
▲ Jefferson Industries Corp .... C 614 879-5300
   West Jefferson *(G-15610)*
La Boit Specialty Vehicles .... D 614 231-7640
   Gahanna *(G-7843)*
Lordstown Ev Corporation .... F 678 428-6558
   Warren *(G-15185)*
Lordstown Motors Corp .... G 312 925-2466
   Mason *(G-10021)*
Magic Dragon Machine Inc .... G 614 539-8004
   Grove City *(G-8103)*
Mobile Solutions LLC .... F 614 286-3944
   Columbus *(G-5575)*
Monarch Plastic Inc .... F 330 683-0822
   Orrville *(G-12137)*
Navistar Inc .... G 513 733-8500
   Cincinnati *(G-3183)*
Navistar Inc .... C 937 390-4776
   Springfield *(G-13610)*
Navistar Inc .... E 937 561-3315
   Springfield *(G-13611)*
▲ Obs Inc .... F 330 453-3725
   Canton *(G-2180)*
◆ Ohio Module Manufacturing .... A 419 729-6700
   Toledo *(G-14409)*
P C Workshop Inc .... F 419 399-4805
   Paulding *(G-12319)*
Paccar Inc .... D 740 774-5111
   Chillicothe *(G-2522)*
Scottrods LLC .... G 419 499-2705
   Monroeville *(G-11125)*
Star Fab Inc .... E 330 482-1601
   Columbiana *(G-5052)*
Subaru of A .... G 614 793-2358
   Dublin *(G-6948)*
Sutphen Corporation .... E 937 969-8851
   Springfield *(G-13640)*
▼ Sutphen Corporation .... C 800 726-7030
   Dublin *(G-6949)*
Thor Industries Inc .... F 937 596-6111
   Jackson Center *(G-8739)*
Toledo Pro Fiberglass Inc .... G 419 241-9390
   Toledo *(G-14503)*
Tpam Inc .... E 567 315-8694
   Toledo *(G-14511)*
Transit Fittings N Amer Inc .... G 330 797-2516
   Youngstown *(G-16458)*
▲ Tremcar USA Inc .... D 330 878-7708
   Strasburg *(G-13750)*
Universal Composite LLC .... F 614 507-1646
   Sunbury *(G-13965)*
Village of Grafton .... F 440 926-2075
   Grafton *(G-8006)*
W&W Automotive & Towing Inc .... F 937 429-1699
   Beavercreek Township *(G-1095)*
Warfighter Fcsed Logistics Inc .... E 740 513-4692
   West Chester *(G-15526)*
Workhorse Technologies Inc .... E 888 646-5205
   Sharonville *(G-13176)*
Wyatt Specialties Inc .... F 614 989-5362
   Circleville *(G-3561)*

3713 Truck and bus bodies

Abutilon Company Inc .... F 419 536-6123
   Toledo *(G-14175)*

Employee Codes: A=Over 500 employees, B=251-500
C=101-250, D=51-100, E=20-50, F=10-19, G=1-9

2024 Harris Ohio Industrial Directory

37 TRANSPORTATION EQUIPMENT

Ace Truck Equipment Co .... E 740 453-0551
  Zanesville *(G-16494)*

◆ Airstream Inc .... B 937 596-6111
  Jackson Center *(G-8729)*

Altec Industries Inc .... F 205 408-2341
  Cuyahoga Falls *(G-6062)*

ARE Inc .... A 330 830-7800
  Massillon *(G-10076)*

▲ Atc Lighting & Plastics Inc .... C 440 466-7670
  Andover *(G-485)*

Bores Manufacturing Inc .... F 419 465-2606
  Monroeville *(G-11123)*

▼ Bosserman Automotive Engrg LLC ... E 419 722-2879
  Findlay *(G-7485)*

▲ Brothers Body and Eqp LLC .... F 419 462-1975
  Galion *(G-7862)*

Brown Industrial Inc .... E 937 693-3838
  Botkins *(G-1542)*

Bush Specialty Vehicles Inc .... F 937 382-5502
  Wilmington *(G-16042)*

Cascade Corporation .... D 937 327-0300
  Springfield *(G-13541)*

Cipted Corp .... D 412 829-2120
  Monroe *(G-11098)*

Composite Panel Tech Co .... G 704 310-5838
  Strongsville *(G-13824)*

Contech Manufacturing Inc .... G 440 946-3322
  Willoughby *(G-15902)*

▲ Cota International Inc .... F 937 526-5520
  Versailles *(G-14978)*

Crane Carrier Company LLC .... C 918 286-2889
  New Philadelphia *(G-11495)*

Crane Carrier Holdings LLC .... C 918 286-2889
  New Philadelphia *(G-11496)*

Custom Truck One Source LP .... E 330 409-7291
  Canton *(G-2085)*

Dan Patrick Enterprises Inc .... G 740 477-1006
  Circleville *(G-3546)*

Elliott Machine Works Inc .... E 419 468-4709
  Galion *(G-7874)*

Field Gymmy Inc .... G 419 538-6511
  Glandorf *(G-7978)*

Friesen Transfer Ltd .... G 614 873-5672
  Plain City *(G-12579)*

▲ Galion-Godwin Truck Bdy Co LLC ... F 330 359-5495
  Dundee *(G-6965)*

Gerich Fiberglass Inc .... F 419 362-4591
  Mount Gilead *(G-11233)*

H & H Truck Parts LLC .... E 216 642-4540
  Cleveland *(G-4160)*

Hendrickson International Corp .... D 740 929-5600
  Hebron *(G-8343)*

▲ Joseph Industries Inc .... D 330 528-0091
  Streetsboro *(G-13776)*

Kaffenbarger Truck Eqp Co .... E 513 772-6800
  Cincinnati *(G-3056)*

◆ Kaffenbarger Truck Eqp Co .... C 937 845-3804
  New Carlisle *(G-11418)*

Kidron Inc .... B 330 857-3011
  Kidron *(G-8915)*

Kilar Manufacturing Inc .... F 330 534-8961
  Hubbard *(G-8567)*

▲ Kimble Custom Chassis Company ... D 877 546-2537
  New Philadelphia *(G-11508)*

▲ Kimble Mixer Company .... D 330 308-6700
  New Philadelphia *(G-11509)*

▲ King Kutter II Inc .... E 740 446-0351
  Gallipolis *(G-7896)*

Kruz Inc .... E 330 878-5595
  Dover *(G-6831)*

Kuka Tledo Prdction Oprtons LL .... C 419 727-5500
  Toledo *(G-14353)*

La Boit Specialty Vehicles .... D 614 231-7640
  Gahanna *(G-7843)*

▼ Lifeline Mobile Inc .... D 614 497-8300
  Obetz *(G-12061)*

Mancor Ohio Inc .... C 937 228-6141
  Dayton *(G-6428)*

Mancor Ohio Inc .... E 937 228-6141
  Dayton *(G-6427)*

Marengo Fabricated Steel Ltd .... F 800 919-2652
  Cardington *(G-2276)*

Martin Sheet Metal Inc .... E 216 377-8200
  Cleveland *(G-4362)*

McNeilus Truck and Mfg Inc .... E 513 874-2022
  Fairfield *(G-7382)*

McNeilus Truck and Mfg Inc .... G 614 868-0760
  Gahanna *(G-7844)*

Meritor Inc .... C 740 348-3270
  Granville *(G-8020)*

Paccar Inc .... D 740 774-5111
  Chillicothe *(G-2522)*

Proform Group Inc .... F 614 332-9654
  Columbus *(G-5694)*

Q T Columbus LLC .... G 800 758-2410
  Columbus *(G-5700)*

▼ QT Equipment Company .... E 330 724-3055
  Akron *(G-289)*

Radar Love Co .... E 419 951-4750
  Findlay *(G-7555)*

Schodorf Truck Body & Eqp Co .... E 614 228-6793
  Columbus *(G-5751)*

Skymark Refuelers LLC .... D 419 957-1709
  Findlay *(G-7562)*

Sutphen Towers Inc .... E 614 876-1262
  Hilliard *(G-8444)*

▲ Tarpstop LLC .... F 419 873-7867
  Perrysburg *(G-12428)*

▲ Truck Cab Manufacturers Inc .... E 513 922-1300
  Cincinnati *(G-3469)*

Unlimted Rcovery Solutions LLC .... E 419 868-4888
  Wauseon *(G-15276)*

Valco Industries LLC .... E 937 399-7400
  Springfield *(G-13653)*

▲ Venco Venturo Industries LLC .... E 513 772 8448
  Cincinnati *(G-3490)*

Vitatoe Industries Inc .... E 740 773-2425
  Chillicothe *(G-2541)*

▲ Wallace Forge Company .... D 330 488-1203
  Canton *(G-2265)*

Willard Machine & Welding Inc .... F 330 467-0642
  Macedonia *(G-9586)*

Wilson Seat Company .... F 513 732-2460
  Batavia *(G-961)*

Youngstown-Kenworth Inc .... F 330 534-9761
  Hubbard *(G-8574)*

Zie Bart Rhino Linings Toledo .... G 419 841-2886
  Toledo *(G-14533)*

3714 Motor vehicle parts and accessories

◆ 31 Inc .... D 740 498-8324
  Newcomerstown *(G-11640)*

5pd Coatings LLC .... G 216 235-6086
  North Royalton *(G-11865)*

A Good Mobile Detailing LLC .... G 513 316-3802
  Cincinnati *(G-2584)*

◆ ABC Technologies Dlhb Inc .... B 330 478-2503
  Canton *(G-2026)*

◆ Accel Performance Group LLC .... C 216 658-6413
  Independence *(G-8651)*

Accuride Corporation .... E 812 962-5000
  Springfield *(G-13527)*

▲ Ach LLC .... G 419 621-5748
  Sandusky *(G-13040)*

◆ Ad Industries Inc .... A 303 744-1911
  Dayton *(G-6183)*

▲ Ada Technologies Inc .... C 419 634-7000
  Ada *(G-2)*

◆ Adelmans Truck Parts Corp .... E 330 456-0206
  Canton *(G-2028)*

Adient US LLC .... C 937 981-2176
  Greenfield *(G-8026)*

Adient US LLC .... C 419 662-4900
  Northwood *(G-11916)*

Adient US LLC .... D 419 394-7800
  Saint Marys *(G-12944)*

◆ Advics Manufacturing Ohio Inc .... A 513 932-7878
  Lebanon *(G-9060)*

◆ Airstream Inc .... B 937 596-6111
  Jackson Center *(G-8729)*

Airtex Industries LLC .... B 330 899-0340
  Toledo *(G-14181)*

Albright Radiator Inc .... G 330 264-8886
  Wooster *(G-16100)*

▲ Alegre Inc .... F 937 885-6786
  Miamisburg *(G-10609)*

All Wright Enterprises LLC .... G 440 259-5656
  Perry *(G-12349)*

Allied Separation Tech Inc .... F 704 736-0420
  Twinsburg *(G-14629)*

Allied Witan Company .... F 440 237-9630
  North Royalton *(G-11866)*

Alta Mira Corporation .... D 330 648-2461
  Spencer *(G-13479)*

American Axle & Mfg Inc .... E 330 863-7500
  Malvern *(G-9608)*

American Axle & Mfg Inc .... E 330 868-5761
  Minerva *(G-11026)*

American Axle & Mfg Inc .... D 330 486-3200
  Twinsburg *(G-14630)*

American Manufacturing & Eqp .... G 513 829-2248
  Fairfield *(G-7335)*

Americana Development Inc .... D 330 633-3278
  Tallmadge *(G-14022)*

Americlean 2 LLC .... F 216 781-3720
  Cleveland *(G-3657)*

Amsoil Inc .... G 614 274-9851
  Urbancrest *(G-14852)*

Amsted Industries Incorporated .... D 614 836-2323
  Groveport *(G-8129)*

Aptiv Services Us LLC .... C 330 367-6000
  Vienna *(G-14994)*

Aptiv Services Us LLC .... B 330 306-1000
  Warren *(G-15142)*

Aptiv Services Us LLC .... B 330 505-3150
  Warren *(G-15143)*

ARE Inc .... A 330 830-7800
  Massillon *(G-10076)*

▲ Areway LLC .... D 216 651-9022
  Brooklyn *(G-1676)*

Arlington Rack & Packaging Co .... F 419 476-7700
  Toledo *(G-14199)*

◆ ASC Industries Inc .... D 800 253-6009
  North Canton *(G-11715)*

Askar Productive Resources LLC ..... G 440 946-0393
  Willoughby *(G-15887)*

▲ Atc Lighting & Plastics Inc .... C 440 466-7670
  Andover *(G-485)*

Atwood Mobile Products LLC .... D 419 258-5531
  Antwerp *(G-492)*

Auria Fremont LLC .... B 419 332-1587
  Fremont *(G-7764)*

Auria Holmesville LLC .... B 330 279-4505
  Holmesville *(G-8542)*

Auria Sidney LLC .... B 937 492-1225
  Sidney *(G-13224)*

37 TRANSPORTATION EQUIPMENT

Austin Parts & Service............................ G 330 253-7791
  Akron *(G-69)*
Autoneum North America Inc................. D 419 690-8924
  Oregon *(G-12102)*
Autoneum North America Inc................. B 419 693-0511
  Oregon *(G-12103)*
B A Malcuit Racing Inc........................... G 330 878-7111
  Strasburg *(G-13743)*
B&C Machine Co LLC............................ E 330 745-4013
  Barberton *(G-859)*
Beach Manufacturing Co........................ C 937 882-6372
  Donnelsville *(G-6806)*
Beijing West Industries........................... F 937 455-5281
  Dayton *(G-6225)*
Bellevue Manufacturing Company.......... D 419 483-3190
  Bellevue *(G-1223)*
◆ Bendix Coml Vhcl Systems LLC.......... B 440 329-9000
  Avon *(G-763)*
Bergstrom Company Ltd Partnr............... E 440 232-2282
  Cleveland *(G-3730)*
Bobbart Industries Inc............................ E 419 350-5477
  Sylvania *(G-13991)*
Boler Company....................................... C 330 445-6728
  Canton *(G-2049)*
Bores Manufacturing Inc........................ F 419 465-2606
  Monroeville *(G-11123)*
Bowden Manufacturing Corp.................. E 440 946-1770
  Willoughby *(G-15891)*
Bpi Ec LLC.. G 216 589-0198
  Cleveland *(G-3752)*
Brake Parts Inc China LLC..................... G 216 589-0198
  Cleveland *(G-3753)*
Buckeye Brake Mfg Inc.......................... F 740 782-1379
  Morristown *(G-11222)*
Buckley Manufacturing Company............ F 513 821-4444
  Cincinnati *(G-2693)*
▲ Bucyrus Precision Tech Inc................ C 419 563-9950
  Bucyrus *(G-1852)*
◆ Buyers Products Company.................. C 440 974-8888
  Mentor *(G-10435)*
Bwi Chassis Dynamics NA Inc............... F 937 455-5100
  Kettering *(G-8902)*
Bwi North America Inc........................... B 937 455-5190
  Kettering *(G-8903)*
▲ Bwi North America Inc....................... E 937 253-1130
  Kettering *(G-8904)*
C&C Indy Cylinder Head LLC................ G 937 708-8563
  Xenia *(G-16254)*
▲ Callies Performance Products Inc....... D 419 435-7448
  Fostoria *(G-7630)*
Capco Automotive Products Corp.......... A 216 523-5000
  Cleveland *(G-3786)*
▲ Cardington Yutaka Tech Inc............... A 419 864-8777
  Cardington *(G-2274)*
◆ Cequent Consumer Products Inc....... D 440 498-0001
  Solon *(G-13327)*
Champion Laboratories Inc.................... F 330 899-0340
  Toledo *(G-14231)*
Champion Spark Plug Cmbrdge Pl........ G 740 432-2393
  Cambridge *(G-1928)*
▲ Champion Spark Plug Company........ D 419 535-2567
  Toledo *(G-14232)*
Chantilly Development Corp................... E 419 243-8109
  Toledo *(G-14233)*
Classic Reproductions............................ G 937 548-9839
  Greenville *(G-8042)*
▲ Cleveland Ignition Co Inc................... G 440 439-3688
  Cleveland *(G-3842)*
Cmbf Products Inc.................................. B 440 528-4000
  Solon *(G-13330)*
◆ CMI Holding Company Crawford........ D 419 468-9122
  Galion *(G-7866)*

▲ Cmt Imports Inc.................................. G 513 615-1851
  Cincinnati *(G-2777)*
Comprehensive Logistics Co Inc............ E 440 934-3517
  Avon *(G-768)*
Connective Design Incorporated............ F 937 746-8252
  Miamisburg *(G-10628)*
Cooper-Standard Automotive Inc........... D 740 342-3523
  New Lexington *(G-11451)*
Crown Div of Allen Gr............................ G 330 263-4919
  Wooster *(G-16111)*
Cummins Filtration Inc........................... C
  Findlay *(G-7500)*
Cummins Inc... E 614 604-6004
  Grove City *(G-8085)*
Custom Cltch Jint Hydrlics Inc................ F 216 431-1630
  Cleveland *(G-3923)*
Custom Floaters LLC.............................. F 216 536-8979
  Brookpark *(G-1710)*
▲ Cvg National Seating Co LLC............ F 219 872-7295
  New Albany *(G-11377)*
◆ Cwd LLC... E 310 218-1082
  Cleveland *(G-3933)*
▲ D-Terra Solutions LLC....................... G 614 450-1040
  Powell *(G-12670)*
▲ Daido Metal Bellefontaine LLC.......... D 937 592-5010
  Bellefontaine *(G-1205)*
Dana.. E 419 887-3000
  Toledo *(G-14259)*
◆ Dana Auto Systems Group LLC........ E 419 887-3000
  Maumee *(G-10176)*
Dana Automotive Mfg Inc...................... D 419 887-3000
  Maumee *(G-10177)*
Dana Brazil Holdings I LLC.................... G 419 887-3000
  Maumee *(G-10178)*
◆ Dana Commercial Vhcl Pdts LLC...... C 419 887-3000
  Maumee *(G-10179)*
▲ Dana Driveshaft Mfg LLC.................. G 419 887-3000
  Maumee *(G-10180)*
▲ Dana Driveshaft Products LLC.......... E 419 887-3000
  Maumee *(G-10181)*
◆ Dana Global Products Inc.................. E 419 887-3000
  Maumee *(G-10182)*
Dana Heavy Vehicle Systems................ D 419 866-3900
  Holland *(G-8502)*
◆ Dana Hvy Vhcl Systems Group LL..... E 419 887-3000
  Maumee *(G-10183)*
Dana Incorporated................................. A 419 887-3000
  Maumee *(G-10184)*
Dana Light Axle Mfg LLC...................... B 419 887-3000
  Toledo *(G-14260)*
▲ Dana Light Axle Mfg LLC.................. G 419 346-4528
  Maumee *(G-10185)*
Dana Limited.. D 419 866-7253
  Holland *(G-8503)*
Dana Limited.. E 419 887-3000
  Maumee *(G-10187)*
Dana Limited.. F 419 887-3000
  Maumee *(G-10188)*
Dana Limited.. D 419 482-2000
  Maumee *(G-10189)*
▲ Dana Limited..................................... B 419 887-3000
  Maumee *(G-10186)*
Dana Off Highway Products LLC........... D 614 864-1116
  Blacklick *(G-1334)*
◆ Dana Off Highway Products LLC...... E 419 887-3000
  Maumee *(G-10190)*
Dana Sac USA Inc................................. E 419 887-3550
  Maumee *(G-10191)*
▲ Dana Sealing Manufacturing LLC...... D
  Maumee *(G-10192)*
▲ Dana Sealing Products LLC.............. F 419 887-3000
  Maumee *(G-10193)*

▼ Dana Structural Mfg LLC................... C 419 887-3000
  Maumee *(G-10194)*
Dana Structural Products LLC................ G 419 887-3000
  Maumee *(G-10195)*
▲ Dana Thermal Products LLC............. F 419 887-3000
  Maumee *(G-10196)*
Dana World Trade Corporation............... F 419 887-3000
  Maumee *(G-10197)*
Davis Cummins Inc................................ G 614 309-6077
  Columbus *(G-5317)*
Dayton Clutch & Joint Inc...................... F 937 236-9770
  Dayton *(G-6276)*
◆ Dbw Fiber Corporation....................... D
  Wooster *(G-16113)*
◆ Dcm Manufacturing Inc..................... E 216 265-8006
  Cleveland *(G-3948)*
Designed Harness Systems Inc............. F 937 599-2485
  Bellefontaine *(G-1206)*
Detroit Toledo Fiber LLC........................ F 248 647-0400
  Toledo *(G-14265)*
Doran Mfg LLC....................................... D 866 816-7233
  Blue Ash *(G-1385)*
Doug Marine Motors Inc........................ E 740 335-3700
  Wshngtn Ct Hs *(G-16230)*
Driveline 1 Inc.. G 614 279-7734
  Columbus *(G-5336)*
Dusty Ductz LLC.................................... G 317 462-9622
  Lebanon *(G-9070)*
Eaton Corporation................................... B 440 523-5000
  Beachwood *(G-985)*
Eaton Corporation................................... C 216 281-2211
  Cleveland *(G-3992)*
Eaton Corporation................................... F 216 523-5000
  Willoughby *(G-15916)*
◆ Eaton Corporation.............................. B 440 523-5000
  Cleveland *(G-3994)*
Ebco Inc.. E 330 562-8265
  Streetsboro *(G-13769)*
Ebog Legacy Inc.................................... D 330 239-4933
  Sharon Center *(G-13166)*
Edgerton Forge Inc................................ D 419 298-2333
  Edgerton *(G-7074)*
Egr Products Company Inc.................... F 330 833-6554
  Dalton *(G-6131)*
Emssons Faurecia Ctrl Systems............ B 937 743-0551
  Franklin *(G-7672)*
▲ Emssons Faurecia Ctrl Systems....... C 812 341-2000
  Toledo *(G-14276)*
Entratech Systems LLC.......................... G 419 433-7683
  Sandusky *(G-13055)*
Ernie Green Industries Inc..................... E 740 420-5252
  Circleville *(G-3550)*
Ernie Green Industries Inc..................... F 614 219-1423
  New Madison *(G-11473)*
Exito Manufacturing LLC........................ G 937 291-9871
  Beavercreek *(G-1073)*
▲ F&P America Mfg Inc........................ E 937 339-0212
  Troy *(G-14567)*
Falls Stamping & Welding Co................ C 330 928-1191
  Cuyahoga Falls *(G-6083)*
Farin Industries Inc................................ F 440 275-2755
  Austinburg *(G-746)*
Faurecia Exhaust Systems Inc.............. B 937 339-0551
  Troy *(G-14568)*
FCA North America Holdings LLC......... C 419 661-3500
  Perrysburg *(G-12380)*
First Brands Group LLC........................ F 248 371-1700
  Cleveland *(G-4062)*
▲ Flaming River Industries Inc............. F 440 826-4488
  Berea *(G-1281)*
Flex Technologies Inc............................ D 330 359-5415
  Mount Eaton *(G-11230)*

Employee Codes: A=Over 500 employees, B=251-500
C=101-250, D=51-100, E=20-50, F=10-19, G=1-9

37 TRANSPORTATION EQUIPMENT

Florida Production Engrg Inc .... D 937 996-4361
  New Madison (G-11474)
▲ Force Control Industries Inc .... E 513 868-0900
  Fairfield (G-7363)
Ford Motor Company .... D 216 676-7918
  Brookpark (G-1715)
Forgeline Motorsports LLC .... E 800 886-0093
  Moraine (G-11181)
Fram Group .... G 479 271-7934
  Cleveland (G-4089)
Fram Group Operations LLC .... E 419 436-5827
  Fostoria (G-7637)
Fremont Plastic Products Inc .... C 419 332-6407
  Fremont (G-7783)
Freudenberg-Nok Sealing Tech .... F 877 331-8427
  Milan (G-10883)
◆ Friction Products Co .... B 330 725-4941
  Medina (G-10328)
Frontier Tank Center Inc .... F 330 659-3888
  Richfield (G-12788)
▲ Ft Precision Inc .... A 740 694-1500
  Fredericktown (G-7748)
Ftd Investments LLC .... A 937 833-2161
  Brookville (G-1737)
▲ Ftech R&D North America Inc .... E 937 339-2777
  Troy (G-14572)
◆ Fuserashi Intl Tech Inc .... E 330 273-0140
  Valley City (G-14870)
Gear Company of America Inc .... D 216 671-5400
  Cleveland (G-4107)
◆ Gear Star American Performance .... G 330 434-5216
  Akron (G-163)
General Aluminum Mfg Company .... C 419 739-9300
  Wapakoneta (G-15115)
General Metals Powder Co LLC .... E 330 633-1226
  Akron (G-166)
General Motors LLC .... A 216 265-5000
  Cleveland (G-4116)
General Motors LLC .... C 330 824-5840
  Warren (G-15173)
Gerich Fiberglass Inc .... F 419 362-4591
  Mount Gilead (G-11233)
GKN Driveline North Amer Inc .... D 419 354-3955
  Bowling Green (G-1568)
God Speed Turbo Innovations .... G 513 307-5584
  West Chester (G-15443)
Goodrich Corporation .... A 937 339-3811
  Troy (G-14574)
▲ Gra-Mag Truck Intr Systems LLC .... E 740 490-1000
  London (G-9388)
▲ Grand-Rock Company Inc .... A 440 639-2000
  Painesville (G-12240)
Green Acquisition LLC .... F 440 930-7600
  Avon (G-776)
Green Rdced Emssons Netwrk LLC .... G 330 340-0941
  Strasburg (G-13746)
Green Tokai Co Ltd .... C 937 237-1630
  Dayton (G-6362)
◆ Green Tokai Co Ltd .... A 937 833-5444
  Brookville (G-1738)
▲ GSW Manufacturing Inc .... B 419 423-7111
  Findlay (G-7516)
Gt Technologies Inc .... D 419 782-8955
  Defiance (G-6680)
Gt Technologies Inc .... D 419 324-7300
  Toledo (G-14304)
Hall-Toledo Inc .... F 419 893-4334
  Maumee (G-10203)
◆ Haltec Corporation .... C 330 222-1501
  Salem (G-12999)
Hanon Systems Usa LLC .... C 313 920-0583
  Carey (G-2279)

Harco Manufacturing Group LLC .... C 937 528-5000
  Moraine (G-11184)
▲ Harco Manufacturing Group LLC .... C 937 528-5000
  Moraine (G-11183)
Hdt Expeditionary Systems Inc .... F 216 438-6111
  Solon (G-13360)
▲ Hdt Tactical Systems Inc .... C 216 438-6111
  Solon (G-13361)
Hendrickson .... F 740 678-8033
  Vincent (G-15008)
Hendrickson International Corp .... D 740 929-5600
  Hebron (G-8343)
Hendrickson Usa LLC .... C 330 456-7288
  Canton (G-2124)
Hendrickson Usa LLC .... B 740 929-5600
  Hebron (G-8344)
Hendrickson Usa LLC .... D 630 910-2800
  North Canton (G-11737)
◆ Hfi LLC .... B 614 491-0700
  Canal Winchester (G-1987)
▲ Hi-Tek Manufacturing Inc .... C 513 459-1094
  Mason (G-10001)
Hilite Intl .... G 216 641-9632
  Cleveland (G-4189)
◆ Hirschvogel Incorporated .... B 614 445-6060
  Columbus (G-5441)
Hitachi Astemo Americas Inc .... C 419 425-1259
  Findlay (G-7523)
Hite Parts Exchange Inc .... F 614 272-5115
  Columbus (G-5442)
Honda Dev & Mfg Amer LLC .... A 937 843-5555
  Russells Point (G-12876)
▲ Honda Transmission Manufa .... A 937 843-5555
  Russells Point (G-12877)
Horizon Global Corporation .... E 734 656-3000
  Cleveland (G-4200)
▲ Hytec-Debartolo LLC .... G 614 527-9370
  Columbus (G-5450)
▲ Ig Watteeuw Usa LLC .... F 740 588-1722
  Zanesville (G-16538)
Igw USA .... F 740 588-1722
  Zanesville (G-16539)
Illinois Tool Works Inc .... C 513 489-7600
  Blue Ash (G-1408)
Illinois Tool Works Inc .... E 262 248-8277
  Bryan (G-1821)
◆ Imasen Bucyrus Technology Inc .... C 419 563-9590
  Bucyrus (G-1862)
▲ Industry Products Co .... B 937 778-0585
  Piqua (G-12526)
Interntnl Auto Cmpnnts Group .... E 419 335-1000
  Wauseon (G-15264)
Interntnl Auto Cmpnnts Group .... A 419 433-5653
  Wauseon (G-15265)
◆ Interstate Diesel Service Inc .... C 216 881-0015
  Cleveland (G-4233)
Inteva Products LLC .... C 937 280-8500
  Vandalia (G-14945)
Jae Tech Inc .... D 330 698-2000
  Apple Creek (G-502)
▲ Jbar A/C Inc .... E 216 447-4294
  Cleveland (G-4252)
Johnson Controls Inc .... E 414 524-1200
  Saint Marys (G-12954)
▲ Joseph Industries Inc .... D 330 528-0091
  Streetsboro (G-13776)
▲ Julie Maynard Inc .... F 937 443-0408
  Dayton (G-6394)
K Wm Beach Mfg Co Inc .... C 937 399-3838
  Springfield (G-13586)
▲ Kalida Manufacturing Inc .... C 419 532-2026
  Kalida (G-8785)

Kasai North America Inc .... E 614 356-1494
  Dublin (G-6903)
Kasai North America Inc .... C 419 209-0399
  Upper Sandusky (G-14812)
Kenley Enterprises LLC .... F 419 630-0921
  Bryan (G-1824)
Kerr Friction Products Inc .... F 330 455-3983
  Canton (G-2138)
Keystone Auto Glass Inc .... D 419 509-0497
  Maumee (G-10211)
KG Medina LLC .... E 256 330-4273
  Medina (G-10343)
Kic Ltd .... G 614 775-9570
  Gahanna (G-7841)
Kilar Manufacturing Inc .... F 330 534-8961
  Hubbard (G-8567)
▲ Knippen Chrysler Ddge Jeep Inc .... E 419 695-4976
  Delphos (G-6767)
▲ Knott Brake Company .... E 800 566-8887
  Lodi (G-9352)
Kongsberg Actation Systems LLC .... E 440 639-9778
  Grand River (G-8012)
▲ Kosei St Marys Corporation .... A 419 394-7840
  Saint Marys (G-12955)
◆ Kth Parts Industries Inc .... A 937 663-5941
  Saint Paris (G-12973)
Ktri Holdings Inc .... F 216 400-9308
  Cleveland (G-4301)
Ktsdi LLC .... G 330 783-2000
  North Lima (G-11808)
KWD Automotive Inc .... G 419 344-8232
  Whitehouse (G-15820)
▲ Kyklos Bearing International Llc .... A 419 627-7000
  Sandusky (G-13072)
L-H Battery Company Inc .... G 937 613-3769
  Jeffersonville (G-8765)
▲ Lacal Equipment Inc .... E 937 596-6106
  Jackson Center (G-8734)
▲ Leadec Corp .... E 513 731-3590
  Blue Ash (G-1420)
Lear Corporation .... C 740 928-4358
  Hebron (G-8347)
Lear Corporation .... E 419 335-6010
  Wauseon (G-15267)
Linamar Strctures USA Mich Inc .... C 260 636-7030
  Edon (G-7088)
Linamar Strctures USA Mich Inc .... C 567 249-0838
  Edon (G-7089)
▲ Linde Hydraulics Corporation .... B 330 533-6801
  Canfield (G-2009)
◆ Lintern Corporation .... E 440 255-9333
  Mentor (G-10494)
Lorain County Auto Systems Inc .... A 248 442-6800
  Lorain (G-9421)
▲ Lorain County Auto Systems Inc ...... E 440 960-7470
  Lorain (G-9422)
Ltf Acquisition LLC .... E 330 533-0111
  Canfield (G-2010)
Lubriquip Inc .... B 216 581-2000
  Cleveland (G-4338)
Lucas Sumitomo Brakes Inc .... E 513 934-0024
  Lebanon (G-9094)
◆ Luk Clutch Systems LLC .... E 330 264-4383
  Wooster (G-16147)
Maags Automotive & Mch Inc .... G 419 626-1539
  Sandusky (G-13076)
Magna International Amer Inc .... C 330 824-3101
  Sheffield Village (G-13185)
Magna International Amer Inc .... D 419 410-4780
  Swanton (G-13977)
▲ Magna Modular Systems LLC .... D 419 324-3387
  Toledo (G-14376)

SIC SECTION
37 TRANSPORTATION EQUIPMENT

Magnaco Industries Inc.............................. E 216 961-3636
  Lodi *(G-9353)*
Mahle Behr Dayton LLC............................ A 937 369-2900
  Dayton *(G-6423)*
Mahle Behr Dayton LLC............................ A 937 356-2001
  Vandalia *(G-14948)*
◆ Mahle Behr Dayton LLC............................D 937 369-2900
  Dayton *(G-6424)*
◆ Mahle Behr Mt Sterling Inc.................... B 740 869-3333
  Mount Sterling *(G-11256)*
Mahle Behr USA Inc................................... C 937 356-2001
  Vandalia *(G-14949)*
Mahle Industries Incorporated.................. E 937 890-2739
  Dayton *(G-6426)*
▲ Maradyne Corporation............................ D 216 362-0755
  Cleveland *(G-4356)*
Marion Industries LLC................................ A 740 223-0075
  Marion *(G-9861)*
◆ Maval Industries LLC...............................C 330 405-1600
  Twinsburg *(G-14692)*
Maxion Wheels Sedalia LLC...................... A 330 794-2300
  Akron *(G-239)*
Meritor Inc... C 740 348-3270
  Granville *(G-8020)*
Midwest Muffler Pros & More.................. G 937 293-2450
  Moraine *(G-11195)*
Milark Industries Inc.................................. D 419 524-7627
  Mansfield *(G-9693)*
Milark Industries Inc.................................. D 419 524-7627
  Mansfield *(G-9694)*
Millat Industries Corp................................ F 937 535-1500
  Dayton *(G-6450)*
▲ Millat Industries Corp.............................. D 937 434-6666
  Dayton *(G-6449)*
▲ Mitec Powertrain Inc............................... C 567 525-5606
  Findlay *(G-7538)*
◆ Mitsubishi Elc Auto Amer Inc................. B 513 573-6614
  Mason *(G-10030)*
▲ Modern Transmission Dev Co............... C
  Valley City *(G-14880)*
Monarch Plastic Inc................................... F 330 683-0822
  Orrville *(G-12137)*
Mrs Electronic Inc..................................... F 937 660-6767
  Dayton *(G-6460)*
◆ Namoh Ohio Holdings Inc......................E
  Norwood *(G-11996)*
Nanogate North America LLC.................. B 419 522-7745
  Mansfield *(G-9701)*
▲ Neaton Auto Products Mfg Inc.............. E 937 456-7103
  Eaton *(G-7066)*
Nebraska Industries Corp......................... F 419 335-6010
  Wauseon *(G-15270)*
New Sabina Industries Inc....................... G 937 584-2433
  Grove City *(G-8111)*
▲ New Sabina Industries Inc..................... E 937 584-2433
  Sabina *(G-12888)*
Newburgh Crankshaft Inc......................... G 440 502-6998
  Cleveland *(G-4455)*
▲ Newman Technology Inc........................ A 419 525-1856
  Mansfield *(G-9704)*
Nippon Stl Intgrted Crnkshaft.................. F 419 435-0411
  Fostoria *(G-7647)*
Nitto Inc.. F 937 773-4820
  Piqua *(G-12539)*
▲ Nitto Inc.. F 937 773-4820
  Piqua *(G-12540)*
Noco Company..D 216 464-8131
  Solon *(G-13399)*
▼ Norlake Manufacturing Company.......... D 440 353-3200
  North Ridgeville *(G-11851)*
◆ Norplas Industries Inc............................. B 419 662-3200
  Northwood *(G-11922)*

North Coast Exotics Inc............................ G 216 651-5512
  Cleveland *(G-4468)*
Northern Stamping Co.............................. F 216 642-8081
  Cleveland *(G-4479)*
Norton Manufacturing Co Inc.................. F 419 435-0411
  Fostoria *(G-7648)*
O D L LLC.. G 419 833-2533
  Bowling Green *(G-1579)*
Oakley Inds Sub Assmbly Div In............. F 419 661-8888
  Northwood *(G-11923)*
Oe Exchange LLC...................................... G 440 266-1639
  Mentor *(G-10514)*
Oerlikon Friction Systems........................ E 937 449-4000
  Dayton *(G-6485)*
◆ Oerlikon Friction Systems........................E 937 449-4000
  Dayton *(G-6486)*
Ohio Auto Supply Company..................... F 330 454-5105
  Canton *(G-2182)*
▲ Ohta Press US Inc.................................... F 937 374-3382
  Xenia *(G-16271)*
OReilly Equipment LLC............................. G 440 564-1234
  Newbury *(G-11633)*
◆ Pacific Industries USA Inc........................E 513 860-3900
  Fairfield *(G-7389)*
▲ Pacific Manufacturing Ohio Inc............. B 513 860-3900
  Fairfield *(G-7390)*
▲ Pako Inc.. C 440 946-8030
  Mentor *(G-10519)*
Park-Ohio Industries Inc.......................... C 216 341-2300
  Newburgh Heights *(G-11620)*
Parker-Hannifin Corporation................... B 440 943-5700
  Wickliffe *(G-15846)*
▲ Pdi Ground Support Systems Inc......... D 216 271-7344
  Solon *(G-13403)*
Performance Motorsports Inc................. F 440 951-6600
  Mentor *(G-10522)*
◆ Pioneer Automotive Tech Inc................. C 937 746-2293
  Miamisburg *(G-10670)*
Piston Automotive LLC............................. A 740 223-0075
  Marion *(G-9872)*
Piston Automotive LLC............................. A 419 464-0250
  Toledo *(G-14437)*
▲ Powers and Sons LLC.............................. C 419 485-3151
  Montpelier *(G-11140)*
Pt Tech LLC.. D 330 239-4933
  Wadsworth *(G-15056)*
Pullman Company..................................... C 419 499-2541
  Milan *(G-10885)*
Pullman Company..................................... C 419 592-2055
  Napoleon *(G-11331)*
▲ Qualitor Inc... A 248 204-8600
  Cleveland *(G-4603)*
Qualitor Subsidiary H Inc......................... C 419 562-7987
  Bucyrus *(G-1865)*
Quality Reproductions Inc....................... G 330 335-5000
  Wadsworth *(G-15058)*
Race Winning Brands Inc........................ B 440 951-6600
  Mentor *(G-10544)*
Radar Love Co... E 419 951-4750
  Findlay *(G-7555)*
◆ Ramco Specialties Inc.............................D 330 653-5135
  Hudson *(G-8609)*
▲ Reactive Resin Products Co................... E 419 666-6119
  Perrysburg *(G-12423)*
▲ Remington Steel Inc................................ D 937 322-2414
  Springfield *(G-13628)*
Restortion Parts Unlimited Inc............... F 513 934-0815
  Lebanon *(G-9108)*
Resz Fabrication Inc................................. G 440 207-0044
  Eastlake *(G-7047)*
▼ Riker Products Inc................................... D 419 729-1626
  Toledo *(G-14451)*

Rochling Automotive USA LLP................ D 330 400-5785
  Akron *(G-307)*
◆ Roki America Co Ltd.................................B 419 424-9713
  Findlay *(G-7556)*
RTC Converters Inc................................... F 937 743-2300
  Franklin *(G-7700)*
Rubber Duck 4x4 Inc................................ G 513 889-1735
  Hamilton *(G-8239)*
Saf-Holland Inc.. G 513 874-7888
  Fairfield *(G-7404)*
▲ Saia-Burgess Lcc..................................... D 937 898-3621
  Vandalia *(G-14958)*
▲ Sanoh America Inc.................................. D 419 425-2600
  Findlay *(G-7558)*
Schaeffler Transm Systems LLC............ A 330 202-6212
  Wooster *(G-16166)*
◆ Schaeffler Transm Systems LLC............E 330 264-4383
  Wooster *(G-16167)*
▲ Schaeffler Transmission Llc................... B 330 264-4383
  Wooster *(G-16168)*
◆ Schafer Driveline LLC...............................F 740 694-2055
  Fredericktown *(G-7753)*
Schott Metal Products Company............ E 330 773-7873
  Akron *(G-326)*
Scs Gearbox Inc.. F 419 483-7278
  Bellevue *(G-1233)*
▲ Seabiscuit Motorsports Inc.................... B 440 951-6600
  Mentor *(G-10551)*
Sew-Eurodrive Inc.................................... D 937 335-0036
  Troy *(G-14609)*
Sfs Group Usa Inc..................................... C 330 239-7100
  Medina *(G-10375)*
Sfs Intec Inc... E 330 239-7100
  Medina *(G-10376)*
Solo Dyna Systems Ltd........................... G 440 871-7112
  Bay Village *(G-967)*
Soundwich Inc.. E 216 249-4900
  Cleveland *(G-4715)*
Soundwich Inc.. D 216 486-2666
  Cleveland *(G-4716)*
Speedline North America Inc.................. G 937 291-7000
  Dayton *(G-6584)*
Spencer Manufacturing Company Inc.... D 330 648-2461
  Spencer *(G-13484)*
▲ Steck Manufacturing Co LLC.................. F 937 222-0062
  Dayton *(G-6594)*
Steer & Gear Inc....................................... F 614 231-4064
  Columbus *(G-5793)*
▲ Steere Enterprises Inc............................ D 330 633-4926
  Tallmadge *(G-14049)*
Stoneridge Inc... A 419 884-1219
  Lexington *(G-9202)*
◆ Sumiriko Ohio Inc.....................................E 419 358-2121
  Bluffton *(G-1507)*
Sumitomo Elc Wirg Systems Inc............. E 937 642-7579
  Marysville *(G-9941)*
▼ Superior Energy Systems LLC................ F 440 236-6009
  Columbia Station *(G-5022)*
▲ Superior Production LLC......................... C 614 444-2181
  Columbus *(G-5800)*
Superior Trim Holdings Limited.............. G 419 425-5555
  Findlay *(G-7572)*
▲ Supertrapp Industries Inc...................... D 216 265-8400
  Cleveland *(G-4754)*
Sutphen Corporation................................ E 937 969-8851
  Springfield *(G-13640)*
◆ Taiho Corporation of America................C 419 443-1645
  Tiffin *(G-14107)*
Teijin Automotive Tech Inc..................... B 419 396-1980
  Carey *(G-2285)*
Teijin Automotive Tech Inc..................... B 419 257-2231
  North Baltimore *(G-11700)*

Employee Codes: A=Over 500 employees, B=251-500
C=101-250, D=51-100, E=20-50, F=10-19, G=1-9

37 TRANSPORTATION EQUIPMENT

Teijin Automotive Tech Inc .... B 419 238-4628
　Van Wert (G-14928)
Tenneco Inc .... F 419 499-2541
　Milan (G-10887)
Tetra Mold & Tool Inc .... E 937 845-1651
　New Carlisle (G-11428)
▲ Tfo Tech Co Ltd .... C 740 426-6381
　Jeffersonville (G-8766)
Thermal Solutions Mfg Inc .... F 800 776-4225
　Brookpark (G-1726)
▲ Thyssenkrupp Bilstein Amer Inc .... C 513 881-7600
　Hamilton (G-8249)
TI Group Auto Systems LLC .... E 740 929-2049
　Hebron (G-8366)
▲ Tigerpoly Manufacturing Inc .... B 614 871-0045
　Grove City (G-8122)
Tko Mfg Services Inc .... E 937 299-1637
　Moraine (G-11215)
▲ Tmg Performance Products LLC .... D 440 891-0999
　Berea (G-1297)
Toledo Molding & Die LLC .... C 419 692-6022
　Delphos (G-6772)
Toledo Molding & Die LLC .... B 419 692-6022
　Delphos (G-6773)
Toledo Pro Fiberglass Inc .... G 419 241-9390
　Toledo (G-14503)
▲ Tom Smith Industries Inc .... D 937 832-1555
　Englewood (G-7245)
▲ Torque 2020 CMA Acqisition LLC .... C 330 874-2900
　Bolivar (G-1539)
Torsion Control Products Inc .... F 248 537-1900
　Wadsworth (G-15070)
Total Engine Airflow .... G 330 634-2155
　Tallmadge (G-14052)
Tower Atmtive Oprtons USA I LL .... C 419 483-1500
　Bellevue (G-1239)
▲ Trailer Component Mfg Inc .... E 440 255-2888
　Mentor (G-10580)
Tri State Corebuyers LLC .... F 513 288-8063
　Amelia (G-468)
Tri-Mac Mfg & Svcs Co .... F 513 896-4445
　Hamilton (G-8251)
Trico Holding Corporation .... G 216 589-0198
　Cleveland (G-4827)
◆ Trico Products Corporation .... C 248 371-1700
　Cleveland (G-4829)
▲ Trim Parts Inc .... E 513 934-0815
　Lebanon (G-9115)
▲ Trim Systems Operating Corp .... D 614 289-5360
　New Albany (G-11392)
▼ Trulil Inc .... C 937 652-1242
　Urbana (G-14849)
▲ TS Tech USA Corporation .... B 614 577-1088
　Reynoldsburg (G-12777)
▲ TS Trim Industries Inc .... B 614 837-4114
　Canal Winchester (G-1993)
▲ UCI International LLC .... E 330 899-0340
　North Canton (G-11772)
UGN Inc .... C 513 360-3500
　Lebanon (G-9118)
Unison Industries LLC .... B 904 667-9904
　Dayton (G-6175)
◆ United Components LLC .... E 330 899-0340
　Toledo (G-14213)
Universal Auto Filter LLC .... G 216 589-0198
　Cleveland (G-4848)
▲ US Kondo Corporation .... F 937 916-3045
　Piqua (G-12557)
US Tsubaki Power Transm LLC .... C 419 626-4560
　Sandusky (G-13102)
Usui International Corporation .... C 513 448-0410
　Sharonville (G-13174)

Usui International Corporation .... D 734 354-3626
　West Chester (G-15523)
▼ Varbros LLC .... D 216 267-5200
　Cleveland (G-4860)
▲ Vari-Wall Tube Specialists Inc .... D 330 482-0000
　Columbiana (G-5053)
Vehicle Systems Inc .... G 330 854-0535
　Massillon (G-10153)
▲ Venco Manufacturing Inc .... F 513 772-8448
　Cincinnati (G-3489)
▲ Venco Venturo Industries LLC .... E 513 772-8448
　Cincinnati (G-3490)
▲ Ventra Sandusky LLC .... B 419 627-3600
　Sandusky (G-13103)
Veoneer Brake Systems LLC .... B 419 425-6725
　Findlay (G-7578)
Viper Acquisition I Inc .... D 216 589-0198
　Cleveland (G-4877)
Walther Engrg & Mfg Co Inc .... E 937 743-8125
　Franklin (G-7710)
▲ Weastec Incorporated .... C 937 393-6800
　Hillsboro (G-8469)
West & Barker Inc .... E 330 652-9923
　Niles (G-11691)
▲ Westbrook Mfg Inc .... B 937 254-2004
　Dayton (G-6650)
Western Branch Diesel LLC .... F 330 454-8800
　Canton (G-2267)
Westfield Steel Inc .... D 937 322-2414
　Springfield (G-13654)
Wheel Group Holdings LLC .... G 614 253-6247
　Columbus (G-5875)
Wheelskins Inc .... G 800 755-2128
　North Royalton (G-11901)
Whirlaway Corporation .... D 440 647-4711
　Wellington (G-15323)
Whirlaway Corporation .... D 440 647-4711
　Wellington (G-15324)
▲ Whirlaway Corporation .... C 440 647-4711
　Wellington (G-15325)
White Mule Company .... E 740 382-9008
　Ontario (G-12097)
▲ Winzeler Stamping Co .... E 419 485-3147
　Montpelier (G-11147)
Woodbridge Group .... C 419 334-3666
　Fremont (G-7820)
Workhorse Group Inc .... D 888 646-5205
　Sharonville (G-13175)
Workhorse Technologies Inc .... E 888 646-5205
　Sharonville (G-13176)
▲ Yachiyo of America Inc .... C 614 876-3220
　Columbus (G-5889)
▲ Yamada North America Inc .... B 937 462-7111
　South Charleston (G-13456)
Yanfeng US Auto Intr Systems I .... D 419 633-1873
　Bryan (G-1847)
Yanfeng US Auto Intr Systems I .... D 616 834-9422
　Bryan (G-13408)
ZF Active Safety & Elec US LLC .... C 216 750-2400
　Cleveland (G-4933)
ZF Active Safety & Elec US LLC .... E 419 726-5599
　Toledo (G-14532)
ZF Active Safety US Inc .... F 419 237-2511
　Fayette (G-7463)
ZF Active Safety US Inc .... G 734 812-6979
　Findlay (G-7584)

3715 Truck trailers

4w Services .... F 614 554-5427
　Hebron (G-8334)
American Mnfctring Oprtons Inc .... G 419 269-1560
　Toledo (G-14190)

Bell Logistics Co .... E 740 702-9830
　Chillicothe (G-2495)
Bruce High Performance Tran .... F 440 357-8964
　Painesville (G-12219)
Diamond Trailers Inc .... F 513 738-4500
　Shandon (G-13160)
East Manufacturing Corporation .... F 330 325-9921
　Randolph (G-12698)
▼ East Manufacturing Corporation .... B 330 325-9921
　Randolph (G-12697)
Engineered MBL Solutions Inc .... F 513 724-0247
　Batavia (G-923)
Gerich Fiberglass Inc .... F 419 362-4591
　Mount Gilead (G-11233)
H & H Equipment Inc .... G 330 264-5400
　Wooster (G-16127)
Haulette Manufacturing Inc .... D 419 586-1717
　Celina (G-2336)
High Tech Prfmce Trlrs Inc .... D 440 357-8964
　Painesville (G-12245)
J & L Body Inc .... F 216 661-2323
　Brooklyn Heights (G-1693)
J W Devers & Son Inc .... F 937 854-3040
　Trotwood (G-14544)
Jsm Express Inc .... G 216 272-4512
　Euclid (G-7278)
Kenan Advantage Group Inc .... G 614 878-4050
　Columbus (G-5506)
Kidron Inc .... B 330 857-3011
　Kidron (G-8915)
Lyons .... G 440 224-0676
　Kingsville (G-8932)
M & W Trailers Inc .... F 419 453-3331
　Ottoville (G-12201)
M R Trailer Sales Inc .... G 330 339-7701
　New Philadelphia (G-11512)
Mac Manufacturing Inc .... C 330 829-1680
　Salem (G-13014)
▲ Mac Manufacturing Inc .... A 330 823-9900
　Alliance (G-408)
Mac Steel Trailer Ltd .... E 330 823-9900
　Alliance (G-409)
Mac Straight Truck Bodies Inc .... F 800 647-9424
　Alliance (G-410)
◆ Mac Trailer Manufacturing Inc .... A 800 795-8454
　Alliance (G-411)
Mac Trailer Service Inc .... E 330 823-9190
　Alliance (G-412)
Martin Allen Trailer LLC .... F 330 942-0217
　Akron (G-238)
Moritz International Inc .... E 419 526-5222
　Mansfield (G-9700)
▼ Nelson Manufacturing Company ...... D 419 523-5321
　Ottawa (G-12185)
Paccar Inc .... D 740 774-5111
　Chillicothe (G-2522)
▲ Pdi Ground Support Systems Inc ..... D 216 271-7344
　Solon (G-13403)
▲ Quick Loadz Container Sys LLC ...... E 888 304-3946
　Athens (G-693)
Saf-Holland Inc .... G 513 874-7888
　Fairfield (G-7404)
Shilling Transport Inc .... G 330 948-1105
　Lodi (G-9356)
Stahl/Scott Fetzer Company .... C 800 277-8245
　Wooster (G-16175)
▼ Trailer One Inc .... F 330 723-7474
　Medina (G-10388)
Trailstar International Inc .... D 330 821-9900
　Alliance (G-433)
Wabash National Corporation .... E 419 434-9409
　Findlay (G-7579)

SIC SECTION
37 TRANSPORTATION EQUIPMENT

3716 Motor homes

Advanced Rv LLC .... E 440 283-0405
　Willoughby (G-15874)
◆ Airstream Inc .... B 937 596-6111
　Jackson Center (G-8729)

3721 Aircraft

Aerovation Tech Holdings LLC .... G 567 208-5525
　Forest (G-7589)
Avari Aero LLC .... G 513 828-0860
　Cincinnati (G-2646)
Boeing Company .... E 740 788-4000
　Heath (G-8318)
Executive Wings Inc .... G 440 254-1812
　Painesville (G-12234)
Goodrich Corporation .... A 937 339-3811
　Troy (G-14574)
Hii Mission Technologies Corp .... G 937 426-3421
　Beavercreek (G-1074)
K&M Aviation LLC .... D 216 261-9000
　Cleveland (G-4270)
Nextant Aerospace LLC .... E 216 898-4800
　Cleveland (G-4456)
Nextant Aircraft LLC .... G 216 261-9000
　Cleveland (G-4457)
Pacer Flight LLC .... G 419 433-5562
　Huron (G-8644)
Ruhe Sales Inc .... F 419 943-3357
　Leipsic (G-9140)
Sea Air Space McHning Mlding L .... F 440 248-3025
　Streetsboro (G-13791)
Snow Aviation Intl Inc .... E 614 588-2452
　Gahanna (G-7849)
Star Jet LLC .... E 614 338-4379
　Columbus (G-5789)
Steel Aviation Aircraft Sales .... G 937 332-7587
　Casstown (G-2317)
Tessec LLC .... D 937 576-0010
　Dayton (G-6615)
Tessec Manufacturing Svcs LLC .... E 937 985-3552
　Dayton (G-6616)
Textron Aviation Inc .... G 330 286-3043
　Canfield (G-2020)
Theiss Uav Solutions LLC .... G 330 584-2070
　North Benton (G-11711)
Toledo Jet Center LLC .... G 419 866-9050
　Swanton (G-13985)

3724 Aircraft engines and engine parts

Advanced Ground Systems .... F 513 402-7226
　Cincinnati (G-2598)
Aero Jet Wash Llc .... F 866 381-7955
　Dayton (G-6186)
American Aero Components Llc .... G 937 367-5068
　Dayton (G-6197)
At Holdings Corporation .... A 216 692-6000
　Cleveland (G-3694)
Avidyne .... G 800 284-3963
　Dublin (G-6865)
Avion Tool Corporation .... F 937 278-0779
　Dayton (G-6220)
Barnes Group Inc .... E 513 779-6888
　West Chester (G-15374)
CFM International Inc .... F 513 563-4180
　Cincinnati (G-2721)
CFM International Inc .... F 513 563-4180
　Cincinnati (G-2722)
CFM International Inc .... E 513 552-2787
　West Chester (G-15389)
Defense Research Assoc Inc .... E 937 431-1644
　Dayton (G-6158)

◆ Dreison International Inc .... C 216 362-0755
　Cleveland (G-3972)
Drt Aerospace LLC .... E 937 492-6121
　Sidney (G-13242)
Eaton Industrial Corporation .... B 216 523-4205
　Cleveland (G-3998)
Enjet Aero Dayton Inc .... E 937 878-3800
　Huber Heights (G-8576)
▲ Ferrotherm Corporation .... C 216 883-9350
　Cleveland (G-4058)
GE Military Systems .... D 513 243-2000
　Cincinnati (G-2938)
General Electric Company .... G 513 948-4170
　Cincinnati (G-2941)
Golden Eagle Aviation LLC .... G 937 308-4709
　Sidney (G-13251)
Heico Aerospace Parts Corp .... B 954 987-6101
　Highland Heights (G-8388)
▲ Henry Tools Inc .... G 216 291-1011
　Cleveland (G-4182)
▲ Hi-Tek Manufacturing Inc .... C 513 459-1094
　Mason (G-10001)
Honeywell International I .... F 513 282-5519
　Mason (G-10002)
Honeywell International Inc .... F 216 459-6048
　Brookpark (G-1718)
Honeywell International Inc .... F 513 745-7200
　Cincinnati (G-3007)
Honeywell International Inc .... E 440 329-9000
　Elyria (G-7157)
▲ Honeywell Lebow Products .... C 614 850-5000
　Columbus (G-5445)
Lsp Technologies Inc .... E 614 718-3000
　Dublin (G-6907)
Magellan Arospc Middletown Inc .... D 513 422-2751
　Middletown (G-10839)
◆ Meyer Tool Inc .... A 513 681-7362
　Cincinnati (G-3160)
▲ Miba Bearings US LLC .... B 740 962-4242
　Mcconnelsville (G-10282)
Optical Display Engrg Inc .... F 440 995-6555
　Highland Heights (G-8390)
Otto Konigslow Mfg Co .... F 216 851-7900
　Cleveland (G-4513)
▲ Pako Inc .... C 440 946-8030
　Mentor (G-10519)
Parker-Hannifin Corporation .... C 440 284-6277
　Elyria (G-7192)
Pas Technologies Inc .... D 937 840-1053
　Hillsboro (G-8464)
PCC Airfoils LLC .... C 440 255-9770
　Mentor (G-10521)
Precision Castparts Corp .... F 440 350-6150
　Painesville (G-12258)
◆ Sifco Industries Inc .... C 216 881-8600
　Cleveland (G-4700)
Snow Aviation Intl Inc .... E 614 588-2452
　Gahanna (G-7849)
Spirit Avionics Ltd .... F 614 237-4271
　Columbus (G-5786)
▲ Superalloy Mfg Solutions Corp .... C 513 489-9800
　Blue Ash (G-1473)
Tessec LLC .... D 937 576-0010
　Dayton (G-6615)
Turbine Eng Cmpnents Tech Corp .... B 216 692-5200
　Cleveland (G-4837)
▲ Turbine Standard Ltd .... G 419 865-0355
　Holland (G-8535)
Warfighter Fcsed Logistics Inc .... E 740 513-4692
　West Chester (G-15526)
▲ Welded Ring Products Co .... D 216 961-3800
　Cleveland (G-4902)

Wp Cpp Holdings LLC .... G 216 453-4800
　Cleveland (G-4924)

3728 Aircraft parts and equipment, nec

17111 Waterview Pkwy LLC .... F 216 706-2960
　Cleveland (G-3569)
Achilles Aerospace Pdts Inc .... E 330 425-8444
　Twinsburg (G-14623)
▼ Advanced Fuel Systems Inc .... G 614 252-8422
　Columbus (G-5103)
Aero Tech Tool & Mold Inc .... G 440 942-3327
　Mentor (G-10406)
Aerospace LLC .... F 937 561-1104
　Moraine (G-11153)
▲ Aerospace Maint Solutions LLC .... E 440 729-7703
　Solon (G-13307)
Aim International .... G 513 831-2938
　Miamiville (G-10710)
Aircraft Ground Services .... G 419 356-5027
　Monclova (G-11092)
Aircraft Wheel & Brake LLC .... D 440 937-6211
　Avon (G-762)
Allen Aircraft Products Inc .... E 330 296-9621
　Ravenna (G-12702)
▲ Allen Aircraft Products Inc .... D 330 296-9621
　Ravenna (G-12704)
American Aero Components Llc .... G 937 367-5068
　Dayton (G-6197)
▲ Apph Wichita Inc .... E 316 943-5752
　Strongsville (G-13808)
Arctos Mission Solutions LLC .... E 813 609-5591
　Beavercreek (G-1040)
At Holdings Corporation .... A 216 692-6000
　Cleveland (G-3694)
Auto-Valve Inc .... E 937 854-3037
　Dayton (G-6217)
Aviation Cmpnent Solutions Inc .... F 440 295-6590
　Richmond Heights (G-12805)
Avtron Aerospace Inc .... C 216 750-5152
　Cleveland (G-3709)
Aws Industries Inc .... E 513 932-7941
　Lebanon (G-9063)
Barnes Group Inc .... E 513 779-6888
　West Chester (G-15373)
◆ Bosserman Aviation Equipment Inc .... E 419 722-2879
　Carey (G-2277)
▲ Columbus Jack Corporation .... E 614 443-7492
　Swanton (G-13971)
Composite Solutions LLC .... G 513 321-7337
　Cincinnati (G-2785)
Ctl-Aerospace Inc .... E 513 874-7900
　West Chester (G-15546)
Ctl-Aerospace Inc .... C 513 874-7900
　West Chester (G-15547)
Danfoss Power Solutions II LLC .... G 419 238-1190
　Van Wert (G-14913)
Dircksen and Associates Inc .... G 614 238-0413
　Columbus (G-5327)
Drone Express Inc .... F 513 577-5152
　Dayton (G-6304)
Drt Aerospace LLC .... E 937 492-6121
　Sidney (G-13242)
Drt Holdings Inc .... D 937 298-7391
　Dayton (G-6305)
Dukes Aerospace Inc .... D 818 998-9811
　Painesville (G-12229)
◆ Eaton Aeroquip LLC .... C 440 523-5000
　Cleveland (G-3991)
Eaton Industrial Corporation .... C 216 692-5456
　Cleveland (G-3997)
Eaton Industrial Corporation .... B 216 523-4205
　Cleveland (G-3998)

Employee Codes: A=Over 500 employees, B=251-500
C=101-250, D=51-100, E=20-50, F=10-19, G=1-9

37 TRANSPORTATION EQUIPMENT

Electronic Concepts Engrg Inc..............F 419 861-9000
  Holland *(G-8509)*
Enjet Aero LLC..............................F 937 878-3800
  Huber Heights *(G-8575)*
Enjet Aero Dayton Inc.....................E 937 878-3800
  Huber Heights *(G-8576)*
▼ Esterline Technologies Corp............E 216 706-2960
  Cleveland *(G-4031)*
Eti Tech LLC..............................F 937 832-4200
  Kettering *(G-8907)*
Exito Manufacturing LLC....................G 937 291-9871
  Beavercreek *(G-1073)*
▲ Federal Equipment Company.............D 513 621-5260
  Cincinnati *(G-2899)*
Ferco Tech LLC............................C 937 746-6696
  Franklin *(G-7674)*
Field Aviation Inc........................E 513 792-2282
  Cincinnati *(G-2903)*
Fluid Power Inc...........................F 330 653-5107
  Hudson *(G-8593)*
◆ Friction Products Co....................B 330 725-4941
  Medina *(G-10328)*
GE Aviation Systems LLC...................B 937 898-5881
  Vandalia *(G-14940)*
GE Engine Services LLC....................B 513 977-1500
  Cincinnati *(G-2936)*
General Dynamics-Ots Inc..................C 937 746-8500
  Springboro *(G-13502)*
General Electric Company..................E 513 977-1500
  Cincinnati *(G-2943)*
Goodrich Aerospace........................G 704 423-7000
  Uniontown *(G-14784)*
Goodrich Corporation......................G 330 374-2358
  North Canton *(G-11732)*
Goodrich Corporation......................A 937 339-3811
  Troy *(G-14574)*
Goodrich Corporation......................F 216 429-4378
  Troy *(G-14575)*
Grimes Aerospace Company..................D 937 484-2000
  Urbana *(G-14831)*
▲ Grimes Aerospace Company...............A 937 484-2000
  Urbana *(G-14830)*
▲ GSE Production and Support LLC........F 419 866-6301
  Swanton *(G-13975)*
◆ Hartzell Propeller Inc..................B 937 778-4200
  Piqua *(G-12523)*
Hdi Landing Gear USA Inc..................E 937 325-1586
  Strongsville *(G-13840)*
Hdi Landing Gear USA Inc..................D 937 325-1586
  Springfield *(G-13572)*
Heller Machine Products Inc...............G 216 281-2951
  Cleveland *(G-4179)*
Heroux-Devtek Inc.........................F 937 325-1586
  Springfield *(G-13575)*
Hydro-Aire Inc............................C 440 323-3211
  Elyria *(G-7158)*
Hydro-Aire Aerospace Corp.................C 440 323-3211
  Elyria *(G-7159)*
Hyfast Aerospace LLC......................G 216 712-4158
  Parma *(G-12291)*
◆ Industrial Mfg Co LLC...................F 440 838-4700
  Brecksville *(G-1621)*
Jay-Em Aerospace Corporation..............E 330 923-0333
  Cuyahoga Falls *(G-6092)*
JCB Arrowhead Products Inc................G 440 546-4288
  Brecksville *(G-1623)*
Kbr Inc...................................F 937 320-2731
  Dayton *(G-6397)*
Kelly Arspc Thrmal Systems LLC............E 440 951-4744
  Willoughby *(G-15938)*
Lincoln Electric Automtn Inc..............B 937 295-2120
  Fort Loramie *(G-7603)*

Lkd Aerospace Holdings Inc................F 216 262-8481
  Cleveland *(G-4333)*
▲ Logan Machine Company..................D 330 633-6163
  Akron *(G-223)*
Long-Lok LLC..............................E 336 343-7319
  Cincinnati *(G-3111)*
Magellan Arospc Middletown Inc............D 513 422-2751
  Middletown *(G-10839)*
Malabar...................................E 419 866-6301
  Swanton *(G-13978)*
Mar-Con Tool Company......................E 937 299-2244
  Moraine *(G-11191)*
Marvin Lewis Enterprises LLC..............E 216 785-8419
  Euclid *(G-7284)*
Master Swaging Inc........................G 937 596-6171
  Jackson Center *(G-8735)*
▲ Maverick Molding Co....................F 513 387-6100
  Blue Ash *(G-1431)*
McKechnie Arospc Holdings Inc.............E 216 706-2960
  Cleveland *(G-4381)*
◆ Meggitt Arcft Brking Systems C.........A 330 796-4400
  Akron *(G-243)*
Meggitt Polymers & Composites.............F 513 851-5550
  Cincinnati *(G-3144)*
Meggitt Rockmart Inc......................E 770 684-7855
  Akron *(G-244)*
Microweld Engineering Inc.................G 614 847-9410
  Worthington *(G-16204)*
Middleton Enterprises Inc.................G 614 885-2514
  Worthington *(G-16205)*
▼ Midwest Aircraft Products Co...........F 419 884-2164
  Mansfield *(G-9692)*
Pacific Piston Ring Co Inc................E 513 387-6100
  Blue Ash *(G-1449)*
▲ Pako Inc...............................C 440 946-8030
  Mentor *(G-10519)*
Parker-Hannifin Corporation...............C 440 937-6211
  Avon *(G-782)*
Parker-Hannifin Corporation...............C 440 284-6277
  Elyria *(G-7192)*
PCC Airfoils LLC..........................B 740 982-6025
  Crooksville *(G-6048)*
▲ Skidmore-Wilhelm Mfg Company...........F 216 481-4774
  Solon *(G-13422)*
Snow Aviation Intl Inc....................E 614 588-2452
  Gahanna *(G-7849)*
Spectrum Textiles Inc.....................F 513 933-8346
  Lebanon *(G-9111)*
Starwin Industries LLC....................E 937 293-8568
  Dayton *(G-6591)*
Summit Aerospace Product Corp.............G 440 652-6829
  Brecksville *(G-1631)*
Summit Avionics Inc.......................F 330 425-1440
  Twinsburg *(G-14739)*
Taylor Manufacturing Co Inc...............F 937 322-8622
  Springfield *(G-13643)*
Tessec Technology Services LLC............E 513 240-5601
  Dublin *(G-6617)*
Test-Fuchs Corporation....................G 440 708-3505
  Brecksville *(G-1635)*
Tracewell Systems Inc.....................D 614 846-6175
  Lewis Center *(G-9182)*
Transdigm Group Incorporated..............B 216 706-2960
  Cleveland *(G-4817)*
Trinity Midwest Aviation LLC..............G 513 583-0519
  Maineville *(G-9603)*
Triumph Thermal Systems LLC...............D 419 273-2511
  Forest *(G-7593)*
◆ Tronair Inc............................C 419 866-6301
  Swanton *(G-13987)*
Truline Industries Inc....................D 440 729-0140
  Wickliffe *(G-15855)*

Turbine Eng Cmpnents Tech Corp............B 216 692-5200
  Cleveland *(G-4837)*
Unison Industries LLC.....................B 904 667-9904
  Dayton *(G-6175)*
US Aeroteam Inc...........................E 937 458-0344
  Dayton *(G-6641)*
◆ US Technology Corporation..............E 330 455-1181
  Canton *(G-2258)*
Weldon Pump LLC...........................E 440 232-2282
  Oakwood Village *(G-12047)*
White Machine Inc.........................G 440 237-3282
  North Royalton *(G-11902)*

3731 Shipbuilding and repairing

Dredger LLC...............................G 513 507-8774
  West Chester *(G-15416)*
Great Lakes Group.........................C 216 621-4854
  Cleveland *(G-4145)*
Ironhead Marine Inc.......................E 419 690-0000
  Toledo *(G-14339)*
Lake Erie Ship Repr Fbrction L............F 440 228-7110
  Jefferson *(G-8752)*
McGinnis Inc..............................C 740 377-4391
  South Point *(G-13470)*
McNational Inc............................D 740 377-4391
  South Point *(G-13471)*
O-Kan Marine Repair Inc...................E 740 446-4686
  Gallipolis *(G-7897)*
◆ Pinney Dock & Transport LLC............D 440 964-7186
  Ashtabula *(G-655)*
Professional Marine Repair LLC............G 440 409-9957
  Ashtabula *(G-656)*
Services Acquisition Co LLC...............F 330 479-9267
  Dennison *(G-6795)*
Superior Marine Ways Inc..................C 740 894-6224
  Proctorville *(G-12687)*
Tack-Anew Inc.............................F 419 734-4212
  Port Clinton *(G-12629)*
The Great Lakes Towing Company............D 216 621-4854
  Cleveland *(G-4784)*

3732 Boatbuilding and repairing

Allmand Boats LLC.........................G 513 805-4673
  Hamilton *(G-8176)*
Brewster Sugarcreek Twp Histo.............F 330 767-0045
  Brewster *(G-1643)*
Ceasars Creek Marine......................G 513 897-2912
  Loveland *(G-9477)*
Checkmate Marine Inc......................F 419 562-3881
  Bucyrus *(G-1853)*
Don Wartko Construction Co................D 330 673-5252
  Kent *(G-8810)*
Dynamic Plastics Inc......................G 937 437-7261
  New Paris *(G-11481)*
Fife Services LLC.........................G 614 829-6285
  Ravenna *(G-12714)*
G M Greco Inc.............................G 614 822-0522
  Dublin *(G-6884)*
Hesseling & Sons LLC......................G 419 642-0013
  Lima *(G-9251)*
Mariners Landing Inc......................F 513 941-3625
  Cincinnati *(G-3131)*
▲ Nauticus Inc...........................G 440 746-1290
  Brecksville *(G-1629)*
O-Kan Marine Repair Inc...................E 740 446-4686
  Gallipolis *(G-7897)*
Racelite Southcoast Inc...................F 216 581-4600
  Maple Heights *(G-9759)*
Samkat Enterprises Inc....................G 937 398-6704
  Medway *(G-10399)*
Screaming Eagle Boats.....................G 937 292-7674
  Bellefontaine *(G-1218)*

Spectre Powerboats LLC.................................G..... 937 292-7674
    Bellefontaine *(G-1220)*

Tugz International LLC..................................F..... 216 621-4854
    Cleveland *(G-4836)*

Underground Eyes II LLC..............................G..... 352 601-1446
    Heath *(G-8332)*

W of Ohio Inc..G..... 614 873-4664
    Plain City *(G-12601)*

3743 Railroad equipment

A Stucki Company..G..... 412 424-0560
    North Canton *(G-11713)*

Aliquippa & Ohio River RR Co.....................G..... 740 622-8092
    Youngstown *(G-16306)*

▲ Alliance Castings Company LLC..............E..... 330 829-5600
    Alliance *(G-391)*

Amsted Industries Incorporated..................D..... 614 836-2423
    Groveport *(G-8129)*

B&C Machine Co LLC...................................E..... 330 745-4013
    Barberton *(G-859)*

◆ Buck Equipment Inc................................E..... 614 539-3039
    Grove City *(G-8081)*

◆ Dayton-Phoenix Group Inc.....................D..... 937 496-3900
    Dayton *(G-6292)*

Engines Inc of Ohio......................................E..... 740 377-9874
    South Point *(G-13466)*

Great Lake Port Corporation........................G..... 330 718-3727
    Poland *(G-12611)*

Gunderson Rail Services LLC......................D..... 330 792-6521
    Youngstown *(G-16376)*

▼ Jk-Co LLC..E..... 419 422-5240
    Findlay *(G-7526)*

Johnson Bros Rubber Co Inc.......................E..... 419 752-4814
    Greenwich *(G-8067)*

K & G Machine Company.............................F..... 216 732-7115
    Cleveland *(G-4268)*

L B Foster Company....................................F..... 330 652-1461
    Mineral Ridge *(G-11022)*

Midwest Rlwy Prsrvtion Soc Inc..................G..... 216 781-3629
    Cleveland *(G-4412)*

Nolan Company...G..... 740 269-1512
    Bowerston *(G-1545)*

Nolan Company...E..... 330 453-7922
    Canton *(G-2173)*

Ohio Valley Trackwork Inc...........................F..... 740 446-0181
    Bidwell *(G-1325)*

Progress Rail Services Corp.......................B..... 216 641-4000
    Cleveland *(G-4591)*

Progress Rail Services Corp.......................E..... 614 850-1730
    Columbus *(G-5695)*

R H Little Co..G..... 330 477-3455
    Canton *(G-2208)*

Ready 2 Ride Trnsp LLC..............................G..... 614 207-2683
    Pickerington *(G-12469)*

Shems Inc...G..... 614 279-2342
    Columbus *(G-5762)*

Transco Railway Products Inc.....................E..... 330 872-0934
    Newton Falls *(G-11659)*

Westinghouse A Brake Tech Corp..............G..... 419 526-5323
    Mansfield *(G-9733)*

Youngstown Belt Railroad Co......................G..... 740 622-8092
    Youngstown *(G-16477)*

3751 Motorcycles, bicycles, and parts

B&D Truck Parts Sls & Svcs LLC................G..... 419 701-7041
    Fostoria *(G-7629)*

Bike Miami Valley Ohio................................G..... 937 496-3825
    Dayton *(G-6229)*

▲ Cmbf Products Inc..................................C..... 440 528-4000
    Medina *(G-10180)*

▲ Cobra Motorcycles Mfg..........................F..... 330 207-3844
    North Lima *(G-11802)*

Colony Machine & Tool Inc..........................G..... 330 225-3410
    Brunswick *(G-1752)*

Custom Assembly Inc..................................E..... 419 622-3040
    Haviland *(G-8309)*

Custom Cycle ACC Mfg Dstrg Inc...............F..... 440 585-2200
    Wickliffe *(G-15830)*

◆ Dco LLC..E..... 419 931-9086
    Perrysburg *(G-12373)*

▲ Ktm North America Inc..........................D..... 855 215-6360
    Amherst *(G-477)*

Milark Industries Inc.....................................D..... 419 524-7627
    Mansfield *(G-9693)*

Milark Industries Inc.....................................E..... 419 524-7627
    Mansfield *(G-9694)*

▲ Newman Technology Inc........................A..... 419 525-1856
    Mansfield *(G-9704)*

Safe Haven Brands LLC..............................F..... 937 550-9407
    Springboro *(G-13519)*

▲ Spiegler Brake Systems USA LLC.......G..... 937 291-1735
    Dayton *(G-6585)*

Sunstar Engrg Americas Inc.......................D..... 937 743-9049
    Franklin *(G-7704)*

▲ Sunstar Engrg Americas Inc.................E..... 937 746-8575
    Springboro *(G-13520)*

◆ Tarantula Performance Racg LLC.........G..... 330 273-3456
    Hinckley *(G-8477)*

Thomas D Epperson....................................G..... 937 855-3300
    Germantown *(G-7954)*

▲ Vari-Wall Tube Specialists Inc..............D..... 330 482-0000
    Columbiana *(G-5053)*

3761 Guided missiles and space vehicles

Starwin Industries LLC..................................E..... 937 293-8568
    Dayton *(G-6591)*

Tessec Manufacturing Svcs LLC.................E..... 937 985-3552
    Dayton *(G-6616)*

3769 Space vehicle equipment, nec

Curtiss-Wright Controls................................E..... 937 252-5601
    Fairborn *(G-7312)*

Defense Co Inc...E..... 413 998-1637
    Cleveland *(G-3950)*

General Electric Company...........................E..... 513 977-1500
    Cincinnati *(G-2943)*

◆ Gleason Metrology Systems Corp........E..... 937 384-8901
    Dayton *(G-6353)*

Grimes Aerospace Company.......................D..... 937 484-2001
    Urbana *(G-14832)*

▲ Industrial Quartz Corporation...............E..... 440 942-0909
    Mentor *(G-10471)*

L3harris Cincinnati Elec Corp......................A..... 513 573-6100
    Mason *(G-10019)*

Lord Corporation...C..... 937 278-9431
    Dayton *(G-6415)*

◆ Metalex Manufacturing Inc....................C..... 513 489-0507
    Blue Ash *(G-1437)*

▲ Millat Industries Corp.............................D..... 937 434-6666
    Dayton *(G-6449)*

Morris Bean & Company..............................C..... 937 767-7301
    Yellow Springs *(G-16285)*

Sunpower Inc..D..... 740 594-2221
    Athens *(G-699)*

Te Connectivity Corporation.........................C..... 419 521-9500
    Mansfield *(G-9725)*

3792 Travel trailers and campers

◆ Airstream Inc..B..... 937 596-6111
    Jackson Center *(G-8729)*

ARE Inc..A..... 330 830-7800
    Massillon *(G-10076)*

Berlin Truck Caps & Tarps Ltd.....................F..... 330 893-2811
    Millersburg *(G-10944)*

Gerich Fiberglass Inc...................................F..... 419 362-4591
    Mount Gilead *(G-11233)*

Xtreme Outdoors LLC..................................E..... 330 731-4137
    Uniontown *(G-14797)*

3795 Tanks and tank components

CSC..G..... 419 221-7037
    Lima *(G-9231)*

General Dynmics Land Systems I..............B..... 419 221-7000
    Lima *(G-9245)*

Integris Composites Inc...............................D..... 740 928-0326
    Hebron *(G-8345)*

Performance Tank Sales Inc.......................G
    Dover *(G-6839)*

Tessec Manufacturing Svcs LLC.................E..... 937 985-3552
    Dayton *(G-6616)*

◆ US Yachiyo Inc...C..... 740 375-4687
    Marion *(G-9888)*

Weldon Pump LLC..E..... 440 232-2282
    Oakwood Village *(G-12047)*

3799 Transportation equipment, nec

All Power Equipment LLC............................F..... 740 593-3279
    Athens *(G-674)*

B & B Industries Inc.....................................E..... 614 871-3883
    Orient *(G-12113)*

Bjs DEMo&hauling LLC................................G..... 216 904-8909
    Garfield Heights *(G-7911)*

Blue Ribbon Trailers Ltd..............................G..... 330 538-4114
    North Jackson *(G-11779)*

Buckeye Trailer & Fab Co LLC....................G..... 330 501-9440
    Damascus *(G-6147)*

Bulk Carriers Service Inc.............................F..... 330 339-3333
    New Philadelphia *(G-11490)*

Cleveland Wheels...G..... 440 937-6211
    Avon *(G-767)*

Fitchville East Corp......................................G..... 419 929-1510
    New London *(G-11462)*

▲ Hawkline Nevada LLC............................G..... 937 444-4295
    Mount Orab *(G-11241)*

Hitch-Hiker Mfg Inc.......................................F..... 330 542-3052
    New Middletown *(G-11478)*

Interstate Truckway Inc................................F..... 614 771-1220
    Columbus *(G-5477)*

Kmj Leasing Ltd..F..... 614 871-3883
    Orient *(G-12115)*

▲ Kolpin Outdoors Corporation................F..... 330 328-0772
    Cuyahoga Falls *(G-6096)*

◆ L & R Racing Inc.....................................E..... 330 220-3102
    Brunswick *(G-1773)*

Loadmaster Trailer Company Ltd...............F..... 419 732-3434
    Port Clinton *(G-12622)*

Malabar..E..... 419 866-6301
    Swanton *(G-13978)*

Midwest Motoplex LLC.................................G..... 740 772-5300
    Chillicothe *(G-2518)*

Otterbacher Trailers LLC.............................F..... 419 462-1975
    Galion *(G-7882)*

Performance Tank Sales Inc.......................G
    Dover *(G-6839)*

Premier Uv Products LLC............................G..... 330 715-2452
    Cuyahoga Falls *(G-6111)*

Prostar LLC...F..... 419 225-8806
    Lima *(G-9306)*

Rankin Mfg Inc..E..... 419 929-8338
    New London *(G-11466)*

Riverside Transportation LLC......................G..... 440 935-3120
    Cleveland *(G-4639)*

Rv Xpress Inc..G..... 937 418-0127
    Piqua *(G-12553)*

Siraj Recovery LLC.......................................G..... 614 893-3507
    Columbus *(G-5774)*

37 TRANSPORTATION EQUIPMENT

Steve Mulcahy .... G 419 229-4801
  Lima *(G-9292)*
Thor Industries Inc .... F 937 596-6111
  Jackson Center *(G-8739)*
◆ Wholecycle Inc .... E 330 929-8123
  Peninsula *(G-12345)*
World Class Carriages LLC .... G 330 857-7811
  Dalton *(G-6145)*

38 MEASURING, PHOTOGRAPHIC, MEDICAL, & OPTICAL GOODS, & CLOCKS

3812 Search and navigation equipment

Accurate Electronics Inc .... C 330 682-7015
  Orrville *(G-12116)*
◆ ADB Safegate Americas LLC .... C 614 861-1304
  Gahanna *(G-7828)*
Aero-Instruments Co LLC .... E 216 071-0130
  Cleveland *(G-3610)*
Alternate Defense LLC .... G 216 225-5889
  Maple Heights *(G-9746)*
Atk Space Systems LLC .... C 937 490-4121
  Beavercreek *(G-1070)*
Atk Systems .... G 937 429-8632
  Beavercreek *(G-1071)*
Atlantic Inertial Systems Inc .... C 740 788-3800
  Heath *(G-8317)*
Boeing Company .... E 740 788-4000
  Heath *(G-8318)*
Btc Inc .... G 740 549-2722
  Lewis Center *(G-9153)*
Btc Technology Services Inc .... G 740 549-2722
  Lewis Center *(G-9154)*
Cedar Elec Holdings Corp .... D 773 804-6288
  West Chester *(G-15388)*
▲ Ceia Usa Ltd .... D 330 310-4741
  Hudson *(G-8588)*
Circle Prime Manufacturing .... E 330 923-0019
  Cuyahoga Falls *(G-6074)*
Decibel Research Inc .... E 256 705-3341
  Beavercreek *(G-1045)*
Dedrone Defense Inc .... F 614 948-2002
  Westerville *(G-15700)*
Defense Surplus LLC .... G 419 460-9906
  Maumee *(G-10198)*
Dragoon Technologies Inc .... G 937 439-9223
  Dayton *(G-6303)*
Drs Advanced Isr LLC .... C 937 429-7408
  Beavercreek *(G-1046)*
Drs Leonardo Inc .... E 937 429-7408
  Beavercreek *(G-1047)*
Drs Leonardo Inc .... E 513 943-1111
  Cincinnati *(G-2557)*
▲ Editencom Ltd .... E 419 865-5877
  Holland *(G-8508)*
Enjet Aero Dayton Inc .... G 937 878-3800
  Huber Heights *(G-8576)*
▲ Escort Inc .... C 513 870-8500
  West Chester *(G-15427)*
▼ Esterline Technologies Corp .... E 216 706-2960
  Cleveland *(G-4031)*
Eti Tech LLC .... F 937 832-4200
  Kettering *(G-8907)*
▲ Ferrotherm Corporation .... C 216 883-9350
  Cleveland *(G-4058)*
GE Aviation Systems LLC .... E 513 470-2889
  Cincinnati *(G-2934)*
GE Aviation Systems LLC .... G 937 898-9500
  Dayton *(G-6347)*

GE Aviation Systems LLC .... B 937 898-5881
  Vandalia *(G-14941)*
GE Aviation Systems LLC .... F 513 779-1910
  West Chester *(G-15435)*
GE Aviation Systems LLC .... F 513 786-4555
  West Chester *(G-15436)*
▲ GE Aviation Systems LLC .... G 937 898-9600
  Cincinnati *(G-2935)*
General Dynmics Mssion Systems ..... F 513 253-4770
  Beavercreek *(G-1051)*
General Electric Company .... A 617 443-3000
  Cincinnati *(G-2942)*
Genpact LLC .... E 513 763-7660
  Cincinnati *(G-2947)*
Grimes Aerospace Company .... D 937 484-2001
  Urbana *(G-14832)*
◆ HBD Industries Inc .... E 614 526-7000
  Dublin *(G-6891)*
Heller Machine Products Inc .... G 216 281-2951
  Cleveland *(O-4179)*
Honeywell International Inc .... A 937 484-2000
  Urbana *(G-14835)*
Hunter Defense Tech Inc .... F 513 943-7880
  Cincinnati *(G-2565)*
IEC Infrared Systems Inc .... E 440 234-8000
  Middleburg Heights *(G-10719)*
IMT Defense Corp .... G 614 891-8812
  Westerville *(G-15659)*
Innovative Products Inc .... G 865 322-9715
  Cleveland *(G-4229)*
L3 Technologies Inc .... G 937 223-3285
  Dayton *(G-6400)*
L3harris Cincinnati Elec Corp .... A 513 573-6100
  Mason *(G-10019)*
L3harris Electrodynamics Inc .... C 847 259-0740
  Cincinnati *(G-2569)*
Lake Shore Cryotronics Inc .... D 614 891-2243
  Westerville *(G-15662)*
Landrum Brown Wrldwide Svcs LL .... F 513 530-5333
  Blue Ash *(G-1418)*
Lockheed Mrtin Intgrted System .... C 330 796-2800
  Akron *(G-222)*
Midwest Precision Holdings Inc .... F 440 497-4086
  Eastlake *(G-7040)*
Mrl Materials Resources LLC .... E 937 531-6657
  Xenia *(G-16269)*
Nhvs International Inc .... B 440 527-8610
  Mentor *(G-10509)*
Northrop Grmman Innvtion Syste ..... C 937 429-9261
  Beavercreek *(G-1076)*
Northrop Grmman Tchncal Svcs I .... F 937 320-3100
  Beavercreek Township *(G-1086)*
Northrop Grumman Systems Corp .... C 937 490-4111
  Beavercreek *(G-1077)*
Northrop Grumman Systems Corp .... D 937 429-6450
  Beavercreek Township *(G-1087)*
Northrop Grumman Systems Corp .... B 513 881-3296
  West Chester *(G-15573)*
Oculii Corp .... E 937 912-9261
  Beavercreek Township *(G-1088)*
Ohio Defense Services Inc .... E 937 608-2371
  Dayton *(G-6487)*
On Guard Defense LLC .... G 740 596-1984
  New Plymouth *(G-11533)*
Parker Aerospace .... G 216 225-2721
  Cleveland *(G-4527)*
PCC Airfoils LLC .... C 216 692-7900
  Cleveland *(G-4537)*
Personal Defense & Tactics LLC .... G 513 571-7163
  Middletown *(G-10849)*
Quasonix Inc .... E 513 942-1987
  West Chester *(G-15491)*

Raven Personal Defense Systems ..... G 419 631-0573
  Ontario *(G-12095)*
Raytheon Company .... F 937 429-5429
  Beavercreek *(G-1059)*
◆ Reuter-Stokes LLC .... B 330 425-3755
  Twinsburg *(G-14724)*
Ryse Aero Holdco Inc .... E 513 318-9907
  Mason *(G-10051)*
S&L Fleet Services Inc .... E 740 549-2722
  Westerville *(G-15677)*
▲ Star Dynamics Corporation .... D 614 334-4510
  Hilliard *(G-8442)*
Sunset Industries Inc .... E 440 306-8284
  Mentor *(G-10570)*
Te Connectivity Corporation .... C 419 521-9500
  Mansfield *(G-9725)*
▲ Thermo Gamma-Metrics LLC .... E 858 450-9811
  Bedford *(G-1157)*
Transdiqm Inc .... G 216 706 2000
  Cleveland *(G-4816)*
Tri-State Jet Mfg LLC .... G 513 896-4538
  Hamilton *(G-8253)*
Trimble Inc .... F 937 233-8921
  Dayton *(G-6634)*
Trimble Inc .... F 937 233-8921
  Tipp City *(G-14160)*
U S Army Corps of Engineers .... G 740 537-2571
  Toronto *(G-14536)*
Valentine Research Inc .... E 513 984-8900
  Blue Ash *(G-1487)*
Vector Electromagnetics LLC .... F 937 478-5904
  Wilmington *(G-16062)*
Wall Colmonoy Corporation .... D 513 842-4200
  Cincinnati *(G-3507)*
Watts Antenna Company .... G 740 797-9380
  The Plains *(G-14060)*
Yost Labs Inc .... F 740 876-4936
  Portsmouth *(G-12661)*

3821 Laboratory apparatus and furniture

Accuscan Instruments Inc .... F 614 878-6644
  Columbus *(G-5097)*
▲ American Isostatic Presses Inc ..... F 614 497-3148
  Columbus *(G-5126)*
▲ American Sterilizer Company .... E 440 392-8328
  Mentor *(G-10415)*
▲ Caron Products and Svcs Inc .... E 740 373-6809
  Marietta *(G-9781)*
Cellular Technology Limited .... E 216 791-5084
  Shaker Heights *(G-13152)*
Center For Excptional Practices .... G 330 523-5240
  Richfield *(G-12782)*
Cheminstruments Inc .... G 513 860-1598
  West Chester *(G-15390)*
Chemsultants International Inc .... G 513 860-1598
  West Chester *(G-15392)*
Chemsultants International Inc .... G 440 974-3080
  Mentor *(G-10437)*
Continntal Hydrdyne Systems In ...... G 330 494-2740
  Canton *(G-2080)*
Cortest Inc .... F 440 942-1235
  Willoughby *(G-15903)*
Denton Atd Inc .... E 567 265-5200
  Huron *(G-8631)*
Dentronix Inc .... D 330 916-7300
  Cuyahoga Falls *(G-6080)*
◆ E R Advanced Ceramics Inc .... E 330 426-9433
  East Palestine *(G-7004)*
Gdj Inc .... G 440 975-0258
  Mentor *(G-10463)*
▲ Gilson Company Inc .... E 740 548-7298
  Lewis Center *(G-9161)*

38 MEASURING, PHOTOGRAPHIC, MEDICAL, & OPTICAL GOODS, & CLOCKS

◆ Global Cooling Inc .... C 740 274-7900
   Athens *(G-685)*
Health Aid of Ohio Inc .... E 216 252-3900
   Cleveland *(G-4174)*
Ies Systems Inc .... E 330 533-6683
   Canfield *(G-2008)*
Ignio Systems LLC .... G 419 708-0503
   Toledo *(G-14326)*
Malta Dynamics LLC .... F 740 749-3512
   Waterford *(G-15238)*
Mettler-Toledo Intl Fin Inc .... F 614 438-4511
   Columbus *(G-5065)*
◆ Mettler-Toledo Intl Inc .... A 614 438-4511
   Columbus *(G-5066)*
◆ Mettler-Toledo LLC .... A 614 438-4511
   Columbus *(G-5067)*
P212121 LLC .... G 253 229-9327
   Toledo *(G-14427)*
◆ Philips Med Systems Clvland In .... B 440 483-3000
   Cleveland *(G-4547)*
Powdermet Powder Prod Inc .... F 216 404-0053
   Euclid *(G-7294)*
Strategic Technology Entp .... F 440 354-2600
   Mentor *(G-10567)*
▲ Tech Pro Inc .... G 330 923-3546
   Akron *(G-350)*
Teledyne Instruments Inc .... E 513 229-7000
   Mason *(G-10063)*
Teledyne Tekmar Company .... E 513 229-7000
   Mason *(G-10064)*
Universal Scientific Inc .... G 440 428-1777
   Madison *(G-9595)*
Waller Brothers Stone Company .... E 740 858-1948
   Mc Dermott *(G-10275)*

3822 Environmental controls

Action Air & Hydraulics Inc .... G 937 372-8614
   Xenia *(G-16247)*
Acutemp Thermal Systems .... F 937 312-0114
   Moraine *(G-11152)*
Ademco Inc .... G 440 439-7002
   Bedford *(G-1098)*
Ademco Inc .... F 513 772-1851
   Blue Ash *(G-1358)*
Air Enterprises Inc .... A 330 794-9770
   Akron *(G-24)*
▲ Alan Manufacturing Inc .... E 330 262-1555
   Wooster *(G-16099)*
◆ Babcock & Wilcox Company .... A 330 753-4511
   Akron *(G-73)*
◆ Bry-Air Inc .... E 740 965-2974
   Sunbury *(G-13951)*
Building Ctrl Integrators LLC .... G 513 247-6154
   Cincinnati *(G-2694)*
Building Ctrl Integrators LLC .... G 513 860-9600
   West Chester *(G-15542)*
Building Ctrl Integrators LLC .... E 614 334-3300
   Powell *(G-12665)*
Certified Labs & Service Inc .... G 419 289-7462
   Ashland *(G-563)*
Cincinnati Air Conditioning Co .... D 513 721-5622
   Cincinnati *(G-2739)*
Columbus Controls Inc .... E 614 882-9029
   Columbus *(G-5264)*
▲ Conery Manufacturing Inc .... F 419 289-1444
   Ashland *(G-567)*
Cool Times .... G 513 608-5201
   Cincinnati *(G-2794)*
Doan/Pyramid Solutions LLC .... D 216 587-9510
   Cleveland *(G-3965)*
▲ Dyoung Enterprise Inc .... C 440 918-0505
   Willoughby *(G-15913)*

Ecopro Solutions LLC .... E 216 232-4040
   Independence *(G-8665)*
Energy & Ctrl Integrators Inc .... G 419 222-0025
   Lima *(G-9240)*
Envirnment Ctrl Sthwest Ohio I .... E 937 669-9900
   Tipp City *(G-14134)*
▼ Estabrook Assembly Svcs Inc .... F 440 243-3350
   Berea *(G-1278)*
Evokes LLC .... E 513 947-8433
   Mason *(G-9992)*
Future Controls Corporation .... E 440 275-3191
   Austinburg *(G-747)*
Grid Sentry LLC .... G 937 490-2101
   Beavercreek *(G-1052)*
Helm Instrument Company Inc .... E 419 893-4356
   Maumee *(G-10205)*
Honeywell International Inc .... A 937 484-2000
   Urbana *(G-14835)*
▼ Hunter Defense Tech Inc .... E 216 438-6111
   Solon *(G-13363)*
Ignio Systems LLC .... G 419 708-0503
   Toledo *(G-14326)*
Integrated Development & Mfg .... F 440 543-2423
   Chagrin Falls *(G-2403)*
Integrated Development & Mfg .... F 440 247-5100
   Chagrin Falls *(G-2380)*
K Davis Inc .... G 419 307-7051
   Fremont *(G-7791)*
Karman Rubber Company .... D 330 864-2161
   Akron *(G-201)*
▲ Logisync Corporation .... F 440 937-0388
   Avon *(G-780)*
Mader Machine Co Inc .... E 440 355-4505
   Lagrange *(G-8951)*
Melink Corporation .... D 513 685-0958
   Milford *(G-10913)*
Mestek Inc .... D 419 288-2703
   Bowling Green *(G-1576)*
Mestek Inc .... F 419 288-2703
   Bradner *(G-1603)*
Ohio Coatings Company .... D 740 859-5500
   Yorkville *(G-16294)*
Parker-Hannifin Corporation .... G 216 433-1795
   Cleveland *(G-4531)*
▲ Pepperl + Fuchs Inc .... C 330 425-3555
   Twinsburg *(G-14709)*
Pepperl + Fuchs Entps Inc .... F 330 425-3555
   Twinsburg *(G-14710)*
▲ Portage Electric Products Inc .... C 330 499-2727
   North Canton *(G-11752)*
Ruskin Manufacturing .... G 937 476-6500
   Dayton *(G-6172)*
Salus North America Inc .... F 888 387-2587
   Mason *(G-10053)*
▲ Sasha Electronics Inc .... F 419 662-8100
   Rossford *(G-12872)*
Sje Rhombus Controls .... G 419 281-5767
   Ashland *(G-614)*
▲ Skuttle Mfg Co .... F 740 373-9169
   Marietta *(G-9825)*
▲ Therm-O-Disc Incorporated .... A 419 525-8500
   Westerville *(G-15681)*
◆ Thermtrol Corporation .... A 330 497-4148
   North Canton *(G-11765)*
▲ Tlt-Babcock Inc .... D 330 867-8540
   Akron *(G-359)*
Tridelta Industries Inc .... G 440 255-1080
   Mentor *(G-10584)*
▲ Ventra Sandusky LLC .... B 419 627-3600
   Sandusky *(G-13103)*
Vib-Iso LLC .... F 800 735-9645
   Wooster *(G-16180)*

Vortec Corporation .... E
   Blue Ash *(G-1489)*
▲ West 6th Products Company .... D 330 467-7446
   Northfield *(G-11915)*
Young Regulator Company Inc .... E 440 232-9452
   Bedford *(G-1161)*

3823 Process control instruments

Adalet/Scott Fetzer Company .... E 440 892-3074
   Cleveland *(G-3596)*
▲ Airmate Co Inc .... D 419 636-3184
   Bryan *(G-1803)*
◆ Alpha Technologies Svcs LLC .... D 330 745-1641
   Hudson *(G-8583)*
▲ Altronic LLC .... C 330 545-9768
   Girard *(G-7960)*
American Water Services Inc .... G 440 243-9840
   Strongsville *(G-13806)*
Aqua Technology Group LLC .... E 513 298-1183
   West Chester *(G-15367)*
▼ Arzel Technology Inc .... E 216 831-6068
   Cleveland *(G-3684)*
Ascon Tecnologic N Amer LLC .... G 216 485-8350
   Cleveland *(G-3686)*
Assetwatch Inc .... C 844 464-5652
   Westerville *(G-15691)*
Automation and Ctrl Tech Inc .... E 614 495-1120
   Dublin *(G-6864)*
Automation Technology Inc .... E 937 233-6084
   Dayton *(G-6219)*
◆ Avure Autoclave Systems Inc .... F 614 891-2732
   Columbus *(G-5167)*
Beaumont Machine LLC .... F 513 701-0421
   Mason *(G-9958)*
Brighton Science .... G 513 469-1800
   Cincinnati *(G-2686)*
◆ Bry-Air Inc .... E 740 965-2974
   Sunbury *(G-13951)*
Bwx Technologies Inc .... E 330 860-1692
   Barberton *(G-863)*
C H Washington Water Plan .... G 740 636-2382
   Wshngtn Ct Hs *(G-16227)*
▲ Caron Products and Svcs Inc .... E 740 373-6809
   Marietta *(G-9781)*
Catacel Corp .... F
   Ravenna *(G-12709)*
Cincinnati Test Systems Inc .... D 513 202-5100
   Harrison *(G-8270)*
◆ Clark-Reliance LLC .... C 440 572-1500
   Strongsville *(G-13821)*
Cleveland Controls Inc .... F 216 398-0330
   Cleveland *(G-3837)*
Cleveland Electric Labs Co .... E 800 447-2207
   Twinsburg *(G-14643)*
Cognex Corp .... G 513 339-0402
   Mason *(G-9981)*
Command Alkon Incorporated .... E 614 799-0600
   Dublin *(G-6876)*
Comtec Incorporated .... F 330 425-8102
   Twinsburg *(G-14644)*
Consoldted Anlytcal Systems In .... F 513 542-1200
   Cincinnati *(G-2787)*
◆ Copeland Access + Inc .... C 937 498-3802
   Sidney *(G-13234)*
▲ Copeland Scroll Compressors LP .... D 937 498-3066
   Sidney *(G-13234)*
▲ Crawford United Corporation .... D 216 541-8060
   Cleveland *(G-3916)*
De Nora Tech Inc .... C 440 285-0100
   Chardon *(G-2448)*
Diamond Power Intl Inc .... F 740 687-4001
   Lancaster *(G-9011)*

38 MEASURING, PHOTOGRAPHIC, MEDICAL, & OPTICAL GOODS, & CLOCKS — SIC SECTION

▲ Dixon Bayco USA .... G 513 874-8499
   Fairfield *(G-7354)*

▲ Doubleday Acquisitions LLC .... E 513 360-7189
   Monroe *(G-11104)*

▲ Dyoung Enterprise Inc .... C 440 918-0505
   Willoughby *(G-15913)*

Emerson Commercial Reside .... F 937 493-2828
   Sidney *(G-13246)*

Emerson Corp .... G 614 841-5498
   Delaware *(G-6719)*

Emerson Electric Co .... C 513 731-2020
   Cincinnati *(G-2865)*

Emerson Helix .... G 937 710-5771
   Dayton *(G-6319)*

Emerson Industrial Automation .... G 216 901-2400
   Cleveland *(G-4011)*

Emerson Professional Tools LLC .... D 740 432-8782
   Cambridge *(G-1934)*

Encompass Atmtn Engrg Tech LLC ...... F 419 873-0000
   Perrysburg *(G-12378)*

Ernst Flow Industries LLC .... E 732 938-5641
   Strongsville *(G-13833)*

Facts Inc .... E 330 928-2332
   Cuyahoga Falls *(G-6082)*

Fisher Controls Intl LLC .... F 513 285-6000
   West Chester *(G-15430)*

Five Star Technologies Ltd .... F 216 447-9422
   Independence *(G-8668)*

Future Controls Corporation .... E 440 275-3191
   Austinburg *(G-747)*

Gem Instrument Company Inc .... F 330 273-6117
   Brunswick *(G-1764)*

Gentherm Medical LLC .... C 513 772-8810
   Cincinnati *(G-2948)*

Geocorp Inc .... E 419 433-1101
   Huron *(G-8632)*

◆ Gleason Metrology Systems Corp ..... E 937 384-8901
   Dayton *(G-6353)*

Glo-Quartz Electric Htr Co Inc .... E 440 255-9701
   Mentor *(G-10464)*

Godfrey & Wing Inc .... F 419 980-4616
   Defiance *(G-6679)*

Gooch & Housego (ohio) LLC .... D 216 486-6100
   Highland Heights *(G-8387)*

H W Fairway International Inc 330 678-2540
   Canton *(G-2119)*

H2flow Controls Inc .... G 419 841-7774
   Toledo *(G-14307)*

Harris Instrument Corporation .... G 740 369-3580
   Delaware *(G-6729)*

Helm Instrument Company Inc .... E 419 893-4356
   Maumee *(G-10205)*

Homeworth Fabrication Mch Inc .... F 330 525-5459
   Homeworth *(G-8554)*

Honeywell International Inc .... A 937 484-2000
   Urbana *(G-14835)*

Hunkar Technologies Inc .... C 513 272-1010
   Cincinnati *(G-3012)*

Innovative Controls Corp .... E 419 691-6684
   Toledo *(G-14333)*

▼ Intek Inc .... F 614 895-0301
   Westerville *(G-15660)*

▲ ITT Torque Systems Inc .... C 216 524-8800
   Cleveland *(G-4241)*

Journey Electronics Corp .... G 513 539-9836
   Monroe *(G-11112)*

▲ Keithley Instruments LLC .... C 440 248-0400
   Solon *(G-13377)*

Koester Corporation .... E 419 599-0291
   Napoleon *(G-11322)*

Kuhlman Instrument Company .... G 419 668-9533
   Norwalk *(G-11976)*

L J Star Incorporated .... E 330 405-3040
   Twinsburg *(G-14684)*

L3harris Cincinnati Elec Corp .... A 513 573-6100
   Mason *(G-10019)*

L3harris Electrodynamics Inc .... C 847 259-0740
   Cincinnati *(G-2569)*

Lake Shore Cryotronics Inc .... D 614 891-2243
   Westerville *(G-15662)*

Liebert Field Services Inc .... C 614 841-5763
   Westerville *(G-15665)*

▲ Logisync Corporation .... F 440 937-0388
   Avon *(G-780)*

LS Starrett Company .... D 440 835-0005
   Westlake *(G-15763)*

M & S Equipment Leasing Co .... F 216 662-8800
   Cleveland *(G-4343)*

M T Systems Inc .... G 330 453-4646
   Canton *(G-2150)*

Machine Applications Corp .... G 419 621-2322
   Sandusky *(G-13011)*

◆ Marlin Manufacturing Corp .... D 216 676-1340
   Cleveland *(G-4360)*

Measurement Computing Corp .... E 440 439-4091
   Cleveland *(G-4386)*

▲ Meech Sttic Elminators USA Inc ...... F 330 564-2000
   Copley *(G-5950)*

Mercury Iron and Steel Co .... F 440 349-1500
   Solon *(G-13385)*

Mettler-Toledo Intl Fin Inc .... E 614 438-4511
   Columbus *(G-5065)*

◆ Mettler-Toledo Intl Inc .... A 614 438-4511
   Columbus *(G-5066)*

◆ Mettler-Toledo LLC .... A 614 438-4511
   Columbus *(G-5067)*

Nextech Materials Ltd .... E 614 842-6606
   Lewis Center *(G-9174)*

Nidec Avtron Automation Corporation .. C 216 642-1230
   Independence *(G-8677)*

Nidec Motor Corporation .... C 216 642-1230
   Cleveland *(G-4458)*

Nidec Motor Corporation .... E 216 642-1230
   Cleveland *(G-4459)*

▲ Noshok Inc .... E 440 243-0888
   Berea *(G-1290)*

Nov Process & Flow Tech US Inc .... E 937 454-3300
   Dayton *(G-6480)*

Overhoff Technology Corp .... F 513 248-2400
   Milford *(G-10916)*

▲ Pacs Industries Inc .... D 740 397-5021
   Mount Vernon *(G-11285)*

Pg Square LLC .... F 216 896-3000
   Cleveland *(G-4545)*

Primex .... E 513 831-9959
   Milford *(G-10919)*

▼ Production Control Units Inc .... D 937 299-5594
   Moraine *(G-11204)*

▲ Q-Lab Corporation .... D 440 835-8700
   Westlake *(G-15776)*

Ram Sensors Inc .... E 440 835-3540
   Cleveland *(G-4613)*

▲ Refractory Specialties Inc .... E 330 938-2101
   Sebring *(G-13125)*

▲ Reuter-Stokes LLC .... B 330 425-3755
   Twinsburg *(G-14724)*

◆ Rhi US Ltd .... G 513 527-6160
   Cincinnati *(G-3335)*

▲ Richards Industrials Inc .... D 513 533-5600
   Cincinnati *(G-3339)*

Rickly Hydrological Co .... E 614 297-9877
   Columbus *(G-5722)*

Roto Tech Inc .... F 937 859-8503
   Moraine *(G-11209)*

Rsa Controls Inc .... G 513 476-6277
   West Chester *(G-15504)*

▲ Rsw Technologies LLC .... F 419 662-8100
   Rossford *(G-12871)*

Sansei Showa Co Ltd .... E 440 248-4440
   Cleveland *(G-4673)*

Schneider Electric Usa Inc .... D 513 777-4445
   West Chester *(G-15506)*

Sealtron Inc .... C 513 733-8400
   Cincinnati *(G-3373)*

Seekirk Inc .... F 614 278-9200
   Columbus *(G-5757)*

▲ Selas Heat Technology Co LLC .... E 800 523-6500
   Streetsboro *(G-13792)*

Sherbrooke Corporation .... E 440 942-3520
   Willoughby *(G-15990)*

Slone Gear International Inc .... G 507 401-4327
   Tipp City *(G-14156)*

▲ Solon Manufacturing Company .... E 440 200-7149
   Chardon *(G-2468)*

Stewart Manufacturing Corp .... E 937 390-3333
   Springfield *(G-13638)*

Stock Fairfield Corporation .... C 440 543-6000
   Solon *(G-13425)*

T E Brown LLC .... F 937 223-2241
   Dayton *(G-6607)*

Tecmark Corporation .... E 440 205-9188
   Mentor *(G-10572)*

▲ Tecmark Corporation .... D 440 205-7600
   Mentor *(G-10573)*

▲ Therm-O-Disc Incorporated .... A 419 525-8500
   Westerville *(G-15681)*

▲ Thermo Gamma-Metrics LLC .... E 858 450-9811
   Bedford *(G-1157)*

Thermo King Corporation .... G 567 280-9243
   Fremont *(G-7814)*

▲ Thk Manufacturing America Inc .... C 740 928-1415
   Hebron *(G-8365)*

Timberlake Automation Inc .... F 330 523-5300
   Richfield *(G-12801)*

Toledo Controls .... G 419 474-2537
   Toledo *(G-14493)*

Toledo Transducers Inc .... E 419 724-4170
   Maumee *(G-10242)*

Tpf Inc .... G 513 761-9968
   Cincinnati *(G-3458)*

Trane Technologies Company LLC ..... E 419 633-6800
   Bryan *(G-1842)*

▲ Unison UCI Inc .... G
   Cleveland *(G-4845)*

United Tool Supply Inc .... G 513 752-6000
   Cincinnati *(G-2576)*

◆ Vanner Holdings Inc .... D 614 771-2718
   Hilliard *(G-8451)*

◆ Vega Americas Inc .... C 513 272-0131
   Lebanon *(G-9119)*

Vertiv Corporation .... C 740 547-5100
   Ironton *(G-8705)*

Visi-Trak Worldwide LLC .... F 216 524-2363
   Cleveland *(G-4878)*

Vitec Inc .... F 216 464-4670
   Bedford *(G-1159)*

WIKA Sensor Technlgy LP .... E 614 430-0683
   Lewis Center *(G-9183)*

Wild Fire Systems .... G 440 442-8999
   Cleveland *(G-4908)*

Xylem Inc .... E 937 767-7241
   Yellow Springs *(G-16287)*

◆ Ysi Incorporated .... D 937 767-7241
   Yellow Springs *(G-16292)*

3824 Fluid meters and counting devices

38 MEASURING, PHOTOGRAPHIC, MEDICAL, & OPTICAL GOODS, & CLOCKS

Aclara Technologies LLC............................ C 440 528-7200
   Solon *(G-13305)*

Aqua Technology Group LLC................... G 513 298-1183
   West Chester *(G-15367)*

Bif Co LLC... F 330 564-0941
   Akron *(G-86)*

Brooks Manufacturing............................... G 419 244-1777
   Toledo *(G-14221)*

Commercial Electric Pdts Corp................. E 216 241-2886
   Cleveland *(G-3889)*

Eaton Corporation..................................... B 440 523-5000
   Beachwood *(G-985)*

Ernst Flow Industries LLC........................ F 732 938-5641
   Strongsville *(G-13833)*

Exact Equipment Corporation.................. F 215 295-2000
   Columbus *(G-5062)*

▲ Graco Ohio Inc...................................... D 330 494-1313
   North Canton *(G-11733)*

L3harris Electrodynamics Inc................... C 847 259-0740
   Cincinnati *(G-2569)*

Lake Shore Cryotronics Inc...................... D 614 891-2243
   Westerville *(G-15662)*

Mill & Motion Properties Ltd.................... F 216 524-4000
   Independence *(G-8674)*

Parking & Traffic Control SEC.................. F 440 243-7565
   Cleveland *(G-4533)*

Reliable Manufacturing LLC..................... E 740 756-9373
   Carroll *(G-2301)*

▲ Thermo Gamma-Metrics LLC................ E 858 450-9811
   Bedford *(G-1157)*

▲ Triplett Bluffton Corporation................. G 419 358-8750
   Bluffton *(G-1509)*

Westmont Inc... G 330 862-3080
   Minerva *(G-11042)*

3825 Instruments to measure electricity

Aclara Technologies LLC............................ C 440 528-7200
   Solon *(G-13305)*

▲ Adams Elevator Equipment Co.............. D 847 581-2900
   Holland *(G-8492)*

Advanced Integration LLC........................ E 614 863-2433
   Reynoldsburg *(G-12748)*

Advanced Kiffer Systems Inc.................... E 216 267-8181
   Cleveland *(G-3606)*

Analytica Usa Inc..................................... F 513 348-2333
   Dayton *(G-6206)*

Andeen-Hagerling Inc................................ F 440 349-0370
   Cleveland *(G-3665)*

Aqua Technology Group LLC................... G 513 298-1183
   West Chester *(G-15367)*

Automation Technology Inc...................... E 937 233-6084
   Dayton *(G-6219)*

Avtron Holdings LLC................................ E 216 642-1230
   Cleveland *(G-3710)*

Battery Unlimited..................................... G 740 452-5030
   Zanesville *(G-16506)*

Bionix Safety Technologies Ltd................ E 419 727-0552
   Maumee *(G-10172)*

▲ Bird Electronic Corporation................... C 440 248-1200
   Solon *(G-13318)*

Bird Technologies Group Inc..................... G 440 248-1200
   Solon *(G-13319)*

CDI Industries Inc..................................... E 440 243-1100
   Cleveland *(G-3802)*

Community Care Network Inc.................. E 216 671-0977
   Cleveland *(G-3890)*

Contact Industries Inc.............................. E 419 884-9788
   Lexington *(G-9200)*

Desco Corporation..................................... G 614 888-8855
   New Albany *(G-11378)*

Dewesoft LLC.. D 855 339-3669
   Whitehouse *(G-15817)*

Drs Signal Technologies Inc..................... E 937 429-7470
   Beavercreek *(G-1048)*

Dss Installations Ltd................................. F 513 761-7000
   Cincinnati *(G-2842)*

▲ Dynamp LLC.. E 614 871-6900
   Grove City *(G-8089)*

Eazytrade Inc... G 513 257-9189
   West Chester *(G-15423)*

Eazytrade Inc... G 513 257-9189
   West Chester *(G-15422)*

F Squared Inc.. G 419 752-7273
   Greenwich *(G-8066)*

Field Apparatus Service & Tstg................ G 513 353-9399
   Cincinnati *(G-2902)*

Fluke Electronics Corporation.................. E 800 850-4608
   Cleveland *(G-4073)*

GE Additive LLC...................................... E 513 341-0597
   West Chester *(G-15434)*

▲ Hana Technologies Inc.......................... D 330 405-4600
   Twinsburg *(G-14671)*

Hannon Company....................................... D 330 456-4728
   Canton *(G-2121)*

Helm Instrument Company Inc................. E 419 893-4356
   Maumee *(G-10205)*

Hughes Corporation................................... E 440 238-2550
   Strongsville *(G-13842)*

▲ Keithley Instruments LLC..................... C 440 248-0400
   Solon *(G-13377)*

Lake Shore Cryotronics Inc...................... D 614 891-2243
   Westerville *(G-15662)*

Lomar Enterprises Inc............................... E 614 409-9104
   Groveport *(G-8151)*

Machine Products Company..................... E 937 890-6600
   Dayton *(G-6420)*

Medina County.. F 330 723-3641
   Medina *(G-10347)*

Morgan Matroc (es)................................... G 440 232-8600
   Bedford *(G-1140)*

Mueller Electric Company Inc.................. F 614 888-8855
   New Albany *(G-11384)*

Nanotronics Imaging Inc........................... G 330 926-9809
   Cuyahoga Falls *(G-6106)*

Nebulatronics Inc...................................... F 440 243-2370
   Olmsted Twp *(G-12089)*

Neptune Equipment Company.................. E 513 851-8008
   Cincinnati *(G-3186)*

Nextech Materials Ltd.............................. D 614 842-6606
   Lewis Center *(G-9174)*

Nu-Di Products Co Inc.............................. D 216 251-9070
   Cleveland *(G-4487)*

Omega Engineering Inc............................. E 740 965-9340
   Sunbury *(G-13962)*

Omegadyne Inc... D 740 965-9340
   Sunbury *(G-13963)*

▲ Opw Engineered Systems Inc............... E 888 771-9438
   West Chester *(G-15471)*

▼ Orton Edward Jr Crmic Fndation.......... E 614 895-2663
   Westerville *(G-15672)*

Paneltech LLC.. F 440 516-1300
   Chagrin Falls *(G-2413)*

▲ Pressco Technology Inc......................... D 440 498-2600
   Cleveland *(G-4585)*

Resonant Sciences LLC............................. E 937 431-8180
   Beavercreek *(G-1080)*

▲ Skidmore-Wilhelm Mfg Company......... F 216 481-4774
   Solon *(G-13422)*

Tacoma Energy LLC................................. E 614 410-9000
   Westerville *(G-15721)*

▲ Tech Pro Inc... G 330 923-3546
   Akron *(G-350)*

Tektronix Inc.. F 248 305-5200
   West Chester *(G-15594)*

◆ Tmsi LLC.. F 888 867-4872
   North Canton *(G-11769)*

▲ Triplett Bluffton Corporation................ G 419 358-8750
   Bluffton *(G-1509)*

Val-Con Inc... G 440 357-1898
   Concord Township *(G-5913)*

▲ Vmetro Inc.. D 281 584-0728
   Fairborn *(G-7326)*

▲ Westerman Inc.. C 800 338-8265
   Bremen *(G-1640)*

▲ Zts Inc... F 513 271-2557
   Cincinnati *(G-3538)*

3826 Analytical instruments

Affymetrix Inc... E 800 321-9322
   Cleveland *(G-3614)*

Affymetrix Inc... E 419 887-1233
   Maumee *(G-10160)*

▲ American Scientific LLC....................... G 614 764-9002
   Columbus *(G-5130)*

Auto Technology Company....................... F 440 572-7800
   Strongsville *(G-13811)*

Bionix Safety Technologies Ltd................ E 419 727-0552
   Maumee *(G-10172)*

Bridge Analyzers Inc................................ F 216 332-0592
   Bedford Heights *(G-1165)*

◆ Bry-Air Inc.. E 740 965-2974
   Sunbury *(G-13951)*

Columbus Instruments LLC..................... E 614 276-0861
   Columbus *(G-5267)*

◆ Columbus Instruments Intl Corp.......... E 614 276-0593
   Columbus *(G-5268)*

Compliant Healthcare Tech LLC.............. E 216 255-9607
   Cleveland *(G-3892)*

Consoldted Anlytcal Systems In............... F 513 542-1200
   Cincinnati *(G-2787)*

Dentronix Inc.. D 330 916-7300
   Cuyahoga Falls *(G-6080)*

Envirnmntal Cmpliance Tech LLC........... F 216 634-0400
   North Royalton *(G-11874)*

Environmental Sample Technology Inc.... E 513 642-0100
   West Chester *(G-15425)*

▲ HEF USA Corporation........................... G 937 323-2556
   Springfield *(G-13574)*

IEC Infrared Systems LLC....................... E 440 234-8000
   Middleburg Heights *(G-10720)*

Kolmer.. G 614 261-0190
   Columbus *(G-5514)*

▲ Laserlinc Inc.. E 937 318-2440
   Fairborn *(G-7318)*

Metron Instruments Inc........................... G 216 332-0592
   Bedford Heights *(G-1176)*

Mettler-Toledo Intl Fin Inc...................... F 614 438-4511
   Columbus *(G-5065)*

◆ Mettler-Toledo Intl Inc......................... A 614 438-4511
   Columbus *(G-5066)*

◆ Mettler-Toledo LLC............................... A 614 438-4511
   Columbus *(G-5067)*

Mettlr-Tledo Globl Hldings LLC............... D 614 438-4511
   Columbus *(G-5068)*

Nanotronics Imaging Inc........................... G 330 926-9809
   Cuyahoga Falls *(G-6106)*

NDC Technologies Inc.............................. C 937 233-9935
   Dayton *(G-6468)*

Northcoast Environmental Labs.............. G 330 342-3377
   Streetsboro *(G-13782)*

Omnitech Electronics Inc......................... F 800 822-1344
   Columbus *(G-5638)*

▼ Orton Edward Jr Crmic Fndation.......... E 614 895-2663
   Westerville *(G-15672)*

PMC Gage Inc... E 440 953-1672
   Willoughby *(G-15973)*

Employee Codes: A=Over 500 employees, B=251-500
C=101-250, D=51-100, E=20-50, F=10-19, G=1-9

38 MEASURING, PHOTOGRAPHIC, MEDICAL, & OPTICAL GOODS, & CLOCKS

Precision Anlytical Instrs Inc .... G 513 984-1600
  Blue Ash (G-1455)
Prospira America Corporation .... F 419 423-9552
  Findlay (G-7553)
Pts Prfssnal Technical Svc Inc .... E 513 642-0111
  West Chester (G-15488)
▲ Q-Lab Corporation .... D 440 835-8700
  Westlake (G-15776)
◆ Reuter-Stokes LLC .... B 330 425-3755
  Twinsburg (G-14724)
◆ Rotex Global LLC .... C 513 541-1236
  Cincinnati (G-3351)
▲ S-Tek Inc .... G 440 439-8232
  Twinsburg (G-14732)
Satelytics Inc .... G 419 372-0160
  Perrysburg (G-12424)
Targeted Cmpund Monitoring LLC .... G 937 825-0842
  Dayton (G-6608)
Tech4imaging LLC .... F 614 214-2655
  Columbus (G-5817)
Teledyne Instruments Inc .... D 603 886-8400
  Mason (G-10062)
Teledyne Instruments Inc .... E 513 229-7000
  Mason (G-10063)
Teledyne Tekmar Company .... E 513 229-7000
  Mason (G-10064)
Test-Fuchs Corporation .... G 440 708-3505
  Brecksville (G-1635)
Thermo Fisher Scientific Inc .... G 800 955-6288
  Cincinnati (G-3451)
Thermo Fsher Scntfic Ashvlle L .... A 740 373-4763
  Marietta (G-9836)
▲ Thermo Gamma-Metrics LLC .... E 858 450-9811
  Bedford (G-1157)
Trek Diagnostics Inc .... F 440 808-0000
  Brooklyn Heights (G-1702)
Viavi Solutions Inc .... G 316 522-4981
  Columbus (G-5073)
▲ Weidmann Electrical Tech Inc .... G 937 508-2112
  Cleveland (G-4900)
Xorb Corporation .... G 419 354-6021
  Bowling Green (G-1597)
Ysi Environmental Inc .... D 937 767-7241
  Yellow Springs (G-16291)
◆ Ysi Incorporated .... D 937 767-7241
  Yellow Springs (G-16292)

3827 Optical instruments and lenses

Cincinnati Eye Inst - Estgate .... F 513 984-5133
  Cincinnati (G-2554)
▲ Cleveland Hoya Corp .... E 440 234-5703
  Berea (G-1269)
Genvac Aerospace Inc .... F 440 646-9986
  Highland Heights (G-8386)
Gooch & Housego (ohio) LLC .... D 216 486-6100
  Highland Heights (G-8387)
Greenlight Optics LLC .... E 513 247-9777
  Loveland (G-9483)
Isomet LLC .... G 937 382-3867
  Wilmington (G-16055)
▼ Krendl Machine Company .... D 419 692-3060
  Delphos (G-6768)
Lear Engineering Corp .... G 937 429-0534
  Beavercreek (G-1054)
Mercury Iron and Steel Co .... F 440 349-1500
  Solon (G-13385)
Miller-Holzwarth Inc .... G 330 342-7224
  Salem (G-13017)
Ncrx Optical Solutions Inc .... G 330 239-5453
  Hudson (G-8607)
Optics Incorporated .... E 800 362-1337
  Brunswick (G-1777)

Punch Components Inc .... E 419 224-1242
  Lima (G-9280)
Seiler Enterprises LLC .... G 614 330-2220
  Hilliard (G-8439)
Sticktite Lenses LLC .... F 571 276-9508
  New Albany (G-11390)
True Vision .... G 740 277-7550
  Lancaster (G-9048)
▲ Volk Optical Inc .... D 440 942-6161
  Mentor (G-10594)
Vsp Lab Columbus .... F 614 409-8900
  Lockbourne (G-9342)
Wilson Optical Labs Inc .... E 440 357-7000
  Mentor (G-10595)

3829 Measuring and controlling devices, nec

1 A Lifesafer Inc .... E 513 651-9560
  Cincinnati (G-2578)
Aclara Technologies LLC .... C 440 528-7200
  Solon (G-13305)
▲ Advanced Indus Msrment Systems .... F 937 320-4930
  Miamisburg (G-10605)
Advanced OEM Solutions LLC .... G 513 407-0140
  West Chester (G-15361)
Advanced Telemetrics Intl .... F 937 862-6948
  Spring Valley (G-13490)
Alsco Meter .... G 740 254-4500
  Gnadenhutten (G-7984)
Amano Cincinnati Incorporated .... F 513 697-9000
  Loveland (G-9474)
American Cube Mold Inc .... G 330 558-0044
  Brunswick (G-1748)
American Thermal Instrs Inc .... E 937 429-2114
  Moraine (G-11156)
Apera Instruments LLC .... G 614 285-3080
  Columbus (G-5148)
◆ Arnco Corporation .... D 800 847-7661
  Elyria (G-7112)
Automation and Ctrl Tech Inc .... E 614 495-1120
  Dublin (G-6864)
Automation Technology Inc .... E 937 233-6084
  Dayton (G-6219)
Babcock & Wilcox Entps Inc .... C 330 753-4511
  Akron (G-74)
Balmac Inc .... G 614 876-1295
  Hilliard (G-8403)
▲ Bilz Vibration Technology Inc .... F 330 468-2459
  Macedonia (G-9538)
Bio Elctrctcal Scence Tech Inc .... G 888 614-1227
  Upper Arlington (G-14799)
Bionix Safety Technologies Ltd .... F 419 727-0552
  Maumee (G-10172)
Blaze Technical Services Inc .... E 330 923-0409
  Stow (G-13688)
Ccsi Inc .... F 800 742-8535
  Akron (G-101)
▲ Ceia Usa Ltd .... D 330 310-4741
  Hudson (G-8588)
▲ Cheminstruments Inc .... G 513 860-1598
  West Chester (G-15391)
Cincinnati Ctrl Dynamics Inc .... G 513 242-7300
  Cincinnati (G-2746)
Clark Fixture Technologies Inc .... E 419 354-1541
  Bowling Green (G-1560)
▲ Controlled Access Inc .... F 330 273-6185
  Brunswick (G-1755)
Crawford United Corporation .... D 216 541-8060
  Cleveland (G-3916)
Daytronic Corporation .... G 937 866-3300
  Miamisburg (G-10635)
Denton Atd Inc .... E 567 265-5200
  Huron (G-8631)

Eagle Composites LLC .... G 513 330-6108
  West Chester (G-15420)
Electric Speed Indicator Co .... F 216 251-2540
  Aurora (G-713)
Excelitas Technologies Corp .... C 866 539-5916
  Miamisburg (G-10639)
◆ Ferry Industries Inc .... D 330 920-9200
  Stow (G-13698)
▲ Fluke Biomedical LLC .... C 440 248-9300
  Solon (G-13351)
▲ Fowler Products Inc .... F 419 683-4057
  Crestline (G-6033)
Gem Instrument Company Inc .... F 330 273-6117
  Brunswick (G-1764)
▲ Gilson Company Inc .... E 740 548-7298
  Lewis Center (G-9161)
Gilson Screen Incorporated .... E 419 256-7711
  Malinta (G-9604)
◆ Gleason Metrology Systems Corp ..... E 937 384-8901
  Dayton (G-6353)
Halliday Technologies Inc .... G 614 504-4150
  Delaware (G-6728)
Harris Instrument Corporation .... G 740 369-3580
  Delaware (G-6729)
Helm Instrument Company Inc .... E 419 893-4356
  Maumee (G-10205)
Heraeus Electro-Nite Co LLC .... G 330 725-1419
  Medina (G-10333)
Honeywell International Inc .... D 302 327-8920
  Columbus (G-5444)
Instrumentors Inc .... G 440 238-3430
  Strongsville (G-13846)
Karman Rubber Company .... D 330 864-2161
  Akron (G-201)
◆ Kinetics Noise Control Inc .... C 614 889-0480
  Dublin (G-6905)
Krumor Inc .... F 216 328-9802
  Cleveland (G-4300)
Kw Acquisition Inc .... G 740 548-7298
  Lewis Center (G-9168)
Lake Shore Cryotronics Inc .... D 614 891-2243
  Westerville (G-15662)
▲ LH Marshall Company .... F 614 294-6433
  Columbus (G-5524)
Lmg Holdings Inc .... E 905 829-3541
  Blue Ash (G-1424)
▲ Logisync Corporation .... F 440 937-0388
  Avon (G-780)
LS Starrett Company .... D 440 835-0005
  Westlake (G-15763)
▲ M&H Medical Holdings Inc .... F 419 727-8421
  Maumee (G-10215)
Magna Three LLC .... G 513 389-0776
  Cincinnati (G-3126)
Magnetic Analysis Corporation .... G 330 758-1367
  Youngstown (G-16394)
Malabar .... E 419 866-6301
  Swanton (G-13978)
Matrix Research Inc .... D 937 427-8433
  Beavercreek (G-1075)
▼ MB Dynamics Inc .... E 216 292-5850
  Cleveland (G-4377)
Measurement Specialties Inc .... E 330 659-3312
  Akron (G-242)
Multi Lapping Service Inc .... F 440 944-7592
  Wickliffe (G-15840)
◆ Multilink Inc .... C 440 366-6966
  Elyria (G-7183)
▲ NDC Technologies Inc .... C 937 233-9935
  Dayton (G-6469)
Nebulatronics Inc .... F 440 243-2370
  Olmsted Twp (G-12089)

SIC SECTION
38 MEASURING, PHOTOGRAPHIC, MEDICAL, & OPTICAL GOODS, & CLOCKS

▲ Newall Electronics Inc .... F 614 771-0213
   Columbus *(G-5596)*

Nidec Avtron Automation Corporation ... C 216 642-1230
   Independence *(G-8677)*

Nidec Motor Corporation .... E 216 642-1230
   Cleveland *(G-4459)*

▲ Nucon International Inc .... F 614 846-5710
   Columbus *(G-5607)*

Omega Engineering Inc .... E 740 965-9340
   Sunbury *(G-13962)*

Omegadyne Inc .... D 740 965-9340
   Sunbury *(G-13963)*

Overhoff Technology Corp .... F 513 248-2400
   Milford *(G-10916)*

PMC Gage Inc .... E 440 953-1672
   Willoughby *(G-15973)*

▲ Portage Electric Products Inc .... C 330 499-2727
   North Canton *(G-11752)*

▲ Pressco Technology Inc .... D 440 498-2600
   Cleveland *(G-4585)*

▼ Production Control Units Inc .... D 937 299-5594
   Moraine *(G-11204)*

▲ Q-Lab Corporation .... D 440 835-8700
   Westlake *(G-15776)*

Quality Controls Inc .... F 513 272-3900
   Cincinnati *(G-3310)*

Quidel Dhi .... F 740 589-3300
   Athens *(G-696)*

Ralston Instruments LLC .... E 440 564-1430
   Newbury *(G-11636)*

◆ Reuter-Stokes LLC .... B 330 425-3755
   Twinsburg *(G-14724)*

Roto Tech Inc .... F 937 859-8503
   Moraine *(G-11209)*

Safe-Grain Inc .... G 513 398-2500
   Loveland *(G-9503)*

Science/Electronics Inc .... F 937 224-4444
   Dayton *(G-6562)*

Sensotec LLC .... G 614 481-8616
   Hilliard *(G-8440)*

▲ Skidmore-Wilhelm Mfg Company .... F 216 481-4774
   Solon *(G-13422)*

Smithers Group Inc .... D 330 833-8548
   Massillon *(G-10145)*

◆ Struers Inc .... D 440 871-0071
   Westlake *(G-15792)*

◆ Sumiriko Ohio Inc .... E 419 358-2121
   Bluffton *(G-1507)*

Super Systems Inc .... E 513 772-0060
   Cincinnati *(G-3432)*

▲ Te-Co Manufacturing LLC .... D 937 836-0961
   Englewood *(G-7244)*

▲ Tech Pro Inc .... G 330 923-3546
   Akron *(G-350)*

Tech Products Corporation .... F 937 438-1100
   Miamisburg *(G-10690)*

Tegam Inc .... E 440 466-6100
   Geneva *(G-7945)*

Teledyne Instruments Inc .... E 513 229-7000
   Mason *(G-10063)*

Teledyne Tekmar Company .... E 513 229-7000
   Mason *(G-10064)*

Teradyne Inc .... F 937 427-1280
   Beavercreek *(G-1065)*

▼ Test Mark Industries Inc .... F 330 426-2200
   East Palestine *(G-7010)*

Test-Fuchs Corporation .... G 440 708-3505
   Brecksville *(G-1635)*

Toledo Transducers Inc .... E 419 724-4170
   Maumee *(G-10242)*

Tool Technologies Van Dyke .... F 937 349-4900
   Marysville *(G-9942)*

◆ UPA Technology Inc .... F 513 755-1380
   West Chester *(G-15522)*

Waygate Technologies Usa LP .... D 866 243-2638
   Cincinnati *(G-3508)*

Welding Consultants Inc .... G 614 258-7018
   Columbus *(G-5870)*

Xcite Systems Corporation .... G 513 965-0300
   Cincinnati *(G-2577)*

Xpansion Instrument LLC .... G 330 618-0062
   Tallmadge *(G-14058)*

3841 Surgical and medical instruments

Abbott Laboratories .... D 847 937-6100
   Columbus *(G-5087)*

Advanced Nanotherapies Inc .... F 415 517-0867
   Cleveland *(G-3607)*

Applied Medical Technology Inc .... E 440 717-4000
   Brecksville *(G-1606)*

▲ Atc Group Inc .... D 440 293-4064
   Andover *(G-484)*

Atricure Inc .... A 513 755-4100
   Mason *(G-9956)*

Avalign - Integrated LLC .... F 440 269-6984
   Mentor *(G-10424)*

Avalign Technologies Inc .... C 419 542-7743
   Hicksville *(G-8372)*

Aws Industries Inc .... E 513 932-7941
   Lebanon *(G-9063)*

Axon Medical Llc .... E 216 276-0262
   Medina *(G-10299)*

Beam Technologies Inc .... B 800 648-1179
   Columbus *(G-5177)*

Becton Dickinson and Company .... G 858 617-4272
   Groveport *(G-8131)*

Bexley Imaging .... G 614 533-6560
   Columbus *(G-5185)*

Boston Scntfc Nrmdlation Corp .... F 513 377-6160
   Mason *(G-9966)*

Boston Scntfc Nrmdlation Corp .... F 330 372-2652
   Warren *(G-15147)*

Bowden Manufacturing Corp .... E 440 946-1770
   Willoughby *(G-15891)*

Buckeye Medical Tech LLC .... G 330 719-9868
   Warren *(G-15149)*

Butler Cnty Surgical Prpts LLC .... G 513 844-2200
   Hamilton *(G-8189)*

Care Fusion .... F 216 521-1220
   Lakewood *(G-8969)*

▲ Casco Mfg Solutions Inc .... D 513 681-0003
   Cincinnati *(G-2706)*

Cmd Medtech LLC .... F 614 364-4243
   Columbus *(G-5257)*

◆ Codonics Inc .... C 800 444-1198
   Cleveland *(G-3881)*

Covidien Holding Inc .... C 513 948-7219
   Cincinnati *(G-2799)*

Cqt Kennedy LLC .... D 419 238-2442
   Van Wert *(G-14912)*

▼ Daavlin Distributing Co .... E 419 636-6304
   Bryan *(G-1815)*

Dentronix Inc .... D 330 916-7300
   Cuyahoga Falls *(G-6080)*

Devicor Med Pdts Holdings Inc .... A 513 864-9000
   Cincinnati *(G-2827)*

Diagnostic Hybrids Inc .... C 740 593-1784
   Athens *(G-681)*

Elite Biomedical Solutions LLC .... F 513 207-0602
   Cincinnati *(G-2558)*

Encore Industries Inc .... C 419 626-8000
   Sandusky *(G-13053)*

▼ Eoi Inc .... F 740 201-3300
   Lewis Center *(G-9160)*

▲ Ethicon Endo-Surgery Inc .... A 513 337-7000
   Blue Ash *(G-1389)*

Ethicon US LLC .... C 513 337-7000
   Blue Ash *(G-1391)*

Eye Surgery Center Ohio Inc .... E 614 228-3937
   Columbus *(G-5368)*

Findlay Amrcn Prsthtic Orthtic .... G 419 424-1622
   Findlay *(G-7505)*

Frantz Medical Development Ltd .... G 440 255-1155
   Mentor *(G-10457)*

◆ General Data Company Inc .... B 513 752-7978
   Cincinnati *(G-2561)*

Gentherm Medical LLC .... C 513 772-8810
   Cincinnati *(G-2948)*

Grimm Scientific Industries .... F 740 374-3412
   Marietta *(G-9797)*

Gyrus Acmi LP .... C 419 668-8201
   Norwalk *(G-11971)*

◆ Haag-Streit Usa Inc .... D 513 398-3937
   Mason *(G-10000)*

Hammill Manufacturing Co .... E 419 476-9125
   Toledo *(G-14311)*

Hdwt Holdings Inc .... D 440 269-6984
   Mentor *(G-10467)*

◆ Hgi Holdings Inc .... A 330 963-6996
   Twinsburg *(G-14672)*

Hickok Waekon LLC .... D 216 541-8060
   Cleveland *(G-4188)*

Howmedica Osteonics Corp .... D 937 291-3900
   Dayton *(G-6374)*

Icad Inc .... F 866 280-2239
   Dayton *(G-6163)*

Innerdyne Holdings Inc .... D 614 757-5000
   Dublin *(G-6898)*

Innovative Stoneworks Inc .... G 440 352-2231
   Concord Township *(G-5907)*

Inspyre Health Systems LLC .... G 440 412-7916
   Grafton *(G-8002)*

▲ Invacare Holdings Corporation .... C 440 329-6000
   Elyria *(G-7169)*

Kinetic Concepts Inc .... F 440 234-8590
   Middleburg Heights *(G-10722)*

Klarity Medical Products LLC .... F 740 788-8107
   Heath *(G-8324)*

▲ KMC Holdings LLC .... C 419 238-2442
   Van Wert *(G-14920)*

Lababidi Enterprises Inc .... G 330 733-2907
   Akron *(G-214)*

Leica Biosystems - TAS .... E 513 864-9671
   Cincinnati *(G-3101)*

Life Sciences - Vandalia LLC .... C 937 387-0880
   Dayton *(G-6407)*

▲ M&H Medical Holdings Inc .... E 419 727-8421
   Maumee *(G-10215)*

Mark W Thruman .... G 614 754-5500
   Columbus *(G-5542)*

Markethtch Inc D/B/A Mh Eye CA .... F 330 376-6363
   Akron *(G-236)*

Medical Quant USA Inc .... F 440 542-0761
   Solon *(G-13384)*

Mediview Xr Inc .... F 419 270-2774
   Cleveland *(G-4388)*

Medtronic Inc .... F 216 642-1977
   Cleveland *(G-4389)*

Medtronic Inc .... G 763 526-2566
   Independence *(G-8672)*

▼ Megadyne Medical Products Inc .... C 801 576-9669
   Blue Ash *(G-1434)*

Meridian LLC .... G 330 995-0371
   Aurora *(G-724)*

Micromd .... G 850 217-7412
   Youngstown *(G-16399)*

Employee Codes: A=Over 500 employees, B=251-500
C=101-250, D=51-100, E=20-50, F=10-19, G=1-9

38 MEASURING, PHOTOGRAPHIC, MEDICAL, & OPTICAL GOODS, & CLOCKS

Midmark Corporation .... G 937 526-3662
  Versailles (G-14986)
◆ Midmark Corporation .... A 937 528-7500
  Miamisburg (G-10661)
▲ Mill-Rose Company .... C 440 255-9171
  Mentor (G-10505)
Minimally Invasive Devices Inc .... G 614 484-5036
  Columbus (G-5572)
Morris Technologies Inc .... E 513 733-1611
  Cincinnati (G-3174)
Morrison Medical Ltd .... G 800 438-6677
  Columbus (G-5581)
▲ National Biological Corp .... E 216 831-0600
  Beachwood (G-1001)
Navigate Crdiac Structures Inc .... G 949 482-5858
  Cleveland (G-4441)
Nelson Labs Fairfield Inc .... E 973 227-6882
  Broadview Heights (G-1663)
Nervive Inc .... F 847 274-1790
  Cleveland (G-4447)
Neurologix Technologies Inc .... F 512 914-7941
  Cleveland (G-4451)
Norman Noble Inc .... E 216 851-4007
  Euclid (G-7289)
▲ Norman Noble Inc .... B 216 761-5387
  Highland Heights (G-8389)
Norwood Medical LLC .... D 937 228-4101
  Dayton (G-6477)
Nuevue Solutions Inc .... G 440 836-4772
  Rootstown (G-12856)
OMI Surgical Products .... F 513 561-2241
  Cincinnati (G-3221)
Optimum Surgical .... F 216 870-8526
  Medina (G-10358)
Optoquest Corporation .... F 216 445-3637
  Cleveland (G-4507)
Patriot Products Inc .... F 419 865-9712
  Holland (G-8522)
Pediavascular Inc .... G 216 236-5533
  Chagrin Falls (G-2414)
Pemco Inc .... E 216 524-2990
  Cleveland (G-4539)
Percuvision LLC .... F 614 891-4800
  Columbus (G-5669)
Peritec Biosciences Ltd .... G 216 445-3756
  Cleveland (G-4541)
Phoenix Quality Mfg LLC .... E 705 279-0538
  Jackson (G-8722)
Pt Solutions LLC .... G 844 786-6300
  Brunswick (G-1784)
Pulse Worldwide Ltd .... G 513 234-7829
  Mason (G-10044)
Quality Electrodynamics LLC .... C 440 638-5106
  Mayfield Village (G-10261)
Realized Mfg LLC .... F 330 535-3887
  Medina (G-10369)
Resonetics LLC .... E 937 865-4070
  Kettering (G-8909)
Respironics Novametrix LLC .... A 800 345-6443
  Columbus (G-5719)
Rhinosystems Inc .... F 216 351-6262
  Brooklyn (G-1681)
Rsb Spine LLC .... G 216 241-2804
  Cleveland (G-4659)
Rultract Inc .... G 330 856-9808
  Warren (G-15204)
Scottcare Corporation .... E 216 362-0550
  Cleveland (G-4680)
Sense Diagnostics Inc .... G 513 702-0376
  Cincinnati (G-3381)
Smiths Medical Asd Inc .... E 800 796-8701
  Dublin (G-6937)

Smiths Medical Asd Inc .... C 614 889-2220
  Dublin (G-6938)
Smiths Medical North America .... G 614 210-7300
  Dublin (G-6939)
◆ Smiths Medical Pm Inc .... F 614 210-7300
  Dublin (G-6940)
Sonogage Inc .... F 216 464-1119
  Cleveland (G-4714)
Southeastern Emergency Eqp Co .... F 919 556-1890
  Dublin (G-6942)
Spartronics Strongsville Inc .... D 440 878-4630
  Strongsville (G-13883)
Spring Hlthcare Dagnostics LLC .... D 866 201-9503
  Jackson (G-8724)
SRI Healthcare LLC .... G 513 398-6406
  Mason (G-10060)
Standard Bariatrics Inc .... E 513 620-7751
  Blue Ash (G-1469)
Steris Corporation .... D 440 354-2600
  Mentor (G-10562)
◆ Steris Corporation .... A 440 354-2600
  Mentor (G-10563)
Steris Instrument MGT Svcs Inc .... C 800 783-9251
  Stow (G-13728)
Summit Online Products LLC .... G 800 326-1972
  Powell (G-12682)
Surgrx Inc .... F 650 482-2400
  Blue Ash (G-1475)
Theken Companies LLC .... F 330 733-7600
  Akron (G-353)
Thermo Fisher Scientific Inc .... E 800 871-8909
  Oakwood Village (G-12044)
Torbot Group Inc .... F 419 724-1475
  Northwood (G-11930)
Troy Innovative Instrs Inc .... E 440 834-9567
  Middlefield (G-10792)
United Medical Supply Company .... F 866 678-8633
  Brunswick (G-1797)
▲ United Sttes Endscopy Group In .... C 440 639-4494
  Mentor (G-10589)
Valensil Technologies LLC .... E 440 937-8181
  Avon (G-790)
Vesco Medical LLC .... G 614 914-5991
  Westerville (G-15723)
Ward Engineering Inc .... G 614 442-8063
  Columbus (G-5863)
◆ Ysi Incorporated .... D 937 767-7241
  Yellow Springs (G-16292)

3842 Surgical appliances and supplies

ABI Orthtc/Prosthetic Labs Ltd .... E 330 758-1143
  Youngstown (G-16299)
Acor Orthopaedic Inc .... F 440 532-0117
  Cleveland (G-3593)
▲ Acor Orthopaedic LLC .... E 216 662-4500
  Cleveland (G-3594)
Akron Orthotic Solutions Inc .... G 330 253-3002
  Akron (G-37)
American Orthopedics Inc .... G 614 291-6454
  Columbus (G-5128)
American Power LLC .... F 937 235-0418
  Dayton (G-6202)
Anatomical Concepts Inc .... F 330 757-3569
  Youngstown (G-16312)
Ansell Healthcare Products LLC .... C 740 622-4369
  Coshocton (G-5969)
Ansell Healthcare Products LLC .... C 740 622-4311
  Coshocton (G-5970)
Avalign Technologies Inc .... C 419 542-7743
  Hicksville (G-8372)
Axon Medical Llc .... E 216 276-0262
  Medina (G-10299)

Bahler Medical Inc .... F 614 873-7600
  Plain City (G-12564)
Barton-Carey Medical Pdts Inc .... E 419 887-1285
  Maumee (G-10169)
▲ Beaufort Rfd Inc .... F 330 239-4331
  Sharon Center (G-13163)
Beeline Purchasing LLC .... G 513 703-3733
  Mason (G-9959)
Beiersdorf Inc .... C 513 682-7300
  West Chester (G-15541)
Benchmark Shield LLC .... G 614 695-6500
  Gahanna (G-7831)
Bracemart LLC .... G 440 353-2830
  North Ridgeville (G-11833)
Capital Prsthtic Orthtic Ctr I .... F 614 451-0446
  Columbus (G-5232)
Cardinal Health Inc .... E 614 553-3830
  Dublin (G-6871)
Cardinal Health Inc .... G 614 757-2863
  Lewis Center (G-9155)
◆ Cardinal Health Inc .... A 614 757-5000
  Dublin (G-6872)
Cleveland Medical Devices Inc .... E 216 619-5928
  Cleveland (G-3846)
Cole Orthotics Prosthetic Ctr .... G 419 476-4248
  Toledo (G-14247)
Columbus Prescr Rehabilitation .... G 614 294-1600
  Westerville (G-15696)
Communications Aid Inc .... F 513 475-8453
  Cincinnati (G-2783)
Dan Allen Surgical LLC .... F 800 261-9953
  Newbury (G-11622)
Deco Tools Inc .... E 419 476-9321
  Toledo (G-14262)
Dentronix Inc .... D 330 916-7300
  Cuyahoga Falls (G-6080)
Doling & Assoc Dntl Lab Inc .... F 937 254-0075
  Dayton (G-6300)
Eddies Iron Lung LLC .... G 614 493-3411
  Columbus (G-5344)
Eleven 10 LLC .... F 888 216-4049
  Westlake (G-15747)
Enespro LLC .... G 630 332-2801
  Cleveland (G-4018)
Ethicon Inc .... C 513 786-7000
  Blue Ash (G-1390)
▲ Faretec Inc .... F 440 350-9510
  Painesville (G-12236)
◆ Ferno-Washington Inc .... C 877 733-0911
  Wilmington (G-16050)
Fidelity Orthopedic Inc .... G 937 228-0682
  Dayton (G-6332)
Findlay Amrcn Prsthtic Orthtic .... G 419 424-1622
  Findlay (G-7505)
Florida Invacare Holdings LLC .... E 800 333-6900
  Elyria (G-7152)
Forceone LLC .... F 513 939-1018
  Hebron (G-8342)
Form5 Prosthetics Inc .... F 614 226-1141
  New Albany (G-11379)
Francisco Jaume .... G 740 622-1200
  Coshocton (G-5978)
▲ Frohock-Stewart Inc .... E 440 329-6000
  North Ridgeville (G-11840)
▲ Gelok International Corp .... E 419 352-1482
  Bowling Green (G-1566)
Gendron Inc .... E 419 636-0848
  Bryan (G-1819)
Gottfried Medical Inc .... F 419 474-2973
  Toledo (G-14301)
▲ Greendale Home Fashions LLC .... D 859 916-5475
  Cincinnati (G-2971)

2024 Harris Ohio Industrial Directory

38 MEASURING, PHOTOGRAPHIC, MEDICAL, & OPTICAL GOODS, & CLOCKS

▲ Guardian Manufacturing Co LLC....... E 419 933-2711
  Willard (G-15859)
Hammill Manufacturing Co................... D 419 476-0789
  Maumee (G-10204)
Hdwt Holdings Inc................................. D 440 269-6984
  Mentor (G-10467)
Healthwares Manufacturing .... F 513 353-3691
  Cleves (G-4954)
Hearingaid Medina Service.................... G 330 725-1060
  Medina (G-10332)
Invacare Canadian Holdings Inc............ E 440 329-6000
  Elyria (G-7161)
Invacare Canadian Holdings LLC.......... F 440 329-6000
  Elyria (G-7162)
Invacare Continuing Care Inc................ G 800 668-2337
  Elyria (G-7163)
Invacare Corporation............................... F 440 329-6000
  Elyria (G-7165)
Invacare Corporation............................... G 800 333-6900
  Elyria (G-7166)
Invacare Corporation............................... F 440 329-6000
  North Ridgeville (G-11846)
◆ Invacare Corporation............................ A 440 329-6000
  Elyria (G-7164)
Invacare Hcs LLC.................................... E 330 634-9925
  Elyria (G-7167)
Invacare Holdings LLC........................... E 440 329-6000
  Elyria (G-7168)
▲ Invacare Holdings Corporation............ C 440 329-6000
  Elyria (G-7169)
Jobskin Div of Torbot Group.................. F 419 724-1475
  Northwood (G-11921)
Jones Metal Products Co LLC............... E 740 545-6381
  West Lafayette (G-15618)
Jones Metal Products Company............ E 740 545-6341
  West Lafayette (G-15619)
▲ Julius Zorn Inc.. D 330 923-4999
  Cuyahoga Falls (G-6094)
Kempf Surgical Appliances Inc.............. F 513 984-5758
  Montgomery (G-11130)
Kuhlmanns Fabrication........................... G 513 967-4617
  Hamilton (G-8226)
Leimkuehler Inc....................................... E 440 899-7842
  Cleveland (G-4319)
Lion First Responder Ppe Inc................ G 937 898-1949
  Dayton (G-6410)
Lower Limb Centers LLC....................... G 440 365-2502
  Elyria (G-7175)
Luminaud Inc... G 440 255-9082
  Mentor (G-10497)
▲ Marlen Manufacturing & Dev Co......... G 216 292-7060
  Bedford (G-1137)
▲ Matplus Ltd.. G 440 352-7201
  Painesville (G-12250)
Medco Labs Inc....................................... E 216 292-7546
  Cleveland (G-4387)
Medical Device Bus Svcs Inc................. E 937 274-5850
  Dayton (G-6434)
Medline Industries LP............................. E 614 879-9728
  West Jefferson (G-15612)
Meridian Industries Inc........................... D 330 673-1011
  Kent (G-8834)
Midmark Corporation.............................. G 937 526-3662
  Versailles (G-14986)
◆ Midmark Corporation............................ A 937 528-7500
  Miamisburg (G-10661)
Morning Pride Mfg LLC.......................... A 937 264-1726
  Dayton (G-6458)
▲ Morning Pride Mfg LLC........................ A 937 264-2662
  Dayton (G-6457)
Motion Mobility & Design Inc................ F 330 244-9723
  North Canton (G-11745)

Mst Inc.. G 419 542-6645
  Hicksville (G-8375)
Mt Pleasant Pharmacy LLC................... G 216 672-4377
  Bedford (G-1141)
Myfootshopcom LLC.............................. G 740 522-5681
  Newark (G-11595)
◆ National Safety Apparel Inc................ D 216 941-1111
  Cleveland (G-4440)
Nmn Spinco Inc....................................... G 800 850-0335
  Columbus (G-5599)
Novagard Solutions Inc........................... C 216 881-8111
  Cleveland (G-4483)
Opc Inc... G 419 531-2222
  Toledo (G-14416)
Orthotic & Prosthetic Spc Inc................. E 216 531-2773
  Euclid (G-7291)
Orthotics Prsthtics Rhblttion................... F 330 856-2553
  Warren (G-15197)
Osteonovus Inc.. G 419 530-5940
  Toledo (G-14418)
Osteonovus Inc.. G 419 530-5940
  Toledo (G-14419)
Osteosymbionics LLC............................. F 216 881-8500
  Cleveland (G-4511)
◆ Philips Med Systems Clvland In........... B 440 483-3000
  Cleveland (G-4547)
Presque Isle Orthtics Prsthtic................. E 216 371-0660
  Cleveland (G-4583)
Reliable Wheelchair Trans..................... G 216 390-3999
  Beachwood (G-1017)
▲ Schaerer Medical Usa Inc.................... F 513 561-2241
  Cincinnati (G-3368)
Soundtrace Inc... G 513 278-5288
  Mason (G-10057)
▼ Southpaw Enterprises Inc.................... E 937 252-7676
  Moraine (G-11212)
Spinal Balance Inc.................................. G 419 530-5935
  Swanton (G-13983)
▲ Sroufe Healthcare Products LLC......... E 260 894-4171
  Wadsworth (G-15067)
Stable Step LLC...................................... C 800 491-1571
  Wadsworth (G-15068)
Steris Corporation................................... C 330 696-9946
  Mentor (G-10564)
Steris Corporation................................... C 440 392-8079
  Mentor (G-10565)
Steris Corporation................................... C 440 354-2600
  Mentor (G-10566)
◆ Steris Corporation................................ A 440 354-2600
  Mentor (G-10563)
Steris-IMS.. F 330 686-4557
  Stow (G-13729)
▲ Surgical Appliance Inds Inc................. C 513 271-4594
  Cincinnati (G-3436)
Theken Spine LLC.................................. F 330 773-7677
  Medina (G-10385)
Thomas Products Co Inc........................ E 513 756-9009
  Cincinnati (G-3453)
▲ Tilt 15 Inc... D 330 239-4192
  Sharon Center (G-13169)
Touch Bionics Inc.................................... G 800 233-6263
  Dublin (G-6953)
Tranzonic Companies............................. D 216 535-4300
  Richmond Heights (G-12811)
▲ Wcm Holdings Inc................................ C 513 705-2100
  Cincinnati (G-3509)
▲ West Chester Holdings LLC................ C 513 705-2100
  Cincinnati (G-3516)
Whiteford Industries Inc......................... F 419 381-1155
  Toledo (G-14524)
◆ Willowwood Global LLC...................... C 740 869-3377
  Mount Sterling (G-11259)

Yanke Bionics Inc.................................... E 330 762-6411
  Akron (G-378)
▲ Zimmer Surgical Inc............................. B 800 321-5533
  Dover (G-6851)

3843 Dental equipment and supplies

◆ Boxout LLC... C 833 462-7746
  Hudson (G-8587)
Dental Ceramics Inc................................ E 330 523-5240
  Richfield (G-12785)
Dental Pure Water Inc............................. F 440 234-0890
  Berea (G-1274)
Dentronix Inc.. D 330 916-7300
  Cuyahoga Falls (G-6080)
Dentsply Sirona Inc................................. D 419 893-5672
  Maumee (G-10199)
Dentsply Sirona Inc................................. E 419 865-9497
  Maumee (G-10200)
Midmark Corporation.............................. G 937 526-3662
  Versailles (G-14986)
◆ Midmark Corporation............................ A 937 528-7500
  Miamisburg (G-10661)
Palm Plastics Ltd..................................... G 561 776-6700
  Bowling Green (G-1581)
Precision Swiss LLC............................... G 513 716-7000
  Cincinnati (G-3271)
Sentage Corporation............................... G 419 842-6730
  Sylvania (G-14013)
United Dental Laboratories..................... E 330 253-1810
  Tallmadge (G-14054)

3844 X-ray apparatus and tubes

Control-X Inc.. G 614 777-9729
  Columbus (G-5290)
Dentsply Sirona Inc................................. E 419 865-9497
  Maumee (G-10200)
General Electric Company..................... E 216 663-2110
  Cleveland (G-4113)
Leisure Time Pdts Design Corp............ G 440 934-1032
  Avon (G-779)
Metro Design Inc..................................... E 440 458-4200
  Elyria (G-7181)
North Coast Medical Eqp Inc................. F 440 243-6189
  Berea (G-1289)
Philips Med Systems Clvland In............ D 617 245-5510
  Beachwood (G-1010)
◆ Philips Med Systems Clvland In........... B 440 483-3000
  Cleveland (G-4547)
Trionix Research Lab Inc....................... G 330 425-9055
  Twinsburg (G-14748)
Waygate Technologies Usa LP.............. D 866 243-2638
  Cincinnati (G-3508)

3845 Electromedical equipment

▼ Alltech Med Systems Amer Inc........... E 440 424-2240
  Solon (G-13310)
Brainmaster Technologies Inc............... G 440 232-6000
  Bedford (G-1107)
Canary Health Technologies Inc.......... F 617 784-4021
  Cleveland (G-3784)
Cardiac Analytics LLC............................ F 614 314-1332
  Powell (G-12667)
Cardioinsight Technologies Inc............. G 216 274-2221
  Independence (G-8655)
Checkpoint Surgical Inc......................... D 216 378-9107
  Independence (G-8657)
Cleveland Medical Devices Inc.............. E 216 619-5928
  Cleveland (G-3846)
Ctl Analyzers LLC................................... E 216 791-5084
  Shaker Heights (G-13153)
Deep Brain Innovations LLC.................. F 216 378-9106
  Beachwood (G-984)

38 MEASURING, PHOTOGRAPHIC, MEDICAL, & OPTICAL GOODS, & CLOCKS

▼ Eoi Inc .... F 740 201-3300
   Lewis Center *(G-9160)*
Great Lkes Nrotechnologies Inc .... E 855 456-3876
   Cleveland *(G-4147)*
Gyrus Acmi LP .... C 419 668-8201
   Norwalk *(G-11971)*
Imalux Corporation .... F 216 502-0755
   Cleveland *(G-4216)*
▲ Lumitex Inc .... D 440 243-8401
   Strongsville *(G-13852)*
Mrpicker .... G 440 354-6497
   Cleveland *(G-4429)*
◆ Ndi Medical LLC .... F 216 378-9106
   Cleveland *(G-4443)*
Neuros Medical Inc .... G 440 951-2565
   Willoughby Hills *(G-16026)*
Neurowave Systems Inc .... G 216 361-1591
   Beachwood *(G-1002)*
Nkh-Safety Inc .... F 513 771-3839
   Cincinnati *(G-3200)*
Norwood Medical LLC .... D 937 228-4101
   Dayton *(G-6477)*
Pemco Inc .... E 216 524-2990
   Cleveland *(G-4539)*
Rapiscan Systems High Enrgy In .... E 937 879-4200
   Fairborn *(G-7321)*
Releveium Labs Inc .... G 614 568-7000
   Oxford *(G-12212)*
Respironics Novametrix LLC .... A 800 345-6443
   Columbus *(G-5719)*
Scallywag Tag .... G 513 922-4999
   Cincinnati *(G-3366)*
Sonosite Inc .... G 425 951-1200
   Hamilton *(G-8244)*
◆ Steris Corporation .... A 440 354-2600
   Mentor *(G-10563)*
Synsei Medical .... G 609 759-1101
   Dublin *(G-6950)*
Torax Medical Inc .... F 651 361-8900
   Blue Ash *(G-1482)*
Valued Relationships Inc .... B 800 860-4230
   Franklin *(G-7708)*
▲ Viewray Inc .... D 440 703-3210
   Oakwood Village *(G-12045)*
Viewray Technologies Inc .... F 440 703-3210
   Oakwood Village *(G-12046)*
Westerville Endoscopy Ctr LLC .... G 614 568-1666
   Westerville *(G-15689)*

3851 Ophthalmic goods

Albright Albright & Schn .... F 614 825-4829
   Worthington *(G-16189)*
▲ Central-1-Optical LLC .... D 330 783-9660
   Youngstown *(G-16334)*
▲ Classic Optical Labs Inc .... C 330 759-8245
   Youngstown *(G-16339)*
▲ Cleveland Hoya Corp .... E 440 234-5703
   Berea *(G-1269)*
Diversified Ophthalmics Inc .... C 803 783-3454
   Cincinnati *(G-2832)*
DMV Corporation .... G 740 452-4787
   Zanesville *(G-16526)*
Essilor Laboratories Amer Inc .... E 614 274-0840
   Columbus *(G-5361)*
Essilor Laboratories Amer Inc .... G 330 425-3003
   Twinsburg *(G-14657)*
Essilor of America Inc .... F 513 765-6000
   Mason *(G-9991)*
Glasses Guy LLC .... E 970 624-9019
   Canton *(G-2113)*
Luxottica North Amer Dist LLC .... G 614 492-5610
   Lockbourne *(G-9338)*
Luxottica of America Inc .... F 614 492-5610
   Lockbourne *(G-9339)*
Malta Dynamics LLC .... F 740 749-3512
   Waterford *(G-15238)*
▲ Nexus Vision Group LLC .... F 866 492-6499
   Grove City *(G-8112)*
Oakley Inc .... F 949 672-6560
   Dayton *(G-6483)*
Steiner Eoptics Inc .... D 937 426-2341
   Miamisburg *(G-10686)*
Sticktite Lenses LLC .... F 571 276-9508
   New Albany *(G-11390)*
Toledo Optical Laboratory Inc .... E 419 248-3384
   Toledo *(G-14501)*
▲ Volk Optical Inc .... D 440 942-6161
   Mentor *(G-10594)*
Wilson Optical Labs Inc .... E 440 357-7000
   Mentor *(G-10595)*
Zenni USA LLC .... D 614 120-0060
   Obetz *(G-12065)*

3861 Photographic equipment and supplies

44toolscom .... G 614 873-4800
   Plain City *(G-12558)*
AGFA Corporation .... G 513 829-6292
   Fairfield *(G-7330)*
▲ American Frame Corporation .... D 419 893-5595
   Maumee *(G-10163)*
Cree Logistics LLC .... G 513 978-1112
   Cincinnati *(G-2802)*
Dupont Specialty Pdts USA LLC .... E 740 474-0220
   Circleville *(G-3548)*
E-Waste Systems (ohio) Inc .... G 614 824-3057
   Columbus *(G-5340)*
Eastman Kodak Company .... E 937 259-3000
   Kettering *(G-8906)*
Eprad Inc .... G 419 666-3266
   Perrysburg *(G-12379)*
Gary Dattilo .... G 513 671-2117
   Cincinnati *(G-2931)*
Gvs Industries Inc .... G 513 851-3606
   Hamilton *(G-8214)*
◆ Horizons Incorporated .... C 216 475-0555
   Cleveland *(G-4201)*
Kay-Zee Inc .... G 330 339-1268
   New Philadelphia *(G-11507)*
◆ Kg63 LLC .... F 216 941-7766
   Cleveland *(G-4287)*
Legrand AV Inc .... E 574 267-8101
   Blue Ash *(G-1422)*
Mediajacked Sound Studio LLC .... G 330 391-3123
   Youngstown *(G-16397)*
Miller-Holzwarth Inc .... D 330 342-7224
   Salem *(G-13017)*
Ohio Hd Video .... F 614 656-1162
   New Albany *(G-11387)*
Plastigraphics Inc .... F 513 771-8848
   Cincinnati *(G-3261)*
Precision Remotes LLC .... F 510 215-6474
   Middleburg Heights *(G-10725)*
◆ Printer Components Inc .... G 585 924-5190
   Fairfield *(G-7397)*
▲ Pulsar Ecoproducts LLC .... F 216 861-8800
   Cleveland *(G-4600)*
Rti Securex LLC .... F 937 859-5290
   Miamisburg *(G-10679)*
Sound Laboratory LLC .... G 330 968-4060
   Kent *(G-8867)*
Stewart Filmscreen Corp .... E 513 753-0800
   Amelia *(G-466)*
▲ Stretchtape Inc .... E 216 486-9400
   Cleveland *(G-4737)*

3873 Watches, clocks, watchcases, and parts

Amano Cincinnati Incorporated .... F 513 697-9000
   Loveland *(G-9474)*
▲ Dimcogray Corporation .... D 937 433-7600
   Centerville *(G-2361)*
◆ I T Verdin Co .... E 513 241-4010
   Cincinnati *(G-3015)*
Sgi Matrix LLC .... D 937 438-9033
   Miamisburg *(G-10681)*

39 MISCELLANEOUS MANUFACTURING INDUSTRIES

3911 Jewelry, precious metal

◆ Associated Premium Corporation ..... E 513 679-4444
   Cincinnati *(G-2637)*
Bensan Jewelers Inc .... G 216 221-1434
   Lakewood *(G-8967)*
Diamond Designs Inc .... G 330 434-6776
   Akron *(G-127)*
Don Basch Jewelers Inc .... E 330 467-2116
   Macedonia *(G-9547)*
Em Es Be Company LLC .... G 216 761-9500
   Cleveland *(G-4008)*
Farah Jewelers Inc .... F 614 438-6140
   Westerville *(G-15656)*
▲ Ginos Awards Inc .... E 216 831-6565
   Warrensville Heights *(G-15229)*
Goyal Enterprises Inc .... F 513 874-9303
   West Chester *(G-15557)*
Gustave Julian Jewelers Inc .... G 440 888-1100
   Cleveland *(G-4157)*
H P Nielsen Inc .... G 440 244-4255
   Lorain *(G-9413)*
Im Greenberg Inc .... G 440 461-4464
   Cleveland *(G-4214)*
James C Free Inc .... G 513 793-0133
   Cincinnati *(G-3035)*
▲ James C Free Inc .... E 937 298-0171
   Dayton *(G-6387)*
Koop Diamond Cutters Inc .... F 513 621-2838
   Cincinnati *(G-3087)*
Lotus Love LLC .... G 614 964-8477
   Columbus *(G-5534)*
M B Saxon Co Inc .... G 440 229-5006
   Cleveland *(G-4345)*
Marfo Company .... D 614 276-3352
   Columbus *(G-5541)*
Markus Jewelers LLC .... G 513 474-4950
   Cincinnati *(G-3132)*
Michael W Hyes Desgr Goldsmith ..... G 440 519-0889
   Solon *(G-13389)*
▲ Prince & Izant LLC .... E 216 362-7000
   Cleveland *(G-4587)*
Rego Manufacturing Co Inc .... D 419 562-0466
   Bucyrus *(G-1867)*
Robert W Johnson Inc .... D 614 336-4545
   Dublin *(G-6931)*
Rosenfeld Jewelry Inc .... G 440 446-0099
   Cleveland *(G-4650)*
Sheiban Jewelry Inc .... F 440 238-0616
   Strongsville *(G-13879)*
Signet Group Inc .... B 330 668-5000
   Fairlawn *(G-7450)*
Signet Group Services US Inc .... G 330 668-5000
   Fairlawn *(G-7451)*
Val Casting Inc .... F 419 562-2499
   Bucyrus *(G-1871)*
Vy Inc .... F 513 421-8100
   Cincinnati *(G-3505)*

39 MISCELLANEOUS MANUFACTURING INDUSTRIES

White Jewelers Inc.................................. G 330 264-3324
  Wooster *(G-16182)*
▲ Whitehouse Bros Inc............................ G 513 621-2259
  Blue Ash *(G-1491)*

3914 Silverware and plated ware

Ahner Fabricating & Shtmtl Inc............... E 419 626-6641
  Sandusky *(G-13042)*
Behrco Inc.. G 419 394-1612
  Saint Marys *(G-12945)*
▲ Ginos Awards Inc................................ E 216 831-6565
  Warrensville Heights *(G-15229)*
Hr Machine llc... G 937 222-7644
  Dayton *(G-6375)*
Professional Award Service..................... G 513 389-3600
  Cincinnati *(G-3301)*
Tempo Manufacturing Company.............. G 937 773-6653
  Piqua *(G-12556)*

3915 Jewelers' materials and lapidary work

Dentsply Sirona Inc.................................. E 419 865-9497
  Maumee *(G-10200)*
Koop Diamond Cutters Inc...................... F 513 621-2838
  Cincinnati *(G-3087)*
▲ Prince & Izant LLC.............................. E 216 362-7000
  Cleveland *(G-4587)*
Sunshine Products.................................. G 303 478-4913
  Toledo *(G-14476)*
The-Fischer-Group.................................. E 513 285-1241
  Fairfield *(G-7419)*
Zero-D Products Inc................................ G 440 942-5005
  Willoughby *(G-16020)*

3931 Musical instruments

▲ A R Schopps Sons Inc....................... E 330 821-8406
  Alliance *(G-386)*
Bbb Music LLC.. G 740 772-2262
  Chillicothe *(G-2494)*
Belco Works Inc...................................... D 740 695-0500
  Saint Clairsville *(G-12897)*
Bell Industries... F 513 353-2355
  Harrison *(G-8265)*
Brooks Manufacturing............................. G 419 244-1777
  Toledo *(G-14221)*
Bunn-Minnick Co..................................... G 614 299-7934
  Columbus *(G-5221)*
Cardinal Percussion Inc.......................... G 330 707-4446
  Girard *(G-7964)*
▼ Commercial Music Service Co........... G 740 746-8500
  Sugar Grove *(G-13915)*
Conn-Selmer Inc..................................... D 440 946-6100
  Willoughby *(G-15901)*
D Picking & Co....................................... G 419 562-6891
  Bucyrus *(G-1856)*
Dangelico Guitars................................... G 513 218-3985
  Cincinnati *(G-2818)*
▲ Earthquaker Devices LLC................... E 330 252-9220
  Akron *(G-136)*
▲ Grover Musical Products Inc.............. E 216 391-1188
  Cleveland *(G-4153)*
◆ I T Verdin Co..................................... E 513 241-4010
  Cincinnati *(G-3015)*
▲ Jatiga Inc... G 859 817-7100
  Blue Ash *(G-1411)*
Loft Violin Shop...................................... F 614 267-7221
  Columbus *(G-5531)*
McHael D Goronok String Instrs............. G 216 421-4227
  Cleveland *(G-4380)*
Muller Pipe Organ Co............................. F 740 893-1700
  Croton *(G-6051)*
Peebles - Herzog Inc............................... G 614 279-2211
  Columbus *(G-5665)*

S I T Strings Co Inc................................. E 330 434-8010
  Akron *(G-321)*
Schantz Organ Company......................... F 330 682-6065
  Orrville *(G-12150)*
▲ Stewart-Macdonald Mfg Co................ E 740 592-3021
  Athens *(G-698)*
The Holtkamp Organ Co.......................... F 216 741-5180
  Cleveland *(G-4786)*
The W L Jenkins Company..................... F 330 477-3407
  Canton *(G-2244)*
Verdin Organ Division............................. G 513 502-2333
  Cincinnati *(G-3495)*
Victor Organ Company............................ G 330 792-1321
  Youngstown *(G-16470)*

3942 Dolls and stuffed toys

Love Yueh LLC....................................... G 614 408-8677
  Pickerington *(G-12463)*
Middleton Llyd Dolls Inc......................... G 740 989-2082
  Coolville *(G-5941)*

3944 Games, toys, and children's vehicles

Advance Novelty Incorporated................ G 419 424-0363
  Findlay *(G-7472)*
▲ Ajj Enterprises LLC............................ F 513 755-9562
  West Chester *(G-15534)*
▲ Anime Palace..................................... G 408 858-1918
  Lewis Center *(G-9149)*
Aog Inc... G 937 436-2412
  Dayton *(G-6208)*
Applied Concepts Inc............................. F 440 229-5033
  Willoughby *(G-15882)*
◆ Arrow International Inc........................ C 216 961-3500
  Cleveland *(G-3676)*
▲ AW Faber-Castell Usa Inc.................. D 216 643-4660
  Independence *(G-8654)*
Berlin Wood Products Inc....................... G 330 893-3281
  Berlin *(G-1304)*
Brown Dave Products Inc....................... G 513 738-1576
  Hamilton *(G-8188)*
Container Graphics Corp........................ E 419 531-5133
  Toledo *(G-14252)*
Cornhole Worldwide LLC........................ G 513 324-2877
  Cleves *(G-4949)*
Evenflo Company Inc.............................. D 937 773-3971
  Troy *(G-14566)*
◆ Foundations Worldwide Inc................. E 330 722-5033
  Medina *(G-10326)*
Fremont Plastic Products Inc................. C 419 332-6407
  Fremont *(G-7783)*
Friends Rocking Horse Center................ G 937 324-1111
  Springfield *(G-13569)*
Hershberger Lawn Structures................. F 330 674-3900
  Millersburg *(G-10957)*
▲ Late For Sky Production Co................ E 513 531-4400
  Cincinnati *(G-3096)*
Lawbre Co.. G 330 637-3363
  Cortland *(G-5965)*
Little Cottage Company........................... F 330 893-4212
  Millersburg *(G-10975)*
▲ Mag-Nif Inc... D 440 255-9366
  Mentor *(G-10498)*
Mahoning Valley Manufacturing.............. E 330 537-4492
  Beloit *(G-1251)*
Michaels Stores Inc................................ F 330 505-1168
  Niles *(G-11676)*
Ohio Model Products LLC...................... F 614 808-4488
  Columbus *(G-5621)*
Pioneer National Latex Inc..................... E 419 289-3300
  Ashland *(G-602)*
Plaid Hat Games..................................... G 419 552-5490
  Ashland *(G-603)*

Plaid Hat Games LLC.............................. G 419 552-5490
  Ashland *(G-604)*
Puzzles & Planeswalkers LLC................. G 937 540-9047
  Englewood *(G-7239)*
◆ Recaro Child Safety LLC.................... G 248 904-1570
  Cincinnati *(G-3326)*
Rocky Hinge Inc..................................... G 330 539-6296
  Girard *(G-7974)*
RPM Consumer Holding Company.......... E 330 273-5090
  Medina *(G-10371)*
◆ S Toys Holdings LLC........................... A 330 656-0440
  Streetsboro *(G-13789)*
Scrambl-Gram Inc................................... G 419 635-2321
  Port Clinton *(G-12628)*
Step2 Company LLC............................... B 419 938-6343
  Perrysville *(G-12449)*
◆ Step2 Company LLC.......................... B 866 429-5200
  Streetsboro *(G-13794)*
The Guardtower Inc................................ F 614 488-4311
  Hilliard *(G-8447)*
◆ The Little Tikes Company.................... A 330 650-3000
  Hudson *(G-8616)*
▲ Watch-Us Inc...................................... E 513 829-8870
  Fairfield *(G-7425)*
Wells Manufacturing Llc......................... F 937 987-2481
  New Vienna *(G-11544)*

3949 Sporting and athletic goods, nec

Al-Co Products Inc................................. G 419 399-3867
  Latty *(G-9053)*
◆ American Heritage Billd LLC............... D 877 998-0908
  Mentor *(G-10413)*
Arem Co.. F 440 974-6740
  Mentor *(G-10423)*
▲ AWC Transition Corporation............... F 614 846-2918
  Columbus *(G-5168)*
Backyard Scoreboards LLC.................... G 513 702-6561
  Middletown *(G-10805)*
Black Wing Shooting Center LLC............ G 740 363-7555
  Delaware *(G-6705)*
Board of Park Commissioners................. F 216 635-3200
  Cleveland *(G-3743)*
Bracemart LLC.. G 440 353-2830
  North Ridgeville *(G-11833)*
Bradley Enterprises Inc........................... G 330 875-1444
  Louisville *(G-9456)*
Brg Sports Inc... G 217 891-1429
  North Ridgeville *(G-11834)*
Buddy Hunting Inc.................................. G 330 353-6850
  Canton *(G-2056)*
▲ Bullseye Dart Shoppe Inc................... G 440 951-9277
  Willoughby *(G-15895)*
Columbus Canvas Products Inc............. F 614 375-1397
  Columbus *(G-5263)*
Corner Alley LLC.................................... D 216 298-4070
  Cleveland *(G-3906)*
Country CLB Rtrment Ctr IV LLC............ G 740 676-2300
  Bellaire *(G-1185)*
Creighton Sports Center Inc................... G 740 865-2521
  New Matamoras *(G-11477)*
▲ Crownplace Brands Ltd...................... G 888 332-5534
  Apple Creek *(G-497)*
Darting Around LLC................................ F 330 639-3990
  Canton *(G-2088)*
Dayton Stencil Works Company.............. F 937 223-3233
  Dayton *(G-6290)*
▲ Done-Rite Bowling Service Co............ E 440 232-3280
  Bedford *(G-1118)*
EJ Weber Ltd.. G 513 759-0103
  West Chester *(G-15424)*
Equipment Guys Inc................................ F 614 871-9220
  Newark *(G-11575)*

39 MISCELLANEOUS MANUFACTURING INDUSTRIES

Fjr Industries Inc... G 859 277-8207
  Painesville (G-12238)
▲ Forrest Enterprises Inc........................... F 937 773-1714
  Piqua (G-12516)
Front Pocket Innovations LLC..................... G 330 441-2365
  Wadsworth (G-15031)
Funtown Playgrounds Inc............................ F 513 871-8585
  Cincinnati (G-2559)
▲ Ghostblind Industries Inc......................... G 740 374-6766
  Belpre (G-1253)
▲ GL International LLC................................ C 330 744-8812
  Youngstown (G-16370)
Golf Car Company Inc.................................. F 614 873-1055
  Plain City (G-12580)
▲ Golf Galaxy Golfworks Inc........................ C 740 328-4193
  Newark (G-11577)
Grip Spritz LLC.. G 440 888-7022
  Cleveland (G-4150)
▲ H & S Distributing Inc.............................. G 800 336-7784
  North Ridgeville (G-11843)
Hendershot Performance LLC...................... G 740 315-0090
  Belpre (G-1254)
Hofmanns Lures Inc.................................... G 937 684-0338
  Arcanum (G-518)
Hoistech LLC... G 440 327-5479
  North Ridgeville (G-11844)
House of Awards Inc.................................... G 419 422-7877
  Findlay (G-7525)
Huffy Sports Washington Inc........................ F 937 865-2800
  Miamisburg (G-10647)
▲ Hunters Manufacturing Co Inc................. E 330 628-9245
  Mogadore (G-11075)
Imperial On-Pece Fibrgls Pools.................... F 740 747-2971
  Ashley (G-622)
Imperial Pools Inc.. F 513 771-1506
  Cincinnati (G-3018)
Jfab LLC... G 740 572-0227
  Jeffersonville (G-8764)
▲ Kent Water Sports LLC............................. D 419 929-7021
  New London (G-11463)
Lake Erie Waterkeeper Inc........................... G 419 691-3788
  Toledo (G-14358)
Leisure Time Pdts Design Corp.................... G 440 934-1032
  Avon (G-779)
▲ Lem Products Holding LLC...................... E 513 202-1188
  West Chester (G-15457)
Lifetime Products Inc................................... G 614 272-1255
  Columbus (G-5526)
Line Drive Sportz-Lcrc LLC.......................... G 419 794-7150
  Maumee (G-10214)
▲ Litehouse Products LLC........................... E 440 638-2350
  Strongsville (G-13851)
Mc Alarney Pool Spas and Billd................... F 740 373-6698
  Marietta (G-9808)
Meridian Industries Inc................................ D 330 359-5447
  Winesburg (G-16081)
Meyer Design Inc... E 330 434-9176
  Akron (G-247)
Mudbrook Golf Ctr At Thndrbird.................. G 419 433-2945
  Huron (G-8640)
Nova Golf Corp... G 419 652-3160
  Nova (G-12004)
▲ Ohio Table Pad Company......................... F 419 872-6400
  Perrysburg (G-12407)
◆ Rain Drop Products Llc............................ E 419 207-1229
  Ashland (G-609)
Raven Concealment Systems LLC............... E 440 508-9000
  North Ridgeville (G-11856)
Red Barakuda LLC....................................... G 614 596-5432
  Columbus (G-5715)
Rogue Bowstrings... G 330 749-9725
  Dover (G-6841)

Shoot-A-Way Inc... F 419 294-4654
  Nevada (G-11361)
Soccer Centre Owners Ltd........................... G 419 893-5425
  Maumee (G-10233)
◆ Sports Imports Incorporated.................... F 614 771-0246
  Worthington (G-16212)
▲ Sunset Golf LLC.. G 419 994-5563
  Tallmadge (G-14051)
Total Tennis Inc.. F 614 488-5004
  Columbus (G-5829)
Total Tennis Inc.. G 614 504-7446
  Plain City (G-12595)
Tuffy Pad Company...................................... F 330 688-0043
  Stow (G-13733)
UGL Inc.. G 630 250-1600
  Dayton (G-6639)
Ultrabilt Play Systems Nova Lt.................... G 234 248-4414
  Chippewa Lake (G-2543)
Ultrabuilt Play Systems Inc......................... F 419 652-2201
  Nova (G-12005)
Uniwall Mfg Co.. F 330 875-1444
  Louisville (G-9472)
Wholesale Bait Co Inc................................. F 513 863-2380
  Fairfield (G-7427)
Wilson Sporting Goods Co........................... C 419 634-9901
  Ada (G-6)
Yakpads Inc... G 419 357-5684
  Huron (G-8646)
◆ Zebec of North America Inc.................... E 513 829-5533
  Fairfield (G-7429)

3952 Lead pencils and art goods

Airbrush Sugar Shack Inc............................ G 614 735-4988
  Columbus (G-5108)
▲ North Shore Strapping Company.............. E 216 661-5200
  Brooklyn Heights (G-1696)
◆ Pulsar Ecoproducts LLC........................... F 216 861-8800
  Cleveland (G-4600)
RPM Consumer Holding Company............... E 330 273-5090
  Medina (G-10371)

3953 Marking devices

Ace Rubber Stamp & Off Sup Co.................. F 216 771-8483
  Cleveland (G-3590)
◆ Akron Paint & Varnish Inc....................... D 330 773-8911
  Akron (G-38)
Bishop Machine Tool & Die.......................... F 740 453-8818
  Zanesville (G-16510)
Dayton Stencil Works Company................... F 937 223-3233
  Dayton (G-6290)
E C Shaw Company of Ohio......................... F 513 721-6334
  Cincinnati (G-2848)
Greg G Wright & Sons LLC.......................... E 513 721-3310
  Cincinnati (G-2972)
Hathaway Stamp Co..................................... E 513 621-1052
  Cincinnati (G-2989)
Hathaway Stamp Idntfction Cncn................ G 513 621-1052
  Cincinnati (G-2990)
Impact Printing and Design LLC................. F 833 522-6200
  Columbus (G-5456)
▲ Infosight Corporation................................ D 740 642-3600
  Chillicothe (G-2512)
Marathon Mfg & Sup Co............................... F 330 343-2656
  New Philadelphia (G-11514)
▲ Mark-All Enterprises LLC........................ E 800 433-3615
  Akron (G-235)
Marking Devices Inc.................................... G 216 861-4498
  Cleveland (G-4359)
Master Marking Company Inc..................... F 330 688-6797
  Cuyahoga Falls (G-6102)
Metal Marker Manufacturing Co.................. F 440 327-2300
  North Ridgeville (G-11850)

▲ Microcom Corporation............................... E 740 548-6262
  Lewis Center (G-9171)
Monode Marking Products Inc..................... F 419 929-0346
  New London (G-11464)
Quality Rubber Stamp Inc........................... G 614 235-2700
  Lancaster (G-9034)
Quick As A Wink Printing Co....................... G 419 224-9786
  Lima (G-9281)
▲ REA Elektronik Inc................................... F 440 232-0555
  Bedford (G-1151)
▲ Royal Acme Corporation........................... E 216 241-1477
  Cleveland (G-4654)
Sprinter Marking Inc................................... G 740 453-1000
  Zanesville (G-16565)
Stakes Manufacturing LLC.......................... D 216 245-4752
  Willowick (G-16035)
System Seals Inc... E 216 220-1800
  Brecksville (G-1632)
▲ System Seals Inc...................................... E 440 735-0200
  Cleveland (G-4763)
▲ Telesis Technologies Inc.......................... C 740 477-5000
  Circleville (G-3558)
Visual Marking Systems Inc........................ D 330 425-7100
  Twinsburg (G-14753)
Volk Corporation.. G 513 621-1052
  Cincinnati (G-3501)
Williams Steel Rule Die Co.......................... F 216 431-3232
  Cleveland (G-4910)

3955 Carbon paper and inked ribbons

▲ All Write Ribbon Inc................................. F 513 753-8300
  Amelia (G-450)
▲ Kroy LLC... C 216 426-5600
  Cleveland (G-4299)
◆ Printer Components Inc........................... G 585 924-5190
  Fairfield (G-7397)
Progressive Ribbon Inc............................... E 513 705-9319
  Middletown (G-10852)
◆ Pubco Corporation.................................... D 216 881-5300
  Cleveland (G-4597)
Wood County Ohio....................................... G 419 353-1227
  Bowling Green (G-1596)

3961 Costume jewelry

Bcp Imports LLC.. G 419 467-0291
  Toledo (G-14208)
Bellas Jewels LLC.. G 216 551-9593
  Cleveland (G-3729)
Benzle Porcelain Company.......................... G 614 876-2159
  Hilliard (G-8404)
Gardella Jewelry LLC.................................. G 440 877-9261
  North Royalton (G-11876)
Pughs Designer Jewelers Inc...................... G 740 344-9259
  Newark (G-11603)
Silly Brandz Global LLC.............................. D 419 697-8324
  Toledo (G-14473)

3965 Fasteners, buttons, needles, and pins

Aspen Fasteners USA................................... G 800 479-0056
  Cleveland (G-3692)
Bamal Corp.. G 937 492-9484
  Sidney (G-13225)
Beckett-Greenhill LLC................................. F 216 861-5730
  Cleveland (G-3728)
Cailin Development LLC.............................. F 216 408-6261
  Cleveland (G-3781)
▲ Cardinal Fstener Specialty Inc................. E 216 831-3800
  Bedford Heights (G-1166)
▲ Catania Medallic Specialty Inc................. E 440 933-9595
  Avon Lake (G-801)
▲ Dimcgray Corporation............................... D 937 433-7600
  Centerville (G-2361)

39 MISCELLANEOUS MANUFACTURING INDUSTRIES

Dubose Nat Enrgy Fas McHned PR........ F 216 362-1700
  Middleburg Heights *(G-10718)*
Efg Holdings Inc................................... A 440 325-4337
  Berea *(G-1275)*
Erico International Corp...................... B 440 248-0100
  Solon *(G-13345)*
▲ ET&f Fastening Systems Inc............ F 800 248-2376
  Solon *(G-13346)*
Global Specialties Inc.......................... G 800 338-0814
  Brunswick *(G-1765)*
Lockfast LLC.. G 800 543-7157
  Loveland *(G-9491)*
Master Bolt LLC................................... E 440 323-5529
  Elyria *(G-7178)*
▲ Midwest Motor Supply Co................ C 800 233-1294
  Columbus *(G-5565)*
▲ Ohashi Technica USA Mfg Inc......... F 740 965-9002
  Sunbury *(G-13961)*
Purebuttonscom LLC.......................... F 330 721-1600
  Medina *(G-10367)*
◆ Ramco Specialties Inc.....................D 330 653-5135
  Hudson *(G-8609)*
▲ Solution Industries LLC.................... F 440 816-9500
  Strongsville *(G-13882)*
Stanley Engineered Fasten................. F 440 657-3537
  Elyria *(G-7205)*
◆ Stelfast LLC.....................................E 440 879-0077
  Strongsville *(G-13886)*
◆ Tfp Corporation............................... F 330 725-7741
  Medina *(G-10384)*
W W Cross Industries Inc................... F 330 588-8400
  Canton *(G-2263)*
Wodin Inc... E 440 439-4222
  Cleveland *(G-4916)*
Youngstown Bolt & Supply Co............ G 330 799-3201
  Youngstown *(G-16479)*

3991 Brooms and brushes

Brushes Inc... E 216 267-8084
  Cleveland *(G-3766)*
D A L E S Corporation........................ G 419 255-5335
  Toledo *(G-14257)*
Deco Tools Inc.................................... E 419 476-9321
  Toledo *(G-14262)*
Delaware Paint Company Ltd............. F 740 368-9981
  Plain City *(G-12574)*
Designetics Inc....................................D 419 866-0700
  Holland *(G-8504)*
Ekco Cleaning Inc............................... C 513 733-8882
  Cincinnati *(G-2860)*
◆ Fimm USA Inc.................................. F 614 568-4874
  Lancaster *(G-9016)*
◆ Malish Corporation..........................D 440 951-5356
  Mentor *(G-10499)*
▲ Mill Rose Laboratories Inc.............. E 440 974-6730
  Mentor *(G-10504)*
▲ Mill-Rose Company......................... C 440 255-9171
  Mentor *(G-10505)*
Precision Brush Co.............................. F 440 542-9600
  Solon *(G-13407)*
Public Works Dept Street Div............. G 740 283-6013
  Steubenville *(G-13675)*
◆ Spiral Brushes Inc........................... E 330 686-2861
  Stow *(G-13725)*
▲ Stephen M Trudick........................... E 440 834-1891
  Burton *(G-1886)*
◆ The Wooster Brush Company..........C 330 264-4440
  Wooster *(G-16177)*
Tod Thin Brushes Inc.......................... F 440 576-6859
  Jefferson *(G-8762)*
Trent Manufacturing Company........... G 216 391-1551
  Mentor *(G-10583)*

Unique Packaging & Printing.............. F 440 785-6730
  Mentor *(G-10588)*
United Rotary Brush Inc...................... E 937 644-3515
  Plain City *(G-12597)*
Wooster Brush Company.................... G 440 322-8081
  Elyria *(G-7219)*

3993 Signs and advertising specialties

1157 Designconcepts LLC.................. E 937 497-1157
  Sidney *(G-13216)*
A & A Safety Inc.................................. F 937 567-9781
  Beavercreek *(G-1068)*
A & A Safety Inc.................................. E 513 943-6100
  Amelia *(G-447)*
A&E Signs and Lighting LLC.............. F 513 541-0024
  Cincinnati *(G-2586)*
Abbott Image Solutions LLC............... F 937 382-6677
  Wilmington *(G-16037)*
ABC Signs Inc..................................... F 513 241-8884
  Cincinnati *(G-2590)*
Accent Signage Systems Inc.............. E 612 377-9156
  Findlay *(G-7470)*
Adcraft Decals Incorporated............... E 216 524-2934
  Cleveland *(G-3598)*
Affinity Disp Expositions Inc............... F 513 771-2339
  Cincinnati *(G-2599)*
▲ Affinity Disp Expositions Inc...........D 513 771-2339
  Cincinnati *(G-2600)*
Agile Sign & Ltg Maint Inc.................. E 440 918-1311
  Eastlake *(G-7017)*
▲ Alberts Screen Print Inc.................. C 330 753-7559
  Norton *(G-11938)*
All Signs of Chillicothe Inc.................. G 740 773-5016
  Chillicothe *(G-2492)*
Allen Industries Inc..............................D 567 408-7538
  Toledo *(G-14182)*
Allied Sign Co...................................... F 614 443-9656
  Columbus *(G-5115)*
Alvin L Roepke.................................... G 419 862-3891
  Elmore *(G-7099)*
American Awards Inc.......................... F 614 875-1850
  Grove City *(G-8077)*
▲ American Led-Gible Inc.................. F 614 851-1100
  Columbus *(G-5127)*
Apex Signs Inc.................................... G 330 952-2626
  Medina *(G-10295)*
Archer Corporation.............................. E 330 455-9995
  Canton *(G-2038)*
Architctral Identification Inc................ F 614 868-8400
  Gahanna *(G-7830)*
◆ Associated Premium Corporation....E 513 679-4444
  Cincinnati *(G-2637)*
Atchley Signs & Graphics LLC........... F 614 421-7446
  Columbus *(G-5162)*
Atlantic Sign Company Inc................. E 513 383-1504
  Cincinnati *(G-2640)*
Auto Dealer Designs Inc..................... E 330 374-7666
  Akron *(G-70)*
Avid Signs Plus LLC........................... G 513 932-7446
  Lebanon *(G-9062)*
Baker Plastics Inc................................ G 330 743-3142
  Youngstown *(G-16317)*
Barnes Advertising Corporation......... E 740 453-6836
  Zanesville *(G-16505)*
Bates Metal Products Inc....................D 740 498-8371
  Port Washington *(G-12631)*
▲ BDS Packaging Inc......................... F 937 643-0530
  Moraine *(G-11161)*
Beebe Worldwide Graphics Sign........ G 513 241-2726
  Blue Ash *(G-1367)*
Behrco Inc... G 419 394-1612
  Saint Marys *(G-12945)*

Belco Works Inc...................................D 740 695-0500
  Saint Clairsville *(G-12897)*
Benchmark Craftsman Inc................... E 866 313-4700
  Seville *(G-13135)*
Best Graphics...................................... G 614 327-7929
  Columbus *(G-5183)*
Blang Acquisition LLC........................ F 937 223-2155
  Dayton *(G-6231)*
Boyer Signs & Graphics Inc................ E 216 383-7242
  Columbus *(G-5206)*
Brainerd Industries Inc........................ E 937 228-0488
  Miamisburg *(G-10622)*
Brandon Screen Printing..................... F 419 229-9837
  Lima *(G-9224)*
Brilliant Electric Sign Co Ltd...............D 216 741-3800
  Brooklyn Heights *(G-1685)*
Brown Cnty Bd Mntal Rtardation........ E 937 378-4891
  Georgetown *(G-7950)*
▲ Buckeye Boxes Inc..........................D 614 274-8484
  Columbus *(G-5219)*
Busch & Thiem Inc.............................. E 419 625-7515
  Sandusky *(G-13047)*
Business Idntfction Systems In........... G 614 841-1255
  Columbus *(G-5223)*
C JS Signs.. G 330 821-7446
  Alliance *(G-397)*
Call Sign Alpha LLC........................... G 330 842-6200
  Salem *(G-12980)*
Campbell Signs & Apparel LLC.......... F 330 386-4768
  East Liverpool *(G-6989)*
▲ Casad Company Inc........................ F 419 586-9457
  Coldwater *(G-4984)*
▲ Catalog Merchandiser Inc............... F
  Cincinnati *(G-2708)*
▲ Cgs Imaging Inc.............................. F 419 897-3000
  Holland *(G-8497)*
Chad Abbott Signs LLC...................... G 937 393-8864
  Hillsboro *(G-8456)*
Chase Sign & Lighting Svc Inc........... G 567 128-3444
  Toledo *(G-14234)*
Cicogna Electric and Sign Co.............D 440 998-2637
  Ashtabula *(G-627)*
Cincinnati Custom Signs Inc............... E 513 322-2559
  Cincinnati *(G-2747)*
Classic Sign Company........................ G 419 420-0058
  Findlay *(G-7495)*
Cleveland E Speedpro Imaging.......... G 216 342-4954
  Cleveland *(G-3839)*
▲ Co Pac Services Inc........................ F 216 688-1780
  Cleveland *(G-3879)*
Columbus Graphics Inc....................... F 614 577-9360
  Reynoldsburg *(G-12759)*
Columbus Sign Company................... E 614 252-3133
  Columbus *(G-5277)*
Communication Exhibits Inc................D 330 854-4040
  Canal Fulton *(G-1970)*
CSP Group Inc.................................... E 513 984-9500
  Cincinnati *(G-2804)*
Cubbison Company.............................D 330 793-2481
  Youngstown *(G-16344)*
Custom Sign & Design LLC................ G 419 202-3633
  Norwalk *(G-11960)*
Custom Sign Center............................ G 614 279-6035
  Columbus *(G-5311)*
Danite Holdings Ltd............................ E 614 444-3333
  Columbus *(G-5316)*
◆ Davis Printing Company..................E 330 745-3113
  Barberton *(G-866)*
Dayton Wire Products Inc................... E 937 236-8000
  Dayton *(G-6291)*
◆ Dee Sign Co.................................... E 513 779-3333
  West Chester *(G-15412)*

39 MISCELLANEOUS MANUFACTURING INDUSTRIES

Dee Sign Usa LLC .... F 513 779-3333
  West Chester *(G-15413)*
▲ Dern Trophies Corp .... F 614 895-3260
  Westerville *(G-15653)*
Design Masters Inc .... G 513 772-7175
  Cincinnati *(G-2826)*
Devries & Associates Inc .... G 614 890-3821
  Westerville *(G-15701)*
DJ Signs MD LLC .... F 330 344-6643
  Akron *(G-131)*
Djmc Partners Inc .... F 614 890-3821
  Westerville *(G-15702)*
Doxie Inc .... G 937 427-3431
  Dayton *(G-6160)*
▲ Dualite Inc .... C 513 724-7100
  Williamsburg *(G-15864)*
E P Gerber & Sons Inc .... D 330 857-2021
  Kidron *(G-8913)*
▲ E-B Display Company Inc .... C 330 833-4101
  Massillon *(G-10092)*
Eaglestone Products LLC .... G 440 463-8715
  Brecksville *(G-1615)*
▲ Eighth Floor Promotions LLC .... C 419 586-6433
  Celina *(G-2330)*
Ellet Neon Sales & Service Inc .... E 330 628-9907
  Akron *(G-137)*
Engravers Gallery & Sign Co .... G 330 830-1271
  Massillon *(G-10094)*
Enlarging Arts Inc .... G 330 434-3433
  Akron *(G-142)*
▲ Etched Metal Company .... E 440 248-0240
  Solon *(G-13347)*
F J Designs Inc .... F 330 264-1377
  Wooster *(G-16117)*
Fair Publishing House Inc .... E 419 668-3746
  Norwalk *(G-11967)*
Fast Signs .... G 614 710-1312
  Hilliard *(G-8411)*
Fast Track Signs LLC .... G 937 593-9990
  Bellefontaine *(G-1209)*
Fastsigns .... G 513 489-8989
  Cincinnati *(G-2896)*
Fastsigns .... G 937 890-6770
  Dayton *(G-6329)*
Fastsigns .... G 513 226-6733
  Liberty Township *(G-9206)*
Fastsigns .... G 330 952-2626
  Medina *(G-10323)*
Fastsigns .... G 440 954-9191
  Mentor *(G-10454)*
Fastsigns .... F 419 843-1073
  Toledo *(G-14284)*
Fdi Cabinetry LLC .... G 513 353-4500
  Cleves *(G-4952)*
Federal Heath Sign Company LLC .... D 740 369-0999
  Delaware *(G-6721)*
Fineline Imprints Inc .... F 740 453-1083
  Zanesville *(G-16530)*
Finn Graphics Inc .... F 513 941-6161
  Cincinnati *(G-2905)*
Flawless Signs & Wraps LLC .... G 937 559-0672
  Troy *(G-14569)*
Folks Creative Printers Inc .... F 740 383-6326
  Marion *(G-9852)*
Forty Nine Degrees LLC .... F 419 678-0100
  Coldwater *(G-4990)*
Fourteen Ventures Group LLC .... G 937 866-2341
  West Carrollton *(G-15354)*
Freds Sign Service Inc .... G 937 335-1901
  Troy *(G-14570)*
Frontier Signs & Displays Inc .... G 513 367-0813
  Harrison *(G-8275)*

Gardner Signs Inc .... F 419 385-6669
  Toledo *(G-14297)*
Gary Lawrence Enterprises Inc .... G 330 833-7181
  Massillon *(G-10099)*
Geograph Industries Inc .... E 513 202-9200
  Harrison *(G-8276)*
Gerber Wood Products Inc .... D 330 857-9007
  Kidron *(G-8914)*
▲ Ginos Awards Inc .... E 216 831-6565
  Warrensville Heights *(G-15229)*
Glavin Industries Inc .... E 440 349-0049
  Solon *(G-13353)*
▲ Global Lighting Tech Inc .... E 440 922-4584
  Brecksville *(G-1618)*
▲ Golf Marketing Group Inc .... G 330 963-5155
  Twinsburg *(G-14669)*
Grady McCauley Inc .... D 330 494-9444
  Akron *(G-172)*
Greg G Wright & Sons LLC .... C 513 721-3310
  Cincinnati *(G-2972)*
Gus Holthaus Signs Inc .... E 513 861-0060
  Cincinnati *(G-2978)*
Hall Company .... E 937 652-1376
  Urbana *(G-14833)*
Ham Signs LLC DBA Fastsigns .... F 937 890-6770
  Dayton *(G-6365)*
Harbor Wraps LLC .... G 614 725-0429
  Columbus *(G-5419)*
Hart Advertising Inc .... F 419 668-1194
  Norwalk *(G-11972)*
Hendricks Vacuum Forming Inc .... F 330 837-2040
  Massillon *(G-10106)*
Highrise Creative LLC .... F 614 890-3821
  Westerville *(G-15708)*
HP Manufacturing Company Inc .... D 216 361-6500
  Cincinnati *(G-4204)*
Hy-Ko Products Company LLC .... E 330 467-7446
  Northfield *(G-11907)*
Identitek Systems Inc .... D 330 832-9844
  Massillon *(G-10111)*
Ike Smart City .... E 614 294-4898
  Columbus *(G-5453)*
Industrial and Mar Eng Svc Co .... F 740 694-0791
  Fredericktown *(G-7749)*
Industrial Electronic Service .... F 937 746-9750
  Carlisle *(G-2288)*
Innomark Group LLC .... G 419 720-8102
  Toledo *(G-14332)*
Insignia Signs Inc .... G 937 866-2341
  Moraine *(G-11186)*
Insta Plak Inc .... F 419 537-1555
  Toledo *(G-14334)*
Integral Design Inc .... F 216 524-0555
  Cleveland *(G-4230)*
Interior Graphic Systems LLC .... G 330 244-0100
  Canton *(G-2132)*
Interstate Sign Products Inc .... G 419 683-1962
  Crestline *(G-6034)*
J Best Inc .... G 513 943-7000
  Cincinnati *(G-2567)*
Johnny Hulsman Signs .... G 513 638-9788
  Cincinnati *(G-3046)*
Jones Old Rustic Sign Company .... G 937 643-1695
  Oakwood *(G-12028)*
Kasper Enterprises Inc .... G 419 841-6656
  Toledo *(G-14345)*
▲ Kdm Signs Inc .... C 513 769-1932
  Cincinnati *(G-3069)*
Kessler Sign Company .... E 740 453-0668
  Zanesville *(G-16542)*
Kinly Signs Corporation .... F 740 451-7446
  South Point *(G-13468)*

Kinoly Signs .... G 740 451-7446
  South Point *(G-13469)*
Kmgrafx Inc .... G 513 248-4100
  Loveland *(G-9490)*
Laad Sign & Lighting Inc .... F 330 379-2297
  Ravenna *(G-12721)*
Lake Erie Graphics Inc .... E 216 575-1333
  Brookpark *(G-1721)*
Lehner Signs Inc .... G 614 258-0500
  Columbus *(G-5523)*
Lettergraphics Inc .... G 330 683-3903
  Orrville *(G-12135)*
License Ad Plate Company .... F 216 265-4200
  Cleveland *(G-4323)*
Lightning Signs and Decals LLC .... G 304 403-1290
  New Philadelphia *(G-11511)*
Long Sign Co .... G 614 294-1057
  Columbus *(G-5532)*
LSI Industries Inc .... B 513 793-3200
  Cincinnati *(G-3115)*
Macray Co LLC .... G 937 325-1726
  Springfield *(G-13598)*
Masterpiece Signs & Graphics .... F 419 358-0077
  Bluffton *(G-1505)*
Mayfair Granite Co Inc .... G 216 382-8150
  Cleveland *(G-4372)*
McRd Enterprises LLC .... F 740 775-2377
  Chillicothe *(G-2517)*
Mel Wacker Signs Inc .... G 330 832-1726
  Massillon *(G-10126)*
Mes Painting and Graphics .... G 614 496-1696
  Westerville *(G-15714)*
Mes Painting and Graphics Ltd .... E 614 496-1696
  Westerville *(G-15715)*
Metalphoto of Cincinnati Inc .... E 513 772-8281
  Cincinnati *(G-3155)*
Metromedia Technologies Inc .... D 330 264-2501
  Wooster *(G-16151)*
Midwest Sign Ctr .... G 330 493-7330
  Canton *(G-2164)*
Mitchell Plastics Inc .... E 330 825-2461
  Barberton *(G-883)*
Moonshine Screen Printing Inc .... G 513 523-7775
  Oxford *(G-12211)*
Morrison Sign Company Inc .... E 614 276-1181
  Columbus *(G-5582)*
Myers and Lasch Inc .... G 440 235-2050
  Westlake *(G-15766)*
National Illmination Sign Corp .... G 419 866-1666
  Holland *(G-8520)*
National Scoreboards LLC .... G 513 791-5244
  Cincinnati *(G-3181)*
▼ National Sign Systems Inc .... D 614 850-2540
  Hilliard *(G-8424)*
Neon Workshop .... G 216 832-5236
  Bedford *(G-1143)*
Nevco Services Ltd .... G 937 603-1500
  Dayton *(G-6470)*
North Coast Theatrical Inc .... G 330 762-1768
  Akron *(G-266)*
North Hill Marble & Granite Co .... F 330 253-2179
  Akron *(G-267)*
Norton Outdoor Advertising .... E 513 631-4864
  Cincinnati *(G-3205)*
Nrka Corp .... F 440 817-0700
  Broadview Heights *(G-1664)*
Obhc Inc .... G 440 236-5112
  Columbia Station *(G-5015)*
▲ Ohio Awning & Manufacturing Co ...... E 216 861-2400
  Cleveland *(G-4494)*
Ohio Displays Inc .... F 216 961-5600
  Elyria *(G-7189)*

SIC SECTION

39 MISCELLANEOUS MANUFACTURING INDUSTRIES

Ohio Shelterall Inc.............................. F 614 882-1110
   Westerville *(G-15717)*

Omni Media Cleveland Inc..................... G 216 687-0077
   Cleveland *(G-4503)*

On Site Signs Ohio Ltd........................... G 614 496-9400
   Hilliard *(G-8428)*

Onestop Signs.. F 513 722-7867
   Goshen *(G-7994)*

Orange Barrel Media LLC..................... D 614 294-4898
   Columbus *(G-5643)*

Painted Hill Inv Group Inc....................... F 937 339-1756
   Troy *(G-14600)*

Patriot Signage Inc................................ G 859 655-9009
   Cincinnati *(G-3239)*

Paul Peterson Safety Div Inc................. E 614 486-4375
   Columbus *(G-5661)*

Pfi Displays Inc...................................... E 330 925-9015
   Rittman *(G-12826)*

Plastigraphics Inc................................... F 513 771-8848
   Cincinnati *(G-3261)*

Precision Signs & Graphics LLC............ G 740 446-1774
   Gallipolis *(G-7898)*

Pro A V of Ohio...................................... G 877 812-5350
   New Philadelphia *(G-11523)*

Pro Image Sign & Design Inc................ E 440 986-8888
   Amherst *(G-482)*

Pro-Decal Inc... G 330 484-0089
   Canton *(G-2203)*

Quality Custom Signs LLC..................... G 614 580-7233
   Worthington *(G-16209)*

Queen Exhibits LLC............................... G 937 615-6051
   Piqua *(G-12551)*

▲ Quikey Manufacturing Co Inc............. C 330 633-8106
   Akron *(G-293)*

Ray Meyer Sign Company Inc................ E 513 984-5446
   Loveland *(G-9500)*

Renoir Visions LLC................................ G 419 586-5679
   Celina *(G-2345)*

Retain Loyalty LLC................................ G 330 830-0839
   Massillon *(G-10139)*

Ripped Vinyl.. G 330 332-5004
   Salem *(G-13027)*

▲ Rocal Inc... D 740 998-2122
   Frankfort *(G-7658)*

Roemer Industries Inc........................... D 330 448-2000
   Masury *(G-10158)*

Rogers Display Inc................................ E 440 951-9200
   Mentor *(G-10547)*

▲ Royal Acme Corporation.................... E 216 241-1477
   Cleveland *(G-4654)*

Ruff Neon & Lighting Maint Inc.............. F 440 350-6267
   Painesville *(G-12263)*

S&S Sign Service................................... G 614 279-9722
   Columbus *(G-5737)*

▲ Sabco Industries Inc......................... E 419 531-5347
   Toledo *(G-14461)*

Scioto Sign Co Inc................................. E 419 673-1261
   Kenton *(G-8900)*

Screen Works Inc.................................. E 937 264-9111
   Dayton *(G-6564)*

Sdmk LLC.. G 330 965-0970
   Youngstown *(G-16435)*

Select Signs.. E 937 262-7095
   Dayton *(G-6173)*

▲ Sensical Inc...................................... D 216 641-1141
   Solon *(G-13420)*

Sideway Signs LLC................................ G 501 400-4013
   Cincinnati *(G-3388)*

Sign America Incorporated.................... F 740 765-5555
   Richmond *(G-12803)*

Sign Connection Inc.............................. F 937 435-4070
   Dayton *(G-6572)*

Sign Design Wooster Inc....................... G 330 262-8838
   Wooster *(G-16172)*

Sign Technologies LLC.......................... G 937 439-3970
   Dayton *(G-6573)*

Sign Write... G 937 559-4388
   Beavercreek *(G-1063)*

Signarama... G 330 468-0556
   Macedonia *(G-9573)*

Signcom Incorporated........................... F 614 228-9999
   Columbus *(G-5770)*

Signs Limited LLC................................. G 740 282-7715
   Steubenville *(G-13677)*

Signs Ohio Inc....................................... G 419 228-7446
   Lima *(G-9289)*

Signs Unlmted The Grphic Advnt........... G 614 836-7446
   Logan *(G-9376)*

Signwire Worldwide Inc......................... G 937 428-6189
   Dayton *(G-6574)*

Speedpro Imaging.................................. F 513 771-4776
   Cincinnati *(G-3407)*

Speedpro Imaging................................. G 513 753-5600
   Milford *(G-10924)*

Standard Signs Incorporated................. G 330 467-2030
   Macedonia *(G-9579)*

Sterling Associates Inc.......................... G 330 630-3500
   Akron *(G-338)*

▲ Stratus Unlimited LLC....................... C 440 209-6200
   Mentor *(G-10568)*

Super Signs Inc..................................... G 480 968-2200
   North Bend *(G-11707)*

Superior Label Systems Inc................... B 513 336-0825
   Mason *(G-10061)*

T&T Graphics Inc................................... D 937 847-6000
   Miamisburg *(G-10688)*

TCS Schindler & Co LLC....................... G 937 836-9473
   Englewood *(G-7243)*

◆ Ternion Inc.. E 216 642-6180
   Cleveland *(G-4777)*

Terry & Jack Neon Sign Co................... G 419 229-0674
   Lima *(G-9297)*

The Hartman Corp................................. G 614 475-5035
   Columbus *(G-5822)*

The Massillon-Cleveland-A.................... C 330 833-3165
   Massillon *(G-10149)*

Toledo Sign Company Inc...................... E 419 244-4444
   Toledo *(G-14504)*

Traffic Cntrl Sgnls Signs & MA.............. G 740 670-7763
   Newark *(G-11609)*

Traffic Detectors & Signs Inc................. G 330 707-9060
   Youngstown *(G-16457)*

Traxx North America Inc....................... F 513 554-4700
   Blue Ash *(G-1485)*

Triangle Sign Co LLC............................ G 513 266-1009
   Hamilton *(G-8254)*

Triumph Signs & Consulting Inc............. E 513 576-8090
   Milford *(G-10926)*

Tusco Limited Partnership..................... C 740 254-4343
   Gnadenhutten *(G-7991)*

United - Maier Signs Inc....................... D 513 681-6600
   Cincinnati *(G-3478)*

▲ Vgu Industries Inc............................. E 216 676-9093
   Cleveland *(G-4867)*

Vision Graphix Inc................................. G 440 835-6540
   Westlake *(G-15800)*

Vista Creations LLC............................... G 440 954-9191
   Mentor *(G-10593)*

Visual Marking Systems Inc................... D 330 425-7100
   Twinsburg *(G-14753)*

▲ Vmi Liquidating Inc........................... E 937 492-3100
   Sidney *(G-13293)*

W C Bunting Co Inc............................... F 330 385-2050
   East Liverpool *(G-7002)*

Wellman Container Corporation............ E 513 860-3040
   Cincinnati *(G-3515)*

▲ West 6th Products Company............. D 330 467-7446
   Northfield *(G-11915)*

Wettle Corp... G 419 865-6923
   Holland *(G-8537)*

Wholesale Channel Letters................... G 440 256-3200
   Kirtland *(G-8942)*

Williams Steel Rule Die Co................... F 216 431-3232
   Cleveland *(G-4910)*

Wilson Seat Company........................... F 513 732-2460
   Batavia *(G-961)*

▲ Wurtec Manufacturing Service........... E 419 726-1066
   Toledo *(G-14528)*

Yesco Sign & Lighting Service.............. G 419 407-6581
   Toledo *(G-14531)*

Zilla.. G 614 763-5311
   Dublin *(G-6960)*

3995 Burial caskets

American Steel Grave Vault Co............. F 419 468-6715
   Galion *(G-7860)*

Case Ohio Burial Co.............................. F 440 779-1992
   Cleveland *(G-3797)*

McCord Products Inc............................. G 419 352-3691
   Bowling Green *(G-1575)*

3996 Hard surface floor coverings, nec

Armstrong World Industries Inc............. E 614 771-9307
   Hilliard *(G-8399)*

▲ Flowcrete North America Inc............. E 936 539-6700
   Cleveland *(G-4071)*

Schlabach Woodworks Ltd.................... E 330 674-7488
   Millersburg *(G-10992)*

3999 Manufacturing industries, nec

212 Scent Studio LLC........................... G 614 906-3673
   Columbus *(G-5076)*

3-D Technical Services Company.......... E 937 746-2901
   Franklin *(G-7659)*

4S Company.. F 330 792-5518
   Youngstown *(G-16296)*

Aajaj Hair Company LLC....................... F 216 309-0816
   Cleveland *(G-3584)*

Absolute Zero Mch & Design LLC......... G 440 370-4172
   Lorain *(G-9400)*

Ace Assembly & Packaging Inc............ G 330 866-9117
   Waynesburg *(G-15292)*

Acoustech Systems LLC....................... G 270 796-5853
   Columbus *(G-5099)*

Actual Industries LLC............................ G 614 379-2739
   Columbus *(G-5101)*

Advance Products................................. F 419 882-8117
   Sylvania *(G-13990)*

Agile Manufacturing Tech LLC.............. F 937 258-3338
   Dayton *(G-6191)*

Al Root Company................................. G 330 725-6677
   Medina *(G-10290)*

▲ Al Root Company.............................. C 330 723-4359
   Medina *(G-10291)*

AK Mansfield.. F 419 755-3011
   Mansfield *(G-9622)*

Alene Candles Midwest LLC................. F 614 933-4005
   New Albany *(G-11364)*

◆ Aluminum Line Products Company....D 440 835-8880
   Westlake *(G-15729)*

Ambrosia Inc... G 419 825-3896
   Swanton *(G-13967)*

AMG Industries Inc............................... G 740 397-4044
   Mount Vernon *(G-11260)*

Amy Industries Inc................................ G 440 942-3478
   Mentor *(G-10416)*

39 MISCELLANEOUS MANUFACTURING INDUSTRIES

▲ Anza Inc..G 513 542-7337
  Cincinnati (G-2629)
◆ Aquatic Technology..............................F 440 236-8330
  Columbia Station (G-5005)
Ariezhair Collection Inc.........................F 614 964-5748
  Columbus (G-5153)
ARS Recycling Systems 2019 LLC........E 330 536-8210
  Lowellville (G-9512)
Aster Industries Inc..............................E 330 762-7965
  Akron (G-66)
Atcpc of Ohio LLC.................................D 330 670-9900
  Akron (G-67)
Automtive Rfnish Clor Sltons I..............E 330 461-6067
  Medina (G-10298)
B&M Underground LLC.........................F 740 505-3096
  Wilmington (G-16040)
Bead Shoppe At Home..........................G 330 479-9598
  Canton (G-2046)
Beaute Asylum LLC...............................F 419 377-9933
  Toledo (G-14209)
Beck Studios Inc..................................E 513 831-6650
  Milford (G-10895)
▲ Bevcorp Industries LLC........................G 513 673-8520
  Blue Ash (G-1368)
Blackstar International Inc...................G 917 510-5482
  Columbus (G-5199)
Brookville Glove Manufacturing............G 812 673-4893
  Uhrichsville (G-14762)
Byron Products Inc..............................G 513 870-9111
  Fairfield (G-7341)
Cairns Industries LLC..........................G 440 255-1190
  Mentor (G-10436)
Candle Coach.......................................G 330 455-4444
  Canton (G-2059)
Candle-Lite Company LLC....................C 513 662-8616
  Cincinnati (G-2699)
Candle-Lite Company LLC....................D 937 780-2563
  Leesburg (G-9122)
Canine Creations Inc..........................G 937 667-8576
  Tipp City (G-14125)
Carroll Hills Industries........................F 330 627-5524
  Carrollton (G-2304)
Cas Laboratories LLC..........................G 740 815-2440
  Columbus (G-5239)
Cbd 4 Real LLC....................................G 419 480-9800
  Toledo (G-14228)
Ccbdd..F 330 424-0404
  Lisbon (G-9310)
Centerless Grinding Service................G 216 251-4100
  Cleveland (G-3803)
Clarity Retail Services LLC..................D 513 800-9369
  West Chester (G-15395)
▲ Clearsonic Manufacturing Inc............G 828 772-9809
  Akron (G-113)
Cleveland Plant and Flower Co............G 614 478-9900
  Columbus (G-5253)
▲ CM Paula Company............................E 513 759-7473
  Mason (G-9980)
CNB Machining and Mfg LLC...............F 330 877-2786
  Hartville (G-8299)
Colby Properties LLC...........................G 937 390-0816
  Springfield (G-13545)
Connelly Industries LLC.......................G 330 468-0675
  Macedonia (G-9542)
Connies Candles..................................G 740 574-1224
  Wheelersburg (G-15808)
Coopers Mill Incorporated...................G 419 562-2878
  Bucyrus (G-1855)
Country Clippins LLC...........................G 740 472-5228
  Woodsfield (G-16086)
Country Lane Custom Buildings..........G 740 485-8481
  Danville (G-6148)

County of Holmes................................G 330 674-2083
  Millersburg (G-10952)
Crochet Kitty LLC................................G 440 340-5152
  Parma (G-12287)
◆ Cropking Incorporated.......................F 330 302-4203
  Lodi (G-9349)
Crownme Coil Care LLC.......................F 937 797-2070
  Trotwood (G-14543)
Csi America Inc...................................G 330 305-1403
  Canton (G-2084)
Cyber Shed Inc...................................G 419 724-5855
  Niles (G-14256)
D Industries Inc..................................G 216 535-4900
  Cleveland (G-3935)
D Jacob Industries LLC........................F 440 292-7277
  Cleveland (G-3936)
Dalamer Industries LLC.......................G 440 855-1368
  Cleveland (G-3939)
Datco Manufacturing LLC....................G 330 755-1414
  Struthers (G-13903)
Dayton Armor LLC................................G 937 723-8675
  Moraine (G-11170)
Denton Atd Inc....................................E 567 265-5200
  Huron (G-8631)
Desco Machine Company LLC.............F 330 405-5181
  Twinsburg (G-14649)
DLAC Industries Inc............................G 330 519-4789
  Canfield (G-2004)
Donlon Manufacturing LLC..................G 847 437-7360
  Brecksville (G-1614)
◆ Downing Enterprises Inc...................D 330 666-3888
  Copley (G-5948)
DP Assembly LLC................................G 740 225-4591
  Richwood (G-12814)
Duraflow Industries Inc.......................G 440 965-5047
  Wakeman (G-15074)
E-Z Shade LLC....................................G 419 340-2185
  Toledo (G-14270)
E5 Chem LLC......................................G 513 204-0173
  Mason (G-9986)
Eagle Industries..................................G 440 376-3885
  Cleveland (G-3988)
Edi Custom Interiors Inc....................G 513 829-3895
  Fairfield (G-7355)
Elaire Corporation..............................G 419 843-2192
  Toledo (G-14271)
Elite Manufacturing Inds LLC..............G 440 934-0920
  Avon (G-773)
Endurance Industries LLC...................G 513 285-8503
  Cincinnati (G-2870)
Erie Street Thea Svcs Inc..................G 216 426-0050
  Cleveland (G-4028)
Essentialware.....................................G 888 975-0405
  Kirtland (G-8939)
Excalibur Barber LLC..........................F 330 729-9006
  Boardman (G-1512)
Fallen Oak Candles Inc......................G 419 204-8162
  Celina (G-2332)
FB Acquisition LLC.............................E 513 459-7782
  Lebanon (G-9074)
Fbr Industries Inc..............................G 330 701-7425
  Mineral Ridge (G-11019)
Fcbdd...D 614 475-6440
  Columbus (G-5372)
Fire Safety Services Inc....................F 937 686-2000
  Huntsville (G-8623)
Firelands Manufacturing LLC..............G 419 687-8237
  Plymouth (G-12608)
Five Star Fabrication LLC..................F 440 666-0427
  Wellington (G-15308)
Flower Manufacturing LLC..................G 888 241-9100
  Fremont (G-7779)

Form Mfg...G 419 763-1030
  Coldwater (G-4989)
Fortress Industries LLC.......................G 614 402-3045
  Johnstown (G-8773)
◆ Foundation Industries Inc..................E 330 564-1250
  Akron (G-157)
Friendly Candle LLC............................G 740 683-0312
  Columbus (G-5390)
Front Pocket Innovations LLC.............G 330 441-2365
  Wadsworth (G-15031)
Gateways Industries Inc.....................G 330 505-0479
  Niles (G-11669)
◆ Gayston Corporation.........................C 937 743-6050
  Miamisburg (G-10640)
Genergy..G 937 477-3628
  Lebanon (G-9078)
Genesis One Industries LLC................G 330 842-9428
  Silver Lake (G-13297)
Gerber Wood Products Inc.................D 330 857-9007
  Kidron (G-8914)
▲ GKN Driveline Bowl Green Inc..........E 419 373-7700
  Bowling Green (G-1567)
Global Manufacturing Assoc Inc..........G 216 938-9056
  Cleveland (G-4128)
Gmx...G 216 641-7502
  Cleveland (G-4131)
Gorant Chocolatier LLC......................C 330 726-8821
  Boardman (G-1513)
Groff Industries..................................F 216 634-9100
  Cleveland (G-4151)
Gumbys LLC..F 740 671-0818
  Bellaire (G-1187)
Hafners Hrdwood Connection LLC......G 419 726-4828
  Toledo (G-14309)
Hartz Mountain Corporation...............D 513 877-2131
  Pleasant Plain (G-12607)
◆ Heading4ward Investment Co..........D 937 293-9994
  Moraine (G-11185)
◆ Henry-Griffitts Limited.....................G 419 482-9095
  Maumee (G-10206)
HK Technologies.................................G 330 337-9710
  Cleveland (G-4192)
Honda Transmission Manufacturi.......F 937 843-5555
  Marysville (G-9919)
Housing & Emrgncy Lgstcs Plnnr.......E 209 201-7511
  Lisbon (G-9315)
▲ Hunters Manufacturing Co Inc.........E 330 628-9245
  Mogadore (G-11075)
Hyggelight LLC....................................G 419 309-6321
  Toledo (G-14323)
▲ Ideal Image Inc................................D 937 832-1660
  Englewood (G-7233)
▲ Identiphoto Co Ltd..........................F 440 306-9000
  Willoughby (G-15930)
Idx Corporation..................................C 937 401-3225
  Dayton (G-6378)
Indispenser Ltd..................................E 419 625-5825
  Sandusky (G-13065)
Inez Essentials LLC............................F 216 701-8360
  Maple Heights (G-9752)
Interarms Manufacturing Ltd.............G 440 201-9850
  Bedford (G-1128)
Item NA..G 216 271-7241
  Akron (G-194)
Jameson Industries LLC.....................G 330 533-5579
  Boardman (G-1515)
Janson Industries..............................D 330 455-7029
  Canton (G-2135)
Jbs Industries Ltd..............................G 513 314-5599
  Columbus (G-5490)
Jones Industries LLC..........................F 440 810-1251
  Olmsted Twp (G-12088)

39 MISCELLANEOUS MANUFACTURING INDUSTRIES

Jrb Industries LLC .... E 567 825-7022
   Greenville *(G-8048)*

Juba Industries Inc .... G 440 655-9960
   Jefferson *(G-8747)*

Julius Patrick Industries LLC .... G 440 600-7369
   Solon *(G-13373)*

JW Manufacturing LLC .... G 419 375-5536
   Fort Recovery *(G-7622)*

K K Tool Co .... E 937 325-1473
   Springfield *(G-13585)*

Kanya Industries LLC .... G 330 722-5432
   Medina *(G-10340)*

Kayden Industries .... G 740 336-7801
   Marietta *(G-9804)*

King Industries LLC .... G 330 733-9106
   Akron *(G-209)*

King Model Company .... E 330 633-0491
   Akron *(G-210)*

Kitto Katsu Inc .... G 818 256-6997
   Clayton *(G-3567)*

KS Technologies & Cstm Mfg LLC .... G 419 426-0172
   Attica *(G-701)*

Kth Industries .... G 614 733-2020
   Plain City *(G-12585)*

LEPD Industries Ltd .... G 614 985-1470
   Powell *(G-12676)*

Lincoln Manufacturing Inc .... F 330 878-7772
   Strasburg *(G-13749)*

Lucys Barkery LLC .... G 419 886-3779
   Bellville *(G-1244)*

▲ Lumi-Lite Candle Company .... D 740 872-3248
   Norwich *(G-11992)*

Lyle Industries Inc .... G 513 233-2803
   Cincinnati *(G-3117)*

M N M Mfg Inc .... F 330 256-5572
   Kent *(G-8829)*

◆ Mace Personal Def & SEC Inc .... E 440 424-5321
   Cleveland *(G-4348)*

◆ Mace Security Intl Inc .... D 440 424-5325
   Cleveland *(G-4349)*

▲ Makergear LLC .... G 216 765-0030
   Beachwood *(G-996)*

Mako Finished Products Inc .... E 740 357-0839
   Lucasville *(G-9523)*

Manitou Candle Co LLC .... G 513 429-5254
   Cincinnati *(G-3129)*

Mansfield Industries .... G 419 785-4510
   Defiance *(G-6690)*

Manufctred Assemblies Corp LLC .... E 937 454-0722
   Vandalia *(G-14950)*

▲ Mark-All Enterprises LLC .... E 800 433-3615
   Akron *(G-235)*

MCS Mfg LLC .... F 419 923-0169
   Lyons *(G-9532)*

Midwest Stamping & Mfg Co .... G 419 298-2394
   Edgerton *(G-7078)*

Millers Aplus Cmpt Svcs LLC .... F 330 620-5288
   Akron *(G-250)*

MODE Industries Inc .... G 614 504-8008
   Columbus *(G-5576)*

Morgan Site Services Inc .... E 330 823-6120
   Alliance *(G-416)*

Morris Technologies Inc .... E 513 733-1611
   Cincinnati *(G-3174)*

Multi-Valve Technology Inc .... G 330 608-4096
   Akron *(G-257)*

My Splash Pad .... G 330 705-1802
   Louisville *(G-9465)*

Myriad Industries Inc .... G 619 232-6700
   Ostrander *(G-12175)*

N2y LLC .... C 419 433-9800
   Huron *(G-8641)*

Natural Beauty Hc Express .... G 440 459-1776
   Mayfield Heights *(G-10252)*

◆ Neff Motivation Inc .... C 937 548-3194
   Greenville *(G-8053)*

New Republic Industries LLC .... G 614 580-9927
   Marysville *(G-9929)*

Nfi Industries Inc .... F 740 928-9522
   Hebron *(G-8352)*

Nhmf LLC .... G 614 444-2184
   Columbus *(G-5598)*

Nicholson Manufacturing Co LLC .... G 978 776-2000
   Lebanon *(G-9101)*

Njf Manufacturing LLC .... G 419 294-0400
   Upper Sandusky *(G-14818)*

Norkaam Industries LLC .... G 330 873-9793
   Akron *(G-265)*

Norris North Manufacturing .... F 330 691-0449
   Canton *(G-2175)*

Noxgear LLC .... F 937 317-0199
   Worthington *(G-16206)*

Octsys Security Corp .... G 614 470-4510
   Columbus *(G-5611)*

Ohio Cbd Guy LLC .... G 513 417-9806
   Cincinnati *(G-3212)*

▲ Ohio Feather Company Inc .... G 513 921-3373
   Cincinnati *(G-3213)*

On Display Ltd .... E 513 841-1600
   Batavia *(G-941)*

On The Mantle LLC .... G 740 702-1803
   Chillicothe *(G-2521)*

OPC Cultivation LLC .... F 419 616-5115
   Huron *(G-8643)*

P & R Mfg .... G 330 674-1431
   Millersburg *(G-10988)*

Pacific Manufacturing Ohio Inc .... E 513 860-3900
   Fairfield *(G-7391)*

▲ Padco Industries LLC .... F 440 564-7160
   Newbury *(G-11634)*

Palmer Donavin Manufacturing .... F 740 527-1111
   Hebron *(G-8355)*

◆ Partners In Recognition Inc .... E 937 420-2150
   Fort Loramie *(G-7605)*

Pavletich Manufacturing .... G 440 382-0997
   Brunswick *(G-1779)*

Perfomance Feed & Seeds Inc .... G 419 496-0531
   Ashland *(G-599)*

Perma Edge Industries LLC .... G 937 623-7819
   Vandalia *(G-14957)*

Platinum Industries LLC .... F 740 285-2641
   Ironton *(G-8699)*

Plumb Builders Inc .... F 937 293-1111
   Dayton *(G-6508)*

Pragmatic Mfg LLC .... F 330 222-6051
   Brunswick *(G-1782)*

Production TI Co Cleveland Inc .... F 330 425-4466
   Twinsburg *(G-14719)*

Proto Prcsion Mfg Slutions LLC .... F 614 771-0080
   Hilliard *(G-8434)*

Pur Hair Extensions LLC .... G 330 786-5772
   Akron *(G-287)*

Pwa Great Northern Corp Ctr LP .... G 412 415-1177
   North Olmsted *(G-11825)*

Pyramid Industries LLC .... F 614 783-1543
   Columbus *(G-5699)*

Quick Tech Business Forms Inc .... F 937 743-5952
   Springboro *(G-13517)*

R & D Industries LLC .... G 937 397-5836
   Medway *(G-10398)*

R&R Candles LLC .... G 614 600-7729
   Columbus *(G-5708)*

Rable Machine Inc .... E 740 689-9009
   Lancaster *(G-9036)*

Ransome AC LLC .... G 234 205-6907
   Akron *(G-297)*

RB Sigma LLC .... D 440 290-0577
   Mentor *(G-10545)*

Rbs Manufacturing Inc .... E 330 426-9486
   East Palestine *(G-7007)*

Resource Recycling Inc .... F 419 222-2702
   Lima *(G-9285)*

▲ Rhc Inc .... E 330 874-3750
   Bolivar *(G-1536)*

RLM & Sqg Industries Inc .... G 513 527-4057
   Cincinnati *(G-3345)*

Ronfeldt Manufacturing .... F 419 382-5641
   Sylvania *(G-14012)*

Rowend Industries Inc .... G 419 333-8300
   Fremont *(G-7806)*

RS&b Industries LLC .... F 330 255-6000
   Wooster *(G-16165)*

Rubber City Industries Inc .... G 330 990-9641
   Wadsworth *(G-15064)*

▲ S & H Industries Inc .... G 216 831-0550
   Cleveland *(G-4665)*

Saint Johnsbury Perfect Scents .... G 330 846-0175
   New Waterford *(G-11559)*

▲ Salon Styling Concepts Ltd .... F 216 539-0437
   Maple Heights *(G-9760)*

Scarefactory Inc .... G 614 565-3590
   Columbus *(G-5750)*

Schell Scenic Studio Inc .... G 614 444-9550
   Millersport *(G-11013)*

Schreiner Manufacturing LLC .... G 419 937-0300
   New Riegel *(G-11537)*

Scott Models Inc .... G 513 771-8005
   Cincinnati *(G-3370)*

Sdi Industries .... G 513 561-4032
   Cincinnati *(G-3372)*

Serving Veterans Mobility Inc .... G 937 746-4788
   Franklin *(G-7701)*

Shafts Mfg .... G 440 942-6012
   Willoughby *(G-15989)*

Silly Brandz Global LLC .... D 419 697-8324
   Toledo *(G-14473)*

Southpaw Industries LLC .... G 714 215-8592
   Westlake *(G-15789)*

◆ Specialty Hardware Inc .... G 216 291-1160
   Cleveland *(G-4720)*

Specialty Mfg & Service .... G 330 821-4675
   Alliance *(G-426)*

Spectre Industries LLC .... G 440 665-2600
   Chagrin Falls *(G-2423)*

◆ Staco Energy Products Co .... G 937 253-1191
   Miamisburg *(G-10685)*

Stevens Industries LLC .... G 937 266-8240
   Dayton *(G-6595)*

Steves Vans ACC Unlimited LLC .... G 740 374-3154
   Marietta *(G-9832)*

T J Davies Company Inc .... G 440 248-5510
   Mantua *(G-9744)*

Tangent Company LLC .... G 440 543-2775
   Chagrin Falls *(G-2427)*

Tango Echo Bravo Mfg Inc .... G 440 353-2605
   North Ridgeville *(G-11861)*

Tasyd Industries LLC .... G 440 352-8019
   Painesville *(G-12266)*

Teamfg LLC .... G 513 313-8855
   Fairfield *(G-7414)*

Teledoor Manufacturing LLC .... G 419 227-3000
   Lima *(G-9296)*

Terracotta Industries LLC .... G 513 313-6215
   Cincinnati *(G-3444)*

Texstone Industries .... G 419 722-4664
   Findlay *(G-7573)*

Employee Codes: A=Over 500 employees, B=251-500
C=101-250, D=51-100, E=20-50, F=10-19, G=1-9

39 MISCELLANEOUS MANUFACTURING INDUSTRIES

Threat Extinguisher LLC.................... G 614 882-2959
  Westerville *(G-15682)*

TI Marie Candle Company LLC............ F 513 746-7798
  Cincinnati *(G-3454)*

Tiffin Candle Co Ltd........................... G 567 268-9015
  Tiffin *(G-14108)*

Tiffin Scenic Studios Inc.................... E 800 445-1546
  Tiffin *(G-14112)*

Tiger Cat Furniture............................. G 330 220-7232
  Brunswick *(G-1794)*

Tiger Inds Oil & Gas Lsg LLC.............. G 330 533-1776
  Canfield *(G-2021)*

▲ TLC Products Inc............................ F 216 472-3030
  Westlake *(G-15797)*

Tmt Inc.. F 419 592-1041
  Perrysburg *(G-12437)*

Trademark Designs Inc...................... E 419 628-3897
  Minster *(G-11063)*

Travis Products Mfg Inc..................... G 234 759-3741
  North Lima *(G-11815)*

Triboro Quilt Mfg Corp....................... G 937 222-2132
  Vandalia *(G-14962)*

Troyridge Mfg..................................... G 330 893-7516
  Millersburg *(G-11001)*

◆ Truck Fax Inc.................................. G 216 921-8866
  Cleveland *(G-4835)*

Ttr Manufacturing LLC...................... G 440 366-5005
  Elyria *(G-7213)*

Tuffy Manufacturing........................... F 330 940-2356
  Cuyahoga Falls *(G-6125)*

Turfware Manufacturing Inc............... G 330 688-8500
  Stow *(G-13734)*

▲ Twin Sisters Productions LLC......... E 330 631-0361
  Stow *(G-13735)*

Twm LLC... G 419 562-9622
  Bucyrus *(G-1870)*

Tyler Industries Inc........................... G 440 578-1104
  Mentor *(G-10586)*

U S Hair Inc.. G 614 235-5190
  Columbus *(G-5842)*

United Candle Company LLC............. G 740 872-3248
  Norwich *(G-11993)*

Universal Manufacturing.................... G 816 396-0101
  Cleveland *(G-4850)*

Vandalia Massage Therapy................ G 937 890-8660
  Vandalia *(G-14965)*

Velocity Concept Dev Group LLC....... G 513 204-2100
  Mason *(G-10067)*

Vic Maroscher.................................... F 330 332-4958
  Salem *(G-13036)*

Vistech Mfg Solutions LLC................. F 513 860-1408
  Fairfield *(G-7424)*

▲ Voo Doo Industries LLC................. G 440 653-5333
  Avon Lake *(G-826)*

VT Industries LLC.............................. G 614 804-6904
  Hilliard *(G-8453)*

Ward Industrial Services Inc............. G 877 459-9272
  Brunswick *(G-1801)*

Waterloo Industries Inc...................... G 800 833-8851
  Cleveland *(G-4895)*

Weaver Industries Propak.................. G 330 475-8160
  Akron *(G-373)*

Weaver Propack - Marc Drive............ G 330 379-3660
  Cuyahoga Falls *(G-6128)*

Woodsage Industries LLC.................. G 419 866-8000
  Holland *(G-8538)*

Wrayco Manufacturing In................... G 330 688-5617
  Stow *(G-13741)*

Yankee Candle Company Inc............. G 413 712-7416
  Etna *(G-7257)*

Yellow Creek Industries...................... G 330 757-1065
  Youngstown *(G-16475)*

Yes Mfg LLC....................................... G 614 296-3553
  Lewis Center *(G-9184)*

Yoder Manufacturing.......................... G 740 504-5028
  Howard *(G-8560)*

Zorich Industries Inc......................... G 330 482-9803
  Columbiana *(G-5058)*

42 MOTOR FREIGHT TRANSPORTATION

4212 Local trucking, without storage

C P S Enterprises Inc........................ G 216 441-7969
  Cleveland *(G-3779)*

Carl E Oeder Sons Sand & Grav......... F 513 494-1555
  Lebanon *(G-9066)*

Corbett R Caudill Chipping Inc.......... G 740 596-5984
  Hamden *(G-8172)*

Dale R Adkins.................................... G 740 682-7312
  Oak Hill *(G-1201)*

Demilta Sand and Gravel Inc............. E 440 942-2015
  Willoughby *(G-15907)*

Glenn Michael Brick........................... F 740 391-5735
  Flushing *(G-7587)*

H Hafner & Sons Inc......................... E 513 321-1895
  Cincinnati *(G-2979)*

Hershberger Manufacturing............... E 440 272-5555
  Windsor *(G-16075)*

Hull Ready Mix Concrete Inc............. F 419 625-8070
  Sandusky *(G-13064)*

Kirby and Sons Inc............................ F 419 927-2260
  Upper Sandusky *(G-14813)*

M & R Redi Mix Inc............................ E 419 445-7771
  Pettisville *(G-12451)*

Mac Oil Field Service Inc.................. E 330 674-7371
  Millersburg *(G-10978)*

Mm Outsourcing LLC......................... F 937 661-4300
  Leesburg *(G-9126)*

Move Ez Inc....................................... D 844 466-8339
  Columbus *(G-5583)*

Parobek Trucking Co......................... G 419 869-7500
  West Salem *(G-15635)*

◆ Pro-Pet LLC.................................... D 419 394-3374
  Saint Marys *(G-12964)*

Rjw Trucking Company Ltd................ E 740 363-5343
  Delaware *(G-6746)*

Roe Transportation Entps Inc............ G 937 497-7161
  Sidney *(G-13278)*

S&M Trucking LLC............................. F 661 310-2585
  Mason *(G-10052)*

Shawn Fleming Ind Trckg LLC........... G 937 707-8539
  Dayton *(G-6568)*

Smith & Thompson Entps LLC.......... F 330 386-9245
  East Liverpool *(G-7000)*

Tk Gas Services Inc.......................... E 740 826-0303
  New Concord *(G-11434)*

Ward Construction Co....................... F 419 943-2450
  Leipsic *(G-9142)*

Werlor Inc.. E 419 784-4285
  Defiance *(G-6698)*

Wonderly Trucking & Excvtg LLC...... F 419 837-6294
  Perrysburg *(G-12446)*

Wooster Abruzzi Company................ E 330 345-3968
  Wooster *(G-16183)*

4213 Trucking, except local

Akron Centl Engrv Mold Mch Inc...... E 330 794-8704
  Akron *(G-29)*

American Power LLC......................... F 937 235-0418
  Dayton *(G-6202)*

B M Machine...................................... E 419 595-2898
  New Riegel *(G-11534)*

◆ Barrett Paving Materials Inc........... E 973 533-1001
  Hamilton *(G-8183)*

Bc Investment Corporation................ G 330 262-3070
  Wooster *(G-16103)*

Buckeye Energy Resources Inc........ G 740 452-9506
  Zanesville *(G-16514)*

Chagrin Vly Stl Erectors Inc............. F 440 975-1556
  Willoughby Hills *(G-16023)*

Custom Built Crates Inc................... E
  Milford *(G-10904)*

◆ Euclid Chemical Company.............. E 800 321-7628
  Cleveland *(G-4032)*

Flegal Brothers Inc........................... E 419 298-3539
  Edgerton *(G-7075)*

Kmj Leasing Ltd................................ F 614 871-3883
  Orient *(G-12115)*

Mpi Logistics and Service Inc........... E 330 832-5309
  Massillon *(G-10130)*

Parobek Trucking Co......................... G 419 869-7500
  West Salem *(G-15635)*

Sandwisch Enterprises Inc............... G 419 944-6446
  Toledo *(G-14462)*

Shawn Fleming Ind Trckg LLC........... G 937 707-8539
  Dayton *(G-6568)*

Tk Gas Services Inc.......................... E 740 826-0303
  New Concord *(G-11434)*

4214 Local trucking with storage

▲ M G Q Inc.. E 419 992-4236
  Tiffin *(G-14092)*

Resource Recycling Inc.................... F 419 222-2702
  Lima *(G-9285)*

4215 Courier services, except by air

Akay Holdings Inc.............................. E 330 753-8458
  Barberton *(G-852)*

Grand Aire Inc................................... E 419 861-6700
  Swanton *(G-13974)*

4221 Farm product warehousing and storage

ES Industries Inc.............................. F 419 643-2625
  Lima *(G-9242)*

▲ The Mennel Milling Company......... E 419 435-8151
  Fostoria *(G-7656)*

4222 Refrigerated warehousing and storage

Pettisville Meats Incorporated........... F 419 445-0921
  Pettisville *(G-12453)*

Produce Packaging Inc...................... C 216 391-6129
  Willoughby Hills *(G-16027)*

Youngs Locker Service Inc............... F 740 599-6833
  Danville *(G-6150)*

4225 General warehousing and storage

▲ Aero Fulfillment Services Corp...... D 800 225-7145
  Mason *(G-9945)*

▲ Alegre Inc....................................... F 937 885-6786
  Miamisburg *(G-10609)*

▲ Cooper Tire Vhcl Test Ctr Inc........ F 419 423-1321
  Findlay *(G-7498)*

Dayton Bag & Burlap Co.................... F 937 253-1722
  Dayton *(G-6273)*

Efco Corp... G 614 876-1226
  Columbus *(G-5347)*

Fuchs Lubricants Co......................... F 330 963-0400
  Twinsburg *(G-14663)*

John D Oil and Gas Company........... G 440 255-6325
  Mentor *(G-10484)*

Klosterman Baking Co....................... F 513 398-2707
  Mason *(G-10017)*

▲ McCrary Metal Polishing Co Inc..... F 937 492-1979
  Port Jefferson *(G-12630)*

SIC SECTION

48 COMMUNICATIONS

▲ Ohio Valley Alloy Services Inc............ E 740 373-1900
  Marietta *(G-9812)*
▲ Performance Packaging Inc................ F 419 478-8805
  Toledo *(G-14433)*
Precision Strip Inc.................................. D 419 674-4186
  Kenton *(G-8897)*
Precision Strip Inc.................................. D 937 667-6255
  Tipp City *(G-14148)*
SH Bell Company.................................. E 412 963-9910
  East Liverpool *(G-6999)*
Taylor Communications Inc.................. F 614 351-6868
  Columbus *(G-5812)*
Trane Technologies Company LLC....... E 419 633-6800
  Bryan *(G-1842)*
◆ Vectra Inc.. C 614 351-6868
  Columbus *(G-5855)*
Victory White Metal Company............... F 216 271-1400
  Cleveland *(G-4875)*
◆ Workflowone LLC................................ A 877 735-4966
  Dayton *(G-6661)*

4226 Special warehousing and storage, nec

Abbott Laboratories................................ D 847 937-6100
  Columbus *(G-5087)*
Ballreich Bros Inc................................... C 419 447-1814
  Tiffin *(G-14078)*
▲ Kuhlman Corporation.......................... E 419 897-6000
  Maumee *(G-10213)*
Lalac One LLC...................................... E 216 432-4422
  Cleveland *(G-4307)*
Littlern Corporation................................ G 330 848-8847
  Fairlawn *(G-7444)*
SH Bell Company................................... E 412 963-9910
  East Liverpool *(G-6999)*

4231 Trucking terminal facilities

Jordankelly LLC...................................... F 216 855-8550
  Akron *(G-197)*

44 WATER TRANSPORTATION

4424 Deep sea domestic transportation of freight

S&M Trucking LLC................................. F 661 310-2585
  Mason *(G-10052)*

4491 Marine cargo handling

McGinnis Inc.. C 740 377-4391
  South Point *(G-13470)*
McNational Inc....................................... D 740 377-4391
  South Point *(G-13471)*
◆ Pinney Dock & Transport LLC............ D 440 964-7186
  Ashtabula *(G-655)*
Rayle Coal Co....................................... F 740 695-2197
  Saint Clairsville *(G-12920)*

4492 Towing and tugboat service

Great Lakes Group................................ C 216 621-4854
  Cleveland *(G-4145)*
Shelly Materials Inc................................ F 740 247-2311
  Racine *(G-12695)*
Shelly Materials Inc................................ D 740 246-6315
  Thornville *(G-14072)*
The Great Lakes Towing Company....... D 216 621-4854
  Cleveland *(G-4784)*

4493 Marinas

Mariners Landing Inc............................. F 513 941-3625
  Cincinnati *(G-3131)*
Tack-Anew Inc....................................... F 419 734-4212
  Port Clinton *(G-12629)*

45 TRANSPORTATION BY AIR

4512 Air transportation, scheduled

Grand Aire Inc....................................... E 419 861-6700
  Swanton *(G-13974)*
Ruhe Sales Inc....................................... F 419 943-3357
  Leipsic *(G-9140)*

4522 Air transportation, nonscheduled

Grand Aire Inc....................................... E 419 861-6700
  Swanton *(G-13974)*

4581 Airports, flying fields, and services

Aero Jet Wash Llc.................................. F 866 381-7955
  Dayton *(G-6186)*
General Electric Company..................... A 617 443-3000
  Cincinnati *(G-2942)*
Grand Aire Inc....................................... E 419 861-6700
  Swanton *(G-13974)*
Malta Dynamics LLC.............................. F 740 749-3512
  Waterford *(G-15238)*
Ruhe Sales Inc....................................... F 419 943-3357
  Leipsic *(G-9140)*
Spirit Avionics Ltd.................................. F 614 237-4271
  Columbus *(G-5786)*
Swagelok Company................................ F 440 442-6611
  Cleveland *(G-4757)*
Toledo Jet Center LLC........................... G 419 866-9050
  Swanton *(G-13985)*
Unison Industries LLC............................ B 904 667-9904
  Dayton *(G-6175)*

47 TRANSPORTATION SERVICES

4731 Freight transportation arrangement

Millwood Natural LLC............................ E 330 393-4400
  Vienna *(G-15002)*
Ogc Industries Inc.................................. F 330 456-1500
  Canton *(G-2181)*
SDS National LLC.................................. G 330 759-8066
  Youngstown *(G-16436)*
Tgs International Inc.............................. E 330 893-4828
  Millersburg *(G-10997)*
◆ Workflowone LLC................................ A 877 735-4966
  Dayton *(G-6661)*

4741 Rental of railroad cars

Andersons Inc.. G 419 536-0460
  Toledo *(G-14194)*
Andersons Inc.. C 419 893-5050
  Maumee *(G-10165)*

4783 Packing and crating

▲ Amerisource Health Svcs LLC........... D 614 492-8177
  Columbus *(G-5131)*
Bates Metal Products Inc....................... D 740 498-8371
  Port Washington *(G-12631)*
▲ Caravan Packaging Inc...................... G 440 243-4100
  Cleveland *(G-3790)*
Cassis Packaging Co............................. F 937 223-8868
  Dayton *(G-6249)*
Eleeo Brands LLC.................................. G 513 572-8100
  Cincinnati *(G-2864)*
Forest City Companies Inc.................... E 216 586-5279
  Cleveland *(G-4081)*
▲ Forrest Enterprises Inc...................... F 937 773-1714
  Piqua *(G-12516)*
Global Packaging & Exports Inc............ G 513 454-2020
  West Chester *(G-15442)*
Lalac One LLC...................................... E 216 432-4422
  Cleveland *(G-4307)*

◆ McNerney & Associates LLC............. E 513 241-9951
  West Chester *(G-15570)*
Overseas Packing LLC.......................... E 440 232-2917
  Bedford *(G-1148)*
Reynolds Industries Inc......................... G 330 889-9466
  West Farmington *(G-15607)*

4789 Transportation services, nec

Andersons Inc.. G 419 536-0460
  Toledo *(G-14194)*
Andersons Inc.. C 419 893-5050
  Maumee *(G-10165)*
Bulk Carriers Service Inc....................... F 330 339-3333
  New Philadelphia *(G-11490)*
▼ Jk-Co LLC... E 419 422-5240
  Findlay *(G-7526)*
Simpson & Sons Inc............................... F 513 367-0152
  Harrison *(G-8292)*
Tmt Inc... F 419 592-1041
  Perrysburg *(G-12437)*

48 COMMUNICATIONS

4812 Radiotelephone communication

911cellular LLC...................................... F 216 283-6100
  Solon *(G-13304)*
Airwave Communications Cons............. G 419 331-1526
  Lima *(G-9218)*
AT&T Corp.. E 614 223-8236
  Columbus *(G-5161)*

4813 Telephone communication, except radio

Airwave Communications Cons............. G 419 331-1526
  Lima *(G-9218)*
AT&T Corp.. G 513 792-9300
  Cincinnati *(G-2639)*
AT&T Corp.. E 614 223-8236
  Columbus *(G-5161)*
Christopher Sweeney............................. G 513 276-4350
  Troy *(G-14554)*
▼ Data Processing Sciences................. D 513 791-7100
  Cincinnati *(G-2820)*
▲ F+w Media Inc.................................... A 513 531-2690
  Blue Ash *(G-1393)*
Great Lakes Telcom Ltd......................... E 330 629-8848
  Youngstown *(G-16373)*
Kraft Electrical Contg Inc....................... E 614 836-9300
  Groveport *(G-8149)*
Kraftmaid Trucking Inc........................... D 440 632-2531
  Middlefield *(G-10762)*
Revolution Group Inc............................. D 614 212-1111
  Westerville *(G-15675)*

4832 Radio broadcasting stations

Franklin Communications Inc................ E 614 459-9769
  Columbus *(G-5386)*
Iheartcommunications Inc..................... G 419 223-2060
  Lima *(G-9254)*
Isaac Foster Mack Co............................ C 419 625-5500
  Sandusky *(G-13067)*
Tomahawk Entrmt Group LLC............... F 216 505-0548
  Euclid *(G-7302)*

4833 Television broadcasting stations

Block Communications Inc.................... F 419 724-6212
  Toledo *(G-14214)*

4841 Cable and other pay television services

Block Communications Inc.................... F 419 724-6212
  Toledo *(G-14214)*
Ohio News Network................................ E 614 460-3700
  Columbus *(G-5622)*

4899 Communication services, nec

Brackish Media LLC .... F 513 394-2871
   Cincinnati *(G-2679)*

Springdot Inc .... D 513 542-4000
   Cincinnati *(G-3411)*

Water Drop Media Inc .... G 234 600-5817
   Vienna *(G-15005)*

49 ELECTRIC, GAS AND SANITARY SERVICES

4911 Electric services

Asidaco LLC .... G 800 204-1544
   Dayton *(G-6215)*

Hexion Inc .... C 888 443-9466
   Columbus *(G-5428)*

National Gas & Oil Corporation .... E 740 344-2102
   Newark *(G-11596)*

Talus Renewables Inc .... E 650 248-5374
   Cleveland Heights *(G-4943)*

4922 Natural gas transmission

◆ Knight Material Tech LLC .... D 330 488-1651
   East Canton *(G-6979)*

National Gas & Oil Corporation .... E 740 344-2102
   Newark *(G-11596)*

▲ Ngo Development Corporation .... E 740 344-3790
   Newark *(G-11598)*

4923 Gas transmission and distribution

Ngo Development Corporation .... B 740 622-9560
   Coshocton *(G-5987)*

4924 Natural gas distribution

City of Lancaster .... E 740 687-6670
   Lancaster *(G-9002)*

National Gas & Oil Corporation .... E 740 344-2102
   Newark *(G-11596)*

4932 Gas and other services combined

National Gas & Oil Corporation .... E 740 344-2102
   Newark *(G-11596)*

4941 Water supply

American Water Services Inc .... G 440 243-9840
   Strongsville *(G-13806)*

Aqua Pennsylvania Inc .... G 440 257-6190
   Mentor On The Lake *(G-10600)*

City of Athens .... E 740 592-3344
   Athens *(G-679)*

City of Middletown .... D 513 425-7781
   Middletown *(G-10807)*

City of Troy .... F 937 339-4826
   Troy *(G-14555)*

Greene County .... G 937 429-0127
   Dayton *(G-6162)*

Victory White Metal Company .... F 216 271-1400
   Cleveland *(G-4875)*

4952 Sewerage systems

City of Ravenna .... G 330 296-5214
   Ravenna *(G-12710)*

4953 Refuse systems

A & B Iron & Metal Co Inc .... G 937 228-1561
   Dayton *(G-6178)*

A-Gas US Holdings Inc .... F 419 867-8990
   Bowling Green *(G-1547)*

Auris Noble LLC .... E 330 321-6649
   Akron *(G-68)*

Capital City Oil Inc .... G 740 397-4483
   Mount Vernon *(G-11266)*

▲ Cirba Solutions Us Inc .... E 740 653-6290
   Lancaster *(G-9000)*

▲ Fpt Cleveland LLC .... C 216 441-3800
   Cleveland *(G-4088)*

▲ Garden Street Iron & Metal Inc .... E 513 721-4660
   Cincinnati *(G-2928)*

Green Vision Materials Inc .... F 440 564-5500
   Newbury *(G-11625)*

H Hafner & Sons Inc .... E 513 321-1895
   Cincinnati *(G-2979)*

Homan Metals LLC .... E 513 721-5010
   Cincinnati *(G-3004)*

▼ Hope Timber Pallet Recycl LLC .... E 740 344-1788
   Newark *(G-11582)*

Innovation Plastics LLC .... E 513 818-1771
   Fostoria *(G-7639)*

Koski Construction Co .... O 440 997-5337
   Ashtabula *(G-644)*

▲ Magnus International Group Inc .... G 216 592-8355
   Painesville *(G-12248)*

Metalico Akron Inc .... F 330 376-1400
   Akron *(G-246)*

Mondo Polymer Technologies Inc .... E 740 376-9396
   Marietta *(G-9810)*

Montgomerys Pallet Service Inc .... G 330 297-6677
   Ravenna *(G-12725)*

▲ Novelis Alr Recycling Ohio LLC .... C 740 922-2373
   Uhrichsville *(G-14767)*

Perma-Fix of Dayton Inc .... F 937 268-6501
   Dayton *(G-6503)*

Polychem LLC .... D 419 547-1400
   Clyde *(G-4975)*

Pratt Paper (oh) LLC .... E 567 320-3353
   Wapakoneta *(G-15129)*

Resource Recycling Inc .... F 419 222-2702
   Lima *(G-9285)*

Roe Transportation Entps Inc .... G 937 497-7161
   Sidney *(G-13278)*

Rumpke Transportation Co LLC .... B 513 242-4600
   Cincinnati *(G-3356)*

Rumpke Transportation Co LLC .... F 513 851-0122
   Cincinnati *(G-3355)*

Synagro Midwest Inc .... F 937 384-0669
   Miamisburg *(G-10687)*

Unlimited Energy Services LLC .... F 304 517-7097
   Beverly *(G-1322)*

Waste Parchment Inc .... F 330 674-6868
   Millersburg *(G-11006)*

Werlor Inc .... E 419 784-4285
   Defiance *(G-6698)*

4959 Sanitary services, nec

Ash Sewer & Drain Service .... G 330 376-9714
   Akron *(G-65)*

Envirnmntal Cmpliance Tech LLC .... F 216 634-0400
   North Royalton *(G-11874)*

Evolution Lawn & Landscape LLC .... G 330 268-5306
   Mineral City *(G-11017)*

Green Impressions LLC .... D 440 240-8508
   Sheffield Village *(G-13182)*

Image Pavement Maintenance .... F 937 833-9200
   Brookville *(G-1739)*

Ioppolo Concrete Corporation .... E 440 439-6606
   Bedford *(G-1130)*

Mapledale Farm Inc .... F 440 286-3389
   Chardon *(G-2458)*

N-Viro International Corp .... F 419 535-6374
   Toledo *(G-14394)*

▲ Samsel Rope & Marine Supply Co ..... E 216 241-0333
   Cleveland *(G-4670)*

Smith & Thompson Entps LLC .... F 330 386-9345
   East Liverpool *(G-7000)*

50 WHOLESALE TRADE - DURABLE GOODS

5012 Automobiles and other motor vehicles

Ace Truck Equipment Co .... E 740 453-0551
   Zanesville *(G-16494)*

Brown Industrial Inc .... E 937 693-3838
   Botkins *(G-1542)*

Btw LLC .... G 419 382-4443
   Toledo *(G-14223)*

Bulk Carrier Trnsp Eqp Co .... E 330 339-3333
   New Philadelphia *(G-11489)*

Cipted Corp .... D 412 829-2120
   Monroe *(G-11098)*

Doug Marine Motors Inc .... E 740 335-3700
   Wshngtn Ct Hs *(G-16230)*

Fire Safety Services Inc .... F 937 686-2000
   Huntsville *(G-8623)*

Interstate Truckway Inc .... F 614 771-1220
   Columbus *(G-5477)*

J W Devers & Son Inc .... F 937 854-3040
   Trotwood *(G-14544)*

Kinstle Truck & Auto Svc Inc .... F 419 738-7493
   Wapakoneta *(G-15120)*

▲ Ktm North America Inc .... D 855 215-6360
   Amherst *(G-477)*

◆ L & R Racing Inc .... E 330 220-3102
   Brunswick *(G-1773)*

M & W Trailers Inc .... F 419 453-3331
   Ottoville *(G-12201)*

M R Trailer Sales Inc .... G 330 339-7701
   New Philadelphia *(G-11512)*

Mac Manufacturing Inc .... C 330 829-1680
   Salem *(G-13014)*

▲ Mac Manufacturing Inc .... A 330 823-9900
   Alliance *(G-408)*

◆ Mac Trailer Manufacturing Inc .... A 800 795-8454
   Alliance *(G-411)*

Midwest Motoplex LLC .... G 740 772-5300
   Chillicothe *(G-2518)*

Schodorf Truck Body & Eqp Co .... E 614 228-6793
   Columbus *(G-5751)*

Subaru of A .... G 614 793-2358
   Dublin *(G-6948)*

Tpam Inc .... F 567 315-8694
   Toledo *(G-14511)*

▲ Venco Venturo Industries LLC .... E 513 772-8448
   Cincinnati *(G-3490)*

Volens LLC .... G 216 544-1200
   Macedonia *(G-9585)*

◆ Wholecycle Inc .... E 330 929-8123
   Peninsula *(G-12345)*

Youngstown-Kenworth Inc .... F 330 534-9761
   Hubbard *(G-8574)*

5013 Motor vehicle supplies and new parts

◆ Accel Performance Group LLC .... C 216 658-6413
   Independence *(G-8651)*

◆ Adelmans Truck Parts Corp .... E 330 456-0206
   Canton *(G-2028)*

▲ Alegre Inc .... F 937 885-6786
   Miamisburg *(G-10609)*

All Power Battery Inc .... G 330 453-5236
   Canton *(G-2033)*

All Wright Enterprises LLC .... G 440 259-5656
   Perry *(G-12349)*

▲ Anest Iwata Usa Inc .... F 513 755-3100
   West Chester *(G-15536)*

50 WHOLESALE TRADE - DURABLE GOODS

ARE Inc.. A 330 830-7800
  Massillon (G-10076)
Autobody Supply Company Inc............... D 614 228-4328
  Columbus (G-5166)
◆ Bendix Coml Vhcl Systems LLC............. B 440 329-9000
  Avon (G-763)
Black Gold Capital LLC............................. E 614 348-7460
  Columbus (G-5196)
Brookville Roadster Inc.............................. F 937 833-4605
  Brookville (G-1730)
◆ Buyers Products Company........................C 440 974-8888
  Mentor (G-10435)
Cedar Elec Holdings Corp......................... D 773 804-6288
  West Chester (G-15388)
▲ Chemspec Usa Inc.................................... D 330 669-8512
  Orrville (G-12121)
Crane Carrier Company LLC....................C 918 286-2889
  New Philadelphia (G-11495)
Crane Carrier Holdings LLC....................C 918 286-2889
  New Philadelphia (G-11496)
D & J Electric Motor Repair Co................ F 330 336-4343
  Wadsworth (G-15025)
D-G Custom Chrome LLC........................G 513 531-1881
  Cincinnati (G-2815)
Dan Patrick Enterprises Inc......................G 740 477-1006
  Circleville (G-3546)
Doran Mfg LLC... D 866 816-7233
  Blue Ash (G-1385)
◆ Dreison International Inc...........................C 216 362-0755
  Cleveland (G-3972)
▲ Durable Corporation................................. D 800 537-1603
  Norwalk (G-11962)
▼ East Manufacturing Corporation.......... B 330 325-9921
  Randolph (G-12697)
▲ Emssons Faurecia Ctrl Systems..............C 812 341-2000
  Toledo (G-14276)
Exide Technologies LLC...........................G 614 863-3866
  Gahanna (G-7835)
Finale Products Inc...................................G 419 874-2662
  Perrysburg (G-12381)
Finishmaster Inc... F 614 228-4328
  Groveport (G-8139)
Frontier Tank Center Inc........................... F 330 659-3888
  Richfield (G-12788)
Fuyao Glass America Inc......................... F 937 496-5777
  Dayton (G-6343)
◆ Gear Star American Performance.........G 330 434-5216
  Akron (G-163)
Gmelectric Inc..G 330 477-3392
  Canton (G-2114)
◆ Goodyear Tire & Rubber Company....... A 330 796-2121
  Akron (G-171)
Herbert E Orr Company Inc.....................C 419 399-4866
  Paulding (G-12313)
Hite Parts Exchange Inc........................... F 614 272-5115
  Columbus (G-5442)
◆ Interstate Diesel Service Inc....................C 216 881-0015
  Cleveland (G-4233)
◆ Kaffenbarger Truck Eqp Co....................C 937 845-3804
  New Carlisle (G-11418)
Keystone Auto Glass Inc.......................... D 419 509-0497
  Maumee (G-10211)
◆ L & R Racing Inc.. E 330 220-3102
  Brunswick (G-1773)
Legacy Supplies Inc..................................G 330 405-4565
  Twinsburg (G-14685)
Lucas Sumitomo Brakes Inc..................... E 513 934-0024
  Lebanon (G-9094)
◆ Mac Trailer Manufacturing Inc................. A 800 795-8454
  Alliance (G-411)
Mader Automotive Center Inc.................. F 937 339-2681
  Troy (G-14595)

◆ Mahle Behr Mt Sterling Inc..................... B 740 869-3333
  Mount Sterling (G-11256)
Martin Diesel Inc....................................... E 419 782-9911
  Defiance (G-6691)
▲ Matco Tools Corporation......................... B 330 929-4949
  Stow (G-13708)
Motionsource International LLC................ F 440 287-7037
  Solon (G-13392)
Myers Industries Inc.................................. E 330 253-5592
  Akron (G-260)
◆ Namoh Ohio Holdings Inc....................... E
  Norwood (G-11996)
Neff Machinery and Supplies.................... F 740 454-0128
  Zanesville (G-16547)
Nu-Di Products Co Inc............................. D 216 251-9070
  Cleveland (G-4487)
▲ Ohashi Technica USA Inc........................ E 740 965-5115
  Sunbury (G-13960)
Ohio Auto Supply Company..................... F 330 454-5105
  Canton (G-2182)
Ohio Trailer Supply Inc.............................G 614 471-9121
  Columbus (G-5629)
OSI Environmental LLC............................ E 440 237-4600
  North Royalton (G-11890)
Perkins Motor Service Ltd........................ F 440 277-1256
  Lorain (G-9430)
◆ Pioneer Automotive Tech Inc..................C 937 746-2293
  Miamisburg (G-10670)
▲ Qualitor Inc..G 248 204-8600
  Cleveland (G-4603)
Qualitor Subsidiary H Inc.........................C 419 562-7987
  Bucyrus (G-1865)
▲ Sims Bros Inc.. D 740 387-9041
  Marion (G-9883)
▲ T A Bacon Co.. E 216 851-1404
  Chesterland (G-2489)
▲ Thyssenkrupp Bilstein Amer Inc.............C 513 881-7600
  Hamilton (G-8249)
◆ Tmsi LLC.. F 888 867-4872
  North Canton (G-11769)
▲ TS Trim Industries Inc............................. B 614 837-4114
  Canal Winchester (G-1993)
Tuffy Manufacturing................................... F 330 940-2356
  Cuyahoga Falls (G-6125)
Ultra-Met Company................................... F 937 653-7133
  Urbana (G-14851)
Vintage Automotive Elc Inc....................... F 419 472-9349
  Toledo (G-14520)
▲ Wis 1985 Inc.. E 423 581-4916
  Dayton (G-6657)
Youngstown-Kenworth Inc........................ F 330 534-9761
  Hubbard (G-8574)

5014 Tires and tubes

Associates Tire and Svc Inc..................... F 937 436-4692
  Centerville (G-2359)
B & S Transport Inc..................................G 330 767-4319
  Navarre (G-11340)
Bell Tire Co.. F 440 234-8022
  Olmsted Falls (G-12076)
Best One Tire & Svc Lima Inc..................G 419 425-3322
  Findlay (G-7484)
▲ Best One Tire & Svc Lima Inc................ E 419 229-2380
  Lima (G-9223)
Bob Sumerel Tire Co Inc.......................... F 614 527-9700
  Columbus (G-5204)
Bob Sumerel Tire Co Inc..........................G 740 432-5200
  Lore City (G-9446)
Bob Sumerel Tire Company Inc...............G 740 927-2811
  Reynoldsburg (G-12755)
Central Ohio Bandag LP........................... F 740 454-9728
  Zanesville (G-16520)

Forklift Tire East Mich Inc......................... F 586 771-1330
  Toledo (G-14292)
▲ Grismer Tire Company............................. E 937 643-2526
  Centerville (G-2363)
Gt Tire Service Inc....................................G 740 927-7226
  Pataskala (G-12298)
L & O Tire Service Inc..............................G 937 394-8462
  Anna (G-490)
Mark Knupp Muffler & Tire Inc................. E 937 773-1334
  Piqua (G-12535)
Myers Industries Inc.................................. E 330 253-5592
  Akron (G-260)
North Coast Tire Co Inc...........................G 216 447-1690
  Cleveland (G-4473)
Pro Tire Inc.. F 614 864-8662
  Columbus (G-5693)
◆ Technical Rubber Company Inc.............C 740 967-9015
  Johnstown (G-8779)
Ziegler Tire and Supply Co......................G 330 434-7126
  Akron (G-381)

5015 Motor vehicle parts, used

Bob Sumerel Tire Co Inc.......................... F 614 527-9700
  Columbus (G-5204)
Cedar Elec Holdings Corp....................... D 773 804-6288
  West Chester (G-15388)
Lucas Sumitomo Brakes Inc..................... E 513 934-0024
  Lebanon (G-9094)
◆ Mac Trailer Manufacturing Inc................. A 800 795-8454
  Alliance (G-411)

5021 Furniture

Ahmf Inc... E 614 921-1223
  Columbus (G-5107)
American Platinum Door LLC...................G 440 497-6213
  Solon (G-13312)
Bailey & Jensen Inc..................................G 937 272-1784
  Centerville (G-2360)
▼ Eoi Inc.. F 740 201-3300
  Lewis Center (G-9160)
Fabcor Inc.. F 419 628-4428
  Minster (G-11052)
Friends Service Co Inc............................. F 800 427-1704
  Dayton (G-6339)
Friends Service Co Inc............................. D 419 427-1704
  Findlay (G-7512)
Furniture Concepts Inc............................. F 216 292-9100
  Cleveland (G-4093)
G & P Construction LLC........................... E 855 494-4830
  North Royalton (G-11875)
Jsc Employee Leasing Corp..................... D 330 773-8971
  Akron (G-199)
▲ KMC Holdings LLC...................................C 419 238-2442
  Van Wert (G-14920)
Millwood Wholesale Inc............................ F 330 359-6109
  Dundee (G-6968)
▲ National Electro-Coatings Inc.................. D 216 898-0080
  Cleveland (G-4436)
Partitions Plus Incorporated..................... E 419 422-2600
  Findlay (G-7550)
◆ Progressive Furniture Inc......................... E 419 446-4500
  Archbold (G-542)
◆ Rize Home LLC... D 800 333-8333
  Solon (G-13415)
Sauder Woodworking Co.......................... F 419 446-2711
  Archbold (G-545)
◆ Sauder Woodworking Co......................... A 419 446-2711
  Archbold (G-546)
Urbn Timber LLC.......................................G 614 981-3043
  Columbus (G-5850)
◆ Wasserstrom Company............................. B 614 228-6525
  Columbus (G-5865)

Employee Codes: A=Over 500 employees, B=251-500
C=101-250, D=51-100, E=20-50, F=10-19, G=1-9

50 WHOLESALE TRADE - DURABLE GOODS

5023 Homefurnishings

Accent Drapery Co Inc .... E 614 488-0741
  Columbus *(G-5092)*

▲ American Frame Corporation .... D 419 893-5595
  Maumee *(G-10163)*

Anchor Hocking Glass Company .... G 740 681-6025
  Lancaster *(G-8988)*

Blind Factory Showroom .... F 614 771-6549
  Hilliard *(G-8405)*

Cincinnati Window Shade Inc .... F 513 631-7200
  Cincinnati *(G-2763)*

Creative Products Inc .... G 419 866-5501
  Holland *(G-8500)*

Custom Blind Corporation .... F 937 643-2907
  Dayton *(G-6270)*

Dale Kestler .... G 513 871-9000
  Cincinnati *(G-2817)*

◆ G & S Metal Products Co Inc .... C 216 441-0700
  Cleveland *(G-4096)*

Ghp II LLC .... F 740 681-6825
  Lancaster *(G-9018)*

Golden Drapery Supply Inc .... E 216 351-3283
  Cleveland *(G-4133)*

◆ Greenway Home Products Inc .... F
  Perrysburg *(G-12387)*

▲ Inside Outfitters Inc .... E 614 798-3500
  Lewis Center *(G-9165)*

Lumenomics Inc .... E 614 798-3500
  Lewis Center *(G-9170)*

Luminex HM Dcor Frgrnce Hldg C .... B 513 563-1113
  Blue Ash *(G-1427)*

▲ Mag Resources LLC .... F 330 294-0494
  Barberton *(G-878)*

Pfpc Enterprises Inc .... F 513 941-6200
  Cincinnati *(G-3253)*

▲ Rhc Inc .... E 330 874-3750
  Bolivar *(G-1536)*

▲ S I Distributing Inc .... F 419 647-4909
  Spencerville *(G-13489)*

◆ Standard Textile Co Inc .... B 513 761-9255
  Cincinnati *(G-3415)*

Style-Line Incorporated .... E 614 291-0600
  Columbus *(G-5796)*

Walter F Stephens Jr Inc .... F 937 746-0521
  Franklin *(G-7709)*

Watershed Mangement LLC .... F 740 852-5607
  Mount Sterling *(G-11258)*

▲ Weavers Furniture Ltd .... F 330 852-2701
  Sugarcreek *(G-13948)*

Yellow Springs Pottery LLC .... F 937 767-1666
  Yellow Springs *(G-16289)*

5031 Lumber, plywood, and millwork

Alumo Extrusions and Mfg Co .... E 330 779-3333
  Youngstown *(G-16308)*

Architctral Mllwk Cbinetry Inc .... G 440 708-0086
  Chagrin Falls *(G-2389)*

▲ Associated Materials LLC .... A 330 929-1811
  Cuyahoga Falls *(G-6069)*

Associated Materials Group Inc .... C 330 929-1811
  Cuyahoga Falls *(G-6070)*

Associated Mtls Holdings LLC .... A 330 929-1811
  Cuyahoga Falls *(G-6071)*

Baillie Lumber Co LP .... E 419 462-2000
  Galion *(G-7861)*

Bison Builders LLC .... F 614 636-0365
  Columbus *(G-5191)*

Blockamerica Corporation .... G 614 274-0700
  Columbus *(G-5201)*

Buckeye Components LLC .... E 330 482-5163
  Columbiana *(G-5029)*

Cabot Lumber Inc .... G 740 545-7109
  West Lafayette *(G-15616)*

Cameo Countertops Inc .... E 419 865-6371
  Holland *(G-8496)*

Cardinal Building Supply LLC .... G 614 706-4499
  Columbus *(G-5237)*

Carter-Jones Lumber Company .... F 330 674-9060
  Millersburg *(G-10950)*

◆ Champion Win Co Cleveland LLC ...... F 440 899-2562
  Macedonia *(G-9541)*

Component Solutions Group Inc .... F 937 434-8100
  Dayton *(G-6261)*

Contract Lumber Inc .... F 614 751-1109
  Columbus *(G-5289)*

Custom Design Cabinets & Tops .... G 440 639-9900
  Painesville *(G-12225)*

◆ Df Supply Inc .... E 330 650-9226
  Twinsburg *(G-14650)*

Double D D Mtls Instlltion Inc .... G 937 898-2534
  Dayton *(G-6302)*

Dublin Millwork Co Inc .... G 614 889-7776
  Dublin *(G-6882)*

▲ Enclosure Suppliers LLC .... E 513 782-3900
  Cincinnati *(G-2868)*

Flagship Trading Corporation .... E
  Cleveland *(G-4066)*

Francis-Schulze Co .... E 937 295-3941
  Russia *(G-12884)*

Gorell Enterprises Inc .... B 724 465-1800
  Streetsboro *(G-13772)*

Great Lakes Stair & Mllwk Co .... G 330 225-2005
  Hinckley *(G-8473)*

Gross Lumber Inc .... F 330 683-2055
  Apple Creek *(G-501)*

▼ Hartzell Hardwoods Inc .... D 937 773-7054
  Piqua *(G-12521)*

Higgins Construction & Supply Co Inc ... F 937 364-2331
  Hillsboro *(G-8458)*

Holmes Lumber & Bldg Ctr Inc .... E 330 479-8314
  Canton *(G-2125)*

Holmes Lumber & Bldg Ctr Inc .... C 330 674-9060
  Millersburg *(G-10967)*

J McCoy Lumber Co Ltd .... F 937 587-3423
  Peebles *(G-12328)*

Jerry Harolds Doors Unlimited .... G 740 635-4949
  Bridgeport *(G-1647)*

Khempco Bldg Sup Co Ltd Partnr .... D 740 549-0465
  Delaware *(G-6733)*

Kitchen Designs Plus Inc .... E 419 536-6605
  Toledo *(G-14348)*

◆ Litco International Inc .... D 330 539-5433
  Vienna *(G-14999)*

M-D Building Products Inc .... F 513 539-2255
  Middletown *(G-10837)*

Mason Structural Steel LLC .... E 440 439-1040
  Walton Hills *(G-15100)*

Modern Builders Supply Inc .... E 419 526-0002
  Mansfield *(G-9698)*

Mssi Group Inc .... D 440 439-1040
  Walton Hills *(G-15102)*

Orrville Trucking & Grading Co .... E 330 682-4010
  Orrville *(G-12144)*

Overhead Door of Pike County .... G 740 289-3925
  Piketon *(G-12481)*

Premier Construction Company .... F 513 874-2611
  Fairfield *(G-7395)*

Provia Holdings Inc .... C 330 852-4711
  Sugarcreek *(G-13935)*

R W Long Lumber & Box Co Inc .... E 513 932-5124
  Lebanon *(G-9106)*

Rockwood Products Ltd .... E 330 893-2392
  Millersburg *(G-10991)*

Roofing Annex LLC .... G 513 942-0555
  West Chester *(G-15581)*

S R Door Inc .... D 740 927-3558
  Hebron *(G-8360)*

Salt Creek Lumber Company Inc .... G 330 695-3500
  Fredericksburg *(G-7733)*

Schwab Industries Inc .... F 330 364-4411
  Dover *(G-6842)*

▲ Sims-Lohman Inc .... E 513 651-3510
  Cincinnati *(G-3395)*

Stark Truss Company Inc .... F 330 478-2100
  Canton *(G-2235)*

▲ Stephen M Trudick .... E 440 834-1891
  Burton *(G-1886)*

The F A Requarth Company .... F 937 224-1141
  Dayton *(G-6618)*

The Galehouse Companies Inc .... E 330 658-2023
  Doylestown *(G-6854)*

Toledo Molding & Die LLC .... B 419 692-6022
  Delphos *(G-6773)*

Toledo Window & Awning Inc .... F 419 474-3396
  Toledo *(G-14509)*

Traichal Construction Company .... E 800 255-3667
  Niles *(G-11689)*

Troymill Manufacturing Inc .... F 440 632-5580
  Middlefield *(G-10793)*

Universal Pallets Inc .... E 614 444-1095
  Columbus *(G-5846)*

Walnut Creek Lumber Co Ltd .... F 330 852-4559
  Dundee *(G-6972)*

Wappoo Wood Products Inc .... E 937 492-1166
  Sidney *(G-13294)*

Youngstown Curve Form Inc .... F 330 744-3028
  Youngstown *(G-16480)*

5032 Brick, stone, and related material

Basetek LLC .... F 877 712-2273
  Middlefield *(G-10733)*

▲ Castelli Marble LLC .... G 216 361-1222
  Cleveland *(G-3799)*

▲ Clay Burley Products Co .... E 740 452-3633
  Roseville *(G-12859)*

Collinwood Shale Brick Sup Co .... E 216 587-2700
  Cleveland *(G-3882)*

Encore Precast LLC .... E 513 726-5678
  Seven Mile *(G-13132)*

▼ Exhibit Concepts Inc .... D 937 890-7000
  Vandalia *(G-14939)*

Grafton Ready Mix Concret Inc .... C 440 926-2911
  Grafton *(G-8001)*

Helmart Company Inc .... G 513 941-3095
  Cincinnati *(G-2992)*

Hilltop Basic Resources Inc .... F 937 859-3616
  Miamisburg *(G-10646)*

Huron Cement Products Company .... E 419 433-4161
  Huron *(G-8633)*

Hy-Grade Corporation .... E 216 341-7711
  Cleveland *(G-4210)*

Jalco Industries Inc .... F 740 286-3808
  Jackson *(G-8717)*

Koltcz Concrete Block Co .... E 440 232-3630
  Bedford *(G-1132)*

▲ Kuhlman Corporation .... E 419 897-6000
  Maumee *(G-10213)*

Lancaster W Side Coal Co Inc .... F 740 862-4713
  Lancaster *(G-9021)*

▲ Lang Stone Company Inc .... E 614 235-4099
  Columbus *(G-5520)*

Mayfair Granite Co Inc .... G 216 382-8150
  Cleveland *(G-4372)*

Michaels Pre-Cast Con Pdts .... F 513 683-1292
  Loveland *(G-9497)*

50 WHOLESALE TRADE - DURABLE GOODS

Modern Builders Supply Inc .... E 419 526-0002
Mansfield *(G-9698)*

Modern Builders Supply Inc .... C 419 241-3961
Toledo *(G-14389)*

Moritz Materials Inc .... E 419 281-0575
Ashland *(G-593)*

▲ Ohio Tile & Marble Co .... E 513 541-4211
Cincinnati *(G-3217)*

OK Brugmann Jr & Sons Inc .... F 330 274-2106
Mantua *(G-9741)*

Olen Corporation .... F 419 294-2611
Upper Sandusky *(G-14819)*

Palmer Bros Transit Mix Con .... F 419 686-2366
Portage *(G-12636)*

Phoenix Asphalt Company Inc .... G 330 339-4935
Magnolia *(G-9597)*

◆ Pinney Dock & Transport LLC .... D 440 964-7186
Ashtabula *(G-655)*

Piqua Granite & Marble Co Inc .... G 937 773-2000
Piqua *(G-12546)*

Quality Block & Supply Inc .... E 330 364-4411
Mount Eaton *(G-11231)*

R W Sidley Incorporated .... C 440 298-3232
Thompson *(G-14062)*

R W Sidley Incorporated .... G 330 793-7374
Youngstown *(G-16426)*

Ridge Township Stone Quarry .... G 419 968-2222
Van Wert *(G-14925)*

Russell Standard Corporation .... G 330 733-9400
Akron *(G-318)*

Schwab Industries Inc .... F 330 364-4411
Dover *(G-6842)*

Sewer Rodding Equipment Co .... C 419 991-2065
Lima *(G-9288)*

Smyrna Ready Mix Concrete LLC .... E 937 855-0410
Germantown *(G-7952)*

Snyder Concrete Products Inc .... G 937 224-1433
Dayton *(G-6577)*

▲ Snyder Concrete Products Inc .... E 937 885-5176
Moraine *(G-11211)*

Stamm Contracting Company Inc .... E 330 274-8230
Mantua *(G-9743)*

Stocker Concrete Company .... F 740 254-4626
Gnadenhutten *(G-7989)*

Stoneco Inc .... E 419 893-7645
Maumee *(G-10236)*

Tamarron Technology Inc .... F 800 277-3207
Cincinnati *(G-3440)*

◆ The D S Brown Company .... C 419 257-3561
North Baltimore *(G-11701)*

The Ideal Builders Supply .... F 216 741-1600
Cleveland *(G-4787)*

Toledo Cut Stone Inc .... F 419 531-1623
Toledo *(G-14494)*

Trumbull Cement Products Co .... G 330 372-4342
Warren *(G-15211)*

Warren Concrete and Supply Co .... E 330 393-1581
Warren *(G-15218)*

William Dauch Concrete Company .... F 419 668-4458
Norwalk *(G-11991)*

5033 Roofing, siding, and insulation

Alside Inc .... D 419 865-0934
Maumee *(G-10161)*

▲ Associated Materials LLC .... A 330 929-1811
Cuyahoga Falls *(G-6069)*

Associated Materials Group Inc .... C 330 929-1811
Cuyahoga Falls *(G-6070)*

Associated Mtls Holdings LLC .... A 330 929-1811
Cuyahoga Falls *(G-6071)*

◆ Denizen Inc .... F 937 615-9561
Piqua *(G-12513)*

Modern Builders Supply Inc .... E 419 526-0002
Mansfield *(G-9698)*

▲ Tlg Cochran Inc .... E 440 914-1122
Twinsburg *(G-14744)*

Vinyl Design Corporation .... E 419 283-4009
Holland *(G-8536)*

5039 Construction materials, nec

A Service Glass Inc .... E 937 426-4920
Beavercreek *(G-1038)*

Active Aeration Systems Inc .... G 614 873-3626
Plain City *(G-12559)*

▲ Agratronix LLC .... E 330 562-2222
Streetsboro *(G-13753)*

Allen Enterprises Inc .... E 740 532-5913
Ironton *(G-8694)*

Alumo Extrusions and Mfg Co .... E 330 779-3333
Youngstown *(G-16308)*

Anderson Glass Co Inc .... E 614 476-4877
Columbus *(G-5145)*

Charles Mfg Co .... F 330 395-3490
Warren *(G-15153)*

Clearvue Insulating Glass Co .... F 216 651-1140
Cleveland *(G-3828)*

Dale Kestler .... G 513 871-9000
Cincinnati *(G-2817)*

Koebbe Products Inc .... D 513 753-4200
Amelia *(G-458)*

Lab-Pro Inc .... G 937 434-9600
Miamisburg *(G-10653)*

Machined Glass Specialist Inc .... F 937 743-6166
Springboro *(G-13509)*

Marysville Steel Inc .... E 937 642-5971
Marysville *(G-9927)*

Morton Buildings Inc .... F 419 675-2311
Kenton *(G-8894)*

Morton Buildings Inc .... E 330 345-6188
Wooster *(G-16153)*

Patio Enclosures .... F 513 733-4646
Cincinnati *(G-3236)*

▲ Richards Whl Fence Co Inc .... E 330 773-0423
Akron *(G-304)*

Security Fence Group Inc .... E 513 681-3700
Cincinnati *(G-3374)*

Trulite GL Alum Solutions LLC .... D 740 929-2443
Hebron *(G-8368)*

Will-Burt Company .... F 330 682-7015
Orrville *(G-12162)*

▲ Will-Burt Company .... C 330 682-7015
Orrville *(G-12163)*

5043 Photographic equipment and supplies

Eastman Kodak Company .... E 937 259-3000
Dayton *(G-6311)*

▲ Identiphoto Co Ltd .... F 440 306-9000
Willoughby *(G-15930)*

5044 Office equipment

Copier Resources Inc .... G 614 268-1100
Columbus *(G-5295)*

Cummins - Allison Corp .... G 440 824-5050
Cleveland *(G-3919)*

Friends Service Co Inc .... F 800 427-1704
Dayton *(G-6339)*

Friends Service Co Inc .... D 419 427-1704
Findlay *(G-7512)*

McIntosh Safe Corp .... F 937 222-7008
Dayton *(G-6432)*

Mpc Inc .... E 440 835-1405
Cleveland *(G-4424)*

Ricoh Usa Inc .... F 412 281-6700
Cleveland *(G-4634)*

Robert Becker Impressions Inc .... F 419 385-5303
Toledo *(G-14456)*

Symatic Inc .... F 330 225-1510
Medina *(G-10381)*

5045 Computers, peripherals, and software

▲ Accretech SBS Inc .... G 513 373-4844
Cincinnati *(G-2594)*

Application Link Incorporated .... F 614 934-1735
Columbus *(G-5150)*

Arctos Mission Solutions LLC .... E 813 609-5591
Beavercreek *(G-1040)*

B & S Transport Inc .... G 330 767-4319
Navarre *(G-11340)*

Black Box Corporation .... G 855 324-9909
Westlake *(G-15738)*

▼ Data Processing Sciences .... D 513 791-7100
Cincinnati *(G-2820)*

Eci Macola/Max LLC .... C 978 539-6186
Dublin *(G-6883)*

Freedom Usa Inc .... E 216 503-6374
Twinsburg *(G-14662)*

▲ Fscreations Corporation .... D 330 746-3015
Youngstown *(G-16360)*

▲ GBS Corp .... C 330 494-5330
North Canton *(G-11729)*

Government Acquisitions Inc .... E 513 721-8700
Cincinnati *(G-2967)*

▲ Identiphoto Co Ltd .... F 440 306-9000
Willoughby *(G-15930)*

Journey Systems LLC .... F 513 831-6200
Milford *(G-10912)*

Legrand North America LLC .... B 937 224-0639
Dayton *(G-6403)*

Magnum Computers Inc .... F 216 781-1757
Cleveland *(G-4351)*

Microplex Inc .... E 330 498-0600
North Canton *(G-11743)*

Miles Midprint Inc .... F 216 860-4770
Cleveland *(G-4413)*

Pemro Corporation .... F 800 440-5441
Cleveland *(G-4540)*

◆ Printer Components Inc .... G 585 924-5190
Fairfield *(G-7397)*

▲ Sarcom Inc .... A 614 854-1300
Lewis Center *(G-9180)*

Smartronix Inc .... F 216 378-3300
Northfield *(G-11910)*

Software Solutions Inc .... E 513 932-6667
Dayton *(G-6578)*

▲ Systemax Manufacturing Inc .... D 937 368-2300
Dayton *(G-6604)*

Vr Assets LLC .... G 440 600-2963
Solon *(G-13443)*

5046 Commercial equipment, nec

Abstract Displays Inc .... F 513 985-9700
Blue Ash *(G-1356)*

Active Aeration Systems Inc .... G 614 873-3626
Plain City *(G-12559)*

Baker Plastics Inc .... G 330 743-3142
Youngstown *(G-16317)*

Behrco Inc .... G 419 394-1612
Saint Marys *(G-12945)*

Cummins - Allison Corp .... G 513 469-2924
Blue Ash *(G-1384)*

Cummins - Allison Corp .... G 440 824-5050
Cleveland *(G-3919)*

▲ Door Fabrication Services Inc .... F 937 454-9207
Vandalia *(G-14938)*

G & P Construction LLC .... E 855 494-4830
North Royalton *(G-11875)*

50 WHOLESALE TRADE - DURABLE GOODS

◆ General Data Company Inc................B 513 752-7978
Cincinnati (G-2561)

▲ Harry C Lobalzo & Sons Inc................ E 330 666-6758
Akron (G-180)

◆ ITW Food Equipment Group LLC............A 937 332-2396
Troy (G-14589)

Joneszylon Company LLC................. G 740 545-6341
West Lafayette (G-15620)

Leiden Cabinet Company LLC................ G 330 425-8555
Strasburg (G-13748)

◆ N Wasserstrom & Sons Inc................C 614 228-5550
Columbus (G-5588)

National Pride Equipment Inc................. G 419 289-2886
Mansfield (G-9703)

Partitions Plus Incorporated................. E 419 422-2600
Findlay (G-7550)

Rayhaven Group Inc................. G 330 659-3183
Richfield (G-12795)

RS Industries Inc................. G 216 351-8200
Brooklyn Heights (G-1699)

Sign America Incorporated................. F 740 765-5555
Richmond (G-12803)

Starks Plastics LLC................. F 513 541-4591
Cincinnati (G-3416)

◆ Ternion Inc................. E 216 642-6180
Cleveland (G-4777)

Tri-State Supply Co Inc................. F 614 272-6767
Columbus (G-5836)

◆ Wasserstrom Company................. B 614 228-6525
Columbus (G-5865)

5047 Medical and hospital equipment

American Power LLC................. F 937 235-0418
Dayton (G-6202)

▲ Axon Medical Llc................. E 216 276-0262
Medina (G-10299)

Beeline Purchasing LLC................. E 513 703-3733
Mason (G-9959)

Berlin Industries Inc................. F 330 549-2100
Youngstown (G-16319)

◆ Boxout LLC................. C 833 462-7746
Hudson (G-8587)

Cardinal Health Inc................. E 614 553-3830
Dublin (G-6871)

Cardinal Health Inc................. G 614 757-2863
Lewis Center (G-9155)

◆ Cardinal Health Inc................. A 614 757-5000
Dublin (G-6872)

Dentronix Inc................. D 330 916-7300
Cuyahoga Falls (G-6080)

Electro-Cap International Inc................. F 937 456-6099
Eaton (G-7058)

▼ Eoi Inc................. F 740 201-3300
Lewis Center (G-9160)

▲ Ethicon Endo-Surgery Inc................. A 513 337-7000
Blue Ash (G-1389)

▲ Faretec Inc................. F 440 350-9510
Painesville (G-12236)

◆ Ferno-Washington Inc................. F 877 733-0911
Wilmington (G-16050)

Homecare Mattress Inc................. F 937 746-2556
Franklin (G-7680)

Jones Metal Products Company............... E 740 545-6341
West Lafayette (G-15619)

▲ Julius Zorn Inc................. D 330 923-4999
Cuyahoga Falls (G-6094)

Kempf Surgical Appliances Inc................. F 513 984-5758
Montgomery (G-11130)

Lion First Responder Ppe Inc................. D 937 898-1949
Dayton (G-6410)

Lion Group Inc................. D 937 898-1949
Dayton (G-6411)

Markethtch Inc D/B/A Mh Eye CA........... F 330 376-6363
Akron (G-236)

▲ Mill Rose Laboratories Inc................. E 440 974-6730
Mentor (G-10504)

Neurowave Systems Inc................. G 216 361-1591
Beachwood (G-1002)

Optum Infusion Svcs 550 LLC................. D 866 442-4679
Cincinnati (G-3227)

◆ Philips Med Systems Clvland In........B 440 483-3000
Cleveland (G-4547)

RB Sigma LLC................. D 440 290-0577
Mentor (G-10545)

Relevium Labs Inc................. G 614 568-7000
Oxford (G-12212)

Smiths Medical North America............ G 614 210-7300
Dublin (G-6939)

◆ Smiths Medical Pm Inc................. F 614 210-7300
Dublin (G-6940)

Stable Step LLC................. O 800 491-1571
Wadsworth (G-15068)

Thermo Fisher Scientific Inc................. E 800 871-8909
Oakwood Village (G-12044)

◆ Tosoh America Inc................. B 614 539-8622
Grove City (G-8124)

Triage Ortho Group................. G 937 653-6431
Urbana (G-14848)

True Vision................. G 740 277-7550
Lancaster (G-9048)

Ultra-Met Company................. F 937 653-7133
Urbana (G-14851)

United Medical Supply Company......... F 866 678-8633
Brunswick (G-1797)

▲ Viewray Inc................. D 440 703-3210
Oakwood Village (G-12045)

5048 Ophthalmic goods

Diversified Ophthalmics Inc................. E 803 783-3454
Cincinnati (G-2832)

◆ Haag-Streit Usa Inc................. D 513 398-3937
Mason (G-10000)

Toledo Optical Laboratory Inc................. E 419 248-3384
Toledo (G-14501)

5049 Professional equipment, nec

Ahner Fabricating & Shtmtl Inc............ E 419 626-6641
Sandusky (G-13042)

Consoldted Anlytcal Systems In............ F 513 542-1200
Cincinnati (G-2787)

Diversified Ophthalmics Inc................. E 803 783-3454
Cincinnati (G-2832)

Erie Street Thea Svcs Inc................. G 216 426-0050
Cleveland (G-4028)

Essilor Laboratories Amer Inc................. E 614 274-0840
Columbus (G-5361)

▲ Gilson Company Inc................. E 740 548-7298
Lewis Center (G-9161)

◆ Hapco Inc................. F 330 678-9353
Kent (G-8817)

▼ ICM Distributing Company Inc............. E 234 212-3030
Twinsburg (G-14675)

Laser Automation Inc................. F 440 543-9291
Chagrin Falls (G-2405)

▲ Lorenz Corporation................. D 937 228-6118
Dayton (G-6416)

Mettler-Toledo Intl Fin Inc................. F 614 438-4511
Columbus (G-5065)

◆ Mettler-Toledo LLC................. A 614 438-4511
Columbus (G-5067)

▲ Monarch Steel Company Inc................. E 216 587-8000
Cleveland (G-4420)

Novak J F Manufacturing Co LLC......... G 216 741-5912
Cleveland (G-4484)

Queen City Reprographics................. C 513 326-2300
Cincinnati (G-3319)

Revvity Health Sciences Inc................. E 330 825-4525
Akron (G-303)

▲ S&V Industries Inc................. E 330 666-1986
Medina (G-10373)

Science/Electronics Inc................. F 937 224-4444
Dayton (G-6562)

Tech4imaging LLC................. F 614 214-2655
Columbus (G-5817)

Teledyne Instruments Inc................. E 513 229-7000
Mason (G-10063)

Teledyne Tekmar Company............... E 513 229-7000
Mason (G-10064)

▼ Test Mark Industries Inc................. F 330 426-2200
East Palestine (G-7010)

US Tsubaki Power Transm LLC............. C 419 626-4560
Sandusky (G-13102)

Zaenkert Surveying Essentials............ G 513 738-2917
Okeana (G-12070)

▲ Zaner-Bloser Inc................. C 614 486-0221
Columbus (G-5892)

5051 Metals service centers and offices

Akron Bldg Closeout Mtls LLC............... G 234 738-0867
Barberton (G-853)

◆ Alanod Westlake Metal Ind Inc............E 440 327-8184
North Ridgeville (G-11826)

Alro Steel Corporation................. E 614 878-7271
Columbus (G-5116)

Alro Steel Corporation................. E 937 253-6121
Dayton (G-6196)

Alro Steel Corporation................. D 419 720-5300
Toledo (G-14184)

Aluminum Bearing Co of America......... G 216 267-8560
Cleveland (G-3643)

◆ Aluminum Line Products Company....D 440 835-8880
Westlake (G-15729)

AM Castle & Co................. F 330 425-7000
Bedford (G-1100)

◆ American Ir Met Cleveland LLC............E 216 266-0509
Cleveland (G-3653)

American Posts LLC................. E 419 720-0652
Toledo (G-14191)

▲ American Tank & Fabricating Co........ D 216 252-1500
Cleveland (G-3656)

▲ Atlas Bolt & Screw Company LLC........ E 419 289-6171
Ashland (G-554)

B&A Ison Steel Inc................. F 216 663-4300
Cleveland (G-3716)

Berkshire Road Holdings Inc............... F 216 883-4200
Cleveland (G-3731)

▲ Bico Akron Inc................. D 330 794-1716
Mogadore (G-11067)

Blackburns Fabrication Inc................. E 614 875-0784
Columbus (G-5198)

Canfield Coating LLC................. E 330 533-3311
Canfield (G-2002)

Canfield Metal Coating Corp............... D 330 702-3876
Canfield (G-2003)

◆ Clifton Steel Company................. D 216 662-6111
Maple Heights (G-9749)

▲ Cmt Imports Inc................. G 513 615-1851
Cincinnati (G-2777)

Conley Group Inc................. E 330 372-2030
Warren (G-15158)

Contractors Steel Company............... D 330 425-3050
Twinsburg (G-14645)

Coventry Steel Services Inc................. F 216 883-4477
Cleveland (G-3909)

Curtis Steel & Supply Inc................. F 330 376-7141
Akron (G-119)

50 WHOLESALE TRADE - DURABLE GOODS

Efco Corp... G 614 876-1226
  Columbus *(G-5347)*
EPI of Cleveland Inc........................... G 330 468-2872
  Twinsburg *(G-14656)*
▲ Ferralloy Inc.. G 440 250-1900
  Cleveland *(G-4057)*
▲ Fpt Cleveland LLC............................. C 216 441-3800
  Cleveland *(G-4088)*
General Steel Corporation................. F 216 883-4200
  Cleveland *(G-4118)*
Graber Metal Works Inc..................... F 440 237-8422
  North Royalton *(G-11877)*
Grenga Machine & Welding............... F 330 743-1113
  Youngstown *(G-16374)*
▲ H & D Steel Service Inc................... E 800 666-3390
  North Royalton *(G-11878)*
◆ Hickman Williams & Company.......F 513 621-1946
  Cincinnati *(G-2998)*
Howard Industries Inc........................ F 614 444-9900
  Columbus *(G-5447)*
JSW Steel USA Ohio Inc.................... B 740 535-8172
  Mingo Junction *(G-11046)*
◆ Kirtland Capital Partners LP............E 216 593-0100
  Beachwood *(G-993)*
Krendl Rack Co Inc............................. G 419 667-4800
  Venedocia *(G-14970)*
Lake Building Products Inc............... E 216 486-1500
  Cleveland *(G-4306)*
Lapham-Hickey Steel Corp................ E 614 443-4881
  Columbus *(G-5521)*
◆ Latrobe Spcialty Mtls Dist Inc..........D 330 609-5137
  Vienna *(G-14997)*
Louis Arthur Steel Company.............. G 440 997-5545
  Geneva *(G-7941)*
◆ Loveman Steel Corporation.............D 440 232-6200
  Bedford *(G-1135)*
M-D Building Products Inc................ F 513 539-2255
  Middletown *(G-10837)*
Major Metals Company....................... E 419 886-4600
  Mansfield *(G-9681)*
Master-Halco Inc................................. F 513 869-7600
  Fairfield *(G-7379)*
McOn Inds Inc..................................... E 937 294-2681
  Moraine *(G-11192)*
McWane Inc.. B 740 622-6651
  Coshocton *(G-5983)*
▲ Merit Brass Co................................... C 216 261-9800
  Cleveland *(G-4394)*
Mid-America Steel Corp..................... E 800 282-3466
  Cleveland *(G-4407)*
Modern Welding Co Ohio Inc............ F 740 344-9425
  Newark *(G-11593)*
▲ Monarch Steel Company Inc........... E 216 587-8000
  Cleveland *(G-4420)*
▲ National Bronze Mtls Ohio Inc........ E 440 277-1226
  Lorain *(G-9425)*
▲ Nimers & Woody II Inc..................... C 937 454-0722
  Vandalia *(G-14955)*
Nucor Steel Marion Inc...................... E 740 383-6068
  Marion *(G-9867)*
◆ Nucor Steel Marion Inc....................B 740 383-4011
  Marion *(G-9868)*
Ohio Metal Processing LLC............... G 740 912-2057
  Jackson *(G-8719)*
Ohio Steel Sheet and Plate Inc......... E 800 827-2401
  Hubbard *(G-8569)*
▲ Oliver Steel Plate Co........................ D 330 425-7000
  Twinsburg *(G-14704)*
Omega 1 Inc... F 216 663-8424
  Willoughby *(G-15965)*
◆ Panacea Products Corporation.......E 614 850-7000
  Columbus *(G-5652)*

▲ Pipe Products Inc.............................. C 513 587-7532
  West Chester *(G-15480)*
Radix Wire Co...................................... D 216 731-9191
  Solon *(G-13411)*
▲ Remington Steel Inc.......................... D 937 322-2414
  Springfield *(G-13628)*
Rex Welding Inc.................................. F 740 387-1650
  Marion *(G-9875)*
▲ Rockwell Metals Company LLC....... F 440 242-2420
  Lorain *(G-9436)*
▲ Samsel Rope & Marine Supply Co.... E 216 241-0333
  Cleveland *(G-4670)*
Samuel Son & Co (usa) Inc................ D 740 522-2500
  Heath *(G-8331)*
▲ Sausser Steel Company Inc............. F 419 422-9632
  Findlay *(G-7559)*
Scot Industries Inc............................. D 330 262-7585
  Wooster *(G-16169)*
Shaq Inc.. D 770 427-0402
  Beachwood *(G-1023)*
▲ Sims Bros Inc..................................... D 740 387-9041
  Marion *(G-9883)*
St Lawrence Holdings LLC................ E 330 562-9000
  Maple Heights *(G-9761)*
◆ St Lawrence Steel Corporation.......E 330 562-9000
  Maple Heights *(G-9762)*
Stamped Steel Products Inc............. F 330 538-3951
  North Jackson *(G-11791)*
Stephens Pipe & Steel LLC............... C 740 869-2257
  Mount Sterling *(G-11257)*
Swagelok Company............................. D 440 349-5934
  Solon *(G-13431)*
The Mansfield Strl & Erct Co............ F 419 522-5911
  Mansfield *(G-9726)*
Thyssenkrupp Materials NA Inc........ D 216 883-8100
  Independence *(G-8687)*
Tomson Steel Company...................... E 513 420-8600
  Middletown *(G-10866)*
◆ Tricor Industrial Inc..........................D 330 264-3299
  Wooster *(G-16178)*
▲ Tsk America Co Ltd.......................... F 513 942-4002
  West Chester *(G-15600)*
Tubular Techniques Inc..................... G 614 529-4130
  Hilliard *(G-8450)*
▲ Universal Steel Company................. D 216 883-4972
  Cleveland *(G-4852)*
Victory White Metal Company........... F 216 641-2575
  Cleveland *(G-4873)*
◆ Watteredge LLC.................................D 440 933-6110
  Avon Lake *(G-828)*
Westfield Steel Inc............................. D 937 322-2414
  Springfield *(G-13654)*
Wheatland Tube LLC........................... C 724 342-6851
  Niles *(G-11692)*
▲ Wieland Metal Svcs Foils LLC........ D 330 823-1700
  Alliance *(G-437)*
Worthington Enterprises Inc............. D 513 539-9291
  Monroe *(G-11121)*
Worthngton Smuel Coil Proc LLC..... E 330 963-3777
  Twinsburg *(G-14758)*
Worthngton Stelpac Systems LLC.... C 614 438-3205
  Columbus *(G-5886)*
Youngstown Specialty Mtls Inc......... G 330 259-1110
  Youngstown *(G-16488)*

5052 Coal and other minerals and ores

B & S Transport Inc............................ G 330 767-4319
  Navarre *(G-11340)*
Graphel Corporation........................... C 513 779-6166
  West Chester *(G-15444)*
◆ Hickman Williams & Company.......F 513 621-1946
  Cincinnati *(G-2998)*

▲ Seaforth Mineral & Ore Co Inc........ F 216 292-5820
  Beachwood *(G-1022)*
◆ Tosoh America Inc............................B 614 539-8622
  Grove City *(G-8124)*

5063 Electrical apparatus and equipment

Accurate Mechanical Inc................... D 740 681-1332
  Lancaster *(G-8985)*
Acorn Technology Corporation......... E 216 663-1244
  Shaker Heights *(G-13149)*
Ademco Inc... G 440 439-7002
  Bedford *(G-1098)*
Ademco Inc... F 513 772-1851
  Blue Ash *(G-1358)*
Akron Foundry Co............................... C 330 745-3101
  Akron *(G-33)*
Allen Fields Assoc Inc....................... E 513 228-1010
  Lebanon *(G-9061)*
Als High Tech Inc............................... F 440 232-7090
  Bedford *(G-1099)*
◆ American De Rosa Lamparts LLC......D
  Cuyahoga Falls *(G-6063)*
Ametek Inc... F 937 440-0800
  Troy *(G-14550)*
Ametek Tchnical Indus Pdts Inc....... D 330 673-3451
  Kent *(G-8799)*
Architectural Busstrut Corp.............. F 614 933-8695
  New Albany *(G-11367)*
Associated Mtls Holdings LLC.......... A 330 929-1811
  Cuyahoga Falls *(G-6071)*
Astro Industries Inc........................... E 937 429-5900
  Beavercreek *(G-1041)*
B2d Solutions Inc............................... G 855 484-1145
  Cleveland *(G-3718)*
Battery Unlimited............................... G 740 452-5030
  Zanesville *(G-16506)*
Bennett Electric Inc........................... F 800 874-5405
  Norwalk *(G-11956)*
◆ Best Lighting Products Inc..............D 740 964-1198
  Etna *(G-7254)*
Big River Electric Inc........................ F 740 446-4360
  Gallipolis *(G-7889)*
Black Box Corporation....................... G 855 324-9909
  Westlake *(G-15738)*
Bornhorst Motor Service Inc............ G 937 773-0426
  Piqua *(G-12507)*
C & S Industrial Ltd........................... G 440 327-2360
  North Ridgeville *(G-11835)*
Cattron Holdings Inc.......................... E 234 806-0018
  Warren *(G-15150)*
Ces Nationwide.................................... G 937 322-0771
  Springfield *(G-13543)*
Clark-Fowler Enterprises Inc............ E 330 262-0906
  Wooster *(G-16110)*
▲ Cleanlife Energy LLC........................ F 800 316-2532
  Cleveland *(G-3827)*
Controllix Corporation....................... F 440 232-8757
  Walton Hills *(G-15097)*
Current Elec & Enrgy Solutions....... G 513 575-4600
  Loveland *(G-9479)*
D C Systems Inc................................... F 330 273-3030
  Brunswick *(G-1756)*
Daycoa Inc.. F 937 849-1315
  Medway *(G-10397)*
Fenton Bros Electric Co..................... E 330 343-0093
  New Philadelphia *(G-11501)*
◆ Filnor Inc..F 330 821-8731
  Alliance *(G-403)*
Gt Industrial Supply Inc.................... F 513 771-7000
  Cincinnati *(G-2976)*
Hackworth Electric Motors Inc......... G 330 345-6049
  Wooster *(G-16128)*

Employee Codes: A=Over 500 employees, B=251-500
C=101-250, D=51-100, E=20-50, F=10-19, G=1-9

50 WHOLESALE TRADE - DURABLE GOODS

Hannon Company .... F 330 343-7758
  Dover (G-6826)
Hannon Company .... F 740 453-0527
  Zanesville (G-16536)
Horner Industrial Services Inc .... F 937 390-6667
  Springfield (G-13579)
Hughes Corporation .... E 440 238-2550
  Strongsville (G-13842)
Ignio Systems LLC .... G 419 708-0503
  Toledo (G-14326)
Industrial Ctrl Dsign Mnt Inc .... F 330 785-9840
  Tallmadge (G-14033)
Industrial Power Systems Inc .... B 419 531-3121
  Rossford (G-12867)
▼ Kirk Key Interlock Company LLC .... E 330 833-8223
  North Canton (G-11740)
Legrand North America LLC .... B 937 224-0639
  Dayton (G-6403)
Lima Armature Works Inc .... G 419 222-4010
  Lima (G-9261)
LSI Industries Inc .... C 913 281-1100
  Blue Ash (G-1425)
▲ LSI Lightron Inc .... A 845 562-5500
  Blue Ash (G-1426)
Machine Drive Company .... D 513 793-7077
  Cincinnati (G-3122)
Mader Elc Mtr Pwr Trnsmssons L .... G 937 325-5576
  Springfield (G-13599)
Masteller Electric Motor Svc .... G 937 492-8500
  Sidney (G-13262)
▼ Matlock Electric Co Inc .... E 513 731-9600
  Cincinnati (G-3134)
▲ Megalight Inc .... E 800 957-1797
  Hudson (G-8604)
Mid-Ohio Electric Co .... E 614 274-8000
  Columbus (G-5563)
Mjo Industries Inc .... D 800 590-4055
  Huber Heights (G-8577)
◆ Multilink Inc .... C 440 366-6966
  Elyria (G-7183)
◆ Noco Company .... D 216 464-8131
  Solon (G-13399)
Ohio Electric Motor Service Center Inc .. F 614 444-1451
  Columbus (G-5617)
One Wish LLC .... F 800 505-6883
  Bedford (G-1147)
▲ Osburn Associates Inc .... F 740 385-5732
  Logan (G-9372)
Peak Electric Inc .... F 419 726-4848
  Toledo (G-14430)
Phillips Electric Co .... F 216 361-0014
  Cleveland (G-4548)
Powell Electrical Systems Inc .... D 330 966-1750
  North Canton (G-11753)
▼ Riverside Drives Inc .... E 216 362-1211
  Cleveland (G-4637)
Rv Mobile Power LLC .... G 855 427-7978
  Columbus (G-5735)
Schneider Electric Usa Inc .... B 513 523-4171
  Oxford (G-12213)
Schneider Electric Usa Inc .... D 513 777-4445
  West Chester (G-15506)
Scott Fetzer Company .... C 216 267-9000
  Cleveland (G-4678)
▲ Shoemaker Electric Company .... E 614 294-5626
  Columbus (G-5764)
Sieb & Meyer America Inc .... F 513 563-5860
  West Chester (G-15585)
▲ Specialty Switch Company LLC .... F 330 427-3000
  Youngstown (G-16444)
Status Solutions LLC .... D 434 296-1789
  Westerville (G-15680)

Stock Fairfield Corporation .... C 440 543-6000
  Solon (G-13425)
Sumitomo Elc Wirg Systems Inc .... E 937 642-7579
  Marysville (G-9941)
Tesa Inc .... G 614 847-8200
  Lewis Center (G-9181)
Total Life Safety LLC .... F 866 955-2318
  West Chester (G-15516)
Warmus and Associates Inc .... F 330 659-4440
  Bath (G-962)
Wes-Garde Components Group Inc ...... G 614 885-0319
  Westerville (G-15724)
Western Branch Diesel LLC .... F 330 454-8800
  Canton (G-2267)
▲ Winkle Industries Inc .... D 330 823-9730
  Alliance (G-438)

5064 Electrical appliances, television and radio

◆ Associated Premium Corporation .... E 513 679-4444
  Cincinnati (G-2637)
◆ GMI Holdings Inc .... B 800 354-3643
  Mount Hope (G-11237)
Great Lakes Telcom Ltd .... E 330 629-8848
  Youngstown (G-16373)
Whirlpool Corporation .... E 740 383-7122
  Marion (G-9889)
World Wide Recyclers Inc .... G 614 554-3296
  Columbus (G-5881)

5065 Electronic parts and equipment, nec

ABC Appliance Inc .... E 419 693-4414
  Oregon (G-12099)
Black Box Corporation .... G 855 324-9909
  Westlake (G-15738)
▼ Cartessa Corp .... F 513 738-4477
  Shandon (G-13159)
Cattron Holdings Inc .... E 234 806-0018
  Warren (G-15150)
Caudabe LLC .... G 513 501-9799
  Blue Ash (G-1376)
Cbst Acquisition LLC .... D 513 361-9600
  Cincinnati (G-2711)
Certified Comparator Products .... G 937 426-9677
  Beavercreek (G-1072)
▲ Cota International Inc .... F 937 526-5520
  Versailles (G-14978)
Db Unlimited LLC .... F 937 401-2602
  Dayton (G-6293)
Electra Sound Inc .... D 216 433-9600
  Avon Lake (G-805)
Electro-Line Inc .... F 937 461-5683
  Dayton (G-6315)
Famous Industries Inc .... E 330 535-1811
  Akron (G-150)
▲ Floyd Bell Inc .... D 614 294-4000
  Columbus (G-5381)
H2flow Controls Inc .... G 419 841-7774
  Toledo (G-14307)
Heilind Electronics Inc .... F 440 473-9600
  Cleveland (G-4177)
Holland Assocts LLC DBA Archou .... F 513 891-0006
  Cincinnati (G-3003)
◆ J & C Group Inc of Ohio .... F 440 205-9658
  Mentor (G-10477)
◆ Kontron America Incorporated .... G 937 324-2420
  Springfield (G-13591)
◆ Mace Personal Def & SEC Inc .... E 440 424-5321
  Cleveland (G-4348)
Mjo Industries Inc .... D 800 590-4055
  Huber Heights (G-8577)

Pemro Corporation .... F 800 440-5441
  Cleveland (G-4540)
▲ Pepperl + Fuchs Inc .... C 330 425-3555
  Twinsburg (G-14709)
Pepperl + Fuchs Entps Inc .... C 330 425-3555
  Twinsburg (G-14710)
◆ Premier Farnell Holding Inc .... E 330 523-4273
  Richfield (G-12794)
Pro Oncall Technologies LLC .... F 614 761-1400
  Dublin (G-6927)
Projects Unlimited Inc .... C 937 918-2200
  Dayton (G-6534)
Quasonix Inc .... E 513 942-1287
  West Chester (G-15491)
Ray Communications Inc .... G 330 686-0226
  Stow (G-13720)
Rixan Associates Inc .... E 937 438-3005
  Dayton (G-6550)
Rpa Electronic Distrs Inc .... G 937 223-7001
  Dayton (G-6553)
▲ S-Tek Inc .... G 440 439-8232
  Twinsburg (G-14732)
Sage Integration Holdings LLC .... E 330 733-8183
  Kent (G-8857)
Securcom Inc .... E 419 628-1049
  Minster (G-11060)
Spirit Avionics Ltd .... F 614 237-4271
  Columbus (G-5786)
▲ Standex Electronics Inc .... D 513 871-3777
  Fairfield (G-7411)
▲ Vmetro Inc .... D 281 584-0728
  Fairborn (G-7326)
Wes-Garde Components Group Inc ...... G 614 885-0319
  Westerville (G-15724)
Wurth Electronics Ics Inc .... E 937 415-7700
  Miamisburg (G-10703)

5072 Hardware

▲ Akko Fastener Inc .... F 513 489-8300
  Middletown (G-10804)
▲ Atlas Bolt & Screw Company LLC .... C 419 289-6171
  Ashland (G-554)
Barnes Group Inc .... C 419 891-9292
  Maumee (G-10168)
Cammel Saw Company .... F 330 477-3764
  Canton (G-2058)
Diy Holster LLC .... G 419 921-2168
  Elyria (G-7132)
DL Schwartz Co LLC .... G 260 692-1464
  Hicksville (G-8373)
Elliott Tool Technologies Ltd .... D 937 253-6133
  Dayton (G-6318)
◆ F & M Mafco Inc .... C 513 367-2151
  Harrison (G-8273)
◆ Facil North America Inc .... C 330 487-2500
  Twinsburg (G-14659)
◆ G & S Metal Products Co Inc .... C 216 441-0700
  Cleveland (G-4096)
Khempco Bldg Sup Co Ltd Partnr .... D 740 549-0465
  Delaware (G-6733)
▲ L E Smith Company .... D 419 636-4555
  Bryan (G-1825)
▲ Matco Tools Corporation .... B 330 929-4949
  Stow (G-13708)
Maumee Machine & Tool Corp .... E 419 385-2501
  Toledo (G-14379)
National Tool & Equipment Inc .... F 330 629-8665
  Youngstown (G-16403)
◆ Noco Company .... D 216 464-8131
  Solon (G-13399)
▲ Norbar Torque Tools Inc .... F 440 953-1175
  Willoughby (G-15959)

SIC SECTION 50 WHOLESALE TRADE - DURABLE GOODS

▲ Ohashi Technica USA Inc.............. E 740 965-5115
   Sunbury *(G-13960)*
▲ Paulin Industries Inc...................... E 216 433-7633
   Parma *(G-12293)*
▲ Shook Manufactured Pdts Inc........ G 330 848-9780
   Akron *(G-330)*
◆ Specialty Hardware Inc.................G 216 291-1160
   Cleveland *(G-4720)*
State Industrial Products Corp.......... D 740 929-6370
   Hebron *(G-8363)*
◆ State Industrial Products Corp........ B 877 747-6986
   Cleveland *(G-4731)*
Superior Caster Inc........................... F 513 539-8980
   Middletown *(G-10861)*
▲ Texmaster Tools Inc...................... F 740 965-8778
   Fredericktown *(G-7755)*
Twin Cities Concrete Co.................... F 330 343-4491
   Dover *(G-6848)*
Twin Ventures Inc............................. F 330 405-3838
   Twinsburg *(G-14749)*
Uhrichsville Carbide Inc.................... F 740 922-9197
   Uhrichsville *(G-14772)*
◆ Waxman Industries Inc..................C 440 439-1830
   Bedford Heights *(G-1181)*

5074 Plumbing and hydronic heating supplies

Accurate Mechanical Inc................... D 740 681-1332
   Lancaster *(G-8985)*
Carter-Jones Lumber Company......... E 440 834-8164
   Middlefield *(G-10739)*
▲ Chandler Systems Incorporated...... D 888 363-9434
   Ashland *(G-564)*
Columbus Pipe and Equipment Co.... F 614 444-7871
   Columbus *(G-5273)*
▲ Empire Brass Co............................ G 216 431-6565
   Cleveland *(G-4012)*
▲ Enting Water Conditioning Inc......... E 937 294-5100
   Moraine *(G-11175)*
Famous Industries Inc....................... E 330 535-1811
   Akron *(G-150)*
Famous Realty Cleveland Inc............ F 740 685-2533
   Byesville *(G-1897)*
Ferguson Enterprises LLC................ G 216 635-2493
   Parma *(G-12289)*
Hess Advanced Solutions Llc............ G 937 829-4794
   Dayton *(G-6368)*
Hombre Capital Inc........................... F 440 838-5335
   Brecksville *(G-1620)*
Indelco Custom Products Inc............ E 216 797-7300
   Euclid *(G-7274)*
Kauffman Lumber & Supply............... F 330 893-9186
   Millersburg *(G-10971)*
◆ Kinetico Incorporated..................... B 440 564-9111
   Newbury *(G-11628)*
◆ Mansfield Plumbing Pdts LLC......... A 419 938-5211
   Perrysville *(G-12447)*
Mason Structural Steel LLC.............. E 440 439-1040
   Walton Hills *(G-15100)*
▲ Merit Brass Co............................... C 216 261-9800
   Cleveland *(G-4394)*
Mssi Group Inc.................................. D 440 439-1040
   Walton Hills *(G-15102)*
▲ Mssk Manufacturing Inc................. E 330 393-6624
   Warren *(G-15192)*
◆ Oatey Supply Chain Svcs Inc......... C 216 267-7100
   Cleveland *(G-4491)*
Parker-Hannifin Corporation.............. C 614 279-7070
   Columbus *(G-5656)*
Parker-Hannifin Corporation.............. D 937 456-5571
   Eaton *(G-7067)*

Pelton Environmental Pdts Inc........... G 440 838-1221
   Lewis Center *(G-9175)*
Ppafco Inc.. E 614 488-7259
   Columbus *(G-5685)*
R D Baker Enterprises Inc................. G 937 461-5225
   Dayton *(G-6537)*
US Water Company LLC................... G 740 453-0604
   Zanesville *(G-16567)*
W A S P Inc....................................... G 740 439-2398
   Cambridge *(G-1960)*
◆ Waxman Industries Inc..................C 440 439-1830
   Bedford Heights *(G-1181)*
◆ Wayne/Scott Fetzer Company........ C 800 237-0987
   Harrison *(G-8296)*
Wolff Bros Supply Inc........................ F 440 327-1650
   North Ridgeville *(G-11864)*
Zekelman Industries Inc.................... C 740 432-2146
   Cambridge *(G-1961)*
Zurn Industries LLC.......................... F 814 455-0921
   Hilliard *(G-8454)*

5075 Warm air heating and air conditioning

▼ Air-Rite Inc.................................... E 216 228-8200
   Cleveland *(G-3617)*
Cincinnati A Flter Sls Svc Inc............. E 513 242-3400
   Cincinnati *(G-2737)*
Controls and Sheet Metal Inc............. E 513 721-3610
   Cincinnati *(G-2793)*
Daikin Applied Americas Inc.............. G 614 351-9862
   Westerville *(G-15697)*
◆ Glt Inc... F 937 237-0055
   Dayton *(G-6358)*
Rel Enterprises Inc............................ E 216 741-1700
   Brooklyn Heights *(G-1698)*
Shape Supply Inc.............................. G 513 863-6695
   Hamilton *(G-8242)*
Style Crest Enterprises Inc................ D 419 355-8586
   Fremont *(G-7811)*
Swift Filters Inc................................. E 440 735-0995
   Oakwood Village *(G-12043)*
▼ Verantis Corporation..................... E 440 243-0700
   Middleburg Heights *(G-10728)*
Weather King Heating & AC.............. G 330 908-0281
   Northfield *(G-11914)*
Yanfeng US Auto Intr Systems I........ E 419 662-4905
   Northwood *(G-11935)*

5078 Refrigeration equipment and supplies

Climate Pros LLC............................. D 216 881-5200
   Cleveland *(G-3878)*
Climate Pros LLC............................. D 330 744-2732
   Youngstown *(G-16340)*
◆ Lvd Acquisition LLC......................D 614 861-1350
   Columbus *(G-5537)*
◆ Modern Ice Equipment & Sup Co... E 513 367-2101
   Cincinnati *(G-3170)*
▲ Slush Puppie................................ F 513 771-0940
   West Chester *(G-15587)*
The Hattenbach Company................. D 216 881-5200
   Cleveland *(G-4785)*

5082 Construction and mining machinery

◆ Advanced Specialty Products........G 419 882-6528
   Bowling Green *(G-1550)*
Bauer Corporation............................. E 800 321-4760
   Wooster *(G-16102)*
Brewpro Inc...................................... G 513 577-7200
   Cincinnati *(G-2682)*
Columbus Pipe and Equipment Co.... F 614 444-7871
   Columbus *(G-5273)*
EZ Grout Corporation Inc.................. E 740 962-2024
   Malta *(G-9607)*

◆ F & M Mafco Inc............................C 513 367-2151
   Harrison *(G-8273)*
Global Energy Partners LLC............. E 419 756-8027
   Mansfield *(G-9660)*
Great Lakes Power Service Co......... G 440 259-0025
   Perry *(G-12351)*
JD Power Systems LLC.................... F 614 317-9394
   Hilliard *(G-8416)*
Koenig Equipment Inc....................... F 937 653-5281
   Urbana *(G-14842)*
La Mfg Inc... G 513 577-7200
   Cincinnati *(G-3094)*
McNeilus Truck and Mfg Inc............... G 614 868-0760
   Gahanna *(G-7844)*
◆ Mesa Industries Inc.......................E 513 321-2950
   Cincinnati *(G-3151)*
▲ Mini Mix Inc.................................. G 513 353-3811
   Cleves *(G-4960)*
Murphy Tractor & Eqp Co Inc............. G 330 220-4999
   Brunswick *(G-1774)*
Murphy Tractor & Eqp Co Inc............. G 330 477-9304
   Canton *(G-2169)*
Murphy Tractor & Eqp Co Inc............. G 614 876-1141
   Columbus *(G-5585)*
Murphy Tractor & Eqp Co Inc............. G 419 221-3666
   Lima *(G-9272)*
Murphy Tractor & Eqp Co Inc............. G 937 898-4198
   Vandalia *(G-14954)*
◆ Npk Construction Equipment Inc....D 440 232-7900
   Bedford *(G-1145)*
◆ Ohio Machinery Co........................C 440 526-6200
   Broadview Heights *(G-1665)*
Petrox Inc... F 330 653-5526
   Streetsboro *(G-13784)*
Shearer Farm Inc.............................. C 330 345-9023
   Wooster *(G-16171)*
Simpson Strong-Tie Company Inc..... C 614 876-8060
   Columbus *(G-5773)*
Terry Asphalt Materials Inc................ E 513 874-6192
   Hamilton *(G-8247)*
The Wagner-Smith Company............ B 866 338-0398
   Moraine *(G-11214)*
Thirion Brothers Eqp Co LLC............ G 440 357-8004
   Painesville *(G-12271)*
Unified Scrning Crshing - OH I.......... G 937 836-3201
   Englewood *(G-7246)*
Waco Scaffolding & Equipment Inc... A 216 749-8900
   Cleveland *(G-4889)*
West Equipment Company Inc.......... G 419 698-1601
   Toledo *(G-14522)*
◆ Winter Equipment Company ....E 440 946-8377
   Willoughby *(G-16019)*

5083 Farm and garden machinery

All Power Equipment LLC................. F 740 593-3279
   Athens *(G-674)*
◆ Arnold Corporation........................C 330 225-2600
   Valley City *(G-14861)*
Bortnick Tractor Sales Inc.................. F 330 924-2555
   Cortland *(G-5960)*
Buckeye Companies.......................... E 740 452-3641
   Zanesville *(G-16513)*
◆ Fort Recovery Equipment Inc........F 419 375-1006
   Fort Recovery *(G-7615)*
Franklin Equipment LLC.................... D 614 228-2014
   Groveport *(G-8143)*
Hawthorne Gardening Company....... E 360 883-8846
   Marysville *(G-9913)*
▲ Hawthorne Hydroponics LLC......... F 888 478-6544
   Marysville *(G-9914)*
J L Wannemacher Sls Svc Inc........... F 419 453-3445
   Ottoville *(G-12200)*

Employee Codes: A=Over 500 employees, B=251-500
C=101-250, D=51-100, E=20-50, F=10-19, G=1-9

50 WHOLESALE TRADE - DURABLE GOODS

Karl Kuemmerling Inc .... F
  Massillon (G-10114)
▲ S I Distributing Inc .... F 419 647-4909
  Spencerville (G-13489)
Schmidt Machine Company .... E 419 294-3814
  Upper Sandusky (G-14823)
Smg Growing Media Inc .... F 937 644-0011
  Marysville (G-9938)

5084 Industrial machinery and equipment

2e Associates Inc .... E 440 975-9955
  Willoughby (G-15871)
A & A Safety Inc .... F 937 567-9781
  Beavercreek (G-1068)
A & A Safety Inc .... E 513 943-6100
  Amelia (G-447)
A & B Deburring Company .... F 513 723-0444
  Cincinnati (G-2582)
▲ Adams Elevator Equipment Co .... D 847 581-2900
  Holland (G-8492)
▲ Addition Manufacturing Te .... C 513 228-7000
  Lebanon (G-9059)
Addup Inc .... E 513 745-4510
  Blue Ash (G-1357)
Advanced Green Tech Inc .... G 614 397-8130
  Plain City (G-12560)
Advanced Tech Utilization Co .... F 440 238-3770
  Strongsville (G-13802)
Aerocontrolex Group Inc .... D 216 291-6025
  South Euclid (G-13457)
◆ Air Technical Industries Inc .... E 440 951-5191
  Mentor (G-10409)
Airgas Usa LLC .... G 937 222-8312
  Moraine (G-11154)
Airgas Usa LLC .... G 440 232-6397
  Twinsburg (G-14625)
Alba Manufacturing Inc .... D 513 874-0551
  Fairfield (G-7332)
Aldrich Chemical .... D 937 859-1808
  Miamisburg (G-10608)
◆ Alfons Haar Inc .... E 937 560-2031
  Springboro (G-13495)
Alkon Corporation .... E 614 799-6650
  Dublin (G-6858)
▲ Alkon Corporation .... D 419 355-9111
  Fremont (G-7762)
◆ American Rescue Technology Inc .... F 937 293-6240
  Dayton (G-6203)
▲ American Solving Inc .... G 440 234-7373
  Brookpark (G-1703)
◆ Ampac Packaging LLC .... C 513 671-1777
  Cincinnati (G-2623)
Anderson & Vreeland Inc .... D 419 636-5002
  Bryan (G-1807)
Anthe Machine Works Inc .... G 859 431-1035
  Cincinnati (G-2552)
ARC Solutions Inc .... E 419 542-9272
  Hicksville (G-8371)
▲ Armour Spray Systems Inc .... F 216 398-3838
  Cleveland (G-3675)
Atlas Machine and Supply Inc .... E 502 584-7262
  Hamilton (G-8182)
▲ Ats Systems Oregon Inc .... C 541 738-0932
  Lewis Center (G-9152)
◆ Avure Autoclave Systems Inc .... F 614 891-2732
  Columbus (G-5167)
Axion International Inc .... G 740 452-2500
  Zanesville (G-16502)
▲ Belle Center Air Tool Co Inc .... G 937 464-7474
  Belle Center (G-1195)
Bickett Machine and Gas Supply .... G 740 353-5710
  Portsmouth (G-12641)

▲ Bilz Vibration Technology Inc .... F 330 468-2459
  Macedonia (G-9538)
Bionix Safety Technologies Ltd .... E 419 727-0552
  Maumee (G-10172)
Bobco Enterprises Inc .... F 419 867-3560
  Toledo (G-14215)
Bollin & Sons Inc .... E 419 693-6573
  Toledo (G-14216)
Breaker Technology Inc .... F 440 248-7168
  Solon (G-13324)
Brown Industrial Inc .... E 937 693-3838
  Botkins (G-1542)
Bud Corp .... G 740 967-9992
  Johnstown (G-8771)
Bulk Carriers Service Inc .... F 330 339-3333
  New Philadelphia (G-11490)
Cascade Corporation .... E 419 425-3675
  Findlay (G-7491)
◆ Chemineer Inc .... O 937 454-3200
  Dayton (G-6254)
Cintas Corporation .... D 513 631-5750
  Cincinnati (G-2770)
◆ Cintas Corporation .... A 513 459-1200
  Cincinnati (G-2769)
Cintas Corporation No 2 .... D 330 966-7800
  Canton (G-2074)
Contitech Usa Inc .... D 937 644-8900
  Marysville (G-9906)
▲ Control Line Equipment Inc .... F 216 433-7766
  Cleveland (G-3903)
Cortest Inc .... F 440 942-1235
  Willoughby (G-15903)
Country Sales & Service LLC .... F 330 683-2500
  Orrville (G-12122)
Ctm Integration Incorporated .... E 330 332-1800
  Salem (G-12988)
Dearing Compressor and Pu .... E 330 783-2258
  Youngstown (G-16348)
Delille Oxygen Company .... G 937 325-9595
  Springfield (G-13553)
▲ Dengensha America Corporation .... F 440 439-8081
  Bedford (G-1115)
▲ Depot Direct Inc .... E 419 661-1233
  Perrysburg (G-12375)
Digilube Systems Inc .... F 937 748-2209
  Springboro (G-13499)
▲ Dura Magnetics Inc .... F 419 882-0591
  Sylvania (G-13995)
Eaton Corporation .... F 216 523-5000
  Willoughby (G-15916)
Electric Dsign For Indust Inc .... E 740 401-4000
  Belpre (G-1252)
Eltool Corporation .... G 513 723-1772
  Mansfield (G-9652)
▲ EMI Corp .... D 937 596-5911
  Jackson Center (G-8733)
Equipment Guys Inc .... F 614 871-9220
  Newark (G-11575)
▲ Equipment Mfrs Intl Inc .... E 216 651-6700
  Cleveland (G-4026)
◆ Esko-Graphics Inc .... D 937 454-1721
  Miamisburg (G-10637)
Exomet Inc .... E 440 593-1161
  Conneaut (G-5917)
Expert Crane Inc .... E 216 451-9900
  Wellington (G-15307)
Fastener Industries Inc .... E 440 891-2031
  Berea (G-1279)
▲ Fastener Industries Inc .... G 440 243-0034
  Berea (G-1280)
▲ Fcx Performance Inc .... E 614 253-1996
  Columbus (G-5373)

Fluid Power Solutions LLC .... G 614 777-8954
  Hilliard (G-8412)
Forte Industrial Equipmen .... E 513 398-2800
  Mason (G-9993)
Freeman Manufacturing & Sup Co .... E 440 934-1902
  Avon (G-775)
G & P Construction LLC .... E 855 494-4830
  North Royalton (G-11875)
G W Cobb Co .... F 216 341-0100
  Cleveland (G-4099)
GE Vernova International LLC .... G 330 963-2066
  Twinsburg (G-14665)
Ged Holdings Inc .... F 330 963-5401
  Twinsburg (G-14666)
◆ General Data Company Inc .... B 513 752-7978
  Cincinnati (G-2561)
Gerow Equipment Company Inc .... G 216 383-8800
  Cleveland (G-4122)
▲ Giant Industries Inc .... E 419 531-4600
  Toledo (G-14300)
Glavin Industries Inc .... E 440 349-0049
  Solon (G-13353)
▲ Gokoh Corporation .... F 937 339-4977
  Troy (G-14573)
Gorman-Rupp Company .... G 419 755-1245
  Mansfield (G-9662)
Grand Harbor Yacht Sales & Svc .... G 440 442-2919
  Cleveland (G-4139)
▲ Great Lakes Power Products Inc .... D 440 951-5111
  Mentor (G-10465)
Grenga Machine & Welding .... F 330 743-1113
  Youngstown (G-16374)
▲ Hammelmann Corporation .... F 937 859-8777
  Miamisburg (G-10642)
Hannon Company .... D 330 456-4728
  Canton (G-2121)
▲ Hawthorne Hydroponics LLC .... F 888 478-6544
  Marysville (G-9914)
Hendrickson International Corp .... D 740 929-5600
  Hebron (G-8343)
◆ Hiab USA Inc .... D 419 482-6000
  Perrysburg (G-12388)
◆ Hickman Williams & Company .... F 513 621-1946
  Cincinnati (G-2998)
Hydraulic Manifolds USA LLC .... E 973 728-1214
  Stow (G-13702)
Hydraulic Parts Store Inc .... E 330 364-6667
  New Philadelphia (G-11505)
Hydro Supply Co .... F 740 454-3842
  Zanesville (G-16537)
◆ Hydrotech Inc .... D 888 651-5712
  West Chester (G-15563)
IBI Brake Products Inc .... G 440 543-7962
  Chagrin Falls (G-2402)
▲ Ic-Fluid Power Inc .... F 419 661-8811
  Rossford (G-12866)
Imco Carbide Tool Inc .... D 419 661-6313
  Perrysburg (G-12390)
◆ Impact Products LLC .... D 419 841-2891
  Toledo (G-14328)
Industrial Parts Depot LLC .... F 440 237-9164
  North Royalton (G-11880)
Instrumentors Inc .... G 440 238-3430
  Strongsville (G-13846)
Intelligrated Inc .... A 513 874-0788
  West Chester (G-15565)
▲ Intelligrated Systems Inc .... A 866 936-7300
  Mason (G-10010)
Intelligrated Systems LLC .... A 513 701-7300
  Mason (G-10011)
◆ Intelligrated Systems Ohio LLC .... A 513 701-7300
  Mason (G-10012)

50 WHOLESALE TRADE - DURABLE GOODS

Interstate Pump Company Inc .... G 330 222-1006
Salem (G-13005)

Interstate Tool Corporation .... E 216 671-1077
Cleveland (G-4234)

J & S Tool Corporation .... F 216 676-8330
Cleveland (G-4243)

J McCaman Enterprises Inc .... G 330 825-2401
New Franklin (G-11437)

▲ Jay Dee Service Corporation .... G 330 425-1546
Macedonia (G-9558)

Jed Industries Inc .... F 440 639-9973
Grand River (G-8011)

▲ Jergens Inc .... C 216 486-5540
Cleveland (G-4253)

Jerrys Welding Supply Inc .... G 937 364-1500
Hillsboro (G-8460)

Jis Distribution LLC .... F 216 706-6552
Cleveland (G-4256)

▲ Joseph Industries Inc .... D 330 528-0091
Streetsboro (G-13776)

JPS Technologies Inc .... F 513 984-6400
Blue Ash (G-1415)

JPS Technologies Inc .... F 513 984-6400
Blue Ash (G-1414)

Jsh International LLC .... G 330 734-0251
Akron (G-200)

Kecamm LLC .... G 330 527-2918
Garrettsville (G-7918)

◆ Kinetics Noise Control Inc .... C 614 889-0480
Dublin (G-6905)

Kingsly Compression Inc .... G 740 439-0772
Cambridge (G-1939)

Kolinahr Systems Inc .... F 513 745-9401
Blue Ash (G-1417)

Krupp Rubber Machinery .... G 330 864-0800
Akron (G-212)

▲ Kyocera SGS Precision Tls Inc .... E 330 688-6667
Cuyahoga Falls (G-6098)

◆ Lawrence Industries Inc .... E 216 518-7000
Cleveland (G-4318)

▲ Lefeld Welding & Stl Sups Inc .... E 419 678-2397
Coldwater (G-4995)

Linde Gas & Equipment Inc .... G 513 821-2192
Cincinnati (G-3107)

Linden-Two Inc .... E 330 928-4064
Cuyahoga Falls (G-6100)

▲ Logitech Inc .... E 614 871-2822
Grove City (G-8102)

Lubrisource Inc .... F 937 432-9292
Middletown (G-10836)

M & S Equipment Leasing Co .... F 216 662-8800
Cleveland (G-4343)

Maag Automatik Inc .... E 330 677-2225
Kent (G-8830)

▲ Maintenance Repair Supply Inc .... F 740 922-3006
Midvale (G-10881)

Marengo Fabricated Steel Ltd .... F 800 919-2652
Cardington (G-2276)

Martin Allen Trailer LLC .... F 330 942-0217
Akron (G-238)

Martin Diesel Inc .... E 419 782-9911
Defiance (G-6691)

Matheson Tri-Gas Inc .... G 419 865-8881
Holland (G-8518)

Matheson Tri-Gas Inc .... G 513 727-9638
Middletown (G-10842)

Mfh Partners Inc .... B 440 461-4100
Cleveland (G-4398)

▲ Mid-State Sales Inc .... G 614 864-1811
Columbus (G-5564)

Midwest Conveyor Products Inc .... E 419 281-1235
Ashland (G-592)

Millwood Inc .... E 513 860-4567
West Chester (G-15464)

Minerva Welding and Fabg Inc .... E 330 868-7731
Minerva (G-11036)

Modern Machine Development .... F 937 253-4576
Dayton (G-6454)

Monaghan & Associates Inc .... F 937 253-7706
Dayton (G-6456)

Monode Marking Products Inc .... E 440 975-8802
Mentor (G-10506)

Motionsource International LLC .... F 440 287-7037
Solon (G-13392)

◆ Multi Products Company .... E 330 674-5981
Millersburg (G-10986)

National Tool & Equipment Inc .... F 330 629-8665
Youngstown (G-16403)

Neff Machinery and Supplies .... F 740 454-0128
Zanesville (G-16547)

Neil R Scholl Inc .... F 740 653-6593
Lancaster (G-9027)

Oak View Enterprises Inc .... E 513 860-4446
Bucyrus (G-1864)

▲ Off Contact Inc .... F 419 255-5546
Toledo (G-14406)

Ohio Hydraulics Inc .... E 513 771-2590
Cincinnati (G-3215)

Otis Elevator Company .... E 216 573-2333
Cleveland (G-4512)

◆ Park Corporation .... B 216 267-4870
Medina (G-10362)

Parker-Hannifin Corporation .... G 216 433-1795
Cleveland (G-4531)

Paul Peterson Company .... G 614 486-4375
Columbus (G-5660)

▲ PE Usa LLC .... F 513 771-7374
Cincinnati (G-3244)

Pfpc Enterprises Inc .... F 513 941-6200
Cincinnati (G-3253)

▲ Pines Manufacturing Inc .... E 440 835-5553
Westlake (G-15775)

◆ Plastic Process Equipment Inc .... E 216 367-7000
Macedonia (G-9566)

Pomacon Inc .... F 330 273-1576
Brunswick (G-1781)

▲ Power Distributors LLC .... D 614 876-3533
Columbus (G-5684)

Powerclean Equipment Company .... F 513 202-0001
Cleves (G-4963)

▲ Princeton Tool Inc .... C 440 290-8666
Mentor (G-10531)

Proampac Orlando Inc .... F 513 671-1777
Cincinnati (G-3279)

Programmable Control Svc Inc .... G 740 927-0744
Pataskala (G-12304)

Progressive Mfg Co Inc .... G 330 784-4717
Akron (G-286)

R & M Fluid Power Inc .... E 330 758-2766
Youngstown (G-16425)

R and J Corporation .... E 440 871-6009
Westlake (G-15777)

Ralph Robinson Inc .... G 740 385-2747
Logan (G-9375)

Rayhaven Group Inc .... G 330 659-3183
Richfield (G-12795)

▲ Ready Technology Inc .... F 937 866-7200
Dayton (G-6544)

◆ Reduction Engineering Inc .... E 330 677-2225
Kent (G-8852)

Rel Enterprises Inc .... E 216 741-1700
Brooklyn Heights (G-1698)

Remtec Engineering .... E 513 860-4299
Mason (G-10047)

Rixan Associates Inc .... E 937 438-3005
Dayton (G-6550)

Rnm Holdings Inc .... F 614 444-5556
Columbus (G-5726)

Rnm Holdings Inc .... F 419 867-8712
Holland (G-8528)

▲ Robeck Fluid Power Co .... D 330 562-1140
Aurora (G-734)

◆ Rolls-Royce Energy Systems Inc .... A 703 834-1700
Mount Vernon (G-11292)

▲ Rubber City Machinery Corp .... E 330 434-3500
Akron (G-312)

Rumpke Transportation Co LLC .... F 513 851-0122
Cincinnati (G-3355)

Ryanworks Inc .... F 937 438-1282
Dayton (G-6555)

Salem Welding & Supply Company .... G 330 332-4517
Salem (G-13029)

Samuel Son & Co (usa) Inc .... D 740 522-2500
Heath (G-8331)

▲ Sausser Steel Company Inc .... F 419 422-9632
Findlay (G-7559)

Schenck Process LLC .... F 513 576-9200
Solon (G-13419)

Sequa Can Machinery Inc .... E 330 493-0444
Canton (G-2221)

▲ Siebtechnik Tema Inc .... E 513 489-7811
Cincinnati (G-3390)

South Shore Controls Inc .... E 440 259-2500
Mentor (G-10557)

Stanley Bittinger .... G 740 942-4302
Cadiz (G-1904)

▼ Stanley Industries Inc .... E 216 475-4000
Cleveland (G-4730)

Stanwade Metal Products Inc .... G 330 772-2421
Hartford (G-8298)

Starkey Machinery Inc .... E 419 468-2560
Galion (G-7885)

Super Systems Inc .... E 513 772-0060
Cincinnati (G-3432)

Suspension Technology Inc .... F 330 458-3058
Canton (G-2240)

System Seals Inc .... E 216 220-1800
Brecksville (G-1632)

▲ System Seals Inc .... E 440 735-0200
Cleveland (G-4763)

T & D Fabricating Inc .... E 440 951-5646
Eastlake (G-7051)

▲ Taiyo America Inc .... F 419 300-8811
Saint Marys (G-12968)

Tech Products Corporation .... F 937 438-1100
Miamisburg (G-10690)

Tilt-Or-Lift Inc .... G 419 893-6944
Maumee (G-10241)

Toga-Pak Inc .... E 937 294-7311
Dayton (G-6626)

Tool Systems Incorporated .... F 440 461-6363
Cleveland (G-4801)

Tooltex Inc .... F 614 539-3222
Grove City (G-8123)

◆ Transducers Direct Llc .... F 513 247-0601
Cincinnati (G-3462)

◆ Trewbric III Inc .... E 614 444-2184
Columbus (G-5835)

Tri State Equipment Company .... G 513 738-7227
Shandon (G-13161)

Tri-Mac Mfg & Svcs Co .... F 513 896-4445
Hamilton (G-8251)

United Hydraulics .... G 440 585-0906
Wickliffe (G-15856)

Valv-Trol LLC .... F 330 686-2800
Stow (G-13736)

50 WHOLESALE TRADE - DURABLE GOODS

▲ Valve Related Controls Inc .... F 513 677-8724
   Loveland *(G-9507)*
▲ Venco Venturo Industries LLC .... E 513 772-8448
   Cincinnati *(G-3490)*
   Venturo Manufacturing Inc .... F 513 772-8448
   Cincinnati *(G-3492)*
   Versatile Automation Tech Corp .... G 330 220-2600
   Brunswick *(G-1798)*
▲ Versatile Automation Tech Ltd .... G 440 589-6700
   Solon *(G-13442)*
   Weld-Action Company Inc .... G 330 372-1063
   Warren *(G-15223)*
   Weldco Inc .... E 513 744-9353
   Cincinnati *(G-3514)*
   Welders Supply Inc .... F 216 241-1696
   Cleveland *(G-4903)*
   Western Branch Diesel LLC .... F 330 454-8800
   Canton *(G-2267)*
   Wolf Machine Company .... E 513 791-5194
   Blue Ash *(G-1493)*
   Worker Automation Inc .... G 937 473-2111
   Dayton *(G-6660)*
   Wright Brothers Inc .... F 513 731-2222
   Cincinnati *(G-3527)*

5085 Industrial supplies

   Airgas Usa LLC .... G 937 222-8312
   Moraine *(G-11154)*
   Airgas Usa LLC .... G 440 232-6397
   Twinsburg *(G-14625)*
   Akron Belting & Supply Company .... G 330 633-8212
   Akron *(G-27)*
   Alb Tyler Holdings Inc .... G 440 946-7171
   Mentor *(G-10410)*
   Alkon Corporation .... E 614 799-6650
   Dublin *(G-6858)*
▲ Alkon Corporation .... D 419 355-9111
   Fremont *(G-7762)*
▲ All Ohio Threaded Rod Co Inc .... E 216 426-1800
   Cleveland *(G-3632)*
◆ Alliance Knife Inc .... E 513 367-9000
   Harrison *(G-8264)*
   Allied Shipping and Packa .... F 937 222-7422
   Moraine *(G-11155)*
   Alro Steel Corporation .... E 614 878-7271
   Columbus *(G-5116)*
   Alro Steel Corporation .... D 419 720-5300
   Toledo *(G-14184)*
▲ Anchor Flange Company .... D 513 527-3512
   Cincinnati *(G-2626)*
   Andre Corporation .... E 574 293-0207
   Mason *(G-9950)*
   Aqua Technology Group LLC .... E 513 298-1183
   West Chester *(G-15367)*
▲ Atlas Bolt & Screw Company LLC .... E 419 289-6171
   Ashland *(G-554)*
▲ Atwood Rope Manufacturing Inc .... E 614 920-0534
   Canal Winchester *(G-1979)*
   B W Grinding Co .... E 419 923-1376
   Lyons *(G-9531)*
   Bearings Manufacturing Company .... F 440 846-5517
   Strongsville *(G-13815)*
   Brimar Packaging Inc .... E 440 934-3080
   Avon *(G-764)*
▲ C B Mfg & Sls Co Inc .... D 937 866-5986
   Miamisburg *(G-10624)*
   Chardon Tool & Supply Co Inc .... E 440 286-6440
   Chardon *(G-2445)*
   Ci Disposition Co .... D 216 587-5200
   Brooklyn Heights *(G-1687)*
   Cincinnati Abrasive Supply Co .... G 513 941-8660
   Cincinnati *(G-2738)*

◆ Cleveland Supplyone Inc .... E 216 514-7000
   Cleveland *(G-3857)*
   Cmt Machining & Fabg LLC .... F 937 652-3740
   Urbana *(G-14827)*
   Commercial Electric Pdts Corp .... E 216 241-2886
   Cleveland *(G-3889)*
   Cornwell Quality Tools Company .... D 330 628-2627
   Mogadore *(G-11068)*
   Crane Pumps & Systems Inc .... C 937 773-2442
   Piqua *(G-12508)*
▲ Crawford Products Inc .... E 614 890-1822
   Columbus *(G-5306)*
▲ Creative Plastic Concepts LLC .... F 419 927-9588
   Sycamore *(G-13988)*
   Dadco Inc .... F 513 489-2244
   Cincinnati *(G-2816)*
◆ Datwyler Sling Sltions USA Inc .... D 937 387-2800
   Vandalia *(G-14937)*
   Dayton Stencil Works Company .... F 937 223-3233
   Dayton *(G-6290)*
   Dearing Compressor and Pu .... E 330 783-2258
   Youngstown *(G-16348)*
   Delille Oxygen Company .... E 614 444-1177
   Columbus *(G-5324)*
   Dixon Valve & Coupling Co LLC .... F 330 425-3000
   Twinsburg *(G-14652)*
   Dynatech Systems Inc .... F 440 365-1774
   Elyria *(G-7135)*
◆ Eagle Industrial Truck Mfg LLC .... E 419 866-6301
   Swanton *(G-13973)*
   Edward W Daniel LLC .... E 440 647-1960
   Wellington *(G-15306)*
   Elyria Spring Spclty Holdg Inc .... F 440 323-5502
   Elyria *(G-7147)*
▲ ET&f Fastening Systems Inc .... F 800 248-2376
   Solon *(G-13346)*
   Evans Adhesive Corporation .... E 614 451-2665
   Columbus *(G-5362)*
◆ F & M Mafco Inc .... C 513 367-2151
   Harrison *(G-8273)*
◆ Facil North America Inc .... C 330 487-2500
   Twinsburg *(G-14659)*
◆ Fcx Performance Inc .... E 614 253-1996
   Columbus *(G-5373)*
   First Francis Company Inc .... E 440 352-8927
   Painesville *(G-12237)*
▲ Forge Industries Inc .... A 330 960-2468
   Youngstown *(G-16359)*
▲ Fouty & Company Inc .... E 419 693-0017
   Oregon *(G-12105)*
◆ Ges Graphite Inc .... E 216 658-6660
   Parma *(G-12290)*
◆ Gokoh Corporation .... F 937 339-4977
   Troy *(G-14573)*
▲ Great Lakes Fasteners Inc .... D 330 425-4488
   Twinsburg *(G-14670)*
▲ Great Lakes Power Products Inc .... D 440 951-5111
   Mentor *(G-10465)*
▲ H & D Steel Service Inc .... E 800 666-3390
   North Royalton *(G-11878)*
   H3d Tool Corporation .... E 740 498-5181
   Newcomerstown *(G-11644)*
◆ Hickman Williams & Company .... F 513 621-1946
   Cincinnati *(G-2998)*
▲ High Quality Tools Inc .... F 440 975-9684
   Eastlake *(G-7036)*
◆ HMS Industries LLC .... F 440 899-0001
   Westlake *(G-15756)*
   Horwitz & Pintis Co .... F 419 666-2220
   Toledo *(G-14320)*
   Hydraulic Manifolds USA LLC .... E 973 728-1214
   Stow *(G-13702)*

   Ig Watteeuw Usa LLC .... F 740 588-1722
   Zanesville *(G-16538)*
   Indelco Custom Products Inc .... E 216 797-7300
   Euclid *(G-7274)*
▼ Industrial Connections Inc .... G 330 274-2155
   Mantua *(G-9737)*
   Industrial Mold Inc .... E 330 425-7374
   Twinsburg *(G-14676)*
   Interstate Pump Company Inc .... G 330 222-1006
   Salem *(G-13005)*
   Interstate Sign Products Inc .... G 419 683-1962
   Crestline *(G-6034)*
▼ Japo Inc .... E 614 263-2850
   Columbus *(G-5488)*
   Jet Rubber Company .... E 330 325-1821
   Rootstown *(G-12853)*
◆ Kaufman Container Company .... C 216 898-2000
   Cleveland *(G-4276)*
▲ Kenag Inc .... E 419 281-1204
   Ashland *(G-586)*
◆ Lawrence Industries Inc .... E 216 518-7000
   Cleveland *(G-4318)*
▲ Logan Clutch Corporation .... E 440 808-4258
   Cleveland *(G-4334)*
   Lynk Packaging Inc .... G 330 562-8080
   Aurora *(G-723)*
▲ Maintenance Repair Supply Inc .... F 740 922-3006
   Midvale *(G-10881)*
   Maumee Hose & Fitting Inc .... G 419 893-7252
   Maumee *(G-10218)*
▲ McNeil Industries Inc .... E 440 951-7756
   Painesville *(G-12251)*
   McWane Inc .... B 740 622-6651
   Coshocton *(G-5983)*
◆ Mesa Industries Inc .... E 513 321-2950
   Cincinnati *(G-3151)*
   Metzger Machine Co .... F 513 241-3360
   Cincinnati *(G-3159)*
▲ Miba Bearings US LLC .... B 740 962-4242
   Mcconnelsville *(G-10282)*
   Mid-State Sales Inc .... G 330 744-2158
   Youngstown *(G-16400)*
▲ Mill-Rose Company .... C 440 255-9171
   Mentor *(G-10505)*
   Modroto .... G 440 998-1202
   Ashtabula *(G-649)*
◆ Namoh Ohio Holdings Inc .... E
   Norwood *(G-11996)*
   Netherland Rubber Company .... F 513 733-0883
   Cincinnati *(G-3187)*
   Newact Inc .... F 513 321-5177
   Batavia *(G-940)*
▲ North Coast Seal Incorporated .... F 216 898-5000
   Brookpark *(G-1722)*
◆ NSK Industries Inc .... D 330 923-4112
   Cuyahoga Falls *(G-6107)*
   Ohio Drill & Tool Co .... E 330 525-7717
   Homeworth *(G-8555)*
   Orbytel Print and Packg Inc .... E 216 267-8734
   Cleveland *(G-4508)*
▲ Pipe Products Inc .... C 513 587-7532
   West Chester *(G-15480)*
◆ Plastic Process Equipment Inc .... E 216 367-7000
   Macedonia *(G-9566)*
◆ Pressure Connections Corp .... D 614 863-6930
   Columbus *(G-5689)*
   Quad Fluid Dynamics Inc .... F 330 220-3005
   Brunswick *(G-1785)*
   R C Musson Rubber Co .... E 330 773-7651
   Akron *(G-294)*
▲ RB&w Manufacturing LLC .... G 234 380-8540
   Streetsboro *(G-13787)*

▲ Sabco Industries Inc.......................... E 419 531-5347
Toledo *(G-14461)*

▲ Samsel Rope & Marine Supply Co..... E 216 241-0333
Cleveland *(G-4670)*

Samuel Son & Co (usa) Inc.................. D 740 522-2500
Heath *(G-8331)*

▲ Save Edge Inc..................................... E 937 376-8268
Xenia *(G-16272)*

Service Spring Corp............................. G 419 867-0212
Maumee *(G-10230)*

Shaq Inc... D 770 427-0402
Beachwood *(G-1023)*

Solo Products Inc................................ F 513 321-7884
Cincinnati *(G-3402)*

▲ SSP Fittings Corp................................ D 330 425-4250
Twinsburg *(G-14736)*

◆ Stafast Products Inc.............................E 440 357-5546
Painesville *(G-12264)*

Steam Trbine Altrntive Rsrces............. E 740 387-5535
Marion *(G-9884)*

▲ Strata-Tac Inc...................................... F 630 879-9388
Troy *(G-14613)*

▼ Stud Welding Associates Inc............... D 440 783-3160
Strongsville *(G-13887)*

▲ Summers Acquisition Corp.................. E 216 941-7700
Cleveland *(G-4745)*

Superior Holding LLC........................... E 216 651-9400
Cleveland *(G-4748)*

Superior Products LLC......................... D 216 651-9400
Cleveland *(G-4751)*

Supply Technologies LLC..................... G 937 898-5795
Dayton *(G-6601)*

◆ Supply Technologies LLC.....................C 440 947-2100
Cleveland *(G-4755)*

▲ TCH Industries Incorporated................ F 330 487-5155
Twinsburg *(G-14741)*

Tenney Tool & Supply Co..................... G 330 666-2807
Barberton *(G-899)*

▲ The Cornwell Quality Tool.................... D 330 336-3506
Wadsworth *(G-15069)*

◆ The Kindt-Collins Company LLC.........D 216 252-4122
Cleveland *(G-4788)*

▲ Timken Company.................................A 234 262-3000
North Canton *(G-11766)*

▲ Tlg Cochran Inc.................................... E 440 914-1122
Twinsburg *(G-14744)*

◆ Tolco Corporation.................................D 419 241-1113
Toledo *(G-14491)*

Toledo Tarp Service Inc........................ E 419 837-5098
Perrysburg *(G-12440)*

Trent Manufacturing Company............ G 216 391-1551
Mentor *(G-10583)*

◆ Tricor Industrial Inc..............................D 330 264-3299
Wooster *(G-16178)*

United Tool Supply Inc......................... G 513 752-6000
Cincinnati *(G-2576)*

Valv-Trol LLC.. F 330 686-2800
Stow *(G-13736)*

▲ Victory White Metal Company............. D 216 271-1400
Cleveland *(G-4874)*

◆ Watteredge LLC...................................D 440 933-6110
Avon Lake *(G-828)*

Wesco Distribution Inc......................... F 419 666-1670
Northwood *(G-11933)*

Wulco Inc.. D 513 379-6115
Hamilton *(G-8259)*

▲ Wulco Inc... D 513 679-2600
Cincinnati *(G-3529)*

Youngstown Bolt & Supply Co.............. G 330 799-3201
Youngstown *(G-16479)*

5087 Service establishment equipment

A-1 Sprinkler Company Inc.................. D 937 859-6198
Miamisburg *(G-10604)*

▲ Action Coupling & Eqp Inc.................. D 330 279-4242
Holmesville *(G-8541)*

AIN Industries Inc................................ G 440 781-0950
Cleveland *(G-3616)*

▲ Alco-Chem Inc...................................... E 330 253-3535
Akron *(G-49)*

Allen Enterprises Inc............................ E 740 532-5913
Ironton *(G-8694)*

Baxter Burial Vault Svc Inc................... F 513 641-1010
Cincinnati *(G-2660)*

Beaute Asylum LLC.............................. F 419 377-9933
Toledo *(G-14209)*

Case Ohio Burial Co............................. F 440 779-1992
Cleveland *(G-3797)*

Chem-Sales Inc.................................... F
Toledo *(G-14235)*

Cooper Enterprises Inc........................ D 419 347-5232
Shelby *(G-13193)*

Cummins - Allison Corp....................... G 440 824-5050
Cleveland *(G-3919)*

Excalibur Barber LLC........................... F 330 729-9006
Boardman *(G-1512)*

Fire Safety Services Inc....................... F 937 686-2000
Huntsville *(G-8623)*

Friends Service Co Inc......................... F 800 427-1704
Dayton *(G-6339)*

Friends Service Co Inc.........................D 419 427-1704
Findlay *(G-7512)*

Gt Industrial Supply Inc....................... F 513 771-7000
Cincinnati *(G-2976)*

◆ Impact Products LLC............................D 419 841-2891
Toledo *(G-14328)*

Jls Funeral Home................................. F 614 625-1220
Columbus *(G-5497)*

Johnsons Fire Equipment Co............... F 740 357-4916
Wellston *(G-15330)*

K-O-K Products Inc.............................. F 740 548-0526
Galena *(G-7855)*

▲ Majestic Manufacturing Inc.................E 330 457-2447
New Waterford *(G-11558)*

Martin-Brower Company LLC.............. C 513 773-2301
West Chester *(G-15462)*

National Pride Equipment Inc.............. G 419 289-2886
Mansfield *(G-9703)*

▲ Pioneer Manufacturing Inc.................. D 216 671-5500
Cleveland *(G-4555)*

Pneumatic Specialties Inc.................... G 440 729-4400
Chesterland *(G-2488)*

Rose Products and Services Inc.......... F 614 443-7647
Columbus *(G-5731)*

Service Station Equipment Co............. G 216 431-6100
Cleveland *(G-4686)*

▼ Sutphen Corporation............................ C 800 726-7030
Dublin *(G-6949)*

◆ Wasserstrom Company........................B 614 228-6525
Columbus *(G-5865)*

5088 Transportation equipment and supplies

17111 Waterview Pkwy LLC.................. F 216 706-2960
Cleveland *(G-3569)*

American Power LLC............................ F 937 235-0418
Dayton *(G-6202)*

Amsted Industries Incorporated.......... D 614 836-2323
Groveport *(G-8129)*

◆ Bendix Coml Vhcl Systems LLC...........B 440 329-9000
Avon *(G-763)*

◆ Buck Equipment Inc.............................E 614 539-3039
Grove City *(G-8081)*

Cleveland Wheels................................. G 440 937-6211
Avon *(G-767)*

Dircksen and Associates Inc................ G 614 238-0413
Columbus *(G-5327)*

▲ Eleet Cryogenics Inc............................ E 330 874-4009
Bolivar *(G-1524)*

General Electric Company................... A 617 443-3000
Cincinnati *(G-2942)*

Grimes Aerospace Company............... D 937 484-2001
Urbana *(G-14832)*

Hydromotive Engineering Co............... G 330 425-4266
Twinsburg *(G-14673)*

Transdigm Group Incorporated........... B 216 706-2960
Cleveland *(G-4817)*

▼ Werner G Smith Inc.............................. F 216 861-3676
Cleveland *(G-4904)*

▲ Ysd Industries Inc................................ E 330 792-6521
Youngstown *(G-16491)*

5091 Sporting and recreation goods

A K Athletic Equipment Inc.................. E 614 920-3069
Canal Winchester *(G-1977)*

▼ Advantage Tent Fittings Inc................. F 740 773-3015
Chillicothe *(G-2491)*

Agean Marble Manufacturing............... F 513 874-1475
West Chester *(G-15533)*

▲ Atwood Rope Manufacturing Inc......... E 614 920-0534
Canal Winchester *(G-1979)*

Berry Investments Inc.......................... G 937 293-0398
Moraine *(G-11162)*

Bradley Enterprises Inc........................ G 330 875-1444
Louisville *(G-9456)*

Cyber Shed Inc..................................... G 419 724-5855
Toledo *(G-14256)*

▲ Done-Rite Bowling Service Co............. E 440 232-3280
Bedford *(G-1118)*

Electra Tarp Inc.................................... G 330 477-7168
Canton *(G-2095)*

Garick LLC... E 216 581-0100
Cleveland *(G-4102)*

▲ Ghostblind Industries Inc..................... G 740 374-6766
Belpre *(G-1253)*

▲ Golf Galaxy Golfworks Inc.................... C 740 328-4193
Newark *(G-11577)*

▲ H & S Distributing Inc.......................... G 800 336-7784
North Ridgeville *(G-11843)*

▲ Hammersmith Bros Invstmnts Inc...... E 513 353-3000
North Bend *(G-11704)*

Hershberger Lawn Structures.............. F 330 674-3900
Millersburg *(G-10957)*

House of Awards Inc............................ G 419 422-7877
Findlay *(G-7525)*

▲ Litehouse Products LLC...................... E 440 638-2350
Strongsville *(G-13851)*

Mc Alarney Pool Spas and Blldd.......... F 740 373-6698
Marietta *(G-9808)*

R & A Sports Inc................................... E 216 289-2254
Euclid *(G-7297)*

Total Tennis Inc.................................... F 614 488-5004
Columbus *(G-5829)*

◆ Zebec of North America Inc................E 513 829-5533
Fairfield *(G-7429)*

5092 Toys and hobby goods and supplies

Advance Novelty Incorporated............. G 419 424-0363
Findlay *(G-7472)*

▲ AW Faber-Castell Usa Inc.................... D 216 643-4660
Independence *(G-8654)*

▲ Bendon Inc... D 419 207-3600
Ashland *(G-556)*

▼ ICM Distributing Company Inc............ E 234 212-3030
Twinsburg *(G-14675)*

Middleton Llyd Dolls Inc...................... G 740 989-2082
Coolville *(G-5941)*

50 WHOLESALE TRADE - DURABLE GOODS

▲ Party Animal Inc .... F 440 471-1030
  Westlake (G-15771)
▲ Twin Sisters Productions LLC .... E 330 631-0361
  Stow (G-13735)
  Wooden Horse .... G 740 503-5243
  Baltimore (G-849)

5093 Scrap and waste materials

  A & B Iron & Metal Co Inc .... G 937 228-1561
  Dayton (G-6178)
◆ Aci Industries Ltd .... E 740 368-4160
  Delaware (G-6699)
  Agmet LLC .... F 216 663-8200
  Cleveland (G-3615)
  Auris Noble LLC .... E 330 321-6649
  Akron (G-68)
  Cohen Brothers Inc .... F 513 217-5200
  Middletown (G-10812)
  Cohen Brothers Inc .... E 513 422-3696
  Middletown (G-10811)
  Edw C Levy Co .... G 330 484-6328
  Canton (G-2094)
▼ Fex LLC .... F 412 604-0400
  Mingo Junction (G-11045)
▲ Fpt Cleveland LLC .... C 216 441-3800
  Cleveland (G-4088)
  Frankes Wood Products LLC .... E 937 642-0706
  Marysville (G-9910)
▲ Franklin Iron & Metal Corp .... C 937 253-8184
  Dayton (G-6338)
  Garick LLC .... E 216 581-0100
  Cleveland (G-4102)
  Homan Metals LLC .... G 513 721-5010
  Cincinnati (G-3004)
  Makers Supply LLC .... G 937 203-8245
  Piqua (G-12534)
  Metalico Akron Inc .... F 330 376-1400
  Akron (G-246)
  Mw Metals Group LLC .... D 937 222-5992
  Dayton (G-6462)
  Nucor Steel Marion Inc .... E 740 383-6068
  Marion (G-9867)
  Oil Works LLC .... G 614 245-3090
  Columbus (G-5635)
  R L S Corporation .... F 740 773-1440
  Chillicothe (G-2530)
  Rm Advisory Group Inc .... E 513 242-2100
  Cincinnati (G-3346)
  Rnw Holdings Inc .... E 330 792-0600
  Youngstown (G-16429)
▲ Sims Bros Inc .... D 740 387-9041
  Marion (G-9883)
◆ Triple Arrow Industries Inc .... G 614 437-5588
  Marysville (G-9943)
  W R G Inc .... E 216 351-8494
  Avon Lake (G-827)

5094 Jewelry and precious stones

  Behrco Inc .... G 419 394-1612
  Saint Marys (G-12945)
▲ Dern Trophies Corp .... F 614 895-3260
  Westerville (G-15653)
  Goyal Enterprises Inc .... F 513 874-9303
  West Chester (G-15557)
  M B Saxon Co Inc .... G 440 229-5006
  Cleveland (G-4345)
  Marfo Company .... D 614 276-3452
  Columbus (G-5541)
  Renoir Visions LLC .... G 419 586-5679
  Celina (G-2345)
  Scholz & Ey Engravers Inc .... F 614 444-8052
  Columbus (G-5752)

  Sharonco Inc .... G 419 882-3443
  Sylvania (G-14014)
  Sheiban Jewelry Inc .... F 440 238-0616
  Strongsville (G-13879)
  Vy Inc .... F 513 421-8100
  Cincinnati (G-3505)

5099 Durable goods, nec

  77 Coach Supply Ltd .... G 330 674-1454
  Millersburg (G-10937)
  A-Gas US Holdings Inc .... F 419 867-8990
  Bowling Green (G-1547)
  All-American Fire Eqp Inc .... F 800 972-6035
  Wshngtn Ct Hs (G-16225)
  Baker Plastics Inc .... G 330 743-3142
  Youngstown (G-16317)
  CD Solutions Inc .... G 937 676-2376
  Pleasant Hill (G-12606)
  Cindoco Wood Products Co .... F 937 444-2504
  Mount Orab (G-11240)
  Club 513 LLC .... G 800 530-2574
  Cincinnati (G-2776)
◆ Evenflo Company Inc .... E 937 415-3300
  Miamisburg (G-10638)
  Fire Safety Services Inc .... F 937 686-2000
  Huntsville (G-8623)
  Gross Lumber Inc .... F 330 683-2055
  Apple Creek (G-501)
▲ Jatiga Inc .... D 859 817-7100
  Blue Ash (G-1411)
  K Ventures Inc .... F 419 678-2308
  Coldwater (G-4994)
▲ Klw Plastics Inc .... G 513 539-2673
  Monroe (G-11114)
  Macray Co LLC .... G 937 325-1726
  Springfield (G-13598)
  McHael D Goronok String Instrs .... G 216 421-4227
  Cleveland (G-4380)
  Netherland Rubber Company .... F 513 733-0883
  Cincinnati (G-3187)
  Quick As A Wink Printing Co .... G 419 224-9786
  Lima (G-9281)
◆ Recaro Child Safety LLC .... G 248 904-1570
  Cincinnati (G-3326)
▼ Resource Mtl Hdlg & Recycl Inc .... E 440 834-0727
  Middlefield (G-10784)
  Samb LLC Services .... G 937 660-0115
  Englewood (G-7241)
▲ TS Tech Americas Inc .... B 614 575-4100
  Reynoldsburg (G-12776)
  Victory Postcards Inc .... G 614 764-8975
  Dublin (G-6957)
  Water Drop Media Inc .... G 234 600-5817
  Vienna (G-15005)
▲ Wcm Holdings Inc .... C 513 705-2100
  Cincinnati (G-3509)
▲ West Chester Holdings LLC .... C 513 705-2100
  Cincinnati (G-3516)

51 WHOLESALE TRADE - NONDURABLE GOODS

5111 Printing and writing paper

  Gvs Industries Inc .... G 513 851-3606
  Hamilton (G-8214)
▲ Microcom Corporation .... E 740 548-6262
  Lewis Center (G-9171)
▲ Millcraft Group LLC .... D 216 441-5500
  Independence (G-8675)

5112 Stationery and office supplies

  American Business Forms Inc .... E 513 312-2522
  West Chester (G-15535)
  Anthony Business Forms Inc .... G 937 253-0072
  Dayton (G-6153)
▲ AW Faber-Castell Usa Inc .... D 216 643-4660
  Independence (G-8654)
  Bay Business Forms Inc .... F 937 322-3000
  Springfield (G-13539)
  Bloch Printing Company .... G 330 576-6760
  Copley (G-5945)
  Envelope Mart of Ohio Inc .... F 440 365-8177
  Elyria (G-7150)
  Equip Business Solutions Co .... G 614 854-9755
  Jackson (G-8715)
  Friends Service Co Inc .... F 800 427-1704
  Dayton (G-6339)
  Friends Service Co Inc .... D 419 427-1704
  Findlay (G-7512)
▲ GBS Corp .... C 330 494-5330
  North Canton (G-11729)
  Gq Business Products Inc .... E 513 792-4750
  Loveland (G-9482)
  Gvs Industries Inc .... G 513 851-3606
  Hamilton (G-8214)
  Highland Computer Forms Inc .... D 937 393-4215
  Hillsboro (G-8459)
  Identity Group LLC .... G 614 337-6167
  Westerville (G-15658)
▲ Jbm Packaging Company .... C 513 933-8333
  Lebanon (G-9090)
▲ Microcom Corporation .... E 740 548-6262
  Lewis Center (G-9171)
  Optimum System Products Inc .... E 614 885-4464
  Westerville (G-15718)
  Pac Worldwide Corporation .... E 800 535-0039
  Monroe (G-11117)
◆ Printer Components Inc .... G 585 924-5190
  Fairfield (G-7397)
▲ Pulsar Ecoproducts LLC .... F 216 861-8800
  Cleveland (G-4600)
  Queen City Office Machine .... F 513 251-7200
  Cincinnati (G-3317)
▼ Quick Tab II Inc .... D 419 448-6622
  Tiffin (G-14101)
▲ REA Elektronik Inc .... F 440 232-0555
  Bedford (G-1151)
▲ Shamrock Companies Inc .... D 440 899-9510
  Westlake (G-15786)
◆ Wasserstrom Company .... B 614 228-6525
  Columbus (G-5865)
  Western States Envelope Co .... E 419 666-7480
  Walbridge (G-15088)
  Westrock Commercial LLC .... D 419 476-9101
  Toledo (G-14523)
  William J Bergen & Co .... G 440 248-6132
  Solon (G-13448)

5113 Industrial and personal service paper

  A To Z Paper Box Company .... G 330 325-8722
  Rootstown (G-12850)
◆ Aci Industries Converting Ltd .... F 740 368-4160
  Delaware (G-6700)
  Acme Steak & Seafood Inc .... F 330 270-8000
  Youngstown (G-16303)
  Adapt-A-Pak Inc .... E 937 845-0386
  Fairborn (G-7307)
  American Made Corrugated Packg ..... F 937 981-2111
  Greenfield (G-8027)
  Argrov Box Co .... F 937 898-1700
  Dayton (G-6212)
▼ Buckeye Paper Co Inc .... E 330 477-5925
  Canton (G-2054)

SIC SECTION

51 WHOLESALE TRADE - NONDURABLE GOODS

Canton Sterilized Wiping Cloth............ G 330 455-5179
  Canton *(G-2068)*

CJ Dannemiller Co............................ E 330 825-7808
  Norton *(G-11939)*

◆ Cleveland Supplyone Inc................... E 216 514-7000
  Cleveland *(G-3857)*

▲ Dazpak Flexible Packaging Corp......... C 614 252-2121
  Columbus *(G-5318)*

Deufol Worldwide Packaging LLC........ E 440 232-1100
  Bedford *(G-1116)*

Gt Industrial Supply Inc..................... F 513 771-7000
  Cincinnati *(G-2976)*

Gvs Industries Inc............................. G 513 851-3606
  Hamilton *(G-8214)*

Lynk Packaging Inc........................... E 330 562-8080
  Aurora *(G-723)*

▲ Millcraft Group LLC......................... D 216 441-5500
  Independence *(G-8675)*

Ohio Paper Tube Co......................... E 330 478-5171
  Canton *(G-2185)*

◆ Polymer Packaging Inc.....................D 330 832-2000
  North Canton *(G-11751)*

Putnam Plastics Inc........................... G 937 866-6261
  Dayton *(G-6535)*

Ray C Sprosty Bag Co Inc.................. F 330 669-0045
  Smithville *(G-13301)*

Ricking Holding Co............................ E 513 825-3551
  Cleveland *(G-4633)*

Solas Ltd... E 650 501-0889
  Avon *(G-788)*

Sonoco Products Company................ D 937 429-0040
  Beavercreek Township *(G-1094)*

▲ Strata-Tac Inc................................. F 630 879-9388
  Troy *(G-14613)*

Systems Pack Inc............................. E 330 467-5729
  Macedonia *(G-9583)*

Truechoicepack Corp......................... F 937 630-3832
  West Chester *(G-15519)*

Zebco Industries Inc.......................... F 740 654-4510
  Lancaster *(G-9049)*

5122 Drugs, proprietaries, and sundries

American Regent Inc......................... D 614 436-2222
  Hilliard *(G-8397)*

◆ Beautyavenues LLC.........................C 614 856-6000
  Reynoldsburg *(G-12754)*

Beiersdorf Inc.................................... C 513 682-7300
  West Chester *(G-15541)*

◆ Boxout LLC......................................C 833 462-7746
  Hudson *(G-8587)*

Buderer Drug Company Inc............... E 419 627-2800
  Sandusky *(G-13046)*

Cardinal Health Inc............................ E 614 553-3830
  Dublin *(G-6871)*

Cardinal Health Inc............................ G 614 757-2863
  Lewis Center *(G-9155)*

◆ Cardinal Health Inc..........................A 614 757-5000
  Dublin *(G-6872)*

Direct Action Co Inc.......................... F 330 364-3219
  Dover *(G-6815)*

▼ ICM Distributing Company Inc......... E 234 212-3030
  Twinsburg *(G-14675)*

▲ Nehemiah Manufacturing Co LLC..... D 513 351-5700
  Cincinnati *(G-3185)*

Omnicare Phrm of Midwest LLC......... D 513 719-2600
  Cincinnati *(G-3222)*

Optum Infusion Svcs 550 LLC............ D 866 442-4679
  Cincinnati *(G-3227)*

River City Pharma............................. F 513 870-1680
  Fairfield *(G-7403)*

Samuels Products Inc........................ E 513 891-4456
  Blue Ash *(G-1464)*

Sysco Guest Supply LLC................... E 440 960-2515
  Lorain *(G-9440)*

Teva Womens Health LLC.................. C 513 731-9900
  Cincinnati *(G-3446)*

Walter F Stephens Jr Inc................... E 937 746-0521
  Franklin *(G-7709)*

5131 Piece goods and notions

▲ Custom Products Corporation.......... D 440 528-7100
  Solon *(G-13334)*

Cyber Shed Inc................................. G 419 724-5855
  Toledo *(G-14256)*

▲ Mmi Textiles Inc.............................. G 440 899-8050
  Brooklyn *(G-1679)*

Purebuttonscom LLC......................... F 330 721-1600
  Medina *(G-10367)*

▲ Strata-Tac Inc................................. F 630 879-9388
  Troy *(G-14613)*

Style-Line Incorporated..................... E 614 291-0600
  Columbus *(G-5796)*

Sysco Guest Supply LLC................... E 440 960-2515
  Lorain *(G-9440)*

▲ Tlg Cochran Inc............................... E 440 914-1122
  Twinsburg *(G-14744)*

5136 Men's and boy's clothing

▲ Barbs Graffiti Inc............................. E 216 881-5550
  Cleveland *(G-3719)*

Cintas Sales Corporation................... B 513 459-1200
  Cincinnati *(G-2771)*

Design Original Inc............................ F 937 596-5121
  Jackson Center *(G-8731)*

Digitek Corp...................................... F 513 794-3190
  Mason *(G-9984)*

▲ Hands On International LLC............ G 513 502-9000
  West Chester *(G-15560)*

Identity Group LLC........................... G 614 337-6167
  Westerville *(G-15658)*

▲ McCc Sportswear Inc....................... G 513 583-9210
  West Chester *(G-15569)*

Precision Imprint............................... G 740 592-5916
  Athens *(G-692)*

R & A Sports Inc............................... E 216 289-2254
  Euclid *(G-7297)*

Rbr Enterprises LLC.......................... F 866 437-9327
  Brecksville *(G-1630)*

Unisport Inc....................................... F 419 529-4727
  Ontario *(G-12096)*

Walter F Stephens Jr Inc................... E 937 746-0521
  Franklin *(G-7709)*

▲ West Chester Holdings LLC............. C 513 705-2100
  Cincinnati *(G-3516)*

5137 Women's and children's clothing

▲ Barbs Graffiti Inc............................. E 216 881-5550
  Cleveland *(G-3719)*

Cintas Sales Corporation................... B 513 459-1200
  Cincinnati *(G-2771)*

Design Original Inc............................ F 937 596-5121
  Jackson Center *(G-8731)*

Digitek Corp...................................... F 513 794-3190
  Mason *(G-9984)*

Fluff Boutique................................... G 513 227-6614
  Cincinnati *(G-2911)*

K Ventures Inc.................................. F 419 678-2308
  Coldwater *(G-4994)*

▲ McCc Sportswear Inc....................... G 513 583-9210
  West Chester *(G-15569)*

◆ Philips Med Systems Clvland In.......B 440 483-3000
  Cleveland *(G-4547)*

Precision Imprint............................... G 740 592-5916
  Athens *(G-692)*

R & A Sports Inc............................... E 216 289-2254
  Euclid *(G-7297)*

Rbr Enterprises LLC.......................... F 866 437-9327
  Brecksville *(G-1630)*

Unisport Inc....................................... F 419 529-4727
  Ontario *(G-12096)*

▲ West Chester Holdings LLC............. C 513 705-2100
  Cincinnati *(G-3516)*

▲ Zimmer Enterprises Inc................... E 937 428-1057
  Dayton *(G-6663)*

5139 Footwear

Careismatic Brands LLC.................... G 561 843-8727
  Groveport *(G-8135)*

Georgia-Boot Inc............................... D 740 753-1951
  Nelsonville *(G-11356)*

Sysco Guest Supply LLC................... E 440 960-2515
  Lorain *(G-9440)*

US Footwear Holdings LLC................ C 740 753-9100
  Nelsonville *(G-11360)*

5141 Groceries, general line

Brantley Partners IV LP..................... G 216 464-8400
  Cleveland *(G-3754)*

Comber Holdings Inc......................... E 216 961-8600
  Cleveland *(G-3886)*

La Perla Inc....................................... G 419 534-2074
  Toledo *(G-14356)*

▲ R S Hanline and Co Inc................... C 419 347-8077
  Shelby *(G-13199)*

Ricking Holding Co............................ E 513 825-3551
  Cleveland *(G-4633)*

The Ellenbee-Leggett Company Inc... C 513 874-3200
  Fairfield *(G-7417)*

5142 Packaged frozen goods

A To Z Portion Ctrl Meats Inc............. E 419 358-2926
  Bluffton *(G-1498)*

Dee-Jays Cstm Btchring Proc LL........ F 740 694-7492
  Fredericktown *(G-7743)*

Foodies Vegan Ltd............................ F 513 487-3037
  Cincinnati *(G-2913)*

Frank Brunckhorst Company LLC...... G 614 662-5300
  Groveport *(G-8142)*

King Kold Inc.................................... E 937 836-2731
  Englewood *(G-7235)*

Lori Holding Co.................................. E 740 342-3230
  New Lexington *(G-11453)*

The Ellenbee-Leggett Company Inc... C 513 874-3200
  Fairfield *(G-7417)*

◆ White Castle System Inc..................B 614 228-5781
  Columbus *(G-5876)*

5143 Dairy products, except dried or canned

Acme Steak & Seafood Inc................ F 330 270-8000
  Youngstown *(G-16303)*

Bfc Inc.. E 330 364-6645
  Dover *(G-6809)*

Borden Dairy Co Cincinnati LLC......... E 513 948-8811
  Cleveland *(G-3748)*

Cheese Holdings Inc......................... E 330 893-2479
  Millersburg *(G-10951)*

Country Parlour Ice Cream Co........... F 440 237-4040
  Cleveland *(G-3908)*

Frank L Harter & Son Inc................... E 513 574-1330
  Cincinnati *(G-2920)*

Grays Orange Barn Inc..................... G 419 568-2718
  Wapakoneta *(G-15116)*

◆ Great Lakes Cheese Co Inc..............B 440 834-2500
  Hiram *(G-8485)*

▲ Hans Rothenbuhler & Son Inc.......... E 440 632-6000
  Middlefield *(G-10753)*

51 WHOLESALE TRADE - NONDURABLE GOODS

Instantwhip Connecticut Inc .... F 614 488-2536
  Columbus *(G-5463)*

Instantwhip Foods Inc .... F 614 488-2536
  Columbus *(G-5464)*

Instantwhip Products Co PA .... F 614 488-2536
  Columbus *(G-5465)*

Instantwhip-Buffalo Inc .... F 614 488-2536
  Columbus *(G-5466)*

Instantwhip-Columbus Inc .... E 614 871-9447
  Grove City *(G-8098)*

▲ Instantwhip-Dayton Inc .... G 937 235-5930
  Dayton *(G-6384)*

Johnsons Real Ice Cream LLC .... C 614 231-0014
  Columbus *(G-5500)*

Lori Holding Co .... E 740 342-3230
  New Lexington *(G-11453)*

Louis Instantwhip-St Inc .... F 614 488-2536
  Columbus *(G-5535)*

Philadelphia Instantwhip Inc .... F 614 488-2536
  Columbus *(G-5672)*

Snowville Creamery LLC .... E 740 698-2301
  Pomeroy *(G-12614)*

United Dairy Farmers Inc .... C 513 396-8700
  Cincinnati *(G-3479)*

Velvet Ice Cream Company .... E 419 562-2009
  Bucyrus *(G-1872)*

▲ Weaver Bros Inc .... D 937 526-3907
  Versailles *(G-14992)*

5144 Poultry and poultry products

▼ Ballas Egg Products Corp .... D 614 453-0386
  Zanesville *(G-16504)*

Bfc Inc .... E 330 364-6645
  Dover *(G-6809)*

Borden Dairy Co Cincinnati LLC .... E 513 948-8811
  Cleveland *(G-3748)*

Frank L Harter & Son Inc .... G 513 574-1330
  Cincinnati *(G-2920)*

Just Natural Provision Company .... G 216 431-7922
  Cleveland *(G-4267)*

▲ Ohio Fresh Eggs LLC .... G 740 893-7200
  Croton *(G-6052)*

Roots Poultry Inc .... F 419 332-0041
  Fremont *(G-7805)*

5145 Confectionery

▲ Bendon Inc .... D 419 207-3600
  Ashland *(G-556)*

Bloomer Candy Co .... C 740 452-7501
  Zanesville *(G-16511)*

CJ Dannemiller Co .... E 330 825-7808
  Norton *(G-11939)*

Esther Price Candies Corporation .... E 937 253-2121
  Dayton *(G-6324)*

Gehm & Sons Limited .... G 330 724-8423
  Akron *(G-164)*

◆ Gold Medal Products Co .... B 513 769-7676
  Cincinnati *(G-2962)*

Gorant Chocolatier LLC .... C 330 726-8821
  Boardman *(G-1513)*

▲ Hayden Valley Foods Inc .... D 614 539-7233
  Urbancrest *(G-14853)*

Hen of Woods LLC .... G 513 954-8871
  Cincinnati *(G-2993)*

Humphrey Popcorn Company .... F 216 662-6629
  Strongsville *(G-13843)*

International Leisure Activities Inc .... G
  Springfield *(G-13582)*

◆ Jml Holdings Inc .... E 419 866-7500
  Holland *(G-8515)*

Jones Potato Chip Co .... E 419 529-9424
  Mansfield *(G-9674)*

Linneas Candy Supplies Inc .... E 330 678-7112
  Kent *(G-8828)*

Mike-Sells Potato Chip Co .... E 937 228-9400
  Dayton *(G-6447)*

Mike-Sells West Virginia Inc .... D 937 228-9400
  Dayton *(G-6448)*

Nuts Are Good Inc .... F 586 619-2400
  Columbus *(G-5608)*

Ohio Hckry Hrvest Brnd Pdts In .... E 330 644-6266
  Coventry Township *(G-6014)*

Robert E McGrath Inc .... F 440 572-7747
  Strongsville *(G-13872)*

◆ Shearers Foods LLC .... A 800 428-6843
  Massillon *(G-10142)*

Sweeties Olympia Treats LLC .... F 440 572-7747
  Strongsville *(G-13888)*

Tarrier Foods Corp .... E 614 876-8594
  Columbus *(G-5810)*

5146 Fish and seafoods

Acme Steak & Seafood Inc .... F 330 270-8000
  Youngstown *(G-16303)*

Alsatian Llc .... G 330 661-0600
  Medina *(G-10293)*

5147 Meats and meat products

Acme Steak & Seafood Inc .... F 330 270-8000
  Youngstown *(G-16303)*

Caven and Sons Meat Packing Co .... F 937 368-3841
  Conover *(G-5935)*

Cheese Holdings Inc .... E 330 893-2479
  Millersburg *(G-10951)*

Empire Packing Company LP .... D 513 942-5400
  West Chester *(G-15551)*

Fink Meat Company Inc .... G 937 390-2750
  Springfield *(G-13564)*

◆ Fresh Mark Inc .... B 330 832-7491
  Massillon *(G-10097)*

John Krusinski .... F 216 441-0100
  Cleveland *(G-4258)*

Lori Holding Co .... E 740 342-3230
  New Lexington *(G-11453)*

Marshallville Packing Co Inc .... F 330 855-2871
  Marshallville *(G-9893)*

North Country Charcuterie LLC .... F 614 670-5726
  Columbus *(G-5602)*

The Ellenbee-Leggett Company Inc ..... C 513 874-3200
  Fairfield *(G-7417)*

Tri-State Beef Co Inc .... F 513 579-1722
  Cincinnati *(G-3464)*

Winner Corporation .... E 419 582-4321
  Yorkshire *(G-16293)*

5148 Fresh fruits and vegetables

Bfc Inc .... E 330 364-6645
  Dover *(G-6809)*

Big Gus Onion Rings Inc .... F 216 883-9045
  Cleveland *(G-3735)*

C J Kraft Enterprises Inc .... G 740 653-9606
  Lancaster *(G-8997)*

Chefs Garden Inc .... C 419 433-4947
  Huron *(G-8630)*

Dno Inc .... D 614 231-3601
  Columbus *(G-5334)*

Dole Fresh Vegetables Inc .... C 937 525-4300
  Springfield *(G-13556)*

Frank L Harter & Son Inc .... G 513 574-1330
  Cincinnati *(G-2920)*

Freshway Foods Company Inc .... D 937 498-4664
  Sidney *(G-13249)*

Grays Orange Barn Inc .... G 419 568-2718
  Wapakoneta *(G-15116)*

Produce Packaging Inc .... C 216 391-6129
  Willoughby Hills *(G-16027)*

5149 Groceries and related products, nec

Acme Steak & Seafood Inc .... F 330 270-8000
  Youngstown *(G-16303)*

American Bottling Company .... C 614 237-4201
  Columbus *(G-5121)*

◆ Amerihua Intl Entps Inc .... G 740 549-0300
  Lewis Center *(G-9148)*

▲ Bendon Inc .... D 419 207-3600
  Ashland *(G-556)*

Bread Kneads Inc .... G 419 422-3863
  Findlay *(G-7486)*

Brew Kettle Inc .... F 440 234-8788
  Strongsville *(G-13817)*

Busken Bakery Inc .... D 513 871-2114
  Cincinnati *(G-2695)*

Cassanos Inc .... E 937 294-8400
  Dayton *(G-6248)*

Central Coca-Cola Btlg Co Inc .... C 419 476-6622
  Toledo *(G-14230)*

Cheese Holdings Inc .... E 330 893-2479
  Millersburg *(G-10951)*

Coopers Mill Inc .... F 419 562-4215
  Bucyrus *(G-1854)*

Distillata Company .... D 216 771-2900
  Cleveland *(G-3962)*

Ditsch Usa LLC .... E 513 782-8888
  Cincinnati *(G-2830)*

Food Plant Engineering LLC .... F 513 618-3165
  Blue Ash *(G-1396)*

G & J Pepsi-Cola Bottlers Inc .... E 740 593-3366
  Athens *(G-683)*

G & J Pepsi-Cola Bottlers Inc .... B 740 354-9191
  Franklin Furnace *(G-7712)*

G & J Pepsi-Cola Bottlers Inc .... E 740 354-9191
  Zanesville *(G-16534)*

Grace Juice Company LLC .... F 614 398-6879
  Westerville *(G-15707)*

▲ Hayden Valley Foods Inc .... D 614 539-7233
  Urbancrest *(G-14853)*

Iron Bean Inc .... F 518 641-9917
  Perrysburg *(G-12393)*

James C Robinson .... G 513 969-7482
  Cincinnati *(G-3036)*

JM Smucker LLC .... D 330 682-3000
  Orrville *(G-12132)*

▲ Kaiser Foods Inc .... E 513 621-2053
  Cincinnati *(G-3058)*

Kerry Inc .... E 760 685-2548
  Byesville *(G-1899)*

Klosterman Baking Co LLC .... D 513 242-5667
  Cincinnati *(G-3081)*

Lifestyle Nutraceuticals Ltd .... G 513 376-7218
  Cincinnati *(G-3105)*

Luxfer Magtech Inc .... E 513 772-3066
  Cincinnati *(G-3116)*

Michael Zakany LLC .... G 740 221-3934
  Zanesville *(G-16545)*

▲ More Than Gourmet Holdings Inc .... E 330 762-6652
  Akron *(G-253)*

Morton Salt Inc .... C 330 925-3015
  Rittman *(G-12825)*

▲ Muscle Feast LLC .... F 740 877-8808
  Nashport *(G-11339)*

▲ National Foods Packaging Inc .... E 216 622-2740
  Cleveland *(G-4437)*

Natures Health Food LLC .... F 419 260-9265
  Mount Victory *(G-11301)*

Norcia Bakery .... F 330 454-1077
  Canton *(G-2174)*

Obhc Inc... G..... 440 236-5112
  Columbia Station (G-5015)
Ohio Coffee Collaborative Ltd................ F..... 614 564-9852
  Columbus (G-5613)
Ohio Hckry Hrvest Brnd Pdts In.............. E..... 330 644-6266
  Coventry Township (G-6014)
Osmans Pies Inc.................................... E..... 330 607-9083
  Stow (G-13716)
Pepsi-Cola Metro Btlg Co Inc................. E..... 937 461-4664
  Dayton (G-6501)
Pepsi-Cola Metro Btlg Co Inc................. F..... 440 323-5524
  Elyria (G-7193)
Pepsi-Cola Metro Btlg Co Inc................. C..... 330 425-8236
  Twinsburg (G-14711)
Rambasek Realty Inc............................. F..... 937 228-1189
  Dayton (G-6540)
Richards Maple Products Inc................. G..... 440 286-4160
  Chardon (G-2466)
▲ Skyline Cem Holdings LLC................ C..... 513 874-1188
  Fairfield (G-7408)
Stumps Converting Inc.......................... F..... 419 492-2542
  New Washington (G-11551)
Tarrier Foods Corp................................ E..... 614 876-8594
  Columbus (G-5810)
Thurns Bakery & Deli............................. F..... 614 221-9246
  Columbus (G-5825)
Tiffin Paper Company............................ F..... 419 447-2121
  Tiffin (G-14111)
Unger Kosher Bakery Inc....................... F..... 216 321-7176
  Cleveland Heights (G-4944)
Walnut Creek Chocolate Co Inc............. E..... 330 893-2995
  Walnut Creek (G-15096)
Wheeling Coffee & Spice Co.................. F..... 304 232-0141
  Saint Clairsville (G-12763)

5153 Grain and field beans

Andersons Inc....................................... G..... 419 536-0460
  Toledo (G-14194)
Andersons Inc....................................... C..... 419 893-5050
  Maumee (G-10165)
Cooper Hatchery Inc............................. C..... 419 594-3325
  Oakwood (G-12030)
Countyline Co-Op Inc............................. F..... 419 287-3241
  Pemberville (G-12334)
Fort Recovery Equity Inc....................... E..... 419 375-4119
  Fort Recovery (G-7616)
Hanby Farms Inc................................... E..... 740 763-3554
  Nashport (G-11337)
Keystone Cooperative Inc..................... G..... 937 884-5526
  Verona (G-14975)
Legacy Farmers Cooperative................. F..... 419 423-2611
  Findlay (G-7528)
Mid-Wood Inc... F..... 419 257-3331
  North Baltimore (G-11696)
Minster Farmers Coop Exch.................. D..... 419 628-4705
  Minster (G-11056)
▼ Mullet Enterprises Inc........................ G..... 330 852-4681
  Sugarcreek (G-13932)
Pettisville Grain Co................................ E..... 419 446-2547
  Pettisville (G-12452)
Premier Feeds LLC................................ G..... 937 584-2411
  Sabina (G-12891)
▲ Simmons Feed & Supply LLC............ E..... 800 754-1228
  Salem (G-13031)
Sunrise Cooperative Inc........................ G..... 419 628-4705
  Minster (G-11062)
Van Tilburg Farms Inc........................... F..... 419 586-3077
  Celina (G-2354)

5154 Livestock

Gardner Lumber Company Inc.............. F..... 740 254-4664
  Tippecanoe (G-14170)

Werling and Sons Inc............................ F..... 937 338-3281
  Burkettsville (G-1879)
Winner Corporation............................... E..... 419 582-4321
  Yorkshire (G-16293)

5159 Farm-product raw materials, nec

G A Wintzer and Son Company.............. F..... 419 739-4900
  Wapakoneta (G-15112)
Griffin Industries LLC............................. F..... 513 549-0041
  Blue Ash (G-1400)
Inland Products Inc............................... E..... 614 443-3425
  Columbus (G-5460)

5162 Plastics materials and basic shapes

Allied Shipping and Packa..................... F..... 937 222-7422
  Moraine (G-11155)
Alro Steel Corporation........................... E..... 614 878-7271
  Columbus (G-5116)
Alro Steel Corporation........................... D..... 419 720-5300
  Toledo (G-14184)
Ampacet Corporation............................. F..... 513 247-5400
  Cincinnati (G-2625)
♦ Avient Corporation.............................. D..... 440 930-1000
  Avon Lake (G-797)
♦ Bay State Polymer Distribution Inc...... F..... 440 892-8500
  Westlake (G-15736)
♦ Carney Plastics Inc............................. G..... 330 746-8273
  Youngstown (G-16331)
♦ Cleveland Supplyone Inc..................... E..... 216 514-7000
  Cleveland (G-3857)
Epsilyte Holdings LLC............................ D..... 937 778-9500
  Piqua (G-12515)
Hexpol Compounding LLC..................... C..... 440 834-4644
  Burton (G-1880)
HP Manufacturing Company Inc............ D..... 216 361-6500
  Cleveland (G-4204)
♦ Network Polymers Inc......................... E..... 330 773-2700
  Akron (G-261)
Plastics Family Holdings Inc.................. F..... 614 272-0777
  Columbus (G-5680)
Plastics R Unique Inc............................. E..... 330 334-4820
  Wadsworth (G-15053)
♦ Polymer Packaging Inc....................... D..... 330 832-2000
  North Canton (G-11751)
Queen City Polymers Inc....................... E..... 513 779-0990
  West Chester (G-15492)
Skybox Packaging LLC........................... C..... 419 525-7209
  Mansfield (G-9719)
Tahoma Enterprises Inc......................... D..... 330 745-9016
  Barberton (G-897)
▼ Tahoma Rubber & Plastics Inc............ D..... 330 745-9016
  Barberton (G-898)
Total Plastics Resources LLC................. G..... 440 891-1140
  Cleveland (G-4810)
United States Plastic Corp..................... D..... 419 228-2242
  Lima (G-9299)
Univar Solutions USA LLC...................... F..... 800 531-7106
  Dublin (G-6956)
UPL International Inc............................. E..... 330 433-2860
  North Canton (G-11773)

5169 Chemicals and allied products, nec

AIN Industries Inc.................................. G..... 440 781-0950
  Cleveland (G-3616)
Airgas Usa LLC...................................... G..... 937 222-8312
  Moraine (G-11154)
Airgas Usa LLC...................................... G..... 440 232-6397
  Twinsburg (G-14625)
♦ Akrochem Corporation........................ D..... 330 535-2100
  Akron (G-26)
Aquablue Incorporated.......................... G..... 330 343-0220
  New Philadelphia (G-11484)

Ashland Chemco Inc.............................. C..... 614 790-3333
  Columbus (G-5156)
Bleachtech LLC..................................... E..... 216 921-1980
  Seville (G-13139)
Brewpro Inc... G..... 513 577-7200
  Cincinnati (G-2682)
▲ Calvary Industries Inc........................ E..... 513 874-1113
  Fairfield (G-7342)
▼ Ccp Industries Inc.............................. B..... 216 535-4227
  Richmond Heights (G-12807)
Chem-Sales Inc...................................... F
  Toledo (G-14235)
Chemcore Inc.. F..... 937 228-6118
  Dayton (G-6253)
▲ Chemical Solvents Inc........................ E..... 216 741-9310
  Cleveland (G-3816)
♦ Chemmasters Inc................................ E..... 440 428-2105
  Madison (G-9589)
Cleaning Lady Inc.................................. G..... 419 589-5566
  Mansfield (G-9638)
Consolidated Coatings Corp.................. A..... 216 514-7596
  Cleveland (G-3898)
Corrugated Chemicals Inc..................... G..... 513 561-7773
  Cincinnati (G-2798)
D W Dickey and Son Inc........................ C..... 330 424-1441
  Lisbon (G-9311)
♦ Dover Chemical Corporation................ C..... 330 343-7711
  Dover (G-6818)
▲ Electro Prime Group LLC..................... D..... 419 476-0100
  Toledo (G-14273)
Environmental Chemical Corp................ F..... 330 453-5200
  Uniontown (G-14782)
Finale Products Inc................................ G..... 419 874-2662
  Perrysburg (G-12381)
Flex Technologies Inc............................ D..... 330 897-6311
  Baltic (G-836)
Formlabs Ohio Inc.................................. E..... 419 837-9783
  Millbury (G-10932)
Gehm & Sons Limited............................ G..... 330 724-8423
  Akron (G-164)
▲ Goldsmith & Eggleton Inc................... F..... 330 336-6616
  Wadsworth (G-15032)
▲ Goldsmith & Eggleton LLC.................. F..... 203 855-6000
  Wadsworth (G-15033)
Hexion Inc.. C..... 888 443-9466
  Columbus (G-5428)
♦ Hickman Williams & Company............. F..... 513 621-1946
  Cincinnati (G-2998)
▲ Imcd Us LLC....................................... E..... 216 228-8900
  Westlake (G-15760)
Jerrys Welding Supply Inc..................... G..... 937 364-1500
  Hillsboro (G-8460)
♦ Knight Material Tech LLC.................... D..... 330 488-1651
  East Canton (G-6979)
Kraton Polymers US LLC........................ B..... 740 423-7571
  Belpre (G-1257)
Love Laugh & Laundry........................... G..... 567 377-1951
  Toledo (G-14370)
Mantaline Corporation........................... G..... 330 274-2264
  Mantua (G-9739)
Maroon Intrmdiate Holdings LLC............ G..... 440 937-1000
  Avon (G-781)
♦ McGill Corporation.............................. F..... 614 829-1200
  Groveport (G-8153)
▲ Mesocoat Inc..................................... F..... 216 453-0866
  Euclid (G-7286)
▲ National Colloid Company................... E..... 740 282-1171
  Steubenville (G-13673)
National Polymer Inc.............................. F..... 440 708-1245
  Chagrin Falls (G-2409)
Netherland Rubber Company................. F..... 513 733-0883
  Cincinnati (G-3187)

51 WHOLESALE TRADE - NONDURABLE GOODS

Novagard Solutions Inc............................ C 216 881-8111
  Cleveland *(G-4483)*

▲ Phoenix Technologies Intl LLC.............. E 419 353-7738
  Bowling Green *(G-1583)*

▼ Polar Inc.. F 937 297-0911
  Moraine *(G-11201)*

Polymer Additives Holdings Inc................ C 216 875-7200
  Independence *(G-8680)*

PVS Chemical Solutions Inc..................... F 330 666-0888
  Copley *(G-5955)*

▲ Quality Borate Co LLC........................... F 216 896-1949
  Cleveland *(G-4604)*

◆ Rhein Chemie Corporation.....................C 440 279-2367
  Chardon *(G-2465)*

◆ Shin-Etsu Silicones of America Inc.......C 330 630-9460
  Akron *(G-328)*

Sigma-Aldrich Corporation........................ D 216 206-5424
  Cleveland *(G-4701)*

▼ Singleton Corporation............................. F 216 651-7800
  Cleveland *(G-4703)*

◆ Tembec Btlsr Inc..................................... E 419 244-5856
  Toledo *(G-14483)*

▲ Toagosei America Inc............................. D 614 718-3855
  West Jefferson *(G-15615)*

◆ Tosoh America Inc.................................. B 614 539-8622
  Grove City *(G-8124)*

◆ Tricor Industrial Inc................................. D 330 264-3299
  Wooster *(G-16178)*

▲ United McGill Corporation....................... E 614 829-1200
  Groveport *(G-8165)*

Univar Solutions USA LLC........................ F 800 531-7106
  Dublin *(G-6956)*

Univar Solutions USA LLC........................ F 513 714-5264
  West Chester *(G-15602)*

▼ Washing Systems LLC............................C 800 272-1974
  Loveland *(G-9509)*

5171 Petroleum bulk stations and terminals

Cincinnati - Vulcan Company.................... D 513 242-5300
  Cincinnati *(G-2736)*

Universal Oil Inc.. E 216 771-4300
  Cleveland *(G-4851)*

5172 Petroleum products, nec

American Ultra Specialties Inc.................. F 330 656-5000
  Hudson *(G-8584)*

Centerra Co-Op... E 419 281-2153
  Ashland *(G-562)*

D W Dickey and Son Inc.......................... C 330 424-1441
  Lisbon *(G-9311)*

Digilube Systems Inc................................ F 937 748-2209
  Springboro *(G-13499)*

Eni USA R&M Co Inc............................... F 330 723-6457
  Medina *(G-10320)*

▼ Functional Products Inc.......................... F 330 963-3060
  Macedonia *(G-9552)*

Gfl Environmental Svcs USA Inc.............. E 614 441-4001
  Columbus *(G-5401)*

Grand Aire Inc... E 419 861-6700
  Swanton *(G-13974)*

◆ Knight Material Tech LLC....................... D 330 488-1651
  East Canton *(G-6979)*

Lubriplate Lubricants Company................ G 419 691-2491
  Toledo *(G-14372)*

◆ Marathon Petroleum Company LP......... F 419 422-2121
  Findlay *(G-7532)*

▲ Marathon Petroleum Corporation.......... A 419 422-2121
  Findlay *(G-7533)*

Minster Farmers Coop Exch..................... D 419 628-4705
  Minster *(G-11056)*

Mplx Terminals LLC.................................. D 330 479-5539
  Canton *(G-2167)*

▼ Polar Inc.. F 937 297-0911
  Moraine *(G-11201)*

Sunrise Cooperative Inc............................ G 419 628-4705
  Minster *(G-11062)*

5181 Beer and ale

Frontwaters Rest & Brewing Co................ G 419 798-8058
  Marblehead *(G-9765)*

Wild Ohio Brewing Company.................... G 614 262-0000
  Columbus *(G-5877)*

5182 Wine and distilled beverages

Blue Collar M LLC..................................... F 216 209-5666
  Solon *(G-13320)*

Old Firehouse Winery Inc......................... E 440 466-9300
  Geneva *(G-7943)*

▲ Paramount Distillers Inc......................... B 216 671-6300
  Cleveland *(G-4522)*

Sandra Weddington.................................... F 740 417-4286
  Delaware *(G-6749)*

Veriano Fine Foods Spirits Ltd.................. F 614 745-7705
  New Albany *(G-11394)*

Watershed Distillery LLC........................... E 614 357-1936
  Columbus *(G-5866)*

Wedco LLC.. G 513 309-0781
  Mount Orab *(G-11247)*

5191 Farm supplies

A Best Trmt & Pest Ctrl Sups................... G 330 434-5555
  Akron *(G-10)*

Andersons Inc.. G 419 536-0460
  Toledo *(G-14194)*

Andersons Inc.. C 419 893-5050
  Maumee *(G-10165)*

Cooper Farms Inc...................................... D 419 375-4116
  Fort Recovery *(G-7614)*

Countyline Co-Op Inc................................ F 419 287-3241
  Pemberville *(G-12334)*

Darling Ingredients Inc.............................. G 216 651-9300
  Cleveland *(G-3940)*

Gerald Grain Center Inc............................ E 419 445-2451
  Archbold *(G-529)*

Granville Milling Co................................... G 740 345-1305
  Newark *(G-11578)*

Green Field Farms Co-Op......................... G 330 263-0246
  Wooster *(G-16126)*

H Hafner & Sons Inc................................. E 513 321-1895
  Cincinnati *(G-2979)*

Hanby Farms Inc....................................... E 740 763-3554
  Nashport *(G-11337)*

Helena Agri-Enterprises LLC.................... G 614 275-4200
  Columbus *(G-5426)*

Helena Agri-Enterprises LLC.................... G 419 596-3806
  Continental *(G-5937)*

▲ Imcd Us LLC... E 216 228-8900
  Westlake *(G-15760)*

K M B Inc... E 330 889-3451
  Bristolville *(G-1652)*

Keynes Bros Inc.. D 740 385-6824
  Logan *(G-9366)*

Keystone Cooperative Inc......................... G 937 884-5526
  Verona *(G-14975)*

Land OLakes Inc....................................... E 330 879-2158
  Massillon *(G-10119)*

Legacy Farmers Cooperative.................... F 419 423-2611
  Findlay *(G-7528)*

Lesco Inc... F 740 633-6366
  Martins Ferry *(G-9899)*

Mennel Milling Company........................... E 740 385-6824
  Logan *(G-9371)*

Minster Farmers Coop Exch..................... D 419 628-4705
  Minster *(G-11056)*

Nutrien AG Solutions Inc.......................... G 614 873-4253
  Milford Center *(G-10929)*

Ohigro Inc.. E 740 726-2429
  Waldo *(G-15090)*

Phillips Ready Mix Co............................... E 937 426-5151
  Beavercreek Township *(G-1090)*

▲ Provimi North America Inc.................... B 937 770-2400
  Lewisburg *(G-9190)*

▼ Republic Mills Inc................................... E 419 758-3511
  Okolona *(G-12071)*

Ridley USA Inc... F 800 837-8222
  Botkins *(G-1543)*

Schlessman Seed Co................................ E 419 499-2572
  Milan *(G-10886)*

Stony Hill Mixing Ltd................................ G 330 674-0814
  Millersburg *(G-10995)*

Sunrise Cooperative Inc............................ G 419 628-4705
  Minster *(G-11062)*

XS Smith Inc... E 252 940-5060
  Cincinnati *(G-3533)*

5192 Books, periodicals, and newspapers

B & S Transport Inc.................................. G 330 767-4319
  Navarre *(G-11340)*

◆ Bookmasters Inc.....................................C 419 281-1802
  Ashland *(G-557)*

CSS Publishing Company......................... E 419 227-1818
  Lima *(G-9232)*

▲ Findaway World LLC.............................. E 440 893-0808
  Solon *(G-13349)*

Hecks Direct Mail & Prtg Svc.................... E 419 661-6028
  Toledo *(G-14314)*

Hubbard Company..................................... E 419 784-4455
  Defiance *(G-6682)*

McGraw-Hill Schl Edcatn Hldngs.............. A 419 207-7400
  Ashland *(G-591)*

▲ Zaner-Bloser Inc..................................... C 614 486-0221
  Columbus *(G-5892)*

5193 Flowers and florists supplies

Cleveland Plant and Flower Co................. G 614 478-9900
  Columbus *(G-5253)*

5194 Tobacco and tobacco products

◆ Scandinavian Tob Group Ln Ltd............C 770 934-4594
  Akron *(G-325)*

5198 Paints, varnishes, and supplies

Autobody Supply Company Inc................. D 614 228-4328
  Columbus *(G-5166)*

◆ Comex North America Inc..................... D 303 307-2100
  Cleveland *(G-3888)*

Finishmaster Inc.. F 614 228-4328
  Groveport *(G-8139)*

▲ Jmac Inc.. E 614 436-2418
  Columbus *(G-5498)*

Matrix Sys Auto Finishes LLC................... B 248 668-8135
  Massillon *(G-10125)*

Sherwin-Williams Mfg Co.......................... F 216 566-2000
  Cleveland *(G-4695)*

▲ Teknol Inc.. D 937 264-0190
  Dayton *(G-6613)*

◆ The Blonder Company.............................C 216 431-3560
  Cleveland *(G-4780)*

5199 Nondurable goods, nec

Ace Plastics Company.............................. G 330 928-7720
  Stow *(G-13680)*

▲ Acor Orthopaedic LLC............................ E 216 662-4500
  Cleveland *(G-3594)*

Ad-Sensations Inc..................................... F 419 841-5395
  Sylvania *(G-13989)*

52 BUILDING MATERIALS, HARDWARE, GARDEN SUPPLIES & MOBILE HOMES

▲ Advanced Poly-Packaging Inc............. C 330 785-4000
　Akron *(G-23)*
◆ Allied Shipping and Packa................... F 937 222-7422
　Moraine *(G-11155)*
　American Business Forms Inc............. E 513 312-2522
　West Chester *(G-15535)*
◆ Aquatic Technology............................ F 440 236-8330
　Columbia Station *(G-5005)*
▼ Armaly LLC.. E 740 852-3621
　London *(G-9381)*
◆ Associated Premium Corporation......E 513 679-4444
　Cincinnati *(G-2637)*
　Auto Dealer Designs Inc..................... E 330 374-7666
　Akron *(G-70)*
　B B Bradley Company Inc................... G 614 777-5600
　Columbus *(G-5171)*
◆ B D G Wrap-Tite Inc............................ E 440 349-5400
　Solon *(G-13315)*
▼ Baggallini Inc....................................... F 800 448-8753
　Pickerington *(G-12456)*
　Baker Plastics Inc................................ G 330 743-3142
　Youngstown *(G-16317)*
　Benchmark Prints................................ F 419 332-7640
　Fremont *(G-7766)*
　Berlin Truck Caps & Tarps Ltd............ F 330 893-2811
　Millersburg *(G-10944)*
　Blang Acquisition LLC.......................... F 937 223-2155
　Dayton *(G-6231)*
▲ Bottomline Ink Corporation............... E 419 897-8000
　Perrysburg *(G-12364)*
　BP 10 Inc... E 513 346-3900
　West Chester *(G-15382)*
　Cal Sales Embroidery.......................... G 440 236-3820
　Columbia Station *(G-5007)*
　Cambridge Packaging Inc................... E 740 432-3351
　Cambridge *(G-1925)*
　Canton Sterilized Wiping Cloth........... G 330 455-5179
　Canton *(G-2068)*
　Capehart Enterprises LLC................... F 614 769-7746
　Columbus *(G-5230)*
　Charizma Corp...................................... G 216 621-2220
　Cleveland *(G-3807)*
▲ Custom Products Corporation........... D 440 528-7100
　Solon *(G-13334)*
　Custom Sportswear Imprints LLC....... G 330 335-8326
　Wadsworth *(G-15024)*
　Diversified Products & Svcs................ F 740 393-6202
　Mount Vernon *(G-11270)*
　Ekco Cleaning Inc................................ C 513 733-8882
　Cincinnati *(G-2860)*
　Eleven 10 LLC....................................... F 888 216-4049
　Westlake *(G-15747)*
　Flashions Sportswear Ltd.................... G 937 323-5885
　Springfield *(G-13565)*
　Gary Lawrence Enterprises Inc........... G 330 833-7181
　Massillon *(G-10099)*
　Global Manufacturing Solutions......... F 937 236-8315
　Dayton *(G-6355)*
▲ Global-Pak Inc...................................... E 330 482-1993
　Lisbon *(G-9312)*
　Gq Business Products Inc................... G 513 792-4750
　Loveland *(G-9482)*
　Gt Industrial Supply Inc...................... G 513 771-7000
　Cincinnati *(G-2976)*
　Home City Ice Company..................... F 614 836-2877
　Groveport *(G-8146)*
▼ ICM Distributing Company Inc........... E 234 212-3030
　Twinsburg *(G-14675)*
　Identity Group LLC.............................. G 614 337-6167
　Westerville *(G-15658)*
　Johnson Bros Rubber Co Inc.............. E 419 752-4814
　Greenwich *(G-8067)*

◆ Johnson Bros Rubber Co..................... D 419 853-4122
　West Salem *(G-15634)*
　Kopco Graphics Inc............................. E 513 874-7230
　West Chester *(G-15456)*
　La Mfg Inc.. G 513 577-7200
　Cincinnati *(G-3094)*
　Lori Holding Co.................................... E 740 342-3230
　New Lexington *(G-11453)*
　Marathon Mfg & Sup Co...................... F 330 343-2656
　New Philadelphia *(G-11514)*
▲ Mazzolini Artcraft Co Inc.................... F 216 431-7529
　Cleveland *(G-4376)*
　Midwestern Bag Co Inc....................... G 419 241-3112
　Toledo *(G-14386)*
▲ Mosser Glass Inc................................. E 740 439-1827
　Cambridge *(G-1944)*
　Mr Emblem Inc...................................... G 419 697-1888
　Oregon *(G-12108)*
◆ Novelty Advertising Co Inc................. E 740 622-3113
　Coshocton *(G-5988)*
▲ Nucon International Inc...................... F 614 846-5710
　Columbus *(G-5607)*
　Ohio State Institute Fin Inc................ G 614 861-8811
　Reynoldsburg *(G-12770)*
▲ Papyrus-Recycled Greetings Inc........ D 773 348-6410
　Westlake *(G-15770)*
◆ Peter Graham Dunn Inc....................... E 330 816-0035
　Dalton *(G-6139)*
◆ Pfp Holdings LLC.................................. A 419 647-4191
　Spencerville *(G-13488)*
▲ Posterservice Incorporated................ G 513 577-7100
　Cincinnati *(G-3268)*
　Protective Packg Solutions LLC......... E 513 769-5777
　Cincinnati *(G-3306)*
　PS Superior Inc..................................... E 216 587-1000
　Cleveland *(G-4596)*
　Publishing Group Ltd.......................... F 614 572-1240
　Columbus *(G-5697)*
　Putnam Plastics Inc............................. G 937 866-6261
　Dayton *(G-6535)*
　Randd Assoc Prtg & Promotions........ G 937 294-1874
　Dayton *(G-6541)*
　Samb LLC Services.............................. G 937 660-0115
　Englewood *(G-7241)*
　Samuel Son & Co (usa) Inc................. D 740 522-2500
　Heath *(G-8331)*
　Scholz & Ey Engravers Inc................. F 614 444-8052
　Columbus *(G-5752)*
　Screen Works Inc................................ E 937 264-9111
　Dayton *(G-6564)*
　Sew & Sew Embroidery Inc................ F 330 676-1600
　Kent *(G-8863)*
▲ Shamrock Companies Inc................... D 440 899-9510
　Westlake *(G-15786)*
　Skybox Packaging LLC........................ C 419 525-7209
　Mansfield *(G-9719)*
　Solar Arts Graphic Designs................. G 330 744-0535
　Youngstown *(G-16441)*
▲ Solo Vino Imports Ltd......................... G 440 714-9591
　Vermilion *(G-14973)*
▲ Storopack Inc....................................... E 513 874-0314
　West Chester *(G-15592)*
　Systems Pack Inc................................ E 330 467-5729
　Macedonia *(G-9583)*
　T & L Custom Screening Inc............... G 937 237-3121
　Dayton *(G-6605)*
　Tahoma Enterprises Inc...................... D 330 745-9016
　Barberton *(G-897)*
▼ Tahoma Rubber & Plastics Inc.......... D 330 745-9016
　Barberton *(G-898)*
　Toga-Pak Inc... E 937 294-7311
　Dayton *(G-6626)*

　Traichal Construction Company......... E 800 255-3667
　Niles *(G-11689)*
　Tri-State Paper Inc.............................. F 937 885-3365
　Dayton *(G-6631)*
▲ Underground Sports Shop Inc........... F 513 751-1662
　Cincinnati *(G-3477)*
　Versa-Pak Ltd....................................... E 419 586-5466
　Celina *(G-2355)*
▲ Weaver Leather LLC............................ D 330 674-7548
　Millersburg *(G-11007)*
　White Tiger Inc..................................... F 740 852-4873
　London *(G-9397)*
　Wholesale Bait Co Inc......................... F 513 863-2380
　Fairfield *(G-7427)*
　Wilsons Country Creations Inc.......... G 330 377-4190
　Killbuck *(G-8926)*

52 BUILDING MATERIALS, HARDWARE, GARDEN SUPPLIES & MOBILE HOMES

5211 Lumber and other building materials

　A L Callahan Door Sales...................... G 419 884-3667
　Mansfield *(G-9620)*
　Ace Lumber Company......................... F 330 744-3167
　Youngstown *(G-16301)*
　Adams Brothers Inc............................. F 740 819-0323
　Zanesville *(G-16496)*
　Agean Marble Manufacturing............. F 513 874-1475
　West Chester *(G-15533)*
　Alside Inc.. D 419 865-0934
　Maumee *(G-10161)*
　American Concrete Products Inc........ F 937 224-1433
　Dayton *(G-6200)*
　American Platinum Door LLC............. G 440 497-6213
　Solon *(G-13312)*
　American Quality Door Co.................. G 330 296-0393
　Ravenna *(G-12705)*
　Architctral Mllwk Cbinetry Inc............ G 440 708-0086
　Chagrin Falls *(G-2389)*
　Associated Associates Inc................. E 330 626-3300
　Mantua *(G-9734)*
　Building Concepts Inc........................ F 419 298-2371
　Edgerton *(G-7072)*
　Cabinet Restylers Inc......................... D 419 281-8449
　Ashland *(G-561)*
　Cardinal Building Supply LLC............. G 614 706-4499
　Columbus *(G-5237)*
　Carter-Jones Lumber Company......... E 440 834-8164
　Middlefield *(G-10739)*
　Carter-Jones Lumber Company......... F 330 674-9060
　Millersburg *(G-10950)*
　Champion Window Co of Toledo....... E 419 841-0154
　Perrysburg *(G-12370)*
　Conover Lumber Company Inc.......... F 937 368-3010
　Conover *(G-5936)*
　Consumeracq Inc................................ E 440 277-9305
　Lorain *(G-9408)*
　Consumers Builders Supply Co......... G 440 277-9306
　Lorain *(G-9409)*
　Contract Lumber Inc............................ F 614 751-1109
　Columbus *(G-5289)*
　Counter Concepts Inc......................... F 330 848-4848
　Doylestown *(G-6853)*
　Cox Wood Product Inc........................ F 740 372-4735
　Otway *(G-12206)*
　Creative Products Inc......................... G 419 866-5501
　Holland *(G-8500)*
　Dale Kestler... G 513 871-9000
　Cincinnati *(G-2817)*

Employee Codes: A=Over 500 employees, B=251-500
C=101-250, D=51-100, E=20-50, F=10-19, G=1-9

52 BUILDING MATERIALS, HARDWARE, GARDEN SUPPLIES & MOBILE HOMES

Dearth Resources Inc .... G 937 325-0651
  Springfield (G-13551)
◆ Df Supply Inc .... E 330 650-9226
  Twinsburg (G-14650)
Double D D Mtls InstlItion Inc .... G 937 898-2534
  Dayton (G-6302)
Dowel Yoder & Molding .... G 330 231-2962
  Fredericksburg (G-7723)
E P Gerber & Sons Inc .... D 330 857-2021
  Kidron (G-8913)
Encore Precast LLC .... E 513 726-5678
  Seven Mile (G-13132)
Ernst Enterprises Inc .... E 614 443-9456
  Columbus (G-5358)
Ernst Enterprises Inc .... E 419 222-2015
  Lima (G-9241)
Euclid Jalousies Inc .... G 440 953-1112
  Cleveland (G-4034)
Everything In America .... G 347 871-6872
  Cleveland (G-4039)
▲ Feather Lite Innovations Inc .... E 937 743-9008
  Springboro (G-13501)
Gillard Construction Inc .... F 740 376-9744
  Marietta (G-9795)
Glen-Gery Corporation .... D 419 845-3321
  Caledonia (G-1915)
Gopowerx Inc .... F 440 707-6029
  Richfield (G-12789)
Grafton Ready Mix Concret Inc .... C 440 926-2911
  Grafton (G-8001)
Great Lakes Window Inc .... A 419 666-5555
  Walbridge (G-15082)
Gregory Stone Co Inc .... G 937 275-7455
  Dayton (G-6363)
Hardwood Store Inc .... G 937 864-2899
  Enon (G-7250)
Hazelbaker Industries Ltd .... F
  Columbus (G-5424)
Higgins Construction & Supply Co Inc ...... F 937 364-2331
  Hillsboro (G-8458)
Holmes Lumber & Bldg Ctr Inc .... E 330 479-8314
  Canton (G-2125)
Holmes Lumber & Bldg Ctr Inc .... C 330 674-9060
  Millersburg (G-10967)
Holmes Panel LLC .... G 330 897-5040
  Baltic (G-838)
Home Stor & Off Solutions Inc .... E 216 362-4660
  Cleveland (G-4199)
Huth Ready Mix & Supply Co .... E 330 833-4191
  Massillon (G-10108)
Jerry Harolds Doors Unlimited .... G 740 635-4949
  Bridgeport (G-1647)
Judy Mills Company Inc .... E 513 271-4241
  Cincinnati (G-3053)
K M B Inc .... E 330 889-3451
  Bristolville (G-1652)
Khempco Bldg Sup Co Ltd Partnr .... D 740 549-0465
  Delaware (G-6733)
Kinsella Manufacturing Co Inc .... F 513 561-5285
  Cincinnati (G-3077)
Koltcz Concrete Block Co .... E 440 232-3630
  Bedford (G-1132)
Laborie Enterprises LLC .... G 419 686-6245
  Portage (G-12634)
Laminate Shop .... F 740 749-3536
  Waterford (G-15237)
Lancaster W Side Coal Co Inc .... E 740 862-4713
  Lancaster (G-9021)
▲ Lang Stone Company Inc .... E 614 235-4099
  Columbus (G-5520)
Mack Industries .... E 419 353-7081
  Bowling Green (G-1572)

Marble Arch Products Inc .... G 937 746-8388
  Franklin (G-7685)
Marsh Industries Inc .... E 330 308-8667
  New Philadelphia (G-11515)
Medina Supply Company .... E 330 723-3681
  Medina (G-10352)
Menard Inc .... C 513 583-1444
  Loveland (G-9496)
Mohler Lumber Company .... E 330 499-5461
  North Canton (G-11744)
Nofziger Door Sales Inc .... F 419 445-2961
  Archbold (G-539)
▼ Nofziger Door Sales Inc .... C 419 337-9900
  Wauseon (G-15271)
▲ Ohio Tile & Marble Co .... E 513 541-4211
  Cincinnati (G-3217)
OK Brugmann Jr & Sons Inc .... F 330 274-2106
  Mantua (G-9741)
▲ Osborne Inc .... E 440 942-7000
  Mentor (G-10517)
Overhead Inc .... G 419 476-9100
  Toledo (G-14420)
P & T Millwork Inc .... F 440 543-2151
  Chagrin Falls (G-2412)
Pickens Window Service Inc .... F 513 931-4432
  Cincinnati (G-3255)
Pleasant Valley Ready Mix Inc .... G 330 852-2613
  Sugarcreek (G-13934)
Portsmouth Block Inc .... E 740 353-4113
  Portsmouth (G-12653)
Prairie Builders Supply Inc .... G 419 332-7546
  Fremont (G-7802)
Quikrete Companies LLC .... E 330 296-6080
  Ravenna (G-12729)
R C Moore Lumber Co .... F 740 732-4950
  Caldwell (G-1912)
Randy Lewis Inc .... F 330 784-0456
  Akron (G-296)
Rockwood Products Ltd .... E 330 893-2392
  Millersburg (G-10991)
◆ Saint-Gobain Norpro Corp .... C 330 673-5860
  Stow (G-13722)
Salem Mill & Cabinet Co .... G 330 337-9568
  Salem (G-13028)
Scioto Ready Mix LLC .... D 740 924-9273
  Pataskala (G-12308)
Seemray LLC .... E 440 536-8705
  Cleveland (G-4685)
Smyrna Ready Mix Concrete LLC .... E 937 855-0410
  Germantown (G-7952)
St Henry Tile Co Inc .... G 937 548-1101
  Greenville (G-8061)
St Henry Tile Co Inc .... E 419 678-4841
  Saint Henry (G-12938)
Stamm Contracting Company Inc .... E 330 274-8230
  Mantua (G-9743)
Stiber Fabricating Inc .... F 216 771-7210
  Cleveland (G-4735)
Stocker Concrete Company .... F 740 254-4626
  Gnadenhutten (G-7989)
T C Redi Mix Youngstown Inc .... E 330 755-2143
  Youngstown (G-16450)
Terry Lumber and Supply Co .... F 330 659-6800
  Peninsula (G-12342)
The F A Requarth Company .... E 937 224-1141
  Dayton (G-6618)
The Galehouse Companies Inc .... E 330 658-2023
  Doylestown (G-6854)
The Ideal Builders Supply .... F 216 741-1600
  Cleveland (G-4787)
▲ Thomas Do-It Center Inc .... E 740 446-2002
  Gallipolis (G-7903)

Toledo Window & Awning Inc .... F 419 474-3396
  Toledo (G-14509)
Tri-County Block and Brick Inc .... E 419 826-7060
  Swanton (G-13986)
Trumbull Cement Products Co .... G 330 372-4342
  Warren (G-15211)
◆ Walnut Creek Planing Ltd .... D 330 893-3244
  Millersburg (G-11005)
Warren Concrete and Supply Co .... E 330 393-1581
  Warren (G-15218)
Waxco International Inc .... F 937 746-4845
  Miamisburg (G-10701)
Westview Concrete Corp .... F 440 458-5800
  Elyria (G-7218)
Westview Concrete Corp .... E 440 235-1800
  Olmsted Falls (G-12084)
Wmg Wood More .... G 440 350-3970
  Painesville (G-12278)
Yoder Lumber Co Inc .... D 330 893-3131
  Sugarcreek (G-13949)
Youngstown Fence Incorporated .... G 330 788-8110
  Youngstown (G-16481)
Zaenkert Surveying Essentials .... G 513 738-2917
  Okeana (G-12070)

5231 Paint, glass, and wallpaper stores

A Service Glass Inc .... E 937 426-4920
  Beavercreek (G-1038)
All State GL Block Fctry Inc .... G 440 205-8410
  Mentor (G-10411)
American Indus Maintenance .... G 937 254-3400
  Dayton (G-6201)
Blockamerica Corporation .... G 614 274-0700
  Columbus (G-5201)
◆ Comex North America Inc .... D 303 307-2100
  Cleveland (G-3888)
Dale Kestler .... G 513 871-9000
  Cincinnati (G-2817)
▲ Franklin Art Glass Studios .... E 614 221-2972
  Columbus (G-5385)
Helios Quartz America Inc .... G 419 882-3377
  Sylvania (G-13999)
Middlefield Glass Incorporated .... F 440 632-5699
  Middlefield (G-10765)
Niles Mirror & Glass Inc .... E 330 652-6277
  Niles (G-11679)
Ohio Trailer Inc .... F 330 392-4444
  Warren (G-15196)
Oldcastle Buildingenvelope Inc .... D 800 537-4064
  Perrysburg (G-12411)
Prints & Paints Flr Cvg Co Inc .... E 419 462-5663
  Galion (G-7883)
Sherwin-Williams Company .... G 330 528-0124
  Hudson (G-8611)
Sherwin-Williams Company .... F 440 846-4328
  Strongsville (G-13880)
Sherwin-Williams Company .... A 216 566-2000
  Cleveland (G-4693)
◆ Sherwn-WIlams Auto Fnshes Corp .... E 216 332-8330
  Cleveland (G-4696)

5251 Hardware stores

Caldwell Lumber & Supply Co .... E 740 732-2306
  Caldwell (G-1908)
Cammel Saw Company .... F 330 477-3764
  Canton (G-2058)
D & M Saw & Tool Inc .... G 513 871-5433
  Cincinnati (G-2811)
E P Gerber & Sons Inc .... D 330 857-2021
  Kidron (G-8913)
Fountain Specialists Inc .... G 513 831-5717
  Milford (G-10906)

SIC SECTION

54 FOOD STORES

Gordon Tool Inc .... F 419 263-3151
   Payne *(G-12321)*

▲ Graco Ohio Inc .... D 330 494-1313
   North Canton *(G-11733)*

Hyde Park Lumber Company .... E 513 271-1500
   Cincinnati *(G-3013)*

Judy Mills Company Inc .... E 513 271-4241
   Cincinnati *(G-3053)*

Lochard Inc .... D 937 492-8811
   Sidney *(G-13261)*

Mapledale Farm Inc .... F 440 286-3389
   Chardon *(G-2458)*

▲ Matco Tools Corporation .... B 330 929-4949
   Stow *(G-13708)*

Mid-Wood Inc .... F 419 257-3331
   North Baltimore *(G-11696)*

National Tool & Equipment Inc .... F 330 629-8665
   Youngstown *(G-16403)*

◆ Oase North America Inc .... G 800 365-3880
   Aurora *(G-728)*

Rocky Hinge Inc .... G 330 539-6296
   Girard *(G-7974)*

S Lehman Central Warehouse .... G 330 828-8828
   Dalton *(G-6142)*

Simonds International LLC .... G 978 424-0100
   Kimbolton *(G-8928)*

Spencer Feed & Supply LLC .... F 330 648-2111
   Spencer *(G-13483)*

Stanley Industrial & Auto LLC .... C 614 755-7089
   Dublin *(G-6943)*

▲ Stanley Industrial & Auto LLC .... D 614 755-7000
   Dublin *(G-6944)*

Terry Lumber and Supply Co .... G 330 659-6800
   Peninsula *(G-12342)*

▲ Thomas Do-It Center Inc .... E 740 446-2002
   Gallipolis *(G-7903)*

Woodsfeld True Vlue HM Ctr Inc .... E 740 472-1651
   Woodsfield *(G-16090)*

5261 Retail nurseries and garden stores

All Power Equipment LLC .... F 740 593-3279
   Athens *(G-674)*

Bortnick Tractor Sales Inc .... F 330 924-2555
   Cortland *(G-5960)*

▼ Buckeye Tractor Corporation .... G 419 659-2162
   Columbus Grove *(G-5896)*

Centerra Co-Op .... E 419 281-2153
   Ashland *(G-562)*

Fountain Specialists Inc .... G 513 831-5717
   Milford *(G-10906)*

Insta-Gro Manufacturing Inc .... G 419 845-3046
   Caledonia *(G-1916)*

K M B Inc .... E 330 889-3451
   Bristolville *(G-1652)*

Karl Kuemmerling Inc .... F
   Massillon *(G-10114)*

Keystone Cooperative Inc .... G 937 884-5526
   Verona *(G-14975)*

Markers Inc .... G 440 933-5927
   Avon Lake *(G-816)*

Mid-Wood Inc .... F 419 257-3331
   North Baltimore *(G-11696)*

New Eezy-Gro Inc .... F 419 927-6110
   Upper Sandusky *(G-14817)*

Nutrien AG Solutions Inc .... G 614 873-4253
   Milford Center *(G-10929)*

Ohigro Inc .... E 740 726-2429
   Waldo *(G-15090)*

Ohio Drill & Tool Co .... E 330 525-7717
   Homeworth *(G-8555)*

Premier Feeds LLC .... G 937 584-2411
   Sabina *(G-12891)*

Riverview Productions Inc .... G 740 441-1150
   Gallipolis *(G-7900)*

▲ The Hc Companies Inc .... E 440 632-3333
   Twinsburg *(G-14743)*

Wilsons Country Creations Inc .... G 330 377-4190
   Killbuck *(G-8926)*

53 GENERAL MERCHANDISE STORES

5311 Department stores

Siemens Industry Inc .... E 513 576-2088
   Milford *(G-10922)*

5399 Miscellaneous general merchandise

▲ Crownplace Brands Ltd .... G 888 332-5534
   Apple Creek *(G-497)*

John Purdum .... G 513 897-9686
   Waynesville *(G-15298)*

Raven Concealment Systems LLC .... E 440 508-9000
   North Ridgeville *(G-11856)*

54 FOOD STORES

5411 Grocery stores

Baltic Country Meats .... G 330 897-7025
   Baltic *(G-834)*

Bread Kneads Inc .... G 419 422-3863
   Findlay *(G-7486)*

Brinkman Turkey Farms Inc .... F 419 365-5127
   Findlay *(G-7487)*

C J Kraft Enterprises Inc .... G 740 653-9606
   Lancaster *(G-8997)*

Dioguardis Italian Foods Inc .... F 330 492-3777
   Canton *(G-2093)*

Fragapane Bakeries Inc .... G 440 779-6050
   North Olmsted *(G-11823)*

Gibson Bros Inc .... F 440 774-2401
   Oberlin *(G-12051)*

Heinens Inc .... C 330 562-5297
   Aurora *(G-718)*

Investors United Inc .... F 419 473-8942
   Toledo *(G-14336)*

Lariccias Italian Foods Inc .... F 330 729-0222
   Youngstown *(G-16388)*

Mumfords Potato Chips & Deli .... G 937 653-3491
   Urbana *(G-14844)*

Nestle Prepared Foods Company .... B 440 349-5757
   Solon *(G-13395)*

▲ Nestle Prepared Foods Company .... A 440 248-3600
   Solon *(G-13396)*

Riesbeck Food Markets Inc .... C 740 695-3401
   Saint Clairsville *(G-12921)*

Tbone Sales LLC .... F 330 897-6131
   Baltic *(G-841)*

Troyers Trail Bologna Inc .... F 330 893-2414
   Dundee *(G-6971)*

Unger Kosher Bakery Inc .... F 216 321-7176
   Cleveland Heights *(G-4944)*

United Dairy Farmers Inc .... C 513 396-8700
   Cincinnati *(G-3479)*

Whitacre Enterprises Inc .... E 740 934-2331
   Graysville *(G-8024)*

Zygo Inc .... G 513 281-0888
   Cincinnati *(G-3539)*

5421 Meat and fish markets

Caven and Sons Meat Packing Co .... F 937 368-3841
   Conover *(G-5935)*

D & H Meats Inc .... G 419 387-7767
   Vanlue *(G-14969)*

Dee-Jays Cstm Btchring Proc LL .... F 740 694-7492
   Fredericktown *(G-7743)*

Duma Meats Inc .... G 330 628-3438
   Mogadore *(G-11070)*

Hoffman Meat Processing .... G 419 864-3994
   Cardington *(G-2275)*

Honeybaked Ham Company .... E 513 583-9700
   Cincinnati *(G-3006)*

John Krusinski .... F 216 441-0100
   Cleveland *(G-4258)*

John Stehlin & Sons Co .... F 513 385-6164
   Cincinnati *(G-3045)*

Lee Williams Meats Inc .... E 419 729-3893
   Toledo *(G-14362)*

Marshallville Packing Co Inc .... F 330 855-2871
   Marshallville *(G-9893)*

Mc Connells Market .... G 740 765-4300
   Richmond *(G-12802)*

North Country Charcuterie LLC .... F 614 670-5726
   Columbus *(G-5602)*

Pettisville Meats Incorporated .... F 419 445-0921
   Pettisville *(G-12453)*

Riesbeck Food Markets Inc .... C 740 695-3401
   Saint Clairsville *(G-12921)*

Winesburg Meats Inc .... G 330 359-5092
   Winesburg *(G-16083)*

5431 Fruit and vegetable markets

Coopers Mill Inc .... F 419 562-4215
   Bucyrus *(G-1854)*

Grays Orange Barn Inc .... G 419 568-2718
   Wapakoneta *(G-15116)*

5441 Candy, nut, and confectionery stores

▲ Anthony-Thomas Candy Company ... C 614 274-8405
   Columbus *(G-5147)*

Brandts Candies Inc .... G 440 942-1016
   Willoughby *(G-15892)*

Chocolate Pig Inc .... G 440 461-4511
   Cleveland *(G-3820)*

Dietsch Brothers Incorporated .... E 419 422-4474
   Findlay *(G-7501)*

Esther Price Candies Corporation .... E 937 253-2121
   Dayton *(G-6324)*

Fannie May Confections Inc .... A 330 494-0833
   North Canton *(G-11726)*

Fawn Confectionery Inc .... F 513 574-9612
   Cincinnati *(G-2897)*

Golden Turtle Chocolate Fctry .... G 513 932-1990
   Lebanon *(G-9085)*

Gorant Chocolatier LLC .... C 330 726-8821
   Boardman *(G-1513)*

Great Lakes Popcorn Company .... G 419 732-3080
   Port Clinton *(G-12620)*

▲ Harry London Candies Inc .... E 330 494-0833
   North Canton *(G-11736)*

Hartville Chocolates Inc .... F 330 877-1999
   Hartville *(G-8300)*

Island Delights Inc .... G 866 887-4100
   Seville *(G-13143)*

◆ Jml Holdings Inc .... E 419 866-7500
   Holland *(G-8515)*

Linneas Candy Supplies Inc .... E 330 678-7112
   Kent *(G-8828)*

▲ Malleys Candies Inc .... D 216 362-8700
   Cleveland *(G-4353)*

Maries Candies LLC .... F 937 465-3061
   West Liberty *(G-15623)*

Piqua Chocolate Company Inc .... G 937 773-1981
   Piqua *(G-12544)*

Robert E McGrath Inc .... F 440 572-7747
   Strongsville *(G-13872)*

54 FOOD STORES

Suzin L Chocolatiers................................G 440 323-3372
  Elyria *(G-7208)*
Sweeties Olympia Treats LLC..................F 440 572-7747
  Strongsville *(G-13888)*
◆ Trophy Nut Co.....................................E 937 667-8478
  Tipp City *(G-14161)*
Walnut Creek Chocolate Co Inc.................E 330 893-2995
  Walnut Creek *(G-15096)*

5451 Dairy products stores

Bunker Hill Cheese Co Inc.......................D 330 893-2131
  Millersburg *(G-10949)*
Food Plant Engineering LLC.....................F 513 618-3165
  Blue Ash *(G-1396)*
Grays Orange Barn Inc............................G 419 568-2718
  Wapakoneta *(G-15116)*
Guggisberg Cheese Inc............................E 330 893-2550
  Millersburg *(G-10956)*
▲ Hans Rothenbuhler & Son Inc................E 440 632-6000
  Middlefield *(G-10753)*
Jenis Splendid Ice Creams LLC.................E 614 488-3224
  Columbus *(G-5492)*
▲ Malleys Candies Inc............................D 216 362-8700
  Cleveland *(G-4353)*
Milk Hney Cndy Soda Shoppe LLC............F 330 492-5884
  Canton *(G-2165)*
Nosh Butters LLC....................................G 773 710-0668
  Cleveland *(G-4482)*
United Dairy Inc.....................................B 740 373-4121
  Marietta *(G-9841)*
United Dairy Farmers Inc........................C 513 396-8700
  Cincinnati *(G-3479)*
Youngs Jersey Dairy Inc..........................B 937 325-0629
  Yellow Springs *(G-16290)*

5461 Retail bakeries

Alfred Nickles Bakery Inc........................E 740 453-6522
  Zanesville *(G-16498)*
Blf Enterprises Inc.................................F 937 642-6425
  Westerville *(G-15694)*
Brooks Pastries Inc................................G 614 274-4880
  Plain City *(G-12567)*
Buns of Delaware Inc.............................E 740 363-2867
  Delaware *(G-6706)*
Busken Bakery Inc.................................D 513 871-2114
  Cincinnati *(G-2695)*
Chestnut Land Company.........................G 330 652-1939
  Niles *(G-11663)*
Cookie Bouquets Inc..............................G 614 888-2171
  Columbus *(G-5293)*
Crispie Creme Chillicothe Inc..................G 740 774-3770
  Chillicothe *(G-2500)*
Crumbs Inc...F 740 592-3803
  Athens *(G-680)*
Dandi Enterprises Inc............................F 419 516-9070
  Solon *(G-13336)*
Evans Bakery Inc...................................F 937 228-4151
  Dayton *(G-6326)*
Fragapane Bakeries Inc..........................G 440 779-6050
  North Olmsted *(G-11823)*
Giminetti Baking Company......................F 513 751-7655
  Cincinnati *(G-2951)*
Great American Cookie Company.............F 419 474-9417
  Toledo *(G-14302)*
I Dream of Cakes...................................G 937 533-6024
  Eaton *(G-7061)*
Investors United Inc...............................F 419 473-8942
  Toledo *(G-14336)*
K & B Acquisitions Inc............................F 937 253-1163
  Dayton *(G-6396)*
Kennedys Bakery Inc..............................F 740 432-2301
  Cambridge *(G-1938)*

Krispy Kreme Doughnut Corp..................E 614 798-0812
  Columbus *(G-5515)*
Krispy Kreme Doughnut Corp..................D 614 876-0058
  Columbus *(G-5516)*
Mary Ann Donut Shoppe Inc...................G 330 478-1655
  Canton *(G-2152)*
McHappys Donuts of Parkersburg............D 740 593-8744
  Athens *(G-687)*
Meeks Pastry Shop.................................G 419 782-4871
  Defiance *(G-6692)*
Minus G LLC...G 440 817-0338
  Newbury *(G-11630)*
Norcia Bakery..F 330 454-1077
  Canton *(G-2174)*
Osmans Pies Inc....................................E 330 607-9083
  Stow *(G-13716)*
Pepperidge Farm Incorporated................G 419 933-2611
  Willard *(G-15863)*
Schulers Bakery Inc...............................E 937 323-4154
  Springfield *(G-13630)*
Schwebel Baking Company.....................G 330 783-2860
  Hebron *(G-8361)*
Thurns Bakery & Deli.............................F 614 221-9246
  Columbus *(G-5825)*
Unger Kosher Bakery Inc........................F 216 321-7176
  Cleveland Heights *(G-4944)*
Wal-Bon of Ohio Inc..............................F 740 423-8178
  Belpre *(G-1262)*

5499 Miscellaneous food stores

Aqua Pennsylvania Inc...........................G 440 257-6190
  Mentor On The Lake *(G-10600)*
Boston Stoker Inc..................................F 937 890-6401
  Vandalia *(G-14934)*
Dental Pure Water Inc...........................F 440 234-0890
  Berea *(G-1274)*
Gold Star Chili Inc.................................E 513 231-4541
  Cincinnati *(G-2963)*
Iron Bean Inc..F 518 641-9917
  Perrysburg *(G-12393)*
McDonalds..F 513 336-0820
  Mason *(G-10028)*
Mustard Seed Health Fd Mkt Inc.............E 440 519-3663
  Solon *(G-13394)*
Nestle Usa Inc......................................D 216 861-8350
  Cleveland *(G-4450)*
Ohio Coffee Collaborative Ltd.................F 614 564-9852
  Columbus *(G-5613)*
Premier Tanning & Nutrition..................G 419 342-6259
  Shelby *(G-13198)*
Roots Poultry Inc..................................F 419 332-0041
  Fremont *(G-7805)*
Wileys Finest LLC..................................C 740 622-1072
  Coshocton *(G-6002)*

55 AUTOMOTIVE DEALERS AND GASOLINE SERVICE STATIONS

5511 New and used car dealers

▲ Bwi North America Inc........................E 937 253-1130
  Kettering *(G-8904)*
Doug Marine Motors Inc........................E 740 335-3700
  Wshngtn Ct Hs *(G-16230)*
Fleetpride Inc.......................................E 740 282-2711
  Steubenville *(G-13667)*
Ford Motor Company.............................C 440 933-1215
  Avon Lake *(G-807)*
Ford Motor Company.............................A 419 226-7000
  Lima *(G-9243)*
Friess Welding Inc................................G 330 644-8160
  Coventry Township *(G-6009)*

General Motors LLC..............................A 216 265-5000
  Cleveland *(G-4116)*
General Motors LLC..............................C 330 824-5840
  Warren *(G-15173)*
Honda Dev & Mfg Amer LLC.................C 937 644-0724
  Marysville *(G-9915)*
▲ Jmac Inc...E 614 436-2418
  Columbus *(G-5498)*
Kinstle Truck & Auto Svc Inc..................F 419 738-7493
  Wapakoneta *(G-15120)*
▲ Knippen Chrysler Ddge Jeep Inc..........E 419 695-4976
  Delphos *(G-6767)*
Mitsubishi Chemical Amer Inc................D 419 483-2931
  Bellevue *(G-1230)*
◆ Mitsubishi Elc Auto Amer Inc...............B 513 573-6614
  Mason *(G-10030)*
Steves Vans ACC Unlimited LLC............G 740 374-3154
  Marietta *(G-9832)*
Subaru of A..G 614 793 2358
  Dublin *(G-6948)*
Tbone Sales LLC...................................F 330 897-6131
  Baltic *(G-841)*
Tiger General LLC................................F 330 239-4949
  Medina *(G-10387)*
▼ Trailer One Inc..................................F 330 723-7474
  Medina *(G-10388)*

5521 Used car dealers

Cars and Parts Magazine........................D 937 498-0803
  Sidney *(G-13232)*
D&D Clssic Auto Rstoration Inc..............F 937 473-2229
  Covington *(G-6021)*
▲ Dawn Enterprises Inc.........................E 216 642-5506
  Cleveland *(G-3943)*
▲ King Kutter II Inc..............................E 740 446-0351
  Gallipolis *(G-7896)*
▲ Knippen Chrysler Ddge Jeep Inc..........E 419 695-4976
  Delphos *(G-6767)*
Suburbanite Inc....................................G 419 756-4390
  Mansfield *(G-9723)*
Tuffy Manufacturing..............................F 330 940-2356
  Cuyahoga Falls *(G-6125)*
▲ United Ignition Wire Corp..................G 216 898-1112
  Cleveland *(G-4847)*

5531 Auto and home supply stores

AB Tire & Repair...................................G 440 543-2929
  Chagrin Falls *(G-2386)*
Abutilon Company Inc...........................F 419 536-6123
  Toledo *(G-14175)*
Ace Truck Equipment Co.......................E 740 453-0551
  Zanesville *(G-16494)*
▲ Allen Aircraft Products Inc.................D 330 296-9621
  Ravenna *(G-12704)*
American Cold Forge LLC......................E 419 836-1062
  Northwood *(G-11917)*
Associates Tire and Svc Inc...................F 937 436-4692
  Centerville *(G-2359)*
Battery Unlimited.................................G 740 452-5030
  Zanesville *(G-16506)*
Bell Tire Co..F 440 234-8022
  Olmsted Falls *(G-12076)*
Best One Tire & Svc Lima Inc................G 419 425-3322
  Findlay *(G-7484)*
▲ Best One Tire & Svc Lima Inc............E 419 229-2380
  Lima *(G-9223)*
▲ Bkt USA Inc......................................F 330 836-1090
  Copley *(G-5944)*
Bob Sumerel Tire Co Inc.......................F 937 235-0062
  Dayton *(G-6233)*
Bob Sumerel Tire Co Inc.......................G 740 432-5200
  Lore City *(G-9446)*

55 AUTOMOTIVE DEALERS AND GASOLINE SERVICE STATIONS

Bob Sumerel Tire Co Inc .... F 330 769-9092
   Seville *(G-13140)*

Bob Sumerel Tire Co Inc .... G 740 454-9728
   Zanesville *(G-16512)*

Bob Sumerel Tire Company .... G 330 262-1220
   Wooster *(G-16105)*

Bob Sumerel Tire Company Inc .... G 740 927-2811
   Reynoldsburg *(G-12755)*

Boy RAD Inc .... F 614 766-1228
   Dublin *(G-6869)*

Bridgestone Ret Operations LLC .... G 740 592-3075
   Athens *(G-677)*

Bridgestone Ret Operations LLC .... G 614 834-3672
   Canal Winchester *(G-1982)*

Bridgestone Ret Operations LLC .... G 330 454-9478
   Canton *(G-2053)*

Bridgestone Ret Operations LLC .... G 513 681-7682
   Cincinnati *(G-2683)*

Bridgestone Ret Operations LLC .... G 513 793-4550
   Cincinnati *(G-2684)*

Bridgestone Ret Operations LLC .... G 513 677-5200
   Cincinnati *(G-2685)*

Bridgestone Ret Operations LLC .... G 440 842-3200
   Cleveland *(G-3756)*

Bridgestone Ret Operations LLC .... G 440 461-4747
   Cleveland *(G-3757)*

Bridgestone Ret Operations LLC .... G 216 229-2550
   Cleveland *(G-3758)*

Bridgestone Ret Operations LLC .... G 216 382-8970
   Cleveland *(G-3759)*

Bridgestone Ret Operations LLC .... F 614 864-3350
   Columbus *(G-5214)*

Bridgestone Ret Operations LLC .... F 614 491-8062
   Columbus *(G-5215)*

Bridgestone Ret Operations LLC .... G 614 224-4221
   Columbus *(G-5216)*

Bridgestone Ret Operations LLC .... G 440 324-3327
   Elyria *(G-7117)*

Bridgestone Ret Operations LLC .... G 440 365-8308
   Elyria *(G-7118)*

Bridgestone Ret Operations LLC .... G 937 548-1197
   Greenville *(G-8039)*

Bridgestone Ret Operations LLC .... G 513 868-7399
   Hamilton *(G-8186)*

Bridgestone Ret Operations LLC .... G 330 673-1700
   Kent *(G-8803)*

Bridgestone Ret Operations LLC .... F 440 299-6126
   Mentor *(G-10431)*

Bridgestone Ret Operations LLC .... F 740 397-5601
   Mount Vernon *(G-11265)*

Bridgestone Ret Operations LLC .... G 614 861-7994
   Reynoldsburg *(G-12756)*

Bridgestone Ret Operations LLC .... G 419 625-6571
   Sandusky *(G-13045)*

Bridgestone Ret Operations LLC .... G 937 325-4638
   Springfield *(G-13540)*

Bridgestone Ret Operations LLC .... G 330 758-0921
   Youngstown *(G-16325)*

Bridgestone Ret Operations LLC .... G 330 759-3697
   Youngstown *(G-16326)*

▲ Bucyrus Precision Tech Inc .... C 419 563-9950
   Bucyrus *(G-1852)*

Canton Bandag Co .... F 330 454-3025
   Canton *(G-2060)*

Capital Tire Inc .... E 330 364-4731
   Toledo *(G-14227)*

◆ Cequent Consumer Products Inc .... D 440 498-0001
   Solon *(G-13327)*

Colyer C & Sons Truck Service .... G 513 563-0663
   Cincinnati *(G-2781)*

◆ Crown Equipment Corporation .... A 419 629-2311
   New Bremen *(G-11400)*

Custom Recapping Inc .... G 937 324-4331
   Springfield *(G-13550)*

Doug Marine Motors Inc .... E 740 335-3700
   Wshngtn Ct Hs *(G-16230)*

Epix Tube Co Inc .... F 937 529-4858
   Dayton *(G-6321)*

Exit 11 Truck Tire Service .... G 330 659-6372
   Richfield *(G-12786)*

Finale Products Inc .... G 419 874-2662
   Perrysburg *(G-12381)*

Front Pocket Innovations LLC .... G 330 441-2365
   Wadsworth *(G-15031)*

▲ Galion-Godwin Truck Bdy Co LLC .... F 330 359-5495
   Dundee *(G-6965)*

Garro Tread Corporation .... G 330 376-3125
   Akron *(G-162)*

Goodyear Tire & Rubber Company .... F 419 643-8273
   Beaverdam *(G-1096)*

Goodyear Tire & Rubber Company .... G 330 966-1274
   Canton *(G-2116)*

Goodyear Tire & Rubber Company .... G 330 759-9343
   Youngstown *(G-16371)*

◆ Goodyear Tire & Rubber Company .... A 330 796-2121
   Akron *(G-171)*

▲ Grismer Tire Company .... E 937 643-2526
   Centerville *(G-2363)*

H & H Truck Parts LLC .... E 216 642-4540
   Cleveland *(G-4160)*

Horizon Global Corporation .... E 734 656-3000
   Cleveland *(G-4200)*

J & J Tire & Alignment .... G 330 424-5200
   Lisbon *(G-9316)*

JTL Enterprises LLC .... E 937 890-8189
   Dayton *(G-6392)*

K-M-S Industries Inc .... F 440 243-6680
   Brookpark *(G-1720)*

Kaffenbarger Truck Eqp Co .... E 513 772-6800
   Cincinnati *(G-3056)*

Keystone Auto Glass Inc .... D 419 509-0497
   Maumee *(G-10211)*

▲ Knippen Chrysler Ddge Jeep Inc .... E 419 695-4976
   Delphos *(G-6767)*

L & O Tire Service Inc .... G 937 394-8462
   Anna *(G-490)*

M Technologies Inc .... F 330 477-9009
   Canton *(G-2151)*

Mader Automotive Center Inc .... F 937 339-2681
   Troy *(G-14595)*

Mark Knupp Muffler & Tire Inc .... E 937 773-1334
   Piqua *(G-12535)*

Martin Diesel Inc .... E 419 782-9911
   Defiance *(G-6691)*

Mid America Tire of Hillsboro Inc .... E 937 393-3520
   Hillsboro *(G-8461)*

Mid-Wood Inc .... F 419 257-3331
   North Baltimore *(G-11696)*

Mitchell Bros Tire Rtread Svc .... G 740 353-1551
   Portsmouth *(G-12649)*

Ntb National Tire and Battery .... G 614 870-8945
   Columbus *(G-5606)*

Ohio Auto Supply Company .... F 330 454-5105
   Canton *(G-2182)*

Ohio Truck Equipment LLC .... F 740 830-6488
   Mount Vernon *(G-11283)*

Overhead Door of Pike County .... G 740 289-3925
   Piketon *(G-12481)*

Pattons Trck & Hvy Eqp Svc Inc .... E 740 385-4067
   Logan *(G-9373)*

Paul Shovlin .... G 330 757-0032
   Youngstown *(G-16416)*

Perkins Motor Service Ltd .... F 440 277-1256
   Lorain *(G-9430)*

Q T Columbus LLC .... G 800 758-2410
   Columbus *(G-5700)*

▼ QT Equipment Company .... E 330 724-3055
   Akron *(G-289)*

River City Body Company .... F 513 772-9317
   Cincinnati *(G-3343)*

Rust Belt Broncos LLC .... E 330 533-0048
   Canfield *(G-2017)*

Shrader Tire & Oil Inc .... G 419 420-8435
   Perrysburg *(G-12426)*

Skinner Firestone Inc .... F 740 984-4247
   Beverly *(G-1321)*

Snider Tire Inc .... E 740 439-2741
   Cambridge *(G-1953)*

Steves Vans ACC Unlimited LLC .... G 740 374-3154
   Marietta *(G-9832)*

▲ Superior Production LLC .... C 614 444-2181
   Columbus *(G-5800)*

Support Svc LLC .... G 419 617-0660
   Lexington *(G-9203)*

Tbc Retail Group Inc .... E 216 267-8040
   Cleveland *(G-4768)*

Tbone Sales LLC .... F 330 897-6131
   Baltic *(G-841)*

Tom Barbour Auto Parts Inc .... F 740 354-4654
   Portsmouth *(G-12659)*

Vintage Automotive Elc Inc .... F 419 472-9349
   Toledo *(G-14520)*

Wayne A Whaley .... G 330 525-7779
   Homeworth *(G-8556)*

Western Branch Diesel LLC .... F 330 454-8800
   Canton *(G-2267)*

X-Treme Finishes Inc .... F 330 474-0614
   North Royalton *(G-11903)*

Ziegler Tire and Supply Co .... G 330 434-7126
   Akron *(G-381)*

Ziegler Tire and Supply Co .... G 330 477-3463
   Canton *(G-2273)*

Ziegler Tire and Supply Co .... E 330 343-7739
   Dover *(G-6850)*

5541 Gasoline service stations

Calvary Christian Ch of Ohio .... F 740 828-9000
   Frazeysburg *(G-7714)*

Plug Power Inc .... G 518 605-5703
   West Carrollton *(G-15356)*

Shelly and Sands Inc .... F 740 453-0721
   Zanesville *(G-16562)*

Tbone Sales LLC .... F 330 897-6131
   Baltic *(G-841)*

United Dairy Farmers Inc .... C 513 396-8700
   Cincinnati *(G-3479)*

5551 Boat dealers

Ceasars Creek Marine .... G 513 897-2912
   Loveland *(G-9477)*

Dynamic Plastics Inc .... G 937 437-7261
   New Paris *(G-11481)*

Hydromotive Engineering Co .... G 330 425-4266
   Twinsburg *(G-14673)*

Mariners Landing Inc .... F 513 941-3625
   Cincinnati *(G-3131)*

Sailors Tailor Inc .... F 937 862-7781
   Spring Valley *(G-13491)*

5561 Recreational vehicle dealers

All Power Equipment LLC .... F 740 593-3279
   Athens *(G-674)*

Mitchs Welding & Hitches .... G 419 893-3117
   Maumee *(G-10223)*

Steves Vans ACC Unlimited LLC .... G 740 374-3154
   Marietta *(G-9832)*

Employee Codes: A=Over 500 employees, B=251-500
C=101-250, D=51-100, E=20-50, F=10-19, G=1-9

55 AUTOMOTIVE DEALERS AND GASOLINE SERVICE STATIONS

5571 Motorcycle dealers

◆ Gear Star American Performance.......G 330 434-5216
   Akron *(G-163)*
▲ Spiegler Brake Systems USA LLC......E 937 291-1735
   Dayton *(G-6585)*
◆ Wholecycle Inc...............................E 330 929-8123
   Peninsula *(G-12345)*

5599 Automotive dealers, nec

Custom Way Welding Inc...................F 937 845-9469
   New Carlisle *(G-11414)*
Golf Car Company Inc.......................F 614 873-1055
   Plain City *(G-12580)*
M R Trailer Sales Inc.........................G 330 339-7701
   New Philadelphia *(G-11512)*
OReilly Equipment LLC......................G 440 564-1234
   Newbury *(G-11633)*

56 APPAREL AND ACCESSORY STORES

5611 Men's and boys' clothing stores

Benchmark Prints.............................F 419 332-7640
   Fremont *(G-7766)*
▲ City Apparel Inc.............................F 419 434-1155
   Findlay *(G-7493)*
Rnp Inc..G
   Dellroy *(G-6758)*
S F Mock & Associates LLC..............F 937 438-0196
   Dayton *(G-6556)*

5621 Women's clothing stores

▲ City Apparel Inc.............................F 419 434-1155
   Findlay *(G-7493)*
Fancy ME Boutique LLC....................G 419 357-8927
   Sandusky *(G-13058)*
Fluff Boutique.................................G 513 227-6614
   Cincinnati *(G-2911)*

5632 Women's accessory and specialty stores

Owl Be Sweatin...............................G 513 260-2026
   Cincinnati *(G-3231)*
Trophy Sports Center LLC................F 937 376-2311
   Xenia *(G-16279)*

5641 Children's and infants' wear stores

Fancy ME Boutique LLC....................G 419 357-8927
   Sandusky *(G-13058)*
Love Laugh & Laundry.....................G 567 377-1951
   Toledo *(G-14370)*

5651 Family clothing stores

Chris Stepp....................................G 513 248-0822
   Milford *(G-10898)*
Fancy ME Boutique LLC....................G 419 357-8927
   Sandusky *(G-13058)*
Ohio Mills Corporation......................G 216 431-3979
   Cleveland *(G-4499)*

5661 Shoe stores

Cobblers Corner LLC........................F 330 482-4005
   Columbiana *(G-5032)*
Rnp Inc..G
   Dellroy *(G-6758)*

5699 Miscellaneous apparel and accessories

Appleheart Inc.................................G 937 384-0430
   Miamisburg *(G-10612)*

Charles Wisvari...............................G 740 671-9960
   Bellaire *(G-1184)*
Deborah Meredith............................G 330 644-0425
   Coventry Township *(G-6008)*
Impact Printing and Design LLC........F 833 522-6200
   Columbus *(G-5456)*
K Ventures Inc................................F 419 678-2308
   Coldwater *(G-4994)*
Karl Kuemmerling Inc.......................F
   Massillon *(G-10114)*
Kip-Craft Incorporated......................D 216 898-5500
   Cleveland *(G-4293)*
LLC Bowman Leather.......................G 330 893-1954
   Millersburg *(G-10976)*
Markt LLC.....................................G 740 397-5900
   Mount Vernon *(G-11278)*
Rbr Enterprises LLC.........................F 866 437-9327
   Brecksville *(G-1630)*
Rnp Inc..C
   Dellroy *(G-6758)*
Shoot-A-Way Inc.............................F 419 294-4654
   Nevada *(G-11361)*
Tee Creations.................................G 937 878-2822
   Fairborn *(G-7325)*
◆ The Fechheimer Brothers Co.........C 513 793-5400
   Blue Ash *(G-1480)*
▲ Totes Isotoner Corporation............D 513 682-8200
   West Chester *(G-15598)*
▲ Totes Isotoner Holdings Corp.........C 513 682-8200
   West Chester *(G-15599)*
Trophy Sports Center LLC................F 937 376-2311
   Xenia *(G-16279)*
Unisport Inc....................................F 419 529-4727
   Ontario *(G-12096)*
Vandalia Sportswear LLC..................G 937 264-3204
   Vandalia *(G-14966)*

57 HOME FURNITURE, FURNISHINGS AND EQUIPMENT STORES

5712 Furniture stores

Ahmf Inc..E 614 921-1223
   Columbus *(G-5107)*
Americas Mdular Off Specialist.........G 614 277-0216
   Grove City *(G-8078)*
◆ Archbold Furniture Co...................E 567 444-4666
   Archbold *(G-523)*
▲ Banner Mattress Co Inc.................D 419 324-7181
   Toledo *(G-14206)*
Bruening Glass Works Inc................G 440 333-4768
   Cleveland *(G-3765)*
Chagrin Valley Custom Furn LLC.......G 440 591-5511
   Warrensville Heights *(G-15227)*
▲ Coconis Furniture Inc....................E 740 452-1231
   South Zanesville *(G-13477)*
COS Blueprint Inc............................E 330 376-0022
   Akron *(G-115)*
▼ Eoi Inc..F 740 201-3300
   Lewis Center *(G-9160)*
▲ Fortner Upholstering Inc................F 614 475-8282
   Columbus *(G-5384)*
▲ Furniture By Otmar Inc..................F 937 435-2039
   Dayton *(G-6342)*
Great Day Improvements LLC..........B 267 223-1289
   Macedonia *(G-9555)*
Hallmark Industries Inc.....................E 937 864-7378
   Springfield *(G-13571)*
Hilltop Glass & Mirror LLC................G 513 931-3688
   Cincinnati *(G-3002)*
Home Stor & Off Solutions Inc..........E 216 362-4660
   Cleveland *(G-4199)*

Homecare Mattress Inc....................F 937 746-2556
   Franklin *(G-7680)*
▲ Litehouse Products LLC................E 440 638-2350
   Strongsville *(G-13851)*
Mel Heitkamp Builders Ltd...............G 419 375-0405
   Fort Recovery *(G-7623)*
▲ Morris Furniture Co Inc.................C 937 874-7100
   Fairborn *(G-7320)*
Newbury Woodworks.......................G 440 564-5273
   Newbury *(G-11632)*
▲ Ohio Table Pad Company..............F 419 872-6400
   Perrysburg *(G-12407)*
▲ Pei Liquidation Company...............C 330 467-4267
   Macedonia *(G-9564)*
Precision Fab Products Inc..............G 937 526-5681
   Versailles *(G-14988)*
Queen City Awning & Tent Co..........E 513 530-9660
   Cincinnati *(G-3315)*
Recycled Systems Furniture Inc.......E 614 880-9110
   Worthington *(G-16210)*
River East Custom Cabinets............E 419 244-3226
   Toledo *(G-14452)*
Sailors Tailor Inc.............................F 937 862-7781
   Spring Valley *(G-13491)*
▲ Senator International Inc...............E 419 887-5806
   Maumee *(G-10229)*
Urbn Timber LLC.............................G 614 981-3043
   Columbus *(G-5850)*

5713 Floor covering stores

Armstrong World Industries Inc........E 614 771-9307
   Hilliard *(G-8399)*
Hardwood Lumber Company Inc......F 440 834-1891
   Middlefield *(G-10754)*
Prints & Paints Flr Cvg Co Inc..........F 419 462-5663
   Galion *(G-7883)*
Shaheen Oriental Rug Co Inc...........F 330 493-9000
   Canton *(G-2222)*
▲ Stanley Steemer Intl Inc................C 614 764-2007
   Dublin *(G-6945)*
Wccv Floor Coverings LLC..............F 330 688-0114
   Peninsula *(G-12344)*

5714 Drapery and upholstery stores

Accent Drapery Co Inc....................E 614 488-0741
   Columbus *(G-5092)*
Elden Draperies of Toledo Inc..........F 419 535-1909
   Toledo *(G-14272)*
Nancys Draperies Inc......................G 330 855-7751
   Marshallville *(G-9894)*

5719 Miscellaneous homefurnishings

All Fired Up Pnt Your Own Pot..........G 330 865-5858
   Copley *(G-5943)*
Blind Factory Showroom..................F 614 771-6549
   Hilliard *(G-8405)*
Bonfoey Co.....................................F 216 621-0178
   Cleveland *(G-3747)*
Bruening Glass Works Inc...............G 440 333-4768
   Cleveland *(G-3765)*
Buckeye BOP LLC...........................G 740 498-9898
   Newcomerstown *(G-11643)*
Cincinnati Window Shade Inc..........F 513 631-7200
   Cincinnati *(G-2763)*
Dale Kestler...................................G 513 871-9000
   Cincinnati *(G-2817)*
▲ Down-Lite International Inc............C 513 229-3696
   Mason *(G-9985)*
Fountain Specialists Inc...................G 513 831-5717
   Milford *(G-10906)*
General Electric Company...............E 440 593-1156
   Mc Donald *(G-10277)*

Great Day Improvements LLC............ B 267 223-1289
  Macedonia (G-9555)
Handy Twine Knife Co...................... G 419 294-3424
  Upper Sandusky (G-14810)
House of 10000 Picture Frames............ G 937 254-5541
  Dayton (G-6373)
▲ Microsun Lamps LLC..................... G 888 328-8701
  Dayton (G-6443)
▲ Morris Furniture Co Inc.................... C 937 874-7100
  Fairborn (G-7320)
▲ Mosser Glass Inc.......................... E 740 439-1827
  Cambridge (G-1944)
Nacco Industries Inc........................... E 440 229-5151
  Cleveland (G-4434)
Overhead Inc.................................... G 419 476-0300
  Toledo (G-14420)
▲ Pei Liquidation Company.................. C 330 467-4267
  Macedonia (G-9564)
Scs Construction Services Inc............... E 513 929-0260
  Cincinnati (G-3371)
◆ The Blonder Company..................... C 216 431-3560
  Cleveland (G-4780)
▲ The Kitchen Collection LLC............... A 740 773-9150
  Chillicothe (G-2538)
◆ Wasserstrom Company.................... B 614 228-6525
  Columbus (G-5865)
Whempys Corp.................................. G 614 888-6670
  Worthington (G-16218)

5722 Household appliance stores

5 Core Inc... F 951 386-6372
  Bellefontaine (G-1199)
ABC Appliance Inc............................. E 419 693-4414
  Oregon (G-12099)
Bolons Custom Kitchens Inc................. G 330 499-0092
  Canton (G-2050)
C-Link Enterprises LLC....................... F 937 222-2829
  Dayton (G-6244)
Carbonless Cut Sheet Forms Inc............ F 740 826-1700
  New Concord (G-11431)
▲ Kitchens By Rutenschroer Inc............ G 513 251-8333
  Cincinnati (G-3080)
Miller Cabinet Ltd.............................. F 614 873-4221
  Plain City (G-12586)
Wolff Bros Supply Inc......................... F 440 327-1650
  North Ridgeville (G-11864)
Z Line Kitchen and Bath LLC................. G 614 777-5004
  Marysville (G-9944)

5731 Radio, television, and electronic stores

ABC Appliance Inc............................. E 419 693-4414
  Oregon (G-12099)
Bender Communications Inc................. F 740 382-0000
  Marion (G-9848)
Dish One Up Satellite Inc..................... D 216 482-3875
  Cleveland (G-3961)
Dss Installations Ltd........................... F 513 761-7000
  Cincinnati (G-2842)
Electra Sound Inc.............................. D 216 433-9600
  Avon Lake (G-805)
◆ Phantom Sound............................. G 513 759-4477
  Mason (G-10038)
◆ TT Electronics Integrated.................. B 440 352-8961
  Perry (G-12357)
Tune Town Car Audio......................... G 419 627-1100
  Sandusky (G-13098)

5734 Computer and software stores

Aztech Printing & Promotions............... G 937 339-0100
  Troy (G-14551)
Bizall Inc.. G 216 939-9580
  Cleveland (G-3738)

Copier Resources Inc......................... G 614 268-1100
  Columbus (G-5295)
Gordons Graphics Inc......................... G 330 863-2322
  Malvern (G-9613)
Journey Systems LLC......................... F 513 831-6200
  Milford (G-10912)
Lantek Systems Inc............................ G 877 805-1028
  Mason (G-10020)
RB Sigma LLC................................... D 440 290-0577
  Mentor (G-10545)
Retalix Inc.. E 937 384-2277
  Miamisburg (G-10676)
Thyme Inc.. F 484 872-8430
  Akron (G-357)

5735 Record and prerecorded tape stores

True Dinero Records & Tech LLC........... G 513 428-4610
  Cincinnati (G-3470)

5736 Musical instrument stores

Bbb Music LLC.................................. G 740 772-2262
  Chilliccthe (G-2494)
Cardinal Percussion Inc....................... G 330 707-4446
  Girard (G-7964)
Loft Violin Shop................................. F 614 267-7221
  Columbus (G-5531)
S I T Strings Co Inc............................ E 330 434-8010
  Akron (G-321)
▲ Stewart-Macdonald Mfg Co.............. E 740 592-3021
  Athens (G-698)
Willis Music Company......................... F 513 671-3288
  Cincinnati (G-3520)

58 EATING AND DRINKING PLACES

5812 Eating places

Amish Door Inc.................................. C 330 359-5464
  Wilmot (G-16065)
Beca House Coffee LLC...................... G 419 731-4961
  Upper Sandusky (G-14804)
Best Bite Grill LLC.............................. F 419 344-7462
  Versailles (G-14977)
Binos Inc.. G 330 938-0888
  Sebring (G-13118)
Breitenbach Wine Cellars Inc................. G 330 343-3603
  Dover (G-6810)
Brewpub Restaurant Corporation........... E 614 228-2537
  Columbus (G-5211)
Brinkman LLC................................... F 419 204-5934
  Lima (G-9225)
Buckeye Valley Pizza Hut Ltd................. E 419 586-5900
  Celina (G-2324)
Bunker Hill Cheese Co Inc.................... D 330 893-2131
  Millersburg (G-10949)
Buns of Delaware Inc.......................... E 740 363-2867
  Delaware (G-6706)
Cassanos Inc..................................... E 937 294-8400
  Dayton (G-6248)
Chestnut Land Company...................... G 330 652-1939
  Niles (G-11663)
Christopher Sweeney.......................... G 513 276-4350
  Troy (G-14554)
Circleville Oil Co................................. G 740 477-3341
  Circleville (G-3544)
Ferrante Wine Farm Inc....................... E 440 466-8466
  Geneva (G-7936)
Frontwaters Rest & Brewing Co............. G 419 798-8058
  Marblehead (G-9765)
Georgetown Vineyards Inc.................... E 740 435-3222
  Cambridge (G-1936)

Glenn Ravens Winery.......................... F 740 545-1000
  West Lafayette (G-15617)
Gold Star Chili Inc.............................. E 513 631-1990
  Cincinnati (G-2964)
Gold Star Chili Inc.............................. E 513 231-4541
  Cincinnati (G-2963)
Grace Juice Company LLC................... F 614 398-6879
  Westerville (G-15707)
◆ Great Lakes Brewing Co................... C 216 771-4404
  Cleveland (G-4142)
Guggisberg Cheese Inc........................ E 330 893-2550
  Millersburg (G-10956)
International Brand Services................. G 513 376-8209
  Cincinnati (G-3028)
Iron Bean Inc.................................... F 518 641-9917
  Perrysburg (G-12393)
John Purdum.................................... G 513 897-9686
  Waynesville (G-15298)
Johnsons Real Ice Cream LLC............... C 614 231-0014
  Columbus (G-5500)
Karrikin Spirits Company LLC................ F 513 561-5000
  Cincinnati (G-3064)
Kenyetta Bagby Enterprise LLC............. F 614 584-3426
  Reynoldsburg (G-12768)
Lbzb Restaurants Inc........................... F 567 413-4700
  Bowling Green (G-1570)
Lloyd F Helber.................................. G 740 756-9607
  Carroll (G-2299)
Magic Wok Inc................................... G 419 531-1818
  Toledo (G-14375)
Mark Grzianis St Treats Ex Inc.............. F 330 414-6266
  Kent (G-8832)
McDonalds....................................... F 513 336-0820
  Mason (G-10028)
Milk Hney Cndy Soda Shoppe LLC......... F 330 492-5884
  Canton (G-2165)
Moyer Vineyards Inc........................... F 937 549-2957
  Mount Orab (G-11243)
Mustard Seed Health Fd Mkt Inc............ E 440 519-3663
  Solon (G-13394)
Ohio Coffee Collaborative Ltd............... F 614 564-9852
  Columbus (G-5613)
▲ Paramount Distillers Inc................... B 216 671-6300
  Cleveland (G-4522)
R & T Estate LLC............................... F 216 862-0822
  Cleveland (G-4611)
Rivals Sports Grille LLC....................... E 216 267-0005
  Middleburg Heights (G-10726)
Robert Barr...................................... G 740 826-7325
  New Concord (G-11433)
Rocky River Brewing Co...................... F 440 895-2739
  Rocky River (G-12842)
Shawadi LLC.................................... E 614 839-0698
  Westerville (G-15720)
▲ Skyline Cem Holdings LLC................ C 513 874-1188
  Fairfield (G-7408)
▲ Solo Vino Imports Ltd..................... F 440 714-9591
  Vermilion (G-14973)
Stella Lou Llc.................................... E 937 935-9536
  Powell (G-12681)
Sweets and Meats LLC........................ F 513 888-4227
  Cincinnati (G-3437)
Tr Boes Holdings Inc.......................... E 419 595-2255
  New Riegel (G-11538)
Velvet Ice Cream Company................... D 740 892-3921
  Utica (G-14859)
Wal-Bon of Ohio Inc........................... F 740 423-6351
  Belpre (G-1261)
White Castle System Inc...................... E 513 563-2290
  Cincinnati (G-3518)
◆ White Castle System Inc................... B 614 228-5781
  Columbus (G-5876)

58 EATING AND DRINKING PLACES

Willoughby Brewing Company LLC....... F 440 975-0202
  Willoughby (G-16016)
Youngs Jersey Dairy Inc.................... B 937 325-0629
  Yellow Springs (G-16290)

5813 Drinking places

Artisan Ales LLC................................ E 216 544-8703
  Cleveland (G-3679)
Bajio Brewing Company LLC............. G 419 410-8275
  Toledo (G-14205)
Brewdog Brewing Company LLC........ F 614 908-3051
  Canal Winchester (G-1981)
▲ District Brewing Company Inc........ E 614 224-3626
  Columbus (G-5331)
◆ Great Lakes Brewing Co................. C 216 771-4404
  Cleveland (G-4142)
Green Room Brewing LLC.................. G 614 421-2337
  Columbus (G-5412)
Lock 15 Brewing Company LLC.......... E 234 900-8277
  Akron (G-221)
Lock 27 Brewing LLC......................... F 937 433-2739
  Dayton (G-6414)
Mansfield Brew Works LLC................. F 419 631-3153
  Mansfield (G-9684)
McDonalds... F 513 336-0820
  Mason (G-10028)
Railroad Brewing Company................ G 440 723-8234
  Avon (G-785)
Rocky River Brewing Co..................... F 440 895-2739
  Rocky River (G-12842)

59 MISCELLANEOUS RETAIL

5912 Drug stores and proprietary stores

Express Pharmacy & Dme LLC........... G 210 981-9690
  Columbus (G-5366)
Omnicare Phrm of Midwest LLC......... D 513 719-2600
  Cincinnati (G-3222)
Riesbeck Food Markets Inc................ C 740 695-3401
  Saint Clairsville (G-12921)
Soleo Health Inc................................. E 844 467-8200
  Dublin (G-6941)

5921 Liquor stores

Currier Richard & James.................... G 440 988-4132
  Amherst (G-474)
Kelleys Island Winery Inc.................... G 419 746-2678
  Kelleys Island (G-8788)
Millersburg Ice Company.................... E 330 674-3016
  Millersburg (G-10983)
Ohio Eagle Distributing LLC............... E 513 539-8483
  West Chester (G-15469)
Old Firehouse Winery Inc................... E 440 466-9300
  Geneva (G-7943)
Sandra Weddington............................ F 740 417-4286
  Delaware (G-6749)
Toledo Spirits Company LLC.............. F 419 704-3705
  Toledo (G-14505)

5932 Used merchandise stores

▲ Crownplace Brands Ltd................... G 888 332-5534
  Apple Creek (G-497)
John Purdum...................................... G 513 897-9680
  Waynesville (G-15298)

5941 Sporting goods and bicycle shops

Area 419 Firearms LLC...................... F 419 830-8353
  Delta (G-6779)
▲ Golf Galaxy Golfworks Inc.............. C 740 328-4193
  Newark (G-11577)
Hershberger Lawn Structures............. F 330 674-3900
  Millersburg (G-10957)
Highpoint Firearms............................. E 419 747-9444
  Mansfield (G-9668)
Lima Sporting Goods Inc.................... E 419 222-1036
  Lima (G-9265)
Peska Inc.. F 440 998-4664
  Ashtabula (G-654)
R & S Monitions Inc............................ G 614 846-0597
  Columbus (G-5706)
Reloading Supplies Corp.................... G 440 228-0367
  Ashtabula (G-658)
◆ Rubber Grinding Inc........................ D 419 692-3000
  Delphos (G-6771)
Sportsmans Haven Inc....................... G 740 432-7243
  Cambridge (G-1955)
▲ Sunset Golf LLC.............................. G 419 994-5563
  Tallmadge (G-14051)
The Hartman Corp.............................. G 614 475-5035
  Columbus (G-5822)
TS Sales LLC..................................... F 727 804-8060
  Akron (G-365)

5942 Book stores

Auguste Moone Enterprises Ltd......... E 216 333-9248
  Cleveland Heights (G-4937)
▼ Bookfactory LLC.............................. E 937 226-7100
  Dayton (G-6234)
Christian Missionary Alliance.............. C 380 208-6200
  Reynoldsburg (G-12758)
Incorprted Trstees of The Gspl........... D 216 749-2100
  Middleburg Heights (G-10721)
Ketman Corporation............................ G 330 262-1688
  Wooster (G-16142)

5943 Stationery stores

Ace Rubber Stamp & Off Sup Co....... F 216 771-8483
  Cleveland (G-3590)
Avon Lake Printing............................. G 440 933-2078
  Avon Lake (G-799)
COS Blueprint Inc.............................. E 330 376-0022
  Akron (G-115)
Gordons Graphics Inc........................ G 330 863-2322
  Malvern (G-9613)
Hathaway Stamp Co.......................... F 513 621-1052
  Cincinnati (G-2989)
Hubbard Company............................. E 419 784-4455
  Defiance (G-6682)
Marsh Industries Inc........................... E 330 308-8667
  New Philadelphia (G-11515)
Murr Corporation................................ F 330 264-2223
  Wooster (G-16154)
O Connor Office Pdts & Prtg.............. G 740 852-2209
  London (G-9392)
Quick Tech Graphics Inc.................... E 937 743-5952
  Springboro (G-13518)
Warren Printing & Off Pdts Inc........... F 419 523-3635
  Ottawa (G-12196)

5944 Jewelry stores

Bensan Jewelers Inc.......................... G 216 221-1434
  Lakewood (G-8967)
Em Es Be Company LLC................... G 216 761-9500
  Cleveland (G-4008)
Farah Jewelers Inc............................. F 614 438-6140
  Westerville (G-15656)
Goyal Enterprises Inc......................... F 513 874-9303
  West Chester (G-15557)
Gustave Julian Jewelers Inc............... G 440 888-1100
  Cleveland (G-4157)
H P Nielsen Inc................................... G 440 244-4255
  Lorain (G-9413)
Handcrafted Jewelry Inc..................... G 330 650-9011
  Hudson (G-8595)
James C Free Inc............................... G 513 793-0133
  Cincinnati (G-3035)
▲ James C Free Inc........................... E 937 298-0171
  Dayton (G-6387)
M B Saxon Co Inc............................... G 440 229-5006
  Cleveland (G-4345)
Markus Jewelers LLC......................... G 513 474-4950
  Cincinnati (G-3132)
Michael W Hyes Desgr Goldsmith..... G 440 519-0889
  Solon (G-13389)
Pughs Designer Jewelers Inc............. G 740 344-9259
  Newark (G-11603)
◆ Quality Gold Inc.............................. B 513 942-7659
  Fairfield (G-7400)
Robert W Johnson Inc........................ D 614 336-4545
  Dublin (G-6931)
Rosenfeld Jewelry Inc........................ G 440 446-0099
  Cleveland (G-4650)
Sheiban Jewelry Inc........................... F 440 238-0616
  Strongsville (G-13879)
White Jewelers Inc............................. G 330 264-3324
  Wooster (G-16182)

5945 Hobby, toy, and game shops

▲ Anime Palace.................................. G 408 858-1918
  Lewis Center (G-9149)
Elite Ceramics and Metals LLC.......... G 330 787-2777
  Warren (G-15166)
▲ Franklin Art Glass Studios.............. E 614 221-2972
  Columbus (G-5385)
Intrism Inc... F 614 733-9304
  Worthington (G-16199)
Little Cottage Company..................... F 330 893-4212
  Millersburg (G-10975)
Michaels Stores Inc............................ F 330 505-1168
  Niles (G-11676)
Middleton Llyd Dolls Inc..................... G 740 989-2082
  Coolville (G-5941)
▲ Ohio Art Company.......................... D 419 636-3141
  Bryan (G-1833)
Scrambl-Gram Inc.............................. G 419 635-2321
  Port Clinton (G-12628)
The Guardtower Inc............................ F 614 488-4311
  Hilliard (G-8447)

5947 Gift, novelty, and souvenir shop

Amish Door Inc................................... C 330 359-5464
  Wilmot (G-16065)
▲ City Apparel Inc.............................. F 419 434-1155
  Findlay (G-7493)
Cookie Bouquets Inc.......................... G 614 888-2171
  Columbus (G-5293)
▲ Crownplace Brands Ltd................. G 888 332-5534
  Apple Creek (G-497)
Down Home.. G 740 393-1186
  Mount Vernon (G-11271)
E Warther & Sons Inc........................ F 330 343-7513
  Dover (G-6823)
Global Manufacturing Solutions......... F 937 236-8315
  Dayton (G-6355)
Golden Turtle Chocolate Fctry........... G 513 932-1990
  Lebanon (G-9085)
Gorant Chocolatier LLC..................... C 330 726-8821
  Boardman (G-1513)
Handcrafted Jewelry Inc.................... G 330 650-9011
  Hudson (G-8595)
Modern China Company Inc.............. E 330 938-6104
  Sebring (G-13123)
Naptime Productions LLC.................. G 419 662-9521
  Rossford (G-12868)
Ohio Designer Craftsmen Entps........ F 614 486-7119
  Columbus (G-5615)

SIC SECTION
59 MISCELLANEOUS RETAIL

Piqua Chocolate Company Inc .... G 937 773-1981
Piqua *(G-12544)*

▲ Pulsar Ecoproducts LLC .... F 216 861-8800
Cleveland *(G-4600)*

R J Manray Inc .... G 330 559-6716
Canfield *(G-2015)*

S-P Company Inc .... D 330 782-5651
Columbiana *(G-5050)*

Scholz & Ey Engravers Inc .... F 614 444-8052
Columbus *(G-5752)*

Shops By Todd Inc .... G 937 458-3192
Beavercreek *(G-1061)*

Suzin L Chocolatiers .... G 440 323-3372
Elyria *(G-7208)*

The Hartman Corp .... G 614 475-5035
Columbus *(G-5822)*

Velvet Ice Cream Company .... D 740 892-3921
Utica *(G-14859)*

▲ Wild Berry Incense Inc .... F 513 523-8583
Oxford *(G-12214)*

Wooden Horse .... G 740 503-5243
Baltimore *(G-849)*

Youngs Jersey Dairy Inc .... B 937 325-0629
Yellow Springs *(G-16290)*

5948 Luggage and leather goods stores

▼ Baggallini Inc .... F 800 448-8753
Pickerington *(G-12456)*

5949 Sewing, needlework, and piece goods

Fabric Square Shop .... G 330 752-3044
Stow *(G-13696)*

Fine Points Inc .... F 216 229-6644
Cleveland *(G-4060)*

Quilting Creations Intl .... G 330 874-4741
Bolivar *(G-1535)*

5961 Catalog and mail-order houses

▲ American Frame Corporation .... D 419 893-5595
Maumee *(G-10163)*

▲ Bendon Inc .... D 419 207-3600
Ashland *(G-556)*

Communication Concepts Inc .... G 937 426-8600
Beavercreek *(G-1043)*

Diy Holster LLC .... G 419 921-2168
Elyria *(G-7132)*

E Retailing Associates LLC .... D 614 300-5785
Columbus *(G-5339)*

E-Z Grader Company .... G 440 247-7511
Chagrin Falls *(G-2375)*

Guggisberg Cheese Inc .... E 330 893-2550
Millersburg *(G-10956)*

Hen of Woods LLC .... G 513 954-8871
Cincinnati *(G-2993)*

Jfab .... G 740 572-0227
Jeffersonville *(G-8764)*

Pardson Inc .... F 740 373-5285
Marietta *(G-9814)*

Sailors Tailor Inc .... F 937 862-7781
Spring Valley *(G-13491)*

Scott Fetzer Company .... A 440 892-3000
Westlake *(G-15784)*

▲ Systemax Manufacturing Inc .... D 937 368-2300
Dayton *(G-6604)*

▲ Twin Sisters Productions LLC .... E 330 631-0361
Stow *(G-13735)*

▲ Universal Drect Flflment Corp .... C 330 650-5000
Hudson *(G-8617)*

◆ Universal Screen Arts Inc .... E 330 650-5000
Hudson *(G-8618)*

5963 Direct selling establishments

Conns Potato Chip Co Inc .... E 740 452-4615
Zanesville *(G-16523)*

Cygnus Home Service LLC .... E 419 222-9977
Lima *(G-9234)*

Fluff Boutique .... G 513 227-6614
Cincinnati *(G-2911)*

P & M Enterprises Group Inc .... G 330 316-0387
Canton *(G-2190)*

Rambasek Realty Inc .... F 937 228-1189
Dayton *(G-6540)*

Smartsoda Holdings Inc .... E 888 998-9668
Cleveland *(G-4708)*

5983 Fuel oil dealers

Centerra Co-Op .... E 419 281-2153
Ashland *(G-562)*

Cincinnati - Vulcan Company .... D 513 242-5300
Cincinnati *(G-2736)*

5984 Liquefied petroleum gas dealers

Brightstar Propane & Fuels .... F 614 891-8395
Westerville *(G-15648)*

Jomac Ltd .... E 330 627-7727
Carrollton *(G-2311)*

Legacy Farmers Cooperative .... F 419 423-2611
Findlay *(G-7528)*

Ngo Development Corporation .... B 740 622-9560
Coshocton *(G-5987)*

Welders Supply Inc .... E 216 267-4470
Brookpark *(G-1727)*

5989 Fuel dealers, nec

▼ Cliffs Logan County Coal LLC .... C 216 694-5700
Cleveland *(G-3871)*

5992 Florists

Cleveland Plant and Flower Co .... G 614 478-9900
Columbus *(G-5253)*

5993 Tobacco stores and stands

Boston Stoker Inc .... F 937 890-6401
Vandalia *(G-14934)*

Smoke Rings Inc .... G 419 420-9966
Findlay *(G-7564)*

5994 News dealers and newsstands

Cruisin Times Magazine .... G 440 331-4615
Rocky River *(G-12837)*

Gazette Publishing Company .... D 419 335-2010
Napoleon *(G-11314)*

Journal Register Company .... D 440 245-6901
Lorain *(G-9416)*

5995 Optical goods stores

▲ Central-1-Optical LLC .... D 330 783-9660
Youngstown *(G-16334)*

Zenni USA LLC .... D 614 439-9850
Obetz *(G-12065)*

5999 Miscellaneous retail stores, nec

A/C Laser Technologies Inc .... F 330 784-3355
Akron *(G-12)*

ABC Appliance Inc .... E 419 693-4414
Oregon *(G-12099)*

Akron Cotton Products Inc .... G 330 434-7171
Akron *(G-32)*

Akron Orthotic Solutions Inc .... G 330 253-3002
Akron *(G-37)*

American Awards Inc .... F 614 875-1850
Grove City *(G-8077)*

Annin & Co Inc .... C 740 622-4447
Coshocton *(G-5968)*

◆ Aquatic Technology .... F 440 236-8330
Columbia Station *(G-5005)*

ARC Solutions Inc .... E 419 542-9272
Hicksville *(G-8371)*

Artistic Rock LLC .... G 216 291-8856
Cleveland *(G-3683)*

◆ Bath & Body Works LLC .... B 614 856-6000
Reynoldsburg *(G-12753)*

Battery Unlimited .... G 740 452-5030
Zanesville *(G-16506)*

Battle Motors Inc .... C 888 328-5443
New Philadelphia *(G-11486)*

◆ Beautyavenues LLC .... C 614 856-6000
Reynoldsburg *(G-12754)*

Beeline Purchasing LLC .... G 513 703-3733
Mason *(G-9959)*

Behrco Inc .... G 419 394-1612
Saint Marys *(G-12945)*

Bell Vault and Monu Works Inc .... E 937 866-2444
Miamisburg *(G-10615)*

▲ Bendon Inc .... D 419 207-3600
Ashland *(G-556)*

Big River Electric Inc .... G 740 446-4360
Gallipolis *(G-7889)*

◆ Black Squirrel Holdings Inc .... E 513 577-7107
Cincinnati *(G-2671)*

Blang Acquisition LLC .... F 937 223-2155
Dayton *(G-6231)*

◆ Boxout LLC .... C 833 462-7746
Hudson *(G-8587)*

Business Idntfction Systems In .... G 614 841-1255
Columbus *(G-5223)*

▲ Catania Medallic Specialty Inc .... E 440 933-9595
Avon Lake *(G-801)*

Centerra Co-Op .... E 419 281-2153
Ashland *(G-562)*

Certified Walk In Tubs .... G 614 436-4848
Columbus *(G-5244)*

Cineen Inc .... G 440 236-3658
Columbia Station *(G-5009)*

Communications Aid Inc .... F 513 475-8453
Cincinnati *(G-2783)*

Copier Resources Inc .... G 614 268-1100
Columbus *(G-5295)*

COS Blueprint Inc .... E 330 376-0022
Akron *(G-115)*

Country Sales & Service LLC .... F 330 683-2500
Orrville *(G-12122)*

▲ Dbhl Inc .... D 216 267-7100
Cleveland *(G-3946)*

▲ DW Hercules LLC .... F 330 830-2498
Massillon *(G-10091)*

E M Service Inc .... F 440 323-3260
Elyria *(G-7137)*

Eastgate Custom Graphics Ltd .... G 513 528-7922
Cincinnati *(G-2854)*

▼ Educational Direction Inc .... G 330 836-8439
Fairlawn *(G-7437)*

▲ Enting Water Conditioning Inc .... E 937 294-5100
Moraine *(G-11175)*

Erosion Control Products Corp .... F 302 815-6500
West Chester *(G-15426)*

Fenwick Gallery of Fine Arts .... G 419 475-1651
Toledo *(G-14286)*

▲ Findaway World LLC .... E 440 893-0808
Solon *(G-13349)*

Fineline Imprints Inc .... F 740 453-1083
Zanesville *(G-16530)*

Flag Lady Inc .... G 614 263-1776
Columbus *(G-5378)*

◆ Foundations Worldwide Inc .... E 330 722-5033
Medina *(G-10326)*

59 MISCELLANEOUS RETAIL

Gerber & Sons Inc .... E 330 897-6201
  Baltic (G-837)
Geygan Enterprises Inc .... F 513 932-4222
  Lebanon (G-9082)
Greg Blume .... G 740 574-2308
  Wheelersburg (G-15809)
Haller Enterprises Inc .... F 330 733-9693
  Akron (G-177)
Hartville Chocolates Inc .... F 330 877-1999
  Hartville (G-8300)
Hathaway Stamp Co .... E 513 621-1052
  Cincinnati (G-2989)
◆ Heading4ward Investment Co ....D 937 293-9994
  Moraine (G-11185)
Health Aid of Ohio Inc .... E 216 252-3900
  Cleveland (G-4174)
Health Nuts Media LLC .... G 818 802-5222
  Cleveland (G-4175)
Hirt Publishing Co Inc .... E 419 946-3010
  Mount Gilead (G-11234)
Hit Trophy Inc .... G 419 445-5356
  Archbold (G-532)
Home City Ice Company .... G 937 461-6028
  Dayton (G-6371)
Home City Ice Company .... F 614 836-2877
  Groveport (G-8146)
House of 10000 Picture Frames .... G 937 254-5541
  Dayton (G-6373)
Incorprted Trstees of The Gspl ....D 216 749-2100
  Middleburg Heights (G-10721)
Indoor Envmtl Specialists Inc .... E 937 433-5202
  Dayton (G-6381)
Jackson Monument Inc .... G 740 286-1590
  Jackson (G-8716)
Johnsons Fire Equipment Co .... F 740 357-4916
  Wellston (G-15330)
K-Mar Structures LLC .... F 231 924-5777
  Junction City (G-8783)
Kathleen Williams .... G 740 360-3515
  Marion (G-9858)
Kempf Surgical Appliances Inc .... F 513 984-5758
  Montgomery (G-11130)
Kriss Kreations .... G 330 405-6102
  Twinsburg (G-14682)
Lazars Art Gllery Crtive Frmng .... G 330 477-8351
  Canton (G-2144)
Leimkuehler Inc .... E 440 899-7842
  Cleveland (G-4319)
Lemsco Inc .... G 419 242-4005
  Toledo (G-14363)
Linde Gas & Equipment Inc .... G 513 821-2192
  Cincinnati (G-3107)
▲ Litehouse Products LLC .... E 440 638-2350
  Strongsville (G-13851)
Love Laugh & Laundry .... G 567 377-1951
  Toledo (G-14370)
M & S AG Solutions LLC .... F 419 598-8675
  Napoleon (G-11323)
Maggard Mmrals Lser Art Tech L .... G 513 282-6969
  Lebanon (G-9095)
Maumee Valley Memorials Inc .... F 419 878-9030
  Waterville (G-15250)
Mayfair Granite Co Inc .... G 216 382-8150
  Cleveland (G-4372)
Mel Wacker Signs Inc .... G 330 832-1726
  Massillon (G-10126)
Michaels Pre-Cast Con Pdts .... F 513 683-1292
  Loveland (G-9497)
Miners Tractor Sales Inc .... F 330 325-9914
  Rootstown (G-12854)
Mixed Logic LLC .... G 440 826-1676
  Valley City (G-14879)

Mt Vernon Machine & Tool Inc .... E 740 397-0311
  Mount Vernon (G-11282)
National Lime and Stone Co .... E 740 387-3485
  Marion (G-9865)
Natural Beauty Products Inc .... F 513 420-9400
  Middletown (G-10847)
North Hill Marble & Granite Co .... F 330 253-2179
  Akron (G-267)
Noxgear LLC .... F 937 317-0199
  Worthington (G-16206)
One Wish LLC .... F 800 505-6883
  Bedford (G-1147)
▲ Osborne Coinage Company LLC ....D 877 480-0456
  Blue Ash (G-1448)
Paul Peterson Safety Div Inc .... E 614 486-4375
  Columbus (G-5661)
PCR Restorations Inc .... F 419 747-7957
  Mansfield (G-9709)
Pettisville Grain Co .... E 419 446-2547
  Pettisville (G-12452)
Piqua Granite & Marble Co Inc .... G 937 773-2000
  Piqua (G-12546)
Plumb Builders Inc .... F 937 293-1111
  Dayton (G-6508)
Pneumatic Specialties Inc .... G 440 729-4400
  Chesterland (G-2488)
Pomacon Inc .... F 330 273-1576
  Brunswick (G-1781)
Precision Replacement LLC .... G 330 908-0410
  Macedonia (G-9569)
Presque Isle Orthtics Prsthtic .... G 216 371-0660
  Cleveland (G-4583)
Primal Life Organics LLC .... E 800 260-4946
  Copley (G-5954)
◆ Printer Components Inc .... G 585 924-5190
  Fairfield (G-7397)
Qualitee Design Sportswear Co .... F 740 333-8337
  Wshngtn Ct Hs (G-16237)
R & J AG Manufacturing Inc .... F 419 962-4707
  Ashland (G-608)
▲ Rainbow Industries Inc .... G 937 323-6493
  Springfield (G-13623)
Ray Communications Inc .... G 330 686-0226
  Stow (G-13720)
Relevium Labs Inc .... G 614 568-7000
  Oxford (G-12212)
▲ Rhc Inc .... E 330 874-3750
  Bolivar (G-1536)
▲ Schaerer Medical Usa Inc .... F 513 561-2241
  Cincinnati (G-3368)
Schenz Theatrical Supply Inc .... F 513 542-6100
  Cincinnati (G-3369)
Schmelzer Industries Inc .... E 740 743-2866
  Somerset (G-13450)
Securcom Inc .... E 419 628-1049
  Minster (G-11060)
Stable Step LLC .... C 800 491-1571
  Wadsworth (G-15068)
Steves Vans ACC Unlimited LLC .... G 740 374-3154
  Marietta (G-9832)
Strictly Stitchery Inc .... F 440 543-7128
  Cleveland (G-4739)
Studgionsgroup LLC .... E 216 804-1561
  Cleveland (G-4743)
Sun Shine Awards .... F 740 425-2504
  Barnesville (G-905)
Tha Presidential Suite LLC .... G 216 338-7287
  Dublin (G-6952)
The Hartman Corp .... G 614 475-5035
  Columbus (G-5822)
▲ Thomas Do-It Center Inc .... E 740 446-2002
  Gallipolis (G-7903)

Toledo Pro Fiberglass Inc .... G 419 241-9390
  Toledo (G-14503)
Town Cntry Technical Svcs Inc .... F 614 866-7700
  Reynoldsburg (G-12775)
Trophy Sports Center LLC .... F 937 376-2311
  Xenia (G-16279)
US Water Company LLC .... G 740 453-0604
  Zanesville (G-16567)
Vandava Inc .... G 614 277-8003
  Grove City (G-8128)
Walter F Stephens Jr Inc .... E 937 746-0521
  Franklin (G-7709)
Water Drop Media Inc .... G 234 600-5817
  Vienna (G-15005)
Welders Supply Inc .... E 216 267-4470
  Brookpark (G-1727)
Welders Supply Inc .... F 216 241-1696
  Cleveland (G-4903)
Western Ohio Graphics .... F 937 335-8769
  Troy (G-14616)
◆ William R Hague Inc ....D 614 836-2115
  Groveport (G-8168)

61 NONDEPOSITORY CREDIT INSTITUTIONS

6141 Personal credit institutions

◆ Mtd Holdings Inc .... B 330 225-2600
  Valley City (G-14882)

6153 Short-term business credit

Lemon Group LLC .... E 614 409-9850
  Obetz (G-12060)

6159 Miscellaneous business credit

Momentum Fleet MGT Group Inc ....D 440 759-2219
  Westlake (G-15765)
◆ Ohio Machinery Co .... C 440 526-6200
  Broadview Heights (G-1665)

62 SECURITY & COMMODITY BROKERS, DEALERS, EXCHANGES & SERVICES

6211 Security brokers and dealers

Western & Southern Lf Insur Co .... A 513 629-1800
  Cincinnati (G-3517)

6282 Investment advice

Linsalata Cpitl Prtners Fund I .... G 440 684-1400
  Cleveland (G-4330)
Schaeffers Investment Research Inc ....D 513 589-3800
  Blue Ash (G-1465)

63 INSURANCE CARRIERS

6311 Life insurance

Western & Southern Lf Insur Co .... A 513 629-1800
  Cincinnati (G-3517)

64 INSURANCE AGENTS, BROKERS AND SERVICE

6411 Insurance agents, brokers, and service

Acu-Serve Corp .... C 330 923-5258
  Akron (G-18)
Beam Technologies Inc .... B 800 648-1179
  Columbus (G-5177)

▲ Forge Industries Inc .... A 330 960-2468
   Youngstown *(G-16359)*

Move Ez Inc .... D 844 466-8339
   Columbus *(G-5583)*

Mxr Imaging Inc .... G 614 219-2011
   Hilliard *(G-8423)*

◆ Safelite Group Inc .... A 614 210-9000
   Columbus *(G-5740)*

65 REAL ESTATE

6512 Nonresidential building operators

Afc Company .... F 330 533-5581
   Canfield *(G-1997)*

Anthony Mining Co Inc .... G 740 282-5301
   Wintersville *(G-16084)*

At Holdings Corporation .... A 216 692-6000
   Cleveland *(G-3694)*

▲ Caravan Packaging Inc .... G 440 243-4100
   Cleveland *(G-3790)*

Garland Industries Inc .... G 216 641-7500
   Cleveland *(G-4104)*

Garland/Dbs Inc .... C 216 641-7500
   Cleveland *(G-4105)*

◆ Park Corporation .... B 216 267-4870
   Medina *(G-10362)*

Perry County Tribune .... F 740 342-4121
   New Lexington *(G-11455)*

◆ Pubco Corporation .... D 216 881-5300
   Cleveland *(G-4597)*

S-P Company Inc .... D 330 782-5651
   Columbiana *(G-5050)*

U S Development Corp .... D 330 673-6900
   Kent *(G-8879)*

Wernli Realty Corporation .... F 937 258-7878
   Beavercreek *(G-1083)*

6515 Mobile home site operators

L C Liming & Sons Inc .... G 513 876-2555
   Felicity *(G-7468)*

6519 Real property lessors, nec

Lloyd F Helber .... G 740 756-9607
   Carroll *(G-2299)*

Prairie Lane Corporation .... G 330 262-3322
   Wooster *(G-16159)*

6531 Real estate agents and managers

EL Ostendorf Inc .... G 440 247-7631
   Chagrin Falls *(G-2377)*

Elite Property Group LLC .... F 216 356-7469
   Elyria *(G-7139)*

Hitti Enterprises Inc .... F 440 243-4100
   Cleveland *(G-4191)*

Kenyetta Bagby Enterprise LLC ..... F 614 584-3426
   Reynoldsburg *(G-12768)*

▲ Lenz Inc .... E 937 277-9364
   Dayton *(G-6405)*

Lloyd F Helber .... G 740 756-9607
   Carroll *(G-2299)*

◆ Nesco Inc .... E 440 461-6000
   Cleveland *(G-4448)*

Rona Enterprises Inc .... G 740 927-9971
   Pataskala *(G-12306)*

Ruscilli Real Estate Services .... F 614 923-6400
   Dublin *(G-6932)*

Sawmill Road Management Co LLC ... E 937 342-9071
   Columbus *(G-5749)*

Stonyridge Inc .... F 937 845-9482
   New Carlisle *(G-11426)*

Wedco LLC .... G 513 309-0781
   Mount Orab *(G-11247)*

6552 Subdividers and developers, nec

Phillips Companies .... E 937 426-5461
   Beavercreek Township *(G-1089)*

Stonyridge Inc .... F 937 845-9482
   New Carlisle *(G-11426)*

67 HOLDING AND OTHER INVESTMENT OFFICES

6719 Holding companies, nec

Akron Brass Holding Corp .... E 330 264-5678
   Wooster *(G-16098)*

◆ Ampac Holdings LLC .... A 513 671-1777
   Cincinnati *(G-2622)*

Armor Consolidated Inc .... A 513 923-5260
   Mason *(G-9952)*

Cpp Group Holdings LLC .... E 216 453-4800
   Cleveland *(G-3912)*

Crane Carrier Holdings LLC .... C 918 286-2889
   New Philadelphia *(G-11496)*

Drt Holdings Inc .... D 937 298-7391
   Dayton *(G-6305)*

Elite Property Group LLC .... F 216 356-7469
   Elyria *(G-7139)*

Hartzell Industries Inc .... F 937 773-6295
   Piqua *(G-12522)*

▼ Hexion Topco LLC .... D 614 225-4000
   Columbus *(G-5430)*

Hexpol Holding Inc .... F 440 834-4644
   Burton *(G-1882)*

Kenyetta Bagby Enterprise LLC ..... F 614 584-3426
   Reynoldsburg *(G-12768)*

Lion Group Inc .... D 937 898-1949
   Dayton *(G-6411)*

Norse Dairy Systems Inc .... C 614 294-4931
   Columbus *(G-5600)*

Vertiv JV Holdings LLC .... A 614 888-0246
   Columbus *(G-5859)*

6726 Investment offices, nec

▲ Westlake Dimex LLC .... C 740 374-3100
   Marietta *(G-9844)*

6794 Patent owners and lessors

Cassanos Inc .... E 937 294-8400
   Dayton *(G-6248)*

Chemstation International Inc .... E 937 294-8265
   Moraine *(G-11166)*

Construction Techniques Inc .... F 216 267-7310
   Cleveland *(G-3900)*

Gold Star Chili Inc .... E 513 231-4541
   Cincinnati *(G-2963)*

Instantwhip Foods Inc .... F 614 488-2536
   Columbus *(G-5464)*

R&D Marketing Group Inc .... G 216 398-9100
   Brooklyn Heights *(G-1697)*

Sakrete Inc .... E 513 242-3644
   Cincinnati *(G-3359)*

▲ Skyline Cem Holdings LLC .... C 513 874-1188
   Fairfield *(G-7408)*

▲ Stanley Steemer Intl Inc .... C 614 764-2007
   Dublin *(G-6945)*

▲ The Cornwell Quality Tool .... D 330 336-3506
   Wadsworth *(G-15069)*

Tomahawk Entrmt Group LLC ...... F 216 505-0548
   Euclid *(G-7302)*

6798 Real estate investment trusts

Infinitaire Industries LLC .... G 216 600-2051
   Euclid *(G-7275)*

6799 Investors, nec

Alpha Zeta Holdings Inc .... G 216 271-1601
   Cleveland *(G-3640)*

Brain Brew Ventures 30 Inc .... F 513 310-6374
   Newtown *(G-11661)*

Brantley Partners IV LP .... G 216 464-8400
   Cleveland *(G-3754)*

Edgewater Capital Partners LP ..... G 216 292-3838
   Independence *(G-8666)*

◆ Kinetico Incorporated .... B 440 564-9111
   Newbury *(G-11628)*

Linsalata Cpitl Prtners Fund I .... G 440 684-1400
   Cleveland *(G-4330)*

Resilience Fund III LP .... E 216 292-0200
   Cleveland *(G-4629)*

70 HOTELS, ROOMING HOUSES, CAMPS, AND OTHER LODGING PLACES

7011 Hotels and motels

Amish Door Inc .... C 330 359-5464
   Wilmot *(G-16065)*

Breitenbach Wine Cellars Inc .... G 330 343-3603
   Dover *(G-6810)*

▲ Continental GL Sls & Inv Group ... E 614 679-1201
   Powell *(G-12669)*

Inns Holdings Ltd .... F 740 345-3700
   Newark *(G-11584)*

John Purdum .... G 513 897-9686
   Waynesville *(G-15298)*

7032 Sporting and recreational camps

Prairie Lane Corporation .... G 330 262-3322
   Wooster *(G-16159)*

7041 Membership-basis organization hotels

American Gild of English Hndbe ... G 937 438-0085
   Cincinnati *(G-2618)*

72 PERSONAL SERVICES

7212 Garment pressing and cleaners' agents

Love Laugh & Laundry .... G 567 377-1951
   Toledo *(G-14370)*

7213 Linen supply

Geauga Group LLC .... G 440 543-8797
   Chagrin Falls *(G-2397)*

7217 Carpet and upholstery cleaning

Image By J & K LLC .... F 888 667-6929
   Maumee *(G-10207)*

Shaheen Oriental Rug Co Inc .... F 330 493-9000
   Canton *(G-2222)*

▲ Stanley Steemer Intl Inc .... C 614 764-2007
   Dublin *(G-6945)*

7218 Industrial launderers

Cintas Corporation .... D 513 631-5750
   Cincinnati *(G-2770)*

◆ Cintas Corporation .... A 513 459-1200
   Cincinnati *(G-2769)*

Cintas Sales Corporation .... B 513 459-1200
   Cincinnati *(G-2771)*

Pneumatic Specialties Inc .... G 440 729-4400
   Chesterland *(G-2488)*

7231 Beauty shops

72 PERSONAL SERVICES

Beaute Asylum LLC .... F 419 377-9933
 Toledo (G-14209)
James C Robinson .... G 513 969-7482
 Cincinnati (G-3036)
Pur Hair Extensions LLC .... G 330 786-5772
 Akron (G-287)
Ransome AC LLC .... G 234 205-6907
 Akron (G-297)

7241 Barber shops

Excalibur Barber LLC .... F 330 729-9006
 Boardman (G-1512)

7251 Shoe repair and shoeshine parlors

Cobblers Corner LLC .... F 330 482-4005
 Columbiana (G-5032)

7261 Funeral service and crematories

Bell Vault and Monu Works Inc .... E 937 866-2444
 Miamisburg (G-10615)
Martin M Hardin .... G 740 282-1234
 Steubenville (G-13671)

7291 Tax return preparation services

Michele Caldwell .... G 937 505-7744
 Dayton (G-6442)
Samb LLC Services .... G 937 660-0115
 Englewood (G-7241)
Steward Edge Bus Solutions .... F 614 826-5305
 Columbus (G-5795)

7299 Miscellaneous personal services

Akron Design & Costume LLC .... G 330 644-0425
 Coventry Township (G-6004)
American Egle Prprty Prsrvtion .... G 855 440-6938
 North Ridgeville (G-11828)
Artisan Constructors LLC .... E 216 800-7641
 Cleveland (G-3680)
B Richardson Inc .... G 330 724-2122
 Akron (G-72)
Buns of Delaware Inc .... E 740 363-2867
 Delaware (G-6706)
Costume Specialists Inc .... E 614 464-2115
 Columbus (G-5298)
D J Klingler Inc .... G 513 891-2284
 Montgomery (G-11129)
Deborah Meredith .... G 330 644-0425
 Coventry Township (G-6008)
Holmes Manufacturing .... G 330 231-6327
 Millersburg (G-10968)
J & G Goecke Clothing LLC .... G 419 692-9981
 Delphos (G-6766)
Mustard Seed Health Fd Mkt Inc .... E 440 519-3663
 Solon (G-13394)
Premier Tanning & Nutrition .... G 419 342-6259
 Shelby (G-13198)
Skyliner .... G 740 738-0874
 Bridgeport (G-1649)
Vandalia Massage Therapy .... G 937 890-8660
 Vandalia (G-14965)
Vulcan Machinery Corporation .... E 330 376-6025
 Akron (G-371)

73 BUSINESS SERVICES

7311 Advertising agencies

Aardvark Screen Prtg & EMB LLC .... F 419 354-6686
 Bowling Green (G-1548)
Advertising Joe LLC Mean .... G 440 247-8200
 Chagrin Falls (G-2367)
▲ Airmate Co Inc .... D 419 636-3184
 Bryan (G-1803)

Black River Group Inc .... E 419 524-6699
 Mansfield (G-9628)
Buckeye Business Forms Inc .... G 614 882-1890
 Westerville (G-15649)
Dee Printing Inc .... F 614 777-8700
 Columbus (G-5322)
Just Business Inc .... F 866 577-3303
 Dayton (G-6395)
Kyle Media Inc .... G 877 775-2538
 Toledo (G-14355)
Mark Advertising Agency Inc .... F 419 626-9000
 Sandusky (G-13079)
Propress Inc .... F 216 631-8200
 Cleveland (G-4593)

7312 Outdoor advertising services

Barnes Advertising Corporation .... E 740 453-6836
 Zanesville (G-16505)
Hart Advertising Inc .... F 419 668-1194
 Norwalk (G-11972)
Ike Smart City .... F 614 294-4898
 Columbus (G-5453)
Kessler Sign Company .... E 740 453-0668
 Zanesville (G-16542)
Norton Outdoor Advertising .... E 513 631-4864
 Cincinnati (G-3205)
Ohio Shelterall Inc .... F 614 882-1110
 Westerville (G-15717)
Orange Barrel Media LLC .... D 614 294-4898
 Columbus (G-5643)

7313 Radio, television, publisher representatives

Agri Communicators Inc .... E 614 273-0465
 Columbus (G-5105)
American City Bus Journals Inc .... B 937 528-4400
 Dayton (G-6199)
Brackish Media LLC .... F 513 394-2871
 Cincinnati (G-2679)
Copley Ohio Newspapers Inc .... C 330 364-5577
 New Philadelphia (G-11493)
Gazette Publishing Company .... D 419 335-2010
 Napoleon (G-11314)
Kyle Media Inc .... G 877 775-2538
 Toledo (G-14355)
News Watchman & Paper .... F 740 947-2149
 Waverly (G-15288)
Ohio Newspaper Services Inc .... G 614 486-6677
 Columbus (G-5623)
Progressor Times .... G 419 396-7567
 Carey (G-2283)
Retain Loyalty LLC .... G 330 830-0839
 Massillon (G-10139)

7319 Advertising, nec

Aztech Printing & Promotions .... G 937 339-0100
 Troy (G-14551)
▲ Cgs Imaging Inc .... F 419 897-3000
 Holland (G-8497)
Design Masters Inc .... G 513 772-7175
 Cincinnati (G-2826)
Digital Color Intl LLC .... F
 Akron (G-130)
Display Dynamics Inc .... E 937 832-2830
 Englewood (G-7229)
Hollywood Imprints LLC .... F 614 501-6040
 Gahanna (G-7838)
Kyle Media Inc .... G 877 775-2538
 Toledo (G-14355)
Malik Media LLC .... F 614 933-0328
 New Albany (G-11383)

SIC SECTION

▲ Performance Packaging Inc .... F 419 478-8805
 Toledo (G-14433)
Sprint Print Inc .... G 740 622-4429
 Coshocton (G-5997)

7322 Adjustment and collection services

C & S Associates Inc .... E 440 461-9661
 Highland Heights (G-8383)
ITM Marketing Inc .... C 740 295-3575
 Coshocton (G-5981)

7331 Direct mail advertising services

▲ Aero Fulfillment Services Corp .... D 800 225-7145
 Mason (G-9945)
American Paper Group Inc .... B 330 758-4545
 Youngstown (G-16309)
Amsive OH LLC .... D 937 885-8000
 Miamisburg (G-10611)
Angstrom Graphics Inc Midwest .... C 216 271-5300
 Cleveland (G-3009)
Baesman Group Inc .... D 614 771-2300
 Hilliard (G-8402)
Bindery & Spc Pressworks Inc .... D 614 873-4623
 Plain City (G-12566)
Brothers Publishing Co LLC .... E 937 548-3330
 Greenville (G-8040)
Buckeye Business Forms Inc .... G 614 882-1890
 Westerville (G-15649)
Cleveland Letter Service Inc .... G 216 781-8300
 Chagrin Falls (G-2371)
▲ Consolidated Graphics Group Inc .... C 216 881-9191
 Cleveland (G-3896)
Cpmm Services Group Inc .... E 614 447-0165
 Columbus (G-5304)
Digital Color Intl LLC .... F
 Akron (G-130)
Directconnectgroup Ltd .... F 216 281-2866
 Cleveland (G-3960)
Eg Enterprise Services Inc .... F 216 431-3300
 Cleveland (G-4001)
▲ Fine Line Graphics Corp .... C 614 486-0276
 Columbus (G-5375)
Franklin Printing Company .... F 740 452-6375
 Zanesville (G-16533)
Gerald L Herrmann Company Inc .... F 513 661-1818
 Cincinnati (G-2949)
Hecks Direct Mail & Prtg Svc .... E 419 661-6028
 Toledo (G-14314)
▲ Hecks Direct Mail Prtg Svc Inc .... F 419 697-3505
 Toledo (G-14315)
Hkm Drect Mkt Cmmnications Inc .... C 800 860-4456
 Cleveland (G-4193)
Laipplys Prtg Mktg Sltions Inc .... G 740 387-9282
 Marion (G-9859)
Macke Brothers Inc .... E 513 771-7500
 Cincinnati (G-3123)
Malik Media LLC .... F 614 933-0328
 New Albany (G-11383)
Master Printing Group Inc .... F 216 351-2246
 Berea (G-1287)
Network Printing & Graphics .... F 614 230-2084
 Columbus (G-5593)
Northcoast Pmm LLC .... F 419 540-8667
 Toledo (G-14399)
Porath Business Services Inc .... F 216 626-0060
 Cleveland (G-4564)
Quez Media Marketing Inc .... F 216 910-0202
 Independence (G-8683)
Retain Loyalty LLC .... G 330 830-0839
 Massillon (G-10139)
Selby Service/Roxy Press Inc .... G 513 241-3445
 Cincinnati (G-3378)

SIC SECTION

73 BUSINESS SERVICES

Traxium LLC... E..... 330 572-8200
 Stow *(G-13732)*

Victory Direct LLC................................... G..... 614 626-0000
 Gahanna *(G-7852)*

Youngstown Letter Shop Inc.................... G..... 330 793-4935
 Youngstown *(G-16484)*

7334 Photocopying and duplicating services

A Grade Notes Inc.................................... G..... 614 299-9999
 Dublin *(G-6856)*

A-A Blueprint Co Inc................................ E..... 330 794-8803
 Akron *(G-11)*

Aztech Printing & Promotions.................. G..... 937 339-0100
 Troy *(G-14551)*

Bethart Enterprises Inc............................ F..... 513 863-6161
 Hamilton *(G-8185)*

Capitol Citicom Inc.................................. E..... 614 472-2679
 Columbus *(G-5234)*

Cincinnati Print Solutions LLC.................. G..... 513 943-9500
 Milford *(G-10900)*

Colortech Graphics & Printing.................. F..... 614 766-2400
 Columbus *(G-5260)*

Corporate Dcment Solutions Inc............... G..... 513 595-8200
 Cincinnati *(G-2797)*

Eg Enterprise Services Inc....................... F..... 216 431-3300
 Cleveland *(G-4001)*

Geygan Enterprises Inc........................... G..... 513 932-4222
 Lebanon *(G-9082)*

Hoster Graphics Company Inc................. F..... 614 299-9770
 Columbus *(G-5446)*

J & J Tire & Alignment.............................. G..... 330 424-5200
 Lisbon *(G-9316)*

Monks Copy Shop Inc.............................. F..... 614 461-6438
 Columbus *(G-5579)*

Morse Enterprises Inc.............................. G..... 513 229-3600
 Mason *(G-10031)*

Northeast Blueprint and Sup Co............... G..... 216 261-7500
 Cleveland *(G-4475)*

Print-Digital Incorporated........................ G..... 330 686-5945
 Stow *(G-13718)*

Printers Devil Inc..................................... E..... 330 650-1218
 Hudson *(G-8608)*

Queen City Reprographics....................... C..... 513 326-2300
 Cincinnati *(G-3319)*

Rhoads Print Center Inc........................... G..... 330 678-2042
 Tallmadge *(G-14045)*

Robert Becker Impressions Inc................. F..... 419 385-5303
 Toledo *(G-14456)*

7335 Commercial photography

Eclipse 3d/Pi LLC.................................... E..... 614 626-8536
 Columbus *(G-5343)*

Queen City Reprographics....................... C..... 513 326-2300
 Cincinnati *(G-3319)*

The Photo-Type Engraving Company........ D..... 513 281-0999
 Cincinnati *(G-3450)*

Tj Metzgers Inc....................................... D..... 419 861-8611
 Toledo *(G-14487)*

Universal Ch Directories LLC................... G..... 419 522-5011
 Mansfield *(G-9729)*

Youngstown ARC Engraving Co............... G..... 330 793-2471
 Youngstown *(G-16476)*

7336 Commercial art and graphic design

Abstract Displays Inc.............................. F..... 513 985-9700
 Blue Ash *(G-1356)*

Academy Graphic Comm Inc.................... E..... 216 661-2550
 Cleveland *(G-3589)*

▲ Alonovus Corp..................................... E..... 330 674-2300
 Millersburg *(G-10940)*

Alvin L Roepke....................................... G..... 419 862-3891
 Elmore *(G-7099)*

Amatech Inc.. E..... 614 252-2506
 Columbus *(G-5119)*

Art-American Printing Plates................... F..... 216 241-4420
 Cleveland *(G-3678)*

Clarity Retail Services LLC...................... D..... 513 800-9369
 West Chester *(G-15395)*

Container Graphics Corp......................... E..... 419 531-5133
 Toledo *(G-14252)*

Converters/Prepress Inc.......................... F..... 937 743-0935
 Carlisle *(G-2287)*

Coyne Graphic Finishing Inc.................... E..... 740 397-6232
 Mount Vernon *(G-11269)*

Digital Color Intl LLC............................... F
 Akron *(G-130)*

Eastgate Custom Graphics Ltd................. G..... 513 528-7922
 Cincinnati *(G-2854)*

Enlarging Arts Inc................................... G..... 330 434-3433
 Akron *(G-142)*

Envoi Design Inc..................................... G..... 513 651-4229
 Cincinnati *(G-2877)*

Eugene Stewart...................................... G..... 937 898-1117
 Dayton *(G-6325)*

Fx Digital Media Inc................................ F..... 216 241-4040
 Cleveland *(G-4095)*

▲ General Theming Contrs LLC................ C..... 614 252-6342
 Columbus *(G-5397)*

Great Lakes Graphics Inc........................ F..... 216 391-0077
 Cleveland *(G-4144)*

Hollywood Imprints LLC........................... F..... 614 501-6040
 Gahanna *(G-7838)*

Insignia Signs Inc................................... G..... 937 866-2341
 Moraine *(G-11186)*

Kent Stow Screen Printing Inc................. G..... 330 923-5118
 Akron *(G-205)*

Kimpton Printing & Spc Co...................... F..... 330 467-1640
 Macedonia *(G-9561)*

Laipplys Prtg Mktg Sltions Inc.................. G..... 740 387-9282
 Marion *(G-9859)*

Malik Media LLC..................................... F..... 614 933-0328
 New Albany *(G-11383)*

Meridian Arts and Graphics..................... F..... 330 759-9099
 Youngstown *(G-16398)*

Midwest Menu Mate Inc.......................... F..... 740 323-2599
 Newark *(G-11592)*

ML Advertising & Design LLC.................. G..... 419 447-6523
 Tiffin *(G-14094)*

Morse Enterprises Inc............................. G..... 513 229-3600
 Mason *(G-10031)*

Mueller Art Cover & Binding Co............... E..... 440 238-3303
 Strongsville *(G-13858)*

Newmast Mktg & Communications........... G..... 614 837-1200
 Columbus *(G-5597)*

ONeil & Associates Inc............................ C..... 937 865-0800
 Miamisburg *(G-10669)*

Painted Hill Inv Group Inc....................... F..... 937 339-1756
 Troy *(G-14600)*

Perrons Printing Company....................... F..... 440 236-8870
 Columbia Station *(G-5016)*

Phantasm Dsgns Sprtsn More Ltd............ G..... 419 538-6737
 Ottawa *(G-12188)*

Professional Screen Printing.................... G..... 740 687-0760
 Lancaster *(G-9033)*

Qualitee Design Sportswear Co................ F..... 740 333-8337
 Wshngtn Ct Hs *(G-16237)*

Quez Media Marketing Inc....................... F..... 216 910-0202
 Independence *(G-8683)*

Rba Inc... G..... 330 336-6700
 Wadsworth *(G-15062)*

Red Barn Screen Printing & EMB.............. F..... 740 474-6657
 Circleville *(G-3555)*

Roban Inc... G..... 330 794-1059
 Lakemore *(G-8958)*

Sanger & EBY Design LLC....................... F..... 513 784-9046
 Cincinnati *(G-3362)*

Schuerholz Inc.. G..... 937 294-5218
 Dayton *(G-6561)*

Screen Works Inc.................................... E..... 937 264-9111
 Dayton *(G-6564)*

▲ Shamrock Companies Inc..................... D..... 440 899-9510
 Westlake *(G-15786)*

Sylvan Studios Inc................................... G..... 419 882-3423
 Sylvania *(G-14016)*

The Photo-Type Engraving Company........ D..... 513 281-0999
 Cincinnati *(G-3450)*

True Dinero Records & Tech LLC............. G..... 513 428-4610
 Cincinnati *(G-3470)*

Visual Art Graphic Services..................... G..... 330 274-2775
 Mantua *(G-9745)*

Western Ohio Graphics........................... F..... 937 335-8769
 Troy *(G-14616)*

White Tiger Inc....................................... F..... 740 852-4873
 London *(G-9397)*

▲ Wis 1985 Inc....................................... F..... 423 581-4916
 Dayton *(G-6657)*

Woodrow Manufacturing Co..................... E..... 937 399-9333
 Springfield *(G-13657)*

Youngstown Pre-Press Inc....................... F..... 330 793-3690
 Youngstown *(G-16486)*

7338 Secretarial and court reporting

Ohio Shelterall Inc.................................. F..... 614 882-1110
 Westerville *(G-15717)*

Sound Communications Inc..................... E..... 614 875-8500
 Grove City *(G-8120)*

7342 Disinfecting and pest control services

A Best Trmt & Pest Ctrl Sups................... G..... 330 434-5555
 Akron *(G-10)*

Hawthorne Gardening Company............... E..... 360 883-8846
 Marysville *(G-9913)*

Image By J & K LLC................................ F..... 888 667-6929
 Maumee *(G-10207)*

▲ Scotts Miracle-Gro Company................ B..... 937 644-0011
 Marysville *(G-9935)*

7349 Building maintenance services, nec

All Pack Services LLC............................. G..... 614 935-0964
 Grove City *(G-8076)*

American Egle Prprty Prsrvtion................ G..... 855 440-6938
 North Ridgeville *(G-11828)*

Bleachtech LLC....................................... E..... 216 921-1980
 Seville *(G-13139)*

▲ Chemical Solvents Inc......................... E..... 216 741-9310
 Cleveland *(G-3816)*

Cincinnati A Flter Sls Svc Inc................... E..... 513 242-3400
 Cincinnati *(G-2737)*

Cleaning Lady Inc................................... G..... 419 589-5566
 Mansfield *(G-9638)*

Contract Lumber Inc............................... F..... 614 751-1109
 Columbus *(G-5289)*

Green Impressions LLC........................... D..... 440 240-8508
 Sheffield Village *(G-13182)*

High-TEC Industrial Services................... D..... 937 667-1772
 Tipp City *(G-14137)*

Image By J & K LLC................................ F..... 888 667-6929
 Maumee *(G-10207)*

Indoor Envmtl Specialists Inc................... E..... 937 433-5202
 Dayton *(G-6381)*

▲ Leadec Corp....................................... E..... 513 731-3590
 Blue Ash *(G-1420)*

Lima Sheet Metal Machine & Mfg............. E..... 419 229-1161
 Lima *(G-9264)*

Link To Success Inc................................ G..... 888 959-4203
 Norwalk *(G-11978)*

Employee Codes: A=Over 500 employees, B=251-500
C=101-250, D=51-100, E=20-50, F=10-19, G=1-9

73 BUSINESS SERVICES

MPW Industrial Svcs Group Inc .... B 740 927-8790
  Hebron *(G-8350)*
Omega Cementing Co .... G 330 695-7147
  Apple Creek *(G-508)*
Omnipresence Cleaning LLC .... F 937 250-4749
  Dayton *(G-6491)*
▲ Paro Services Co .... F 330 467-1300
  Twinsburg *(G-14707)*
Phase II Enterprises Inc .... G 330 484-2113
  Canton *(G-2196)*
Primo Services LLC .... F 513 725-7888
  Cincinnati *(G-3276)*
Richland Newhope Inds Inc .... C 419 774-4400
  Mansfield *(G-9712)*
RT Industries Inc .... G 937 335-5784
  Troy *(G-14606)*
Sand PROperties&landscaping .... G 440 360-7386
  Westlake *(G-15781)*
Whempys Corp .... G 614 888-6670
  Worthington *(G-16218)*

7352 Medical equipment rental

Columbus Prescr Rehabilitation .... G 614 294-1600
  Westerville *(G-15696)*
Health Aid of Ohio Inc .... E 216 252-3900
  Cleveland *(G-4174)*
Kempf Surgical Appliances Inc .... F 513 984-5758
  Montgomery *(G-11130)*

7353 Heavy construction equipment rental

Brewpro Inc .... G 513 577-7200
  Cincinnati *(G-2682)*
Dover Fabrication and Burn Inc .... G 330 339-1057
  Dover *(G-6819)*
Efco Corp .... G 614 876-1226
  Columbus *(G-5347)*
▲ Eleet Cryogenics Inc .... E 330 874-4009
  Bolivar *(G-1524)*
◆ F & M Mafco Inc .... C 513 367-2151
  Harrison *(G-8273)*
Ioppolo Concrete Corporation .... E 440 439-6606
  Bedford *(G-1130)*
▲ Lefeld Welding & Stl Sups Inc .... E 419 678-2397
  Coldwater *(G-4995)*
◆ Ohio Machinery Co .... C 440 526-6200
  Broadview Heights *(G-1665)*
Phillips Ready Mix Co .... E 937 426-5151
  Beavercreek Township *(G-1090)*
Pollock Research & Design Inc .... E 330 332-3300
  Salem *(G-13023)*
Rnm Holdings Inc .... F 614 444-5556
  Columbus *(G-5726)*
The Wagner-Smith Company .... B 866 338-0398
  Moraine *(G-11214)*

7359 Equipment rental and leasing, nec

A & A Safety Inc .... F 937 567-9781
  Beavercreek *(G-1068)*
A & A Safety Inc .... E 513 943-6100
  Amelia *(G-447)*
ABC Signs Inc .... F 513 241-8884
  Cincinnati *(G-2590)*
BJ Equipment Ltd .... E 614 497-1188
  Columbus *(G-5193)*
Brinkman LLC .... F 419 204-5934
  Lima *(G-9225)*
Cattron Holdings Inc .... E 234 806-0018
  Warren *(G-15150)*
Certon Technologies Inc .... F 440 786-7185
  Bedford *(G-1111)*
Copier Resources Inc .... G 614 268-1100
  Columbus *(G-5295)*

Cuyahoga Vending Co Inc .... C 440 353-9595
  North Ridgeville *(G-11837)*
◆ De Nora Tech LLC .... D 440 710-5334
  Concord Township *(G-5905)*
Dearing Compressor and Pu .... E 330 783-2258
  Youngstown *(G-16348)*
Eaton Leasing Corporation .... B 216 382-2292
  Beachwood *(G-986)*
Elliott Tool Technologies Ltd .... D 937 253-6133
  Dayton *(G-6318)*
Galion Canvas Products .... G 419 468-5333
  Galion *(G-7876)*
Glawe Manufacturing Co Inc .... F 937 754-0064
  Fairborn *(G-7317)*
Golf Car Company Inc .... F 614 873-1055
  Plain City *(G-12580)*
Great Lakes Crushing Ltd .... D 440 944-5500
  Wickliffe *(G-15833)*
Hansen Scaffolding LLC .... F 513 574-9000
  West Chester *(G-15561)*
Higgins Construction & Supply Co Inc .. F 937 364-2331
  Hillsboro *(G-8458)*
Hull Ready Mix Concrete Inc .... F 419 625-8070
  Sandusky *(G-13064)*
Importers Direct LLC .... F 330 436-3260
  Akron *(G-189)*
Loft Violin Shop .... F 614 267-7221
  Columbus *(G-5531)*
Paul Peterson Company .... F 614 486-4375
  Columbus *(G-5660)*
Paul Peterson Safety Div Inc .... E 614 486-4375
  Columbus *(G-5661)*
Powerclean Equipment Company .... F 513 202-0001
  Cleves *(G-4963)*
▲ Rainbow Industries Inc .... F 937 323-6493
  Springfield *(G-13623)*
Rambasek Realty Inc .... F 937 228-1189
  Dayton *(G-6540)*
South Akron Awning Co .... F 330 848-7611
  Akron *(G-333)*
Tarpco Inc .... F 330 677-8277
  Kent *(G-8871)*
▲ Thomas Do-It Center Inc .... E 740 446-2002
  Gallipolis *(G-7903)*
▼ Trailer One Inc .... F 330 723-7474
  Medina *(G-10388)*
Tri State Equipment Company .... G 513 738-7227
  Shandon *(G-13161)*
Waco Scaffolding & Equipment Inc .... A 216 749-8900
  Cleveland *(G-4889)*
West Equipment Company Inc .... G 419 698-1601
  Toledo *(G-14522)*
Williams Scotsman Inc .... D 614 449-8675
  Columbus *(G-5878)*
Wolf G T Awning & Tent Co .... F 937 548-4161
  Greenville *(G-8065)*

7363 Help supply services

Aqua Technology Group LLC .... G 513 298-1183
  West Chester *(G-15367)*
▲ Channel Products Inc .... D 440 423-0113
  Solon *(G-13328)*
▲ Cima Inc .... G 513 382-8976
  Hamilton *(G-8192)*
Fluff Boutique .... G 513 227-6614
  Cincinnati *(G-2911)*
Industrial Repair and Mfg .... F 419 822-0314
  Delta *(G-6786)*
▲ Industrial Repair and Mfg .... E 419 822-4232
  Delta *(G-6787)*
Theiss Uav Solutions LLC .... G 330 584-2070
  North Benton *(G-11711)*

Upshift Work LLC .... C 513 813-5695
  Cincinnati *(G-3485)*

7371 Custom computer programming services

Aclara Technologies LLC .... C 440 528-7200
  Solon *(G-13305)*
Advanced Prgrm Resources Inc .... E 614 761-9994
  Dublin *(G-6857)*
Airwave Communications Cons .... G 419 331-1526
  Lima *(G-9218)*
American Power LLC .... F 937 235-0418
  Dayton *(G-6202)*
Analytica Usa Inc .... F 513 348-2333
  Dayton *(G-6206)*
Application Link Incorporated .... F 614 934-1735
  Columbus *(G-5150)*
Armada Power LLC .... G 614 721-4844
  Columbus *(G-5154)*
Associated Software Cons Inc .... F 440 826-1010
  Lakewood *(G-8966)*
Atr Distributing Company .... G 513 353-1800
  Cincinnati *(G-2641)*
Brainmaster Technologies Inc .... G 440 232-6000
  Bedford *(G-1107)*
Brown Dave Products Inc .... G 513 738-1576
  Hamilton *(G-8188)*
Cerkl Incorporated .... D 513 813-8425
  Blue Ash *(G-1378)*
Cerner Corporation .... D 740 826-7678
  New Concord *(G-11432)*
Chatterbox Sports LLC .... F 513 545-4754
  Hamilton *(G-8190)*
Cimx LLC .... E 513 248-7700
  Cincinnati *(G-2735)*
Command Alkon Incorporated .... E 614 799-0600
  Dublin *(G-6876)*
Computer Allied Technology Co .... G 614 457-2292
  Columbus *(G-5284)*
Computer Workshop Inc .... E 614 798-9505
  Dublin *(G-6877)*
Corporate Elevator LLC .... G 614 288-1847
  Columbus *(G-5297)*
Cott Systems Inc .... D 614 847-4405
  Columbus *(G-5299)*
Datcomedia LLC .... G 419 866-6301
  Swanton *(G-13972)*
Deemsys Inc .... D 614 322-9928
  Gahanna *(G-7833)*
Drb Holdings LLC .... B 330 645-3299
  Akron *(G-134)*
Drb Systems LLC .... B 330 645-3299
  Akron *(G-135)*
Drs Signal Technologies Inc .... E 937 429-7470
  Beavercreek *(G-1048)*
Eci Macola/Max LLC .... C 978 539-6186
  Dublin *(G-6883)*
Electronic Concepts Engrg Inc .... F 419 861-9000
  Holland *(G-8509)*
Embedded Planet Inc .... F 216 245-4180
  Solon *(G-13342)*
Empyracom Inc .... F 330 744-5570
  Boardman *(G-1511)*
Facts Inc .... E 330 928-2332
  Cuyahoga Falls *(G-6082)*
Forcam Inc .... F 513 878-2780
  Cincinnati *(G-2914)*
Foundation Software LLC .... B 330 220-8383
  Strongsville *(G-13834)*
▲ Fscreations Corporation .... D 330 746-3015
  Youngstown *(G-16360)*

SIC SECTION

73 BUSINESS SERVICES

Ganymede Technologies Corp............... G 419 562-5522
  Bucyrus (G-1860)
Gb Liquidating Company Inc................ E 513 248-7600
  Milford (G-10907)
Generic Systems Inc............................... F 419 841-8460
  Holland (G-8510)
Global Realms LLC................................ G 614 828-7284
  Gahanna (G-7836)
▼ Gracie Plum Investments Inc............ E 740 355-9029
  Portsmouth (G-12645)
H Mack Charles & Associates Inc....... E 513 791-4456
  Blue Ash (G-1402)
Hab Inc.. E 608 785-7650
  Solon (G-13358)
Health Nuts Media LLC......................... G 818 802-5222
  Cleveland (G-4175)
Intelligrated Inc..................................... A 513 874-0788
  West Chester (G-15565)
▲ Intelligrated Systems Inc................... A 866 936-7300
  Mason (G-10010)
Intelligrated Systems LLC.................... A 513 701-7300
  Mason (G-10011)
IPA Ltd.. F 614 523-3974
  Columbus (G-5479)
Jasstek Inc... F 614 808-3600
  Dublin (G-6902)
▲ Keithley Instruments LLC................... C 440 248-0400
  Solon (G-13377)
Lantek Systems Inc............................... G 877 805-1028
  Mason (G-10020)
Leidos Inc... D 937 656-8433
  Beavercreek (G-1055)
Link Systems Inc................................... F 800 321-8770
  Solon (G-13381)
Malik Media LLC.................................... F 614 933-0328
  New Albany (G-11383)
▲ Masterbrand Cabinets LLC................ B 812 482-2527
  Beachwood (G-999)
Miles Midprint Inc.................................. F 216 860-4770
  Cleveland (G-4413)
Navistone Inc... E 844 677-3667
  Cincinnati (G-3184)
NCR Technology Center....................... G 937 445-1936
  Dayton (G-6466)
Online Mega Sellers Corp..................... G 888 384-6468
  Toledo (G-14415)
Pathfinder Cmpt Systems Inc.............. G 330 928-1961
  Barberton (G-889)
Proficient Info Tech Inc........................ G 937 470-1300
  Dayton (G-6531)
Profound Logic Software Inc.............. E 937 439-7925
  Dayton (G-6532)
Pwi Inc.. G 732 212-8110
  New Albany (G-11389)
Qc Software LLC.................................. E 513 469-1424
  Cincinnati (G-3308)
Quez Media Marketing Inc.................. F 216 910-0202
  Independence (G-8683)
Qxsoft LLC... G 740 777-9609
  Lewis Center (G-9177)
Rockhead Group Usa LLC.................... G 216 310-1569
  Beachwood (G-1019)
Sanctuary Software Studio Inc........... E 330 666-9690
  Fairlawn (G-7448)
Santec Resources Inc.......................... F 614 664-9540
  Columbus (G-5746)
▲ Sarcom Inc.. A 614 854-1300
  Lewis Center (G-9180)
Sest Inc.. F 440 777-9777
  Westlake (G-15785)
Sightgain Inc... F 202 494-9317
  Mason (G-10056)

Signalysis Inc.. F 513 528-6164
  Cincinnati (G-3392)
Simplevms LLC..................................... F 888 255-8918
  Cincinnati (G-3393)
Soaring Software Solutions Inc.......... F 419 442-7676
  Swanton (G-13982)
Stellar Systems Inc............................... G 513 921-8748
  Cincinnati (G-3421)
Steward Edge Bus Solutions............... F 614 826-5305
  Columbus (G-5795)
Tata America Intl Corp......................... B 513 677-6500
  Milford (G-10925)
▲ Teachers Publishing Group................ F 614 486-0631
  Hilliard (G-8445)
Tech4imaging LLC................................ F 614 214-2655
  Columbus (G-5817)
Technosoft Inc...................................... F 513 985-9877
  Blue Ash (G-1478)
Thyme Inc.. F 484 872-8430
  Akron (G-357)
▲ Timekeeping Systems Inc.................. F 216 595-0890
  Solon (G-13439)
Triad Governmental Systems.............. E 937 376-5446
  Xenia (G-16278)
◆ Truck Fax Inc....................................... G 216 921-8866
  Cleveland (G-4835)
Virtual Hold Tech Slutions LLC............ E 330 670-2200
  Akron (G-370)
Wentworth Solutions............................ F 440 212-7696
  Hinckley (G-8479)

7372 Prepackaged software

911cellular LLC..................................... F 216 283-6100
  Solon (G-13304)
About Time Software Inc..................... G 614 759-6295
  Pickerington (G-12454)
Acclaimd Inc.. F 614 219-9519
  Columbus (G-5093)
Acu-Serve Corp..................................... C 330 923-5258
  Akron (G-18)
Ad Company Holdings Inc................... E 404 256-3544
  Akron (G-19)
Advanced Prgrm Resources Inc.......... E 614 761-9994
  Dublin (G-6857)
Advant-E Corporation.......................... F 937 429-4288
  Beavercreek (G-1039)
Agile Global Solutions Inc.................. E 916 655-7745
  Independence (G-8652)
AMD Services.. G 614 571-7190
  Dublin (G-6859)
Application Link Incorporated............ F 614 934-1735
  Columbus (G-5150)
Associated Software Cons Inc............ F 440 826-1010
  Lakewood (G-8966)
Atr Distributing Company.................... F 513 353-1800
  Cincinnati (G-2642)
Atr Distributing Company.................... G 513 353-1800
  Cincinnati (G-2641)
Automation Software & Engrg............ F 330 405-2990
  Twinsburg (G-14632)
Avt Technology Solutions LLC........... D 727 539-7429
  Groveport (G-8130)
Big River Online.................................... G 855 244-7487
  Cleveland (G-3736)
Bjond Inc... G 614 537-7246
  Columbus (G-5194)
Building Block Performance LLC........ G 614 918-7476
  Plain City (G-12568)
Butler Tech.. E 513 867-1028
  Fairfield Township (G-7430)
Bybe Inc... G 614 706-3050
  Columbus (G-5224)

Cake LLC.. G 614 592-7681
  Dublin (G-6870)
Capitol Citicom Inc............................... E 614 472-2679
  Columbus (G-5234)
Cayosoft Inc.. E 614 423-6718
  Westerville (G-15650)
Cbts Technology Solutions LLC.......... B 440 569-2300
  Cleveland (G-3800)
CCA Youngstown.................................. G 615 263-3000
  Youngstown (G-16332)
Cequence Security Inc........................ C 650 437-6338
  Blue Ash (G-1377)
Cerkl Incorporated............................... D 513 813-8425
  Blue Ash (G-1378)
Cerner Corporation.............................. D 740 826-7678
  New Concord (G-11432)
Check Point Software Tech Inc........... E 440 748-0900
  Cleveland (G-3814)
Cherrybend Custom Aplicat LLC......... G 937 584-4269
  Wilmington (G-16044)
Cimx LLC.. E 513 248-7700
  Cincinnati (G-2735)
Clinicl Otcms Mngmnt Syst LLC......... D 330 650-9900
  Broadview Heights (G-1658)
Cluster Software Inc............................ G 614 760-9380
  Columbus (G-5256)
Coffing Corporation.............................. E 513 919-2813
  Liberty Twp (G-9212)
Colburn Patterson LLC......................... G 419 866-5544
  Holland (G-8499)
Columbus Incontact............................. F 801 245-8369
  Columbus (G-5266)
Columbus International Corp.............. F 614 917-2274
  Lewis Center (G-9156)
Columbus International Corp.............. G 614 323-1086
  Columbus (G-5269)
Computer Enterprise Inc...................... G 216 228-7156
  Lakewood (G-8972)
Concept Xxi Inc..................................... G 216 831-2121
  Beachwood (G-981)
Corporate Elevator LLC....................... G 614 288-1847
  Columbus (G-5297)
Creative Microsystems Inc.................. D 937 836-4499
  Englewood (G-7227)
Crimson Gate Consulting Co............... G 614 805-0897
  Dublin (G-6878)
Csg Software.. G 614 986-2600
  Columbus (G-5309)
Custom Information Systems Inc....... F 614 875-2245
  Grove City (G-8086)
D+h USA Corporation.......................... C 513 381-9400
  Cincinnati (G-2814)
Dakota Software Corporation............. D 216 765-7100
  Cleveland (G-3937)
Datatrak International Inc.................... E 440 443-0082
  Beachwood (G-983)
Datcomedia LLC.................................... G 419 866-6301
  Swanton (G-13972)
Delphia Consulting LLC........................ E 614 421-2000
  Columbus (G-5325)
Delta Media Group Inc......................... D 330 493-0350
  North Canton (G-11720)
Digisoft Systems Corporation............. G 937 833-5016
  Brookville (G-1734)
Dr Dave Solutions LLC......................... G 614 219-6543
  Dublin (G-6880)
Drb Holdings LLC.................................. B 330 645-3299
  Akron (G-134)
Drb Systems LLC.................................. B 330 645-3299
  Akron (G-135)
E Ventus Corporation........................... F 216 643-6840
  Independence (G-8664)

73 BUSINESS SERVICES

Eagle Software Corp .... G 937 630-4548
   Oakwood *(G-12027)*

Echo Mobile Solutions LLC .... G 614 282-3756
   Pickerington *(G-12460)*

Eci Macola/Max LLC .... C 978 539-6186
   Dublin *(G-6883)*

Eclipse .... G 419 564-7482
   Galion *(G-7873)*

Edict Systems Inc .... E 937 429-4288
   Beavercreek *(G-1049)*

Elytus Ltd .... F 614 824-4985
   Columbus *(G-5350)*

Empyracom Inc .... F 330 744-5570
   Boardman *(G-1511)*

◆ Esko-Graphics Inc .... D 937 454-1721
   Miamisburg *(G-10637)*

Espline LLC .... G 401 234-4520
   Columbus *(G-5360)*

Ewebschedule .... G 614 882-0726
   Westerville *(G-15655)*

Explorys Inc .... E 216 767-4700
   Cleveland *(G-4042)*

Exponentia US Inc .... G 614 944-5103
   Columbus *(G-5365)*

Facilities Management Ex LLC .... D 614 519-2186
   Columbus *(G-5370)*

Fifth Third Proc Solutions Inc .... F 800 972-3030
   Cincinnati *(G-2904)*

Flexnova Inc .... F 216 288-6961
   Cleveland *(G-4068)*

Flypaper Studio Inc .... F 602 801-2208
   Cincinnati *(G-2912)*

Forcam Inc .... F 513 878-2780
   Cincinnati *(G-2914)*

Foundation Software LLC .... B 330 220-8383
   Strongsville *(G-13834)*

▲ Fscreations Corporation .... D 330 746-3015
   Youngstown *(G-16360)*

Fusion Software Inc .... G 330 723-2957
   Medina *(G-10329)*

Gaslight Holdings LLC .... E 513 470-3525
   Cincinnati *(G-2933)*

Glance Software LLC .... F 844 383-2500
   Hamilton *(G-8213)*

▼ Gracie Plum Investments Inc .... E 740 355-9029
   Portsmouth *(G-12645)*

H Mack Charles & Associates Inc .... E 513 791-4456
   Blue Ash *(G-1402)*

Hab Inc .... E 608 785-7650
   Solon *(G-13358)*

Health Nuts Media LLC .... G 818 802-5222
   Cleveland *(G-4175)*

Honeywell International Inc .... G 513 745-7200
   Cincinnati *(G-3007)*

Hyland Software Inc .... A 440 788-5000
   Westlake *(G-15757)*

ICC Systems Inc .... G 614 524-0299
   Sunbury *(G-13956)*

Ideal Integrations LLC .... E 614 786-7100
   Worthington *(G-16197)*

Idialogs LLC .... G 937 372-2890
   Xenia *(G-16264)*

Igel Technology America LLC .... E 954 739-9990
   Cincinnati *(G-3016)*

Ignyte Assurance Platform .... E 833 446-9831
   Dayton *(G-6380)*

Incessant Software Inc .... G 614 206-2211
   Lancaster *(G-9019)*

Innerapps LLC .... G 419 467-3110
   Perrysburg *(G-12392)*

Integrity Group Consulting Inc .... F 614 759-9148
   Reynoldsburg *(G-12767)*

Intellinetics Inc .... F 614 388-8908
   Columbus *(G-5470)*

Iot Diagnostics LLC .... G 844 786-7631
   West Chester *(G-15449)*

Ireportsource .... F 888 294-9578
   Cincinnati *(G-3031)*

Ivy Ventures LLC .... G 513 259-3307
   Fairfield *(G-7373)*

Janova LLC .... G 614 638-6785
   New Albany *(G-11381)*

Jasstek Inc .... F 614 808-3600
   Dublin *(G-6902)*

Jda Software Group Inc .... F 480 308-3000
   Akron *(G-195)*

Jenzabar Inc .... F 513 563-4542
   Blue Ash *(G-1412)*

Jst LLC .... G 614 423-7815
   Westerville *(G-15661)*

Kapios LLC .... G 567 661-0772
   Toledo *(G-14344)*

Lantek Systems Inc .... G 877 805-1028
   Mason *(G-10020)*

Learn21 A Flxble Lrng Cllbrtiv .... F 513 402-2121
   Blue Ash *(G-1421)*

Lectora .... G 513 929-0188
   Cincinnati *(G-3098)*

Liminal Esports LLC .... G 440 423-5856
   Gates Mills *(G-7928)*

Linestream Technologies Inc .... G 216 862-7874
   Cleveland *(G-4329)*

Link Systems Inc .... F 800 321-8770
   Solon *(G-13381)*

Lost Technology LLP .... G 513 685-0054
   West Chester *(G-15459)*

Manuvis Corp .... G 440 352-6261
   Painesville *(G-12249)*

Matrix Management Solutions .... E 330 470-3700
   Canton *(G-2154)*

McAfee LLC .... G 440 892-0173
   Cleveland *(G-4379)*

Miami Valley Eductl Cmpt Assn .... F 937 767-1468
   Yellow Springs *(G-16284)*

Michele Caldwell .... G 937 505-7744
   Dayton *(G-6442)*

Microsoft Corporation .... G 216 986-1440
   Cleveland *(G-4404)*

Miles Midprint Inc .... F 216 860-4770
   Cleveland *(G-4413)*

Mim Software Inc .... C 216 455-0600
   Beachwood *(G-1000)*

Mirus Adapted Tech LLC .... E 614 402-4585
   Dublin *(G-6910)*

Move Ez Inc .... D 844 466-8339
   Columbus *(G-5583)*

Msm Fundraising LLC .... G 740 369-8160
   Delaware *(G-6738)*

Navistore Inc .... E 844 677-3667
   Cincinnati *(G-3184)*

Newton Software .... F 714 469-5773
   Cincinnati *(G-3192)*

Nextmed Systems Inc .... E 216 674-0511
   Cincinnati *(G-3195)*

Northrop Grmmn Spce & Mssn Sys .... D 937 259-4956
   Dayton *(G-6474)*

Nsa Technologies LLC .... G 330 576-4600
   Akron *(G-269)*

Nuance Company .... F 740 964-0367
   Granville *(G-8022)*

▲ Ohio Cllbrtive Lrng Sltons Inc .... E 216 595-5289
   Strongsville *(G-13862)*

Ohio Distinctive Enterprises .... E 614 459-0453
   Columbus *(G-5616)*

One Cloud Services LLC .... G 513 231-9500
   Cincinnati *(G-3223)*

Onguard Systems LLC .... F 614 325-0551
   Dublin *(G-6918)*

Onx Acquisition LLC .... B 440 569-2300
   Mayfield Heights *(G-10253)*

Onx Holdings LLC .... D 866 587-2287
   Cincinnati *(G-3226)*

Open Text Inc .... E 614 658-3588
   Hilliard *(G-8429)*

Oracle LLC .... F 724 979-2269
   Youngstown *(G-16407)*

Organalytix LLC .... G 908 938-6711
   West Chester *(G-15473)*

Osb Software Inc .... F 440 542-9145
   Solon *(G-13401)*

Pakra LLC .... F 614 477-6965
   Columbus *(G-5651)*

Pamee LLC .... E 216 232-9255
   Rocky River *(G-12841)*

Parallel Technologies Inc .... D 614 798-9700
   Dublin *(G-6920)*

Pathfinder Cmpt Systems Inc .... G 330 928-1961
   Barberton *(G-889)*

Patrick J Burke & Co .... E 513 455-8200
   Cincinnati *(G-3237)*

Patriot Software LLC .... G 877 968-7147
   Canton *(G-2193)*

Paycor Hcm Inc .... F 800 381-0053
   Cincinnati *(G-3243)*

Perdatum Inc .... G 614 761-1578
   Hilliard *(G-8430)*

Perfect Probate .... G 513 791-4100
   Cincinnati *(G-3246)*

Phantom Technology LLC .... G 614 710-0074
   Hilliard *(G-8431)*

Posm Software LLC .... F 859 274-0041
   Mansfield *(G-9710)*

Proficient Info Tech Inc .... G 937 470-1300
   Dayton *(G-6531)*

Profound Logic Software Inc .... E 937 439-7925
   Dayton *(G-6532)*

Projitech Inc .... G 970 333-9727
   Cleveland *(G-4592)*

Pwi Inc .... G 732 212-8110
   New Albany *(G-11389)*

Qc Software LLC .... E 513 469-1424
   Cincinnati *(G-3308)*

Quest Software Inc .... E 614 336-9223
   Dublin *(G-6929)*

Qxsoft LLC .... G 740 777-9609
   Lewis Center *(G-9177)*

R & H Enterprises Llc .... G 216 702-4449
   Richmond Heights *(G-12810)*

R & L Software LLC .... G 513 847-4942
   Monroe *(G-11118)*

Realeflow LLC .... G 855 545-2095
   Brunswick *(G-1787)*

Rebiz LLC .... E 844 467-3249
   Cleveland *(G-4618)*

Retail Management Products Ltd .... F 740 548-1725
   Lewis Center *(G-9178)*

Retalix Inc .... E 937 384-2277
   Miamisburg *(G-10676)*

Revolution Group Inc .... D 614 212-1111
   Westerville *(G-15675)*

Rina Systems LLC .... G 513 469-7462
   Cincinnati *(G-3341)*

Rivals Sports Grille LLC .... E 216 267-0005
   Middleburg Heights *(G-10726)*

Ross Group Inc .... G 937 427-3069
   Blue Ash *(G-1461)*

SIC SECTION
73 BUSINESS SERVICES

Samegoal Inc .... G 216 766-5713
   Beachwood *(G-1021)*

Sanctuary Software Studio Inc .... E 330 666-9690
   Fairlawn *(G-7448)*

Sanger & EBY Design LLC .... F 513 784-9046
   Cincinnati *(G-3362)*

▲ Sarcom Inc .... A 614 854-1300
   Lewis Center *(G-9180)*

Savi Corporation Inc .... G 330 277-3300
   Salem *(G-13030)*

SC Strategic Solutions LLC .... C 567 424-6054
   Norwalk *(G-11988)*

Sest Inc .... F 440 777-9777
   Westlake *(G-15785)*

Sightgain Inc .... F 202 494-9317
   Mason *(G-10056)*

Sigmatek Systems LLC .... D 513 674-0005
   Cincinnati *(G-3391)*

Signal Interactive .... G 614 360-3938
   Columbus *(G-5767)*

Simplevms LLC .... F 888 255-8918
   Cincinnati *(G-3393)*

Snap-On Business Solutions Inc .... B 330 659-1600
   Richfield *(G-12799)*

Soaring Software Solutions Inc .... F 419 442-7676
   Swanton *(G-13982)*

Software Solutions Inc .... E 513 932-6667
   Dayton *(G-6578)*

Souzza LLC .... G 330 479-9500
   Massillon *(G-10147)*

Spearfysh Inc .... G 330 487-0300
   Hudson *(G-8613)*

Stac Enterprises LLC .... G 513 574-7822
   Cincinnati *(G-3413)*

Stack Construction Tech Inc .... F 513 445-5122
   Blue Ash *(G-1468)*

Starwin Industries LLC .... E 937 293-8568
   Dayton *(G-6591)*

Sterling Commerce LLC .... A 614 798-2192
   Dublin *(G-6947)*

Steward Edge Bus Solutions .... F 614 826-5305
   Columbus *(G-5795)*

Sylvania Mose Ldge No 1579 Lya .... F 419 885-4953
   Sylvania *(G-14017)*

Syntec LLC .... F 440 229-6262
   Rocky River *(G-12845)*

Tarigma Corporation .... F 614 436-3734
   Columbus *(G-5809)*

Tata America Intl Corp .... B 513 677-6500
   Milford *(G-10925)*

Technosoft Inc .... F 513 985-9877
   Blue Ash *(G-1478)*

Telehealth Care Solutions LLC .... G 440 823-6023
   Brecksville *(G-1633)*

▲ Timekeeping Systems Inc .... F 216 595-0890
   Solon *(G-13439)*

To Scale Software LLC .... E 513 253-0053
   Mason *(G-10066)*

TOA Technologies Inc .... C 216 925-5950
   Beachwood *(G-1028)*

Tracker Management Systems .... G 800 445-2438
   Brecksville *(G-1636)*

Trapeze Software Group Inc .... F 905 629-8727
   Beachwood *(G-1029)*

Triad Governmental Systems .... E 937 376-5446
   Xenia *(G-16278)*

Trimble Trnsp Entp Sltions Inc .... C 216 831-6606
   Mayfield Heights *(G-10255)*

True Dinero Records & Tech LLC .... G 513 428-4610
   Cincinnati *(G-3470)*

◆ Turning Technologies LLC .... C 330 746-3015
   Youngstown *(G-16462)*

Tyler Technologies Inc .... F 800 800-2581
   Moraine *(G-11217)*

Ultraedit Inc .... D 216 464-7465
   Hamilton *(G-8255)*

Uninterrupted LLC .... F 216 771-2323
   Akron *(G-366)*

Upshift Work LLC .... C 513 813-5695
   Cincinnati *(G-3485)*

Veeam Government Solutions LLC .... E 614 339-8200
   Columbus *(G-5071)*

Veeam Software Corporation .... A 614 339-8200
   Columbus *(G-5072)*

Vertical Data LLC .... F 330 289-0313
   Akron *(G-369)*

Virtual Hold Tech Slutions LLC .... E 330 670-2200
   Akron *(G-370)*

Vista Community Church .... F 614 718-2294
   Plain City *(G-12600)*

Vndly LLC .... E 513 572-2500
   Mason *(G-10068)*

Vurvey Labs Inc .... F 513 379-3595
   Cincinnati *(G-3504)*

Waylens Inc .... G 513 445-8684
   Mason *(G-10070)*

Wentworth Solutions .... F 440 212-7696
   Hinckley *(G-8479)*

Whatifsportscom Inc .... G 513 333-0313
   Blue Ash *(G-1490)*

Zipscene LLC .... D 513 201-5174
   Cincinnati *(G-3536)*

Zullix LLC .... E 440 536-9300
   Rocky River *(G-12846)*

7373 Computer integrated systems design

Aclara Technologies LLC .... C 440 528-7200
   Solon *(G-13305)*

Advanced Prgrm Resources Inc .... E 614 761-9994
   Dublin *(G-6857)*

Applied Experience LLC .... G 614 943-2970
   Plain City *(G-12562)*

Bcs Technologies Ltd .... F 513 829-4577
   Fairfield *(G-7337)*

CHI Corporation .... G 440 498-2300
   Cleveland *(G-3818)*

Cincinnati Ctrl Dynamics Inc .... G 513 242-7300
   Cincinnati *(G-2746)*

Cott Systems Inc .... D 614 847-4405
   Columbus *(G-5299)*

Creative Microsystems Inc .... D 937 836-4499
   Englewood *(G-7227)*

▼ Data Processing Sciences .... D 513 791-7100
   Cincinnati *(G-2820)*

David Chojnacki .... E 303 905-1918
   Westerville *(G-15699)*

Deemsys Inc .... D 614 322-9928
   Gahanna *(G-7833)*

Dewesoft LLC .... D 855 339-3669
   Whitehouse *(G-15817)*

Drb Holdings LLC .... B 330 645-3299
   Akron *(G-134)*

Drb Systems LLC .... B 330 645-3299
   Akron *(G-135)*

Eaj Services LLC .... F 513 792-3400
   Blue Ash *(G-1387)*

Electronic Concepts Engrg Inc .... F 419 861-9000
   Holland *(G-8509)*

Freedom Usa Inc .... E 216 503-6374
   Twinsburg *(G-14662)*

Generic Systems Inc .... F 419 841-8460
   Holland *(G-8510)*

Industrial Screen Prcess Svc I .... F 419 255-4900
   Toledo *(G-14330)*

IPA Ltd .... F 614 523-3974
   Columbus *(G-5479)*

◆ Kc Robotics Inc .... E 513 860-4442
   West Chester *(G-15452)*

Lantek Systems Inc .... G 877 805-1028
   Mason *(G-10020)*

Leidos Inc .... D 937 656-8433
   Beavercreek *(G-1055)*

▲ Logisync Corporation .... F 440 937-0388
   Avon *(G-780)*

M T Systems Inc .... G 330 453-4646
   Canton *(G-2150)*

Matrix Management Solutions .... E 330 470-3700
   Canton *(G-2154)*

Millers Aplus Cmpt Svcs LLC .... F 330 620-5288
   Akron *(G-250)*

Northrop Grmman Tchncal Svcs I .... D 937 320-3100
   Beavercreek Township *(G-1086)*

Online Mega Sellers Corp .... G 888 384-6468
   Toledo *(G-14415)*

▲ Pinnacle Data Systems Inc .... C 614 748-1150
   Groveport *(G-8158)*

R & L Software LLC .... G 513 847-4942
   Monroe *(G-11118)*

▲ Sarcom Inc .... A 614 854-1300
   Lewis Center *(G-9180)*

Sentient Studios Ltd .... E 330 204-8636
   Fairlawn *(G-7449)*

Sest Inc .... F 440 777-9777
   Westlake *(G-15785)*

Sgi Matrix LLC .... D 937 438-9033
   Miamisburg *(G-10681)*

Sightgain Inc .... F 202 494-9317
   Mason *(G-10056)*

Smartronix Inc .... F 216 378-3300
   Northfield *(G-11910)*

Software Solutions Inc .... E 513 932-6667
   Dayton *(G-6578)*

Sutter Llc .... F 513 891-2261
   Blue Ash *(G-1476)*

Syntec LLC .... F 440 229-6262
   Rocky River *(G-12845)*

▲ Systemax Manufacturing Inc .... D 937 368-2300
   Dayton *(G-6604)*

Tata America Intl Corp .... B 513 677-6500
   Milford *(G-10925)*

Thyme Inc .... F 484 872-8430
   Akron *(G-357)*

Town Cntry Technical Svcs Inc .... F 614 866-7700
   Reynoldsburg *(G-12775)*

Worker Automation Inc .... G 937 473-2111
   Dayton *(G-6660)*

7374 Data processing and preparation

▲ Aero Fulfillment Services Corp .... D 800 225-7145
   Mason *(G-9945)*

Amsive OH LLC .... D 937 885-8000
   Miamisburg *(G-10611)*

CD Solutions Inc .... G 937 676-2376
   Pleasant Hill *(G-12606)*

Cpmm Services Group Inc .... E 614 447-0165
   Columbus *(G-5304)*

Datatrak International Inc .... E 440 443-0082
   Beachwood *(G-983)*

▼ Gracie Plum Investments Inc .... E 740 355-9029
   Portsmouth *(G-12645)*

Great Lakes Publishing Company .... D 216 771-2833
   Cleveland *(G-4146)*

IPA Ltd .... F 614 523-3974
   Columbus *(G-5479)*

ITM Marketing Inc .... C 740 295-3575
   Coshocton *(G-5981)*

73 BUSINESS SERVICES

Miami Valley Eductl Cmpt Assn............. F 937 767-1468
　Yellow Springs (G-16284)
NCR Technology Center........................ G 937 445-1936
　Dayton (G-6466)
Northrop Grmmn Spce & Mssn Sys....... D 937 259-4956
　Dayton (G-6474)
Quez Media Marketing Inc.................... F 216 910-0202
　Independence (G-8683)
Rebiz LLC... E 844 467-3249
　Cleveland (G-4618)
▲ Sarcom Inc.. A 614 854-1300
　Lewis Center (G-9180)
SC Strategic Solutions LLC................... C 567 424-6054
　Norwalk (G-11988)
Sightgain Inc... F 202 494-9317
　Mason (G-10056)
Vndly LLC.. E 513 572-2500
　Mason (G-10068)

7375 Information retrieval services

Advant-E Corporation............................ F 937 429-4288
　Beavercreek (G-1039)
AGS Custom Graphics Inc..................... D 330 963-7770
　Macedonia (G-9534)
Hkm Drect Mkt Cmmnications Inc.......... C 800 860-4456
　Cleveland (G-4193)
▲ Lexisnexis Group.............................. C 937 865-6800
　Miamisburg (G-10654)
Promatch Solutions LLC....................... F 877 299-0185
　Moraine (G-11205)
▲ Repro Acquisition Company LLC...... F 216 738-3800
　Cleveland (G-4626)
Sightgain Inc... F 202 494-9317
　Mason (G-10056)
Welch Publishing Co............................. E 419 874-2528
　Perrysburg (G-12444)

7376 Computer facilities management

Park Place Technologies LLC................ C 877 778-8707
　Cleveland (G-4523)

7377 Computer rental and leasing

▼ Data Processing Sciences .... D 513 791-7100
　Cincinnati (G-2820)

7378 Computer maintenance and repair

Eaj Services LLC................................... F 513 792-3400
　Blue Ash (G-1387)
Government Acquisitions Inc................ E 513 721-8700
　Cincinnati (G-2967)
Magnum Computers Inc........................ E 216 781-1757
　Cleveland (G-4351)
Park Place Technologies LLC................ C 877 778-8707
　Cleveland (G-4523)
▲ Pinnacle Data Systems Inc............... C 614 748-1150
　Groveport (G-8158)
Programmable Control Svc Inc.............. G 740 927-0744
　Pataskala (G-12304)
Smartronix Inc....................................... F 216 378-3500
　Northfield (G-11910)
Vr Assets LLC.. G 440 600-2963
　Solon (G-13443)

7379 Computer related services, nec

Advanced Prgrm Resources Inc............ E 614 761-9994
　Dublin (G-6857)
American Power LLC............................ F 937 235-0418
　Dayton (G-6202)
Arctos Mission Solutions LLC............... E 813 609-5491
　Beavercreek (G-1040)
Cbts Technology Solutions LLC............ B 440 569-2300
　Cleveland (G-3800)

Concept Xxi Inc..................................... G 216 831-2121
　Beachwood (G-981)
David Chojnacki..................................... E 303 905-1918
　Westerville (G-15699)
Empyracom Inc...................................... F 330 744-5570
　Boardman (G-1511)
Freedom Usa Inc.................................... E 216 503-6374
　Twinsburg (G-14662)
▲ Fscreations Corporation.................... D 330 746-3015
　Youngstown (G-16360)
Glance Software LLC............................. F 844 383-2500
　Hamilton (G-8213)
Jasstek Inc.. F 614 808-3600
　Dublin (G-6902)
Link Systems Inc................................... F 800 321-8770
　Solon (G-13381)
NCR Technology Center........................ G 937 445-1936
　Dayton (G-6466)
Onx Acquisition LLC.............................. B 440 569-2300
　Mayfield Heights (G-10253)
Onx Holdings LLC.................................. D 866 587-2287
　Cincinnati (G-3226)
Park Place Technologies LLC................ C 877 778-8707
　Cleveland (G-4523)
◆ Phase Array Company LLC................ G 513 785-0801
　West Chester (G-15475)
Proficient Info Tech Inc......................... G 937 470-1300
　Dayton (G-6531)
Profound Logic Software Inc................. E 937 439-7925
　Dayton (G-6532)
Revolution Group Inc............................ D 614 212-1111
　Westerville (G-15675)
Santec Resources Inc........................... F 614 664-9540
　Columbus (G-5746)
▲ Sarcom Inc.. A 614 854-1300
　Lewis Center (G-9180)
Syntec LLC.. F 440 229-6262
　Rocky River (G-12845)
Vr Assets LLC.. G 440 600-2963
　Solon (G-13443)
Wild Fire Systems.................................. G 440 442-8999
　Cleveland (G-4908)
Wolters Kluwer Clinical D...................... D 330 650-6506
　Hudson (G-8619)

7382 Security systems services

Fellhauer Mechanical Systems.............. E 419 734-3674
　Port Clinton (G-12617)
Johnson Controls Inc............................ F 513 671-6338
　Cincinnati (G-3049)
Sage Integration Holdings LLC............. E 330 733-8183
　Kent (G-8857)
▲ Say Security Group USA LLC........... F 419 634-0004
　Ada (G-5)
Securcom Inc.. E 419 628-1049
　Minster (G-11060)
Sound Communications Inc.................. E 614 875-8500
　Grove City (G-8120)

7383 News syndicates

Ohio News Network.............................. E 614 460-3700
　Columbus (G-5622)

7384 Photofinish laboratories

Enlarging Arts Inc................................. G 330 434-3433
　Akron (G-142)

7389 Business services, nec

3-D Technical Services Company.......... E 937 746-2901
　Franklin (G-7659)
A Good Mobile Detailing LLC................ G 513 316-3802
　Cincinnati (G-2584)

Abstract Displays Inc............................ F 513 985-9700
　Blue Ash (G-1356)
Ace Assembly & Packaging Inc............ G 330 866-9117
　Waynesburg (G-15292)
Acreo Inc... E 513 734-3327
　Amelia (G-448)
ADSr Ent LLC.. F 773 280-2129
　Columbus (G-5102)
Advanced Cryogenic Entps LLC............ G 330 922-0750
　Akron (G-22)
◆ Advanced Specialty Products........... G 419 882-6528
　Bowling Green (G-1550)
Afc Company... F 330 533-5581
　Canfield (G-1997)
▲ Amos Media Company...................... C 937 638-0967
　Sidney (G-13221)
Amros Industries Inc............................. E 216 433-0010
　Cleveland (G-3659)
Appalachia Freeze Dry Co LLC............. F 740 412-0169
　Richmond Dale (G-12804)
Appetzers R US St Eats 2 Go LL........... G 937 460-1470
　Springfield (G-13534)
Applied Experience LLC........................ G 614 943-2970
　Plain City (G-12562)
As Clean As It Gets Off Brkroo.............. E 216 256-1143
　South Euclid (G-13459)
Asist Translation Services..................... F 614 451-6744
　Columbus (G-5158)
▲ Asm International............................. D 440 338-5151
　Novelty (G-12007)
Atchley Signs & Graphics LLC.............. F 614 421-7446
　Columbus (G-5162)
Atlantic Welding LLC............................ F 937 570-5094
　Piqua (G-12505)
Aubrey Rose Apparel LLC..................... G 513 728-2681
　Cincinnati (G-2644)
Automted Cmpnent Spcalists LLC........ E 513 335-4285
　Cincinnati (G-2645)
Azsr Technologies Distr LLC................. G 216 315-8285
　Brookpark (G-1705)
◆ Baumfolder Corporation.................... E 937 492-1281
　Sidney (G-13226)
▲ BDS Packaging Inc........................... F 937 643-0530
　Moraine (G-11161)
Benchmark Craftsman Inc..................... E 866 313-4700
　Seville (G-13135)
▲ Bernard Laboratories Inc.................. E 513 681-7373
　Cincinnati (G-2666)
Bjond Inc... G 614 537-7246
　Columbus (G-5194)
Bjs DEMo&hauling LLC......................... G 216 904-8909
　Garfield Heights (G-7911)
Bollin & Sons Inc................................... E 419 693-6573
　Toledo (G-14216)
◆ Bookmasters Inc................................ C 419 281-1802
　Ashland (G-557)
Bridgits Bath LLC.................................. G 937 259-1960
　Dayton (G-6236)
Brown Company of Findlay Ltd............. E 419 425-3002
　Findlay (G-7488)
Capitol Citicom Inc................................ E 614 472-2679
　Columbus (G-5234)
◆ CIP International Inc......................... D 513 874-9925
　West Chester (G-15394)
▲ City Apparel Inc................................ F 419 434-1155
　Findlay (G-7493)
Clarity Retail Services LLC................... D 513 800-9369
　West Chester (G-15395)
Clovernook Ctr For Blind Vslly.............. C 513 522-3860
　Cincinnati (G-2775)
▲ CMC Group Inc.................................. D 419 354-2591
　Bowling Green (G-1561)

73 BUSINESS SERVICES

Coffing Corporation .... E 513 919-2813
 Liberty Twp *(G-9212)*

Compliant Healthcare Tech LLC .... E 216 255-9607
 Cleveland *(G-3892)*

Controls Inc .... E 330 239-4345
 Medina *(G-10312)*

▲ Conversion Tech Intl Inc .... E 419 924-5566
 West Unity *(G-15638)*

Country Lane Custom Buildings .... G 740 485-8481
 Danville *(G-6148)*

Crain Communications Inc .... E 330 836-9180
 Cuyahoga Falls *(G-6077)*

Crane Consumables Inc .... E 513 539-9980
 Middletown *(G-10814)*

Creative Fabrication Ltd .... G 740 262-5789
 Richwood *(G-12813)*

Crest Products Inc .... F 440 942-5770
 Mentor *(G-10446)*

Custom Built Crates Inc .... E
 Milford *(G-10904)*

Custom Information Systems Inc .... F 614 875-2245
 Grove City *(G-8086)*

▲ Custom Products Corporation .... D 440 528-7100
 Solon *(G-13334)*

Custom Sporstwear Imprints LLC .... G 330 335-8326
 Wadsworth *(G-15024)*

D&D Clssic Auto Rstoration Inc .... F 937 473-2229
 Covington *(G-6021)*

Dale R Adkins .... G 740 682-7312
 Oak Hill *(G-12017)*

Darlenes Kitchen LLC .... G 910 633-9744
 Toledo *(G-14261)*

Dbcr Inc .... E 330 920-1900
 Cuyahoga Falls *(G-6078)*

DCW Acquisition Inc .... E 216 451-0666
 Cleveland *(G-3949)*

▲ Depot Direct Inc .... E 419 661-1233
 Perrysburg *(G-12375)*

Display Dynamics Inc .... E 937 832-2830
 Englewood *(G-7229)*

Dollars N Cent Inc .... F 971 381-0406
 Cleveland *(G-3966)*

Domino Foods Inc .... C 216 432-3222
 Cleveland *(G-3968)*

◆ Downing Enterprises Inc .... D 330 666-3888
 Copley *(G-5948)*

Echo Mobile Solutions LLC .... G 614 282-3756
 Pickerington *(G-12460)*

Electrovations Inc .... G 330 274-3558
 Solon *(G-13341)*

Elite Biomedical Solutions LLC .... F 513 207-0602
 Cincinnati *(G-2558)*

Endless Home Improvements LLC .... G 614 599-1799
 Columbus *(G-5353)*

Engravers Gallery & Sign Co .... G 330 830-1271
 Massillon *(G-10094)*

▲ Ergo Desktop LLC .... E 567 890-3746
 Celina *(G-2331)*

Essential Provisions LLC .... G 937 271-0381
 Wilmington *(G-16049)*

Everything In America .... G 347 871-6872
 Cleveland *(G-4039)*

▲ Exact Cutting Service Inc .... E 440 546-1319
 Brecksville *(G-1616)*

▼ Exhibit Concepts Inc .... D 937 890-7000
 Vandalia *(G-14939)*

Expo Packaging Inc .... G 216 267-9700
 Cleveland *(G-4043)*

Express Ground Services Inc .... G 216 870-9374
 Cleveland *(G-4044)*

Fabstar Tanks Inc .... G 419 587-3639
 Grover Hill *(G-8169)*

Facility Service Pros LLC .... G 419 577-6123
 Collins *(G-5004)*

Fire Safety Services Inc .... F 937 686-2000
 Huntsville *(G-8623)*

▲ First Choice Packaging Inc .... C 419 333-4100
 Fremont *(G-7778)*

Flexsys Inc .... B 212 605-6000
 Akron *(G-156)*

Freds Sign Service Inc .... G 937 335-1901
 Troy *(G-14570)*

G and J Automatic Systems Inc .... E 216 741-6070
 Cleveland *(G-4097)*

G H Cutter Services Inc .... G 419 476-0476
 Toledo *(G-14296)*

G S K Inc .... G 937 547-1611
 Greenville *(G-8046)*

Gdw Woodworking LLC .... G 513 494-3041
 South Lebanon *(G-13461)*

Geauga Highway Co .... F 440 834-4580
 Hiram *(G-8484)*

Gencraft Designs LLC .... E 330 359-6251
 Navarre *(G-11342)*

▲ General Theming Contrs LLC .... C 614 252-6342
 Columbus *(G-5397)*

Geneva Liberty Steel Ltd .... E 330 740-0103
 Youngstown *(G-16366)*

Genius Solutions Engrg Co .... E 419 794-9914
 Maumee *(G-10202)*

Gerdau McSteel Atmsphere Annli .... E 330 478-0314
 Canton *(G-2112)*

GL Industries Inc .... E 513 874-1233
 Hamilton *(G-8212)*

Groff Industries .... F 216 634-9100
 Cleveland *(G-4151)*

Groundhogs 2000 LLC .... G 440 653-1647
 Bedford *(G-1122)*

Hafners Hrdwood Connection LLC .... G 419 726-4828
 Toledo *(G-14309)*

▲ Hands On International LLC .... G 513 502-9000
 West Chester *(G-15560)*

Health Nuts Media LLC .... G 818 802-5222
 Cleveland *(G-4175)*

Herman Machine Inc .... F 330 633-3261
 Tallmadge *(G-14032)*

Hochstetler Milling LLC .... E 419 368-0004
 Loudonville *(G-9449)*

Holly Robakowski .... G 440 854-9317
 Cleveland *(G-4196)*

Howard Industries Inc .... F 614 444-9900
 Columbus *(G-5447)*

▼ Htec Systems Inc .... F 937 438-3010
 Dayton *(G-6376)*

Hunt Products Inc .... G 440 667-2457
 Newburgh Heights *(G-11617)*

Hutnik Company .... G 330 336-9700
 Wadsworth *(G-15035)*

IBI Brake Products Inc .... G 440 543-7962
 Chagrin Falls *(G-2402)*

Ideal Drapery Company Inc .... F 330 745-9873
 Barberton *(G-874)*

IEC Infrared Systems LLC .... E 440 234-8000
 Middleburg Heights *(G-10720)*

Ies Systems Inc .... E 330 533-6683
 Canfield *(G-2008)*

Impact Printing and Design LLC .... F 833 522-6200
 Columbus *(G-5456)*

Industrial Power Systems Inc .... B 419 531-3121
 Rossford *(G-12867)*

◆ Ineos ABS (usa) LLC .... C 513 467-2400
 Addyston *(G-8)*

◆ Interscope Manufacturing Inc .... E 513 423-8866
 Middletown *(G-10832)*

ITM Marketing Inc .... C 740 295-3575
 Coshocton *(G-5981)*

Jls Funeral Home .... F 614 625-1220
 Columbus *(G-5497)*

Jnp Group LLC .... F 800 735-9645
 Wooster *(G-16137)*

Joseph G Pappas .... G 330 383-2917
 East Liverpool *(G-6995)*

Joseph T Snyder Industries Inc .... G 216 883-6900
 Cleveland *(G-4260)*

Kaylo Enterprises LLC .... G 330 535-1860
 Akron *(G-202)*

◆ Kent Adhesive Products Co .... D 330 678-1626
 Kent *(G-8821)*

Konecranes Inc .... F 440 461-8400
 Broadview Heights *(G-1660)*

Kts Cstm Lgs/Xclsvely You Inc .... G 440 285-9803
 Chardon *(G-2456)*

▲ Kyocera Senco Indus Tls Inc .... D 513 388-2000
 Cincinnati *(G-3093)*

Laserflex Corporation .... D 614 850-9600
 Hilliard *(G-8418)*

Leak Finder Inc .... G 440 735-0130
 Hudson *(G-8602)*

Liminal Esports LLC .... G 440 423-5856
 Gates Mills *(G-7928)*

Link Systems Inc .... F 800 321-8770
 Solon *(G-13381)*

Link To Success Inc .... G 888 959-4203
 Norwalk *(G-11978)*

Love Laugh & Laundry .... G 567 377-1951
 Toledo *(G-14370)*

Love Yueh LLC .... G 614 408-8677
 Pickerington *(G-12463)*

Magnaco Industries Inc .... E 216 961-3636
 Lodi *(G-9353)*

Marie Noble Wine Company .... E 216 633-0025
 Euclid *(G-7282)*

Mark Grzianis St Treats Ex Inc .... F 330 414-6266
 Kent *(G-8832)*

Metal Shredders Inc .... F 937 866-0777
 Miamisburg *(G-10656)*

Mettler Footwear Inc .... G 330 703-0079
 Hudson *(G-8605)*

Metzenbaum Sheltered Inds Inc .... D 440 729-1919
 Chesterland *(G-2485)*

Michele Caldwell .... G 937 505-7744
 Dayton *(G-6442)*

Micro Products Co Inc .... E 440 943-0258
 Willoughby Hills *(G-16025)*

Millers Aplus Cmpt Svcs LLC .... F 330 620-5288
 Akron *(G-205)*

Momma Js Blazing Kitchen LLC .... G 216 551-8791
 Cleveland Heights *(G-4941)*

National Wldg Tanker Repr LLC .... G 614 875-3399
 Grove City *(G-8110)*

Natures Health Food LLC .... F 419 260-9265
 Mount Victory *(G-11301)*

Natures Way Bird Products LLC .... E 440 554-6166
 Chagrin Falls *(G-2410)*

Neurologix Technologies Inc .... F 512 914-7941
 Cleveland *(G-4451)*

◆ New Path International LLC .... E 614 410-3974
 Powell *(G-12679)*

▲ Nordic Light America Inc .... F 614 981-9497
 Canal Winchester *(G-1991)*

North Shore Printing LLC .... G 740 876-9066
 Portsmouth *(G-12651)*

Ogonek Custom Hardwood Inc .... G 833 718-2531
 Barberton *(G-885)*

◆ Ohio Gasket and Shim Co Inc .... E 330 630-0626
 Akron *(G-270)*

Employee Codes: A=Over 500 employees, B=251-500
C=101-250, D=51-100, E=20-50, F=10-19, G=1-9

73 BUSINESS SERVICES

▲ Ohio Laminating & Binding Inc......... F 614 771-4868
  Hilliard *(G-8426)*
Ohio Shelterall Inc............................... F 614 882-1110
  Westerville *(G-15717)*
Olde Man Granola LLC...................... F 419 819-9576
  Findlay *(G-7545)*
P & L Precision Grinding Llc............. F 330 746-8081
  Youngstown *(G-16410)*
P C Workshop Inc.............................. F 419 399-4805
  Paulding *(G-12319)*
Pactiv LLC.. D 614 771-5400
  Columbus *(G-5650)*
Park Press Direct.............................. F 419 626-4426
  Sandusky *(G-13086)*
Paul Shovlin...................................... G 330 757-0032
  Youngstown *(G-16416)*
Pentagear Products LLC.................. F 937 660-8182
  Dayton *(G-6500)*
▲ Performance Packaging Inc........... F 419 478-8805
  Toledo *(G-14433)*
Pioneer Solutions LLC..................... E 216 383-3400
  Euclid *(G-7292)*
Pollock Research & Design Inc........ E 330 332-3300
  Salem *(G-13023)*
Precision Cut Fabricating Inc........... F 440 877-1260
  North Royalton *(G-11891)*
Printing Services................................ F 440 708-1999
  Chagrin Falls *(G-2417)*
◆ Pro-Pet LLC..................................... D 419 394-3374
  Saint Marys *(G-12964)*
Professional Award Service............. G 513 389-3600
  Cincinnati *(G-3301)*
Prospect Rock LLC........................... F 740 512-0542
  Saint Clairsville *(G-12919)*
PS Superior Inc................................ E 216 587-1000
  Cleveland *(G-4596)*
Publishing Group Ltd........................ F 614 572-1240
  Columbus *(G-5697)*
Pughs Designer Jewelers Inc........... G 740 344-9259
  Newark *(G-11603)*
Pur Hair Extensions LLC.................. G 330 786-5772
  Akron *(G-287)*
Quality Durable Indus Floors........... F 937 696-2833
  Farmersville *(G-7460)*
Queen City Spirit LLC....................... F 513 533-2662
  Cincinnati *(G-3320)*
Quest Technologies Inc.................... F 937 743-1200
  Franklin *(G-7696)*
Quick As A Wink Printing Co............ G 419 224-9786
  Lima *(G-9281)*
Quintus Technologies LLC.............. E 614 891-2732
  Lewis Center *(G-9176)*
R & H Enterprises Llc...................... G 216 702-4449
  Richmond Heights *(G-12810)*
R and J Corporation......................... E 440 871-6009
  Westlake *(G-15777)*
R J K Enterprises Inc....................... F 440 257-6018
  Mentor *(G-10542)*
R J Manray Inc.................................. G 330 559-6716
  Canfield *(G-2015)*
Ransome AC LLC............................. G 234 205-6907
  Akron *(G-297)*
RE Connors Construction Ltd......... G 740 644-0261
  Thornville *(G-14068)*
Red Barakuda LLC........................... G 614 596-5432
  Columbus *(G-5715)*
Rex Welding Inc................................ F 740 387-1650
  Marion *(G-9875)*
▲ Richardson Printing Corp.............. D 800 848-9752
  Marietta *(G-9820)*
Richland Newhope Inds Inc............. C 419 774-4400
  Mansfield *(G-9712)*

Rock Iron Corporation...................... F 419 529-9411
  Crestline *(G-6037)*
Romans Mobile Welding LLC.......... G 513 603-0961
  Amelia *(G-462)*
Ryder Engraving Inc......................... G 740 927-7193
  Pataskala *(G-12307)*
▲ S C Industries Inc........................... E 216 732-9000
  Euclid *(G-7300)*
Safecor Health LLC.......................... G 614 351-6117
  Columbus *(G-5738)*
Safecor Health LLC.......................... F 781 933-8780
  Columbus *(G-5739)*
Sandwisch Enterprises Inc.............. G 419 944-6446
  Toledo *(G-14462)*
Scot Industries Inc........................... D 330 262-7585
  Wooster *(G-16169)*
Scottrods LLC.................................... G 419 499-2705
  Monroeville *(G-11125)*
Screen Works Inc............................. F 937 264 0111
  Dayton *(G-6564)*
Sew & Sew Embroidery Inc............. F 330 676-1600
  Kent *(G-8863)*
▲ Shamrock Companies Inc.............. D 440 899-9510
  Westlake *(G-15786)*
Shear Service Inc............................. G 216 341-2700
  Cleveland *(G-4689)*
Shoot-A-Way Inc............................... F 419 294-4654
  Nevada *(G-11361)*
Shousha Trucking LLC..................... G 937 270-4471
  Dayton *(G-6571)*
Signalysis Inc.................................... F 513 528-6164
  Cincinnati *(G-3392)*
Signs Unlmted The Grphic Advnt.... G 614 836-7446
  Logan *(G-9376)*
Simply Unique Snacks LLC.............. G 513 223-7736
  Cincinnati *(G-3394)*
Siraj Recovery LLC........................... G 614 893-3507
  Columbus *(G-5774)*
Southwood Pallet LLC..................... D 330 682-3747
  Orrville *(G-12158)*
◆ Standard Textile Co Inc.................. B 513 761-9255
  Cincinnati *(G-3415)*
Standard Wellness Company LLC... C 330 931-1037
  Cleveland *(G-4729)*
STI Liquidation Inc........................... E 614 733-0099
  Plain City *(G-12592)*
Struggle Grind Success LLC........... G 330 834-6738
  Boardman *(G-1518)*
Stutzman Manufacturing Ltd........... G 330 674-4359
  Millersburg *(G-10996)*
Supplier Inspection Svcs Inc........... F 877 263-7097
  Dayton *(G-6600)*
Swagg Productions2015llc............... F 614 601-7414
  Worthington *(G-16213)*
Systems Pack Inc............................. E 330 467-5729
  Macedonia *(G-9583)*
Tekni-Plex Inc.................................... E 419 491-2399
  Holland *(G-8532)*
Teva Womens Health LLC............... C 513 731-9900
  Cincinnati *(G-3446)*
TI Marie Candle Company LLC....... F 513 746-7798
  Cincinnati *(G-3454)*
Timmys Sandwich Shop................... G 419 350-8267
  Toledo *(G-14486)*
Tiny Lion Music Groups................... G 419 874-7353
  Perrysburg *(G-12435)*
Tipp Machine & Tool Inc.................. C 937 890-8428
  Dayton *(G-6625)*
Tko Mfg Services Inc....................... E 937 299-1637
  Moraine *(G-11215)*
Tomahawk Entrmt Group LLC........ F 216 505-0948
  Euclid *(G-7302)*

Total Call Center Solutions.............. F 330 869-9844
  Akron *(G-361)*
Triangle Sign Co LLC....................... G 513 266-1009
  Hamilton *(G-8254)*
Tugz International LLC..................... F 216 621-4854
  Cleveland *(G-4836)*
▲ Twin Sisters Productions LLC....... E 330 631-0361
  Stow *(G-13735)*
▲ Ultra Tech Machinery Inc................ E 330 929-5544
  Cuyahoga Falls *(G-6126)*
▲ Underground Sports Shop Inc........ F 513 751-1662
  Cincinnati *(G-3477)*
Unique Packaging & Printing........... F 440 785-6730
  Mentor *(G-10588)*
Universal Dsign Fbrication LLC....... F 419 202-5269
  Sandusky *(G-13101)*
Universal Packg Systems Inc.......... C 513 732-2000
  Batavia *(G-957)*
Universal Packg Systems Inc.......... C 513 735-4777
  Batavia *(G-958)*
Universal Packg Systems Inc.......... C 513 674-9400
  Cincinnati *(G-3483)*
▲ Urban Industries of Ohio Inc........... E 419 468-3578
  Galion *(G-7886)*
US Water Company LLC.................. G 740 453-0604
  Zanesville *(G-16567)*
Valley View Pallets LLC................... G 740 599-0010
  Danville *(G-6149)*
Walter North...................................... F 937 204-6050
  Dayton *(G-6646)*
Welch Packaging Group Inc............ C 614 870-2000
  Columbus *(G-5869)*
◆ Whole Shop Inc................................ F 330 630-5305
  Tallmadge *(G-14057)*
◆ William R Hague Inc........................ D 614 836-2115
  Groveport *(G-8168)*
Worthngton Smuel Coil Proc LLC... E 330 963-3777
  Twinsburg *(G-14758)*

75 AUTOMOTIVE REPAIR, SERVICES AND PARKING

7513 Truck rental and leasing, without drivers

▲ Knippen Chrysler Ddge Jeep Inc.... E 419 695-4976
  Delphos *(G-6767)*
◆ Ohio Machinery Co.......................... C 440 526-6200
  Broadview Heights *(G-1665)*

7514 Passenger car rental

Precision Coatings Systems............. E 937 642-4727
  Marysville *(G-9931)*

7519 Utility trailer rental

Advanced Rv LLC............................. E 440 283-0405
  Willoughby *(G-15874)*
▲ Eleet Cryogenics Inc....................... E 330 874-4009
  Bolivar *(G-1524)*
Lloyd F Helber.................................. G 740 756-9607
  Carroll *(G-2299)*

7521 Automobile parking

Integrity Parking LLC........................ F 440 543-4123
  Aurora *(G-720)*
Youngstown Letter Shop Inc............. G 330 793-4935
  Youngstown *(G-16484)*

7532 Top and body repair and paint shops

ABRA Auto Body & Glass LP........... G 513 247-3400
  Cincinnati *(G-2592)*

SIC SECTION
75 AUTOMOTIVE REPAIR, SERVICES AND PARKING

ABRA Auto Body & Glass LP................ G 513 367-9200
  Harrison *(G-8263)*
ABRA Auto Body & Glass LP................ F 513 755-7709
  West Chester *(G-15359)*
Advanced Rv LLC...................................... E 440 283-0405
  Willoughby *(G-15874)*
Bobbart Industries Inc............................... E 419 350-5477
  Sylvania *(G-13991)*
Chardon Square Auto & Body Inc........... F 440 286-7600
  Chardon *(G-2444)*
D&D Clssic Auto Rstoration Inc................ F 937 473-2229
  Covington *(G-6021)*
Design Masters Inc.................................... G 513 772-7175
  Cincinnati *(G-2826)*
Ham Signs LLC DBA Fastsigns................ F 937 890-6770
  Dayton *(G-6365)*
Michael W Newton...................................... G 740 352-9334
  Lucasville *(G-9525)*
Mobile Conversions Inc............................. F 513 797-1991
  Amelia *(G-460)*
National Fleet Svcs Ohio LLC................... F 440 930-5177
  Avon Lake *(G-818)*
Newbury Sndblst & Pntg Inc..................... G 440 564-7204
  Newbury *(G-11631)*
▲ Obs Inc... F 330 453-3725
  Canton *(G-2180)*
Precision Coatings Systems..................... E 937 642-4727
  Marysville *(G-9931)*
Q T Columbus LLC..................................... G 800 758-2410
  Columbus *(G-5700)*
▼ QT Equipment Company......................... E 330 724-3055
  Akron *(G-289)*
Steves Vans ACC Unlimited LLC............. G 740 374-3154
  Marietta *(G-9832)*
W&W Automotive & Towing Inc................ F 937 429-1699
  Beavercreek Township *(G-1095)*
Webers Body & Frame Inc........................ G 937 839-5946
  West Alexandria *(G-15346)*
Willard Machine & Welding Inc................ F 330 467-0642
  Macedonia *(G-9586)*

7533 Auto exhaust system repair shops

Mark Knupp Muffler & Tire Inc.................. E 937 773-1334
  Piqua *(G-12535)*

7534 Tire retreading and repair shops

AB Tire & Repair.. G 440 543-2929
  Chagrin Falls *(G-2386)*
Associates Tire and Svc Inc..................... F 937 436-4692
  Centerville *(G-2359)*
Bell Tire Co... F 440 234-8022
  Olmsted Falls *(G-12076)*
Best One Tire & Svc Lima Inc................... G 419 425-3322
  Findlay *(G-7484)*
▲ Best One Tire & Svc Lima Inc................. E 419 229-2380
  Lima *(G-9223)*
Big Oki LLC.. E 513 874-1111
  Fairfield *(G-7338)*
Bob Sumerel Tire Co Inc........................... F 614 527-9700
  Columbus *(G-5204)*
Bob Sumerel Tire Co Inc........................... F 937 235-0062
  Dayton *(G-6233)*
Bob Sumerel Tire Co Inc........................... G 740 432-5200
  Lore City *(G-9446)*
Bob Sumerel Tire Co Inc........................... F 330 769-9092
  Seville *(G-13140)*
Bob Sumerel Tire Co Inc........................... G 740 454-9728
  Zanesville *(G-16512)*
Bob Sumerel Tire Company...................... G 330 262-1220
  Wooster *(G-16105)*
Bob Sumerel Tire Company Inc................ G 740 927-2811
  Reynoldsburg *(G-12755)*

Boy RAD Inc... F 614 766-1228
  Dublin *(G-6869)*
Bridgestone Ret Operations LLC............ G 740 592-3075
  Athens *(G-677)*
Bridgestone Ret Operations LLC............ G 614 834-3672
  Canal Winchester *(G-1982)*
Bridgestone Ret Operations LLC............ G 330 454-9478
  Canton *(G-2053)*
Bridgestone Ret Operations LLC............ G 513 681-7682
  Cincinnati *(G-2683)*
Bridgestone Ret Operations LLC............ G 513 793-4550
  Cincinnati *(G-2684)*
Bridgestone Ret Operations LLC............ G 513 677-5200
  Cincinnati *(G-2685)*
Bridgestone Ret Operations LLC............ G 440 842-3200
  Cleveland *(G-3756)*
Bridgestone Ret Operations LLC............ G 440 461-4747
  Cleveland *(G-3757)*
Bridgestone Ret Operations LLC............ G 216 229-2550
  Cleveland *(G-3758)*
Bridgestone Ret Operations LLC............ G 216 382-8970
  Cleveland *(G-3759)*
Bridgestone Ret Operations LLC............ F 614 864-3350
  Columbus *(G-5214)*
Bridgestone Ret Operations LLC............ F 614 491-8062
  Columbus *(G-5215)*
Bridgestone Ret Operations LLC............ G 614 224-4221
  Columbus *(G-5216)*
Bridgestone Ret Operations LLC............ G 440 324-3927
  Elyria *(G-7117)*
Bridgestone Ret Operations LLC............ G 440 365-8308
  Elyria *(G-7118)*
Bridgestone Ret Operations LLC............ G 937 548-1197
  Greenville *(G-8039)*
Bridgestone Ret Operations LLC............ G 513 868-7399
  Hamilton *(G-8186)*
Bridgestone Ret Operations LLC............ G 330 673-1700
  Kent *(G-8803)*
Bridgestone Ret Operations LLC............ F 440 299-6126
  Mentor *(G-10431)*
Bridgestone Ret Operations LLC............ F 740 397-5601
  Mount Vernon *(G-11265)*
Bridgestone Ret Operations LLC............ G 614 861-7994
  Reynoldsburg *(G-12756)*
Bridgestone Ret Operations LLC............ G 419 625-6571
  Sandusky *(G-13045)*
Bridgestone Ret Operations LLC............ G 937 325-4638
  Springfield *(G-13540)*
Bridgestone Ret Operations LLC............ G 330 758-0921
  Youngstown *(G-16325)*
Bridgestone Ret Operations LLC............ G 330 759-3697
  Youngstown *(G-16326)*
Canton Bandag Co..................................... F 330 454-3025
  Canton *(G-2060)*
Capital Tire Inc.. E 330 364-4731
  Toledo *(G-14227)*
Central Ohio Bandag LP............................ F 740 454-9728
  Zanesville *(G-16520)*
Chardon Square Auto & Body Inc........... F 440 286-7600
  Chardon *(G-2444)*
Cims Incorporated..................................... E 330 794-8102
  Akron *(G-110)*
Colyer C & Sons Truck Service................ G 513 563-0663
  Cincinnati *(G-2781)*
Custom Recapping Inc............................... G 937 324-4331
  Springfield *(G-13550)*
Exit 11 Truck Tire Service.......................... G 330 659-6372
  Richfield *(G-12786)*
Firestone Complete Auto Care................. G 937 528-2496
  Centerville *(G-2362)*
Fleet Relief Company................................. F 419 525-2625
  Mansfield *(G-9657)*

Forklift Tire East Mich Inc......................... F 586 771-1330
  Toledo *(G-14292)*
Goodyear Tire & Rubber Company......... F 419 643-8273
  Beaverdam *(G-1096)*
Goodyear Tire & Rubber Company......... G 330 966-1274
  Canton *(G-2116)*
Goodyear Tire & Rubber Company......... G 330 759-9343
  Youngstown *(G-16371)*
◆ Goodyear Tire & Rubber Company......... A 330 796-2121
  Akron *(G-171)*
▲ Grismer Tire Company............................. E 937 643-2526
  Centerville *(G-2363)*
Gt Tire Service Inc..................................... G 740 927-7226
  Pataskala *(G-12298)*
Heartland Retreaders Inc......................... F 740 472-0558
  Woodsfield *(G-16087)*
Heisley Tire & Brake Inc........................... F 440 357-9797
  Mentor *(G-10468)*
J & J Tire & Alignment................................ G 330 424-5200
  Lisbon *(G-9316)*
JTL Enterprises LLC.................................. E 937 890-8189
  Dayton *(G-6392)*
K S Bandag Inc... E 330 264-9237
  Wooster *(G-16139)*
L & O Tire Service Inc............................... G 937 394-8462
  Anna *(G-490)*
Liberty Tire Recycling LLC....................... E 614 871-8097
  Grove City *(G-8101)*
Lonny Eugene Horst................................... G 330 846-0057
  New Waterford *(G-11557)*
Mark Knupp Muffler & Tire Inc.................. E 937 773-1334
  Piqua *(G-12535)*
Mid America Tire of Hillsboro Inc............ E 937 393-3520
  Hillsboro *(G-8461)*
Mitchell Bros Tire Rtread Svc.................. G 740 353-1551
  Portsmouth *(G-12649)*
North Coast Tire Co Inc............................ G 216 447-1690
  Cleveland *(G-4473)*
Ntb National Tire and Battery.................. G 614 870-8945
  Columbus *(G-5606)*
Ohio Made Tires LLC................................. G 740 421-4934
  Woodsfield *(G-16089)*
Paul Shovlin... G 330 757-0032
  Youngstown *(G-16416)*
Philip Radke... G 614 475-6788
  Columbus *(G-5673)*
Premier Bandag 8 Inc................................ F 330 823-3822
  Alliance *(G-420)*
Premier Bandag Inc.................................... F 513 248-8850
  Milford *(G-10918)*
Pro Tire Inc.. F 614 864-8662
  Columbus *(G-5693)*
Shrader Tire & Oil Inc................................ G 419 420-8435
  Perrysburg *(G-12426)*
Skinner Firestone Inc................................ F 740 984-4247
  Beverly *(G-1321)*
Snider Tire Inc.. E 740 439-2741
  Cambridge *(G-1953)*
Swiss Valley Tire LLC................................ G 330 231-6187
  Wilmot *(G-16069)*
Tbc Retail Group Inc.................................. E 216 267-8040
  Cleveland *(G-4768)*
Tires Plus 7061... G 513 851-1900
  Cincinnati *(G-3455)*
Wayne A Whaley.. G 330 525-7779
  Homeworth *(G-8556)*
Ziegler Tire and Supply Co....................... G 330 434-7126
  Akron *(G-381)*
Ziegler Tire and Supply Co....................... G 330 477-3463
  Canton *(G-2273)*
Ziegler Tire and Supply Co....................... E 330 343-7739
  Dover *(G-6850)*

Employee Codes: A=Over 500 employees, B=251-500
C=101-250, D=51-100, E=20-50, F=10-19, G=1-9

2024 Harris Ohio
Industrial Directory

75 AUTOMOTIVE REPAIR, SERVICES AND PARKING

7536 Automotive glass replacement shops

A Service Glass Inc .... E 937 426-4920
  Beavercreek (G-1038)
J W Goss Company .... F 330 395-0739
  Warren (G-15179)
Keystone Auto Glass Inc .... D 419 509-0497
  Maumee (G-10211)
◆ Safelite Group Inc .... A 614 210-9000
  Columbus (G-5740)
Support Svc LLC .... G 419 617-0660
  Lexington (G-9203)
Webers Body & Frame Inc .... G 937 839-5946
  West Alexandria (G-15346)

7537 Automotive transmission repair shops

Bob Sumerel Tire Co Inc .... F 330 769-9092
  Seville (G-13140)
Bob Sumerel Tire Company .... G 330 262-1220
  Wooster (G-16105)
Mikes Transm & Auto Svc LLC .... F 330 799-8266
  Youngstown (G-16401)
Power Acquisition LLC .... D 614 228-5000
  Dublin (G-6925)
Rumpke Transportation Co LLC .... F 513 851-0122
  Cincinnati (G-3355)
▲ Tri-W Group Inc .... A 614 228-5000
  Columbus (G-5837)
W W Williams Company LLC .... D 614 228-5000
  Dublin (G-6958)

7538 General automotive repair shops

Abutilon Company Inc .... F 419 536-6123
  Toledo (G-14175)
Automtive Rfnish Clor Sltons I .... E 330 461-6067
  Medina (G-10298)
Bob Sumerel Tire Co Inc .... F 330 769-9092
  Seville (G-13140)
Bridgestone Ret Operations LLC .... F 440 299-6126
  Mentor (G-10431)
Bridgestone Ret Operations LLC .... G 419 625-6571
  Sandusky (G-13045)
Carl E Oeder Sons Sand & Grav .... F 513 494-1555
  Lebanon (G-9066)
Colyer C & Sons Truck Service .... G 513 563-0663
  Cincinnati (G-2781)
Dan Patrick Enterprises Inc .... G 740 477-1006
  Circleville (G-3546)
Doug Marine Motors Inc .... E 740 335-3700
  Wshngtn Ct Hs (G-16230)
Firestone Complete Auto Care .... G 937 528-2496
  Centerville (G-2362)
Fleetpride Inc .... E 740 282-2711
  Steubenville (G-13667)
◆ Goodyear Tire & Rubber Company .... A 330 796-2121
  Akron (G-171)
▲ Grismer Tire Company .... E 937 643-2526
  Centerville (G-2363)
Heisley Tire & Brake Inc .... F 440 357-9797
  Mentor (G-10468)
Hutter Racing Engines Ltd .... F 440 285-2175
  Chardon (G-2453)
J & J Tire & Alignment .... G 330 424-5200
  Lisbon (G-9316)
Kaffenbarger Truck Eqp Co .... E 513 772-6800
  Cincinnati (G-3056)
Kinstle Truck & Auto Svc Inc .... F 419 738-7493
  Wapakoneta (G-15120)
Kirbys Auto and Truck Repr Inc .... G 513 934-3999
  Lebanon (G-9093)
▲ Knippen Chrysler Ddge Jeep Inc .... E 419 695-4976
  Delphos (G-6767)

L & O Tire Service Inc .... G 937 394-8462
  Anna (G-490)
M & W Trailers Inc .... F 419 453-3331
  Ottoville (G-12201)
Maags Automotive & Mch Inc .... G 419 626-1539
  Sandusky (G-13076)
Nice Body Automotive LLC .... G 440 752-5568
  Elyria (G-7185)
Ohio Trailer Inc .... F 330 392-4444
  Warren (G-15196)
Pattons Trck & Hvy Eqp Svc Inc .... E 740 385-4067
  Logan (G-9373)
Power Acquisition LLC .... D 614 228-5000
  Dublin (G-6925)
Sammy S Auto Detail .... F 614 263-2728
  Columbus (G-5743)
Sutphen Towers Inc .... D 614 876-1262
  Hilliard (G-8444)
▲ Tri-W Group Inc .... A 614 228-5000
  Columbus (G-5837)
W W Williams Company LLC .... D 614 228-5000
  Dublin (G-6958)
Youngstown-Kenworth Inc .... F 330 534-9761
  Hubbard (G-8574)

7539 Automotive repair shops, nec

Albright Radiator Inc .... G 330 264-8886
  Wooster (G-16100)
Bob Sumerel Tire Co Inc .... F 330 769-9092
  Seville (G-13140)
Bob Sumerel Tire Company .... G 330 262-1220
  Wooster (G-16105)
Bridgestone Ret Operations LLC .... F 614 491-8062
  Columbus (G-5215)
Brock RAD Wldg Fabrication Inc .... G 740 773-2540
  Chillicothe (G-2496)
Chardon Square Auto & Body Inc .... F 440 286-7600
  Chardon (G-2444)
▲ Cincinnati Radiator Inc .... F 513 874-5555
  Hamilton (G-8193)
Circleville Oil Co .... G 740 477-3341
  Circleville (G-3544)
▼ East Manufacturing Corporation .... B 330 325-9921
  Randolph (G-12697)
Entratech Systems LLC .... G 419 433-7683
  Sandusky (G-13055)
Friess Welding Inc .... G 330 644-8160
  Coventry Township (G-6009)
◆ Goodyear Tire & Rubber Company .... A 330 796-2121
  Akron (G-171)
Heisley Tire & Brake Inc .... F 440 357-9797
  Mentor (G-10468)
J & J Tire & Alignment .... G 330 424-5200
  Lisbon (G-9316)
J & L Body Inc .... F 216 661-2323
  Brooklyn Heights (G-1693)
Jordon Auto Service & Tire Inc .... G 216 214-6528
  Cleveland (G-4259)
M & W Trailers Inc .... F 419 453-3331
  Ottoville (G-12201)
Maags Automotive & Mch Inc .... G 419 626-1539
  Sandusky (G-13076)
◆ Mac Trailer Manufacturing Inc .... A 800 795-8454
  Alliance (G-411)
Mark Knupp Muffler & Tire Inc .... E 937 773-1334
  Piqua (G-12535)
▲ Mc Machine Llc .... E 216 398-3666
  Cleveland (G-4378)
Midwest Muffler Pros & More .... G 937 293-2450
  Moraine (G-11195)
Mikes Transm & Auto Svc LLC .... F 330 799-8266
  Youngstown (G-16401)

▲ Miscor Group Ltd .... B 330 830-3500
  Massillon (G-10129)
▼ Nelson Manufacturing Company .... D 419 523-5321
  Ottawa (G-12185)
Nice Body Automotive LLC .... G 440 752-5568
  Elyria (G-7185)
Perkins Motor Service Ltd .... F 440 277-1256
  Lorain (G-9430)
◆ RL Best Company .... E 330 758-8601
  Boardman (G-1517)
Support Svc LLC .... G 419 617-0660
  Lexington (G-9203)
▲ Tuf-Tug Inc .... F 937 299-1213
  Moraine (G-11216)
Vintage Automotive Elc Inc .... F 419 472-9349
  Toledo (G-14520)

7549 Automotive services, nec

▲ Afg Industries Inc .... D 614 322-4580
  Grove City (G-8074)
J & L Body Inc .... F 216 661-2323
  Brooklyn Heights (G-1693)
Johns Welding & Towing Inc .... F 419 447-8937
  Tiffin (G-14089)
Mikes Transm & Auto Svc LLC .... F 330 799-8266
  Youngstown (G-16401)
Mpi Logistics and Service Inc .... E 330 832-5309
  Massillon (G-10130)
Precision Coatings Systems .... E 937 642-4727
  Marysville (G-9931)
Tbone Sales LLC .... F 330 897-6131
  Baltic (G-841)
X-Treme Finishes Inc .... F 330 474-0614
  North Royalton (G-11903)

76 MISCELLANEOUS REPAIR SERVICES

7622 Radio and television repair

Cattron Holdings Inc .... E 234 806-0018
  Warren (G-15150)
Cbst Acquisition LLC .... D 513 361-9600
  Cincinnati (G-2711)
Central USA Wireless LLC .... F 513 469-1500
  Cincinnati (G-2719)
Dss Installations Ltd .... F 513 761-7000
  Cincinnati (G-2842)
Electra Sound Inc .... D 216 433-9600
  Avon Lake (G-805)
Industrial Electronic Service .... F 937 746-9750
  Carlisle (G-2288)

7623 Refrigeration service and repair

▼ Air-Rite Inc .... E 216 228-8200
  Cleveland (G-3617)
Bell Industrial Services LLC .... F 937 507-9193
  Sidney (G-13227)
Northeastern Rfrgn Corp .... E 440 942-7676
  Willoughby (G-15960)
Weather King Heating & AC .... G 330 908-0281
  Northfield (G-11914)

7629 Electrical repair shops

Allied Machine Works Inc .... G 740 454-2534
  Zanesville (G-16499)
▲ Amko Service Company .... E 330 364-8857
  Midvale (G-10875)
Bentronix Corp .... G 440 632-0606
  Middlefield (G-10734)
Cbst Acquisition LLC .... D 513 361-9600
  Cincinnati (G-2711)

SIC SECTION

76 MISCELLANEOUS REPAIR SERVICES

◆ Ceramic Holdings Inc............................C 216 362-3900
  Brookpark *(G-1707)*

Copier Resources Inc............................G 614 268-1100
  Columbus *(G-5295)*

Cornerstone Wauseon Inc......................C 419 337-0940
  Wauseon *(G-15259)*

D & J Electric Motor Repair Co..............F 330 336-4343
  Wadsworth *(G-15025)*

DTE Inc..E 419 522-3428
  Mansfield *(G-9647)*

Electric Service Co Inc..........................E 513 271-6387
  Cincinnati *(G-2861)*

Emerson Network Power........................E 614 841-8054
  Ironton *(G-8697)*

▲ Enprotech Industrial Tech LLC..........E 216 883-3220
  Cleveland *(G-4019)*

General Electric Company......................E 513 977-1500
  Cincinnati *(G-2943)*

General Electric Company......................E 216 883-1000
  Cleveland *(G-4115)*

Hannon Company....................................F 330 343-7758
  Dover *(G-6826)*

▲ Instrmntation Ctrl Systems Inc..........E 513 662-2600
  Cincinnati *(G-3024)*

Interface Logic Systems Inc..................G 614 236-8388
  Columbus *(G-5472)*

▲ J-C-R Tech Inc....................................F 937 783-2296
  Blanchester *(G-1351)*

Kcn Technologies LLC............................G 440 439-4219
  Bedford *(G-1131)*

Kiemle-Hankins Company......................E 419 661-2430
  Perrysburg *(G-12395)*

Mid-Ohio Electric Co..............................E 614 274-8000
  Columbus *(G-5563)*

▲ Miscor Group Ltd..............................B 330 830-3500
  Massillon *(G-10129)*

Narrow Way Custom Tech Inc................E 937 743-1611
  Carlisle *(G-2290)*

◆ Niktec Inc..G 513 282-3747
  Franklin *(G-7689)*

Oaks Welding Inc....................................G 330 482-4216
  Columbiana *(G-5047)*

Precision Assemblies Inc......................F 330 549-2630
  North Lima *(G-11809)*

Queen City Office Machine....................F 513 251-7200
  Cincinnati *(G-3317)*

▲ Rubber City Machinery Corp............E 330 434-3500
  Akron *(G-312)*

▲ Sasha Electronics Inc........................F 419 662-8100
  Rossford *(G-12872)*

Spirit Avionics Ltd..................................F 614 237-4271
  Columbus *(G-5786)*

▲ Steel Eqp Specialists Inc..................D 330 823-8260
  Alliance *(G-427)*

▲ Stein LLC..F 440 526-9301
  Independence *(G-8685)*

Tegam Inc..E 440 466-6100
  Geneva *(G-7945)*

Town Cntry Technical Svcs Inc..............F 614 866-7700
  Reynoldsburg *(G-12775)*

Vacuum Electric Switch Co Inc..............F 330 374-5156
  Mogadore *(G-11089)*

Vertiv Corporation..................................G 614 888-0246
  Lockbourne *(G-9341)*

◆ Vertiv Corporation..............................A 614 888-0246
  Westerville *(G-15686)*

◆ Vertiv Energy Systems Inc................A 440 288-1122
  Lorain *(G-9443)*

Vertiv Group Corporation......................G 440 288-1122
  Lorain *(G-9444)*

7631 Watch, clock, and jewelry repair

Bensan Jewelers Inc..............................G 216 221-1434
  Lakewood *(G-8967)*

Don Basch Jewelers Inc........................E 330 467-2116
  Macedonia *(G-9547)*

Gustave Julian Jewelers Inc..................G 440 888-1100
  Cleveland *(G-4157)*

H P Nielsen Inc......................................G 440 244-4255
  Lorain *(G-9413)*

Im Greenberg Inc....................................G 440 461-4464
  Cleveland *(G-4214)*

Koop Diamond Cutters Inc....................F 513 621-2838
  Cincinnati *(G-3087)*

Michael W Hyes Desgr Goldsmith........G 440 519-0889
  Solon *(G-13389)*

Pughs Designer Jewelers Inc................G 740 344-9259
  Newark *(G-11603)*

Sheiban Jewelry Inc..............................F 440 238-0616
  Strongsville *(G-13879)*

White Jewelers Inc................................G 330 264-3324
  Wooster *(G-16182)*

7641 Reupholstery and furniture repair

American Office Services Inc................G 440 899-6888
  Westlake *(G-15731)*

▲ Casco Mfg Solutions Inc....................D 513 681-0003
  Cincinnati *(G-2706)*

Custom Craft Collection Inc..................F 440 998-3000
  Ashtabula *(G-630)*

▲ Fortner Upholstering Inc....................F 614 475-8282
  Columbus *(G-5384)*

Furniture Concepts Inc..........................F 216 292-9100
  Cleveland *(G-4093)*

Mielke Furniture Repair Inc..................G 419 625-4572
  Sandusky *(G-13082)*

▲ National Electro-Coatings Inc............D 216 898-0080
  Cleveland *(G-4436)*

Office Magic Inc....................................F 510 782-6100
  Medina *(G-10357)*

Recycled Systems Furniture Inc............E 614 880-9110
  Worthington *(G-16210)*

Robert Mayo Industries..........................G 330 426-2587
  East Palestine *(G-7008)*

Soft Touch Wood LLC............................E 330 545-4204
  Girard *(G-7975)*

7692 Welding repair

3-B Welding Ltd....................................G 740 819-4329
  New Concord *(G-11430)*

A & C Welding Inc................................E 330 762-4777
  Peninsula *(G-12337)*

▲ A & G Manufacturing Co Inc............E 419 468-7433
  Galion *(G-7858)*

A Tech Welding Products Inc................G 614 296-1573
  Valley City *(G-14860)*

Abbott Tool Inc......................................E 419 476-6742
  Toledo *(G-14174)*

▲ Active Metal and Molds Inc..............F 419 281-9623
  Ashland *(G-549)*

Advanced Welding Inc..........................E 937 746-6800
  Franklin *(G-7662)*

Advanced Wldg Fabrication Inc............F 440 724-9165
  Sheffield Lake *(G-13178)*

Albright Radiator Inc............................G 330 264-8886
  Wooster *(G-16100)*

All - Do Weld & Fab LLC......................F 740 477-2133
  Circleville *(G-3540)*

All Ohio Welding Inc............................G 937 663-7116
  Saint Paris *(G-12970)*

All-Type Welding & Fabrication............E 440 439-3990
  Cleveland *(G-3635)*

Allied Fabricating & Wldg Co................E 614 751-6664
  Columbus *(G-5113)*

Almandrey Fabricating Tech..................G 937 408-0054
  Springfield *(G-13531)*

Amptech Machining & Welding............G 419 652-3444
  Nova *(G-12002)*

Apollo Welding & Fabg Inc....................E 440 942-0227
  Willoughby *(G-15881)*

ARC Solutions Inc..................................E 419 542-9272
  Hicksville *(G-8371)*

Arctech Fabricating Inc..........................E 937 525-9353
  Springfield *(G-13535)*

Athens Mold and Machine Inc..............D 740 593-6613
  Athens *(G-675)*

B & R Fabricators & Maint Inc..............F 513 641-2222
  Cincinnati *(G-2650)*

Bamf Welding & Fabrication LLC..........G 440 862-8286
  Novelty *(G-12008)*

Baughman Machine & Weld Sp Inc......G 330 866-9243
  Waynesburg *(G-15293)*

Bayloff Stmped Pdts Knsman Inc..........D 330 876-4511
  Kinsman *(G-8935)*

Bear Welding Services LLC..................F 740 630-7538
  Caldwell *(G-1907)*

Blackwood Sheet Metal Inc..................G 614 291-3115
  Columbus *(G-5200)*

Blevins Metal Fabrication Inc................E 419 522-6082
  Mansfield *(G-9629)*

Bob Lanes Welding Inc..........................G 740 373-3567
  Marietta *(G-9779)*

Brad Grizer On Spot Welding................G 740 516-3436
  Whipple *(G-15813)*

Breitinger Company................................C 419 526-4255
  Mansfield *(G-9631)*

Brock RAD Wldg Fabrication Inc..........G 740 773-2540
  Chillicothe *(G-2496)*

Brown Industrial Inc..............................E 937 693-3838
  Botkins *(G-1542)*

Buckeye State Wldg & Fabg Inc............G 440 322-0344
  Elyria *(G-7119)*

Buckeye Welding..................................G 330 674-0944
  Millersburg *(G-10948)*

▲ Byron Products Inc............................D 513 870-9111
  Fairfield *(G-7340)*

C & R Inc..E 614 497-1130
  Groveport *(G-8134)*

C-N-D Industries Inc..............................E 330 478-8811
  Massillon *(G-10080)*

Camelot Manufacturing Inc....................F 419 678-2603
  Coldwater *(G-4983)*

Cardinal Welding Inc............................G 330 426-2404
  East Palestine *(G-7003)*

Carter Manufacturing Co Inc................E 513 398-7303
  Mason *(G-9968)*

▲ Case-Maul Manufacturing Co............F 419 524-1061
  Mansfield *(G-9635)*

Ccr Fabrications LLC............................G 937 667-6632
  Tipp City *(G-14128)*

◆ Ceramic Holdings Inc........................C 216 362-3900
  Brookpark *(G-1707)*

Certified Welding Co..............................E 216 961-5410
  Cleveland *(G-3804)*

Chore Anden..F 330 695-2300
  Fredericksburg *(G-7719)*

City Machine Technologies Inc............F 330 747-2639
  Youngstown *(G-16336)*

Clemens Mobile Welding LLC..............E 419 782-4220
  Defiance *(G-6674)*

Cleveland Jsm Inc..................................E 440 876-3050
  Strongsville *(G-13822)*

Clipsons Metal Working Inc..................G 513 772-6393
  Cincinnati *(G-2774)*

Cmt Machining & Fabg LLC..................F 937 652-3740
  Urbana *(G-14827)*

Employee Codes: A=Over 500 employees, B=251-500
C=101-250, D=51-100, E=20-50, F=10-19, G=1-9

76 MISCELLANEOUS REPAIR SERVICES

Company	Code	Phone
Columbus Mobile Welding LLC	G	614 352-6052
Centerburg (G-2357)		
Columbus Pipe and Equipment Co	F	614 444-7871
Columbus (G-5273)		
▲ Combs Manufacturing Inc	D	330 784-3151
Akron (G-114)		
Complete Metal Services	G	740 694-0000
Fredericktown (G-7740)		
Complete Stud Welding Inc	G	216 533-8482
Chagrin Falls (G-2372)		
Compton Metal Products Inc	F	937 382-2403
Wilmington (G-16045)		
Comptons Precision Machine	F	937 325-9139
Springfield (G-13546)		
Connaughton Wldg & Fence LLC	G	513 867-0230
Hamilton (G-8195)		
CRA Welding LLC	G	330 317-2007
Fredericksburg (G-7721)		
Creative Fab & Welding LLC	E	937 780-5000
Leesburg (G-9123)		
Creative Fabrication Ltd	G	740 262-5789
Richwood (G-12813)		
Creative Mold and Machine Inc	E	440 338-5146
Newbury (G-11621)		
Crest Bending Inc	E	419 492-2108
New Washington (G-11546)		
Custom Machine Inc	E	419 986-5122
Tiffin (G-14082)		
Custom Way Welding Inc	G	937 845-9469
New Carlisle (G-11414)		
Custom Weld & Machine Corp	F	330 452-3935
Canton (G-2086)		
Danny L Boyle	G	330 206-1448
Salem (G-12990)		
Dayton Brick Company Inc	F	937 293-4189
Moraine (G-11171)		
Dbcr Inc	E	330 920-1900
Cuyahoga Falls (G-6078)		
Dover Fabrication and Burn Inc	G	330 339-1057
Dover (G-6819)		
Dover Machine Co	F	330 343-4123
Dover (G-6821)		
Drabik Manufacturing Inc	F	216 267-1616
Cleveland (G-3971)		
Dragonfly Cstm Fabrication LLC	G	614 522-9618
Blacklick (G-1336)		
Drj Welding Services LLC	F	740 229-7428
New Philadelphia (G-11499)		
Ds Welding LLC	G	330 893-4049
Millersburg (G-10953)		
Duco Tool & Die Inc	F	419 628-2031
Minster (G-11050)		
Duray Machine Company Inc	F	440 277-4119
Amherst (G-475)		
Dynamic Weld Corporation	E	419 582-2900
Osgood (G-12173)		
E & M Liberty Welding Inc	G	330 866-2338
Waynesburg (G-15294)		
E & R Welding Inc	G	440 329-9387
Berlin Heights (G-1313)		
Eagle Welding & Fabg Inc	E	440 946-0692
Willoughby (G-15914)		
▲ East End Welding LLC	C	330 677-6000
Kent (G-8811)		
Fabrication Shop Inc	F	419 435-7934
Fostoria (G-7631)		
Falls Stamping & Welding Co	C	330 928-1191
Cuyahoga Falls (G-6083)		
Finely Tuned Fabrications LLC	G	216 513-6731
Lagrange (G-8947)		
Fleetpride Inc	E	740 282-2711
Steubenville (G-13667)		
Fredrick Welding & Machining	F	614 866-9650
Reynoldsburg (G-12766)		
Friess Welding Inc	G	330 644-8160
Coventry Township (G-6009)		
G & R Welding Service LLC	G	937 245-2341
Middletown (G-10825)		
G-Rod Welding & Fabg LLC	G	740 588-0609
Chandlersville (G-2439)		
Gabel Welding Inc	G	567 201-8217
Port Clinton (G-12619)		
Garland Welding Co Inc	F	330 536-6506
Lowellville (G-9515)		
Gaspar Inc	D	330 477-2222
Canton (G-2110)		
▲ General Technologies Inc	E	419 747-1800
Mansfield (G-9659)		
▲ General Tool Company	C	513 733-5500
Cincinnati (G-2946)		
George Steel Fabricating Inc	E	513 932-2887
Lebanon (G-9000)		
Gilson Machine & Tool Co Inc	E	419 592-2911
Napoleon (G-11316)		
▲ Glenridge Machine Co	E	440 975-1055
Solon (G-13354)		
Gmp Welding & Fabrication Inc	G	513 825-7861
Cincinnati (G-2961)		
Gorski Welding LLC	G	440 412-7910
North Ridgeville (G-11841)		
Greber Machine Tool Inc	G	440 322-3685
Elyria (G-7156)		
Griffiths Mobile Welding	G	937 750-3711
New Carlisle (G-11415)		
H & H Machine Shop Akron Inc	E	330 773-3327
Akron (G-175)		
Habco Tool and Dev Co Inc	E	440 946-5546
Mentor (G-10466)		
Harris Welding and Machine Co	F	419 281-8351
Ashland (G-577)		
Harrison Welding Services LLC	G	513 405-6581
Amelia (G-456)		
HI Tecmetal Group Inc	E	216 881-8100
Wickliffe (G-15835)		
▲ Hi-Tek Manufacturing Inc	C	513 459-1094
Mason (G-10001)		
Highs Welding Inc	G	937 464-3029
Belle Center (G-1197)		
Hobart Bros Stick Electrode	F	937 332-5375
Troy (G-14578)		
Holdren Brothers Inc	F	937 465-7050
West Liberty (G-15622)		
Holdsworth Industrial Fabg LLC	G	330 874-3945
Bolivar (G-1527)		
Holmview Welding LLC	F	330 359-5315
Fredericksburg (G-7725)		
Independent Machine & Wldg Inc	G	937 339-7330
Troy (G-14586)		
▲ Industry Products Co	B	937 778-0585
Piqua (G-12526)		
J & S Industrial Mch Pdts Inc	D	419 691-1380
Toledo (G-14341)		
J A B Welding Service Inc	F	740 453-5868
Zanesville (G-16540)		
J&J Precision Fabricators Ltd	F	330 482-4964
Columbiana (G-5043)		
Jerl Machine Inc	D	419 873-0270
Perrysburg (G-12394)		
Jerrys Welding Supply Inc	F	937 364-1500
Hillsboro (G-8460)		
JMw Welding and Mfg Inc	E	330 484-2428
Canton (G-2136)		
Johns Welding & Towing Inc	F	419 447-8937
Tiffin (G-14089)		
JP Suggins Mobile Wldg Inc	F	216 566-7131
Cleveland (G-4265)		
Jrs MBL Wldg Fabrication LLC	G	567 307-5460
Ashland (G-581)		
K & J Machine Inc	G	740 425-3282
Barnesville (G-903)		
K-M-S Industries Inc	F	440 243-6680
Brookpark (G-1720)		
Kda Manufacturing LLC	F	330 590-7431
Norton (G-11947)		
Kellers Fine Line Welding LLC	G	903 348-8304
Tallmadge (G-14035)		
Kellys Wldg & Fabrication Ltd	G	440 593-6040
Conneaut (G-5922)		
Kendel Welding & Fabrication	G	330 834-2429
Massillon (G-10115)		
Kings Welding and Fabg Inc	F	330 738-3592
Mechanicstown (G-10287)		
Kinninger Prod Wldg Co Inc	D	419 629-3491
New Bremen (G-11403)		
Kirbys Auto and Truck Repr Inc	G	513 934-3999
Lebanon (G-9093)		
▲ Kottler Metal Products Co Inc	E	440 946-7473
Willoughby (G-15940)		
Kramer Power Equipment Co	F	937 456-2232
Eaton (G-7063)		
KS Welding & Fabrication LLC	G	937 420-2270
Fort Loramie (G-7602)		
Lakecraft Inc	G	419 734-2828
Port Clinton (G-12621)		
Laserflex Corporation	D	614 850-9600
Hilliard (G-8418)		
Lima Sheet Metal Machine & Mfg	E	419 229-1161
Lima (G-9264)		
Lincoln Electric Automtn Inc	B	937 295-2120
Fort Loramie (G-7603)		
Logan Welding Inc	G	740 385-9651
Logan (G-9370)		
▲ Long-Stanton Mfg Company	E	513 874-8020
West Chester (G-15458)		
Lostcreek Tool & Machine Inc	F	937 773-6022
Piqua (G-12533)		
Lunar Tool & Mold Inc	E	440 237-2141
North Royalton (G-11884)		
M & M Certified Welding Inc	F	330 467-1729
Macedonia (G-9562)		
M & M Concepts Inc	G	937 355-1115
West Mansfield (G-15626)		
Majestic Tool and Machine Inc	F	440 248-5058
Solon (G-13383)		
Marengo Fabricated Steel Ltd	F	800 919-2652
Cardington (G-2276)		
Marsam Metalfab Inc	E	330 405-1520
Twinsburg (G-14691)		
Martin Welding LLC	F	937 687-3602
New Lebanon (G-11450)		
Matcor Metal Fabrication Inc	G	419 298-2394
Edgerton (G-7076)		
Mc Elwain Industries Inc	F	419 532-3126
Ottawa (G-12184)		
▲ Mc Machine Llc	E	216 398-3666
Cleveland (G-4378)		
▲ McGregor Mtal Leffel Works LLC	D	937 325-5561
Springfield (G-13603)		
Mdb Fabricating Inc	G	216 799-7017
Cleveland (G-4385)		
Meta Manufacturing Corporation	E	513 793-6382
Blue Ash (G-1435)		
Microweld Engineering Inc	G	614 847-9410
Worthington (G-16204)		
Mike Loppe	F	937 969-8102
Tremont City (G-14538)		

Millwrght Wldg Fbrication Svcs............. G 740 533-1510
  Kitts Hill *(G-8944)*
Mk Welding & Fabrication Inc............... G 937 603-4430
  Waynesville *(G-15299)*
Modern Machine Development............. F 937 253-4576
  Dayton *(G-6454)*
Montgomery & Montgomery LLC........... G 330 858-9533
  Akron *(G-252)*
Morrison Custom Welding Inc............... G 330 464-1637
  Fredericksburg *(G-7727)*
Ms Welding LLC.................................... G 419 925-4141
  Maria Stein *(G-9773)*
Mt Vernon Mold Works Inc..................... E 618 242-6040
  Akron *(G-255)*
Nation Welding LLC............................... G 419 466-2241
  Delta *(G-6790)*
National Wldg Tanker Repr LLC............. G 614 875-3399
  Grove City *(G-8110)*
Northwind Industries Inc........................ E 216 433-0666
  Cleveland *(G-4481)*
Oaks Welding Inc.................................. G 330 482-4216
  Columbiana *(G-5047)*
Ohio Hydraulics Inc................................ E 513 771-2590
  Cincinnati *(G-3215)*
Ohio Trailer Inc...................................... F 330 392-4444
  Warren *(G-15196)*
Ohio Trailer Supply Inc.......................... G 614 471-9121
  Columbus *(G-5629)*
Ottawa Defense Logistics LLC.............. F 419 596-3202
  Ottawa *(G-12186)*
Patriot Stainless Welding....................... F 740 297-6040
  Zanesville *(G-16553)*
Paul Wilke & Son Inc............................. F 513 921-3163
  Cincinnati *(G-3241)*
Paulo Products Company....................... E 440 942-0153
  Willoughby *(G-15969)*
◆ Pentaflex Inc....................................... C 937 325-5551
  Springfield *(G-13617)*
Perkins Motor Service Ltd..................... F 440 277-1256
  Lorain *(G-9430)*
Perry Welding Service Inc..................... F 330 425-2211
  Twinsburg *(G-14714)*
Phillips Mfg and Tower Co..................... D 419 347-1720
  Shelby *(G-13197)*
Phoenix Inds & Apparatus Inc............... F 513 722-1085
  Loveland *(G-9498)*
Piscione Welding................................... G 440 653-3985
  Burbank *(G-1877)*
Pr-Weld & Manufacturing Ltd................ G 419 633-9204
  West Unity *(G-15642)*
Precision Assemblies Inc...................... F 330 549-2630
  North Lima *(G-11809)*
Precision Mtal Fabrication Inc............... D 937 235-9261
  Dayton *(G-6516)*
Precision Reflex Inc.............................. F 419 629-2603
  New Bremen *(G-11407)*
Precision Weld Fab............................... G 440 576-5800
  Jefferson *(G-8756)*
Precision Welding.................................. G 740 627-7320
  Howard *(G-8559)*
Precision Welding & Mfg Inc.................. F 937 444-6925
  Mount Orab *(G-11245)*
Precision Welding Corporation.............. E 216 524-6110
  Cleveland *(G-4577)*
▲ Prince & Izant LLC.............................. E 216 362-7000
  Cleveland *(G-4587)*
Process Eqp Co Wldg Svcs LLC........... G 937 667-4451
  Tipp City *(G-14149)*
Prout Boiler Htg & Wldg Inc................... F 330 744-0293
  Youngstown *(G-16423)*
Quality Welding Inc............................... G 419 483-6067
  Bellevue *(G-1231)*

Quality Wldg & Fabrication LLC............ G 567 220-6639
  Tiffin *(G-14100)*
Quick Service Welding & Mch Co.......... F 330 673-3818
  Kent *(G-8851)*
▲ R K Industries Inc............................... D 419 523-5001
  Ottawa *(G-12190)*
Rbm Environmental & Cnstr Inc............ F 419 693-5840
  Oregon *(G-12110)*
Rex Welding Inc.................................... F 740 387-1650
  Marion *(G-9875)*
RI Alto Mfg Inc...................................... F 740 914-4230
  Marion *(G-9876)*
Ridge Engineering Inc........................... G 513 681-5500
  Cincinnati *(G-3340)*
Ridge Machine & Welding Co................ G 740 537-2821
  Toronto *(G-14534)*
Rodney Wells.. G 740 425-2266
  Barnesville *(G-904)*
Roetmans Welding LLC........................ G 216 385-5938
  Akron *(G-308)*
Romar Metal Fabricating Inc................. G 740 682-7731
  Oak Hill *(G-12025)*
Rose Metal Industries LLC.................... F 216 881-3355
  Cleveland *(G-4648)*
Rsv Wlding Fbrction McHning In........... F 419 592-0993
  Napoleon *(G-11333)*
Salem Welding & Supply Company....... G 330 332-4517
  Salem *(G-13029)*
Sauerwein Welding................................ G 513 563-2979
  Cincinnati *(G-3364)*
Schmidt Machine Company................... E 419 294-3814
  Upper Sandusky *(G-14823)*
▲ Semtorq Inc.. F 330 487-0600
  Twinsburg *(G-14734)*
Simpson & Sons Inc.............................. F 513 367-0152
  Harrison *(G-8292)*
Sky Climber Fabricating LLC................. F 740 990-9430
  Delaware *(G-6750)*
Smp Welding LLC.................................. F 440 205-9353
  Mentor *(G-10556)*
Somerville Manufacturing Inc................ E 740 336-7847
  Marietta *(G-9829)*
Spradlin Bros Welding Co..................... F 800 219-2182
  Springfield *(G-13634)*
Stan-Kell LLC.. E 440 998-1116
  Ashtabula *(G-661)*
State Metal Hose Inc............................. G 614 527-4700
  Hilliard *(G-8443)*
Steve Vore Welding and Steel.............. F 419 375-4087
  Fort Recovery *(G-7624)*
Steven Crumbaker Jr............................ G 740 995-0613
  Zanesville *(G-16566)*
Stud Welding Associates...................... G 216 392-7808
  Elyria *(G-7207)*
Superior Weld and Fabg Co Inc............ G 216 249-5122
  Cleveland *(G-4753)*
Systech Handling Inc............................ F 419 445-8226
  Archbold *(G-547)*
▼ T & R Welding Systems Inc............... F 937 228-7517
  Dayton *(G-6606)*
Tbone Sales LLC................................... F 330 897-6131
  Baltic *(G-841)*
Techniweld.. G 412 357-2176
  Youngstown *(G-16452)*
Temperature Controls Co Inc................ F 330 773-6633
  New Franklin *(G-11444)*
Terex Services...................................... G 440 262-3200
  Brecksville *(G-1634)*
Toney Tool Manufacturing Inc............... F 937 890-8535
  Dayton *(G-6627)*
Tonys Wldg & Fabrication LLC.............. E 740 333-4000
  Wshngtn Ct Hs *(G-16242)*

Tri-State Plating & Polishing.................. G 304 529-2579
  Proctorville *(G-12688)*
Tri-Weld Inc... G 216 281-6009
  Cleveland *(G-4823)*
Triangle Precision Industries................. D 937 299-6776
  Dayton *(G-6632)*
Tru-Fab Technology Inc......................... F 440 954-9760
  Willoughby *(G-16009)*
Turn-Key Industrial Svcs LLC................ D 614 274-1128
  Grove City *(G-8127)*
United Abrasives & Welding Inc............. G 304 996-1490
  Canton *(G-2252)*
US Welding Training LLC...................... G 440 669-9380
  Fairport Harbor *(G-7459)*
Valley Machine Tool Inc......................... E 513 899-2737
  Morrow *(G-11227)*
Viking Fabricators Inc............................ E 740 374-5246
  Marietta *(G-9843)*
Ways Cstm Wldg & Fabrication.............. G 440 354-1350
  Painesville *(G-12276)*
Webers Body & Frame Inc..................... G 937 839-5946
  West Alexandria *(G-15346)*
Welders Supply Inc................................ E 216 267-4470
  Brookpark *(G-1727)*
Welding Consultants Inc........................ G 614 258-7018
  Columbus *(G-5870)*
Welding Consultants LLC...................... G 614 258-7018
  Columbus *(G-5871)*
Weldments Inc....................................... F 937 235-9261
  Dayton *(G-6649)*
Wengerds Welding & Repair LLC......... G 740 599-9071
  Butler *(G-1891)*
Wenrick Machine and Tool Corp........... F 937 667-7307
  Tipp City *(G-14166)*
Whitt Machine Inc.................................. F 513 423-7624
  Middletown *(G-10872)*
Worthington Industries Inc..................... E 614 438-3028
  Columbus *(G-5883)*
Wpc Successor Inc............................... F 937 233-6141
  Tipp City *(G-14167)*

7694 Armature rewinding shops

▲ 3-D Service Ltd.................................. C 330 830-3500
  Massillon *(G-10072)*
Als High Tech Inc.................................. F 440 232-7090
  Bedford *(G-1099)*
Bennett Electric Inc............................... F 800 874-5405
  Norwalk *(G-11956)*
Big River Electric Inc............................. G 740 446-4360
  Gallipolis *(G-7889)*
Bornhorst Motor Service Inc.................. G 937 773-0426
  Piqua *(G-12507)*
City Machine Technologies Inc.............. F 330 747-2639
  Youngstown *(G-16336)*
Clark-Fowler Enterprises Inc................. E 330 262-0906
  Wooster *(G-16110)*
D & J Electric Motor Repair Co............. F 330 336-4343
  Wadsworth *(G-15025)*
E M Service Inc..................................... F 440 323-3260
  Elyria *(G-7137)*
E-Z Electric Motor Svc Corp.................. E 216 581-8820
  Cleveland *(G-3986)*
Fenton Bros Electric Co......................... G 330 343-0093
  New Philadelphia *(G-11501)*
Hackworth Electric Motors Inc............... G 330 345-6049
  Wooster *(G-16128)*
Hannon Company.................................. F 330 343-7758
  Dover *(G-6826)*
Hannon Company.................................. F 740 453-0527
  Zanesville *(G-16536)*
Hennings Quality Service Inc................ F 216 941-9120
  Cleveland *(G-4181)*

76 MISCELLANEOUS REPAIR SERVICES

Horner Industrial Services Inc .... F 937 390-6667
  Springfield (G-13579)
Horner Industrial Services Inc .... G 513 874-8722
  West Chester (G-15562)
Integrated Power Services LLC .... D 216 433-7808
  Cleveland (G-4231)
Integrated Power Services LLC .... E 513 863-8816
  Hamilton (G-8221)
Kcn Technologies LLC .... G 440 439-4219
  Bedford (G-1131)
Kiemle-Hankins Company .... E 419 661-2430
  Perrysburg (G-12395)
Lemsco Inc .... G 419 242-4005
  Toledo (G-14363)
Lima Armature Works Inc .... G 419 222-4010
  Lima (G-9261)
Mader Elc Mtr Pwr Trnsmssons L .... G 937 325-5576
  Springfield (G-13599)
▲ Magnetech Industrial Svcs Inc .... D 330 830-3500
  Massillon (G-10121)
Masteller Electric Motor Svc .... G 937 492-8500
  Sidney (G-13262)
▼ Matlock Electric Co Inc .... E 513 731-9600
  Cincinnati (G-3134)
Mid-Ohio Electric Co .... E 614 274-8000
  Columbus (G-5563)
◆ National Electric Coil Inc .... B 614 488-1151
  Columbus (G-5589)
Ohio Electric Motor Service Center Inc .... F 614 444-1451
  Columbus (G-5617)
Ohio Electric Motor Svc LLC .... F 614 444-1451
  Columbus (G-5618)
Phillips Electric Co .... F 216 361-0014
  Cleveland (G-4548)
Rel Enterprises Inc .... E 216 741-1700
  Brooklyn Heights (G-1698)
▲ Shoemaker Electric Company .... E 614 294-5626
  Columbus (G-5764)
Whelco Industrial Ltd .... D 419 385-4627
  Perrysburg (G-12445)
Yaskawa America Inc .... C 937 847-6200
  Miamisburg (G-10704)

7699 Repair services, nec

▲ 3-D Service Ltd .... C 330 830-3500
  Massillon (G-10072)
A L Callahan Door Sales .... G 419 884-3667
  Mansfield (G-9620)
A/C Laser Technologies Inc .... F 330 784-3355
  Akron (G-12)
AB Bonded Locksmiths Inc .... G 513 531-7334
  Cincinnati (G-2589)
Abj Equipfix LLC .... E 419 684-5236
  Castalia (G-2318)
Able Pallet Mfg & Repr .... G 614 444-2115
  Columbus (G-5091)
Accu-Grind Inc .... G 330 677-2225
  Kent (G-8792)
▼ Air-Rite Inc .... E 216 228-8200
  Cleveland (G-3617)
◆ Ajax Tocco Magnethermic Corp .... C 800 547-1527
  Warren (G-15135)
All Power Battery Inc .... G 330 453-5236
  Canton (G-2033)
▲ American Frame Corporation .... D 419 893-5595
  Maumee (G-10163)
▲ American Hydraulic Svcs Inc .... D 606 739-8680
  Ironton (G-8695)
▲ Amko Service Company .... E 330 364-8857
  Midvale (G-10875)
▲ Apph Wichita Inc .... E 316 943-5752
  Strongsville (G-13808)

ARC Solutions Inc .... E 419 542-9272
  Hicksville (G-8371)
ARS Recycling Systems LLC .... F 330 536-8210
  Lowellville (G-9511)
B M Machine .... E 419 595-2898
  New Riegel (G-11534)
◆ Babcock & Wilcox Company .... A 330 753-4511
  Akron (G-73)
Battery Unlimited .... G 740 452-5030
  Zanesville (G-16506)
Beaumont Machine LLC .... F 513 701-0421
  Mason (G-9958)
Beckman Environmental Svcs Inc .... F 513 752-3570
  Batavia (G-912)
Bunn-Minnick Co .... G 614 299-7934
  Columbus (G-5221)
Cammel Saw Company .... F 330 477-3764
  Canton (G-2058)
Canvas Specialty Mfg Co .... G 216 881-0647
  Cleveland (G-3785)
Certified Labs & Service Inc .... E 419 289-7462
  Ashland (G-563)
Certon Technologies Inc .... F 440 786-7185
  Bedford (G-1111)
Cleveland Electric Labs Co .... E 800 447-2207
  Twinsburg (G-14643)
Cleveland Jsm Inc .... E 440 876-3050
  Strongsville (G-13822)
Commercial Electric Pdts Corp .... E 216 241-2886
  Cleveland (G-3889)
Compton Metal Products Inc .... F 937 382-2403
  Wilmington (G-16045)
Conviber Inc .... F 330 723-6006
  Medina (G-10313)
Corrotec Inc .... F 937 325-3585
  Springfield (G-13547)
Csg Software .... G 614 986-2600
  Columbus (G-5309)
Custom Metal Works Inc .... F 419 668-7831
  Norwalk (G-11959)
Custom Services and Designs .... G 937 866-7636
  Miamisburg (G-10630)
Cuyahoga Machine Company LLC .... F 216 267-3560
  Brookpark (G-1711)
D & M Saw & Tool Inc .... G 513 871-5433
  Cincinnati (G-2811)
D C Systems Inc .... F 330 273-3030
  Brunswick (G-1756)
Dayton Machine Tool Company .... E 937 222-6444
  Dayton (G-6282)
Dearing Compressor and Pu .... F 330 783-2258
  Youngstown (G-16348)
Diamond Machinery LLC .... G 216 312-1235
  Cleveland (G-3956)
Division Overhead Door Inc .... F 513 872-0888
  Cincinnati (G-2834)
DNC Hydraulics LLC .... F 419 963-2800
  Rawson (G-12743)
Eaton Industrial Corporation .... C 216 692-5456
  Cleveland (G-3997)
Electric Speed Indicator Co .... F 216 251-2540
  Aurora (G-713)
Elite Biomedical Solutions LLC .... F 513 207-0602
  Cincinnati (G-2558)
Evoqua Water Technologies LLC .... G 614 491-5917
  Groveport (G-8138)
Expert Crane Inc .... F 216 451-9900
  Wellington (G-15307)
Fawcett Co Inc .... G 330 659-4187
  Richfield (G-12787)
Fire Foe Corp .... E 330 759-9834
  Girard (G-7968)

Fluid System Service Inc .... G 216 651-2450
  Cleveland (G-4072)
▲ Forge Industries Inc .... A 330 960-2468
  Youngstown (G-16359)
Fox Tool Co Inc .... F 330 928-3402
  Cuyahoga Falls (G-6085)
Frontier Tank Center Inc .... F 330 659-3888
  Richfield (G-12788)
Glen D Lala .... G 937 274-7770
  Dayton (G-6354)
Glenn Michael Brick .... F 740 391-5735
  Flushing (G-7587)
Graphic Systems Services Inc .... E 937 746-0708
  Springboro (G-13503)
Grimes Aerospace Company .... D 937 484-2001
  Urbana (G-14832)
◆ Grob Systems Inc .... A 419 358-9015
  Bluffton (G-1504)
▲ Hamilton Industrial Grinding Inc .... E 513 863-1221
  Hamilton (G-8218)
Handcrafted Jewelry Inc .... G 330 650-9011
  Hudson (G-8595)
Hannon Company .... F 330 343-7758
  Dover (G-6826)
Hannon Company .... F 740 453-0527
  Zanesville (G-16536)
▲ Harry C Lobalzo & Sons Inc .... E 330 666-6758
  Akron (G-180)
Hendershot Performance LLC .... F 740 315-0090
  Belpre (G-1254)
▲ Hunger Hydraulics CC Ltd .... F 419 666-4510
  Rossford (G-12865)
Hunter Hydraulics Inc .... G 330 455-3983
  Canton (G-2126)
Hy-Blast Inc .... E 513 424-0704
  Middletown (G-10829)
Hydraulic Specialists Inc .... F 740 922-3343
  Midvale (G-10879)
Hydro Supply Co .... F 740 454-3842
  Zanesville (G-16537)
▲ Ic-Fluid Power Inc .... F 419 661-8811
  Rossford (G-12866)
Industrial Ctrl Dsign Mint Inc .... F 330 785-9840
  Tallmadge (G-14033)
▲ Industrial Repair and Mfg .... E 419 822-4232
  Delta (G-6787)
Instrumentors Inc .... G 440 238-3430
  Strongsville (G-13846)
J & J Performance Inc .... F 330 567-2455
  Shreve (G-13211)
J L Wannemacher Sls Svc Inc .... F 419 453-3445
  Ottoville (G-12200)
JJ&pl Services-Consulting LLC .... E 330 923-5783
  Cuyahoga Falls (G-6093)
Jonmar Gear and Machine Inc .... G 330 854-6500
  Canal Fulton (G-1971)
K & J Machine Inc .... F 740 425-3282
  Barnesville (G-903)
Kars Ohio LLC .... G 614 655-1099
  Pataskala (G-12300)
L M Equipment & Design Inc .... F 330 332-9951
  Salem (G-13009)
Langstons Ultmate Clg Svcs Inc .... F 330 298-9150
  Ravenna (G-12722)
Laserflex Corporation .... D 614 850-9600
  Hilliard (G-8418)
◆ Lawrence Industries Inc .... E 216 518-7000
  Cleveland (G-4318)
Loadmaster Trailer Company Ltd .... F 419 732-3434
  Port Clinton (G-12622)
Loft Violin Shop .... F 614 267-7221
  Columbus (G-5531)

Lubrisource Inc... F 937 432-9292
  Middletown (G-10836)
Lyco Corporation.. E 412 973-9176
  Lowellville (G-9517)
Machine Tool Design & Fab LLC............... F 419 435-7676
  Fostoria (G-7641)
McNational Inc... D 740 377-4391
  South Point (G-13471)
MCS Midwest LLC...................................... G 513 217-0805
  Franklin (G-7686)
Mechanical Dynamics Analis LLC............ E 440 946-0082
  Euclid (G-7285)
▲ Mesocoat Inc... F 216 453-0866
  Euclid (G-7286)
Metro Design Inc....................................... E 440 458-4200
  Elyria (G-7181)
Mettler-Toledo Intl Fin Inc......................... F 614 438-4511
  Columbus (G-5065)
◆ Mettler-Toledo LLC................................. A 614 438-4511
  Columbus (G-5067)
Miami Valley Punch & Mfg......................... F 937 237-0533
  Dayton (G-6440)
Midwest Knife Grinding Inc....................... F 330 854-1030
  Canal Fulton (G-1973)
Midwest Rlwy Prsrvtion Soc Inc................ G 216 781-3629
  Cleveland (G-4412)
Mjcj Holdings Inc....................................... G 937 885-0800
  Miamisburg (G-10663)
Mpi Logistics and Service Inc.................... E 330 832-5309
  Massillon (G-10130)
National Tool & Equipment Inc................. F 330 629-8665
  Youngstown (G-16403)
National Wldg Tanker Repr LLC................ G 614 875-3399
  Grove City (G-8110)
Nbw Inc... E 216 377-1700
  Cleveland (G-4442)
Nice Body Automotive LLC........................ G 440 752-5568
  Elyria (G-7185)
North Coast Exotics Inc............................. G 216 651-5512
  Cleveland (G-4468)
Northwood Industries Inc.......................... F 419 666-2100
  Perrysburg (G-12404)
Obr Cooling Towers Inc............................. E 419 243-3443
  Northwood (G-11924)
Odyssey Machine Company Ltd................ G 419 455-6621
  Perrysburg (G-12406)
▼ Ohio Broach & Machine Company..... E 440 946-1040
  Willoughby (G-15963)
Ohio Hydraulics Inc................................... E 513 771-2590
  Cincinnati (G-3215)
◆ Ohio Machinery Co................................ C 440 526-6200
  Broadview Heights (G-1665)
◆ OKL Can Line Inc.................................... E
  Cincinnati (G-3220)
Optimum Surgical...................................... F 216 870-8526
  Medina (G-10358)
P & L Precision Grinding Llc..................... F 330 746-8081
  Youngstown (G-16410)
Pas Technologies Inc................................. D 937 840-1053
  Hillsboro (G-8464)
Peebles - Herzog Inc................................. G 614 279-2211
  Columbus (G-5665)
Perkins Motor Service Ltd......................... F 440 277-1256
  Lorain (G-9430)
Pickens Window Service Inc..................... F 513 931-4432
  Cincinnati (G-3255)
Precision Gage & Tool Company............... E 937 866-9666
  Dayton (G-6512)
Quad Fluid Dynamics Inc........................... F 330 220-3005
  Brunswick (G-1785)
Quality Components Inc............................ F 440 255-0606
  Mentor (G-10540)

Quality Cutter Grinding Co........................ E 216 362-6444
  Cleveland (G-4605)
Quintus Technologies LLC........................ E 614 891-2732
  Lewis Center (G-9176)
Rbm Environmental & Cnstr Inc............... F 419 693-5840
  Oregon (G-12110)
Rudd Equipment Company Inc................ D 513 321-7833
  Cincinnati (G-3354)
▲ Sabco Industries Inc.............................. E 419 531-5347
  Toledo (G-14461)
▲ Save Edge Inc... E 937 376-8268
  Xenia (G-16272)
Schaeffer Metal Products Inc.................... G 330 296-6226
  Ravenna (G-12732)
Schindler Elevator Corporation................ F 419 861-5900
  Holland (G-8529)
Seilkop Industries Inc................................ E 513 761-1035
  Cincinnati (G-3377)
Slater Road Mills Inc................................. E 330 332-9951
  Salem (G-13032)
Sportsmans Haven Inc............................... G 740 432-7243
  Cambridge (G-1955)
▲ Steel Eqp Specialists Inc....................... D 330 823-8260
  Alliance (G-427)
▲ Stein LLC... F 440 526-9301
  Independence (G-8685)
Superior Marine Ways Inc......................... C 740 894-6224
  Proctorville (G-12687)
Superior Soda Service LLC....................... G 937 657-9700
  Beavercreek (G-1081)
T E Brown LLC... F 937 223-2241
  Dayton (G-6607)
Taft Tool & Production Co......................... F 419 385-2576
  Toledo (G-14481)
▲ Tech Pro Inc.. G 330 923-3546
  Akron (G-350)
Tektronix Inc.. F 248 305-5200
  West Chester (G-15594)
Thirion Brothers Eqp Co LLC..................... G 440 357-8004
  Painesville (G-12271)
Tpf Inc.. G 513 761-9968
  Cincinnati (G-3458)
Tri State Equipment Company.................. G 513 738-7227
  Shandon (G-13161)
U S Molding Machinery Co Inc................. E 440 918-1701
  Willoughby (G-16012)
Uhrichsville Carbide Inc............................ F 740 922-9197
  Uhrichsville (G-14772)
Unified Scrning Crshing - OH I.................. G 937 836-3201
  Englewood (G-7246)
Unison Industries LLC............................... F 937 426-0621
  Alpha (G-439)
◆ UPA Technology Inc............................... F 513 755-1380
  West Chester (G-15522)
Victor Organ Company.............................. G 330 792-1321
  Youngstown (G-16470)
◆ Walker National Inc............................... E 614 492-1614
  Columbus (G-5862)
Weather King Heating & AC...................... G 330 908-0281
  Northfield (G-11914)
West Equipment Company Inc................. G 419 698-1601
  Toledo (G-14522)
▲ Winkle Industries Inc............................. D 330 823-9730
  Alliance (G-438)
Wm Plotz Machine and Forge Co.............. E 216 861-0441
  Cleveland (G-4915)
◆ Wood Graphics Inc................................. E 513 771-6300
  Cincinnati (G-3525)

78 MOTION PICTURES

7812 Motion picture and video production

▲ Master Communications Inc.................. G 208 821-3473
  Cincinnati (G-3133)
World Harvest Church Inc......................... C 614 837-1990
  Canal Winchester (G-1994)

7819 Services allied to motion pictures
Swagg Productions2015llc......................... F 614 601-7414
  Worthington (G-16213)

7822 Motion picture and tape distribution
Allied Shipping and Packa......................... F 937 222-7422
  Moraine (G-11155)

7841 Video tape rental
Ohio Hd Video.. F 614 656-1162
  New Albany (G-11387)

79 AMUSEMENT AND RECREATION SERVICES

7922 Theatrical producers and services
North Coast Theatrical Inc........................ G 330 762-1768
  Akron (G-266)
▲ Scenic Solutions Ltd Lblty Co............... G 937 866-5062
  Dayton (G-6560)
Schell Scenic Studio Inc........................... G 614 444-9550
  Millersport (G-11013)
Schenz Theatrical Supply Inc.................... F 513 542-6100
  Cincinnati (G-3369)

7929 Entertainers and entertainment groups
American Gild of English Hndbe............... G 937 438-0085
  Cincinnati (G-2618)
Club 513 LLC.. G 800 530-2574
  Cincinnati (G-2776)
Kenyetta Bagby Enterprise LLC................ F 614 584-3426
  Reynoldsburg (G-12768)
Status Entertainment Group LLC............. G 216 252-2243
  Cleveland (G-4732)
Swagg Productions2015llc........................ F 614 601-7414
  Worthington (G-16213)
Tomahawk Entrmt Group LLC................... F 216 505-0548
  Euclid (G-7302)

7933 Bowling centers
Greater Cincinnati Bowl Assn................... E 513 761-7387
  Cincinnati (G-2970)

7992 Public golf courses
McClelland Inc... E 740 452-3036
  Zanesville (G-16544)

7993 Coin-operated amusement devices
Glenn Michael Brick.................................. F 740 391-5735
  Flushing (G-7587)

7997 Membership sports and recreation clubs
Hilltop Recreation Inc............................... F 937 549-2904
  Manchester (G-9619)
Lake Township Trustees........................... E 419 836-1143
  Millbury (G-10934)

7999 Amusement and recreation, nec
▲ Asm International................................... D 440 338-5151
  Novelty (G-12007)
Black Wing Shooting Center LLC............. G 740 363-7555
  Delaware (G-6705)
Building Block Performance LLC.............. G 614 918-7476
  Plain City (G-12568)

79 AMUSEMENT AND RECREATION SERVICES

Giuseppes Concessions LLC.................F 614 554-2551
  Marengo (G-9768)
▲ Jmac Inc..E 614 436-2418
  Columbus (G-5498)
Kelblys Rifle Range Inc....................G 330 683-4674
  North Lawrence (G-11798)
Melinz Industries Inc.........................F 440 946-3512
  Willoughby (G-15951)
◆ Park Corporation.............................B 216 267-4870
  Medina (G-10362)
Soccer Centre Owners Ltd................G 419 893-5425
  Maumee (G-10233)
X-Press Tool Inc...............................F 330 225-8748
  Brunswick (G-1802)
Youngs Jersey Dairy Inc...................B 937 325-0629
  Yellow Springs (G-16290)

80 HEALTH SERVICES

8011 Offices and clinics of medical doctors

Community Action Program Corp.........F 740 374-8501
  Marietta (G-9786)
Dayton Laser & Aesthetic Medic..........G 937 208-8282
  Dayton (G-6280)
Evokes LLC..E 513 947-8433
  Mason (G-9992)
Eye Surgery Center Ohio Inc..............E 614 228-3937
  Columbus (G-5368)
Francisco Jaume.................................G 740 622-1200
  Coshocton (G-5978)
Lababidi Enterprises Inc.....................G 330 733-2907
  Akron (G-214)
Nutritional Medicinals LLC..................F 937 433-4673
  West Chester (G-15467)
Orthotics Prsthtics Rhblttion................F 330 856-2553
  Warren (G-15197)
Presque Isle Orthtics Prsthtic.............G 216 371-0660
  Cleveland (G-4583)
▲ Volk Optical Inc..............................D 440 942-6161
  Mentor (G-10594)
Westerville Endoscopy Ctr LLC...........G 614 568-1666
  Westerville (G-15689)

8041 Offices and clinics of chiropractors

◆ Boxout LLC....................................C 833 462-7746
  Hudson (G-8587)

8042 Offices and clinics of optometrists

True Vision..G 740 277-7550
  Lancaster (G-9048)

8049 Offices of health practitioner

◆ Boxout LLC....................................C 833 462-7746
  Hudson (G-8587)
Cincinnati Eye Inst - Estgate................F 513 984-5133
  Cincinnati (G-2554)
True Vision..G 740 277-7550
  Lancaster (G-9048)

8051 Skilled nursing care facilities

Ohio Home & Leisure Products I........G 614 833-4144
  Pickerington (G-12465)
Optum Infusion Svcs 550 LLC............D 866 442-4679
  Cincinnati (G-3227)

8052 Intermediate care facilities

Bittersweet Inc...................................D 419 875-6986
  Whitehouse (G-15816)
▲ Cardinal Health 414 LLC................C 614 757-5000
  Dublin (G-6873)

8062 General medical and surgical hospitals

Dan Allen Surgical LLC......................F 800 261-9953
  Newbury (G-11622)
Optoquest Corporation.......................F 216 445-3637
  Cleveland (G-4507)

8071 Medical laboratories

Cellular Technology Limited................E 216 791-5084
  Shaker Heights (G-13152)
Mp Biomedicals LLC..........................C 440 337-1200
  Solon (G-13393)
Personnel Selection Services..............F 440 835-3255
  Cleveland (G-4542)
Quest Diagnostics Incorporated..........G 513 229-5500
  Mason (G-10045)
Smithers Group Inc.............................D 330 833-8548
  Massillon (G-10145)

8072 Dental laboratories

Dental Ceramics Inc...........................E 330 523-5240
  Richfield (G-12785)
Doling & Assoc Dntl Lab Inc...............F 937 254-0075
  Dayton (G-6300)
Sentage Corporation..........................G 419 842-6730
  Sylvania (G-14013)
United Dental Laboratories.................E 330 253-1810
  Tallmadge (G-14054)

8093 Specialty outpatient clinics, nec

Community Action Program Corp.........F 740 374-8501
  Marietta (G-9786)

8099 Health and allied services, nec

Bio-Blood Components Inc.................C 614 294-3183
  Columbus (G-5189)
Kapios LLC..G 567 661-0772
  Toledo (G-14344)

81 LEGAL SERVICES

8111 Legal services

Akron Legal News Inc........................F 330 296-7578
  Akron (G-35)
General Bar Inc..................................F 440 835-2000
  Westlake (G-15753)
Gongwer News Service Inc................F 614 221-1992
  Columbus (G-5407)
Perfect Probate..................................G 513 791-4100
  Cincinnati (G-3246)
Petro Quest Inc..................................G 740 593-3800
  Athens (G-690)

82 EDUCATIONAL SERVICES

8211 Elementary and secondary schools

Butler Tech..E 513 867-1028
  Fairfield Township (G-7430)
Society of The Precious Blood............E 419 925-4516
  Celina (G-2349)

8222 Junior colleges

Borman Enterprises Inc.......................F 216 459-9292
  Cleveland (G-3749)

8243 Data processing schools

Computer Workshop Inc......................E 614 798-9505
  Dublin (G-6877)
Corporate Elevator LLC......................G 614 288-1847
  Columbus (G-5297)
Millers Aplus Cmpt Svcs LLC..............F 330 620-5288
  Akron (G-250)

8249 Vocational schools, nec

▲ Flightsafety International Inc...........C 614 324-3500
  Columbus (G-5380)
M R I Education Foundation...............E 513 281-3400
  Cincinnati (G-3119)
Pakra LLC...F 614 477-6965
  Columbus (G-5651)
▲ Zaner-Bloser Inc............................C 614 486-0221
  Columbus (G-5892)

8299 Schools and educational services

Auguste Moone Enterprises Ltd..........E 216 333-9248
  Cleveland Heights (G-4937)
Deemsys Inc......................................D 614 322-9928
  Gahanna (G-7833)
Dietrich Von Hldbrand Lgacy PR.........G 703 496-7821
  Steubenville (G-13666)
Equipping Ministries Intl Inc................G 513 742-1100
  Cincinnati (G-2882)
Health Sense Inc................................G 440 354-8057
  Painesville (G-12244)
Studio Arts and Glass Inc...................F 330 494-9779
  Canton (G-2237)
Tangible Solutions Inc........................E 937 912-4603
  Fairborn (G-7324)
Toastmasters International..................F 937 429-2680
  Dayton (G-6174)
Wooden Horse....................................G 740 503-5243
  Baltimore (G-849)

83 SOCIAL SERVICES

8322 Individual and family services

▲ Cincinnati Assn For The Blind........C 513 221-8558
  Cincinnati (G-2740)
Clovernook Ctr For Blind Vslly............C 513 522-3860
  Cincinnati (G-2775)
County of Lake...................................F 440 269-2193
  Willoughby (G-15904)
Jeffco Sheltered Workshop.................F 740 264-4608
  Steubenville (G-13669)
Omnipresence Cleaning LLC..............F 937 250-4749
  Dayton (G-6491)
Trumbull Mobile Meals.......................F 330 394-2538
  Warren (G-15212)

8331 Job training and related services

Belco Works Inc.................................D 740 695-0500
  Saint Clairsville (G-12897)
Boundless Cmnty Pathways Inc.........A 937 461-0034
  West Carrollton (G-15351)
Brown Cnty Bd Mntal Rtardation........E 937 378-4891
  Georgetown (G-7950)
Carroll Hills Industries.........................F 330 627-5524
  Carrollton (G-2304)
▲ Cincinnati Assn For The Blind........C 513 221-8558
  Cincinnati (G-2740)
County of Lake...................................F 440 269-2193
  Willoughby (G-15904)
▲ Findaway World LLC.....................E 440 893-0808
  Solon (G-13349)
▼ Hunter Defense Tech Inc...............E 216 438-6111
  Solon (G-13363)
Jeffco Sheltered Workshop.................F 740 264-4608
  Steubenville (G-13669)
Metzenbaum Sheltered Inds Inc.........D 440 729-1919
  Chesterland (G-2485)
Pakra LLC...F 614 477-6965
  Columbus (G-5651)
Quadco Rehabilitation Ctr Inc..............E 419 445-1950
  Archbold (G-543)
Quadco Rehabilitation Ctr Inc..............B 419 682-1011
  Stryker (G-13912)

Richland Newhope Inds Inc.................. C 419 774-4400
 Mansfield *(G-9712)*
RT Industries Inc................................. G 937 335-5784
 Troy *(G-14606)*
Sandco Industries................................ E 419 547-3273
 Clyde *(G-4978)*
TAC Industries Inc............................... B 937 328-5200
 Springfield *(G-13642)*
Vgs Inc... C 216 431-7800
 Cleveland *(G-4866)*
Vocational Services Inc....................... E 216 431-8085
 Cleveland *(G-4880)*

8351 Child day care services

Learn21 A Flxble Lrng Cllbrtiv................ F 513 402-2121
 Blue Ash *(G-1421)*

8361 Residential care

Bittersweet Inc..................................... D 419 875-6986
 Whitehouse *(G-15816)*
RT Industries Inc................................. G 937 335-5784
 Troy *(G-14606)*

8399 Social services, nec

Community Action Program Corp......... F 740 374-8501
 Marietta *(G-9786)*

84 MUSEUMS, ART GALLERIES AND BOTANICAL AND ZOOLOGICAL GARDENS

8412 Museums and art galleries

Brewster Sugarcreek Twp Histo............ F 330 767-0045
 Brewster *(G-1643)*
Velvet Ice Cream Company.................. D 740 892-3921
 Utica *(G-14859)*

86 MEMBERSHIP ORGANIZATIONS

8611 Business associations

▲ Hirzel Canning Company................... E 419 693-0531
 Northwood *(G-11919)*
Interstate Contractors LLC.................. E 513 372-5393
 Mason *(G-10013)*
▲ Precision Metalforming Assn............. E 216 901-8800
 Independence *(G-8681)*

8621 Professional organizations

American Ceramic Society................... E 614 890-4700
 Westerville *(G-15647)*

8641 Civic and social associations

Family Motor Coach Assn Inc.............. E 513 474-3622
 Cincinnati *(G-2894)*
Sylvania Mose Ldge No 1579 Lya........ F 419 885-4953
 Sylvania *(G-14017)*

8661 Religious organizations

Calvary Christian Ch of Ohio................ F 740 828-9000
 Frazeysburg *(G-7714)*
Christian Missionary Alliance............... C 380 208-6200
 Reynoldsburg *(G-12758)*
Incorprted Trstees of The Gspl............ D 216 749-2100
 Middleburg Heights *(G-10721)*
Saint Ctherines Metalworks Inc........... G 216 409-0576
 Cleveland *(G-4668)*
Society of The Precious Blood............. E 419 925-4516
 Celina *(G-2349)*
Temple Israel....................................... G 330 762-8617
 Akron *(G-351)*

Vista Community Church...................... F 614 718-2294
 Plain City *(G-12600)*

8699 Membership organizations, nec

American Gild of English Hndbe........... G 937 438-0085
 Cincinnati *(G-2618)*
Greater Cincinnati Bowl Assn............... E 513 761-7387
 Cincinnati *(G-2970)*

87 ENGINEERING, ACCOUNTING, RESEARCH, AND MANAGEMENT SERVICES

8711 Engineering services

A+ Engineering Fabrication Inc............ F 419 832-0748
 Grand Rapids *(G-8008)*
ACC Automation Co Inc....................... E 330 928-3821
 Akron *(G-14)*
▲ Advanced Design Industries Inc........ E 440 277-4141
 Sheffield Village *(G-13180)*
▲ Advanced Engrg Solutions Inc.......... D 937 743-6900
 Springboro *(G-13493)*
Aerovation Tech Holdings LLC............. G 567 208-5525
 Forest *(G-7589)*
◆ Alfons Haar Inc.................................. E 937 560-2031
 Springboro *(G-13495)*
▲ American Controls Inc....................... E 440 944-9735
 Wickliffe *(G-15824)*
Applied Experience LLC...................... G 614 943-2970
 Plain City *(G-12562)*
Atmos360 Inc....................................... E 513 772-4777
 West Chester *(G-15539)*
Automted Cmpnent Spcalists LLC....... E 513 335-4285
 Cincinnati *(G-2645)*
Autotec Corporation............................. E 419 885-2529
 Toledo *(G-14201)*
B&N Coal Inc....................................... E 740 783-3575
 Dexter City *(G-6802)*
Babcock & Wilcox Holdings Inc........... A 704 625-4900
 Akron *(G-75)*
Barr Engineering Incorporated............. E 614 714-0299
 Columbus *(G-5175)*
Bender Engineering Company............. G 330 938-2355
 Beloit *(G-1250)*
Beringer Plating Inc............................. G 330 633-8409
 Akron *(G-82)*
▲ Cbn Westside Technologies Inc......... B 513 772-7000
 West Chester *(G-15387)*
▲ Cecil C Peck Co................................ F 330 785-0781
 Akron *(G-103)*
Ceso Inc... E 937 435-8584
 Miamisburg *(G-10626)*
Circle Prime Manufacturing.................. E 330 923-0019
 Cuyahoga Falls *(G-6074)*
Clarkwestern Dietrich Building............. E 330 372-5564
 Warren *(G-15154)*
▼ Clarkwstern Dtrich Bldg System....... C 513 870-1100
 West Chester *(G-15396)*
Cleveland Roll Forming En................... F 440 899-3888
 Westlake *(G-15744)*
Coal Services Inc................................. B 740 795-5220
 Powhatan Point *(G-12684)*
Coating Systems Group Inc................. F 440 816-9306
 Middleburg Heights *(G-10717)*
Comtec Incorporated........................... F 330 425-8102
 Twinsburg *(G-14644)*
Consoldted Anlytcal Systems In........... F 513 542-1200
 Cincinnati *(G-2787)*
Control Electric Co............................... E 216 671-8010
 Columbia Station *(G-5011)*

Corrpro Companies Inc........................ E 330 725-6681
 Medina *(G-10314)*
CPI Group Limited............................... F 216 525-0046
 Cleveland *(G-3911)*
Crown Solutions Co LLC..................... C 937 890-4075
 Vandalia *(G-14936)*
Crowne Group LLC.............................. F 216 589-0198
 Cleveland *(G-3917)*
Curtiss-Wright Controls........................ E 937 252-5601
 Fairborn *(G-7312)*
Custom Craft Controls Inc................... F 330 630-9599
 Akron *(G-120)*
DA Precision Products Inc................... F 513 459-1113
 West Chester *(G-15411)*
David Chojnacki.................................... E 303 905-1918
 Westerville *(G-15699)*
Davis Technologies Inc........................ F 330 823-2544
 Alliance *(G-401)*
Decision Systems Inc.......................... F 330 456-7600
 Canton *(G-2090)*
Dillin Engineered Systems Corp.......... E 419 666-6789
 Perrysburg *(G-12376)*
Dlz Ohio Inc... C 614 888-0040
 Columbus *(G-5332)*
◆ Dms Inc... C 440 951-9838
 Willoughby *(G-15910)*
Donald E Didion II................................ F 419 483-2226
 Bellevue *(G-1226)*
Electrovations Inc................................ G 330 274-3558
 Solon *(G-13341)*
◆ Empire Systems Inc.......................... F 440 653-9300
 Avon Lake *(G-806)*
▲ Enprotech Industrial Tech LLC.......... E 216 883-3220
 Cleveland *(G-4019)*
EP Ferris & Associates Inc.................. E 614 299-2999
 Columbus *(G-5357)*
Eti Tech LLC....................................... F 937 832-4200
 Kettering *(G-8907)*
Ever Secure SEC Systems Inc............ F 937 369-8294
 Dayton *(G-6327)*
Field Apparatus Service & Tstg............ G 513 353-9399
 Cincinnati *(G-2902)*
Fishel Company................................... C 614 850-4400
 Columbus *(G-5377)*
Forte Industrial Equipmen.................... E 513 398-2800
 Mason *(G-9993)*
Frost Engineering Inc........................... E 513 541-6330
 Cincinnati *(G-2923)*
General Precision Corporation............. G 440 951-9380
 Willoughby *(G-15925)*
Genius Solutions Engrg Co.................. E 419 794-9914
 Maumee *(G-10202)*
Genpact LLC.. E 513 763-7660
 Cincinnati *(G-2947)*
Hahn Automation Group Us Inc........... D 937 886-3232
 Miamisburg *(G-10641)*
Halliday Technologies Inc.................... G 614 504-4150
 Delaware *(G-6728)*
▲ Hamilton Manufacturing Corp........... E 419 867-4858
 Holland *(G-8511)*
Hess Advanced Solutions Llc.............. G 937 829-4794
 Dayton *(G-6368)*
Hexion Inc.. C 888 443-9466
 Columbus *(G-5428)*
Hii Mission Technologies Corp............. G 937 426-3421
 Beavercreek *(G-1074)*
▼ Htec Systems Inc.............................. F 937 438-3010
 Dayton *(G-6376)*
▼ Hunter Defense Tech Inc.................. E 216 438-6111
 Solon *(G-13363)*
▲ Hydro-Dyne Inc.................................. E 330 832-5076
 Massillon *(G-10109)*

87 ENGINEERING, ACCOUNTING, RESEARCH, AND MANAGEMENT SERVICES

Imax Industries Inc .... F 440 639-0242
  Painesville (G-12246)
Innovative Controls Corp .... E 419 691-6684
  Toledo (G-14333)
Inovent Engineering Inc .... G 330 468-0019
  Macedonia (G-9557)
Integris Composites Inc .... D 740 928-0326
  Hebron (G-8345)
JB Industries Ltd .... F 330 856-4587
  Warren (G-15181)
Jet Di Inc .... G 330 607-7913
  Brunswick (G-1772)
Johnson Mfg Systems LLC .... F 937 866-4744
  Miamisburg (G-10650)
Jotco Inc .... G 513 721-4943
  Mansfield (G-9675)
◆ Keuchel & Associates Inc .... E 330 945-9455
  Cuyahoga Falls (G-6095)
L-3 Cmmncations Nova Engrg Inc .... C 877 282-1168
  Mason (G-10018)
Latanick Equipment Inc .... E 419 433-2200
  Huron (G-8638)
Lintech Electronics LLC .... F 513 528-6190
  Cincinnati (G-2571)
Matrix Research Inc .... D 937 427-8433
  Beavercreek (G-1075)
◆ Maval Industries LLC .... C 330 405-1600
  Twinsburg (G-14692)
Melink Corporation .... D 513 685-0958
  Milford (G-10913)
◆ Mendenhall Technical Services Inc .... E 513 860-1280
  Fairfield (G-7383)
Mercury Iron and Steel Co .... F 440 349-1500
  Solon (G-13385)
Micro Industries Corporation .... D 740 548-7878
  Westerville (G-15716)
Mid-Ohio Electric Co .... E 614 274-8000
  Columbus (G-5563)
Mill & Motion Inc .... F 216 524-4000
  Independence (G-8673)
Morris Technologies Inc .... E 513 733-1611
  Cincinnati (G-3174)
Mound Manufacturing Center Inc .... F 937 236-8387
  Dayton (G-6459)
Mrl Materials Resources LLC .... E 937 531-6657
  Xenia (G-16269)
◆ Nesco Inc .... E 440 461-6000
  Cleveland (G-4448)
Neundorfer Inc .... E 440 942-8990
  Willoughby (G-15957)
New Dawn Labs LLC .... F 203 675-5644
  Union (G-14773)
◆ New Path International LLC .... E 614 410-3974
  Powell (G-12679)
Northrop Grmman Tchncal Svcs I .... D 937 320-3100
  Beavercreek Township (G-1086)
Northwood Industries Inc .... F 419 666-2100
  Perrysburg (G-12404)
▲ Nucon International Inc .... F 614 846-5710
  Columbus (G-5607)
Ohio Blow Pipe Company .... E 216 681-7379
  Cleveland (G-4496)
Onpower Inc .... E 513 228-2100
  Lebanon (G-9103)
Owens Corning Sales LLC .... F 330 633-6735
  Tallmadge (G-14042)
Panelmatic Inc .... E 330 782-8007
  Youngstown (G-16412)
Panelmatic Cincinnati Inc .... E 513 829-1960
  Fairfield (G-7392)
Parking & Traffic Control SEC .... F 440 243-7565
  Cleveland (G-4533)

▲ Performnce Plymr Solutions Inc .... F 937 298-3713
  Moraine (G-11196)
Pioneer Solutions LLC .... E 216 383-3400
  Euclid (G-7292)
Plate-All Metal Company Inc .... G 330 633-6166
  Akron (G-277)
PMC Systems Limited .... E 330 538-2268
  North Jackson (G-11789)
Pollock Research & Design Inc .... E 330 332-3300
  Salem (G-13023)
▼ Projects Designed & Built .... E 419 726-7400
  Toledo (G-14443)
Providence REES Inc .... F 614 833-6231
  Columbus (G-5696)
Qcsm LLC .... G 216 650-8731
  Cleveland (G-4602)
▲ Quality Plating Co .... G 216 361-0151
  Cleveland (G-4607)
Ra Consultants LLC .... E 513 469-6600
  Blue Ash (G-1459)
▲ RAD-Con Inc .... E 440 871-5720
  Lakewood (G-8981)
Resonant Sciences LLC .... E 937 431-8180
  Beavercreek (G-1080)
◆ Rolls-Royce Energy Systems Inc .... A 703 834-1700
  Mount Vernon (G-11292)
Sest Inc .... F 440 777-9777
  Westlake (G-15785)
Sgi Matrix LLC .... D 937 438-9033
  Miamisburg (G-10681)
Signalysis Inc .... F 513 528-6164
  Cincinnati (G-3392)
Sponseller Group Inc .... G 937 492-9949
  Sidney (G-13289)
Sponseller Group Inc .... E 419 861-3000
  Holland (G-8531)
Star Distribution and Mfg LLC .... E 513 860-3573
  West Chester (G-15590)
Stock Fairfield Corporation .... C 440 543-6000
  Solon (G-13425)
Storetek Engineering Inc .... E 330 294-0678
  Tallmadge (G-14050)
Straight 72 Inc .... D 740 943-5730
  Marysville (G-9940)
Sunpower Inc .... D 740 594-2221
  Athens (G-699)
Support Svc LLC .... G 419 617-0660
  Lexington (G-9203)
Systech Handling Inc .... F 419 445-8226
  Archbold (G-547)
Systems Kit LLC MB .... E 330 945-4500
  Akron (G-343)
Tangent Company LLC .... G 440 543-2775
  Chagrin Falls (G-2427)
Tangible Solutions Inc .... E 937 912-4603
  Fairborn (G-7324)
Tech4imaging LLC .... F 614 214-2655
  Columbus (G-5817)
▲ Technology House Ltd .... G 440 248-3025
  Streetsboro (G-13795)
Tekworx LLC .... F 513 533-4777
  Blue Ash (G-1479)
Tfi Manufacturing LLC .... G 440 290-9411
  Mentor (G-10575)
Thermal Treatment Center Inc .... E 216 881-8100
  Wickliffe (G-15854)
▲ Timekeeping Systems Inc .... F 216 595-0890
  Solon (G-13439)
TL Industries Inc .... C 419 666-8144
  Perrysburg (G-12436)
Torsion Control Products Inc .... F 248 537-1900
  Wadsworth (G-15070)

U S Army Corps of Engineers .... G 740 537-2571
  Toronto (G-14536)
Ultra-Met Company .... F 937 653-7133
  Urbana (G-14851)
Uvonics Co .... F 614 458-1163
  Columbus (G-5852)
Vector Electromagnetics LLC .... F 937 478-5904
  Wilmington (G-16062)
Warmus and Associates Inc .... F 330 659-4440
  Bath (G-962)
Welding Consultants Inc .... G 614 258-7018
  Columbus (G-5870)
Werks Kraft Engineering LLC .... F 330 721-7374
  Medina (G-10394)
◆ Wrc Holdings Inc .... F 330 733-6662
  Akron (G-377)
◆ Xaloy LLC .... C 330 726-4000
  Austintown (G-757)
Xcite Systems Corporation .... E 513 965-0300
  Cincinnati (G-2577)
Youngstown Plastic Tooling .... F 330 783-7222
  Youngstown (G-16485)

8712 Architectural services

Ceso Inc .... E 937 435-8584
  Miamisburg (G-10626)
Dlz Ohio Inc .... C 614 888-0040
  Columbus (G-5332)
Garland Industries Inc .... G 216 641-7500
  Cleveland (G-4104)
Garland/Dbs Inc .... C 216 641-7500
  Cleveland (G-4105)
Golden Angle Archtctral Group .... G 614 531-7932
  Columbus (G-5406)
Russell Group United LLC .... F 614 353-6853
  Columbus (G-5734)

8713 Surveying services

Barr Engineering Incorporated .... E 614 714-0299
  Columbus (G-5175)
Dlz Ohio Inc .... C 614 888-0040
  Columbus (G-5332)

8721 Accounting, auditing, and bookkeeping

Colburn Patterson LLC .... G 419 866-5544
  Holland (G-8499)
Kent Information Services Inc .... G 330 672-2110
  Kent (G-8824)
Lipari Foods Operating Co LLC .... E 330 893-2479
  Millersburg (G-10973)
Michele Caldwell .... G 937 505-7744
  Dayton (G-6442)
Patrick J Burke & Co .... E 513 455-8200
  Cincinnati (G-3237)
Samb LLC Services .... G 937 660-0115
  Englewood (G-7241)
Steward Edge Bus Solutions .... F 614 826-5305
  Columbus (G-5795)
Watson Haran & Company Inc .... G 937 436-1414
  Dayton (G-6648)

8731 Commercial physical research

Applied Medical Technology Inc .... E 440 717-4000
  Brecksville (G-1606)
Applied Sciences Inc .... F 937 766-2020
  Cedarville (G-2322)
Barco Inc .... E 937 372-7579
  Xenia (G-16250)
BASF Catalysts LLC .... C 216 360-5005
  Cleveland (G-3723)
◆ Borchers Americas Inc .... D 440 899-2950
  Westlake (G-15741)

Circle Prime Manufacturing................. E 330 923-0019
  Cuyahoga Falls *(G-6074)*
Copernicus Therapeutics Inc................ F 216 231-0227
  Cleveland *(G-3904)*
Curtiss-Wright Controls........................ E 937 252-5601
  Fairborn *(G-7312)*
Defense Research Assoc Inc................ E 937 431-1644
  Dayton *(G-6158)*
Electronic Concepts Engrg Inc............. F 419 861-9000
  Holland *(G-8509)*
EMD Millipore Corporation................... C 513 631-0445
  Norwood *(G-11995)*
◆ Flexsys America LP............................. D 330 666-4111
  Akron *(G-155)*
▲ Ftech R&D North America Inc............ E 937 339-2777
  Troy *(G-14572)*
Global Realms LLC............................... G 614 828-7284
  Gahanna *(G-7836)*
Guild Associates Inc............................. G 843 573-0095
  Dublin *(G-6889)*
▲ Guild Associates Inc........................... D 614 798-8215
  Dublin *(G-6888)*
▲ Heraeus Epurio LLC............................ E 937 264-1000
  Vandalia *(G-14942)*
Iconic Labs LLC..................................... F 216 759-4040
  Westlake *(G-15758)*
Ion Vacuum Ivac Tech Corp.................. F 216 662-5158
  Cleveland *(G-4235)*
KS Technologies & Cstm Mfg LLC...... G 419 426-0172
  Attica *(G-701)*
Leidos Inc... D 937 656-8433
  Beavercreek *(G-1055)*
Lifestyle Nutraceuticals Ltd.................. G 513 376-7218
  Cincinnati *(G-3105)*
Lyondell Chemical Company................ C 513 530-4000
  Cincinnati *(G-3118)*
Medpace Holdings Inc.......................... C 513 579-9911
  Cincinnati *(G-3142)*
Microweld Engineering Inc................... G 614 847-9410
  Worthington *(G-16204)*
Morris Technologies Inc........................ E 513 733-1611
  Cincinnati *(G-3174)*
Mp Biomedicals LLC............................. C 440 337-1200
  Solon *(G-13393)*
Northcoast Environmental Labs........... G 330 342-3377
  Streetsboro *(G-13782)*
Nsa Technologies LLC.......................... G 330 576-4600
  Akron *(G-269)*
Open Additive LLC................................ F 937 306-6140
  Dayton *(G-6492)*
Owens Corning Sales LLC................... G 330 633-6735
  Tallmadge *(G-14202)*
▲ Performnce Plymr Solutions Inc....... F 937 298-3713
  Moraine *(G-11196)*
Range Impact Inc................................... G 216 304-6556
  Cleveland *(G-4615)*
Ronald T Dodge Co................................ F 937 439-4497
  Dayton *(G-6552)*
Sierra Nevada Corporation................... C 937 431-2800
  Beavercreek *(G-1062)*
Steiner Eoptics Inc................................. D 937 426-2341
  Miamisburg *(G-10686)*
Sunpower Inc... D 740 594-2221
  Athens *(G-699)*
Tacoma Energy LLC.............................. E 614 410-9000
  Westerville *(G-15721)*
◆ Trico Products Corporation................C 248 371-1700
  Cleveland *(G-4829)*
Vehicle Systems Inc.............................. G 330 854-0535
  Massillon *(G-10153)*
Velocys Inc... D 614 733-3300
  Plain City *(G-12599)*

▲ Wiley Companies................................ C 740 622-0755
  Coshocton *(G-6000)*

8732 Commercial nonphysical research

▼ Intek Inc... F 614 895-0301
  Westerville *(G-15660)*
Liminal Esports LLC.............................. G 440 423-5856
  Gates Mills *(G-7928)*
Quality Solutions Inc............................. E 440 933-9946
  Cleveland *(G-4608)*
Steward Edge Bus Solutions................ F 614 826-5305
  Columbus *(G-5795)*

8733 Noncommercial research organizations

Mp Biomedicals LLC............................. C 440 337-1200
  Solon *(G-13393)*
▲ Performnce Plymr Solutions Inc....... F 937 298-3713
  Moraine *(G-11196)*
Quasonix Inc.. E 513 942-1287
  West Chester *(G-15491)*
Sdg Inc.. F 440 893-0771
  Cleveland *(G-4682)*
Sunpower Inc... D 740 594-2221
  Athens *(G-699)*
Tangent Company LLC......................... G 440 543-2775
  Chagrin Falls *(G-2427)*
Valensil Technologies LLC................... F 440 937-8181
  Avon *(G-790)*

8734 Testing laboratories

Agrana Fruit Us Inc............................... C 937 693-3821
  Anna *(G-488)*
Balancing Company Inc........................ E 937 898-9111
  Vandalia *(G-14933)*
Barr Engineering Incorporated............ E 614 714-0299
  Columbus *(G-5175)*
Chemsultants International Inc............ G 440 974-3080
  Mentor *(G-10437)*
Curtiss-Wright Flow Ctrl Corp.............. D 513 528-7900
  Cincinnati *(G-2556)*
Global Manufacturing Solutions........... F 937 236-8315
  Dayton *(G-6355)*
▲ Godfrey & Wing Inc............................ E 330 562-1440
  Aurora *(G-716)*
Jci Jones Chemicals Inc....................... F 330 825-2531
  New Franklin *(G-11438)*
◆ Kaplan Industries Inc......................... D 856 779-8181
  Harrison *(G-8282)*
Metcut Research Associates Inc......... D 513 271-5100
  Cincinnati *(G-3156)*
Mjcj Holdings Inc................................... G 937 885-0800
  Miamisburg *(G-10663)*
Mrl Materials Resources LLC.............. E 937 531-6657
  Xenia *(G-16269)*
National Polymer Inc............................. F 440 708-1245
  Chagrin Falls *(G-2409)*
Nelson Labs Fairfield Inc...................... E 973 227-6882
  Broadview Heights *(G-1663)*
▲ Nucon International Inc..................... F 614 846-5710
  Columbus *(G-5607)*
Phymet Inc.. F 937 743-8061
  Springboro *(G-13515)*
R D Baker Enterprises Inc.................... G 937 461-5225
  Dayton *(G-6537)*
Ream and Haager Laboratory Inc........ F 330 343-3711
  Dover *(G-6840)*
Sample Machining Inc........................... E 937 258-3338
  Dayton *(G-6558)*
Smithers Group Inc................................ D 330 833-8548
  Massillon *(G-10145)*
Tangent Company LLC......................... G 440 543-2775
  Chagrin Falls *(G-2427)*

◆ Trico Products Corporation................C 248 371-1700
  Cleveland *(G-4829)*
US Tubular Products Inc....................... D 330 832-1734
  North Lawrence *(G-11800)*
Wallover Enterprises Inc....................... E 440 238-9250
  Strongsville *(G-13893)*
Welding Consultants Inc....................... G 614 258-7018
  Columbus *(G-5870)*
Yoder Industries Inc............................... C 937 278-5769
  Dayton *(G-6662)*

8741 Management services

◆ Babcock & Wilcox Company.............. A 330 753-4511
  Akron *(G-73)*
Cardinal Health Inc................................ E 614 553-3830
  Dublin *(G-6871)*
Cardinal Health Inc................................ G 614 757-2863
  Lewis Center *(G-9155)*
◆ Cardinal Health Inc............................. A 614 757-5000
  Dublin *(G-6872)*
Central Coca-Cola Btlg Co Inc............. E 330 875-1487
  Akron *(G-105)*
Central Coca-Cola Btlg Co Inc............. E 740 474-2180
  Circleville *(G-3543)*
CFM Religion Pubg Group LLC........... D 513 931-4050
  Cincinnati *(G-2723)*
Coal Services Inc................................... B 740 795-5220
  Powhatan Point *(G-12684)*
◆ Dco LLC.. E 419 931-9086
  Perrysburg *(G-12373)*
▲ Eleet Cryogenics Inc.......................... E 330 874-4009
  Bolivar *(G-1524)*
Elite Property Group LLC..................... F 216 356-7469
  Elyria *(G-7139)*
Eric Allshouse LLC............................... G 330 533-4258
  Canfield *(G-2005)*
Ingle-Barr Inc... D 740 702-6117
  Chillicothe *(G-2513)*
Instantwhip Foods Inc........................... F 614 488-2536
  Columbus *(G-5464)*
Instantwhip-Columbus Inc.................... G 614 871-9447
  Grove City *(G-8098)*
Integrated Resources Inc...................... E 419 885-7122
  Sylvania *(G-14002)*
Ironhawk Industrial Dist LLC................ G 216 502-3700
  Euclid *(G-7276)*
▲ Jmac Inc... E 614 436-2418
  Columbus *(G-5498)*
Kenyetta Bagby Enterprise LLC.......... F 614 584-3426
  Reynoldsburg *(G-12768)*
▲ Kurtz Bros Compost Services........... F 330 864-2621
  Akron *(G-213)*
▲ Leadec Corp... E 513 731-3590
  Blue Ash *(G-1420)*
Mel Heitkamp Builders Ltd................... G 419 375-0405
  Fort Recovery *(G-7623)*
Momentum Fleet MGT Group Inc........ D 440 759-2219
  Westlake *(G-15765)*
▲ Ohio Cllbrtive Lrng Sltons Inc........... E 216 595-5289
  Strongsville *(G-13862)*
Ohio Designer Craftsmen Entps.......... F 614 486-7119
  Columbus *(G-5615)*
Organalytix LLC..................................... G 908 938-6711
  West Chester *(G-15473)*
Pf Management Inc................................ G 513 874-8741
  West Chester *(G-15575)*
Protective Industrial Polymers............. F 440 327-0015
  North Ridgeville *(G-11854)*
RB Sigma LLC.. D 440 290-0577
  Mentor *(G-10545)*
Revolution Group Inc............................ D 614 212-1111
  Westerville *(G-15675)*

87 ENGINEERING, ACCOUNTING, RESEARCH, AND MANAGEMENT SERVICES

Sand PROperties&landscaping............ G 440 360-7386
  Westlake (G-15781)
Steward Edge Bus Solutions............... F 614 826-5305
  Columbus (G-5795)
TAC Industries Inc............................... B 937 328-5200
  Springfield (G-13642)

8742 Management consulting services

5me LLC... E 513 719-1600
  Cincinnati (G-2544)
Advanced Prgrm Resources Inc........... E 614 761-9994
  Dublin (G-6857)
Akron Centl Engrv Mold Mch Inc.......... E 330 794-8704
  Akron (G-29)
Alloy Extrusion Company..................... E 330 677-4946
  Kent (G-8798)
American Egle Prprty Prsrvtion............ G 855 440-6938
  North Ridgeville (G-11828)
◆ Amerihua Intl Entps Inc..................... G 740 549-0300
  Lewis Center (G-9148)
▲ Applied Marketing Services Inc.......... E 440 716-9962
  Westlake (G-15733)
◆ Applied Specialties Inc....................... E 440 933-9442
  Avon Lake (G-796)
Capehart Enterprises LLC................... F 614 769-7746
  Columbus (G-5230)
Chemsultants International Inc............ G 440 974-3080
  Mentor (G-10437)
Clarity Retail Services LLC.................. D 513 800-9369
  West Chester (G-15395)
◆ Comex North America Inc................. D 303 307-2100
  Cleveland (G-3888)
Crimson Gate Consulting Co................ G 614 805-0897
  Dublin (G-6878)
Delphia Consulting LLC....................... E 614 421-2000
  Columbus (G-5325)
◆ Dms Inc.. C 440 951-9838
  Willoughby (G-15910)
Electronic Imaging Svcs Inc................ F 740 549-2487
  Lewis Center (G-9159)
Elite Property Group LLC.................... F 216 356-7469
  Elyria (G-7139)
Eltool Corporation............................... E 513 723-1772
  Mansfield (G-9652)
EP Ferris & Associates Inc.................. E 614 299-2999
  Columbus (G-5357)
Equip Business Solutions Co................ G 614 854-9755
  Jackson (G-8715)
Frankes Wood Products LLC............... E 937 642-0706
  Marysville (G-9910)
Health Sense Inc................................ G 440 354-8057
  Painesville (G-12244)
Honda Dev & Mfg Amer LLC............... C 937 644-0724
  Marysville (G-9915)
Infinitaire Industries LLC..................... G 216 600-2051
  Euclid (G-7275)
Integrity Parking LLC......................... F 440 543-4123
  Aurora (G-720)
ITM Marketing Inc.............................. C 740 295-3575
  Coshocton (G-5981)
Just Business Inc................................ F 866 577-3303
  Dayton (G-6395)
Ketman Corporation............................ G 330 262-1688
  Wooster (G-16142)
Kitto Katsu Inc.................................... G 818 256-6997
  Clayton (G-3567)
Leidos Inc... D 937 656-8433
  Beavercreek (G-1055)
Link To Success Inc............................ G 888 959-4203
  Norwalk (G-11978)
▲ Mag Resources LLC......................... F 330 294-0494
  Barberton (G-878)

◆ Malco Products Inc........................... C 330 753-0361
  Barberton (G-879)
Malik Media LLC................................. F 614 933-0328
  New Albany (G-11383)
Michele Caldwell................................. G 937 505-7744
  Dayton (G-6442)
▲ Midwest Motor Supply Co................. C 800 233-1294
  Columbus (G-5565)
Millers Aplus Cmpt Svcs LLC............... F 330 620-5288
  Akron (G-250)
Neurologix Technologies Inc............... F 512 914-7941
  Cleveland (G-4451)
Nsa Technologies LLC......................... G 330 576-4600
  Akron (G-269)
One Wish LLC..................................... F 800 505-6883
  Bedford (G-1147)
Organalytix LLC.................................. G 908 938-6711
  West Chester (G-15473)
Page One Group................................. G 740 397-4240
  Mount Vernon (G-11286)
Pakra LLC... F 614 477-6965
  Columbus (G-5651)
Paycor Hcm Inc.................................. F 800 381-0053
  Cincinnati (G-3243)
Proficient Info Tech Inc....................... G 937 470-1300
  Dayton (G-6531)
▼ Projects Designed & Built................. E 419 726-7400
  Toledo (G-14443)
Pwi Inc... G 732 212-8110
  New Albany (G-11389)
Quality Solutions Inc........................... E 440 933-9946
  Cleveland (G-4608)
▲ Quarrymasters Inc........................... G 330 612-0474
  Akron (G-292)
Quez Media Marketing Inc................... F 216 910-0202
  Independence (G-8683)
Recognition Robotics Inc..................... F 440 590-0499
  Elyria (G-7200)
Russell Group United LLC.................... F 614 353-6853
  Columbus (G-5734)
Salient Systems Inc............................ E 614 792-5800
  Dublin (G-6934)
Santec Resources Inc.......................... F 614 664-9540
  Columbus (G-5746)
Sightgain Inc...................................... F 202 494-9317
  Mason (G-10056)
Simplevms LLC................................... F 888 255-8918
  Cincinnati (G-3393)
▲ SSP Industrial Group Inc.................. G 330 665-2900
  Fairlawn (G-7452)
Star Distribution and Mfg LLC.............. F 513 860-3573
  West Chester (G-15590)
Streamside Materials Llc..................... G 419 423-1290
  Findlay (G-7570)
Telex Communications Inc.................. G 419 865-0972
  Toledo (G-14482)
Tha Presidential Suite LLC................... G 216 338-7287
  Dublin (G-6952)
Tomahawk Entrmt Group LLC.............. F 216 505-0548
  Euclid (G-7302)
Tramonte & Sons LLC.......................... F 513 770-5501
  Lebanon (G-9114)
Trophy Sports Center LLC................... F 937 376-2311
  Xenia (G-16279)
Vehicle Systems Inc........................... G 330 854-0535
  Massillon (G-10153)
Welding Consultants Inc..................... G 614 258-7018
  Columbus (G-5870)

8743 Public relations services

Marketing Essentials LLC..................... E 419 629-0080
  New Bremen (G-11404)

8744 Facilities support services

Facility Service Pros LLC..................... G 419 577-6123
  Collins (G-5004)
▼ Fex LLC... F 412 604-0400
  Mingo Junction (G-11045)
Indoor Envmtl Specialists Inc.............. E 937 433-5202
  Dayton (G-6381)
MPW Industrial Svcs Group Inc........... B 740 927-8790
  Hebron (G-8350)
Radon Eliminator LLC.......................... F 330 844-0703
  North Canton (G-11755)
Taylor Communications Inc................. E 937 221-1000
  Dayton (G-6609)

8748 Business consulting, nec

Aeroseal LLC...................................... E 937 428-9300
  Dayton (G-6187)
▲ Aeroseal LLC................................... E 937 428-9300
  Miamisburg (G-10607)
◆ Alpha Technologies Svcs LLC........... D 330 745-1641
  Hudson (G-8583)
Apex Control Systems Inc................... D 330 938-2588
  Sebring (G-13117)
Architctral Identification Inc................ F 614 868-8400
  Gahanna (G-7830)
▲ Athens Technical Specialists............ F 740 592-2874
  Athens (G-676)
D M L Steel Tech................................ G 513 737-9911
  Liberty Twp (G-9213)
Deemsys Inc....................................... D 614 322-9928
  Gahanna (G-7833)
Defense Research Assoc Inc................ E 937 431-1644
  Dayton (G-6158)
E Retailing Associates LLC.................. D 614 300-5785
  Columbus (G-5339)
Estone Group LLC............................... E 888 653-2246
  Toledo (G-14280)
Great Lakes Mfg Group Ltd................. G 440 391-8266
  Rocky River (G-12838)
Infinitaire Industries LLC..................... G 216 600-2051
  Euclid (G-7275)
▲ Interactive Engineering Corp........... E 330 239-6888
  Medina (G-10337)
Jasstek Inc... F 614 808-3600
  Dublin (G-6902)
Ktsdi LLC.. G 330 783-2000
  North Lima (G-11808)
Lake Publishing Inc............................ G 440 299-8500
  Mentor (G-10490)
Magnum Computers Inc...................... F 216 781-1757
  Cleveland (G-4351)
Melink Corporation.............................. D 513 685-0958
  Milford (G-10913)
Millers Aplus Cmpt Svcs LLC............... F 330 620-5288
  Akron (G-250)
Nkh-Safety Inc................................... F 513 771-3839
  Cincinnati (G-3200)
Optum Infusion Svcs 550 LLC.............. D 866 442-4679
  Cincinnati (G-3227)
▼ Orton Edward Jr Crmic Fndation...... E 614 895-2663
  Westerville (G-15672)
Qlog Corp... G 513 874-1211
  Hamilton (G-8238)
Radon Eliminator LLC.......................... F 330 844-0703
  North Canton (G-11755)
Ream and Haager Laboratory Inc......... F 330 343-3711
  Dover (G-6840)
Russell Group United LLC.................... F 614 353-6853
  Columbus (G-5734)
Sentek Corporation............................. G 614 586-1123
  Columbus (G-5759)

Simplevms LLC............................. F..... 888 255-8918
 Cincinnati *(G-3393)*
Sutter Llc.. F..... 513 891-2261
 Blue Ash *(G-1476)*
Tangible Solutions Inc.................. E..... 937 912-4603
 Fairborn *(G-7324)*
Tekworx LLC.................................. F..... 513 533-4777
 Blue Ash *(G-1479)*
Telex Communications Inc............ G..... 419 865-0972
 Toledo *(G-14482)*

89 SERVICES, NOT ELSEWHERE CLASSIFIED

8999 Services, nec

4w Services..................................... F..... 614 554-5427
 Hebron *(G-8334)*
Advanced Green Tech Inc............. G..... 614 397-8130
 Plain City *(G-12560)*
Auguste Moone Enterprises Ltd.... E..... 216 333-9248
 Cleveland Heights *(G-4937)*
B&D Truck Parts Sls & Svcs LLC... G..... 419 701-7041
 Fostoria *(G-7629)*
Bonfoey Co..................................... F..... 216 621-0178
 Cleveland *(G-3747)*
Kyle Media Inc................................ G..... 877 775-2538
 Toledo *(G-14355)*
Mrl Materials Resources LLC........ E..... 937 531-6657
 Xenia *(G-16269)*
▲ **Nucon International Inc**.............. F..... 614 846-5710
 Columbus *(G-5607)*

ONeil & Associates Inc................... C..... 937 865-0800
 Miamisburg *(G-10669)*
Those Chrcters From Clvland LL.... F..... 216 252-7300
 Cleveland *(G-4795)*
Whitney Stained GL Studio Inc...... G..... 216 348-1616
 Cleveland *(G-4907)*

91 EXECUTIVE, LEGISLATIVE & GENERAL GOVERNMENT, EXCEPT FINANCE

9111 Executive offices

City of Canton................................. D..... 330 489-3370
 Canton *(G-2075)*
County of Holmes........................... G..... 330 674-2083
 Millersburg *(G-10952)*
Lake Township Trustees................ E..... 419 836-1143
 Millbury *(G-10934)*
Liverpool Township........................ G..... 330 483-4747
 Valley City *(G-14876)*

9199 General government, nec

City of Cleveland............................ E..... 216 664-3013
 Cleveland *(G-3822)*
Turtlecreek Township..................... F..... 513 932-4080
 Lebanon *(G-9117)*
Village of Ansonia.......................... E..... 937 337-5741
 Greenville *(G-8063)*

92 JUSTICE, PUBLIC ORDER AND SAFETY

9221 Police protection

Ohio Department Public Safety....... G..... 440 943-5545
 Willowick *(G-16033)*

96 ADMINISTRATION OF ECONOMIC PROGRAMS

9621 Regulation, administration of transportation

National Wldg Tanker Repr LLC..... G..... 614 875-3399
 Grove City *(G-8110)*
Ohio Department Transportation... E..... 614 351-2898
 Columbus *(G-5614)*

9661 Space research and technology

Weldon Pump LLC........................... E..... 440 232-2282
 Oakwood Village *(G-12047)*

97 NATIONAL SECURITY AND INTERNATIONAL AFFAIRS

9711 National security

Dla Document Services................... F..... 937 257-6014
 Dayton *(G-6159)*

ALPHABETIC SECTION

R & R Sealants (HQ)..999 999-9999
   651 Tally Blvd, Yourtown (99999) *(G-458)*
Ready Box Co...999 999-9999
   704 Lawrence Rd, Anytown (99999) *(G-1723)*
Rendall Mfg Inc, Anytown Also Called RMI *(G-1730)*

- Address, city & ZIP
- Designates this location as a headquarters
- Business phone
- Geographic Section entry number where full company information appears

See footnotes for symbols and codes identification.
- Companies listed alphabetically.
- Complete physical or mailing address.

(Mcgregor Metal Yellow Springs Works Llc, Springfield, OH), Springfield Also Called: McGregor Mtal Innsfllen Wrks L *(G-13602)*

1 & 1 Property Preservation, North Ridgeville Also Called: American Egle Prprty Prsrvtion *(G-11828)*

1 888 U Pitch It...440 796-9028
   7176 Fillmore Ct Mentor (44060) *(G-10401)*

1 A Lifesafer Inc (PA)...513 651-9560
   3630 Park 42 Dr Ste 140c Cincinnati (45241) *(G-2578)*

1 Emc LLC..216 990-2586
   1931 Tiffin Ave Findlay (45840) *(G-7469)*

1-2-3 Gluten Free Inc..216 378-9233
   125 Orange Tree Dr Chagrin Falls (44022) *(G-2365)*

1-800-Usa-home.com, Columbus Also Called: Owens Corning *(G-5648)*

1010 Magapp LLC..210 701-1754
   242 E Liberty St Wooster (44691) *(G-16093)*

10155 Broadview Business...440 546-1901
   10155 Broadview Rd Broadview Heights (44147) *(G-1654)*

1062 Technologies Inc..303 453-9251
   1062 Ohio Works Dr Youngstown (44510) *(G-16295)*

11 92 Holdings LLC..216 920-7790
   8 E Washington St Ste 200 Chagrin Falls (44022) *(G-2366)*

1157 Designconcepts LLC..937 497-1157
   210 S Lester Ave Sidney (45365) *(G-13216)*

1200 Feet Limited..419 827-6061
   41 County Road 2350 Lakeville (44638) *(G-8962)*

16363 Sca Inc..330 448-0000
   7800 Addison Rd Masury (44438) *(G-10155)*

17111 Waterview Pkwy LLC...216 706-2960
   The Tower At Erieview 1301 East 9th St Ste 3000 Cleveland (44114) *(G-3569)*

1923 W 25th St Inc..216 696-7529
   1923 W 25th St Cleveland (44113) *(G-3570)*

1one Stop Printing Inc...614 216-1438
   1509 Blatt Blvd Ste 8303 Columbus (43230) *(G-5074)*

1st Choice Contractor, Elyria Also Called: Elite Property Group LLC *(G-7139)*

1st Impressions Plus LLC..330 696-7605
   1868 Akron Peninsula Rd Akron (44313) *(G-9)*

2 Retrievers LLC...216 200-9040
   2515 Jay Ave Cleveland (44113) *(G-3571)*

2 Tones Brewing Co..740 412-0845
   145 N Hamilton Rd Columbus (43213) *(G-5075)*

2-M Manufacturing Company Inc.....................................440 269-1270
   34560 Lakeland Blvd Eastlake (44095) *(G-7016)*

20/20 Custom Molded Plas LLC (PA)...............................419 485-2020
   14620 Selwyn Dr Montpelier (43543) *(G-11133)*

212 Scent Studio LLC...614 906-3673
   950 Vernon Rd Columbus (43209) *(G-5076)*

277 Northfield Inc..440 439-1029
   277 Northfield Rd Bedford (44146) *(G-1097)*

2c Transport LLC..513 799-5278
   2344 Kemper Ln Cincinnati (45206) *(G-2579)*

2checkout, Columbus Also Called: Verifone Inc *(G-5857)*

2cravealloys, Dalton Also Called: J Horst Manufacturing Co *(G-6133)*

2e Associates Inc..440 975-9955
   38363 Airport Pkwy Willoughby (44094) *(G-15871)*

3 Sigma LLC..937 440-3400
   1985 W Stanfield Rd Troy (45373) *(G-14548)*

3-B Welding Ltd..740 819-4329
   2580 Holmes Rd New Concord (43762) *(G-11430)*

3-D Service Ltd (PA)...330 830-3500
   800 Nave Rd Se Massillon (44646) *(G-10072)*

3-D Technical Services Company....................................937 746-2901
   255 Industrial Dr Franklin (45005) *(G-7659)*

3-Dmed, Franklin Also Called: 3-D Technical Services Company *(G-7659)*

31 Inc...740 498-8324
   100 Enterprise Dr Newcomerstown (43832) *(G-11640)*

3249 Inc..937 294-5692
   3249 Dryden Rd Moraine (45439) *(G-11150)*

3359 Kingston LLC..614 871-8989
   1111 London Groveport Rd Grove City (43123) *(G-8071)*

360 Wrapz, Columbus Also Called: Atchley Signs & Graphics LLC *(G-5162)*

3d Partners LLC..330 323-6453
   1817 20th St Ne Canton (44714) *(G-2023)*

3d Printing..501 248-0468
   7139 Trillium Dr Lewis Center (43035) *(G-9143)*

3d Sales & Consulting Inc...513 422-1198
   408 Vanderveer St Middletown (45044) *(G-10800)*

3d Systems, Euclid Also Called: Village Plastics Co *(G-7306)*

3i Solutions, Wooster Also Called: Ingredient Innovations Intl Co *(G-16132)*

3jd Inc..513 324-9655
   2823 Northlawn Ave Moraine (45439) *(G-11151)*

3M, Medina Also Called: 3M Company *(G-10288)*

3M Company..330 725-1444
   1030 Lake Rd Medina (44256) *(G-10288)*

4 Over LLC..937 610-0629
   7801 Technology Blvd Dayton (45424) *(G-6177)*

4-B Wood Custom Cabinets, Seville Also Called: 4-B Wood Specialties Inc *(G-13133)*

4-B Wood Specialties Inc..330 769-2188
   255 W Greenwich Rd Seville (44273) *(G-13133)*

400 SW 7th Street Partners Ltd.......................................440 826-4700
   3825 Edwards Rd Ste 800 Cincinnati (45209) *(G-2580)*

400 SW 7th Street Partners Ltd (PA)...............................772 781-2144
   3825 Edwards Rd Ste 800 Cincinnati (45209) *(G-2581)*

44stronger LLC...440 371-6455
   1019 Commerce Dr Grafton (44044) *(G-7996)*

44toolscom...614 873-4800
   7640 Commerce Pl Plain City (43064) *(G-12558)*

48 Hr Books Inc..330 374-6917
   1909 Summit Commerce Park Twinsburg (44087) *(G-14620)*

48hr Books, Twinsburg Also Called: Printing System Inc *(G-14718)*

4blar LLC...513 576-0441
   5948 Shallow Creek Dr Milford (45150) *(G-10889)*

4d Screenprinting Ltd...513 353-1070
   5833 Hamilton Cleves Rd Cleves (45002) *(G-4945)*

(PA)=Parent Co (HQ)=Headquarters (DH)=Div Headquarters

ALPHABETIC SECTION

4matic Valve Automtn Ohio LLC.. 614 806-1221
4993 Cleveland Ave Columbus (43231) *(G-5077)*

4S Company.. 330 792-5518
3730 Mahoning Ave Youngstown (44515) *(G-16296)*

4w Services.. 614 554-5427
7901 Minecaster Rd Hebron (43025) *(G-8334)*

4wallscom LLC.. 216 432-1400
4700 Lakeside Ave E Unit 173a Cleveland (44114) *(G-3572)*

5 BS Inc (PA).. 740 454-8453
1000 5 Bs Dr Zanesville (43701) *(G-16493)*

5 Core Inc.. 951 386-6372
1221 W Sandusky Ave Bellefontaine (43311) *(G-1199)*

5 S Inc.. 440 968-0212
9755 Plank Rd Montville (44064) *(G-11148)*

5-Acre Mill, Hicksville *Also Called: Adroit Thinking Inc (G-8370)*

5me LLC.. 513 719-1600
4270 Ivy Pointe Blvd Ste 100 Cincinnati (45245) *(G-2544)*

5pd Coatings LLC.. 216 235-6086
12650 N Star Dr North Royalton (44133) *(G-11865)*

5th Element Fitness LLC.. 614 537-6038
6124 Busch Blvd Columbus (43229) *(G-5078)*

614 Cupcakes LLC.. 614 245-8800
4045 Chelsea Grn W New Albany (43054) *(G-11363)*

614 Magazine, Columbus *Also Called: 614 Media Group LLC (G-5079)*

614 Media Group LLC.. 614 488-4400
458 E Main St Columbus (43215) *(G-5079)*

64 Metals, Saint Louisville *Also Called: C Green & Sons Incorporated (G-12942)*

696 Ledgerock Cir.. 330 289-0996
2950 Westway Dr Brunswick (44212) *(G-1745)*

7 7 Print Solutions LLC.. 513 600-4597
6601 Dixie Hwy Ste C Fairfield (45014) *(G-7328)*

7 Up / R C/Canada Dry Btlg Co, Columbus *Also Called: American Bottling Company (G-5121)*

7 Up Bottling Co, Lima *Also Called: American Bottling Company (G-9220)*

7 Up Bottling Co, Midvale *Also Called: American Bottling Company (G-10874)*

7 Up/ Royal Crown, Cincinnati *Also Called: American Bottling Company (G-2616)*

717 Inc.. 440 925-0402
13000 Athens Ave Ste 110 Lakewood (44107) *(G-8965)*

717 Ink, Lakewood *Also Called: 717 Inc (G-8965)*

72 Chocolate Collection, The, Cleveland *Also Called: 72 Chocolate LLC (G-3573)*

72 Chocolate LLC.. 216 672-6040
1806 W 52nd St Cleveland (44102) *(G-3573)*

77 Coach Supply Ltd.. 330 674-1454
7426 County Road 77 Millersburg (44654) *(G-10937)*

7signal Inc (PA).. 216 777-2900
6155 Rockside Rd Ste 110 Independence (44131) *(G-8650)*

911cellular LLC.. 216 283-6100
6001 Cochran Rd Ste 200 Solon (44139) *(G-13304)*

9444 Ohio Holding Co.. 330 359-6291
1658 Us Route 62 E Winesburg (44690) *(G-16077)*

9729 Flagstone Way LLC.. 513 239-1950
5425 Timber Trail Pl Milford (45150) *(G-10890)*

A A S Amels Sheet Meta L Inc.. 330 793-9326
222 Steel St Youngstown (44509) *(G-16297)*

A - Y Machining LLC.. 216 404-0400
18504 Syracuse Ave Cleveland (44110) *(G-3576)*

A & A Quality Paving & Cem LLC.. 440 886-9595
13938a Cedar Rd Ste 250 Cleveland (44118) *(G-3574)*

A & A Safety Inc (PA).. 513 943-6100
1126 Ferris Rd Amelia (45102) *(G-447)*

A & A Safety Inc.. 937 567-9781
4080 Industrial Ln Beavercreek (45430) *(G-1068)*

A & B, Cincinnati *Also Called: A & B Deburring Company (G-2582)*

A & B Deburring Company.. 513 723-0444
525 Carr St Cincinnati (45203) *(G-2582)*

A & B Foundry LLC (PA).. 937 369-3007
835 N Main St Franklin (45005) *(G-7660)*

A & B Foundry LLC.. 937 412-1900
4754 Us Route 40 Tipp City (45371) *(G-14118)*

A & B Iron & Metal Co Inc.. 937 228-1561
329 Washington St Dayton (45402) *(G-6178)*

A & B Machine Inc.. 937 492-8662
2040 Commerce Dr Sidney (45365) *(G-13217)*

A & B Printing, Fort Loramie *Also Called: Sharp Enterprises Inc (G-7609)*

A & B Tool & Manufacturing.. 419 382-0215
2921 South Ave Toledo (43609) *(G-14172)*

A & C Welding Inc.. 330 762-4777
80 Cuyahoga Falls Industrial Pkwy Peninsula (44264) *(G-12337)*

A & D Wood Products Inc (PA).. 419 331-8859
4220 Sherrick Rd Elida (45807) *(G-7093)*

A & E Powder Coating Ltd.. 937 525-3750
1511 Sheridan Ave Springfield (45505) *(G-13526)*

A & F Machine Products Co.. 440 826-0959
454 Geiger St Berea (44017) *(G-1263)*

A & G Manufacturing Co Inc.. 419 468-7433
165 Gelsanliter Rd Galion (44833) *(G-7857)*

A & G Manufacturing Co Inc (PA).. 419 468-7433
280 Gelsanliter Rd Galion (44833) *(G-7858)*

A & I Metal Finishing, Vermilion *Also Called: Architctral Indus Met Fnshg LL (G-14971)*

A & J Woodworking Inc.. 419 695-5655
808 Ohio St Delphos (45833) *(G-6759)*

A & L Inds Machining & Repr, Oregon *Also Called: A & L Industries (G-12098)*

A & L Industries.. 419 698-3733
2054 Grange St Oregon (43616) *(G-12098)*

A & L Metal Processing, Sandusky *Also Called: Equinox Enterprises LLC (G-13056)*

A & M Pallet.. 937 295-3093
3860 Rangeline Rd Russia (45363) *(G-12881)*

A & M Pallet Shop Inc.. 440 632-1941
14550 Madison Rd Middlefield (44062) *(G-10729)*

A & M Refractories Inc.. 740 456-8020
202 West Ave New Boston (45662) *(G-11396)*

A & P Technology Inc.. 513 688-3200
4622 E Tech Dr Cincinnati (45245) *(G-2545)*

A & P Technology Inc.. 513 688-3200
4578 E Tech Dr Cincinnati (45245) *(G-2546)*

A & P Technology Inc.. 513 688-3200
4624 E Tech Dr Cincinnati (45245) *(G-2547)*

A & P Technology Inc.. 513 688-3200
4599 E Tech Dr Cincinnati (45245) *(G-2548)*

A & P Technology Inc (PA).. 513 688-3200
4595 E Tech Dr Cincinnati (45245) *(G-2549)*

A & R Machine Co Inc.. 330 832-4631
13212 Vega St Sw Massillon (44647) *(G-10073)*

A & W Table Pad Co.. 800 541-0271
6520 Carnegie Ave Cleveland (44103) *(G-3575)*

A A E, Canton *Also Called: American Aluminum Extrusions (G-2035)*

A Aabaco Plastics Inc.. 216 663-9494
9520 Midwest Ave Cleveland (44125) *(G-3577)*

A and R Logging LLC.. 740 352-6182
222 Enley Rd Mc Dermott (45652) *(G-10273)*

A and V Grinding Inc.. 937 444-4141
1115 Straight St 17 Cincinnati (45214) *(G-2583)*

A B B Electric Systems, Westerville *Also Called: ABB Inc (G-15646)*

A B P Induction, Massillon *Also Called: Abp Induction LLC (G-10075)*

A Best Trmt & Pest Ctrl Sups.. 330 434-5555
891 Gorge Blvd Akron (44310) *(G-10)*

A C F, Lima *Also Called: Allen County Fabrication Inc (G-9219)*

A C Hadley - Printing Inc.. 937 426-0952
1530 Marsetta Dr Beavercreek (45432) *(G-1037)*

A C Williams Co Inc (PA).. 330 296-6110
700 N Walnut St Ravenna (44266) *(G-12699)*

A E F Inc.. 216 360-9800
24050 Commerce Park Fl 2 Cleveland (44122) *(G-3578)*

A E T, Maumee *Also Called: Applied Energy Tech Inc (G-10166)*

A E Wilson Holdings Inc.. 330 405-0316
2307 E Aurora Rd Twinsburg (44087) *(G-14621)*

A F Krainz Co.. 216 431-4341
1364 E 47th St Cleveland (44103) *(G-3579)*

A G Industries Inc.. 330 220-0050
2963 Interstate Pkwy Brunswick (44212) *(G-1746)*

A G Industries Inc.. 216 252-7300
1 American Rd Cleveland (44144) *(G-3580)*

ALPHABETIC SECTION

A G Mercury, Galion Also Called: A & G Manufacturing Co Inc **(G-7858)**

A G S Ohio, Macedonia Also Called: AGS Custom Graphics Inc **(G-9534)**

A Gatehouse Media Company.. 330 580-8579
  500 Market Ave S Canton (44702) **(G-2024)**

A Good Mobile Detailing LLC.. 513 316-3802
  2464 8 Mile Rd Cincinnati (45244) **(G-2584)**

A Grade Notes Inc (PA)... 614 299-9999
  6385 Shier Rings Rd Ste 1 Dublin (43016) **(G-6856)**

A I P, Columbus Also Called: American Isostatic Presses Inc **(G-5126)**

A J C Hatchet Co, Hudson Also Called: A JC Inc **(G-8581)**

A J Construction Co.. 330 539-9544
  870 Shannon Rd Girard (44420) **(G-7958)**

A J Rose Mfg Co (PA)... 216 631-4645
  38000 Chester Rd Avon (44011) **(G-758)**

A Jacks Manufacturing Co.. 216 531-1010
  1441 Chardon Rd Cleveland (44117) **(G-3581)**

A JC Inc... 800 428-2438
  5145 Hudson Dr Hudson (44236) **(G-8581)**

A K Athletic Equipment Inc.. 614 920-3069
  8015 Howe Industrial Pkwy Canal Winchester (43110) **(G-1977)**

A L Callahan Door Sales.. 419 884-3667
  35 Industrial Dr Mansfield (44904) **(G-9620)**

A L D Precast Corp (PA)... 614 449-3366
  400 Frank Rd Columbus (43207) **(G-5080)**

A M C P, Greenfield Also Called: American Made Corrugated Packg **(G-8027)**

A M D.. 440 918-8930
  4580 Beidler Rd Willoughby (44094) **(G-15872)**

A M I, Olmsted Falls Also Called: Affiliated Metal Industries Inc **(G-12075)**

A M W, Columbus Also Called: Assembly Machining Wire Pdts **(G-5160)**

A P S, Dayton Also Called: Aps-Materials Inc **(G-6210)**

A P T, Middlefield Also Called: American Plastic Tech Inc **(G-10731)**

A Park Ohio Company, Wickliffe Also Called: PMC Industries Corp **(G-15848)**

A Plus Machining & Tooling, New Carlisle Also Called: Custom Threading Systems LLC **(G-11413)**

A Plus Powder Coaters Inc.. 330 482-4389
  1384 Kauffman Ave Columbiana (44408) **(G-5025)**

A Quick Copy Center, Cleveland Also Called: Theb Inc **(G-4790)**

A R E Logistics LLC.. 330 327-7315
  400 Nave Rd Se Massillon (44646) **(G-10074)**

A R Schopps Sons Inc.. 330 821-8406
  14536 Oyster Rd Alliance (44601) **(G-386)**

A S C, Lakewood Also Called: Associated Software Cons Inc **(G-8966)**

A S D, Dayton Also Called: Automation Systems Design Inc **(G-6218)**

A Schulman, Conneaut Also Called: Lyondllbsell Advnced Plymers I **(G-5927)**

A Schulman Compression, Geneva Also Called: Lyondllbsell Advnced Plymers I **(G-7942)**

A Service Glass Inc.. 937 426-4920
  1363 N Fairfield Rd Beavercreek (45432) **(G-1038)**

A Simona Group Company, Newcomerstown Also Called: Simona Boltaron Inc **(G-11651)**

A Stucki Company.. 412 424-0560
  5335 Mayfair Rd North Canton (44720) **(G-11713)**

A T & F Co, Cleveland Also Called: American Tank & Fabricating Co **(G-3656)**

A T C, Westlake Also Called: American Tchnical Coatings Inc **(G-15732)**

A T I, Spring Valley Also Called: Advanced Telemetrics Intl **(G-13490)**

A T P, Milford Center Also Called: Advanced Technology Products Inc **(G-10927)**

A Tech Welding Products Inc... 614 296-1573
  5977 Boston Rd Valley City (44280) **(G-14860)**

A To Z Paper Box Company... 330 325-8722
  4477 Tallmadge Rd Rootstown (44272) **(G-12850)**

A To Z Portion Ctrl Meats Inc... 419 358-2926
  201 N Main St Bluffton (45817) **(G-1498)**

A V C, Canton Also Called: Assocted Vsual Cmmncations Inc **(G-2040)**

A W Taylor Lumber Incorporated... 440 577-1889
  1114 State Route 7 S Pierpont (44082) **(G-12473)**

A Westlake Axiall Co... 614 754-3677
  1441 Universal Rd Columbus (43207) **(G-5081)**

A Z Printing Inc (PA)... 513 733-3900
  10122 Reading Rd Cincinnati (45241) **(G-2585)**

A-1 Fabricators Finishers LLC.. 513 724-0383
  4220 Curliss Ln Batavia (45103) **(G-906)**

A-1 Resources Ltd.. 330 695-9351
  8241 Tr 601 Fredericksburg (44627) **(G-7717)**

A-1 Sprinkler Company Inc.. 937 859-6198
  2383 Northpointe Dr Miamisburg (45342) **(G-10604)**

A-1 Welding & Fabrication.. 440 233-8474
  4909 Oak Point Rd Lorain (44053) **(G-9399)**

A-A Blueprint Co Inc... 330 794-8803
  2757 Gilchrist Rd Akron (44305) **(G-11)**

A-Best Termite and Pest Ctrl, Akron Also Called: A Best Trmt & Pest Ctrl Sups **(G-10)**

A-Display Service Corp.. 614 469-1230
  541 Dana Ave Columbus (43223) **(G-5082)**

A-Gas Americas, Bowling Green Also Called: A-Gas US Holdings Inc **(G-1547)**

A-Gas US Holdings Inc (DH)... 419 867-8990
  1100 Haskins Rd Bowling Green (43402) **(G-1547)**

A-Kobak Container Company Inc.. 330 225-7791
  1701 W 130th St Hinckley (44233) **(G-8471)**

A-Wall, Cleveland Also Called: Component Systems Inc **(G-3893)**

A-Z Discount Printing, Cincinnati Also Called: A Z Printing Inc **(G-2585)**

A.I.M., Aurora Also Called: Advanced Innovative Mfg Inc **(G-705)**

A.V.E.C., Heath Also Called: American Veneer Edgebanding Co **(G-8316)**

A/C Laser Technologies Inc... 330 784-3355
  471 Rutland Ave Akron (44305) **(G-12)**

A&B Fndry McHning Fabrications, Tipp City Also Called: A & B Foundry LLC **(G-14118)**

A&B Foundry & Machining LLC... 937 746-3634
  835 N Main St Franklin (45005) **(G-7661)**

A&D Machining LLC.. 330 786-0964
  1464 Waterloo Rd Barberton (44203) **(G-850)**

A&E Signs and Lighting LLC.. 513 541-0024
  1030 Straight St Cincinnati (45214) **(G-2586)**

A&M Cheese Co.. 419 476-8369
  253 Waggoner Blvd Toledo (43612) **(G-14173)**

A+ Engineering Fabrication Inc... 419 832-0748
  17562 Beech St Grand Rapids (43522) **(G-8008)**

A1 Industrial Painting Inc.. 330 750-9441
  894 Coitsville Hubbard Rd Youngstown (44505) **(G-16298)**

AA Hand Sanitizer.. 513 506-7575
  2230 Park Ave Ste 202 Cincinnati (45206) **(G-2587)**

AA Pallets LLC.. 216 856-2614
  4326 W 48th St Cleveland (44144) **(G-3582)**

AAA, Perrysburg Also Called: Industrial Hardwood Inc **(G-12391)**

AAA Galvanizing - Joliet Inc.. 513 871-5700
  4454 Steel Pl Cincinnati (45209) **(G-2588)**

AAA Laminating & Bindery, Fairfield Also Called: AAA Laminating and Bindery Inc **(G-7329)**

AAA Laminating and Bindery Inc... 513 860-2680
  7209 Dixie Hwy Fairfield (45014) **(G-7329)**

AAA Plastics & Pallets Inc... 330 844-2556
  246 N Cleveland Ave Mogadore (44260) **(G-11065)**

AAA Stamping Inc... 216 749-4494
  4001 Pearl Rd Uppr Cleveland (44109) **(G-3583)**

Aag Glass LLC.. 513 286-8268
  760 Kent Rd Batavia (45103) **(G-907)**

Aajaj Hair Company LLC.. 216 309-0816
  3905 W 18th St Cleveland (44109) **(G-3584)**

Aalberts Surface Technologies, Kenton Also Called: Atmosphere Annealing LLC **(G-8880)**

AAM Mold and Machine Inc... 440 998-2040
  1015 Westwood Dr Ashtabula (44004) **(G-625)**

AAM Mtal Frmng-Mlvern Opration, Malvern Also Called: American Axle & Mfg Inc **(G-9608)**

Aardvark Screen Prtg & EMB LLC... 419 354-6686
  123 S Main St Bowling Green (43402) **(G-1548)**

Aat USA LLC.. 614 388-8866
  1850 Denune Ave Columbus (43211) **(G-5083)**

AB Bonded Locksmiths Inc.. 513 531-7334
  4344 Montgomery Rd Cincinnati (45212) **(G-2589)**

AB Plastics Inc.. 513 576-6333
  1287 Us Route 50 Milford (45150) **(G-10891)**

AB Resources LLC.. 440 922-1098
  6802 W Snowville Rd Ste E Brecksville (44141) **(G-1604)**

AB Tire & Repair... 440 543-2929
  9685 Washington St Chagrin Falls (44023) **(G-2386)**

Abacus Biodiesel Complex, Columbus Also Called: Citi 2 Citi Logistics **(G-5250)**

ALPHABETIC SECTION

Abanaki Corporation (PA) 440 543-7400
17387 Munn Rd Chagrin Falls (44023) *(G-2387)*

Abatement Lead Tstg Risk Assss 330 785-6420
404 Abbyshire Rd Akron (44319) *(G-13)*

ABB Autoclave Systems, Columbus *Also Called: Avure Autoclave Systems Inc (G-5167)*

ABB Inc 614 818-6300
579 Executive Campus Dr Frnt Westerville (43082) *(G-15646)*

Abbey Carpet, Canton *Also Called: Shaheen Oriental Rug Co Inc (G-2222)*

Abbott 608 931-1057
923 Dennison Ave Columbus (43201) *(G-5084)*

Abbott Image Solutions LLC 937 382-6677
185 Park Dr Ste A Wilmington (45177) *(G-16037)*

Abbott Laboratories 614 624-3191
585 Cleveland Ave Columbus (43215) *(G-5085)*

Abbott Laboratories 614 624-3192
350 N 5th St Columbus (43215) *(G-5086)*

Abbott Laboratories 847 937-6100
2900 Easton Square Pl Columbus (43219) *(G-5087)*

Abbott Laboratories 800 551-5838
625 Cleveland Ave Columbus (43215) *(G-5088)*

Abbott Laboratories 614 024-7077
3300 Stelzer Rd Columbus (43219) *(G-5089)*

Abbott Laboratories 937 503-3405
1 Abbott Park Way Tipp City (45371) *(G-14119)*

Abbott Nutrition, Columbus *Also Called: Abbott Laboratories (G-5085)*

Abbott Tool Inc 419 476-6742
405 Dura Ave Toledo (43612) *(G-14174)*

ABC, Oregon *Also Called: ABC Appliance Inc (G-12099)*

ABC Appliance Inc 419 693-4414
3012 Navarre Ave Oregon (43616) *(G-12099)*

ABC Materials, Barberton *Also Called: Akron Bldg Closeout Mtls LLC (G-853)*

ABC Plastics Inc 330 948-3322
140 West Dr Lodi (44254) *(G-9344)*

ABC Signs Inc 513 241-8884
38 W Mcmicken Ave Cincinnati (45202) *(G-2590)*

ABC Technologies Dlhb Inc 330 479-7595
2310 Leo Ave Sw Canton (44706) *(G-2025)*

ABC Technologies Dlhb Inc (DH) 330 478-2503
2422 Leo Ave Sw Canton (44706) *(G-2026)*

ABC Technologies Dlhb Inc 330 488-0716
336 Wood St S East Canton (44730) *(G-6977)*

Abco Bar & Tube Cutng Svc Inc 513 697-9487
7685 S State Route 48 Ste 1 Maineville (45039) *(G-9598)*

Abco Services, Toledo *Also Called: Abutilon Company Inc (G-14175)*

Abel Manufacturing Company 513 681-5000
3474 Beekman St Cincinnati (45223) *(G-2591)*

Abel Metal Processing Inc 216 881-4156
2105 E 77th St Cleveland (44103) *(G-3585)*

Abeona, Cleveland *Also Called: Abeona Therapeutics Inc (G-3586)*

Abeona Therapeutics Inc (PA) 646 813-4701
6555 Carnegie Ave 4th Fl Cleveland (44103) *(G-3586)*

ABI, Cleveland *Also Called: ABI Inc (G-3587)*

ABI Inc 800 847-8950
5350 Transportation Blvd Ste 18b Cleveland (44125) *(G-3587)*

ABI Orthtc/Prosthetic Labs Ltd 330 758-1143
930 Trailwood Dr Youngstown (44512) *(G-16299)*

Abitec Corporation (HQ) 614 429-6464
501 W 1st Ave Columbus (43215) *(G-5090)*

Abj, Castalia *Also Called: Abj Equipfix LLC (G-2318)*

Abj Equipfix LLC 419 684-5236
202 Lucas St W Castalia (44824) *(G-2318)*

Abl Products Inc 216 281-2400
3726 Ridge Rd Cleveland (44144) *(G-3588)*

Able Applied Technologies, Columbus *Also Called: Aat USA LLC (G-5083)*

Able One's Moving Company, Cleveland *Also Called: C P S Enterprises Inc (G-3779)*

Able Pallet Mfg & Repr 614 444-2115
1271 Harmon Ave Columbus (43223) *(G-5091)*

Ableprint / Toucan Inc 419 522-9742
26 W 6th St Mansfield (44902) *(G-9621)*

About Golf, Maumee *Also Called: Henry-Griffitts Limited (G-10206)*

About Time Software Inc (PA) 614 759-6295
12790 Pickerington Rd Pickerington (43147) *(G-12454)*

Abp Induction LLC (PA) 262 878-6390
607 1st St Sw Massillon (44646) *(G-10075)*

ABRA Auto Body & Glass LP 513 247-3400
6947 E Kemper Rd Cincinnati (45249) *(G-2592)*

ABRA Auto Body & Glass LP 513 367-9200
10106 Harrison Ave Harrison (45030) *(G-8263)*

ABRA Auto Body & Glass LP 513 755-7709
8445 Cincinnati Columbus Rd West Chester (45069) *(G-15359)*

ABRA Autobody & Glass, Cincinnati *Also Called: ABRA Auto Body & Glass LP (G-2592)*

ABRA Autobody & Glass, Harrison *Also Called: ABRA Auto Body & Glass LP (G-8263)*

ABRA Autobody & Glass, West Chester *Also Called: ABRA Auto Body & Glass LP (G-15359)*

Abrasive Leaders & Innovators, Fairborn *Also Called: Ali Industries LLC (G-7308)*

Abrasive Products 513 502-9150
1028 Rosetree Ln Cincinnati (45230) *(G-2593)*

Abrasive Source Inc 937 526-9753
211 W Main St Russia (45363) *(G-12882)*

Abrasive Supply Company Inc 330 894-2818
25240 State Route 172 Minerva (44657) *(G-11025)*

Abrasive Technology LLC (PA) 740 548-4100
8400 Green Meadows Dr N Lewis Center (43035) *(G-9144)*

Abrasive Technology Lapidary 740 548-4855
8400 Green Meadows Dr N Lewis Center (43035) *(G-9145)*

ABS Materials Inc 330 234-7999
1909 Old Mansfield Rd Ste C Wooster (44691) *(G-16094)*

Absolute Impressions Inc 614 840-0599
281 Enterprise Dr Lewis Center (43035) *(G-9146)*

Absolute Zero Mch & Design LLC 440 370-4172
6042 White Tail Ln Lorain (44053) *(G-9400)*

Absorbent Products Company Inc 419 352-5353
455 W Woodland Cir Bowling Green (43402) *(G-1549)*

Abstract Displays Inc 513 985-9700
6465 Creek Rd Blue Ash (45242) *(G-1356)*

Abutilon Company Inc 419 536-6123
701 N Westwood Ave Toledo (43607) *(G-14175)*

AC Green LLC 740 292-2604
6648 Hudnell Rd Athens (45701) *(G-672)*

Aca Millworks Inc 419 339-7600
16330 Waynesfield Rd Waynesfield (45896) *(G-15295)*

Academy Graphic Comm Inc 216 661-2550
1000 Brookpark Rd Cleveland (44109) *(G-3589)*

Acadia Scientific LLC 267 980-1644
27100 Oakmead Dr Perrysburg (43551) *(G-12358)*

ACC Automation Co Inc 330 928-3821
475 Wolf Ledges Pkwy Akron (44311) *(G-14)*

Accel Color, Avon *Also Called: Accel Corporation (G-759)*

Accel Color, Avon *Also Called: Accel Corporation (G-760)*

Accel Corporation (DH) 440 934-7711
38620 Chester Rd Avon (44011) *(G-759)*

Accel Corporation 440 327-7418
38620 Chester Rd Avon (44011) *(G-760)*

Accel Group Inc (PA) 330 336-0317
325 Quadral Dr Wadsworth (44281) *(G-15014)*

Accel Performance Group LLC (DH) 216 658-6413
6100 Oak Tree Blvd Ste 200 Independence (44131) *(G-8651)*

Accent Drapery Co Inc 614 488-0741
1180 Goodale Blvd Columbus (43212) *(G-5092)*

Accent Drapery Supply Co, Columbus *Also Called: Accent Drapery Co Inc (G-5092)*

Accent Manufacturing Inc 330 724-7704
80 Cole Ave Akron (44301) *(G-15)*

Accent Manufacturing Inc (PA) 330 724-7704
1026 Gardner Blvd Norton (44203) *(G-11936)*

Accent Showroom & Design Ctr, Norton *Also Called: Accent Manufacturing Inc (G-11936)*

Accent Signage Systems Inc 612 377-9156
5409 Hamlet Dr Findlay (45840) *(G-7470)*

Accents By Renoir, Celina *Also Called: Renoir Visions LLC (G-2345)*

Access Envelope Inc 513 889-0888
2903 Terry Dr Middletown (45042) *(G-10801)*

Access Midstream 330 679-2019
10 E Main St Salineville (43945) *(G-13037)*

ALPHABETIC SECTION — Acoustech Systems LLC

Acclaimd Inc.. 614 219-9519
1275 Kinnear Rd Columbus (43212) *(G-5093)*

Accretech SBS Inc (PA).................................... 513 373-4844
8790 Governors Hill Dr Cincinnati (45249) *(G-2594)*

Accro-Cast Corporation.................................. 937 228-0497
4147 Gardendale Ave Dayton (45417) *(G-6179)*

Accu Grind, Kent Also Called: Reduction Engineering Inc *(G-8852)*

Accu-Grind & Mfg Co Inc................................. 937 224-3303
272 Leo St Dayton (45404) *(G-6180)*

Accu-Grind Inc... 330 677-2225
4430 Crystal Pkwy Kent (44240) *(G-8792)*

Accu-Rite Tool & Die Co Corp.......................... 330 497-9959
7295 Sunset Strip Ave Nw Canton (44720) *(G-2027)*

Accu-Tech Manufacturing Co........................... 330 848-8100
195 Olivet Ave Coventry Township (44319) *(G-6003)*

Accu-Tek Tool & Die Inc.................................. 330 726-1946
1390 Allen Rd Bldg 1 Salem (44460) *(G-12975)*

Accu-Tool Inc.. 937 667-5878
9765 Julie Ct Tipp City (45371) *(G-14120)*

Accuform Manufacturing Inc........................... 330 797-9291
2750 Intertech Dr Youngstown (44509) *(G-16300)*

Acculon Energy Inc.. 614 259-7792
1275 Kinnear Rd Columbus (43212) *(G-5094)*

Accurate, Painesville Also Called: Accurate Metal Machining Inc *(G-12215)*

Accurate Electronics Inc................................. 330 682-7015
169 S Main St Orrville (44667) *(G-12116)*

Accurate Fab LLC.. 330 562-3140
760 Deep Woods Dr Aurora (44202) *(G-703)*

Accurate Fab LLC
1400 Miller Pkwy Streetsboro (44241) *(G-13752)*

Accurate Gear Manufacturing Co..................... 513 761-3220
16 E 73rd St Cincinnati (45216) *(G-2595)*

Accurate Insulation LLC................................. 302 241-0940
495 S High St Ste 50 Columbus (43215) *(G-5095)*

Accurate Manufacturing Company.................. 614 878-6510
1940 Lone Eagle St Columbus (43228) *(G-5096)*

Accurate Mechanical Inc................................ 740 681-1332
566 Mill Park Dr Lancaster (43130) *(G-8985)*

Accurate Metal Machining Inc......................... 440 350-8225
882 Callendar Blvd Painesville (44077) *(G-12215)*

Accurate Plastics LLC................................... 330 701-0019
4430 Crystal Pkwy Kent (44240) *(G-8793)*

Accurate Products Company........................... 740 498-7202
98 Elizabeth St Newcomerstown (43832) *(G-11641)*

Accurate Tech, Mentor Also Called: Accurate Tech Inc *(G-10402)*

Accurate Tech Inc.. 440 951-9153
7230 Industrial Park Blvd Mentor (44060) *(G-10402)*

Accuride Corporation..................................... 812 962-5000
4800 Gateway Blvd Springfield (45502) *(G-13527)*

Accuscan Instruments Inc.............................. 614 878-6644
5098 Trabue Rd Columbus (43228) *(G-5097)*

Accushred LLC... 419 244-7473
1114 W Central Ave Toledo (43610) *(G-14176)*

Accutech Plastic Molding Inc.......................... 937 233-0017
5015 Kitridge Rd Dayton (45424) *(G-6181)*

Ace American Wire Die Co.............................. 330 425-7269
9041 Dutton Dr Twinsburg (44087) *(G-14622)*

Ace Assembly & Packaging Inc....................... 330 866-9117
133 N Mill St Waynesburg (44688) *(G-15292)*

Ace Boiler & Welding Co Inc........................... 330 745-4443
2891 Newpark Dr Barberton (44203) *(G-851)*

Ace Equipment Company, Strongsville Also Called: Armature Coil Equipment Inc *(G-13809)*

Ace Grinding Co Inc....................................... 440 951-6760
37518 N Industrial Pkwy Willoughby (44094) *(G-15873)*

Ace Hydraulics, Bedford Also Called: Kcn Technologies LLC *(G-1131)*

Ace Lumber Company.................................... 330 744-3167
1039 Poland Ave Youngstown (44502) *(G-16301)*

Ace Manufacturing Company.......................... 513 541-2490
5219 Muhlhauser Rd West Chester (45011) *(G-15360)*

Ace Metal Stamping Company, Bedford Also Called: Continental Business Entps Inc *(G-1113)*

Ace Plastics Company................................... 330 928-7720
122 E Tuscarawas Ave Stow (44224) *(G-13680)*

Ace Precision Industries Inc........................... 330 633-8523
925 Moe Dr Akron (44310) *(G-16)*

Ace Products & Consulting LLC...................... 330 577-4088
6800 N Chestnut St Ste 3 Ravenna (44266) *(G-12700)*

Ace Ready Mix Concrete Co Inc...................... 330 745-8125
3826 Summit Rd Norton (44203) *(G-11937)*

Ace Rubber Products Division, Akron Also Called: Garro Tread Corporation *(G-162)*

Ace Rubber Stamp & Off Sup Co..................... 216 771-8483
3110 Payne Ave Cleveland (44114) *(G-3590)*

Ace Sanitary, West Chester Also Called: Ace Manufacturing Company *(G-15360)*

Ace Transfer Company................................... 937 398-1103
1020 Hometown St Springfield (45504) *(G-13528)*

Ace Truck Equipment Co................................ 740 453-0551
1130 Newark Rd Zanesville (43701) *(G-16494)*

Ach LLC... 419 621-5748
3020 Tiffin Ave Sandusky (44870) *(G-13040)*

Ach Sandusky Plastics, Sandusky Also Called: Ach LLC *(G-13040)*

Achilles Aerospace Pdts Inc........................... 330 425-8444
2100 Enterprise Pkwy Twinsburg (44087) *(G-14623)*

Achilles Aerospace Products, Twinsburg Also Called: Achilles Aerospace Pdts Inc *(G-14623)*

Aci Industries Ltd (PA)................................... 740 368-4160
970 Pittsburgh Dr Frnt Delaware (43015) *(G-6699)*

Aci Industries Converting Ltd (HQ).................. 740 368-4160
970 Pittsburgh Dr Delaware (43015) *(G-6700)*

Aci Services Inc (PA)..................................... 740 435-0240
125 Steubenville Ave Cambridge (43725) *(G-1918)*

Acid Development LLC.................................. 330 502-4164
5700 Patriot Blvd Youngstown (44515) *(G-16302)*

Ackerman.. 440 246-2034
1138 W 19th St Lorain (44052) *(G-9401)*

Aclara Technologies LLC............................... 440 528-7200
30400 Solon Rd Solon (44139) *(G-13305)*

Acm, Brunswick Also Called: American Cube Mold Inc *(G-1748)*

Acm Ohio, Waverly Also Called: News Watchman & Paper *(G-15288)*

Acme Duplicating Co Inc................................ 216 241-1241
1565 Greenleaf Cir Westlake (44145) *(G-15727)*

Acme Fence & Lumber, Akron Also Called: Randy Lewis Inc *(G-296)*

Acme Home Improvement Co Inc..................... 614 252-2129
2909 E 4th Ave Columbus (43219) *(G-5098)*

Acme Industrial Group Inc.............................. 330 821-3900
540 N Freedom Ave Alliance (44601) *(G-387)*

Acme Lifting Products Inc.............................. 440 838-4430
6892 W Snowville Rd Ste 2 Cleveland (44141) *(G-3591)*

Acme Machine Automatics Inc........................ 419 453-0010
111 Progressive Dr Ottoville (45876) *(G-12197)*

Acme Paper Tube, Cleveland Also Called: Acme Spirally Wound Paper Pdts *(G-3592)*

Acme Printing, Westlake Also Called: Acme Duplicating Co Inc *(G-15727)*

Acme Printing Co Inc..................................... 419 626-4426
2143 Sherman St Sandusky (44870) *(G-13041)*

Acme Spirally Wound Paper Pdts.................... 216 267-2950
4810 W 139th St Cleveland (44135) *(G-3592)*

Acme Steak & Seafood Inc.............................. 330 270-8000
31 Bissell Ave Youngstown (44505) *(G-16303)*

Acme Surface Dynamics Inc........................... 330 821-3900
555 N Freedom Ave Alliance (44601) *(G-388)*

Acmi LLC... 330 501-0728
229 N Four Mile Run Rd Ste A Youngstown (44515) *(G-16304)*

Aco Inc (DH)... 440 639-7230
9470 Pinecone Dr Mentor (44060) *(G-10403)*

Acon Inc.. 513 276-2111
11408 Dogleg Rd Tipp City (45371) *(G-14121)*

Acor Orthopaedic Inc.................................... 440 532-0117
18700 S Miles Rd Cleveland (44128) *(G-3593)*

Acor Orthopaedic LLC (PA)............................ 216 662-4500
18530 S Miles Rd Cleveland (44128) *(G-3594)*

Acorn Rubber, Atwater Also Called: Curtis Hilbruner *(G-702)*

Acorn Technology Corporation....................... 216 663-1244
3176 Morley Rd Shaker Heights (44122) *(G-13149)*

Acoustech Systems LLC................................ 270 796-5853
1250 Arthur E Adams Dr Columbus (43221) *(G-5099)*

Acpo, Oak Harbor *Also Called: Acpo Ltd (G-12009)*

Acpo Ltd... 419 898-8273
8035 W Lake Winds Dr Oak Harbor (43449) *(G-12009)*

Acreo Inc.. 513 734-3327
3209 Marshall Dr Amelia (45102) *(G-448)*

Acro Tool & Die Company.. 330 773-5173
325 Morgan Ave Akron (44311) *(G-17)*

Acromet Metal Fabricators.. 440 237-8745
21693 Drake Rd Strongsville (44149) *(G-13800)*

Acromet Metal Fabricators, Cleveland *Also Called: G T Metal Fabricators Inc (G-4098)*

ACS Commercial Graphics, Columbus *Also Called: American Colorscans Inc (G-5122)*

ACS Industries Inc.. 330 678-2511
2151 Mogadore Rd Kent (44240) *(G-8794)*

ACS Publications LLC.. 330 686-3082
3934 Cardinal Cir Stow (44224) *(G-13681)*

Act, Dublin *Also Called: Automation and Ctrl Tech Inc (G-6864)*

Action, Strongsville *Also Called: Action Industries Ltd (G-13801)*

Action Air & Hydraulics Inc... 937 372-8614
1087 Bellbrook Ave Xenia (45385) *(G-16247)*

Action Coupling & Eqp Inc.. 330 279-4242
8248 County Road 245 Holmesville (44633) *(G-8541)*

Action Express Inc.. 929 351-3620
100 E Campus View Blvd Ste 250 Columbus (43235) *(G-5100)*

Action Group Inc.. 614 868-8868
411 Reynoldsburg New Albany Rd Blacklick (43004) *(G-1330)*

Action Industries Ltd (PA).. 216 252-7800
13325 Darice Pkwy Strongsville (44149) *(G-13801)*

Action Machine & Mfg Inc... 513 899-3889
6788 E Us Highway 22 And 3 Morrow (45152) *(G-11223)*

Action Precision Products Inc... 419 737-2348
100 E North Ave Pioneer (43554) *(G-12488)*

Action Rubber Co Inc... 937 866-5975
601 Fame Rd Dayton (45449) *(G-6182)*

Action Specialty Packaging LLC (DH)   4758 Devitt Dr West Chester (45246) *(G-15530)*

Action Super Abrasive Pdts Inc.. 330 673-7333
945 Greenbriar Pkwy Kent (44240) *(G-8795)*

Active Aeration Systems Inc... 614 873-3626
7245 Industrial Pkwy Plain City (43064) *(G-12559)*

Active Chemical Systems Inc... 440 543-7755
16755 Park Circle Dr Chagrin Falls (44023) *(G-2388)*

Active Daily Living LLC.. 513 607-6769
3308 Bishop St Cincinnati (45220) *(G-2596)*

Active Metal and Molds Inc... 419 281-9623
2219 Cottage St Ashland (44805) *(G-549)*

Activities Press Inc.. 440 953-1200
7181 Industrial Park Blvd Mentor (44060) *(G-10404)*

Actual Industries LLC... 614 379-2739
655 N James Rd Columbus (43219) *(G-5101)*

Acu-Serve Corp (PA).. 330 923-5258
121 S Main St Ste 102 Akron (44308) *(G-18)*

Acuity Brands Lighting Inc... 800 754-0463
3825 Columbus Rd Bldg A Granville (43023) *(G-8014)*

Acuity Brands Lighting Inc... 740 349-4343
214 Oakwood Ave Newark (43055) *(G-11560)*

Acuity Brands Lighting Inc... 740 892-2011
140 Carey St Utica (43080) *(G-14856)*

Acutemp, Monroe *Also Called: Doubleday Acquisitions LLC (G-11104)*

Acutemp Thermal Systems... 937 312-0114
2900 Dryden Rd Moraine (45439) *(G-11152)*

Ad Choice Inc.. 419 697-8889
1532 Bury Rd Oregon (43616) *(G-12100)*

Ad Company Holdings Inc... 404 256-3544
3245 Pickle Rd Akron (44312) *(G-19)*

Ad Industries Inc.. 303 744-1911
6450 Poe Ave Ste 109 Dayton (45414) *(G-6183)*

Ad Piston Ring, Cleveland *Also Called: Ad Piston Ring LLC (G-3595)*

Ad Piston Ring LLC.. 216 781-5200
3145 Superior Ave E Cleveland (44114) *(G-3595)*

Ad-Sensations Inc.. 419 841-5395
3315 Centennial Rd Ste C Sylvania (43560) *(G-13989)*

Ada Extrusions Inc.. 440 285-7653
505 W Wilbeth Rd Akron (44314) *(G-20)*

Ada Solutions Inc... 440 576-0423
901 Footville Richmond Rd E Jefferson (44047) *(G-8744)*

Ada Technologies Inc (HQ)... 419 634-7000
805 E North Ave Ada (45810) *(G-2)*

Adalet/Scott Fetzer Company... 440 892-3074
10920 Madison Ave Cleveland (44102) *(G-3596)*

Adams Automatic Inc.. 440 235-4416
26070 N Depot St Olmsted Falls (44138) *(G-12074)*

Adams Bros Concrete Pdts Ltd.. 740 452-7566
3401 East Pike Zanesville (43701) *(G-16495)*

Adams Brothers Inc... 740 819-0323
1501 Woodlawn Ave Zanesville (43701) *(G-16496)*

Adams Elevator Equipment Co (DH)... 847 581-2900
1530 Timber Wolf Dr Holland (43528) *(G-8492)*

Adams Publishing Group LLC (HQ).. 740 592-6612
9300 Johnson Hollow Rd Athens (45701) *(G-673)*

Adams Signs, Massillon *Also Called: Identitek Systems Inc (G-10111)*

Adams Street Publishing Co Inc... 419 244-9859
1120 Adams St Toledo (43604) *(G-14177)*

Adapt Oil.. 330 658-1482
188 N Portage St Doylestown (44230) *(G-6852)*

Adapt-A-Pak Inc.. 937 845-0386
678 Yellow Springs Fairfield Rd Ste 100 Fairborn (45324) *(G-7307)*

Adaptall America Inc... 330 425-4114
9047 Dutton Dr Twinsburg (44087) *(G-14624)*

Adapted Tech, Dublin *Also Called: Mirus Adapted Tech LLC (G-6910)*

Adare Pharmaceuticals Inc (DH).. 937 898-9669
845 Center Dr Vandalia (45377) *(G-14931)*

ADB, Gahanna *Also Called: ADB Safegate Americas LLC (G-7828)*

ADB Safegate Americas LLC.. 614 861-1304
700 Science Blvd Gahanna (43230) *(G-7828)*

Adchem Adhesives Inc.. 440 526-1976
4111 E Royalton Rd Cleveland (44147) *(G-3597)*

Adcraft Decals Incorporated.. 216 524-2934
7708 Commerce Park Oval Cleveland (44131) *(G-3598)*

Adcura Mfg.. 937 222-3800
1314 Farr Dr Dayton (45404) *(G-6184)*

Adcura Mfg, Dayton *Also Called: Rct Industries Inc (G-6543)*

Add-A-Trap LLC.. 330 750-0417
488 Como St Struthers (44471) *(G-13898)*

Added Edge Assembly Inc.. 216 464-4305
26800 Fargo Ave Ste A Cleveland (44146) *(G-3599)*

Addisonmckee, Lebanon *Also Called: Addition Manufacturing Technologies LLC (G-9059)*

Addition Manufacturing Technologies LLC.................................. 513 228-7000
1637 Kingsview Dr Lebanon (45036) *(G-9059)*

Additive Metal Alloys... 419 215-5800
427 W Dussel Dr Maumee (43537) *(G-10159)*

Additive Metal Alloys Ltd.. 800 687-6110
1421 Holloway Rd Ste B Holland (43528) *(G-8493)*

Addivant.. 440 352-1719
10641 Buckingham Pl Concord Township (44077) *(G-5900)*

Addup Inc.. 513 745-4510
5101 Creek Rd Blue Ash (45242) *(G-1357)*

Adelman's Truck Sales, Canton *Also Called: Adelmans Truck Parts Corp (G-2028)*

Adelmans Truck Parts Corp (PA).. 330 456-0206
2000 Waynesburg Dr Se Canton (44707) *(G-2028)*

Adelphia, Wellington *Also Called: Forest City Technologies Inc (G-15311)*

Ademco Inc... 440 439-7002
7710 First Pl Ste A Bedford (44146) *(G-1098)*

Ademco Inc... 513 772-1851
5601 Creek Rd Ste A Blue Ash (45242) *(G-1358)*

Adept Manufacturing Corp... 937 222-7110
1710 E 1st St Dayton (45403) *(G-6185)*

Adex International, Cincinnati *Also Called: Affinity Disp Expositions Inc (G-2599)*

Adex International, Cincinnati *Also Called: Affinity Disp Expositions Inc (G-2600)*

Adgo Incorporated... 513 752-6880
3988 Mcmann Rd Cincinnati (45245) *(G-2550)*

Adh Industries Inc.. 330 283-5822
2854 Morrison St Akron (44312) *(G-21)*

Adherex Group (PA)... 201 440-3806
3100 Hamilton Ave Cleveland (44114) *(G-3600)*

ALPHABETIC SECTION

Adhesives Lab USA North LLC.. 567 825-2004
1040 Findlay Rd Lima (45801) *(G-9217)*

Adhesves Sealants Coatings Div, Blue Ash *Also Called: HB Fuller Company (G-1404)*

ADI, Sheffield Village *Also Called: Advanced Design Industries Inc (G-13180)*

ADI Global Distribution, Bedford *Also Called: Ademco Inc (G-1098)*

ADI Global Distribution, Blue Ash *Also Called: Ademco Inc (G-1358)*

ADI Machining Inc.. 440 277-4141
4686 French Creek Rd Sheffield Village (44054) *(G-13179)*

Adidas North America Inc.. 330 562-4689
549 S Chillicothe Rd Aurora (44202) *(G-704)*

Adidas Outlet Store Aurora, Aurora *Also Called: Adidas North America Inc (G-704)*

Adient US LLC.. 937 981-2176
1147 N Washington St Greenfield (45123) *(G-8026)*

Adient US LLC.. 419 662-4900
7560 Arbor Dr Northwood (43619) *(G-11916)*

Adient US LLC.. 419 394-7800
1111 Mckinley Rd Saint Marys (45885) *(G-12944)*

Adkins & Sons, Oak Hill *Also Called: Denver Adkins (G-12018)*

Adkins, Dale Logging, Oak Hill *Also Called: Dale R Adkins (G-12017)*

Adler & Company Inc.. 513 248-1500
6801 Shawnee Run Rd Cincinnati (45243) *(G-2597)*

Adler Team Sports, Euclid *Also Called: R & A Sports Inc (G-7297)*

ADM, Fostoria *Also Called: Archer-Daniels-Midland Company (G-7628)*

ADM, Sugarcreek *Also Called: Archer-Daniels-Midland Company (G-13918)*

ADM, Toledo *Also Called: Archer-Daniels-Midland Company (G-14197)*

Adma Products, Hudson *Also Called: Advance Materials Products Inc (G-8582)*

Admark Printing Inc.. 937 833-5111
310 Sycamore St Brookville (45309) *(G-1728)*

Admj Holdings LLC.. 216 588-0038
5260 Commerce Pkwy W Cleveland (44130) *(G-3601)*

Adohio, Columbus *Also Called: Ohio Newspaper Services Inc (G-5623)*

Adr Fuel Inc.. 419 872-2178
353 Elm St Perrysburg (43551) *(G-12359)*

Adria Scientific GL Works Co.. 440 474-6691
2683 State Route 534 S Geneva (44041) *(G-7929)*

Adroit Thinking Inc.. 419 542-9363
10860 State Route 2 Hicksville (43526) *(G-8370)*

ADS.. 419 422-6521
401 Olive St Findlay (45840) *(G-7471)*

ADS, Hilliard *Also Called: Advanced Drainage Systems Inc (G-8396)*

ADS, London *Also Called: Advanced Drainage Systems Inc (G-9379)*

ADS International.. 513 896-2094
2650 Hamilton Eaton Rd Hamilton (45011) *(G-8174)*

ADS International Inc.. 614 658-0050
4640 Trueman Blvd Hilliard (43026) *(G-8392)*

ADS Machinery Corp.. 330 399-3601
1201 Vine Ave Ne Ste 1 Warren (44483) *(G-15134)*

ADS Ventures Inc (HQ).. 614 658-0050
4640 Trueman Blvd Hilliard (43026) *(G-8393)*

ADS Worldwide Inc (HQ).. 614 658-0050
4640 Trueman Blvd Hilliard (43026) *(G-8394)*

Adsetting Service, Cleveland *Also Called: Royal Acme Corporation (G-4654)*

ADSr Ent LLC.. 773 280-2129
1888 Noe Bixby Rd Columbus (43232) *(G-5102)*

Advance Apex Inc (PA).. 614 539-3000
2375 Harrisburg Pike Grove City (43123) *(G-8072)*

Advance Bronze Inc (PA).. 330 948-1231
139 Ohio St Lodi (44254) *(G-9345)*

Advance Bronzehubco Div (HQ).. 304 232-4414
139 Ohio St Lodi (44254) *(G-9346)*

Advance Cnc Machining, Grove City *Also Called: Advance Apex Inc (G-8072)*

Advance Door Co., Cleveland *Also Called: Admj Holdings LLC (G-3601)*

Advance Graphics, Columbus *Also Called: Hoster Graphics Company Inc (G-5446)*

Advance Industrial Mfg Inc.. 614 871-3333
1996 Longwood Ave Grove City (43123) *(G-8073)*

Advance Industries Group LLC.. 216 741-1800
3636 W 58th St Cleveland (44102) *(G-3602)*

Advance Lens Labs, Berea *Also Called: Cleveland Hoya Corp (G-1269)*

Advance Manufacturing Corp.. 216 333-1684
6800 Madison Ave Cleveland (44102) *(G-3603)*

Advance Materials Products Inc.. 330 650-4000
1890 Georgetown Rd Hudson (44236) *(G-8582)*

Advance Metal Products Inc.. 216 741-1800
3636 W 58th St Cleveland (44102) *(G-3604)*

Advance Novelty Incorporated.. 419 424-0363
101 Stanford Pkwy Findlay (45840) *(G-7472)*

Advance Products.. 419 882-8117
6041 Angleview Dr Sylvania (43560) *(G-13990)*

Advance Trans Inc.. 330 572-0390
4833 Darrow Rd Ste 105 Stow (44224) *(G-13682)*

Advance Wire Forming Inc.. 216 432-3250
3636 W 58th St Cleveland (44102) *(G-3605)*

Advanced Bar Technology, Canton *Also Called: Gerdau McSteel Atmsphere Annli (G-2112)*

Advanced Biological Mktg Inc.. 419 232-2461
375 Bonnewitz Ave Van Wert (45891) *(G-14904)*

Advanced Composites Inc (DH).. 937 575-9800
1062 S 4th Ave Sidney (45365) *(G-13218)*

Advanced Cryogenic Entps LLC.. 330 922-0750
1034 Home Ave Akron (44310) *(G-22)*

Advanced Design Industries, Sheffield Village *Also Called: ADI Machining Inc (G-13179)*

Advanced Design Industries Inc.. 440 277-4141
4686 French Creek Rd Sheffield Village (44054) *(G-13180)*

Advanced Drainage of Ohio Inc.. 614 658-0050
4640 Trueman Blvd Hilliard (43026) *(G-8395)*

Advanced Drainage Systems Inc.. 419 424-8222
12370 Hancock County Rd Findlay (45840) *(G-7473)*

Advanced Drainage Systems Inc.. 419 424-8324
401 Olive St Findlay (45840) *(G-7474)*

Advanced Drainage Systems Inc.. 513 863-1384
2650 Hamilton Eaton Rd Hamilton (45011) *(G-8175)*

Advanced Drainage Systems Inc (PA).. 614 658-0050
4640 Trueman Blvd Hilliard (43026) *(G-8396)*

Advanced Drainage Systems Inc.. 740 852-2980
400 E High St London (43140) *(G-9379)*

Advanced Drainage Systems Inc.. 419 599-9565
1075 Independence Dr Napoleon (43545) *(G-11308)*

Advanced Drainage Systems Inc.. 330 264-4949
3113 W Old Lincoln Way Wooster (44691) *(G-16095)*

Advanced Engrg Solutions Inc.. 937 743-6900
250 Advanced Dr Springboro (45066) *(G-13493)*

Advanced Equipment Systems LLC.. 216 289-6505
22800 Lakeland Blvd Euclid (44132) *(G-7258)*

Advanced Fiber LLC.. 419 562-1337
100 Crossroads Blvd Bucyrus (44820) *(G-1849)*

Advanced FME Products Inc.. 440 953-0700
9413 Hamilton Dr Mentor (44060) *(G-10405)*

Advanced Fuel Systems Inc.. 614 252-8422
841 Alton Ave Columbus (43219) *(G-5103)*

Advanced Green Tech Inc.. 614 397-8130
8059 Corporate Blvd Ste A Plain City (43064) *(G-12560)*

Advanced Ground Systems.. 513 402-7226
1650 Magnolia Dr Cincinnati (45215) *(G-2598)*

Advanced Holding Designs Inc.. 330 928-4456
3332 Cavalier Trl Cuyahoga Falls (44224) *(G-6060)*

Advanced Incentives Inc.. 419 471-9088
1732 W Alexis Rd Toledo (43613) *(G-14178)*

Advanced Indus Machining Inc (PA).. 614 596-4183
3982 Powell Rd Ste 218 Powell (43065) *(G-12662)*

Advanced Indus Msrment Systems (PA).. 937 320-4930
2580 Kohnle Dr Miamisburg (45342) *(G-10605)*

Advanced Innovative Mfg Inc.. 330 562-2468
116 Lena Dr Aurora (44202) *(G-705)*

Advanced Integration LLC.. 614 863-2433
6880 Tussing Rd Reynoldsburg (43068) *(G-12748)*

Advanced Intr Solutions Inc.. 937 550-0065
250 Advanced Dr Springboro (45066) *(G-13494)*

Advanced Kiffer Systems Inc.. 216 267-8181
4905 Rocky River Dr Cleveland (44135) *(G-3606)*

Advanced Lighting Tech LLC (PA).. 888 440-2358
6675 Parkland Blvd Solon (44139) *(G-13306)*

Advanced Nanotherapies Inc.. 415 517-0867
10000 Cedar Ave Cleveland (44106) *(G-3607)*

Advanced OEM Solutions LLC — ALPHABETIC SECTION

Advanced OEM Solutions LLC..513 407-0140
9472 Meridian Way West Chester (45069) *(G-15361)*

Advanced Paper Tube Inc..216 281-5691
1951 W 90th St Cleveland (44102) *(G-3608)*

Advanced Plastic Systems Inc..614 759-6550
990 Gahanna Pkwy Gahanna (43230) *(G-7829)*

Advanced Plastics Inc..330 336-6681
590 Corporate Pkwy Wadsworth (44281) *(G-15015)*

Advanced Poly-Packaging Inc (PA)...330 785-4000
1331 Emmitt Rd Akron (44306) *(G-23)*

Advanced Polymer Coatings Ltd..440 937-6218
951 Jaycox Rd Avon (44011) *(G-761)*

Advanced Prgrm Resources Inc (PA)......................................614 761-9994
2715 Tuller Pkwy Dublin (43017) *(G-6857)*

Advanced Recycling Systems, Lowellville *Also Called: ARS Recycling Systems LLC (G-9511)*

Advanced Rv LLC...440 283-0405
4590 Hamann Pkwy Willoughby (44094) *(G-15874)*

Advanced Specialty Products..419 882-6528
428 Clough St Bowling Green (43402) *(G-1550)*

Advanced Surface Technology...216 476-0600
12211 Sobieski Ave Cleveland (44135) *(G-3609)*

Advanced Tech Utilization Co..440 238-3770
12005 Prospect Rd Unit 1 Strongsville (44149) *(G-13802)*

Advanced Technical Pdts Sup Co..513 851-6858
6186 Centre Park Dr West Chester (45069) *(G-15362)*

Advanced Technology, Strongsville *Also Called: Advanced Tech Utilization Co (G-13802)*

Advanced Technology Corp...440 293-4064
101 Parker Dr Andover (44003) *(G-483)*

Advanced Technology Products Inc (PA)...............................937 349-4055
190 N Mill St Milford Center (43045) *(G-10927)*

Advanced Telemetrics Intl..937 862-6948
2361 Darnell Dr Spring Valley (45370) *(G-13490)*

Advanced Visual Solutions, Hilliard *Also Called: National Sign Systems Inc (G-8424)*

Advanced Welding Inc..937 746-6800
901 N Main St Franklin (45005) *(G-7662)*

Advanced Wldg Fabrication Inc (PA)......................................440 724-9165
821 Lafayette Blvd Sheffield Lake (44054) *(G-13178)*

Advancepierre, West Chester *Also Called: Advancperre Foods Holdings Inc (G-15532)*

Advancepierre Foods Inc (DH)...513 874-8741
9990 Princeton Glendale Rd West Chester (45246) *(G-15531)*

Advancperre Foods Holdings Inc (HQ)...................................513 428-5699
9990 Princeton Glendale Rd West Chester (45246) *(G-15532)*

Advant-E Corporation (PA)..937 429-4288
2434 Esquire Dr Beavercreek (45431) *(G-1039)*

Advantage Machine Shop..330 337-8377
777 S Ellsworth Ave Salem (44460) *(G-12976)*

Advantage Mold Inc..419 691-5676
525 N Wheeling St Toledo (43605) *(G-14179)*

Advantage Powder Coating Inc (PA)......................................419 782-2363
2090 E 2nd St Ste 102 Defiance (43512) *(G-6667)*

Advantage Print Solutions LLC...614 519-2392
79 Acton Rd Columbus (43214) *(G-5104)*

Advantage Products Corporation (PA)..................................513 489-2283
11559 Grooms Rd Blue Ash (45242) *(G-1359)*

Advantage Tent Fittings Inc..740 773-3015
11661 Pleasant Valley Rd Chillicothe (45601) *(G-2491)*

Advantage Truck Trailers, Columbus *Also Called: Kenan Advantage Group Inc (G-5506)*

Advantic Building Group LLC..513 290-4796
511 Byers Rd Miamisburg (45342) *(G-10606)*

Advent Designs, Logan *Also Called: Signs Unlmted The Grphic Advnt (G-9376)*

Advertiser-Tribune, The, Tiffin *Also Called: Ogden Newspapers Ohio Inc (G-14097)*

Advertising Joe LLC Mean...440 247-8200
33 River St Ste 7 Chagrin Falls (44022) *(G-2367)*

Advertising Specialty Co, East Liverpool *Also Called: W C Bunting Co Inc (G-7002)*

Advetech Inc (PA)...330 533-2227
445 W Main St Canfield (44406) *(G-1995)*

Advetech Inc...330 533-2227
451 W Main St Canfield (44406) *(G-1996)*

Advics, Lebanon *Also Called: Advics Manufacturing Ohio Inc (G-9060)*

Advics Manufacturing Ohio Inc...513 932-7878
1650 Kingsview Dr Lebanon (45036) *(G-9060)*

Advint, Reynoldsburg *Also Called: Advanced Integration LLC (G-12748)*

Aecom Energy & Cnstr Inc..419 698-6277
4001 Cedar Point Rd Oregon (43616) *(G-12101)*

Aero Fluid Products, Painesville *Also Called: Dukes Aerospace Inc (G-12229)*

Aero Fulfillment Services Corp (PA)......................................800 225-7145
3900 Aero Dr Mason (45040) *(G-9945)*

Aero Instruments, Cleveland *Also Called: Aero-Instruments Co LLC (G-3610)*

Aero Jet Wash Llc..866 381-7955
450 Gargrave Rd Dayton (45449) *(G-6186)*

Aero Pallets Inc..330 260-7107
348 Raley Ave Se Carrollton (44615) *(G-2303)*

Aero Tech Tool & Mold Inc..440 942-3327
7224 Industrial Park Blvd Mentor (44060) *(G-10406)*

Aero-Instruments Co LLC...216 671-3133
4223 Monticello Blvd Cleveland (44121) *(G-3610)*

Aerobarrier, Dayton *Also Called: Aeroseal LLC (G-6187)*

Aerocase Incorporated..440 617-9294
1061 Bradley Rd Westlake (44145) *(G-15728)*

Aerocontrolex, Cleveland *Also Called: Transdigm Inc (G-4815)*

Aerocontrolex, South Euclid *Also Called: Aerocontrolex Group Inc (G-13457)*

Aerocontrolex Group Inc..216 201-0025
4223 Monticello Blvd South Euclid (44121) *(G-13457)*

Aerodyne, Chagrin Falls *Also Called: Abanaki Corporation (G-2387)*

Aeroflex Powell, Hilliard *Also Called: Star Dynamics Corporation (G-8442)*

Aerontics Systems Arspc Strctr, Beavercreek *Also Called: Northrop Grumman Systems Corp (G-1077)*

Aeropact Manufacturing LLC...419 373-1711
435 W Woodland Cir Bowling Green (43402) *(G-1551)*

Aeroquip Corp...419 238-1190
1225 W Main St Van Wert (45891) *(G-14905)*

Aeroscena LLC..800 671-1890
10000 Cedar Ave Cleveland (44106) *(G-3611)*

Aeroseal LLC...937 428-9300
1851 S Metro Pkwy Dayton (45459) *(G-6187)*

Aeroseal LLC (PA)..937 428-9300
225 Byers Rd # 1 Miamisburg (45342) *(G-10607)*

Aeroserv Inc..513 932-9227
201 Industrial Row Dr Mason (45040) *(G-9946)*

Aerospace LLC..937 561-1104
3300 Encrete Ln Moraine (45439) *(G-11153)*

Aerospace Logistics, Moraine *Also Called: Aerospace LLC (G-11153)*

Aerospace Maint Solutions LLC..440 729-7703
29401 Ambina Dr Solon (44139) *(G-13307)*

Aerospace Simulations, Akron *Also Called: Lockheed Mrtin Intgrted System (G-222)*

Aerotech Enterprise...440 729-2616
8511 Mulberry Rd Chesterland (44026) *(G-2478)*

Aerotorque Corporation, Sharon Center *Also Called: Atc Legacy Inc (G-13162)*

Aerovation Tech Holdings LLC..567 208-5525
11651 Township Rd 81 Forest (45843) *(G-7589)*

Aerowave Inc...440 731-8464
361 Windward Dr Elyria (44035) *(G-7104)*

Aerpio Therapeutics LLC...513 985-1920
9987 Carver Rd Ste 420 Blue Ash (45242) *(G-1360)*

AES, Cincinnati *Also Called: Aluminum Extruded Shapes Inc (G-2613)*

AES Beaver Valley LLC
1065 Woodman Dr Dayton (45432) *(G-6151)*

Aesi, Springboro *Also Called: Advanced Engrg Solutions Inc (G-13493)*

Aesthetic Finishers Inc..937 778-8777
1502 S Main St Piqua (45356) *(G-12501)*

Aesthetic Powder Coating LLC..330 360-2422
281 Ohltown Rd Youngstown (44515) *(G-16305)*

Aetna Plating Co...216 341-9111
6511 Morgan Ave Cleveland (44127) *(G-3612)*

Aexcel Corporation (PA)..440 974-3800
7373 Production Dr Mentor (44060) *(G-10407)*

Afc Company...330 533-5581
5183 W Western Reserve Rd Canfield (44406) *(G-1997)*

Afc Stamping & Production Inc...937 275-8700
4900 Webster St Dayton (45414) *(G-6188)*

Afc Tool Co Inc...937 275-8700
4900 Webster St Dayton (45414) *(G-6189)*

ALPHABETIC SECTION

Affiliated Metal Industries... 216 267-0155
16110 Brookpark Rd Cleveland (44135) *(G-3613)*

Affiliated Metal Industries Inc.. 440 235-3345
25600 Chapin St Olmsted Falls (44138) *(G-12075)*

Affinity Disp Expositions Inc... 513 771-2339
1375 Spring Park Walk Cincinnati (45215) *(G-2599)*

Affinity Disp Expositions Inc (PA)...................................... 513 771-2339
1301 Glendale Milford Rd Cincinnati (45215) *(G-2600)*

Affordable Barn Co Ltd.. 330 674-3001
4260 Township Road 617 Millersburg (44654) *(G-10938)*

Affordable Cabinet Doors... 513 734-9663
205 S Main St Bethel (45106) *(G-1318)*

Affordable Tire, Canton *Also Called: Ziegler Tire and Supply Co (G-2273)*

Affymetrix Inc... 800 321-9322
26111 Miles Rd Cleveland (44128) *(G-3614)*

Affymetrix Inc... 419 887-1233
434 W Dussel Dr Maumee (43537) *(G-10160)*

Afg Industries Inc... 614 322-4580
4000 Gantz Rd Ste A Grove City (43123) *(G-8074)*

Aframian Partnership LLC.. 614 868-8634
7719 Taylor Rd Sw Reynoldsburg (43068) *(G-12749)*

Afs Technology LLC... 937 545-0627
6649 Deer Bluff Dr Dayton (45424) *(G-6190)*

AG Antenna Group LLC (PA)... 513 289-6521
11923 Montgomery Rd Cincinnati (45249) *(G-2601)*

Agb LLC... 419 924-5216
15188 Us Highway 127 West Unity (43570) *(G-15636)*

AGC Automotive Americas, Grove City *Also Called: Afg Industries Inc (G-8074)*

AGE Graphics LLC (PA)... 740 989-0006
678 Collins Rd Little Hocking (45742) *(G-9332)*

Agean Marble Manufacturing... 513 874-1475
9756 Princeton Glendale Rd West Chester (45246) *(G-15533)*

Agents of Gaming, Dayton *Also Called: Aog Inc (G-6208)*

AGFA Corporation.. 513 829-6292
6104 Monastery Dr Fairfield (45014) *(G-7330)*

Agile Global Solutions Inc... 916 655-7745
5755 Granger Rd Ste 610 Independence (44131) *(G-8652)*

Agile Manufacturing Tech LLC.. 937 258-3338
220 N Jersey St Dayton (45403) *(G-6191)*

Agile Sign & Ltg Maint Inc.. 440 918-1311
35280 Lakeland Blvd Eastlake (44095) *(G-7017)*

Agmet LLC.. 216 663-8200
5533 Dunham Rd Cleveland (44137) *(G-3615)*

Agmet Metals Inc... 440 439-7400
7800 Medusa Rd Oakwood Village (44146) *(G-12035)*

Agnone-Kelly Enterprises Inc... 800 634-6503
11658 Baen Rd Cincinnati (45242) *(G-2602)*

AGR Consulting Inc... 440 974-4030
35400 Lakeland Blvd Eastlake (44095) *(G-7018)*

Agrana Fruit Us Inc.. 937 693-3821
16197 County Road 25a Anna (45302) *(G-488)*

Agrana Fruit Us Inc (DH).. 440 546-1199
6850 Southpointe Pkwy Brecksville (44141) *(G-1605)*

Agrati - Medina LLC (DH)... 330 725-8853
941 Lake Rd 955 Medina (44256) *(G-10289)*

Agrati - Tiffin LLC.. 419 447-2221
1988 S County Road 593 Tiffin (44883) *(G-14074)*

Agratronix LLC... 330 562-2222
1790 Miller Pkwy Streetsboro (44241) *(G-13753)*

Agrauxine By Lesaffre, Van Wert *Also Called: Advanced Biological Mktg Inc (G-14904)*

Agri Communicators Inc.. 614 273-0465
280 N High St Fl 6 Columbus (43215) *(G-5105)*

Agricool Veg & Fruits LLC.. 310 625-0024
310 S Green Rd South Euclid (44121) *(G-13458)*

Agridry LLC... 419 459-4399
3460 Us Highway 20 Edon (43518) *(G-7085)*

Agrium Advanced Tech US Inc... 614 276-5103
701 Kaderly Dr Columbus (43228) *(G-5106)*

AGS Custom Graphics, Macedonia *Also Called: Custom Graphics Inc (G-9543)*

AGS Custom Graphics Inc.. 330 963-7770
8107 Bavaria Dr E Macedonia (44056) *(G-9534)*

Agse Tooling, Cincinnati *Also Called: Advanced Ground Systems (G-2598)*

Ahalogy.. 314 974-5599
1140 Main St # 3 Cincinnati (45202) *(G-2603)*

Ahd, Cuyahoga Falls *Also Called: Advanced Holding Designs Inc (G-6060)*

Ahkeo Labs LLC... 216 406-1919
6685 Beta Dr Mayfield Village (44143) *(G-10258)*

Ahmf Inc (PA).. 614 921-1223
2245 Wilson Rd Columbus (43228) *(G-5107)*

Ahner Fabricating & Shtmtl Inc... 419 626-6641
2001 E Perkins Ave Sandusky (44870) *(G-13042)*

Ahresty Wilmington Corporation... 937 382-6112
2627 S South St Wilmington (45177) *(G-16038)*

Ai Life LLC.. 513 605-1079
4680 Parkway Dr Ste 300 Mason (45040) *(G-9947)*

Ai Root Company.. 330 725-6677
234 S State Rd Medina (44256) *(G-10290)*

Ai Root Company (PA).. 330 723-4359
623 W Liberty St Medina (44256) *(G-10291)*

Ai Wellness, Mason *Also Called: Ai Life LLC (G-9947)*

Aida-America Corporation (HQ).. 937 237-2382
7660 Center Point 70 Blvd Dayton (45424) *(G-6192)*

Ailes Millwork Inc... 330 678-4300
1520 Enterprise Way Kent (44240) *(G-8796)*

Aim Attachments... 614 539-3030
1720 Feddern Ave Grove City (43123) *(G-8075)*

Aim International... 513 831-2938
264 Center St Miamiville (45147) *(G-10710)*

Aim Media Midwest Oper LLC.. 740 354-6621
1437 Layton Dr Portsmouth (45662) *(G-12640)*

Aim Services Company... 800 321-9038
1500 Trumbull Ave Girard (44420) *(G-7959)*

Aims-CMI Technology LLC... 937 832-2000
65 Haas Dr Englewood (45322) *(G-7221)*

AIN Industries Inc.. 440 781-0950
13901 Aspinwall Ave Cleveland (44110) *(G-3616)*

Air Craft Wheels LLC.. 440 937-7903
700 N Walnut St Ravenna (44266) *(G-12701)*

Air Enterprises Inc... 330 794-9770
735 Glaser Pkwy Akron (44306) *(G-24)*

Air Heater Seal Company Inc... 740 984-2146
15710 Waterford Rd Waterford (45786) *(G-15235)*

Air Locke Dock Seal Division, Youngstown *Also Called: ONeals Tarpaulin & Awning Co (G-16406)*

Air Power Dynamics LLC... 440 701-2100
7350 Corporate Blvd Mentor (44060) *(G-10408)*

Air Rite Service Supply, Cleveland *Also Called: Air-Rite Inc (G-3617)*

Air Supply Co, Twinsburg *Also Called: Allied Separation Tech Inc (G-14628)*

Air Technical Industries Inc... 440 951-5191
7501 Clover Ave Mentor (44060) *(G-10409)*

Air-Rite Inc.. 216 228-8200
1290 W 117th St Cleveland (44107) *(G-3617)*

Air-Tech Mechanical Inc... 419 292-0074
4444 Monroe St Toledo (43613) *(G-14180)*

Airam Press, Covington *Also Called: Airam Press Co Ltd (G-6016)*

Airam Press Co Ltd.. 937 473-5672
2065 Industrial Ct Covington (45318) *(G-6016)*

Airbase Industries LLC.. 937 540-1140
1000 Cass Dr Englewood (45315) *(G-7222)*

Airbrush Sugar Shack Inc... 614 735-4988
3480 Cleveland Ave Columbus (43224) *(G-5108)*

Aircraft & Auto Fittings Co.. 216 486-0047
17120 Saint Clair Ave Cleveland (44110) *(G-3618)*

Aircraft Ground Services.. 419 356-5027
4449 Weckerly Rd Monclova (43542) *(G-11092)*

Aircraft Wheel & Brake LLC.. 440 937-6211
1160 Center Rd Avon (44011) *(G-762)*

Aircraft Wheels and Breaks, Avon *Also Called: Cleveland Wheels (G-767)*

Aircraft-Refuelers.com, Findlay *Also Called: Bosserman Automotive Engrg LLC (G-7485)*

Airecon Manufacturing Corp.. 513 561-5522
5271 Brotherton Rd Cincinnati (45227) *(G-2604)*

Airfasco Inc.. 330 430-6190
2655 Harrison Ave Sw Canton (44706) *(G-2029)*

Airfasco Inds Fstner Group LLC 330 430-6190
2655 Harrison Ave Sw Canton (44706) *(G-2030)*

Airgas Usa LLC 330 454-1330
2505 Shepler Ave Sw Canton (44706) *(G-2031)*

Airgas Usa LLC 937 222-8312
2400 Sandridge Dr Moraine (45439) *(G-11154)*

Airgas Usa LLC 440 232-6397
9155 Dutton Dr Twinsburg (44087) *(G-14625)*

Airmate Co Inc 419 636-3184
16280 County Road D Bryan (43506) *(G-1803)*

Airplaco Equipment Company, Cincinnati *Also Called: Mesa Industries Inc (G-3151)*

Airsources Inc 610 983-0102
950 Honeysuckle Cir Ne North Canton (44720) *(G-11714)*

Airstream Inc (HQ) 937 596-6111
1001 W Pike St Jackson Center (45334) *(G-8729)*

Airtech 419 269-1000
6898 Commodore Dr Walbridge (43465) *(G-15078)*

Airtex Industries LLC 330 899-0340
6056 Deer Park Ct Toledo (43614) *(G-14181)*

Airtx International Ltd 513 631-0660
6320 Wiehe Rd Cincinnati (45237) *(G-2605)*

Airwave Communications Cons 419 331-1526
1209 Allentown Rd Lima (45805) *(G-9218)*

Airwaves LLC 740 548-1200
7750 Green Meadows Dr Ste A Lewis Center (43035) *(G-9147)*

Aitken, Geneva *Also Called: Aitken Products Inc (G-7930)*

Aitken Products Inc 440 466-5711
566 N Eagle St Geneva (44041) *(G-7930)*

Aj Enterprise LLC 740 231-2205
2300 National Rd Zanesville (43701) *(G-16497)*

Ajax Tocco Magnethermic Corp (HQ) 800 547-1527
1745 Overland Ave Ne Warren (44483) *(G-15135)*

Ajax-Ceco 440 295-0244
1500 E 219th St Euclid (44117) *(G-7259)*

AJD Holding Co (PA) 330 405-4477
2181 Enterprise Pkwy Twinsburg (44087) *(G-14626)*

Ajinomoto Hlth Ntrtn N Amer In 330 762-6652
929 Home Ave Akron (44310) *(G-25)*

Ajj Enterprises LLC 513 755-9562
10073 Commerce Park Dr West Chester (45246) *(G-15534)*

AK Fabrication Inc 330 458-1037
1500 Allen Ave Se Canton (44707) *(G-2032)*

AK Mansfield 419 755-3011
913 Bowman St Mansfield (44903) *(G-9622)*

AK Ready Mix LLC 740 286-8900
441 Dixon Run Rd Jackson (45640) *(G-8707)*

AK Steel Door 360, Middletown *Also Called: Matheson Tri-Gas Inc (G-10842)*

Ak-Isg Steel Coating Company 216 429-6901
3531 Campbell Rd Cleveland (44105) *(G-3619)*

Akalina Associates Inc 440 992-2195
2751 West Ave Ashtabula (44004) *(G-626)*

Akay Holdings Inc 330 753-8458
1031 Lambert St Barberton (44203) *(G-852)*

Akers Packaging Service Inc (PA) 513 422-6312
2820 Lefferson Rd Middletown (45044) *(G-10802)*

Akers Packaging Service Group, Middletown *Also Called: Akers Packaging Service Inc (G-10802)*

Akers Packaging Service Group, Middletown *Also Called: Akers Packaging Solutions Inc (G-10803)*

Akers Packaging Solutions Inc (PA) 513 422-6312
2820 Lefferson Rd Middletown (45044) *(G-10803)*

Akko Fastener Inc (PA) 513 489-8300
1225 Hook Dr Middletown (45042) *(G-10804)*

Akland Printing, Macedonia *Also Called: Gaspar Services LLC (G-9554)*

Akro Tool Co Inc 513 858-1555
240 Donald Dr Fairfield (45014) *(G-7331)*

Akro Tool Company, Fairfield *Also Called: Deffren Machine Tool Svc Inc (G-7351)*

Akro-Plastics, Kent *Also Called: U S Development Corp (G-8879)*

Akrochem Corporation (PA) 330 535-2100
3770 Embassy Pkwy Akron (44333) *(G-26)*

Akron Anodizing & Coating Div, Akron *Also Called: Russell Products Co Inc (G-315)*

Akron Belting & Supply Company 330 633-8212
1244 Home Ave Akron (44310) *(G-27)*

Akron Bldg Closeout Mtls LLC 234 738-0867
425 Fairview Ave Barberton (44203) *(G-853)*

Akron Brass Company 614 529-7230
3656 Paragon Dr Columbus (43228) *(G-5109)*

Akron Brass Company 800 228-1161
1615 Old Mansfield Rd Wooster (44691) *(G-16096)*

Akron Brass Company (DH) 330 264-5678
343 Venture Blvd Wooster (44691) *(G-16097)*

Akron Brass Holding Corp (HQ) 330 264-5678
343 Venture Blvd Wooster (44691) *(G-16098)*

Akron Canton Waste Oil, Canton *Also Called: Emaxx Northeast Ohio LLC (G-2096)*

Akron Centl Engrv Mold Mch Inc 330 475-1388
2680 Cory Ave Akron (44314) *(G-28)*

Akron Centl Engrv Mold Mch Inc 330 794-8704
1625 Massillon Rd Akron (44312) *(G-29)*

Akron Coating Adhesives Co Inc 330 724-4716
365 Stanton Ave Akron (44301) *(G-30)*

Akron Coca-Cola Bottling Co 330 784-2653
1560 Triplett Blvd Akron (44306) *(G-31)*

Akron Cotton Products Inc 330 404-7171
437 W Cedar St Akron (44307) *(G-32)*

Akron Crematory, Akron *Also Called: Akron Vault Company Inc (G-48)*

Akron Design & Costume LLC 330 644-0425
888 Tippecanoe Dr Coventry Township (44319) *(G-6004)*

Akron Dispersions Inc 330 666-0045
3291 Sawmill Rd Copley (44321) *(G-5942)*

Akron Equipment Company 330 645-3780
3522 Manchester Rd Ste B Coventry Township (44319) *(G-6005)*

Akron Foundry Co (PA) 330 745-3101
2728 Wingate Ave Akron (44314) *(G-33)*

Akron Gasket & Packg Entps Inc 330 633-3742
445 Northeast Ave Tallmadge (44278) *(G-14021)*

Akron Gear & Engineering Inc 330 773-6608
501 Morgan Ave Akron (44311) *(G-34)*

Akron Jewelry Rubber, Willoughby *Also Called: Zero-D Products Inc (G-16020)*

Akron Legal News Inc 330 296-7578
60 S Summit St Akron (44308) *(G-35)*

Akron Life, Akron *Also Called: Baker Media Group LLC (G-77)*

Akron Litho-Print Company Inc 330 434-3145
1026 S Main St Akron (44311) *(G-36)*

Akron Orthotic Solutions Inc 330 253-3002
582 W Market St Akron (44303) *(G-37)*

Akron Paint & Varnish Inc 330 773-8911
1390 Firestone Pkwy Akron (44301) *(G-38)*

Akron Plating Co Inc 330 773-6878
1774 Hackberry St Akron (44301) *(G-39)*

Akron Polymer Products Inc (PA) 330 628-5551
1471 Exeter Rd Akron (44306) *(G-40)*

Akron Porcelain & Plastic Co, Akron *Also Called: Akron Porcelain & Plastics Co (G-41)*

Akron Porcelain & Plastics Co (PA) 330 745-2159
2739 Cory Ave Akron (44314) *(G-41)*

Akron Products Company 330 576-1750
6600 Ridge Rd Wadsworth (44281) *(G-15016)*

Akron Rebar Co (PA)   809 W Waterloo Rd Akron (44314) *(G-42)*

Akron Special Machinery Inc (PA) 330 753-1077
2740 Cory Ave Akron (44314) *(G-43)*

Akron Steel Fabricators Co 330 644-0616
3291 Manchester Rd Akron (44319) *(G-44)*

Akron Steel Treating Co 330 773-8211
336 Morgan Ave Akron (44311) *(G-45)*

Akron Thermography Inc 330 896-9712
3506 Fortuna Dr Akron (44312) *(G-46)*

Akron Thermography Inc 330 896-9712
3406 Fortuna Dr Akron (44312) *(G-47)*

Akron Tool and Die, Akron *Also Called: Diamond America Corporation (G-126)*

Akron Vault Company Inc 330 784-5475
2399 Gilchrist Rd Akron (44305) *(G-48)*

Akzo Nobel Coatings Inc 614 294-3361
1313 Windsor Ave Ste 1313 Columbus (43211) *(G-5110)*

ALPHABETIC SECTION — Alkermes Inc

Akzo Nobel Coatings Inc 419 433-9143
300 Sprowl Rd Huron (44839) *(G-8625)*

Akzo Nobel Coatings Inc 937 322-2671
1550 Progress Rd Springfield (45505) *(G-13529)*

Akzo Nobel Paints LLC 440 297-8000
8381 Pearl Rd Strongsville (44136) *(G-13803)*

Al Fe Heat Treating-Ohio Inc 330 336-0211
979 Seville Rd Wadsworth (44281) *(G-15017)*

Al Yoder Construction Co 330 359-5726
3375 County Road 160 Millersburg (44654) *(G-10939)*

Al-Cast Mold & Pattern 330 968-4490
3865 Poplar Ln Kent (44240) *(G-8797)*

Al-Co Products Inc 419 399-3867
485 2nd St Latty (45855) *(G-9053)*

Al-Fe Heat Treating LLC 419 782-7200
2066 E 2nd St Defiance (43512) *(G-6668)*

Al's Electric Motor Service, Bedford Also Called: Als High Tech Inc *(G-1099)*

Alabama Sling Center Inc 440 239-7000
21000 Aerospace Pkwy Cleveland (44142) *(G-3620)*

Alacriant Inc (PA) 330 562-7191
1760 Miller Pkwy Streetsboro (44241) *(G-13754)*

Alacriant Inc 330 562-7191
2500 Crane Centre Dr Streetsboro (44241) *(G-13755)*

Alan Bortree 937 585-6962
8176 State Route 508 De Graff (43318) *(G-6664)*

Alan Manufacturing Inc 330 262-1555
3927 E Lincoln Way Wooster (44691) *(G-16099)*

Alanod Westlake Metal Ind Inc 440 327-8184
36696 Sugar Ridge Rd North Ridgeville (44039) *(G-11826)*

Alb Tyler Holdings Inc 440 946-7171
7255 Industrial Park Blvd Ste A Mentor (44060) *(G-10410)*

Alba Manufacturing Inc 513 874-0551
8950 Seward Rd Fairfield (45011) *(G-7332)*

Albanese Concessions LLC 614 402-4937
6983 Greensview Village Dr Canal Winchester (43110) *(G-1978)*

Albany Screen Printing LLC 614 585-3279
7049 Trillium Ln Reynoldsburg (43068) *(G-12750)*

Albco Foundry Inc 330 424-7716
230 Maple St Lisbon (44432) *(G-9307)*

Albeco, Cleveland Also Called: Aluminum Bearing Co of America *(G-3643)*

Albemarle Amendments LLC (HQ) 330 425-2354
1664 Highland Rd Ste 3 Twinsburg (44087) *(G-14627)*

Albert Freytag Inc 419 628-2018
306 Executive Dr Minster (45865) *(G-11047)*

Albert Screenprint, Norton Also Called: Alberts Screen Print Inc *(G-11938)*

Alberts Screen Print Inc 330 753-7559
3704 Summit Rd Norton (44203) *(G-11938)*

Albion Industries Inc 440 238-1955
20246 Progress Dr Strongsville (44149) *(G-13804)*

Albion Machine & Tool Co Inc 216 267-9627
13200 Enterprise Ave Cleveland (44135) *(G-3621)*

Albright Albright & Schn 614 825-4829
89 E Wilson Bridge Rd Ste D Worthington (43085) *(G-16189)*

Albright Radiator, Wooster Also Called: Albright Radiator Inc *(G-16100)*

Albright Radiator Inc 330 264-8886
331 N Hillcrest Dr Wooster (44691) *(G-16100)*

Alcan Corporation (HQ) 440 460-3307
6060 Parkland Blvd Cleveland (44124) *(G-3622)*

Alcan Primary Products Corp
6055 Rockside Woods Blvd N Ste 180 Independence (44131) *(G-8653)*

Alchem Aluminum Europe Inc 216 910-3400
25825 Science Park Dr Ste 400 Beachwood (44122) *(G-972)*

Alchem Corporation 330 725-2436
525 W Liberty St Medina (44256) *(G-10292)*

Alchemical Transmutation Corp 216 313-8674
314 E 195th St Cleveland (44119) *(G-3623)*

Alcm, Cleveland Also Called: Aluminum Coating Manufacturers *(G-3644)*

Alco, Akron Also Called: Alco-Chem Inc *(G-49)*

Alco Manufacturing Corp LLC (PA) 440 458-5165
10584 Middle Ave Elyria (44035) *(G-7105)*

Alco-Chem Inc (PA) 330 253-3535
45 N Summit St Akron (44308) *(G-49)*

Alcoa Inc 937 492-8915
2900 Campbell Rd Sidney (45365) *(G-13219)*

Alcoa Titanium Engineered Pdts, Niles Also Called: Rti International Metals Inc *(G-11687)*

Alcohol & Drug Addiction Svcs 216 348-4830
2012 W 25th St Ste 600 Cleveland (44113) *(G-3624)*

Alcon, Akron Also Called: Alcon Tool Company *(G-51)*

Alcon Inc (HQ) 513 722-1037
1132 Ferris Rd Amelia (45102) *(G-449)*

Alcon Connectors, Amelia Also Called: Sanreed Management Group LLC *(G-464)*

Alcon Industries Inc 216 961-1100
7990 Baker Ave Cleveland (44102) *(G-3625)*

Alcon Tool Co Ltd 330 773-9171
561 Lafollette St Akron (44311) *(G-50)*

Alcon Tool Company 330 773-9171
565 Lafollette St Akron (44311) *(G-51)*

Alden Excavating, Cuyahoga Falls Also Called: Alden Sand & Gravel Co Inc *(G-6061)*

Alden Sand & Gravel Co Inc 330 928-3249
2486 Northampton Rd Cuyahoga Falls (44223) *(G-6061)*

Alderwoods (oklahoma) Inc 903 597-6611
311 Elm St Ste 1000 Cincinnati (45202) *(G-2606)*

Aldrich Chemical 937 859-1808
3858 Benner Rd Miamisburg (45342) *(G-10608)*

Aldridge Folders, Wadsworth Also Called: Deshea Printing Company *(G-15026)*

Aldridge Folders, Wadsworth Also Called: Keeler Enterprises Inc *(G-15039)*

Alegre Inc 937 885-6786
3101 W Tech Blvd Miamisburg (45342) *(G-10609)*

Alegre Global Supply Solutions, Miamisburg Also Called: Alegre Inc *(G-10609)*

Alektronics Inc 937 429-2118
4095 Executive Dr Beavercreek (45430) *(G-1069)*

Alene Candles Midwest LLC 614 933-4005
8860 Smiths Mill Rd Ste 100 New Albany (43054) *(G-11364)*

Aleris Rm Inc 216 910-3400
25825 Science Park Dr Ste 400 Beachwood (44122) *(G-973)*

Alert Safety Lite Products Co 440 232-5020
24500 Solon Rd Cleveland (44146) *(G-3626)*

Alex Products, Inc., Ridgeville Corners Also Called: Nasg Sting Rdgvlle Corners LLC *(G-12816)*

Alexander Pierce Corp 330 798-9840
1874 Englewood Ave Akron (44312) *(G-52)*

Alexander Wilbert Vault Co (PA) 419 468-3477
1263 State Hwy 598 Galion (44833) *(G-7859)*

Alexis Concrete Enterprise Inc 440 366-0031
672 Sugar Ln Elyria (44035) *(G-7106)*

Alfa Green Supreme, Ottawa Also Called: Verhoff Alfalfa Mills Inc *(G-12195)*

Alfagreen Supreme, Toledo Also Called: Ohio Blenders Inc *(G-14407)*

Alfalight Inc 608 240-4800
676 Alpha Dr Cleveland (44143) *(G-3627)*

Alfman Logging LLC 740 982-6227
4499 Township Road 448 Ne Crooksville (43731) *(G-6043)*

Alfons Haar Inc 937 560-2031
150 Advanced Dr Springboro (45066) *(G-13495)*

Alfrebro LLC 513 539-7373
1055 Reed Dr Monroe (45050) *(G-11093)*

Alfred Machine Co (HQ) 440 248-4600
29500 Solon Rd Cleveland (44139) *(G-3628)*

Alfred Nickles Bakery Inc 740 453-6522
1147 Newark Rd Zanesville (43701) *(G-16498)*

Algix LLC 706 207-3425
3916 Clock Pointe Trl Ste 103 Stow (44224) *(G-13683)*

Ali Industries LLC 937 878-3946
747 E Xenia Dr Fairborn (45324) *(G-7308)*

Alimento Ventures Inc 855 510-2866
10001 Alliance Rd Blue Ash (45242) *(G-1361)*

Alin Machining Company Inc 740 223-0200
875 E Mark St Marion (43302) *(G-9847)*

ALIN MACHINING COMPANY, INC., Marion Also Called: Alin Machining Company Inc *(G-9847)*

Aliquippa & Ohio River RR Co 740 622-8092
123 Division Street Ext Youngstown (44510) *(G-16306)*

Alkermes Inc 937 382-5642
265 Olinger Cir Wilmington (45177) *(G-16039)*

Alkid Corporation 216 896-3000
6035 Parkland Blvd Cleveland (44124) *(G-3629)*

Alkon Corporation 614 799-6650
6750 Crosby Ct Dublin (43016) *(G-6858)*

Alkon Corporation (PA) 419 355-9111
728 Graham Dr Fremont (43420) *(G-7762)*

All - Do Weld & Fab LLC 740 477-2133
28155 River Dr Circleville (43113) *(G-3540)*

All About Plastics LLC 937 547-0098
5339 State Route 571 Greenville (45331) *(G-8035)*

All American Fire Equiptment, Wshngtn Ct Hs *Also Called: All-American Fire Eqp Inc*
(G-16225)

All Around Primo Logistics LLC 513 725-7888
6027 Magnolia Woods Way Cincinnati (45247) *(G-2607)*

All Coatings Co Inc 330 821-3806
510 W Ely St Alliance (44601) *(G-389)*

All Craft Manufacturing Co 513 661-3383
6500 Glenway Ave Side 2 Cincinnati (45211) *(G-2608)*

All Cstom Fabricators Erectors, Cleveland *Also Called: Varmland Inc (G-4861)*

All Fired Up Pnt Your Own Pot 330 865-5858
30 Rothrock Loop Copley (44321) *(G-5943)*

All Foam Pdts Safety Foam Proc, Middlefield *Also Called: All Foam Products Co (G-10730)*

All Foam Products Co (PA) 330 849-3636
15005 Enterprise Way Middlefield (44062) *(G-10730)*

All Metal Fabricators Inc 216 267-0033
15400 Commerce Park Dr Cleveland (44142) *(G-3630)*

All Ohio Companies Inc 216 420-9274
2735 Scranton Rd Cleveland (44113) *(G-3631)*

All Ohio Ready Mix Concrete 419 841-3838
622 Eckel Rd Perrysburg (43551) *(G-12360)*

All Ohio Threaded Rod Co Inc 216 426-1800
5349 Saint Clair Ave Cleveland (44103) *(G-3632)*

All Ohio Welding Inc 937 663-7116
3833 State Route 235 N Saint Paris (43072) *(G-12970)*

All Pack Services LLC 614 935-0964
3442 Grant Ave Grove City (43123) *(G-8076)*

All Points Printing Inc 440 585-1125
1330 Lloyd Rd Wickliffe (44092) *(G-15823)*

All Power Battery Inc 330 453-5236
1387 Clarendon Ave Sw Ste 6 Canton (44710) *(G-2033)*

All Power Equipment LLC (PA) 740 593-3279
8880 United Ln Athens (45701) *(G-674)*

All Pro Ovrhd Door Systems LLC 614 444-3667
1985 Oakland Park Ave Columbus (43224) *(G-5111)*

All Seal 740 852-2628
141 Sharp Ave London (43140) *(G-9380)*

All Signs, Chillicothe *Also Called: All Signs of Chillicothe Inc (G-2492)*

All Signs of Chillicothe Inc 740 773-5016
12035 Pleasant Valley Rd Chillicothe (45601) *(G-2492)*

All Srvice Plastic Molding Inc 937 415-3674
611 Yellow Springs Fairfield Rd Fairborn (45324) *(G-7309)*

All Srvice Plastic Molding Inc (PA) 937 890-0322
850 Falls Creek Dr Vandalia (45377) *(G-14932)*

All State GL Block Fctry Inc 440 205-8410
8781 East Ave Mentor (44060) *(G-10411)*

All Streets Auto LLC 330 714-7717
15317 Chatfield Ave Cleveland (44111) *(G-3633)*

All Trades Contractors LLC 440 850-5693
9920 Olivet Ave Cleveland (44108) *(G-3634)*

All Ways Green Lawn & Turf LLC 937 763-4766
1856 Greenbrier Rd Seaman (45679) *(G-13114)*

All Wright Enterprises LLC 440 259-5656
4285 Main St Perry (44081) *(G-12349)*

All Write Ribbon Inc 513 753-8300
3916 Bach Buxton Rd Amelia (45102) *(G-450)*

All-American Fire Eqp Inc 800 972-6035
5101 Us Highway 22 Sw Wshngtn Ct Hs (43160) *(G-16225)*

All-In Nutritionals LLC 888 400-0333
5060 S Charleston Pike Springfield (45502) *(G-13530)*

All-Line Truck Sales, Hubbard *Also Called: Youngstown-Kenworth Inc (G-8574)*

All-Plant Liquid Plant Food, Ashland *Also Called: R & J AG Manufacturing Inc (G-608)*

All-Tech Manufacturing Ltd 330 633-1095
1477 Industrial Pkwy Akron (44310) *(G-53)*

All-Type Welding & Fabrication 440 439-3990
7690 Bond St Cleveland (44139) *(G-3635)*

Allega Concrete Corp 216 447-0814
5146 Allega Way Richfield (44286) *(G-12781)*

Allegion Access Tech LLC 440 461-5500
5335 Avion Park Dr Cleveland (44143) *(G-3636)*

Allegra Marketing Print Mail, Blue Ash *Also Called: Dsk Imaging LLC (G-1386)*

Allegra Print, Findlay *Also Called: Allegra Print & Imaging (G-7475)*

Allegra Print & Imaging 419 427-8095
701 W Sandusky St Findlay (45840) *(G-7475)*

Allen Aircraft Products Inc 330 296-9621
312 E Lake St Ravenna (44266) *(G-12702)*

Allen Aircraft Products Inc 330 296-1531
4879 Newton Falls Rd Ravenna (44266) *(G-12703)*

Allen Aircraft Products Inc (PA) 330 296-9621
6168 Woodbine Rd Ravenna (44266) *(G-12704)*

Allen County Fabrication Inc 419 227-7447
999 Industry Ave Lima (45804) *(G-9219)*

Allen Enterprises Inc 740 532-5913
2900 S 9th St Ironton (45638) *(G-8694)*

Allen Fields Assoc Inc 513 228-1010
3525 Grant Ave Ste D Lebanon (45036) *(G-9061)*

Allen Graphics Inc 440 349-4100
27100 Richmond Rd Ste 6 Solon (44139) *(G-13308)*

Allen Industrial Company 440 327-4100
7650 Race Rd North Ridgeville (44039) *(G-11827)*

Allen Industries Inc 567 408-7538
7844 W Central Ave Toledo (43617) *(G-14182)*

Allen Randall Enterprises Inc 330 374-9850
70 E Miller Ave Akron (44301) *(G-54)*

Allergan, Cincinnati *Also Called: Allergan Sales LLC (G-2609)*

Allergan Sales LLC 513 271-6800
5000 Brotherton Rd Cincinnati (45209) *(G-2609)*

Allergan Sales LLC 513 271-6800
3941 Brotherton Rd Cincinnati (45209) *(G-2610)*

Allermuir, Maumee *Also Called: Senator International Inc (G-10229)*

Alley Cat Designs Inc 937 291-8803
919 Senate Dr Dayton (45459) *(G-6193)*

Allfab Inc 614 491-4944
2273 Williams Rd Columbus (43207) *(G-5112)*

Allgaier Process Technology 513 402-2566
9780 Windisch Rd West Chester (45069) *(G-15363)*

Allgeier & Son Inc (PA) 513 574-3735
6386 Bridgetown Rd Cincinnati (45248) *(G-2611)*

Alliance Abrasives LLC 330 823-7957
23649 State Route 62 Alliance (44601) *(G-390)*

Alliance Automation LLC 419 238-2520
1100 John Brown Rd Van Wert (45891) *(G-14906)*

Alliance Carpet Cushion Co 740 966-5001
143 Commerce Blvd Johnstown (43031) *(G-8768)*

Alliance Castings Company LLC 330 829-5600
1001 E Broadway St Alliance (44601) *(G-391)*

Alliance Equipment Company Inc 330 821-2291
1000 N Union Ave Alliance (44601) *(G-392)*

Alliance Forging Group LLC 330 680-4861
847 Pier Dr # 1000 Akron (44307) *(G-55)*

Alliance Knife Inc 513 367-9000
124 May Dr Harrison (45030) *(G-8264)*

Alliance Publishing Co Inc (HQ) 330 453-1304
40 S Linden Ave Alliance (44601) *(G-393)*

Alliance Redi-Mix Inc 330 821-9244
22138 Hartley Rd Alliance (44601) *(G-394)*

Alliance, The, Reynoldsburg *Also Called: Christian Missionary Alliance (G-12758)*

Allied Coating Corporation 937 615-0391
220 Fox Dr Piqua (45356) *(G-12502)*

Allied Consolidated Inds Inc (PA) 330 744-0808
2100 Poland Ave Youngstown (44502) *(G-16307)*

Allied Corp Inc 330 626-3401
8505 State Route 14 Streetsboro (44241) *(G-13756)*

ALPHABETIC SECTION — Altec Industries Inc

Allied Fabricating & Wldg Co 614 751-6664
5699 Chantry Dr Columbus (43232) *(G-5113)*

Allied Machine & Engrg Corp (PA) 330 343-4283
120 Deeds Dr Dover (44622) *(G-6807)*

Allied Machine Works Inc 740 454-2534
120 Graham St Zanesville (43701) *(G-16499)*

Allied Mask and Tooling Inc 419 470-2555
6051 Telegraph Rd Ste 6 Toledo (43612) *(G-14183)*

Allied Mineral Products LLC (PA) 614 876-0244
2700 Scioto Pkwy Columbus (43221) *(G-5114)*

Allied Motion At Dayton 937 228-3171
2275 Stanley Ave Dayton (45404) *(G-6194)*

Allied Moulded Products Inc (PA) 419 636-4217
222 N Union St Bryan (43506) *(G-1804)*

Allied Nutrients, Brunswick *Also Called: Turf Care Supply LLC (G-1796)*

Allied Pdstal Boom Systems LLC 419 663-0279
405 Industrial Pkwy Norwalk (44857) *(G-11952)*

Allied Pedestal Boom Sys LLC 419 663-0279
75 Norwalk Commons Dr Norwalk (44857) *(G-11953)*

Allied Polymers 330 975-4200
21 Mill St Seville (44273) *(G-13134)*

Allied Separation Tech Inc (PA) 704 732-8034
2300 E Enterprise Pkwy Twinsburg (44087) *(G-14628)*

Allied Separation Tech Inc 704 736-0420
2300 E Enterprise Pkwy Twinsburg (44087) *(G-14629)*

Allied Shipping and Packaging Supplies Inc 937 222-7422
3681 Vance Rd Moraine (45439) *(G-11155)*

Allied Sign Co 614 443-9656
818 Marion Rd Columbus (43207) *(G-5115)*

Allied Silk Screen Inc 937 223-4921
2740 Thunderhawk Ct Dayton (45414) *(G-6195)*

Allied Supplied Company, Twinsburg *Also Called: Allied Separation Tech Inc (G-14629)*

Allied Tool & Die Inc 216 941-6196
16146 Puritas Ave Cleveland (44135) *(G-3637)*

Allied Tube & Conduit Corp 740 928-1018
250 Capital Dr Hebron (43025) *(G-8335)*

Allied Witan Company 440 237-9630
13805 Progress Pkwy North Royalton (44133) *(G-11866)*

Allite Inc 937 200-0831
8889 Gander Creek Dr Miamisburg (45342) *(G-10610)*

Allmand Boats LLC 513 805-4673
1000 Forest Ave Hamilton (45015) *(G-8176)*

Alloy Engineering Company (PA) 440 243-6800
844 Thacker St Berea (44017) *(G-1264)*

Alloy Extrusion Company 330 677-4946
4211 Karg Industrial Pkwy Kent (44240) *(G-8798)*

Alloy Fabricators Inc 330 948-3535
700 Wooster St Lodi (44254) *(G-9347)*

Alloy Machining and Fabg Inc 330 482-5543
1028 Lower Elkton Rd Columbiana (44408) *(G-5026)*

Alloy Precision Tech Inc 440 266-7700
6989 Lindsay Dr Mentor (44060) *(G-10412)*

Alloy Welding & Fabricating 440 914-0650
30340 Solon Industrial Pkwy Ste B Solon (44139) *(G-13309)*

Allpass Corporation 440 998-6300
222 N Lake St Madison (44057) *(G-9587)*

Alltech Med Systems Amer Inc 440 424-2240
28900 Fountain Pkwy Solon (44139) *(G-13310)*

Almandrey Fabricating Tech 937 408-0054
107 Tremont City Rd Springfield (45502) *(G-13531)*

Almira Tire & Supply Div, Olmsted Falls *Also Called: Bell Tire Co (G-12076)*

Almo Process Technology, West Chester *Also Called: Allgaier Process Technology (G-15363)*

Almondina Brand Biscuits, Maumee *Also Called: Yz Enterprises Inc (G-10246)*

Alonovus Corp 330 674-2300
7368 County Road 623 Millersburg (44654) *(G-10940)*

Alpco, Westlake *Also Called: Aluminum Line Products Company (G-15729)*

Alpha Inc 419 996-7355
3320 Fort Shawnee Industrial Dr Lima (45806) *(G-9303)*

Alpha Coatings Inc 419 435-5111
622 S Corporate Dr W Fostoria (44830) *(G-7627)*

Alpha Container, Marysville *Also Called: Larsen Packaging Products Inc (G-9923)*

Alpha Control LLC 740 377-3400
1042 County Road 60 South Point (45680) *(G-13463)*

Alpha Control Fabg & Mfg, South Point *Also Called: Alpha Control LLC (G-13463)*

Alpha Ctrl Fabrication & Mfg 740 377-3400
1042 County Road 60 South Point (45680) *(G-13464)*

Alpha Omega Import Export LLC 740 885-9155
1135 Browns Rd Marietta (45750) *(G-9774)*

Alpha Packaging Holdings Inc 216 252-5595
14801 Emery Ave Cleveland (44135) *(G-3638)*

Alpha Strike, Kent *Also Called: Primal Screen Inc (G-8848)*

Alpha Technologies Svcs LLC (DH) 330 745-1641
6279 Hudson Crossing Pkwy Ste 200 Hudson (44236) *(G-8583)*

Alpha Tool & Mold Inc 440 473-2343
83 Alpha Park Cleveland (44143) *(G-3639)*

Alpha Water Conditioning Co, Dayton *Also Called: R D Baker Enterprises Inc (G-6537)*

Alpha Zeta Holdings Inc (PA) 216 271-1601
2981 Independence Rd Cleveland (44115) *(G-3640)*

Alphabet Inc (HQ) 330 856-3366
8640 E Market St Warren (44484) *(G-15136)*

Alphabet Embroidery Studios 937 372-6557
1291 Bellbrook Ave Xenia (45385) *(G-16248)*

AlphaGraphics 513 204-6070
7288 Central Parke Blvd Mason (45040) *(G-9948)*

AlphaGraphics, Cincinnati *Also Called: Banbury Investments Inc (G-2655)*

AlphaGraphics, Cleveland *Also Called: Swimmer Printing Inc (G-4761)*

AlphaGraphics, Columbus *Also Called: Headlee Enterprises Ltd (G-5063)*

AlphaGraphics, Columbus *Also Called: DC Reprographics Co (G-5319)*

AlphaGraphics, Strongsville *Also Called: AlphaGraphics 507 Inc (G-13805)*

AlphaGraphics 507 Inc 440 878-9700
14765 Pearl Rd Strongsville (44136) *(G-13805)*

AlphaGraphics Cincinnati, Mason *Also Called: Morse Enterprises Inc (G-10031)*

AlphaGraphics Strongsville, Strongsville *Also Called: Blue Crescent Enterprises Inc (G-13816)*

AlphaGraphics Valley View, Cleveland *Also Called: Image Concepts Inc (G-4215)*

AlphaGraphics Westlake, Westlake *Also Called: Vision Graphix Inc (G-15800)*

Alpine Cabinets 330 359-5724
7932 Township Road 662 Dundee (44624) *(G-6962)*

Alpine Dairy LLC 330 359-6291
1658 Township Road 660 Dundee (44624) *(G-6963)*

Alpine Gage Inc 937 669-8665
4325 Lisa Dr Tipp City (45371) *(G-14122)*

Alpla Inc 419 991-9484
3320 Fort Shawnee Industrial Dr Lima (45806) *(G-9304)*

Alro Steel Corporation 614 878-7271
555 Hilliard Rome Rd Columbus (43228) *(G-5116)*

Alro Steel Corporation 937 253-6121
821 Springfield St Dayton (45403) *(G-6196)*

Alro Steel Corporation 419 720-5300
3003 Airport Hwy Toledo (43609) *(G-14184)*

Alron 330 477-3405
805 Margo Dr Sw Strasburg (44680) *(G-13742)*

Als High Tech Inc (PA) 440 232-7090
135 Northfield Rd Bedford (44146) *(G-1099)*

Alsatian Llc 330 661-0600
985 Boardman Aly Medina (44256) *(G-10293)*

Alsco Meter 740 254-4500
260 Echo Rd Sw Gnadenhutten (44629) *(G-7984)*

Alsher APM 216 496-8288
7601 Detour Ave Cleveland (44103) *(G-3641)*

Alside Inc 419 865-0934
3510 Briarfield Blvd Maumee (43537) *(G-10161)*

Alside Supply Center, Cuyahoga Falls *Also Called: Associated Materials LLC (G-6069)*

Alstart Enterprises LLC 330 533-3222
451 W Main St Canfield (44406) *(G-1998)*

Alta Mira Corporation 330 648-2461
225 N Main St Spencer (44275) *(G-13479)*

Altec Industries 419 289-6066
1236 Township Road 1175 Ashland (44805) *(G-550)*

Altec Industries Inc 614 295-4895
1667 Watkins Rd Columbus (43207) *(G-5117)*

(PA)=Parent Co (HQ)=Headquarters (DH)=Div Headquarters

Altec Industries Inc... 205 408-2341
  307 Munroe Falls Ave Cuyahoga Falls (44221) *(G-6062)*
Altenloh Brinck & Co Inc... 419 636-6715
  2105 County Road 12c Bryan (43506) *(G-1805)*
Altenloh Brinck & Co US Inc (DH)............................... 419 636-6715
  2105 County Road 12c Bryan (43506) *(G-1806)*
Altenloh Brinck & Co US Inc.. 419 737-2381
  302 Clark St Pioneer (43554) *(G-12489)*
Altera Polymers LLC.. 864 973-7000
  222 S Sycamore St Jefferson (44047) *(G-8745)*
Alternate Defense LLC... 216 225-5889
  19101 Watercrest Ave Maple Heights (44137) *(G-9746)*
Alternative Flash Inc.. 330 334-6111
  1734 Wall Rd Ste B Wadsworth (44281) *(G-15018)*
Alternative Surface Grinding....................................... 330 273-3443
  1093 Industrial Pkwy N Brunswick (44212) *(G-1747)*
Alterntive Sltons Innvtion Dev, Dayton *Also Called: Asidaco LLC (G-6215)*
Alterra Energy LLC... 800 569-6061
  1200 E Waterloo Rd Akron (44306) *(G-56)*
Althar LLC... 216 408-9860
  5432 Broadway Ave Cleveland (44127) *(G-3642)*
Altier Brothers Inc... 740 347-4329
  155 Walnut St Corning (43730) *(G-5957)*
Altivia Petrochemicals LLC... 740 532-3420
  1019 Haverhill Ohio Furnace Rd Haverhill (45636) *(G-8308)*
Altivity Packaging, Middletown *Also Called: Graphic Packaging Intl LLC (G-10828)*
Altivity Packaging, Solon *Also Called: Graphic Packaging Intl LLC (G-13357)*
Altman, Sandra L, Dayton *Also Called: Past Patterns (G-6498)*
Alton Products Inc... 419 893-0201
  425 W Sophia St Maumee (43537) *(G-10162)*
Altraserv LLC.. 614 889-2500
  8495 Estates Ct Plain City (43064) *(G-12561)*
Altronic LLC (DH)... 330 545-9768
  712 Trumbull Ave Girard (44420) *(G-7960)*
Aluchem Inc (PA).. 513 733-8519
  1 Landy Ln Ste 1 Cincinnati (45215) *(G-2612)*
Aluchem of Jackson Inc.. 740 286-2455
  14782 Beaver Pike Jackson (45640) *(G-8708)*
Alufab, Cincinnati *Also Called: Alufab Inc (G-2551)*
Alufab Inc.. 513 528-7281
  1018 Seabrook Way Cincinnati (45245) *(G-2551)*
Alumetal Manufacturing Company............................. 419 268-2311
  4555 Sr 127 Coldwater (45828) *(G-4981)*
Aluminum Bearing Co of America.............................. 216 267-8560
  4775 W 139th St Cleveland (44135) *(G-3643)*
Aluminum Coating Manufacturers............................. 216 341-2000
  7301 Bessemer Ave Cleveland (44127) *(G-3644)*
Aluminum Color Industries Inc (PA).......................... 330 536-6295
  369 W Wood St Lowellville (44436) *(G-9510)*
Aluminum Extruded Shapes Inc................................. 513 563-2205
  10549 Reading Rd Cincinnati (45241) *(G-2613)*
Aluminum Extrusion Tech, Canfield *Also Called: Aluminum Extrusion Tech LLC (G-1999)*
Aluminum Extrusion Tech LLC................................... 330 533-3994
  6155 State Route 446 Canfield (44406) *(G-1999)*
Aluminum Line Products Company (PA).................... 440 835-8880
  24460 Sperry Cir Westlake (44145) *(G-15729)*
Alumo Extrusions and Mfg Co.................................... 330 779-3333
  3749 Mahoning Ave Ste 2 Youngstown (44515) *(G-16308)*
Alvin L Roepke... 419 862-3891
  329 Rice St Elmore (43416) *(G-7099)*
Alvito Custom Imprints LLC.. 614 207-1004
  726 E Lincoln Ave Columbus (43229) *(G-5118)*
Alwitco, North Royalton *Also Called: Allied Witan Company (G-11866)*
AM Castle & Co.. 330 425-7000
  26800 Miles Rd Bedford (44146) *(G-1100)*
AM Warren LLC... 330 841-2800
  2234 Main Ave. S.W. Warren (44481) *(G-15137)*
Amac Enterprises Inc.. 216 362-1880
  5925 W 130th St Cleveland (44130) *(G-3645)*
Amac Enterprises Inc (PA).. 216 362-1880
  5909 W 130th St Parma (44130) *(G-12286)*

Amaltech Inc... 440 248-7500
  30670 Bainbridge Rd Solon (44139) *(G-13311)*
Amanda Bent Bolt Company....................................... 740 385-6893
  1120 C I C Dr Logan (43138) *(G-9358)*
Amanda Manufacturing, Logan *Also Called: Amanda Bent Bolt Company (G-9358)*
Amani Vines LLC.. 440 335-5432
  3100 E 45th St Ste 512 Cleveland (44127) *(G-3646)*
Amano Cincinnati Incorporated.................................. 513 697-9000
  130 Commerce Dr Loveland (45140) *(G-9474)*
Amano USA Holdings Inc.. 973 403-1900
  130 Commerce Dr Loveland (45140) *(G-9475)*
Amantea Nonwovens LLC.. 513 842-6600
  6715 Steger Dr Cincinnati (45237) *(G-2614)*
Amarok Industries LLC.. 216 898-1948
  6895 Dogwood Cir Cleveland (44130) *(G-3647)*
Amaroq Inc.. 419 747-2110
  648 N Trimble Rd Mansfield (44906) *(G-9623)*
Amatech Inc.. 614 252-2506
  1633 Woodland Ave Columbus (43219) *(G-5119)*
Ambaflex Inc... 330 478-1858
  1530 Raff Rd Sw Canton (44710) *(G-2034)*
Ambrosia Inc... 419 825-3896
  395 W Airport Hwy Swanton (43558) *(G-13967)*
AMC, Wooster *Also Called: ABS Materials Inc (G-16094)*
Amcan Stair & Rail LLC... 937 781-3084
  20 Zischler St Springfield (45504) *(G-13532)*
Amclo, North Royalton *Also Called: Amclo Group Inc (G-11867)*
Amclo Group Inc.. 216 791-8400
  9721 York Alpha Dr North Royalton (44133) *(G-11867)*
Amco Products Inc.. 937 433-7982
  500 N Smithville Rd Dayton (45431) *(G-6152)*
Amcor Rigid Packaging Usa LLC............................... 419 483-4343
  975 W Main St Bellevue (44811) *(G-1221)*
Amcraft Inc.. 419 729-7900
  5144 Enterprise Blvd Toledo (43612) *(G-14185)*
Amcraft Manufacturing, Toledo *Also Called: Amcraft Inc (G-14185)*
AMD Fabricators Inc.. 440 946-8855
  4580 Beidler Rd Willoughby (44094) *(G-15875)*
AMD Plastics Inc (PA).. 216 289-4862
  27600 Lakeland Blvd Euclid (44132) *(G-7260)*
AMD Services... 614 571-7190
  6000 Buffalo Head Trl Dublin (43017) *(G-6859)*
AME Nutrition Ingredients, Columbus *Also Called: Kantner Ingredients Inc (G-5503)*
Ameco USA Met Fbrction Sltons................................. 440 899-9400
  4600 W 160th St Cleveland (44135) *(G-3648)*
Amelia Plastics... 513 386-4926
  3202 Marshall Dr Bldg 8 Amelia (45102) *(G-451)*
Amerascrew Inc.. 419 522-2232
  653 Lida St Mansfield (44903) *(G-9624)*
Ameri-Kart Corp... 800 232-0847
  1293 S Main St Akron (44301) *(G-57)*
American Advnced Assmblies LLC............................. 937 339-6267
  37 Harolds Way Troy (45373) *(G-14549)*
American Aero Components Llc................................. 937 367-5068
  2601 W Stroop Rd Ste 62 Dayton (45439) *(G-6197)*
American Agritech LLC.. 480 777-2000
  14111 Scottslawn Rd Marysville (43040) *(G-9904)*
American Airless Inc.. 614 552-0146
  7095 Americana Pkwy Reynoldsburg (43068) *(G-12751)*
American Alloy Corporation.. 216 642-9638
  9501 Allen Dr Cleveland (44125) *(G-3649)*
American Aluminum Extrusions.................................. 330 458-0300
  4416 Louisville St Ne Canton (44705) *(G-2035)*
American Augers, West Salem *Also Called: Charles Machine Works Inc (G-15633)*
American Awards Inc... 614 875-1850
  2380 Harrisburg Pike Grove City (43123) *(G-8077)*
American Axle & Mfg Inc... 330 863-7500
  3255 Alliance Rd Nw Malvern (44644) *(G-9608)*
American Axle & Mfg Inc... 330 868-5761
  461 Knox Ct Minerva (44657) *(G-11026)*
American Axle & Mfg Inc... 330 486-3200
  8001 Bavaria Rd Twinsburg (44087) *(G-14630)*

ALPHABETIC SECTION — American Manufacturing & Eqp

American Baler Co 419 483-5790
  800 E Center St Bellevue (44811) *(G-1222)*

American Belleville, Concord Township *Also Called: Zsi Manufacturing Inc (G-5915)*

American Bottling Company 330 733-3830
  1259 George Washington Blvd Akron (44312) *(G-58)*

American Bottling Company 513 381-4891
  125 E Court St Ste 820 Cincinnati (45202) *(G-2615)*

American Bottling Company 513 242-5151
  5151 Fischer Ave Cincinnati (45217) *(G-2616)*

American Bottling Company 614 237-4201
  960 Stelzer Rd Columbus (43219) *(G-5120)*

American Bottling Company 614 237-4201
  950 Stelzer Rd Columbus (43219) *(G-5121)*

American Bottling Company 937 236-0333
  3131 Transportation Rd Dayton (45404) *(G-6198)*

American Bottling Company 419 229-7777
  2350 Central Point Pkwy Lima (45804) *(G-9220)*

American Bottling Company 740 423-9230
  871 State Route 618 Little Hocking (45742) *(G-9333)*

American Bottling Company 740 922-5253
  Old Rte #250 Midvale (44653) *(G-10874)*

American Bottling Company 740 377-4371
  2531 County Road 1 South Point (45680) *(G-13465)*

American Bottling Company 419 535-0777
  224 N Byrne Rd Toledo (43607) *(G-14186)*

American Brass, Cleveland *Also Called: Empire Brass Co (G-4012)*

American Brass Mfg Co 216 431-6565
  5000 Superior Ave Cleveland (44103) *(G-3650)*

American Brick & Block, Dayton *Also Called: American Concrete Products Inc (G-6200)*

American Bronze Corporation 216 341-7800
  2941 Broadway Ave Cleveland (44115) *(G-3651)*

American Brzing Div Paulo Pdts, Willoughby *Also Called: Paulo Products Company (G-15969)*

American Buffing, Carlisle *Also Called: Qibco Buffing Pads Inc (G-2292)*

American Business Forms Inc 513 312-2522
  10000 International Blvd West Chester (45246) *(G-15535)*

American Canvas Products Inc 419 382-8450
  2925 South Ave Toledo (43609) *(G-14187)*

American Ceramic Society (PA) 614 890-4700
  550 Polaris Pkwy Ste 510 Westerville (43082) *(G-15647)*

American City Bus Journals Inc 513 337-9450
  120 E 4th St Ste 230 Cincinnati (45202) *(G-2617)*

American City Bus Journals Inc 937 528-4400
  40 N Main St Ste 810 Dayton (45423) *(G-6199)*

American Cnsld Ntral Rsrces In (PA) 740 338-3100
  46226 National Rd Saint Clairsville (43950) *(G-12894)*

American Coal Company 740 338-3334
  46226 National Rd Saint Clairsville (43950) *(G-12895)*

American Cold Forge LLC 419 836-1062
  5650 Woodville Rd Northwood (43619) *(G-11917)*

American Colors Inc (PA) 419 621-4000
  4602 Timber Commons Dr Sandusky (44870) *(G-13043)*

American Colorscans, Columbus *Also Called: West-Camp Press Inc (G-5872)*

American Colorscans Inc 614 895-0233
  5178 Sinclair Rd Columbus (43229) *(G-5122)*

American Community Newspapers 614 888-4567
  5255 Sinclair Rd Columbus (43229) *(G-5123)*

American Concrete Products Inc 937 224-1433
  1433 S Euclid Ave Dayton (45417) *(G-6200)*

American Confections Co LLC 614 888-8838
  90 Logan Pkwy Coventry Township (44319) *(G-6006)*

American Controls Inc 440 944-9735
  1340 Lloyd Rd Wickliffe (44092) *(G-15824)*

American Corrugated Products Inc 614 870-2000
  4700 Alkire Rd Columbus (43228) *(G-5124)*

American Coupler Systems, Kent *Also Called: ACS Industries Inc (G-8794)*

American Cube Mold Inc 330 558-0044
  1636 W 130th St Brunswick (44212) *(G-1748)*

American Culvert, Cambridge *Also Called: American Culvert & Fabg Co (G-1919)*

American Culvert & Fabg Co 740 432-6334
  201 Wheeling Ave Cambridge (43725) *(G-1919)*

American Custom Industries, Sylvania *Also Called: Bobbart Industries Inc (G-13991)*

American Custom Polishing, Cincinnati *Also Called: Charles J Meyers (G-2726)*

American De Rosa Lamparts LLC (HQ) 370 Falls Commerce Pkwy Cuyahoga Falls (44224) *(G-6063)*

American Diesel, Cleveland *Also Called: Interstate Diesel Service Inc (G-4233)*

American Egle Prprty Prsrvtion 855 440-6938
  39050 Center Ridge Rd North Ridgeville (44039) *(G-11828)*

American Electric Furnace Co, Cleveland *Also Called: A E F Inc (G-3578)*

American Energy Pdts Inc Ind, Mount Vernon *Also Called: Capital City Oil Inc (G-11266)*

American Fan, Fairfield *Also Called: FM AF LLC (G-7362)*

American Fan Company 513 874-2400
  2933 Symmes Rd Fairfield (45014) *(G-7333)*

American Fine Sinter Co Ltd 419 443-8880
  957 N County Road 11 Tiffin (44883) *(G-14075)*

American Fluid Power Inc 440 773-7462
  7407 Tattersall Dr Chesterland (44026) *(G-2479)*

American Fluid Power Inc 877 223-8742
  144 Reaser Ct Elyria (44035) *(G-7107)*

American Frame Corporation (PA) 419 893-5595
  400 Tomahawk Dr Maumee (43537) *(G-10163)*

American Gild of English Hndbe 937 438-0085
  201 E 5th St Cincinnati (45202) *(G-2618)*

American Greetings, Cleveland *Also Called: American Greetings Corporation (G-3652)*

American Greetings Corporation (HQ) 216 252-7300
  1 American Blvd Cleveland (44145) *(G-3652)*

American Health Packaging, Columbus *Also Called: Amerisource Health Svcs LLC (G-5131)*

American Heat Treating, Dayton *Also Called: Pride Investments LLC (G-6519)*

American Heritage Blld LLC 877 998-0908
  9248 Headlands Rd Mentor (44060) *(G-10413)*

American Highway Products LLC 330 874-3270
  11723 Strasburg Bolivar Rd Nw Bolivar (44612) *(G-1522)*

American Hvy Plate Sltions LLC 740 331-4620
  42722 State Route 7 Ste 12 Clarington (43915) *(G-3562)*

American Hydraulic Svcs Inc 606 739-8680
  1912 S 1st St Ironton (45638) *(G-8695)*

American Imprssions Sportswear 614 848-6677
  5523 Mercer St Columbus (43235) *(G-5125)*

American Imprssions Sportswear, Columbus *Also Called: American Imprssions Sportswear (G-5125)*

American Indus Maintenance 937 254-3400
  605 Springfield St Dayton (45403) *(G-6201)*

American Inks and Coatings Co 513 552-7200
  575 Quality Blvd Fairfield (45014) *(G-7334)*

American Insulation Tech LLC 513 733-4248
  6071 Branch Hill Guinea Pike Ste A Milford (45150) *(G-10892)*

American Ir Met Cleveland LLC 216 266-0509
  1240 Marquette St Cleveland (44114) *(G-3653)*

American Isostatic Presses Inc 614 497-3148
  1205 S Columbus Airport Rd Columbus (43207) *(G-5126)*

American Laser & Machine LLC 419 930-9303
  362 N Westwood Ave Toledo (43607) *(G-14188)*

American Lawyers Co Inc (PA) 440 333-5190
  853 Westpoint Pkwy Ste 710 Westlake (44145) *(G-15730)*

American Lawyers Quarterly, Westlake *Also Called: American Lawyers Co Inc (G-15730)*

American Led-Gible Inc 614 851-1100
  1776 Lone Eagle St Columbus (43228) *(G-5127)*

American Legal Publishing Corp 513 421-4248
  525 Vine St Ste 300 Cincinnati (45202) *(G-2619)*

American Light Metals LLC 330 908-3065
  635 Highland Rd E Macedonia (44056) *(G-9535)*

American Made Bags LLC 330 475-1385
  999 Sweitzer Akron (44311) *(G-59)*

American Made Corrugated Packg 937 981-2111
  1100 N 5th St Greenfield (45123) *(G-8027)*

American Made Fuels Inc 330 417-7663
  717 Warner Rd Se Canton (44707) *(G-2036)*

American Manufacturing Inc (PA) 419 531-9471
  2375 Dorr St Ste F Toledo (43607) *(G-14189)*

American Manufacturing & Eqp 513 829-2248
  4990 Factory Dr Fairfield (45014) *(G-7335)*

(PA)=Parent Co (HQ)=Headquarters (DH)=Div Headquarters

American Metal Coatings Inc   **ALPHABETIC SECTION**

American Metal Coatings Inc (PA) 216 451-3131
   7700 Tyler Blvd Mentor (44060) *(G-10414)*

American Metal Fabricating LLC 440 277-5600
   7516 W Ridge Rd Elyria (44035) *(G-7108)*

American Metal Fabricators, Dayton Also Called: Innovative Mech Systems LLC *(G-6164)*

American Metal Stamping Co LLC 216 531-3100
   20900 Saint Clair Ave Euclid (44117) *(G-7261)*

American Metal Treating Co 216 431-4492
   1043 E 62nd St Cleveland (44103) *(G-3654)*

American Micro Products Inc (PA) 513 732-2674
   4288 Armstrong Blvd Batavia (45103) *(G-908)*

American Mine Door, Cleveland Also Called: Zen Industries Inc *(G-4932)*

American Mnfctring Oprtons Inc 419 269-1560
   1931 E Manhattan Blvd Toledo (43608) *(G-14190)*

American Molded Plastics Inc 330 872-3838
   3876 Newton Falls Bailey Rd Newton Falls (44444) *(G-11652)*

American Molding Company Inc 330 620-6799
   711 Wooster Rd W Barberton (44203) *(G-854)*

American Office Services Inc 440 899-6888
   30257 Clemens Rd Ste C Westlake (44145) *(G-15731)*

American Orginal Bldg Pdts LLC 330 786-3000
   1000 Arlington Cir Akron (44306) *(G-60)*

American Orthopedics Inc (PA) 614 291-6454
   1151 W 5th Ave Columbus (43212) *(G-5128)*

American Paint Recyclers, Lima Also Called: Brinkman LLC *(G-9225)*

American Pan Company (PA) 937 652-3232
   417 E Water St Urbana (43078) *(G-14825)*

American Pan Company, Sunbury Also Called: Russell T Bundy Associates Inc *(G-13964)*

American Paper Group Inc 330 758-4545
   8401 Southern Blvd Youngstown (44512) *(G-16309)*

American Paper Products Co Div, Youngstown Also Called: American Paper Group Inc *(G-16309)*

American Plastech LLC 330 538-0576
   11635 Mahoning Ave North Jackson (44451) *(G-11777)*

American Plastic Tech Inc 440 632-5203
   15229 S State Ave Middlefield (44062) *(G-10731)*

American Plastics LLC 419 423-1213
   814 W Lima St Findlay (45840) *(G-7476)*

American Platinum Door LLC 440 497-6213
   30335 Solon Industrial Pkwy Solon (44139) *(G-13312)*

American Polymers Corporation (PA) 330 666-6048
   231 Springside Dr Ste 145 Akron (44333) *(G-61)*

American Posts LLC (PA) 419 720-0652
   810 Chicago St Toledo (43611) *(G-14191)*

American Power LLC 937 235-0418
   1819 Troy St Dayton (45404) *(G-6202)*

American Power Pull Corp 419 335-7050
   2022 S Defiance St Archbold (43502) *(G-520)*

American Precision Spindles 267 436-6000
   670 Alpha Dr Cleveland (44143) *(G-3655)*

American Printing Inc 330 630-1121
   1121 Tower Dr Akron (44305) *(G-62)*

American Printing & Lithog Co (PA) 513 867-0602
   528 S 7th St Hamilton (45011) *(G-8177)*

American Pro-Mold Inc 330 336-4111
   350 State St # 7 Wadsworth (44281) *(G-15019)*

American Products, Waterville Also Called: Duvall Woodworking Inc *(G-15242)*

American Publishers, Huron Also Called: American Publishers LLC *(G-8626)*

American Publishers LLC 419 626-0623
   2401 Sawmill Pkwy Huron (44839) *(G-8626)*

American Punch Co 216 731-4501
   1655 Century Corners Pkwy Euclid (44132) *(G-7262)*

American Quality Door Co 330 296-0393
   6193 Courtesy Blvd Ravenna (44266) *(G-12705)*

American Quality Stripping Inc 419 625-6288
   1750 5th St Sandusky (44870) *(G-13044)*

American Quicksilver Company 513 871-4517
   646 Rushton Rd Cincinnati (45226) *(G-2620)*

American Ramp Systems 440 336-4988
   4327 Coe Ave North Olmsted (44070) *(G-11816)*

American Regent Inc 614 436-2222
   960 Crupper Ave Columbus (43229) *(G-5129)*

American Regent Inc 614 436-2222
   4150 Lyman Dr Hilliard (43026) *(G-8397)*

American Regent Inc 614 436-2222
   6610 New Albany Rd E New Albany (43054) *(G-11365)*

American Rescue Technology Inc 937 293-6240
   2780 Culver Ave Dayton (45429) *(G-6203)*

American Rodpump Ltd 440 987-9457
   5201 Indian Hill Rd Dublin (43017) *(G-6860)*

American Roll Formed Pdts Corp (DH) 440 352-0753
   3805 Hendricks Rd Ste A Youngstown (44515) *(G-16310)*

American Rubber Pdts Co Inc 440 461-0900
   30775 Solon Industrial Pkwy Solon (44139) *(G-13313)*

American Rugged Enclosures Inc (PA) 513 942-3004
   4 Standen Dr Hamilton (45015) *(G-8178)*

American Sand & Gravel Div, Massillon Also Called: Kenmore Construction Co Inc *(G-10116)*

American Scientific LLC 614 764-9002
   6420 Fiesta Dr Columbus (43235) *(G-5130)*

American Solutions For Bus, West Chester Also Called: American Business Forms Inc *(G-15535)*

American Solving Inc 440 234-7373
   6519 Eastland Rd Ste 5 Brookpark (44142) *(G-1703)*

American Spring Wire Corp (PA) 216 292-4620
   26300 Miles Rd Bedford Heights (44146) *(G-1163)*

American Standard Brands, Mansfield Also Called: As America Inc *(G-9626)*

American Steel & Alloys LLC 330 847-0487
   4000 Mahoning Ave Nw Warren (44483) *(G-15138)*

American Steel Assod Pdts Inc 419 531-9471
   2375 Dorr St Ste F Toledo (43607) *(G-14192)*

American Steel Grave Vault Co 419 468-6715
   799 Newberry Dr Galion (44833) *(G-7860)*

American Steel LLC 330 482-4299
   326 Blueberry Dr Columbiana (44408) *(G-5027)*

American Steel Treating Inc 419 874-2044
   29200 Glenwood Rd Perrysburg (43551) *(G-12361)*

American Sterilizer Company (PA) 440 392-8328
   5960 Heisley Rd Mentor (44060) *(G-10415)*

American Stirrup, Holmesville Also Called: Holmes Wheel Shop Inc *(G-8548)*

American Stirways Cstm Railing 513 367-6700
   2991 Triplecrown Dr North Bend (45052) *(G-11703)*

American Tank & Fabricating Co (PA) 216 252-1500
   12314 Elmwood Ave Cleveland (44111) *(G-3656)*

American Tchnical Coatings Inc 440 401-2270
   28045 Ranney Pkwy Ste H Westlake (44145) *(G-15732)*

American Thermal Instrs Inc (PA) 937 429-2114
   2400 E River Rd Moraine (45439) *(G-11156)*

American Tool & Manufacturing, Mansfield Also Called: American Tool & Mfg Co *(G-9625)*

American Tool & Mfg Co 419 522-2452
   211 Newman St Mansfield (44902) *(G-9625)*

American Tool and Die Inc 419 726-5394
   2024 Champlain St Toledo (43611) *(G-14193)*

American Tool Works Inc 513 844-6363
   160 Hancock Ave Hamilton (45011) *(G-8179)*

American Tower, Shelby Also Called: Amto Acquisition Corp *(G-13190)*

American Trim, Lima Also Called: Superior Metal Products Inc *(G-9294)*

American Trim LLC (HQ) 419 228-1145
   1005 W Grand Ave Lima (45801) *(G-9221)*

American Trim LLC 419 228-1145
   1501 Michigan St Ste 1 Sidney (45365) *(G-13220)*

American Trim LLC 419 739-4349
   217 Krein Ave Wapakoneta (45895) *(G-15105)*

American Turf Recycling LLC 440 323-0306
   860 Taylor St Elyria (44035) *(G-7109)*

American Ultra Specialties Inc 330 656-5000
   6855 Industrial Pkwy Hudson (44236) *(G-8584)*

American Veneer Edgebanding Co 740 928-2700
   1700 James Pkwy Heath (43056) *(G-8316)*

American Water Services Inc 440 243-9840
   17449 W Sprague Rd Strongsville (44136) *(G-13806)*

American Way Exteriors LLC 937 221-8860
   7666 Mcewen Rd Dayton (45459) *(G-6204)*

American Way Manufacturing Inc 330 824-2353
   1871 Henn Pkwy Sw Warren (44481) *(G-15139)*

ALPHABETIC SECTION

American Wire & Cable Company (PA) 440 235-1140
7951 Bronson Rd Olmsted Twp (44138) *(G-12085)*

American Wire Shapes LLC 330 744-2905
81 S Bridge St Struthers (44471) *(G-13899)*

American Wood Fibers Inc 740 420-3233
2500 Owens Rd Circleville (43113) *(G-3541)*

American Wood Reface Inc (PA) 440 944-3750
854 Medina Rd Medina (44256) *(G-10294)*

Americana Development Inc 330 633-3278
342 West Ave Tallmadge (44278) *(G-14022)*

Americana Glass Co Inc 330 938-6135
356 E Maryland Ave Sebring (44672) *(G-13116)*

Americas Best Cstm Digitizing, Xenia Also Called: Alphabet Embroidery Studios *(G-16248)*

Americas Components, Springfield Also Called: Konecranes Inc *(G-13589)*

Americas Mdular Off Specialist 614 277-0216
4423 Broadway Ste A Grove City (43123) *(G-8078)*

Americas Styrenics LLC 740 302-8667
925 County Road 1a Ironton (45638) *(G-8696)*

Americhem, Cuyahoga Falls Also Called: Americhem Inc *(G-6065)*

Americhem Inc (PA) 330 929-4213
2000 Americhem Way Cuyahoga Falls (44221) *(G-6064)*

Americhem Inc 330 926-3185
155 E Steels Corners Rd Cuyahoga Falls (44224) *(G-6065)*

Americlean 2 LLC 216 781-3720
2061 Gehring Ave Cleveland (44113) *(G-3657)*

Americraft Bronze Co, Waterville Also Called: Maumee Valley Memorials Inc *(G-15250)*

Americraft Carton Inc 419 668-1006
201 Republic St Norwalk (44857) *(G-11954)*

Americraft Mfg Co Inc 513 489-1047
7937 School Rd Cincinnati (45249) *(G-2621)*

Amerihua Intl Entps Inc 740 549-0300
707 Radio Dr Lewis Center (43035) *(G-9148)*

Amerimold Inc 800 950-8020
595 Waterloo Rd Ste A Mogadore (44260) *(G-11066)*

Amerimulch, Independence Also Called: Chromascape LLC *(G-8658)*

Amerisource Health Svcs LLC 614 492-8177
2550 John Glenn Ave Ste A Columbus (43217) *(G-5131)*

Ameritech Publishing Inc 614 895-6123
2550 Corporate Exchange Dr Ste 310 Columbus (43231) *(G-5132)*

Ameritech Publishing Inc 330 896-6037
1530 Corporate Woods Pkwy Ste 100 Uniontown (44685) *(G-14780)*

Ameriwater LLC 937 461-8833
3345 Stop 8 Rd Dayton (45414) *(G-6205)*

Ameriwood Industries, Tiffin Also Called: Dorel Home Furnishings Inc *(G-14083)*

Amerix Ntra-Pharmaceutical Inc 567 204-7756
904 N Cable Rd Lima (45805) *(G-9222)*

Ames Companies Inc 740 783-2535
21460 Ames Ln Dexter City (45727) *(G-6801)*

Ametco Manufacturing Corp 440 951-4300
4326 Hamann Pkwy Willoughby (44094) *(G-15876)*

Ametek Inc 937 440-0800
66 Industry Ct Ste F Troy (45373) *(G-14550)*

Ametek Electromechanical Group, Kent Also Called: Ametek Tchnical Indus Pdts Inc *(G-8799)*

Ametek HDR Power Systems, Worthington Also Called: HDR Power Systems LLC *(G-16196)*

Ametek Micro-Poise Measurement, Streetsboro Also Called: Micro-Pise Msrment Systems LLC *(G-13779)*

Ametek Presto Light Power, Troy Also Called: Ametek Inc *(G-14550)*

Ametek Solidstate Controls, Columbus Also Called: Solidstate Controls LLC *(G-5775)*

Ametek Tchnical Indus Pdts Inc (HQ) 330 673-3451
100 E Erie St Ste 130 Kent (44240) *(G-8799)*

Amex Dies Inc 330 545-9766
932 N State St Girard (44420) *(G-7961)*

AMF Burns 330 650-6500
1797 Georgetown Rd Hudson (44236) *(G-8585)*

Amfm Inc 440 953-4545
38373 Pelton Rd Willoughby (44094) *(G-15877)*

AMG Aluminum, Cambridge Also Called: AMG Aluminum North America LLC *(G-1920)*

AMG Aluminum North America LLC (HQ) 659 348-3620
60790 Southgate Rd Cambridge (43725) *(G-1920)*

AMG Industries Inc 740 397-4044
300 Commerce Dr Mount Vernon (43050) *(G-11260)*

AMG Industries LLC 740 397-4044
200 Commerce Dr Mount Vernon (43050) *(G-11261)*

AMG Products LLC 614 507-7749
1375 Newark Rd Mount Vernon (43050) *(G-11262)*

AMG Trailer and Equipment, Akron Also Called: Martin Allen Trailer LLC *(G-238)*

Amh Holdings II Inc 330 929-1811
3773 State Rd Cuyahoga Falls (44223) *(G-6066)*

Amherst Party Shop, Amherst Also Called: Currier Richard & James *(G-474)*

Amidac Wind, Elyria Also Called: Amidac Wind Corporation *(G-7110)*

Amidac Wind Corporation 213 973-4000
151 Innovation Dr Elyria (44035) *(G-7110)*

Amir Foods Inc 440 646-9388
761 Beta Dr Ste A Cleveland (44143) *(G-3658)*

Amir International Foods Inc 614 332-1742
3504 Broadway Grove City (43123) *(G-8079)*

Amish Country Soap Co 866 687-1724
4826 E Main St Berlin (44610) *(G-1302)*

Amish Country Soaps & Sundries, Berlin Also Called: Amish Country Soap Co *(G-1302)*

Amish Door Inc (PA) 330 359-5464
1210 Winesburg St Wilmot (44689) *(G-16065)*

Amish Door Restaurant, Wilmot Also Called: Amish Door Inc *(G-16065)*

Amish Heritg WD Floors & Furn, Middlefield Also Called: Cherokee Hardwoods Inc *(G-10741)*

Amish Wedding Foods Inc 330 674-9199
316 S Mad Anthony St Millersburg (44654) *(G-10941)*

Amko Service Company (DH) 330 364-8857
3211 Brightwood Rd Midvale (44653) *(G-10875)*

Amko Service Company, Midvale Also Called: Fiba Technologies Inc *(G-10877)*

Aml Industries Inc 330 399-5000
520 Pine Ave Se Ste 1 Warren (44483) *(G-15140)*

Amon Inc 513 734-1700
3214 Marshall Dr Amelia (45102) *(G-452)*

Amos Media Company (PA) 937 638-0967
1660 Campbell Rd Ste A Sidney (45365) *(G-13221)*

AMP Plastics of Ohio LLC
1815 Magda Dr Montpelier (43543) *(G-11134)*

Ampac, Cincinnati Also Called: Ampac Packaging LLC *(G-2623)*

Ampac, Cincinnati Also Called: Ampac Plastics LLC *(G-2624)*

Ampac Holdings LLC (HQ) 513 671-1777
12025 Tricon Rd Cincinnati (45246) *(G-2622)*

Ampac Packaging LLC (HQ) 513 671-1777
12025 Tricon Rd Cincinnati (45246) *(G-2623)*

Ampac Plastics LLC 513 671-1777
12025 Tricon Rd Cincinnati (45246) *(G-2624)*

Ampacet Corp 513 247-5403
4705 Duke Dr Ste 400 Mason (45040) *(G-9949)*

Ampacet Corporation 513 247-5400
4705 Duke Dr # 400 Cincinnati (45249) *(G-2625)*

Ampacet Corporation 740 929-5521
1855 James Pkwy Newark (43056) *(G-11561)*

Ampex Metal Products Company (PA) 216 267-9242
5581 W 164th St Brookpark (44142) *(G-1704)*

Ampp, Perrysburg Also Called: Ampp Incorporated *(G-12362)*

Ampp Incorporated 419 666-4747
28271 Cedar Park Blvd Ste 5 Perrysburg (43551) *(G-12362)*

Ampsco Division 614 444-2181
2301 Fairwood Ave Columbus (43207) *(G-5133)*

Amptech Machining & Welding 419 652-3444
910 County Road 40 Nova (44859) *(G-12002)*

Amresco, LLC, Solon Also Called: VWR Part of Avantor *(G-13445)*

Amrican Spring Wire, Bedford Heights Also Called: Aswpengg LLC *(G-1164)*

Amrod Bridge & Iron LLC
105 Ohio Ave Mc Donald (44437) *(G-10276)*

Amros Industries Inc 216 433-0010
14701 Industrial Pkwy Cleveland (44135) *(G-3659)*

AMS, Strongsville Also Called: Automated Mfg Solutions Inc *(G-13812)*

AMS Global Ltd 937 620-1036
119 E Dayton St West Alexandria (45381) *(G-15339)*

Amsive OH LLC 937 885-8000
3303 W Tech Blvd Miamisburg (45342) *(G-10611)*

Amsoil Inc 614 274-9851
3389 Urbancrest Industrial Dr Urbancrest (43123) *(G-14852)*

Amsted Industries Incorporated 614 836-2323
3900 Bixby Rd Groveport (43125) *(G-8129)*

Amt, Brecksville *Also Called: Applied Medical Technology Inc (G-1606)*

Amt Machine Systems Limited 740 965-2693
1760 Zollinger Rd Ste 2 Columbus (43221) *(G-5134)*

Amt Machine Systems Ltd 614 635-8050
50 W Broad St Ste 1200 Columbus (43215) *(G-5135)*

Amtank Armor 440 268-7735
22555 Ascoa Ct Strongsville (44149) *(G-13807)*

Amtekco, Columbus *Also Called: Amtekco Industries LLC (G-5136)*

Amtekco Industries LLC (HQ) 614 228-6590
2300 Lockbourne Rd Columbus (43207) *(G-5136)*

Amtekco Industries Inc 614 228-6525
33 W Hinman Ave Columbus (43207) *(G-5137)*

AMTEKCO INDUSTRIES INC, Columbus *Also Called: Amtekco Industries Inc (G-5137)*

Amthor Steel Inc 330 759-0200
5019 Belmont Ave Youngstown (44505) *(G-16311)*

Amto Acquisition Corp 419 347-1185
5085 State Route 39 W Shelby (44875) *(G-13190)*

Amy Electric 740 349-9484
46 N 4th St Newark (43055) *(G-11562)*

Amy Industries Inc 440 942-3478
8790 Twinbrook Rd Mentor (44060) *(G-10416)*

Amylin Ohio 512 592-8710
8814 Trade Port Dr West Chester (45011) *(G-15364)*

Anadem Inc 614 262-2539
3620 N High St Ste 201 Columbus (43214) *(G-5138)*

Anaheim Manufacturing Company 800 767-6293
25300 Al Moen Dr North Olmsted (44070) *(G-11817)*

Analiza Inc (PA) 216 432-9050
3615 Superior Ave E Ste 4407b Cleveland (44114) *(G-3660)*

Analytica Usa Inc (PA) 513 348-2333
711 E Monument Ave Ste 309 Dayton (45402) *(G-6206)*

Ananda Anani LLC 440 406-6086
1769 E Waterford Ct Apt 912 Akron (44313) *(G-63)*

Anatomical Concepts Inc 330 757-3569
1399 E Western Reserve Rd Youngstown (44514) *(G-16312)*

Anchi Inc 740 653-2527
1115 W 5th Ave Lancaster (43130) *(G-8986)*

Anchor Die Technologies, Cleveland *Also Called: Condor Tool & Die Inc (G-3895)*

Anchor Fabricators Inc 937 836-5117
386 Talmadge Rd Clayton (45315) *(G-3563)*

Anchor Flange Company (PA) 513 527-3512
5553 Murray Ave Cincinnati (45227) *(G-2626)*

Anchor Fluid Power, Cincinnati *Also Called: Anchor Flange Company (G-2626)*

Anchor Glass Container Corp 740 452-2743
1206 Brandywine Blvd Ste C Zanesville (43701) *(G-16500)*

Anchor Hocking, Lancaster *Also Called: Anchi Inc (G-8986)*

Anchor Hocking LLC (HQ) 740 687-2500
1600 Dublin Rd Ste 200 Columbus (43215) *(G-5139)*

Anchor Hocking Company, The, Columbus *Also Called: Anchor Hocking LLC (G-5139)*

Anchor Hocking Consmr GL Corp 740 653-2527
1115 W 5th Ave Lancaster (43130) *(G-8987)*

Anchor Hocking Corporation 614 633-4247
1600 Dublin Rd Columbus (43215) *(G-5140)*

Anchor Hocking Glass Company 740 681-6025
1115 W 5th Ave Lancaster (43130) *(G-8988)*

Anchor Hocking Glass Corp PA 740 681-6275
519 N Pierce Ave Lancaster (43130) *(G-8989)*

Anchor Hocking Holdings Inc (PA) 740 687-2500
1600 Dublin Rd Ste 200 Columbus (43215) *(G-5141)*

Anchor Hocking Indus GL Div, Lancaster *Also Called: Ghp II LLC (G-9017)*

Anchor Industries Incorporated 440 473-1414
30775 Solon Industrial Pkwy Cleveland (44139) *(G-3661)*

Anchor Manufacturing Group, Cleveland *Also Called: Anchor Tool & Die Co (G-3664)*

Anchor Metal Processing Inc 216 362-6463
12200 Brookpark Rd Cleveland (44130) *(G-3662)*

Anchor Metal Processing Inc (PA) 216 362-1850
11830 Brookpark Rd Cleveland (44130) *(G-3663)*

Anchor Pattern Company 614 443-2221
748 Frebis Ave Columbus (43206) *(G-5142)*

Anchor Tool & Die Co 216 362-1850
12200 Brookpark Rd Cleveland (44130) *(G-3664)*

Ancom Business Products, Medina *Also Called: Symatic Inc (G-10381)*

Andal Woodworking 330 897-8059
1411 Township Road 151 Baltic (43804) *(G-833)*

Andeen-Hagerling Inc 440 349-0370
31200 Bainbridge Rd Ste 2 Cleveland (44139) *(G-3665)*

Andelyn Biosciences Inc (HQ) 844 228-2366
1180 Arthur E Adams Dr Columbus (43221) *(G-5143)*

Andelyn Biosciences Inc 614 332-0554
5185 Blazer Pkwy Dublin (43017) *(G-6861)*

Andelyn Development Center, Dublin *Also Called: Andelyn Biosciences Inc (G-6861)*

Anderson & Vreeland Inc 419 636-5002
15348 Us Highway 127 Ew Bryan (43506) *(G-1807)*

Anderson Brothers Entps Inc 440 269-3920
38180 Airport Pkwy Willoughby (44094) *(G-15878)*

Anderson Concrete Corp 614 443-0123
400 Frank Rd Columbus (43207) *(G-5144)*

Anderson Door Co 216 475-5700
18090 Miles Rd Cleveland (44128) *(G-3666)*

Anderson Energy Inc 740 678-8608
12959 State Route 550 Fleming (45729) *(G-7585)*

Anderson Glass Co Inc 614 476-4877
2816 Morse Rd Columbus (43231) *(G-5145)*

Anderson Graphics Inc 330 745-2165
711 Wooster Rd W Barberton (44203) *(G-855)*

Anderson International Corp 216 641-1112
4545 Boyce Pkwy Stow (44224) *(G-13684)*

Anderson Pallet & Packg Inc 937 962-2614
210 Western Ave Lewisburg (45338) *(G-9185)*

Anderson Pallet Service, Lewisburg *Also Called: Anderson Pallet & Packg Inc (G-9185)*

Anderson Vreeland Midwest, Bryan *Also Called: Anderson & Vreeland Inc (G-1807)*

Andersons Inc 419 891-2930
415 Illinois Ave Maumee (43537) *(G-10164)*

Andersons Inc (PA) 419 893-5050
1947 Briarfield Blvd Maumee (43537) *(G-10165)*

Andersons Inc 419 536-0460
801 S Reynolds Rd Toledo (43615) *(G-14194)*

Andersons Mrathon Holdings LLC 937 316-3700
5728 Sebring Warner Rd N Greenville (45331) *(G-8036)*

Andersons, The, Maumee *Also Called: Andersons Inc (G-10165)*

Andersound PA Service 216 401-4631
15911 Harvard Ave Cleveland (44128) *(G-3667)*

Andre Corporation 574 293-0207
4600 N Mason Montgomery Rd Mason (45040) *(G-9950)*

Andrew M Farnham 419 298-4300
2112 County Road C60 Edgerton (43517) *(G-7071)*

Andrin Enterprises Inc 937 276-7794
3350 Kettering Blvd Moraine (45439) *(G-11157)*

Andritz Inc 513 677-5620
6680 Miami Woods Dr Loveland (45140) *(G-9476)*

Androm Industries Inc 614 408-9067
9960 Butler Rd Newark (43055) *(G-11563)*

Andy McGough Tom Vantassel, Gambier *Also Called: Ghost Logging LLC (G-7906)*

Andys Mdterranean Fd Pdts LLC 513 281-9791
906 Nassau St Cincinnati (45206) *(G-2627)*

Anest Iwata Americas Inc 513 755-3100
9525 Glades Dr West Chester (45011) *(G-15365)*

Anest Iwata Usa Inc 513 755-3100
10148 Commerce Park Dr West Chester (45246) *(G-15536)*

Angels Landing Inc 513 687-3681
3430 S Dixie Dr Ste 301 Moraine (45439) *(G-11158)*

Angels Uniform & Print Sp LLC 330 707-6506
840 Woodford Ave Youngstown (44511) *(G-16313)*

Angleboard, Loveland *Also Called: Signode Industrial Group LLC (G-9505)*

Angstrom Fiber Englewood LLC (PA) 734 756-1164
300 Lau Pkwy Englewood (45315) *(G-7223)*

Angstrom Graphics Inc (PA) 216 271-5300
4437 E 49th St Cleveland (44125) *(G-3668)*

Angstrom Graphics Inc Midwest (HQ)..................216 271-5300
4437 E 49th St Cleveland (44125) *(G-3669)*

Angstrom Precision Metals LLC..........................440 255-6700
8229 Tyler Blvd Mentor (44060) *(G-10417)*

Anheuser-Busch, Canton Also Called: Anheuser-Busch LLC *(G-2037)*

Anheuser-Busch, Columbus Also Called: Anheuser-Busch LLC *(G-5146)*

Anheuser-Busch LLC..330 438-2036
1611 Marietta Ave Se Canton (44707) *(G-2037)*

Anheuser-Busch LLC..614 847-6213
700 Schrock Rd Columbus (43229) *(G-5146)*

Anime Palace...408 858-1918
8185 Green Meadows Dr N Ste M Lewis Center (43035) *(G-9149)*

Ankim Enterprises Incorporated..........................937 599-1121
2005 Campbell Rd Sidney (45365) *(G-13222)*

Annarino Foods Ltd...937 274-3663
2787 Armstrong Ln Dayton (45414) *(G-6207)*

Annin & Co..740 498-5008
100 State Route 258 Newcomerstown (43832) *(G-11642)*

Annin & Co Inc..740 622-4447
700 S 3rd St Coshocton (43812) *(G-5968)*

ANNIN & CO., Newcomerstown Also Called: Annin & Co *(G-11642)*

Anodizing Specialists Inc...................................440 951-0257
7547 Tyler Blvd Mentor (44060) *(G-10418)*

Anomatic Corporation (DH)................................740 522-2203
8880 Innovation Campus Way New Albany (43054) *(G-11366)*

Anomatic Corporation..740 522-2203
1650 Tamarack Rd Newark (43055) *(G-11564)*

Anomatic Opportunity, New Albany Also Called: Anomatic Corporation *(G-11366)*

Ansco Machine Company....................................330 929-8181
60 Cuyahoga Falls Industrial Pkwy Peninsula (44264) *(G-12338)*

Ansell Edmont Div, Coshocton Also Called: Ansell Healthcare Products LLC *(G-5969)*

Ansell Healthcare Products LLC.........................740 622-4369
925 Chestnut St Coshocton (43812) *(G-5969)*

Ansell Healthcare Products LLC.........................740 622-4311
925 Chestnut St Coshocton (43812) *(G-5970)*

Antero Resources Corporation............................303 357-7310
44510 Marietta Rd Caldwell (43724) *(G-1906)*

Antero Resources Corporation............................740 760-1000
27841 State Route 7 Marietta (45750) *(G-9775)*

Anthe Machine Works Inc...................................859 431-1035
2 Locust Hill Rd Cincinnati (45245) *(G-2552)*

Anthony Business Forms Inc...............................937 253-0072
3160 Plainfield Rd Dayton (45432) *(G-6153)*

Anthony Flottemesch & Son Inc..........................513 561-1212
8201 Camargo Rd Ste 1 Cincinnati (45243) *(G-2628)*

Anthony Mining Co Inc.......................................740 282-5301
72 Airport Rd Wintersville (43953) *(G-16084)*

Anthony W Hilderbrant......................................740 682-1035
1701 Monroe Hollow Rd Oak Hill (45656) *(G-12016)*

Anthony-Thomas Candy Company (PA)..............614 274-8405
1777 Arlingate Ln Columbus (43228) *(G-5147)*

Anthony-Thomas Candy Shoppes, Columbus Also Called: Anthony-Thomas Candy Company *(G-5147)*

Antique Auto Sheet Metal Inc.............................937 833-4422
718 Albert Rd Brookville (45309) *(G-1729)*

Antwerp Tool & Die Inc.......................................419 258-5271
3167 County Road 424 Antwerp (45813) *(G-491)*

Anza Inc..513 542-7337
3265 Colerain Ave Ste 2 Cincinnati (45225) *(G-2629)*

Aog Inc...937 436-2412
7672 Mcewen Rd Dayton (45459) *(G-6208)*

Aot Inc..937 323-9669
4800 Gateway Blvd Springfield (45502) *(G-13533)*

AP Direct, Mentor Also Called: Activities Press Inc *(G-10404)*

AP Services LLC..216 267-3200
18001 Sheldon Rd Middleburg Heights (44130) *(G-10715)*

AP Tech Group Inc...513 761-8111
5130 Rialto Rd West Chester (45069) *(G-15366)*

Apache Acquisitions LLC...................................419 782-8003
1008 Jackson Ave Defiance (43512) *(G-6669)*

Apeks LLC..740 809-1174
31 Greenscape Ct Johnstown (43031) *(G-8769)*

Apeks Supercritical, Johnstown Also Called: Apeks LLC *(G-8769)*

Apera Instruments LLC......................................614 285-3080
6656 Busch Blvd Columbus (43229) *(G-5148)*

Apex Advanced Technologies LLC......................216 898-1595
4857 W 130th St A Cleveland (44135) *(G-3670)*

Apex Aluminum Die Cast Co Inc..........................937 773-0432
8877 Sherry Dr Piqua (45356) *(G-12503)*

Apex Bag Company, Wapakoneta Also Called: Brady Ruck Company *(G-15108)*

Apex Bag Company, Wapakoneta Also Called: Gateway Packaging Company LLC *(G-15114)*

Apex Bolt & Machine Company...........................419 729-3741
5324 Enterprise Blvd Toledo (43612) *(G-14195)*

Apex Bulk Handlers, Bedford Also Called: Apex Welding Incorporated *(G-1101)*

Apex Control Systems Inc..................................330 938-2588
751 N Johnson Rd Sebring (44672) *(G-13117)*

Apex Metal Fabricating & Mch, Toledo Also Called: Apex Bolt & Machine Company *(G-14195)*

Apex Metals, Cleveland Also Called: Erieview Metal Treating Co *(G-4029)*

Apex Signs Inc..330 952-2626
2755 Medina Rd Medina (44256) *(G-10295)*

Apex Specialty Co Inc..330 725-6663
620 E Smith Rd Ste E7 Medina (44256) *(G-10296)*

Apex Tool Group LLC...937 222-7871
762 W Stewart St Dayton (45417) *(G-6209)*

Apex Welding Incorporated................................440 232-6770
1 Industry Dr Bedford (44146) *(G-1101)*

Apf Legacy Subs LLC (DH).................................513 682-7173
9990 Princeton Glendale Rd West Chester (45246) *(G-15537)*

Apg Media of Ohio, Athens Also Called: Adams Publishing Group LLC *(G-673)*

API Pattern Works Inc..440 269-1766
4456 Hamann Pkwy Willoughby (44094) *(G-15879)*

Apogee Plastics Corp...937 864-1966
8300 Dayton Springfield Rd Fairborn (45324) *(G-7310)*

Apollo GL Mirror Win Screen Co, Cincinnati Also Called: Dale Kestler *(G-2817)*

Apollo Manufacturing Co LLC.............................440 951-9972
7911 Enterprise Dr Mentor (44060) *(G-10419)*

Apollo Plastic, Mentor Also Called: Skribs Tool and Die Inc *(G-10555)*

Apollo Plastics Inc...440 951-7774
7555 Tyler Blvd Ste 11 Mentor (44060) *(G-10420)*

Apollo Products Inc...440 269-8551
4456 Hamann Pkwy Willoughby (44094) *(G-15880)*

Apollo Welding & Fabg Inc (PA).........................440 942-0227
35600 Curtis Blvd Willoughby (44095) *(G-15881)*

Apowermedia, Dayton Also Called: American Power LLC *(G-6202)*

Appalachia Freeze Dry Co LLC............................740 412-0169
659 Jackson St Richmond Dale (45673) *(G-12804)*

Appalachian Fuels LLC (PA)...............................606 928-0460
6375 Riverside Dr Ste 200 Dublin (43017) *(G-6862)*

Appalachian Oilfield Svcs LLC............................337 216-0066
34602 State Route 7 Sardis (43946) *(G-13110)*

Appalachian Solvents LLC.................................740 680-3649
5041 Skyline Dr Cambridge (43725) *(G-1921)*

Appalachian Well Surveys Inc............................740 255-7652
10291 Ohio Ave Cambridge (43725) *(G-1922)*

Appetzers R US St Eats 2 Go LL.........................937 460-1470
2019 Ontario Ave Springfield (45505) *(G-13534)*

Apph, Strongsville Also Called: Apph Wichita Inc *(G-13808)*

Apph Wichita Inc...316 943-5752
15900 Foltz Pkwy Strongsville (44149) *(G-13808)*

Appian Manufacturing Corp................................614 445-2230
2025 Camaro Ave Columbus (43207) *(G-5149)*

Apple, Cincinnati Also Called: Apple of His Eye Inc *(G-2630)*

Apple, Lewis Center Also Called: Apple & Apple LLC *(G-9150)*

Apple & Apple LLC...740 972-2209
1767 Westwood Dr Lewis Center (43035) *(G-9150)*

Apple of His Eye Inc..513 521-0655
796 Denier Pl Cincinnati (45224) *(G-2630)*

Appleheart, Miamisburg Also Called: Appleheart Inc *(G-10612)*

Appleheart Inc..937 384-0430
2240 E Central Ave Miamisburg (45342) *(G-10612)*

Application Link Incorporated............................614 934-1735
4449 Easton Way Fl 2 Columbus (43219) *(G-5150)*

ALPHABETIC SECTION

Applied Automation Entp Inc.................................. 419 929-2428
  24 Cedar St New London (44851) *(G-11460)*
Applied Bingo Mate, Willoughby *Also Called: Applied Concepts Inc (G-15882)*
Applied Collegiate Systems Div, Hudson *Also Called: Griffin Technology Inc (G-8594)*
Applied Concepts Inc... 440 229-5033
  36445 Biltmore Pl Ste E Willoughby (44094) *(G-15882)*
Applied Energy Tech Inc....................................... 419 537-9052
  1720 Indian Wood Cir Ste E Maumee (43537) *(G-10166)*
Applied Engneered Surfaces Inc.............................. 440 366-0440
  535 Ternes Ln Rear Elyria (44035) *(G-7111)*
Applied Experience LLC....................................... 614 943-2970
  7780 Corporate Blvd Plain City (43064) *(G-12562)*
Applied Marketing Services Inc (HQ)........................ 440 716-9962
  28825 Ranney Pkwy Westlake (44145) *(G-15733)*
Applied Materials Finshg Ltd.................................. 330 336-5645
  1040 Valley Belt Rd Brooklyn Heights (44131) *(G-1682)*
Applied Medical Technology Inc............................... 440 717-4000
  8006 Katherine Blvd Brecksville (44141) *(G-1606)*
Applied Metals Tech Ltd....................................... 216 741-3236
  1040 Valley Belt Rd Brooklyn Heights (44131) *(G-1683)*
Applied Sciences Inc (PA)..................................... 937 766-2020
  141 W Xenia Ave Cedarville (45314) *(G-2322)*
Applied Specialties Inc.. 440 933-9442
  33555 Pin Oak Pkwy Avon Lake (44012) *(G-796)*
Applied Vision Corporation (PA).............................. 330 926-2222
  2020 Vision Ln Cuyahoga Falls (44223) *(G-6067)*
Approved Plbg & Sewer Clg Co, Cleveland *Also Called: Approved Plumbing Co (G-3671)*
Approved Plumbing Co... 216 663-5063
  770 Ken Mar Industrial Pkwy Cleveland (44147) *(G-3671)*
Appvion Inc.. 717 731-7522
  1025 Logistics Way Monroe (45044) *(G-11094)*
Appvion Inc (PA)... 937 859-8262
  1030 W Alex Bell Rd West Carrollton (45449) *(G-15349)*
Apr Tool, Willoughby *Also Called: Askar Productive Resources LLC (G-15887)*
Apr Tool Inc... 440 946-0393
  4712 Beidler Rd Ste A Willoughby (44094) *(G-15883)*
Aprecia Pharmaceuticals LLC (HQ)........................... 513 984-5000
  10901 Kenwood Rd Blue Ash (45242) *(G-1362)*
Aps-Materials Inc (PA)....................................... 937 278-6547
  4011 Riverside Dr Dayton (45405) *(G-6210)*
Apsx LLC.. 513 716-5992
  11121 Kenwood Rd Blue Ash (45242) *(G-1363)*
Aptiv Services Us LLC.. 330 367-6000
  3400 Aero Park Dr Vienna (44473) *(G-14994)*
Aptiv Services Us LLC.. 330 373-7614
  1265 N River Rd Ne Warren (44483) *(G-15141)*
Aptiv Services Us LLC.. 330 306-1000
  4551 Research Pkwy Nw Warren (44483) *(G-15142)*
Aptiv Services Us LLC.. 330 505-3150
  1265 N River Rd Ne Warren (44483) *(G-15143)*
Aptiv Services Us LLC.. 330 373-3568
  1265 N River Rd Ne # Fr11 Warren (44483) *(G-15144)*
APV Engineered Coatings, Akron *Also Called: Akron Paint & Varnish Inc (G-38)*
Aqua Lily Products LLC....................................... 951 322-0981
  4505 Beidler Rd Willoughby (44094) *(G-15884)*
Aqua Marine Supply, Millersport *Also Called: Hefty Hoist Inc (G-11012)*
Aqua Ohio, Mentor On The Lake *Also Called: Aqua Pennsylvania Inc (G-10600)*
Aqua Ohio Inc... 740 867-8700
  32 Private Dr 11100 Chesapeake (45619) *(G-2472)*
Aqua Pennsylvania Inc.. 440 257-6190
  7748 Twilight Dr Mentor On The Lake (44060) *(G-10600)*
Aqua Precision LLC... 937 912-9582
  165 Janney Rd Dayton (45404) *(G-6211)*
Aqua Science Inc.. 614 252-5000
  1877 E 17th Ave Columbus (43219) *(G-5151)*
Aqua Technology Group LLC.................................. 513 298-1183
  8104 Beckett Center Dr West Chester (45069) *(G-15367)*
Aquablok Ltd.. 419 402-4170
  230 W Airport Hwy Swanton (43558) *(G-13968)*
Aquablok Ltd (PA).. 419 825-1325
  175 Woodland Ave Swanton (43558) *(G-13969)*

Aquablue Incorporated.. 330 343-0220
  1776 Tech Park Dr Ne New Philadelphia (44663) *(G-11484)*
Aquapro Systems LLC... 877 278-2797
  223 Telford Ave Oakwood (45419) *(G-12026)*
Aquatic Technology... 440 236-8330
  26966 Royalton Rd Columbia Station (44028) *(G-5005)*
Aquent Studios.. 216 266-7551
  33433 Curtis Blvd Willoughby (44095) *(G-15885)*
Aquila Pharmatech LLC....................................... 419 386-2527
  8225 Farnsworth Rd Ste A7 Waterville (43566) *(G-15239)*
Aracor, Fairborn *Also Called: Rapiscan Systems High Enrgy In (G-7321)*
Arbenz Inc.. 614 274-6800
  1777 Mckinley Ave Columbus (43222) *(G-5152)*
Arbor Foods Inc... 419 698-4442
  3332 Saint Lawrence Dr Bldg C Toledo (43605) *(G-14196)*
Arbor Industries Inc.. 440 255-4720
  6830 Patterson Dr Mentor (44060) *(G-10421)*
Arboris LLC... 740 522-9350
  1780 Tamarack Rd Newark (43055) *(G-11565)*
Arbortech, Wooster *Also Called: Stahl/Scott Fetzer Company (G-16175)*
ARC Drilling Inc (PA).. 216 525-0920
  9551 Corporate Cir Cleveland (44125) *(G-3672)*
ARC Elec.. 440 774-2800
  18637 State Route 511 Wellington (44090) *(G-15303)*
ARC Metal Stamping LLC.................................... 517 448-8954
  447 E Walnut St Wauseon (43567) *(G-15256)*
ARC Rubber Inc.. 440 466-4555
  100 Water St Geneva (44041) *(G-7931)*
ARC Solutions Inc.. 419 542-9272
  605 Industrial Dr Hicksville (43526) *(G-8371)*
Arcadian Ohio, Lima *Also Called: Pcs Nitrogen Inc (G-9275)*
Arcani Coil Care, Trotwood *Also Called: Crownme Coil Care LLC (G-14543)*
Arcelormittal Tubular Pdts USA, Shelby *Also Called: Arcelrmttal Tblar Pdts Shlby L (G-13191)*
Arcelormittal Warren, Warren *Also Called: AM Warren LLC (G-15137)*
Arcelrmttal Tblar Pdts Shlby L............................... 419 347-2424
  132 W Main St Shelby (44875) *(G-13191)*
Arcelrmttal Tblar Pdts USA LLC.............................. 419 347-2424
  132 W Main St Shelby (44875) *(G-13192)*
Arch Angle Window and Door LLC........................... 800 548-0214
  6979 Wooster Pike Medina (44256) *(G-10297)*
Arch Cutng Tls Cincinnati LLC................................ 513 851-6363
  133 Circle Freeway Dr West Chester (45246) *(G-15538)*
Arch Cutting Tls - Mentor LLC............................... 440 350-9393
  9332 Pinecone Dr Mentor (44060) *(G-10422)*
Arch Polymers, Marysville *Also Called: Triple Arrow Industries Inc (G-9943)*
Archbold Buckeye Inc.. 419 445-4466
  207 N Defiance St Archbold (43502) *(G-521)*
Archbold Container Corp..................................... 800 446-2520
  800 W Barre Rd Archbold (43502) *(G-522)*
Archbold Furniture Co.. 567 444-4666
  733 W Barre Rd Archbold (43502) *(G-523)*
Archem America Inc (DH).................................... 419 294-6304
  245 Commerce Way Upper Sandusky (43351) *(G-14803)*
Archer Corporation... 330 455-9995
  1917 Henry Ave Sw Canton (44706) *(G-2038)*
Archer Counter Design Inc................................... 513 396-7526
  4433 Verne Ave Cincinnati (45209) *(G-2631)*
Archer Custom Chrome LLC.................................. 216 441-2795
  25703 Rustic Ln Westlake (44145) *(G-15734)*
Archer Publishing LLC.. 440 338-5233
  27101 E Oviatt Rd Bay Village (44140) *(G-963)*
Archer Sign, Canton *Also Called: Archer Corporation (G-2038)*
Archer-Daniels-Midland Company............................ 419 435-6633
  608 Findlay St Fostoria (44830) *(G-7628)*
Archer-Daniels-Midland Company............................ 330 852-3025
  554 Pleasant Valley Rd Nw Sugarcreek (44681) *(G-13918)*
Archer-Daniels-Midland Company............................ 419 705-3292
  1308 Miami St Toledo (43605) *(G-14197)*
Archies Too... 419 427-2663
  2145 S Lake Ct Findlay (45840) *(G-7477)*
Architctral Identification Inc (PA)............................ 614 868-8400
  1170 Claycraft Rd Gahanna (43230) *(G-7830)*

ALPHABETIC SECTION — Arrowhead Industries

Architctral Indus Met Fnshg LL.. 440 963-0410
  1091 Sunnyside Rd Vermilion (44089) *(G-14971)*

Architctral Mllwk Cbinetry Inc.. 440 708-0086
  16715 W Park Circle Dr Chagrin Falls (44023) *(G-2389)*

Architechual Etc, Cortland *Also Called: Lawbre Co (G-5965)*

Architectural Busstrut Corp.. 614 933-8695
  4311 Brompton Ct New Albany (43054) *(G-11367)*

Architectural Fiberglass Inc.. 216 641-8300
  8300 Bessemer Ave Cleveland (44127) *(G-3673)*

Architectural Metal Maint, Cleves *Also Called: Metal Maintenance Inc (G-4959)*

Archoustics Mid-America, Cincinnati *Also Called: Holland Assocts LLC DBA Archou (G-3003)*

Arclin USA LLC.. 419 726-5013
  6175 American Rd Toledo (43612) *(G-14198)*

Arconic.. 330 471-1844
  1935 Warner Rd Se Canton (44707) *(G-2039)*

Arctech Fabricating Inc (PA).. 937 525-9353
  1317 Lagonda Ave Springfield (45503) *(G-13535)*

Arctos Mission Solutions LLC.. 813 609-5591
  2601 Mission Point Blvd Beavercreek (45431) *(G-1040)*

Arden J Neer Sr.. 937 585-6733
  4859 Township Road 45 Bellefontaine (43311) *(G-1200)*

ARE Inc.. 330 830-7800
  400 Nave Rd Sw Massillon (44646) *(G-10076)*

Area 419, Delta *Also Called: Area 419 Firearms LLC (G-6779)*

Area 419 Firearms LLC.. 419 830-8353
  4750 County Road 5 Delta (43515) *(G-6779)*

Arem Co.. 440 974-6740
  7234 Justin Way Mentor (44060) *(G-10423)*

Arena Eye Surgeons, Columbus *Also Called: Eye Surgery Center Ohio Inc (G-5368)*

Arens Corporation (PA).. 937 473-2028
  395 S High St Covington (45318) *(G-6017)*

Arens Corporation.. 937 473-2028
  22 N High St Covington (45318) *(G-6018)*

Arens Publications & Printing, Covington *Also Called: Arens Corporation (G-6018)*

Ares Inc.. 419 635-2175
  818 Front St Lake Erie Business Park Port Clinton (43452) *(G-12615)*

Ares Sportswear Ltd.. 614 767-1950
  3700 Lacon Rd Ste A Hilliard (43026) *(G-8398)*

Areway, Cleveland *Also Called: Epsilon Management Corporation (G-4025)*

Areway Acquisition Inc.. 216 651-9022
  8525 Clinton Rd Brooklyn (44144) *(G-1675)*

Areway LLC.. 216 651-9022
  8525 Clinton Rd Brooklyn (44144) *(G-1676)*

Arf, Youngstown *Also Called: American Roll Formed Pdts Corp (G-16310)*

Argo Tech Fluid Elec Dist Div, Cleveland *Also Called: Eaton Industrial Corporation (G-3997)*

Argo Tool Corporation.. 330 425-2407
  9138 Jody Lynn Ln Twinsburg (44087) *(G-14631)*

Argrov Box Co.. 937 898-1700
  6030 Webster St Dayton (45414) *(G-6212)*

ARI Phoenix Inc (PA).. 513 229-3750
  11163 Woodward Ln Sharonville (45241) *(G-13170)*

Ariel Corporation.. 330 896-2660
  3360 Miller Park Rd Akron (44312) *(G-64)*

Ariel Corporation.. 740 397-0311
  8405 Blackjack Rd Mount Vernon (43050) *(G-11263)*

Ariel Corporation (PA).. 740 397-0311
  35 Blackjack Road Ext Mount Vernon (43050) *(G-11264)*

Ariezhair Collection LLC.. 614 964-5748
  1747 Olentangy River Rd Columbus (43212) *(G-5153)*

Arisdyne Systems Inc.. 216 458-1991
  17830 Englewood Dr Ste 11 Cleveland (44130) *(G-3674)*

Arizona Beverages, Cincinnati *Also Called: Hornell Brewing Co Inc (G-3009)*

Ark Operations Inc.. 419 871-1186
  2700 Kettg Tower 40n Main St Dayton (45423) *(G-6213)*

Arkansas Face Veneer Co Inc (HQ).. 937 773-6295
  1025 S Roosevelt Ave Piqua (45356) *(G-12504)*

Arkay Industries Inc (PA).. 513 360-0390
  240 American Way Monroe (45050) *(G-11095)*

Arkay Plastics Alabama Inc (HQ).. 513 360-0390
  220 American Way Monroe (45050) *(G-11096)*

Arku Inc.. 513 985-0500
  7251 E Kemper Rd Cincinnati (45249) *(G-2632)*

Arlington Rack & Packaging Co.. 419 476-7700
  6120 N Detroit Ave Toledo (43612) *(G-14199)*

Arlington Valley Farms LLC (PA).. 216 426-5000
  5369 Hudson Dr Hudson (44236) *(G-8586)*

Arlington-Blaine Lumber Co, Delaware *Also Called: Khempco Bldg Sup Co Ltd Partnr (G-6733)*

ARM (usa) Inc.. 740 264-6599
  1506 Fernwood Rd Wintersville (43953) *(G-16085)*

Arm & Hammer, London *Also Called: Church & Dwight Co Inc (G-9384)*

Armada Power LLC.. 614 721-4844
  230 West St Ste 150 Columbus (43215) *(G-5154)*

Armaly Brands, London *Also Called: Armaly LLC (G-9381)*

Armaly LLC.. 740 852-3621
  110 W 1st St London (43140) *(G-9381)*

Armature Coil Equipment Inc.. 216 267-6366
  22269 Horseshoe Ln Strongsville (44149) *(G-13809)*

Armco Inc.. 740 829-3000
  17400 State Route 16 Coshocton (43812) *(G-5971)*

Armoloy of Ohio Inc.. 937 323-8702
  1950 E Leffel Ln Springfield (45505) *(G-13536)*

Armor.. 614 459-1414
  2218 Bristol Rd Columbus (43221) *(G-5155)*

Armor Aftermarket Inc.. 513 923-5600
  4600 N Mason Montgomery Rd Oh Mason (45040) *(G-9951)*

Armor Consolidated Inc (PA).. 513 923-5260
  4600 N Mason Montgomery Rd Mason (45040) *(G-9952)*

Armor Metal Group Elkhart Inc.. 800 672-6373
  4600 N Mason Montgomery Rd Mason (45040) *(G-9953)*

Armor Metal Group Mason Inc (HQ).. 513 769-0700
  4600 N Mason Montgomery Rd Mason (45040) *(G-9954)*

Armormetal, Mason *Also Called: Armor Metal Group Mason Inc (G-9954)*

Armorsource LLC.. 740 928-0070
  3600 Hebron Rd Hebron (43025) *(G-8336)*

Armour Spray Systems Inc.. 216 398-3838
  210 Hayes Dr Ste I Cleveland (44131) *(G-3675)*

Armstrong Custom Moulding Inc.. 740 922-5931
  6408 State Route 800 Se Uhrichsville (44683) *(G-14761)*

Armstrong World, Hilliard *Also Called: Armstrong World Industries Inc (G-8399)*

Armstrong World Industries Inc.. 614 771-9307
  4241 Leap Rd Bldg A Hilliard (43026) *(G-8399)*

Arnco Corporation.. 800 847-7661
  860 Garden St Elyria (44035) *(G-7112)*

Arnett Tool Inc.. 937 437-0361
  217 W Main St New Paris (45347) *(G-11480)*

Arnold Company, Valley City *Also Called: Arnold Corporation (G-14861)*

Arnold Corporation.. 330 225-2600
  5965 Grafton Rd Valley City (44280) *(G-14861)*

Arnold Gauge Co Inc (PA).. 877 942-4243
  9823 Harwood Ct West Chester (45014) *(G-15368)*

Arnold Machine, Tiffin *Also Called: Arnold Machine Inc (G-14076)*

Arnold Machine Inc.. 419 443-1818
  19 Heritage Dr Tiffin (44883) *(G-14076)*

Arnold Magnetic Technologies, Marietta *Also Called: Flexmag Industries Inc (G-9793)*

Arnold's Candies, Akron *Also Called: Dauphin Holdings Inc (G-124)*

Aromair Fine Fragrance Company.. 614 984-2900
  8860 Smiths Mill Rd Ste 500 New Albany (43054) *(G-11368)*

Array Telepresence Inc.. 800 779-7480
  9480 Meridian Way West Chester (45069) *(G-15369)*

Arrow Fabricating Co.. 216 641-0490
  7355 Calley Ln Novelty (44072) *(G-12006)*

Arrow International Inc (PA).. 216 961-3500
  9900 Clinton Rd Cleveland (44144) *(G-3676)*

Arrow Print & Copy, Sylvania *Also Called: Kevin K Tidd (G-14003)*

Arrow Tru-Line Inc (PA).. 419 446-2785
  2211 S Defiance St Archbold (43502) *(G-524)*

Arrow Tru-Line Inc.. 419 636-7013
  720 E Perry St Bryan (43506) *(G-1808)*

Arrowhead Industries, Cleveland *Also Called: Scovil Hanna LLC (G-4681)*

Arrowhead Pallet LLC 440 693-4241
7851 Parkman Mespo Rd Middlefield (44062) *(G-10732)*

Arrowstrip Inc 740 633-2609
1st & Locust St S Martins Ferry (43935) *(G-9895)*

ARS Recycling Systems LLC (PA) 330 536-8210
4000 Mccartney Rd Lowellville (44436) *(G-9511)*

ARS Recycling Systems 2019 LLC 330 536-8210
4000 Mccartney Rd Lowellville (44436) *(G-9512)*

Arsco Custom Metals LLC 513 385-0555
3330 E Kemper Rd Cincinnati (45241) *(G-2633)*

Arsco Manufacturing Company, Cincinnati Also Called: Arsco Custom Metals LLC *(G-2633)*

Art Galvanizing Works Inc 216 749-0020
3935 Valley Rd Cleveland (44109) *(G-3677)*

Art Guild Binders Inc 513 242-3000
1068 Meta Dr Cincinnati (45237) *(G-2634)*

Art Iron Inc 419 241-1261
860 Curtis St Toledo (43609) *(G-14200)*

Art Metals Group, Hamilton Also Called: Art Technologies LLC *(G-8180)*

Art Tech, Chillicothe Also Called: McRd Enterprises LLC *(G-2517)*

Art Technologies LLC 513 942-8800
3795 Symmes Rd Hamilton (45015) *(G-8180)*

Art Woodworking & Mfg Co 513 681-2986
4238 Dane Ave Cincinnati (45223) *(G-2635)*

Art-American Printing Plates 216 241-4420
1138 W 9th St Fl 4 Cleveland (44113) *(G-3678)*

Artco LLC 740 493-2901
1729 Jasper Rd Piketon (45661) *(G-12475)*

Arte Limited, Cleveland Also Called: Lawrence Industries Inc *(G-4317)*

Artesian of Pioneer Inc (PA) 419 737-2352
50 Industrial Ave Pioneer (43554) *(G-12490)*

Artex Energy Group LLC 740 373-3313
2337 State Route 821 Marietta (45750) *(G-9776)*

Artex Oil Company 740 373-3313
2337 State Route 821 Marietta (45750) *(G-9777)*

Arthur Corporation 419 433-7202
1305 Huron Avery Rd Huron (44839) *(G-8627)*

Arthur Louis Steel Co, Geneva Also Called: Louis Arthur Steel Company *(G-7940)*

Artiflex Manufacturing Inc (HQ) 330 262-2015
1425 E Bowman St Wooster (44691) *(G-16101)*

Artiflex Manufacturing, LLC, Wooster Also Called: Artiflex Manufacturing Inc *(G-16101)*

Artisan Ales LLC 216 544-8703
17448 Lorain Ave Cleveland (44111) *(G-3679)*

Artisan Constructors LLC 216 800-7641
600 Superior Ave E Cleveland (44114) *(G-3680)*

Artisan Equipment Inc 740 756-9135
5770 Winchester Rd Carroll (43112) *(G-2294)*

Artisan Grinding Service Inc 937 667-7383
1300 Stanley Ave Dayton (45404) *(G-6214)*

Artisan Renovations, Cleveland Also Called: Artisan Constructors LLC *(G-3680)*

Artisan Tool & Die Corp 216 883-2769
4911 Grant Ave Cleveland (44125) *(G-3681)*

Artistic Finishes Inc 440 951-7850
38357 Apollo Pkwy Willoughby (44094) *(G-15886)*

Artistic Metal Spinning Inc 216 961-3336
4700 Lorain Ave Cleveland (44102) *(G-3682)*

Artistic Photography Prtg Inc 813 310-6965
1119 Broadway Ave Bedford (44146) *(G-1102)*

Artistic Rock LLC 216 291-8856
3786 Fairoaks Rd Cleveland (44121) *(G-3683)*

Arvinmrtor Commerical Vhcl Sys, Granville Also Called: Meritor Inc *(G-8020)*

Arzel Technology Inc 216 831-6068
4801 Commerce Pkwy Cleveland (44128) *(G-3684)*

Arzel Zoning Technology, Cleveland Also Called: Arzel Technology Inc *(G-3684)*

As America Inc 419 522-4211
41 Cairns Rd Mansfield (44903) *(G-9626)*

As America Inc 330 332-9954
605 S Ellsworth Ave Salem (44460) *(G-12977)*

As Clean As It Gets Off Brkroo 216 256-1143
4099 Lowden Rd South Euclid (44121) *(G-13459)*

ASAP, Moraine Also Called: Allied Shipping and Packaging Supplies Inc *(G-11155)*

ASAP Ready Mix Inc 513 797-1774
250 Mount Holly Rd Amelia (45102) *(G-453)*

ASC, North Canton Also Called: ASC Industries Inc *(G-11715)*

ASC Industries Inc (DH) 800 253-6009
2100 International Pkwy North Canton (44720) *(G-11715)*

Ascents, Cleveland Also Called: Aeroscena LLC *(G-3611)*

Asco Power Technologies LP 216 573-7600
6255 Halle Dr Cleveland (44125) *(G-3685)*

Ascon Tecnologic, Cleveland Also Called: Ascon Tecnologic N Amer LLC *(G-3686)*

Ascon Tecnologic N Amer LLC 216 485-8350
1111 Brookpark Rd Cleveland (44109) *(G-3686)*

Ascot Valley Foods Ltd 330 376-9411
205 Ascot Pkwy Cuyahoga Falls (44223) *(G-6068)*

ASG 216 486-6163
15700 S Waterloo Rd Cleveland (44110) *(G-3687)*

Asg Division Jergens Inc 888 486-6163
15700 S Waterloo Rd Jergens Way Cleveland (44110) *(G-3688)*

Ash Sewer & Drain Service 330 376-9714
451 E North St Akron (44304) *(G-65)*

Ashcraft Machine & Supply Inc 740 349-8110
185 Wilson St Newark (43055) *(G-11566)*

Ashland Chemco Inc 216 961-4690
2191 W 110th St Cleveland (44102) *(G-3689)*

Ashland Chemco Inc 614 790-3333
1979 Atlas St Columbus (43228) *(G-5156)*

Ashland Conveyor Products, Ashland Also Called: Midwest Conveyor Products Inc *(G-592)*

Ashland Distribution, Columbus Also Called: Ashland Chemco Inc *(G-5156)*

Ashland Precision Tooling LLC 419 289-1736
1750 S Baney Rd Ashland (44805) *(G-551)*

Ashland Publishing Co 419 281-0581
40 E 2nd St Ashland (44805) *(G-552)*

Ashland Spcalty Ingredients GP 614 529-3311
1979 Atlas St Columbus (43228) *(G-5157)*

Ashland Times Gazette, Ashland Also Called: Ashland Publishing Co *(G-552)*

Ashland Water Group Inc (PA) 877 326-3561
1899 Cottage St Ashland (44805) *(G-553)*

Ashley F Ward Inc (PA) 513 398-1414
7490 Easy St Mason (45040) *(G-9955)*

Ashta Enterprises Ltd Lblty Co 216 252-7620
3001 W 121st St Cleveland (44111) *(G-3690)*

Ashta Forge & Machine Inc 216 252-7000
3001 W 121st St Cleveland (44111) *(G-3691)*

Ashton Custom Prtg & Gift Sp, Pickerington Also Called: Ashton LLC *(G-12455)*

Ashton LLC 614 833-4165
77 E Columbus St Pickerington (43147) *(G-12455)*

Asi Chemical Company, Avon Lake Also Called: Applied Specialties Inc *(G-796)*

Asi Sign Systems, Loveland Also Called: Kmgrafx Inc *(G-9490)*

Asia For Kids, Cincinnati Also Called: Master Communications Inc *(G-3133)*

Asidaco LLC (PA) 800 204-1544
400 Linden Ave Ste 95 Dayton (45403) *(G-6215)*

Asist Translation Services 614 451-6744
4891 Sawmill Rd Ste 200 Columbus (43235) *(G-5158)*

Asist Translation Services, Columbus Also Called: Asist Translation Services *(G-5158)*

Ask Chemicals, Cleveland Also Called: Ashland Chemco Inc *(G-3689)*

ASK Chemicals LLC 800 848-7485
495 Metro Pl S Dublin (43017) *(G-6863)*

Ask Chemicals LP 614 763-0248
4400 Easton Cmns Columbus (43219) *(G-5159)*

Askar Productive Resources LLC 440 946-0393
4712a Beidler Rd Willoughby (44094) *(G-15887)*

Aslan Worldwide 513 671-0671
8583 Rupp Farm Dr West Chester (45069) *(G-15370)*

Asm International 440 338-5151
9639 Kinsman Rd Novelty (44073) *(G-12007)*

Aspec Inc 513 561-9922
5810 Carothers St Cincinnati (45227) *(G-2636)*

Aspen Fasteners USA 800 479-0056
1028 E 134th St Cleveland (44110) *(G-3692)*

Aspen Machine and Plastics 937 526-4644
257 Baker Rd Versailles (45380) *(G-14976)*

Asphalt, Cincinnati *Also Called: Valley Asphalt Corporation (G-3486)*
Asphalt Fabrics & Specialties.. 440 786-1077
7710 Bond St Solon (44139) *(G-13314)*
Assembleis Co, Mansfield *Also Called: Mansfield Engineered Components LLC (G-9685)*
Assembly Division, Walbridge *Also Called: Riverside Mch & Automtn Inc (G-15086)*
Assembly Machining Wire Pdts.. 614 443-1110
2375 Refugee Park Columbus (43207) *(G-5160)*
Assembly Specialty Pdts Inc.. 216 676-5600
14700 Brookpark Rd Cleveland (44135) *(G-3693)*
Assembly Tool Specialists, Twinsburg *Also Called: Production Tl Co Cleveland Inc (G-14719)*
Assembly Works Inc.. 419 433-5010
1705 Sawmill Pkwy Huron (44839) *(G-8628)*
Assembly Works Matrix Automtn, Huron *Also Called: Assembly Works Inc (G-8628)*
Assetwatch Inc... 844 464-5652
60 Collegeview Rd Westerville (43081) *(G-15691)*
Associated Associates Inc.. 330 626-3300
9551 Elliman Rd Mantua (44255) *(G-9734)*
Associated Hygienic Pdts LLC... 770 497-9800
2332 Us Highway 42 S Delaware (43015) *(G-6701)*
Associated Materials LLC (PA).. 330 929-1811
3773 State Rd Cuyahoga Falls (44223) *(G-6069)*
Associated Materials Group Inc (PA).. 330 929-1811
3773 State Rd Cuyahoga Falls (44223) *(G-6070)*
Associated Mtls Holdings LLC... 330 929-1811
3773 State Rd Cuyahoga Falls (44223) *(G-6071)*
Associated Plastics Corp.. 419 634-3910
502 Eric Wolber Dr Ada (45810) *(G-3)*
Associated Premium Corporation.. 513 679-4444
1870 Summit Rd Cincinnati (45237) *(G-2637)*
Associated Press Repair Inc... 216 881-2288
7547 Brigham Rd Gates Mills (44040) *(G-7927)*
Associated Ready Mix Concrete, Mantua *Also Called: Associated Associates Inc (G-9734)*
Associated Software Cons Inc... 440 826-1010
1101 Forest Rd Lakewood (44107) *(G-8966)*
Associates Tire and Svc Inc.. 937 436-4692
1099 S Main St Centerville (45458) *(G-2359)*
Assocted Vsual Cmmncations Inc.. 330 452-4449
7000 Firestone Ave Ne Canton (44721) *(G-2040)*
Aster Industries Inc.. 330 762-7965
275 N Arlington St Ste B Akron (44305) *(G-66)*
Astrazeneca Pharmaceuticals LP... 513 645-2600
8814 Trade Port Dr West Chester (45011) *(G-15371)*
Astro Aluminum Enterprises Inc.. 330 755-1414
65 Main St Struthers (44471) *(G-13900)*
Astro Industries Inc... 937 429-5900
4403 Dayton Xenia Rd Beavercreek (45432) *(G-1041)*
Astro Manufacturing & Design, Eastlake *Also Called: Astro Manufacturing & Design Inc (G-7019)*
Astro Manufacturing & Design Inc (PA)...................................... 888 215-1746
34459 Curtis Blvd Eastlake (44095) *(G-7019)*
Astro Met Inc (PA).. 513 772-1242
9974 Springfield Pike Cincinnati (45215) *(G-2638)*
Astro Model Development Corp.. 440 946-8855
34459 Curtis Blvd Eastlake (44095) *(G-7020)*
Astro Shapes.. 330 755-1414
4605 Lake Park Rd Youngstown (44512) *(G-16314)*
Astro Shapes LLC.. 330 755-1414
65 Main St Struthers (44471) *(G-13901)*
Astro Technical Services Inc
2401 Parkman Rd Nw Warren (44485) *(G-15145)*
Astro-Coatings Inc.. 330 755-1414
65 Main St Struthers (44471) *(G-13902)*
Astro-TEC Mfg Inc.. 330 854-2209
550 Elm Ridge Ave Canal Fulton (44614) *(G-1967)*
Asw, Bedford Heights *Also Called: American Spring Wire Corp (G-1163)*
Aswpengg LLC.. 216 292-4620
26300 Miles Rd Bedford Heights (44146) *(G-1164)*
At Holdings Corporation.. 216 692-6000
23555 Euclid Ave Cleveland (44117) *(G-3694)*
At Your Service... 513 498-9392
61 Betty Dr Hamilton (45013) *(G-8181)*

AT&f Advanced Metals LLC (PA)... 330 684-1122
12314 Elmwood Ave Cleveland (44111) *(G-3695)*
AT&f Advanced Metals LLC... 330 684-1122
95 N Swinehart Rd Orrville (44667) *(G-12117)*
AT&T, Cincinnati *Also Called: AT&T Corp (G-2639)*
AT&T, Columbus *Also Called: AT&T Corp (G-5161)*
AT&T Corp.. 513 792-9300
7875 Montgomery Rd Ofc Cincinnati (45236) *(G-2639)*
AT&T Corp.. 614 223-8236
150 E Gay St Ste 4a Columbus (43215) *(G-5161)*
Atama Tech LLC... 614 763-0399
9485 Gibson Dr Powell (43065) *(G-12663)*
Atc Group Inc (PA)... 440 293-4064
101 Parker Dr Andover (44003) *(G-484)*
Atc Legacy Inc.. 330 590-8105
1441 Wolf Creek Trail Sharon Center (44274) *(G-13162)*
Atc Lighting & Plastics, Andover *Also Called: Atc Group Inc (G-484)*
Atc Lighting & Plastics Inc (HQ).. 440 466-7670
101 Parker Dr Andover (44003) *(G-485)*
Atchley Signs & Graphics LLC.. 614 421-7446
1616 Transamerica Ct Columbus (43228) *(G-5162)*
Atcpc of Ohio LLC.. 330 670-9900
1055 Home Ave Akron (44310) *(G-67)*
Atech Fire Services, West Chester *Also Called: Total Life Safety LLC (G-15516)*
Atelierkopii LLC.. 216 559-0815
11811 Shaker Blvd Ste 204 Cleveland (44120) *(G-3696)*
Athens Foods Inc... 216 676-8500
13600 Snow Rd Cleveland (44142) *(G-3697)*
Athens Messenger, The, Athens *Also Called: Messenger Publishing Company (G-688)*
Athens Mold and Machine Inc... 740 593-6613
180 Mill St Athens (45701) *(G-675)*
Athens Technical Specialists.. 740 592-2874
8157 Us Highway 50 Athens (45701) *(G-676)*
ATI, Batavia *Also Called: Auto Temp Inc (G-909)*
ATI, Toledo *Also Called: Abbott Tool Inc (G-14174)*
ATI Flat Rlled Pdts Hldngs LLC... 330 875-2244
1500 W Main St Louisville (44641) *(G-9455)*
ATI Flat Rolled Products, Louisville *Also Called: ATI Flat Rlled Pdts Hldngs LLC (G-9455)*
ATI Solutions Properties LLC.. 937 609-7681
8801 Sugarcreek Pt Dayton (45458) *(G-6216)*
Atk Space Systems LLC.. 937 490-4121
1365 Technology Ct Beavercreek (45430) *(G-1070)*
Atk Systems.. 937 429-8632
1365 Technology Ct Beavercreek (45430) *(G-1071)*
Atkins Custom Framing Ltd.. 740 816-1501
3116 Troy Rd Delaware (43015) *(G-6702)*
Atlanta Rotomolding Inc.. 404 328-1004
4429 Crystal Pkwy Kent (44240) *(G-8800)*
Atlantic and Prfmce Rigging, Tiffin *Also Called: Tiffin Scenic Studios Inc (G-14112)*
Atlantic Co.. 440 944-8988
26651 Curtiss Wright Pkwy Willoughby Hills (44092) *(G-16021)*
Atlantic Inertial Systems Inc... 740 788-3800
781 Irving Wick Dr W Ste 01 Heath (43056) *(G-8317)*
Atlantic Sign Company Inc... 513 383-1504
2328 Florence Ave Cincinnati (45206) *(G-2640)*
Atlantic Tool & Die Company (PA)... 440 238-6931
19963 Progress Dr Strongsville (44149) *(G-13810)*
Atlantic Veal & Lamb LLC.. 330 435-6400
2416 E West Salem Rd Creston (44217) *(G-6038)*
Atlantic Water Gardens, Aurora *Also Called: Meridienne International Inc (G-725)*
Atlantic Welding LLC... 937 570-5094
1708 Commerce Dr Piqua (45356) *(G-12505)*
Atlantis Sportswear Inc.. 937 773-0680
344 Fox Dr Piqua (45356) *(G-12506)*
Atlas America Inc... 330 339-3155
1026a Cookson Ave Se New Philadelphia (44663) *(G-11485)*
Atlas Bolt & Screw Company LLC (DH)...................................... 419 289-6171
1628 Troy Rd Ashland (44805) *(G-554)*
Atlas Dowel & Wood Products Co, Harrison *Also Called: Puttmann Industries Inc (G-8287)*
Atlas Fasteners For Cnstr, Ashland *Also Called: Atlas Bolt & Screw Company LLC (G-554)*

Atlas Industrial Contractors

ALPHABETIC SECTION

Atlas Industrial Contractors, Columbus *Also Called: Atlas Industrial Contrs LLC (G-5163)*
Atlas Industrial Contrs LLC (HQ)... 614 841-4500
  5275 Sinclair Rd Columbus (43229) *(G-5163)*
Atlas Industries Inc... 419 355-1000
  1750 E State St Fremont (43420) *(G-7763)*
Atlas Machine and Supply Inc.. 502 584-7262
  8556 Trade Center Dr # 250 Hamilton (45011) *(G-8182)*
Atlas Machine Products Co... 216 228-3688
  44800 Us Highway 20 Oberlin (44074) *(G-12048)*
Atlas Portable Space Solutions, Oberlin *Also Called: Atlas Machine Products Co (G-12048)*
Atlas Roofing Corporation... 937 746-9941
  675 Oxford Rd Franklin (45005) *(G-7663)*
Atm Nerds LLC.. 614 983-3056
  175 S 3rd St Ste 200 Columbus (43215) *(G-5164)*
Atmos 360 A Systems Solutions, West Chester *Also Called: Atmos360 Inc (G-15539)*
Atmos360 Inc.. 513 772-4777
  4690 Interstate Dr Ste A West Chester (45246) *(G-15539)*
Atmosphere Annealing LLC.. 330 478-0314
  1501 Raff Rd Sw Kenton (43326) *(G-8880)*
Atom Blasting & Finishing Inc... 440 235-4765
  24933 Sprague Rd Columbia Station (44028) *(G-5006)*
Atr Automation, Cincinnati *Also Called: Atr Distributing Company (G-2641)*
Atr Distributing Company (PA)... 513 353-1800
  11857 Kemper Springs Dr Cincinnati (45240) *(G-2641)*
Atr Distributing Company... 513 353-1800
  11857 Kemper Springs Dr Cincinnati (45240) *(G-2642)*
Atra Metal Spinning Inc... 440 354-9525
  572 S Saint Clair St Painesville (44077) *(G-12216)*
Atricure, Mason *Also Called: Atricure Inc (G-9956)*
Atricure Inc (PA).. 513 755-4100
  7555 Innovation Way Mason (45040) *(G-9956)*
Atrium At Anna Maria Inc.. 330 562-7777
  849 N Aurora Rd Aurora (44202) *(G-706)*
Atrium Centers Inc.. 513 830-5014
  1400 Mallard Cove Dr Cincinnati (45246) *(G-2643)*
Ats Machine & Tool Co... 440 255-1120
  37033 Lake Shore Blvd Eastlake (44095) *(G-7021)*
Ats Ohio Inc.. 614 888-2344
  7115 Green Meadows Dr Lewis Center (43035) *(G-9151)*
Ats Systems Oregon Inc... 541 738-0932
  425 Enterprise Dr Lewis Center (43035) *(G-9152)*
Atsi, Athens *Also Called: Athens Technical Specialists (G-676)*
Attends Healthcare Pdts Inc.. 740 368-7880
  2332 Us Highway 42 S Delaware (43015) *(G-6703)*
Attia Applied Sciences Inc.. 740 369-1891
  548 W Central Ave Delaware (43015) *(G-6704)*
Attindas Hygiene Partners, Delaware *Also Called: Attends Healthcare Pdts Inc (G-6703)*
Atv Insider... 740 282-7102
  742 Sunshine Park Rd Steubenville (43953) *(G-13660)*
ATW, Hamilton *Also Called: American Tool Works Inc (G-8179)*
Atwood Mobile Products LLC.. 419 258-5531
  5406 County Road 424 Antwerp (45813) *(G-492)*
Atwood Rope Manufacturing Inc... 614 920-0534
  121 N Trine St Canal Winchester (43110) *(G-1979)*
Atwood Rope Manufacturing Inc... 614 920-0534
  2185 Refugee St Millersport (43046) *(G-11010)*
Atx Networks.. 440 427-9036
  27036 Waterside Dr Olmsted Twp (44138) *(G-12086)*
Aubrey Rose Apparel LLC.. 513 728-2681
  3862 Race Rd Cincinnati (45211) *(G-2644)*
Auburn Metal Processing LLC (PA)...................................... 315 253-2565
  4550 Darrow Rd Stow (44224) *(G-13685)*
Audimute Sndprfing Mdic Bttrie, Bedford *Also Called: One Wish LLC (G-1147)*
Audion Automation Ltd.. 216 267-1911
  775 Berea Industrial Pkwy Berea (44017) *(G-1265)*
Audion Automation Ltd (PA).. 216 267-1911
  775 Berea Industrial Pkwy Berea (44017) *(G-1266)*
Audit Forms, Cleveland *Also Called: Foote Printing Company Inc (G-4079)*
Auglaize Erie Machine Company.. 419 629-2068
  07148 Quellhorst Rd New Bremen (45869) *(G-11398)*

Augusta Sportswear Inc.. 937 497-7575
  600 N Stolle Ave Sidney (45365) *(G-13223)*
Auguste Moone Enterprises Ltd.. 216 333-9248
  3355 Tullamore Rd Cleveland Heights (44118) *(G-4937)*
Aukerman J F Steel Rule Die.. 937 456-4498
  5582 Ozias Rd Eaton (45320) *(G-7054)*
Auld Corporation... 614 454-1010
  1569 Westbelt Dr Columbus (43228) *(G-5165)*
Auntie Anne's, Niles *Also Called: Chestnut Land Company (G-11663)*
Auria Fremont LLC... 419 332-1587
  400 S Stone St Fremont (43420) *(G-7764)*
Auria Holmesville LLC.. 330 279-4505
  8281 County Road 245 Holmesville (44633) *(G-8542)*
Auria Sidney LLC.. 937 492-1225
  2000 Schlater Dr Sidney (45365) *(G-13224)*
Auria Solutions, Fremont *Also Called: Auria Fremont LLC (G-7764)*
Auris Noble LLC (PA)... 330 321-6649
  160 E Voris St Akron (44311) *(G-68)*
Aurora Balloon Company, Malvern *Also Called: Perfect Products Company (G-9614)*
Aurora Material Solutions, Streetsboro *Also Called: Aurora Plastics LLC (G-13757)*
Aurora Plastics LLC (HQ)... 330 422-0700
  9280 Jefferson St Streetsboro (44241) *(G-13757)*
Austin Parts & Service.. 330 253-7791
  56 N Union St Akron (44304) *(G-69)*
Austin Powder, Findlay *Also Called: Austin Powder Company (G-7478)*
Austin Powder Company (DH).. 216 464-2400
  25800 Science Park Dr Ste 300 Cleveland (44122) *(G-3698)*
Austin Powder Company... 419 299-3347
  3518 Township Road 142 Findlay (45840) *(G-7478)*
Austin Powder Company... 740 596-5286
  430 Powder Plant Rd Mc Arthur (45651) *(G-10262)*
Austin Powder Company... 740 968-1555
  74200 Edwards Rd Saint Clairsville (43950) *(G-12896)*
Austin Powder Holdings Company (HQ)............................... 216 464-2400
  25800 Science Park Dr Ste 300 Cleveland (44122) *(G-3699)*
Austin Tape and Label Inc.. 330 928-7999
  3350 Cavalier Trl Stow (44224) *(G-13686)*
Austinburg Machine Inc.. 440 275-2001
  2899 Industrial Park Dr Austinburg (44010) *(G-741)*
Austintown Metal Works Inc.. 330 259-4673
  45 Victoria Rd Youngstown (44515) *(G-16315)*
Auto Bolt and Nut Company, The, Cleveland *Also Called: Auto Bolt Company (G-3700)*
Auto Bolt Company... 216 881-3913
  4740 Manufacturing Ave Cleveland (44135) *(G-3700)*
Auto Data, Akron *Also Called: Ad Company Holdings Inc (G-19)*
Auto Dealer Designs Inc... 330 374-7666
  303 W Bartges St Akron (44307) *(G-70)*
Auto Technology Company... 440 572-7800
  20026 Progress Dr Strongsville (44149) *(G-13811)*
Auto Temp Inc... 513 732-6969
  950 Kent Rd Batavia (45103) *(G-909)*
Auto-Tap Inc... 216 671-1043
  3317 W 140th St Cleveland (44111) *(G-3701)*
Auto-Valve Inc.. 937 854-3037
  1707 Guenther Rd Dayton (45417) *(G-6217)*
Autobody Supply Company, Groveport *Also Called: Finishmaster Inc (G-8139)*
Autobody Supply Company Inc... 614 228-4328
  212 N Grant Ave Columbus (43215) *(G-5166)*
Autogate Inc.. 419 588-2796
  7306 Driver Rd Berlin Heights (44814) *(G-1312)*
Automated Bldg Components Inc (PA)................................. 419 257-2152
  2359 Grant Rd North Baltimore (45872) *(G-11694)*
Automated Laser Fabrication Co.. 330 562-7200
  1 Singer Dr Streetsboro (44241) *(G-13758)*
Automated Mfg Solutions Inc.. 440 878-3711
  19706 Progress Dr Strongsville (44149) *(G-13812)*
Automated Packaging Systems LLC (HQ)............................ 330 528-2000
  10175 Philipp Pkwy Streetsboro (44241) *(G-13759)*
AUTOMATED PACKAGING SYSTEMS, INC., Cleveland *Also Called: Automated Packg Systems Inc (G-3702)*
AUTOMATED PACKAGING SYSTEMS, INC., Streetsboro *Also Called: Automated Packg Systems Inc (G-13760)*

Automated Packg Systems Inc 330 342-2000
25900 Solon Rd Bedford (44146) *(G-1103)*

Automated Packg Systems Inc 216 663-2000
13555 Mccracken Rd Cleveland (44125) *(G-3702)*

Automated Packg Systems Inc 330 626-2313
600 Mondial Pkwy Streetsboro (44241) *(G-13760)*

Automated Packg Systems Inc, Streetsboro Also Called: Automated Packaging Systems LLC *(G-13759)*

Automated Wheel LLC 216 651-9022
8525 Clinton Rd Cleveland (44144) *(G-3703)*

Automatic Parts 419 524-5841
433 Springmill St Mansfield (44903) *(G-9627)*

Automatic Parts, Mansfield Also Called: McDaniel Products Inc *(G-9688)*

Automatic Parts, Mansfield Also Called: McDaniel Products Inc *(G-9689)*

Automatic Stamp Products Inc 216 781-7933
1822 Columbus Rd Cleveland (44113) *(G-3704)*

Automation and Ctrl Tech Inc 614 495-1120
6141 Avery Rd Dublin (43016) *(G-6864)*

Automation Finishing, Cleveland Also Called: Automation Finishing Inc *(G-3705)*

Automation Finishing Inc 216 251-8805
3206 W 121st St Cleveland (44111) *(G-3705)*

Automation Plastics Corp 330 562-5148
150 Lena Dr Aurora (44202) *(G-707)*

Automation Software & Engrg (PA) 330 405-2990
9321 Ravenna Rd Ste A Twinsburg (44087) *(G-14632)*

Automation Systems Design Inc 937 387-0351
3540 Vance Rd Dayton (45439) *(G-6218)*

Automation Technology Inc 937 233-6084
1900 Troy St Dayton (45404) *(G-6219)*

Automation Tool & Die Inc 330 558-8128
3005 Interstate Pkwy Brunswick (44212) *(G-1749)*

Automation Tool & Die Inc 330 225-8336
5576 Innovation Dr Valley City (44280) *(G-14862)*

Automation Tooling Systems, Lewis Center Also Called: Ats Ohio Inc *(G-9151)*

Automator Marking Systems Inc 740 983-0157
475 Douglas Ave Chillicothe (45601) *(G-2493)*

Automotive Industries Division, Wauseon Also Called: Interntnal Auto Cmpnnts Group *(G-15265)*

Automted Cmpnent Spcalists LLC 513 335-4285
7740 Reinhold Dr Cincinnati (45237) *(G-2645)*

Automtive Rfnish Clor Sltons I 330 461-6067
2771 Sunburst Dr Medina (44256) *(G-10298)*

Autoneum North America Inc 419 690-8924
4131 Spartan Dr Oregon (43616) *(G-12102)*

Autoneum North America Inc 419 693-0511
645 N Lallendorf Rd Oregon (43616) *(G-12103)*

Autoplas Division, Bellevue Also Called: Windsor Mold USA Inc *(G-1240)*

Autotec Corporation 419 885-2529
6155 Brent Dr Toledo (43611) *(G-14201)*

Autotec Systems, Toledo Also Called: Autotec Corporation *(G-14201)*

Autotool Inc 614 733-0222
7875 Corporate Blvd Plain City (43064) *(G-12563)*

Autotx Inc 216 510-6666
4635 Northfield Rd Cleveland (44128) *(G-3706)*

Autowax Inc 440 334-4417
15015 Foltz Pkwy Strongsville (44149) *(G-13813)*

Avadirect.com, Twinsburg Also Called: Freedom Usa Inc *(G-14662)*

Avalign - Integrated LLC 440 269-6984
7124 Industrial Park Blvd Mentor (44060) *(G-10424)*

Avalign Technologies Inc 419 542-7743
801 Industrial Dr Hicksville (43526) *(G-8372)*

Avalon, Cleveland Also Called: Xapc Co *(G-4926)*

Avari Aero LLC 513 828-0860
7711 Affinity Pl Cincinnati (45231) *(G-2646)*

Avari Aerospace, Cincinnati Also Called: Avari Aero LLC *(G-2646)*

Avc Inc 513 458-2600
4625 Red Bank Rd Ste 200 Cincinnati (45227) *(G-2647)*

Avcom Smt Inc 614 882-8176
213 E Broadway Ave Westerville (43081) *(G-15692)*

Avecia, Cincinnati Also Called: Girindus America Inc *(G-2952)*

Avenue Fabricating Inc 513 752-1911
1281 Clough Pike Batavia (45103) *(G-910)*

Avery Dennison, Mentor Also Called: Avery Dennison Corporation *(G-10426)*

Avery Dennison Corporation 513 682-7500
11101 Mosteller Rd Ste 2 Cincinnati (45241) *(G-2648)*

Avery Dennison Corporation 216 267-8700
15939 Industrial Pkwy Cleveland (44135) *(G-3707)*

Avery Dennison Corporation 440 358-4691
7600 Auburn Rd Bldg 18 Concord Township (44077) *(G-5901)*

Avery Dennison Corporation 440 534-6527
8100 Tyler Blvd Mentor (44060) *(G-10425)*

Avery Dennison Corporation (PA) 440 534-6000
8080 Norton Pkwy Mentor (44060) *(G-10426)*

Avery Dennison Corporation 440 639-3900
5750 Heisley Rd Mentor (44060) *(G-10427)*

Avery Dennison Corporation 440 358-2828
7100 Lindsay Dr Mentor (44060) *(G-10428)*

Avery Dennison Corporation 937 865-2439
200 Monarch Ln Miamisburg (45342) *(G-10613)*

Avery Dennison Corporation 419 898-8273
8035 W Lake Winds Dr Oak Harbor (43449) *(G-12010)*

Avery Dennison Corporation 440 358-3466
670 Hardy Rd Painesville (44077) *(G-12217)*

Avery Dennison Corporation 440 358-2564
250 Chester St Bldg 3 Painesville (44077) *(G-12218)*

Avery Dennison Corporation 440 878-7000
17700 Foltz Pkwy Strongsville (44149) *(G-13814)*

Avery Dnnison G Holdings I LLC 440 534-6000
8080 Norton Pkwy Mentor (44060) *(G-10429)*

Aviary, Cleveland Also Called: Hinterland Cof Strategies LLC *(G-4190)*

Aviation Cmpnent Solutions Inc 440 295-6590
26451 Curtiss Wright Pkwy Ste 106 Richmond Heights (44143) *(G-12805)*

Avid Signs Plus LLC 513 932-7446
495 Lakeside Dr Lebanon (45036) *(G-9062)*

Avidyne 800 284-3963
5980 Wilcox Pl Ste I Dublin (43016) *(G-6865)*

Avient, Avon Lake Also Called: Avient Corporation *(G-797)*

Avient Corporation (PA) 440 930-1000
33587 Walker Rd Avon Lake (44012) *(G-797)*

Avient Corporation 440 930-3727
33587 Walker Rd # Rdb-418 Avon Lake (44012) *(G-798)*

Avient Corporation 800 727-4338
1050 Landsdowne Ave Greenville (45331) *(G-8037)*

Avient Corporation 330 834-3812
1675 Navarre Rd Se Massillon (44646) *(G-10077)*

Avient Corporation 419 668-4844
80 N West St Norwalk (44857) *(G-11955)*

Aviles Construction Co Inc 216 939-1084
7011 Clark Ave Cleveland (44102) *(G-3708)*

Avion Tool Corporation 937 278-0779
3620 Lenox Dr Dayton (45429) *(G-6220)*

Aviva Metals, Lorain Also Called: National Bronze Mtls Ohio Inc *(G-9425)*

Avon, Cleveland Also Called: Wallseye Concrete Corp *(G-4892)*

Avon Concrete, Elyria Also Called: Westview Concrete Corp *(G-7218)*

Avon Lake Printing 440 933-2078
227 Miller Rd Avon Lake (44012) *(G-799)*

Avon Lake Sheet Metal Co 440 933-3505
33574 Pin Oak Pkwy Avon Lake (44012) *(G-800)*

Avt Beckett Elevators USA Inc 844 360-0288
30130 Industrial Park Dr Logan (43138) *(G-9359)*

Avt Technology Solutions LLC 727 539-7429
5350 Centerpoint Pkwy Groveport (43125) *(G-8130)*

Avtek International Inc 330 633-7500
382 Commerce St Tallmadge (44278) *(G-14023)*

Avtron Aerospace Inc 216 750-5152
7900 E Pleasant Valley Rd Cleveland (44131) *(G-3709)*

Avtron Holdings LLC 216 642-1230
7900 E Pleasant Valley Rd Cleveland (44131) *(G-3710)*

Avtron Industrial Automation, Independence Also Called: Nidec Avtron Automation Corporation *(G-8677)*

Avtron Loadbank Inc 216 573-7600
6255 Halle Dr Cleveland (44125) *(G-3711)*

Avure Autoclave Systems Inc

Avure Autoclave Systems Inc (DH).. 614 891-2732
   3721 Corp Dr Columbus (43231) *(G-5167)*

AW Faber-Castell Usa Inc.. 216 643-4660
   9000 Rio Nero Dr Independence (44131) *(G-8654)*

Awardcraft, Celina *Also Called: Eighth Floor Promotions LLC (G-2330)*

AWC Transition Corporation... 614 846-2918
   6540 Huntley Rd Columbus (43229) *(G-5168)*

Awning Fabri Caters Inc.. 216 476-4888
   10237 Lorain Ave Cleveland (44111) *(G-3712)*

Aws Industries Inc... 513 932-7941
   2600 Henkle Dr Lebanon (45036) *(G-9063)*

Awu Corp... 740 504-8448
   325 Huntsford Dr Macedonia (44056) *(G-9536)*

Axalt Powde Coati Syste Usa I.. 614 921-8000
   4150 Lyman Dr Hilliard (43026) *(G-8400)*

Axalt Powde Coati Syste Usa I.. 614 600-4104
   4130 Lyman Dr Hilliard (43026) *(G-8401)*

Axess International LLC.. 330 460-4840
   4641 Stag Thicket Ln Brunswick (44212) *(G-1750)*

Axiom Engineered Systems LLC (PA).. 416 435-7313
   1 Seagate Fl 27 Toledo (43604) *(G-14202)*

Axiom International Inc... 330 396-5942
   3517 Embassy Pkwy Ste 150 Akron (44333) *(G-71)*

Axiom Tool Group Inc... 844 642-4902
   270 Broad St Westerville (43081) *(G-15693)*

Axion International Holdings Inc... 740 452-2500
   4005 All American Way Zanesville (43701) *(G-16501)*

Axion International Inc.. 740 452-2500
   4005 All American Way Zanesville (43701) *(G-16502)*

Axion Strl Innovations LLC (PA)... 740 452-2500
   1100 Brandywine Blvd Ste H Zanesville (43701) *(G-16503)*

Axis Corporation.. 937 592-1958
   314 Water Ave Bellefontaine (43311) *(G-1201)*

Axium Packaging LLC (PA)... 614 706-5955
   9005 Smiths Mill Rd New Albany (43054) *(G-11369)*

Axium Plastics, New Albany *Also Called: Axium Packaging LLC (G-11369)*

Axle Machine Services Ltd... 419 827-2000
   41 County Road 2350 Lakeville (44638) *(G-8963)*

Axon Medical Llc.. 216 276-0262
   1484 Medina Rd Ste 117 Medina (44256) *(G-10299)*

Axxess LLC... 330 861-0911
   61 E State St Barberton (44203) *(G-856)*

Ayers Limestone Quarry Inc... 740 633-2958
   2002 Colerain Pike Martins Ferry (43935) *(G-9896)*

Ayling and Reichert Co Consent... 419 898-2471
   411 S Railroad St Oak Harbor (43449) *(G-12011)*

Azsr Technologies Distr LLC.. 216 315-8285
   14380 Gallatin Blvd Brookpark (44142) *(G-1705)*

Aztec Manufacturing Inc... 330 783-9747
   4325 Simon Rd Youngstown (44512) *(G-16316)*

Aztech Printing & Promotions... 937 339-0100
   402 E Main St Troy (45373) *(G-14551)*

Aztlan Communications, Toledo *Also Called: La Prensa Publications Inc (G-14357)*

Azz Galvanizing - Cincinnati, Cincinnati *Also Called: AAA Galvanizing - Joliet Inc (G-2588)*

Azz Inc... 330 456-3241
   1723 Cleveland Ave Sw Canton (44707) *(G-2041)*

B & A Holistic Fd & Herbs LLC... 614 747-2200
   4550 Heaton Rd Ste B7 Columbus (43229) *(G-5169)*

B & B Box Company Inc.. 419 872-5600
   26490 Southpoint Rd Perrysburg (43551) *(G-12363)*

B & B Gear and Machine Co Inc... 937 687-1771
   440 W Main St New Lebanon (45345) *(G-11448)*

B & B Industries, Orient *Also Called: Kmj Leasing Ltd (G-12115)*

B & B Industries Inc... 614 871-3883
   7001 Harrisburg Pike Orient (43146) *(G-12113)*

B & B Molded Products Inc... 419 592-8700
   1250 Ottawa Ave Defiance (43512) *(G-6670)*

B & B Paper Converters Inc.. 216 941-8100
   12500 Elmwood Ave Frnt Cleveland (44111) *(G-3713)*

B & B Printing Graphics Inc.. 419 893-7068
   1689 Lance Pointe Rd Maumee (43537) *(G-10167)*

ALPHABETIC SECTION

B & C Research, Barberton *Also Called: B & C Research Inc (G-857)*

B & C Research Inc.. 330 848-4000
   842 Norton Ave Barberton (44203) *(G-857)*

B & D Commissarys LLC... 740 743-3890
   5705 State Route 204 Ne Mount Perry (43760) *(G-11249)*

B & D Machinists Inc... 513 831-8588
   1350 Us Route 50 Milford (45150) *(G-10893)*

B & F Manufacturing Co.. 216 518-0333
   19050 Cranwood Pkwy Warrensville Heights (44128) *(G-15226)*

B & G Tool Company... 614 451-2538
   4832 Kenny Rd Columbus (43220) *(G-5170)*

B & H Machine Inc... 330 868-6425
   15001 Lincoln St Se Minerva (44657) *(G-11027)*

B & J Baking Company.. 513 541-2386
   4056 Colerain Ave Cincinnati (45223) *(G-2649)*

B & P Company Inc.. 937 298-0265
   97 Compark Rd Dayton (45459) *(G-6221)*

B & P Polishing Inc.. 330 753-4202
   123 9th St Nw Barberton (44203) *(G-858)*

B & P Spring Production Co.. 216 486-4260
   19520 Nottingham Rd Cleveland (44110) *(G-3714)*

B & R Custom Chrome.. 419 500-7216
   469 Dearborn Ave Toledo (43605) *(G-14203)*

B & R Fabricators & Maint Inc... 513 641-2222
   4524 W Mitchell Ave Cincinnati (45232) *(G-2650)*

B & R Machine Co.. 216 961-7370
   2216 W 65th St Cleveland (44102) *(G-3715)*

B & S Transport Inc (PA)... 330 767-4319
   11325 Lawndell Rd Sw Navarre (44662) *(G-11340)*

B & T Welding and Machine Co.. 740 687-1908
   423 S Mount Pleasant Ave Lancaster (43130) *(G-8990)*

B A Malcuit Racing Inc.. 330 878-7111
   707 S Wooster Ave Strasburg (44680) *(G-13743)*

B B & H Tool Company.. 614 868-8634
   7719 Taylor Rd Sw Reynoldsburg (43068) *(G-12752)*

B B Bradley Company Inc... 614 777-5600
   2699 Scioto Pkwy Columbus (43221) *(G-5171)*

B B Bradley Company Inc (PA)... 440 354-2005
   7755 Crile Rd Concord Township (44077) *(G-5902)*

B C I, Fairlawn *Also Called: Buckeye Corrugated Inc (G-7434)*

B C I, Powell *Also Called: Building Ctrl Integrators LLC (G-12665)*

B C T, Akron *Also Called: Akron Thermography Inc (G-46)*

B C T, Akron *Also Called: Akron Thermography Inc (G-47)*

B D G Wrap-Tite Inc (PA)... 440 349-5400
   6200 Cochran Rd Solon (44139) *(G-13315)*

B Exterior Coatings LLC... 937 561-2654
   515 Anthony Ln Miamisburg (45342) *(G-10614)*

B J Pallett.. 419 447-9665
   324 4th Ave Tiffin (44883) *(G-14077)*

B K Plastics Inc.. 937 473-2087
   1400 Mote Dr Covington (45318) *(G-6019)*

B M Machine (PA).. 419 595-2898
   11722 W County Road 6 Alvada (44802) *(G-440)*

B M Machine.. 419 595-2898
   27 S Perry St New Riegel (44853) *(G-11534)*

B O K Inc.. 937 322-9588
   508 W Main St Springfield (45504) *(G-13537)*

B P Oil Company.. 513 671-4107
   1201 Omniplex Dr Cincinnati (45240) *(G-2651)*

B P T, Bucyrus *Also Called: Bucyrus Precision Tech Inc (G-1852)*

B R Printers Inc.. 513 271-6035
   3962 Virginia Ave Cincinnati (45227) *(G-2652)*

B Richardson Inc... 330 724-2122
   25 Elinor Ave Akron (44305) *(G-72)*

B S F Inc (PA).. 937 890-6121
   8895 N Dixie Dr Dayton (45414) *(G-6222)*

B S F Inc.. 937 890-6121
   320b S 5th St Tipp City (45371) *(G-14123)*

B V Grinding Machining Inc.. 440 918-1884
   1438 E 363rd St Willoughby (44095) *(G-15888)*

B V Mfg Inc.. 330 549-5331
   13426 Woodworth Rd New Springfield (44443) *(G-11539)*

ALPHABETIC SECTION   Ballastshop

B W Grinding Co 419 923-1376
15048 County Rd 10-3 Lyons (43533) *(G-9531)*

B-K Tool & Design Inc 419 532-3890
480 W Main St Kalida (45853) *(G-8784)*

B-R-O-T Incorporated 216 267-5335
4730 Briar Rd Cleveland (44135) *(G-3717)*

B-Wear Sportswear, Zanesville Also Called: 5 BS Inc *(G-16493)*

B&A Ison Steel Inc 216 663-4300
3238 E 82nd St Cleveland (44104) *(G-3716)*

B&B Distributors LLC 440 324-1293
811 Taylor St Elyria (44035) *(G-7113)*

B&C Machine Co LLC 330 745-4013
401 Newell St Barberton (44203) *(G-859)*

B&D Truck Parts Sls & Svcs LLC 419 701-7041
1498 Perrysburg Rd Fostoria (44830) *(G-7629)*

B&D Water Inc 330 771-3318
69478 Fairground Rd Quaker City (43773) *(G-12691)*

B&G Contractors Supply, Coventry Township Also Called: Kuhlman Corporation *(G-6012)*

B&G Foods Inc 513 482-8226
5204 Spring Grove Ave Cincinnati (45217) *(G-2653)*

B&L Services 740 390-4272
28 Zent Ave Fredericktown (43019) *(G-7738)*

B&M Underground LLC 740 505-3096
1403 Gurneyville Rd Wilmington (45177) *(G-16040)*

B&N Coal Inc 740 783-3575
38455 Marietta Rt Dexter City (45727) *(G-6802)*

B2d Solutions Inc 855 484-1145
3558 Lee Rd Cleveland (44120) *(G-3718)*

B5 Systems Inc 937 372-4768
1463 Bellbrook Ave Xenia (45385) *(G-16249)*

Babbert Real Estate Inv Co Ltd (PA) 614 837-8444
7415 Diley Rd Canal Winchester (43110) *(G-1980)*

Babcock & Wilcox Co, Lancaster Also Called: Babcock & Wilcox Company *(G-8991)*

Babcock & Wilcox Company (HQ) 330 753-4511
1200 E Market St Ste 650 Akron (44305) *(G-73)*

Babcock & Wilcox Company 330 753-4511
91 Stirling Ave Barberton (44203) *(G-860)*

Babcock & Wilcox Company 740 687-6500
2600 E Main St Lancaster (43130) *(G-8991)*

Babcock & Wilcox Entps Inc (PA) 330 753-4511
1200 E Market St Ste 650 Akron (44305) *(G-74)*

Babcock & Wilcox Entps Inc 740 687-4370
2560 E Main St Lancaster (43130) *(G-8992)*

Babcock & Wilcox Holdings Inc 704 625-4900
1200 E Market St Ste 650 Akron (44305) *(G-75)*

Babcox Media Inc 330 670-1234
3550 Embassy Pkwy Akron (44333) *(G-76)*

Back In Black Co 419 425-5555
2100 Fostoria Ave Findlay (45840) *(G-7479)*

Backattack Snacks 216 236-4580
5121 W 161st St Brookpark (44142) *(G-1706)*

Backyard Scoreboards LLC 513 702-6561
431 Kenridge Dr Middletown (45042) *(G-10805)*

Badboy Blasters Incorporated 330 454-2699
1720 Wallace Ave Ne Canton (44705) *(G-2042)*

Badlime Promo and Apparel LLC 330 425-7100
2146 E Aurora Rd Twinsburg (44087) *(G-14633)*

Bae Systems Survivability Systems LLC 513 881-9800
9113 Le Saint Dr West Chester (45014) *(G-15372)*

Baerlocher, Dover Also Called: Baerlocher Usa LLC *(G-6808)*

Baerlocher Production Usa LLC 513 482-6300
5890 Highland Ridge Dr Cincinnati (45232) *(G-2654)*

Baerlocher Usa LLC (DH) 330 364-6000
3676 Davis Rd Nw Dover (44622) *(G-6808)*

Baesman Group Inc (PA) 614 771-2300
4477 Reynolds Dr Hilliard (43026) *(G-8402)*

Bag & Bottle Manufacturing, Ashland Also Called: Liqui-Box Corporation *(G-589)*

Bag, The, Lancaster Also Called: Dispatch Consumer Services *(G-9013)*

Baggallini Inc 800 448-8753
13405 Yarmouth Dr Pickerington (43147) *(G-12456)*

Bagpack, West Chester Also Called: BP 10 Inc *(G-15382)*

Bahler Medical Inc 614 873-7600
8910 Warner Rd Plain City (43064) *(G-12564)*

Bailee Logging LLC 330 881-4688
36575 Dinch Rd Salineville (43945) *(G-13038)*

Bailey & Jensen Inc 937 272-1784
442 Yankee Tr Centerville (45458) *(G-2360)*

Baillie Lumber Co LP 419 462-2000
3953 County Road 51 Galion (44833) *(G-7861)*

Bainbridge419 Inc 937 228-2181
6142 American Rd Toledo (43612) *(G-14204)*

Bainter Machining Company (PA) 740 653-2422
1230 Rainbow Dr Ne Lancaster (43130) *(G-8993)*

Bainter Machining Company 740 756-4598
842 N Columbus St Lancaster (43130) *(G-8994)*

Baird Brothers Sawmill Inc 330 533-3122
7060 Crory Rd Canfield (44406) *(G-2000)*

Baird Concrete Products Inc 740 623-8600
15 Locust St Coshocton (43812) *(G-5972)*

Bajio Brewing Company LLC 419 410-8275
2959 Nebraska Ave Toledo (43607) *(G-14205)*

Bakelite Chemicals LLC 404 652-4000
1975 Watkins Rd Columbus (43207) *(G-5172)*

Bakelite N Sumitomo Amer Inc 419 675-1282
13717 Us Highway 68 Kenton (43326) *(G-8881)*

Bakemark USA LLC 440 323-5100
6325 Gateway Blvd S Elyria (44035) *(G-7114)*

Baker & Taylor Publisher Svcs, Ashland Also Called: Bookmasters Inc *(G-557)*

Baker & Taylor Publisher Svcs, Ashland Also Called: Follett Hgher Edcatn Group Inc *(G-574)*

Baker McMillen Co (PA) 330 923-8300
3688 Wyoga Lake Rd Stow (44224) *(G-13687)*

Baker Media Group LLC 330 253-0056
1653 Merriman Rd Ste 116 Akron (44313) *(G-77)*

Baker Plastics Inc 330 743-3142
900 Mahoning Ave Youngstown (44502) *(G-16317)*

Baker Store Equipment Company
23449 Laureldale Rd Shaker Heights (44122) *(G-13150)*

Baker-Shindler Builders Sup Co, Defiance Also Called: Baker-Shindler Contracting Co *(G-6671)*

Baker-Shindler Contracting Co (PA) 419 782-5080
525 Cleveland Ave Defiance (43512) *(G-6671)*

Bakers Welding, Zanesville Also Called: J A B Welding Service Inc *(G-16540)*

Bakerwell Inc (PA) 330 276-2161
10420 County Road 620 Killbuck (44637) *(G-8916)*

Bakerwell Service Rigs Inc (HQ) 330 276-2161
10420 County Road 620 Killbuck (44637) *(G-8917)*

Balancing Company Inc (PA) 937 898-9111
898 Center Dr Vandalia (45377) *(G-14933)*

Baldwin, Hilliard Also Called: Mxr Imaging Inc *(G-8423)*

Baleco International, North Bend Also Called: Hammersmith Bros Invstmnts Inc *(G-11704)*

Ball Aerosol And Specialty Container Inc., Hubbard Also Called: Ball Arosol Specialty Cont Inc *(G-8561)*

Ball Arosol Specialty Cont Inc 330 534-1903
644 Myron St Hubbard (44425) *(G-8561)*

Ball Corporation 234 360-2141
2121 Warner Rd Se Canton (44707) *(G-2043)*

Ball Corporation 614 771-9112
2690 Charter St Columbus (43228) *(G-5173)*

Ball Corporation 419 423-3071
1800 Production Dr Findlay (45840) *(G-7480)*

Ball Corporation 330 244-2313
3075 Brookline Rd North Canton (44720) *(G-11716)*

Ball Jackets LLC 937 572-1114
5120 Waynesville Jamestown Rd Jamestown (45335) *(G-8740)*

Ball Metal Beverage Cont Corp 419 423-3071
12340 Township Rd 99 E Findlay (45840) *(G-7481)*

Ball Metal Beverage Cont Div, Findlay Also Called: Ball Metal Beverage Cont Corp *(G-7481)*

Ball Metal Food Container, Columbus Also Called: Ball Corporation *(G-5173)*

Ballas Egg Products, Zanesville Also Called: BE Products Inc *(G-16507)*

Ballas Egg Products Corp 614 453-0386
40 N 2nd St Zanesville (43701) *(G-16504)*

Ballastshop, Cleveland Also Called: B2d Solutions Inc *(G-3718)*

Ballinger Industries Inc

ALPHABETIC SECTION

Ballinger Industries Inc (PA)..419 422-4533
2500 Fostoria Ave Findlay (45840) *(G-7482)*

Ballinger Industries Inc...419 421-4704
616 N Blanchard St Findlay (45840) *(G-7483)*

Ballreich Bros Inc..419 447-1814
186 Ohio Ave Tiffin (44883) *(G-14078)*

Ballreichs Potato Chips Snacks, Tiffin *Also Called: Ballreich Bros Inc (G-14078)*

Balmac Inc...614 876-1295
4010 Main St Hilliard (43026) *(G-8403)*

Baltic Country Meats...330 897-7025
3320 State Route 557 Baltic (43804) *(G-834)*

Baltic Meats, Baltic *Also Called: Baltic Country Meats (G-834)*

Bam Fuel Inc..740 397-6674
21191 Floralwood Dr Howard (43028) *(G-8558)*

Bamal Corp..937 492-9484
2580 Ross St Sidney (45365) *(G-13225)*

Bamberger Polymers Inc...614 718-9104
9374 Culross Ct Dublin (43017) *(G-6866)*

Bamf Welding & Fabrication LLC..440 862-8286
9988 Kinsman Rd Novelty (44072) *(G-12008)*

Ban Inc..937 325 6539
619 S Belmont Ave Springfield (45505) *(G-13538)*

Banbury Investments Inc..513 677-4500
9160 Union Cemetery Rd Cincinnati (45249) *(G-2655)*

Banco Die Inc..330 821-8511
11322 Union Ave Ne Alliance (44601) *(G-395)*

Bandages & Boo-Boos Press LLC..614 271-6193
4101 Williamsburg Ct Medina (44256) *(G-10300)*

Banks Manufacturing Company..440 458-8661
40259 Banks Rd Grafton (44044) *(G-7997)*

Banner Mattress & Furniture Co, Toledo *Also Called: Banner Mattress Co Inc (G-14206)*

Banner Mattress Co Inc..419 324-7181
2544 N Reynolds Rd Toledo (43615) *(G-14206)*

Banner Metals Group Inc..614 291-3105
1308 Holly Ave Columbus (43212) *(G-5174)*

BAP Manufacturing Inc..419 332-5041
601 N Stone St Ste 1 Fremont (43420) *(G-7765)*

Bar Processing Corporation...330 872-0914
1000 Windham Rd Newton Falls (44444) *(G-11653)*

Bar Processing Corporation...440 943-0094
1271 E 289th St Wickliffe (44092) *(G-15825)*

Barbara A Lieurance..937 382-2864
180 E Sugartree St Wilmington (45177) *(G-16041)*

Barbasol LLC..419 903-0738
2011 Ford Dr Ashland (44805) *(G-555)*

Barbco, East Canton *Also Called: Barbco Inc (G-6978)*

Barbco Inc...330 488-9400
315 Pekin Dr Se East Canton (44730) *(G-6978)*

Barberton Facility, Barberton *Also Called: Babcock & Wilcox Company (G-860)*

Barberton Herald, Barberton *Also Called: Richardson Publishing Company (G-894)*

Barberton Steel Industries Inc..330 745-6837
240 E Huston St Barberton (44203) *(G-861)*

Barbour Auto Parts, Portsmouth *Also Called: Tom Barbour Auto Parts Inc (G-12659)*

Barbs Graffiti Inc (PA)..216 881-5550
3111 Carnegie Ave Cleveland (44115) *(G-3719)*

Barco Inc...937 372-7579
600 Bellbrook Ave Xenia (45385) *(G-16250)*

Barcon LLC...866 883-4804
47161 State Route 558 New Waterford (44445) *(G-11553)*

Bard Manufacturing Company Inc (PA).................................419 636-1194
1914 Randolph Dr Bryan (43506) *(G-1809)*

Bardes Corporation...513 533-6200
4730 Madison Rd Cincinnati (45227) *(G-2656)*

Bardons & Oliver Inc (PA)..440 498-5800
5800 Harper Rd Solon (44139) *(G-13316)*

Bardwell Winery, Mount Orab *Also Called: Wedco LLC (G-11247)*

Barfections LLC (PA)...330 759-3100
1598 Motor Inn Dr Girard (44420) *(G-7962)*

Barfections LLC...330 759-3100
6105 W Liberty St Hubbard (44425) *(G-8562)*

Barfections LLC...330 759-3100
4718 Belmont Ave Youngstown (44505) *(G-16318)*

Bargain Hunter, Millersburg *Also Called: Alonovus Corp (G-10940)*

Bargmann Management, L.L.C., Elyria *Also Called: Invacare Hcs LLC (G-7167)*

Barile Precision Grinding Inc..216 267-6500
12320 Plaza Dr Cleveland (44130) *(G-3720)*

Barium & Chemicals Inc...740 282-9776
515 Kingsdale Rd Steubenville (43952) *(G-13661)*

Barker Products Company
1028 E 134th St Cleveland (44110) *(G-3721)*

Barkman Products LLC..330 893-2520
2550 Township Road 121 Millersburg (44654) *(G-10942)*

Barlamy Supply, Wapakoneta *Also Called: Jewett Supply (G-15119)*

Barley's Brewing Company, Columbus *Also Called: Brewpub Restaurant Corporation (G-5211)*

Barn Small Engine Repa..419 583-6595
10295 State Route 108 Wauseon (43567) *(G-15257)*

Barnes Advertising Corporation...740 453-6836
1580 Fairview Rd Zanesville (43701) *(G-16505)*

Barnes Group Inc...440 526-5900
10367 Brecksville Rd Brecksville (44141) *(G-1607)*

Barnes Group Inc...419 891-9292
370 W Dussel Dr Ste A Maumee (43537) *(G-10168)*

Barnes Group Inc...513 770-6888
9826 Crescent Park Dr West Chester (45069) *(G-15373)*

Barnes Group Inc...513 779-6888
9826 Crescent Park Dr West Chester (45069) *(G-15374)*

Barnes International LLC..419 352-7501
555 Van Camp Rd Bowling Green (43402) *(G-1552)*

Barnes Services LLC...440 319-2088
20677 Centuryway Rd Maple Heights (44137) *(G-9747)*

Barneys Hot Shot Service LLC..740 517-9593
22905 Caldwell Rd Quaker City (43773) *(G-12692)*

Barnhart Printing Corp...330 456-2279
1107 Melchoir Pl Sw Canton (44707) *(G-2044)*

Barnhart Publishing, Canton *Also Called: Barnhart Printing Corp (G-2044)*

Barr Engineering Incorporated (PA)......................................614 714-0299
2800 Corporate Exchange Dr Ste 240 Columbus (43231) *(G-5175)*

Barr Laboratories Inc...513 731-9900
5040 Duramed Rd Cincinnati (45213) *(G-2657)*

Barracuda Technologies Inc...216 469-1566
2900 State Route 82 Aurora (44202) *(G-708)*

Barrel Run Crssing Wnery Vnyrd..330 325-1075
3272 Industry Rd Rootstown (44272) *(G-12851)*

Barrett Paving Materials Inc (DH)..973 533-1001
8590 Bilstein Blvd Hamilton (45015) *(G-8183)*

Barrett Paving Materials Inc...937 293-9033
2701 W Dorothy Ln Moraine (45439) *(G-11159)*

Barry-Wehmiller Companies Inc..330 923-0491
4485 Allen Rd Cuyahoga Falls (44224) *(G-6072)*

Barsplice Products Inc..937 275-8700
4900 Webster St Dayton (45414) *(G-6223)*

Barth Industries Co LLC (PA)..216 267-1950
12650 Brookpark Rd Cleveland (44130) *(G-3722)*

Barton-Carey Medical Pdts Inc (PA)......................................419 887-1285
1331 Conant St Ste 102 Maumee (43537) *(G-10169)*

Barudan, Solon *Also Called: Barudan America Inc (G-13317)*

Barudan America Inc (HQ)..440 248-8770
30901 Carter St Frnt A Solon (44139) *(G-13317)*

Basco Manufacturing Company (PA)....................................513 573-1900
7201 Snider Rd Mason (45040) *(G-9957)*

Basco Shower Enclosures, Mason *Also Called: Basco Manufacturing Company (G-9957)*

Basetek LLC (PA)..877 712-2273
14975 White Rd Middlefield (44062) *(G-10733)*

BASF..419 408-5398
522 Crawford Rd Arlington (45814) *(G-548)*

BASF, Cleveland *Also Called: BASF Catalysts LLC (G-3723)*

BASF Catalysts LLC..216 360-5005
23800 Mercantile Rd Cleveland (44122) *(G-3723)*

BASF Catalysts LLC..440 322-3741
120 Pine St Elyria (44035) *(G-7115)*

BASF Corp..513 681-9100
3131 Spring Grove Ave Cincinnati (45225) *(G-2658)*

BASF Corporation 513 482-3000
4900 Este Ave Cincinnati (45232) *(G-2659)*

BASF Corporation 614 662-5682
9565 Logistics Ct Columbus (43217) *(G-5176)*

BASF Corporation 440 329-2525
120 Pine St Elyria (44035) *(G-7116)*

BASF Corporation 937 547-6700
1175 Martin St Greenville (45331) *(G-8038)*

BASF Corporation 419 877-5308
6125 Industrial Pkwy Whitehouse (43571) *(G-15815)*

Basic Cases Inc 216 662-3900
19561 Miles Rd Cleveland (44128) *(G-3724)*

Basic Coatings LLC 419 241-2156
400 Van Camp Rd Bowling Green (43402) *(G-1553)*

Basic Grain Products Inc 419 678-2304
300 E Vine St 310 Coldwater (45828) *(G-4982)*

Basilius Inc 419 536-5810
4338 South Ave Toledo (43615) *(G-14207)*

Bassett Nut Company, Holland *Also Called: Jml Holdings Inc (G-8515)*

Bates Metal Products Inc 740 498-8371
403 E Mn St Port Washington (43837) *(G-12631)*

Bates Printing Inc 330 833-5830
150 23rd St Se Massillon (44646) *(G-10078)*

Bath & Body Works, Reynoldsburg *Also Called: Bath & Body Works LLC (G-12753)*

Bath & Body Works LLC (HQ) 614 856-6000
7 Limited Pkwy E Reynoldsburg (43068) *(G-12753)*

Bath and Body Works, Reynoldsburg *Also Called: Beautyavenues LLC (G-12754)*

Battery Unlimited 740 452-5030
1080 Linden Ave Zanesville (43701) *(G-16506)*

Battle Motors Inc 888 328-5443
1951 Reiser Ave Se New Philadelphia (44663) *(G-11486)*

Bauer Corporation (PA) 800 321-4760
2540 Progress Dr Wooster (44691) *(G-16102)*

Bauer Ladder, Wooster *Also Called: Bauer Corporation (G-16102)*

Baughman Machine & Weld Sp Inc 330 866-9243
6498 June Rd Nw Waynesburg (44688) *(G-15293)*

Baughman Tile Company 800 837-3160
8516 Road 137 Paulding (45879) *(G-12311)*

Baumfolder Corporation (DH) 937 492-1281
1660 Campbell Rd Sidney (45365) *(G-13226)*

Baumgardner Products Co 330 376-2466
295 Silver St Akron (44303) *(G-78)*

Bautec N Technoform Amer Inc 330 487-6600
1755 Enterprise Pkwy Ste 300 Twinsburg (44087) *(G-14634)*

Baxter Burial Vault Svc Inc 513 641-1010
909 E Ross Ave Cincinnati (45217) *(G-2660)*

Baxter Holdings Inc 513 860-3593
3370 Port Union Rd Hamilton (45014) *(G-8184)*

Baxter-Wilbert Burial Vault, Cincinnati *Also Called: Baxter Burial Vault Svc Inc (G-2660)*

Baxters LLC 234 678-5484
1259 Ashford Ln Akron (44313) *(G-79)*

Baxters North America Inc 513 552-7463
4700 Creek Rd Blue Ash (45242) *(G-1364)*

Baxters North America Inc 513 552-7400
10825 Kenwood Rd Blue Ash (45242) *(G-1365)*

Baxters North America Inc 513 552-7728
4602 Ilmenau Way Blue Ash (45242) *(G-1366)*

Baxters North America Inc (DH) 513 552-7485
4700 Creek Rd Cincinnati (45242) *(G-2661)*

Baxters North America Inc 513 552-7718
9756 International Blvd West Chester (45246) *(G-15540)*

Bay Business Forms Inc 937 322-3000
1803 W Columbia St Springfield (45504) *(G-13539)*

Bay Controls LLC 419 891-4390
6528 Weatherfield Ct Maumee (43537) *(G-10170)*

Bay Corporation 440 835-2212
867 Canterbury Rd Westlake (44145) *(G-15735)*

Bay Packing, Lancaster *Also Called: C J Kraft Enterprises Inc (G-8997)*

Bay State Polymer, Westlake *Also Called: Bay State Polymer Distribution Inc (G-15736)*

Bay State Polymer Distribution Inc 440 892-8500
27540 Detroit Rd Ste 102 Westlake (44145) *(G-15736)*

Bayard Inc 937 293-1415
2621 Dryden Rd Ste 300 Moraine (45439) *(G-11160)*

Bayer 513 336-6600
700 Nilles Rd Fairfield (45014) *(G-7336)*

Bayloff Stmped Pdts Knsman Inc 330 876-4511
8091 State Route 5 Kinsman (44428) *(G-8935)*

Bayou Steel Group, Cleveland *Also Called: Bd Laplace LLC (G-3725)*

Bbb Music LLC 740 772-2262
643 Central Ctr Chillicothe (45601) *(G-2494)*

BBC Technology Solutions, Blue Ash *Also Called: Sutter Llc (G-1476)*

Bbm Fairway Inc 330 899-2200
3515 Massillon Rd Ste 200 Uniontown (44685) *(G-14781)*

Bc Investment Corporation (PA) 330 262-3070
1505 E Bowman St Wooster (44691) *(G-16103)*

Bc Machine Services Corp 513 428-0327
3104 Wayne Madison Rd Trenton (45067) *(G-14539)*

BCI, Toledo *Also Called: Block Communications Inc (G-14214)*

BCi and V Investments Inc 330 538-0660
11675 Mahoning Ave North Jackson (44451) *(G-11778)*

BCI International, Dublin *Also Called: Smiths Medical Pm Inc (G-6940)*

Bcmr Publications LLC 740 441-7778
430 2nd Ave Gallipolis (45631) *(G-7888)*

Bcp Imports LLC 419 467-0291
146 Main St Toledo (43605) *(G-14208)*

Bcs Technologies Ltd 513 829-4577
1041 Tedia Way Fairfield (45014) *(G-7337)*

BCT Alarm Services Inc 440 669-8153
5064 Oberlin Ave Lorain (44053) *(G-9402)*

Bcte, New Philadelphia *Also Called: Bulk Carriers Service Inc (G-11490)*

Bd Laplace LLC (PA) 985 652-4900
28026 Gates Mills Blvd Cleveland (44124) *(G-3725)*

BD Oil Gathering Corp 740 374-9355
649 Mitchells Ln Marietta (45750) *(G-9778)*

Bdi, Canton *Also Called: Bdi Inc (G-2045)*

Bdi Inc 330 498-4980
417 Applegrove St Nw Canton (44720) *(G-2045)*

Bdl Supply, South Charleston *Also Called: Buckeye Diamond Logistics Inc (G-13454)*

Bdp Services Inc 740 828-9685
8255 Blackrun Rd Nashport (43830) *(G-11335)*

BDS Packaging Inc 937 643-0530
3155 Elbee Rd Ste 201 Moraine (45439) *(G-11161)*

Bdu Holdings Inc 330 374-1810
467 Dan St Akron (44310) *(G-80)*

BE Products Inc 740 453-0386
40 N 2nd St Zanesville (43701) *(G-16507)*

Bea-Ecc Apparels Inc 216 650-6336
1287 W 76th St Cleveland (44102) *(G-3726)*

Beach City Lumber Llc 330 878-4097
5177 Austin Ln Nw Strasburg (44680) *(G-13744)*

Beach Company 740 622-0905
240 Browns Ln Coshocton (43812) *(G-5973)*

Beach Manufacturing Co 937 882-6372
118 N Hampton Rd Donnelsville (45319) *(G-6806)*

Beach Mfg Plastic Molding Div 937 882-6400
7816 W National Rd New Carlisle (45344) *(G-11411)*

Beachs Trees, Cincinnati *Also Called: Beachs Trees Slctive Hrvstg LL (G-2553)*

Beachs Trees Slctive Hrvstg LL 513 289-5976
915 Wilma Cir Cincinnati (45245) *(G-2553)*

Beachy Barns Ltd 614 873-4193
8720 Amish Pike Plain City (43064) *(G-12565)*

Beacon Metal Fabricators Inc 216 391-7444
5425 Hamilton Ave Ste D Cleveland (44114) *(G-3727)*

Bead Shoppe At Home 330 479-9598
2872 Whipple Ave Nw Canton (44708) *(G-2046)*

Beam Technologies Inc 800 648-1179
80 E Rich St Ste 400 Columbus (43215) *(G-5177)*

Bean Bag City, Spring Valley *Also Called: Sailors Tailor Inc (G-13491)*

Bear Welding Services LLC 740 630-7538
18210 Myrtle Ake Rd Caldwell (43724) *(G-1907)*

Bearing & Transm Sup Co Div, Macedonia *Also Called: Jay Dee Service Corporation (G-9558)*

ALPHABETIC SECTION

Bearing Precious Seed Intl Inc (PA) 513 575-1706
1369 Woodville Pike Unit B Milford (45150) *(G-10894)*

Bearings Manufacturing Company (PA) 440 846-5517
15157 Foltz Pkwy Strongsville (44149) *(G-13815)*

Beaufort Rfd Inc 330 239-4331
1420 Wolf Creek Trl Sharon Center (44274) *(G-13163)*

Beaumont Bros Stoneware Inc 740 982-0055
410 Keystone St Crooksville (43731) *(G-6044)*

Beaumont Brothers Pottery, Crooksville Also Called: Beaumont Bros Stoneware Inc *(G-6044)*

Beaumont Machine, Mason Also Called: Beaumont Machine LLC *(G-9958)*

Beaumont Machine LLC 513 383-5061
4001 Borman Dr Batavia (45103) *(G-911)*

Beaumont Machine LLC 513 701-0421
7697 Innovation Way Ste 1100 Mason (45040) *(G-9958)*

Beaute Asylum LLC 419 377-9933
2011 Glendale Ave Toledo (43614) *(G-14209)*

Beauty Cft Met Fabricators Inc 440 439-0710
5439 Perkins Rd Bedford (44146) *(G-1104)*

Beautyavenues LLC (HQ) 614 856-6000
7 Limited Pkwy E Reynoldsburg (43068) *(G-12754)*

Beaver Productions 330 352-4603
2251 Cooledge Ave Akron (44305) *(G-81)*

Beaver Wood Products 740 226-6211
190 Buck Hollow Rd Beaver (45613) *(G-1035)*

Beaverson Machine Inc 419 923-8064
11600 County Road 10 2 Delta (43515) *(G-6780)*

Beazer East Inc 740 474-3169
200 E Corwin St Circleville (43113) *(G-3542)*

Beazer East Inc 937 364-2311
4281 Roush Rd Hillsboro (45133) *(G-8455)*

Beazer East Inc 740 947-4677
9978 State Route 220 Waverly (45690) *(G-15278)*

Beca House Coffee LLC 419 731-4961
965 E Wyandot Ave Upper Sandusky (43351) *(G-14804)*

Beck Aluminum Alloys Ltd 216 861-4455
6150 Parkland Blvd # 260 Mayfield Heights (44124) *(G-10247)*

Beck Energy Corporation 330 297-6891
160 N Chestnut St Ravenna (44266) *(G-12706)*

Beck Sand & Gravel Inc 330 626-3863
2820 Webb Rd Ravenna (44266) *(G-12707)*

Beck Studios Inc 513 831-6650
1001 Tech Dr Milford (45150) *(G-10895)*

Becker Gllagher Legal Pubg Inc 513 677-5044
8790 Governors Hill Dr Ste 102 Cincinnati (45249) *(G-2662)*

Beckermills Inc 419 738-3450
15286 State Route 67 Wapakoneta (45895) *(G-15106)*

Beckers Bake Shop Inc 216 752-4161
436 Countryside Dr Broadview Heights (44147) *(G-1655)*

Beckett Air Incorporated (PA) 440 327-9999
37850 Taylor Pkwy North Ridgeville (44039) *(G-11829)*

Beckett Gas Inc (HQ) 440 327-3141
38000 Taylor Pkwy North Ridgeville (44039) *(G-11830)*

Beckett Thermal Solutions, North Ridgeville Also Called: Beckett Gas Inc *(G-11830)*

Beckett-Greenhill LLC 216 861-5730
1800 E 30th St Cleveland (44114) *(G-3728)*

Beckman & Gast Company (PA) 419 678-4195
282 W Kremer Hoying Rd Saint Henry (45883) *(G-12934)*

Beckman Environmental Svcs Inc 513 752-3570
4259 Armstrong Blvd Batavia (45103) *(G-912)*

Beckman Machine LLC 513 242-2700
4684 Paddock Rd Cincinnati (45229) *(G-2663)*

Beckman Xmo 614 864-2232
376 Morrison Rd Ste D Columbus (43213) *(G-5178)*

Beckman Xmo, Columbus Also Called: S Beckman Print Grphic Sltons *(G-5736)*

Becton Dickinson and Company 858 617-4272
2727 London Groveport Rd Groveport (43125) *(G-8131)*

Bedford Gear, Solon Also Called: Joy Global Underground Min LLC *(G-13371)*

Bedford Laboratories, Bedford Also Called: Ben Venue Laboratories Inc *(G-1105)*

Bee Valve, Elyria Also Called: Plastic Enterprises Inc *(G-7196)*

Beebe Worldwide Graphics Sign 513 241-2726
9933 Alliance Rd Ste 2 Blue Ash (45242) *(G-1367)*

Beech Engineering & Mfg, New Philadelphia Also Called: Miller Products Inc *(G-11518)*

Beehex Inc 512 633-5304
1130 Gahanna Pkwy Columbus (43230) *(G-5179)*

Beehex LLC 512 633-5304
1130 Gahanna Pkwy Columbus (43230) *(G-5180)*

Beelighting Inc 937 296-4460
347 Leo St Dayton (45404) *(G-6224)*

Beeline Purchasing LLC 513 703-3733
4454 N Mallard Cv Mason (45040) *(G-9959)*

Beemer Machine Company Inc 330 678-3822
1530 Enterprise Way Kent (44240) *(G-8801)*

Bef Foods Inc 937 372-4493
640 Birch Rd Xenia (45385) *(G-16251)*

Behrco Inc 419 394-1612
1865 Celina Rd Saint Marys (45885) *(G-12945)*

Beiersdorf Inc 513 682-7300
5232 E Provident Dr West Chester (45246) *(G-15541)*

Beijing West Industries 937 455-5281
3100 Research Blvd Ste 10 Dayton (45420) *(G-6225)*

Beitner Tire, Toledo Also Called: Capital Tire Inc *(G-14227)*

Bekaert Corporation (DH) 330 867-3325
3200 W Market St Ste 303 Fairlawn (44333) *(G-7433)*

Bekaert Corporation 330 683-5060
510 Collins Blvd Orrville (44667) *(G-12118)*

Bekaert Corporation 330 683-5060
322 E Pine St Orrville (44667) *(G-12119)*

Bekaert Orrville, Orrville Also Called: Bekaert Corporation *(G-12118)*

Bel-Air Mattress Company, Columbus Also Called: Solstice Sleep Products Inc *(G-5777)*

Belanger Inc (DH) 517 870-3206
9393 Princeton Glendale Rd West Chester (45011) *(G-15375)*

BELCO WORKS, Saint Clairsville Also Called: Belco Works Inc *(G-12897)*

Belco Works Inc 740 695-0500
68425 Hammond Rd Saint Clairsville (43950) *(G-12897)*

Belden Brick Company LLC 330 456-0031
700 Edelweiss Dr Sugarcreek (44681) *(G-13919)*

Belden Brick Company LLC 330 265-2030
690 Dover Rd Ne Sugarcreek (44681) *(G-13920)*

Belden Brick Plant 3, Sugarcreek Also Called: Belden Brick Company LLC *(G-13920)*

Belem Group LLC 614 604-6870
6012 E Main St Columbus (43213) *(G-5181)*

Bell Binders LLC 419 242-3201
320 21st St Toledo (43604) *(G-14210)*

Bell Industrial Services LLC 937 507-9193
1553 Target Dr Sidney (45365) *(G-13227)*

Bell Industries 513 353-2355
9843 New Haven Rd Harrison (45030) *(G-8265)*

Bell Logistics Co 740 702-9830
27311 Old Route 35 Chillicothe (45601) *(G-2495)*

Bell Ohio, Inc., Groveport Also Called: Gpi Ohio LLC *(G-8145)*

Bell Optical, Twinsburg Also Called: Essilor Laboratories Amer Inc *(G-14657)*

Bell Tire Co (PA) 440 234-8022
27003 Oakwood Cir Apt 107 Olmsted Falls (44138) *(G-12076)*

Bell Vault and Monu Works Inc 937 866-2444
1019 S Main St Miamisburg (45342) *(G-10615)*

Bellas Jewels LLC 216 551-9593
975 Parkwood Dr 10ste1 Cleveland (44108) *(G-3729)*

Belle Center Air Tool Co Inc 937 464-7474
202 N Elizabeth St Belle Center (43310) *(G-1195)*

Bellevue Manufacturing Company (PA) 419 483-3190
520 Goodrich Rd Bellevue (44811) *(G-1223)*

Bellisio 740 286-5505
100 E Broadway St Jackson (45640) *(G-8709)*

Bellisio Foods Inc 740 286-5505
100 E Bdwy Jackson (45640) *(G-8710)*

Belmont Community Health Ctr, Bellaire Also Called: Belmont Community Hospital *(G-1183)*

Belmont Community Hospital 740 671-1216
4697 Harrison St Bellaire (43906) *(G-1183)*

Belmont Stamping, Shadyside Also Called: Knight Manufacturing Co Inc *(G-13146)*

Belocal, Columbus Also Called: Creative Nest LLC *(G-5307)*

Beloit Fuel LLC 330 584-1915
9379 First East St North Benton (44449) *(G-11709)*

Belot Concrete Block, Tiltonsville *Also Called: Walden Industries Inc (G-14117)*

Below Zero Inc... 419 973-2366
3324 Secor Rd Ste 23 Toledo (43606) *(G-14211)*

Belton Foods, Dayton *Also Called: Belton Foods LLC (G-6226)*

Belton Foods LLC.. 937 890-7768
2701 Thunderhawk Ct Dayton (45414) *(G-6226)*

Ben Venue Laboratories Inc... 800 989-3320
300 Northfield Rd Bedford (44146) *(G-1105)*

Bench Made Woodworking LLC.. 513 702-2698
5150 Kieley Pl Cincinnati (45217) *(G-2664)*

Benchmark Archtectural Systems.. 614 444-0110
720 Marion Rd Columbus (43207) *(G-5182)*

Benchmark Craftsman Inc.. 866 313-4700
4700 Greenwich Rd Seville (44273) *(G-13135)*

Benchmark Craftsmen, Seville *Also Called: Benchmark Craftsman Inc (G-13135)*

Benchmark Education Co LLC.. 845 215-9808
6295 Commerce Center Dr Ste B Groveport (43125) *(G-8132)*

Benchmark Land Management LLC... 513 310-7850
9431 Butler Warren Rd West Chester (45069) *(G-15376)*

Benchmark Prints... 419 332-7640
2252 W State St Fremont (43420) *(G-7766)*

Benchmark Shield LLC... 614 695-6500
950 Claycraft Rd Gahanna (43230) *(G-7831)*

Benchmark-Cabinets LLC... 740 694-1144
97 Mount Vernon Ave Fredericktown (43019) *(G-7739)*

Bendco Machine & Tool Inc... 419 628-3802
283 W 1st St Minster (45865) *(G-11048)*

Bender Communications Inc (PA).. 740 382-0000
1541 Harding Hwy E Marion (43302) *(G-9848)*

Bender Engineering Company.. 330 938-2355
17934 Mill St Beloit (44609) *(G-1250)*

Bendix, Avon *Also Called: Bendix Coml Vhcl Systems LLC (G-763)*

Bendix Coml Vhcl Systems LLC (DH)... 440 329-9000
35500 Chester Rd Avon (44011) *(G-763)*

Bendon Inc (PA)... 419 207-3600
1840 S Baney Rd Ashland (44805) *(G-556)*

Bendon Publishing Intl, Ashland *Also Called: Bendon Inc (G-556)*

Benjamin Media Inc... 330 467-7588
10050 Brecksville Rd Brecksville (44141) *(G-1608)*

Benjamin P Forbes Company... 440 838-4400
800 Ken Mar Industrial Pkwy Broadview Heights (44147) *(G-1656)*

Benko Products Inc... 440 934-2180
5350 Evergreen Pkwy Sheffield Village (44054) *(G-13181)*

Benmit Division, North Lawrence *Also Called: US Tubular Products Inc (G-11800)*

Bennett & Bennett Inc (PA).. 937 324-1100
888 Dayton St Yellow Springs (45387) *(G-16282)*

Bennett Displays, Geneva *Also Called: Dwayne Bennett Industries (G-7934)*

Bennett Electric Inc.. 800 874-5405
211 Republic St Norwalk (44857) *(G-11956)*

Bennett Machine & Stamping Co... 440 415-0401
150 D Termination Ave Geneva (44041) *(G-7932)*

Bensan Jewelers Inc.. 216 221-1434
14410 Madison Ave Lakewood (44107) *(G-8967)*

Bent Wood Solutions LLC.. 330 674-1454
7426 County Road 77 Millersburg (44654) *(G-10943)*

Bentronix Corp... 440 632-0606
14999 Madison Rd Middlefield (44062) *(G-10734)*

Benvic Trinity LLC.. 609 520-0000
600 Oak St West Unity (43570) *(G-15637)*

Benzle Porcelain Company... 614 876-2159
6100 Hayden Run Rd Hilliard (43026) *(G-8404)*

Berea Manufacturing Inc.. 440 260-0590
480 Geiger St Berea (44017) *(G-1267)*

Berea Printing Company.. 440 243-1080
95 Pelret Industrial Pkwy Berea (44017) *(G-1268)*

Bergen, W J & Co, Solon *Also Called: William J Bergen & Co (G-13448)*

Berghausen Corporation.. 513 591-4491
4524 Este Ave Cincinnati (45232) *(G-2665)*

Bergholz 7, Bergholz *Also Called: Rosebud Mining Company (G-1301)*

Bergstrom Company Ltd Partnr.. 440 232-2282
640 Golden Oak Pkwy Cleveland (44146) *(G-3730)*

Beringer Plating Inc... 330 633-8409
1211 Devalera St Akron (44310) *(G-82)*

Berkshire Road Holdings Inc.. 216 883-4200
3344 E 80th St Cleveland (44127) *(G-3731)*

Berlekamp Plastics Inc... 419 334-4481
2587 County Road 99 Fremont (43420) *(G-7767)*

Berlin Gardens Gazebos Ltd.. 330 893-3411
5045 State Rte 39 Berlin (44610) *(G-1303)*

Berlin Inds Protector Pdts, Youngstown *Also Called: Berlin Industries Inc (G-16319)*

Berlin Industries Inc... 330 549-2100
1275 Boardman Poland Rd Ste 1 Youngstown (44514) *(G-16319)*

Berlin Parts, Millersburg *Also Called: Berlin Truck Caps & Tarps Ltd (G-10944)*

Berlin Truck Caps & Tarps Ltd... 330 893-2811
4560 State Route 39 Millersburg (44654) *(G-10944)*

Berlin Wood Products Inc.. 330 893-3281
5039 County Rd 120 Berlin (44610) *(G-1304)*

Berlin Woodworking LLC.. 330 893-3234
4575 Township Road 366 Millersburg (44654) *(G-10945)*

Bernard Engraving Corp... 419 478-5610
414 N Erie St Ste 100 Toledo (43604) *(G-14212)*

Bernard Laboratories Inc... 513 681-7373
1738 Townsend St Cincinnati (45223) *(G-2666)*

Berran Industrial Group Inc... 330 253-5800
570 Wolf Ledges Pkwy Akron (44311) *(G-83)*

Berry Company.. 513 768-7800
312 Plum St Ste 600 Cincinnati (45202) *(G-2667)*

Berry Film Products Co Inc (DH).. 800 225-6729
8585 Duke Blvd Mason (45040) *(G-9960)*

Berry Global Inc.. 419 887-1602
1695 Indian Wood Cir Maumee (43537) *(G-10171)*

Berry Global Inc.. 419 465-2291
311 Monroe St Monroeville (44847) *(G-11122)*

Berry Global Inc.. 330 896-6700
1275 Ethan Ave Streetsboro (44241) *(G-13761)*

Berry Investments Inc... 937 293-0398
3055 Kettering Blvd Ste 418 Moraine (45439) *(G-11162)*

Berry Plastics, Monroeville *Also Called: Berry Global Inc (G-11122)*

Berry Plastics Filmco Inc... 330 562-6111
1450 S Chillicothe Rd Aurora (44202) *(G-709)*

Besa Lighting Co Inc... 614 475-7046
6695 Taylor Rd Blacklick (43004) *(G-1331)*

Bescast Inc.. 440 946-5300
4600 E 355th St Willoughby (44094) *(G-15889)*

Besco, Batavia *Also Called: Beckman Environmental Svcs Inc (G-912)*

Besi Manufacturing Inc.. 513 874-1460
9445 Sutton Pl West Chester (45011) *(G-15377)*

Besi Manufacturing Inc (PA).. 513 874-0232
9087 Sutton Pl West Chester (45011) *(G-15378)*

Bessamaire Sales Inc.. 440 439-1200
1869 E Aurora Rd Ste 700 Twinsburg (44087) *(G-14635)*

Bessamaire Sales Intl LLC... 800 321-5992
1869 E Aurora Rd Twinsburg (44087) *(G-14636)*

Best Bite Grill LLC.. 419 344-7462
22 N Center St Versailles (45380) *(G-14977)*

Best Controls Company, Ashland *Also Called: Chandler Systems Incorporated (G-564)*

Best Equipment Co Inc.. 440 237-3515
12620 York Delta Dr North Royalton (44133) *(G-11868)*

Best Fab Co., Elyria *Also Called: Stays Lighting Inc (G-7206)*

Best Glass, West Alexandria *Also Called: Kimmatt Corp (G-15342)*

Best Graphics.. 614 327-7929
3760 Snouffer Rd Ste B Columbus (43235) *(G-5183)*

Best Graphics & Printing Inc.. 513 535-3529
11836 Stone Mill Rd Cincinnati (45251) *(G-2668)*

Best Inc.. 419 394-2745
State Rte 116 Saint Marys (45885) *(G-12946)*

Best Lighting Products, Etna *Also Called: Best Lighting Products Inc (G-7254)*

Best Lighting Products Inc (HQ)... 740 964-1198
1213 Etna Pkwy Etna (43062) *(G-7254)*

Best Mold & Manufacturing Inc.. 330 896-9988
1546 E Turkeyfoot Lake Rd Akron (44312) *(G-84)*

Best One Tire & Svc Lima Inc.. 419 425-3322
10456 W Us Route 224 Unit 1 Findlay (45840) *(G-7484)*

Best One Tire & Svc Lima Inc

Best One Tire & Svc Lima Inc (PA)..419 229-2380
 701 E Hanthorn Rd Lima (45804) *(G-9223)*

Best One Tire of Hillsboro, Hillsboro *Also Called: Mid America Tire of Hillsboro Inc (G-8461)*

Best Performance Inc...419 394-2299
 14381 State Route 116 Saint Marys (45885) *(G-12947)*

Best Plating Rack Corp...440 944-3270
 428 E 314th St Willowick (44095) *(G-16030)*

Best Process Solutions Inc...330 220-1440
 26780 Gershwin Dr Westlake (44145) *(G-15737)*

Best Result Marketing Inc..234 212-1194
 7730 First Pl Ste E Bedford (44146) *(G-1106)*

Besten Equipment Inc..216 581-1166
 388 S Main St Ste 700 Akron (44311) *(G-85)*

Besten Inc..216 910-2880
 4416 Lee Rd Cleveland (44128) *(G-3732)*

Bestlight Led Corporation..440 205-1552
 8909 East Ave Mentor (44060) *(G-10430)*

Bestwood Cabinetry LLC..937 661-9621
 117 W Main St Xenia (45385) *(G-16252)*

Beta Industries Inc (PA)..937 299-7385
 2860 Culver Ave Dayton (45429) *(G-0227)*

Betco Corporation Ltd (HQ)..419 241-2156
 400 Van Camp Rd Bowling Green (43402) *(G-1554)*

Bethart Enterprises Inc (PA)...513 863-6161
 531 Main St Hamilton (45013) *(G-8185)*

Bethart Printing Services, Hamilton *Also Called: Bethart Enterprises Inc (G-8185)*

Bethel Engineering, New Hampshire *Also Called: Bethel Engineering and Eqp Inc (G-11445)*

Bethel Engineering and Eqp Inc..419 568-1100
 13830 Mcbeth Rd New Hampshire (45870) *(G-11445)*

Better Banner Printing, New Philadelphia *Also Called: Pro A V of Ohio (G-11523)*

Better Foam Insulation, South Point *Also Called: Pyro-Chem Corporation (G-13474)*

Better Living Concepts Inc...330 494-2213
 7233 Freedom Ave Nw Canton (44720) *(G-2047)*

Betts Co DBA Betts Hd..330 533-0111
 430 W Main St Canfield (44406) *(G-2001)*

Bevcorp Industries LLC..513 673-8520
 10885 Millington Ct Blue Ash (45242) *(G-1368)*

Bevcorp Properties, Eastlake *Also Called: Miconvi Properties Inc (G-7039)*

Beverage Engineering Inc..216 641-6678
 4705 Van Epps Rd Brooklyn Heights (44131) *(G-1684)*

Beverage Mch & Fabricators Inc..216 252-5100
 13301 Lakewood Heights Blvd Cleveland (44107) *(G-3733)*

Beverages Holdings LLC...513 483-3300
 10300 Alliance Rd Ste 500 Blue Ash (45242) *(G-1369)*

Beverly Dove Inc..740 495-5200
 43 E Front St New Holland (43145) *(G-11446)*

Bexley Fabrics Inc..614 231-7272
 2476 E Main St Columbus (43209) *(G-5184)*

Bexley Imaging...614 533-6560
 2222 Welcome Pl Columbus (43209) *(G-5185)*

BF & CD Roberts RE Imprv..937 277-2632
 3336 Highcrest Ct Dayton (45405) *(G-6228)*

Bfc Inc (PA)...330 364-6645
 1213 E 3rd St Dover (44622) *(G-6809)*

Bfs Supply, Cincinnati *Also Called: Frederick Steel Company LLC (G-2922)*

Bgh Specialty Steel Inc...330 467-0324
 8190 Roll And Hold Pkwy Ste A Macedonia (44056) *(G-9537)*

Bharat Trading, West Chester *Also Called: Goyal Enterprises Inc (G-15557)*

Bhi Transition Inc...937 663-4152
 8801 Us Highway 36 Saint Paris (43072) *(G-12971)*

Bhl International Inc..216 458-8472
 10533 Baltic Rd Cleveland (44102) *(G-3734)*

Bi-Con Services Inc..740 685-2542
 10901 Clay Pike Rd Derwent (43733) *(G-6798)*

Bianchi Usa Inc...440 801-1083
 31336 Industrial Pkwy Ste 3 North Olmsted (44070) *(G-11818)*

Bic Manufacturing Inc..216 531-9393
 26420 Century Corners Pkwy Euclid (44132) *(G-7263)*

Blc Precision Machine Co Inc...937 783-1406
 3004 Cherry St Blanchester (45107) *(G-1347)*

Bickers Metal Products Inc..513 353-4000
 5825 State Rte128 Miamitown (45041) *(G-10705)*

Bickett Machine and Gas Supply..740 353-5710
 1411 Robinson Ave Portsmouth (45662) *(G-12641)*

Bico Akron Inc..330 794-1716
 3100 Gilchrist Rd Mogadore (44260) *(G-11067)*

Bico Steel Service Centers, Mogadore *Also Called: Bico Akron Inc (G-11067)*

Bidwell Family Corporation (HQ)......................................513 988-6351
 400 E State St Trenton (45067) *(G-14540)*

Biedenbach Logging...740 732-6477
 48443 Seneca Lake Rd Sarahsville (43779) *(G-13105)*

Bif Co LLC..330 564-0941
 1405 Home Ave Akron (44310) *(G-86)*

Bif, LLC, Akron *Also Called: Bif Co LLC (G-86)*

Big Chief Manufacturing Ltd..513 934-3888
 250 Harmon Ave Lebanon (45036) *(G-9064)*

Big Gus Onion Rings Inc..216 883-9045
 4500 Turney Rd Cleveland (44105) *(G-3735)*

Big Kahuna Graphics, Canton *Also Called: Big Kahuna Graphics LLC (G-2048)*

Big Kahuna Graphics LLC..330 455-2625
 1255 Prospect Ave Sw Canton (44706) *(G-2048)*

Big Mouth Egg Rolls LLC...614 404-3607
 737 Parkwood Ave Columbus (43219) *(G-5186)*

Big Noodle LLC...614 550-7170
 687 Kenwick Rd Columbus (43209) *(G-5187)*

Big Oki LLC...513 874-1111
 6500 Dixie Hwy # 4 Fairfield (45014) *(G-7338)*

Big Productions Inc..440 775-0015
 45300b Us Highway 20 Oberlin (44074) *(G-12049)*

Big River Electric, Gallipolis *Also Called: Big River Electric Inc (G-7889)*

Big River Electric Inc...740 446-4360
 299 Upper River Rd Gallipolis (45631) *(G-7889)*

Big River Online..855 244-7487
 2509 Euclid Heights Blvd Cleveland (44106) *(G-3736)*

Big Sky Petroleum, New Concord *Also Called: Robert Barr (G-11433)*

Big Wheels Leasing LLC...330 769-1594
 4970 Park Ave W Seville (44273) *(G-13136)*

Bijoe Development Inc...330 674-5981
 7188 State Rte 62 & 39 Millersburg (44654) *(G-10946)*

Bike Miami Valley Ohio...937 496-3825
 929 S Perry St Dayton (45402) *(G-6229)*

Bil-Jac Foods Inc (PA)..330 722-7888
 3337 Medina Rd Medina (44256) *(G-10301)*

Bil-Jax, Archbold *Also Called: Haulotte US Inc (G-531)*

Bil-Jax Inc (DH)..419 445-8915
 125 Taylor Pkwy Archbold (43502) *(G-525)*

Bilco Company..740 455-9020
 3400 Jim Granger Dr Zanesville (43701) *(G-16508)*

Biljax Scaffolding, Archbold *Also Called: Bil-Jax Inc (G-525)*

Bill Davis Stadium..614 292-2624
 650 Borror Dr Columbus (43210) *(G-5188)*

Bill's Counter Tops, Saint Clairsville *Also Called: D Lewis Inc (G-12901)*

Billerud Americas Corporation (HQ)..................................877 855-7243
 8540 Gander Creek Dr Miamisburg (45342) *(G-10616)*

Billerud Americas Corporation..901 369-4105
 9025 Centre Pointe Dr West Chester (45069) *(G-15379)*

Billerud Commercial LLC...877 855-7243
 8540 Gander Creek Dr Miamisburg (45342) *(G-10617)*

Billerud Escanaba LLC...877 855-7243
 8540 Gander Creek Dr Miamisburg (45342) *(G-10618)*

Billerud US Prod Holdg LLC (DH).....................................877 855-7243
 8540 Gander Creek Dr Miamisburg (45342) *(G-10619)*

Billington Company Inc...440 647-3039
 143 Erie St Wellington (44090) *(G-15304)*

Billock, John N Cpo, Warren *Also Called: Orthotics Prsthtics Rhblttion (G-15197)*

Bilz Vibration Technology Inc..330 468-2459
 895 Highland Rd E Ste F Macedonia (44056) *(G-9538)*

Bimac, Moraine *Also Called: Santos Industrial Ltd (G-11210)*

Bimbo Bkries USA Clvland Hts D......................................216 641-5700
 4570 E 71st St Cleveland (44105) *(G-3737)*

Bimbo Qsr Us LLC..740 562-4188
 750 Airport Rd Zanesville (43701) *(G-16509)*

ALPHABETIC SECTION — Blair Logging

Bindery & Spc Pressworks Inc.. 614 873-4623
351 W Bigelow Ave Plain City (43064) *(G-12566)*

Bindery Tech Inc.. 440 934-3247
35205 Center Ridge Rd North Ridgeville (44039) *(G-11831)*

Bindtech LLC... 615 834-0404
8212 Bavaria Dr E Macedonia (44056) *(G-9539)*

Bindusa... 513 247-3000
6819 Ashfield Dr Blue Ash (45242) *(G-1370)*

Binkley, Geoffrey, Columbus *Also Called: Signme LLC (G-5771)*

Binos Inc... 330 938-0888
700 W Ohio Ave Sebring (44672) *(G-13118)*

Bio Elctrctcal Scence Tech Inc.. 888 614-1227
2025 Riverside Dr Upper Arlington (43221) *(G-14799)*

Bio-Blood Components Inc.. 614 294-3183
1393 N High St Columbus (43201) *(G-5189)*

Bio-Systems Corporation.. 608 365-9550
400 Van Camp Rd Bowling Green (43402) *(G-1555)*

Biobent Holdings LLC... 513 658-5560
1275 Kinnear Rd Ste 239 Columbus (43212) *(G-5190)*

Biobent Polymers, Columbus *Also Called: Biobent Holdings LLC (G-5190)*

Biofit Engineered Products Limited Partnership (PA)............... 419 823-1089
15500 Bio Fit Way Bowling Green (43402) *(G-1556)*

Bionix Radiation Therapy, Maumee *Also Called: M&H Medical Holdings Inc (G-10215)*

Bionix Safety Technologies Ltd (HQ)...................................... 419 727-0552
1670 Indian Wood Cir Maumee (43537) *(G-10172)*

Biosortia Pharmaceuticals Inc.. 614 636-4850
4266 Tuller Rd Dublin (43017) *(G-6867)*

Biothane Coated Webbing Corp... 440 327-0485
31393 Industrial Pkwy Bldg 2 North Olmsted (44070) *(G-11819)*

Biothane Coated Webbing Corp... 440 327-0485
34655 Mills Rd North Ridgeville (44039) *(G-11832)*

Biowish, Cincinnati *Also Called: Biowish Technologies Inc (G-2669)*

Biowish Technologies Inc.. 312 572-6700
2724 Erie Ave Ste B Cincinnati (45208) *(G-2669)*

Biowish Technologies Inc.. 312 572-6700
2717 Erie Ave Cincinnati (45208) *(G-2670)*

Bip Printing Solutions LLC... 216 832-5673
24755 Highpoint Rd Beachwood (44122) *(G-974)*

Bird Control International... 330 425-2377
1393 Highland Rd Twinsburg (44087) *(G-14637)*

Bird Electronic Corporation... 440 248-1200
30303 Aurora Rd Solon (44139) *(G-13318)*

Bird Equipment LLC... 330 549-1004
11950 South Ave North Lima (44452) *(G-11801)*

Bird Technologies Group Inc (PA).. 440 248-1200
30303 Aurora Rd Solon (44139) *(G-13319)*

Bird Watcher's Digest, Marietta *Also Called: Pardson Inc (G-9814)*

Birds Eye Foods Inc... 330 854-0818
611 Elm Ridge Ave Canal Fulton (44614) *(G-1968)*

Biro Manufacturing Company (PA).. 419 798-4451
1114 W Main St Marblehead (43440) *(G-9764)*

Biro Manufacturing Company.. 419 798-4451
6658 Promway Ave Nw North Canton (44720) *(G-11717)*

Biro Manufacturing Company, Marblehead *Also Called: Biro Manufacturing Company (G-9764)*

Bis Printing... 440 951-2606
35401 Euclid Ave Willoughby (44094) *(G-15890)*

Biscotti Winery LLC.. 440 466-1248
1520 Harpersfield Rd Geneva (44041) *(G-7933)*

Bishop Machine Shop, Zanesville *Also Called: Bishop Machine Tool & Die (G-16510)*

Bishop Machine Tool & Die... 740 453-8818
2304 Hoge Ave Zanesville (43701) *(G-16510)*

Bishop Well Services Corp.. 330 264-2023
416 N Bauer Rd Wooster (44691) *(G-16104)*

Bishops Daily Blessings LLC.. 724 624-3779
5 Maplewood Dr Apt 15 Steubenville (43952) *(G-13662)*

Bismark Lawncare LLC... 440 361-5561
4057 State Route 307 Austinburg (44010) *(G-742)*

Bison Builders LLC... 614 636-0365
6999 Huntley Rd Ste M Columbus (43229) *(G-5191)*

Bison Leather Co... 419 517-1737
7409 W Central Ave Toledo (43617) *(G-14213)*

Bitec, Dayton *Also Called: Sample Machining Inc (G-6558)*

BITTERSWEET FARMS, Whitehouse *Also Called: Bittersweet Inc (G-15816)*

Bittersweet Inc (PA)... 419 875-6986
12660 Archbold Whitehouse Rd Whitehouse (43571) *(G-15816)*

Bittinger Carbide, Cadiz *Also Called: Stanley Bittinger (G-1904)*

Bizall Inc... 216 939-9580
1935 W 96th St Ste H Cleveland (44102) *(G-3738)*

Bizzy Bee Printing Inc.. 614 771-1222
1500 W 3rd Ave Ste 106 Columbus (43212) *(G-5192)*

BJ Equipment Ltd.. 614 497-1188
4522 Lockbourne Rd Columbus (43207) *(G-5193)*

Bjond Inc... 614 537-7246
1463 Briarmeadow Dr Columbus (43235) *(G-5194)*

Bjs DEMo&hauling LLC... 216 904-8909
4937 E 88th St Garfield Heights (44125) *(G-7911)*

Bk Tool Company Inc... 513 870-9622
300 Security Dr Fairfield (45014) *(G-7339)*

Bkt, Copley *Also Called: Bkt USA Inc (G-5944)*

Bkt USA Inc... 330 836-1090
202 Montrose West Ave Ste 240 Copley (44321) *(G-5944)*

Black & Decker, Cleveland *Also Called: Black & Decker Corporation (G-3739)*

Black & Decker (us) Inc.. 614 895-3112
1948 Schrock Rd Columbus (43229) *(G-5195)*

Black & Decker Corporation.. 440 842-9100
12100 Snow Rd Ste 1 Cleveland (44130) *(G-3739)*

Black Box Corporation.. 800 676-8850
6650 W Snowville Rd Ste R Brecksville (44141) *(G-1609)*

Black Box Corporation.. 800 837-7777
5400 Frantz Rd Ste 240 Dublin (43016) *(G-6868)*

Black Box Corporation.. 855 324-9909
26100 1st St Westlake (44145) *(G-15738)*

Black Box Network Services, Westlake *Also Called: Black Box Corporation (G-15738)*

Black Gate Blinds LLC.. 937 402-6158
1053 Purcell Rd Peebles (45660) *(G-12325)*

Black Gold Capital LLC... 614 348-7460
2121 Bethel Rd Ste A Columbus (43220) *(G-5196)*

Black Lab Custom Products, Chardon *Also Called: Kona Blackbird Inc (G-2455)*

Black Lion Products LLC... 234 232-3680
3710 Hendricks Rd Youngstown (44515) *(G-16320)*

Black Machining & Tech Inc.. 513 752-8625
4020 Bach Buxton Rd Batavia (45103) *(G-913)*

Black Radish Creamery Ltd... 614 517-9520
59 Spruce St Columbus (43215) *(G-5197)*

Black River Display Group, Mansfield *Also Called: Black River Group Inc (G-9628)*

Black River Group Inc (PA)... 419 524-6699
195 E 4th St Mansfield (44902) *(G-9628)*

Black Squirrel Holdings Inc... 513 577-7107
225 Northland Blvd Cincinnati (45246) *(G-2671)*

Black Wing Shooting Center LLC... 740 363-7555
3722 Marysville Rd Delaware (43015) *(G-6705)*

Blackburns Fabrication Inc.. 614 875-0784
2467 Jackson Pike Columbus (43223) *(G-5198)*

Blackfish Sealcoating LLC... 419 647-4010
404 N Elizabeth St Spencerville (45887) *(G-13485)*

Blackhawk Machine LLC... 419 779-3958
300 Warner St Walbridge (43465) *(G-15079)*

Blacklick Machine Company.. 614 866-9300
265 North St Blacklick (43004) *(G-1332)*

Blackmer Pump.. 616 248-9239
9393 Princeton Glendale Rd West Chester (45011) *(G-15380)*

Blackstar International Inc.. 917 510-5482
361 Indian Mound Rd Columbus (43213) *(G-5199)*

Blackthorn LLC.. 937 836-9296
6113 Brookville Salem Rd Clayton (45315) *(G-3564)*

Blackwood Sheet Metal Inc... 614 291-3115
844 Kerr St Columbus (43215) *(G-5200)*

Blade Manufacturing Co, The, Columbus *Also Called: Callahan Cutting Tools Inc (G-5227)*

Blains Folding Service Inc... 216 631-4700
4103 Detroit Ave Cleveland (44113) *(G-3740)*

Blair Logging... 740 934-2730
30530 Lebanon Rd Lower Salem (45745) *(G-9519)*

Blair Rubber, Seville *Also Called: Blair Sales Inc (G-13138)*
Blair Rubber Company.. 330 769-5583
5020 Enterprise Pkwy Seville (44273) *(G-13137)*
Blair Sales Inc... 330 769-5586
5020 Enterprise Pkwy Seville (44273) *(G-13138)*
Blair's Cnc, Dayton *Also Called: Blairs Cnc Turning Inc (G-6230)*
Blairs Cnc Turning Inc.. 937 461-1100
245 Leo St Dayton (45404) *(G-6230)*
Blako Industries Inc... 419 246-6172
10850 Middleton Pike Dunbridge (43414) *(G-6961)*
Blanchester Foundry Co Inc
2121 S State Route 133 Blanchester (45107) *(G-1348)*
Blaney Hardwoods Ohio Inc... 740 678-8288
425 Timberline Dr Vincent (45784) *(G-15006)*
Blang Acquisition LLC... 937 223-2155
7464 Webster St Dayton (45414) *(G-6231)*
Blankenship Logging LLC.. 740 372-3833
433 Curtis Smith Rd Otway (45657) *(G-12205)*
Blaster Corporation... 216 901-5800
775 W Smith Rd Medina (44256) *(G-10302)*
BLaster Holdings LLC (PA).. 216 901-5800
8500 Sweet Valley Dr Cleveland (44125) *(G-3741)*
BLaster LLC (PA).. 216 901-5800
8500 Sweet Valley Dr Cleveland (44125) *(G-3742)*
Blastwrap, Columbus *Also Called: Highcom Global Security Inc (G-5434)*
Blaze Technical Services Inc... 330 923-0409
1445 Commerce Dr Stow (44224) *(G-13688)*
Bld Pharmatech Co Limited... 330 333-6550
10999 Reed Hartman Hwy Ste 304b Blue Ash (45242) *(G-1371)*
Bleachtech LLC... 216 921-1980
320 Ryan Rd Seville (44273) *(G-13139)*
Blend of Seven Winery, Delaware *Also Called: Sandra Weddington (G-6749)*
Blesco Services... 614 871-4900
8905 Mckendree Rd Mount Sterling (43143) *(G-11253)*
Blevins Fabrication, Mansfield *Also Called: Blevins Metal Fabrication Inc (G-9629)*
Blevins Metal Fabrication Inc.. 419 522-6082
288 Illinois Ave S Mansfield (44905) *(G-9629)*
Blf Enterprises Inc... 937 642-6425
445 S State St Westerville (43081) *(G-15694)*
Blind Factory Showroom.. 614 771-6549
3670 Parkway Ln Ste M Hilliard (43026) *(G-8405)*
Blinged & Bronzed... 330 631-1255
2303 Manchester Rd Akron (44314) *(G-87)*
Blingflingforever LLC.. 216 215-6955
7383 Dahlia Dr Mentor On The Lake (44060) *(G-10601)*
Blink Marketing Logistics, Perrysburg *Also Called: Bottomline Ink Corporation (G-12364)*
Blink Print & Mail, Toledo *Also Called: Northcoast Pmm LLC (G-14299)*
Bloch Printing Company... 330 576-6760
3569 Copley Rd Copley (44321) *(G-5945)*
Block Communications Inc (PA)..................................... 419 724-6212
405 Madison Ave Ste 2100 Toledo (43604) *(G-14214)*
Blockamerica Corporation... 614 274-0700
750 Kaderly Dr Columbus (43228) *(G-5201)*
Blonde Swan... 419 307-8591
307 W State St Fremont (43420) *(G-7768)*
Blonder Home Accents, Cleveland *Also Called: The Blonder Company (G-4780)*
Bloom Industries Inc.. 330 898-3878
1052 Mahoney Ave Nw Warren (44483) *(G-15146)*
Bloomer Candy Co.. 740 452-7501
3610 National Rd Zanesville (43701) *(G-16511)*
Blooming Services, Dennison *Also Called: Blooms Printing Inc (G-6793)*
Bloomngburg Spring Wire Form I................................... 740 437-7614
83 Main St Bloomingburg (43106) *(G-1353)*
Blooms Printing Inc... 740 922-1765
4792 N 4th Street Ext Se Dennison (44621) *(G-6793)*
Blu Bird LLC.. 513 271-5646
4820 Stafford St Cincinnati (45227) *(G-2672)*
Blu Bird LLC (PA).. 614 276-3585
1736 Mckinley Ave Columbus (43222) *(G-5202)*
Blue Ash Tool & Die Co Inc... 513 793-4530
4245 Creek Rd Blue Ash (45241) *(G-1372)*

Blue Chip Manufacturing & Sales Inc............................... 614 475-3853
3155 Lamb Ave Columbus (43219) *(G-5203)*
Blue Chip Tool Inc... 513 489-3561
11511 Goldcoast Dr Cincinnati (45249) *(G-2673)*
Blue Collar M LLC.. 216 209-5666
31005 Bainbridge Rd Ste 2 Solon (44139) *(G-13320)*
Blue Creek Enterprises Inc... 937 222-9969
2153 Winners Cir Dayton (45404) *(G-6232)*
Blue Crescent Enterprises Inc... 440 878-9700
17295 Foltz Pkwy Ste B Strongsville (44149) *(G-13816)*
Blue Engineered Products LLC.. 937 247-5537
47 Pierce St West Carrollton (45449) *(G-15350)*
Blue Grass Cooperage - Jackson, Wellston *Also Called: Brown-Forman Corporation (G-15326)*
Blue Racer Midstream LLC... 740 630-7556
11388 E Pike Rd Unit B Cambridge (43725) *(G-1923)*
Blue Ribbon Trailers Ltd.. 330 538-4114
12800 Leonard Pkwy North Jackson (44451) *(G-11779)*
Blue Ridge Paper Products LLC...................................... 440 235-7200
7920 Mapleway Dr Olmsted Falls (44138) *(G-12077)*
Blue Skies Operating Corp... 877 330-2354
1661 Saint Marys Rd Sidney (45065) *(G-13228)*
Bluffton News Pubg & Prtg Co.. 419 358-4610
103 N Main St Bluffton (45817) *(G-1499)*
Bluffton Precast Concrete Co... 419 358-6946
8950 Dixie Hwy Bluffton (45817) *(G-1500)*
Bluffton Stone Co.. 419 358-6941
310 Quarry Dr Bluffton (45817) *(G-1501)*
BMC, Strongsville *Also Called: Bearings Manufacturing Company (G-13815)*
BMC Growth Fund LLC... 937 291-4110
2991 Newmark Dr Miamisburg (45342) *(G-10620)*
Bmca Insulation Products Inc... 330 335-2501
270 Main St Wadsworth (44281) *(G-15020)*
Bmf Devices Inc.. 937 866-3451
510 S Riverview Ave Miamisburg (45342) *(G-10621)*
Bnoat Oncology.. 330 285-2537
411 Wolf Ledges Pkwy Ste 105 Akron (44311) *(G-88)*
Board of Park Commissioners.. 216 635-3200
4101 Fulton Pkwy Cleveland (44144) *(G-3743)*
Boardman Molded Intl LLC... 800 233-4575
1110 Thalia Ave Youngstown (44512) *(G-16321)*
Boardman Molded Products Inc (PA).............................. 330 788-2400
1110 Thalia Ave Youngstown (44512) *(G-16322)*
Boardman News.. 330 758-6397
8302 Southern Blvd Ste 2 Boardman (44512) *(G-1510)*
Boardman Steel Inc... 330 758-0951
156 Nulf Dr Columbiana (44408) *(G-5028)*
Boat Decor LLC... 216 831-1889
3700 Park East Dr Beachwood (44122) *(G-975)*
Bob Evans, Bidwell *Also Called: Bob Evans Farms Inc (G-1324)*
Bob Evans, Xenia *Also Called: Bef Foods Inc (G-16251)*
Bob Evans Farms Inc... 740 245-5305
791 Farmview Rd Bidwell (45614) *(G-1324)*
Bob Lanes Welding Inc.. 740 373-3567
5151 Warren Chapel Rd Marietta (45750) *(G-9779)*
Bob Sumerel Tire Co Inc.. 614 527-9700
2807 International St Columbus (43228) *(G-5204)*
Bob Sumerel Tire Co Inc.. 937 235-0062
7711 Center Point 70 Blvd Dayton (45424) *(G-6233)*
Bob Sumerel Tire Co Inc.. 740 432-5200
63303 Institute Rd Lore City (43755) *(G-9446)*
Bob Sumerel Tire Co Inc.. 330 769-9092
8692 Lake Rd Seville (44273) *(G-13140)*
Bob Sumerel Tire Co Inc.. 740 454-9728
1140 Newark Rd Zanesville (43701) *(G-16512)*
Bob Sumerel Tire Company.. 330 262-1220
519 Madison Ave Wooster (44691) *(G-16105)*
Bob Sumerel Tire Company Inc....................................... 740 927-2811
67 Klema Dr N Ste D Reynoldsburg (43068) *(G-12755)*
Bobbart Industries Inc... 419 350-5477
5035 Alexis Rd Ste 1 Sylvania (43560) *(G-13991)*

ALPHABETIC SECTION — Bottomline Ink Corporation

Bobco Enterprises Inc... 419 867-3560
2910 Glanzman Rd Toledo (43614) *(G-14215)*

Bocchi Laboratories Ohio LLC.. 614 741-7458
9200 Smiths Mill Rd N New Albany (43054) *(G-11370)*

Bodied Beauties LLC... 216 971-1155
4820 Geraldine Rd Richmond Heights (44143) *(G-12806)*

Bodnar Printing Co Inc.. 440 277-8295
3480 Colorado Ave Lorain (44052) *(G-9403)*

Bodor Vents Inc... 513 348-3853
400 Murray Rd Cincinnati (45217) *(G-2674)*

Bodycote Imt Inc... 740 852-5000
443 E High St London (43140) *(G-9382)*

Bodycote Kolsterising, London *Also Called: Bodycote Thermal Proc Inc (G-9383)*

Bodycote Srfc Tech Prperty LLC..................................... 513 770-4900
8118 Corporate Way Ste 201 Mason (45040) *(G-9961)*

Bodycote Srfc Tech Wrtburg Inc (DH)............................ 513 770-4900
8093 Columbia Rd Ste 201 Mason (45040) *(G-9962)*

Bodycote Surface Tech Inc (DH)..................................... 513 770-4922
8118 Corporate Way Ste 201 Mason (45040) *(G-9963)*

Bodycote Surfc Tech Group Inc (HQ)............................. 513 770-4900
8118 Corporate Way Ste 201 Mason (45040) *(G-9964)*

Bodycote Surfc Tech Mexico LLC................................... 513 770-4900
8118 Corporate Way Ste 201 Mason (45040) *(G-9965)*

Bodycote Thermal Proc Inc... 513 921-2300
710 Burns St Cincinnati (45204) *(G-2675)*

Bodycote Thermal Proc Inc... 440 473-2020
5475 Avion Park Dr Cleveland (44143) *(G-3744)*

Bodycote Thermal Proc Inc... 740 852-4955
443 E High St London (43140) *(G-9383)*

Boehm Inc (PA).. 614 875-9010
2050 Hardy Pkwy St Grove City (43123) *(G-8080)*

Boehm Pressed Steel Company...................................... 330 220-8000
5440 Wegman Dr Valley City (44280) *(G-14863)*

Boehrnger Inglheim Phrmcctcals.................................... 440 286-5667
11540 Autumn Ridge Dr Chardon (44024) *(G-2440)*

Boeing, Heath *Also Called: Boeing Company (G-8318)*

Boeing Company.. 740 788-4000
801 Irving Wick Dr W Heath (43056) *(G-8318)*

Boes, Wilbert J, New Riegel *Also Called: Tr Boes Holdings Inc (G-11538)*

Bogie Industries Inc Ltd.. 330 745-3105
1100 Home Ave Akron (44310) *(G-89)*

Bohlender Engravg, Cincinnati *Also Called: Bohlender Engraving Company (G-2676)*

Bohlender Engraving Company....................................... 513 621-4095
1599 Central Pkwy Cincinnati (45214) *(G-2676)*

Boivin Machine.. 330 928-3942
400 Lombard St Akron (44310) *(G-90)*

Boler Company.. 330 445-6728
2070 Industrial Pl Se Canton (44707) *(G-2049)*

Bolger... 440 979-9577
4200 W 229th St Cleveland (44126) *(G-3745)*

Bollari/Davis Inc.. 330 296-4445
5292 S Prospect St Ravenna (44266) *(G-12708)*

Bollin & Sons Inc... 419 693-6573
6001 Brent Dr Toledo (43611) *(G-14216)*

Bollin Label Systems, Toledo *Also Called: Bollin & Sons Inc (G-14216)*

Bollinger Tool & Die Inc.. 419 866-5180
959 Hamilton Dr Holland (43528) *(G-8494)*

Bolons Custom Kitchens Inc... 330 499-0092
6287 Promler St Nw Canton (44720) *(G-2050)*

Boltech Incorporated... 330 746-6881
1201 Crescent St Youngstown (44502) *(G-16323)*

Bolttech Mannings Inc... 614 836-0021
351 Lowery Ct Ste 3 Groveport (43125) *(G-8133)*

Bolttech Mannings, Inc., Groveport *Also Called: Bolttech Mannings Inc (G-8133)*

Bomat Inc... 216 692-8382
19218 Redwood Rd Cleveland (44110) *(G-3746)*

Bond Chemicals Inc... 330 725-5935
1154 W Smith Rd Medina (44256) *(G-10303)*

Bond Distributing LLC... 440 461-7920
35585 Curtis Blvd Unit D Eastlake (44095) *(G-7022)*

Bond Machine Company Inc... 937 746-4941
921 N Main St Franklin (45005) *(G-7664)*

Bonfoey Co... 216 621-0178
1710 Euclid Ave Cleveland (44115) *(G-3747)*

Bonne Bell Company, The, Westlake *Also Called: Bonne Bell Inc (G-15739)*

Bonne Bell Inc.. 440 835-2440
1006 Crocker Rd Westlake (44145) *(G-15739)*

Bonne Bell LLC (PA).. 440 835-2440
1006 Crocker Rd Westlake (44145) *(G-15740)*

Bonnot Company... 330 896-6544
1301 Home Ave Akron (44310) *(G-91)*

Bonsal American Inc.. 513 398-7300
5155 Fischer Ave Cincinnati (45217) *(G-2677)*

Boogie Wipes, Cincinnati *Also Called: Eleeo Brands LLC (G-2863)*

Bookfactory LLC... 937 226-7100
2302 S Edwin C Moses Blvd Dayton (45417) *(G-6234)*

Bookmasters Inc (HQ)... 419 281-1802
30 Amberwood Pkwy Ashland (44805) *(G-557)*

Boomerang Rubber Inc.. 937 693-4611
105 Dinsmore St Botkins (45306) *(G-1541)*

Bor-It Mfg Co Inc... 419 289-6639
1687 Cleveland Rd Ashland (44805) *(G-558)*

Borchers Americas Inc (HQ)... 440 899-2950
811 Sharon Dr Westlake (44145) *(G-15741)*

Borden Dairy Co Cincinnati LLC (DH)............................ 513 948-8811
3068 W 106th St Cleveland (44111) *(G-3748)*

Border Lumber & Logging Ltd.. 330 897-0177
31181 County Road 10 Fresno (43824) *(G-7821)*

Bores Manufacturing Inc... 419 465-2606
300 Sandusky St Monroeville (44847) *(G-11123)*

Bores, J F Mfg, Monroeville *Also Called: Bores Manufacturing Inc (G-11123)*

Borke Mold Specialist Inc.. 513 870-8000
9541 Glades Dr West Chester (45011) *(G-15381)*

Borman Enterprises Inc... 216 459-9292
1311 Brookpark Rd Cleveland (44109) *(G-3749)*

Bornhorst Motor Service Inc... 937 773-0426
8270 N Dixie Dr Piqua (45356) *(G-12507)*

Bornhorst Printing Company Inc..................................... 419 738-5901
10139 County Road 25a Wapakoneta (45895) *(G-15107)*

Boro Drive-Thru LLC.. 937 743-1700
115 S Pioneer Blvd Springboro (45066) *(G-13496)*

Bortnick Tractor Sales Inc... 330 924-2555
6192 Warren Rd Cortland (44410) *(G-5960)*

Bosca Accesories, Springfield *Also Called: Hugo Bosca Company Inc (G-13581)*

Bosch Rexroth Corporation... 330 263-3300
290 E Milltown Rd Wooster (44691) *(G-16106)*

Boscott, Bradford *Also Called: Boscott Metals Inc (G-1599)*

Boscott Metals Inc... 937 448-2018
138 S Miami Ave Bradford (45308) *(G-1599)*

Boscowood Ventures Inc... 440 429-5669
7425 Industrial Parkway Dr Lorain (44053) *(G-9404)*

Boss Industries Inc.. 330 273-2266
5478 Grafton Rd Valley City (44280) *(G-14864)*

Bosserman Automotive Engrg LLC................................. 419 722-2879
18919 Olympic Dr Findlay (45840) *(G-7485)*

Bosserman Aviation Equipment Inc................................ 419 722-2879
2327 State Highway 568 Carey (43316) *(G-2277)*

Bostik Inc... 419 289-9588
1745 Cottage St Ashland (44805) *(G-559)*

Bostik Inc... 614 232-8510
802 Harmon Ave Columbus (43223) *(G-5205)*

Boston Beer Company... 267 240-4429
1625 Central Pkwy Cincinnati (45214) *(G-2678)*

Boston Scntfic Nrmdlation Corp..................................... 513 377-6160
4267 S Haven Dr Mason (45040) *(G-9966)*

Boston Scntfic Nrmdlation Corp..................................... 330 372-2652
2174 Sarkies Dr Ne Warren (44483) *(G-15147)*

Boston Stoker, Vandalia *Also Called: Boston Stoker Inc (G-14934)*

Boston Stoker Inc (PA).. 937 890-6401
10855 Engle Rd Vandalia (45377) *(G-14934)*

Botanicare, Marysville *Also Called: American Agritech LLC (G-9904)*

Bottomline Ink Corporation... 419 897-8000
7829 Ponderosa Rd Perrysburg (43551) *(G-12364)*

Boundless Cmnty Pathways Inc   **ALPHABETIC SECTION**

Boundless Cmnty Pathways Inc (PA) 937 461-0034
700 Liberty Ln West Carrollton (45449) *(G-15351)*

Bourbon Plastics Inc 574 342-0893
111 Stow Ave Ste 100 Cuyahoga Falls (44221) *(G-6073)*

Boville Indus Coatings Inc 330 669-8558
7459 Leichty Rd Smithville (44677) *(G-13298)*

Bowden Manufacturing Corp 440 946-1770
4590 Beidler Rd Willoughby (44094) *(G-15891)*

Bowdil Company 800 356-8663
2030 Industrial Pl Se Canton (44707) *(G-2051)*

Bowerston Shale Company (PA) 740 269-2921
515 Main St Bowerston (44695) *(G-1544)*

Bowerston Shale Company 740 763-3921
1329 Seven Hills Rd Newark (43055) *(G-11567)*

Bowes Manufacturing Inc 216 378-2110
30340 Solon Industrial Pkwy Ste B Solon (44139) *(G-13321)*

Bowne of Columbus, Columbus *Also Called: RR Donnelley & Sons Company (G-5733)*

Bows Barrettes & Baubles 440 247-2697
4180 Chagrin River Rd Moreland Hills (44022) *(G-11218)*

Boxit Corporation (HQ) 216 631-6900
5555 Walworth Ave Cleveland (44102) *(G-3750)*

Boxit Corporation 216 416-9475
3000 Quigley Rd B Cleveland (44113) *(G-3751)*

Boxout LLC (PA) 833 462-7746
6333 Hudson Crossing Pkwy Hudson (44236) *(G-8587)*

Boy RAD Inc 614 766-1228
7742 Sawmill Rd Dublin (43016) *(G-6869)*

Boyce Machine Inc 330 678-3210
3609 Mogadore Rd Kent (44240) *(G-8802)*

Boyds Mch & Met Finshg Inc 937 698-5623
7650 S Kessler Frederick Rd West Milton (45383) *(G-15629)*

Boyer Signs & Graphics Inc 216 383-7242
3200 Valleyview Dr Columbus (43204) *(G-5206)*

BP, Cincinnati *Also Called: B P Oil Company (G-2651)*

BP 10 Inc 513 346-3900
9486 Sutton Pl West Chester (45011) *(G-15382)*

BP Products North America Inc 419 698-6400
4001 Cedar Point Rd Oregon (43616) *(G-12104)*

BP Products North America Inc 419 537-9540
2450 Hill Ave Toledo (43607) *(G-14217)*

Bpi Ec LLC 216 589-0198
127 Public Sq Ste 5110 Cleveland (44114) *(G-3752)*

Bpi Energy Holdings Inc 281 556-6200
30775 Bainbridge Rd Ste 280 Solon (44139) *(G-13322)*

Bpr-Rico Equipment Inc (PA) 330 723-4050
691 W Liberty St Medina (44256) *(G-10304)*

Bpr-Rico Manufacturing Inc 330 723-4050
691 W Liberty St Medina (44256) *(G-10305)*

Bpr/Rico, Medina *Also Called: Bpr-Rico Manufacturing Inc (G-10305)*

Bprex Halthcare Brookville Inc (DH) 847 541-9700
1899 N Wilkinson Way Perrysburg (43551) *(G-12365)*

Bprex Plastic Packaging Inc (PA) 419 247-5000
1 Seagate Toledo (43604) *(G-14218)*

Bprex Plastic Services Co Inc 419 247-5000
1 Seagate Toledo (43604) *(G-14219)*

BR Ohio, Cincinnati *Also Called: B R Printers Inc (G-2652)*

BR Pallet Inc 419 427-2200
21395 County Road 7 Alvada (44802) *(G-441)*

Bracemart LLC 440 353-2830
36097 Westminster Ave North Ridgeville (44039) *(G-11833)*

Brackish Media LLC 513 394-2871
2662 Mckinley Ave Cincinnati (45211) *(G-2679)*

Brad Grizer On Spot Welding 740 516-3436
1532 Nichols Rd Whipple (45788) *(G-15813)*

Braden-Sutphin Ink Company, Cleveland *Also Called: Red Tie Group Inc (G-4621)*

Bradley Enterprises Inc (PA) 330 875-1444
3750 Beck Ave Louisville (44641) *(G-9456)*

Bradley Stone Industries LLC 440 519-3277
30801 Carter St Solon (44139) *(G-13323)*

Brady Ruck Company 419 738-5126
253 Indl Dr Wapakoneta (45895) *(G-15108)*

Brain Brew Ventures 30 Inc 513 310-6374
3849 Edwards Rd Newtown (45244) *(G-11661)*

Brain Child Products LLC 419 698-4020
146 Main St Toledo (43605) *(G-14220)*

Brainard Rivet Company 330 545-4931
222 Harry St Girard (44420) *(G-7963)*

Brainerd Industries Inc (PA) 937 228-0488
680 Precision Ct Miamisburg (45342) *(G-10622)*

Brainmaster Technologies Inc 440 232-6000
195 Willis St # 3 Bedford (44146) *(G-1107)*

Brake Parts Inc China LLC (DH) 216 589-0198
127 Public Sq Ste 5110 Cleveland (44114) *(G-3753)*

Brake Products, Chagrin Falls *Also Called: IBI Brake Products Inc (G-2402)*

Bramkamp Printing Company Inc 513 241-1865
9933 Alliance Rd Ste 2 Blue Ash (45242) *(G-1373)*

Branch & Bone Artisan Ales LLC 937 723-7608
905 Wayne Ave Dayton (45410) *(G-6235)*

Branch 49, Columbus *Also Called: Plastics Family Holdings Inc (G-5680)*

Brand Printer LLC 614 404-2615
7260 Cook Rd Powell (43065) *(G-12664)*

Brand5 LLC 614 920-9254
106 Cool Spring Ct Pickerington (43147) *(G-12457)*

Brandon Screen Printing 419 229-9837
1755 Shawnee Rd Lima (45805) *(G-9224)*

Brands' Marina, Port Clinton *Also Called: Tack-Anew Inc (G-12629)*

Brandts Candies Inc 440 942-1016
1238 Lost Nation Rd Willoughby (44094) *(G-15892)*

Brandts Custom Machining LLC 419 566-3192
1183 Stewart Rd N Mansfield (44905) *(G-9630)*

Brantley Partners IV LP 216 464-8400
3550 Lander Rd Ste 160 Cleveland (44124) *(G-3754)*

Brass & Bronze Ingot Division, Cincinnati *Also Called: G A Avril Company (G-2925)*

Brass Bull 1 LLC 740 335-8030
1020 Leesburg Ave Wshngtn Ct Hs (43160) *(G-16226)*

Brass Lantern Antiques, Waynesville *Also Called: John Purdum (G-15298)*

Brassgate Industries Inc 937 339-2192
650 Olympic Dr Troy (45373) *(G-14552)*

Brat Printing, Cincinnati *Also Called: Randy Gray (G-3324)*

Brattiegirlz LLC 513 607-4757
175 S 3rd St Ste 200 Columbus (43215) *(G-5207)*

Braun Industries Inc 419 232-7020
1170 Production Dr Van Wert (45891) *(G-14907)*

Bravo LLC (HQ) 866 922-9222
2425 W Dorothy Ln Moraine (45439) *(G-11163)*

Bravo Pet Foods, Moraine *Also Called: Bravo LLC (G-11163)*

Bread Kneads Inc 419 422-3863
510 S Blanchard St Findlay (45840) *(G-7486)*

Breaker Technology Inc 440 248-7168
30625 Solon Industrial Pkwy Solon (44139) *(G-13324)*

Breaking Bread Pizza Company 614 754-4777
8824 Commerce Loop Dr Columbus (43240) *(G-5059)*

Breakthrough Media Ministries, Canal Winchester *Also Called: World Harvest Church Inc (G-1994)*

Breakwall Publishing LLC 813 575-2570
3593 Medina Rd # 117 Medina (44256) *(G-10306)*

Breckenridge Paper & Packaging, Huron *Also Called: Central Ohio Paper & Packg Inc (G-8629)*

Brecksvll-Brdview Hts Gztte In 440 526-7977
7014 Mill Rd Brecksville (44141) *(G-1610)*

Breining Mech Systems Inc (PA) 216 391-2400
883 Addison Rd Cleveland (44103) *(G-3755)*

Breitenbach Bed & Breakfast, Dover *Also Called: Breitenbach Wine Cellars Inc (G-6810)*

Breitenbach Wine Cellars Inc 330 343-3603
5934 Old Route 39 Nw Dover (44622) *(G-6810)*

Breitinger Company 419 526-4255
595 Oakenwaldt St Mansfield (44905) *(G-9631)*

Brekkie Shack Grandview LLC 614 306-5618
2 Miranova Pl Ste 700 Columbus (43215) *(G-5208)*

Brendel Producing Company 330 854-4151
8215 Arlington Ave Nw Canton (44720) *(G-2052)*

Brendons Fiber Works 614 353-6599
306 E Jeffrey Pl Columbus (43214) *(G-5209)*

Brenmar Construction Inc.. 740 286-2151
900 Morton St Jackson (45640) *(G-8711)*

Brennan Inds Clvland Mfg Group, Euclid *Also Called: Bic Manufacturing Inc (G-7263)*

Brenner International, Newark *Also Called: I G Brenner Inc (G-11583)*

Brentwood Originals Inc.. 330 793-2255
1309 N Meridian Rd Youngstown (44509) *(G-16324)*

Brentwood Printing & Sty.. 513 522-2679
8630 Winton Rd Cincinnati (45231) *(G-2680)*

Brew Cleveland LLC.. 440 455-9218
23489 Greenwood Ln North Olmsted (44070) *(G-11820)*

Brew Kettle Inc.. 440 234-8788
8377 Pearl Rd Strongsville (44136) *(G-13817)*

Brew Kettle Strongsville LLC.. 440 915-7074
3520 Longwood Dr Medina (44256) *(G-10307)*

Brewdog, Canal Winchester *Also Called: Brewdog Brewing Company LLC (G-1981)*

Brewdog Brewing Company LLC (PA)..................................614 908-3051
96 Gender Rd Canal Winchester (43110) *(G-1981)*

Brewer Company.. 513 576-6300
7300 Main St Cincinnati (45244) *(G-2681)*

Brewer Company (PA).. 800 394-0017
25 Whitney Dr Ste 104 Milford (45150) *(G-10896)*

Brewer Products, Cincinnati *Also Called: La Mfg Inc (G-3094)*

Brewer Products Co, Cincinnati *Also Called: Brewpro Inc (G-2682)*

Brewercote, Milford *Also Called: Brewer Company (G-10896)*

Brewery Real Estate Partnr.. 614 224-9023
467 N High St Columbus (43215) *(G-5210)*

Brewpro Inc.. 513 577-7200
9483 Reading Rd Cincinnati (45215) *(G-2682)*

Brewpub Restaurant Corporation.. 614 228-2537
467 N High St Columbus (43215) *(G-5211)*

Brewster Cheese, Brewster *Also Called: Brewster Cheese Company (G-1642)*

Brewster Cheese Company (PA).. 330 767-3492
800 Wabash Ave S Brewster (44613) *(G-1642)*

BREWSTER HISTORICAL SOCIETY, Brewster *Also Called: Brewster Sugarcreek Twp Histo (G-1643)*

Brewster Sugarcreek Twp Histo.. 330 767-0045
45 Wabash Ave S Brewster (44613) *(G-1643)*

Brg Sports Inc.. 217 891-1429
7501 Performance Ln North Ridgeville (44039) *(G-11834)*

Briar Hill Stone Co Inc.. 216 377-5100
12470 State Route 520 Glenmont (44628) *(G-7980)*

Briar Hill Stone Company.. 330 377-5100
12470 State Route 520 Glenmont (44628) *(G-7981)*

Bricker Plating Inc.. 419 636-1990
612 E Edgerton St Bryan (43506) *(G-1810)*

Bridge Analyzers Inc.. 216 332-0592
5198 Richmond Rd Bedford Heights (44146) *(G-1165)*

Bridge Components Incorporated.. 614 873-0777
3476 Millikin Ct Columbus (43228) *(G-5212)*

Bridge Components Inds Inc.. 614 873-0777
3476 Millikin Ct Columbus (43228) *(G-5213)*

Bridges Sheet Metal.. 330 339-3185
2244 Goshen Valley Dr Se New Philadelphia (44663) *(G-11487)*

Bridgestone Ret Operations LLC.. 740 592-3075
820 E State St Athens (45701) *(G-677)*

Bridgestone Ret Operations LLC.. 614 834-3672
6574 Winchester Blvd Canal Winchester (43110) *(G-1982)*

Bridgestone Ret Operations LLC.. 330 454-9478
3032 Atlantic Blvd Ne Canton (44705) *(G-2053)*

Bridgestone Ret Operations LLC.. 513 681-7682
272 W Mitchell Ave Cincinnati (45232) *(G-2683)*

Bridgestone Ret Operations LLC.. 513 793-4550
7800 Montgomery Rd Unit 18 Cincinnati (45236) *(G-2684)*

Bridgestone Ret Operations LLC.. 513 677-5200
9107 Fields Ertel Rd Cincinnati (45249) *(G-2685)*

Bridgestone Ret Operations LLC.. 440 842-3200
6874 Pearl Rd Cleveland (44130) *(G-3756)*

Bridgestone Ret Operations LLC.. 440 461-4747
5117 Wilson Mills Rd Cleveland (44143) *(G-3757)*

Bridgestone Ret Operations LLC.. 216 229-2550
12420 Cedar Rd Cleveland (44106) *(G-3758)*

Bridgestone Ret Operations LLC.. 216 382-8970
700 Richmond Rd Cleveland (44143) *(G-3759)*

Bridgestone Ret Operations LLC.. 614 864-3350
4015 E Broad St Columbus (43213) *(G-5214)*

Bridgestone Ret Operations LLC.. 614 491-8062
35 Great Southern Blvd Columbus (43207) *(G-5215)*

Bridgestone Ret Operations LLC.. 614 224-4221
180 N 3rd St Columbus (43215) *(G-5216)*

Bridgestone Ret Operations LLC.. 440 324-3327
1951 Midway Blvd Elyria (44035) *(G-7117)*

Bridgestone Ret Operations LLC.. 440 365-8308
520 Abbe Rd S Elyria (44035) *(G-7118)*

Bridgestone Ret Operations LLC.. 937 548-1197
425 Walnut St Greenville (45331) *(G-8039)*

Bridgestone Ret Operations LLC.. 513 868-7399
33 N Brookwood Ave Hamilton (45013) *(G-8186)*

Bridgestone Ret Operations LLC.. 330 673-1700
202 E Main St Kent (44240) *(G-8803)*

Bridgestone Ret Operations LLC.. 440 299-6126
7495 Mentor Ave Mentor (44060) *(G-10431)*

Bridgestone Ret Operations LLC.. 740 397-5601
855 Coshocton Ave Ste 21 Mount Vernon (43050) *(G-11265)*

Bridgestone Ret Operations LLC.. 614 861-7994
7085 E Main St Reynoldsburg (43068) *(G-12756)*

Bridgestone Ret Operations LLC.. 419 625-6571
4320 Milan Rd Sandusky (44870) *(G-13045)*

Bridgestone Ret Operations LLC.. 937 325-4638
1475 Upper Valley Pike Springfield (45504) *(G-13540)*

Bridgestone Ret Operations LLC.. 330 758-0921
7401 Market St Rear Youngstown (44512) *(G-16325)*

Bridgestone Ret Operations LLC.. 330 759-3697
3335 Belmont Ave Youngstown (44505) *(G-16326)*

Bridgetek, Dayton *Also Called: Contech Bridge Solutions LLC (G-6263)*

Bridgetek, West Chester *Also Called: Contech Bridge Solutions LLC (G-15400)*

Bridgits Bath LLC.. 937 259-1960
1226 Pursell Ave Dayton (45420) *(G-6236)*

Bridgestone Amrcas Tire Oprtons.. 330 379-3714
1670 Firestone Pkwy Akron (44301) *(G-92)*

Bright Holdco LLC (PA)..................................614 741-7458
9002 Smith's Mill Rd N New Albany (43054) *(G-11371)*

Bright Innovation Labs, New Albany *Also Called: Bright Holdco LLC (G-11371)*

Bright Star Books Inc.. 330 888-2156
1357 Home Ave Akron (44310) *(G-93)*

Bright-On Polishing & Mfg LLC.. 937 489-3985
10160 Lochard Rd Sidney (45365) *(G-13229)*

Brightguy Inc.. 440 942-8318
38205b Stevens Blvd Willoughby (44094) *(G-15893)*

Brighton Mills, Cincinnati *Also Called: H Nagel & Son Co (G-2981)*

Brighton Science.. 513 469-1800
4914 Gray Rd Cincinnati (45232) *(G-2686)*

Brightpet Nutrition Group LLC (PA).. 330 424-1431
38251 Industrial Park Rd Lisbon (44432) *(G-9308)*

Brightstar Propane & Fuels.. 614 891-8395
6190 Frost Rd Westerville (43082) *(G-15648)*

Brilex Industries Inc.. 330 744-1114
101 Andrews Ave Youngstown (44503) *(G-16327)*

Brilex Industries Inc (PA).. 330 744-1114
1201 Crescent St Youngstown (44502) *(G-16328)*

Brilex Tech Services, Youngstown *Also Called: Brilex Industries Inc (G-16328)*

Brilista Foods Company Inc (PA).. 614 299-4132
1000 Goodale Blvd Columbus (43212) *(G-5217)*

Brilliant Electric Sign Co Ltd.. 216 741-3800
4811 Van Epps Rd Brooklyn Heights (44131) *(G-1685)*

Brimar Packaging Inc.. 440 934-3080
37520 Colorado Ave Avon (44011) *(G-764)*

Brinkley Technology Group LLC.. 330 830-2498
2770 Erie St S Massillon (44646) *(G-10079)*

Brinkman LLC.. 419 204-5934
1524 Adak Ave Lima (45805) *(G-9225)*

Brinkman Turkey Farms Inc (PA)..................................419 365-5127
16314 State Route 68 Findlay (45840) *(G-7487)*

Brinkman's Country Corner — ALPHABETIC SECTION

Brinkman's Country Corner, Findlay *Also Called: Brinkman Turkey Farms Inc* **(G-7487)**

Brio Coffee Co, Plain City *Also Called: Altraserv LLC* **(G-12561)**

Briskheat Corporation (DH) 614 294-3376
4800 Hilton Corporate Dr Columbus (43232) **(G-5218)**

Brittany Stamping LLC 216 267-0850
50 Public Sq Ste 4000 Cleveland (44113) **(G-3760)**

BROADBAND HOSPITALITY, Youngstown *Also Called: Great Lakes Telcom Ltd* **(G-16373)**

Broadview Journal, The, Richfield *Also Called: Scriptype Publishing Inc* **(G-12796)**

Broadway Printing LLC 513 621-3429
530 Reading Rd Cincinnati (45202) **(G-2687)**

Broadway Sand and Gravel LLC 937 853-5555
130 W 2nd St Ste 2000 Dayton (45402) **(G-6237)**

Brocar Products Inc 513 922-2888
4335 River Rd Cincinnati (45204) **(G-2688)**

Brock Corporation (PA) 440 235-1806
26000 Sprague Rd Olmsted Falls (44138) **(G-12078)**

Brock RAD Wldg Fabrication Inc 740 773-2540
370 Douglas Ave Chillicothe (45601) **(G-2496)**

Brocker Machine Inc 330 744-5858
1530 Poland Ave Youngstown (44502) **(G-16329)**

Brocks RAD Wldg Fabrication I, Chillicothe *Also Called: Brock RAD Wldg Fabrication Inc* **(G-2496)**

Broco Products Inc 216 531-0880
8510 Bessemer Ave Cleveland (44127) **(G-3761)**

Brodwill LLC 513 258-2716
3900 Rose Hill Ave Ste C Cincinnati (45229) **(G-2689)**

Broestl & Wallis Fine Jewelers, Lakewood *Also Called: Bensan Jewelers Inc* **(G-8967)**

Broke Boys Sealcoating LLC 614 477-0322
10698 Baldwin Rd Mount Sterling (43143) **(G-11254)**

Broken Spinning Wheel 419 825-1609
14230 Monclova Rd Swanton (43558) **(G-13970)**

Bronco Machine Inc 440 951-5015
38411 Apollo Pkwy Willoughby (44094) **(G-15894)**

Bront Machining Inc 937 228-4551
2601 W Dorothy Ln Moraine (45439) **(G-11164)**

Bronx Taylor Wilson, North Canton *Also Called: Fives Bronx Inc* **(G-11727)**

Broodle Brands LLC 855 276-6353
8361 Broadwell Rd Ste 100 Cincinnati (45244) **(G-2690)**

Brook & Whittle Limited 513 860-2457
4000 Hamilton Middletown Rd Hamilton (45011) **(G-8187)**

Brooker Bros Forging Co Inc 419 668-2535
102 Jefferson St Norwalk (44857) **(G-11957)**

Brooklyn Machine & Mfg Co Inc 216 341-1846
5180 Grant Ave Cleveland (44125) **(G-3762)**

Brooks Manufacturing 419 244-1777
1102 N Summit St Toledo (43604) **(G-14221)**

Brooks Pastries Inc 614 274-4880
8205 Estates Pkwy Ste F Plain City (43064) **(G-12567)**

Brookville Glove Manufacturing 812 673-4893
1020 W 1st St Uhrichsville (44683) **(G-14762)**

Brookville Roadster Inc 937 833-4605
718 Albert Rd Brookville (45309) **(G-1730)**

Brookwood Group Inc 513 791-3030
3210 Wasson Rd Cincinnati (45209) **(G-2691)**

Broshco Fabricated Products, Mansfield *Also Called: Jay Industries Inc* **(G-9671)**

Brost Foundry Company (PA) 216 641-1131
2934 E 55th St Cleveland (44127) **(G-3763)**

Brost Foundry Company 419 522-1133
198 Wayne St Mansfield (44902) **(G-9632)**

Brothers Body and Eqp LLC 419 462-1975
352 South St Door 26 Galion (44833) **(G-7862)**

Brothers Printing Co Inc 216 621-6050
2000 Euclid Ave Cleveland (44115) **(G-3764)**

Brothers Publishing Co LLC 937 548-3330
100 Washington Ave Greenville (45331) **(G-8040)**

Brothers Tool and Mfg Ltd 513 353-9700
8300 Harrison Ave Miamitown (45041) **(G-10706)**

Brown Box Company, Findlay *Also Called: Square One Solutions LLC* **(G-7567)**

Brown Cnc Machining Inc 937 865-9191
433 E Maple Ave Miamisburg (45342) **(G-10623)**

Brown Cnty Bd Mntal Rtardation 937 378-4891
325 W State St Bldg A Georgetown (45121) **(G-7950)**

Brown Company of Findlay Ltd 419 425-3002
225 Stanford Pkwy Findlay (45840) **(G-7488)**

Brown Dave Products Inc 513 738-1576
4560 Layhigh Rd Hamilton (45013) **(G-8188)**

Brown Fired Heater Div, Berea *Also Called: Es Thermal Inc* **(G-1277)**

Brown Industrial Inc 937 693-3838
311 W South St Botkins (45306) **(G-1542)**

Brown Publishing, Jackson *Also Called: Brown Publishing Co Inc* **(G-8712)**

Brown Publishing Co Inc (PA) 740 286-2187
1 Acy Ave Ste D Jackson (45640) **(G-8712)**

Brown Publishing Inc LLC 513 794-5040
4229 Saint Andrews Pl Blue Ash (45236) **(G-1374)**

Brown Wood Products Company 330 339-8000
7783 Crooked Run Rd Sw New Philadelphia (44663) **(G-11488)**

Brown-Forman Corporation 740 384-3027
468 Salem Church Rd Wellston (45692) **(G-15326)**

Browns Handyman Remodeling 330 766-0925
2721 Montclair St Ne Warren (44483) **(G-15148)**

Brp Manufacturing Company 800 858-0482
637 N Jackson St Lima (45801) **(G-9226)**

RRT Extrusions Inc 330 544-0177
1818 N Main St Unit 1 Niles (44446) **(G-11662)**

Brubaker Metalcrafts Inc 937 456-5834
209 N Franklin St Eaton (45320) **(G-7055)**

Bruce High Performance Tran 440 357-8964
1 High Tech Ave Painesville (44077) **(G-12219)**

Brueneman Sales Inc 513 520-3377
11583 Carolina Trace Rd Harrison (45030) **(G-8266)**

Bruening Glass Works Inc 440 333-4768
20157 Lake Rd Cleveland (44116) **(G-3765)**

Bruewer Woodwork Mfg Co 513 353-3505
10000 Cilley Rd Cleves (45002) **(G-4946)**

Brumall Manufacturing Corp 440 974-2622
7850 Division Dr Mentor (44060) **(G-10432)**

Brushes Inc 216 267-8084
5400 Smith Rd Cleveland (44142) **(G-3766)**

Brushes Inc 216 267-8084
5400 Smith Rd Cleveland (44142) **(G-3767)**

Brw Tool Inc 419 394-3371
502 Scott St Saint Marys (45885) **(G-12948)**

Brx, Rootstown *Also Called: Barrel Run Crssing Wnery Vnyrd* **(G-12851)**

Bry Air Inc 614 839-0250
8415 Pulsar Pl Ste 200 Columbus (43240) **(G-5060)**

Bry-Air Inc 740 965-2974
10793 E State Route 37 Sunbury (43074) **(G-13951)**

Bryan Die-Cast Products Ltd 419 252-6208
4 Seagate Ste 803 Toledo (43604) **(G-14222)**

Bryan Publishing Company (PA) 419 636-1111
211 W High St Ste A Bryan (43506) **(G-1811)**

Bryan West Main Stop 419 636-1616
1310 W High St Bryan (43506) **(G-1812)**

Brydet Development Corporation 740 623-0455
16867 State Route 83 Coshocton (43812) **(G-5974)**

BSC Environmental, Bowling Green *Also Called: Bio-Systems Corporation* **(G-1555)**

Bsfc LLC (HQ) 419 447-1814
186 Ohio Ave Tiffin (44883) **(G-14079)**

BSI Group, The, Derwent *Also Called: Bi-Con Services Inc* **(G-6798)**

BT 4 LLC 513 771-2739
11276 Chester Rd Cincinnati (45246) **(G-2692)**

BTA of Motorcars Inc 440 716-1000
27500 Lorain Rd North Olmsted (44070) **(G-11821)**

Btc Inc 740 549-2722
8842 Whitney Dr Lewis Center (43035) **(G-9153)**

Btc Technology Services Inc 740 549-2722
617 Carle Ave Lewis Center (43035) **(G-9154)**

BTR Enterprises LLC 740 975-2526
7371 Stewart Rd Newark (43055) **(G-11568)**

Btw LLC 419 382-4443
2226 Greenlawn Dr Toledo (43614) **(G-14223)**

Bucher Printing 937 228-2022
26 N Clinton St Dayton (45402) **(G-6238)**

ALPHABETIC SECTION — Budget Newspaper, The

Buck Equipment Inc 614 539-3039
1720 Feddern Ave Grove City (43123) *(G-8081)*

Buckeye Abrasive Inc 330 753-1041
1020 Eagon St Barberton (44203) *(G-862)*

Buckeye Blow Out Preventer, Newcomerstown Also Called: Buckeye BOP LLC *(G-11643)*

Buckeye BOP LLC 740 498-9898
401 Enterprise Dr Newcomerstown (43832) *(G-11643)*

Buckeye Boxes Inc (PA) 614 274-8484
601 N Hague Ave Columbus (43204) *(G-5219)*

Buckeye Brake Mfg Inc 740 782-1379
40168 National Rd W Morristown (43759) *(G-11222)*

Buckeye Building Products, Reynoldsburg Also Called: Buckeye Ready-Mix LLC *(G-12757)*

Buckeye Business Forms Inc 614 882-1890
7307 Red Bank Rd Westerville (43082) *(G-15649)*

Buckeye Business Products, Cleveland Also Called: Kroy LLC *(G-4299)*

Buckeye Companies (PA) 740 452-3641
999 Zane St Zanesville (43701) *(G-16513)*

Buckeye Components LLC 330 482-5163
1340 State Route 14 Columbiana (44408) *(G-5029)*

Buckeye Container Division, Wooster Also Called: Buckeye Corrugated Inc *(G-16107)*

Buckeye Corrugated Inc (PA) 330 576-0590
822 Kumho Dr Ste 400 Fairlawn (44333) *(G-7434)*

Buckeye Corrugated Inc 330 264-6336
3350 Long Rd Wooster (44691) *(G-16107)*

Buckeye Custom Fabrication LLC 330 831-5619
7573 State Route 45 Lisbon (44432) *(G-9309)*

Buckeye Design & Engr Svc LLC 419 375-4241
2600 Wabash Rd Fort Recovery (45846) *(G-7613)*

Buckeye Diamond Logistics Inc (PA) 937 462-8361
15 Sprague Rd South Charleston (45368) *(G-13454)*

Buckeye Energy Resources Inc 740 452-9506
999 Zane St Zanesville (43701) *(G-16514)*

Buckeye Fabric Finishers Inc 740 622-3251
1260 E Main St Coshocton (43812) *(G-5975)*

Buckeye Fabric Finishing Co, Coshocton Also Called: Buckeye Fabric Finishers Inc *(G-5975)*

Buckeye Fabricating Company 937 746-9822
245 S Pioneer Blvd Springboro (45066) *(G-13497)*

Buckeye Fasteners Company, Berea Also Called: Fastener Industries Inc *(G-1280)*

BUCKEYE FASTENERS COMPANY, Streetsboro Also Called: Joseph Industries Inc *(G-13776)*

Buckeye Franklin Co 330 859-2465
3471 New Zoarville Rd Ne Zoarville (44656) *(G-16575)*

Buckeye Lake Winery 614 439-7576
13750 Rosewood Dr Ne Thornville (43076) *(G-14065)*

Buckeye Machining Inc 216 731-9535
25020 Lakeland Blvd Euclid (44132) *(G-7264)*

Buckeye Mch Fabricators Inc (PA) 419 273-2521
610 E Lima St Forest (45843) *(G-7590)*

Buckeye Medical Tech LLC 330 719-9868
405 Niles Cortland Rd Se Ste 202 Warren (44484) *(G-15149)*

Buckeye Metal Works Inc 614 239-8000
3240 Petzinger Rd Columbus (43232) *(G-5220)*

Buckeye Metals, Avon Lake Also Called: W R G Inc *(G-827)*

Buckeye Metals Industries, Cleveland Also Called: B&A Ison Steel Inc *(G-3716)*

Buckeye Oil Equipment Co 937 387-0671
20 Innovation Ct Dayton (45414) *(G-6239)*

Buckeye Oil Producing Co 330 264-8847
544 E Liberty St Wooster (44691) *(G-16108)*

Buckeye Packaging Co Inc 330 935-0301
12223 Marlboro Ave Ne Alliance (44601) *(G-396)*

Buckeye Paper Co Inc 330 477-5925
5233 Southway St Sw Ste 523 Canton (44706) *(G-2054)*

Buckeye Pipe Inspection LLC 440 476-8369
10770 Mayfield Rd Chardon (44024) *(G-2441)*

Buckeye Ready Mix, Columbus Also Called: Anderson Concrete Corp *(G-5144)*

Buckeye Ready Mix Concrete 330 798-5511
1562 Massillon Rd Akron (44312) *(G-94)*

Buckeye Ready-Mix LLC 740 967-4801
7720 Johnstown Alexandria Rd Johnstown (43031) *(G-8770)*

Buckeye Ready-Mix LLC 614 879-6316
6600 State Route 29 West Jefferson (43162) *(G-15608)*

Buckeye Ready-Mix LLC 740 654-4423
1750 Logan Lancaster Rd Se Lancaster (43130) *(G-8995)*

Buckeye Ready-Mix LLC 937 642-2951
838 N Main St Marysville (43040) *(G-9905)*

Buckeye Ready-Mix LLC (PA) 614 575-2132
7657 Taylor Rd Sw Reynoldsburg (43068) *(G-12757)*

Buckeye Rocker, Millersburg Also Called: M H Woodworking LLC *(G-10977)*

Buckeye Rubber Products, Lima Also Called: Brp Manufacturing Company *(G-9226)*

Buckeye Seating LLC 330 893-7700
6945 Co Rd 672 Millersburg (44654) *(G-10947)*

Buckeye Smoothies LLC 740 589-2900
145 Columbus Rd Athens (45701) *(G-678)*

Buckeye Sports Bulletin, Columbus Also Called: Columbus-Sports Publications *(G-5282)*

Buckeye State Wldg & Fabg Inc 440 322-0344
175 Woodford Ave Elyria (44035) *(G-7119)*

Buckeye State Wldg & Fabg Inc (PA) 440 322-0319
131 Buckeye St Elyria (44035) *(G-7120)*

Buckeye Steel Inc 740 425-2306
607 Watt Ave Barnesville (43713) *(G-902)*

Buckeye Terminals 330 453-4170
807 Hartford Ave Se Canton (44707) *(G-2055)*

Buckeye Tractor Corporation 419 659-2162
11313 Slabtown Rd Columbus Grove (45830) *(G-5896)*

Buckeye Trailer & Fab Co LLC 330 501-9440
14779 French St Damascus (44619) *(G-6147)*

Buckeye Valley Pizza Hut Ltd 419 586-5900
1152 E Market St Celina (45822) *(G-2324)*

Buckeye Welding 330 674-0944
2507 Township Road 110 Millersburg (44654) *(G-10948)*

Buckeye Woodworking 330 698-1070
5556 Mount Hope Rd Apple Creek (44606) *(G-495)*

Buckingham Coal Company LLC
11 N 4th St Zanesville (43701) *(G-16515)*

Buckingham Src Inc 216 941-6115
3425 Service Rd Cleveland (44111) *(G-3768)*

Buckler Industries Inc 419 589-6134
861 Expressview Dr Mansfield (44905) *(G-9633)*

Buckley Manufacturing Company 513 821-4444
148 Caldwell Dr Cincinnati (45216) *(G-2693)*

Buckman Ltd 419 420-1687
1413 Forest Park Findlay (45840) *(G-7489)*

Buckys Machine and Fab Ltd 419 981-5050
8376 S County Road 47 Mc Cutchenville (44844) *(G-10272)*

Bucyrus Blades Inc (DH) 419 562-6015
260 E Beal Ave Bucyrus (44820) *(G-1850)*

Bucyrus Extruded Composites, Bloomville Also Called: Buecomp Inc *(G-1354)*

Bucyrus Graphics Inc 419 562-2906
214 W Liberty St Bucyrus (44820) *(G-1851)*

Bucyrus Ice Company, Bucyrus Also Called: Velvet Ice Cream Company *(G-1872)*

Bucyrus Precision Tech Inc 419 563-9950
200 Crossroads Blvd Bucyrus (44820) *(G-1852)*

Bud Corp 740 967-9992
158 Commerce Blvd Johnstown (43031) *(G-8771)*

Bud May Inc 216 676-8850
16850 Hummel Rd Cleveland (44142) *(G-3769)*

Budd Co Plastics Div 419 238-4332
1276 Industrial Dr Van Wert (45891) *(G-14908)*

Budde Precision Machining Corp 937 278-1962
2608 Nordic Rd Dayton (45414) *(G-6240)*

Budde Sheet Metal Works Inc (PA) 937 224-0868
305 Leo St Dayton (45404) *(G-6241)*

Buddy Hunting Inc 330 353-6850
3440 Overhill Dr Nw Canton (44718) *(G-2056)*

Buddy RC, Columbus Also Called: Ohio Model Products LLC *(G-5621)*

Buderer Drug Company Inc (PA) 419 627-2800
633 Hancock St Sandusky (44870) *(G-13046)*

Budget Dumpsters 419 690-9896
120 N Howard Rd Curtice (43412) *(G-6056)*

Budget Molders Supply Inc 216 367-7050
8303 Corporate Park Dr Macedonia (44056) *(G-9540)*

Budget Newspaper, The, Sugarcreek Also Called: Sugarcreek Budget Publishers *(G-13940)*

Budzar Industries — ALPHABETIC SECTION

Budzar Industries, Willoughby Also Called: Dyoung Enterprise Inc (G-15913)

Buecomp Inc 419 284-3840
7016 S State Route 19 Bloomville (44818) (G-1354)

Buffalo Abrasives Inc 614 891-6450
1093 Smoke Burr Dr Westerville (43081) (G-15695)

Buffalo Peanuts, Columbus Also Called: Nuts Are Good Inc (G-5608)

Buffex Metal Finishing Inc 216 631-2202
1935 W 96th St Ste L Cleveland (44102) (G-3770)

Builder Tech Wholesale LLC 419 535-7606
2931 South Ave Toledo (43609) (G-14224)

Builder Tech Windows, Toledo Also Called: Builder Tech Wholesale LLC (G-14224)

Builders Straight Edge, Elyria Also Called: B&B Distributors LLC (G-7113)

Building Block Performance LLC 614 918-7476
7920 Corporate Blvd Ste C Plain City (43064) (G-12568)

Building Concepts Inc (PA) 419 298-2371
444 N Michigan Ave Edgerton (43517) (G-7072)

Building Ctrl Integrators LLC 513 247-6154
300 E Business Way Ste 200 Cincinnati (45241) (G-2694)

Building Ctrl Integrators LLC (PA) 614 334-3300
383 N Liberty St Powell (43065) (G-12665)

Building Ctrl Integrators LLC 513 860-9600
10174 International Blvd West Chester (45246) (G-15542)

Building Rlationships Together, Niles Also Called: BRT Extrusions Inc (G-11662)

Built-Rite Box & Crate Inc 330 263-0936
608 Freedlander Rd Wooster (44691) (G-16109)

Bula Defense Systems, Cleveland Also Called: Bula Forge & Machine Inc (G-3771)

Bula Forge & Machine Inc (PA) 216 252-7600
3001 W 121st St Cleveland (44111) (G-3771)

Bula Forge Machine 216 252-7600
12117 Berea Rd Ste 1 Cleveland (44111) (G-3772)

Bulk Apothecary, Streetsboro Also Called: Natural Essentials Inc (G-13781)

Bulk Carrier Trnsp Eqp Co 330 339-3333
2743 Brightwood Rd Se New Philadelphia (44663) (G-11489)

Bulk Carriers Service Inc 330 339-3333
2743 Brightwood Rd Se New Philadelphia (44663) (G-11490)

Bulk Handling Equipment Co 330 468-5703
28 W Aurora Rd Northfield (44067) (G-11904)

Bullen, Eaton Also Called: Bullen Ultrasonics Inc (G-7056)

Bullen Ultrasonics Inc 937 456-7133
1301 Miller Williams Rd Eaton (45320) (G-7056)

Bullseye, Willoughby Also Called: Bullseye Dart Shoppe Inc (G-15895)

Bullseye Dart Shoppe Inc 440 951-9277
950c Erie Rd Willoughby (44095) (G-15895)

Bully Tools Inc 740 282-5834
14 Technology Way Steubenville (43952) (G-13663)

Bummin Beaver Brewery LLC 440 543-9900
11610 Washington St Chagrin Falls (44023) (G-2390)

Bunge North America East LLC 419 483-5340
605 Goodrich Rd Bellevue (44811) (G-1224)

Bunker Hill Cheese Co Inc 330 893-2131
6005 County Road 77 Millersburg (44654) (G-10949)

Bunn-Minnick Co 614 299-7934
875 Michigan Ave Columbus (43215) (G-5221)

Bunnell Hill Construction Inc 513 932-6010
3000g Henkle Dr Lebanon (45036) (G-9065)

Buns of Delaware Inc 740 363-2867
14 W Winter St Delaware (43015) (G-6706)

Buns Restaurant & Bakery, Delaware Also Called: Buns of Delaware Inc (G-6706)

Bunting Bearings LLC (PA) 419 866-7000
1001 Holland Park Blvd Holland (43528) (G-8495)

Bunting Bearings LLC 419 522-3323
153 E 5th St Mansfield (44902) (G-9634)

Burdens Machine & Welding Inc 740 345-9246
94 S 5th St Newark (43055) (G-11569)

Burghardt Manufacturing Inc 330 253-7590
1524 Massillon Rd Akron (44306) (G-95)

Burghardt Metal Fabg Inc 330 794-1830
1638 Mcchesney Rd Akron (44306) (G-96)

Burial Vaults By Neher, Springfield Also Called: Neher Burial Vault Company (G-13612)

Burke & Company, Cincinnati Also Called: Patrick J Burke & Co (G-3237)

Burke Products Inc 937 372-3516
1355 Enterprise Ln Xenia (45385) (G-16253)

Burkettsville Stockyard, Burkettsville Also Called: Werling and Sons Inc (G-1879)

Burkholder Woodworking Llc 440 313-8203
15078 Georgia Rd Middlefield (44062) (G-10735)

Burrrows Paper Corroc Div, Franklin Also Called: Novolex Holdings Inc (G-7690)

Burt Manufacturing Company Inc 330 762-0061
44 E South St Akron (44311) (G-97)

Burton Industries Inc 440 974-1700
7875 Division Dr Mentor (44060) (G-10433)

Burton Metal Finishing Inc 614 252-9523
1711 Woodland Ave Columbus (43219) (G-5222)

Burton Mtal Fnshg Inc Pwdr Cti, Columbus Also Called: Burton Metal Finishing Inc (G-5222)

Burton Rubber Processing, Burton Also Called: Hexpol Compounding LLC (G-1880)

Busch & Thiem Inc 419 625-7515
1316 Cleveland Rd Sandusky (44870) (G-13047)

Buschman Corporation 216 431-6633
1740 E 43rd St Cleveland (44103) (G-3773)

Buschman Corporation 216 431-6633
4100 Payne Ave Ste 1 Cleveland (44103) (G-3774)

Bush Inc 216 362-6700
15901 Industrial Pkwy Cleveland (44135) (G-3775)

Bush Integrated, Cleveland Also Called: PJ Bush Associates Inc (G-4556)

Bush Specialty Vehicles Inc 937 382-5502
80 Park Dr Wilmington (45177) (G-16042)

Bushong Auto Service, Troy Also Called: Mader Automotive Center Inc (G-14595)

Bushworks Incorporated 937 767-1713
1280 Grinnell Dr Unit 1 Yellow Springs (45387) (G-16283)

Business Idntfction Systems In 614 841-1255
6185 Huntley Rd Ste M Columbus (43229) (G-5223)

Business Journal 330 744-5023
25 E Boardman St Ste 306 Youngstown (44503) (G-16330)

Busken Bakery Inc (PA) 513 871-2114
2675 Madison Rd Cincinnati (45208) (G-2695)

Busse Combat Knives, Wauseon Also Called: Busse Knife Co (G-15258)

Busse Knife Co 419 923-6471
11651 County Road 12 Wauseon (43567) (G-15258)

Butech Bliss, Salem Also Called: Butech Inc (G-12979)

Butech Inc 330 337-0000
633 S Broadway Ave Salem (44460) (G-12978)

Butech Inc (PA) 330 337-0000
550 S Ellsworth Ave Salem (44460) (G-12979)

Butler Cnty Surgical Prpts LLC 513 844-2200
213 Dayton St Hamilton (45011) (G-8189)

Butler Tech 513 867-1028
3611 Hamilton Middletown Rd Fairfield Township (45011) (G-7430)

Butt Hut, Findlay Also Called: Smoke Rings Inc (G-7564)

Butt Kickn Creamery Inc 419 482-6610
26383 Carronade Dr Perrysburg (43551) (G-12366)

Buttkicker, Columbus Also Called: Guitammer Company (G-5413)

Buyers Products Company 440 974-8888
8120 Tyler Blvd Mentor (44060) (G-10434)

Buyers Products Company (PA) 440 974-8888
9049 Tyler Blvd Mentor (44060) (G-10435)

Buzz Seating Inc (PA) 877 263-5737
4774 Interstate Dr West Chester (45246) (G-15543)

Bw Supply Co., Lyons Also Called: B W Grinding Co (G-9531)

Bway Corporation 513 388-2200
8200 Broadwell Rd Cincinnati (45244) (G-2696)

Bwaypackaging, Cincinnati Also Called: Bway Corporation (G-2696)

Bwi Chassis Dynamics NA Inc 937 455-5100
3100 Research Blvd Kettering (45420) (G-8902)

Bwi Group, Kettering Also Called: Bwi North America Inc (G-8904)

Bwi North America Inc 937 455-5190
3100 Research Blvd Ste 210 Kettering (45420) (G-8903)

Bwi North America Inc (DH) 937 253-1130
3100 Research Blvd Ste 240 Kettering (45420) (G-8904)

Bwx Technologies Inc 330 860-1692
91 Stirling Ave Barberton (44203) (G-863)

Bwx Technologies Inc 740 687-4180
2600 E Main St Lancaster (43130) (G-8996)

ALPHABETIC SECTION — Caesarcreek Pallets Ltd

Bwxt Nclear Oprtions Group Inc.. 216 912-3000
24703 Euclid Ave Cleveland (44117) *(G-3776)*

Bybe Inc.. 614 706-3050
107 S High St Columbus (43215) *(G-5224)*

Byg Industries Inc.. 216 961-5436
8003 Clinton Rd Cleveland (44144) *(G-3777)*

Byler Truss.. 330 465-5412
1271 State Route 96 Ashland (44805) *(G-560)*

Byron Products Inc.. 513 870-9111
3781 Port Union Rd Fairfield (45014) *(G-7340)*

Byron Products Inc.. 513 870-9111
250 Osborne Dr Fairfield (45014) *(G-7341)*

C & C Industries, Vandalia Also Called: Sinbon Ohio LLC *(G-14959)*

C & C Metal Products, Wooster Also Called: Global Body & Equipment Co *(G-16124)*

C & F Fabrications Inc... 937 666-3234
3100 State St East Liberty (43319) *(G-6984)*

C & H Enterprises Ltd... 510 226-6083
2121 Bright Rd Findlay (45840) *(G-7490)*

C & K Machine Co Inc... 419 237-3203
604 N Park St Fayette (43521) *(G-7461)*

C & L Erectors & Riggers Inc.. 740 332-7185
16412 Thompson Ridge Rd Laurelville (43135) *(G-9054)*

C & L Supply, Logan Also Called: Kilbarger Construction Inc *(G-9367)*

C & M Rubber Co Inc... 937 299-2782
414 Littell Ave Dayton (45419) *(G-6242)*

C & R Inc (PA).. 614 497-1130
5600 Clyde Moore Dr Groveport (43125) *(G-8134)*

C & S Associates Inc... 440 461-9661
729 Miner Rd Highland Heights (44143) *(G-8383)*

C & S Industrial Ltd... 440 327-2360
5120 Mills Industrial Pkwy North Ridgeville (44039) *(G-11835)*

C & W Custom Wdwkg Co Inc... 513 891-6340
11949 Tramway Dr Cincinnati (45241) *(G-2697)*

C A Joseph Co (PA)... 330 385-6869
13712 Old Fredericktown Rd East Liverpool (43920) *(G-6988)*

C A Joseph Co.. 330 532-4646
170 Broadway St Irondale (43932) *(G-8693)*

C A Litzler Co Inc... 216 267-8020
4800 W 160th St Cleveland (44135) *(G-3778)*

C B Mfg & Sls Co Inc... 937 866-5986
4475 Infirmary Rd Dayton (45449) *(G-6243)*

C B Mfg & Sls Co Inc (PA).. 937 866-5986
4455 Infirmary Rd Miamisburg (45342) *(G-10624)*

C C M Wire Inc.. 330 425-3421
1920 Case Pkwy S Twinsburg (44087) *(G-14638)*

C D I, Miamisburg Also Called: Connective Design Incorporated *(G-10628)*

C Dcap Modem Line.. 419 748-7409
232 S East St Mc Clure (43534) *(G-10265)*

C DI Services LLC... 440 354-1433
831 Callendar Blvd Painesville (44077) *(G-12220)*

C E Electronics Inc.. 419 636-6705
2107 Industrial Dr Bryan (43506) *(G-1813)*

C E White Co (HQ).. 419 492-2157
417 N Kibler St New Washington (44854) *(G-11545)*

C F Poeppelman Inc (PA)... 937 448-2191
4755 N State Route 721 Bradford (45308) *(G-1600)*

C G S, Cleveland Also Called: Centerless Grinding Service *(G-3803)*

C Green & Sons Incorporated... 740 745-2998
9020 Mount Vernon Rd Saint Louisville (43071) *(G-12942)*

C H T, Cleveland Also Called: Compliant Healthcare Tech LLC *(G-3892)*

C H Washington Water Plan... 740 636-2382
220 Park Ave Wshngtn Ct Hs (43160) *(G-16227)*

C I P, Canton Also Called: Sequa Can Machinery Inc *(G-2221)*

C Imperial Inc... 937 669-5620
1322 Commerce Park Dr Tipp City (45371) *(G-14124)*

C J Kraft Enterprises Inc.. 740 653-9606
301 S Maple St Lancaster (43130) *(G-8997)*

C J Woodworking Inc.. 330 607-4221
8676 Markley Dr Wadsworth (44281) *(G-15021)*

C JS Signs... 330 821-7446
1670 Charl Ann Dr Alliance (44601) *(G-397)*

C L W Inc... 740 374-8443
1201 Gilman Ave Marietta (45750) *(G-9780)*

C L Woodworking LLC.. 440 487-7940
15841 Chipmunk Ln Middlefield (44062) *(G-10736)*

C M C, Cleveland Also Called: ITT Torque Systems Inc *(G-4241)*

C M M S - Re LLC... 513 489-5111
6130 Interstate Cir Blue Ash (45242) *(G-1375)*

C Massouh Printing, Canal Fulton Also Called: C Massouh Printing Co Inc *(G-1969)*

C Massouh Printing Co Inc.. 330 408-7330
590 Elm Ridge Ave Canal Fulton (44614) *(G-1969)*

C Nelson Mfg Co.. 419 898-3305
265 N Lake Winds Pkwy Oak Harbor (43449) *(G-12012)*

C P P, Cleveland Also Called: Consolidated Foundries Inc *(G-3899)*

C P S Enterprises Inc.. 216 441-7969
9815 Reno Ave Cleveland (44105) *(G-3779)*

C Q Printing, Strongsville Also Called: J & J Bechke Inc *(G-13847)*

C S I, Harrison Also Called: Coating Systems Inc *(G-8271)*

C S I, Toledo Also Called: Chem-Sales Inc *(G-14235)*

C T I Audio Inc.. 440 593-1111
220 Eastview Dr Ste 1 Brooklyn Heights (44131) *(G-1686)*

C V G, New Albany Also Called: Cvg National Seating Co LLC *(G-11377)*

C W Ohio, Conneaut Also Called: Cascade Ohio Inc *(G-5916)*

C-Link Enterprises LLC.. 937 222-2829
1825 Webster St Dayton (45404) *(G-6244)*

C-Mold Inc
22251 Mccauley Rd Shaker Heights (44122) *(G-13151)*

C-N-D Industries Inc... 330 478-8811
359 State Ave Nw Massillon (44647) *(G-10080)*

C-Tech Industries, West Chester Also Called: Tvh Parts Co *(G-15521)*

C.T.L. Steel Division, Columbus Also Called: Clark Grave Vault Company *(G-5251)*

C&C Fabrication LLC.. 419 592-1408
13226 County Road R Napoleon (43545) *(G-11309)*

C&C Indy Cylinder Head LLC... 937 708-8563
1031 Cincinnati Ave Xenia (45385) *(G-16254)*

C&W Swiss Inc.. 937 832-2889
100 Lau Pkwy Englewood (45315) *(G-7224)*

C2g, Dayton Also Called: Legrand North America LLC *(G-6403)*

CA Litzler Holding Company (PA).. 216 267-8020
4800 W 160th St Cleveland (44135) *(G-3780)*

Cabconnect Inc.. 773 282-3565
714 E Monument Ave Ste 107 Dayton (45402) *(G-6245)*

Cabinet and Granite Depot LLC... 513 874-2100
8730 N Pavillion West Chester (45069) *(G-15383)*

Cabinet Concepts Inc... 440 232-4644
590 Golden Oak Pkwy Unit B Oakwood Village (44146) *(G-12036)*

Cabinet Creat By Lillibridge.. 419 476-6838
5344 Jackman Rd Ste A Toledo (43613) *(G-14225)*

Cabinet Guys, The, Columbus Also Called: Bison Builders LLC *(G-5191)*

Cabinet Restylers, Ashland Also Called: Cabinet Restylers Inc *(G-561)*

Cabinet Restylers Inc... 419 281-8449
419 E 8th St Ashland (44805) *(G-561)*

Cabinet Shop.. 614 885-9676
9075 Antares Ave Columbus (43240) *(G-5061)*

Cabinet Specialties Inc.. 330 695-3463
10738 Criswell Rd Fredericksburg (44627) *(G-7718)*

Cabinetworks Group Mich LLC... 440 247-3091
25 N Franklin St Chagrin Falls (44022) *(G-2368)*

Cabinetworks Group Mich LLC... 440 632-2547
15535 S State Ave Middlefield (44062) *(G-10737)*

Cabintwrks Group Mddlfield LLC (HQ)................................. 888 562-7744
15535 S State Ave Middlefield (44062) *(G-10738)*

Cablecraft Motion Controls, Bolivar Also Called: Torque 2020 CMA Acqisition LLC *(G-1539)*

Cabletek Wiring Products Inc.. 800 562-9378
1150 Taylor St Elyria (44035) *(G-7121)*

Cabot Lumber Inc... 740 545-7109
304 E Union Ave West Lafayette (43845) *(G-15616)*

Cadbury Schweppes Bottling.. 614 238-0469
950 Stelzer Rd Columbus (43219) *(G-5225)*

Cadillac Papers, Hamilton Also Called: Gvs Industries Inc *(G-8214)*

Caesarcreek Pallets Ltd... 937 416-4447
4392 Shawnee Trl Jamestown (45335) *(G-8741)*

Cafco Filter

ALPHABETIC SECTION

Cafco Filter, Cincinnati *Also Called: Cincinnati A Flter Sls Svc Inc (G-2737)*

Cage Gear & Machine LLC 330 452-1532
1776 Gateway Blvd Se Canton (44707) *(G-2057)*

Cahill Services Inc 216 410-5595
13000 Athens Ave Ste 104e Lakewood (44107) *(G-8968)*

Cailin Development LLC 216 408-6261
896 E 70th St Cleveland (44103) *(G-3781)*

Cairns Industries LLC 440 255-1190
7667 Jenther Dr Mentor (44060) *(G-10436)*

Cake House Cleveland LLC 216 870-4659
1536 Saint Clair Ave Ne Ste 65 Cleveland (44114) *(G-3782)*

Cake LLC 614 592-7681
6724 Perimeter Loop Rd Unit 254 Dublin (43017) *(G-6870)*

Cal Sales Embroidery 440 236-3820
13975 Station Rd Columbia Station (44028) *(G-5007)*

Cal-Maine Foods Inc 937 337-9576
3078 Washington Rd Rossburg (45362) *(G-12861)*

Cal-Maine Foods Inc 937 968-4874
1039 Zumbrum Rd Union City (45390) *(G-14776)*

Caldwell Lumber & Supply Co 740 732-2306
17990 Woodsfield Rd Caldwell (43724) *(G-1908)*

Calgon Carbon Corporation 614 258-9501
835 N Cassady Ave Columbus (43219) *(G-5226)*

Caliber Mold and Machine Inc 330 633-8171
2200 Massillon Rd Akron (44312) *(G-98)*

California Creamery Operators 440 264-5351
30003 Bainbridge Rd Solon (44139) *(G-13325)*

Call & Post, Cleveland *Also Called: King Media Enterprises Inc (G-4290)*

Call Sign Alpha LLC 330 842-6200
2789 E State St Ste 10 Salem (44460) *(G-12980)*

Callahan AMS Machine Company, Blue Ash *Also Called: Omya Inc (G-1446)*

Callahan Cutting Tools Inc 614 294-1649
915 Distribution Dr Ste A Columbus (43228) *(G-5227)*

Callender Group, The, Mentor *Also Called: Lake Publishing Inc (G-10490)*

Callies Performance Products Inc 419 435-7448
901 S Union St Fostoria (44830) *(G-7630)*

Calm Distributors LLC 614 678-5554
1084 Rarig Ave Columbus (43219) *(G-5228)*

Calmego Specialized Pdts LLC 937 669-5620
1569 Martindale Rd Greenville (45331) *(G-8041)*

Calorplast USA LLC 513 576-6333
1287 Us Route 50 Milford (45150) *(G-10897)*

Calvary Christian Ch of Ohio 740 828-9000
338 W 3rd St Frazeysburg (43822) *(G-7714)*

Calvary Industries Inc (PA) 513 874-1113
9233 Seward Rd Fairfield (45014) *(G-7342)*

Calvert Wire & Cable Corp 330 494-3248
4276 Strausser Street, Applegrove Ext North Canton (44720) *(G-11718)*

Calvin J Magsig 419 862-3311
343 Clinton St Elmore (43416) *(G-7100)*

Calvin W Lafferty 740 498-6566
72628 Hopewell Rd Kimbolton (43749) *(G-8927)*

Calzurocom 800 257-9472
8055 Corporate Blvd Unit B Plain City (43064) *(G-12569)*

CAM Machine Inc 937 663-5000
513 S Springfield St Saint Paris (43072) *(G-12972)*

CAM-Lem Inc 216 391-7750
1768 E 25th St Cleveland (44114) *(G-3783)*

Camaco LLC 440 288-4444
3400 River Industrial Park Rd Lorain (44052) *(G-9405)*

Camaco Lorain, Lorain *Also Called: Camaco LLC (G-9405)*

Camargo Construction, Cincinnati *Also Called: Adler & Company Inc (G-2597)*

Camargo Phrm Svcs LLC (DH) 513 561-3329
1 E 4th St Ste 1400 Cincinnati (45202) *(G-2698)*

Cambrdge Ohio Prod Assmbly Cor 740 432-6383
1521 Morton Ave Cambridge (43725) *(G-1924)*

Cambridge Box & Gift Shop, Cambridge *Also Called: Cambridge Packaging Inc (G-1925)*

Cambridge Mill Products Inc 330 863-1121
6005 Alliance Rd Nw Malvern (44644) *(G-9609)*

Cambridge Packaging Inc 740 432-3351
60794 Southgate Rd Cambridge (43725) *(G-1925)*

Camden Ready Mix, West Alexandria *Also Called: Wysong Gravel Co Inc (G-15347)*

Camden Ready Mix Co (PA) 937 456-4539
478 Camden College Corner Rd Camden (45311) *(G-1962)*

Camelot Cellars Winery 614 441-8860
7780 Corporate Blvd Plain City (43064) *(G-12570)*

Camelot Manufacturing Inc 419 678-2603
210 Butler St Coldwater (45828) *(G-4983)*

Camelot Printing, Lodi *Also Called: Stephen Andrews Inc (G-9357)*

Cameo Inc 419 661-9611
995 3rd St - Ampoint Perrysburg (43551) *(G-12367)*

Cameo Countertops Inc (PA) 419 865-6371
1610 Kieswetter Rd Holland (43528) *(G-8496)*

Cameron Drilling Co Inc 740 453-3300
3636 Adamsville Rd Zanesville (43701) *(G-16516)*

Cameron International Corp 740 654-4260
471 Quarry Rd Se Lancaster (43130) *(G-8998)*

Cameron Packaging Inc 419 222-9404
250 E Hanthorn Rd Lima (45804) *(G-9227)*

Cameron Valve & Measurement, Lancaster *Also Called: Cameron International Corp (G-8998)*

Cammel Saw Company 330 477-3764
4898 Hills And Dales Rd Nw Canton (44708) *(G-2058)*

Campbell Group, Cincinnati *Also Called: Cn Transition Company LLC (G-2724)*

Campbell Signs & Apparel LLC 330 386-4768
47366 Y And O Rd East Liverpool (43920) *(G-6989)*

Campion Pipe Fitting 740 627-1125
4205 State Route 213 Steubenville (43952) *(G-13664)*

Canadus Power Systems LLC 216 831-6600
9347 Ravenna Rd Ste A Twinsburg (44087) *(G-14639)*

Canal Winchester Facility, Canal Winchester *Also Called: Nifco America Corporation (G-1990)*

Canary Health Technologies Inc 617 784-4021
5005 Rockside Rd Ste 600 Cleveland (44131) *(G-3784)*

Canberra Corporation 419 724-4300
3610 N Holland Sylvania Rd Toledo (43615) *(G-14226)*

Candle Coach 330 455-4444
1501 Perry Dr Sw Canton (44710) *(G-2059)*

Candle-Lite, Leesburg *Also Called: Candle-Lite Company LLC (G-9122)*

Candle-Lite Company LLC 513 662-8616
6252 Glenway Ave Cincinnati (45211) *(G-2699)*

Candle-Lite Company LLC (HQ) 937 780-2563
250 Eastern Ave Leesburg (45135) *(G-9122)*

Canfield Coating LLC 330 533-3311
460 W Main St Canfield (44406) *(G-2002)*

Canfield Industrial Park, Canfield *Also Called: Afc Company (G-1997)*

Canfield Manufacturing Co Inc 330 533-3333
489 Rosemont Rd North Jackson (44451) *(G-11780)*

Canfield Metal Coating Corp 330 702-3876
460 W Main St Canfield (44406) *(G-2003)*

Canine Creations Inc 937 667-8576
120b W Broadway St # A Tipp City (45371) *(G-14125)*

Cannon Salt & Supply Inc 440 232-1700
26041 Cannon Rd Bedford (44146) *(G-1108)*

Canron Manufacturing Inc 330 497-1131
3979 State Street N W Greentown (44630) *(G-8034)*

Cantelli Block and Brick Inc 419 433-0102
1602 Milan Rd Sandusky (44870) *(G-13048)*

Cantex Inc 330 995-3665
11444 Chamberlain Rd # 1 Aurora (44202) *(G-710)*

Canton Bandag Co 330 454-3025
922 Benskin Ave Sw Canton (44710) *(G-2060)*

Canton Carnival Wheels Inc 330 837-3878
2407 Tanglewood Dr Ne Massillon (44646) *(G-10081)*

Canton Drop Forge, Canton *Also Called: Canton Drop Forge Inc (G-2061)*

Canton Drop Forge Inc 330 477-4511
4575 Southway St Sw Canton (44706) *(G-2061)*

Canton Elevator Inc 330 833-3600
2575 Greensburg Rd North Canton (44720) *(G-11719)*

Canton Galvanizing 330 685-7316
2300 Allen Ave Se Canton (44707) *(G-2062)*

Canton Galvanizing LLC 330 685-9060
1821 Moore Ave Se Canton (44707) *(G-2063)*

Canton Gear Mfg Designing Inc 330 455-2771
1600 Tuscarawas St E Canton (44707) *(G-2064)*

ALPHABETIC SECTION — Cardinal Products Inc

Canton Hot Rolled Plant, Canton *Also Called: Republic Steel (G-2213)*

Canton Manufacturing, Valley City *Also Called: Greenfield Die & Mfg Corp (G-14871)*

Canton OH Rubber Speclty Prods 330 454-3847
1387 Clarendon Ave Sw Bldg 13 Canton (44710) *(G-2065)*

Canton Oil Well Service Inc 330 494-1221
7793 Pittsburg Ave Nw Canton (44720) *(G-2066)*

Canton Plating Co Inc 330 452-7808
903 9th St Ne Canton (44704) *(G-2067)*

Canton Sterilized Wiping Cloth 330 455-5179
1401 Waynesburg Dr Se Canton (44707) *(G-2068)*

Canton Tool, Canton *Also Called: Stolle Machinery Company LLC (G-2236)*

Cantrell Rfinery Sls Trnsp Inc 937 695-0318
18856 State Route 136 Winchester (45697) *(G-16072)*

Canvas Specialty Mfg Co 216 881-0647
4045 Saint Clair Ave Cleveland (44103) *(G-3785)*

Canvus Inc 216 340-7500
18500 Lake Rd Rocky River (44116) *(G-12836)*

Canyon Run Engineering, Troy *Also Called: Slimline Surgical Devices LLC (G-14611)*

Cap & Associates Inc 614 863-3363
445 Mccormick Blvd Columbus (43213) *(G-5229)*

Cap Fixtures, Columbus *Also Called: Cap & Associates Inc (G-5229)*

Caparo Bull Moose Inc 330 448-4878
1433 Standard Ave Masury (44438) *(G-10156)*

Capco Automotive Products Corp 216 523-5000
1111 Superior Ave Eaton Ctr Cleveland (44114) *(G-3786)*

Capehart Enterprises LLC 614 769-7746
1724 Northwest Blvd Ste B Columbus (43212) *(G-5230)*

Capital City Awning Company 614 221-5404
577 N 4th St Columbus (43215) *(G-5231)*

Capital City Oil Inc 740 397-4483
375 Columbus Rd Mount Vernon (43050) *(G-11266)*

Capital Precision Machine & Tl 937 258-1176
1865 Radio Rd Dayton (45431) *(G-6154)*

Capital Prsthtic Orthtic Ctr I (PA) 614 451-0446
4678 Larwell Dr Columbus (43220) *(G-5232)*

Capital Resin Corporation 614 445-7177
324 Dering Ave Columbus (43207) *(G-5233)*

Capital Spring, Columbus *Also Called: Matthew Warren Inc (G-5547)*

Capital Tire Inc 330 364-4731
516 E Hudson St Toledo (43608) *(G-14227)*

Capital Toe Grinding, Columbus *Also Called: HI Lite Plastic Products (G-5432)*

Capital Tool Company 216 661-5750
1110 Brookpark Rd Cleveland (44109) *(G-3787)*

Capitol Aluminum & Glass Corp 800 331-8268
1276 W Main St Bellevue (44811) *(G-1225)*

Capitol Citicom Inc 614 472-2679
2225 Citygate Dr Ste A Columbus (43219) *(G-5234)*

Capitol Square Printing Inc 614 221-2850
59 E Gay St Columbus (43215) *(G-5235)*

Caps Inc 513 377-0800
2170 Struble Rd Cincinnati (45231) *(G-2700)*

Capsa Solutions LLC 800 437-6633
8170 Dove Pkwy Canal Winchester (43110) *(G-1983)*

Capt, Celina *Also Called: Celina Alum Precision Tech Inc (G-2325)*

Captor Corporation 937 667-8484
5040 S County Road 25a Tipp City (45371) *(G-14126)*

Car Brite, Perrysburg *Also Called: Finale Products Inc (G-12381)*

Car Bros Inc 440 232-1840
7177 Northfield Rd Bedford (44146) *(G-1109)*

Caraustar, Copley *Also Called: Caraustar Industries Inc (G-5946)*

Caraustar Indus Cnsmr Pdts Gro 330 868-4111
460 Knox Ct Minerva (44657) *(G-11028)*

Caraustar Industries Inc 740 862-4167
310 W Water St Baltimore (43105) *(G-843)*

Caraustar Industries Inc 513 871-7112
5500 Wooster Pike Cincinnati (45226) *(G-2701)*

Caraustar Industries Inc 216 961-5060
3400 Vega Ave Cleveland (44113) *(G-3788)*

Caraustar Industries Inc 216 939-3001
7960 Lorain Ave Cleveland (44102) *(G-3789)*

Caraustar Industries Inc 330 665-7700
202 Montrose West Ave Ste 315 Copley (44321) *(G-5946)*

Caraustar Industries Inc 937 298-9969
2601 E River Rd Moraine (45439) *(G-11165)*

Caravan Packaging Inc (PA) 440 243-4100
6427 Eastland Rd Cleveland (44142) *(G-3790)*

Carbide Probes Inc 937 429-9123
1328 Research Park Dr Beavercreek (45432) *(G-1042)*

Carbide Specialist Inc 440 951-4027
36430 Reading Ave Ste 10 Willoughby (44094) *(G-15896)*

Carbo Forge Inc 419 334-9788
150 State Route 523 Fremont (43420) *(G-7769)*

Carbon Group, The, Solon *Also Called: Cmbf Products Inc (G-13330)*

Carbon Polymers Company 330 948-3007
104 Lee St Lodi (44254) *(G-9348)*

Carbon Products, West Chester *Also Called: Graphel Corporation (G-15444)*

Carbon Web Print LLC 216 402-3504
38033 Dodds Hill Dr Willoughby Hills (44094) *(G-16022)*

Carbonklean Llc 614 980-9515
24 Village Pointe Dr Powell (43065) *(G-12666)*

Carbonless Cut Sheet Forms Inc 740 826-1700
1948 John Glenn Hwy New Concord (43762) *(G-11431)*

Carbonless On Demandcom LLC 330 837-8611
332 Erie St S Massillon (44646) *(G-10082)*

Carborundum, Logan *Also Called: Carborundum Grinding Wheel Company (G-9360)*

Carborundum Grinding Wheel Company 740 385-2171
1011 E Front St Logan (43138) *(G-9360)*

Carco America LLC 216 928-5409
1100 Superior Ave E Ste 1100 Cleveland (44114) *(G-3791)*

Carden Door Company LLC 513 459-2233
1224 Castle Dr Mason (45040) *(G-9967)*

Cardiac Analytics LLC 614 314-1332
5683 Liberty Rd N Powell (43065) *(G-12667)*

Cardinal Aggregate Inc 419 872-4380
8026 Fremont Pike Perrysburg (43551) *(G-12368)*

Cardinal Air Design LLC 440 638-4717
8527 Ridge Rd North Royalton (44133) *(G-11869)*

Cardinal Builders Inc 614 237-1000
4409 E Main St Columbus (43213) *(G-5236)*

Cardinal Building Supply LLC 614 706-4499
1000 Edgehill Rd Ste B Columbus (43212) *(G-5237)*

Cardinal CT Company 740 892-2324
140 Carey St Utica (43080) *(G-14857)*

Cardinal Fastener, Bedford Heights *Also Called: Cardinal Fstener Specialty Inc (G-1166)*

Cardinal Fstener Specialty Inc 216 831-3800
5185 Richmond Rd Bedford Heights (44146) *(G-1166)*

Cardinal Glass Industries Inc 740 892-2324
140 Carey St Utica (43080) *(G-14858)*

Cardinal Health, Dublin *Also Called: Cardinal Health Tech LLC (G-6874)*

Cardinal Health Inc 614 553-3830
7200 Cardinal Pl W Dublin (43017) *(G-6871)*

Cardinal Health Inc (PA) 614 757-5000
7000 Cardinal Pl Dublin (43017) *(G-6872)*

Cardinal Health Inc 614 757-2863
850 Corduroy Rd Ste 100 Lewis Center (43035) *(G-9155)*

Cardinal Health 414 LLC (HQ) 614 757-5000
7000 Cardinal Pl Dublin (43017) *(G-6873)*

Cardinal Health 414 LLC 513 759-1900
9866 Windisch Rd Bldg 3 West Chester (45069) *(G-15384)*

Cardinal Health Tech LLC (HQ) 614 757-5000
7000 Cardinal Pl Dublin (43017) *(G-6874)*

Cardinal Hlth Nclear Prcsion H, Lewis Center *Also Called: Cardinal Health Inc (G-9155)*

Cardinal Machine Company 440 238-7050
14459 Foltz Pkwy Strongsville (44149) *(G-13818)*

Cardinal Operating Company 614 846-5757
6677 Busch Blvd Columbus (43229) *(G-5238)*

Cardinal Percussion Inc 330 707-4446
1690 Tibbetts Wick Rd Ste 1 Girard (44420) *(G-7964)*

Cardinal Printing Inc 330 773-7300
112 W Wilbeth Rd Akron (44301) *(G-99)*

Cardinal Products Inc 440 237-8280
11929 Abbey Rd Ste D North Royalton (44133) *(G-11870)*

Cardinal Pumps Exchangers Inc | ALPHABETIC SECTION

Cardinal Pumps Exchangers Inc (DH) 330 332-8558
1425 Quaker Ct Salem (44460) *(G-12981)*

Cardinal Rubber Company 330 745-2191
939 Wooster Rd N Barberton (44203) *(G-864)*

Cardinal Truss & Components, Edgerton *Also Called: Building Concepts Inc (G-7072)*

Cardinal Welding Inc 330 426-2404
895 E Taggart St East Palestine (44413) *(G-7003)*

Cardinalhealth, Dublin *Also Called: Cardinal Health Inc (G-6872)*

Cardington Yutaka Tech Inc (DH) 419 864-8777
575 W Main St Cardington (43315) *(G-2274)*

Cardioinsight Technologies Inc 216 274-2221
3 Summit Park Dr Ste 400 Independence (44131) *(G-8655)*

Cardpak Incorporated 440 542-3100
29601 Solon Rd Solon (44139) *(G-13326)*

Care Fusion 216 521-1220
14414 Detroit Ave Ste 205 Lakewood (44107) *(G-8969)*

Care Industries 614 584-6595
6137 Enterprise Pkwy Grove City (43123) *(G-8082)*

Carefusion, Groveport *Also Called: Becton Dickinson and Company (G-8131)*

Careismatic Brands LLC 561 843-8727
6625 Port Rd Groveport (43125) *(G-8135)*

Carepoint Partners, Canfield *Also Called: Molorokalin Inc (G-2012)*

Carey Color Inc 330 239-1835
6835 Ridge Rd Sharon Center (44274) *(G-13164)*

Carey Precast Concrete Company 419 396-7142
3420 Township Highway 98 Carey (43316) *(G-2278)*

Cargill, Akron *Also Called: Cargill Incorporated (G-100)*

Cargill, Cleveland *Also Called: Cargill Incorporated (G-3792)*

Cargill, Dayton *Also Called: Cargill Incorporated (G-6246)*

Cargill, Saint Marys *Also Called: Cargill Incorporated (G-12949)*

Cargill Incorporated 330 745-0031
2065 Manchester Rd Akron (44314) *(G-100)*

Cargill Incorporated 513 941-7400
5204 River Rd Cincinnati (45233) *(G-2702)*

Cargill Incorporated 216 651-7200
2400 Ships Channel Cleveland (44113) *(G-3792)*

Cargill Incorporated 937 236-1971
3201 Needmore Rd Dayton (45414) *(G-6246)*

Cargill Incorporated 419 394-3374
1400 Mckinley Rd Saint Marys (45885) *(G-12949)*

Cargill Incorporated 937 497-4848
701 S Vandemark Rd Sidney (45365) *(G-13230)*

Cargill Incorporated 937 498-4555
2400 Industrial Dr Sidney (45365) *(G-13231)*

Cargill Premix and Nutrition, Lewisburg *Also Called: Provimi North America Inc (G-9190)*

Carl E Oeder Sons Sand & Grav 513 494-1555
1000 Mason Morrow Millgrove Rd Lebanon (45036) *(G-9066)*

Carl Rittberger Sr Inc 740 452-2767
1900 Lutz Ln Zanesville (43701) *(G-16517)*

Carlisle and Finch Company 513 681-6080
4562 W Mitchell Ave Cincinnati (45232) *(G-2703)*

Carlisle Oak 330 852-8734
3872 Township Road 162 Sugarcreek (44681) *(G-13921)*

Carlisle Plastics Company 937 845-9411
320 Ohio Ave New Carlisle (45344) *(G-11412)*

Carlisle Prtg Walnut Creek Ltd 330 852-9922
2673 Township Road 421 Sugarcreek (44681) *(G-13922)*

Carmel Publishing Inc 330 478-9200
4501 Hills And Dales Rd Nw Canton (44708) *(G-2069)*

Carmens Installation Co 216 321-4040
2865 Mayfield Rd Cleveland (44118) *(G-3793)*

Carmeuse Lime Inc 419 986-5200
1967 W County Rd 42 Bettsville (44815) *(G-1319)*

Carmeuse Lime Inc 419 638-2511
3964 County Road 41 Millersville (43435) *(G-11016)*

Carmeuse Lime Inc 419 986-2000
1967 W County Rd 42 Tiffin (44883) *(G-14080)*

Carmeuse Lime & Stone, Millersville *Also Called: Carmeuse Lime Inc (G-11016)*

Carmeuse Natural Chemicals, Bettsville *Also Called: Carmeuse Lime Inc (G-1319)*

Carnaudmetalbox Machinery USA 740 681-6788
1765 W Fair Ave Lancaster (43130) *(G-8999)*

Carney Plastics Inc 330 746-8273
1010 W Rayen Ave Youngstown (44502) *(G-16331)*

Carolina Knife Services, Hamilton *Also Called: Hamilton Industrial Grinding Inc (G-8218)*

Carolina Stair Supply Inc (PA) 740 922-3333
316 Herrick St Uhrichsville (44683) *(G-14763)*

Carolina Stamping Company 216 271-5100
5405 Avion Park Dr Highland Heights (44143) *(G-8384)*

Caron Products and Svcs Inc 740 373-6809
27640 State Route 7 Marietta (45750) *(G-9781)*

CARONDELET FOUNDRY, Sandusky *Also Called: Sandusky International Inc (G-13090)*

Carpe Diem Industries LLC 419 358-0129
505 E Jefferson St Bluffton (45817) *(G-1502)*

Carpe Diem Industries LLC (PA) 419 659-5639
4599 Campbell Rd Columbus Grove (45830) *(G-5897)*

Carper Well Service Inc 740 374-2567
30745 State Route 7 Marietta (45750) *(G-9782)*

Carr Bros Inc 440 232-3700
7177 Northfield Rd Bedford (44146) *(G-1110)*

Carr Bros Bldrs Sup & Coal Co 440 232-3700
7177 Northfield Rd Cleveland (44146) *(G-3794)*

Carr Tool Company 513 825-2900
575 Security Dr Fairfield (45014) *(G-7343)*

Carrera Holdings Inc 216 687-1311
101 W Prospect Ave Cleveland (44115) *(G-3795)*

Carrillo Pallets LLC 513 942-2210
1292 Glendale Milford Rd Cincinnati (45215) *(G-2704)*

Carroll Hills Industries 330 627-5524
540 High St Nw Carrollton (44615) *(G-2304)*

Carrollton Publishing Company 330 627-5591
43 E Main St Carrollton (44615) *(G-2305)*

Carruth Studio Inc (PA) 419 878-3060
1178 Farnsworth Rd Waterville (43566) *(G-15240)*

Cars and Parts Magazine 937 498-0803
911 S Vandemark Rd Sidney (45365) *(G-13232)*

Carson Industries LLC 419 592-2309
1675 Industrial Dr Napoleon (43545) *(G-11310)*

Carson-Saeks Inc (PA) 937 278-5311
2601 Timber Ln Dayton (45414) *(G-6247)*

Carter Carburetor LLC 216 314-2711
127 Public Sq Ste 5300 Cleveland (44114) *(G-3796)*

Carter Lumber, Middlefield *Also Called: Carter-Jones Lumber Company (G-10739)*

Carter Manufacturing Co Inc 513 398-7303
4220 State Route 42 Mason (45040) *(G-9968)*

Carter Scott-Browne 513 398-3970
4220 State Route 42 Mason (45040) *(G-9969)*

Carter-Jones Lumber Company 440 834-8164
14601 Kinsman Rd Middlefield (44062) *(G-10739)*

Carter-Jones Lumber Company 330 674-9060
6139 State Route 39 Millersburg (44654) *(G-10950)*

Cartessa Corp 513 738-4477
4825 Cincinnati Brookville Rd Shandon (45063) *(G-13159)*

Caruso Foods LLC 513 860-9200
3465 Hauck Rd Cincinnati (45241) *(G-2705)*

Cas, Cincinnati *Also Called: Consoldted Anlytcal Systems In (G-2787)*

Cas Laboratories LLC 740 815-2440
6361 Nicholas Dr Columbus (43235) *(G-5239)*

Casa Di Sassi, Apple Creek *Also Called: Rock Decor Company (G-510)*

Casa Di Vino Winery and 440 494-7878
28932 Euclid Ave Wickliffe (44092) *(G-15826)*

Casad Company Inc 419 586-9457
450 S 2nd St Coldwater (45828) *(G-4984)*

Cascade Corporation 419 425-3675
2000 Production Dr Findlay (45840) *(G-7491)*

Cascade Corporation 937 327-0300
2501 Sheridan Ave Springfield (45505) *(G-13541)*

Cascade Ohio Inc 440 593-5800
1209 Maple Ave Conneaut (44030) *(G-5916)*

Cascade Pattern Company Inc 440 323-4300
519 Ternes Ln Elyria (44035) *(G-7122)*

Cascade Unlimited LLC 440 352-7995
2510 Hale Rd Painesville (44077) *(G-12221)*

ALPHABETIC SECTION

Casco Mfg Solutions Inc 513 681-0003
   3107 Spring Grove Ave Cincinnati (45225) *(G-2706)*
Case Crafters Inc 937 667-9473
   211 S 1st St Tipp City (45371) *(G-14127)*
Case Farms 330 452-0230
   3436 Lesh St Ne Canton (44705) *(G-2070)*
Case Farms LLC 330 832-0030
   4001 Millennium Blvd Se Massillon (44646) *(G-10083)*
Case Farms Chicken, Winesburg *Also Called: Case Farms of Ohio Inc (G-16078)*
Case Farms of Ohio Inc 330 878-7118
   1225 Hensel Ave Ne Strasburg (44680) *(G-13745)*
Case Farms of Ohio Inc (HQ) 330 359-7141
   1818 County Rd 160 Winesburg (44690) *(G-16078)*
Case Maul Clamps Inc 419 668-6563
   69 N West St Norwalk (44857) *(G-11958)*
Case Ohio Burial Co (PA) 440 779-1992
   1720 Columbus Rd Cleveland (44113) *(G-3797)*
Case-Maul Manufacturing Co 419 524-1061
   30 Harker St Mansfield (44903) *(G-9635)*
Cashen Ready Mix 440 354-3227
   225 W Prospect St Painesville (44077) *(G-12222)*
Cashman Kiosk, Bedford *Also Called: Best Result Marketing Inc (G-1106)*
Cass Frames Inc 419 468-2863
   6052 State Route 19 Galion (44833) *(G-7863)*
Cass Woodworking, Galion *Also Called: Cass Woodworking Inc (G-7864)*
Cass Woodworking Inc 800 589-8841
   6052 State Route 19 Galion (44833) *(G-7864)*
Cassady Woodworks Inc 937 256-7948
   446 N Smithville Rd Dayton (45431) *(G-6155)*
Cassano's Pizza & Subs, Dayton *Also Called: Cassanos Inc (G-6248)*
Cassanos Inc (PA) 937 294-8400
   1700 E Stroop Rd Dayton (45429) *(G-6248)*
Cassis Packaging Co 937 223-8868
   1235 Mccook Ave Dayton (45404) *(G-6249)*
Cast Metals Incorporated 419 278-2010
   104 W North St Deshler (43516) *(G-6799)*
Cast Metals Technology Inc 937 968-5460
   305 Se Deerfield Rd Union City (45390) *(G-14777)*
Cast Nylons, Willoughby *Also Called: Cast Nylons Co Ltd (G-15897)*
Cast Nylons Co Ltd (PA) 440 269-2300
   4300 Hamann Pkwy Willoughby (44094) *(G-15897)*
Cast Plus Inc 937 743-7278
   415 Oxford Rd Franklin (45005) *(G-7665)*
Cast-Fab Technologies Inc (PA) 513 758-1000
   3040 Forrer St Cincinnati (45209) *(G-2707)*
Castalia Trenching & Rdymx LLC 419 684-5502
   4814 State Route 269 S Castalia (44824) *(G-2319)*
Castalia Trenching & Ready Mix 419 684-5502
   4814 State Route 269 S Castalia (44824) *(G-2320)*
Castalloy Inc 216 961-7990
   7990 Baker Ave Cleveland (44102) *(G-3798)*
Castco Inc 440 365-2333
   527 Ternes Ln Elyria (44035) *(G-7123)*
Castek Inc 440 365-2333
   527 Ternes Ln Elyria (44035) *(G-7124)*
Castelli Marble LLC (PA) 216 361-1222
   3958 Superior Ave E Cleveland (44114) *(G-3799)*
Casting Solutions LLC 740 452-9371
   2345 Licking Rd Zanesville (43701) *(G-16518)*
Castings Usa Inc 330 339-3611
   2061 Brightwood Rd Se New Philadelphia (44663) *(G-11491)*
Castle Blinds and Draperies, Dayton *Also Called: Custom Blind Corporation (G-6270)*
Castle Printing Inc 740 439-2208
   139 N 7th St Cambridge (43725) *(G-1926)*
Castruction Company Inc 330 332-9622
   1588 Salem Pkwy Salem (44460) *(G-12982)*
Cat-Wood Metalworks, Moraine *Also Called: Rolling Enterprises Inc (G-11208)*
Cat's Meow Village, The, Wooster *Also Called: F J Designs Inc (G-16117)*
Catacel Corp
   785 N Freedom St Ravenna (44266) *(G-12709)*
Catalog Merchandiser Inc
   10525 Chester Rd Ste A Cincinnati (45215) *(G-2708)*

Catania Medallic Specialities, Avon Lake *Also Called: Catania Medallic Specialty Inc (G-801)*
Catania Medallic Specialty Inc 440 933-9595
   668 Moore Rd Avon Lake (44012) *(G-801)*
Cateringstone 513 410-1064
   6119 Kenwood Rd Cincinnati (45243) *(G-2709)*
Caterpillar Authorized Dealer, Broadview Heights *Also Called: Ohio Machinery Co (G-1665)*
Caterpillar Industrial Inc 440 247-8484
   45 E Washington St Ste 203 Chagrin Falls (44022) *(G-2369)*
Catexel Nease LLC 513 738-1255
   10740 Paddys Run Rd Harrison (45030) *(G-8267)*
Catexel Nease LLC (DH) 513 587-2800
   9774 Windisch Rd West Chester (45069) *(G-15385)*
Catholic Diocese of Columbus 614 224-5195
   197 E Gay St Ste 4 Columbus (43215) *(G-5240)*
Catholic Times, Columbus *Also Called: Catholic Diocese of Columbus (G-5240)*
Catstrap, Whitehouse *Also Called: KWD Automotive Inc (G-15820)*
Cattron Holdings Inc (HQ) 234 806-0018
   655 N River Rd Nw Ste A Warren (44483) *(G-15150)*
Cattron North America Inc (DH) 234 806-0018
   655 N River Rd Nw Ste A Warren (44483) *(G-15151)*
Caudabe LLC 513 501-9799
   4480 Lake Forest Dr Ste 304 Blue Ash (45242) *(G-1376)*
Cave Tool & Mfg Inc 937 324-0662
   20 Walnut St Springfield (45505) *(G-13542)*
Caven and Sons Meat Packing Co 937 368-3841
   7850 E Us Rte 36 Conover (45317) *(G-5935)*
Cayosoft Inc (PA) 614 423-6718
   470 Olde Worthington Rd Ste 200 Westerville (43082) *(G-15650)*
Cbc Global 330 482-3373
   200 W Railroad St Columbiana (44408) *(G-5030)*
Cbd 4 Real LLC 419 480-9800
   1026 N Holland Sylvania Rd Toledo (43615) *(G-14228)*
Cbd Relieve ME Inc 216 544-1696
   22420 Tracy Ave Euclid (44123) *(G-7265)*
Cbf, Medina *Also Called: Cmbf Products Inc (G-10310)*
Cbn Westside Holdings Inc 513 772-7000
   8800 Global Way West Chester (45069) *(G-15386)*
Cbn Westside Technologies Inc 513 772-7000
   8800 Global Way West Chester (45069) *(G-15387)*
Cbp Co Inc 513 860-9053
   6545 Wiehe Rd Cincinnati (45237) *(G-2710)*
Cbr Express LLC 440 293-4744
   7737 Shady Ln Williamsfield (44093) *(G-15868)*
CBs Boring and Mch Co Inc 419 784-9500
   2064 E 2nd St Defiance (43512) *(G-6672)*
Cbst Acquisition LLC 513 361-9600
   6900 Steger Dr Cincinnati (45237) *(G-2711)*
Cbts Technology Solutions LLC 440 569-2300
   5910 Landerbrook Dr Ste 250 Cleveland (44124) *(G-3800)*
Cbus Inc 614 327-6971
   13799 Nantucket Ave Pickerington (43147) *(G-12458)*
CCA Youngstown 615 263-3000
   2240 Hubbard Rd Youngstown (44505) *(G-16332)*
Ccbdd 330 424-0404
   35947 State Route 172 Lisbon (44432) *(G-9310)*
CCL Design, Strongsville *Also Called: CCL Label Inc (G-13819)*
CCL Design Electronics, Strongsville *Also Called: CCL Label Inc (G-13820)*
CCL Label Inc 216 676-2703
   15939 Industrial Pkwy Cleveland (44135) *(G-3801)*
CCL Label Inc 856 273-0700
   8600 Innovation Campus Way W New Albany (43054) *(G-11372)*
CCL Label Inc 440 878-7000
   17890 Foltz Pkwy Strongsville (44149) *(G-13819)*
CCL Label Inc 440 878-7277
   17700 Foltz Pkwy Strongsville (44149) *(G-13820)*
Ccp Industries, Richmond Heights *Also Called: Ccp Industries Inc (G-12807)*
Ccp Industries Inc 216 535-4227
   26301 Curtiss Wright Pkwy Ste 200 Richmond Heights (44143) *(G-12807)*
Ccp Newco LLC 419 448-1700
   1780 S County Road 1 Tiffin (44883) *(G-14081)*
Ccpi Inc (PA) 937 783-2476
   838 Cherry St Blanchester (45107) *(G-1349)*

Ccr Fabrications LLC 937 667-6632
40 Ginghamsburg Rd Tipp City (45371) *(G-14128)*

CCS International Circuits LLC 440 563-3462
2593 Cardinal Dr Roaming Shores (44084) *(G-12830)*

Ccsi Inc 800 742-8535
1868 Akron Peninsula Rd Akron (44313) *(G-101)*

CD / Dvd Distribution, Dayton Also Called: Chaos Entertainment *(G-6251)*

CD Company LLC 419 332-2693
215 N Stone St Fremont (43420) *(G-7770)*

CD Solutions Inc 937 676-2376
100 W Monument St Pleasant Hill (45359) *(G-12606)*

Cdc Corporation 715 532-5548
1445 Holland Rd Maumee (43537) *(G-10173)*

Cdc Fab Co 419 866-7705
1445 Holland Rd Maumee (43537) *(G-10174)*

Cdc Publishing 772 770-6003
3825 Edwards Rd Ste 800 Cincinnati (45209) *(G-2712)*

Cdh Custom Roll Form LLC 330 984-0555
1300 Phoenix Rd Ne Warren (44483) *(G-15152)*

Cdh Liquidation Inc 419 720-4096
1343 Miami St Toledo (43605) *(G-14229)*

CDI Industries Inc 440 243-1100
6800 Lake Abrams Dr Cleveland (44130) *(G-3802)*

CDK Perforating LLC 817 862-9834
2167 State Route 821 Marietta (45750) *(G-9783)*

Cdss Inc 614 626-8747
950 Taylor Station Rd Ste U Gahanna (43230) *(G-7832)*

Ceasars Creek Marine 513 897-2912
11840 Carter Grove Ln Loveland (45140) *(G-9477)*

CEC Electronics Corp 330 916-8100
1739 Akron Peninsula Rd Akron (44313) *(G-102)*

Cecil C Peck Co 330 785-0781
1029 Arlington Cir Akron (44306) *(G-103)*

Cecil Peck Co, Akron Also Called: Summit Machine Solutions LLC *(G-340)*

Ceco Environmental Corp 513 874-8915
9759 Inter Ocean Dr West Chester (45246) *(G-15544)*

Ceco Filters Inc 513 458-2600
4625 Red Bank Rd Ste 200 Cincinnati (45227) *(G-2713)*

Ceco Group Global Holdings LLC (HQ) 513 458-2600
4625 Red Bank Rd Ste 200 Cincinnati (45227) *(G-2714)*

CED Process Minerals Inc (PA) 330 666-5500
863 N Cleveland Massillon Rd Akron (44333) *(G-104)*

Cedar Craft Products Inc 614 759-1600
776 Reynoldsburg New Albany Rd Blacklick (43004) *(G-1333)*

Cedar Elec Holdings Corp 773 804-6288
5440 W Chester Rd West Chester (45069) *(G-15388)*

Cedar Woodworking, Delaware Also Called: Cedee Cedar Inc *(G-6707)*

Cedee Cedar Inc (PA) 740 363-3148
3903 Us Highway 42 S Delaware (43015) *(G-6707)*

Ceia USA, Hudson Also Called: Ceia Usa Ltd *(G-8588)*

Ceia Usa Ltd 330 310-4741
6336 Hudson Crossing Pkwy Hudson (44236) *(G-8588)*

Celina Alum Precision Tech Inc 419 586-2278
7059 Staeger Rd Celina (45822) *(G-2325)*

Celina Percision Machine 419 586-9222
1201 Havemann Rd Celina (45822) *(G-2326)*

Celina Tent Inc 419 586-3610
5373 State Route 29 Celina (45822) *(G-2327)*

Cell 4less, Lima Also Called: Airwave Communications Cons *(G-9218)*

Cell-O-Core Co 330 239-4370
6935 Ridge Rd Sharon Center (44274) *(G-13165)*

Cell-O-Core Co 800 239-4370
276 College St Wadsworth (44281) *(G-15022)*

Cellular Technology Limited 216 791-5084
20521 Chagrin Blvd Ste 200 Shaker Heights (44122) *(G-13152)*

Cellular Technology Ltd, Shaker Heights Also Called: Ctl Analyzers LLC *(G-13153)*

Cemco Construction Corporation 440 567-7708
10176 Page Dr Concord Township (44060) *(G-5903)*

Cement Products Inc 419 524-4342
389 Park Ave E Mansfield (44905) *(G-9636)*

Cemex Cement Inc 937 873-9858
4410 State Rt 235 Fairborn (45324) *(G-7311)*

Cemex Materials LLC 330 654-2501
4200 Universal Dr Diamond (44412) *(G-6804)*

Cemplex Group NC LLC 513 671-3300
3195 Profit Dr Fairfield (45014) *(G-7344)*

Cengage Learning, Mason Also Called: Cengage Lrng Holdings II Inc *(G-9973)*

Cengage Learning Inc 513 234-5967
770 Broadway Mason (45036) *(G-9970)*

Cengage Learning Inc (HQ) 617 289-7700
5191 Natorp Blvd Lowr Mason (45040) *(G-9971)*

Cengage Learning Inc 415 839-2300
5191 Natorp Blvd Lowr Mason (45040) *(G-9972)*

Cengage Lrng Holdings II Inc (PA) 617 289-7700
5191 Natorp Blvd Mason (45040) *(G-9973)*

Cenmac Metalworks, Marion Also Called: Central Machinery Company LLC *(G-9849)*

Censtar Coatings Inc 330 723-8000
11829 Jeffrey Rd West Salem (44287) *(G-15632)*

Cent-Roll Products Inc 513 829-5201
4866 Factory Dr Fairfield (45014) *(G-7345)*

Centaur Tool & Die Inc 419 352-7704
2019 Wood Bridge Blvd Bowling Green (43402) *(G-1557)*

Centennial Barn 513 761-1697
110 Compton Rd Cincinnati (45215) *(G-2715)*

Center Concrete Inc 419 782-2495
24187 Jewell Rd Defiance (43512) *(G-6673)*

Center Concrete Inc (PA) 800 453-4224
8790 Us Highway 6 Edgerton (43517) *(G-7073)*

Center For Excptonal Practices 330 523-5240
3404 Brecksville Rd Richfield (44286) *(G-12782)*

Center For Inquiry Inc 330 671-7192
6413 Riverview Rd Peninsula (44264) *(G-12339)*

Center Street Technologies, Youngstown Also Called: 1062 Technologies Inc *(G-16295)*

Centerless Grinding Service 216 251-4100
19500 S Miles Rd Cleveland (44128) *(G-3803)*

Centerless Grinding Solutions 216 520-4612
8440 Tower Dr Twinsburg (44087) *(G-14640)*

Centerra Co-Op (PA) 419 281-2153
813 Clark Ave Ashland (44805) *(G-562)*

Centor Inc 800 321-3391
5091 County Rd 120 Berlin (44610) *(G-1305)*

Centor Inc (HQ) 567 336-8094
1899 N Wilkinson Way Perrysburg (43551) *(G-12369)*

Central Allied Enterprises Inc (PA) 330 477-6751
1243 Raff Rd Sw Canton (44710) *(G-2071)*

Central Aluminum Company LLC 614 491-5700
2045 Broehm Rd Obetz (43207) *(G-12057)*

Central Coated Products Inc 330 821-9830
2025 Mccrea St Alliance (44601) *(G-398)*

Central Coca-Cola Btlg Co Inc 330 875-1487
1560 Triplett Blvd Akron (44306) *(G-105)*

Central Coca-Cola Btlg Co Inc 740 474-2180
387 Walnut St Circleville (43113) *(G-3543)*

Central Coca-Cola Btlg Co Inc 614 863-7200
4500 Groves Rd Columbus (43232) *(G-5241)*

Central Coca-Cola Btlg Co Inc 440 324-3335
1410 Lake Ave Elyria (44035) *(G-7125)*

Central Coca-Cola Btlg Co Inc 419 522-2653
100 Industrial Pkwy Mansfield (44903) *(G-9637)*

Central Coca-Cola Btlg Co Inc 419 476-6622
3970 Catawba St Toledo (43612) *(G-14230)*

Central Coca-Cola Btlg Co Inc 330 425-4401
1882 Highland Rd Twinsburg (44087) *(G-14641)*

Central Coca-Cola Btlg Co Inc 440 269-1433
4800 E 355th St Willoughby (44094) *(G-15898)*

Central Coca-Cola Btlg Co Inc 330 783-1982
531 E Indianola Ave Youngstown (44502) *(G-16333)*

Central Coca-Cola Btlg Co Inc 740 452-3608
154 S 7th St Zanesville (43701) *(G-16519)*

Central Investment LLC (PA) 513 563-4700
7265 Kenwood Rd Ste 240 Cincinnati (45236) *(G-2716)*

Central Machinery Company LLC 740 387-1289
1339 E Fairground Rd Marion (43302) *(G-9849)*

Central Machinery Company LLC.. 740 387-1289
116 S Main St Marion (43302) *(G-9850)*

Central Market Specialty Meats, Columbus *Also Called: Karn Meats Inc (G-5504)*

Central Ohio Bandag LP.. 740 454-9728
1600 S Point Dr Zanesville (43701) *(G-16520)*

Central Ohio Bldg Components, Newark *Also Called: Columbus Roof Trusses Inc (G-11571)*

Central Ohio Fabricators LLC.. 740 393-3892
105 Progress Dr Mount Vernon (43050) *(G-11267)*

Central Ohio Met Stmping Fbrct.. 614 861-3332
4361 Brompton Ct New Albany (43054) *(G-11373)*

Central Ohio Paper & Packg Inc (PA).. 419 621-9239
2350 University Dr E Huron (44839) *(G-8629)*

Central Ohio Welding, Columbus *Also Called: COW Industries Inc (G-5301)*

Central Oil Asphalt Corp (PA).. 614 224-8111
8 E Long St Ste 400 Columbus (43215) *(G-5242)*

Central Power Systems, Columbus *Also Called: Power Distributors LLC (G-5684)*

Central Ready Mix LLC (PA).. 513 402-5001
6310 E Kemper Rd Ste 125 Cincinnati (45241) *(G-2717)*

Central Ready-Mix of Ohio LLC.. 614 252-3452
6310 E Kemper Rd Ste 125 Cincinnati (45241) *(G-2718)*

Central State Enterprises Inc.. 419 468-8191
1331 Freese Works Pl (Galion Indl Pk) Galion (44833) *(G-7865)*

Central USA Wireless LLC.. 513 469-1500
11210 Montgomery Rd Cincinnati (45249) *(G-2719)*

Central-1-Optical LLC.. 330 783-9660
6981 Southern Blvd Ste B Youngstown (44512) *(G-16334)*

Centrex Plastics, Findlay *Also Called: American Plastics LLC (G-7476)*

Centria Inc.. 740 432-7351
530 N 2nd St Cambridge (43725) *(G-1927)*

Centria Coil Coating Services, Cambridge *Also Called: Metal Coaters (G-1942)*

Centric Parts, Cleveland *Also Called: Cwd LLC (G-3933)*

Century Container LLC.. 330 457-2367
32 W Railroad St Columbiana (44408) *(G-5031)*

Century Container LLC (HQ).. 330 457-2367
5331 State Route 7 New Waterford (44445) *(G-11554)*

Century Container Corporation.. 330 457-2367
5331 State Route 7 New Waterford (44445) *(G-11555)*

Century Graphics Inc.. 614 895-7698
9101 Hawthorne Pt Westerville (43082) *(G-15651)*

Century Industries Corporation.. 330 457-2367
5331 State Route 7 New Waterford (44445) *(G-11556)*

Century Marketing Corporation.. 419 354-2591
1145 Fairview Ave Bowling Green (43402) *(G-1558)*

Century Mold Company Inc.. 513 539-9283
55 Wright Dr Middletown (45044) *(G-10806)*

Century Tool & Stamping Co.. 216 241-2032
24600 Center Ridge Rd Ste 140 Westlake (44145) *(G-15742)*

Cequence Security Inc.. 650 437-6338
10805 Indeco Dr Ste B Blue Ash (45241) *(G-1377)*

Cequent Consumer Products, Solon *Also Called: Cequent Consumer Products Inc (G-13327)*

Cequent Consumer Products Inc.. 440 498-0001
29000 Aurora Rd Ste 2 Solon (44139) *(G-13327)*

Ceramic Holdings Inc (DH).. 216 362-3900
20600 Sheldon Rd Brookpark (44142) *(G-1707)*

Cerelia USA Corp.. 614 471-9994
430 N Yearling Rd Columbus (43213) *(G-5243)*

Cerkl, Blue Ash *Also Called: Cerkl Incorporated (G-1378)*

Cerkl Incorporated.. 513 813-8425
11126 Kenwood Rd Blue Ash (45242) *(G-1378)*

Cermet Technologies, Cleveland *Also Called: Postle Industries Inc (G-4565)*

Cerner Corporation.. 740 826-7678
140 S Friendship Dr New Concord (43762) *(G-11432)*

Certainteed LLC.. 419 499-2581
11519 Us Highway 250 N Milan (44846) *(G-10882)*

Certified Comparator Products.. 937 426-9677
1174 Grange Hall Rd Beavercreek (45430) *(G-1072)*

Certified Heat Treating Inc (PA).. 937 866-0245
4475 Infirmary Rd Dayton (45449) *(G-6250)*

Certified Labs & Service Inc.. 419 289-7462
535 E 7th St Ashland (44805) *(G-563)*

Certified Tool & Grinding Inc.. 937 865-5934
4455 Infirmary Rd Miamisburg (45342) *(G-10625)*

Certified Walk In Tubs.. 614 436-4848
926 Freeway Dr N Columbus (43229) *(G-5244)*

Certified Welding Co.. 216 961-5410
9603 Clinton Rd Cleveland (44144) *(G-3804)*

Certon Technologies Inc (PA).. 440 786-7185
60 S Park St Bedford (44146) *(G-1111)*

Ces Nationwide.. 937 322-0771
567 E Leffel Ln Springfield (45505) *(G-13543)*

Cesgroup, Hamilton *Also Called: Cryogenic Equipment & Svcs Inc (G-8196)*

Ceso, Miamisburg *Also Called: Ceso Inc (G-10626)*

Ceso Inc (PA).. 937 435-8584
3601 Rigby Rd Ste 300 Miamisburg (45342) *(G-10626)*

Cetek, Brookpark *Also Called: Ceramic Holdings Inc (G-1707)*

Ceutix Pharma Inc.. 614 388-8800
2041 Builders Pl Columbus (43204) *(G-5245)*

CF Industries Inc.. 330 385-5424
425 River Rd East Liverpool (43920) *(G-6990)*

CF Tools LLC.. 740 294-0419
52025 Township Road 509 Fresno (43824) *(G-7822)*

Cfgsc LLC.. 513 772-5920
5927 Belmont Ave Cincinnati (45224) *(G-2720)*

CFM International Inc.. 513 563-4180
111 Merchant St Cincinnati (45246) *(G-2721)*

CFM International Inc.. 513 563-4180
1 Neumann Way Cincinnati (45215) *(G-2722)*

CFM International Inc (PA).. 513 552-2787
6440 Aviation Way West Chester (45069) *(G-15389)*

CFM Religion Pubg Group LLC (PA).. 513 931-4050
8805 Governors Hill Dr Ste 400 Cincinnati (45249) *(G-2723)*

Cfo Ntic.. 216 450-5700
23205 Mercantile Rd Beachwood (44122) *(G-976)*

Cft Systems, Fairport Harbor *Also Called: George Whalley Company (G-7454)*

Cg Industries, Fairfield *Also Called: Cincinnati Grinding Technologies Inc (G-7347)*

Cgas Exploration Inc (HQ).. 614 436-4631
110 E Wilson Bridge Rd Ste 250 Worthington (43085) *(G-16190)*

Cgas Inc (PA).. 614 975-4697
110 E Wilson Bridge Rd Ste 250 Worthington (43085) *(G-16191)*

Cgi Group Benefits LLC.. 440 246-6191
1374 E 28th St Lorain (44055) *(G-9406)*

Cgs, Medina *Also Called: Commercial Grinding Svcs Inc (G-10311)*

Cgs Imaging Inc.. 419 897-3000
6950 Hall St Holland (43528) *(G-8497)*

Cgs Liquidation Company LLC.. 614 878-6041
1875 Lone Eagle St Columbus (43228) *(G-5246)*

Ch Mack, Blue Ash *Also Called: H Mack Charles & Associates Inc (G-1402)*

Ch Transition Company LLC (DH).. 800 543-6400
225 Pictoria Dri Ste 210 Cincinnati (45246) *(G-2724)*

Chad Abbott Signs LLC.. 937 393-8864
439 N West St Hillsboro (45133) *(G-8456)*

Chad M Marsh.. 419 994-0587
16104 State Route 39 Loudonville (44842) *(G-9448)*

Chagrin Valley Custom Furn LLC.. 440 591-5511
26309 Miles Rd Ste 6 Warrensville Heights (44128) *(G-15227)*

Chagrin Valley Publishing Co.. 440 247-5335
525 Washington St Chagrin Falls (44022) *(G-2370)*

Chagrin Valley Times, Chagrin Falls *Also Called: Chagrin Valley Publishing Co (G-2370)*

Chagrin Vly Stl Erectors Inc.. 440 975-1556
2278 River Rd Willoughby Hills (44094) *(G-16023)*

Chalet Debonne, Madison *Also Called: Chalet Debonne Vineyards Inc (G-9588)*

Chalet Debonne Vineyards Inc.. 440 466-3485
7840 Doty Rd Madison (44057) *(G-9588)*

Chalet In The Valley, Millersburg *Also Called: Guggisberg Cheese Inc (G-10956)*

Chalfant Loading Dock Eqp, Cleveland *Also Called: Chalfant Sew Fabricators Inc (G-3805)*

Chalfant Manufacturing Company (DH).. 330 273-3510
1050 Jaycox Rd Avon (44011) *(G-765)*

Chalfant Sew Fabricators Inc.. 216 521-7922
11525 Madison Ave Cleveland (44102) *(G-3805)*

Challenger Hardware Company.. 216 591-1141
800 Resource Dr Ste 8 Independence (44131) *(G-8656)*

Cham Cor Industries Inc   **ALPHABETIC SECTION**

Cham Cor Industries Inc... 740 967-9015
117 W Coshocton St Johnstown (43031) *(G-8772)*

Champion, Cincinnati *Also Called: Enclosure Suppliers LLC (G-2868)*

Champion, Springfield *Also Called: Champion Company (G-13544)*

Champion Bridge Company... 937 382-2521
261 E Sugartree St Wilmington (45177) *(G-16043)*

Champion Company... 937 324-5681
1100 Kenton St Springfield (45505) *(G-13544)*

CHAMPION INDUSTRIES DIV, Troy *Also Called: RT Industries Inc (G-14606)*

Champion International.. 440 235-7200
7920 Mapleway Dr Olmsted Falls (44138) *(G-12079)*

Champion Laboratories Inc... 330 899-0340
6056 Deer Park Ct Toledo (43614) *(G-14231)*

Champion Opco LLC (DH)... 513 327-7338
12121 Champion Way Cincinnati (45241) *(G-2725)*

Champion Plating Inc... 216 881-1050
5200 Superior Ave Cleveland (44103) *(G-3806)*

Champion Spark Plug Cmbrdge Pl....................................... 740 432-2393
6420 Glenn Hwy Cambridge (43725) *(G-1928)*

Champion Spark Plug Company... 419 535-2567
900 Upton Ave Toledo (43607) *(G-14232)*

Champion Strapping Pdts Inc... 614 527-1454
1819 Walcutt Rd Ste 13 Columbus (43228) *(G-5247)*

Champion Win Co Cleveland LLC.. 440 899-2562
9011 Freeway Dr Ste 1 Macedonia (44056) *(G-9541)*

Champion Window Co of Toledo.. 419 841-0154
7546 Ponderosa Rd Ste A Perrysburg (43551) *(G-12370)*

Champion Windows, Cincinnati *Also Called: Champion Opco LLC (G-2725)*

Chandler Machine Company... 330 688-7615
4960 Hudson Dr Stow (44224) *(G-13689)*

Chandler Machine Company... 330 688-5585
4960 Hudson Dr Stow (44224) *(G-13690)*

Chandler Mch & Prod Gear & Bro, Stow *Also Called: Chandler Machine Company (G-13689)*

Chandler Systems Incorporated... 888 363-9434
710 Orange St Ashland (44805) *(G-564)*

Chang Audio, Toledo *Also Called: China Enterprises Inc (G-14238)*

Channel Products Inc (PA)... 440 423-0113
30700 Solon Industrial Pkwy Solon (44139) *(G-13328)*

Chantilly Development Corp.. 419 243-8109
3101 Monroe St Toledo (43606) *(G-14233)*

Chaos Entertainment.. 937 520-5260
7570 Mount Whitney St Dayton (45424) *(G-6251)*

Chapin Customer Molding Inc... 440 458-6550
635 Oberlin Elyria Rd Elyria (44035) *(G-7126)*

Chaplet & Chill Division, Canton *Also Called: The W L Jenkins Company (G-2244)*

Chappell Door Company, Washington Court Hou *Also Called: Courthouse Manufacturing LLC (G-15232)*

Characters Inc... 937 335-1976
190 Peters Ave Ste A Troy (45373) *(G-14553)*

Chardon Custom Polymers LLC... 440 285-2161
373 Washington St Chardon (44024) *(G-2442)*

Chardon Metal Products Co... 440 285-2147
206 5th Ave Chardon (44024) *(G-2443)*

Chardon Square Auto & Body Inc (PA)............................. 440 286-7600
525 Water St Chardon (44024) *(G-2444)*

Chardon Tire and Brake, Chardon *Also Called: Chardon Square Auto & Body Inc (G-2444)*

Chardon Tool & Supply Co Inc... 440 286-6440
115 Parker Ct Chardon (44024) *(G-2445)*

Charger Press Inc.. 513 542-3113
6088 Rte128 Miamitown (45041) *(G-10707)*

Charizma Corp... 216 621-2220
1400 E 30th St Ste 201 Cleveland (44114) *(G-3807)*

Charles Auto Electric Co Inc.. 330 535-6269
600 Grant St Akron (44311) *(G-106)*

Charles Brent Nichols.. 513 772-7000
5041 Tanglewood Park Dr Cleves (45002) *(G-4947)*

Charles C Lewis Company.. 440 439-3150
1 W Interstate St Ste 200 Cleveland (44146) *(G-3808)*

Charles Costa Inc... 330 376-3636
924 Home Ave Akron (44310) *(G-107)*

Charles Huffman & Associates... 216 295-0850
19214 Gladstone Rd Warrensville Heights (44122) *(G-15228)*

Charles J Meyers.. 513 922-2866
866 Suncreek Ct Cincinnati (45238) *(G-2726)*

Charles Machine Works Inc... 800 324-4930
135 State Route 42 West Salem (44287) *(G-15633)*

Charles Messina... 216 663-3344
16645 Granite Rd Cleveland (44137) *(G-3809)*

Charles Mfg Co.. 330 395-3490
3021 Sferra Ave Nw Warren (44483) *(G-15153)*

Charles Rewinding Div, Canton *Also Called: Hannon Company (G-2121)*

Charles Svec Inc.. 216 662-5200
5470 Dunham Rd Maple Heights (44137) *(G-9748)*

Charles Wisvari.. 740 671-9960
3266 Guernsey St Bellaire (43906) *(G-1184)*

Charleston Ordnance Center, Medina *Also Called: Park Corporation (G-10362)*

Charqui Jerky Co... 614 286-2938
130 E Olentangy St Powell (43065) *(G-12668)*

Chart Asia Inc.. 440 753-1490
1 Infinity Corporate Centre Dr Cleveland (44125) *(G-3810)*

Chart Industries Inc... 440 753-1490
5885 Landerbrook Dr Ste 150 Cleveland (44124) *(G-3811)*

Chart International Inc (HQ).. 440 753-1490
1 Infinity Corporate Centre Dr Cleveland (44125) *(G-3812)*

Chart-Tech Tool Inc... 937 667-3543
4060 Lisa Dr Tipp City (45371) *(G-14129)*

Charter Manufacturing Co Inc... 216 883-3800
4300 E 49th St Cleveland (44125) *(G-3813)*

Charter Nex Films, Delaware *Also Called: Charter Nex Films - Delaware Oh Inc (G-6708)*

Charter Nex Films - Delaware Oh Inc................................ 740 369-2770
1188 S Houk Rd Delaware (43015) *(G-6708)*

Charter Next Generation Inc... 740 369-2770
1188 S Houk Rd Delaware (43015) *(G-6709)*

Charter Next Generation Inc... 419 884-8150
165 Industrial Dr Lexington (44904) *(G-9195)*

Charter Next Generation Inc... 419 884-8150
1450 State Route 97 Lexington (44904) *(G-9196)*

Charter Next Generation Inc... 419 884-8150
235 Industrial Dr Lexington (44904) *(G-9197)*

Charter Next Generation Inc... 419 884-8150
145 Frecka Dr Lexington (44904) *(G-9198)*

Charter Next Generation Inc... 419 884-8150
215 Industrial Dr Lexington (44904) *(G-9199)*

Charter Next Generation Inc... 330 830-6030
8333 Navarre Rd Se Massillon (44646) *(G-10084)*

Chase Industries Inc... 513 603-2936
11502 Century Blvd Cincinnati (45246) *(G-2727)*

Chase Sign & Lighting Svc Inc... 567 128-3444
5924 American Rd E Toledo (43612) *(G-14234)*

Chassis Division, Springfield *Also Called: Sutphen Corporation (G-13640)*

Chattanooga Laser Cutting LLC... 513 779-7200
891 Redna Ter Cincinnati (45215) *(G-2728)*

Chatterbox Sports LLC... 513 545-4754
6 S 2nd St Ste 205 Hamilton (45011) *(G-8190)*

Chc Fabricating Corp (PA)... 513 821-7757
10270 Wayne Ave Cincinnati (45215) *(G-2729)*

Chc Manufacturing Inc (PA)... 513 821-7757
10270 Wayne Ave Cincinnati (45215) *(G-2730)*

Check Point Software Tech Inc.. 440 748-0900
6100 Oak Tree Blvd Ste 200 Cleveland (44131) *(G-3814)*

Checkered Express Inc... 330 530-8169
2501 W Liberty St Girard (44420) *(G-7965)*

Checkmate Marine Inc... 419 562-3881
3691 State Route 4 Bucyrus (44820) *(G-1853)*

Checkpoint Surgical Inc.. 216 378-9107
6050 Oak Tree Blvd Ste 360 Independence (44131) *(G-8657)*

Checkpoint Surgical Instrs Inc, Independence *Also Called: Checkpoint Surgical Inc (G-8657)*

Checkpoint Systems Inc.. 330 456-7776
1510 4th St Se Canton (44707) *(G-2072)*

Cheese Holdings Inc... 330 893-2479
6597 County Road 625 Millersburg (44654) *(G-10951)*

Chef 2 Chef Foods LLC... 216 696-0080
1893 E 55th St Cleveland (44103) *(G-3815)*

Chef Ink LLC 937 474-2032
1131 Benfield Dr Dayton (45429) *(G-6252)*

Chefs Garden Inc 419 433-4947
9009 Huron Avery Rd Huron (44839) *(G-8630)*

Chelsea House Fabrics, Columbus Also Called: Style-Line Incorporated *(G-5796)*

Chem Instruments, West Chester Also Called: Chemsultants International Inc *(G-15392)*

Chem Technologies Ltd 440 632-9311
14875 Bonner Dr Middlefield (44062) *(G-10740)*

Chem-Materials Inc 440 455-9465
24700 Center Ridge Rd Ste 280 Westlake (44145) *(G-15743)*

Chem-Materials Co, Westlake Also Called: Chem-Materials Inc *(G-15743)*

Chem-Sales Inc
3860 Dorr St Toledo (43607) *(G-14235)*

Chemcore Inc (PA) 937 228-6118
20 Madison St Dayton (45402) *(G-6253)*

Chemequip Sales Inc 330 724-8300
1004 Swartz Rd Coventry Township (44319) *(G-6007)*

Chemical Instruments, West Chester Also Called: Cheminstruments Inc *(G-15390)*

Chemical Methods Incorporated 216 476-8400
2853 Westway Dr # A Brunswick (44212) *(G-1751)*

Chemical Solvents Inc (PA) 216 741-9310
3751 Jennings Rd Cleveland (44109) *(G-3816)*

Chemical Technologies, Swanton Also Called: Magna International Amer Inc *(G-13977)*

Chemineer, Dayton Also Called: National Oilwell Varco LP *(G-6464)*

Chemineer, Dayton Also Called: Nov Inc *(G-6479)*

Chemineer Inc 937 454-3200
5870 Poe Ave Dayton (45414) *(G-6254)*

Cheminstruments Inc 513 860-1598
510 Commercial Dr West Chester (45014) *(G-15390)*

Cheminstruments Inc (PA) 513 860-1598
510 Commercial Dr West Chester (45014) *(G-15391)*

Chemionics Corporation 330 733-8834
390 Munroe Falls Rd Tallmadge (44278) *(G-14024)*

Chemmasters Inc 440 428-2105
300 Edwards St Madison (44057) *(G-9589)*

Chempace Corporation 419 535-0101
339 Arco Dr Toledo (43607) *(G-14236)*

Chemres Trinity, West Unity Also Called: Benvic Trinity LLC *(G-15637)*

Chemron Corp 419 352-5565
1142 N Main St Bowling Green (43402) *(G-1559)*

Chemspec Ltd (DH) 330 896-0355
4450 Belden Village St Nw Ste 507 Canton (44718) *(G-2073)*

Chemspec Ltd 330 364-4422
419 Tuscarawas Ave Nw New Philadelphia (44663) *(G-11492)*

Chemspec Polymer Additives, Canton Also Called: Chemspec Ltd *(G-2073)*

Chemspec Usa LLC 330 669-8512
9287 Smucker Rd Orrville (44667) *(G-12120)*

Chemspec Usa Inc 330 669-8512
9287 Smucker Rd Orrville (44667) *(G-12121)*

Chemstation, Moraine Also Called: Chemstation International Inc *(G-11166)*

Chemstation International Inc (PA) 937 294-8265
3400 Encrete Ln Moraine (45439) *(G-11166)*

Chemsultants International Inc (PA) 440 974-3080
9079 Tyler Blvd Mentor (44060) *(G-10437)*

Chemsultants International Inc 513 860-1598
510 Commercial Dr West Chester (45014) *(G-15392)*

Chemtrade Chemicals US LLC 419 255-0193
1661 Campbell St Toledo (43607) *(G-14237)*

Chemtrade Logistics Inc 216 566-8070
2545 W 3rd St Cleveland (44113) *(G-3817)*

Chemtrade Refinery Svcs Inc 419 641-4151
7680 Ottawa Rd Cairo (45820) *(G-1905)*

Chemtreat 937 644-2525
11000 State Route 347 East Liberty (43319) *(G-6985)*

Cheney Pulp and Paper Company 937 746-9991
1000 Anderson St Franklin (45005) *(G-7666)*

Chep (usa) Inc 614 497-9448
2130 New World Dr Columbus (43207) *(G-5248)*

Cherokee Hardwoods Inc (PA) 440 632-0322
16741 Newcomb Rd Middlefield (44062) *(G-10741)*

Cherokee Manufacturing LLC 800 777-5030
3891 Shepard Rd Perry (44081) *(G-12350)*

Cherrybend Custom Aplicat LLC 937 584-4269
2326 Cherrybend Rd Wilmington (45177) *(G-16044)*

Cheryl & Co 614 776-1500
4465 Industrial Center Dr Obetz (43207) *(G-12058)*

Chester Labs Inc 513 458-3871
900 Section Rd Ste A Cincinnati (45237) *(G-2731)*

Chesterland News, Chesterland Also Called: Chesterland News Inc *(G-2480)*

Chesterland News Inc 440 729-7667
8389 Mayfield Rd Ste B-4 Chesterland (44026) *(G-2480)*

Chestnut Land Company 330 652-1939
5555 Youngstown Warren Rd Unit 637 Niles (44446) *(G-11663)*

CHI Corporation (PA) 440 498-2300
5265 Naiman Pkwy Ste H Cleveland (44139) *(G-3818)*

CHI Storage Solutions Corp, Cleveland Also Called: CHI Corporation *(G-3818)*

Chica Bands LLC 513 871-4300
6216 Madison Rd Cincinnati (45227) *(G-2732)*

Chicago Pneumatic Tool Co LLC 704 883-3500
9100 Market Pl Rear Broadview Heights (44147) *(G-1657)*

Chick Master Incubator Company (PA) .. 330 722-5591
1093 Medina Rd Medina (44256) *(G-10308)*

Chickasaw Machine & TI Co Inc 419 925-4325
3050 Chickasaw Rd Chickasaw (45826) *(G-2490)*

Chieffos Frozen Foods Inc 330 652-1222
406 S Main St Niles (44446) *(G-11664)*

Chilcote Company 216 781-6000
4600 Tiedeman Rd Cleveland (44144) *(G-3819)*

Chillicothe Facility, Chillicothe Also Called: Glatfelter Corporation *(G-2508)*

Chillicothe Packaging Corp 740 773-5800
4168 State Route 159 Chillicothe (45601) *(G-2497)*

Chillicothe Packing, Chillicothe Also Called: Churmac Industries Inc *(G-2498)*

Chilltex LLC 937 710-3308
7440 Hoying Rd Anna (45302) *(G-489)*

Chime Master Systems, Sugar Grove Also Called: Commercial Music Service Co *(G-13915)*

China Enterprises Inc 419 885-1485
5151 Monroe St Toledo (43623) *(G-14238)*

Chippewa Tool and Mfg Co 419 849-2790
1101 Oak St Woodville (43469) *(G-16091)*

Chips Manufacturing Inc 440 946-3666
35720 Lakeland Blvd Willoughby (44095) *(G-15899)*

Cho Bedford Inc (PA) 330 343-8896
2997 Progress St Dover (44622) *(G-6811)*

Cho Bedford Inc 330 343-8896
2997 Progress St Dover (44622) *(G-6812)*

Chocolate Ecstasy Inc 330 434-4199
879 Home Ave Akron (44310) *(G-108)*

Chocolate Pig Inc (PA) 440 461-4511
5338 Mayfield Rd Cleveland (44124) *(G-3820)*

Choice Adhesives, Cincinnati Also Called: Choice Brands Adhesives Ltd *(G-2733)*

Choice Ballast Solutions LLC 440 973-9841
11700 Station Rd Columbia Station (44028) *(G-5008)*

Choice Brands Adhesives Ltd 800 330-5566
666 Redna Ter Ste 500 Cincinnati (45215) *(G-2733)*

Choice Marketing 614 638-8404
5130 Transamerica Dr Columbus (43228) *(G-5249)*

Chore Anden 330 695-2300
11461 Salt Creek Rd Fredericksburg (44627) *(G-7719)*

Chris Erhart Foundry & Mch Co 513 421-6550
1240 Mehring Way Cincinnati (45203) *(G-2734)*

Chris Haughey 937 652-3338
1463 S Us Highway 68 Urbana (43078) *(G-14826)*

Chris Stepp 513 248-0822
927 Business 28 Unit B Milford (45150) *(G-10898)*

Christian Blue Pages (PA) 937 847-2583
521 Byers Rd Ste 102 Miamisburg (45342) *(G-10627)*

Christian Missionary Alliance (PA) 380 208-6200
6421 E Main St Reynoldsburg (43068) *(G-12758)*

Christopher Sweeney 513 276-4350
924 E Main St Troy (45373) *(G-14554)*

Christopher Tool & Mfg Co 440 248-8080
30500 Carter St Frnt Solon (44139) *(G-13329)*

Christy Catalytics LLC ... 740 982-1302
713 Keystone St Crooksville (43731) *(G-6045)*

Christy Machine Company ... 419 332-6451
118 Birchard Ave Fremont (43420) *(G-7771)*

Chroma Color Corporation ... 740 363-6622
100 Colomet Dr Delaware (43015) *(G-6710)*

Chromaflo, Ashtabula *Also Called: Vibrantz Color Solutions Inc (G-664)*

Chromalloy Corporation ... 937 890-3775
7425 Webster St Dayton (45414) *(G-6255)*

Chromascape LLC (PA) ... 330 998-7574
7555 E Pleasant Valley Rd Ste 100 Independence (44131) *(G-8658)*

Chrome Deposit Corporation ... 330 773-7800
1566 Firestone Pkwy Akron (44301) *(G-109)*

Chrome Deposit Corporation ... 513 539-8486
341 Lawton Ave Monroe (45050) *(G-11097)*

Chromium Corporation ... 216 271-4910
8701 Union Ave Cleveland (44105) *(G-3821)*

Chronicle Telegram ... 330 725-4166
885 W Liberty St Medina (44256) *(G-10309)*

Chuck Meadors Plastics Co ... 440 813-4466
150 S Cucumber St Jefferson (44047) *(G-8746)*

Church & Dwight Co Inc ... 740 852-3621
110 W 1st St London (43140) *(G-9384)*

Church & Dwight Co Inc ... 419 992-4244
2501 E County Rd 34 Old Fort (44861) *(G-12072)*

Church Budget Monthly Inc ... 330 337-1122
157 W Pershing St Salem (44460) *(G-12983)*

Church-Budget Envelope Company ... 800 446-9780
271 S Ellsworth Ave Salem (44460) *(G-12984)*

Churchill Steel Plate Ltd ... 330 425-9000
7851 Bavaria Rd Twinsburg (44087) *(G-14642)*

Churmac Industries, Chillicothe *Also Called: Chillicothe Packaging Corp (G-2497)*

Churmac Industries Inc ... 740 773-5800
4168 State Route 159 Chillicothe (45601) *(G-2498)*

Ci Disposition Co ... 216 587-5200
1000 Valley Belt Rd Brooklyn Heights (44131) *(G-1687)*

Cicogna, Ashtabula *Also Called: Cicogna Electric and Sign Co (G-627)*

Cicogna Electric and Sign Co (PA) ... 440 998-2637
4330 N Bend Rd Ashtabula (44004) *(G-627)*

Cil Isotope Separations LLC ... 937 376-5413
1689 Burnett Dr Xenia (45385) *(G-16255)*

Cima, Hamilton *Also Called: Wulco Inc (G-8259)*

Cima Inc ... 513 382-8976
1010 Eaton Ave Ste B Hamilton (45013) *(G-8191)*

Cima Inc ... 513 382-8976
1010 Eaton Ave Ste B Hamilton (45013) *(G-8192)*

Cima Plastics Group, Twinsburg *Also Called: Stewart Acquisition LLC (G-14738)*

Cimbar Performance Mnrl WV LLC ... 330 532-2034
2400 Clark Ave Wellsville (43968) *(G-15334)*

Cims Incorporated ... 330 794-8102
2701 Gilchrist Rd Akron (44305) *(G-110)*

Cimx LLC ... 513 248-7700
2368 Victory Pkwy Ste 120 Cincinnati (45206) *(G-2735)*

Cimx Software, Cincinnati *Also Called: Cimx LLC (G-2735)*

Cinchempro Inc ... 513 724-6111
458 W Main St Batavia (45103) *(G-914)*

Cinci Cnc LLC ... 513 722-6756
1139 Fox Run Rd Milford (45150) *(G-10899)*

Cincinnati - Vulcan Company ... 513 242-5300
5353 Spring Grove Ave Cincinnati (45217) *(G-2736)*

Cincinnati A Flter Sls Svc Inc ... 513 242-3400
4815 Para Dr Cincinnati (45237) *(G-2737)*

Cincinnati Abrasive Supply Co ... 513 941-8866
5700 Hillside Ave Cincinnati (45233) *(G-2738)*

Cincinnati Air Conditioning Co ... 513 721-5622
2080 Northwest Dr Cincinnati (45231) *(G-2739)*

Cincinnati Assn For The Blind ... 513 221-8558
2045 Gilbert Ave Cincinnati (45202) *(G-2740)*

Cincinnati Babbitt Inc ... 513 942-5088
9217 Seward Rd Fairfield (45014) *(G-7346)*

Cincinnati Beverage Company ... 513 904-8910
242 W Mcmicken Ave Cincinnati (45214) *(G-2741)*

Cincinnati Bindery & Packg Inc ... 859 816-0282
2838 Spring Grove Ave Cincinnati (45225) *(G-2742)*

Cincinnati Biorefining Corp (HQ) ... 513 482-8800
470 Este Ave Cincinnati (45232) *(G-2743)*

Cincinnati Business Courier, Cincinnati *Also Called: American City Bus Journals Inc (G-2617)*

Cincinnati Chemical Processing, Batavia *Also Called: Cinchempro Inc (G-914)*

Cincinnati Convertors Inc ... 513 731-6600
1730 Cleneay Ave Cincinnati (45212) *(G-2744)*

Cincinnati Crane & Hoist LLC ... 513 202-1408
10860 Paddys Run Rd Harrison (45030) *(G-8268)*

Cincinnati Crt Index Press Inc ... 513 241-1450
119 W Central Pkwy Cincinnati (45202) *(G-2745)*

Cincinnati Ctrl Dynamics Inc ... 513 242-7300
4924 Para Dr Cincinnati (45237) *(G-2746)*

Cincinnati Custom Signs Inc ... 513 322-2559
417 Northland Blvd Cincinnati (45240) *(G-2747)*

Cincinnati Dowel & WD Pdts Co ... 937 444-2502
135 Oak St Mount Orab (45154) *(G-11239)*

Cincinnati Enquirer ... 513 721-2700
312 Elm St Fl 18 Cincinnati (45202) *(G-2748)*

Cincinnati Eye Inst - Estgate ... 513 984-5133
601 Ivy Gbwy Ste 301 Cincinnati (45245) *(G-2554)*

Cincinnati Family Magazine ... 513 842-0077
10945 Reed Hartman Hwy Ste 221 Blue Ash (45242) *(G-1379)*

Cincinnati Fan, Mason *Also Called: Cincinnati Fan & Ventilator Company Inc (G-9974)*

Cincinnati Fan & Ventilator Company Inc (DH) ... 513 573-0600
7697 Snider Rd Mason (45040) *(G-9974)*

Cincinnati Flame Hardening Co, Fairfield *Also Called: Detroit Flame Hardening Co (G-7352)*

Cincinnati Ftn Sq News Inc ... 513 421-4049
8739 S Shore Pl Mason (45040) *(G-9975)*

Cincinnati Gasket & Indus GL, Cincinnati *Also Called: Cincinnati Gasket Pkg Mfg Inc (G-2749)*

Cincinnati Gasket Pkg Mfg Inc ... 513 761-3458
40 Illinois Ave Cincinnati (45215) *(G-2749)*

Cincinnati Gearing Systems Inc ... 513 527-8634
301 Milford Pkwy Cincinnati (45227) *(G-2750)*

Cincinnati Gearing Systems Inc (PA) ... 513 527-8600
5757 Mariemont Ave Cincinnati (45227) *(G-2751)*

Cincinnati Gilbert Mch TI LLC ... 513 541-4815
3366 Beekman St Cincinnati (45223) *(G-2752)*

Cincinnati GL Blck Dyton GL Bl, Cincinnati *Also Called: G L Pierce Inc (G-2927)*

Cincinnati Grinding Technologies Inc ... 866 983-1097
300 Distribution Cir Ste G Fairfield (45014) *(G-7347)*

Cincinnati Heat Exchangers Inc ... 513 770-0777
6404 Thornberry Ct Ste 440 Mason (45040) *(G-9976)*

Cincinnati Incorporated (PA) ... 513 367-7100
7420 Kilby Rd Harrison (45030) *(G-8269)*

Cincinnati Industrial McHy Inc ... 513 923-5600
4600 N Mason Montgomery Rd Mason (45040) *(G-9977)*

Cincinnati Laser Cutting LLC ... 513 779-7200
891 Redna Ter Cincinnati (45215) *(G-2753)*

Cincinnati Machines Inc ... 513 536-2432
4165 Half Acre Rd Batavia (45103) *(G-915)*

Cincinnati Magazine, Cincinnati *Also Called: Cincinnati Media LLC (G-2754)*

Cincinnati Mechanical Svcs LLC, Blue Ash *Also Called: Complete Mechanical Svcs LLC (G-1382)*

Cincinnati Media LLC ... 513 562-2755
1818 Race St Ste 301 Cincinnati (45202) *(G-2754)*

Cincinnati Metal Fabricating, Cincinnati *Also Called: Cincinnati Laser Cutting LLC (G-2753)*

Cincinnati Mine Machinery Co (PA) ... 513 522-7777
2950 Jonrose Ave Cincinnati (45239) *(G-2755)*

Cincinnati Mtals Fbrcation Inc ... 513 382-2988
6305 Lisbon Ave Cincinnati (45213) *(G-2756)*

Cincinnati Paperboard, Cincinnati *Also Called: Caraustar Industries Inc (G-2701)*

Cincinnati Pattern Company ... 513 241-9872
2405 Spring Grove Ave Cincinnati (45214) *(G-2757)*

Cincinnati Phone, Troy *Also Called: Christopher Sweeney (G-14554)*

Cincinnati Precision McHy Inc ... 513 860-4133
9083 Sutton Pl West Chester (45011) *(G-15393)*

Cincinnati Premier Candy Llc ... 513 253-0079
5141 Fischer Ave Cincinnati (45217) *(G-2758)*

ALPHABETIC SECTION — CJ Dannemiller Co

Cincinnati Print Solutions LLC 513 943-9500
2002 Ford Cir. Ste G Milford (45150) *(G-10900)*

Cincinnati Prof Door Sls Div, Cincinnati *Also Called: Division Overhead Door Inc (G-2834)*

Cincinnati Radiator Inc 513 874-5555
3400 Port Union Rd Hamilton (45014) *(G-8193)*

Cincinnati Renewable Fuels LLC 513 482-8800
4700 Este Ave Cincinnati (45232) *(G-2759)*

Cincinnati Retread Systems, Fairfield *Also Called: American Manufacturing & Eqp (G-7335)*

Cincinnati Site Solutions LLC 513 373-5001
36 E 7th St Ste 1650 Cincinnati (45202) *(G-2760)*

Cincinnati Stair & Handrail 513 722-3947
1220 Hill Smith Dr Ste C Cincinnati (45215) *(G-2761)*

Cincinnati Stl Treating Co LLC 513 271-3173
5701 Mariemont Ave Cincinnati (45227) *(G-2762)*

Cincinnati Test Systems Inc (HQ) 513 202-5100
10100 Progress Way Harrison (45030) *(G-8270)*

Cincinnati Thermal Spray Inc 513 793-1037
5901 Creek Rd Blue Ash (45242) *(G-1380)*

Cincinnati Thermal Spray Inc (PA) 513 793-0670
10904 Deerfield Rd Blue Ash (45242) *(G-1381)*

Cincinnati Transfer Station, Cincinnati *Also Called: Darling Ingredients Inc (G-2819)*

Cincinnati Window Decor, Cincinnati *Also Called: Cincinnati Window Shade Inc (G-2763)*

Cincinnati Window Shade Inc (PA) 513 631-7200
3004 Harris Ave Cincinnati (45212) *(G-2763)*

Cincinnatti Processing, West Chester *Also Called: Empire Packing Company LP (G-15551)*

Cincy Cupcakes LLC 513 985-4440
7940 Hosbrook Rd, Cincinnati (45243) *(G-2764)*

Cincy Deli & Carryout, Cincinnati *Also Called: Zygo Inc (G-3539)*

Cincy Glass Inc 513 241-0455
3249 Fredonia Ave Cincinnati (45229) *(G-2765)*

Cincy Safe Company 513 900-9152
5372 Galley Hill Rd Milford (45150) *(G-10901)*

Cindee Shivers LLC 419 385-0503
2603 Airport Hwy Toledo (43609) *(G-14239)*

Cindoco Wood Products Co 937 444-2504
410 Mount Clifton Dr Mount Orab (45154) *(G-11240)*

Cindus Corporation 513 948-9951
515 Station Ave Cincinnati (45215) *(G-2766)*

Cineen Inc 440 236-3658
25011 Royalton Rd Columbia Station (44028) *(G-5009)*

Cinex Inc 513 921-2825
2641 Cummins St Cincinnati (45225) *(G-2767)*

Cinfab, Cincinnati *Also Called: Cinfab LLC (G-2768)*

Cinfab LLC 513 396-6100
5240 Lester Rd Cincinnati (45213) *(G-2768)*

Cinncinati Bindery, Cincinnati *Also Called: Spring Grove Manufacturing Inc (G-3410)*

Cintas, Canton *Also Called: Cintas Corporation No 2 (G-2074)*

Cintas, Cincinnati *Also Called: Cintas Corporation (G-2769)*

Cintas, Cincinnati *Also Called: Cintas Sales Corporation (G-2771)*

Cintas Corporation (PA) 513 459-1200
6800 Cintas Blvd Cincinnati (45262) *(G-2769)*

Cintas Corporation 513 631-5750
5570 Ridge Ave Cincinnati (45213) *(G-2770)*

Cintas Corporation No 2 .... 330 966-7800
3865 Highland Park Nw Canton (44720) *(G-2074)*

Cintas Sales Corporation (HQ) 513 459-1200
6800 Cintas Blvd Cincinnati (45262) *(G-2771)*

Cintas Uniforms AP Fcilty Svcs, Cincinnati *Also Called: Cintas Corporation (G-2770)*

Cioffi Holdings LLC 330 794-9448
1001 Eastwood Ave Akron (44305) *(G-111)*

CIP International Inc 513 874-9925
9575 Le Saint Dr West Chester (45014) *(G-15394)*

Cipted Corp 412 829-2120
301 Lawton Ave Monroe (45050) *(G-11098)*

Cirba Solutions Us Inc (PA) 740 653-6290
265 Quarry Rd Se Lancaster (43130) *(G-9000)*

Cirba Solutions Us Inc 740 653-6290
265 Quarry Rd Se Lancaster (43130) *(G-9001)*

Circle Machine Rolls Inc 330 938-9010
245 W Kentucky Ave Sebring (44672) *(G-13119)*

Circle Mold & Machine Co, Tallmadge *Also Called: Circle Mold Incorporated (G-14025)*

Circle Mold Incorporated 330 633-7017
85 S Thomas Rd Tallmadge (44278) *(G-14025)*

Circle Prime Manufacturing 330 923-0019
2114 Front St Cuyahoga Falls (44221) *(G-6074)*

Circleville Glass Operations, Circleville *Also Called: Technicolor Usa Inc (G-3557)*

Circleville Oil Co 740 477-3341
224 Lancaster Pike Circleville (43113) *(G-3544)*

Circuit Board Mining LLC 419 348-1057
23546 Us Highway 224 Alvada (44802) *(G-442)*

Circuit Center 513 435-2131
4738 Gateway Cir Dayton (45440) *(G-6256)*

Cirigliano Enterprises LLC 567 525-4571
2410 Foxfire Ln Findlay (45840) *(G-7492)*

Cisco Systems, Richfield *Also Called: Cisco Systems Inc (G-12783)*

Cisco Systems Inc 330 523-2000
4125 Highlander Pkwy Richfield (44286) *(G-12783)*

Citadel Plastics, Fairlawn *Also Called: Hggc Citadel Plas Holdings Inc (G-7441)*

Citi 2 Citi Logistics 614 306-4109
6031 E Main St Columbus (43213) *(G-5250)*

Citicom, Columbus *Also Called: Capitol Citicom Inc (G-5234)*

City Apparel Inc 419 434-1155
116 E Main Cross St Findlay (45840) *(G-7493)*

City Concrete LLc 330 743-2825
151 Old Division St Youngstown (44510) *(G-16335)*

City Elyria Communication 440 322-3329
851 Garden St Elyria (44035) *(G-7127)*

City Machine Technologies Inc (PA) 330 747-2639
773 W Rayen Ave Youngstown (44502) *(G-16336)*

City of Ashland 419 289-8728
310 W 12th St Ashland (44805) *(G-565)*

City of Athens 740 592-3344
395 W State St Athens (45701) *(G-679)*

City of Canton 330 489-3370
2436 30th St Ne Canton (44705) *(G-2075)*

City of Chardon 440 286-2657
201 N Hambden St Chardon (44024) *(G-2446)*

City of Cleveland 216 664-3013
1735 Lakeside Ave E Cleveland (44114) *(G-3822)*

City of Cleveland 216 664-2711
500 Lakeside Ave E Cleveland (44114) *(G-3823)*

City of Lancaster 740 687-6670
1424 Campground Rd Lancaster (43130) *(G-9002)*

City of Middletown 513 425-7781
805 Columbia Ave Middletown (45042) *(G-10807)*

City of Mount Vernon 740 393-9508
1550 Old Delaware Rd Mount Vernon (43050) *(G-11268)*

City of Newark 740 349-6765
164 Waterworks Rd Newark (43055) *(G-11570)*

City of Newark, Newark *Also Called: Traffic Cntrl Sgnls Signs & MA (G-11609)*

City of Ravenna 330 296-5214
3722 Hommon Rd Ravenna (44266) *(G-12710)*

City of Troy 937 339-4826
300 E Staunton Rd Troy (45373) *(G-14555)*

City of Xenia 937 376-7269
1831 Us Route 68 N Xenia (45385) *(G-16256)*

City Plating, Cleveland *Also Called: City Plating and Polishing LLC (G-3824)*

City Plating and Polishing LLC 216 267-8158
4821 W 130th St Cleveland (44135) *(G-3824)*

City Printing Co Inc 330 747-5691
122 Oak Hill Ave Youngstown (44502) *(G-16337)*

Cityscapes International Inc 614 850-2540
4200 Lyman Ct Hilliard (43026) *(G-8406)*

Citywide Materials Inc 513 533-1111
5263 Wooster Pike Cincinnati (45226) *(G-2772)*

Citywide Ready Mix, Cincinnati *Also Called: Citywide Materials Inc (G-2772)*

Civacon, West Chester *Also Called: Knappco Corporation (G-15455)*

Civica CMI, Englewood *Also Called: Creative Microsystems Inc (G-7227)*

Civitas Media, Miamisburg *Also Called: Heartland Publications LLC (G-10645)*

CJ Dannemiller Co 330 825-7808
5300 S Hametown Rd Norton (44203) *(G-11939)*

CJ Salt World 440 343-5661
29149 Euclid Ave Wickliffe (44092) *(G-15827)*

CK Technologies, Montpelier *Also Called: Creative Liquid Coatings Inc (G-11135)*

Cks Solution Incorporated (PA) 513 947-1277
4293 Muhlhauser Rd Fairfield (45014) *(G-7348)*

Claflin Co. 330 650-0582
5270 Hudson Dr Hudson (44236) *(G-8589)*

Claflin Co, Hudson *Also Called: Howard B Claflin Co (G-8596)*

Claflin Company, Hudson *Also Called: Claflin Co (G-8589)*

Clampco, Wadsworth *Also Called: Clampco Products Inc (G-15023)*

Clampco Products Inc (PA) 330 336-8857
1743 Wall Rd Wadsworth (44281) *(G-15023)*

Clancey Printing Inc 740 275-4070
263 Main St Steubenville (43953) *(G-13665)*

Clancys Cabinets LLC 419 445-4455
3751 County Road 26 Archbold (43502) *(G-526)*

Clapp & Haney Brazed TI Co Inc 740 922-3515
901 Race St Dennison (44621) *(G-6794)*

Clarios LLC 419 636-4211
918 S Union St Bryan (43506) *(G-1814)*

Clarios LLC 419 865-0542
10300 Industrial St Holland (43528) *(G-8498)*

Clarios LLC 440 205-7221
7780 Metric Dr Mentor (44060) *(G-10438)*

Clarity Retail Services LLC 513 800-9369
5115 Excello Ct West Chester (45069) *(G-15395)*

Clark & Son, East Sparta *Also Called: Clark Son Actn Liquidation Inc (G-7013)*

Clark Dietrich Building, Warren *Also Called: Clarkwestern Dietrich Building (G-15154)*

Clark Fixture Technologies Inc 419 354-1541
410 N Dunbridge Rd Bowling Green (43402) *(G-1560)*

Clark Grave Vault Company (PA) 614 294-3761
375 E 5th Ave Columbus (43201) *(G-5251)*

Clark Oil & Chemical Division, Cleveland *Also Called: Cochem Inc (G-3880)*

Clark Optimization LLC 330 417-2164
1222 Easton St Ne Canton (44721) *(G-2076)*

Clark Rm Inc 419 425-9889
400 Crystal Ave Findlay (45840) *(G-7494)*

Clark Rubber & Plastic Company 440 255-9793
8888 East Ave Mentor (44060) *(G-10439)*

Clark Rubber & Plastics, Mentor *Also Called: Clark Rubber & Plastic Company (G-10439)*

Clark Son Actn Liquidation Inc 330 866-9330
10233 Sandyville Ave Se East Sparta (44626) *(G-7013)*

Clark Substations, Canton *Also Called: Clark Substations LLC (G-2077)*

Clark Substations LLC 330 452-5200
2240 Allen Ave Se Canton (44707) *(G-2077)*

Clark-Fowler Elc Mtr & Sups, Wooster *Also Called: Clark-Fowler Enterprises Inc (G-16110)*

Clark-Fowler Enterprises Inc 330 262-0906
510 W Henry St Wooster (44691) *(G-16110)*

Clark-Reliance LLC (PA) 440 572-1500
16633 Foltz Pkwy Strongsville (44149) *(G-13821)*

Clarkdietrich, West Chester *Also Called: Clarkwstrn Dtrich Bldg System (G-15396)*

Clarke Fire Protection Product, Cincinnati *Also Called: Clarke Power Services Inc (G-2773)*

Clarke Fire Prtection Pdts Inc 513 771-2200
133 Circle Freeway Dr West Chester (45246) *(G-15545)*

Clarke Power Services Inc 513 771-2200
3133 E Kemper Rd Cincinnati (45241) *(G-2773)*

Clarke-Boxit Corporation 716 487-1950
5601 Walworth Ave Cleveland (44102) *(G-3825)*

Clarksville Stave & Veneer Co 740 947-4159
9329 State Route 220 Ste A Waverly (45690) *(G-15279)*

Clarkwestern Dietrich Building 330 372-5564
1985 N River Rd Ne Warren (44483) *(G-15154)*

Clarkwstern Dtrich Bldg System 330 372-4014
1455 Ridge Rd Vienna (44473) *(G-14995)*

Clarkwstern Dtrich Bldg System (HQ) 513 870-1100
9050 Centre Pointe Dr Ste 400 West Chester (45069) *(G-15396)*

Classic Coatings 330 421-3703
6074 Pebblebrook Ln North Olmsted (44070) *(G-11822)*

Classic Countertops LLC 330 882-4220
1519 Kenmore Blvd Akron (44314) *(G-112)*

Classic Delight, Saint Marys *Also Called: Old Classic Delight Inc (G-12959)*

Classic Fuel Injection LLC 330 757-7171
2750 Intertech Dr Youngstown (44509) *(G-16338)*

Classic Laminations Inc 440 735-1333
7703 First Pl Ste B Oakwood Village (44146) *(G-12037)*

Classic Metal Roofing Systems, Piqua *Also Called: Isaiah Industries Inc (G-12527)*

Classic Monuments, Piqua *Also Called: Piqua Granite & Marble Co Inc (G-12546)*

Classic Optical Labs Inc 330 759-8245
3710 Belmont Ave Youngstown (44505) *(G-16339)*

Classic Reproductions 937 548-9839
5315 Meeker Rd Greenville (45331) *(G-8042)*

Classic Sign Company 419 420-0058
3230 Township Road 232 Findlay (45840) *(G-7495)*

Classic Stone Company Inc 614 833-3946
4090 Janitrol Rd Columbus (43228) *(G-5252)*

Clay Burley Products Co (PA) 740 452-3633
455 Gordon St Roseville (43777) *(G-12859)*

Clay Logan Products Company 740 385-2184
201 S Walnut St Logan (43138) *(G-9361)*

Claycor Inc 419 318-7290
5924 American Rd E Toledo (43612) *(G-14240)*

Clayton Homes 937 592-3039
2720 Us Highway 68 S Bellefontaine (43311) *(G-1202)*

Clcb LLC 316 284-0401
66920 S Ray Rd Saint Clairsville (43950) *(G-12898)*

Cle Pickles Inc 440 473-3740
6727 Bonnieview Rd Cleveland (44143) *(G-3826)*

Clean Remedies LLC 440 670-2112
1431 Lear Industrial Pkwy Ste A Avon (44011) *(G-766)*

Cleancut, West Chester *Also Called: Safeway Safety Step LLC (G-15505)*

Cleaning Lady Inc 419 589-5566
190 Stewart Rd N Mansfield (44905) *(G-9638)*

Cleaning Technologies Grp, Tiffin *Also Called: Nmgg Ctg LLC (G-14096)*

Cleanlife Energy LLC 800 316-2532
7620 Hub Pkwy Cleveland (44125) *(G-3827)*

Cleanlife Products, Springboro *Also Called: No Rinse Laboratories LLC (G-13512)*

Clear Channel, Lima *Also Called: Iheartcommunications Inc (G-9254)*

Clear Creek Screw Machine Co 740 969-2113
4900 Julian Rd Sw Amanda (43102) *(G-445)*

Clear Images LLC 419 241-9347
121 11th St Toledo (43604) *(G-14241)*

Clear Skies Ahead LLC (PA) 440 632-3157
15626 W High St Middlefield (44062) *(G-10742)*

Clearpath Utility Solutions LLC 740 661-4240
8155 Ridge Rd Zanesville (43701) *(G-16521)*

Clearsonic Manufacturing Inc 828 772-9809
1025 Evans Ave Akron (44305) *(G-113)*

Clearvue Insulating Glass Co 216 651-1140
14735 Lorain Ave Ste 1 Cleveland (44111) *(G-3828)*

Clearvue Products LLC 440 871-4209
24620 Wolf Rd Bay Village (44140) *(G-964)*

Cleary Machine Company Inc 937 839-4278
4858 Us Route 35 E West Alexandria (45381) *(G-15340)*

Clecorr Inc 216 961-5500
10610 Berea Rd Rear Cleveland (44102) *(G-3829)*

Clecorr Packaging, Cleveland *Also Called: Clecorr Inc (G-3829)*

Clemens License Agency 614 288-8007
12825 Wheaton Ave Pickerington (43147) *(G-12459)*

Clemens Mobile Welding LLC 419 782-4220
25239 Commerce Dr Defiance (43512) *(G-6674)*

Clermont Steel Fabricators LLC 513 732-6033
2565 Old State Route 32 Batavia (45103) *(G-916)*

Cleveland Activist 888 817-3777
1223 W 6th St Cleveland (44113) *(G-3830)*

Cleveland AEC West LLC 216 362-6000
14000 Keystone Pkwy Cleveland (44135) *(G-3831)*

Cleveland Bean Sprout Inc 216 881-2112
2675 E 40th St Cleveland (44115) *(G-3832)*

Cleveland Black Oxide, Cleveland *Also Called: Tatham Schulz Incorporated (G-4767)*

Cleveland Black Oxide Inc 216 861-4431
11400 Brookpark Rd Cleveland (44130) *(G-3833)*

ALPHABETIC SECTION — Cleveland-Cliffs Steel Corp

Cleveland Black Pages, Cleveland Also Called: Lanier & Associates Inc *(G-4311)*
Cleveland Cabinets LLC... 216 459-7676
19389 Lorain Rd Cleveland (44126) *(G-3834)*
Cleveland Canvas Goods Mfg Co... 216 361-4567
1960 E 57th St Cleveland (44103) *(G-3835)*
Cleveland Church Supply, Cleveland Also Called: Novak J F Manufacturing Co LLC *(G-4484)*
Cleveland Circuits Corp... 216 267-9020
15516 Industrial Pkwy Cleveland (44135) *(G-3836)*
Cleveland City Forge Inc... 440 647-5400
46950 State Route 18 Wellington (44090) *(G-15305)*
Cleveland Coatings Inc... 330 467-4326
51 Meadow Ln Northfield (44067) *(G-11905)*
Cleveland Coca-Cola Btlg Inc... 216 690-2653
25000 Miles Rd Bedford Heights (44146) *(G-1167)*
Cleveland Controls, Cleveland Also Called: UCI Controls Inc *(G-4843)*
Cleveland Controls Inc... 216 398-0330
1111 Brookpark Rd Cleveland (44109) *(G-3837)*
Cleveland Coretec Inc... 314 727-2087
12080 Debartolo Dr North Jackson (44451) *(G-11781)*
Cleveland Cstm Pallet & Crate, Cleveland Also Called: Millwood Inc *(G-4416)*
Cleveland Die & Mfg, Middleburg Heights Also Called: Cleveland Die & Mfg Co *(G-10716)*
Cleveland Die & Mfg Co (PA).. 440 243-3404
20303 1st Ave Middleburg Heights (44130) *(G-10716)*
Cleveland Digital Imaging Svcs, Cleveland Also Called: Caraustar Industries Inc *(G-3789)*
Cleveland Drapery Stitch Inc.. 216 252-3857
12890 Berea Rd Cleveland (44111) *(G-3838)*
Cleveland E Speedpro Imaging.. 216 342-4954
26851 Miles Rd Cleveland (44128) *(G-3839)*
Cleveland Electric Labs, Twinsburg Also Called: Cleveland Electric Labs Co *(G-14643)*
Cleveland Electric Labs Co (PA)... 800 447-2207
1776 Enterprise Pkwy Twinsburg (44087) *(G-14643)*
Cleveland Elevator Inc... 216 924-0505
121 E Ascot Ln Cuyahoga Falls (44223) *(G-6075)*
Cleveland Gear Company Inc (DH).. 216 641-9000
3249 E 80th St Cleveland (44104) *(G-3840)*
Cleveland Granite & Marble LLC... 216 291-7637
4121 Carnegie Ave Cleveland (44103) *(G-3841)*
Cleveland Hoya Corp... 440 234-5703
94 Pelret Industrial Pkwy Berea (44017) *(G-1269)*
Cleveland Ignition Co Inc... 440 439-3688
600 Golden Oak Pkwy Cleveland (44146) *(G-3842)*
Cleveland Indus Training Ctr... 216 531-3446
706 E 163rd St Cleveland (44110) *(G-3843)*
Cleveland Indus Training Ctr, Cleveland Also Called: Borman Enterprises Inc *(G-3749)*
Cleveland Jewish News, Cleveland Also Called: Cleveland Jewish Publ Co *(G-3844)*
Cleveland Jewish Publ Co... 216 454-8300
23880 Commerce Park Ste 1 Cleveland (44122) *(G-3844)*
Cleveland Jewish Publ Co Fdn... 216 454-8300
23800 Commerce Park Beachwood (44122) *(G-977)*
Cleveland Jsm Inc... 440 876-3050
11792 Alameda Dr Strongsville (44149) *(G-13822)*
Cleveland Letter Service Inc.. 216 781-8300
8351 Clover Ln Chagrin Falls (44022) *(G-2371)*
Cleveland LLC... 216 249-3098
13602 Kelso Ave Cleveland (44110) *(G-3845)*
Cleveland Magazine, Cleveland Also Called: Great Lakes Publishing Company *(G-4146)*
Cleveland Medical Devices Inc... 216 619-5928
4415 Euclid Ave Ste 400 Cleveland (44103) *(G-3846)*
Cleveland Menu Printing Inc... 216 241-5256
1441 E 17th St Cleveland (44114) *(G-3847)*
Cleveland Metal Processing Inc (PA)..................................... 440 243-3404
20303 1st Ave Cleveland (44130) *(G-3848)*
Cleveland Metal Stamping Co... 440 234-0010
1231 W Bagley Rd Ste 1 Berea (44017) *(G-1270)*
Cleveland Mica Co.. 216 226-1360
1360 Hird Ave Lakewood (44107) *(G-8970)*
Cleveland Plant and Flower Co... 614 478-9900
2370 Marilyn Park Ln Columbus (43219) *(G-5253)*
Cleveland Plating LLC... 216 249-0300
1028 E 134th St Cleveland (44110) *(G-3849)*

Cleveland Press... 440 289-3227
30628 Detroit Road Cleveland (44145) *(G-3850)*
Cleveland Press... 440 442-5101
452 Bishop Rd Cleveland (44143) *(G-3851)*
Cleveland Prosthetic Center, Cleveland Also Called: Acor Orthopaedic Inc *(G-3593)*
Cleveland Punch and Die Co, Ravenna Also Called: True Industries Inc *(G-12740)*
Cleveland Quarries, Vermilion Also Called: Irg Operating LLC *(G-14972)*
Cleveland Range LLC (DH)... 216 481-4900
760 Beta Dr Ste G Cleveland (44143) *(G-3852)*
Cleveland Rebabbitting Svc Inc... 216 433-0123
15593 Brookpark Rd Cleveland (44142) *(G-3853)*
Cleveland Rebar, Akron Also Called: Akron Rebar Co *(G-42)*
Cleveland Reclaim Inds Inc (PA).. 440 282-4917
7400 Industrial Parkway Dr Lorain (44053) *(G-9407)*
Cleveland Recycling Plant, Cleveland Also Called: Caraustar Industries Inc *(G-3788)*
Cleveland Roll Forming Co... 216 281-0202
3170 W 32nd St Cleveland (44109) *(G-3854)*
Cleveland Roll Forming Environmental Division Inc................ 440 899-3888
27881 Clemens Rd Westlake (44145) *(G-15744)*
Cleveland Shutters Inc... 440 234-7600
204 Depot St Berea (44017) *(G-1271)*
Cleveland Special Tool Inc... 440 944-1600
1351 E 286th St Wickliffe (44092) *(G-15828)*
Cleveland Specialty Pdts Inc... 216 281-8300
2130 W 110th St Cleveland (44102) *(G-3855)*
Cleveland Steel Container Corp... 330 544-2271
412 Mason St Niles (44446) *(G-11665)*
Cleveland Steel Container Corp... 330 656-5600
10048 Aurora Hudson Rd Streetsboro (44241) *(G-13762)*
Cleveland Steel Container Corporation (PA)........................... 440 349-8000
100 Executive Pkwy Hudson (44236) *(G-8590)*
Cleveland Steel Specialty Co.. 216 464-9400
26001 Richmond Rd Bedford Heights (44146) *(G-1168)*
Cleveland Steel Tool Company... 216 681-7400
474 E 105th St Cleveland (44108) *(G-3856)*
Cleveland Supplyone Inc (DH)... 216 514-7000
26801b Fargo Ave Cleveland (44146) *(G-3857)*
Cleveland Tool and Machine Inc... 216 267-6010
4717 Hinckley Industrial Pkwy Cleveland (44109) *(G-3858)*
Cleveland Track Material, Cleveland Also Called: Progress Rail Services Corp *(G-4591)*
Cleveland Vibrator Company.. 800 221-3298
4544 Hinckley Industrial Pkwy Cleveland (44109) *(G-3859)*
Cleveland Wheels.. 440 937-6211
1160 Center Rd Avon (44011) *(G-767)*
Cleveland Wind Company LLC.. 216 269-7667
4176 Hinsdale Rd Cleveland (44121) *(G-3860)*
Cleveland Wire Cloth Mfg LLC.. 216 341-1832
3573 E 78th St Cleveland (44105) *(G-3861)*
Cleveland-Cliffs, Cleveland Also Called: Cleveland-Cliffs Steel Corp *(G-3864)*
Cleveland-Cliffs Columbus LLC... 614 492-8287
4300 Alum Creek Dr Columbus (43207) *(G-5254)*
Cleveland-Cliffs Columbus LLC (DH)..................................... 614 492-6800
4020 Kinross Lakes Pkwy Ste 101 Richfield (44286) *(G-12784)*
Cleveland-Cliffs Inc (PA).. 216 694-5700
200 Public Sq Ste 3300 Cleveland (44114) *(G-3862)*
Cleveland-Cliffs Inc... 419 243-8198
811 Madison Ave Fl 7 Toledo (43604) *(G-14242)*
Cleveland-Cliffs Inc... 216 694-5700
330 Millard Ave Toledo (43605) *(G-14243)*
Cleveland-Cliffs Intl Holdg Co... 216 694-5700
1100 Superior Ave E Fl 18 Cleveland (44114) *(G-3863)*
Cleveland-Cliffs Steel Corp (DH)... 216 694-5700
200 Public Sq Ste 3300 Cleveland (44114) *(G-3864)*
Cleveland-Cliffs Steel Corp... 419 755-3011
913 Bowman St Mansfield (44903) *(G-9639)*
Cleveland-Cliffs Steel Corp... 513 425-3593
622 Box Middletown (45042) *(G-10808)*
Cleveland-Cliffs Steel Corp... 513 425-5000
1801 Crawford St Middletown (45044) *(G-10809)*
Cleveland-Cliffs Steel Corp... 513 425-3694
801 Crawford St Middletown (45044) *(G-10810)*

(PA)=Parent Co (HQ)=Headquarters (DH)=Div Headquarters

Clevelandcom

Clevelandcom 216 862-7159
4800 Tiedeman Rd Cleveland (44144) *(G-3865)*

Clevelandcrystals, Highland Heights Also Called: Gooch & Housego (ohio) LLC *(G-8387)*

Clevelnd-Clffs Clvland Wrks LL (HQ) 216 429-6000
3060 Eggers Ave Cleveland (44105) *(G-3866)*

Clevelnd-Clffs Clvland Wrks LL 216 429-6000
3100 E 4th St Cleveland (44127) *(G-3867)*

Clevelnd-Clffs Mddletown Works, Middletown Also Called: Cleveland-Cliffs Steel Corp *(G-10809)*

Clevelnd-Clffs Tblar Cmpnnts L (DH) 419 661-4150
30400 E Broadway St Walbridge (43465) *(G-15080)*

Clevelnd-Clffs Tling Stmping H (DH) 519 969-4632
9227 Centre Pointe Dr West Chester (45069) *(G-15397)*

Clevelnd-Clffs Toling Stamping (DH) 216 694-5700
9227 Centre Pointe Dr West Chester (45069) *(G-15398)*

Clevelnd-Cliffs Stl Holdg Corp (DH) 216 694-5700
200 Public Sq Ste 3300 Cleveland (44114) *(G-3868)*

Clevemed, Cleveland Also Called: Cleveland Medical Devices Inc *(G-3846)*

Clicks Document Management, Cleveland Also Called: Marcus Uppe Inc *(G-4357)*

Clientrax Software, Grove City Also Called: Custom Information Systems Inc *(G-8086)*

Cliffs, Cleveland Also Called: Cleveland-Cliffs Inc *(G-3862)*

Cliffs & Associates Ltd 216 694-5700
1100 Superior Ave E Ste 1500 Cleveland (44114) *(G-3869)*

Cliffs Empire Inc 216 694-5700
200 Public Sq Ste 3300 Cleveland (44114) *(G-3870)*

Cliffs Logan County Coal LLC 216 694-5700
200 Public Sq Ste 3300 Cleveland (44114) *(G-3871)*

Cliffs Mining Company 216 694-5700
200 Public Sq Ste 3300 Cleveland (44114) *(G-3872)*

Cliffs Mining Holding Sub Co 216 694-5700
200 Public Sq Ste 3300 Cleveland (44114) *(G-3873)*

Cliffs Mining Services Company 218 262-5913
1100 Superior Ave E Ste 1500 Cleveland (44114) *(G-3874)*

Cliffs Natural Resources Explo 216 694-5700
200 Public Sq Ste 3300 Cleveland (44114) *(G-3875)*

Cliffs Steel Inc (HQ) 216 694-5700
200 Public Sq Ste 3300 Cleveland (44114) *(G-3876)*

Cliffs UTAC Holding LLC 216 694-5700
200 Public Sq Ste 3300 Cleveland (44114) *(G-3877)*

Clifton Steel Company (HQ) 216 662-6111
16500 Rockside Rd Maple Heights (44137) *(G-9749)*

Climate Pros LLC 216 881-5200
5309 Hamilton Ave Cleveland (44114) *(G-3878)*

Climate Pros LLC 330 744-2732
52 E Myrtle Ave Youngstown (44507) *(G-16340)*

Climax Metal Products Company 440 943-8898
8141 Tyler Blvd Mentor (44060) *(G-10440)*

Climax Packaging Machinery, Hamilton Also Called: GL Industries Inc *(G-8212)*

Cline Fire LLC 419 571-4119
161 N Trimble Rd Mansfield (44906) *(G-9640)*

Cline Machine and Automtn Inc 740 474-4237
1050 Tarlton Rd Circleville (43113) *(G-3545)*

Clinical Specialties Inc (HQ) 888 873-7888
6288 Hudson Crossing Pkwy Hudson (44236) *(G-8591)*

Clinicl Otcms Mngmnt Syst LLC 330 650-9900
9200 S Hills Blvd Ste 200 Broadview Heights (44147) *(G-1658)*

Clinton Foundry Ltd 419 243-6885
1202 W Bancroft St Toledo (43606) *(G-14244)*

Clinton Machine Co Inc 330 882-2060
6270 Van Buren Rd New Franklin (44216) *(G-11435)*

Clinton Pattern Works Inc 419 243-0855
1215 W Bancroft St Toledo (43606) *(G-14245)*

Clipper Products, Cincinnati Also Called: Clipper Products Inc *(G-2555)*

Clipper Products Inc 513 688-7300
675 Cincinnati Batavia Pike Cincinnati (45245) *(G-2555)*

Clipson S Metalworking, Cincinnati Also Called: Clipsons Metal Working Inc *(G-2774)*

Clipsons Metal Working Inc 513 772-6393
127 Novner Dr Cincinnati (45215) *(G-2774)*

Clockingme LLC 614 400-9727
3280 Morse Rd Columbus (43231) *(G-5255)*

Clopay, Mason Also Called: Berry Film Products Co Inc *(G-9960)*

Clopay Building Pdts Co Inc (DH) 513 770-4800
8585 Duke Blvd Mason (45040) *(G-9978)*

Clopay Corporation (HQ) 800 282-2260
8585 Duke Blvd Mason (45040) *(G-9979)*

Closet Factory, The, Cleveland Also Called: Home Stor & Off Solutions Inc *(G-4199)*

Closets By Mike 740 607-2212
517 Winton Ave Zanesville (43701) *(G-16522)*

Clouth Sprenger LLC 937 642-8390
1425 Kingsview Dr Lebanon (45036) *(G-9067)*

Clovernook Ctr For Blind Vslly (PA) 513 522-3860
7000 Hamilton Ave Cincinnati (45231) *(G-2775)*

Clovervale Farms LLC (DH) 440 960-0146
8133 Cooper Foster Park Rd Amherst (44001) *(G-473)*

Clovervale Foods, Amherst Also Called: Clovervale Farms LLC *(G-473)*

Clp Services, Bolivar Also Called: Slm LLC *(G-1537)*

CLS Finishing Inc 330 784-4134
409 Munroe Falls Rd Tallmadge (44278) *(G-14026)*

Club 513 LLC 800 530-2574
201 E 5th St 19th Fl Cincinnati (45202) *(G-2776)*

Cluster Software Inc 614 760-9380
2674 Billingsley Rd Columbus (43235) *(G-5256)*

Clutch Mov 740 525-5510
100 Dayton Rd Marietta (45750) *(G-9784)*

Clyde Foam, Clyde Also Called: Clyde Tool & Die Inc *(G-4971)*

Clyde Tool & Die Inc 419 547-9574
524 S Church St Clyde (43410) *(G-4971)*

CM Paula Company (PA) 513 759-7473
6049 Hi Tek Ct Mason (45040) *(G-9980)*

CM Slicechief Co 419 241-7647
3333 Maple St Toledo (43608) *(G-14246)*

Cmbf Products Inc (HQ) 440 528-4000
920 Lake Rd Medina (44256) *(G-10310)*

Cmbf Products Inc 440 528-4000
29001 Solon Rd Solon (44139) *(G-13330)*

CMC Consulting, Solon Also Called: CMC Pharmaceuticals Inc *(G-13331)*

CMC Group Inc (PA) 419 354-2591
12836 S Dixie Hwy Bowling Green (43402) *(G-1561)*

CMC Pharmaceuticals Inc (PA) 216 600-9430
30625 Solon Rd Ste G Solon (44139) *(G-13331)*

Cmd Medtech LLC 614 364-4243
3585 Interchange Rd Columbus (43204) *(G-5257)*

Cmg Company Plant 2, West Mansfield Also Called: M & M Concepts Inc *(G-15626)*

CMI, Galion Also Called: CMI Holding Company Crawford *(G-7866)*

CMI Holding Company Crawford 419 468-9122
1310 Freese Works Pl Galion (44833) *(G-7866)*

CMI Industry Americas Inc (HQ) 330 332-4661
435 W Wilson St Salem (44460) *(G-12985)*

CMI Technology Inc 937 832-2000
65 Haas Dr Englewood (45322) *(G-7225)*

Cmt Imports Inc (PA) 513 615-1851
2930 Glendale Milford Rd Ste 330 Cincinnati (45241) *(G-2777)*

Cmt Machining & Fabg LLC 937 652-3740
1411 Kennard Kingscreek Rd Urbana (43078) *(G-14827)*

CNB Machining and Mfg LLC 330 877-2786
1052 Manning Rd Nw Hartville (44632) *(G-8299)*

Cnc Painting Inc 513 662-1018
3244 Vittmer Ave Cincinnati (45238) *(G-2778)*

Cnc Precision Machine Inc 440 548-3880
18360 Industrial Cir Parkman (44080) *(G-12283)*

Cnd Machine, Massillon Also Called: C-N-D Industries Inc *(G-10080)*

CNG, Lexington Also Called: Charter Next Generation Inc *(G-9196)*

Co Pac Services Inc 216 688-1780
3113 W 110th St Cleveland (44111) *(G-3879)*

Co-Ax Technology Inc 440 914-9200
30301 Emerald Valley Pkwy Solon (44139) *(G-13332)*

Coach Tool & Die LLC 937 890-4716
235 S Pioneer Blvd Springboro (45066) *(G-13498)*

Coachella Trotting & Prtg Ltd 614 326-1009
1625 Bethel Rd Columbus (43220) *(G-5258)*

Coal Resources Inc (PA) 216 765-1240
46226 National Rd Saint Clairsville (43950) *(G-12899)*

ALPHABETIC SECTION

Coal Services Inc 740 795-5220
155 Highway 7 S Powhatan Point (43942) *(G-12684)*

Coal Services Group, Powhatan Point *Also Called: Coal Services Inc (G-12684)*

Coastal Diamond, Mentor *Also Called: Performance Superabrasives LLC (G-10523)*

Coating Systems Inc 513 367-5600
150 Sales Ave Harrison (45030) *(G-8271)*

Coating Systems Group Inc 440 816-9306
6909 Engle Rd Bldg C Middleburg Heights (44130) *(G-10717)*

Coatings & Colorants, Cincinnati *Also Called: Evonik Corporation (G-2889)*

Coaxial Dynamics, Cleveland *Also Called: CDI Industries Inc (G-3802)*

Cobblers Corner LLC 330 482-4005
1115 Village Plz Columbiana (44408) *(G-5032)*

Coblentz Brothers Inc 330 857-7211
7101 S Kohler Rd Apple Creek (44606) *(G-496)*

Coblentz Chocolate Co, Walnut Creek *Also Called: Walnut Creek Chocolate Co Inc (G-15096)*

Cobra Motorcycles Mfg 330 207-3844
11511 Springfield Rd North Lima (44452) *(G-11802)*

Coburn Inc (PA) 419 368-4051
636 Ashland County Rd 30 A Hayesville (44838) *(G-8315)*

Coca Cola 513 898-7709
6560 Meadowbrook Ct West Chester (45069) *(G-15399)*

Coca Cola Offices 678 327-8959
4343 Cooper Rd Cincinnati (45242) *(G-2779)*

Coca-Cola 937 446-4644
136 Fairview Ave Sardinia (45171) *(G-13106)*

Coca-Cola, Akron *Also Called: Akron Coca-Cola Bottling Co (G-31)*

Coca-Cola, Akron *Also Called: Central Coca-Cola Btlg Co Inc (G-105)*

Coca-Cola, Bedford Heights *Also Called: Cleveland Coca-Cola Btlg Inc (G-1167)*

Coca-Cola, Cincinnati *Also Called: Coca-Cola Consolidated Inc (G-2780)*

Coca-Cola, Circleville *Also Called: Central Coca-Cola Btlg Co Inc (G-3543)*

Coca-Cola, Columbus *Also Called: Central Coca-Cola Btlg Co Inc (G-5241)*

Coca-Cola, Columbus *Also Called: Coca-Cola Company (G-5259)*

Coca-Cola, Dayton *Also Called: Coca-Cola Consolidated Inc (G-6257)*

Coca-Cola, Elyria *Also Called: Central Coca-Cola Btlg Co Inc (G-7125)*

Coca-Cola, Lima *Also Called: Coca-Cola Consolidated Inc (G-9228)*

Coca-Cola, Mansfield *Also Called: Central Coca-Cola Btlg Co Inc (G-9637)*

Coca-Cola, Portsmouth *Also Called: Coca-Cola Consolidated Inc (G-12642)*

Coca-Cola, Sardinia *Also Called: Coca-Cola (G-13106)*

Coca-Cola, Toledo *Also Called: Central Coca-Cola Btlg Co Inc (G-14230)*

Coca-Cola, Twinsburg *Also Called: Central Coca-Cola Btlg Co Inc (G-14641)*

Coca-Cola, West Chester *Also Called: Coca Cola (G-15399)*

Coca-Cola, Willoughby *Also Called: Central Coca-Cola Btlg Co Inc (G-15898)*

Coca-Cola, Youngstown *Also Called: Central Coca-Cola Btlg Co Inc (G-16333)*

Coca-Cola, Zanesville *Also Called: Central Coca-Cola Btlg Co Inc (G-16519)*

Coca-Cola Company 614 491-6305
2455 Watkins Rd Columbus (43207) *(G-5259)*

Coca-Cola Consolidated Inc 513 527-6600
5100 Duck Creek Rd Cincinnati (45227) *(G-2780)*

Coca-Cola Consolidated Inc 937 878-5000
1000 Coca Cola Blvd Dayton (45424) *(G-6257)*

Coca-Cola Consolidated Inc 419 422-3743
201 N Shore Dr Lima (45801) *(G-9228)*

Coca-Cola Consolidated Inc 740 353-3133
5050 Old Scioto Trl Portsmouth (45662) *(G-12642)*

Cochem Inc 216 341-8914
7555 Bessemer Ave Cleveland (44127) *(G-3880)*

Cochran 6573 LLC 440 349-4900
6573 Cochran Rd Ste I Solon (44139) *(G-13333)*

Coconis Furniture Inc (PA) 740 452-1231
4 S Maysville Ave South Zanesville (43701) *(G-13477)*

Codonics Inc (PA) 800 444-1198
17991 Englewood Dr Ste B Cleveland (44130) *(G-3881)*

Coffee News 614 679-2967
3027 Landen Farm Rd W Hilliard (43026) *(G-8407)*

Coffey and Associates, West Chester *Also Called: D C Controls LLC (G-15548)*

Coffing Corporation (PA) 513 919-2813
5336 Lesourdsville West Chester Rd Liberty Twp (45011) *(G-9212)*

Coffman Media LLC 614 956-7015
5995 Wilcox Pl Ste A Dublin (43016) *(G-6875)*

Cognex Corp 513 339-0402
4178 Meadowbrook Ln Mason (45040) *(G-9981)*

Cohen Brothers Inc (PA) 513 422-3696
1520 14th Ave Middletown (45044) *(G-10811)*

Cohen Brothers Inc 513 217-5200
1300 Lafayette Ave Middletown (45044) *(G-10812)*

Cohen Brothers Inc Lafayette, Middletown *Also Called: Cohen Brothers Inc (G-10812)*

Cohesant Inc (PA) 216 910-1700
3601 Green Rd Ste 308 Beachwood (44122) *(G-978)*

Coil Specialty Chemicals LLC 740 236-2407
2375 Glendale Rd Marietta (45750) *(G-9785)*

Coin World, Sidney *Also Called: Amos Media Company (G-13221)*

Col-Pump Company Inc 330 482-1029
131 E Railroad St Columbiana (44408) *(G-5033)*

Colbleu Vodka, Solon *Also Called: Blue Collar M LLC (G-13320)*

Colburn Patterson LLC (PA) 419 866-5544
1100 S Holland Sylvania Rd Holland (43528) *(G-8499)*

Colby Properties LLC 937 390-0816
2071 N Bechtle Ave Springfield (45504) *(G-13545)*

Colby Woodworking Inc 937 224-7676
1912 Lucille Dr Dayton (45404) *(G-6258)*

Cold Headed Fas Assemblies Inc 330 833-0800
1875 Harsh Ave Se Ste 3 Massillon (44646) *(G-10085)*

Cold Jet, Loveland *Also Called: Cold Jet International LLC (G-9478)*

Cold Jet International LLC (PA) 513 831-3211
455 Wards Corner Rd Loveland (45140) *(G-9478)*

Coldstone Creamery, Powell *Also Called: Stella Lou Llc (G-12681)*

Coldwater Machine Company LLC 419 678-4877
911 N 2nd St Coldwater (45828) *(G-4985)*

Cole Orthotics Prosthetic Ctr 419 476-4248
723 Phillips Ave Bldg F Toledo (43612) *(G-14247)*

Cole Tool & Die Company 419 522-1272
466 State Rte 314 N Ontario (44903) *(G-12090)*

Colepak LLC 937 652-3910
1030 S Edgewood Ave Urbana (43078) *(G-14828)*

Colfor Manufacturing Inc (DH) 330 470-6207
3255 Alliance Rd Nw Malvern (44644) *(G-9610)*

Colfor Manufacturing Inc 330 863-0404
461 Knox Ct Minerva (44657) *(G-11029)*

Colgate-Palmolive, Cambridge *Also Called: Colgate-Palmolive Company (G-1929)*

Colgate-Palmolive Company 212 310-2000
8800 Guernsey Industrial Blvd Cambridge (43725) *(G-1929)*

Collective Arts Network 216 235-3564
1372 Edwards Ave Lakewood (44107) *(G-8971)*

College Issue, Piqua *Also Called: Atlantis Sportswear Inc (G-12506)*

Collins & Venco Venturo, Cincinnati *Also Called: Venco Manufacturing Inc (G-3489)*

Collins Aerospace, Troy *Also Called: Goodrich Corporation (G-14574)*

Collinwood Shale Brick Sup Co (PA) 216 587-2700
16219 Saranac Rd Cleveland (44110) *(G-3882)*

Collotype Labels Usa Inc 513 381-1480
4053 Clough Woods Dr Batavia (45103) *(G-917)*

Colonial Cabinets Inc 440 355-9663
337 S Center St Lagrange (44050) *(G-8946)*

Colonial Machine Company Inc 330 673-5859
1041 Mogadore Rd Kent (44240) *(G-8804)*

Colonial Patterns Inc 330 673-6475
920 Overholt Rd Kent (44240) *(G-8805)*

Colonial Rubber Company (PA) 330 296-2831
706 Oakwood St Ravenna (44266) *(G-12711)*

Colonial Surface Solutions, Columbus Grove *Also Called: Carpe Diem Industries LLC (G-5897)*

Colony Hardware, Cleveland *Also Called: Beckett-Greenhill LLC (G-3728)*

Colony Machine & Tool Inc 330 225-3410
1300 Industrial Pkwy N Brunswick (44212) *(G-1752)*

Color 3 Embroidery Inc 330 652-9495
2927 Mahoning Ave Nw Warren (44483) *(G-15155)*

Color Bar Printing Centers Inc 216 595-3939
4576 Renaissance Pkwy Cleveland (44128) *(G-3883)*

Color Process Inc 440 268-7100
13900 Prospect Rd Strongsville (44149) *(G-13823)*

Color Products Inc... 513 860-2749
  36 Standen Dr Hamilton (45015) *(G-8194)*
Color Resolutions International LLC................................ 513 552-7200
  575 Quality Blvd Fairfield (45014) *(G-7349)*
Coloramic Process Inc... 440 275-1199
  2883 Industrial Park Dr Austinburg (44010) *(G-743)*
Coloramics LLC.. 614 876-1171
  4077 Weaver Ct S Hilliard (43026) *(G-8408)*
Coloring Book Solutions LLC... 419 281-9641
  426 E 8th St Ashland (44805) *(G-566)*
Colormatrix Corporation (HQ).. 216 622-0100
  680 N Rocky River Dr Berea (44017) *(G-1272)*
Colortech Graphics & Printing (PA).................................. 614 766-2400
  4000 Business Park Dr Columbus (43204) *(G-5260)*
Columbia, Vandalia *Also Called: Datwyler Sling Sltions USA Inc (G-14937)*
Columbia Chemical Corporation...................................... 330 225-3200
  1000 Western Dr Brunswick (44212) *(G-1753)*
Columbia Industrial Pdts Inc.. 216 431-6633
  4100 Payne Ave Cleveland (44103) *(G-3884)*
Columbia Industries, Cleveland *Also Called: Qcsm LLC (G-4602)*
Columbia Industries, Solon *Also Called: Skidmore Wilhelm Mfg Company (G-13422)*
Columbia Stamping Inc.. 440 236-6677
  13676 Station Rd Columbia Station (44028) *(G-5010)*
Columbiana Boiler Company, LLC, Columbiana *Also Called: Cbc Global (G-5030)*
Columbiana Foundry Company... 330 482-3336
  501 Lisbon St Columbiana (44408) *(G-5034)*
Columbus Apparel Studio, Columbus *Also Called: Columbus Apparel Studio LLC (G-5261)*
Columbus Apparel Studio LLC... 614 706-7292
  757 Garden Rd Ste 110 Columbus (43214) *(G-5261)*
Columbus Art Memorial Inc.. 614 221-9333
  606 W Broad St Columbus (43215) *(G-5262)*
Columbus Brewing Company, Columbus *Also Called: District Brewing Company Inc (G-5331)*
Columbus Canvas Products, Columbus *Also Called: Columbus Canvas Products Inc (G-5263)*
Columbus Canvas Products Inc....................................... 614 375-1397
  577 N 4th St Columbus (43215) *(G-5263)*
Columbus Castings, Columbus *Also Called: Columbus Steel Castings Co (G-5278)*
Columbus Controls Inc... 614 882-9029
  3573 Johnny Appleseed Ct Columbus (43231) *(G-5264)*
Columbus Gasket & Supply, Columbus *Also Called: James K Green Enterprises Inc (G-5487)*
Columbus Graphics Inc.. 614 577-9360
  7295 Rickly St Reynoldsburg (43068) *(G-12759)*
Columbus Heating & Vent Co.. 614 274-1177
  182 N Yale Ave Columbus (43222) *(G-5265)*
Columbus Incontact.. 801 245-8369
  555 S Front St Columbus (43215) *(G-5266)*
Columbus Industries Inc (HQ).. 740 983-2552
  2938 State Route 752 Ashville (43103) *(G-667)*
Columbus Industries One LLC... 740 983-2552
  2938 State Route 752 Ashville (43103) *(G-668)*
Columbus Instruments, Columbus *Also Called: Columbus Instruments Intl Corp (G-5268)*
Columbus Instruments LLC... 614 276-0861
  950 N Hague Ave Columbus (43204) *(G-5267)*
Columbus Instruments Intl Corp...................................... 614 276-0593
  950 N Hague Ave Columbus (43204) *(G-5268)*
Columbus International Corp (PA).................................... 614 323-1086
  200 E Campus View Blvd Ste 200 Columbus (43235) *(G-5269)*
Columbus International Corp.. 614 917-2274
  8876 Whitney Dr Lewis Center (43035) *(G-9156)*
Columbus Jack Corporation.. 614 443-7492
  1 Air Cargo Pkwy E Swanton (43558) *(G-13971)*
Columbus Jack Regent, Swanton *Also Called: Columbus Jack Corporation (G-13971)*
Columbus Jewish News.. 216 342-5184
  23880 Commerce Park Ste 1 Beachwood (44122) *(G-979)*
Columbus Kombucha Company LLC................................ 614 262-0000
  930 Freeway Dr N Columbus (43229) *(G-5270)*
Columbus Machine Works Inc... 614 409-0244
  2491 Fairwood Ave Columbus (43207) *(G-5271)*
Columbus Messenger Company (PA).............................. 614 272-5422
  3500 Sullivant Ave Columbus (43204) *(G-5272)*

Columbus Mobile Welding LLC....................................... 614 352-6052
  110 S Preston St Centerburg (43011) *(G-2357)*
Columbus Pipe and Equipment Co................................. 614 444-7871
  763 E Markison Ave Columbus (43207) *(G-5273)*
Columbus Podcast Company LLC................................... 614 405-8298
  105 N Cassingham Rd Columbus (43209) *(G-5274)*
Columbus Prescr Rehabilitation....................................... 614 294-1600
  975 Eastwind Dr Ste 155 Westerville (43081) *(G-15696)*
COLUMBUS PUBLIC SCHOOL DISTRICT, Columbus *Also Called: Columbus Public School Dst (G-5275)*
Columbus Public School Dst.. 614 365-6517
  300 E Livingston Ave Columbus (43215) *(G-5275)*
Columbus Roof Trusses Inc (PA)..................................... 614 272-6464
  2525 Fisher Rd Columbus (43204) *(G-5276)*
Columbus Roof Trusses Inc... 740 763-3000
  400 Marne Dr Newark (43055) *(G-11571)*
Columbus Sign Company (PA)... 614 252-3133
  1515 E 5th Ave Columbus (43219) *(G-5277)*
Columbus Steel Castings Co... 614 444-2121
  2211 Parsons Ave Columbus (43207) *(G-5278)*
Columbus SteelMasters Inc... 614 231-2141
  660 Concrea Rd Columbus (43219) *(G-5279)*
Columbus Underground, Columbus *Also Called: Evans Creative Group LLC (G-5364)*
Columbus V&S Galvanizing LLC...................................... 614 449-8281
  987 Buckeye Park Rd Columbus (43207) *(G-5280)*
Columbus Washboard Company Ltd................................ 740 380-3828
  4 E Main St Logan (43138) *(G-9362)*
Columbus Water Section Permit...................................... 614 645-8039
  910 Dublin Rd Columbus (43215) *(G-5281)*
Columbus Winter Fair, Columbus *Also Called: Ohio Designer Craftsmen Entps (G-5615)*
Columbus-Sports Publications... 614 486-2202
  1200 Chambers Rd Columbus (43212) *(G-5282)*
Colyer C & Sons Truck Service.. 513 563-0663
  11536 Reading Rd Cincinnati (45241) *(G-2781)*
Com-Corp Industries Inc.. 216 431-6266
  7601 Bittern Ave Cleveland (44103) *(G-3885)*
Com-Fab Inc... 740 857-1107
  4657 Price Hilliards Rd Plain City (43064) *(G-12571)*
Com-Net Software Specialists, Miamisburg *Also Called: Signature Technologies Inc (G-10683)*
Comber Holdings Inc.. 216 961-8600
  3304 W 67th Pl Cleveland (44102) *(G-3886)*
Combi Packaging Systems Llc....................................... 330 456-9333
  6299 Dressler Rd Nw Canton (44720) *(G-2078)*
Combined Containerboard Inc.. 513 530-5700
  7741 School Rd Cincinnati (45249) *(G-2782)*
Combs Manufacturing Inc... 330 784-3151
  380 Kennedy Rd Akron (44305) *(G-114)*
Comcorp Inc (HQ)... 718 981-1234
  1801 Superior Ave E Cleveland (44114) *(G-3887)*
Comdess Company Inc.. 330 769-2094
  8733 Wooster Pike Rd Seville (44273) *(G-13141)*
Comex Group, Cleveland *Also Called: Comex North America Inc (G-3888)*
Comex North America Inc (HQ)....................................... 303 307-2100
  101 W Prospect Ave Ste 1020 Cleveland (44115) *(G-3888)*
Comfort Line Ltd.. 419 729-8520
  5500 Enterprise Blvd Toledo (43612) *(G-14248)*
Comm Steel Inc.. 216 881-4600
  8043 Corporate Cir Ste 2 North Royalton (44133) *(G-11871)*
Command Alkon Incorporated.. 614 799-0600
  6750 Crosby Ct Dublin (43016) *(G-6876)*
Command Plastic Corporation.. 800 321-8001
  22475 Aurora Rd Bedford (44146) *(G-1112)*
Commconnect.. 937 414-0505
  5747 Executive Blvd Dayton (45424) *(G-6259)*
Commercial Anodizing Co.. 440 942-8384
  38387 Apollo Pkwy Willoughby (44094) *(G-15900)*
Commercial Cnstr Group LLC.. 513 722-1357
  5902 Montclair Blvd Milford (45150) *(G-10902)*
Commercial Decal Ohio Inc.. 330 385-7178
  46686 Y And O Rd East Liverpool (43920) *(G-6991)*

ALPHABETIC SECTION — Concrete Sealants Inc

Commercial Dock & Door Inc.................................440 951-1210
7653 Saint Clair Ave Mentor (44060) *(G-10441)*

Commercial Electric Pdts Corp (PA)........................216 241-2886
1821 E 40th St Cleveland (44103) *(G-3889)*

Commercial Fluid Power, Dover *Also Called: Commercial Honing LLC (G-6813)*

Commercial Grinding Svcs Inc................................330 273-5040
1155 Industrial Pkwy Unit 1 Medina (44258) *(G-10311)*

Commercial Honing LLC (DH)................................330 343-8896
2997 Progress St Dover (44622) *(G-6813)*

Commercial Interior Products, West Chester *Also Called: CIP International Inc (G-15394)*

Commercial Metal Forming, Youngstown *Also Called: Star Manufacturing LLC (G-16447)*

Commercial Metal Forming, Youngstown *Also Called: Steel Forming Inc (G-16448)*

Commercial Minerals Inc.....................................330 549-2165
10900 South Ave North Lima (44452) *(G-11803)*

Commercial Mtal Fbricators Inc..............................937 233-4911
150 Commerce Park Dr Dayton (45404) *(G-6260)*

Commercial Music Service Co................................740 746-8500
6312 Goss Rd Sugar Grove (43155) *(G-13915)*

Commercial Press, Canton *Also Called: Wernet Inc (G-2266)*

Commercial Printing Co, Greenville *Also Called: Commercial Prtg Greenville Inc (G-8043)*

Commercial Prtg Greenville Inc..............................937 548-3835
314 S Broadway St Greenville (45331) *(G-8043)*

Commercial Turf Products Ltd...............................330 995-7000
1777 Miller Pkwy Streetsboro (44241) *(G-13763)*

Commercial Vehicle Group Inc (PA)..........................614 289-5360
7800 Walton Pkwy New Albany (43054) *(G-11374)*

Commonwealth Aluminum Mtls LLC..............................216 910-3400
25825 Science Park Dr Ste 400 Beachwood (44122) *(G-980)*

Communication Concepts Inc.................................937 426-8600
508 Mill Stone Dr Beavercreek (45434) *(G-1043)*

Communication Exhibits Inc..................................330 854-4040
1119 Milan St N Canal Fulton (44614) *(G-1970)*

Communication Resources Inc................................800 992-2144
4786 Dressler Rd Nw Ste 309 Canton (44718) *(G-2079)*

Communications Aid Inc.....................................513 475-8453
222 Piedmont Ave Ste 5200 Cincinnati (45219) *(G-2783)*

Communicator Needs...614 781-1160
90 W Campus View Blvd Columbus (43235) *(G-5283)*

Community Action Program Corp..............................740 374-8501
696 Wayne St Marietta (45750) *(G-9786)*

Community Action Wic Hlth Svc, Marietta *Also Called: Community Action Program Corp (G-9786)*

Community Care Network Inc (PA)............................216 671-0977
4614 Prospect Ave Ste 240 Cleveland (44103) *(G-3890)*

Community Care On Wheels...................................330 882-5506
2 Kauffmans Crk Clinton (44216) *(G-4968)*

Community Mirror, The, Maumee *Also Called: Mirror (G-10221)*

Compass, Moraine *Also Called: Angels Landing Inc (G-11158)*

Compass Electronics Solutions, Vandalia *Also Called: Mac Its LLC (G-14947)*

Compass Energy LLC..866 665-2225
17877 Saint Clair Ave Ste 1 Cleveland (44110) *(G-3891)*

Compass S&S, Norton *Also Called: Compass Systems & Sales LLC (G-11940)*

Compass Systems & Sales LLC................................330 733-2111
5185 New Haven Cir Norton (44203) *(G-11940)*

Compco Columbiana Company (HQ)..............................330 482-0200
400 W Railroad St Columbiana (44408) *(G-5035)*

Compco Industries, Columbiana *Also Called: Compco Columbiana Company (G-5035)*

Compco Industries, Columbiana *Also Called: Compco Youngstown Company (G-5036)*

Compco Quaker Mfg Inc......................................330 482-0200
187 Georgetown Rd Salem (44460) *(G-12986)*

Compco Youngstown Company..................................330 482-6488
400 W Railroad St Columbiana (44408) *(G-5036)*

Competetive Carbide Inc....................................440 350-9393
5879 Shore Dr Madison (44057) *(G-9590)*

Competitive Carbide, Madison *Also Called: Competetive Carbide Inc (G-9590)*

Complete Cylinder Service Inc...............................513 772-1500
1240 Glendale Milford Rd Cincinnati (45215) *(G-2784)*

Complete Energy Services Inc................................440 577-1070
7338 Us Route 6 Pierpont (44082) *(G-12474)*

Complete Mechanical Svcs LLC................................513 489-3080
11399 Grooms Rd Blue Ash (45242) *(G-1382)*

Complete Metal Services....................................740 694-0000
18581 Divelbiss Rd Fredericktown (43019) *(G-7740)*

Complete Stud Welding Inc...................................216 533-8482
3700 Chagrin River Rd Chagrin Falls (44022) *(G-2372)*

Compliant Healthcare Tech LLC (PA)..........................216 255-9607
7123 Pearl Rd Ste 305 Cleveland (44130) *(G-3892)*

Component Mfg & Design.....................................330 225-8080
3121 Interstate Pkwy Brunswick (44212) *(G-1754)*

Component Solutions Group Inc (HQ)..........................937 434-8100
7755 Paragon Rd Ste 104 Dayton (45459) *(G-6261)*

Component Systems Inc......................................216 252-9292
5350 Tradex Pkwy Cleveland (44102) *(G-3893)*

Composite Group, The, Fairlawn *Also Called: Hpc Holdings LLC (G-7442)*

Composite Panel Tech Co.....................................704 310-5838
21944 Drake Rd Strongsville (44149) *(G-13824)*

Composite Solutions LLC....................................513 321-7337
3415 Paxton Ave Cincinnati (45208) *(G-2785)*

Composite Technologies Co LLC...............................937 228-2880
401 N Keowee St Dayton (45404) *(G-6262)*

Compounded Eps, Piqua *Also Called: Epsilyte Holdings LLC (G-12515)*

Comprehensive Logistics Co Inc..............................440 934-3517
1200 A Chester Industrial Pkwy Avon (44011) *(G-768)*

Compton Metal Products Inc.................................937 382-2403
416 Steele Rd Wilmington (45177) *(G-16045)*

Comptons Precision Machine..................................937 325-9139
224 Dayton Ave Springfield (45506) *(G-13546)*

Compu-Print, Canton *Also Called: Better Living Concepts Inc (G-2047)*

Computer Allied Technology Co...............................614 457-2292
3385 Somerford Rd Columbus (43221) *(G-5284)*

Computer Enterprise Inc....................................216 228-7156
1530 Saint Charles Ave Lakewood (44107) *(G-8972)*

Computer Stitch Designs Inc.................................330 856-7826
1414 Henn Hyde Rd Ne Warren (44484) *(G-15156)*

Computer Workshop Inc (PA)..................................614 798-9505
5200 Upper Metro Pl Ste 140 Dublin (43017) *(G-6877)*

Coms Interactive, Broadview Heights *Also Called: Clinicl Otcms Mngmnt Syst LLC (G-1658)*

Comtec Incorporated...330 425-8102
1800 Enterprise Pkwy Twinsburg (44087) *(G-14644)*

Comturn Manufacturing LLC...................................219 267-6911
13704 Enterprise Ave Cleveland (44135) *(G-3894)*

Con-AG, Saint Marys *Also Called: Conag Inc (G-12950)*

Con-Belt Inc..330 273-2003
5656 Innovation Dr Valley City (44280) *(G-14865)*

Con-Cure, Pioneer *Also Called: Premiere Con Solutions LLC (G-12496)*

Conag Inc..419 394-8870
16672 County Road 66a Saint Marys (45885) *(G-12950)*

Conagra Brands Inc..419 445-8015
901 Stryker St Archbold (43502) *(G-527)*

Conagra Fods Pckaged Foods LLC..............................937 440-2800
801 Dye Mill Rd Troy (45373) *(G-14556)*

Concentrix Cvg LLC (DH)....................................972 454-8000
201 E 4th St Cincinnati (45202) *(G-2786)*

Concept 9 Inc...614 294-3743
1604 Clara St Columbus (43211) *(G-5285)*

Concept Machine & Tool Inc..................................937 473-3334
2065 Industrial Ct Covington (45318) *(G-6020)*

Concept Xxi Inc...216 831-2121
23600 Mercantile Rd Ste 101 Beachwood (44122) *(G-981)*

Concord Fabricators Inc.....................................614 875-2500
6511 Seeds Rd Grove City (43123) *(G-8083)*

Concord Road Equipment Mfg Inc..............................440 357-5344
348 Chester St Painesville (44077) *(G-12223)*

Concord Road Equipment Mfg LLC..............................440 357-5344
8200 Tyler Blvd Ste H Mentor (44060) *(G-10442)*

Concord Steel of Ohio, Warren *Also Called: Conley Group Inc (G-15158)*

Concrete Material Supply LLC................................419 261-6404
875 E Main St Woodville (43469) *(G-16092)*

Concrete One Construction LLC...............................740 595-9680
755 Us Highway 23 N Ste E Delaware (43015) *(G-6711)*

Concrete Sealants Inc.......................................937 845-8776
9325 State Route 201 Tipp City (45371) *(G-14130)*

(PA)=Parent Co (HQ)=Headquarters (DH)=Div Headquarters

2024 Harris Ohio Industrial Directory

Condevco Inc 740 373-5302
44403 State Route 7 New Matamoras (45767) *(G-11476)*

Condo Incorporated 330 609-6021
3869 Niles Rd Se Warren (44484) *(G-15157)*

Condor Tool & Die Inc 216 671-6000
4541 Industrial Pkwy Cleveland (44135) *(G-3895)*

Conduit Pipe Products Company 614 879-9114
1501 W Main St West Jefferson (43162) *(G-15609)*

Conery Manufacturing Inc 419 289-1444
1380 Township Road 743 Ashland (44805) *(G-567)*

Conform Automotive LLC 937 492-2708
1630 Ferguson Ct Sidney (45365) *(G-13233)*

Conforming Matrix Corporation 419 729-3777
6255 Suder Ave Toledo (43611) *(G-14249)*

Conley Group Inc 330 372-2030
197 W Market St Ste 202 Warren (44481) *(G-15158)*

Conn-Selmer Inc 440 946-6100
34199 Curtis Blvd Willoughby (44095) *(G-15901)*

Connaughton Welding & Fence, Hamilton *Also Called: Connaughton Wldg & Fence LLC (G-8195)*

Connaughton Wldg & Fence LLC 513 867-0230
440 Vine St Hamilton (45011) *(G-8195)*

Connect Housing Blocks LLC 614 503-4344
577 W Nationwide Blvd Ste 600 Columbus (43215) *(G-5286)*

Connect Television 614 876-4402
4811 Northwest Pkwy Hilliard (43026) *(G-8409)*

Connective Design Incorporated 937 746-8252
3010 S Tech Blvd Miamisburg (45342) *(G-10628)*

Connectors Unlimited Inc (PA) 440 357-1161
1359 W Jackson St Painesville (44077) *(G-12224)*

Connectronics Corp (DH) 419 537-0020
2745 Avondale Ave Toledo (43607) *(G-14250)*

Connelly Industries LLC 330 468-0675
9651 N Bedford Rd Macedonia (44056) *(G-9542)*

Connies Candles 740 574-1224
9103 Ohio River Rd Wheelersburg (45694) *(G-15808)*

Conns Potato Chip Co Inc 614 252-2150
1271 Alum Creek Dr Columbus (43209) *(G-5287)*

Conns Potato Chip Co Inc (PA) 740 452-4615
1805 Kemper Ct Zanesville (43701) *(G-16523)*

Conover Lumber Company Inc 937 368-3010
7960 Alcony Conover Rd. Rt 36 Conover (45317) *(G-5936)*

Conquest Industries Inc 330 926-9236
4488 Allen Rd Stow (44224) *(G-13691)*

Conquest Maps LLC 614 654-1627
5696 Westbourne Ave Columbus (43213) *(G-5288)*

Conseal, Tipp City *Also Called: Concrete Sealants Inc (G-14130)*

Consoldated Graphics Group Inc 216 881-9191
1614 E 40th St Cleveland (44103) *(G-3896)*

Consoldted Anlytcal Systems In 513 542-1200
2629 Spring Grove Ave Cincinnati (45214) *(G-2787)*

Consoldted Precision Pdts Corp (PA) 216 453-4800
1621 Euclid Ave Ste 1850 Cleveland (44115) *(G-3897)*

Consoldted Precision Pdts Corp 440 953-0053
34000 Lakeland Blvd Eastlake (44095) *(G-7023)*

Consolidated Biscuit Company 419 293-2911
312 Rader Rd Mc Comb (45858) *(G-10268)*

Consolidated Biscuit Company, Mc Comb *Also Called: Hearthside Food Solutions LLC (G-10270)*

Consolidated Bottling Company 419 227-3541
1750 Greely Chapel Rd Lima (45804) *(G-9229)*

Consolidated Ceramic Products, Blanchester *Also Called: Ccpi Inc (G-1349)*

Consolidated Coatings Corp 216 514-7596
3735 Green Rd Cleveland (44122) *(G-3898)*

Consolidated Foundries Inc (HQ) 909 595-2252
1621 Euclid Ave Ste 1850 Cleveland (44115) *(G-3899)*

Consolidated Gas Coop Inc 419 946-6600
5255 State Route 95 Mount Gilead (43338) *(G-11232)*

Consolidated Graphics Inc 740 654-2112
3950 Lancaster New Lexington Rd Se Lancaster (43130) *(G-9003)*

Consolidated Metal Pdts Inc (PA) 513 251-2624
1028 Depot St Cincinnati (45204) *(G-2788)*

Consolidated Metco Inc 740 772-6758
351 Chamber Dr Chillicothe (45601) *(G-2499)*

Consolidated Precision Pdts, Eastlake *Also Called: Esco Turbine Technologies - Cleveland Inc (G-7031)*

Consolidated Solutions, Cleveland *Also Called: Consolidated Graphics Group Inc (G-3896)*

Consolidated Vehicle Converter, Dayton *Also Called: Julie Maynard Inc (G-6394)*

Constar International, Hebron *Also Called: Plastipak Packaging Inc (G-8356)*

Constrction Adhsves Slants Div, Columbus *Also Called: Franklin International Inc (G-5387)*

Constrction Aggrgtes Corp Mich 616 842-7900
3 Summit Park Dr Ste 700 Independence (44131) *(G-8659)*

Construction, Solon *Also Called: American Platinum Door LLC (G-13312)*

Construction Journal, Cincinnati *Also Called: 400 SW 7th Street Partners Ltd (G-2581)*

Construction Techniques Inc (HQ) 216 267-7310
15887 Snow Rd Ste 100 Cleveland (44142) *(G-3900)*

Consulting, Aurora *Also Called: Integrity Parking LLC (G-720)*

Consumer Guild Foods Inc 419 726-3406
5035 Enterprise Blvd Toledo (43612) *(G-14251)*

Consumeracq Inc (PA) 440 277-9305
2509 N Ridge Rd E Lorain (44055) *(G-9408)*

Consumers Builders Supply Co (PA) 440 277-9306
2509 N Ridge Rd E Lorain (44055) *(G-9409)*

Consun Food Industries Inc 440 322-6301
123 Gateway Blvd N Elyria (44035) *(G-7128)*

Contact Control Interfaces LLC 609 333-3264
231 W 12th St Ste 201c Cincinnati (45202) *(G-2789)*

Contact Industries Inc 419 884-9788
25 Industrial Dr Lexington (44904) *(G-9200)*

Container Graphics Corp 937 746-5666
1 Miller St Franklin (45005) *(G-7667)*

Container Graphics Corp 419 531-5133
305 Ryder Rd Toledo (43607) *(G-14252)*

Contech Bridge Solutions LLC 937 878-2170
7941 New Carlisle Pike Dayton (45424) *(G-6263)*

Contech Bridge Solutions LLC (DH) 513 645-7000
9025 Centre Pointe Dr Ste 400 West Chester (45069) *(G-15400)*

Contech Cnstr Pdts Hldings Inc 513 645-7000
9025 Centre Pointe Dr Ste 400 West Chester (45069) *(G-15401)*

Contech Engnered Solutions Inc (HQ) 513 645-7000
9025 Centre Pointe Dr Ste 400 West Chester (45069) *(G-15402)*

Contech Engnered Solutions LLC (HQ) 513 645-7000
9025 Centre Pointe Dr Ste 400 West Chester (45069) *(G-15403)*

Contech Manufacturig Inc 440 946-3322
38134 Western Pkwy Willoughby (44094) *(G-15902)*

Contech Strmwter Solutions LLC 513 645-7000
9025 Centre Pointe Dr Ste 400 West Chester (45069) *(G-15404)*

Contemprary Image Labeling Inc 513 583-5699
2034 Mckinley Blvd Lebanon (45036) *(G-9068)*

Continental Business Entps Inc (PA) 440 439-4400
7311 Northfield Rd Bedford (44146) *(G-1113)*

Continental Cast Stone East, West Chester *Also Called: Russell Cast Stone Inc (G-15582)*

Continental Coatings LLC 216 429-1843
3007 E Overlook Rd Cleveland Heights (44118) *(G-4938)*

Continental Contitech, Fairlawn *Also Called: Contitech Usa Inc (G-7436)*

Continental Contitech, Marysville *Also Called: Contitech Usa Inc (G-9906)*

Continental GL Sls & Inv Group 614 679-1201
315 Ashmoore Cir W Powell (43065) *(G-12669)*

Continental Group, Powell *Also Called: Continental GL Sls & Inv Group (G-12669)*

Continental Metal Proc Co (PA) 216 268-0000
18711 Cleveland Ave Cleveland (44110) *(G-3901)*

Continental Metal Proc Co 216 268-0000
14919 Saranac Rd Cleveland (44110) *(G-3902)*

Continental Mineral Processing Corporation 513 771-7190
11817 Mosteller Rd Cincinnati (45241) *(G-2790)*

Continntal Hydrdyne Systems In 330 494-2740
2216 Glenmont Dr Nw Canton (44708) *(G-2080)*

Contitech North America Inc (DH) 330 664-7180
703 S Cleveland Massillon Rd Fairlawn (44333) *(G-7435)*

Contitech Usa Inc (DH) 330 664-7000
703 S Cleveland Massillon Rd Fairlawn (44333) *(G-7436)*

Contitech Usa Inc 937 644-8900
13601 Industrial Pkwy Marysville (43040) *(G-9906)*

ALPHABETIC SECTION

Contour Forming Inc 740 345-9777
215 Oakwood Ave Newark (43055) *(G-11572)*

Contour Tool Inc 440 365-7333
38830 Taylor Pkwy North Ridgeville (44035) *(G-11836)*

Contours, Orrville *Also Called: Bekaert Corporation (G-12119)*

Contract Lumber Inc 614 751-1109
200 Schofield Dr Columbus (43213) *(G-5289)*

Contractors Steel Company 330 425-3050
8383 Boyle Pkwy Twinsburg (44087) *(G-14645)*

Control Craft LLC 513 674-0056
1123 Hickorywood Ct Cincinnati (45233) *(G-2791)*

Control Electric Co 216 671-8010
12130 Eaton Commerce Pkwy Columbia Station (44028) *(G-5011)*

Control Industries Inc 937 653-7694
614 Central Ave Findlay (45840) *(G-7496)*

Control Interface Inc 513 874-2062
517 Commercial Dr West Chester (45014) *(G-15405)*

Control Line Equipment Inc 216 433-7766
14750 Industrial Pkwy Cleveland (44135) *(G-3903)*

Control Transformer Inc 330 637-6015
3701 Warren Meadville Rd Cortland (44410) *(G-5961)*

Control-X Inc 614 777-9729
3546 Rosburg Dr Columbus (43228) *(G-5290)*

Controlled Access Inc 330 273-6185
1535 Industrial Pkwy Brunswick (44212) *(G-1755)*

Controlled Release Society Inc 513 948-8000
110 E 69th St Cincinnati (45216) *(G-2792)*

Controllix Corporation 440 232-8757
21415 Alexander Rd Walton Hills (44146) *(G-15097)*

Controls and Sheet Metal Inc (PA) 513 721-3610
1051 Sargent St Cincinnati (45203) *(G-2793)*

Controls Inc 330 239-4345
5204 Portside Dr Medina (44256) *(G-10312)*

Convault of Ohio Inc 614 252-8422
841 Alton Ave Columbus (43219) *(G-5291)*

Converge Group Inc 419 281-0000
1850 S Baney Rd Ashland (44805) *(G-568)*

Conversion Tech Intl Inc 419 924-5566
700 Oak St West Unity (43570) *(G-15638)*

Convertapax, Midvale *Also Called: Maintenance Repair Supply Inc (G-10881)*

Converters/Prepress Inc 937 743-0935
301 Industry Dr Carlisle (45005) *(G-2287)*

Conveyor Guard Corp 614 337-1727
187 W Johnstown Rd Columbus (43230) *(G-5292)*

Conveyor Metal Works Inc 740 477-8700
2717 Bush Mill Rd Frankfort (45628) *(G-7657)*

Conveyor Solutions LLC 513 367-4845
6705 Dry Fork Rd Cleves (45002) *(G-4948)*

Conveyor Technologies Ltd 513 248-0663
501 Techne Center Dr Ste B Milford (45150) *(G-10903)*

Conviber Inc 330 723-6006
1066 Industrial Pkwy Medina (44256) *(G-10313)*

Conway Greene Co Inc 440 230-2627
17325 Parkside Dr North Royalton (44133) *(G-11872)*

Cookie Bouquet, Columbus *Also Called: Cookie Bouquets Inc (G-5293)*

Cookie Bouquets Inc 614 888-2171
6665 Huntley Rd Ste F Columbus (43229) *(G-5293)*

Cookie Cupboard, Cleveland *Also Called: Mid American Ventures Inc (G-4405)*

Cool Machines Inc 419 232-4871
740 Fox Rd Van Wert (45891) *(G-14909)*

Cool Seal Usa LLC 419 666-1111
232 J St Perrysburg (43551) *(G-12371)*

Cool Times 513 608-5201
6127 Fairway Dr Cincinnati (45212) *(G-2794)*

Coolant Control Inc (HQ) 513 471-8770
5353 Spring Grove Ave Cincinnati (45217) *(G-2795)*

Cooper, Bowling Green *Also Called: Cooper-Standard Automotive Inc (G-1562)*

Cooper, Findlay *Also Called: Cooper Tire & Rubber Co LLC (G-7497)*

Cooper, Findlay *Also Called: Cooper Tire Vhcl Test Ctr Inc (G-7498)*

Cooper Enterprises Inc 419 347-5232
89 Curtis Dr Shelby (44875) *(G-13193)*

Cooper Farms, Oakwood *Also Called: Cooper Hatchery Inc (G-12030)*

Cooper Farms, Saint Henry *Also Called: V H Cooper & Co Inc (G-12940)*

Cooper Farms Inc (PA) 419 375-4116
2321 State Route 49 Fort Recovery (45846) *(G-7614)*

Cooper Farms Cooked Meat, Van Wert *Also Called: Cooper Foods (G-14910)*

Cooper Farms Cooked Meats, Van Wert *Also Called: Cooper Hatchery Inc (G-14911)*

Cooper Foods 419 232-2440
6893 Us Route 127 Van Wert (45891) *(G-14910)*

Cooper Foods, Fort Recovery *Also Called: V H Cooper & Co Inc (G-7626)*

Cooper Hatchery Inc (PA) 419 594-3325
22348 Rd 140 Oakwood (45873) *(G-12030)*

Cooper Hatchery Inc 419 238-4869
6793 Us Route 127 Van Wert (45891) *(G-14911)*

Cooper Lighting LLC 800 334-6871
Columbus (43218) *(G-5294)*

Cooper Lighting Solutions, Columbus *Also Called: Cooper Lighting LLC (G-5294)*

Cooper Tire & Rubber Co LLC (HQ) 419 423-1321
701 Lima Ave Findlay (45840) *(G-7497)*

Cooper Tire Vhcl Test Ctr Inc (DH) 419 423-1321
701 Lima Ave Findlay (45840) *(G-7498)*

Cooper-Standard Automotive Inc 419 352-3533
1175 N Main St Bowling Green (43402) *(G-1562)*

Cooper-Standard Automotive Inc 740 342-3523
2378 State Route 345 Ne New Lexington (43764) *(G-11451)*

Coopers Mill Inc 419 562-4215
1414 N Sandusky Ave Bucyrus (44820) *(G-1854)*

Coopers Mill Incorporated 419 562-2878
115 Crossroads Blvd Bucyrus (44820) *(G-1855)*

Copac, Cambridge *Also Called: Cambrdge Ohio Prod Assmbly Cor (G-1924)*

Copeland, Sidney *Also Called: Copeland LP (G-13235)*

Copeland Access + Inc 937 498-3802
1675 Campbell Rd Sidney (45365) *(G-13234)*

Copeland LP (HQ) 937 498-3011
1675 W Campbell Rd Sidney (45365) *(G-13235)*

Copeland LP 937 498-3011
756 Brooklyn Ave Sidney (45365) *(G-13236)*

Copeland LP 937 498-3587
1351 N Vandemark Rd Sidney (45365) *(G-13237)*

Copeland Scroll Compressors LP (DH) 937 498-3066
1675 Campbell Rd Sidney (45365) *(G-13238)*

Coperion Food Equipment LLC (DH) 937 492-4158
500 S Vandemark Rd Sidney (45365) *(G-13239)*

Copernicus Therapeutics Inc 216 231-0227
11000 Cedar Ave Ste 145 Cleveland (44106) *(G-3904)*

Copier Resources Inc 614 268-1100
4800 Evanswood Dr Columbus (43229) *(G-5295)*

Copley Fire & Rescue Assn 330 666-6464
1540 S Cleveland Massillon Rd Copley (44321) *(G-5947)*

Copley Ohio Newspapers Inc (HQ) 585 598-0030
500 Market Ave S Canton (44702) *(G-2081)*

Copley Ohio Newspapers Inc 330 364-5577
629 Wabash Ave Nw New Philadelphia (44663) *(G-11493)*

Copley Township Fire Dept, Copley *Also Called: Copley Fire & Rescue Assn (G-5947)*

Copperloy, Twinsburg *Also Called: Jh Industries Inc (G-14677)*

Copy King Inc 216 861-3377
3333 Chester Ave Cleveland (44114) *(G-3905)*

Copy Print, Tallmadge *Also Called: Rhoads Print Center Inc (G-14045)*

Corbett R Caudill Chipping Inc 740 596-5984
35887 State Route 324 Hamden (45634) *(G-8172)*

Cordier Group Holdings Inc 330 477-4511
4575 Southway St Sw Canton (44706) *(G-2082)*

Core Composites Cincinnati LLC 513 724-6111
4174 Half Acre Rd Batavia (45103) *(G-918)*

Core Manufacturing, Mentor *Also Called: Core Manufacturing LLC (G-10443)*

Core Manufacturing LLC 440 946-8002
8878 East Ave Mentor (44060) *(G-10443)*

Core Molding Technologies Inc (PA) 614 870-5000
800 Manor Park Dr Columbus (43228) *(G-5296)*

Core Optix Inc 855 267-3678
821 Melbourne St Cincinnati (45229) *(G-2796)*

Core Technology Inc — 440 934-9935
1260 Moore Rd Ste E Avon (44011) *(G-769)*

Core-Tech Enterprises LLC — 440 946-8324
7850 Enterprise Dr Mentor (44060) *(G-10444)*

Coreworth Holdings LLC — 419 468-7100
3396 Sr 309 Iberia (43325) *(G-8647)*

Corner Alley LLC — 216 298-4070
402 Euclid Ave Cleveland (44114) *(G-3906)*

Cornerstone Bldg Brands Inc — 937 584-3300
2400 Yankee Rd Middletown (45044) *(G-10813)*

Cornerstone Brands Inc — 866 668-5962
5568 W Chester Rd West Chester (45069) *(G-15406)*

Cornerstone Manufacturing Inc — 937 456-5930
861 Us Route 35 Eaton (45320) *(G-7057)*

Cornerstone Wauseon Inc — 419 337-0940
995 Enterprise Ave Wauseon (43567) *(G-15259)*

Cornhole Worldwide LLC — 513 324-2777
5337 Hamilton Cleves Rd Cleves (45002) *(G-4949)*

Cornwell Quality Tools, Mogadore *Also Called: Cornwell Quality Tools Company (G-11068)*

CORNWELL QUALITY TOOLS, Van Wert *Also Called: Cqt Kennedy LLC (G-14912)*

Cornwell Quality Tools, Wadsworth *Also Called: The Cornwell Quality Tools Company (G-15069)*

Cornwell Quality Tools Company — 330 628-2627
200 N Cleveland Ave Mogadore (44260) *(G-11068)*

Coronado Steel Co — 330 744-1143
2360 Funston Dr Youngstown (44510) *(G-16341)*

Corpad Company Inc — 419 522-7818
555 Park Ave E Mansfield (44905) *(G-9641)*

Corporate Dcment Solutions Inc (PA) — 513 595-8200
11120 Ashburn Rd Cincinnati (45240) *(G-2797)*

Corporate Elevator LLC — 614 288-1847
35 E Gay St Ste 218 Columbus (43215) *(G-5297)*

Corporate Raw Materials, Solon *Also Called: Swagelok Company (G-13427)*

Corrchoice, Delaware *Also Called: Greif Packaging LLC (G-6726)*

Corrchoice Cincinnati — 330 833-2884
777 3rd St Nw Massillon (44647) *(G-10086)*

Corrotec Inc — 937 325-3585
1125 W North St Springfield (45504) *(G-13547)*

Corrpro Companies Inc — 330 725-6681
1055 W Smith Rd Medina (44256) *(G-10314)*

Corrpro Companies Intl Inc — 330 723-5082
1055 W Smith Rd Medina (44256) *(G-10315)*

Corrpro Waterworks, Medina *Also Called: Corrpro Companies Inc (G-10314)*

Corrugated Chemicals, Cincinnati *Also Called: Corrugated Chemicals Inc (G-2798)*

Corrugated Chemicals Inc — 513 561-7773
3865 Virginia Ave Cincinnati (45227) *(G-2798)*

Cors Products, Canton *Also Called: Canton OH Rubber Speclty Prods (G-2065)*

Cortape Inc — 330 929-6700
60 Marc Dr Cuyahoga Falls (44223) *(G-6076)*

Cortest, Willoughby *Also Called: Cortest Inc (G-15903)*

Cortest Inc (PA) — 440 942-1235
38322 Apollo Pkwy Willoughby (44094) *(G-15903)*

Cortina Leathers, Conneaut *Also Called: Leather Resource of America Inc (G-5923)*

Corvac Composites LLC — 248 807-0969
1025 N Washington St Greenfield (45123) *(G-8028)*

COS Blueprint Inc — 330 376-0022
590 N Main St Akron (44310) *(G-115)*

Coshocton Ethanol LLC — 740 623-3046
18137 County Road 271 Coshocton (43812) *(G-5976)*

Coshocton Orthopedic Center, Coshocton *Also Called: Francisco Jaume (G-5978)*

Coshocton Pallet & Door Co, Coshocton *Also Called: Thomas J Weaver Inc (G-5998)*

Cosmetic Technologies LLC — 614 656-1130
8825 Smiths Mill Rd New Albany (43054) *(G-11375)*

Cosmo, Cleveland *Also Called: Cosmo Plastics Company (G-3907)*

Cosmo Plastics Co, Wilmot *Also Called: Cosmo Plastics Company (G-16066)*

Cosmo Plastics Company (HQ) — 440 498-7500
30201 Aurora Rd Cleveland (44139) *(G-3907)*

Cosmo Plastics Company — 330 359-5429
211 Winesburg St Wilmot (44689) *(G-16066)*

Costa Machine, Akron *Also Called: Charles Costa Inc (G-107)*

Costume Specialists Inc — 614 464-2115
1801 Lone Eagle St Columbus (43228) *(G-5298)*

Cota International Inc — 937 526-5520
67 Industrial Pkwy Versailles (45380) *(G-14978)*

Cotsworks Inc (PA) — 440 446-8800
749 Miner Rd Highland Heights (44143) *(G-8385)*

Cott Systems Inc — 614 847-4405
2800 Corporate Exchange Dr Ste 300 Columbus (43231) *(G-5299)*

Couch Business Development Inc — 937 253-1099
32 Bates St Dayton (45402) *(G-6264)*

Counter Concepts Inc — 330 848-4848
15535 Portage St Doylestown (44230) *(G-6853)*

Counter-Advice Inc — 937 291-1600
7002 State Route 123 Franklin (45005) *(G-7668)*

Countertop Sales — 614 626-4476
5767 Westbourne Ave Columbus (43213) *(G-5300)*

Countertops Helmart, Cincinnati *Also Called: Helmart Company Inc (G-2992)*

Country CLB Rtrment Ctr IV LLC — 740 676-2300
55801 Conno Mara Dr Bellaire (43906) *(G-1185)*

Country Clippins LLC — 740 472-5228
114 S Main St Woodsfield (43793) *(G-16086)*

Country Comfart Wdwkg LLC — 330 695-4408
2 Mi Sw Of Mt Eaton Fredericksburg (44627) *(G-7720)*

Country Crust Bakery — 888 860-2940
4918 State Route 41 S Bainbridge (45612) *(G-830)*

Country Lane Custom Buildings — 740 485-8481
21318 Pealer Mill Rd Danville (43014) *(G-6148)*

Country Manufacturing Inc — 740 694-9926
333 Salem Ave Ext Fredericktown (43019) *(G-7741)*

Country Mile Woodworking — 740 668-2452
6345 Woods Church Rd Walhonding (43843) *(G-15091)*

Country Outdoor WD Stoves Cows — 740 967-0315
6040 Castle Rd Alexandria (43001) *(G-383)*

Country Parlour Ice Cream Co — 440 237-4040
12905 York Delta Dr Ste C Cleveland (44133) *(G-3908)*

Country Pure Foods Inc (PA) — 330 753-2293
222 S Main St Ste 401 Akron (44308) *(G-116)*

Country Sales & Service LLC — 330 683-2500
255 Tracy Bridge Rd Orrville (44667) *(G-12122)*

Countryside Cabinets — 740 397-6488
18720 Butler Rd Fredericktown (43019) *(G-7742)*

Countryside Construction, Danville *Also Called: Country Lane Custom Buildings (G-6148)*

County Classifieds — 937 592-8847
117 E Patterson Ave Bellefontaine (43311) *(G-1203)*

County Line, Bryan *Also Called: Bryan Publishing Company (G-1811)*

County Line Wood Working LLC — 330 316-3057
1482 County Road 600 Baltic (43804) *(G-835)*

County of Holmes — 330 674-2083
75 E Clinton St Ste 112 Millersburg (44654) *(G-10952)*

County of Lake — 440 428-1794
7815 Cashen Rd Madison (44057) *(G-9591)*

County of Lake — 440 269-2193
2100 Joseph Lloyd Pkwy Willoughby (44094) *(G-15904)*

Countyline Co-Op Inc (PA) — 419 287-3241
425 E Front St Pemberville (43450) *(G-12334)*

Courier, The, Findlay *Also Called: Ogden News Publishing Ohio Inc (G-7544)*

Courier, The, Sandusky *Also Called: Ogden News Publishing Ohio Inc (G-13083)*

Course Technology, Mason *Also Called: Cengage Learning Inc (G-9971)*

Courthouse Manufacturing LLC — 740 335-2727
1730 Washington Avenue, Solar Lane Washington Court Hou (43160) *(G-15232)*

Coventry Steel Services Inc — 216 883-4477
4200 E 71st St Ste 1 Cleveland (44105) *(G-3909)*

Coventya Inc — 315 768-6635
4639 Van Epps Rd Frnt Brooklyn Heights (44131) *(G-1688)*

COVENTYA, INC., Brooklyn Heights *Also Called: Coventya Inc (G-1688)*

Covert, Galion *Also Called: Covert Manufacturing Inc (G-7868)*

Covert Manufacturing Inc — 419 468-1761
303 E Parson St Galion (44833) *(G-7867)*

Covert Manufacturing Inc (PA) — 419 468-1761
328 S East St Galion (44833) *(G-7868)*

Covestro LLC — 740 929-2015
1111 O Neill Dr Hebron (43025) *(G-8337)*

ALPHABETIC SECTION — Creamer Metal Products Inc

Covia Holdings LLC (PA) 800 255-7263
3 Summit Park Dr Ste 700 Independence (44131) *(G-8660)*

Covia Solutions Inc (HQ) 404 214-3200
3 Summit Park Dr Ste 700 Independence (44131) *(G-8661)*

Covidien, Cincinnati *Also Called: Covidien Holding Inc (G-2799)*

Covidien Holding Inc 513 948-7219
2111 E Galbraith Rd Cincinnati (45237) *(G-2799)*

COW Industries Inc (PA) 614 443-6537
1875 Progress Ave Columbus (43207) *(G-5301)*

Cowles Industrial Tool, Austintown *Also Called: Cowles Industrial Tool Co LLC (G-751)*

Cowles Industrial Tool Co LLC 330 799-9100
185 N Four Mile Run Rd Austintown (44515) *(G-751)*

Cox Inc 740 858-4400
11201 State Route 104 Lucasville (45648) *(G-9521)*

Cox Interior Inc 614 473-9169
2220 Citygate Dr Columbus (43219) *(G-5302)*

Cox Interior Inc 270 789-3129
4080 Webster Ave Norwood (45212) *(G-11994)*

Cox Media Group, Dayton *Also Called: Ohio Newspapers Inc (G-6490)*

Cox Newspapers LLC 937 866-3331
230 S 2nd St Miamisburg (45342) *(G-10629)*

Cox Ohio Publishing 937 743-6700
5000 Commerce Center Dr Franklin (45005) *(G-7669)*

Cox Ohio Publishing - Dayton 937 328-0300
202 N Limestone St Springfield (45503) *(G-13548)*

Cox Painting, Wilmington *Also Called: Cox Printing Company (G-16046)*

Cox Precast, Lucasville *Also Called: Cox Inc (G-9521)*

Cox Printing Company 937 382-2312
1087 Wayne Rd Wilmington (45177) *(G-16046)*

Cox Publishing Hq 937 225-2000
1611 S Main St Dayton (45409) *(G-6265)*

Cox Wood Product Inc 740 372-4735
5715 State Route 348 Otway (45657) *(G-12206)*

Cox's Interior Supply, Columbus *Also Called: Cox Interior Inc (G-5302)*

Coyne Finishing, Mount Vernon *Also Called: Coyne Graphic Finishing Inc (G-11269)*

Coyne Graphic Finishing Inc 740 397-6232
1301 Newark Rd Mount Vernon (43050) *(G-11269)*

Cozmyk Enterprises, Columbus *Also Called: Unity Enterprises Inc (G-5844)*

Cozmyk Enterprises Inc 614 231-1370
3757 Courtright Ct Columbus (43227) *(G-5303)*

CP Chemicals Group LP 440 833-3000
28960 Lakeland Blvd Wickliffe (44092) *(G-15829)*

CP Industries Inc 740 763-2886
11047 Lambs Ln Newark (43055) *(G-11573)*

CP Trading Group, Wickliffe *Also Called: CP Chemicals Group LP (G-15829)*

CPC Holding Inc 216 383-3932
2926 Chester Ave Cleveland (44114) *(G-3910)*

Cpg - Ohio LLC (HQ) 513 825-4800
470 Northland Blvd Cincinnati (45240) *(G-2800)*

Cpg International LLC 937 655-8766
894 Prairie Rd Wilmington (45177) *(G-16047)*

Cpg Printing & Graphics, Toledo *Also Called: Culaine Inc (G-14254)*

CPI, Holland *Also Called: Creative Products Inc (G-8500)*

CPI Group Limited 216 525-0046
13858 Tinkers Creek Rd Cleveland (44125) *(G-3911)*

CPI Industrial Co 614 445-0800
299 Yankeetown St Mount Sterling (43143) *(G-11255)*

Cpic Automotive Inc 740 587-3262
1226 Weaver Dr Granville (43023) *(G-8015)*

CPM Tool Co LLC 937 258-1176
1865 Radio Rd Dayton (45431) *(G-6156)*

Cpmm Services Group Inc 614 447-0165
3785 Indianola Ave Columbus (43214) *(G-5304)*

Cpp, Cleveland *Also Called: Consoldted Precision Pdts Corp (G-3897)*

Cpp Cleveland, Eastlake *Also Called: Consoldted Precision Pdts Corp (G-7023)*

Cpp Group Holdings LLC (PA) 216 453-4800
1621 Euclid Ave Ste 1850 Cleveland (44115) *(G-3912)*

Cpp-Cleveland Inc (DH) 216 453-4800
1621 Euclid Ave Ste 1850 Cleveland (44115) *(G-3913)*

Cpp-Cleveland Inc 440 953-0053
34000 Lakeland Blvd Eastlake (44095) *(G-7024)*

Cql Mfg LLC 330 482-5846
187 Georgetown Rd Salem (44460) *(G-12987)*

Cqt Kennedy LLC 419 238-2442
1260 Industrial Dr Van Wert (45891) *(G-14912)*

Cr Holding Inc 513 860-5039
9100 Centre Pointe Dr Ste 200 West Chester (45069) *(G-15407)*

CRA Welding LLC 330 317-2007
8728 Criswell Rd Fredericksburg (44627) *(G-7721)*

Crack Corn Ltd 440 467-0108
7993 Hills And Dales Rd Ne Massillon (44646) *(G-10087)*

Craco Embroidery Inc 513 563-6999
37 Techview Dr Cincinnati (45215) *(G-2801)*

Crafco Inc 330 270-3034
912 Salt Springs Rd Youngstown (44509) *(G-16342)*

Crafted Elements LLC 816 739-1307
742 Oak St Nw New Philadelphia (44663) *(G-11494)*

Crafted Surface and Stone LLC 440 658-3799
16625 Wren Rd Chagrin Falls (44023) *(G-2391)*

Craftwood, Mount Orab *Also Called: Cindoco Wood Products Co (G-11240)*

Craig Saylor 740 352-8363
53020 State Route 124 Portland (45770) *(G-12638)*

Crain Communications Inc 216 522-1383
700 W Saint Clair Ave Ste 310 Cleveland (44113) *(G-3914)*

Crain Communications Inc 330 836-9180
2291 Riverfront Pkwy Ste 1000 Cuyahoga Falls (44221) *(G-6077)*

Crain's Cleveland Business, Cleveland *Also Called: Crain Communications Inc (G-3914)*

Cramers Inc 330 477-4571
4944 Southway St Sw Canton (44706) *(G-2083)*

Crane 1 Services Inc (HQ) 937 704-9900
9075 Centre Pointe Dr West Chester (45069) *(G-15408)*

Crane Blending Center 614 542-1199
2141 Fairwood Ave Columbus (43207) *(G-5305)*

Crane Carrier Company LLC (HQ) 918 286-2889
1951 Reiser Ave Se New Philadelphia (44663) *(G-11495)*

Crane Carrier Holdings LLC 918 286-2889
1951 Reiser Ave Se New Philadelphia (44663) *(G-11496)*

Crane Chempharma & Energy, Cincinnati *Also Called: Xomox Corporation (G-3531)*

Crane Consumables Inc 513 539-9980
155 Wright Dr Middletown (45044) *(G-10814)*

Crane Plumbing LLC 419 522-4211
41 Cairns Rd Mansfield (44903) *(G-9642)*

Crane Pro Services 937 525-5555
4401 Gateway Blvd Springfield (45502) *(G-13549)*

Crane Pro Services, Broadview Heights *Also Called: Konecranes Inc (G-1660)*

Crane Pro Services, Toledo *Also Called: Konecranes Inc (G-14350)*

Crane Pro Services, West Chester *Also Called: Konecranes Inc (G-15567)*

Crane Pumps & Systems Inc 937 773-2442
420 3rd St Piqua (45356) *(G-12508)*

Crane Pumps & Systems Inc (HQ) 937 773-2442
420 3rd St Piqua (45356) *(G-12509)*

Crane Pumps & Systems Inc 937 778-8947
1950 Covington Ave Piqua (45356) *(G-12510)*

Crane Xomox, Blue Ash *Also Called: Xomox Corporation (G-1497)*

Crase Communications Inc 419 468-1173
120 Harding Way E Ste 104 Galion (44833) *(G-7869)*

Crawford Acquisition Corp 216 486-0702
16130 Saint Clair Ave Cleveland (44110) *(G-3915)*

Crawford Ae LLC 330 794-9770
735 Glaser Pkwy Akron (44306) *(G-117)*

Crawford Computer Center, Solon *Also Called: Swagelok Company (G-13430)*

Crawford Products Inc 614 890-1822
3637 Corporate Dr Columbus (43231) *(G-5306)*

Crawford United Corporation (PA) 216 541-8060
10514 Dupont Ave Cleveland (44108) *(G-3916)*

Crayex Corporation (PA) 937 773-7000
1747 Commerce Dr Piqua (45356) *(G-12511)*

Crazy Monkey Baking Inc 419 903-0403
1191 Commerce Pkwy Ashland (44805) *(G-569)*

Crazy Richards, Plain City *Also Called: Krema Group Inc (G-12584)*

Creamer Metal Products Inc (PA) 740 852-1752
77 S Madison Rd London (43140) *(G-9385)*

Created Hardwood Ltd
ALPHABETIC SECTION

Created Hardwood Ltd 330 556-1825
   8454 State Route 93 Nw Dundee (44624) *(G-6964)*

Creative Cabinets Ltd 740 689-0603
   1807 Snoke Rd Sw Lancaster (43130) *(G-9004)*

Creative Canvas LLC 740 359-3173
   132 Wood St Flushing (43977) *(G-7586)*

Creative Coatings LLC 216 226-9058
   1634 Waterbury Rd Lakewood (44107) *(G-8973)*

Creative Countertops, Englewood *Also Called: Creative Countertops Ohio Inc* *(G-7226)*

Creative Countertops Ohio Inc 937 540-9450
   477 E Wenger Rd Englewood (45322) *(G-7226)*

Creative Edge Cbnets Wdwkg LLC 419 453-3416
   188 Nw Canal St Ottoville (45876) *(G-12198)*

Creative Edge Group, Canton *Also Called: Superior Dairy Inc* *(G-2239)*

Creative Extruded Products 937 335-3336
   101 Dye Mill Rd Troy (45373) *(G-14557)*

Creative Fab & Welding LLC 937 780-5000
   9691 Stafford Rd Leesburg (45135) *(G-9123)*

Creative Fabrication Ltd 740 262-5789
   20110 Predmore Rd Richwood (43344) *(G-12813)*

Creative Foam Dayton Mold 937 279-9987
   3337 N Dixie Dr Dayton (45414) *(G-6266)*

Creative Ip LLC 234 571-2466
   1653 Merriman Rd Ste L1 Akron (44313) *(G-118)*

Creative Liquid Coatings Inc 419 485-1110
   1701 Magda Dr Montpelier (43543) *(G-11135)*

Creative Microsystems Inc 937 836-4499
   52 Hillside Ct Englewood (45322) *(G-7227)*

Creative Millwork Ohio Inc 440 992-3566
   1801 W 47th St Ashtabula (44004) *(G-628)*

Creative Mold and Machine Inc 440 338-5146
   10385 Kinsman Rd Newbury (44065) *(G-11621)*

Creative Nest LLC 614 216-8102
   3885 Barley Cir Columbus (43207) *(G-5307)*

Creative Packaging LLC 740 452-8497
   1781 Kemper Ct Zanesville (43701) *(G-16524)*

Creative Plastic Concepts LLC (HQ) 419 927-9588
   206 S Griffith St Sycamore (44882) *(G-13988)*

Creative Plastics Intl 937 596-6769
   18163 Snider Rd Jackson Center (45334) *(G-8730)*

Creative Processing Inc 440 834-4070
   17540 Rapids Rd Mantua (44255) *(G-9735)*

Creative Products Inc 513 727-9872
   2705 Carmody Blvd Middletown (45042) *(G-10815)*

Creative Products Inc 419 866-5501
   1430 Kieswetter Rd Holland (43528) *(G-8500)*

Creative Tool & Die LLC 614 836-0080
   244 Main St Groveport (43125) *(G-8136)*

Creativity For Kids, Independence *Also Called: AW Faber-Castell Usa Inc* *(G-8654)*

Cree Logistics LLC 513 978-1112
   7439 Wooster Pike Cincinnati (45227) *(G-2802)*

Creek Smoothies LLC 937 429-1519
   3195 Dayton Xenia Rd Beavercreek (45434) *(G-1044)*

Creighton Sports Center Inc (PA) 740 865-2521
   205 Broadway Ave New Matamoras (45767) *(G-11477)*

Cremation Association Shawnee, Cincinnati *Also Called: Alderwoods (oklahoma) Inc* *(G-2606)*

Cres Cor, Mentor *Also Called: Crescent Metal Products Inc* *(G-10445)*

Crescent & Sprague 740 373-2331
   1100 Greene St Marietta (45750) *(G-9787)*

Crescent Blades, Fremont *Also Called: Crescent Manufacturing Company* *(G-7772)*

Crescent Manufacturing Company (PA) 419 332-6484
   1310 Majestic Dr Fremont (43420) *(G-7772)*

Crescent Metal Products Inc (PA) 440 350-1100
   5925 Heisley Rd Mentor (44060) *(G-10445)*

Crescent Services LLC 405 603-1200
   11137 E Pike Rd Cambridge (43725) *(G-1930)*

Cresset Chemical Co Inc (PA) 419 669-2041
   13255 Main St Weston (43569) *(G-15804)*

Cresset Chemical Co Inc 419 669-2041
   13490 Silver St Weston (43569) *(G-15805)*

Crest Aluminum Products, Mentor *Also Called: Crest Products Inc* *(G-10446)*

Crest Bending Inc 419 492-2108
   108 John St New Washington (44854) *(G-11546)*

Crest Craft Co 513 271-4858
   4460 Lake Forest Dr Ste 232 Blue Ash (45242) *(G-1383)*

Crest Products Inc 440 942-5770
   8287 Tyler Blvd Mentor (44060) *(G-10446)*

Crestar Crusts Inc 740 335-4813
   1104 Clinton Ave Wshngtn Ct Hs (43160) *(G-16228)*

Crestar Foods, Wshngtn Ct Hs *Also Called: Crestar Crusts Inc* *(G-16228)*

Crg Plastics Inc 937 298-2025
   2661 Culver Ave Dayton (45429) *(G-6267)*

Crh US 216 642-3920
   6925 Granger Rd Independence (44131) *(G-8662)*

Cri, Fairfield *Also Called: Color Resolutions International LLC* *(G-7349)*

Cri Digital, Columbus *Also Called: Copier Resources Inc* *(G-5295)*

Cricket, Blacklick *Also Called: Wireless Retail LLC* *(G-1345)*

Crimson Gate Consulting Co (PA) 614 805-0897
   6457 Reflections Dr S200 Dublin (43017) *(G-6878)*

Crimson Oak Grove Rsources LLC 740 338-3100
   46226 National Rd Saint Clairsville (43950) *(G-12900)*

Crispie Creme Chillicothe Inc 740 774-3770
   47 N Bridge St Chillicothe (45601) *(G-2500)*

Criswell Furniture LLC 330 695-2082
   8139 Criswell Rd Fredericksburg (44627) *(G-7722)*

Criterion Instrument, Brookpark *Also Called: Criterion Tool & Die Inc* *(G-1708)*

Criterion Tool & Die Inc 216 267-1733
   5349 W 161st St Brookpark (44142) *(G-1708)*

Critical Ctrl Enrgy Svcs Inc 330 539-4267
   1688 Shannon Rd Girard (44420) *(G-7966)*

Criticalaire LLC 513 475-3800
   350 Worthington Rd Ste G Westerville (43082) *(G-15652)*

Crmd LLC 440 225-7179
   1190 N High St Columbus (43201) *(G-5308)*

Crochet Kitty, Parma *Also Called: Crochet Kitty LLC* *(G-12287)*

Crochet Kitty LLC 440 340-5152
   12100 Snow Rd Ste 1 Parma (44130) *(G-12287)*

Croft & Son Mfg Inc 740 859-2200
   509 Highland Ave Tiltonsville (43963) *(G-14116)*

Crook Miller Company, Stow *Also Called: Baker McMillen Co* *(G-13687)*

Cropking Incorporated 330 302-4203
   134 West Dr Lodi (44254) *(G-9349)*

Crosco Wood Products, Fredericksburg *Also Called: Miller Crist* *(G-7726)*

Crosscreek Pallet Co 440 632-1940
   14530 Madison Rd Middlefield (44062) *(G-10743)*

Crossroads Machine Inc 937 832-2000
   65 Haas Dr Englewood (45322) *(G-7228)*

Crow Works LLC 888 811-2769
   9595 Us-62 Killbuck (44637) *(G-8918)*

Crowe Manufacturing Services 800 831-1893
   2731 Walnut Ridge Dr Troy (45373) *(G-14558)*

Crowes Cabinets Inc 330 729-9911
   590 E Western Reserve Rd Bldg 8 Youngstown (44514) *(G-16343)*

Crowley Blue Wtr Partners LLC 419 422-2121
   539 S Main St Findlay (45840) *(G-7499)*

Crown Battery, Fremont *Also Called: Crown Battery Manufacturing Co* *(G-7773)*

Crown Battery Manufacturing Co (PA) 419 334-7181
   1445 Majestic Dr Fremont (43420) *(G-7773)*

Crown Battery Manufacturing Co 330 425-3308
   1750 Highland Rd Ste 3 Twinsburg (44087) *(G-14646)*

Crown Closures Machinery 740 681-6593
   1765 W Fair Ave Lancaster (43130) *(G-9005)*

Crown Closures Machinery, Lancaster *Also Called: Carnaudmetalbox Machinery USA* *(G-8999)*

Crown Cork & Seal Usa Inc 740 681-3000
   940 Mill Park Dr Lancaster (43130) *(G-9006)*

Crown Cork & Seal Usa Inc 740 681-6593
   1765 W Fair Ave Lancaster (43130) *(G-9007)*

Crown Cork & Seal Usa Inc 330 833-1011
   700 16th St Se Massillon (44646) *(G-10088)*

Crown Cork & Seal Usa Inc 937 299-2027
5005 Springboro Pike Moraine (45439) *(G-11167)*

Crown Cork & Seal Usa Inc 419 727-8201
5201 Enterprise Blvd Toledo (43612) *(G-14253)*

Crown Credit Company 419 629-2311
44 S Washington St New Bremen (45869) *(G-11399)*

Crown Div of Allen Gr 330 263-4919
1654 Old Mansfield Rd Wooster (44691) *(G-16111)*

Crown Electric Engrg & Mfg LLC 513 539-7394
175 Edison Dr Middletown (45044) *(G-10816)*

Crown Equipment Corporation 419 586-1100
410 Grand Lake Rd Celina (45822) *(G-2328)*

Crown Equipment Corporation 513 874-2600
10685 Medallion Dr Cincinnati (45241) *(G-2803)*

Crown Equipment Corporation 937 295-4062
300 Tower Dr Fort Loramie (45845) *(G-7596)*

Crown Equipment Corporation 614 274-7700
2100 Southwest Blvd Grove City (43123) *(G-8084)*

Crown Equipment Corporation (PA) 419 629-2311
44 S Washington St New Bremen (45869) *(G-11400)*

Crown Equipment Corporation 419 629-2311
624 W Monroe St New Bremen (45869) *(G-11401)*

Crown Equipment Corporation 419 629-2311
510 W Monroe St New Bremen (45869) *(G-11402)*

Crown Equipment Corporation 937 454-7545
750 Center Dr Vandalia (45377) *(G-14935)*

Crown Group Co (HQ) 586 575-9800
1340 Neubrecht Rd Lima (45801) *(G-9230)*

Crown Lift Trucks, Celina *Also Called: Crown Equipment Corporation (G-2328)*

Crown Lift Trucks, Cincinnati *Also Called: Crown Equipment Corporation (G-2803)*

Crown Lift Trucks, Fort Loramie *Also Called: Crown Equipment Corporation (G-7596)*

Crown Lift Trucks, Grove City *Also Called: Crown Equipment Corporation (G-8084)*

Crown Lift Trucks, New Bremen *Also Called: Crown Equipment Corporation (G-11400)*

Crown Lift Trucks, New Bremen *Also Called: Crown Equipment Corporation (G-11401)*

Crown Lift Trucks, New Bremen *Also Called: Crown Equipment Corporation (G-11402)*

Crown Lift Trucks, Vandalia *Also Called: Crown Equipment Corporation (G-14935)*

Crown Mats & Mating, Fremont *Also Called: Ludlow Composites Corporation (G-7796)*

Crown Place Brands, Apple Creek *Also Called: Crownplace Brands Ltd (G-497)*

Crown Plastics Co LLC 513 367-0238
116 May Dr Harrison (45030) *(G-8272)*

Crown Solutions, Vandalia *Also Called: Crown Solutions Co LLC (G-14936)*

Crown Solutions Co LLC 937 890-4075
913 Industrial Park Dr Vandalia (45377) *(G-14936)*

Crowne Group LLC (PA) 216 589-0198
127 Public Sq Ste 5110 Cleveland (44114) *(G-3917)*

Crownme Coil Care LLC 937 797-2070
4910 Denlinger Rd Trotwood (45426) *(G-14543)*

Crownover Lumber Company Inc (PA) 740 596-5229
501 Fairview Ave Mc Arthur (45651) *(G-10263)*

Crownplace Brands Ltd 888 332-5534
13110 Emerson Rd Apple Creek (44606) *(G-497)*

Cruisin Times Holdings LLC 234 646-2095
5239 Lake Rd W Ashtabula (44004) *(G-629)*

Cruisin Times Magazine 440 331-4615
20545 Center Ridge Rd Ste Ll40 Rocky River (44116) *(G-12837)*

Crum Manufacturing Inc 419 878-9779
1265 Waterville Monclova Rd Waterville (43566) *(G-15241)*

Crumbs Inc 740 592-3803
94 Columbus Rd Athens (45701) *(G-680)*

Crumbs Bakery, Athens *Also Called: Crumbs Inc (G-680)*

Crumley Racing Stable LLC 216 513-0334
9675 Chatham Rd Spencer (44275) *(G-13480)*

Crushed Stone Sandusky 419 483-4390
9220 Portland Rd Castalia (44824) *(G-2321)*

Crushproof Tubing Co 419 293-2111
100 North St Mc Comb (45858) *(G-10269)*

Cryogenic Equipment & Svcs Inc 513 761-4200
4583 Brate Dr Hamilton (45011) *(G-8196)*

Cryogenic Technical Services, Plain City *Also Called: Drivetrain USA Inc (G-12576)*

Cryovac LLC 513 771-7770
7410 Union Centre Blvd West Chester (45014) *(G-15409)*

Crystal Water Company, Dayton *Also Called: Rambasek Realty Inc (G-6540)*

Crystalite, Lewis Center *Also Called: Abrasive Technology Lapidary (G-9145)*

Csa Nutrition Services Inc 800 257-3788
10 Nutrition Way Brookville (45309) *(G-1731)*

Csafe, Monroe *Also Called: Csafe LLC (G-11099)*

Csafe LLC 513 360-7189
675 Gateway Blvd Monroe (45050) *(G-11099)*

CSC 419 221-7037
1161 Buckeye Rd Lima (45804) *(G-9231)*

CSC Worldwide, Columbus *Also Called: The Columbus Show Case Company (G-5820)*

Csg Software 614 986-2600
700 Taylor Ave Columbus (43219) *(G-5309)*

Csi America Inc 330 305-1403
121 14th St Se Canton (44707) *(G-2084)*

Csi Infusion Services, Hudson *Also Called: Clinical Specialties Inc (G-8591)*

CSM Concepts LLC 330 483-1320
6450 Grafton Rd Valley City (44280) *(G-14866)*

CSM Horvath Ledgebrook Inc 419 522-1133
198 Wayne St Mansfield (44902) *(G-9643)*

CSP Carey, Carey *Also Called: Teijin Automotive Tech Inc (G-2285)*

CSP Group Inc 513 984-9500
7141 E Kemper Rd Cincinnati (45249) *(G-2804)*

CSP North Baltimore, North Baltimore *Also Called: Teijin Automotive Tech Inc (G-11700)*

CSP Van Wert, Van Wert *Also Called: Teijin Automotive Tech Inc (G-14928)*

CSS Publishing Company 419 227-1818
5450 N Dixie Hwy Lima (45807) *(G-9232)*

Csw Inc 413 589-1311
3545 Silica Rd Unit E Sylvania (43560) *(G-13992)*

CT Specialty Polymers Ltd 440 632-9311
14875 Bonner Dr Middlefield (44062) *(G-10744)*

Ctc / Roach Studios, Columbus *Also Called: Roach Studios LLC (G-5727)*

Ctc East, Dayton *Also Called: Ctc Plastics (G-6268)*

Ctc Plastics 937 281-4002
943 Woodley Rd Dayton (45403) *(G-6268)*

Ctc Plastics (HQ) 937 228-9184
401 N Keowee St Dayton (45404) *(G-6269)*

Ctek Tool & Machine Company 513 742-0423
11310 Southland Rd Cincinnati (45240) *(G-2805)*

Ctg, Miamisburg *Also Called: Certified Tool & Grinding Inc (G-10625)*

Ctl Analyzers, Shaker Heights *Also Called: Cellular Technology Limited (G-13152)*

Ctl Analyzers LLC (PA) 216 791-5084
20521 Chagrin Blvd Ste 200 Shaker Heights (44122) *(G-13153)*

Ctl-Aerospace Inc 513 874-7900
9970 International Blvd West Chester (45246) *(G-15546)*

Ctl-Aerospace Inc (PA) 513 874-7900
5616 Spellmire Dr West Chester (45246) *(G-15547)*

Ctm Integration Incorporated 330 332-1800
1318 Quaker Cir Salem (44460) *(G-12988)*

Ctm Labeling Systems 330 332-1800
1318 Quaker Cir Salem (44460) *(G-12989)*

CTS, Blue Ash *Also Called: Cincinnati Thermal Spray Inc (G-1381)*

CTS National Corporation 216 566-2000
101 W Prospect Ave Ste 1020 Cleveland (44115) *(G-3918)*

CTS Waterjet LLC 513 641-0600
2865 Compton Rd Cincinnati (45251) *(G-2806)*

Cub Cadet Corporation Sales 330 273-4550
614 Liverpool Dr Valley City (44280) *(G-14867)*

Cubbison Company (PA) 330 793-2481
380 Victoria Rd Youngstown (44515) *(G-16344)*

Culaine Inc 419 345-4984
1036 W Laskey Rd Toledo (43612) *(G-14254)*

Culinary Standards, Blue Ash *Also Called: Rsw Distributors LLC (G-1462)*

Culligan, Fairfield *Also Called: Waterco of The Central States (G-7426)*

Culligan, Zanesville *Also Called: US Water Company LLC (G-16567)*

Cultured Marble Inc 330 549-2282
213 N Main St Poland (44514) *(G-12610)*

Cumberland Limestone LLC 740 638-3942
53681 Spencer Rd Cumberland (43732) *(G-6054)*

Cummins, Blue Ash *Also Called: Cummins - Allison Corp (G-1384)*

Cummins, Cleveland Also Called: Cummins - Allison Corp (G-3919)
  Cummins - Allison Corp... 513 469-2924
    11256 Cornell Park Dr Blue Ash (45242) (G-1384)
  Cummins - Allison Corp... 440 824-5050
    6777 Engle Rd Ste H Cleveland (44130) (G-3919)
Cummins Filtration Inc
  2150 Industrial Dr Findlay (45840) (G-7500)
Cummins Inc... 614 604-6004
  2297 Southwest Blvd Ste K Grove City (43123) (G-8085)
Cupboard Distributing, Urbana Also Called: Chris Haughey (G-14826)
  Current Inc... 330 392-5151
    455 N River Rd Nw Warren (44483) (G-15159)
Current Elec & Enrgy Solutions................................... 513 575-4600
  1527 State Route 28 Loveland (45140) (G-9479)
Current Electrical & Lighting, Loveland Also Called: Current Elec & Enrgy Solutions (G-9479)
Current Lighting Solutions LLC (HQ)........................... 216 462-4700
  25825 Science Park Dr Ste 400 Beachwood (44122) (G-982)
Current Lighting Solutions LLC..................................... 216 266-4416
  1099 Ivanhoe Rd Cleveland (44110) (G-3920)
Currier Richard & James... 440 988-4132
  540 Mcintosh Ln Amherst (44001) (G-474)
Curtis Hilbruner... 330 947-3527
  1315 Bank St Atwater (44201) (G-702)
Curtis Industries.. 216 430-5759
  1301 E 9th St Ste 700 Cleveland (44114) (G-3921)
Curtis Steel & Supply Inc... 330 376-7141
  1210 Curtis St Akron (44301) (G-119)
Curtiss-Wright Controls... 937 252-5601
  2600 Paramount Pl Ste 200 Fairborn (45324) (G-7312)
Curtiss-Wright Controls, Fairborn Also Called: Curtiss-Wright Controls (G-7312)
Curtiss-Wright Flow Control... 440 838-7690
  10195 Brecksville Rd Brecksville (44141) (G-1611)
Curtiss-Wright Flow Ctrl Corp..................................... 513 528-7900
  4600 E Tech Dr Cincinnati (45245) (G-2556)
Curtiss-Wright Flow Ctrl Corp..................................... 216 267-3200
  18001 Sheldon Rd Cleveland (44130) (G-3922)
Curves and More Woodworking................................... 614 239-7837
  2002 Zettler Rd Columbus (43232) (G-5310)
Cushman Foundry Div, Cincinnati Also Called: Jrm 2 Company (G-3052)
Custar Stone Co.. 419 669-4327
  9072 County Road 424 Napoleon (43545) (G-11311)
Custom Assembly Inc... 419 622-3040
  2952 Road 107 Haviland (45851) (G-8309)
Custom Blast, Lima Also Called: Custom Blast & Coat Inc (G-9233)
Custom Blast & Coat Inc... 419 225-6024
  1511 S Dixie Hwy Lima (45804) (G-9233)
Custom Blind Corporation... 937 643-2907
  2895 Culver Ave Dayton (45429) (G-6270)
Custom Built Crates Inc
  1700 Victory Park Dr Milford (45150) (G-10904)
Custom Canvas & Boat Repr Inc................................. 419 732-3314
  29 S Bridge Rd Lakeside (43440) (G-8959)
Custom Canvas & Upholstery, Lakeside Also Called: Custom Canvas & Boat Repr Inc (G-8959)
Custom Carving Source LLC....................................... 513 407-1008
  3182 Beekman St Cincinnati (45223) (G-2807)
Custom Chassis Inc... 440 839-5574
  52826 State Route 303 Wakeman (44889) (G-15073)
Custom Chemical Packaging LLC............................... 330 331-7416
  4086 Watercourse Dr Medina (44256) (G-10316)
Custom Cltch Jint Hydrlics Inc (PA)............................. 216 431-1630
  3417 Saint Clair Ave Ne Cleveland (44114) (G-3923)
Custom Coil & Transformer Co................................... 740 452-5211
  2900 Newark Rd Zanesville (43701) (G-16525)
Custom Connector Corporation................................... 216 241-1679
  1821 E 40th St Cleveland (44103) (G-3924)
Custom Control Specialists, Norton Also Called: Sdk Associates Inc (G-11948)
Custom Craft, Akron Also Called: Custom Craft Controls Inc (G-120)
Custom Craft Collection Inc... 440 998-3000
  5422 Main Ave Ashtabula (44004) (G-630)
Custom Craft Controls Inc... 330 630-9599
  1620 Triplett Blvd Akron (44306) (G-120)

Custom Crankshaft Inc... 330 382-1200
  1730 Annesley Rd East Liverpool (43920) (G-6992)
Custom Cycle ACC Mfg Dstrg Inc............................... 440 585-2200
  29110 Anderson Rd Wickliffe (44092) (G-15830)
Custom Deco, Toledo Also Called: Cdh Liquidation Inc (G-14229)
Custom Deco LLC.. 419 698-2900
  1345 Miami St Toledo (43605) (G-14255)
Custom Design Cabinets & Tops................................. 440 639-9900
  379 Fountain Ave Painesville (44077) (G-12225)
Custom Design Kitchen & Bath, Painesville Also Called: Custom Design Cabinets & Tops (G-12225)
Custom Dsign Chakra Reiki Jwly, Columbus Also Called: Lotus Love LLC (G-5534)
Custom Fab By Fisher LLC... 513 738-4600
  5009 Cincinnati Brookville Rd Hamilton (45013) (G-8197)
Custom Fabrication By Fisher..................................... 513 738-4600
  100 Weaver Rd Okeana (45053) (G-12066)
Custom Floaters LLC... 216 337-9118
  5161 W 161st St Brookpark (44142) (G-1709)
Custom Floaters LLC... 216 536-8979
  6519 Eastland Rd Ste 101 Brookpark (44142) (G-1710)
Custom Foam Products Inc (PA)................................. 937 295-2700
  900 Tower Dr Fort Loramie (45845) (G-7597)
Custom Formed Products, Miamisburg Also Called: Customformed Products Inc (G-10631)
Custom Glass Solutions LLC (PA).............................. 248 340-1800
  600 Lakeview Plaza Blvd Ste A Worthington (43085) (G-16192)
Custom Glass Solutions Upper S................................. 419 294-4921
  12688 State Highway 67 Upper Sandusky (43351) (G-14805)
Custom Graphics Inc... 330 963-7770
  8107 Bavaria Dr E Macedonia (44056) (G-9543)
Custom Hitch & Trailer, Piketon Also Called: Overhead Door of Pike County (G-12481)
Custom Hoists Inc (HQ).. 419 368-4721
  771 County Road 30a Ashland (44805) (G-570)
Custom Imprint... 440 238-4488
  19573 Progress Dr Strongsville (44149) (G-13825)
Custom Information Systems Inc................................ 614 875-2245
  3347 Mcdowell Rd Grove City (43123) (G-8086)
Custom Kerf Woodworking LLC................................. 330 745-7651
  927 Raymond Ave Barberton (44203) (G-865)
Custom Machine Inc... 419 986-5122
  3315 W Township Road 158 Tiffin (44883) (G-14082)
Custom Manufacturing Solutions (PA)........................ 937 372-0777
  479 Bellbrook Ave Xenia (45385) (G-16257)
Custom Material Hdlg Eqp LLC................................... 513 235-5336
  7868 Gapstow Brg Cincinnati (45231) (G-2808)
Custom Metal Products Inc... 614 855-2263
  5037 Babbitt Rd New Albany (43054) (G-11376)
Custom Metal Works Inc (PA)..................................... 419 668-7831
  193 Akron Rd Norwalk (44857) (G-11959)
Custom Millcraft Corp... 513 874-7080
  9092 Le Saint Dr West Chester (45014) (G-15410)
Custom Millwork Designs, Oakwood Village Also Called: Cabinet Concepts Inc (G-12036)
Custom Molded Products LLC................................... 937 382-1070
  92 Grant St Wilmington (45177) (G-16048)
Custom Needle-Print LLC... 330 432-5506
  670 Orchard Ave Nw New Philadelphia (44663) (G-11497)
Custom Nickel LLC... 937 222-1995
  45 N Clinton St Dayton (45402) (G-6271)
Custom Palet Manufacturing....................................... 440 693-4603
  9291 N Girdle Rd Middlefield (44062) (G-10745)
Custom Paper Tubes Inc... 216 362-2964
  6030 Carey Dr Cleveland (44125) (G-3925)
Custom Poly Bag LLC... 330 935-2408
  9465 Edison St Ne Alliance (44601) (G-399)
Custom Powdr Coating By Greber, Elyria Also Called: Greber Machine Tool Inc (G-7156)
Custom Products Corporation (PA)............................. 440 528-7100
  7100 Cochran Rd Solon (44139) (G-13334)
Custom Pultrusions Inc (HQ)..................................... 330 562-5201
  1331 S Chillicothe Rd Aurora (44202) (G-711)
Custom Quality Products Inc
  1645 Blue Rock St Cincinnati (45223) (G-2809)
Custom Recapping Inc... 937 324-4331
  126 Linden Ave Springfield (45505) (G-13550)

ALPHABETIC SECTION

Custom Rubber Corporation.. 216 391-2928
1274 E 55th St Cleveland (44103) *(G-3926)*

Custom Services and Designs (PA)....................................... 937 866-7636
7075 Jamaica Rd Miamisburg (45342) *(G-10630)*

Custom Sign & Design LLC... 419 202-3633
911 Meadow Ln N Norwalk (44857) *(G-11960)*

Custom Sign Center.. 614 279-6035
400 N Wilson Rd Columbus (43204) *(G-5311)*

Custom Sportswear Imprints LLC.. 330 335-8326
238 High St Wadsworth (44281) *(G-15024)*

Custom Surfaces Inc... 440 439-2310
26185 Broadway Ave Bedford (44146) *(G-1114)*

Custom Surroundings Inc... 913 839-0100
6450 Grafton Rd Valley City (44280) *(G-14868)*

Custom Tarpaulin Products Inc.. 330 758-1801
8095 Southern Blvd Youngstown (44512) *(G-16345)*

Custom Threading Systems LLC... 937 846-1405
1833 N Dayton Lakeview Rd New Carlisle (45344) *(G-11413)*

Custom Tire, Springfield Also Called: Custom Recapping Inc *(G-13550)*

Custom Tooling Company... 513 733-5790
603 Wayne Park Dr Cincinnati (45215) *(G-2810)*

Custom Truck One Source LP... 330 409-7291
3522 Middlebranch Ave Ne Canton (44705) *(G-2085)*

Custom Way Welding Inc... 937 845-9469
2217 N Dayton Lakeview Rd New Carlisle (45344) *(G-11414)*

Custom Weld & Machine Corp... 330 452-3935
1500 Henry Ave Sw Canton (44706) *(G-2086)*

Custom Woodworking Inc... 419 456-3330
214 S Main St Ottawa (45875) *(G-12177)*

Customformed Products Inc... 937 388-0480
645 Precision Ct Miamisburg (45342) *(G-10631)*

Customized Girl, Columbus Also Called: E Retailing Associates LLC *(G-5339)*

Customworks Inc... 614 262-1002
330 Lenappe Dr Columbus (43214) *(G-5312)*

Cutter Equipment Company, Canton Also Called: Randall Richard & Moore LLC *(G-2210)*

Cutter Solutins Intl LLC.. 850 725-5600
2614 Foxden Hudson (44236) *(G-8592)*

Cuttercroix LLC... 330 289-6185
7251 Engle Rd Ste 350 Cleveland (44130) *(G-3927)*

Cutting Dynamics Inc... 440 249-4666
35050 Avon Commerce Pkwy Avon (44011) *(G-770)*

Cutting Dynamics Inc... 440 930-2862
33597 Pin Oak Pkwy Avon Lake (44012) *(G-802)*

Cutting Edge Countertops Inc.. 419 873-9500
1300 Flagship Dr Perrysburg (43551) *(G-12372)*

Cutting Edge Manufacturing LLC.. 419 355-0921
220 Sullivan Rd Fremont (43420) *(G-7774)*

Cutting Edge Roofing Products, Tallmadge Also Called: Trans-Foam Inc *(G-14053)*

Cutting Edge Technologies Inc... 216 574-4759
1241 Superior Ave E Cleveland (44114) *(G-3928)*

Cutting Systems Inc... 216 928-0500
15593 Brookpark Rd Cleveland (44142) *(G-3929)*

Cuyahoga Fence LLC.. 216 830-2200
3100 E 45th St Ste 504 Cleveland (44127) *(G-3930)*

Cuyahoga Group, The, North Ridgeville Also Called: Cuyahoga Vending Co Inc *(G-11837)*

Cuyahoga Machine Company LLC.. 216 267-3560
5250 W 137th St Brookpark (44142) *(G-1711)*

Cuyahoga Molded Plastics Co... 216 261-2744
9351 Mercantile Dr Mentor (44060) *(G-10447)*

Cuyahoga Molded Plastics Co (inc) (PA)............................. 216 261-2744
1265 Babbitt Rd Euclid (44132) *(G-7266)*

Cuyahoga Plastics, Euclid Also Called: Cuyahoga Molded Plastics Co (inc) *(G-7266)*

Cuyahoga Rebuilders Inc.. 216 635-0659
5111 Brookpark Rd Cleveland (44134) *(G-3931)*

Cuyahoga Vending Co Inc.. 440 353-9595
39405 Taylor Pkwy North Ridgeville (44035) *(G-11837)*

Cvc Thermoset Specialties, Akron Also Called: Huntsman Corporation *(G-187)*

Cvg National Seating Co LLC.. 219 872-7295
7800 Walton Pkwy New Albany (43054) *(G-11377)*

Cvg Trim Systems, New Albany Also Called: Trim Systems Operating Corp *(G-11392)*

Cw Liquidation Inc
1801 E 9th St Ste 1100 Cleveland (44114) *(G-3932)*

CW Machine Worx Ltd... 740 654-5304
4805 Scooby Ln Carroll (43112) *(G-2295)*

Cwd LLC (DH)... 310 218-1082
127 Public Sq Ste 5110 Cleveland (44114) *(G-3933)*

Cwh Graphics LLC... 866 241-8515
23196 Miles Rd Ste A Bedford Heights (44128) *(G-1169)*

Cyber Shed Inc... 419 724-5855
5221 Tractor Rd Toledo (43612) *(G-14256)*

Cyberutility LLC.. 216 291-8723
1599 Maywood Rd Cleveland (44121) *(G-3934)*

Cycle Electric Inc.. 937 884-7300
8734 Dayton Greenville Pike Brookville (45309) *(G-1732)*

Cygnus Home Service LLC... 419 222-9977
2545 Saint Johns Rd Lima (45804) *(G-9234)*

Cylinders and Valves Inc... 440 238-7343
20811 Westwood Dr Strongsville (44149) *(G-13826)*

Cypress Court, Reynoldsburg Also Called: Mulch Manufacturing Inc *(G-12769)*

Cypress Valley Log Homes, Marietta Also Called: Gillard Construction Inc *(G-9795)*

Cyril-Scott Company, The, Lancaster Also Called: Consolidated Graphics Inc *(G-9003)*

Cyrpress Wine Cellars... 419 295-2124
37 E 4th St Mansfield (44902) *(G-9644)*

D & B Industries Inc.. 937 253-8658
5031 Linden Ave Ste B Dayton (45432) *(G-6157)*

D & D Mining Co Inc.. 330 549-3127
3379 E Garfield Rd New Springfield (44443) *(G-11540)*

D & E Electric Inc.. 513 738-1172
7055 Okeana Drewersburg Rd Okeana (45053) *(G-12067)*

D & E Machine Co... 513 932-2184
962 S Us Route 42 Lebanon (45036) *(G-9069)*

D & H Meats Inc.. 419 387-7767
400 Blanchard St Vanlue (45890) *(G-14969)*

D & J Distributing & Mfg.. 419 865-2552
1302 Holloway Rd Holland (43528) *(G-8501)*

D & J Electric Motor Repair Co.. 330 336-4343
1734 Wall Rd Office Wadsworth (44281) *(G-15025)*

D & J Machine Shop.. 937 256-2730
1296 S Patton St Xenia (45385) *(G-16258)*

D & J Printing Inc.. 330 678-5868
3765 Sunnybrook Rd Kent (44240) *(G-8806)*

D & L Energy Inc... 330 270-1201
3930 Fulton Dr Nw Ste 200 Canton (44718) *(G-2087)*

D & L Excavating Ltd... 419 271-0635
969 N Rymers Rd Port Clinton (43452) *(G-12616)*

D & L Machine Co.. 330 785-0781
1029 Arlington Cir Akron (44306) *(G-121)*

D & M Printing, Massillon Also Called: David A and Mary A Mathis *(G-10089)*

D & M Saw & Tool Inc.. 513 871-5433
2974 P G Graves Ln Cincinnati (45241) *(G-2811)*

D & M Welding, Moraine Also Called: Dayton Brick Company Inc *(G-11171)*

D 4 Industries Inc... 419 523-9555
685 Woodland Dr Ottawa (45875) *(G-12178)*

D A Fitzgerald Co Inc.. 937 548-0511
1045 Sater St Greenville (45331) *(G-8044)*

D A L E S Corporation.. 419 255-5335
1402 Jackson St Toledo (43604) *(G-14257)*

D and D Plastics Inc.. 330 376-0668
581 E Tallmadge Ave Akron (44310) *(G-122)*

D B S Stinless Stl Fabricators... 513 856-9600
21 Standen Dr Hamilton (45015) *(G-8198)*

D C, Cleveland Also Called: Die-Cut Products Co *(G-3958)*

D C Controls LLC.. 513 225-0813
4836 Duff Dr Ste E West Chester (45246) *(G-15548)*

D C G, Cleveland Also Called: Directconnectgroup Ltd *(G-3960)*

D C I, Akron Also Called: Digital Color Intl LLC *(G-130)*

D C Morrison Company Inc... 859 581-7511
11959 Tramway Dr Cincinnati (45241) *(G-2812)*

D C Systems Inc.. 330 273-3030
1251 Industrial Pkwy N Brunswick (44212) *(G-1756)*

D D D Hams Inc... 440 487-9572
34234 Aurora Rd Solon (44139) *(G-13335)*

D F Electronics Inc.. 513 772-7792
200 Novner Dr Cincinnati (45215) *(G-2813)*

D G M Inc
1668 Kessinger School Rd Jackson (45640) *(G-8713)* 740 286-2131

D H Bowman & Sons Inc 419 886-2711
1201 Mill Rd Bellville (44813) *(G-1241)*

D H S LLC 937 599-2485
220 Reynolds Ave Bellefontaine (43311) *(G-1204)*

D Industries Inc 216 535-4900
1350 Euclid Ave Ste 1500 Cleveland (44115) *(G-3935)*

D J Klingler Inc 513 891-2284
9999 Montgomery Rd Montgomery (45242) *(G-11129)*

D Jacob Industries LLC 440 292-7277
13995 Enterprise Ave Cleveland (44135) *(G-3936)*

D K Manufacturing 740 654-5566
2118 Commerce St Lancaster (43130) *(G-9008)*

D L T, Cincinnati Also Called: Dominion Liquid Tech LLC *(G-2836)*

D Lewis Inc 740 695-2615
52235 National Rd Saint Clairsville (43950) *(G-12901)*

D M I, Reynoldsburg Also Called: Dimensional Metals Inc *(G-12761)*

D M L Steel Tech 513 737-9911
6974 Zenith Ct Liberty Twp (45011) *(G-9213)*

D M Tool & Plastics Inc 937 962-4140
11150 Baltimore Phillipsburg Rd Brookville (45309) *(G-1733)*

D M Tool & Plastics Inc (PA) 937 962-4140
4140 Us Route 40 E Lewisburg (45338) *(G-9186)*

D M U, Dayton Also Called: Dayton Molded Urethanes LLC *(G-6283)*

D Martone Industries Inc 440 632-5800
15060 Madison Rd Middlefield (44062) *(G-10746)*

D N A, Plain City Also Called: Daily Needs Assistance Inc *(G-12572)*

D P I, Toledo Also Called: Decorative Panels Intl Inc *(G-14264)*

D P Products Inc 440 834-9663
14790 Berkshire Ind. Pkwy. Middlefield (44062) *(G-10747)*

D Picking & Co 419 562-6891
119 S Walnut St Bucyrus (44820) *(G-1856)*

D W Dickey, Lisbon Also Called: D W Dickey and Son Inc *(G-9311)*

D W Dickey and Son Inc (PA) 330 424-1441
7896 Dickey Dr Lisbon (44432) *(G-9311)*

D-G Custom Chrome LLC 513 531-1881
5200 Lester Rd Cincinnati (45213) *(G-2815)*

D-Terra Solutions Inc 614 450-1040
35 Clairedan Dr Powell (43065) *(G-12670)*

D. A. Surgical, Newbury Also Called: Dan Allen Surgical LLC *(G-11622)*

D&D Classic Restoration, Covington Also Called: D&D Clssic Auto Rstoration Inc *(G-6021)*

D&D Clssic Auto Rstoration Inc 937 473-2229
2300 Mote Dr Covington (45318) *(G-6021)*

D&D Design Concepts Inc 513 752-2191
4360 Winding Creek Blvd Batavia (45103) *(G-919)*

D&D Ingredient Distrs Inc 419 692-2667
1610 S Acadia Rd Spencerville (45887) *(G-13486)*

D&D Ingredients LLC, Spencerville Also Called: D&D Ingredient Distrs Inc *(G-13486)*

D&D Quality Machining Co Inc 440 942-2772
36495 Reading Ave Ste 1 Willoughby (44094) *(G-15905)*

D+h USA Corporation 513 381-9400
312 Plum St Ste 500 Cincinnati (45202) *(G-2814)*

Da Investments Inc 330 781-6100
4605 Lake Park Rd Youngstown (44512) *(G-16346)*

DA Precision Products Inc 513 459-1113
9052 Goldpark Dr West Chester (45011) *(G-15411)*

Daavlin, Bryan Also Called: Daavlin Distributing Co *(G-1815)*

Daavlin Distributing Co 419 636-6304
205 W Bement St Bryan (43506) *(G-1815)*

Dabar Industries LLC 614 873-3949
7630 Copper Glen St Columbus (43235) *(G-5313)*

Dac, Dover Also Called: Direct Action Co Inc *(G-6815)*

Dacraft, Miamisburg Also Called: Waxco International Inc *(G-10701)*

Dadco Inc 513 489-2244
10111 Evendale Commons Dr Cincinnati (45241) *(G-2816)*

Daddy Katz LLC 937 296-0347
3250 Kettering Blvd Moraine (45439) *(G-11168)*

Dai Ceramics LLC 440 946-6964
38240 Airport Pkwy Willoughby (44094) *(G-15906)*

Daido Metal Bellefontaine LLC 937 592-5010
1215 S Greenwood St Bellefontaine (43311) *(G-1205)*

Daifuku America Corporation (DH) 614 863-1888
6700 Tussing Rd Reynoldsburg (43068) *(G-12760)*

Daikin Applied Americas Inc 614 351-9862
192 Heatherdown Dr Westerville (43081) *(G-15697)*

Daily Chief Union 419 294-2331
111 W Wyandot Ave Upper Sandusky (43351) *(G-14806)*

Daily Fantasy Circuit Inc 614 989-8689
5 E Long St Ste 603 Columbus (43215) *(G-5314)*

Daily Globe, Shelby Also Called: Shelby Daily Globe Inc *(G-13200)*

Daily Growler Inc 614 656-2337
2812 Fishinger Rd Upper Arlington (43221) *(G-14800)*

Daily Needs Assistance Inc 614 824-8340
340 W Main St Plain City (43064) *(G-12572)*

Daily Record, The, Millersburg Also Called: Holmes County Hub Inc *(G-10965)*

Daily Reporter 614 224-4835
580 S High St Ste 316 Columbus (43215) *(G-5315)*

Daily Standard The, Celina Also Called: Standard Printing Co Inc *(G-2350)*

Dairy Clean, Delaware Also Called: Frischco Inc *(G-6723)*

Dairy Farmers America Inc 330 670-7800
1035 Medina Rd Ste 300 Medina (44256) *(G-10317)*

Dairy Pak Div, Olmsted Falls Also Called: Blue Ridge Paper Products LLC *(G-12077)*

Dairy Shed 937 848-3504
55 Bellbrook Plz Bellbrook (45305) *(G-1191)*

Daisy Brand LLC 330 202-4410
3049 Daisy Way Wooster (44691) *(G-16112)*

Daisyfield Pork LLC 419 626-2251
4413 W Bogart Rd Sandusky (44870) *(G-13049)*

Dak Enterprises Inc (PA) 740 828-3291
18062 Timber Trails Rd Marysville (43040) *(G-9907)*

Dakkota Integrated Systems LLC 517 694-6500
315 Matzinger Rd Unit G Toledo (43612) *(G-14258)*

Dakota Software Corporation (PA) 216 765-7100
1375 Euclid Ave Ste 500 Cleveland (44115) *(G-3937)*

Dal-Little Fabricating Inc 216 883-3323
11707 Putnam Ave Cleveland (44105) *(G-3938)*

Dalaco, Liberty Twp Also Called: Dm2018 LLC *(G-9214)*

Dalamer Industries LLC 440 855-1368
6701 Hubbard Ave Cleveland (44127) *(G-3939)*

Dale Kestler 513 871-9000
3475 Cardiff Ave Cincinnati (45209) *(G-2817)*

Dale R Adkins 740 682-7312
106 Smith St Oak Hill (45656) *(G-12017)*

Dalton Corporation 419 682-6328
310 Ellis St Stryker (43557) *(G-13907)*

Dalton Stryker McHining Fcilty 419 682-6328
310 Ellis St Stryker (43557) *(G-13908)*

Dalton US Inc 440 878-7661
15830 Foltz Pkwy Strongsville (44149) *(G-13827)*

Damak 1 LLC 513 858-6004
33 Donald Dr Fairfield (45014) *(G-7350)*

Damar Products Inc 937 492-9023
516 Park St Sidney (45365) *(G-13240)*

Damon Industries Inc (PA) 330 821-5310
12435 Rockhill Ave Ne Alliance (44601) *(G-400)*

Dan Allen Surgical LLC 800 261-9953
11110 Kinsman Rd Unit 10 Newbury (44065) *(G-11622)*

Dan K Williams Inc 419 893-3251
1350 Ford St Maumee (43537) *(G-10175)*

Dan Patrick Enterprises Inc 740 477-1006
8564 Zane Trail Rd Circleville (43113) *(G-3546)*

Dan-Mar Company Inc 419 660-8830
200 Bluegrass Dr E Norwalk (44857) *(G-11961)*

Dana 419 887-3000
3044 Jeep Pkwy Toledo (43610) *(G-14259)*

Dana, Maumee Also Called: Dana Commercial Vhcl Pdts LLC *(G-10179)*

Dana, Maumee Also Called: Dana Incorporated *(G-10184)*

Dana, Maumee Also Called: Dana Off Highway Products LLC *(G-10190)*

Dana, Maumee Also Called: Dana Sac USA Inc *(G-10191)*

ALPHABETIC SECTION

Dana Auto Systems Group LLC (DH) 419 887-3000
  3939 Technology Dr Maumee (43537) *(G-10176)*
Dana Automotive Aftermarket,, Maumee *Also Called: Dana Automotive Mfg Inc (G-10177)*
Dana Automotive Mfg Inc (HQ) 419 887-3000
  3939 Technology Dr Maumee (43537) *(G-10177)*
Dana Automotive Systems, Maumee *Also Called: Dana Limited (G-10188)*
Dana Brazil Holdings I LLC (DH) 419 887-3000
  3939 Technology Dr Maumee (43537) *(G-10178)*
Dana Commercial Vhcl Pdts LLC (DH) 419 887-3000
  3939 Technology Dr Maumee (43537) *(G-10179)*
Dana Driveshaft Mfg LLC (DH) 419 887-3000
  6515 Maumee Western Rd Maumee (43537) *(G-10180)*
Dana Driveshaft Products, Maumee *Also Called: Dana Driveshaft Mfg LLC (G-10180)*
Dana Driveshaft Products, Maumee *Also Called: Dana Driveshaft Products LLC (G-10181)*
Dana Driveshaft Products LLC (DH) 419 887-3000
  3939 Technology Dr Maumee (43537) *(G-10181)*
Dana Global Products Inc (DH) 419 887-3000
  3939 Technology Dr Maumee (43537) *(G-10182)*
Dana Heavy Vehicle Systems 419 866-3900
  6936 Airport Hwy Holland (43528) *(G-8502)*
Dana Heavy Vhcl Systems Group, Maumee *Also Called: Dana Hvy Vhcl Systems Group LL (G-10183)*
Dana Hvy Vhcl Systems Group LL (DH) 419 887-3000
  3939 Technology Dr Maumee (43537) *(G-10183)*
Dana Incorporated (PA) 419 887-3000
  3939 Technology Dr Maumee (43537) *(G-10184)*
Dana Information Technology, Maumee *Also Called: Dana Limited (G-10189)*
Dana Light Axle Mfg LLC (DH) 419 346-4528
  3939 Technology Dr Maumee (43537) *(G-10185)*
Dana Light Axle Mfg LLC 419 887-3000
  3044 Jeep Pkwy Toledo (43610) *(G-14260)*
Dana Light Axle Products, Maumee *Also Called: Dana Light Axle Mfg LLC (G-10185)*
Dana Limited 419 866-7253
  6201 Trust Dr Holland (43528) *(G-8503)*
Dana Limited (HQ) 419 887-3000
  3939 Technology Dr Maumee (43537) *(G-10186)*
Dana Limited 419 887-3000
  6515 Maumee Western Rd Maumee (43537) *(G-10187)*
Dana Limited 419 887-3000
  6515 Maumee Western Rd Maumee (43537) *(G-10188)*
Dana Limited 419 482-2000
  580 Longbow Dr Maumee (43537) *(G-10189)*
Dana Off Highway Products LLC 614 864-1116
  6635 Taylor Rd Blacklick (43004) *(G-1334)*
Dana Off Highway Products LLC (DH) 419 887-3000
  3939 Technology Dr Maumee (43537) *(G-10190)*
Dana Sac USA Inc 419 887-3550
  3939 Technology Dr Maumee (43537) *(G-10191)*
Dana Sealing Manufacturing LLC (DH) 3939 Technology Dr Maumee (43537) *(G-10192)*
Dana Sealing Products LLC (DH) 419 887-3000
  3939 Technology Dr Maumee (43537) *(G-10193)*
Dana Spicer Service Parts, Holland *Also Called: Dana Heavy Vehicle Systems (G-8502)*
Dana Structural Mfg LLC 419 887-3000
  3939 Technology Dr Maumee (43537) *(G-10194)*
Dana Structural Products, Maumee *Also Called: Dana Structural Mfg LLC (G-10194)*
Dana Structural Products, Maumee *Also Called: Dana Structural Products LLC (G-10195)*
Dana Structural Products LLC (DH) 419 887-3000
  3939 Technology Dr Maumee (43537) *(G-10195)*
Dana Supply Chain Mgmt, Holland *Also Called: Dana Limited (G-8503)*
Dana Thermal Products, Maumee *Also Called: Dana Thermal Products LLC (G-10196)*
Dana Thermal Products LLC (DH) 419 887-3000
  3939 Technology Dr Maumee (43537) *(G-10196)*
Dana World Trade Corporation (DH) 419 887-3000
  3939 Technology Dr Maumee (43537) *(G-10197)*
Danco Metal Products LLC 440 871-2300
  760 Moore Rd Avon Lake (44012) *(G-803)*
Dandi Enterprises Inc 419 516-9070
  6353 Som Center Rd Solon (44139) *(G-13336)*
Dandy Products Inc (PA) 513 625-3000
  3314 State Route 131 Goshen (45122) *(G-7992)*
Danfoss, Van Wert *Also Called: Danfoss Power Solutions II LLC (G-14913)*
Danfoss Power Solutions II LLC 419 238-1190
  1225 W Main St Van Wert (45891) *(G-14913)*
Dangelico Guitars 513 218-3985
  10346 Evendale Dr Cincinnati (45241) *(G-2818)*
Daniels Amish Collection LLC 330 276-0110
  100 Straits Ln Killbuck (44637) *(G-8919)*
Danite Holdings Ltd 614 444-3333
  1640 Harmon Ave Columbus (43223) *(G-5316)*
Danite Sign Co, Columbus *Also Called: Danite Holdings Ltd (G-5316)*
Danmarco, Norwalk *Also Called: Dan-Mar Company Inc (G-11961)*
Danny L Boyle 330 206-1448
  14156 Duck Creek Rd Salem (44460) *(G-12990)*
Danone Us LLC 513 229-0092
  7577 Central Parke Blvd Mason (45040) *(G-9982)*
Danone Us LLC 419 628-1295
  216 Southgate Minster (45865) *(G-11049)*
Danos and Curole 740 609-3599
  305 N 1st St Martins Ferry (43935) *(G-9897)*
Dap Products Inc 937 667-4461
  875 N 3rd St Tipp City (45371) *(G-14131)*
Dapsco 937 294-5331
  3110 Kettering Blvd Moraine (45439) *(G-11169)*
Darana Hybrid Inc (PA) 513 860-4490
  903 Belle Ave Hamilton (45015) *(G-8199)*
Darby Creek Millwork LLC 614 873-3267
  10001 Plain City Georgesville Rd Ne Plain City (43064) *(G-12573)*
Dare Electronics Inc 937 335-0031
  3245 S County Road 25a Troy (45373) *(G-14559)*
Darifill Inc 614 890-3274
  750 Green Crest Dr Westerville (43081) *(G-15698)*
Darin Jordan 740 819-3525
  3460 Gorsuch Rd Nashport (43830) *(G-11336)*
Darke Precision Inc 937 548-2232
  291 Fox Dr Piqua (45356) *(G-12512)*
Darlenes Kitchen LLC 910 633-9744
  2629 Greenway St Toledo (43607) *(G-14261)*
Darling Ingredients Inc 972 717-0300
  3105 Spring Grove Ave Cincinnati (45225) *(G-2819)*
Darling Ingredients Inc 216 651-9300
  1002 Peltnine Ave Cleveland (44109) *(G-3940)*
Darling Ingredients Inc 216 351-3440
  1002 Belt Line Ave Cleveland (44109) *(G-3941)*
Darpro Storage Solutions LLC 567 233-3190
  1089 County Road 26 Marengo (43334) *(G-9766)*
Darrah Electric Company (PA) 216 631-0912
  5914 Merrill Ave Cleveland (44102) *(G-3942)*
Darting Around LLC 330 639-3990
  3058 Cromer Ave Nw Canton (44709) *(G-2088)*
Darusta Woodlife Division, Tipp City *Also Called: Dap Products Inc (G-14131)*
Das Deutsch Cheese, Middlefield *Also Called: Middlfeld Original Cheese Coop (G-10768)*
Data Cooling Technologies LLC 330 954-3800
  3092 Euclid Heights Blvd Cleveland Heights (44118) *(G-4939)*
Data Image 740 763-7008
  2345 Gratiot Rd Se Heath (43056) *(G-8319)*
Data Processing Sciences Corporation 513 791-7100
  2 Camargo Cyn Cincinnati (45243) *(G-2820)*
Datamax Oneil Printer Supplies, West Chester *Also Called: Pioneer Labels Inc (G-15479)*
Dataq Instruments Inc 330 668-1444
  241 Springside Dr Akron (44333) *(G-123)*
Datatrak International Inc 440 443-0082
  3690 Orange Pl Ste 375 Beachwood (44122) *(G-983)*
Datco Manufacturing LLC 330 755-1414
  65 Main St Struthers (44471) *(G-13903)*
Datcomedia LLC 419 866-6301
  1 Air Cargo Pkwy E Swanton (43558) *(G-13972)*
Datono Products, Dayton *Also Called: Dayton Stencil Works Company (G-6290)*
Datwyler Sling Sltions USA Inc 937 387-2800
  875 Center Dr Vandalia (45377) *(G-14937)*
Daubenmires Printing Co LLC 513 425-7223
  1527 Central Ave Middletown (45044) *(G-10817)*

(PA)=Parent Co (HQ)=Headquarters (DH)=Div Headquarters

Dauphin Holdings Inc

ALPHABETIC SECTION

Dauphin Holdings Inc 330 733-4022
931 High Grove Blvd Akron (44312) *(G-124)*

Dave Krissinger 440 669-9957
12335 Old State Rd Chardon (44024) *(G-2447)*

Davenport Rolling Mill, Beachwood Also Called: Novelis Alr Aluminum LLC *(G-1004)*

Davey Drill, Kent Also Called: Davey Kent Inc *(G-8807)*

Davey Kent Inc 330 673-5400
200 W Williams St Kent (44240) *(G-8807)*

David A and Mary A Mathis 330 837-8611
332 Erie St S Massillon (44646) *(G-10089)*

David Adkins Logging 740 533-0297
1260 Township Road 256 Kitts Hill (45645) *(G-8943)*

David Bixel 440 474-4410
2683 State Route 534 Rock Creek (44084) *(G-12831)*

David Chojnacki 303 905-1918
5471 Camlin Pl E Westerville (43081) *(G-15699)*

David E Easterday and Co Inc 330 359-0700
1225 Us Route 62 Unit C Wilmot (44689) *(G-16067)*

David Moore 614 836-9331
733 Blacklick St Groveport (43125) *(G-8137)*

David R Hill Inc 740 685-5168
132 S 2nd St Byesville (43723) *(G-1893)*

David Round Company, The, Streetsboro Also Called: Drc Acquisition Inc *(G-13767)*

Davidson Meat Processing Plant, Waynesville Also Called: Patrick M Davidson *(G-15302)*

Davis Cummins Inc 614 309-6077
3679 E Livingston Ave Columbus (43227) *(G-5317)*

Davis Fabricators Inc 419 898-5297
15765 W State Route 2 Oak Harbor (43449) *(G-12013)*

Davis Graphic Comm Solutions, Barberton Also Called: Davis Printing Company *(G-866)*

Davis Machine Products Inc 440 474-0247
74 Sapphire Ln Streetsboro (44241) *(G-13764)*

Davis Printing Company 330 745-3113
101 Robinson Ave Barberton (44203) *(G-866)*

Davis Technologies Inc 330 823-2544
837 W Main St Alliance (44601) *(G-401)*

Dawn Enterprises Inc (PA) 216 642-5506
9155 Sweet Valley Dr Cleveland (44125) *(G-3943)*

Dawsduke Ltd 614 270-6278
9655 Salem Church Rd Canal Winchester (43110) *(G-1984)*

Day-Glo Color Corp (DH) 216 391-7070
4515 Saint Clair Ave Cleveland (44103) *(G-3944)*

Day-Glo Color Corp 216 391-7070
4518 Hamilton Ave Cleveland (44114) *(G-3945)*

Day-Glo Color Corp 216 391-7070
1570 Highland Rd Twinsburg (44087) *(G-14647)*

Day-Hio Products Inc 937 445-0782
709 Webster St Dayton (45404) *(G-6272)*

Day-TEC Tool & Mfg Inc 937 847-0022
4900 Lyons Rd Unit A Miamisburg (45342) *(G-10632)*

Daycoa Inc 937 849-1315
50 Walnut Rd Medway (45341) *(G-10397)*

Daycoa Lighting, Medway Also Called: Daycoa Inc *(G-10397)*

Daylay Egg Farm Inc 937 355-6531
11177 Township Road 133 West Mansfield (43358) *(G-15625)*

Dayton Armor LLC 937 723-8675
2360 W Dorothy Ln Ste 107 Moraine (45439) *(G-11170)*

Dayton Bag & Burlap Co 937 253-1722
448 Huffman Ave Dayton (45403) *(G-6273)*

Dayton Bag & Burlap Co 419 733-7108
4248 Display Ln Kettering (45429) *(G-8905)*

Dayton Bindery Service Inc 937 235-3111
3757 Inpark Dr Dayton (45414) *(G-6274)*

Dayton Brewery & Pub, Dayton Also Called: Lock 27 Brewing LLC *(G-6414)*

Dayton Brick Company Inc 937 293-4189
2300 Arbor Blvd Moraine (45439) *(G-11171)*

Dayton Business Journal, Dayton Also Called: American City Bus Journals Inc *(G-6199)*

Dayton City Paper Group Llc 937 222-8855
126 N Main St Ste 240 Dayton (45402) *(G-6275)*

Dayton Clutch & Joint Inc (PA) 937 236-9770
2005 Troy St 1 Dayton (45404) *(G-6276)*

Dayton Coating Tech LLC 937 278-2060
1926 E Siebenthaler Ave Dayton (45414) *(G-6277)*

Dayton Forging Heat Treating 937 253-4126
215 N Findlay St Dayton (45403) *(G-6278)*

Dayton Gear and Tool Co 937 866-4327
500 Fame Rd Dayton (45449) *(G-6279)*

Dayton Heidelberg Distrg Co 440 989-1027
5901 Baumhart Rd Lorain (44053) *(G-9410)*

DAYTON HEIDELBERG DISTRIBUTING CO., Lorain Also Called: Dayton Heidelberg Distrg Co *(G-9410)*

Dayton Laser & Aesthetic Medic 937 208-8282
6611 Clyo Rd Ste E Dayton (45459) *(G-6280)*

Dayton Legal Blank Inc 937 435-4405
875 Congress Park Dr Dayton (45459) *(G-6281)*

Dayton Machine Tool Company 937 222-6444
1314 Webster St Dayton (45404) *(G-6282)*

Dayton Manufacturing Company, Dayton Also Called: Delma Corp *(G-6296)*

Dayton Molded Urethanes LLC 937 279-9987
3337 N Dixie Dr Dayton (45414) *(G-6283)*

Dayton Molded Urethanes LLC 937 279-1910
6400 Sand Lake Rd Dayton (45414) *(G-6284)*

Dayton One LLC 937 265-0227
212 Heid Ave Dayton (45404) *(G-6285)*

Dayton Pattern Inc 937 277-0761
5591 Wadsworth Rd Dayton (45414) *(G-6286)*

Dayton Polymeric Products Inc 937 279-9987
3337 N Dixie Dr Dayton (45414) *(G-6287)*

Dayton Progress Corporation (DH) 937 859-5111
500 Progress Rd Dayton (45449) *(G-6288)*

Dayton Progress Intl Corp 937 859-5111
500 Progress Rd Dayton (45449) *(G-6289)*

Dayton Rogers of Ohio Inc 614 491-1477
2309 Mcgaw Rd W Obetz (43207) *(G-12059)*

Dayton Stencil Works Company 937 223-3233
113 E 2nd St Dayton (45402) *(G-6290)*

Dayton Superior Corporation (DH) 937 866-0711
1125 Byers Rd Miamisburg (45342) *(G-10633)*

Dayton Superior Corporation 937 682-4015
270 Rush St Rushsylvania (43347) *(G-12874)*

Dayton Superior Pdts Co Inc 937 332-1930
1370 Lytle Rd Troy (45373) *(G-14560)*

Dayton Systems Group Inc 937 885-5665
3003 S Tech Blvd Miamisburg (45342) *(G-10634)*

Dayton Technologies 513 539-5474
351 N Garver Rd Monroe (45050) *(G-11100)*

Dayton Wire Products Inc 937 236-8000
7 Dayton Wire Pkwy Dayton (45404) *(G-6291)*

Dayton-Phoenix Group Inc (PA) 937 496-3900
1619 Kuntz Rd Dayton (45404) *(G-6292)*

Daytronic, Miamisburg Also Called: Daytronic Corporation *(G-10635)*

Daytronic Corporation (HQ) 937 866-3300
965 Capstone Cir Miamisburg (45342) *(G-10635)*

Dazpak Flexible Packaging Corp (PA) 614 252-2121
2901 E 4th Ave Columbus (43219) *(G-5318)*

Db Parent Inc 513 475-3265
3630 E Kemper Rd Cincinnati (45241) *(G-2821)*

Db Products USA, Dayton Also Called: Db Unlimited LLC *(G-6293)*

Db Unlimited LLC 937 401-2602
61 Marco Ln Dayton (45458) *(G-6293)*

Dbcr Inc 330 920-1900
3400 Cavalier Trl Cuyahoga Falls (44224) *(G-6078)*

Dbh Asscates - Ohio Ltd Partnr 330 676-2006
3765 Sunnybrook Rd Kent (44240) *(G-8808)*

Dbhl Inc (HQ) 216 267-7100
4700 W 160th St Cleveland (44135) *(G-3946)*

Dbw Fiber Corporation
1720 Enterprise Corporation Wooster (44691) *(G-16113)*

DC Legacy Corp 330 896-4220
3300 Massillon Rd Akron (44312) *(G-125)*

DC Orrville Inc 330 683-0646
229 W Market St Orrville (44667) *(G-12123)*

DC Printing LLC 937 640-1957
2149 N Gettysburg Ave Dayton (45406) *(G-6294)*

ALPHABETIC SECTION — Dei Fratelli

DC Reprographics Co. 614 297-1200
1254 Courtland Ave Columbus (43201) *(G-5319)*

Dc- Digital, Carlisle *Also Called: Industrial Electronic Service (G-2288)*

DCA Construction Products LLC 330 527-4308
10421 Industrial Dr Garrettsville (44231) *(G-7912)*

Dcd Technologies Inc 216 481-0056
17920 S Waterloo Rd Cleveland (44119) *(G-3947)*

Dcm Manufacturing Inc (HQ) 216 265-8006
4540 W 160th St Cleveland (44135) *(G-3948)*

Dcm Soundex Inc 937 522-0371
1901 E 5th St Dayton (45403) *(G-6295)*

Dco LLC (DH) 419 931-9086
900 E Boundary St Ste 8a Perrysburg (43551) *(G-12373)*

DCW Acquisition Inc 216 451-0666
10646 Leuer Ave Cleveland (44108) *(G-3949)*

Dd Foundry Inc (PA) 216 362-4100
15583 Brookpark Rd Brookpark (44142) *(G-1712)*

Ddi North Jackson Corp 330 538-3900
12080 Debartolo Dr North Jackson (44451) *(G-11782)*

Ddp Specialty Electronic MA 937 839-4612
10 Electric St West Alexandria (45381) *(G-15341)*

De Angelo Instrument Inc 330 929-7266
1431 Falls Ave Cuyahoga Falls (44223) *(G-6079)*

De Bra - Kuempel, Cincinnati *Also Called: Debra-Kuempel Inc (G-2822)*

De Kay Fabricators Inc 330 793-0826
295 S Meridian Rd Youngstown (44509) *(G-16347)*

De Nora Holdings Us Inc 440 710-5300
7590 Discovery Ln Concord Township (44077) *(G-5904)*

De Nora North America Inc 440 357-4000
7590 Discovery Ln Painesville (44077) *(G-12226)*

De Nora Tech Inc 440 285-0100
464 Center St Chardon (44024) *(G-2448)*

De Nora Tech LLC (DH) 440 710-5334
7590 Discovery Ln Concord Township (44077) *(G-5905)*

De Nora Tech LLC 440 285-0368
7661 Crile Rdunit 1 Bldg 2 Painesville (44077) *(G-12227)*

De Vore Engraving Co 330 454-6820
1017 Tuscarawas St E Canton (44707) *(G-2089)*

Deadbolts Plus 614 405-2117
1509 Lockbourne Rd Columbus (43206) *(G-5320)*

Deangelo Instrument Inc 330 654-9264
3200 Mcclintocksburg Rd Diamond (44412) *(G-6805)*

Dearborn Inc 440 234-1353
678 Front St Berea (44017) *(G-1273)*

Dearfoams Div, Pickerington *Also Called: R G Barry Corporation (G-12468)*

Dearing Compressor and Pump Company (PA) 330 783-2258
3974 Simon Rd Youngstown (44512) *(G-16348)*

Dearth Resources Inc (PA) 937 325-0651
2301 Sheridan Ave Springfield (45505) *(G-13551)*

Dearth Resources Inc 937 663-4171
8801 State Route 36 Springfield (45501) *(G-13552)*

Deborah Meredith 330 644-0425
3425 Manchester Rd Coventry Township (44319) *(G-6008)*

Debra-Kuempel Inc (HQ) 513 271-6500
3976 Southern Ave Cincinnati (45227) *(G-2822)*

Deca Manufacturing, Mansfield *Also Called: Malabar Properties LLC (G-9682)*

Deca Mfg Co 419 884-0071
300 S Mill St Mansfield (44904) *(G-9645)*

Decaplus, Middletown *Also Called: Natural Beauty Products Inc (G-10847)*

Decaria Brothers Inc 330 385-0825
104 E 5th St East Liverpool (43920) *(G-6993)*

Decent Hill Press, Hilliard *Also Called: Decent Hill Publishers LLC (G-8410)*

Decent Hill Publishers LLC 216 548-1255
2825 Wynneleaf St Hilliard (43026) *(G-8410)*

Deceuninck North America LLC (HQ) 513 539-4444
351 N Garver Rd Monroe (45050) *(G-11101)*

Decibel Research Inc 256 705-3341
2661 Commons Blvd Ste 136 Beavercreek (45431) *(G-1045)*

DECIBEL RESEARCH, INC, Beavercreek *Also Called: Decibel Research Inc (G-1045)*

Decision Systems Inc 330 456-7600
2935 Woodcliff Dr Nw Canton (44718) *(G-2090)*

Decked LLC 208 806-0251
25401 Elliott Rd Defiance (43512) *(G-6675)*

Decker Custom Wood Llc 419 332-3464
505 W Mcgormley Rd Fremont (43420) *(G-7775)*

Decker Custom Wood Working, Fremont *Also Called: Decker Custom Wood Llc (G-7775)*

Decker Drilling Inc 740 749-3939
11565 State Route 676 Vincent (45784) *(G-15007)*

Decko Products Inc (PA) 419 626-5757
2105 Superior St Sandusky (44870) *(G-13050)*

Deco Crete Supply 614 372-5142
700 Harrison Dr Columbus (43204) *(G-5321)*

Deco Plas Properties LLC 419 485-0632
700 Randolph St Montpelier (43543) *(G-11136)*

Deco Tools Inc 419 476-9321
1541 Coining Dr Toledo (43612) *(G-14262)*

Decoma Systems Integration Gro 419 324-3387
1800 Nathan Dr Toledo (43611) *(G-14263)*

Decora, Beachwood *Also Called: Masterbrand Cabinets LLC (G-999)*

Decorative Panels Intl Inc (DH) 419 535-5921
2900 Hill Ave Toledo (43607) *(G-14264)*

Dedrone Defense Inc 614 948-2002
735 Ceramic Pl Ste 110 Westerville (43081) *(G-15700)*

Dedtru, Stow *Also Called: Total Repair Express Mich LLC (G-13731)*

Dee Printing Inc 614 777-8700
4999 Transamerica Dr Columbus (43228) *(G-5322)*

Dee Sign Co (PA) 513 779-3333
6163 Allen Rd West Chester (45069) *(G-15412)*

Dee Sign Usa LLC 513 779-3333
6163 Allen Rd West Chester (45069) *(G-15413)*

Dee-Jays Cstm Btchring Proc LL 740 694-7492
17460 Ankneytown Rd Fredericktown (43019) *(G-7743)*

Deemsys Inc (PA) 614 322-9928
800 Cross Pointe Rd Ste A Gahanna (43230) *(G-7833)*

Deep Brain Innovations LLC 216 378-9106
22901 Millcreek Blvd Ste 10 Beachwood (44122) *(G-984)*

Deer Creek Honey Farms Ltd 740 852-0899
551 E High St London (43140) *(G-9386)*

Deer's Leap Winery, Geneva *Also Called: Biscotti Winery LLC (G-7933)*

Deerfield Digital, Cincinnati *Also Called: Laurenee Ltd (G-3097)*

Deerfield Manufacturing Inc 513 398-2010
320 N Mason Montgomery Rd Mason (45040) *(G-9983)*

Deerfield Ventures Inc 614 875-0688
2224 Stringtown Rd Grove City (43123) *(G-8087)*

Dees Family Raceway LLC 740 772-5431
906 Charleston Pike Chillicothe (45601) *(G-2501)*

Defabco Inc 614 231-2700
3765 E Livingston Ave Columbus (43227) *(G-5323)*

Defense Co Inc 413 998-1637
600 Superior Ave E Cleveland (44114) *(G-3950)*

Defense Research Assoc Inc 937 431-1644
3915 Germany Ln Ste 102 Dayton (45431) *(G-6158)*

Defense Surplus LLC 419 460-9906
706 Waite Ave Maumee (43537) *(G-10198)*

Deffren Machine Tool Svc Inc 513 858-1555
240 Donald Dr Fairfield (45014) *(G-7351)*

Defiance Crescent News, The, Defiance *Also Called: Defiance Publishing Co Ltd (G-6677)*

Defiance Metal Products Co (HQ) 419 784-5332
21 Seneca St Defiance (43512) *(G-6676)*

Defiance Operations, Defiance *Also Called: Gt Technologies Inc (G-6680)*

Defiance Publishing Co Ltd 419 784-5441
624 W 2nd St Defiance (43512) *(G-6677)*

Defiance Stamping Co 419 782-5781
800 Independence Dr Napoleon (43545) *(G-11312)*

Deflecto LLC 330 602-0840
303 Oxford St Ste A Dover (44622) *(G-6814)*

Degussa, Akron *Also Called: Evonik Corporation (G-145)*

Degussa Construction, Beachwood *Also Called: Master Builders LLC (G-998)*

Degussa Incorporated 513 733-5111
620 Shepherd Dr Cincinnati (45215) *(G-2823)*

Dei Fratelli, Northwood *Also Called: Hirzel Canning Company (G-11919)*

Deimling/Jeliho Plastics Inc   ALPHABETIC SECTION

Deimling/Jeliho Plastics Inc 513 752-6653
   4010 Bach Buxton Rd Amelia (45102) *(G-454)*

Delafoil, Perrysburg *Also Called: Delafoil Pennsylvania Inc (G-12374)*

Delafoil Pennsylvania Inc 610 327-9565
   1775 Progress Dr Perrysburg (43551) *(G-12374)*

Delaware City Vineyard 740 362-6383
   32 Troy Rd Delaware (43015) *(G-6712)*

Delaware Company, Cleveland *Also Called: Tremont Electric Incorporated (G-4820)*

Delaware Data Products 740 369-5449
   216 London Rd Delaware (43015) *(G-6713)*

Delaware Gazette Company 740 363-1161
   40 N Sandusky St Ste 202 Delaware (43015) *(G-6714)*

Delaware Paint Company Ltd 740 368-9981
   8455 Rausch Dr Plain City (43064) *(G-12574)*

Delhi Welding Co, Cincinnati *Also Called: Ridge Engineering Inc (G-3340)*

Delille Oxygen Company (PA) 614 444-1177
   772 Marion Rd Columbus (43207) *(G-5324)*

Delille Oxygen Company 937 325-9595
   1101 W Columbia St Springfield (45504) *(G-13553)*

Dell Inc 614 491-4603
   3795 Creekside Pkwy Lockbourne (43137) *(O-0331)*

Delma Corp 937 253-2142
   3327 Elkton Ave Dayton (45403) *(G-6296)*

Delo Screw Products, Delaware *Also Called: Supply Technologies LLC (G-6754)*

Delohio Tech 740 816-5628
   2061 State Route 521 Delaware (43015) *(G-6715)*

Deloscrew Products 740 363-1971
   700 London Rd Delaware (43015) *(G-6716)*

Delphi, Vandalia *Also Called: Mahle Behr USA Inc (G-14949)*

Delphi, Vienna *Also Called: Aptiv Services Us LLC (G-14994)*

Delphi, Warren *Also Called: Aptiv Services Us LLC (G-15142)*

Delphi, Warren *Also Called: Aptiv Services Us LLC (G-15143)*

Delphi Pckard Eea - Wrren Plan, Warren *Also Called: Aptiv Services Us LLC (G-15141)*

Delphi-T - Vandalia Ptc, Dayton *Also Called: Mahle Industries Incorporated (G-6426)*

Delphia Consulting LLC 614 421-2000
   250 E Broad St Ste 1150 Columbus (43215) *(G-5325)*

Delphos Herald Inc (PA) 419 695-0015
   405 N Main St Delphos (45833) *(G-6760)*

Delphos Herald Inc 419 399-4015
   113 S Williams St Paulding (45879) *(G-12312)*

Delphos Plant 2, Delphos *Also Called: Toledo Molding & Die LLC (G-6773)*

Delphos Rubber Company 419 692-3000
   1450 N Main St Delphos (45833) *(G-6761)*

Delphos Tent and Awning Inc 419 692-5776
   1454 N Main St Delphos (45833) *(G-6762)*

Delta H Technologies LLC (PA) 740 756-7676
   62 High St Carroll (43112) *(G-2296)*

Delta Manufacturing Inc 330 386-1270
   49207 Calcutta Smithferry Rd East Liverpool (43920) *(G-6994)*

Delta Media Group Inc 330 493-0350
   7015 Sunset Strip Ave Nw North Canton (44720) *(G-11720)*

Delta Power Supply Inc 513 771-3835
   10330 Chester Rd Cincinnati (45215) *(G-2824)*

Delta Systems Inc 330 626-2811
   1734 Frost Rd Streetsboro (44241) *(G-13765)*

Delta Tool & Die, Delta *Also Called: Delta Tool & Die Stl Block Inc (G-6781)*

Delta Tool & Die Stl Block Inc 419 822-5939
   5226 County Road 6 Delta (43515) *(G-6781)*

Deltacraft, Independence *Also Called: Millcraft Group LLC (G-8675)*

Deltec Incorporated 513 732-0800
   4230 Grissom Dr Batavia (45103) *(G-920)*

Deltech Polymers LLC 937 339-3150
   1250 Union St Troy (45373) *(G-14561)*

Deltech Polymers Opco LLC 225 358-3306
   1250 Union St Troy (45373) *(G-14562)*

Deluxe Business Systems, Streetsboro *Also Called: Deluxe Corporation (G-13766)*

Deluxe Corporation 330 342-1500
   10030 Philipp Pkwy Streetsboro (44241) *(G-13766)*

Dem Manufacturing, Newbury *Also Called: Padco Industries LLC (G-11634)*

Demag Cranes & Components Corp (DH) 440 248-2400
   6675 Parkland Blvd Ste 200 Solon (44139) *(G-13337)*

Demark, Wauseon *Also Called: E & J Demark Inc (G-15260)*

Dematic Corp 440 526-2770
   6930 Treeline Dr Brecksville (44141) *(G-1612)*

Demilta Sand and Gravel Inc 440 942-2015
   921 Erie Rd Willoughby (44095) *(G-15907)*

Demmy Sand and Gravel LLC
   4324 Fairfield Pike Springfield (45502) *(G-13554)*

Denbro Plastics Company, Toledo *Also Called: Claycor Inc (G-14240)*

Dendratec Ltd 330 473-4878
   1417 Zuercher Rd Dalton (44618) *(G-6130)*

Dengensha America, Bedford *Also Called: Dengensha America Corporation (G-1115)*

Dengensha America Corporation 440 439-8081
   7647 First Pl Bedford (44146) *(G-1115)*

Denim6729 Inc 216 854-3634
   6729 Denison Ave Cleveland (44102) *(G-3951)*

Denizen Inc 937 615-9561
   130 Fox Dr Piqua (45356) *(G-12513)*

Denman Tire Corporation 330 675-4242
   400 Diehl South Rd Leavittsburg (44430) *(G-9057)*

Dennelli Custom Wdwkg Inc 740 927-1900
   1886 Ivywood Ct Pataskala (43062) *(G-12296)*

Denney Plastics Machining LLC 330 308-5300
   149 Stonecreek Rd Nw New Philadelphia (44663) *(G-11498)*

Denny Printing LLC 417 825-4936
   3423 Mcginn Dr Apt 211 Grove City (43123) *(G-8088)*

Denoon Lumber Company LLC (PA) 740 768-2220
   571 County Road 52 Bergholz (43908) *(G-1300)*

Dental Ceramics Inc 330 523-5240
   3404 Brecksville Rd Richfield (44286) *(G-12785)*

Dental Pure Water Inc 440 234-0890
   336 Daisy Ave Ste 102b Berea (44017) *(G-1274)*

Dental Services Group, Sylvania *Also Called: Sentage Corporation (G-14013)*

Denton & Anderson Mktg Div, Hubbard *Also Called: Taylor - Winfield Corporation (G-8571)*

Denton Atd Inc (PA) 567 265-5200
   900 Denton Dr Huron (44839) *(G-8631)*

Dentronix Inc 330 916-7300
   235 Ascot Pkwy Cuyahoga Falls (44223) *(G-6080)*

Dentsply Sirona Inc 419 893-5672
   520 Illinois Ave Maumee (43537) *(G-10199)*

Dentsply Sirona Inc 419 865-9497
   3535 Briarfield Blvd Maumee (43537) *(G-10200)*

Denver Adkins 740 682-3123
   642 Phillip Kuhn Rd Oak Hill (45656) *(G-12018)*

Dependable Stamping Company 216 486-5522
   1160 E 222nd St Cleveland (44117) *(G-3952)*

Depot Direct Inc 419 661-1233
   487 J St Perrysburg (43551) *(G-12375)*

Derma Glow Med Spa Corp 440 641-1406
   22237 Lorain Rd Cleveland (44126) *(G-3953)*

Dermamed Coatin 330 474-3786
   271 Progress Blvd Kent (44240) *(G-8809)*

Dern Trophies Corp 614 895-3260
   6225 Frost Rd Westerville (43082) *(G-15653)*

Dern Trophy Mfg, Westerville *Also Called: Dern Trophies Corp (G-15653)*

Derrick Company Inc 513 321-8122
   4560 Kellogg Ave Cincinnati (45226) *(G-2825)*

Derrick Petroleum Inc 740 668-5711
   Market Street Bladensburg (43005) *(G-1346)*

Deruijter Intl USA Inc 419 678-3909
   120 Harvest Dr Coldwater (45828) *(G-4986)*

DES Machine Services Inc 330 633-6897
   4115 Baird Rd Stow (44224) *(G-13692)*

Des Tech, Troy *Also Called: Design Technologies & Mfg Co (G-14563)*

Desco Corporation (PA) 614 888-8855
   7795 Walton Pkwy Ste 175 New Albany (43054) *(G-11378)*

Desco Equipment Corp 330 405-1581
   1903 Case Pkwy Twinsburg (44087) *(G-14648)*

Desco Machine Company LLC 330 405-5181
   1903 Case Pkwy Twinsburg (44087) *(G-14649)*

Deshazo 513 402-7466
   60 American Way Ste B Monroe (45050) *(G-11102)*

ALPHABETIC SECTION — Diamonite Plant

Deshea Printing Company 330 336-7601
924 Seville Rd Wadsworth (44281) *(G-15026)*

Design and Fabrication Inc 419 294-2414
400 Malabar Dr Upper Sandusky (43351) *(G-14807)*

Design Concrete Surfaces, Kent *Also Called: Don Wartko Construction Co (G-8810)*

Design Masters Inc 513 772-7175
800 Redna Ter Cincinnati (45215) *(G-2826)*

Design Molded Products LLC (PA) 330 963-4400
8220 Bavaria Dr E Macedonia (44056) *(G-9544)*

Design Molded Products LLC 330 963-4400
8272 Bavaria Dr E Macedonia (44056) *(G-9545)*

Design Original Inc 937 596-5121
402 Jackson St Jackson Center (45334) *(G-8731)*

Design Pattern Works Inc 937 252-0797
2312 E 3rd St Dayton (45403) *(G-6297)*

Design Technologies & Mfg Co 937 335-0757
2000 Corporate Dr Troy (45373) *(G-14563)*

Design Wheel and Hub, Akron *Also Called: Schott Metal Products Company (G-326)*

Designed Harness Systems Inc 937 599-2485
227 Water Ave Bellefontaine (43311) *(G-1206)*

Designed Images Inc 440 708-2526
10121 Stafford Rd Ste C Chagrin Falls (44023) *(G-2392)*

Designer Cntemporary Laminates 440 946-8207
1700 Sheffield Ter Painesville (44077) *(G-12228)*

Designer Doors Inc 330 772-6391
4810 State Route 7 Burghill (44404) *(G-1878)*

Designer Stone Co 740 492-1300
303 E Main St Port Washington (43837) *(G-12632)*

Designer Window Treatments Inc 419 822-4967
302 Superior St Delta (43515) *(G-6782)*

Designetics Inc (PA) 419 866-0700
1624 Eber Rd Holland (43528) *(G-8504)*

Desmond-Stephan Mfgcompany 937 653-7181
121 W Water St Urbana (43078) *(G-14829)*

Dester Corporation (DH) 419 362-8020
1200 E Kibby St Bldg 32 Lima (45804) *(G-9235)*

Dester Corporation 419 362-8020
1200 E Kibby St Bldg 6 Lima (45804) *(G-9236)*

Destin Die Casting LLC 937 347-1111
851 Bellbrook Ave Xenia (45385) *(G-16259)*

Destiny Manufacturing Inc 330 273-9000
2974 Interstate Pkwy Brunswick (44212) *(G-1757)*

Detailed Machining Inc 937 492-1264
2490 Ross St Sidney (45365) *(G-13241)*

Detrex Corporation (DH) 216 749-2605
1000 Belt Line Ave Cleveland (44109) *(G-3954)*

Detrick Design Fabrication LLC 937 620-6736
425 Wisteria Dr Troy (45373) *(G-14564)*

Detroit Desl Rmnfctrng-Ast Inc 740 439-7701
60703 Country Club Rd Byesville (43723) *(G-1894)*

Detroit Desl Rmnufacturing LLC 740 439-7701
8475 Reitler Rd Cambridge (43725) *(G-1931)*

Detroit Diesl Specialty TI Inc 740 435-4452
60703 Country Club Rd Byesville (43723) *(G-1895)*

Detroit Flame Hardening Co 513 942-1400
375 Security Dr Fairfield (45014) *(G-7352)*

Detroit Toledo Fiber LLC 248 647-0400
1245 E Manhattan Blvd Toledo (43608) *(G-14265)*

Deuce Machining LLC 513 875-2291
3088 Us Highway 50 Fayetteville (45118) *(G-7464)*

Deufol Worldwide Packaging LLC 440 232-1100
19800 Alexander Rd Bedford (44146) *(G-1116)*

Devault Machine & Mould Co LLC 740 654-5925
2294 Commerce St Lancaster (43130) *(G-9009)*

Devco Oil Inc 740 439-3833
2522 Glenn Hwy Cambridge (43725) *(G-1932)*

Devco Trucking, Cambridge *Also Called: Devco Oil Inc (G-1932)*

Devicor Med Pdts Holdings Inc 513 864-9000
300 E Business Way Fl 5 Cincinnati (45241) *(G-2827)*

Devilbiss Ransburg 419 470-2000
320 Phillips Ave Toledo (43612) *(G-14266)*

Devries & Associates Inc 614 890-3821
654 Brooksedge Blvd Ste A Westerville (43081) *(G-15701)*

Dewesoft, Whitehouse *Also Called: Dewesoft LLC (G-15817)*

Dewesoft LLC 855 339-3669
10730 Logan St Whitehouse (43571) *(G-15817)*

Dewitt Inc 216 662-0800
14450 Industrial Ave N Maple Heights (44137) *(G-9750)*

Df Supply, Twinsburg *Also Called: Df Supply Inc (G-14650)*

Df Supply Inc 330 650-9226
8500 Hadden Rd Twinsburg (44087) *(G-14650)*

Dfa Dairy Brands Ice Cream LLC 419 473-9621
4117 Fitch Rd Toledo (43613) *(G-14267)*

Dgl Woodworking Inc 937 837-7091
5931 Wolf Creek Pike Dayton (45426) *(G-6298)*

DH, Cincinnati *Also Called: D+h USA Corporation (G-2814)*

Dhpp, Dover *Also Called: Dover High Prfmce Plas Inc (G-6820)*

Dhs Innovations, Bellefontaine *Also Called: Designed Harness Systems Inc (G-1206)*

Di Iorio Sheet Metal Inc 216 961-3703
5002 Clark Ave Cleveland (44102) *(G-3955)*

Diagnostic Hybrids Inc 740 593-1784
2005 E State St Ste 100 Athens (45701) *(G-681)*

Diamant Polymers Inc 513 979-4011
3495 Mustafa Dr Cincinnati (45241) *(G-2828)*

Diamond Aluminum Co, Middletown *Also Called: John H Hosking Co (G-10834)*

Diamond America Corporation 330 762-9269
96 E Miller Ave Akron (44301) *(G-126)*

Diamond Cellar, The, Dublin *Also Called: Robert W Johnson Inc (G-6931)*

Diamond Child Clothing Co LLC 614 575-6238
7647 Schneider Way Blacklick (43004) *(G-1335)*

Diamond Designs Inc 330 434-6776
231 Springside Dr Ste 145 Akron (44333) *(G-127)*

Diamond Door Limited, Fredericksburg *Also Called: Ohio Custom Door LLC (G-7730)*

Diamond Electronics, Lancaster *Also Called: Diamond Power Intl Inc (G-9011)*

Diamond Electronics Inc 740 652-9222
1858 Cedar Hill Rd Lancaster (43130) *(G-9010)*

Diamond Hard Chrome Co Inc 216 391-3618
7536 Monterey Bay Dr Unit 1 Mentor On The Lake (44060) *(G-10602)*

Diamond Heavy Haul, Shandon *Also Called: Diamond Trailers Inc (G-13160)*

Diamond Innovations Inc (PA) 614 438-2000
6325 Huntley Rd Columbus (43229) *(G-5326)*

Diamond Machine and Mfg, Bluffton *Also Called: Carpe Diem Industries LLC (G-1502)*

Diamond Machinery Company, Cleveland *Also Called: Diamond Machinery LLC (G-3956)*

Diamond Machinery LLC 216 312-1235
19525 Hilliard Blvd Unit 16729 Cleveland (44116) *(G-3956)*

Diamond Mfg Bluffton Ltd 419 358-0129
505 E Jefferson St Bluffton (45817) *(G-1503)*

Diamond Mold & Die Inc 330 633-5682
109 E Garwood Dr Tallmadge (44278) *(G-14027)*

Diamond Oilfield Tech LLC 234 806-4185
106 E Market St Fl 2 Warren (44481) *(G-15160)*

Diamond Polymers Incorporated 330 773-2700
1353 Exeter Rd Akron (44306) *(G-128)*

Diamond Power Intl Inc 740 687-4001
2530 E Main St Lancaster (43130) *(G-9011)*

Diamond Power Intl Inc (DH) 740 687-6500
2600 E Main St Lancaster (43130) *(G-9012)*

Diamond Power Specialty, Lancaster *Also Called: Diamond Power Intl Inc (G-9012)*

Diamond Products Limited 440 323-4616
1111 Taylor St Elyria (44035) *(G-7129)*

Diamond Products Limited (DH) 440 323-4616
333 Prospect St Elyria (44035) *(G-7130)*

Diamond Reserve Inc 440 892-7877
801 Sharon Dr Westlake (44145) *(G-15745)*

Diamond Trailers Inc 513 738-4500
5045 Cincinnati-Brookville Rd Shandon (45063) *(G-13160)*

Diamond Wipes Intl Inc 419 562-3575
1375 Isaac Beal Rd Bucyrus (44820) *(G-1857)*

Diamonds Products Inc 440 323-4616
1250 E Broad St Elyria (44035) *(G-7131)*

Diamonite Plant, Shreve *Also Called: I Cerco Inc (G-13210)*

(PA)=Parent Co (HQ)=Headquarters (DH)=Div Headquarters

Diana Food, Elyria Also Called: Symrise Inc *(G-7209)*

Diano Construction and Sup Co..330 456-7229
1000 Warner Rd Se Canton (44707) *(G-2091)*

Diano Supply Co, Canton Also Called: Diano Construction and Sup Co *(G-2091)*

Diasome Pharmaceuticals Inc..216 444-7110
10000 Cedar Ave Ste 6 Cleveland (44106) *(G-3957)*

Dickens Foundry, Arcadia Also Called: Maass Midwest Mfg Inc *(G-516)*

Didion's Mechanical, Bellevue Also Called: Donald E Didion II *(G-1226)*

Die Co Inc..440 942-8856
1889 E 337th St Eastlake (44095) *(G-7025)*

Die Guys Inc..330 239-3437
5238 Portside Dr Medina (44256) *(G-10318)*

Die-Cut Products Co..216 771-6994
1801 E 30th St Cleveland (44114) *(G-3958)*

Die-Gem Co Inc..330 784-7400
394 Greenwood Ave Akron (44320) *(G-129)*

Die-Matic Corporation..216 749-4656
201 Eastview Dr Brooklyn Heights (44131) *(G-1689)*

Die-Mension Corporation..330 273-5872
3020 Nationwide Pkwy Brunswick (44212) *(G-1758)*

Diebold, North Canton Also Called: Diebold Nixdorf Incorporated *(G-11721)*

Diebold Nixdorf, North Canton Also Called: Diebold Nixdorf Incorporated *(G-11722)*

Diebold Nixdorf Incorporated..330 490-4000
818 Mulberry Rd Se Canton (44707) *(G-2092)*

Diebold Nixdorf Incorporated..740 928-0200
1050 O Neill Dr Hebron (43025) *(G-8338)*

Diebold Nixdorf Incorporated..740 928-1010
511 Milliken Dr Hebron (43025) *(G-8339)*

Diebold Nixdorf Incorporated..336 662-1115
334 Orchard Ave Ne North Canton (44720) *(G-11721)*

Diebold Nixdorf Incorporated (PA)..330 490-4000
350 Orchard Ave Ne North Canton (44720) *(G-11722)*

Diemaster Tool & Mold Inc..330 467-4281
895 Highland Rd E # 5 Macedonia (44056) *(G-9546)*

Dietrich Industries Inc..330 372-4014
1300 Phoenix Rd Ne Warren (44483) *(G-15161)*

Dietrich Industries Inc..330 372-2868
1985 N River Rd Ne Warren (44483) *(G-15162)*

Dietrich Industries Inc (HQ)..800 873-2604
200 W Old Wilson Bridge Rd Worthington (43085) *(G-16193)*

Dietrich Metal Framing, Warren Also Called: Dietrich Industries Inc *(G-15161)*

Dietrich Von Hldbrand Lgacy PR..703 496-7821
1235 University Blvd Steubenville (43952) *(G-13666)*

Dietsch Brothers Incorporated (PA)..419 422-4474
400 W Main Cross St Findlay (45840) *(G-7501)*

Digicom Inc..216 642-3838
5405 Valley Belt Rd Ste A Brooklyn Heights (44131) *(G-1690)*

Digilube Systems Inc..937 748-2209
216 E Mill St Springboro (45066) *(G-13499)*

Digisoft Systems Corporation..937 833-5016
4520 Clayton Rd Brookville (45309) *(G-1734)*

Digital & Analog Design, Dublin Also Called: Pro Oncall Technologies LLC *(G-6927)*

Digital Color Intl LLC
1653 Merriman Rd Ste 211 Akron (44313) *(G-130)*

Digital Technologies, Rossford Also Called: Sasha Electronics Inc *(G-12872)*

Digitek Corp..513 794-3190
3785 Marble Ridge Ln Mason (45040) *(G-9984)*

Dilco Industries Inc..330 337-6732
300 Benton Rd Salem (44460) *(G-12991)*

Diletto Winery LLC..440 991-6217
8578 Market St Youngstown (44512) *(G-16349)*

Dillen Products, Middlefield Also Called: Myers Industries Inc *(G-10774)*

Diller Metals Inc..419 943-3364
507 S Eastom St Leipsic (45856) *(G-9132)*

Dillin Engineered Systems Corp..419 666-6789
8030 Broadstone Rd Perrysburg (43551) *(G-12376)*

Dillon Manufacturing Inc..937 325-8482
2115 Progress Rd Springfield (45505) *(G-13555)*

Dimco Gray..937 291-4720
8200 S Suburban Dr Dayton (45458) *(G-6299)*

Dimco-Gray Company, Centerville Also Called: Dimcogray Corporation *(G-2361)*

Dimcogray Corporation (PA)..937 433-7600
900 Dimco Way Centerville (45458) *(G-2361)*

Dimension Hardwood Veneers Inc..419 272-2245
509 Woodville St Edon (43518) *(G-7086)*

Dimension Industries Inc..440 236-3265
27335 Royalton Rd Columbia Station (44028) *(G-5012)*

Dimensional Metals Inc (PA)..740 927-3633
58 Klema Dr N Reynoldsburg (43068) *(G-12761)*

Dimex LLC, Marietta Also Called: Westlake Dimex LLC *(G-9844)*

Dinesol Building Products Ltd..330 270-0212
168 N Meridian Rd Youngstown (44509) *(G-16350)*

Dinesol Plastics, Niles Also Called: Dinesol Plastics Inc *(G-11666)*

Dinesol Plastics Inc..330 544-7171
195 E Park Ave Niles (44446) *(G-11666)*

Dinol US Inc..740 548-1656
8520 Cotter St Lewis Center (43035) *(G-9157)*

Diocesan Publications Inc (PA)..614 718-9500
6161 Wilcox Rd Dublin (43016) *(G-6879)*

Dioguardis Italian Foods Inc..330 492-3777
3116 Market Ave N Canton (44714) *(G-2093)*

Dip Coal Customs LLC..513 503-1243
2303 Beechmont Ave Cincinnati (45230) *(G-2829)*

Diplomat Spclty Infusion Group, Cincinnati Also Called: Optum Infusion Svcs 550 LLC *(G-3227)*

Dips Publishing Inc..216 801-7886
4229 E 124th St Cleveland (44105) *(G-3959)*

Dircksen and Associates Inc..614 238-0413
743 S Front St Columbus (43206) *(G-5327)*

Direct Action Co Inc..330 364-3219
6668 Old Route 39 Nw Dover (44622) *(G-6815)*

Direct Digital Graphics Inc..330 405-3770
1716 Enterprise Pkwy Twinsburg (44087) *(G-14651)*

Direct Disposables LLC..440 717-3335
10605 Snowville Rd Brecksville (44141) *(G-1613)*

Direct Tool LLC..614 687-3111
5953 Pleasant Chapel Rd Mechanicsburg (43044) *(G-10285)*

Direct Wire Service LLP..937 526-4447
100 Subler Dr Versailles (45380) *(G-14979)*

Directconnectgroup Ltd..216 281-2866
5501 Cass Ave Cleveland (44102) *(G-3960)*

Directional One Svcs Inc USA..740 371-5031
2163a-1 Gwb Complex 2 Bldg 6 State Route 821 Marietta (45750) *(G-9788)*

Discount Smokes & Gifts Xenia..937 372-0259
37 E Main St Xenia (45385) *(G-16260)*

Discover Publications..877 872-3080
6425 Busch Blvd Columbus (43229) *(G-5328)*

Dish One Up Satellite Inc..216 482-3875
3634 Euclid Ave Ste 100 Cleveland (44115) *(G-3961)*

Diskin Enterprises LLC..330 527-4308
10421 Industrial Dr Garrettsville (44231) *(G-7913)*

Dismat Corporation..419 531-8963
336 N Westwood Ave Toledo (43607) *(G-14268)*

Dispatch Consumer Services..740 687-1893
3160 W Fair Ave Lancaster (43130) *(G-9013)*

Dispatch Printing Company (PA) 62 E Broad St Columbus (43215) *(G-5329)*

Display Dynamics Inc..937 832-2830
1 Display Point Dr Englewood (45315) *(G-7229)*

Distillata Company (PA)..216 771-2900
1608 E 24th St Cleveland (44114) *(G-3962)*

Distinct Advantage Cabinetry, Toledo Also Called: Online Mega Sellers Corp *(G-14415)*

Distinctive Marble & Gran Inc..614 760-0003
7635 Commerce Pl Plain City (43064) *(G-12575)*

Distinctive Surfaces LLC..614 431-0898
4600 Bridgeway Ave Columbus (43219) *(G-5330)*

Distribution Center, West Chester Also Called: Martin-Brower Company LLC *(G-15462)*

Distributor Graphics Inc..440 260-0024
6909 Engle Rd Ste 13 Cleveland (44130) *(G-3963)*

District Brewing Company Inc..614 224-3626
2555 Harrison Rd Columbus (43204) *(G-5331)*

Distrubutors, Cincinnati Also Called: Ecopac LLC *(G-2858)*

Ditsch Usa LLC... 513 782-8888
    311 Northland Blvd Cincinnati (45246) *(G-2830)*
Ditty Printing LLC.. 614 893-7439
    6306 Crystal Valley Dr Galena (43021) *(G-7853)*
Ditz Designs, Norwalk *Also Called: Hen House Inc (G-11973)*
Divelbiss Corporation.. 800 245-2327
    9778 Mount Gilead Rd Fredericktown (43019) *(G-7744)*
Diverse Mfg Solutions LLC... 740 363-3600
    970 Pittsburgh Dr Ste 22 Delaware (43015) *(G-6717)*
Diversey Taski Inc (PA)... 419 531-2121
    3115 Frenchmens Rd Toledo (43607) *(G-14269)*
Diverseylever Inc.. 513 554-4200
    3630 E Kemper Rd Cincinnati (45241) *(G-2831)*
Diversfied Mch Pdts Gnsvlle GA, Columbus *Also Called: Prime Equipment Group LLC (G-5690)*
Diversified Air Systems, Brooklyn Heights *Also Called: Rel Enterprises Inc (G-1698)*
Diversified Brands.. 216 595-8777
    26300 Fargo Ave Bedford (44146) *(G-1117)*
Diversified Honing Inc.. 330 874-4663
    11036 Industrial Pkwy Nw Bolivar (44612) *(G-1523)*
Diversified Mch Components LLC.................................. 440 942-5701
    34099 Melinz Pkwy Unit D Eastlake (44095) *(G-7026)*
Diversified Mold & Castings Co, Cleveland *Also Called: Diversified Mold Castings LLC (G-3964)*
Diversified Mold and Castings, Cleveland *Also Called: Plaster Process Castings Co (G-4559)*
Diversified Mold Castings LLC...................................... 216 663-1814
    19800 Miles Rd Cleveland (44128) *(G-3964)*
Diversified Ophthalmics Inc.. 803 783-3454
    250 Mccullough St Cincinnati (45226) *(G-2832)*
Diversified Production LLC... 740 373-8771
    111 Industry Rd Unit 206 Marietta (45750) *(G-9789)*
Diversified Products & Svcs.. 740 393-6202
    1250 Vernonview Dr Mount Vernon (43050) *(G-11270)*
Diversified Ready Mix Ltd... 330 628-3355
    1680 Southeast Ave Tallmadge (44278) *(G-14028)*
Diversified SE Division, Cincinnati *Also Called: Diversified Ophthalmics Inc (G-2832)*
Diversified Sign, West Chester *Also Called: Dee Sign Co (G-15412)*
Diversipak Inc... 513 321-7884
    838 Reedy St Cincinnati (45202) *(G-2833)*
Diversity-Vuteq LLC.. 614 490-5034
    1015 Taylor Rd Gahanna (43230) *(G-7834)*
Division of Selling Materials, Dover *Also Called: Smith Concrete Co (G-6843)*
Division Overhead Door Inc (PA)................................... 513 872-0888
    861 Dellway St Cincinnati (45229) *(G-2834)*
Dixie Container Corporation... 513 860-1145
    3840 Port Union Rd Fairfield (45014) *(G-7353)*
Dixie Machinery Inc... 513 360-0091
    845 Todhunter Rd Monroe (45050) *(G-11103)*
Dixitech Cnc, Monroe *Also Called: Dixie Machinery Inc (G-11103)*
Dixon Bayco USA... 513 874-8499
    7280 Union Centre Blvd Fairfield (45014) *(G-7354)*
Dixon Valve & Coupling Co LLC................................... 330 425-3000
    1900 Enterprise Pkwy Twinsburg (44087) *(G-14652)*
Diy Holster, Elyria *Also Called: Diy Holster LLC (G-7132)*
Diy Holster LLC.. 419 921-2168
    781 Finwood Ct Elyria (44035) *(G-7132)*
Dj S Weld... 330 432-2206
    424 N Main St Uhrichsville (44683) *(G-14764)*
DJ Signs MD LLC... 330 344-6643
    224 W Exchange St Ste 290 Akron (44302) *(G-131)*
DJM Plastics Ltd... 419 424-5250
    1530 Harvard Ave Findlay (45840) *(G-7502)*
Djmc Partners Inc.. 614 890-3821
    654 Brooksedge Blvd Ste A Westerville (43081) *(G-15702)*
Djsc Inc... 740 928-2697
    1001 O Neill Dr Hebron (43025) *(G-8340)*
DK Bicycles, Springboro *Also Called: Safe Haven Brands LLC (G-13519)*
DK Manfcturing Frazeysburg Inc (HQ)........................... 740 828-3291
    119 W 2nd St Frazeysburg (43822) *(G-7715)*
DK Manufacturing, Frazeysburg *Also Called: DK Manfcturing Frazeysburg Inc (G-7715)*
DK Manufacturing Lancaster Inc.................................. 740 654-5566
    2118 Commerce St Lancaster (43130) *(G-9014)*
DL Schwartz Co LLC.. 260 692-1464
    9737 State Route 49 Hicksville (43526) *(G-8373)*
Dla Document Services.. 937 257-6014
    4165 Communications Blvd, Ste 2, Bldg 281, Door 18 Dayton (45433) *(G-6159)*
DLAC Industries Inc... 330 519-4789
    3755 Sugarbush Dr Canfield (44406) *(G-2004)*
Dlg Woodworks & Finishing Inc................................... 513 649-1245
    330 Industry Dr Franklin (45005) *(G-7670)*
Dlh Enterprises LLC... 330 253-6960
    2086 Romig Rd Ste 2 Akron (44320) *(G-132)*
Dlhbowles, Inc., Canton *Also Called: ABC Technologies Dlhb Inc (G-2026)*
DLM Plastics, Findlay *Also Called: DJM Plastics Ltd (G-7502)*
Dlz Ohio Inc (HQ).. 614 888-0040
    6121 Huntley Rd Columbus (43229) *(G-5332)*
DM Machine Co... 440 946-0771
    38338 Apollo Pkwy Ste 1a Willoughby (44094) *(G-15908)*
Dm Pallet Service, Columbus *Also Called: Ohio Wood Recycling Inc (G-5631)*
DM Pallet Service Inc... 614 491-0881
    2019 Rathmell Rd Columbus (43207) *(G-5333)*
Dm2018 LLC... 513 893-5483
    4805 Hamilton Middletown Rd Ste A Liberty Twp (45011) *(G-9214)*
Dmax, Moraine *Also Called: Dmax Ltd (G-11172)*
Dmax Ltd (DH).. 937 425-9700
    3100 Dryden Rd Moraine (45439) *(G-11172)*
Dmg Mori... 513 808-4842
    300 E Business Way Ste 200 Cincinnati (45241) *(G-2835)*
Dmg Mori Usa Inc.. 440 546-7088
    9415 Meridian Way West Chester (45069) *(G-15414)*
DMG Tool & Die LLC... 937 407-0810
    1215 S Greenwood St Bellefontaine (43311) *(G-1207)*
Dmi Manufacturing Inc.. 800 238-5384
    7177 Industrial Park Blvd Mentor (44060) *(G-10448)*
Dmi Manufacturing Inc.. 440 975-8645
    4780 Beidler Rd Willoughby (44094) *(G-15909)*
Dmk Industries Inc.. 513 727-4549
    1801 Made Dr Middletown (45044) *(G-10818)*
Dms Inc... 440 951-9838
    37121 Euclid Ave Ste 1 Willoughby (44094) *(G-15910)*
DMV Corporation... 740 452-4787
    1024 Military Rd Zanesville (43701) *(G-16526)*
DNC Hydraulics LLC.. 419 963-2800
    5219 County Road 313 Rawson (45881) *(G-12743)*
Dnd Emulsions Inc... 419 525-4988
    270 Park Ave E Mansfield (44902) *(G-9646)*
Dnh Mixing Inc.. 330 296-6327
    3939a Mogadore Industrial Pkwy Mogadore (44260) *(G-11069)*
Dno Inc... 614 231-3601
    3650 E 5th Ave Columbus (43219) *(G-5334)*
Do 210, Cleveland *Also Called: Euclid Media Group LLC (G-4035)*
Do All Sheet Metal, New Albany *Also Called: Custom Metal Products Inc (G-11376)*
Do Duds, Kent *Also Called: Embroidery Network Inc (G-8813)*
Do It Best, Caldwell *Also Called: Caldwell Lumber & Supply Co (G-1908)*
Do It Best, Cincinnati *Also Called: Hyde Park Lumber Company (G-3013)*
Do It Best, Sidney *Also Called: Lochard Inc (G-13261)*
Doak Laser.. 740 374-0090
    2801 Waterford Rd Marietta (45750) *(G-9790)*
Doan/Pyramid Solutions LLC....................................... 216 587-9510
    5069 Corbin Dr Cleveland (44128) *(G-3965)*
Docmann Printing & Assoc Inc..................................... 440 975-1775
    5275 Naiman Pkwy Ste E Solon (44139) *(G-13338)*
Document Concepts Inc... 330 575-5685
    607 S Main St # A North Canton (44720) *(G-11723)*
Docustar, Cincinnati *Also Called: Vya Inc (G-3506)*
Dodge Company, Dayton *Also Called: Ronald T Dodge Co (G-6552)*
Dofasco Tubular Products.. 419 342-1371
    132 W Main St Shelby (44875) *(G-13194)*
Dolana Group LLC.. 440 622-8615
    8870 Darrow Rd Ste F104 Twinsburg (44087) *(G-14653)*

Dole

Dole, Springfield *Also Called: Dole Fresh Vegetables Inc (G-13556)*

Dole Fresh Vegetables Inc..937 525-4300
600 Benjamin Dr Springfield (45502) *(G-13556)*

Doling & Assoc Dntl Lab Inc..937 254-0075
3318 Successful Way Dayton (45414) *(G-6300)*

Doll Inc..419 586-7880
1901 Havemann Rd Celina (45822) *(G-2329)*

Doll Printing, Celina *Also Called: Doll Inc (G-2329)*

Dollars N Cent Inc..971 381-0406
1057 S Belvoir Blvd Cleveland (44121) *(G-3966)*

Dom Tube Corp..412 299-2616
640 Keystone St Alliance (44601) *(G-402)*

Dome Drilling Company (PA)..440 892-9434
2001 Crocker Rd Ste 420 Westlake (44145) *(G-15746)*

Dome Resources, Westlake *Also Called: Dome Drilling Company (G-15746)*

Domestic Casting Company LLC..717 532-6615
620 Liberty Rd Delaware (43015) *(G-6718)*

Dometic Sanitation, Big Prairie *Also Called: Dometic Sanitation Corporation (G-1328)*

Dometic Sanitation Corporation..330 439-5550
13128 State Route 226 Big Prairie (44611) *(G-1328)*

Dominion Enterprises..216 472-1870
26301 Curtiss Wright Pkwy Cleveland (44143) *(G-3967)*

Dominion Liquid Tech LLC..513 272-2824
3965 Virginia Ave Cincinnati (45227) *(G-2836)*

Domino Foods Inc..216 432-3222
2075 E 65th St Cleveland (44103) *(G-3968)*

Domino Sugar, Cleveland *Also Called: Domino Foods Inc (G-3968)*

Domtar Corporation...937 859-8262
820 S Alex Rd West Carrollton (45449) *(G-15352)*

Domtar Corporation...937 859-8261
1030 W Alex Bell Rd West Carrollton (45449) *(G-15353)*

Domtar Paper Company LLC..740 333-0003
1803 Lowes Blvd Wshngtn Ct Hs (43160) *(G-16229)*

Don Basch Jewelers Inc..330 467-2116
8210 Macedonia Commons Blvd Unit 36 Macedonia (44056) *(G-9547)*

Don Puckett Lumber Inc..740 887-4191
31263 Beech Grove Rd Londonderry (45647) *(G-9398)*

Don Wartko Construction Co...330 673-5252
975 Tallmadge Rd Kent (44240) *(G-8810)*

Don-Ell Corporation (PA)..419 841-7114
8450 Central Ave Sylvania (43560) *(G-13993)*

Don-Ell Corporation..419 841-7114
8456 Central Ave Sylvania (43560) *(G-13994)*

Donahue's Hilltop Supply, Cambridge *Also Called: Donohues Hilltop Ice Co Ltd (G-1933)*

Donald E Didion II..419 483-2226
1027b County Road 308 Bellevue (44811) *(G-1226)*

Donald E Dornon...740 926-9144
44592 Game Ridge Rd Beallsville (43716) *(G-1034)*

Done-Rite Bowling Service Co (PA)...................................440 232-3280
20434 Krick Rd Bedford (44146) *(G-1118)*

Dongan Electric Mfg Co..419 737-2304
500 Cedar St Pioneer (43554) *(G-12491)*

Donlon Manufacturing LLC...847 437-7360
10680 Springhill Dr Brecksville (44141) *(G-1614)*

Donohues Hilltop Ice Co Ltd...740 432-3348
1112 Highland Ave Cambridge (43725) *(G-1933)*

Donprint Inc..847 573-7777
17700 Foltz Pkwy Strongsville (44149) *(G-13828)*

Donut Place Kings Inc...937 829-9725
100 N James H Mcgee Blvd Dayton (45402) *(G-6301)*

Door Engineering and Mfg, Cincinnati *Also Called: Senneca Holdings Inc (G-3380)*

Door Fabrication Services Inc...937 454-9207
3250 Old Springfield Rd Ste 1 Vandalia (45377) *(G-14938)*

Doors Unlimited, Bridgeport *Also Called: Jerry Harolds Doors Unlimited (G-1647)*

Doran Manufacturing Co., Blue Ash *Also Called: Osborne Coinage Company LLC (G-1448)*

Doran Mfg LLC...866 816-7233
4362 Glendale Milford Rd Blue Ash (45242) *(G-1385)*

Dorel Home Furnishings Inc...419 447-7448
458 2nd Ave Tiffin (44883) *(G-14083)*

Dorex LLC..216 271-7064
4420 Gamma Ave Newburgh Heights (44105) *(G-11613)*

Doris Kimble..330 343-1226
3596 State Route 39 Nw Dover (44622) *(G-6816)*

Dorn Color LLC..216 634-2252
11555 Berea Rd Cleveland (44102) *(G-3969)*

Dosmatic USA Inc (PA)..972 245-9765
3798 Round Bottom Rd Cincinnati (45244) *(G-2837)*

Dotcentral LLC..330 809-0112
1650 Deerford Ave Sw Massillon (44647) *(G-10090)*

Double D D Mtls Instllation In, Dayton *Also Called: Double D D Mtls Instlition Inc (G-6302)*

Double D D Mtls Instlition Inc...937 898-2534
7733 N Main St Dayton (45415) *(G-6302)*

Double Dippin Inc..937 847-2572
949 Blanche Dr Miamisburg (45342) *(G-10636)*

Double Eagle Golf, Lima *Also Called: Lima Armature Works Inc (G-9261)*

Doubleday Acquisitions LLC (PA)......................................513 360-7189
675 Gateway Blvd Monroe (45050) *(G-11104)*

Doug Marine Motors Inc..740 335-3700
1120 Clinton Ave Wshngtn Ct Hs (43160) *(G-16230)*

Douglas W & B C Richardson..440 247-5262
62 Wychwood Dr Chagrin Falls (44022) *(G-2373)*

Douthit Communications Inc..419 855-7465
1550 Woodville Rd Millbury (43447) *(G-10930)*

Douthit Communications Inc (PA).....................................419 625-6625
520 Warren St Sandusky (44870) *(G-13051)*

Dove Die and Stamping Company.....................................216 267-3720
15665 Brookpark Rd Cleveland (44142) *(G-3970)*

Dover Cabinet Industries Inc...330 343-9074
1568 State Route 39 Nw Dover (44622) *(G-6817)*

Dover Chemical Corporation (HQ)....................................330 343-7711
3676 Davis Rd Nw Dover (44622) *(G-6818)*

Dover Conveyor Inc..740 922-9390
3323 Brightwood Rd Midvale (44653) *(G-10876)*

Dover Corporation..513 870-3206
9393 Princeton Glendale Rd West Chester (45011) *(G-15415)*

Dover Cryogenics, Midvale *Also Called: Amko Service Company (G-10875)*

Dover Fabrication and Burn Inc (HQ)................................330 339-1057
2996 Progress St Dover (44622) *(G-6819)*

Dover High Prfmce Plas Inc...330 343-3477
140 Williams Dr Nw Dover (44622) *(G-6820)*

Dover Machine Co..330 343-4123
2208 State Route 516 Nw Dover (44622) *(G-6821)*

Dover Phila Heating & Cooling, Dover *Also Called: Hvac Inc (G-6827)*

Dover Tank and Plate Company..330 343-4443
5725 Crown Rd Nw Dover (44622) *(G-6822)*

Dover Wipes Company..513 983-1100
1 Procter And Gamble Plz Cincinnati (45202) *(G-2838)*

Dow Cameron Oil & Gas LLC..740 452-1568
5555 Eden Park Dr Zanesville (43701) *(G-16527)*

Dow Chemical, Hebron *Also Called: Transcendia Inc (G-8367)*

Dow Jones, Bowling Green *Also Called: Dow Jones & Company Inc (G-1563)*

Dow Jones & Company Inc..419 352-4696
1100 Brim Rd Bowling Green (43402) *(G-1563)*

Dowa Tht America Inc..419 354-4144
2130 S Woodland Cir Bowling Green (43402) *(G-1564)*

Dowco LLC..330 773-6654
1374 Markle St Akron (44306) *(G-133)*

Dowel Yoder & Molding...330 231-2962
4754 Township Road 613 Fredericksburg (44627) *(G-7723)*

Down Decor, Cincinnati *Also Called: Downhome Inc (G-2840)*

Down Decor Ohio Feather, Cincinnati *Also Called: Downhome Inc (G-2839)*

Down Home...740 393-1186
9 N Main St Mount Vernon (43050) *(G-11271)*

Down Home Leather, Mount Vernon *Also Called: Down Home (G-11271)*

Down-Lite International Inc (PA)......................................513 229-3696
8153 Duke Blvd Mason (45040) *(G-9985)*

Downhome Inc..513 921-3373
1910 South St Cincinnati (45204) *(G-2839)*

Downhome Inc (PA)...513 921-3373
1 Kovach Dr Cincinnati (45215) *(G-2840)*

Downing Enterprises Inc...330 666-3888
1287 Centerview Cir Copley (44321) *(G-5948)*

ALPHABETIC SECTION

Downing Exhibits, Copley *Also Called: Downing Enterprises Inc (G-5948)*
Downlite, Mason *Also Called: Down-Lite International Inc (G-9985)*
Doxie Inc.. 937 427-3431
3197 Beaver Vu Dr Dayton (45434) *(G-6160)*
Doyle Manufacturing Inc.. 419 865-2548
1440 Holloway Rd Holland (43528) *(G-8505)*
Doyle Systems, Norton *Also Called: J E Doyle Company (G-11945)*
DP Assembly LLC.. 740 225-4591
113 N Franklin St Richwood (43344) *(G-12814)*
Dpsciences, Cincinnati *Also Called: Data Processing Sciences Corporation (G-2820)*
Dr Dave Solutions LLC... 614 219-6543
6233 Riverside Dr Dublin (43017) *(G-6880)*
Dr JS Print Shop Ltd... 513 571-6553
21 East Ave Monroe (45050) *(G-11105)*
Dr Pepper, Lima *Also Called: Dr Pepper Snapple Group (G-9237)*
Dr Pepper, Youngstown *Also Called: Dr Pepper Bottlers Associates (G-16351)*
Dr Pepper, Zanesville *Also Called: Dr Pepper Bottling Company (G-16528)*
Dr Pepper Bottlers Associates.................................. 330 746-7651
500 Pepsi Pl Youngstown (44502) *(G-16351)*
Dr Pepper Bottling Company.................................... 740 452-2721
335 N 6th St Zanesville (43701) *(G-16528)*
Dr Pepper Snapple Group.. 419 223-0072
2480 Saint Johns Rd Lima (45804) *(G-9237)*
Dr Pepper/Seven Up Inc... 513 875-2466
3943 Us Highway 50 Fayetteville (45118) *(G-7465)*
Dr Pepper/Seven Up Inc... 419 229-7777
2350 Central Point Pkwy Lima (45804) *(G-9238)*
Dr Z Amplification, Maple Heights *Also Called: Dr Z Amps Inc (G-9751)*
Dr Z Amps Inc... 216 475-1444
17011 Broadway Ave Maple Heights (44137) *(G-9751)*
Dr. Pepper 7 Up Columbus, Columbus *Also Called: American Bottling Company (G-5120)*
Drabik Manufacturing Inc.. 216 267-1616
15601 Commerce Park Dr Cleveland (44142) *(G-3971)*
Dracool, Franklin *Also Called: Dracool-Usa Inc (G-7671)*
Dracool-Usa Inc (PA).. 937 743-5899
331 Industrial Dr Franklin (45005) *(G-7671)*
Dragon Products LLC... 330 345-3968
3310 Columbus Rd Wooster (44691) *(G-16114)*
Dragonfly Cstm Fabrication LLC............................... 614 522-9618
179 Malloy Ln Blacklick (43004) *(G-1336)*
Dragoon Technologies Inc (PA)................................ 937 439-9223
900 Senate Dr Dayton (45459) *(G-6303)*
Dragoonitcn, Dayton *Also Called: Dragoon Technologies Inc (G-6303)*
Drainage Pipe & Fittings LLC................................... 419 538-6337
450 Tile Company St Ottawa (45875) *(G-12179)*
Drainage Products Inc... 419 622-6951
100 Main St Haviland (45851) *(G-8310)*
Drake Brothers Ltd... 415 819-4941
1215 Forsythe Ave Columbus (43201) *(G-5335)*
Drake Manufacturing, Warren *Also Called: Drake Manufacturing LLC (G-15163)*
Drake Manufacturing LLC.. 330 847-7291
4371 N Leavitt Rd Nw Warren (44485) *(G-15163)*
Drake Manufacturing Services Co........................... 330 847-7291
4371 N Leavitt Rd Nw Warren (44485) *(G-15164)*
Drapery Stitch, Cleveland *Also Called: Cleveland Drapery Stitch Inc (G-3838)*
Drapery Stitch, Delphos *Also Called: Drapery Stitch of Delphos (G-6763)*
Drapery Stitch of Delphos.. 419 692-3921
50 Summers Ln Delphos (45833) *(G-6763)*
Drapery Sttch - Cincinnati Inc.................................. 513 561-2443
5601 Wooster Pike Cincinnati (45227) *(G-2841)*
Drb Holdings LLC... 330 645-3299
3245 Pickle Rd Akron (44312) *(G-134)*
Drb Systems LLC (HQ)... 330 645-3299
3245 Pickle Rd Akron (44312) *(G-135)*
Drb Tunnel Solutions, Akron *Also Called: Drb Systems LLC (G-135)*
Drc Acquisition Inc... 330 656-1600
10200 Wellman Rd Streetsboro (44241) *(G-13767)*
Dreamscape Media, Holland *Also Called: Dreamscape Media LLC (G-8506)*
Dreamscape Media LLC.. 877 983-7326
1417 Timber Wolf Dr Holland (43528) *(G-8506)*

Dreco Inc.. 440 327-6021
7887 Root Rd North Ridgeville (44039) *(G-11838)*
Dredger LLC.. 513 507-8774
5698 Sage Meadow Ct West Chester (45069) *(G-15416)*
Dreison International Inc (PA).................................. 216 362-0755
4540 W 160th St Cleveland (44135) *(G-3972)*
Dri Rubber, Coldwater *Also Called: Deruijter Intl USA Inc (G-4986)*
Dribble Creek Inc.. 440 439-8650
8333 Boyle Pkwy Twinsburg (44087) *(G-14654)*
Drifter Marine Inc.. 419 666-8144
28271 Cedar Park Blvd Ste 6 Perrysburg (43551) *(G-12377)*
Drink Modern Technologies LLC.............................. 216 577-1536
4125 Lorain Ave 2nd Fl Cleveland (44113) *(G-3973)*
Drive Components LLC... 440 234-6200
19668 Progress Dr Strongsville (44149) *(G-13829)*
Driveline 1 Inc... 614 279-7734
1369 Frank Rd Columbus (43223) *(G-5336)*
Drivetrain USA Inc.. 614 733-0940
8445 Rausch Dr Plain City (43064) *(G-12576)*
Drj Welding Services LLC....................................... 740 229-7428
936 Front Ave Sw New Philadelphia (44663) *(G-11499)*
Drone Express Inc (PA).. 513 577-5152
123 Webster St Dayton (45402) *(G-6304)*
Drr USA, Brunswick *Also Called: L & R Racing Inc (G-1773)*
Drs Advanced Isr LLC (DH).................................... 937 429-7408
2601 Mission Point Blvd Ste 250 Beavercreek (45431) *(G-1046)*
Drs Leonardo Inc.. 937 429-7408
2601 Mission Point Blvd Ste 250 Beavercreek (45431) *(G-1047)*
Drs Leonardo Inc.. 513 943-1111
4043 Mcmann Rd Cincinnati (45245) *(G-2557)*
Drs Signal Technologies Inc................................... 937 429-7470
4393 Dayton Xenia Rd Beavercreek (45432) *(G-1048)*
Drt, Dayton *Also Called: Drt Mfg Co LLC (G-6307)*
Drt Aerospace LLC (HQ).. 937 492-6121
1950 Campbell Rd Sidney (45365) *(G-13242)*
Drt Holdings Inc (PA).. 937 298-7391
618 Greenmount Blvd Dayton (45419) *(G-6305)*
Drt Holdings LLC.. 937 297-6676
9025 Centre Pointe Dr Ste 120 West Chester (45069) *(G-15417)*
Drt Mfg Co LLC... 937 298-7391
618 Greenmount Blvd Dayton (45419) *(G-6306)*
Drt Mfg Co LLC (HQ).. 937 297-6670
4201 Little York Rd Dayton (45414) *(G-6307)*
Drt Precision Mfg LLC (HQ)................................... 937 507-4308
1985 Campbell Rd Sidney (45365) *(G-13243)*
Drum Parts, Cleveland *Also Called: Group Industries Inc (G-4152)*
Drum Parts Inc... 216 271-0702
7580 Garfield Blvd Cleveland (44125) *(G-3974)*
Drummond Corporation.. 440 834-9660
14990 Berkshire Industrial Pkwy Middlefield (44062) *(G-10748)*
Drummond Dolomite Inc... 440 942-7000
7954 Reynolds Rd Mentor (44060) *(G-10449)*
Drummond Dolomite Quarry, Mentor *Also Called: Drummond Dolomite Inc (G-10449)*
Drycal Inc... 440 974-1999
7355 Production Dr Mentor (44060) *(G-10450)*
Dryden Shafts LLC... 937 365-7420
3249 Dryden Rd Moraine (45439) *(G-11173)*
DS Techstar Inc.. 419 424-0888
1219 W Main Cross St Ste 204 Findlay (45840) *(G-7503)*
Ds Welding LLC.. 330 893-4049
3982 State Route 39 Millersburg (44654) *(G-10953)*
Ds World LLC... 925 200-4985
4652 Lakes Edge Apt 5 West Chester (45069) *(G-15418)*
DSC Supply Company LLC..................................... 614 891-1100
237 E Broadway Ave Ste A Westerville (43081) *(G-15703)*
Dsg-Canusa, Loveland *Also Called: Mattr US Inc (G-9495)*
Dsk Imaging LLC.. 513 554-1797
6839 Ashfield Dr Blue Ash (45242) *(G-1386)*
DSM Industries Inc... 440 585-1100
1340 E 289th St Wickliffe (44092) *(G-15831)*
Dss Installations Ltd... 513 761-7000
6721 Montgomery Rd Ste 1 Cincinnati (45236) *(G-2842)*

(PA)=Parent Co (HQ)=Headquarters (DH)=Div Headquarters

Dss/Drect Tv/Rfs/Ms/rmediation, Cincinnati Also Called: Dss Installations Ltd (G-2842)

Dswdwk LLC 513 853-5021
4831 Spring Grove Ave Cincinnati (45232) (G-2843)

DTE Inc 419 522-3428
110 Baird Pkwy Mansfield (44903) (G-9647)

Dti, Alliance Also Called: Davis Technologies Inc (G-401)

DTR Equipment Inc 419 692-3000
1430 N Main St Delphos (45833) (G-6764)

Dualite Inc (PA) 513 724-7100
1 Dualite Ln Williamsburg (45176) (G-15864)

Dublin Embroiderer Inc 614 789-1898
7215 Sawmill Rd Ste 50 Dublin (43016) (G-6881)

Dublin Millwork Co Inc 614 889-7776
7575 Fishel Dr S Dublin (43016) (G-6882)

Dublin Plastics Inc 216 641-5904
9202 Reno Ave Cleveland (44105) (G-3975)

Dubose Nat Enrgy Fas McHned PR 216 362-1700
18737 Sheldon Rd Middleburg Heights (44130) (G-10718)

Dubose Strapping Inc 419 221-0626
1221 Stewart Rd Lima (45801) (G-9239)

Duca Manufacturing & Consulting Inc (PA) 330 758-0828
761 Mcclurg Rd Youngstown (44512) (G-16352)

Duca Mfg & Consulting Inc 330 726-7175
697 Mcclurg Rd Youngstown (44512) (G-16353)

Duco Tool & Die Inc 419 628-2031
19 S Main St Minster (45865) (G-11050)

Duct Fabricators Inc 216 391-2400
883 Addison Rd Cleveland (44103) (G-3976)

Ducts Inc 216 391-2400
883 Addison Rd Cleveland (44103) (G-3977)

Dudick Inc 330 562-1970
1818 Miller Pkwy Streetsboro (44241) (G-13768)

Duff Quarry, Huntsville Also Called: Duff Quarry Inc (G-8622)

Duff Quarry Inc 419 273-2518
3798 State Route 53 Forest (45843) (G-7591)

Duff Quarry Inc (PA) 937 686-2811
9042 State Route 117 Huntsville (43324) (G-8622)

Duffee Finishing Inc 740 965-4848
4860 N County Line Rd Sunbury (43074) (G-13952)

Dugan Drilling Inc 740 668-3811
27238 New Guilford Rd Walhonding (43843) (G-15092)

Duke Graphics Inc 440 946-0606
33212 Lakeland Blvd Willoughby (44095) (G-15911)

Duke Manufacturing Inc 440 942-6537
38205 Western Pkwy Willoughby (44094) (G-15912)

Duke Printing, Willoughby Also Called: Duke Graphics Inc (G-15911)

Dukes Aerospace Inc 818 998-9811
313 Gillett St Painesville (44077) (G-12229)

Duma Meats Inc 330 628-3438
857 Randolph Rd Mogadore (44260) (G-11070)

Dumas Deer Processing LLC 330 805-3429
831 Waterloo Rd Mogadore (44260) (G-11071)

Duncan Press Corporation 330 477-4529
5122 Strausser St Nw North Canton (44720) (G-11724)

Duncan Tool Inc 937 667-9364
9790 Julie Ct Tipp City (45371) (G-14132)

Dunham Machine Inc 216 398-4500
1311 E Schaaf Rd Bldg A Independence (44131) (G-8663)

Dunham Products Inc 440 232-0885
7400 Northfield Rd Walton Hills (44146) (G-15098)

Dunkelberger Fuel LLC 513 726-1999
2304 Somerville Rd Somerville (45064) (G-13452)

Dunkin' Donuts, Solon Also Called: Dandi Enterprises Inc (G-13336)

Dunn Industrial Services 513 738-4999
5009 Cincinnati Brookville Rd Hamilton (45013) (G-8200)

Dunstone Company Inc 704 841-1380
17930 Great Lakes Pkwy Hiram (44234) (G-8481)

Duo-Corp 330 549-2149
280 Miley Rd North Lima (44452) (G-11804)

Duplex Mill & Manufacturing Co 937 325-5555
415 Sigler St Springfield (45506) (G-13557)

Dupli-Systems Inc 440 234-9415
8260 Dow Cir Strongsville (44136) (G-13830)

Dupont 740 412-9752
15804 Matville Rd Orient (43146) (G-12114)

Dupont, Avon Also Called: Eidp Inc (G-772)

Dupont, Circleville Also Called: Dupont Specialty Pdts USA LLC (G-3548)

Dupont Electronic Polymers LP 937 268-3411
1515 Nicholas Rd Dayton (45417) (G-6308)

Dupont Specialty Pdts USA LLC 740 474-0635
800 Dupont Rd Circleville (43113) (G-3547)

Dupont Specialty Pdts USA LLC 740 474-0220
Rt 23 S Dupont Rd Circleville (43113) (G-3548)

Dupont Specialty Pdts USA LLC 216 901-3600
6200 Hillcrest Dr Cleveland (44125) (G-3978)

Dupont Vespel Parts and Shapes, Circleville Also Called: Dupont Specialty Pdts USA LLC (G-3547)

Dupont Vespel Parts and Shapes, Cleveland Also Called: Dupont Specialty Pdts USA LLC (G-3978)

Dupps, Germantown Also Called: The Dupps Company (G-7953)

Dura Magnetics Inc 419 882-0591
5500 Schultz Dr Sylvania (43560) (G-13995)

Dura-Line Corporation 440 322-1000
860 Garden St Elyria (44035) (G-7133)

DURA-LINE CORPORATION, Elyria Also Called: Dura-Line Corporation (G-7133)

Dura-Line Services LLC 440 322-1000
669 Sugar Ln Elyria (44035) (G-7134)

Durable Corporation 800 537-1603
75 N Pleasant St Norwalk (44857) (G-11962)

Durable Plating Co 216 391-2132
4404 Saint Clair Ave Cleveland (44103) (G-3979)

Duracoat Powder Finishing Inc (PA) 419 636-3111
1012 E Wilson St Bryan (43506) (G-1816)

Duracorp LLC (PA) 740 549-3336
7787 Graphics Way Lewis Center (43035) (G-9158)

Duracote Corporation 330 296-9600
350 N Diamond St Ravenna (44266) (G-12712)

Duraflow Industries Inc 440 965-5047
15706 Garfield Rd Wakeman (44889) (G-15074)

Duramax Global Corp 440 834-5400
17990 Great Lakes Pkwy Hiram (44234) (G-8482)

Duramax Marine, Hiram Also Called: Duramax Global Corp (G-8482)

Duramax Marine LLC 440 834-5400
17990 Great Lakes Pkwy Hiram (44234) (G-8483)

Durango Boot, Nelsonville Also Called: Georgia-Boot Inc (G-11356)

Durashield, Urbana Also Called: American Pan Company (G-14825)

Duray Machine Company Inc 440 277-4119
400 Ravenglass Blvd Amherst (44001) (G-475)

Duray Plating Company Inc 216 941-5540
13701 Triskett Rd Cleveland (44111) (G-3980)

Dure Foods Us LLC 614 409-9030
6967 Alum Creek Dr Columbus (43217) (G-5337)

Durez, Kenton Also Called: Durez Corporation (G-8882)

Durez Corporation 567 295-6400
13717 Us Highway 68 Kenton (43326) (G-8882)

Durivage Pattern and Mfg Inc 419 836-8655
20522 State Route 579 W Williston (43468) (G-15870)

Duro Dyne Midwest Corp 513 870-6000
3825 Symmes Rd Hamilton (45015) (G-8201)

Durox Company 440 238-5350
12312 Alameda Dr Strongsville (44149) (G-13831)

DUrso Bakery Inc 330 652-4741
212 S Cedar Ave Niles (44446) (G-11667)

Dusty Ductz LLC 317 462-9622
518 Terrace Creek Ct Lebanon (45036) (G-9070)

Dutch Country Kettles Ltd 937 780-6718
6732 Pavey Rd Leesburg (45135) (G-9124)

Dutch Heritage Woodcraft 330 893-2211
4363 State Route 39 Berlin (44610) (G-1306)

Dutch Quality Stone Inc 877 359-7866
18012 Dover Rd Mount Eaton (44659) (G-11229)

Dutch Valley Woodworking Inc 330 852-4319
State Rte 39 Sugarcreek (44681) (G-13923)

Dutchcraft Truss Component Inc 330 862-2220
  2212 Fox Ave Se Minerva (44657) *(G-11030)*

Duvall Woodworking Inc 419 878-9581
  7551 Dutch Rd Waterville (43566) *(G-15242)*

Dvuv LLC 216 741-5511
  4641 Hinckley Industrial Pkwy Cleveland (44109) *(G-3981)*

DW Hercules LLC 330 830-2498
  2770 Erie St S Massillon (44646) *(G-10091)*

Dwayne Bennett Industries 440 466-5724
  6708 N Ridge Rd W Geneva (44041) *(G-7934)*

Dwd2 Inc 513 563-0070
  10200 Wayne Ave Cincinnati (45215) *(G-2844)*

Dwyer Companies Inc (PA) 513 777-0998
  6083 Schumacher Park Dr West Chester (45069) *(G-15419)*

Dwyer Concrete Lifting, West Chester Also Called: Dwyer Companies Inc *(G-15419)*

Dybrook Products Inc 330 392-7665
  5232 Tod Ave Sw Ste 23 Warren (44481) *(G-15165)*

Dyco Manufacturing Inc 419 485-5525
  12708 State Route 576 Montpelier (43543) *(G-11137)*

Dyenamo Distributing LLC 419 462-9474
  6124 State Route 19 Galion (44833) *(G-7870)*

Dyna-Flex Inc 440 946-9424
  1000 Bacon Rd Painesville (44077) *(G-12230)*

Dyna-Vac Plastics Inc 937 773-0092
  921 S Downing St Piqua (45356) *(G-12514)*

Dynalab Ems Inc 614 866-9999
  555 Lancaster Ave Reynoldsburg (43068) *(G-12762)*

Dynalab Ff Inc 614 866-9999
  555 Lancaster Ave Reynoldsburg (43068) *(G-12763)*

Dynalab Inc (PA) 614 866-9999
  555 Lancaster Ave Reynoldsburg (43068) *(G-12764)*

Dynamat, Hamilton Also Called: Dynamat Inc *(G-8202)*

Dynamat Inc (PA) 513 860-5094
  3042 Symmes Rd Hamilton (45015) *(G-8202)*

Dynamic Control, Hamilton Also Called: Dynamic Control North Amer Inc *(G-8203)*

Dynamic Control North Amer Inc (PA) 513 860-5094
  3042 Symmes Rd Hamilton (45015) *(G-8203)*

Dynamic Design & Systems Inc 440 708-1010
  7639 Washington St Chagrin Falls (44023) *(G-2393)*

Dynamic Dies Inc 513 705-9524
  1310 Hook Dr Middletown (45042) *(G-10819)*

Dynamic Dies Inc (PA) 419 865-0249
  1705 Commerce Rd Holland (43528) *(G-8507)*

Dynamic Industries Inc 513 861-6767
  3611 Woodburn Ave Cincinnati (45207) *(G-2845)*

Dynamic Machine Works 419 564-7925
  139 Illinois Ave S Mansfield (44905) *(G-9648)*

Dynamic Plastics Inc 937 437-7261
  8207 H W Rd New Paris (45347) *(G-11481)*

Dynamic Tool & Mold Inc 440 237-8665
  12126 York Rd Unit N Cleveland (44133) *(G-3982)*

Dynamic Weld, Osgood Also Called: Dynamic Weld Corporation *(G-12173)*

Dynamic Weld Corporation 419 582-2900
  242 N St Osgood (45351) *(G-12173)*

Dynamp, Grove City Also Called: Dynamp LLC *(G-8089)*

Dynamp LLC 614 871-6900
  3735 Gantz Rd Ste D Grove City (43123) *(G-8089)*

Dynapoint Technologies Inc 937 859-5193
  475 Progress Rd Dayton (45449) *(G-6309)*

Dynatech Systems Inc 440 365-1774
  161 Reaser Ct Elyria (44035) *(G-7135)*

Dyneon LLC 859 334-4500
  2165 Cablecar Ct Cincinnati (45244) *(G-2846)*

Dynus Technologies, Cincinnati Also Called: Cbst Acquisition LLC *(G-2711)*

Dyoung Enterprise Inc 440 918-0505
  38241 Willoughby Pkwy Willoughby (44094) *(G-15913)*

Dysinger Incorporated (PA) 937 297-7761
  4316 Webster St Dayton (45414) *(G-6310)*

E - I Corp 614 899-2282
  214 Hoff Rd Unit M Westerville (43082) *(G-15654)*

E & E Nameplates Inc 419 468-3617
  760 E Walnut St Galion (44833) *(G-7871)*

E & E Parts Machining, Strongsville Also Called: Stefra Inc *(G-13885)*

E & I, Westerville Also Called: McNish Corporation *(G-15667)*

E & J Demark Inc 419 337-5866
  1115 N Ottokee St Wauseon (43567) *(G-15260)*

E & J Gallo Winery 513 381-4050
  125 E Court St Cincinnati (45202) *(G-2847)*

E & K Products Co Inc 216 631-2510
  3520 Cesko Ave Cleveland (44109) *(G-3983)*

E & M Liberty Welding Inc 330 866-2338
  141 James St Waynesburg (44688) *(G-15294)*

E & R Welding Inc 440 329-9387
  32 South St Berlin Heights (44814) *(G-1313)*

E A Cox Inc 740 858-4400
  11201 State Route 104 Lucasville (45648) *(G-9522)*

E B P Inc 216 241-2550
  29125 Hall St Solon (44139) *(G-13339)*

E Bee Printing Inc 614 224-0416
  70 S 4th St Columbus (43215) *(G-5338)*

E C Babbert Inc 614 837-8444
  7415 Diley Rd Canal Winchester (43110) *(G-1985)*

E C E, Holland Also Called: Electronic Concepts Engrg Inc *(G-8509)*

E C S Corp 440 323-1707
  8015 Murray Ridge Rd Elyria (44035) *(G-7136)*

E C Shaw Company of Ohio 513 721-6334
  1242 Mehring Way Cincinnati (45203) *(G-2848)*

E D I, Belpre Also Called: Electrnic Dsign For Indust Inc *(G-1252)*

E D M Fastar Inc 216 676-0100
  13410 Enterprise Ave Cleveland (44135) *(G-3984)*

E D M Star-One Inc 440 647-0600
  6831 Ridge Rd Wadsworth (44281) *(G-15027)*

E H T Company, Euclid Also Called: Euclid Heat Treating Co *(G-7269)*

E I Ceramics LLC 513 772-7001
  2600 Commerce Blvd Cincinnati (45241) *(G-2849)*

E J Skok Industries (PA) 216 292-7533
  26901 Richmond Rd Bedford (44146) *(G-1119)*

E L Mustee & Sons Inc (PA) 216 267-3100
  5431 W 164th St Brookpark (44142) *(G-1713)*

E L Stone Company 330 825-4565
  2998 Eastern Rd Norton (44203) *(G-11941)*

E M E C, Marysville Also Called: Engineered Mfg & Eqp Co *(G-9908)*

E M I, Cleveland Also Called: Equipment Mfrs Intl Inc *(G-4026)*

E M I Plastic Equipment, Jackson Center Also Called: EMI Corp *(G-8733)*

E M S, Batavia Also Called: Engineered MBL Solutions Inc *(G-923)*

E M Service Inc 440 323-3260
  600 Lowell St Elyria (44035) *(G-7137)*

E M Wave, Cleveland Also Called: Electro-Magwave Inc *(G-4004)*

E P Gerber & Sons Inc 330 857-2021
  4918 Kidron Rd Kidron (44636) *(G-8913)*

E P P Inc 440 322-8577
  710 Taylor St Elyria (44035) *(G-7138)*

E P S Specialists Ltd Inc 513 489-3676
  7875 School Rd Cincinnati (45249) *(G-2850)*

E Pompili Sons Inc 216 581-8080
  12307 Broadway Ave Cleveland (44125) *(G-3985)*

E R Advanced Ceramics Inc 330 426-9433
  600 E Clark St East Palestine (44413) *(G-7004)*

E Retailing Associates LLC 614 300-5785
  2282 Westbrooke Dr Columbus (43228) *(G-5339)*

E S C, Akron Also Called: Ellet Neon Sales & Service Inc *(G-137)*

E S S, North Canton Also Called: Environmental Sampling Sup Inc *(G-11725)*

E Systems Design & Automtn Inc 419 443-0220
  226 Heritage Dr Tiffin (44883) *(G-14084)*

E T I, Mansfield Also Called: Energy Technologies Inc *(G-9653)*

E Technologies Inc 440 247-7000
  300 Industrial Pkwy Ste A Chagrin Falls (44022) *(G-2374)*

E Ventus Corporation 216 643-6840
  5005 Rockside Rd Independence (44131) *(G-8664)*

E Warther & Sons Inc 330 343-7513
  924 N Tuscarawas Ave Dover (44622) *(G-6823)*

E Z Grout Corporation 740 749-3512
  1833 N Riverview Rd Malta (43758) *(G-9606)*

ALPHABETIC SECTION

E Z Machine Inc 330 784-3363
298 Northeast Ave Tallmadge (44278) *(G-14029)*

E-1 (2012) Holdings Inc 330 482-3900
41969 State Route 344 Columbiana (44408) *(G-5037)*

E-B Display Company Inc 330 833-4101
1369 Sanders Ave Sw Massillon (44647) *(G-10092)*

E-B Wire Works Inc 330 833-4101
1350 Sanders Ave Sw Massillon (44647) *(G-10093)*

E-Beam Services Inc 513 933-0031
2775 Henkle Dr Unit B Lebanon (45036) *(G-9071)*

E-Pak Manufacturing LLC 330 264-0825
1109 Pittsburgh Ave Wooster (44691) *(G-16115)*

E-Waste Systems (ohio) Inc 614 824-3057
1033 Brentnell Ave Ste 300 Columbus (43219) *(G-5340)*

E-Z Electric Motor Svc Corp 216 581-8820
8510 Bessemer Ave Cleveland (44127) *(G-3986)*

E-Z Grader Company 440 247-7511
300 Industrial Pkwy Ste A Chagrin Falls (44022) *(G-2375)*

E-Z Label Co, Brookfield *Also Called: E-Z Stop Service Center (G-1668)*

E-Z Shade LLC 419 340-2185
2720 Centennial Rd Toledo (43617) *(G-14270)*

E-Z Stop Service Center 330 448-2236
354 Bedford Rd Se Brookfield (44403) *(G-1668)*

E.C. Kitzel & Sons, Cleveland *Also Called: Schumann Enterprises Inc (G-4675)*

E&O Fbn Inc 513 241-5150
2230 Gilbert Ave Cincinnati (45206) *(G-2851)*

E5 Chem LLC 513 204-0173
4834 Socialville Foster Rd Mason (45040) *(G-9986)*

Eagle Chemicals Inc 513 868-9662
2550 Bobmeyer Rd Hamilton (45015) *(G-8204)*

Eagle Coach Company, West Chester *Also Called: Federaleagle LLC (G-15552)*

Eagle Composites LLC 513 330-6108
8494 Firebird Dr West Chester (45014) *(G-15420)*

Eagle Creek Inc 513 385-4442
9799 Prechtel Rd Cincinnati (45252) *(G-2852)*

EAGLE CREEK, INC., Cincinnati *Also Called: Eagle Creek Inc (G-2852)*

Eagle Crusher Co Inc 419 562-1183
521 E Southern Ave Bucyrus (44820) *(G-1858)*

Eagle Crusher Co Inc (PA) 419 468-2288
525 S Market St Galion (44833) *(G-7872)*

Eagle Elastomer Inc 330 923-7070
70 Cuyahoga Falls Industrial Pkwy Peninsula (44264) *(G-12340)*

Eagle Family Foods Group LLC (PA) 330 382-3725
1975 E 61st St Cleveland (44103) *(G-3987)*

Eagle Hardwoods, Windsor *Also Called: Hershberger Manufacturing (G-16075)*

Eagle Industrial Truck Mfg LLC 419 866-6301
1 Air Cargo Pkwy E Swanton (43558) *(G-13973)*

Eagle Industries 440 376-3885
16911 Saint Clair Ave Cleveland (44110) *(G-3988)*

Eagle Machinery & Supply Inc 330 852-1300
422 Dutch Vly Dr Ne Sugarcreek (44681) *(G-13924)*

Eagle Machining LLC 419 237-1366
705 N Fayette St Fayette (43521) *(G-7462)*

Eagle Precision Products LLC 440 582-9393
13800 Progress Pkwy Ste J North Royalton (44133) *(G-11873)*

Eagle Print, Delphos *Also Called: Delphos Herald Inc (G-6760)*

Eagle Software Corp 937 630-4548
1201 Hathaway Rd Oakwood (45419) *(G-12027)*

Eagle Specialty Materials LLC 216 401-6075
233 Erie Rd Columbus (43214) *(G-5341)*

Eagle Tugs, Swanton *Also Called: Eagle Industrial Truck Mfg LLC (G-13973)*

Eagle Welding, Willoughby *Also Called: Eagle Welding & Fabg Inc (G-15914)*

Eagle Welding & Fabg Inc 440 946-0692
1766 Joseph Lloyd Pkwy Willoughby (44094) *(G-15914)*

Eagleburgmann Industries LP 513 563-7325
3478 Hauck Rd Ste A Cincinnati (45241) *(G-2853)*

Eaglehead Manufacturing Co 440 951-0400
35280 Lakeland Blvd Ste K Eastlake (44095) *(G-7027)*

Eagles Nest Holdings LLC 419 526-4123
1111 N Main St Mansfield (44903) *(G-9649)*

Eaglestone Products LLC 440 463-8715
8057 Amber Ln Brecksville (44141) *(G-1615)*

Eaj Services LLC 513 792-3400
4350 Glendale Milford Rd Ste 170 Blue Ash (45242) *(G-1387)*

Early Bird, The, Greenville *Also Called: Brothers Publishing Co LLC (G-8040)*

Earnie Green Industries, Circleville *Also Called: Ernie Green Industries Inc (G-3550)*

Earth and Atmospheric Sciences, Dayton *Also Called: Science/Electronics Inc (G-6562)*

Earth Dreams Jewelry, North Royalton *Also Called: Gardella Jewelry LLC (G-11876)*

Earthley Wellness 614 625-1064
320 Outerbelt St Ste J Columbus (43213) *(G-5342)*

Earthquaker Devices, Akron *Also Called: Earthquaker Devices LLC (G-136)*

Earthquaker Devices LLC 330 252-9220
350 W Bowery St Akron (44307) *(G-136)*

Easi, Berea *Also Called: Estabrook Assembly Svcs Inc (G-1278)*

East Chemical Plant, Marysville *Also Called: Scotts Miracle-Gro Company (G-9936)*

East End Welding LLC 330 677-6000
357 Tallmadge Rd Kent (44240) *(G-8811)*

East Manufacturing Corporation (PA) 330 325-9921
1871 State Rte 44 Randolph (44265) *(G-12697)*

East Manufacturing Corporation 330 325-9921
3865 Waterloo Rd Randolph (44265) *(G-12698)*

East Oberlin Cabinets LLC 440 775-1166
13184 Hale Rd Oberlin (44074) *(G-12050)*

East Palestine China Dctg LLC 330 426-9600
870 W Main St East Palestine (44413) *(G-7005)*

East Side Fuel Plus Operations 419 563-0777
1505 N Sandusky Ave Bucyrus (44820) *(G-1859)*

East West Copolymer, Cleveland *Also Called: East West Copolymer LLC (G-3989)*

East West Copolymer LLC (PA) 225 267-3400
28026 Gates Mills Blvd Cleveland (44124) *(G-3989)*

East Woodworking Company 216 791-5950
2044 Random Rd Cleveland (44106) *(G-3990)*

Easterday & Co, Wilmot *Also Called: David E Easterday and Co Inc (G-16067)*

Eastern Automated Piping 740 535-8184
424 State St Mingo Junction (43938) *(G-11044)*

Eastern Enterprise, Springfield *Also Called: Comptons Precision Machine (G-13546)*

Eastern Ohio Newspapers Inc 740 633-1131
200 S 4th St Martins Ferry (43935) *(G-9898)*

Eastern Sheet Metal Inc (DH) 513 793-3440
8959 Blue Ash Rd Blue Ash (45242) *(G-1388)*

Eastgate Custom Graphics Ltd 513 528-7922
4459 Mount Carmel Tobasco Rd Cincinnati (45244) *(G-2854)*

Eastlake Machine Products LLC 440 953-1014
1956 Joseph Lloyd Pkwy Willoughby (44094) *(G-15915)*

Eastlake Mfg Facility, Willoughby *Also Called: Conn-Selmer Inc (G-15901)*

Eastman Kodak Company 937 259-3000
3000 Research Blvd Dayton (45420) *(G-6311)*

Eastman Kodak Company 937 259-3000
3100 Research Blvd Ste 250 Kettering (45420) *(G-8906)*

Easy Way Leisure Company LLC (PA) 513 731-5640
8950 Rossash Rd Cincinnati (45236) *(G-2855)*

Easy Way Products, Cincinnati *Also Called: Easy Way Leisure Company LLC (G-2855)*

Eaton, Cleveland *Also Called: Eaton Corporation (G-3994)*

Eaton Aeroquip LLC (HQ) 440 523-5000
1000 Eaton Blvd Cleveland (44122) *(G-3991)*

Eaton Aeroquip LLC 419 891-7775
1660 Indian Wood Cir Maumee (43537) *(G-10201)*

Eaton Compressor & Fabrication, Englewood *Also Called: Airbase Industries LLC (G-7222)*

Eaton Comprsr Fabrication Inc 877 283-7614
1000 Cass Dr Englewood (45315) *(G-7230)*

Eaton Corporation 330 274-0743
115 Lena Dr Aurora (44202) *(G-712)*

Eaton Corporation 440 523-5000
1000 Eaton Blvd Beachwood (44122) *(G-985)*

Eaton Corporation 216 281-2211
9919 Clinton Rd Cleveland (44144) *(G-3992)*

Eaton Corporation 440 826-1115
6055 Rockside Woods Blvd N Cleveland (44131) *(G-3993)*

Eaton Corporation (HQ) 440 523-5000
1000 Eaton Blvd Cleveland (44122) *(G-3994)*

Eaton Corporation 419 238-1190
1225 W Main St Van Wert (45891) *(G-14914)*

Eaton Corporation.. 513 387-2000
9902 Windisch Rd West Chester (45069) *(G-15421)*

Eaton Corporation.. 216 523-5000
34899 Curtis Blvd Willoughby (44095) *(G-15916)*

Eaton Electric Holdings LLC (HQ).................................... 440 523-5000
1000 Eaton Blvd Cleveland (44122) *(G-3995)*

Eaton Electrical.. 787 257-4470
23555 Euclid Ave Cleveland (44117) *(G-3996)*

Eaton Fabricating Company Inc....................................... 440 926-3121
1009 Mcalpin Ct Grafton (44044) *(G-7998)*

Eaton Global Hose, Cleveland *Also Called: Eaton Aeroquip LLC (G-3991)*

Eaton Industrial Corporation.. 216 692-5456
1000 Eaton Blvd Cleveland (44122) *(G-3997)*

Eaton Industrial Corporation (HQ)................................... 216 523-4205
23555 Euclid Ave Cleveland (44117) *(G-3998)*

Eaton Leasing Corporation... 216 382-2292
1000 Eaton Blvd Beachwood (44122) *(G-986)*

Eazytrade, West Chester *Also Called: Eazytrade Inc (G-15422)*

Eazytrade Inc (PA)... 513 257-9189
9743 Crescent Park Dr West Chester (45069) *(G-15422)*

Eazytrade Inc... 513 257-9189
7503 Overglen Dr West Chester (45069) *(G-15423)*

Ebco Inc... 330 562-8265
3500 Crane Centre Dr Streetsboro (44241) *(G-13769)*

Ebel Tape & Label, Cincinnati *Also Called: Ebel-Binder Printing Co Inc (G-2856)*

Ebel-Binder Printing Co Inc... 513 471-1067
1630 Dalton Ave # 1 Cincinnati (45214) *(G-2856)*

Ebner Furnaces Inc.. 330 335-2311
224 Quadral Dr Wadsworth (44281) *(G-15028)*

Ebnerfab, Wadsworth *Also Called: Ebner Furnaces Inc (G-15028)*

Ebo Group, Inc., Sharon Center *Also Called: Ebog Legacy Inc (G-13166)*

Ebog Legacy Inc (HQ).. 330 239-4933
1441 Wolf Creek Trail Sharon Center (44274) *(G-13166)*

Ebsco Industries Inc.. 513 398-3695
4680 Parkway Dr Ste 200 Mason (45040) *(G-9987)*

Ecc Company, Groveport *Also Called: Lomar Enterprises Inc (G-8151)*

Eccles Saw & Tool, Cincinnati *Also Called: D & M Saw & Tool Inc (G-2811)*

Echo Environmental Waverly LLC.................................... 740 710-7901
479 Industrial Park Dr Waverly (45690) *(G-15280)*

Echo Mobile Solutions LLC.. 614 282-3756
108 Leasure Dr Pickerington (43147) *(G-12460)*

Echopress Ltd.. 216 373-7560
444 Avon Point Ave Avon Lake (44012) *(G-804)*

Eci Macola/Max LLC (DH)... 978 539-6186
5455 Rings Rd Ste 100 Dublin (43017) *(G-6883)*

Ecil Met TEC, Brookpark *Also Called: Reliacheck Manufacturing Inc (G-1724)*

Eckart Aluminum, Painesville *Also Called: Eckart America Corporation (G-12231)*

Eckart America, Painesville *Also Called: Obron Atlantic Corporation (G-12252)*

Eckart America Corporation (DH)..................................... 440 954-7600
830 E Erie St Painesville (44077) *(G-12231)*

Eclipse.. 419 564-7482
126 N Union St Galion (44833) *(G-7873)*

Eclipse 3d/Pi LLC... 614 626-8536
825 Taylor Rd Columbus (43230) *(G-5343)*

Eclipse Resources - Ohio LLC.. 740 452-4503
4900 Boggs Rd Zanesville (43701) *(G-16529)*

Ecm Industries LLC.. 513 533-6242
3898 Duck Creek Rd Cincinnati (45227) *(G-2857)*

Ecm Industries, Llc, Cincinnati *Also Called: Ecm Industries LLC (G-2857)*

Eco Energy International LLC... 419 544-5000
233 Park Ave E Mansfield (44902) *(G-9650)*

Eco Fuel Solution LLC.. 440 282-8592
779 Sunrise Dr Amherst (44001) *(G-476)*

Eco-Groupe Inc (PA).. 937 898-2603
6161 Ventnor Ave Dayton (45414) *(G-6312)*

Ecochem Alternative Fuels LLC.. 614 764-3835
7304 Town St Plain City (43064) *(G-12577)*

Ecolab Inc... 513 932-0830
726 E Main St Ste F Lebanon (45036) *(G-9072)*

Economy Flame Hardening Inc.. 216 431-9333
896 E 70th St Cleveland (44103) *(G-3999)*

Economy Forms, Columbus *Also Called: Efco Corp (G-5347)*

Ecopac LLC... 732 715-0236
8100 Reading Rd Cincinnati (45237) *(G-2858)*

Ecopro Solutions LLC... 216 232-4040
5617 E Schaaf Rd Independence (44131) *(G-8665)*

Ecp Corporation... 440 934-0444
1305 Chester Industrial Pkwy Avon (44011) *(G-771)*

Ect, North Royalton *Also Called: Envirnmntal Cmpliance Tech LLC (G-11874)*

Ecu Corporation (PA)... 513 898-9294
11500 Goldcoast Dr Cincinnati (45249) *(G-2859)*

Edac Composites, Cincinnati *Also Called: Meggitt (erlanger) LLC (G-3143)*

Edc Liquidating Inc.. 330 467-0750
635 Highland Rd E Macedonia (44056) *(G-9548)*

Edco Tool & Die, Toledo *Also Called: Exco Engineering USA Inc (G-14281)*

Eddies Iron Lung LLC... 614 493-3411
2490 Eastcleft Dr Columbus (43221) *(G-5344)*

Eden Cryogenics LLC... 614 873-3949
7630 Copper Glen St Columbus (43235) *(G-5345)*

Edfa LLC... 937 222-1415
90 Vermont Ave Dayton (45404) *(G-6313)*

Edge 247 Corp.. 216 771-7000
2765 E 55th St Ste 7 Cleveland (44104) *(G-4000)*

Edge Adhesives Inc.. 614 875-6343
3709 Grove City Rd Grove City (43123) *(G-8090)*

Edge Adhesives-Oh, Grove City *Also Called: Rubex Inc (G-8118)*

Edge Exponential LLC.. 614 226-4421
1140 Gahanna Pkwy Columbus (43230) *(G-5346)*

Edge Plastics Inc (PA).. 419 522-6696
449 Newman St Mansfield (44902) *(G-9651)*

Edgeenergy, Cincinnati *Also Called: One Three Energy Inc (G-3224)*

Edgepark Medical Supplies, Twinsburg *Also Called: Hgi Holdings Inc (G-14672)*

Edgerton Forge Inc (HQ).. 419 298-2333
257 E Morrison St Edgerton (43517) *(G-7074)*

Edgewater Capital Partners LP (PA)................................. 216 292-3838
5005 Rockside Rd Ste 840 Independence (44131) *(G-8666)*

Edgewell Per Care Brands LLC... 330 527-2191
10545 Freedom St Garrettsville (44231) *(G-7914)*

Edgewell Personal Care LLC.. 937 492-1057
1810 Progress Way Sidney (45365) *(G-13244)*

Edgewell Personal Care Company................................... 740 374-1905
Marietta (45750) *(G-9791)*

Edi Custom Interiors Inc... 513 829-3895
5648 Lindenwood Ln Fairfield (45014) *(G-7355)*

Edible Arrangement, Twinsburg *Also Called: Kriss Kreations (G-14682)*

Edict Systems Inc.. 937 429-4288
2434 Esquire Dr Beavercreek (45431) *(G-1049)*

Edinburg Fixture and Mch Inc.. 330 947-1700
3101 State Route 14 Rootstown (44272) *(G-12852)*

Edison Branch, Edison *Also Called: Hord Elevator LLC (G-7084)*

Editencom Ltd... 419 865-5877
7134 Railroad St Holland (43528) *(G-8508)*

Edl Displays Inc.. 937 429-7423
1304 Research Park Dr Beavercreek (45432) *(G-1050)*

Edmar Chemical Company... 440 247-9560
539 Washington St Chagrin Falls (44022) *(G-2376)*

Edsal Sandusky Corporation.. 419 626-5465
117 E Washington Row Sandusky (44870) *(G-13052)*

EDSAL SANDUSKY CORPORATION, Sandusky *Also Called: Edsal Sandusky Corporation (G-13052)*

Educational Direction Inc... 330 836-8439
150 N Miller Rd Ste 200 Fairlawn (44333) *(G-7437)*

Educational Equipment, Kent *Also Called: Michael Kaufman Companies Inc (G-8836)*

Edw C Levy Co.. 330 484-6328
3715 Whipple Ave Sw Canton (44706) *(G-2094)*

Edward D Segen & Co LLC... 937 295-3672
100 Enterprise Dr Fort Loramie (45845) *(G-7598)*

Edward W Daniel LLC... 440 647-1960
46950 State Route 18 Ste B Wellington (44090) *(G-15306)*

Edwards Culvert Co, Fredericktown *Also Called: Edwards Sheet Metal Works Inc (G-7745)*

Edwards Machine Service Inc.. 937 295-2929
8800 State Route 66 Fort Loramie (45845) *(G-7599)*

Edwards Sheet Metal Works Inc 740 694-0010
  10439 Sparta Rd Fredericktown (43019) *(G-7745)*
Edwards Steel, Columbus *Also Called: Arbenz Inc (G-5152)*
Edwards Vacuum LLC 440 248-4453
  7905 Cochran Rd Ste 100 Solon (44139) *(G-13340)*
Eei Acquisition Corp 440 564-5484
  15175 Kinsman Rd Middlefield (44062) *(G-10749)*
Efco Corp 614 876-1226
  3900 Zane Trace Dr Columbus (43228) *(G-5347)*
Efficient Machine Pdts Corp 440 268-0205
  12133 Alameda Dr Strongsville (44149) *(G-13832)*
Effox-Flextor-Mader Inc (HQ) 513 874-8915
  9759 Inter Ocean Dr West Chester (45246) *(G-15549)*
Efg Holdings Inc 440 325-4337
  777 W Bagley Rd Berea (44017) *(G-1275)*
EFG HOLDINGS, INC., Berea *Also Called: Efg Holdings Inc (G-1275)*
Eg Enterprise Services Inc 216 431-3300
  5000 Euclid Ave Ste 100 Cleveland (44103) *(G-4001)*
Eg Industries, Circleville *Also Called: Florida Production Engrg (G-3551)*
Eg Industries, New Madison *Also Called: Ernie Green Industries Inc (G-11473)*
Egc Enterprises, Chardon *Also Called: Egc Operating Company LLO (G-2110)*
Egc Operating Company LLC (PA) 440 285-5835
  140 Parker Ct Chardon (44024) *(G-2449)*
Egr Products Company Inc (PA) 330 833-6554
  55 Eckard Rd Dalton (44618) *(G-6131)*
Egypt Structural Steel Proc 419 628-2375
  480 Osterloh Rd Minster (45865) *(G-11051)*
Ei Ceramics 513 881-2000
  3 Standen Dr Hamilton (45015) *(G-8205)*
Eia, Cleveland *Also Called: Everything In America (G-4039)*
Eidp Inc 440 934-6444
  38620 Chester Rd Avon (44011) *(G-772)*
Eighth Floor Promotions LLC 419 586-6433
  1 Visions Pkwy Celina (45822) *(G-2330)*
Einstruction Corporation, Youngstown *Also Called: Fscreations Corporation (G-16360)*
Eisenhauer Mfg Co LLC 419 238-0081
  409 Center St Van Wert (45891) *(G-14915)*
Eitle Machine Tool Inc 419 935-8753
  6036 Coder Rd Attica (44807) *(G-700)*
Ej Usa Inc 614 871-2436
  1855 Feddern Ave Grove City (43123) *(G-8091)*
Ej Usa Inc 216 692-3001
  4160 Glenridge Rd South Euclid (44121) *(G-13460)*
Ej Usa Inc 330 782-3900
  4150 Simon Rd Youngstown (44512) *(G-16354)*
EJ Weber Ltd 513 759-0103
  7331 Charter Cup Ln West Chester (45069) *(G-15424)*
Ekco Cleaning Inc 513 733-8882
  4055 Executive Park Dr Ste 240 Cincinnati (45241) *(G-2860)*
El Nuevo Naranjo 614 863-4212
  6142 Glenworth Ct Galloway (43119) *(G-7904)*
EL Ostendorf Inc 440 247-7631
  3425 Roundwood Rd Chagrin Falls (44022) *(G-2377)*
Elaire Corporation 419 843-2192
  7944 W Central Ave Ste 10 Toledo (43617) *(G-14271)*
Elan Designs Inc 614 985-5600
  10 E Schrock Rd # 110 Westerville (43081) *(G-15704)*
Elastostar Rubber Corp 614 841-4400
  8475 Rausch Dr Plain City (43064) *(G-12578)*
Elastotec Div, Independence *Also Called: Robin Industries Inc (G-8684)*
Elbex, Kent *Also Called: Elbex Corporation (G-8812)*
Elbex Corporation 330 673-3233
  300 Martinel Dr Kent (44240) *(G-8812)*
Elco, Cleveland *Also Called: Elco Corporation (G-4002)*
Elco Corporation 440 997-6131
  1100 State Rd Ashtabula (44004) *(G-631)*
Elco Corporation (DH) 800 321-0467
  1000 Belt Line Ave Cleveland (44109) *(G-4002)*
Elden Draperies of Toledo Inc 419 535-1909
  1845 N Reynolds Rd Toledo (43615) *(G-14272)*

Eldorado National Kansas Inc 937 596-6849
  419 W Pike St Jackson Center (45334) *(G-8732)*
Eldorado Stone LLC 330 698-3931
  167 Maple St Apple Creek (44606) *(G-498)*
Electr-Gnral Plas Corp Clumbus 614 871-2915
  6200 Enterprise Pkwy Grove City (43123) *(G-8092)*
Electra - Cord, Inc., Massillon *Also Called: Rah Investment Holding Inc (G-10138)*
Electra Sound Inc (PA) 216 433-9600
  32483 English Turn Avon Lake (44012) *(G-805)*
Electra Tarp Inc 330 477-7168
  2900 Perry Dr Sw Canton (44706) *(G-2095)*
Electraform Industries Div, Vandalia *Also Called: Wentworth Mold Inc Electra (G-14967)*
Electrasound TV & Appl Svc, Avon Lake *Also Called: Electra Sound Inc (G-805)*
Electric Cord Sets Inc (PA) 216 261-1000
  4700 Manufacturing Ave Cleveland (44135) *(G-4003)*
Electric Eel Mfg Co Inc 937 323-4644
  501 W Leffel Ln Springfield (45506) *(G-13558)*
Electric Motor Service, Piqua *Also Called: Bornhorst Motor Service Inc (G-12507)*
Electric Service Co Inc 513 271-6387
  5331 Hetzell St Cincinnati (45227) *(G-2861)*
Electric Speed Indicator Co 216 251-2540
  650 Cedar Bark Dr Aurora (44202) *(G-713)*
Electrical Insulation Company, Delta *Also Called: Workman Electronic Pdts Inc (G-6792)*
Electripack Inc 937 433-2602
  2985 Springboro W Moraine (45439) *(G-11174)*
Electrnic Dsign For Indust Inc 740 401-4000
  100 Ayers Blvd Belpre (45714) *(G-1252)*
Electro Controls Inc 866 497-1717
  1625 Ferguson Ct Sidney (45365) *(G-13245)*
Electro Plasma Incorporated 419 838-7365
  4400 Moline Martin Rd Millbury (43447) *(G-10931)*
Electro Polish Company 937 222-3611
  332 Vermont Ave Dayton (45404) *(G-6314)*
Electro Prime, Toledo *Also Called: Electro Prime Group LLC (G-14273)*
Electro Prime Assembly Inc 419 476-0100
  63 Dixie Hwy Ste 7 Rossford (43460) *(G-12863)*
Electro Prime Group LLC 419 666-5000
  63 Dixie Hwy Ste 7 Rossford (43460) *(G-12864)*
Electro Prime Group LLC (PA) 419 476-0100
  4510 Lint Ave Ste B Toledo (43612) *(G-14273)*
Electro-Cap International Inc 937 456-6099
  1011 W Lexington Rd Eaton (45320) *(G-7058)*
Electro-Line Inc 937 461-5683
  118 S Terry St Dayton (45403) *(G-6315)*
Electro-Magwave Inc 216 453-1160
  10221 Sweet Valley Dr Ste 1 Cleveland (44125) *(G-4004)*
Electro-Metallics Co 513 423-8091
  3004 Lefferson Rd Middletown (45044) *(G-10820)*
Electro-Plating & Fabricating, Cleveland *Also Called: Roberts Demand No 3 Corp (G-4641)*
Electroburr, Wellington *Also Called: Rochester Manufacturing Inc (G-15321)*
Electrocoat, Medina *Also Called: Office Magic Inc (G-10357)*
Electrocraft Arkansas Inc 501 268-4203
  250 Mccormick Rd Gallipolis (45631) *(G-7890)*
Electrocraft Ohio Inc 740 441-6200
  250 Mccormick Rd Gallipolis (45631) *(G-7891)*
Electrodata Inc 216 663-3333
  23400 Aurora Rd Ste 5 Bedford Heights (44146) *(G-1170)*
Electrodynamics, Inc., Cincinnati *Also Called: L3harris Electrodynamics Inc (G-2569)*
Electrodyne Company Inc 513 732-2822
  4188 Taylor Rd Batavia (45103) *(G-921)*
Electrolizing Corp of Ohio (PA) 800 451-8655
  1325 E 152nd St Cleveland (44112) *(G-4005)*
ELECTROLIZING CORPORATION OF OHIO, Cleveland *Also Called: Electrolizing Corporation Ohio (G-4006)*
Electrolizing Corporation Ohio 216 451-8653
  1655 Collamer Ave Cleveland (44110) *(G-4006)*
Electromotive Inc (PA) 330 688-6494
  4880 Hudson Dr Stow (44224) *(G-13693)*
Electronauts LLC 859 261-3600
  621 Wilmer Ave Cincinnati (45226) *(G-2862)*

ALPHABETIC SECTION

Electronic Concepts Engrg Inc.. 419 861-9000
1465 Timber Wolf Dr Holland (43528) *(G-8509)*

Electronic Imaging Svcs Inc.. 740 549-2487
8273 Green Meadows Dr N Ste 400 Lewis Center (43035) *(G-9159)*

Electronic Printing Pdts Inc.. 800 882-4050
4560 Darrow Rd Stow (44224) *(G-13694)*

Electronics & Communications, Dayton *Also Called: General Dynmcs Mssion Systems* *(G-6350)*

Electrovations Inc... 330 274-3558
30333 Emerald Valley Pkwy Solon (44139) *(G-13341)*

Electrowind... 937 229-0101
1960 Troy St Dayton (45404) *(G-6316)*

Eleeo Brands LLC
212 E 3rd St Cincinnati (45202) *(G-2863)*

Eleeo Brands LLC.. 513 572-8100
2150 Winchell Ave Cincinnati (45214) *(G-2864)*

Eleet Cryogenics Inc (PA).. 330 874-4009
11132 Industrial Pkwy Nw Bolivar (44612) *(G-1524)*

Element 41 Inc (PA).. 216 410-5646
141 Main St Chardon (44024) *(G-2450)*

Element 41 Inc.. 440 579-5531
1932 Pinewood Ln Painesville (44077) *(G-12232)*

Element Machinery LLC.. 855 447-7648
4801 Bennett Rd Toledo (43612) *(G-14274)*

Elements Hr Inc... 614 488-6944
2845 Canterbury Ln Columbus (43221) *(G-5348)*

Elemetal Refining LLC... 740 286-6457
16064 Beaver Pike Jackson (45640) *(G-8714)*

Elevator Cncepts By Wurtec LLC.. 734 246-4700
6200 Brent Dr Toledo (43611) *(G-14275)*

Eleven 10 LLC... 888 216-4049
975 Bassett Rd Ste B Westlake (44145) *(G-15747)*

Elgin Fastener Group... 440 239-1165
6519 Eastland Rd Brookpark (44142) *(G-1714)*

Eliason Corporation... 800 828-3655
10021 Commerce Park Dr West Chester (45246) *(G-15550)*

Eliokem Inc (DH)... 330 734-1100
175 Ghent Rd Fairlawn (44333) *(G-7438)*

Elite Biomedical Solutions LLC.. 513 207-0602
756 Cincinnati Batavia Pike Ste C Cincinnati (45245) *(G-2558)*

Elite Ceramics and Metals LLC... 330 787-2777
5390 Copeland Ave Nw Warren (44483) *(G-15166)*

Elite Enclosure Company, Sidney *Also Called: Mk Trempe Corporation (G-13267)*

Elite Industrial Controls Inc... 567 234-1057
7308 Driver Rd Berlin Heights (44814) *(G-1314)*

Elite Industrial Controls Inc... 440 477-6923
38045 Crook St Grafton (44044) *(G-7999)*

Elite Manufacturing Inds LLC... 440 934-0920
2395 Muirwood Rd Avon (44011) *(G-773)*

Elite Property Group LLC.. 216 356-7469
1036 N Pasadena Ave Elyria (44035) *(G-7139)*

Elk Technologies LLC.. 937 902-4165
390 Signalfire Dr Dayton (45458) *(G-6317)*

Elkhead Gas & Oil Co... 740 763-3966
12163 Marne Rd Newark (43055) *(G-11574)*

Ellet Neon Sales & Service Inc.. 330 628-9907
3041 E Waterloo Rd Akron (44312) *(G-137)*

Elliott, Dayton *Also Called: Elliott Tool Technologies Ltd (G-6318)*

Elliott Machine Works Inc... 419 468-4709
1351 Freese Works Pl Galion (44833) *(G-7874)*

Elliott Tool Technologies Ltd (PA)....................................... 937 253-6133
1760 Tuttle Ave Dayton (45403) *(G-6318)*

Ellis & Watts Global Inds Inc... 513 752-9000
4400 Glen Willow Lake Ln Batavia (45103) *(G-922)*

Ellis Brothers Inc Upg.. 740 397-9191
14220 Parrott Ext Mount Vernon (43050) *(G-11272)*

Ellis Laundry and Lin Sup Inc.. 330 339-4941
213 8th Street Ext Sw New Philadelphia (44663) *(G-11500)*

Ellison Surface Tech - W LLC (DH)..................................... 513 770-4900
8093 Columbia Rd Ste 201 Mason (45040) *(G-9988)*

Ellison Surface Technologies, Mason *Also Called: Bodycote Surface Tech Inc (G-9963)*

Ellison Surfc Technologies-Tn, Mason *Also Called: Bodycote Srfc Tech Wrtburg Inc (G-9962)*

Elloras Cave Publishing Inc... 330 253-3521
1056 Home Ave Akron (44310) *(G-138)*

Ellwood Engineered Castings Co... 330 568-3000
7158 Hubbard Masury Rd Hubbard (44425) *(G-8563)*

Elmers Products Inc.. 614 225-4000
180 E Broad St Fl 4 Columbus (43215) *(G-5349)*

Elmet Euclid LLC... 216 692-3990
21801 Tungsten Rd Euclid (44117) *(G-7267)*

Elmet Technologies Inc... 216 692-3990
21801 Tungsten Rd Cleveland (44117) *(G-4007)*

Elmore Mfg Co, Elmore *Also Called: Calvin J Magsig (G-7100)*

Elra Industries Inc... 513 868-6228
550 S Erie Hwy Hamilton (45011) *(G-8206)*

Elster Perfection, Geneva *Also Called: Honeywell Smart Energy (G-7939)*

Elster Perfection Corporation (DH)..................................... 440 428-1171
436 N Eagle St Geneva (44041) *(G-7935)*

Eltech Systems Corporation (PA)....................................... 440 285-0380
7590 Discovery Ln Concord Township (44077) *(G-5906)*

Eltool Corporation... 513 723-1772
1400 Park Ave E Mansfield (44905) *(G-9652)*

Elugen Pharmaceuticals, Cleveland *Also Called: 2 Retrievers LLC (G-3571)*

Ely Road Reel Company Ltd.. 330 683-1818
9081 Ely Rd Apple Creek (44606) *(G-499)*

Elyria Concrete Inc.. 440 322-2750
400 Lowell St Elyria (44035) *(G-7140)*

Elyria Concrete Step Company, Elyria *Also Called: E C S Corp (G-7136)*

Elyria Foundry Company LLC (PA)..................................... 440 322-4657
120 Filbert St Elyria (44035) *(G-7141)*

Elyria Manufacturing Corp (PA).. 440 365-4171
145 Northrup St Elyria (44035) *(G-7142)*

Elyria Metal Spinning Fabg Co.. 440 323-8068
7511 W River Rd S Elyria (44035) *(G-7143)*

Elyria Pattern Co Inc... 440 323-1526
6785 W River Rd S Elyria (44035) *(G-7144)*

Elyria Plastic Products, Elyria *Also Called: E P P Inc (G-7138)*

Elyria Plating Corporation... 440 365-8300
118 Olive St Elyria (44035) *(G-7145)*

Elyria Spring & Specialty Inc... 440 323-5502
123 Elbe St Elyria (44035) *(G-7146)*

Elyria Spring Spclty Holdg Inc... 440 323-5502
123 Elbe St Elyria (44035) *(G-7147)*

Elytus Ltd.. 614 824-4985
601 S High St Columbus (43215) *(G-5350)*

Em Es Be Company LLC.. 216 761-9500
18210 Saint Clair Ave Cleveland (44110) *(G-4008)*

Em4 Inc... 608 240-4800
676 Alpha Dr Cleveland (44143) *(G-4009)*

Em4 Inc... 410 987-5600
676 Alpha Dr Cleveland (44143) *(G-4010)*

Emaxx Northeast Ohio LLC... 844 645-6299
1701 Sherrick Rd Se Canton (44707) *(G-2096)*

EMB Designs, Coldwater *Also Called: K Ventures Inc (G-4994)*

Embedded Planet Inc.. 216 245-4180
31225 Bainbridge Rd Ste N Solon (44139) *(G-13342)*

Emblem Athletic LLC.. 614 743-6955
106 Gainsway Ct Powell (43065) *(G-12671)*

Embroidery Design Group LLC... 614 798-8152
2564 Billingsley Rd Columbus (43235) *(G-5351)*

Embroidery Network Inc.. 330 678-4887
4693 Kent Rd Kent (44240) *(G-8813)*

Embroidme.. 330 484-8484
3611 Cleveland Ave S Canton (44707) *(G-2097)*

Embroidme, Gahanna *Also Called: Cdss Inc (G-7832)*

EMC Precision Machining, Elyria *Also Called: Elyria Manufacturing Corp (G-7142)*

EMC Precision Machining II LLC (PA)................................. 440 365-4171
145 Northrup St Elyria (44035) *(G-7148)*

EMD Millipore Corporation.. 513 631-0445
2909 Highland Ave Norwood (45212) *(G-11995)*

Emergency Products & RES Inc.. 330 673-5003
890 W Main St Kent (44240) *(G-8814)*

Emergency Training Inst Div, Fairlawn Also Called: Educational Direction Inc (G-7437)
Emerson, Cincinnati Also Called: Emerson Electric Co (G-2865)
Emerson Commercial Reside..937 493-2828
1675 Campbell Rd Sidney (45365) (G-13246)
Emerson Corp..614 841-5498
975 Pittsburgh Dr Delaware (43015) (G-6719)
Emerson Electric Co...513 731-2020
6000 Fernview Ave Cincinnati (45212) (G-2865)
Emerson Helix...937 710-5771
40 W Stewart St Dayton (45409) (G-6319)
Emerson Industrial Automation..216 901-2400
7800 Hub Pkwy Cleveland (44125) (G-4011)
Emerson Network Power..614 841-8054
3040 S 9th St Ironton (45638) (G-8697)
Emerson Network Power System, Westerville Also Called: Liebert Field Services Inc (G-15665)
Emerson Process Management..419 529-4311
2500 Park Ave W Ontario (44906) (G-12091)
Emerson Professional Tools LLC..740 432-8782
9877 Brick Church Rd Cambridge (43725) (G-1934)
Emery, Cincinnati Also Called: Emery Oleochemicals LLC (C-2866)
Emery Cnty Coal Resources Inc..740 338-3100
46226 National Rd Saint Clairsville (43950) (G-12902)
Emery Oleochemicals LLC (HQ)...513 762-2500
4900 Este Ave Cincinnati (45232) (G-2866)
Emes Supply LLC..216 400-8025
35622 Vine St Willowick (44095) (G-16031)
Emh Inc (PA)..330 220-8600
550 Crane Dr Valley City (44280) (G-14869)
EMI Corp (PA)..937 596-5511
801 W Pike St Jackson Center (45334) (G-8733)
Eminent Transport, Cleveland Also Called: Express Ground Services Inc (G-4044)
Emmco Inc..216 429-2020
19199 Saint Clair Ave Euclid (44117) (G-7268)
Emmert Grains, Cincinnati Also Called: The F L Emmert Co Inc (G-3448)
Empanadas Aqui LLC...513 312-9566
8749 Surrey Pl Maineville (45039) (G-9599)
Empire Brass Co..216 431-6565
5000 Superior Ave Cleveland (44103) (G-4012)
Empire Die Casting Co, Macedonia Also Called: Edc Liquidating Inc (G-9548)
Empire Die Casting Company, Macedonia Also Called: American Light Metals LLC (G-9535)
Empire Diecasting, Macedonia Also Called: SRS Die Casting Holdings LLC (G-9577)
Empire Machine LLC..937 506-7793
222 N 6th St Tipp City (45371) (G-14133)
Empire Packing Company LP..901 948-4788
4780 Alliance Dr Mason (45040) (G-9989)
Empire Packing Company LP..513 942-5400
113 Circle Freeway Dr West Chester (45246) (G-15551)
Empire Plow Company Inc (DH)..216 641-2290
343 W Bagley Rd Ste 214 Berea (44017) (G-1276)
Empire Printing Inc...513 242-3900
9560 Le Saint Dr Fairfield (45014) (G-7356)
Empire Systems Inc..440 653-9300
33683 Walker Rd Avon Lake (44012) (G-806)
Empire Tire Inc..330 983-4176
445 Munroe Falls Rd Tallmadge (44278) (G-14030)
Empirical Manufacturing Co Inc..513 948-1616
7616 Reinhold Dr Cincinnati (45237) (G-2867)
Empress Royalty Ltd..614 943-1903
236 Fairway Dr Columbus (43214) (G-5352)
Empyracom Inc (PA)..330 744-5570
7510 Market St Ste 8 Boardman (44512) (G-1511)
Emroid ME...614 789-1898
6065 Shreven Dr Westerville (43081) (G-15705)
Emssons Faurecia Ctrl Systems...937 743-0551
2301 Commerce Center Dr Franklin (45005) (G-7672)
Emssons Faurecia Ctrl Systems (DH)...812 341-2000
543 Matzinger Rd Toledo (43612) (G-14276)
Emx Industries Inc (HQ)..216 518-9888
5660 Transportation Blvd Cleveland (44125) (G-4013)
En-Hanced Products Inc..614 882-7400
14111 Chambers Rd Sunbury (43074) (G-13953)

Enamelac Company..216 481-8878
18103 Roseland Rd Cleveland (44112) (G-4014)
Encapsulation Technologies LLC...419 819-6319
2937 Industrial Park Dr Austinburg (44010) (G-744)
Enclosure Suppliers LLC...513 782-3900
12119 Champion Way Cincinnati (45241) (G-2868)
Encompass Atmtn Engrg Tech LLC...419 873-0000
622 Eckel Rd Perrysburg (43551) (G-12378)
Encompass Woodworking LLC..513 569-2841
1303 Monmouth St Cincinnati (45225) (G-2869)
Encon, Dayton Also Called: Encon Inc (G-6320)
Encon Inc...937 898-2603
6161 Ventnor Ave Dayton (45414) (G-6320)
Encore Industries Inc...419 626-8000
319 Howard Dr Sandusky (44870) (G-13053)
Encore Industries Inc (DH)..419 626-8000
725 Water St Cambridge (43725) (G-1935)
Encore Plastics, Cambridge Also Called: Encore Industries Inc (G-1935)
Encore Plastics Southeast LLC..419 626-8000
319 Howard Dr Sandusky (44870) (G-13054)
Encore Precast LLC..513 726-5678
416 W Ritter Seven Mile (45062) (C-13133)
Endless Home Improvements LLC..614 599-1799
3897 Fergus Rd Columbus (43207) (G-5353)
Endurance Industries LLC...513 285-8503
5055 Madison Rd Cincinnati (45227) (G-2870)
Endurance Manufacturing Inc...330 628-2600
1615 E Market St Akron (44305) (G-139)
Enduro Rubber Company..330 296-9603
685 S Chestnut St Ravenna (44266) (G-12713)
Enerco Group Inc (PA)...216 916-3000
4560 W 160th St Cleveland (44135) (G-4015)
Enerco Technical Products Inc...216 916-3000
4560 W 160th St Cleveland (44135) (G-4016)
Enerfab Inc...513 771-2300
11861 Mosteller Rd Cincinnati (45241) (G-2871)
Enerfab LLC (PA)..513 641-0500
4430 Chickering Ave Cincinnati (45232) (G-2872)
Energizer Battery Inc (HQ)..440 835-7500
25225 Detroit Rd Westlake (44145) (G-15748)
Energizer Manufacturing Inc
25225 Detroit Rd Westlake (44145) (G-15749)
Energy & Ctrl Integrators Inc (PA)..419 222-0025
1130 E Albert St Lima (45804) (G-9240)
Energy Corportive, Coshocton Also Called: Ngo Development Corporation (G-5987)
Energy Focus, Solon Also Called: Energy Focus Inc (G-13343)
Energy Focus Inc (PA)...440 715-1300
32000 Aurora Rd Ste B Solon (44139) (G-13343)
Energy Hbr Nclear Gnration LLC...888 254-6359
168 E Market St Akron (44308) (G-140)
Energy Manufacturing Ltd...419 355-9304
1830 Oak Harbor Rd Fremont (43420) (G-7776)
Energy Resources, Saint Clairsville Also Called: Mill Creek Mining Company (G-12913)
Energy Technologies Inc...419 522-4444
219 Park Ave E Mansfield (44902) (G-9653)
Enersys...216 252-4242
12690 Elmwood Ave Cleveland (44111) (G-4017)
Enespro LLC..630 332-2801
15825 Industrial Pkwy Cleveland (44135) (G-4018)
Enespro Ppe..800 553-0672
10601 Memphis Ave Brooklyn (44144) (G-1677)
Engelhard Corp..440 322-3741
120 Pine St Elyria (44035) (G-7149)
Engineered Conductive Mtl LLC...740 362-4444
132 Johnson Dr Delaware (43015) (G-6720)
Engineered Endeavors, Middlefield Also Called: Eei Acquisition Corp (G-10749)
Engineered Endeavors Inc...440 564-5484
10975 Kinsman Rd Newbury (44065) (G-11623)
Engineered Films Division Inc..419 884-8150
230 Industrial Dr Lexington (44904) (G-9201)
Engineered Imaging LLC...419 255-1283
110 E Woodruff Ave Toledo (43604) (G-14277)

ALPHABETIC SECTION — Epg Inc

Engineered Marble Inc.. 614 308-0041
4064 Fisher Rd Columbus (43228) *(G-5354)*

Engineered Material Handling, Valley City *Also Called: Emh Inc (G-14869)*

Engineered MBL Solutions Inc....................................... 513 724-0247
4155 Taylor Rd Batavia (45103) *(G-923)*

Engineered Mfg & Eqp Co... 937 642-7776
11611 Industrial Pkwy Marysville (43040) *(G-9908)*

Engineered Plastics Corp.. 330 376-7700
420 Kenmore Blvd Akron (44301) *(G-141)*

Engineered Polymer Systems LLC................................. 216 255-2116
2600 Medina Rd Medina (44256) *(G-10319)*

Engineered Products, Twinsburg *Also Called: EPI of Cleveland Inc (G-14656)*

Engineered Profiles LLC.. 614 754-3700
2141 Fairwood Ave Columbus (43207) *(G-5355)*

Engineered Wire Products Inc (DH)............................... 419 294-3817
1200 N Warpole St Upper Sandusky (43351) *(G-14808)*

Engineered Wire Products Inc....................................... 330 469-6958
3121 W Market St Warren (44485) *(G-15167)*

Engineering Chain Div, Sandusky *Also Called: US Tsubaki Power Transm LLC (G-13102)*

Engineering Dept, Troy *Also Called: Hobart LLC (G-14581)*

Engines Inc of Ohio.. 740 377-9874
101 Commerce Dr South Point (45680) *(G-13466)*

Enginetics, Huber Heights *Also Called: Mpe Aeroengines Inc (G-8578)*

Enginetics Aero Space, Huber Heights *Also Called: Enjet Aero Dayton Inc (G-8576)*

Engler Printing Co.. 419 332-2181
808 W State St Fremont (43420) *(G-7777)*

Englewood Precision Inc.. 937 836-1910
375 Union Rd Englewood (45315) *(G-7231)*

English Oak LLC... 614 600-8038
8280 Lariat Ct Powell (43065) *(G-12672)*

Engraved In Usa LLC... 513 301-7760
93 Arndt Ct Fairfield (45014) *(G-7357)*

Engravers Gallery & Sign Co.. 330 830-1271
10 Lincoln Way E Massillon (44646) *(G-10094)*

Engstrom Manufacturing Inc... 513 573-0010
4503 State Route 42 Ste B Mason (45040) *(G-9990)*

Eni USA R&M Co Inc.. 330 723-6457
740 S Progress Dr Medina (44256) *(G-10320)*

Enjet Aero LLC... 937 878-3800
7700 New Carlisle Pike Huber Heights (45424) *(G-8575)*

Enjet Aero Dayton, Huber Heights *Also Called: Enjet Aero LLC (G-8575)*

Enjet Aero Dayton Inc (DH)... 937 878-3800
7700 New Carlisle Pike Huber Heights (45424) *(G-8576)*

Enlarging Arts Inc.. 330 434-3433
161 Tarbell St Akron (44303) *(G-142)*

Ennis Inc.. 800 537-8648
4444 N Detroit Ave Toledo (43612) *(G-14278)*

Enon Sand and Gravel LLC.. 513 771-0820
11641 Mosteller Rd Ste 2 Cincinnati (45241) *(G-2873)*

Enpac LLC... 440 975-0070
34355 Melinz Pkwy Eastlake (44095) *(G-7028)*

Enpress LLC.. 440 510-0108
34899 Curtis Blvd Eastlake (44095) *(G-7029)*

Enpro, West Chester *Also Called: Hydrotech Inc (G-15563)*

Enprotech Industrial Tech LLC (DH)............................... 216 883-3220
4259 E 49th St Cleveland (44125) *(G-4019)*

Enprotech Mechanical Services, Cleveland *Also Called: Enprotech Industrial Tech LLC (G-4019)*

Enquirer Printing Co Inc.. 513 241-1956
7188 Main St Cincinnati (45244) *(G-2874)*

Enquirer Printing Company... 513 241-1956
7188 Main St Cincinnati (45244) *(G-2875)*

Enrevo Pyro LLC.. 203 517-5002
6874 Strimbu Dr Brookfield (44403) *(G-1669)*

Ensign Product Company Inc.. 216 341-5911
3528 E 76th St Cleveland (44105) *(G-4020)*

Entec International Systems, Lakewood *Also Called: RAD-Con Inc (G-8981)*

Enterprise Electric, Lakewood *Also Called: Computer Enterprise Inc (G-8972)*

Enterprise Tool & Die Company.................................... 216 351-1300
4940 Schaaf Ln Cleveland (44131) *(G-4021)*

Enterprise Welding & Fabg Inc...................................... 440 354-4128
6257 Heisley Rd Mentor (44060) *(G-10451)*

Enterprise Welding Fbrctn... 440 354-3868
9280 Pineneedle Dr Mentor (44060) *(G-10452)*

Enterpriseid Inc... 330 963-0064
9321 Ravenna Rd Ste C Twinsburg (44087) *(G-14655)*

Entertrainment Junction.. 513 326-1100
2721 E Sharon Rd Cincinnati (45241) *(G-2876)*

Enting Water Conditioning Inc (PA)............................... 937 294-5100
3211 Dryden Rd Frnt Moraine (45439) *(G-11175)*

Entratech Systems, Sandusky *Also Called: Entratech Systems LLC (G-13055)*

Entratech Systems LLC (PA).. 419 433-7683
202 Fox Rd Sandusky (44870) *(G-13055)*

Entrochem Inc... 614 946-7602
1245 Kinnear Rd Columbus (43212) *(G-5356)*

Envases Media Inc.. 419 636-5461
1 Toy St Bryan (43506) *(G-1817)*

Envelope 1, Columbiana *Also Called: E-1 (2012) Holdings Inc (G-5037)*

Envelope 1 Inc (PA)... 330 482-3900
41969 State Route 344 Columbiana (44408) *(G-5038)*

Envelope Mart of Ohio Inc... 440 365-8177
1540 Lowell St Elyria (44035) *(G-7150)*

Enviri Corporation... 740 367-7322
5486 State Rte 7 Cheshire (45620) *(G-2477)*

Enviri Corporation... 216 961-1570
7900 Hub Pkwy Cleveland (44125) *(G-4022)*

Enviri Corporation... 740 387-1150
3477 Harding Hwy E Marion (43302) *(G-9851)*

Enviri Corporation... 330 372-1781
101 Tidewater St Ne Warren (44483) *(G-15168)*

Envirnment Ctrl Sthwest Ohio I..................................... 937 669-9900
7939 S County Road 25a Tipp City (45371) *(G-14134)*

Envirnmntal Cmpliance Tech LLC.................................. 216 634-0400
13953 Progress Pkwy North Royalton (44133) *(G-11874)*

Envirofab Inc... 216 651-1767
7914 Lake Ave Cleveland (44102) *(G-4023)*

Envirokure Incorporated.. 215 289-9800
9408 Rosedale Rd Hicksville (43526) *(G-8374)*

Environmental Chemical Corp....................................... 330 453-5200
2167 Prestwick Dr Uniontown (44685) *(G-14782)*

Environmental Doctor, Dayton *Also Called: Indoor Envmtl Specialists Inc (G-6381)*

Environmental Growth Chambers, Chagrin Falls *Also Called: Integrated Development & Mfg (G-2380)*

Environmental Products Div, Sheffield Village *Also Called: Benko Products Inc (G-13181)*

Environmental Sample Technology Inc.......................... 513 642-0100
503 Commercial Dr West Chester (45014) *(G-15425)*

Environmental Sampling Sup Inc (DH)........................... 330 497-9396
4101 Shuffel St Nw North Canton (44720) *(G-11725)*

Envirozyme, Bowling Green *Also Called: Envirozyme LLC (G-1565)*

Envirozyme LLC... 800 232-2847
400 Van Camp Rd Bowling Green (43402) *(G-1565)*

Envoi Design Inc.. 513 651-4229
1332 Main St Frnt Cincinnati (45202) *(G-2877)*

Eoi Inc... 740 201-3300
8377 Green Meadows Dr N Ste C Lewis Center (43035) *(G-9160)*

Eos Technology Inc.. 216 281-2999
8525 Clinton Rd Cleveland (44144) *(G-4024)*

Ep Bollinger LLC.. 513 941-1101
2664 Saint Georges Ct Cincinnati (45233) *(G-2878)*

EP Ferris & Associates Inc... 614 299-2999
2130 Quarry Trails Dr # 2 Columbus (43228) *(G-5357)*

Epanel Plus Ltd.. 513 772-0888
271 Northland Blvd Cincinnati (45246) *(G-2879)*

Epc-Columbia Inc.. 740 420-5252
30627 Orr Rd Circleville (43113) *(G-3549)*

Epco, Germantown *Also Called: Thomas D Epperson (G-7954)*

Epco Extrusion Painting Co... 330 781-6100
4605 Lake Park Rd Youngstown (44512) *(G-16355)*

Epcor Foundries, Cincinnati *Also Called: Seilkop Industries Inc (G-3377)*

Epg Inc.. 330 995-5125
500 Lena Dr Aurora (44202) *(G-714)*

Epg Inc (DH) 330 995-9725
1780 Miller Pkwy Streetsboro (44241) *(G-13770)*

Epi Global, Millbury *Also Called: Electro Plasma Incorporated (G-10931)*

Epi Global, Millbury *Also Called: Levison Enterprises LLC (G-10935)*

EPI of Cleveland Inc 330 468-2872
2224 E Enterprise Pkwy Twinsburg (44087) *(G-14656)*

Epic Steel, Solon *Also Called: E B P Inc (G-13339)*

Epiroc USA LLC 844 437-4762
7171 E Pleasant Valley Rd Independence (44131) *(G-8667)*

Epix Tube Co Inc (PA) 937 529-4858
5800 Wolf Creek Pike Dayton (45426) *(G-6321)*

Epluno LLC 800 249-5275
420 Heatherwoode Cir Springboro (45066) *(G-13500)*

Epoxy Systems Blstg Cating Inc 513 924-1800
5640 Morgan Rd Cleves (45002) *(G-4950)*

Epr, Kent *Also Called: Emergency Products & RES Inc (G-8814)*

EPRAD, Perrysburg *Also Called: Eprad Inc (G-12379)*

Eprad Inc 419 666-3266
28271 Cedar Park Blvd Ste 1 Perrysburg (43551) *(G-12379)*

Eps Specialties Ltd Inc 513 489-3676
7875 School Rd # 77 Cincinnati (45249) *(G-2880)*

Epsilon Management Corporation 216 634-2500
8525 Clinton Rd Cleveland (44144) *(G-4025)*

Epsilyte, Piqua *Also Called: Polysource LLC (G-12549)*

Epsilyte Holdings LLC 937 778-9500
555 E Statler Rd Piqua (45356) *(G-12515)*

Eqm Technologies & Energy Inc (PA) 513 825-7500
1800 Carillion Blvd Cincinnati (45240) *(G-2881)*

Equinox Enterprises LLC 419 627-0022
1920 George St Sandusky (44870) *(G-13056)*

Equip Business Solutions Co (PA) 614 854-9755
120 Twin Oaks Dr Jackson (45640) *(G-8715)*

Equipment Guys Inc 614 871-9220
185 Westgate Dr Newark (43055) *(G-11575)*

Equipment Mfrs Intl Inc 216 651-6700
16151 Puritas Ave Cleveland (44135) *(G-4026)*

Equipping Ministries Intl Inc 513 742-1100
3908 Plainville Rd # 200 Cincinnati (45227) *(G-2882)*

Equistar, Fairport Harbor *Also Called: Lyondell Chemical Company (G-7455)*

Equistar Chemicals LP 513 530-4000
11530 Northlake Dr Cincinnati (45249) *(G-2883)*

Equitrans Midstream Corpo 304 626-7934
252 W Main St Ste D Saint Clairsville (43950) *(G-12903)*

ERAMET MARIETTA INC 740 374-1000
16705 State Route 7 Marietta (45750) *(G-9792)*

Erath Veneer, Granville *Also Called: Erath Veneer Corp Virginia (G-8016)*

Erath Veneer Corp Virginia 540 483-5223
2825 Hallie Ln # B Granville (43023) *(G-8016)*

Erdie Industries Inc 440 288-0166
1205 Colorado Ave Lorain (44052) *(G-9411)*

Ergo Desktop LLC 567 890-3746
457 Grand Lake Rd Celina (45822) *(G-2331)*

Ergocan, Toledo *Also Called: Mon-Say Corp (G-14390)*

Erhart Foundry, Cincinnati *Also Called: Chris Erhart Foundry & Mch Co (G-2734)*

Eric Allshouse LLC 330 533-4258
9666 Lisbon Rd Canfield (44406) *(G-2005)*

Erichsen Inc 734 474-1471
815 Crocker Rd Ste 9 Westlake (44145) *(G-15750)*

Erico, Cleveland *Also Called: Erico Products Inc (G-4027)*

Erico Global Company 440 248-0100
31700 Solon Rd Solon (44139) *(G-13344)*

Erico International Corp 440 248-0100
34600 Solon Rd Solon (44139) *(G-13345)*

Erico Products Inc 440 248-0100
34600 Solon Rd Cleveland (44139) *(G-4027)*

Ericson Manufacturing Co 440 951-8000
4323 Hamann Pkwy Willoughby (44094) *(G-15917)*

Erie Steel Ltd 419 478-3743
5540 Jackman Rd Toledo (43613) *(G-14279)*

Erie Street Thea Svcs Inc 216 426-0050
1621 E 41st St Cleveland (44103) *(G-4028)*

Erieview Metal Treating Co 216 663-1780
4465 Johnston Pkwy Cleveland (44128) *(G-4029)*

Ernest Industries Inc 937 325-9851
4000 Mccartney Rd Lowellville (44436) *(G-9513)*

Ernest Industries Inc 937 325-9851
1221 Groop Rd Springfield (45504) *(G-13559)*

Ernie Green Industries Inc 740 420-5252
30627 Orr Rd Circleville (43113) *(G-3550)*

Ernie Green Industries Inc 614 219-1423
1855 State Rd Ste 121n New Madison (45346) *(G-11473)*

Ernst America Inc 937 434-3133
2920 Kreitzer Rd Moraine (45439) *(G-11176)*

Ernst Concrete, Cleves *Also Called: Ernst Enterprises Inc (G-4951)*

Ernst Concrete, Dayton *Also Called: Ernst Enterprises Inc (G-6322)*

Ernst Enterprises Inc 937 848-6811
2181 Ferry Rd Bellbrook (45305) *(G-1192)*

Ernst Enterprises Inc 937 866-9441
4710 Soldiers Home Rd Carrollton (44615) *(G-2306)*

Ernst Enterprises Inc 513 367-1939
7340 Dry Fork Rd Cleves (45002) *(G-4951)*

Ernst Enterprises Inc 614 443-9456
711 Stimmel Rd Columbus (40223) *(G-5358)*

Ernst Enterprises Inc 614 308-0063
569 N Wilson Rd Columbus (43204) *(G-5359)*

Ernst Enterprises Inc (PA) 937 233-5555
3361 Successful Way Dayton (45414) *(G-6322)*

Ernst Enterprises Inc 937 878-9378
5325 Medway Rd Fairborn (45324) *(G-7313)*

Ernst Enterprises Inc 513 874-8300
4250 Columbia Rd Lebanon (45036) *(G-9073)*

Ernst Enterprises Inc 419 222-2015
377 S Central Ave Lima (45804) *(G-9241)*

Ernst Enterprises Inc 513 422-3651
2504 S Main St Middletown (45044) *(G-10821)*

Ernst Enterprises Inc 937 339-6249
805 Union St Troy (45373) *(G-14565)*

Ernst Flow Industries LLC 732 938-5641
16633 Foltz Pkwy Strongsville (44149) *(G-13833)*

Ernst Metal Technologies LLC 937 434-3133
3031 Dryden Rd Moraine (45439) *(G-11177)*

Ernst Metal Technologies LLC (DH) 937 434-3133
2920 Kreitzer Rd Moraine (45439) *(G-11178)*

Ernst Ready Mix Division, Lima *Also Called: Ernst Enterprises Inc (G-9241)*

Erosion Control Products Corp 302 815-6500
9281 Le Saint Dr West Chester (45014) *(G-15426)*

ES Industries Inc (PA) 419 643-2625
110 Brookview Ct Lima (45801) *(G-9242)*

Es Steiner Dairy, Baltic *Also Called: Tri State Dairy LLC (G-842)*

Es Thermal Inc 440 323-3291
388 Cranston Dr Berea (44017) *(G-1277)*

ES&w, Lakewood *Also Called: Euclid Steel & Wire Inc (G-8974)*

ESAB Group Incorporated 440 813-2506
3325 Middle Rd Ashtabula (44004) *(G-632)*

Escher Division, Toledo *Also Called: Maumee Valley Fabricators Inc (G-14380)*

Esco Turbine Tech Cleveland 440 953-0053
34000 Lakeland Blvd Eastlake (44095) *(G-7030)*

Esco Turbine Technologies - Cleveland Inc 440 953-0053
34000 Lakeland Blvd Eastlake (44095) *(G-7031)*

Escort Inc 513 870-8500
5440 W Chester Rd West Chester (45069) *(G-15427)*

Esi-Extrusion Services Inc 330 374-3388
305 W North St Akron (44303) *(G-143)*

Esko-Graphics Inc (HQ) 937 454-1721
8535 Gander Creek Dr Miamisburg (45342) *(G-10637)*

Eskoartwork, Miamisburg *Also Called: Esko-Graphics Inc (G-10637)*

Esmet Inc 330 452-9132
1406 5th St Sw Canton (44702) *(G-2098)*

ESP Akron Sub LLC 330 374-2242
240 W Emerling Ave Akron (44301) *(G-144)*

Espi Enterprises Inc (PA) 440 543-8108
10145 Queens Way Chagrin Falls (44023) *(G-2394)*

ALPHABETIC SECTION

Espline LLC.. 401 234-4520
1810 Grace Ln Columbus (43220) *(G-5360)*

Ess, Dayton *Also Called: Ever Secure SEC Systems Inc (G-6327)*

Essc Group Inc.. 330 317-3566
3340 Burbank Rd Wooster (44691) *(G-16116)*

Essential Elements Usa LLC....................... 513 482-5700
4775 Paddock Rd Cincinnati (45229) *(G-2884)*

Essential Learning Products, Hilliard *Also Called: Teachers Publishing Group (G-8445)*

Essential Provisions LLC........................... 937 271-0381
292 Inwood Rd Wilmington (45177) *(G-16049)*

Essential Sealing Products, Chagrin Falls *Also Called: Espi Enterprises Inc (G-2394)*

Essentialware... 888 975-0405
7637 Euclid Chardon Rd Kirtland (44094) *(G-8939)*

Essi Acoustical Products............................ 216 251-7888
11750 Berea Rd Ste 1 Cleveland (44111) *(G-4030)*

Essilor Laboratories Amer Inc..................... 614 274-0840
3671 Interchange Rd Columbus (43204) *(G-5361)*

Essilor Laboratories Amer Inc..................... 330 425-3003
9221 Ravenna Rd # 3 Twinsburg (44087) *(G-14657)*

Essilor of America Inc................................. 513 765-6000
4000 Luxottica Pl Mason (45040) *(G-9991)*

Essity Operations Wausau LLC................... 513 217-3644
700 Columbia Ave Middletown (45042) *(G-10822)*

Essity Prof Hygiene N Amer LLC................. 513 217-3644
700 Columbia Ave Middletown (45042) *(G-10823)*

ESSITY PROFESSIONAL HYGIENE NORTH AMERICA LLC, Middletown *Also Called: Essity Prof Hygiene N Amer LLC (G-10823)*

Est, Walton Hills *Also Called: Intigral Inc (G-15099)*

Est Analytical, West Chester *Also Called: Pts Prfssnal Technical Svc Inc (G-15488)*

Estabrook Assembly Svcs Inc..................... 440 243-3350
700 W Bagley Rd Berea (44017) *(G-1278)*

Estee 2 Inc.. 937 224-7853
612 Linden Ave Dayton (45403) *(G-6323)*

Esterle Mold & Machine Co Inc (PA)........... 330 686-1685
1539 Commerce Dr Stow (44224) *(G-13695)*

Esterline, Cleveland *Also Called: Esterline Technologies Corp (G-4031)*

Esterline & Sons Mfg Co LLC..................... 937 265-5278
6508 Old Clifton Rd Springfield (45502) *(G-13560)*

Esterline Technologies Corp (HQ).............. 216 706-2960
1301 E 9th St Ste 3000 Cleveland (44114) *(G-4031)*

Esther Price Candies & Gifts, Dayton *Also Called: Esther Price Candies Corporation (G-6324)*

Esther Price Candies Corporation (PA)....... 937 253-2121
1709 Wayne Ave Dayton (45410) *(G-6324)*

Estone Group LLC....................................... 888 653-2246
2900 Carskaddon Ave # 200 Toledo (43606) *(G-14280)*

ET&f Fastening Systems Inc....................... 800 248-2376
29019 Solon Rd Solon (44139) *(G-13346)*

Etc Lighting and Plastic, Andover *Also Called: K-D Lamp Company (G-486)*

Etched Metal Company............................... 440 248-0240
30200 Solon Industrial Pkwy Solon (44139) *(G-13347)*

Etchworks.. 330 274-8345
9769 State Route 44 Mantua (44255) *(G-9736)*

Ethicon Endo - Surgery, Blue Ash *Also Called: Ethicon Inc (G-1390)*

Ethicon Endo-Surgery Inc (HQ)................. 513 337-7000
4545 Creek Rd Blue Ash (45242) *(G-1389)*

Ethicon Inc.. 513 786-7000
10123 Alliance Rd Blue Ash (45242) *(G-1390)*

Ethicon US LLC (DH).................................. 513 337-7000
4545 Creek Rd # 3 Blue Ash (45242) *(G-1391)*

Ethima Inc... 419 626-4912
1528 First St Sandusky (44870) *(G-13057)*

Eti Tech LLC... 937 832-4200
3387 Woodman Dr Kettering (45429) *(G-8907)*

Etko Machine Inc.. 330 745-4033
2796 Barber Rd Norton (44203) *(G-11942)*

Etl Performance Products Inc..................... 234 575-7226
1717 Pennsylvania Ave Salem (44460) *(G-12992)*

Etna Products Incorporated........................ 440 543-9845
16824 Park Circle Dr Chagrin Falls (44023) *(G-2395)*

Ets Schaefer LLC (DH)............................... 330 468-6600
3700 Park East Dr Ste 300 Beachwood (44122) *(G-987)*

Ets Schaefer LLC....................................... 330 468-6600
8050 Highland Pointe Pkwy Macedonia (44056) *(G-9549)*

Euclid Chemical Company (DH).................. 800 321-7628
19215 Redwood Rd Cleveland (44110) *(G-4032)*

Euclid Coffee Co Inc................................... 216 481-3330
17230 S Waterloo Rd Cleveland (44110) *(G-4033)*

Euclid Design and Mfg Inc.......................... 440 942-0066
38333 Willoughby Pkwy Willoughby (44094) *(G-15918)*

Euclid Heat Treating Co.............................. 216 481-8444
1408 E 222nd St Euclid (44117) *(G-7269)*

Euclid Jalousies Inc.................................... 440 953-1112
490 E 200th St Cleveland (44119) *(G-4034)*

Euclid Media Group LLC (PA)...................... 216 241-7550
737 Bolivar Rd Cleveland (44115) *(G-4035)*

Euclid Precision Grinding Co...................... 440 946-8888
35400 Lakeland Blvd Eastlake (44095) *(G-7032)*

Euclid Refinishing Compnay Inc.................. 440 275-3356
2937 Industrial Park Dr Austinburg (44010) *(G-745)*

Euclid Spring Co... 440 943-3213
30006 Lakeland Blvd Wickliffe (44092) *(G-15832)*

Euclid Steel & Wire Inc............................... 216 731-6744
13000 Athens Ave Ste 101 Lakewood (44107) *(G-8974)*

Euclid Welding Company Inc...................... 216 289-0714
29956 White Rd Willoughby Hills (44092) *(G-16024)*

Eugene Stewart.. 937 898-1117
5671 Webster St Dayton (45414) *(G-6325)*

Eureka Screw Machine Co, Cleveland *Also Called: Eureka Screw Machine Pdts Co (G-4036)*

Eureka Screw Machine Pdts Co................... 216 883-1715
3960 E 91st St Cleveland (44105) *(G-4036)*

Eurocase Archtctral Cbnets Mll................... 330 674-0681
6086 State Route 241 Millersburg (44654) *(G-10954)*

Eurostampa North America Inc................... 513 821-2275
1440 Seymour Ave Cincinnati (45237) *(G-2885)*

Eurotherm, Westlake *Also Called: Gc Controls Inc (G-15752)*

Evans Adhesive Corporation (HQ).............. 614 451-2665
925 Old Henderson Rd Columbus (43220) *(G-5362)*

Evans Adhesive Corporation Ltd................. 614 451-2665
925 Old Henderson Rd Columbus (43220) *(G-5363)*

Evans Bakery Inc....................................... 937 228-4151
700 Troy St Dayton (45404) *(G-6326)*

Evans Creative Group LLC.......................... 614 657-9439
11 E Gay St Columbus (43215) *(G-5364)*

Evans Food Group Ltd................................ 626 636-8110
406 Barklow Extension Rd Portsmouth (45662) *(G-12643)*

Evans Food Group Ltd................................ 740 285-3078
2310 8th St Portsmouth (45662) *(G-12644)*

Evans Industries Inc................................... 330 453-1122
606 Walnut Ave Ne Canton (44702) *(G-2099)*

Even Cut Abrasive Company....................... 216 881-9595
850 E 72nd St Cleveland (44103) *(G-4037)*

Evenflo, Miamisburg *Also Called: Evenflo Company Inc (G-10638)*

Evenflo Company Inc (DH)......................... 937 415-3300
3131 Newmark Dr Ste 300 Miamisburg (45342) *(G-10638)*

Evenflo Company Inc................................. 937 773-3971
1801 W Main St Troy (45373) *(G-14566)*

Evening Leader, The, Saint Marys *Also Called: Horizon Ohio Publications Inc (G-12953)*

Ever Roll Specialties Co............................. 937 964-1302
3988 Lawrenceville Dr Springfield (45504) *(G-13561)*

Ever Secure SEC Systems Inc..................... 937 369-8294
5523 Salem Ave Ste 134 Dayton (45426) *(G-6327)*

Eveready Printing Inc.................................. 216 587-2389
20700 Miles Pkwy Cleveland (44128) *(G-4038)*

Everett Industries LLC............................... 330 372-3700
3601 Larchmont Ave Ne Warren (44483) *(G-15169)*

Everflow Eastern Partners LP (PA).............. 330 533-2692
585 W Main St Canfield (44406) *(G-2006)*

Everflow Eastern Partners LP..................... 330 537-3863
29093 Salem Alliance Rd Salem (44460) *(G-12993)*

Evergreen Midwest, Clyde *Also Called: Evergreen Recycling LLC (G-4972)*

Evergreen Plastics, Clyde *Also Called: Polychem LLC (G-4975)*

Evergreen Recycling LLC (DH)................... 419 547-1400
202 Watertower Dr Clyde (43410) *(G-4972)*

Everhard, Canton *Also Called: Everhard Products Inc (G-2100)*
Everhard Products Inc (PA).. 330 453-7786
  1016 9th St Sw Canton (44707) *(G-2100)*
Evers Enterprises Inc.. 513 541-7200
  1210 Ellis St Cincinnati (45223) *(G-2886)*
Evers Welding Co Inc... 513 385-7352
  4849 Blue Rock Rd Cincinnati (45247) *(G-2887)*
Evertz Technology Svc USA Inc.. 513 422-8400
  2601 S Verity Pkwy Bldg 102 Middletown (45044) *(G-10824)*
Everyday Technologies Inc.. 937 497-7774
  324 Adams St Bldg 1 Sidney (45365) *(G-13247)*
Everyday Technologies Inc.. 419 739-6104
  751 Industrial Dr Wapakoneta (45895) *(G-15109)*
Everyday Technologies Inc (PA)... 937 492-4171
  2005 Campbell Rd Sidney (45365) *(G-13248)*
Everything In America.. 347 871-6872
  4141 Stilmore Rd Cleveland (44121) *(G-4039)*
Everythings Image Inc... 513 469-6727
  9933 Alliance Rd Ste 2 Blue Ash (45242) *(G-1392)*
Evokes LLC.. 513 947-8433
  8118 Corporate Way Ste 212 Mason (45040) *(G-9992)*
Evolution Crtive Solutions Inc... 513 681-4450
  7107 Shona Dr Cincinnati (45237) *(G-2888)*
Evolution Lawn & Landscape LLC....................................... 330 268-5306
  4389 Tabor Ridge Rd Ne Mineral City (44656) *(G-11017)*
Evolve Solutions LLC.. 440 357-8964
  1 High Tech Ave Painesville (44077) *(G-12233)*
Evonik Corporation... 330 668-2235
  3500 Embassy Pkwy Ste 100 Akron (44333) *(G-145)*
Evonik Corporation... 513 554-8969
  620 Shepherd Dr Cincinnati (45215) *(G-2889)*
Evoqua Water Technologies LLC... 614 491-5917
  6300 Commerce Center Dr Groveport (43125) *(G-8138)*
Evoqua Water Technologies LLC... 614 861-5440
  1154 Hill Rd N Pickerington (43147) *(G-12461)*
Evp International LLC... 513 761-7614
  2701 Short Vine St # 200 Cincinnati (45219) *(G-2890)*
Ewart-Ohlson Machine Company... 330 928-2171
  1435 Main St Cuyahoga Falls (44221) *(G-6081)*
Ewebschedule... 614 882-0726
  180 Commerce Park Dr Westerville (43082) *(G-15655)*
Ewh Spectrum LLC... 937 593-8010
  221 W Chillicothe Ave Bellefontaine (43311) *(G-1208)*
Exact Cutting Service Inc.. 440 546-1319
  6892 W Snowville Rd Ste 108 Brecksville (44141) *(G-1616)*
Exact Equipment Corporation (HQ)..................................... 215 295-2000
  1900 Polaris Pkwy Columbus (43240) *(G-5062)*
Exact-Tool & Die Inc... 216 676-9140
  5425 W 140th St Cleveland (44142) *(G-4040)*
Exair Corporation.. 513 671-3322
  11510 Goldcoast Dr Cincinnati (45249) *(G-2891)*
Excalibur Barber LLC... 330 729-9006
  7401 Market St Boardman (44512) *(G-1512)*
Excel Loading Systems LLC.. 513 504-1069
  1051 Belle Ave Hamilton (45015) *(G-8207)*
Excel Machine & Tool Inc.. 419 678-3318
  212 Butler St Coldwater (45828) *(G-4987)*
Excelitas Technologies Corp.. 866 539-5916
  1100 Vanguard Blvd Miamisburg (45342) *(G-10639)*
Excellent Tool & Die Inc... 216 671-9222
  10921 Briggs Rd Cleveland (44111) *(G-4041)*
Excello Fabric Finishers Inc.. 740 622-7444
  802 S 2nd St Coshocton (43812) *(G-5977)*
Excelsior Marking, Akron *Also Called: Mark-All Enterprises LLC (G-235)*
Excelsior Printing Co.. 740 927-2934
  1014 Putnam Rd Sw Pataskala (43062) *(G-12297)*
Exco Engineering USA Inc (HQ).. 419 726-1595
  5244 Enterprise Blvd Toledo (43612) *(G-14281)*
Exco Resources (pa) LLC.. 740 796-5231
  4100 Valley Rd Adamsville (43802) *(G-7)*
Exco Resources LLC... 740 254-4061
  3618 Fallen Timber Rd Se Tippecanoe (44699) *(G-14169)*

Executive Sweets East Inc... 440 359-9866
  7603 First Pl Oakwood Village (44146) *(G-12038)*
Executive Wings Inc.. 440 254-1812
  13550 Carter Rd Painesville (44077) *(G-12234)*
Exhibit Concepts Inc (PA)... 937 890-7000
  700 Crossroads Ct Vandalia (45377) *(G-14939)*
Exhibit Design International, Fairfield *Also Called: Edi Custom Interiors Inc (G-7355)*
Exide Technologies LLC.. 614 863-3866
  861 Taylor Rd Unit G Gahanna (43230) *(G-7835)*
Exit 11 Truck Tire Service... 330 659-6372
  5219 Brecksville Rd Ste B Richfield (44286) *(G-12786)*
Exito Manufacturing LLC... 937 291-9871
  4120 Industrial Ln Ste B Beavercreek (45430) *(G-1073)*
Exomet Inc.. 440 593-1161
  1100 Maple Ave Conneaut (44030) *(G-5917)*
Exothermics
  5040 Enterprise Blvd Toledo (43612) *(G-14282)*
Exotica Fresheners Co, Holland *Also Called: D & J Distributing & Mfg (G-8501)*
Exp Fuels Inc.. 419 382-7713
  3070 Airport Hwy Toledo (43609) *(G-14283)*
Experimental Machine, Brecksville *Also Called: Exact Cutting Service Inc (G-1616)*
Expert Crane, Wellington *Also Called: Expert Crane Inc (G-15307)*
Expert Crane Inc... 216 451-9900
  720 Shiloh Ave Wellington (44090) *(G-15307)*
Explorys Inc.. 216 767-4700
  1111 Superior Ave E Cleveland (44114) *(G-4042)*
Expo Machinery, Cleveland *Also Called: Expo Packaging Inc (G-4043)*
Expo Packaging Inc... 216 267-9700
  4832 Ridge Rd Cleveland (44144) *(G-4043)*
Exponentia US Inc (PA).. 614 944-5103
  424 Beecher Rd Ste A Columbus (43230) *(G-5365)*
Express Ground Services Inc... 216 870-9374
  1241 E 172nd St Cleveland (44119) *(G-4044)*
Express Grphics Prtg Dsign Inc... 513 728-3344
  9695 Hamilton Ave Cincinnati (45231) *(G-2892)*
Express Pharmacy & Dme LLC.. 210 981-9690
  2750 S Hamilton Rd Ste 19 Columbus (43232) *(G-5366)*
Express Trading Pins LLC... 419 394-2550
  105 Marbello Ct Saint Marys (45885) *(G-12951)*
Extendit Company.. 330 743-4343
  14150 Beaver Springfield Rd New Springfield (44443) *(G-11541)*
Exterior Portfolio LLC.. 614 754-3400
  1441 Universal Rd Columbus (43207) *(G-5367)*
Extol of Ohio Inc (PA)... 419 668-2072
  208 Republic St Norwalk (44857) *(G-11963)*
Extol of Ohio Inc... 419 668-2072
  208 Republic St Norwalk (44857) *(G-11964)*
Extra Seal, Newcomerstown *Also Called: 31 Inc (G-11640)*
Extreme Caster Services Inc.. 330 637-9030
  3333 Niles Cortland Rd Ne Cortland (44410) *(G-5962)*
Extreme Microbial Tech LLC.. 844 885-0088
  2800 E River Rd Moraine (45439) *(G-11179)*
Extreme Microbial Technologies, Moraine *Also Called: Extreme Microbial Tech LLC (G-11179)*
Extruded Silicone Products, Mogadore *Also Called: S P E Inc (G-11082)*
Extruded Slcone Pdts Gskets In.. 330 733-0101
  3300 Gilchrist Rd Mogadore (44260) *(G-11072)*
Extrudex, Painesville *Also Called: Extrudex Limited Partnership (G-12235)*
Extrudex Aluminum Inc... 330 538-4444
  12051 Mahoning Ave North Jackson (44451) *(G-11783)*
Extrudex Limited Partnership (PA)..................................... 440 352-7101
  310 Figgie Dr Painesville (44077) *(G-12235)*
Eye Surgery Center Ohio Inc (PA)...................................... 614 228-3937
  262 Neil Ave Ste 320 Columbus (43215) *(G-5368)*
Eyescience, Powell *Also Called: Eyescience Labs LLC (G-12673)*
Eyescience Labs LLC.. 614 885-7100
  493 Village Park Dr Powell (43065) *(G-12673)*
EZ Brite Brands Inc.. 440 871-7817
  806 Sharon Dr Ste C Cleveland (44145) *(G-4045)*
EZ Grout Corporation Inc.. 740 962-2024
  1833 N Riverview Rd Malta (43758) *(G-9607)*

ALPHABETIC SECTION

Ezg Manufacturing, Malta *Also Called: E Z Grout Corporation (G-9606)*

Ezg Manufacturing, Malta *Also Called: EZ Grout Corporation Inc (G-9607)*

Ezurio LLC (PA)...330 434-7929
  50 S Main St Ste 1100 Akron (44308) *(G-146)*

F & F Shtmtl & Fabrication LLC...419 618-3171
  3601 County Road 14 New Riegel (44853) *(G-11535)*

F & F Shtmtl & Fabrication LLC...567 938-8788
  4720 W Us Highway 224 Tiffin (44883) *(G-14085)*

F & G Tool and Die Co..937 746-3658
  130 Industrial Dr Franklin (45005) *(G-7673)*

F & G Tool and Die Co (PA)..937 294-1405
  3024 Dryden Rd Moraine (45439) *(G-11180)*

F & M Mafco Inc (HQ)...513 367-2151
  9149 Dry Fork Rd Harrison (45030) *(G-8273)*

F & S Hydraulics Inc...513 575-1600
  6071 Branch Hill Guinea Pike Ste B Milford (45150) *(G-10905)*

F A S T, Cincinnati *Also Called: Field Apparatus Service & Tstg (G-2902)*

F A Tech Corp...513 942-1920
  9065 Sutton Pl West Chester (45011) *(G-15428)*

F C Brengman and Assoc LLC..740 756-4308
  86 High St Carroll (43112) *(G-2297)*

F H Bonn Co Inc..937 323-7024
  4300 Gateway Blvd Springfield (45502) *(G-13562)*

F I C, Akron *Also Called: Foundation Industries Inc (G-157)*

F I T, Valley City *Also Called: Fuserashi Intl Tech Inc (G-14870)*

F J Designs Inc...330 264-1377
  2163 Great Trails Dr Wooster (44691) *(G-16117)*

F M Machine Co..330 773-8237
  1114 Triplett Blvd Akron (44306) *(G-147)*

F M P Inc..330 628-1118
  3555 Gilchrist Rd Mogadore (44260) *(G-11073)*

F S A, Canton *Also Called: Foundation Systems Anchors Inc (G-2104)*

F Squared Inc...419 752-7273
  9 Sunset Dr Greenwich (44837) *(G-8066)*

F&P America Mfg Inc (HQ)...937 339-0212
  2101 Corporate Dr Troy (45373) *(G-14567)*

F+w Media Inc..513 531-2690
  9912 Carver Rd Ste 100 Blue Ash (45242) *(G-1393)*

Fab Form, Mentor *Also Called: V K C Inc (G-10590)*

Fab-Steel Co Inc...419 666-5100
  240 W Andrus Rd Northwood (43619) *(G-11918)*

Fab3 Group, Cleveland *Also Called: Duct Fabricators Inc (G-3976)*

Fabacraft Inc..513 677-0500
  201 Grandin Rd Maineville (45039) *(G-9600)*

Fabacraft Co, Maineville *Also Called: Fabacraft Inc (G-9600)*

Fabco Inc (HQ)..419 422-4533
  2500 Fostoria Ave Findlay (45840) *(G-7504)*

Fabcon Companies LLC...614 875-8601
  3400 Jackson Pike Grove City (43123) *(G-8093)*

Fabcor Inc..419 628-4428
  350 S Ohio St Minster (45865) *(G-11052)*

Fabohio Inc..740 922-4233
  521 E 7th St Uhrichsville (44683) *(G-14765)*

Fabric Forms Inc..513 281-6300
  1320 Bates Ave Cincinnati (45225) *(G-2893)*

Fabric Square Shop..330 752-3044
  2091 Liberty Rd Stow (44224) *(G-13696)*

Fabricating Machine Tools Ltd..440 666-9187
  12360 Plaza Dr Cleveland (44130) *(G-4046)*

Fabricating Solutions Inc..330 486-0998
  7920 Bavaria Rd Twinsburg (44087) *(G-14658)*

Fabrication and Welding, Sandusky *Also Called: Universal Dsign Fbrication LLC (G-13101)*

Fabrication Division, Maumee *Also Called: Andersons Inc (G-10164)*

Fabrication Shop Inc..419 435-7934
  1395 Buckley St Fostoria (44830) *(G-7631)*

Fabriweld Corporation..419 663-0279
  360 Eastpark Dr Norwalk (44857) *(G-11965)*

Fabriweld Corporation (PA)..419 668-3358
  405 Industrial Pkwy Norwalk (44857) *(G-11966)*

Fabstar Tanks Inc...419 587-3639
  20302 Road 48 Grover Hill (45849) *(G-8169)*

Fabtech Ohio Inc..308 532-1860
  5451 Grace Dr Mentor (44060) *(G-10453)*

Fabx LLC..614 565-5835
  1819 Walcutt Rd Ste 100 Columbus (43228) *(G-5369)*

Facemyer Lumber Co Inc (PA)...740 992-5965
  31940 Bailey Run Rd Pomeroy (45769) *(G-12613)*

Facil North America Inc (HQ)...330 487-2500
  2242 Pinnacle Pkwy Ste 100 Twinsburg (44087) *(G-14659)*

Facilities Management Ex LLC...614 519-2186
  800 Yard St Ste 115 Columbus (43212) *(G-5370)*

Facility Service Pros LLC...419 577-6123
  3206 Townsend Angling Rd Collins (44826) *(G-5004)*

Factory Direct, Cincinnati *Also Called: Candle-Lite Company LLC (G-2699)*

Facts Inc..330 928-2332
  2737 Front St Cuyahoga Falls (44221) *(G-6082)*

Facultatieve Tech Americas Inc.......................................330 723-6339
  940 Lake Rd Medina (44256) *(G-10321)*

Fair Publishing House Inc..419 668-3746
  15 Schauss Ave Norwalk (44857) *(G-11967)*

Fairborn Cement Company LLC.......................................937 879-8393
  3250 Linebaugh Rd Xenia (45385) *(G-16261)*

Fairborn Cement Plant..937 879-8466
  3250 Linebaugh Rd Fairborn (45324) *(G-7314)*

Fairborn USA Inc (PA)..419 294-4987
  205 Broadview St Upper Sandusky (43351) *(G-14809)*

Fairfield Machined Pdts Inc..740 756-4409
  6215 Columbus Lancaster Rd Nw Carroll (43112) *(G-2298)*

Fairfield Manufacturing Inc...513 642-0081
  8585 Seward Rd Fairfield (45011) *(G-7358)*

Fairfield Wood Works Ltd...740 689-1953
  1612 E Main St Lancaster (43130) *(G-9015)*

Fairmount Minerals, Independence *Also Called: Covia Solutions Inc (G-8661)*

Fairview Log Homes, Millersburg *Also Called: Al Yoder Construction Co (G-10939)*

Faith Tool & Manufacturing..440 951-5934
  36575 Reading Ave Willoughby (44094) *(G-15919)*

Falcon, Medina *Also Called: Falcon Industries Inc (G-10322)*

Falcon Foundry Company...330 536-6221
  96 6th St Lowellville (44436) *(G-9514)*

Falcon Industries Inc (PA)..330 723-0099
  180 Commerce Dr Medina (44256) *(G-10322)*

Falcon Innovations Inc...216 252-0676
  3316 W 118th St Cleveland (44111) *(G-4047)*

Falcon Tool & Machine Inc...937 534-9999
  2795 Lance Dr Dayton (45409) *(G-6328)*

Falholt Division, Akron *Also Called: Russell Products Co Inc (G-317)*

Fallen Oak Candles Inc..419 204-8162
  917 Lilac St Celina (45822) *(G-2332)*

Fallon Pharaohs..216 990-2746
  3911 Grosvenor Rd Cleveland (44118) *(G-4048)*

Falls Filtration Tech Inc..330 928-4100
  115 E Steels Corners Rd Stow (44224) *(G-13697)*

Falls Mtal Fbrctors Indus Svcs..330 253-7181
  380 Kennedy Rd Akron (44305) *(G-148)*

Falls Stamping & Welding Co...216 771-9635
  1720 Fall St Cleveland (44113) *(G-4049)*

Falls Stamping & Welding Co (PA)...................................330 928-1191
  2900 Vincent St Cuyahoga Falls (44221) *(G-6083)*

Falls Tool and Die Inc...330 633-4884
  1416 Piedmont Ave Akron (44310) *(G-149)*

Family Fun, Louisville *Also Called: Bradley Enterprises Inc (G-9456)*

Family Motor Coach Assn Inc (PA)...................................513 474-3622
  8291 Clough Pike Cincinnati (45244) *(G-2894)*

Family Motor Coaching, Cincinnati *Also Called: Family Motor Coaching Inc (G-2895)*

Family Motor Coaching Inc...513 474-3622
  8291 Clough Pike Cincinnati (45244) *(G-2895)*

Family Packaging Inc (PA)...937 325-4106
  504 W Euclid Ave Springfield (45506) *(G-13563)*

Famous Industries Inc (DH)...330 535-1811
  2620 Ridgewood Rd Ste 200 Akron (44313) *(G-150)*

Famous Industries Inc..740 685-2592
  356 Main St Byesville (43723) *(G-1896)*

Famous Kiss-N-Korn Shop, Cleveland Also Called: Crawford Acquisition Corp (G-3915)
Famous Realty Cleveland Inc 740 685-2533
354 Main St Byesville (43723) *(G-1897)*
Famous Supply, Byesville Also Called: Famous Realty Cleveland Inc (G-1897)
Fanci Forms, Upper Sandusky Also Called: Mar-Metal Mfg Inc (G-14815)
Fancy ME Boutique LLC 419 357-8927
133 E Market St Sandusky (44870) *(G-13058)*
Fannie May Confections Inc 330 494-0833
5353 Lauby Rd North Canton (44720) *(G-11726)*
Fannin Machine Company LLC 419 524-9525
76 Atenway St Mansfield (44902) *(G-9654)*
Fantasia Enterprises LLC 330 400-8741
625 Erie St S Massillon (44646) *(G-10095)*
Fantasy Candies, Cleveland Also Called: Chocolate Pig Inc (G-3820)
Far Corner 330 767-3734
13189 Mount Eaton St Sw Navarre (44662) *(G-11341)*
Farah Jewelers Inc 614 438-6140
5965 Medallion Dr E Westerville (43082) *(G-15656)*
Farasey Steel Fabricators Inc 216 641-1853
4000 Iron Ct Cleveland (44115) *(G-4050)*
Faretec Inc 440 350-9510
1610 W Jackson St Unit 6 Painesville (44077) *(G-12236)*
Farin Industries Inc 440 275-2755
2844 Industrial Park Dr Austinburg (44010) *(G-746)*
Farm & Dairy, Salem Also Called: Lyle Printing & Publishing Co (G-13013)
Farm Elevator, Upper Sandusky Also Called: Mennel Milling Company (G-14816)
Farm Products Division, Dayton Also Called: Putnam Plastics Inc (G-6535)
Farmer Hub, Wooster Also Called: Wooster Daily Record Inc LLC (G-16184)
Farmer Smiths Market, Dover Also Called: Bfc Inc (G-6809)
Farmerstown Meats 330 897-7972
2933 Township Road 163 Sugarcreek (44681) *(G-13925)*
Farr Automation Inc 419 289-1883
58 Sugarbush Ct Ashland (44805) *(G-571)*
Farsight Management Inc 330 602-8338
6790 Middle Run Rd Nw Dover (44622) *(G-6824)*
Fast Signs 614 710-1312
4469 Cemetery Rd Hilliard (43026) *(G-8411)*
Fast Track Signs LLC 937 593-9990
813 N Main St Bellefontaine (43311) *(G-1209)*
Fastener Industries Inc 440 891-2031
33 Lou Groza Blvd Berea (44017) *(G-1279)*
Fastener Industries Inc (PA) 440 243-0034
1 Berea Cmns Ste 209 Berea (44017) *(G-1280)*
Fastfeed Corporation 330 948-7333
124 S Academy St Lodi (44254) *(G-9350)*
Fastformingcom LLC 330 927-3277
300 Morning Star Dr Rittman (44270) *(G-12821)*
Fastsigns 513 489-8989
12125 Montgomery Rd Cincinnati (45249) *(G-2896)*
Fastsigns 937 890-6770
6020 N Dixie Dr Dayton (45414) *(G-6329)*
Fastsigns 513 226-6733
6681 Woodland Trace Ct Liberty Township (45044) *(G-9206)*
Fastsigns 330 952-2626
2736 Medina Rd Ste 109 Medina (44256) *(G-10323)*
Fastsigns 440 954-9191
7538 Mentor Ave Mentor (44060) *(G-10454)*
Fastsigns 419 843-1073
1100 N Mccord Rd Ste A Toledo (43615) *(G-14284)*
Fastsigns, Akron Also Called: Sterling Associates Inc (G-338)
Fastsigns, Broadview Heights Also Called: Nrka Corp (G-1664)
Fastsigns, Cincinnati Also Called: J Best Inc (G-2567)
Fastsigns, Cincinnati Also Called: Fastsigns (G-2896)
Fastsigns, Dayton Also Called: Fastsigns (G-6329)
Fastsigns, Hilliard Also Called: Fast Signs (G-8411)
Fastsigns, Liberty Township Also Called: Fastsigns (G-9206)
Fastsigns, Medina Also Called: Apex Signs Inc (G-10295)
Fastsigns, Medina Also Called: Fastsigns (G-10323)
Fastsigns, Mentor Also Called: Vista Creations LLC (G-10593)

Fastsigns, Toledo Also Called: Fastsigns (G-14284)
Fastsigns, Westerville Also Called: Djmc Partners Inc (G-15702)
Fastsigns, Westerville Also Called: Highrise Creative LLC (G-15708)
Fastsigns, Youngstown Also Called: Sdmk LLC (G-16435)
Fate Industries Inc 440 327-1770
36682 Sugar Ridge Rd North Ridgeville (44039) *(G-11839)*
Faull & Son LLC 330 652-4341
515 Holford Ave Niles (44446) *(G-11668)*
Faurecia Exhaust Systems Inc 937 339-0551
1255 Archer Dr Troy (45373) *(G-14568)*
FAURECIA EXHAUST SYSTEMS, INC., Troy Also Called: Faurecia Exhaust Systems Inc (G-14568)
Fawcett Co Inc 330 659-4187
3863 Congress Pkwy Richfield (44286) *(G-12787)*
Fawn Confectionery Inc (PA) 513 574-9612
4271 Harrison Ave Cincinnati (45211) *(G-2897)*
FB Acquisition LLC 513 459-7782
2025 Mckinley Blvd Lebanon (45036) *(G-9074)*
FB Ins, Fostoria Also Called: Fostoria Bushings Inc (G-7634)
FBC Chemical Corporation 216 341-2000
7301 Bessemer Ave Cleveland (44127) *(G-4051)*
Fbf Limited 513 541-6300
2980 Spring Grove Ave Cincinnati (45225) *(G-2898)*
Fbg Bottling Group LLC 614 580-7063
818 S Yearling Rd Columbus (43213) *(G-5371)*
Fbr Industries Inc 330 701-7425
1336 Seaborn St Ste 7 Mineral Ridge (44440) *(G-11019)*
Fc Industries Inc (PA) 937 275-8700
4900 Webster St Dayton (45414) *(G-6330)*
FCA North America Holdings LLC 419 661-3500
8000 Chrysler Dr Perrysburg (43551) *(G-12380)*
Fcbdd 614 475-6440
2879 Johnstown Rd Columbus (43219) *(G-5372)*
Fci Inc 216 251-5200
4801 W 160th St Cleveland (44135) *(G-4052)*
Fcx Performance Inc (HQ) 614 253-1996
3000 E 14th Ave Columbus (43219) *(G-5373)*
Fd Machinery, Solon Also Called: Fd Rolls Corp (G-13348)
Fd Rolls Corp 216 916-1922
30400 Solon Industrial Pkwy Solon (44139) *(G-13348)*
Fdc Machine Repair Inc 216 362-1082
5585 Venture Dr Parma (44130) *(G-12288)*
Fdi, Cleves Also Called: Fdi Cabinetry LLC (G-4952)
Fdi Cabinetry LLC 513 353-4500
5555 Dry Fork Rd Cleves (45002) *(G-4952)*
Fdi Enterprises 440 269-8282
17700 Saint Clair Ave Cleveland (44110) *(G-4053)*
Feather Lite Innovations Inc 513 893-5483
4805 Hamilton Middletown Rd Liberty Twp (45011) *(G-9215)*
Feather Lite Innovations Inc (PA) 937 743-9008
650 Pleasant Valley Dr Springboro (45066) *(G-13501)*
Fecon LLC 513 696-4430
1087b Mane Way Lebanon (45036) *(G-9075)*
Fecon LLC (PA) 513 696-4430
3460 Grant Ave Lebanon (45036) *(G-9076)*
Federal Equipment Company (DH) 513 621-5260
5298 River Rd Cincinnati (45233) *(G-2899)*
Federal Gear, Eastlake Also Called: Tymoca Partners LLC (G-7052)
Federal Heath Sign Company LLC 740 369-0999
1020 Pittsburgh Dr Ste A Delaware (43015) *(G-6721)*
Federal Hose Manufacturing, Painesville Also Called: First Francis Company Inc (G-12237)
Federal Hose Manufacturing LLC 800 346-4673
10514 Dupont Ave Cleveland (44108) *(G-4054)*
Federal Iron Works Company 330 482-5910
42082 State Route 344 Columbiana (44408) *(G-5039)*
Federal Metal Co, Bedford Also Called: Oakwood Industries Inc (G-1146)
Federal Metal Company (HQ) 440 232-8700
7250 Division St Bedford (44146) *(G-1120)*
Federal Parkway Diesel Co LLC 614 571-0388
1879 Federal Pkwy Ste 100 Columbus (43207) *(G-5374)*

Federaleagle LLC 513 797-4100
64 Circle Freeway Dr West Chester (45246) *(G-15552)*

FedPro Inc (HQ) 216 464-6440
4520 Richmond Rd Cleveland (44128) *(G-4055)*

Feedall Inc 440 942-8100
38379 Pelton Rd Willoughby (44094) *(G-15920)*

Feilhauers Machine Shop Inc 513 202-0545
421 Industrial Dr Harrison (45030) *(G-8274)*

Feiner Pattern Works Inc 513 851-9800
7823 Seward Rd Fairfield (45011) *(G-7359)*

Feintool Cincinnati Inc (DH) 513 247-0110
11280 Cornell Park Dr Blue Ash (45242) *(G-1394)*

Feintool US Operations Inc (DH) 513 247-0110
11280 Cornell Park Dr Cincinnati (45242) *(G-2900)*

Feitl Manufacturing Co Inc 330 405-6600
8406 Bavaria Dr E Macedonia (44056) *(G-9550)*

Felicity Plastics Machinery 513 876-7003
892 Neville Penn Schoolhouse Rd Felicity (45120) *(G-7467)*

Feller Tool Co 440 324-6277
6285 Lake Ave Elyria (44035) *(G-7151)*

Fellhauer In-Focus, Port Clinton Also Called: Fellhauer Mechanical Systems *(G-12617)*

Fellhauer Mechanical Systems 419 734-3674
2435 E Gill Rd Port Clinton (43452) *(G-12617)*

Femc, Bedford Heights Also Called: Food Equipment Mfg Corp *(G-1172)*

Fence One Inc 216 441-2600
11111 Broadway Ave Cleveland (44125) *(G-4056)*

Fenix LLC (HQ) 419 739-3400
820 Willipie St Wapakoneta (45895) *(G-15110)*

Fenix Fabrication Inc 330 745-8731
2689 Wingate Ave Akron (44314) *(G-151)*

Fenner Dnlop Engnred Cnvyor Sl, Port Clinton Also Called: Fenner Dunlop Port Clinton LLC *(G-12618)*

Fenner Dunlop (toledo) LLC 419 531-5300
146 S Westwood Ave Toledo (43607) *(G-14285)*

Fenner Dunlop Port Clinton LLC 419 635-2191
5225 W Lakeshore Dr Ste 320 Port Clinton (43452) *(G-12618)*

Fenton Bros Electric Co 330 343-0093
235 Ray Ave Ne New Philadelphia (44663) *(G-11501)*

Fenton's Festival of Lights, New Philadelphia Also Called: Fenton Bros Electric Co *(G-11501)*

Fenwick Frame Shppe Art Gllery, Toledo Also Called: Fenwick Gallery of Fine Arts *(G-14286)*

Fenwick Gallery of Fine Arts (PA) 419 475-1651
3433 W Alexis Rd Frnt Toledo (43623) *(G-14286)*

Ferco Tech LLC 937 746-6696
291 Conover Dr Franklin (45005) *(G-7674)*

Ferguson Enterprises LLC 216 635-2493
2415 Brookpark Rd Parma (44134) *(G-12289)*

Fernandes Enterprises LLC (PA) 937 890-6444
2801 Ontario Ave Dayton (45414) *(G-6331)*

Ferno, Wilmington Also Called: Ferno-Washington Inc *(G-16050)*

Ferno-Washington Inc (PA) 877 733-0911
70 Weil Way Wilmington (45177) *(G-16050)*

Ferralloy Inc 440 250-1900
28001 Ranney Pkwy Cleveland (44145) *(G-4057)*

Ferrante Wine Farm Inc 440 466-8466
5585 State Route 307 Geneva (44041) *(G-7936)*

Ferriot Inc 330 786-3000
1000 Arlington Cir Akron (44306) *(G-152)*

Ferro, Mayfield Heights Also Called: Vibrantz Corporation *(G-10256)*

Ferro Corp 800 245-8225
416 Maple Ave Crooksville (43731) *(G-6046)*

Ferro Corporation 216 577-7144
7050 Krick Rd Bedford (44146) *(G-1121)*

Ferro Corporation 330 682-8015
1560 N Main St Orrville (44667) *(G-12124)*

Ferro International Svcs Inc (DH) 216 875-5600
6060 Parkland Blvd Ste 250 Mayfield Heights (44124) *(G-10248)*

Ferroglobe USA Mtllurgical Inc (DH) 740 984-2361
1595 Sparling Rd Waterford (45786) *(G-15236)*

Ferrotherm Corporation 216 883-9350
4758 Warner Rd Cleveland (44125) *(G-4058)*

Ferrous Processing and Trading, Cleveland Also Called: Fpt Cleveland LLC *(G-4088)*

Ferrum Industries Inc (HQ) 440 519-1768
1831 Highland Rd Twinsburg (44087) *(G-14660)*

Ferry & Quintax, Stow Also Called: Ferry Industries Inc *(G-13698)*

Ferry Industries Inc (PA) 330 920-9200
4445 Allen Rd Ste A Stow (44224) *(G-13698)*

Few Atmtive GL Applcations Inc 234 249-1880
1720 Enterprise Pkwy Wooster (44691) *(G-16118)*

Fex LLC (PA) 412 604-0400
1058 Commercial St Mingo Junction (43938) *(G-11045)*

Fex Group, Mingo Junction Also Called: Fex LLC *(G-11045)*

Fgs-Wi LLC 630 375-8597
37 S Park Pl Newark (43055) *(G-11576)*

Fiba Technologies Inc 330 602-7300
3211 Brightwood Road Midvale (44653) *(G-10877)*

Fiber -Tech Industries Inc 740 335-9400
2000 Kenskill Ave Wshngtn Ct Hs (43160) *(G-16231)*

Fiber Frame, Toledo Also Called: Comfort Line Ltd *(G-14248)*

Fiber Systems, Dayton Also Called: Industrial Fiberglass Spc Inc *(G-6382)*

Fibercorr Mills LLC 330 837-5151
670 17th St Nw Massillon (44647) *(G-10096)*

Fiberglass Engineering Co, Cleveland Also Called: Hanlon Industries Inc *(G-4168)*

Fiberglass Technology Inds Inc 740 335-9400
2000 Kenskill Ave Wshngtn Ct Hs (43160) *(G-16232)*

Fibertech Networks 614 436-3565
720 Lakeview Plaza Blvd Worthington (43085) *(G-16194)*

Fibre Glast Dvlpments Corp LLC 937 833-5200
385 Carr Dr Brookville (45309) *(G-1735)*

Fibreboard Corporation (DH) 419 248-8000
1 Owens Corning Pkwy Toledo (43659) *(G-14287)*

Fidelity Orthopedic Inc 937 228-0682
8514 N Main St Dayton (45415) *(G-6332)*

Fiedeldey Stl Fabricators Inc 513 353-3300
8487 E Miami River Rd Cincinnati (45247) *(G-2901)*

Field Apparatus Service & Tstg 513 353-9399
4040 Rev Dr Cincinnati (45232) *(G-2902)*

Field Aviation Inc (PA) 513 792-2282
8044 Montgomery Rd Ste 530 Cincinnati (45236) *(G-2903)*

Field Gymmy Inc 419 538-6511
138-143 S Main St Glandorf (45848) *(G-7978)*

Field Stone Inc 937 898-3236
2750 Us Route 40 Tipp City (45371) *(G-14135)*

Fields Process Technology Inc 216 781-4787
1849 W 24th St Cleveland (44113) *(G-4059)*

Fife Services LLC 614 829-6285
9004 Emily Ct Ravenna (44266) *(G-12714)*

Fifth Avenue Lumber Co 614 833-6655
5200 Winchester Pike Canal Winchester (43110) *(G-1986)*

Fifth Third Proc Solutions Inc 800 972-3030
38 Fountain Square Plz Cincinnati (45202) *(G-2904)*

Fifty West Brewing Company LLC 740 775-2337
1 N Paint St Chillicothe (45601) *(G-2502)*

File 13 Inc 937 642-4855
232 N Main St Ste K Marysville (43040) *(G-9909)*

Fill-Rite Company (HQ) 419 755-1011
600 S Airport Rd Mansfield (44903) *(G-9655)*

Filmtec Fabrications LLC 419 435-1819
1120 Sandusky St Fostoria (44830) *(G-7632)*

Filnor Inc (PA) 330 821-8731
227 N Freedom Ave Alliance (44601) *(G-403)*

Filter Technology Inc 614 921-9801
11885 Paddock View Ct Nw Baltimore (43105) *(G-844)*

Fimm USA Inc 614 568-4874
4155 Brook Rd Nw Lancaster (43130) *(G-9016)*

Fin Pan Inc (PA) 513 870-9200
3255 Symmes Rd Hamilton (45015) *(G-8208)*

Finale Products Inc 419 874-2662
301 Walnut St Perrysburg (43551) *(G-12381)*

Findaway World LLC (PA) 440 893-0808
31999 Aurora Rd Solon (44139) *(G-13349)*

Findlay Amrcn Prsthtic Orthtic 419 424-1622
12474 County Road 99 Findlay (45840) *(G-7505)*

Findlay Machine & Tool LLC 419 434-3100
2000 Industrial Dr Findlay (45840) *(G-7506)*

Findlay Pallet Inc 419 423-0511
300 Bell Ave Findlay (45840) *(G-7507)*

Findlay Pallet Inc 419 423-0511
102 Crystal Ave Findlay (45840) *(G-7508)*

Findlay Party Mart, Findlay *Also Called: Ottawa Oil Co Inc (G-7548)*

Findlay Products Corporation 419 423-3324
2045 Industrial Dr Findlay (45840) *(G-7509)*

Fine Line Excvtg & Ldscpg LLC 330 541-0590
9251 Newton Falls Rd Ravenna (44266) *(G-12715)*

Fine Line Graphics, Columbus *Also Called: Fine Line Graphics Corp (G-5375)*

Fine Line Graphics Corp 614 486-0276
2364 Featherwood Dr Columbus (43228) *(G-5375)*

Fine Lines, Wadsworth *Also Called: Quality Reproductions Inc (G-15058)*

Fine Points Inc 216 229-6644
12602 Larchmere Blvd Cleveland (44120) *(G-4060)*

Fineline Imprints Inc 740 453-1083
516 State St Zanesville (43701) *(G-16530)*

Finelli Architectural Iron Co, Cleveland *Also Called: Finelli Ornamental Iron Co (G-4061)*

Finelli Ornamental Iron Co 440 248-0050
30815 Solon Rd Cleveland (44139) *(G-4061)*

Finely Tuned Fabrications LLC 216 513-6731
129 Commerce Dr Lagrange (44050) *(G-8947)*

Finish Line Binderies, Macedonia *Also Called: Bindtech LLC (G-9539)*

Finishing Brands, Toledo *Also Called: Finishing Brands Holdings Inc (G-14288)*

Finishing Brands Holdings Inc 260 665-8800
320 Phillips Ave Toledo (43612) *(G-14288)*

Finishing Department 419 737-3334
201 Ohio St Pioneer (43554) *(G-12492)*

Finishmaster Inc 614 228-4328
5830 Green Pointe Dr S Groveport (43125) *(G-8139)*

Finite Fibers, Akron *Also Called: Dowco LLC (G-133)*

Fink Meat Company Inc 937 390-2750
2475 Troy Rd Springfield (45504) *(G-13564)*

Finn Corporation (HQ) 513 874-2818
9281 Le Saint Dr West Chester (45014) *(G-15429)*

Finn Graphics Inc 513 941-6161
220 Stille Dr Cincinnati (45233) *(G-2905)*

Finzer Roller Inc 937 746-4069
315 Industrial Dr Franklin (45005) *(G-7675)*

Fioritto of Wooster LLC 330 466-3776
2500 Carrie Ln Wooster (44691) *(G-16119)*

Fire & Iron 937 470-8536
538 Maple Hill Dr W Carrollton (45449) *(G-15013)*

Fire Department, Grafton *Also Called: Village of Grafton (G-8006)*

Fire Fab Corp 330 759-9834
999 Trumbull Ave Girard (44420) *(G-7967)*

Fire Foe Corp 330 759-9834
999 Trumbull Ave Girard (44420) *(G-7968)*

Fire From Ice Ventures LLC 419 944-6705
30333 Emerald Valley Pkwy Solon (44139) *(G-13350)*

Fire Safety Services Inc 937 686-2000
6228 Township Road 95 Huntsville (43324) *(G-8623)*

Fire-Dex LLC (PA) 330 723-0000
780 S Progress Dr Medina (44256) *(G-10324)*

Fire-End & Croker Corp 513 870-0517
4690 Interstate Dr Ste P West Chester (45246) *(G-15553)*

FIRE-END & CROKER CORP., West Chester *Also Called: Fire-End & Croker Corp (G-15553)*

Firehouse Foods 614 592-8115
917 E Whittier St Columbus (43206) *(G-5376)*

Firelands Fabrication 419 929-0680
201 N Main St New London (44851) *(G-11461)*

Firelands Farmer, The, New London *Also Called: Sdg News Group Inc (G-11468)*

Firelands Manufacturing LLC 419 687-8237
500 Industrial Park Dr Plymouth (44865) *(G-12608)*

Firelands Media Group LLC (PA) 440 543-8566
16759 W Park Circle Dr Chagrin Falls (44023) *(G-2396)*

Firelands Scientific, Huron *Also Called: OPC Cultivation LLC (G-8643)*

Fireline Inc (PA) 330 743-1164
300 Andrews Ave Youngstown (44505) *(G-16356)*

Fireline Tcon, Youngstown *Also Called: Fireline Inc (G-16356)*

Firestone, Athens *Also Called: Bridgestone Ret Operations LLC (G-677)*

Firestone, Beverly *Also Called: Skinner Firestone Inc (G-1321)*

Firestone, Canal Winchester *Also Called: Bridgestone Ret Operations LLC (G-1982)*

Firestone, Canton *Also Called: Bridgestone Ret Operations LLC (G-2053)*

Firestone, Cincinnati *Also Called: Bridgestone Ret Operations LLC (G-2684)*

Firestone, Cincinnati *Also Called: Bridgestone Ret Operations LLC (G-2685)*

Firestone, Cleveland *Also Called: Bridgestone Ret Operations LLC (G-3756)*

Firestone, Cleveland *Also Called: Bridgestone Ret Operations LLC (G-3757)*

Firestone, Cleveland *Also Called: Bridgestone Ret Operations LLC (G-3758)*

Firestone, Cleveland *Also Called: Bridgestone Ret Operations LLC (G-3759)*

Firestone, Columbus *Also Called: Bridgestone Ret Operations LLC (G-5214)*

Firestone, Columbus *Also Called: Bridgestone Ret Operations LLC (G-5215)*

Firestone, Columbus *Also Called: Bridgestone Ret Operations LLC (G-5216)*

Firestone, Elyria *Also Called: Bridgestone Ret Operations LLC (G-7117)*

Firestone, Elyria *Also Called: Bridgestone Ret Operations LLC (G-7118)*

Firestone, Greenville *Also Called: Bridgestone Ret Operations LLC (G-8039)*

Firestone, Hamilton *Also Called: Bridgestone Ret Operations LLC (G-8186)*

Firestone, Kent *Also Called: Bridgestone Ret Operations LLC (G-8803)*

Firestone, Mentor *Also Called: Bridgestone Ret Operations LLC (G-10431)*

Firestone, Mount Vernon *Also Called: Bridgestone Ret Operations LLC (G-11265)*

Firestone, Reynoldsburg *Also Called: Bridgestone Ret Operations LLC (G-12756)*

Firestone, Sandusky *Also Called: Bridgestone Ret Operations LLC (G-13045)*

Firestone, Springfield *Also Called: Bridgestone Ret Operations LLC (G-13540)*

Firestone, Youngstown *Also Called: Bridgestone Ret Operations LLC (G-16325)*

Firestone, Youngstown *Also Called: Bridgestone Ret Operations LLC (G-16326)*

Firestone Complete Auto Care 937 528-2496
199 E Alex Bell Rd Centerville (45459) *(G-2362)*

Firestone Laser and Mfg LLC 330 337-9551
14000 W Middletown Rd Salem (44460) *(G-12994)*

Firestone Machine, North Lima *Also Called: Precision Assemblies Inc (G-11809)*

Firestone Polymers LLC (PA) 330 379-7000
381 W Wilbeth Rd Akron (44301) *(G-153)*

First Brands Group LLC (DH) 248 371-1700
127 Public Sq Ste 5300 Cleveland (44114) *(G-4062)*

First Brnds Group Holdings LLC (PA) 216 589-0198
127 Public Sq Ste 5110 Cleveland (44114) *(G-4063)*

First Brnds Group Intrmdate LL (HQ) 216 589-0198
127 Public Sq Ste 5110 Cleveland (44114) *(G-4064)*

First Choice Packaging Inc (PA) 419 333-4100
1501 W State St Fremont (43420) *(G-7778)*

First Choice Packg Solutions, Fremont *Also Called: First Choice Packaging Inc (G-7778)*

First Francis Company Inc (HQ) 440 352-8927
25 Florence Ave Painesville (44077) *(G-12237)*

First Impression Wear LLC 937 456-3900
120 E Main St Eaton (45320) *(G-7059)*

First Machine & Tool Corp 440 269-8644
38181 Airport Pkwy Willoughby (44094) *(G-15921)*

First Solar Inc 419 661-1478
28101 Cedar Park Blvd Perrysburg (43551) *(G-12382)*

First Solar Electric, Perrysburg *Also Called: First Solar Inc (G-12382)*

First Tool Corp (PA) 937 254-6197
612 Linden Ave Dayton (45403) *(G-6333)*

Firth Rixson Inc 860 760-1040
1616 Harvard Ave Ste 53 Newburgh Heights (44105) *(G-11614)*

Fischer Global Enterprises LLC 513 583-4900
155 Commerce Dr Loveland (45140) *(G-9480)*

Fischer Special Tooling Corp 440 951-8411
7219 Commerce Dr Mentor (44060) *(G-10455)*

Fishburn Tank Truck Service 419 253-6031
5012 State Route 229 Marengo (43334) *(G-9767)*

Fishel Company 614 850-4400
1600 Walcutt Rd Columbus (43228) *(G-5377)*

Fisher Controls Intl LLC 513 285-6000
5453 W Chester Rd West Chester (45069) *(G-15430)*

Fisher Metal Fabricating LLC 419 838-7200
27953 E Broadway St Walbridge (43465) *(G-15081)*

Fisher Sand & Gravel Inc 330 745-9239
3322 Clark Mill Rd Norton (44203) *(G-11943)*

ALPHABETIC SECTION — Flour Management LLC

Fiske Brothers Refining Co... 419 691-2491
  1500 Oakdale Ave Toledo (43605) *(G-14289)*

Fitchville East Corp.. 419 929-1510
  1732 Us Highway 250 S New London (44851) *(G-11462)*

Fitchville East Storage, New London *Also Called: Fitchville East Corp (G-11462)*

Fithian-Wilbert Burial Vlt Co... 330 758-2327
  6234 Market St Youngstown (44512) *(G-16357)*

Five Handicap Inc (PA)... 419 525-2511
  127 N Walnut St Mansfield (44902) *(G-9656)*

Five Points Distillery LLC.. 937 776-4634
  122 Van Buren St Dayton (45402) *(G-6334)*

Five Star Fabrication LLC.. 440 666-0427
  18308 Quarry Rd Wellington (44090) *(G-15308)*

Five Star Foodies, Cincinnati *Also Called: Foodies Vegan Ltd (G-2913)*

Five Star Healthy Vending LLC.. 330 549-6011
  388 S Main St Ste 440 Akron (44311) *(G-154)*

Five Star Technologies Ltd.. 216 447-9422
  6801 Brecksville Rd Ste 200 Independence (44131) *(G-8668)*

Five Vines Winery LLC... 419 657-2675
  12179 Buckland Holden Rd Wapakoneta (45895) *(G-15111)*

Fivepoint LLC... 937 374-3193
  825 Bellbrook Ave Unit B Xenia (45385) *(G-16262)*

Fives Bronx Inc.. 330 244-1960
  8817 Pleasantwood Ave Nw North Canton (44720) *(G-11727)*

Fives N Amercn Combustn Inc (DH)..................................... 216 271-6000
  4455 E 71st St Cleveland (44105) *(G-4065)*

Fives St Corp... 234 217-9070
  1 Park Centre Dr Ste 210 Wadsworth (44281) *(G-15029)*

Fixture Dimensions Inc... 513 360-7512
  5660 Liberty Woods Dr Liberty Twp (45011) *(G-9216)*

Fjr Industries Inc... 859 277-8207
  5436 Stoney Ln Painesville (44077) *(G-12238)*

Fki Logistex, West Chester *Also Called: Intelligrated Systems Ohio LLC (G-15566)*

Fki Logistex Automation Inc... 513 881-5251
  10045 International Blvd West Chester (45246) *(G-15554)*

Flag Lady Inc... 614 263-1776
  4567 N High St Columbus (43214) *(G-5378)*

Flag Lady's Flag Store, The, Columbus *Also Called: Flag Lady Inc (G-5378)*

Flagship Trading Corporation
  734 Alpha Dr Ste J Cleveland (44143) *(G-4066)*

Flambeau Inc... 440 632-6131
  15981 Valplast St Middlefield (44062) *(G-10750)*

Flaming River Industries Inc.. 440 826-4488
  800 Poertner Dr Berea (44017) *(G-1281)*

Flash Industrial Tech Ltd.. 440 786-8979
  30 Industry Dr Cleveland (44146) *(G-4067)*

Flashions Sportswear Ltd... 937 323-5885
  1002 N Bechtle Ave Springfield (45504) *(G-13565)*

Flatiron Crane Oper Co LLC... 330 332-3300
  1134 Salem Pkwy Salem (44460) *(G-12995)*

Flavor Producers LLC... 513 771-0777
  2429 E Kemper Rd Cincinnati (45241) *(G-2906)*

Flavor Systems Intl Inc (HQ)... 513 870-4900
  5404 Duff Dr Cincinnati (45246) *(G-2907)*

Flavorseal LLC.. 440 937-3900
  35179 Avon Commerce Pkwy Avon (44011) *(G-774)*

Flawless Logistics LLC... 330 201-7070
  5010 Quincy St Nw Canton (44708) *(G-2101)*

Flawless Signs & Wraps LLC... 937 559-0672
  66 Industry Ct Ste C Troy (45373) *(G-14569)*

Fleet Graphics Inc.. 937 252-2552
  1701 Thomas Paine Pkwy Dayton (45459) *(G-6335)*

Fleet Relief Company... 419 525-2625
  550 N Main St Mansfield (44902) *(G-9657)*

Fleetchem LLC.. 513 539-1111
  651 N Garver Rd Monroe (45050) *(G-11106)*

Fleetmaster Express Inc.. 866 425-0666
  5250 Distribution Dr Findlay (45840) *(G-7510)*

Fleetpride Inc.. 740 282-2711
  620 South St Steubenville (43952) *(G-13667)*

Flegal Brothers Inc... 419 298-3539
  104 Industrial Dr Edgerton (43517) *(G-7075)*

Fleming Construction Co.. 740 494-2177
  5298 Marion Marysville Rd Prospect (43342) *(G-12689)*

Flesher Sand & Gravel, Norton *Also Called: Fisher Sand & Gravel Inc (G-11943)*

Flex Core Division, Hilliard *Also Called: Morlan & Associates Inc (G-8421)*

Flex Technologies Inc... 330 897-6311
  3430 State Route 93 Baltic (43804) *(G-836)*

Flex Technologies Inc... 330 359-5415
  16183 East Main St Mount Eaton (44659) *(G-11230)*

Flex Technologies Inc (PA)... 740 922-5992
  5479 Gundy Dr Midvale (44653) *(G-10878)*

Flex-Core Division, Hilliard *Also Called: Morlan & Associates Inc (G-8422)*

Flex-E-On Inc... 330 928-4496
  3332 Cavalier Trl Cuyahoga Falls (44224) *(G-6084)*

Flex-Strut Inc... 330 372-9999
  2900 Commonwealth Ave Ne Warren (44483) *(G-15170)*

Flexarm, Wapakoneta *Also Called: Midwest Specialties Inc (G-15127)*

Flexmag Industries Inc (DH)... 740 373-3492
  107 Industry Rd Marietta (45750) *(G-9793)*

Flexnova Inc (PA).. 216 288-6961
  6100 Oak Tree Blvd Ste 200 Cleveland (44131) *(G-4068)*

Flexomation LLC... 513 825-0555
  11701 Chesterdale Rd Cincinnati (45246) *(G-2908)*

Flexoparts Com... 513 932-2060
  1054 Monroe Rd Lebanon (45036) *(G-9077)*

Flexoplate Inc.. 513 489-0433
  6504 Corporate Dr Blue Ash (45242) *(G-1395)*

Flexotech Graphics Inc (PA)... 330 929-4743
  4830 Hudson Dr Stow (44224) *(G-13699)*

Flexrack By Qcells LLC (PA).. 216 998-5988
  23000 Harvard Rd Ste B Cleveland (44122) *(G-4069)*

Flexsys America, Akron *Also Called: Flexsys America LP (G-155)*

Flexsys America LP (HQ)... 330 666-4111
  260 Springside Dr Akron (44333) *(G-155)*

Flexsys America LP.. 618 482-6371
  1658 Williams Rd Columbus (43207) *(G-5379)*

Flexsys Inc (PA).. 212 605-6000
  260 Springside Dr Akron (44333) *(G-156)*

Flextronics Intl USA Inc.. 513 755-2500
  6224 Windham Ct Liberty Township (45044) *(G-9207)*

Flight Bright Ltd.. 216 663-6677
  23100 Miles Rd Cleveland (44128) *(G-4070)*

Flight Operations, Cleveland *Also Called: Parker-Hannifin Corporation (G-4531)*

Flight Operations, Cleveland *Also Called: Swagelok Company (G-4757)*

Flight Specialties Components, Highland Heights *Also Called: Heico Aerospace Parts Corp (G-8388)*

Flightsafety International Inc (HQ)....................................... 614 324-3500
  3100 Easton Square Pl Ste 100 Columbus (43219) *(G-5380)*

Flint CPS Inks North Amer LLC... 513 619-2089
  410 Glendale Milford Rd Cincinnati (45215) *(G-2909)*

Flint Group US LLC... 513 552-7232
  575 Quality Blvd Fairfield (45014) *(G-7360)*

Flohr Machine Company Inc.. 330 745-3030
  1028 Coventry Rd Barberton (44203) *(G-867)*

Flohrmachine.com, Barberton *Also Called: Flohr Machine Company Inc (G-867)*

Flood Heliarc, Groveport *Also Called: Flood Heliarc Inc (G-8140)*

Flood Heliarc Inc... 614 835-3929
  4181 Venture Pl Groveport (43125) *(G-8140)*

Florida Invacare Holdings LLC... 800 333-6900
  1 Invacare Way Elyria (44035) *(G-7152)*

Florida Production Engrg Inc... 740 420-5252
  30627 Orr Rd Circleville (43113) *(G-3551)*

Florida Production Engrg Inc... 937 996-4361
  1855 State Route 121 N New Madison (45346) *(G-11474)*

Flossys Sweet Tooth LLC... 614 425-7939
  5888 Marietta Rd Chillicothe (45601) *(G-2503)*

Floturn Inc (PA)... 513 860-8040
  4236 Thunderbird Ln Fairfield (45014) *(G-7361)*

Flour Management LLC.. 216 910-9019
  26800 Fargo Ave Ste E Bedford Heights (44146) *(G-1171)*

Flour Management LLC (PA).. 216 910-9019
  34205 Chagrin Blvd Moreland Hills (44022) *(G-11219)*

(PA)=Parent Co (HQ)=Headquarters (DH)=Div Headquarters

Flour Pasta Company

ALPHABETIC SECTION

Flour Pasta Company, Bedford Heights *Also Called: Flour Management LLC (G-1171)*
Flour Pasta Company, Moreland Hills *Also Called: Flour Management LLC (G-11219)*
Flow Control US Holding Corp... 419 289-1144
  1101 Myers Pkwy Ashland (44805) *(G-572)*
Flow Dry Technology Inc (HQ)... 937 833-2161
  379 Albert Rd Brookville (45309) *(G-1736)*
Flow Technology Inc.. 513 745-6000
  4444 Cooper Rd Cincinnati (45242) *(G-2910)*
Flow-Liner Systems Ltd.. 800 348-0020
  4830 Northpointe Dr Zanesville (43701) *(G-16531)*
Flowcrete North America Inc... 936 539-6700
  19218 Redwood Rd Cleveland (44110) *(G-4071)*
Flower Manufacturing LLC... 888 241-9109
  423 Knapp St Fremont (43420) *(G-7779)*
Flowers Baking Co Ohio LLC... 937 260-4412
  1791 Stanley Ave Dayton (45404) *(G-6336)*
Flowers Baking Co Ohio LLC (HQ)... 419 269-9202
  325 W Alexis Rd Ste 1 Toledo (43612) *(G-14290)*
Flowserve Corporation... 937 226-4000
  2200 E Monument Ave Dayton (45402) *(G-6337)*
Flowserve Corporation... 513 874-6990
  422 Wards Corner Rd Unit F Loveland (45140) *(G-9481)*
Floyd Bell Inc (PA)... 614 294-4000
  720 Dearborn Park Ln Columbus (43085) *(G-5381)*
Fluff Boutique... 513 227-6614
  6539 Harrison Ave Cincinnati (45247) *(G-2911)*
Fluid Applied Roofing LLC.. 855 860-2300
  830 Space Dr Beavercreek Township (45434) *(G-1084)*
Fluid Automation Inc... 248 912-1970
  8400 Port Jackson Ave Nw North Canton (44720) *(G-11728)*
Fluid Handling Dynamics Ltd.. 419 633-0560
  815 Navarre Ave Bryan (43506) *(G-1818)*
Fluid Power Inc... 330 653-5107
  1300 Hudson Gate Dr Hudson (44236) *(G-8593)*
Fluid Power Plant, Beachwood *Also Called: Eaton Corporation (G-985)*
Fluid Power Solutions LLC (PA)... 614 777-8954
  4400 Edgewyn Ave Hilliard (43026) *(G-8412)*
Fluid Quip Custom MA... 937 324-0662
  20 Walnut St Springfield (45505) *(G-13566)*
Fluid Quip Ks LLC... 937 324-0352
  1940 S Yellow Springs St Ste 2 Springfield (45506) *(G-13567)*
Fluid System Service Inc.. 216 651-2450
  13825 Triskett Rd Cleveland (44111) *(G-4072)*
Fluidpower Assembly Inc... 419 394-7486
  313 S Park Dr Saint Marys (45885) *(G-12952)*
Fluke Biomedical LLC (DH).. 440 248-9300
  28775 Aurora Rd Solon (44139) *(G-13351)*
Fluke Electronics Corporation... 800 850-4608
  28775 Aurora Rd Cleveland (44139) *(G-4073)*
Fluvitex USA Inc... 614 610-1199
  6510 Pontius Rd Groveport (43125) *(G-8141)*
Fly Race Fuels LLC.. 419 744-9402
  1905 Maple Ridge Rd North Fairfield (44855) *(G-11776)*
Flying Dutchman Inc... 330 669-2297
  6631 Egypt Rd Smithville (44677) *(G-13299)*
Flynn Inc.. 419 478-3743
  5540 Jackman Rd Toledo (43613) *(G-14291)*
Flypaper Studio Inc... 602 801-2208
  311 Elm St Ste 200 Cincinnati (45202) *(G-2912)*
FM, Bedford *Also Called: Federal Metal Company (G-1120)*
FM AF LLC.. 866 771-6266
  2933 Symmes Rd Fairfield (45014) *(G-7362)*
FM Systems... 330 273-3000
  4295 Center Rd Brunswick (44212) *(G-1759)*
Fmt, Findlay *Also Called: Findlay Machine & Tool LLC (G-7506)*
Foam Concepts & Design Inc.. 513 860-5589
  4602 Mulhauser Rd W Chester Township West Chester (45011) *(G-15431)*
Foam Pac Materials Company, West Chester *Also Called: Storopack Inc (G-15592)*
Foam Seal, Cleveland *Also Called: Novagard Solutions Inc (G-4483)*
Foam Seal Inc... 216 881-8111
  5109 Hamilton Ave Cleveland (44114) *(G-4074)*
Foam-Tex Solutions Corp... 216 889-2702
  13981 W Parkway Rd Cleveland (44135) *(G-4075)*
Focal Point Communications, West Chester *Also Called: Greenworld Enterprises Inc (G-15559)*
Foghorn Designs... 419 706-3861
  98 E Main St Norwalk (44857) *(G-11968)*
Foil Tapes LLC.. 216 255-6655
  1700 London Rd Cleveland (44112) *(G-4076)*
Foldedpak Inc... 740 527-1090
  263 Milliken Dr Hebron (43025) *(G-8341)*
Folding Carton Service Inc... 419 281-4099
  608 Westlake Dr Ashland (44805) *(G-573)*
Folger Coffee Company (HQ)... 800 937-9745
  1 Strawberry Ln Orrville (44667) *(G-12125)*
Folgers, Orrville *Also Called: Folger Coffee Company (G-12125)*
Folio Photonics Inc... 440 420-4500
  6864 Cochran Rd Solon (44139) *(G-13352)*
Folks Creative Printers Inc... 740 383-6326
  101 E George St Marion (43302) *(G-9852)*
Follett Hgher Edcatn Group Inc.. 419 281-5100
  30 Amberwood Pkwy Ashland (44805) *(G-574)*
Follow Print Club On Facebook.. 216 707-2579
  11150 East Blvd Cleveland (44106) *(G-4077)*
Foltz Machine LLC.. 330 453-9235
  2030 Allen Ave Se Canton (44707) *(G-2102)*
Fom USA Incorporated.. 234 248-4400
  1065 Medina Rd Ste 800 Medina (44256) *(G-10325)*
Fontaine Pieciak Engrg Inc.. 413 592-2273
  2300 E Enterprise Pkwy Twinsburg (44087) *(G-14661)*
Food 4 Your Soul.. 330 402-4073
  3957 S Schenley Ave Youngstown (44511) *(G-16358)*
Food Designs Inc.. 216 651-9221
  5299 Crayton Ave Cleveland (44104) *(G-4078)*
Food Equipment Mfg Corp... 216 672-5859
  22201 Aurora Rd Bedford Heights (44146) *(G-1172)*
Food Furniture, Lebanon *Also Called: Schmidt Progressive LLC (G-9110)*
Food Plant Engineering LLC... 513 618-3165
  10816 Millington Ct Ste 110 Blue Ash (45242) *(G-1396)*
Foodies Vegan Ltd.. 513 487-3037
  4524 Este Ave Cincinnati (45232) *(G-2913)*
Foote Foundry LLC... 740 694-1595
  283 N Main St Fredericktown (43019) *(G-7746)*
Foote Printing Company Inc.. 216 431-1757
  2800 E 55th St Cleveland (44104) *(G-4079)*
For Call Inc.. 330 863-0404
  3255 Alliance Rd Nw Malvern (44644) *(G-9611)*
Forbes Chocolate, Broadview Heights *Also Called: Benjamin P Forbes Company (G-1656)*
Forcam Inc... 513 878-2780
  3825 Edwards Rd Cincinnati (45209) *(G-2914)*
Force Control Industries Inc... 513 868-0900
  3660 Dixie Hwy Fairfield (45014) *(G-7363)*
Force Robots Inc.. 216 881-8360
  1768 E 25th St Ste 315 Cleveland (44114) *(G-4080)*
Forceone LLC... 513 939-1018
  3600 Hebron Rd Hebron (43025) *(G-8342)*
Ford, Avon Lake *Also Called: Ford Motor Company (G-807)*
Ford, Brookpark *Also Called: Ford Motor Company (G-1715)*
Ford, Lima *Also Called: Ford Motor Company (G-9243)*
Ford, Wellington *Also Called: Kts Equipment Inc (G-15316)*
Ford Motor Company... 440 933-1215
  650 Miller Rd Avon Lake (44012) *(G-807)*
Ford Motor Company... 216 676-7918
  17601 Brookpark Rd Brookpark (44142) *(G-1715)*
Ford Motor Company... 419 226-7000
  1155 Bible Rd Lima (45801) *(G-9243)*
Fordyce Custom Finishing, Dayton *Also Called: Couch Business Development Inc (G-6264)*
Forepleasure.. 330 821-1293
  14461 Gaskill Dr Ne Alliance (44601) *(G-404)*
Forest City Companies Inc.. 216 586-5279
  3607 W 56th St Cleveland (44102) *(G-4081)*
Forest City Packaging, Cleveland *Also Called: Forest City Companies Inc (G-4081)*

ALPHABETIC SECTION — Four Natures Keepers Inc

Forest City Tech Plant 4, Wellington *Also Called: Forest City Technologies Inc (G-15310)*

Forest City Technologies, Wellington *Also Called: Forest City Technologies Inc (G-15309)*

Forest City Technologies Inc 440 647-2115
232 Maple St Wellington (44090) *(G-15309)*

Forest City Technologies Inc 440 647-2115
401 Magyar St Wellington (44090) *(G-15310)*

Forest City Technologies Inc 440 647-2115
299 Clay St Wellington (44090) *(G-15311)*

Forest City Technologies Inc (PA) 440 647-2115
299 Clay St Wellington (44090) *(G-15312)*

Forest Converting Co Inc 513 631-4190
4701 Forest Ave Cincinnati (45212) *(G-2915)*

Forest Hill Publishing LLC 216 761-8316
13200 Forest Hill Ave Cleveland (44112) *(G-4082)*

Forge Biologics Inc 216 401-7611
3900 Gantz Rd Grove City (43123) *(G-8094)*

Forge Industries Inc (PA) 330 960-2468
4450 Market St Youngstown (44512) *(G-16359)*

Forge Products Corporation 216 231-2600
9503 Woodland Ave Cleveland (44104) *(G-4083)*

Forged Products, Cleveland *Also Called: Forge Products Corporation (G-4083)*

Forgeline Motorsports, Moraine *Also Called: Forgeline Motorsports LLC (G-11181)*

Forgeline Motorsports LLC 800 886-0093
3522 Kettering Blvd Moraine (45439) *(G-11181)*

Forklift Solutions LLC 419 717-9496
425 Oxford St Napoleon (43545) *(G-11313)*

Forklift Tire East Mich Inc 586 771-1330
4934 Lewis Ave Toledo (43612) *(G-14292)*

Form Manufacturing Llc 419 678-1400
149 Harvest Dr Coldwater (45828) *(G-4988)*

Form Mfg 419 763-1030
149 Harvest Dr Coldwater (45828) *(G-4989)*

Form5 Prosthetics Inc 614 226-1141
6560 New Albany Condit Rd New Albany (43054) *(G-11379)*

Formasters Corporation 440 639-9206
5959 Pinecone Dr Mentor (44060) *(G-10456)*

Formatech Inc 330 273-2800
3024 Interstate Pkwy Brunswick (44212) *(G-1760)*

Formation Cementing Inc 740 453-6926
1800 Timber Port Dr Zanesville (43701) *(G-16532)*

Formco, Canton *Also Called: Mdi of Ohio Inc (G-2158)*

Formco Inc 330 966-2111
5175 Stoneham Rd Canton (44720) *(G-2103)*

Formica Corporation (DH) 513 786-3400
10155 Reading Rd Cincinnati (45241) *(G-2916)*

Formlabs Ohio Inc 419 837-9783
27800 Lemoyne Rd Ste J Millbury (43447) *(G-10932)*

Formtek Inc (DH) 216 292-4460
4899 Commerce Pkwy Cleveland (44128) *(G-4084)*

Formtek International, Cleveland *Also Called: Formtek Inc (G-4084)*

Formtek Metal Forming Inc 216 292-4460
4899 Commerce Pkwy Cleveland (44128) *(G-4085)*

Forre Sports Accessories, Piqua *Also Called: Forrest Enterprises Inc (G-12516)*

Forrest Enterprises Inc 937 773-1714
510 W Statler Rd Piqua (45356) *(G-12516)*

Forrest Machine Pdts Co Ltd 419 589-3774
145 Industrial Dr Mansfield (44904) *(G-9658)*

Forrest Scrw Machine, Mansfield *Also Called: Forrest Machine Pdts Co Ltd (G-9658)*

Fort Recovery Equipment Inc 419 375-1006
1201 Industrial Dr Fort Recovery (45846) *(G-7615)*

Fort Recovery Equity Inc (PA) 419 375-4119
2351 Wabash Rd Fort Recovery (45846) *(G-7616)*

Fort Recovery Equity Exchange 937 338-8901
13243 Cochran Rd Rossburg (45362) *(G-12862)*

Fort Recovery Industries Inc (PA) 419 375-4121
2440 State Route 49 Fort Recovery (45846) *(G-7617)*

Fort Recovery Industries Inc 419 375-3005
1200 Industrial Park Dr Fort Recovery (45846) *(G-7618)*

Forte Industrial Equipment Systems Inc 513 398-2800
6037 Commerce Ct Mason (45040) *(G-9993)*

Forte Industries, Mason *Also Called: Forte Industrial Equipment Systems Inc (G-9993)*

Fortec Medical Lithotripsy LLC 330 656-4301
10125 Wellman Rd Streetsboro (44241) *(G-13771)*

Forterra Pipe & Precast LLC 614 445-3830
1500 Haul Rd Columbus (43207) *(G-5382)*

Forterra Pipe & Precast LLC 330 467-7890
7925 Empire Pkwy Macedonia (44056) *(G-9551)*

Fortin Ironworks, Columbus *Also Called: Fortin Welding & Mfg Inc (G-5383)*

Fortin Welding & Mfg Inc 614 291-4342
944 W 5th Ave Columbus (43212) *(G-5383)*

Fortis Energy Services Inc 248 283-7100
66999 Executive Dr Saint Clairsville (43950) *(G-12904)*

Fortis Plastics LLC 937 382-0966
185 Park Dr Wilmington (45177) *(G-16051)*

Fortner Upholstering Inc 614 475-8282
2050 S High St Columbus (43207) *(G-5384)*

Fortress Industries LLC 614 402-3045
15710 Center Village Rd Johnstown (43031) *(G-8773)*

Forty Nine Degrees LLC 419 678-0100
149 Harvest Dr Coldwater (45828) *(G-4990)*

Forum III Inc 513 961-5123
436 Mcgregor Ave Cincinnati (45206) *(G-2917)*

Forum Works LLC 937 349-8685
77 Brown St Milford Center (43045) *(G-10928)*

Forward Day By Day, Cincinnati *Also Called: Forward Movement Publications (G-2918)*

Forward Movement Publications 513 721-6659
412 Sycamore St Fl 2 Cincinnati (45202) *(G-2918)*

Forward Technologies, Blue Ash *Also Called: C M M S - Re LLC (G-1375)*

Forzza Corporation (PA) 440 998-6300
222 N Lake St Madison (44057) *(G-9592)*

Foster Canning Inc 419 841-6755
6725 W Central Ave Ste T Toledo (43617) *(G-14293)*

Foster Transformer Company 513 681-2420
3820 Colerain Ave Cincinnati (45223) *(G-2919)*

Fostoria Bshngs Inslators Corp 419 435-7514
602 S Corporate Dr W Ste D Fostoria (44830) *(G-7633)*

Fostoria Bushings Inc 419 435-7514
602 S Corporate Dr W Fostoria (44830) *(G-7634)*

Fostoria Concrete, Bowling Green *Also Called: Palmer Bros Transit Mix Con (G-1582)*

Fostoria Focus Inc 419 435-6397
112 N Main St Fostoria (44830) *(G-7635)*

Fostoria MT&f Corp 419 435-7676
1401 Sandusky St Fostoria (44830) *(G-7636)*

Foundation Industries Inc (PA) 330 564-1250
880 W Waterloo Rd Ste B Akron (44314) *(G-157)*

Foundation Software LLC (PA) 330 220-8383
17999 Foltz Pkwy Strongsville (44149) *(G-13834)*

Foundation Systems Anchors Inc (PA) 330 454-1700
2300 Allen Ave Se Canton (44707) *(G-2104)*

Foundation Wellness 330 335-1571
961 Seville Rd Wadsworth (44281) *(G-15030)*

Foundation Wellness, Upper Arlington *Also Called: Remington Products Company (G-14802)*

Foundations, Medina *Also Called: Foundations Worldwide Inc (G-10326)*

Foundations Worldwide Inc (PA) 330 722-5033
5216 Portside Dr Medina (44256) *(G-10326)*

Founder's Service Co, Deerfield *Also Called: Founders Service & Mfg Inc (G-6666)*

Founders Service & Mfg Inc (PA) 330 584-7759
879 State Route 14 Deerfield (44411) *(G-6666)*

Foundry Artists Inc 216 391-9030
4404 Perkins Ave Cleveland (44103) *(G-4086)*

Foundry Sand Service LLC 330 823-6152
20455 Lake Park Blvd Sebring (44672) *(G-13120)*

Fount LLC 216 855-8751
2570 Superior Ave E Ste 504 Cleveland (44114) *(G-4087)*

Fountain News, Mason *Also Called: Cincinnati Ftn Sq News Inc (G-9975)*

Fountain Nook Woodcraft 330 473-2162
5528 Fountain Nook Rd Apple Creek (44606) *(G-500)*

Fountain Specialists Inc 513 831-5717
226 Main St Milford (45150) *(G-10906)*

Four Elements Inc 330 591-4505
4328 Remsen Rd Medina (44256) *(G-10327)*

Four Natures Keepers Inc 740 363-8007
4651 Marysville Rd Delaware (43015) *(G-6722)*

Four Seasons Manufacturing

ALPHABETIC SECTION

Four Seasons Manufacturing, Garrettsville Also Called: Diskin Enterprises LLC *(G-7913)*

Fouremans Sand & Gravel Inc... 937 547-1005
2791 Wildcat Rd Greenville (45331) *(G-8045)*

Fourjay Industries, Dayton Also Called: Fernandes Enterprises LLC *(G-6331)*

Fourteen Ventures Group LLC... 937 866-2341
3131 W Alex Bell Rd West Carrollton (45449) *(G-15354)*

Fouty & Company Inc... 419 693-0017
5003 Bayshore Rd Oregon (43616) *(G-12105)*

Fowler Products Inc... 419 683-4057
810 Colby Rd Crestline (44827) *(G-6033)*

Fox Lite Inc... 937 864-1966
8300 Dayton Springfield Rd Fairborn (45324) *(G-7315)*

Fox Tool Co Inc... 330 928-3402
1471 Main St Cuyahoga Falls (44221) *(G-6085)*

FOXCONN EV SYSTEM LLC... 234 285-4001
2300 Hallock Young Rd Sw Warren (44481) *(G-15171)*

FP Holdco Inc... 614 729-7205
13405 Yarmouth Dr Pickerington (43147) *(G-12462)*

Fpe Inc... 740 420-5252
30627 Orr Rd Circleville (43113) *(G-3552)*

Fpt Cleveland LLC (NH)... 216 441-3800
8550 Aetna Rd Cleveland (44105) *(G-4088)*

Fq Sale Inc (PA) 1940 S Yellow Springs St Springfield (45506) *(G-13568)*

Fragapane Bakeries Inc (PA)... 440 779-6050
28625 Lorain Rd North Olmsted (44070) *(G-11823)*

Fragapane Bakery & Deli, North Olmsted Also Called: Fragapane Bakeries Inc *(G-11823)*

Fram Group... 479 271-7934
127 Public Sq Ste 5110 Cleveland (44114) *(G-4089)*

Fram Group Operations LLC... 419 436-5827
1600 N Union St Fostoria (44830) *(G-7637)*

Frame Usa, Inc., Cincinnati Also Called: Black Squirrel Holdings Inc *(G-2671)*

Frame Warehouse... 614 861-4582
7502 E Main St Reynoldsburg (43068) *(G-12765)*

Framework Industries LLC... 234 759-2080
80 Eastgate Industrial Dr North Lima (44452) *(G-11805)*

Francis Manufacturing Company... 937 526-4551
500 E Mn St Russia (45363) *(G-12883)*

Francis-Schulze Co... 937 295-3941
3880 Rangeline Rd Russia (45363) *(G-12884)*

Francisco Jaume... 740 622-1200
311 S 15th St Ste 206 Coshocton (43812) *(G-5978)*

Franck and Fric Incorporated... 216 524-4451
7919 Old Rockside Rd Cleveland (44131) *(G-4090)*

Frank Brunckhorst Company LLC... 614 662-5300
2225 Spiegel Dr Groveport (43125) *(G-8142)*

Frank Csapo... 330 435-4458
157 Myers St Creston (44217) *(G-6039)*

Frank Csapo Oil & Gas Producer, Creston Also Called: Frank Csapo *(G-6039)*

Frank L Harter & Son Inc... 513 574-1330
3778 Frondorf Ave Cincinnati (45211) *(G-2920)*

Frankes Wood Products LLC... 937 642-0706
825 Collins Ave Marysville (43040) *(G-9910)*

Franklin... 419 699-5757
747 Michigan Ave Waterville (43566) *(G-15243)*

Franklin Art Glass Studios... 614 221-2972
222 E Sycamore St Columbus (43206) *(G-5385)*

Franklin Brazing Met Treating, Lebanon Also Called: Kando of Cincinnati Inc *(G-9092)*

Franklin Cabinet Company Inc... 937 743-9606
2500 Commerce Center Dr Franklin (45005) *(G-7676)*

Franklin Communications Inc... 614 459-9769
4401 Carriage Hill Ln Columbus (43220) *(G-5386)*

Franklin County Coal Company... 740 338-3100
46226 National Rd Saint Clairsville (43950) *(G-12905)*

Franklin Covey Co... 513 680-0975
7875 Montgomery Rd Spc 1202 Cincinnati (45236) *(G-2921)*

Franklin Equipment LLC (HQ)... 614 228-2014
4141 Hamilton Square Blvd Groveport (43125) *(G-8143)*

Franklin Gas & Oil Company LLC... 330 264-8739
1615 W Old Lincoln Way Wooster (44691) *(G-16120)*

Franklin International Inc (PA)... 614 443-0241
2020 Bruck St Columbus (43207) *(G-5387)*

Franklin Iron & Metal Corp... 937 253-8184
1939 E 1st St Dayton (45403) *(G-6338)*

Franklin Mfg Div, Franklin Also Called: Emssons Faurecia Ctrl Systems *(G-7672)*

Franklin Printing Company... 740 452-6375
984 Beverly Ave Zanesville (43701) *(G-16533)*

Franklin's Printing, Zanesville Also Called: Franklin Printing Company *(G-16533)*

Franks Sawmill Inc... 419 682-3831
Rd 1950 Stryker (43557) *(G-13909)*

Frantz Grinding Co... 330 343-8689
1879 E High Ave New Philadelphia (44663) *(G-11502)*

Frantz Medical Development Ltd (PA)... 440 255-1155
7740 Metric Dr Mentor (44060) *(G-10457)*

Frantz Well Servicing Inc... 419 992-4564
7227 N County Road 33 Tiffin (44883) *(G-14086)*

Frazeysburg Restaurant & Bky, Frazeysburg Also Called: Calvary Christian Ch of Ohio *(G-7714)*

Frazier Machine and Prod Inc... 419 874-7321
26489 Southpoint Rd Perrysburg (43551) *(G-12383)*

Frd, Kent Also Called: Furukawa Rock Drill USA Co Ltd *(G-8816)*

Frecon Technologies Inc... 513 874-8981
9319 Princeton Glendale Rd West Chester (45011) *(G-15432)*

Fred D Pfening Company... 614 294-5361
1075 W 5th Ave Columbus (43212) *(G-5388)*

Fred D Pfening Company (PA)... 614 294-5361
1075 W 5th Ave Columbus (43212) *(G-5389)*

Frederick Steel Company LLC... 513 821-6400
630 Glendale Milford Rd Cincinnati (45215) *(G-2922)*

Fredericksburg Facility, Fredericksburg Also Called: Robin Industries Inc *(G-7732)*

Fredericktown Tomato Show... 740 694-4816
Fredericktown (43019) *(G-7747)*

Fredon Corporation... 440 951-5200
8990 Tyler Blvd Mentor (44060) *(G-10458)*

Fredrick Ramond, Avon Lake Also Called: Hinkley Lighting Inc *(G-812)*

Fredrick Welding & Machining... 614 866-9650
6840 Americana Pkwy Reynoldsburg (43068) *(G-12766)*

Freds Sign Service Inc... 937 335-1901
3055 S County Road 25a Troy (45373) *(G-14570)*

Freds Woodworking & Remodelin... 330 802-8646
665 Fairview Ave Barberton (44203) *(G-868)*

Free Press Standard, Carrollton Also Called: Carrollton Publishing Company *(G-2305)*

Freedom Forklift Sales LLC... 330 289-0879
1114 Garman Rd Akron (44313) *(G-158)*

Freedom Health LLC... 330 562-0888
65 Aurora Industrial Pkwy Aurora (44202) *(G-715)*

Freedom Homes... 740 446-3093
208 Upper River Rd Gallipolis (45631) *(G-7892)*

Freedom Usa Inc... 216 503-6374
2045 Midway Dr Twinsburg (44087) *(G-14662)*

Freeman, Fremont Also Called: The Louis G Freeman Company LLC *(G-7813)*

Freeman Enclosure Systems LLC... 877 441-8555
4160 Half Acre Rd Batavia (45103) *(G-924)*

Freeman Manufacturing & Sup Co (PA)... 440 934-1902
1101 Moore Rd Avon (44011) *(G-775)*

Freeport Press Inc (PA)... 330 308-3300
2127 Reiser Ave Se New Philadelphia (44663) *(G-11503)*

Freeway Corporation (PA)... 216 524-9700
9301 Allen Dr Cleveland (44125) *(G-4091)*

Fremar Industries Inc... 330 220-3700
2808 Westway Dr Brunswick (44212) *(G-1761)*

Fremont, Fremont Also Called: Fremont Company *(G-7780)*

Fremont, Rockford Also Called: Fremont Company *(G-12833)*

Fremont Company (PA)... 419 334-8995
802 N Front St Fremont (43420) *(G-7780)*

Fremont Company... 419 363-2924
150 Hickory St Rockford (45882) *(G-12833)*

Fremont Cutting Dies Inc... 419 334-5153
3179 Us 20 E Fremont (43420) *(G-7781)*

Fremont Flask Co... 419 332-2231
1000 Wolfe Ave Fremont (43420) *(G-7782)*

Fremont Plastic Products Inc... 419 332-6407
2101 Cedar St Fremont (43420) *(G-7783)*

ALPHABETIC SECTION — Furn Tech

Fremont Printing Inc.. 480 272-3443
1208 Dickinson St Fremont (43420) *(G-7784)*

French Oil Mill Machinery Co (PA)........................... 937 773-3420
1035 W Greene St Piqua (45356) *(G-12517)*

French Transit LLC... 650 431-3959
7588 Central Parke Blvd Ste 220 Mason (45040) *(G-9994)*

French USA, Piqua Also Called: French Oil Mill Machinery Co *(G-12517)*

Frepeg Industries Inc.. 440 255-8595
8624 East Ave Mentor (44060) *(G-10459)*

Fresh and Limited, Sidney Also Called: Freshway Foods Company Inc *(G-13249)*

Fresh Mark Inc... 330 455-5253
1600 Harmont Ave Ne Canton (44705) *(G-2105)*

Fresh Mark Inc (PA)... 330 832-7491
1888 Southway St Sw Massillon (44646) *(G-10097)*

Fresh Mark Inc... 330 332-8508
1735 S Lincoln Ave Salem (44460) *(G-12996)*

Fresh Products LLC.. 419 531-9741
30600 Oregon Rd Perrysburg (43551) *(G-12384)*

Fresh Vegetable Technology, Columbus Also Called: National Frt Vgtable Tech Corp *(G-5590)*

Freshway Foods Company Inc (DH)....................... 937 498-4664
601 Stolle Ave Sidney (45365) *(G-13249)*

Freudenberg-Nok Findlay, Findlay Also Called: Freudenberg-Nok General Partnr *(G-7511)*

Freudenberg-Nok General Partnr........................... 419 427-5221
555 Marathon Blvd Findlay (45840) *(G-7511)*

Freudenberg-Nok General Partnr........................... 937 335-3306
1275 Archer Dr Troy (45373) *(G-14571)*

Freudenberg-Nok Sealing Tech.............................. 877 331-8427
11617 State Route 13 Milan (44846) *(G-10883)*

Freudenberg-Nok Sealing Tech, Troy Also Called: Freudenberg-Nok General Partnr *(G-14571)*

Frezerve Inc... 440 661-4037
1218 Lake Ave Ashtabula (44004) *(G-633)*

Friction Products Co.. 330 725-4941
920 Lake Rd Medina (44256) *(G-10328)*

Friendly Candle LLC.. 740 683-0312
1160 Corrugated Way Columbus (43201) *(G-5390)*

Friends Business Source, Findlay Also Called: Friends Service Co Inc *(G-7512)*

Friends Rocking Horse Center................................. 937 324-1111
651 S Limestone St Springfield (45505) *(G-13569)*

Friends Service Co Inc.. 800 427-1704
4604 Salem Ave Dayton (45416) *(G-6339)*

Friends Service Co Inc (PA).................................... 419 427-1704
2300 Bright Rd Findlay (45840) *(G-7512)*

Fries Machine & Tool Inc.. 937 898-6432
5729 Webster St Dayton (45414) *(G-6340)*

Friesen Transfer Ltd... 614 873-5672
9280 Iams Rd Plain City (43064) *(G-12579)*

Friess Welding Inc... 330 644-8160
3342 S Main St Coventry Township (44319) *(G-6009)*

Frisby Printing Company... 330 665-4565
3571 Brookwall Dr Unit C Fairlawn (44333) *(G-7439)*

Frischco Inc.. 740 363-7537
715 Sunbury Rd Delaware (43015) *(G-6723)*

Frito-Lay, Canton Also Called: Frito-Lay North America Inc *(G-2106)*

Frito-Lay, Wooster Also Called: Frito-Lay North America Inc *(G-16121)*

Frito-Lay North America Inc.................................... 330 477-7009
4030 16th St Sw Canton (44710) *(G-2106)*

Frito-Lay North America Inc.................................... 972 334-7000
1626 Old Mansfield Rd Wooster (44691) *(G-16121)*

Fritzie Freeze Inc... 419 727-0818
5137 N Summit St Unit 1 Toledo (43611) *(G-14294)*

Frog Ranch Foods Ltd... 740 767-3705
5 S High St Glouster (45732) *(G-7983)*

Frohn North America Inc.. 770 819-0089
23800 Corbin Dr Ste B Bedford Heights (44128) *(G-1173)*

Frohock-Stewart Inc.. 440 329-6000
39400 Taylor Pkwy North Ridgeville (44035) *(G-11840)*

Front and Center MGT Group LLC......................... 740 383-5176
381 W Center St Marion (43302) *(G-9853)*

Front Pocket Innovations LLC................................. 330 441-2365
471 E Bergey St Ste C Wadsworth (44281) *(G-15031)*

Frontier Signs & Displays Inc................................. 513 367-0813
525 New Biddinger Rd Harrison (45030) *(G-8275)*

Frontier Tank Center Inc... 330 659-3888
3800 Congress Pkwy Richfield (44286) *(G-12788)*

Frontwaters Brewing Company, Marblehead Also Called: Frontwaters Rest & Brewing Co *(G-9765)*

Frontwaters Rest & Brewing Co............................. 419 798-8058
8660 E Bayshore Rd Marblehead (43440) *(G-9765)*

Frost Engineering Inc.. 513 541-6330
3408 Beekman St Cincinnati (45223) *(G-2923)*

Frostop, Columbus Also Called: Fbg Bottling Group LLC *(G-5371)*

Frozen Specialties Inc.. 419 445-9015
720 W Barre Rd Archbold (43502) *(G-528)*

Frutarom, West Chester Also Called: Frutarom USA Inc *(G-15556)*

Frutarom USA Holding Inc (DH)............................. 201 861-9500
5404 Duff Dr West Chester (45246) *(G-15555)*

Frutarom USA Inc (HQ)... 513 870-4900
5404 Duff Dr West Chester (45246) *(G-15556)*

Fry Foods Inc... 419 448-0831
99 Maule Rd Tiffin (44883) *(G-14087)*

Fryburg Door Inc... 330 674-5252
6086 State Route 241 Millersburg (44654) *(G-10955)*

Fscreations Corporation (HQ)................................. 330 746-3015
255 W Federal St Youngstown (44503) *(G-16360)*

FSI, Archbold Also Called: Frozen Specialties Inc *(G-528)*

FSRc Tanks Inc.. 234 221-2015
11029 Industrial Pkwy Nw Bolivar (44612) *(G-1525)*

Ft Precision Inc.. 740 694-1500
9731 Mount Gilead Rd Fredericktown (43019) *(G-7748)*

Ftd Investments LLC... 937 833-2161
379 Albert Rd Brookville (45309) *(G-1737)*

Ftech R&D North America Inc (HQ)....................... 937 339-2777
1191 Horizon West Ct Troy (45373) *(G-14572)*

Ftp, Fredericktown Also Called: Ft Precision Inc *(G-7748)*

Fuchs Franklin Div, Twinsburg Also Called: Fuchs Lubricants Co *(G-14663)*

Fuchs Lubricants Co... 330 963-0400
8036 Bavaria Rd Twinsburg (44087) *(G-14663)*

Fuel America.. 419 586-5609
204 E Market St Celina (45822) *(G-2333)*

Fukuvi Usa Inc... 937 236-7288
7631 Progress Ct Dayton (45424) *(G-6341)*

Full Circle Oil Field Svcs Inc.................................. 740 371-5422
7585 State Route 821 Whipple (45788) *(G-15814)*

Fullgospel Publishing.. 216 339-1973
16781 Chagrin Blvd Ste 134 Shaker Heights (44120) *(G-13154)*

Fully Involved Printing Co LLC............................... 440 635-6858
9819 Johnnycake Ridge Rd Mentor (44060) *(G-10460)*

Fully Promoted, Canton Also Called: Fully Promoted of Canton *(G-2107)*

Fully Promoted of Canton....................................... 330 484-8484
3611 Cleveland Ave S Canton (44707) *(G-2107)*

Fulton, Wauseon Also Called: Fulton Industries Inc *(G-15261)*

Fulton County Expositor, Napoleon Also Called: Gazette Publishing Company *(G-11314)*

Fulton County Processing Ltd................................ 419 822-9266
7800 State Route 109 Delta (43515) *(G-6783)*

Fulton Equipment Co (PA)...................................... 419 290-5393
823 Hamilton St Toledo (43607) *(G-14295)*

Fulton Industries Inc (PA)....................................... 419 335-3015
135 E Linfoot St Wauseon (43567) *(G-15261)*

Fulton Manufacturing Inds LLC
6600 W Snowville Rd # 6500 Brecksville (44141) *(G-1617)*

Fulton Sign & Decal Inc.. 440 951-1515
7144 Industrial Park Blvd Mentor (44060) *(G-10461)*

Functional Formularies, West Chester Also Called: Nutritional Medicinals LLC *(G-15467)*

Functional Products Inc... 330 963-3060
8282 Bavaria Dr E Macedonia (44056) *(G-9552)*

Funky Ink Prints LLC... 330 241-7291
1736 W 130th St Ste 110 Brunswick (44212) *(G-1762)*

Funny Times Inc... 216 371-8600
2176 Lee Rd Cleveland (44118) *(G-4092)*

Funtown Playgrounds Inc.. 513 871-8585
839 Cypresspoint Ct Cincinnati (45245) *(G-2559)*

Furn Tech, Waterville Also Called: Furnace Technologies Inc *(G-15244)*

Furnace Technologies Inc... 419 878-2100
1070 Disher Dr Waterville (43566) *(G-15244)*

Furniture By Otmar Inc (PA)... 937 435-2039
301 Miamisburg Centerville Rd Dayton (45459) *(G-6342)*

Furniture Concepts Inc.. 216 292-9100
4925 Galaxy Pkwy Ste G Cleveland (44128) *(G-4093)*

Furntech, Waterville Also Called: Labcraft Inc *(G-15249)*

Furukawa Rock Drill, Kent Also Called: Furukawa Rock Drill Usa Inc *(G-8815)*

Furukawa Rock Drill Usa Inc (HQ)................................ 330 673-5826
805 Lake St Kent (44240) *(G-8815)*

Furukawa Rock Drill USA Co Ltd (PA)........................... 330 673-5826
711 Lake St Kent (44240) *(G-8816)*

Fuserashi Intl Tech Inc.. 330 273-0140
5401 Innovation Dr Valley City (44280) *(G-14870)*

Fusion Ceramics Inc (PA).. 330 627-5821
160 Scio Rd Se Carrollton (44615) *(G-2307)*

Fusion Incorporated (PA)... 440 946-3300
4658 E 355th St Willoughby (44094) *(G-15922)*

Fusion Metal Fabrication LLC..................................... 937 753-1090
974 E Broadway St Covington (45318) *(G-6022)*

Fusion Needle Company Inc... 740 589-5511
30 E Union St Athens (45701) *(G-682)*

Fusion Software Inc.. 330 723-2957
5235 Linda Dr Medina (44256) *(G-10329)*

Future Controls Corporation....................................... 440 275-3191
1419 State Route 45 Austinburg (44010) *(G-747)*

Future Finishes Inc... 513 860-0020
40 Standen Dr Hamilton (45015) *(G-8209)*

Future Molding Inc... 419 281-0000
1850 S Baney Rd Ashland (44805) *(G-575)*

Future Polytech Inc (PA).. 614 942-1209
2215 Citygate Dr Ste D Columbus (43219) *(G-5391)*

Fuyao Glass America Inc (HQ)..................................... 937 496-5777
2801 W Stroop Rd Dayton (45439) *(G-6343)*

Fuzzy Ten LLC.. 614 276-4738
3375 En Joie Dr Columbus (43228) *(G-5392)*

Fwy Machine Company LLC.. 216 533-7515
2495 Stony Hill Rd Hinckley (44233) *(G-8472)*

Fx Digital Media Inc... 216 241-4040
2400 Superior Ave E Ste 100 Cleveland (44114) *(G-4094)*

Fx Digital Media Inc (PA).. 216 241-4040
1600 E 23rd St Cleveland (44114) *(G-4095)*

G & C Raw LLC... 937 827-0010
225 N West St Versailles (45380) *(G-14980)*

G & C Raw Dog Food, Versailles Also Called: G & C Raw LLC *(G-14980)*

G & J Extrusions Inc... 330 753-0162
1580 Turkeyfoot Lake Rd New Franklin (44203) *(G-11436)*

G & J Packaging, Cleveland Also Called: G and J Automatic Systems Inc *(G-4097)*

G & J Pepsi-Cola Bottlers Inc...................................... 740 593-3366
2001 E State St Athens (45701) *(G-683)*

G & J Pepsi-Cola Bottlers Inc...................................... 740 774-2148
400 E 7th St Chillicothe (45601) *(G-2504)*

G & J Pepsi-Cola Bottlers Inc (PA)............................... 513 785-6060
9435 Waterstone Blvd Ste 390 Cincinnati (45249) *(G-2924)*

G & J Pepsi-Cola Bottlers Inc...................................... 866 647-2734
870 N 22nd St Columbus (43219) *(G-5393)*

G & J Pepsi-Cola Bottlers Inc...................................... 614 253-8771
1241 Gibbard Ave Columbus (43219) *(G-5394)*

G & J Pepsi-Cola Bottlers Inc...................................... 740 354-9191
4587 Gallia Pike Franklin Furnace (45629) *(G-7712)*

G & J Pepsi-Cola Bottlers Inc...................................... 513 896-3700
2580 Bobmeyer Rd Hamilton (45015) *(G-8210)*

G & J Pepsi-Cola Bottlers Inc...................................... 740 354-9191
336 N Sixth St Zanesville (43701) *(G-16534)*

G & L Machining Inc... 513 724-2600
299 N 3rd St Williamsburg (45176) *(G-15865)*

G & P Construction LLC... 855 494-4830
10139 Royalton Rd Ste D North Royalton (44133) *(G-11875)*

G & R Welding Service LLC... 937 245-2341
1350 Hook Dr Middletown (45042) *(G-10825)*

G & S Custom Tooling LLC... 419 286-2888
18406 Road 20 Fort Jennings (45844) *(G-7595)*

G & S Metal Products Co Inc (PA)................................ 216 441-0700
3330 E 79th St Cleveland (44127) *(G-4096)*

G & S Titanium Inc... 330 263-0564
4000 E Lincoln Way Wooster (44691) *(G-16122)*

G & T Manufacturing Co.. 440 639-7777
6085 Pinecone Dr Mentor (44060) *(G-10462)*

G A Avril Company (PA).. 513 641-0566
4445 Kings Run Dr Cincinnati (45232) *(G-2925)*

G A Avril Company... 513 731-5133
2108 Eagle Ct Cincinnati (45237) *(G-2926)*

G A Wintzer and Son Company (PA)............................ 419 739-4900
204 W Auglaize St Wapakoneta (45895) *(G-15112)*

G A Wintzer and Son Company................................... 419 739-4913
12279 S Dixey Hwy Wapakoneta (45895) *(G-15113)*

G and J Automatic Systems Inc................................... 216 741-6070
14701 Industrial Pkwy Cleveland (44135) *(G-4097)*

G Big Inc (PA).. 740 867-5758
441 Rockwood Ave Chesapeake (45619) *(G-2473)*

G Denver and Co LLC... 937 498-2555
211 E Russell Rd Sidney (45365) *(G-13250)*

G E S, Parma Also Called: Ges Graphite Inc *(G-12290)*

G F Frank and Sons Inc.. 513 870-9075
9075 Le Saint Dr West Chester (45014) *(G-15433)*

G Fordyce Co... 937 393-3241
210 Hobart Dr Hillsboro (45133) *(G-8457)*

G Grafton Machine & Rubber...................................... 330 297-1062
640 Cleveland Rd Ravenna (44266) *(G-12716)*

G H Cutter Services Inc.. 419 476-0476
6203 N Detroit Ave Toledo (43612) *(G-14296)*

G I Plastek Inc... 440 230-1942
24700 Center Ridge Rd Ste 8 Westlake (44145) *(G-15751)*

G L Pierce Inc.. 513 772-7202
12100 Mosteller Rd Ste 500 Cincinnati (45241) *(G-2927)*

G M Greco Inc.. 614 822-0522
6500 Emerald Pkwy Ste 100 Dublin (43016) *(G-6884)*

G M R Technology Inc... 440 992-6003
2131 Aetna Rd Ashtabula (44004) *(G-634)*

G P Manufacturing Inc.. 937 544-3190
376 Buckeye St Peebles (45660) *(G-12326)*

G S K Inc... 937 547-1611
915 Front St Greenville (45331) *(G-8046)*

G S S, Barberton Also Called: Glass Surface Systems Inc *(G-870)*

G S S, Springboro Also Called: Graphic Systems Services Inc *(G-13503)*

G T Automotive Service Center, Pataskala Also Called: Gt Tire Service Inc *(G-12298)*

G T Metal Fabricators Inc... 440 237-8745
12126 York Rd Unit E Cleveland (44133) *(G-4098)*

G W Cobb Co.. 216 341-0100
3914 Broadway Ave 16 Cleveland (44115) *(G-4099)*

G W Steffen Bookbinders Inc...................................... 330 963-0300
8212 Bavaria Dr E Macedonia (44056) *(G-9553)*

G W Tool & Die Co, Fort Loramie Also Called: Schmitmeyer Inc *(G-7607)*

G-M-I Inc... 440 953-8811
4822 E 355th St Willoughby (44094) *(G-15923)*

G-Rod Welding & Fabg LLC... 740 588-0609
5065 Chandlersville Rd Chandlersville (43727) *(G-2439)*

G.S. Steel Company, Cuyahoga Falls Also Called: Dbcr Inc *(G-6078)*

G&H Baltimore, Cleveland Also Called: Em4 Inc *(G-4010)*

G&O Resources Ltd.. 330 253-2525
96 E Crosier St Akron (44311) *(G-159)*

G2 Materials LLC... 216 293-4211
17325 Euclid Ave Ste 3038 Cleveland (44112) *(G-4100)*

G3 Packaging LLC.. 334 799-0015
4273 Salzman Rd Monroe (45044) *(G-11107)*

Gabel Welding Inc.. 567 201-8217
2400 W Sandy Ln Port Clinton (43452) *(G-12619)*

Gabriel Logan LLC (PA).. 740 380-6809
4141 Hamilton Square Blvd Groveport (43125) *(G-8144)*

Gabriel Performance Products, Akron Also Called: Huntsman Advnced Mtls Amrcas L *(G-186)*

Gabriel Phenoxies Inc (PA)... 704 499-9801
240 W Emerling Ave Akron (44301) *(G-160)*

Galapagos Inc (PA)... 937 890-3068
3345 Old Salem Rd Dayton (45415) *(G-6344)*

Galaxy Outdoor, Miamisburg Also Called: Hearth Products Controls Co *(G-10644)*
Galehouse Lumber, Doylestown Also Called: The Galehouse Companies Inc *(G-6854)*
Galena Vault Ltd.. 740 965-2200
4909 Harlem Rd Galena (43021) *(G-7854)*
Galenas LLC.. 330 208-9423
1956 S Main St Akron (44301) *(G-161)*
Galion LLC.. 419 468-5214
515 N East St Galion (44833) *(G-7875)*
Galion Canvas Products (PA).. 419 468-5333
385 S Market St Galion (44833) *(G-7876)*
Galion Dump Bodies, Dundee Also Called: Galion-Godwin Truck Bdy Co LLC *(G-6965)*
Galion-Godwin Truck Bdy Co LLC....................................... 330 359-5495
7415 Township Road 666 Dundee (44624) *(G-6965)*
Galipols Reduction Co, Rio Grande Also Called: Inland Products Inc *(G-12818)*
Galley Printing Inc.. 330 220-5577
2892 Westway Dr Brunswick (44212) *(G-1763)*
Galley Printing Company, Brunswick Also Called: Galley Printing Inc *(G-1763)*
Galt Alloys, Canton Also Called: Rmi Titanium Company LLC *(G-2216)*
Galt Alloys Enterprise... 330 309-8194
1550 Marietta Ave Se Canton (44707) *(G-2108)*
Galt Alloys Inc Main Ofc.. 330 453-4678
122 Central Plz N Canton (44702) *(G-2109)*
Gamco, Ravenna Also Called: General Aluminum Mfg LLC *(G-12718)*
Gameday Vision.. 330 830-4550
1147 Oberlin Ave Sw Massillon (44647) *(G-10098)*
Ganeden, Mayfield Heights Also Called: Ganeden Biotech Inc *(G-10249)*
Ganeden Biotech Inc.. 440 229-5200
5800 Landerbrook Dr Ste 300 Mayfield Heights (44124) *(G-10249)*
Gannett Stllite Info Ntwrk LLC.. 419 334-1012
1800 E State St Ste B Fremont (43420) *(G-7785)*
Gannett Stllite Info Ntwrk LLC.. 304 485-1891
700 Channel Ln Marietta (45750) *(G-9794)*
Ganymede Technologies Corp.. 419 562-5522
1685 Marion Rd Bucyrus (44820) *(G-1860)*
Ganzcorp Investments Inc.. 330 963-5400
2300 Pinnacle Pkwy Twinsburg (44087) *(G-14664)*
Garage Scenes Ltd... 614 407-6094
7385 State Route 3 Unit 112 Westerville (43082) *(G-15657)*
Garber Farms, Greenville Also Called: Russell L Garber *(G-8058)*
Gardella Jewelry LLC.. 440 877-9261
7432 Julia Dr North Royalton (44133) *(G-11876)*
Garden Street Iron & Metal Inc (PA).................................. 513 721-4660
2885 Spring Grove Ave Cincinnati (45225) *(G-2928)*
Gardner Inc (PA).. 614 456-4000
3641 Interchange Rd Columbus (43204) *(G-5395)*
Gardner Business Media Inc.. 513 527-8800
6925 Valley Ln Cincinnati (45244) *(G-2929)*
Gardner Business Media Inc (PA)...................................... 513 527-8800
6915 Valley Ln Cincinnati (45244) *(G-2930)*
Gardner Lumber Company Inc.. 740 254-4664
5805 Laurel Creek Rd Se Tippecanoe (44699) *(G-14170)*
Gardner Pie Company... 330 245-2030
191 Logan Pkwy Coventry Township (44319) *(G-6010)*
Gardner Signs Inc (PA).. 419 385-6669
3800 Airport Hwy Toledo (43615) *(G-14297)*
Gareth Stevens Publishing, Strongsville Also Called: Gareth Stevens Publishing LP *(G-13835)*
Gareth Stevens Publishing LP.. 800 542-2595
23221 Morgan Ct Strongsville (44149) *(G-13835)*
Garfield Alloys Inc (PA)... 216 587-4843
4878 Chaincraft Rd Cleveland (44125) *(G-4101)*
Garick LLC (HQ)... 216 581-0100
8400 Sweet Valley Dr Ste 408 Cleveland (44125) *(G-4102)*
Garland Commercial Industries LLC.................................. 800 338-2204
1333 E 179th St Cleveland (44110) *(G-4103)*
Garland Industries Inc (PA)... 216 641-7500
3800 E 91st St Cleveland (44105) *(G-4104)*
Garland Welding Co Inc.. 330 536-6506
804 E Liberty St Lowellville (44436) *(G-9375)*
Garland/Dbs Inc... 216 641-7500
3800 E 91st St Cleveland (44105) *(G-4105)*

Garro Tread Corporation (PA).. 330 376-3125
100 Beech St Akron (44308) *(G-162)*
Garvey Corporation... 330 779-0700
1019 Ohio Works Dr Youngstown (44510) *(G-16361)*
Garvin Industries Div, Strongsville Also Called: Guarantee Specialties Inc *(G-13838)*
Gary Dattilo... 513 671-2117
1329 E Kemper Rd Cincinnati (45246) *(G-2931)*
Gary I Teach Jr.. 614 582-7483
4855 Rosedale Milford Center Rd London (43140) *(G-9387)*
Gary L Gast... 419 626-5915
2024 Campbell St Sandusky (44870) *(G-13059)*
Gary Lawrence Enterprises Inc... 330 833-7181
21 Charles Ave Sw Massillon (44646) *(G-10099)*
Garys Chesecakes Fine Desserts....................................... 513 574-1700
5285 Crookshank Rd Side Cincinnati (45238) *(G-2932)*
Gas Assist Injction Mlding Exp.. 440 632-5203
15285 S State Ave Middlefield (44062) *(G-10751)*
Gas Products, Cambridge Also Called: Aci Services Inc *(G-1918)*
Gas Turbine Fuel Systems, Mentor Also Called: Parker-Hannifin Corporation *(G-10520)*
Gasdorf Tool and Mch Co Inc.. 419 227-0103
445 N Mcdonel St Lima (45801) *(G-9244)*
Gasflux Company... 440 365-1941
32 Hawthorne St Elyria (44035) *(G-7153)*
Gasgas North America, Amherst Also Called: Ktm North America Inc *(G-477)*
Gasko Fabricated Products LLC (HQ)................................ 330 239-1781
4049 Ridge Rd Medina (44256) *(G-10330)*
Gaslight, Cincinnati Also Called: Gaslight Holdings LLC *(G-2933)*
Gaslight Holdings LLC... 513 470-3525
5910 Hamilton Ave Cincinnati (45224) *(G-2933)*
Gasoila Thred-Taper, Cleveland Also Called: FedPro Inc *(G-4055)*
Gaspar, Canton Also Called: Gaspar Inc *(G-2110)*
Gaspar Inc... 330 477-2222
1545 Whipple Ave Sw Canton (44710) *(G-2110)*
Gaspar Services LLC... 330 467-8292
7791 Capital Blvd Ste 2 Macedonia (44056) *(G-9554)*
Gasser Chair Co Inc (PA)... 330 534-2234
4136 Logan Way Youngstown (44505) *(G-16362)*
Gasser Chair Co Inc.. 330 759-2234
2457 Logan Ave Youngstown (44505) *(G-16363)*
Gate West Coast Ventures LLC... 513 891-1000
4901 Hunt Rd Ste 200 Blue Ash (45242) *(G-1397)*
Gatekeeper Press LLC... 866 535-0913
2167 Stringtown Rd Ste 109 Grove City (43123) *(G-8095)*
Gatesair Inc (HQ).. 513 459-3400
5300 Kings Island Dr Ste 101 Mason (45040) *(G-9995)*
Gateway Con Forming Svcs Inc.. 513 353-2000
5938 Hamilton-Cleves Rd Miamitown (45041) *(G-10708)*
Gateway Industrial Pdts Inc.. 440 324-4112
160 Freedom Ct Elyria (44035) *(G-7154)*
Gateway Packaging Company LLC.................................... 419 738-5126
253 Indl Dr Wapakoneta (45895) *(G-15114)*
Gateway Printing, Wadsworth Also Called: Rohrer Corporation *(G-15063)*
Gateways Industries Inc.. 330 505-0479
1200 Youngstown Warren Rd Niles (44446) *(G-11669)*
Gatton Packaging Inc.. 419 886-2577
99 East St Bellville (44813) *(G-1242)*
Gawa Traders Wholesale & Dist....................................... 614 697-1440
250 West St Columbus (43215) *(G-5396)*
Gaydash Enterprises Inc... 330 896-4811
3640 Tabs Dr Uniontown (44685) *(G-14783)*
Gaydash Industries, Uniontown Also Called: Gaydash Enterprises Inc *(G-14783)*
Gayson Silicon Dispersions Inc... 330 848-8422
33587 Walker Rd Avon Lake (44012) *(G-808)*
Gayston Corporation.. 937 743-6050
721 Richard St Miamisburg (45342) *(G-10640)*
Gazette Publishing, Conneaut Also Called: The Gazette Printing Co Inc *(G-5934)*
Gazette Publishing Company.. 419 335-2010
595 E Riverview Ave Napoleon (43545) *(G-11314)*
Gb, Delta Also Called: Gb Manufacturing Company *(G-6784)*
Gb Fabrication Company... 419 347-1835
2510 Taylortown Rd Shelby (44875) *(G-13195)*

Gb Fabrication Company (HQ)... 419 896-3191
  60 Scott St Shiloh (44878) *(G-13203)*
Gb Liquidating Company Inc.. 513 248-7600
  22 Whitney Dr Milford (45150) *(G-10907)*
Gb Manufacturing Company (PA).. 419 822-5323
  1120 E Main St Delta (43515) *(G-6784)*
Gbc International LLC.. 513 943-7283
  1091 Ohio Pike Cincinnati (45245) *(G-2560)*
Gbr Property Maintenance LLC... 937 879-0200
  1260 Spangler Rd Bldg 1 Fairborn (45324) *(G-7316)*
GBS Corp... 330 863-1828
  224 Morges Rd Malvern (44644) *(G-9612)*
GBS Corp (PA)... 330 494-5330
  7233 Freedom Ave Nw North Canton (44720) *(G-11729)*
GBS Filing Solutions, Malvern Also Called: GBS Corp *(G-9612)*
GBS Filing Solutions, North Canton Also Called: GBS Corp *(G-11729)*
Gc Controls Inc... 440 779-4777
  30311 Clemens Rd Westlake (44145) *(G-15752)*
Gcc, Monroe Also Called: Glass Coatings & Concepts LLC *(G-11108)*
GCI Metals Inc.. 937 835-7123
  7660 W 3rd St Dayton (45417) *(G-6345)*
Gconsent LLC... 614 886-2416
  5412 Talladega Dr Dublin (43016) *(G-6885)*
Gconsent Logistics, Dublin Also Called: Gconsent LLC *(G-6885)*
Gdc Inc... 574 533-3128
  1700 Old Mansfield Rd Wooster (44691) *(G-16123)*
Gdc Industries LLC.. 937 367-7229
  170 Gracewood Dr Dayton (45458) *(G-6346)*
Gdj Inc... 440 975-0258
  7585 Tyler Blvd Mentor (44060) *(G-10463)*
Gdw Woodworking LLC.. 513 494-3041
  120 Vista Ridge Dr South Lebanon (45065) *(G-13461)*
Gdy Installations Inc... 419 467-0036
  302 Arco Dr Toledo (43607) *(G-14298)*
GE, Aurora Also Called: USA Instruments Inc *(G-739)*
GE, Bucyrus Also Called: General Electric Company *(G-1861)*
GE, Canton Also Called: General Electric Company *(G-2111)*
GE, Cincinnati Also Called: GE Engine Services LLC *(G-2936)*
GE, Cincinnati Also Called: General Electric Company *(G-2941)*
GE, Cincinnati Also Called: General Electric Company *(G-2943)*
GE, Cleveland Also Called: GE Lighting Inc *(G-4106)*
GE, Cleveland Also Called: General Electric Company *(G-4112)*
GE, Cleveland Also Called: General Electric Company *(G-4113)*
GE, Cleveland Also Called: General Electric Company *(G-4114)*
GE, Cleveland Also Called: General Electric Company *(G-4115)*
GE, Coshocton Also Called: General Electric Company *(G-5979)*
GE, Logan Also Called: General Electric Company *(G-9363)*
GE, Mc Donald Also Called: General Electric Company *(G-10277)*
GE, Twinsburg Also Called: GE Vernova International LLC *(G-14665)*
GE, Twinsburg Also Called: General Electric Company *(G-14668)*
GE, Warren Also Called: General Electric Company *(G-15172)*
GE, West Chester Also Called: General Electric Company *(G-15440)*
GE Additive, West Chester Also Called: General Electric Company *(G-15439)*
GE Additive LLC.. 513 341-0597
  5115 Excello Ct West Chester (45069) *(G-15434)*
GE Aviation, Cincinnati Also Called: GE Aviation Systems LLC *(G-2934)*
GE Aviation, Cincinnati Also Called: GE Aviation Systems LLC *(G-2935)*
GE Aviation, Springdale Also Called: GE Aviation Systems LLC *(G-13525)*
GE Aviation, West Chester Also Called: GE Aviation Systems LLC *(G-15435)*
GE Aviation, West Chester Also Called: GE Aviation Systems LLC *(G-15436)*
GE Aviation Systems LLC... 513 470-2889
  10270 Saint Rita Ln Cincinnati (45215) *(G-2934)*
GE Aviation Systems LLC (HQ).. 937 898-9600
  1 Neumann Way Cincinnati (45215) *(G-2935)*
GE Aviation Systems LLC... 937 898-9600
  6800 Poe Ave Dayton (45414) *(G-6347)*
GE Aviation Systems LLC... 620 218-5237
  183 Progress Pl Springdale (45246) *(G-13525)*

GE Aviation Systems LLC... 937 898-5881
  740 E National Rd Vandalia (45377) *(G-14940)*
GE Aviation Systems LLC... 937 898-5881
  740 E National Rd Vandalia (45377) *(G-14941)*
GE Aviation Systems LLC... 513 779-1910
  9647 Roundhouse Dr West Chester (45069) *(G-15435)*
GE Aviation Systems LLC... 513 786-4555
  7831 Ashford Glen Ct West Chester (45069) *(G-15436)*
GE Aviation Systems LLC... 513 889-5150
  5223 Muhlhauser Rd West Chester (45011) *(G-15437)*
GE Current, Cleveland Also Called: Current Lighting Solutions LLC *(G-3920)*
GE Current, A Daintree Company, Beachwood Also Called: Current Lighting Solutions LLC *(G-982)*
GE Engine Services LLC... 513 977-1500
  201 W Crescentville Rd Cincinnati (45246) *(G-2936)*
GE Healthcare Inc... 513 241-5955
  346 Gest St Cincinnati (45203) *(G-2937)*
GE Honda Aero Engines LLC.. 513 552-4322
  9050 Centre Pointe Dr Ste 200 West Chester (45069) *(G-15438)*
GE Lighting Inc.. 216 266-2121
  1975 Noble Rd Cleveland (44112) *(G-4106)*
GE Lighting, A Savant Company, East Cleveland Also Called: Savant Technologies LLC *(G-6983)*
GE Military Systems... 513 243-2000
  1 Neumann Way Cincinnati (45215) *(G-2938)*
GE Rolls Royce Fighter.. 513 243-2787
  One Neumann Way, Md H318 A Cincinnati (45215) *(G-2939)*
GE Vernova International LLC.. 330 963-2066
  8941 Dutton Dr Twinsburg (44087) *(G-14665)*
Gear Company of America Inc... 216 671-5400
  14300 Lorain Ave Cleveland (44111) *(G-4107)*
Gear Star American Performance.. 330 434-5216
  132 N Howard St Akron (44308) *(G-163)*
Gear Wash, Medina Also Called: Fire-Dex LLC *(G-10324)*
Geartec Inc... 440 953-3900
  4245 Hamann Pkwy Willoughby (44094) *(G-15924)*
Geauga Coatings LLC... 440 221-7286
  15120 Sisson Rd Chardon (44024) *(G-2451)*
Geauga Concrete Inc.. 440 338-4915
  10509 Kinsman Rd Newbury (44065) *(G-11624)*
Geauga Counting Logging LLC.. 440 478-7896
  12038 Prentiss Rd Garrettsville (44231) *(G-7915)*
Geauga Group LLC... 440 543-8797
  11024 Wingate Dr Chagrin Falls (44023) *(G-2397)*
Geauga Highway Co... 440 834-4580
  14126 Main Market Rd Hiram (44234) *(G-8484)*
Geauga Publishing Company Ltd.. 419 625-5825
  520 Warren St Sandusky (44870) *(G-13060)*
Gebauer Company.. 216 581-3030
  4444 E 153rd St Cleveland (44128) *(G-4108)*
Ged Holdings Inc.. 330 963-5401
  9280 Dutton Dr Twinsburg (44087) *(G-14666)*
Gehm & Sons Limited.. 330 724-8423
  825 S Arlington St Akron (44306) *(G-164)*
Gei of Columbiana Inc.. 330 783-0270
  4040 Lake Park Rd Youngstown (44512) *(G-16364)*
Geist, Westerville Also Called: Vertiv Corporation *(G-15686)*
Gelok International Corp... 419 352-1482
  20189 Pine Lake Rd Bowling Green (43402) *(G-1566)*
Gem Beverages Inc.. 740 384-2411
  106 E 11th St Wellston (45692) *(G-15327)*
Gem City, Dayton Also Called: Gem City Metal Tech LLC *(G-6349)*
Gem City Engineering Co (DH).. 937 223-5544
  401 Leo St Dayton (45404) *(G-6348)*
Gem City Metal Tech LLC.. 937 252-8998
  1825 E 1st St Dayton (45403) *(G-6349)*
Gem Coatings Ltd... 740 589-2998
  5840 Industrial Park Rd Athens (45701) *(G-684)*
Gem Instrument Company Inc... 330 273-6117
  2832 Nationwide Pkwy Brunswick (44212) *(G-1764)*
Gem Tool LLC... 216 771-8444
  17000 Saint Clair Ave Ste 102 Cleveland (44110) *(G-4109)*

Gemco Pacific Energy LLC.. 216 937-1371
200 Public Sq Cleveland (44114) *(G-4110)*

Gemini Fiber Corporation... 330 874-4131
11145 Industrial Pkwy Nw Bolivar (44612) *(G-1526)*

Gempco, Akron *Also Called: General Metals Powder Co LLC (G-166)*

Gen Digital Inc... 330 252-1171
159 S Main St Akron (44308) *(G-165)*

Gen X Sports, Miamisburg *Also Called: Huffy Sports Washington Inc (G-10647)*

Gen-Rubber LLC... 440 655-3643
352 South St Galion (44833) *(G-7877)*

Genco.. 419 207-7648
1250 George Rd Ashland (44805) *(G-576)*

Genco, Lockbourne *Also Called: Dell Inc (G-9334)*

Gencraft Designs LLC.. 330 359-6251
7412 Massillon Rd Sw Navarre (44662) *(G-11342)*

Gendron Inc... 419 636-0848
520 W Mulberry St Ste 100 Bryan (43506) *(G-1819)*

General Aluminum Mfg Company.. 440 593-6225
1370 Chamberlain Blvd Conneaut (44030) *(G-5918)*

General Aluminum Mfg Company.. 330 297-1020
5159 S Prospect St Ravenna (44266) *(G-12717)*

General Aluminum Mfg Company.. 419 739-9300
13663 Short Rd Wapakoneta (45895) *(G-15115)*

General Aluminum Mfg LLC (HQ)... 330 297-1225
5159 S Prospect St Ravenna (44266) *(G-12718)*

GENERAL ALUMINUM MFG. COMPANY, Conneaut *Also Called: General Aluminum Mfg Company (G-5918)*

General Awning Company Inc.. 216 749-0110
1350 E Granger Rd Cleveland (44131) *(G-4111)*

General Bar Inc.. 440 835-2000
25000 Center Ridge Rd Ste 3 Westlake (44145) *(G-15753)*

General Book Binding, Chesterland *Also Called: Hf Group LLC (G-2482)*

General Chain & Mfg Corp... 513 541-6005
3274 Beekman St Cincinnati (45223) *(G-2940)*

General Color Investments Inc... 330 868-4161
250 Bridge St Minerva (44657) *(G-11031)*

General Contractor, Columbus *Also Called: Golden Angle Archtctral Group (G-5406)*

General Cutlery Inc (PA).. 419 332-2316
1918 N County Road 232 Fremont (43420) *(G-7786)*

General Data Company Inc (PA).. 513 752-7978
4354 Ferguson Dr Cincinnati (45245) *(G-2561)*

General Data Healthcare Inc.. 513 752-7978
4043 Mcmann Rd Cincinnati (45245) *(G-2562)*

General Die Casters Inc... 330 467-6700
6212 Akron Peninsula Rd Northfield (44067) *(G-11906)*

General Die Casters Inc (HQ).. 330 678-2528
2150 Highland Rd Twinsburg (44087) *(G-14667)*

General Dynamics, Springboro *Also Called: General Dynamics-Ots Inc (G-13502)*

General Dynamics-Ots Inc.. 937 746-8500
200 S Pioneer Blvd Springboro (45066) *(G-13502)*

General Dynmics Land Systems I.. 419 221-7000
1161 Buckeye Rd Lima (45804) *(G-9245)*

General Dynmics Lima Army Tank, Lima *Also Called: General Dynmics Land Systems I (G-9245)*

General Dynmics Mssion Systems.. 513 253-4770
2673 Commons Blvd Ste 200 Beavercreek (45431) *(G-1051)*

General Dynmics Mssion Systems.. 937 723-2001
1900 Founders Dr Ste 106 Dayton (45420) *(G-6350)*

General Electric, Cincinnati *Also Called: General Electric Company (G-2942)*

General Electric Company.. 419 563-1200
1250 S Walnut St Bucyrus (44820) *(G-1861)*

General Electric Company.. 330 458-3200
5555 Massillon Rd Bldg D Canton (44720) *(G-2111)*

General Electric Company.. 513 948-4170
445 S Cooper Ave Cincinnati (45215) *(G-2941)*

General Electric Company (PA).. 617 443-3000
1 Aviation Way Cincinnati (45215) *(G-2942)*

General Electric Company.. 513 977-1500
201 W Crescentville Rd Cincinnati (45246) *(G-2943)*

General Electric Company.. 216 391-8741
1814 E 45th St Cleveland (44103) *(G-4112)*

General Electric Company.. 216 663-2110
18683 S Miles Rd Cleveland (44128) *(G-4113)*

General Electric Company.. 216 268-3846
1099 Ivanhoe Rd Cleveland (44110) *(G-4114)*

General Electric Company.. 216 883-1000
4477 E 49th St Cleveland (44125) *(G-4115)*

General Electric Company.. 740 623-5379
1350 S 2nd St Coshocton (43812) *(G-5979)*

General Electric Company.. 740 385-2114
State Route 93 N Logan (43138) *(G-9363)*

General Electric Company.. 440 593-1156
3159 Wildwood Dr Mc Donald (44437) *(G-10277)*

General Electric Company.. 330 425-3755
8499 Darrow Rd Twinsburg (44087) *(G-14668)*

General Electric Company.. 330 373-1400
1210 Park Warren (44483) *(G-15172)*

General Electric Company.. 513 341-0214
8556 Trade Center Dr Ste 100 West Chester (45011) *(G-15439)*

General Electric Company.. 714 668-0951
9701 Windisch Rd West Chester (45069) *(G-15440)*

General Engine Products LLC.. 937 704-0160
2000 Watkins Glen Dr Franklin (45005) *(G-7677)*

General Envmtl Science Corp... 216 464-0680
3659 Green Rd Ste 306 Beachwood (44122) *(G-988)*

General Extrusions Intl LLC.. 330 783-0270
4040 Lake Park Rd Youngstown (44512) *(G-16365)*

General Fabrications Corp.. 419 625-6055
7777 Milan Rd Sandusky (44870) *(G-13061)*

General Films Inc... 888 436-3456
645 S High St Covington (45318) *(G-6023)*

General Intl Pwr Pdts LLC.. 419 877-5234
6243 Industrial Pkwy Whitehouse (43571) *(G-15818)*

General Ionics, Cincinnati *Also Called: Veolia Wts Systems Usa Inc (G-3494)*

General Ionics, Stow *Also Called: Veolia Wts Systems Usa Inc (G-13737)*

General Machine & Saw Company.. 740 382-1104
305 Davids St Marion (43302) *(G-9854)*

General Machine and Mould Co, Lancaster *Also Called: Devault Machine & Mould Co LLC (G-9009)*

General Metals Powder Co LLC (PA)................................... 330 633-1226
1195 Home Ave Akron (44310) *(G-166)*

General Mills, Toledo *Also Called: General Mills Inc (G-14299)*

General Mills, Wellston *Also Called: General Mills Inc (G-15328)*

General Mills Inc... 513 771-8200
11301 Mosteller Rd Cincinnati (45241) *(G-2944)*

General Mills Inc... 419 269-3100
1250 W Laskey Rd Toledo (43612) *(G-14299)*

General Mills Inc... 740 286-2170
2403 S Pennsylvania Ave Wellston (45692) *(G-15328)*

General Motors, Defiance *Also Called: General Motors LLC (G-6678)*

General Motors, Warren *Also Called: General Motors LLC (G-15173)*

General Motors LLC... 216 265-5000
5400 Chevrolet Blvd Cleveland (44130) *(G-4116)*

General Motors LLC... 419 782-7010
26427 State Route 281 Defiance (43512) *(G-6678)*

General Motors LLC... 330 824-5840
2369 Ellsworth Bailey Rd Sw Warren (44481) *(G-15173)*

General Plastics North Corp.. 800 542-2466
5220 Vine St Cincinnati (45217) *(G-2945)*

General Plug and Mfg Co (PA)... 440 926-2411
455 Main St Grafton (44044) *(G-8000)*

General Polymers... 330 896-7126
567 E Turkeyfoot Lake Rd Akron (44319) *(G-167)*

General Precision Corporation... 440 951-9380
4553 Beidler Rd Willoughby (44094) *(G-15925)*

General Sheave Company Inc... 216 781-8120
1335 Main Ave Cleveland (44113) *(G-4117)*

General Steel Corporation... 216 883-4200
3344 E 80th St Cleveland (44127) *(G-4118)*

General Technologies Inc... 419 747-1800
855 W Longview Ave Mansfield (44906) *(G-9659)*

General Theming Contrs LLC... 614 252-6342
3750 Courtright Ct Columbus (43227) *(G-5397)*

General Tool Company (PA) 513 733-5500
101 Landy Ln Cincinnati (45215) *(G-2946)*

Generals Books 614 870-1861
522 Norton Rd Columbus (43228) *(G-5398)*

Generations Ace Inc 440 835-4872
29121 Inverness Dr Bay Village (44140) *(G-965)*

Genergy 937 477-3628
1623 Kirby Rd Lebanon (45036) *(G-9078)*

Generic Systems Inc 419 841-8460
10560 Geiser Rd Holland (43528) *(G-8510)*

Genesis Lamp Corp 440 354-0095
375 N Saint Clair St Painesville (44077) *(G-12239)*

Genesis One Industries LLC 330 842-9428
2976 Millboro Rd Silver Lake (44224) *(G-13297)*

Geneva Gear & Machine Inc 937 866-0318
339 Progress Rd Dayton (45449) *(G-6351)*

Geneva Liberty Steel Ltd (PA) 330 740-0103
947 Martin Luther King Jr Blvd Youngstown (44502) *(G-16366)*

Geneva Rubber Company, Cortland *Also Called: Control Transformer Inc (G-5961)*

Genex Tool and Die Inc 330 788-2466
4000 Lake Park Rd Youngstown (44512) *(G-16367)*

Genie Company, The, Mount Hope *Also Called: GMI Holdings Inc (G-11237)*

Genie Repros Inc 216 696-6677
2211 Hamilton Ave Cleveland (44114) *(G-4119)*

Genius Solutions Engrg Co (HQ) 419 794-9914
6421 Monclova Rd Maumee (43537) *(G-10202)*

Genmak Geneva Liberty, Youngstown *Also Called: Geneva Liberty Steel Ltd (G-16366)*

Genoa Healthcare LLC 513 727-0471
1036 S Verity Pkwy Middletown (45044) *(G-10826)*

Genpact LLC 513 763-7660
100 Tri County Pkwy Ste 200 Cincinnati (45246) *(G-2947)*

Genpak LLC 614 276-5156
845 Kaderly Dr Columbus (43228) *(G-5399)*

Gent Machine Company 216 481-2334
12315 Kirby Ave Cleveland (44108) *(G-4120)*

Gentek Building Products Inc (HQ) 800 548-4542
3773 State Rd Cuyahoga Falls (44223) *(G-6086)*

Gentherm Medical LLC (HQ) 513 772-8810
12011 Mosteller Rd Cincinnati (45241) *(G-2948)*

Gentzler Tool & Die Corp (PA) 330 896-1941
3903 Massillon Rd Akron (44312) *(G-168)*

Genvac Aerospace Inc 440 646-9986
110 Alpha Park Highland Heights (44143) *(G-8386)*

Geo-Tech Polymers LLC 614 797-2300
479 Industrial Park Dr Waverly (45690) *(G-15281)*

Geocentral, Mason *Also Called: CM Paula Company (G-9980)*

Geocorp Inc 419 433-1101
9010 River Rd Huron (44839) *(G-8632)*

Geodyne One, Columbus *Also Called: Mori Shuji (G-5580)*

Geograph Industries Inc 513 202-9200
475 Industrial Dr Harrison (45030) *(G-8276)*

Geon Company 216 447-6000
6100 Oak Tree Blvd Cleveland (44131) *(G-4121)*

Geon Performance Solutions LLC 440 930-1000
556 Moore Rd Avon Lake (44012) *(G-809)*

Geon Performance Solutions LLC 440 987-4553
835 Leo Bullocks Pkwy Elyria (44035) *(G-7155)*

Geon Performance Solutions LLC (DH) 800 438-4366
25777 Detroit Rd Ste 200 Westlake (44145) *(G-15754)*

George A Mitchell Company 330 758-5777
557 Mcclurg Rd Youngstown (44512) *(G-16368)*

George Manufacturing Inc 513 932-1067
160 Harmon Ave Lebanon (45036) *(G-9079)*

George Steel Fabricating Inc 513 932-2887
1207 Us Route 42 S Lebanon (45036) *(G-9080)*

George Whalley Company 216 453-0099
1180 High St Ste 1 Fairport Harbor (44077) *(G-7454)*

Georgetown Vineyards, Cambridge *Also Called: Georgetown Vineyards Inc (G-1936)*

Georgetown Vineyards Inc 740 435-3222
62920 Georgetown Rd Cambridge (43725) *(G-1936)*

Georgia-Boot Inc 740 753-1951
39 E Canal St Nelsonville (45764) *(G-11356)*

Georgia-Pacific, Circleville *Also Called: Georgia-Pacific LLC (G-3553)*

Georgia-Pacific, Columbus *Also Called: Georgia-Pacific LLC (G-5400)*

Georgia-Pacific, Mogadore *Also Called: Georgia-Pacific LLC (G-11074)*

Georgia-Pacific, West Chester *Also Called: Georgia-Pacific LLC (G-15441)*

Georgia-Pacific LLC 740 477-3347
2850 Owens Rd Circleville (43113) *(G-3553)*

Georgia-Pacific LLC 614 491-9100
1975 Watkins Rd Columbus (43207) *(G-5400)*

Georgia-Pacific LLC 330 794-4444
3265 Gilchrist Rd Mogadore (44260) *(G-11074)*

Georgia-Pacific LLC 513 942-4800
9048 Port Union Rialto Rd West Chester (45069) *(G-15441)*

Georgia-Pacific Pcpi Inc 513 932-9855
1899 Kingsview Dr Lebanon (45036) *(G-9081)*

Gerald D Damron 740 894-3680
197 Township Road 1156 Chesapeake (45619) *(G-2474)*

Gerald Grain Center Inc 419 445-2451
3265 County Road 24 Archbold (43502) *(G-529)*

Gerald L Herrmann Company Inc 513 661-1818
3325 Harrison Ave Cincinnati (45211) *(G-2949)*

Gerber & Sons, Baltic *Also Called: Gerber & Sons Inc (G-837)*

Gerber & Sons Inc (PA) 330 697-0201
201 E Main St Baltic (43804) *(G-837)*

Gerber Farm Division Inc 800 362-7381
133 Collins Blvd Orrville (44667) *(G-12126)*

Gerber Lumber & Hardware, Kidron *Also Called: E P Gerber & Sons Inc (G-8913)*

Gerber Wood Products Inc 330 857-9007
6075 Kidron Rd Kidron (44636) *(G-8914)*

Gerdau Ameristeel US Inc 740 671-9410
5310 Guernsey St Bellaire (43906) *(G-1186)*

Gerdau Ameristeel US Inc 513 869-7660
2175 Schlichter Dr Hamilton (45015) *(G-8211)*

Gerdau McSteel Atmsphere Annli 330 478-0314
1501 Raff Rd Sw Canton (44710) *(G-2112)*

Gergel-Kellem Company Inc 216 398-2000
8707 Forest View Dr Olmsted Falls (44138) *(G-12080)*

Gerich Fiberglass Inc 419 362-4591
7004 Us Highway 42 Mount Gilead (43338) *(G-11233)*

Gerken Materials Inc (PA) 419 533-2421
9072 County Road 424 Napoleon (43545) *(G-11315)*

Gerling and Associates Inc 740 965-6200
200 Kintner Pkwy Sunbury (43074) *(G-13954)*

Germ Guardian, Euclid *Also Called: Guardian Technologies LLC (G-7270)*

Germ-Busters Solutions LLC 330 610-0480
3649 Northwood Ave Youngstown (44511) *(G-16369)*

Gerow Equipment Company Inc 216 383-8800
706 E 163rd St Cleveland (44110) *(G-4122)*

Gerstenslager Construction 330 832-3604
343 16th St Se Massillon (44646) *(G-10100)*

Gerstenslager Hardwood Pdts, Massillon *Also Called: Gerstenslager Construction (G-10100)*

Gerstner International, Dayton *Also Called: H Gerstner & Sons Inc (G-6364)*

Ges AGM 216 658-6528
12300 Snow Rd Cleveland (44130) *(G-4123)*

Ges Graphite Inc (PA) 216 658-6660
12300 Snow Rd Parma (44130) *(G-12290)*

Gew Inc 440 237-4439
11941 Abbey Rd Ste X Cleveland (44133) *(G-4124)*

Geygan Enterprises Inc 513 932-4222
101 Dave Ave Ste E Lebanon (45036) *(G-9082)*

Gfl Environmental Svcs USA Inc 614 441-4001
4001 E 5th Ave Columbus (43219) *(G-5401)*

Gfl Environmental Svcs USA Inc 281 486-4182
4376 State Route 601 Norwalk (44857) *(G-11969)*

GFS Chemicals, Powell *Also Called: GFS Chemicals Inc (G-12674)*

GFS Chemicals Inc 614 351-5347
800 Kaderly Dr Columbus (43228) *(G-5402)*

GFS Chemicals Inc 614 224-5345
851 Mckinley Ave Columbus (43222) *(G-5403)*

GFS Chemicals Inc (PA) 740 881-5501
155 Hidden Ravines Dr Powell (43065) *(G-12674)*

ALPHABETIC SECTION — Glenn Ravens Winery

Ggb US Holdco LLC (HQ) 234 262-3000
  4500 Mount Pleasant St Nw North Canton (44720) *(G-11730)*

Ghent Manufacturing, Lebanon *Also Called: GMI Companies Inc (G-9083)*

Ghost Logging LLC 740 504-1819
  17459 Glen Rd Gambier (43022) *(G-7906)*

Ghostblind Industries Inc 740 374-6766
  801 Ashberry Dr Belpre (45714) *(G-1253)*

Ghp II LLC (DH) 740 687-2500
  1115 W 5th Ave Lancaster (43130) *(G-9017)*

Ghp II LLC 740 681-6825
  2893 W Fair Ave Lancaster (43130) *(G-9018)*

Giannios Candy Co Inc (PA) 330 755-7000
  430 Youngstown Poland Rd Struthers (44471) *(G-13904)*

Giant Industries Inc 419 531-4600
  900 N Westwood Ave Toledo (43607) *(G-14300)*

Gibbco, Cincinnati *Also Called: Trans Ash Inc (G-3461)*

Gibson Bakery, Oberlin *Also Called: Gibson Bros Inc (G-12051)*

Gibson Bros Inc 440 774-2401
  23 W College St Oberlin (44074) *(G-12051)*

Gideon Owen Wine, Port Clinton *Also Called: Quinami LLC (G-12626)*

Gie Media Inc (PA) 800 456-0707
  5811 Canal Rd Cleveland (44125) *(G-4125)*

Giles Logging LLC 406 855-5284
  7340 Richman Rd Spencer (44275) *(G-13481)*

Gillard Construction Inc 740 376-9744
  1308 Greene St Marietta (45750) *(G-9795)*

Gillette, Cincinnati *Also Called: Gillette Company LLC (G-2950)*

Gillette Company LLC 513 983-1100
  1 Procter And Gamble Plz Cincinnati (45202) *(G-2950)*

Gillig Custom Winery Inc 419 202-6057
  1720 Northridge Rd Findlay (45840) *(G-7513)*

Gills Petroleum Llc 740 702-2600
  213 S Paint St Chillicothe (45601) *(G-2505)*

Gilson Company Inc (PA) 740 548-7298
  7975 N Central Dr Lewis Center (43035) *(G-9161)*

Gilson Machine & Tool Co Inc 419 592-2911
  529 Freedom Dr Napoleon (43545) *(G-11316)*

Gilson Screen Incorporated 419 256-7711
  8-810 K-2 Rd Malinta (43535) *(G-9604)*

Giminetti Baking Company 513 751-7655
  2900 Gilbert Ave Cincinnati (45206) *(G-2951)*

Ginko Systems, Dayton *Also Called: Ginko Voting Systems LLC (G-6352)*

Ginko Voting Systems LLC 937 291-4060
  600 Progress Rd Dayton (45449) *(G-6352)*

Gino's Jewelers & Trophy Mfrs, Warrensville Heights *Also Called: Ginos Awards Inc (G-15229)*

Ginos Awards Inc 216 831-6565
  4701 Richmond Rd Ste 200 Warrensville Heights (44128) *(G-15229)*

Girard Machine Company Inc 330 545-9731
  700 Dot St Girard (44420) *(G-7969)*

Girindus America Inc 513 679-3000
  10608 Deercreek Ln Cincinnati (45249) *(G-2952)*

Giuseppes Concessions LLC 614 554-2551
  5383 Township Road 187 Marengo (43334) *(G-9768)*

Givaudan, Cincinnati *Also Called: Givaudan Flavors Corporation (G-2955)*

Givaudan Flavors Corporation 513 948-3428
  100 E 69th St Cincinnati (45216) *(G-2953)*

Givaudan Flavors Corporation 513 786-0124
  110 E 69th St Cincinnati (45216) *(G-2954)*

Givaudan Flavors Corporation (DH) 513 948-8000
  1199 Edison Dr 1-2 Cincinnati (45216) *(G-2955)*

Givaudan Flavors Corporation 513 948-8000
  110 E 70th St Cincinnati (45216) *(G-2956)*

Givaudan Fragrances Corp 513 948-3428
  100 E 69th St Cincinnati (45216) *(G-2957)*

Givaudan Fragrances Corp (DH) 513 948-8000
  1199 Edison Dr Ste 1-2 Cincinnati (45216) *(G-2958)*

Gizmo, Chagrin Falls *Also Called: Whip Guide Co (G-2434)*

GKN Driveline Bowl Green Inc (DH) 419 373-7700
  2223 Wood Bridge Blvd Bowling Green (43402) *(G-1567)*

GKN Driveline Bowling Green, Bowling Green *Also Called: GKN Driveline North Amer Inc (G-1568)*

GKN Driveline North Amer Inc 419 354-3955
  2223 Wood Bridge Blvd Bowling Green (43402) *(G-1568)*

GKN PLC 740 446-9211
  2160 Eastern Ave Gallipolis (45631) *(G-7893)*

GKN Sinter Metals, Gallipolis *Also Called: GKN PLC (G-7893)*

GKN Sinter Metals LLC 740 441-3203
  2160 Eastern Ave Gallipolis (45631) *(G-7894)*

GL Heller Co Inc 419 877-5122
  6246 Industrial Pkwy Whitehouse (43571) *(G-15819)*

GL Industries Inc 513 874-1233
  25 Standen Dr Hamilton (45015) *(G-8212)*

GL International LLC 330 744-8812
  215 Sinter Ct Youngstown (44510) *(G-16370)*

Glance Software LLC 844 383-2500
  1340 Missy Ct Hamilton (45013) *(G-8213)*

Glas Ornamental Metals Inc 330 753-0215
  1559 Waterloo Rd Barberton (44203) *(G-869)*

Glascraft Inc 330 966-3000
  8400 Port Jackson Ave Nw North Canton (44720) *(G-11731)*

Glass Block Headquarters Inc 216 941-5470
  3535 W 140th St Ste B Cleveland (44111) *(G-4126)*

Glass Block Warehouse, The, Columbus *Also Called: Blockamerica Corporation (G-5201)*

Glass City Machining and Fab, Lancaster *Also Called: Ted M Figgins (G-9042)*

Glass Coatings & Concepts LLC 513 539-5300
  300 Lawton Ave Monroe (45050) *(G-11108)*

Glass Surface Systems Inc 330 745-8500
  24 Brown St Barberton (44203) *(G-870)*

Glasses Guy LLC 970 624-9019
  5151 Tuscarawas St W Canton (44708) *(G-2113)*

Glassline Corporation (PA) 419 666-9712
  28905 Glenwood Rd Perrysburg (43551) *(G-12385)*

Glasstech Inc (PA) 419 661-9500
  995 4th St Perrysburg (43551) *(G-12386)*

Glatfelter Corporation 740 772-3893
  353 S Paint St Chillicothe (45601) *(G-2506)*

Glatfelter Corporation 740 775-6119
  311 Caldwell St Chillicothe (45601) *(G-2507)*

Glatfelter Corporation 740 772-3111
  232 E 8th St Chillicothe (45601) *(G-2508)*

Glatfelter Corporation 419 333-6700
  2275 Commerce Dr Fremont (43420) *(G-7787)*

Glatfelter Corporation 740 289-5100
  200 Schuster Rd Piketon (45661) *(G-12476)*

Glavin Industries Inc 440 349-0049
  6835 Cochran Rd Ste A Solon (44139) *(G-13353)*

Glavin Specialty Co, Solon *Also Called: Glavin Industries Inc (G-13353)*

Glawe Awnings, Fairborn *Also Called: Glawe Manufacturing Co Inc (G-7317)*

Glawe Manufacturing Co Inc 937 754-0064
  851 Zapata Dr Fairborn (45324) *(G-7317)*

Glaxosmithkline LLC 330 608-2365
  4273 Ridge Crest Dr Copley (44321) *(G-5949)*

Gleason M & M Precision, Dayton *Also Called: Gleason Metrology Systems Corp (G-6353)*

Gleason Metrology Systems Corp (HQ) 937 384-8901
  300 Progress Rd Dayton (45449) *(G-6353)*

Gledhill Road Machinery Co 419 468-4400
  765 Portland Way S Galion (44833) *(G-7878)*

Glen D Lala 937 274-7770
  2610 Willowburn Ave Dayton (45417) *(G-6354)*

Glen-Gery Caledonia Plant, Caledonia *Also Called: Glen-Gery Corporation (G-1915)*

Glen-Gery Corporation 419 845-3321
  5692 Rinker Rd Caledonia (43314) *(G-1915)*

Glen-Gery Corporation 419 468-4890
  3785 Cardington Iberia Rd Galion (44833) *(G-7879)*

Glen-Gery Corporation 419 468-5002
  County Rd 9 Iberia (43325) *(G-8648)*

Glenn Hunter & Associates Inc 419 533-0925
  1222 County Road 6 Delta (43515) *(G-6785)*

Glenn Michael Brick 740 391-5735
  108 Wood St Flushing (43977) *(G-7587)*

Glenn Ravens Winery 740 545-1000
  56183 County Road 143 West Lafayette (43845) *(G-15617)*

(PA)=Parent Co (HQ)=Headquarters (DH)=Div Headquarters

Glenridge Machine Co — ALPHABETIC SECTION

Glenridge Machine Co.. 440 975-1055
37435 Fawn Path Dr Solon (44139) *(G-13354)*

Glenrock Company.. 513 489-6710
10852 Millington Ct Blue Ash (45242) *(G-1398)*

Glenwood Erectors Inc.. 330 652-9616
251 Durst Dr Nw Warren (44483) *(G-15174)*

Glf International Inc (PA).. 216 621-6901
3690 Orange Pl Ste 495 Cleveland (44122) *(G-4127)*

Gli, Stow Also Called: Gli Holdings Inc *(G-13701)*

Gli Holdings Inc.. 440 892-7760
4484 Allen Rd Stow (44224) *(G-13700)*

Gli Holdings Inc (PA).. 216 651-1500
4246 Hudson Dr Stow (44224) *(G-13701)*

Gli Pool Products, Youngstown Also Called: GL International LLC *(G-16370)*

Glidden Professional Paint Ctr, Strongsville Also Called: Akzo Nobel Paints LLC *(G-13803)*

Glister Inc.. 614 252-6400
830 Harmon Ave Columbus (43223) *(G-5404)*

Glo-Quartz Electric Htr Co Inc.. 440 255-9701
7084 Maple St Mentor (44060) *(G-10464)*

Global Body & Equipment Co.. 330 264-6640
2061 Sylvan Rd Wooster (44691) *(G-16124)*

Global Coal Sales Group LLC.. 614 221-0101
6641 Dublin Center Dr Dublin (43017) *(G-6886)*

Global Cooling Inc.. 740 274-7900
6000 Poston Rd Athens (45701) *(G-685)*

Global Energy Partners LLC.. 419 756-8027
3401 State Route 13 Mansfield (44904) *(G-9660)*

Global Laser Tek LLC.. 513 701-0452
7697 Innovation Way Ste 700 Mason (45040) *(G-9996)*

Global Lighting Tech Inc.. 440 922-4584
55 Andrews Cir Ste 1 Brecksville (44141) *(G-1618)*

Global Manufacturing Assoc Inc.. 216 938-9056
1750 E 39th St Cleveland (44114) *(G-4128)*

Global Manufacturing Solutions.. 937 236-8315
2001 Kuntz Rd Dayton (45404) *(G-6355)*

Global Metal Services Ltd.. 440 591-1264
8401 Chagrin Rd Ste 14a Chagrin Falls (44023) *(G-2398)*

Global Packaging & Exports Inc (PA).. 513 454-2020
9166 Sutton Pl West Chester (45011) *(G-15442)*

Global Plastic Tech Inc.. 330 963-6830
7762 Sunstone Dr Brecksville (44141) *(G-1619)*

Global Plastic Tech Inc.. 440 879-6045
1657 Bdwy Ave Lorain (44052) *(G-9412)*

Global Precision Parts, East Liberty Also Called: Harding Machine Acquisition Co *(G-6987)*

Global Precision Parts, Ottoville Also Called: Acme Machine Automatics Inc *(G-12197)*

Global Precision Parts Inc.. 260 563-9030
7600 Us Route 127 Van Wert (45891) *(G-14916)*

Global Principals, Kirtland Also Called: Essentialware *(G-8939)*

Global Realms LLC.. 614 828-7284
81 Mill St Ste 300 Gahanna (43230) *(G-7836)*

Global Security Tech Inc.. 614 890-6400
132 Dorchester Sq S Ste 200 Westerville (43081) *(G-15706)*

Global Specialties Inc.. 800 338-0814
2950 Westway Dr Ste 110 Brunswick (44212) *(G-1765)*

Global Specialty Machines LLC (PA).. 513 701-0452
7697 Innovation Way Ste 700 Mason (45040) *(G-9997)*

Global Srcing Support Svcs LLC.. 800 645-2986
260 E University Ave Cincinnati (45219) *(G-2959)*

Global TBM Company (HQ).. 440 248-3303
29100 Hall St Solon (44139) *(G-13355)*

Global Technology Center, Holland Also Called: Tekni-Plex Inc *(G-8532)*

Global Tool, Dayton Also Called: Ovase Manufacturing LLC *(G-6496)*

Global Trucking LLC.. 614 598-6264
3723 Ellerdale Dr Columbus (43230) *(G-5405)*

Global-Pak Inc (PA).. 330 482-1993
9636 Elkton Rd Lisbon (44432) *(G-9312)*

Globe Metallurgical Inc., Waterford Also Called: Ferroglobe USA Mtlurgical Inc *(G-15236)*

Globe Motors, Dayton Also Called: Globe Motors Inc *(G-6356)*

Globe Motors Inc (HQ).. 334 983-3742
2275 Stanley Ave Dayton (45404) *(G-6356)*

Globe Pipe Hanger Products Inc.. 216 362-6300
14601 Industrial Pkwy Cleveland (44135) *(G-4129)*

Globe Products Inc (PA).. 937 233-0233
5051 Kitridge Rd Dayton (45424) *(G-6357)*

Globus Printing & Packg Co Inc (PA).. 419 628-2381
1 Exec Pkwy Minster (45865) *(G-11053)*

Glt Inc (PA).. 937 237-0055
3341 Successful Way Dayton (45414) *(G-6358)*

Glunt Industries Inc.. 330 399-7585
319 N River Rd Nw Warren (44483) *(G-15175)*

Glx Power Systems Inc.. 440 338-6526
46 Chagrin Plaza Ste 201 Chagrin Falls (44022) *(G-2378)*

GM Mechanical Inc (PA).. 937 473-3006
4263 N State Route 48 Covington (45318) *(G-6024)*

GM Pallets Company.. 859 408-1781
121 Citycentre Dr Unit 2 Cincinnati (45216) *(G-2960)*

Gmd Industries LLC.. 937 252-3643
1414 E 2nd St Dayton (45403) *(G-6359)*

Gmelectric Inc.. 330 477-3392
4606 Southway St Sw Canton (44706) *(G-2114)*

Gmerecords, Worthington Also Called: Swagg Productions2015llc *(G-16213)*

GMI Companies Inc.. 937 981-0244
512 S Washington St Greenfield (45123) *(G-8029)*

GMI Companies Inc.. 937 981-7724
512 S Washington St Greenfield (45123) *(G-8030)*

GMI Companies Inc (PA).. 513 932-3445
2999 Henkle Dr Lebanon (45036) *(G-9083)*

GMI Companies Inc.. 513 932-3445
2999 Henkle Dr Lebanon (45036) *(G-9084)*

GMI Holdings Inc (DH).. 800 354-3643
1 Door Dr Mount Hope (44660) *(G-11237)*

Gmp Welding & Fabrication Inc.. 513 825-7861
11175 Adwood Dr Cincinnati (45240) *(G-2961)*

GMR Furniture Services Ltd.. 216 244-5072
1801 E 9th St Ste 1100 Cleveland (44114) *(G-4130)*

Gmx.. 216 641-7502
3800 E 91st St Cleveland (44105) *(G-4131)*

Gnw Aluminum Inc.. 330 821-7955
1356 Beeson St Ne Alliance (44601) *(G-405)*

Go For Broke Amusement, Flushing Also Called: Glenn Michael Brick *(G-7587)*

God Speed Turbo Innovations.. 513 307-5584
9862 Crescent Park Dr West Chester (45069) *(G-15443)*

Godfrey & Wing Inc (PA).. 330 562-1440
220 Campus Dr Aurora (44202) *(G-716)*

Godfrey & Wing Inc.. 419 980-4616
2066 E 2nd St Defiance (43512) *(G-6679)*

Gofs, Mansfield Also Called: Global Energy Partners LLC *(G-9660)*

Going My Way Trnsp Svcs LLC.. 423 623-3802
4655 Queen Mary Dr Cleveland (44121) *(G-4132)*

Gojo, Akron Also Called: Gojo Industries Inc *(G-170)*

Gojo Canada Inc.. 330 255-6000
1 Gojo Plz Ste 500 Akron (44311) *(G-169)*

Gojo Industries Inc (PA).. 330 255-6000
1 Gojo Plz Ste 500 Akron (44311) *(G-170)*

Gojo Industries Inc.. 330 255-6000
3783 State Rd Cuyahoga Falls (44223) *(G-6087)*

Gojo Industries Inc.. 330 255-6527
3783 State Rd Cuyahoga Falls (44223) *(G-6088)*

Gojo Industries Inc.. 330 255-6000
4676 Erie Ave Sw Navarre (44662) *(G-11343)*

Gokoh Corporation (HQ).. 937 339-4977
1280 Archer Dr Troy (45373) *(G-14573)*

Gold Key Processing Inc.. 440 632-0901
14910 Madison Rd Middlefield (44062) *(G-10752)*

Gold Medal Products Co (PA).. 513 769-7676
10700 Medallion Dr Cincinnati (45241) *(G-2962)*

Gold Medal-Carolina, Cincinnati Also Called: Gold Medal Products Co *(G-2962)*

Gold Rush Jerky, Litchfield Also Called: Medina Foods Inc *(G-9328)*

Gold Star Chili, Cincinnati Also Called: Gold Star Chili Inc *(G-2963)*

Gold Star Chili, Cincinnati Also Called: Gold Star Chili Inc *(G-2964)*

Gold Star Chili Inc (PA).. 513 231-4541
650 Lunken Park Dr Cincinnati (45226) *(G-2963)*

ALPHABETIC SECTION — Graeters Ice Cream Company

Gold Star Chili Inc 513 631-1990
5420 Ridge Ave Cincinnati (45213) *(G-2964)*

Golden Angle Archtctral Group 614 531-7932
4207 E Broad St Ste C Columbus (43213) *(G-5406)*

Golden Drapery Supply Inc 216 351-3283
2500 Brookpark Rd Unit 3 Cleveland (44134) *(G-4133)*

Golden Eagle, Upper Sandusky *Also Called: New Eezy-Gro Inc (G-14817)*

Golden Eagle Aviation LLC 937 308-4709
14833 Sidney Plattsville Rd Sidney (45365) *(G-13251)*

Golden Giant Inc 419 674-4038
13300 S Vision Dr Kenton (43326) *(G-8883)*

Golden Giants Building System, Kenton *Also Called: Golden Giant Inc (G-8883)*

Golden Jersey Inn, Yellow Springs *Also Called: Youngs Jersey Dairy Inc (G-16290)*

Golden Spring Company Inc 937 848-2513
2143 Ferry Rd Bellbrook (45305) *(G-1193)*

Golden Turtle Chocolate Fctry 513 932-1990
120 S Broadway St Ste 1 Lebanon (45036) *(G-9085)*

Golden Window Fashions, Cleveland *Also Called: Golden Drapery Supply Inc (G-4133)*

Goldsmith & Eggleton Inc 330 336-6616
300 1st St Wadsworth (44281) *(G-15032)*

Goldsmith & Eggleton LLC 203 855-6000
300 1st St Wadsworth (44281) *(G-15033)*

Golf Car Company Inc 614 873-1055
8899 Memorial Dr Plain City (43064) *(G-12580)*

Golf Design Screcards Unlimited, Columbus *Also Called: Scorecards Unlimited LLC (G-5755)*

Golf Galaxy Golfworks Inc 740 328-4193
4820 Jacksontown Rd Newark (43056) *(G-11577)*

Golf Marketing Group Inc 330 963-5155
9221 Ravenna Rd Ste 7 Twinsburg (44087) *(G-14669)*

Golfworks, The, Newark *Also Called: Golf Galaxy Golfworks Inc (G-11577)*

Golias Publishing Company Inc 330 425-4744
7271 Lonesome Pine Trl Medina (44256) *(G-10331)*

Gomez Salsa LLC 513 314-1978
8575 Coolwood Ct Cincinnati (45236) *(G-2965)*

Gonda Wood Products, Grafton *Also Called: Joe Gonda Company Incorporated (G-8003)*

Gongwer News Service Inc (PA) 614 221-1992
175 S 3rd St Columbus (43215) *(G-5407)*

Gonzoil Inc 330 497-5888
5260 Fulton Dr Nw Canton (44718) *(G-2115)*

Gooch & Housego (ohio) LLC 216 486-6100
676 Alpha Dr Highland Heights (44143) *(G-8387)*

Good Fortunes Inc 440 942-2888
1486 E 361st St Willoughby (44095) *(G-15926)*

Good Greens, Oakwood Village *Also Called: Good Nutrition LLC (G-12039)*

Good News, Middlefield *Also Called: Suburban Communications Inc (G-10791)*

Good Nutrition LLC 216 534-6617
7710 First Pl Oakwood Village (44146) *(G-12039)*

Goodrich Aerospace 704 423-7000
1555 Corporate Woods Pkwy Uniontown (44685) *(G-14784)*

Goodrich Corporation 330 374-2358
6051 N Airport Dr North Canton (44720) *(G-11732)*

Goodrich Corporation 937 339-3811
101 Waco St Troy (45373) *(G-14574)*

Goodrich Corporation 216 429-4378
101 Walton St Troy (45373) *(G-14575)*

Goodyear, Akron *Also Called: Goodyear Tire & Rubber Company (G-171)*

Goodyear, Beaverdam *Also Called: Goodyear Tire & Rubber Company (G-1096)*

Goodyear, Canton *Also Called: Goodyear Tire & Rubber Company (G-2116)*

Goodyear, Dublin *Also Called: Boy RAD Inc (G-6869)*

Goodyear, Youngstown *Also Called: Goodyear Tire & Rubber Company (G-16371)*

Goodyear Tire & Rubber Company (PA) 330 796-2121
200 E Innovation Way Akron (44316) *(G-171)*

Goodyear Tire & Rubber Company 419 643-8273
415 E Main St Beaverdam (45808) *(G-1096)*

Goodyear Tire & Rubber Company 330 966-1274
6850 Frank Ave Nw Canton (44720) *(G-2116)*

Goodyear Tire & Rubber Company 330 759-9343
3651 Belmont Ave Youngstown (44505) *(G-16371)*

Gopowerx Inc 440 707-6029
3850 Sawbridge Dr Unit 24 Richfield (44286) *(G-12789)*

Gorant Chocolatier LLC (PA) 330 726-8821
8301 Market St Boardman (44512) *(G-1513)*

Gorant's Yum Yum Tree, Boardman *Also Called: Gorant Chocolatier LLC (G-1513)*

Gordon Brothers Btlg Group Inc 330 337-8754
776 N Ellsworth Ave Salem (44460) *(G-12997)*

Gordon Tool Inc 419 263-3151
1301 State Route 49 Payne (45880) *(G-12321)*

Gordons Graphics Inc 330 863-2322
123 S Reed Ave Malvern (44644) *(G-9613)*

Gorell Enterprises Inc (DH) 724 465-1800
10250 Philipp Pkwy Streetsboro (44241) *(G-13772)*

Gorell Windows & Doors, Streetsboro *Also Called: Gorell Enterprises Inc (G-13772)*

Gorilla Joe Printing Co LLC 234 719-1861
31 Woodbine Ave E Youngstown (44505) *(G-16372)*

Gorman-Rupp Company 419 755-1011
305 Bowman St Mansfield (44903) *(G-9661)*

Gorman-Rupp Company 419 755-1245
100 Rupp Rd Mansfield (44903) *(G-9662)*

Gorman-Rupp Company (PA) 419 755-1011
600 S Airport Rd Mansfield (44903) *(G-9663)*

Gorski Welding LLC 440 412-7910
37190 Sugar Ridge Rd North Ridgeville (44039) *(G-11841)*

Gosun Inc 888 868-6154
5151 Fischer Ave Cincinnati (45217) *(G-2966)*

Got Graphix Llc 330 703-9047
3265 W Market St Fairlawn (44333) *(G-7440)*

Gottfried Medical Inc 419 474-2973
2920 Centennial Rd Toledo (43617) *(G-14301)*

Gould Fire Protection Inc 419 957-2416
633 Bristol Dr Findlay (45840) *(G-7514)*

Government Acquisitions Inc 513 721-8700
2060 Reading Rd Fl 4 Cincinnati (45202) *(G-2967)*

Goyal Enterprises Inc 513 874-9303
4836 Business Center Way West Chester (45246) *(G-15557)*

Gpi Ohio LLC 605 332-6721
6300 Commerce Center Dr Ste 100 Groveport (43125) *(G-8145)*

GPM, Franklin *Also Called: Greenpoint Metals Inc (G-7678)*

Gq Business Products Inc 513 792-4750
142 Commerce Dr Loveland (45140) *(G-9482)*

Gr Golf, New Washington *Also Called: Wurms Woodworking Company (G-11552)*

Gr8 News Packaging LLC 314 739-1202
3657 Tradeport Ct Lockbourne (43137) *(G-9335)*

Gra-Mag Truck Intr Systems LLC (DH) 740 490-1000
470 E High St London (43140) *(G-9388)*

Graber Metal Works Inc 440 237-8422
9664 Akins Rd Ste 1 North Royalton (44133) *(G-11877)*

Grabo Interiors Inc 216 391-6677
3605 Perkins Ave Cleveland (44114) *(G-4134)*

Grace Juice Company LLC 614 398-6879
6318 E Dublin Granville Rd Westerville (43081) *(G-15707)*

Gracie International Corp 717 725-9138
6314 Olivia Ct Dublin (43016) *(G-6887)*

Gracie Plum Investments, Portsmouth *Also Called: Gracie Plum Investments Inc (G-12645)*

Gracie Plum Investments Inc 740 355-9029
609 2nd St Unit 2 Portsmouth (45662) *(G-12645)*

Graco Ohio Inc (HQ) 330 494-1313
8400 Port Jackson Ave Nw North Canton (44720) *(G-11733)*

Gradall, New Philadelphia *Also Called: Gradall Industries LLC (G-11504)*

Gradall Industries Inc 540 819-6638
6307 Barkley Rd Se Uhrichsville (44683) *(G-14766)*

Gradall Industries LLC (DH) 330 339-2211
406 Mill Ave Sw New Philadelphia (44663) *(G-11504)*

Gradeworks 440 487-4201
7913 Euclid Chardon Rd Ste 10 Kirtland (44094) *(G-8940)*

Grady McCauley Inc 330 494-9444
5127 Boyer Pkwy Akron (44312) *(G-172)*

Grae-Con Process Piping LLC 740 282-6830
300 Commerce Dr Marietta (45750) *(G-9796)*

Graeter's Ice Cream, Cincinnati *Also Called: International Brand Services (G-3028)*

Graeters Ice Cream Company (PA) 513 721-3323
1175 Regina Graeter Way Cincinnati (45216) *(G-2968)*

Graffiti Co, Cleveland *Also Called: Barbs Graffiti Inc (G-3719)*

Graffiti Foods Limited... 614 759-1921
333 Outerbelt St Columbus (43213) *(G-5408)*

Grafisk Maskinfabrik Amer LLC.................................... 630 432-4370
603 Norgal Dr Ste F Lebanon (45036) *(G-9086)*

Grafisk Msknfabrik-America LLC, Lebanon *Also Called: Grafisk Maskinfabrik Amer LLC (G-9086)*

Grafix, Cleveland *Also Called: Graphic Art Systems Inc (G-4140)*

Graftech Global Entps Inc... 216 676-2000
12900 Snow Rd Cleveland (44130) *(G-4135)*

Graftech Holdings Inc.. 216 676-2000
6100 Oak Tree Blvd Ste 300 Independence (44131) *(G-8669)*

Graftech International, Brooklyn Heights *Also Called: Graftech International Ltd (G-1691)*

Graftech International Ltd (PA).................................... 216 676-2000
982 Keynote Cir Ste 6 Brooklyn Heights (44131) *(G-1691)*

Graftech Intl Holdings Inc (HQ).................................... 216 676-2000
982 Keynote Cir Ste 6 Brooklyn Heights (44131) *(G-1692)*

Graftech Intl Trdg Inc.. 216 676-2000
12900 Snow Rd Cleveland (44130) *(G-4136)*

Graftech NY Inc... 216 676-2000
12000 Snow Rd Cleveland (44130) *(G-4137)*

Grafton Ready Mix Concret Inc.................................... 440 926-2911
1155 Elm St Grafton (44044) *(G-8001)*

Graham Electric... 614 231-8500
2855 Banwick Rd Columbus (43232) *(G-5409)*

Graham Packaging Pet Tech Inc................................... 419 334-4197
725 Industrial Dr Fremont (43420) *(G-7788)*

Graham Packaging Pet Tech Inc................................... 513 398-5000
1225 Castle Dr Mason (45040) *(G-9998)*

Graham Packg Plastic Pdts Inc..................................... 419 421-8037
170 Stanford Pkwy 7 Findlay (45840) *(G-7515)*

Graminex LLC... 419 278-1023
2300 County Road C Deshler (43516) *(G-6800)*

Gramke Enterprises Ltd.. 614 252-8711
3021 E 4th Ave Ste B Columbus (43219) *(G-5410)*

Grand Aire Inc (PA)... 419 861-6700
11777 W Airport Service Rd Swanton (43558) *(G-13974)*

Grand Architect, Cleveland *Also Called: Grand Archt Etrnl Eye 314 LLC (G-4138)*

Grand Archt Etrnl Eye 314 LLC.................................... 800 377-8147
10413 Nelson Ave Cleveland (44105) *(G-4138)*

Grand Harbor Yacht Sales & Svc................................. 440 442-2919
706 Alpha Dr Cleveland (44143) *(G-4139)*

Grand River Railway Company, Poland *Also Called: Great Lake Port Corporation (G-12611)*

Grand River Rubber & Plastics Company.................... 440 998-2900
2029 Aetna Rd Ashtabula (44004) *(G-635)*

Grand-Rock Company Inc.. 440 639-2000
395 Fountain Ave Painesville (44077) *(G-12240)*

Grandinroad Catalog, West Chester *Also Called: Cornerstone Brands Inc (G-15406)*

Grandpa Jack's, Chillicothe *Also Called: Crispie Creme Chillicothe Inc (G-2500)*

Granex Industries Inc (PA)... 440 248-4915
32400 Aurora Rd Ste 4 Solon (44139) *(G-13356)*

GRANGER PLASTICS CO THE.................................... 513 424-1955
1600 Made Industrial Dr Middletown (45044) *(G-10827)*

Grant Street Pallet Inc... 330 424-0355
39196 Grant St Lisbon (44432) *(G-9313)*

Granville Milling Co... 740 345-1305
145 N Cedar St Newark (43055) *(G-11578)*

Granville Milling Drive-Thru, Newark *Also Called: Granville Milling Co (G-11578)*

Graphel Corporation... 513 779-6166
6115 Centre Park Dr West Chester (45069) *(G-15444)*

Graphic Art Systems Inc... 216 581-9050
5800 Pennsylvania Ave Cleveland (44137) *(G-4140)*

Graphic Industries, Alliance *Also Called: Sams Graphic Industries (G-422)*

Graphic Info Systems Inc... 513 948-1300
7177 Central Parke Blvd Mason (45040) *(G-9999)*

Graphic Packaging Intl LLC... 419 673-0711
1300 S Main St Kenton (43326) *(G-8884)*

Graphic Packaging Intl LLC... 513 424-4200
407 Charles St Middletown (45042) *(G-10828)*

Graphic Packaging Intl LLC... 419 668-1106
209 Republic St Norwalk (44857) *(G-11970)*

Graphic Packaging Intl LLC... 440 248-4370
6385 Cochran Rd Solon (44139) *(G-13357)*

Graphic Paper Products Corp (HQ)............................. 937 325-5503
6069 Yeazell Rd Springfield (45502) *(G-13570)*

Graphic Print Solutions Inc... 513 948-3344
7633 Production Dr Cincinnati (45237) *(G-2969)*

Graphic Publications Inc... 330 343-4377
123 W 3rd St Dover (44622) *(G-6825)*

Graphic Stitch Inc.. 937 642-6707
169 Grove St Rm A Marysville (43040) *(G-9911)*

Graphic Systems Services Inc...................................... 937 746-0708
400 S Pioneer Blvd Springboro (45066) *(G-13503)*

Graphic Village LLC... 513 241-1865
4440 Creek Rd Blue Ash (45242) *(G-1399)*

Graphite Sales Inc (PA).. 419 652-3388
220 Township Road 791 Nova (44859) *(G-12003)*

Graphix Network... 740 941-3771
122 N High St Waverly (45690) *(G-15282)*

Graphix One Corporation... 513 870-0512
4690 Interstate Dr Ste F West Chester (45246) *(G-15558)*

Graphtech Communications Inc.................................. 216 676-1020
2892 Westway Dr Brunswick (44212) *(G-1766)*

Grassroots Strategies LLC.. 614 783-6515
5990 E Livingston Ave Columbus (43232) *(G-5411)*

Gravel Doctor of Ohio... 844 472-8353
2985 Canal Dr Millersport (43046) *(G-11011)*

Gray America Corp (PA).. 937 293-9313
3050 Dryden Rd Moraine (45439) *(G-11182)*

Gray Area Bistro Ultra Lounge, Cleveland *Also Called: R & T Estate LLC (G-4611)*

Gray Tech International, Cleveland *Also Called: Hephaestus Technologies LLC (G-4183)*

Gray-Eering Ltd... 740 498-8816
3158 Sandy Ridge Rd Se Tippecanoe (44699) *(G-14171)*

Graymont Dolime (oh) Inc... 419 855-8682
21880 State Route 163 Genoa (43430) *(G-7947)*

Grays Orange Barn Inc.. 419 568-2718
14286 State Rte 196 Wapakoneta (45895) *(G-15116)*

Graywacke Inc... 419 884-7014
300 S Mill St Mansfield (44904) *(G-9664)*

GRB Holdings Inc... 937 236-3250
131 Janney Rd Dayton (45404) *(G-6360)*

Gre'n Disc, Strasburg *Also Called: Green Rdced Emssons Netwrk LLC (G-13746)*

Great American Cookie Co, Toledo *Also Called: Great American Cookie Company (G-14302)*

Great American Cookie Company................................ 419 474-9417
5001 Monroe St Ste Fc13 Toledo (43623) *(G-14302)*

Great Day Improvements LLC (HQ)............................ 267 223-1289
700 Highland Rd E Macedonia (44056) *(G-9555)*

Great Harvest Bread, Westerville *Also Called: Blf Enterprises Inc (G-15694)*

Great Lake Fence, Cleveland *Also Called: Fence One Inc (G-4056)*

Great Lake Port Corporation.. 330 718-3727
213 Diana Dr Poland (44514) *(G-12611)*

Great Lakes Assemblies LLC..................................... 937 645-3900
11590 Township Road 298 East Liberty (43319) *(G-6986)*

Great Lakes Brewing Co... 216 771-4404
1947 W 28th St Cleveland (44113) *(G-4141)*

Great Lakes Brewing Co... 216 771-4404
2516 Market Ave Cleveland (44113) *(G-4142)*

Great Lakes Brewing Co... 216 771-4404
13675 Darice Pkwy Strongsville (44149) *(G-13836)*

Great Lakes Cheese Co Inc (PA)................................ 440 834-2500
17825 Great Lakes Pkwy Hiram (44234) *(G-8485)*

Great Lakes Crushing Ltd... 440 944-5500
30831 Euclid Ave Wickliffe (44092) *(G-15833)*

Great Lakes Etching Finshg Co.................................. 440 439-3624
7010 Krick Rd Cleveland (44146) *(G-4143)*

Great Lakes Fasteners Inc (PA)................................. 330 425-4488
2204 E Enterprise Pkwy Twinsburg (44087) *(G-14670)*

Great Lakes Fasteners & Sup Co, Twinsburg *Also Called: Great Lakes Fasteners Inc (G-14670)*

Great Lakes Glasswerks Inc... 440 358-0460
360 W Prospect St Painesville (44077) *(G-12241)*

Great Lakes Graphics Inc... 216 391-0077
3354 Superior Ave E Cleveland (44114) *(G-4144)*

Great Lakes Group 216 621-4854
  4500 Division Ave Cleveland (44102) *(G-4145)*
Great Lakes Mfg Group Ltd 440 391-8266
  19035 Old Detroit Rd Rocky River (44116) *(G-12838)*
Great Lakes Polymer Proc Inc (PA) 313 655-4024
  1210 Massillon Rd Akron (44306) *(G-173)*
Great Lakes Popcorn Company 419 732-3080
  60 Madison St Port Clinton (43452) *(G-12620)*
Great Lakes Power Products Inc (PA) 440 951-5111
  7455 Tyler Blvd Mentor (44060) *(G-10465)*
Great Lakes Power Service Co 440 259-0025
  3691 Shepard Rd Perry (44081) *(G-12351)*
Great Lakes Printing Inc 440 993-8781
  2926 Lake Ave Ashtabula (44004) *(G-636)*
Great Lakes Publishing Company (PA) 216 771-2833
  1422 Euclid Ave Ste 730 Cleveland (44115) *(G-4146)*
Great Lakes Scuttlebutt, Toledo Also Called: Kyle Media Inc *(G-14355)*
Great Lakes Shipyard, Cleveland Also Called: The Great Lakes Towing Company *(G-4784)*
Great Lakes Stair & Mllwk Co 330 225-2005
  1545 W 130th St Ste A1 Hinckley (44233) *(G-8473)*
Great Lakes Telcom Ltd (PA) 330 629-8848
  590 E Western Reserve Rd Bldg 9c Youngstown (44514) *(G-16373)*
Great Lakes Towing, Cleveland Also Called: Great Lakes Group *(G-4145)*
Great Lakes Window Inc 419 666-5555
  30499 Tracy Rd Walbridge (43465) *(G-15082)*
Great Lkes Nrotechnologies Inc 855 456-3876
  6100 Rockside Woods Blvd N Ste 415 Cleveland (44131) *(G-4147)*
Greater Cincinnati Bowl Assn 513 761-7387
  611 Mercury Dr Cincinnati (45244) *(G-2970)*
Greater Cleve Pipe Ftting Fund 216 524-8334
  6305 Halle Dr Cleveland (44125) *(G-4148)*
Greater Cleveland FCC 440 333-5984
  4440 W 210th St Cleveland (44126) *(G-4149)*
Greber Machine Tool Inc 440 322-3685
  313 Clark St Elyria (44035) *(G-7156)*
Green Acquisition LLC 440 930-7600
  1141 Jaycox Rd Avon (44011) *(G-776)*
Green Bay Packaging Inc 419 332-5593
  2323 Commerce Dr Fremont (43420) *(G-7789)*
Green Bay Packaging Inc 513 489-8700
  760 Kingsview Dr Lebanon (45036) *(G-9087)*
Green Bearing Co, Avon Also Called: Green Acquisition LLC *(G-776)*
Green Corp Magnetic Inc 614 801-4000
  4342 Mcdowell Rd Grove City (43123) *(G-8096)*
Green County Wtr Sup & Trtmnt, Dayton Also Called: Greene County *(G-6162)*
Green Energy Inc 330 262-5112
  4489 E Lincoln Way Wooster (44691) *(G-16125)*
Green Field Farms Co-Op (PA) 330 263-0246
  6464 Fredericksburg Rd Wooster (44691) *(G-16126)*
Green Gourmet Foods LLC 740 400-4212
  515 N Main St Baltimore (43105) *(G-845)*
Green Harvest Energy LLC 330 716-3068
  1340 State Route 14 Columbiana (44408) *(G-5040)*
Green Impressions LLC 440 240-8508
  842 Abbe Rd Sheffield Village (44054) *(G-13182)*
Green Leaf Printing and Design 937 222-3634
  1001 E 2nd St Ste 2485 Dayton (45402) *(G-6361)*
Green Machine Tool Inc 937 253-0771
  1865 Radio Rd Dayton (45431) *(G-6161)*
Green Meadows Paper Company 330 837-5151
  670 17th St Nw Massillon (44647) *(G-10101)*
Green Rdced Emssons Netwrk LLC 330 340-0941
  5029 Hilltop Dr Nw Strasburg (44680) *(G-13746)*
Green Room Brewing LLC 614 421-2337
  1101 N 4th St Columbus (43201) *(G-5412)*
Green Technologies Ohio LLC 330 630-3350
  460 Tacoma Ave Ste B Tallmadge (44278) *(G-14031)*
Green Tokai Co Ltd (DH) 937 833-5444
  55 Robert Wright Dr Brookville (45309) *(G-1738)*
Green Tokai Co Ltd 937 237-1630
  3700 Inpark Dr Dayton (45414) *(G-6362)*
Green Vision Materials Inc 440 564-5500
  11220 Kinsman Rd Newbury (44065) *(G-11625)*
Greenbridge, Mentor Also Called: Polychem LLC *(G-10526)*
Greenbrier Rail Services, Youngstown Also Called: Gunderson Rail Services LLC *(G-16376)*
Greendale Home Fashions LLC 859 916-5475
  5500 Muddy Creek Rd Cincinnati (45238) *(G-2971)*
Greene County 937 429-0127
  1122 Beaver Valley Rd Dayton (45434) *(G-6162)*
Greenfield Die & Mfg Corp (HQ) 734 454-4000
  880 Steel Dr Valley City (44280) *(G-14871)*
Greenfield Precision Plas LLC 937 803-0328
  175 Industrial Park Dr Greenfield (45123) *(G-8031)*
Greenfield Research Inc (PA) 937 981-7763
  347 Edgewood Ave Greenfield (45123) *(G-8032)*
Greenfield Solar Corp 216 535-9200
  7881 Root Rd North Ridgeville (44039) *(G-11842)*
Greenhart Rstoration Mllwk LLC 330 502-6050
  6001 Southern Blvd Ste 105 Boardman (44512) *(G-1514)*
Greenkote Usa Inc 440 243-2865
  6435 Eastland Rd Brookpark (44142) *(G-1716)*
Greenlight Optics LLC 513 247-9777
  8940 Glendale Milford Rd Loveland (45140) *(G-9483)*
Greenpoint Metals Inc 937 743-4075
  301 Shotwell Dr Franklin (45005) *(G-7678)*
Greens Pure Coatings LLC 513 907-2765
  1186 Sycamore Ln Amelia (45102) *(G-455)*
Greenville Technology Inc 937 642-6744
  15000 Industrial Pkwy Marysville (43040) *(G-9912)*
Greenway Home Products Inc
  1270 Flagship Dr Perrysburg (43551) *(G-12387)*
Greenwood Printing, Toledo Also Called: Greenwood Prtg & Graphics Inc *(G-14303)*
Greenwood Prtg & Graphics Inc 419 727-3275
  3615 Stickney Ave Toledo (43608) *(G-14303)*
Greenworld Enterprises Inc 800 525-6999
  61 Circle Freeway Dr West Chester (45246) *(G-15559)*
Greer & Whitehead Cnstr Inc (PA) 513 202-1757
  510 S State St Ste D Harrison (45030) *(G-8277)*
Greg Blume 740 574-2308
  7459 Ohio River Rd Wheelersburg (45694) *(G-15809)*
Greg G Wright & Sons LLC 513 721-3310
  10200 Springfield Pike Cincinnati (45215) *(G-2972)*
Gregory Industries Inc (PA) 330 477-4800
  4100 13th St Sw Canton (44710) *(G-2117)*
Gregory Roll Form Inc 330 477-4800
  4100 13th St Sw Canton (44710) *(G-2118)*
Gregory Stone Co Inc 937 275-7455
  1860 N Gettysburg Ave Dayton (45417) *(G-6363)*
Greif, Delaware Also Called: Greif Inc *(G-6724)*
Greif Inc (PA) 740 549-6000
  425 Winter Rd Delaware (43015) *(G-6724)*
Greif Inc 740 657-6500
  366 Greif Pkwy Delaware (43015) *(G-6725)*
Greif Inc 330 879-2936
  787 Warmington Rd Se Massillon (44646) *(G-10102)*
Greif Inc 419 238-0565
  975 Glenn St Van Wert (45891) *(G-14917)*
Greif Packaging LLC (HQ) 740 549-6000
  366 Greif Pkwy Delaware (43015) *(G-6726)*
Greif USA LLC (DH) 740 549-6000
  366 Greif Pkwy Delaware (43015) *(G-6727)*
Grenada Stamping Assembly Inc (HQ) 419 842-3600
  3810 Herr Rd Sylvania (43560) *(G-13996)*
Grenga Machine & Welding 330 743-1113
  56 Wayne Ave Youngstown (44502) *(G-16374)*
Gress Gas & Oil, Coshocton Also Called: Gress Oil & Gas Inc *(G-5980)*
Gress Oil & Gas Inc 740 622-8356
  3984 County Road 271 Coshocton (43812) *(G-5980)*
Greyden Press, Springboro Also Called: Jk Digital Publishing LLC *(G-13506)*
Grid Industrial Heating Inc 330 332-9931
  1108 Salem Pkwy Salem (44460) *(G-12998)*
Grid Sentry LLC 937 490-2101
  3915 Germany Ln Beavercreek (45431) *(G-1052)*

Grief Brothers, Delaware *Also Called: Greif Inc (G-6725)*

Griffin Fisher Co Inc... 513 961-2110
   1126 William Howard Taft Rd Cincinnati (45206) *(G-2973)*

Griffin Industries LLC.. 513 549-0041
   11315 Reed Hartman Hwy Blue Ash (45241) *(G-1400)*

Griffin Technology Inc.. 585 924-7121
   50 Executive Pkwy Hudson (44236) *(G-8594)*

Griffiths Mobile Welding... 937 750-3711
   411 S Dayton Lakeview Rd New Carlisle (45344) *(G-11415)*

Grimes Aerospace Company (HQ)..................................... 937 484-2000
   550 State Route 55 Urbana (43078) *(G-14830)*

Grimes Aerospace Company... 937 484-2000
   515 N Russell St Urbana (43078) *(G-14831)*

Grimes Aerospace Company... 937 484-2001
   550 State Route 55 Urbana (43078) *(G-14832)*

Grimm Scientific Industries... 740 374-3412
   1403 Pike St Marietta (45750) *(G-9797)*

Grind-All Corporation.. 330 220-1600
   1113 Industrial Pkwy N Brunswick (44212) *(G-1767)*

Grinding Equipment & McHy LLC... 330 747-2313
   15 S Worthington St Youngstown (44502) *(G-16375)*

Grip Spritz LLC... 440 888-7022
   5747 W 44th St Cleveland (44134) *(G-4150)*

Grippo Foods Inc (PA)... 513 923-1900
   6750 Colerain Ave Cincinnati (45239) *(G-2974)*

Grippo Potato Chip Co Inc.. 513 923-1900
   6750 Colerain Ave Cincinnati (45239) *(G-2975)*

Grismer Tire, Centerville *Also Called: Associates Tire and Svc Inc (G-2359)*

Grismer Tire Company (PA)... 937 643-2526
   1099 S Main St Centerville (45458) *(G-2363)*

Grob Systems Inc... 419 358-9015
   1070 Navajo Dr Bluffton (45817) *(G-1504)*

Groeneveld Atlantic South.. 330 225-4949
   1130 Industrial Pkwy N Ste 7 Brunswick (44212) *(G-1768)*

Groff Industries.. 216 634-9100
   2201 W 110th St Cleveland (44102) *(G-4151)*

Groovemaster Music, Perrysburg *Also Called: Tiny Lion Music Groups (G-12435)*

Gross & Sons Custom Millwork.. 419 227-0214
   1219 Grant St Lima (45801) *(G-9246)*

Gross Lumber Inc.. 330 683-2055
   8848 Ely Rd Apple Creek (44606) *(G-501)*

Grote, Columbus *Also Called: JE Grote Company Inc (G-5491)*

Groundhogs 2000 LLC... 440 653-1647
   33 Industry Dr Bedford (44146) *(G-1122)*

Group Endeavor LLC... 234 571-5096
   1750 Canton Rd Akron (44312) *(G-174)*

Group Industries Inc (PA).. 216 271-0702
   7580 Garfield Blvd Cleveland (44125) *(G-4152)*

Grouper Acquisition Co LLC... 248 299-7500
   880 Steel Dr Valley City (44280) *(G-14872)*

Grouper Acquisition Co LLC... 330 558-2600
   350 Maple St Wellington (44090) *(G-15313)*

Grove Engineered Products... 419 659-5939
   201 E Cross St Columbus Grove (45830) *(G-5898)*

Grover Musical Products Inc (PA)....................................... 216 391-1188
   9287 Midwest Ave Cleveland (44125) *(G-4153)*

Grover Trophy Musical Products, Cleveland *Also Called: Grover Musical Products Inc (G-4153)*

Growco Inc... 419 886-4628
   844 Kochheiser Rd Mansfield (44904) *(G-9665)*

Growers Choice Ltd... 330 262-8754
   5505 S Elyria Rd Shreve (44676) *(G-13208)*

Grypmat Inc... 419 953-7607
   6886 Nancy Ave Celina (45822) *(G-2334)*

Gs Engineering, Maumee *Also Called: Genius Solutions Engrg Co (G-10202)*

Gsdi, Massillon *Also Called: Gsdi Specialty Dispersions Inc (G-10103)*

Gsdi Specialty Dispersions Inc... 330 848-9200
   1675 Navarre Rd Se Massillon (44646) *(G-10103)*

GSE Production and Support LLC (DH)............................... 419 866-6301
   1 Air Cargo Pkwy E Swanton (43558) *(G-13975)*

GSE Spares, Swanton *Also Called: GSE Production and Support LLC (G-13975)*

Gsh Industries Inc.. 440 238-3009
   15242 Foltz Pkwy Strongsville (44149) *(G-13837)*

Gsi of Ohio LLC... 216 431-3344
   3820 Lakeside Ave E Cleveland (44114) *(G-4154)*

GSW Manufacturing Inc (DH).. 419 423-7111
   1801 Production Dr Findlay (45840) *(G-7516)*

Gt Industrial Supply, Cincinnati *Also Called: Gt Industrial Supply Inc (G-2976)*

Gt Industrial Supply Inc... 513 771-7000
   7775 E Kemper Rd Cincinnati (45249) *(G-2976)*

Gt Technlgies Tledo Operations, Toledo *Also Called: Gt Technologies Inc (G-14304)*

Gt Technologies Inc... 419 782-8955
   1125 Precision Way Defiance (43512) *(G-6680)*

Gt Technologies Inc... 419 324-7300
   99 N Fearing Blvd Toledo (43607) *(G-14304)*

Gt Tire Service Inc... 740 927-7226
   15 W Broad St Pataskala (43062) *(G-12298)*

GTC, Brookville *Also Called: Green Tokai Co Ltd (G-1738)*

GTC Artist With Machines, Columbus *Also Called: General Theming Contrs LLC (G-5397)*

Gtlp Holdings LLC (PA)... 513 489-6700
   7911 School Rd Cincinnati (45249) *(G-2977)*

Guarantee Specialties Inc.. 216 451-9744
   21693 Drake Rd Strongsville (44149) *(G-13838)*

Guaranteed Fnshg Unlimited Inc.. 216 252-8200
   3200 W 121st St Cleveland (44111) *(G-4155)*

Guardian Energy Holdings LLC... 567 940-9500
   2485 Houx Pkwy Lima (45804) *(G-9247)*

Guardian Fabrication LLC... 419 855-7706
   24145 W Moline Martin Rd Millbury (43447) *(G-10933)*

Guardian Gloves, Willard *Also Called: Guardian Manufacturing Co LLC (G-15859)*

Guardian Lima LLC.. 567 940-9500
   2485 Houx Pkwy Lima (45804) *(G-9248)*

Guardian Manufacturing Co LLC.. 419 933-2711
   302 S Conwell Ave Willard (44890) *(G-15859)*

Guardian Mfg., Hudson *Also Called: Fluid Power Inc (G-8593)*

Guardian Millbury, Millbury *Also Called: Guardian Fabrication LLC (G-10933)*

Guardian Publications Inc.. 216 621-5005
   55 Public Sq Ste 2075 Cleveland (44113) *(G-4156)*

Guardian Technologies LLC... 866 603-5900
   26251 Bluestone Blvd Ste 7 Euclid (44132) *(G-7270)*

Guerin-Zimmerman Co, Cleveland *Also Called: Byg Industries Inc (G-3777)*

Guetle Die & Stamping, Mansfield *Also Called: Amaroq Inc (G-9623)*

Guggisberg Cheese Inc (PA)... 330 893-2550
   5060 State Route 557 Millersburg (44654) *(G-10956)*

Guild Associates Inc (PA).. 614 798-8215
   5750 Shier Rings Rd Dublin (43016) *(G-6888)*

Guild Associates Inc.. 843 573-0095
   4412 Tuller Rd Dublin (43017) *(G-6889)*

Guild Biosciences, Dublin *Also Called: Guild Associates Inc (G-6889)*

Guitammer Company... 614 898-9370
   7099 Huntley Rd Ste 108 Columbus (43229) *(G-5413)*

Gumbys LLC.. 740 671-0818
   2300 Belmont St Bellaire (43906) *(G-1187)*

Gunderson Rail Services LLC.. 330 792-6521
   3710 Hendricks Rd Bldg 2a Youngstown (44515) *(G-16376)*

Gundlach, Cincinnati *Also Called: Rotex Global LLC (G-3351)*

Gundlach Sheet Metal Works Inc (PA)................................ 419 626-4525
   910 Columbus Ave Sandusky (44870) *(G-13062)*

Gunk, Cleveland *Also Called: BLaster Holdings LLC (G-3741)*

Gunnison Associates Llc... 330 562-5230
   114 Barrington Town Square Dr # 11 Aurora (44202) *(G-717)*

Gus Holthaus Signs Inc... 513 861-0060
   817 Ridgeway Ave Cincinnati (45229) *(G-2978)*

Gushen America Inc.. 708 664-2852
   701 International Dr Heath (43056) *(G-8320)*

Gustave Julian Jewelers Inc.. 440 888-1100
   7432 State Rd Cleveland (44134) *(G-4157)*

Gutter Logic Charlotte LLC.. 833 714-5479
   7901 Cleveland Ave Nw Ste A North Canton (44720) *(G-11734)*

Guttman Oil, Westerville *Also Called: Brightstar Propane & Fuels (G-15648)*

Guyer Precision Inc... 440 354-8024
   280 W Prospect St Painesville (44077) *(G-12242)*

ALPHABETIC SECTION — Hague Quality Water Intl

Gvr Warehouse and Packg LLC.. 440 272-1005
4814 State Route 322 Orwell (44076) *(G-12164)*

Gvs Filtration Inc (DH)... 419 423-9040
2150 Industrial Dr Findlay (45840) *(G-7517)*

Gvs Industries Inc.. 513 851-3606
1030 Beissinger Rd Hamilton (45013) *(G-8214)*

Gwj Liquidation Inc... 216 475-5770
16153 Libby Rd Cleveland (44137) *(G-4158)*

Gwp Holdings Inc.. 513 860-4050
8675 Seward Rd Fairfield (45011) *(G-7364)*

Gws Levi Up Home Solutions LLC.. 419 667-6041
6020 W Bancroft St Unit 350061 Toledo (43615) *(G-14305)*

Gyrus Acmi LP.. 419 668-8201
93 N Pleasant St Norwalk (44857) *(G-11971)*

H & B Machine & Tool Inc.. 216 431-3254
1390 E 40th St Cleveland (44103) *(G-4159)*

H & C Building Supplies, Huron Also Called: Huron Cement Products Company *(G-8633)*

H & D Steel Service Inc.. 800 666-3390
9960 York Alpha Dr North Royalton (44133) *(G-11878)*

H & D Steel Service Center, North Royalton Also Called: H & D Steel Service Inc *(G-11878)*

H & G Equipment Inc (PA)... 513 761-2060
10837 Millington Ct Blue Ash (45242) *(G-1401)*

H & H Engineered Molded Pdts... 440 415-1814
436 N Eagle St Geneva (44041) *(G-7937)*

H & H Equipment Inc.. 330 264-5400
6247 Ashland Rd Wooster (44691) *(G-16127)*

H & H Industries Inc... 740 682-7721
5400 State Route 93 Oak Hill (45656) *(G-12019)*

H & H Machine Shop Akron Inc... 330 773-3327
955 Grant St Akron (44311) *(G-175)*

H & H Quick Machine Inc.. 330 935-0944
7816 Edison St Ne Louisville (44641) *(G-9457)*

H & H Sailcraft, New Paris Also Called: Dynamic Plastics Inc *(G-11481)*

H & H Truck Parts LLC.. 216 642-4540
5500s Cloverleaf Pkwy Cleveland (44125) *(G-4160)*

H & K Pallet Services... 937 608-1140
1039 Jasper Ave Xenia (45385) *(G-16263)*

H & M Machine Shop Inc... 419 453-3414
290 State Route 189 Ottoville (45876) *(G-12199)*

H & M Metal Processing Co (HQ)... 330 745-3075
1414 Kenmore Blvd Akron (44314) *(G-176)*

H & R Metal Finishing Inc.. 440 942-6656
1052 E 347th St Eastlake (44095) *(G-7033)*

H & S Company Inc.. 419 394-4444
7219 Harris Rd Celina (45822) *(G-2335)*

H & S Distributing Inc.. 800 336-7784
35478 Lorain Rd North Ridgeville (44039) *(G-11843)*

H & S Operating Company Inc.. 330 830-8178
2581 County Rd 160 Winesburg (44690) *(G-16079)*

H & S Precision Screw Pdts Inc.. 937 437-0316
8205 H W Rd New Paris (45347) *(G-11482)*

H & S Tool Inc... 330 335-1536
715 Weber Dr Wadsworth (44281) *(G-15034)*

H & W Screw Products Inc... 937 866-2577
335 Industrial Dr Franklin (45005) *(G-7679)*

H & W Tool Co.. 216 795-5520
1363 Chardon Rd Ste 3 Euclid (44117) *(G-7271)*

H B Chemical, Twinsburg Also Called: Ravago Chemical Dist Inc *(G-14723)*

H D C, Miamisburg Also Called: The Hooven - Dayton Corp *(G-10694)*

H Duane Leis Acquisitions... 937 835-5621
443 S Diamond Mill Rd New Lebanon (45345) *(G-11449)*

H Gerstner & Sons Inc... 937 228-1662
20 Gerstner Way Dayton (45402) *(G-6364)*

H Hafner & Sons Inc.. 513 321-1895
5445 Wooster Pike Cincinnati (45226) *(G-2979)*

H Hansen Industries, Toledo Also Called: Riverside Marine Inds Inc *(G-14453)*

H I T, Painesville Also Called: Hardy Industrial Tech LLC *(G-12243)*

H K K Machining Co... 419 924-5116
1201 Oak St West Unity (43570) *(G-15639)*

H K M, Cleveland Also Called: Hkm Drect Mkt Cmmnications Inc *(G-4193)*

H K M Drect Mktg Cmmunications, Sheffield Village Also Called: Hkm Drect Mkt Cmmnications Inc *(G-13183)*

H Lee Philippi Co.. 513 321-5330
3660 Hyde Park Ave Cincinnati (45208) *(G-2980)*

H Machining Inc.. 419 636-6890
720 Commerce Dr Bryan (43506) *(G-1820)*

H Mack Charles & Associates Inc... 513 791-4456
10101 Alliance Rd Ste 10 Blue Ash (45242) *(G-1402)*

H Nagel & Son Co.. 513 665-4550
2641 Spring Grove Ave Cincinnati (45214) *(G-2981)*

H P E Inc (PA).. 330 833-3161
2025 Harsh Ave Se Massillon (44646) *(G-10104)*

H P Manufacturing Co.. 216 361-6500
3740 Prospect Ave E Cleveland (44115) *(G-4161)*

H P Nielsen Inc.. 440 244-4255
753 Broadway Lorain (44052) *(G-9413)*

H W Chair Co, Millersburg Also Called: Hochstetler Wood *(G-10961)*

H W Fairway International Inc.. 330 678-2540
1016 9th St Sw Canton (44707) *(G-2119)*

H Y O Inc... 614 488-2861
2550 W 5th Ave Columbus (43204) *(G-5414)*

H-P Products Inc.. 330 875-7193
2000 W Main St Louisville (44641) *(G-9458)*

H-P Products Inc (PA).. 330 875-5556
512 W Gorgas St Louisville (44641) *(G-9459)*

H. Meyer Dairy, Cleveland Also Called: Borden Dairy Co Cincinnati LLC *(G-3748)*

H.O.t, Northwood Also Called: HOT Graphic Services Inc *(G-11920)*

H&G Legacy Co (PA)... 513 921-1075
1085 Summer St Cincinnati (45204) *(G-2982)*

H&H Machine Shop Ravenna LL... 330 296-4445
5292 S Prospect St Ravenna (44266) *(G-12719)*

H&M Machine & Tool LLC... 419 776-9220
3823 Seiss Ave Toledo (43612) *(G-14306)*

H&M Mtal Stamping Assembly Inc.. 216 898-9030
5325 W 140th St Brookpark (44142) *(G-1717)*

H2flow Controls Inc.. 419 841-7774
7629 New West Rd Toledo (43617) *(G-14307)*

H3d Tool Corporation... 740 498-5181
295 Enterprise Dr Newcomerstown (43832) *(G-11644)*

Ha-International LLC.. 419 537-0096
4243 South Ave Toledo (43615) *(G-14308)*

Ha-Ste Manufacturing Co Inc... 937 968-4858
119 E Elm St Union City (45390) *(G-14778)*

Haag-Streit Usa Inc (DH)... 513 398-3937
3535 Kings Mills Rd Mason (45040) *(G-10000)*

Haas Door Company... 419 337-9900
320 Sycamore St Wauseon (43567) *(G-15262)*

Haas Doors, Wauseon Also Called: Nofziger Door Sales Inc *(G-15271)*

Hab Computer Services, Solon Also Called: Hab Inc *(G-13358)*

Hab Inc... 608 785-7650
28925 Fountain Pkwy Solon (44139) *(G-13358)*

Habco Tool and Dev Co Inc... 440 946-5546
7725 Metric Dr Mentor (44060) *(G-10466)*

Hacker Wood Products Inc.. 513 737-4462
2144 Jackson Rd Hamilton (45011) *(G-8215)*

Hackman Frames LLC... 614 841-0007
502 Schrock Rd Columbus (43229) *(G-5415)*

Hackworth Electric Motors Inc.. 330 345-6049
500 E Henry St Wooster (44691) *(G-16128)*

Hadley Printing, Beavercreek Also Called: A C Hadley - Printing Inc *(G-1037)*

Hadronics Inc.. 513 321-9350
4570 Steel Pl Cincinnati (45209) *(G-2983)*

Haeco Inc (PA)... 513 722-1030
6504 Snider Rd Loveland (45140) *(G-9484)*

Haessly Lumber Sales Co (PA)... 740 373-6681
25 Sheets Run Rd Marietta (45750) *(G-9798)*

Hafco-Case Inc... 216 267-4644
12212 Sprecher Ave Cleveland (44135) *(G-4162)*

Hafners Hrdwood Connection LLC... 419 726-4828
2845 111th St Toledo (43611) *(G-14309)*

Hagen Well Service LLC.. 330 264-7500
474 Industrial Blvd Wooster (44691) *(G-16129)*

Hague Quality Water Intl, Groveport Also Called: William R Hague Inc *(G-8168)*

(PA)=Parent Co (HQ)=Headquarters (DH)=Div Headquarters

Hahn Automation Group Us Inc 937 886-3232
10909 Industry Ln Miamisburg (45342) *(G-10641)*

Hahn Manufacturing Company 216 391-9300
5332 Hamilton Ave Cleveland (44114) *(G-4163)*

Haines Criss Cross (PA) 330 494-9111
8050 Freedom Ave Nw North Canton (44720) *(G-11735)*

Haines Publishing Inc 330 494-9111
8050 Freedom Ave Nw Canton (44720) *(G-2120)*

Hake Head LLC 614 291-2244
1855 E 17th Ave Columbus (43219) *(G-5416)*

Halcore Group Inc (HQ) 614 539-8181
3800 Mcdowell Rd Grove City (43123) *(G-8097)*

Hale Manufacturing LLC 937 382-2127
1065 Wayne Rd Wilmington (45177) *(G-16052)*

Hale Performance Coatings Inc 419 244-6451
2282 Albion St Toledo (43606) *(G-14310)*

Halex, A Scott Fetzer Company, Harrison Also Called: Halex/Scott Fetzer Company *(G-8278)*

Halex/Scott Fetzer Company (HQ) 800 749-3261
101 Production Dr Harrison (45030) *(G-8278)*

Hall Acquisition LLC 330 627-2119
1209 N Lisbon St Carrollton (44615) *(G-2308)*

Hall Closet, East Liverpool Also Called: The China Hall Company *(G-7001)*

Hall Company 937 652-1376
420 E Water St Urbana (43078) *(G-14833)*

Hall-Toledo Inc 419 893-4334
525 W Sophia St Maumee (43537) *(G-10203)*

Haller Enterprises Inc 330 733-9693
1621 E Market St Akron (44305) *(G-177)*

Halliburton Energy Svcs Inc 740 617-2917
4999 E Pointe Dr Zanesville (43701) *(G-16535)*

Halliday Holdings Inc 740 335-1430
1544 Old Us 35 Se Wshngtn Ct Hs (43160) *(G-16233)*

Halliday Technologies Inc 614 504-4150
105 Innovation Ct Ste F Delaware (43015) *(G-6728)*

Hallmark Industries Inc (PA) 937 864-7378
2233 N Limestone St Springfield (45503) *(G-13571)*

Halman Inc
3901 N Bend Rd Ashtabula (44004) *(G-637)*

Halo Metal Prep Inc 216 741-0506
5712 Brookpark Rd Unit C Cleveland (44129) *(G-4164)*

Haltec Corporation 330 222-1501
32585 N Price Rd Salem (44460) *(G-12999)*

Halvorsen Company 216 341-7500
7500 Grand Division Ave Ste 1 Cleveland (44125) *(G-4165)*

Halvorsons LLC 440 503-1162
4780 W 220th St Cleveland (44126) *(G-4166)*

Ham Signs LLC DBA Fastsigns 937 890-6770
6020 N Dixie Dr Dayton (45414) *(G-6365)*

Haman Enterprises Inc 614 888-7574
75 W Southington Ave Columbus (43085) *(G-5417)*

Haman Midwest, Columbus Also Called: Haman Enterprises Inc *(G-5417)*

Hamilton Brass & Alum Castings
706 S 8th St Hamilton (45011) *(G-8216)*

Hamilton Casework Solutions, Fairfield Also Called: Workstream Inc *(G-7428)*

Hamilton Custom Molding Inc 513 844-6643
1365 Shuler Ave Hamilton (45011) *(G-8217)*

Hamilton Industrial Grinding Inc (PA) 513 863-1221
240 N B St Hamilton (45013) *(G-8218)*

Hamilton Journal News Inc 513 863-8200
7320 Yankee Rd Liberty Township (45044) *(G-9208)*

Hamilton Manufacturing Corp 419 867-4858
1026 Hamilton Dr Holland (43528) *(G-8511)*

Hamilton Mold & Machine Co 216 732-8200
25016 Lakeland Blvd Rear Cleveland (44132) *(G-4167)*

Hamilton Products Group Inc (DH) 800 876-6066
1030 Round Bottom Rd Milford (45150) *(G-10908)*

Hamilton Safe, Milford Also Called: Hamilton Security Products Co *(G-10910)*

Hamilton Safe Co (DH) 513 874-3733
1030 Round Bottom Rd Milford (45150) *(G-10909)*

Hamilton Safe Company, Milford Also Called: Hamilton Safe Co *(G-10909)*

Hamilton Security Products Co 513 874-3733
1030 Round Bottom Rd Milford (45150) *(G-10910)*

Hamilton Tanks LLC 614 445-8446
2200 Refugee Rd Columbus (43207) *(G-5418)*

Hamlet Protein Inc 567 525-5627
5289 Hamlet Dr Findlay (45840) *(G-7518)*

Hamlin Newco LLC 330 753-7791
2741 Wingate Ave Akron (44314) *(G-178)*

Hamlin Steel Products LLC 330 753-7791
2741 Wingate Ave Akron (44314) *(G-179)*

Hammelmann Corporation (HQ) 937 859-8777
436 Southpointe Dr Miamisburg (45342) *(G-10642)*

Hammer Jammer LLC 937 549-4062
700 Brush Creek Rd Manchester (45144) *(G-9617)*

Hammersmith Bros Invstmnts Inc 513 353-3000
3200 State Line Rd North Bend (45052) *(G-11704)*

Hammill Manufacturing Co (PA) 419 476-0789
360 Tomahawk Dr Maumee (43537) *(G-10204)*

Hammill Manufacturing Co 419 476-9125
1517 Coining Dr Toledo (43612) *(G-14311)*

Hammond Kinetics, Dublin Also Called: Kinetics Noise Control Inc *(G-6905)*

Hampshire Co 937 773-3493
9225 State Route 66 Piqua (45356) *(G-12518)*

Hana Technologies Inc 330 405-4600
2061 Case Pkwy S Twinsburg (44087) *(G-14671)*

Hanby Farms Inc 740 763-3554
10790 Newark Rd Nashport (43830) *(G-11337)*

Hanchett Paper Company 513 782-4440
12121 Best Pl Cincinnati (45241) *(G-2984)*

Hancock Structural Steel LLC 419 424-1217
813 E Bigelow Ave Findlay (45840) *(G-7519)*

Hancor Inc 419 424-8222
12370 Jackson Township Rd Findlay (45839) *(G-7520)*

Hancor Inc 419 424-8225
433 Olive St Findlay (45840) *(G-7521)*

Hancor Inc (HQ) 614 658-0050
4640 Trueman Blvd Hilliard (43026) *(G-8413)*

Handcrafted Jewelry Inc 330 650-9011
116 N Main St Hudson (44236) *(G-8595)*

Handlebar & Grill On Main LLC 740 746-2077
201 S Main St Sugar Grove (43155) *(G-13916)*

Hands On, West Chester Also Called: Hands On International LLC *(G-15560)*

Hands On International LLC 513 502-9000
9776 Inter Ocean Dr West Chester (45246) *(G-15560)*

Handy Twine Knife Co 419 294-3424
5676 County Highway 330 Upper Sandusky (43351) *(G-14810)*

Hanline Fresh, Shelby Also Called: R S Hanline and Co Inc *(G-13199)*

Hanlon Composites LLC 216 261-7056
21611 Tungsten Rd Euclid (44117) *(G-7272)*

Hanlon Industries Inc 216 261-7056
1280 E 286th St Cleveland (44132) *(G-4168)*

Hann Manufacturing Inc 740 962-3752
4678 N State Route 60 Nw Mcconnelsville (43756) *(G-10281)*

Hannecard Roller Coatings Inc 330 753-8458
1031 Lambert St Barberton (44203) *(G-871)*

Hannibal Company Inc 614 846-5060
6536 Proprietors Rd Worthington (43085) *(G-16195)*

Hannon Company (PA) 330 456-4728
1605 Waynesburg Dr Se Canton (44707) *(G-2121)*

Hannon Company 330 343-7758
801 Commercial Pkwy Dover (44622) *(G-6826)*

Hannon Company 740 453-0527
218 Adams St Zanesville (43701) *(G-16536)*

Hanon Systems Usa LLC 313 920-0583
581 Arrowhead Dr Carey (43316) *(G-2279)*

Hans Rothenbuhler & Son Inc 440 632-6000
15815 Nauvoo Rd Middlefield (44062) *(G-10753)*

Hansa Brewery LLC 216 631-6585
2717 Lorain Ave Cleveland (44113) *(G-4169)*

Hansen Scaffolding LLC (PA) 513 574-9000
193 Circle Freeway Dr West Chester (45246) *(G-15561)*

Hanser Music Group, Blue Ash Also Called: Jatiga Inc *(G-1411)*

Hanson Aggregates, Sandusky Also Called: Wagner Quarries Company *(G-13104)*

ALPHABETIC SECTION   Hathaway Stamp Identification

Hanson Aggregates Eagle Quarry, Winchester *Also Called: Heidelberg Materials Us Inc* **(G-16073)**

Hanson Aggregates East.. 513 353-1100
7000 Dry Fork Rd Cleves (45002) **(G-4953)**

Hanson Aggrgates Plum Run Quar, Peebles *Also Called: Heidelberg Materials Us Inc* **(G-12327)**

Hantech, Findlay *Also Called: Hancor Inc* **(G-7521)**

Hapco Inc... 330 678-9353
390 Portage Blvd Kent (44240) **(G-8817)**

Happy Booker, Cincinnati *Also Called: Art Guild Binders Inc* **(G-2634)**

Happy Grape LLC... 419 884-9463
300 E Main St Mansfield (44904) **(G-9666)**

Happy Trails Rv, Cleveland *Also Called: Electric Cord Sets Inc* **(G-4003)**

Har Adhesive Technologies, Bedford *Also Called: Certon Technologies Inc* **(G-1111)**

Har Equipment Sales Inc... 440 786-7189
60 S Park St Bedford (44146) **(G-1123)**

Harbor Castings Inc (PA).. 330 499-7178
2508 Bailey Rd Cuyahoga Falls (44221) **(G-6089)**

Harbor Industrial Corp... 440 599-8366
859 W Jackson St Conneaut (44030) **(G-5919)**

Harbor Wraps LLC.. 614 725-0429
341 S 3rd St Ste 100 Columbus (43215) **(G-5419)**

Harco Manufacturing Group LLC (PA)... 937 528-5000
3535 Kettering Blvd Moraine (45439) **(G-11183)**

Harco Manufacturing Group LLC... 937 528-5000
3535 Kettering Blvd # 200 Moraine (45439) **(G-11184)**

Hardcore Offroad Tires, Youngstown *Also Called: Warrior Imports Inc* **(G-16474)**

Hardin County Publishing Co (HQ).. 419 674-4066
201 E Columbus St Kenton (43326) **(G-8885)**

Hardin Creek Machine & TI Inc... 419 678-4913
200 Hardin St Coldwater (45828) **(G-4991)**

Harding Machine Acquisition Co.. 937 666-3031
13060 State Route 287 East Liberty (43319) **(G-6987)**

Hardline International Inc... 419 924-9556
1107 Oak St West Unity (43570) **(G-15640)**

Hardwood Connection, The, Toledo *Also Called: Hafners Hrdwood Connection LLC* **(G-14309)**

Hardwood Lumber Co, Burton *Also Called: Stephen M Trudick* **(G-1886)**

Hardwood Lumber Company Inc... 440 834-1891
13813 Station Rd Middlefield (44062) **(G-10754)**

Hardwood Solutions... 330 359-5755
112 E Main St Wilmot (44689) **(G-16068)**

Hardwood Store Inc.. 937 864-2899
350 Enon Rd Enon (45323) **(G-7250)**

Hardy Industrial Tech LLC... 440 350-6300
679 Hardy Rd Painesville (44077) **(G-12243)**

Harknesservices, Norwalk *Also Called: Link To Success Inc* **(G-11978)**

Harlan Graphic Arts Svcs Inc... 513 251-5700
4752 River Rd Cincinnati (45233) **(G-2985)**

Harmon Homes.. 513 602-6896
5476 Camelot Dr Apt 40 Fairfield (45014) **(G-7365)**

Harmon Sign Company, Toledo *Also Called: Kasper Enterprises Inc* **(G-14345)**

Harmony Systems and Svc Inc... 937 778-1082
1711 Commerce Dr Piqua (45356) **(G-12519)**

Harper Engraving & Printing Co (PA)... 614 276-0700
2626 Fisher Rd Columbus (43204) **(G-5420)**

Harray LLC.. 888 568-8371
266 W Mitchell Ave Cincinnati (45232) **(G-2986)**

Harris Broadcast, Mason *Also Called: Imagine Communications Corp* **(G-10006)**

Harris Calorific Inc... 216 383-4107
22801 Saint Clair Ave Cleveland (44117) **(G-4170)**

Harris Instrument Corporation... 740 369-3580
155 Johnson Dr Delaware (43015) **(G-6729)**

Harris Paper Crafts Inc... 614 299-2141
266 E 5th Ave Columbus (43201) **(G-5421)**

Harris Products Group, The, Mason *Also Called: J W Harris Co Inc* **(G-10014)**

Harris Welding and Machine Co... 419 281-8351
2219 Cottage St Ashland (44805) **(G-577)**

Harrison County Coal Company (HQ)... 740 338-3100
46226 National Rd Saint Clairsville (43950) **(G-12906)**

Harrison Hub, Scio *Also Called: M3 Midstream LLC* **(G-13111)**

Harrison Mch & Plastic Corp (PA)... 330 527-5641
11614 State Route 88 Garrettsville (44231) **(G-7916)**

Harrison News Herald Inc.. 740 942-2118
144 S Main St Lowr Cadiz (43907) **(G-1903)**

Harrison Paint, Canton *Also Called: Harrison Paint Company* **(G-2122)**

Harrison Paint Company (PA)... 330 455-5120
1329 Harrison Ave Sw Canton (44706) **(G-2122)**

Harrison Plant, Canton *Also Called: Metallus Inc* **(G-2162)**

Harrison Welding Services LLC... 513 405-6581
3462 Winter Holly Dr Amelia (45102) **(G-456)**

Harrop Industries Inc.. 614 231-3621
3470 E 5th Ave Columbus (43219) **(G-5422)**

Harry C Lobalzo & Sons Inc.. 330 666-6758
61 N Cleveland Massillon Rd Unit A Akron (44333) **(G-180)**

Harry London Candies Inc (DH)... 330 494-0833
5353 Lauby Rd North Canton (44720) **(G-11736)**

Harry London Chocolates, North Canton *Also Called: Harry London Candies Inc* **(G-11736)**

Hart & Cooley LLC... 937 832-7800
1 Lau Pkwy Englewood (45315) **(G-7232)**

Hart Advertising Inc... 419 668-1194
69 E Seminary St 75 Norwalk (44857) **(G-11972)**

Hartco Printing Company (PA).. 614 761-1292
4106 Delancy Park Dr Dublin (43016) **(G-6890)**

Hartco Products, The, Dublin *Also Called: Hartco Printing Company* **(G-6890)**

Hartline Products Coinc... 216 851-7189
15035 Woodworth Rd Ste 3 Cleveland (44110) **(G-4171)**

Hartman Distributing LLC.. 740 616-7764
1262 Bluejack Ln Heath (43056) **(G-8321)**

Hartman Trophies, Columbus *Also Called: The Hartman Corp* **(G-5822)**

Hartmann Electronic, Springfield *Also Called: Kontron America Incorporated* **(G-13591)**

Hartmann Inc.. 513 276-7318
4615 Carlynn Dr Blue Ash (45241) **(G-1403)**

Hartsgrove Machine, Rock Creek *Also Called: David Bixel* **(G-12831)**

Hartville Chocolate Factory, Hartville *Also Called: Hartville Chocolates Inc* **(G-8300)**

Hartville Chocolates Inc... 330 877-1999
114 S Prospect Ave Hartville (44632) **(G-8300)**

Hartz Mountain Corporation.. 513 877-2131
5374 Long Spurling Rd Pleasant Plain (45162) **(G-12607)**

Hartzell Fan Inc (PA)... 937 773-7411
910 S Downing St Piqua (45356) **(G-12520)**

Hartzell Hardwoods Inc (PA)... 937 773-7054
1025 S Roosevelt Ave Piqua (45356) **(G-12521)**

Hartzell Industries Inc (PA).. 937 773-6295
1025 S Roosevelt Ave Piqua (45356) **(G-12522)**

Hartzell Mfg Co LLC... 937 859-5955
2533 Technical Dr Miamisburg (45342) **(G-10643)**

Hartzell Propeller Inc... 937 778-4200
1 Propeller Pl Piqua (45356) **(G-12523)**

Harvard Coil Processing Inc.. 216 883-6366
5400 Harvard Ave Cleveland (44105) **(G-4172)**

Harvest Commissary LLC... 513 706-1951
3825 Columbus Rd Bldg J Granville (43023) **(G-8017)**

Harvey Brothers Inc (PA)... 513 541-2622
3492 Spring Grove Ave Cincinnati (45223) **(G-2987)**

Harwood Entp Holdings Inc.. 330 923-3256
1365 Orlen Ave Cuyahoga Falls (44221) **(G-6090)**

Harwood Rubber Products, Akron *Also Called: M7 Hrp LLC* **(G-232)**

Harwood Screw Products, Springfield *Also Called: Ban Inc* **(G-13538)**

Hashier & Hashier Mfg... 440 933-4883
644 Moore Rd Avon Lake (44012) **(G-810)**

Hason USA Corp.. 513 248-0287
1080 Nimitzview Dr Ste 402 Cincinnati (45230) **(G-2988)**

Hatchery, Strasburg *Also Called: Case Farms of Ohio Inc* **(G-13745)**

Hatfield Industries LLC... 513 225-0456
9717 Flagstone Way West Chester (45069) **(G-15445)**

Hathaway, Cincinnati *Also Called: Volk Corporation* **(G-3501)**

Hathaway Stamp, Cincinnati *Also Called: Hathaway Stamp Co* **(G-2989)**

Hathaway Stamp Co... 513 621-1052
304 E 8th St Cincinnati (45202) **(G-2989)**

Hathaway Stamp Identification, Cincinnati *Also Called: Hathaway Stamp Idntfction Cncn* **(G-2990)**

Hathaway Stamp Idntfction Cncn............513 621-1052
304 E 8th St Cincinnati (45202) *(G-2990)*

Hattenbach, Cleveland *Also Called: The Hattenbach Company (G-4785)*

Haulette Manufacturing Inc............419 586-1717
8271 Us Route 127 Celina (45822) *(G-2336)*

Haulotte North America Mfg Inc............567 444-4159
125 Taylor Pkwy Archbold (43502) *(G-530)*

Haulotte US Inc (DH)............419 445-8915
125 Taylor Pkwy Archbold (43502) *(G-531)*

Hauser Landscaping, Middlefield *Also Called: Hauser Services Llc (G-10755)*

Hauser Services Llc............440 632-5126
15668 Old State Rd Middlefield (44062) *(G-10755)*

Haviland Culvert Company............419 622-6951
100 Main St Haviland (45851) *(G-8311)*

Haviland Drainage Products Co (PA)............800 860-6294
100 Main St Haviland (45851) *(G-8312)*

Haviland Plastic Products Co............419 622-3110
119 Main St Haviland (45851) *(G-8313)*

Hawk Performance, Medina *Also Called: Friction Products Co (G-10328)*

Hawkins Machine Shop Inc............937 335-8737
1112 Race Dr Troy (45373) *(G-14576)*

Hawkline Nevada LLC............937 444-4295
200 Front St Mount Orab (45154) *(G-11241)*

Hawks & Associates Inc............513 752-4311
1029 Seabrook Way Cincinnati (45245) *(G-2563)*

Hawks Tag, Cincinnati *Also Called: Hawks & Associates Inc (G-2563)*

Hawthorne Collective Inc............937 644-0011
4400 Easton Cmns Ste 125 Columbus (43219) *(G-5423)*

Hawthorne Gardening Co., Marysville *Also Called: Hawthorne Gardening Company (G-9913)*

Hawthorne Gardening Company (HQ)............360 883-8846
14111 Scottslawn Rd Marysville (43040) *(G-9913)*

Hawthorne Hydrophonics Botanic, Marysville *Also Called: Hawthorne Hydroponics LLC (G-9914)*

Hawthorne Hydroponics LLC (DH)............888 478-6544
14111 Scottslawn Rd Marysville (43040) *(G-9914)*

Hawthorne Tool LLC............440 516-1891
1340 Lloyd Rd Ste C Wickliffe (44092) *(G-15834)*

Hawthorne Wire Ltd............216 712-4747
13000 Athens Ave Ste 101 Lakewood (44107) *(G-8975)*

Hawthorne-Seving Inc............419 643-5531
320 W Main St Cridersville (45806) *(G-6041)*

Haybner Sheet Metal Inc............440 623-0194
18819 Hearthstone Dr Strongsville (44136) *(G-13839)*

Hayden Valley Foods Inc (PA)............614 539-7233
3150 Urbancrest Industrial Dr Urbancrest (43123) *(G-14853)*

Hayes Bros Ornamental Ir Works............419 531-1491
1830 N Reynolds Rd Toledo (43615) *(G-14312)*

Hayes, Michael Designer, Solon *Also Called: Michael W Hyes Desgr Goldsmith (G-13389)*

Hayford Technologies Inc............419 524-7627
500 S Airport Rd Mansfield (44903) *(G-9667)*

Haynes Manufacturing Company, Westlake *Also Called: R and J Corporation (G-15777)*

Hays Cleveland, Cleveland *Also Called: Unison UCI Inc (G-4845)*

Hazelbaker Industries Ltd
1661 Old Henderson Rd Columbus (43220) *(G-5424)*

Hazenstab Machine Inc............330 337-1865
1575 Salem Pkwy Salem (44460) *(G-13000)*

HB Fuller Company............833 672-1482
400 N Buckeye St Bellevue (44811) *(G-1227)*

HB Fuller Company............513 719-3600
4450 Malsbary Rd Blue Ash (45242) *(G-1404)*

HB Fuller Company............513 719-3600
4440 Malsbary Rd Blue Ash (45242) *(G-1405)*

HB Fuller Company............440 708-1212
17340 Munn Rd Chagrin Falls (44023) *(G-2399)*

HBD Industries Inc (PA)............614 526-7000
5200 Upper Metro Pl Ste 110 Dublin (43017) *(G-6891)*

Hbd/Thermoid Inc............937 593-5010
1301 W Sandusky Ave Bellefontaine (43311) *(G-1210)*

Hbd/Thermoid Inc (HQ)............614 526-7000
5200 Upper Metro Pl Ste 110 Dublin (43017) *(G-6892)*

HBE Machine Incorporated............419 668-9426
1100 State Route 61 N Monroeville (44847) *(G-11124)*

HCC Holdings Inc............800 203-1155
4700 W 160th St Cleveland (44135) *(G-4173)*

HCC/Sealtron (DH)............513 733-8400
9705 Reading Rd Cincinnati (45215) *(G-2991)*

Hdi Landing Gear USA Inc (HQ)............937 325-1586
663 Montgomery Ave Springfield (45506) *(G-13572)*

Hdi Landing Gear USA Inc............937 325-1586
663 Montgomery Ave Strongsville (44149) *(G-13840)*

HDR Power Systems LLC............614 308-5500
530 Lakeview Plaza Blvd Ste C Worthington (43085) *(G-16196)*

Hdt Ep Inc............216 438-6111
30500 Aurora Rd Ste 100 Solon (44139) *(G-13359)*

Hdt Expeditionary Systems Inc............513 943-1111
1032 Seabrook Way Cincinnati (45245) *(G-2564)*

Hdt Expeditionary Systems Inc............440 466-6640
5455 Route 307 West Geneva (44041) *(G-7938)*

Hdt Expeditionary Systems Inc............216 438-6111
30500 Aurora Rd Ste 100 Solon (44139) *(G-13360)*

Hdt Global, Solon *Also Called: Hunter Defense Tech Inc (G-13363)*

Hdt Tactical Systems Inc............216 438-6111
30525 Aurora Rd Solon (44139) *(G-13361)*

Hdwt Holdings Inc............440 269-6984
7124 Industrial Park Blvd Mentor (44060) *(G-10467)*

Heading4ward Investment Co (PA)............937 293-9994
2425 W Dorothy Ln Moraine (45439) *(G-11185)*

Headlee Enterprises Ltd............614 785-1476
9015 Antares Ave Columbus (43240) *(G-5063)*

Headwaters Incorporated............989 671-1500
745 Us Highway 52 Manchester (45144) *(G-9618)*

Health Aid of Ohio Inc (PA)............216 252-3900
5230 Hauserman Rd Ste B Cleveland (44130) *(G-4174)*

Health Care Products Inc............419 678-9620
410 Nisco St Coldwater (45828) *(G-4992)*

Health Nuts Media LLC............818 802-5222
4225 W 229th St Cleveland (44126) *(G-4175)*

Health Sense Inc............440 354-8057
433 S State St Painesville (44077) *(G-12244)*

Health-Mor, Brooklyn *Also Called: Hmi Industries Inc (G-1678)*

Healthsense, Painesville *Also Called: Health Sense Inc (G-12244)*

Healthwares Manufacturing............513 353-3691
5838b Hamilton Cleves Rd Cleves (45002) *(G-4954)*

Hearingaid Medina Service............330 725-1060
799 N Court St Medina (44256) *(G-10332)*

Hearn Plating Co Ltd............419 473-9773
3184 Bellevue Rd Toledo (43606) *(G-14313)*

Heart Healthy Homes Corp............216 521-6029
11860 Clifton Blvd Lakewood (44107) *(G-8976)*

Hearth and Home At Urbana............937 653-5263
1579 E State Route 29 Urbana (43078) *(G-14834)*

Hearth Products Controls Co............937 436-9800
2225 Lyons Rd Miamisburg (45342) *(G-10644)*

Hearthside Food Solutions LLC............419 293-2911
312 Rader Rd Mc Comb (45858) *(G-10270)*

Heartland Bread & Roll, Worthington *Also Called: Hannibal Company Inc (G-16195)*

Heartland Communications Div, Pataskala *Also Called: Pataskala Post (G-12303)*

Heartland Education Cmnty Inc............330 684-3034
200 N Main St Orrville (44667) *(G-12127)*

Heartland Group Holdings LLC............614 441-4001
4001 E 5th Ave Columbus (43219) *(G-5425)*

Heartland Petroleum, Columbus *Also Called: Gfl Environmental Svcs USA Inc (G-5401)*

Heartland Publications LLC............860 664-1075
4500 Lyons Rd Miamisburg (45342) *(G-10645)*

Heartland Retreaders Inc............740 472-0558
103 N Sycamore St Woodsfield (43793) *(G-16087)*

Heartland Stairways Inc............330 279-2554
7964 Township Road 565 Holmesville (44633) *(G-8543)*

Heartland Stairways Inc (PA)............330 279-2554
8230 County Road 245 Holmesville (44633) *(G-8544)*

Heat & Sensor, Lebanon *Also Called: Heat Sensor Technologie LLC (G-9088)*

Heat Exchange Applied Tech Inc............330 682-4328
150 B Allen Ave Orrville (44667) *(G-12128)*

Heat Precision Machining Inc 937 233-3140
2796 Culver Ave Dayton (45429) *(G-6366)*

Heat Sensor Technologie LLC 513 228-0481
627 Norgal Dr Lebanon (45036) *(G-9088)*

Heat Treating Inc (PA) 937 325-3121
1762 W Pleasant St Springfield (45506) *(G-13573)*

Heat Treating Equipment Inc 740 549-3700
8185 Green Meadows Dr N Lewis Center (43035) *(G-9162)*

Heat Treating Inc 614 759-9963
675 Cross Pointe Rd Gahanna (43230) *(G-7837)*

Heat Treating Technologies 419 224-8324
1799 E 4th St Lima (45804) *(G-9249)*

Heatermeals, Cincinnati *Also Called: Luxfer Magtech Inc (G-3116)*

Heating & Cooling Products, Mount Vernon *Also Called: Royal Metal Products LLC (G-11293)*

Heatmax Heaters, Mentor *Also Called: Glo-Quartz Electric Htr Co Inc (G-10464)*

Heatstar, Cleveland *Also Called: Mr Heater Inc (G-4427)*

Heavenly Creamery Inc 440 593-6080
264 Sandusky St Conneaut (44030) *(G-5920)*

Hec Investments Inc 937 278-9123
4800 Wadsworth Rd Dayton (45414) *(G-6367)*

Heck's Diamond Printing, Toledo *Also Called: Hecks Direct Mail & Prtg Svc (G-14314)*

Hecks Direct Mail & Prtg Svc 419 661-6028
202 W Florence Ave Toledo (43605) *(G-14314)*

Hecks Direct Mail Prtg Svc Inc (PA) 419 697-3505
417 Main St Toledo (43605) *(G-14315)*

Hedalloy Die Corporation 216 341-3768
3266 E 49th St Cleveland (44127) *(G-4176)*

Hedges Selective TI & Prod Inc 419 478-8670
702 W Laskey Rd Toledo (43612) *(G-14316)*

Hedstrom Injection, Ashland *Also Called: Future Molding Inc (G-575)*

Hedstrom Plastics LLC 419 289-9310
100 Hedstrom Dr Ashland (44805) *(G-578)*

Heeter Printing Company Inc 440 946-0606
33212 Lakeland Blvd Eastlake (44095) *(G-7034)*

HEF USA Corporation (PA) 937 323-2556
2015 Progress Rd Springfield (45505) *(G-13574)*

Hefty Hoist Inc 740 467-2515
2397a Refugee St Millersport (43046) *(G-11012)*

Heico Aerospace Parts Corp (DH) 954 987-6101
375 Alpha Park Highland Heights (44143) *(G-8388)*

Heidelberg Materials Us Inc 937 587-2671
848 Plum Run Rd Peebles (45660) *(G-12327)*

Heidelberg Materials Us Inc 937 442-6009
13526 Overstake Rd Winchester (45697) *(G-16073)*

Heidelberg Mtls Mdwest Agg Inc 419 983-2211
4575 S County Road 49 Bloomville (44818) *(G-1355)*

Heidelberg Mtls Mdwest Agg Inc 419 882-0123
8130 Brint Rd Sylvania (43560) *(G-13997)*

Heidelberg Mtls Mdwest Agg Inc 419 878-2006
600 S River Rd Waterville (43566) *(G-15245)*

Heidelberg Mtls US Cem LLC 330 499-9100
8282 Middlebranch Rd Middlebranch (44652) *(G-10714)*

Heidelberg Mtls US Cem LLC 972 653-5500
8130 Brint Rd Sylvania (43560) *(G-13998)*

Heidtman Steel, Toledo *Also Called: Heidtman Steel Products Inc (G-14317)*

Heidtman Steel Products Inc (HQ) 419 691-4646
2401 Front St Toledo (43605) *(G-14317)*

Heilind Electronics Inc 440 473-9600
5300 Avion Park Dr Cleveland (44143) *(G-4177)*

Heim Sheet Metal Inc 330 424-7820
905 N Market St Lisbon (44432) *(G-9314)*

Heinemann Saw Company 330 456-4721
2017 Navarre Rd Sw Canton (44706) *(G-2123)*

Heinen's 8, Aurora *Also Called: Heinens Inc (G-718)*

Heinens Inc 330 562-5297
115 N Chillicothe Rd Aurora (44202) *(G-718)*

Heinis Cheese Chalet, Millersburg *Also Called: Bunker Hill Cheese Co Inc (G-10949)*

Heintz Conveying Belt Service, Medina *Also Called: Conviber Inc (G-10313)*

Heintz Farms Enterprise Partnr 937 464-2535
4367 State Route 273 W Belle Center (43310) *(G-1196)*

Heinz, Coshocton *Also Called: Kraft Heinz Foods Company (G-5982)*

Heinz, Fremont *Also Called: Kraft Heinz Foods Company (G-7792)*

Heinz Foreign Investment Co 330 837-8331
1301 Oberlin Ave Sw Massillon (44647) *(G-10105)*

Heinz Frozen Foods, Massillon *Also Called: HJ Heinz Company LP (G-10107)*

Heirloom Woodworks LLC 937 430-0394
5930 Rudy Rd Tipp City (45371) *(G-14136)*

Heisler Tool Company 440 951-2424
38228 Western Pkwy Willoughby (44094) *(G-15927)*

Heisley Tire & Brake Inc 440 357-9797
5893 Heisley Rd Mentor (44060) *(G-10468)*

Helena Agri-Enterprises LLC 614 275-4200
800 Distribution Dr Columbus (43228) *(G-5426)*

Helena Agri-Enterprises LLC 419 596-3806
200 N Main St Continental (45831) *(G-5937)*

Helical Line Products Co 440 933-9263
659 Miller Rd Avon Lake (44012) *(G-811)*

Helios Quartz, Sylvania *Also Called: Helios Quartz America Inc (G-13999)*

Helios Quartz America Inc 419 882-3377
7345 Sylvania Ave Sylvania (43560) *(G-13999)*

Helium Seo 513 563-3065
11311 Cornell Park Dr Blue Ash (45242) *(G-1406)*

Helix Linear Technologies Inc 216 485-2263
23200 Commerce Park Beachwood (44122) *(G-989)*

Helix Operating Company LLC 855 435-4958
23200 Commerce Park Beachwood (44122) *(G-990)*

Hellan Strainer Company 216 206-4200
3249 E 80th St Cleveland (44104) *(G-4178)*

Heller Machine Products Inc 216 281-2951
1971 W 90th St Cleveland (44102) *(G-4179)*

Heller Sports Center, Montpelier *Also Called: W C Heller & Co Inc (G-11145)*

Helm Instrument Company Inc 419 893-4356
361 W Dussel Dr Maumee (43537) *(G-10205)*

Helmart Company Inc 513 941-3095
4960 Hillside Ave Cincinnati (45233) *(G-2992)*

Hematite, Englewood *Also Called: Woodbridge Englewood Inc (G-7249)*

Hemmelrath, Lima *Also Called: Hemmelrath Coatings Inc (G-9250)*

Hemmelrath Coatings Inc
1340 Neubrecht Rd Lima (45801) *(G-9250)*

Hen House Inc 419 663-3377
100 N West St Norwalk (44857) *(G-11973)*

Hen of Woods LLC 513 954-8871
2116 Colerain Ave Cincinnati (45214) *(G-2993)*

Hendershot Performance LLC 740 315-0090
3015 State Route 339 Belpre (45714) *(G-1254)*

Henderson Trucking, Delaware *Also Called: Rjw Trucking Company Ltd (G-6746)*

Hendrckson Trlr Coml Vhcl Syst, Canton *Also Called: Hendrickson Usa LLC (G-2124)*

Hendricks Vacuum Forming Inc 330 837-2040
3500 17th St Sw Massillon (44647) *(G-10106)*

Hendrickson 740 678-8033
1051 Windy Ridge Rd Vincent (45784) *(G-15008)*

Hendrickson Auxiliary Axles, Hebron *Also Called: Hendrickson International Corp (G-8343)*

Hendrickson International Corp 740 929-5600
277 N High St Hebron (43025) *(G-8343)*

Hendrickson Usa LLC 330 456-7288
2070 Industrial Pl Se Canton (44707) *(G-2124)*

Hendrickson Usa LLC 740 929-5600
277 N High St Hebron (43025) *(G-8344)*

Hendrickson Usa LLC 630 910-2800
9260 Pleasantwood Ave Nw North Canton (44720) *(G-11737)*

Henkel Surface Technologies, Delaware *Also Called: Henkel US Operations Corp (G-6730)*

Henkel US Operations Corp 513 830-0260
9435 Waterstone Blvd Cincinnati (45249) *(G-2994)*

Henkel US Operations Corp 216 475-3600
18731 Cranwood Pkwy Cleveland (44128) *(G-4180)*

Henkel US Operations Corp 740 363-1351
421 London Rd Delaware (43015) *(G-6730)*

Henkel US Operations Corp 440 255-8900
7405 Production Dr Mentor (44060) *(G-10469)*

Henkel US Operations Corp 440 250-7700
26235 1st St Westlake (44145) *(G-15755)*

Hennings Quality Service Inc 216 941-9120
  3115 Berea Rd Cleveland (44111) *(G-4181)*
Henny Penny Corporation (PA) 937 456-8400
  1219 U S 35 W Eaton (45320) *(G-7060)*
Henry Filters, Bowling Green *Also Called: Barnes International LLC (G-1552)*
Henry Tools Inc 216 291-1011
  498 S Belvoir Blvd Cleveland (44121) *(G-4182)*
Henry-Griffitts Limited (HQ) 419 482-9095
  352 Tomahawk Dr Maumee (43537) *(G-10206)*
Henthorne Jr Jay Mary Beth 330 264-1049
  3927 Cleveland Rd Wooster (44691) *(G-16130)*
Henty Usa LLC 513 984-5590
  7260 Edington Dr Cincinnati (45249) *(G-2995)*
Hephaestus Technologies LLC 216 252-0430
  3811 W 150th St Cleveland (44111) *(G-4183)*
Heraeus Electro-Nite Co LLC 330 725-1419
  6469 Fenn Rd Medina (44256) *(G-10333)*
Heraeus Epurio LLC 937 264-1000
  970 Industrial Park Dr Vandalia (45377) *(G-14942)*
Heraeus Prcous Mtls N Amer Dyc, Vandalia *Also Called: Heraeus Epurio LLC (G-14942)*
Herald Inc 419 492-2133
  625 S Kibler St New Washington (44854) *(G-11547)*
Herald Reflector Inc (PA) 419 668-3771
  61 E Monroe St Norwalk (44857) *(G-11974)*
Herbert E Orr Company Inc 419 399-4866
  335 W Wall St Paulding (45879) *(G-12313)*
Herbert Usa Inc 330 929-4297
  1480 Industrial Pkwy Akron (44310) *(G-181)*
Herco Inc 740 498-5181
  295 Enterprise Dr Newcomerstown (43832) *(G-11645)*
Hercules, Wickliffe *Also Called: Universal Metal Products Inc (G-15857)*
Hercules Engine, Massillon *Also Called: Brinkley Technology Group LLC (G-10079)*
Hercules Engine Components, Massillon *Also Called: DW Hercules LLC (G-10091)*
Hercules Industries Inc 740 494-2620
  7194 Prospect Delaware Rd Prospect (43342) *(G-12690)*
Hercules Stamping Co, Pemberville *Also Called: JA Acquisition Corp (G-12335)*
Herd, Cleveland *Also Called: Herd Manufacturing Inc (G-4184)*
Herd Manufacturing Inc 216 651-4221
  9227 Clinton Rd Cleveland (44144) *(G-4184)*
Heritage Cooperative Inc 740 828-2215
  10790 Newark Rd Nashport (43830) *(G-11338)*
Heritage Group Inc 330 875-5566
  303 S Chapel St Louisville (44641) *(G-9460)*
Heritage Hill LLC 513 237-0240
  11563 Grooms Rd Blue Ash (45242) *(G-1407)*
Heritage Industrial Finshg Inc 330 798-9840
  1874 Englewood Ave Akron (44312) *(G-182)*
Heritage Marble of Ohio Inc 614 436-1464
  7086 Huntley Rd Columbus (43229) *(G-5427)*
Heritage Marbles, Columbus *Also Called: Heritage Marble of Ohio Inc (G-5427)*
Heritage Plastics, Carrollton *Also Called: Heritage Plastics Liquidation Inc (G-2309)*
Heritage Plastics Liquidation Inc 330 627-8002
  861 N Lisbon St Carrollton (44615) *(G-2309)*
Heritage Truck Equipment Inc 330 699-4491
  661 Powell Ave Hartville (44632) *(G-8301)*
Herman Machine Inc 330 633-3261
  298 Northeast Ave Tallmadge (44278) *(G-14032)*
Herman Manufacturing LLC 216 251-6400
  13825 Triskett Rd Cleveland (44111) *(G-4185)*
Hermetic Seal Technology Inc 513 851-4899
  2150 Schappelle Ln Cincinnati (45240) *(G-2996)*
Herold Salads Inc 216 991-7500
  17512 Miles Ave Cleveland (44128) *(G-4186)*
Heroux Devtek Landing Gear Div, Strongsville *Also Called: Hdi Landing Gear USA Inc (G-13840)*
Heroux-Devtek Inc 937 325-1586
  663 Montgomery Ave Springfield (45506) *(G-13575)*
Heroux-Devtek Springfield, Springfield *Also Called: Heroux-Devtek Inc (G-13575)*
Herr Foods Incorporated 740 773-8282
  476 E 7th St Chillicothe (45601) *(G-2509)*

Herr Foods Incorporated 800 344-3777
  104 S Mcarthur St Chillicothe (45601) *(G-2510)*
Hershberger Lawn Structures 330 674-3900
  8990 State Route 39 Millersburg (44654) *(G-10957)*
Hershberger Manufacturing 440 272-5555
  7584 Rockwood Rd Windsor (44099) *(G-16075)*
Hershy Way Ltd 330 893-2809
  5918 County Road 201 Millersburg (44654) *(G-10958)*
Heskamp Printing Co Inc 513 871-6770
  5514 Fair Ln Cincinnati (45227) *(G-2997)*
Hess Advanced Solutions Llc 937 829-4794
  7415 Chambersburg Rd Dayton (45424) *(G-6368)*
Hess Corporation 740 266-7835
  4525 Sunset Blvd Steubenville (43952) *(G-13668)*
Hess Print Solutions, Kent *Also Called: D & J Printing Inc (G-8806)*
Hess Print Solutions, Kent *Also Called: Dbh Asscates - Ohio Ltd Partnr (G-8808)*
Hess Print Solutions, Kent *Also Called: Press of Ohio Inc (G-8847)*
Hess Print Solutions, Kent *Also Called: The D B Hess Company (G-8874)*
Hess Print Solutions, Kent *Also Called: Tpo Hess Holdings Inc (G-8876)*
Hess Print Solutions - OH, Kent *Also Called: The Press of Ohio Inc (G-8875)*
Hesseling & Sons LLC 419 642-0013
  2818 Elida Rd Ste 1 Lima (45805) *(G-9251)*
Heule Tool Corporation 513 860-9900
  131 Commerce Dr Loveland (45140) *(G-9485)*
Hexa Americas Inc 937 497-7900
  1150 S Vandemark Rd Sidney (45365) *(G-13252)*
Hexagon Industries Inc 216 249-0200
  1135 Ivanhoe Rd Cleveland (44110) *(G-4187)*
Hexion, Columbus *Also Called: Hexion Inc (G-5428)*
Hexion Inc (PA) 888 443-9466
  180 E Broad St Columbus (43215) *(G-5428)*
Hexion LLC (HQ) 614 225-4000
  180 E Broad St Fl 26 Columbus (43215) *(G-5429)*
Hexion Topco LLC (PA) 614 225-4000
  180 E Broad St Columbus (43215) *(G-5430)*
Hexion US Finance Corp 614 225-4000
  180 E Broad St Columbus (43215) *(G-5431)*
Hexpol Compounding LLC 440 682-4038
  1497 Exeter Rd Akron (44306) *(G-183)*
Hexpol Compounding LLC 440 834-4644
  14330 Kinsman Rd Burton (44021) *(G-1880)*
Hexpol Compounding LLC (DH) 440 834-4644
  14330 Kinsman Rd Burton (44021) *(G-1881)*
Hexpol Compounding LLC 440 632-1962
  14910 Madison Rd Middlefield (44062) *(G-10756)*
Hexpol Holding Inc (HQ) 440 834-4644
  14330 Kinsman Rd Burton (44021) *(G-1882)*
Hexpol Middlefield, Middlefield *Also Called: Gold Key Processing Inc (G-10752)*
Hexpol Polymers, Burton *Also Called: Hexpol Compounding LLC (G-1881)*
Hexpol Silicone, Akron *Also Called: Hexpol Compounding LLC (G-183)*
Hey 9 Inc 919 259-2884
  7794 Eagle Creek Ct Willoughby (44094) *(G-15928)*
Hf Group LLC (PA) 440 729-2445
  400 Aurora Commons Cir Unit 74 Aurora (44202) *(G-719)*
Hf Group LLC 440 729-9411
  8844 Mayfield Rd Chesterland (44026) *(G-2481)*
Hf Group LLC 440 729-9411
  8844 Mayfield Rd Chesterland (44026) *(G-2482)*
Hfi LLC (PA) 614 491-0700
  59 Gender Rd Canal Winchester (43110) *(G-1987)*
Hggc Citadel Plas Holdings Inc 330 666-3751
  3637 Ridgewood Rd Fairlawn (44333) *(G-7441)*
Hgi Holdings Inc 330 963-6996
  1810 Summit Commerce Park Twinsburg (44087) *(G-14672)*
Hh Robertsons Flooring, Cambridge *Also Called: Centria Inc (G-1927)*
Hhi, Canton *Also Called: Hunter Hydraulics Inc (G-2126)*
Hi Carb Corp 216 486-5000
  1857 E 337th St # A Eastlake (44095) *(G-7035)*
Hi Lite Plastic Products 614 235-9050
  3760 E 5th Ave Columbus (43219) *(G-5432)*

ALPHABETIC SECTION

HI Standard Machine Co, De Graff *Also Called: Alan Bortree* **(G-6664)**
HI Tech Printing Co Inc... 513 874-5325
   3741 Port Union Rd Fairfield (45014) **(G-7366)**
HI Tecmetal Group Inc (PA)... 216 881-8100
   28910 Lakeland Blvd Wickliffe (44092) **(G-15835)**
Hi-Point Firearms, Mansfield *Also Called: Highpoint Firearms* **(G-9668)**
Hi-Point Graphics LLC... 937 407-6524
   127 E Chillicothe Ave Bellefontaine (43311) **(G-1211)**
Hi-Stat A Stoneridge Co, Lexington *Also Called: Stoneridge Inc* **(G-9202)**
Hi-Tech Wire Inc.. 419 678-8376
   631 E Washington St Saint Henry (45883) **(G-12935)**
Hi-Tek Manufacturing Inc.. 513 459-1094
   6050 Hi Tek Ct Mason (45040) **(G-10001)**
HI-Vac Corporation (PA)... 740 374-2306
   117 Industry Rd Marietta (45750) **(G-9799)**
Hiab USA Inc (HQ)... 419 482-6000
   12233 Williams Rd Perrysburg (43551) **(G-12388)**
Hickman Williams & Company (PA)............................... 513 621-1946
   250 E 5th St Ste 300 Cincinnati (45202) **(G-2998)**
Hickmans Construction Co LLC...................................... 866 271-2565
   21150 Morris Ave Euclid (44123) **(G-7273)**
Hickok Ae LLC, Akron *Also Called: Crawford Ae LLC* **(G-117)**
Hickok Waekon LLC... 216 541-8060
   10514 Dupont Ave Cleveland (44108) **(G-4188)**
Hickory Harvest Foods, Coventry Township *Also Called: Ohio Hckry Hrvest Brnd Pdts In* **(G-6014)**
Hickory Lane Welding, Fredericksburg *Also Called: Chore Anden* **(G-7719)**
Hidaka Usa Inc.. 614 889-8611
   5761 Shier Rings Rd Dublin (43016) **(G-6893)**
Higgins Construction & Supply Co Inc........................... 937 364-2331
   3801 Us Highway 50 Hillsboro (45133) **(G-8458)**
Higgins Tool Rental, Hillsboro *Also Called: Higgins Construction & Supply Co Inc* **(G-8458)**
High Concrete Group LLC.. 937 748-2412
   95 Mound Park Dr Springboro (45066) **(G-13504)**
High Definition Tooling, Newcomerstown *Also Called: H3d Tool Corporation* **(G-11644)**
High Life... 330 978-4124
   2792 Ivy Hill Cir Cortland (44410) **(G-5963)**
High Low Winery.. 844 466-4456
   3867 Medina Rd Akron (44333) **(G-184)**
High Production Technology LLC.................................... 419 599-1511
   13068 County Road R Napoleon (43545) **(G-11317)**
High Production Technology LLC (DH).......................... 419 591-7000
   476 E Riverview Ave Napoleon (43545) **(G-11318)**
High Quality Plastics Inc... 419 422-8290
   2000 Fostoria Ave Findlay (45840) **(G-7522)**
High Quality Tools, Eastlake *Also Called: High Quality Tools Inc* **(G-7036)**
High Quality Tools Inc (PA).. 440 975-9684
   34940 Lakeland Blvd Eastlake (44095) **(G-7036)**
High Ridge Brands Co... 614 497-1660
   1654 Williams Rd Columbus (43207) **(G-5433)**
High Tech Castings.. 937 845-1204
   12170 Milton Carlisle Rd New Carlisle (45344) **(G-11416)**
High Tech Elastomers Inc (PA).. 937 236-6575
   885 Scholz Dr Vandalia (45377) **(G-14943)**
High Tech Metal Products Inc.. 419 227-9414
   1900 Garland Ave Lima (45804) **(G-9252)**
High Tech Prfmce Trlrs Inc... 440 357-8964
   1 High Tech Ave Painesville (44077) **(G-12245)**
High Temperature Systems Inc.. 440 543-8271
   16755 Park Circle Dr Chagrin Falls (44023) **(G-2400)**
High-TEC Industrial Services... 937 667-1772
   15 Industry Park Ct Tipp City (45371) **(G-14137)**
High-Tech Mold & Machine Inc.. 330 896-4466
   3771 Tabs Dr Uniontown (44685) **(G-14785)**
Highcom Global Security Inc (HQ).................................. 727 592-9400
   2901 E 4th Ave Unit J Columbus (43219) **(G-5434)**
Higher Ground Ministries, Springfield *Also Called: Rebecca Benston* **(G-13625)**
Highland Computer Forms Inc (PA)................................ 937 393-4215
   1025 W Main St Hillsboro (45133) **(G-8459)**
Highland Products Corp.. 440 352-4777
   9331 Mercantile Dr Mentor (44060) **(G-10470)**

Highlights Consumer Svcs Inc... 570 253-1164
   1800 Watermark Dr Columbus (43215) **(G-5435)**
Highlights For Children Inc (PA)...................................... 614 486-0631
   1800 Watermark Dr Columbus (43215) **(G-5436)**
Highlights For Children Publr, Columbus *Also Called: Highlights For Children Inc* **(G-5436)**
Highpoint Firearms.. 419 747-9444
   1015 Springmill St Mansfield (44906) **(G-9668)**
Highrise Creative LLC... 614 890-3821
   654 Brooksedge Blvd Ste A Westerville (43081) **(G-15708)**
Highs Welding Inc.. 937 464-3029
   3065 County Road 150 Belle Center (43310) **(G-1197)**
Highway Safety Corp... 740 387-6991
   473 W Fairground St Marion (43302) **(G-9855)**
HIGHWAY SAFETY CORP., Marion *Also Called: Highway Safety Corp* **(G-9855)**
Hii Mission Technologies Corp.. 937 426-3421
   1430 Oak Ct Beavercreek (45430) **(G-1074)**
Hikma Labs Inc... 614 276-4000
   1900 Arlingate Ln Columbus (43228) **(G-5437)**
Hikma Labs Inc (DH)... 614 276-4000
   1809 Wilson Rd Columbus (43216) **(G-5438)**
Hikma Pharmaceuticals, Columbus *Also Called: West-Ward Columbus Inc* **(G-5873)**
Hikma Pharmaceuticals USA Inc..................................... 732 542-1191
   300 Northfield Rd Bedford (44146) **(G-1124)**
Hikma Pharmaceuticals USA Inc..................................... 614 276-4000
   1809 Wilson Rd Columbus (43228) **(G-5439)**
Hikma Pharmaceuticals USA Inc..................................... 732 542-1191
   2130 Rohr Rd Lockbourne (43137) **(G-9336)**
Hikma Specialty USA Inc.. 856 489-2110
   1900 Arlingate Ln Columbus (43228) **(G-5440)**
Hilcorp Energy Co.. 330 536-6406
   8066 S State Line Rd Lowellville (44436) **(G-9516)**
Hilcorp Energy Co.. 330 532-9300
   2406 Clark Ave Wellsville (43968) **(G-15335)**
Hildreth Mfg LLC.. 740 375-5832
   1657 Cascade Dr Marion (43302) **(G-9856)**
Hilite Intl... 216 641-9632
   7750 Hub Pkwy Cleveland (44125) **(G-4189)**
Hill Bryce Concrete, Springfield *Also Called: Dearth Resources Inc* **(G-13551)**
Hill Manufacturing Inc... 419 335-5006
   318 W Chestnut St Wauseon (43567) **(G-15263)**
Hillman Precision Inc... 419 289-1557
   462 E 9th St Ste 1 Ashland (44805) **(G-579)**
Hillside Winery.. 419 456-3108
   221 Main St Gilboa (45875) **(G-7957)**
Hillside Wood Ltd... 330 359-5991
   8413 Township Road 652 Millersburg (44654) **(G-10959)**
Hilltop Basic Resources Inc... 937 795-2020
   8030 Rte 52 Us Aberdeen (45101) **(G-1)**
Hilltop Basic Resources Inc... 513 242-8400
   900 Kieley Pl Cincinnati (45217) **(G-2999)**
Hilltop Basic Resources Inc... 513 621-1500
   511 W Water St Cincinnati (45202) **(G-3000)**
Hilltop Basic Resources Inc... 937 859-3616
   4710 Soldiers Home W Carrollton Rd Miamisburg (45342) **(G-10646)**
Hilltop Basic Resources Inc... 937 882-6357
   1665 Enon Rd Springfield (45502) **(G-13576)**
Hilltop Big Bend Quarry LLC.. 513 651-5000
   1 W 4th St Ste 1100 Cincinnati (45202) **(G-3001)**
Hilltop Cmpnies St Brnard Rdym, Cincinnati *Also Called: Hilltop Basic Resources Inc* **(G-2999)**
Hilltop Concrete, Cincinnati *Also Called: Hilltop Basic Resources Inc* **(G-3000)**
Hilltop Energy Inc.. 330 859-2108
   6978 Lindentree Rd Ne Mineral City (44656) **(G-11018)**
Hilltop Glass & Mirror LLC... 513 931-3688
   7612 Hamilton Ave Cincinnati (45231) **(G-3002)**
Hilltop Golf Course, Manchester *Also Called: Hilltop Recreation Inc* **(G-9619)**
Hilltop Printing.. 419 782-9898
   1815 Baltimore St Defiance (43512) **(G-6681)**
Hilltop Recreation Inc... 937 549-2904
   1649 Brown Hill Rd Manchester (45144) **(G-9619)**
Hinchcliff Lumber Company (PA).................................... 440 238-5200
   13550 Falling Water Rd Ste 105 Strongsville (44136) **(G-13841)**

Hinchcliff Products, Strongsville *Also Called: Hinchcliff Lumber Company (G-13841)*

Hinckley Wood Products Ltd 330 220-9999
1545 W 130th St Hinckley (44233) *(G-8474)*

Hine Racing Equipment, Kinsman *Also Called: R E H Inc (G-8937)*

Hines Builders Inc 937 335-4586
1587 Lytle Rd Troy (45373) *(G-14577)*

Hines Specialty Vehicle Group, New Philadelphia *Also Called: Kimble Mixer Company (G-11509)*

Hinkle Fine Foods Inc 937 836-3665
4800 Wadsworth Rd Dayton (45414) *(G-6369)*

Hinkle Manufacturing, Perrysburg *Also Called: Orbis Corporation (G-12413)*

Hinkle Manufacturing Inc 419 666-5550
348 5th St Perrysburg (43551) *(G-12389)*

Hinkley Lighting Inc (PA) 440 653-5500
33000 Pin Oak Pkwy Avon Lake (44012) *(G-812)*

Hinterland Cof Strategies LLC 440 829-5604
6515 Saint Clair Ave Cleveland (44103) *(G-4190)*

Hipsy LLC 513 403-5333
4951 Dixie Hwy Fairfield (45014) *(G-7367)*

Hirschvogel Incorporated 614 445-6060
2230 S 3rd St Columbus (43207) *(G-5441)*

Hirt Publishing Co Inc 419 946-3010
245 Neal Ave Ste A Mount Gilead (43338) *(G-11234)*

Hirzel Canning Company (PA) 419 693-0531
411 Lemoyne Rd Northwood (43619) *(G-11919)*

Hirzel Canning Company 419 523-3225
325 E Williamstown Rd Ottawa (45875) *(G-12180)*

Hit Trophy Inc 419 445-5356
4989 State Route 66 Archbold (43502) *(G-532)*

Hitachi Astemo Americas Inc 937 783-4961
960 Cherry St Blanchester (45107) *(G-1350)*

Hitachi Astemo Americas Inc 419 425-1259
1901 Industrial Dr Findlay (45840) *(G-7523)*

Hitachi Astemo Americas Inc 740 965-1133
707 W Cherry St Sunbury (43074) *(G-13955)*

Hitachi Automation Ohio Inc 937 753-1148
2000 Industrial Ct Covington (45318) *(G-6025)*

Hitch-Hiker Mfg Inc 330 542-3052
10065 Rapp Rd New Middletown (44442) *(G-11478)*

Hite Parts Exchange Inc 614 272-5115
2235 Mckinley Ave Columbus (43204) *(G-5442)*

Hitech Shapes & Designs, Cincinnati *Also Called: Seilkop Industries Inc (G-3376)*

Hitti Enterprises Inc 440 243-4100
6427 Eastland Rd Cleveland (44142) *(G-4191)*

HJ Heinz Company LP (DH) 330 837-8331
1301 Oberlin Ave Sw Massillon (44647) *(G-10107)*

Hj Systems Inc 614 351-9777
230 N Central Ave Columbus (43222) *(G-5443)*

HK Cooperative Inc 419 626-2551
4413 W Bogart Rd Sandusky (44870) *(G-13063)*

HK Coprative Inc/J H Routh Pkg, Sandusky *Also Called: HK Cooperative Inc (G-13063)*

HK Logging & Lumber Ltd 440 632-1997
16465 Farley Rd Middlefield (44062) *(G-10757)*

HK Technologies 330 337-9710
4544 Hinckley Industrial Pkwy Cleveland (44109) *(G-4192)*

Hkm Drect Mkt Cmmnications Inc (PA) 800 860-4456
5501 Cass Ave Cleveland (44102) *(G-4193)*

Hkm Drect Mkt Cmmnications Inc 440 934-3060
2931 Abbe Rd Sheffield Village (44054) *(G-13183)*

Hkm Drect Mkt Cmmnications Inc 330 395-9538
387 Chestnut Ave Ne Warren (44483) *(G-15176)*

Hmi Industries Inc (PA) 440 846-7800
1 American Rd Ste 1250 Brooklyn (44144) *(G-1678)*

HMS Industries, Westlake *Also Called: HMS Industries LLC (G-15756)*

HMS Industries LLC 440 899-0001
27995 Ranney Pkwy Westlake (44145) *(G-15756)*

Hobart, Troy *Also Called: Hobart LLC (G-14582)*

Hobart, Troy *Also Called: ITW Food Equipment Group LLC (G-14589)*

Hobart Bros Stick Electrode 937 332-5375
101 Trade Sq E Troy (45373) *(G-14578)*

Hobart Brothers LLC 937 332-5953
8585 Industry Park Dr Piqua (45356) *(G-12524)*

Hobart Brothers LLC (HQ) 937 332-5439
101 Trade Sq E Troy (45373) *(G-14579)*

Hobart Cabinet Company 937 335-4666
1100 Wayne St Ste 1 Troy (45373) *(G-14580)*

Hobart LLC 937 332-2797
8515 Industry Park Dr Piqua (45356) *(G-12525)*

Hobart LLC 937 332-3000
401 S Market St Troy (45373) *(G-14581)*

Hobart LLC (DH) 937 332-3000
701 S Ridge Ave Troy (45373) *(G-14582)*

Hobart Sales & Service, Akron *Also Called: Harry C Lobalzo & Sons Inc (G-180)*

Hobby Hill Wood Working 330 893-4518
6559 County Road 77 Millersburg (44654) *(G-10960)*

Hochstetler Milling LLC 419 368-0004
552 State Route 95 Loudonville (44842) *(G-9449)*

Hochstetler Wood 330 893-2384
6291 County Road 77 Millersburg (44654) *(G-10961)*

Hochstetler Wood Ltd 330 893-1601
6791 County Road 77 Millersburg (44654) *(G-10962)*

Hocker Tool and Die Inc 937 274-3443
5161 Webster St Dayton (45414) *(G-6370)*

Hocking Hills Hardwoods, Laurelville *Also Called: T & D Thompson Inc (G-9056)*

Hocking Hlls Enrgy Well Svcs L 740 385-6690
32919 Logan Horns Mill Rd Logan (43138) *(G-9364)*

Hocking Valley Concrete Inc 740 592-5335
748 W Union St Athens (45701) *(G-686)*

Hocking Valley Concrete Inc (PA) 740 385-2165
35255 Hocking Dr Logan (43138) *(G-9365)*

Hocking Valley Concrete Inc 740 342-1948
1500 Commerce Dr New Lexington (43764) *(G-11452)*

Hofacker Prcsion Machining LLC 937 832-7712
7560 Jacks Ln Clayton (45315) *(G-3565)*

Hoffman Meat Processing 419 864-3994
157 S 4th St Cardington (43315) *(G-2275)*

Hofmanns Lures Inc 937 684-0338
3937 Kilbourn Rd Arcanum (45304) *(G-518)*

Hog Slat Incorporated 937 968-3890
200 N Grandview St Union City (45390) *(G-14779)*

Hoge Brush, New Knoxville *Also Called: Hoge Lumber Company (G-11447)*

Hoge Lumber Company (PA) 419 753-2263
701 S Main St State New Knoxville (45871) *(G-11447)*

Hoist Equipment Co Inc (PA) 440 232-0300
26161 Cannon Rd Bedford Heights (44146) *(G-1174)*

Hoistech LLC 440 327-5379
32960 Fern Tree Ln North Ridgeville (44039) *(G-11844)*

Holcim (us) Inc 216 781-9330
2500 Elm St Cleveland (44113) *(G-4194)*

Holcim (us) Inc 419 399-4861
11435 Road 176 Paulding (45879) *(G-12314)*

Holcim Quarries Ny Inc 216 566-0545
560 Harrison Street Cleveland (44113) *(G-4195)*

HOLCIM QUARRIES NY, INC., Cleveland *Also Called: Holcim Quarries Ny Inc (G-4195)*

Holding Company, Olmsted Twp *Also Called: Jones Industries LLC (G-12088)*

Holdren Brothers Inc 937 465-7050
301 Runkle St West Liberty (43357) *(G-15622)*

Holdsworth Industrial Fabg LLC 330 874-3945
10407 Welton Rd Ne Bolivar (44612) *(G-1527)*

Holes Custom Woodworking 419 586-8171
6875 Nancy Ave Celina (45822) *(G-2337)*

Holgate Metal Fab Inc 419 599-2000
555 Independence Dr Napoleon (43545) *(G-11319)*

Holistic Botanicals, Bellville *Also Called: Natural Optons Armatherapy LLC (G-1245)*

Holistic Foods Herbs and Books, Columbus *Also Called: B & A Holistic Fd & Herbs LLC (G-5169)*

Holland Assocts LLC DBA Archou 513 891-0006
316 W 4th St Ste 201 Cincinnati (45202) *(G-3003)*

Holland Engineering Co, Toledo *Also Called: Holland Engraving Company (G-14318)*

Holland Engraving Company 419 865-2765
7340 Dorr St Toledo (43615) *(G-14318)*

Holland Grills Distributing, Spencerville *Also Called: S I Distributing Inc (G-13489)*

Holloway Sportswear Inc (DH) 937 497-7575
2633 Campbell Rd Sidney (45365) *(G-13253)*

Holly Robakowski.. 440 854-9317
  641 E 185th St Cleveland (44119) *(G-4196)*
Hollywood Dance Jams... 419 234-0746
  8402 Hoaglin Center Rd Van Wert (45891) *(G-14918)*
Hollywood Imprints LLC.. 614 501-6040
  1000 Morrison Rd Ste D Gahanna (43230) *(G-7838)*
Holmco Division, Winesburg *Also Called: Robin Industries Inc (G-16082)*
Holmes By-Products Co Inc... 330 893-2322
  3175 Township Road 411 Millersburg (44654) *(G-10963)*
Holmes Cheese Co... 330 674-6451
  9444 State Route 39 Millersburg (44654) *(G-10964)*
Holmes County Gis, Millersburg *Also Called: County of Holmes (G-10952)*
Holmes County Hub Inc... 330 674-1811
  6 W Jackson St Ste C Millersburg (44654) *(G-10965)*
Holmes Custom Moulding Ltd... 330 893-3598
  5039 County Road 120 Millersburg (44654) *(G-10966)*
Holmes Limestone Co (PA)... 330 893-2721
  4255 State Rte 39 Berlin (44610) *(G-1307)*
Holmes Lumber & Bldg Ctr Inc... 330 479-8314
  1532 Perry Dr Sw Canton (44710) *(G-2125)*
Holmes Lumber & Bldg Ctr Inc (PA).. 330 674-9060
  6139 S R 39 Millersburg (44654) *(G-10967)*
Holmes Lumber & Supply, Millersburg *Also Called: Holmes Lumber & Bldg Ctr Inc (G-10967)*
Holmes Made Foods LLC... 216 618-5043
  21315 Fairmount Blvd Cleveland (44118) *(G-4197)*
Holmes Manufacturing.. 330 231-6327
  6775 County Road 624 Millersburg (44654) *(G-10968)*
Holmes Panel LLC... 330 897-5040
  3052 State Route 557 Baltic (43804) *(G-838)*
Holmes Printing, Springfield *Also Called: Holmes W & Sons Printing (G-13577)*
Holmes Printing Solutions LLC... 330 234-9699
  8757 County Road 77 Fredericksburg (44627) *(G-7724)*
Holmes Redimix Inc.. 330 674-0865
  7571 State Route 83 Holmesville (44633) *(G-8545)*
Holmes Stair Parts Ltd... 330 279-2797
  8614 Township Road 561 Holmesville (44633) *(G-8546)*
Holmes Supply Corp.. 330 279-2634
  7571 State Route 83 Holmesville (44633) *(G-8547)*
Holmes W & Sons Printing... 937 325-1509
  401 E Columbia St Springfield (45503) *(G-13577)*
Holmes Wheel Shop Inc... 330 279-2891
  7969 County Road 189 Holmesville (44633) *(G-8548)*
Holmview Welding LLC... 330 359-5315
  4041 Township Road 606 Fredericksburg (44627) *(G-7725)*
Holophane, Granville *Also Called: Holophane Corporation (G-8018)*
Holophane Corporation... 330 823-5535
  12720 Beech St Ne Alliance (44601) *(G-406)*
Holophane Corporation (HQ)... 866 759-1577
  3825 Columbus Rd Bldg A Granville (43023) *(G-8018)*
Holophane Corporation... 740 349-4194
  515 Mckinley Ave Newark (43055) *(G-11579)*
Holtgreven Scale & Elec Corp... 419 422-4779
  420 E Lincoln St Findlay (45840) *(G-7524)*
Holthaus Lackner Signs, Cincinnati *Also Called: Gus Holthaus Signs Inc (G-2978)*
Homan Metals LLC.. 513 721-5010
  1253 Knowlton St Cincinnati (45223) *(G-3004)*
Hombre Capital Inc... 440 838-5335
  5945 W Snowville Rd Brecksville (44141) *(G-1620)*
Home Asb & Mold Removal Inc... 216 661-6696
  4407 Brookpark Rd Cleveland (44134) *(G-4198)*
Home Bakery.. 419 678-3018
  109 W Main St Coldwater (45828) *(G-4993)*
Home City Ice Company.. 513 851-4040
  11920 Kemper Springs Dr Cincinnati (45240) *(G-3005)*
Home City Ice Company.. 937 461-6028
  1020 Gateway Dr Dayton (45404) *(G-6371)*
Home City Ice Company.. 419 562-4953
  150 Johnson Dr Delaware (43015) *(G-6731)*
Home City Ice Company.. 614 836-2877
  4505 S Hamilton Rd Groveport (43125) *(G-8146)*
Home City Ice Company.. 513 353-9346
  5709 State Rte 128 Harrison (45030) *(G-8279)*
Home City Ice Company.. 513 598-3000
  8131 Bronson Rd Olmsted Twp (44138) *(G-12087)*
Home Idea Center Inc... 419 375-4951
  1100 Commerce St Fort Recovery (45846) *(G-7619)*
Home Pro, Columbus *Also Called: Certified Walk In Tubs (G-5244)*
Home Stor & Off Solutions Inc.. 216 362-4660
  5305 Commerce Pkwy W Cleveland (44130) *(G-4199)*
Homecare Mattress Inc.. 937 746-2556
  303 Conover Dr Franklin (45005) *(G-7680)*
Homestretch Sportswear Inc.. 419 678-4282
  491 S Eastern Ave Saint Henry (45883) *(G-12936)*
Homeworth Fabrication Mch Inc... 330 525-5459
  23094 Georgetown Rd Homeworth (44634) *(G-8554)*
Homeworth Sales Service Div, Homeworth *Also Called: Ohio Drill & Tool Co (G-8555)*
Honda... 937 524-5177
  1501 Michael Dr Troy (45373) *(G-14583)*
Honda Dev & Mfg Amer LLC.. 937 644-0724
  19900 State Route 739 Marysville (43040) *(G-9915)*
Honda Dev & Mfg Amer LLC (DH).. 937 642-5000
  24000 Honda Pkwy Marysville (43040) *(G-9916)*
Honda Dev & Mfg Amer LLC.. 937 642-5000
  25000 Honda Pkwy Marysville (43040) *(G-9917)*
Honda Dev & Mfg Amer LLC.. 937 843-5555
  6964 State Route 235 N Russells Point (43348) *(G-12876)*
Honda Engineering N Amer Inc, Marysville *Also Called: Honda Engineering North America LLC (G-9918)*
Honda Engineering North America LLC.................................. 937 642-5000
  24000 Honda Pkwy Marysville (43040) *(G-9918)*
Honda Support Office, Marysville *Also Called: Honda Dev & Mfg Amer LLC (G-9915)*
Honda Transmission Manufacturi... 937 843-5555
  25000 Honda Pkwy Marysville (43040) *(G-9919)*
Honda Transmission Manufacturing of America Inc............ 937 843-5555
  6964 State Route 235 N Russells Point (43348) *(G-12877)*
Hones Harbor House Gifts... 216 334-9836
  720 E 6th St Ashtabula (44004) *(G-638)*
Honey Cell Inc Mid West.. 513 360-0280
  6480 Hamilton Lebanon Rd Monroe (45044) *(G-11109)*
Honeybaked, Holland *Also Called: Honeybaked Foods Inc (G-8512)*
Honeybaked Foods Inc.. 567 703-0002
  6145 Merger Dr Holland (43528) *(G-8512)*
Honeybaked Ham Company (PA).. 513 583-9700
  11935 Mason Montgomery Rd Ste 200 Cincinnati (45249) *(G-3006)*
Honeycomb Midwest.. 513 360-0280
  6480 Hamilton Lebanon Rd Monroe (45044) *(G-11110)*
Honeymoon Paper Products Inc.. 513 755-7200
  7100 Dixie Hwy Fairfield (45014) *(G-7368)*
Honeywell, Brookpark *Also Called: Honeywell International Inc (G-1718)*
Honeywell, Cincinnati *Also Called: Honeywell International Inc (G-3007)*
Honeywell, Columbus *Also Called: Honeywell International Inc (G-5444)*
Honeywell, Elyria *Also Called: Honeywell International Inc (G-7157)*
Honeywell, Lancaster *Also Called: Diamond Electronics Inc (G-9010)*
Honeywell, Urbana *Also Called: Grimes Aerospace Company (G-14830)*
Honeywell, Urbana *Also Called: Grimes Aerospace Company (G-14832)*
Honeywell, West Chester *Also Called: Honeywell International Inc (G-15446)*
Honeywell Authorized Dealer, Anna *Also Called: Chilltex LLC (G-489)*
Honeywell Authorized Dealer, Cincinnati *Also Called: Cincinnati Air Conditioning Co (G-2739)*
Honeywell Authorized Dealer, Cincinnati *Also Called: Wine Cellar Innovations LLC (G-3522)*
Honeywell Authorized Dealer, Sandusky *Also Called: Gundlach Sheet Metal Works Inc (G-13062)*
Honeywell First Responder Pdts... 937 264-1726
  4978 Riverton Dr Dayton (45414) *(G-6372)*
Honeywell First Responder Pdts, Dayton *Also Called: Morning Pride Mfg LLC (G-6457)*
Honeywell Intelligrated, Mason *Also Called: Intelligrated Systems Inc (G-10010)*
Honeywell Intelligrated, West Chester *Also Called: Intelligrated Systems Inc (G-15448)*
Honeywell International I... 513 282-5519
  7901 Innovation Way Mason (45040) *(G-10002)*
Honeywell International Inc.. 216 459-6048
  2100 Apollo Dr Brookpark (44142) *(G-1718)*
Honeywell International Inc.. 513 745-7200
  1280 Kemper Meadow Dr Cincinnati (45240) *(G-3007)*

Honeywell International Inc

Honeywell International Inc 302 327-8920
2080 Arlingate Ln Columbus (43228) *(G-5444)*

Honeywell International Inc 440 329-9000
Elyria (44036) *(G-7157)*

Honeywell International Inc 937 484-2000
550 State Route 55 Urbana (43078) *(G-14835)*

Honeywell International Inc 513 874-5882
9290 Le Saint Dr West Chester (45014) *(G-15446)*

Honeywell Lebow Products 614 850-5000
2080 Arlingate Ln Columbus (43228) *(G-5445)*

Honeywell Lightning & Elec, Urbana *Also Called: Grimes Aerospace Company (G-14831)*

Honeywell Senfopec, Columbus *Also Called: Honeywell Lebow Products (G-5445)*

Honeywell Smart Energy 440 415-1606
436 N Eagle St Geneva (44041) *(G-7939)*

Honeywell Smart Energy, Geneva *Also Called: Elster Perfection Corporation (G-7935)*

Hood Packaging Corporation 937 382-6681
1961 Rombach Ave Wilmington (45177) *(G-16053)*

Hoot and Holler,, Cincinnati *Also Called: Owl Be Sweatin (G-3231)*

Hoover & Wells Inc 419 691-9220
2011 Seaman St Toledo (43605) *(G-14319)*

Hoover Fabrication Ltd 330 575-1118
1789 N Lincoln Ave Salem (44460) *(G-13001)*

Hope Timber, Newark *Also Called: Hope Timber Pallet Recycl LLC (G-11582)*

Hope Timber & Marketing Group (PA) 740 344-1788
141 Union St Newark (43055) *(G-11580)*

Hope Timber Mulch LLC 740 344-1788
141 Union St Newark (43055) *(G-11581)*

Hope Timber Pallet Recycl LLC 740 344-1788
141 Union St Newark (43055) *(G-11582)*

Hopewell Oil and Gas, Columbus *Also Called: Zane Petroleum Inc (G-5891)*

Hopewood Inc 330 359-5656
8087 Township Road 652 Millersburg (44654) *(G-10969)*

Hoppel Fabrication Specialties 330 823-5700
9481 Columbus Rd Ne Ste 1 Louisville (44641) *(G-9461)*

Hopscotch Magazine, Bluffton *Also Called: Bluffton News Pubg & Prtg Co (G-1499)*

Hord Elevator LLC 419 562-1198
6775 Township Road 66 Edison (43320) *(G-7084)*

Horizon Global Corporation (DH) 734 656-3000
127 Public Sq Cleveland (44114) *(G-4200)*

Horizon Industries Corporation 937 323-0801
1801 W Columbia St Springfield (45504) *(G-13578)*

Horizon Metals Inc 440 235-3338
8059 Lewis Rd Ste 102 Berea (44017) *(G-1282)*

Horizon Ohio Publications Inc (HQ) 419 394-7414
102 E Spring St Saint Marys (45885) *(G-12953)*

Horizon Ohio Publications Inc 419 738-2128
520 Industrial Dr Wapakoneta (45895) *(G-15117)*

Horizons Incorporated (PA) 216 475-0555
18531 S Miles Rd Cleveland (44128) *(G-4201)*

Hormel, Cincinnati *Also Called: Hormel Foods Corp Svcs LLC (G-3008)*

Hormel Foods Corp Svcs LLC 513 563-0211
4055 Executive Park Dr Ste 300 Cincinnati (45241) *(G-3008)*

Hornell Brewing Co Inc 516 812-0384
644 Linn St Ste 318 Cincinnati (45203) *(G-3009)*

Horner Industrial Services Inc 937 390-6667
5330 Prosperity Dr Springfield (45502) *(G-13579)*

Horner Industrial Services Inc 513 874-8722
4721 Interstate Dr West Chester (45246) *(G-15562)*

Horrorhound Ltd 513 239-7263
1706 Republic St Cincinnati (45202) *(G-3010)*

Horsburgh & Scott Co (PA) 216 431-3900
5114 Hamilton Ave Cleveland (44114) *(G-4202)*

Horseshoe Express Inc 330 692-1209
8045 Camden Way Canfield (44406) *(G-2007)*

Horton Emergency Vehicles, Grove City *Also Called: Halcore Group Inc (G-8097)*

Horwitz & Pintis Co 419 666-2220
1604 Tracy St Toledo (43605) *(G-14320)*

Hose Master LLC (PA) 216 481-2020
1233 E 222nd St Cleveland (44117) *(G-4203)*

Hospeco, Richmond Heights *Also Called: Tranzonic Companies (G-12811)*

Hostar International Inc (PA) 440 564-5362
31005 Solon Rd Solon (44139) *(G-13362)*

Hoster Graphics Company Inc 614 299-9770
2580 Westbelt Dr Columbus (43228) *(G-5446)*

Hot Brass Inc 440 564-5179
15140 Munn Rd Newbury (44065) *(G-11626)*

Hot Cards.com, Cleveland *Also Called: Fx Digital Media Inc (G-4094)*

HOT Graphic Services Inc 419 242-7000
2595 Tracy Rd Northwood (43619) *(G-11920)*

Hot Mama Foods Inc 419 474-3402
5839 Secor Rd Toledo (43623) *(G-14321)*

Hotcards, Chagrin Falls *Also Called: HP Acquisition II LLC (G-2379)*

Hotcards of Akron, Akron *Also Called: Dlh Enterprises LLC (G-132)*

House of 10000 Picture Frames 937 254-5541
2210 Wilmington Pike Dayton (45420) *(G-6373)*

House of Awards Inc 419 422-7877
419 N Main St Findlay (45840) *(G-7525)*

House of Plastics, Cleveland *Also Called: HP Manufacturing Company Inc (G-4204)*

Housing & Emrgncy Lgstcs Plnnr 209 201-7511
36905 State Route 30 Lisbon (44432) *(G-9315)*

Houston Machine Products Inc 937 322-8022
1065 W Leffel Ln Springfield (45500) *(G-13580)*

Howard B Claflin Co 330 928-1704
5270 Hudson Dr Hudson (44236) *(G-8596)*

Howard Industries Inc 614 444-9900
1840 Progress Ave Columbus (43207) *(G-5447)*

Howden, Fairfield *Also Called: Howden USA Company (G-7370)*

Howden North America, Fairfield *Also Called: Howden North America Inc (G-7369)*

Howden North America Inc 513 874-2400
2933 Symmes Rd Fairfield (45014) *(G-7369)*

Howden North America Inc 330 721-7374
935 Heritage Dr Medina (44256) *(G-10334)*

Howden North America Inc 330 867-8540
411 Independence Dr Medina (44256) *(G-10335)*

Howden USA Company (DH) 513 874-2400
2933 Symmes Rd Fairfield (45014) *(G-7370)*

Howland Machine Corp 330 544-4029
947 Summit Ave Niles (44446) *(G-11670)*

Howland Printing Inc 330 637-8255
3117 Niles Cortland Rd Ne Cortland (44410) *(G-5964)*

Howling Print and Promo Inc 440 363-4999
10974 Leader Rd Chardon (44024) *(G-2452)*

Howmedica Osteonics Corp 937 291-3900
474 Windsor Park Dr Dayton (45459) *(G-6374)*

Howmet Aerospace Inc 330 848-4000
842 Norton Ave Barberton (44203) *(G-872)*

Howmet Aerospace Inc 216 641-3600
1600 Harvard Ave Newburgh Heights (44105) *(G-11615)*

Howmet Aerospace Inc 330 544-7633
1000 Warren Ave Niles (44446) *(G-11671)*

Howmet Aerospace Inc 330 222-1501
32585 N Price Rd Salem (44460) *(G-13002)*

HOWMET AEROSPACE INC, Barberton *Also Called: Howmet Aerospace Inc (G-872)*

HOWMET AEROSPACE INC, Newburgh Heights *Also Called: Howmet Aerospace Inc (G-11615)*

HOWMET AEROSPACE INC, Niles *Also Called: Howmet Aerospace Inc (G-11671)*

Howmet Aerospace Inc, Salem *Also Called: Howmet Aerospace Inc (G-13002)*

Howmet Aluminum Casting Inc (HQ) 216 641-4340
1600 Harvard Ave Newburgh Heights (44105) *(G-11616)*

HP Acquisition II LLC 216 241-4040
22 N Main St Fl 2 Chagrin Falls (44022) *(G-2379)*

HP Enterprise Inc 800 232-7950
10008 State Route 43 Streetsboro (44241) *(G-13773)*

HP Industries Inc 419 478-0695
400 E State Line Rd Toledo (43612) *(G-14322)*

HP Liquidating Inc 614 861-1791
725 Reynoldsburg New Albany Rd Blacklick (43004) *(G-1337)*

HP Manufacturing Company Inc (PA) 216 361-6500
3705 Carnegie Ave Cleveland (44115) *(G-4204)*

Hpc Holdings LLC (HQ) 330 666-3751
3637 Ridgewood Rd Fairlawn (44333) *(G-7442)*

ALPHABETIC SECTION

Hpc Holdings LLC.. 440 224-7204
3365 East Center St North Kingsville (44068) *(G-11796)*

HPM North America Corp, Iberia *Also Called: Yizumi-HPM Corporation (G-8649)*

Hr Graphics... 216 455-0534
5246 E 98th St Cleveland (44125) *(G-4205)*

Hr Machine llc... 937 222-7644
1934 Stanley Ave Dayton (45404) *(G-6375)*

Hrh Door Corp... 513 674-9300
2136 Stapleton Ct Cincinnati (45240) *(G-3011)*

Hrh Door Corp... 330 828-2291
14512 Lincoln Way E Dalton (44618) *(G-6132)*

Hrh Door Corp (PA).. 850 208-3400
One Door Dr Mount Hope (44660) *(G-11238)*

Hs Services, Westlake *Also Called: Imcd Us LLC (G-15760)*

Hsm Solutions Inc... 513 898-9586
4370 Ashfield Pl Mason (45040) *(G-10003)*

HSP Bedding Solutions LLC................................. 440 437-4425
243 Staley Rd Orwell (44076) *(G-12165)*

Hst, Cincinnati *Also Called: Hermetic Seal Technology Inc (G-2996)*

Htci Co.. 937 845-1204
12170 Milton Carlisle Rd New Carlisle (45344) *(G-11417)*

Htec Systems Inc.. 937 438-3010
561 Congress Park Dr Dayton (45459) *(G-6376)*

Hubbard Company.. 419 784-4455
612 Clinton St Defiance (43512) *(G-6682)*

Hubbard Feeds, Botkins *Also Called: Ridley USA Inc (G-1543)*

Hubbard Publishing Co... 937 592-3060
127 E Chillicothe Ave Bellefontaine (43311) *(G-1212)*

Hubbell Machine Tooling Inc................................ 216 524-1797
7507 Exchange St Cleveland (44125) *(G-4206)*

Hudco Manufacturing Inc..................................... 440 951-4040
38250 Western Pkwy Willoughby (44094) *(G-15929)*

Hudson Extrusions Inc.. 330 653-6015
1255 Norton Rd Hudson (44236) *(G-8597)*

Hudson Feeds, Okolona *Also Called: Republic Mills Inc (G-12071)*

Hudson Hines Hill Company................................. 330 562-1970
1818 Millers Pkwy Streetsboro (44241) *(G-13774)*

Hudson Supply Company Inc................................ 216 518-3000
4500 Lee Rd Ste 120 Cleveland (44128) *(G-4207)*

Hudson Workwear, Brecksville *Also Called: Rbr Enterprises LLC (G-1630)*

HUFFMAN, CHARLES & ASSOCIATES, Warrensville Heights *Also Called: Charles Huffman & Associates (G-15228)*

Huffy Sports Washington Inc............................... 937 865-2800
225 Byers Rd Miamisburg (45342) *(G-10647)*

Hughes Corporation (PA)..................................... 440 238-2550
16900 Foltz Pkwy Strongsville (44149) *(G-13842)*

Hughes-Peters, Huber Heights *Also Called: Mjo Industries Inc (G-8577)*

Hughey & Phillips LLC... 937 652-3500
240 W Twain Ave Urbana (43078) *(G-14836)*

Hugo Bosca Company Inc (PA)............................ 937 323-5523
1905 W Jefferson St Springfield (45506) *(G-13581)*

Hugo Sand Company.. 216 570-1212
7055 State Route 43 Kent (44240) *(G-8818)*

Huhtamaki Inc.. 513 201-1525
1985 James E Sauls Sr Dr Batavia (45103) *(G-925)*

Huhtamaki Inc.. 937 746-9700
4000 Commerce Center Dr Franklin (45005) *(G-7681)*

Hull Builders Supply, Sandusky *Also Called: Hull Ready Mix Concrete Inc (G-13064)*

Hull Ready Mix Concrete Inc................................ 419 625-8070
4419 Tiffin Ave Sandusky (44870) *(G-13064)*

Humbert Screen Graphix, Canton *Also Called: Tim L Humbert (G-2245)*

Humongous Fan, Cleveland *Also Called: Humongous Holdings Llc (G-4208)*

Humongous Holdings Llc..................................... 216 663-8830
23103 Miles Rd Cleveland (44128) *(G-4208)*

Humphrey Popcorn Company (PA)....................... 216 662-6629
11606 Pearl Rd Strongsville (44136) *(G-13843)*

Humtown Pattern Company................................. 330 482-5555
44708 Columbiana Waterford Rd Columbiana (44408) *(G-5041)*

Humtown Products, Columbiana *Also Called: Humtown Pattern Company (G-5041)*

Hunger Hydraulics CC Ltd.................................... 419 666-4510
63 Dixie Hwy Ste 1 Rossford (43460) *(G-12865)*

Hunger Industrial Complex, Rossford *Also Called: Hunger Hydraulics CC Ltd (G-12865)*

Hunkar Technologies Inc (PA).............................. 513 272-1010
2368 Victory Pkwy Ste 210 Cincinnati (45206) *(G-3012)*

Hunt Imaging LLC (PA)... 440 826-0433
210 Sheldon Rd Berea (44017) *(G-1283)*

Hunt Products Inc.. 440 667-2457
3982 E 42nd St Newburgh Heights (44105) *(G-11617)*

Hunt Valve Actuator LLC...................................... 330 337-9535
1913 E State St Salem (44460) *(G-13003)*

Hunt Valve Company Inc (DH)............................. 330 337-9535
1913 E State St Salem (44460) *(G-13004)*

Hunter Defense Tech Inc..................................... 513 943-7880
1032 Seabrook Way Cincinnati (45245) *(G-2565)*

Hunter Defense Tech Inc (PA)............................. 216 438-6111
30500 Aurora Rd Ste 100 Solon (44139) *(G-13363)*

Hunter Environmental Corp................................. 440 248-6111
30525 Aurora Rd Solon (44139) *(G-13364)*

Hunter Eureka Pipeline LLC................................. 740 374-2940
125 Putnam St Marietta (45750) *(G-9800)*

Hunter Hydraulics Inc.. 330 455-3983
2512 Columbus Rd Ne Canton (44705) *(G-2126)*

Hunter Manufacturing Company, Solon *Also Called: Hunter Environmental Corp (G-13364)*

Hunters Manufacturing Co Inc (PA)..................... 330 628-9245
1325 Waterloo Rd Mogadore (44260) *(G-11075)*

Huntsman Advnced Mtls Amrcas L...................... 330 374-2424
240 W Emerling Ave Akron (44301) *(G-185)*

Huntsman Advnced Mtls Amrcas L...................... 866 800-2436
240 W Emerling Ave Akron (44301) *(G-186)*

Huntsman Corporation... 330 374-2418
240 W Emerling Ave Akron (44301) *(G-187)*

Huron Cement Products Company (PA).............. 419 433-4161
617 Main St Huron (44839) *(G-8633)*

Husky Energy, Dublin *Also Called: Husky Marketing and Supply Co (G-6894)*

Husky Lima Refinery.. 419 226-2300
1150 S Metcalf St Lima (45804) *(G-9253)*

Husky Marketing and Supply Co.......................... 614 210-2300
5550 Blazer Pkwy Ste 200 Dublin (43017) *(G-6894)*

Husqvarna Construction Pdts, Cleveland *Also Called: Husqvarna US Holding Inc (G-4209)*

Husqvarna US Holding Inc (HQ).......................... 216 898-1800
20445 Emerald Pkwy Ste 205 Cleveland (44135) *(G-4209)*

Huth Ready Mix & Supply Co............................... 330 833-4191
501 5th St Nw Massillon (44647) *(G-10108)*

Huth Ready-Mix & Supply Co, Massillon *Also Called: Huth Ready Mix & Supply Co (G-10108)*

Hutnik Company... 330 336-9700
350 State St Ste 5 Wadsworth (44281) *(G-15035)*

Hutter Racing Engines Ltd................................... 440 285-2175
12550 Gar Hwy Chardon (44024) *(G-2453)*

Hv Coil.. 330 260-4126
700 Newport St Newcomerstown (43832) *(G-11646)*

Hvac, Akron *Also Called: Lowry Furnace Co Inc (G-224)*

Hvac Inc.. 330 343-5511
133 W 3rd St Dover (44622) *(G-6827)*

Hvac Mech Cntrcto Plbg Ppfttin, Cincinnati *Also Called: Jfdb Ltd (G-3042)*

Hvfi, Massillon *Also Called: Hendricks Vacuum Forming Inc (G-10106)*

Hy-Blast Inc.. 513 424-0704
70 Enterprise Dr Middletown (45044) *(G-10829)*

Hy-Grade Corporation (PA).................................. 216 341-7711
3993 E 93rd St Cleveland (44105) *(G-4210)*

Hy-Ko Products Company LLC............................. 330 467-7446
60 Meadow Ln Northfield (44067) *(G-11907)*

Hy-Production Inc.. 330 273-2400
6000 Grafton Rd Valley City (44280) *(G-14873)*

Hy-Tech Controls Inc... 440 232-4040
7411 First Pl Bedford (44146) *(G-1125)*

Hycom Inc.. 330 753-2330
374 5th St Nw Barberton (44203) *(G-873)*

Hydac Technology Corp....................................... 610 266-0100
4265 E Lincoln Way Unit C Wooster (44691) *(G-16131)*

Hyde Brothers Printing Co, Marietta *Also Called: Pen-Ann Corporation (G-9816)*

Hyde Brothers Prtg & Mktg LLC (PA).................. 740 373-2054
2343 State Route 821 Ste A Marietta (45750) *(G-9801)*

Hyde Park Lumber Company........................ 513 271-1500
  3360 Red Bank Rd Cincinnati (45227) *(G-3013)*
Hydralyte LLC.. 844 301-2109
  27070 Miles Rd Ste A Solon (44139) *(G-13365)*
Hydranamics Inc..................................... 419 468-3530
  820 Edward St Galion (44833) *(G-7880)*
Hydranamics Div Carter Mch Co, Galion *Also Called: Hydranamics Inc (G-7880)*
Hydraulic Manifolds USA LLC..................... 973 728-1214
  4540 Boyce Pkwy Stow (44224) *(G-13702)*
Hydraulic Parts Store Inc......................... 330 364-6667
  145 1st Dr Ne New Philadelphia (44663) *(G-11505)*
Hydraulic Specialists Inc......................... 740 922-3343
  5655 Gundy Dr Midvale (44653) *(G-10879)*
Hydro Aluminum Fayetteville..................... 937 492-9194
  401 N Stolle Ave Sidney (45365) *(G-13254)*
Hydro Extrusion Usa LLC........................... 888 935-5759
  401 N Stolle Ave Sidney (45365) *(G-13255)*
Hydro Supply Co..................................... 740 454-3842
  3112 East Pike Zanesville (43701) *(G-16537)*
Hydro Systems Company........................... 513 271-8800
  9393 Princeton Glendale Rd West Chester (45011) *(G-15447)*
Hydro Tube Enterprises Inc (PA)................. 440 774-1022
  137 Artino St Oberlin (44074) *(G-12052)*
Hydro-Aire Inc...................................... 440 323-3211
  241 Abbe Rd S Elyria (44035) *(G-7158)*
Hydro-Aire Aerospace Corp (HQ)................. 440 323-3211
  249 Abbe Rd S Elyria (44035) *(G-7159)*
Hydro-Dyne Inc..................................... 330 832-5076
  225 Wetmore Ave Se Massillon (44646) *(G-10109)*
Hydro-Thrift Corporation......................... 330 837-5141
  1301 Sanders Ave Sw Massillon (44647) *(G-10110)*
Hydro-Vac, Wickliffe *Also Called: HI Tecmetal Group Inc (G-15835)*
Hydrodec Inc (PA)................................... 330 454-8202
  2021 Steinway Blvd Se Canton (44707) *(G-2127)*
Hydrodec of North America LLC.................. 330 454-8202
  2021 Steinway Blvd Se Canton (44707) *(G-2128)*
Hydrofresh Ltd..................................... 567 765-1010
  1571 Gressel Dr Delphos (45833) *(G-6765)*
Hydrofresh Hpp, Delphos *Also Called: Hydrofresh Ltd (G-6765)*
Hydromatic Pumps Inc............................. 419 289-1144
  1101 Myers Pkwy Ashland (44805) *(G-580)*
Hydromotive Engineering Co..................... 330 425-4266
  9261 Ravenna Rd Bldg B1 Twinsburg (44087) *(G-14673)*
Hydrotech Inc (PA)................................. 888 651-5712
  10052 Commerce Park Dr West Chester (45246) *(G-15563)*
Hydrothrift, Massillon *Also Called: Hydro-Thrift Corporation (G-10110)*
Hyfast Aerospace LLC............................. 216 712-4158
  12313 Plaza Dr Parma (44130) *(G-12291)*
Hygenic Company LLC............................. 330 633-8460
  1245 Home Ave Akron (44310) *(G-188)*
Hyggelight LLC...................................... 419 309-6321
  902 N Superior St # A Toledo (43604) *(G-14323)*
Hyland Machine Company......................... 937 233-8600
  1900 Kuntz Rd Dayton (45404) *(G-6377)*
Hyland Screw Machine Products, Dayton *Also Called: Hyland Machine Company (G-6377)*
Hyland Software Inc (HQ)......................... 440 788-5000
  28105 Clemens Rd Westlake (44145) *(G-15757)*
Hyload Inc (DH)..................................... 330 336-6604
  5020 Enterprise Pkwy Seville (44273) *(G-13142)*
Hynes Holding Company (HQ).................... 330 799-3221
  3805 Hendricks Rd Youngstown (44515) *(G-16377)*
Hynes Industries, Youngstown *Also Called: Hynes Holding Company (G-16377)*
Hynes Industries Inc (PA)........................ 800 321-9257
  3805 Hendricks Rd Youngstown (44515) *(G-16378)*
Hyo Seong America Corporation................. 513 682-6182
  275 Northpointe Dr Fairfield (45014) *(G-7371)*
Hype Socks LLC..................................... 855 497-3769
  204 S Front St Apt 400 Columbus (43215) *(G-5448)*
Hyper Tech Research Inc......................... 614 481-8050
  539 Industrial Mile Rd Columbus (43228) *(G-5449)*
Hyper Tool Company............................... 440 543-5151
  16829 Park Circle Dr Chagrin Falls (44023) *(G-2401)*

Hyperion, Columbus *Also Called: Diamond Innovations Inc (G-5326)*
Hyponex Corporation (DH)........................ 937 644-0011
  14111 Scottslawn Rd Marysville (43040) *(G-9920)*
Hyponex Corporation.............................. 330 262-1300
  3875 S Elyria Rd Shreve (44676) *(G-13209)*
Hyradix Inc.. 847 391-1200
  8445 Rausch Dr Plain City (43064) *(G-12581)*
Hyson Products, Brecksville *Also Called: Barnes Group Inc (G-1607)*
Hyster, Cleveland *Also Called: Hyster-Yale Materials Hdlg Inc (G-4211)*
Hyster-Yale Materials Hdlg Inc (PA).............. 440 449-9600
  5875 Landerbrook Dr Ste 300 Cleveland (44124) *(G-4211)*
Hytec Automotive, Columbus *Also Called: Hytec-Debartolo LLC (G-5450)*
Hytec-Debartolo LLC............................... 614 527-9370
  4419 Equity Dr Columbus (43228) *(G-5450)*
Hytech Silicone Products Inc.................... 330 297-1888
  6112 Knapp Rd Ravenna (44266) *(G-12720)*
I 5S of Huron Inc................................... 419 433-9075
  356 Main St Huron (44839) *(G-8634)*
I AM King Apparel Llc............................. 513 284-9195
  8778 Planet Dr Cincinnati (45231) *(G-3014)*
I B-Tech, Bucyrus *Also Called: Imasen Bucyrus Technology Inc (G-1862)*
I Cerco Inc... 740 082-2050
  416 Maple Ave Crooksville (43731) *(G-6047)*
I Cerco Inc (PA).................................... 330 567-2145
  453 W Mcconkey St Shreve (44676) *(G-13210)*
I D I, Wapakoneta *Also Called: Ingredia Inc (G-15118)*
I Dream of Cakes.................................. 937 533-6024
  995 Camden Rd Eaton (45320) *(G-7061)*
I E C, Bolivar *Also Called: Inventive Extrusions Corp (G-1528)*
I E R Industries, Macedonia *Also Called: Ier Fujikura Inc (G-9556)*
I G Brenner Inc.................................... 740 345-8845
  1806 Stonewall Dr Newark (43055) *(G-11583)*
I Jalcite Inc.. 216 622-5000
  25 W Prospect Ave Cleveland (44115) *(G-4212)*
I L S, Cleveland *Also Called: Supply Technologies LLC (G-4755)*
I L S, Hamilton *Also Called: Innovtive Lbling Solutions Inc (G-8220)*
I P D, North Royalton *Also Called: Industrial Parts Depot LLC (G-11880)*
I P S, Rossford *Also Called: Industrial Power Systems Inc (G-12867)*
I S I, Lewis Center *Also Called: Industrial Solutions Inc (G-9163)*
I Schumann & Co, Bedford *Also Called: I Schumann & Co LLC (G-1126)*
I Schumann & Co LLC.............................. 440 439-2300
  22500 Alexander Rd Bedford (44146) *(G-1126)*
I T Verdin Co (PA).................................. 513 241-4010
  444 Reading Rd Cincinnati (45202) *(G-3015)*
I T W Automotive Finishing...................... 419 470-2000
  320 Phillips Ave Toledo (43612) *(G-14324)*
I V Miller & Sons................................... 732 493-4040
  940 Lafayette Rd Medina (44256) *(G-10336)*
I-Convert, Caldwell *Also Called: Interntnal Cnvrter Cldwell Inc (G-1909)*
I-M-A Enterprises Inc............................. 330 948-3535
  700 Wooster St Lodi (44254) *(G-9351)*
I-Plus Inc... 216 432-9200
  4501 Lakeside Ave E Cleveland (44114) *(G-4213)*
I.T. Plastics, Mentor *Also Called: Industrial Thermoset Plas Inc (G-10472)*
I2, Hubbard *Also Called: Independence 2 LLC (G-8564)*
Iabf Inc.. 614 279-4498
  1890 Mckinley Ave Columbus (43222) *(G-5451)*
Ibi, Chillicothe *Also Called: Ingle-Barr Inc (G-2513)*
IBI Brake Products Inc........................... 440 543-7962
  16751 Hilltop Park Pl Chagrin Falls (44023) *(G-2402)*
Ibidltd-Blue Green Energy....................... 909 547-5160
  1456 N Summit St Toledo (43604) *(G-14325)*
Ibiza Holdings Inc................................. 513 701-7300
  7901 Innovation Way Mason (45040) *(G-10004)*
IBM, Cincinnati *Also Called: International Bus Mchs Corp (G-3029)*
Ibycorp.. 330 425-8226
  8968 Dutton Dr Twinsburg (44087) *(G-14674)*
Ibycorp Tool & Die, Twinsburg *Also Called: Ibycorp (G-14674)*
Ic Roofing, Mason *Also Called: Interstate Contractors LLC (G-10013)*

ALPHABETIC SECTION
Image Group Inc

Ic Scientific Solutions, Westlake *Also Called: Iconic Labs LLC* ***(G-15758)***

Ic-Fluid Power Inc 419 661-8811
63 Dixie Hwy Rossford (43460) ***(G-12866)***

Icad Inc 866 280-2239
2689 Commons Blvd Ste 100 Dayton (45431) ***(G-6163)***

ICC, Brecksville *Also Called: Integrated Chem Concepts Inc* ***(G-1622)***

ICC Safety Service Inc 614 261-4557
1070 Leona Ave Columbus (43201) ***(G-5452)***

ICC Systems Inc 614 524-0299
5665 Blue Church Rd Ste 202 Sunbury (43074) ***(G-13956)***

Iccnexergy, Dublin *Also Called: Inventus Power (ohio) Inc* ***(G-6901)***

Ice Industries Inc 513 398-2010
320 N Mason Montgomery Rd Mason (45040) ***(G-10005)***

Ice Industries Inc (PA) 419 842-3600
3810 Herr Rd Sylvania (43560) ***(G-14000)***

Ice Industries Columbus Inc 614 475-3853
3810 Herr Rd Sylvania (43560) ***(G-14001)***

Ice Industries Deerfield, Mason *Also Called: Deerfield Manufacturing Inc* ***(G-9983)***

Ice Industries Grenada, Sylvania *Also Called: Grenada Stamping Assembly Inc* ***(G-13996)***

Ice Industries Ronfeldt, Toledo *Also Called: Ronfeldt Manufacturing LLC* ***(G-14460)***

Icecap LLC 216 548-4145
514 Arcadia Rd Wadsworth (44281) ***(G-15036)***

ICEE USA 513 771-0630
44 Carnegie Way West Chester (45246) ***(G-15564)***

ICM Distributing Company Inc 234 212-3030
1755 Enterprise Pkwy Ste 200 Twinsburg (44087) ***(G-14675)***

ICO Products LLC 419 867-3900
6415 Angola Rd Holland (43528) ***(G-8513)***

Icomold By Fathom, Holland *Also Called: ICO Products LLC* ***(G-8513)***

Icon Machining LLC 740 532-6739
987 Township Road 145 Ironton (45638) ***(G-8698)***

Iconic Labs LLC 216 759-4040
909 Canterbury Rd Ste G Westlake (44145) ***(G-15758)***

ICP Adhesives and Sealants Inc (HQ) 330 753-4585
2775 Barber Rd Norton (44203) ***(G-11944)***

Ics Electrical Services, Cincinnati *Also Called: Instrmntation Ctrl Systems Inc* ***(G-3024)***

Ics-Cargo Clean, Cincinnati *Also Called: Industrial Container Svcs LLC* ***(G-3020)***

Ics-Cargo Clean, Cincinnati *Also Called: Industrial Container Svcs LLC* ***(G-3021)***

Ict Sales, Cincinnati *Also Called: Industrial Coating Tech Inc* ***(G-3019)***

ID Images Inc 330 220-7300
1120 W 130th St Brunswick (44212) ***(G-1769)***

ID Images LLC (PA) 330 220-7300
1120 W 130th St Brunswick (44212) ***(G-1770)***

ID Plastech Engraving, Cincinnati *Also Called: Professional Award Service* ***(G-3301)***

Idea Works, Sugarcreek *Also Called: Middaugh Enterprises Inc* ***(G-13930)***

Ideal Branding, Englewood *Also Called: Ideal Image Inc* ***(G-7233)***

Ideal Door, Mason *Also Called: Clopay Building Pdts Co Inc* ***(G-9978)***

Ideal Drapery Company Inc 330 745-9873
1024 Wooster Rd N Barberton (44203) ***(G-874)***

Ideal Electric, Mansfield *Also Called: Ideal Electric Power Co* ***(G-9669)***

Ideal Electric Power Co 419 522-3611
330 E 1st St Mansfield (44902) ***(G-9669)***

Ideal Image Inc 937 832-1660
115 Haas Dr Englewood (45322) ***(G-7233)***

Ideal Integrations LLC 614 786-7100
7420 Worthington Galena Rd Worthington (43085) ***(G-16197)***

Identiphoto Co Ltd 440 306-9000
1810 Joseph Lloyd Pkwy Willoughby (44094) ***(G-15930)***

Identitek Systems Inc 330 832-9844
1100 Industrial Ave Sw Massillon (44647) ***(G-10111)***

Identity Group LLC 614 337-6167
6111c Maxtown Rd Westerville (43082) ***(G-15658)***

Identity Syncronizer, Perrysburg *Also Called: Innerapps LLC* ***(G-12392)***

Idex Corporation 419 526-7222
800 N Main St Mansfield (44902) ***(G-9670)***

Idialogs LLC 937 372-2890
121 Pawleys Plantation Ct Xenia (45385) ***(G-16264)***

IDM Computer Solutions, Hamilton *Also Called: Ultraedit Inc* ***(G-8255)***

Idx Corporation 937 401-3225
2875 Needmore Rd Dayton (45414) ***(G-6378)***

Idx Dayton LLC 937 401-3460
2875 Needmore Rd Dayton (45414) ***(G-6379)***

IEC, Middleburg Heights *Also Called: IEC Infrared Systems Inc* ***(G-10719)***

IEC, Middleburg Heights *Also Called: IEC Infrared Systems LLC* ***(G-10720)***

IEC Infrared Systems Inc 440 234-8000
7803 Freeway Cir Middleburg Heights (44130) ***(G-10719)***

IEC Infrared Systems LLC 440 234-8000
7803 Freeway Cir Middleburg Heights (44130) ***(G-10720)***

Ieg Plastics LLC 937 565-4211
223 Lock And Load Rd Bellefontaine (43311) ***(G-1213)***

Ier Fujikura Inc (PA) 330 425-7121
8271 Bavaria Dr E Macedonia (44056) ***(G-9556)***

Ies Systems Inc 330 533-6683
464 Lisbon St Canfield (44406) ***(G-2008)***

Ig Watteeuw Usa LLC 740 588-1722
1000 Linden Ave Zanesville (43701) ***(G-16538)***

Igc Software, Reynoldsburg *Also Called: Integrity Group Consulting Inc* ***(G-12767)***

Igel Technology America LLC 954 739-9990
2106 Florence Ave Cincinnati (45206) ***(G-3016)***

Igloo Press LLC 614 787-5528
39 W New England Ave Worthington (43085) ***(G-16198)***

Ignio Systems LLC 419 708-0503
444 W Laskey Rd Ste V Toledo (43612) ***(G-14326)***

Ignition Interlock, Cincinnati *Also Called: 1 A Lifesafer Inc* ***(G-2578)***

Ignition Systems Inc 330 653-9674
6751 Evergreen Rd Hudson (44236) ***(G-8598)***

Ignyte Assurance Platform 833 446-9831
714 E Monument Ave Dayton (45402) ***(G-6380)***

Igw USA 740 588-1722
1000 Linden Ave Zanesville (43701) ***(G-16539)***

Iheartcommunications Inc 419 223-2060
667 W Market St Lima (45801) ***(G-9254)***

Ihi Connectors R, Mentor *Also Called: International Hydraulics Inc* ***(G-10475)***

Iiot World LLC 440 715-0564
25985 Rustic Ln Westlake (44145) ***(G-15759)***

Ike Smart City 614 294-4898
250 N Hartford Ave Columbus (43222) ***(G-5453)***

Ikiriska LLC 614 389-8994
16 Village Pointe Dr Powell (43065) ***(G-12675)***

Iko, Franklin *Also Called: Iko Production Inc* ***(G-7682)***

Iko Production Inc 937 746-4561
1200 S Main St Franklin (45005) ***(G-7682)***

Illinois Tool Works Inc 216 292-7161
26101 Fargo Ave Bedford (44146) ***(G-1127)***

Illinois Tool Works Inc 513 489-7600
6600 Cornell Rd Blue Ash (45242) ***(G-1408)***

Illinois Tool Works Inc 262 248-8277
730 E South St Bryan (43506) ***(G-1821)***

Illinois Tool Works Inc 419 633-3236
730 E South St Bryan (43506) ***(G-1822)***

Illinois Tool Works Inc 419 636-3161
730 E South St Bryan (43506) ***(G-1823)***

Illinois Tool Works Inc 440 914-3100
6875 Parkland Blvd Solon (44139) ***(G-13366)***

Illinois Tool Works Inc 937 332-2839
750 Lincoln Ave Troy (45373) ***(G-14584)***

Illinois Tool Works Inc 937 335-7171
701 S Ridge Ave Troy (45374) ***(G-14585)***

Ilsco, Cincinnati *Also Called: Bardes Corporation* ***(G-2656)***

Ilsco LLC (HQ) 513 533-6200
4730 Madison Rd Cincinnati (45227) ***(G-3017)***

Im Greenberg Inc 440 461-4464
5470 Mayfield Rd Cleveland (44124) ***(G-4214)***

Image, Maumee *Also Called: Image By J & K LLC* ***(G-10207)***

Image By J & K LLC 888 667-6929
1575 Henthorne Dr Maumee (43537) ***(G-10207)***

Image Concepts Inc 216 524-9000
8200 Sweet Valley Dr Ste 107 Cleveland (44125) ***(G-4215)***

Image Graphics, Columbia Station *Also Called: Perrons Printing Company* ***(G-5016)***

Image Group Inc 419 866-3300
1255 Corporate Dr Holland (43528) ***(G-8514)***

ALPHABETIC

Image Pavement Maintenance 937 833-9200
425 Carr Dr Brookville (45309) *(G-1739)*

Image Print Inc 614 776-3985
6019 Jamesport Dr Westerville (43081) *(G-15709)*

Imagen Brands, Mason *Also Called: Ebsco Industries Inc* *(G-9987)*

Imagine Communications Corp 513 459-3400
5300 Kings Island Dr Ste 101 Mason (45040) *(G-10006)*

Imagine This Renovations 330 833-6739
4220 Alabama Ave Sw Navarre (44662) *(G-11344)*

Imaging Sciences LLC 440 975-9640
38174 Willoughby Pkwy Willoughby (44094) *(G-15931)*

Imalux Corporation 216 502-0755
11000 Cedar Ave Ste 250 Cleveland (44106) *(G-4216)*

Imasen Bucyrus Technology Inc 419 563-9590
260 Crossroads Blvd Bucyrus (44820) *(G-1862)*

Imax Industries Inc 440 639-0242
117 W Walnut Ave Painesville (44077) *(G-12246)*

Imcd Us LLC (HQ) 216 228-8900
2 Equity Way Ste 210 Westlake (44145) *(G-15760)*

Imco Carbide Tool Inc 419 661-6313
28170 Cedar Park Blvd Perrysburg (43551) *(G-12390)*

Imco Recycling, Uhrichsville *Also Called: Novelis Alr Recycling Ohio LLC* *(G-14787)*

Imco Recycling of Indiana Inc 216 910-3400
25825 Science Park Dr Ste 400 Beachwood (44122) *(G-991)*

Imeldas Baking Company LLC 937 484-5405
964 N Main St Urbana (43078) *(G-14837)*

Imesco, Fredericktown *Also Called: Industrial and Mar Eng Svc Co* *(G-7749)*

Imet Corporation 440 799-3135
13400 Glenside Rd Cleveland (44110) *(G-4217)*

IMG, Cleveland *Also Called: Im Greenberg Inc* *(G-4214)*

IMH LLC 513 800-9830
160 Easton Town Ctr Columbus (43219) *(G-5454)*

IMH LLC (PA) 614 436-0991
7020 Huntley Rd Ste C Columbus (43229) *(G-5455)*

IMI Precision, Brookville *Also Called: Norgren Inc* *(G-1742)*

IMI-Irving Materials Inc 513 844-8444
600 Augspurger Rd Hamilton (45011) *(G-8219)*

Iml Containers Ohio Inc 330 754-1066
5365 E Center Dr Ne Canton (44721) *(G-2129)*

Impac Hi-Performance Machining 419 726-7100
5515 Enterprise Blvd Toledo (43612) *(G-14327)*

Impact Armor Technologies LLC 216 706-2024
17000 Saint Clair Ave Ste 106 Cleveland (44110) *(G-4218)*

Impact Cutoff Div, Maumee *Also Called: Hammill Manufacturing Co* *(G-10204)*

Impact Industries Inc 440 327-2360
5120 Mills Industrial Pkwy North Ridgeville (44039) *(G-11845)*

Impact Printing and Design LLC 833 522-6200
4670 Groves Rd Columbus (43232) *(G-5456)*

Impact Products LLC (HQ) 419 841-2891
2840 Centennial Rd Toledo (43617) *(G-14328)*

Impact Weekly, Dayton *Also Called: Dayton City Paper Group Llc* *(G-6275)*

Impaction Co 440 349-5652
6100 Cochran Rd Solon (44139) *(G-13367)*

Imperial Castings, Tipp City *Also Called: C Imperial Inc* *(G-14124)*

Imperial Conveying Systems LLC 330 491-3200
4155 Martindale Rd Ne Canton (44705) *(G-2130)*

Imperial Die & Mfg Co 440 268-9080
22930 Royalton Rd Strongsville (44149) *(G-13844)*

Imperial Electric Company 330 734-3600
2575 Greensburg Rd North Canton (44720) *(G-11738)*

Imperial Family Inc 330 927-5065
80 Industrial St Rittman (44270) *(G-12822)*

Imperial Metal Solutions LLC 216 781-4094
2284 Scranton Rd Cleveland (44113) *(G-4219)*

Imperial Metal Spinning Co 216 524-5020
7600 Exchange St Cleveland (44125) *(G-4220)*

Imperial On-Pece Fibrgls Pools 740 747-2971
255 S Franklin St Ashley (43003) *(G-622)*

Imperial Orthodontics, Urbana *Also Called: Triage Ortho Group* *(G-14848)*

Imperial Pools Inc 513 771-1506
12090 Best Pl Cincinnati (45241) *(G-3018)*

Imperial Stucco LLC 614 787-5888
Dublin (43017) *(G-6895)*

Importers Direct LLC 330 436-3260
1559 S Main St Akron (44301) *(G-189)*

Imprint LLC 216 233-0066
3654 W 104th St Cleveland (44111) *(G-4221)*

Imprints 330 650-0467
77 Maple Dr Hudson (44236) *(G-8599)*

Improv Electronics, Kent *Also Called: Kent Displays Inc* *(G-8822)*

IMT Defense, Westerville *Also Called: IMT Defense Corp* *(G-15659)*

IMT Defense Corp 614 891-8812
5386 Club Dr Westerville (43082) *(G-15659)*

In Sttches Ctr For Ltrgcal Art, Cleveland *Also Called: Strictly Stitchery Inc* *(G-4739)*

Inc., K.I.W.I., Twinsburg *Also Called: Kiwi Promotional AP & Prtg Co* *(G-14681)*

Inca Presswood-Pallets Ltd (PA) 330 343-3361
3005 Progress St Dover (44622) *(G-6828)*

Incessant Software Inc 614 206-2211
8577 Ohio Wesleyan Ct Nw Lancaster (43130) *(G-9019)*

Incinerator Specialists, Medina *Also Called: Facultatieve Tech Americas Inc* *(G-10321)*

Incorprted Trstees of The Gspl 216 749-1428
1980 Brookpark Rd Cleveland (44109) *(G-4222)*

Incorprted Trstees of The Gspl 216 749-2100
19695 Commerce Pkwy Middleburg Heights (44130) *(G-10721)*

Incredible Plastics, Warren *Also Called: Bloom Industries Inc* *(G-15146)*

Incredible Solutions Inc 330 898-3878
1052 Mahoning Ave Nw Warren (44483) *(G-15177)*

Indelco Custom Products Inc 216 797-7300
25861 Tungsten Rd Euclid (44132) *(G-7274)*

Independence 2 LLC 800 414-0545
623 W Liberty St Hubbard (44425) *(G-8564)*

Independent Can Company 440 593-5300
1049 Chamberlain Blvd Conneaut (44030) *(G-5921)*

Independent Machine & Wldg Inc 937 339-7330
710 Boone Dr Troy (45373) *(G-14586)*

Independent Power Cons Inc 419 476-8383
6051 Telegraph Rd Ste 19 Toledo (43612) *(G-14329)*

Independent Stamping Inc 216 251-3500
12025 Zelis Rd Cleveland (44135) *(G-4223)*

Index Inc 440 632-5400
16582 Kinsman Rd Middlefield (44062) *(G-10758)*

Indian Bear Winery Ltd 740 507-3322
3483 Mccament Rd Walhonding (43843) *(G-15093)*

Indian Creek Fabricators Inc 937 667-7214
1350 Commerce Park Dr Tipp City (45371) *(G-14138)*

Indian Creek Structures, Rome *Also Called: J Aaron Weaver* *(G-12848)*

Indian Lake Raceway LLC 937 837-7533
6341 Silverbell Ct Clayton (45315) *(G-3566)*

Indian Lake Shoppers Edge 937 843-6600
204 1/2 Lincoln Blvd Russells Point (43348) *(G-12878)*

Indispenser Ltd 419 625-5825
520 Warren St Sandusky (44870) *(G-13065)*

Indoor Envmtl Specialists Inc 937 433-5202
438 Windsor Park Dr Dayton (45459) *(G-6381)*

Induction Management Svcs LLC 440 947-2000
1745 Overland Ave Ne Warren (44483) *(G-15178)*

Induction Tooling Inc 440 237-0711
12510 York Delta Dr North Royalton (44133) *(G-11879)*

Industrial Aluminum Foundry, Columbus *Also Called: Iabf Inc* *(G-5451)*

Industrial and Mar Eng Svc Co 740 694-0791
13843 Armentrout Rd Fredericktown (43019) *(G-7749)*

Industrial Ceramic Products Inc 937 642-3897
14401 Suntra Way Marysville (43040) *(G-9921)*

Industrial Coating Tech Inc 513 376-9945
1011 Sunset Ave Cincinnati (45205) *(G-3019)*

Industrial Connections Inc 330 274-2155
11730 Timber Point Trl Mantua (44255) *(G-9737)*

Industrial Container Svcs LLC 614 864-1900
1385 Blatt Blvd Gahanna Indsutrial Pk Blacklick (43004) *(G-1338)*

Industrial Container Svcs LLC 513 921-2056
1258 Knowlton St Cincinnati (45223) *(G-3020)*

Industrial Container Svcs LLC 513 921-8811
837 Depot St Cincinnati (45204) *(G-3021)*

Industrial Ctrl Design & Maint, Tallmadge Also Called: Industrial Ctrl Dsign Mint Inc *(G-14033)*
Industrial Ctrl Dsign Mint Inc... 330 785-9840
311 Geneva Ave Tallmadge (44278) *(G-14033)*
Industrial Electronic Service.. 937 746-9750
325 Industry Dr Carlisle (45005) *(G-2288)*
Industrial Fabrication and Mch... 330 454-7644
3216 Kuemerle Ct Ne Canton (44705) *(G-2131)*
Industrial Fabricators Inc.. 614 882-7423
265 E Broadway Ave Westerville (43081) *(G-15710)*
Industrial Farm Tank Inc... 937 843-2972
10676 Township Road 80 Lewistown (43333) *(G-9194)*
Industrial Fiberglass Spc Inc.. 937 222-9000
351 Deeds Ave Dayton (45404) *(G-6382)*
Industrial Fluid MGT Inc.. 419 748-7460
2926 Us Highway 6 Mc Clure (43534) *(G-10266)*
Industrial Hardwood Inc.. 419 666-2503
521 F St Perrysburg (43551) *(G-12391)*
Industrial Machining Services.. 937 295-2022
700 Tower Dr Fort Loramie (45845) *(G-7600)*
Industrial Mfg Co Intl LLC... 440 838-4555
3366 Riverside Dr Ste 103 Upper Arlington (43221) *(G-14801)*
Industrial Mfg Co LLC (HQ).. 440 838-4700
8223 Brecksville Rd Ste 100 Brecksville (44141) *(G-1621)*
Industrial Mill Maintenance... 330 746-1155
1609 Wilson Ave Ste 2 Youngstown (44506) *(G-16379)*
Industrial Millwright Svcs LLC.. 419 523-9147
1024 Heritage Trl Ottawa (45875) *(G-12181)*
Industrial Mold Inc.. 330 425-7374
2057 E Aurora Rd Twinsburg (44087) *(G-14676)*
Industrial Molded Plastics.. 330 673-1464
425 1/2 W Grant St Kent (44240) *(G-8819)*
Industrial Nut Corp.. 419 625-8543
1425 Tiffin Ave Sandusky (44870) *(G-13066)*
Industrial Paint & Strip Inc... 419 568-2222
1000 Commerce Ct Waynesfield (45896) *(G-15296)*
Industrial Paper Shredders Inc.. 888 637-4733
12037 South Ave North Lima (44452) *(G-11806)*
Industrial Parts Depot LLC... 440 237-9164
11266 Royalton Rd North Royalton (44133) *(G-11880)*
Industrial Pattern & Mfg Co.. 614 252-0934
899 N 20th St Columbus (43219) *(G-5457)*
Industrial Power Systems Inc.. 419 531-3121
146 Dixie Hwy Rossford (43460) *(G-12867)*
Industrial Prfctn Mold & Mch, Twinsburg Also Called: Industrial Mold Inc *(G-14676)*
Industrial Profile Systems, Akron Also Called: Systems Kit LLC MB *(G-343)*
Industrial Quartz Corporation... 440 942-0909
7552 Saint Clair Ave Ste D Mentor (44060) *(G-10471)*
Industrial Repair and Mfg... 419 822-0314
265 Rogers Rd Delta (43515) *(G-6786)*
Industrial Repair and Mfg (PA)... 419 822-4232
1140 E Main St Delta (43515) *(G-6787)*
Industrial Rlblity Spclsts Inc (PA).. 800 800-6345
370 Douglas Ave Chillicothe (45601) *(G-2511)*
Industrial Screen Prcess Svc I (PA)..................................... 419 255-4900
17 17th St Toledo (43604) *(G-14330)*
Industrial Solutions Inc... 614 431-8118
8333 Green Meadows Dr N Ste A Lewis Center (43035) *(G-9163)*
Industrial Tank & Containment... 330 448-4876
411 State Route 7 Se Ste 3 Brookfield (44403) *(G-1670)*
Industrial Technologies Inc.. 330 434-2033
1643 Massillon Rd Akron (44312) *(G-190)*
Industrial Thermal Systems Inc... 513 561-2100
3914 Virginia Ave Cincinnati (45227) *(G-3022)*
Industrial Thermoset Plas Inc.. 440 975-0411
7675 Jenther Dr Mentor (44060) *(G-10472)*
Industrial Timber & Land Co.. 740 596-5294
35748 State Route 93 Hamden (45634) *(G-8173)*
Industrial Timber & Lumber Co, Cleveland Also Called: Itl Corp *(G-4240)*
Industrial Timber and Lumber, Beachwood Also Called: Itl LLC *(G-992)*
Industrial WD Prts Fabrication, Archbold Also Called: Liechty Specialties Inc *(G-534)*
Industry Products Co (PA)... 937 778-0585
500 W Statler Rd Piqua (45356) *(G-12526)*

Ineos, Addyston Also Called: Ineos ABS (usa) LLC *(G-8)*
Ineos LLC (PA).. 419 226-1200
1900 Fort Amanda Rd Lima (45804) *(G-9255)*
Ineos ABS (usa) LLC... 513 467-2400
356 Three Rivers Pkwy Addyston (45001) *(G-8)*
Ineos Composites Us LLC (DH)... 614 790-9299
955 Yard St # 400 Columbus (43212) *(G-5458)*
INEOS KOH INC... 440 997-5221
3509 Middle Rd Ashtabula (44004) *(G-639)*
Ineos Neal LLC... 610 790-3333
5220 Blazer Pkwy Dublin (43017) *(G-6896)*
Ineos Nitriles USA LLC (DH).. 281 535-6600
1900 Fort Amanda Rd Lima (45804) *(G-9256)*
Ineos Pigments Asu LLC.. 440 994-1999
2501 Middle Rd Ashtabula (44004) *(G-640)*
Ineos Pigments USA Inc... 440 994-1400
2900 Middle Rd Ashtabula (44004) *(G-641)*
Ineos Solvents Sales US Corp.. 614 790-3333
5220 Blazer Pkwy Dublin (43017) *(G-6897)*
Inez Essentials LLC.. 216 701-8360
5333 Cato St Maple Heights (44137) *(G-9752)*
Infinit Nutrition LLC.. 513 791-3500
11240 Cornell Park Dr Ste 110 Blue Ash (45242) *(G-1409)*
Infinitaire Industries, Euclid Also Called: Infinitaire Industries LLC *(G-7275)*
Infinitaire Industries LLC... 216 600-2051
24370 Hartland Dr Euclid (44123) *(G-7275)*
Infinite Energy Mfg LLC.. 440 759-5920
4517 Industrial Pkwy Cleveland (44135) *(G-4224)*
Infinium Wall Systems Inc.. 440 572-5000
21000 Infinium Way Strongsville (44149) *(G-13845)*
Inflatable Images, Brunswick Also Called: Scherba Industries Inc *(G-1790)*
Informa Media Inc... 216 696-7000
1300 E 9th St Cleveland (44114) *(G-4225)*
Infosight Corporation... 740 642-3600
20700 Us Highway 23 Chillicothe (45601) *(G-2512)*
Ingersoll Rand... 440 277-7100
2199 E 28th St Lorain (44055) *(G-9414)*
Ingersoll Rand, Holland Also Called: Trane Company *(G-8534)*
Ingersoll-Rand, Bryan Also Called: Trane Technologies Company LLC *(G-1842)*
Ingersoll-Rand, Cincinnati Also Called: Trane Technologies Company LLC *(G-3459)*
Ingle-Barr Inc (PA)... 740 702-6117
20 Plyleys Ln Chillicothe (45601) *(G-2513)*
Ingredia Inc.. 419 738-4060
625 Commerce Rd Wapakoneta (45895) *(G-15118)*
Ingredient Innovations Intl Co.. 330 262-4440
146 S Bever St Wooster (44691) *(G-16132)*
Ingredient Masters Inc.. 513 231-7432
377 E Main St Batavia (45103) *(G-926)*
Inhance Technologies LLC... 614 846-6400
6575 Huntley Rd Ste D Columbus (43229) *(G-5459)*
Initial Designs Inc... 419 475-3900
2453 Tremainsville Rd Unit 2 Toledo (43613) *(G-14331)*
Injection Alloys Incorporated... 513 422-8819
2601 S Verity Pkwy Bldg 1 Middletown (45044) *(G-10830)*
Ink Slingers LLC... 740 867-3528
1564 County Road 36 Chesapeake (45619) *(G-2475)*
Ink Technology Corporation.. 216 486-6720
18320 Lanken Ave Cleveland (44119) *(G-4226)*
Ink Well, Bedford Heights Also Called: Cwh Graphics LLC *(G-1169)*
Ink Well, Grove City Also Called: Deerfield Ventures Inc *(G-8087)*
Inkscape Print and Promos LLC... 330 893-0160
5991 County Road 77 Millersburg (44654) *(G-10970)*
Inland Hardwood Corporation... 740 373-7187
25 Sheets Run Rd Marietta (45750) *(G-9802)*
Inland Paperboard Pkg.. 562 946-6127
Milford (45150) *(G-10911)*
Inland Products Inc (PA)... 614 443-3425
599 Frank Rd Columbus (43223) *(G-5460)*
Inland Products Inc... 740 245-5514
Rio Grande (45674) *(G-12818)*
Inland Tarp & Liner LLC... 419 436-6001
1600 N Main St Fostoria (44830) *(G-7638)*

Inland Wood Products, Marietta *Also Called: Inland Hardwood Corporation (G-9802)*

Inline Underground Hdd, Bremen *Also Called: Inline Undgrd Hrzntal Drctnal (G-1638)*

Inline Undgrd Hrzntal Drctnal... 740 808-0316
5440 Marietta Rd Sw Bremen (43107) *(G-1638)*

Inn Maid Products, Westerville *Also Called: Tmarzetti Company (G-15683)*

Inneractiv, Dublin *Also Called: Onguard Systems LLC (G-6918)*

Innerapps LLC... 419 467-3110
28350 Kensington Ln Ste 200 Perrysburg (43551) *(G-12392)*

Innerdyne Holdings Inc (HQ)... 614 757-5000
7000 Cardinal Pl Dublin (43017) *(G-6898)*

Innerwood & Company... 513 677-2229
688 Elizabeth Ln Loveland (45140) *(G-9486)*

Innocomp.. 440 248-5104
33195 Wagon Wheel Dr Solon (44139) *(G-13368)*

Innomark Communications LLC.. 513 285-1040
375 Northpointe Dr Fairfield (45014) *(G-7372)*

Innomark Communications LLC.. 937 454-5555
3233 S Tech Blvd Miamisburg (45342) *(G-10648)*

Innomark Group LLC... 419 720-8102
1218 Madison Ave Toledo (43604) *(G-14332)*

Innoplast Inc (PA)... 440 543-8660
5718 Transportation Blvd Cleveland (44125) *(G-4227)*

Innovar Systems Limited.. 330 538-3942
12155 Commissioner Dr North Jackson (44451) *(G-11784)*

Innovated Health LLC.. 330 858-0651
2241 Front St 1st Fl Cuyahoga Falls (44221) *(G-6091)*

Innovation Plastics LLC.. 513 818-1771
1150 State St Fostoria (44830) *(G-7639)*

Innovations In Plastic Inc... 216 541-6060
1643 Eddy Rd Cleveland (44112) *(G-4228)*

Innovative Assembly Svcs LLC.. 419 399-3886
400 W Wall St Paulding (45879) *(G-12315)*

Innovative Computer Forms, Columbus *Also Called: Bizzy Bee Printing Inc (G-5192)*

Innovative Control Systems... 513 894-3712
5870 Fairham Rd Fairfield Township (45011) *(G-7431)*

Innovative Controls Corp... 419 691-6684
1354 E Bdwy St Toledo (43605) *(G-14333)*

Innovative Creations, Dayton *Also Called: Glen D Lala (G-6354)*

Innovative Displays, Columbus *Also Called: Retail Project Management Inc (G-5721)*

Innovative Food Processors Inc.. 507 334-2730
136 Fox Run Dr Defiance (43512) *(G-6683)*

Innovative Graphics Ltd... 877 406-3636
2580 Westbelt Dr Columbus (43228) *(G-5461)*

Innovative Mech Systems LLC... 937 813-8713
3100 Plainfield Rd Ste A Dayton (45432) *(G-6164)*

Innovative Plastic Molders LLC... 937 898-3775
10451 Dog Leg Rd Ste 200 Vandalia (45377) *(G-14944)*

Innovative Products Inc... 865 322-9715
3201 E Royalton Rd Ste 5 Cleveland (44147) *(G-4229)*

Innovative Sport Surfacing LLC... 440 205-0875
8425 Station St Mentor (44060) *(G-10473)*

Innovative Stiching, North Baltimore *Also Called: Truck Stop Embroidery (G-11702)*

Innovative Stoneworks Inc... 440 352-2231
6815 Edinboro Pl Concord Township (44077) *(G-5907)*

Innovative Tool & Die Inc.. 419 599-0492
1700 Industrial Dr Napoleon (43545) *(G-11320)*

Innovative Vend Solutions LLC.. 866 931-9413
740 Royal Ridge Dr Dayton (45449) *(G-6383)*

Innovative Woodworking Inc.. 513 531-1940
1901 Ross Ave Cincinnati (45212) *(G-3023)*

Innovest Energy Group LLC... 440 644-1027
8834 Mayfield Rd Ste A Chesterland (44026) *(G-2483)*

Innovtive Cnfction Sltions LLC... 440 835-8001
28025 Ranney Pkwy Westlake (44145) *(G-15761)*

Innovtive Engnred Slutions Inc.. 937 382-6710
2695 Progress Way Wilmington (45177) *(G-16054)*

Innovtive Lbling Solutions Inc
4000 Hamilton Middletown Rd Hamilton (45011) *(G-8220)*

Inns Holdings Ltd... 740 345-3700
29 W Locust St Newark (43055) *(G-11584)*

Inovent Engineering Inc.. 330 468-0019
8877 Freeway Dr Macedonia (44056) *(G-9557)*

Inpower LLC... 740 548-0965
8311 Green Meadows Dr N Lewis Center (43035) *(G-9164)*

Ins Robotics Inc... 888 293-5325
3600 Parkway Ln Hilliard (43026) *(G-8414)*

Inservco Inc (DH)... 847 855-9600
110 Commerce Dr Lagrange (44050) *(G-8948)*

Inside Outfitters, Lewis Center *Also Called: Lumenomics Inc (G-9170)*

Inside Outfitters Inc... 614 798-3500
8333 Green Meadows Dr N Ste B Lewis Center (43035) *(G-9165)*

Insights Sccess Media Tech LLC....................................... 614 602-1754
555 Metro Pl N Ste 100 Dublin (43017) *(G-6899)*

Insignia Signs Inc.. 937 866-2341
2265 Dryden Rd Moraine (45439) *(G-11186)*

Inskeep Brothers Inc... 614 898-6620
3193 E Dublin Granville Rd Columbus (43231) *(G-5462)*

Inskeep Brothers Printers, Columbus *Also Called: Inskeep Brothers Inc (G-5462)*

Insource Tech Inc... 419 399-3600
12124 Road 111 Paulding (45879) *(G-12316)*

Inspirtec LLC... 614 571-7130
10203 Christian Rd Versailles (45380) *(G-14981)*

Inspyre Health Systems LLC.. 440 412-7916
1004 Commerce Dr Grafton (44044) *(G-8002)*

Insta Plak Inc (PA)... 419 537-1555
5025 Dorr St Toledo (43615) *(G-14334)*

Insta-Gro Manufacturing Inc.. 419 845-3046
8217 Linn Hipsher Rd Caledonia (43314) *(G-1916)*

Insta-Plak, Toledo *Also Called: Insta Plak Inc (G-14334)*

Instant Graphications Inc.. 330 819-5267
1025 Bloomfield Ave Akron (44302) *(G-191)*

Instant Replay Ltd... 937 592-0534
334 E Columbus Ave Bellefontaine (43311) *(G-1214)*

Instant Surface Solutions Inc.. 513 266-1667
3572 Calumet Dr Cincinnati (45245) *(G-2566)*

Instantwhip Connecticut Inc (PA)...................................... 614 488-2536
2200 Cardigan Ave Columbus (43215) *(G-5463)*

Instantwhip Foods Inc (PA).. 614 488-2536
2200 Cardigan Ave Columbus (43215) *(G-5464)*

Instantwhip of Pennsylvania, Columbus *Also Called: Instantwhip Products Co PA (G-5465)*

Instantwhip Products Co PA (HQ)...................................... 614 488-2536
2200 Cardigan Ave Columbus (43215) *(G-5465)*

Instantwhip-Buffalo Inc (HQ)... 614 488-2536
2200 Cardigan Ave Columbus (43215) *(G-5466)*

Instantwhip-Chicago Inc (PA)... 614 488-2536
2200 Cardigan Ave Columbus (43215) *(G-5467)*

Instantwhip-Columbus Inc (HQ)... 614 871-9447
3855 Marlane Dr Grove City (43123) *(G-8098)*

Instantwhip-Dayton Inc (PA)... 937 235-5930
5820 Executive Blvd Dayton (45424) *(G-6384)*

Instantwhip-Dayton Inc... 937 435-4371
967 Senate Dr Dayton (45459) *(G-6385)*

Instantwhip-Syracuse Inc (PA)... 614 488-2536
2200 Cardigan Ave Columbus (43215) *(G-5468)*

Instrmntation Ctrl Systems Inc.. 513 662-2600
11355 Sebring Dr Cincinnati (45240) *(G-3024)*

Instrumatics, Cleveland *Also Called: Cleveland Circuits Corp (G-3836)*

Instrumentors Inc.. 440 238-3430
22077 Drake Rd Strongsville (44149) *(G-13846)*

Insulpro Inc... 614 262-3768
4650 Indianola Ave Columbus (43214) *(G-5469)*

Integra, Willoughby *Also Called: Integra Enclosures Inc (G-15932)*

Integra Enclosures Inc (PA).. 440 269-4966
7750 Pyler Blvd Willoughby (44094) *(G-15932)*

Integra Enclosures Limited.. 440 269-4966
8989 Tyler Blvd Mentor (44060) *(G-10474)*

Integral Design Inc.. 216 524-0555
7670 Hub Pkwy Cleveland (44125) *(G-4230)*

Integrated Chem Concepts Inc.. 440 838-5666
6650 W Snowville Rd Ste F Brecksville (44141) *(G-1622)*

Integrated Development & Mfg (PA).................................. 440 247-5100
510 Washington St Chagrin Falls (44022) *(G-2380)*

Integrated Development & Mfg.. 440 543-2423
8401 Washington St Chagrin Falls (44023) *(G-2403)*

ALPHABETIC SECTION

Integrated Power Services LLC.. 216 433-7808
5325 W 130th St Cleveland (44130) *(G-4231)*

Integrated Power Services LLC.. 513 863-8816
2175a Schlichter Dr Hamilton (45015) *(G-8221)*

Integrated Resources Inc... 419 885-7122
7901 Sylvania Ave Sylvania (43560) *(G-14002)*

Integris Composites Inc.. 740 928-0326
1051 O Neill Dr Hebron (43025) *(G-8345)*

Integrity Group Consulting Inc.. 614 759-9148
6432 E Main St Ste 201 Reynoldsburg (43068) *(G-12767)*

Integrity Industrial Equipment... 937 335-5658
18 E Water St Troy (45373) *(G-14587)*

Integrity Manufacturing Corp.. 937 233-6792
3723 Inpark Dr Dayton (45414) *(G-6386)*

Integrity Parking LLC... 440 543-4123
400 Aurora Commons Cir Unit 438 Aurora (44202) *(G-720)*

Intek Inc... 614 895-0301
751 Intek Way Westerville (43082) *(G-15660)*

Intel Interpeace... 330 922-4450
1342 Easton Dr Akron (44310) *(G-192)*

Intelacomm Inc... 888 610-9250
12375 Kinsman Rd Newbury (44065) *(G-11627)*

Intelitool Mfg Svcs Inc... 440 953-1071
36335 Reading Ave Ste 4 Willoughby (44094) *(G-15933)*

Intelligent Signal Tech Intl.. 614 530-4784
6318 Dustywind Ln Loveland (45140) *(G-9487)*

Intelligrated Inc (HQ).. 866 936-7300
7901 Innovation Way Mason (45040) *(G-10007)*

Intelligrated Inc... 513 874-0788
10045 International Blvd West Chester (45246) *(G-15565)*

Intelligrated Headquarters LLC... 866 936-7300
7901 Innovation Way Mason (45040) *(G-10008)*

Intelligrated Products LLC.. 740 490-0300
475 E High St London (43140) *(G-9389)*

Intelligrated Sub Holdings Inc.. 513 701-7300
7901 Innovation Way Mason (45040) *(G-10009)*

Intelligrated Systems Inc (HQ)... 866 936-7300
7901 Innovation Way Mason (45040) *(G-10010)*

Intelligrated Systems Inc.. 513 881-5136
4436 Muhlhauser Rd Ste 300 West Chester (45011) *(G-15448)*

Intelligrated Systems LLC... 513 701-7300
7901 Innovation Way Mason (45040) *(G-10011)*

Intelligrated Systems Ohio LLC (DH)....................................... 513 701-7300
7901 Innovation Way Mason (45040) *(G-10012)*

Intelligrated Systems Ohio LLC.. 513 682-6600
10045 International Blvd West Chester (45246) *(G-15566)*

Intellinetics Inc (PA)... 614 388-8908
2190 Dividend Dr Columbus (43228) *(G-5470)*

Intellitarget Marketing Svcs, Coshocton Also Called: ITM Marketing Inc *(G-5981)*

Intelliworks Ht LLC... 419 660-9050
61 Saint Marys St Norwalk (44857) *(G-11975)*

Inter American Products Inc (HQ)... 800 645-2233
1240 State Ave Cincinnati (45204) *(G-3025)*

Interactive Engineering Corp.. 330 239-6888
884 Medina Rd Medina (44256) *(G-10337)*

Interactive Products Corp... 513 313-3397
5346 Roden Park Dr Monroe (45050) *(G-11111)*

Interarms Manufacturing Ltd... 440 201-9850
7400 Northfield Rd Bedford (44146) *(G-1128)*

Interbake Foods LLC (HQ)... 614 294-4931
1740 Joyce Ave Columbus (43219) *(G-5471)*

Interco Division 10 Ohio Inc... 614 875-2959
3600 Brookham Dr Ste D Grove City (43123) *(G-8099)*

Intercontinental Chemical Corp (PA)....................................... 513 541-7100
4660 Spring Grove Ave Cincinnati (45232) *(G-3026)*

Interface Logic Systems Inc... 614 236-8388
1020 Taylor Station Rd Ste F Columbus (43230) *(G-5472)*

Interior Dnnage Spcialites Inc.. 614 291-0900
470 E Starr Ave Columbus (43201) *(G-5473)*

Interior Graphic Systems LLC.. 330 244-0100
4550 Aultman Rd Canton (44720) *(G-2132)*

Interior Products Co Inc... 216 641-1919
3615 Superior Ave E Ste 3104f Cleveland (44114) *(G-4232)*

Interlake Stamping Ohio Inc.. 440 942-0800
4732 E 355th St Willoughby (44094) *(G-15934)*

Interlube Corporation... 513 531-1777
4646 Baker St Cincinnati (45212) *(G-3027)*

International Automotive Compo... 330 279-6557
8281 County Road 245 Holmesville (44633) *(G-8549)*

International Bellows.. 937 294-6261
2 Ferrari Ct Englewood (45315) *(G-7234)*

International Brand Services.. 513 376-8209
3397 Erie Ave Apt 215 Cincinnati (45208) *(G-3028)*

International Bus Mchs Corp... 513 826-1001
1 Procter And Gamble Plz Cincinnati (45202) *(G-3029)*

International Confections Company LLC................................. 800 288-8002
1855 E 17th Ave Columbus (43219) *(G-5474)*

International Hydraulics Inc... 440 951-7186
7700 Saint Clair Ave Mentor (44060) *(G-10475)*

International Jump Rope Union... 937 409-1006
1103 Lakemont Dr Springboro (45066) *(G-13505)*

International Leisure Activities Inc
107 Tremont City Rd Springfield (45502) *(G-13582)*

International Machining Inc... 330 225-1963
2885 Nationwide Pkwy Brunswick (44212) *(G-1771)*

International Metal Hose Co.. 419 483-7690
520 Goodrich Rd Bellevue (44811) *(G-1228)*

International Metal Supply LLC.. 330 764-1004
3995 Medina Rd Ste 200 Medina (44256) *(G-10338)*

International Noodle Company.. 614 888-0665
341 Enterprise Dr Lewis Center (43035) *(G-9166)*

International Paper, Eaton Also Called: International Paper Company *(G-7062)*
International Paper, Kenton Also Called: Graphic Packaging Intl LLC *(G-8884)*
International Paper, Loveland Also Called: International Paper Company *(G-9488)*
International Paper, Marion Also Called: International Paper Company *(G-9857)*
International Paper, Marysville Also Called: International Paper Company *(G-9922)*
International Paper, Middletown Also Called: International Paper Company *(G-10831)*
International Paper, Streetsboro Also Called: International Paper Company *(G-13775)*

International Paper Company... 740 369-7691
875 Pittsburgh Dr Delaware (43015) *(G-6732)*

International Paper Company... 937 456-4131
900 Us Route 35 Eaton (45320) *(G-7062)*

International Paper Company... 513 248-6319
6283 Tri Ridge Blvd Loveland (45140) *(G-9488)*

International Paper Company... 740 383-4061
1600 Cascade Dr Marion (43302) *(G-9857)*

International Paper Company... 937 578-7718
13307 Industrial Pkwy Marysville (43040) *(G-9922)*

International Paper Company... 800 473-0830
912 Nelbar St Middletown (45042) *(G-10831)*

International Paper Company... 740 397-5215
8800 Granville Rd Mount Vernon (43050) *(G-11273)*

International Paper Company... 330 626-7300
700 Mondial Pkwy Streetsboro (44241) *(G-13775)*

International Paper Company... 330 264-1322
689 Palmer St Wooster (44691) *(G-16133)*

International Sources Inc... 440 735-9890
380 Golden Oak Pkwy Bedford (44146) *(G-1129)*

Interntnal Auto Cmpnnts Group.. 419 335-1000
555 W Linfoot St Wauseon (43567) *(G-15264)*

Interntnal Auto Cmpnnts Group.. 419 433-5653
555 W Linfoot St Wauseon (43567) *(G-15265)*

Interntnal Cnvrter Cldwell Inc.. 740 732-5665
17153 Industrial Hwy Caldwell (43724) *(G-1909)*

Interntnal Pckg Pallets Crates, Sidney Also Called: Wappoo Wood Products Inc *(G-13294)*

Interntnal Pdts Srcing Group I.. 614 334-1500
2701 Charter St Ste A Columbus (43228) *(G-5475)*

Interntnal Tchncal Catings Inc... 800 567-6592
845 E Markison Ave Columbus (43207) *(G-5476)*

Interntnal Tchncal Plymr Syste.. 330 505-1218
852 Ann Ave Niles (44446) *(G-11672)*

Interpak Inc... 440 974-8999
7278 Justin Way Mentor (44060) *(G-10476)*

(PA)=Parent Co (HQ)=Headquarters (DH)=Div Headquarters

Interscope Manufacturing Inc 513 423-8866
  2901 Carmody Blvd Middletown (45042) *(G-10832)*

Interstate Contractors LLC 513 372-5393
  762 Reading Rd # G Mason (45040) *(G-10013)*

Interstate Diesel Service Inc (PA) 216 881-0015
  5300 Lakeside Ave E Cleveland (44114) *(G-4233)*

Interstate Gas Supply, Dublin *Also Called: Interstate Gas Supply LLC (G-6900)*

Interstate Gas Supply LLC (PA) 877 995-4447
  6100 Emerald Pkwy Dublin (43016) *(G-6900)*

Interstate Pump Company Inc (PA) 330 222-1006
  33370 Winona Rd Salem (44460) *(G-13005)*

Interstate Sign Products Inc 419 683-1962
  432 E Main St Crestline (44827) *(G-6034)*

Interstate Tool Corporation 216 671-1077
  4538 W 130th St Cleveland (44135) *(G-4234)*

Interstate Truckway Inc 614 771-1220
  5440 Renner Rd Columbus (43228) *(G-5477)*

Intertape Polymer Corp 704 279-3011
  1800 E Pleasant St Springfield (45505) *(G-13583)*

Intertec Corporation (PA) 419 537-9711
  3400 Exec Pkwy Toledo (43606) *(G-14335)*

Intertek LLC 440 323-3325
  6805 W River Rd S Elyria (44035) *(G-7160)*

Interweave Press LLC 513 531-2690
  10151 Carver Rd Ste 200 Blue Ash (45242) *(G-1410)*

Inteva Products LLC 937 280-8500
  707 Crossroads Ct Vandalia (45377) *(G-14945)*

Intier Sting Systems-Lordstown, Sheffield Village *Also Called: Magna International Amer Inc (G-13185)*

Intigral Inc (PA) 440 439-0980
  7850 Northfield Rd Walton Hills (44146) *(G-15099)*

Intigral Inc 440 439-0980
  45 Karago Ave Youngstown (44512) *(G-16380)*

Intrepid Co 440 355-6089
  15815 Diagonal Rd Lagrange (44050) *(G-8949)*

Intrism Inc 614 733-9304
  6969 Worthington Galena Rd Ste J Worthington (43085) *(G-16199)*

Invacare, Elyria *Also Called: Invacare Corporation (G-7164)*

Invacare Canadian Holdings Inc 440 329-6000
  1 Invacare Way Elyria (44035) *(G-7161)*

Invacare Canadian Holdings LLC 440 329-6000
  1 Invacare Way Elyria (44035) *(G-7162)*

Invacare Continuing Care Inc 800 668-2337
  1 Invacare Way Elyria (44035) *(G-7163)*

Invacare Corporation (PA) 440 329-6000
  1 Invacare Way Elyria (44035) *(G-7164)*

Invacare Corporation 440 329-6000
  1200 Taylor St Elyria (44035) *(G-7165)*

Invacare Corporation 800 333-6900
  1320 Taylor St Elyria (44035) *(G-7166)*

Invacare Corporation 440 329-6000
  38683 Taylor Pkwy North Ridgeville (44035) *(G-11846)*

Invacare Hcs LLC 330 634-9925
  1 Invacare Way Elyria (44035) *(G-7167)*

Invacare Hme, North Ridgeville *Also Called: Invacare Corporation (G-11846)*

Invacare Holdings LLC 440 329-6000
  1 Invacare Way Elyria (44035) *(G-7168)*

Invacare Holdings Corporation 440 329-6000
  1 Invacare Way Elyria (44035) *(G-7169)*

Invacare It & Financial Svcs, Elyria *Also Called: Invacare Corporation (G-7166)*

Inventive Extrusions Corp 330 874-3000
  10882 Fort Laurens Rd Nw Bolivar (44612) *(G-1528)*

Inventory Controlled Mdsg, Twinsburg *Also Called: ICM Distributing Company Inc (G-14675)*

Inventus Power (ohio) Inc (DH) 614 351-2191
  5115 Parkcenter Ave Ste 275 Dublin (43017) *(G-6901)*

Investors United Inc (PA) 419 473-8942
  4215 Monroe St Toledo (43606) *(G-14336)*

Invirsa Inc 614 344-1765
  1275 Kinnear Rd Ste 217 Columbus (43212) *(G-5478)*

Invue Security Products Inc 330 456-7776
  1510 4th St Se Canton (44707) *(G-2133)*

INX International Ink Co 707 693-2990
  350 Homan Rd Lebanon (45036) *(G-9089)*

INX INTERNATIONAL INK CO, Lebanon *Also Called: INX International Ink Co (G-9089)*

Ion Vacuum Ivac Tech Corp 216 662-5158
  18678 Cranwood Pkwy Cleveland (44128) *(G-4235)*

Ion Vacuum Technologies, Cleveland *Also Called: Ion Vacuum Ivac Tech Corp (G-4235)*

Ionbond LLC 216 831-0880
  24700 Highpoint Rd Cleveland (44122) *(G-4236)*

Ioppolo Concrete Corporation 440 439-6606
  10 Industry Dr Bedford (44146) *(G-1130)*

Iosil Energy Corporation
  5700 Green Pointe Dr N Ste A Groveport (43125) *(G-8147)*

Iot Diagnostics LLC 844 786-7631
  9361 Allen Rd West Chester (45069) *(G-15449)*

Iotech, Cleveland *Also Called: Measurement Computing Corp (G-4386)*

Iowa Quality Meats Ltd 515 225-6868
  805 E Kemper Rd Cincinnati (45246) *(G-3030)*

IPA Ltd 614 523-3974
  199 Mckenna Creek Dr Columbus (43230) *(G-5479)*

IPL Dayton Inc
  1765 W County Line Rd Urbana (43078) *(G-14838)*

Ips, Wadsworth *Also Called: Parker-Hannifin Corporation (G-15052)*

Ips Treatments Inc 419 241-5955
  3254 Hill Ave Toledo (43607) *(G-14337)*

Ipsco Tubulars Inc 330 448-6772
  6880 Parkway Dr Brookfield (44403) *(G-1671)*

IPSCO TUBULARS, INC., Brookfield *Also Called: Ipsco Tubulars Inc (G-1671)*

Ipsg, Columbus *Also Called: Interntnal Pdts Srcing Group I (G-5475)*

Iptc, Troy *Also Called: Ishmael Precision Tool Corp (G-14588)*

Ireportsource 888 294-9578
  7864 Camargo Rd Cincinnati (45243) *(G-3031)*

Irg Operating LLC 440 963-4008
  850 W River Rd Vermilion (44089) *(G-14972)*

Irok Inc 330 819-3612
  753 N Main St Akron (44310) *(G-193)*

Iron Bean Inc 518 641-9917
  25561 Fort Meigs Rd Ste E Perrysburg (43551) *(G-12393)*

Iron Gate Industries LLC 330 264-0626
  1435 S Honeytown Rd Wooster (44691) *(G-16134)*

Iron Horse Engineering, Parkman *Also Called: Montville Plastics & Rbr LLC (G-12284)*

Iron Works Inc 937 420-2100
  62 Elm St Ste A Fort Loramie (45845) *(G-7601)*

Ironfab LLC 614 443-3900
  1771 Progress Ave Columbus (43207) *(G-5480)*

Ironhawk Industrial, Euclid *Also Called: Ironhawk Industrial Dist LLC (G-7276)*

Ironhawk Industrial Dist LLC 216 502-3700
  1261 Babbitt Rd Ste B Euclid (44132) *(G-7276)*

Ironhead Fabg & Contg Inc 419 690-0000
  2245 Front St Toledo (43605) *(G-14338)*

Ironhead Marine Inc 419 690-0000
  2245 Front St Toledo (43605) *(G-14339)*

Ironics Inc 330 652-0583
  750 S Main St Niles (44446) *(G-11673)*

Ironunits LLC 216 694-5303
  200 Public Sq Ste 3300 Cleveland (44114) *(G-4237)*

Irr, Chillicothe *Also Called: Industrial Rlblity Spclsts Inc (G-2511)*

Irvine Wood Recovery Inc (PA) 513 831-0060
  110 Glendale Milford Rd Miamiville (45147) *(G-10711)*

Irving Materials Inc 513 769-3666
  2792 Glendale Milford Rd Cincinnati (45241) *(G-3032)*

Irving Materials Inc 513 844-8444
  600 Augspurger Rd Hamilton (45011) *(G-8222)*

Irwin Engraving & Printing Co 216 391-7300
  5318 Saint Clair Ave Ste 1 Cleveland (44103) *(G-4238)*

Isaac Foster Mack Co (PA) 419 625-5500
  314 W Market St Sandusky (44870) *(G-13067)*

Isaiah Industries Inc (PA) 937 773-9840
  8510 Industry Park Dr Piqua (45356) *(G-12527)*

Ishikawa Gasket America Inc 419 353-7300
  1745 Indian Wood Cir Ste 125 Maumee (43537) *(G-10208)*

Ishmael Precision Tool Corp 937 335-8070
55 Industry Ct Troy (45373) *(G-14588)*

Ishos Bros Fuel Ventures 419 913-5718
2446 W Alexis Rd Toledo (43613) *(G-14340)*

ISK Americas Incorporated (HQ) 440 357-4600
7474 Auburn Rd Concord Township (44077) *(G-5908)*

Island Aseptics LLC 740 685-2548
100 Hope Ave Byesville (43723) *(G-1898)*

Island Delights Inc 866 887-4100
240 W Greenwich Rd Seville (44273) *(G-13143)*

ISO Technologies Inc 740 928-0084
1870 James Pkwy Heath (43056) *(G-8322)*

ISO Technologies Inc (PA) 740 928-0084
200 Milliken Dr Hebron (43025) *(G-8346)*

Isochem Incorporated 614 775-9328
3 Highgrove New Albany (43054) *(G-11380)*

Isofoton North America Inc 419 591-4330
800 Independence Dr Napoleon (43545) *(G-11321)*

Isomet LLC 937 382-3867
2149 S Us Highway 68 Wilmington (45177) *(G-16055)*

Isotoner, West Chester *Also Called: Totes Isotoner Corporation (G-15598)*

Isp Chemicals LLC 614 876-3637
1979 Atlas St Columbus (43228) *(G-5481)*

Isp Lima LLC 419 998-8700
12220 S Metcalf St Lima (45804) *(G-9257)*

Isps, Toledo *Also Called: Industrial Screen Prcess Svc I (G-14330)*

Ist International, Loveland *Also Called: Intelligent Signal Tech Intl (G-9487)*

Italmatch Sc LLC 216 749-2605
1000 Belt Line Ave Cleveland (44109) *(G-4239)*

Itc Manufacturing, Columbus *Also Called: Interntnal Tchncal Catings Inc (G-5476)*

Item NA 216 271-7241
925 Glaser Pkwy Akron (44306) *(G-194)*

Iten Industries Inc (PA) 440 997-6134
4602 Benefit Ave Ashtabula (44004) *(G-642)*

Iten Industries Inc 440 997-6134
3500 N Ridge Rd W Ashtabula (44004) *(G-643)*

Itl LLC 216 831-3140
23925 Commerce Park Rd Beachwood (44122) *(G-992)*

Itl Corp (HQ) 216 831-3140
23925 Commerce Park Cleveland (44122) *(G-4240)*

ITM Marketing Inc 740 295-3575
331 Main St Coshocton (43812) *(G-5981)*

Itps, Niles *Also Called: Interntnal Tchncal Plymr Syste (G-11672)*

ITT Torque Systems Inc 216 524-8800
7550 Hub Pkwy Cleveland (44125) *(G-4241)*

ITW Evercoat, Blue Ash *Also Called: Illinois Tool Works Inc (G-1408)*

ITW Filtration Products, Bryan *Also Called: Illinois Tool Works Inc (G-1821)*

ITW Food Equipment Group LLC (HQ) 937 332-2396
701 S Ridge Ave Troy (45374) *(G-14589)*

ITW Hobart, Troy *Also Called: Illinois Tool Works Inc (G-14584)*

ITW Hobart Brothers, Troy *Also Called: Hobart Brothers LLC (G-14579)*

ITW Powertrain Components, Bryan *Also Called: Illinois Tool Works Inc (G-1822)*

IVEX Protective Packaging LLC (PA) 937 498-9298
2600 Campbell Rd Sidney (45365) *(G-13256)*

Ivi Mining Group Ltd 740 418-7745
72116 Grey Rd Vinton (45686) *(G-15011)*

Ivies Wholistic Dynamics 216 469-3103
2390 Cardinal Court Apt D Wooster (44691) *(G-16135)*

Ivostud LLC 440 925-4227
6430 Eastland Rd Ste C Brookpark (44142) *(G-1719)*

Ivy Ventures LLC 513 259-3307
39 Citadel Dr Apt 2 Fairfield (45014) *(G-7373)*

Iwata Bolt USA Inc 513 942-5050
102 Iwata Dr Fairfield (45014) *(G-7374)*

J & C Group Inc of Ohio 440 205-9658
6781 Hopkins Rd Mentor (44060) *(G-10477)*

J & C Industries Inc 216 362-8867
4808 W 130th St Cleveland (44135) *(G-4242)*

J & D Mining Inc 330 339-4935
3497 University Dr Ne New Philadelphia (44663) *(G-11506)*

J & D Steel Service Center LLC 330 759-7430
3030 Gale Dr Hubbard (44425) *(G-8565)*

J & D Wood Ltd 937 778-9663
401 S College St Piqua (45356) *(G-12528)*

J & E Publications LLC 614 457-7989
3307 Kirkham Rd Columbus (43221) *(G-5482)*

J & G Goecke Clothing LLC 419 692-9981
22877 Spieles Rd Delphos (45833) *(G-6766)*

J & H Manufacturing LLC 330 482-2636
1652 Columbiana Lisbon Rd Columbiana (44408) *(G-5042)*

J & H Mfg, Columbiana *Also Called: J & H Manufacturing LLC (G-5042)*

J & J Bechke Inc (PA) 440 238-1441
12931 Pearl Rd Strongsville (44136) *(G-13847)*

J & J Performance Inc 330 567-2455
410 E Wood St Shreve (44676) *(G-13211)*

J & J Performance Paintball, Shreve *Also Called: J & J Performance Inc (G-13211)*

J & J Tire & Alignment 330 424-5200
12649 State Route 45 Lisbon (44432) *(G-9316)*

J & J Tool & Die Inc 330 343-4721
203 W 4th St Dover (44622) *(G-6829)*

J & K Cabinetry Inc 513 860-3461
8800 Global Way # 200 West Chester (45069) *(G-15450)*

J & K Pallet Inc 937 526-5117
30 Subler Dr Versailles (45380) *(G-14982)*

J & K Powder Coating 330 540-6145
1336 Seaborn St Mineral Ridge (44440) *(G-11020)*

J & L Body Inc 216 661-2323
4848 Van Epps Rd Brooklyn Heights (44131) *(G-1693)*

J & L Management Corporation 440 205-1199
8634 Station St Mentor (44060) *(G-10478)*

J & L Specialty Steel Inc 330 875-6200
1500 W Main St Louisville (44641) *(G-9462)*

J & L Wood Products Inc (PA) 937 667-4064
155 Lightner Rd Tipp City (45371) *(G-14139)*

J & M Fabrications LLC 330 860-4346
3000 S 1st St Clinton (44216) *(G-4969)*

J & M Industries Inc 440 951-1985
7775 Division Dr Mentor (44060) *(G-10479)*

J & M Manufacturing Co Inc 419 375-2376
284 Railroad St Fort Recovery (45846) *(G-7620)*

J & M Precision Die Cast Inc, Elyria *Also Called: J&M Precision Die Casting LLC (G-7170)*

J & O Plastics Inc 330 927-3169
12475 Sheets Rd Rittman (44270) *(G-12823)*

J & P Products Inc 440 974-2830
8865 East Ave Mentor (44060) *(G-10480)*

J & R Pallet Ltd 740 226-1112
1100 Travis Rd Waverly (45690) *(G-15283)*

J & S Industrial Mch Pdts Inc 419 691-1380
123 Oakdale Ave Toledo (43605) *(G-14341)*

J & S Tool Corporation 216 676-8330
15330 Brookpark Rd Cleveland (44135) *(G-4243)*

J A B Welding Service Inc 740 453-5868
2820 S River Rd Zanesville (43701) *(G-16540)*

J A McMahon Incorporated 330 652-2588
6 E Park Ave Niles (44446) *(G-11674)*

J Aaron Weaver 440 474-9185
5759 Us Highway 6 Rome (44085) *(G-12848)*

J and J Sales, Delaware *Also Called: Aci Industries Converting Ltd (G-6700)*

J and N Incorporated 234 759-3741
80 Eastgate Dr North Lima (44452) *(G-11807)*

J B Manufacturing Inc 330 676-9744
4465 Crystal Pkwy Kent (44240) *(G-8820)*

J B Stamping Inc 216 631-0013
7413 Associate Ave Cleveland (44144) *(G-4244)*

J Best Inc 513 943-7000
4476 Glen Este Withamsville Rd Cincinnati (45245) *(G-2567)*

J C L S Enterprises LLC 740 472-0314
742 Lewisville Rd Woodsfield (43793) *(G-16088)*

J C Robinson Products, Cincinnati *Also Called: James C Robinson (G-3036)*

J C Whitlam Manufacturing Co 330 334-2524
200 W Walnut St Wadsworth (44281) *(G-15037)*

J D Drilling Company — ALPHABETIC SECTION

J D Drilling Company 740 949-2512
   107 S 3rd St Racine (45771) *(G-12693)*

J D Hydraulic Inc 419 686-5234
   Rte 25 Portage (43451) *(G-12633)*

J D Indoor Comfort Duct Clg, Sheffield Village *Also Called: J D Indoor Comfort Inc (G-13184)*

J D Indoor Comfort Inc 440 949-8758
   4040 Colorado Ave Sheffield Village (44054) *(G-13184)*

J E Doyle Company 330 564-0743
   5186 New Haven Cir Norton (44203) *(G-11945)*

J E Nicolozakes Co 740 310-1606
   62920 Georgetown Rd Cambridge (43725) *(G-1937)*

J G Pads, Akron *Also Called: Markethtch Inc D/B/A Mh Eye CA (G-236)*

J H Plastics Inc 419 937-2035
   4720 W Us Highway 224 Tiffin (44883) *(G-14088)*

J H Routh Packing Company 419 626-2251
   4413 W Bogart Rd Sandusky (44870) *(G-13068)*

J Henry Holland, Cleveland *Also Called: Mazzella Jhh Company Inc (G-4374)*

J Horst Manufacturing Co 330 828-2216
   279 E Main St Dalton (44618) *(G-6133)*

J I C, West Jefferson *Also Called: Jefferson Industries Corp (G-15610)*

J I T Pallets Inc 330 424-0355
   39196 Grant St Lisbon (44432) *(G-9317)*

J K Plastics Co 440 632-1482
   14135 Madison Rd Middlefield (44062) *(G-10759)*

J K Precast, Wshngtn Ct Hs *Also Called: James Kimmey (G-16235)*

J K Precast LLC 740 335-2188
   1001 Armbrust Ave Wshngtn Ct Hs (43160) *(G-16234)*

J L R Products Inc 330 832-9557
   1212 Oberlin Ave Sw Massillon (44647) *(G-10112)*

J L Wannemacher Sls Svc Inc 419 453-3445
   26992 Us 224 W Ottoville (45876) *(G-12200)*

J M C Rollmasters, Mentor *Also Called: Johnston Mfg Co Inc (G-10485)*

J M Machinery, New Franklin *Also Called: J McCaman Enterprises Inc (G-11437)*

J M Mold Inc 937 778-0077
   1707 Commerce Dr Piqua (45356) *(G-12529)*

J M Smucker Company (PA) 330 682-3000
   1 Strawberry Ln Orrville (44667) *(G-12129)*

J M Smucker Flight Dept 330 497-0073
   5430 Lauby Rd Bldg 7 North Canton (44720) *(G-11739)*

J McCaman Enterprises Inc 330 825-2401
   3032 Franks Rd New Franklin (44216) *(G-11437)*

J McCoy Lumber Co Ltd (PA) 937 587-3423
   6 N Main St Peebles (45660) *(G-12328)*

J P Industrial Products Inc 330 627-1377
   755 N Lisbon St Carrollton (44615) *(G-2310)*

J P Industrial Products Inc 330 424-3388
   State Rte 518 Lisbon (44432) *(G-9318)*

J P Industrial Products Inc (PA) 330 424-1110
   11988 State Route 45 Lisbon (44432) *(G-9319)*

J P Sand & Gravel Company 614 497-0083
   5911 Lockbourne Rd Lockbourne (43137) *(G-9337)*

J Pappas, East Liverpool *Also Called: Joseph G Pappas (G-6995)*

J R Custom Unlimited Inc 513 894-9800
   2620 Bobmeyer Rd Hamilton (45015) *(G-8223)*

J R M Chemical Inc 216 475-8488
   4881 Neo Pkwy Cleveland (44128) *(G-4245)*

J R Tool & Die, Wooster *Also Called: McCann Tool & Die Inc (G-16150)*

J Rettenmaier USA LP 937 652-2101
   1228 Muzzy Rd Urbana (43078) *(G-14839)*

J S C Publishing 614 424-6911
   958 King Ave Columbus (43212) *(G-5483)*

J Schrader Company 216 961-2890
   4603 Fenwick Ave Cleveland (44102) *(G-4246)*

J Solutions LLC 614 732-4857
   216 E Hinman Ave Columbus (43207) *(G-5484)*

J T M, Solon *Also Called: Jtm Products Inc (G-13372)*

J Tek Tool & Mold Inc 419 547-9476
   304 Elm St Clyde (43410) *(G-4973)*

J W Devers & Son Inc 937 854-3040
   5 N Broadway St Trotwood (45426) *(G-14544)*

J W Goss Company (PA) 330 395-0739
   410 South St Sw Warren (44483) *(G-15179)*

J W Harris Co Inc (HQ) 513 754-2000
   4501 Quality Pl Mason (45040) *(G-10014)*

J W Harwood Co (PA) 216 531-6230
   18001 Roseland Rd Cleveland (44112) *(G-4247)*

J W P, Urbana *Also Called: Trulil Inc (G-14849)*

J-C-R Tech Inc 937 783-2296
   936 Cherry St Blanchester (45107) *(G-1351)*

J-Lenco Inc 740 499-2260
   664 N High St Morral (43337) *(G-11221)*

J-Mak Industries, Columbus *Also Called: Panacea Products Corporation (G-5652)*

J-Well Service Inc 330 824-2718
   6345 Tod Ave Sw Warren (44481) *(G-15180)*

J&D Wood Enterprises, Piqua *Also Called: J & D Wood Ltd (G-12528)*

J&I Duct Fab Llc 937 473-2121
   7502 W State Route 41 Covington (45318) *(G-6026)*

J&J Precision Fabrication, Columbiana *Also Called: J&J Precision Fabricators Ltd (G-5043)*

J&J Precision Fabricators Ltd 330 482-4964
   1341 Heck Rd Columbiana (44408) *(G-5043)*

J&M Precision Die Casting LLC 440 365-7388
   1329 Taylor St Elyria (44035) *(G-7170)*

J3 Point-Of-Sale, Bucyrus *Also Called: Ganymede Technologies Corp (G-1860)*

JA Acquisition Corp 419 287-3223
   850 W Front St Pemberville (43450) *(G-12335)*

Jack Huffman 740 384-5178
   1210 Hiram West Rd Wellston (45692) *(G-15329)*

Jack Pine Studio LLC 740 332-2223
   21397 State Route 180 Laurelville (43135) *(G-9055)*

Jack Walker Printing Co 440 352-4222
   9517 Jackson St Mentor (44060) *(G-10481)*

Jack Walters & Sons Corp 937 653-8986
   5045 N Us Highway 68 Urbana (43078) *(G-14840)*

Jackson Monument Inc 740 286-1590
   14 Fairmount St Jackson (45640) *(G-8716)*

Jackson Tube Service Inc (PA) 937 773-8550
   8210 Industry Park Dr Piqua (45356) *(G-12530)*

Jackson Wells Services 419 886-2017
   1201 Mill Rd Bellville (44813) *(G-1243)*

Jacksonlea, Hamilton *Also Called: Jason Incorporated (G-8224)*

Jaco Manufacturing Company 440 234-4000
   90 Karl St Berea (44017) *(G-1284)*

Jaco Manufacturing Company (PA) 440 234-4000
   468 Geiger St Berea (44017) *(G-1285)*

Jaco Products, Middlefield *Also Called: D Martone Industries Inc (G-10746)*

Jaco Products LLC 614 219-1670
   3659 Parkway Ln Ste A Hilliard (43026) *(G-8415)*

Jacob & Levis Ltd 330 852-7600
   1689 State Route 39 Sugarcreek (44681) *(G-13926)*

Jacobi Carbons Inc 215 546-3900
   432 Mccormick Blvd Columbus (43213) *(G-5485)*

Jacobs, Cincinnati *Also Called: Jacobs Mechanical Co (G-3033)*

Jacobs Mechanical Co 513 681-6800
   4500 W Mitchell Ave Cincinnati (45232) *(G-3033)*

Jacodar Inc 330 832-9557
   1212 Oberlin Ave Sw Massillon (44647) *(G-10113)*

Jacodar Fsa LLC 330 454-1832
   2300 Allen Ave Se Canton (44707) *(G-2134)*

JAD Machine Company Inc 419 256-6332
   10620 County Road J Malinta (43535) *(G-9605)*

Jade Products Inc 440 352-1700
   9309 Mercantile Dr Mentor (44060) *(G-10482)*

Jade Tool Company 937 376-4740
   1280 Burnett Dr Xenia (45385) *(G-16265)*

Jae Nail 216 225-3743
   3657 E 53rd St Cleveland (44105) *(G-4248)*

Jae Tech Inc 330 698-2000
   32 Hunter St Apple Creek (44606) *(G-502)*

Jaf Usa LLC 919 935-2726
   2825 Hallie Ln Granville (43023) *(G-8019)*

Jaf USA LLC Veneers, Granville *Also Called: Jaf Usa LLC (G-8019)*

ALPHABETIC SECTION — Jed Industries Inc

Jafe Decorating Inc 937 547-1888
  1250 Martin St Greenville (45331) *(G-8047)*

Jails Correctional Products, Minster Also Called: Fabcor *(G-11052)*

Jain America Foods Inc (HQ) 614 850-9400
  1819 Walcutt Rd Ste I Columbus (43228) *(G-5486)*

Jain Americas, Columbus Also Called: Jain America Foods Inc *(G-5486)*

Jakes Woodshop 937 672-4964
  2734 E State Route 73 Waynesville (45068) *(G-15297)*

Jakmar Incorporated 513 631-4303
  3280 Hageman Ave Cincinnati (45241) *(G-3034)*

Jakprints Inc 877 246-3132
  3133 Chester Ave Cleveland (44114) *(G-4249)*

Jakprints Inc 216 246-3132
  34440 Vine St Willowick (44095) *(G-16032)*

Jalco Industries Inc 740 286-3808
  330 Athens St Jackson (45640) *(G-8717)*

Jamac Inc 419 625-9790
  422 Buchanan St Sandusky (44870) *(G-13069)*

Jamar Precision Grinding Co 330 220-0099
  2661 Center Rd Hinckley (44233) *(G-8475)*

Jamen Tool & Die Co (PA) 330 788-6521
  4450 Lake Park Rd Youngstown (44512) *(G-16381)*

Jamen Tool & Die Co 330 782-6731
  914 E Indianola Ave Youngstown (44502) *(G-16382)*

James Bunnell Inc 513 353-1100
  7000 Dry Fork Rd Cleves (45002) *(G-4955)*

James C Free Inc 513 793-0133
  9555 Main St Ste 1 Cincinnati (45242) *(G-3035)*

James C Free Inc (PA) 937 298-0171
  3100 Far Hills Ave Dayton (45429) *(G-6387)*

James C Robinson 513 969-7482
  442 Chestnut St Apt 1 Cincinnati (45203) *(G-3036)*

James Free Jewelers, Dayton Also Called: James C Free Inc *(G-6387)*

James Free Jewellers, Cincinnati Also Called: James C Free Inc *(G-3035)*

James K Green Enterprises Inc 614 878-6041
  1875 Lone Eagle St Columbus (43228) *(G-5487)*

James Kimmey 740 335-5746
  1000 Armbrust Ave Wshngtn Ct Hs (43160) *(G-16235)*

James L Deckebach LLC 513 321-3733
  4575 Eastern Ave Cincinnati (45226) *(G-3037)*

James O Emert Jr 330 650-6990
  7920 Princewood Dr Hudson (44236) *(G-8600)*

James R Smail Inc 330 264-7500
  2285 Eagle Pass Ste B Wooster (44691) *(G-16136)*

Jameson Industries LLC 330 533-5579
  7997 Hitchcock Rd Boardman (44512) *(G-1515)*

Jamestown Cont Cleveland Inc 216 831-3700
  4500 Renaissance Pkwy Cleveland (44128) *(G-4250)*

Jamestown Industries Inc 330 779-0670
  650 N Meridian Rd Ste 3 Youngstown (44509) *(G-16383)*

Jamesway Chick Mstr Incubator, Medina Also Called: Chick Master Incubator Company *(G-10308)*

Jamies Tire & Service 937 372-9254
  213 W Main St Xenia (45385) *(G-16266)*

Jan S Kleinman 440 473-9776
  136 Stonecreek Dr Mayfield Hts (44143) *(G-10257)*

Janorpot LLC 330 564-0232
  3175 Gilchrist Rd Mogadore (44260) *(G-11076)*

Janova LLC 614 638-6785
  7570 N Goodrich Sq New Albany (43054) *(G-11381)*

Janson Industries 330 455-7029
  1200 Garfield Ave Sw Canton (44706) *(G-2135)*

Japo Inc 614 263-2850
  3902 Indianola Ave Columbus (43214) *(G-5488)*

Jasa Asphalt Russell Standard, Akron Also Called: Russell Standard Corporation *(G-318)*

Jasmine Distributing Ltd 216 251-9420
  12117 Berea Rd Cleveland (44111) *(G-4251)*

Jason C Gibson 740 663-4520
  414 Bethel Rd Chillicothe (45601) *(G-2514)*

Jason Incorporated 513 860-3400
  3440 Symmes Rd Hamilton (45015) *(G-8224)*

Jasper Paula 740 559-3983
  2425 Ervin Ln Pennsville (43787) *(G-12348)*

Jasstek Inc 614 808-3600
  555 Metro Pl N Ste 100 Dublin (43017) *(G-6902)*

Jatiga Inc (PA) 859 817-7100
  9933 Alliance Rd Ste 1 Blue Ash (45242) *(G-1411)*

Jatrodiesel, Miamisburg Also Called: Jatrodiesel Inc *(G-10649)*

Jatrodiesel Inc
  845 N Main St Miamisburg (45342) *(G-10649)*

Javanation 419 584-1705
  108 S Main St Celina (45822) *(G-2338)*

Jax Wax Inc 614 476-6769
  3145 E 17th Ave Columbus (43219) *(G-5489)*

Jay Dee Service Corporation 330 425-1546
  1320 Highland Rd E Macedonia (44056) *(G-9558)*

Jay Industries Inc 419 747-4161
  1595 W Longview Ave Mansfield (44906) *(G-9671)*

Jay Mid-South LLC 256 439-6600
  150 Longview Ave E Mansfield (44903) *(G-9672)*

Jay Tees LLC 740 405-1579
  8941 Somerset Rd Thornville (43076) *(G-14066)*

Jay-Em Aerospace Corporation 330 923-0333
  75 Marc Dr Cuyahoga Falls (44223) *(G-6092)*

Jayna Inc (PA) 937 335-8922
  15 Marybill Dr S Troy (45373) *(G-14590)*

Jaytee Division, Mentor Also Called: Arem Co *(G-10423)*

JB Entrprses Prts Dtailing LLC 440 309-4984
  860 Taylor St Elyria (44035) *(G-7171)*

JB Industries Ltd (PA) 330 856-4587
  160 Clifton Dr Ne Ste 4 Warren (44484) *(G-15181)*

JB Machining Concepts LLC 419 523-0096
  995 Sugar Mill Dr Ottawa (45875) *(G-12182)*

JB Pavers and Hardscapes LLC 937 454-1145
  812 E National Rd Vandalia (45377) *(G-14946)*

JB Polymers Inc 216 941-7041
  55 S Main St Ste 204 Oberlin (44074) *(G-12053)*

Jbar, Cleveland Also Called: Jbar A/C Inc *(G-4252)*

Jbar A/C Inc 216 447-4294
  15501 Chatfield Ave Cleveland (44111) *(G-4252)*

Jbc Technologies Inc (PA) 440 327-4522
  7887 Bliss Pkwy North Ridgeville (44039) *(G-11847)*

Jbj Technologies Inc 216 469-7297
  185 E 280th St Euclid (44132) *(G-7277)*

Jbk Manufacturing, Dayton Also Called: Premier Aerospace Group LLC *(G-6518)*

Jbm Packaging, Lebanon Also Called: Jbm Packaging Company *(G-9090)*

Jbm Packaging Company 513 933-8333
  2850 Henkle Dr Lebanon (45036) *(G-9090)*

Jbnovember LLC 513 272-7000
  3950 Virginia Ave Cincinnati (45227) *(G-3038)*

Jbs Industries Ltd 513 314-5599
  1001 Atlantic Ave Apt 783 Columbus (43229) *(G-5490)*

Jbt Foodtech, Sandusky Also Called: John Bean Technologies Corp *(G-13070)*

JC Carter LLC (DH) 440 569-1818
  26451 Curtiss Wright Pkwy Ste 106 Richmond Heights (44143) *(G-12808)*

JC Carter Nozzles, Richmond Heights Also Called: JC Carter LLC *(G-12808)*

JC Electric Llc 330 760-2915
  9717 State Route 88 Garrettsville (44231) *(G-7917)*

JCB Arrowhead Products Inc 440 546-4288
  8223 Brecksville Rd Ste 100 Brecksville (44141) *(G-1623)*

Jci Jones Chemicals Inc 330 825-2531
  2500 Vanderhoof Rd New Franklin (44203) *(G-11438)*

JD Power Systems LLC 614 317-9394
  3979 Parkway Ln Hilliard (43026) *(G-8416)*

Jda Software Group Inc 480 308-3000
  308 N Cleveland Massillon Rd Akron (44333) *(G-195)*

JDA SOFTWARE GROUP, INC., Akron Also Called: Jda Software Group Inc *(G-195)*

Jdh Holdings Inc 330 963-4400
  8220 Bavaria Dr E Macedonia (44056) *(G-9559)*

JE Grote Company Inc (PA) 614 868-8414
  1160 Gahanna Pkwy Columbus (43230) *(G-5491)*

Jed Industries Inc 440 639-9973
  320 River St Grand River (44045) *(G-8011)*

Jeff Bonham Electric Inc 937 233-7662
  3647 Wright Way Rd Dayton (45424) *(G-6388)*
Jeff Lori Jed Holdings Inc 513 423-0319
  1500 S University Blvd Middletown (45044) *(G-10833)*
Jeffco Sheltered Workshop 740 264-4608
  256 John Scott Hwy Steubenville (43952) *(G-13669)*
Jefferson Industries Corp (HQ) 614 879-5300
  6670 State Route 29 West Jefferson (43162) *(G-15610)*
Jefferson Logging Company LLC 304 634-9203
  148 Wells Run Rd Crown City (45623) *(G-6053)*
Jefferson Manufacturing Div, Valley City *Also Called: Shl Liquidation Jefferson Inc (G-14894)*
Jefferson Smurfit Corporation 440 248-4370
  6385 Cochran Rd Solon (44139) *(G-13369)*
Jeffrey D Layton 513 706-4352
  6788 High Meadows Dr Cincinnati (45230) *(G-3039)*
Jeg Associates, Westerville *Also Called: Jeg Associates Inc (G-15711)*
Jeg Associates Inc 614 882-1295
  509 S Otterbein Ave Ste 7 Westerville (43081) *(G-15711)*
Jeld-Wen Inc 740 964-1431
  91 Heritage Dr Etna (43062) *(G-7255)*
Jeld-Wen Inc 740 397-1144
  1201 Newark Rd Mount Vernon (43050) *(G-11274)*
Jeld-Wen Inc 740 397-3403
  335 Commerce Dr Mount Vernon (43050) *(G-11275)*
Jeld-Wen Millwork Masters, Etna *Also Called: Jeld-Wen Inc (G-7255)*
Jeld-Wen Windows, Mount Vernon *Also Called: Jeld-Wen Inc (G-11274)*
Jen-Coat Inc (DH) 513 671-1777
  12025 Tricon Rd Cincinnati (45246) *(G-3040)*
Jena Tool Inc 937 296-1122
  5219 Springboro Pike Moraine (45439) *(G-11187)*
Jenis Splendid Ice Creams LLC (PA) 614 488-3224
  401 N Front St Ste 300 Columbus (43215) *(G-5492)*
Jennmar McSweeney LLC 740 377-3354
  235 Commerce Dr South Point (45680) *(G-13467)*
Jentgen Steel Services LLC 614 268-6340
  611 E Weber Rd Ste 201 Columbus (43211) *(G-5493)*
Jenzabar Inc 513 563-4542
  10300 Alliance Rd Ste 200 Blue Ash (45242) *(G-1412)*
Jergens Inc (PA) 216 486-5540
  15700 S Waterloo Rd Cleveland (44110) *(G-4253)*
Jerguson, Strongsville *Also Called: Clark-Reliance LLC (G-13821)*
Jerico Industries, Wadsworth *Also Called: Jerico Plastic Industries Inc (G-15038)*
Jerico Plastic Industries Inc (PA) 330 868-4600
  7970 Boneta Rd Wadsworth (44281) *(G-15038)*
Jerl Machine Inc 419 873-0270
  11140 Avenue Rd Perrysburg (43551) *(G-12394)*
Jerry Harolds Doors Unlimited 740 635-4949
  415 Hall St Bridgeport (43912) *(G-1647)*
Jerry Offenberger Cnstr LLC 740 374-2578
  575 Bramblewood Heights Rd Marietta (45750) *(G-9803)*
Jerry Tools Inc 513 242-3211
  6200 Vine St Cincinnati (45216) *(G-3041)*
Jerry's Welding Supply ICN, Hillsboro *Also Called: Jerrys Welding Supply Inc (G-8460)*
Jerrys Welding Supply Inc 937 364-1500
  5367 Us Highway 50 Hillsboro (45133) *(G-8460)*
JES Foods Inc (PA) 216 883-8987
  865 W Liberty St Ste 200 Medina (44256) *(G-10339)*
JES Foods/Celina Inc 419 586-7446
  1800 Industrial Dr Celina (45822) *(G-2339)*
Jet Container Company 614 444-2133
  1033 Brentnell Ave Ste 100 Columbus (43219) *(G-5494)*
Jet Di Inc 330 607-7913
  1736 W 130th St Ste 200 Brunswick (44212) *(G-1772)*
Jet Dock Systems Inc 216 750-2264
  9601 Corporate Cir Cleveland (44125) *(G-4254)*
Jet Fuel Strategies LLC 440 323-4220
  44050 Russia Rd Elyria (44035) *(G-7172)*
Jet Fuel Tech Inc 614 463-1986
  100 E Broad St Fl 16 Columbus (43215) *(G-5495)*
Jet Inc 440 461-2000
  750 Alpha Dr Cleveland (44143) *(G-4255)*

Jet Machine, Cincinnati *Also Called: Wulco Inc (G-3530)*
Jet Machine & Manufacturing, Cincinnati *Also Called: Wulco Inc (G-3529)*
Jet Products Incorporated 937 866-7969
  535 E Dixie Dr Dayton (45449) *(G-6389)*
Jet Rubber Company 330 325-1821
  4457 Tallmadge Rd Rootstown (44272) *(G-12853)*
Jet Stream International Inc 330 505-9988
  644 Myron St Hubbard (44425) *(G-8566)*
Jetcoat, Columbus *Also Called: Jetcoat LLC (G-5496)*
Jetcoat LLC 800 394-0047
  472 Brehl Ave Columbus (43223) *(G-5496)*
Jewelry Art, Hudson *Also Called: Handcrafted Jewelry Inc (G-8595)*
Jewett Supply 419 738-9882
  607 N Water St Wapakoneta (45895) *(G-15119)*
Jewish Federation of Cinti 513 487-4900
  4380 Malsbary Road Ste 150 Blue Ash (45242) *(G-1413)*
Jewish Synagogue, Akron *Also Called: Temple Israel (G-351)*
Jfab LLC 740 572-0227
  14514 State Route 729 Jeffersonville (43128) *(G-8764)*
Jfdb Ltd 513 870-0601
  10036 Springfield Pike Cincinnati (45215) *(G-3042)*
Jh Industries Inc 330 963-4106
  1981 E Aurora Rd Twinsburg (44087) *(G-14677)*
Jh Instruments, Columbus *Also Called: Fcx Performance Inc (G-5373)*
Jh Woodworking LLC 330 276-7600
  11259 Township Road 71 Killbuck (44637) *(G-8920)*
Jilco, Akron *Also Called: Jilco Precision Mold Mch Inc (G-196)*
Jilco Precision Mold Mch Inc 330 633-9645
  1245 Devalera St Akron (44310) *(G-196)*
Jim Nier Construction Inc (PA) 740 289-3925
  340 Bailey Chapel Rd Piketon (45661) *(G-12477)*
Jis Distribution LLC (HQ) 216 706-6552
  15700 S Waterloo Rd Cleveland (44110) *(G-4256)*
Jit Company Ohio 614 529-8010
  5908 Heritage Lakes Dr Hilliard (43026) *(G-8417)*
Jit Milrob, Aurora *Also Called: Lynk Packaging Inc (G-723)*
Jj Seville LLC 330 769-2071
  22 Milton St Seville (44273) *(G-13144)*
Jj Sleeves Inc 440 205-1055
  6850 Patterson Dr Mentor (44060) *(G-10483)*
JJ&pl Services-Consulting LLC 330 923-5783
  1474 Main St Cuyahoga Falls (44221) *(G-6093)*
Jk Digital Publishing LLC 937 299-0185
  20 Heatherwoode Cir Springboro (45066) *(G-13506)*
Jk-Co LLC 419 422-5240
  16960 E State Route 12 Findlay (45840) *(G-7526)*
Jkrg Construction Services, West Chester *Also Called: Clarity Retail Services LLC (G-15395)*
Jlc Industrial LLC 513 236-0462
  3048 Bachelier Rd Amelia (45102) *(G-457)*
Jlg Industries Inc 330 684-0132
  2927 E Paradise Street Ext Orrville (44667) *(G-12130)*
Jlg Industries Inc 330 684-0200
  600 E Chestnut St Orrville (44667) *(G-12131)*
Jls Funeral Home 614 625-1220
  2322 Randy Ct Columbus (43232) *(G-5497)*
JM Hamilton Group Inc 419 229-4010
  1700 Elida Rd Lima (45805) *(G-9258)*
JM Logging Inc 740 441-0941
  1624 Graham School Rd Gallipolis (45631) *(G-7895)*
JM Smucker LLC (HQ) 330 682-3000
  1 Strawberry Ln Orrville (44667) *(G-12132)*
Jmac Inc (PA) 614 436-2418
  200 W Nationwide Blvd Unit 1 Columbus (43215) *(G-5498)*
JMB Energy Inc 330 505-9610
  3729 Union St Mineral Ridge (44440) *(G-11021)*
Jml Holdings Inc 419 866-7500
  6210 Merger Dr Holland (43528) *(G-8515)*
Jmp Industries 216 749-6030
  2906 Maplecrest Ave Cleveland (44134) *(G-4257)*
JMS Composites, Springfield *Also Called: JMS Industries Inc (G-13584)*

JMS Industries Inc 937 325-3502
 3240 E National Rd Springfield (45505) *(G-13584)*

JMw Welding and Mfg Inc 330 484-2428
 512 45th St Sw Canton (44706) *(G-2136)*

Jnc,, Piketon *Also Called: Jim Nier Construction Inc (G-12477)*

Jnp Group LLC 800 735-9645
 449 Freedlander Rd Wooster (44691) *(G-16137)*

Jobap Assembly Inc 440 632-5393
 16090 Industrial Pkwy Unit 9 Middlefield (44062) *(G-10760)*

Jobskin Div of Torbot Group 419 724-1475
 3461 Curtice Rd Northwood (43619) *(G-11921)*

Jobskin Division, Northwood *Also Called: Torbot Group Inc (G-11930)*

Joe Fuller Inc 740 886-6182
 1132 Tinker Ln Proctorville (45669) *(G-12686)*

Joe Gonda Company Incorporated 440 458-6000
 50000 Gondawood Dr Grafton (44044) *(G-8003)*

Joe Rees Welding 937 652-4067
 326 W Twain Ave Urbana (43078) *(G-14841)*

Joe The Printer Guy LLC 216 651-3880
 1590 Parkwood Rd Lakewood (44107) *(G-8977)*

Joey Elliott Logging LLC 740 626-0061
 8040 Upper Twin Rd South Salem (45681) *(G-13475)*

Johannings Inc 330 875-1706
 3244 South Nickel Plate Street Louisville (44641) *(G-9463)*

John Adams 614 564-9307
 3375 En Joie Dr Columbus (43228) *(G-5499)*

John Bean Technologies Corp 419 626-0304
 1622 First St Sandusky (44870) *(G-13070)*

John C Meier Grape Juice Co, Cincinnati *Also Called: Meiers Wine Cellars Inc (G-3146)*

John Christ Winery Inc 440 933-9672
 32421 Walker Rd Avon Lake (44012) *(G-813)*

John D Oil and Gas Company 440 255-6325
 7001 Center St Mentor (44060) *(G-10484)*

John Deere Authorized Dealer, Brunswick *Also Called: Murphy Tractor & Eqp Co Inc (G-1774)*

John Deere Authorized Dealer, Canton *Also Called: Murphy Tractor & Eqp Co Inc (G-2169)*

John Deere Authorized Dealer, Canton *Also Called: Western Branch Diesel LLC (G-2267)*

John Deere Authorized Dealer, Columbus *Also Called: Murphy Tractor & Eqp Co Inc (G-5585)*

John Deere Authorized Dealer, Hilliard *Also Called: JD Power Systems LLC (G-8416)*

John Deere Authorized Dealer, Lima *Also Called: Murphy Tractor & Eqp Co Inc (G-9272)*

John Deere Authorized Dealer, Mentor *Also Called: Great Lakes Power Products Inc (G-10465)*

John Deere Authorized Dealer, Perry *Also Called: Great Lakes Power Service Co (G-12351)*

John Deere Authorized Dealer, Urbana *Also Called: Koenig Equipment Inc (G-14842)*

John Deere Authorized Dealer, Vandalia *Also Called: Murphy Tractor & Eqp Co Inc (G-14954)*

John Deere Authorized Dealer, Wooster *Also Called: Shearer Farm Inc (G-16171)*

John Frieda Prof Hair Care Inc (DH) 800 521-3189
 2535 Spring Grove Ave Cincinnati (45214) *(G-3043)*

John H Hosking Co 513 422-9425
 4665 Emerald Way Middletown (45044) *(G-10834)*

John Krizay Inc 330 332-5607
 1777 Pennsylvania Ave Salem (44460) *(G-13006)*

John Krusinski 216 441-0100
 6300 Heisley Ave Cleveland (44105) *(G-4258)*

John L Garber Materials Corp 419 884-1567
 2745 Gass Rd Mansfield (44904) *(G-9673)*

John Purdum 513 897-9686
 100 S Main St Waynesville (45068) *(G-15298)*

John R Jurgensen Co (PA) 513 771-0820
 11641 Mosteller Rd Cincinnati (45241) *(G-3044)*

John Stehlin & Sons Co 513 385-6164
 10134 Colerain Ave Cincinnati (45251) *(G-3045)*

John Zidian Company 330 965-8455
 382 Rosemont Rd North Jackson (44451) *(G-11785)*

John Zidian Company (PA) 330 743-6050
 574 Mcclurg Rd Youngstown (44512) *(G-16384)*

Johndow Industries Inc 330 753-6895
 151 Snyder Ave Barberton (44203) *(G-875)*

Johnny Hulsman Signs 513 638-9788
 2955 Spring Grove Ave Cincinnati (45225) *(G-3046)*

Johnny Johnson Sports, Ontario *Also Called: Unisport Inc (G-12096)*

Johns Manville Corporation 419 782-0180
 1410 Columbus Ave Defiance (43512) *(G-6684)*

Johns Manville Corporation 419 784-7000
 925 Carpenter Rd Defiance (43512) *(G-6685)*

Johns Manville Corporation 419 784-7000
 3rd And Perry Defiance (43512) *(G-6686)*

Johns Manville Corporation 419 878-8111
 408 Perry St Defiance (43512) *(G-6687)*

Johns Manville Corporation 419 467-8189
 1020 Ford St Maumee (43537) *(G-10209)*

Johns Manville Corporation 419 499-1400
 49 Lockwood Rd Milan (44846) *(G-10884)*

Johns Manville Corporation 419 878-8111
 7500 Dutch Rd Waterville (43566) *(G-15246)*

Johns Manville Corporation 419 878-8112
 6050 N River Rd Waterville (43566) *(G-15247)*

Johns Welding & Towing Inc 419 447-8937
 850 N County Road 11 Tiffin (44883) *(G-14089)*

Johnson & Johnson Services LLC 513 289-4514
 273 Mccormick Pl Cincinnati (45219) *(G-3047)*

Johnson Bros Greenwich, Greenwich *Also Called: Johnson Bros Rubber Co Inc (G-8067)*

Johnson Bros Rubber Co (PA) 419 853-4122
 42 W Buckeye St West Salem (44287) *(G-15634)*

Johnson Bros Rubber Co Inc 419 752-4814
 41 Center St Greenwich (44837) *(G-8067)*

Johnson Contrls Authorized Dlr, Akron *Also Called: Famous Industries Inc (G-150)*

Johnson Contrls Authorized Dlr, Dayton *Also Called: Glt Inc (G-6358)*

Johnson Contrls Authorized Dlr, Northwood *Also Called: Yanfeng US Auto Intr Systems I (G-11935)*

Johnson Controls, Brecksville *Also Called: Johnson Controls Inc (G-1624)*

Johnson Controls, Bryan *Also Called: Clarios LLC (G-1814)*

Johnson Controls, Cincinnati *Also Called: Johnson Controls Inc (G-3048)*

Johnson Controls, Cincinnati *Also Called: Johnson Controls Inc (G-3049)*

Johnson Controls, Holland *Also Called: Clarios LLC (G-8498)*

Johnson Controls, Mentor *Also Called: Clarios LLC (G-10438)*

Johnson Controls, Saint Marys *Also Called: Johnson Controls Inc (G-12954)*

Johnson Controls, Westerville *Also Called: Johnson Controls Inc (G-15712)*

Johnson Controls, Youngstown *Also Called: Johnson Controls Inc (G-16385)*

Johnson Controls Inc 216 587-0100
 6650 W Snowville Rd Brecksville (44141) *(G-1624)*

Johnson Controls Inc 513 489-0950
 7863 Palace Dr Cincinnati (45249) *(G-3048)*

Johnson Controls Inc 513 671-6338
 11648 Springfield Pike Cincinnati (45246) *(G-3049)*

Johnson Controls Inc 414 524-1200
 1111 Mckinley Road Saint Marys (45885) *(G-12954)*

Johnson Controls Inc 614 895-6600
 835 Green Crest Dr Westerville (43081) *(G-15712)*

Johnson Controls Inc 330 270-4385
 1044 N Meridian Rd Ste A Youngstown (44509) *(G-16385)*

Johnson Metall Inc 440 245-6826
 1305 Oberlin Ave Lorain (44052) *(G-9415)*

Johnson Mfg Systems LLC 937 866-4744
 4505 Infirmary Rd Miamisburg (45342) *(G-10650)*

Johnson Plastic Plus, Findlay *Also Called: Rowmark LLC (G-7557)*

Johnson Prcision Machining Inc 513 353-4252
 5919 Hamilton Cleves Rd Cleves (45002) *(G-4956)*

Johnson-Nash Metal Pdts Inc 513 874-7022
 9265 Seward Rd Fairfield (45014) *(G-7375)*

Johnsonite, Solon *Also Called: Tarkett USA Inc (G-13434)*

Johnsonite Inc 440 632-3441
 16035 Industrial Pkwy Middlefield (44062) *(G-10761)*

Johnsonite Inc 440 543-8916
 30000 Aurora Rd Solon (44139) *(G-13370)*

Johnsonite Rubber Flooring, Middlefield *Also Called: Johnsonite Inc (G-10761)*

Johnsons Emrgncy Vhcl Slutions, Wellston *Also Called: Johnsons Fire Equipment Co (G-15330)*

Johnsons Fire Equipment Co 740 357-4916
 20213 State Route 93 Wellston (45692) *(G-15330)*

Johnsons Real Ice Cream LLC 614 231-0014
 2728 E Main St Columbus (43209) *(G-5500)*

Johnston Mfg Co Inc   **ALPHABETIC SECTION**

Johnston Mfg Co Inc 440 269-1420
7611 Saint Clair Ave Mentor (44060) *(G-10485)*

Joining Metals Inc 440 259-1790
3314 Blackmore Rd Perry (44081) *(G-12352)*

Jolly Pats, Streetsboro Also Called: HP Enterprise Inc *(G-13773)*

Jomac Ltd 330 627-7727
182 Scio Rd Se Carrollton (44615) *(G-2311)*

Jonashtons LLC 419 488-2363
12485 State Route 634 Cloverdale (45827) *(G-4970)*

Jones Industries LLC 440 810-1251
8543 Evergreen Trl Olmsted Twp (44138) *(G-12088)*

Jones Metal Products Co LLC (PA) 740 545-6381
200 N Center St West Lafayette (43845) *(G-15618)*

Jones Metal Products Company 740 545-6341
305 N Center St West Lafayette (43845) *(G-15619)*

Jones Old Rustic Sign Company 937 643-1695
343 Beverly Pl Oakwood (45419) *(G-12028)*

Jones Potato Chip Co (PA) 419 529-9424
823 Bowman St Mansfield (44903) *(G-9674)*

Jones Propane Supply, Carrollton Also Called: Jomac Ltd *(G-2311)*

Jones Signs, Oakwood Also Called: Jones Old Rustic Sign Company *(G-12028)*

Jones-Hamilton Co (PA) 419 666-9838
30354 Tracy Rd Walbridge (43465) *(G-15083)*

Jones-Hamilton Co., Walbridge Also Called: Jones-Hamilton Co *(G-15083)*

Joneszylon Company LLC 740 545-6341
300 N Center St West Lafayette (43845) *(G-15620)*

Jonmar Gear and Machine Inc 330 854-6500
13786 Warwick Dr Nw Canal Fulton (44614) *(G-1971)*

Jordan Valve 513 533-5600
3170 Wasson Rd Cincinnati (45209) *(G-3050)*

Jordan Young International, London Also Called: Textiles Inc *(G-9395)*

Jordankelly LLC 216 855-8550
165 Ira Ave Akron (44301) *(G-197)*

Jordon Auto Service & Tire Inc 216 214-6528
5201 Carnegie Ave Cleveland (44103) *(G-4259)*

Jos Berning Printing Co 513 721-0781
1850 Dalton Ave Cincinnati (45214) *(G-3051)*

Jose Madrid Salsa, Zanesville Also Called: Michael Zakany LLC *(G-16545)*

Joseph Adams Corp 330 225-9125
5740 Grafton Rd Valley City (44280) *(G-14874)*

Joseph G Pappas 330 383-2917
3197 Forest Hills Dr East Liverpool (43920) *(G-6995)*

Joseph Industries, Cleveland Also Called: Charles Messina *(G-3809)*

Joseph Industries Inc 330 528-0091
10039 Aurora Hudson Rd Streetsboro (44241) *(G-13776)*

Joseph Sabatino 330 332-5879
1834 Depot Rd Salem (44460) *(G-13007)*

Joseph T Snyder Industries Inc 216 883-6900
9210 Loren Ave Cleveland (44105) *(G-4260)*

Joslyn Hi-Voltage Company LLC 216 271-6600
4000 E 116th St Cleveland (44105) *(G-4261)*

Joslyn Manufacturing Company 330 467-8111
9400 Valley View Rd Macedonia (44056) *(G-9560)*

Jotco Inc 513 721-4943
1400 Park Ave E Mansfield (44905) *(G-9675)*

Joules Angstrom Uv Prtg Inks C (PA) 740 964-9113
104 Heritage Dr Pataskala (43062) *(G-12299)*

Journal News 513 829-7900
5120 Dixie Hwy Fairfield (45014) *(G-7376)*

Journal Register Company 440 245-6901
401 Broadway Ste B Lorain (44052) *(G-9416)*

Journal Register Company 440 951-0000
36625 Vine St Willoughby (44094) *(G-15935)*

Journey Electronics Corp 513 539-9836
902 N Garver Rd Monroe (45050) *(G-11112)*

Journey Systems LLC 513 831-6200
25 Whitney Dr Ste 100 Milford (45150) *(G-10912)*

Joy Global Underground Min LLC 440 248-7970
6160 Cochran Rd Cleveland (44139) *(G-4262)*

Joy Global Underground Min LLC 440 248-7970
6160 Cochran Rd Solon (44139) *(G-13371)*

Joyce Dayton LLC 440 449-3333
6449 Wilson Mills Rd Cleveland (44143) *(G-4263)*

Joyce Manufacturing Co 440 239-9100
1125 Berea Industrial Pkwy Berea (44017) *(G-1286)*

Joyce Windows, Berea Also Called: Joyce Manufacturing Co *(G-1286)*

Joyce/Dayton Corp (HQ) 937 294-6261
3300 S Dixie Dr Ste 101 Dayton (45439) *(G-6390)*

Joyce/Dayton Corp 937 294-6261
Dayton (45401) *(G-6391)*

JP Cabinets LLC 440 232-9780
20910 Miles Pkwy Cleveland (44128) *(G-4264)*

JP Industrial, Lisbon Also Called: J P Industrial Products Inc *(G-9319)*

JP Suggins Mobile Wldg Inc 216 566-7131
2020 Saint Clair Ave Ne Cleveland (44114) *(G-4265)*

Jpc Llc 513 310-1608
215 Kings Mills Rd Mason (45040) *(G-10015)*

Jpi Coastal LLC 330 424-1110
11988 State Route 45 Lisbon (44432) *(G-9320)*

JPS Technologies Inc (PA) 513 984-6400
11110 Deerfield Rd Blue Ash (45242) *(G-1414)*

JPS Technologies Inc 513 984-6400
11110 Deerfield Rd Blue Ash (45242) *(G-1415)*

JR Manufacturing Inc (PA) 419 375-8021
900 Industrial Dr W Fort Recovery (45846) *(G-7621)*

Jrb Attachments LLC (DH) 330 734-3000
820 Glaser Pkwy Akron (44306) *(G-198)*

Jrb Family Holdings Inc
4255 E Lincoln Way Wooster (44691) *(G-16138)*

Jrb Industries LLC 567 825-7022
3425 State Route 571 Greenville (45331) *(G-8048)*

Jrm 2 Company 513 554-1700
425 Shepherd Ave Cincinnati (45215) *(G-3052)*

Jrp Solutions Llc 330 825-5989
3764 Golf Course Dr Norton (44203) *(G-11946)*

Jrs MBL Wldg Fabrication LLC 567 307-5460
992 County Road 601 Ashland (44805) *(G-581)*

Js Fabrications Inc 419 333-0323
1400 E State St Fremont (43420) *(G-7790)*

Jsc Employee Leasing Corp (PA) 330 773-8971
1560 Firestone Pkwy Akron (44301) *(G-199)*

Jsh International LLC 330 734-0251
124 Darrow Rd Ste 5 Akron (44305) *(G-200)*

Jsm Express Inc 216 272-4512
27301 Markbarry Ave Euclid (44132) *(G-7278)*

Jst LLC 614 423-7815
6240 Frost Rd Ste C Westerville (43082) *(G-15661)*

JSW Steel USA Ohio Inc 740 535-8172
1500 Commercial St Mingo Junction (43938) *(G-11046)*

Jsw USA, Mingo Junction Also Called: JSW Steel USA Ohio Inc *(G-11046)*

JT Plus Well Service LLC 740 347-0070
140 E Main St Corning (43730) *(G-5958)*

Jt Premier Printing Corp 216 831-8785
18780 Cranwood Pkwy Cleveland (44128) *(G-4266)*

JTL Enterprises LLC (PA) 937 890-8189
5700 Webster St Dayton (45414) *(G-6392)*

Jtm Food Group, Harrison Also Called: Jtm Provisions Company Inc *(G-8280)*

Jtm Food Group, Harrison Also Called: Jtm Provisions Company Inc *(G-8281)*

Jtm Products Inc 440 287-2302
31025 Carter St Solon (44139) *(G-13372)*

Jtm Provisions Company Inc (PA) 513 367-4900
200 Sales Ave Harrison (45030) *(G-8280)*

Jtm Provisions Company Inc 513 367-4900
270 Industrial Dr Harrison (45030) *(G-8281)*

Juba Industries Inc 440 655-9960
126 W Jefferson St Jefferson (44047) *(G-8747)*

Judith Leiber LLC (PA) 614 449-4217
4300 E 5th Ave Columbus (43219) *(G-5501)*

Judo Steel, Dayton Also Called: Judo Steel Company Inc *(G-6393)*

Judo Steel Company Inc
1526 Nicholas Rd Dayton (45417) *(G-6393)*

Judy Mills Company Inc (PA) 513 271-4241
3360 Red Bank Rd Cincinnati (45227) *(G-3053)*

ALPHABETIC SECTION — Kam Manufacturing Inc

Julie Maynard Inc 937 443-0408
4991 Hempstead Station Dr Dayton (45429) *(G-6394)*

Julius Patrick Industries LLC 440 600-7369
5845 Elm Hill Dr Solon (44139) *(G-13373)*

Julius Zorn Inc 330 923-4999
3690 Zorn Dr Cuyahoga Falls (44223) *(G-6094)*

Juno Enterprises LLC 419 448-9350
8146 Us Highway 224 New Riegel (44853) *(G-11536)*

Jupmode 419 318-2029
2022 Adams St Toledo (43604) *(G-14342)*

Just Business Inc 866 577-3303
1612 Prosser Ave Ste 100 Dayton (45409) *(G-6395)*

Just Name It Inc 614 626-8662
110 Hedstrom Dr Ashland (44805) *(G-582)*

Just Natural Provision Company 216 431-7922
4800 Crayton Ave Cleveland (44104) *(G-4267)*

Just Plastics Inc 419 468-5506
869 Smith St Galion (44833) *(G-7881)*

Just-Ink-Tees, Jamestown Also Called: Ball Jackets LLC *(G-8740)*

Justins Delight LLC 567 234-3575
101 W Park St Toledo (43608) *(G-14343)*

Juzo USA, Cuyahoga Falls Also Called: Julius Zorn Inc *(G-6094)*

JW Manufacturing LLC 419 375-5536
317 Watkins Rd Fort Recovery (45846) *(G-7622)*

K & B Acquisitions Inc 937 253-1163
3013 Linden Ave Dayton (45290) *(G-6396)*

K & B Molded Products, Brookville Also Called: Kuhns Mold & Tool Co Inc *(G-1740)*

K & G Machine Company 216 732-7115
26981 Tungsten Rd Cleveland (44132) *(G-4268)*

K & H Industries LLC 513 921-6770
1041 Evans St Cincinnati (45204) *(G-3054)*

K & J Machine Inc 740 425-3282
326 Fairmont Ave Barnesville (43713) *(G-903)*

K & K Auto & Truck Parts, Logan Also Called: Pattons Trck & Hvy Eqp Svc Inc *(G-9373)*

K & K Precision Inc 513 336-0032
5001 N Mason Montgomery Rd Mason (45040) *(G-10016)*

K & L Ready Mix Inc 419 293-2937
5511 State Route 613 Mc Comb (45858) *(G-10271)*

K & L Ready Mix Inc (PA) 419 523-4376
10391 State Route 15 Ottawa (45875) *(G-12183)*

K & L Tool Inc 419 258-2086
5141 County Road 424 Antwerp (45813) *(G-493)*

K A P C O, Kent Also Called: Kent Adhesive Products Co *(G-8821)*

K A Ventures Inc 513 860-3340
9418 Sutton Pl West Chester (45011) *(G-15451)*

K B I, Sandusky Also Called: Kyklos Bearing International Llc *(G-13072)*

K B Machine & Tool Inc 937 773-1624
1500 S Main St Piqua (45356) *(G-12531)*

K C P, Beachwood Also Called: Kirtland Capital Partners LP *(G-993)*

K D C, Johnstown Also Called: Tri-Tech Laboratories Inc *(G-8780)*

K Davis Inc 419 307-7051
206 Lynn St Fremont (43420) *(G-7791)*

K F T Inc 513 241-5910
726 Mehring Way Cincinnati (45203) *(G-3055)*

K G M, Cincinnati Also Called: Knoble Glass & Metal Inc *(G-3084)*

K K Tool Co 937 325-1373
115 S Center St Springfield (45502) *(G-13585)*

K L M Manufacturing Company 740 666-5171
56 Huston St Ostrander (43061) *(G-12174)*

K M B Inc 330 889-3451
1306 State Route 88 Bristolville (44402) *(G-1652)*

K M I, Cincinnati Also Called: United Tool Supply Inc *(G-2576)*

K Petroleum Inc (PA) 614 532-5420
905 Creekside Plz Gahanna (43230) *(G-7839)*

K S Bandag Inc 330 264-9237
737 Industrial Blvd Wooster (44691) *(G-16139)*

K S Machine Inc 216 687-0459
3215 Superior Ave E Cleveland (44114) *(G-4269)*

K Ventures Inc 419 678-2308
211 E Main St Coldwater (45828) *(G-4994)*

K Wm Beach Mfg Co Inc 937 399-3838
4655 Urbana Rd Springfield (45502) *(G-13586)*

K-D Lamp Company 440 293-4064
101 Parker Dr Andover (44003) *(G-486)*

K-J Kustom Powder Coat 740 961-5267
3015 Scioto Trl Portsmouth (45662) *(G-12646)*

K-M-S Industries Inc 440 243-6680
6519 Eastland Rd Ste 1 Brookpark (44142) *(G-1720)*

K-Mar Structures LLC 231 924-5777
1825 Flagdale Rd S Junction City (43748) *(G-8783)*

K-O-K Products Inc 740 548-0526
700 S 3 Bs And K Rd Galena (43021) *(G-7855)*

K-Sha Press Inc 216 252-0037
13613 Tyler Ave Cleveland (44111) *(G-4271)*

K.M.I. Printing, Chardon Also Called: Key Maneuvers Inc *(G-2454)*

K.M.S., Brookpark Also Called: K-M-S Industries Inc *(G-1720)*

K/H Enterprises, Fairfield Also Called: Kaaa/Hamilton Enterprises Inc *(G-7377)*

K&M Aviation LLC 216 261-9000
355 Richmond Rd Cleveland (44143) *(G-4270)*

Kaaa/Hamilton Enterprises Inc 513 874-5874
3143 Production Dr Fairfield (45014) *(G-7377)*

Kabab-G Inc 216 476-3335
6676 Rochelle Blvd Cleveland (44130) *(G-4272)*

Kadant Black Clawson Inc (HQ) 513 229-8100
1425 Kingsview Dr Lebanon (45036) *(G-9091)*

Kadee Industries, Twinsburg Also Called: Dribble Creek Inc *(G-14654)*

Kaeden Books, Westlake Also Called: Kaeden Publishing *(G-15762)*

Kaeden Publishing 440 617-1400
24700 Center Ridge Rd Ste 170 Westlake (44145) *(G-15762)*

Kaeper Machine Inc 440 974-1010
8680 Twinbrook Rd Mentor (44060) *(G-10486)*

Kaffenbarger Truck Eqp Co 513 772-6800
3260 E Kemper Rd Cincinnati (45241) *(G-3056)*

Kaffenbarger Truck Eqp Co (PA) 937 845-3804
10100 Ballentine Pike New Carlisle (45344) *(G-11418)*

Kahiki, Gahanna Also Called: Kahiki Foods Inc *(G-7840)*

Kahiki Foods Inc 614 322-3180
1100 Morrison Rd Gahanna (43230) *(G-7840)*

Kahny Printing Inc 513 251-2911
4766 River Rd Cincinnati (45233) *(G-3057)*

Kaiser Aluminum Fab Pdts LLC 740 522-1151
600 Kaiser Dr Heath (43056) *(G-8323)*

Kaiser Aluminum Newark Works, Heath Also Called: Kaiser Aluminum Fab Pdts LLC *(G-8323)*

Kaiser Foods Inc (PA) 513 621-2053
500 York St Cincinnati (45214) *(G-3058)*

Kaiser Pickles LLC (HQ) 513 621-2053
500 York St Cincinnati (45214) *(G-3059)*

Kaiser Pickles LLC 513 621-2053
422 York St Cincinnati (45214) *(G-3060)*

Kaivac, Hamilton Also Called: Kaivac Inc *(G-8225)*

Kaivac Inc 513 887-4600
2680 Van Hook Ave Hamilton (45015) *(G-8225)*

Kalcor Coatings Company 440 946-4700
37721 Stevens Blvd Willoughby (44094) *(G-15936)*

Kaliburn Inc 843 695-4073
22801 Saint Clair Ave Cleveland (44117) *(G-4273)*

Kalida Manufacturing Inc 419 532-2026
801 Ottawa St Kalida (45853) *(G-8785)*

Kalinich Fence Company Inc 440 238-6127
12223 Prospect Rd Strongsville (44149) *(G-13848)*

Kalmbach, Upper Sandusky Also Called: Kalmbach Feeds Inc *(G-14811)*

Kalmbach Feeds Inc (PA) 419 294-3838
7148 State Highway 199 Upper Sandusky (43351) *(G-14811)*

Kalron LLC 440 647-3039
143 Erie St Wellington (44090) *(G-15314)*

Kalron LLC 440 647-3039
775 Shiloh Ave Wellington (44090) *(G-15315)*

Kalt Manufacturing Company 440 327-2102
36700 Sugar Ridge Rd North Ridgeville (44039) *(G-11848)*

Kam Manufacturing Inc 419 238-6037
1197 Grill Rd Van Wert (45891) *(G-14919)*

Kamco Industries Inc — ALPHABETIC SECTION

Kamco Industries Inc (HQ) 419 924-5511
1001 E Jackson St West Unity (43570) *(G-15641)*

Kamps Inc 937 526-9333
10709 Reed Rd Versailles (45380) *(G-14983)*

Kamps Pallets 616 818-4323
2132 Refugee Rd Columbus (43207) *(G-5502)*

Kanan Enterprises Inc (PA) 440 248-8484
31900 Solon Rd Solon (44139) *(G-13374)*

Kanan Enterprises Inc 440 248-8484
30600 Carter St Solon (44139) *(G-13375)*

Kanan Enterprises Inc 440 349-0719
6401 Davis Industrial Pkwy Solon (44139) *(G-13376)*

Kando of Cincinnati Inc 513 459-7782
2025 Mckinley Blvd Lebanon (45036) *(G-9092)*

Kangaroo Brand Mops, Union City Also Called: Ha-Ste Manufacturing Co Inc *(G-14778)*

Kantner Ingredients Inc 614 766-3638
975 Worthington Woods Loop Rd Columbus (43085) *(G-5503)*

Kanya Industries LLC 330 722-5432
694 W Liberty St Medina (44256) *(G-10340)*

KAO Brands Company 513 977-2931
1231 Draper St Cincinnati (45214) *(G-3061)*

KAO USA Inc (HQ) 513 421-1400
2535 Spring Grove Ave Cincinnati (45214) *(G-3062)*

KAO USA Inc 513 629-5210
312 Plum St Cincinnati (45202) *(G-3063)*

Kap Signs, Dayton Also Called: Blang Acquisition LLC *(G-6231)*

Kapios LLC 567 661-0772
2865 N Reynolds Rd Ste 220d Toledo (43615) *(G-14344)*

Kapios Health, Toledo Also Called: Kapios LLC *(G-14344)*

Kaplan Industries Inc 856 779-8181
6255 Kilby Rd Harrison (45030) *(G-8282)*

Kaps, Willoughby Also Called: Kelly Arspc Thrmal Systems LLC *(G-15938)*

Kar-Del Plastics Inc 419 289-9739
1177 Faultless Dr Ashland (44805) *(G-583)*

Kard Bridge Products, Minster Also Called: Kard Welding Inc *(G-11054)*

Kard Welding Inc 419 628-2598
480 Osterloh Rd Minster (45865) *(G-11054)*

Kardol Quality Products LLC (PA) 513 933-8206
9933 Alliance Rd Ste 2 Blue Ash (45242) *(G-1416)*

Karen Carson Creations, Dayton Also Called: Carson-Saeks Inc *(G-6247)*

Karg Corporation 330 633-4916
241 Southwest Ave Tallmadge (44278) *(G-14034)*

Karl Kuemmerling Inc
129 Edgewater Ave Nw Massillon (44646) *(G-10114)*

Karlco, Jefferson Also Called: Karlco Oilfield Services Inc *(G-8748)*

Karlco Oilfield Services Inc 440 576-3415
141 E Jefferson St Jefferson (44047) *(G-8748)*

Karma Metal Products Inc 419 524-4371
556 Caldwell Ave Mansfield (44905) *(G-9676)*

Karman Rubber Company 330 864-2161
2331 Copley Rd Akron (44320) *(G-201)*

Karn Meats Inc 614 252-3712
922 Taylor Ave Columbus (43219) *(G-5504)*

Karol-Warner, Lewis Center Also Called: Kw Acquisition Inc *(G-9168)*

Karrikin Spirits Company LLC 513 561-5000
3717 Jonlen Dr Cincinnati (45227) *(G-3064)*

Kars Ohio LLC 614 655-1099
6359 Summit Rd Sw Pataskala (43062) *(G-12300)*

Karyall-Telday Inc 216 281-4063
8221 Clinton Rd Cleveland (44144) *(G-4274)*

Kasai North America Inc 614 356-1494
655 Metro Pl S Ste 560 Dublin (43017) *(G-6903)*

Kasai North America Inc 419 209-0399
1111 N Warpole St Upper Sandusky (43351) *(G-14812)*

Kase Equipment Corporation 216 642-9040
7400 Hub Pkwy Cleveland (44125) *(G-4275)*

Kasel Engineering LLC 937 854-8775
5911 Wolf Creek Pike Trotwood (45426) *(G-14545)*

Kaskell, Springboro Also Called: Kaskell Manufacturing Inc *(G-13507)*

Kaskell Manufacturing Inc 937 704-9700
240 Hiawatha Trl Springboro (45066) *(G-13507)*

Kasper Enterprises Inc 419 841-6656
7844 W Central Ave Toledo (43617) *(G-14345)*

Katch Kitchen LLC 513 537-8056
4172 Hamilton Ave Cincinnati (45223) *(G-3065)*

Kathleen Williams 740 360-3515
354 Pearl St Marion (43302) *(G-9858)*

Kathom Manufacturing Co Inc 513 868-8890
1301 Hook Dr Middletown (45042) *(G-10835)*

Kathys Krafts and Kollectibles 423 787-3709
3303 Hamilton Rd Medina (44256) *(G-10341)*

Katies Light House LLC 419 645-5451
300 Dupler Ave Cridersville (45806) *(G-6042)*

Katimex USA Inc 440 338-3500
15241 Hemlock Point Rd Chagrin Falls (44022) *(G-2381)*

Kauffman Lumber & Supply 330 893-9186
4051 Us Route 62 Millersburg (44654) *(G-10971)*

Kaufman Container Company (PA) 216 898-2000
1000 Keystone Pkwy Ste 100 Cleveland (44135) *(G-4276)*

Kaufman Engineered Systems Inc 419 878-9727
1260 Waterville Monclova Rd Waterville (43566) *(G-15248)*

Kavon Filter Products Co 732 938-3135
837 E 79th St Cleveland (44103) *(G-4277)*

Kawneer Company Inc 216 252-3203
4536 Industrial Pkwy Cleveland (44135) *(G-4278)*

Kaws Inc 513 521-8292
2680 Civic Center Dr Cincinnati (45231) *(G-3066)*

Kay Toledo Tag Inc 419 729-5479
6050 Benore Rd Toledo (43612) *(G-14346)*

Kay-Zee Inc 330 339-1268
1279 Crestview Ave Sw New Philadelphia (44663) *(G-11507)*

Kayden Industries 740 336-7801
2167 State Route 821 Marietta (45750) *(G-9804)*

Kaydon Corporation 231 755-3741
1500 Nagel Rd Avon (44011) *(G-777)*

Kaylo Enterprises LLC 330 535-1860
540 S Main St Ste 115 Akron (44311) *(G-202)*

Kbr, Cincinnati Also Called: Kitchens By Rutenschroer Inc *(G-3080)*

Kbr Inc 937 320-2731
2700 Indian Ripple Rd Dayton (45440) *(G-6397)*

Kc Marketing LLC 513 471-8770
5353 Spring Grove Ave Cincinnati (45217) *(G-3067)*

Kc Robotics Inc 513 860-4442
9000 Le Saint Dr West Chester (45014) *(G-15452)*

Kci, Middleburg Heights Also Called: Kinetic Concepts Inc *(G-10722)*

Kci Holding USA Inc (DH) 937 525-5533
4401 Gateway Blvd Springfield (45502) *(G-13587)*

Kci Works, Canal Winchester Also Called: Kellogg Cabinets Inc *(G-1988)*

Kcn Technologies LLC 440 439-4219
1 W Interstate St # 13 Bedford (44146) *(G-1131)*

Kcox Enterprises LLC 574 952-5084
7353 Preserve Pl West Chester (45069) *(G-15453)*

Kcs Cleaning Service 740 418-5479
7550 State Route 93 Oak Hill (45656) *(G-12020)*

Kda Manufacturing LLC 330 590-7431
5221 S Cleveland Massillon Rd Norton (44203) *(G-11947)*

Kdae Inc 844 543-8339
7750 Green Meadows Dr Ste A Lewis Center (43035) *(G-9167)*

Kdc Lynchburg, Groveport Also Called: Kdc US Holdings Inc *(G-8148)*

Kdc One 614 984-2871
8825 Smiths Mill Rd New Albany (43054) *(G-11382)*

Kdc US Holdings Inc (DH) 434 845-7073
4400 S Hamilton Rd Groveport (43125) *(G-8148)*

Kdc/One, New Albany Also Called: Tri-Tech Laboratories LLC *(G-11391)*

KDI Med Supply, Fremont Also Called: K Davis Inc *(G-7791)*

Kdlamp Company, Andover Also Called: Atc Lighting & Plastics Inc *(G-485)*

Kdm Screen Printing, Cincinnati Also Called: Kdm Signs Inc *(G-3069)*

Kdm Signs Inc 513 554-1393
2996 Exon Ave Cincinnati (45241) *(G-3068)*

Kdm Signs Inc (PA) 513 769-1932
10450 N Medallion Dr Cincinnati (45241) *(G-3069)*

Kdm Signs Inc 513 769-3900
3000 Exon Ave Cincinnati (45241) *(G-3070)*

ALPHABETIC SECTION — Kent Corporation

Keb Industries Inc.. 440 953-4623
2166 Joseph Lloyd Pkwy Willoughby (44094) *(G-15937)*

Keban Industries Inc... 216 446-0159
1263 Royalwood Rd Broadview Heights (44147) *(G-1659)*

Kebco Prcision Fabricators Inc.................................. 330 456-0808
2006 Allen Ave Se Canton (44707) *(G-2137)*

Kec America, Covington Also Called: Hitachi Automation Ohio Inc *(G-6025)*

Kecamm LLC... 330 527-2918
10404 Industrial Dr Garrettsville (44231) *(G-7918)*

Kecoat LLC... 330 527-0215
10610 Freedom St Garrettsville (44231) *(G-7919)*

Kecy Metal Technologies, Wauseon Also Called: ARC Metal Stamping LLC *(G-15256)*

Keebler, Cincinnati Also Called: Keebler Company *(G-3071)*

Keebler Company.. 513 271-3500
1 Trade St Cincinnati (45227) *(G-3071)*

Keeler Enterprises Inc... 330 336-7601
924 Seville Rd Wadsworth (44281) *(G-15039)*

Keen Pump, Ashland Also Called: Keen Pump Company Inc *(G-584)*

Keen Pump Company Inc.. 419 207-9400
471 E State Rte 250 E Ashland (44805) *(G-584)*

Keene Building Products Co (PA).............................. 440 605-1020
2926 Chester Ave Cleveland (44114) *(G-4279)*

Keene Village Plastics Ltd....................................... 330 753-0100
23610 Saint Clair Ave Euclid (44117) *(G-7279)*

Keener, Cleveland Also Called: Keener Printing Inc *(G-4280)*

Keener Printing Inc.. 216 531-7595
401 E 200th St Cleveland (44119) *(G-4280)*

Keener Rubber Company.. 330 821-1880
14700 Commerce St Ne Alliance (44601) *(G-407)*

KEffs Inc.. 614 443-0586
2117 S High St Columbus (43207) *(G-5505)*

Kehl-Kolor Inc... 419 281-3107
824 Us Highway 42 Ashland (44805) *(G-585)*

Keith O King... 419 339-5028
4095 Pioneer Rd Lima (45807) *(G-9259)*

Keithley Instruments LLC (DH)................................ 440 248-0400
28775 Aurora Rd Solon (44139) *(G-13377)*

Kel-Eez, Akron Also Called: Die-Gem Co Inc *(G-129)*

Kel-Mar Inc.. 419 806-4600
436 N Enterprise St Bowling Green (43402) *(G-1569)*

Kelbly's, North Lawrence Also Called: Kelblys Rifle Range Inc *(G-11798)*

Kelblys Rifle Range Inc.. 330 683-4674
7222 Dalton Fox Lake Rd North Lawrence (44666) *(G-11798)*

Kelchner Inc (DH)... 937 704-9890
50 Advanced Dr Springboro (45066) *(G-13508)*

Kelic, Waterville Also Called: Rimer Enterprises Inc *(G-15251)*

Kellanova... 513 271-3500
1 Trade St Cincinnati (45227) *(G-3072)*

Kellanova... 614 879-9659
125 Enterprise Pkwy West Jefferson (43162) *(G-15611)*

Kellanova... 740 453-5501
1675 Fairview Rd Zanesville (43701) *(G-16541)*

Kellermyer Bergensons Svcs LLC............................. 419 867-4300
1575 Henthorne Dr Maumee (43537) *(G-10210)*

Kellers Fine Line Welding LLC................................. 903 348-8304
440 Southeast Ave Tallmadge (44278) *(G-14035)*

Kelley Bible Books, Dayton Also Called: Kelley Communication Dev *(G-6398)*

Kelley Communication Dev..................................... 937 298-6132
2312 Candlewood Dr Dayton (45419) *(G-6398)*

Kelleys Island Winery Inc....................................... 419 746-2678
418 Woodford Rd Kelleys Island (43438) *(G-8788)*

Kellog, Cincinnati Also Called: Kellanova *(G-3072)*

Kellog, West Jefferson Also Called: Kellanova *(G-15611)*

Kellog, Zanesville Also Called: Kellanova *(G-16541)*

Kellogg Cabinets Inc... 614 833-9596
7711 Diley Rd Canal Winchester (43110) *(G-1988)*

Kellogg Co... 330 306-1500
655 N River Rd Nw Warren (44483) *(G-15182)*

Kellstone, Kelleys Island Also Called: Kellstone Inc *(G-8789)*

Kellstone Inc.. 419 746-2396
Lake Shore Drive Kelleys Island (43438) *(G-8789)*

Kelly Arspc Thrmal Systems LLC............................. 440 951-4744
1625 Lost Nation Rd Willoughby (44094) *(G-15938)*

Kelly Duplex, Springfield Also Called: Duplex Mill & Manufacturing Co *(G-13557)*

Kelly Foods Corporation (PA).................................. 330 722-8855
3337 Medina Rd Medina (44256) *(G-10342)*

Kelly Plating Co.. 216 961-1080
10316 Madison Ave Cleveland (44102) *(G-4281)*

Kelly-Creswell Company, Springfield Also Called: Ernest Industries Inc *(G-13559)*

Kellys Wldg & Fabrication Ltd................................. 440 593-6040
285 N Amboy Rd Conneaut (44030) *(G-5922)*

Keltec Inc (PA)... 330 425-3100
2300 E Enterprise Pkwy Twinsburg (44087) *(G-14678)*

Keltec-Technolab, Twinsburg Also Called: Keltec Inc *(G-14678)*

Kem Advertising and Prtg LLC................................ 330 818-5061
564 W Tuscarawas Ave Ste 104 Barberton (44203) *(G-876)*

Kempf Surgical Appliances Inc................................ 513 984-5758
10567 Montgomery Rd Montgomery (45242) *(G-11130)*

Ken Beaverson Inc.. 330 264-0378
3501 W Old Lincoln Way Wooster (44691) *(G-16140)*

Ken Emerick Machine Products............................... 440 834-4501
14504 Main Market Rd Burton (44021) *(G-1883)*

Ken Forging Inc.. 440 993-8091
1049 Griggs Rd Jefferson (44047) *(G-8749)*

Ken Ganley Kia, Medina Also Called: KG Medina LLC *(G-10343)*

Ken-Dal Corporation.. 330 644-7118
644 Killian Rd Coventry Township (44319) *(G-6011)*

Ken-Tools, Akron Also Called: Summit Tool Company *(G-341)*

Kenag Inc.. 419 281-1204
101 E 7th St Ashland (44805) *(G-586)*

Kenakore Solutions, Perrysburg Also Called: Depot Direct Inc *(G-12375)*

Kenamerican Resources Inc.................................... 740 338-3100
46226 National Rd Saint Clairsville (43950) *(G-12907)*

Kenan Advantage Group Inc................................... 614 878-4050
500 Manor Park Dr Columbus (43228) *(G-5506)*

Kenco Products Co Inc.. 216 351-7610
3204 Sackett Ave Cleveland (44109) *(G-4282)*

Kendall Holdings Ltd (PA)..................................... 614 486-4750
2111 Builders Pl Columbus (43204) *(G-5507)*

Kendall/Hunt Publishing Co.................................... 877 275-4725
8805 Governors Hill Dr Ste 400 Cincinnati (45249) *(G-3073)*

Kendel Welding & Fabrication................................. 330 834-2429
1700 Navarre Rd Se Massillon (44646) *(G-10115)*

Kenics, Dayton Also Called: Chemineer Inc *(G-6254)*

Kenlake Foods, Cincinnati Also Called: Inter American Products Inc *(G-3025)*

Kenley Enterprises LLC... 419 630-0921
418 N Lynn St Bryan (43506) *(G-1824)*

Kenmore Construction Co Inc................................. 330 832-8888
9500 Forty Corners Rd Nw Massillon (44647) *(G-10116)*

Kenmore Development & Mch Co............................ 330 753-2274
1395 Kenmore Blvd Akron (44314) *(G-203)*

Kenmore Gear & Machine Co Inc............................ 330 753-6671
2129 Jennifer St Akron (44313) *(G-204)*

Kennametal Inc.. 440 437-5131
180 Penniman Rd Orwell (44076) *(G-12166)*

Kennametal Inc.. 440 349-5151
6865 Cochran Rd Solon (44139) *(G-13378)*

Kennedy Group Incorporated (PA).......................... 440 951-7660
38601 Kennedy Pkwy Willoughby (44094) *(G-15939)*

Kennedy Ink Company Inc (PA)............................. 513 871-2515
5230 Wooster Pike Cincinnati (45226) *(G-3074)*

Kennedy Manufacturing, Van Wert Also Called: KMC Holdings LLC *(G-14920)*

Kennedys Bakery Inc.. 740 432-2301
1025 Wheeling Ave Cambridge (43725) *(G-1938)*

Kenoil Inc.. 330 262-1144
1537 Blachleyville Rd Wooster (44691) *(G-16141)*

Kensington Plant, Kensington Also Called: M3 Midstream LLC *(G-8790)*

Kent Adhesive Products Co.................................... 330 678-1626
1000 Cherry St Kent (44240) *(G-8821)*

Kent Corporation.. 440 582-3400
9601 York Alpha Dr North Royalton (44133) *(G-11881)*

Kent Displays Inc — ALPHABETIC SECTION

Kent Displays Inc (PA) 330 673-8784
343 Portage Blvd Kent (44240) *(G-8822)*

Kent Elastomer Products, Kent *Also Called: Meridian Industries Inc (G-8834)*

Kent Elastomer Products, Winesburg *Also Called: Meridian Industries Inc (G-16081)*

Kent Elastomer Products Inc (HQ) 330 673-1011
1500 Saint Clair Ave Kent (44240) *(G-8823)*

Kent Elastomer Products Inc 800 331-4762
3890 Mogadore Industrial Pkwy Mogadore (44260) *(G-11077)*

Kent Information Services Inc 330 672-2110
6185 2nd Ave Kent (44240) *(G-8824)*

Kent Mold and Manufacturing Co 330 673-3469
1190 W Main St Kent (44240) *(G-8825)*

Kent Post Acquisition Inc 330 678-6343
449 Dodge St Kent (44240) *(G-8826)*

Kent Stow Screen Printing Inc 330 923-5118
1340 Home Ave Ste F Akron (44310) *(G-205)*

Kent Water Sports, New London *Also Called: Kent Water Sports LLC (G-11463)*

Kent Water Sports LLC (PA) 419 929-7021
433 Park Ave New London (44851) *(G-11463)*

Kentak Products Company 330 386-3700
1308 Railroad St East Liverpool (43920) *(G-6996)*

Kentak Products Company (PA) 330 382-2000
1230 Railroad St Ste 1 East Liverpool (43920) *(G-6997)*

Kenton Iron Products Inc (PA) 419 674-4178
13510 S Vision Dr Kenton (43326) *(G-8886)*

Kenton Strl & Orn Ir Works 419 674-4025
100 Cleveland Ave Kenton (43326) *(G-8887)*

Kenton Times, The, Kenton *Also Called: Hardin County Publishing Co (G-8885)*

Kentrox Inc (HQ) 614 798-2000
5800 Innovation Dr Dublin (43016) *(G-6904)*

Kenwel Printers Inc 614 261-1011
4272 Indianola Ave Columbus (43214) *(G-5508)*

Kenyetta Bagby Enterprise LLC 614 584-3426
6629 Penick Dr Reynoldsburg (43068) *(G-12768)*

Kenyon Co, Coshocton *Also Called: Novelty Advertising Co Inc (G-5988)*

Kepcor Inc 330 868-6434
215 Bridge St Minerva (44657) *(G-11032)*

Kerber Sheetmetal Works Inc 937 339-6366
104 Foss Way Troy (45373) *(G-14591)*

Kerek Industries Ltd Lblty Co
750 Beta Dr Ste A Cleveland (44143) *(G-4283)*

Kern Inc 440 930-7315
755 Alpha Dr Cleveland (44143) *(G-4284)*

Kern-Liebers Texas Inc 419 865-2437
1510 Albon Rd Holland (43528) *(G-8516)*

Kern-Liebers Usa Inc (HQ) 419 865-2437
1510 Albon Rd Holland (43528) *(G-8517)*

Kernells Autmtc Machining Inc 419 588-2164
10511 State Rte 61 N Berlin Heights (44814) *(G-1315)*

Kerr Friction Products Inc 330 455-3983
2512 Columbus Rd Ne Canton (44705) *(G-2138)*

Kerr Lakeside Inc 216 261-2100
26841 Tungsten Rd Euclid (44132) *(G-7280)*

Kerry Flavor Systems Us LLC 513 539-7373
1055 Reed Dr Monroe (45050) *(G-11113)*

Kerry Inc 760 685-2548
100 Hope Ave Byesville (43723) *(G-1899)*

Kerry Inc 440 229-5200
29136 Norman Ave Wickliffe (44092) *(G-15836)*

Kerry Ingredients, Byesville *Also Called: Kerry Inc (G-1899)*

Kerry Ingredients & Flavours, Monroe *Also Called: Kerry Flavor Systems Us LLC (G-11113)*

Kessler Outdoor Advertising, Zanesville *Also Called: Kessler Sign Company (G-16542)*

Kessler Sign Company (PA) 740 453-0668
2669 National Rd Zanesville (43701) *(G-16542)*

Ketco Inc 937 426-9331
1348 Research Park Dr Beavercreek (45432) *(G-1053)*

Ketman Corporation 330 262-1688
205 W Liberty St Wooster (44691) *(G-16142)*

Kettering Monogramming, Dayton *Also Called: Zimmer Enterprises Inc (G-6663)*

Kettering Roofing & Shtmtl Inc 513 281-6413
3210 Jefferson Ave Ste 1 Cincinnati (45220) *(G-3075)*

Kettle Creations LLC 567 940-9401
651 Commerce Pkwy Lima (45804) *(G-9260)*

Keuchel & Associates Inc 330 945-9455
175 Muffin Ln Cuyahoga Falls (44223) *(G-6095)*

Keurig Dr Pepper Inc 614 237-4201
950 Stelzer Rd Columbus (43219) *(G-5509)*

Kevin K Tidd 419 885-5603
5505 Roan Rd Sylvania (43560) *(G-14003)*

Key Finishes LLC 614 351-8393
727 Harrison Dr Columbus (43204) *(G-5510)*

Key Maneuvers Inc (PA) 440 285-0774
10639 Grant St Ste C Chardon (44024) *(G-2454)*

Key Resin Company (DH) 513 943-4225
4050 Clough Woods Dr Batavia (45103) *(G-927)*

Keyah International Trdg LLC (PA) 937 399-3140
4655 Urbana Rd Springfield (45502) *(G-13588)*

Keyline, North Olmsted *Also Called: Bianchi Usa Inc (G-11818)*

Keynes Bros Inc 740 385-6824
1 W Front St Logan (43138) *(G-9366)*

Keys Cheesecakes and Pies LLC 513 356-1221
9519 Triangle Dr West Chester (45011) *(G-15454)*

Keysco Tools, Cleveland *Also Called: S & H Industries Inc (G-4664)*

Keystone Auto Glass Inc 419 509-0497
2255 Linden Ct Maumee (43537) *(G-10211)*

Keystone Bolt & Nut Company 216 524-9626
7600 Hub Pkwy Cleveland (44125) *(G-4285)*

Keystone Cooperative Inc 937 884-5526
141 S Commerce St Verona (45378) *(G-14975)*

Keystone Foods LLC 419 257-2341
2208 Grant Rd North Baltimore (45872) *(G-11695)*

Keystone Press Inc 419 243-7326
1801 Broadway St Toledo (43609) *(G-14347)*

Keystone Threaded Products, Cleveland *Also Called: Keystone Bolt & Nut Company (G-4285)*

Keytel Systems, Reynoldsburg *Also Called: Town Cntry Technical Svcs Inc (G-12775)*

KG Medina LLC 256 330-4273
2925 Medina Rd Medina (44256) *(G-10343)*

Kg63 LLC 216 941-7766
15501 Chatfield Ave Cleveland (44111) *(G-4286)*

Kg63 LLC 216 941-7766
15501 Chatfield Ave Cleveland (44111) *(G-4287)*

Kgi Holdings, Cincinnati *Also Called: Kost Usa Inc (G-3088)*

Khempco Bldg Sup Co Ltd Partnr (PA) 740 549-0465
130 Johnson Dr Delaware (43015) *(G-6733)*

Kic Ltd 614 775-9570
1129 Brookhouse Ln Gahanna (43230) *(G-7841)*

Kichler Lighting, Solon *Also Called: Kichler Lighting LLC (G-13379)*

Kichler Lighting LLC (HQ) 216 573-1000
30455 Solon Rd Solon (44139) *(G-13379)*

Kidron Inc 330 857-3011
13442 Emerson Rd Kidron (44636) *(G-8915)*

Kiemle-Hankins, Perrysburg *Also Called: Kiemle-Hankins Company (G-12395)*

Kiemle-Hankins Company (PA) 419 661-2430
94 H St Perrysburg (43551) *(G-12395)*

Kiffer Industries Inc (PA) 216 267-1818
4905 Rocky River Dr Cleveland (44135) *(G-4288)*

Kilar Manufacturing Inc 330 534-8961
2616 N Main St Hubbard (44425) *(G-8567)*

Kilbarger Construction Inc 740 385-6019
450 Gallagher Ave Logan (43138) *(G-9367)*

Kiley Machine Company 513 875-3223
4196 Anderson State Rd Fayetteville (45118) *(G-7466)*

Killbuck Creek Oil Co LLC 330 601-0921
2098 Portage Rd Ste 250 Wooster (44691) *(G-16143)*

Killbuck Oil and Gas LLC 330 447-8423
52 Marvin Ave Akron (44302) *(G-206)*

Killer Brownie Ltd 937 535-5690
650 Precision Ct Miamisburg (45342) *(G-10651)*

Killian Latex Inc 330 644-6746
2064 Killian Rd Akron (44312) *(G-207)*

Kilroy Company (PA) 440 951-8700
17325 Euclid Ave Ste 2042 Cleveland (44112) *(G-4289)*

ALPHABETIC SECTION

Kiltex Corporation.. 330 644-6746
  2064 Killian Rd Akron (44312) *(G-208)*
Kimball Midwest, Columbus *Also Called: Midwest Motor Supply Co (G-5565)*
Kimble Clay & Limestone, Dover *Also Called: Kimble Company (G-6830)*
Kimble Company (PA).. 330 343-1226
  3596 State Route 39 Nw Dover (44622) *(G-6830)*
Kimble Custom Chassis Company.. 877 546-2537
  1951 Reiser Ave Se New Philadelphia (44663) *(G-11508)*
Kimble Machines Inc... 419 485-8449
  124 S Jonesville St Montpelier (43543) *(G-11138)*
Kimble Manufacturing Company, New Philadelphia *Also Called: Kimble Custom Chassis Company (G-11508)*
Kimble Mixer Company.. 330 308-6700
  1951 Reiser Ave Se New Philadelphia (44663) *(G-11509)*
Kimmatt Corp... 937 228-3811
  4459 Preble County Line Rd S West Alexandria (45381) *(G-15342)*
Kimpton Printing & Spc Co... 330 467-1640
  400 Highland Rd E Macedonia (44056) *(G-9561)*
Kimpton Prtg & Specialities, Macedonia *Also Called: Kimpton Printing & Spc Co (G-9561)*
Kinetic Concepts Inc.. 440 234-8590
  6751 Engle Rd Middleburg Heights (44130) *(G-10722)*
Kinetico Incorporated (HQ).. 440 564-9111
  10845 Kinsman Rd Newbury (44065) *(G-11628)*
Kinetics Noise Control Inc (PA).. 614 889-0480
  6300 Irelan Pl Dublin (43016) *(G-6905)*
King Bag and Manufacturing Co (PA)...................................... 513 541-5440
  1500 Spring Lawn Ave Cincinnati (45223) *(G-3076)*
King Bros Feed & Supply, Bristolville *Also Called: K M B Inc (G-1652)*
King Castings, Akron *Also Called: King Model Company (G-210)*
King Force & Machine, Twinsburg *Also Called: King Forge and Machine Company (G-14679)*
King Forge and Machine Company... 330 963-0600
  8250 Boyle Pkwy Twinsburg (44087) *(G-14679)*
King Industries LLC... 330 733-9106
  1324 Newton St Akron (44305) *(G-209)*
King Kold Inc.. 937 836-2731
  331 N Main St Englewood (45322) *(G-7235)*
King Kutter II Inc... 740 446-0351
  2150 Eastern Ave Gallipolis (45631) *(G-7896)*
King Limestone Inc.. 740 638-3942
  53681 Spencer Rd Cumberland (43732) *(G-6055)*
King Luminaire, Jefferson *Also Called: Stress-Crete Company (G-8759)*
King Luminaire Company Inc (HQ)... 440 576-9073
  1153 State Route 46 N Jefferson (44047) *(G-8750)*
King Machine and Tool Co... 330 833-7217
  1237 Sanders Ave Sw Massillon (44647) *(G-10117)*
King Media Enterprises Inc.. 216 588-6700
  11800 Shaker Blvd Cleveland (44120) *(G-4290)*
King Model Company... 330 633-0491
  365 Kenmore Blvd Akron (44301) *(G-210)*
King Nut Companies, Solon *Also Called: Kanan Enterprises Inc (G-13374)*
King Nut Companies, Solon *Also Called: Kanan Enterprises Inc (G-13375)*
King Nut Companies, Plant 2, Solon *Also Called: Kanan Enterprises Inc (G-13376)*
King of The Road, Troy *Also Called: Crowe Manufacturing Services (G-14558)*
King-Indiana Forge Inc... 330 425-4250
  8250 Boyle Pkwy Twinsburg (44087) *(G-14680)*
Kings Command Foods 2022 LLC... 937 827-7131
  770 N Center St Versailles (45380) *(G-14984)*
Kings Welding and Fabg Inc.. 330 738-3592
  5259 Bane Rd Ne Mechanicstown (44651) *(G-10287)*
Kingscote Chemicals Inc... 330 523-5300
  3778 Timberlake Dr Richfield (44286) *(G-12790)*
Kingsly Compression, Cambridge *Also Called: Kingsly Compression Inc (G-1939)*
Kingsly Compression Inc... 740 439-0772
  3956 Glenn Hwy Cambridge (43725) *(G-1939)*
Kingspan Benchmark, Columbus *Also Called: Benchmark Archtectural Systems (G-5182)*
Kingswood Company, The, Columbus *Also Called: Glister Inc (G-5404)*
Kinko's, Cleveland *Also Called: Kinkos Inc (G-4291)*
Kinkos Inc.. 216 661-9950
  4832 Ridge Rd Cleveland (44144) *(G-4291)*
Kinly Signs Corporation.. 740 451-7446
  2485 County Road 1 South Point (45680) *(G-13468)*

Kinnemeyers Cornerstone Cab Co, Cleves *Also Called: Kinnemyers Cornerstone Cab Inc (G-4957)*
Kinnemyers Cornerstone Cab Inc.. 513 353-3030
  6000 Hamilton Cleves Rd Cleves (45002) *(G-4957)*
Kinninger Prod Wldg Co Inc.. 419 629-3491
  710 Kuenzel Dr New Bremen (45869) *(G-11403)*
Kinoly Signs... 740 451-7446
  2485 County Road 1 South Point (45680) *(G-13469)*
Kinsella Manufacturing Co Inc... 513 561-5285
  7880 Camargo Rd Cincinnati (45243) *(G-3077)*
Kinstle Strlng/Wstern Star Trc, Wapakoneta *Also Called: Kinstle Truck & Auto Svc Inc (G-15120)*
Kinstle Truck & Auto Svc Inc... 419 738-7493
  1770 Wapakoneta Fisher Rd Wapakoneta (45895) *(G-15120)*
Kinzua Environmental Inc.. 216 881-4040
  1176 E 38th St Ste 1 Cleveland (44114) *(G-4292)*
Kip-Craft Incorporated (PA)... 216 898-5500
  4747 W 160th St Cleveland (44135) *(G-4293)*
Kipps Gravel Company Inc.. 513 732-1024
  30464 Jackson Rd Kingston (45644) *(G-8931)*
Kipton Properties Inc... 440 315-3699
  14647 State Route 511 Oberlin (44074) *(G-12054)*
Kiraly Tool and Die Inc.. 330 744-5773
  1250 Crescent St Youngstown (44502) *(G-16386)*
Kirby and Sons Inc.. 419 927-2260
  4876 County Highway 43 Upper Sandusky (43351) *(G-14813)*
Kirby Sand & Gravel, Upper Sandusky *Also Called: Kirby and Sons Inc (G-14813)*
Kirbys Auto and Truck Repr Inc... 513 934-3999
  875 Columbus Ave Lebanon (45036) *(G-9093)*
Kirchhoff Auto Waverly Inc (DH).. 740 947-7763
  611 W 2nd St Waverly (45690) *(G-15284)*
Kirk & Blum Manufacturing Co (DH)... 513 458-2600
  4625 Red Bank Rd Ste 200 Cincinnati (45227) *(G-3078)*
Kirk Key Interlock Company LLC... 330 833-8223
  9048 Meridian Cir Nw North Canton (44720) *(G-11740)*
Kirk Williams Company Inc.. 614 875-9023
  2734 Home Rd Grove City (43123) *(G-8100)*
Kirkwood Holding Inc (PA)... 216 267-6200
  1239 Rockside Rd Cleveland (44134) *(G-4294)*
Kirtland Capital Partners LP (PA).. 216 593-0100
  3201 Enterprise Pkwy Ste 200 Beachwood (44122) *(G-993)*
Kirtland Plastics Inc.. 440 951-4466
  7955 Euclid Chardon Rd Kirtland (44094) *(G-8941)*
Kirtley Mold Inc... 330 472-2427
  1986 Manchester Rd Akron (44314) *(G-211)*
Kirwan Industries Inc... 513 333-0766
  8390 Ridge Rd Cincinnati (45236) *(G-3079)*
Kish Company Inc (PA)... 440 205-9970
  8020 Tyler Blvd Ste 100 Mentor (44060) *(G-10487)*
Kiss Custom Coatings LLC.. 440 941-5002
  4503 Fenwick Ave Cleveland (44102) *(G-4295)*
Kissicakes-N-Sweets LLC... 614 940-2779
  7660 Silver Fox Dr Columbus (43235) *(G-5511)*
Kitchen Designs Plus Inc... 419 536-6605
  2725 N Reynolds Rd Toledo (43615) *(G-14348)*
Kitchenaid Inc... 937 316-4782
  1700 Kitchen Aid Way Greenville (45331) *(G-8049)*
Kitchens By Java... 419 621-7677
  1903 Cleveland Rd Sandusky (44870) *(G-13071)*
Kitchens By Rutenschroer Inc (PA)... 513 251-8333
  950 Laidlaw Ave Cincinnati (45237) *(G-3080)*
Kitto Katsu Inc.. 818 256-6997
  7445 Lockwood St Clayton (45315) *(G-3567)*
Kittyhawk Molding Company Inc... 937 746-3663
  10 Eagle Ct Carlisle (45005) *(G-2289)*
Kiwi Promotional AP & Prtg Co... 330 487-5115
  2170 E Aurora Rd Twinsburg (44087) *(G-14681)*
Kkr LLC.. 440 564-7168
  14905 Cross Creek Pkwy Newbury (44065) *(G-11629)*
Klarity Medical Products LLC.. 740 788-8107
  600 Industrial Pkwy Ste A Heath (43056) *(G-8324)*

Kleen Polymers Inc

ALPHABETIC SECTION

Kleen Polymers Inc
145 Rainbow St Wadsworth (44281) *(G-15040)*

Kleen Test Products, Beach City Also Called: Meridian Industries Inc *(G-968)*

Kleen Test Products Corp.. 330 878-5586
216 12th St Ne Strasburg (44680) *(G-13747)*

Kleenline LLC.. 800 259-5973
6279 Tri Ridge Blvd Ste 410 Loveland (45140) *(G-9489)*

Klenk, Canton Also Called: Klenk Industries Inc *(G-2139)*

Klenk Industries Inc... 330 453-7857
1016 9th St Sw Canton (44707) *(G-2139)*

Klinger Agency Inc... 419 893-9759
1760 Manley Rd Maumee (43537) *(G-10212)*

Klingshirn Winery Inc... 440 933-6666
33050 Webber Rd Avon Lake (44012) *(G-814)*

Klingstedt Brothers Company... 330 456-8319
425 Schroyer Ave Sw Canton (44702) *(G-2140)*

Klosterman, Cincinnati Also Called: Klosterman Baking Co LLC *(G-3082)*

Klosterman Baking Co.. 513 398-2707
1130 Reading Rd Mason (45040) *(G-10017)*

Klosterman Baking Co LLC.. 513 242-5667
1000 E Ross Ave Cincinnati (45217) *(G-3081)*

Klosterman Baking Co LLC (PA)..................................... 513 242-1004
4760 Paddock Rd Cincinnati (45229) *(G-3082)*

KLOSTERMAN BAKING CO., Mason Also Called: Klosterman Baking Co *(G-10017)*

Klutch Cannabis, Akron Also Called: Atcpc of Ohio LLC *(G-67)*

Klw Plastics Inc (DH)... 513 539-2673
980 Deneen Ave Monroe (45050) *(G-11114)*

Klx Energy Services LLC.. 740 922-1155
3571 Brighwood Rd Midvale (44653) *(G-10880)*

Kmak Group LLC... 937 308-1023
480 E High St London (43140) *(G-9390)*

KMC Holdings LLC... 419 238-2442
1260 Industrial Dr Van Wert (45891) *(G-14920)*

Kmgrafx Inc... 513 248-4100
394 Wards Corner Rd Ste 100 Loveland (45140) *(G-9490)*

Kmi Processing LLC.. 330 862-2185
15441 Lisbon St Ne Minerva (44657) *(G-11033)*

Kmj Leasing Ltd... 614 871-3883
7001 Harrisburg Pike Orient (43146) *(G-12115)*

Kml Acquisitions Ltd... 614 732-9777
10325 Spicebrush Dr Plain City (43064) *(G-12582)*

KMS 2000 Inc (PA).. 330 454-9444
315 12th St Nw Canton (44703) *(G-2141)*

Kn Rubber LLC (HQ)... 419 739-4200
1400 Lunar Dr Wapakoneta (45895) *(G-15121)*

Kn8designs LLC... 859 380-5926
4016 Allston St Cincinnati (45209) *(G-3083)*

Knape Industries Inc... 614 885-3016
6592 Proprietors Rd Worthington (43085) *(G-16200)*

Knapke Cabinets Inc... 937 335-8383
2 E Main St Troy (45373) *(G-14592)*

Knapke Custom Cabinetry, Versailles Also Called: Knapke Custom Cabinetry Ltd *(G-14985)*

Knapke Custom Cabinetry Ltd.. 937 459-8866
9306 Kelch Rd Versailles (45380) *(G-14985)*

Knappco Corporation... 513 870-3100
9393 Princeton Glendale Rd West Chester (45011) *(G-15455)*

Knb Tools of America Inc.. 614 733-0400
8440 Rausch Dr Plain City (43064) *(G-12583)*

Knh Industries Inc (PA)... 330 235-1235
3844 Oneida St Stow (44224) *(G-13703)*

Knh Industries Inc... 330 510-8390
3900 Darrow Rd Unit 2732 Stow (44224) *(G-13704)*

Knight Industries Corp.. 419 478-8550
5949 Telegraph Rd Toledo (43612) *(G-14349)*

Knight Line Signature AP Corp....................................... 330 545-8108
16 W Liberty St Girard (44420) *(G-7970)*

Knight Manufacturing Co Inc.. 740 676-5516
E 40th St Shadyside (43947) *(G-13146)*

Knight Manufacturing Co Inc (PA)................................. 740 676-9532
399 E 40th St Shadyside (43947) *(G-13147)*

Knight Material Tech LLC (PA)....................................... 330 488-1651
5385 Orchardview Dr Se East Canton (44730) *(G-6979)*

Knippen Chrysler Ddge Jeep Inc.................................... 419 695-4976
800 W 5th St Delphos (45833) *(G-6767)*

Knippen Chrysler Dodge Jeep, Delphos Also Called: Knippen Chrysler Ddge Jeep Inc *(G-6767)*

Knisley Lumber.. 740 634-2935
160 Potts Hill Rd Bainbridge (45612) *(G-831)*

Knitting Machinery Corp.. 937 548-2338
607 Riffle Ave Greenville (45331) *(G-8050)*

KNITTING MACHINERY CORP., Greenville Also Called: Knitting Machinery Corp *(G-8050)*

Knoble Glass & Metal Inc (PA)....................................... 513 753-1246
8650 Green Rd Cincinnati (45255) *(G-3084)*

Knott Brake Company.. 800 566-8887
144 West Dr Lodi (44254) *(G-9352)*

Knowlton Machine Inc... 419 281-6802
726 Virginia Ave Ashland (44805) *(G-587)*

Knowlton Manufacturing Co Inc..................................... 513 631-7353
2524 Leslie Ave Cincinnati (45212) *(G-3085)*

Knowlton Packaging, Groveport Also Called: Tri-Tech Laboratories LLC *(G-8164)*

Knox Energy Inc (PA)... 740 927-6731
11072 Worthington Rd Nw Pataskala (43062) *(G-12301)*

Knox Energy Inc.. 614 885-4828
795 Old Woods Rd Columbus (43235) *(G-5512)*

Knox Machine & Tool.. 740 392-3133
250 Columbus Rd Mount Vernon (43050) *(G-11276)*

Knudsen & Sons Inc... 330 682-3000
1 Strawberry Ln Orrville (44667) *(G-12133)*

Knutsen Machine Products Inc...................................... 216 751-6500
15020 Miles Ave Cleveland (44128) *(G-4296)*

Kobelco Stewart Bolling Inc... 330 655-3111
1600 Terex Rd Hudson (44236) *(G-8601)*

Kodak, Dayton Also Called: Eastman Kodak Company *(G-6311)*

Kodak, Kettering Also Called: Eastman Kodak Company *(G-8906)*

Kodiak Chemical, Cincinnati Also Called: Kc Marketing LLC *(G-3067)*

Koebbe Products Inc (PA)... 513 753-4200
1132 Ferris Rd Amelia (45102) *(G-458)*

Koebbe Products Inc.. 513 735-1400
4226 Grissom Dr Batavia (45103) *(G-928)*

Koenig Equipment Inc... 937 653-5281
3130 E Us Highway 36 Urbana (43078) *(G-14842)*

Koester Corporation (PA)... 419 599-0291
813 N Perry St Napoleon (43545) *(G-11322)*

Koester Machined Products Co...................................... 419 782-0291
136 Fox Run Dr Defiance (43512) *(G-6688)*

Kohl & Madden Inc.. 513 326-6900
5000 Spring Grove Ave Cincinnati (45232) *(G-3086)*

KOHLER COATING, Canton Also Called: Kohler Coating Inc *(G-2142)*

Kohler Coating Inc... 330 499-1407
1205 5th St Sw Canton (44707) *(G-2142)*

Kohler Coating Inc... 330 499-1407
10995 Wright Rd Nw Uniontown (44685) *(G-14786)*

Kokosing Materials Inc... 740 694-5872
11624 Hyatt Rd Fredericktown (43019) *(G-7750)*

Kokosing Materials Inc... 419 522-2715
215 Oak St Mansfield (44907) *(G-9677)*

Kokosing Materials Inc... 740 745-3341
9134 Mount Vernon Rd Saint Louisville (43071) *(G-12943)*

Kokosing Materials Inc... 614 491-1199
4755 S High St Columbus (43207) *(G-5513)*

Kokosing Materials Inc (HQ).. 740 694-9585
17531 Waterford Rd Fredericktown (43019) *(G-7751)*

Kol-Cap Manufacturing Co, Brunswick Also Called: Walest Incorporated *(G-1800)*

Kolhfab Cstm Plstic Fbrication....................................... 937 237-2098
2025 Webster St Dayton (45404) *(G-6399)*

Kolinahr Systems Inc.. 513 745-9401
6840 Ashfield Dr Blue Ash (45242) *(G-1417)*

Kolmer.. 614 261-0190
3851 N High St Ste B Columbus (43214) *(G-5514)*

Kolpin Outdoors Corporation.. 330 328-0772
3479 State Rd Cuyahoga Falls (44223) *(G-6096)*

ALPHABETIC SECTION — Kse Manufacturing

Koltcz Concrete Block Co 440 232-3630
7660 Oak Leaf Rd Bedford (44146) *(G-1132)*

Komatsu Mining Corp 216 503-5029
981 Keynote Cir Ste 8 Independence (44131) *(G-8670)*

Kona Blackbird Inc 440 285-3189
11730 Ravenna Rd Chardon (44024) *(G-2455)*

Konecranes Inc 440 461-8400
331 Treeworth Blvd Broadview Heights (44147) *(G-1660)*

Konecranes Inc 614 863-0150
1110 Claycraft Rd Ste C Gahanna (43230) *(G-7842)*

Konecranes Inc 937 328-5100
4505 Gateway Blvd Springfield (45502) *(G-13589)*

Konecranes Inc (HQ) 937 525-5533
4401 Gateway Blvd Springfield (45502) *(G-13590)*

Konecranes Inc 419 382-7575
2221 Tedrow Rd Toledo (43614) *(G-14350)*

Konecranes Inc 513 755-2800
4866 Duff Dr West Chester (45246) *(G-15567)*

Koneta Inc 419 739-4200
1400 Lunar Dr Wapakoneta (45895) *(G-15122)*

Koneta Rubber, Wapakoneta Also Called: Kn Rubber LLC *(G-15121)*

Kongsberg Actation Systems LLC 440 639-8778
301 Olive St Grand River (44045) *(G-8012)*

Kongsberg Automotive, Grand River Also Called: Kongsberg Actation Systems LLC *(G-8012)*

Kongsberg Prcsion Ctng Systems 937 800-2169
1983 Byers Rd Miamisburg (45342) *(G-10652)*

Kontron America Incorporated 937 324-2420
202 N Limestone St Springfield (45503) *(G-13591)*

Konys, Mark Glass Design, Cleveland Also Called: Bruening Glass Works Inc *(G-3765)*

Koop Diamond Cutters Inc 513 621-2838
214 E 8th St Fl 4 Cincinnati (45202) *(G-3087)*

Kopco Graphics Inc (PA) 513 874-7230
9750 Crescent Prk Dr West Chester (45069) *(G-15456)*

Korda Manufacturing Inc 330 262-1555
3927 E Lincoln Way Wooster (44691) *(G-16144)*

Korff Holdings LLC 330 332-1566
310 E Euclid Ave Salem (44460) *(G-13008)*

Kosei St Marys Corporation 419 394-7840
1100 Mckinley Rd Saint Marys (45885) *(G-12955)*

Koski Construction Co (PA) 440 997-5337
5841 Woodman Ave Ashtabula (44004) *(G-644)*

Kost Usa Inc (DH) 513 583-7070
1000 Tennessee Ave Cincinnati (45229) *(G-3088)*

Kotobuki-Reliable Die Casting Inc 937 347-1111
851 Bellbrook Ave Xenia (45385) *(G-16267)*

Kottler Metal Products Co Inc 440 946-7473
1595 Lost Nation Rd Willoughby (44094) *(G-15940)*

Kowalski Heat Treating Co 216 631-4411
3611 Detroit Ave Cleveland (44113) *(G-4297)*

Krafft and Associates Inc 937 325-4671
991 W Leffel Ln Springfield (45506) *(G-13592)*

Kraft Electrical Contg Inc 614 836-9300
4407 Professional Pkwy Groveport (43125) *(G-8149)*

Kraft Heinz Company 330 837-8331
1301 Oberlin Ave Sw Massillon (44647) *(G-10118)*

Kraft Heinz Company, Massillon Also Called: Kraft Heinz Company *(G-10118)*

Kraft Heinz Foods Company 740 622-0523
1660 S 2nd St Coshocton (43812) *(G-5982)*

Kraft Heinz Foods Company 419 334-5724
1301 N River Rd Fremont (43420) *(G-7792)*

Kraft Heinz Foods Company 419 332-7357
1200n N 5th St Fremont (43420) *(G-7793)*

Kraftmaid Cabinetry, Middlefield Also Called: Cabintwrks Group Mddlfield LLC *(G-10738)*

Kraftmaid Trucking Inc (PA) 440 632-2531
16052 Industrial Pkwy Middlefield (44062) *(G-10762)*

Krafts Exotika LLC 216 563-1178
3553 Bosworth Rd Cleveland (44111) *(G-4298)*

Kram Precision Machining Inc 937 849-1301
1751 Dalton Dr New Carlisle (45344) *(G-11419)*

Kramer & Kiefer Inc 330 336-8742
2662 Valley Side Ave Wadsworth (44281) *(G-15041)*

Kramer Graphics Inc 937 296-9600
2408 W Dorothy Ln Moraine (45439) *(G-11188)*

Kramer Power Equipment Co 937 456-2232
2388 State Route 726 N Eaton (45320) *(G-7063)*

Kramer Printing, Mentor Also Called: J & L Management Corporation *(G-10478)*

Kraton Corporation 740 423-7571
2419 State Route 618 Belpre (45714) *(G-1255)*

Kraton Emplyees Recreation CLB 740 423-7571
2419 State Route 618 Belpre (45714) *(G-1256)*

Kraton Polymers, Belpre Also Called: Kraton Polymers US LLC *(G-1257)*

Kraton Polymers US LLC 740 423-7571
2419 State Route 618 Belpre (45714) *(G-1257)*

Krausher Machining Inc 440 839-2828
4267 Butler Rd Wakeman (44889) *(G-15075)*

Krazy Glue, West Jefferson Also Called: Toagosei America Inc *(G-15615)*

Kreager Co LLC 740 345-1605
1045 Brice St Newark (43055) *(G-11585)*

Kreate Extrusion LLC 419 683-4057
2000 Industrial Dr Findlay (45840) *(G-7527)*

Krehbiel Holdings Inc
3962 Virginia Ave Cincinnati (45227) *(G-3089)*

Kreider Corp 937 325-8787
400 Harrison St Springfield (45505) *(G-13593)*

Krema Group Inc 614 889-4824
8415 Rausch Dr Plain City (43064) *(G-12584)*

Krema Nut Co, Columbus Also Called: Brilista Foods Company Inc *(G-5217)*

Krendl Machine Company 419 692-3060
1201 Spencerville Rd Delphos (45833) *(G-6768)*

Krendl Rack Co Inc 419 667-4800
18413 Haver Rd Venedocia (45894) *(G-14970)*

Krengel Equipment LLC 440 946-3570
34580 Lakeland Blvd Eastlake (44095) *(G-7037)*

Krengel Manufacturing, Eastlake Also Called: Krengel Equipment LLC *(G-7037)*

Krenz Precision Machining Inc 440 237-1800
9801 York Alpha Dr North Royalton (44133) *(G-11882)*

Krieg Rev 2 Inc 513 542-1522
10600 Chester Rd Cincinnati (45215) *(G-3090)*

Krin USA, Lakeville Also Called: 1200 Feet Limited *(G-8962)*

Krisdale, Valley City Also Called: Krisdale Inc *(G-14875)*

Krisdale Inc 330 225-2392
649 Marks Rd Valley City (44280) *(G-14875)*

Krispy Kreme, Columbus Also Called: Krispy Kreme Doughnut Corp *(G-5516)*

Krispy Kreme 322, Columbus Also Called: Krispy Kreme Doughnut Corp *(G-5515)*

Krispy Kreme Doughnut Corp 614 798-0812
3690 W Dublin Granville Rd Columbus (43235) *(G-5515)*

Krispy Kreme Doughnut Corp 614 876-0058
2557 Westbelt Dr Columbus (43228) *(G-5516)*

Kriss Kreations 330 405-6102
9224 Darrow Rd Twinsburg (44087) *(G-14682)*

Krista Messer 734 459-1952
15301 E State Route 37 Sunbury (43074) *(G-13957)*

Kroner Publications Inc (PA) 330 544-5500
1123 W Park Ave Niles (44446) *(G-11675)*

Kroy LLC 216 426-5600
3830 Kelley Ave Cleveland (44114) *(G-4299)*

Krumor Inc 216 328-9802
7655 Hub Pkwy Ste 206 Cleveland (44125) *(G-4300)*

Krupp Rubber Machinery 330 864-0800
103 Western Ave Akron (44313) *(G-212)*

Krusinski's Meat Market, Cleveland Also Called: John Krusinski *(G-4258)*

Kruz Inc 330 878-5595
6332 Columbia Rd Nw Dover (44622) *(G-6831)*

KS Technologies & Cstm Mfg LLC 419 426-0172
12178 E County Road 6 Attica (44807) *(G-701)*

KS Welding & Fabrication LLC 937 420-2270
7820 Dawson Rd Fort Loramie (45845) *(G-7602)*

KSA Limited Partnership 740 776-3238
6501 Pershing Ave Portsmouth (45662) *(G-12647)*

Kse Manufacturing 937 409-9831
175 S Lester Ave Sidney (45365) *(G-13257)*

Ksm Metal Fabrication 937 339-6366
  104 Foss Way Troy (45373) *(G-14593)*
Ksm Metal Fabrications, Troy *Also Called: Kerber Sheetmetal Works Inc (G-14591)*
Kth Industries 614 733-2020
  8205 Business Way Plain City (43064) *(G-12585)*
Kth Parts Industries Inc (HQ) 937 663-5941
  1111 N State Rte 235 Saint Paris (43072) *(G-12973)*
Ktm North America Inc (PA) 855 215-6360
  1119 Milan Ave Amherst (44001) *(G-477)*
Ktri Holdings Inc (HQ) 216 400-9308
  127 Public Sq Ste 5110 Cleveland (44114) *(G-4301)*
Kts Cstm Lgs/Xclsvely You Inc 440 285-9803
  602 South St Ste C-2 Chardon (44024) *(G-2456)*
Kts Custom Logos 440 285-9803
  602 South St Ste C-2 Chardon (44024) *(G-2457)*
Kts Equipment Inc 440 647-2015
  47117 State Route 18 Wellington (44090) *(G-15316)*
Kts Met-Bar Products Inc 440 288-9308
  967 G St Lorain (44052) *(G-9417)*
Ktsdi LLC 330 783-2000
  801 E Middletown Rd North Lima (44452) *(G-11808)*
Kubota Authorized Dealer, Athens *Also Called: All Power Equipment LLC (G-374)*
Kubota Tractor Corporation 614 835-3800
  6300 At One Kubota Way Groveport (43125) *(G-8150)*
Kuhlman Construction Products, Maumee *Also Called: Kuhlman Corporation (G-10213)*
Kuhlman Corporation 330 724-9900
  999 Swartz Rd Coventry Township (44319) *(G-6012)*
Kuhlman Corporation (PA) 419 897-6000
  1845 Indian Wood Cir Maumee (43537) *(G-10213)*
Kuhlman Corporation 419 321-1670
  444 Kuhlman Dr Toledo (43609) *(G-14351)*
Kuhlman Engineering Co 419 243-2196
  840 Champlain St Toledo (43604) *(G-14352)*
Kuhlman Instrument Company 419 668-9533
  54 Summit St Norwalk (44857) *(G-11976)*
Kuhlmanns Fabrication 513 967-4617
  1753 Millville Oxford Rd Hamilton (45013) *(G-8226)*
Kuhls Hot Sportspot 513 474-2282
  6701 Beechmont Ave Cincinnati (45230) *(G-3091)*
Kuhn Fabricating Inc 440 277-4182
  1637 E 28th St Lorain (44055) *(G-9418)*
Kuhns Mold & Tool Co Inc 937 833-2178
  9360 National Rd Brookville (45309) *(G-1740)*
Kuka Tledo Prdction Oprtons LL 419 727-5500
  3770 Stickney Ave Toledo (43608) *(G-14353)*
Kundel, Vienna *Also Called: Kundel Industries Inc (G-14996)*
Kundel Industries Inc (PA) 330 469-6147
  1510 Ridge Rd Vienna (44473) *(G-14996)*
Kurome Therapeutics Inc 513 445-3852
  3536 Edwards Rd Ste 100 Cincinnati (45208) *(G-3092)*
Kurtz Bros Compost Services 330 864-2621
  2677 Riverview Rd Akron (44313) *(G-213)*
Kurtz Tool & Die Co Inc 330 755-7723
  164 State St Struthers (44471) *(G-13905)*
Kurz-Kasch, Newcomerstown *Also Called: Kurz-Kasch Inc (G-11647)*
Kurz-Kasch Inc (DH) 740 498-8343
  199 E State St Newcomerstown (43832) *(G-11647)*
Kutol Products Company Inc (PA) 513 527-5500
  100 Partnership Way Sharonville (45241) *(G-13171)*
Kutol Products Company Inc 513 527-5500
  11955 Enterprise Dr Sharonville (45241) *(G-13172)*
Kutrite Manufacturing, Tremont City *Also Called: Mike Loppe (G-14538)*
Kuzma Industries LLC 419 701-7005
  1541 N Township Road 101 Fostoria (44830) *(G-7640)*
Kw Acquisition Inc 740 548-7298
  7975 N Central Dr Lewis Center (43035) *(G-9168)*
KWD Automotive Inc 419 344-8232
  6700 Cemetery Rd Whitehouse (43571) *(G-15820)*
Kween and Co 440 724-4342
  994 Valley Belt Rd Brooklyn Heights (44131) *(G-1694)*
Kwik Kopy Printing, Blue Ash *Also Called: Larmax Inc (G-1419)*

Kyklos Bearing International Llc 419 627-7000
  2509 Hayes Ave Sandusky (44870) *(G-13072)*
Kyle Media Inc 419 754-4234
  2611 Montebello Rd Toledo (43607) *(G-14354)*
Kyle Media Inc 877 775-2538
  7862 W Central Ave Ste F Toledo (43617) *(G-14355)*
Kyntrol Holdings Inc 440 220-5990
  34700 Lakeland Blvd Eastlake (44095) *(G-7038)*
Kyntronics Inc (PA) 440 220-5990
  6565 Davis Industrial Pkwy Ste R Solon (44139) *(G-13380)*
Kyocera Hardcoating Tech Ltd 330 686-2136
  220 Marc Dr Cuyahoga Falls (44223) *(G-6097)*
Kyocera Precision Tools, Cuyahoga Falls *Also Called: Kyocera SGS Precision Tls Inc (G-6098)*
Kyocera Senco Indus Tls Inc (HQ) 513 388-2000
  8450 Broadwell Rd Cincinnati (45244) *(G-3093)*
Kyocera SGS Precision Tls Inc (PA) 330 688-6667
  150 Marc Dr Cuyahoga Falls (44223) *(G-6098)*
Kyocera SGS Precision Tls Inc 330 922-1953
  238 Marc Dr Cuyahoga Falls (44223) *(G-6099)*
Kyron Tool & Machine Co Inc 614 231-6000
  2900 Banwick Rd Columbus (43232) *(G-5517)*
L & F Products 937 498-4710
  1810 Progress Way Sidney (45365) *(G-13258)*
L & J Cable Inc 937 526-9445
  102 Industrial Dr Russia (45363) *(G-12885)*
L & J Drive Thru LLC 330 767-2185
  212 Wabash Ave N Brewster (44613) *(G-1644)*
L & L Machine Inc 419 272-5000
  2919 County Road 2l Edon (43518) *(G-7087)*
L & L Ornamental Iron Co 513 353-1930
  6024 Hamilton Cleves Rd Cleves (45002) *(G-4958)*
L & L Plastics, Felicity *Also Called: L C Liming & Sons Inc (G-7468)*
L & L Railings, Cleves *Also Called: L & L Ornamental Iron Co (G-4958)*
L & M Mineral Co 330 852-3696
  2010 County Road 144 Sugarcreek (44681) *(G-13927)*
L & M Processing LLC 330 405-0615
  1900 Case Pkwy S Twinsburg (44087) *(G-14683)*
L & O Tire Service Inc 937 394-8462
  14555 State Route 119 E Anna (45302) *(G-490)*
L & R Racing Inc 330 220-3102
  1261 Industrial Pkwy N Ste 1a Brunswick (44212) *(G-1773)*
L & S Home Improvement 330 906-3199
  549 Saunders Ave Coventry Township (44319) *(G-6013)*
L & T Collins Inc 740 345-4494
  44 S 4th St Newark (43055) *(G-11586)*
L & W Inc 734 397-6300
  1190 Jaycox Rd Avon (44011) *(G-778)*
L & W Investments Inc 937 492-4171
  2005 Campbell Rd Sidney (45365) *(G-13259)*
L and J Woodworking 330 359-3216
  9035 Senff Rd Dundee (44624) *(G-6966)*
L B Foster Company 330 652-1461
  1193 Salt Springs Rd Mineral Ridge (44440) *(G-11022)*
L B L Printing, Painesville *Also Called: LBL Lithographers Inc (G-12247)*
L B Manufacturing, Byesville *Also Called: Famous Industries Inc (G-1896)*
L C F Inc 330 877-3322
  114 S Prospect Ave Hartville (44632) *(G-8302)*
L C Liming & Sons Inc 513 876-2555
  3200 State Route 756 Felicity (45120) *(G-7468)*
L D C, Independence *Also Called: Liquid Development Company (G-8671)*
L E Smith Company (PA) 419 636-4555
  1030 E Wilson St Bryan (43506) *(G-1825)*
L E Sommer Kidron Inc 330 857-2031
  6856 Kidron Rd Apple Creek (44606) *(G-503)*
L Haberny Co Inc 440 543-5999
  10115 Queens Way Chagrin Falls (44023) *(G-2404)*
L J Manufacturing Inc 440 352-1979
  9436 Mercantile Dr Mentor (44060) *(G-10488)*
L J Minor Corp 216 861-8350
  2621 W 25th St Cleveland (44113) *(G-4302)*

ALPHABETIC SECTION

L J Publishing LLC 888 749-5994
 1287 Ridge Rd Ste B Hinckley (44233) *(G-8476)*

L J Star Incorporated 330 405-3040
 2396 Edison Blvd Twinsburg (44087) *(G-14684)*

L M Animal Farms, Pleasant Plain *Also Called: Hartz Mountain Corporation (G-12607)*

L M Engineering Inc 330 270-2400
 3760 Oakwood Ave Austintown (44515) *(G-752)*

L M Equipment & Design Inc 330 332-9951
 11000 Youngstown Salem Rd Salem (44460) *(G-13009)*

L N Brut Manufacturing Co 330 833-9045
 7300 State Route 754 Shreve (44676) *(G-13212)*

L P S I, Cleveland *Also Called: Laser Printing Solutions Inc (G-4315)*

L T V Steel Company Inc 216 622-5000
 200 Public Sq Cleveland (44114) *(G-4303)*

L-3 Cmmncations Nova Engrg Inc 877 282-1168
 4393 Digital Way Mason (45040) *(G-10018)*

L-H Battery Company Inc (PA) 937 613-3769
 One Innovation Way Jeffersonville (43128) *(G-8765)*

L.A.m Wldg & Met Fabrication, East Sparta *Also Called: William Niccum (G-7015)*

L.E.M. Products, West Chester *Also Called: Lem Products Holding LLC (G-15457)*

L&H Threaded Rods Corp 937 294-6666
 3050 Dryden Rd Moraine (45439) *(G-11189)*

L&W Cleveland, Avon *Also Called: L & W Inc (G-778)*

L3 Technologies Inc 513 943-2000
 3975 Mcmann Rd Cincinnati (45245) *(G-2568)*

L3 Technologies Inc 937 257-8501
 47 Alf/ Raythoen Arospace Bld 201 Area C 5 Dayton (45433) *(G-6165)*

L3 Technologies Inc 937 223-3285
 3155 Research Blvd Ste 101 Dayton (45420) *(G-6400)*

L3harris Cincinnati Elec Corp (DH) 513 573-6100
 7500 Innovation Way Mason (45040) *(G-10019)*

L3harris Electrodynamics Inc 847 259-0740
 3975 Mcmann Rd Cincinnati (45245) *(G-2569)*

L3harris Fzing Ord Systems Inc 513 943-2000
 3975 Mc Mann Rd Cincinnati (45245) *(G-2570)*

La Boit Specialty Vehicles 614 231-7640
 700 Cross Pointe Rd Gahanna (43230) *(G-7843)*

La Ganke & Sons Stamping Co 216 451-0278
 13676 Station Rd Columbia Station (44028) *(G-5013)*

La Grange Elec Assemblies Co 440 355-5388
 349 S Center St Lagrange (44050) *(G-8950)*

La Mfg Inc 513 577-7200
 9483 Reading Rd Cincinnati (45215) *(G-3094)*

La Perla Inc (PA) 419 534-2074
 2742 Hill Ave Toledo (43607) *(G-14356)*

La Prensa Publications Inc 419 870-6565
 616 Adams St Toledo (43604) *(G-14357)*

LA Rose Paving Co 440 632-0330
 16590 Nauvoo Rd Middlefield (44062) *(G-10763)*

Laad Sign & Lighting Inc 330 379-2297
 3097 State Route 59 Ravenna (44266) *(G-12721)*

Lab Quality Machining Inc 513 625-0219
 6311 Roudebush Rd Goshen (45122) *(G-7993)*

Lab-Pro Inc 937 434-9600
 845 N Main St Miamisburg (45342) *(G-10653)*

Lababidi Enterprises Inc 330 733-2907
 2167 Forest Oak Dr Akron (44312) *(G-214)*

Labcraft Inc 419 878-4400
 1070 Disher Dr Waterville (43566) *(G-15249)*

Label Aid, Huron *Also Called: Label Aid Inc (G-8635)*

Label Aid Inc 419 433-2888
 608 Rye Beach Rd Huron (44839) *(G-8635)*

Label Print Technologies, LLC, Mogadore *Also Called: Tpl Holdings LLC (G-11088)*

Label Technique Southeast LLC 440 951-7660
 38601 Kennedy Pkwy Willoughby (44094) *(G-15941)*

Labeltek Inc 330 335-3110
 985 Seville Rd Wadsworth (44281) *(G-15042)*

Laborie Enterprises, Portage *Also Called: Laborie Enterprises LLC (G-12634)*

Laborie Enterprises LLC 419 686-6245
 10892 S Dixie Hwy Portage (43451) *(G-12634)*

Lacal Equipment Inc 937 596-6106
 901 W Pike St Jackson Center (45334) *(G-8734)*

Lachina Creative Inc 216 292-7959
 3791 Green Rd Cleveland (44122) *(G-4304)*

Lad Technology Inc 561 543-9858
 7830 Hermitage Rd Concord Township (44077) *(G-5909)*

Lafarge Holcim 419 798-4866
 831 S Quarry Rd Lakeside Marblehead (43440) *(G-8960)*

Lafferty Chipping, Kimbolton *Also Called: Calvin W Lafferty (G-8927)*

Lagonda Investments III Inc 937 325-7305
 2145 Airpark Dr Springfield (45502) *(G-13594)*

Lahlouh Inc 650 692-6600
 150 Lawton Ave Monroe (45050) *(G-11115)*

Lahm Tool, Dayton *Also Called: Lahm-Trosper Inc (G-6401)*

Lahm-Trosper Inc 937 252-8791
 1030 Springfield St Dayton (45403) *(G-6401)*

Laipplys Prtg Mktg Sltions Inc 740 387-9282
 270 E Center St Marion (43302) *(G-9859)*

Laird Technologies, Cleveland *Also Called: Thermagon Inc (G-4791)*

Laird Technologies Inc 330 434-7929
 50 S Main St Ste 1100 Akron (44308) *(G-215)*

Laird Technologies Inc 216 939-2300
 4707 Detroit Ave Cleveland (44102) *(G-4305)*

Laird Technologies Inc 234 806-0105
 655 N River Rd Nw Warren (44483) *(G-15183)*

Lake Building Products Inc 216 486-1500
 1361 Chardon Rd Ste 4 Cleveland (44117) *(G-4306)*

Lake Building Products Ltd 216 486-1500
 1361 Chardon Rd Ste 4 Euclid (44117) *(G-7281)*

Lake City Plating, Ashtabula *Also Called: Lake City Plating LLC (G-645)*

Lake City Plating LLC (PA) 440 964-3555
 1701 Lake Ave Ashtabula (44004) *(G-645)*

Lake City Plating LLC 440 964-3555
 108 S Sycamore St Jefferson (44047) *(G-8751)*

Lake Cnty Dprtmntal Rtrdtion D, Willoughby *Also Called: County of Lake (G-15904)*

Lake Community News 440 946-2577
 36081 Lake Shore Blvd Ste 5 Willoughby (44095) *(G-15942)*

Lake County Plating Corp 440 255-8835
 7790 Division Dr Mentor (44060) *(G-10489)*

Lake Erie Aggregates Inc 419 541-0130
 720 Gloucester Dr Huron (44839) *(G-8636)*

Lake Erie Frozen Foods Mfg Co 419 289-9204
 1830 Orange Rd Ashland (44805) *(G-588)*

Lake Erie Graphics Inc 216 575-1333
 5372 W 130th St Brookpark (44142) *(G-1721)*

Lake Erie Interlock Inc 440 918-9898
 2132 Lost Nation Rd Unit 3 Willoughby (44094) *(G-15943)*

Lake Erie Iron and Metal, Cleveland *Also Called: Welders Supply Inc (G-4903)*

Lake Erie Ship Repr Fbrction L 440 228-7110
 1459 State Route 46 S Jefferson (44047) *(G-8752)*

Lake Erie Steel & Fabrication 440 232-6200
 5455 Perkins Rd Bedford Heights (44146) *(G-1175)*

Lake Erie Waterkeeper Inc 419 691-3788
 3900 N Summit St Toledo (43611) *(G-14358)*

Lake Metals, Ravenna *Also Called: A C Williams Co Inc (G-12699)*

Lake Park Tool & Machine, Youngstown *Also Called: Lake Park Tool & Machine LLC (G-16387)*

Lake Park Tool & Machine LLC 330 788-2437
 1221 Velma Ct Youngstown (44512) *(G-16387)*

Lake Publishing Inc 440 299-8500
 9853 Johnnycake Ridge Rd Ste 107 Mentor (44060) *(G-10490)*

Lake Region Oil Inc 330 828-8420
 26 N Cochran St Dalton (44618) *(G-6134)*

Lake Screen Printing Inc 440 244-5707
 1924 Broadway Lorain (44052) *(G-9419)*

Lake Shore Cryotronics Inc (PA) 614 891-2243
 575 Mccorkle Blvd Westerville (43082) *(G-15662)*

Lake Shore Graphic Inds Inc 419 626-8631
 2111 Cleveland Rd Sandusky (44870) *(G-13073)*

Lake Township Trustees 419 836-1143
 3800 Ayers Rd Millbury (43447) *(G-10934)*

Lakecraft, Port Clinton *Also Called: Lakecraft Inc (G-12621)*

Lakecraft Inc (PA) 419 734-2828
 1010 W Lakeshore Dr Port Clinton (43452) *(G-12621)*

Lakepark Industries Inc — ALPHABETIC SECTION

Lakepark Industries Inc 419 752-4471
  40 Seminary St Greenwich (44837) *(G-8068)*

Lakeside Sand & Gravel Inc 330 274-2569
  3498 Frost Rd Mantua (44255) *(G-9738)*

Lakeview Farms LLC (PA) 419 695-9925
  1600 Gressel Dr Delphos (45833) *(G-6769)*

Lakeway Mfg Inc (PA) 419 433-3030
  730 River Rd Huron (44839) *(G-8637)*

Lakewood Observer Inc 216 712-7070
  14900 Detroit Ave Ste 205 Lakewood (44107) *(G-8978)*

Lako Tool & Manufacturing Inc 419 662-5256
  7400 Ponderosa Rd Perrysburg (43551) *(G-12396)*

Lalac One LLC 216 432-4422
  18451 Euclid Ave Cleveland (44112) *(G-4307)*

Lam Pro Inc 216 426-0661
  4701 Crayton Ave Ste A Cleveland (44104) *(G-4308)*

Lam Research, Eaton *Also Called: Lam Research Corporation (G-7064)*

Lam Research Corporation 937 472-3311
  960 S Franklin St Eaton (45320) *(G-7064)*

Lam Tech, Tiffin *Also Called: Laminate Technologies Inc (G-14090)*

Lambert Sheet Metal Inc 614 237-0384
  3776 E 5th Ave Columbus (43219) *(G-5518)*

Laminate Shop 740 749-3536
  1145 Klinger Rd Waterford (45786) *(G-15237)*

Laminate Technologies Inc (PA) 800 231-2523
  161 Maule Rd Tiffin (44883) *(G-14090)*

Laminated Concepts Inc 216 475-4141
  14300 Industrial Ave N Maple Heights (44137) *(G-9753)*

Lamports Filter Media, Cleveland *Also Called: Lamports Filter Media Inc (G-4309)*

Lamports Filter Media Inc 216 881-2050
  837 E 79th St Cleveland (44103) *(G-4309)*

Lancaster Colony Corporation 614 792-9774
  280 Cramer Creek Ct Dublin (43017) *(G-6906)*

Lancaster Colony Corporation (PA) 614 224-7141
  380 Polaris Pkwy Ste 400 Westerville (43082) *(G-15663)*

Lancaster Colony Design Group, Dublin *Also Called: Lancaster Colony Corporation (G-6906)*

Lancaster Glass Corporation 614 224-7141
  380 Polaris Pkwy Ste 400 Westerville (43082) *(G-15664)*

Lancaster Metal Products Inc 740 653-3421
  520 Slocum St Lancaster (43130) *(G-9020)*

Lancaster Municipal Gas, Lancaster *Also Called: City of Lancaster (G-9002)*

Lancaster W Side Coal Co Inc (PA) 740 862-4713
  700 Van Buren Ave Lancaster (43130) *(G-9021)*

Lancer Dispersions Inc
  1680 E Market St Akron (44305) *(G-216)*

Land O'Lakes, Kent *Also Called: Land OLakes Inc (G-8827)*

Land O'Lakes, Massillon *Also Called: Land OLakes Inc (G-10119)*

Land OLakes Inc 330 678-1578
  2001 Mogadore Rd Kent (44240) *(G-8827)*

Land OLakes Inc 330 879-2158
  8485 Navarre Rd Sw Massillon (44646) *(G-10119)*

Land Specialties LLC 330 663-6974
  2293 Ullet St Sw East Sparta (44626) *(G-7014)*

Landerwood Industries Inc 440 233-4234
  4245 Hamann Pkwy Willoughby (44094) *(G-15944)*

Landis Machine Division, Cleveland *Also Called: Barth Industries Co LLC (G-3722)*

Landmark Plastic Corporation (PA) 330 785-2200
  1331 Kelly Ave Akron (44306) *(G-217)*

Landoll Publishing, Strongsville *Also Called: Landoll Publishing Sjs LLC (G-13849)*

Landoll Publishing Sjs LLC 330 353-2688
  14800 Foltz Pkwy Strongsville (44149) *(G-13849)*

Landon Vault Company 614 443-5505
  1477 Frebis Ave Columbus (43206) *(G-5519)*

Landrum & Brown, Blue Ash *Also Called: Landrum Brown Wrldwide Svcs LL (G-1418)*

Landrum Brown Wrldwide Svcs LL 513 530-5333
  4445 Lake Forest Dr # 700 Blue Ash (45242) *(G-1418)*

Lane Field Materials Inc 330 526-8082
  530 Walnut Ave Ne Canton (44702) *(G-2143)*

Lang Stone Company Inc (PA) 614 235-4099
  4099 E 5th Ave Columbus (43219) *(G-5520)*

Langa Tool & Machine Inc 440 953-1138
  36430 Reading Ave Ste 1 Willoughby (44094) *(G-15945)*

Langdon Inc 513 733-5955
  9865 Wayne Ave Cincinnati (45215) *(G-3095)*

Lange Grinding & Machining Inc 330 463-3500
  10165 Philipp Pkwy Streetsboro (44241) *(G-13777)*

Langenau Manufacturing Company 216 651-3400
  7306 Madison Ave Cleveland (44102) *(G-4310)*

Langstons Ultmate Clg Svcs Inc 330 298-9150
  3764 Summit Rd Ravenna (44266) *(G-12722)*

Lanier & Associates Inc 216 391-7735
  1814 E 40th St Ste 1c Cleveland (44103) *(G-4311)*

Lanko Industries Inc 440 269-1641
  7301 Industrial Park Blvd Mentor (44060) *(G-10491)*

Lanly Company 216 731-1115
  26201 Tungsten Rd Cleveland (44132) *(G-4312)*

Lansing Bros Sawmill 937 588-4291
  897 Chenoweth Fork Rd Piketon (45661) *(G-12478)*

Lantek Systems Inc (DH) 877 805-1028
  5412 Courseview Dr Ste 205 Mason (45040) *(G-10020)*

Lapel Pins Unlimited LLC 614 562-3218
  5649 Ketch St Lewis Center (43035) *(G-9169)*

Lapham-Hickey Steel Corp 614 443-4881
  753 Marion Rd Columbus (43207) *(G-5521)*

Lapham-Hickey Steel Corp 419 399-4803
  815 W Gasser Rd Paulding (45879) *(G-12317)*

Larcom and Mitchell LLC 740 595-3750
  1800 Pittsburgh Dr Delaware (43015) *(G-6734)*

Lariccias Italian Foods Inc 330 729-0222
  7438 Southern Blvd Youngstown (44512) *(G-16388)*

Larmax Inc 513 984-0783
  10945 Reed Hartman Hwy Ste 210 Blue Ash (45242) *(G-1419)*

Larmco Windows Inc (PA) 216 502-2832
  8400 Sweet Valley Dr Ste 404 Cleveland (44125) *(G-4313)*

Larsen Cusotm Cabinetry 614 282-3929
  5660 Westbourne Ave Columbus (43213) *(G-5522)*

Larsen Packaging Products Inc 937 644-5511
  16789 Square Dr Marysville (43040) *(G-9923)*

Las Americas Inc 440 459-2030
  5722 Mayfield Rd Cleveland (44124) *(G-4314)*

Lasenor Usa LLC 800 754-1228
  600 Snyder Rd Salem (44460) *(G-13010)*

Laser Automation Inc 440 543-9291
  16771 Hilltop Park Pl Chagrin Falls (44023) *(G-2405)*

Laser Cartridge Express, Bowling Green *Also Called: Wood County Ohio (G-1596)*

Laser Graphics 419 433-2509
  4606 Mason Rd Berlin Heights (44814) *(G-1316)*

Laser Label Technologies, Stow *Also Called: Electronic Printing Pdts Inc (G-13694)*

Laser Printing Solutions Inc 216 351-4444
  6040 Hillcrest Dr Cleveland (44125) *(G-4315)*

Laserfab Technologies Inc 937 493-0800
  2339 Industrial Dr Sidney (45365) *(G-13260)*

Laserflex, Hilliard *Also Called: Laserflex Corporation (G-8418)*

Laserflex Corporation (HQ) 614 850-9600
  3649 Parkway Ln Hilliard (43026) *(G-8418)*

Laserlinc Inc 937 318-2440
  777 Zapata Dr Fairborn (45324) *(G-7318)*

Laspina Tool and Die Inc 330 923-9996
  4282 Hudson Dr Stow (44224) *(G-13705)*

Last Arrow Manufacturing LLC 330 683-7777
  8991 Lincoln Way E Orrville (44667) *(G-12134)*

Last Word, The, Port Clinton *Also Called: Scrambl-Gram Inc (G-12628)*

Lastar Inc 937 224-0639
  3555 Kettering Blvd Moraine (45439) *(G-11190)*

Laszeray Technology LLC 440 582-8430
  12315 York Delta Dr North Royalton (44133) *(G-11883)*

Latanick Equipment Inc 419 433-2200
  720 River Rd Huron (44839) *(G-8638)*

Late For Sky Production Co 513 531-4400
  1292 Glendale Milford Rd Cincinnati (45215) *(G-3096)*

Latham Limestone LLC 740 493-2677
  6424 State Route 124 Latham (45646) *(G-9051)*

Latham Lumber & Pallet Co.. 740 493-2707
  9445 Street Rte 124 Latham (45646) *(G-9052)*

Latrobe Spcialty Mtls Dist Inc (HQ)..................................... 330 609-5137
  1551 Vienna Pkwy Vienna (44473) *(G-14997)*

Latrobe Specialty Mtls Co LLC... 419 335-8010
  14614 County Road H Wauseon (43567) *(G-15266)*

Lattice Composites LLC.. 440 543-7526
  10095 Queens Way Chagrin Falls (44023) *(G-2406)*

Lau Holdings LLC (HQ)... 216 486-4000
  16900 S Waterloo Rd Cleveland (44110) *(G-4316)*

Lau Holdings LLC... 937 476-6500
  4509 Springfield St Dayton (45431) *(G-6166)*

Lau Industries Inc... 216 894-3903
  4509 Springfield St Dayton (45431) *(G-6167)*

Lauber Manufacturing Co... 419 446-2450
  3751 County Road 26 Archbold (43502) *(G-533)*

Lauren International Ltd (PA).. 234 303-2400
  143 Garland Dr Sw New Philadelphia (44663) *(G-11510)*

Laurenco Systems of Ohio LLC
  4255 W Market St Leavittsburg (44430) *(G-9058)*

Laurenee Ltd.. 513 662-2225
  3509 Harrison Ave Cincinnati (45211) *(G-3097)*

Laurentia Winery.. 440 296-9170
  6869 River Rd Madison (44057) *(G-9593)*

Lawbre Co... 330 637-3363
  3311 Warren Meadville Rd Cortland (44410) *(G-5965)*

Lawn Aid Inc... 417 533-5555
  480 Hathaway Trl Tipp City (45371) *(G-14140)*

Lawrence Industries Inc... 216 518-1400
  4500 Lee Rd Ste 120 Cleveland (44128) *(G-4317)*

Lawrence Industries Inc (PA).. 216 518-7000
  4500 Lee Rd Ste 120 Cleveland (44128) *(G-4318)*

Lawrence Machine, Massillon Also Called: Gary Lawrence Enterprises Inc *(G-10099)*

Layerzero Power Systems Inc... 440 399-9000
  1500 Danner Dr Aurora (44202) *(G-721)*

Lazars Art Gllery Crtive Frmng.. 330 477-8351
  2940 Woodlawn Ave Nw Canton (44708) *(G-2144)*

Lba Custom Printing.. 419 535-3151
  207 Arco Dr Toledo (43607) *(G-14359)*

LBC Clay Co LLC... 330 674-0674
  4501 Township Road 307 Millersburg (44654) *(G-10972)*

LBL Lithographers Inc... 440 350-0106
  365 W Prospect St Painesville (44077) *(G-12247)*

Lbzb Restaurants Inc... 567 413-4700
  132 E Wooster St Bowling Green (43402) *(G-1570)*

Lc, Cleveland Also Called: Logan Clutch Corporation *(G-4334)*

Lcas, Lorain Also Called: Lorain County Auto Systems Inc *(G-9422)*

Le Gourmet Chef, Chillicothe Also Called: The Kitchen Collection LLC *(G-2538)*

Leadec Corp (DH)... 513 731-3590
  9395 Kenwood Rd Ste 200 Blue Ash (45242) *(G-1420)*

Leadec Services, Blue Ash Also Called: Leadec Corp *(G-1420)*

Leader Engnrng-Fabrication Inc.. 419 636-1731
  County Rd D-50 Bryan (43506) *(G-1826)*

Leader Publications Inc... 330 665-9595
  3075 Smith Rd Ste 204 Fairlawn (44333) *(G-7443)*

Leak Finder Inc... 440 735-0130
  6583 Wooded View Dr Hudson (44236) *(G-8602)*

Lear Corporation.. 740 928-4358
  180 N High St Hebron (43025) *(G-8347)*

Lear Corporation.. 419 335-6010
  447 E Walnut St Wauseon (43567) *(G-15267)*

Lear Engineering Corp... 937 429-0534
  2942 Stauffer Dr Beavercreek (45434) *(G-1054)*

Lear Mfg Co Inc.. 440 324-1111
  147 Freedom Ct Elyria (44035) *(G-7173)*

Lear Romec, Elyria Also Called: Hydro-Aire Inc *(G-7158)*

Learn21 A Flxble Lrng Cllbrtiv... 513 402-2121
  5959 Hagewa Dr Blue Ash (45242) *(G-1421)*

Leather Resource of America Inc.. 440 262-5761
  494 E Main Rd Conneaut (44030) *(G-5923)*

Lectora.. 513 929-0188
  311 Elm St Ste 200 Cincinnati (45202) *(G-3098)*

Lectroetch Company, The, Mentor Also Called: Monode Marking Products Inc *(G-10506)*

Led Lighting Center Inc (PA).. 714 271-2633
  5500 Enterprise Blvd Toledo (43612) *(G-14360)*

Led Lighting Center LLC.. 888 988-6533
  5500 Enterprise Blvd Toledo (43612) *(G-14361)*

Led-Andon, Columbus Also Called: American Led-Gible Inc *(G-5127)*

Ledbetter Partners LLC.. 937 253-5311
  214 W Monument Ave Dayton (45402) *(G-6402)*

Ledex & Dormeyer Products, Vandalia Also Called: Saia-Burgess Lcc *(G-14958)*

Lee Corporation.. 513 771-3602
  12055 Mosteller Rd Cincinnati (45241) *(G-3099)*

Lee Plastic Company LLC.. 937 456-5720
  1100 Us Route 35 Eaton (45320) *(G-7065)*

Lee Printers, Cincinnati Also Called: Lee Corporation *(G-3099)*

Lee Saylor Logging LLC... 740 682-0479
  565 Cress Rd Oak Hill (45656) *(G-12021)*

Lee Williams Meats Inc (PA).. 419 729-3893
  3002 131st St Toledo (43611) *(G-14362)*

Lees Grinding Inc... 440 572-4610
  15620 Foltz Pkwy Strongsville (44149) *(G-13850)*

Leesburg Loom & Supply, Van Wert Also Called: Leesburg Looms Incorporated *(G-14921)*

Leesburg Looms Incorporated... 419 238-2738
  201 N Cherry St Van Wert (45891) *(G-14921)*

Leetonia Tool Company.. 330 427-6944
  142 Main St Leetonia (44431) *(G-9127)*

Lefeld Supplies Rental, Coldwater Also Called: Lefeld Welding & Stl Sups Inc *(G-4995)*

Lefeld Welding & Stl Sups Inc (PA)..................................... 419 678-2397
  600 N 2nd St Coldwater (45828) *(G-4995)*

Legacy Farmers Cooperative (PA)....................................... 419 423-2611
  6566 County Road 236 Findlay (45840) *(G-7528)*

Legacy Finishing Inc.. 937 743-7278
  415 Oxford Rd Franklin (45005) *(G-7683)*

Legacy Supplies Inc... 330 405-4565
  8252 Darrow Rd Ste E Twinsburg (44087) *(G-14685)*

Legalcraft Inc.. 330 494-1261
  302 Hallum St Sw Canton (44720) *(G-2145)*

Legatum Project Inc... 216 533-8843
  15820 Van Aken Blvd # 102 Shaker Heights (44120) *(G-13155)*

Legends Auto Spa LLC... 216 333-8030
  600 Turney Rd Apt 219 Bedford (44146) *(G-1133)*

Legrand AV Inc... 574 267-8101
  11500 Williamson Rd Blue Ash (45241) *(G-1422)*

Legrand North America LLC.. 937 224-0639
  6500 Poe Ave Dayton (45414) *(G-6403)*

Lehigh Portland Cement.. 513 769-3666
  2792 Glendale Milford Rd Cincinnati (45241) *(G-3100)*

Lehman's, Dalton Also Called: Robura Inc *(G-6141)*

Lehner Screw Machine LLC... 330 688-6616
  1169 Brittain Rd Akron (44305) *(G-218)*

Lehner Signs Inc.. 614 258-0500
  2983 Switzer Ave Columbus (43219) *(G-5523)*

Lehr Awning Co, Mansfield Also Called: PCR Restorations Inc *(G-9709)*

Leica Biosystems - TAS.. 513 864-9671
  300 E Business Way Fl 5 Cincinnati (45241) *(G-3101)*

Leiden Cabinet Co.. 330 425-8555
  1842 Enterprise Pkwy Twinsburg (44087) *(G-14686)*

Leiden Cabinet Company LLC... 330 425-8555
  1230 Hensel Ave Ne Strasburg (44680) *(G-13748)*

Leiden Cabinet Company LLC (PA)..................................... 330 425-8555
  2385 Edison Blvd Twinsburg (44087) *(G-14687)*

Leiden Company, Twinsburg Also Called: Leiden Cabinet Company LLC *(G-14687)*

Leidos Inc.. 937 656-8433
  3745 Pentagon Blvd Beavercreek (45431) *(G-1055)*

Leimkuehler Inc (PA).. 440 899-7842
  4625 Detroit Ave Cleveland (44102) *(G-4319)*

Leisure Time Pdts Design Corp... 440 934-1032
  1284 Miller Rd Avon (44011) *(G-779)*

Leitner Fabrication LLC.. 330 721-7374
  935 Heritage Dr Medina (44256) *(G-10344)*

Leland-Gifford Inc.. 330 785-9730
  1029 Arlington Cir Akron (44306) *(G-219)*

Lem Products Holding LLC (PA)..........513 202-1188
4440 Muhlhauser Rd Ste 300 West Chester (45011) *(G-15457)*

Lemon Group LLC..........614 409-9850
2195 Broehm Rd Obetz (43207) *(G-12060)*

Lemsco Inc..........419 242-4005
2056 Canton Ave Toledo (43620) *(G-14363)*

Lemsco-Girkins, Toledo Also Called: Lemsco Inc *(G-14363)*

Lenco Industries Inc..........937 277-9364
3301 Klepinger Rd Dayton (45406) *(G-6404)*

Lennox, Cleveland Also Called: Lennox Industries Inc *(G-4320)*

Lennox Industries Inc..........216 739-1909
4562 Hinckley Industrial Pkwy Unit 8 Cleveland (44109) *(G-4320)*

Lennox Machine Inc..........419 525-1020
1471 Sprang Pkwy Mansfield (44903) *(G-9678)*

Lennox Machine Shop, Mansfield Also Called: Lennox Machine Inc *(G-9678)*

Lenz Inc..........937 277-9364
3301 Klepinger Rd Dayton (45406) *(G-6405)*

Lenz Company, Dayton Also Called: Lenz Inc *(G-6405)*

Leon Newswanger..........419 896-3336
7828 Planktown North Rd Shiloh (44878) *(G-13204)*

Leonardo Drs Arbr Intllgnce Sy, Beavercreek Also Called: Drs Leonardo Inc *(G-1047)*

Leonhardt Plating Company..........513 242-1410
5753 Este Ave Cincinnati (45232) *(G-3102)*

LEPD Industries Ltd..........614 985-1470
2292 Clairborne Dr Powell (43065) *(G-12676)*

Lerner Assoc..........330 348-0360
665 E Homestead Dr Aurora (44202) *(G-722)*

Leroi Compressors, Sidney Also Called: G Denver and Co LLC *(G-13250)*

Lesch Boat Cover Canvas Co LLC..........419 668-6374
43 1/2 Saint Marys St Norwalk (44857) *(G-11977)*

Lesco Inc..........740 633-6366
100 Picoma Rd Martins Ferry (43935) *(G-9899)*

Lesco Inc..........614 848-3712
7917 Schoolside Dr Westerville (43081) *(G-15713)*

Lesco Service Center, Martins Ferry Also Called: Lesco Inc *(G-9899)*

Lesco Service Center, Westerville Also Called: Lesco Inc *(G-15713)*

Lesher Printers Inc..........419 332-8253
810 N Wilson Ave Fremont (43420) *(G-7794)*

Lester Miller, Owner, West Farmington Also Called: Millertech Energy Solutions *(G-15606)*

Lettergraphics Inc..........330 683-3905
400 W Market St Orrville (44667) *(G-12135)*

Letterman Printing Inc..........513 523-1111
316 S College Ave Oxford (45056) *(G-12210)*

Lettermans, Wooster Also Called: Lettermans LLC *(G-16145)*

Lettermans LLC..........330 345-2628
344 Beall Ave Wooster (44691) *(G-16145)*

Levan Enterprises Inc (PA)..........330 923-9797
4585 Allen Rd Stow (44224) *(G-13706)*

Levison Enterprises LLC..........419 838-7365
4470 Moline Martin Rd Millbury (43447) *(G-10935)*

Lewark Metal Spinning Inc..........937 275-3303
2746 Keenan Ave Dayton (45414) *(G-6406)*

Lewart Plastics LLC..........216 281-2333
3562 W 69th St Cleveland (44102) *(G-4321)*

Lewco Inc (PA)..........419 625-4014
706 Lane St Sandusky (44870) *(G-13074)*

Lewis Unlimited Inc..........216 514-8282
3690 Orange Pl Ste 340 Beachwood (44122) *(G-994)*

Lewisburg Container Company (DH)..........937 962-2681
275 W Clay St Lewisburg (45338) *(G-9187)*

Lexington Concrete & Sup Inc (PA)..........419 529-3232
362 N Trimble Rd Mansfield (44906) *(G-9679)*

Lexington Rubber Group Inc (PA)..........330 425-8472
1700 Highland Rd Twinsburg (44087) *(G-14688)*

Lexisnexis, Miamisburg Also Called: Relx Inc *(G-10674)*

Lexisnexis Group (DH)..........937 865-6800
9443 Springboro Pike Miamisburg (45342) *(G-10654)*

Lexisnexis Group, Miamisburg Also Called: Lexisnexis Group *(G-10654)*

Lextech Industries Ltd..........216 883-7900
6800 Union Ave Cleveland (44105) *(G-4322)*

Ley Industries Inc..........419 238-6742
121 S Walnut St Van Wert (45891) *(G-14922)*

Lfe Instruments, Bluffton Also Called: Triplett Bluffton Corporation *(G-1509)*

Lfg Specialties LLC..........419 424-4999
16406 E Us Route 224 Findlay (45840) *(G-7529)*

Lg Chem Ohio Petrochemical Inc..........470 792-5127
310 Rayann Pkwy Ravenna (44266) *(G-12723)*

LH Marshall Company..........614 294-6433
1601 Woodland Ave Columbus (43219) *(G-5524)*

Lhpc Inc (PA)..........330 527-2696
11964 State Route 88 Garrettsville (44231) *(G-7920)*

Lib Therapeutics Inc..........859 240-7764
5375 Medpace Way Cincinnati (45227) *(G-3103)*

Libbey, Toledo Also Called: Libbey Glass LLC *(G-14364)*

Libbey, Toledo Also Called: Libbey Inc *(G-14366)*

Libbey America, Toledo Also Called: Libbey Glass LLC *(G-14365)*

Libbey Glass LLC (HQ)..........419 325-2100
300 Madison Ave Toledo (43604) *(G-14364)*

Libbey Glass LLC..........419 727-2211
940 Ash St Toledo (43611) *(G-14365)*

Libbey Inc (PA)..........419 325-2100
300 Madison Ave Toledo (43604) *(G-14366)*

Liberty Casting Company LLC (PA)..........740 363-1941
550 Liberty Rd Delaware (43015) *(G-6735)*

Liberty Iron & Metal Inc..........724 347-4534
27 Furnace Ln Girard (44420) *(G-7971)*

Liberty Pattern and Mold Inc..........330 788-9463
1131 Meadowbrook Ave Youngstown (44512) *(G-16389)*

Liberty Sportswear LLC..........513 755-8740
5573 Eureka Dr Hamilton (45011) *(G-8227)*

Liberty Steel Pressed Pdts LLC..........330 538-2236
11650 Mahoning Ave North Jackson (44451) *(G-11786)*

Liberty Tax Service, Englewood Also Called: Samb LLC Services *(G-7241)*

Liberty Tire Recycling LLC..........614 871-8097
3041 Jackson Pike Grove City (43123) *(G-8101)*

LIBERTY TIRE RECYCLING, LLC, Grove City Also Called: Liberty Tire Recycling LLC *(G-8101)*

Libra Guaymas LLC..........440 974-7770
7770 Division Dr Mentor (44060) *(G-10492)*

Libra Industries, Dayton Also Called: Gem City Engineering Co *(G-6348)*

Libra Industries LLC (DH)..........440 974-7770
7770 Division Dr Mentor (44060) *(G-10493)*

License Ad Plate Company..........216 265-4200
13110 Enterprise Ave Side B Cleveland (44135) *(G-4323)*

Lidsen Publishing Inc..........216 378-7542
2000 Auburn Dr Ste 200 Beachwood (44122) *(G-995)*

Liebert Field Services Inc..........614 841-5763
610 Executive Campus Dr Westerville (43082) *(G-15665)*

Liechty Specialties, Archbold Also Called: Nef Ltd *(G-538)*

Liechty Specialties Inc..........419 445-6696
1901 S Defiance St Archbold (43502) *(G-534)*

Liette L & S Express LLC..........419 394-7077
2286 Celina Rd Saint Marys (45885) *(G-12956)*

Life Is Sweet LLC (PA)..........330 342-0172
6926 Main St Cincinnati (45244) *(G-3104)*

Life Sciences - Vandalia LLC (HQ)..........937 387-0880
4201 Little York Rd Dayton (45414) *(G-6407)*

Life Support Development Ltd..........614 221-1765
777 Dearborn Park Ln Ste R Columbus (43085) *(G-5525)*

Lifeformations, Bowling Green Also Called: Lifeformations Inc *(G-1571)*

Lifeformations Inc..........419 352-2101
2029 Wood Bridge Blvd Bowling Green (43402) *(G-1571)*

Lifeline Mobile Inc..........614 497-8300
2050 Mcgaw Rd Obetz (43207) *(G-12061)*

Lifestyle Nutraceuticals Ltd..........513 376-7218
5911 Turpin Hills Dr Ste 101 Cincinnati (45244) *(G-3105)*

Lifetime Fenders, Canfield Also Called: Ltf Acquisition LLC *(G-2010)*

Lifetime Products Inc..........614 272-1255
4364 Sullivant Ave Columbus (43228) *(G-5526)*

Lift-Tech International Inc..........330 424-7248
240 Pennsylvania Ave Salem (44460) *(G-13011)*

ALPHABETIC SECTION — Liquid Control

Light Craft Direct, Fremont *Also Called: Light Craft Manufacturing Inc (G-7795)*
Light Craft Manufacturing Inc 419 332-0536
220 Sullivan Rd Fremont (43420) *(G-7795)*

Light Vision 513 351-9444
1776 Mentor Ave Cincinnati (45212) *(G-3106)*

Lighting Products Inc 440 293-4064
101 Parker Dr Andover (44003) *(G-487)*

Lighting Systems Inc 513 372-3332
10000 Alliance Rd Blue Ash (45242) *(G-1423)*

Lightning Bolt Fastners, Mount Gilead *Also Called: Lilly Industries Inc (G-11235)*
Lightning Mold & Machine, Conneaut *Also Called: Lightning Mold & Machine Inc (G-5924)*
Lightning Mold & Machine Inc 440 593-6460
509 W Main Rd Conneaut (44030) *(G-5924)*

Lightning Signs and Decals LLC 304 403-1290
205 S Broadway St New Philadelphia (44663) *(G-11511)*

Lil Turtles 330 897-6400
504 N Ray St Baltic (43804) *(G-839)*

Lilienthal/Southeastern Inc 740 439-1640
1609 N 11th St Cambridge (43725) *(G-1940)*

Lilly Industries Inc (PA) 419 946-7908
6437 County Road 20 Mount Gilead (43338) *(G-11235)*

Lily Ann Cabinets 419 360-2455
2939 Douglas Rd Toledo (43606) *(G-14367)*

Lima Armature Works Inc 419 222-4010
142 E Pearl St Lima (45801) *(G-9261)*

Lima Millwork Inc 419 331-3303
4251 East Rd Elida (45807) *(G-7094)*

Lima Pallet Company Inc 419 229-5736
1470 Neubrecht Rd Lima (45801) *(G-9262)*

Lima Refining Company (HQ) 419 226-2300
1150 S Metcalf St Lima (45804) *(G-9263)*

Lima Sheet Metal, Lima *Also Called: Lima Sheet Metal Machine & Mfg (G-9264)*
Lima Sheet Metal Machine & Mfg 419 229-1161
1001 Bowman Rd Lima (45804) *(G-9264)*

Lima Sporting Goods Inc 419 222-1036
1404 Allentown Rd Lima (45805) *(G-9265)*

Liminal Data, Gates Mills *Also Called: Liminal Esports LLC (G-7928)*
Liminal Esports LLC 440 423-5856
1500 Chagrin River Rd Unit 361 Gates Mills (44040) *(G-7928)*

Linamar Strctures USA Mich Inc 260 636-7030
507 W Indiana St Edon (43518) *(G-7088)*

Linamar Strctures USA Mich Inc 567 249-0838
201 Leanne St Edon (43518) *(G-7089)*

Lincoln Center Manufacturing, Cardington *Also Called: Marengo Fabricated Steel Ltd (G-2276)*

Lincoln Electric Automtn Inc 419 678-4877
911 N 2nd St Coldwater (45828) *(G-4996)*

Lincoln Electric Automtn Inc 614 471-5926
1700 Jetway Blvd Columbus (43219) *(G-5527)*

Lincoln Electric Automtn Inc (HQ) 937 295-2120
407 S Main St Fort Loramie (45845) *(G-7603)*

Lincoln Electric Company (HQ) 216 481-8100
22801 Saint Clair Ave Cleveland (44117) *(G-4324)*

Lincoln Electric Holdings Inc (PA) 216 481-8100
22801 Saint Clair Ave Cleveland (44117) *(G-4325)*

Lincoln Foodservice Products, Cleveland *Also Called: Lincoln Foodservice Products LLC (G-4326)*

Lincoln Foodservice Products LLC 260 459-8200
1333 E 179th St Cleveland (44110) *(G-4326)*

Lincoln Manufacturing Inc 330 878-7772
310 Railroad Ave Se Strasburg (44680) *(G-13749)*

LINCOLN MANUFACTURING, INC., Strasburg *Also Called: Lincoln Manufacturing Inc (G-13749)*

Lincoln Way Vineyards Inc 330 804-9463
9050 W Old Lincoln Way Wooster (44691) *(G-16146)*

Linda & Ray's Machine Service, Oberlin *Also Called: Ray Muro (G-12056)*
Linde Gas & Equipment Inc 513 821-2192
8376 Reading Rd Cincinnati (45237) *(G-3107)*

Linde Gas & Equipment Inc 614 846-7048
7029 Huntley Rd Columbus (43229) *(G-5528)*

Linde Gas & Equipment Inc 614 443-7687
450 Greenlawn Ave Columbus (43223) *(G-5529)*

Linde Gas & Equipment Inc 419 729-7732
6055 Brent Dr Toledo (43611) *(G-14368)*

Linde Gas & Equipment Inc 440 944-8844
1140 Lloyd Rd Wickliffe (44092) *(G-15837)*

Linde Gas North America, Columbus *Also Called: Linde Gas & Equipment Inc (G-5528)*
Linde Gas USA LLC 330 425-3989
2045 E Aurora Rd Twinsburg (44087) *(G-14689)*

Linde Hydraulics Corporation (DH) 330 533-6801
5089 W Western Reserve Rd Canfield (44406) *(G-2009)*

Linde Inc 440 994-1000
3102 Lake Rd E Ashtabula (44004) *(G-646)*

Linde Inc 330 825-4449
4805 Fairland Rd Barberton (44203) *(G-877)*

Linde Inc 440 237-8690
14788 York Rd Cleveland (44133) *(G-4327)*

Linde Inc 419 698-8005
3742 Cedar Point Rd Oregon (43616) *(G-12106)*

Linden-Two Inc 330 928-4064
137 Ascot Pkwy Cuyahoga Falls (44223) *(G-6100)*

Lindev Investors Group Inc 440 856-9201
9215 Madison Rd Montville (44064) *(G-11149)*

Lindsay Precast LLC (PA) 800 837-7788
6845 Erie Ave Nw Canal Fulton (44614) *(G-1972)*

Line Drive Sportz-Lcrc LLC 419 794-7150
2901 Key St Ste 1 Maumee (43537) *(G-10214)*

Line-X of Akron/Medina, North Royalton *Also Called: X-Treme Finishes Inc (G-11903)*
Linear Acoustic Inc 717 735-3611
1241 Superior Ave E Cleveland (44114) *(G-4328)*

Linear Asics Inc 330 474-3920
2061 Case Pkwy S Twinsburg (44087) *(G-14690)*

Linear It Solutions LLC 614 306-0761
639 Gallop Ln Marysville (43040) *(G-9924)*

Linestream Technologies Inc 216 862-7874
1468 W 9th St Ste 435 Cleveland (44113) *(G-4329)*

Link Systems Inc 800 321-8770
28925 Fountain Pkwy Solon (44139) *(G-13381)*

Link To Success Inc 888 959-4203
52 Summit St Ste 3 Norwalk (44857) *(G-11978)*

Linnea's, Kent *Also Called: Linneas Candy Supplies Inc (G-8828)*
Linneas Candy Supplies Inc (PA) 330 678-7112
4149 Karg Industrial Pkwy Kent (44240) *(G-8828)*

Linsalata Cpitl Prtners Fund I 440 684-1400
5900 Landerbrook Dr Ste 280 Cleveland (44124) *(G-4330)*

Lintech Electronics LLC 513 528-6190
4435 Aicholtz Rd Ste 500 Cincinnati (45245) *(G-2571)*

Lintern Corporation (PA) 440 255-9333
8685 Station St Mentor (44060) *(G-10494)*

Lion Apparel Inc (DH) 937 898-1949
7200 Poe Ave Ste 400 Dayton (45414) *(G-6408)*

Lion Apparel Inc 937 898-1949
6450 Poe Ave Ste 300 Dayton (45414) *(G-6409)*

Lion Clothing, Delphos *Also Called: J & G Goecke Clothing LLC (G-6766)*
Lion First Responder Ppe Inc 937 898-1949
7200 Poe Ave Ste 400 Dayton (45414) *(G-6410)*

Lion Group Inc (HQ) 937 898-1949
7200 Poe Ave Ste 400 Dayton (45414) *(G-6411)*

Lion Industries LLC 740 676-1100
423 53rd St Bellaire (43906) *(G-1188)*

Lipari Foods Operating Co LLC 330 893-2479
6597 County Road 625 Millersburg (44654) *(G-10973)*

Lipari Foods Operating Co LLC 330 674-9199
316 S Mad Anthony St Millersburg (44654) *(G-10974)*

Lipo Technologies Inc 937 264-1222
707 Harco Dr Englewood (45315) *(G-7236)*

Lippincott and Peto Inc 330 864-2122
1741 Akron Peninsula Rd Akron (44313) *(G-220)*

Liqui-Box Corporation 419 289-9696
1817 Masters Ave Ashland (44805) *(G-589)*

Liqui-Box Corporation 419 294-3884
519 Raybestos Dr Upper Sandusky (43351) *(G-14814)*

Liquid Control, North Canton *Also Called: Graco Ohio Inc (G-11733)*

Liquid Development Company (PA) 216 641-9366
 5708 E Schaaf Rd Independence (44131) *(G-8671)*

Liquid Image Corp America 216 458-9800
 3700 Prospect Ave E Cleveland (44115) *(G-4331)*

Liquid Luggers LLC 330 426-2538
 183 Edgeworth Ave East Palestine (44413) *(G-7006)*

Liquid Manufacturing Solutions 937 401-0821
 401 Shotwell Dr Franklin (45005) *(G-7684)*

Lisbon Powder Coating 234 567-1324
 6191 Lisbon Rd Lisbon (44432) *(G-9321)*

Listermann Brewery Supply, Cincinnati Also Called: Listermann Mfg Co Inc *(G-3108)*

Listermann Mfg Co Inc 513 731-1130
 4120 Forest Ave Cincinnati (45212) *(G-3108)*

Litco Corner Protection LLC 330 539-5433
 1000 Tuscarawas St E Vienna (44473) *(G-14998)*

Litco Cornerguard, LLC, Vienna Also Called: Litco Corner Protection LLC *(G-14998)*

Litco International Inc (PA) 330 539-5433
 1 Litco Dr Vienna (44473) *(G-14999)*

Litco Manufacturing LLC 330 539-5433
 1512 Phoenix Rd Ne Warren (44483) *(G-15184)*

Litco Wood Products, Apple Creek Also Called: Millwood Inc *(G-505)*

Lite Metals Company 330 296-6110
 700 N Walnut St Ravenna (44266) *(G-12724)*

Liteflex Disc LLC 937 836-7025
 3251 Mccall St Dayton (45417) *(G-6412)*

Litehouse Pools & Spas, Strongsville Also Called: Litehouse Products LLC *(G-13851)*

Litehouse Products LLC (PA) 440 638-2350
 10883 Pearl Rd Ste 301 Strongsville (44136) *(G-13851)*

Lithchem, Lancaster Also Called: Cirba Solutions Us Inc *(G-9000)*

Lithchem Intl Toxco Inc 740 653-6290
 265 Quarry Rd Se Lancaster (43130) *(G-9022)*

Lithium Innovations Co LLC 419 725-3525
 3171 N Republic Blvd Ste 101 Toledo (43615) *(G-14369)*

Litho-Print Ltd 937 222-4351
 848 E Monument Ave Dayton (45402) *(G-6413)*

Little Cottage Company (PA) 330 893-4212
 4070 State Route 39 Millersburg (44654) *(G-10975)*

Little Mountain Precision LLC 440 290-2903
 8677 Tyler Blvd Mentor (44060) *(G-10495)*

Little Printing Company 937 773-4595
 4317 W Us Route 36 Piqua (45356) *(G-12532)*

Little Tikes, Hudson Also Called: The Little Tikes Company *(G-8616)*

Littlern Corporation 330 848-8847
 1006 Bunker Dr Apt 207 Fairlawn (44333) *(G-7444)*

Liturgical Publications Inc 216 325-6825
 4560 E 71st St Cleveland (44105) *(G-4332)*

Live Off Loyalty Inc 513 413-2401
 12019 Hitchcock Dr Cincinnati (45240) *(G-3109)*

Liverpool Manufacturing, Valley City Also Called: Shl Liquidation Automotive Inc *(G-14891)*

Liverpool Township 330 483-4747
 6700 Center Rd Valley City (44280) *(G-14876)*

Lj Manfcturing Inc Mentor Ohio 440 953-3726
 6345 Carnegie St Mentor (44060) *(G-10496)*

Lkd Aerospace Holdings Inc (PA) 216 262-8481
 25101 Chagrin Blvd Ste 350 Cleveland (44122) *(G-4333)*

LLC Bowman Leather 330 893-1954
 6705 Private Road 387 Millersburg (44654) *(G-10976)*

LLC Ring Masters 330 832-1511
 240 6th St Nw Massillon (44647) *(G-10120)*

Lld Gas & Oil Corp 330 364-6331
 137 E Iron Ave Dover (44622) *(G-6832)*

Lloyd F Helber 740 756-9607
 3820 Columbus Lancaster Rd Nw Carroll (43112) *(G-2299)*

Lm Cases, Austintown Also Called: L M Engineering Inc *(G-752)*

LMC, Akron Also Called: Logan Machine Company *(G-223)*

Lmg Holdings Inc (PA) 905 829-3541
 4290 Glendale Milford Rd Blue Ash (45242) *(G-1424)*

Lmp Machine LLC 740 596-4559
 115 E Chestnut St Zaleski (45698) *(G-16492)*

Load32 LLC 614 984-6648
 265 N Oakley Ave Columbus (43204) *(G-5530)*

Loadmaster Scale, Findlay Also Called: Holtgreven Scale & Elec Corp *(G-7524)*

Loadmaster Trailer Company Ltd 419 732-3434
 2354 East Harbor Rd Port Clinton (43452) *(G-12622)*

Loadmaster Trailers Mfg, Port Clinton Also Called: Loadmaster Trailer Company Ltd *(G-12622)*

Lochard Inc 937 492-8811
 903 Wapakoneta Ave Sidney (45365) *(G-13261)*

Lock 15 Brewing Company LLC 234 900-8277
 21 W North St Akron (44304) *(G-221)*

Lock 27 Brewing LLC 937 433-2739
 1024 Quail Run Dr Dayton (45458) *(G-6414)*

Lock Joint Tube Ohio LLC 210 278-3757
 135 Penniman Rd Orwell (44076) *(G-12167)*

Lockfast LLC 800 543-7157
 107 Northeast Dr Loveland (45140) *(G-9491)*

Lockheed Mrtin Intgrted System 330 796-2800
 1210 Massillon Rd Akron (44315) *(G-222)*

Lockrey Manufacturing, Toledo Also Called: Raka Corporation *(G-14449)*

Loctite, Westlake Also Called: Henkel US Operations Corp *(G-15755)*

Loft Violin Shop 614 267-7221
 4604 N High St Columbus (43214) *(G-5531)*

Logan Clutch Corporation 440 808-4258
 28855 Ranney Pkwy Cleveland (44145) *(G-4334)*

Logan Coatings LLC 740 380-0047
 2255 E Front St Logan (43138) *(G-9368)*

Logan Foundry & Machine, Logan Also Called: Clay Logan Products Company *(G-9361)*

Logan Glass Technologies LLC 740 385-2114
 12680 State Route 93 N Logan (43138) *(G-9369)*

Logan Machine Company (PA) 330 633-6163
 1405 Home Ave Akron (44310) *(G-223)*

Logan Welding Inc 740 385-9651
 37062 Hocking Dr Logan (43138) *(G-9370)*

Logisync, Avon Also Called: Logisync Corporation *(G-780)*

Logisync Corporation 440 937-0388
 1313 Lear Industrial Pkwy Avon (44011) *(G-780)*

Logitech Inc 614 871-2822
 6423 Seeds Rd Grove City (43123) *(G-8102)*

Logo This 419 445-1355
 301 Ditto St Ste E Archbold (43502) *(G-535)*

Lokring Technology LLC 440 942-0880
 38376 Apollo Pkwy Willoughby (44094) *(G-15946)*

Lomar Enterprises Inc 614 409-9104
 5905 Green Pointe Dr S Ste G Groveport (43125) *(G-8151)*

Lombardo Gelato Company 480 274-1018
 552 Turney Rd Apt A Bedford (44146) *(G-1134)*

Lone Star Industries Inc 513 467-0430
 6381 River Rd Cincinnati (45233) *(G-3110)*

Long Sign Co 614 294-1057
 979 E 5th Ave Columbus (43201) *(G-5532)*

Long View Steel Corp 419 747-1108
 1555 W Longview Ave Mansfield (44906) *(G-9680)*

Long-Lok LLC (PA) 336 343-7319
 10630 Chester Rd Cincinnati (45215) *(G-3111)*

Long-Lok Fasteners Corporation 513 772-1880
 10630 Chester Rd Cincinnati (45215) *(G-3112)*

Long-Stanton Mfg Company 513 874-8020
 9388 Sutton Pl West Chester (45011) *(G-15458)*

Lonny Eugene Horst 330 846-0057
 2239 Waterford Rd New Waterford (44445) *(G-11557)*

Lonolife Inc 614 296-2250
 432 W 2nd Ave Columbus (43201) *(G-5533)*

Lonz Winery, Cleveland Also Called: Paramount Distillers Inc *(G-4522)*

Lonz Winery LLC 419 625-5474
 917 Bardshar Rd Sandusky (44870) *(G-13075)*

Lopaus Point LLC 614 302-7242
 4395 Marketing Pl Groveport (43125) *(G-8152)*

Lorain Apples 440 282-4471
 1051 Meister Rd Lorain (44052) *(G-9420)*

Lorain County Auto Systems Inc 248 442-6800
 3400 River Industrial Park Rd Lorain (44052) *(G-9421)*

Lorain County Auto Systems Inc (HQ) 440 960-7470
 7470 Industrial Parkway Dr Lorain (44053) *(G-9422)*

ALPHABETIC SECTION — Ludowici Roof Tile Inc

Lorain Modern Pattern Inc.. 440 365-6780
159 Woodbury St Elyria (44035) *(G-7174)*

Lorain Rled Die Pdts Indus Sup.. 440 281-8607
6287 Lear Nagle Rd Ste 4 North Ridgeville (44039) *(G-11849)*

Lord Corporation.. 937 278-9431
4644 Wadsworth Rd Dayton (45414) *(G-6415)*

Lordstown, Mason *Also Called: Lordstown Motors Corp (G-10021)*

Lordstown Ev Corporation (PA).. 678 428-6558
2300 Hallock Young Rd Sw Warren (44481) *(G-15185)*

Lordstown Motors Corp.. 312 925-2466
7588 Central Parke Blvd Ste 321 Mason (45040) *(G-10021)*

Lorenz Corporation (PA).. 937 228-6118
501 E 3rd St Dayton (45402) *(G-6416)*

Lori Holding Co (PA).. 740 342-3230
1400 Commerce Dr New Lexington (43764) *(G-11453)*

Loroco Industries Inc.. 513 891-9544
10600 Evendale Dr Cincinnati (45241) *(G-3113)*

Losantiville Winery LLC.. 513 918-3015
38 W Mcmicken Ave Cincinnati (45202) *(G-3114)*

Lost Nation Fuel.. 440 951-9088
3525 Lost Nation Rd Willoughby (44094) *(G-15947)*

Lost Tech, West Chester *Also Called: Lost Technology LLP (G-15459)*

Lost Technology LLP.. 513 685-0054
9501 Woodland Hills Dr West Chester (45011) *(G-15459)*

Lostcreek Tool & Machine Inc.. 937 773-6022
1150 S Main St Piqua (45356) *(G-12533)*

Lotus Love LLC.. 614 964-8477
1091 Fountain Ln Apt B Columbus (43213) *(G-5534)*

Lotus Pipes & Rockdrills USA.. 516 209-6995
1700 E 12th St Cleveland (44114) *(G-4335)*

Lou's Sausage, Cleveland *Also Called: Lous Sausage Ltd (G-4336)*

Louis Arthur Steel Company.. 440 997-5545
200 North Ave E Geneva (44041) *(G-7940)*

Louis Arthur Steel Company (PA).................................... 440 997-5545
185 Water St Geneva (44041) *(G-7941)*

Louis G Freeman Co.. 513 263-1720
4064 Clough Woods Dr Batavia (45103) *(G-929)*

Louis Instantwhip-St Inc.. 614 488-2536
2200 Cardigan Ave Columbus (43215) *(G-5535)*

Lous Machine Company Inc.. 513 856-9199
102 Hastings Ave Hamilton (45011) *(G-8228)*

Lous Sausage Ltd.. 216 752-5060
14723 Miles Ave Cleveland (44128) *(G-4336)*

Love Laugh & Laundry.. 567 377-1951
5333 Secor Rd Toledo (43623) *(G-14370)*

Love Chocolate Factory, Hartville *Also Called: L C F Inc (G-8302)*

Love Yueh LLC.. 614 408-8677
9126 Calverton Ter Pickerington (43147) *(G-12463)*

Love. Laugh. Laundry., Toledo *Also Called: Love Laugh & Laundry (G-14370)*

Loveland Graphics, Cincinnati *Also Called: Eastgate Custom Graphics Ltd (G-2854)*

Loveman Steel Corporation.. 440 232-6200
5455 Perkins Rd Bedford (44146) *(G-1135)*

Loving Choice Adoption-Prntng...................................... 330 994-1451
625 Cleveland Ave Nw Canton (44702) *(G-2146)*

Lower Investments LLC.. 765 825-4151
4072 Pimlico Ct Mason (45040) *(G-10022)*

Lower Limb Centers LLC.. 440 365-2502
1100 Abbe Rd N Ste D Elyria (44035) *(G-7175)*

Lowry Furnace Co Inc.. 330 745-4822
663 Flora Ave Akron (44314) *(G-224)*

Lowry Tool & Die Inc.. 330 332-1722
986 Salem Pkwy Salem (44460) *(G-13012)*

LPI, Cleveland *Also Called: Liturgical Publications Inc (G-4332)*

Lrb Tool & Die Ltd.. 330 898-5783
3303 Parkman Rd Nw Warren (44481) *(G-15186)*

Lrbg Chemicals USA Inc.. 419 244-5856
2112 Sylvan Ave Toledo (43606) *(G-14371)*

Lri Post-Acquisition Inc (PA).. 419 227-2200
893 Shawnee Rd Lima (45805) *(G-9266)*

Lrp Solutions Inc.. 419 678-3909
120 Harvest Dr Coldwater (45828) *(G-4997)*

LS Starrett Company.. 440 835-0005
24500 Detroit Rd Westlake (44145) *(G-15763)*

Lsc Communications Inc.. 419 935-0111
1145 S Conwell Ave Willard (44890) *(G-15860)*

LSc Service Corp.. 440 331-1359
20665 Lorain Rd Cleveland (44126) *(G-4337)*

LSI Graphic Solutions Plus, Akron *Also Called: Grady McCauley Inc (G-172)*

LSI Industries, Cincinnati *Also Called: LSI Industries Inc (G-3115)*

LSI Industries Inc.. 913 281-1100
10000 Alliance Rd Blue Ash (45242) *(G-1425)*

LSI Industries Inc (PA).. 513 793-3200
10000 Alliance Rd Cincinnati (45242) *(G-3115)*

LSI Lightron Inc.. 845 562-5500
10000 Alliance Rd Blue Ash (45242) *(G-1426)*

Lsmi, Columbus *Also Called: Lambert Sheet Metal Inc (G-5518)*

Lsp Technologies Inc.. 614 718-3000
6161 Shamrock Ct Dublin (43016) *(G-6907)*

Lsp Tubes Inc.. 216 378-2092
135 Penniman Rd Orwell (44076) *(G-12168)*

Lsq Manufacturing Inc.. 330 725-4905
1140 Industrial Pkwy Medina (44256) *(G-10345)*

Lt Enterprises of Ohio LLC.. 330 526-6908
334 Orchard Ave Ne North Canton (44720) *(G-11741)*

Lt Moses Willard Inc.. 513 248-5500
3972 Bach Buxton Rd Amelia (45102) *(G-459)*

Lt Wright Handcrafted Knife Co...................................... 740 317-1404
130 Warren Ln Unit B Steubenville (43953) *(G-13670)*

Ltf Acquisition LLC.. 330 533-0111
430 W Main St Canfield (44406) *(G-2010)*

LTI Power Systems Inc.. 440 327-5050
10800 Middle Ave Hngr B Elyria (44035) *(G-7176)*

Lube & Chem Products, Cincinnati *Also Called: Interlube Corporation (G-3027)*

Luberfiner, Cleveland *Also Called: First Brnds Group Intrmdate LL (G-4064)*

Lubricant Additives, Wickliffe *Also Called: The Lubrizol Corporation (G-15853)*

Lubriplate Lubricants Company.. 419 691-2491
1500 Oakdale Ave Toledo (43605) *(G-14372)*

Lubriquip Inc.. 216 581-2000
18901 Cranwood Pkwy Cleveland (44128) *(G-4338)*

Lubrisource Inc.. 937 432-9292
2900 Cincinnati Dayton Rd Middletown (45044) *(G-10836)*

Lubrizol, Cleveland *Also Called: Lubrizol Global Management Inc (G-4339)*

Lubrizol Advanced Mtls Inc (HQ).................................... 216 447-5000
9911 Brecksville Rd Brecksville (44141) *(G-1625)*

Lubrizol Corporation.. 216 447-5447
9921 Brecksville Rd Brecksville (44141) *(G-1626)*

Lubrizol Global Management Inc.................................... 440 933-0400
550 Moore Rd Avon Lake (44012) *(G-815)*

Lubrizol Global Management Inc (DH).......................... 216 447-5000
9911 Brecksville Rd Cleveland (44141) *(G-4339)*

Lubrizol Holdings LLC.. 440 943-4200
29400 Lakeland Blvd Wickliffe (44092) *(G-15838)*

Lubrizol Production Plant, Painesville *Also Called: The Lubrizol Corporation (G-12270)*

Luc Ice Inc.. 419 734-2201
10020 River Rd Huron (44839) *(G-8639)*

Lucas Specialty Products LLC.. 419 290-6168
1101 Pelee St Toledo (43607) *(G-14373)*

Lucas Sumitomo Brakes Inc.. 513 934-0024
1650 Kingsview Dr Lebanon (45036) *(G-9094)*

Lucius Fence and Decking, New Riegel *Also Called: Juno Enterprises LLC (G-11536)*

Lucky Thirteen Inc.. 216 631-0013
7413 Associate Ave Cleveland (44144) *(G-4340)*

Lucky Thirteen Laser, Cleveland *Also Called: Lucky Thirteen Inc (G-4340)*

Luckys Bottles Inc.. 614 447-9522
2401 Mac Ct Columbus (43235) *(G-5536)*

Lucys Barkery LLC.. 419 886-3779
5527 Etzwiler Rd Bellville (44813) *(G-1244)*

Ludlow Composites Corporation...................................... 419 332-5531
2100 Commerce Dr Fremont (43420) *(G-7796)*

Ludowici Roof Tile Inc.. 740 342-1995
4757 Tile Plant Rd Se New Lexington (43764) *(G-11454)*

Ludy Greenhouse Mfg Corp (PA) 800 255-5839
 122 Railroad St New Madison (45346) *(G-11475)*

Luk Clutch Systems, Wooster *Also Called: Luk Clutch Systems LLC (G-16147)*

Luk Clutch Systems LLC (DH) 330 264-4383
 3401 Old Airport Rd Wooster (44691) *(G-16147)*

Luke Engineering & Mfg, Wadsworth *Also Called: Luke Engineering & Mfg Corp (G-15043)*

Luke Engineering & Mfg Corp 330 925-3344
 11 Pipestone Rd Rittman (44270) *(G-12824)*

Luke Engineering & Mfg Corp (PA) 330 335-1501
 456 South Blvd Wadsworth (44281) *(G-15043)*

Lukens Inc 937 440-2500
 1040 S Dorset Rd Troy (45373) *(G-14594)*

Lukjan Metal Pdts Holdg Co Inc 440 599-8127
 645 Industry Rd Conneaut (44030) *(G-5925)*

Lukjan Metal Products Inc (PA) 440 599-8127
 645 Industry Rd Conneaut (44030) *(G-5926)*

Lumacurve Airfield Signs, Macedonia *Also Called: Standard Signs Incorporated (G-9579)*

Lumenforce Led LLC 330 330-8962
 5411 Market St Youngstown (44512) *(G-16390)*

Lumenomics Inc 614 798-3500
 8333 Green Meadows Dr N Ste B Lewis Center (43035) *(G-9170)*

Lumi Craft, Norwich *Also Called: Lumi-Lite Candle Company (G-11992)*

Lumi-Lite Candle Company 740 872-3248
 102 Sundale Rd Norwich (43767) *(G-11992)*

Luminance, Cuyahoga Falls *Also Called: American De Rosa Lamparts LLC (G-6063)*

Luminaud Inc 440 255-9082
 8688 Tyler Blvd Mentor (44060) *(G-10497)*

Luminex HD&f Company, Blue Ash *Also Called: Luminex HM Dcor Frgrnce Hldg C (G-1427)*

Luminex HM Dcor Frgrnce Hldg C (PA) 513 563-1113
 10521 Millington Ct Blue Ash (45242) *(G-1427)*

Lumitex, Strongsville *Also Called: Lumitex Inc (G-13852)*

Lumitex Inc (PA) 440 243-8401
 8443 Dow Cir Strongsville (44136) *(G-13852)*

Lunar Tool & Mold Inc 440 237-2141
 9860 York Alpha Dr North Royalton (44133) *(G-11884)*

Lund Equipment Company 330 659-4800
 2400 N Cleveland Massillon Rd Akron (44333) *(G-225)*

Lustrous Metal Coatings Inc 330 478-4653
 1541 Raff Rd Sw Canton (44710) *(G-2147)*

Luther Machine Inc 440 259-5014
 4604 Davis Rd Perry (44081) *(G-12353)*

Luvata, Delaware *Also Called: Luvata Ohio Inc (G-6736)*

Luvata Ohio Inc (HQ) 740 363-1981
 1376 Pittsburgh Dr Delaware (43015) *(G-6736)*

Luxaire Cushion Co 330 872-0995
 2410 S Center St Newton Falls (44444) *(G-11654)*

Luxco Inc 216 671-6300
 3116 Berea Rd Cleveland (44111) *(G-4341)*

Luxcraft LLC 330 852-1036
 1221 County Road 144 Sugarcreek (44681) *(G-13928)*

Luxfer Magtech Inc (HQ) 513 772-3066
 2940 Highland Ave Ste 210 Cincinnati (45212) *(G-3116)*

Luxottica North Amer Dist LLC 614 492-5610
 2150 Bixby Rd Lockbourne (43137) *(G-9338)*

Luxottica of America Inc 614 492-5610
 2150 Bixby Rd Lockbourne (43137) *(G-9339)*

Luxottica Rx Operations, Lockbourne *Also Called: Luxottica of America Inc (G-9339)*

Luxus Arms, Mount Orab *Also Called: Luxus Products LLC (G-11242)*

Luxus Products LLC 937 444-6500
 222 Homan Way Mount Orab (45154) *(G-11242)*

Lvd Acquisition LLC (HQ) 614 861-1350
 222 E Campus View Blvd Columbus (43235) *(G-5537)*

Lyco Corporation 412 973-9176
 1089 N Hubbard Rd Lowellville (44436) *(G-9517)*

Lyle Industries Inc 513 233-2803
 6633 Wyndwatch Dr Cincinnati (45230) *(G-3117)*

Lyle Printing & Publishing Co (PA) 330 337-3419
 185 E State St Salem (44460) *(G-13013)*

Lyle Tate 937 698-6526
 5573 State Route 55 Ludlow Falls (45339) *(G-9528)*

Lynk Packaging Inc (PA) 330 562-8080
 1250 Page Rd Aurora (44202) *(G-723)*

Lynn Electronics, Springboro *Also Called: Nyle LLC (G-13513)*

Lynx Precision Products Corp 866 305-9012
 6636 Rosemont Ln Mason (45040) *(G-10023)*

Lyondell Chemical Company 513 530-4000
 11530 Northlake Dr Cincinnati (45249) *(G-3118)*

Lyondell Chemical Company 440 352-9393
 110 3rd St Fairport Harbor (44077) *(G-7455)*

Lyondllbsell Advnced Plymers I 330 773-2700
 1353 Exeter Rd Akron (44306) *(G-226)*

Lyondllbsell Advnced Plymers I 330 630-0308
 790 E Tallmadge Ave Akron (44310) *(G-227)*

Lyondllbsell Advnced Plymers I 330 630-3315
 1183 Home Ave Akron (44310) *(G-228)*

Lyondllbsell Advnced Plymers I 330 498-4840
 1353 Exeter Rd Akron (44306) *(G-229)*

Lyondllbsell Advnced Plymers I 440 224-7291
 3365 E Center St Conneaut (44030) *(G-5927)*

Lyondllbsell Advnced Plymers I 440 224-7544
 110 N Eagle St Geneva (44041) *(G-7942)*

Lyondllbsell Advnced Plymers I 419 872-1408
 12600 Eckel Rd Perrysburg (43551) *(G-12397)*

Lyondllbsell Advnced Plymers I 419 682-3311
 103 Railroad Ave Stryker (43557) *(G-13910)*

Lyons 440 224-0676
 5231 State Route 193 Kingsville (44048) *(G-8932)*

M & B Asphalt Company Inc 419 992-4236
 1525 W County Road 42 Old Fort (44861) *(G-12073)*

M & B Asphalt Company Inc (PA) 419 992-4235
 1525 W County Road 42 Tiffin (44883) *(G-14091)*

M & H Fabricating Co Inc (PA) 937 325-8708
 717 Mound St Springfield (45505) *(G-13595)*

M & H Fabricating Co Inc 937 325-8708
 823 Mound St Springfield (45505) *(G-13596)*

M & H Screen Printing 740 522-1957
 1486 Hebron Rd Newark (43056) *(G-11587)*

M & J Machine Company 330 645-0042
 2420 Pickle Rd Akron (44312) *(G-230)*

M & J Tooling, Dayton *Also Called: M & J Tooling Ltd (G-6417)*

M & J Tooling Ltd 937 951-3527
 420 Davis Ave Dayton (45403) *(G-6417)*

M & M Certified Welding Inc 330 467-1729
 556 Highland Rd E Ste 3 Macedonia (44056) *(G-9562)*

M & M Concepts Inc 937 355-1115
 2633 State Route 292 West Mansfield (43358) *(G-15626)*

M & M Dies Inc 216 883-6628
 3502 Beyerle Rd Cleveland (44105) *(G-4342)*

M & M Fabrication Inc 740 779-3071
 18828 Us Highway 50 Chillicothe (45601) *(G-2515)*

M & M Hardwoods, Sugarcreek *Also Called: Tusco Hardwoods LLC (G-13946)*

M & R Phillips Enterprises 740 323-0580
 6242 Jacksontown Rd Newark (43056) *(G-11588)*

M & R Redi Mix Inc (PA) 419 445-7771
 521 Commercial St Pettisville (43553) *(G-12451)*

M & S AG Solutions LLC 419 598-8675
 755 American Rd Napoleon (43545) *(G-11323)*

M & S Equipment Leasing Co 216 662-8800
 17700 Miles Rd Cleveland (44128) *(G-4343)*

M & W Trailers Inc 419 453-3331
 525 East Main St Ottoville (45876) *(G-12201)*

M A C, Vandalia *Also Called: Nimers & Woody II Inc (G-14955)*

M A C Machine 410 944-6171
 1111 Faircrest St Se Canton (44707) *(G-2148)*

M A Harrison Mfg Co Inc 440 965-4306
 14307 State Route 113 Wakeman (44889) *(G-15076)*

M Argueso & Co Inc 216 252-4122
 12651 Elmwood Ave Cleveland (44111) *(G-4344)*

M B Saxon Co Inc 440 229-5006
 47 Alpha Park Cleveland (44143) *(G-4345)*

M B Trucking, Dover *Also Called: Sugarcreek Lime Service (G-6845)*

ALPHABETIC SECTION — Machine Products Company

M C D Plastics & Manufacturing, Piqua *Also Called: Miami Specialties Inc* *(G-12536)*

M D Tool, Dayton *Also Called: Dayton Machine Tool Company* *(G-6282)*

M F Y Inc 330 747-1334
1640 Wilson Ave Youngstown (44506) *(G-16391)*

M G Q Inc 419 992-4236
1525 W County Road 42 Tiffin (44883) *(G-14092)*

M H Woodworking LLC 330 893-3929
2789 County Rd Ste 600 Millersburg (44654) *(G-10977)*

M I P Inc 330 744-0215
701 Jones St Youngstown (44502) *(G-16392)*

M K Metals 330 482-3351
41659 Esterly Dr Leetonia (44431) *(G-9128)*

M K Morse Company (PA) 330 453-8187
1101 11th St Se Canton (44707) *(G-2149)*

M L B Molded Urethane Pdts LLC 419 825-9140
1680 Us Highway 20a Swanton (43558) *(G-13976)*

M N A, Toledo *Also Called: Ohio Module Manufacturing Company LLC* *(G-14409)*

M N M Mfg Inc 330 256-5572
449 Dodge St Kent (44240) *(G-8829)*

M P G, Maumee *Also Called: Magnesium Products Group Inc* *(G-10216)*

M P I Label Systems, Sebring *Also Called: Miller Products Inc* *(G-13122)*

M P I Labeltek, Wadsworth *Also Called: Miller Products Inc* *(G-15046)*

M P I Logistics, Massillon *Also Called: Mpi Logistics and Service Inc* *(G-10130)*

M PI Label Systems 330 938-2134
450 Courtney Rd Sebring (44672) *(G-13121)*

M R Echo-E Inc 937 322-4972
2755 Columbus Rd Springfield (45503) *(G-13597)*

M R I Education Foundation 513 281-3400
5400 Kennedy Ave Cincinnati (45213) *(G-3119)*

M R S, Columbus *Also Called: MRS Industrial Inc* *(G-5584)*

M R T, Middletown *Also Called: 3d Sales & Consulting Inc* *(G-10800)*

M R Trailer Sales Inc 330 339-7701
1565 Steel Hill Rd Nw New Philadelphia (44663) *(G-11512)*

M Rosenthal Company 513 563-0081
3125 Exon Ave Cincinnati (45241) *(G-3120)*

M S B Machine Inc 330 686-7740
36 Castle Dr Munroe Falls (44262) *(G-11303)*

M S International Inc 513 712-5300
8556 Trade Center Dr Ste 300 West Chester (45011) *(G-15460)*

M T, Elmore *Also Called: Machining Technologies Inc* *(G-7101)*

M T D Service Division, Shelby *Also Called: Mtd Products Inc* *(G-13196)*

M T M Molded Products Company 937 890-7461
3370 Obco Ct Dayton (45414) *(G-6418)*

M T O, Saint Marys *Also Called: Murotech Ohio Corporation* *(G-12958)*

M T S I, Fairfield *Also Called: Mendenhall Technical Services Inc* *(G-7383)*

M T Systems Inc 330 453-4646
400 Schroyer Ave Sw Canton (44702) *(G-2150)*

M Technologies Inc 330 477-9009
1818 Hopple Ave Sw Canton (44706) *(G-2151)*

M W Solutions LLC 419 782-1611
1802 Baltimore St Ste B Defiance (43512) *(G-6689)*

M-D Building Products Inc 513 539-2255
100 Westheimer Dr Middletown (45044) *(G-10837)*

M-D Building Products Inc 513 539-2255
100 Westheimer Dr Middletown (45044) *(G-10838)*

M-D Metal Source, Middletown *Also Called: M-D Building Products Inc* *(G-10837)*

M. A. I., Delaware *Also Called: Midwest Acoust-A-Fiber Inc* *(G-6737)*

M.S. Barkin Company, Cleveland *Also Called: Em Es Be Company LLC* *(G-4008)*

M/W International Inc 440 526-6900
3839 Heron Dr Lorain (44053) *(G-9423)*

M&D Machine LLC 419 214-0201
42 W Sylvania Ave Toledo (43612) *(G-14374)*

M&H Medical Holdings Inc (PA) 419 727-8421
1670 Indian Wood Cir Maumee (43537) *(G-10215)*

M&Ms Autosales LLC 234 334-7022
2203 Manchester Rd Akron (44314) *(G-231)*

M&S Machine and Manufacturing, Cincinnati *Also Called: Modern Manufacturing Inc* *(G-3171)*

M21 Industries LLC 937 781-1377
721 Springfield St Dayton (45403) *(G-6419)*

M2m Imaging Corporation 440 684-9690
5427 Wilson Mills Rd Cleveland (44143) *(G-4346)*

M3 Midstream LLC 330 223-2220
11543 State Route 644 Kensington (44427) *(G-8790)*

M3 Midstream LLC 330 679-5580
10 E Main St Salineville (43945) *(G-13039)*

M3 Midstream LLC 740 945-1170
37950 Crimm Rd Scio (43988) *(G-13111)*

M3 Technologies Inc 216 898-9936
13910 Enterprise Ave Cleveland (44135) *(G-4347)*

M7 Hrp LLC 330 923-3256
75 E Market St Akron (44308) *(G-232)*

M7 Technologies, Youngstown *Also Called: Garvey Corporation* *(G-16361)*

MA Workwear LLC 800 459-4405
2048 Akron Peninsula Rd Akron (44313) *(G-233)*

Maag Automatik Inc 330 677-2225
235 Progress Blvd Kent (44240) *(G-8830)*

Maag Reduction Inc 704 716-9000
235 Progress Blvd Kent (44240) *(G-8831)*

Maag Reduction Engineering, Kent *Also Called: Maag Automatik Inc* *(G-8830)*

Maag's Automotive, Sandusky *Also Called: Maags Automotive & Mch Inc* *(G-13076)*

Maags Automotive & Mch Inc 419 626-1539
1640 Columbus Ave Sandusky (44870) *(G-13076)*

Maass Midwest Mfg Inc 419 894-6424
19710 State Route 12 Arcadia (44804) *(G-516)*

Mabsc, Akron *Also Called: Meggitt Arcft Brking Systems C* *(G-243)*

Mac, Alliance *Also Called: Mac Manufacturing Inc* *(G-408)*

Mac Instruments, Sandusky *Also Called: Machine Applications Corp* *(G-13077)*

Mac Its LLC (PA) 937 454-0722
1625 Fieldstone Way Vandalia (45377) *(G-14947)*

Mac Lean J S Co 614 878-5454
5454 Alkire Rd Columbus (43228) *(G-5538)*

Mac Manufacturing Inc (HQ) 330 823-9900
14599 Commerce St Ne Alliance (44601) *(G-408)*

Mac Manufacturing Inc 330 829-1680
1453 Allen Rd Salem (44460) *(G-13014)*

Mac Mfg and Test Facilities, Youngstown *Also Called: Magnetic Analysis Corporation* *(G-16394)*

Mac Oil Field Service Inc 330 674-7371
7861 Township Road 306 Millersburg (44654) *(G-10978)*

Mac Steel Trailer Ltd 330 823-9900
14599 Commerce St Ne Alliance (44601) *(G-409)*

Mac Straight Truck Bodies Inc 800 647-9424
14599 Commerce St Ne Alliance (44601) *(G-410)*

Mac Tools, Dublin *Also Called: Stanley Industrial & Auto LLC* *(G-6943)*

Mac Tools, Dublin *Also Called: Stanley Industrial & Auto LLC* *(G-6944)*

Mac Tools Inc 614 755-7039
505 N Cleveland Ave Ste 200 Westerville (43082) *(G-15666)*

Mac Trailer Manufacturing Inc (PA) 800 795-8454
14599 Commerce St Ne Alliance (44601) *(G-411)*

Mac Trailer Service Inc 330 823-9190
14504 Commerce St Ne Alliance (44601) *(G-412)*

Macdivitt Rubber Company LLC 440 259-5937
3291 Center Rd Perry (44081) *(G-12354)*

Mace, Cleveland *Also Called: Mace Security Intl Inc* *(G-4349)*

Mace Personal Def & SEC Inc (HQ) 440 424-5321
4400 Carnegie Ave Cleveland (44103) *(G-4348)*

Mace Security Intl Inc (PA) 440 424-5325
4400 Carnegie Ave Cleveland (44103) *(G-4349)*

Machine Applications Corp 419 621-2322
3410 Tiffin Ave Sandusky (44870) *(G-13077)*

Machine Concepts Inc 419 628-3498
2167 State Route 66 Minster (45865) *(G-11055)*

Machine Development Corp 513 825-5885
7707 Affinity Dr Cincinnati (45231) *(G-3121)*

Machine Drive Company 513 793-7077
2513 Crescentville Rd Cincinnati (45241) *(G-3122)*

Machine Products, Loveland *Also Called: Macpro Inc* *(G-9492)*

Machine Products Company 937 890-6600
5660 Webster St Dayton (45414) *(G-6420)*

Machine Shop — ALPHABETIC SECTION

Machine Shop, Toledo *Also Called: M&D Machine LLC* *(G-14374)*

Machine Tek Systems Inc 330 527-4450
10400 Industrial Dr Garrettsville (44231) *(G-7921)*

Machine Tool Design & Fab LLC 419 435-7676
1401 Sandusky St Fostoria (44830) *(G-7641)*

Machine Tool Division, Bluffton *Also Called: Grob Systems Inc* *(G-1504)*

Machine Tools Supply, Huber Heights *Also Called: Updike Supply Company* *(G-8580)*

Machine-Pro Technologies Inc 419 584-0086
1321 W Market St Celina (45822) *(G-2340)*

Machined Glass Specialist Inc 937 743-6166
245 Hiawatha Trl Springboro (45066) *(G-13509)*

Machining Solutions LLC 419 593-0038
425 Enterprise Ave Wauseon (43567) *(G-15268)*

Machining Technologies Inc (PA) 419 862-3110
468 Maple St Elmore (43416) *(G-7101)*

Machintek Co 513 551-1000
3721 Port Union Rd Fairfield (45014) *(G-7378)*

Mack Concrete Industries Inc 330 784-7008
124 Darrow Rd Ste 7 Akron (44305) *(G-234)*

Mack Concrete Industries Inc (HQ) 330 483-3111
201 Columbia Rd Valley City (44280) *(G-14877)*

Mack Industries 419 353-7081
507 Derby Ave Bowling Green (43402) *(G-1572)*

Mack Industries Inc 740 393-1121
400 Howard St Mount Vernon (43050) *(G-11277)*

Mack Industries PA Inc (HQ) 330 483-3111
201 Columbia Rd Valley City (44280) *(G-14878)*

Mack Industries PA Inc 330 638-7680
2207 Sodom Hutchings Rd Ne Vienna (44473) *(G-15000)*

Mack Iron Works Company 419 626-3712
124 Warren St Sandusky (44870) *(G-13078)*

Mack Ready-Mix, Akron *Also Called: Mack Concrete Industries Inc* *(G-234)*

Macke Brothers Inc 513 771-7500
10355 Spartan Dr Cincinnati (45215) *(G-3123)*

Macpherson & Company, Warren *Also Called: Macpherson Engineering Inc* *(G-15187)*

Macpherson Engineering Inc 440 243-6565
2809 Mahoning Ave Nw Warren (44483) *(G-15187)*

Macpro Inc 513 575-3000
1456 Fay Rd Unit B Loveland (45140) *(G-9492)*

Macray Co LLC 937 325-1726
100 W North St Springfield (45504) *(G-13598)*

Macro Meric, Aurora *Also Called: Saco Aei Polymers Inc* *(G-735)*

Mactac, Stow *Also Called: Mactac Americas LLC* *(G-13707)*

Mactac, Stow *Also Called: Morgan Adhesives Company LLC* *(G-13709)*

Mactac Americas LLC (DH) 800 762-2822
4560 Darrow Rd Stow (44224) *(G-13707)*

Macton Corporation 330 259-8555
3200 Innovation Pl Youngstown (44509) *(G-16393)*

Mad River Steel Ltd 937 845-4046
2141 N Dayton Lakeview Rd New Carlisle (45344) *(G-11420)*

Mad River Steel Company, New Carlisle *Also Called: Mad River Steel Ltd* *(G-11420)*

Made Men Circle LLC 216 501-0414
2883 Mayfield Rd Apt 2 Cleveland Heights (44118) *(G-4940)*

Mader Automotive Center Inc (PA) 937 339-2681
225 S Walnut St Troy (45373) *(G-14595)*

Mader Dampers, Lagrange *Also Called: Mader Machine Co Inc* *(G-8951)*

Mader Elc Mtr Pwr Trnsmssons L 937 325-5576
205 E Main St Springfield (45503) *(G-13599)*

Mader Machine Co Inc 440 355-4505
422 Commerce Dr E Lagrange (44050) *(G-8951)*

Madison Electric Products Inc (HQ) 216 391-7776
30575 Bainbridge Rd Ste 130 Solon (44139) *(G-13382)*

Madison Messenger, Columbus *Also Called: Columbus Messenger Company* *(G-5272)*

Madison Mine Supply Co, Jackson *Also Called: Waterloo Coal Company Inc* *(G-8727)*

Madison Property Holdings Inc 800 215-3210
5055 Madison Rd Cincinnati (45227) *(G-3124)*

Madisono's Gelato, Cincinnati *Also Called: Cfgsc LLC* *(G-2720)*

Madsen Wire Products Inc 937 829-6561
101 Madison St Dayton (45402) *(G-6421)*

Mae Materials LLC 740 778-2242
8336 Bennett School House Rd South Webster (45682) *(G-13476)*

Mag Resources LLC 330 294-0494
711 Wooster Rd W Barberton (44203) *(G-878)*

Mag-Nif Inc 440 255-9366
8820 East Ave Mentor (44060) *(G-10498)*

Magellan Arospc Middletown Inc (HQ) 513 422-2751
2320 Wedekind Dr Middletown (45042) *(G-10839)*

Maggard Mmrals Lser Art Tech L 513 282-6969
19 N Sycamore St Lebanon (45036) *(G-9095)*

Magic Dragon Machine Inc 614 539-8004
3451 Grant Ave Grove City (43123) *(G-8103)*

Magic Molding Inc 937 778-0836
6460 W Piqua Clayton Rd Covington (45318) *(G-6027)*

Magic Wok Inc (PA) 419 531-1818
3352 W Laskey Rd Toledo (43623) *(G-14375)*

Magic Wok Enterprises, Toledo *Also Called: Magic Wok Inc* *(G-14375)*

Magna, Northwood *Also Called: Norplas Industries Inc* *(G-11922)*

Magna International Amer Inc 330 824-3101
3637 Mallard Run Sheffield Village (44054) *(G-13185)*

Magna International Amer Inc 419 410-4780
428 Church St Swanton (43558) *(G-13977)*

Magna Machine Co (PA) 513 851-6900
11180 Southland Rd Cincinnati (45240) *(G-3125)*

Magna Modular Systems LLC (DH) 419 324-3387
1800 Jason St Toledo (43611) *(G-14376)*

Magna Products, Grafton *Also Called: Sulo Enterprises Inc* *(G-8005)*

Magna Three LLC 513 389-0776
2668 Cyclorama Dr Cincinnati (45211) *(G-3126)*

Magnaco Industries Inc 216 961-3636
140 West Dr Lodi (44254) *(G-9353)*

Magneco/Metrel Inc 330 426-9468
51365 State Route 154 Negley (44441) *(G-11354)*

Magneforce Inc 330 856-9300
155 Shaffer Dr Ne Warren (44484) *(G-15188)*

Magnesium Products Group Inc 310 971-5799
3928 Azalea Cir Maumee (43537) *(G-10216)*

Magnesium Refining Technologies Inc 419 483-9199
29695 Pettibone Rd Cleveland (44139) *(G-4350)*

Magnet Engineering Inc 513 248-4578
2690 Riggs Ln Batavia (45103) *(G-930)*

Magnetech, Massillon *Also Called: 3-D Service Ltd* *(G-10072)*

Magnetech Industrial Services, Massillon *Also Called: Magnetech Industrial Svcs Inc* *(G-10121)*

Magnetech Industrial Svcs Inc (DH) 330 830-3500
800 Nave Rd Se Massillon (44646) *(G-10121)*

Magnetic Analysis Corporation 330 758-1367
675 Mcclurg Rd Youngstown (44512) *(G-16394)*

Magnetic Screw Machine Pdts 937 348-2807
23241 State Route 37 Marysville (43040) *(G-9925)*

Magnetic Source, Marietta *Also Called: Master Magnetics Inc* *(G-9807)*

Magnext Ltd 614 433-0011
7100 Huntley Rd Ste 100 Columbus (43229) *(G-5539)*

Magni Fab & Magnetic, Wooster *Also Called: Magni-Power Company* *(G-16148)*

Magni-Power Company (PA) 330 264-3637
5511 E Lincoln Way Wooster (44691) *(G-16148)*

Magnum Asset Acquisition LLC 330 915-2382
5675 Hudson Industrial Pkwy # 3 Hudson (44236) *(G-8603)*

Magnum Computers Inc 216 781-1757
868 Montford Rd Cleveland (44121) *(G-4351)*

Magnum Inks & Coatings, Marietta *Also Called: Magnum Magnetics Corporation* *(G-9805)*

Magnum Innovations, Hudson *Also Called: Magnum Asset Acquisition LLC* *(G-8603)*

Magnum Magnetics Corporation 740 516-6237
17289 Industrial Hwy Caldwell (43724) *(G-1910)*

Magnum Magnetics Corporation (PA) 740 373-7770
801 Masonic Park Rd Marietta (45750) *(G-9805)*

Magnum Magnetics Corporation 513 360-0790
355 Wright Dr Middletown (45044) *(G-10840)*

Magnum Piering Inc 513 759-3348
156 Circle Freeway Dr West Chester (45246) *(G-15568)*

Magnum Press, Columbus *Also Called: Resilient Holdings Inc* *(G-5718)*

Magnum Tapes Films 877 460-8402
17289 Industrial Hwy Caldwell (43724) *(G-1911)*

Magnum Tool Corp 937 228-0900
1407 Stanley Ave Dayton (45404) *(G-6422)*

Magnus Engineered Eqp LLC 440 942-8488
4500 Beidler Rd Willoughby (44094) *(G-15948)*

Magnus Equipment, Willoughby *Also Called: Reid Asset Management Company (G-15982)*

Magnus International Group Inc (PA) 216 592-8355
679 Hardy Rd Painesville (44077) *(G-12248)*

Mahan Packing Co 330 889-2454
6540 State Route 45 Bristolville (44402) *(G-1653)*

Mahle Behr Dayton LLC 937 369-2900
1720 Webster St Dayton (45404) *(G-6423)*

Mahle Behr Dayton LLC (DH) 937 369-2900
1600 Webster St Dayton (45404) *(G-6424)*

Mahle Behr Dayton LLC 937 369-2000
1600 Webster St Dayton (45404) *(G-6425)*

Mahle Behr Dayton LLC 937 356-2001
250 Northwoods Blvd Bldg 47 Vandalia (45377) *(G-14948)*

Mahle Behr Mt Sterling Inc 740 869-3333
10500 Oday Harrison Rd Mount Sterling (43143) *(G-11256)*

Mahle Behr USA Inc 937 356-2001
250 Northwoods Blvd Bldg 47 Vandalia (45377) *(G-14949)*

Mahle Behr USA Inc 937 369-2610
1003 Bellbrook Ave Xenia (45385) *(G-16268)*

Mahle Industries Incorporated 937 890-2739
1600 Webster St Dayton (45404) *(G-6426)*

Mahoning Valley Manufacturing 330 537-4492
17796 Rte 62 Beloit (44609) *(G-1251)*

Mahoning Valley Tool & Mch LLC 330 482-0870
1380 Wardingley Ave Columbiana (44408) *(G-5044)*

MAI Manufacturing, Marysville *Also Called: Straight 72 Inc (G-9940)*

MAI-Weave LLC 937 322-1698
1800 E Pleasant St Springfield (45505) *(G-13600)*

Mailposts By Mike, Cleveland *Also Called: Stiber Fabricating Inc (G-4735)*

Main Awning & Tent Inc 513 621-6947
415 W Seymour Ave Cincinnati (45216) *(G-3127)*

Main Street Cambritt Cookies, Cuyahoga Falls *Also Called: Main Street Gourmet LLC (G-6101)*

Main Street Gourmet LLC 330 929-0000
170 Muffin Ln Cuyahoga Falls (44223) *(G-6101)*

Main Street Lighting Standards, Medina *Also Called: Msls Group LLC (G-10355)*

Maine Rubber Preforms LLC 216 387-1268
14481 Butternut Rd Burton (44021) *(G-1884)*

Mainstream Waterjet LLC 513 683-5426
108 Northeast Dr Loveland (45140) *(G-9493)*

Maintenance + Inc 330 264-6262
1051 W Liberty St Wooster (44691) *(G-16149)*

Maintenance Repair Supply Inc 740 922-3006
5539 Gundy Dr Midvale (44653) *(G-10881)*

Maiweave, Springfield *Also Called: Intertape Polymer Corp (G-13583)*

Majestic Fireplace Distr 440 439-1040
7500 Northfield Rd Bedford (44146) *(G-1136)*

Majestic Manufacturing Inc 330 457-2447
4536 State Route 7 New Waterford (44445) *(G-11558)*

Majestic Plastics Inc 937 593-9500
811 N Main St Bellefontaine (43311) *(G-1215)*

Majestic Tool and Machine Inc 440 248-5058
30700 Carter St Ste C Solon (44139) *(G-13383)*

Major Metals Company 419 886-4600
844 Kochheiser Rd Mansfield (44904) *(G-9681)*

MAK Fabricating Inc 330 747-0040
1609 Wilson Ave Youngstown (44506) *(G-16395)*

Makergear LLC 216 765-0030
23632 Mercantile Rd Ste I Beachwood (44122) *(G-996)*

Makers Supply LLC 937 203-8245
6665 N Spiker Rd Piqua (45356) *(G-12534)*

Makino Inc (HQ) 513 573-7200
7680 Innovation Way Mason (45040) *(G-10024)*

Mako Finished Products Inc 740 357-0839
708 Fairground Rd Lucasville (45648) *(G-9523)*

Malabar 419 866-6301
1 Air Cargo Pkwy E Swanton (43558) *(G-13978)*

Malabar International, Swanton *Also Called: Malabar (G-13978)*

Malabar Properties LLC 419 884-0071
300 S Mill St Mansfield (44904) *(G-9682)*

Malco Products, Barberton *Also Called: Malco Products Inc (G-879)*

Malco Products Inc (PA) 330 753-0361
361 Fairview Ave Barberton (44203) *(G-879)*

Malcuit Racing Engines, Strasburg *Also Called: B A Malcuit Racing Inc (G-13743)*

Malik Media LLC 614 933-0328
7591 Lambton Park Rd New Albany (43054) *(G-11383)*

Malin Co, Cleveland *Also Called: Malin Wire Co (G-4352)*

Malin Company, Cleveland *Also Called: Brushes Inc (G-3767)*

Malin Wire Co 216 267-9080
5400 Smith Rd Cleveland (44142) *(G-4352)*

Malish, Mentor *Also Called: Malish Corporation (G-10499)*

Malish Corporation (PA) 440 951-5356
7333 Corporate Blvd Mentor (44060) *(G-10499)*

Malley's Chocolates, Cleveland *Also Called: Malleys Candies Inc (G-4353)*

Malleys Candies Inc (PA) 216 362-8700
13400 Brookpark Rd Cleveland (44135) *(G-4353)*

Mallory Pattern Works Inc 419 726-8001
5340 Enterprise Blvd Toledo (43612) *(G-14377)*

Malta Dynamics LLC (PA) 740 749-3512
405 Watertown Rd Waterford (45786) *(G-15238)*

Mama Jo Homestyle Pies, Amherst *Also Called: Papa Joes Pies Inc (G-481)*

Mama Rosas's, Sidney *Also Called: Schwans Mama Rosass LLC (G-13282)*

Mamabees HM Gds Lifestyle LLC 419 277-2914
2186 Mccutchenville Rd Fostoria (44830) *(G-7642)*

Mameco International Inc 216 752-4400
4475 E 175th St Cleveland (44128) *(G-4354)*

Mammana Custom Woodworking Inc 216 581-9059
14400 Industrial Ave N Maple Heights (44137) *(G-9754)*

Mammoth Labels & Packaging, Grove City *Also Called: Boehm Inc (G-8080)*

Manairco Inc 419 524-2121
28 Industrial Pkwy Mansfield (44903) *(G-9683)*

Manco Manufacturing Co 419 925-4152
2411 Rolfes Rd Maria Stein (45860) *(G-9771)*

Mancor Ohio Inc (HQ) 937 228-6141
1008 Leonhard St Dayton (45404) *(G-6427)*

Mancor Ohio Inc 937 228-6141
600 Kiser St Dayton (45404) *(G-6428)*

Mandrax Technologies, Westerville *Also Called: David Chojnacki (G-15699)*

Mandrel Group LLC 330 881-1266
105 Ohio Ave Mc Donald (44437) *(G-10278)*

Mane Inc 513 248-9876
10261 Chester Rd Cincinnati (45215) *(G-3128)*

Mane Inc (DH) 513 248-9876
2501 Henkle Dr Lebanon (45036) *(G-9096)*

Mane Calafornia, Lebanon *Also Called: Mane Inc (G-9096)*

Manitou Candle Co LLC 513 429-5254
7 W 7th St Ste 1400 Cincinnati (45202) *(G-3129)*

Manitwoc Ovens Advnced Cooking, Cleveland *Also Called: Cleveland Range LLC (G-3852)*

Mannings Packing Co 937 446-3278
100 College Ave Sardinia (45171) *(G-13107)*

Manoranjan Shaffer & Heidkamp, Dayton *Also Called: Watson Haran & Company Inc (G-6648)*

Mansfield Brass & Aluminum Corporation 419 492-2154
636 S Center St New Washington (44854) *(G-11548)*

Mansfield Brew Works LLC 419 631-3153
131 N Diamond St Mansfield (44902) *(G-9684)*

Mansfield Castings, New Washington *Also Called: Mansfield Brass & Aluminum Corporation (G-11548)*

Mansfield Engineered Components LLC 419 524-1331
1776 Harrington Memorial Rd Mansfield (44903) *(G-9685)*

Mansfield Fabricated Products, Mansfield *Also Called: The Mansfield Strl & Erct Co (G-9726)*

Mansfield Graphics, Mansfield *Also Called: Five Handicap Inc (G-9656)*

Mansfield Industries 419 785-4510
844 N Clinton St Lot C17 Defiance (43512) *(G-6690)*

Mansfield Industries Inc 419 524-1300
1776 Harrington Memorial Rd Mansfield (44903) *(G-9686)*

Mansfield Journal Co 330 364-8641
629 Wabash Ave Nw New Philadelphia (44663) *(G-11513)*

Mansfield Operations, Mansfield *Also Called: Cleveland-Cliffs Steel Corp (G-9639)*

Mansfield Paint Co Inc.. 330 725-2436
525 W Liberty St Medina (44256) *(G-10346)*

Mansfield Plumbing Pdts LLC (HQ).................................. 419 938-5211
150 E 1st St Perrysville (44864) *(G-12447)*

Mansfield Welding Service LLC.. 419 594-2738
20027 State Route 613 Oakwood (45873) *(G-12031)*

Mansion Homes, Bryan *Also Called: Manufactured Housing Entps Inc (G-1827)*

Mantaline, Hiram *Also Called: Mantaline Corporation (G-8486)*

Mantaline Corporation... 330 569-3147
6969 Constance Rd Hiram (44234) *(G-8486)*

Mantaline Corporation... 330 274-2264
4754 E High St Mantua (44255) *(G-9739)*

Mantaline Corporation (PA).. 330 274-2264
4754 E High St Mantua (44255) *(G-9740)*

Mantra Haircare LLC.. 440 526-3304
305 Ken Mar Industrial Pkwy Broadview Heights (44147) *(G-1661)*

Mantua Bed Frames, Solon *Also Called: Rize Home LLC (G-13415)*

Mantych Metalworking Inc.. 937 258-1373
3175 Plainfield Rd Dayton (45432) *(G-6168)*

Manufactured Housing Entps Inc....................................... 419 636-4511
9302 Us Highway 6 Bryan (43506) *(G-1827)*

Manufacturers Equipment Co... 513 424-3573
35 Enterprise Dr Middletown (45044) *(G-10841)*

Manufacturers Repdirect Distr, Hudson *Also Called: Starbright Lighting USA LLC (G-8615)*

Manufacturers Service Inc.. 216 267-3771
11440 Brookpark Rd Cleveland (44130) *(G-4355)*

Manufacturers Wholesale Lumber, Cleveland *Also Called: Flagship Trading Corporation (G-4066)*

Manufacturing, Beavercreek Township *Also Called: Fluid Applied Roofing LLC (G-1084)*

Manufacturing, Twinsburg *Also Called: Phoenix Mtal Sls Fbrcation LLC (G-14715)*

Manufacturing, West Chester *Also Called: DA Precision Products Inc (G-15411)*

Manufacturing Animal Food Phrm, Batavia *Also Called: Ingredient Masters Inc (G-926)*

Manufacturing Concepts... 330 784-9054
409 Munroe Falls Rd Tallmadge (44278) *(G-14036)*

Manufacturing Division, Willard *Also Called: Lsc Communications Inc (G-15860)*

Manufacturing Process Tech, Ashland *Also Called: Mp Technologies Inc (G-594)*

Manufctred Assemblies Corp LLC..................................... 937 454-0722
1625 Fieldstone Way Vandalia (45377) *(G-14950)*

Manufctring Bus Dev Sltons LLC....................................... 419 294-1313
1950 Industrial Dr Findlay (45840) *(G-7530)*

Manuvis Corp.. 440 352-6261
1 Victoria Pl Ste 309 Painesville (44077) *(G-12249)*

Mapco, Mansfield *Also Called: Midwest Aircraft Products Co (G-9692)*

Mapcs, Akron *Also Called: Millers Aplus Cmpt Svcs LLC (G-250)*

Maple City Rubber Co, Norwalk *Also Called: MCR of Norwalk Inc (G-11979)*

Maple Grove Companies, Tiffin *Also Called: M G Q Inc (G-14092)*

Maple Grove Materials Inc... 419 992-4235
1525 W City Rd Ste 42 Tiffin (44883) *(G-14093)*

Maple Grove Stone, Old Fort *Also Called: M & B Asphalt Company Inc (G-12073)*

Maple Hill Woodworking LLC... 330 674-2500
2726 Trl 128 Millersburg (44654) *(G-10979)*

Maple Valley Cleaners, Akron *Also Called: Norkaam Industries LLC (G-265)*

Mapledale Farm Inc... 440 286-3389
12613 Woodin Rd Chardon (44024) *(G-2458)*

Mapledale Landscaping, Chardon *Also Called: Mapledale Farm Inc (G-2458)*

Mar-Bal Inc (PA)... 440 543-7526
10095 Queens Way Chagrin Falls (44023) *(G-2407)*

Mar-Bal Pultrusion Inc... 440 953-0456
38310 Apollo Pkwy Willoughby (44094) *(G-15949)*

Mar-Con Tool Company.. 937 299-2244
2301 Arbor Blvd Moraine (45439) *(G-11191)*

Mar-Metal Mfg Inc.. 419 447-1102
420 N Warpole St Upper Sandusky (43351) *(G-14815)*

Mar-Vel Tool Co.. 937 223-2137
858 Hall Ave Dayton (45404) *(G-6429)*

Mar-Zane Inc (HQ)... 740 453-0721
3570 S River Rd Zanesville (43701) *(G-16543)*

Mar-Zane Materials, Zanesville *Also Called: Mar-Zane Inc (G-16543)*

Maradyne Corporation (HQ)... 216 362-0755
4540 W 160th St Cleveland (44135) *(G-4356)*

Maramor Chocolates, Columbus *Also Called: Hake Head LLC (G-5416)*

Marathon At Sawmill.. 614 734-0836
7200 Sawmill Rd Columbus (43235) *(G-5540)*

Marathon Canton Refinery, Canton *Also Called: Mplx Terminals LLC (G-2167)*

Marathon Industrial Cntrs Inc... 440 324-2748
100 Freedom Ct Elyria (44035) *(G-7177)*

Marathon Mfg & Sup Co... 330 343-2656
5165 Main St Ne New Philadelphia (44663) *(G-11514)*

Marathon Oil, Bryan *Also Called: Bryan West Main Stop (G-1812)*

Marathon Oil, Doylestown *Also Called: Adapt Oil (G-6852)*

Marathon Oil Company... 419 422-2121
539 S Main St Findlay (45840) *(G-7531)*

Marathon Petroleum, Findlay *Also Called: Marathon Petroleum Corporation (G-7533)*

Marathon Petroleum Company LP (HQ)........................... 419 422-2121
539 S Main St Findlay (45840) *(G-7532)*

Marathon Petroleum Corporation (PA)............................. 419 422-2121
539 S Main St Findlay (45840) *(G-7533)*

Marathon Ptro Cnada Trdg Sup U..................................... 419 422-2121
539 S Main St Findlay (45840) *(G-7534)*

Marathon Special Products Corp...................................... 419 352-0441
427 Van Camp Rd Bowling Green (43402) *(G-1573)*

Marbee Inc.. 419 422-9441
2703 N Main St Ste 1 Findlay (45840) *(G-7535)*

Marbee Printing & Graphic Art, Findlay *Also Called: Marbee Inc (G-7535)*

Marble Arch Products Inc... 937 746-8388
263 Industrial Dr Franklin (45005) *(G-7685)*

Marble Cliff Block & Bldrs Sup, Lockbourne *Also Called: J P Sand & Gravel Company (G-9337)*

Marble Cliff Limestone Inc.. 614 488-3030
2650 Old Dublin Rd Hilliard (43026) *(G-8419)*

March First Brewing, Cincinnati *Also Called: March First Manufacturing LLC (G-3130)*

March First Manufacturing LLC (PA)................................ 513 266-3076
7885 E Kemper Rd Cincinnati (45249) *(G-3130)*

Marco Printed Products Co.. 937 433-7030
25 W Whipp Rd Dayton (45459) *(G-6430)*

Marco's Papers, Dayton *Also Called: Marco Printed Products Co (G-6430)*

Marcus Jewelers, Cincinnati *Also Called: Markus Jewelers LLC (G-3132)*

Marcus Uppe Inc.. 216 263-4000
815 Superior Ave E Ste 714 Cleveland (44114) *(G-4357)*

Marengo Fabricated Steel Ltd (PA)................................... 800 919-2652
2896 State Route 61 Cardington (43315) *(G-2276)*

Marfo Company (PA)... 614 276-3352
799 N Hague Ave Columbus (43204) *(G-5541)*

Margo Tool Technology Inc.. 740 653-8115
2616 Setter Ct Nw Lancaster (43130) *(G-9023)*

Maric Drilling Co.. 330 830-8178
2581 County Rd 160 Winesburg (44690) *(G-16080)*

Marich Machine and Tool Co.. 216 391-5502
3815 Lakeside Ave E Cleveland (44114) *(G-4358)*

Marie Noble Wine Company... 216 633-0025
1891 Idlehurst Dr Euclid (44117) *(G-7282)*

Marie's Candies, West Liberty *Also Called: Maries Candies LLC (G-15623)*

Maries Candies LLC.. 937 465-3061
311 Zanesfield Rd West Liberty (43357) *(G-15623)*

Marietta Coal Co (PA)... 740 695-2197
67705 Friends Church Rd Saint Clairsville (43950) *(G-12908)*

Marietta Martin Materials Inc.. 740 247-2211
50427 State Route 124 Racine (45771) *(G-12694)*

Marietta Martin Materials Inc.. 937 335-8313
250 Dye Mill Rd Troy (45373) *(G-14596)*

Marietta Resources Corporation....................................... 740 373-6305
704 Pike St Marietta (45750) *(G-9806)*

Marietta Times, Marietta *Also Called: Gannett Stllite Info Ntwrk LLC (G-9794)*

Marik Spring Inc... 330 564-0617
121 Northeast Ave Tallmadge (44278) *(G-14037)*

Marine Development, Cincinnati *Also Called: Machine Development Corp (G-3121)*

Marine Jet Power Inc... 614 759-9000
6740 Commerce Court Dr Blacklick (43004) *(G-1339)*

ALPHABETIC SECTION — Mary Ann Donut Shoppe Inc

Mariner's Landing Marina, Cincinnati Also Called: Mariners Landing Inc *(G-3131)*
Mariners Landing Inc.. 513 941-3625
  7405 Forbes Rd Cincinnati (45233) *(G-3131)*
Marino Maintenance Co, Canton Also Called: Phase II Enterprises Inc *(G-2196)*
Marion Cnty Coal Resources Inc................................ 740 338-3100
  46226 National Rd Saint Clairsville (43950) *(G-12909)*
Marion County Coal Company................................... 740 338-3100
  46226 National Rd Saint Clairsville (43950) *(G-12910)*
Marion Dofasco Inc.. 740 382-3979
  686 W Fairground St Marion (43302) *(G-9860)*
Marion Industries LLC.. 740 223-0075
  999 Kellogg Pkwy Marion (43302) *(G-9861)*
Marion Star... 740 328-8542
  22 N 1st St Newark (43055) *(G-11589)*
Mariotti Printing Co LLC... 440 245-4120
  513 E 28th St Lorain (44055) *(G-9424)*
Mark Advertising Agency Inc..................................... 419 626-9000
  1600 5th St Sandusky (44870) *(G-13079)*
Mark Andronis.. 740 259-5613
  50 Mcnamer Brown Rd Lucasville (45648) *(G-9524)*
Mark Grzianis St Treats Ex Inc (PA)......................... 330 414-6266
  1294 Windward Ln Kent (44240) *(G-8832)*
Mark Knupp Muffler & Tire Inc................................... 937 773-1334
  950 S College St Piqua (45356) *(G-12535)*
Mark W Thruman... 614 754-5500
  85 Mcnaughten Rd Columbus (43213) *(G-5542)*
Mark-All Enterprises LLC... 800 433-3615
  888 W Waterloo Rd Akron (44314) *(G-235)*
Markers Inc... 440 933-5927
  33490 Pin Oak Pkwy Avon Lake (44012) *(G-816)*
Market Media Creations, Coshocton Also Called: Sprint Print Inc *(G-5997)*
Market Ready... 513 289-9231
  1129 Avalon Dr Maineville (45039) *(G-9601)*
Markethtch Inc D/B/A Mh Eye CA.............................. 330 376-6363
  91 E Voris St Akron (44311) *(G-236)*
Marketing Essentials LLC.. 419 629-0080
  14 N Washington St New Bremen (45869) *(G-11404)*
Markham Converting Limited..................................... 419 353-2458
  12830 S Dixie Hwy Bowling Green (43402) *(G-1574)*
Markham Machine Company Inc............................... 330 762-7676
  160 N Union St Akron (44304) *(G-237)*
Marking Devices Inc... 216 861-4498
  3110 Payne Ave Cleveland (44114) *(G-4359)*
Markt LLC... 740 397-5900
  314 W Burgess St Mount Vernon (43050) *(G-11278)*
Markus Jewelers LLC.. 513 474-4950
  2022 8 Mile Rd Cincinnati (45244) *(G-3132)*
Markwest Utica Emg LLC.. 740 942-4810
  46700 Giacobbi Rd Jewett (43986) *(G-8767)*
Markwith Tool Company Inc...................................... 937 548-6808
  5261 S State Route 49 Greenville (45331) *(G-8051)*
Marlboro Manufacturing Inc....................................... 330 935-2221
  11750 Marlboro Ave Ne Alliance (44601) *(G-413)*
Marlen, Bedford Also Called: Marlen Manufacturing & Dev Co *(G-1137)*
Marlen Manufacturing & Dev Co (PA)....................... 216 292-7060
  5150 Richmond Rd Bedford (44146) *(G-1137)*
Marlin Manufacturing Corp (PA)................................ 216 676-1340
  12800 Corporate Dr Cleveland (44130) *(G-4360)*
Marlin Thermocouple Wire Inc.................................. 440 835-1950
  847 Canterbury Rd Westlake (44145) *(G-15764)*
Marlite Inc (DH).. 330 343-6621
  1 Marlite Dr Dover (44622) *(G-6833)*
Marmax Machine Co.. 937 698-9900
  2425 S State Route 48 Ludlow Falls (45339) *(G-9529)*
Marne Plastics LLC.. 614 732-4666
  3655 Brookham Dr Ste F Grove City (43123) *(G-8104)*
Maroon Intrmdiate Holdings LLC............................... 440 937-1000
  1390 Jaycox Rd Avon (44011) *(G-781)*
Marpro, Cincinnati Also Called: Cincinnati Premier Candy Llc *(G-2758)*
Marrow County Sentinel, Mount Gilead Also Called: Hirt Publishing Co Inc *(G-11234)*
Mars Horsecare, Dalton Also Called: Mars Horsecare Us Inc *(G-6135)*

Mars Horsecare Us Inc.. 330 828-2251
  330 E Schultz St Dalton (44618) *(G-6135)*
Mars Petcare Us Inc.. 419 943-4280
  3700 State Route 65 Leipsic (45856) *(G-9133)*
Marsam Metalfab Inc... 330 405-1520
  1870 Enterprise Pkwy Twinsburg (44087) *(G-14691)*
Marsh Composites LLC.. 937 350-1214
  1691 Spaulding Rd Dayton (45432) *(G-6169)*
Marsh Industries Inc... 330 308-8667
  1117 Bowers Ave Nw New Philadelphia (44663) *(G-11515)*
Marsh Industries Inc (PA).. 800 426-4244
  2301 E High Ave New Philadelphia (44663) *(G-11516)*
Marsh Technologies Inc... 330 545-0085
  30 W Main St Ste A Girard (44420) *(G-7972)*
Marshall Plastics Inc.. 937 653-4740
  590 S Edgewood Ave Urbana (43078) *(G-14843)*
Marshalltown Packaging Inc...................................... 641 753-5272
  601 N Hague Ave Columbus (43204) *(G-5543)*
Marshallville Packing Co Inc..................................... 330 855-2871
  50 E Market St Marshallville (44645) *(G-9893)*
Marshas Buckeyes LLC.. 419 872-7666
  25631 Fort Meigs Rd Ste E Perrysburg (43551) *(G-12398)*
Marsulex Inc.. 419 698-8181
  1400 Otter Creek Rd Oregon (43616) *(G-12107)*
Mart Plus Fuel... 216 261-0420
  21820 Lake Shore Blvd Euclid (44123) *(G-7283)*
Martin Allen Trailer LLC... 330 942-0217
  837 N Cleveland Massillon Rd Akron (44333) *(G-238)*
Martin Cab Div, Cleveland Also Called: Martin Sheet Metal Inc *(G-4362)*
Martin Diesel Inc... 419 782-9911
  27809 County Road 424 Defiance (43512) *(G-6691)*
Martin Industries Inc... 419 862-2694
  473 Maple St Elmore (43416) *(G-7102)*
Martin M Hardin.. 740 282-1234
  411 N 7th St Steubenville (43952) *(G-13671)*
Martin Machine, Bowling Green Also Called: Aeropact Manufacturing LLC *(G-1551)*
Martin Marietta Aggregate, West Chester Also Called: Martin Marietta Materials Inc *(G-15461)*
Martin Marietta Aggregates, Mason Also Called: Martin Marietta Materials Inc *(G-10025)*
Martin Marietta Aggregates, Racine Also Called: Marietta Martin Materials Inc *(G-12694)*
Martin Marietta Materials Inc..................................... 513 701-1120
  4900 Parkway Dr Mason (45040) *(G-10025)*
Martin Marietta Materials Inc..................................... 513 701-1140
  9277 Centre Pointe Dr Ste 250 West Chester (45069) *(G-15461)*
Martin Mohr... 740 727-2233
  3521 Rhodes Ave New Boston (45662) *(G-11397)*
Martin Paper Products Inc... 740 756-9271
  5907 Columbus Lancaster Rd Nw Carroll (43112) *(G-2300)*
Martin Pultrusion Group Inc....................................... 440 439-9130
  20801 Miles Rd Ste B Cleveland (44128) *(G-4361)*
Martin Sheet Metal Inc... 216 377-8200
  7108 Madison Ave Cleveland (44102) *(G-4362)*
Martin Welding LLC (PA)... 937 687-3602
  1472 W Main St New Lebanon (45345) *(G-11450)*
Martin Wheel, Tallmadge Also Called: Americana Development Inc *(G-14022)*
Martin-Brower Company LLC.................................... 513 773-2301
  4260 Port Union Rd West Chester (45011) *(G-15462)*
Martin-Palmer Tool, Dayton Also Called: Edfa LLC *(G-6313)*
Martina Metal LLC.. 614 291-9700
  1575 Shawnee Ave Columbus (43211) *(G-5544)*
Martindale Electric Company..................................... 216 521-8567
  1375 Hird Ave Cleveland (44107) *(G-4363)*
Martinez Food Products LLC..................................... 419 720-6973
  1220 Belmont Ave Toledo (43607) *(G-14378)*
Martins Partitions, Lancaster Also Called: Thorwald Holdings Inc *(G-9044)*
Martins Steel Fabrication Inc..................................... 330 882-4311
  2115 Center Rd New Franklin (44216) *(G-11439)*
Marvin Lewis Enterprises LLC................................... 216 785-8419
  27801 Euclid Ave Euclid (44132) *(G-7284)*
Marwil, Fort Loramie Also Called: Rol - Tech Inc *(G-7606)*
Mary Ann Donut Shoppe Inc (PA)............................. 330 478-1655
  5032 Yukon St Nw Canton (44708) *(G-2152)*

(PA)=Parent Co (HQ)=Headquarters (DH)=Div Headquarters

Mary Ann Donuts

ALPHABETIC SECTION

Mary Ann Donuts, Canton *Also Called: Mary Ann Donut Shoppe Inc (G-2152)*

Marysville Auto Plant, Marysville *Also Called: Honda Dev & Mfg Amer LLC (G-9916)*

Marysville Newspaper Inc (PA)................................. 937 644-9111
207 N Main St Marysville (43040) *(G-9926)*

Marysville Steel Inc... 937 642-5971
323 E 8th St Marysville (43040) *(G-9927)*

Marz Direct, Monroe *Also Called: R & L Software LLC (G-11118)*

Marzano Inc.. 216 459-2051
4147 Pearl Rd Cleveland (44109) *(G-4364)*

Mascot Shop, The, Akron *Also Called: Kent Stow Screen Printing Inc (G-205)*

Masheen Specialties... 330 652-7535
3519 Union St Mineral Ridge (44440) *(G-11023)*

Mason Color Works Inc.. 330 385-4400
250 E 2nd St East Liverpool (43920) *(G-6998)*

Mason Company LLC.. 937 780-2321
260 Depot Ln Leesburg (45135) *(G-9125)*

Mason Steel, Walton Hills *Also Called: Mssi Group Inc (G-15102)*

Mason Structural Steel LLC..................................... 440 439-1040
7500 Northfield Rd Walton Hills (44146) *(G-15100)*

Masonite Corporation... 937 454-9207
3260 Old Springfield Rd Ste 1 Vandalia (45377) *(G-14951)*

Masonite International Corp..................................... 937 454-9308
875 Center Dr Vandalia (45377) *(G-14952)*

Masons Sand and Gravel Co.................................... 614 491-3611
2385 Rathmell Rd Obetz (43207) *(G-12062)*

Massageblocks.com, Powell *Also Called: Summit Online Products LLC (G-12682)*

Massillon Container Co.. 330 879-5653
49 Ohio St Sw Navarre (44662) *(G-11345)*

Massillon Feed Mill, Massillon *Also Called: Case Farms LLC (G-10083)*

Massillon Machine & Die Inc................................... 330 833-8913
3536 17th St Sw Massillon (44647) *(G-10122)*

Massillon Materials Inc (PA)................................... 330 837-4767
26 N Cochran St Dalton (44618) *(G-6136)*

Massillon Metaphysics... 330 837-1653
912 Amherst Rd Ne Massillon (44646) *(G-10123)*

Mast Farm Service Ltd.. 330 893-2972
3585 State Rte 39 Walnut Creek (44687) *(G-15094)*

Mast Mini Barn, Junction City *Also Called: K-Mar Structures LLC (G-8783)*

Masteller Electric Motor Svc.................................... 937 492-8500
122 Lane St Sidney (45365) *(G-13262)*

Master Bldrs Sltons Admxtres U (HQ)..................... 216 839-7500
23700 Chagrin Blvd Beachwood (44122) *(G-997)*

Master Bldrs Sltons Cnstr Syst, Beachwood *Also Called: Sika Mbcc US LLC (G-1024)*

Master Bolt LLC.. 440 323-5529
811 Taylor St Elyria (44035) *(G-7178)*

Master Builders LLC (HQ)....................................... 800 228-3318
23700 Chagrin Blvd Beachwood (44122) *(G-998)*

Master Carbide Tools Company............................... 440 352-1112
3529 Lane Rd Ext Perry (44081) *(G-12355)*

Master Caster Company, Cleveland *Also Called: Master Mfg Co Inc (G-4367)*

Master Chemical Corporation (PA).......................... 419 874-7902
501 W Boundary St Perrysburg (43551) *(G-12399)*

Master Chrome Service Inc..................................... 216 961-2012
5709 Herman Ave Cleveland (44102) *(G-4365)*

Master Communications Inc.................................... 208 821-3473
2692 Madison Rd Ste N1-307 Cincinnati (45208) *(G-3133)*

Master Craft Products Inc.. 216 281-5910
10621 Briggs Rd Cleveland (44111) *(G-4366)*

Master Draw Lubricants, Chagrin Falls *Also Called: Etna Products Incorporated (G-2395)*

Master Fluid Solutions, Perrysburg *Also Called: Master Chemical Corporation (G-12399)*

Master Magnetics Inc... 740 373-0909
108 Industry Rd Marietta (45750) *(G-9807)*

Master Marking Company Inc.................................. 330 688-6797
2260 Stone Creek Trl Cuyahoga Falls (44223) *(G-6102)*

Master Mfg Co Inc.. 216 641-0500
9200 Inman Ave Cleveland (44105) *(G-4367)*

Master Print Center, Cincinnati *Also Called: Gerald L Herrmann Company Inc (G-2949)*

Master Printing & Mailing, Berea *Also Called: Master Printing Group Inc (G-1287)*

Master Printing Group Inc....................................... 216 351-2246
95 Pelret Industrial Pkwy Berea (44017) *(G-1287)*

Master Products Company....................................... 216 341-1740
6400 Park Ave Cleveland (44105) *(G-4368)*

Master Swaging Inc.. 937 596-6171
210 Washington St Jackson Center (45334) *(G-8735)*

Master-Halco Inc.. 513 869-7600
620 Commerce Center Dr Fairfield (45011) *(G-7379)*

Masterbrand Cabinets LLC (HQ)............................. 812 482-2527
3300 Enterprise Pkwy Ste 300 Beachwood (44122) *(G-999)*

Masterpiece Signs & Graphics................................ 419 358-0077
902 N Main St Bluffton (45817) *(G-1505)*

Masters Pharmaceutical Inc.................................... 513 290-2969
8695 Seward Rd Fairfield (45011) *(G-7380)*

Masters Prcision Machining Inc.............................. 330 419-1933
4465 Crystal Pkwy Kent (44240) *(G-8833)*

Mastertech Diamond Products Co, Perry *Also Called: Master Carbide Tools Company (G-12355)*

Mastropietro Winery Inc.. 330 547-2151
14558 Ellsworth Rd Berlin Center (44401) *(G-1309)*

Mat Basics Incorporated... 513 793-0313
4546 Cornell Rd Blue Ash (45241) *(G-1428)*

Matalco (us) Inc (DH).. 330 452-4760
4420 Louisville St Ne Canton (44705) *(G-2153)*

Matalco (us) Inc.. 234 806-0600
5120 Tod Ave Sw Warren (44481) *(G-15189)*

Match Mold & Machine Inc...................................... 330 830-5503
1100 Nova Dr Se Massillon (44646) *(G-10124)*

Matco Tools, Stow *Also Called: Matco Tools Corporation (G-13708)*

Matco Tools Corporation (HQ)................................ 330 929-4949
4403 Allen Rd Stow (44224) *(G-13708)*

Matcor Metal Fabrication Inc................................... 419 298-2394
228 E Morrison St Edgerton (43517) *(G-7076)*

Matdan Corporation... 513 794-0500
10855 Millington Ct Blue Ash (45242) *(G-1429)*

Material Holdings Inc... 513 583-5500
185 Commerce Dr Loveland (45140) *(G-9494)*

Material Processing & Hdlg Co............................... 419 436-9562
1150 State St Fostoria (44830) *(G-7643)*

Material Sciences Corporation................................ 330 702-3882
460 W Main St Canfield (44406) *(G-2011)*

Material Sciences Corporation................................ 419 661-5905
30610 E Broadway St Walbridge (43465) *(G-15084)*

Materials Processing Inc... 330 730-5959
120 Deeds Dr Dover (44622) *(G-6834)*

Materials Science Intl Inc.. 614 870-0400
1660 Georgesville Rd Columbus (43228) *(G-5545)*

Materion, Mayfield Heights *Also Called: Materion Brush Inc (G-10250)*

Materion Brush Inc.. 419 862-2745
14710 W Portage River South Rd Elmore (43416) *(G-7103)*

Materion Brush Inc (HQ)... 216 486-4200
6070 Parkland Blvd Ste 1 Mayfield Heights (44124) *(G-10250)*

Materion Corporation (PA)...................................... 216 486-4200
6070 Parkland Blvd Mayfield Heights (44124) *(G-10251)*

Matern Metal Works Inc.. 419 529-3100
210 N Adams St Mansfield (44902) *(G-9687)*

Matheson Tri-Gas Inc... 419 865-8881
1720 Trade Rd Holland (43528) *(G-8518)*

Matheson Tri-Gas Inc... 513 727-9638
1801 Crawford St Middletown (45044) *(G-10842)*

Mathews Printing Company..................................... 614 444-1010
1250 S Front St Columbus (43206) *(G-5546)*

Matlock Electric Co Inc... 513 731-9600
2780 Highland Ave Cincinnati (45212) *(G-3134)*

Matplus, Painesville *Also Called: Matplus Ltd (G-12250)*

Matplus Ltd.. 440 352-7201
76 Burton St Painesville (44077) *(G-12250)*

Matrix Management Solutions................................ 330 470-3700
5200 Stoneham Rd Canton (44720) *(G-2154)*

Matrix Meats Inc.. 614 602-1846
5164 Blazer Pkwy Dublin (43017) *(G-6908)*

Matrix Research Inc... 937 427-8433
3844 Research Blvd Beavercreek (45430) *(G-1075)*

ALPHABETIC SECTION — McCann Plastics LLC

Matrix Sys Auto Finishes LLC 248 668-8135
600 Nova Dr Se Massillon (44646) *(G-10125)*

Matrix Tool & Machine Inc 440 255-0300
7870 Division Dr Mentor (44060) *(G-10500)*

Matsu Ohio Inc 419 298-2394
228 E Morrison St Edgerton (43517) *(G-7077)*

Matteo Aluminum Inc 440 585-5213
1261 E 289th St Wickliffe (44092) *(G-15839)*

Matthew Bender & Company, Miamisburg *Also Called: Matthew Bender & Company Inc*
(G-10655)

Matthew Bender & Company Inc 518 487-3000
9443 Springboro Pike Miamisburg (45342) *(G-10655)*

Matthew Warren Inc 614 418-0250
2000 Jetway Blvd Columbus (43219) *(G-5547)*

Matting Products Div, Fairlawn *Also Called: Rjf International Corporation (G-7447)*

Mattmark Drilling Company, Cambridge *Also Called: Mattmark Partners Inc (G-1941)*

Mattmark Partners Inc 740 439-3109
61234 Southgate Rd Cambridge (43725) *(G-1941)*

Mattr US Inc 513 683-7800
173 Commerce Dr Loveland (45140) *(G-9495)*

Mattress Mart, Plain City *Also Called: Quilting Inc (G-12591)*

Matus Winery Inc 440 774-9463
15674 Gore Orphanage Rd Wakeman (44889) *(G-15077)*

Maumee Assembly & Stamping LLC 419 304-2887
920 Illinois Ave Maumee (43537) *(G-10217)*

Maumee Hose & Belting Co, Maumee *Also Called: Maumee Hose & Fitting Inc (G-10218)*

Maumee Hose & Fitting Inc 419 893-7252
720 Illinois Ave Ste H Maumee (43537) *(G-10218)*

Maumee Machine & Tool Corp 419 385-2501
2960 South Ave Toledo (43609) *(G-14379)*

Maumee Valley Fabricators Inc 419 476-1411
4801 Bennett Rd Toledo (43612) *(G-14380)*

Maumee Valley Memorials Inc (DH) 419 878-9030
111 Anthony Wayne Trl Waterville (43566) *(G-15250)*

Mauser Usa LLC 513 398-1300
1229 Castle Dr Mason (45040) *(G-10026)*

Maval Industries LLC (PA) 330 405-1600
1555 Enterprise Pkwy Twinsburg (44087) *(G-14692)*

Maval Manufacturing, Twinsburg *Also Called: Maval Industries LLC (G-14692)*

Maverick Corporation 513 469-9919
11285 Grooms Rd Blue Ash (45242) *(G-1430)*

Maverick Electronics, Cleveland *Also Called: Heilind Electronics Inc (G-4177)*

Maverick Innvtive Slutions LLC 419 281-7944
532 County Road 1600 Ashland (44805) *(G-590)*

Maverick Molding Co 513 387-6100
11359 Grooms Rd Blue Ash (45242) *(G-1431)*

Maverick Nail & Staple Ltd 513 843-5270
1680 Autumn Oak Dr Ste 100 Batavia (45103) *(G-931)*

Mavericks Stainless, Mansfield *Also Called: Mk Metal Products Entps Inc (G-9697)*

Max - Pro Tools Inc 800 456-0931
8999 W Pleasant Valley Rd Cleveland (44130) *(G-4369)*

Max Roush 937 288-2557
661 Polo Woods Dr Cincinnati (45244) *(G-3135)*

Maxfield Candy Company, Columbus *Also Called: International Confections Company LLC*
(G-5474)

Maxim Integrated Products LLC 216 375-1057
9000 Yale Ave Cleveland (44108) *(G-4370)*

Maxion Wheels Sedalia LLC 330 794-2300
428 Seiberling St Akron (44306) *(G-239)*

Maxx Iron LLC 614 753-9697
287 E North St Worthington (43085) *(G-16201)*

May Conveyor Inc 440 237-8012
9981 York Theta Dr North Royalton (44133) *(G-11885)*

May Industries of Ohio Inc 440 237-8012
9981 York Theta Dr North Royalton (44133) *(G-11886)*

May Lin Silicone Products Inc 330 825-9019
955 Wooster Rd W Barberton (44203) *(G-880)*

May Tool & Die Co 440 237-8012
9981 York Theta Dr Ste 1 Cleveland (44133) *(G-4371)*

Mayco Colors, Hilliard *Also Called: Coloramics LLC (G-8408)*

Mayfair Granite Co Inc 216 382-8150
4202 Mayfield Rd Cleveland (44121) *(G-4372)*

Mayfair Memorial, Cleveland *Also Called: Mayfair Granite Co Inc (G-4372)*

Mayfran International Inc (HQ) 440 461-4100
6650 Beta Dr Cleveland (44143) *(G-4373)*

Maynard Company, The, Cleveland *Also Called: Bud May Inc (G-3769)*

Mayo, R A Industries, East Palestine *Also Called: Robert Mayo Industries (G-7008)*

Maysville Materials LLC 740 849-0474
6535 Old Town Rd Mount Perry (43760) *(G-11250)*

Maysville Ready Mix Con Co, Aberdeen *Also Called: Hilltop Basic Resources Inc (G-1)*

Mazzella Jhh Company Inc 440 239-7000
21000 Aerospace Pkwy Cleveland (44142) *(G-4374)*

Mazzella Lifting Tech Inc (HQ) 440 239-7000
21000 Aerospace Pkwy Cleveland (44142) *(G-4375)*

Mazzolini Artcraft Co Inc 216 431-7529
1607 E 41st St Cleveland (44103) *(G-4376)*

MB Dynamics Inc 216 292-5850
25865 Richmond Rd Cleveland (44146) *(G-4377)*

MB Manufacturing Corp 513 682-1461
2904 Symmes Rd Fairfield (45014) *(G-7381)*

MB Renovations & Designs LLC 614 772-6139
4449 Easton Way Ste 200 Columbus (43219) *(G-5548)*

MB Woodworking Llc 330 808-5122
5175 Stroups Hickox Rd West Farmington (44491) *(G-15605)*

MBA Design, Peninsula *Also Called: X44 Corp (G-12347)*

Mbas Printing Inc 513 489-3000
11401 Deerfield Rd Blue Ash (45242) *(G-1432)*

Mbcc Group, Beachwood *Also Called: Master Bldrs Sltons Admxtres U (G-997)*

Mbds, Findlay *Also Called: Manufctring Bus Dev Sltons LLC (G-7530)*

Mbs Acquisition, Mason *Also Called: Remtec Engineering (G-10047)*

Mc Alarney Pool Spas and Blld 740 373-6698
908 Pike St Marietta (45750) *(G-9808)*

Mc Alister Woodworking 614 989-6264
6035 Huntley Rd Columbus (43229) *(G-5549)*

Mc Brown Industries Inc 419 963-2800
10534 Township Road 128 Findlay (45840) *(G-7536)*

Mc Cartney Industries, Mentor *Also Called: Semper Quality Industry Inc (G-10552)*

Mc Concepts Llc 330 933-6402
2459 55th St Ne Canton (44721) *(G-2155)*

Mc Connells Market 740 765-4300
2189 State Route 43 Richmond (43944) *(G-12802)*

Mc Elwain Industries Inc 419 532-3126
17941 Road L Ottawa (45875) *(G-12184)*

Mc Graw-Hill Educational Pubg, Ashland *Also Called: McGraw-Hill Schl Edcatn Hldngs*
(G-591)

Mc Group, Mentor *Also Called: Stratus Unlimited LLC (G-10568)*

Mc Happy's Bake Shoppe, Belpre *Also Called: Wal-Bon of Ohio Inc (G-1262)*

Mc Happys Donuts, Athens *Also Called: McHappys Donuts of Parkersburg (G-687)*

Mc Machine Llc 216 398-3666
9000 Brookpark Rd Cleveland (44129) *(G-4378)*

MCA Industries, Massillon *Also Called: The Massillon-Cleveland-Akronsign Company*
(G-10149)

McAfee LLC 440 892-0173
1050 Tollis Pkwy Apt 307 Cleveland (44147) *(G-4379)*

McAfee Tool & Die Inc 330 896-9555
1717 Boettler Rd Uniontown (44685) *(G-14787)*

McAlarney Pols Spas Blld More, Marietta *Also Called: Mc Alarney Pool Spas and Blld*
(G-9808)

McAlear Winery LLC 567 703-1281
3415 Briarfield Blvd Maumee (43537) *(G-10219)*

McBmrdd 937 910-7301
5450 Salem Ave Dayton (45426) *(G-6431)*

McC - Mason W&S (DH) 513 459-1100
5510 Courseview Dr Mason (45040) *(G-10027)*

McC Label, Batavia *Also Called: Multi-Color Corporation (G-939)*

McC-Norway LLC 513 381-1480
4053 Clough Woods Dr Batavia (45103) *(G-932)*

McCann, Canton *Also Called: McCann Plastics LLC (G-2157)*

McCann Color Inc 330 498-4840
8562 Port Jackson Ave Nw Canton (44720) *(G-2156)*

McCann Plastics LLC 330 499-1515
5600 Mayfair Rd Canton (44720) *(G-2157)*

McCann Tool & Die Inc.. 330 264-8820
  3230 Columbus Rd Wooster (44691) *(G-16150)*

McCc Sportswear Inc (PA).. 513 583-9210
  9944 Princeton Glendale Rd West Chester (45246) *(G-15569)*

McClelland Inc (PA)... 740 452-3036
  98 E La Salle St Zanesville (43701) *(G-16544)*

McConnell Ready Mix.. 440 458-4325
  37500 Butternut Ridge Rd Elyria (44039) *(G-7179)*

McConnell's Farm Market, Richmond *Also Called: Mc Connells Market (G-12802)*

McCord Monuments, Bowling Green *Also Called: McCord Products Inc (G-1575)*

McCord Products Inc.. 419 352-3691
  1135 N Main St Bowling Green (43402) *(G-1575)*

McCoy Group Inc... 330 753-1041
  1020 Eagon St Barberton (44203) *(G-881)*

McCrary, Port Jefferson *Also Called: McCrary Metal Polishing Co Inc (G-12630)*

McCrary Metal Polishing Co Inc... 937 492-1979
  207 Pasco Montra Rd Port Jefferson (45360) *(G-12630)*

McCullough Industries, Kenton *Also Called: McI Inc (G-8890)*

McCullough Industries Inc... 419 673-0767
  13047 County Road 175 Kenton (43326) *(G-8888)*

McDaniel Envelope Company Inc... 330 868-5929
  1400 Union Ave Se Minerva (44657) *(G-11034)*

McDaniel Products Inc (PA)... 419 524-5841
  50 Industrial Pkwy Mansfield (44903) *(G-9688)*

McDaniel Products Inc.. 419 524-5841
  433 Springmill St Mansfield (44903) *(G-9689)*

McDonald Steel Corporation (PA)... 330 530-9118
  100 Ohio Ave Mc Donald (44437) *(G-10279)*

McDonald's, Mason *Also Called: McDonalds (G-10028)*

McDonalds... 513 336-0820
  5301 Kings Island Dr Mason (45040) *(G-10028)*

McElroy Coal Company (DH).. 724 485-4000
  46226 National Rd Saint Clairsville (43950) *(G-12911)*

McF Industries... 330 526-6337
  1206 N Main St North Canton (44720) *(G-11742)*

McFlusion Inc.. 800 341-8616
  2112 Case Pkwy Ste 8 Twinsburg (44087) *(G-14693)*

McGean, Newburgh Heights *Also Called: McGean-Rohco Inc (G-11619)*

McGean-Rohco Inc.. 216 441-4900
  2910 Harvard Ave Newburgh Heights (44105) *(G-11618)*

McGean-Rohco Inc (PA).. 216 441-4900
  2910 Harvard Ave Newburgh Heights (44105) *(G-11619)*

McGill Airclean, Columbus *Also Called: McGill Airclean LLC (G-5550)*

McGill Airclean LLC.. 614 829-1200
  1777 Refugee Rd Columbus (43207) *(G-5550)*

McGill Airflow LLC.. 614 829-1200
  2400 Fairwood Ave Columbus (43207) *(G-5551)*

McGill Corporation (PA).. 614 829-1200
  1 Mission Park Groveport (43125) *(G-8153)*

McGill Septic Tank Co.. 330 876-2171
  8913 State St Kinsman (44428) *(G-8936)*

McGinnis Inc (HQ).. 740 377-4391
  502 2nd St E South Point (45680) *(G-13470)*

McGlennon Metal Products Inc.. 614 252-7114
  940 N 20th St Columbus (43219) *(G-5552)*

McGovney Ready Mix Inc.. 740 353-4111
  55 River Ave Portsmouth (45662) *(G-12648)*

McGovney River Terminal, Portsmouth *Also Called: McGovney Ready Mix Inc (G-12648)*

McGraw-Hill Global Educatn LLC... 614 755-4151
  860 Taylor Station Rd Blacklick (43004) *(G-1340)*

McGraw-Hill Global Educatn LLC... 800 338-3987
  4400 Easton Commons Columbus (43219) *(G-5553)*

McGraw-Hill Learning Group, Columbus *Also Called: McGraw-Hill Global Educatn LLC (G-5553)*

McGraw-Hill Schl Edcatn Hldngs.. 419 207-7400
  1250 George Rd Ashland (44805) *(G-591)*

McGraw-Hill Schl Edcatn Hldngs.. 614 430-4000
  8787 Orion Pl Columbus (43240) *(G-5064)*

McGregor & Associates Inc... 937 833-6768
  365 Carr Dr Brookville (45309) *(G-1741)*

McGregor Metal National Works LLC.. 937 882-6347
  5573 W National Rd Springfield (45504) *(G-13601)*

McGregor Metalworking, Springfield *Also Called: McGregor Mtal Yllow Sprng Wrks (G-13604)*

McGregor Mtal Innsfllen Wrks L... 937 322-3880
  1305 Innisfallen Ave Springfield (45506) *(G-13602)*

McGregor Mtal Leffel Works LLC... 937 325-5561
  900 W Leffel Ln Springfield (45506) *(G-13603)*

McGregor Mtal Yllow Sprng Wrks (PA)..................................... 937 325-5561
  2100 S Yellow Springs St Springfield (45506) *(G-13604)*

McGuire Machine,, North Lawrence *Also Called: Sjk Machine LLC (G-11799)*

McHael D Goronok String Instrs.. 216 421-4227
  10823 Magnolia Dr Cleveland (44106) *(G-4380)*

McHale Group Ltd.. 330 923-7070
  338 Remington Rd Cuyahoga Falls (44224) *(G-6103)*

McHappys Donuts of Parkersburg.. 740 593-8744
  384 Richland Ave Athens (45701) *(G-687)*

McI Inc.. 800 245-9490
  13047 County Road 175 Kenton (43326) *(G-8889)*

McI Inc.. 800 245-9490
  13047 County Road 175 Kenton (43326) *(G-8890)*

McIntosh Manufacturing LLC... 513 424-5307
  3350 Yankee Rd Middletown (45044) *(G-10843)*

McIntosh Safe Corp.. 937 222-7008
  607 Lee St Dayton (45404) *(G-6432)*

McKay-Gross Division... 330 683-2055
  8848 Ely Rd Apple Creek (44606) *(G-504)*

McKechnie Arospc Holdings Inc... 216 706-2960
  1301 E 9th St Ste 3000 Cleveland (44114) *(G-4381)*

McKinley Leather, Marion *Also Called: Williams Leather Products Inc (G-9890)*

McKinley Packaging Company... 216 663-3344
  16645 Granite Rd Maple Heights (44137) *(G-9755)*

McKnight Industries Inc.. 937 592-9010
  Orchard & Elm Street Bellefontaine (43311) *(G-1216)*

McL Inc... 614 861-6259
  5240 E Main St Columbus (43213) *(G-5554)*

McL Whitehall, Columbus *Also Called: McL Inc (G-5554)*

McLeod Bar Group LLC... 614 299-2099
  234 King Ave Columbus (43201) *(G-5555)*

McM Ind Co Inc (PA).. 216 292-4506
  22901 Millcreek Blvd Ste 250 Cleveland (44122) *(G-4382)*

McM Ind Co Inc... 216 641-6300
  7800 Finney Ave Cleveland (44105) *(G-4383)*

McM Industries, Cleveland *Also Called: McM Ind Co Inc (G-4382)*

McM Precision Castings Inc.. 419 669-3226
  13133 Beech St Weston (43569) *(G-15806)*

McNational Inc (PA)... 740 377-4391
  502 2nd St E South Point (45680) *(G-13471)*

McNeal Enterprises LLC.. 740 703-7108
  807 E 2nd St Chillicothe (45601) *(G-2516)*

McNeil & Nrm Inc (HQ)... 330 761-1855
  96 E Crosier St Akron (44311) *(G-240)*

McNeil & Nrm Intl Inc (PA).. 330 253-2525
  96 E Crosier St Akron (44311) *(G-241)*

McNeil Group Inc... 614 298-0300
  1701 Woodland Ave Columbus (43219) *(G-5556)*

McNeil Holdings LLC.. 614 298-0300
  1701 Woodland Ave Columbus (43219) *(G-5557)*

McNeil Industries Inc... 440 951-7756
  835 Richmond Rd Ste 2 Painesville (44077) *(G-12251)*

McNeilus Truck and Mfg Inc.. 513 874-2022
  8997 Le Saint Dr Fairfield (45014) *(G-7382)*

McNeilus Truck and Mfg Inc.. 614 868-0760
  1130 Morrison Rd Gahanna (43230) *(G-7844)*

McNerney & Associates LLC... 513 241-9951
  5443 Duff Dr West Chester (45246) *(G-15570)*

McNish Corporation.. 614 899-2282
  214 Hoff Rd Unit M Westerville (43082) *(G-15667)*

McO Inc (PA)... 216 341-8914
  7555 Bessemer Ave Cleveland (44127) *(G-4384)*

McOn Inds Inc (HQ)... 937 294-2681
  2221 Arbor Blvd Moraine (45439) *(G-11192)*

McPp, Bellevue *Also Called: Mitsubishi Chemical Amer Inc (G-1230)*

McPp-Detroit, Bellevue *Also Called: Mitsubishi Chemical Amer Inc (G-1229)*

ALPHABETIC SECTION

MCR of Norwalk Inc.. 419 668-8261
55 Newton St Norwalk (44857) *(G-11979)*

McRd Enterprises LLC.. 740 775-2377
337 E Main St Chillicothe (45601) *(G-2517)*

McRon Finance Corp.. 513 487-5000
3010 Disney St Cincinnati (45209) *(G-3136)*

MCS Mfg LLC... 419 923-0169
15210 County Road 10 3 Lyons (43533) *(G-9532)*

MCS Midwest LLC (PA)... 513 217-0805
3876 Hendrickson Rd Franklin (45005) *(G-7686)*

McSwain Manufacturing LLC....................................... 513 619-1222
189 Container Pl Cincinnati (45246) *(G-3137)*

McSweeneys Inc... 740 894-3353
235 Commerce Dr South Point (45680) *(G-13472)*

McWane Inc... 740 622-6651
2266 S 6th St Coshocton (43812) *(G-5983)*

Mdb Fabricating Inc... 216 799-7017
8600 E Pleasant Valley Rd Cleveland (44131) *(G-4385)*

MDE Energy Transfer.. 330 788-5747
5017 Lynn St Youngstown (44512) *(G-16396)*

Mdf Tool, North Royalton Also Called: Mdf Tool Corporation *(G-11887)*

Mdf Tool Corporation... 440 237-2277
10166 Royalton Rd North Royalton (44133) *(G-11887)*

Mdi of Ohio Inc.. 937 866-2345
5175 Stoneham Rd Canton (44720) *(G-2158)*

Meador Supply Company Inc....................................... 330 405-4403
20437 Hannan Pkwy Ste 5 Walton Hills (44146) *(G-15101)*

Meadow Burke Products, West Chester Also Called: Merchants Metals LLC *(G-15463)*

Measurement Computing Corp (DH)........................... 440 439-4091
25971 Cannon Rd Cleveland (44146) *(G-4386)*

Measurement Specialties, Miamisburg Also Called: Advanced Indus Msrment Systems *(G-10605)*

Measurement Specialties Inc....................................... 330 659-3312
2236 N Cleveland Massillon Rd Ste A Akron (44333) *(G-242)*

Measurement Specialties Inc....................................... 937 427-1231
2670 Indian Ripple Rd Dayton (45440) *(G-6433)*

Meccas Lounge LLC.. 419 239-6918
2614 Pioneer Trl Apt 606 Sandusky (44870) *(G-13080)*

Mechanical Dynamics Analis LLC............................... 440 946-0082
1250 E 222nd St Euclid (44117) *(G-7285)*

Mechanical Finishers Inc LLC..................................... 513 641-5419
6350 Este Ave Cincinnati (45232) *(G-3138)*

Mechanical Finishing Inc... 513 641-5419
6350 Este Ave Cincinnati (45232) *(G-3139)*

Mechanical Galv-Plating Corp..................................... 937 492-3143
933 Oak Ave Sidney (45365) *(G-13263)*

Mechanical Rubber Ohio LLC..................................... 845 986-2271
12312 Alameda Dr Strongsville (44149) *(G-13853)*

Mechanicsburg Sand & Gravel.................................... 937 834-2606
5734 State Route 4 Mechanicsburg (43044) *(G-10286)*

Meco, Middletown Also Called: Manufacturers Equipment Co *(G-10841)*

Medal Components LLC.. 864 561-9464
515 Richholt St Holgate (43527) *(G-8489)*

Medallion... 513 936-0597
6100 Hagewa Dr Blue Ash (45242) *(G-1433)*

Medco Adhesive Coated Products, Cleveland Also Called: Medco Labs Inc *(G-4387)*

Medco Labs Inc.. 216 292-7546
5156 Richmond Rd Cleveland (44146) *(G-4387)*

Meder Special-Tees Ltd.. 513 921-3800
618 Delhi Ave Cincinnati (45204) *(G-3140)*

Medex, Dublin Also Called: Saint-Gobain Prfmce Plas Corp *(G-6933)*

Media, Hamilton Also Called: Chatterbox Sports LLC *(G-8190)*

Mediajacked Sound Studio LLC................................... 330 391-3123
2903 Mahoning Ave Youngstown (44509) *(G-16397)*

Medical & Home Health, Westlake Also Called: Applied Marketing Services Inc *(G-15733)*

Medical Device Bus Svcs Inc....................................... 937 274-5850
2747 Armstrong Ln Dayton (45414) *(G-6434)*

Medical Quant USA Inc.. 440 542-0761
6521 Davis Industrial Pkwy Solon (44139) *(G-13384)*

Medical Resources, Lewis Center Also Called: Eoi Inc *(G-9160)*

Medina County... 330 723-3641
144 N Broadway St Ste 117 Medina (44256) *(G-10347)*

Medina County Recorders, Medina Also Called: Medina County *(G-10347)*

Medina Foods Inc... 330 725-1390
9706 Crow Rd Litchfield (44253) *(G-9328)*

Medina Hntngton RE Group II LL............................... 330 591-2777
635 N Huntington St Medina (44256) *(G-10348)*

Medina Powder Coating Corp..................................... 330 952-1977
930 Lafayette Rd Unit C Medina (44256) *(G-10349)*

Medina Powder Group Inc... 330 952-2711
910 Lake Rd Ste B Medina (44256) *(G-10350)*

Medina Supply Co, Twinsburg Also Called: Medina Supply Company *(G-14694)*

Medina Supply Company... 330 364-4411
820 W Smith Rd Medina (44256) *(G-10351)*

Medina Supply Company (DH)................................... 330 723-3681
230 E Smith Rd Medina (44256) *(G-10352)*

Medina Supply Company... 330 425-0752
1516 Highland Rd Twinsburg (44087) *(G-14694)*

Medina Tool & Die, Wadsworth Also Called: Kramer & Kiefer Inc *(G-15041)*

Medinutra LLC... 614 292-6848
8050 Simfield Rd Dublin (43016) *(G-6909)*

Mediview Xr Inc.. 419 270-2774
10000 Cedar Ave Cleveland (44106) *(G-4388)*

Medline Industries LP... 614 879-9728
1040 Enterprise Pkwy West Jefferson (43162) *(G-15612)*

MEDPACE, Cincinnati Also Called: Medpace Holdings Inc *(G-3142)*

Medpace Core Laboratories LLC................................. 513 579-9911
5375 Medpace Way Cincinnati (45227) *(G-3141)*

Medpace Holdings Inc (PA).. 513 579-9911
5375 Medpace Way Cincinnati (45227) *(G-3142)*

Medrano USA, Columbus Also Called: Medrano Usa Inc *(G-5558)*

Medrano Usa Inc (PA).. 614 272-5856
4311 Janitrol Rd Ste 500 Columbus (43228) *(G-5558)*

Medtrace, Akron Also Called: Vertical Data LLC *(G-369)*

Medtronic, Cleveland Also Called: Medtronic Inc *(G-4389)*

Medtronic, Independence Also Called: Cardioinsight Technologies Inc *(G-8655)*

Medtronic, Independence Also Called: Medtronic Inc *(G-8672)*

Medtronic Inc.. 216 642-1977
5005 Rockside Rd Ste 1160 Cleveland (44131) *(G-4389)*

Medtronic Inc.. 763 526-2566
3 Summit Park Dr Ste 400 Independence (44131) *(G-8672)*

Medway Tool Corp... 937 335-7717
2100 Corporate Dr Troy (45373) *(G-14597)*

Meech Sttic Elminators USA Inc................................. 330 564-2000
1298 Centerview Cir Copley (44321) *(G-5950)*

Meeks Pastry Shop.. 419 782-4871
315 Clinton St Defiance (43512) *(G-6692)*

Meese Inc.. 440 998-1202
4920 State Rd Ashtabula (44004) *(G-647)*

Mega Bright LLC.. 216 712-4689
4979 W 130th St Cleveland (44135) *(G-4390)*

Mega Bright LLC.. 330 577-8859
2251 Front St Ste 200 Cuyahoga Falls (44221) *(G-6104)*

Mega Plastics Co... 330 527-2211
10610 Freedom St Garrettsville (44231) *(G-7922)*

Mega Techway Inc (PA).. 440 605-0700
760 Beta Dr Ste F Cleveland (44143) *(G-4391)*

Megadyne Medical Products Inc................................. 801 576-9669
4545 Creek Rd Blue Ash (45242) *(G-1434)*

Megalight Inc.. 800 957-1797
581 Boston Mills Rd Ste 500 Hudson (44236) *(G-8604)*

Meggitt (erlanger) LLC... 513 851-5550
10293 Burlington Rd Cincinnati (45231) *(G-3143)*

Meggitt Arcft Brking Systems C (DH)......................... 330 796-4400
1204 Massillon Rd Akron (44306) *(G-243)*

Meggitt Polymers & Composites................................. 513 851-5550
10293 Burlington Rd Cincinnati (45231) *(G-3144)*

Meggitt Rockmart Inc.. 770 684-7855
1204 Massillon Rd Akron (44306) *(G-244)*

Megna Plastics, Cleveland Also Called: Dal-Little Fabricating Inc *(G-3938)*

Mehaffie Pie Company, Dayton Also Called: K & B Acquisitions Inc *(G-6396)*

MEI, Wapakoneta Also Called: Midwest Elastomers Inc *(G-15124)*

Meierjohan-Wengler Inc 513 771-6074
  10340 Julian Dr Cincinnati (45215) *(G-3145)*

Meiers Wine Cellars Inc 513 891-2900
  6955 Plainfield Rd Cincinnati (45236) *(G-3146)*

Meigs County Coal Company 740 338-3100
  46226 National Rd Saint Clairsville (43950) *(G-12912)*

Meiring Precision, Ludlow Falls *Also Called: Marmax Machine Co (G-9529)*

Meister Media Worldwide, Willoughby *Also Called: Meister Media Worldwide Inc (G-15950)*

Meister Media Worldwide Inc (PA) 440 942-2000
  37733 Euclid Ave Willoughby (44094) *(G-15950)*

Meistermatic Inc 216 481-7773
  12446 Bentbrook Dr Chesterland (44026) *(G-2484)*

Mek Van Wert Inc 419 203-4902
  595 Fox Rd Van Wert (45891) *(G-14923)*

Mel Heitkamp Builders Ltd 419 375-0405
  635 Secret Judy Rd Fort Recovery (45846) *(G-7623)*

Mel Wacker Signs Inc 330 832-1726
  13076 Barrs St Sw Massillon (44647) *(G-10126)*

Melaluca, Worthington *Also Called: Rod or Tammy Whitlatch (G-16211)*

Meldrum Mechanical Services 419 535-3500
  4455 South Ave Toledo (43615) *(G-14381)*

Melin Tool Company Inc 216 362-4200
  5565 Venture Dr Ste C Cleveland (44130) *(G-4392)*

Melink Corporation 513 685-0958
  5140 River Valley Rd Milford (45150) *(G-10913)*

Melinz Industries Inc (PA) 440 946-3512
  34099 Melinz Pkwy Unit D Willoughby (44095) *(G-15951)*

Mellott Bronze Inc 330 435-6304
  4634 E Sterling Rd Creston (44217) *(G-6040)*

Melnor Graphics LLC 419 476-8808
  5225 Telegraph Rd Toledo (43612) *(G-14382)*

Melvin Stone Co LLC 513 771-0820
  11641 Mosteller Rd Ste 2 Cincinnati (45241) *(G-3147)*

Memphis Smokehouse Inc 216 351-5321
  8463 Memphis Ave Cleveland (44144) *(G-4393)*

Menard Inc 513 250-4566
  2789 Cunningham Rd Cincinnati (45241) *(G-3148)*

Menard Inc 419 998-4348
  2614 N Eastown Rd Lima (45807) *(G-9267)*

Menard Inc 513 583-1444
  3787 W State Route 22 3 Loveland (45140) *(G-9496)*

Menards, Loveland *Also Called: Menard Inc (G-9496)*

Menasha, West Jefferson *Also Called: Menasha Packaging Company LLC (G-15613)*

Menasha Packaging Company LLC 614 202-4084
  131 Enterprise Pkwy West Jefferson (43162) *(G-15613)*

Mendenhall Technical Services Inc 513 860-1280
  9175 Seward Rd Fairfield (45014) *(G-7383)*

Mennel Milling Company 419 436-5130
  320 Findlay St Fostoria (44830) *(G-7644)*

Mennel Milling Company 740 385-6824
  1 W Front St Logan (43138) *(G-9371)*

Mennel Milling Company 419 294-2337
  7097 County Highway 47 Upper Sandusky (43351) *(G-14816)*

Mennel Milling Logan, Logan *Also Called: Mennel Milling Company (G-9371)*

Mentorbio LLC 440 796-2995
  9122 Hendricks Rd Mentor (44060) *(G-10501)*

Mercer Color Corporation 419 678-8273
  425 Hardin St Coldwater (45828) *(G-4998)*

Mercer Tool Corporation 419 394-7277
  311 S Park Dr Saint Marys (45885) *(G-12957)*

Merchants Metals LLC 513 942-0268
  8760 Global Way Bldg 1 West Chester (45069) *(G-15463)*

Mercury Iron and Steel Co 440 349-1500
  6275 Cochran Rd Solon (44139) *(G-13385)*

Mercury Machine Co 440 349-3222
  30250 Carter St Solon (44139) *(G-13386)*

Mercury Plastics LLC 440 632-5281
  15760 Madison Rd Middlefield (44062) *(G-10764)*

Meriam Instrument, Cleveland *Also Called: Adalet/Scott Fetzer Company (G-3596)*

Meridian, Aurora *Also Called: Meridian LLC (G-724)*

Meridian Arts and Graphics 330 759-9099
  16 Belgrade St Youngstown (44505) *(G-16398)*

Meridian Bioscience, Cincinnati *Also Called: Meridian Bioscience Inc (G-3149)*

Meridian Bioscience Inc (PA) 513 271-3700
  3471 River Hills Dr Cincinnati (45244) *(G-3149)*

Meridian Industries Inc 330 359-5809
  9901 Chestnut Ridge Rd Nw Beach City (44608) *(G-968)*

Meridian Industries Inc 330 673-1011
  1500 Saint Clair Ave Kent (44240) *(G-8834)*

Meridian Industries Inc 330 359-5447
  7369 Peabody Kent Rd Winesburg (44690) *(G-16081)*

Meridian Life Science Inc (HQ) 513 271-3700
  3471 River Hills Dr Cincinnati (45244) *(G-3150)*

Meridian LLC 330 995-0371
  325 Harris Dr Aurora (44202) *(G-724)*

Meridienne International Inc 330 274-8317
  125 Lena Dr Aurora (44202) *(G-725)*

Meristem Crop Prfmce Group LLC 833 637-4783
  575 W 1st Ave Apt 100 Columbus (43215) *(G-5559)*

Merit Brass, Cleveland *Also Called: Merit Brass Co (G-4394)*

Merit Brass Co (PA) 216 261-9800
  1 Merit Dr Cleveland (44143) *(G-4394)*

Meritech, Painesville *Also Called: Ohio Associated Entps LLC (G-12253)*

Meritor Inc 740 348-3270
  4009 Columbus Rd Unit 111 Granville (43023) *(G-8020)*

Merksteijn, Warren *Also Called: Reinforcement Systems of Ohio LLC (G-15202)*

Merle Norman Cosmetics Inc 419 282-0630
  893 Park Ave W Mansfield (44906) *(G-9690)*

Merritt, Mentor *Also Called: Profac Inc (G-10532)*

Merritt Woodwork, Mentor *Also Called: Profac Inc (G-10533)*

Merryweather, Barberton *Also Called: Merryweather Foam Inc (G-882)*

Merryweather Foam Inc (PA) 330 753-0353
  11 Brown St Barberton (44203) *(G-882)*

Mes Painting and Graphics 614 496-1696
  8298 Harlem Rd Westerville (43081) *(G-15714)*

Mes Painting and Graphics Ltd 614 496-1696
  8298 Harlem Rd Westerville (43081) *(G-15715)*

Mesa Industries Inc (PA) 513 321-2950
  4027 Eastern Ave Cincinnati (45226) *(G-3151)*

Mesa Industries Inc 513 999-9781
  4141 Airport Rd Cincinnati (45226) *(G-3152)*

Mesocoat Inc 216 453-0866
  24112 Rockwell Dr Euclid (44117) *(G-7286)*

Mesocoat Advanced Coating Tech, Euclid *Also Called: Mesocoat Inc (G-7286)*

Messenger Publishing Company 740 592-6612
  9300 Johnson Hollow Rd Athens (45701) *(G-688)*

Messer LLC 216 533-7256
  6300 Halle Dr Cleveland (44125) *(G-4395)*

Messer LLC 419 822-3909
  6744 County Road 10 Delta (43515) *(G-6788)*

Messer LLC 614 539-2259
  1699 Feddern Ave Grove City (43123) *(G-8105)*

Messer LLC 419 227-9585
  961 Industry Ave Lima (45804) *(G-9268)*

Messer LLC 419 221-5043
  1680 Buckeye Rd Lima (45804) *(G-9269)*

Messer LLC 513 831-4742
  State Road 126160 Glendale-Milford Road Miamiville (45147) *(G-10712)*

Messer LLC 330 608-3008
  4179 Meadow Wood Ln Uniontown (44685) *(G-14788)*

Messer LLC 330 394-4541
  2000 Pine Ave Se Warren (44483) *(G-15190)*

Messinger Press, Celina *Also Called: Society of The Precious Blood (G-2349)*

Mestek Inc 419 288-2703
  219 S Church St # 200 Bowling Green (43402) *(G-1576)*

Mestek Inc 419 288-2703
  120 Plin St Bradner (43406) *(G-1603)*

Met Fab Fabrication and Mch 513 724-3715
  2974 Waitensburg Pike Batavia (45103) *(G-933)*

Met-Pro Technologies LLC (HQ) 513 458-2600
  4625 Red Bank Rd Cincinnati (45227) *(G-3153)*

Meta Manufacturing Corporation 513 793-6382
  8901 Blue Ash Rd Ste 1 Blue Ash (45242) *(G-1435)*

Metal & Wire Products Company 330 332-1015
1069 Salem Pkwy Salem (44460) *(G-13015)*

Metal & Wire Products Company (PA) 330 332-9448
1065 Salem Pkwy Salem (44460) *(G-13016)*

Metal Building Intr Pdts Co 440 322-6500
750 Adams St Elyria (44035) *(G-7180)*

Metal Coaters 740 432-7351
530 N 2nd St Cambridge (43725) *(G-1942)*

Metal Coating Company, Lima *Also Called: JM Hamilton Group Inc (G-9258)*

Metal Fabricating Corporation 216 631-8121
10408 Berea Rd Cleveland (44102) *(G-4396)*

Metal Finishers Inc 937 492-9175
2600 Fair Rd Sidney (45365) *(G-13264)*

Metal Finishing Divison, Ravenna *Also Called: Allen Aircraft Products Inc (G-12703)*

Metal Finishing Needs Ltd 216 561-6334
7550 Lucerne Dr Ste 400 Middleburg Heights (44130) *(G-10723)*

Metal Forming & Coining LLC (PA) 419 893-8748
1007 Illinois Ave Maumee (43537) *(G-10220)*

Metal Improvement Company LLC 513 489-6484
11131 Luschek Dr Blue Ash (45241) *(G-1436)*

Metal Improvement Company LLC 330 425-1490
1652 Highland Rd Twinsburg (44087) *(G-14695)*

Metal Maintenance Inc 513 661-3300
322 N Finley St Cleves (45002) *(G-4959)*

Metal Man Inc 614 830-0968
4681 Homer Ohio Ln Ste A Groveport (43125) *(G-8154)*

Metal Manufacturing, Elyria *Also Called: Elyria Metal Spinning Fabg Co (G-7143)*

Metal Marker Manufacturing, North Ridgeville *Also Called: Metal Marker Manufacturing Co (G-11850)*

Metal Marker Manufacturing Co 440 327-2300
6225 Lear Nagle Rd North Ridgeville (44039) *(G-11850)*

Metal Merchants Usa Inc 330 723-3228
445 W Liberty St Medina (44256) *(G-10353)*

Metal Mnkey Wldg Fbrcation LLC 330 231-1490
806 W Main St Sugarcreek (44681) *(G-13929)*

Metal Panel Systems, West Chester *Also Called: Mp Acquisition Group LLC (G-15466)*

Metal Polishing Spc L L C 513 321-0363
5170 Wooster Pike Cincinnati (45226) *(G-3154)*

Metal Products Company (PA) 330 652-2558
9455 Concord Rd Powell (43065) *(G-12677)*

Metal Sales Manufacturing Corp 440 319-3779
352 E Erie St Jefferson (44047) *(G-8753)*

Metal Seal & Products Inc 440 946-8500
7333 Corporate Blvd Mentor (44060) *(G-10502)*

Metal Seal Precision Ltd (PA) 440 255-8888
8687 Tyler Blvd Mentor (44060) *(G-10503)*

Metal Seal Precision Ltd 440 255-8888
4369 Hamann Pkwy Willoughby (44094) *(G-15952)*

Metal Shredders Inc 937 866-0777
5101 Farmersville W Carrollton Rd Miamisburg (45342) *(G-10656)*

Metal Stamping, Cleveland *Also Called: Precision Metal Products Inc (G-4575)*

Metal Stampings Unlimited Inc 937 328-0206
552 W Johnny Lytle Ave Springfield (45506) *(G-13605)*

Metal-Max Inc 330 673-9926
1540 Enterprise Way Kent (44240) *(G-8835)*

Metalbrite Polishing LLC 937 278-9739
2445 Neff Rd Unit 4 Dayton (45414) *(G-6435)*

Metalcraft Industries, Northfield *Also Called: Nor-Fab Inc (G-11908)*

Metalcraft Solutions, Akron *Also Called: Acro Tool & Die Company (G-17)*

Metalcrafts, Youngstown *Also Called: P & L Metalcrafts LLC (G-16409)*

Metalctting Spclists Group Ltd 330 962-4980
468 Molane Ave Akron (44313) *(G-245)*

Metalex Manufacturing Inc (PA) 513 489-0507
5750 Cornell Rd Blue Ash (45242) *(G-1437)*

Metalfab Group 440 543-6234
10145 Philipp Pkwy Streetsboro (44241) *(G-13778)*

Metalico Akron Inc (HQ) 330 376-1400
943 Hazel St Akron (44305) *(G-246)*

Metalico Annaco, Akron *Also Called: Metalico Akron Inc (G-246)*

Metallic Resources Inc 330 425-3155
2368 E Enterprise Pkwy Twinsburg (44087) *(G-14696)*

Metallics, Cleveland *Also Called: Ironunits LLC (G-4237)*

Metallurgical Service Inc 937 294-2681
2221 Arbor Blvd Moraine (45439) *(G-11193)*

Metallus Inc (PA) 330 471-7000
1835 Dueber Ave Sw Canton (44706) *(G-2159)*

Metallus Inc 216 825-2533
2311 Shepler Church Ave Sw Canton (44706) *(G-2160)*

Metallus Inc 800 967-1218
4748 Navarre Rd Canton (44706) *(G-2161)*

Metallus Inc 330 471-7000
1835 Dueber Ave Sw Canton (44706) *(G-2162)*

Metallus Inc 330 471-7000
4511 Faircrest St Sw Canton (44706) *(G-2163)*

Metalphoto of Cincinnati Inc 513 772-8281
1080 Skillman Dr Cincinnati (45215) *(G-3155)*

Metaltek Industries Inc 937 342-1750
829 Pauline St Springfield (45503) *(G-13606)*

Metaltek International, Sandusky *Also Called: Metaltek International Inc (G-13081)*

Metaltek International Inc 419 626-5340
615 W Market St Sandusky (44870) *(G-13081)*

Metalworking Group, The, Cincinnati *Also Called: Mwgh LLC (G-3178)*

Metaullics Systems, Solon *Also Called: Metaullics Systems LP (G-13387)*

Metaullics Systems LP 509 926-6212
31935 Aurora Rd Solon (44139) *(G-13387)*

Metcut Research Associates Inc (PA) 513 271-5100
3980 Rosslyn Dr Cincinnati (45209) *(G-3156)*

Metcut Research, Inc., Cincinnati *Also Called: Metcut Research Associates Inc (G-3156)*

Meteor Automotive, Dover *Also Called: Meteor Sealing Systems LLC (G-6835)*

Meteor Creative Inc (DH) 800 273-1535
1414 Commerce Park Dr Tipp City (45371) *(G-14141)*

Meteor Sealing Systems LLC 330 343-9595
400 S Tuscarawas Ave Dover (44622) *(G-6835)*

Metlweb Ltd 513 563-8822
3330 E Kemper Rd Cincinnati (45241) *(G-3157)*

Metokote Corporation 937 233-1565
8040 Center Point 70 Blvd Dayton (45424) *(G-6436)*

Metokote Corporation (HQ) 419 996-7800
1340 Neubrecht Rd Lima (45801) *(G-9270)*

Metro Containers Inc 513 351-6800
4927 Beech St Cincinnati (45212) *(G-3158)*

Metro Design Inc 440 458-4200
10740 Middle Ave Elyria (44035) *(G-7181)*

Metro Flex Inc 937 299-5360
3304 Encrete Ln Moraine (45439) *(G-11194)*

Metro Press, Millbury *Also Called: Douthit Communications Inc (G-10930)*

Metromedia Technologies Inc 330 264-2501
1061 Venture Blvd Wooster (44691) *(G-16151)*

Metron Instruments Inc 216 332-0592
5198 Richmond Rd Bedford Heights (44146) *(G-1176)*

Mettler Footwear Inc 330 703-0079
704 Westbrook Way Hudson (44236) *(G-8605)*

Mettler-Toledo LLC 614 841-7300
6600 Huntley Rd Columbus (43229) *(G-5560)*

Mettler-Toledo LLC 614 438-4511
720 Dearborn Park Ln Worthington (43085) *(G-16202)*

Mettler-Toledo LLC 614 438-4390
1150 Dearborn Dr Worthington (43085) *(G-16203)*

Mettler-Toledo Intl Fin Inc (DH) 614 438-4511
1900 Polaris Pkwy Columbus (43240) *(G-5065)*

Mettler-Toledo Intl Inc (PA) 614 438-4511
1900 Polaris Pkwy Columbus (43240) *(G-5066)*

Mettler-Toledo LLC (HQ) 614 438-4511
1900 Polaris Pkwy Columbus (43240) *(G-5067)*

Mettlr-Tledo Globl Hldings LLC (HQ) 614 438-4511
1900 Polaris Pkwy Columbus (43240) *(G-5068)*

Metzenbaum Sheltered Inds Inc 440 729-1919
8090 Cedar Rd Chesterland (44026) *(G-2485)*

Metzger Machine Co 513 241-3360
2165 Spring Grove Ave Cincinnati (45214) *(G-3159)*

Metzgers 419 861-8611
150 Arco Dr Toledo (43607) *(G-14383)*

Metzgers, Toledo Also Called: Tj Metzgers Inc *(G-14487)*
Mexichem Specialty Resins Inc (HQ).. 440 930-1435
  33653 Walker Rd Avon Lake (44012) *(G-817)*
Meyer Company (PA).. 216 587-3400
  7180 Sugar Bush Ln Chagrin Falls (44022) *(G-2382)*
Meyer Design Inc... 330 434-9176
  100 N High St Akron (44308) *(G-247)*
Meyer Products LLC... 216 486-1313
  18513 Euclid Ave Cleveland (44112) *(G-4397)*
Meyer Products LLC... 216 486-1313
  324 N 7th St Steubenville (43952) *(G-13672)*
Meyer Tool Inc (PA)... 513 681-7362
  3055 Colerain Ave Cincinnati (45225) *(G-3160)*
Meyerpt, Hudson Also Called: Boxout LLC *(G-8587)*
Meyers Printing & Design Inc... 937 461-6000
  254 Leo St Dayton (45404) *(G-6437)*
Mfg Composite Systems Company... 440 997-5851
  2925 Mfg Pl Ashtabula (44004) *(G-648)*
Mfg CSC, Ashtabula Also Called: Mfg Composite Systems Company *(G-648)*
Mfh Partners Inc (PA)... 440 461-4100
  6650 Beta Dr Cleveland (44143) *(G-4398)*
Mfi, Cincinnati Also Called: Mechanical Finishers Inc LLC *(G-3138)*
Mfm Building Products Corp... 740 622-2645
  425 Brewer Ln Coshocton (43812) *(G-5984)*
Mfm Building Products Corp (PA)... 740 622-2645
  525 Orange St Coshocton (43812) *(G-5985)*
Mfs Supply LLC (PA).. 800 607-0541
  31100 Solon Rd Ste 16 Solon (44139) *(G-13388)*
MGF Sourcing, Columbus Also Called: MGF Sourcing US LLC *(G-5561)*
MGF Sourcing US LLC (HQ).. 614 904-3300
  4200 Regent St Ste 205 Columbus (43219) *(G-5561)*
MGM Construction Inc... 440 234-7660
  1480 W Bagley Rd Ste 1 Berea (44017) *(G-1288)*
MGM Roofing, Berea Also Called: MGM Construction Inc *(G-1288)*
Mhi, Cincinnati Also Called: Micropyretics Heaters Intl Inc *(G-3162)*
Mhp Flooring, Millersburg Also Called: Mount Hope Planing *(G-10984)*
Miami Control Systems Inc... 937 233-8146
  4433 Interpoint Blvd Dayton (45424) *(G-6438)*
Miami Ice Machine Inc... 513 863-6707
  4251 Riverside Dr Overpeck (45055) *(G-12208)*
Miami Machine, Cleves Also Called: Pohl Machining Inc *(G-4962)*
Miami Machine Corporation.. 513 863-6707
  4251 Riverside Dr Overpeck (45055) *(G-12209)*
Miami Specialties Inc.. 937 778-1850
  172 Robert M Davis Pkwy Piqua (45356) *(G-12536)*
Miami Valley Eductl Cmpt Assn... 937 767-1468
  888 Dayton St Unit 102 Yellow Springs (45387) *(G-16284)*
Miami Valley Lighting LLC.. 937 224-6000
  1065 Woodman Dr Dayton (45432) *(G-6170)*
Miami Valley Meals Inc... 937 938-7141
  428 S Edwin C Moses Blvd Dayton (45402) *(G-6439)*
Miami Valley Plastics Inc... 937 273-3200
  310 S Main St Eldorado (45321) *(G-7092)*
Miami Valley Polishing LL.. 937 498-1634
  1317 Pinetree Ct Sidney (45365) *(G-13265)*
Miami Valley Polishing LLC.. 937 615-9353
  211 S Lester Ave Sidney (45365) *(G-13266)*
Miami Valley Precision Inc.. 937 866-1804
  1944 Byers Rd Miamisburg (45342) *(G-10657)*
Miami Valley Publishing LLC.. 937 879-5678
  678 Yellow Springs Fairfield Rd Fairborn (45324) *(G-7319)*
Miami Valley Punch & Mfg.. 937 237-0533
  1540 Thomas Farm Ct Dayton (45458) *(G-6440)*
Miami Valley Spray Foam LLC.. 419 295-6536
  3428 Wysong Rd Lewisburg (45338) *(G-9188)*
Miami Vly Counters & Spc Inc... 937 865-0562
  8515 Dayton Cincinnati Pike Miamisburg (45342) *(G-10658)*
Miami Vly Mfg & Assembly Inc.. 937 254-6665
  1889 Radio Rd Dayton (45431) *(G-6171)*
Miami Vly Packg Solutions Inc.. 937 224-1800
  1752 Stanley Ave Dayton (45404) *(G-6441)*

Miami-Cast Inc.. 937 866-2951
  901 N Main St Miamisburg (45342) *(G-10659)*
Miamisburg Coating.. 937 866-1323
  925 N Main St Miamisburg (45342) *(G-10660)*
Miamisburg News, Miamisburg Also Called: Cox Newspapers LLC *(G-10629)*
Miba Bearings US LLC... 740 962-4242
  5037 N State Route 60 Nw Mcconnelsville (43756) *(G-10282)*
Miba Sinter USA LLC.. 740 962-4242
  5045 N State Route 60 Nw Mcconnelsville (43756) *(G-10283)*
Mic-Ray Metal Products Inc.. 216 791-2206
  9016 Manor Ave Cleveland (44104) *(G-4399)*
Micc Manufacturing Corporation.. 567 331-0101
  26695 Eckel Rd Perrysburg (43551) *(G-12400)*
Miceli Dairy Products Co (PA).. 216 791-6222
  2721 E 90th St Cleveland (44104) *(G-4400)*
Michael Byrne Manufacturing Co Inc... 419 525-1214
  1855 Earth Boring Rd Mansfield (44903) *(G-9691)*
Michael Day Enterprises LLC.. 330 335-5100
  9774 Trease Rd Wadsworth (44281) *(G-15044)*
Michael Kaufman Companies Inc... 330 673-4881
  845 Overholt Rd Kent (44240) *(G-8836)*
Michael W Hyes Desgr Goldsmith.. 440 519-0889
  28200 Miles Rd Unit F Solon (44139) *(G-13309)*
Michael W Newton... 740 352-9334
  768 Fairground Rd Lucasville (45648) *(G-9525)*
Michael Zakany LLC.. 740 221-3934
  601 Putnam Ave Zanesville (43701) *(G-16545)*
Michaels 9837, Niles Also Called: Michaels Stores Inc *(G-11676)*
Michaels Pre-Cast Con Pdts... 513 683-1292
  1917 Adams Rd Loveland (45140) *(G-9497)*
Michaels Stores Inc.. 330 505-1168
  5555 Youngstown Warren Rd Unit 914 Niles (44446) *(G-11676)*
Michalek Manufacturing LLC.. 740 763-0910
  160 Obannon Ave Newark (43055) *(G-11590)*
Michel Tires Plus 227565, Cincinnati Also Called: Bridgestone Ret Operations LLC *(G-2683)*
Michele Caldwell.. 937 505-7744
  3421 Olive Rd Dayton (45426) *(G-6442)*
Michelman, Blue Ash Also Called: Michelman Inc *(G-1438)*
Michelman Inc (PA).. 513 793-7766
  9080 Shell Rd Blue Ash (45236) *(G-1438)*
Michigan Silkscreen Inc.. 419 885-1163
  5354 Whiteford Rd Sylvania (43560) *(G-14004)*
Michigan Sugar Company.. 419 332-9931
  1101 N Front St Fremont (43420) *(G-7797)*
Mickes Quality Machining LLC.. 614 746-6639
  488 Trade Rd Columbus (43204) *(G-5562)*
Miconvi Properties Inc... 440 954-3500
  37200 Research Dr Eastlake (44095) *(G-7039)*
Micro Industries Corporation (PA)... 740 548-7878
  8399 Green Meadows Dr N Westerville (43081) *(G-15716)*
Micro Lapping & Grinding Co.. 216 267-6500
  12320 Plaza Dr Cleveland (44130) *(G-4401)*
Micro Machine Ltd.. 330 438-7078
  275 7th St Sw Brewster (44613) *(G-1645)*
Micro Machine Works Inc... 740 678-8471
  8900 State Route 339 Vincent (45784) *(G-15009)*
Micro Metal Finishing LLC.. 513 541-3095
  3448 Spring Grove Ave Cincinnati (45225) *(G-3161)*
Micro Products Co Inc... 440 943-0258
  26653 Curtiss Wright Pkwy Willoughby Hills (44092) *(G-16025)*
Micro Tool Service, New Lebanon Also Called: H Duane Leis Acquisitions *(G-11449)*
Micro-Pise Msrment Systems LLC.. 330 541-9100
  555 Mondial Pkwy Streetsboro (44241) *(G-13779)*
Microcom Corporation... 740 548-6262
  855 Corduroy Rd Lewis Center (43035) *(G-9171)*
Microfinish, Vandalia Also Called: Microfinish LLC *(G-14953)*
Microfinish LLC... 937 264-1598
  865 Scholz Dr Vandalia (45377) *(G-14953)*
Micromd... 850 217-7412
  790 Boardman Canfield Rd Youngstown (44512) *(G-16399)*
Micron Manufacturing Inc... 440 355-4200
  186 Commerce Dr Lagrange (44050) *(G-8952)*

Microplex Inc 330 498-0600
7568 Whipple Ave Nw North Canton (44720) *(G-11743)*

Microplex Printware Corp 440 374-2424
30300 Solon Industrial Pkwy Ste E Solon (44139) *(G-13390)*

Micropure Filtration Inc 952 472-2323
837 E 79th St Cleveland (44103) *(G-4402)*

Micropyretics Heaters Intl Inc 513 772-0404
750 Redna Ter Cincinnati (45215) *(G-3162)*

Microsheen Corporation 216 481-5610
1100 E 222nd St Ste 1 Cleveland (44117) *(G-4403)*

Microsoft, Cleveland Also Called: Microsoft Corporation *(G-4404)*

Microsoft Corporation 216 986-1440
6050 Oak Tree Blvd Ste 300 Cleveland (44131) *(G-4404)*

Microsun Lamps LLC 888 328-8701
7890 Center Point 70 Blvd Dayton (45424) *(G-6443)*

Microtek Finishing LLC 513 766-5600
5579 Spellmire Dr West Chester (45246) *(G-15571)*

Microweld Engineering Inc 614 847-9410
7451 Oakmeadows Dr Worthington (43085) *(G-16204)*

Mid, Columbus Also Called: Minimally Invasive Devices Inc *(G-5572)*

Mid America Tire of Hillsboro Inc 937 393-3520
108 Willetsville Pike Hillsboro (45133) *(G-8461)*

Mid American Ventures Inc 216 524-0974
7600 Wall St Ste 205 Cleveland (44125) *(G-4405)*

Mid Ohio Net, Delaware Also Called: Delaware Gazette Company *(G-6714)*

Mid Ohio Wood Products Inc 740 323-0427
535 Franklin Ave Newark (43056) *(G-11591)*

Mid Ohio Wood Recycling Inc 419 673-8470
16289 State Route 31 Kenton (43326) *(G-8891)*

Mid West Fabricating Co, Amanda Also Called: Mid-West Fabricating Co *(G-446)*

Mid-America Chemical Corp 216 749-0100
4701 Spring Rd Cleveland (44131) *(G-4406)*

Mid-America Packaging LLC 330 963-4199
2127 Reiser Ave Se New Philadelphia (44663) *(G-11517)*

Mid-America Stainless, Cleveland Also Called: Mid-America Steel Corp *(G-4407)*

Mid-America Steel Corp 800 282-3466
20900 Saint Clair Ave Rear Cleveland (44117) *(G-4407)*

Mid-America Store Fixtures, Obetz Also Called: Lemon Group LLC *(G-12060)*

Mid-Continent Minerals Corp (PA) 216 283-5700
20600 Chagrin Blvd Ste 850 Cleveland (44122) *(G-4408)*

Mid-Ohio Electric Co 614 274-8000
1170 Mckinley Ave Columbus (43222) *(G-5563)*

Mid-Ohio Finishing LLC 330 466-9117
96 County Road 2575 Lakeville (44638) *(G-8964)*

Mid-Ohio Screen Print Inc 614 875-1774
4163 Kelnor Dr Grove City (43123) *(G-8106)*

Mid-State Sales, Columbus Also Called: Mid-State Sales Inc *(G-5564)*

Mid-State Sales Inc 330 744-2158
519 N Meridian Rd Youngstown (44509) *(G-16400)*

Mid-State Sales Inc (PA) 614 864-1811
1101 Gahanna Pkwy Columbus (43230) *(G-5564)*

Mid-West Fabricating Co (PA) 740 969-4411
313 N Johns St Amanda (43102) *(G-446)*

Mid-West Fabricating Co 740 277-7021
885 Mill Park Dr Lancaster (43130) *(G-9024)*

Mid-West Forge Corporation (PA) 216 481-3030
2778 Som Center Rd Ste 200 Willoughby (44094) *(G-15953)*

Mid-Wood Inc 419 257-3331
101 E State St North Baltimore (45872) *(G-11696)*

Mid's Spaghetti Sauce, Navarre Also Called: RC Industries Inc *(G-11352)*

Middaugh Enterprises Inc 330 852-2471
211 Yoder Ave Ne Sugarcreek (44681) *(G-13930)*

Middlebury Cheese Company LLC 330 893-2500
5060 State Route 557 Millersburg (44654) *(G-10980)*

Middlefield Glass Incorporated 440 632-5699
17447 Kinsman Rd Middlefield (44062) *(G-10765)*

Middlefield Pallet Inc 440 632-0553
15940 Burton Windsor Rd Middlefield (44062) *(G-10766)*

Middlefield Plastics Inc 440 834-4638
15235 Burton Windsor Rd Middlefield (44062) *(G-10767)*

Middleton Llyd Dolls Inc (PA) 740 989-2082
23689 Mountain Bell Rd Coolville (45723) *(G-5941)*

Middleton Enterprises Inc 614 885-2514
7100 N High St Worthington (43085) *(G-16205)*

Middleton Printing Co Inc 614 294-7277
81 Mill St Ste 300 Gahanna (43230) *(G-7845)*

Middletown License Agency Inc 513 422-7225
3232 Roosevelt Blvd Middletown (45044) *(G-10844)*

Middlfeld Original Cheese Coop 440 632-5567
16942 Kinsman Rd Middlefield (44062) *(G-10768)*

Middlton Lloyd Doll Fctry Outl, Coolville Also Called: Middleton Llyd Dolls Inc *(G-5941)*

Midlake Products & Mfg Co 330 875-4202
819 N Nickelplate St Louisville (44641) *(G-9464)*

Midland Engineering, Canton Also Called: Decision Systems Inc *(G-2090)*

Midmark Corporation (PA) 937 528-7500
10170 Penny Ln Ste 300 Miamisburg (45342) *(G-10661)*

Midmark Corporation 937 526-3662
60 Vista Dr Versailles (45380) *(G-14986)*

Midmark Corporation 937 526-8387
160 Industrial Parkway Versailles (45380) *(G-14987)*

Midstate Machine, Cincinnati Also Called: McSwain Manufacturing LLC *(G-3137)*

Midstate Machine Ohio Facility 513 619-1222
189 Container Pl Cincinnati (45246) *(G-3163)*

Midtown Pallet & Recycling Inc 419 241-1311
1987 Hawthorne St Toledo (43606) *(G-14384)*

Midway Machining Inc 740 373-8976
1060 Gravel Bank Rd Marietta (45750) *(G-9809)*

Midway Products, Findlay Also Called: P & A Industries Inc *(G-7549)*

Midway Products Group, Greenwich Also Called: Lakepark Industries Inc *(G-8068)*

Midway Products Group Inc 419 422-7070
2045 Industrial Drive Findlay (45840) *(G-7537)*

Midwest Acoust-A-Fiber Inc (PA) 740 369-3624
759 Pittsburgh Dr Delaware (43015) *(G-6737)*

Midwest Aircraft Products Co 419 884-2164
125 S Mill St Mansfield (44904) *(G-9692)*

Midwest Bath Salt Company LLC 513 770-9177
8251 Arbor Square Dr Mason (45040) *(G-10029)*

Midwest Box Company 216 281-9021
9801 Walford Ave Ste C Cleveland (44102) *(G-4409)*

Midwest Centerless Grinding, Cincinnati Also Called: A and V Grinding Inc *(G-2583)*

Midwest Commercial Mllwk Inc 419 224-5001
514 N Union St Lima (45801) *(G-9271)*

Midwest Composites LLC 419 738-2431
302 Krein Ave Wapakoneta (45895) *(G-15123)*

Midwest Compost Inc 419 547-7979
7250 State Route 101 E Clyde (43410) *(G-4974)*

Midwest Container Corporation 513 870-3000
1899 Kingsview Dr Lebanon (45036) *(G-9097)*

Midwest Conveyor Products Inc 419 281-1235
1919 Cellar Dr Ashland (44805) *(G-592)*

Midwest Curtainwalls Inc 216 641-7900
5171 Grant Ave Cleveland (44125) *(G-4410)*

Midwest Cylinder, Harrison Also Called: Kaplan Industries Inc *(G-8282)*

Midwest Die Supply Company 419 729-7141
6240 American Rd Ste A Toledo (43612) *(G-14385)*

Midwest Distribution Center, Columbus Also Called: BASF Corporation *(G-5176)*

Midwest Division, Hebron Also Called: Diebold Nixdorf Incorporated *(G-8339)*

Midwest Elastomers Inc 419 738-8844
700 Industrial Dr Wapakoneta (45895) *(G-15124)*

Midwest Fabrications Inc 330 633-0191
516 Commerce St Tallmadge (44278) *(G-14038)*

Midwest Filtration LLC 513 874-6510
9775 International Blvd West Chester (45246) *(G-15572)*

Midwest Fuel LLC 740 753-5960
1155 Chestnut St Nelsonville (45764) *(G-11357)*

Midwest Glycol Services LLC 419 946-3326
116 Lawrence Ave Marion (43302) *(G-9862)*

Midwest Knife Grinding Inc 330 854-1030
492 Elm Ridge Ave Ste 4 Canal Fulton (44614) *(G-1973)*

Midwest Laser Systems Inc 419 424-0062
4777 S Us Highway 23 Alvada (44802) *(G-443)*

Midwest Machine Service Inc 216 631-8151
4700 Train Ave Ste 1 Cleveland (44102) *(G-4411)*

Midwest Marketing — ALPHABETIC SECTION

Midwest Marketing, Newark Also Called: Midwest Menu Mate Inc (G-11592)

Midwest Menu Mate Inc.. 740 323-2599
1065 Lizabeth Cir Newark (43056) *(G-11592)*

Midwest Metal Fabricators... 419 739-7077
712 Maple St Wapakoneta (45895) *(G-15125)*

Midwest Metal Fabricators Ltd.. 419 739-7077
712 Maple St Wapakoneta (45895) *(G-15126)*

Midwest Metal Products LLC... 614 539-7322
3945 Brookham Dr Grove City (43123) *(G-8107)*

Midwest Mold & Texture Corp.. 513 732-1300
4270 Armstrong Blvd Batavia (45103) *(G-934)*

Midwest Motoplex LLC.. 740 772-5300
98 Consumer Center Dr Chillicothe (45601) *(G-2518)*

Midwest Motor Supply Co (PA)... 800 233-1294
4800 Roberts Rd Columbus (43228) *(G-5565)*

Midwest Muffler Pros & More.. 937 293-2450
3061 Dryden Rd Moraine (45439) *(G-11195)*

Midwest Precision... 216 658-0058
1000 Valley Belt Rd Brooklyn Heights (44131) *(G-1695)*

Midwest Precision Holdings Inc (HQ).................................... 440 497-4086
34700 Lakeland Blvd Eastlake (44095) *(G-7040)*

Midwest Precision LLC.. 440 951-2333
34700 Lakeland Blvd Eastlake (44095) *(G-7041)*

Midwest Quality Bedding Inc... 614 504-5971
3860 Morse Rd Columbus (43219) *(G-5566)*

Midwest Rlwy Prsrvtion Soc Inc.. 216 781-3629
2800 W 3rd St Cleveland (44113) *(G-4412)*

Midwest Security Services.. 937 853-9000
4050 Benfield Dr Dayton (45429) *(G-6444)*

Midwest Service, Middletown Also Called: Vail Rubber Works Inc (G-10869)

Midwest Sign Center, Canton Also Called: Midwest Sign Ctr (G-2164)

Midwest Sign Ctr... 330 493-7330
4210 Cleveland Ave Nw Canton (44709) *(G-2164)*

Midwest Specialties Inc.. 800 837-2503
705 Commerce Rd Wapakoneta (45895) *(G-15127)*

Midwest Specialty Pdts Co Inc... 513 874-7070
280 Northpointe Dr Fairfield (45014) *(G-7384)*

Midwest Stamping & Mfg Co... 419 298-2394
228 E Morrison St Edgerton (43517) *(G-7078)*

Midwest Steel Fabricators Inc... 937 437-0371
8155 State Route 121 N New Paris (45347) *(G-11483)*

Midwest Strapping Products... 614 527-1454
1819 Walcutt Rd Ste 13 Columbus (43228) *(G-5567)*

Midwest Tool & Engineering Co
112 Webster St Dayton (45402) *(G-6445)*

Midwest Wood Trim Inc... 419 592-3389
1650 Commerce Dr Napoleon (43545) *(G-11324)*

Midwest Woodworking Co Inc.. 513 631-6684
4019 Montgomery Rd Cincinnati (45212) *(G-3164)*

Midwestern Bag Co Inc... 419 241-3112
3230 Monroe St Toledo (43606) *(G-14386)*

Midwestern Industries Inc (PA).. 330 837-4203
915 Oberlin Ave Sw Massillon (44647) *(G-10127)*

Mielke Furniture Repair Inc... 419 625-4572
3209 Columbus Ave Sandusky (44870) *(G-13082)*

Miiler Brewing Company... 513 896-9200
2525 Wayne Madison Rd Trenton (45067) *(G-14541)*

Mika Metal Fabricating, Willoughby Also Called: Weybridge LLC (G-16015)

Mike Loppe.. 937 969-8102
2 W Main St Tremont City (45372) *(G-14538)*

Mike-Sells Potato Chip Co... 937 228-9400
1610 Stanley Ave Dayton (45404) *(G-6446)*

Mike-Sells Potato Chip Co (HQ).. 937 228-9400
333 Leo St Dayton (45404) *(G-6447)*

Mike-Sells Potato Chip Co... 937 228-9400
155 N College St Sabina (45169) *(G-12887)*

Mike-Sells West Virginia Inc (PA).. 937 228-9400
333 Leo St Dayton (45404) *(G-6448)*

Mikes Transm & Auto Svc LLC... 330 799-8266
202 S Meridian Rd Youngstown (44509) *(G-16401)*

Mikesells Snack Fd Co Dist Ctr, Dayton Also Called: Mike-Sells Potato Chip Co (G-6446)

Mikron Industries Inc (HQ).. 713 961-4600
388 S Main St Ste 700 Akron (44311) *(G-248)*

Mil-Mar Century Corporation... 937 275-4860
8641 Washington Church Rd Miamisburg (45342) *(G-10662)*

Milacron, Batavia Also Called: Milacron Holdings Corp (G-935)

Milacron Holdings Corp (HQ).. 513 487-5000
4165 Half Acre Rd Batavia (45103) *(G-935)*

Milacron LLC (DH)... 513 487-5000
10200 Alliance Rd Ste 200 Blue Ash (45242) *(G-1439)*

Milacron Marketing Company LLC (DH)............................... 513 536-2000
4165 Half Acre Rd Batavia (45103) *(G-936)*

Milacron Plas Tech Group LLC (DH)..................................... 513 536-2000
4165 Half Acre Rd Batavia (45103) *(G-937)*

Milark Industries, Mansfield Also Called: Hayford Technologies Inc (G-9667)

Milark Industries Inc.. 419 524-7627
520 S Airport Rd Mansfield (44903) *(G-9693)*

Milark Industries Inc (PA).. 419 524-7627
536 S Airport Rd Mansfield (44903) *(G-9694)*

Milathan Wholesalers.. 614 697-1458
423 N Front St 237 Columbus (43215) *(G-5568)*

Miles Folding Box Co Div, Cleveland Also Called: Sobel Corrugated Containers Inc (G-4712)

Miles Midprint Inc... 216 860-4770
1215 W 10th St Ste B Cleveland (44113) *(G-4413)*

Miles Rubber & Packing Company (PA)............................... 330 425-3888
9020 Dutton Dr Twinsburg (44087) *(G-14697)*

Milestone Services Corp.. 330 374-9988
551 Beacon St Akron (44311) *(G-249)*

Milford Printers (PA).. 513 831-6630
317 Main St Milford (45150) *(G-10914)*

Military Spec Packaging, Columbus Also Called: Tri-W Group Inc (G-5837)

Milk Hney Cndy Soda Shoppe LLC.. 330 492-5884
3400 Cleveland Ave Nw Ste 1 Canton (44709) *(G-2165)*

Mill & Motion Inc... 216 524-4000
5415 E Schaaf Rd Independence (44131) *(G-8673)*

Mill & Motion Properties Ltd... 216 524-4000
5415 E Schaaf Rd Independence (44131) *(G-8674)*

Mill Creek Mining Company (HQ)... 216 765-1240
46226 National Rd W Saint Clairsville (43950) *(G-12913)*

Mill Rose Laboratories Inc.. 440 974-6730
7310 Corp Blvd Mentor (44060) *(G-10504)*

Mill-Rose, Mentor Also Called: Mill-Rose Company (G-10505)

Mill-Rose Company (PA).. 440 255-9171
7995 Tyler Blvd Mentor (44060) *(G-10505)*

Millat Industries Corp (PA)... 937 434-6666
4901 Croftshire Dr Dayton (45440) *(G-6449)*

Millat Industries Corp... 937 535-1500
7611 Center Point 70 Blvd Dayton (45424) *(G-6450)*

Millcraft Group LLC (PA)... 216 441-5500
9000 Rio Nero Dr Independence (44131) *(G-8675)*

Millcraft Purchasing Corp... 216 441-5505
6800 Grant Ave Cleveland (44105) *(G-4414)*

Millennium, Ashtabula Also Called: Ineos Pigments USA Inc (G-641)

Millennium Adhesive Pdts LLC.. 440 708-1212
178 E Washington St Ste 1 Chagrin Falls (44022) *(G-2383)*

Millennium Cell Inc.. 614 688-5160
1250 Arthur E Adams Dr Columbus (43221) *(G-5569)*

Millennium Machine Tech LLC... 440 269-8080
38323 Apollo Pkwy Ste 7 Willoughby (44094) *(G-15954)*

Millennium Plant, Massillon Also Called: Shearers Foods LLC (G-10143)

Millennium Printing LLC.. 513 489-3000
11401 Deerfield Rd Blue Ash (45242) *(G-1440)*

Miller and Slay Wdwkg LLC... 513 265-3816
4140 E Foster Maineville Rd Morrow (45152) *(G-11224)*

Miller Bearing Company Inc.. 330 678-8844
420 Portage Blvd Kent (44240) *(G-8837)*

Miller Bros Paving Inc (HQ)... 419 445-1015
1613 S Defiance St Archbold (43502) *(G-536)*

Miller Cabinet Ltd.. 614 873-4221
6217 Converse Huff Rd Plain City (43064) *(G-12586)*

Miller Castings Inc... 330 482-2923
1634 Lower Elkton Rd Columbiana (44408) *(G-5045)*

Miller Consolidated Inds Inc, Moraine *Also Called: McOn Inds Inc (G-11192)*

Miller Core II Inc 330 359-0500
9823 Chestnut Ridge Rd Nw Beach City (44608) *(G-969)*

Miller Crist 330 359-7877
10258 S Kansas Rd Fredericksburg (44627) *(G-7726)*

Miller Energy LLC 614 367-1812
3812 Zephyr Pl Columbus (43232) *(G-5570)*

Miller Engine & Machine Co, Springfield *Also Called: Muller Engine & Machine Co (G-13607)*

Miller Express Inc 330 714-6751
828 Dogwood Ter Copley (44321) *(G-5951)*

Miller Fabrication and Welding 419 884-0459
125 S Mill St Mansfield (44904) *(G-9695)*

Miller Logging 440 693-4001
5327 Parks West Rd Middlefield (44062) *(G-10769)*

Miller Logging Inc 330 279-4721
8373 State Route 83 Holmesville (44633) *(G-8550)*

Miller Lumber Co Inc 330 674-0273
7101 State Route 39 Millersburg (44654) *(G-10981)*

Miller Manufacturing Inc 330 852-0689
2705 Shetler Rd Nw Sugarcreek (44681) *(G-13931)*

Miller Plating LLC 330 952-2550
940 Lafayette Rd Medina (44256) *(G-10354)*

Miller Precision Manufacturing Industries Inc 419 453-3251
131 Progressive Dr Ottoville (45876) *(G-12202)*

Miller Printing Co, Springfield *Also Called: Graphic Paper Products Corp (G-13570)*

Miller Products Inc 330 308-5934
642 Wabash Ave Nw New Philadelphia (44663) *(G-11518)*

Miller Products Inc 330 335-3110
985 Seville Rd Wadsworth (44281) *(G-15045)*

Miller Products Inc 330 335-3110
985 Seville Rd Wadsworth (44281) *(G-15046)*

Miller Products Inc (PA) 330 938-2134
450 Courtney Rd Sebring (44672) *(G-13122)*

Miller Studio Inc 330 339-1100
734 Fair Ave Nw New Philadelphia (44663) *(G-11519)*

Miller Weldmaster Corporation (PA) 330 833-6739
4220 Alabama Ave Sw Navarre (44662) *(G-11346)*

Miller Wood Design, Sugarcreek *Also Called: Miller Manufacturing Inc (G-13931)*

Miller-Holzwarth Inc 330 342-7224
450 W Pershing St Salem (44460) *(G-13017)*

Miller, Jim Furniture, Springfield *Also Called: Hallmark Industries Inc (G-13571)*

Millers Aplus Cmpt Svcs LLC 330 620-5288
1067 Mercer Ave Akron (44320) *(G-250)*

Millers Liniments Llc 440 548-5800
17150 Bundysburg Rd Middlefield (44062) *(G-10770)*

Millers Storage Barns LLC 330 893-3293
4230 State Route 39 Millersburg (44654) *(G-10982)*

Millersburg Ice Company 330 674-3016
25 S Grant St Millersburg (44654) *(G-10983)*

Millertech Energy Solutions 855 629-5484
17795 Farmington Rd West Farmington (44491) *(G-15606)*

Millmcrawley, Greenville *Also Called: Markwith Tool Company Inc (G-8051)*

Millprint, Blue Ash *Also Called: Millennium Printing LLC (G-1440)*

Mills Custom Coatings 330 280-0633
2976 Kipling Ave Nw Massillon (44646) *(G-10128)*

Mills Customs Woodworks 216 407-3600
3950 Prospect Ave E Cleveland (44115) *(G-4415)*

Mills Metal Finishing, Columbus *Also Called: Mmf Incorporated (G-5574)*

Mills Partition Company LLC 740 375-0770
3007 Harding Hwy E Bldg 201 Marion (43302) *(G-9863)*

Mills Pride Premier Inc 740 941-1300
423 Hopewell Rd Waverly (45690) *(G-15285)*

Millstone Coffee Inc (HQ) 513 983-1100
1 Procter And Gamble Plz Cincinnati (45202) *(G-3165)*

Milltree Lumber Holdings 740 226-2090
535 Coal Dock Rd Waverly (45690) *(G-15286)*

Millwood Inc 330 857-3075
8208 S Kohler Rd Apple Creek (44606) *(G-505)*

Millwood Inc 216 881-1414
4201 Lakeside Ave E Cleveland (44114) *(G-4416)*

Millwood Inc 330 359-5220
18279 Dover Rd Dundee (44624) *(G-6967)*

Millwood Inc 440 914-0540
30311 Emerald Valley Pkwy Ste 300 Solon (44139) *(G-13391)*

Millwood Inc 330 609-0220
1328 Ridge Rd Vienna (44473) *(G-15001)*

Millwood Inc 740 226-2090
535 Coal Dock Rd Waverly (45690) *(G-15287)*

Millwood Inc 513 860-4567
4438 Muhlhauser Rd Ste 100 West Chester (45011) *(G-15464)*

Millwood Incorporated 330 704-6707
13407 Dover Rd Apple Creek (44606) *(G-506)*

Millwood Logging, Gnadenhutten *Also Called: Millwood Lumber Inc (G-7985)*

Millwood Lumber Inc 740 254-4681
2400 Larson Rd Se Gnadenhutten (44629) *(G-7985)*

Millwood Natural LLC 330 393-4400
3708 International Blvd Vienna (44473) *(G-15002)*

Millwood Pallet Co, Dundee *Also Called: Millwood Inc (G-6967)*

Millwood Wholesale Inc 330 359-6109
7969 Township Road 662 Dundee (44624) *(G-6968)*

Millwork Elements LLC 614 905-8163
6663 Huntley Rd Ste A Columbus (43229) *(G-5571)*

Millwork Enterprises LLC (PA) 216 644-1481
25418 Tyndall Falls Dr Olmsted Falls (44138) *(G-12081)*

Millwrght Wldg Fbrication Svcs 740 533-1510
1590 County Road 105 Kitts Hill (45645) *(G-8944)*

Milo Family Vineyards Ltd 440 922-0190
8869 Brecksville Rd Ste A Brecksville (44141) *(G-1627)*

Milos Kitchen LLC 330 682-3000
1 Strawberry Ln Orrville (44667) *(G-12136)*

Milos Whole World Gourmet LLC 740 589-6456
296 S Harper St Nelsonville (45764) *(G-11358)*

Milsek Furniture Polish Inc 330 542-2700
1351 Quaker Cir Salem (44460) *(G-13018)*

Mim Software Inc (PA) 216 455-0600
25800 Science Park Dr Ste 180 Beachwood (44122) *(G-1000)*

Minco Group, The, Dayton *Also Called: Minco Tool and Mold Inc (G-6451)*

Minco Tool and Mold Inc (PA) 937 890-7905
5690 Webster St Dayton (45414) *(G-6451)*

Mindful, Akron *Also Called: Virtual Hold Tech Slutions LLC (G-370)*

Miner's Bishop Tractor Sales, Rootstown *Also Called: Miners Tractor Sales Inc (G-12854)*

Mineral Processing Company 419 396-3501
1855 County Highway 99 Carey (43316) *(G-2280)*

Miners Tractor Sales Inc (PA) 330 325-9914
6941 Tallmadge Rd Rootstown (44272) *(G-12854)*

Minerva Dairy Inc 330 868-4196
430 Radloff Ave Minerva (44657) *(G-11035)*

Minerva Maid, Minerva *Also Called: Minerva Dairy Inc (G-11035)*

Minerva Manufacturing Facility, Minerva *Also Called: American Axle & Mfg Inc (G-11026)*

Minerva Operations, Minerva *Also Called: Colfor Manufacturing Inc (G-11029)*

Minerva Tube Plant, Minerva *Also Called: Caraustar Indus Cnsmr Pdts Gro (G-11028)*

Minerva Welding and Fabg Inc 330 868-7731
22133 Us Route 30 Minerva (44657) *(G-11036)*

Mini Mix Inc 513 353-3811
7432 Hamilton Cleves Rd Cleves (45002) *(G-4960)*

Minimally Invasive Devices Inc 614 484-5036
1275 Kinnear Rd Columbus (43212) *(G-5572)*

Mining and Reclamation Inc 740 327-5555
15953 State Route 60 S Dresden (43821) *(G-6855)*

Minnich Manufacturing Co Inc 419 903-0010
1444 State Route 42 Mansfield (44903) *(G-9696)*

Minster Farmers, Minster *Also Called: Sunrise Cooperative Inc (G-11062)*

Minster Farmers Co-Op Exchange, Minster *Also Called: Minster Farmers Coop Exch (G-11056)*

Minster Farmers Coop Exch 419 628-4705
292 W 4th St Minster (45865) *(G-11056)*

Minster Machine, Minster *Also Called: NIDEC MINSTER CORPORATION (G-11057)*

Minteq International Inc 419 636-4561
719 E High St Bryan (43506) *(G-1828)*

Minteq International Inc 330 343-8821
5864 Crown Street Ext Nw Dover (44622) *(G-6836)*

Minus G LLC 440 817-0338
12300 Kinsman Rd Unit A-1 Newbury (44065) *(G-11630)*

Minuteman of Heath, Newark *Also Called: L & T Collins Inc (G-11586)*

Minuteman Press.. 937 701-7100
2599 Needmore Rd Dayton (45414) *(G-6452)*

Minuteman Press.. 513 454-7318
223 Court St Hamilton (45011) *(G-8229)*

Minuteman Press.. 937 451-8222
120 W Water St Piqua (45356) *(G-12537)*

Minuteman Press, Cincinnati *Also Called: Minuteman Press Inc (G-3166)*

Minuteman Press, Cincinnati *Also Called: Mmp Printing Inc (G-3168)*

Minuteman Press, Columbus *Also Called: Capehart Enterprises LLC (G-5230)*

Minuteman Press, Fairlawn *Also Called: Frisby Printing Company (G-7439)*

Minuteman Press, Hamilton *Also Called: Minuteman Press (G-8229)*

Minuteman Press, Lebanon *Also Called: Geygan Enterprises Inc (G-9082)*

Minuteman Press, Maumee *Also Called: Stepping Stone Enterprises Inc (G-10235)*

Minuteman Press Inc.. 513 741-9056
9904 Colerain Ave Cincinnati (45251) *(G-3166)*

Miracle, Moraine *Also Called: Heading4ward Investment Co (G-11185)*

Miracle Air, Franklin *Also Called: Miracle Welding Inc (G-7687)*

Miracle Welding Inc.. 937 746-9977
141 Industrial Dr Ste 200 Franklin (45005) *(G-7687)*

Mirion Technologies Ist Corp... 614 367 2050
12954 Stonecreek Dr Ste C Pickerington (43147) *(G-12464)*

Mirror... 419 893-8135
113 W Wayne St Maumee (43537) *(G-10221)*

Mirror Publishing Co Inc.. 419 893-8135
113 W Wayne St Maumee (43537) *(G-10222)*

Mirror, The, Maumee *Also Called: Mirror Publishing Co Inc (G-10222)*

Mirus Adapted Tech LLC.. 614 402-4585
288 Cramer Creek Ct Dublin (43017) *(G-6910)*

Mis, Ashland *Also Called: Maverick Innvtive Slutions LLC (G-590)*

Miscellnous Mtals Fbrction Inc....................................... 740 779-3071
18828 Us Highway 50 Chillicothe (45601) *(G-2519)*

Misco Refractometer, Solon *Also Called: Mercury Iron and Steel Co (G-13385)*

Miscor Group Ltd.. 330 830-3500
800 Nave Rd Se Massillon (44646) *(G-10129)*

Miswest Ambrodery.. 513 661-2770
8060 Reading Rd Cincinnati (45237) *(G-3167)*

Mitchell, Youngstown *Also Called: George A Mitchell Company (G-16368)*

Mitchell Bros Tire Rtread Svc... 740 353-1551
1205 Findlay St Portsmouth (45662) *(G-12649)*

Mitchell Brothers Retread Svc, Portsmouth *Also Called: Mitchell Bros Tire Rtread Svc (G-12649)*

Mitchell Piping LLC.. 330 245-0258
1101 Sunnyside St Sw Hartville (44632) *(G-8303)*

Mitchell Plastics Inc... 330 825-2461
130 31st St Nw Barberton (44203) *(G-883)*

Mitchellace Inc (PA)... 740 354-2813
830 Murray St Portsmouth (45662) *(G-12650)*

Mitchs Welding & Hitches.. 419 893-3117
802 Kingsbury St Maumee (43537) *(G-10223)*

Mitec Powertrain Inc.. 567 525-5606
4000 Fostoria Ave Findlay (45840) *(G-7538)*

Mitsubishi Chemical Amer Inc....................................... 586 755-1660
350 N Buckeye St Bellevue (44811) *(G-1229)*

Mitsubishi Chemical Amer Inc....................................... 419 483-2931
350 N Buckeye St Bellevue (44811) *(G-1230)*

Mitsubishi Elc Auto Amer Inc (DH)............................... 513 573-6614
4773 Bethany Rd Mason (45040) *(G-10030)*

Mix Marketing LLC.. 614 791-0489
5675 Kentfield Dr Dublin (43016) *(G-6911)*

Mixed Logic LLC.. 440 826-1676
5907 E Law Rd Valley City (44280) *(G-14879)*

Mj Bornhorst Enterprises LLC....................................... 937 295-3469
400 Enterprise Dr Fort Loramie (45845) *(G-7604)*

MJB Toledo Inc (HQ)... 419 531-2121
3115 Frenchmens Rd Toledo (43607) *(G-14387)*

Mjc Enterprise Inc... 330 669-3744
7820 Blough Rd Sterling (44276) *(G-13659)*

Mjcj Holdings Inc... 937 885-0600
2580 Kohnle Dr Miamisburg (45342) *(G-10663)*

MJM Industries Inc.. 440 350-1230
1200 East St Fairport Harbor (44077) *(G-7456)*

Mjo Industries Inc (PA)... 800 590-4055
8000 Technology Blvd Huber Heights (45424) *(G-8577)*

Mk Metal Products Inc.. 330 669-2631
301 W Prospect St Smithville (44677) *(G-13300)*

Mk Metal Products Entps Inc (PA)............................... 419 756-3644
90 Sawyer Pkwy Mansfield (44903) *(G-9697)*

Mk Trempe Corporation.. 937 492-3548
2349 Industrial Dr Sidney (45365) *(G-13267)*

Mk Welding & Fabrication Inc...................................... 937 603-4430
1824 E Lower Springboro Rd Waynesville (45068) *(G-15299)*

Mkfour Inc... 620 629-1120
108 Hawks Cove Ct Granville (43023) *(G-8021)*

Mkgs Corp.. 937 254-8181
1712 Springfield St Ste 2 Dayton (45403) *(G-6453)*

ML Advertising & Design LLC...................................... 419 447-6523
185 Jefferson St Tiffin (44883) *(G-14094)*

ML Erectors LLC... 440 328-3227
827 Walnut St Elyria (44035) *(G-7182)*

Mlad Graphic Design Services, Tiffin *Also Called: ML Advertising & Design LLC (G-14094)*

MLS Systems, Alvada *Also Called: Midwest Laser Systems Inc (G-443)*

Mm Industries Inc... 800 002 0017
36135 Salem Grange Rd Salem (44460) *(G-13019)*

Mm Outsourcing LLC... 937 661-4300
355 S South St Leesburg (45135) *(G-9126)*

Mmei, Middlefield *Also Called: Molten Mtal Eqp Innvations LLC (G-10771)*

Mmf Inc.. 614 252-2522
1977 Mcallister Ave Columbus (43205) *(G-5573)*

Mmf Incorporated (PA).. 614 252-0078
1977 Mcallister Ave Columbus (43205) *(G-5574)*

Mmi Textiles Inc (PA).. 440 899-8050
1 American Rd Ste 950 Brooklyn (44144) *(G-1679)*

Mmp Printing, Moraine *Also Called: Andrin Enterprises Inc (G-11157)*

Mmp Printing Inc.. 513 381-0990
10570 Chester Rd Cincinnati (45215) *(G-3168)*

Mmp Toledo... 419 472-0505
5847 Secor Rd Toledo (43623) *(G-14388)*

Mn8-Foxfire, Cincinnati *Also Called: Evp International LLC (G-2890)*

Mo-Trim Inc.. 740 439-2725
240 Steubenville Ave Cambridge (43725) *(G-1943)*

Mob Apparel, Grove City *Also Called: Vandava Inc (G-8128)*

Mobex Global, Edon *Also Called: Linamar Strctures USA Mich Inc (G-7088)*

Mobex Global, Edon *Also Called: Linamar Strctures USA Mich Inc (G-7089)*

Mobile Conversions Inc.. 513 797-1991
3354 State Route 132 Amelia (45102) *(G-460)*

Mobile Operations, Van Wert *Also Called: Eaton Corporation (G-14914)*

Mobile Solutions LLC... 614 286-3944
149 N Hamilton Rd Columbus (43213) *(G-5575)*

Mock Woodworking Company LLC.............................. 740 452-2701
4400 West Pike Zanesville (43701) *(G-16546)*

MODE Industries Inc.. 614 504-8008
3000 E Main St Ste 134 Columbus (43209) *(G-5576)*

Model Graphics, West Chester *Also Called: Model GRaphics& Media Inc (G-15465)*

Model GRaphics& Media Inc... 513 541-2355
2614 Crescentville Rd West Chester (45069) *(G-15465)*

Model Medical LLC.. 216 972-0573
3429 Lee Rd Apt 12 Shaker Heights (44120) *(G-13156)*

Model Pattern & Foundry Co....................................... 513 542-2322
3242 Spring Grove Ave Cincinnati (45225) *(G-3169)*

Modern Builders Supply Inc.. 419 526-0002
85 Smith Ave Mansfield (44905) *(G-9698)*

Modern Builders Supply Inc (PA)............................... 419 241-3961
3500 Phillips Ave Toledo (43608) *(G-14389)*

Modern China Company Inc (PA)............................... 330 938-6104
550 E Ohio Ave Sebring (44672) *(G-13123)*

Modern Designs Inc... 330 644-1771
310 Killian Rd Green (44232) *(G-8025)*

Modern Engineering Inc.. 440 593-5414
527 W Adams St Conneaut (44030) *(G-5928)*

ALPHABETIC SECTION — Mondo Polymer Technologies Inc

Modern Ice Equipment & Sup Co (PA) 513 367-2101
5709 Harrison Ave Cincinnati (45248) *(G-3170)*

Modern Industries Inc 216 432-2855
6610 Metta Ave Cleveland (44103) *(G-4417)*

Modern Machine Development 937 253-4576
400 Linden Ave Ste 3 Dayton (45403) *(G-6454)*

Modern Manufacturing Inc (PA) 513 251-3600
240 Stille Dr Cincinnati (45233) *(G-3171)*

Modern Methods Brewing Co LLC 330 506-4613
197 Washington St Nw Warren (44483) *(G-15191)*

Modern Mold Corporation 440 236-9600
27684 Royalton Rd Columbia Station (44028) *(G-5014)*

Modern Pipe Supports Corp 216 361-1666
4734 Commerce Ave Cleveland (44103) *(G-4418)*

Modern Plastics Recovery Inc 419 622-4611
100 Main St Haviland (45851) *(G-8314)*

Modern Retail Solutions LLC 330 527-4308
10421 Industrial Dr Garrettsville (44231) *(G-7923)*

Modern Safety Techniques, Hicksville *Also Called: Mst Inc (G-8375)*

Modern Sheet Metal Works Inc 513 353-3666
6037 State Rte 128 Cleves (45002) *(G-4961)*

Modern Time Dealer, Uniontown *Also Called: Bbm Fairway Inc (G-14781)*

Modern Tour, Cincinnati *Also Called: Modern Ice Equipment & Sup Co (G-3170)*

Modern Transmission Dev Co
5903 Grafton Rd Valley City (44280) *(G-14880)*

Modern Welding Co Ohio Inc 740 344-9425
1 Modern Way Newark (43055) *(G-11593)*

Modernfold, Youngstown *Also Called: W B Becherer Inc (G-16473)*

Modroto 440 998-1202
4920 State Rd Ashtabula (44004) *(G-649)*

Modular Assmbly Innvations LLC (PA) 614 389-4860
600 Stonehenge Pkwy Ste 100 Dublin (43017) *(G-6912)*

Module 21 Bldg Company, Dayton *Also Called: M21 Industries LLC (G-6419)*

Moeller Brew Barn LLC 937 400-8628
416 E 1st St Dayton (45402) *(G-6455)*

Moeller Brew Barn LLC (PA) 419 925-3005
8016 Marion Dr Maria Stein (45860) *(G-9772)*

Moeller Brew Barn LLC 937 400-8626
6550 Hamilton Lebanon Rd Monroe (45044) *(G-11416)*

Moen, North Olmsted *Also Called: Moen Incorporated (G-11824)*

Moen Incorporated (HQ) 800 289-6636
25300 Al Moen Dr North Olmsted (44070) *(G-11824)*

Mohawk 11 Inc 614 771-0327
5529 Mirage Dr Hilliard (43026) *(G-8420)*

Mohawk Industries Inc 800 837-3812
3565 Urbancrest Industrial Dr Grove City (43123) *(G-8108)*

Mohawk Manufacturing Inc 860 632-2345
306 E Gambier St Mount Vernon (43050) *(G-11279)*

Mohican Industries Inc 330 869-0500
1225 W Market St Akron (44313) *(G-251)*

Mohler Lumber Company 330 499-5461
4214 Portage St Nw North Canton (44720) *(G-11744)*

Mohr Stamping Inc 440 647-4316
22038 Fairgrounds Rd Wellington (44090) *(G-15317)*

Mojonnier Usa LLC 844 665-6664
10325 State Route 43 Ste N Streetsboro (44241) *(G-13780)*

Mok Industries LLC 614 934-1734
4449 Easton Way Columbus (43219) *(G-5577)*

Mold Masters Inc 216 561-6653
18224 Fernway Rd Shaker Heights (44122) *(G-13157)*

Mold Masters Intl LLC 440 953-0220
34000 Melinz Pkwy Eastlake (44095) *(G-7042)*

Mold Shop Inc 419 829-2041
8520 Central Ave Sylvania (43560) *(G-14005)*

Mold Surface Textures Inc 330 678-8590
4485 Crystal Pkwy Ste 300 Kent (44240) *(G-8838)*

Mold Tech, Painesville *Also Called: Xponet Inc (G-12279)*

Mold-Rite Plastics LLC 330 405-7739
2222 Highland Rd Twinsburg (44087) *(G-14698)*

Mold-Rite Plastics LLC 330 405-7739
2300 Highland Rd Twinsburg (44087) *(G-14699)*

Molded Extruded 216 475-5491
23940 Miles Rd Bedford Heights (44128) *(G-1177)*

Molded Fiber Glass Companies (PA) 440 997-5851
2925 Mfg Pl Ashtabula (44004) *(G-650)*

Molded Fiber Glass Companies 440 997-5851
4401 Benefit Ave Ashtabula (44004) *(G-651)*

Molded Fiber Glass Companies 440 994-5100
1315 W 47th St Ashtabula (44004) *(G-652)*

Molders World Inc 513 469-6653
11471 Deerfield Rd Blue Ash (45242) *(G-1441)*

Molding Dynamics Inc 440 786-8100
7009 Krick Rd Bedford (44146) *(G-1138)*

Molding Technologies, Hebron *Also Called: Molding Technologies Ltd (G-8348)*

Molding Technologies, Hebron *Also Called: MTI Acquisition LLC (G-8351)*

Molding Technologies Ltd 740 929-2065
85 N. High Street Hebron (43025) *(G-8348)*

Moldmakers Inc 419 673-0902
13608 Us Highway 68 Kenton (43326) *(G-8892)*

Molorokalin Inc (DH) 330 629-1332
4137 Boardman Canfield Rd Ste Ll04 Canfield (44406) *(G-2012)*

Molson Coors Bev Co USA LLC 513 896-9200
2525 Wayne Madison Rd Trenton (45067) *(G-14542)*

Molten Metals, Middlefield *Also Called: Pckd Enterprises Inc (G-10779)*

Molten Mtal Eqp Innvations LLC 440 632-9119
15510 Old State Rd Middlefield (44062) *(G-10771)*

Molten North America Corp (DH) 419 425-2700
1835 Industrial Dr Findlay (45840) *(G-7539)*

Momentive Perf Mtrls Quartz 408 436-6221
22557 Lunn Rd Strongsville (44149) *(G-13854)*

Momentive Performance Mtls, Richmond Heights *Also Called: Momentive Performance Mtls Inc (G-12809)*

Momentive Performance Mtls Inc 614 986-2495
180 E Broad St Columbus (43215) *(G-5578)*

Momentive Performance Mtls Inc 740 928-7010
611 O Neill Dr Hebron (43025) *(G-8349)*

Momentive Performance Mtls Inc 440 878-5705
24400 Highland Rd Richmond Heights (44143) *(G-12809)*

Momentive Performance Mtls Inc 740 929-8732
4901 Campbell Rd Willoughby (44094) *(G-15955)*

Momentive Prfmce Mtls Qrtz Inc (HQ) 440 878-5700
22557 Lunn Rd Strongsville (44149) *(G-13855)*

Momentive Technologies, Strongsville *Also Called: Momentive Prfmce Mtls Qrtz Inc (G-13855)*

Momentum Fleet MGT Group Inc 440 759-2219
24481 Detroit Rd Westlake (44145) *(G-15765)*

Momma Js Blazing Kitchen LLC 216 551-8791
2281 S Overlook Rd Cleveland Heights (44106) *(G-4941)*

Momq Holding Company (PA) 440 878-5700
22557 Lunn Rd Strongsville (44149) *(G-13856)*

Mon-Say Corp 419 720-0163
2735 Dorr St Toledo (43607) *(G-14390)*

Monaco Plating Inc 216 206-2360
3555 E 91st St Cleveland (44105) *(G-4419)*

Monaghan & Associates Inc 937 253-7706
30 N Clinton St Dayton (45402) *(G-6456)*

Monaghan Tooling Group, Dayton *Also Called: Monaghan & Associates Inc (G-6456)*

Monarch, Cleveland *Also Called: Integrated Power Services LLC (G-4231)*

Monarch, Cleveland *Also Called: Monarch Steel Company Inc (G-4420)*

Monarch Engraving Inc 440 638-1500
8293 Dow Cir Strongsville (44136) *(G-13857)*

Monarch Plastic Inc 330 683-0822
516 Jefferson Ave Orrville (44667) *(G-12137)*

Monarch Products Co 330 868-7717
105 Short St Minerva (44657) *(G-11037)*

Monarch Steel Company Inc 216 587-8000
4650 Johnston Pkwy Cleveland (44128) *(G-4420)*

Monarch Water Systems Inc 937 426-5773
689 Greystone Dr Beavercreek (45434) *(G-1056)*

Mondi Pakaging 541 686-2665
3165 Wilson Rd Lancaster (43130) *(G-9025)*

Mondo Polymer Technologies Inc 740 376-9396
27620 State Route 7 Marietta (45750) *(G-9810)*

Monique Bath and Body Ltd 513 440-7370
6545 Market Ave N Canton (44721) *(G-2166)*

Monitor Mold & Machine Co. 330 697-7800
3393 Industry Rd Rootstown (44272) *(G-12855)*

Monks Copy Shop Inc 614 461-6438
47 E Gay St Columbus (43215) *(G-5579)*

Monode Marking Products Inc (PA) 440 975-8802
9200 Tyler Blvd Mentor (44060) *(G-10506)*

Monode Marking Products Inc 419 929-0346
149 High St New London (44851) *(G-11464)*

Monode Steel Stamp Inc 440 975-8802
7620 Tyler Blvd Mentor (44060) *(G-10507)*

Monroe Tool and Mfg Co 216 883-7360
3900 E 93rd St Cleveland (44105) *(G-4421)*

Monsanto, Greenville Also Called: Monsanto Company *(G-8052)*

Monsanto Company 937 548-7858
1051 Landsdowne Ave Greenville (45331) *(G-8052)*

Montgomery & Montgomery LLC 330 858-9533
80 N Pershing Ave Akron (44313) *(G-252)*

Montgomery License Bureau, Montgomery Also Called: D J Klingler Inc *(G-11129)*

Montgomery Mch Fabrication Inc 740 286-2863
206 Watts Blevins Rd Jackson (45640) *(G-8710)*

Montgomerys Pallet Service Inc 330 297-6677
7937 State Route 44 Ravenna (44266) *(G-12725)*

Monti Incorporated (PA) 513 761-7775
4510 Reading Rd Cincinnati (45229) *(G-3172)*

Montville Plastics, Parkman Also Called: Montville Plastics & Rubber Inc *(G-12285)*

Montville Plastics & Rbr LLC 440 548-2005
15567 Main Market Rd Parkman (44080) *(G-12284)*

Montville Plastics & Rubber Inc 440 548-3211
15567 Main Market Rd Parkman (44080) *(G-12285)*

Moog Inc 330 682-0010
1701 N Main St Orrville (44667) *(G-12138)*

Moonlight Woodworks LLC 440 836-3738
17607 Egbert Rd Bedford (44146) *(G-1139)*

Moonshine Screen Printing Inc 513 523-7775
23 N College Ave Oxford (45056) *(G-12211)*

Moorchild LLC 513 649-8867
6 S Broad St Middletown (45044) *(G-10845)*

Moore Mc Millen Holdings (PA) 330 745-3075
1850 Front St Cuyahoga Falls (44221) *(G-6105)*

Moore Chrome Products Company 419 843-3510
3525 Silica Rd Sylvania (43560) *(G-14006)*

Moore Industries Inc 419 485-5572
1317 Henricks Dr Montpelier (43543) *(G-11139)*

Moore Metal Finishing, Sylvania Also Called: Moore Chrome Products Company *(G-14006)*

Moore Mr Specialty Company 330 332-1229
1050 Pennsylvania Ave Salem (44460) *(G-13020)*

Moore Outdoor Sign Craftsman, Westerville Also Called: Ohio Shelterall Inc *(G-15717)*

Moore Well Services Inc 330 650-4443
246 N Cleveland Ave Mogadore (44260) *(G-11078)*

MOORE, R C LUMBER CO (INC), Caldwell Also Called: R C Moore Lumber Co *(G-1912)*

Mor-X Plastics, Youngstown Also Called: Jamen Tool & Die Co *(G-16382)*

Morbark LLC 330 264-8699
4255 E Lincoln Way Wooster (44691) *(G-16152)*

Mordies Inc 330 758-8050
556 Bev Rd Youngstown (44512) *(G-16402)*

More Manufacturing LLC 937 233-3898
4025 Lisa Dr Ste A Tipp City (45371) *(G-14142)*

More Than Gourmet, Akron Also Called: Ajinomoto Hlth Ntrtn N Amer In *(G-25)*

More Than Gourmet Holdings Inc 330 762-6652
929 Home Ave Akron (44310) *(G-253)*

Morehouse Logging LLC 740 501-0256
13494 Sand Hollow Rd Thornville (43076) *(G-14067)*

Morel Landscaping LLC 216 551-4395
3684 Forest Run Dr Richfield (44286) *(G-12791)*

Morgan Adhesives Company LLC (DH) 330 688-1111
4560 Darrow Rd Stow (44224) *(G-13709)*

Morgan Advanced Ceramics Inc 330 405-1033
2181 Pinnacle Pkwy Twinsburg (44087) *(G-14700)*

Morgan Advanced Materials 419 435-8182
200 N Town St Fostoria (44830) *(G-7645)*

Morgan Advanced Materials, Twinsburg Also Called: Morgan Advanced Ceramics Inc *(G-14700)*

Morgan AM&t 419 435-8182
200 N Town St Fostoria (44830) *(G-7646)*

Morgan County Herald, Mcconnelsville Also Called: Morgan County Publishing Co *(G-10284)*

Morgan County Publishing Co 740 962-3377
25 N 5th St Mcconnelsville (43756) *(G-10284)*

Morgan Engineering Systems Inc 330 821-4721
1182 E Summit St Alliance (44601) *(G-414)*

Morgan Engineering Systems Inc (PA) 330 823-6130
1049 S Mahoning Ave Alliance (44601) *(G-415)*

Morgan Engineering Systems Inc 330 545-9731
700 Dot St Girard (44420) *(G-7973)*

Morgan Litho, Cleveland Also Called: T D Dynamics Inc *(G-4765)*

Morgan Matroc (es) 440 232-8600
232 Forbes Rd Bedford (44146) *(G-1140)*

Morgan Mfg Plant No 3, Girard Also Called: Morgan Engineering Systems Inc *(G-7973)*

Morgan Site Services Inc 330 823-6120
1049 S Mahoning Ave Alliance (44601) *(G-416)*

Morgan Wood Products Inc 614 336-4000
9761 Fairway Dr Powell (43065) *(G-12678)*

Morgan4140 LLC 513 873-1426
4760 Paddock Rd Ste B Cincinnati (45229) *(G-3173)*

Mori Shuji 614 459-1296
3755 Mountview Rd Columbus (43220) *(G-5580)*

Moriroku Technology N Amer Inc (HQ) 937 548-3217
15000 Industrial Pkwy Marysville (43040) *(G-9928)*

Moritz Concrete Inc 419 529-3232
362 N Trimble Rd Mansfield (44906) *(G-9699)*

Moritz International Inc 419 526-5222
665 N Main St Mansfield (44902) *(G-9700)*

Moritz Materials Inc (PA) 419 281-0575
859 Faultless Dr Ashland (44805) *(G-593)*

Moritz Ready Mix Inc 419 253-0001
4083 Bennington Way Marengo (43334) *(G-9769)*

Morlan & Associates Inc 614 889-6152
4970 Scioto Darby Rd Ste D Hilliard (43026) *(G-8421)*

Morlan & Associates Inc (PA) 614 889-6152
4970 Scioto Darby Rd Ste D Hilliard (43026) *(G-8422)*

Morlock Asphalt Ltd 419 686-4601
9362 Mermill Rd Portage (43451) *(G-12635)*

Morning Journal, Lisbon Also Called: Ogden Newspapers Ohio Inc *(G-9322)*

Morning Journal, The, Lorain Also Called: Journal Register Company *(G-9416)*

Morning Pride Mfg LLC (HQ) 937 264-2662
1 Innovation Ct Dayton (45414) *(G-6457)*

Morning Pride Mfg LLC 937 264-1726
4978 Riverton Dr Dayton (45414) *(G-6458)*

Morningstar Cstm Woodworks LLC 740 508-7178
53611 Sandy Desert Rd Portland (45770) *(G-12639)*

Morris Bean & Company 937 767-7301
777 E Hyde Rd Yellow Springs (45387) *(G-16285)*

Morris Furniture Co Inc (PA) 937 874-7100
2377 Commerce Center Blvd Ste A Fairborn (45324) *(G-7320)*

Morris Home Furnishing, Fairborn Also Called: Morris Furniture Co Inc *(G-7320)*

Morris Technologies Inc 513 733-1611
11988 Tramway Dr Cincinnati (45241) *(G-3174)*

Morrison Custom Welding, Wooster Also Called: Iron Gate Industries LLC *(G-16134)*

Morrison Custom Welding Inc 330 464-1637
4399 E Moreland Rd Fredericksburg (44627) *(G-7727)*

Morrison Medical Ltd 800 438-6677
3735 Paragon Dr Columbus (43228) *(G-5581)*

Morrison Products Inc (PA) 216 486-4000
16900 S Waterloo Rd Cleveland (44110) *(G-4422)*

Morrison Sign Company Inc 614 276-1181
2757 Scioto Pkwy Columbus (43221) *(G-5582)*

Morrow Gravel, Morrow Also Called: Valley Asphalt Corporation *(G-11226)*

Morrow Gravel Company Inc (PA) 513 771-0820
11641 Mosteller Rd Cincinnati (45241) *(G-3175)*

Morse Enterprises Inc 513 229-3600
6678 Tri Way Dr Mason (45040) *(G-10031)*

Morton Buildings Inc 419 399-4549
14623 State Route 31 Kenton (43326) *(G-8893)*

ALPHABETIC SECTION

Morton Buildings Inc 419 675-2311
14483 State Route 31 Kenton (43326) *(G-8894)*

Morton Buildings Inc 330 345-6188
1055 Columbus Avenue Ext Wooster (44691) *(G-16153)*

Morton Buildings Plant, Kenton *Also Called: Morton Buildings Inc (G-8894)*

Morton Salt, Cincinnati *Also Called: Morton Salt Inc (G-3176)*

Morton Salt Inc 513 941-1578
5336 River Rd Cincinnati (45233) *(G-3176)*

Morton Salt Inc 216 664-0728
2100 W 3rd St Cleveland (44113) *(G-4423)*

Morton Salt Inc 330 925-3015
151 Industrial Ave Rittman (44270) *(G-12825)*

Mos International Inc 330 329-0905
3213 Peterboro Dr Stow (44224) *(G-13710)*

Mosher Machine & Tool Co Inc 937 258-8070
2201 Valley Springs Rd Beavercreek Township (45434) *(G-1085)*

Mosser Glass Inc 740 439-1827
9279 Cadiz Rd Cambridge (43725) *(G-1944)*

Mossing Machine and Tool Inc 419 476-5657
5225 Telegraph Rd Toledo (43612) *(G-14391)*

Motion Mobility & Design Inc 330 244-9723
6490 Promler St Nw North Canton (44720) *(G-11745)*

Motionsource International LLC 440 287-7037
31200 Solon Rd Ste 7 Solon (44139) *(G-13392)*

Motorola Solutions Inc 330 664-1610
3875 Embassy Pkwy Ste 280 Akron (44333) *(G-254)*

Motors & Drives Division, Norwood *Also Called: Siemens Industry Inc (G-12000)*

Mound Laser Photonics Center, Kettering *Also Called: Resonetics LLC (G-8909)*

Mound Manufacturing Center Inc 937 236-8387
33 Commerce Park Dr Dayton (45404) *(G-6459)*

Mound Printing Company Inc 937 866-2872
2455 Belvo Rd Miamisburg (45342) *(G-10664)*

Mound Steel Corp 937 748-2937
25 Mound Park Dr Springboro (45066) *(G-13510)*

Mound Technologies Inc 937 748-2937
25 Mound Park Dr Springboro (45066) *(G-13511)*

Moundbuilders Babe Ruth Basbal 740 345-6830
429 Ohio St Newark (43055) *(G-11594)*

Mount Eaton Division, Mount Eaton *Also Called: Flex Technologies Inc (G-11230)*

Mount Hope Planing 330 359-0538
7598 Tr652 Millersburg (44654) *(G-10984)*

Mount Vernon News, Mount Vernon *Also Called: Progrssive Communications Corp (G-11290)*

Mount Vernon Packaging Inc 740 397-3221
135 Progress Dr Mount Vernon (43050) *(G-11280)*

Mount Vernon Steel, Mount Vernon *Also Called: Mt Vernon Machine & Tool Inc (G-11282)*

Mountain Tarp, Ravenna *Also Called: Tarped Out Inc (G-12738)*

Mountain Top Frozen Pies Div, Columbus *Also Called: Quality Bakery Company Inc (G-5702)*

Mountaineer Industries LLC 740 676-1100
5310 Guernsey St Bellaire (43906) *(G-1189)*

Move Ez Inc 844 466-8339
855 Grandview Ave Ste 140 Columbus (43215) *(G-5583)*

Moveeasy, Columbus *Also Called: Move Ez Inc (G-5583)*

Mowhawk Lumber Ltd 330 698-5333
2931 S Carr Rd Apple Creek (44606) *(G-507)*

Moyer Vineyards Inc 937 549-2957
16765 Malady Rd Mount Orab (45154) *(G-11243)*

Moyer Winery & Restaurant, Mount Orab *Also Called: Moyer Vineyards Inc (G-11243)*

Mp Acquisition Group LLC 513 554-6120
9283 Sutton Pl West Chester (45011) *(G-15466)*

Mp Biomedicals LLC 440 337-1200
29525 Fountain Pkwy Solon (44139) *(G-13393)*

Mp Technologies Inc 440 838-4466
532 County Road 1600 Ashland (44805) *(G-594)*

Mpac Switchback, Cleveland *Also Called: Switchback Group Inc (G-4762)*

Mpc Inc 440 835-1405
5350 Tradex Pkwy Cleveland (44102) *(G-4424)*

MPC Plastics Inc 216 881-7220
1859 E 63rd St Cleveland (44103) *(G-4425)*

MPC Plating LLC 216 881-7220
9921 Clinton Rd Cleveland (44144) *(G-4426)*

Mpc Plating Inc 216 881-7220
9921 Clinton Rd Brooklyn (44144) *(G-1680)*

Mpe Aeroengines Inc 937 878-3800
7700 New Carlisle Pike Huber Heights (45424) *(G-8578)*

Mpi Label Systems., Sebring *Also Called: Mpi Labels of Baltimore Inc (G-13124)*

Mpi Labels of Baltimore Inc (HQ) 330 938-2134
450 Courtney Rd Sebring (44672) *(G-13124)*

Mpi Logistics and Service Inc 330 832-5309
1414 Industrial Ave Sw Massillon (44647) *(G-10130)*

Mplx GP LLC 419 422-2121
539 S Main St Findlay (45840) *(G-7540)*

Mplx Terminals LLC 330 479-5539
2408 Gambrinus Ave Sw Canton (44706) *(G-2167)*

MPW Industrial Svcs Group Inc (PA) 740 927-8790
9711 Lancaster Rd Hebron (43025) *(G-8350)*

Mr Box, Mansfield *Also Called: Skybox Packaging LLC (G-9719)*

Mr Emblem Inc 419 697-1888
3209 Navarre Ave Oregon (43616) *(G-12108)*

Mr Heater, Cleveland *Also Called: Enerco Group Inc (G-4015)*

Mr Heater Inc 216 916-3000
4560 W 160th St Cleveland (44135) *(G-4427)*

Mr Label Inc 513 681-2088
5018 Gray Rd Cincinnati (45232) *(G-3177)*

Mr O Fficials LLC 216 240-2534
4408 Brooks Rd Cleveland (44105) *(G-4428)*

Mr. Heater, Cleveland *Also Called: Enerco Technical Products Inc (G-4016)*

MRC & Associates, Dayton *Also Called: Michele Caldwell (G-6442)*

Mrd Solutions LLC 440 942-6969
34201 Melinz Pkwy Unit A Eastlake (44095) *(G-7043)*

Mrl, Xenia *Also Called: Mrl Materials Resources LLC (G-16269)*

Mrl Materials Resources LLC 937 531-6657
123 Fairground Rd Xenia (45385) *(G-16269)*

Mro Built LLC 330 526-0555
6410 Promway Ave Nw North Canton (44720) *(G-11746)*

Mro Built, Inc., North Canton *Also Called: Mro Built LLC (G-11746)*

Mrpicker 440 354-6497
595 Miner Rd Cleveland (44143) *(G-4429)*

Mrs Electronic Inc 937 660-6767
6680 Poe Ave Ste 100 Dayton (45414) *(G-6460)*

MRS Industrial Inc 614 308-1070
2583 Harrison Rd Columbus (43204) *(G-5584)*

Mrs Mllers Hmmade Noodles Ltd 330 694-5814
9140 County Road 192 Fredericksburg (44627) *(G-7728)*

Mrt LLC 330 533-0721
5670 Mission Hills Dr Canfield (44406) *(G-2013)*

Ms Murcko & Sons LLC 724 854-4907
8090 Chestnut Ridge Rd Hubbard (44425) *(G-8568)*

Ms Welding LLC 419 925-4141
8070 Flyer Dr Maria Stein (45860) *(G-9773)*

MSC Industries Inc 440 474-8788
5131 Ireland Rd Rome (44085) *(G-12849)*

MSC Walbridge Coatings Inc 419 666-6130
30610 E Broadway St Walbridge (43465) *(G-15085)*

Msf Acres LLC 330 857-0257
2600 Kidron Rd Orrville (44667) *(G-12139)*

Msg Premier Molded Fiber, Ashtabula *Also Called: Molded Fiber Glass Companies (G-651)*

MSI, Chesterland *Also Called: Metzenbaum Sheltered Inds Inc (G-2485)*

MSI Surfaces, West Chester *Also Called: M S International Inc (G-15460)*

Msk Trencher Mfg Inc 419 394-4444
7219 Harris Rd Celina (45822) *(G-2341)*

Msls Group LLC 330 723-4431
1080 Industrial Pkwy Medina (44256) *(G-10355)*

Msm Fundraising LLC 740 369-8160
2083 Klondike Rd Delaware (43015) *(G-6738)*

Mssi Group Inc 440 439-1040
7500 Northfield Rd Walton Hills (44146) *(G-15102)*

Mssk Manufacturing Inc 330 393-6624
400 Dietz Rd Ne Warren (44483) *(G-15192)*

MST, Kent *Also Called: Mold Surface Textures Inc (G-8838)*

Mst Inc 419 542-6645
11370 Breininger Rd Hicksville (43526) *(G-8375)*

Mt Eaton Pallet Ltd 330 893-2986
   4761 County Road 207 Millersburg (44654) *(G-10985)*

Mt Perry Foods Inc 740 743-3890
   5705 State Route 204 Ne Mount Perry (43760) *(G-11251)*

Mt Pleasant Blacktopping Inc 513 874-3777
   3199 Production Dr Fairfield (45014) *(G-7385)*

Mt Pleasant Pharmacy LLC 216 672-4377
   631 Lee Rd Apt 1228 Bedford (44146) *(G-1141)*

Mt Vernon Cy Wastewater Trtmnt 740 393-9502
   3 Cougar Dr Unit 3 Mount Vernon (43050) *(G-11281)*

Mt Vernon Machine & Tool Inc 740 397-0311
   8585 Blackjack Road Ext Mount Vernon (43050) *(G-11282)*

Mt Vernon Mold Works Inc 618 242-6040
   2200 Massillon Rd Akron (44312) *(G-255)*

Mt.pleasant Blacktopping, Fairfield *Also Called: Mt Pleasant Blacktopping Inc (G-7385)*

Mtc Electroceramics 440 232-8600
   232 Forbes Rd Bedford (44146) *(G-1142)*

Mtd Consumer Group Inc (DH) 330 225-2600
   5965 Grafton Rd Valley City (44280) *(G-14881)*

Mtd Consumer Products Supply, Valley City *Also Called: Mtd Products Inc (G-14885)*

Mtd Holdings Inc (HQ) 330 225-2600
   5965 Grafton Rd Valley City (44280) *(G-14882)*

Mtd International Operations (DH) 330 225-2600
   5965 Grafton Rd Valley City (44280) *(G-14883)*

Mtd Products Inc 419 342-6455
   305 Mansfield Ave Shelby (44875) *(G-13196)*

Mtd Products Inc (DH) 330 225-2600
   5965 Grafton Rd Valley City (44280) *(G-14884)*

Mtd Products Inc 330 225-1940
   5903 Grafton Rd Valley City (44280) *(G-14885)*

Mtd Products Inc 330 225-9127
   680 Liverpool Dr Valley City (44280) *(G-14886)*

Mtd Products Inc 419 951-9779
   810 Theo Moll Dr Willard (44890) *(G-15861)*

Mtd Products Inc 419 935-6611
   979 S Conwell Ave Willard (44890) *(G-15862)*

MTI Acquisition LLC 740 929-2065
   85 N High St Hebron (43025) *(G-8351)*

Mto Suncoke, Middletown *Also Called: Suncoke Energy Inc (G-10860)*

Mudbrook Golf Ctr At Thndrbird 419 433-2945
   1609 Mudbrook Rd Huron (44839) *(G-8640)*

Mueller Art Cover & Binding Co 440 238-3303
   12005 Alameda Dr Strongsville (44149) *(G-13858)*

Mueller Electric Company Inc (HQ) 216 771-5225
   2850 Gilchrist Rd Ste 5 Akron (44305) *(G-256)*

Mueller Electric Company Inc 614 888-8855
   7795 Walton Pkwy Ste 175 New Albany (43054) *(G-11384)*

Muhlenberg County Coal Co LLC 740 338-3100
   46226 National Rd Saint Clairsville (43950) *(G-12914)*

Muir Graphics Inc 419 882-7993
   5454 Alger Dr Ste A Sylvania (43560) *(G-14007)*

Mulch Manufacturing Inc (HQ) 614 864-4004
   6747 Taylor Rd Sw Reynoldsburg (43068) *(G-12769)*

Mulch Masters of Ohio, Miamisburg *Also Called: Gayston Corporation (G-10640)*

Mulhern Belting Inc 201 337-5700
   310 Osborne Dr Fairfield (45014) *(G-7386)*

Mull Iron, Rittman *Also Called: Rittman Inc (G-12827)*

Muller Engine & Machine Co 937 322-1861
   1414 S Yellow Springs St Springfield (45506) *(G-13607)*

Muller Pipe Organ Co 740 893-1700
   122 N High St Croton (43013) *(G-6051)*

Muller Pipe Organ Company, Croton *Also Called: Muller Pipe Organ Co (G-6051)*

Mullet Enterprises Inc (PA) 330 852-4681
   138 2nd St Nw Sugarcreek (44681) *(G-13932)*

Mullins Rubber Products Inc 937 233-4211
   2949 Valley Pike Dayton (45404) *(G-6461)*

Multi Cast LLC 419 335-0010
   225 E Linfoot St Wauseon (43567) *(G-15269)*

Multi Galvanizing LLC 330 453-1441
   825 Navarre Rd Sw Canton (44707) *(G-2168)*

Multi Lapping Service Inc 440 944-7592
   30032 Lakeland Blvd Wickliffe (44092) *(G-15840)*

Multi Products Company 330 674-5981
   7188 State Route 39 Millersburg (44654) *(G-10986)*

Multi Radiance Medical, Solon *Also Called: Medical Quant USA Inc (G-13384)*

Multi-Color, Batavia *Also Called: Verstrete In Mold Lbels USA In (G-959)*

Multi-Color, Mason *Also Called: McC - Mason W&S (G-10027)*

Multi-Color Australia LLC (DH) 513 381-1480
   4053 Clough Woods Dr Batavia (45103) *(G-938)*

Multi-Color Corporation (HQ) 513 381-1480
   4053 Clough Woods Dr Batavia (45103) *(G-939)*

Multi-Color Corporation 513 459-3283
   5510 Courseview Dr Mason (45040) *(G-10032)*

Multi-Craft Litho Inc 859 581-2754
   4440 Creek Rd Blue Ash (45242) *(G-1442)*

Multi-Form Plastics, Batavia *Also Called: Plastikos Corporation (G-943)*

Multi-Plastics Inc (PA) 740 548-4894
   7770 N Central Dr Lewis Center (43035) *(G-9172)*

Multi-Valve Technology Inc 330 608-4096
   1100 Triplett Blvd Akron (44306) *(G-257)*

Multi-Wing America Inc 440 834-9400
   15030 Berkshire Industrial Pkwy Middlefield (44062) *(G-10772)*

Multibase Inc 330 666-0505
   3835 Conley Rd Copley (44321) *(G-5952)*

Multifab, Elyria *Also Called: Multilink Inc (G-7183)*

Multilink Inc 440 366-6966
   580 Ternes Ln Elyria (44035) *(G-7183)*

Multiple Products Company, Cleveland *Also Called: Kg63 LLC (G-4286)*

Multiple Products Company, Cleveland *Also Called: Kg63 LLC (G-4287)*

Mum Industries Inc (PA) 440 269-4966
   8989 Tyler Blvd Mentor (44060) *(G-10508)*

Mumford's Potato Chip, Urbana *Also Called: Mumfords Potato Chips & Deli (G-14844)*

Mumfords Potato Chips & Deli 937 653-3491
   325 N Main St Urbana (43078) *(G-14844)*

Muncy Corporation 937 346-0800
   2020 Progress Rd Springfield (45505) *(G-13608)*

Municipal Brew Works LLC 513 889-8369
   306 Ashley Brook Dr Hamilton (45013) *(G-8230)*

Munson Machine Company Inc 740 967-6867
   80 E College Ave Johnstown (43031) *(G-8774)*

Murotech Ohio Corporation 419 394-6529
   550 Mckinley Rd Saint Marys (45885) *(G-12958)*

Murphy Dog LLC 614 755-4278
   225 Business Center Dr Blacklick (43004) *(G-1341)*

Murphy Tractor & Eqp Co Inc 330 220-4999
   1550 Industrial Pkwy Brunswick (44212) *(G-1774)*

Murphy Tractor & Eqp Co Inc 330 477-9304
   1509 Raff Rd Sw Canton (44710) *(G-2169)*

Murphy Tractor & Eqp Co Inc 614 876-1141
   2121 Walcutt Rd Columbus (43228) *(G-5585)*

Murphy Tractor & Eqp Co Inc 419 221-3666
   3550 Saint Johns Rd Lima (45804) *(G-9272)*

Murphy Tractor & Eqp Co Inc 937 898-4198
   1015 Industrial Park Dr Vandalia (45377) *(G-14954)*

Murphy's Landing Casual Dining, Middletown *Also Called: Moorchild LLC (G-10845)*

Murr Corporation 330 264-2223
   201 N Buckeye St Wooster (44691) *(G-16154)*

Murr Printing and Graphics, Wooster *Also Called: Murr Corporation (G-16154)*

Murray American Energy Inc (DH) 740 338-3100
   46226 National Rd Saint Clairsville (43950) *(G-12915)*

Murray Display Fixtures Ltd 614 875-1594
   2300 Southwest Blvd Grove City (43123) *(G-8109)*

Murray Fabrics Inc (PA) 216 881-4041
   837 E 79th St Cleveland (44103) *(G-4430)*

Murray Machine and Tool Inc 216 267-1126
   17801 Sheldon Rd Side Cleveland (44130) *(G-4431)*

Murrubber Technologies Inc 330 688-4881
   1350 Commerce Dr Stow (44224) *(G-13711)*

Muscle Feast LLC (PA) 740 877-8808
   1320 Boston Rd Nashport (43830) *(G-11339)*

Muskingum Grinding and Mch Co 740 622-4741
   2155 Otsego Ave Coshocton (43812) *(G-5986)*

Mustang Dynamometer, Twinsburg *Also Called: Ganzcorp Investments Inc (G-14664)*

Mustang Printing.. 419 592-2746
119 W Washington St Napoleon (43545) *(G-11325)*

Mustard Seed Health Fd Mkt Inc.. 440 519-3663
6025 Kruse Dr Ste 100 Solon (44139) *(G-13394)*

Muster Rdu Inc... 614 537-5440
1450 E Walnut St Lancaster (43130) *(G-9026)*

Mutual Tool LLC.. 937 667-5818
1350 Commerce Park Dr Tipp City (45371) *(G-14143)*

Mveca, Yellow Springs *Also Called: Miami Valley Eductl Cmpt Assn (G-16284)*

Mvp Pharmacy.. 614 449-8000
1931 Parsons Ave Columbus (43207) *(G-5586)*

Mvp Plastics Inc (PA)... 440 834-1790
15005 Enterprise Way Middlefield (44062) *(G-10773)*

Mw Metals Group LLC.. 937 222-5992
461 Homestead Ave Dayton (45417) *(G-6462)*

Mwgh LLC... 513 521-4114
9070 Pippin Rd Cincinnati (45251) *(G-3178)*

Mwi Dmntable Office Partitions, Lorain *Also Called: M/W International Inc (G-9423)*

Mxr Imaging Inc.. 614 219-2011
4770 Northwest Pkwy Hilliard (43026) *(G-8423)*

My Alarm, Franklin *Also Called: Valued Relationships Inc (G-7708)*

My Floors By Prints and Paints, Galion *Also Called: Prints & Paints Flr Cvg Co Inc (G-7883)*

My Second Home Early Lrng Schl, Marysville *Also Called: New Republic Industries LLC (G-9929)*

My Soaps LLC... 614 832-4634
250 W Coshocton St Johnstown (43031) *(G-8775)*

My Splash Pad.. 330 705-1802
9897 Byers Ave Louisville (44641) *(G-9465)*

My Way Home Finder Magazine.. 419 841-6201
5215 Monroe St Ste 14 Toledo (43623) *(G-14392)*

Mye Automotive Inc... 330 253-5592
1293 S Main St Akron (44301) *(G-258)*

Myers.. 419 727-2010
1500 E Alexis Rd Toledo (43612) *(G-14393)*

Myers and Lasch Inc... 440 235-2050
2530 Wyndgate Ct Westlake (44145) *(G-15766)*

Myers Controlled Power LLC.. 909 923-1800
133 Taft Ave Ne Canton (44720) *(G-2170)*

Myers FSI, North Canton *Also Called: Myers Power Products Inc (G-11747)*

Myers Industries, Akron *Also Called: Myers Industries Inc (G-260)*

Myers Industries Inc.. 330 253-5592
1293 S Main St Akron (44301) *(G-259)*

Myers Industries Inc (PA).. 330 253-5592
1293 S Main St Akron (44301) *(G-260)*

Myers Industries Inc.. 330 821-4700
2290 W Main St Alliance (44601) *(G-417)*

Myers Industries Inc.. 440 632-1006
15150 Madison Rd Middlefield (44062) *(G-10774)*

Myers Industries Inc.. 330 336-6621
250 Seville Rd Wadsworth (44281) *(G-15047)*

Myers Machining Inc.. 330 874-3005
11789 Strasburg Bolivar Rd Nw Bolivar (44612) *(G-1529)*

Myers Power Products Inc (PA).. 330 834-3200
219 E Maple St Ste 100/200e North Canton (44720) *(G-11747)*

Myers Precision Grinding Inc... 216 587-3737
19500 S Miles Rd Cleveland (44128) *(G-4432)*

Myfootshopcom LLC... 740 522-5681
1159 Cherry Valley Rd Se Newark (43055) *(G-11595)*

Myriad Industries Inc... 619 232-6700
6011 Houseman Rd Ostrander (43061) *(G-12175)*

Myrlen, Cincinnati *Also Called: Ep Bollinger LLC (G-2878)*

Mysta Equipment Co... 330 879-5353
6434 Werstler Ave Sw Navarre (44662) *(G-11347)*

Mystic Chemical Products Co... 216 251-4416
3561 W 105th St Cleveland (44111) *(G-4433)*

N & G Takhar Oil LLC... 937 604-0012
4365 Lisa Dr Tipp City (45371) *(G-14144)*

N & W Machining & Fabg Inc.. 937 695-5582
8 Mathias Rd Winchester (45697) *(G-16074)*

N A C, Findlay *Also Called: Nichidai America Corporation (G-7542)*

N A D, Cincinnati *Also Called: National Access Design LLC (G-3179)*

N E C Columbus, Columbus *Also Called: National Electric Coil Inc (G-5589)*

N F M, Massillon *Also Called: Nfm/Welding Engineers Inc (G-10131)*

N G C, North Royalton *Also Called: Next Gerenation Crimping (G-11888)*

N J E M A Magazine, Cincinnati *Also Called: Sesh Communications (G-3384)*

N M Hansen Machine and Tool, Toledo *Also Called: Rogar International Inc (G-14458)*

N N I, Cleveland *Also Called: Norman Noble Inc (G-4464)*

N S B, Cincinnati *Also Called: National Scoreboards LLC (G-3181)*

N W P Manufacturing, Waldo *Also Called: Nwp Manufacturing Inc (G-15089)*

N Wasserstrom & Sons Inc.. 614 737-5410
862 E Jenkins Ave Columbus (43207) *(G-5587)*

N Wasserstrom & Sons Inc (HQ).. 614 228-5550
2300 Lockbourne Rd Columbus (43207) *(G-5588)*

N-Molecular Inc.. 440 439-5356
7650 First Pl Ste B Oakwood Village (44146) *(G-12040)*

N-Viro, Toledo *Also Called: N-Viro International Corp (G-14394)*

N-Viro International Corp... 419 535-6374
2254 Centennial Rd Toledo (43617) *(G-14394)*

N2 Publishing.. 937 641-8277
3634 Watertower Ln Ste 4 West Carrollton (45449) *(G-15355)*

N2 Publishing, Pickerington *Also Called: Cbus Inc (G-12458)*

N2y LLC... 419 433-9800
909 University Dr S Huron (44839) *(G-8641)*

NA Financial Service Center, Cleveland *Also Called: Eaton Corporation (G-3993)*

Nabco Entrances, Sylvania *Also Called: Nabco Entrances Inc (G-14008)*

Nabco Entrances Inc... 419 842-0484
3407 Silica Rd Sylvania (43560) *(G-14008)*

Nabors & Nabors Ltd.. 440 846-0000
627 Redstone Cir Brunswick (44212) *(G-1775)*

Nacco Industries Inc (PA).. 440 229-5151
5875 Landerbrook Dr Ste 220 Cleveland (44124) *(G-4434)*

Nachurs Alpine Solutions LLC (HQ)... 740 382-5701
421 Leader St Marion (43302) *(G-9864)*

Nachurs Alpine Solutions Corp, Marion *Also Called: Nachurs Alpine Solutions LLC (G-9864)*

Nagase Chemtex America LLC... 740 362-4444
100 Innovation Ct Delaware (43015) *(G-6739)*

Nalk Woods LLC.. 216 548-0994
832 Sioux Ln Macedonia (44056) *(G-9563)*

Namoh Ohio Holdings Inc (PA)   5612 Carthage Ave Norwood (45212) *(G-11996)*

Nancy Blanket, Mount Sterling *Also Called: Watershed Mangement LLC (G-11258)*

Nancys Draperies Inc... 330 855-7751
57 S Main St Marshallville (44645) *(G-9894)*

Nanofiber Solutions LLC.. 614 319-3075
5164 Blazer Pkwy Dublin (43017) *(G-6913)*

Nanogate North America LLC.. 419 522-7745
515 Newman St Mansfield (44902) *(G-9701)*

Nanogate North America LLC.. 419 747-1096
1555 W Longview Ave Mansfield (44906) *(G-9702)*

Nanolap Technologies LLC.. 877 658-4949
85 Harrisburg Dr Englewood (45322) *(G-7237)*

Nanosperse LLC.. 937 296-5030
2000 Composite Dr Kettering (45420) *(G-8908)*

Nanotronics, Cuyahoga Falls *Also Called: Nanotronics Imaging Inc (G-6106)*

Nanotronics Imaging Inc (PA)... 330 926-9809
2251 Front St Ste 110 Cuyahoga Falls (44221) *(G-6106)*

Napoleon Inc... 419 592-5055
595 E Riverview Ave Napoleon (43545) *(G-11326)*

Napoleon Machine LLC.. 419 591-7010
476 E Riverview Ave Napoleon (43545) *(G-11327)*

Napoleon Spring Works Inc (HQ)... 419 445-1010
111 Weires Dr Archbold (43502) *(G-537)*

Napoli's Pizza, Belpre *Also Called: Wal-Bon of Ohio Inc (G-1261)*

Naprotek, Independence *Also Called: Naprotek Holdings LLC (G-8676)*

Naprotek Holdings LLC.. 408 830-5000
5005 Rockside Rd Ste 840 Independence (44131) *(G-8676)*

Naptime Productions LLC.. 419 662-9521
107 Hidden Cove St Rossford (43460) *(G-12868)*

Narrow Way Custom Tech Inc... 937 743-1611
100 Industry Dr Carlisle (45005) *(G-2290)*

ALPHABETIC SECTION

Nasg Auto-Seat Tec LLC.. 419 359-5954
19911 County Rd T Ridgeville Corners (43555) *(G-12815)*

Nasg Ohio LLC.. 419 634-3125
605 E Montford Ave Ada (45810) *(G-4)*

Nasg Seating Bryan LLC.. 419 633-0662
633 Commerce Dr Bryan (43506) *(G-1829)*

Nasg Sting Rdgvlle Corners LLC (HQ).. 419 267-5240
19911 County Rd T Ridgeville Corners (43555) *(G-12816)*

Nasg Tooling and Automtn LLC.. 419 359-5954
19963 County Rd T Ridgeville Corners (43555) *(G-12817)*

Nat2 Inc.. 614 270-2507
1675 James Pkwy Heath (43056) *(G-8325)*

Nat2 Inc (PA).. 614 270-2507
8754 Cotter St Lewis Center (43035) *(G-9173)*

Nate's Nectar, De Graff *Also Called: Nates Nectar LLC (G-6665)*

Nates Nectar LLC.. 937 935-3289
4684 Township Road 53 De Graff (43318) *(G-6665)*

Nation Tool & Die Ltd.. 419 822-5939
5226 County Road 6 Delta (43515) *(G-6789)*

Nation Welding LLC.. 419 466-2241
5226 County Road 6 Delta (43515) *(G-6790)*

National Access Design LLC.. 513 351-3400
1871 Summit Rd Cincinnati (45237) *(G-3179)*

National Aerospace Proc LLC.. 234 900-6497
1330 Commerce Dr Stow (44224) *(G-13712)*

National Aviation Products Inc (DH).. 330 688-6494
4880 Hudson Dr Stow (44224) *(G-13713)*

National Beef Ohio LLC.. 800 449-2333
2208 Grant Rd North Baltimore (45872) *(G-11697)*

National Beef Packing Co LLC.. 419 257-5500
2208 Grant Rd North Baltimore (45872) *(G-11698)*

National Beverage, Obetz *Also Called: Shasta Beverages Inc (G-12064)*

National Beverage Corp.. 614 491-5415
4685 Groveport Rd Obetz (43207) *(G-12063)*

National Bias Fabric Co.. 216 361-0530
4516 Saint Clair Ave Cleveland (44103) *(G-4435)*

National Biological Corp.. 216 831-0600
23700 Mercantile Rd Beachwood (44122) *(G-1001)*

National Bronze Mtls Ohio Inc.. 440 277-1226
5311 W River Rd Lorain (44055) *(G-9425)*

National Carton & Coating Company.. 937 347-1042
1439 Lavelle Dr Xenia (45385) *(G-16270)*

National Colloid Company.. 740 282-1171
906 Adams St Steubenville (43952) *(G-13673)*

National Compressor Svcs LLC (PA).. 419 868-4980
10349 Industrial St Holland (43528) *(G-8519)*

National Con Burial Vlt Assn.. 407 788-1996
136 S Keowee St Dayton (45402) *(G-6463)*

National Diamond Tl & Coating, Westlake *Also Called: Diamond Reserve Inc (G-15745)*

National Door and Trim Inc.. 419 238-9345
1189 Grill Rd Van Wert (45891) *(G-14924)*

National Electric Coil Inc (PA).. 614 488-1151
800 King Ave Columbus (43212) *(G-5589)*

National Electro-Coatings Inc.. 216 898-0080
15655 Brookpark Rd Cleveland (44142) *(G-4436)*

National Engrg Archtctral Svcs, Columbus *Also Called: Barr Engineering Incorporated (G-5175)*

National Extrusion & Mfg Co, Bellefontaine *Also Called: McKnight Industries Inc (G-1216)*

National Fleet Svcs Ohio LLC.. 440 930-5177
607 Miller Rd Avon Lake (44012) *(G-818)*

National Foods Packaging Inc.. 216 622-2740
8200 Madison Ave Cleveland (44102) *(G-4437)*

National Frt Vgtable Tech Corp.. 740 400-4055
250 Civic Center Dr Columbus (43215) *(G-5590)*

National Gas & Oil Corporation (DH).. 740 344-2102
1500 Granville Rd Newark (43055) *(G-11596)*

National Glass Service Group, Dublin *Also Called: National Glass Svc Group LLC (G-6914)*

National Glass Svc Group LLC.. 614 652-3699
5500 Frantz Rd Ste 120 Dublin (43017) *(G-6914)*

National Illmination Sign Corp.. 419 866-1666
6525 Angola Rd Holland (43528) *(G-8520)*

National Indus Concepts Inc.. 615 989-9101
170 N Park Dr Chillicothe (45601) *(G-2520)*

National Lien Digest, Highland Heights *Also Called: C & S Associates Inc (G-8383)*

National Lime and Stone Co.. 419 562-0771
4580 Bethel Rd Bucyrus (44820) *(G-1863)*

National Lime and Stone Co.. 419 396-7671
370 N Patterson St Carey (43316) *(G-2281)*

National Lime and Stone Co.. 740 548-4206
2406 S Section Line Rd Delaware (43015) *(G-6740)*

National Lime and Stone Co.. 419 423-3400
9860 County Road 313 Findlay (45840) *(G-7541)*

National Lime and Stone Co.. 419 228-3434
1314 Findlay Rd Lima (45801) *(G-9273)*

National Lime and Stone Co.. 614 497-0083
5911 Lockbourne Rd Lockbourne (43137) *(G-9340)*

National Lime and Stone Co.. 740 387-3485
700 Likens Rd Marion (43302) *(G-9865)*

National Lime and Stone Co.. 330 966-4836
5377 Lauby Rd North Canton (44720) *(G-11748)*

National Lime and Stone Co.. 419 657-6745
18430 Main Street Rd Wapakoneta (45895) *(G-15128)*

National Lime Stone Clmbus Reg, Delaware *Also Called: National Lime and Stone Co (G-6740)*

National Machine Company (HQ).. 330 688-6494
4880 Hudson Dr Stow (44224) *(G-13714)*

National Machine Company, Mansfield *Also Called: Buckler Industries Inc (G-9633)*

National Machine Tool Company.. 513 541-6682
2013 E Galbraith Rd Cincinnati (45215) *(G-3180)*

National Machinery LLC (HQ).. 419 447-5211
161 Greenfield St Tiffin (44883) *(G-14095)*

National Metal Shapes Inc.. 740 363-9559
425 S Sandusky St Ste 1 Delaware (43015) *(G-6741)*

National Office Services, Cleveland *Also Called: National Electro-Coatings Inc (G-4436)*

National Oil Products, Hamilton *Also Called: Wallover Oil Hamilton Inc (G-8257)*

National Oilwell Varco LP.. 937 454-4660
5870 Poe Ave Dayton (45414) *(G-6464)*

National Pallet & Mulch LLC.. 937 237-1643
3550 Intercity Dr Dayton (45424) *(G-6465)*

National Pattern Mfgco.. 330 682-6871
1200 N Main St Orrville (44667) *(G-12140)*

National Peening.. 216 342-9155
23800 Corbin Dr Unit B Bedford Heights (44128) *(G-1178)*

National Plating Corporation.. 216 341-6707
6701 Hubbard Ave Ste 1 Cleveland (44127) *(G-4438)*

National Polishing Systems Inc.. 330 659-6547
9299 Market Pl Broadview Heights (44147) *(G-1662)*

National Polymer Dev Co Inc.. 440 708-1245
10200 Gottschalk Pkwy Ste 4 Chagrin Falls (44023) *(G-2408)*

National Polymer Inc.. 440 708-1245
10200 Gottschalk Pkwy Chagrin Falls (44023) *(G-2409)*

National Power Coating Ohio.. 330 405-5587
2020 Case Pkwy Twinsburg (44087) *(G-14701)*

National Pride Equipment, Mansfield *Also Called: National Pride Equipment Inc (G-9703)*

National Pride Equipment Inc.. 419 289-2886
905 Hickory Ln Ste 101 Mansfield (44905) *(G-9703)*

National Production, Newark *Also Called: Ngo Development Corporation (G-11598)*

National Pwdr Coating Ohio LLC.. 330 405-5587
2060 Case Pkwy Twinsburg (44087) *(G-14702)*

National Rolled Thread Die Co.. 440 232-8101
7051 Krick Rd Cleveland (44146) *(G-4439)*

National Roller Die Inc.. 440 951-3850
4750 Beidler Rd Unit 4 Willoughby (44094) *(G-15956)*

National Safety Apparel Inc (PA).. 216 941-1111
15825 Industrial Pkwy Cleveland (44135) *(G-4440)*

National Scoreboards LLC.. 513 791-5244
8044 Montgomery Rd Ste 700 Cincinnati (45236) *(G-3181)*

National Screen Production, Cleveland *Also Called: Charizma Corp (G-3807)*

National Sign Systems Inc.. 614 850-2540
4200 Lyman Ct Hilliard (43026) *(G-8424)*

National Smallwares, Columbus *Also Called: Wasserstrom Company (G-5865)*

National Staffing Services LLC.. 785 731-2540
5151 Monroe St Ste 101 Toledo (43623) *(G-14395)*

National Stair Corp...... 937 325-1347
20 Zischler St Springfield (45504) *(G-13609)*

National Super Service Co, Toledo *Also Called: MJB Toledo Inc (G-14387)*

National Tool & Equipment Inc...... 330 629-8665
60 Karago Ave Youngstown (44512) *(G-16403)*

National Welding, Grove City *Also Called: National Wldg Tanker Repr LLC (G-8110)*

National Wldg Tanker Repr LLC...... 614 875-3399
2036 Hendrix Dr Grove City (43123) *(G-8110)*

Nationwide Chemical Products...... 419 714-7075
24851 E Broadway Rd Perrysburg (43551) *(G-12401)*

Natreeola Soap Company LLC...... 513 390-2247
2367 Bendel Dr Middletown (45044) *(G-10846)*

Natural Beauty Hc Express...... 440 459-1776
6809 Mayfield Rd Apt 550 Mayfield Heights (44124) *(G-10252)*

Natural Beauty Products Inc...... 513 420-9400
104 Charles St Middletown (45042) *(G-10847)*

Natural Essentials Inc...... 330 562-8022
115 Lena Dr Aurora (44202) *(G-726)*

Natural Essentials Inc (PA)...... 330 562-8022
1830 Miller Pkwy Streetsboro (44241) *(G-13781)*

Natural Optons Armatherapy LLC...... 419 886-3736
610 State Route 97 W Bellville (44813) *(G-1245)*

Nature Pure LLC (PA)...... 937 358-2364
26586 State Route 739 Raymond (43067) *(G-12746)*

Nature Pure LLC...... 937 358-2364
26560 Storms Rd West Mansfield (43358) *(G-15627)*

Natures Health Food LLC...... 419 260-9265
21561 County Road 190 Mount Victory (43340) *(G-11301)*

Natures Mark LLC...... 513 557-3200
415 Greenwell Ave Cincinnati (45238) *(G-3182)*

Natures Own Source LLC...... 440 838-5135
7033 Mill Rd Brecksville (44141) *(G-1628)*

Natures Way Bird Products LLC...... 440 554-6166
9054 Washington St Chagrin Falls (44023) *(G-2410)*

Nauticus Inc...... 440 746-1290
8080 Snowville Rd Brecksville (44141) *(G-1629)*

Nauvoo Machine LLC...... 440 632-1990
16254 Nauvoo Rd Middlefield (44062) *(G-10775)*

Navage, Brooklyn *Also Called: Rhinosystems Inc (G-1681)*

NAVIDEA, Dublin *Also Called: Navidea Biopharmaceuticals Inc (G-6915)*

Navidea Biopharmaceuticals Inc (PA)...... 614 793-7500
4995 Bradenton Ave Ste 240 Dublin (43017) *(G-6915)*

Navigate Crdiac Structures Inc...... 949 482-5858
9500 Euclid Ave Cleveland (44195) *(G-4441)*

Navistar, Cincinnati *Also Called: Navistar Inc (G-3183)*

Navistar, Springfield *Also Called: Navistar Inc (G-13610)*

Navistar Inc...... 513 733-8500
11775 Highway Dr Cincinnati (45241) *(G-3183)*

Navistar Inc...... 937 390-4776
6125 Urbana Rd Springfield (45502) *(G-13610)*

Navistar Inc...... 937 561-3315
811 N Murray St Springfield (45503) *(G-13611)*

Navistone Inc...... 844 677-3667
231 W 12th St Ste 200w Cincinnati (45202) *(G-3184)*

Nbbi...... 614 888-8320
1055 Crupper Ave Columbus (43229) *(G-5591)*

Nbw Inc...... 216 377-1700
4556 Industrial Pkwy Cleveland (44135) *(G-4442)*

NC Works Inc...... 937 514-7781
3500 Commerce Center Dr Franklin (45005) *(G-7688)*

Ncc, Cleveland *Also Called: North Coast Container LLC (G-4466)*

Nccd, Wooster *Also Called: North Central Con Designs Inc (G-16155)*

NCM, Cleveland *Also Called: North Coast Media LLC (G-4471)*

NCR Technology Center...... 937 445-1936
1560 S Patterson Blvd Dayton (45409) *(G-6466)*

Ncrformscom...... 800 709-1938
137 Owen Brown St Hudson (44236) *(G-8606)*

Ncrx Optical Solutions Inc (PA)...... 330 239-5353
105 Executive Pkwy Ste 401 Hudson (44236) *(G-8607)*

Ncs, Brookpark *Also Called: North Coast Seal Incorporated (G-1722)*

Nct Technologies Group, New Carlisle *Also Called: Nct Technologies Group Inc (G-11421)*

Nct Technologies Group Inc (PA)...... 937 882-6800
7867 W National Rd New Carlisle (45344) *(G-11421)*

ND Paper Inc...... 937 528-3822
7777 Washington Village Dr Ste 210 Dayton (45459) *(G-6467)*

NDC Technologies, Dayton *Also Called: NDC Technologies Inc (G-6469)*

NDC Technologies Inc...... 937 233-9935
8001 Technology Blvd Dayton (45424) *(G-6468)*

NDC Technologies Inc (HQ)...... 937 233-9935
8001 Technology Blvd Dayton (45424) *(G-6469)*

Ndi Medical LLC (PA)...... 216 378-9106
22901 Millcreek Blvd Ste 110 Cleveland (44122) *(G-4443)*

Ndw Textiles, Brooklyn *Also Called: Mmi Textiles Inc (G-1679)*

Nease Co. LLC, West Chester *Also Called: Catexel Nease LLC (G-15385)*

Nease Performance Chemicals, Harrison *Also Called: Catexel Nease LLC (G-8267)*

Neatlysmart, Lima *Also Called: United States Plastic Corp (G-9299)*

Neaton Auto Products Mfg Inc (HQ)...... 937 456-7103
975 S Franklin St Eaton (45320) *(G-7066)*

Nebraska Industries Corp...... 419 335-6010
447 E Walnut St Wauseon (43567) *(G-15270)*

Nebulatronics Inc...... 440 243-2370
24542 Nobottom Rd Olmsted Twp (44138) *(G-12089)*

Neer's Engineering Labs, Bellefontaine *Also Called: Arden J Neer Sr (G-1200)*

Nef Ltd...... 419 445-6696
1901 S Defiance St Archbold (43502) *(G-538)*

Neff Machinery and Supplies...... 740 454-0128
112 S Shawnee Ave Zanesville (43701) *(G-16547)*

Neff Motivation Inc (DH)...... 937 548-3194
645 Pine St Greenville (45331) *(G-8053)*

Neff Parts, Zanesville *Also Called: Neff Machinery and Supplies (G-16547)*

Neff-Perkins Company (PA)...... 440 632-1658
16080 Industrial Pkwy Middlefield (44062) *(G-10776)*

Nehemiah Manufacturing Co LLC...... 513 351-5700
1907 South St Cincinnati (45204) *(G-3185)*

Neher Burial Vault Company...... 937 399-4494
1903 Saint Paris Pike Springfield (45504) *(G-13612)*

Neider, F A Co, Norwood *Also Called: Namoh Ohio Holdings Inc (G-11996)*

Neil R Scholl Inc...... 740 653-6593
54 Snoke Hill Rd Ne Lancaster (43130) *(G-9027)*

Nelson, Oak Harbor *Also Called: C Nelson Mfg Co (G-12012)*

Nelson Aluminum Foundry Inc...... 440 543-1941
17093 Munn Rd Chagrin Falls (44023) *(G-2411)*

Nelson Company...... 614 444-1164
2160 Refugee Rd Columbus (43207) *(G-5592)*

Nelson Labs Fairfield Inc...... 973 227-6882
9100 S Hills Blvd Broadview Heights (44147) *(G-1663)*

Nelson Manufacturing Company...... 419 523-5321
6448 State Route 224 Ottawa (45875) *(G-12185)*

Nelson Sand & Gravel Inc...... 440 224-0198
5720 State Route 193 Kingsville (44048) *(G-8933)*

Nelson Stud Welding Inc (HQ)...... 440 329-0400
7900 W Ridge Rd Elyria (44035) *(G-7184)*

Nelson Tool Corporation...... 740 965-1894
388 N County Line Rd Sunbury (43074) *(G-13958)*

Nemco Food Equipment Ltd (PA)...... 419 542-7751
301 Meuse Argonne St Hicksville (43526) *(G-8376)*

Neograf Solutions LLC...... 216 529-3777
11709 Madison Ave Lakewood (44107) *(G-8979)*

Neon...... 216 541-5600
15201 Euclid Ave Cleveland (44112) *(G-4444)*

Neon City...... 440 301-2000
11500 Madison Ave Cleveland (44102) *(G-4445)*

Neon Health Services Inc...... 216 231-7700
4800 Payne Ave Cleveland (44103) *(G-4446)*

Neon Workshop...... 216 832-5236
21417 Aurora Rd Bedford (44146) *(G-1143)*

Neptune Equipment Company...... 513 851-8008
11082 Southland Rd Cincinnati (45240) *(G-3186)*

Nervive, Cleveland *Also Called: Nervive Inc (G-4447)*

Nervive Inc...... 847 274-1790
5900 Landerbrook Dr Ste 350 Cleveland (44124) *(G-4447)*

Nes Corp 440 834-0438
18031 Claridon Troy Rd Hiram (44234) *(G-8487)*

Nesco Inc (PA) 440 461-6000
6140 Parkland Blvd Ste 110 Cleveland (44124) *(G-4448)*

Nesco Resource, Cleveland *Also Called: Nesco Inc (G-4448)*

Nestaway LLC 216 587-1500
9100 Bank St Ste 1 Cleveland (44125) *(G-4449)*

Nestle, Solon *Also Called: Nestle Prepared Foods Company (G-13396)*

Nestle Brands Company, Solon *Also Called: Nestle Usa Inc (G-13398)*

Nestle Food Service Factory, Cleveland *Also Called: Nestle Usa Inc (G-4450)*

Nestle Prepared Foods Company 440 349-5757
5750 Harper Rd Solon (44139) *(G-13395)*

Nestle Prepared Foods Company (DH) 440 248-3600
30003 Bainbridge Rd Solon (44139) *(G-13396)*

Nestle Purina Petcare Company 740 454-8575
5 N 2nd St Zanesville (43701) *(G-16548)*

Nestle Usa Inc 216 861-8350
2621 W 25th St Cleveland (44113) *(G-4450)*

Nestle Usa Inc 440 349-5757
30003 Bainbridge Rd Solon (44139) *(G-13397)*

Nestle Usa Inc 440 264-6600
30000 Bainbridge Rd Solon (44139) *(G-13398)*

Net Braze LLC 937 444-1444
351 Apple St Mount Orab (45154) *(G-11244)*

Netform, Maumee *Also Called: Metal Forming & Coining LLC (G-10220)*

Netherland Rubber Company (PA) 513 733-0883
2931 Exon Ave Cincinnati (45241) *(G-3187)*

Nettleton Steel Treating Div, Wickliffe *Also Called: Thermal Treatment Center Inc (G-15854)*

Neturen America Corporation 513 863-1900
2995 Moser Ct Hamilton (45011) *(G-8231)*

Network Polymers Inc 330 773-2700
1353 Exeter Rd Akron (44306) *(G-261)*

Network Printing & Graphics 614 230-2084
443 Crestview Rd Columbus (43202) *(G-5593)*

Network Technologies Inc 330 562-7070
1275 Danner Dr Aurora (44202) *(G-727)*

Neundorfer Inc 440 942-8990
4590 Hamann Pkwy Willoughby (44094) *(G-15957)*

Neundorfer Engineering Service, Willoughby *Also Called: Neundorfer Inc (G-15957)*

Neurologix Technologies Inc 512 914-7941
10000 Cedar Ave Ste 3-160 Cleveland (44106) *(G-4451)*

Neuronoff Inc 216 505-1818
11000 Cedar Ave Ste 290 Cleveland (44106) *(G-4452)*

Neuros Medical Inc 440 951-2565
35010 Chardon Rd Ste 210 Willoughby Hills (44094) *(G-16026)*

Neurowave Systems Inc 216 361-1591
25825 Science Park Dr Ste 250 Beachwood (44122) *(G-1002)*

Nevco Services Ltd 937 603-1500
3620 Old Salem Rd Dayton (45415) *(G-6470)*

New Age Design & Tool Inc 440 355-5400
162 Commerce Dr Lagrange (44050) *(G-8953)*

New Aqua LLC 614 265-9000
3707 Interchange Rd Columbus (43204) *(G-5594)*

NEW AQUA LLC, Columbus *Also Called: New Aqua LLC (G-5594)*

New Bltmore Ice Cream Pdts Inc 330 904-6687
2932 Clearview Ave Nw Canton (44718) *(G-2171)*

New Bremen Machine & Tool Co 419 629-3295
705 Kuenzel Dr New Bremen (45869) *(G-11405)*

New Burlington Woodworks 937 488-3503
2581 New Burlington Rd Wilmington (45177) *(G-16056)*

New Castings Inc 330 645-6653
2200 Massillon Rd Akron (44312) *(G-262)*

New Cumberland Lock & Dam, Toronto *Also Called: U S Army Corps of Engineers (G-14536)*

New Cut Tool and Mfg Corp 740 676-1666
1 New Cut Road Shadyside (43947) *(G-13148)*

New Dairy Cincinnati LLC 214 258-1200
415 John St Cincinnati (45215) *(G-3188)*

New Dairy Ohio LLC 214 258-1200
3068 W 106th St Cleveland (44111) *(G-4453)*

New Dairy Ohio Transport LLC 214 258-1200
3068 W 106th St Cleveland (44111) *(G-4454)*

New Dawn Labs LLC 203 675-5644
102 S Main St Union (45322) *(G-14773)*

New Die Inc 419 726-7581
2828 E Manhattan Blvd Toledo (43611) *(G-14396)*

New Diry Cincinnati Trnspt LLC 214 258-1200
415 John St Cincinnati (45215) *(G-3189)*

New Eezy-Gro Inc 419 927-6110
9841 County Highway 49 Upper Sandusky (43351) *(G-14817)*

New Horizons Baking Co LLC (PA) 419 668-8226
211 Woodlawn Ave Norwalk (44857) *(G-11980)*

New Horizons Fd Solutions LLC (PA) 614 861-3639
3455 Millennium Ct Columbus (43219) *(G-5595)*

New London Regalia Mfg Co 419 929-1516
1 Harmony Pl New London (44851) *(G-11465)*

New Mansfield Brass & Alum Co 419 492-2166
636 S Center St New Washington (44854) *(G-11549)*

New Page Corporation 877 855-7243
8540 Gander Creek Dr Miamisburg (45342) *(G-10665)*

New Path International LLC 614 410-3974
1476 Manning Pkwy Ste A Powell (43065) *(G-12679)*

New Pme Inc 513 671-1717
518 W Crescentville Rd Cincinnati (45246) *(G-3190)*

New Publishing Holdings LLC 513 531-2690
10151 Carver Rd Ste 200 Blue Ash (45242) *(G-1443)*

New Republic Industries LLC (PA) 614 580-9927
497 Bridle Dr Marysville (43040) *(G-9929)*

New Sabina Industries Inc 937 584-2433
3650 Brookham Dr Ste A Grove City (43123) *(G-8111)*

New Sabina Industries Inc (HQ) 937 584-2433
12555 Us Highway 22 And 3 Sabina (45169) *(G-12888)*

New Stone Age, North Ridgeville *Also Called: Rock Hard Industries LLC (G-11859)*

New Tech Plastics Inc 937 473-3011
1300 Mote Dr Covington (45318) *(G-6028)*

New Waste Concepts Inc 877 736-6924
26624 Glenwood Rd Perrysburg (43551) *(G-12402)*

New Wayne Inc 740 453-3454
1555 Ritchey Pkwy Zanesville (43701) *(G-16549)*

New World Energy Resources (PA) 740 344-4087
1500 Granville Rd Newark (43055) *(G-11597)*

New World Solutions Inc 614 271-6233
6444 S Old 3c Hwy Westerville (43082) *(G-15668)*

New York Frozen Foods Inc (DH) 216 292-5655
25900 Fargo Ave Bedford (44146) *(G-1144)*

New York Frozen Foods Inc 614 846-2232
380 Polaris Pkwy Ste 400 Westerville (43082) *(G-15669)*

New York Frozen Foods Inc 626 338-3000
380 Polaris Pkwy Ste 400 Westerville (43082) *(G-15670)*

Newact Inc 513 321-5177
2084 James E Sauls Sr Dr Batavia (45103) *(G-940)*

Newall Electronics Inc 614 771-0213
1803 Obrien Rd Columbus (43228) *(G-5596)*

Newark Water Plant, Newark *Also Called: City of Newark (G-11570)*

Neway Stamping & Mfg Inc 440 951-8500
4820 E 345th St Willoughby (44094) *(G-15958)*

Newberry Sheet Metal LLC 513 807-7385
5405 State Route 133 Williamsburg (45176) *(G-15866)*

Newberry Wood Enterprises Inc (PA) 440 238-6127
12223 Prospect Rd Strongsville (44149) *(G-13859)*

Newburgh Crankshaft Inc 440 502-6998
13304 Gilmore Ave Cleveland (44135) *(G-4455)*

Newbury Sandblasting & Pntg, Newbury *Also Called: Newbury Sndblst & Pntg Inc (G-11631)*

Newbury Sndblst & Pntg Inc 440 564-7204
9992 Kinsman Rd Newbury (44065) *(G-11631)*

Newbury Woodworks 440 564-5273
10958 Kinsman Rd Unit 2 Newbury (44065) *(G-11632)*

Newco Industries 717 566-9560
4057 Glenmoor Rd Nw Canton (44718) *(G-2172)*

Newell - Psn LLC (PA) 304 387-2700
235 E State Route 14 Ste 104 Columbiana (44408) *(G-5046)*

Newell Brands Inc 330 733-1184
212 Progress Blvd Kent (44240) *(G-8839)*

Newell Brands Inc..330 733-7771
3200 Gilchrist Rd Mogadore (44260) *(G-11079)*

Newell Holdings Delaware Inc............................740 681-6461
1115 W 5th Ave Lancaster (43130) *(G-9028)*

Newell Rubbermaid, Mogadore Also Called: Newell Brands Inc *(G-11079)*

Newhouse Printing Company, Stow Also Called: R & J Printing Enterprises Inc *(G-13719)*

Newman Brothers Inc
5609 Center Hill Ave Cincinnati (45216) *(G-3191)*

Newman Diaphragms LLC....................................513 932-7379
964 W Main St Lebanon (45036) *(G-9098)*

Newman International Inc......................................513 932-7379
964 W Main St Lebanon (45036) *(G-9099)*

Newman Sanitary Gasket, Lebanon Also Called: Newman International Inc *(G-9099)*

Newman Sanitary Gasket Company....................513 932-7379
964 W Main St Lebanon (45036) *(G-9100)*

Newman Technology Inc (HQ)..............................419 525-1856
100 Cairns Rd Mansfield (44903) *(G-9704)*

Newmast Mktg & Communications......................614 837-1200
2060 Integrity Dr N Columbus (43209) *(G-5597)*

Newpage Group Inc..937 242-9500
8540 Gander Creek Dr Miamisburg (45342) *(G-10666)*

News Gazette Printing Company..........................419 227-2527
324 W Market St Lima (45801) *(G-9274)*

News Tribune, Hicksville Also Called: Tribune Printing Inc *(G-8382)*

News Watchman & Paper......................................740 947-2149
860 W Emmitt Ave Ste 5 Waverly (45690) *(G-15288)*

Newsafe Transport Service Inc..............................740 387-1679
979 Pole Lane Rd Marion (43302) *(G-9866)*

Newsome & Work Metalizing Co..........................330 376-7144
258 Kenmore Blvd Akron (44301) *(G-263)*

Newspaper Network Central OH..........................419 524-3545
70 W 4th St Mansfield (44903) *(G-9705)*

Newswanger Machine, Shiloh Also Called: Leon Newswanger *(G-13204)*

Newton Materion Inc..216 692-3990
21801 Tungsten Rd Euclid (44117) *(G-7287)*

Newton Software..714 469-5773
4811 Montgomery Rd Cincinnati (45212) *(G-3192)*

Newton's Paint & Body, Lucasville Also Called: Michael W Newton *(G-9525)*

Nexceris, Lewis Center Also Called: Nextech Materials Ltd *(G-9174)*

Next, Cincinnati Also Called: Nilpeter Usa Inc *(G-3198)*

Next Generation Hearing Case.............................513 451-0360
4223 Harrison Ave Cincinnati (45211) *(G-3193)*

Next Generation Plastics LLC..............................330 668-1200
3075 Smith Rd Ste 101 Fairlawn (44333) *(G-7445)*

Next Gerenation Crimping....................................440 237-6300
9880 York Alpha Dr North Royalton (44133) *(G-11888)*

Next Resins, Sylvania Also Called: Next Specialty Resins Inc *(G-14009)*

Next Sales LLC..330 704-4126
3258 Dogwood Ln Nw Dover (44622) *(G-6837)*

Next Specialty Resins Inc (PA)............................419 843-4600
3315 Centennial Rd Ste J Sylvania (43560) *(G-14009)*

Next Surface Inc..440 576-0194
223 S Spruce St Jefferson (44047) *(G-8754)*

Next Wave Automation LLC................................419 491-4520
600 W Boundary St Perrysburg (43551) *(G-12403)*

Nextant Aerospace, Cleveland Also Called: Nextant Aerospace LLC *(G-4456)*

Nextant Aerospace LLC..216 898-4800
18601 Cleveland Pkwy Dr Cleveland (44135) *(G-4456)*

Nextant Aerospace Holdings LLC, Cleveland Also Called: K&M Aviation LLC *(G-4270)*

Nextant Aircraft LLC..216 261-9000
355 Richmond Rd Cleveland (44143) *(G-4457)*

Nextech Materials Ltd..614 842-6606
404 Enterprise Dr Lewis Center (43035) *(G-9174)*

Nextgen Fiber Optics LLC (PA)............................513 549-4691
720 E Pete Rose Way Ste 410 Cincinnati (45202) *(G-3194)*

Nextmed Systems Inc (PA)..................................216 674-0511
16 Triangle Park Dr Cincinnati (45246) *(G-3195)*

Nextstep Networking, Blue Ash Also Called: Eaj Services LLC *(G-1387)*

Nexus Vision Group LLC......................................866 492-6499
2156 Southwest Blvd Grove City (43123) *(G-8112)*

Neyra Interstate Inc (PA)......................................513 733-1000
10700 Evendale Dr Cincinnati (45241) *(G-3196)*

Nfi Industries Inc..740 928-9522
111 Enterprise Dr Hebron (43025) *(G-8352)*

Nfm/Welding Engineers Inc (PA)..........................330 837-3868
577 Oberlin Ave Sw Massillon (44647) *(G-10131)*

Ngo Development Corporation............................740 622-9560
504 N 3rd St Coshocton (43812) *(G-5987)*

Ngo Development Corporation (HQ)..................740 344-3790
1500 Granville Rd Newark (43055) *(G-11598)*

Ngp Printing Professional, Lima Also Called: News Gazette Printing Company *(G-9274)*

Ngts, Beavercreek Township Also Called: Northrop Grmman Tchncal Svcs I *(G-1086)*

Nhmf LLC..614 444-2184
1701 Moler Rd Columbus (43207) *(G-5598)*

Nhvs International Inc..440 527-8610
7600 Tyler Blvd Mentor (44060) *(G-10509)*

Niagara Bottling LLC..614 751-7420
1700 Eastgate Pkwy Gahanna (43230) *(G-7846)*

Niagara Custombilt Mfg, Cleveland Also Called: S A Langmack Company *(G-4666)*

Nic Global, Chillicothe Also Called: National Indus Concepts Inc *(G-2520)*

Nice Body Automotive, Elyria Also Called: Nice Body Automotive LLC *(G-7185)*

Nice Body Automotive LLC..................................440 752-5568
818 Cleveland St Elyria (44035) *(G-7185)*

Nichidai America Corporation..............................419 423-7511
15630 E State Route 12 Ste 4 Findlay (45840) *(G-7542)*

Nichols Mold Inc..330 297-9719
222 W Lake St Ravenna (44266) *(G-12726)*

Nicholson Manufacturing Co LLC........................978 776-2000
1425 Kingsview Dr Lebanon (45036) *(G-9101)*

Nick Kostecki Excavating Inc..............................330 242-0706
10644 Chatham Rd Spencer (44275) *(G-13482)*

Nickel Plate Railcar LLC......................................440 382-6580
6730 N Palmerston Dr Mentor (44060) *(G-10510)*

Nickels Marketing Group Inc................................440 835-1532
4016 Brewster Dr Westlake (44145) *(G-15767)*

Nicklaus Group LLC..740 277-5700
1649 River Valley Cir N Lancaster (43130) *(G-9029)*

Nickles Bakery 45, Zanesville Also Called: Alfred Nickles Bakery Inc *(G-16498)*

Nickolas Plastics LLC..419 423-1213
814 W Lima St Findlay (45840) *(G-7543)*

Nicks Plating Co..937 773-3175
6980 Free Rd Piqua (45356) *(G-12538)*

Nidec Avtron Automation Corporation................216 642-1230
7555 E Pleasant Valley Rd Independence (44131) *(G-8677)*

Nidec Industrial Solutions, Cleveland Also Called: Nidec Motor Corporation *(G-4458)*

Nidec Industrial Solutions, Cleveland Also Called: Nidec Motor Corporation *(G-4459)*

NIDEC MINSTER CORPORATION (DH)..............419 628-2331
240 W 5th St Minster (45865) *(G-11057)*

Nidec Motor Corporation......................................575 434-0633
3030 Gilchrist Rd Akron (44305) *(G-264)*

Nidec Motor Corporation......................................216 642-1230
243 Tuxedo Ave Cleveland (44131) *(G-4458)*

Nidec Motor Corporation......................................216 642-1230
7555 E Pleasant Valley Rd Cleveland (44131) *(G-4459)*

Nielsen Jewelers, Lorain Also Called: H P Nielsen Inc *(G-9413)*

Niese Farms..419 347-1204
7506 Cole Rd Crestline (44827) *(G-6035)*

Nifco America Corporation (HQ)..........................614 920-6800
8015 Dove Pkwy Canal Winchester (43110) *(G-1989)*

Nifco America Corporation..................................614 836-3808
7877 Robinett Way Canal Winchester (43110) *(G-1990)*

Nifco America Corporation..................................614 836-8691
4485 S Hamilton Rd Groveport (43125) *(G-8155)*

Niftech, Mentor Also Called: R J K Enterprises Inc *(G-10542)*

Niftech Inc..440 257-6018
5565 Wilson Dr Mentor (44060) *(G-10511)*

Niftech Precision Race Pdts, Mentor Also Called: Niftech Inc *(G-10511)*

Nifty Promo Products, Middletown Also Called: Backyard Scoreboards LLC *(G-10805)*

Nigerian Assn Pharmacists & PH........................513 861-2329
483 Northland Blvd Cincinnati (45240) *(G-3197)*

Night Lightscapes LLC — ALPHABETIC SECTION

Night Lightscapes LLC 419 304-2486
 3303 Herr Rd Sylvania (43560) *(G-14010)*

Nightrider Overnite Copy Svc, Cleveland Also Called: Ricoh Usa Inc *(G-4634)*

Nihon Company, Urbana Also Called: Parker Trutec Incorporated *(G-14846)*

Nikola Labs, Westerville Also Called: Assetwatch Inc *(G-15691)*

Niktec Inc 513 282-3747
 127 Industrial Dr Franklin (45005) *(G-7689)*

Niles Building Products Company (PA) 330 544-0880
 1600 Hunter Ave Niles (44446) *(G-11677)*

Niles Expanded Metals & Plas, Niles Also Called: Nmc Metals Inc *(G-11681)*

Niles Manufacturing & Finshg 330 544-0402
 465 Walnut St Niles (44446) *(G-11678)*

Niles Mirror & Glass Inc 330 652-6277
 234 Robbins Ave Ste 1 Niles (44446) *(G-11679)*

Niles Roll Service Inc (PA) 330 544-0026
 704 Warren Ave Niles (44446) *(G-11680)*

Nilodor Inc 800 443-4321
 10966 Industrial Pkwy Nw Bolivar (44612) *(G-1530)*

Nilpeter Usa Inc 513 489-4400
 11550 Goldcoast Dr Cincinnati (45249) *(G-3198)*

Nimers & Woody II Inc (PA) 937 454-0722
 1625 Fieldstone Way Vandalia (45377) *(G-14955)*

Nine Downhole Technologies LLC (PA) 817 862-9834
 2345 State Route 821 Marietta (45750) *(G-9811)*

Nine Giant Brewing LLC 510 220-5104
 6095 Montgomery Rd Cincinnati (45213) *(G-3199)*

Niobium Microsystems Inc 937 203-8117
 444 E 2nd St Dayton (45402) *(G-6471)*

Nippon Paint America, Cleveland Also Called: Nippon Paint Auto Americas Inc *(G-4460)*

Nippon Paint Auto Americas Inc (DH) 201 692-1111
 11110 Berea Rd Ste 1 Cleveland (44102) *(G-4460)*

Nippon Stl Intgrted Crnkshaft 419 435-0411
 1815 Sandusky St Fostoria (44830) *(G-7647)*

Nissen Chemitec America, London Also Called: Nissen Chemitec America Inc *(G-9391)*

Nissen Chemitec America Inc 740 852-3200
 350 E High St London (43140) *(G-9391)*

Nissin Precision N Amer Inc 937 836-1910
 375 Union Rd Englewood (45315) *(G-7238)*

Nitrojection 440 729-2711
 8430 Mayfield Rd Chesterland (44026) *(G-2486)*

Nitto Inc 937 773-4820
 220 Fox Dr Piqua (45356) *(G-12539)*

Nitto Inc 937 773-4820
 1620 S Main St Piqua (45356) *(G-12540)*

Njf Manufacturing LLC 419 294-0400
 7387 Township Highway 104 Upper Sandusky (43351) *(G-14818)*

Njm Furniture Outlet Inc 330 893-3514
 6899 County Road 672 Millersburg (44654) *(G-10987)*

Nk Machine Inc 513 737-8035
 1550 Pleasant Ave Hamilton (45015) *(G-8232)*

Nkh-Safety Inc 513 771-3839
 1375 Kemper Meadow Dr Ste 12 Cincinnati (45240) *(G-3200)*

Nmc Metals Inc (PA) 330 652-2501
 310 N Pleasant Ave Niles (44446) *(G-11681)*

Nmg Aerospace, Stow Also Called: National Machine Company *(G-13714)*

Nmgg Ctg LLC (HQ) 419 447-5211
 161 Greenfield St Tiffin (44883) *(G-14096)*

Nmn Spinco Inc 800 850-0335
 330 W Spring St Ste 303 Columbus (43215) *(G-5599)*

Nn Inc 440 647-4711
 125 Bennett St Wellington (44090) *(G-15318)*

Nn Autocam Precision Component 440 647-4711
 125 Bennett St Wellington (44090) *(G-15319)*

Nn Metal Stampings LLC (PA) 419 737-2311
 510 S Maple St Pioneer (43554) *(G-12493)*

Nnodum Pharmaceuticals Corp 513 861-2329
 483 Northland Blvd Cincinnati (45240) *(G-3201)*

No Burn Inc 330 336-1500
 1392 High St Ste 211 Wadsworth (44281) *(G-15048)*

No Burn North America Inc 419 841-6055
 2930 Centennial Rd Toledo (43617) *(G-14397)*

No Name Lumber LLC 740 289-3722
 165 No Name Rd Piketon (45661) *(G-12479)*

No Rinse Laboratories LLC 937 746-7357
 868 Pleasant Valley Dr Springboro (45066) *(G-13512)*

No-Bull Tactical & Machine LLC 937 470-7687
 444 Lammes Ln New Carlisle (45344) *(G-11422)*

Noble Beast Brewing LLC 570 809-6405
 1864 W 45th St Cleveland (44102) *(G-4461)*

Noble Denim Workshop 513 560-5640
 2929 Spring Grove Ave Cincinnati (45225) *(G-3202)*

Noble Tool Corp 937 461-4040
 1535 Stanley Ave Dayton (45404) *(G-6472)*

Nock and Son Company 740 682-7741
 4138 Monroe Hollow Rd Oak Hill (45656) *(G-12022)*

Noco, Solon Also Called: Noco Company *(G-13399)*

Noco Company (PA) 216 464-8131
 30339 Diamond Pkwy Ste 102 Solon (44139) *(G-13399)*

Nof Metal Coatings N Amer Inc (HQ) 440 285-2231
 275 Industrial Pkwy Chardon (44024) *(G-2459)*

Nofziger Door Sales Inc 419 445-2961
 111 Taylor Pkwy Archbold (43502) *(G-539)*

Nofziger Door Sales Inc (PA) 419 337-9900
 320 Sycamore St Wauseon (43567) *(G-15271)*

Noi Enhancements LLC 216 218-4136
 2554 Claver Rd University Heights (44118) *(G-14798)*

Nolan Company 740 269-1512
 300 Boyce Dr Bowerston (44695) *(G-1545)*

Nolan Company (HQ) 330 453-7922
 1016 9th St Sw Canton (44707) *(G-2173)*

Nolte Precise Manufacturing Inc 513 923-3100
 6850 Colerain Ave Cincinnati (45239) *(G-3203)*

Nomac Drilling LLC 330 476-7040
 1258 Panda Rd Se Carrollton (44615) *(G-2312)*

Nomac Drilling LLC 724 324-2205
 67090 Executive Dr Saint Clairsville (43950) *(G-12916)*

Nomah Naturals Inc 330 212-8785
 200 Public Sq Ste 2300 Cleveland (44114) *(G-4462)*

Non-Ferrous Casting Company 937 228-1162
 736 Albany St Dayton (45417) *(G-6473)*

Non-Ferrous Heat Treating, Maple Heights Also Called: Dewitt Inc *(G-9750)*

Non-Injectable Manufacturing, Columbus Also Called: Hikma Pharmaceuticals USA Inc *(G-5439)*

Nook Industries LLC (DH) 216 271-7900
 4950 E 49th St Cleveland (44125) *(G-4463)*

Nor-Fab Inc 330 467-6580
 231 Beechwood Dr Northfield (44067) *(G-11908)*

Noramco, Euclid Also Called: North American Plas Chem Inc *(G-7290)*

Noramco Inc 216 531-3400
 1400 E 222nd St Euclid (44117) *(G-7288)*

Norbar Torque Tools Inc 440 953-1175
 36400 Biltmore Pl Willoughby (44094) *(G-15959)*

Norcia Bakery 330 454-1077
 624 Belden Ave Ne Canton (44704) *(G-2174)*

Norcold LLC (HQ) 800 543-1219
 1440 N Vandemark Rd Sidney (45365) *(G-13268)*

Nordec Inc 330 940-3700
 900 Hampshire Rd Stow (44224) *(G-13715)*

Norden Mfg LLC 440 693-4630
 4210 Kinsman Rd Nw North Bloomfield (44450) *(G-11712)*

Nordic Light America Inc 614 981-9497
 6320 Winchester Blvd Canal Winchester (43110) *(G-1991)*

Nordson, Westlake Also Called: Nordson Corporation *(G-15768)*

Nordson Corporation 440 985-4496
 300 Nordson Dr Amherst (44001) *(G-478)*

Nordson Corporation 440 985-4458
 444 Gordon Ave Dock C1-C3 Amherst (44001) *(G-479)*

Nordson Corporation 440 985-4000
 100 Nordson Dr M 81 Amherst (44001) *(G-480)*

Nordson Corporation (PA) 440 892-1580
 28601 Clemens Rd Westlake (44145) *(G-15768)*

Nordson MCS, Dayton Also Called: NDC Technologies Inc *(G-6468)*

Nordson Medical Corporation 440 892-1580
28601 Clemens Rd Westlake (44145) *(G-15769)*

Norgren Inc 937 833-4033
325 Carr Dr Brookville (45309) *(G-1742)*

Noritake Co Inc 513 234-0770
4990 Alliance Dr Mason (45040) *(G-10033)*

Norkaam Industries LLC 330 873-9793
1477 Copley Rd Akron (44320) *(G-265)*

Norlab, Lorain Also Called: Norlab Inc *(G-9426)*

Norlab Inc 440 282-5265
7465 Industrial Parkway Dr Lorain (44053) *(G-9426)*

Norlake, North Ridgeville Also Called: Norlake Manufacturing Company *(G-11851)*

Norlake Manufacturing Company (PA) 440 353-3200
39301 Taylor Pkwy North Ridgeville (44035) *(G-11851)*

Norman Noble Inc 216 761-5387
5507 Avion Park Dr Cleveland (44143) *(G-4464)*

Norman Noble Inc 216 851-4007
931 E 228th St Euclid (44123) *(G-7289)*

Norman Noble Inc (PA) 216 761-5387
5507 Avion Park Dr Highland Heights (44143) *(G-8389)*

Normandy Products Co 440 632-5050
16125 Industrial Pkwy Middlefield (44062) *(G-10777)*

Norplas Industries Inc (DH) 419 662-3200
7825 Caple Blvd Northwood (43619) *(G-11922)*

Norrenbrock Company Inc 513 316-1383
249 Wood Forge Cir Lebanon (45036) *(G-9102)*

Norris Manufacturing LLC 330 602-5005
317 E Broadway St Dover (44622) *(G-6838)*

Norris North Manufacturing 330 691-0449
1500 Henry Ave Sw Canton (44706) *(G-2175)*

Norse Dairy Systems, Columbus Also Called: Interbake Foods LLC *(G-5471)*

Norse Dairy Systems Inc 614 294-4931
1700 E 17th Ave Columbus (43219) *(G-5600)*

Norse Dairy Systems LP 614 294-4931
1740 Joyce Ave Columbus (43219) *(G-5601)*

North Amercn Kit Solutions Inc (PA) 800 854-3267
172 Reaser Ct Elyria (44035) *(G-7186)*

North American Assemblies LLC 843 420-5354
600 Stonehenge Pkwy Dublin (43017) *(G-6916)*

North American Cast Stone Inc 440 286-1999
11546 Claridon Troy Rd Chardon (44024) *(G-2460)*

North American Coating Labs, Mentor Also Called: Wilson Optical Labs Inc *(G-10595)*

North American Composites 440 930-0602
33660 Pin Oak Pkwy Avon Lake (44012) *(G-819)*

North American Dist Ctr, Cambridge Also Called: Ridge Tool Company *(G-1951)*

North American Plas Chem Inc (PA) 216 531-3400
1400 E 222nd St Euclid (44117) *(G-7290)*

North American Stamping Group, Ada Also Called: Nasg Ohio LLC *(G-4)*

North Amrcn Stamping Group LLC 419 633-0662
633 Commerce Dr Bryan (43506) *(G-1830)*

North Canton Plastics Inc 330 497-0071
6658 Promway Ave Nw Canton (44720) *(G-2176)*

North Canton Tool Co 330 452-0545
1156 Marion Ave Sw Canton (44707) *(G-2177)*

North Cape Manufacturing, Streetsboro Also Called: Technology House Ltd *(G-13795)*

North Central Con Designs Inc 419 606-1908
3331 E Lincoln Way Wooster (44691) *(G-16155)*

North Central Insulation Inc (PA) 419 886-2030
7539 State Route 13 Bellville (44813) *(G-1246)*

North Coast Composites Inc 216 398-8550
4605 Spring Rd Cleveland (44131) *(G-4465)*

North Coast Container LLC (HQ) 216 441-6214
8806 Crane Ave Cleveland (44105) *(G-4466)*

North Coast Custom Molding Inc 419 905-6447
211 W Geneva St Dunkirk (45836) *(G-6976)*

North Coast Dumpster Svcs LLC 216 644-5647
3740 Carnegie Ave Cleveland (44115) *(G-4467)*

North Coast Exotics Inc 216 651-5512
3159 W 68th St Cleveland (44102) *(G-4468)*

North Coast Instruments Inc 216 251-2353
14615 Lorain Ave Cleveland (44111) *(G-4469)*

North Coast Litho Inc 216 881-1952
4701 Manufacturing Ave Cleveland (44135) *(G-4470)*

North Coast Media LLC 216 706-3700
1360 E 9th St Ste 1070 Cleveland (44114) *(G-4471)*

North Coast Medical Eqp Inc 440 243-6189
96 Lincoln Ave Berea (44017) *(G-1289)*

North Coast Minority Media LLC 216 407-4327
1360 E 9th St Cleveland (44114) *(G-4472)*

North Coast Publications, Cleveland Also Called: North Coast Minority Media LLC *(G-4472)*

North Coast Rivet Inc 440 366-6829
700 Sugar Ln Elyria (44035) *(G-7187)*

North Coast Seal Incorporated 216 898-5000
5163 W 137th St Brookpark (44142) *(G-1722)*

North Coast Theatrical Inc 330 762-1768
2181 Killian Rd Akron (44312) *(G-266)*

North Coast Tire Co Inc 216 447-1690
7810 Old Rockside Rd Cleveland (44131) *(G-4473)*

North Coatings Inc 330 896-7126
4782 Mars Rd Uniontown (44685) *(G-14789)*

North Country Charcuterie LLC 614 670-5726
1145 Chesapeake Ave Ste E Columbus (43212) *(G-5602)*

North East Fuel Inc 330 264-4454
3927 Cleveland Rd Wooster (44691) *(G-16156)*

North End Press Incorporated 740 653-6514
235 S Columbus St Lancaster (43130) *(G-9030)*

North Hill Marble & Granite Co 330 253-2179
448 N Howard St Akron (44310) *(G-267)*

North Ridge Enterprises Inc 440 965-5300
62 Firelands Blvd Norwalk (44857) *(G-11981)*

North Shore Printing LLC 740 876-9066
1105 Gallia St Portsmouth (45662) *(G-12651)*

North Shore Safety, Mentor Also Called: Tecmark Corporation *(G-10572)*

North Shore Strapping Company (PA) 216 661-5200
1400 Valley Belt Rd Brooklyn Heights (44131) *(G-1696)*

North Toledo Graphics LLC 419 476-8808
5225 Telegraph Rd Toledo (43612) *(G-14398)*

Northast Ohio Nghbrhood Hlth S 216 751-3100
13301 Miles Ave Cleveland (44105) *(G-4474)*

Northcoast Environmental Labs 330 342-3377
10100 Wellman Rd Streetsboro (44241) *(G-13782)*

Northcoast Pmm LLC 419 540-8667
4725 Southbridge Rd Toledo (43623) *(G-14399)*

Northcoast Valve and Gate Inc 440 392-9910
9437 Mercantile Dr Mentor (44060) *(G-10512)*

Northcoast Woodcraft Inc 330 677-1189
939 Treat Blvd Tallmadge (44278) *(G-14039)*

Northeast Blueprint and Sup Co 216 261-7500
1230 E 286th St Cleveland (44132) *(G-4475)*

Northeast Box Company 440 992-5500
1726 Griswold Ave Ashtabula (44004) *(G-653)*

Northeast Cabinet Co LLC 614 759-0800
6063 Taylor Rd Columbus (43230) *(G-5603)*

Northeast Coatings Inc 330 784-7773
415 Munroe Falls Rd Tallmadge (44278) *(G-14040)*

Northeast Fabricators LLC 330 747-3484
365 E Boardman St Youngstown (44503) *(G-16404)*

Northeast Logging & Lumber LLC 440 272-5100
8641 Fletcher Rd Middlefield (44062) *(G-10778)*

Northeast Tubular Inc 330 567-2690
426 S Grant St Wooster (44691) *(G-16157)*

Northeastern Oilfield Svcs LLC (PA) 330 581-3304
1537 Waynesburg Dr Se Canton (44707) *(G-2178)*

Northeastern Plastics Inc 330 453-5925
112 Navarre Rd Sw Canton (44707) *(G-2179)*

Northeastern Process Cooling, Willoughby Also Called: Nrc Inc *(G-15961)*

Northeastern Rfrgn Corp 440 942-7676
38274 Western Pkwy Willoughby (44094) *(G-15960)*

Northern Bank Note Company, Harrison Also Called: Sekuworks LLC *(G-8290)*

Northern Chem Blnding Corp Inc 216 781-7799
360 Literary Rd Cleveland (44113) *(G-4476)*

Northern Concrete Pipe Inc 419 841-3361
3756 Centennial Rd Sylvania (43560) *(G-14011)*

Northern Manufacturing Co Inc — 419 898-2821
150 N Lake Winds Pkwy Oak Harbor (43449) *(G-12014)*

Northern Mobile Electric, Canton *Also Called: M Technologies Inc (G-2151)*

Northern Precision Inc — 513 860-4701
3245 Production Dr Fairfield (45014) *(G-7387)*

Northern Stamping Co — 216 883-8888
5900 Harvard Ave Cleveland (44105) *(G-4477)*

Northern Stamping Co (HQ) — 216 883-8888
6600 Chapek Pkwy Cleveland (44125) *(G-4478)*

Northern Stamping Co — 216 642-8081
7750 Hub Pkwy Cleveland (44125) *(G-4479)*

Northern Stamping Plant 2, Cleveland *Also Called: Northern Stamping Co (G-4479)*

Northern Stamping, Inc., Cleveland *Also Called: Northern Stamping Co (G-4478)*

Northfield — 440 949-1815
5190 Oster Rd Sheffield Village (44054) *(G-13186)*

Northfield Block Co — 513 242-3644
5155 Fischer Ave Cincinnati (45217) *(G-3204)*

Northfield Propane LLC — 330 854-4320
10355 Lincoln Way E Orrville (44667) *(G-12141)*

Northhill T-Shirt Print Dsign — 330 208-0338
509 E Glenwood Ave Akron (44310) *(G-268)*

Northlake Steel Corporation — 330 220-7717
5455 Wegman Dr Valley City (44280) *(G-14887)*

Northrop Grmman Innvtion Syste — 937 429-9261
1365 Technology Ct Beavercreek (45430) *(G-1076)*

Northrop Grmman Tchncal Svcs I — 937 320-3100
4065 Colonel Glenn Hwy Beavercreek Township (45431) *(G-1086)*

Northrop Grmmn Spce & Mssn Sys — 937 259-4956
1900 Founders Dr Ste 202 Dayton (45420) *(G-6474)*

Northrop Grumman Systems Corp — 937 490-4111
1365 Technology Ct Beavercreek (45430) *(G-1077)*

Northrop Grumman Systems Corp — 937 429-6450
4065 Colonel Glenn Hwy Beavercreek Township (45431) *(G-1087)*

Northrop Grumman Systems Corp — 513 881-3296
460 W Crescentville Rd West Chester (45246) *(G-15573)*

Northshore Mold Inc — 440 838-8212
2861 E Royalton Rd Cleveland (44147) *(G-4480)*

Northstar Asphalt, Canton *Also Called: Stark Materials Inc (G-2232)*

Northstar Publishing Inc — 330 721-9126
437 Lafayette Rd Ste 310 Medina (44256) *(G-10356)*

Northwest Molded Plastics — 419 459-4414
14372 County Road 4 Edon (43518) *(G-7090)*

NORTHWEST PRODUCTS, Stryker *Also Called: Quadco Rehabilitation Ctr Inc (G-13912)*

Northwest Products Div, Archbold *Also Called: Quadco Rehabilitation Ctr Inc (G-543)*

Northwest Signal, Napoleon *Also Called: Napoleon Inc (G-11326)*

Northwestern Tools Inc — 937 298-9994
4800 Hempstead Station Dr Dayton (45429) *(G-6475)*

Northwind Industries Inc — 216 433-0666
11324 Brookpark Rd Cleveland (44130) *(G-4481)*

Northwood Energy Corporation — 614 457-1024
941 Chatham Ln Ste 100 Columbus (43221) *(G-5604)*

Northwood Industries Inc — 419 666-2100
7650 Ponderosa Rd Perrysburg (43551) *(G-12404)*

Norton Industries Inc — 888 357-2345
1366 W 117th St Lakewood (44107) *(G-8980)*

Norton Manufacturing Co Inc — 419 435-0411
455 W 4th St Fostoria (44830) *(G-7648)*

Norton Outdoor Advertising — 513 631-4864
5280 Kennedy Ave Cincinnati (45213) *(G-3205)*

Norvin Hill Machinery LLC — 419 752-0278
4497 Edwards Rd Greenwich (44837) *(G-8069)*

Norwalk Concrete Inds Inc (PA) — 419 668-8167
80 Commerce Dr Norwalk (44857) *(G-11982)*

Norwalk Precast Molds, Inc., Norwalk *Also Called: Precast Products LLC (G-11986)*

Norwalk Reflector, Norwalk *Also Called: Herald Reflector Inc (G-11974)*

Norwalk Reflector, Norwalk *Also Called: Ogden News Publishing Ohio Inc (G-11984)*

Norwalk Wastewater Eqp Co — 419 668-4471
220 Republic St Norwalk (44857) *(G-11983)*

Norweco, Norwalk *Also Called: Norwalk Wastewater Eqp Co (G-11983)*

Norwesco Inc — 740 654-6402
3111 Wilson Rd Lancaster (43130) *(G-9031)*

Norwood Medical, Dayton *Also Called: Norwood Medical LLC (G-6477)*

Norwood Medical LLC — 937 228-4101
2101 Winners Cir Dayton (45404) *(G-6476)*

Norwood Medical LLC (DH) — 937 228-4101
2122 Winners Cir Dayton (45404) *(G-6477)*

Norwood Tool Company — 937 228-4101
2055 Winners Cir Dayton (45404) *(G-6478)*

NORWOOD TOOL COMPANY, Dayton *Also Called: Norwood Tool Company (G-6478)*

Nosh Butters LLC — 773 710-0668
1274 W 65th St Cleveland (44102) *(G-4482)*

Noshok Inc (PA) — 440 243-0888
1010 W Bagley Rd Berea (44017) *(G-1290)*

Noster Rubber Company — 419 299-3387
1481 Township Road 229 Van Buren (45889) *(G-14903)*

Nostrum Laboratories Inc — 419 636-1168
705 E Mulberry St Bryan (43506) *(G-1831)*

Nov Inc — 937 454-3200
5870 Poe Ave Dayton (45414) *(G-6479)*

Nov Process & Flow Tech US Inc — 937 454-3300
5870 Poe Ave Dayton (45414) *(G-6480)*

Nova, Middleburg Heights *Also Called: Nova Machine Products Inc (G-10724)*

Nova Golf Corp — 419 652-3160
63 State Route 511 Nova (44859) *(G-12004)*

Nova Machine Products Inc — 216 267-3200
18001 Sheldon Rd Middleburg Heights (44130) *(G-10724)*

Nova Metal Products, Mentor *Also Called: Nova Metal Products Inc (G-10513)*

Nova Metal Products Inc — 440 269-1741
7500 Clover Ave Mentor (44060) *(G-10513)*

Novacel Inc — 937 335-5611
421 Union St Troy (45373) *(G-14598)*

Novacel Prfmce Coatings Inc — 937 552-4932
421 Union St Troy (45373) *(G-14599)*

Novagard Solutions Inc (PA) — 216 881-8111
5109 Hamilton Ave Cleveland (44114) *(G-4483)*

Novak J F Manufacturing Co LLC — 216 741-5112
2701 Meyer Ave Cleveland (44109) *(G-4484)*

Novartis Corporation — 919 577-5000
1880 Waycross Rd Cincinnati (45240) *(G-3206)*

Novartis Vaccines & Diagnostic, Cincinnati *Also Called: Novartis Corporation (G-3206)*

Novatex North America Inc — 419 282-4264
1070 Faultless Dr Ashland (44805) *(G-595)*

Novation Solutions LLC — 330 620-6721
25 Foundation Pl Barberton (44203) *(G-884)*

Novavision LLC (PA) — 419 354-1427
524 E Woodland Cir Bowling Green (43402) *(G-1577)*

Novel Writing Workshop, Blue Ash *Also Called: F+w Media Inc (G-1393)*

Novelis Alr Almnum-Alabama LLC — 256 353-1550
25825 Science Park Dr Ste 400 Beachwood (44122) *(G-1003)*

Novelis Alr Aluminum LLC — 216 910-3400
25825 Science Park Dr Ste 400 Beachwood (44122) *(G-1004)*

Novelis Alr Recycling Ohio LLC — 740 922-2373
7335 Newport Rd Se Uhrichsville (44683) *(G-14767)*

Novelis Alr Rolled Pdts LLC — 740 983-2571
1 Reynolds Rd Ashville (43103) *(G-669)*

Novelis Alr Rolled Pdts LLC (DH) — 216 910-3400
25825 Science Park Dr Ste 400 Beachwood (44122) *(G-1005)*

Novelis Corporation — 740 983-2571
1 Reynolds Rd Ashville (43103) *(G-670)*

Novelis Corporation — 330 841-3456
390 Griswold St Ne Warren (44483) *(G-15193)*

Novelty Advertising Co Inc — 740 622-3113
1148 Walnut St Coshocton (43812) *(G-5988)*

Noveon Fcc Inc — 440 943-4200
29400 Lakeland Blvd Wickliffe (44092) *(G-15841)*

Novex Operating Company LLC — 330 335-2371
258 Main St Wadsworth (44281) *(G-15049)*

Novex Products Inc — 440 244-3330
2707 Toledo Ave Ste A Lorain (44055) *(G-9427)*

Novo Manufacturing LLC (DH) — 740 269-2221
35280 Scio Bowerston Rd Bowerston (44695) *(G-1546)*

Novoco LLC — 330 359-5315
4041 Township Road 606 Fredericksburg (44627) *(G-7729)*

ALPHABETIC SECTION — Oakes Foundry Inc

Novolex Holdings Inc.. 937 746-1933
2000 Commerce Center Dr Franklin (45005) *(G-7690)*

Novolyte Performance, Cleveland *Also Called: Novolyte Technologies Inc (G-4485)*

Novolyte Technologies Inc.. 216 867-1040
8001 E Pleasant Valley Rd Cleveland (44131) *(G-4485)*

Noxgear LLC.. 937 248-1860
2264 Green Island Dr Columbus (43228) *(G-5605)*

Noxgear LLC.. 937 317-0199
966 Proprietors Rd Worthington (43085) *(G-16206)*

Npa Coatings, Cleveland *Also Called: Npa Coatings Inc (G-4486)*

Npa Coatings Inc... 216 651-5900
11110 Berea Rd Ste 1 Cleveland (44102) *(G-4486)*

Npas Inc... 614 595-6916
2090 Harrington Memorial Rd Mansfield (44903) *(G-9706)*

Npk Construction Equipment Inc (HQ)..................... 440 232-7900
7550 Independence Dr Bedford (44146) *(G-1145)*

Npk LLC... 740 927-2801
13390 Morse Rd Sw New Albany (43054) *(G-11385)*

NPS, Broadview Heights *Also Called: National Polishing Systems Inc (G-1662)*

Nrc Inc... 440 975-9449
38160 Western Pkwy Willoughby (44094) *(G-15961)*

NRG Industrial Lighting Mfg Co................................. 419 354-8207
7458 Linwood Rd Bowling Green (43402) *(G-1578)*

Nrka Corp.. 440 817-0700
1100 W Royalton Rd Ste A Broadview Heights (44147) *(G-1664)*

Nsa Technologies LLC... 330 576-4600
3867 Medina Rd Ste 256 Akron (44333) *(G-269)*

Nsg Glass North America Inc.................................... 734 755-5816
21705 Pemberville Rd Luckey (43443) *(G-9527)*

Nsg Glass North America Inc (PA)............................ 419 247-4800
811 Madison Ave Toledo (43604) *(G-14400)*

Nsi Crankshaft, Fostoria *Also Called: Nippon Stl Intgrted Crnkshaft (G-7647)*

NSK Industries Inc (PA).. 330 923-4112
150 Ascot Pkwy Cuyahoga Falls (44223) *(G-6107)*

NSM, Cleveland *Also Called: Flexrack By Qcells LLC (G-4069)*

Nt, Toledo *Also Called: North Toledo Graphics LLC (G-14398)*

Nta Graphics Inc... 419 476-8808
5225 Telegraph Rd Toledo (43612) *(G-14401)*

Ntb, Cleveland *Also Called: Tbc Retail Group Inc (G-4768)*

Ntb National Tire and Battery.................................... 614 870-8945
1640 Holt Rd Columbus (43228) *(G-5606)*

Ntech Industries Inc... 707 467-3747
5475 Kellenburger Rd Dayton (45424) *(G-6481)*

Nu Pet Company (HQ).. 330 682-3000
1 Strawberry Ln Orrville (44667) *(G-12142)*

Nu Risers Stair Company.. 937 322-8100
2748 Columbus Rd Springfield (45503) *(G-13613)*

Nu Stream Filtration Inc... 937 949-3174
1257 Stanley Ave Dayton (45404) *(G-6482)*

Nu-Di, Cleveland *Also Called: Nu-Di Products Co Inc (G-4487)*

Nu-Di Products Co Inc... 216 251-9070
12730 Triskett Rd Cleveland (44111) *(G-4487)*

Nu-Tech Polymers Co Inc.. 513 942-6003
3220 E Sharon Rd Cincinnati (45241) *(G-3207)*

Nuance Company... 740 964-0367
17 Amanda Dr Granville (43023) *(G-8022)*

Nucam, Twinsburg *Also Called: Semtorq Inc (G-14734)*

Nucon International Inc (PA)..................................... 614 846-5710
7000 Huntley Rd Columbus (43229) *(G-5607)*

Nucor Corporation.. 937 390-2300
3000 Presidential Dr Ste 110 Beavercreek (45324) *(G-1057)*

Nucor Corporation.. 407 855-2990
Cincinnati (45201) *(G-3208)*

Nucor Corporation.. 901 275-3826
300 Pike St Fl 4 Cincinnati (45202) *(G-3209)*

Nucor Load Center, Cincinnati *Also Called: Nucor Corporation (G-3209)*

Nucor Steel Marion Inc... 740 383-6068
400 Bartram Ave Marion (43302) *(G-9867)*

Nucor Steel Marion Inc (HQ)..................................... 740 383-4011
912 Cheney Ave Marion (43302) *(G-9868)*

Nuevue Solutions Inc... 440 836-4772
4209 State Route 44 D-134 Rootstown (44272) *(G-12856)*

Nufacturing Inc.. 330 814-5259
2845 Center Rd Brunswick (44212) *(G-1776)*

Nuflux LLC... 330 399-1122
2395 State Route 5 Cortland (44410) *(G-5966)*

Numerics Unlimited Inc... 937 849-0100
1700 Dalton Dr New Carlisle (45344) *(G-11423)*

Nunzios Cabinet Shop, Cleveland *Also Called: Marzano Inc (G-4364)*

Nupco Inc.. 419 629-2259
06561 County Road 66a New Bremen (45869) *(G-11406)*

Nupro Company.. 440 951-9729
4800 E 345th St Willoughby (44094) *(G-15962)*

Nutone Inc... 888 336-3948
9825 Kenwood Rd Ste 301 Blue Ash (45242) *(G-1444)*

Nutrien AG Solutions Inc... 614 873-4253
9972 State Route 38 Milford Center (43045) *(G-10929)*

Nutrien AG Solutions Inc... 513 941-4100
10743 Brower Rd North Bend (45052) *(G-11705)*

Nutritional Medicinals LLC....................................... 937 433-4673
9277 Centre Pointe Dr Ste 220 West Chester (45069) *(G-15467)*

Nutro Corporation.. 440 572-3800
11515 Alameda Dr Strongsville (44149) *(G-13860)*

Nutro Inc.. 440 572-3800
11515 Alameda Dr Strongsville (44149) *(G-13861)*

Nutro Machinery, Strongsville *Also Called: Nutro Corporation (G-13860)*

Nuts Are Good Inc (PA).. 586 619-2400
Busch Blvd Columbus (43229) *(G-5608)*

Nutz4coffee Ltd... 216 236-5292
2800 Euclid Ave Ste 150 Cleveland (44115) *(G-4488)*

Nwp Manufacturing Inc... 419 894-6871
2862 County Road 146 Waldo (43356) *(G-15089)*

Nyle LLC.. 888 235-2097
283 Sharts Dr Springboro (45066) *(G-13513)*

O C I, Waverly *Also Called: Oak Chips Inc (G-15289)*

O Connor Office Pdts & Prtg..................................... 740 852-2209
60 W High St London (43140) *(G-9392)*

O D L LLC.. 419 833-2533
19260 Dunbridge Rd Bowling Green (43402) *(G-1579)*

O D M, Mason *Also Called: Oakley Die & Mold Co (G-10034)*

O E Meyer Co.. 614 428-5656
5677 Chantry Dr Columbus (43232) *(G-5609)*

O E Meyer Co.. 419 332-6931
1005 Everett Rd Fremont (43420) *(G-7798)*

O G Bell, Avon Lake *Also Called: Wolff Tool & Mfg Company Inc (G-829)*

O Gauge Railroading, Hilliard *Also Called: Ogr Publishing Inc (G-8425)*

O K Coal & Concrete, Zanesville *Also Called: McClelland Inc (G-16544)*

O S C, Columbus *Also Called: Octsys Security Corp (G-5611)*

O-1, Perrysburg *Also Called: Owens-Illinois General Inc (G-12415)*

O-I, Perrysburg *Also Called: O-I Glass Inc (G-12405)*

O-I Glass Inc (PA)... 567 336-5000
1 Michael Owens Way Perrysburg (43551) *(G-12405)*

O-Kan Marine Repair Inc... 740 446-4686
267 Upper River Rd Gallipolis (45631) *(G-7897)*

O'Reilly Precision Tool, Russia *Also Called: OReilly Precision Pdts Inc (G-12886)*

Oak Chips Inc.. 740 947-4159
9329 State Route 220 Ste A Waverly (45690) *(G-15289)*

Oak Hills Carton Co... 513 948-4200
6310 Este Ave Cincinnati (45232) *(G-3210)*

Oak Industrial Inc... 440 263-2780
12955 York Delta Dr Ste G North Royalton (44133) *(G-11889)*

Oak Pointe LLC... 740 498-9820
96 New Pace Rd Newcomerstown (43832) *(G-11648)*

Oak Tree Intl Holdings Inc... 702 462-7295
1209 Lowell St Elyria (44035) *(G-7188)*

Oak View Enterprises Inc.. 513 860-4446
100 Crossroads Blvd Bucyrus (44820) *(G-1864)*

Oakbridge Timber Framing....................................... 419 994-1052
9001 Township Road 461 Loudonville (44842) *(G-9450)*

Oakes Foundry Inc... 330 372-4010
700 Bronze Rd Ne Warren (44483) *(G-15194)*

Oakley Inc
ALPHABETIC SECTION

Oakley Inc 949 672-6560
   1421 Springfield St Unit 2 Dayton (45403) *(G-6483)*

Oakley Die & Mold Co 513 754-8500
   4393 Digital Way Mason (45040) *(G-10034)*

Oakley Inds Sub Assmbly Div In 419 661-8888
   6317 Fairfield Dr Northwood (43619) *(G-11923)*

Oaks Welding Inc 330 482-4216
   201 Prospect St Columbiana (44408) *(G-5047)*

Oaktree Wireline LLC 330 352-7250
   1825 E High Ave New Philadelphia (44663) *(G-11520)*

Oakwood Industries Inc (PA) 440 232-8700
   7250 Division St Bedford (44146) *(G-1146)*

Oakwood Laboratories LLC (PA) 440 359-0000
   7670 First Pl Ste A Oakwood Village (44146) *(G-12041)*

Oakwood Laboratories LLC 440 505-2011
   27070 Miles Rd Solon (44139) *(G-13400)*

Oakwood Register, The, Dayton Also Called: Winkler Co Inc *(G-6655)*

Oase North America Inc 800 365-3880
   125 Lena Dr Aurora (44202) *(G-728)*

Oasis Consumer Healthcare LLC 216 394-0544
   425 Literary Rd Apt 100 Cleveland (44113) *(G-4489)*

Oasis International, Columbus Also Called: Lvd Acquisition LLC *(G-5537)*

Oasis Mditerranean Cuisine Inc 419 269-1459
   1520 W Laskey Rd Toledo (43612) *(G-14402)*

Oatey, Cleveland Also Called: Oatey Supply Chain Svcs Inc *(G-4491)*

Oatey Co (PA) 800 203-1755
   20600 Emerald Pkwy Cleveland (44135) *(G-4490)*

Oatey Supply Chain Svcs Inc (HQ) 216 267-7100
   20600 Emerald Pkwy Cleveland (44135) *(G-4491)*

Obars Machine and Tool Company (PA) 419 535-6307
   115 N Westwood Ave # 125 Toledo (43607) *(G-14403)*

Obars Welding & Fabg Div, Toledo Also Called: Obars Machine and Tool Company *(G-14403)*

Oberfields LLC 614 252-0955
   1165 Alum Creek Dr Columbus (43209) *(G-5610)*

Oberfields LLC (HQ) 740 369-7644
   528 London Rd Delaware (43015) *(G-6742)*

Oberfields LLC 740 369-7644
   471 Kintner Pkwy Sunbury (43074) *(G-13959)*

Obhc Inc 440 236-5112
   33549 E Royalton Rd Unit 9 Columbia Station (44028) *(G-5015)*

Obic LLC 419 633-3147
   525 Winzeler Dr # 1 Bryan (43506) *(G-1832)*

Obr Cooling Towers Inc 419 243-3443
   2845 Crane Way Northwood (43619) *(G-11924)*

Obron Atlantic Corporation 440 954-7600
   830 E Erie St Painesville (44077) *(G-12252)*

Obs Inc 330 453-3725
   1324 Tuscarawas St W Canton (44702) *(G-2180)*

Obs Specialty Vehicles, Canton Also Called: Obs Inc *(G-2180)*

Occassionaly Yours, Beavercreek Also Called: Shops By Todd Inc *(G-1061)*

Occidental Chemical Corp 513 242-2900
   4701 Paddock Rd Cincinnati (45229) *(G-3211)*

Occidental Chemical Durez 419 675-1310
   13717 Us Highway 68 Kenton (43326) *(G-8895)*

Occv1 Inc 419 248-8000
   1 Owens Corning Pkwy Toledo (43659) *(G-14404)*

Occv2 LLC 419 248-8000
   1 Owens Corning Prkwy Toledo (43659) *(G-14405)*

Ochc, Cleveland Also Called: Oasis Consumer Healthcare LLC *(G-4489)*

Ocm LLC 937 247-2700
   4500 Lyons Rd Miamisburg (45342) *(G-10667)*

Ocs Intellitrak Inc 513 742-5600
   8660 Seward Rd Fairfield (45011) *(G-7388)*

Ocsial LLC (PA) 415 906-5271
   950 Taylor Station Rd Ste W Gahanna (43230) *(G-7847)*

Octal Extrusion Corp 513 881-6100
   5399 E Provident Dr West Chester (45246) *(G-15574)*

Octopus Express Inc 614 412-1222
   470 Olde Worthington Rd Westerville (43082) *(G-15671)*

Octsys Security Corp 614 470-4510
   341 S 3rd St Ste 100-42 Columbus (43215) *(G-5611)*

Oculii Corp 937 912-9261
   829 Space Dr Beavercreek Township (45434) *(G-1088)*

Odawara Automation Inc 937 667-8433
   4805 S County Road 25a Tipp City (45371) *(G-14145)*

Odell Electronic Cleaning Stns, Westlake Also Called: Aerocase Incorporated *(G-15728)*

Odi, Elyria Also Called: Ohio Displays Inc *(G-7189)*

Odom, Milford Also Called: Odom Industries Inc *(G-10915)*

Odom Industries Inc 513 248-0287
   1262 Us Hwy 50 Milford (45150) *(G-10915)*

Odyssey Machine Company Ltd 419 455-6621
   26675 Eckel Rd # 5 Perrysburg (43551) *(G-12406)*

Odyssey Press Inc 614 410-0356
   913 Superior Dr Huron (44839) *(G-8642)*

Oe Exchange LLC (PA) 440 266-1639
   7750 Tyler Blvd Mentor (44060) *(G-10514)*

OEM, West Chester Also Called: Ctl-Aerospace Inc *(G-15547)*

Oerlikon Frction Systems US In 937 233-9191
   240 Detrick St Dayton (45404) *(G-6484)*

Oerlikon Friction Systems 937 449-4000
   14 Heid Ave Dayton (45404) *(G-6485)*

Oerlikon Friction Systems (HQ) 937 449-4000
   240 Detrick St Dayton (45404) *(G-6486)*

Ofco Inc 740 622-5922
   111 N 14th St Coshocton (43812) *(G-5989)*

Off Contact Inc 419 255-5546
   4756 W Bancroft St Toledo (43615) *(G-14406)*

Off Contact Productions, Toledo Also Called: Off Contact Inc *(G-14406)*

Office Furniture Solution, North Canton Also Called: Document Concepts Inc *(G-11723)*

Office Magic Inc (PA) 510 782-6100
   2290 Wilbur Rd Medina (44256) *(G-10357)*

Ogc Industries Inc 330 456-1500
   934 Wells Ave Nw Canton (44703) *(G-2181)*

Ogden News Publishing Ohio Inc 419 422-5151
   701 W Sandusky St Findlay (45840) *(G-7544)*

Ogden News Publishing Ohio Inc 567 743-9843
   34 E Main St Norwalk (44857) *(G-11984)*

Ogden News Publishing Ohio Inc (DH) 419 625-5500
   314 W Market St Sandusky (44870) *(G-13083)*

Ogden Newspapers Inc 304 748-0606
   401 Herald Sq Steubenville (43952) *(G-13674)*

Ogden Newspapers Ohio Inc (DH) 330 424-9541
   308 Maple St Lisbon (44432) *(G-9322)*

Ogden Newspapers Ohio Inc 419 448-3200
   320 Nelson St Tiffin (44883) *(G-14097)*

Ogg Garick, Cleveland Also Called: Garick LLC *(G-4102)*

Oglebay Norton Mar Svcs Co LLC 216 861-3300
   1001 Lakeside Ave E 15th Fl Cleveland (44114) *(G-4492)*

Ogonek Custom Hardwood Inc (PA) 833 718-2531
   61 E State St Barberton (44203) *(G-885)*

Ogr Publishing Inc 330 757-3020
   5825 Redsand Rd Hilliard (43026) *(G-8425)*

Ogs Industries, Akron Also Called: Ohio Gasket and Shim Co Inc *(G-270)*

OH Road LLC 614 582-4765
   2636 Berwyn Rd Columbus (43221) *(G-5612)*

Ohashi Technica USA Inc (HQ) 740 965-5115
   111 Burrer Dr Sunbury (43074) *(G-13960)*

Ohashi Technica USA Mfg Inc 740 965-9002
   99 Burrer Dr Sunbury (43074) *(G-13961)*

Ohigro Inc (PA) 740 726-2429
   6720 Gillette Rd Waldo (43356) *(G-15090)*

Ohio Aluminum Chemicals LLC 513 860-3842
   4544 Mulhauser Rd West Chester (45011) *(G-15468)*

Ohio Aluminum Industries Inc 216 641-8865
   4840 Warner Rd Cleveland (44125) *(G-4493)*

Ohio Art Company (PA) 419 636-3141
   1 Toy St Bryan (43506) *(G-1833)*

Ohio Asphaltic Limestone Corp 937 364-2191
   8591 Mad River Rd Hillsboro (45133) *(G-8462)*

Ohio Associated Entps LLC 440 354-3148
   72 Corwin Dr Painesville (44077) *(G-12253)*

Ohio Associated Entps LLC 440 354-3148
   1359 W Jackson St Painesville (44077) *(G-12254)*

Ohio Auto Supply Company..330 454-5105
1128 Tuscarawas St W Canton (44702) *(G-2182)*

Ohio Awning & Manufacturing Co..............................216 861-2400
5777 Grant Ave Cleveland (44105) *(G-4494)*

Ohio Beef USA LLC...419 257-5536
2208 Grant Rd North Baltimore (45872) *(G-11699)*

Ohio Belt Control Supply Co, Wadsworth Also Called: D & J Electric Motor Repair Co *(G-15025)*

Ohio Beverage Systems Inc..216 475-3900
9200 Midwest Ave Cleveland (44125) *(G-4495)*

Ohio Biosystems Coop Inc..419 980-7663
134 S Adams St Loudonville (44842) *(G-9451)*

Ohio Blenders Inc (PA)..419 726-2655
2404 N Summit St Toledo (43611) *(G-14407)*

Ohio Blow Pipe, Cleveland Also Called: Ohio Blow Pipe Company *(G-4496)*

Ohio Blow Pipe Company (PA)...................................216 681-7379
446 E 131st St Cleveland (44108) *(G-4496)*

Ohio Box & Crate Inc..440 526-3133
16751 Tavern Rd Burton (44021) *(G-1885)*

Ohio Box and Crate Co, Burton Also Called: Ohio Box & Crate Inc *(G-1885)*

Ohio Bridge Corporation...740 432-6334
201 Wheeling Ave Cambridge (43725) *(G-1945)*

Ohio Broach & Machine Company............................440 946-1040
35264 Topps Industrial Pkwy Willoughby (44094) *(G-15963)*

Ohio Brush Works, Plain City Also Called: Delaware Paint Company Ltd *(G-12574)*

Ohio Building Restoration Inc (PA)...........................419 244-7372
830 Mill St Toledo (43609) *(G-14408)*

Ohio Carbon Blank Inc..440 953-9302
38403 Pelton Rd Willoughby (44094) *(G-15964)*

Ohio Cbd Guy LLC..513 417-9806
7875 Montgomery Rd Cincinnati (45236) *(G-3212)*

Ohio City Pasta, Cleveland Also Called: Food Designs Inc *(G-4078)*

Ohio Cllbrtive Lrng Sltons Inc (PA)...........................216 595-5289
17171 Golden Star Dr Strongsville (44136) *(G-13862)*

Ohio Coatings Company...740 859-5500
2100 Tin Plate Pl Yorkville (43971) *(G-16294)*

Ohio Coffee Collaborative Ltd...................................614 564-9852
745 N High St Columbus (43215) *(G-5613)*

Ohio Community Media, Miamisburg Also Called: Ocm LLC *(G-10667)*

Ohio Construction News, Cincinnati Also Called: 400 SW 7th Street Partners Ltd *(G-2580)*

Ohio Crafted Malt House LLC....................................614 961-7805
8000 Walton Pkwy Ste 200 New Albany (43054) *(G-11386)*

Ohio Crankshaft Div, Newburgh Heights Also Called: Park-Ohio Industries Inc *(G-11620)*

Ohio Custom Dies LLC..330 538-3396
293 Rosemont Rd North Jackson (44451) *(G-11787)*

Ohio Custom Door LLC...330 695-6301
9141 County Road 201 Fredericksburg (44627) *(G-7730)*

Ohio Cut Sheet, Strongsville Also Called: Dupli-Systems Inc *(G-13830)*

Ohio Dalley Press, Belpre Also Called: Ovp Inc *(G-1259)*

Ohio Decorative Products LLC (PA)..........................419 647-9033
220 S Elizabeth St Spencerville (45887) *(G-13487)*

Ohio Defense Services Inc...937 608-2371
143 S Monmouth St Dayton (45403) *(G-6487)*

Ohio Department Public Safety................................440 943-5545
31517 Vine St Willowick (44095) *(G-16033)*

Ohio Department Transportation.............................614 351-2898
1606 W Broad St Columbus (43223) *(G-5614)*

Ohio Dermatological Assn...330 465-8281
698 Dalton Fox Lake Rd Dalton (44618) *(G-6137)*

Ohio Designer Craftsmen Entps (HQ)......................614 486-7119
1665 W 5th Ave Columbus (43212) *(G-5615)*

Ohio Displays Inc..216 961-5600
825 Leona St Elyria (44035) *(G-7189)*

Ohio Distinctive Enterprises.....................................614 459-0453
6500 Fiesta Dr Columbus (43235) *(G-5616)*

Ohio Distinctive Software, Columbus Also Called: Ohio Distinctive Enterprises *(G-5616)*

Ohio Drill & Tool Co (PA)..330 525-7717
23255 Georgetown Rd Homeworth (44634) *(G-8555)*

Ohio Eagle Distributing LLC......................................513 539-8483
9300 Allen Rd West Chester (45069) *(G-15469)*

Ohio Electric Control, Ashland Also Called: Precision Design Inc *(G-605)*

Ohio Electric Motor Service Center Inc....................614 444-1451
1854 S High St Columbus (43207) *(G-5617)*

Ohio Electric Motor Svc LLC (PA)..............................614 444-1451
1909 E Livingston Ave Columbus (43209) *(G-5618)*

Ohio Embroidery LLC..330 479-0029
1321 Davis St Sw Canton (44706) *(G-2183)*

Ohio Engineering and Mfg Co, Wadsworth Also Called: Hutnik Company *(G-15035)*

Ohio Envelope Manufacturing Co............................216 267-2920
5161 W 164th St Cleveland (44142) *(G-4497)*

Ohio Esc Print Shop..419 774-2512
890 W 4th St Ontario (44906) *(G-12092)*

Ohio Fabricators, Coshocton Also Called: Ofco Inc *(G-5989)*

Ohio Fabricators Company..740 622-5922
1321 Elm St Coshocton (43812) *(G-5990)*

Ohio Feather Company Inc.......................................513 921-3373
1 Kovach Dr Cincinnati (45215) *(G-3213)*

Ohio Fire Suppression LLC.......................................216 269-6032
10481 Maryland St Aurora (44202) *(G-729)*

Ohio Flame Hardening Company (PA)....................513 336-6160
3944 Miami Rd Apt 106 Cincinnati (45227) *(G-3214)*

Ohio Flexible Packaging Co......................................513 494-1800
512 S Main St South Lebanon (45065) *(G-13462)*

Ohio Foam Corporation...614 252-4877
1513 Alum Creek Dr Columbus (43209) *(G-5619)*

Ohio Foam Corporation...419 492-2151
529 S Kibler St New Washington (44854) *(G-11550)*

Ohio Foam Corporation...330 799-4553
1201 Ameritech Blvd Youngstown (44509) *(G-16405)*

Ohio Fresh Eggs LLC (PA)...740 893-7200
11212 Croton Rd Croton (43013) *(G-6052)*

Ohio Galvanizing LLC..740 387-6474
467 W Fairground St Marion (43302) *(G-9869)*

Ohio Gasket and Shim Co Inc (PA)..........................330 630-0626
976 Evans Ave Akron (44305) *(G-270)*

Ohio Gratings Inc (PA)..800 321-9800
5299 Southway St Sw Canton (44706) *(G-2184)*

Ohio Gratings Inc...330 479-4292
6355 Lattasburg Rd Wooster (44691) *(G-16158)*

Ohio Gravure Technologies, Miamisburg Also Called: Ohio Gravure Technologies Inc *(G-10668)*

Ohio Gravure Technologies Inc................................937 439-1582
4401 Lyons Rd Miamisburg (45342) *(G-10668)*

Ohio Guitar Shows Inc..740 592-4614
23 Curtis St Athens (45701) *(G-689)*

Ohio Guns, Ashtabula Also Called: Reloading Supplies Corp *(G-658)*

Ohio Hckry Hrvest Brnd Pdts In...............................330 644-6266
90 Logan Pkwy Coventry Township (44319) *(G-6014)*

Ohio Hd Video...614 656-1162
1355 Bingham Mills Dr New Albany (43054) *(G-11387)*

Ohio Heat Transfer..513 870-5323
3400 Port Union Rd Hamilton (45014) *(G-8233)*

Ohio Heat Transfer Ltd...740 695-0635
66721 Executive Dr Saint Clairsville (43950) *(G-12917)*

Ohio Home & Leisure Products I.............................614 833-4144
569 Pickerington Hills Dr Pickerington (43147) *(G-12465)*

Ohio Hydraulics Inc...513 771-2590
2510 E Sharon Rd Cincinnati (45241) *(G-3215)*

Ohio Industrial Coating Corp...................................567 230-6719
880 S Bon Aire Ave Tiffin (44883) *(G-14098)*

Ohio Irish American News..216 647-1144
14615 Triskett Rd Cleveland (44111) *(G-4498)*

Ohio Label Inc...614 777-0180
5005 Transamerica Dr Columbus (43228) *(G-5620)*

Ohio Laminating & Binding Inc...............................614 771-4868
4364 Reynolds Dr Hilliard (43026) *(G-8426)*

Ohio Laser LLC...614 873-7030
8260 Estates Pkwy Plain City (43064) *(G-12587)*

Ohio Luxury Builders, Austintown Also Called: Ohio Luxury Builders LLC *(G-753)*

Ohio Luxury Builders LLC..330 881-0073
4958 Mahoning Ave Austintown (44515) *(G-753)*

Ohio Machinery Co   **ALPHABETIC SECTION**

Ohio Machinery Co (PA) 440 526-6200
   3993 E Royalton Rd Broadview Heights (44147) *(G-1665)*

Ohio Made Tires LLC 740 421-4934
   47063 Black Walnut Pkwy Woodsfield (43793) *(G-16089)*

Ohio Magnetics Inc 216 662-8484
   5400 Dunham Rd Maple Heights (44137) *(G-9756)*

Ohio Metal Fabricating Inc 937 233-2400
   6057 Milo Rd Dayton (45414) *(G-6488)*

Ohio Metal Processing LLC 740 912-2057
   16064 Beaver Pike Jackson (45640) *(G-8719)*

Ohio Metal Products Company 937 228-6101
   35 Bates St Dayton (45402) *(G-6489)*

Ohio Metal Technologies Inc 740 928-8288
   470 John Alford Pkwy Hebron (43025) *(G-8353)*

Ohio Metallurgical Service Inc 440 365-4104
   1033 Clark St Elyria (44035) *(G-7190)*

Ohio Mill Supply, Cleveland Also Called: Ohio Mills Corporation *(G-4499)*

Ohio Mills Corporation (PA) 216 431-3979
   1719 E 39th St Cleveland (44114) *(G-4499)*

Ohio Mirror Technologies Inc (PA) 419 399-5903
   114 W Jackson St Paulding (45879) *(G-12318)*

Ohio Model Products LLC 614 808-4488
   4180 Fisher Rd Columbus (43228) *(G-5621)*

Ohio Module Manufacturing Company LLC 419 729-6700
   3900 Stickney Ave Toledo (43608) *(G-14409)*

Ohio Moulding Corporation (HQ) 440 944-2100
   30396 Lakeland Blvd Wickliffe (44092) *(G-15842)*

Ohio News Network 614 460-3700
   770 Twin Rivers Dr Columbus (43215) *(G-5622)*

Ohio News Network, Columbus Also Called: Ohio News Network *(G-5622)*

Ohio Newspaper Services Inc 614 486-6677
   1335 Dublin Rd Ste 216b Columbus (43215) *(G-5623)*

Ohio Newspapers Inc (DH) 937 225-2000
   1611 S Main St Dayton (45409) *(G-6490)*

Ohio Newspapers Foundation 614 486-6677
   1335 Dublin Rd Ste 216b Columbus (43215) *(G-5624)*

Ohio Nitrogen LLC 216 839-5485
   25800 Science Park Dr Beachwood (44122) *(G-1006)*

Ohio Nut & Bolt Company Div, Berea Also Called: Fastener Industries Inc *(G-1279)*

Ohio Ordnance Works Inc 440 285-3481
   310 Park Dr Chardon (44024) *(G-2461)*

Ohio Packing Company 614 445-0627
   1306 Harmon Ave Columbus (43223) *(G-5625)*

Ohio Paper Tube Co 330 478-5171
   3422 Navarre Rd Sw Canton (44706) *(G-2185)*

Ohio Pet Foods Inc (HQ) 330 424-1431
   38251 Industrial Park Rd Lisbon (44432) *(G-9323)*

Ohio Pickling & Processing, Toledo Also Called: Ohio Steel Processing LLC *(G-14410)*

Ohio Plastics & Belting Co LLC 330 882-6764
   6140 Manchester Rd New Franklin (44319) *(G-11440)*

Ohio Power Systems LLC 419 396-4041
   807 E Findlay St Carey (43316) *(G-2282)*

Ohio Precision Inc 330 453-9710
   1239 Market Ave S Canton (44707) *(G-2186)*

Ohio Precision Molding Inc 330 745-9393
   122 E Tuscarawas Ave Barberton (44203) *(G-886)*

Ohio Pulp Mills Inc 513 631-7400
   2100 Losantiville Ave Ste 3 Cincinnati (45237) *(G-3216)*

Ohio Pure Foods Inc (HQ) 330 753-2293
   681 W Waterloo Rd Akron (44314) *(G-271)*

Ohio Refining Company LLC 614 210-2300
   5550 Blazer Pkwy Ste 200 Dublin (43017) *(G-6917)*

Ohio Report, Columbus Also Called: Gongwer News Service Inc *(G-5407)*

Ohio Rights Group 614 300-0529
   1021 E Broad St Columbus (43205) *(G-5626)*

Ohio River Valley Cabinet 740 975-8846
   4 Waterworks Rd Newark (43055) *(G-11599)*

Ohio Roll Grinding Inc 330 453-1884
   5165 Louisville St Louisville (44641) *(G-9466)*

Ohio Rotational Molding LLC 419 608-5040
   503 Joe E Brown Ave Holgate (43527) *(G-8490)*

Ohio Screw Products Inc 440 322-6341
   818 Lowell St Elyria (44035) *(G-7191)*

Ohio Select Imprinted Fabrics, Reynoldsburg Also Called: Ohio State Institute Fin Inc *(G-12770)*

Ohio Semitronics Inc 614 777-1005
   4242 Reynolds Dr Hilliard (43026) *(G-8427)*

Ohio Shelterall Inc 614 882-1110
   6060 Westerville Rd Westerville (43081) *(G-15717)*

Ohio Specialty Dies LLC 330 538-3396
   293 Rosemont Rd North Jackson (44451) *(G-11788)*

Ohio Standard Bread, Medina Also Called: Trogdon Publishing Inc *(G-10389)*

Ohio Star Forge Co (HQ) 330 847-6360
   3991 Mahoning Ave Nw Warren (44483) *(G-15195)*

Ohio State Institute Fin Inc 614 861-8811
   7394 E Main St Reynoldsburg (43068) *(G-12770)*

Ohio State Pallet Corp 614 332-3961
   2175 Broehm Rd Homer (43027) *(G-8552)*

Ohio State Plastics 614 299-5618
   1917 Joyce Ave Columbus (43219) *(G-5627)*

Ohio Steel Industries Inc 740 927-9500
   13792 Broad St Sw Pataskala (43062) *(G-12302)*

Ohio Steel Industries Inc (PA) 614 471-4800
   2575 Ferris Rd Columbus (43224) *(G-5628)*

Ohio Steel Processing LLC 419 241-9601
   1149 Campbell St Toledo (43607) *(G-14410)*

Ohio Steel Sheet and Plate Inc 800 827-2401
   7845 Chestnut Ridge Rd Hubbard (44425) *(G-8569)*

Ohio Table Pad Co Georgia Div, Perrysburg Also Called: Ohio Table Pad Company *(G-12407)*

Ohio Table Pad Company (PA) 419 872-6400
   350 3 Meadows Dr Perrysburg (43551) *(G-12407)*

Ohio Table Pad Company 419 872-6400
   350 3 Meadows Dr Perrysburg (43551) *(G-12408)*

Ohio Table Pad of Indiana 419 872-6400
   350 3 Meadows Dr Perrysburg (43551) *(G-12409)*

Ohio Tile & Marble Co 513 541-4211
   3809 Spring Grove Ave Cincinnati (45223) *(G-3217)*

Ohio Timberland Products Inc 419 682-6322
   102 Railroad Ave Stryker (43557) *(G-13911)*

Ohio Tool & Jig Grind Inc 937 415-0692
   6948 Clearview Ct Springboro (45066) *(G-13514)*

Ohio Tool Works LLC 419 281-3700
   1374 Township Road 743 Ashland (44805) *(G-596)*

Ohio Trailer Inc 330 392-4444
   1899 Tod Ave Sw Warren (44485) *(G-15196)*

Ohio Trailer Supply Inc 614 471-9121
   2966 Westerville Rd Columbus (43224) *(G-5629)*

Ohio Transitional Machine & Tl 419 476-0820
   3940 Castener St Toledo (43612) *(G-14411)*

Ohio Truck Equipment LLC 740 830-6488
   8920 Columbus Rd Mount Vernon (43050) *(G-11283)*

Ohio Valley Alloy Services Inc 740 373-1900
   100 Westview Ave Marietta (45750) *(G-9812)*

Ohio Valley Coal Company 740 926-1351
   46226 National Rd Saint Clairsville (43950) *(G-12918)*

Ohio Valley Manufacturing Inc 419 522-5818
   1501 Harrington Memorial Rd Mansfield (44903) *(G-9707)*

Ohio Valley Sand LLC 740 661-4240
   513 Mill Ave Se New Philadelphia (44663) *(G-11521)*

Ohio Valley Sand LLC 330 440-6495
   100 E State St Newcomerstown (43832) *(G-11649)*

Ohio Valley Specialty Company 740 373-2276
   115 Industry Rd Marietta (45750) *(G-9813)*

Ohio Valley Stave Inc 740 259-6222
   18253 State Route 73 Mc Dermott (45652) *(G-10274)*

Ohio Valley Trackwork Inc 740 446-0181
   39 Fairview Rd Bidwell (45614) *(G-1325)*

Ohio Valley Truss Company (PA) 937 393-3995
   6000 Us Highway 50 Hillsboro (45133) *(G-8463)*

Ohio Valley Veneer Inc (PA) 740 493-2901
   16523 State Route 124 Piketon (45661) *(G-12480)*

Ohio Valley Veneer Co, Piketon Also Called: Ohio Valley Veneer Inc *(G-12480)*

Ohio Vertical Heat Treat Inc.. 330 456-7176
  2030 Industrial Pl Se Canton (44707) *(G-2187)*

Ohio Vly Stmpng-Assemblies Inc.. 419 522-0983
  500 Newman St Mansfield (44902) *(G-9708)*

Ohio Willow Wood Company, The, Mount Sterling Also Called: Willowwood Global LLC *(G-11259)*

Ohio Windmill & Pump Co Inc... 330 547-6300
  8389 S Pricetown Rd Berlin Center (44401) *(G-1310)*

Ohio Wire Cloth, Englewood Also Called: Unified Scrning Crshing - OH I *(G-7246)*

Ohio Wire Form & Spring Co... 614 444-3676
  2270 S High St Columbus (43207) *(G-5630)*

Ohio Wire Harness LLC.. 937 292-7355
  225 Lincoln Ave Bellefontaine (43311) *(G-1217)*

Ohio Wood Connection LLC... 513 581-0361
  8805 Lancaster Ave Cincinnati (45242) *(G-3218)*

Ohio Wood Fabrication, Sandusky Also Called: Gary L Gast *(G-13059)*

Ohio Wood Recycling Inc.. 614 491-0881
  2019 Rathmell Rd Columbus (43207) *(G-5631)*

Ohio Woodworking Co Inc.. 513 631-0870
  5035 Beech St Cincinnati (45212) *(G-3219)*

Ohio's Country Journal, Columbus Also Called: Agri Communicators Inc *(G-5105)*

Ohiomet, Elyria Also Called: Ohio Metallurgical Service Inc *(G-7190)*

Ohios Best Juice Company LLC... 440 258-0834
  299 Pathfinder Dr Ste 103 Reynoldsburg (43068) *(G-12771)*

Ohlheiser Corp... 860 953-7632
  1900 Jetway Blvd Columbus (43219) *(G-5632)*

Ohlinger Dev & Editorial Co.. 614 261-5360
  28 W Henderson Rd Columbus (43214) *(G-5633)*

Ohlinger Publishing Svcs Inc.. 614 261-5360
  28 W Henderson Rd Columbus (43214) *(G-5634)*

Ohlinger Studios, Columbus Also Called: Ohlinger Dev & Editorial Co *(G-5633)*

Ohlinger Studios, Columbus Also Called: Ohlinger Publishing Svcs Inc *(G-5634)*

Ohmart Vega, Lebanon Also Called: Vega Americas Inc *(G-9119)*

Ohta Press US Inc... 937 374-3382
  1125 S Patton St Xenia (45385) *(G-16271)*

Oi, Perrysburg Also Called: Owens-Illinois Inc *(G-12417)*

Oi California Containers Inc (HQ)... 567 336-5000
  1 Michael Owens Way Perrysburg (43551) *(G-12410)*

Oi Castalia STS Inc... 419 247-5000
  1 Seagate Toledo (43604) *(G-14412)*

Oil Enterprises, Logan Also Called: Ralph Robinson Inc *(G-9375)*

Oil Skimmers, North Royalton Also Called: OSI Environmental LLC *(G-11890)*

Oil Tooling and Stamping, Ontario Also Called: Cole Tool & Die Company *(G-12090)*

Oil Works LLC... 614 245-3090
  1611 Integrity Dr E Columbus (43209) *(G-5635)*

OK Brugmann Jr & Sons Inc.. 330 274-2106
  4083 Mennonite Rd Mantua (44255) *(G-9741)*

OK Industries Inc... 419 435-2361
  2307 W Corporate Dr W Fostoria (44830) *(G-7649)*

Okamoto Sandusky Mfg LLC.. 419 626-1633
  3130 W Monroe St Sandusky (44870) *(G-13084)*

Okamoto USA, Sandusky Also Called: Okamoto Sandusky Mfg LLC *(G-13084)*

OKL Can Line Inc
  11235 Sebring Dr Cincinnati (45240) *(G-3220)*

Okolona Iron & Metal LLC... 419 758-3701
  18641 County Rd N Napoleon (43545) *(G-11328)*

Okuley Hvac & Met Fabrication.. 419 478-4699
  50 W Sylvania Ave Toledo (43612) *(G-14413)*

Olay LLC.. 787 535-2191
  11530 Reed Hartman Hwy Blue Ash (45241) *(G-1445)*

Olberding Brand Family, Cincinnati Also Called: The Photo-Type Engraving Company *(G-3450)*

Old Classic Delight Inc.. 419 394-7955
  310 S Park Dr Saint Marys (45885) *(G-12959)*

Old Firehouse Cellars, Geneva Also Called: Old Firehouse Winery Inc *(G-7943)*

Old Firehouse Winery Inc... 440 466-9300
  5499 Lake Rd E Geneva (44041) *(G-7943)*

Old Mason Winery Inc... 937 698-1122
  4199 S Iddings Rd West Milton (45383) *(G-15630)*

Old Mill Winery Inc.. 440 466-5560
  403 S Broadway Geneva (44041) *(G-7944)*

Old Rar Inc... 216 545-7249
  3700 Park East Dr Ste 300 Beachwood (44122) *(G-1007)*

Old Smo Inc.. 419 394-3346
  323 S Park Dr Saint Marys (45885) *(G-12960)*

Old Smo Inc (PA).. 419 394-3346
  405 E South St Saint Marys (45885) *(G-12961)*

Old Trail Printing Co, Columbus Also Called: Old Trail Printing Company *(G-5636)*

Old Trail Printing Company.. 614 443-4852
  100 Fornoff Rd Columbus (43207) *(G-5636)*

Old West Woods, Waynesfield Also Called: Aca Millworks Inc *(G-15295)*

Old World Stones... 330 299-1128
  4791 Richman Rd Litchfield (44253) *(G-9329)*

Oldcastle Apg Midwest Inc... 440 949-1815
  5190 Oster Rd Sheffield Village (44054) *(G-13187)*

Oldcastle Buildingenvelope Inc.. 800 537-4064
  291 M St Perrysburg (43551) *(G-12411)*

Oldcastle Infrastructure Inc... 419 592-2309
  1675 Industrial Dr Napoleon (43545) *(G-11329)*

Olde Man Granola LLC.. 419 819-9576
  7227 W State Route 12 Findlay (45840) *(G-7545)*

Olde Wood Ltd.. 330 866-1441
  7557 Willowdale Ave Se Magnolia (44643) *(G-9596)*

Olen Corporation... 419 294-2611
  6326 County Highway 61 Upper Sandusky (43351) *(G-14819)*

Olive Romanum Oil Inc.. 330 554-4102
  1881 Brady Lake Rd Kent (44240) *(G-8840)*

Oliver Healthcare Packaging Co.. 513 860-6880
  3840 Symmes Rd Hamilton (45015) *(G-8234)*

Oliver Printing & Packg Co LLC (PA)...................................... 330 425-7890
  1760 Enterprise Pkwy Twinsburg (44087) *(G-14703)*

Oliver Rubber Co... 419 420-6235
  701 Lima Ave Findlay (45840) *(G-7546)*

Oliver Steel Plate, Bedford Also Called: AM Castle & Co *(G-1100)*

Oliver Steel Plate Co... 330 425-7000
  7851 Bavaria Rd Twinsburg (44087) *(G-14704)*

Oliver-Tolas Healthcare Packg, Hamilton Also Called: Oliver Healthcare Packaging Co *(G-8234)*

Olson Sheet Metal Cnstr Co... 330 745-8225
  465 Glenn St Barberton (44203) *(G-887)*

Olympia Candies, Strongsville Also Called: Robert E McGrath Inc *(G-13872)*

Olympic Forest Products Co.. 216 421-2775
  2280 W 11th St Cleveland (44113) *(G-4500)*

Olympus Surgical Technologies, Norwalk Also Called: Gyrus Acmi LP *(G-11971)*

Om Group, Westlake Also Called: Borchers Americas Inc *(G-15741)*

Om Group Inc... 216 781-0083
  127 Public Sq Ste 3900 Cleveland (44114) *(G-4501)*

Omco Holdings Inc (PA)... 440 944-2100
  30396 Lakeland Blvd Wickliffe (44092) *(G-15843)*

Omco Solar Inc... 216 621-6633
  1300 E 9th St Cleveland (44114) *(G-4502)*

Omco Usa LLC.. 740 588-1722
  1000 Linden Ave Zanesville (43701) *(G-16550)*

Omega 1 Inc... 216 663-8424
  38373 Pelton Rd Willoughby (44094) *(G-15965)*

Omega Cementing Co... 330 695-7147
  3776 S Millborne Rd Apple Creek (44606) *(G-508)*

Omega Engineering Inc... 740 965-9340
  149 Stelzer Ct Sunbury (43074) *(G-13962)*

Omega Machine & Tool Inc... 440 946-6846
  7590 Jenther Dr Mentor (44060) *(G-10515)*

Omega Polymer Technologies Inc (PA).................................... 330 562-5201
  1331 S Chillicothe Rd Aurora (44202) *(G-730)*

Omega Pultrusions Incorporated... 330 562-5201
  1331 S Chillicothe Rd Aurora (44202) *(G-731)*

Omegadyne, Sunbury Also Called: Omega Engineering Inc *(G-13962)*

Omegadyne, Sunbury Also Called: Omegadyne Inc *(G-13963)*

Omegadyne Inc... 740 965-9340
  149 Stelzer Ct Sunbury (43074) *(G-13963)*

Omegaone, Willoughby Also Called: Amfm Inc *(G-15877)*

Omer J Smith Inc... 513 921-4717
  9112 Le Saint Dr West Chester (45014) *(G-15470)*

Ometek Inc..614 861-6729
  790 Cross Pointe Rd Columbus (43230) *(G-5637)*
OMI Surgical Products..513 561-2241
  4900 Charlemar Dr Cincinnati (45227) *(G-3221)*
Omni Manufacturing Inc (PA)...419 394-7424
  901 Mckinley Rd Saint Marys (45885) *(G-12962)*
Omni Manufacturing Inc...419 394-7424
  220 Cleveland Ave Saint Marys (45885) *(G-12963)*
Omni Media Cleveland Inc..216 687-0077
  1375 E 9th St Ste 1250 Cleveland (44114) *(G-4503)*
Omni Systems Inc (PA)..216 377-5160
  701 Beta Dr Ste 31 Mayfield Village (44143) *(G-10259)*
Omni Tech Electronics, Columbus *Also Called: Accuscan Instruments Inc (G-5097)*
Omni Technical Products Inc..216 433-1970
  15300 Industrial Pkwy Cleveland (44135) *(G-4504)*
Omni USA Inc...330 830-5500
  1100 Nova Dr Se Massillon (44646) *(G-10132)*
Omnicare Phrm of Midwest LLC (DH)..............................513 719-2600
  201 E 4th St Ste 900 Cincinnati (45202) *(G-3222)*
Omnipresence Cleaning LLC..937 250-4749
  302 W Fairview Ave Dayton (45405) *(G-6491)*
Omnitec, Painesville *Also Called: Ohio Associated Entps LLC (G-12254)*
Omnitech Electronics Inc...800 822-1344
  5090 Trabue Rd Columbus (43228) *(G-5638)*
Omnova North America, Inc., Solon *Also Called: Surteco North America Inc (G-13426)*
Omnova Wallcovering USA Inc..216 682-7000
  25435 Harvard Rd Beachwood (44122) *(G-1008)*
Omwp Company...330 453-8438
  3620 Progress St Ne Canton (44705) *(G-2188)*
Omya, Mason *Also Called: Omya Industries Inc (G-10036)*
Omya Distribution LLC (DH)..513 387-4600
  4605 Duke Dr Mason (45040) *(G-10035)*
Omya Inc (DH)..513 387-4600
  9987 Carver Rd Ste 300 Blue Ash (45242) *(G-1446)*
Omya Industries Inc (HQ)...513 387-4600
  4605 Duke Dr Mason (45040) *(G-10036)*
On Display Ltd...513 841-1600
  1250 Clough Pike Batavia (45103) *(G-941)*
On Guard Defense LLC..740 596-1984
  66211 Bethel Rd New Plymouth (45654) *(G-11533)*
On Site Signs Ohio Ltd..614 496-9400
  2970 Carlsbad Dr Hilliard (43026) *(G-8428)*
On The Mantle LLC..740 702-1803
  20 E Water St Chillicothe (45601) *(G-2521)*
On US LLC...330 286-3436
  315 Gougler Ave Kent (44240) *(G-8841)*
Onbase, Westlake *Also Called: Hyland Software Inc (G-15757)*
Onco Wva Inc...216 861-3700
  1001 Lakeside Ave E 15th Fl Cleveland (44114) *(G-4505)*
One Cloud Services LLC...513 231-9500
  1080 Nimitzview Dr Ste 400 Cincinnati (45230) *(G-3223)*
One Line Coffee, Columbus *Also Called: Ohio Coffee Collaborative Ltd (G-5613)*
One Orijin LLC..630 362-5291
  4300 E 5th Ave Columbus (43219) *(G-5639)*
One Styling, Maple Heights *Also Called: Salon Styling Concepts Ltd (G-9760)*
One Three Energy Inc...513 996-6973
  5460 Muddy Creek Rd Cincinnati (45238) *(G-3224)*
One Time, Eastlake *Also Called: Bond Distributing LLC (G-7022)*
One Tortilla Co...614 570-9312
  1724 Northwest Blvd Columbus (43212) *(G-5640)*
One Wish LLC...800 505-6883
  23700 Aurora Rd Bedford (44146) *(G-1147)*
ONeals Tarpaulin & Awning Co...330 788-6504
  549 W Indianola Ave Youngstown (44511) *(G-16406)*
Oneida Consumer LLC..740 687-2500
  1600 Dublin Rd Ste 200 Columbus (43215) *(G-5641)*
Oneil, Miamisburg *Also Called: ONeil & Associates Inc (G-10669)*
ONeil & Associates Inc (PA)...937 865-0800
  495 Byers Rd Miamisburg (45342) *(G-10669)*
Onesource Water LLC..866 917-7873
  812 Warehouse Rd Ste F Toledo (43615) *(G-14414)*

Onestop Signs...513 722-7867
  2502 State Route 131 Goshen (45122) *(G-7994)*
Onetouchpoint East Corp..513 421-1600
  1441 Western Ave Cincinnati (45214) *(G-3225)*
Onguard Systems LLC...614 325-0551
  5992 Trafalgar Ct Dublin (43016) *(G-6918)*
Onix Corporation...800 844-0076
  27100 Oakmead Dr Perrysburg (43551) *(G-12412)*
Online Mega Sellers Corp (PA)...888 384-6468
  4236 W Alexis Rd Toledo (43623) *(G-14415)*
Onpower Inc...513 228-2100
  3525 Grant Ave Ste A Lebanon (45036) *(G-9103)*
Onq Solutions Inc...234 542-0289
  2213 Romig Rd Akron (44320) *(G-272)*
Onstage Publications, Dayton *Also Called: Just Business Inc (G-6395)*
Ontex Inc..216 861-3300
  1001 Lakeside Ave E 15th Fl Cleveland (44114) *(G-4506)*
Onx Acquisition LLC...440 569-2300
  5910 Landerbrook Dr Ste 250 Mayfield Heights (44124) *(G-10253)*
Onx Enterprise Solutions, Cincinnati *Also Called: Onx Holdings LLC (G-3226)*
Onx Enterprise Solutions, Mayfield Heights *Also Called: Onx Acquisition LLC (G-10253)*
Onx Holdings LLC (DH)..866 587-2287
  221 E 4th St Cincinnati (45202) *(G-3226)*
Ooteksofpak, Columbus *Also Called: Tarigma Corporation (G-5809)*
Opal Diamond LLC..330 653-5876
  20033 Detroit Rd N Ridge Annex 2nd Fl Rocky River (44116) *(G-12839)*
Opc Inc...419 531-2222
  419 N Reynolds Rd Toledo (43615) *(G-14416)*
OPC Cultivation LLC...419 616-5115
  2300 University Dr E Huron (44839) *(G-8643)*
OPC Polymers, Columbus *Also Called: OPC Polymers LLC (G-5642)*
OPC Polymers LLC..614 253-8511
  1920 Leonard Ave Columbus (43219) *(G-5642)*
Open Additive LLC..937 306-6140
  2750 Indian Ripple Rd Dayton (45440) *(G-6492)*
Open Text, Hilliard *Also Called: Open Text Inc (G-8429)*
Open Text Inc...614 658-3588
  3671 Ridge Mill Dr Hilliard (43026) *(G-8429)*
Operational Support Svcs LLC...419 425-0889
  1850 Industrial Dr Findlay (45840) *(G-7547)*
Opm, Barberton *Also Called: Ohio Precision Molding Inc (G-886)*
Opp, Toledo *Also Called: Opp Dissolution LLC (G-14417)*
Opp Dissolution LLC...419 241-9601
  1149 Campbell St Toledo (43607) *(G-14417)*
Ops Wireless, Carey *Also Called: Ohio Power Systems LLC (G-2282)*
Optem, Medina *Also Called: Ovation Plymr Tech Engnred Mtl (G-10359)*
Opti, Aurora *Also Called: Omega Polymer Technologies Inc (G-730)*
Optical Display Engrg Inc..440 995-6555
  375 Alpha Park Highland Heights (44143) *(G-8390)*
Optics Incorporated..800 362-1337
  2936 Westway Dr Brunswick (44212) *(G-1777)*
Optimal Led, Toledo *Also Called: Led Lighting Center Inc (G-14360)*
Optimalled, Toledo *Also Called: Led Lighting Center LLC (G-14361)*
Optimum Graphics, Westerville *Also Called: Optimum System Products Inc (G-15718)*
Optimum Surgical..216 870-8526
  2524 Medina Rd Ste 600 Medina (44256) *(G-10358)*
Optimum System Products Inc (PA)...............................614 885-4464
  921 Eastwind Dr Ste 133 Westerville (43081) *(G-15718)*
Option Advisor, The, Blue Ash *Also Called: Schaeffers Investment Research Inc (G-1465)*
Options Plus, Fredericktown *Also Called: Options Plus Incorporated (G-7752)*
Options Plus Incorporated..740 694-9811
  143 Tuttle Ave Fredericktown (43019) *(G-7752)*
Optoquest Corporation...216 445-3637
  10000 Cedar Ave Cleveland (44106) *(G-4507)*
Optum Infusion Svcs 550 LLC (DH)................................866 442-4679
  7167 E Kemper Rd Cincinnati (45249) *(G-3227)*
Opw Engineered Systems, West Chester *Also Called: Opw Fueling Components Inc (G-15472)*
Opw Engineered Systems Inc (DH)................................888 771-9438
  9393 Princeton Glendale Rd West Chester (45011) *(G-15471)*

Opw Fueling Components Inc (HQ) 800 422-2525
9393 Princeton Glendale Rd West Chester (45011) *(G-15472)*

Or-Tec Inc 216 475-5225
5445 Dunham Rd Maple Heights (44137) *(G-9757)*

Oracle, Youngstown *Also Called: Oracle LLC (G-16407)*

Oracle LLC 724 979-2269
4144 Helena Ave Youngstown (44512) *(G-16407)*

Orange Barrel Media LLC 614 294-4898
250 N Hartford Ave Columbus (43222) *(G-5643)*

Orange Blossom Press Inc 216 781-8655
38005 Brown Ave Willoughby (44094) *(G-15966)*

Orange Frazer Press Inc 937 382-3196
37 1/2 W Main St Wilmington (45177) *(G-16057)*

Orbis Corporation 262 560-5000
232 J St Perrysburg (43551) *(G-12413)*

Orbis Corporation 937 652-1361
200 Elm St Urbana (43078) *(G-14845)*

Orbis Rpm LLC 419 307-8511
592 Claycraft Rd Columbus (43230) *(G-5644)*

Orbis Rpm LLC 419 355-8310
2100 Cedar St Fremont (43420) *(G-7799)*

Orbit Manufacturing Inc 513 732-6097
4291 Armstrong Blvd Batavia (45103) *(G-942)*

Orbytel, Cleveland *Also Called: Orbytel Print and Packg Inc (G-4508)*

Orbytel Print and Packg Inc 216 267-8734
4901 Johnston Pkwy Cleveland (44128) *(G-4508)*

Orchem Corporation 513 874-9700
130 W 2nd St Ste 2030 Dayton (45402) *(G-6493)*

Oregon Printing, Dayton *Also Called: Oregon Vlg Print Shoppe Inc (G-6494)*

Oregon Vlg Print Shoppe Inc 937 222-9418
29 N June St Dayton (45403) *(G-6494)*

Oregonia Valley Metalworks LLC 513 967-5190
184 N Main St Waynesville (45068) *(G-15300)*

OReilly Equipment LLC 440 564-1234
14555 Ravenna Rd Newbury (44065) *(G-11633)*

OReilly Precision Pdts Inc 937 526-4677
560 E Main St Russia (45363) *(G-12886)*

Oren Elliot Products LLC 419 298-0015
113 Industrial Dr Edgerton (43517) *(G-7079)*

Orflex Inc
470 West Northland Blvd Cincinnati (45240) *(G-3228)*

Organalytix LLC 908 938-6711
4695 Guildford Ln West Chester (45069) *(G-15473)*

Organic Technologies, Coshocton *Also Called: Wiley Companies (G-6000)*

Organic Technologies, Coshocton *Also Called: Wiley Organics Inc (G-6001)*

Organized Lightning LLC 407 965-2730
5601 Belleview Ave Blue Ash (45242) *(G-1447)*

Organized Living 513 277-3700
12115 Ellington Ct Cincinnati (45249) *(G-3229)*

Organized Living, Cincinnati *Also Called: Organized Living Inc (G-3230)*

Organized Living Inc (PA) 513 489-9300
3100 E Kemper Rd Cincinnati (45241) *(G-3230)*

Organon Inc 440 729-2290
7407 Cedar Rd Chesterland (44026) *(G-2487)*

Orick Stamping Inc 419 331-0600
614 E Kiracofe Ave Elida (45807) *(G-7095)*

Original Beverage Holder Co, Columbia Station *Also Called: Obhc Inc (G-5015)*

Original Mattress Factory, Columbus *Also Called: Ahmf Inc (G-5107)*

Orion Engineered Carbons LLC 740 423-9571
11135 State Route 7 Belpre (45714) *(G-1258)*

Orlando, Cleveland *Also Called: Orlando Baking Company (G-4509)*

Orlando Baking Company (PA) 216 361-1872
7777 Grand Ave Cleveland (44104) *(G-4509)*

Ormet Corporation 740 483-1381
43840 State Rte 7 Hannibal (43931) *(G-8261)*

Ormet Primary Aluminum Corp 740 483-1381
43840 State Rt 7 Hannibal (43931) *(G-8262)*

ORourke Sales Co 877 599-6548
3319 Southwest Blvd Grove City (43123) *(G-8113)*

Orrville Bronze & Aluminum Co 330 682-4015
Central Ct Orrville (44667) *(G-12143)*

Orrville Trucking & Grading Co (PA) 330 682-4010
475 Orr St Orrville (44667) *(G-12144)*

Orrvilon Inc 330 684-9400
1400 Dairy Ln Orrville (44667) *(G-12145)*

Orthotic & Prosthetic Spc Inc 216 531-2773
20650 Lakeland Blvd Euclid (44119) *(G-7291)*

Orthotics Prsthtics Rhblttion 330 856-2553
700 Howland Wilson Rd Se Warren (44484) *(G-15197)*

Orton Edward Jr Crmic Fndation 614 895-2663
6991 S Old 3c Hwy Westerville (43082) *(G-15672)*

Orval Kent Food Company LLC 419 695-5015
1600 Gressel Dr Delphos (45833) *(G-6770)*

Orwell Printing 440 285-2233
10639 Grant St Ste C Chardon (44024) *(G-2462)*

OS Kelly Corporation 937 322-4921
318 E North St Springfield (45503) *(G-13614)*

Osair Inc (PA) 440 974-6500
7001 Center St Mentor (44060) *(G-10516)*

Osb Software Inc 440 542-9145
6240 Som Center Rd Ste 230 Solon (44139) *(G-13401)*

Osborne Inc 440 232-1440
26481 Cannon Rd Cleveland (44146) *(G-4510)*

Osborne Inc (PA) 440 942-7000
7954 Reynolds Rd Mentor (44060) *(G-10517)*

Osborne Co 440 942-7000
7954 Reynolds Rd Mentor (44060) *(G-10518)*

Osborne Coinage Company LLC (PA) 877 480-0456
4362 Glendale Milford Rd Blue Ash (45242) *(G-1448)*

Osburn Associates Inc (PA) 740 385-5732
9383 Vanatta Rd Logan (43138) *(G-9372)*

Oscar Brugmann Sand & Gravel 330 274-8224
3828 Dudley Rd Mantua (44255) *(G-9742)*

Osco Industries Inc 740 286-5004
165 Athens St Jackson (45640) *(G-8720)*

Osco Industries Inc (PA) 740 354-3183
734 11th St Portsmouth (45662) *(G-12652)*

Osg-Sterling Die Inc 216 267-1300
12502 Plaza Dr Parma (44130) *(G-12292)*

OSI, Hilliard *Also Called: Ohio Semitronics Inc (G-8427)*

OSI Environmental LLC 440 237-4600
12800 York Rd North Royalton (44133) *(G-11890)*

OSI Global Sourcing LLC 614 471-4800
2575 Ferris Rd Columbus (43224) *(G-5645)*

Osmans Pies Inc 330 607-9083
3678 Elm Rd Stow (44224) *(G-13716)*

Osram Sylvania Inc 800 463-9275
6400 Rockside Rd Independence (44131) *(G-8678)*

Ossid Inc 724 463-3232
5695 Avery Rd Ste E Dublin (43016) *(G-6919)*

Osteonovus Inc 419 530-5940
1510 N Westwood Ave Ste 1080 Toledo (43606) *(G-14418)*

Osteonovus Inc 419 530-5940
1510 N Westwood Ave # 2040 Toledo (43606) *(G-14419)*

Osteosymbionics LLC 216 881-8500
1768 E 25th St Ste 316 Cleveland (44114) *(G-4511)*

Oster Enterprises, Massillon *Also Called: Oster Sand and Gravel Inc (G-10133)*

Oster Sand and Gravel Inc 330 874-3322
3467 Dover Zoar Rd Ne Bolivar (44612) *(G-1531)*

Oster Sand and Gravel Inc (PA) 330 494-5472
5947 Whipple Ave Nw Canton (44720) *(G-2189)*

Oster Sand and Gravel Inc 330 833-2649
1955 Riverside Dr Nw Massillon (44647) *(G-10133)*

Otc Industrial Technologies (PA) 800 837-6827
1900 Jetway Blvd Columbus (43219) *(G-5646)*

Otc Services Inc 330 871-2444
1776 Constitution Ave Louisville (44641) *(G-9467)*

Other Styles - See Operation, Cleveland *Also Called: Lubriquip Inc (G-4338)*

Otis Elevator Company 216 573-2333
9800 Rockside Rd Ste 1200 Cleveland (44125) *(G-4512)*

Otp Holding LLC 614 733-0979
8000 Corporate Blvd Plain City (43064) *(G-12588)*

Ots ALPHABETIC SECTION

Ots, Columbus Also Called: Ohio Trailer Supply Inc **(G-5629)**

Ottawa Defense Logistics LLC.. 419 596-3202
   804 N Pratt St Ottawa (45875) **(G-12186)**

Ottawa Oil Co Inc.. 419 425-3301
   1100 Trenton Ave Findlay (45840) **(G-7548)**

Ottawa Products Co... 419 836-5115
   1602 N Curtice Rd Ste A Curtice (43412) **(G-6057)**

Ottawa Rubber Company (PA).. 419 865-1378
   1600 Commerce Rd Holland (43528) **(G-8521)**

Otterbacher Trailers LLC... 419 462-1975
   352 South St Galion (44833) **(G-7882)**

Otto Konigslow Mfg Co.. 216 851-7900
   13300 Coit Rd Cleveland (44110) **(G-4513)**

Ottokee Group Inc... 419 636-1932
   17768 County Road H 50 Bryan (43506) **(G-1834)**

Outfit Good LLC.. 419 565-3770
   1145 Chesapeake Ave Ste G Columbus (43212) **(G-5647)**

Outhouse Paper Etc Inc... 937 382-2800
   319 Collett Rd Waynesville (45068) **(G-15301)**

Outlook Tool Inc... 937 235-6330
   360 Fame Rd Dayton (45449) **(G-6495)**

Outotec North America, Strongsville Also Called: Outotec Oyj **(G-13863)**

Outotec Oyj.. 440 783-3336
   11288 Alameda Dr Strongsville (44149) **(G-13863)**

Ovase Manufacturing LLC... 937 275-0617
   1990 Berwyck Ave Dayton (45414) **(G-6496)**

Ovation Plymr Tech Engnred Mtl... 330 723-5686
   1030 W Smith Rd Medina (44256) **(G-10359)**

Overhead Door Company, Toledo Also Called: Overhead Inc **(G-14420)**

Overhead Door Corporation.. 440 593-5226
   1001 Chamberlain Blvd Conneaut (44030) **(G-5929)**

Overhead Door Corporation.. 740 383-6376
   1332 E Fairground Rd Marion (43302) **(G-9870)**

Overhead Door Corporation.. 419 294-3874
   781 Rt 30w Upper Sandusky (43351) **(G-14820)**

Overhead Door of Pike County.. 740 289-3925
   4237 Us Highway 23 Piketon (45661) **(G-12481)**

Overhead Inc.. 419 476-0300
   340 New Towne Square Dr Toledo (43612) **(G-14420)**

Overhoff Technology Corp.. 513 248-2400
   1160 Us Route 50 Milford (45150) **(G-10916)**

Overly Hautz Company, Lebanon Also Called: Overly Hautz Motor Base Co **(G-9104)**

Overly Hautz Motor Base Co... 513 932-0025
   285 S West St Lebanon (45036) **(G-9104)**

Overseas Packing LLC.. 440 232-2917
   19800 Alexander Rd Bedford (44146) **(G-1148)**

Ovp Inc.. 740 423-5171
   305 Washington Blvd Belpre (45714) **(G-1259)**

Ovs Knife Co., Akron Also Called: Wise Edge LLC **(G-376)**

Owens Corning... 614 754-4098
   2050 Integrity Dr S Columbus (43209) **(G-5648)**

Owens Corning... 419 248-8000
   9318 Erie Ave Sw Navarre (44662) **(G-11348)**

Owens Corning (PA)... 419 248-8000
   1 Owens Corning Pkwy Toledo (43659) **(G-14421)**

Owens Corning, Ashville Also Called: Owens Corning Sales LLC **(G-671)**

Owens Corning, Grove City Also Called: Owens Corning Sales LLC **(G-8114)**

Owens Corning, Hebron Also Called: Owens Corning Sales LLC **(G-8354)**

Owens Corning, Mount Vernon Also Called: Owens Corning Sales LLC **(G-11284)**

Owens Corning, Swanton Also Called: Owens Corning Sales LLC **(G-13979)**

Owens Corning, Tallmadge Also Called: Owens Corning Sales LLC **(G-14042)**

Owens Corning, Toledo Also Called: Owens Corning **(G-14421)**

Owens Corning Ht Inc... 419 248-8000
   Owens Corning World Headquar Toledo (43659) **(G-14422)**

Owens Corning Roofg & Asp LLC.. 330 764-7800
   890 W Smith Rd Medina (44256) **(G-10360)**

Owens Corning Roofg & Asp LLC (HQ).................................... 877 858-3855
   1 Owens Corning Pkwy Toledo (43659) **(G-14423)**

Owens Corning Sales LLC.. 740 983-1300
   1 Reynolds Rd Ashville (43103) **(G-671)**

Owens Corning Sales LLC.. 614 539-0830
   3750 Brookham Dr Ste K Grove City (43123) **(G-8114)**

Owens Corning Sales LLC.. 740 928-6620
   341 O Neill Dr Bldg 6 Hebron (43025) **(G-8354)**

Owens Corning Sales LLC.. 614 399-3915
   100 Blackjack Road Ext Mount Vernon (43050) **(G-11284)**

Owens Corning Sales LLC.. 419 248-5751
   11451 W Airport Service Rd Swanton (43558) **(G-13979)**

Owens Corning Sales LLC.. 330 634-0460
   170 South Ave Tallmadge (44278) **(G-14041)**

Owens Corning Sales LLC.. 330 633-6735
   275 Southwest Ave Tallmadge (44278) **(G-14042)**

Owens Corning Sales LLC (HQ).. 419 248-8000
   1 Owens Corning Pkwy Toledo (43659) **(G-14424)**

Owens Crning Inslting Systm... 740 328-2300
   400 Case Ave Newark (43055) **(G-11600)**

Owens Crning Tchncal Fbrics LL.. 419 248-5535
   1 Owens Corning Pkwy Toledo (43659) **(G-14425)**

Owens Foods Inc
   8111 Smiths Mill Rd New Albany (43054) **(G-11388)**

Owens-Brockway Glass Cntrs, Perrysburg Also Called: Owens-Brockway Glass Cont Inc **(G-12414)**

Owens-Brockway Glass Cont Inc (DH).................................... 567 336-8449
   1 Michael Owens Way Perrysburg (43551) **(G-12414)**

Owens-Brockway Glass Cont Inc.. 740 455-4516
   1700 State St Zanesville (43701) **(G-16551)**

Owens-Corning Fibrgls Trumbull, Medina Also Called: Owens Corning Roofg & Asp LLC **(G-10360)**

Owens-Illinois General Inc... 567 336-5000
   1 Michael Owens Way Perrysburg (43551) **(G-12415)**

Owens-Illinois Group Inc (HQ).. 567 336-5000
   1 Michael Owens Way Perrysburg (43551) **(G-12416)**

Owens-Illinois Inc.. 567 336-5000
   1 Michael Owens Way Perrysburg (43551) **(G-12417)**

Owl Be Sweatin... 513 260-2026
   4914 Ridge Ave Cincinnati (45209) **(G-3231)**

Oxford Mining Company Inc (DH)... 740 622-6302
   544 Chestnut St Coshocton (43812) **(G-5991)**

Oxford Mining Company Inc... 740 588-0190
   1855 Kemper Ct Zanesville (43701) **(G-16552)**

Oxford Mining Company LLC (DH).. 740 622-6302
   544 Chestnut St Coshocton (43812) **(G-5992)**

Oxford Mining Company - KY LLC.. 740 622-6302
   544 Chestnut St Coshocton (43812) **(G-5993)**

Oxford Resources Inc.. 614 873-7955
   7858 Industrial Pkwy Plain City (43064) **(G-12589)**

Oxyrase Inc... 419 589-8800
   3000 Park Ave W Ontario (44906) **(G-12093)**

P & A Industries Inc (HQ).. 419 422-7070
   600 Crystal Ave Findlay (45840) **(G-7549)**

P & C Metal Polishing Inc.. 513 771-9143
   9766 Pinto Ct Cincinnati (45242) **(G-3232)**

P & J Industries Inc (PA)... 419 726-2675
   4934 Lewis Ave Toledo (43612) **(G-14426)**

P & L Heat Trting Grinding Inc... 330 746-1339
   313 E Wood St Youngstown (44503) **(G-16408)**

P & L Metalcrafts LLC.. 330 793-2178
   1050 Ohio Works Dr Youngstown (44510) **(G-16409)**

P & L Precision Grinding Llc.. 330 746-8081
   948 Poland Ave Youngstown (44502) **(G-16410)**

P & M Enterprises Group Inc.. 330 316-0387
   1900 Mahoning Rd Ne Canton (44705) **(G-2190)**

P & P Machine Tool Inc... 440 232-7404
   26189 Broadway Ave Cleveland (44146) **(G-4514)**

P & P Mold & Die Inc... 330 784-8333
   1034 S Munroe Rd Tallmadge (44278) **(G-14043)**

P & R Mfg.. 330 674-1431
   5935 County Road 349 Millersburg (44654) **(G-10988)**

P & R Specialty Inc.. 937 773-0263
   1835 W High St Piqua (45356) **(G-12541)**

P & T Millwork Inc... 440 543-2151
   10090 Queens Way Chagrin Falls (44023) **(G-2412)**

ALPHABETIC SECTION

P & T Products Inc.. 419 621-1966
472 Industrial Pkwy Sandusky (44870) *(G-13085)*

P A I, Blue Ash *Also Called: Precision Anlytical Instrs Inc (G-1455)*

P C M Co (PA).. 330 336-8040
291 W Bergey St Wadsworth (44281) *(G-15050)*

P C S, Pataskala *Also Called: Programmable Control Svc Inc (G-12304)*

P C Workshop Inc.. 419 399-4805
900 W Caroline St Paulding (45879) *(G-12319)*

P G I, Cleveland *Also Called: Pinnacle Graphics Imaging Inc (G-4553)*

P Graham Dunn Inc.. 330 828-2105
630 Henry St Dalton (44618) *(G-6138)*

P H I, Toledo *Also Called: Pilkington Holdings Inc (G-14435)*

P J McNerney & Associates, West Chester *Also Called: McNerney & Associates LLC (G-15570)*

P J Tool Company Inc... 937 254-2817
1115 Springfield St Dayton (45403) *(G-6497)*

P L M Corporation... 216 341-8008
1400 Brookpark Rd Cleveland (44109) *(G-4515)*

P M C, Blue Ash *Also Called: Plastic Moldings Company Llc (G-1451)*

P M C, Wickliffe *Also Called: Precision McHning Cnnction LLC (G-15849)*

P M I Food Equipment Group, Piqua *Also Called: Hobart LLC (G-12525)*

P M Motor -Fan Blade Company, North Ridgeville *Also Called: P M Motor Company (G-11852)*

P M Motor Company.. 440 327-9999
37850 Taylor Pkwy North Ridgeville (44039) *(G-11852)*

P O McIntire Company (PA).. 440 269-1848
29191 Anderson Rd Wickliffe (44092) *(G-15844)*

P P C Greatstuff Co, Mansfield *Also Called: Shelly Fisher (G-9717)*

P P F, Bradford *Also Called: Production Paint Finishers Inc (G-1601)*

P P G, Milford *Also Called: PPG Industries Inc (G-10917)*

P P G Refinishing Group, Delaware *Also Called: PPG Industries Inc (G-6743)*

P P I Graphics, Canton *Also Called: KMS 2000 Inc (G-2141)*

P Q Corp... 216 621-0840
2380 W 3rd St Cleveland (44113) *(G-4516)*

P R Machine Works Inc.. 419 529-5748
1825 Nussbaum Pkwy Ontario (44906) *(G-12094)*

P S Awards, Cleveland *Also Called: PS Superior Inc (G-4596)*

P S C Inc... 216 531-3375
21761 Tungsten Rd Cleveland (44117) *(G-4517)*

P S Graphics Inc.. 440 356-9656
20284 Orchard Grove Ave Rocky River (44116) *(G-12840)*

P S P Inc... 330 283-5635
7337 Westview Rd Kent (44240) *(G-8842)*

P S Plastics Inc... 614 262-7070
2020 Britains Ln Columbus (43224) *(G-5649)*

P T C, Lima *Also Called: Precison Thrmplstic Cmpnnts In (G-9305)*

P T I Inc.. 419 445-2800
100 Taylor Pkwy Archbold (43502) *(G-540)*

P-Americas LLC... 513 948-5100
2121 Sunnybrook Dr Cincinnati (45237) *(G-3233)*

P-Mac Ltd.. 419 235-2245
14208 Cross Creek Rd Bowling Green (43402) *(G-1580)*

P.E. Labellers, Cincinnati *Also Called: PE Usa LLC (G-3244)*

P&G, Cincinnati *Also Called: Procter & Gamble Company (G-3280)*

P&The Mfg Acquisition LLC... 937 492-4134
815 Oak Ave Sidney (45365) *(G-13269)*

P212121 LLC... 253 229-9327
2027 Bretton Pl Toledo (43606) *(G-14427)*

P2p Manufacturing, Cleveland *Also Called: P2p Mfg LLC (G-4518)*

P2p Mfg LLC... 216 282-4110
4911 Grant Ave Cleveland (44125) *(G-4518)*

P3 Infrastructure Inc... 330 408-9504
2146 Entp Pkwy Ste C Twinsburg (44087) *(G-14705)*

PA MA Inc... 440 846-3799
11288 Alameda Dr Strongsville (44149) *(G-13864)*

Paarlo Plastics Inc... 330 494-3798
7720 Tim Ave Nw North Canton (44720) *(G-11749)*

Pac Manufacturing, Monroe *Also Called: Pac Worldwide Corporation (G-11117)*

Pac Worldwide Corporation.. 800 535-0039
575 Gateway Blvd Monroe (45050) *(G-11117)*

Paccar Inc... 740 774-5111
65 Kenworth Dr Chillicothe (45601) *(G-2522)*

Pace Consolidated Inc (PA)... 440 942-1234
4800 Beidler Rd Willoughby (44094) *(G-15967)*

Pace Engineering, Willoughby *Also Called: Pace Consolidated Inc (G-15967)*

Pace Engineering Inc... 440 942-1234
4800 Beidler Rd Willoughby (44094) *(G-15968)*

Pacer Flight LLC.. 419 433-5562
3306 Fox Rd Huron (44839) *(G-8644)*

Pacific Atlantic Provs Inc... 330 467-0150
8051 Vesta Ave Northfield (44067) *(G-11909)*

Pacific Highway Products LLC.. 740 914-5217
324 Barnhart St Marion (43302) *(G-9871)*

Pacific Industries USA Inc... 513 860-3900
8955 Seward Rd Fairfield (45011) *(G-7389)*

Pacific Manufacturing Ohio Inc.. 513 860-3900
8955 Seward Rd Fairfield (45011) *(G-7390)*

Pacific Manufacturing Ohio Inc.. 513 860-3900
8935 Seward Rd Fairfield (45011) *(G-7391)*

Pacific Manufacturing Tenn Inc.. 513 900-7862
555 Smith Ln Jackson (45640) *(G-8721)*

Pacific Piston Ring Co Inc... 513 387-6100
11379 Grooms Rd Blue Ash (45242) *(G-1449)*

Pacific Tool & Die Co... 330 273-7363
1035 Western Dr Brunswick (44212) *(G-1778)*

Pacific Valve, Piqua *Also Called: Crane Pumps & Systems Inc (G-12508)*

Pack Line Corp.. 212 564-0664
22900 Miles Rd Cleveland (44128) *(G-4519)*

Packaging Corporation America.. 419 282-5809
929 Faultless Dr Ashland (44805) *(G-597)*

Packaging Corporation America.. 330 644-9542
708 Killian Rd Coventry Township (44319) *(G-6015)*

Packaging Corporation America.. 513 424-3542
1824 Baltimore St Middletown (45044) *(G-10848)*

Packaging Corporation America.. 740 344-1126
205 S 21st St Newark (43055) *(G-11601)*

Packaging Department, Ashland *Also Called: Pioneer National Latex Inc (G-602)*

Packaging Materials Inc.. 740 432-6337
62805 Bennett Ave Cambridge (43725) *(G-1946)*

Packaging Specialties Inc.. 330 723-6000
300 Lake Rd Medina (44256) *(G-10361)*

Pacs Industries Inc.. 740 397-5021
8405 Blackjack Rd Mount Vernon (43050) *(G-11285)*

Pactiv LLC... 614 771-5400
2120 Westbelt Dr Columbus (43228) *(G-5650)*

Padco Industries LLC... 440 564-7160
10357 Kinsman Rd Newbury (44065) *(G-11634)*

Paddock Enterprises LLC (HQ).. 567 336-5000
1 Michael Owens Way 2 Perrysburg (43551) *(G-12418)*

Page One Group.. 740 397-4240
10 E Vine St Ste C Mount Vernon (43050) *(G-11286)*

Page Slotting Saw Co Inc.. 419 476-7475
3820 Lagrange St Toledo (43612) *(G-14428)*

Pahl Ready Mix Concrete, Bryan *Also Called: Pahl Ready Mix Concrete Inc (G-1835)*

Pahl Ready Mix Concrete Inc (PA)... 419 636-4238
14586 Us Highway 127 Ew Bryan (43506) *(G-1835)*

Paine Falls Centerpin LLC.. 440 867-4954
6342 Ledge Rd Thompson (44086) *(G-14061)*

Painesville Pride, Willoughby *Also Called: Lake Community News (G-15942)*

Painesville Publishing Inc.. 440 354-4142
2883 Industrial Park Dr Austinburg (44010) *(G-748)*

Painted Hill Inv Group Inc... 937 339-1756
402 E Main St Troy (45373) *(G-14600)*

Pak Master LLC... 330 523-5319
3778 Timberlake Dr Richfield (44286) *(G-12792)*

Pakfab USA Engnred Sltions Inc.. 937 547-0413
5963 Jaysville Saint Johns Rd Greenville (45331) *(G-8054)*

Paklab, Batavia *Also Called: Universal Packg Systems Inc (G-957)*

Paklab, Cincinnati *Also Called: Universal Packg Systems Inc (G-3483)*

Pako Inc... 440 946-8030
7615 Jenther Dr Mentor (44060) *(G-10519)*

Pakra LLC   **ALPHABETIC SECTION**

Pakra LLC 614 477-6965
   449 E Mound St Columbus (43215) *(G-5651)*

Paleomd LLC 248 854-0031
   26245 Broadway Ave Ste B Bedford (44146) *(G-1149)*

Palisin & Associates Inc (PA) 216 252-3930
   10003 Memphis Ave Cleveland (44144) *(G-4520)*

Pallet Distributors Inc 330 852-3531
   10343 Copperhead Rd Nw Sugarcreek (44681) *(G-13933)*

Pallet Source Inc 419 660-8882
   55 N Garfield St Norwalk (44857) *(G-11985)*

Pallet Specs Plus LLC 513 351-3200
   1701 Mills Ave Norwood (45212) *(G-11997)*

Pallet World Inc 419 874-9333
   8272 Fremont Pike Perrysburg (43551) *(G-12419)*

Pallets & Crates Inc 330 527-4534
   9294 State Route 305 Garrettsville (44231) *(G-7924)*

Pallets-Fam-In-place-packaging, Versailles *Also Called: Kamps Inc (G-14983)*

Palm Harbor Homes Inc 937 725-9465
   11004 State Route 28 New Vienna (45159) *(G-11543)*

Palm Plastics Ltd 561 776-6700
   843 Miller Dr Bowling Green (43402) *(G-1581)*

Palmer Bros Transit Mix Con (PA) 419 352-4681
   12205 E Gypsy Lane Rd Bowling Green (43402) *(G-1582)*

Palmer Bros Transit Mix Con 419 332-6363
   210 N Stone St Fremont (43420) *(G-7800)*

Palmer Bros Transit Mix Con 419 686-2366
   12580 Greensburg Pike Portage (43451) *(G-12636)*

Palmer Bros Transit Mix Con 419 447-2018
   1900 S County Road 1 Tiffin (44883) *(G-14099)*

Palmer Donavin Manufacturing 740 527-1111
   1120 O Neill Dr Hebron (43025) *(G-8355)*

Palmer Products, Akron *Also Called: Palmer Products Inc (G-273)*

Palmer Products Inc 330 630-9397
   920 Moe Dr Akron (44310) *(G-273)*

Palpac Industries Inc 419 523-3230
   610 N Agner St Ottawa (45875) *(G-12187)*

Pama Tool & Die, Strongsville *Also Called: PA MA Inc (G-13864)*

Pamee LLC 216 232-9255
   18500 Lake Rd Rocky River (44116) *(G-12841)*

Pamton 3d Printing LLC 330 792-5503
   904 S Hazelwood Ave Youngstown (44509) *(G-16411)*

Pan-Glo, Mansfield *Also Called: Russell T Bundy Associates Inc (G-9716)*

Panacea Products Corporation (PA) 614 850-7000
   2711 International St Columbus (43228) *(G-5652)*

Panacea Products Corporation 614 429-6320
   1825 Joyce Ave Columbus (43219) *(G-5653)*

Panam Imaging Systems, Cleveland *Also Called: Horizons Incorporated (G-4201)*

Pandrol Inc 419 592-5050
   25 Interstate Dr Napoleon (43545) *(G-11330)*

Panel Master LLC 440 355-4442
   191 Commerce Dr Lagrange (44050) *(G-8954)*

Panel-Fab Inc 513 771-1462
   10520 Taconic Ter Cincinnati (45215) *(G-3234)*

Panelmatic Inc 330 782-8007
   1125 Meadowbrook Ave Youngstown (44512) *(G-16412)*

Panelmatic Bldg Solutions Inc 330 619-5235
   6882 Parkway Dr Brookfield (44403) *(G-1672)*

Panelmatic Cincinnati Inc 513 829-1960
   258 Donald Dr Fairfield (45014) *(G-7392)*

Panelmatic Youngstown, Youngstown *Also Called: Panelmatic Inc (G-16412)*

Panelmatic Youngstown Inc 330 782-8007
   1125 Meadowbrook Ave Youngstown (44512) *(G-16413)*

Paneltech LLC 440 516-1300
   17525 Haskins Rd Chagrin Falls (44023) *(G-2413)*

Pang Rubber Company, Johnstown *Also Called: Truflex Rubber Products Co (G-8782)*

Panhandle Olfld Svc Cmpnies In 330 340-9525
   62787 Philips Rd Cambridge (43725) *(G-1947)*

Pantrybag 614 927-8744
   769 Sullivant Ave Columbus (43222) *(G-5654)*

Papa Joes Pies Inc (PA) 440 960-7437
   1969 Cooper Foster Park Rd Amherst (44001) *(G-481)*

Papel Couture 614 848-5700
   6522 Singletree Dr Columbus (43229) *(G-5655)*

Paper Products Company, West Chester *Also Called: Omer J Smith Inc (G-15470)*

Paper Service Inc 330 227-3546
   12022 Leslie Rd Lisbon (44432) *(G-9324)*

Paper Systems Incorporated, Springboro *Also Called: Psix LLC (G-13516)*

Papertech, Findlay *Also Called: Pressed Paperboard Tech LLC (G-7552)*

Papyrus-Recycled Greetings Inc 773 348-6410
   1 American Blvd Westlake (44145) *(G-15770)*

Paradigm International Inc 740 370-2428
   4239 Us Highway 23 Piketon (45661) *(G-12482)*

Paragon Integrated Svcs Group, Newcomerstown *Also Called: Paragon Intgrted Svcs Group LL (G-11650)*

Paragon Intgrted Svcs Group LL 724 639-5126
   200 Enterprise Dr Newcomerstown (43832) *(G-11650)*

Paragon Machine Company, Bedford *Also Called: Done-Rite Bowling Service Co (G-1118)*

Paragon Plastics 330 542-9825
   5551 E Calla Rd New Middletown (44442) *(G-11479)*

Paragon Robotics LLC 216 313-9299
   2234 E Enterprise Pkwy Twinsburg (44087) *(G-14706)*

Paragraphics Inc 330 493-1074
   2011 29th St Nw Canton (44709) *(G-2191)*

Parallel Technologies Inc 614 798-9700
   4868 Blazer Pkwy Dublin (43017) *(G-6920)*

Paramelt, Cleveland *Also Called: M Argueso & Co Inc (G-4344)*

Paramelt, Cleveland *Also Called: Paramelt Argueso Kindt Inc (G-4521)*

Paramelt Argueso Kindt Inc 216 252-4122
   12651 Elmwood Ave Cleveland (44111) *(G-4521)*

Paramont Machine Company LLC 330 339-3489
   963 Commercial Ave Se New Philadelphia (44663) *(G-11522)*

Paramount Distillers, Cleveland *Also Called: Luxco Inc (G-4341)*

Paramount Distillers Inc 216 671-6300
   3116 Berea Rd Cleveland (44111) *(G-4522)*

Paratus Supply Inc 330 745-3600
   30 2nd St Sw Barberton (44203) *(G-888)*

Pardson Inc 740 373-5285
   149 Acme St Marietta (45750) *(G-9814)*

Park Corporation (PA) 216 267-4870
   3555 Reserve Commons Dr Medina (44256) *(G-10362)*

Park Place Technologies LLC (PA) 877 778-8707
   5910 Landerbrook Dr Ste 300 Cleveland (44124) *(G-4523)*

Park PLC Prntg Cpyg & Dgtl IMG 330 799-1739
   3410 Canfield Rd Ste B Youngstown (44511) *(G-16414)*

Park Press Direct 419 626-4426
   2143 Sherman St Sandusky (44870) *(G-13086)*

Park-Ohio, Cleveland *Also Called: Park-Ohio Industries Inc (G-4525)*

Park-Ohio Holdings Corp (PA) 440 947-2000
   6065 Parkland Blvd Ste 1 Cleveland (44124) *(G-4524)*

Park-Ohio Industries Inc (HQ) 440 947-2000
   6065 Parkland Blvd Ste 1 Cleveland (44124) *(G-4525)*

Park-Ohio Industries Inc 216 341-2300
   3800 Harvard Ave Newburgh Heights (44105) *(G-11620)*

Park-Ohio Products Inc 216 961-7200
   7000 Denison Ave Cleveland (44102) *(G-4526)*

Parker, Cleveland *Also Called: Parker-Hannifin Corporation (G-4532)*

Parker Aerospace 216 225-2721
   19600 Five Points Rd Cleveland (44135) *(G-4527)*

Parker Hannifin, Berlin Center *Also Called: Parker-Hannifin Corporation (G-1311)*

Parker Hannifin Partner B LLC 216 896-3000
   6035 Parkland Blvd Cleveland (44124) *(G-4528)*

Parker Royalty Partnership 216 896-3000
   6035 Parkland Blvd Cleveland (44124) *(G-4529)*

Parker Rst-Proof Cleveland Inc 216 481-6680
   1688 Arabella Rd Cleveland (44112) *(G-4530)*

Parker Trutec, Springfield *Also Called: Parker Trutec Incorporated (G-13615)*

Parker Trutec Incorporated (HQ) 937 323-8833
   4700 Gateway Blvd Springfield (45502) *(G-13615)*

Parker Trutec Incorporated 937 653-8500
   4795 Upper Valley Pike Urbana (43078) *(G-14846)*

Parker-Hannifin Corporation 440 937-6211
   1160 Center Rd Avon (44011) *(G-782)*

ALPHABETIC SECTION — Pavletich Manufacturing

Parker-Hannifin Corporation 330 261-1618
14010 Ellsworth Rd Berlin Center (44401) *(G-1311)*

Parker-Hannifin Corporation 216 433-1795
19600 Five Points Rd Cleveland (44135) *(G-4531)*

Parker-Hannifin Corporation (PA) 216 896-3000
6035 Parkland Blvd Cleveland (44124) *(G-4532)*

Parker-Hannifin Corporation 614 279-7070
3885 Gateway Blvd Columbus (43228) *(G-5656)*

Parker-Hannifin Corporation 937 456-5571
725 N Beech St Eaton (45320) *(G-7067)*

Parker-Hannifin Corporation 440 284-6277
711 Taylor St Elyria (44035) *(G-7192)*

Parker-Hannifin Corporation 419 542-6611
373 Meuse Argonne St Hicksville (43526) *(G-8377)*

Parker-Hannifin Corporation 937 644-3915
14249 Industrial Pkwy Marysville (43040) *(G-9930)*

Parker-Hannifin Corporation 440 266-2300
8940 Tyler Blvd Mentor (44060) *(G-10520)*

Parker-Hannifin Corporation 419 644-4311
16810 County Road 2 Metamora (43540) *(G-10603)*

Parker-Hannifin Corporation 330 336-3511
135 Quadral Dr Wadsworth (44281) *(G-15051)*

Parker-Hannifin Corporation 330 335-6740
135 Quadral Dr Wadsworth (44281) *(G-15052)*

Parker-Hannifin Corporation 704 637-1190
30240 Lakeland Blvd Wickliffe (44092) *(G-15845)*

Parker-Hannifin Corporation 440 943-5700
30240 Lakeland Blvd Wickliffe (44092) *(G-15846)*

Parking & Traffic Control SEC 440 243-7565
13651 Newton Rd Cleveland (44130) *(G-4533)*

Parking Facilities, Cleveland Also Called: City of Cleveland *(G-3823)*

Parkn Manufacturing LLC 330 723-8172
8035 Norwalk Rd Ste 107 Litchfield (44253) *(G-9330)*

Parkohio Worldwide LLC (HQ) 440 947-2000
6065 Parkland Blvd Ste 1 Cleveland (44124) *(G-4534)*

Parlex USA LLC (DH) 937 898-3621
801 Scholz Dr Vandalia (45377) *(G-14956)*

Parma Heights License Bureau 440 888-0388
6339 Olde York Rd Cleveland (44130) *(G-4535)*

Parma Seven Hills Gazette, Brecksville Also Called: Brecksvll-Brdview Hts Gztte In *(G-1610)*

Paro Services Co (PA) 330 467-1300
1755 Enterprise Pkwy Ste 100 Twinsburg (44087) *(G-14707)*

Parobek Trucking Co 419 869-7500
192 State Route 42 West Salem (44287) *(G-15635)*

Parry Co 740 884-4893
33630 Old Route 35 Chillicothe (45601) *(G-2523)*

Part 2 Screen Prtg Design Inc 614 294-4429
935 King Ave Columbus (43212) *(G-5657)*

Partitions Plus Incorporated 419 422-2600
12517 County Road 99 Findlay (45840) *(G-7550)*

Partners In Recognition Inc 937 420-2150
405 S Main St Fort Loramie (45845) *(G-7605)*

Party Animal Inc 440 471-1030
909 Crocker Rd Westlake (44145) *(G-15771)*

Pas Technologies Inc 937 840-1053
214 Hobart Dr Hillsboro (45133) *(G-8464)*

Past Patterns 937 223-3722
128 Grafton Ave Dayton (45406) *(G-6498)*

Pataskala Post 740 964-6226
190 E Broad St Ste 2 # E Pataskala (43062) *(G-12303)*

Patent Construction Systems, Marion Also Called: Enviri Corporation *(G-9851)*

Path Robotics Inc (PA) 330 808-2788
528 Maier Pl Columbus (43215) *(G-5658)*

Path Robotics Inc 614 816-1991
3950 Business Park Dr Columbus (43204) *(G-5659)*

Path Technologies Inc 440 358-1500
437 W Prospect St Painesville (44077) *(G-12255)*

Patheon Pharmaceuticals Inc 513 948-9111
4750 Lake Forest Dr Blue Ash (45242) *(G-1450)*

Patheon Pharmaceuticals Inc 513 948-9111
2110 E Galbraith Rd Cincinnati (45237) *(G-3235)*

Pathfinder Cmpt Systems Inc 330 928-1961
345 5th St Ne Barberton (44203) *(G-889)*

Patio Enclosures (PA) 513 733-4646
11949 Tramway Dr Cincinnati (45241) *(G-3236)*

Patio Enclsures Stanek Windows, Macedonia Also Called: Great Day Improvements LLC *(G-9555)*

Patricia M Bokesch 330 793-4682
5360 Nashua Dr Youngstown (44515) *(G-16415)*

Patrick J Burke & Co 513 455-8200
901 Adams Crossing Fl 1 Cincinnati (45202) *(G-3237)*

Patrick M Davidson 513 897-2971
6490 Corwin Ave Waynesville (45068) *(G-15302)*

Patrick Products Inc 419 943-4137
150 S Werner St Leipsic (45856) *(G-9134)*

Patrigraphica Ltd 513 460-5380
2249 Townsend Rd Cincinnati (45238) *(G-3238)*

Patriot Armor, West Chester Also Called: Patriot Armored Systems LLC *(G-15474)*

Patriot Armored Systems LLC 413 637-1060
9113 Le Saint Dr West Chester (45014) *(G-15474)*

Patriot Mfg Group Inc 937 746-2117
512 Linden Ave Carlisle (45005) *(G-2291)*

Patriot Mobility, Holland Also Called: Patriot Products Inc *(G-8522)*

Patriot Precision Products 330 966-7177
8817 Pleasantwood Ave Nw Canton (44720) *(G-2192)*

Patriot Products Inc 419 865-9712
1133 Corporate Dr Ste B Holland (43528) *(G-8522)*

Patriot Signage Inc 859 655-9009
5725 Dragon Way Cincinnati (45227) *(G-3239)*

Patriot Software LLC 877 968-7147
4883 Dressler Rd Nw Ste 301 Canton (44718) *(G-2193)*

Patriot Special Metals Inc 330 580-9600
2201 Harrison Ave Sw Canton (44706) *(G-2194)*

Patriot Stainless Welding 740 297-6040
1555 Fairview Rd Zanesville (43701) *(G-16553)*

Patterson Prcision Fabrication 937 631-8198
33 Walnut St Springfield (45505) *(G-13616)*

Patton Aluminum Products Inc 937 845-9404
65 Quick Rd New Carlisle (45344) *(G-11424)*

Pattons Trck & Hvy Eqp Svc Inc 740 385-4067
35640 Hocking Dr Logan (43138) *(G-9373)*

Paul Blausey Farms, Genoa Also Called: Rcr Partnership *(G-7948)*

Paul H Rohe Company Inc 513 326-6789
11641 Mosteller Rd Cincinnati (45241) *(G-3240)*

Paul J Tatulinski Ltd 330 584-8251
1595 W Main St North Benton (44449) *(G-11710)*

Paul Martin and Sons, Napoleon Also Called: M & S AG Solutions LLC *(G-11323)*

Paul Peterson Company (PA) 614 486-4375
950 Dublin Rd Columbus (43215) *(G-5660)*

Paul Peterson Safety Div Inc 614 486-4375
950 Dublin Rd Columbus (43215) *(G-5661)*

Paul R Lipp & Son Inc 330 227-9614
47563 Pancake Clarkson Rd Rogers (44455) *(G-12847)*

Paul Shovlin 330 757-0032
807 Mulberry Ln Youngstown (44512) *(G-16416)*

Paul Wilke & Son Inc 513 921-3163
1965 Grand Ave Cincinnati (45214) *(G-3241)*

Paul Yoder 740 439-5811
13051 Deerfield Rd Senecaville (43780) *(G-13130)*

Paulin Industries Inc 216 433-7633
12400 Plaza Dr U1 Parma (44130) *(G-12293)*

Paulo Products Company 440 942-0153
4428 Hamann Pkwy Willoughby (44094) *(G-15969)*

Pauls Tire Company, Youngstown Also Called: Paul Shovlin *(G-16416)*

Paus North America Inc 775 778-5980
29001 Solon Rd Unit L Solon (44139) *(G-13402)*

Pave Technology Co 937 890-1100
2751 Thunderhawk Ct Dayton (45414) *(G-6499)*

Pavestone LLC 513 474-3783
8479 Broadwell Rd Cincinnati (45244) *(G-3242)*

Pavletich Manufacturing 440 382-0997
2774 Nationwide Pkwy Brunswick (44212) *(G-1779)*

Pawnee Maintenance Inc 740 373-6861
101 Rathbone Rd Marietta (45750) *(G-9815)*

Paws & Remember NW Ohio LLC 419 662-9000
2121 Tracy Rd Northwood (43619) *(G-11925)*

Pax Corrugated Products, Inc., Lebanon *Also Called: Georgia-Pacific Pcpi Inc (G-9081)*

Pax Machine Works Inc 419 586-2337
5139 Monroe Rd Celina (45822) *(G-2342)*

Pax Products Inc 419 586-2337
5097 Monroe Rd Celina (45822) *(G-2343)*

Pax Steel Products Inc 419 678-1481
104 E Vine St Coldwater (45828) *(G-4999)*

Paxos Plating Inc 330 479-0022
4631 Navarre Rd Sw Canton (44706) *(G-2195)*

Paycor, Cincinnati *Also Called: Paycor Hcm Inc (G-3243)*

Paycor Hcm Inc (HQ) 800 381-0053
4811 Montgomery Rd Cincinnati (45212) *(G-3243)*

Payday 124 Inc 614 509-1080
2246 Citygate Dr Columbus (43219) *(G-5662)*

PB Fbrction Mech Contrs Corp 419 478-4869
750 W Laskey Rd Toledo (43612) *(G-14429)*

PBM Covington LLC 937 473-2050
400 Hazel St Covington (45318) *(G-6029)*

PC, Columbus *Also Called: Papel Couture (G-5655)*

PC Campana Inc 800 321-0151
3000 Leavitt Rd Frnt Lorain (44052) *(G-9428)*

PC Campana Inc (PA) 800 321-0151
6155 Park Square Dr Ste 1 Lorain (44053) *(G-9429)*

PC Molding LLC 614 873-7712
7680 Commerce Pl Plain City (43064) *(G-12590)*

PCA/Akron 312, Coventry Township *Also Called: Packaging Corporation America (G-6015)*

Pca/Ashland 307, Ashland *Also Called: Packaging Corporation America (G-597)*

Pca/Fairfielde 329, Fairfield *Also Called: Dixie Container Corporation (G-7353)*

Pca/Middletown 353, Middletown *Also Called: Packaging Corporation America (G-10848)*

PCA/Newark 365, Newark *Also Called: Packaging Corporation America (G-11601)*

PCC, Painesville *Also Called: Precision Castparts Corp (G-12258)*

PCC Airfoils LLC (DH) 216 831-3590
3401 Enterprise Pkwy Ste 200 Cleveland (44122) *(G-4536)*

PCC Airfoils LLC 216 766-6206
25201 Chagrin Blvd Ste 290 Beachwood (44122) *(G-1009)*

PCC Airfoils LLC 216 692-7900
1781 Octavia Rd Cleveland (44112) *(G-4537)*

PCC Airfoils LLC 740 982-6025
101 China St Crooksville (43731) *(G-6048)*

PCC Airfoils LLC 440 585-8247
34300 Melinz Pkwy Eastlake (44095) *(G-7044)*

PCC Airfoils LLC 440 255-9770
8607 Tyler Blvd Mentor (44060) *(G-10521)*

PCC Airfoils LLC 330 868-6441
3860 Union Ave Se Minerva (44657) *(G-11038)*

PCC Airfoils LLC 440 350-6150
870 Renaissance Pkwy Painesville (44077) *(G-12256)*

PCC AIRFOILS LLC, Crooksville *Also Called: PCC Airfoils LLC (G-6048)*

PCC AIRFOILS LLC, Eastlake *Also Called: PCC Airfoils LLC (G-7044)*

PCC AIRFOILS LLC, Painesville *Also Called: PCC Airfoils LLC (G-12256)*

PCC Ceramic Group 1 .... 440 516-3672
1470 E 289th St Wickliffe (44092) *(G-15847)*

Pchem LLC 419 699-1582
2533 Tracy Rd Northwood (43619) *(G-11926)*

PCI, West Chester *Also Called: Professional Case Inc (G-15578)*

Pckd Enterprises Inc 440 632-9119
15510 Old State Rd Middlefield (44062) *(G-10779)*

Pcna, Cincinnati *Also Called: Peter Cremer North America LP (G-3251)*

PCR Restorations Inc 419 747-7957
933 W Longview Ave Mansfield (44906) *(G-9709)*

Pcs Nitrogen Inc 419 226-1200
1900 Fort Amanda Rd Lima (45804) *(G-9275)*

Pcs Nitrogen Ohio LP 419 879-8989
2200 Fort Amanda Rd Lima (45804) *(G-9276)*

Pcs Phosphate Company Inc 513 738-1261
10818 Paddys Run Rd Harrison (45030) *(G-8283)*

PD&b, Toledo *Also Called: Projects Designed & Built (G-14443)*

Pdi Ground Support Systems Inc 216 271-7344
6225 Cochran Rd Solon (44139) *(G-13403)*

Pdi Group, The, Solon *Also Called: Pdi Ground Support Systems Inc (G-13403)*

PDQ Installation Co, Cleveland *Also Called: GMR Furniture Services Ltd (G-4130)*

PDQ Printing Service 216 241-5443
29003 Brockway Dr Westlake (44145) *(G-15772)*

PDQ Technologies Inc 937 274-4958
2500 Us Route 40 Tipp City (45371) *(G-14146)*

Pdsi, Groveport *Also Called: Pinnacle Data Systems Inc (G-8158)*

Pdsi Technical Services, Dayton *Also Called: Production Design Services Inc (G-6529)*

PE Usa LLC 513 771-7374
89 Partnership Way Cincinnati (45241) *(G-3244)*

Peabody Coal Company 740 450-2420
2810 East Pike Apt 3 Zanesville (43701) *(G-16554)*

Peak Electric, Toledo *Also Called: Peak Electric Inc (G-14430)*

Peak Electric Inc 419 726-4848
320 N Byrne Rd Toledo (43607) *(G-14430)*

Peak Foods Llc 937 440-0707
1903 W Main St Troy (45373) *(G-14601)*

Pearl Valley Cheese Inc 740 545-6002
54760 Township Road 90 Fresno (43824) *(G-7823)*

Pearson Education Inc 614 876-0371
4350 Equity Dr Columbus (43228) *(G-5663)*

Pearson Education Inc 614 841-3700
800 N High St Columbus (43215) *(G-5664)*

Pease Industies Inc 513 870-3600
7100 Dixie Hwy Fairfield (45014) *(G-7393)*

PEC Biofuels LLC 419 542-8210
210 Wendell Ave Hicksville (43526) *(G-8378)*

Peco, Westlake *Also Called: Cleveland Roll Forming Environmental Division Inc (G-15744)*

Peco Holdings Corp (PA) 937 667-5705
6555 S State Route 202 Tipp City (45371) *(G-14147)*

Peco Welding Services LLC, Tipp City *Also Called: Process Eqp Co Wldg Svcs LLC (G-14149)*

Pedagogy Furniture 888 394-8484
745 South St Chardon (44024) *(G-2463)*

Pedestrian Press 419 244-6488
2233 Robinwood Ave Toledo (43620) *(G-14431)*

Pediavascular Inc 216 236-5533
7181 Chagrin Rd Ste 250 Chagrin Falls (44023) *(G-2414)*

Peebles - Herzog Inc 614 279-2211
50 Hayden Ave Columbus (43222) *(G-5665)*

Peebles Messenger Newspaper 937 587-1451
58 S Main St Peebles (45660) *(G-12329)*

Peerless Food Equipment LLC, Sidney *Also Called: Coperion Food Equipment LLC (G-13239)*

Peerless Foods Inc 937 492-4158
500 S Vandemark Rd Sidney (45365) *(G-13270)*

Peerless Foods Equipment, Sidney *Also Called: Peerless Foods Inc (G-13270)*

Peerless Laser Processors Inc 614 836-5790
4353 Directors Blvd Groveport (43125) *(G-8156)*

Peerless Metal Products Inc 216 431-6905
6017 Superior Ave Cleveland (44103) *(G-4538)*

Peerless Printing Company 513 721-4657
2250 Gilbert Ave Ste 1 Cincinnati (45206) *(G-3245)*

Peerless Prof Cooking Eqp, Sandusky *Also Called: Peerless Stove & Mfg Co (G-13087)*

Peerless Pump Clveland Svc Ctr, Cleveland *Also Called: Wm Plotz Machine and Forge Co (G-4915)*

Peerless Saw Company (PA) 614 836-5790
4353 Directors Blvd Groveport (43125) *(G-8157)*

Peerless Stove & Mfg Co 419 625-4514
334 Harrison St Sandusky (44870) *(G-13087)*

Peerless-Winsmith Inc 330 399-3651
5200 Upper Metro Pl Ste 110 Dublin (43017) *(G-6921)*

Pei Liquidation Company 330 467-4267
700 Highland Rd E Macedonia (44056) *(G-9564)*

Pelletier Brothers Mfg Inc 740 774-4704
4000 Sulphur Lick Rd Chillicothe (45601) *(G-2524)*

Pelton Environmental Pdts Inc 440 838-1221
8638 Cotter St Lewis Center (43035) *(G-9175)*

Pemco Inc... 216 524-2990
5663 Brecksville Rd Cleveland (44131) *(G-4539)*

Pemco North Canton Division, North Canton *Also Called: Powell Electrical Systems Inc* *(G-11753)*

Pemjay Inc.. 740 254-4591
318 E Tuscarawas Ave Gnadenhutten (44629) *(G-7986)*

Pemro Corporation.. 800 440-5441
125 Alpha Park Cleveland (44143) *(G-4540)*

Pemro Distribution, Cleveland *Also Called: Pemro Corporation (G-4540)*

Pen-Ann Corporation.. 740 373-2054
2343 State Route 821 Ste A Marietta (45750) *(G-9816)*

Penguin Enterprises Inc... 440 899-5112
869 Canterbury Rd Ste 2 Westlake (44145) *(G-15773)*

Pengywn, Columbus *Also Called: H Y O Inc (G-5414)*

Peninsula Publishing LLC.. 330 524-3359
2 Summit Park Dr Ste 300 Independence (44131) *(G-8679)*

Penn Machine Company LLC.. 814 288-1547
2182 E Aurora Rd Twinsburg (44087) *(G-14708)*

Pennant, Pioneer *Also Called: Nn Metal Stampings LLC (G-12493)*

Pennant Inc... 937 584-5411
401 N Front St Ste 350 Columbus (43215) *(G-5666)*

Pennant Companies (PA).. 614 451-1782
12381 Us Highway 22 And 3 Sabina (45169) *(G-12889)*

Pennant Manufacturing, Columbus *Also Called: Pennant Inc (G-5666)*

Pennant Moldings Inc... 937 584-5411
12381 Us Highway 22 And 3 Sabina (45169) *(G-12890)*

Pennex Aluminum Company LLC..................................... 330 427-6704
1 Commerce Ave Leetonia (44431) *(G-9129)*

Penny Fab, Columbus *Also Called: Penny Fab LLC (G-5667)*

Penny Fab LLC.. 740 967-3669
1055 Gibbard Ave Columbus (43201) *(G-5667)*

Pentaflex Inc... 937 325-5551
4981 Gateway Blvd Springfield (45502) *(G-13617)*

Pentagear Products LLC.. 937 660-8182
6161 Webster St Dayton (45414) *(G-6500)*

Pentagon Protection Usa LLC.. 614 734-7240
5500 Frantz Rd Ste 120 Dublin (43017) *(G-6922)*

Pentair.. 440 248-0100
34600 Solon Rd Solon (44139) *(G-13404)*

Pentair Pump Group Inc... 419 281-9918
740 E 9th St Ashland (44805) *(G-598)*

Pentair Water Ashland Oper, Ashland *Also Called: Flow Control US Holding Corp (G-572)*

Penwood Mfg... 330 359-5600
30505 Township Road 212 Fresno (43824) *(G-7824)*

Pepcon Concrete, Bradford *Also Called: C F Poeppelman Inc (G-1600)*

Pepi, North Canton *Also Called: Portage Electric Products Inc (G-11752)*

Pepperidge Farm Incorporated.. 419 933-2611
3320 State Route 103 E Willard (44890) *(G-15863)*

Pepperl + Fuchs Inc (DH)... 330 425-3555
1600 Enterprise Pkwy Twinsburg (44087) *(G-14709)*

Pepperl + Fuchs Entps Inc (HQ)....................................... 330 425-3555
1600 Enterprise Pkwy Twinsburg (44087) *(G-14710)*

Pepsi Cola Bottling Co, Lima *Also Called: Consolidated Bottling Company (G-9229)*

Pepsi-Cola, Athens *Also Called: G & J Pepsi-Cola Bottlers Inc (G-683)*

Pepsi-Cola, Cincinnati *Also Called: G & J Pepsi-Cola Bottlers Inc (G-2924)*

Pepsi-Cola, Dayton *Also Called: Pepsi-Cola Metro Btlg Co Inc (G-6501)*

Pepsi-Cola, Elyria *Also Called: Pepsi-Cola Metro Btlg Co Inc (G-7193)*

Pepsi-Cola, Hamilton *Also Called: G & J Pepsi-Cola Bottlers Inc (G-8210)*

Pepsi-Cola, Springfield *Also Called: Pepsi-Cola Metro Btlg Co Inc (G-13618)*

Pepsi-Cola, Twinsburg *Also Called: Pepsi-Cola Metro Btlg Co Inc (G-14711)*

Pepsi-Cola Metro Btlg Co Inc... 614 261-8193
2553 N High St Columbus (43202) *(G-5668)*

Pepsi-Cola Metro Btlg Co Inc... 937 461-4664
526 Milburn Ave Dayton (45404) *(G-6501)*

Pepsi-Cola Metro Btlg Co Inc... 440 323-5524
925 Lorain Blvd Elyria (44035) *(G-7193)*

Pepsi-Cola Metro Btlg Co Inc... 937 328-6750
233 Dayton Ave Springfield (45506) *(G-13618)*

Pepsi-Cola Metro Btlg Co Inc... 419 534-2186
3245 Hill Ave Toledo (43607) *(G-14432)*

Pepsi-Cola Metro Btlg Co Inc... 330 425-8236
1999 Enterprise Pkwy Twinsburg (44087) *(G-14711)*

Pepsi-Cola Metro Btlg Co Inc... 330 963-5300
1999 Enterprise Pkwy Twinsburg (44087) *(G-14712)*

Pepsico.. 513 229-3046
5181 Natorp Blvd Ste 450 Mason (45040) *(G-10037)*

Pepsico, Chillicothe *Also Called: G & J Pepsi-Cola Bottlers Inc (G-2504)*

Pepsico, Cincinnati *Also Called: P-Americas LLC (G-3233)*

Pepsico, Columbus *Also Called: G & J Pepsi-Cola Bottlers Inc (G-5393)*

Pepsico, Columbus *Also Called: G & J Pepsi-Cola Bottlers Inc (G-5394)*

Pepsico, Columbus *Also Called: Pepsi-Cola Metro Btlg Co Inc (G-5668)*

Pepsico, Franklin Furnace *Also Called: G & J Pepsi-Cola Bottlers Inc (G-7712)*

Pepsico, Mason *Also Called: Pepsico (G-10037)*

Pepsico, Toledo *Also Called: Pepsi-Cola Metro Btlg Co Inc (G-14432)*

Pepsico, Twinsburg *Also Called: Pepsi-Cola Metro Btlg Co Inc (G-14712)*

Pepsico, Zanesville *Also Called: G & J Pepsi-Cola Bottlers Inc (G-16534)*

Percuvision LLC.. 614 891-4800
2030 Dividend Dr Columbus (43228) *(G-5669)*

Perdatum Inc... 614 761-1578
4098 Main St Hilliard (43026) *(G-8430)*

Perennial Vineyards LLC.. 330 832-3677
11877 Poorman St Sw Navarre (44662) *(G-11349)*

Perfect Prcision Machining Ltd.. 330 475-0324
920 Clay St Akron (44311) *(G-274)*

Perfect Probate... 513 791-4100
2036 8 Mile Rd Cincinnati (45244) *(G-3246)*

Perfect Products Company
265 Morges Rd Malvern (44644) *(G-9614)*

Perfect Score, The, Bedford Heights *Also Called: the Perfect Score Company (G-1179)*

Perfection Fabricators Inc.. 440 365-5850
680 Sugar Ln Elyria (44035) *(G-7194)*

Perfection Fine Products, Cleveland *Also Called: Gwj Liquidation Inc (G-4158)*

Perfection Finishers Inc... 419 337-8015
1151 N Ottokee St Wauseon (43567) *(G-15272)*

Perfection In Carbide, Canfield *Also Called: Advetech Inc (G-1995)*

Perfection Mold & Machine Co... 330 784-5435
2057 E Aurora Rd Ste Hi Twinsburg (44087) *(G-14713)*

Perfection Printing.. 513 874-2173
9560 Le Saint Dr Fairfield (45014) *(G-7394)*

Perfecto Industries Inc... 937 778-1900
1729 W High St Piqua (45356) *(G-12542)*

Perfomance Feed & Seeds Inc.. 419 496-0531
1379 Township Road 1353 Ashland (44805) *(G-599)*

Performace Diesel Inc.. 740 392-3693
16901 Mcvay Rd Mount Vernon (43050) *(G-11287)*

Performance Elastomers, Ravenna *Also Called: Performance Elastomers Corporation (G-12727)*

Performance Elastomers Corporation.............................. 330 297-2255
7162 State Route 88 Ravenna (44266) *(G-12727)*

Performance Electronics Ltd.. 513 777-5233
11529 Goldcoast Dr Cincinnati (45249) *(G-3247)*

Performance Health, Akron *Also Called: Hygenic Company LLC (G-188)*

Performance Motorsports Inc... 440 951-6600
7201 Industrial Park Blvd Mentor (44060) *(G-10522)*

Performance Packaging Inc.. 419 478-8805
5219 Telegraph Rd Toledo (43612) *(G-14433)*

Performance Plastics, Cincinnati *Also Called: Performance Plastics Ltd (G-3248)*

Performance Plastics Ltd... 513 321-8404
4435 Brownway Ave Cincinnati (45209) *(G-3248)*

Performance Research Inc... 614 475-8300
3328 Westerville Rd Columbus (43224) *(G-5670)*

Performance Superabrasives LLC.................................... 440 946-7171
7255 Industrial Park Blvd Ste A Mentor (44060) *(G-10523)*

Performance Tank Sales Inc
424 W 3rd St Dover (44622) *(G-6839)*

Performance Technologies LLC.. 330 875-1216
3690 Tulane Ave Louisville (44641) *(G-9468)*

Performanx Specialty Chem LLC..................................... 614 300-7001
479 Industrial Park Dr Waverly (45690) *(G-15290)*

Performnce Plymr Solutions Inc...................................... 937 298-3713
2711 Lance Dr Moraine (45409) *(G-11196)*

Periflo/Px Pumps USA, Loveland *Also Called: Fischer Global Enterprises LLC (G-9480)*
Peritec Biosciences, Cleveland *Also Called: Peritec Biosciences Ltd (G-4541)*
Peritec Biosciences Ltd 216 445-3756
   3291 Bremerton Rd Cleveland (44124) *(G-4541)*
Perkins Motor Service Ltd (PA) 440 277-1256
   1864 E 28th St Lorain (44055) *(G-9430)*
Perma Edge Industries LLC 937 623-7819
   800 Scholz Dr Vandalia (45377) *(G-14957)*
Perma Edge Paver Edging 844 334-4464
   420 Davis Ave Dayton (45403) *(G-6502)*
Perma-Fix of Dayton Inc 937 268-6501
   300 Cherokee Dr Dayton (45417) *(G-6503)*
Permatex, Solon *Also Called: Illinois Tool Works Inc (G-13366)*
Permco Inc 330 626-2801
   1500 Frost Rd Streetsboro (44241) *(G-13783)*
Permian Oil & Gas Division, Newark *Also Called: National Gas & Oil Corporation (G-11596)*
Perrigo 937 473-2050
   400 Hazel St Covington (45318) *(G-6030)*
Perrons Printing Company 440 236-8870
   27500 Royalton Rd Ste D Columbia Station (44028) *(G-5016)*
Perry County Tribune 740 342-4121
   399 Lincoln Park Dr Ste A New Lexington (43764) *(G-11456)*
Perry Welding Service Inc 330 425-2211
   2075 Case Pkwy S Twinsburg (44087) *(G-14714)*
Perrysburg Messenger-Journal, Perrysburg *Also Called: Welch Publishing Co (G-12444)*
Persistence of Vision Inc 440 591-5443
   16715 W Park Circle Dr Chagrin Falls (44023) *(G-2415)*
Personal Defense & Tactics LLC 513 571-7163
   2200 Ernestine Dr Middletown (45042) *(G-10849)*
Personal Plumber Service Corp 440 324-4321
   42343 N Ridge Rd Elyria (44035) *(G-7195)*
Personnel Selection Services 440 835-3255
   31517 Walker Rd Cleveland (44140) *(G-4542)*
Perstorp Polyols Inc 419 729-5448
   600 Matzinger Rd Toledo (43612) *(G-14434)*
Pesce Bakery Company Ltd 330 746-6537
   45 N Hine St Youngstown (44506) *(G-16417)*
Peska Inc (PA) 440 998-4664
   3600 N Ridge Rd E Ashtabula (44004) *(G-654)*
Pet Goods Mfg, Columbus *Also Called: Tarahill Inc (G-5808)*
Pet Processors LLc 440 354-4321
   1350 Bacon Rd Painesville (44077) *(G-12257)*
Pete Gaietto & Associates Inc 513 771-0903
   1900 Section Rd Cincinnati (45237) *(G-3249)*
Peter Cremer N Amer Enrgy Inc 513 557-3943
   3131 River Rd Cincinnati (45204) *(G-3250)*
Peter Cremer North America, Cincinnati *Also Called: Peter Cremer N Amer Enrgy Inc (G-3250)*
Peter Cremer North America LP (DH) 513 471-7200
   3131 River Rd Cincinnati (45204) *(G-3251)*
Peter Graham Dunn Inc 330 816-0035
   1417 Zuercher Rd Dalton (44618) *(G-6139)*
Peter LI Education Group, Moraine *Also Called: Pjl Enterprise Inc (G-11199)*
Peters Family Enterprises Inc 419 339-0555
   5959 Allentown Rd Elida (45807) *(G-7096)*
Peterson American Corporation 419 867-8711
   1625 Commerce Rd Holland (43528) *(G-8523)*
Petnet Solutions Inc 865 218-2000
   2139 Auburn Ave Cincinnati (45219) *(G-3252)*
Petnet Solutions Cleveland LLC 865 218-2000
   2035 E 86th St Rm Jb-122 Cleveland (44106) *(G-4543)*
Petrition LLC 717 572-5665
   705 Medina St Lodi (44254) *(G-9354)*
Petro Gear Corporation (PA) 216 431-2820
   3901 Hamilton Ave Cleveland (44114) *(G-4544)*
Petro Quest Inc (PA) 740 593-3800
   3 W Stimson Ave Athens (45701) *(G-690)*
Petro Ware Inc 740 982-1302
   713 Keystone St Crooksville (43731) *(G-6049)*
Petroleum Holdings LLC 443 676-0150
   445 Prospect St Salem (44460) *(G-13021)*

Petrox Inc 330 653-5526
   10005 Ellsworth Rd Streetsboro (44241) *(G-13784)*
Petry Power Systems, Kent *Also Called: P S P Inc (G-8842)*
Pettigrew Pumping Inc 330 297-7900
   4171 Sandy Lake Rd Ravenna (44266) *(G-12728)*
Pettisville Grain Co (PA) 419 446-2547
   18251 County Road D-E Pettisville (43553) *(G-12452)*
Pettisville Meats Incorporated 419 445-0921
   3082 Main St Pettisville (43553) *(G-12453)*
Pettits Pallets Inc 614 351-4920
   1891 Dauphin Dr Galloway (43119) *(G-7905)*
Pf Management Inc 513 874-8741
   9990 Princeton Glendale Rd West Chester (45246) *(G-15575)*
Pfi Displays Inc (PA) 330 925-9015
   40 Industrial St Rittman (44270) *(G-12826)*
Pfi Precision Inc 937 845-3563
   2011 N Dayton Lakeview Rd New Carlisle (45344) *(G-11425)*
Pfi Precision Machining, New Carlisle *Also Called: Pfi Precision Inc (G-11425)*
Pfi USA 937 547-0413
   5963 Jaysville Saint Johns Rd Greenville (45331) *(G-8055)*
Pfizer, Franklin *Also Called: Pfizer Inc (G-7691)*
Pfizer Inc 937 746-3603
   160 Industrial Dr Franklin (45005) *(G-7691)*
Pflaum Publishing Group 937 293-1415
   3055 Kettering Blvd Ste 100 Moraine (45439) *(G-11197)*
Pfmi, West Chester *Also Called: Pf Management Inc (G-15575)*
Pfp Holdings LLC 419 647-4191
   220 S Elizabeth St Spencerville (45887) *(G-13488)*
Pfpc Enterprises Inc 513 941-6200
   5750 Hillside Ave Cincinnati (45233) *(G-3253)*
Pg Square LLC 216 896-3000
   6035 Parkland Blvd Cleveland (44124) *(G-4545)*
Pgc Feeds, Pettisville *Also Called: Pettisville Grain Co (G-12452)*
PGT Healthcare LLP (HQ) 513 983-1100
   1 Procter And Gamble Plz Cincinnati (45202) *(G-3254)*
Phantasm Dsgns Sprtsn More Ltd 419 538-6737
   112 W Main St Ottawa (45875) *(G-12188)*
Phantom Fireworks, Youngstown *Also Called: Phantom Fireworks Wstn Reg LLC (G-16418)*
Phantom Fireworks Wstn Reg LLC 330 746-1064
   2445 Belmont Ave Youngstown (44505) *(G-16418)*
Phantom Sound 513 759-4477
   104 Reading Rd Mason (45040) *(G-10038)*
Phantom Technology LLC 614 710-0074
   4179 Lyman Dr Hilliard (43026) *(G-8431)*
Pharmacia Hepar LLC 937 746-3603
   160 Industrial Dr Franklin (45005) *(G-7692)*
Pharmacy Solutions Group of WV, Blue Ash *Also Called: WV CHS Pharmacy Services LLC (G-1496)*
Pharmaforce Inc
   960 Crupper Ave Columbus (43229) *(G-5671)*
Phase Array Company LLC 513 785-0801
   9472 Meridian Way West Chester (45069) *(G-15475)*
Phase II Enterprises Inc 330 484-2113
   2154 Bolivar Rd Sw Canton (44706) *(G-2196)*
PHC Divison Bic Manufacturing, Euclid *Also Called: Precision Hydrlic Cnnctors Inc (G-7296)*
Phe Manufacturing, Franklin *Also Called: Phe Manufacturing Inc (G-7693)*
Phe Manufacturing Inc 937 790-1582
   331 Industrial Dr Franklin (45005) *(G-7693)*
Phelps Creek Wood Works Llc 440 693-4314
   9445 State Route 534 Middlefield (44062) *(G-10780)*
PHI Werkes LLC 419 586-9222
   1201 Havemann Rd Celina (45822) *(G-2344)*
Phil Vedda & Sons Inc 216 671-2222
   12000 Berea Rd Cleveland (44111) *(G-4546)*
Phil-Matic Screw Products Inc 440 942-7290
   1457 E 357th St Willoughby (44095) *(G-15970)*
Philadelphia Instantwhip Inc 614 488-2536
   2200 Cardigan Ave Columbus (43215) *(G-5672)*
Philip Radke 614 475-6788
   1184 Bonham Ave Columbus (43211) *(G-5673)*
Philips Healthcare, Cleveland *Also Called: Philips Med Systems Clvland In (G-4547)*

ALPHABETIC SECTION — Pines Technology

Philips Med Systems Clvland In 617 245-5510
100 Park Ave Ste 300 Beachwood (44122) *(G-1010)*

Philips Med Systems Clvland In (HQ) 440 483-3000
595 Miner Rd Cleveland (44143) *(G-4547)*

Phillips Companies (PA) 937 426-5461
620 Phillips Dr Beavercreek Township (45434) *(G-1089)*

Phillips Electric, Cleveland *Also Called: Phillips Electric Co (G-4548)*

Phillips Electric Co 216 361-0014
4126 Saint Clair Ave Cleveland (44103) *(G-4548)*

Phillips Manufacturing Co 330 652-4335
504 Walnut St Niles (44446) *(G-11682)*

Phillips Mch & Stamping Corp 330 882-6714
5290 S Main St New Franklin (44319) *(G-11441)*

Phillips Meat Processing LLC 740 453-3337
2790 Ridge Rd Zanesville (43701) *(G-16555)*

Phillips Mfg & Mch Corp 330 823-9178
118 1/2 E Ely St Alliance (44601) *(G-418)*

Phillips Mfg and Tower Co (PA) 419 347-1720
5578 State Route 61 N Shelby (44875) *(G-13197)*

Phillips Ready Mix Co 937 426-5151
620 Phillips Dr Beavercreek Township (45434) *(G-1090)*

Phillips Syrup, Westlake *Also Called: Innovtive Cnfction Sltions LLC (G-15761)*

Phillips Syrup LLC 440 835-8001
28025 Ranney Pkwy Westlake (44145) *(G-15774)*

Phillips Tube Group Inc 205 338-4771
2201 Trine St Middletown (45044) *(G-10850)*

Phillips Tube Group, LLC, Middletown *Also Called: Phillips Tube Group Inc (G-10850)*

Philpott Rubber and Plastics, Aurora *Also Called: Philpott Rubber LLC (G-732)*

Philpott Rubber Company, Brunswick *Also Called: Philpott Rubber LLC (G-1780)*

Philpott Rubber LLC 330 225-3344
375 Gentry Dr Aurora (44202) *(G-732)*

Philpott Rubber LLC (HQ) 330 225-3344
1010 Industrial Pkwy N Brunswick (44212) *(G-1780)*

Philway Products Inc 419 281-7777
521 E 7th St Ashland (44805) *(G-600)*

Pho & Rice LLC 216 563-1122
1780 Coventry Rd Cleveland Heights (44118) *(G-4942)*

Phoenix, Twinsburg *Also Called: Stellar Process Inc (G-14737)*

Phoenix Asphalt Company Inc 330 339-4935
18025 Imperial Rd Magnolia (44643) *(G-9597)*

Phoenix Associates 440 543-9701
16760 W Park Circle Dr Chagrin Falls (44023) *(G-2416)*

Phoenix Brewing, Mansfield *Also Called: Mansfield Brew Works LLC (G-9684)*

Phoenix Forge Group LLC 800 848-6125
1501 W Main St West Jefferson (43162) *(G-15614)*

Phoenix Grphics Communications 330 697-4171
99 Laurel Blvd Munroe Falls (44262) *(G-11304)*

Phoenix Hydraulic Presses Inc 614 850-8940
4329 Reynolds Dr Hilliard (43026) *(G-8432)*

Phoenix Inds & Apparatus Inc 513 722-1085
6466 Snider Rd Apt C Loveland (45140) *(G-9498)*

Phoenix Inkjet Clour Sltons LL 937 602-8486
707 Miamisburg Centerville Rd Ste 128 Dayton (45459) *(G-6504)*

Phoenix Mtal Sls Fbrcation LLC 330 562-0585
2201 Pinnacle Pkwy Ste A Twinsburg (44087) *(G-14715)*

Phoenix Quality Mfg LLC 705 279-0538
16064 Beaver Pike # 888 Jackson (45640) *(G-8722)*

Phoenix Safety Outfitters LLC 614 361-0544
110 W Leffel Ln Springfield (45506) *(G-13619)*

Phoenix Technologies Intl LLC (HQ) 419 353-7738
1098 Fairview Ave Bowling Green (43402) *(G-1583)*

Phoenix Tool Company 330 372-4627
1351 Phoenix Rd Ne Warren (44483) *(G-15198)*

Photo Journals, Sandusky *Also Called: Douthit Communications Inc (G-13051)*

Photo-Type Engraving Company 614 308-1900
2500 Harrison Rd Columbus (43204) *(G-5674)*

Photography and Publishing, Mansfield *Also Called: Universal Ch Directories LLC (G-9729)*

Phpk Technologies, Columbus *Also Called: Kendall Holdings Ltd (G-5507)*

Phunkenship - Platform Beer Co 216 417-7743
3137 Sackett Ave Cleveland (44109) *(G-4549)*

Phyllis Ann's, Columbus *Also Called: Roy Retrac Incorporated (G-5732)*

Phymet Inc 937 743-8061
75 N Pioneer Blvd Springboro (45066) *(G-13515)*

Pi-Tech, Dayton *Also Called: Proficient Info Tech Inc (G-6531)*

Pickens Plastics Inc 440 576-4001
149 S Cucumber St Jefferson (44047) *(G-8755)*

Pickens Window Service Inc 513 931-4432
7824 Hamilton Ave Cincinnati (45231) *(G-3255)*

Pickett Concrete, Chesapeake *Also Called: G Big Inc (G-2473)*

Pieco Inc (PA) 419 422-5335
2151 Industrial Dr Findlay (45840) *(G-7551)*

Pieco Inc 937 399-5100
5225 Prosperity Dr Springfield (45502) *(G-13620)*

Piedmont Chemical Company Inc 937 428-6640
1516 Silver Lake Dr Dayton (45458) *(G-6505)*

Piedmont Water Services LLC 216 554-4747
21400 Lorain Rd Cleveland (44126) *(G-4550)*

Pier Tool & Die Inc 440 236-3188
27369 Royalton Rd Columbia Station (44028) *(G-5017)*

Pierce-Wright Precision Inc 216 362-2870
13606 Enterprise Ave Cleveland (44135) *(G-4551)*

Pierre Holding Corp (HQ) 513 874-8741
9990 Princeton Glendale Rd West Chester (45246) *(G-15576)*

Pierres Ice Cream Company Inc 216 432-1144
6200 Euclid Ave Cleveland (44103) *(G-4552)*

Piersante and Associates Inc 330 533-9904
230 Russo Dr Canfield (44406) *(G-2014)*

Pietra Naturale Inc 937 438-8882
2425 Stanley Ave Dayton (45404) *(G-6506)*

Pigments Division, Cincinnati *Also Called: Sun Chemical Corporation (G-3431)*

Pilington Libbey-Owens-Ford Co, Rossford *Also Called: Pilkington North America Inc (G-12869)*

Pilkington Holdings Inc (DH) 811 Madison Ave Fl 1 Toledo (43604) *(G-14435)*

Pilkington North America Inc 800 547-9280
2401 E Broadway St Northwood (43619) *(G-11927)*

Pilkington North America Inc 419 247-3211
140 Dixie Hwy Rossford (43460) *(G-12869)*

Pilkington North America Inc (DH) 419 247-3731
811 Madison Ave Fl 3 Toledo (43604) *(G-14436)*

Pilkington North America Inc 419 247-3731
3440 Centerpoint Dr Urbancrest (43123) *(G-14854)*

Pillar Induction 262 317-5300
1745 Overland Ave Ne Warren (44483) *(G-15199)*

Pillsbury, Caledonia *Also Called: Pillsbury Company LLC (G-1917)*

Pillsbury, Wellston *Also Called: Pillsbury Company LLC (G-15331)*

Pillsbury Company LLC 419 845-3751
4136 Martel Rd Caledonia (43314) *(G-1917)*

Pillsbury Company LLC 740 286-2170
2403 S Pennsylvania Ave Wellston (45692) *(G-15331)*

Pilorusso Construction Div, Lowellville *Also Called: Lyco Corporation (G-9517)*

Pilot Chemical, Newark *Also Called: CP Industries Inc (G-11573)*

Pilot Chemical Company, West Chester *Also Called: Pilot Chemical Company Ohio (G-15476)*

Pilot Chemical Company Ohio (PA) 513 326-0600
9075 Centre Pointe Dr Ste 400 West Chester (45069) *(G-15476)*

Pilot Chemical Corp 513 424-9700
3439 Yankee Rd Middletown (45044) *(G-10851)*

Pilot Chemical Corp (HQ) 513 326-0600
9075 Centre Pointe Dr Ste 400 West Chester (45069) *(G-15477)*

Pilot Plastics, Peninsula *Also Called: Preformed Line Products Co (G-12341)*

Pilot Polymer Technologies 412 735-4799
9075 Centre Pointe Dr Ste 400 West Chester (45069) *(G-15478)*

Pima Valve LLC 330 337-9535
1913 E State St Salem (44460) *(G-13022)*

Pin Oak Development LLC 440 933-9862
32329 Orchard Park Dr Avon Lake (44012) *(G-820)*

Pin Oak Energy Partners LLC (PA) 888 748-0763
388 S Main St Ste 401b Akron (44311) *(G-275)*

Pines Manufacturing Inc (PA) 440 835-5553
29100 Lakeland Blvd Westlake (44145) *(G-15775)*

Pines Technology, Westlake *Also Called: Pines Manufacturing Inc (G-15775)*

Pines Technology, Westlake *Also Called: Risk Industries LLC (G-15779)*
Pink Pages, Cincinnati *Also Called: Printery Inc (G-3277)*

Pinnacle Data Systems Inc 614 748-1150
6600 Port Rd Groveport (43125) *(G-8158)*

Pinnacle Graphics Imaging Inc 216 781-1800
17920 S Waterloo Rd Cleveland (44119) *(G-4553)*

Pinnacle Industrial Entps Inc 419 352-8688
513 Napoleon Rd Bowling Green (43402) *(G-1584)*

Pinnacle Metal Products, Columbus *Also Called: McNeil Group Inc (G-5556)*
Pinnacle Plastic Products, Bowling Green *Also Called: Pinnacle Industrial Entps Inc (G-1584)*

Pinnacle Press Inc 330 453-7060
2960 Harrisburg Rd Ne Canton (44705) *(G-2197)*

Pinnacle Roller Co 513 369-4830
2147 Spring Grove Ave Cincinnati (45214) *(G-3256)*

Pinney Dock & Transport LLC 440 964-7186
1149 E 5th St Ashtabula (44004) *(G-655)*

Pioneer Athletics, Cleveland *Also Called: Pioneer Manufacturing Inc (G-4555)*

Pioneer Automotive Tech Inc (DH) 937 746-2293
10100 Innovation Dr Miamisburg (45342) *(G-10670)*

Pioneer City Casting Company 740 423-7533
904 Campus Dr Belpre (45714) *(G-1260)*

Pioneer Cldding Glzing Systems 216 816-4242
2550 Brookpark Rd Cleveland (44134) *(G-4554)*

Pioneer Corp 330 857-0267
16875 Jericho Rd Dalton (44618) *(G-6140)*

Pioneer Custom Coating LLC 419 737-3152
255 Industrial Ave Bldg D Pioneer (43554) *(G-12494)*

Pioneer Custom Molding Inc 419 737-3252
3 Kexon Dr Pioneer (43554) *(G-12495)*

Pioneer Frge A Div Pwers Sons, Montpelier *Also Called: Powers and Sons LLC (G-11140)*
Pioneer Group, Marietta *Also Called: Pioneer Pipe Inc (G-9817)*

Pioneer Industrial Systems LLC (PA) 419 737-9506
16442 Us Highway 20 Alvordton (43501) *(G-444)*

Pioneer Labels Inc 618 546-5418
9290 Le Saint Dr West Chester (45014) *(G-15479)*

Pioneer Machine Inc 330 948-6500
104 S Prospect St Lodi (44254) *(G-9355)*

Pioneer Manufacturing Inc (PA) 216 671-5500
4529 Industrial Pkwy Cleveland (44135) *(G-4555)*

Pioneer National Latex Inc 419 289-3300
114 E 7th St Ashland (44805) *(G-601)*

Pioneer National Latex Inc 419 289-3300
244 Commercial Ave Ashland (44805) *(G-602)*

Pioneer Packing Co 419 352-5283
510 Napoleon Rd Bowling Green (43402) *(G-1585)*

Pioneer Pipe Inc 740 376-2400
2021 Hanna Rd Marietta (45750) *(G-9817)*

Pioneer Plastics Corporation 330 896-2356
3330 Massillon Rd Akron (44312) *(G-276)*

Pioneer Solutions LLC 216 383-3400
24800 Rockwell Dr Euclid (44117) *(G-7292)*

Pioneer Table Pad, Cleveland *Also Called: A & W Table Pad Co (G-3575)*

PIP Printing 513 245-0590
5628 Cheviot Rd Cincinnati (45247) *(G-3257)*

PIP Printing, Cincinnati *Also Called: PIP Printing (G-3257)*
PIP Printing, Columbus *Also Called: Preisser Inc (G-5688)*

Pipe Line Development Company 440 871-5700
11792 Alameda Dr Strongsville (44149) *(G-13865)*

Pipe Products Inc 513 587-7532
5122 Rialto Rd West Chester (45069) *(G-15480)*

Piqua, Piqua *Also Called: Piqua Champion Foundry Inc (G-12543)*

Piqua Champion Foundry Inc
918 S Main St Piqua (45356) *(G-12543)*

Piqua Chocolate Company Inc (PA) 937 773-1981
124 N Main St Piqua (45356) *(G-12544)*

Piqua Emery Cutter & Fndry Co 937 773-4134
821 S Downing St Piqua (45356) *(G-12545)*

Piqua Emery Foundry, Piqua *Also Called: Piqua Emery Cutter & Fndry Co (G-12545)*

Piqua Granite & Marble Co Inc 937 773-2000
123 N Main St Piqua (45356) *(G-12546)*

Piqua Materials Inc (PA) 513 771-0820
11641 Mosteller Rd Ste 1 Cincinnati (45241) *(G-3258)*

Piqua Materials Inc 937 773-4824
1750 W Statler Rd Piqua (45356) *(G-12547)*

Piqua Mineral Division, Piqua *Also Called: Piqua Materials Inc (G-12547)*

Piqua Paper Box Company 937 773-0313
616 Covington Ave Piqua (45356) *(G-12548)*

Pique Stripping Division, Moraine *Also Called: Rack Processing Company Inc (G-11207)*

Piscione Welding 440 653-3985
10147 Franchester Rd Burbank (44214) *(G-1877)*

Piston Automotive LLC 740 223-0075
999 Kellogg Pkwy Marion (43302) *(G-9872)*

Piston Automotive LLC 419 464-0250
1212 E Alexis Rd Toledo (43612) *(G-14437)*

Piston Group, Toledo *Also Called: Piston Automotive LLC (G-14437)*

Pita Wrap LLC 330 886-8091
4721 Market St Boardman (44512) *(G-1516)*

Pitt Plastics Inc (DH) 614 868-8660
3980 Groves Rd Ste A Columbus (43232) *(G-5675)*

Pittman Engineering Inc 330 821-4365
15835 Armour St Ne Alliance (44601) *(G-419)*

Pittsburg Corning Corp Di 724 327-6100
1 Owens Corning Pkwy Toledo (43659) *(G-14438)*

Pittsburgh Corning LLC (HQ) 724 327-6100
1 Owens Corning Pkwy Toledo (43659) *(G-14439)*

Pixelle Specialty Solutions LLC 740 772-3111
232 E 8th St Chillicothe (45601) *(G-2525)*

Pixelle Specialty Solutions LLC 419 333-6700
2275 Commerce Dr Fremont (43420) *(G-7801)*

Pizza Hut, Celina *Also Called: Buckeye Valley Pizza Hut Ltd (G-2324)*

PJ Bush Associates Inc 216 362-6700
15901 Industrial Pkwy Cleveland (44135) *(G-4556)*

Pjl Enterprise Inc 937 293-1415
2019 Springboro W Moraine (45439) *(G-11198)*

Pjl Enterprise Inc (DH) 937 293-1415
3055 Kettering Blvd Ste 100 Moraine (45439) *(G-11199)*

Pjs Corrugated Inc 419 644-3383
2330 Us Highway 20 Swanton (43558) *(G-13980)*

Pjs Wholesale Inc 614 402-9363
2551 Westbelt Dr Columbus (43228) *(G-5676)*

Pk Controls, Plain City *Also Called: Otp Holding LLC (G-12588)*

Pki Inc 513 832-8749
4500 Reading Rd Cincinnati (45229) *(G-3259)*

Plabell Rubber Products Corp (PA) 419 691-5878
300 S Saint Clair St # 324 Toledo (43604) *(G-14440)*

Placecrete Inc 937 298-2121
2475 Arbor Blvd Moraine (45439) *(G-11200)*

Plaid Hat Games 419 552-5490
1172 State Route 96 Ashland (44805) *(G-603)*

Plaid Hat Games LLC 419 552-5490
1172 State Route 96 Ashland (44805) *(G-604)*

Plain Dealer Publishing Co (HQ) 216 999-5000
4800 Tiedeman Rd Cleveland (44144) *(G-4557)*

Plain Dealer, The, Cleveland *Also Called: Plain Dealer Publishing Co (G-4557)*
Plant 1, Celina *Also Called: S & K Products Company (G-2347)*
Plant 2, Ashtabula *Also Called: Iten Industries Inc (G-642)*
Plant 2, Columbus *Also Called: Fred D Pfening Company (G-5388)*
Plant 2, Wooster *Also Called: Wooster Products Inc (G-16187)*
Plant 5, Dayton *Also Called: Oerlikon Frction Systems US In (G-6484)*
Plant 8, Sugarcreek *Also Called: Belden Brick Company LLC (G-13919)*
Plant Maintenance Engineering, Cincinnati *Also Called: New Pme Inc (G-3190)*

Plant Plant Co 303 809-9588
630 Kaiser Dr Heath (43056) *(G-8326)*

Plant Two, Cleveland *Also Called: Falls Stamping & Welding Co (G-4049)*

Plas-Mac Corp 440 349-3222
30250 Carter St Solon (44139) *(G-13405)*

Plas-Tanks Industries Inc (PA) 513 942-3800
39 Standen Dr Hamilton (45015) *(G-8235)*

Plas-TEC Corp 419 272-2731
601 W Indiana St Edon (43518) *(G-7091)*

ALPHABETIC SECTION — Pmp Industries Inc

Plaskolite LLC.. 614 294-3281
400 W Nationwide Blvd Ste 400 Columbus (43215) *(G-5677)*

Plaskolite LLC (PA)... 614 294-3281
400 W Nationwide Blvd Ste 400 Columbus (43215) *(G-5678)*

Plaskolite LLC.. 740 450-1109
1175 5 Bs Dr Zanesville (43701) *(G-16556)*

Plasman AB LP... 216 252-2995
3000 W 121st St Cleveland (44111) *(G-4558)*

Plasman Cleveland Mfg, Cleveland Also Called: Plasman AB LP *(G-4558)*

Plaster Process Castings Co............................. 216 663-1814
19800 Miles Rd Cleveland (44128) *(G-4559)*

Plasti-Kote Co Inc... 330 725-4511
1000 Lake Rd Medina (44256) *(G-10363)*

Plastic Card Inc (PA)... 330 896-5555
3711 Boettler Oaks Dr Uniontown (44685) *(G-14790)*

Plastic Color Division, Minerva Also Called: General Color Investments Inc *(G-11031)*

Plastic Compounders Inc................................. 740 432-7371
1125 Utica Dr Cambridge (43725) *(G-1948)*

Plastic Enterprises Inc..................................... 440 366-0220
1150 Taylor St Elyria (44035) *(G-7196)*

Plastic Enterprises Inc (PA).............................. 440 324-3240
41520 Schadden Rd Elyria (44035) *(G-7197)*

Plastic Extrusion Tech Ltd............................... 440 632-5611
15229 S State Ave Middlefield (44062) *(G-10781)*

Plastic Forming Company Inc........................... 330 830-5167
201 Vista Ave Se Massillon (44646) *(G-10134)*

Plastic Materials Inc... 330 468-5706
775 Highland Rd E Macedonia (44056) *(G-9565)*

Plastic Mold Technology Inc............................. 330 848-4921
40 Stuver Pl Barberton (44203) *(G-890)*

Plastic Moldings Company Llc (PA)................. 513 921-5040
9825 Kenwood Rd Ste 302 Blue Ash (45242) *(G-1451)*

Plastic Pallet and Container............................ 330 631-4664
2305 Chestnut Blvd Cuyahoga Falls (44223) *(G-6108)*

Plastic Process Equipment Inc (PA)................. 216 367-7000
8303 Corporate Park Dr Macedonia (44056) *(G-9566)*

Plastic Suppliers Inc (PA)................................ 614 471-9100
2400 Marilyn Ln Columbus (43219) *(G-5679)*

Plastic Works Inc... 440 331-5575
19851 Ingersoll Dr Cleveland (44116) *(G-4560)*

Plasticards Inc (PA)... 330 896-5555
3711 Boettler Oaks Dr Uniontown (44685) *(G-14791)*

Plasticraft Usa LLC.. 513 761-2999
3101 Exon Ave Cincinnati (45241) *(G-3260)*

Plastics Cnvrting Slutions Ltd......................... 330 722-2537
5341 River Styx Rd Medina (44256) *(G-10364)*

Plastics Division, Stow Also Called: Esterle Mold & Machine Co Inc *(G-13695)*

Plastics Family Holdings Inc........................... 614 272-0777
2220 International St Columbus (43228) *(G-5680)*

Plastics Machinery Magazine, Independence Also Called: Peninsula Publishing LLC *(G-8679)*

Plastics Mentor LLC... 440 352-1357
6160 Brownstone Ct Mentor (44060) *(G-10524)*

Plastics R Unique Inc...................................... 330 334-4820
330 Grandview Ave Wadsworth (44281) *(G-15053)*

Plastiform Tool & Die, Port Clinton Also Called: Rexles Inc *(G-12627)*

Plastigraphics Inc.. 513 771-8848
722 Redna Ter Cincinnati (45215) *(G-3261)*

Plastikos Corporation...................................... 513 732-0961
700 Kent Rd Batavia (45103) *(G-943)*

Plastilene Inc... 614 592-8699
1010 Mead St Wshngtn Ct Hs (43160) *(G-16236)*

Plastipak Packaging Inc.................................. 740 928-4435
610 O Neill Dr Bldg 22 Hebron (43025) *(G-8356)*

Plastipak Packaging Inc.................................. 937 596-6142
18015 State Route 65 Jackson Center (45334) *(G-8736)*

Plate Engraving Corporation........................... 330 239-2155
2324 Sharon Copley Rd Medina (44256) *(G-10365)*

Plate-All Metal Company Inc............................ 330 633-6166
1210 Devalera St Akron (44310) *(G-277)*

Platform Beer, Cleveland Also Called: Platform Beers LLC *(G-4561)*

Platform Beers LLC.. 440 539-3245
4125 Lorain Ave Cleveland (44113) *(G-4561)*

Plating Process Systems Inc
7561 Tyler Blvd Ste 5 Mentor (44060) *(G-10525)*

Plating Technology Inc..................................... 937 268-6882
1525 W River Rd Dayton (45417) *(G-6507)*

Platinum Industries, Ironton Also Called: Platinum Industries LLC *(G-8699)*

Platinum Industries LLC.................................. 740 285-2641
541 Private Road 908 Ironton (45638) *(G-8699)*

Play Mor, Millersburg Also Called: Hershberger Lawn Structures *(G-10957)*

Playtex Manufacturing Inc............................... 937 498-4710
1905 Progress Way Sidney (45365) *(G-13271)*

Pleasant Hill Vineyards LLC............................ 740 502-3567
5015 Pleasant Hill Rd Athens (45701) *(G-691)*

Pleasant Precision Inc..................................... 419 675-0556
13840 Us Highway 68 Kenton (43326) *(G-8896)*

Pleasant Valley Ready Mix Inc......................... 330 852-2613
559 Pleasant Valley Rd Nw Sugarcreek (44681) *(G-13934)*

Plextrusions Inc... 330 668-2587
38870 Taylor Pkwy North Ridgeville (44035) *(G-11853)*

Plibrico Company LLC..................................... 740 682-7755
1627 Pyro Rd Oak Hill (45656) *(G-12023)*

Plidco Ppline Repr Ppline Mint, Strongsville Also Called: Pipe Line Development Company *(G-13865)*

Plug Power Inc... 518 605-5703
219 S Alex Rd West Carrollton (45449) *(G-15356)*

Plumb Builders Inc.. 937 293-1111
2367 S Dixie Dr Dayton (45409) *(G-6508)*

Plus Mark LLC... 216 252-6770
1 American Rd Cleveland (44144) *(G-4562)*

Ply-Trim Inc (PA).. 330 799-7876
550 N Meridian Rd Youngstown (44509) *(G-16419)*

Plymouth Foam LLC.. 740 254-1188
1 Southern Gateway Dr Gnadenhutten (44629) *(G-7987)*

Plymouth Locomotive Svc LLC........................ 419 896-2854
48 E Main St Shiloh (44878) *(G-13205)*

PM Coal Company LLC.................................... 440 256-7624
9717 Chillicothe Rd Willoughby (44094) *(G-15971)*

PM Graphics Inc.. 330 650-0861
10170 Philipp Pkwy Streetsboro (44241) *(G-13785)*

PM Machine Inc... 440 942-6537
38205 Western Pkwy Willoughby (44094) *(G-15972)*

PM Motor Fan Blade Company, North Ridgeville Also Called: Beckett Air Incorporated *(G-11829)*

PM Power Products LLC.................................. 614 652-6509
4393 Tuller Rd Ste A Dublin (43017) *(G-6923)*

Pmbp Legacy Co Inc (PA)................................. 330 253-8148
485 Kenmore Blvd Akron (44301) *(G-278)*

Pmbp Legacy Co Inc.. 330 253-8148
219 E Miller Ave Akron (44301) *(G-279)*

PMC Gage Inc (PA)... 440 953-1672
38383 Willoughby Pkwy Willoughby (44094) *(G-15973)*

PMC Industries Corp....................................... 440 943-3300
29100 Lakeland Blvd Wickliffe (44092) *(G-15848)*

PMC Lonestar, Willoughby Also Called: PMC Gage Inc *(G-15973)*

PMC Mercury... 440 953-3300
38383 Willoughby Pkwy Willoughby (44094) *(G-15974)*

PMC Smart Solutions LLC............................... 513 921-5040
9825 Kenwood Rd Ste 300 Blue Ash (45242) *(G-1452)*

PMC Specialties Group Inc (DH)...................... 513 242-3300
501 Murray Rd Cincinnati (45217) *(G-3262)*

PMC Specialties Group Inc.............................. 513 242-3300
5220 Vine St Cincinnati (45217) *(G-3263)*

PMC Systems Limited..................................... 330 538-2268
12155 Commissioner Dr North Jackson (44451) *(G-11789)*

Pmcsg, Cincinnati Also Called: PMC Specialties Group Inc *(G-3262)*

PME of Ohio Inc (PA)....................................... 513 671-1717
518 W Crescentville Rd Cincinnati (45246) *(G-3264)*

PME- Babbit Bearings, Cincinnati Also Called: PME of Ohio Inc *(G-3264)*

PMG Cincinnati Inc... 513 421-7275
570 N High St Columbus (43215) *(G-5681)*

Pmp Industries Inc.. 513 563-3028
4460 Lake Forest Dr Ste 228 Blue Ash (45242) *(G-1453)*

(PA)=Parent Co (HQ)=Headquarters (DH)=Div Headquarters

Pneumatic Scale Angelus, Cuyahoga Falls Also Called: Pneumatic Scale Corporation *(G-6109)*

Pneumatic Scale Corporation (DH).. 330 923-0491
10 Ascot Pkwy Cuyahoga Falls (44223) *(G-6109)*

Pneumatic Specialties Inc.. 440 729-4400
11677 Chillicothe Rd Unit 1 Chesterland (44026) *(G-2488)*

Poc Hydraulic Technologies LLC... 614 761-8555
5201 Indian Hill Rd Dublin (43017) *(G-6924)*

Podnar Plastics Inc... 330 673-2255
343 Portage Blvd Unit 3 Kent (44240) *(G-8843)*

Podnar Plastics Inc (PA)... 330 673-2255
1510 Mogadore Rd Kent (44240) *(G-8844)*

Poet Biorefining, Marion Also Called: Poet Biorefining Marion LLC *(G-9873)*

Poet Biorefining - Leipsic LLC... 419 943-7447
3875 State Route 65 Leipsic (45856) *(G-9135)*

Poet Biorefining Marion LLC.. 740 383-4400
1660 Hillman Ford Rd Marion (43302) *(G-9873)*

Poet Biorefining-Leipsic, Leipsic Also Called: Poet Biorefining - Leipsic LLC *(G-9135)*

Poet Borefining - Fostoria LLC... 419 436-0954
2111 Sandusky St Fostoria (44830) *(G-7650)*

Poet Brfining- Fostoria 23200, Fostoria Also Called: Poet Borefining - Fostoria LLC *(G-7650)*

Pohl Machining Inc (PA)... 513 353-2929
4901 Hamilton Cleves Rd Cleves (45002) *(G-4962)*

Pohlman, Massillon Also Called: Pohlman Precision LLC *(G-10135)*

Pohlman Precision LLC... 636 537-1909
999 Oberlin Ave Sw Massillon (44647) *(G-10135)*

Poland Print Shop, North Lima Also Called: Print Factory PII *(G-11810)*

Polar Inc.. 937 297-0911
2297 N Moraine Dr Moraine (45439) *(G-11201)*

Polar Air, Englewood Also Called: Eaton Comprsr Fabrication Inc *(G-7230)*

Polaris Technologies, Toledo Also Called: Modern Builders Supply Inc *(G-14389)*

Polarpics, Etna Also Called: Yankee Candle Company Inc *(G-7257)*

Pole/Zero Acquisition, Inc., West Chester Also Called: Pole/Zero LLC *(G-15481)*

Pole/Zero LLC... 513 870-9060
5558 Union Centre Dr West Chester (45069) *(G-15481)*

Polimeros Usa LLC... 216 591-0175
26210 Emery Rd Ste 202 Warrensville Heights (44128) *(G-15230)*

Poling Group, Akron Also Called: Akron Steel Fabricators Co *(G-44)*

Poling Group, The, Akron Also Called: Akron Special Machinery Inc *(G-43)*

Pollock Research & Design Inc... 330 332-3300
1134 Salem Pkwy Salem (44460) *(G-13023)*

Poly Flex, Baltic Also Called: Flex Technologies Inc *(G-836)*

Poly Products Inc.. 216 391-7659
837 E 79th St Cleveland (44103) *(G-4563)*

Poly TEC East Inc.. 330 799-7876
550 N Meridian Rd Youngstown (44509) *(G-16420)*

Poly-Carb Inc.. 440 248-1223
9456 Freeway Dr Macedonia (44056) *(G-9567)*

Poly-Met Inc... 330 630-9006
1997 Nolt Dr Akron (44312) *(G-280)*

Polycase Division, Avon Also Called: Ecp Corporation *(G-771)*

Polychem LLC... 419 547-1400
202 Watertower Dr Clyde (43410) *(G-4975)*

Polychem LLC (HQ).. 440 357-1500
6277 Heisley Rd Mentor (44060) *(G-10526)*

Polychem Dispersions Inc... 800 545-3530
16066 Industrial Pkwy Middlefield (44062) *(G-10782)*

Polychem Oms Systems LLC... 330 427-1230
5555 Massillon Rd North Canton (44720) *(G-11750)*

Polyfill LLC.. 937 493-0041
960 N Vandemark Rd Sidney (45365) *(G-13272)*

Polyflex, Willoughby Also Called: Polyflex LLC *(G-15975)*

Polyflex LLC.. 440 946-0758
4803 E 345th St Willoughby (44094) *(G-15975)*

Polymer & Steel Tech Inc.. 440 510-0108
34899 Curtis Blvd Eastlake (44095) *(G-7045)*

Polymer Additives Holdings Inc (PA).. 216 875-7200
7500 E Pleasant Valley Rd Independence (44131) *(G-8680)*

Polymer Concepts Inc... 440 953-9605
7555 Tyler Blvd Ste 1 Mentor (44060) *(G-10527)*

Polymer Diagnostics Inc... 440 930-1361
33587 Walker Rd Avon Lake (44012) *(G-821)*

Polymer Packaging Inc (PA)... 330 832-2000
7755 Freedom Ave Nw North Canton (44720) *(G-11751)*

Polymer Stamping Tech LLC (PA).. 616 371-4004
1860 State Route 718 Troy (45373) *(G-14602)*

Polymer Tech & Svcs Inc (HQ).. 740 929-5500
1835 James Pkwy Heath (43056) *(G-8327)*

Polymera Inc.. 740 527-2069
511 Milliken Dr Hebron (43025) *(G-8357)*

Polymerics Inc (PA)... 330 928-2210
2828 2nd St Cuyahoga Falls (44221) *(G-6110)*

Polymerics Inc... 330 677-1131
1540 Saint Clair Ave Kent (44240) *(G-8845)*

Polymet Corporation... 513 874-3586
7397 Union Centre Blvd West Chester (45014) *(G-15482)*

Polymet Recovery LLC... 330 630-9006
1280 Devalera St Akron (44310) *(G-281)*

Polynew Inc.. 330 897-3202
3557 State Rte 93 Baltic (43804) *(G-840)*

Polynt Composites USA Inc.. 816 391-6000
1321 First St Sandusky (44870) *(G-13088)*

Polyone, Greenville Also Called: Avient Corporation *(G-0037)*

Polyone Corporation.. 330 467-8108
775 Highland Rd E Macedonia (44056) *(G-9568)*

Polyone Funding Corporation.. 440 930-1000
33587 Walker Rd Avon Lake (44012) *(G-822)*

Polyone LLC... 440 930-1000
33587 Walker Rd Avon Lake (44012) *(G-823)*

Polyplastex International, Kent Also Called: Schneller LLC *(G-8858)*

Polyquest Inc.. 330 888-9448
762 Valley Brook Cir Sagamore Hills (44067) *(G-12893)*

Polyshield Corporation... 614 755-7674
8643 Chateau Dr Pickerington (43147) *(G-12466)*

Polysource LLC.. 937 778-9500
555 E Statler Rd Piqua (45356) *(G-12549)*

Polystar Inc.. 330 963-5100
1676 Commerce Dr Stow (44224) *(G-13717)*

Polytech Component Corp... 330 726-3235
8469 Southern Blvd Youngstown (44512) *(G-16421)*

Pomacon Inc... 330 273-1576
2996 Interstate Pkwy Brunswick (44212) *(G-1781)*

Pompili Precast Concrete, Cleveland Also Called: E Pompili Sons Inc *(G-3985)*

Pool Office Manager, Hilliard Also Called: Phantom Technology LLC *(G-8431)*

Pops Printed Apparel LLC.. 614 372-5651
1758 N High St Unit 2 Columbus (43201) *(G-5682)*

Porath Business Services Inc... 216 626-0060
21000 Miles Pkwy Cleveland (44128) *(G-4564)*

Porath Printing, Cleveland Also Called: Porath Business Services Inc *(G-4564)*

Porcelain Enamels, Cleveland Also Called: Vibrantz Corporation *(G-4871)*

Porcelain Steel Buildings Company.. 614 228-5781
555 W Goodale St Columbus (43215) *(G-5683)*

Port Clinton Manufacturing LLC... 419 734-2141
328 W Perry St Port Clinton (43452) *(G-12623)*

Portable Crushing LLC... 330 618-5251
4237 State Park Dr New Franklin (44319) *(G-11442)*

Portage Electric Products Inc... 330 499-2727
7700 Freedom Ave Nw North Canton (44720) *(G-11752)*

Portage Knife Company, Akron Also Called: Portage Machine Concepts Inc *(G-282)*

Portage Machine Concepts Inc... 330 628-2343
75 Skelton Rd Akron (44312) *(G-282)*

Porter, Cincinnati Also Called: Porter Precision Products Co *(G-3265)*

Porter Precision Products Co (PA)... 513 385-1569
2734 Banning Rd Cincinnati (45239) *(G-3265)*

Porter-Guertin Co Inc... 513 241-7663
2150 Colerain Ave Cincinnati (45214) *(G-3266)*

Porters Welding Inc (PA).. 740 452-4181
601 Linden Ave Zanesville (43701) *(G-16557)*

Portico Merchandising, Cincinnati Also Called: Catalog Merchandiser Inc *(G-2708)*

Portion Pac Inc (DH).. 513 398-0400
7325 Snider Rd Mason (45040) *(G-10039)*

ALPHABETIC SECTION — Praxair

Portsmouth Block Inc... 740 353-4113
2700 Gallia St Portsmouth (45662) *(G-12653)*

Portsmouth Block & Brick, Portsmouth *Also Called: Portsmouth Block Inc (G-12653)*

Portsmouth Division, Portsmouth *Also Called: Osco Industries Inc (G-12652)*

Positech Corp... 513 942-7411
11310 Williamson Rd Blue Ash (45241) *(G-1454)*

Positrol Inc.. 513 272-0500
3890 Virginia Ave Cincinnati (45227) *(G-3267)*

Positrol Workholding, Cincinnati *Also Called: Positrol Inc (G-3267)*

Posm Software LLC... 859 274-0041
2145 Millsboro Rd Mansfield (44906) *(G-9710)*

Post... 513 768-8000
312 Elm St Reading (45215) *(G-12747)*

Post Printing Co (PA)... 859 254-7714
205 W 4th St Minster (45865) *(G-11058)*

Post Products Inc.. 330 678-0048
1600 Franklin Ave Kent (44240) *(G-8846)*

Posterservice Incorporated (PA)... 513 577-7100
225 Northland Blvd Cincinnati (45246) *(G-3268)*

Postle Industries Inc (PA)... 216 265-9000
5500 W 164th St Cleveland (44142) *(G-4565)*

Potemkin Industries Inc (PA).. 740 397-4888
8043 Columbus Rd Mount Vernon (43050) *(G-11288)*

Potters Industries LLC.. 216 621-0840
2380 W 3rd St Cleveland (44113) *(G-4566)*

Pounce Signs & Print Wear... 408 377-4680
1040 Spring Valley Rd London (43140) *(G-9393)*

Pov Print Communications, Chagrin Falls *Also Called: Persistence of Vision Inc (G-2415)*

Powder Alloy Corporation... 513 984-4016
101 Northeast Dr Loveland (45140) *(G-9499)*

Powder Coating Plus LLC... 419 446-0089
2010 S Defiance St Archbold (43502) *(G-541)*

Powder Coatings, Strongsville *Also Called: PPG Industries Inc (G-13867)*

Powder Kote Industries, Cincinnati *Also Called: Pki Inc (G-3259)*

Powdermet Inc (PA).. 216 404-0053
24112 Rockwell Dr Euclid (44117) *(G-7293)*

Powdermet Powder Prod Inc... 216 404-0053
24112 Rockwell Dr Ste D Euclid (44117) *(G-7294)*

Powell Electrical Systems Inc... 330 966-1750
8967 Pleasantwood Ave Nw North Canton (44720) *(G-11753)*

Powell Logging.. 740 372-6131
7593 State Route 348 Otway (45657) *(G-12207)*

Powell Valve, Cincinnati *Also Called: William Powell Company (G-3519)*

Power Acquisition LLC (HQ).. 614 228-5000
5025 Bradenton Ave Ste 130 Dublin (43017) *(G-6925)*

Power Distributors LLC (PA)... 614 876-3533
3700 Paragon Dr Columbus (43228) *(G-5684)*

Power Shelf LLC.. 419 775-6125
500 Industrial Park Dr Plymouth (44865) *(G-12609)*

Powerbuff Inc.. 419 241-2156
1001 Brown Ave Toledo (43607) *(G-14441)*

Powerclean Equipment Company... 513 202-0001
5945 Dry Fork Rd Cleves (45002) *(G-4963)*

Powerex, Harrison *Also Called: Powerex-Iwata Air Tech Inc (G-8284)*

Powerex-Iwata Air Tech Inc.. 888 769-7979
150 Production Dr Harrison (45030) *(G-8284)*

Powermount Systems Inc... 740 499-4330
1602 Larue Marseilles Rd La Rue (43332) *(G-8945)*

Powers and Sons LLC (DH)... 419 485-3151
1613 Magda Dr Montpelier (43543) *(G-11140)*

Powersonic Industries LLC... 513 429-2329
5406 Spellmire Dr West Chester (45246) *(G-15577)*

Powersteps, Wadsworth *Also Called: Stable Step LLC (G-15068)*

Powertech Inc... 901 850-9393
25805 Fairmount Blvd Apt 203 Beachwood (44122) *(G-1011)*

Powrkleen, Medina *Also Called: Woodbine Products Company (G-10395)*

Ppafco Inc... 614 488-7259
1096 Ridge St Columbus (43215) *(G-5685)*

Ppe, Macedonia *Also Called: Plastic Process Equipment Inc (G-9566)*

PPG Aerospace, Chillicothe *Also Called: PPG Industries Inc (G-2528)*

PPG AF US, Strongsville *Also Called: PPG Industries Ohio Inc (G-13868)*

PPG Architectural Coatings LLC.. 440 297-8000
15885 W Sprague Rd Strongsville (44136) *(G-13866)*

PPG Architectural Finishes Inc.. 513 242-3050
4600 Reading Rd Cincinnati (45229) *(G-3269)*

PPG Architectural Finishes Inc.. 513 563-0220
2960 Exon Ave Cincinnati (45241) *(G-3270)*

PPG Chillicothe, Chillicothe *Also Called: PPG Industries Inc (G-2526)*

PPG Coating Services, Lima *Also Called: Crown Group Co (G-9230)*

PPG Deco USA, Cleveland *Also Called: PPG Industries Ohio Inc (G-4569)*

PPG Industries Inc.. 330 825-0831
4829 Fairland Rd Barberton (44203) *(G-891)*

PPG Industries Inc.. 740 774-8734
7012 Chillicoth Chillicothe (45601) *(G-2526)*

PPG Industries Inc.. 740 774-7600
848 Southern Ave Chillicothe (45601) *(G-2527)*

PPG Industries Inc.. 740 774-7600
848 Southern Ave Chillicothe (45601) *(G-2528)*

PPG Industries Inc.. 740 474-3161
559 Pittsburgh Rd Circleville (43113) *(G-3554)*

PPG Industries Inc.. 216 671-7793
14800 Emery Ave Cleveland (44135) *(G-4567)*

PPG Industries Inc.. 740 363-9610
760 Pittsburgh Dr Delaware (43015) *(G-6743)*

PPG Industries Inc.. 419 331-2011
2599 Shawnee Industrial Dr Lima (45804) *(G-9277)*

PPG Industries Inc.. 513 576-0360
500 Techne Center Dr Milford (45150) *(G-10917)*

PPG Industries Inc.. 440 572-2800
19699 Progress Dr Strongsville (44149) *(G-13867)*

PPG Industries Ohio Inc (HQ).. 216 671-0050
3800 W 143rd St Cleveland (44111) *(G-4568)*

PPG Industries Ohio Inc.. 412 434-3888
Cleveland (44101) *(G-4569)*

PPG Industries Ohio Inc.. 740 363-9610
760 Pittsburgh Dr Delaware (43015) *(G-6744)*

PPG Industries Ohio Inc.. 412 434-1542
23000 Saint Clair Ave Euclid (44117) *(G-7295)*

PPG Industries Ohio Inc.. 440 572-6777
9699 Progress Dr Strongsville (44149) *(G-13868)*

PPG Oak Creek, Cleveland *Also Called: PPG Industries Ohio Inc (G-4568)*

PPG Regional Support Center, Chillicothe *Also Called: PPG Industries Inc (G-2527)*

Ppg-Metokote, Lima *Also Called: Metokote Corporation (G-9270)*

Ppl Holding Company.. 216 514-1840
25201 Chagrin Blvd # 360 Cleveland (44122) *(G-4570)*

Pr-Weld & Manufacturing Ltd.. 419 633-9204
18258 County Road H50 West Unity (43570) *(G-15642)*

Pragmatic Mfg LLC... 330 222-6051
2774 Nationwide Pkwy Unit 18 Brunswick (44212) *(G-1782)*

Prairie Builders Supply Inc... 419 332-7546
2114 Hayes Ave Fremont (43420) *(G-7802)*

Prairie Lane Corporation.. 330 262-3322
4489 Prairie Ln Wooster (44691) *(G-16159)*

Prairie Lane Gravel Co, Wooster *Also Called: Prairie Lane Corporation (G-16159)*

Prasco LLC (PA).. 513 204-1100
6125 Commerce Ct Mason (45040) *(G-10040)*

Prasco Laboratories, Mason *Also Called: Prasco LLC (G-10040)*

Pratt (jet Corr) Inc.. 937 390-7100
1515 Baker Rd Springfield (45504) *(G-13621)*

Pratt (target Container) Inc... 513 770-0851
4700 Duke Dr Ste 140 Mason (45040) *(G-10041)*

Pratt Industries Inc... 513 262-6253
98 Quality Ln Dayton (45449) *(G-6509)*

Pratt Industries Inc... 937 583-4990
301 W Clay St Lewisburg (45338) *(G-9189)*

Pratt Industries USA, Springfield *Also Called: Pratt (jet Corr) Inc (G-13621)*

Pratt Paper (oh) LLC.. 567 320-3353
602 Leon Pratt Dr Wapakoneta (45895) *(G-15129)*

Praxair, Barberton *Also Called: Linde Inc (G-877)*

Praxair, Cincinnati *Also Called: Linde Gas & Equipment Inc (G-3107)*

Praxair, Oregon *Also Called: Linde Inc (G-12106)*
Praxair, Toledo *Also Called: Linde Gas & Equipment Inc (G-14368)*
Praxair, Wickliffe *Also Called: Linde Gas & Equipment Inc (G-15837)*
Prc-Saltillo, Wooster *Also Called: Prentke Romich Company (G-16160)*

Prcc Holdings Inc 330 798-4790
175 Montrose West Ave Ste 200 Copley (44321) *(G-5953)*

Precast Products LLC 419 668-1639
205 Industrial Pkwy Norwalk (44857) *(G-11986)*

Precious Metal Plating Co 440 585-7117
33125 Cannon Rd Solon (44139) *(G-13406)*

Precious Mmories Cstm Prtg Inc 216 721-3909
7512 Lexington Ave Cleveland (44103) *(G-4571)*

Precise Custom Millwork Inc 614 539-7855
6145 Enterprise Pkwy Grove City (43123) *(G-8115)*

Precise Metal Form Inc 419 636-5221
810 Commerce Dr Bryan (43506) *(G-1836)*

Precise Tool & Die Company Inc 440 951-9173
38128 Willoughby Pkwy Willoughby (44094) *(G-15976)*

Precise Tool & Mfg Corp 216 524-1500
5755 Canal Rd Cleveland (44125) *(G-4572)*

Precision Aggregates, Portage *Also Called: Palmer Bros Transit Mix Con (G-12636)*

Precision Aircraft Components 937 278-0203
2787 Armstrong Ln Dayton (45414) *(G-6510)*

Precision Anlytical Instrs Inc 513 984-1600
10857 Millington Ct Blue Ash (45242) *(G-1455)*

Precision Assemblies Inc 330 549-2630
11233 South Ave North Lima (44452) *(G-11809)*

Precision Bending Tech Inc (PA) 440 974-2500
7350 Production Dr Mentor (44060) *(G-10528)*

Precision Brush Co 440 542-9600
6700 Parkland Blvd Solon (44139) *(G-13407)*

Precision Business Solutions 419 661-8700
668 1st St Perrysburg (43551) *(G-12420)*

Precision Castparts Corp 440 350-6150
870 Renaissance Pkwy Painesville (44077) *(G-12258)*

Precision Cnc 614 496-1048
192 Fox Glen Dr E Pickerington (43147) *(G-12467)*

Precision Cnc LLC 740 689-9009
1858 Cedar Hill Rd Lancaster (43130) *(G-9032)*

Precision Coatings Inc 216 441-0805
3289 E 80th St Cleveland (44104) *(G-4573)*

Precision Coatings Systems 937 642-4727
948 Columbus Ave Marysville (43040) *(G-9931)*

Precision Component & Mch Inc 740 867-6366
17 Rosslyn Rd Chesapeake (45619) *(G-2476)*

Precision Component Inds LLC 330 477-6287
5325 Southway St Sw Canton (44706) *(G-2198)*

Precision Cut Fabricating Inc 440 877-1260
9921 York Alpha Dr North Royalton (44133) *(G-11891)*

Precision Cutoff LLC 419 866-8000
7400 Airport Hwy Holland (43528) *(G-8524)*

Precision Design Inc 419 289-1553
2221 Ford Dr Ashland (44805) *(G-605)*

Precision Details Inc 937 596-0068
104 Washington St Jackson Center (45334) *(G-8737)*

Precision Die & Stamping Inc 513 942-8220
9800 Harwood Ct West Chester (45014) *(G-15483)*

Precision Die Masters Inc 440 255-1204
8724 East Ave Mentor (44060) *(G-10529)*

Precision Duct Fabrication LLC 614 580-9385
182 N Yale Ave Columbus (43222) *(G-5686)*

Precision Engineered Plas Inc 216 334-1105
7000 Denison Ave Cleveland (44102) *(G-4574)*

Precision Engineered Components 614 436-0392
7030 Wrthington Galena Rd Worthington (43085) *(G-16207)*

Precision Engrg Components, Worthington *Also Called: Precision Engneered Components (G-16207)*

Precision Fab Products Inc 937 526-5681
10061 Old State Route 121 Versailles (45380) *(G-14988)*

Precision Fabg & Stamping Inc 740 453-7310
1755 Kemper Ct Zanesville (43701) *(G-16558)*

Precision Fabricators Inc 513 288-3358
707 Enterprise Dr Harrison (45030) *(G-8285)*

Precision Finishing Systems 937 415-5794
6101 Webster St Dayton (45414) *(G-6511)*

Precision Fittings LLC 440 647-4143
709 N Main St Wellington (44090) *(G-15320)*

Precision Foam Fabrication Inc 330 270-2440
3760 Oakwood Ave Ste B Austintown (44515) *(G-754)*

Precision Forged Products, Gallipolis *Also Called: GKN Sinter Metals LLC (G-7894)*

Precision Gage & Tool Company 937 866-9666
375 Gargrave Rd Dayton (45449) *(G-6512)*

Precision Gear LLC 330 487-0888
1900 Midway Dr Twinsburg (44087) *(G-14716)*

Precision Geophysical Inc (PA) 330 674-2198
2695 State Route 83 Millersburg (44654) *(G-10989)*

Precision Graphic Services Inc 419 241-5189
4612 Corey Rd Toledo (43623) *(G-14442)*

Precision Hydrlic Cnnctors Inc 440 953-3778
26420 Century Corners Pkwy Euclid (44132) *(G-7296)*

Precision Impacts LLC 937 530-8254
721 Richard St Miamisburg (45342) *(G-10671)*

Precision Imprint 740 592-5916
26 E State St Athens (45701) *(G-092)*

Precision Laser & Forming Inc 419 943-4350
6500 Road 5 Leipsic (45856) *(G-9136)*

Precision Machi Ne Tool 614 564-9360
1625 W Mound St Columbus (43223) *(G-5687)*

Precision Machine & Tool Co 419 334-8405
142 W Wilcox Rd Port Clinton (43452) *(G-12624)*

Precision Machining Services 937 222-4608
365 Leo St Dayton (45404) *(G-6513)*

Precision Manufacturing Co Inc 937 236-2170
2149 Valley Pike Dayton (45404) *(G-6514)*

Precision McHning Cnnction LLC 440 943-3300
29100 Lakeland Blvd Wickliffe (44092) *(G-15849)*

Precision McHning Srfacing Inc 440 439-9850
20637 Krick Rd Bedford (44146) *(G-1150)*

Precision Metal Products Inc 216 447-1900
5745 Canal Rd Cleveland (44125) *(G-4575)*

Precision Metal Products Inc 614 526-7000
5200 Upper Metro Pl Dublin (43017) *(G-6926)*

Precision Metal Products Inc 216 447-1900
9005 Bank St Cleveland (44125) *(G-4576)*

Precision Metalforming Assn 216 901-8800
6363 Oak Tree Blvd Independence (44131) *(G-8681)*

Precision Metals Group LLC 440 255-8888
8687 Tyler Blvd Mentor (44060) *(G-10530)*

Precision Mfg & Assembly LLC 937 252-3507
2240 Richard St Dayton (45403) *(G-6515)*

Precision Mtal Fabrication Inc (PA) 937 235-9261
191 Heid Ave Dayton (45404) *(G-6516)*

Precision of Ohio Inc 330 793-0900
3850 Hendricks Rd Youngstown (44515) *(G-16422)*

Precision Polymer Casting 440 205-1900
4304 Maple St Ste 3 Perry (44081) *(G-12356)*

Precision Polymer Casting LLC 440 343-0461
140 Greentree Rd Moreland Hills (44022) *(G-11220)*

Precision Polymers Inc 614 322-9951
6919 Americana Pkwy Reynoldsburg (43068) *(G-12772)*

Precision Powder Coating Inc 330 478-0741
1530 Raff Rd Sw Canton (44710) *(G-2199)*

Precision Pressed Powdered Met 937 433-6802
1522 Manchester Rd Dayton (45449) *(G-6517)*

Precision Production, Strongsville *Also Called: Precision Production LLC (G-13869)*

Precision Production LLC 216 252-0372
8250 Dow Cir Strongsville (44136) *(G-13869)*

Precision Quincy Inds Inc 888 312-5442
4600 N Mason Montgomery Rd Mason (45040) *(G-10042)*

Precision Reflex Inc 419 629-2603
710 Streine Dr New Bremen (45869) *(G-11407)*

Precision Remotes LLC 510 215-6474
7803 Freeway Cir Middleburg Heights (44130) *(G-10725)*

ALPHABETIC SECTION — Pressure Technology Ohio Inc

Precision Replacement LLC.. 330 908-0410
9009 Freeway Dr Unit 7 Macedonia (44056) *(G-9569)*

Precision Sheetrock LLC.. 440 477-7803
17080 Mayfield Rd Huntsburg (44046) *(G-8620)*

Precision Signs & Graphics LLC.. 740 446-1774
161 Upper River Rd Gallipolis (45631) *(G-7898)*

Precision Strip Inc.. 419 674-4186
190 Bales Rd Kenton (43326) *(G-8897)*

Precision Strip Inc.. 937 667-6255
315 Park Ave Tipp City (45371) *(G-14148)*

Precision Swiss LLC... 513 716-7000
9580 Wayne Ave Cincinnati (45215) *(G-3271)*

Precision Tek Manufacturing, Mason *Also Called: Ashley F Ward Inc (G-9955)*

Precision Temp, Cincinnati *Also Called: RAD Technologies Incorporated (G-3323)*

Precision Tool Grinding Inc... 419 339-9959
216 S Greenlawn Ave Ste 5a Elida (45807) *(G-7097)*

Precision Weld Fab... 440 576-5800
971 Footville Richmond Rd W Jefferson (44047) *(G-8756)*

Precision Welding... 740 627-7320
123 Jonathon Dr Howard (43028) *(G-8559)*

Precision Welding & Mfg Inc (PA).. 937 444-6925
101 Day Rd Mount Orab (45154) *(G-11245)*

Precision Welding Corporation... 216 524-6110
7900 Exchange St Cleveland (44125) *(G-4577)*

Precision Wldg & Installation, Zanesville *Also Called: Steven Crumbaker Jr (G-16566)*

Precision Wood Products Inc (PA)... 937 787-3523
2456 Aukerman Creek Rd Camden (45311) *(G-1963)*

Precision Works Machine LLC... 330 863-0871
6056 Alliance Rd Nw Malvern (44644) *(G-9615)*

Precisions Paint Systems LLC... 740 894-6224
5852 County Road 1 South Point (45680) *(G-13473)*

Precison Coating Technology, Cleveland *Also Called: Precision Coatings Inc (G-4573)*

Precison Thrmplstic Cmpnnts In.. 419 227-4500
3765 Saint Johns Rd Lima (45806) *(G-9305)*

Predicor LLC... 419 460-1831
2728 Euclid Ave Ste 300 Cleveland (44115) *(G-4578)*

Preferred Compounding, Barberton *Also Called: Preferred Compounding Corp (G-892)*

Preferred Compounding, Copley *Also Called: Prcc Holdings Inc (G-5953)*

Preferred Compounding Corp (HQ)....................................... 330 798-4790
1020 Lambert St Barberton (44203) *(G-892)*

Preferred Printing (PA).. 937 492-6961
3700 Michigan St Sidney (45365) *(G-13273)*

Preferred Solutions Inc... 216 642-1200
5000 Rockside Rd Ste 230 Independence (44131) *(G-8682)*

Preformed Line Products Co (PA)... 440 461-5200
660 Beta Dr Mayfield Village (44143) *(G-10260)*

Preformed Line Products Co... 330 920-1718
200 Cuyahoga Falls Industrial Pkwy Peninsula (44264) *(G-12341)*

Preisser Inc.. 614 345-0199
3560 Millikin Ct Ste A Columbus (43228) *(G-5688)*

Premere Enterprises Inc... 330 874-3000
10882 Fort Laurens Rd Nw Bolivar (44612) *(G-1532)*

Premere Precast Products.. 740 533-3333
317 Hecla St Ironton (45638) *(G-8700)*

Premier Aerospace Group LLC.. 937 233-8300
2127 Troy St Dayton (45404) *(G-6518)*

Premier Bandag 8 Inc... 330 823-3822
1469 W Main St Alliance (44601) *(G-420)*

Premier Bandag Inc... 513 248-8850
5997 Meijer Dr Milford (45150) *(G-10918)*

Premier Building Solutions LLC (PA).................................... 330 244-2907
480 Nova Dr Se Massillon (44646) *(G-10136)*

Premier Chemicals... 440 234-4600
7251 Engle Rd Cleveland (44130) *(G-4579)*

Premier Coatings Ltd... 513 942-1070
9390 Le Saint Dr West Chester (45014) *(G-15484)*

Premier Construction Company.. 513 874-2611
9361 Seward Rd Fairfield (45014) *(G-7395)*

Premier Container, Cleveland *Also Called: Premier Container Inc (G-4580)*

Premier Container Inc (PA)... 800 230-7132
4500 Crayton Ave Cleveland (44104) *(G-4580)*

Premier Farnell Corp (HQ)... 330 659-0459
4180 Highlander Pkwy Richfield (44286) *(G-12793)*

Premier Farnell Holding Inc (DH).. 330 523-4273
4180 Highlander Pkwy Richfield (44286) *(G-12794)*

Premier Feeds LLC (HQ)... 937 584-2411
292 N Howard St Sabina (45169) *(G-12891)*

Premier Grain LLC (PA)... 937 584-6552
1 Solutions Ave Sabina (45169) *(G-12892)*

Premier Industries Inc.. 513 271-2550
5721 Dragon Way Ste 113 Cincinnati (45227) *(G-3272)*

Premier Ink Systems Inc (PA).. 513 367-2300
10420 N State St Harrison (45030) *(G-8286)*

Premier Inv Cast Group LLC... 937 299-7333
3034 Dryden Rd Moraine (45439) *(G-11202)*

Premier Manufacturing Corp (HQ).. 216 941-9700
3003 Priscilla Ave Cleveland (44134) *(G-4581)*

Premier O.E.M., Cuyahoga Falls *Also Called: Kolpin Outdoors Corporation (G-6096)*

Premier Packaging Systems LLC.. 419 439-1900
1711 Stonemore Dr Defiance (43512) *(G-6693)*

Premier Pallet and Recycl Inc... 330 767-2221
11361 Lawndell Ave Sw Navarre (44662) *(G-11350)*

Premier Printing, Cleveland *Also Called: Jt Premier Printing Corp (G-4266)*

Premier Printing Corporation.. 216 478-9720
18780 Cranwood Pkwy Cleveland (44128) *(G-4582)*

Premier Prtg Centl Ohio Ltd.. 937 642-0988
16710 Square Dr Marysville (43040) *(G-9932)*

Premier Shot Company.. 330 405-0583
1666 Enterprise Pkwy Twinsburg (44087) *(G-14717)*

Premier Southern Ticket, Cincinnati *Also Called: Gtlp Holdings LLC (G-2977)*

Premier Southern Ticket Co Inc... 513 489-6700
7911 School Rd Cincinnati (45249) *(G-3273)*

Premier Tanning & Nutrition... 419 342-6259
35 Mansfield Ave Shelby (44875) *(G-13198)*

Premier Uv Products LLC.. 330 715-2452
1738 Front St Cuyahoga Falls (44221) *(G-6111)*

Premiere Con Solutions LLC... 419 737-9808
508 Cedar St Pioneer (43554) *(G-12496)*

Premiere Mold and Machine Co.. 330 874-3000
10882 Fort Laurens Rd Nw Bolivar (44612) *(G-1533)*

Premium Balloon ACC Inc... 330 239-4547
6935 Ridge Rd Wadsworth (44281) *(G-15054)*

Premium Balloon Accessories, Wadsworth *Also Called: Premium Balloon ACC Inc (G-15054)*

Premium Wood & Garden Products, Jackson *Also Called: Summers Organization LLC (G-8725)*

Premix-Hadlock Composites LLC.. 440 335-4301
3365 E Center St Conneaut (44030) *(G-5930)*

Premix-Hadlock Composites LLC, Conneaut *Also Called: Premix-Hadlock Composites LLC (G-5930)*

Prentke Romich Company (PA)... 330 262-1984
1022 Heyl Rd Wooster (44691) *(G-16160)*

Presque Isle Medical Tech, Cleveland *Also Called: Presque Isle Orthtics Prsthtic (G-4583)*

Presque Isle Orthtics Prsthtic... 216 371-0660
14055 Cedar Rd Ste 107 Cleveland (44118) *(G-4583)*

Presrite Corporation (PA).. 216 441-5990
3665 E 78th St Cleveland (44105) *(G-4584)*

Presrite Corporation.. 440 576-0015
322 S Cucumber St Jefferson (44047) *(G-8757)*

Press of Ohio Inc... 330 678-5868
3765 Sunnybrook Rd Kent (44240) *(G-8847)*

Press Technology & Mfg Inc... 937 327-0755
1401 Fotler St Springfield (45504) *(G-13622)*

Pressco, Cleveland *Also Called: Pressco Technology Inc (G-4585)*

Pressco Technology Inc (PA)... 440 498-2600
29200 Aurora Rd Cleveland (44139) *(G-4585)*

Pressed Paperboard Tech LLC... 419 423-4030
115 Bentley Ct Findlay (45840) *(G-7552)*

Presslers Meats Inc.. 330 644-5636
2553 Pressler Rd Akron (44312) *(G-283)*

Pressure Connections Corp... 614 863-6930
610 Claycraft Rd Columbus (43230) *(G-5689)*

Pressure Technology Ohio Inc.. 215 628-1975
7996 Auburn Rd Concord Township (44077) *(G-5910)*

Pressure Washer Mfrs Assn Inc — ALPHABETIC SECTION

Pressure Washer Mfrs Assn Inc 216 241-7333
1300 Sumner Ave Cleveland (44115) *(G-4586)*

Pressworks, Plain City *Also Called: Bindery & Spc Pressworks Inc (G-12566)*

Prestige Display and Packaging LLC 513 285-1040
420 Distribution Cir Fairfield (45014) *(G-7396)*

Prestige Enterprise Intl Inc 513 469-6044
11343 Grooms Rd Blue Ash (45242) *(G-1456)*

Prestige Store Interiors Inc 419 476-2106
427 W Dussel Dr # 209 Maumee (43537) *(G-10224)*

Presto Labels, Tipp City *Also Called: Repacorp Inc (G-14152)*

Preston 740 788-8208
42 Sandalwood Dr Newark (43055) *(G-11602)*

Prestress Services Inds LLC (PA) 859 299-0461
3400 Southwest Blvd Grove City (43123) *(G-8116)*

Pretreatment & Specialty Pdts, Euclid *Also Called: PPG Industries Ohio Inc (G-7295)*

Pretzelhaus Bakery LLC 513 906-2017
8800 Global Way # 31 West Chester (45069) *(G-15485)*

PRI Marine, Columbus *Also Called: Performance Research Inc (G-5670)*

Price Farms Organics Ltd 740 369-1000
4838 Warrensburg Rd Delaware (43015) *(G-6745)*

Pride 821 LLC 330 754-6320
401 Cherry Ave Ne Canton (44702) *(G-2200)*

Pride Cast Metals Inc 513 541-1295
2737 Colerain Ave Cincinnati (45225) *(G-3274)*

Pride Investments LLC 937 461-1121
1346 Morris Ave Dayton (45417) *(G-6519)*

Pride of The Hills Manufacturing Inc 330 567-3108
8275 State Route 514 Big Prairie (44611) *(G-1329)*

Pridecraft Enterprises, Cincinnati *Also Called: Standard Textile Co Inc (G-3415)*

Priest Services Inc (PA) 440 333-1123
1127 Linda St 5885 Landerbrook Dr Ste 140 Mayfield Heights (44124) *(G-10254)*

Prigge Woodworking 419 274-1005
520 E Edgerton St Hamler (43524) *(G-8260)*

Primal Life Organics LLC 800 260-4946
405 Rothrock Rd Ste 105 Copley (44321) *(G-5954)*

Primal Screen Inc 330 677-1766
1021 Mason Ave Kent (44240) *(G-8848)*

Primary Pdts Ingrdnts Amrcas L 937 236-5906
5600 Brentlinger Dr Dayton (45414) *(G-6520)*

Primary Pdts Ingrdnts Amrcas L 937 235-4074
5584 Webster St Dayton (45414) *(G-6521)*

Primax Coating 513 455-0629
2101 E Kemper Rd Cincinnati (45241) *(G-3275)*

Prime Conduit Inc (PA) 216 464-3400
23240 Chagrin Blvd Ste 405 Beachwood (44122) *(G-1012)*

Prime Engineered Plastics Corp 330 452-5110
1505 Howington Cir Se Canton (44707) *(G-2201)*

Prime Equipment Group LLC 614 253-8590
2001 Courtright Rd Columbus (43232) *(G-5690)*

Prime Industries Inc
1817 Iowa Ave Lorain (44052) *(G-9431)*

Prime Printing Inc (PA) 937 438-3707
8929 Kingsridge Dr Dayton (45458) *(G-6522)*

Primex 513 831-9959
400 Techne Center Dr Ste 104 Milford (45150) *(G-10919)*

Primo Services LLC 513 725-7888
1937 Clarion Ave Cincinnati (45207) *(G-3276)*

Primrose School of Marysville 937 642-2125
115 N Plum St Marysville (43040) *(G-9933)*

Prince & Izant LLC (PA) 216 362-7000
12999 Plaza Dr Cleveland (44130) *(G-4587)*

Princeton Precision Group, Mentor *Also Called: Princeton Tool Inc (G-10531)*

Princeton Tool Inc (PA) 440 290-8666
7830 Division Dr Mentor (44060) *(G-10531)*

Principle Business Entps Inc (PA) 419 352-1551
20189 Pine Lake Rd Bowling Green (43402) *(G-1586)*

Principled Dynamics Inc 419 351-6303
6920 Hall St Holland (43528) *(G-8525)*

Print Centers of Ohio Inc 419 526-4139
36 W 3rd St Mansfield (44902) *(G-9711)*

Print Digital, Stow *Also Called: Print-Digital Incorporated (G-13718)*

Print Direct For Less 2 Inc 440 236-8870
27500 Royalton Rd Columbia Station (44028) *(G-5018)*

Print Factory PII 330 549-9640
11471 South Ave North Lima (44452) *(G-11810)*

Print Marketing Inc 330 625-1500
11820 Black River School Rd Homerville (44235) *(G-8553)*

Print Shop of Canton Inc 330 497-3212
6536 Promler St Nw Canton (44720) *(G-2202)*

Print Shop, The, Wshngtn Ct Hs *Also Called: Brass Bull 1 LLC (G-16226)*

Print Syndicate Inc 617 290-9550
2282 Westbrooke Dr Columbus (43228) *(G-5691)*

Print Syndicate LLC 614 519-0341
901 W 3rd Ave Ste A Columbus (43212) *(G-5692)*

Print-Digital Incorporated 330 686-5945
4688 Darrow Rd Stow (44224) *(G-13718)*

Printed Image, The, Columbus *Also Called: V & C Enterprises Co (G-5853)*

Printeesweet 888 410-2160
312 Blackburn Rd Hopedale (43976) *(G-8557)*

Printer Components Inc 585 924-5190
4236 Thunderbird Ln Fairfield (45014) *(G-7397)*

Printers Bindery, Batavia *Also Called: Printers Bindery Services Inc (G-944)*

Printers Bindery Services Inc 513 821-8039
4564 Winners Cir Batavia (45103) *(G-944)*

Printers Devil Inc 330 650-1218
77 Maple Dr Hudson (44236) *(G-8608)*

Printers Edge Inc 330 372-2232
4965 Mahoning Ave Nw Warren (44483) *(G-15200)*

Printery Inc 513 574-1099
4460 Bridgetown Rd Cincinnati (45211) *(G-3277)*

Printex Incorporated (PA) 740 773-0088
185 E Main St Chillicothe (45601) *(G-2529)*

Printex-Same Day Printing, Chillicothe *Also Called: Printex Incorporated (G-2529)*

Printing & Reproduction Div, Cleveland *Also Called: City of Cleveland (G-3822)*

Printing Arts Press Inc 740 397-6106
8028 Newark Rd Mount Vernon (43050) *(G-11289)*

Printing Company, The, Columbus *Also Called: Newmast Mktg & Communications (G-5597)*

Printing Concepts, Stow *Also Called: Traxium LLC (G-13732)*

Printing Connection Inc 216 898-4878
5205 W 161st St Brookpark (44142) *(G-1723)*

Printing Dimensions Inc 937 256-0044
500 N Irwin St Dayton (45403) *(G-6523)*

Printing Express 937 276-7794
3350 Kettering Blvd Moraine (45439) *(G-11203)*

Printing Express Inc 740 533-9217
918b Center St Ironton (45638) *(G-8701)*

Printing Graphics, Maumee *Also Called: B & B Printing Graphics Inc (G-10167)*

Printing Partners, Solon *Also Called: Allen Graphics Inc (G-13308)*

Printing Plant, Fairfield *Also Called: Tech/III Inc (G-7415)*

Printing Resources Inc 216 881-7660
4713 Manufacturing Ave Cleveland (44135) *(G-4588)*

Printing Service Company 937 425-6100
3233 S Tech Blvd Miamisburg (45342) *(G-10672)*

Printing Services 440 708-1999
16750 Park Circle Dr Chagrin Falls (44023) *(G-2417)*

Printing System Inc 330 375-9128
1909 Summit Commerce Park Twinsburg (44087) *(G-14718)*

Printing Unlimited Inc 419 874-9828
325 W Indiana Ave Rear Perrysburg (43551) *(G-12421)*

Printink Inc 513 943-0599
3976 Bach Buxton Rd Amelia (45102) *(G-461)*

Printpoint Inc 937 223-9041
150 S Patterson Blvd Dayton (45402) *(G-6524)*

Prints & Paints Flr Cvg Co Inc 419 462-5663
888 Bucyrus Rd Galion (44833) *(G-7883)*

Priority Custom Molding Inc 937 431-8770
2628 Colonial Pkwy Beavercreek (45434) *(G-1058)*

Privacyware, New Albany *Also Called: Pwi Inc (G-11389)*

Pro A V of Ohio 877 812-5350
120 6th Dr Sw New Philadelphia (44663) *(G-11523)*

Pro Audio 513 752-7500
671 Cincinnati Batavia Pike Cincinnati (45245) *(G-2572)*

ALPHABETIC SECTION
Production Manufacturing Inc

Pro Cal, Twinsburg *Also Called: The Hc Companies Inc* *(G-14743)*

Pro Choice Cabinetry LLC.. 937 313-9297
  5700 Far Hills Ave Dayton (45429) *(G-6525)*

Pro Hardware 13074, Sugarcreek *Also Called: Stony Point Hardwoods LLC* *(G-13939)*

Pro Image Sign & Design Inc.. 440 986-8888
  8087 Leavitt Rd Amherst (44001) *(G-482)*

Pro Lighting LLC... 614 561-0089
  5864 Hunting Haven Dr Hilliard (43026) *(G-8433)*

Pro Line Collision and Pnt LLC (PA)....................................... 937 223-7611
  1 Armor Pl Dayton (45417) *(G-6526)*

Pro Mach Inc... 513 771-7374
  89 Partnership Way Cincinnati (45241) *(G-3278)*

Pro Oncall Technologies LLC.. 614 761-1400
  4374 Tuller Rd Ste B Dublin (43017) *(G-6927)*

Pro Tire Inc... 614 864-8662
  61 N Brice Rd Columbus (43213) *(G-5693)*

Pro-Decal Inc.. 330 484-0089
  3638 Cleveland Ave S Canton (44707) *(G-2203)*

Pro-Fab Inc.. 330 644-0044
  2570 Pressler Rd Akron (44312) *(G-284)*

Pro-Gram Engineering Corp... 330 745-1004
  1680 Hampton Rd Akron (44305) *(G-285)*

Pro-Pak Industries Inc (PA)... 419 729-0751
  1125 Ford St Maumee (43537) *(G-10225)*

Pro-Pet LLC.. 419 394-3374
  1601 Mckinley Rd Saint Marys (45885) *(G-12964)*

Pro-TEC Coating Company Inc (PA)..................................... 419 943-1211
  5500 Protec Pkwy Leipsic (45856) *(G-9137)*

Pro-TEC Coating Company LLC... 419 943-1100
  4500 Protec Pkwy Leipsic (45856) *(G-9138)*

Pro-TEC Coating Company LLC... 419 943-1100
  5000 Pro Tec Pkwy Leipsic (45856) *(G-9139)*

Pro-tec Coating Company, Llc, Leipsic *Also Called: Pro-TEC Coating Company LLC* *(G-9138)*

Pro-tec Coating Company, Llc, Leipsic *Also Called: Pro-TEC Coating Company LLC* *(G-9139)*

Pro-TEC Industries Inc.. 440 937-4142
  1384 Lear Industrial Pkwy Avon (44011) *(G-783)*

Pro-Tech Manufacturing Inc... 937 444-6484
  14944 Hillcrest Rd Mount Orab (45154) *(G-11246)*

Proampac, Cincinnati *Also Called: Ampac Holdings LLC* *(G-2622)*

Proampac Orlando Inc (PA)... 513 671-1777
  12025 Tricon Rd Cincinnati (45246) *(G-3279)*

Process Development Corp.. 937 890-3388
  6060 Milo Rd Dayton (45414) *(G-6527)*

Process Eqp Co Wldg Svcs LLC... 937 667-4451
  319 S 1st St Tipp City (45371) *(G-14149)*

Process Technology, Willoughby *Also Called: Tom Richards Inc* *(G-16007)*

Procoat Painting Inc... 513 735-2500
  601 W Main St Batavia (45103) *(G-945)*

Procter & Gamble, Blue Ash *Also Called: Procter & Gamble Company* *(G-1457)*
Procter & Gamble, Cincinnati *Also Called: Procter & Gamble Company* *(G-3281)*
Procter & Gamble, Cincinnati *Also Called: Procter & Gamble Company* *(G-3282)*
Procter & Gamble, Cincinnati *Also Called: Procter & Gamble Company* *(G-3283)*
Procter & Gamble, Cincinnati *Also Called: Procter & Gamble Company* *(G-3284)*
Procter & Gamble, Cincinnati *Also Called: Procter & Gamble Company* *(G-3286)*
Procter & Gamble, Cincinnati *Also Called: Procter & Gamble Company* *(G-3287)*
Procter & Gamble, Cincinnati *Also Called: Procter & Gamble Company* *(G-3288)*
Procter & Gamble, Cincinnati *Also Called: Procter & Gamble Company* *(G-3289)*
Procter & Gamble, Cincinnati *Also Called: Procter & Gamble Company* *(G-3290)*
Procter & Gamble, Cincinnati *Also Called: Procter & Gamble Company* *(G-3291)*
Procter & Gamble, Cincinnati *Also Called: Procter & Gamble Company* *(G-3292)*
Procter & Gamble, Cincinnati *Also Called: Procter & Gamble Mfg Co* *(G-3298)*
Procter & Gamble, Cincinnati *Also Called: Procter & Gamble Paper Pdts Co* *(G-3299)*
Procter & Gamble, Cincinnati *Also Called: Procter & Gamble Paper Pdts Co* *(G-3300)*
Procter & Gamble, Lima *Also Called: Procter & Gamble Mfg Co* *(G-9278)*
Procter & Gamble, Mason *Also Called: Procter & Gamble Company* *(G-10043)*
Procter & Gamble, Union *Also Called: Procter & Gamble Distrg LLC* *(G-14774)*
Procter & Gamble, West Chester *Also Called: Procter & Gamble Company* *(G-15486)*
Procter & Gamble, West Chester *Also Called: Procter & Gamble Company* *(G-15487)*

Procter & Gamble Company.. 513 626-2500
  11530 Reed Hartman Hwy Blue Ash (45241) *(G-1457)*

Procter & Gamble Company (PA)... 513 983-1100
  1 Procter And Gamble Plz Cincinnati (45202) *(G-3280)*

Procter & Gamble Company.. 513 983-1100
  6210 Center Hill Ave Cincinnati (45224) *(G-3281)*

Procter & Gamble Company.. 513 266-4375
  5280 Vine St Cincinnati (45217) *(G-3282)*

Procter & Gamble Company.. 513 871-7557
  654 Wilmer Ave Hngr 4 Cincinnati (45226) *(G-3283)*

Procter & Gamble Company.. 513 983-1100
  5299 Spring Grove Ave Cincinnati (45217) *(G-3284)*

Procter & Gamble Company.. 513 634-2070
  6110 Center Hill Ave Cincinnati (45224) *(G-3285)*

Procter & Gamble Company.. 513 482-6789
  4460 Kings Run Rd. Cincinnati (45232) *(G-3286)*

Procter & Gamble Company.. 513 634-5069
  6300 Center Hill Ave Fl 2 Cincinnati (45224) *(G-3287)*

Procter & Gamble Company.. 513 983-3000
  1 Plaza Cincinnati (45246) *(G-3288)*

Procter & Gamble Company.. 513 627-7115
  5348 Vine St Cincinnati (45217) *(G-3289)*

Procter & Gamble Company.. 513 658-9853
  1340 Clay St Cincinnati (45202) *(G-3290)*

Procter & Gamble Company.. 513 983-1100
  2 Procter And Gamble Plz Cincinnati (45202) *(G-3291)*

Procter & Gamble Company.. 513 945-0340
  6280 Center Hill Ave Cincinnati (45224) *(G-3292)*

Procter & Gamble Company.. 513 242-5752
  5289 Vine St Cincinnati (45217) *(G-3293)*

Procter & Gamble Company.. 513 622-1000
  8700 S Mason Montgomery Rd Mason (45040) *(G-10043)*

Procter & Gamble Company.. 513 634-9600
  8256 Union Centre Blvd West Chester (45069) *(G-15486)*

Procter & Gamble Company.. 513 634-9110
  8611 Beckett Rd West Chester (45069) *(G-15487)*

Procter & Gamble Distrg Co.. 513 983-1100
  1 Procter And Gamble Plz Cincinnati (45202) *(G-3294)*

Procter & Gamble Distrg LLC... 937 387-5189
  1800 Union Airpark Blvd Union (45377) *(G-14774)*

Procter & Gamble Far East Inc (HQ).................................... 513 983-1100
  One Procter & Gamble Plz Cincinnati (45202) *(G-3295)*

Procter & Gamble Hair Care LLC... 513 983-4502
  1 Procter And Gamble Plz Cincinnati (45202) *(G-3296)*

Procter & Gamble Mexico Inc.. 513 983-1100
  1 Procter And Gamble Plz Cincinnati (45202) *(G-3297)*

Procter & Gamble Mfg Co (HQ).. 513 983-1100
  1 Procter And Gamble Plz Cincinnati (45202) *(G-3298)*

Procter & Gamble Mfg Co.. 419 226-5500
  3875 Reservoir Rd Lima (45801) *(G-9278)*

Procter & Gamble Paper Pdts Co (HQ)................................ 513 983-1100
  1 Procter And Gamble Plz Cincinnati (45202) *(G-3299)*

Procter & Gamble Paper Pdts Co.. 513 983-2222
  301 E 6th St Cincinnati (45202) *(G-3300)*

Procter Gamble Olay Co - Cayey, Blue Ash *Also Called: Olay LLC* *(G-1445)*

Prodeva Inc.. 937 596-6713
  100 Jerry Dr Jackson Center (45334) *(G-8738)*

Prodigy Print Inc
  884 Valley St Dayton (45404) *(G-6528)*

Prodigy Print Ink, Dayton *Also Called: Prodigy Print Inc* *(G-6528)*

Produce Packaging Inc.. 216 391-6129
  27853 Chardon Rd Willoughby Hills (44092) *(G-16027)*

Producers Service Corporation.. 740 454-6253
  109 Graham St Zanesville (43701) *(G-16559)*

Production, Cuyahoga Falls *Also Called: Gojo Industries Inc* *(G-6087)*

Production Control Units Inc... 937 299-5594
  2280 W Dorothy Ln Moraine (45439) *(G-11204)*

Production Design Services Inc (PA).................................... 937 866-3377
  313 Mound St Dayton (45402) *(G-6529)*

Production Div, Youngstown *Also Called: Gasser Chair Co Inc* *(G-16363)*

Production Manufacturing Inc.. 513 892-2331
  870 Hanover St Bldg A Hamilton (45011) *(G-8236)*

Production Paint Finishers Inc   **ALPHABETIC SECTION**

Production Paint Finishers Inc.. 937 448-2627
   140 Center St Bradford (45308) *(G-1601)*
Production Pattern Company, Cleveland *Also Called: TW Manufacturing Co (G-4838)*
Production Plant, Dayton *Also Called: U S Chrome Corporation Ohio (G-6638)*
Production Products Inc.. 734 241-7242
   200 Sugar Grove Ln Columbus Grove (45830) *(G-5899)*
Production Screw Machine, Dayton *Also Called: Gmd Industries LLC (G-6359)*
Production TI Co Cleveland Inc... 330 425-4466
   9002 Dutton Dr Twinsburg (44087) *(G-14719)*
Production Tube Cutting... 937 299-7144
   43 Briar Hill Rd Oakwood (45419) *(G-12029)*
Production Tube Cutting Inc... 937 254-6138
   1100 S Smithville Rd Dayton (45403) *(G-6530)*
Products Chemical Company LLC... 216 218-1155
   4005 Clark Ave Cleveland (44109) *(G-4589)*
Profac Inc (PA)... 440 942-0205
   7198 Industrial Park Blvd Mentor (44060) *(G-10532)*
Profac Inc.. 440 942-0205
   7171 Industrial Park Blvd Mentor (44060) *(G-10533)*
Professional Award Service.. 513 389-3600
   3901 N Bend Rd Cincinnati (45211) *(G-3301)*
Professional Case Inc... 513 682-2520
   4954 Provident Dr West Chester (45246) *(G-15578)*
Professional Detailing Pdts, Canton *Also Called: Ohio Auto Supply Company (G-2182)*
Professional Marine Repair LLC... 440 409-9957
   1453 Dover Cntr Rd Ashtabula (44004) *(G-656)*
Professional Plastics Corp.. 614 336-2498
   4863 Rays Cir Dublin (43016) *(G-6928)*
Professional Screen Printing.. 740 687-0760
   731 N Pierce Ave Lancaster (43130) *(G-9033)*
Professional Supply Inc.. 419 332-7373
   504 Liberty St Fremont (43420) *(G-7803)*
Proficient Info Tech Inc... 937 470-1300
   301 W 1st St Dayton (45402) *(G-6531)*
Proficient Machining Co.. 440 942-4942
   7522 Tyler Blvd Unit B-G Mentor (44060) *(G-10534)*
Proficient Plastics Inc.. 440 205-9700
   7777 Saint Clair Ave Mentor (44060) *(G-10535)*
Profile Grinding Inc... 216 351-0600
   4593 Spring Rd Cleveland (44131) *(G-4590)*
Profile Plastics Inc.. 330 452-7000
   1226 Prospect Ave Sw Canton (44706) *(G-2204)*
Profile Rubber Corporation... 330 239-1703
   6784 Ridge Rd Wadsworth (44281) *(G-15055)*
Profiles In Design Inc.. 513 751-2212
   860 Dellway St Cincinnati (45229) *(G-3302)*
Profiles In Diversity Journal, Westlake *Also Called: Rector Inc (G-15778)*
Proform Group Inc.. 614 332-9654
   1715 Georgesville Rd Columbus (43228) *(G-5694)*
Proforma, Cortland *Also Called: Howland Printing Inc (G-5964)*
Proforma Buckeye, Westerville *Also Called: Buckeye Business Forms Inc (G-15649)*
Proforma Echopress, Avon Lake *Also Called: Echopress Ltd (G-804)*
Proforma Prana... 440 345-6466
   1400 Lloyd Rd Unit 472 Wickliffe (44092) *(G-15850)*
Proforma Signature Solutions, Brooklyn Heights *Also Called: R&D Marketing Group Inc (G-1697)*
Proforma Systems Advantage.. 419 224-8747
   1207 Findlay Rd Lima (45801) *(G-9279)*
Profound Logic Software Inc (PA).. 937 439-7925
   396 Congress Park Dr Dayton (45459) *(G-6532)*
Proft & Gamble... 513 945-0340
   6280 Center Hill Ave Cincinnati (45224) *(G-3303)*
Profusion Industries LLC (PA).. 800 938-2858
   822 Kumho Dr Ste 202 Fairlawn (44333) *(G-7446)*
Profusion Industries LLC.. 740 374-6400
   700 Bf Goodrich Rd Marietta (45750) *(G-9818)*
Progage, Mentor *Also Called: Progage Inc (G-10536)*
Progage Inc.. 440 951-4477
   7555 Tyler Blvd Ste 6 Mentor (44060) *(G-10536)*
Program Managers Inc... 937 431-1982
   1138 Richfield Ctr Beavercreek (45430) *(G-1078)*

Programmable Control Svc Inc... 740 927-0744
   6900 Blacks Rd Sw Pataskala (43062) *(G-12304)*
Progress Rail Services Corp... 216 641-4000
   6600 Bessemer Ave Cleveland (44127) *(G-4591)*
Progress Rail Services Corp... 614 850-1730
   2351 Westbelt Dr Columbus (43228) *(G-5695)*
Progress Tool & Stamping Inc.. 419 628-2384
   207 Southgate Minster (45865) *(G-11059)*
Progress Tool Co, Minster *Also Called: Progress Tool & Stamping Inc (G-11059)*
Progressive Foam Tech Inc... 330 756-3200
   6753 Chestnut Ridge Rd Nw Beach City (44608) *(G-970)*
Progressive Furniture Inc (HQ).. 419 446-4500
   502 Middle St Archbold (43502) *(G-542)*
Progressive International, Archbold *Also Called: Progressive Furniture Inc (G-542)*
Progressive Mfg Co Inc... 330 784-4717
   300 Massillon Rd Akron (44312) *(G-286)*
Progressive Molding Tech... 330 220-7030
   5234 Portside Dr Medina (44256) *(G-10366)*
Progressive Plastics, Cleveland *Also Called: Alpha Packaging Holdings Inc (G-3638)*
Progressive Powder Coating Inc... 440 974-3478
   7742 Tyler Blvd Mentor (44060) *(G-10537)*
Progressive Printers Inc.. 937 222-1267
   6700 Homestretch Rd Dayton (45414) *(G-6533)*
Progressive Ribbon Inc (PA)... 513 705-9319
   1533 Central Ave Middletown (45044) *(G-10852)*
Progressive Stamping Inc... 419 453-1111
   200 Progressive Dr Ottoville (45876) *(G-12203)*
Progressive Supply LLC... 570 688-9636
   38601 Kennedy Pkwy Willoughby (44094) *(G-15977)*
Progressive Tool Division, Delphos *Also Called: Van Wert Machine Inc (G-6777)*
Progressor Times.. 419 396-7567
   1198 E Findlay St Carey (43316) *(G-2283)*
Progrssive Communications Corp... 740 397-5333
   18 E Vine St Mount Vernon (43050) *(G-11290)*
Progrssive Molding Bolivar Inc.. 330 874-3000
   10882 Fort Laurens Rd Nw Bolivar (44612) *(G-1534)*
Progrssive Mtllizing Machining, Akron *Also Called: Progressive Mfg Co Inc (G-286)*
Prohos Inc... 419 877-0153
   10755 Logan St Whitehouse (43571) *(G-15821)*
Prohos Manufacturing Co Inc... 419 877-0153
   10755 Logan St Whitehouse (43571) *(G-15822)*
Project Engineering Company.. 937 743-9114
   9874 Eby Rd Germantown (45327) *(G-7951)*
Projects Designed & Built... 419 726-7400
   5949 American Rd E Toledo (43612) *(G-14443)*
Projects Unlimited Inc (PA)... 937 918-2200
   6300 Sand Lake Rd Dayton (45414) *(G-6534)*
Projitech Inc.. 970 333-9727
   2310 Superior Ave E Ste 200 Cleveland (44114) *(G-4592)*
Proklean Services LLC (PA)... 330 273-0122
   3041 Nationwide Pkwy Brunswick (44212) *(G-1783)*
Prolamina, Cincinnati *Also Called: Jen-Coat Inc (G-3040)*
Prolease, Solon *Also Called: Link Systems Inc (G-13381)*
Proline Finishing, Dayton *Also Called: Pro Line Collision and Pnt LLC (G-6526)*
Proline Truss... 419 895-9980
   29 Free Rd Shiloh (44878) *(G-13206)*
Promac Inc.. 937 864-1961
   350 Conley Dr Enon (45323) *(G-7251)*
Promatch Solutions LLC... 877 299-0185
   2251 Arbor Blvd Moraine (45439) *(G-11205)*
Prominence Energy Corporation... 513 818-8329
   1325 Spring St Cincinnati (45202) *(G-3304)*
Promise Machining LLC.. 937 305-8011
   24 Rebecca Dr West Alexandria (45381) *(G-15343)*
Promo Costumes, Marion *Also Called: Front and Center MGT Group LLC (G-9853)*
Promold Inc... 330 633-3532
   487 Commerce St Tallmadge (44278) *(G-14044)*
Promold Gauer, Tallmadge *Also Called: Promold Inc (G-14044)*
Promospark Inc... 513 844-2211
   1120 Hicks Blvd Ste 201 Fairfield (45014) *(G-7398)*

Promospark Inc 513 844-2211
300 Osborne Dr Fairfield (45014) *(G-7399)*

Promote-U-Graphics, Cleveland *Also Called:* Bizall Inc *(G-3738)*

Promotional Fixtures, Rittman *Also Called:* Pfi Displays Inc *(G-12826)*

Promotional Spring, Miamisburg *Also Called:* Mound Printing Company Inc *(G-10664)*

Proof RES Advnced Cmpsites Div, Moraine *Also Called:* Performnce Plymr Solutions Inc *(G-11196)*

Propress Inc 216 631-8200
3135 Berea Rd Ste 1 Cleveland (44111) *(G-4593)*

Prospect Rock LLC 740 512-0542
98 N Market St Ste 4 Saint Clairsville (43950) *(G-12919)*

Prospiant Inc (HQ) 513 242-0310
5513 Vine St Cincinnati (45217) *(G-3305)*

Prospira America Corporation (DH) 419 423-9552
2030 Production Dr Findlay (45839) *(G-7553)*

Prospira America Corporation 419 294-6989
235 Commerce Way Upper Sandusky (43351) *(G-14821)*

Prostar LLC 419 225-8806
4610 S Dixie Hwy Ste D Lima (45806) *(G-9306)*

Protech Industries, Avon *Also Called:* Pro-TEC Industries Inc *(G-783)*

Protech Pet LLC 419 552-4617
3595 State Route 51 Gibsonburg (43431) *(G-7955)*

Protech Powder Coatings Inc 216 244-2761
11110 Berea Rd Ste 1 Cleveland (44102) *(G-4594)*

Protective Coating Tech LLC 419 340-8645
3600 Boulder Ridge Dr Maumee (43537) *(G-10226)*

Protective Industrial Polymers 440 327-0015
7875 Bliss Pkwy North Ridgeville (44039) *(G-11854)*

Protective Packg Solutions LLC 513 769-5777
10345 S Medallion Dr Cincinnati (45241) *(G-3306)*

Protectoplas Div, Streetsboro *Also Called:* Ebco Inc *(G-13769)*

Protein Technologies Ltd 513 769-0840
4015 Executive Park Dr Cincinnati (45241) *(G-3307)*

Proteus Electronics Inc 419 886-2296
161 Spayde Rd Bellville (44813) *(G-1247)*

Proto Machine & Mfg Inc 330 677-1700
2190 State Route 59 Kent (44240) *(G-8849)*

Proto Plastics Inc 937 667-8416
316 Park Ave Tipp City (45371) *(G-14150)*

Proto Prcsion Mfg Slutions LLC 614 771-0080
4101 Leap Rd Hilliard (43026) *(G-8434)*

Proto Precision Fabricators, Hilliard *Also Called:* Proto Prcsion Mfg Slutions LLC *(G-8434)*

Proto Precision Fabricators, Hilliard *Also Called:* Vicart Prcsion Fabricators Inc *(G-8452)*

Proto-Mold Products Co Inc 937 778-1959
1750 Commerce Dr Piqua (45356) *(G-12550)*

Prototype Fabricators Co 216 252-0080
10911 Briggs Rd Cleveland (44111) *(G-4595)*

Prout Boiler Htg & Wldg Inc 330 744-0293
3124 Temple St Youngstown (44510) *(G-16423)*

Proveyance Group, Holland *Also Called:* Woodsage LLC *(G-8539)*

Provia - Heritage Stone, Sugarcreek *Also Called:* Provia Holdings Inc *(G-13935)*

Provia Holdings Inc (PA) 330 852-4711
2150 State Route 39 Sugarcreek (44681) *(G-13935)*

Providence REES Inc 614 833-6231
2111 Builders Pl Columbus (43204) *(G-5696)*

Provimi North America Inc (HQ) 937 770-2400
6571 State Route 503 N Lewisburg (45338) *(G-9190)*

Provimi North America Inc 937 770-2400
6531 State Route 503 N Lewisburg (45338) *(G-9191)*

Provimi North America Inc 937 770-2400
6571 State Route 503 N Lewisburg (45338) *(G-9192)*

PRU Industries Inc 937 746-8702
8401 Claude Thomas Rd Ste 57 Franklin (45005) *(G-7694)*

PS Copy, Westlake *Also Called:* Penguin Enterprises Inc *(G-15773)*

PS Pinchot-Swogger Pubg LLC 330 448-1742
8122 Warren Sharon Rd Masury (44438) *(G-10157)*

PS Superior Inc 216 587-1000
9257 Midwest Ave Cleveland (44125) *(G-4596)*

Psb Company, Columbus *Also Called:* Porcelain Steel Buildings Company *(G-5683)*

PSC 272 TRC Pbf 419 466-7129
1819 Woodville Rd Oregon (43616) *(G-12109)*

PSC Holdings Inc (PA) 740 454-6253
109 Graham St Zanesville (43701) *(G-16560)*

PSI, Chesterland *Also Called:* Pneumatic Specialties Inc *(G-2488)*

Psix LLC 937 746-6841
185 S Pioneer Blvd Springboro (45066) *(G-13516)*

PSK Steel Corp 330 759-1251
2960 Gale Dr Hubbard (44425) *(G-8570)*

Pt Metals LLC 330 767-3003
10384 Navarre Rd Sw Navarre (44662) *(G-11351)*

Pt Solutions LLC 844 786-6300
2985 Nationwide Pkwy Brunswick (44212) *(G-1784)*

Pt Tech LLC (HQ) 330 239-4933
1441 Wolf Creek Trl Wadsworth (44281) *(G-15056)*

Ptc Alliance LLC 330 821-5700
640 Keystone St Alliance (44601) *(G-421)*

Ptc Industries, Cleveland *Also Called:* Parking & Traffic Control SEC *(G-4533)*

Pti, Bowling Green *Also Called:* Phoenix Technologies Intl LLC *(G-1583)*

Ptmj Enterprises Inc 440 543-8000
32000 Aurora Rd Solon (44139) *(G-13408)*

Ptp of Mississippi, Cincinnati *Also Called:* Cindus Corporation *(G-2766)*

Pts, Heath *Also Called:* Polymer Tech & Svcs Inc *(G-8327)*

Pts Prfssnal Technical Svc Inc (PA) 513 642-0111
503 Commercial Dr West Chester (45014) *(G-15488)*

Pubco Corporation (PA) 216 881-5300
3830 Kelley Ave Cleveland (44114) *(G-4597)*

Public Works Dept Street Div 740 283-6013
238 S Lake Erie St Steubenville (43952) *(G-13675)*

Publishing Group Ltd 614 572-1240
781 Northwest Blvd Ste 202 Columbus (43212) *(G-5697)*

Pucel Enterprises Inc 216 881-4604
1440 E 36th St Cleveland (44114) *(G-4598)*

Pucel Enterprises Inc 800 336-4986
1401 E 34th St Cleveland (44114) *(G-4599)*

Puehler Agco Inc 419 388-6614
3304 State Route 108 Wauseon (43567) *(G-15273)*

Pughs Designer Jewelers Inc 740 344-9259
12 W Main St Newark (43055) *(G-11603)*

Pukka Inc (PA) 419 429-7808
337 S Main St Fl 4 Findlay (45840) *(G-7554)*

Pukka Headwear, Findlay *Also Called:* Pukka Inc *(G-7554)*

Pullman Company 419 499-2541
33 Lockwood Rd Milan (44846) *(G-10885)*

Pullman Company 419 592-2055
11800 County Road 424 Napoleon (43545) *(G-11331)*

Pulsar Ecoproducts LLC 216 861-8800
3615 Superior Ave E Ste 4402a Cleveland (44114) *(G-4600)*

Pulsar Products, Cleveland *Also Called:* Pulsar Ecoproducts LLC *(G-4600)*

Pulse Journal 513 829-7900
7320 Yankee Rd Liberty Township (45044) *(G-9209)*

Pulse Worldwide Ltd 513 234-7829
7554 Central Parke Blvd Mason (45040) *(G-10044)*

Pumpco Concrete Pumping LLC 740 809-1473
7230 Johnstown Utica Rd Johnstown (43031) *(G-8776)*

Pumps Group, Toledo *Also Called:* Airtex Industries LLC *(G-14181)*

Pun-U, Cincinnati *Also Called:* Lifestyle Nutraceuticals Ltd *(G-3105)*

Punch Components Inc 419 224-1242
505 N Cable Rd Lima (45805) *(G-9280)*

Pur Hair Extensions LLC 330 786-5772
1088 E Tallmadge Ave Akron (44310) *(G-287)*

Pure Foods LLC 303 358-8375
675 Alpha Dr Ste E Highland Heights (44143) *(G-8391)*

Pure Safety Group Inc 614 436-0700
7007 N High St Worthington (43085) *(G-16208)*

Pure Water Technology NW Ohio, Toledo *Also Called:* Onesource Water LLC *(G-14414)*

Purebuttonscom LLC 330 721-1600
4930 Chippewa Rd Unit A Medina (44256) *(G-10367)*

Puremonics, Cleveland *Also Called:* CPI Group Limited *(G-3911)*

Pureti Group LLC 513 708-3631
10931 Reed Hartman Hwy Ste C Blue Ash (45242) *(G-1458)*

Purina Mills, Orrville *Also Called:* Purina Mills LLC *(G-12146)*

Purina Mills LLC..330 682-1951
635 Collins Blvd Orrville (44667) *(G-12146)*

Puritas Metal Products Inc..440 353-1917
39097 Center Ridge Rd North Ridgeville (44039) *(G-11855)*

Purple Orchid Boutique LLC..614 554-7686
1535 Cunard Rd Columbus (43227) *(G-5698)*

Purushealth LLC...800 601-0580
3558 Lee Rd Shaker Heights (44120) *(G-13158)*

Purvi Oil Inc..419 207-8234
654 Us Highway 250 E Ashland (44805) *(G-606)*

Putnam Aggregrates Co..419 523-6004
7053 Road M Ottawa (45875) *(G-12189)*

Putnam Plastics Inc...937 866-6261
255 S Alex Rd Dayton (45449) *(G-6535)*

Puttmann Industries Inc..513 202-9444
320 N State St Harrison (45030) *(G-8287)*

Puzzles & Planeswalkers LLC...937 540-9047
7 N Main St Englewood (45322) *(G-7239)*

Pvc Industries Inc...518 877-8670
2921 Mcbride Ct Hamilton (45011) *(G-8237)*

Pvm Incorporated...614 871-0302
3515 Grove City Rd Grove City (43123) *(G-8117)*

PVS Chemical Solutions Inc...330 666-0888
3149 Copley Rd Copley (44321) *(G-5955)*

PVS Plastics Technology Corp...937 233-4376
6290 Executive Blvd Huber Heights (45424) *(G-8579)*

Pwa Great Northern Corp Ctr LP..412 415-1177
25050 Country Club Blvd Ste 200 North Olmsted (44070) *(G-11825)*

Pwi Inc..732 212-8110
5195 Hampsted Village Center Way New Albany (43054) *(G-11389)*

Pwp Inc..216 251-2181
532 County Road 1600 Ashland (44805) *(G-607)*

Pyramid Industries LLC..614 783-1543
327 Briarwood Dr Columbus (43213) *(G-5699)*

Pyramid Mold & Machine Co Inc..330 673-5200
222 Martinel Dr Kent (44240) *(G-8850)*

Pyramid Mold & Machine Company, Kent Also Called: Pyramid Mold & Machine Co Inc *(G-8850)*

Pyramid Plastics Inc..216 641-5904
9202 Reno Ave Cleveland (44105) *(G-4601)*

Pyro-Chem Corporation..740 377-2244
2491 County Road 1 South Point (45680) *(G-13474)*

Pyrograf Products Inc..937 766-2020
154 W Xenia Ave Cedarville (45314) *(G-2323)*

Pyromatics Corp (PA)..440 352-3500
9321 Pineneedle Dr Mentor (44060) *(G-10538)*

Pyros Pharmaceuticals Inc...201 743-9468
470 Olde Worthington Rd Westerville (43082) *(G-15673)*

Q Holding Company (HQ)...440 903-1827
1700 Highland Rd Twinsburg (44087) *(G-14720)*

Q Holding Mexico, Twinsburg Also Called: Q Holding Company *(G-14720)*

Q M P, Cleves Also Called: Stock Mfg & Design Co Inc *(G-4965)*

Q Model Inc..330 733-6545
3414 E Waterloo Rd Akron (44312) *(G-288)*

Q S I Fabrication...419 832-1680
10333 S River Rd Grand Rapids (43522) *(G-8009)*

Q T Columbus LLC..800 758-2410
1330 Stimmel Rd Columbus (43223) *(G-5700)*

Q-Lab, Westlake Also Called: Q-Lab Corporation *(G-15776)*

Q-Lab Corporation (PA)...440 835-8700
800 Canterbury Rd Westlake (44145) *(G-15776)*

Q&D Indrustrial Floors, Farmersville Also Called: Quality Durable Indus Floors *(G-7460)*

Qaf Technologies Inc..440 941-4348
1212 E Dublin Granville Rd Ste 105 Columbus (43229) *(G-5701)*

Qc LLC..847 682-9072
730 Miley Rd North Lima (44452) *(G-11811)*

Qc Software LLC...513 469-1424
50 E Business Way Cincinnati (45241) *(G-3308)*

Qca Inc..513 681-8400
2832 Spring Grove Ave Cincinnati (45225) *(G-3309)*

Qcforge.com, Cincinnati Also Called: Queen City Forging Company *(G-2573)*

Qcp, Holland Also Called: Quality Care Products LLC *(G-8526)*

Qcp Pallet Services, Cincinnati Also Called: Queen City Pallets Inc *(G-3318)*

Qcsm LLC...216 650-8731
9335 Mccracken Blvd Cleveland (44125) *(G-4602)*

Qfm Stamping Inc...330 337-3311
400 W Railroad St Ste 1 Columbiana (44408) *(G-5048)*

Qibco Buffing Pads Inc (PA)..937 743-0805
301 Industry Dr Ste B Carlisle (45005) *(G-2292)*

Qlog Corp...513 874-1211
33 Standen Dr Hamilton (45015) *(G-8238)*

Qnnect LLC (PA)...864 275-8970
1382 W Jackson St Painesville (44077) *(G-12259)*

Qol Meds, Middletown Also Called: Genoa Healthcare LLC *(G-10826)*

Qqe Summit LLC...937 236-3250
802 Orchard Ln Beavercreek Township (45434) *(G-1091)*

Qrp Inc..910 371-0700
1000 W Bagley Rd Ste 101 Berea (44017) *(G-1291)*

Qsi, Fairport Harbor Also Called: Quartz Scientific Inc *(G-7457)*

Qsr, Twinsburg Also Called: Lexington Rubber Group Inc *(G-14688)*

QT Equipment Company (PA)...330 724-3055
151 W Dartmore Ave Akron (44301) *(G-289)*

Quad Fluid Dynamics Inc...330 220-3005
2826 Westway Dr Brunswick (44212) *(G-1785)*

Quadco Rehabilitation Ctr Inc..419 445-1950
600 Oak St Archbold (43502) *(G-543)*

Quadco Rehabilitation Ctr Inc (PA)..419 682-1011
427 N Defiance St Stryker (43557) *(G-13912)*

Quadrel Inc..440 602-4700
7670 Jenther Dr Mentor (44060) *(G-10539)*

Quadrel Labeling Systems, Mentor Also Called: Quadrel Inc *(G-10539)*

Quadriga Americas LLC (PA)..614 890-6090
480 Olde Worthington Rd Ste 350 Westerville (43082) *(G-15674)*

Quaker Chemical Corporation (HQ)......................................513 422-9600
3431 Yankee Rd Middletown (45044) *(G-10853)*

Quaker City Casting, Salem Also Called: Korff Holdings LLC *(G-13008)*

Quaker City Concrete Pdts LLC..330 427-2239
290 E High St Leetonia (44431) *(G-9130)*

Quaker Houghton, Middletown Also Called: Quaker Chemical Corporation *(G-10853)*

Quaker Mfg, Salem Also Called: Quaker Mfg Corp *(G-13024)*

Quaker Mfg Corp..330 332-4631
187 Georgetown Rd Salem (44460) *(G-13024)*

Qual-Fab Inc...440 327-5000
34250 Mills Rd Avon (44011) *(G-784)*

Qualiform Inc..330 336-6777
689 Weber Dr Wadsworth (44281) *(G-15057)*

Qualitee Design Sportswear Co (PA)......................................740 333-8337
1270 Us Highway 22 Nw Ste 9 Wshngtn Ct Hs (43160) *(G-16237)*

Qualitor Inc (DH)..248 204-8600
127 Public Sq Ste 5300 Cleveland (44114) *(G-4603)*

Qualitor Subsidiary H Inc...419 562-7987
1232 Whetstone St Bucyrus (44820) *(G-1865)*

Qualiturn Inc...513 868-3333
9081 Le Saint Dr West Chester (45014) *(G-15489)*

Quality Architectural and Fabr...937 743-2923
8 Shotwell Dr Franklin (45005) *(G-7695)*

Quality Assurance, Fremont Also Called: Kraft Heinz Foods Company *(G-7793)*

Quality Bakery Company Inc..614 224-1424
50 N Glenwood Ave Columbus (43222) *(G-5702)*

Quality Bar Inc...330 755-0000
17 Union St Ste 7 Struthers (44471) *(G-13906)*

Quality Block & Supply Inc (DH)..330 364-4411
Rte 250 Mount Eaton (44659) *(G-11231)*

Quality Blow Molding Inc..440 458-6550
635 Oberlin Elyria Rd Elyria (44035) *(G-7198)*

Quality Borate Co LLC...216 896-1949
3690 Orange Pl Ste 495 Cleveland (44122) *(G-4604)*

Quality Care Products LLC..734 847-2704
6920 Hall St Holland (43528) *(G-8526)*

Quality Castings Company (PA)...330 682-6010
1200 N Main St Orrville (44667) *(G-12147)*

ALPHABETIC SECTION — Queen City Office Machine

Quality CNC Machining Inc 440 953-0723
38195 Airport Pkwy Willoughby (44094) *(G-15978)*

Quality Components Inc 440 255-0606
8825 East Ave Mentor (44060) *(G-10540)*

Quality Concepts Telecom Ltd 740 385-2003
19485 Harble Rd Logan (43138) *(G-9374)*

Quality Controls Inc 513 272-3900
3411 Church St Cincinnati (45244) *(G-3310)*

Quality Craft Machine Inc 330 928-4064
137 Ascot Pkwy Cuyahoga Falls (44223) *(G-6112)*

Quality Custom Signs LLC 614 580-7233
651 Lakeview Plaza Blvd Ste F Worthington (43085) *(G-16209)*

Quality Cutter Grinding Co 216 362-6444
15501 Commerce Park Dr Cleveland (44142) *(G-4605)*

Quality Design Machining Inc 440 352-7290
64 Penniman Rd Orwell (44076) *(G-12169)*

Quality Durable Indus Floors 937 696-2833
5005 Farmersville Germantn Pike Farmersville (45325) *(G-7460)*

Quality Electrodynamics LLC 440 638-5106
6655 Beta Dr Ste 100 Mayfield Village (44143) *(G-10261)*

Quality Envelope Inc 513 942-7578
9792 Inter Ocean Dr West Chester (45246) *(G-15579)*

Quality Extractions Group LLC 567 698-9802
2533 Tracy Rd Northwood (43619) *(G-11928)*

Quality Fabricated Metals Inc 330 332-7008
14000 W Middletown Rd Salem (44460) *(G-13025)*

Quality Forms, Piqua *Also Called: Little Printing Company* *(G-12532)*

Quality Gold, Fairfield *Also Called: Quality Gold Inc* *(G-7400)*

Quality Gold Inc (PA) 513 942-7659
500 Quality Blvd Fairfield (45014) *(G-7400)*

Quality Industries Inc 216 961-5566
3716 Clark Ave Cleveland (44109) *(G-4606)*

Quality Liquid Feeds Inc 330 532-4635
2402 Clark Ave Wellsville (43968) *(G-15336)*

Quality Machining and Mfg Inc 419 899-2543
14168 State Route 18 Sherwood (43556) *(G-13202)*

Quality Match Plate Co Inc 330 889-2462
4211 State Route 534 Southington (44470) *(G-13478)*

Quality Mechanicals Inc 513 559-0998
1225 Streng St Cincinnati (45223) *(G-3311)*

Quality Mfg Company Inc 513 921-4500
4323 Spring Grove Ave Cincinnati (45223) *(G-3312)*

Quality Molded, Akron *Also Called: New Castings Inc* *(G-262)*

Quality Office Products, Dayton *Also Called: SPAOS Inc* *(G-6580)*

Quality Plastics, Fredericksburg *Also Called: Yoders Produce Inc* *(G-7736)*

Quality Plating Co 216 361-0151
1443 E 40th St Cleveland (44103) *(G-4607)*

Quality Pllets Recyclables LLC 419 396-3244
410 E Findlay St Carey (43316) *(G-2284)*

Quality Printing Co, Bucyrus *Also Called: Bucyrus Graphics Inc* *(G-1851)*

Quality Quartz Engineering Inc 937 236-3250
802 Orchard Ln Beavercreek Township (45434) *(G-1092)*

Quality Quartz Engineering Inc (PA) 510 791-1013
802 Orchard Ln Beavercreek Township (45434) *(G-1093)*

Quality Quick Print, Troy *Also Called: Western Ohio Graphics* *(G-14616)*

Quality Ready Mix Inc (PA) 419 394-8870
16672 County Road 66a Saint Marys (45885) *(G-12965)*

Quality Reproductions Inc 330 335-5000
127 Hartman Rd Wadsworth (44281) *(G-15058)*

Quality Rubber Stamp Inc 614 235-2700
1777 Victor Rd Nw Lancaster (43130) *(G-9034)*

Quality Solutions Inc 440 933-9946
Cleveland (44140) *(G-4608)*

QUALITY SOLUTIONS INC, Cleveland *Also Called: Quality Solutions Inc* *(G-4608)*

Quality Specialists Inc 440 946-9129
1428 E 363rd St Willoughby (44095) *(G-15979)*

Quality Stamping, Toledo *Also Called: Quality Tool Company* *(G-14444)*

Quality Stamping Products Co (PA) 216 441-2700
5322 Bragg Rd Cleveland (44127) *(G-4609)*

Quality Steel Fabrication 937 492-9503
2500 Fair Rd Sidney (45365) *(G-13274)*

Quality Switch Inc 330 872-5707
715 Arlington Blvd Newton Falls (44444) *(G-11655)*

Quality Synthetic Rubber Co, Twinsburg *Also Called: TAC Materials Inc* *(G-14740)*

Quality Tool Company 419 476-8228
577 Mel Simon Dr Toledo (43612) *(G-14444)*

Quality Welding Inc 419 483-6067
104 Ronald Ln Bellevue (44811) *(G-1231)*

Quality Wldg & Fabrication LLC 567 220-6639
82 N Washington St Tiffin (44883) *(G-14100)*

Quality Woodproducts LLC 330 279-2217
8216 Township Road 568 Fredericksburg (44627) *(G-7731)*

Qualtech NP, Cincinnati *Also Called: Curtiss-Wright Flow Ctrl Corp* *(G-2556)*

Qualtech Technologies Inc 440 946-8081
1685b Joseph Lloyd Pkwy Willoughby (44094) *(G-15980)*

Qualtek Electronics Corp 440 951-3300
7610 Jenther Dr Mentor (44060) *(G-10541)*

Quanex Building Products, Akron *Also Called: Quanex Ig Systems Inc* *(G-291)*

Quanex Building Products, Cambridge *Also Called: Quanex Ig Systems Inc* *(G-1950)*

Quanex Building Products Corp 360 345-1241
388 S Main St Ste 700 Akron (44311) *(G-290)*

Quanex Custom Mixing, Cambridge *Also Called: Quanex Ig Systems Inc* *(G-1949)*

Quanex Ig Systems Inc (HQ) 216 910-1500
388 S Main St Ste 700 Akron (44311) *(G-291)*

Quanex Ig Systems Inc 740 435-0444
804 Byesville Rd Cambridge (43725) *(G-1949)*

Quanex Ig Systems Inc 740 439-2338
800 Cochran Ave Cambridge (43725) *(G-1950)*

Quanex Screens LLC 419 662-5001
7597 Broadmoor Rd Perrysburg (43551) *(G-12422)*

Quanta International LLC 513 354-3639
1 Landy Ln Cincinnati (45215) *(G-3313)*

Quantum 740 328-2548
400 Case Ave Newark (43055) *(G-11604)*

Quantum Commerce LLC 513 777-0737
6748 Dimmick Rd West Chester (45069) *(G-15490)*

Quantum Energy LLC (PA) 440 285-7381
10405 Locust Grove Dr Chardon (44024) *(G-2464)*

Quantum Integration Llc 330 609-0355
1980 Niles Cortland Rd Ne Cortland (44410) *(G-5967)*

Quantum Solutions Group 614 442-0664
1555 Bethel Rd Columbus (43220) *(G-5703)*

Quarrymasters Inc 330 612-0474
1644 Berna Rd Akron (44312) *(G-292)*

Quarter Century Design LLC 937 434-5127
2555 S Dixie Dr Ste 232 Dayton (45409) *(G-6536)*

Quartz, Mentor *Also Called: Aco Inc* *(G-10403)*

Quartz Scientific Inc (PA) 360 574-6254
819 East St Fairport Harbor (44077) *(G-7457)*

Quasonix, West Chester *Also Called: Quasonix Inc* *(G-15491)*

Quasonix Inc (PA) 513 942-1287
6025 Schumacher Park Dr West Chester (45069) *(G-15491)*

Quass Sheet Metal Inc 330 477-4841
5018 Yukon St Nw Canton (44708) *(G-2205)*

Qube Corporation 440 543-2393
16744 W Park Circle Dr Chagrin Falls (44023) *(G-2418)*

Quebecor World Johnson Hardin 614 326-0299
3600 Red Bank Rd Cincinnati (45227) *(G-3314)*

Queen Beanery Coffeehouse LLC 937 798-4023
25675 State Route 41 Peebles (45660) *(G-12330)*

Queen City Awning, Cincinnati *Also Called: Queen City Awning & Tent Co* *(G-3315)*

Queen City Awning & Tent Co 513 530-9660
7225 E Kemper Rd Cincinnati (45249) *(G-3315)*

Queen City Carpets LLC 513 823-8238
6539 Harrison Ave 304 Cincinnati (45247) *(G-3316)*

Queen City Forging Company 513 321-2003
1019 Seabrook Way Cincinnati (45245) *(G-2573)*

Queen City Laser 513 696-4444
3460 Grant Ave Lebanon (45036) *(G-9105)*

Queen City Mascots and Logos, Cincinnati *Also Called: Queen City Spirit LLC* *(G-3320)*

Queen City Office Machine 513 251-7200
3984 Trevor Ave Cincinnati (45211) *(G-3317)*

Queen City Pallets Inc

ALPHABETIC SECTION

Queen City Pallets Inc.. 513 821-6700
7744 Reinhold Dr Cincinnati (45237) *(G-3318)*

Queen City Polymers Inc (PA)...................................... 513 779-0990
6101 Schumacher Park Dr West Chester (45069) *(G-15492)*

Queen City Reprographics... 513 326-2300
2863 E Sharon Rd Cincinnati (45241) *(G-3319)*

Queen City Spirit LLC.. 513 533-2662
8211 Blue Ash Rd Cincinnati (45236) *(G-3320)*

Queen City Steel Treating Co, Cincinnati *Also Called: Fbf Limited (G-2898)*

Queen City Tool Works Inc.. 513 874-0111
125 Constitution Dr Ste 2 Fairfield (45014) *(G-7401)*

Queen Exhibits LLC... 937 615-6051
1707 Commerce Dr Piqua (45356) *(G-12551)*

Ques Industries Inc... 216 267-8989
5420 W 140th St Cleveland (44142) *(G-4610)*

Quest Diagnostics, Mason *Also Called: Quest Diagnostics Incorporated (G-10045)*

Quest Diagnostics Incorporated................................. 513 229-5500
4690 Parkway Dr Mason (45040) *(G-10045)*

Quest Lasercut, Franklin *Also Called: Quest Technologies Inc (G-7696)*

Quest Service Labs, Twinsburg *Also Called: A E Wilson Holdings Inc (G-14621)*

Quest Service Labs Inc... 330 405-0316
2307 E Aurora Rd Unit B10 Twinsburg (44087) *(G-14621)*

Quest Software Inc... 614 336-9223
6500 Emerald Pkwy Ste 400 Dublin (43016) *(G-6929)*

Quest Technologies Inc.. 937 743-1200
600 Commerce Center Dr Franklin (45005) *(G-7696)*

Questline Inc.. 614 255-3166
5500 Frantz Rd Ste 156 Dublin (43017) *(G-6930)*

Quez Media, Independence *Also Called: Quez Media Marketing Inc (G-8683)*

Quez Media Marketing Inc.. 216 910-0202
6100 Oak Tree Blvd Ste 200 Independence (44131) *(G-8683)*

Quick As A Wink Printing Co....................................... 419 224-9786
321 W High St Lima (45801) *(G-9281)*

Quick Loadz Container Sys LLC................................. 888 304-3946
5850 Industrial Park Rd Athens (45701) *(G-693)*

Quick Print, Cambridge *Also Called: Taylor Quick Print (G-1957)*

Quick Print, Canton *Also Called: USA Quickprint Inc (G-2259)*

Quick Service Welding & Mch Co................................ 330 673-3818
117 E Summit St Kent (44240) *(G-8851)*

Quick Tab II Inc (PA).. 419 448-6622
241 Heritage Dr Tiffin (44883) *(G-14101)*

Quick Tech Business Forms Inc................................. 937 743-5952
408 Sharts Dr Springboro (45066) *(G-13517)*

Quick Tech Graphics Inc... 937 743-5952
408 Sharts Dr Frnt Springboro (45066) *(G-13518)*

Quickdraft Inc... 330 477-4574
1525 Perry Dr Sw Canton (44710) *(G-2206)*

Quickloadz, Athens *Also Called: Quick Loadz Container Sys LLC (G-693)*

Quicksilver Die Casting Svc.. 330 757-1160
33 Delaware Ave Youngstown (44514) *(G-16424)*

Quidel Corporation... 858 552-1100
2005 E State St # 100 Athens (45701) *(G-694)*

Quidel Corporation... 740 589-3300
1055 E State St Ste 100 Athens (45701) *(G-695)*

Quidel Dhi... 740 589-3300
2005 E State St Athens (45701) *(G-696)*

Quikey Manufacturing Co Inc (PA).............................. 330 633-8106
1500 Industrial Pkwy Akron (44310) *(G-293)*

Quikrete Cincinnati, Harrison *Also Called: Quikrete Companies LLC (G-8288)*

Quikrete Companies LLC.. 614 885-4406
6225 Huntley Rd Columbus (43229) *(G-5704)*

Quikrete Companies LLC.. 513 367-6135
5425 Kilby Rd Harrison (45030) *(G-8288)*

Quikrete Companies LLC.. 330 296-6080
2693 Lake Rockwell Rd Ravenna (44266) *(G-12729)*

Quikrete Companies LLC.. 419 241-1148
873 Western Ave Toledo (43609) *(G-14445)*

Quikrete of Cleveland, Ravenna *Also Called: Quikrete Companies LLC (G-12729)*

Quikspray, Port Clinton *Also Called: Quikstir Inc (G-12625)*

Quikstir Inc... 419 732-2601
2105 W Lakeshore Dr Port Clinton (43452) *(G-12625)*

Quilting Inc (PA)... 614 504-5971
7600 Industrial Pkwy Plain City (43064) *(G-12591)*

Quilting Creations Intl.. 330 874-4741
8778 Towpath Rd Ne Bolivar (44612) *(G-1535)*

Quinami LLC... 419 797-4445
3845 E Wine Cellar Rd Port Clinton (43452) *(G-12626)*

Quintus Technologies LLC.. 614 891-2732
8270 Green Meadows Dr N Lewis Center (43035) *(G-9176)*

Qxsoft LLC.. 740 777-9609
759 Carle Ave Lewis Center (43035) *(G-9177)*

R & A Sports Inc... 216 289-2254
23780 Lakeland Blvd Euclid (44132) *(G-7297)*

R & C Monument Company LLC................................. 216 297-5444
5146 Warrensville Center Rd Maple Heights (44137) *(G-9758)*

R & D Custom Machine & Tl Inc.................................. 419 727-1700
5961 American Rd E Toledo (43612) *(G-14446)*

R & D Equipment Inc.. 419 668-8439
206 Republic St Norwalk (44857) *(G-11987)*

R & D Hilltop Lumber Inc.. 740 342-3051
2126 State Route 93 Se New Lexington (43764) *(G-11456)*

R & D Industries LLC.. 937 397-5836
1313 Lakeshore Dr Medway (45341) *(G-10398)*

R & D Logging LLC... 740 259-6127
2218 Cramer Rd Lucasville (45648) *(G-9526)*

R & D Machine Inc.. 937 339-2545
1204 S Crawford St Troy (45373) *(G-14603)*

R & D Nestle Center Inc.. 440 349-5757
5750 Harper Rd Solon (44139) *(G-13409)*

R & F Franchise Group LLC.. 440 942-7140
37333 Euclid Ave Willoughby (44094) *(G-15981)*

R & H Enterprises Llc... 216 702-4449
4933 Karen Isle Dr Richmond Heights (44143) *(G-12810)*

R & J AG Manufacturing Inc....................................... 419 962-4707
821 State Route 511 Ashland (44805) *(G-608)*

R & J Bardon Inc... 614 457-5500
4676 Larwell Dr Columbus (43220) *(G-5705)*

R & J Cylinder & Machine Inc..................................... 330 364-8263
464 Robinson Dr Se New Philadelphia (44663) *(G-11524)*

R & J Printing Enterprises Inc.................................... 330 343-1242
4246 Hudson Dr Stow (44224) *(G-13719)*

R & J Tool Inc.. 937 833-3200
10550 Upper Lewisburg Salem Rd Brookville (45309) *(G-1743)*

R & L Software LLC (PA)... 513 847-4942
421 Breaden Dr Ste 3 Monroe (45050) *(G-11118)*

R & L Truss Inc... 419 587-3440
17985 Road 60 Grover Hill (45849) *(G-8170)*

R & M Fluid Power Inc.. 330 758-2766
7953 Southern Blvd Youngstown (44512) *(G-16425)*

R & R Engine & Machine, Coventry Township *Also Called: Chemequip Sales Inc (G-6007)*

R & R Fabrications Inc.. 419 678-4831
601 E Washington St Saint Henry (45883) *(G-12937)*

R & R Tool Inc... 937 783-8665
1449a Middleboro Rd Blanchester (45107) *(G-1352)*

R & S Data Products, Hillsboro *Also Called: Highland Computer Forms Inc (G-8459)*

R & S Label, Oberlin *Also Called: R R Donnelley & Sons Company (G-12055)*

R & S Monitions Inc.. 614 846-0597
181 Rosslyn Ave Columbus (43214) *(G-5706)*

R & T Estate LLC.. 216 862-0822
17001 Euclid Ave Cleveland (44112) *(G-4611)*

R A Hamed International Inc...................................... 330 247-0190
8400 Darrow Rd Twinsburg (44087) *(G-14722)*

R A Heller Company.. 513 771-6100
10530 Chester Rd Cincinnati (45215) *(G-3321)*

R A M Plastics Co Inc... 330 549-3107
11401 South Ave North Lima (44452) *(G-11812)*

R A M Precision Tool, Dayton *Also Called: Ram Precision Industries Inc (G-6538)*

R and J Corporation... 440 871-6009
24142 Detroit Rd Westlake (44145) *(G-15777)*

R and S Technologies Inc... 419 483-3691
2474 State Route 4 Bellevue (44811) *(G-1232)*

R Anthony Enterprises LLC.. 419 341-0961
2626 Whetstone River Rd S Marion (43302) *(G-9874)*

ALPHABETIC SECTION

R C M, Akron *Also Called: Rubber City Machinery Corp (G-312)*

R C Moore Lumber Co 740 732-4950
820 Miller St Caldwell (43724) *(G-1912)*

R C Musson Rubber Co 330 773-7651
1320 E Archwood Ave Akron (44306) *(G-294)*

R D Baker Enterprises Inc 937 461-5225
765 Liberty Ln Dayton (45449) *(G-6537)*

R D Holder Oil Co Inc 740 522-3136
1000 Keller Dr Heath (43056) *(G-8328)*

R E H Inc 330 876-2775
St Rt 5 Kinsman (44428) *(G-8937)*

R E May Inc 216 771-6332
1401 E 24th St Cleveland (44114) *(G-4612)*

R F Cook Manufacturing Co, Stow *Also Called: Levan Enterprises Inc (G-13706)*

R F I 740 654-4502
276 Bremen Rd Lancaster (43130) *(G-9035)*

R F W, Cleveland *Also Called: RFW Holdings Inc (G-4631)*

R G Barry Corporation 212 244-3145
13405 Yarmouth Dr Pickerington (43147) *(G-12468)*

R G Smith Company (PA) 330 456-3415
1249 Dueber Ave Sw Canton (44706) *(G-2207)*

R H Little Co 330 477-3455
4434 Southway St Sw Canton (44706) *(G-2208)*

R Holdings 2500 Co 800 883-7876
2500 E 5th Ave Columbus (43219) *(G-5707)*

R J K Enterprises Inc 440 257-6018
5565 Wilson Dr Mentor (44060) *(G-10542)*

R J Manray Inc 330 559-6716
7320 Akron Canfield Rd Ste B Canfield (44406) *(G-2015)*

R K Industries Inc 419 523-5001
725 N Locust St Ottawa (45875) *(G-12190)*

R K Metals Ltd 513 874-6055
3235 Homeward Way Fairfield (45014) *(G-7402)*

R L Industries Inc 513 874-2800
9355 Le Saint Dr West Chester (45014) *(G-15493)*

R L Rush Tool & Pattern Inc 419 562-9849
1620 Whetstone St Bucyrus (44820) *(G-1866)*

R L S Corporation 740 773-1440
990 Eastern Ave Chillicothe (45601) *(G-2530)*

R L S Recycling, Chillicothe *Also Called: R L S Corporation (G-2530)*

R L Torbeck Industries Inc 513 367-0080
355 Industrial Dr Harrison (45030) *(G-8289)*

R L Waller Construction Inc 740 772-6185
645 Alum Cliff Rd Chillicothe (45601) *(G-2531)*

R M Tool & Die Inc 440 238-6459
19768 Progress Dr Strongsville (44149) *(G-13870)*

R P A, Dayton *Also Called: Rpa Electronic Distrs Inc (G-6553)*

R R Donnelley, Hebron *Also Called: R R Donnelley & Sons Company (G-8358)*

R R Donnelley, Streetsboro *Also Called: R R Donnelley & Sons Company (G-13786)*

R R Donnelley & Sons Company 740 928-6110
190 Milliken Dr Hebron (43025) *(G-8358)*

R R Donnelley & Sons Company 440 774-2101
450 Sterns Rd Oberlin (44074) *(G-12055)*

R R Donnelley & Sons Company 330 562-5250
10400 Danner Dr Streetsboro (44241) *(G-13786)*

R R Donnelley & Sons Company 513 552-1512
8720 Global Way West Chester (45069) *(G-15494)*

R R Donnelley & Sons Company 513 870-4040
8740 Global Way West Chester (45069) *(G-15495)*

R R R Development Co (PA) 330 966-8855
8817 Pleasantwood Ave Nw North Canton (44720) *(G-11754)*

R S C, Columbus *Also Called: Safecor Health LLC (G-5739)*

R S Hanline and Co Inc (PA) 419 347-8077
17 Republic Ave Shelby (44875) *(G-13199)*

R T & T Machining, Mentor *Also Called: R T & T Machining Co Inc (G-10543)*

R T & T Machining Co Inc 440 974-8479
8195 Tyler Blvd Mentor (44060) *(G-10543)*

R Vandewalle Inc 513 921-2657
4030 Delhi Ave Cincinnati (45204) *(G-3322)*

R W Long Lumber & Box Co Inc 513 932-5124
1840 Cornett Rd Ste 1 Lebanon (45036) *(G-9106)*

R W Machine & Tool Inc 330 296-5211
7944 State Route 44 Ravenna (44266) *(G-12730)*

R W Screw Products Inc 330 837-9211
999 Oberlin Ave Sw Massillon (44647) *(G-10137)*

R W Sidley Inc 440 224-2664
3062 E Center St Kingsville (44068) *(G-8934)*

R W Sidley Incorporated 330 499-5616
7545 Pittsburg Ave Nw Canton (44720) *(G-2209)*

R W Sidley Incorporated 440 564-2221
10688 Kinsman Rd Newbury (44065) *(G-11635)*

R W Sidley Incorporated (PA) 440 352-9343
436 Casement Ave Painesville (44077) *(G-12260)*

R W Sidley Incorporated 440 352-9343
436 Casement Ave Painesville (44077) *(G-12261)*

R W Sidley Incorporated 440 298-3232
6900 Madison Rd Thompson (44086) *(G-14062)*

R W Sidley Incorporated 440 298-3232
7123 Madison Rd Thompson (44086) *(G-14063)*

R W Sidley Incorporated 330 392-2721
425 N River Rd Nw Warren (44483) *(G-15201)*

R W Sidley Incorporated 330 793-7374
3424 Oregon Ave Youngstown (44509) *(G-16426)*

R-K Electronics Inc 513 204-6060
7405 Industrial Row Dr Mason (45040) *(G-10046)*

R. W. Sidley, Painesville *Also Called: R W Sidley Incorporated (G-12260)*

R.W., Willoughby *Also Called: Spence Technologies Inc (G-15996)*

R&D Marketing Group Inc 216 398-9100
4597 Van Epps Rd Brooklyn Heights (44131) *(G-1697)*

R&R Candles LLC 614 600-7729
6745 Mcvey Blvd Columbus (43235) *(G-5708)*

R&R Sanitation 419 561-8090
317 N Wiley St Crestline (44827) *(G-6036)*

Ra Consultants LLC 513 469-6600
10856 Kenwood Rd Blue Ash (45242) *(G-1459)*

Raber Lumber Co 330 893-2797
4112 State Rte 557 Charm (44617) *(G-2471)*

Rable Machine Inc 740 689-9009
1858 Cedar Hill Rd Lancaster (43130) *(G-9036)*

Race Winning Brands Inc (PA) 440 951-6600
7201 Industrial Park Blvd Mentor (44060) *(G-10544)*

Racelite Southcoast Inc 216 581-4600
16518 Broadway Ave Maple Heights (44137) *(G-9759)*

Raceway, Lorain *Also Called: Raceway Petroleum Inc (G-9432)*

Raceway Beverage LLC 513 932-2214
11 S Broadway St Lebanon (45036) *(G-9107)*

Raceway Petroleum Inc 440 989-2660
3040 Oberlin Ave Lorain (44052) *(G-9432)*

Rack Coating Service Inc 330 854-2869
5760 Erie Ave Nw Canal Fulton (44614) *(G-1974)*

Rack Processing Company Inc (PA) 937 294-1911
2350 Arbor Blvd Moraine (45439) *(G-11206)*

Rack Processing Company Inc 937 294-1911
2350 Arbor Blvd Moraine (45439) *(G-11207)*

RAD Technologies Incorporated 513 641-0523
3428 Hauck Rd Ste G Cincinnati (45241) *(G-3323)*

RAD-Con Inc (PA) 440 871-5720
13001 Athens Ave Ste 300 Lakewood (44107) *(G-8981)*

Radar Love Co 419 951-4750
5500 Fostoria Ave Findlay (45840) *(G-7555)*

Radcliffe Steel, Berea *Also Called: Rads LLC (G-1292)*

Radco Fire Protection Inc 419 476-0102
444 W Laskey Rd Ste S Toledo (43612) *(G-14447)*

Radco Industries Inc 419 531-4731
3226 Frenchmens Rd Toledo (43607) *(G-14448)*

Radici Plastics Usa Inc (DH) 330 336-7611
960 Seville Rd Wadsworth (44281) *(G-15059)*

Radix Wire, Solon *Also Called: Radix Wire & Cable LLC (G-13410)*

Radix Wire & Cable LLC 216 731-9191
30333 Emerald Valley Pkwy Solon (44139) *(G-13410)*

Radix Wire Co 330 995-3677
350 Harris Dr Aurora (44202) *(G-733)*

Radix Wire Co (PA) 216 731-9191
30333 Emerald Valley Pkwy Solon (44139) *(G-13411)*

Radix Wire Co 216 731-9191
30333 Emerald Valley Pkwy Solon (44139) *(G-13412)*

Radix Wire Company, The, Solon Also Called: Radix Wire Co *(G-13411)*

Radocy Inc 419 666-4400
30652 East River Rd Rossford (43551) *(G-12870)*

Radon Eliminator LLC 330 844-0703
5046 Stoney Creek Ln North Canton (44720) *(G-11755)*

Rads LLC 330 671-0464
135 Blaze Industrial Pkwy Berea (44017) *(G-1292)*

Raf Acquisition Co 440 572-5999
5478 Grafton Rd Valley City (44280) *(G-14888)*

Rafter Equipment Corporation 440 572-3700
12430 Alameda Dr Strongsville (44149) *(G-13871)*

Rage Corporation (PA) 614 771-4771
3949 Lyman Dr Hilliard (43026) *(G-8435)*

Rage Plastics, Hilliard Also Called: Rage Corporation *(G-8435)*

Ragon House Collection, Bolivar Also Called: Rhc Inc *(G-1536)*

Rah Investment Holding Inc 330 832-8124
1320 Sanders Ave Sw Massillon (44647) *(G-10138)*

Rail Bearing Service Inc, North Canton Also Called: Rail Bearing Service LLC *(G-11756)*

Rail Bearing Service LLC 234 262-3000
4500 Mount Pleasant St Nw North Canton (44720) *(G-11756)*

Railroad Brewing Company 440 723-8234
1010 Center Rd Avon (44011) *(G-785)*

Railtech Matweld Inc 419 592-5050
15 Interstate Dr Napoleon (43545) *(G-11332)*

Rain Drop Products Llc 419 207-1229
2121 Cottage St Ashland (44805) *(G-609)*

Rainbow Cultured Marble 330 225-3400
1442 W 130th St Brunswick (44212) *(G-1786)*

Rainbow Industries Inc 937 323-6493
5975 E National Rd Springfield (45505) *(G-13623)*

Rainbow Master Mixing Inc 330 374-1810
467 Dan St Akron (44310) *(G-295)*

Rainbow Printing, Uniontown Also Called: Plastic Card Inc *(G-14790)*

Rainbow Printing, Uniontown Also Called: Plasticards Inc *(G-14791)*

Rainbow Tarp, Springfield Also Called: Rainbow Industries Inc *(G-13623)*

Rainin Instrument LLC 510 564-1600
1900 Polaris Pkwy Columbus (43240) *(G-5069)*

Rains Plastics Inc 330 283-3768
873 Kings Cross Dr Wadsworth (44281) *(G-15060)*

Raka Corporation 419 476-6572
203 Matzinger Rd Toledo (43612) *(G-14449)*

Ralph Robinson Inc 740 385-2747
700 Ohio Ave Logan (43138) *(G-9375)*

Ralphie Gianni Mfg & Co Ltd 216 507-3873
250 E 271st St Euclid (44132) *(G-7298)*

Ralston Food, Lancaster Also Called: Treehouse Private Brands Inc *(G-9046)*

Ralston Instruments LLC 440 564-1430
15035 Cross Creek Pkwy Newbury (44065) *(G-11636)*

Ram Innovative Tech LLC 330 956-4056
3969 Jeffries Cir Louisville (44641) *(G-9469)*

Ram Machining Inc 740 333-5522
806 Delaware St Wshngtn Ct Hs (43160) *(G-16238)*

Ram Plastics Inc 330 549-3342
1837 Celeste Cir Youngstown (44511) *(G-16427)*

Ram Precision Industries Inc 937 885-7700
11125 Yankee St Ste A Dayton (45458) *(G-6538)*

Ram Products Inc 614 443-4634
1091 Stimmel Rd Columbus (43223) *(G-5709)*

Ram Sensors Inc 440 835-3540
875 Canterbury Rd Cleveland (44145) *(G-4613)*

Ram Tool Inc 937 277-0717
1944 Neva Dr Dayton (45414) *(G-6539)*

Rambasek Realty Inc 937 228-1189
827 S Patterson Blvd Dayton (45402) *(G-6540)*

Ramco Electric Motors Inc 937 548-2525
5763 Jaysville Saint Johns Rd Greenville (45331) *(G-8056)*

Ramco Specialties Inc (PA) 330 653-5135
5445 Hudson Industrial Pkwy Hudson (44236) *(G-8609)*

Ramp Creek III Ltd 740 522-0660
1100 Thornwood Dr Lot 1 Heath (43056) *(G-8329)*

Rampe Manufacturing Company 440 352-8995
1246 High St Fairport Harbor (44077) *(G-7458)*

Rampp Company (PA) 740 373-7886
20445 State Route 550 Ofc Marietta (45750) *(G-9819)*

Ramsey Stairs & Wdwkg LLC 614 694-2101
4134 Little Pine Dr Columbus (43230) *(G-5710)*

Rance Industries Inc 330 482-1745
1361 Heck Rd Columbiana (44408) *(G-5049)*

Randall, Lima Also Called: Randall Bearings Inc *(G-9282)*

Randall Richard & Moore LLC 330 455-8873
3710 Progress St Ne Canton (44705) *(G-2210)*

Randall Bearings Inc 419 678-2486
821 Weis St Coldwater (45828) *(G-5000)*

Randall Bearings Inc (DH) 419 223-1075
240 Jay Begg Pkwy Lima (45804) *(G-9282)*

Randall Brothers LLC 419 395-1764
30361 Defiance Aversville Holgate (43527) *(G-8491)*

Randd Assoc Prtg & Promotions 937 294-1874
330 Progress Rd Dayton (45449) *(G-6541)*

Randolph Tool Company Inc 330 877-4923
750 Wales Dr Hartville (44632) *(G-0304)*

Randy Carter Logging Inc 740 634-2604
1100 Schmidt Rd Bainbridge (45612) *(G-832)*

Randy Gray 513 533-3200
4142 Airport Rd Unit 1 Cincinnati (45226) *(G-3324)*

Randy Lewis Inc 330 784-0456
1053 Bank St Akron (44305) *(G-296)*

Randys Pickles LLC 440 864-6611
2203 Superior Ave E Cleveland (44114) *(G-4614)*

Raneys Beef Jerky LLC 606 694-1054
81 Township Road 1326 Ironton (45638) *(G-8702)*

Range Impact Inc (PA) 216 304-6556
200 Park Ave Ste 400 Cleveland (44122) *(G-4615)*

Range Kleen Mfg Inc 419 331-8000
4240 East Rd Elida (45807) *(G-7098)*

Rankin Mfg Inc 419 929-8338
201 N Main St New London (44851) *(G-11466)*

Ranpak Holdings Corp (HQ) 440 354-4445
7990 Auburn Rd Concord Township (44077) *(G-5911)*

Ransom & Randolph LLC (PA) 419 865-9497
3535 Briarfield Blvd Maumee (43537) *(G-10227)*

Ransome AC LLC 234 205-6907
1235 Tioga Ave Akron (44305) *(G-297)*

Rantek Products LLC 419 485-2421
1826 Magda Dr Ste A Montpelier (43543) *(G-11141)*

Rapid Machine Inc 419 737-2377
610 N State St Pioneer (43554) *(G-12497)*

Rapid Mr International Inc 614 486-6300
1500 Lake Shore Dr Ste 310 Columbus (43204) *(G-5711)*

Rapid Quality Manufacturing, West Chester Also Called: GE Aviation Systems LLC *(G-15437)*

Rapiscan Systems High Enrgy In 937 879-4200
514 E Dayton Yellow Springs Rd Fairborn (45324) *(G-7321)*

Ratliff Metal Spinning Company 937 836-3900
40 Harrisburg Dr Englewood (45322) *(G-7240)*

Rauh Polymers Inc 330 376-1120
420 Kenmore Blvd Akron (44301) *(G-298)*

Ravago Americas LLC 330 825-2505
5192 Lake Rd Medina (44256) *(G-10368)*

Ravago Americas LLC 419 924-9090
600 Oak St West Unity (43570) *(G-15643)*

Ravago Chemical Dist Inc 330 920-8023
1665 Enterprise Pkwy Twinsburg (44087) *(G-14723)*

Ravana Industries Inc 330 536-4015
6170 Center Rd Lowellville (44436) *(G-9518)*

Raven Concealment Systems LLC 440 508-9000
7889 Root Rd North Ridgeville (44039) *(G-11856)*

Raven Personal Defense Systems 419 631-0573
1237 W 4th St Ontario (44906) *(G-12095)*

Ravens Sales & Service, Dover Also Called: Kruz Inc *(G-6831)*

ALPHABETIC SECTION

Ravenworks Deer Skin... 937 354-5151
34477 Shertzer Rd Mount Victory (43340) *(G-11302)*

Rawac Plating Company... 937 322-7491
125 N Bell Ave Springfield (45504) *(G-13624)*

Ray C Sprosty Bag Co Inc... 330 669-0045
5857 Applecreek Rd Smithville (44677) *(G-13301)*

Ray Communications Inc... 330 686-0226
1337 Commerce Dr Ste 11 Stow (44224) *(G-13720)*

Ray Fogg Construction Inc... 216 351-7976
981 Keynote Cir Ste 15 Cleveland (44131) *(G-4616)*

Ray H Miller Logging Lumb... 330 683-2055
8848 Ely Rd Apple Creek (44606) *(G-509)*

Ray Lewis Enterprises LLC... 330 424-9585
7235 State Route 45 Lisbon (44432) *(G-9325)*

Ray Meyer Sign Company Inc... 513 984-5446
8942 Glendale Milford Rd Loveland (45140) *(G-9500)*

Ray Muro... 440 984-8845
176 N Main St Oberlin (44074) *(G-12056)*

Ray-Tech Industries LLC... 419 923-0169
15210 County Road 10 3 Lyons (43533) *(G-9533)*

Raydar Inc of Ohio... 330 334-6111
1734 Wall Rd Ste B Wadsworth (44281) *(G-15061)*

Rayhaven Group, Richfield Also Called: Rayhaven Group Inc *(G-12795)*

Rayhaven Group Inc... 330 659-3183
3842 Congress Pkwy Ste A Richfield (44286) *(G-12795)*

Rayle Coal Co... 740 695-2197
67705 Friends Church Rd Saint Clairsville (43950) *(G-12920)*

Raymar Holdings Corporation... 614 497-3033
3700 Lockbourne Rd Columbus (43207) *(G-5712)*

Raymath, Troy Also Called: Raymath Company *(G-14604)*

Raymath Company... 937 335-1860
2323 W State Route 55 Troy (45373) *(G-14604)*

Raymond J Detweiler... 440 632-1255
16747 Nauvoo Rd Middlefield (44062) *(G-10783)*

Raymond Robinson... 937 890-1886
507 Jana Cir Dayton (45415) *(G-6542)*

Raymond W Reisiger... 740 400-4090
11885 Paddock View Ct Nw Baltimore (43105) *(G-846)*

Rays Sausage Inc... 216 921-8782
3146 E 123rd St Cleveland (44120) *(G-4617)*

Raytec Systems, Stow Also Called: Ray Communications Inc *(G-13720)*

Raytheon, Beavercreek Also Called: Raytheon Company *(G-1059)*

Raytheon, Dayton Also Called: L3 Technologies Inc *(G-6165)*

Raytheon Company... 937 429-5429
2970 Presidential Dr Ste 300 Beavercreek (45324) *(G-1059)*

RB Sigma LLC... 440 290-0577
6111 Heisley Rd Mentor (44060) *(G-10545)*

RB Tool & Mfg. Co., Cincinnati Also Called: Kaws Inc *(G-3066)*

RB&w Manufacturing LLC (HQ)... 234 380-8540
10080 Wellman Rd Streetsboro (44241) *(G-13787)*

Rba Inc... 330 336-6700
487 College St Wadsworth (44281) *(G-15062)*

Rbb Systems Inc... 330 263-4502
1909 Old Mansfield Rd Wooster (44691) *(G-16161)*

Rbm Environmental & Cnstr Inc... 419 693-5840
4526 Bayshore Rd Oregon (43616) *(G-12110)*

Rbr Enterprises LLC... 866 437-9327
6910 Miller Rd Brecksville (44141) *(G-1630)*

Rbs Manufacturing Inc... 330 426-9486
145 E Martin St East Palestine (44413) *(G-7007)*

RC Industries Inc... 330 879-5486
620 Main St N Navarre (44662) *(G-11352)*

RCE Heat Exchangers LLC... 330 627-0300
3165 Folsam Rd Nw Carrollton (44615) *(G-2313)*

Rcf Kitchens Indiana LLC... 765 478-6600
87 Shelford Way Beavercreek (45440) *(G-1079)*

Rci, Sidney Also Called: Ross Casting & Innovation LLC *(G-13280)*

Rcl Benziger, Cincinnati Also Called: Kendall/Hunt Publishing Co *(G-3073)*

Rcl Publishing Group LLC... 972 390-6400
8805 Governors Hill Dr Ste 400 Cincinnati (45249) *(G-3325)*

RCM Engineering Company... 330 666-0575
2089 N Cleveland Massillon Rd Akron (44333) *(G-299)*

Rcr Partnership... 419 340-1202
424 N Martin Williston Rd Genoa (43430) *(G-7948)*

Rcs Cross Woods Maple LLC... 614 825-0670
222 E Campus View Blvd Columbus (43235) *(G-5713)*

Rct Industries Inc... 937 602-1100
1314 Farr Dr Dayton (45404) *(G-6543)*

Rd Holder Oil Co... 740 653-4031
238 N Pierce Ave Lancaster (43130) *(G-9037)*

Rda Group LLC... 440 724-4347
2131 Clifton Way Avon (44011) *(G-786)*

RE Connors Construction Ltd... 740 644-0261
13352 Forrest Rd Ne Thornville (43076) *(G-14068)*

REA Elektronik Inc... 440 232-0555
7307 Young Dr Ste B Bedford (44146) *(G-1151)*

REA Polishing Inc... 419 470-0216
1606 W Laskey Rd Toledo (43612) *(G-14450)*

Reactive Resin Products Co... 419 666-6119
327 5th St Perrysburg (43551) *(G-12423)*

Reading Rock Incorporated (PA)... 513 874-2345
4600 Devitt Dr West Chester (45246) *(G-15580)*

Ready 2 Ride Trnsp LLC... 614 207-2683
12435 Thoroughbred Dr Pickerington (43147) *(G-12469)*

Ready Field Solutions LLC... 330 562-0550
1240 Ethan Ave Streetsboro (44241) *(G-13788)*

Ready For Flight, Westerville Also Called: Garage Scenes Ltd *(G-15657)*

Ready Rigs LLC... 740 963-9203
2321 Taylor Park Dr Reynoldsburg (43068) *(G-12773)*

Ready Robotics Corporation... 833 732-3967
1080 Steelwood Rd Columbus (43212) *(G-5714)*

Ready Technology Inc (HQ)... 937 866-7200
333 Progress Rd Dayton (45449) *(G-6544)*

Real Alloy Recycling LLC (HQ)... 216 755-8900
3700 Park East Dr Ste 300 Beachwood (44122) *(G-1013)*

Real Alloy Specialty Pdts LLC (DH)... 216 755-8836
3700 Park East Dr Ste 300 Beachwood (44122) *(G-1014)*

Real Alloy Specialty Pdts LLC (DH)... 216 755-8836
3700 Park East Dr Ste 300 Beachwood (44122) *(G-1015)*

Real Alloy Specialty Pdts LLC... 440 322-0072
320 Huron St Elyria (44035) *(G-7199)*

Real Alloy Specialty Pdts LLC... 440 563-3487
2639 E Water St Rock Creek (44084) *(G-12832)*

Real Alloy Specification LLC (DH)... 216 755-8900
3700 Park East Dr Ste 300 Beachwood (44122) *(G-1016)*

Realeflow LLC... 855 545-2095
150 Pearl Rd Brunswick (44212) *(G-1787)*

Realized Mfg LLC... 330 535-3887
879 S Progress Dr Ste A Medina (44256) *(G-10369)*

Really Cool Foods, Beavercreek Also Called: Rcf Kitchens Indiana LLC *(G-1079)*

Ream and Haager Laboratory Inc... 330 343-3711
179 W Broadway St Dover (44622) *(G-6840)*

Rebecca Benston... 937 360-0669
2130 W Possum Rd Springfield (45506) *(G-13625)*

Rebiltco Inc... 513 424-2024
8775 Thomas Rd Middletown (45042) *(G-10854)*

Rebiz LLC... 844 467-3249
1925 Saint Clair Ave Ne Cleveland (44114) *(G-4618)*

Rebsco Inc... 937 548-2246
4362 Us Route 36 Greenville (45331) *(G-8057)*

Recaro, Cincinnati Also Called: Recaro Child Safety LLC *(G-3326)*

Recaro Child Safety LLC... 248 904-1570
4921 Para Dr Cincinnati (45237) *(G-3326)*

Reclamation Technologies Inc... 800 372-1301
1100 Haskins Rd Bowling Green (43402) *(G-1587)*

Recob Great Lakes Express Inc... 216 265-7940
20600 Sheldon Rd Cleveland (44142) *(G-4619)*

Recognition Robotics Inc (PA)... 440 590-0499
141 Innovation Dr Pmb 306 Elyria (44035) *(G-7200)*

Recon... 740 609-3050
54382 National Rd Bridgeport (43912) *(G-1648)*

Recon Systems LLC... 330 488-0368
330 Wood St S East Canton (44730) *(G-6980)*

Record Herald — ALPHABETIC SECTION

Record Herald, Cincinnati Also Called: Record Herald Publishing Co (G-3327)
Record Herald Publishing Co (DH).................... 717 762-1151
  5050 Kingsley Dr Cincinnati (45227) (G-3327)
Recovery Rm Canvas & Uphl LLC.................... 740 246-6086
  14935 Rustic Ln Thornville (43076) (G-14069)
Recto Molded Products Inc.................... 513 871-5544
  4425 Appleton St Cincinnati (45209) (G-3328)
Rector Inc.................... 440 892-0444
  1991 Crocker Rd Ste 320 Westlake (44145) (G-15778)
Recycled Polymer Solutions LLC.................... 937 821-4020
  750 Buckeye Rd Lima (45804) (G-9283)
Recycled Systems Furniture Inc.................... 614 880-9110
  401 E Wilson Bridge Rd Worthington (43085) (G-16210)
Recycling Eqp Solutions Corp.................... 330 920-1500
  276 Remington Rd Ste C Cuyahoga Falls (44224) (G-6113)
Red Barakuda LLC.................... 614 596-5432
  4439 Shoupmill Dr Columbus (43230) (G-5715)
Red Barn Cabinet Co.................... 937 884-9800
  8046 State Route 722 Arcanum (45304) (G-519)
Red Barn Screen Printing & EMB.................... 740 474-6657
  1144 Northridge Rd Circleville (43113) (G-3555)
Red Barn, The, Circleville Also Called: Red Barn Screen Printing & EMB (G-3555)
Red Diamond Plant, Mc Arthur Also Called: Austin Powder Company (G-10262)
Red Head Brass, Shreve Also Called: Rhba Acquisitions LLC (G-13214)
Red Head Brass Inc.................... 330 567-2903
  643 Legion Dr Shreve (44676) (G-13213)
Red Hill Development Company, Dover Also Called: Doris Kimble (G-6816)
Red Seal Electric Company.................... 216 941-3900
  3835 W 150th St Cleveland (44111) (G-4620)
Red Tie Group Inc (PA)   4521 Industrial Pkwy Cleveland (44135) (G-4621)
Redex Industries Inc (PA).................... 800 345-7339
  1176 Salem Pkwy Salem (44460) (G-13026)
Redhawk Energy Systems LLC.................... 740 927-8244
  10340 Palmer Rd Sw Pataskala (43062) (G-12305)
Reds Auto Glass Shop, Warren Also Called: J W Goss Company (G-15179)
Reduction Engineering Inc.................... 330 677-2225
  235 Progress Blvd Kent (44240) (G-8852)
Reece Brothers Inc.................... 419 212-9226
  1 Toy St Bryan (43506) (G-1837)
Reese Machine Company Inc.................... 440 992-3942
  2501 State Rd Ashtabula (44004) (G-657)
Refocus Holdings Inc.................... 216 751-8384
  2310 Superior Ave E Ste 210 Cleveland (44114) (G-4622)
Refractory Coating Tech Inc.................... 800 807-7464
  2421 E 28th St Lorain (44055) (G-9433)
Refractory Specialties Inc.................... 330 938-2101
  230 W California Ave Sebring (44672) (G-13125)
Refresco North America, Carlisle Also Called: Refresco Us Inc (G-2293)
Refresco Us Inc.................... 937 790-1400
  300 Industry Dr Carlisle (45005) (G-2293)
Refurb-World LLC.................... 440 471-9030
  33888 Center Ridge Rd North Ridgeville (44039) (G-11857)
Regal, Tipp City Also Called: Regal Beloit America Inc (G-14151)
Regal Beloit America Inc.................... 419 352-8441
  427 Van Camp Rd Bowling Green (43402) (G-1588)
Regal Beloit America Inc.................... 608 364-8800
  200 E Chapman Rd Lima (45801) (G-9284)
Regal Beloit America Inc.................... 937 667-2431
  531 N 4th St Tipp City (45371) (G-14151)
Regal Diamond Products Corp.................... 440 944-7700
  1405 E 286th St Wickliffe (44092) (G-15851)
Regal Metal Products Co (PA).................... 330 868-6343
  3615 Union Ave Se Minerva (44657) (G-11039)
Regalia Products Inc.................... 614 579-8399
  2117 S High St Columbus (43207) (G-5716)
Regency Office Furniture, Akron Also Called: Regency Seating Inc (G-300)
Regency Seating Inc.................... 330 848-3700
  2375 Romig Rd Akron (44320) (G-300)
Regency Steel Supplies, Eastlake Also Called: Regency Steel Supply Inc LLC (G-7046)
Regency Steel Supply Inc LLC.................... 440 306-0269
  1662 E 361st St Unit 6a Eastlake (44095) (G-7046)

Register Herald Office.................... 937 456-5553
  200 Eaton Lewisburg Rd Ste 105 Eaton (45320) (G-7068)
Rego Manufacturing Co Inc.................... 419 562-0466
  1870 E Mansfield St Bucyrus (44820) (G-1867)
Regol-G Industries, Cleveland Also Called: DCW Acquisition Inc (G-3949)
Rehn Co, Toledo Also Called: Whiteford Industries Inc (G-14524)
Reid Asset Management Company.................... 440 942-8488
  4500 Beidler Rd Willoughby (44094) (G-15982)
Reifel Industries Inc.................... 419 737-2138
  201 Ohio St Pioneer (43554) (G-12498)
Reighart Steel Products, Willoughby Also Called: Sticker Corporation (G-15998)
Reiki Ladi.................... 513 235-7515
  9693 Loralinda Dr Cincinnati (45251) (G-3329)
Reilloc Machine Co Inc.................... 330 601-0379
  1457 Fox Lake Rd Wooster (44691) (G-16162)
Reilly-Duerr Tank Co.................... 513 554-1022
  698 W Columbia Ave Cincinnati (45215) (G-3330)
Reinalt-Thomas Corporation.................... 330 863-1936
  5125 Canton Rd Nw Carrollton (44615) (G-2314)
Reinforcement Systems of Ohio LLC.................... 330 469-6958
  3121 W Market St Warren (44485) (G-15202)
Reinke Company Inc.................... 614 570-2578
  1616 Tremont Rd Columbus (43212) (G-5717)
Reisbeck Fd Mkts St Clirsville, Saint Clairsville Also Called: Riesbeck Food Markets Inc (G-12921)
Reiter Dairy, Springfield Also Called: Reiter Dairy of Akron Inc (G-13627)
Reiter Dairy LLC Dean Foods.................... 937 323-5777
  1941 Commerce Cir Springfield (45504) (G-13626)
Reiter Dairy of Akron Inc.................... 937 323-5777
  1961 Commerce Cir Springfield (45504) (G-13627)
Rek Associates LLC.................... 419 294-3838
  11218 County Highway 44 Upper Sandusky (43351) (G-14822)
Rel Enterprises Inc (DH).................... 216 741-1700
  4760 Van Epps Rd Brooklyn Heights (44131) (G-1698)
Reladyne Reliability Svcs Inc (HQ).................... 888 478-6996
  3713 Progress St Ne Canton (44705) (G-2211)
Related Metals Inc.................... 330 799-4866
  6011 Deer Spring Run Canfield (44406) (G-2016)
Relay Rail Div., Mineral Ridge Also Called: L B Foster Company (G-11022)
Relevium Labs Inc (PA).................... 614 568-7000
  4663 Katie Ln Ste O Oxford (45056) (G-12212)
Reliable Castings Corporation (PA)   3530 Spring Grove Ave Cincinnati (45223) (G-3331)
Reliable Castings Corporation.................... 937 497-5217
  1521 W Michigan St Sidney (45365) (G-13275)
Reliable Coating Svc Co Inc.................... 513 217-4680
  1301 Hook Dr Middletown (45042) (G-10855)
Reliable Hermetic Seals LLC.................... 888 747-3250
  4156 Dayton Xenia Rd Beavercreek (45432) (G-1060)
Reliable Manufacturing LLC.................... 740 756-9373
  5594 Winchester Rd Carroll (43112) (G-2301)
Reliable Metal Buildings LLC.................... 419 737-1300
  16570 Us Highway 20ns Pioneer (43554) (G-12499)
Reliable Mfg Co LLC.................... 740 756-9373
  4411 Carroll Southern Rd Carroll (43112) (G-2302)
Reliable Pattern Works Inc.................... 440 232-8820
  590 Golden Oak Pkwy Cleveland (44146) (G-4623)
Reliable Printing Solutions.................... 937 486-5031
  8177 N State Route 134 Wilmington (45177) (G-16058)
Reliable Products Co.................... 419 394-5854
  315 S Park Dr Saint Marys (45885) (G-12966)
Reliable Ready Mix Co.................... 330 453-8266
  1606 Allen Ave Se Canton (44707) (G-2212)
Reliable Wheelchair Trans.................... 216 390-3999
  28899 Harvard Rd Beachwood (44122) (G-1017)
Reliacheck Manufacturing Inc.................... 440 933-6162
  6550 Eastland Rd Brookpark (44142) (G-1724)
Reliance Medical Products, Mason Also Called: Haag-Streit Usa Inc (G-10000)
Reliant Worth Corp.................... 440 232-1422
  20638 Krick Rd Bedford (44146) (G-1152)
Reloading Supplies Corp.................... 440 228-0367
  3916 Edgewater Dr Ashtabula (44004) (G-658)

Relx Inc... 937 865-6800
4700 Lyons Rd Miamisburg (45342) *(G-10673)*

Relx Inc... 937 865-6800
9333 Springboro Pike Miamisburg (45342) *(G-10674)*

Rely-On Manufacturing Inc............................. 937 254-0118
955 Springfield St Dayton (45403) *(G-6545)*

Remel Products, Oakwood Village *Also Called: Thermo Fisher Scientific Inc (G-12044)*

Remington Engrg Machining Inc........................ 513 965-8999
5105 River Valley Rd Milford (45150) *(G-10920)*

Remington Products Company (PA).................... 330 335-1571
3366 Riverside Dr Ste 103 Upper Arlington (43221) *(G-14802)*

Remington Steel, Springfield *Also Called: Westfield Steel Inc (G-13654)*

Remington Steel Inc..................................... 937 322-2414
1120 S Burnett Rd Springfield (45505) *(G-13628)*

Remodeling, Cincinnati *Also Called: Superior Property Restoration (G-3433)*

Remram Recovery LLC (PA)............................ 740 667-0092
49705 East Park Dr Tuppers Plains (45783) *(G-14618)*

Remtec Engineering..................................... 513 860-4299
6049 Hi Tek Ct Mason (45040) *(G-10047)*

Remtec International, Bowling Green *Also Called: Reclamation Technologies Inc (G-1587)*

Remtron, Warren *Also Called: Cattron North America Inc (G-15151)*

Renee Grace Bridal, Cincinnati *Also Called: Renee Grace LLC (G-3332)*

Renee Grace LLC.. 513 399-5616
11176 Main St Cincinnati (45241) *(G-3332)*

Renegade Brands LLC.................................. 216 342-4347
3201 Enterprise Pkwy Ste 490 Cleveland (44122) *(G-4624)*

Renegade Brands LLC.................................. 216 789-0535
5351 Naiman Pkwy Ste A Solon (44139) *(G-13413)*

Renegade Materials Corp............................... 513 469-9919
11379 Grooms Rd Blue Ash (45242) *(G-1460)*

Renegade Materials Corporation....................... 937 350-5274
3363 S Tech Blvd Miamisburg (45342) *(G-10675)*

Renewal By Andersen LLC.............................. 614 781-9600
400 Lazelle Rd Ste 1 Columbus (43240) *(G-5070)*

Renewal Parts Maintenance, Euclid *Also Called: Mechanical Dynamics Analis LLC (G-7285)*

Renite Lubrication Engineers, Columbus *Also Called: R Holdings 2500 Co (G-5707)*

Rennco Automation Systems Inc....................... 419 861-2340
971 Hamilton Dr Holland (43528) *(G-8527)*

Reno Machine.. 419 836-3093
11532 Rachel Rd Curtice (43412) *(G-6058)*

Renoir Visions LLC..................................... 419 586-5679
1 Visions Pkwy Celina (45822) *(G-2345)*

Renosol Seating, Hebron *Also Called: Lear Corporation (G-8347)*

Rent-A-John, Columbus *Also Called: BJ Equipment Ltd (G-5193)*

Rent-A-Mom Inc... 216 901-9599
4531 Hillside Rd Seven Hills (44131) *(G-13131)*

Repacorp Inc (PA)....................................... 937 667-8496
31 Industry Park Ct Tipp City (45371) *(G-14152)*

Repko Machine Inc...................................... 216 267-1144
5081 W 164th St Cleveland (44142) *(G-4625)*

Replex Mirror Company................................. 740 397-5535
11 Mount Vernon Ave Mount Vernon (43050) *(G-11291)*

Replex Plastics, Mount Vernon *Also Called: Replex Mirror Company (G-11291)*

Reporter Newspaper Inc................................ 330 535-7061
1088 S Main St Akron (44301) *(G-301)*

Repository, Canton *Also Called: Copley Ohio Newspapers Inc (G-2081)*

Repro Acquisition Company LLC....................... 216 738-3800
25001 Rockwell Dr Cleveland (44117) *(G-4626)*

Reprocenter, The, Cleveland *Also Called: Repro Acquisition Company LLC (G-4626)*

Republic Anode Fabricators, Valley City *Also Called: Raf Acquisition Co (G-14888)*

Republic Engineered Products......................... 440 277-2000
1807 E 28th St Lorain (44055) *(G-9434)*

Republic Metals, Cleveland *Also Called: Vwm-Republic Inc (G-4886)*

Republic Mills Inc....................................... 419 758-3511
888 School St Okolona (43545) *(G-12071)*

Republic Powdered Metals Inc (HQ).................. 330 225-3192
2628 Pearl Rd Medina (44256) *(G-10370)*

Republic Steel.. 330 438-5533
2633 8th St Ne Canton (44704) *(G-2213)*

Republic Steel (DH)..................................... 330 438-5435
2633 8th St Ne Canton (44704) *(G-2214)*

Republic Steel.. 440 277-2000
1807 E 28th St Lorain (44055) *(G-9435)*

Republic Steel, Lorain *Also Called: Republic Engineered Products (G-9434)*

Republic Steel Wire Proc LLC.......................... 440 996-0740
31000 Solon Rd Solon (44139) *(G-13414)*

Republic Storage Systems LLC........................ 330 438-5800
1038 Belden Ave Ne Canton (44705) *(G-2215)*

Republic Technology Corp.............................. 216 622-5000
200 Public Sq Cleveland (44114) *(G-4627)*

Republic Wire Inc....................................... 513 860-1800
5525 Union Centre Dr West Chester (45069) *(G-15496)*

Requarth Lumber Co., Dayton *Also Called: The F A Requarth Company (G-6618)*

Resco Products Inc..................................... 330 488-1226
6878 Osnaburg St Se East Canton (44730) *(G-6981)*

Resco Products Inc..................................... 740 682-7794
3542 State Route 93 Oak Hill (45656) *(G-12024)*

Research & Development Div, Bedford *Also Called: Hikma Pharmaceuticals USA Inc (G-1124)*

Research & Development II, Mentor *Also Called: Steris Corporation (G-10562)*

Research Abrasive Products Inc....................... 440 944-3200
1400 E 286th St Wickliffe (44092) *(G-15852)*

Research Organics LLC................................. 216 883-8025
4353 E 49th St Cleveland (44125) *(G-4628)*

Research Technologies Intl, Cleveland *Also Called: Detrex Corporation (G-3954)*

Reserve Energy Exploration Co........................ 440 543-0770
10155 Gottschalk Pkwy Ste 1 Chagrin Falls (44023) *(G-2419)*

Reserve Industries, Bay Village *Also Called: Reserve Industries Inc (G-966)*

Reserve Industries Inc.................................. 440 871-2796
386 Lake Park Dr Bay Village (44140) *(G-966)*

Reserve Millwork LLC................................... 216 531-6982
26881 Cannon Rd Bedford (44146) *(G-1153)*

Resilience Fund III LP (PA)............................. 216 292-0200
25101 Chagrin Blvd Ste 350 Cleveland (44122) *(G-4629)*

Resilience Us Inc.. 513 645-2600
8814 Trade Port Dr West Chester (45011) *(G-15497)*

Resilient Holdings Inc................................... 614 847-5600
6155 Huntley Rd Ste F Columbus (43229) *(G-5718)*

Resinoid Engineering Corp (PA)....................... 740 928-6115
251 O Neill Dr Hebron (43025) *(G-8359)*

Resonant Sciences LLC................................. 937 431-8180
3975 Research Blvd Beavercreek (45430) *(G-1080)*

Resonetics LLC.. 937 865-4070
2941 College Dr Kettering (45420) *(G-8909)*

Resource America Inc.................................. 330 896-8510
3500 Massillon Rd Ste 100 Uniontown (44685) *(G-14792)*

Resource Mtl Hdlg & Recycl Inc (PA)................. 440 834-0727
14970 Berkshire Industrial Pkwy Middlefield (44062) *(G-10784)*

Resource Recycling Inc................................. 419 222-2702
1596 Neubrecht Rd Lima (45801) *(G-9285)*

Resource Systems, New Concord *Also Called: Cerner Corporation (G-11432)*

Respironics Novametrix LLC........................... 800 345-6443
9570 Logistics Ct Columbus (43217) *(G-5719)*

Response Metal Fabricators............................ 937 222-9000
521 Kiser St Dayton (45404) *(G-6546)*

Restortion Parts Unlimited Inc (PA)................... 513 934-0815
2175 Deerfield Rd Lebanon (45036) *(G-9108)*

Restricted Key.. 614 405-2109
635 E Weber Rd Columbus (43211) *(G-5720)*

Resz Fabrication Inc.................................... 440 207-0044
35280 Lakeland Blvd Eastlake (44095) *(G-7047)*

Retail Display Group, Columbus *Also Called: Plaskolite LLC (G-5677)*

Retail Management Products Ltd...................... 740 548-1725
8851 Whitney Dr Lewis Center (43035) *(G-9178)*

Retail Project Management Inc........................ 614 299-9880
2580 Westbelt Dr Columbus (43228) *(G-5721)*

Retain Loyalty LLC..................................... 330 830-0839
1250 Sanders Ave Sw Massillon (44647) *(G-10139)*

Retalix Inc.. 937 384-2277
2490 Technical Dr Miamisburg (45342) *(G-10676)*

Retention Knob Supply & Mfg Co...................... 937 686-6405
4905 State Route 274 W Huntsville (43324) *(G-8624)*

Retterbush Fiberglass Corp............................ 937 778-1936
719 Long St Piqua (45356) *(G-12552)*

Retterbush Graphics Packg Corp 513 779-4466
  6392 Gano Rd West Chester (45069) *(G-15498)*

Return Polymers Inc 419 289-1998
  400 Westlake Dr Ashland (44805) *(G-610)*

Reuter-Stokes LLC 330 425-3755
  8499 Darrow Rd Ste 1 Twinsburg (44087) *(G-14724)*

Reuther Mold & Manufacturing, Cuyahoga Falls *Also Called: Reuther Mold & Mfg Co Inc* *(G-6114)*

Reuther Mold & Mfg Co Inc 330 923-5266
  1225 Munroe Falls Ave Cuyahoga Falls (44221) *(G-6114)*

Rev38 LLC 937 572-4000
  8888 Beckett Ridge West Chester (45069) *(G-15499)*

Revair LLC 440 462-6100
  1333 Highland Rd E Ste E Macedonia (44056) *(G-9570)*

Revel Otr Urban Winery 513 929-4263
  111 E 12th St Cincinnati (45202) *(G-3333)*

Revere Building Products, Cuyahoga Falls *Also Called: Gentek Building Products Inc* *(G-6086)*

Revere Plas Systems Group LLC (HQ) 419 547-6918
  401 Elm St Clyde (43410) *(G-4976)*

Revere Plastics Systems LLC 573 785-0871
  401 Elm St Clyde (43410) *(G-4977)*

Review, The, Alliance *Also Called: Alliance Publishing Co Inc (G-393)*

Revlis Corporation (PA) 330 535-2100
  255 Fountain St Akron (44304) *(G-302)*

Revlis Corporation 330 535-2108
  2845 Newpark Dr Barberton (44203) *(G-893)*

Revlon, Barberton *Also Called: Revlis Corporation (G-893)*

Revolution Group Inc 614 212-1111
  670 Meridian Way Westerville (43082) *(G-15675)*

Revolution Machine Works Inc 706 505-6525
  5613 Cloverleaf Pkwy Cleveland (44125) *(G-4630)*

Revvity Health Sciences Inc 330 825-4525
  520 S Main St Ste 2423 Akron (44311) *(G-303)*

Rex American Resources, Dayton *Also Called: Rex American Resources Corp (G-6547)*

Rex American Resources Corp (PA) 937 276-3931
  7720 Paragon Rd Dayton (45459) *(G-6547)*

Rex International USA Inc 800 321-7950
  3744 Jefferson Rd Ashtabula (44004) *(G-659)*

Rex Welding Inc 740 387-1650
  1410 E Center St Marion (43302) *(G-9875)*

Rexam Closure Systems, Perrysburg *Also Called: Bprex Halthcare Brookville Inc (G-12365)*

Rexam Plastic Packaging, Toledo *Also Called: Bprex Plastic Packaging Inc (G-14218)*

Rexam PLC 330 893-2451
  5091 County Road 120 Millersburg (44654) *(G-10990)*

Rexarc International Inc 937 839-4604
  35 E 3rd St West Alexandria (45381) *(G-15344)*

Rexles Inc 419 732-8188
  1850 W Lakeshore Dr Port Clinton (43452) *(G-12627)*

Rexon Components Inc 216 292-7373
  24500 Highpoint Rd Beachwood (44122) *(G-1018)*

Reymond Products Intl Inc 330 339-3583
  2066 Brightwood Rd Se New Philadelphia (44663) *(G-11525)*

Reynolds and Reynolds Company 419 584-7000
  824 Murlin Ave Celina (45822) *(G-2346)*

Reynolds Cabinetry & Millwork, Cincinnati *Also Called: Village Cabinet Shop Inc (G-3499)*

Reynolds Industries Inc 330 889-9466
  380 W Main St West Farmington (44391) *(G-15607)*

Reynolds Industries Group LLC 614 363-9149
  97 Hallowell Dr Blacklick (43004) *(G-1342)*

Reynolds Machinery Inc 937 847-8121
  760 Liberty Ln Dayton (45449) *(G-6548)*

Reynoldsburg Trophy, Grove City *Also Called: American Awards Inc (G-8077)*

Rez Stone, Toledo *Also Called: Hoover & Wells Inc (G-14319)*

Rez-Tech Corporation 330 673-4009
  1510 Mogadore Rd Kent (44240) *(G-8853)*

Rezkem Chemicals LLC 330 653-9104
  56 Milford Dr Ste 100 Hudson (44236) *(G-8610)*

RFW Holdings Inc 440 331-8300
  1200 Smith Ct Cleveland (44116) *(G-4631)*

Rgs, Canton *Also Called: R G Smith Company (G-2207)*

Rh Enterprises, Richmond Heights *Also Called: R & H Enterprises Llc (G-12810)*

Rh Seals, Beavercreek *Also Called: Reliable Hermetic Seals LLC (G-1060)*

Rhba Acquisitions LLC 330 567-2903
  643 Legion Dr Shreve (44676) *(G-13214)*

Rhc Inc 330 874-3750
  10841 Fisher Rd Nw Bolivar (44612) *(G-1536)*

Rheaco Builders Inc 330 425-3090
  1941 E Aurora Rd Twinsburg (44087) *(G-14725)*

Rhein Chemie Corporation 440 279-2367
  145 Parker Ct Chardon (44024) *(G-2465)*

Rhenium Alloys, North Ridgeville *Also Called: Rhenium Alloys Inc (G-11858)*

Rhenium Alloys Inc (PA) 440 365-7388
  38683 Taylor Pkwy North Ridgeville (44035) *(G-11858)*

Rhetech Colors, Sandusky *Also Called: Thermocolor LLC (G-13095)*

Rhgs Company 513 721-6299
  1150 W 8th St Ste 111 Cincinnati (45203) *(G-3334)*

Rhi US Ltd (DH) 513 527-6160
  3956 Virginia Ave Cincinnati (45227) *(G-3335)*

Rhinegeist Holding Company Inc 513 381-1367
  1910 Elm St Cincinnati (45202) *(G-3336)*

Rhinestahl AMG, Mason *Also Called: Rhinestahl Corporation (G-10048)*

Rhinestahl Corporation (PA) 513 489-1317
  1111 Western Row Rd Mason (45040) *(G-10048)*

Rhinestahl Corporation 513 229-5300
  7687 Innovation Way Mason (45040) *(G-10049)*

Rhinestahl CTS, Mason *Also Called: Rhinestahl Corporation (G-10049)*

Rhino Linings, Toledo *Also Called: Zie Bart Rhino Linings Toledo (G-14533)*

Rhinosystems Inc 216 351-6262
  One American Way Ste 1100 Brooklyn (44144) *(G-1681)*

Rhk Hardwoods LLC 740 835-1097
  9188 Chenoweth Fork Rd Piketon (45661) *(G-12483)*

Rhoads Print Center Inc 330 678-2042
  564 Washburn Rd Tallmadge (44278) *(G-14045)*

Rhodes Manufacturing Co Inc 740 743-2614
  7045 Buckeye Valley Rd Ne Somerset (43783) *(G-13449)*

RI Alto Mfg Inc 740 914-4230
  1632 Cascade Dr Marion (43302) *(G-9876)*

Ribbon Technology Corporation 614 864-5444
  825 Taylor Station Rd Gahanna (43230) *(G-7848)*

Ribs King Inc 513 791-1942
  9406 Main St Cincinnati (45242) *(G-3337)*

Ribtec, Gahanna *Also Called: Ribbon Technology Corporation (G-7848)*

Riceland Cabinet Inc 330 601-1071
  326 N Hillcrest Dr Wooster (44691) *(G-16163)*

Riceland Cabinet Corporation 330 601-1071
  326 N Hillcrest Dr Ste A Wooster (44691) *(G-16164)*

Rich Industries Inc 330 339-4113
  2384 Brightwood Rd Se New Philadelphia (44663) *(G-11526)*

Rich Products Corporation 614 771-1117
  4600 Northwest Pkwy Hilliard (43026) *(G-8436)*

Richard A Scott 937 898-1592
  8000 Allison Ave Dayton (45415) *(G-6549)*

Richard Benhase & Assoc Inc 513 772-1896
  11741 Chesterdale Rd Cincinnati (45246) *(G-3338)*

Richard Klinger Inc 937 498-2222
  2350 Campbell Rd Sidney (45365) *(G-13276)*

Richard Steel Company Inc 216 520-6390
  11110 Avon Ave Cleveland (44105) *(G-4632)*

Richard Wright 740 829-2127
  15345 County Road 274 Coshocton (43812) *(G-5994)*

Richard's Fence Company, Akron *Also Called: Richards Whl Fence Co Inc (G-304)*

Richards Industrials, Cincinnati *Also Called: Richards Industrials Inc (G-3339)*

Richards Industrials Inc (PA) 513 533-5600
  3170 Wasson Rd Cincinnati (45209) *(G-3339)*

Richards Intrors Bldg Cmpnents, Youngstown *Also Called: Youngstown Shade & Alum LLC (G-16487)*

Richards Maple Products Inc 440 286-4160
  545 Water St Chardon (44024) *(G-2466)*

Richards Whl Fence Co Inc 330 773-0423
  1600 Firestone Pkwy Akron (44301) *(G-304)*

ALPHABETIC SECTION — Riverside Transportation LLC

Richardson Printing Corp (PA) 800 848-9752
201 Acme St Marietta (45750) *(G-9820)*

Richardson Publishing Company 330 753-1068
70 4th St Nw Ste 1 Barberton (44203) *(G-894)*

Richardson Woodworking 614 893-8850
3834 Mann Rd Blacklick (43004) *(G-1343)*

Richelieu Foods Inc 740 335-4813
1104 Clinton Ave Wshngtn Ct Hs (43160) *(G-16239)*

Richland Laminated Columns LLC 419 895-0036
8252 State Route 13 Greenwich (44837) *(G-8070)*

Richland Newhope Inds Inc (PA) 419 774-4400
150 E 4th St Mansfield (44902) *(G-9712)*

Richland Screw Mch Pdts Inc 419 524-1272
531 Grant St Mansfield (44903) *(G-9713)*

Richland Source 419 610-2100
40 W 4th St Mansfield (44902) *(G-9714)*

Richland Township Bd Trustees 419 358-4897
8435 Dixie Hwy Bluffton (45817) *(G-1506)*

Richmond Builders Supply, Saint Henry Also Called: St Henry Tile Co Inc *(G-12938)*

Richmond Machine Co 419 485-5740
1528 Travis Dr Montpelier (43543) *(G-11142)*

Richtech Industries Inc 440 937-4401
34000 Lear Industrial Pkwy Avon (44011) *(G-787)*

Richwood Gazette, Marysville Also Called: Marysville Newspaper Inc *(G-9926)*

Rick Alan Custom Woodworks Inc 513 394-6957
4455 Bethany Rd Mason (45040) *(G-10050)*

Ricking Holding Co 513 825-3551
5800 Grant Ave Cleveland (44105) *(G-4633)*

Rickly Hydrological Co 614 297-9877
1700 Joyce Ave Columbus (43219) *(G-5722)*

Ricoh Usa Inc 412 281-6700
5575 Venture Dr Ste A Cleveland (44130) *(G-4634)*

Ridgco Pallet LLC 330 340-0048
138 W Main St Gnadenhutten (44629) *(G-7988)*

Ridge Corporation (PA) 614 421-7434
1201 Etna Pkwy Etna (43062) *(G-7256)*

Ridge Engineering Inc 513 681-5500
1700 Blue Rock St Cincinnati (45223) *(G-3340)*

Ridge Machine & Welding Co 740 537-2821
1015 Railroad St Toronto (43964) *(G-14534)*

Ridge Tool Company 740 432-8782
9877 Brick Church Rd Cambridge (43725) *(G-1951)*

Ridge Tool Company 440 329-4737
321 Sumner St Elyria (44035) *(G-7201)*

Ridge Tool Company (HQ) 440 323-5581
400 Clark St Elyria (44035) *(G-7202)*

Ridge Tool Manufacturing Co 440 323-5581
400 Clark St Elyria (44035) *(G-7203)*

Ridge Township Stone Quarry 419 968-2222
16905 Middle Point Rd Van Wert (45891) *(G-14925)*

Ridgid, Elyria Also Called: Ridge Tool Company *(G-7202)*

Ridley USA Inc 800 837-8222
104 Oak St Botkins (45306) *(G-1543)*

Riesbeck Food Markets Inc 740 695-3401
104 Plaza Dr Saint Clairsville (43950) *(G-12921)*

Rieter Automotive-Oregon Plant, Oregon Also Called: Autoneum North America Inc *(G-12103)*

Riffle & Sons, Chillicothe Also Called: Riffle Machine Works Inc *(G-2532)*

Riffle Machine Works Inc (PA) 740 775-2838
5746 State Route 159 Chillicothe (45601) *(G-2532)*

Right Away Division, Blue Ash Also Called: Baxters North America Inc *(G-1364)*

Right Restoration LLC 440 614-0480
405 N Brice Rd Blacklick (43004) *(G-1344)*

Riker Products Inc 419 729-1626
4901 Stickney Ave Toledo (43612) *(G-14451)*

Rimeco Products Inc 440 918-1220
2002 Joseph Lloyd Pkwy Willoughby (44094) *(G-15983)*

Rimer Enterprises Inc 419 878-8156
916 Rimer Dr Waterville (43566) *(G-15251)*

Rimm Kleen Systems, West Unity Also Called: Hardline International Inc *(G-15640)*

Rimrock Corporation 614 471-5926
1700 Jetway Blvd Columbus (43219) *(G-5723)*

Rimrock Holdings Corporation 614 471-5926
1700 Jetway Blvd Columbus (43219) *(G-5724)*

Rina Systems LLC 513 469-7462
8180 Corporate Park Dr Ste 140 Cincinnati (45242) *(G-3341)*

Ring Container Tech LLC 937 492-0961
603 Oak Ave Sidney (45365) *(G-13277)*

Ring Masters, Brunswick Also Called: Alternative Surface Grinding *(G-1747)*

Ring Snack LLC 216 334-4356
850 Euclid Ave Ste 819 Cleveland (44114) *(G-4635)*

Ringer LLC 216 228-1442
12906 Arliss Dr Lakewood (44107) *(G-8982)*

Ringer Screen Print, North Kingsville Also Called: Wholesale Imprints Inc *(G-11797)*

Ringneck Brewing Company, Strongsville Also Called: Brew Kettle Inc *(G-13817)*

Rinos Woodworking Shop Inc 440 946-1718
36475 Biltmore Pl Willoughby (44094) *(G-15984)*

Ripley Metalworks LLC 937 392-4992
111 Waterworks Rd Ripley (45167) *(G-12819)*

Ripped Vinyl 330 332-5004
550 Fair Ave Salem (44460) *(G-13027)*

Ripper Woodwork Inc 513 922-1944
6450 Mapleton Ave Cincinnati (45233) *(G-3342)*

Risher & Co 216 732-8351
27011 Tungsten Rd Euclid (44132) *(G-7299)*

Risk Industries LLC 440 835-5553
30505 Clemens Rd Westlake (44145) *(G-15779)*

Rita of Miamisburg LLC (PA) 937 247-5244
6164 State Route 122 Franklin (45005) *(G-7697)*

Rita of Miamisburg LLC 937 247-5244
726 N Heincke Rd Miamisburg (45342) *(G-10677)*

Rite Track, West Chester Also Called: Rite Track Equipment Services LLC *(G-15500)*

Rite Track Equipment Services LLC (PA) 513 881-7820
8655 Rite Track Way West Chester (45069) *(G-15500)*

Riten Industries Incorporated 740 335-5353
1100 Lakeview Ave Wshngtn Ct Hs (43160) *(G-16240)*

Ritime Incorporated 330 273-3443
6363 York Rd Ste 104 Cleveland (44130) *(G-4636)*

Rittman Inc 330 927-6855
10 Mull Dr Rittman (44270) *(G-12827)*

Rivals Sports Grille LLC 216 267-0005
6710 Smith Rd Middleburg Heights (44130) *(G-10726)*

River Cities Signarama, South Point Also Called: Kinly Signs Corporation *(G-13468)*

River City Body Company 513 772-9317
2660 Commerce Blvd Cincinnati (45241) *(G-3343)*

River City Leather Inc 740 645-5044
314 2nd Ave Gallipolis (45631) *(G-7899)*

River City Pharma 513 870-1680
8695 Seward Rd Fairfield (45011) *(G-7403)*

River East Custom Cabinets 419 244-3226
221 S Saint Clair St Toledo (43604) *(G-14452)*

River Valley Paper, Akron Also Called: River Valley Paper Company LLC *(G-305)*

River Valley Paper Company LLC 330 535-1001
131 N Summit St Akron (44304) *(G-305)*

Riverbend Sand Rock and Gravel, Miamisburg Also Called: Hilltop Basic Resources Inc *(G-10646)*

Riverside, Genoa Also Called: Riverside Mch & Automtn Inc *(G-7949)*

Riverside Cnstr Svcs Inc 513 723-0900
218 W Mcmicken Ave Cincinnati (45214) *(G-3344)*

Riverside Drives, Cleveland Also Called: Riverside Drives Inc *(G-4637)*

Riverside Drives Inc 216 362-1211
4509 W 160th St Cleveland (44135) *(G-4637)*

Riverside Marine Inds Inc 419 729-1621
2824 N Summit St Toledo (43611) *(G-14453)*

Riverside Mch & Automtn Inc (PA) 419 855-8308
1240 N Genoa Clay Center Rd Genoa (43430) *(G-7949)*

Riverside Mch & Automtn Inc 419 855-8308
28701 E Broadway St Walbridge (43465) *(G-15086)*

Riverside Mfg Acquisition LLC 585 458-2090
5344 Bragg Rd Cleveland (44127) *(G-4638)*

Riverside Steel Inc 330 856-5299
3102 Warren Sharon Rd Vienna (44473) *(G-15003)*

Riverside Transportation LLC 440 935-3120
9718 Heath Ave Cleveland (44104) *(G-4639)*

Riverview Indus WD Pdts Inc (PA) 330 669-8509
179 S Gilbert Dr Smithville (44677) *(G-13302)*

Riverview Packaging Inc 937 743-9530
101 Shotwell Dr Franklin (45005) *(G-7698)*

Riverview Productions Inc 740 441-1150
652 Jackson Pike Gallipolis (45631) *(G-7900)*

Riverview Raquetball Club, Willoughby Also Called: Melinz Industries Inc *(G-15951)*

Riverview Transport LLC 330 669-8509
179 Gilbert Dr Smithville (44677) *(G-13303)*

Riverview Transport, Inc., Smithville Also Called: Riverview Transport LLC *(G-13303)*

Riwco Corp 937 322-6521
2330 Columbus Rd Springfield (45503) *(G-13629)*

Rixan Associates Inc 937 438-3005
7560 Paragon Rd Dayton (45459) *(G-6550)*

Rize Home LLC (PA) 800 333-8333
31050 Diamond Pkwy Solon (44139) *(G-13415)*

Rj Canvas Works Inc 216 337-6099
3980 Jennings Rd Cleveland (44109) *(G-4640)*

Rjf International Corporation 330 668-2069
3875 Embassy Pkwy Fairlawn (44333) *(G-7447)*

Rjm Stamping Co 614 443-1191
1641 Universal Rd Columbus (43207) *(G-5725)*

Rjs, Akron Also Called: Rjs Corporation *(G-306)*

Rjs Corporation 330 896-2387
3400 Massillon Rd Akron (44312) *(G-306)*

Rjs Machine Shop Services LLC 937 927-0137
720 Pondlick Rd Seaman (45679) *(G-13115)*

Rjw Trucking Company Ltd 740 363-5343
124 Henderson Ct Delaware (43015) *(G-6746)*

Rki Inc (PA) 888 953-9400
8901 Tyler Blvd Mentor (44060) *(G-10546)*

RL Best Company 330 758-8601
723 Bev Rd Boardman (44512) *(G-1517)*

RL Craig Inc 330 424-1525
6496 State Route 45 Lisbon (44432) *(G-9326)*

Rl Smith Graphics, Youngstown Also Called: Rl Smith Graphics LLC *(G-16428)*

Rl Smith Graphics LLC 330 629-8616
493 Bev Rd Bldg 7b Youngstown (44512) *(G-16428)*

RLM & Sqg Industries Inc 513 527-4057
3714 Jonlen Dr Cincinnati (45227) *(G-3345)*

RLM Fabricating Inc 419 729-6130
4801 Bennett Rd Toledo (43612) *(G-14454)*

RLM Fabricating Inc 419 476-1411
5425 Enterprise Blvd Toledo (43612) *(G-14455)*

Rm Advisory Group Inc 513 242-2100
5300 Vine St Cincinnati (45217) *(G-3346)*

RMC USA Incorporation 440 992-4906
149 S Cucumber St Jefferson (44047) *(G-8758)*

Rmi Titanium Company LLC 330 471-1844
208 15th St Sw Canton (44707) *(G-2216)*

Rmi Titanium Company LLC 330 453-2118
1550 Marietta Ave Se Canton (44707) *(G-2217)*

Rmi Titanium Company LLC 330 455-4010
1935 Warner Rd Se Canton (44707) *(G-2218)*

Rmi Titanium Company LLC 330 544-9470
2000 Warren Ave Niles (44446) *(G-11683)*

Rmi Titanium Company LLC (HQ) 330 652-9952
1000 Warren Ave Niles (44446) *(G-11684)*

Rmi Titanium Company LLC 330 652-9955
1000 Warren Ave Niles (44446) *(G-11685)*

RMS Equipment LLC 330 564-1360
1 Vision Ln Cuyahoga Falls (44223) *(G-6115)*

RMS Equipment Company, Cuyahoga Falls Also Called: RMS Equipment LLC *(G-6115)*

Rmt Acquisition Inc 513 241-5566
3111 Spring Grove Ave Cincinnati (45225) *(G-3347)*

Rmt Corporation 937 274-2121
2552 Titus Ave Dayton (45414) *(G-6551)*

Rmt Holdings Inc 419 221-1168
1025 Findlay Rd Lima (45801) *(G-9286)*

Rnm Holdings Inc 614 444-5556
2350 Refugee Park Columbus (43207) *(G-5726)*

Rnm Holdings Inc (PA) 937 704-9900
550 Conover Dr Franklin (45005) *(G-7699)*

Rnm Holdings Inc 419 867-8712
1810 Eber Rd Ste C Holland (43528) *(G-8528)*

Rnp Inc ....
8014 Linden Dr Sw Dellroy (44620) *(G-6758)*

Rnr Enterprises LLC 330 852-3022
1361 County Road 108 Sugarcreek (44681) *(G-13936)*

Rnr Tire Express, Fairfield Also Called: Big Oki LLC *(G-7338)*

Rnw Holdings Inc 330 792-0600
200 Division Street Ext Youngstown (44510) *(G-16429)*

Ro-MAI Industries Inc 330 425-9090
1605 Enterprise Pkwy Twinsburg (44087) *(G-14726)*

Roach Studios LLC 614 725-1405
441 E Hudson St Columbus (43202) *(G-5727)*

Roach Wood Products & Plas Inc 740 532-4855
25 Township Road 328 Ironton (45638) *(G-8703)*

Road Apple Music 513 217-4444
65 S Main St Middletown (45044) *(G-10856)*

Roadsafe Traffic Systems Inc 614 274-9782
1350 Stimmel Rd Columbus (43223) *(G-5728)*

Roban Inc 330 794-1059
1010 Main St Lakemore (44250) *(G-8958)*

Robbins Inc (PA) 513 871-8988
4777 Eastern Ave Cincinnati (45226) *(G-3348)*

Robbins Company, The, Solon Also Called: Global TBM Company *(G-13355)*

Robbins Sports Surfaces, Cincinnati Also Called: Robbins Inc *(G-3348)*

Robeck, Aurora Also Called: Robeck Fluid Power Co *(G-734)*

Robeck Fluid Power Co 330 562-1140
350 Lena Dr Aurora (44202) *(G-734)*

Roberds Converting Co Inc 513 683-6667
113 Northeast Dr Loveland (45140) *(G-9501)*

Robert Barr 740 826-7325
1245 Friendship Dr New Concord (43762) *(G-11433)*

Robert Becker Impressions Inc 419 385-5303
4646 Angola Rd Toledo (43615) *(G-14456)*

Robert E McGrath Inc 440 572-7747
11606 Pearl Rd Strongsville (44136) *(G-13872)*

Robert Long Manufacturing Co 330 678-0911
4192 Karg Industrial Pkwy Kent (44240) *(G-8854)*

Robert Mayo Industries 330 426-2587
157 E Martin St East Palestine (44413) *(G-7008)*

Robert Rothschild Farm LLC 855 969-8050
9958 Crescent Park Dr West Chester (45069) *(G-15501)*

Robert Rothschild Market Cafe, West Chester Also Called: Robert Rothschild Farm LLC *(G-15501)*

Robert Smart Inc 330 454-8881
1100 High Ave Sw Canton (44707) *(G-2219)*

Robert Turner 937 434-1346
8116 Julian Pl Centerville (45458) *(G-2364)*

Robert W Johnson Inc (PA) 614 336-4545
6280 Sawmill Rd Dublin (43017) *(G-6931)*

Robert's Men's Shop, Dellroy Also Called: Rnp Inc *(G-6758)*

Roberts Demand No 3 Corp 216 641-0660
4008 E 89th St Cleveland (44105) *(G-4641)*

Roberts Machine Products LLC 937 682-4015
270 Rush St Rushsylvania (43347) *(G-12875)*

Roberts Manufacturing Co Inc 419 594-2712
24338 Road 148 Oakwood (45873) *(G-12032)*

Roberts Screw Products, Rushsylvania Also Called: Dayton Superior Corporation *(G-12874)*

Robertson Cabinets Inc 937 698-3755
1090 S Main St West Milton (45383) *(G-15631)*

Robertson Manufacturing Co 216 531-8222
10150 Colton Ave Concord Township (44077) *(G-5912)*

Robey Tool Inc 614 251-0412
1593 E 5th Ave Columbus (43219) *(G-5729)*

Robin Enterprises Company 614 891-0250
111 N Otterbein Ave Westerville (43081) *(G-15719)*

Robin Industries Inc 330 893-3501
5200 County Rd 120 Berlin (44610) *(G-1308)*

Robin Industries Inc 330 695-9300
300 W Clay St Fredericksburg (44627) *(G-7732)*

ALPHABETIC SECTION

Robin Industries Inc.. 330 359-5418
7227 State Route 515 Winesburg (44690) *(G-16082)*

Robin Industries Inc (PA).. 216 631-7000
6500 Rockside Rd Ste 230 Independence (44131) *(G-8684)*

Robinson Fin Machines Inc....................................... 419 674-4152
13670 Us Highway 68 Kenton (43326) *(G-8898)*

Robinson Inc.. 614 898-0654
2948 Granada Hills Dr Columbus (43231) *(G-5730)*

Robura Inc... 330 857-7404
3328 S Kohler Rd Orrville (44667) *(G-12148)*

Robura Inc (PA).. 800 438-5346
4779 Kidron Rd Dalton (44618) *(G-6141)*

Rocal Inc (PA).. 740 998-2122
3186 County Road 550 Frankfort (45628) *(G-7658)*

Rochester Manufacturing Inc.................................. 440 647-2463
24765 Quarry Rd Wellington (44090) *(G-15321)*

Rochling Automotive USA LLP................................ 330 400-5785
2275 Picton Pkwy Akron (44312) *(G-307)*

Rochling Glastic Composites, Cleveland *Also Called: Roechling Indus Cleveland LP (G-4645)*

Rock Decor Company... 330 830-9760
167 Maple Street Apple Creek (44606) *(G-510)*

Rock Em Sock Em Retro LLC (PA)........................ 419 575-9309
5902 Moline Martin Rd Walbridge (43465) *(G-15087)*

Rock Hard Industries LLC..................................... 440 327-3077
34555 Mills Rd North Ridgeville (44039) *(G-11859)*

Rock Iron Corporation.. 419 529-9411
1221 Warehouse Dr Crestline (44827) *(G-6037)*

Rock Lite, Maple Heights *Also Called: Charles Svec Inc (G-9748)*

Rock Solid Cut Stone & Sup Inc............................ 330 877-2775
12989 Market Ave N Hartville (44632) *(G-8305)*

Rockbrook Business Svcs LLC............................... 234 817-8107
507 Oak Hill Ave Youngstown (44502) *(G-16430)*

Rocket Ventures LLC... 419 530-6083
300 Madison Ave Ste 270 Toledo (43604) *(G-14457)*

Rockhead Group Usa LLC...................................... 216 310-1569
25370 Letchworth Rd Beachwood (44122) *(G-1019)*

Rockport Ready Mix, Cleveland *Also Called: Rockport Ready Mix Inc (G-4642)*

Rockport Ready Mix Inc.. 216 432-9465
3092 Rockefeller Ave Cleveland (44115) *(G-4642)*

Rocks General Maintenance LLC............................ 740 323-4711
10019 Jacksontown Rd Thornville (43076) *(G-14070)*

Rockstedt Tool & Die Inc...................................... 330 273-9000
2974 Interstate Pkwy Brunswick (44212) *(G-1788)*

Rocktenn Merchandising Display, West Chester *Also Called: Westrock Rkt LLC (G-15527)*

Rockwell Automation Inc...................................... 440 646-7900
6680 Beta Dr Cleveland (44143) *(G-4643)*

Rockwell Automation Inc...................................... 440 646-5000
1 Allen Bradley Dr Cleveland (44124) *(G-4644)*

Rockwell Automation Inc...................................... 330 425-3211
8440 Darrow Rd Twinsburg (44087) *(G-14727)*

Rockwell Automation Inc...................................... 513 942-9828
9355 Allen Rd West Chester (45069) *(G-15502)*

Rockwell Metals Company LLC............................ 440 242-2420
3709 W Erie Ave Lorain (44053) *(G-9436)*

Rockwood Door & Millwork, Millersburg *Also Called: Rockwood Products Ltd (G-10991)*

Rockwood Products Ltd.. 330 893-2392
5264 Township Road 401 Millersburg (44654) *(G-10991)*

Rocky Brands Inc (PA).. 740 753-9100
39 E Canal St Nelsonville (45764) *(G-11359)*

Rocky Hinge Inc.. 330 539-6296
1660 Harding Ave Girard (44420) *(G-7974)*

Rocky Mountain Logging Co LLC......................... 440 313-8574
5880 State Route 82 Hiram (44234) *(G-8488)*

Rocky River Brewing Co...................................... 440 895-2739
21290 Center Ridge Rd Rocky River (44116) *(G-12842)*

Rocla Concrete Tie Inc... 740 776-3238
6501 Pershing Ave Portsmouth (45662) *(G-12654)*

ROCLA CONCRETE TIE, INC, Portsmouth *Also Called: Rocla Concrete Tie Inc (G-12654)*

Roco Industries, Painesville *Also Called: Ropama Inc (G-12262)*

Roconex Corporation... 937 339-2616
2444 Sydneys Bend Dr Miamisburg (45342) *(G-10678)*

Rod or Tammy Whitlatch..................................... 614 848-5198
1411 Abbeyhill Dr Worthington (43085) *(G-16211)*

Rodney Wells.. 740 425-2266
34225 Holland Rd Barnesville (43713) *(G-904)*

Rods Welding and Rebuilding, Barnesville *Also Called: Rodney Wells (G-904)*

Roe Transportation Entps Inc............................... 937 497-7161
3680 Michigan St Sidney (45365) *(G-13278)*

Roechling Indus Cleveland LP (DH)..................... 216 486-0100
4321 Glenridge Rd Cleveland (44121) *(G-4645)*

Roemer Industries Inc.. 330 448-2000
1555 Masury Rd Masury (44438) *(G-10158)*

Roerig Machine... 440 647-4718
27348 State Route 511 New London (44851) *(G-11467)*

Roetmans Welding LLC.. 216 385-5938
155 Beaver St Akron (44304) *(G-308)*

Roettger Hardwood Inc.. 937 693-6811
17066 Kettlersville Rd Kettlersville (45336) *(G-8912)*

Rogar International Inc....................................... 419 476-5500
4015 Dewey St Toledo (43612) *(G-14458)*

Roger Schweitzer Sons.. 513 241-4423
150 Breaden Dr Monroe (45050) *(G-11119)*

Rogers Company, The, Mentor *Also Called: Rogers Display Inc (G-10547)*

Rogers Display Inc (HQ)..................................... 440 951-9200
7550 Tyler Blvd Mentor (44060) *(G-10547)*

Rogers Industrial Products Inc............................ 330 535-3331
532 S Main St Akron (44311) *(G-309)*

Rogue Bowstrings... 330 749-9725
2140 Gordon Rd Nw Dover (44622) *(G-6841)*

Rohrer Corporation (HQ).................................... 330 335-1541
717 Seville Rd Wadsworth (44281) *(G-15063)*

Roki America Co Ltd... 419 424-9713
2001 Production Dr Findlay (45840) *(G-7556)*

Rol - Tech Inc.. 214 905-8050
4814 Calvert Dr Fort Loramie (45845) *(G-7606)*

Rol- Fab Inc... 216 662-2500
4949 Johnston Pkwy Cleveland (44128) *(G-4646)*

Rolcon Inc.. 513 821-7259
510 Station Ave Cincinnati (45215) *(G-3349)*

Roll-In Saw Inc.. 216 459-9001
15851 Commerce Park Dr Brookpark (44142) *(G-1725)*

Roll-Kraft, Mentor *Also Called: Rki Inc (G-10546)*

Roller Source Inc... 440 748-4033
34100 E Royalton Rd Columbia Station (44028) *(G-5019)*

Rolling Enterprises Inc.. 937 866-4917
2701 Lance Dr Moraine (45409) *(G-11208)*

Rolls-Royce Energy Systems Inc......................... 703 834-1700
105 N Sandusky St Mount Vernon (43050) *(G-11292)*

Roman Tool & Die... 440 503-5271
Strongsville (44136) *(G-13873)*

Romans Mobile Welding LLC............................. 513 603-0961
1238 Nottingham Rd Amelia (45102) *(G-462)*

Romar Metal Fabricating Inc.............................. 740 682-7731
201 Zane Oak Rd Oak Hill (45656) *(G-12025)*

Romline Express LLC... 234 855-1905
1572 Brownlee Ave Youngstown (44514) *(G-16431)*

Ron Toelke... 513 598-1881
4377 Oakville Dr Cincinnati (45211) *(G-3350)*

Ron-Al Mold & Machine Inc............................... 330 673-7919
1057 Mason Ave Kent (44240) *(G-8855)*

Rona Enterprises Inc... 740 927-9971
30 W Broad St Pataskala (43062) *(G-12306)*

Ronald T Dodge Co... 937 439-4497
55 Westpark Rd Dayton (45459) *(G-6552)*

Rondy & Co., Barberton *Also Called: Tahoma Rubber & Plastics Inc (G-898)*

Ronfeldt Associates Inc...................................... 419 382-5641
2345 S Byrne Rd Toledo (43614) *(G-14459)*

Ronfeldt Manufacturing..................................... 419 382-5641
3810 Herr Rd Sylvania (43560) *(G-14012)*

Ronfeldt Manufacturing LLC (HQ)................... 419 382-5641
2345 S Byrne Rd Toledo (43614) *(G-14460)*

Ronlen Industries Inc... 330 273-6468
2809 Nationwide Pkwy Brunswick (44212) *(G-1789)*

Roof Maxx, Westerville *Also Called: Roof Maxx Technologies LLC (G-15676)*
Roof Maxx Technologies LLC.. 855 766-3629
 7385 State Route 3 Westerville (43082) *(G-15676)*
Roof To Road LLC... 740 986-6923
 27910 Chillicothe Pike Williamsport (43164) *(G-15869)*
Roofing Annex LLC.. 513 942-0555
 4866 Duff Dr Ste E West Chester (45246) *(G-15581)*
Root Candles, Medina *Also Called: Al Root Company (G-10290)*
Roots Meat Market LLC.. 419 332-0041
 3721 W State St Fremont (43420) *(G-7804)*
Roots Poultry Inc... 419 332-0041
 3721 W State St Fremont (43420) *(G-7805)*
Ropama Inc... 440 358-1304
 380 W Prospect St Painesville (44077) *(G-12262)*
Roppe Corporation.. 419 435-8546
 1602 N Union St Fostoria (44830) *(G-7651)*
Roppe Holding Company... 419 435-6601
 106 N Main St Fostoria (44830) *(G-7652)*
Roppe Holding Company (PA)... 419 435-8546
 1602 N Union St Fostoria (44830) *(G-7653)*
Rose Metal Industries, Cleveland *Also Called: Rose Properties Inc (G-4649)*
Rose Metal Industries LLC.. 216 426-8615
 1155 Marquette St Cleveland (44114) *(G-4647)*
Rose Metal Industries LLC (PA)... 216 881-3355
 1536 E 43rd St Cleveland (44103) *(G-4648)*
Rose Products and Services Inc.. 614 443-7647
 545 Stimmel Rd Columbus (43223) *(G-5731)*
Rose Properties Inc... 216 881-6000
 1536 E 43rd St Cleveland (44103) *(G-4649)*
Rose Remington.. 513 755-1695
 7562 Bales St Liberty Township (45069) *(G-9210)*
Rosebud Mining Company... 740 768-2275
 9076 County Road 53 Bergholz (43908) *(G-1301)*
Rosebud Mining Company... 740 658-4217
 28490 Birmingham Rd Freeport (43973) *(G-7761)*
Rosebud's Real Food, Covington *Also Called: Rosebuds Ranch and Garden LLC (G-6031)*
Rosebuds Ranch and Garden LLC.. 937 214-1801
 473 E Troy Pike Covington (45318) *(G-6031)*
Rosenfeld Jewelry Inc... 440 446-0099
 5668 Mayfield Rd Cleveland (44124) *(G-4650)*
Ross Aluminum, Sidney *Also Called: P&The Mfg Acquisition LLC (G-13269)*
Ross Aluminum Castings LLC.. 937 492-4134
 815 Oak Ave Sidney (45365) *(G-13279)*
Ross Casting & Innovation LLC.. 937 497-4500
 402 S Kuther Rd Sidney (45365) *(G-13280)*
Ross County License Bureau, Willowick *Also Called: Ohio Department Public Safety (G-16033)*
Ross Group Inc... 937 427-3069
 4555 Lake Forest Dr Ste 650 Blue Ash (45242) *(G-1461)*
Ross Hx, Middletown *Also Called: Ross Hx LLC (G-10857)*
Ross Hx LLC (PA)... 513 217-1565
 2722 Cincinnati Dayton Rd Middletown (45044) *(G-10857)*
Ross Special Products Inc... 937 335-8406
 2500 W State Route 55 Troy (45373) *(G-14605)*
Ross-Co Redi-Mix Co Inc (PA).. 740 775-4466
 6430 State Route 159 Chillicothe (45601) *(G-2533)*
Rossborough Automotive Corp.. 216 941-6115
 3425 Service Rd Cleveland (44111) *(G-4651)*
Rossborough Supply Co.. 216 941-6115
 3425 Service Rd Cleveland (44111) *(G-4652)*
Rost Boundry, Mansfield *Also Called: CSM Horvath Ledgebrook Inc (G-9643)*
Rotadyne, Franklin *Also Called: Finzer Roller Inc (G-7675)*
Rotary Forms Press Inc (PA).. 937 393-3426
 835 S High St Hillsboro (45133) *(G-8465)*
Rotary Products Inc.. 740 747-2623
 202 W High St Ashley (43003) *(G-623)*
Rotary Products Inc (PA)... 740 747-2623
 117 E High St Ashley (43003) *(G-624)*
Rotary Smer Spcalist Group LLC.. 330 299-8210
 635 Wooster Rd W Barberton (44203) *(G-895)*
Rotek, Aurora *Also Called: Thyssenkrupp Rothe Erde USA Inc (G-736)*

Rotex Global LLC.. 513 541-1236
 1230 Knowlton St Cincinnati (45223) *(G-3351)*
Rothenbhler Whey Ingrdents Inc.. 440 632-0157
 15815 Nauvoo Rd Middlefield (44062) *(G-10785)*
Rothenbuhler Cheese Chalet LLC... 800 327-9477
 15815 Nauvoo Rd Middlefield (44062) *(G-10786)*
Rothenbuhler Holding Company... 440 632-6000
 15815 Nauvoo Rd Middlefield (44062) *(G-10787)*
Roto Met Rice, West Chester *Also Called: Roto-Die Company Inc (G-15503)*
Roto Mold, Mentor *Also Called: Interpak Inc (G-10476)*
Roto Solutions Inc... 330 279-2424
 8300 County Rd 189 Holmesville (44633) *(G-8551)*
Roto Tech Inc.. 937 859-8503
 2651 E River Rd Moraine (45439) *(G-11209)*
Roto-Die Company Inc... 513 942-3500
 4430 Mulhauser Rd West Chester (45011) *(G-15503)*
Rotocast Technologies Inc.. 330 798-9091
 1900 Englewood Ave Akron (44312) *(G-310)*
Rotoline USA LLC.. 330 677-3223
 4429 Crystal Pkwy Ste B Kent (44240) *(G-8856)*
Rotopolymers.. 216 645-0333
 26210 Emery Rd Ste 202 Cleveland (44128) *(G-4653)*
Rotopolymers, Warrensville Heights *Also Called: Polimeros Usa LLC (G-15230)*
Rotosolutions Inc... 419 903-0800
 1401 Jacobson Ave Ashland (44805) *(G-611)*
Rough Brothers Mfg Inc... 513 242-0310
 5513 Vine St Cincinnati (45217) *(G-3352)*
Roughcut LLC... 505 686-3615
 117 Pinecrest Dr Saint Clairsville (43950) *(G-12922)*
Round Mate Systems.. 419 675-3334
 13840 Us Highway 68 Kenton (43326) *(G-8899)*
Rouster Lfting Rgging A Mzzlla, Cleveland *Also Called: Mazzella Lifting Tech Inc (G-4375)*
Route 62... 740 548-5418
 795 W Coshocton St Johnstown (43031) *(G-8777)*
Rowe Premix Inc.. 937 678-9015
 10107 Us Rr 127 N West Manchester (45382) *(G-15624)*
Rowend Industries Inc.. 419 333-8300
 1035 Napoleon St Ste 101 Fremont (43420) *(G-7806)*
Rowmark LLC (PA).. 419 425-8974
 5409 Hamlet Dr Findlay (45840) *(G-7557)*
Roxane Laboratories, Columbus *Also Called: Hikma Labs Inc (G-5437)*
Roy I Kaufman Inc... 740 382-0643
 1672 Marion Upper Sandusky Rd Marion (43302) *(G-9877)*
Roy Retrac Incorporated... 740 564-5552
 100 E Campus View Blvd Ste 250 Columbus (43235) *(G-5732)*
Royal Acme, Cleveland *Also Called: Ace Rubber Stamp & Off Sup Co (G-3590)*
Royal Acme Corporation (PA).. 216 241-1477
 3110 Payne Ave Cleveland (44114) *(G-4654)*
Royal Adhesives.. 440 708-1212
 10255 Queens Way Chagrin Falls (44023) *(G-2420)*
Royal Adhesives & Sealants LLC.. 440 708-1212
 17340 Munn Rd Chagrin Falls (44023) *(G-2421)*
Royal Appliance Intl Co.. 440 996-2000
 7005 Cochran Rd Cleveland (44139) *(G-4655)*
Royal Cabinet Design Co Inc... 216 267-5330
 15800 Commerce Park Dr Cleveland (44142) *(G-4656)*
Royal Chemical Company Ltd... 330 467-1300
 1755 Enterprise Pkwy Ste 100 Twinsburg (44087) *(G-14728)*
Royal Chemical Company Ltd (HQ)... 330 467-1300
 8679 Freeway Dr Macedonia (44056) *(G-9571)*
Royal Docks Brewing Co LLC.. 330 353-9103
 5646 Wales Ave Nw Massillon (44646) *(G-10140)*
Royal Group, The, Marion *Also Called: Schwarz Partners Packaging LLC (G-9879)*
Royal Metal Products LLC.. 740 397-8842
 325 Commerce Dr Mount Vernon (43050) *(G-11293)*
Royal Pad Products, Cincinnati *Also Called: Loroco Industries Inc (G-3113)*
Royal Plastics Inc... 440 352-1357
 9410 Pineneedle Dr Mentor (44060) *(G-10548)*
Royal Powder Corporation.. 216 898-0074
 4800 Briar Rd Cleveland (44135) *(G-4657)*
Royal Wire Products Inc (PA)... 440 237-8787
 13450 York Delta Dr North Royalton (44133) *(G-11892)*

Royalton Archtctral Fbrication.. 440 582-0400
13155 York Delta Dr North Royalton (44133) *(G-11893)*

Royalton Foodservice Eqp Co... 440 237-0806
9981 York Theta Dr North Royalton (44133) *(G-11894)*

Royalton Industries Inc... 440 748-9900
12450 Eaton Commerce Pkwy Ste 1 Columbia Station (44028) *(G-5020)*

Royalton Manufacturing Inc.. 440 237-2233
1169 Brittain Rd Akron (44305) *(G-311)*

Royster-Clark Inc... 513 941-4100
10743 Brower Rd North Bend (45052) *(G-11706)*

Rozzi Company, Loveland *Also Called: Rozzi Company Inc (G-9502)*

Rozzi Company Inc (PA)... 513 683-0620
10059 Loveland Madeira Rd Loveland (45140) *(G-9502)*

Rozzi Company Inc... 513 683-0620
6047 State Route 350 Martinsville (45146) *(G-9902)*

RP Hoskins Inc... 216 631-1000
3033 W 44th St Cleveland (44113) *(G-4658)*

Rpa Electronic Distrs Inc.. 937 223-7001
122 S Terry St Dayton (45403) *(G-6553)*

Rpg Industries Inc.. 937 698-9801
3571 Ginghamsburg Frederick Rd Tipp City (45371) *(G-14153)*

RPI Color Service Inc.. 513 471-4040
1950 Radcliff Dr Cincinnati (45204) *(G-3353)*

RPI Graphic Data Solutions, Cincinnati *Also Called: RPI Color Service Inc (G-3353)*

RPM, Arcadia *Also Called: RPM Carbide Die Inc (G-517)*

RPM Carbide Die Inc... 419 894-6426
202 E South St Arcadia (44804) *(G-517)*

RPM Consumer Holding Company (HQ).................................... 330 273-5090
2628 Pearl Rd Medina (44256) *(G-10371)*

RPM International Inc (PA)... 330 273-5090
2628 Pearl Rd Medina (44256) *(G-10372)*

Rpmi, Lebanon *Also Called: Rpmi Packaging Inc (G-9109)*

Rpmi Packaging Inc.. 513 398-4040
3899 S Us Route 42 Lebanon (45036) *(G-9109)*

Rpp Containers, Cincinnati *Also Called: Dadco Inc (G-2816)*

Rpui, Lebanon *Also Called: Restortion Parts Unlimited Inc (G-9108)*

RR Donnelley, West Chester *Also Called: R R Donnelley & Sons Company (G-15494)*

RR Donnelley & Sons Company.. 614 221-8385
41 S High St Ste 3750 Columbus (43215) *(G-5733)*

Rrysburg Sunoco, Waterville *Also Called: Franklin (G-15243)*

RS Imprints LLC... 330 872-5905
5 S Milton Blvd Newton Falls (44444) *(G-11656)*

RS Industries Inc... 216 351-8200
1455 E Schaaf Rd Brooklyn Heights (44131) *(G-1699)*

Rs Manufacturing Inc... 440 946-8002
8878 East Ave Mentor (44060) *(G-10549)*

RS&b Industries LLC.. 330 255-6000
1147 Akron Rd Wooster (44691) *(G-16165)*

Rsa Controls Inc... 513 476-6277
6422 Fountains Blvd West Chester (45069) *(G-15504)*

Rsb Spine LLC.. 216 241-2804
2530 Superior Ave E Ste 703 Cleveland (44114) *(G-4659)*

Rsfi Office Furniture, Worthington *Also Called: Recycled Systems Furniture Inc (G-16210)*

RSI Company (PA).. 216 360-9800
24050 Commerce Park Ste 200 Beachwood (44122) *(G-1020)*

Rsl LLC... 330 392-8900
1160 Paige Ave Ne Warren (44483) *(G-15203)*

Rsp Industries Inc.. 440 823-4502
415 Hazelwood Dr Chagrin Falls (44022) *(G-2384)*

Rss Maclin, Barberton *Also Called: Rotary Smer Spcalist Group LLC (G-895)*

Rsv Wlding Fbrction McHning In... 419 592-0993
M063 County Road 12 Napoleon (43545) *(G-11333)*

Rsw Distributors LLC... 502 587-8877
4700 Ashwood Dr Ste 200 Blue Ash (45241) *(G-1462)*

Rsw Technologies LLC.. 419 662-8100
135 Dixie Hwy Rossford (43460) *(G-12871)*

RT Industries Inc (PA).. 937 335-5784
110 Foss Way Troy (45373) *(G-14606)*

RTC Converters Inc.. 937 743-2300
300 Shotwell Dr Franklin (45005) *(G-7700)*

RTD Electronics Inc.. 330 487-0716
1632 Enterprise Pkwy Ste D Twinsburg (44087) *(G-14729)*

Rti, Niles *Also Called: Rmi Titanium Company LLC (G-11683)*

Rti Alloys... 330 652-9952
1000 Warren Ave Niles (44446) *(G-11686)*

Rti Alloys, Canton *Also Called: Rmi Titanium Company LLC (G-2217)*

Rti Alloys Tpd, Canton *Also Called: Rmi Titanium Company LLC (G-2218)*

Rti International Metals Inc
1000 Warren Ave Niles (44446) *(G-11687)*

Rti Niles, Niles *Also Called: Rmi Titanium Company LLC (G-11684)*

Rti Remmele Engineering Inc... 651 635-4179
5801 Postal Rd Cleveland (44181) *(G-4660)*

Rti Securex LLC.. 937 859-5290
20 S 1st St Miamisburg (45342) *(G-10679)*

RTS Companies (us) Inc... 440 275-3077
2900 Industrial Park Dr Austinburg (44010) *(G-749)*

Rtsi LLC.. 440 542-3066
6161 Cochran Rd Ste G Solon (44139) *(G-13416)*

Rtx Corporation.. 330 784-5477
6051 W Airport Dr North Canton (44720) *(G-11757)*

RTZ Manufacturing Co.. 614 848-8366
12755 Fairview Rd Heath (43056) *(G-8330)*

Rubber & Plastics News, Cuyahoga Falls *Also Called: Crain Communications Inc (G-6077)*

Rubber Associates Inc.. 330 745-2186
1522 Turkeyfoot Lake Rd New Franklin (44203) *(G-11443)*

Rubber City Industries Inc... 330 990-9641
471 E Bergey St Wadsworth (44281) *(G-15064)*

Rubber City Machinery Corp... 330 434-3500
One Thousand Sweitzer Avenue Akron (44311) *(G-312)*

Rubber Duck 4x4 Inc.. 513 889-1735
1622 Smith Rd Hamilton (45013) *(G-8239)*

Rubber Grinding Inc... 419 692-3000
1430 N Main St Delphos (45833) *(G-6771)*

Rubber Seal Products, Dayton *Also Called: Teknol Inc (G-6613)*

Rubber World Magazine, Akron *Also Called: Lippincott and Peto Inc (G-220)*

Rubber World Magazine Inc... 330 864-2122
1741 Akron Peninsula Rd Akron (44313) *(G-313)*

Rubber-Tech Inc... 937 274-1114
5208 Wadsworth Rd Dayton (45414) *(G-6554)*

Rubbermaid, Kent *Also Called: Newell Brands Inc (G-8839)*

Rubbermaid, Mogadore *Also Called: Rubbermaid Home Products (G-11080)*

Rubbermaid Home Products... 330 733-7771
3200 Gilchrist Rd Mogadore (44260) *(G-11080)*

Rubbermaid Incorporated... 330 733-7771
3200 Gilchrist Rd Mogadore (44260) *(G-11081)*

Rubberset Company... 800 345-4939
101 W Prospect Ave Cleveland (44115) *(G-4661)*

Rubbertec Industrial Pdts Co... 740 657-3345
7580 Commerce Ct Lewis Center (43035) *(G-9179)*

Rubex Inc.. 614 875-6343
3709 Grove City Rd Grove City (43123) *(G-8118)*

Rudd Equipment Company Inc... 513 321-7833
11807 Enterprise Dr Cincinnati (45241) *(G-3354)*

Rudolph Foods, Lima *Also Called: Rudolph Foods Company Inc (G-9287)*

Rudolph Foods Company Inc (PA).. 909 383-7463
6575 Bellefontaine Rd Lima (45804) *(G-9287)*

Rudy's Strudel & Bakery, Cleveland *Also Called: Rudys Strudel Shop (G-4662)*

Rudys Strudel Shop.. 440 886-4430
5580 Ridge Rd Cleveland (44129) *(G-4662)*

Ruff Neon & Lighting Maint Inc.. 440 350-6267
295 W Prospect St Painesville (44077) *(G-12263)*

Ruhe Sales Inc (PA)... 419 943-3357
5450 State Route 109 Leipsic (45856) *(G-9140)*

Rultract Inc... 330 856-9808
8598 Kimblewick Ln Ne Warren (44484) *(G-15204)*

Rumford Paper Company.. 937 242-9230
8540 Gander Creek Dr Miamisburg (45342) *(G-10680)*

Rumpke Container Service, Cincinnati *Also Called: Rumpke Transportation Co LLC (G-3356)*

Rumpke Transportation Co LLC (HQ)....................................... 513 851-0122
10795 Hughes Rd Cincinnati (45251) *(G-3355)*

Rumpke Transportation Co LLC ... 513 242-4600
553 Vine St Cincinnati (45202) *(G-3356)*

Runkles Sawmill LLC ... 937 663-0115
2534 Dialton Rd Saint Paris (43072) *(G-12974)*

Ruple Trucking, Willoughby Hills Also Called: Chagrin Vly Stl Erectors Inc *(G-16023)*

Ruscilli Real Estate Services ... 614 923-6400
5100 Parkcenter Ave Ste 100 Dublin (43017) *(G-6932)*

Rusco Design Center, Youngstown Also Called: Rusco Products Inc *(G-16432)*

Rusco Products Inc ... 330 758-0378
423 E Western Reserve Rd Youngstown (44514) *(G-16432)*

Ruscoe, Akron Also Called: Pmbp Legacy Co Inc *(G-278)*

Ruscoe Company ... 330 253-8148
485 Kenmore Blvd Akron (44301) *(G-314)*

Rush Fixture & Millwork Co ... 216 241-9100
1978 W 3rd St Cleveland (44113) *(G-4663)*

Rush Woodworks ... 419 569-2370
2116 Kings Corners Rd E Mansfield (44904) *(G-9715)*

Rush, R L Tool & Pattern, Bucyrus Also Called: R L Rush Tool & Pattern Inc *(G-1866)*

Ruskin Manufacturing ... 937 476-6500
4509 Springfield St Dayton (45431) *(G-6172)*

Russ Jr Enterprises Inc ... 440 237-4642
6165 Royalton Rd North Royalton (44133) *(G-11035)*

Russel Hunt Total Land Care, Steubenville Also Called: Russell Hunt *(G-13676)*

Russel Upholstery, Ashtabula Also Called: Custom Craft Collection Inc *(G-630)*

Russell Cast Stone Inc ... 856 753-4000
4600 Devitt Dr West Chester (45246) *(G-15582)*

Russell Group United LLC ... 614 353-6853
1250 Arthur E Adams Dr Ste 205 Columbus (43221) *(G-5734)*

Russell Hunt ... 740 264-1196
175 Detmar Rd Steubenville (43953) *(G-13676)*

Russell L Garber (PA) ... 937 548-6224
4891 Clark Station Rd Greenville (45331) *(G-8058)*

Russell Products Co Inc ... 330 535-3391
1066 Home Ave Akron (44310) *(G-315)*

Russell Products Co Inc ... 330 535-9246
275 N Forge St Ste 1 Akron (44304) *(G-316)*

Russell Products Co Inc (PA) ... 330 535-9246
275 N Forge St Akron (44304) *(G-317)*

Russell Standard Corporation ... 330 733-9400
990 Hazel St Akron (44305) *(G-318)*

Russell T Bundy Associates Inc ... 419 526-4454
1711 N Main St Mansfield (44903) *(G-9716)*

Russell T Bundy Associates Inc ... 740 965-3008
601 W Cherry St Sunbury (43074) *(G-13964)*

Russos Ravioli LLC ... 513 833-7700
5950 Montgomery Rd Cincinnati (45213) *(G-3357)*

Rust Belt Broncos LLC ... 330 533-0048
6145 State Route 446 Canfield (44406) *(G-2017)*

Rustic Cheesecake LLC ... 419 680-6156
1029 Miller St Fremont (43420) *(G-7807)*

Rutland Township ... 740 742-2805
33325 Jessie Creek Rd Bidwell (45614) *(G-1326)*

Rv Mobile Power LLC ... 855 427-7978
830 Kinnear Rd Columbus (43212) *(G-5735)*

Rv Xpress Inc ... 937 418-0127
501 East St Piqua (45356) *(G-12553)*

Rvtronix Corporation ... 440 359-7200
34099 Melinz Pkwy Unit E Eastlake (44095) *(G-7048)*

RW Beckett Corporation (PA) ... 440 327-1060
38251 Center Ridge Rd North Ridgeville (44039) *(G-11860)*

Rw Screw LLC ... 330 837-9211
999 Oberlin Ave Sw Massillon (44647) *(G-10141)*

Rxscan, Lewis Center Also Called: Retail Management Products Ltd *(G-9178)*

Ryan Development Corporation ... 937 587-2266
1 Ryan Rd Peebles (45660) *(G-12331)*

Ryanworks Inc ... 937 438-1282
175 E Alex Bell Rd Ste 264 Dayton (45459) *(G-6555)*

Ryder Engraving Inc ... 740 927-7193
1029 Hazelton Etna Rd Sw Pataskala (43062) *(G-12307)*

Ryder-Heil Bronze Inc ... 419 562-2841
126 E Irving St Bucyrus (44820) *(G-1868)*

Ryman Grinders Inc ... 330 652-5080
704 Warren Ave Niles (44446) *(G-11688)*

Ryse Aero Holdco Inc ... 513 318-9907
6951 Cintas Blvd Mason (45040) *(G-10051)*

S & A Industries Corporation ... 330 733-6040
1500 Exeter Rd Akron (44306) *(G-319)*

S & A Industries Corporation (DH) ... 330 733-6040
1471 Exeter Rd Akron (44306) *(G-320)*

S & D Architectural Metals ... 440 582-2560
12955 York Delta Dr North Royalton (44133) *(G-11896)*

S & G Manufacturing Group LLC (PA) ... 614 529-0100
4830 Northwest Pkwy Hilliard (43026) *(G-8437)*

S & H Industries Inc ... 216 831-0550
5200 Richmond Rd Cleveland (44146) *(G-4664)*

S & H Industries Inc (PA) ... 216 831-0550
5200 Richmond Rd Bedford (44146) *(G-1154)*

S & H Industries Inc ... 216 831-0550
14577 Lorain Ave Cleveland (44111) *(G-4665)*

S & J Lumber, Thurman Also Called: S & J Lumber Company LLC *(G-14073)*

S & J Lumber Company LLC ... 740 245-5804
3667 Garners Ford Rd Thurman (45685) *(G-14073)*

S & K Metal Polsg & Buffing ... 513 732-6662
4194 Taylor Rd Batavia (45103) *(G-940)*

S & K Products Company ... 419 268-2244
4540 St Rt 127 Celina (45822) *(G-2347)*

S & R Egg, Rossburg Also Called: Fort Recovery Equity Exchange *(G-12862)*

S & S Aggregates Inc ... 419 938-5604
4540 State Route 39 Perrysville (44864) *(G-12448)*

S & S Aggregates Inc (HQ) ... 740 453-0721
3570 S River Rd Zanesville (43701) *(G-16561)*

S & S Wldg Fabg Machining Inc ... 330 392-7878
2587 Miller Graber Rd Newton Falls (44444) *(G-11657)*

S & W Express Inc ... 330 683-2747
8849 Lincoln Way E Orrville (44667) *(G-12149)*

S A Langmack Company ... 216 541-0500
13400 Glenside Rd Cleveland (44110) *(G-4666)*

S A Oma-U Inc ... 330 487-0602
9329 Ravenna Rd Ste A Twinsburg (44087) *(G-14730)*

S A S Rubber, Painesville Also Called: Yokohama Tire Corporation *(G-12281)*

S and S Tool Inc ... 440 593-4000
576 Blair St Conneaut (44030) *(G-5931)*

S Beckman Print Grphic Sltons ... 614 864-2232
376 Morrison Rd Ste D Columbus (43213) *(G-5736)*

S C Fastening Systems, Macedonia Also Called: SC Fire Protection Ltd *(G-9572)*

S C Industries Inc ... 216 732-9000
24460 Lakeland Blvd Euclid (44132) *(G-7300)*

S DH Flow Contro Ls LLC ... 513 834-8432
1118 Ferris Rd Amelia (45102) *(G-463)*

S E Johnson Companies Inc (DH) ... 419 893-8731
1360 Ford St Maumee (43537) *(G-10228)*

S F Mock & Associates LLC ... 937 438-0196
105 Westpark Rd Dayton (45459) *(G-6556)*

S Holley Lumber LLC ... 440 272-5315
7143 Noble Rd Windsor (44099) *(G-16076)*

S I Distributing Inc ... 419 647-4909
13540 Spencerville Rd Spencerville (45887) *(G-13489)*

S I T Strings Co Inc ... 330 434-8010
2493 Romig Rd Akron (44320) *(G-321)*

S J Roth Enterprises Inc ... 513 543-1140
900 Kieley Pl Cincinnati (45217) *(G-3358)*

S J T Enterprises Inc ... 440 617-1100
28045 Ranney Pkwy Ste B Westlake (44145) *(G-15780)*

S Lehman Central Warehouse ... 330 828-8828
289 Kurzen Rd N Dalton (44618) *(G-6142)*

S M C, Upper Sandusky Also Called: Schmidt Machine Company *(G-14823)*

S O S Shades, Lewis Center Also Called: Inside Outfitters Inc *(G-9165)*

S P E Inc ... 330 733-0101
3300 Gilchrist Rd Mogadore (44260) *(G-11082)*

S R Door Inc (PA) ... 740 927-3558
1120 O Neill Dr Hebron (43025) *(G-8360)*

S R P M Inc ... 440 248-8440
30300 Bruce Industrial Pkwy Ste B Cleveland (44139) *(G-4667)*

ALPHABETIC SECTION

S T C, Canton *Also Called: Stark Truss Company Inc (G-2235)*

S T Tool & Design Inc..440 357-1250
9452 Mercantile Dr Mentor (44060) *(G-10550)*

S Toys Holdings LLC...330 656-0440
10010 Aurora Hudson Rd Streetsboro (44241) *(G-13789)*

S-P Company Inc (PA)...330 782-5651
400 W Railroad St Ste 1 Columbiana (44408) *(G-5050)*

S-Tek Inc (PA)..440 439-8232
2095 Midway Dr Twinsburg (44087) *(G-14732)*

S.E.S. Engineering, Alliance *Also Called: Steel Eqp Specialists Inc (G-427)*

S&B Metal Pdts Twinsburg LLC (PA)...330 487-5790
2060 Case Pkwy Twinsburg (44087) *(G-14731)*

S&G Distribution, Hilliard *Also Called: S & G Manufacturing Group LLC (G-8437)*

S&L Fleet Services Inc...740 549-2722
670 Meridian Way Ste 252 Westerville (43082) *(G-15677)*

S&M Trucking LLC...661 310-2585
5700 Gateway Ste 400 Mason (45040) *(G-10052)*

S&Ps, Warren *Also Called: Aptiv Services Us LLC (G-15144)*

S&R Lumber LLC...740 352-6135
207 Sugar Run Rd Piketon (45661) *(G-12484)*

S&S Sign Service..614 279-9722
485 Ternstedt Ln Columbus (43228) *(G-5737)*

S&V Industries Inc (PA)..330 666-1986
5054 Paramount Dr Medina (44256) *(G-10373)*

Sabatino Cabinet, Salem *Also Called: Joseph Sabatino (G-13007)*

Sabco Industries Inc...419 531-5347
5242 Angola Rd Ste 150 Toledo (43615) *(G-14461)*

Sabin Robbins Paper Company, Mansfield *Also Called: Eagles Nest Holdings LLC (G-9649)*

Sabre Industries Inc..419 542-1420
761 W High St Hicksville (43526) *(G-8379)*

Saco Aei Polymers Inc..330 995-1600
1395 Danner Dr Aurora (44202) *(G-735)*

Saco Lowell Parts LLC...330 794-1535
1395 Triplett Blvd Akron (44306) *(G-322)*

Sadaf Oil & Gas Inc...330 448-6631
7257 Warren Sharon Rd Brookfield (44403) *(G-1673)*

Saehwa IMC Na Inc (PA)...330 645-6653
2200 Massillon Rd Akron (44312) *(G-323)*

Saf-Holland Inc..513 874-7888
105 Mercantile Dr Fairfield (45014) *(G-7404)*

Safc Cleveland, Cleveland *Also Called: Research Organics LLC (G-4628)*

Safe Grain Max Tronix, Dayton *Also Called: Safe-Grain Inc (G-6557)*

Safe Haven Brands LLC..937 550-9407
217 S Pioneer Blvd Springboro (45066) *(G-13519)*

Safe-Grain Inc...513 398-2500
10522 Success Ln Dayton (45458) *(G-6557)*

Safe-Grain Inc (PA)...513 398-2500
417 Wards Corner Rd Ste B Loveland (45140) *(G-9503)*

Safecor Health LLC...614 351-6117
4000 Business Park Dr Columbus (43204) *(G-5738)*

Safecor Health LLC (PA)...781 933-8780
4060 Business Pk Dr Ste B Columbus (43204) *(G-5739)*

Safeguard, Streetsboro *Also Called: Safeguard Technology Inc (G-13790)*

Safeguard Technology Inc..330 995-5200
1460 Miller Pkwy Streetsboro (44241) *(G-13790)*

Safelite Autoglass, Columbus *Also Called: Safelite Group Inc (G-5740)*

Safelite Group Inc (DH)..614 210-9000
7400 Safelite Way Columbus (43235) *(G-5740)*

Safeway Packaging Inc (PA)...419 629-3200
300 White Mountain Dr New Bremen (45869) *(G-11408)*

Safeway Safety Step LLC..513 942-7837
5242 Rialto Rd West Chester (45069) *(G-15505)*

Safran Usa Inc...513 247-7000
300 E Business Way Sharonville (45241) *(G-13173)*

Sage Integration Holdings LLC (PA)..330 733-8183
4075 Karg Industrial Pkwy Ste B Kent (44240) *(G-8857)*

Sagequest LLC..216 896-7243
31500 Bainbridge Rd Ste 1 Solon (44139) *(G-13417)*

Saia-Burgess Lcc..937 898-3621
801 Scholz Dr Vandalia (45377) *(G-14958)*

Saica, Hamilton *Also Called: Saica Pack US LLC (G-8240)*

Saica Pack US LLC..513 399-5602
2995 Mcbride Ct Hamilton (45011) *(G-8240)*

Sailors Tailor Inc..937 862-7781
1480 Spring Valley Painters Rd Spring Valley (45370) *(G-13491)*

Saint Ctherines Metalworks Inc..216 409-0576
1985 W 68th St Cleveland (44102) *(G-4668)*

Saint Gobain Crystals, Newbury *Also Called: Saint-Gobain Ceramics Plas Inc (G-11637)*

Saint Johnsbury Perfect Scents..330 846-0175
3324 State Route 7 New Waterford (44445) *(G-11559)*

Saint-Gobain Ceramics Plas Inc..440 542-2712
12359 Kinsman Rd Newbury (44065) *(G-11637)*

Saint-Gobain Ceramics Plas Inc..330 673-5860
3840 Fishcreek Rd Stow (44224) *(G-13721)*

Saint-Gobain Hycomp LLC..440 234-2002
17960 Englewood Dr Cleveland (44130) *(G-4669)*

Saint-Gobain Norpro, Stow *Also Called: Saint-Gobain Ceramics Plas Inc (G-13721)*

Saint-Gobain Norpro Corp (HQ)..330 673-5860
3840 Fishcreek Rd Stow (44224) *(G-13722)*

Saint-Gobain Prfmce Plas Corp...330 798-6981
2664 Gilchrist Rd Akron (44305) *(G-324)*

Saint-Gobain Prfmce Plas Corp...614 889-2220
6250 Shier Rings Rd Dublin (43016) *(G-6933)*

Saint-Gobain Prfmce Plas Corp...330 296-9948
335 N Diamond St Ravenna (44266) *(G-12731)*

Saint-Gobain Prfmce Plas Corp...440 836-6900
31500 Solon Rd Solon (44139) *(G-13418)*

Sairam Oil Inc..440 289-8232
4610 Milford Ave Parma (44134) *(G-12294)*

Sajar Plastics, Inc., Middlefield *Also Called: SPI Liquidation Inc (G-10790)*

Sakamura USA Inc...740 223-7777
970 Kellogg Pkwy Marion (43302) *(G-9878)*

Sakrete Inc...513 242-3644
5155 Fischer Ave Cincinnati (45217) *(G-3359)*

Salco Machine Inc...330 456-8281
3822 Victory Ave Louisville (44641) *(G-9470)*

Salem Manufacturing & Sls Inc...614 572-4242
171 N Hamilton Rd Columbus (43213) *(G-5741)*

Salem Mill & Cabinet Co..330 337-9568
1455 Quaker Cir Salem (44460) *(G-13028)*

Salem Welding & Supply Company...330 332-4517
475 Prospect St Salem (44460) *(G-13029)*

Sales Office Rob Jordan Vp Sls, Hilliard *Also Called: Textiles Inc (G-8446)*

Salient Systems Inc...614 792-5800
4393 Tuller Rd Ste K Dublin (43017) *(G-6934)*

Salindia LLC...614 501-4799
2756 Eastland Mall Columbus (43232) *(G-5742)*

Salineville Office, Salineville *Also Called: M3 Midstream LLC (G-13039)*

Salon Styling Concepts Ltd..216 539-0437
20900 Libby Rd Maple Heights (44137) *(G-9760)*

Salsa Rica II LLC..740 616-9918
3744 Fishinger Blvd Hilliard (43026) *(G-8438)*

Salt Creek Lumber Company Inc...330 695-3500
11657 Salt Creek Rd Fredericksburg (44627) *(G-7733)*

Salted Dough...216 288-2124
9174 Broadview Rd Broadview Heights (44147) *(G-1666)*

Salus Enterprises North Amer, Mason *Also Called: Salus North America Inc (G-10053)*

Salus North America Inc...888 387-2587
4700 Duke Dr Ste 200 Mason (45040) *(G-10053)*

Sam Americas Inc...330 628-1118
3555 Gilchrist Rd Mogadore (44260) *(G-11083)*

Sam Dong America Inc..740 363-1985
801 Pittsburgh Dr Delaware (43015) *(G-6747)*

Sam Dong Ohio Inc...740 363-1985
801 Pittsburgh Dr Delaware (43015) *(G-6748)*

Samb LLC Services...937 660-0115
504 Sorna Dr Englewood (45322) *(G-7241)*

Samegoal Inc...216 766-5713
3401 Enterprise Pkwy Ste 340 Beachwood (44122) *(G-1021)*

Samhain Publishing Ltd (llc)...513 453-4688
11821 Mason Montgomery Rd # 2 Cincinnati (45249) *(G-3360)*

Samkat Enterprises Inc 937 398-6704
　10811 Schiller Rd Medway (45341) *(G-10399)*

Sammy S Auto Detail 614 263-2728
　3514 Cleveland Ave Columbus (43224) *(G-5743)*

Sample Machining Inc 937 258-3338
　220 N Jersey St Dayton (45403) *(G-6558)*

Sams Graphic Industries 330 821-4710
　611 Homeworth Rd Alliance (44601) *(G-422)*

Samsel Rope & Marine Supply Co (PA) 216 241-0333
　1285 Old River Rd Uppr Cleveland (44113) *(G-4670)*

Samsel Supply Company, Cleveland *Also Called: Samsel Rope & Marine Supply Co (G-4670)*

Samson 614 504-8038
　772 N High St Ste 101 Columbus (43215) *(G-5744)*

Samuel Son & Co (usa) Inc 740 522-2500
　1455 James Pkwy Heath (43056) *(G-8331)*

Samuel Adams Brewery Company Ltd 513 412-3200
　1625 Central Pkwy Cincinnati (45214) *(G-3361)*

Samuel L Peters LLC 513 745-1500
　10001 Alliance Rd Ste 1 Blue Ash (45242) *(G-1463)*

Samuel Steel Pickling Company, Twinsburg *Also Called: Worthngton Smuel Coil Proc LLC (G-14758)*

Samuels Products Inc 513 891-4456
　9851 Redhill Dr Blue Ash (45242) *(G-1464)*

San-Fab Conveyor and Automtn, Sandusky *Also Called: Sandusky Fabricating & Sls Inc (G-13089)*

Sancap Liner Technology Inc 330 821-1166
　16125 Armour St Ne Alliance (44601) *(G-423)*

Sancast Inc 740 622-8660
　535 Clow Ln Coshocton (43812) *(G-5995)*

Sanctuary Software Studio Inc 330 666-9690
　3090 W Market St Ste 300 Fairlawn (44333) *(G-7448)*

Sand & Gravel, Lebanon *Also Called: Carl E Oeder Sons Sand & Grav (G-9066)*

Sand PROperties&landscaping 440 360-7386
　933 Dover Center Rd Westlake (44145) *(G-15781)*

Sand Rock Enterprises Inc 740 407-2735
　14033 Sand Rock Rd Glenford (43739) *(G-7979)*

Sandco Industries 419 547-3273
　567 Premier Dr Clyde (43410) *(G-4978)*

Sandpiper, Mansfield *Also Called: Warren Rupp Inc (G-9730)*

Sandra Weddington 740 417-4286
　1400 Stratford Rd Delaware (43015) *(G-6749)*

Sands Hill Mining LLC 740 384-4211
　948 State Route 7 N Gallipolis (45631) *(G-7901)*

Sandusky Fabricating & Sls Inc (PA) 419 626-4465
　2000 Superior St Sandusky (44870) *(G-13089)*

Sandusky International Inc 419 626-5340
　510 W Water St Sandusky (44870) *(G-13090)*

Sandusky Machine & Tool Inc 419 626-8359
　2223 Tiffin Ave Sandusky (44870) *(G-13091)*

Sandusky Newspaper Group, Sandusky *Also Called: Isaac Foster Mack Co (G-13067)*

Sandusky Packaging Corporation 419 626-8520
　2016 George St Sandusky (44870) *(G-13092)*

Sandusky Technologies LLC 419 332-8484
　2107 Hayes Ave Fremont (43420) *(G-7808)*

Sandvik Inc 614 438-6579
　6325 Huntley Rd Columbus (43229) *(G-5745)*

Sandvik Hyperion, Columbus *Also Called: Sandvik Inc (G-5745)*

Sandvik Rock Proc Sltons N AME 216 431-2600
　1214 Marquette St Cleveland (44114) *(G-4671)*

Sandvik Rock Proc Sltons N AME (HQ) 216 431-2600
　3900 Kelley Ave Cleveland (44114) *(G-4672)*

Sandwisch Enterprises Inc (PA) 419 944-6446
　1644 Campbell St Toledo (43607) *(G-14462)*

Sanger & EBY Design LLC 513 784-9046
　501 Chestnut St Cincinnati (45203) *(G-3362)*

Sangraf International Inc 216 543-3288
　159 Crocker Park Blvd Ste 100 Westlake (44145) *(G-15782)*

Sanoh America Inc (HQ) 419 425-2600
　1849 Industrial Dr Findlay (45840) *(G-7558)*

Sanreed Management Group LLC 513 722-1037
　1132 Ferris Rd Amelia (45102) *(G-464)*

Sansei Showa Co Ltd 440 248-4440
　31000 Bainbridge Rd Cleveland (44139) *(G-4673)*

Santec Resources Inc 614 664-9540
　2324 Myrtle Valley Dr Columbus (43228) *(G-5746)*

Santos Industrial Ltd (PA) 937 299-7333
　3034 Dryden Rd Moraine (45439) *(G-11210)*

Sapphire Creek Wnery Grdns LLC 440 543-7777
　16965 Park Circle Dr Chagrin Falls (44023) *(G-2422)*

Sara Wood Pharmaceuticals, Mason *Also Called: Sara Wood Pharmaceuticals LLC (G-10054)*

Sara Wood Pharmaceuticals LLC 513 833-5502
　4518 Margaret Ct Mason (45040) *(G-10054)*

Saraga International Food, Columbus *Also Called: Saraga Northern Lights LLC (G-5747)*

Saraga Northern Lights LLC 614 928-3100
　3353 Cleveland Ave Columbus (43224) *(G-5747)*

Sarahs Vineyard Inc 330 929-8057
　1204 W Steels Corners Rd Cuyahoga Falls (44223) *(G-6116)*

Sarasota Quality Products 440 899-9820
　27330 Center Ridge Rd Westlake (44145) *(G-15783)*

Sarcom Inc 614 854-1300
　8337a Green Meadows Dr N Lewis Center (43035) *(G-9180)*

Sardinia Concrete Company (PA) 513 248-0090
　911 Us Route 50 Milford (45150) *(G-10921)*

Sardinia Ready Mix Inc 937 446-2523
　9 Oakdale Ave Sardinia (45171) *(G-13108)*

Sare Plastics, Alliance *Also Called: Stuchell Products LLC (G-428)*

Sarepta Therapeutics 614 766-3296
　5200 Blazer Pkwy Dublin (43017) *(G-6935)*

Sarica, Urbana *Also Called: Sarica Manufacturing Company (G-14847)*

Sarica Manufacturing Company 937 484-4030
　240 W Twain Ave Urbana (43078) *(G-14847)*

Sarka Bros Machining Inc 419 532-2393
　607 Ottawa St Kalida (45853) *(G-8786)*

Sarka Conveyor, Tiffin *Also Called: Sarka Shtmtl & Fabrication Inc (G-14102)*

Sarka Shtmtl & Fabrication Inc 419 447-4377
　70 Clinton Ave Tiffin (44883) *(G-14102)*

Sasha Electronics Inc 419 662-8100
　135 Dixie Hwy Rossford (43460) *(G-12872)*

Satco Inc 513 707-6150
　457 Wards Corner Rd Loveland (45140) *(G-9504)*

Satellite Data Inc 440 926-9300
　577 Main St Grafton (44044) *(G-8004)*

Satelytics Inc 419 372-0160
　6330 Levis Commons Blvd Perrysburg (43551) *(G-12424)*

Sattler Companies Inc 330 239-2552
　1455 Wolf Creek Trl Wadsworth (44281) *(G-15065)*

Sattler Machine Products, Wadsworth *Also Called: Sattler Companies Inc (G-15065)*

Saturday Knight Ltd (PA) 513 641-1400
　4330 Winton Rd Cincinnati (45232) *(G-3363)*

Sauder, Archbold *Also Called: Sauder Woodworking Co (G-546)*

Sauder Manufacturing Co (HQ) 419 445-7670
　930 W Barre Rd Archbold (43502) *(G-544)*

Sauder Manufacturing Co 419 682-3061
　201 Horton St Stryker (43557) *(G-13913)*

Sauder Woodworking Co 419 446-2711
　330 N Clydes Way Archbold (43502) *(G-545)*

Sauder Woodworking Co (PA) 419 446-2711
　502 Middle St Archbold (43502) *(G-546)*

Sauerwein Welding 513 563-2979
　605 Wayne Park Dr Cincinnati (45215) *(G-3364)*

Sausser Steel Company Inc 419 422-9632
　230 Crystal Ave Findlay (45840) *(G-7559)*

Savant Technologies LLC 800 435-4448
　1975 Noble Rd East Cleveland (44112) *(G-6983)*

Save Edge Inc 937 376-8268
　360 W Church St Xenia (45385) *(G-16272)*

Save Edge USA, Xenia *Also Called: Save Edge Inc (G-16272)*

Savi Corporation Inc 330 277-3300
　31257 Salem Alliance Rd Salem (44460) *(G-13030)*

Savor Seasonings LLC 513 732-2333
　4292 Armstrong Blvd Batavia (45103) *(G-947)*

Savory Foods Inc 740 354-6655
　2240 6th St Portsmouth (45662) *(G-12655)*

ALPHABETIC SECTION — Schoolbelles

Savvy Mtngs Special Events Ltd..916 774-3838
  281 Bonds Pkwy Berea (44017) *(G-1293)*

Saw Dust Ltd..740 862-0612
  4799 Refugee Rd Nw Baltimore (43105) *(G-847)*

Sawmill 9721 LLC...614 937-4400
  9721 Sawmill Rd Powell (43065) *(G-12680)*

Sawmill Commons 4420...614 764-7878
  209 E State St Columbus (43215) *(G-5748)*

Sawmill Marathon, Columbus *Also Called: Marathon At Sawmill (G-5540)*

Sawmill Road Management Co LLC (PA)......................................937 342-9071
  370 S 5th St Columbus (43215) *(G-5749)*

Sawyer Crystal Systems, Willoughby *Also Called: Sawyer Technical Materials LLC (G-15985)*

Sawyer Technical Materials LLC (HQ)..440 951-8770
  35400 Lakeland Blvd Willoughby (44095) *(G-15985)*

Saxon Jewelers, Cleveland *Also Called: M B Saxon Co Inc (G-4345)*

Saxon Products Inc...419 241-6771
  2283 Fulton St Toledo (43620) *(G-14463)*

Say Security Group USA LLC (PA)...419 634-0004
  520 E Montford Ave Ada (45810) *(G-5)*

Saylor Products Corporation..419 832-2125
  17484 Saylor Ln Grand Rapids (43522) *(G-8010)*

Sb Trans LLC..407 477-2545
  300 E Business Way Ste 200 Cincinnati (45241) *(G-3365)*

SBC, Columbus *Also Called: Ameritech Publishing Inc (G-5132)*

SBC, Uniontown *Also Called: Ameritech Publishing Inc (G-14780)*

SC Fire Protection Ltd...330 468-3300
  8531 Freeway Dr Macedonia (44056) *(G-9572)*

SC Liquidation Company LLC (DH)...937 332-6500
  550 Summit Ave Troy (45373) *(G-14607)*

SC Strategic Solutions LLC...567 424-6054
  600 Industrial Pkwy Norwalk (44857) *(G-11988)*

Scallywag Tag..513 922-4999
  5055 Glencrossing Way Cincinnati (45238) *(G-3366)*

Scanacon Incorporated..330 877-7600
  950 Wales Dr Hartville (44632) *(G-8306)*

Scandinavian Tob Group Ln Ltd...770 934-4594
  1424 Diagonal Rd Akron (44320) *(G-325)*

Scarefactory Inc..614 565-3590
  350 Mccormick Blvd # C Columbus (43213) *(G-5750)*

Scarlett Kitty LLC..678 438-3796
  2786 Wilmington Pike Dayton (45419) *(G-6559)*

Scarlett Ktty Bath Made Pretty, Dayton *Also Called: Scarlett Kitty LLC (G-6559)*

Scenic Solutions Ltd Lblty Co..937 866-5062
  355 Gargrave Rd Dayton (45449) *(G-6560)*

Scenic Wood Products, Sugarcreek *Also Called: Pallet Distributors Inc (G-13933)*

Scepter Publishers...212 354-0670
  21510 Drake Rd Strongsville (44149) *(G-13874)*

Scepter Supply LLC..307 634-6074
  1500 Greene St Marietta (45750) *(G-9821)*

Schaaf Co Inc..513 241-7044
  2440 Spring Grove Ave Cincinnati (45214) *(G-3367)*

Schaefer Box & Pallet Co..513 738-2500
  11875 Paddys Run Rd Hamilton (45013) *(G-8241)*

Schaefer Equipment Inc...330 372-4006
  1590 Phoenix Rd Ne Warren (44483) *(G-15205)*

Schaeffer Metal Products Inc..330 296-6226
  357 Commerce St Ravenna (44266) *(G-12732)*

Schaeffers Investment Research Inc..513 589-3800
  5151 Pfeiffer Rd Ste 450 Blue Ash (45242) *(G-1465)*

Schaeffler Group USA Inc..800 274-5001
  5370 Wegman Dr Valley City (44280) *(G-14889)*

Schaeffler Transm Systems LLC...330 202-6212
  3177 Old Airport Rd Wooster (44691) *(G-16166)*

Schaeffler Transm Systems LLC (DH)..330 264-4383
  3401 Old Airport Rd Wooster (44691) *(G-16167)*

Schaeffler Transmission Llc (DH)..330 264-4383
  3401 Old Airport Rd Wooster (44691) *(G-16168)*

Schaerer Medical Usa Inc..513 561-2241
  675 Wilmer Ave Cincinnati (45226) *(G-3368)*

Schafer Driveline LLC (HQ)..740 694-2055
  123 Phoenix Pl Fredericktown (43019) *(G-7753)*

Schafer Industries, Fredericktown *Also Called: Schafer Driveline LLC (G-7753)*

Schaffer Grinding Co Inc...323 724-4476
  8470 Chamberlin Rd Twinsburg (44087) *(G-14733)*

Schantz Custom Woodworking, Orrville *Also Called: Schantz Organ Company (G-12150)*

Schantz Organ Company (PA)...330 682-6065
  626 S Walnut St Orrville (44667) *(G-12150)*

Schauer Battery Chargers, Cincinnati *Also Called: Brookwood Group Inc (G-2691)*

Scheel Publishing LLC..216 731-8616
  5900 Som Center Rd Willoughby (44094) *(G-15986)*

Scheiders Foods LLC (PA)...740 404-6641
  5705 State Route 204 Mount Perry (43760) *(G-11252)*

Schell Scenic Studio Inc...614 444-9550
  2140 Refugee St Millersport (43046) *(G-11013)*

Schenck Process LLC...513 576-9200
  30825 Aurora Rd # 150 Solon (44139) *(G-13419)*

Schenz Theatrical Supply Inc..513 542-6100
  2959 Colerain Ave Cincinnati (45225) *(G-3369)*

Scherba Industries Inc...330 273-3200
  2880 Interstate Pkwy Brunswick (44212) *(G-1790)*

Scherer Industrial Group, Springfield *Also Called: Horner Industrial Services Inc (G-13579)*

Schilling Graphics Inc (PA)...419 468-1037
  275 Gelsanliter Rd Galion (44833) *(G-7884)*

Schilling Truss Inc...740 984-2396
  230 Stony Run Rd Beverly (45715) *(G-1320)*

Schindler, Sidney *Also Called: Schindler Elevator Corporation (G-13281)*

Schindler Elevator, Holland *Also Called: Schindler Elevator Corporation (G-8529)*

Schindler Elevator Corporation...419 861-5900
  1530 Timber Wolf Dr Ste B Holland (43528) *(G-8529)*

Schindler Elevator Corporation...937 492-3186
  920 S Vandemark Rd Sidney (45365) *(G-13281)*

Schindler Logistics Center, Holland *Also Called: Adams Elevator Equipment Co (G-8492)*

Schlabach Printers, Sugarcreek *Also Called: Schlabach Printers LLC (G-13937)*

Schlabach Printers LLC...330 852-4687
  798 State Route 93 Nw Sugarcreek (44681) *(G-13937)*

Schlabach Woodworks Ltd...330 674-7488
  6678 State Route 241 Millersburg (44654) *(G-10992)*

Schlessman Seed Co (PA)...419 499-2572
  11513 Us Highway 250 N Milan (44846) *(G-10886)*

Schloss Media, Cadiz *Also Called: Harrison News Herald Inc (G-1903)*

Schmelzer Industries Inc...740 743-2866
  7970 Wesley Chapel Rd Ne Somerset (43783) *(G-13450)*

Schmidt Machine Company..419 294-3814
  7013 State Highway 199 Upper Sandusky (43351) *(G-14823)*

Schmidt Progressive LLC..513 934-2600
  360 Harmon Ave Lebanon (45036) *(G-9110)*

Schmitmeyer Inc..937 295-2091
  195 Ben St Fort Loramie (45845) *(G-7607)*

Schneider Automation Inc...612 426-0709
  5855 Union Centre Blvd Fairfield (45014) *(G-7405)*

Schneider Electric, Oxford *Also Called: Schneider Electric Usa Inc (G-12213)*

Schneider Electric, West Chester *Also Called: Schneider Electric Usa Inc (G-15506)*

Schneider Electric Usa Inc..513 523-4171
  5735 College Corner Pike Oxford (45056) *(G-12213)*

Schneider Electric Usa Inc..513 777-4445
  9870 Crescent Park Dr West Chester (45069) *(G-15506)*

Schneller LLC (HQ)..330 676-7183
  6019 Powdermill Rd Kent (44240) *(G-8858)*

Schnider Pallet LLC..440 632-5346
  9782 Bundysburg Rd Middlefield (44062) *(G-10788)*

Schnipke Engraving Co Inc (PA)...419 453-3376
  14223 Rd 24 Ottoville (45876) *(G-12204)*

Schodorf Truck Body & Eqp Co...614 228-6793
  885 Harmon Ave Columbus (43223) *(G-5751)*

Scholz & Ey Engravers Inc..614 444-8052
  1558 Parsons Ave Columbus (43207) *(G-5752)*

School Pride Limited...614 568-0697
  3511 Johnny Appleseed Ct Columbus (43231) *(G-5753)*

School Uniforms and More Inc..216 365-1957
  13721 Lorain Ave Cleveland (44111) *(G-4674)*

Schoolbelles, Cleveland *Also Called: Kip-Craft Incorporated (G-4293)*

Schoonover Industries Inc... 419 289-8332
1440 Simonton Rd Ashland (44805) *(G-612)*

Schott Metal Products Company........................... 330 773-7873
2225 Lee Dr Akron (44306) *(G-326)*

Schreiner Manufacturing LLC................................ 419 937-0300
1997 Township Road 66 New Riegel (44853) *(G-11537)*

Schrock John... 937 544-8457
99 Fugate Rd Peebles (45660) *(G-12332)*

Schuck Mtal Fbrction Dsign Inc............................. 419 586-1054
8319 Us 127 N Celina (45822) *(G-2348)*

Schuerholz Inc.. 937 294-5218
3540 Marshall Rd Dayton (45429) *(G-6561)*

Schulers Bakery Inc (PA)... 937 323-4154
1911 S Limestone St Springfield (45505) *(G-13630)*

Schumann Enterprises Inc....................................... 216 267-6850
12340 Plaza Dr Cleveland (44130) *(G-4675)*

Schutz Container Systems Inc............................... 419 872-2477
2105 S Wilkinson Way Perrysburg (43551) *(G-12425)*

Schwab Industries Inc (HQ).................................... 330 364-4411
2301 Progress St Dover (44622) *(G-6842)*

Schwab Machine Inc... 419 626-0245
3120 Venice Rd Sandusky (44870) *(G-13093)*

Schwan's Home Service, Lima *Also Called: Cygnus Home Service LLC (G-9234)*

Schwans Mama Rosass LLC (DH)........................ 937 498-4511
1910 Fair Rd Sidney (45365) *(G-13282)*

Schwarz Partners Packaging LLC.......................... 740 387-3700
2135 Innovation Dr Marion (43302) *(G-9879)*

Schwarz Partners Packaging LLC.......................... 317 290-1140
2450 Campbell Rd Sidney (45365) *(G-13283)*

Schwebel Baking Company..................................... 330 783-2860
121 O Neill Dr Hebron (43025) *(G-8361)*

Schwebel Baking Company..................................... 330 926-9410
7382 Whipple Ave Nw North Canton (44720) *(G-11758)*

Schwebel Baking Company..................................... 440 846-1921
22626 Royalton Rd Strongsville (44149) *(G-13875)*

Schwebel Baking Company (PA)........................... 330 783-2860
965 E Midlothian Blvd Youngstown (44502) *(G-16433)*

Schwebel Baking Company..................................... 330 783-2860
920 E Midlothian Blvd Youngstown (44502) *(G-16434)*

Schwebel Bkg Co N Canton Agcy, North Canton *Also Called: Schwebel Baking Company (G-11758)*

Schweizer Dipple Inc.. 440 786-8090
7227 Division St Cleveland (44146) *(G-4676)*

SCI, Columbus *Also Called: SCI Engineered Materials Inc (G-5754)*

SCI Engineered Materials Inc................................. 614 486-0261
2839 Charter St Columbus (43228) *(G-5754)*

Science/Electronics Inc... 937 224-4444
521 Kiser St Dayton (45404) *(G-6562)*

Scientific Plastics Ltd.. 305 557-3737
7154 State Route 88 Ravenna (44266) *(G-12733)*

Scio Laminated Products Inc................................. 740 945-1321
117 Fowler Ave Scio (43988) *(G-13112)*

Scioto Industrial Coatings Inc............................... 740 352-1011
38 Burro St Minford (45653) *(G-11043)*

Scioto Ready Mix LLC... 740 924-9273
6214 Taylor Rd Sw Pataskala (43062) *(G-12308)*

Scioto Sand & Gravel, Prospect *Also Called: Fleming Construction Co (G-12689)*

Scioto Sign Co Inc... 419 673-1261
6047 Us Highway 68 Kenton (43326) *(G-8900)*

Scorecards Unlimited LLC.. 614 885-0796
1820 W Dublin Granville Rd Columbus (43085) *(G-5755)*

Scot Industries Inc.. 330 262-7585
6578 Ashland Rd Wooster (44691) *(G-16169)*

Scott Bader Inc.. 330 920-4410
4280 Hudson Dr Stow (44224) *(G-13723)*

Scott Fetzer Company... 216 252-1190
3881 W 150th St Cleveland (44111) *(G-4677)*

Scott Fetzer Company... 216 267-9000
4801 W 150th St Cleveland (44135) *(G-4678)*

Scott Fetzer Company... 440 892-3000
28800 Clemens Rd Westlake (44145) *(G-15784)*

Scott Francis Antique Prints.................................. 216 737-0873
2826 Franklin Blvd Cleveland (44113) *(G-4679)*

Scott Models Inc.. 513 771-8005
607 Redna Ter Ste 400 Cincinnati (45215) *(G-3370)*

Scott Molders Incorporated.................................... 330 673-5777
7180 State Route 43 Kent (44240) *(G-8859)*

Scott Port-A-Fold Inc.. 419 748-8880
5963 State Route 110 Napoleon (43545) *(G-11334)*

Scott Process Systems Inc..................................... 330 877-2350
1160 Sunnyside St Sw Hartville (44632) *(G-8307)*

Scott Thomas Furniture, Twinsburg *Also Called: R A Hamed International Inc (G-14722)*

Scottcare Corporation (HQ).................................... 216 362-0550
4791 W 150th St Cleveland (44135) *(G-4680)*

Scottcare Crdvscular Solutions, Cleveland *Also Called: Scottcare Corporation (G-4680)*

Scottdel Cushion Inc.. 419 825-0432
400 Church St Swanton (43558) *(G-13981)*

Scottrods LLC... 419 499-2705
2512 Higbee Rd Monroeville (44847) *(G-11125)*

Scotts Company LLC... 937 454-2782
20 Innovation Ct Dayton (45414) *(G-6563)*

Scotts Company LLC (HQ)....................................... 937 644-0011
14111 Scottslawn Rd Marysville (43040) *(G-9934)*

Scotts Miracle-Gro, Marysville *Also Called: Scotts Miracle Gro Company (G-9935)*

Scotts Miracle-Gro Company (PA)......................... 937 644-0011
14111 Scottslawn Rd Marysville (43040) *(G-9935)*

Scotts Miracle-Gro Company................................... 937 578-5065
14101 Industrial Pkwy Marysville (43040) *(G-9936)*

Scotts Miracle-Gro Products, Marysville *Also Called: Scotts Company LLC (G-9934)*

Scotts Temecula Operations LLC........................... 800 221-1760
14111 Scottslawn Rd Marysville (43040) *(G-9937)*

Scotts- Hyponex, Marysville *Also Called: Hyponex Corporation (G-9920)*

Scotts- Hyponex, Shreve *Also Called: Hyponex Corporation (G-13209)*

Scovil Hanna LLC.. 216 581-1500
4545 Johnston Pkwy Cleveland (44128) *(G-4681)*

Scram Systems, Blue Ash *Also Called: Lmg Holdings Inc (G-1424)*

Scrambl-Gram Inc... 419 635-2321
5225 W Lakeshore Dr Ste 340 Port Clinton (43452) *(G-12628)*

Scratch Off Works LLC... 440 333-4302
19537 Lake Rd Rocky River (44116) *(G-12843)*

Screaming Eagle Boats... 937 292-7674
227 Water Ave Bellefontaine (43311) *(G-1218)*

Screen Machine, Pataskala *Also Called: SMI Holdings Inc (G-12309)*

Screen Works Inc (PA).. 937 264-9111
3970 Image Dr Dayton (45414) *(G-6564)*

Scriptel Corporation.. 877 848-6824
2222 Dividend Dr Columbus (43228) *(G-5756)*

Scriptype Publishing Inc.. 330 659-0303
4300 W Streetsboro Rd Richfield (44286) *(G-12796)*

Scroll Compressors LLC, Sidney *Also Called: Copeland Scroll Compressors LP (G-13238)*

Scs Construction Services Inc............................... 513 929-0260
2130 Western Ave Cincinnati (45214) *(G-3371)*

Scs Gearbox Inc.. 419 483-7278
739 W Main St Bellevue (44811) *(G-1233)*

Scsrm Concrete Company Ltd................................ 937 533-1001
4723 Hardin Wapakoneta Rd Sidney (45365) *(G-13284)*

Sdg Inc... 440 893-0771
10000 Cedar Ave Cleveland (44106) *(G-4682)*

Sdg News Group Inc... 419 929-3411
43 E Main St New London (44851) *(G-11468)*

Sdi Industries... 513 561-4032
8561 New England Ct Cincinnati (45236) *(G-3372)*

Sdk Associates Inc... 330 745-3648
2044 Wadsworth Rd Unit B Norton (44203) *(G-11948)*

Sdmk LLC.. 330 965-0970
7340 Market St Youhgstown (44512) *(G-16435)*

Sdo Sports Ltd.. 440 546-9998
10250 Brecksville Rd Cleveland (44141) *(G-4683)*

SDS Logistics Services, Youngstown *Also Called: SDS National LLC (G-16436)*

SDS National LLC.. 330 759-8066
19 Colonial Dr Ste 27 Youngstown (44505) *(G-16436)*

ALPHABETIC SECTION — Seneca

Sea Air Space McHning Mlding L.. 440 248-3025
10036 Aurora Hudson Rd Streetsboro (44241) *(G-13791)*

Sea Bird Publications Inc... 513 869-2200
311 Nilles Rd Ste B Fairfield (45014) *(G-7406)*

Seabiscuit Motorsports Inc (HQ).. 440 951-6600
7201 Industrial Park Blvd Mentor (44060) *(G-10551)*

Seacor Painting Corporation.. 330 755-6361
98 Creed Cir Campbell (44405) *(G-1966)*

Seaforth Mineral & Ore Co Inc (PA).. 216 292-5820
3690 Orange Pl Ste 495 Beachwood (44122) *(G-1022)*

Seagate Plastics, Waterville *Also Called: Seagate Plastics Company LLC (G-15252)*

Seagate Plastics Company LLC (PA).. 419 878-5010
1110 Disher Dr Waterville (43566) *(G-15252)*

Seal Div Natl.. 419 238-0030
150 Fisher Ave Van Wert (45891) *(G-14926)*

Seal Master Corporation.. 330 673-8410
340 Martinel Dr Kent (44240) *(G-8860)*

Seal Master Corporation (PA)... 330 673-8410
368 Martinel Dr Kent (44240) *(G-8861)*

Seal Masters LLC.. 216 860-7710
5935 State Rd Parma (44134) *(G-12295)*

Seal Tite, Hillsboro *Also Called: Seal Tite LLC (G-8466)*

Seal Tite LLC... 937 393-4268
120 Moore Rd Hillsboro (45133) *(G-8466)*

Seal-Rite Door, Hebron *Also Called: S R Door Inc (G-8360)*

Sealco, Uhrichsville *Also Called: Sealco Inc (G-14768)*

Sealco Inc.. 740 922-4122
6566 Superior Rd Se Uhrichsville (44683) *(G-14768)*

Sealmaster, Kent *Also Called: Seal Master Corporation (G-8860)*

Sealmaster, Kent *Also Called: Seal Master Corporation (G-8861)*

Sealmaster, Sandusky *Also Called: Thorworks Industries Inc (G-13096)*

Sealtron Inc... 513 733-8400
9705 Reading Rd Cincinnati (45215) *(G-3373)*

Sealy Mattress Mfg Co LLC... 800 697-3259
1070 Lake Rd Medina (44256) *(G-10374)*

Seaman Corporation (PA).. 330 262-1111
1000 Venture Blvd Wooster (44691) *(G-16170)*

Sean Ison Logging LLC... 740 835-7222
1740 State Route 321 Sardinia (45171) *(G-13109)*

Seaport Mold & Casting Company... 419 243-1422
1309 W Bancroft St Toledo (43606) *(G-14464)*

Seaside Retailer, Medina *Also Called: Breakwall Publishing LLC (G-10306)*

Seaway, Columbia Station *Also Called: Seaway Bolt And Specials Company (G-5021)*

Seaway Bolt And Specials Company....................................... 440 236-5015
11561 Station Rd Columbia Station (44028) *(G-5021)*

Seaway Enterprises, Toledo *Also Called: Initial Designs Inc (G-14331)*

Seaway Pattern Mfg Inc... 419 865-5724
5749 Angola Rd Toledo (43615) *(G-14465)*

Seawin Inc.. 419 355-9111
728 Graham Dr Fremont (43420) *(G-7809)*

Sebring Fluid Power Corp... 330 938-9984
513 N Johnson Rd Sebring (44672) *(G-13126)*

Seco Machine Inc... 330 499-2150
5335 Mayfair Rd North Canton (44720) *(G-11759)*

Second Oil Ltd.. 419 830-4688
N695 County Road 6 Mc Clure (43534) *(G-10267)*

Secondary Machining Svcs Inc.. 440 593-3040
539 Center Rd Conneaut (44030) *(G-5932)*

Securastock LLC.. 330 957-5711
11470 Euclid Ave Cleveland (44106) *(G-4684)*

Securcom, Minster *Also Called: Securcom Inc (G-11060)*

Securcom Inc.. 419 628-1049
307 W 1st St Minster (45865) *(G-11060)*

Secure Pak, Perrysburg *Also Called: Glassline Corporation (G-12385)*

Security Designs, Cleveland *Also Called: Technlgy Install Partners LLC (G-4774)*

Security Fence Group Inc (PA)... 513 681-3700
4260 Dane Ave Cincinnati (45223) *(G-3374)*

Securtex International Inc.. 937 312-1414
982 Senate Dr Dayton (45459) *(G-6565)*

See Ya There Inc.. 614 856-9037
12710 W Bank Dr Ne Millersport (43046) *(G-11014)*

See Ya There Vacation and Trvl, Millersport *Also Called: See Ya There Inc (G-11014)*

Seebach Inc... 937 275-3565
2622 Keenan Ave Dayton (45414) *(G-6566)*

Seebach Tools & Molds Mfg, Dayton *Also Called: Seebach Inc (G-6566)*

Seekirk Inc... 614 278-9200
2420 Scioto Harper Dr Columbus (43204) *(G-5757)*

Seemless Printing LLC... 513 871-2366
717 Linn St Cincinnati (45203) *(G-3375)*

Seemray LLC... 440 536-8705
261 Alpha Park Cleveland (44143) *(G-4685)*

Seepex Inc... 937 864-7150
511 Speedway Dr Enon (45323) *(G-7252)*

Segna Inc... 937 335-6700
1316 Barnhart Rd Ste 1316 Troy (45373) *(G-14608)*

Seiler Enterprises LLC... 614 330-2220
5397 Whispering Oak Blvd Hilliard (43026) *(G-8439)*

Seilkop Industries Inc.. 513 679-5680
7211 Market Pl Cincinnati (45216) *(G-3376)*

Seilkop Industries Inc (PA)... 513 761-1035
425 W North Bend Rd Cincinnati (45216) *(G-3377)*

Seilkop Industries Inc.. 513 353-3090
5927 State Route 128 Miamitown (45041) *(G-10709)*

Seislove Brial Vlts Sptic Tnks, Tiffin *Also Called: Seislove Vault & Septic Tanks (G-14103)*

Seislove Vault & Septic Tanks.. 419 447-5473
2168 S State Route 100 Tiffin (44883) *(G-14103)*

Sekuworks LLC... 513 202-1210
9487 Dry Fork Rd Harrison (45030) *(G-8290)*

Selas Heat Technology Co LLC (HQ)....................................... 800 523-6500
11012 Aurora Hudson Rd Streetsboro (44241) *(G-13792)*

Selby Service/Roxy Press Inc... 513 241-3445
2020 Elm St Cincinnati (45202) *(G-3378)*

Selco Industries Inc... 419 861-0336
1590 Albon Rd Ste 1 Holland (43528) *(G-8530)*

Select Industries Corporation.. 937 233-9191
60 Heid Ave Dayton (45404) *(G-6567)*

Select Logging.. 419 564-0361
5739 Township Road 21 Marengo (43334) *(G-9770)*

Select Machine Inc... 330 678-7676
4125 Karg Industrial Pkwy Kent (44240) *(G-8862)*

Select Seating, Columbus *Also Called: N Wasserstrom & Sons Inc (G-5587)*

Select Signs.. 937 262-7095
1755 Spaulding Rd Dayton (45432) *(G-6173)*

Select Tool & Production, Toledo *Also Called: Hedges Selective Tl & Prod Inc (G-14316)*

Select-Arc Inc (PA)... 937 295-5215
600 Enterprise Dr Fort Loramie (45845) *(G-7608)*

Selecteon Corporation... 614 710-1132
2041 Arlingate Ln Columbus (43228) *(G-5758)*

Self Made Holdings LLC.. 330 477-1052
5325 Southway St Sw Canton (44706) *(G-2220)*

Self-Srvice PDT Dist Shipg Ctr, Hebron *Also Called: Diebold Nixdorf Incorporated (G-8338)*

Selling Precision, Stow *Also Called: Hydraulic Manifolds USA LLC (G-13702)*

Selling Precision Inc.. 973 728-1214
4540 Boyce Pkwy Stow (44224) *(G-13724)*

Selmco Metal Fabricators Inc... 937 498-1331
1615 Ferguson Ct Sidney (45365) *(G-13285)*

Sem-Com Company Inc (PA).. 419 537-8813
1040 N Westwood Ave Toledo (43607) *(G-14466)*

Semco Inc.. 800 848-5764
1025 Pole Lane Rd Marion (43302) *(G-9880)*

Semco Carbon, Lorain *Also Called: Sentinel Management Inc (G-9437)*

Semco Ceramics, Uhrichsville *Also Called: Stebbins Engineering & Mfg Co (G-14770)*

Semper Quality Industry Inc... 440 352-8111
9411 Mercantile Dr Mentor (44060) *(G-10552)*

Semtec Inc... 330 497-7224
7750 Strausser St Nw North Canton (44720) *(G-11760)*

Semtorq Inc... 330 487-0600
1780 Enterprise Pkwy Twinsburg (44087) *(G-14734)*

Senator International Inc (HQ).. 419 887-5806
4111 N Jerome Rd Maumee (43537) *(G-10229)*

Seneca, Bellevue *Also Called: Seneca Railroad & Mining Co (G-1234)*

Seneca Enterprises Inc — 814 432-7890
4053 Clough Woods Dr Batavia (45103) *(G-948)*

Seneca Environmental Products Inc — 419 447-1282
1685 S County Road 1 Tiffin (44883) *(G-14104)*

Seneca Label Inc — 440 237-1600
1120 W 130th St Brunswick (44212) *(G-1791)*

Seneca Millwork Inc — 419 435-6671
300 Court Pl Fostoria (44830) *(G-7654)*

Seneca Petroleum Co Inc — 419 691-3581
2563 Front St Toledo (43605) *(G-14467)*

Seneca Petroleum Co Inc — 419 691-3581
1441 Woodville Rd Toledo (43605) *(G-14468)*

Seneca Railroad & Mining Co — 419 483-7764
1075 W Main St Bellevue (44811) *(G-1234)*

Seneca Sheet Metal Company — 419 447-8434
277 Water Street Tiffin (44883) *(G-14105)*

Seneca Wire & Manufacturing Co Inc (HQ) — 419 435-9261
319 S Vine St Fostoria (44830) *(G-7655)*

Seneca Wires, Fostoria Also Called: Seneca Wire & Manufacturing Co Inc *(G-7655)*

Senior Impact Publications LLC — 513 791-8800
5980 Kugler Mill Rd Cincinnati (45236) *(G-3379)*

Senneca Holdings Inc (HQ) — 800 543-4455
11502 Century Blvd Cincinnati (45246) *(G-3380)*

Sense Diagnostics Inc — 513 702-0376
1776 Mentor Ave Ste 426 Cincinnati (45212) *(G-3381)*

Sensible Products Inc — 330 659-4212
3857 Brecksville Rd Richfield (44286) *(G-12797)*

Sensical Inc — 216 641-1141
31115 Aurora Rd Solon (44139) *(G-13420)*

Sensience, Westerville Also Called: Therm-O-Disc Incorporated *(G-15681)*

Sensor Technology Systems, Miamisburg Also Called: Steiner Eoptics Inc *(G-10686)*

Sensorwerks, Hilliard Also Called: Sensotec LLC *(G-8440)*

Sensory Robotics Inc — 513 545-9501
9711 Winton Hills Ln Cincinnati (45215) *(G-3382)*

Sensoryffcts Powdr Systems Inc — 419 783-5518
136 Fox Run Dr Defiance (43512) *(G-6694)*

Sensotec LLC — 614 481-8616
3450 Cemetery Rd Hilliard (43026) *(G-8440)*

Sensus LLC — 513 892-7100
2991 Hamilton Mason Rd Fairfield Township (45011) *(G-7432)*

Sentage Corporation — 419 842-6730
8730 Resource Park Dr Sylvania (43560) *(G-14013)*

Sentek Corporation — 614 586-1123
1300 Memory Ln N Columbus (43209) *(G-5759)*

Sentient Studios Ltd — 330 204-8636
2894 Chamberlain Rd Apt 6 Fairlawn (44333) *(G-7449)*

Sentinel Daily — 740 992-2155
825 3rd Ave Gallipolis (45631) *(G-7902)*

Sentinel Management Inc — 440 821-7372
3000 Leavitt Rd Unit 1 Lorain (44052) *(G-9437)*

Sentrilock LLC — 513 618-5800
7701 Service Center Dr West Chester (45069) *(G-15507)*

Sentro Tech Corporation — 440 260-0364
21294 Drake Rd Strongsville (44149) *(G-13876)*

Sentronic, Brunswick Also Called: Controlled Access Inc *(G-1755)*

Sentry Products, Canton Also Called: Canton Sterilized Wiping Cloth *(G-2068)*

Sepma Technologies LLC — 937 660-3783
2000 Composite Dr Kettering (45420) *(G-8910)*

Sepmatech, Kettering Also Called: Sepma Technologies LLC *(G-8910)*

Seppi M SPA — 513 443-6339
8880 Beckett Rd West Chester (45069) *(G-15508)*

Septic Products Inc — 419 282-5933
1378 Township Road 743 Ashland (44805) *(G-613)*

Sequa Can Machinery Inc — 330 493-0444
4150 Belden Village St Nw Ste 504 Canton (44718) *(G-2221)*

Serappers Gallery, Newark Also Called: M & R Phillips Enterprises *(G-11588)*

Sergeant Stone Inc — 740 452-7434
1425 State Route 555 Ne Corning (43730) *(G-5959)*

Sermatech International — 513 489-9800
11495 Deerfield Rd Blue Ash (45242) *(G-1466)*

Sermonix Pharmaceuticals Inc — 614 864-4919
250 E Broad St Ste 250 Columbus (43215) *(G-5760)*

Sertek LLC — 614 504-5828
6399 Shier Rings Rd Dublin (43016) *(G-6936)*

Servatii Inc — 513 271-5040
3774 Paxton Ave Cincinnati (45209) *(G-3383)*

Service Express LLC — 513 942-6170
10004 International Blvd West Chester (45246) *(G-15583)*

Service Spring Corp — 419 867-0212
6615 Maumee Western Rd Maumee (43537) *(G-10230)*

Service Spring Corp (PA) — 419 838-6081
1703 Toll Gate Dr Maumee (43537) *(G-10231)*

Service Stampings Inc — 440 946-2330
4700 Hamann Pkwy Willoughby (44094) *(G-15987)*

Service Station Equipment Co (PA) — 216 431-6100
1294 E 55th St Cleveland (44103) *(G-4686)*

Services Acquisition Co LLC — 330 479-9267
4412 Pleasant Valley Rd Se Dennison (44621) *(G-6795)*

Serving Veterans Mobility Inc — 937 746-4788
303 Conover Dr Franklin (45005) *(G-7701)*

Sesh Communications — 513 851-1693
3440 Burnet Ave Ste 130 Cincinnati (45229) *(G-3384)*

Sest Inc — 440 777-9777
24509 Annie Ln Westlake (44145) *(G-15785)*

Setco Industries Inc — 513 941-5110
5880 Hillside Ave Cincinnati (45233) *(G-3385)*

Setex Inc — 419 394-7800
1111 Mckinley Rd Saint Marys (45885) *(G-12967)*

Seth Enterprises, Zanesville Also Called: Buckeye Energy Resources Inc *(G-16514)*

Seven Lakeway Refractories LLC — 419 433-3030
730 River Rd Huron (44839) *(G-8645)*

Seven Mile Creek Corporation — 937 456-3320
315 S Beech St Eaton (45320) *(G-7069)*

Seven Ranges Mfg Corp — 330 627-7155
330 Industrial Dr Sw Carrollton (44615) *(G-2315)*

Seventh Son Brewing, Columbus Also Called: Green Room Brewing LLC *(G-5412)*

Severn River Publishing LLC — 703 819-4686
Kings Mills (45034) *(G-8929)*

Seville Bronze, Seville Also Called: Jj Seville LLC *(G-13144)*

Seville Sand & Gravel Inc — 330 948-0168
12663 Bristol Ln Strongsville (44149) *(G-13877)*

Sew & Sew Embroidery Inc — 330 676-1600
881 Tallmadge Rd Ste C Kent (44240) *(G-8863)*

Sew It Seams, Woodsfield Also Called: J C L S Enterprises LLC *(G-16088)*

Sew-Eurodrive Inc — 937 335-0036
2001 W Main St Troy (45373) *(G-14609)*

Sewah Studios Inc — 740 373-2087
190 Mill Creek Rd Marietta (45750) *(G-9822)*

Sewer Rodding Equipment Co — 419 991-2065
3434 S Dixie Hwy Lima (45804) *(G-9288)*

Sewline Products Inc — 419 929-1114
30 S Railroad St New London (44851) *(G-11469)*

Sexton Industrial Inc — 513 530-5555
366 Circle Freeway Dr West Chester (45246) *(G-15584)*

Seyekcub Inc — 330 324-1394
615 W 4th St Uhrichsville (44683) *(G-14769)*

Sfc Graphic Arts Div, Toledo Also Called: Sfc Graphics Cleveland Ltd *(G-14469)*

Sfc Graphics Cleveland Ltd — 419 255-1283
110 E Woodruff Ave Toledo (43604) *(G-14469)*

SFM Corp — 440 951-5500
4530 Hamann Pkwy Willoughby (44094) *(G-15988)*

Sfs Group Usa Inc — 330 239-7100
5201 Portside Dr Medina (44256) *(G-10375)*

Sfs Intec, Medina Also Called: Sfs Group Usa Inc *(G-10375)*

Sfs Intec Inc — 330 239-7100
5201 Portside Dr Medina (44256) *(G-10376)*

Sfs Truck Sales & Parts, Gallipolis Also Called: King Kutter II Inc *(G-7896)*

SGB Usa Inc (DH) — 330 472-1187
180 South Ave Tallmadge (44278) *(G-14046)*

Sgi Matrix LLC (PA) — 937 438-9033
1041 Byers Rd Miamisburg (45342) *(G-10681)*

Sgl Carbon Technic LLC — 440 572-3600
21945 Drake Rd Strongsville (44149) *(G-13878)*

ALPHABETIC SECTION — Shelly Materials Inc

Sgm Co Inc 440 255-1190
9000 Tyler Blvd Mentor (44060) *(G-10553)*

SGS Cincinnati, Cincinnati Also Called: Stevenson Color Inc *(G-3422)*

SH Bell Company 412 963-9910
2217 Michigan Ave East Liverpool (43920) *(G-6999)*

Shacks Stop N Go LLC 614 296-9292
107 Fox Glen Dr W Pickerington (43147) *(G-12470)*

Shafer Valve Company, Ontario Also Called: Emerson Process Management *(G-12091)*

Shaffer Metal Fab Inc 937 492-1384
2031 Commerce Dr Sidney (45365) *(G-13286)*

Shafts Mfg 440 942-6012
1585 E 361st St Unit G1 Willoughby (44095) *(G-15989)*

Shaheen Oriental Rug Co Inc (PA) 330 493-9000
4120 Whipple Ave Nw Canton (44718) *(G-2222)*

Shaker Numeric Mfg, Euclid Also Called: Tech-Med Inc *(G-7301)*

Shaker Workshops, Blue Ash Also Called: Tappan Chairs LLC *(G-1477)*

Shalix Inc 216 941-3546
10910 Briggs Rd Cleveland (44111) *(G-4687)*

Shalmet Corporation 440 236-8840
164 Freedom Ct Elyria (44035) *(G-7204)*

Shamrock Acquisition Company, Westlake Also Called: Shamrock Companies Inc *(G-15786)*

Shamrock Companies Inc (PA) 440 899-9510
24090 Detroit Rd Westlake (44145) *(G-15786)*

Shamrock Molded Products, Holland Also Called: Doyle Manufacturing Inc *(G-8505)*

Shamrock Printing LLC 740 349-2244
82 S 3rd St Newark (43055) *(G-11605)*

Shanafelt Manufacturing Co (PA) 330 455-0315
2633 Winfield Way Ne Canton (44705) *(G-2223)*

Shape Supply Inc 513 863-6695
700 S Erie Hwy Hamilton (45011) *(G-8242)*

Shaq Inc 770 427-0402
22901 Millcreek Blvd Ste 650 Beachwood (44122) *(G-1023)*

Sharon Manufacturing Inc 330 239-1561
6867 Ridge Rd Sharon Center (44274) *(G-13167)*

Sharon Stone Inc 740 732-7100
44895 Sharon Stone Rd Caldwell (43724) *(G-1913)*

Sharonco Inc 419 882-3443
5651 Main St Sylvania (43560) *(G-14014)*

Sharp Enterprises Inc 937 295-2965
400 Enterprise Dr Fort Loramie (45845) *(G-7609)*

Sharp Tool Service Inc 330 273-4144
4735 W 150th St Unit H Cleveland (44135) *(G-4688)*

Sharps Valet Parking Svc Inc 574 223-5230
11650 Greenhaven Ct Cincinnati (45251) *(G-3386)*

Shasta Beverages 614 409-2965
3219 Rohr Rd Groveport (43125) *(G-8159)*

Shasta Beverages Inc 614 491-5415
4685 Groveport Rd Obetz (43207) *(G-12064)*

Shasta Beverges, Obetz Also Called: National Beverage Corp *(G-12063)*

Shaw Industries Inc 513 942-3692
8580 Seward Rd Ste 400 Fairfield (45011) *(G-7407)*

Shaw Stainless, Beachwood Also Called: Shaq Inc *(G-1023)*

Shawadi LLC 614 839-0698
20 S State St Ste B Westerville (43081) *(G-15720)*

Shawn Fleming Ind Trckg LLC 937 707-8539
4982 Aquilla Dr Dayton (45415) *(G-6568)*

Shawne Springs Winery 740 623-0744
20093 County Road 6 Coshocton (43812) *(G-5996)*

Shawnee Systems Inc 513 561-9932
4221 Brandonmore Dr Cincinnati (45255) *(G-3387)*

Shear Service Inc 216 341-2700
3175 E 81st St Cleveland (44104) *(G-4689)*

Shear Service, The, Cleveland Also Called: Shear Service Inc *(G-4689)*

Shearer Farm Inc 330 345-9023
7762 Cleveland Rd Wooster (44691) *(G-16171)*

Shearer's Snacks, Brewster Also Called: Shearers Foods LLC *(G-1646)*

Shearer's Snacks, Massillon Also Called: Shearers Foods LLC *(G-10142)*

Shearers Foods LLC 330 767-3426
692 Wabash Ave N Brewster (44613) *(G-1646)*

Shearers Foods LLC (HQ) 800 428-6843
100 Lincoln Way E Massillon (44646) *(G-10142)*

Shearers Foods LLC 330 767-7969
4100 Millennium Blvd Se Massillon (44646) *(G-10143)*

Sheds Direct Inc 330 674-3001
4260 Township Road 617 Millersburg (44654) *(G-10993)*

Sheet Metal Fabricator, Tiffin Also Called: Seneca Sheet Metal Company *(G-14105)*

Sheet Metal Products Co Inc 440 392-9000
5950 Pinecone Dr Mentor (44060) *(G-10554)*

Sheetmetal Crafters 330 452-6700
435 Walnut Ave Se Canton (44702) *(G-2224)*

Sheetmetal Crafters Inc 330 452-6700
325 5th St Se Canton (44702) *(G-2225)*

Sheffield Bronze Paint Corp 216 481-8330
17814 S Waterloo Rd Cleveland (44119) *(G-4690)*

Sheffield Metals Cleveland LLC (PA) 800 283-5262
5467 Evergreen Pkwy Sheffield Village (44054) *(G-13188)*

Sheffield Metals International, Sheffield Village Also Called: Sheffield Metals Cleveland LLC *(G-13188)*

Sheffield Metals Intl Inc 440 934-8500
5467 Evergreen Pkwy Sheffield Village (44054) *(G-13189)*

Sheffield Oldcastle, Sheffield Village Also Called: Oldcastle Apg Midwest Inc *(G-13187)*

Sheiban Jewelry Inc 440 238-0616
16938 Pearl Rd Strongsville (44136) *(G-13879)*

Shelar Inc 419 729-9756
5335 Enterprise Blvd Toledo (43612) *(G-14470)*

Shelby Company 440 871-9901
865 Canterbury Rd Westlake (44145) *(G-15787)*

Shelby County Review, Wapakoneta Also Called: Horizon Ohio Publications Inc *(G-15117)*

Shelby Daily Globe Inc 419 342-4276
37 W Main St Shelby (44875) *(G-13200)*

Shelby Printing Partners LLC 419 342-3171
325 S Martin Dr Shelby (44875) *(G-13201)*

Shelby Welded Tube Div, Shelby Also Called: Phillips Mfg and Tower Co *(G-13197)*

Shelley Company, Maumee Also Called: Stoneco Inc *(G-10236)*

Shelli R McMurray 614 275-4381
1360 Louvaine Dr Rear Columbus (43223) *(G-5761)*

Shelly & Sands Zanesville OH, Perrysville Also Called: S & S Aggregates Inc *(G-12448)*

Shelly and Sands Inc 740 859-2104
1731 Old State Route 7 Rayland (43943) *(G-12745)*

Shelly and Sands Inc (PA) 740 453-0721
3570 S River Rd Zanesville (43701) *(G-16562)*

Shelly Company 216 688-0684
4431 W 130th St Cleveland (44135) *(G-4691)*

Shelly Company, The, Thornville Also Called: Shelly Materials Inc *(G-14072)*

Shelly Fisher 419 522-6696
449 Newman St Mansfield (44902) *(G-9717)*

Shelly Liquid Division, Toledo Also Called: Shelly Materials Inc *(G-14471)*

Shelly Materials Inc 740 775-4567
1177 Hopetown Rd Chillicothe (45601) *(G-2534)*

Shelly Materials Inc 419 622-2101
2364 Richey Rd Convoy (45832) *(G-5940)*

Shelly Materials Inc 614 871-6704
3300 Jackson Pike Grove City (43123) *(G-8119)*

Shelly Materials Inc 330 723-3681
820 W Smith Rd Medina (44256) *(G-10377)*

Shelly Materials Inc 740 666-5841
8328 Watkins Rd Ostrander (43061) *(G-12176)*

Shelly Materials Inc 740 247-2311
49947 State Route 338 Racine (45771) *(G-12695)*

Shelly Materials Inc 937 325-7386
4301 S Charleston Pike Springfield (45502) *(G-13631)*

Shelly Materials Inc 740 246-5009
8775 Blackbird Ln Thornville (43076) *(G-14071)*

Shelly Materials Inc 740 246-6315
352 George Hardy Dr Toledo (43605) *(G-14471)*

Shelly Materials Inc 330 963-5180
1749 Highland Rd Twinsburg (44087) *(G-14735)*

Shelly Materials Inc 937 358-2224
20620 Spangler Rd West Mansfield (43358) *(G-15628)*

Shelly Materials Inc 419 273-2510
3798 State Route 53 Forest (45843) *(G-7592)*

Shelly Materials Inc (DH) 740 246-6315
80 Park Dr Thornville (43076) *(G-14072)*

Shelter Studios, Blue Ash *Also Called: Organized Lightning LLC (G-1447)*

Sheltervision LLC.. 419 852-7788
3584 Mercer Auglaize County Rd Minster (45865) *(G-11061)*

Shelves West LLC.. 928 692-1449
510 S Main St Findlay (45840) *(G-7560)*

Shems Inc.. 614 279-2342
154 N Hague Ave Columbus (43204) *(G-5762)*

Shepherd Material Science Co (PA)............................ 513 731-1110
4900 Beech St Norwood (45212) *(G-11998)*

Shepherd Widnes Ltd.. 513 731-1110
4900 Beech St Norwood (45212) *(G-11999)*

Sherbrooke Corporation... 440 942-3520
36490 Reading Ave Willoughby (44094) *(G-15990)*

Sherbrooke Metals.. 440 542-3066
37552 N Industrial Pkwy Willoughby (44094) *(G-15991)*

Sheridan Mfg, Wauseon *Also Called: Lear Corporation (G-15267)*

Sheridan One Stop Carryout Inc................................. 740 687-1300
1510 Sheridan Dr Lancaster (43130) *(G-9038)*

Sheridan Woodworks Inc.. 216 663-9333
17801 S Miles Rd Cleveland (44128) *(G-4692)*

Sherwin-Williams, Cleveland *Also Called: Sherwin-Williams Company (G-4693)*

Sherwin-Williams, Cleveland *Also Called: Sherwin-Williams Company (G-4694)*

Sherwin-Williams, Hudson *Also Called: Sherwin-Williams Company (G-8611)*

Sherwin-Williams, Strongsville *Also Called: Sherwin-Williams Company (G-13880)*

Sherwin-Williams Company (PA)................................ 216 566-2000
101 W Prospect Ave Ste 1020 Cleveland (44115) *(G-4693)*

Sherwin-Williams Company.. 216 566-2000
6012 Orchard Grove Ave Cleveland (44144) *(G-4694)*

Sherwin-Williams Company.. 330 528-0124
5860 Darrow Rd Hudson (44236) *(G-8611)*

Sherwin-Williams Company.. 330 830-6000
600 Nova Dr Se Massillon (44646) *(G-10144)*

Sherwin-Williams Company.. 440 846-4328
11410 Alameda Dr Strongsville (44149) *(G-13880)*

Sherwin-Williams Mfg Co... 216 566-2000
101 W Prospect Ave Ste 1020 Cleveland (44115) *(G-4695)*

Sherwn-Wllams Auto Fnshes Corp (HQ)..................... 216 332-8330
4440 Warrensville Center Rd Cleveland (44128) *(G-4696)*

Sherwood Refractores, Cleveland *Also Called: PCC Airfoils LLC (G-4537)*

Sherwood Rtm Corp.. 330 875-7151
4043 Beck Ave Louisville (44641) *(G-9471)*

Sherwood Valve LLC... 216 264-5023
7900 Hub Pkwy Cleveland (44125) *(G-4697)*

Shield Laminating, Hilliard *Also Called: The Guardtower Inc (G-8447)*

Shields Wright Rubber Co.. 216 741-8200
4800 Van Epps Rd Ste 104 Brooklyn Heights (44131) *(G-1700)*

Shiffler Equipment Sales Inc (PA).............................. 440 285-9175
745 S St Chardon (44024) *(G-2467)*

Shilling Transport Inc... 330 948-1105
9718 Avon Lake Rd Lodi (44254) *(G-9356)*

Shiloh Inds Inc Mdina Blnking, Valley City *Also Called: Shl Liquidation Medina Inc (G-14895)*

Shiloh Inds Wellington Mfg Div, Wellington *Also Called: Shl Liquidation Industries Inc (G-15322)*

Shiloh Industries, Valley City *Also Called: Shl Liquidation Industries Inc (G-14893)*

Shiloh Industries Inc... 937 236-5100
5988 Executive Blvd Ste B Dayton (45424) *(G-6569)*

Shiloh Industries Inc... 330 558-2000
5569 Innovation Dr Valley City (44280) *(G-14890)*

Shiloh Industries, LLC, Valley City *Also Called: Grouper Acquisition Co LLC (G-14872)*

Shiloh Industries, LLC, Wellington *Also Called: Grouper Acquisition Co LLC (G-15313)*

Shim Shack.. 877 557-3930
105 May Dr Harrison (45030) *(G-8291)*

Shin-Etsu Silicones Amer Inc..................................... 330 630-9860
963 Evans Ave Akron (44305) *(G-327)*

Shin-Etsu Silicones of America Inc (HQ).................. 330 630-9460
1150 Damar Dr Akron (44305) *(G-328)*

Shinagawa, Mogadore *Also Called: Shinagawa Inc (G-11084)*

Shinagawa Inc... 330 628-1118
3555 Gilchrist Rd Mogadore (44260) *(G-11084)*

Shinano Pneumatic Inds USA Inc............................... 614 529-6600
1571 Westbelt Dr Columbus (43228) *(G-5763)*

Shincor Silicones Inc.. 330 630-9460
1030 Evans Ave Akron (44305) *(G-329)*

Shirley KS LLC.. 740 331-7934
1150 Newark Rd Zanesville (43701) *(G-16563)*

Shirley KS Storage Trays LLC.................................... 740 868-8140
1150 Newark Rd Zanesville (43701) *(G-16564)*

Shl Liquidation Automotive Inc.................................. 330 558-2600
880 Steel Dr Valley City (44280) *(G-14891)*

Shl Liquidation Inc Dickson (HQ)............................... 615 446-7725
880 Steel Dr Valley City (44280) *(G-14892)*

Shl Liquidation Industries Inc (PA)............................ 248 299-7500
880 Steel Dr Valley City (44280) *(G-14893)*

Shl Liquidation Industries Inc.................................... 440 647-2100
350 Maple St Wellington (44090) *(G-15322)*

Shl Liquidation Jefferson Inc (HQ) 880 Steel Dr Valley City (44280) *(G-14894)*

Shl Liquidation Medina Inc (PA) 5580 Wegman Dr Valley City (44280) *(G-14895)*

Shl Liquidation Mfg LLC (HQ).................................... 330 558-2600
880 Steel Dr Valley City (44280) *(G-14896)*

Shl Liquidation Sectional Co...................................... 330 558-2600
880 Steel Dr Valley City (44280) *(G-14897)*

Shl Liquidation Stamping Inc (HQ)............................ 330 558-2600
880 Steel Dr Valley City (44280) *(G-14898)*

Shoemaker Electric Company..................................... 614 294-5626
831 Bonham Ave Columbus (43211) *(G-5764)*

Shoemaker Industrial Solutions, Columbus *Also Called: Shoemaker Electric Company (G-5764)*

Shook Manufactured Pdts Inc (PA)............................ 330 848-9780
1017 Kenmore Blvd Akron (44314) *(G-330)*

Shook Manufactured Pdts Inc.................................... 440 247-9130
3801 Wiltshire Rd Chagrin Falls (44022) *(G-2385)*

Shoot-A-Way Inc... 419 294-4654
7157 County Highway 134 Nevada (44849) *(G-11361)*

Shops By Todd Inc (PA)... 937 458-3192
2727 Fairfield Commons Blvd Spc W273 Beavercreek (45431) *(G-1061)*

Shore Precision LLC... 330 704-0552
3043 Rockingham St Nw Uniontown (44685) *(G-14793)*

Shore To Shore Inc (DH)... 937 866-1908
8170 Washington Village Dr Dayton (45458) *(G-6570)*

Shoreline Machine Products Co (PA)........................ 216 481-8033
19301 Saint Clair Ave Cleveland (44117) *(G-4698)*

Shorr Packaging, Cincinnati *Also Called: Hanchett Paper Company (G-2984)*

Short Run Machine Products Inc............................... 440 969-1313
4744 Kister Ct Ashtabula (44004) *(G-660)*

Shot Selector, Twinsburg *Also Called: Golf Marketing Group Inc (G-14669)*

Shousha Trucking LLC... 937 270-4471
3695 Barbarosa Dr Dayton (45416) *(G-6571)*

Shout Out Loud Prints... 614 432-8990
809 Phillipi Rd Columbus (43228) *(G-5765)*

Show Ready Professionals... 614 817-5849
7299 Fall Creek Ln Columbus (43235) *(G-5766)*

Show What You Know, Dayton *Also Called: Lorenz Corporation (G-6416)*

Shrader Tire & Oil Inc.. 419 420-8435
3511 Genoa Rd Perrysburg (43551) *(G-12426)*

Shrader Tire Oil Fleet Tire S, Perrysburg *Also Called: Shrader Tire & Oil Inc (G-12426)*

Shreiner Company... 800 722-9915
50 Straits Ln Killbuck (44637) *(G-8921)*

Shreiner Sole Company Inc.. 330 276-6135
1 Taylor Dr Killbuck (44637) *(G-8922)*

Shreve Printing LLC.. 330 567-2341
390 E Wood St Shreve (44676) *(G-13215)*

Shuler Pewter, Chagrin Falls *Also Called: EL Ostendorf Inc (G-2377)*

Shupert Manufacturing Inc... 937 859-7492
3660 Benner Rd Miamisburg (45342) *(G-10682)*

Shur-Fit Distributors Inc... 937 746-0567
221 N Main St Franklin (45005) *(G-7702)*

Shur-Form Laminates Division, Franklin *Also Called: Shur-Fit Distributors Inc (G-7702)*

Sibg, Cleveland *Also Called: Snyder Intl Brewing Group LLC (G-4711)*

Sid-Mar Foods Inc... 330 743-0112
1481 South Ave Ste 182 Youngstown (44502) *(G-16437)*

Sidari's Italian Foods, Cleveland *Also Called: Gsi of Ohio LLC (G-4154)*

Sideway Signs LLC 501 400-4013
4842 Hanley Rd Cincinnati (45247) *(G-3388)*

Sidley Truck & Equipment, Thompson *Also Called: R W Sidley Incorporated (G-14063)*

Sidney Alive 937 210-2539
101 S Ohio Ave Sidney (45365) *(G-13287)*

Sidney Manufacturing Company 937 492-4154
405 N Main Ave Sidney (45365) *(G-13288)*

Sidney Plant, Sidney *Also Called: Advanced Composites Inc (G-13218)*

Sidwell Materials Inc 740 968-4313
72607 Gun Club Rd Saint Clairsville (43950) *(G-12923)*

Sieb & Meyer America Inc 513 563-0860
4884 Duff Dr Ste D West Chester (45246) *(G-15585)*

Sieb & Meyer America USA, West Chester *Also Called: Sieb & Meyer America Inc (G-15585)*

Siebtechnik Tema Inc 513 489-7811
7806 Redsky Dr Cincinnati (45249) *(G-3389)*

Siebtechnik Tema Inc 513 489-7811
7806 Redsky Dr Cincinnati (45249) *(G-3390)*

Siemens AG 513 576-2451
6693 Summer Field Dr Mason (45040) *(G-10055)*

Siemens Energy Inc 740 393-8200
607 W Chestnut St Mount Vernon (43050) *(G-11294)*

Siemens Energy Inc 740 393-8897
105 N Sandusky St Mount Vernon (43050) *(G-11295)*

Siemens Energy Inc 740 504-1947
105 N Sandusky St Mount Vernon (43050) *(G-11296)*

Siemens Industry Inc 937 593-6010
811 N Main St Bellefontaine (43311) *(G-1219)*

Siemens Industry Inc 513 576-2088
2000 Eastman Dr Milford (45150) *(G-10922)*

Siemens Industry Inc 513 841-3100
4620 Forest Ave Norwood (45212) *(G-12000)*

Siemens Power and Gas, Mount Vernon *Also Called: Siemens Energy Inc (G-11296)*

Siemer Distributing, New Lexington *Also Called: Lori Holding Co (G-11453)*

Sierra Nevada Corporation 937 431-2800
2611 Commons Blvd Beavercreek (45431) *(G-1062)*

SIFCO, Cleveland *Also Called: Sifco Industries Inc (G-4700)*

Sifco Applied Srfc Cncepts LLC (PA) 216 524-0099
5708 E Schaaf Rd Cleveland (44131) *(G-4699)*

Sifco ASC, Cleveland *Also Called: Sifco Applied Srfc Cncepts LLC (G-4699)*

Sifco Industries Inc (PA) 216 881-8600
970 E 64th St Cleveland (44103) *(G-4700)*

Sightgain, Mason *Also Called: Sightgain Inc (G-10056)*

Sightgain Inc 202 494-9317
5325 Deerfield Blvd Mason (45040) *(G-10056)*

Sigma Div, Newburgh Heights *Also Called: Howmet Aluminum Casting Inc (G-11616)*

Sigma T E K, Cincinnati *Also Called: Sigmatek Systems LLC (G-3391)*

Sigma Tube Company 419 729-9756
1050 Progress Ave Toledo (43612) *(G-14472)*

Sigma-Aldrich, Miamisburg *Also Called: Aldrich Chemical (G-10608)*

Sigma-Aldrich Corporation 216 206-5424
4353 E 49th St Cleveland (44125) *(G-4701)*

Sigman Cladding Inc 330 497-5200
7630 Freedom Ave Nw North Canton (44720) *(G-11761)*

Sigmatek Systems LLC (HQ) 513 674-0005
1445 Kemper Meadow Dr Cincinnati (45240) *(G-3391)*

Sign America Incorporated 740 765-5555
3887 State Route 43 Richmond (43944) *(G-12803)*

Sign Connection Inc 937 435-4070
90 Compark Rd Ste B Dayton (45459) *(G-6572)*

Sign Design, Wooster *Also Called: Sign Design Wooster Inc (G-16172)*

Sign Design Wooster Inc 330 262-8838
1537 W Old Lincoln Way Wooster (44691) *(G-16172)*

Sign Technologies LLC 937 439-3970
2001 Kuntz Rd Dayton (45404) *(G-6573)*

Sign Write 937 559-4388
3348 Dayton Xenia Rd Beavercreek (45432) *(G-1063)*

Sign-A-Rama, Columbus *Also Called: Business Idntfction Systems In (G-5223)*

Sign-A-Rama, Macedonia *Also Called: Signarama (G-9573)*

Sign-A-Rama, South Point *Also Called: Kinoly Signs (G-13469)*

Signal Interactive 614 360-3938
401 W Town St # B Columbus (43215) *(G-5767)*

Signalysis Inc 513 528-6164
539 Glenrose Ln Cincinnati (45244) *(G-3392)*

Signarama 330 468-0556
9862 Freeway Dr Macedonia (44056) *(G-9573)*

Signature 4 Image, Coldwater *Also Called: Signature Partners Inc (G-5001)*

Signature Cabinetry Inc 614 252-2227
1285 Alum Creek Dr Columbus (43209) *(G-5768)*

Signature Control Systems, Columbus *Also Called: Tiba LLC (G-5826)*

Signature Flexible Packg LLC 614 252-2121
2901 E 4th Ave Columbus (43219) *(G-5769)*

Signature Mold and Fabrication, Akron *Also Called: Kirtley Mold Inc (G-211)*

Signature Partners Inc 419 678-1400
149 Harvest Dr Coldwater (45828) *(G-5001)*

Signature Printing, Dayton *Also Called: Dayton Legal Blank Inc (G-6281)*

Signature Sign Co Inc 216 426-1234
1776 E 43rd St Cleveland (44103) *(G-4702)*

Signature Stitch LLC 440 382-1388
27519 Detroit Rd Westlake (44145) *(G-15788)*

Signature Store Fixtures, Columbus *Also Called: A-Display Service Corp (G-5082)*

Signature Technologies Inc (DH) 937 859-6323
3728 Benner Rd Miamisburg (45342) *(G-10683)*

Signcom Incorporated 614 228-9999
527 W Rich St Columbus (43215) *(G-5770)*

Signet Enterprises LLC (PA) 330 762-9102
19 N High St Akron (44308) *(G-331)*

Signet Group Inc 330 668-5000
375 Ghent Rd Fairlawn (44333) *(G-7450)*

Signet Group Services US Inc 330 668-5000
375 Ghent Rd Fairlawn (44333) *(G-7451)*

Signetics, Dayton *Also Called: Sign Technologies LLC (G-6573)*

Signme LLC 614 221-7803
39 E Gay St Columbus (43215) *(G-5771)*

Signode Industrial Group LLC 513 248-2990
396 Wards Corner Rd Ste 100 Loveland (45140) *(G-9505)*

Signs Limited LLC 740 282-7715
356 Technology Way Steubenville (43952) *(G-13677)*

Signs Now Dayton, Dayton *Also Called: Doxie Inc (G-6160)*

Signs Ohio Inc 419 228-7446
57 Town Sq Lima (45801) *(G-9289)*

Signs Unlmted The Grphic Advnt (PA) 614 836-7446
21313 State Route 93 S Logan (43138) *(G-9376)*

Signwire Worldwide Inc 937 428-6189
2781 Thunderhawk Ct Dayton (45414) *(G-6574)*

Signwire.com, Dayton *Also Called: Signwire Worldwide Inc (G-6574)*

Sika Mbcc US LLC 216 839-7500
23700 Chagrin Blvd Beachwood (44122) *(G-1024)*

Silcor Oilfield Services Inc 330 448-8500
6874 Strimbu Dr Brookfield (44403) *(G-1674)*

Siler Excavation Services 513 400-8628
6025 Catherine Dr Milford (45150) *(G-10923)*

Silfex Inc (HQ) 937 472-3311
950 S Franklin St Eaton (45320) *(G-7070)*

Silfex Inc 937 324-2487
1000 Titus Rd Springfield (45502) *(G-13632)*

Silgan, Ottawa *Also Called: Silgan Plastics LLC (G-12191)*

Silgan Dispensing Systems Corp 330 425-4260
1244 Highland Rd E Macedonia (44056) *(G-9574)*

Silgan Plastics LLC 419 523-3737
690 Woodland Dr Ottawa (45875) *(G-12191)*

Silicon Processors Inc 740 373-2252
1988 Masonic Park Rd Marietta (45750) *(G-9823)*

Silicone Solutions Inc 330 920-3125
338 Remington Rd Cuyahoga Falls (44224) *(G-6117)*

Silly Brandz Global LLC 419 697-8324
148 Main St Toledo (43605) *(G-14473)*

Silmarillion Partners Inc (PA) 330 821-4700
2290 W Main St Alliance (44601) *(G-424)*

Silmix Division, Canton *Also Called: Wacker Chemical Corporation (G-2264)*

Silver Line Building Pdts LLC 740 382-5595
2549 Innovation Dr Marion (43302) *(G-9881)*

Silver Machine Co, Elyria *Also Called: Ultra Machine Inc (G-7214)*

Silvesco Inc 740 373-6661
2985 State Route 26 Marietta (45750) *(G-9824)*

Simco Gas Ohio 2005 Partne 330 799-2268
200 Victoria Rd Bldg 4 Youngstown (44515) *(G-16438)*

Simcote Inc 740 382-5000
250 N Greenwood St Marion (43302) *(G-9882)*

Simcote of Ohio Division, Marion *Also Called: Simcote Inc (G-9882)*

Simet, Hudson *Also Called: Sintered Metal Industries Inc (G-8612)*

Simmers Crane Design & Svcs, Salem *Also Called: Flatiron Crane Oper Co LLC (G-12995)*

Simmons Feed & Supply LLC 800 754-1228
600 Snyder Rd Salem (44460) *(G-13031)*

Simmons Grain Company, Salem *Also Called: Simmons Feed & Supply LLC (G-13031)*

Simon De Young Corporation 440 834-3000
15010 Berkshire Industrial Pkwy Middlefield (44062) *(G-10789)*

Simon Ellis Superabrasives Inc 937 226-0683
501 Progress Rd Dayton (45449) *(G-6575)*

Simon Roofing, Youngstown *Also Called: Simon Roofing and Shtmtl Corp (G-16439)*

Simon Roofing and Shtmtl Corp (PA) 330 629-7392
70 Karago Ave Youngstown (44512) *(G-16439)*

Simona Boltaron Inc 740 498-5900
1 General St Newcomerstown (43832) *(G-11651)*

Simona PMC LLC 419 429-0042
2040 Industrial Dr Findlay (45840) *(G-7561)*

Simonds International LLC 978 424-0100
76000 Old Twenty One Rd Kimbolton (43749) *(G-8928)*

Simple Times LLC 614 504-3551
750 Cross Pointe Rd Ste M Columbus (43230) *(G-5772)*

Simplevms LLC 888 255-8918
7373 Beechmont Ave Ste 130 Cincinnati (45230) *(G-3393)*

Simply Bags, Canfield *Also Called: R J Manray Inc (G-2015)*

Simply Unique Snacks LLC 513 223-7736
4420 Haight Ave Cincinnati (45223) *(G-3394)*

Simpson & Sons Inc 513 367-0152
10220 Harrison Ave Harrison (45030) *(G-8292)*

Simpson Strong-Tie Company Inc 614 876-8060
2600 International St Columbus (43228) *(G-5773)*

Sims Bros Inc (PA) 740 387-9041
1011 S Prospect St Marion (43302) *(G-9883)*

Sims Brothers Recycling, Marion *Also Called: Sims Bros Inc (G-9883)*

Sims-Lohman Inc 440 799-8285
1500 Valley Belt Rd Brooklyn Heights (44131) *(G-1701)*

Sims-Lohman Inc (PA) 513 651-3510
6325 Este Ave Cincinnati (45232) *(G-3395)*

Sims-Lohman Fine Kitchens Gran, Cincinnati *Also Called: Sims-Lohman Inc (G-3395)*

Sinbon Ohio LLC 937 415-2070
815 S Brown School Rd Vandalia (45377) *(G-14959)*

Sinbon Usa LLC 937 667-8999
4265 Gibson Dr Tipp City (45371) *(G-14154)*

Sinel Company Inc 937 433-4772
4811 Pamela Sue Dr Dayton (45429) *(G-6576)*

Singleton Corporation 216 651-7800
3280 W 67th Pl Cleveland (44102) *(G-4703)*

Singleton Reels Inc 330 274-2961
4612 Lynn Rd Rootstown (44272) *(G-12857)*

Sinico Mtm US Inc 216 264-8344
7007 Engle Rd Ste C Middleburg Heights (44130) *(G-10727)*

Sintered Metal Industries Inc 330 650-4000
1890 Georgetown Rd Hudson (44236) *(G-8612)*

Sir Steak Machinery Inc 419 526-9181
40 Baird Pkwy Mansfield (44903) *(G-9718)*

Siraj Recovery LLC 614 893-3507
4088 Seigman Ave Columbus (43213) *(G-5774)*

Sirrus Inc 513 448-0308
422 Wards Corner Rd Loveland (45140) *(G-9506)*

Sister Schbrts Hmmade Rlls Inc (DH) 334 335-2232
380 Polaris Pkwy Ste 400 Westerville (43082) *(G-15678)*

Sister Schubert's, Westerville *Also Called: Sister Schbrts Hmmade Rlls Inc (G-15678)*

Sit Inc 330 758-8468
1305 Boardman Canfield Rd Youngstown (44512) *(G-16440)*

Six C Fabrication Inc 330 296-5594
5245 S Prospect St Ravenna (44266) *(G-12734)*

Sixteen Brcks Artsan Bakehouse, Cincinnati *Also Called: Morgan4140 LLC (G-3173)*

Sjbs, Akron *Also Called: Standard Jig Boring Svc LLC (G-334)*

Sje Rhombus Controls 419 281-5767
2221 Ford Dr Ashland (44805) *(G-614)*

Sjk Machine LLC 330 868-3072
1862 Ben Fulton Rd North Lawrence (44666) *(G-11799)*

Sk, Cincinnati *Also Called: Sk Textile Inc (G-3396)*

Sk Mold & Tool Inc (PA) 937 339-0299
955 N 3rd St Tipp City (45371) *(G-14155)*

Sk Mold & Tool Inc 937 339-0299
2120 Corporate Dr Troy (45373) *(G-14610)*

Sk Screen Printing Inc 330 475-0286
89 Monroe Ave Akron (44301) *(G-332)*

Sk Tech Inc 937 836-3535
200 Metro Dr Englewood (45315) *(G-7242)*

Sk Textile Inc 800 888-9112
1 Knollcrest Dr Cincinnati (45237) *(G-3396)*

SK Wellman Corp 440 528-4000
6180 Cochran Rd Solon (44139) *(G-13421)*

SKF Machine Tool Services, Cleveland *Also Called: SKF USA Inc (G-4704)*

SKF Machine Tools Service, Cleveland *Also Called: American Precision Spindlee (G-3655)*

SKF USA Inc 440 720-0275
670 Alpha Dr Cleveland (44143) *(G-4704)*

Skid Guard, Cleveland *Also Called: Sure-Foot Industries Corp (G-4756)*

Skidmore-Wilhelm Mfg Company 216 481-4774
30340 Solon Industrial Pkwy Ste B Solon (44139) *(G-13422)*

Skiff Craft, Plain City *Also Called: W of Ohio Inc (G-12601)*

Skinner Firestone Inc 740 984-4247
226 Fifth St Beverly (45715) *(G-1321)*

Skinner Machining Co 216 486-6636
38127 Willoughby Pkwy Willoughby (44094) *(G-15992)*

Skl Home, Cincinnati *Also Called: Saturday Knight Ltd (G-3363)*

Skladany Enterprises Inc 614 823-6882
695 Mccorkle Blvd Westerville (43082) *(G-15679)*

Skladany Printing Center, Westerville *Also Called: Skladany Enterprises Inc (G-15679)*

Skok Industries, Bedford *Also Called: E J Skok Industries (G-1119)*

Skribs Tool and Die Inc 440 951-7774
7555 Tyler Blvd Ste 11 Mentor (44060) *(G-10555)*

Skrl Die Casting Inc 440 946-7200
34580 Lakeland Blvd Willoughby (44095) *(G-15993)*

Skuld LLC 330 423-7339
2864 Columbus Rd Springfield (45503) *(G-13633)*

Skuttle Indoor Air Qulty Pdts, Marietta *Also Called: Skuttle Mfg Co (G-9825)*

Skuttle Mfg Co 740 373-9169
101 Margaret St Marietta (45750) *(G-9825)*

Sky Climber Fabricating LLC 740 990-9430
1600 Pittsburgh Dr Delaware (43015) *(G-6750)*

Sky Climber Wind Solutions LLC 740 203-3900
1800 Pittsburgh Dr Delaware (43015) *(G-6751)*

Skybox Packaging LLC 419 525-7209
1275 Pollock Pkwy Mansfield (44905) *(G-9719)*

Skylift Inc 440 960-2100
3000 Leavitt Rd Ste 6 Lorain (44052) *(G-9438)*

Skyline Cem Holdings LLC (PA) 513 874-1188
4180 Thunderbird Ln Fairfield (45014) *(G-7408)*

Skyline Chili, Fairfield *Also Called: Skyline Cem Holdings LLC (G-7408)*

Skyline Corporation 330 852-2483
580 Mill St Nw Sugarcreek (44681) *(G-13938)*

SKYLINE CORPORATION, Sugarcreek *Also Called: Skyline Corporation (G-13938)*

Skyline Material Sales LLC 937 661-1770
12325 Pommert Rd Greenfield (45123) *(G-8033)*

Skyline Trisource Exhibits, Cleveland *Also Called: Ternion Inc (G-4777)*

Skyliner 740 738-0874
225 Main St Bridgeport (43912) *(G-1649)*

Skymark Refuelers LLC 419 957-1709
1525 Lima Ave Findlay (45840) *(G-7562)*

Skyridge Roofing & Masnry LLC 440 628-1983
34880 Vine St Willowick (44095) *(G-16034)*

ALPHABETIC SECTION

Skyway Cement Company LLC.. 513 478-0034
3155 Homeward Way Fairfield (45014) *(G-7409)*

SL Endmills Inc.. 513 851-6363
133 Circle Freeway Dr West Chester (45246) *(G-15586)*

Slabe... 440 298-3693
8000 Plank Rd Thompson (44086) *(G-14064)*

Slabe Machine Products LLC... 440 946-6555
4659 Hamann Pkwy Willoughby (44094) *(G-15994)*

Slater Builders Supply, The Plains *Also Called: Tyjen Inc (G-14059)*

Slater Road Mills Inc... 330 332-9951
11000 Youngstown Salem Rd Salem (44460) *(G-13032)*

Slicechief, Toledo *Also Called: CM Slicechief Co (G-14246)*

Slimans Printery Inc... 330 454-9141
624 5th St Nw Canton (44703) *(G-2226)*

Slimline Surgical Devices LLC.. 937 335-0496
1990 W Stanfield Rd Troy (45373) *(G-14611)*

Slm LLC.. 330 874-7131
125 Canal St Ne Bolivar (44612) *(G-1537)*

Sloat Inc.. 440 951-9554
34099 Melinz Pkwy Unit A Willoughby (44095) *(G-15995)*

Slone Gear International Inc.. 507 401-4327
207 S 1st St Tipp City (45371) *(G-14156)*

Slush Puppie.. 513 771-0940
44 Carnegie Way West Chester (45246) *(G-15587)*

Sluterbeck Tool & Die Co Inc.. 937 836-5736
7540 Jacks Lane Clayton (45315) *(G-3568)*

Sluterbeck Tool Co, Clayton *Also Called: Sluterbeck Tool & Die Co Inc (G-3568)*

Sly Inc (PA).. 800 334-2957
8300 Dow Cir Ste 600 Strongsville (44136) *(G-13881)*

Small Business Products... 800 553-6485
8603 Winton Rd Cincinnati (45231) *(G-3397)*

Small Sand & Gravel Inc... 740 427-3130
10229 Killduff Rd Gambier (43022) *(G-7907)*

Small's Ready-Mixed Concrete, Gambier *Also Called: Smalls Inc (G-7909)*

Smalls Asphalt Paving Inc.. 740 427-4096
10229 Killduff Rd Gambier (43022) *(G-7908)*

Smalls Inc.. 740 427-3633
10229 Killduff Rd Gambier (43022) *(G-7909)*

Smart Business Magazine, Cleveland *Also Called: Smart Business Network Inc (G-4705)*

Smart Business Network Inc (PA)....................................... 440 250-7000
835 Sharon Dr Ste 200 Cleveland (44145) *(G-4705)*

Smart Force LLC.. 216 481-8100
22801 Saint Clair Ave Cleveland (44117) *(G-4706)*

Smart Snic Stencil Clg Systems, Cleveland *Also Called: Smart Sonic Corporation (G-4707)*

Smart Solutions, Strongsville *Also Called: Ohio Cllbrtive Lrng Sltons Inc (G-13862)*

Smart Sonic Corporation... 818 610-7900
837 E 79th St Cleveland (44103) *(G-4707)*

Smartbill Ltd.. 740 928-6909
1050 O Neill Dr Hebron (43025) *(G-8362)*

Smartronix Inc... 216 378-3300
416 Apple Hill Dr Northfield (44067) *(G-11910)*

Smartsoda Holdings Inc (PA)... 888 998-9668
6095 Parkland Blvd Cleveland (44124) *(G-4708)*

Smashray Ltd... 989 620-7507
6450 Weatherfield Ct Maumee (43537) *(G-10232)*

SMC Corporation of America.. 330 659-2006
4160 Highlander Pkwy Ste 200 Richfield (44286) *(G-12798)*

Smead Manufacturing Company.. 740 385-5601
851 Smead Rd Logan (43138) *(G-9377)*

Smg Growing Media Inc (HQ)... 937 644-0011
14111 Scottslawn Rd Marysville (43040) *(G-9938)*

Smgm LLC.. 937 644-0011
14111 Scottslawn Rd Marysville (43040) *(G-9939)*

SMI Holdings Inc... 740 927-3464
10685 Columbus Pkwy Pataskala (43062) *(G-12309)*

Smith & Thompson Entps LLC.. 330 386-9345
46368 Y And O Rd East Liverpool (43920) *(G-7000)*

Smith and Thompson Enterprise, East Liverpool *Also Called: Smith & Thompson Entps LLC (G-7000)*

Smith Brothers Erection Inc.. 740 373-3575
101 Industry Rd Marietta (45750) *(G-9826)*

Smith Carl E Cnslting Engneers, Bath *Also Called: Warmus and Associates Inc (G-962)*

Smith Concrete.. 740 439-7714
61539 Southgate Rd Cambridge (43725) *(G-1952)*

Smith Concrete Co... 740 593-5633
5240 Hebbardsville Rd Athens (45701) *(G-697)*

Smith Concrete Co (PA).. 740 373-7441
2301 Progress St Dover (44622) *(G-6843)*

Smith Electro Chemical Co.. 513 351-7227
5936 Carthage Ct Cincinnati (45212) *(G-3398)*

Smith Machine Inc.. 330 821-9898
20651 Lake Park Blvd Alliance (44601) *(G-425)*

Smith Pallet LLC... 937 564-6492
9855 State Route 121 Versailles (45380) *(G-14989)*

Smith Rn Sheet Metal Shop Inc.. 740 653-5011
1312 Campground Rd Lancaster (43130) *(G-9039)*

Smith-Lustig Paper Box Mfg Co... 216 621-0453
22475 Aurora Rd Bedford (44146) *(G-1155)*

Smithers Group Inc... 330 833-8548
1845 Harsh Ave Se Massillon (44646) *(G-10145)*

Smithers-Oasis Company.. 330 673-5831
919 Marvin St Bldg Dc Kent (44240) *(G-8864)*

Smithers-Oasis Company (PA)... 330 945-5100
295 S Water St Ste 201 Kent (44240) *(G-8865)*

Smithersoasis North America, Kent *Also Called: Smithers-Oasis Company (G-8865)*

Smithfield Direct LLC.. 419 422-2233
4411 Township Road 142 Findlay (45840) *(G-7563)*

Smithfield Packaged Meats Corp (DH)............................... 513 782-3800
805 E Kemper Rd Cincinnati (45246) *(G-3399)*

Smithfoods Inc (PA).. 330 683-8710
1381 Dairy Ln Orrville (44667) *(G-12151)*

Smithfoods Orrville Inc.. 330 683-8710
1381 Dairy Ln Orrville (44667) *(G-12152)*

Smiths Medical Asd Inc.. 800 796-8701
5200 Upper Metro Pl Ste 200 Dublin (43017) *(G-6937)*

Smiths Medical Asd Inc.. 614 889-2220
6250 Shier Rings Rd Dublin (43016) *(G-6938)*

Smiths Medical North America... 614 210-7300
5200 Upper Metro Pl Ste 200 Dublin (43017) *(G-6939)*

Smiths Medical Pm Inc (PA)... 614 210-7300
5200 Upper Metro Pl Ste 200 Dublin (43017) *(G-6940)*

Smithville Mfg Co... 330 345-5818
6563 Cleveland Rd Wooster (44691) *(G-16173)*

Smoke Rings Inc... 419 420-9966
1928 Tiffin Ave Findlay (45840) *(G-7564)*

Smp Welding LLC... 440 205-9353
8171 Tyler Blvd Mentor (44060) *(G-10556)*

SMS Technologies Inc.. 419 465-4175
3531 Everingin Rd Monroeville (44847) *(G-11126)*

Smucker Foodservice Inc... 877 858-3855
1 Strawberry Ln Orrville (44667) *(G-12153)*

Smucker International Inc... 330 682-3000
1 Strawberry Ln Orrville (44667) *(G-12154)*

Smucker Manufacturing Inc... 888 550-9555
1 Strawberry Ln Orrville (44667) *(G-12155)*

Smucker Natural Foods Inc.. 330 682-3000
Strawberry Lane Orrville (44667) *(G-12156)*

Smucker Retail Foods Inc... 330 682-3000
1 Strawberry Ln Orrville (44667) *(G-12157)*

SMUCKER'S, Orrville *Also Called: J M Smucker Company (G-12129)*

Smucker's, Orrville *Also Called: Smucker International Inc (G-12154)*

Smyrna Ready Mix Concrete LLC....................................... 937 855-0410
9151 Township Park Dr Germantown (45327) *(G-7952)*

Smyrna Ready Mix Concrete LLC....................................... 937 773-0841
8395 Piqua Lockington Rd Piqua (45356) *(G-12554)*

Smyrna Ready Mix Concrete LLC....................................... 937 698-7229
555 Old Springfield Rd Vandalia (45377) *(G-14960)*

Snack Alliance Inc (DH).. 330 767-3426
100 Lincoln Way E Massillon (44646) *(G-10146)*

Snap Rite Manufacturing Inc... 910 897-4080
14300 Darley Ave Cleveland (44110) *(G-4709)*

Snap-On Business Solutions Inc (HQ)................................ 330 659-1600
4025 Kinross Lakes Pkwy Richfield (44286) *(G-12799)*

Snaps Inc.. 419 477-5100
2557 Township Road 35 Mount Cory (45868) *(G-11228)*

Sneller Machine Tool Division, Cleveland Also Called: Grand Harbor Yacht Sales & Svc *(G-4139)*

Snider General Tire, Cambridge Also Called: Snider Tire Inc *(G-1953)*

Snider Tire Inc... 740 439-2741
9501 Sunrise Rd Cambridge (43725) *(G-1953)*

Snow Aviation Intl Inc... 614 588-2452
949 Creek Dr Gahanna (43230) *(G-7849)*

Snow Dragon LLC.. 440 295-0238
1441 Chardon Rd Cleveland (44117) *(G-4710)*

Snow Printing Co Inc.. 419 229-7669
1000 W Grand Ave Frnt Lima (45801) *(G-9290)*

Snows Wood Shop Inc (PA)... 419 836-3805
7220 Brown Rd Oregon (43616) *(G-12111)*

Snowville Creamery LLC... 740 698-2301
32623 State Route 143 Pomeroy (45769) *(G-12614)*

Snyder Brick and Block, Dayton Also Called: Snyder Concrete Products Inc *(G-6577)*

Snyder Brick and Block, Moraine Also Called: Snyder Concrete Products Inc *(G-11211)*

Snyder Concrete Products Inc.. 937 224-1433
1433 S Euclid Ave Dayton (45417) *(G-6577)*

Snyder Concrete Products Inc (PA).. 937 885-5176
2301 W Dorothy Ln Moraine (45439) *(G-11211)*

Snyder Hot Shot, Wooster Also Called: H & H Equipment Inc *(G-16127)*

Snyder Intl Brewing Group LLC (PA).. 216 619-7424
1940 E 6th St Ste 200 Cleveland (44114) *(G-4711)*

Snyder Manufacturing Inc... 330 343-4456
3001 Progress St Dover (44622) *(G-6844)*

Soapyfluffs, Hamilton Also Called: Soapyfluffs LLC *(G-8243)*

Soapyfluffs LLC.. 937 823-0015
1600 Nw Washington Blvd Hamilton (45013) *(G-8243)*

Soaring Software Solutions Inc.. 419 442-7676
110 W Airport Hwy Ste 1 Swanton (43558) *(G-13982)*

Sobel Corrugated Containers Inc... 216 475-2100
1111 Superior Ave E Ste 1111 Cleveland (44114) *(G-4712)*

Socar of Ohio Inc (PA)... 419 596-3100
21739 Road E16 Continental (45831) *(G-5938)*

Soccer Centre Owners Ltd... 419 893-5425
1620 Market Place Dr Ste 1 Maumee (43537) *(G-10233)*

Society of The Precious Blood... 419 925-4516
2860 Us Route 127 Celina (45822) *(G-2349)*

Soelter Corporation... 800 838-8984
385 Carr Dr Brookville (45309) *(G-1744)*

Soemhejee Inc... 419 298-2306
128 W Vine St Edgerton (43517) *(G-7080)*

Soffseal Inc... 513 934-0815
11735 Chesterdale Rd Cincinnati (45246) *(G-3400)*

Sofie, Oakwood Village Also Called: N-Molecular Inc *(G-12040)*

Soft Touch Wood LLC... 330 545-4204
1560 S State St Girard (44420) *(G-7975)*

Soft Tuch Furn Repr Rfinishing, Girard Also Called: Soft Touch Wood LLC *(G-7975)*

Softbox Systems Inc.. 864 630-7860
675 Gateway Blvd Monroe (45050) *(G-11120)*

Software In Reach, Dublin Also Called: Dr Dave Solutions LLC *(G-6880)*

Software Solutions Inc (PA).. 513 932-6667
8534 Yankee St Ste 2b Dayton (45458) *(G-6578)*

Sojourners Truth Inc.. 419 243-0007
7 E Bancroft St Toledo (43620) *(G-14474)*

Solae LLC.. 419 483-0400
300 Great Lakes Pkwy Bellevue (44811) *(G-1235)*

Solae Central Soya, Bellevue Also Called: Solae LLC *(G-1235)*

Solae LLC.. 419 483-5340
605 Goodrich Rd Bellevue (44811) *(G-1236)*

Solar Arts Graphic Designs.. 330 744-0535
824 Tod Ave Youngstown (44502) *(G-16441)*

Solas Ltd... 650 501-0889
33587 Streamview Dr Avon (44011) *(G-788)*

Solas Global Solutions, Avon Also Called: Solas Ltd *(G-788)*

Sole Choice Inc.. 740 354-2813
2415 Scioto Trl Portsmouth (45662) *(G-12656)*

Soleo Health Inc.. 844 467-8200
6190 Shamrock Ct Ste 100 Dublin (43016) *(G-6941)*

Solid Dimensions Inc... 419 663-1134
720 Townline Road 151 Norwalk (44857) *(G-11989)*

Solid Dimensions Line, Norwalk Also Called: Solid Dimensions Inc *(G-11989)*

Solid Surface Concepts Inc... 513 948-8677
7660 Production Dr Cincinnati (45237) *(G-3401)*

Solid Surfaces Plus, Cleveland Also Called: Wdi Group Inc *(G-4898)*

Solidstate Controls LLC (HQ)... 614 846-7500
875 Dearborn Dr Columbus (43085) *(G-5775)*

Sollis Therapeutics Inc.. 614 701-9894
1274 Kinnear Rd Columbus (43212) *(G-5776)*

Solmet Drilling Solutions LLC.. 330 455-4328
2025 Dueber Ave Sw Canton (44706) *(G-2227)*

Solmet Technologies Inc... 330 915-4160
2716 Shepler Church Ave Sw Canton (44706) *(G-2228)*

Solo Dyna Systems Ltd... 440 871-7112
24220 Bruce Rd Bay Village (44140) *(G-967)*

Solo Products Inc.. 513 321-7884
838 Reedy St Cincinnati (45202) *(G-3402)*

Solo Vino Imports LLC.. 440 714-9591
450 Nicholson Rd Vermilion (44089) *(G-14973)*

Solon.. 440 498-1798
38235 Mcdowell Dr Solon (44139) *(G-13423)*

Solon Glass Center Inc... 440 248-5018
33001 Station St Cleveland (44139) *(G-4713)*

Solon Glass Ctr, Cleveland Also Called: Solon Glass Center Inc *(G-4713)*

Solon Manufacturing Company.. 440 286-7149
425 Center St Chardon (44024) *(G-2468)*

Solon Specialty Wire Co.. 440 248-7600
30000 Solon Rd Solon (44139) *(G-13424)*

Solstice Sleep Products Inc (PA).. 614 279-8850
3720 W Broad St Columbus (43228) *(G-5777)*

Solsys Inc.. 419 886-4683
96 Vanderbilt Rd Mansfield (44904) *(G-9720)*

Solut, Lewis Center Also Called: Duracorp LLC *(G-9158)*

Solution Industries LLC... 440 816-9500
21555 Drake Rd Strongsville (44149) *(G-13882)*

Solution Ventures Inc.. 330 858-1111
368 Vinewood Ave Tallmadge (44278) *(G-14047)*

Solutions In Polycarbonate LLC... 330 572-2860
6353 Norwalk Rd Medina (44256) *(G-10378)*

Solvay Advanced Polymers LLC.. 740 373-9242
17005 State Route 7 Marietta (45750) *(G-9827)*

Solvay Spclty Polymers USA LLC.. 740 373-9242
17005 State Route 7 Marietta (45750) *(G-9828)*

Solvent Solutions LLC... 937 648-4962
5014 Lausanne Dr Dayton (45458) *(G-6579)*

Somerville Manufacturing Inc... 740 336-7847
15 Townhall Rd Marietta (45750) *(G-9829)*

Sonalysts Inc.. 937 429-9711
2940 Presidential Dr Ste 160 Beavercreek (45324) *(G-1064)*

Sonoco Products Company.. 937 429-0040
761 Space Dr Beavercreek Township (45434) *(G-1094)*

Sonoco Products Company.. 614 759-8470
444 Mccormick Blvd Columbus (43213) *(G-5778)*

Sonoco Products Company.. 330 688-8247
59 N Main St Munroe Falls (44262) *(G-11305)*

Sonoco Products Company.. 513 870-3985
4633 Dues Dr West Chester (45246) *(G-15588)*

Sonoco Prtective Solutions Inc.. 419 420-0029
1900 Industrial Dr Findlay (45840) *(G-7565)*

Sonogage Inc.. 216 464-1119
26650 Renaissance Pkwy Ste 3 Cleveland (44128) *(G-4714)*

Sonosite Inc.. 425 951-1200
236 High St Hamilton (45011) *(G-8244)*

Soondook LLC.. 614 389-5757
6344 Nicholas Dr Columbus (43235) *(G-5779)*

Soprema USA Inc (HQ).. 330 334-0066
310 Quadral Dr Wadsworth (44281) *(G-15066)*

Sorbothane Inc (PA)... 330 678-9444
2144 State Route 59 Kent (44240) *(G-8866)*

ALPHABETIC SECTION — Specialty Packg Licensing Ltd

Soterra LLC 740 549-6072
425 Winter Rd Delaware (43015) *(G-6752)*

Sound Communications Inc 614 875-8500
3474 Park St Grove City (43123) *(G-8120)*

Sound Laboratory LLC 330 968-4060
109 S Water St Kent (44240) *(G-8867)*

Soundex Communications Group, Dayton Also Called: Dcm Soundex Inc *(G-6295)*

Soundtrace Inc 513 278-5288
408 4th Ave Mason (45040) *(G-10057)*

Soundwich Inc 216 249-4900
17000 Saint Clair Ave Cleveland (44110) *(G-4715)*

Soundwich Inc (PA) 216 486-2666
881 Wayside Rd Cleveland (44110) *(G-4716)*

Soundworks Inc 408 219-5737
7951 W Erie Ave Lorain (44053) *(G-9439)*

Source3media Inc 330 467-9003
9085 Freeway Dr Macedonia (44056) *(G-9575)*

South Akron Awning Co (PA) 330 848-7611
763 Kenmore Blvd Akron (44314) *(G-333)*

South Central Industrial LLC 740 333-5401
1825 Old Us 35 Se Wshngtn Ct Hs (43160) *(G-16241)*

South Plant, Barberton Also Called: PPG Industries Inc *(G-891)*

South Shore Controls Inc 440 259-2500
9395 Pinecone Dr Mentor (44060) *(G-10557)*

South Shore Finishers Inc 216 664-1792
1720 Willey Ave Cleveland (44113) *(G-4717)*

South Side Drive Thru 937 295-2927
9204 Hilgefort Rd Fort Loramie (45845) *(G-7610)*

Southast Diesl Acquisition Sub, Greenville Also Called: Stateline Power Corp *(G-8062)*

Southeast Health Center, Cleveland Also Called: Northast Ohio Nghbrhood Hlth S *(G-4474)*

Southeastern Container Inc 419 352-6300
307 Industrial Pkwy Bowling Green (43402) *(G-1589)*

Southeastern Emergency Eqp Co 919 556-1890
5000 Tuttle Crossing Blvd Dublin (43016) *(G-6942)*

Southeastern Shafting Mfg Inc 740 342-4629
402 W Broadway St New Lexington (43764) *(G-11457)*

Southern Bag, Wilmington Also Called: Hood Packaging Corporation *(G-16053)*

Southern Cabinetry Inc 740 245-5992
41 International Blvd Bidwell (45614) *(G-1327)*

Southern Champion Tray LP 513 755-7200
7100 Dixie Hwy Fairfield (45014) *(G-7410)*

Southern Champion Tray, L.P., Fairfield Also Called: Southern Champion Tray LP *(G-7410)*

Southern Division, Perrysburg Also Called: Ohio Table Pad Company *(G-12408)*

Southern Graphic Systems LLC 513 648-4641
9435 Waterstone Blvd Ste 300 Cincinnati (45249) *(G-3403)*

Southern Ohio Kitchens, Dayton Also Called: C-Link Enterprises LLC *(G-6244)*

Southern Ohio Lumber, Peebles Also Called: Southern Ohio Lumber LLC *(G-12333)*

Southern Ohio Lumber LLC 614 436-4472
11855 State Route 73 Peebles (45660) *(G-12333)*

Southern Ohio Mfg Inc 513 943-2555
3214 Marshall Dr Amelia (45102) *(G-465)*

Southern Ohio Printing 513 241-5150
2230 Gilbert Ave Cincinnati (45206) *(G-3404)*

Southern Ohio Vault Co Inc 740 456-5898
502 Shale Dr Portsmouth (45662) *(G-12657)*

Southern Wholesale, Millersburg Also Called: Affordable Barn Co Ltd *(G-10938)*

Southpaw Enterprises Inc 937 252-7676
2350 Dryden Rd Moraine (45439) *(G-11212)*

Southpaw Industries LLC 714 215-8592
1304 Cedarwood Dr Apt C1 Westlake (44145) *(G-15789)*

Southside Wolfies 419 422-5450
546 6th St Findlay (45840) *(G-7566)*

Southstern McHning Feld Svc In (PA) 740 689-1147
500 Lincoln Ave Lancaster (43130) *(G-9040)*

Southwest Ohio Computer Assn, Fairfield Township Also Called: Butler Tech *(G-7430)*

Southwood Pallet LLC 330 682-3747
8849 Lincoln Way E Orrville (44667) *(G-12158)*

Souzza LLC 330 479-9500
3315 Lincoln Way E Massillon (44646) *(G-10147)*

Sovac, Portsmouth Also Called: Southern Ohio Vault Co Inc *(G-12657)*

Sovereign Circuits Inc 330 538-3900
12080 Debartolo Dr North Jackson (44451) *(G-11790)*

SP Mount Printing Company 216 881-3316
1306 E 55th St Cleveland (44103) *(G-4718)*

Sp3 Winco LLC 937 667-4476
835 N Hyatt St Tipp City (45371) *(G-14157)*

Space & Sensors, Mason Also Called: L3harris Cincinnati Elec Corp *(G-10019)*

Space-Links Inc 330 788-2401
1110 Thalia Ave Youngstown (44512) *(G-16442)*

Spacelinks Enterprises Inc 330 788-2401
1110 Thalia Ave Youngstown (44512) *(G-16443)*

Spalding 440 286-5717
12860 Mayfield Rd Chardon (44024) *(G-2469)*

Spallinger Millwright Svc Co 419 225-5830
1155 E Hanthorn Rd Lima (45804) *(G-9291)*

Spalinger Atclave Systms/US MI, Lima Also Called: Spallinger Millwright Svc Co *(G-9291)*

Spang & Company 440 350-6108
9305 Progress Pkwy Mentor (44060) *(G-10558)*

Spangler Candy Company (PA) 419 636-4221
400 N Portland St Bryan (43506) *(G-1838)*

SPAOS Inc (PA) 937 890-0783
6012 N Dixie Dr Dayton (45414) *(G-6580)*

Sparks Belting Company Inc 216 398-7774
4653 Spring Rd Cleveland (44131) *(G-4719)*

Sparoom, Bedford Heights Also Called: Unitrex Ltd *(G-1180)*

Spartech LLC 937 548-1395
1050 Landsdowne Ave Greenville (45331) *(G-8059)*

Spartech LLC 419 399-4050
925 W Gasser Rd Paulding (45879) *(G-12320)*

Spartech Mexico Holding Co Two 440 930-3619
33587 Walker Rd Avon Lake (44012) *(G-824)*

Spartech Plastics, Paulding Also Called: Spartech LLC *(G-12320)*

Sparton Enterprises LLC 877 772-7866
3717 Clark Mill Rd Barberton (44203) *(G-896)*

Spartronics Strongsville Inc 440 878-4630
22740 Lunn Rd Strongsville (44149) *(G-13883)*

Spear Application Systems, Mason Also Called: Spear Inc *(G-10058)*

Spear Inc 513 459-1100
5510 Courseview Dr Mason (45040) *(G-10058)*

Spear Stone Press 513 899-7337
2691 Blackgold Ct Morrow (45152) *(G-11225)*

Spearfysh Inc 330 487-0300
60 W Streetsboro St Ste 5 Hudson (44236) *(G-8613)*

Special Design Products Inc 614 272-6700
520 Industrial Mile Rd Columbus (43228) *(G-5780)*

Special Machined Components 513 459-1113
7626 Easy St Mason (45040) *(G-10059)*

Special Metal Stamping, Columbia Station Also Called: Triad Capital Group LLC *(G-5023)*

Special Pack Inc 330 458-3204
5555 Massillon Rd Canton (44720) *(G-2229)*

Specialized Castings Ltd 937 669-5620
1569 Martindale Rd Greenville (45331) *(G-8060)*

Specialties Unlimited, Mentor Also Called: J & P Products Inc *(G-10480)*

Specialty America Inc 516 252-2438
8351 N High St Ste 285 Columbus (43235) *(G-5781)*

Specialty Ceramics Inc 330 482-0800
41995 State Route 344 Columbiana (44408) *(G-5051)*

Specialty Fab, North Lima Also Called: Bird Equipment LLC *(G-11801)*

Specialty Films Inc 614 471-9100
2887 Johnstown Rd Columbus (43219) *(G-5782)*

Specialty Hardware Inc 216 291-1160
2200 Kerwin Rd Apt 710 Cleveland (44118) *(G-4720)*

Specialty Lithographing Co 513 621-0222
1035 W 7th St Cincinnati (45203) *(G-3405)*

Specialty Machines Inc 937 837-8852
5370 Salem Ave Dayton (45426) *(G-6581)*

Specialty Metals Proc Inc 330 656-2767
837 Seasons Rd Hudson (44224) *(G-8614)*

Specialty Mfg & Service 330 821-4675
12280 Rockhill Ave Ne Alliance (44601) *(G-426)*

Specialty Packg Licensing Ltd, Toledo Also Called: Bprex Plastic Services Co Inc *(G-14219)*

Specialty Polymer Product — ALPHABETIC SECTION

Specialty Polymer Product.. 216 281-8300
Rocky River (44116) *(G-12844)*

Specialty Printing and Proc.. 614 322-9035
4670 Groves Rd Columbus (43232) *(G-5783)*

Specialty Svcs Cabinetry Inc.. 614 421-1599
1253 Essex Ave Columbus (43201) *(G-5784)*

Specialty Switch Company LLC.................................... 330 427-3000
525 Mcclurg Rd Youngstown (44512) *(G-16444)*

Specialty Trans Components, Youngstown Also Called: Specialty Switch Company LLC *(G-16444)*

Specialty Wine-Spirits, Sandusky Also Called: Lonz Winery LLC *(G-13075)*

Specialty Wood Products, Cincinnati Also Called: Wjf Enterprises LLC *(G-3523)*

Spectex LLC.. 603 330-3334
6156 Wesselman Rd Cincinnati (45248) *(G-3406)*

Spectra Group Limited Inc... 419 837-9783
27800 Lemoyne Rd Ste J Millbury (43447) *(G-10936)*

Spectra Photopolymers, Millbury Also Called: Formlabs Ohio Inc *(G-10932)*

Spectra Photopolymers, Millbury Also Called: Spectra Group Limited Inc *(G-10936)*

Spectra-Tech Manufacturing Inc................................... 513 735-9300
4013 Borman Dr Batavia (45103) *(G-949)*

Spectracam Ltd... 937 223-3805
1112 East Race Dr Dayton (45404) *(G-8582)*

Spectre Industries LLC... 440 665-2600
10185 Gottschalk Pkwy Ste 1 Chagrin Falls (44023) *(G-2423)*

Spectre Powerboats LLC.. 937 292-7674
227 Water Ave Bellefontaine (43311) *(G-1220)*

Spectre Sensors Inc... 440 250-0372
2392 Georgia Dr Westlake (44145) *(G-15790)*

Spectron Inc.. 937 461-5590
132 S Terry St Dayton (45403) *(G-6583)*

Spectrum Adhesives Inc... 740 763-2886
11047 Lambs Ln Newark (43055) *(G-11606)*

Spectrum Brands Inc.. 567 998-7930
2800 Concorde Dr Vandalia (45377) *(G-14961)*

Spectrum Brnds Globl Auto Care, Vandalia Also Called: Spectrum Brands Inc *(G-14961)*

Spectrum Machine Inc (PA).. 330 626-3666
1668 Frost Rd Streetsboro (44241) *(G-13793)*

Spectrum Metal Finishing Inc....................................... 330 758-8358
535 Bev Rd Youngstown (44512) *(G-16445)*

Spectrum News Ohio... 614 384-2640
580 N 4th St Ste 350 Columbus (43215) *(G-5785)*

Spectrum Plastics Corporation..................................... 330 926-9766
99 E Ascot Ln Cuyahoga Falls (44223) *(G-6118)*

Spectrum Printing & Design, Dayton Also Called: Eugene Stewart *(G-6325)*

Spectrum Publications.. 740 439-3531
831 Wheeling Ave Cambridge (43725) *(G-1954)*

Spectrum Surgical Instruments, Stow Also Called: Steris Instrument MGT Svcs Inc *(G-13728)*

Spectrum Textiles Inc... 513 933-8346
5883 Casaway Rd Lebanon (45036) *(G-9111)*

Speed North America Inc... 330 202-7775
1700a Old Mansfield Rd Wooster (44691) *(G-16174)*

Speed-O-Print, Crooksville Also Called: Temple Oil and Gas LLC *(G-6050)*

Speedline North America Inc....................................... 937 291-7000
7887 Washington Village Dr Dayton (45459) *(G-6584)*

Speedpro Imaging... 513 771-4776
2888 E Kemper Rd Cincinnati (45241) *(G-3407)*

Speedpro Imaging... 513 753-5600
2000 Ford Cir Ste G Milford (45150) *(G-10924)*

Speedpro Imaging, Cleveland Also Called: Cleveland E Speedpro Imaging *(G-3839)*

Spence Technologies Inc.. 440 946-3035
4752 Topps Industrial Pkwy Willoughby (44094) *(G-15996)*

Spencer Feed & Supply LLC.. 330 648-2111
227 N Main St Spencer (44275) *(G-13483)*

Spencer Forge & Manufacturing, Spencer Also Called: Alta Mira Corporation *(G-13479)*

Spencer Forge & Manufacturing, Spencer Also Called: Spencer Manufacturing Company Inc *(G-13484)*

Spencer Manufacturing Company Inc.......................... 330 648-2461
225 N Main St Spencer (44275) *(G-13484)*

Sperry & Rice, Killbuck Also Called: Sperry & Rice LLC *(G-8924)*

Sperry & Rice LLC.. 330 276-2801
1088 N Main St Killbuck (44637) *(G-8923)*

Sperry & Rice LLC (PA).. 765 647-4141
1088 N Main St Killbuck (44637) *(G-8924)*

SPI Liquidation Inc
15285 S State Ave Middlefield (44062) *(G-10790)*

SPI Mailing, Canton Also Called: Slimans Printery Inc *(G-2226)*

Spicy Olive LLC... 513 376-9061
9901 Montgomery Rd Montgomery (45242) *(G-11131)*

Spicy Olive LLC (PA).. 513 847-4397
7671 Cox Ln West Chester (45069) *(G-15509)*

Spiegelberg Manufacturing Inc (HQ)............................ 440 324-3042
12200 Alameda Dr Strongsville (44149) *(G-13884)*

Spiegler Brake Systems USA, Dayton Also Called: Spiegler Brake Systems USA LLC *(G-6585)*

Spiegler Brake Systems USA LLC................................ 937 291-1735
1699 Thomas Paine Pkwy Dayton (45459) *(G-6585)*

Spikes Beverage Company Inc..................................... 513 429-5134
245 Northland Blvd Unit D Cincinnati (45246) *(G-3408)*

Spinal Balance Inc.. 419 530-5935
11360 S Airfield Rd Swanton (43558) *(G-13983)*

Spinnaker Coating, Troy Also Called: SC Liquidation Company LLC *(G-14607)*

Spinnker Prssure Snstive Pdts..................................... 800 543-9452
550 Summit Ave Troy (45373) *(G-14612)*

Spintech, Miamisburg Also Called: Spintech Holdings Inc *(G-10684)*

Spintech Holdings Inc... 937 912-3250
1964 Byers Rd Miamisburg (45342) *(G-10684)*

Spiral Brushes Inc... 330 686-2861
1355 Commerce Dr Stow (44224) *(G-13725)*

Spiral Publishing LLC.. 614 876-4347
4149 Maystar Way Hilliard (43026) *(G-8441)*

Spiralcool Company.. 419 483-2510
186 Sheffield St Ste 188 Bellevue (44811) *(G-1237)*

Spirex Corporation.. 330 726-1166
375 Victoria Rd Ste 1 Youngstown (44515) *(G-16446)*

Spirit Aeronautics, Columbus Also Called: Spirit Avionics Ltd *(G-5786)*

Spirit Avionics Ltd (PA)... 614 237-4271
465 Waterbury Ct Ste C Columbus (43230) *(G-5786)*

Spirol Shim Corporation (DH)...................................... 330 920-3655
321 Remington Rd Stow (44224) *(G-13726)*

Splendid LLC... 614 396-6481
1415 E Dublin Granville Rd Ste 219 Columbus (43229) *(G-5787)*

Spoerr Precast Concrete Inc.. 419 625-9132
2020 Caldwell St Sandusky (44870) *(G-13094)*

Sponseller Group Inc (PA)... 419 861-3000
1600 Timber Wolf Dr Holland (43528) *(G-8531)*

Sponseller Group Inc... 937 492-9949
1516 Target Dr Sidney (45365) *(G-13289)*

Sports & Sports, Ashtabula Also Called: Peska Inc *(G-654)*

Sports Art, Nashport Also Called: Bdp Services Inc *(G-11335)*

Sports Imports Incorporated.. 614 771-0246
6950 Worthington Galena Rd Worthington (43085) *(G-16212)*

Sportsco Imprinting.. 513 641-5111
8277 Wicklow Ave Cincinnati (45236) *(G-3409)*

Sportsmans Haven Inc.. 740 432-7243
14695 E Pike Rd Cambridge (43725) *(G-1955)*

Sportsmaster... 440 257-3900
9140 Lake Shore Blvd Mentor (44060) *(G-10559)*

Sportwing, Cleveland Also Called: Dawn Enterprises Inc *(G-3943)*

Sposie LLC.. 888 977-2229
4064 Technology Dr Maumee (43537) *(G-10234)*

Spot On Main LLC.. 740 285-0411
91 Harding Ave Jackson (45640) *(G-8723)*

Spot On Main Coffee Roastery, Jackson Also Called: Spot On Main LLC *(G-8723)*

Spotlight Writing LLC.. 216 751-6889
3344 Elsmere Rd Cleveland (44120) *(G-4721)*

Spradlin Bros Welding Co... 800 219-2182
2131 Quality Ln Springfield (45505) *(G-13634)*

Sprague Products, Brecksville Also Called: Curtiss-Wright Flow Control *(G-1611)*

Spring Grove Manufacturing Inc................................... 513 542-6900
2838 Spring Grove Ave Cincinnati (45225) *(G-3410)*

Spring Hlthcare Dagnostics LLC................................... 866 201-9503
16064 Beaver Pike Jackson (45640) *(G-8724)*

ALPHABETIC SECTION

Spring Team Inc... 440 275-5981
2851 Industrial Park Dr Austinburg (44010) *(G-750)*

Spring Works Incorporated.. 614 351-9345
3201 Alberta St Columbus (43204) *(G-5788)*

Springco Metal Coatings Inc.. 216 941-0020
12500 Elmwood Ave Cleveland (44111) *(G-4722)*

Springdot, Cincinnati Also Called: Springdot Inc *(G-3411)*

Springdot Inc (PA)... 513 542-4000
2611 Colerain Ave Cincinnati (45214) *(G-3411)*

Springfield News Sun, Springfield Also Called: Springfield Newspapers Inc *(G-13635)*

Springfield Newspapers Inc... 937 323-5533
137 E Main St Springfield (45502) *(G-13635)*

Springfield Plastics Inc... 937 322-6071
15 N Bechtle Ave Springfield (45504) *(G-13636)*

Springhill Dimensions... 330 317-1926
4530 Mount Eaton Rd S Dalton (44618) *(G-6143)*

Springseal Inc.. 330 626-0673
800 Enterprise Pkwy Ravenna (44266) *(G-12735)*

Sprint Print Inc... 740 622-4429
520 Main St Coshocton (43812) *(G-5997)*

Sprinter Marking Inc... 740 453-1000
1805 Chandlersville Rd Zanesville (43701) *(G-16565)*

Sprosty, Smithville Also Called: Ray C Sprosty Bag Co Inc *(G-13301)*

Spsi, Hartville Also Called: Scott Process Systems Inc *(G-8307)*

Spunfab, Cuyahoga Falls Also Called: Keuchel & Associates Inc *(G-6095)*

Spurlino Materials LLC... 513 202-1111
6600 Dry Fork Rd Cleves (45002) *(G-4964)*

Spurlino Materials LLC (PA)... 513 705-0111
4000 Oxford State Rd Middletown (45044) *(G-10858)*

Spz Machine Company Inc.. 330 848-3286
2871 Newpark Dr Norton (44203) *(G-11949)*

Square D Services... 440 526-9070
2525 E Royalton Rd Ste 6 Broadview Heights (44147) *(G-1667)*

Square One Solutions LLC.. 419 425-5445
130 Bentley Ct Findlay (45840) *(G-7567)*

Squeaky Clean Cincinnati Inc.. 513 729-2712
1500 Goodman Ave Cincinnati (45224) *(G-3412)*

Squeaky Clean Off & Coml Clg, Cincinnati Also Called: Squeaky Clean Cincinnati Inc *(G-3412)*

Sr Products.. 330 998-6500
1380 Highland Rd E Macedonia (44056) *(G-9576)*

SRC Liquidation LLC (PA)... 937 221-1000
111 W 1st St Dayton (45402) *(G-6586)*

SRC Worldwide, Cleveland Also Called: Buckingham Src Inc *(G-3768)*

SRC Worldwide Inc (HQ)... 216 941-6115
3425 Service Rd Cleveland (44111) *(G-4723)*

Sreco Flexible, Lima Also Called: Sewer Rodding Equipment Co *(G-9288)*

SRI Healthcare LLC... 513 398-6406
7086 Industrial Row Dr Mason (45040) *(G-10060)*

SRI Ohio Inc... 740 653-5800
1061 Mill Park Dr Lancaster (43130) *(G-9041)*

Srm Concrete, Piqua Also Called: Smyrna Ready Mix Concrete LLC *(G-12554)*

Sroufe Healthcare Products LLC.. 260 894-4171
961 Seville Rd Wadsworth (44281) *(G-15067)*

SRS Die Casting Holdings LLC (HQ)..................................... 330 467-0750
635 Highland Rd E Macedonia (44056) *(G-9577)*

SRS Light Metals Inc (PA)... 330 467-0750
635 Highland Rd E Macedonia (44056) *(G-9578)*

SRS Manufacturing Corp... 937 746-3086
395 Industrial Dr Franklin (45005) *(G-7703)*

Srt Sales & Service LLC.. 330 620-0681
2917 Reserve Ave Copley (44321) *(G-5956)*

Ss Industries, Dayton Also Called: Stanco Precision Mfg Inc *(G-6589)*

SSC Controls Company... 440 205-1600
8909 East Ave Mentor (44060) *(G-10560)*

Sseco Solutions, Cleveland Also Called: Service Station Equipment Co *(G-4686)*

Ssi Manufacturing Inc... 513 761-7557
9615 Inter Ocean Dr West Chester (45246) *(G-15589)*

Ssi Tiles, Minerva Also Called: Kepcor Inc *(G-11032)*

SSP, Twinsburg Also Called: SSP Fittings Corp *(G-14736)*

SSP Fittings Corp (PA)... 330 425-4250
8250 Boyle Pkwy Twinsburg (44087) *(G-14736)*

SSP Industrial Group Inc.. 330 665-2900
3560 W Market St Ste 300 Fairlawn (44333) *(G-7452)*

Ssr Community Dev Group LLC... 216 466-2674
3957 Princeton Blvd Cleveland (44121) *(G-4724)*

St Clairsville Dairy Queen.. 740 635-1800
178 E Main St Saint Clairsville (43950) *(G-12924)*

St Henry Tile Co Inc... 937 548-1101
5410 S State Route 49 Greenville (45331) *(G-8061)*

St Henry Tile Co Inc... 419 678-4841
281 W Washington St Saint Henry (45883) *(G-12938)*

St Lawrence Holdings LLC.. 330 562-9000
16500 Rockside Rd Maple Heights (44137) *(G-9761)*

St Lawrence Steel Corporation.. 330 562-9000
16500 Rockside Rd Maple Heights (44137) *(G-9762)*

St Media Group International, Blue Ash Also Called: St Media Group Intl Inc *(G-1467)*

St Media Group Intl Inc.. 513 421-2050
11262 Cornell Park Dr Blue Ash (45242) *(G-1467)*

St Paul Park Refining Co... 419 422-2121
539 S Main St Findlay (45840) *(G-7568)*

STA-Warm Electric Company.. 330 296-6461
553 N Chestnut St Ravenna (44266) *(G-12736)*

Staber Industries Inc.. 614 836-5995
4800 Homer Ohio Ln Groveport (43125) *(G-8160)*

Stable Step LLC... 800 491-1571
961 Seville Rd Wadsworth (44281) *(G-15068)*

Stac Enterprises LLC... 513 574-7822
4211 Marcrest Dr Cincinnati (45211) *(G-3413)*

Staci Holdings Inc.. 440 284-2500
110 Commerce Dr Lagrange (44050) *(G-8955)*

Staci Lagrange, Lagrange Also Called: Inservco Inc *(G-8948)*

Stack Construction Tech Inc (PA).. 513 445-5122
9999 Carver Rd Blue Ash (45242) *(G-1468)*

Stack Constructyion Technology, Mason Also Called: To Scale Software LLC *(G-10066)*

Staco Energy Products Co.. 937 253-1191
301 Gaddis Blvd Dayton (45403) *(G-6587)*

Staco Energy Products Co (HQ).. 937 253-1191
2425 Technical Dr Miamisburg (45342) *(G-10685)*

Stacy Equipment Co.. 419 447-6903
325 Hall St Tiffin (44883) *(G-14106)*

Stadco Inc.. 937 878-0911
632 Yellow Springs Fairfield Rd Fairborn (45324) *(G-7322)*

Stadco Automatics, Fairborn Also Called: Stadco Inc *(G-7322)*

Staely Custom Crating, Conover Also Called: Conover Lumber Company Inc *(G-5936)*

Stafast Products Inc (PA).. 440 357-5546
505 Lakeshore Blvd Painesville (44077) *(G-12264)*

Stafast West, Painesville Also Called: Stafast Products Inc *(G-12264)*

Stafford Gage & Tool Inc... 937 277-9944
4606 Webster St Dayton (45414) *(G-6588)*

Stafford Gravel Inc... 419 298-2440
4225 Co Rd 79 Edgerton (43517) *(G-7081)*

Stahl Gear & Machine Co.. 216 431-2820
3901 Hamilton Ave Cleveland (44114) *(G-4725)*

Stahl/Scott Fetzer Company (HQ)... 800 277-8245
3201 W Old Lincoln Way Wooster (44691) *(G-16175)*

Stainless Automation.. 216 961-4550
1978 W 74th St Cleveland (44102) *(G-4726)*

Stainless Specialties Inc.. 440 942-4242
33240 Lakeland Blvd Eastlake (44095) *(G-7049)*

Stakes Manufacturing LLC.. 216 245-4752
34440 Vine St Willowick (44095) *(G-16035)*

Stakes Mfg, Willowick Also Called: Stakes Manufacturing LLC *(G-16035)*

Stalder Spring Works Inc... 937 322-6120
2345 Springfield Xenia Rd Springfield (45506) *(G-13637)*

Stallion Oilfield Cnstr LLC... 330 868-2083
3361 Baird Ave Se Paris (44669) *(G-12282)*

Stam, Mentor Also Called: Precision Bending Tech Inc *(G-10528)*

Stam, Mentor Also Called: Stam Inc *(G-10561)*

Stam Inc... 440 974-2500
7350 Production Dr Mentor (44060) *(G-10561)*

Stamco Industries Inc 216 731-9333
26650 Lakeland Blvd Cleveland (44132) *(G-4727)*

Stamm Contracting Company Inc 330 274-8230
4566 Orchard St Mantua (44255) *(G-9743)*

Stamped Steel Products Inc 330 538-3951
151 S Bailey Rd North Jackson (44451) *(G-11791)*

Stamtex Metal Stampings, Powell Also Called: Metal Products Company *(G-12677)*

Stan-Kell LLC 440 998-1116
2621 West Ave Ashtabula (44004) *(G-661)*

Stanco Precision Mfg Inc 937 274-1785
1 Walbrook Ave Dayton (45405) *(G-6589)*

Standard Advertising Co, Coshocton Also Called: Beach Company *(G-5973)*

Standard Aero Inc 937 840-1053
214 Hobart Dr Hillsboro (45133) *(G-8467)*

Standard Bariatrics Inc 513 620-7751
4300 Glendale Milford Rd Blue Ash (45242) *(G-1469)*

Standard Die Supply, Dayton Also Called: Ready Technology Inc *(G-6544)*

Standard Engineering Group Inc 330 494-4300
3516 Highland Park Nw North Canton (44720) *(G-11762)*

Standard Jig Boring Svc LLC (HQ) 330 896-9530
3360 Miller Park Rd Akron (44312) *(G-334)*

Standard Jig Boring Svc LLC 330 644-5405
3194 Massillon Rd Akron (44312) *(G-335)*

Standard Machine Inc 216 631-4440
1952 W 93rd St Cleveland (44102) *(G-4728)*

Standard Printing Co Inc 419 586-2371
123 E Market St Celina (45822) *(G-2350)*

Standard Printing Co of Canton 330 453-8247
1115 Cherry Ave Ne Canton (44704) *(G-2230)*

Standard Printing Company, Canton Also Called: Standard Printing Co of Canton *(G-2230)*

Standard Publishing LLC 513 931-4050
8805 Governors Hill Dr Ste 400 Cincinnati (45249) *(G-3414)*

Standard Register, Coldwater Also Called: Taylor Communications Inc *(G-5002)*

Standard Register Technologies 937 443-1000
600 Albany St Dayton (45417) *(G-6590)*

Standard Signs Incorporated (PA) 330 467-2030
9115 Freeway Dr Macedonia (44056) *(G-9579)*

Standard Technologies, Fremont Also Called: Standard Technologies LLC *(G-7810)*

Standard Technologies LLC 419 332-6434
2641 Hayes Ave Fremont (43420) *(G-7810)*

Standard Textile Co Inc (PA) 513 761-9255
1 Knollcrest Dr Cincinnati (45237) *(G-3415)*

Standard Welding & Lift Truck, Lorain Also Called: Perkins Motor Service Ltd *(G-9430)*

Standard Wellness Company LLC 330 931-1037
425 Literary Rd Apt 100 Cleveland (44113) *(G-4729)*

Standard Wldg & Stl Pdts Inc 330 273-2777
260 S State Rd Medina (44256) *(G-10379)*

Standardaero, Hillsboro Also Called: Pas Technologies Inc *(G-8464)*

Standby Screw Machine Pdts Co 440 243-8200
1122 W Bagley Rd Berea (44017) *(G-1294)*

Standex Electronics Inc (HQ) 513 871-3777
4150 Thunderbird Ln Fairfield (45014) *(G-7411)*

Standex International Corp 513 533-7111
4150 Thunderbird Ln Fairfield (45014) *(G-7412)*

Standex-Meder Electronics, Fairfield Also Called: Standex Electronics Inc *(G-7411)*

Standout Stickers Inc 877 449-7703
2991 Interstate Pkwy Brunswick (44212) *(G-1792)*

Standridge Color Corporation 770 464-3362
1122 Integrity Dr Defiance (43512) *(G-6695)*

Stanek E F and Assoc Inc 216 341-7700
700 Highland Rd E Macedonia (44056) *(G-9580)*

Stanek Windows, Macedonia Also Called: Stanek E F and Assoc Inc *(G-9580)*

Stanley Bittinger 740 942-4302
81331 Hines Rd Cadiz (43907) *(G-1904)*

Stanley Electric US Co Inc (HQ) 740 852-5200
420 E High St London (43140) *(G-9394)*

Stanley Engineered Fasten 440 657-3537
7900 W Ridge Rd Elyria (44035) *(G-7205)*

Stanley Industrial & Auto LLC 614 755-7089
5195 Blazer Pkwy Dublin (43017) *(G-6943)*

Stanley Industrial & Auto LLC (HQ) 614 755-7000
5195 Blazer Pkwy Dublin (43017) *(G-6944)*

Stanley Industries Inc 216 475-4000
19120 Cranwood Pkwy Cleveland (44128) *(G-4730)*

Stanley Steemer Carpet Cleaner, Dublin Also Called: Stanley Steemer Intl Inc *(G-6945)*

Stanley Steemer Intl Inc (PA) 614 764-2007
5800 Innovation Dr Dublin (43016) *(G-6945)*

Stansley Mineral Resources Inc (PA) 419 843-2813
3793 Silica Rd # B Sylvania (43560) *(G-14015)*

Stanwade Metal Products Inc 330 772-2421
6868 State Rt 305 Hartford (44424) *(G-8298)*

Stanwade Tanks and Equipment, Hartford Also Called: Stanwade Metal Products Inc *(G-8298)*

Star, Marion Also Called: Steam Trbine Altrntive Rsrces *(G-9884)*

Star Brite Express Car WA 330 674-0062
887 S Washington St Millersburg (44654) *(G-10994)*

Star City Press LLC 740 500-0320
931 E Water St Chillicothe (45601) *(G-2535)*

Star Distribution and Mfg LLC 513 860-3573
10179 Commerce Park Dr West Chester (45246) *(G-15590)*

Star Dynamics Corporation (PA) 614 334-4510
4455 Reynolds Dr Hilliard (43026) *(G-8442)*

Star Extruded Shapes Inc 330 533-9863
7055 Herbert Rd Canfield (44406) *(G-2018)*

Star Fab Inc (PA) 330 533-9863
7055 Herbert Rd Canfield (44406) *(G-2019)*

Star Fab Inc 330 482-1601
400 W Railroad St Ste 8 Columbiana (44408) *(G-5052)*

Star Fire Distributing, Akron Also Called: Thermo-Rite Mfg Company *(G-356)*

Star Jet LLC 614 338-4379
4130 E 5th Ave Columbus (43219) *(G-5789)*

Star Manufacturing LLC 330 740-8300
1775 Logan Ave Youngstown (44505) *(G-16447)*

Star Manufacturring, West Chester Also Called: Star Distribution and Mfg LLC *(G-15590)*

Star Metal Products Co Inc 440 899-7000
30405 Clemens Rd Westlake (44145) *(G-15791)*

Star Printing Company Inc 330 376-0514
125 N Union St Akron (44304) *(G-336)*

Star-Tjcm Inc 740 342-3514
701 Madison St New Lexington (43764) *(G-11458)*

Starbright Lighting USA LLC 330 650-2000
5136 Darrow Rd Hudson (44236) *(G-8615)*

Starecasing, Columbus Also Called: Starecasing Systems Inc *(G-5790)*

Starecasing Systems Inc 312 203-5632
2822 Fisher Rd Columbus (43204) *(G-5790)*

Stark Cnty Fdrtion Cnsrvtion C 330 268-1652
6323 Richville Dr Sw Canton (44706) *(G-2231)*

Stark Forest Products, Canton Also Called: Stark Truss Company Inc *(G-2233)*

Stark Industrial LLC 330 966-8108
5103 Stoneham Rd North Canton (44720) *(G-11763)*

Stark Materials Inc 330 497-1648
7345 Sunset Strip Ave Nw Canton (44720) *(G-2232)*

Stark Truss Beach City Lumber, Beach City Also Called: Stark Truss Company Inc *(G-971)*

Stark Truss Company Inc 330 756-3050
6855 Chestnut Ridge Rd Nw Beach City (44608) *(G-971)*

Stark Truss Company Inc 330 478-2100
4933 Southway St Sw Canton (44706) *(G-2233)*

Stark Truss Company Inc 330 478-6063
1601 Perry Dr Sw Canton (44706) *(G-2234)*

Stark Truss Company Inc (PA) 330 478-2100
109 Miles Ave Sw Canton (44710) *(G-2235)*

Stark Truss Company Inc 419 298-3777
400 Component Dr Edgerton (43517) *(G-7082)*

Stark Truss Company Inc 740 335-4156
2000 Landmark Blvd Washington Court Hou (43160) *(G-15233)*

Starkey Machinery Inc 419 468-2560
254 S Washington St Galion (44833) *(G-7885)*

Starks Plastics LLC 513 541-4591
11236 Sebring Dr Cincinnati (45240) *(G-3416)*

Starpoint 20 LLC 330 825-2373
3985 Eastern Rd Ste C Norton (44203) *(G-11950)*

Starr Fabricating Inc 330 394-9891
4175 Warren Sharon Rd Vienna (44473) *(G-15004)*

Starr Services Inc 513 241-7708
3625 Spring Grove Ave Cincinnati (45223) *(G-3417)*

Starr Wheel Group Inc 954 935-5536
2887 N Salem Warren Rd Warren (44481) *(G-15206)*

Starrett Communications Inc 614 798-0606
7437 Christie Chapel Rd Dublin (43017) *(G-6946)*

Start Printing Co LLC 513 424-2121
3140 Cincinnati Dayton Rd Middletown (45044) *(G-10859)*

Starwin Industries LLC 937 293-8568
3387 Woodman Dr Dayton (45429) *(G-6591)*

Stat Index Tab, Chillicothe *Also Called: Stat Industries Inc (G-2536)*

Stat Index Tab Company, Chillicothe *Also Called: Stat Industries Inc (G-2537)*

Stat Industries Inc (PA) 740 779-6561
137 Stone Rd Chillicothe (45601) *(G-2536)*

Stat Industries Inc 740 779-6561
137 Stone Rd Chillicothe (45601) *(G-2537)*

Stat Industries Inc 513 860-4482
3269 Profit Dr Hamilton (45014) *(G-8245)*

State 8 Motorcycle & Atv, Peninsula *Also Called: Wholecycle Inc (G-12345)*

State Chemical Manufacturing, Cleveland *Also Called: State Industrial Products Corp (G-4731)*

State Chemical Manufacturing, Hebron *Also Called: State Industrial Products Corp (G-8363)*

State Industrial Products Corp (PA) 877 747-6986
5915 Landerbrook Dr Ste 300 Cleveland (44124) *(G-4731)*

State Industrial Products Corp 740 929-6370
383 N High St Hebron (43025) *(G-8363)*

State Metal Hose Inc 614 527-4700
4171 Lyman Dr Hilliard (43026) *(G-8443)*

State of Ohio Dayton Raceway 937 237-7802
777 Hollywood Blvd Dayton (45414) *(G-6592)*

State Printing 614 995-1740
4200 Surface Rd Columbus (43228) *(G-5791)*

Stateline Power Corp 937 547-1006
650 Pine St Greenville (45331) *(G-8062)*

Status Entertainment Group LLC 216 252-2243
17005 Larchwood Ave Cleveland (44135) *(G-4732)*

Status Mens Accessories 440 786-9394
7650 First Pl Ste F Oakwood Village (44146) *(G-12042)*

Status Solutions, Westerville *Also Called: Status Solutions LLC (G-15680)*

Status Solutions LLC 434 296-1789
999 County Line Rd W # A Westerville (43082) *(G-15680)*

Staub Laser Cutting Inc 937 890-4486
2501 Thunderhawk Ct Dayton (45414) *(G-6593)*

Staub Manufacturing Solutions, Dayton *Also Called: Staub Laser Cutting Inc (G-6593)*

Staufs Coffee Roasters Limited 614 486-4479
705 Hadley Dr Columbus (43228) *(G-5792)*

Stays Lighting Inc 440 328-3254
936 Taylor St Elyria (44035) *(G-7206)*

STC International Co Ltd (PA) 561 308-6002
1499 Shaker Run Blvd Lebanon (45036) *(G-9112)*

Std Liquidation Inc 937 492-6121
1950 Campbell Rd Sidney (45365) *(G-13290)*

Stealth Arms LLC 419 925-7005
4939 Kittle Rd Celina (45822) *(G-2351)*

Steam Trbine Altrntive Rsrces 740 387-5535
370 W Fairground St Marion (43302) *(G-9884)*

Stebbins Engineering & Mfg Co 740 922-3012
4778 Belden Dr Se Uhrichsville (44683) *(G-14770)*

Steck Manufacturing Co LLC 937 222-0062
1200 Leo St Dayton (45404) *(G-6594)*

Steel & Alloy Utility Pdts Inc 330 530-2220
110 Ohio Ave Mc Donald (44437) *(G-10280)*

Steel Aviation Aircraft Sales 937 332-7587
4433 E State Route 55 Casstown (45312) *(G-2317)*

Steel Ceilings Inc 740 967-1063
451 E Coshocton St Johnstown (43031) *(G-8778)*

Steel City Corporation (PA) 330 792-7663
1000 Hedstrom Dr Ashland (44805) *(G-615)*

Steel Dynamics LLC
15 Townhall Rd Marietta (45750) *(G-9830)*

Steel Eqp Specialists Inc (PA) 330 823-8260
1507 Beeson St Ne Alliance (44601) *(G-427)*

Steel Forming Inc 714 532-6321
1775 Logan Ave Youngstown (44505) *(G-16448)*

Steel It LLC 513 253-3111
250 Mccullough St Cincinnati (45226) *(G-3418)*

Steel Products Corp Akron 330 688-6633
2288 Samira Rd Stow (44224) *(G-13727)*

Steel Quest Inc 513 772-5030
8180 Corporate Park Dr Ste 250 Cincinnati (45242) *(G-3419)*

Steel Structures of Ohio LLC 330 374-9900
1324 Firestone Pkwy Unit A Akron (44301) *(G-337)*

Steel Technologies LLC 419 523-5199
740 E Williamstown Rd Ottawa (45875) *(G-12192)*

Steel Technologies LLC 440 946-8666
2220 Joseph Lloyd Pkwy Willoughby (44094) *(G-15997)*

Steel Valley Tank & Welding 740 598-4994
24 County Road 7e Brilliant (43913) *(G-1651)*

Steel Vly Indus Coatings LLC 330 519-4348
558 Thornberry Trl North Lima (44452) *(G-11813)*

Steel Warehouse Division, Columbus *Also Called: Columbus Pipe and Equipment Co (G-5273)*

Steelastic Company LLC 330 633-0505
1 Vision Ln Cuyahoga Falls (44223) *(G-6119)*

Steeles 5 Acre Mill Inc 419 542-9363
10860 State Route 2 Hicksville (43526) *(G-8380)*

Steelial Cnstr Met Fabrication, Vinton *Also Called: Steelial Wldg Met Fbrction Inc (G-15012)*

Steelial Wldg Met Fbrction Inc 740 669-5300
70764 State Route 124 Vinton (45686) *(G-15012)*

Steeltec Products LLC 216 681-1114
13000 Saint Clair Ave Cleveland (44108) *(G-4733)*

Steer & Gear Inc 614 231-4064
1000 Barnett Rd Columbus (43227) *(G-5793)*

Steer & Geer, Columbus *Also Called: Steer & Gear Inc (G-5793)*

Steer America, Uniontown *Also Called: Steeramerica Inc (G-14794)*

Steeramerica Inc 330 563-4407
1525 Corporate Woods Pkwy Ste 500 Uniontown (44685) *(G-14794)*

Steere Enterprises Inc 330 633-4926
303 Tacoma Ave Tallmadge (44278) *(G-14048)*

Steere Enterprises Inc (PA) 330 633-4926
285 Commerce St Tallmadge (44278) *(G-14049)*

Stefan Restoration, Broadview Heights *Also Called: Keban Industries Inc (G-1659)*

Stefra Inc 440 846-8240
18021 Cliffside Dr Strongsville (44136) *(G-13885)*

Stegemeyer Machine Inc 513 321-5651
212 Mccullough St Cincinnati (45226) *(G-3420)*

Stehlin, John & Sons Meats, Cincinnati *Also Called: John Stehlin & Sons Co (G-3045)*

Steimel Metal Fab LLC 513 863-5310
2478 Morgan Ross Rd Hamilton (45013) *(G-8246)*

Stein LLC 216 883-7444
2032 Campbell Rd Cleveland (44105) *(G-4734)*

Stein LLC (DH) 440 526-9301
3 Summit Park Dr Ste 425 Independence (44131) *(G-8685)*

Stein Holdings Inc 440 526-9301
3 Summit Park Dr Ste 425 Independence (44131) *(G-8686)*

Stein Inc 419 747-2611
1490 Old Bowman St Mansfield (44903) *(G-9721)*

Stein-Palmer Printing Co 740 633-3894
1 Westwood Dr Unit 202 Saint Clairsville (43950) *(G-12925)*

Stein-Way Equipment 330 857-8700
12335 Emerson Rd Apple Creek (44606) *(G-511)*

Steinbarger Precision Cnc Inc 937 376-0322
634 Cincinnati Ave Xenia (45385) *(G-16273)*

Steiner Eoptics Inc (PA) 937 426-2341
3475 Newmark Dr Miamisburg (45342) *(G-10686)*

Steinert Industries Inc 330 678-0028
1507 Franklin Ave Kent (44240) *(G-8868)*

Stelfast LLC (HQ) 440 879-0077
22979 Stelfast Pkwy Strongsville (44149) *(G-13886)*

Stella Lou Llc 937 935-9536
3939 Hickory Rock Dr Powell (43065) *(G-12681)*

Stellar Group Inc — ALPHABETIC SECTION

Stellar Group Inc 330 769-8484
   4935 Enterprise Pkwy Seville (44273) *(G-13145)*

Stellar Process Inc 866 777-4725
   3238 Darien Ln Twinsburg (44087) *(G-14737)*

Stellar Systems Inc 513 921-8748
   1944 Harrison Ave Cincinnati (45214) *(G-3421)*

Stelter and Brinck Inc 513 367-9300
   201 Sales Ave Harrison (45030) *(G-8293)*

Step 2, Streetsboro *Also Called: Step2 Company LLC (G-13794)*

Step In Time, Youngstown *Also Called: Sit Inc (G-16440)*

Step2 Company LLC 419 938-6343
   2 Step 2 Dr Perrysville (44864) *(G-12449)*

Step2 Company LLC (HQ) 866 429-5200
   10010 Aurora Hudson Rd Streetsboro (44241) *(G-13794)*

Stephen Andrews Inc 330 725-2672
   7634 Lafayette Rd Lodi (44254) *(G-9357)*

Stephen M Trudick 440 834-1891
   13813 Station Road Burton (44021) *(G-1886)*

Stephens Pipe & Steel LLC 740 869-2257
   10732 Schadel Ln Mount Sterling (43143) *(G-11257)*

Stepp Sewing Service, Milford *Also Called: Chris Stepp (G-10898)*

Stepping Stone Enterprises Inc 419 472-0505
   1689 Lance Pointe Rd Maumee (43537) *(G-10235)*

Sterilite, Massillon *Also Called: Sterilite Corporation (G-10148)*

Sterilite Corporation 330 830-2204
   4495 Sterilite St Se Massillon (44646) *(G-10148)*

Steris Corporation 440 354-2600
   5900 Heisley Rd Mentor (44060) *(G-10562)*

Steris Corporation (DH) 440 354-2600
   5960 Heisley Rd Mentor (44060) *(G-10563)*

Steris Corporation 330 696-9946
   6515 Hopkins Rd Mentor (44060) *(G-10564)*

Steris Corporation 440 392-8079
   6100 Heisley Rd Mentor (44060) *(G-10565)*

Steris Corporation 440 354-2600
   9325 Pinecone Dr Mentor (44060) *(G-10566)*

Steris Instrument MGT Svcs Inc 800 783-9251
   4575 Hudson Dr Stow (44224) *(G-13728)*

Steris-IMS 330 686-4557
   4575 Hudson Dr Stow (44224) *(G-13729)*

Sterling Associates Inc 330 630-3500
   1783 Brittain Rd Akron (44310) *(G-338)*

Sterling Coating 513 942-4900
   9048 Port Union Rialto Rd West Chester (45069) *(G-15510)*

Sterling Commerce LLC 614 798-2192
   4600 Lakehurst Ct Dublin (43016) *(G-6947)*

Sterling Industries Inc 419 523-3788
   740 E Main St Ottawa (45875) *(G-12193)*

Sterling Mining Corporation (HQ) 330 549-2165
   10900 South Ave North Lima (44452) *(G-11814)*

Sterling Pipe & Tube, Toledo *Also Called: Sigma Tube Company (G-14472)*

Sterling Process Equipment & Services Inc (PA) 614 868-5151
   333 Mccormick Blvd Columbus (43213) *(G-5794)*

Stevco, Wellsville *Also Called: Stevenson Mfg Co (G-15337)*

Steve Mulcahy 419 229-4801
   1700 Shawnee Rd Lima (45805) *(G-9292)*

Steve Vore Welding and Steel 419 375-4087
   3234 State Route 49 Fort Recovery (45846) *(G-7624)*

Steve's Vans Auto Sales, Marietta *Also Called: Steves Vans ACC Unlimited LLC (G-9832)*

Steven Crumbaker Jr 740 995-0613
   3445 Church Hill Rd Zanesville (43701) *(G-16566)*

Stevens Industries LLC 937 266-8240
   2613 Millbridge Ct Dayton (45440) *(G-6595)*

Stevens Oil & Gas LLC 740 374-4542
   110 Lynch Church Rd Marietta (45750) *(G-9831)*

Stevenson Color Inc 513 321-7500
   535 Wilmer Ave Cincinnati (45226) *(G-3422)*

Stevenson Mfg Co 330 532-1581
   1 1st St Wellsville (43968) *(G-15337)*

Steves Sports Inc 440 735-0044
   10333 Northfield Rd Unit 136 Northfield (44067) *(G-11911)*

Steves Vans ACC Unlimited LLC 740 374-3154
   221 Pike St Marietta (45750) *(G-9832)*

Steward Edge Bus Solutions 614 826-5305
   23 N Westgate Ave Columbus (43204) *(G-5795)*

Stewart Acquisition LLC (PA) 330 963-0322
   2146 Enterprise Pkwy Twinsburg (44087) *(G-14738)*

Stewart Filmscreen Corp 513 753-0800
   3919 Bach Buxton Rd Amelia (45102) *(G-466)*

Stewart Manufacturing Corp 937 390-3333
   5230 Prosperity Dr Springfield (45502) *(G-13638)*

Stewart McDnalds Guitar Sp Sup, Athens *Also Called: Stewart-Macdonald Mfg Co (G-698)*

Stewart-Macdonald Mfg Co (PA) 740 592-3021
   21 N Shafer St Athens (45701) *(G-698)*

Stg Lane, Akron *Also Called: Scandinavian Tob Group Ln Ltd (G-325)*

STI Liquidation Inc 614 733-0099
   7710 Corporate Blvd Plain City (43064) *(G-12592)*

Stiber Fabricating Inc 216 771-7210
   1678 Leonard St Cleveland (44113) *(G-4735)*

Sticker Corporation (PA) 440 946-2100
   37877 Elm St Willoughby (44094) *(G-15998)*

Sticker Corporation 440 942-4700
   37941 Elm St Willoughby (44094) *(G-15999)*

Sticktite Lenses LLC 571 276-9508
   5195 Hampsted Vlg Ctr Way New Albany (43054) *(G-11390)*

Stiger Pre Cast Inc 740 482-2313
   17793 State Highway 231 Nevada (44849) *(G-11362)*

Stingray Pressure Pumping LLC (PA) 405 648-4177
   42739 National Rd Belmont (43718) *(G-1249)*

Stirling Ultracold, Athens *Also Called: Global Cooling Inc (G-685)*

Stitches Usa LLC 330 852-0500
   3149 State Rte 39 Walnut Creek (44687) *(G-15095)*

Stitchgrrl LLC 216 269-4398
   10252 Berea Rd Cleveland (44102) *(G-4736)*

Stitching Gluing Solutions LLC 513 588-3168
   9848 Redhill Dr Blue Ash (45242) *(G-1470)*

Stock, Chagrin Falls *Also Called: Stock Equipment Company Inc (G-2424)*

Stock Equipment Company, Solon *Also Called: Stock Fairfield Corporation (G-13425)*

Stock Equipment Company Inc 440 543-6000
   16490 Chillicothe Rd Chagrin Falls (44023) *(G-2424)*

Stock Fairfield Corporation 440 543-6000
   30825 Aurora Rd # 150 Solon (44139) *(G-13425)*

Stock Mfg & Design Co Inc (PA) 513 353-3600
   10040 Cilley Rd Cleves (45002) *(G-4965)*

Stocker Concrete Company 740 254-4626
   7574 Us Hwy 36 Se Gnadenhutten (44629) *(G-7989)*

Stocker Sand & Gravel Co (PA) 740 254-4635
   Rte 36 Gnadenhutten (44629) *(G-7990)*

Stoepfel Drilling Co 419 532-3307
   12245 State Route 115 Ottawa (45875) *(G-12194)*

Stolle Machinery Company LLC 330 244-0555
   1007 High Ave Sw Canton (44707) *(G-2236)*

Stolle Machinery Company LLC 937 497-5400
   7425 Webster St Dayton (45414) *(G-6596)*

Stolle Machinery Company LLC 937 497-5400
   2900 Campbell Rd Sidney (45365) *(G-13291)*

Stolle Machinery-Sidney, Sidney *Also Called: Stolle Machinery Company LLC (G-13291)*

Stolle Milk Biologics Inc 513 489-7997
   4735 Devitt Dr West Chester (45246) *(G-15591)*

Stolle Properties Inc 513 932-8664
   6954 Cornell Rd Ste 100 Blue Ash (45242) *(G-1471)*

Stone Center, Cincinnati *Also Called: Blu Bird LLC (G-2672)*

Stone Center, Columbus *Also Called: Blu Bird LLC (G-5202)*

Stone Center of Dayton, Moraine *Also Called: 3jd Inc (G-11151)*

Stone Statements Incorporated 513 489-7866
   7451 Fields Ertel Rd Cincinnati (45241) *(G-3423)*

Stonebridge Oilfield Svcs LLC 740 373-6134
   406 Colegate Dr Marietta (45750) *(G-9833)*

Stoneco, Carey *Also Called: Wyandot Dolomite Inc (G-2286)*

Stoneco Inc (DH) 419 422-8854
   1700 Fostoria Ave Ste 200 Findlay (45840) *(G-7569)*

Stoneco Inc 419 893-7645
1360 Ford St Maumee (43537) *(G-10236)*

Stoneco Inc 419 393-2555
13762 Road 179 Oakwood (45873) *(G-12033)*

Stoneco Inc 419 686-3311
11580 S Dixie Hwy Portage (43451) *(G-12637)*

Stoneco Inc 419 693-3933
352 George Hardy Dr Toledo (43605) *(G-14475)*

Stonecote, Norton Also Called: E L Stone Company *(G-11941)*

Stoner Glass Act Studio LLC 330 360-3294
30 W Broad St Newton Falls (44444) *(G-11658)*

Stoneridge Inc 419 884-1219
345 S Mill St Lexington (44904) *(G-9202)*

Stony Hill Mixing Ltd 330 674-0814
5526 Township Road 127 Millersburg (44654) *(G-10995)*

Stony Point Hardwoods LLC 330 852-4512
7842 Stony Point Rd Nw Sugarcreek (44681) *(G-13939)*

Stonyridge Inc 937 845-9482
570 S Dayton Lakeview Rd New Carlisle (45344) *(G-11426)*

Stop Stick Ltd 513 202-5500
365 Industrial Dr Harrison (45030) *(G-8294)*

Stop Stick, Liability Company, Harrison Also Called: Stop Stick Ltd *(G-8294)*

Storad Label Co 740 382-6440
126 Blaine Ave Marion (43302) *(G-9885)*

Storetek Engineering Inc 330 294-0678
399 Commerce St Tallmadge (44278) *(G-14050)*

Storopack Inc (DH) 513 874-0314
4758 Devitt Dr West Chester (45246) *(G-15592)*

Stoutheart Corporation 800 556-6470
7205 Chagrin Rd Ste 4 Chagrin Falls (44023) *(G-2425)*

Stover International LLC 740 363-5251
222 Stover Dr Delaware (43015) *(G-6753)*

Straight 72 Inc 740 943-5730
20078 State Route 4 Marysville (43040) *(G-9940)*

Straight Creek Bushman LLC 513 732-1698
202 E Main St Batavia (45103) *(G-950)*

Straightaway Fabrications Ltd 419 281-9440
481us Highway 250 E Ashland (44805) *(G-616)*

Strassells Machine Inc 419 747-1088
1015 Springmill St Mansfield (44906) *(G-9722)*

Strata Mine Services Inc 740 695-6880
68000 Bayberry Dr Unit 103 Saint Clairsville (43950) *(G-12926)*

Strata Mine Services LLC 740 695-0488
67925 Bayberry Dr Saint Clairsville (43950) *(G-12927)*

Strata-Tac Inc 630 879-9388
1985 W Stanfield Rd Troy (45373) *(G-14613)*

Stratagraph Ne Inc 740 373-3091
116 Ellsworth Ave Marietta (45750) *(G-9834)*

Strategic Materials Inc 740 349-9523
101 S Arch St Newark (43055) *(G-11607)*

Strategic Technology Entp 440 354-2600
5960 Heisley Rd Mentor (44060) *(G-10567)*

Stratton Creek Wood Works LLC 330 876-0005
5915 Burnett East Rd Kinsman (44428) *(G-8938)*

Stratus Unlimited LLC (PA) 440 209-6200
8959 Tyler Blvd Mentor (44060) *(G-10568)*

Strawn Oil Field Service, Salem Also Called: Everflow Eastern Partners LP *(G-12993)*

Strawser Steel Drum Ohio Ltd 614 856-5982
219 Commerce Dr Mount Vernon (43050) *(G-11297)*

Streamline Excavating LLC 330 495-8617
6090 Citrus Rd Nw Malvern (44644) *(G-9616)*

Streamline Media & Pubg LLC 614 822-1817
2699 Prendergast Pl Reynoldsburg (43068) *(G-12774)*

Streamside Materials, Findlay Also Called: Streamside Materials Llc *(G-7570)*

Streamside Materials Llc 419 423-1290
7440 Township Road 95 Findlay (45840) *(G-7570)*

Streetpops, Cincinnati Also Called: Streetpops Inc *(G-3424)*

Streetpops Inc 513 446-7505
4720 Vine St Cincinnati (45217) *(G-3424)*

Streetsboro Operations, Twinsburg Also Called: Facil North America Inc *(G-14659)*

Stress-Crete Company 440 576-9073
1153 State Route 46 N Jefferson (44047) *(G-8759)*

Stresscrete, Jefferson Also Called: King Luminaire Company Inc *(G-8750)*

Stretchtape Inc 216 486-9400
3100 Hamilton Ave Cleveland (44114) *(G-4737)*

Stricker Refinishing Inc 216 696-2906
2060 Hamilton Ave Cleveland (44114) *(G-4738)*

Strictly Stitchery Inc 440 543-7128
13801 Shaker Blvd Apt 4a Cleveland (44120) *(G-4739)*

Stride Out Rnch N Rodeo Sp LLC 937 539-1537
4122 Laybourne Rd Springfield (45505) *(G-13639)*

Stride Tool LLC 440 247-4600
30333 Emerald Valley Pkwy Glenwillow (44139) *(G-7982)*

Striker Hydraulic Breakers, Willoughby Also Called: Toku America Inc *(G-16006)*

Stripmatic Products Inc 216 241-7143
5301 Grant Ave Ste 200 Cleveland (44125) *(G-4740)*

Strohecker Incorporated 330 426-9496
213 N Pleasant Dr East Palestine (44413) *(G-7009)*

Strong Bindery Inc 216 231-0001
13015 Larchmere Blvd Cleveland (44120) *(G-4741)*

Strong-Coat LLC 440 299-2068
4420 Sherwin Rd Willoughby (44094) *(G-16000)*

Structural Steel Fabrication, Pataskala Also Called: Ohio Steel Industries Inc *(G-12302)*

Struers Inc (DH) 440 871-0071
24766 Detroit Rd Westlake (44145) *(G-15792)*

Struggle Grind Success LLC 330 834-6738
6414 Market St Boardman (44512) *(G-1518)*

Stryker Plant, Stryker Also Called: Sauder Manufacturing Co *(G-13913)*

Stryver Mfg Inc 937 854-3048
15 N Broadway St Trotwood (45426) *(G-14546)*

Stuart Burial Vault Co Inc 740 569-4158
527 Ford St Bremen (43107) *(G-1639)*

Stuart Company 513 621-9462
2160 Patterson St Cincinnati (45214) *(G-3425)*

Stuart-Dean Co Inc 412 765-2752
2615 Saint Clair Ave Ne Cleveland (44114) *(G-4742)*

Stuchell Products LLC 330 821-4299
12240 Rockhill Ave Ne Alliance (44601) *(G-428)*

Stud Welding, Strongsville Also Called: Stud Welding Associates Inc *(G-13887)*

Stud Welding Associates 216 392-7808
101 Liberty Ct Elyria (44035) *(G-7207)*

Stud Welding Associates, Strongsville Also Called: Spiegelberg Manufacturing Inc *(G-13884)*

Stud Welding Associates Inc 440 783-3160
12200 Alameda Dr Strongsville (44149) *(G-13887)*

Studgionsgroup LLC 216 804-1561
10413 Way Ave Cleveland (44105) *(G-4743)*

Studio Arts and Glass Inc 330 494-9779
7495 Strauss Ave Nw Canton (44720) *(G-2237)*

Studio Eleven Inc (PA) 937 295-2225
301 S Main St Fort Loramie (45845) *(G-7611)*

Studio Foundry, Cleveland Also Called: Foundry Artists Inc *(G-4086)*

Studio Vertu Inc 513 241-9038
1208 Central Pkwy # 1 Cincinnati (45202) *(G-3426)*

Stull Woodworks Inc 937 698-8181
155 Marybill Dr S Troy (45373) *(G-14614)*

Stumps Converting Inc 419 492-2542
742 W Mansfield St New Washington (44854) *(G-11551)*

Stumptown Lbr Pallet Mills Ltd 740 757-2275
55613 Washington St Somerton (43713) *(G-13451)*

Stutzman Manufacturing Ltd 330 674-4359
7727 Township Road 604 Millersburg (44654) *(G-10996)*

Style Crest Enterprises Inc (PA) 419 355-8586
2450 Enterprise St Fremont (43420) *(G-7811)*

Style-Line Incorporated (PA) 614 291-0600
901 W 3rd Ave Ste A Columbus (43212) *(G-5796)*

Subaru of A 614 793-2358
565 Metro Pl S Ste 150 Dublin (43017) *(G-6948)*

Subtropolis Mine, Petersburg Also Called: Subtropolis Mining Co *(G-12450)*

Subtropolis Mining Co 330 549-2165
5455 E Garfield Rd Petersburg (44454) *(G-12450)*

Suburban Communications Inc 440 632-0130
14905 N State Ave Middlefield (44062) *(G-10791)*

Suburban Manufacturing Co 440 953-2024
1924 E 337th St Eastlake (44095) *(G-7050)*

Suburban Metal Products   ALPHABETIC SECTION

Suburban Metal Products, Circleville *Also Called: Cline Machine and Automtn Inc (G-3545)*
Suburban Plastics Co (PA) 847 741-4900
   509 Water St Sw Bolivar (44612) *(G-1538)*
Suburban Press Incorporated 216 961-0766
   3818 Lorain Ave Cleveland (44113) *(G-4744)*
Suburban Steel of Indiana, Columbus *Also Called: Suburban Stl Sup Co Ltd Partnr (G-5797)*
Suburban Steel Supply Co Limited Partnership (PA) 614 737-5501
   1900 Deffenbaugh Ct Gahanna (43230) *(G-7850)*
Suburban Stl Sup Co Ltd Partnr 317 783-6555
   1900 Deffenbaugh Ct Columbus (43230) *(G-5797)*
Suburbanite Inc 419 756-4390
   1552 W Cook Rd Mansfield (44906) *(G-9723)*
Subway, Circleville *Also Called: Circleville Oil Co (G-3544)*
Sucurtex Digital, Dayton *Also Called: Securtex International Inc (G-6565)*
Suelos Sweetz LLC 440 478-1301
   35560 Vine St Willowick (44095) *(G-16036)*
Sugar Creek, Blue Ash *Also Called: Sugar Creek Packing Co (G-1472)*
Sugar Creek Packing Co (PA) 740 335-3586
   4350 Indeco Ct Blue Ash (45241) *(G-1472)*
Sugar Creek Packing Co 937 268-6601
   1241 N Gettysburg Ave Dayton (45417) *(G-6597)*
Sugarcreek Budget Publishers 330 852-4034
   134 Factory St Ne Sugarcreek (44681) *(G-13940)*
Sugarcreek Lime Service 330 364-4460
   2068 Gordon Rd Nw Dover (44622) *(G-6845)*
Sugarcreek Pallet Ltd 330 852-9812
   681 Belden Pkwy Ne Sugarcreek (44681) *(G-13941)*
Sugarcreek Ready Mix, Bellbrook *Also Called: Ernst Enterprises Inc (G-1192)*
Sugarcreek Shavings LLC 330 763-4239
   3121 Winklepleck Rd Nw Sugarcreek (44681) *(G-13942)*
Sulecki Precision Products Inc 440 255-5454
   8785 East Ave Mentor (44060) *(G-10569)*
Sulo Enterprises Inc 440 926-3322
   1017 Commerce Dr Grafton (44044) *(G-8005)*
Sumiriko Ohio Inc (HQ) 419 358-2121
   320 Snider Rd Bluffton (45817) *(G-1507)*
Sumitomo Elc Carbide Mfg Inc (DH) 440 354-0600
   210 River St Grand River (44045) *(G-8013)*
Sumitomo Elc Wirg Systems Inc 937 642-7579
   14800 Industrial Pkwy Marysville (43040) *(G-9941)*
Summer Garden Food Mfg, Boardman *Also Called: Zidian Manufacturing Inc (G-1521)*
Summers Acquisition Corp (DH) 216 941-7700
   12555 Berea Rd Cleveland (44111) *(G-4745)*
Summers Organization LLC 740 286-1322
   345 E Main St Ste H Jackson (45640) *(G-8725)*
Summers Rubber Company, Cleveland *Also Called: Summers Acquisition Corp (G-4745)*
Summit Aerospace Product Corp 440 652-6829
   10250 Brecksville Rd Brecksville (44141) *(G-1631)*
Summit Avionics Inc 330 425-1440
   2225 E Enterprise Pkwy # 1a Twinsburg (44087) *(G-14739)*
Summit Container Corporation (PA) 719 481-8400
   8080 Beckett Center Dr Ste 203 West Chester (45069) *(G-15511)*
Summit Design and Tech Inc 330 733-6662
   1147 Sweitzer Ave Akron (44301) *(G-339)*
Summit Engineered Products Inc 330 854-5388
   516 Elm Ridge Ave Canal Fulton (44614) *(G-1975)*
Summit Machine Ltd 330 628-2663
   3991 Mogadore Rd Mogadore (44260) *(G-11085)*
Summit Machine Solutions LLC 330 785-0781
   1029 Arlington Cir Akron (44306) *(G-340)*
Summit Machining Co Ltd 330 628-2663
   3991 Mogadore Rd Mogadore (44260) *(G-11086)*
Summit Millwork LLC 330 920-4000
   1619 Main St Cuyahoga Falls (44221) *(G-6120)*
Summit Online Products LLC 800 326-1972
   3982 Powell Rd Ste 137 Powell (43065) *(G-12682)*
Summit Packaging Solutions LLC (PA) 719 481-8400
   8080 Beckett Center Dr Ste 203 West Chester (45069) *(G-15512)*
Summit Plastic Company 330 633-3668
   3175 Gilchrist Rd Mogadore (44260) *(G-11087)*
Summit Polymers LLC 330 506-7715
   1900 Hubbard Rd Youngstown (44505) *(G-16449)*

Summit Research Group 330 689-1778
   4466 Darrow Rd Ste 15 Stow (44224) *(G-13730)*
Summit Street News Inc 330 609-5600
   645 Summit St Nw Warren (44485) *(G-15207)*
Summit Tool Company (HQ) 330 535-7177
   768 E North St Akron (44305) *(G-341)*
Summit Trailer Sales & Svcs, Coventry Township *Also Called: Friess Welding Inc (G-6009)*
Summitville Laboratories, Summitville *Also Called: Summitville Tiles Inc (G-13950)*
Summitville Labs, Minerva *Also Called: Summitville Tiles Inc (G-11040)*
Summitville Tiles Inc 330 868-6463
   81 Arbor Rd Ne Minerva (44657) *(G-11040)*
Summitville Tiles Inc 330 868-6771
   1310 Alliance Rd Nw Minerva (44657) *(G-11041)*
Summitville Tiles Inc (PA) 330 223-1511
   15364 State Rte 644 Summitville (43962) *(G-13950)*
Sun America LLC 330 821-6300
   46 N Rockhill Ave Alliance (44601) *(G-429)*
Sun Chemical Corporation 513 753-9550
   3922 Bach Buxton Rd Amelia (45102) *(G-467)*
Sun Chemical Corporation 513 671-0407
   12049 Centron Pl Cincinnati (45246) *(G-3427)*
Sun Chemical Corporation 513 681-5950
   5020 Spring Grove Ave Cincinnati (45232) *(G-3428)*
Sun Chemical Corporation 513 681-5950
   5020 Spring Grove Ave Cincinnati (45232) *(G-3429)*
Sun Chemical Corporation 513 830-8667
   5000 Spring Grove Ave Cincinnati (45232) *(G-3430)*
Sun Chemical Corporation 513 681-5950
   4526 Chickering Ave Cincinnati (45232) *(G-3431)*
Sun Chemical Corporation 419 891-3514
   1380 Ford St Maumee (43537) *(G-10237)*
Sun Chemical US Rycoline, Cincinnati *Also Called: Sun Chemical Corporation (G-3428)*
Sun Newspaper Div, Cleveland *Also Called: Comcorp Inc (G-3887)*
Sun Polishing Corp 440 237-5525
   13800 Progress Pkwy Ste E Cleveland (44133) *(G-4746)*
Sun Shine Awards 740 425-2504
   36099 Bethesda Street Ext Barnesville (43713) *(G-905)*
Sun State Plastics Inc 330 494-5220
   4045 Kevin St Nw Canton (44720) *(G-2238)*
Sunamericaconverting LLC 330 821-6300
   46 N Rockhill Ave Alliance (44601) *(G-430)*
Suncoke Energy Inc 513 727-5571
   3353 Yankee Rd Middletown (45044) *(G-10860)*
Sunfield Inc 740 928-0405
   116 Enterprise Dr Hebron (43025) *(G-8364)*
Sunless, Macedonia *Also Called: Sunless Inc (G-9581)*
Sunless Inc (PA) 440 836-0199
   8909 Freeway Dr Ste A Macedonia (44056) *(G-9581)*
Sunnest Service LLC 740 283-2815
   619 Slack St Steubenville (43952) *(G-13678)*
Sunny Brook Prest Concrete Co 330 673-7667
   3586 Sunnybrook Rd Kent (44240) *(G-8869)*
Sunpower Inc 740 594-2221
   2005 E State St Ste 104 Athens (45701) *(G-699)*
Sunrise Cooperative Inc 419 628-4705
   292 W 4th St Minster (45865) *(G-11062)*
Sunrise Foods, Columbus *Also Called: Sunrise Foods Inc (G-5798)*
Sunrise Foods Inc 614 276-2880
   2097 Corvair Blvd Columbus (43207) *(G-5798)*
Sunset Golf LLC 419 994-5563
   71 West Ave Ste 6 Tallmadge (44278) *(G-14051)*
Sunset Industries Inc 440 306-8284
   7567 Tyler Blvd Mentor (44060) *(G-10570)*
Sunshine Farms Dairy, Elyria *Also Called: Consun Food Industries Inc (G-7128)*
Sunshine Products 303 478-4913
   760 Warehouse Rd Ste O Toledo (43615) *(G-14476)*
Sunstar, Springboro *Also Called: Sunstar Engrg Americas Inc (G-13520)*
Sunstar Engrg Americas Inc 937 743-9049
   700 Watkins Glen Dr Franklin (45005) *(G-7704)*
Sunstar Engrg Americas Inc (HQ) 937 746-8575
   85 S Pioneer Blvd Springboro (45066) *(G-13520)*

ALPHABETIC SECTION

Sunstar Sprockets, Franklin *Also Called: Sunstar Engrg Americas Inc (G-7704)*

Sup-R-Die, Cleveland *Also Called: Palisin & Associates Inc (G-4520)*

Super Signs Inc 480 968-2200
  9890 Mount Nebo Rd North Bend (45052) *(G-11707)*

Super Suppers, Bay Village *Also Called: Generations Ace Inc (G-965)*

Super Systems Inc (PA) 513 772-0060
  7205 Edington Dr Cincinnati (45249) *(G-3432)*

Superalloy Mfg Solutions Corp 513 489-9800
  11230 Deerfield Rd Blue Ash (45242) *(G-1473)*

Superalloy Mfg Solutions Corp 513 605-8380
  11495 Deerfield Rd Blue Ash (45242) *(G-1474)*

Superb Industries Inc 330 852-0500
  330 3rd St Nw Sugarcreek (44681) *(G-13943)*

Superfine Manufacturing Inc 330 897-9024
  33715 County Road 10 Fresno (43824) *(G-7825)*

Superfinishers Inc 330 467-2125
  380 Highland Rd E Macedonia (44056) *(G-9582)*

Superion Inc 937 374-0033
  1285 S Patton St Xenia (45385) *(G-16274)*

Superior Bar Products Inc 419 784-2590
  1710 Spruce St Defiance (43512) *(G-6696)*

Superior Caster Inc 513 539-8980
  455 Wright Dr Middletown (45044) *(G-10861)*

Superior Casters, Middletown *Also Called: Superior Caster Inc (G-10861)*

Superior Dairy Inc 330 477-4515
  4719 Navarre Rd Sw Canton (44706) *(G-2239)*

Superior Die 937 225-6369
  7796 John Elwood Dr Dayton (45459) *(G-6598)*

Superior Die Tool & Machine Co, Columbus *Also Called: Superior Production LLC (G-5800)*

Superior Energy Group Ltd 216 282-4440
  34469 Scotch Ln Apt 4 Willoughby Hills (44094) *(G-16028)*

Superior Energy Systems LLC 440 236-6009
  13660 Station Rd Columbia Station (44028) *(G-5022)*

Superior Fibers Inc 740 394-2491
  9702 Iron Point Rd Se Shawnee (43782) *(G-13177)*

Superior Flux & Mfg Co 440 349-3000
  6615 Parkland Blvd Cleveland (44139) *(G-4747)*

Superior Forge & Steel Corp (PA) 419 222-4412
  1820 Mcclain Rd Lima (45804) *(G-9293)*

Superior Hardwoods Cambridge, Cambridge *Also Called: Superior Hardwoods Ohio Inc (G-1956)*

Superior Hardwoods of Ohio 740 384-6862
  78 Jackson Hill Rd Jackson (45640) *(G-8726)*

Superior Hardwoods of Ohio 740 596-2561
  62581 Us Highway 50 Mc Arthur (45651) *(G-10264)*

Superior Hardwoods Ohio Inc 740 439-2727
  9911 Ohio Ave Cambridge (43725) *(G-1956)*

Superior Hardwoods Ohio Inc (PA) 740 384-5677
  134 Wellston Industrial Park Rd Wellston (45692) *(G-15332)*

Superior Holding LLC (DH) 216 651-9400
  3786 Ridge Rd Cleveland (44144) *(G-4748)*

Superior Image Embroidery LLC 513 991-7543
  10152 International Blvd West Chester (45246) *(G-15593)*

Superior Impressions Inc 419 244-8676
  327 12th St Toledo (43604) *(G-14477)*

Superior Label Systems Inc (DH) 513 336-0825
  7500 Industrial Row Dr Mason (45040) *(G-10061)*

Superior Machine Co, Canton *Also Called: Robert Smart Inc (G-2219)*

Superior Machine Systems, Mason *Also Called: Superior Label Systems Inc (G-10061)*

Superior Machine Tool Inc 419 675-2363
  13606 Us Highway 68 Kenton (43326) *(G-8901)*

Superior Machining Inc 937 236-9619
  2946 Lindale Ave Dayton (45414) *(G-6599)*

Superior Marine Ways Inc 740 894-6224
  5852 County Rd 1 Suoth Pt Proctorville (45669) *(G-12687)*

Superior Metal Products Inc (PA) 419 228-1145
  1005 W Grand Ave Lima (45801) *(G-9294)*

Superior Metal Worx LLC 614 879-9400
  1239 Alum Creek Dr Columbus (43209) *(G-5799)*

Superior Mold & Die Co 330 688-8251
  449 N Main St Munroe Falls (44262) *(G-11306)*

Superior Packaging 419 380-3335
  2930 Airport Hwy Toledo (43609) *(G-14478)*

Superior Plastics Inc 614 733-0307
  8163 Business Way Plain City (43064) *(G-12593)*

Superior Plastics Inc (PA) 614 733-0307
  8175 Business Way Plain City (43064) *(G-12594)*

Superior Plastics Intl Inc 419 424-3113
  1116 Glen Meadow Dr Findlay (45840) *(G-7571)*

Superior Pneumatic & Mfg Inc 440 871-8780
  871 Canterbury Rd Ste E Westlake (44145) *(G-15793)*

Superior Precision Products 216 881-3696
  968 E 69th Pl Cleveland (44103) *(G-4749)*

Superior Printing Ink Co Inc 216 328-1720
  7655 Hub Pkwy Ste 205 Cleveland (44125) *(G-4750)*

Superior Production LLC (PA) 614 444-2181
  2301 Fairwood Ave Columbus (43207) *(G-5800)*

Superior Products LLC 216 651-9400
  3786 Ridge Rd Cleveland (44144) *(G-4751)*

Superior Property Restoration 513 509-6849
  2144 Schappelle Ln Cincinnati (45240) *(G-3433)*

Superior Quality Machine Co 330 527-7146
  10500 Industrial Dr Garrettsville (44231) *(G-7925)*

Superior Soda Service LLC 937 657-9700
  3626 Napanee Dr Beavercreek (45430) *(G-1081)*

Superior Steel Service LLC 513 724-7888
  2760 Old State Route 32 Batavia (45103) *(G-951)*

Superior Structures Inc 513 942-5954
  320 N State St Harrison (45030) *(G-8295)*

Superior Tool Company, Cleveland *Also Called: Superior Tool Corporation (G-4752)*

Superior Tool Corporation 216 398-8600
  100 Hayes Dr Ste C Cleveland (44131) *(G-4752)*

Superior Trim, Findlay *Also Called: Pieco Inc (G-7551)*

Superior Trim Formed Products, Findlay *Also Called: Radar Love Co (G-7555)*

Superior Trim Holdings Limited 419 425-5555
  2100 Fostoria Ave Findlay (45840) *(G-7572)*

Superior Trims Springfield Div, Springfield *Also Called: Pieco Inc (G-13620)*

Superior Water Conditioning Co, Moraine *Also Called: Enting Water Conditioning Inc (G-11175)*

Superior Weld and Fabg Co Inc 216 249-5122
  15002 Woodworth Rd Cleveland (44110) *(G-4753)*

Superior Welding Co 614 252-8539
  906 S Nelson Rd Columbus (43205) *(G-5801)*

Superior's Brand Meats, Massillon *Also Called: Fresh Mark Inc (G-10097)*

Superkids Reading Program, Columbus *Also Called: Zaner-Bloser Inc (G-5892)*

Supertrapp, Cleveland *Also Called: Supertrapp Industries Inc (G-4754)*

Supertrapp Industries Inc 216 265-8400
  4540 W 160th St Cleveland (44135) *(G-4754)*

Supplier Inspection Svcs Inc (PA) 877 263-7097
  2941 S Gettysburg Ave Dayton (45439) *(G-6600)*

Supply One Corporation 937 297-1111
  4146 Woodedge Dr Bellbrook (45305) *(G-1194)*

Supply Technologies LLC (HQ) 440 947-2100
  6065 Parkland Blvd Ste 1 Cleveland (44124) *(G-4755)*

Supply Technologies LLC 614 759-9939
  590 Claycraft Rd Columbus (43230) *(G-5802)*

Supply Technologies LLC 937 898-5795
  4704 Wadsworth Rd Dayton (45414) *(G-6601)*

Supply Technologies LLC 740 363-1971
  700 London Rd Delaware (43015) *(G-6754)*

Supplyone Retail, Cleveland *Also Called: Cleveland Supplyone Inc (G-3857)*

Support Service, Lexington *Also Called: Support Svc LLC (G-9203)*

Support Svc LLC 419 617-0660
  25 Walnut St Ste 4 Lexington (44904) *(G-9203)*

Supreme Fan/Industrial Air, Dayton *Also Called: Lau Industries Inc (G-6167)*

Supro Spring & Wire Forms Inc 330 722-5628
  6440 Norwalk Rd Ste N Medina (44256) *(G-10380)*

Sur-Seal LLC (PA) 513 574-8500
  6156 Wesselman Rd Cincinnati (45248) *(G-3434)*

Sure Tool & Manufacturing Co 937 253-9111
  429 Winston Ave Dayton (45403) *(G-6602)*

(PA)=Parent Co (HQ)=Headquarters (DH)=Div Headquarters

Sure-Foot Industries Corp 440 234-4446
  20260 1st Ave Cleveland (44130) *(G-4756)*
Surenergy LLC 419 626-8000
  9500 W Moonlight Bay Ln Oak Harbor (43449) *(G-12015)*
Surface Combustion Inc (PA) 419 891-7150
  1700 Indian Wood Cir Maumee (43537) *(G-10238)*
Surface Enhancement Tech LLC 513 561-1520
  3929 Virginia Ave Cincinnati (45227) *(G-3435)*
Surface Enterprises Inc 419 476-5670
  1465 W Alexis Rd Toledo (43612) *(G-14479)*
Surface Recovery Tech LLC 937 879-5864
  833 Zapata Dr Fairborn (45324) *(G-7323)*
Surftech, Austinburg *Also Called: Euclid Refinishing Compnay Inc (G-745)*
Surgical Appliance Inds Inc (PA) 513 271-4594
  3960 Rosslyn Dr Cincinnati (45209) *(G-3436)*
Surgrx Inc 650 482-2400
  4545 Creek Rd Blue Ash (45242) *(G-1475)*
Surili Couture LLC 440 600-1456
  29961 Persimmon Dr Westlake (44145) *(G-15794)*
Surplus Freight Inc (PA) 614 235-7660
  501 Morrison Rd Ste 100 Gahanna (43230) *(G-7851)*
Surteco North America Inc (DH) 843 848-3000
  32125 Solon Rd Ste 15 Solon (44139) *(G-13426)*
Survitec Group (usa) Inc (DH) 330 239-4331
  1420 Wolfcreek Trl Sharon Center (44274) *(G-13168)*
Susan Hill Hams 440 543-5967
  1900 Barton Springs Road Unit 5032 Chagrin Falls (44023) *(G-2426)*
Susan Products, Cleveland *Also Called: Mystic Chemical Products Co (G-4433)*
Sushi On The Roll, Medina *Also Called: Alsatian Llc (G-10293)*
Suspension Feeder Corporation 419 763-1377
  482 State Route 119 Fort Recovery (45846) *(G-7625)*
Suspension Technology Inc 330 458-3058
  1424 Scales St Sw Canton (44706) *(G-2240)*
Sustainment Actions LLC 330 805-3468
  20 S 3rd St Ste 210 Columbus (43215) *(G-5803)*
Sutphen, Dublin *Also Called: Sutphen Corporation (G-6949)*
Sutphen Corporation (PA) 800 726-7030
  6450 Eiterman Rd Dublin (43016) *(G-6949)*
Sutphen Corporation 937 969-8851
  1701 W County Line Rd Springfield (45502) *(G-13640)*
Sutphen Towers Inc 614 876-1262
  4500 Sutphen Ct Hilliard (43026) *(G-8444)*
Sutter Llc 513 891-2261
  11105 Deerfield Rd Blue Ash (45242) *(G-1476)*
Sutterlin Machine & TI Co Inc 440 357-0817
  9445 Pineneedle Dr Mentor (44060) *(G-10571)*
Suzin L Chocolatiers 440 323-3372
  230 Broad St Elyria (44035) *(G-7208)*
Swagelok Co, Willoughby Hills *Also Called: Swagelok Company (G-16029)*
Swagelok Company 440 442-6611
  328 Bishop Rd Cleveland (44143) *(G-4757)*
Swagelok Company 440 473-1050
  318 Bishop Rd Cleveland (44143) *(G-4758)*
Swagelok Company 440 461-7714
  358 Bishop Rd Cleveland (44143) *(G-4759)*
Swagelok Company 440 248-4600
  31400 Aurora Rd Solon (44139) *(G-13427)*
Swagelok Company (PA) 440 248-4600
  29500 Solon Rd Solon (44139) *(G-13428)*
Swagelok Company 440 349-5652
  6100 Cochran Rd Solon (44139) *(G-13429)*
Swagelok Company 440 349-5836
  29495 F A Lennon Dr Solon (44139) *(G-13430)*
Swagelok Company 440 349-5934
  29495 F A Lennon Dr Solon (44139) *(G-13431)*
Swagelok Company 440 248-4600
  26653 Curtiss Wright Pkwy Willoughby Hills (44092) *(G-16029)*
Swagelok Zalo 216 524-8950
  6090 Cochran Rd Solon (44139) *(G-13432)*
Swagg Productions2015llc 614 601-7414
  628 Arborway Ct Worthington (43085) *(G-16213)*

Swan Creek Candle Co., Swanton *Also Called: Ambrosia Inc (G-13967)*
Swanton Wldg Machining Co Inc (PA) 419 826-4816
  407 Bdwy Ave Swanton (43558) *(G-13984)*
Swapil Inc
  2740 Airport Dr Ste 310 Columbus (43219) *(G-5804)*
Sweet Manufacturing Company 937 325-1511
  2000 E Leffel Ln Springfield (45505) *(G-13641)*
Sweet Persuasions LLC 614 216-9052
  9636 Circle Dr Pickerington (43147) *(G-12471)*
Sweeties Olympia Treats LLC 440 572-7747
  11606 Pearl Rd Strongsville (44136) *(G-13888)*
Sweets & Meats Bbq, Cincinnati *Also Called: Sweets and Meats LLC (G-3437)*
Sweets and Meats LLC 513 888-4227
  2249 Beechmont Ave Cincinnati (45230) *(G-3437)*
Swift Filters Inc (PA) 440 735-0995
  24040 Forbes Rd Oakwood Village (44146) *(G-12043)*
Swift Manufacturing Co Inc 740 237-4405
  700 Lorain St Ironton (45638) *(G-8704)*
Swiger Coil Systems Ltd 216 362-7500
  4677 Manufacturing Ave Cleveland (44135) *(G-4760)*
Swihart Industries Inc 937 277-4796
  5111 Webster St Dayton (45414) *(G-6603)*
Swimmer Printing Inc 216 623-1005
  1215 Superior Ave E Ste 110 Cleveland (44114) *(G-4761)*
Swingle Drilling, Crooksville *Also Called: Petro Ware Inc (G-6049)*
Swiss Heritage Winery 330 343-4108
  6011 Old Route 39 Nw Dover (44622) *(G-6846)*
Swiss Valley Tire LLC 330 231-6187
  1900 Us Route 62 Wilmot (44689) *(G-16069)*
Swiss Woodcraft Inc 330 925-1807
  15 Industrial St Rittman (44270) *(G-12828)*
Switchback Group Inc (HQ) 216 290-6040
  5638 Transportation Blvd Cleveland (44125) *(G-4762)*
Swp Legacy Ltd 330 340-9663
  10143 Copperhead Rd Nw Sugarcreek (44681) *(G-13944)*
Sy Logging Llc 440 437-5744
  3104 Winters Rd Orwell (44076) *(G-12170)*
Sylvan Studio, Sylvania *Also Called: Sharonco Inc (G-14014)*
Sylvan Studios Inc 419 882-3423
  5651 Main St Sylvania (43560) *(G-14016)*
SYLVANIA MOOSE LODGE 1579, Sylvania *Also Called: Sylvania Mose Ldge No 1579 Lya (G-14017)*
Sylvania Mose Ldge No 1579 Lya 419 885-4953
  6072 Main St Sylvania (43560) *(G-14017)*
Symantec, Akron *Also Called: Gen Digital Inc (G-165)*
Symatic Inc 330 225-1510
  803 E Washington St Ste 200 Medina (44256) *(G-10381)*
Symbol Tool & Die Inc 440 582-5989
  11000 Industrial First Ave North Royalton (44133) *(G-11897)*
Syme Inc (PA) 330 723-6000
  300 Lake Rd Medina (44256) *(G-10382)*
Symmes Creek Mining LLC 740 353-1509
  538 6th St Portsmouth (45662) *(G-12658)*
Symrise Inc 440 324-6060
  110 Liberty Ct Elyria (44035) *(G-7209)*
Synagro Midwest Inc 937 384-0669
  4515 Infirmary Rd Miamisburg (45342) *(G-10687)*
Synergy Manufacturing LLC 740 352-5933
  4239 Us Highway 23 Piketon (45661) *(G-12485)*
Synsei Medical 609 759-1101
  6474 Weston Cir W Dublin (43016) *(G-6950)*
Syntec LLC 440 229-6262
  20525 Center Ridge Rd Ste 512 Rocky River (44116) *(G-12845)*
Synteko, Strongsville *Also Called: PPG Architectural Coatings LLC (G-13866)*
Synthomer Inc 330 734-1237
  1380 Tech Way Akron (44306) *(G-342)*
Synthomer Inc (HQ) 216 682-7000
  25435 Harvard Rd Beachwood (44122) *(G-1025)*
Synthomer USA LLC (HQ) 678 400-6655
  25435 Harvard Rd Beachwood (44122) *(G-1026)*
Syracuse China Company, Toledo *Also Called: Syracuse China LLC (G-14480)*

ALPHABETIC SECTION

Syracuse China LLC (DH).. 419 325-2100
300 Madison Ave Toledo (43604) *(G-14480)*

Sysco Guest Supply LLC.. 440 960-2515
7395 Industrial Parkway Dr Lorain (44052) *(G-9440)*

Systech Handling Inc.. 419 445-8226
120 Taylor Pkwy Archbold (43502) *(G-547)*

Systecon LLC.. 513 777-7722
6121 Schumacher Park Dr West Chester (45069) *(G-15513)*

System EDM of Ohio, Mason Also Called: Hi-Tek Manufacturing Inc *(G-10001)*

System Packaging of Glassline....................................... 419 666-9712
28905 Glenwood Rd Perrysburg (43551) *(G-12427)*

System Seals Inc... 216 220-1800
6600 W Snowville Rd Brecksville (44141) *(G-1632)*

System Seals Inc (HQ).. 440 735-0200
9505 Midwest Ave Cleveland (44125) *(G-4763)*

Systemax Manufacturing Inc... 937 368-2300
6450 Poe Ave Ste 200 Dayton (45414) *(G-6604)*

Systems Advantage, Lima Also Called: Proforma Systems Advantage *(G-9279)*

Systems Kit LLC MB.. 330 945-4500
925 Glaser Pkwy Akron (44306) *(G-343)*

Systems Pack Inc.. 330 467-5729
649 Highland Rd E Macedonia (44056) *(G-9583)*

T & B Foundry Company... 216 391-4200
2469 E 71st St Cleveland (44104) *(G-4764)*

T & CS Repairs & Retail LLC... 704 964-7325
1153 Marcy St Akron (44301) *(G-344)*

T & D Fabricating, Eastlake Also Called: T & D Fabricating Inc *(G-7051)*

T & D Fabricating Inc.. 440 951-5646
1489 E 363rd St Eastlake (44095) *(G-7051)*

T & D Thompson Inc... 740 332-8515
15952 State Route 56 E Laurelville (43135) *(G-9056)*

T & L Custom Screening Inc... 937 237-3121
3464 Successful Way Dayton (45414) *(G-6605)*

T & R Welding Systems Inc... 937 228-7517
1 Janney Rd Dayton (45404) *(G-6606)*

T & S Machine Inc... 419 453-2101
712 Maple St Wapakoneta (45895) *(G-15130)*

T & W Forge, Alliance Also Called: T & W Forge Inc *(G-431)*

T & W Forge Inc...
562 W Ely St Alliance (44601) *(G-431)*

T A Bacon Co.. 216 851-1404
11655 Chillicothe Rd Chesterland (44026) *(G-2489)*

T A C, Hilliard Also Called: Thermoplastic Accessories Corp *(G-8448)*

T A W Inc.. 330 339-1212
2565 Mathias Raceway Rd Sw New Philadelphia (44663) *(G-11527)*

T and W Stamping Acquisition (PA)................................. 330 821-5777
930 W Ely St Alliance (44601) *(G-432)*

T C F C, Cleveland Also Called: Those Chrcters From Clvland LL *(G-4795)*

T C Redi Mix Youngstown Inc (PA).................................. 330 755-2143
2400 Poland Ave Youngstown (44502) *(G-16450)*

T C Service Co.. 440 954-7500
38285 Pelton Rd Willoughby (44094) *(G-16001)*

T D Dynamics Inc.. 216 881-0800
4101 Commerce Ave Cleveland (44103) *(G-4765)*

T E Brown LLC (PA)... 937 223-2241
1205 Lamar St Dayton (45404) *(G-6607)*

T E Q HI Inc.. 877 448-3701
1525 Alum Creek Dr Columbus (43209) *(G-5805)*

T F O, Jeffersonville Also Called: Tfo Tech Co Ltd *(G-8766)*

T J Davies Company Inc.. 440 248-5510
11823 State Route 44 Mantua (44255) *(G-9744)*

T J F Inc.. 419 878-4400
1070 Disher Dr Waterville (43566) *(G-15253)*

T L Squire and Company Inc... 330 668-2604
4040 Embassy Pkwy Ste 300 Akron (44333) *(G-345)*

T S I, Englewood Also Called: Tom Smith Industries Inc *(G-7245)*

T W Corporation... 440 461-3234
99 South Seiberling Street Akron (44305) *(G-346)*

T-Mac Machine Inc... 330 673-0621
924 Overholt Rd Kent (44240) *(G-8870)*

T-N-T Rgulatory Compliance Inc..................................... 513 442-2464
731 Dorgene Ln Cincinnati (45244) *(G-3438)*

T-Shirt Co... 513 821-7100
413 Northland Blvd Cincinnati (45240) *(G-3439)*

T.E.A.M. Systems, Toledo Also Called: Magna Modular Systems LLC *(G-14376)*

T&A Pallets Inc... 330 968-4743
2849 Denny Rd Ravenna (44266) *(G-12737)*

T&R Wood Products, Middle Point Also Called: Traveling Recycle WD Pdts Inc *(G-10713)*

T&T Graphics Inc.. 937 847-6000
2563 Technical Dr Miamisburg (45342) *(G-10688)*

T&T Machine Inc... 440 354-0605
892 Callendar Blvd Painesville (44077) *(G-12265)*

T&W Stamping Inc.. 330 270-0891
207 N Four Mile Run Rd Austintown (44515) *(G-755)*

Taasi, Delaware Also Called: Attia Applied Sciences Inc *(G-6704)*

Tabco, Chesterland Also Called: T A Bacon Co *(G-2489)*

Tablox Inc... 440 953-1951
4821 E 345th St Willoughby (44094) *(G-16002)*

Tabtronics, Dayton Also Called: Blue Creek Enterprises Inc *(G-6232)*

TAC Industries Inc (PA).. 937 328-5200
2160 Old Selma Rd Springfield (45505) *(G-13642)*

TAC Materials Inc... 330 425-8472
1700 Highland Rd Twinsburg (44087) *(G-14740)*

Tack-Anew Inc.. 419 734-4212
451 W Lakeshore Dr Port Clinton (43452) *(G-12629)*

Tacoma Energy LLC... 614 410-9000
697 Green Crest Dr Westerville (43081) *(G-15721)*

Tadd Spring Co Inc... 440 572-1313
15060 Foltz Pkwy Strongsville (44149) *(G-13889)*

Taft Tool & Production Co... 419 385-2576
756 S Byrne Rd Ste 1 Toledo (43609) *(G-14481)*

Taft's Brewpourium Cincinnati, Cincinnati Also Called: Dswdwk LLC *(G-2843)*

Tahoma Engineered Solutions, Ashland Also Called: Tahoma Engineered Solutions Inc *(G-617)*

Tahoma Engineered Solutions Inc.................................. 330 345-6169
532 County Road 1600 Ashland (44805) *(G-617)*

Tahoma Enterprises Inc (PA).. 330 745-9016
255 Wooster Rd N Barberton (44203) *(G-897)*

Tahoma Machining Ltd... 330 952-2410
950 Lake Rd Medina (44256) *(G-10383)*

Tahoma Rubber & Plastics Inc (HQ)............................... 330 745-9016
255 Wooster Rd N Barberton (44203) *(G-898)*

Taiho, Tiffin Also Called: Taiho Corporation of America *(G-14107)*

Taiho Corporation of America.. 419 443-1645
194 Heritage Dr Tiffin (44883) *(G-14107)*

Taikisha Usa Inc... 614 444-5602
1939 Refugee Rd Columbus (43207) *(G-5806)*

Tailored Systems Inc.. 937 299-3900
2853 Springboro W Moraine (45439) *(G-11213)*

Tailwind Technologies Inc (PA)...................................... 937 778-4200
1 Propeller Pl Piqua (45356) *(G-12555)*

Taiyo America Inc (HQ)... 419 300-8811
1702 E Spring St Saint Marys (45885) *(G-12968)*

Take It For Granite LLC... 513 735-0555
3898 Mcmann Rd Cincinnati (45245) *(G-2574)*

Takk Industries Inc.. 513 353-4306
5838a Hamilton Cleves Rd Cleves (45002) *(G-4966)*

Takumi Stamping Inc.. 513 642-0081
8585 Seward Rd Fairfield (45011) *(G-7413)*

Talan Products Inc.. 216 458-0170
18800 Cochran Ave Cleveland (44110) *(G-4766)*

Talent Tool & Die Inc... 440 239-8777
777 Berea Industrial Pkwy Berea (44017) *(G-1295)*

Talisman Racing, Cincinnati Also Called: All Craft Manufacturing Co *(G-2608)*

Talk of Town Silkscreen & EMB, Akron Also Called: B Richardson Inc *(G-72)*

Tallmadge Finishing Co Inc... 330 633-7466
879 Moe Dr Ste C20 Akron (44310) *(G-347)*

Tallmadge Spinning & Metal Co...................................... 330 794-2277
2783 Gilchrist Rd Unit A Akron (44305) *(G-348)*

Tally Ho Slipcovers... 614 448-6170
2019 Andover Rd Columbus (43212) *(G-5807)*

Talus Renewables Inc... 650 248-5374
3762 Bainbridge Rd Cleveland Heights (44118) *(G-4943)*

Tamarron Technology Inc   ALPHABETIC SECTION

Tamarron Technology Inc 800 277-3207
   8044 Montgomery Rd Cincinnati (45236) *(G-3440)*

Tambrands Sales Corp (HQ) 513 983-1100
   1 Procter And Gamble Plz Cincinnati (45202) *(G-3441)*

Tampax, Cincinnati *Also Called: Tambrands Sales Corp (G-3441)*

Tangent Air Inc 740 474-1114
   127 Edison Ave Circleville (43113) *(G-3556)*

Tangent Company LLC 440 543-2775
   10175 Queens Way Ste 1 Chagrin Falls (44023) *(G-2427)*

Tangible Solutions Inc 937 912-4603
   678 Yellow Springs Fairfield Rd Fairborn (45324) *(G-7324)*

Tango Echo Bravo Mfg Inc 440 353-2605
   4915 Mills Industrial Pkwy North Ridgeville (44039) *(G-11861)*

Tank Services, Dennison *Also Called: Services Acquisition Co LLC (G-6795)*

Tap Packaging Solutions, Cleveland *Also Called: Chilcote Company (G-3819)*

Tappan Chairs LLC 800 840-9121
   9115 Blue Ash Rd Blue Ash (45242) *(G-1477)*

Tarahill Inc 706 864-0808
   3985 Groves Rd Columbus (43232) *(G-5808)*

Tarantula Performance Racg LLC 330 273-3456
   1669 W 130th St Ste 301 Hinckley (44233) *(G-8477)*

Targeted Cmpund Monitoring LLC 937 025-0042
   2790 Indian Ripple Rd Ste A Dayton (45440) *(G-6608)*

Tarigma Corporation 614 436-3734
   6161 Busch Blvd Ste 110 Columbus (43229) *(G-5809)*

Tark Inc (PA) 937 434-6766
   9273 Byers Rd Miamisburg (45342) *(G-10689)*

Tarkett Inc 440 543-8916
   16910 Munn Rd Chagrin Falls (44023) *(G-2428)*

Tarkett Inc (DH) 800 899-8916
   30000 Aurora Rd Solon (44139) *(G-13433)*

Tarkett North America, Solon *Also Called: Tarkett Inc (G-13433)*

Tarkett USA, Solon *Also Called: Johnsonite Inc (G-13370)*

Tarkett USA Inc 440 543-8916
   16910 Munn Rd Chagrin Falls (44023) *(G-2429)*

Tarkett USA Inc (DH) 877 827-5388
   30000 Aurora Rd Solon (44139) *(G-13434)*

Tarman Machine Company Inc 614 834-4010
   8215 Dove Pkwy Canal Winchester (43110) *(G-1992)*

Tarpco, Kent *Also Called: Hapco Inc (G-8817)*

Tarpco Inc 330 677-8277
   390 Portage Blvd Kent (44240) *(G-8871)*

Tarped Out Inc 330 325-7722
   4442 State Route 14 Ravenna (44266) *(G-12738)*

Tarpstop LLC (PA) 419 873-7867
   12000 Williams Rd Perrysburg (43551) *(G-12428)*

Tarrier, Columbus *Also Called: Tarrier Foods Corp (G-5810)*

Tarrier Foods Corp 614 876-8594
   2700 International St Columbus (43228) *(G-5810)*

Tarrier Steel Company Inc 614 444-4000
   1379 S 22nd St Columbus (43206) *(G-5811)*

Tastemorr Snacks, Coldwater *Also Called: Basic Grain Products Inc (G-4982)*

Tasyd Industries LLC 440 352-8019
   466 W Jackson St Painesville (44077) *(G-12266)*

Tat Machine & Tool Ltd 419 836-7706
   1313 S Cousino Rd Curtice (43412) *(G-6059)*

Tata America Intl Corp 513 677-6500
   1000 Summit Dr Unit 1 Milford (45150) *(G-10925)*

Tata Consultancy Services, Milford *Also Called: Tata America Intl Corp (G-10925)*

Tate & Lyle, Dayton *Also Called: Primary Pdts Ingrdnts Amrcas L (G-6521)*

Tatham Schulz Incorporated 216 861-4431
   11400 Brookpark Rd Cleveland (44130) *(G-4767)*

Tatum Petroleum Corporation 740 819-6810
   667 Lkview Plz Blvd Ste E Worthington (43085) *(G-16214)*

Tavens Container Inc 216 883-3333
   22475 Aurora Rd Bedford (44146) *(G-1156)*

Tavens Packg Display Solutions, Bedford *Also Called: Tavens Container Inc (G-1156)*

Taylor - Winfield Corporation 330 259-8500
   3200 Innovation Place Hubbard (44425) *(G-8571)*

Taylor & Moore Co 513 733-5730
   807 Wachendorf St Cincinnati (45215) *(G-3442)*

Taylor Communications Inc 419 678-6000
   515 W Sycamore St Coldwater (45828) *(G-5002)*

Taylor Communications Inc 614 351-6868
   3950 Business Park Dr Columbus (43204) *(G-5812)*

Taylor Communications Inc 937 221-1000
   600 Albany St Dayton (45417) *(G-6609)*

Taylor Communications Inc 732 356-0081
   7755 Paragon Road Ste 101 Dayton (45459) *(G-6610)*

Taylor Communications Inc 937 221-3347
   3545 Urbancrest Industrial Dr Grove City (43123) *(G-8121)*

Taylor Communications Inc 216 265-1800
   4125 Highlander Pkwy Ste 230 Richfield (44286) *(G-12800)*

Taylor Communications Inc 614 277-7500
   3125 Lewis Centre Way Urbancrest (43123) *(G-14855)*

Taylor Lumber, Piketon *Also Called: Taylor Lumber Worldwide Inc (G-12486)*

Taylor Lumber Worldwide Inc 740 259-6222
   16523 State Route 124 Piketon (45661) *(G-12486)*

Taylor Made Glass Systems, Payne *Also Called: Taylor Products Inc (G-12323)*

Taylor Manufacturing Co Inc 937 322-8622
   1101 W Main St Springfield (45504) *(G-13643)*

Taylor Metal 614 401-8007
   6400 Huntley Rd Ste 102 Columbus (43229) *(G-5813)*

Taylor Metal Products Co 419 522-3471
   700 Springmill St Mansfield (44903) *(G-9724)*

Taylor Mtl Hdlg & Conveyor, Toledo *Also Called: Bobco Enterprises Inc (G-14215)*

Taylor Products Inc 419 263-2313
   230 S Laura St Payne (45880) *(G-12322)*

Taylor Products Inc 419 263-2313
   407 N Maple St Payne (45880) *(G-12323)*

Taylor Quick Print 740 439-2208
   1008 Woodlawn Ave # A Cambridge (43725) *(G-1957)*

Taylor Tool & Die Inc 937 845-1491
   306 N Main St New Carlisle (45344) *(G-11427)*

Taylor Winfield Indus Wldg Eqp, Youngstown *Also Called: Taylor-Winfield Tech Inc (G-16451)*

Taylor-Winfield Tech Inc 330 259-8500
   3200 Innovation Pl Youngstown (44509) *(G-16451)*

Tb Backstop Inc 330 434-4442
   4478 Regal Dr Akron (44321) *(G-349)*

Tbc Retail Group Inc 216 267-8040
   5370 W 130th St Cleveland (44142) *(G-4768)*

Tbec, Painesville *Also Called: Thirion Brothers Eqp Co LLC (G-12271)*

Tbk Holdings LLC (PA) 313 584-0400
   232 J St Perrysburg (43551) *(G-12429)*

Tbone Sales, Baltic *Also Called: Tbone Sales LLC (G-841)*

Tbone Sales LLC 330 897-6131
   410 N Ray St Baltic (43804) *(G-841)*

Tbt Hauling LLC 904 635-7631
   500 Lehman Ave Ste 103 Bowling Green (43402) *(G-1590)*

Tca Graphics, Fairborn *Also Called: Tee Creations (G-7325)*

Tcb Automation LLC 330 556-6444
   601 W 15th St Dover (44622) *(G-6847)*

TCH Industries Incorporated 330 487-5155
   2307 E Aurora Rd Twinsburg (44087) *(G-14741)*

TCS Schindler & Co LLC 937 836-9473
   36 Haas Dr Englewood (45322) *(G-7243)*

TD Landscape Inc 740 694-0244
   16780 Pinkley Rd Fredericktown (43019) *(G-7754)*

Td Synnex Corporation 614 669-6889
   5350 Centerpoint Pkwy Groveport (43125) *(G-8161)*

Td Synnex Corporation, Groveport *Also Called: Td Synnex Corporation (G-8161)*

Tdi, Mentor *Also Called: Tridelta Industries Inc (G-10584)*

TDS Custom Cabinets LLC 614 517-2220
   1819 Walcutt Rd Ste 9 Columbus (43228) *(G-5814)*

TDS-Bf/Ls Holdings Inc 440 327-5800
   38900 Taylor Industrial Pkwy North Ridgeville (44039) *(G-11862)*

Te Connectivity Corporation 419 521-9500
   175 N Diamond St Mansfield (44902) *(G-9725)*

Te-Co Inc 937 836-0961
   100 Quinter Farm Rd Union (45322) *(G-14775)*

Te-Co Manufacturing LLC 937 836-0961
   100 Quinter Farm Rd Englewood (45322) *(G-7244)*

ALPHABETIC SECTION — Teikuro Corporation

Teachers Publishing Group.. 614 486-0631
   4200 Parkway Ct Hilliard (43026) *(G-8445)*

Team Inc.. 614 263-1808
   3005 Silver Dr Columbus (43224) *(G-5815)*

Team Amity Mlds Plstic Injctio.. 937 667-7856
   1435 Commerce Park Dr Tipp City (45371) *(G-14158)*

Team Cobra Products, North Ridgeville *Also Called: H & S Distributing Inc (G-11843)*

Team Plastics Inc... 216 251-8270
   3901 W 150th St Cleveland (44111) *(G-4769)*

Team Ppi, Kenton *Also Called: Pleasant Precision Inc (G-8896)*

Team Remington Cadillac, Canton *Also Called: McCann Color Inc (G-2156)*

Team Systems, Toledo *Also Called: Decoma Systems Integration Gro (G-14263)*

Team Wendy LLC... 216 738-2518
   17000 Saint Clair Ave Bldg 1 Cleveland (44110) *(G-4770)*

Teamfg LLC... 513 313-8855
   2052 Bohlke Blvd Fairfield (45014) *(G-7414)*

TEC Design & Manufacturing Inc.. 937 435-2147
   4549 Gateway Cir Dayton (45440) *(G-6611)*

Teca, Dayton *Also Called: Troy Engnred Cmpnnts Assmblies (G-6635)*

Tech Data, Groveport *Also Called: Vertiv Corporation (G-8166)*

Tech Development, Dayton *Also Called: GE Aviation Systems LLC (G-6347)*

Tech Dynamics Inc... 419 666-1666
   361 D St Ste B Perrysburg (43551) *(G-12430)*

Tech Industries Inc... 216 861-7337
   1313 Washington Ave Cleveland (44113) *(G-4771)*

Tech International, Johnstown *Also Called: Technical Rubber Company Inc (G-8779)*

Tech Mold and Tool Co... 937 667-8851
   4333 Lisa Dr Tipp City (45371) *(G-14159)*

Tech Pro Inc.. 330 923-3546
   3030 Gilchrist Rd Akron (44305) *(G-350)*

Tech Products Corporation (DH).. 937 438-1100
   2215 Lyons Rd Miamisburg (45342) *(G-10690)*

Tech Ready Mix Inc.. 216 361-5000
   5000 Crayton Ave Cleveland (44104) *(G-4772)*

Tech Systems Inc... 419 878-2100
   1070 Disher Dr Waterville (43566) *(G-15254)*

Tech-Med Inc... 216 486-0900
   1080 E 222nd St Euclid (44117) *(G-7301)*

Tech-Sonic Inc... 614 792-3117
   2710 Sawbury Blvd Columbus (43235) *(G-5816)*

Tech-Way Industries Inc.. 937 746-1004
   301 Industrial Dr Franklin (45005) *(G-7705)*

Tech/III Inc... 513 482-7500
   2594 Mack Rd Fairfield (45014) *(G-7415)*

Tech4imaging LLC.. 614 214-2655
   1910 Crown Park Ct Columbus (43235) *(G-5817)*

Techmetals Inc (PA)... 937 253-5311
   345 Springfield St Dayton (45403) *(G-6612)*

Techneglas Inc... 419 873-2000
   25875 Dixie Hwy Bldg 52 Perrysburg (43551) *(G-12431)*

Techneglas LLC (HQ)... 419 873-2000
   2100 N Wilkinson Way Perrysburg (43551) *(G-12432)*

TECHNEGLAS, INC., Perrysburg *Also Called: Techneglas Inc (G-12431)*

Technibus Inc... 330 479-4202
   1501 Raff Rd Sw Ste 6 Canton (44710) *(G-2241)*

Technical Glass Products Inc (PA)..................................... 440 639-6399
   881 Callendar Blvd Painesville (44077) *(G-12267)*

Technical Glass Products Inc.. 425 396-8420
   7460 Ponderosa Rd Perrysburg (43551) *(G-12433)*

Technical Machine Products Inc
   5500 Walworth Ave Cleveland (44102) *(G-4773)*

Technical Rubber Company Inc (PA).................................. 740 967-9015
   200 E Coshocton St Johnstown (43031) *(G-8779)*

Technical Tool & Gauge Inc... 330 273-1778
   2914 Westway Dr Brunswick (44212) *(G-1793)*

Technicolor Usa Inc.. 614 474-8821
   24200 Us Highway 23 S Circleville (43113) *(G-3557)*

Technicote, Miamisburg *Also Called: Technicote Inc (G-10691)*

Technicote Inc.. 330 928-1476
   70 Marc Dr Cuyahoga Falls (44223) *(G-6121)*

Technicote Inc (PA).. 800 358-4448
   222 Mound Ave Miamisburg (45342) *(G-10691)*

Technicote Westfield Inc... 937 859-4448
   222 Mound Ave Miamisburg (45342) *(G-10692)*

Technidrill Systems Inc... 330 678-9980
   429 Portage Blvd Kent (44240) *(G-8872)*

Technifab Inc (PA).. 440 934-8324
   1355 Chester Industrial Pkwy Avon (44011) *(G-789)*

Technifab Engineered Products, Avon *Also Called: Technifab Inc (G-789)*

Techniplate Inc... 216 486-8825
   796 Carriage Park Oval Westlake (44145) *(G-15795)*

Techniques Surfaces Usa Inc.. 937 323-2556
   2015 Progress Rd Springfield (45505) *(G-13644)*

Techniweld.. 412 357-2176
   1120 Oak Hill Ave Youngstown (44502) *(G-16452)*

Technlgy Install Partners LLC.. 888 586-7040
   13701 Enterprise Ave Cleveland (44135) *(G-4774)*

Techno Adhesives Co... 513 771-1584
   12113 Mosteller Rd Cincinnati (45241) *(G-3443)*

Technoform GL Insul N Amer Inc....................................... 330 487-6600
   1755 Enterprise Pkwy Ste 300 Twinsburg (44087) *(G-14742)*

Technology Explortation Pdts, Mentor *Also Called: Gdj Inc (G-10463)*

Technology House Ltd... 440 248-3025
   30700 Carter St Solon (44139) *(G-13435)*

Technology House Ltd (PA).. 440 248-3025
   10036 Aurora Hudson Rd Streetsboro (44241) *(G-13795)*

Technosoft Inc... 513 985-9877
   11180 Reed Hartman Hwy Ste 200 Blue Ash (45242) *(G-1478)*

Techstar, Findlay *Also Called: DS Techstar Inc (G-7503)*

Techtron Systems Inc... 440 505-2990
   29500 Fountain Pkwy Solon (44139) *(G-13436)*

Tecmark Corporation.. 440 205-9188
   7335 Production Dr Mentor (44060) *(G-10572)*

Tecmark Corporation (PA).. 440 205-7600
   7745 Metric Dr Mentor (44060) *(G-10573)*

Tecnocap LLC.. 330 392-7222
   2100 Griswold Street Ext Ne Warren (44483) *(G-15208)*

Teco, Toledo *Also Called: Toledo Engineering Co Inc (G-14495)*

Tectum Inc... 740 345-9691
   105 S 6th St Newark (43055) *(G-11608)*

Tecumseh Packg Solutions Inc.. 419 238-1122
   1275 Industrial Dr Van Wert (45891) *(G-14927)*

Ted Bolle Millwork Inc... 937 325-8779
   2834 Hustead Rd Springfield (45502) *(G-13645)*

Ted J & Janice Hlavaty... 440 256-8524
   8814 Foxhill Dr Willoughby (44094) *(G-16003)*

Ted M Figgins... 740 277-3750
   347 S Columbus St Pmb 634 Lancaster (43130) *(G-9042)*

Tedia Company LLC... 513 874-5340
   1000 Tedia Way Fairfield (45014) *(G-7416)*

Tee Creations.. 937 878-2822
   701 N Broad St Ste C Fairborn (45324) *(G-7325)*

Tee Hee Co Inc.. 614 515-5581
   740 Lakeview Plaza Blvd Ste 125 Worthington (43085) *(G-16215)*

Tegam, Geneva *Also Called: Tegam Inc (G-7945)*

Tegam Inc (HQ).. 440 466-6100
   10 Tegam Way Geneva (44041) *(G-7945)*

Tegr Inc... 419 678-4991
   191 N Eastern Ave Saint Henry (45883) *(G-12939)*

Teijin Automotive Tech Inc.. 419 396-1980
   2915 County Highway 96 Carey (43316) *(G-2285)*

Teijin Automotive Tech Inc.. 440 945-4800
   333 Gore Rd Conneaut (44030) *(G-5933)*

Teijin Automotive Tech Inc.. 419 257-2231
   100 S Poe Rd North Baltimore (45872) *(G-11700)*

Teijin Automotive Tech Inc.. 419 238-4628
   1276 Industrial Dr Van Wert (45891) *(G-14928)*

Teikoku USA Inc... 304 699-1156
   27881 State Route 7 Marietta (45750) *(G-9835)*

Teikuro Corporation.. 937 327-3955
   4500 Gateway Blvd Springfield (45502) *(G-13646)*

Tek Gear & Machine Inc   **ALPHABETIC SECTION**

Tek Gear & Machine Inc 330 455-3331
   1220 Camden Ave Sw Canton (44706) *(G-2242)*

Tek Group International 330 706-0000
   567 Elm Ridge Ave Canal Fulton (44614) *(G-1976)*

Tek Manufacturing, Canal Fulton *Also Called: Tek Group International (G-1976)*

Tekfor Inc 330 202-7420
   3690 Long Rd Wooster (44691) *(G-16176)*

Tekfor USA, Wooster *Also Called: Tekfor Inc (G-16176)*

Tekmar-Dohrmann, Mason *Also Called: Teledyne Tekmar Company (G-10064)*

Tekni-Plex Inc 419 491-2399
   1445 Timber Wolf Dr Holland (43528) *(G-8532)*

Teknol Inc (PA) 937 264-0190
   5751 Webster St Dayton (45414) *(G-6613)*

Tekraft Industries Inc 440 352-8321
   244 Latimore St Painesville (44077) *(G-12268)*

Tektronix, West Chester *Also Called: Tektronix Inc (G-15594)*

Tektronix Inc 248 305-5200
   9639 Inter Ocean Dr West Chester (45246) *(G-15594)*

Tekus, L Sweater Design, Cleveland *Also Called: Fine Points Inc (G-4060)*

Tekworx LLC 513 533-4777
   4538 Cornell Rd Blue Ash (45241) *(G-1479)*

Telcon LLC 330 562-5566
   1677 Miller Pkwy Streetsboro (44241) *(G-13796)*

Teledoor LLC 419 227-3000
   1075 Prosperity Rd Lima (45801) *(G-9295)*

Teledoor Manufacturing LLC 419 227-3000
   1075 Prosperity Rd Lima (45801) *(G-9296)*

Teledyne Instruments Inc 603 886-8400
   4736 Socialville Foster Rd Mason (45040) *(G-10062)*

Teledyne Instruments Inc 513 229-7000
   4736 Socialville Foster Rd Mason (45040) *(G-10063)*

Teledyne Leeman Labs, Mason *Also Called: Teledyne Instruments Inc (G-10062)*

Teledyne Tekmar, Mason *Also Called: Teledyne Instruments Inc (G-10063)*

Teledyne Tekmar Company (DH) 513 229-7000
   4736 Socialville Foster Rd Mason (45040) *(G-10064)*

Telehealth Care Solutions LLC 440 623-6023
   2551 Sweetwater Dr Brecksville (44141) *(G-1633)*

Telempu N Hayashi Amer Corp 513 932-9319
   1500 Kingsview Dr Lebanon (45036) *(G-9113)*

Telesis Marking Systems, Circleville *Also Called: Telesis Technologies Inc (G-3558)*

Telesis Technologies Inc (DH) 740 477-5000
   28181 River Dr Circleville (43113) *(G-3558)*

Telex Communications Inc 419 865-0972
   5660 Southwyck Blvd Ste 150 Toledo (43614) *(G-14482)*

Telling Industries LLC 740 435-8900
   2105 Larrick Rd Cambridge (43725) *(G-1958)*

Telling Industries LLC (PA) 440 974-3370
   4420 Sherwin Rd Willoughby (44094) *(G-16004)*

Telos Systems, Cleveland *Also Called: Cutting Edge Technologies Inc (G-3928)*

Tembec Btlsr Inc 419 244-5856
   2112 Sylvan Ave Toledo (43606) *(G-14483)*

Tempcraft Corporation 216 391-3885
   3960 S Marginal Rd Cleveland (44114) *(G-4775)*

Temperature Controls Co Inc 330 773-6633
   5729 Dailey Rd New Franklin (44319) *(G-11444)*

Tempest Inc 216 883-6500
   12750 Berea Rd Cleveland (44111) *(G-4776)*

Temple Inland 513 425-0830
   912 Nelbar St Middletown (45042) *(G-10862)*

Temple Israel 330 762-8617
   91 Springside Dr Akron (44333) *(G-351)*

Temple Oil and Gas LLC 740 452-7878
   6626 Ceramic Rd Ne Crooksville (43731) *(G-6050)*

Tempo Manufacturing Company 937 773-6613
   727 E Ash St Piqua (45356) *(G-12556)*

Tempo Trophy Mfg, Piqua *Also Called: Tempo Manufacturing Company (G-12556)*

Temprecision Intl Corp (PA) 855 891-7732
   777 Stow St Kent (44240) *(G-8873)*

Ten Dogs Global Industries LLC 513 752-9000
   4400 Glen Willow Lake Ln Batavia (45103) *(G-952)*

Ten Mfg LLC 440 487-1100
   7675 Saint Clair Ave Mentor (44060) *(G-10574)*

Tenacity Manufacturing Company 513 821-0201
   4455 Mulhauser Rd West Chester (45011) *(G-1514)*

Tencom Ltd 419 865-5877
   7134 Railroad St Holland (43528) *(G-8533)*

Tenk Machine, Strongsville *Also Called: Cleveland Jsm Inc (G-13822)*

Tenneco, Milan *Also Called: Pullman Company (G-10885)*

Tenneco, Milan *Also Called: Tenneco Inc (G-10887)*

Tenneco, Napoleon *Also Called: Pullman Company (G-11331)*

Tenneco Inc 419 499-2541
   33 Lockwood Rd Milan (44846) *(G-10887)*

Tennessee Rand, Fort Loramie *Also Called: Lincoln Electric Automtn Inc (G-7603)*

Tenney Tool & Supply Co 330 666-2807
   973 Wooster Rd N Barberton (44203) *(G-899)*

Tenpoint Crossbow Technologies, Mogadore *Also Called: Hunters Manufacturing Co Inc (G-11075)*

Teradata Operations Inc 937 866-0032
   2461 Rosina Dr Miamisburg (45342) *(G-10693)*

Teradyne Inc 937 427-1280
   2689 Commons Blvd Ste 201 Beavercreek (45431) *(G-1065)*

Terex Services 440 262-3200
   6400 W Snowville Rd Ste 1 Brecksville (44141) *(G-1634)*

Terex USA, Solon *Also Called: Demag Cranes & Components Corp (G-13337)*

Terex Utilities Inc 419 470-8408
   25661 Fort Meigs Rd Ste A Perrysburg (43551) *(G-12434)*

Terminal Equipment Inds Inc 330 468-0322
   64 Privet Ln Northfield (44067) *(G-11912)*

Terminal Ready-Mix Inc 440 288-0181
   524 Colorado Ave Lorain (44052) *(G-9441)*

Ternion Inc (PA) 216 642-6180
   7635 Hub Pkwy Ste A Cleveland (44125) *(G-477)*

Teron Lighting, Fairfield *Also Called: Damak 1 LLC (G-7350)*

Terra Coat LLC 216 254-8157
   500 W Aurora Rd Ste 140 Northfield (44067) *(G-11913)*

Terra Surfaces LLC 937 836-1900
   6350 Frederick Pike Dayton (45414) *(G-6614)*

Terracotta Industries LLC 513 313-6215
   5517 Fair Ln Cincinnati (45227) *(G-3444)*

Terradyn Corporation 614 805-0897
   6457 Reflections Dr Ste 200 Dublin (43017) *(G-6951)*

Terrasmart LLC 239 362-0211
   1000 Buckeye Park Rd Columbus (43207) *(G-5818)*

Terreal North America LLC 888 582-9052
   4757 Tile Plant Rd Se New Lexington (43764) *(G-11459)*

Terry & Jack Neon Sign Co 419 229-0674
   225 S Collins Ave Lima (45804) *(G-9297)*

Terry Asphalt Materials Inc (DH) 513 874-6192
   8600 Bilstein Blvd Hamilton (45015) *(G-8247)*

Terry G Sickles 740 286-8880
   2207 Boy Scout Rd Ray (45672) *(G-12744)*

Terry Lumber and Supply Co 330 659-6800
   1710 Mill St W Peninsula (44264) *(G-12342)*

Terydon Inc 330 879-2448
   7260 Erie Ave Sw Navarre (44662) *(G-11353)*

Tes Therapy, Fairlawn *Also Called: Total Education Solutions Inc (G-7453)*

Tesa Inc 614 847-8200
   544 Enterprise Dr Ste A Lewis Center (43035) *(G-9181)*

Tessa Precision Product Inc 440 392-3470
   850 Callendar Blvd Painesville (44077) *(G-1269)*

Tessec, Dayton *Also Called: Tessec Manufacturing Svcs LLC (G-6616)*

Tessec LLC 937 576-0010
   5621 Webster St Dayton (45414) *(G-6615)*

Tessec Manufacturing Svcs LLC 937 985-3552
   5621 Webster St Dayton (45414) *(G-6616)*

Tessec Technology Services LLC 513 240-5601
   5621 Webster St Dayton (45414) *(G-6617)*

Test Mark Industries Inc 330 426-2200
   995 N Market St East Palestine (44413) *(G-7010)*

Test Measurement Systems Inc 888 867-4872
   9073 Pleasantwood Ave Nw North Canton (44720) *(G-11764)*

ALPHABETIC SECTION

Test-Fuchs Corporation 440 708-3505
   10325 Brecksville Rd Brecksville (44141) *(G-1635)*

Testlink Usa Inc 513 272-1081
   11445 Century Cir W Cincinnati (45246) *(G-3445)*

Tetra Mold & Tool Inc 937 845-1651
   51 Quick Rd New Carlisle (45344) *(G-11428)*

Tetrad Electronics Inc (PA) 440 946-6443
   2048 Joseph Lloyd Pkwy Willoughby (44094) *(G-16005)*

Teva Womens Health LLC (DH) 513 731-9900
   5040 Duramed Rd Cincinnati (45213) *(G-3446)*

Tex-Tyler Corporation 419 729-4951
   5148 Stickney Ave Toledo (43612) *(G-14484)*

Texas Tile Manufacturing LLC 713 869-5811
   30000 Aurora Rd Solon (44139) *(G-13437)*

Texmaster Tools Inc 740 965-8778
   143 Tuttle Ave Fredericktown (43019) *(G-7755)*

Texstone Industries 419 722-4664
   433 Oak Ave Findlay (45840) *(G-7573)*

Textiles Inc 614 529-8642
   5892 Heritage Lakes Dr Hilliard (43026) *(G-8446)*

Textiles Inc (PA) 740 852-0782
   23 Old Springfield Rd London (43140) *(G-9395)*

Textron Aviation Inc 330 286-3043
   449 Greenmont Dr Canfield (44406) *(G-2020)*

Tez Tool & Fabrication Inc 440 323-2300
   115 Buckeye St Elyria (44035) *(G-7210)*

Tfi Manufacturing LLC 440 290-9411
   8989 Tyler Blvd Mentor (44060) *(G-10575)*

Tfo Tech Co Ltd 740 426-6381
   221 State St Jeffersonville (43128) *(G-8766)*

Tfp Corporation (PA) 330 725-7741
   460 Lake Rd Medina (44256) *(G-10384)*

Tfr Printing, Marion *Also Called: Tree Free Resources LLC (G-9887)*

Tgm LLC 419 636-8567
   401 N Union St Bryan (43506) *(G-1839)*

Tgm Holdings Company 419 885-3769
   5439 Roan Rd Sylvania (43560) *(G-14018)*

Tgs Industries Inc 330 339-2211
   406 Mill Ave Sw New Philadelphia (44663) *(G-11528)*

Tgs International Inc 330 893-4828
   4464 State Route 39 Millersburg (44654) *(G-10997)*

Tgs Systems LLC 614 431-6927
   1060 Kingsmill Pkwy Columbus (43229) *(G-5819)*

Th Magnesium Inc 513 285-7568
   9435 Waterstone Blvd Ste 290 Cincinnati (45249) *(G-3447)*

Th Manufacturing Inc 330 893-3572
   4674 County Road 120 Millersburg (44654) *(G-10998)*

Th Plastics Inc 419 352-2770
   843 Miller Dr Bowling Green (43402) *(G-1591)*

Th Plastics Inc 419 425-5821
   101 Bentley Ct Findlay (45840) *(G-7574)*

Tha Presidential Suite LLC 216 338-7287
   2957 Christopher John Dr Unit 308 Dublin (43017) *(G-6952)*

Thaler Machine Company LLC 937 550-2400
   216 Tahlequah Trl Springboro (45066) *(G-13521)*

Thaler Machine Holdings LLC (PA) 937 550-2400
   216 Tahlequah Trl Springboro (45066) *(G-13522)*

The Andersons Clymers Ethanol LLC 574 722-2627
   1947 Briarfield Blvd Maumee (43537) *(G-10239)*

The Apex Paper Box Company (PA) 216 631-4000
   5601 Walworth Ave Cleveland (44102) *(G-4778)*

The Armor Group Inc (PA) 513 923-5260
   4600 N Mason Montgomery Rd Mason (45040) *(G-10065)*

The Basic Aluminum Castings Co 216 481-5606
   1325 E 168th St Cleveland (44110) *(G-4779)*

The Belden Brick Company LLC (HQ) 330 456-0031
   700 Tuscarawas St W Uppr Canton (44702) *(G-2243)*

The Blind Factory, Hilliard *Also Called: Blind Factory Showroom (G-8405)*

The Blonder Company 216 431-3560
   3950 Prospect Ave E Cleveland (44115) *(G-4780)*

The Champion Companies, Springfield *Also Called: The Champion Company (G-13647)*

The Champion Company (PA) 937 324-5681
   400 Harrison St Springfield (45505) *(G-13647)*

The China Hall Company 330 385-2900
   1 Anna St East Liverpool (43920) *(G-7001)*

The Cleveland Jewish Publ Co 216 454-8300
   23880 Commerce Park Ste 1 Beachwood (44122) *(G-1027)*

The Cleveland-Cliffs Iron Co 216 694-5700
   1100 Superior Ave E Ste 1500 Cleveland (44114) *(G-4781)*

The Columbus Show Case Company
   4401 Equity Dr Columbus (43228) *(G-5820)*

The Cornwell Quality Tools Company (PA) 330 336-3506
   667 Seville Rd Wadsworth (44281) *(G-15069)*

The County Classified's, Bellefontaine *Also Called: County Classifieds (G-1203)*

The Crane Group Companies Limited (HQ) 614 754-3000
   330 W Spring St Ste 200 Columbus (43215) *(G-5821)*

The Cyril-Scott Company 740 654-2112
   3950 Lancaster New Lexington Rd Se Lancaster (43130) *(G-9043)*

The D B Hess Company 330 678-5868
   3765 Sunnybrook Rd Kent (44240) *(G-8874)*

The D S Brown Company (HQ) 419 257-3561
   300 E Cherry St North Baltimore (45872) *(G-11701)*

The Dupps Company (PA) 937 855-6555
   548 N Cherry St Germantown (45327) *(G-7953)*

The Ellenbee-Leggett Company Inc 513 874-3200
   3765 Port Union Rd Fairfield (45014) *(G-7417)*

The F A Requarth Company 937 224-1141
   447 E Monument Ave Dayton (45402) *(G-6618)*

The F L Emmert Co Inc 513 721-5808
   2007 Dunlap St Cincinnati (45214) *(G-3448)*

The Fechheimer Brothers Co (HQ) 513 793-5400
   4545 Malsbary Rd Blue Ash (45242) *(G-1480)*

The Fischer & Jirouch Company 216 361-3840
   4821 Superior Ave Cleveland (44103) *(G-4782)*

The Florand Company 330 747-8986
   4404 Lake Park Rd Youngstown (44512) *(G-16453)*

The Fremont Kraut Company 419 332-6481
   724 N Front St Fremont (43420) *(G-7812)*

The Galehouse Companies Inc 330 658-2023
   12667 Portage St Doylestown (44230) *(G-6854)*

The Garland Company Inc (HQ) 216 641-7500
   3800 E 91st St Cleveland (44105) *(G-4783)*

The Gazette Printing Co Inc 440 593-6030
   218 Washington St Conneaut (44030) *(G-5934)*

The Gazette Printing Co Inc (PA) 440 576-9125
   46 W Jefferson St Jefferson (44047) *(G-8760)*

The General's Books, Columbus *Also Called: Generals Books (G-5398)*

The Great Lakes Towing Company (PA) 216 621-4854
   4500 Division Ave Cleveland (44102) *(G-4784)*

The Guardtower Inc 614 488-4311
   5514 Nike Dr Hilliard (43026) *(G-8447)*

The Hamilton Caster & Mfg Company 513 863-3300
   1637 Dixie Hwy Hamilton (45011) *(G-8248)*

The Hartman Corp 614 475-5035
   3216 Morse Rd Columbus (43231) *(G-5822)*

The Hattenbach Company 216 881-5200
   5309 Hamilton Ave Cleveland (44114) *(G-4785)*

The Hc Companies Inc (DH) 440 632-3333
   2450 Edison Blvd Ste 3 Twinsburg (44087) *(G-14743)*

The Holtkamp Organ Co 216 741-5180
   2909 Meyer Ave Cleveland (44109) *(G-4786)*

The Hooven - Dayton Corp 937 233-4473
   511 Byers Rd Miamisburg (45342) *(G-10694)*

The Ideal Builders Supply & Fuel Co Inc (PA) 216 741-1600
   4720 Brookpark Rd Cleveland (44134) *(G-4787)*

The Kindt-Collins Company LLC 216 252-4122
   12651 Elmwood Ave Cleveland (44111) *(G-4788)*

The Kitchen Collection LLC 740 773-9150
   71 E Water St Chillicothe (45601) *(G-2538)*

The Kordenbrock Tool and Die Co 513 326-4390
   10250 Wayne Ave Cincinnati (45215) *(G-3449)*

The Label Team Inc 330 332-1067
   1251 Quaker Cir Salem (44460) *(G-13033)*

The Little Tikes Company (PA) 330 650-3000
  2180 Barlow Rd Hudson (44236) *(G-8616)*
The Louis G Freeman Company LLC (DH) 419 334-9709
  911 Graham Dr Fremont (43420) *(G-7813)*
The Lubrizol Corporation 440 357-7064
  155 Freedom Rd Painesville (44077) *(G-12270)*
The Lubrizol Corporation (HQ) 440 943-4200
  29400 Lakeland Blvd Wickliffe (44092) *(G-15853)*
The Mansfield Strl & Erct Co (PA) 419 522-5911
  429 Park Ave E Mansfield (44905) *(G-9726)*
The Massillon-Cleveland-Akronsign Company 330 833-3165
  681 1st St Sw Massillon (44646) *(G-10149)*
The Mead Corporation 937 495-6323
  4751 Hempstead Station Dr Dayton (45429) *(G-6619)*
The Mennel Milling Company (PA) 419 435-8151
  319 S Vine St Fostoria (44830) *(G-7656)*
The Mobility Store, Westerville Also Called: Columbus Prescr Rehabilitation *(G-15696)*
The National Lime and Stone Company (PA) 419 422-4341
  551 Lake Cascade Pkwy Findlay (45840) *(G-7575)*
The National Telephone Supply Company 216 361-0221
  5100 Superior Ave Cleveland (44103) *(G-4789)*
The Olen Corporation (PA) 614 491-1515
  4755 S High St Columbus (43207) *(G-5823)*
the Perfect Score Company 440 439-9320
  25801 Solon Rd Bedford Heights (44146) *(G-1179)*
The Photo-Type Engraving Company (PA) 513 281-0999
  2141 Gilbert Ave Cincinnati (45206) *(G-3450)*
The Press of Ohio Inc 330 678-5868
  3765 Sunnybrook Rd Kent (44240) *(G-8875)*
The R C A Rubber Company 330 784-1291
  1833 E Market St Akron (44305) *(G-352)*
The Ransohoff Company 513 870-0100
  4933 Provident Dr West Chester (45246) *(G-15595)*
The Reliable Spring Wire Frms 440 365-7400
  910 Taylor St Elyria (44035) *(G-7211)*
The Schaefer Group Inc (PA) 937 253-3342
  1300 Grange Hall Rd Beavercreek (45430) *(G-1082)*
The Sharon Companies Ltd 614 438-3210
  200 W Old Wilson Bridge Rd Worthington (43085) *(G-16216)*
The Sheffer Corporation (HQ) 513 489-9770
  6990 Cornell Rd Blue Ash (45242) *(G-1481)*
The Shepherd Chemical Company (HQ) 513 731-1110
  4900 Beech St Norwood (45212) *(G-12001)*
The Shepherd Color Company (PA) 513 874-0714
  4539 Dues Dr West Chester (45246) *(G-15596)*
The Smead Manufacturing Company, Logan Also Called: Smead Manufacturing Company *(G-9377)*
The Stouffer Corporation (DH) 440 349-5757
  30003 Bainbridge Rd Solon (44139) *(G-13438)*
The Vindicator Printing Company (PA) 330 747-1471
  107 Vindicator Sq Youngstown (44503) *(G-16454)*
The Vulcan Tool Company 937 253-6194
  730 Lorain Ave Dayton (45410) *(G-6620)*
The W L Jenkins Company 330 477-3407
  1445 Whipple Ave Sw Canton (44710) *(G-2244)*
The Wagner-Smith Company 866 338-0398
  3201 Encrete Ln Moraine (45439) *(G-11214)*
The Western States Machine Company 513 863-4758
  625 Commerce Center Dr Fairfield (45011) *(G-7418)*
The Wooster Brush Company (PA) 330 264-4440
  604 Madison Ave Wooster (44691) *(G-16177)*
The-Fischer-Group 513 285-1281
  2028- 2052 Bohlke Blvd Fairfield (45014) *(G-7419)*
The419 .... 855 451-1018
  201 W Market St Lima (45801) *(G-9298)*
Theb Inc 216 391-4800
  3700 Kelley Ave Cleveland (44114) *(G-4790)*
Thees Machine & Tool Company 419 586-4766
  2007 State Route 703 Celina (45822) *(G-2352)*
Theiss Uav Solutions LLC 330 584-2070
  10881 Johnson Rd North Benton (44449) *(G-11711)*

Theken Companies LLC 330 733-7600
  1800 Triplett Blvd Akron (44306) *(G-353)*
Theken Port Park LLC 330 733-7600
  1800 Triplett Blvd Akron (44306) *(G-354)*
Theken Spine LLC 330 773-7677
  1153 Medina Rd Ste 100 Medina (44256) *(G-10385)*
Therm-All, Westlake Also Called: Therm-All Inc *(G-15796)*
Therm-All Inc (PA) 440 779-9494
  830 Canterbury Rd Ste A Westlake (44145) *(G-15796)*
Therm-O-Disc Incorporated (HQ) 419 525-8500
  570 Polaris Pkwy Ste 500 Westerville (43082) *(G-15681)*
Therm-O-Link Inc (PA) 330 527-2124
  10513 Freedom St Garrettsville (44231) *(G-7926)*
Therm-O-Link Inc 330 393-7600
  621 Dana St Ne Ste 5 Warren (44483) *(G-15209)*
Therm-O-Vent, Medina Also Called: Thermo Vent Manufacturing Inc *(G-10386,*
Thermafab Alloy Inc 216 861-0540
  25367 Water St Olmsted Falls (44138) *(G-12082)*
Thermafiber Inc (HQ) 260 563-2111
  1 Owens Corning Pkwy Toledo (43659) *(G-14485)*
Thermagon Inc 216 939-2300
  4707 Detroit Ave Cleveland (44102) *(G-4791)*
Thermal Solutions Inc 614 263-1808
  3005 Silver Dr Columbus (43224) *(G-5824)*
Thermal Solutions Mfg Inc 800 776-4225
  15600 Commerce Park Dr Brookpark (44142) *(G-1726)*
Thermal Treatment Center Inc (HQ) 216 881-8100
  28910 Lakeland Blvd Wickliffe (44092) *(G-15854)*
Thermalgraphics, Cincinnati Also Called: Agnone-Kelly Enterprises Inc *(G-2602)*
Thermelectricity LLC 330 972-8054
  411 Wolf Ledges Pkwy Ste 100 Akron (44311) *(G-355)*
Thermeq Co, Waterville Also Called: T J F Inc *(G-15253)*
Thermo Fisher Scientific Inc 800 955-6288
  2110 E Galbraith Rd Cincinnati (45237) *(G-3451)*
Thermo Fisher Scientific Inc 800 871-8909
  1 Thermo Fisher Way Oakwood Village (44146) *(G-12044)*
Thermo Fsher Scntfic Ashvlle L 740 373-4763
  401 Mill Creek Rd Marietta (45750) *(G-9836)*
Thermo Gamma-Metrics LLC (HQ) 858 450-9811
  1 Thermo Fisher Way Bedford (44146) *(G-1157)*
Thermo King Corporation 567 280-9243
  1750 E State St Fremont (43420) *(G-7814)*
Thermo King Corporation, Fremont Also Called: Thermo King Corporation *(G-7814)*
Thermo Systems Technology Inc 216 292-8250
  2000 Auburn Dr Ste 200 Cleveland (44122) *(G-4792)*
Thermo Vent Manufacturing Inc 330 239-0239
  1213 Medina Rd Medina (44256) *(G-10386)*
Thermo-Rite Mfg Company 330 633-8680
  1355 Evans Ave Akron (44305) *(G-356)*
Thermocolor LLC (DH) 419 626-5677
  2901 W Monroe St Sandusky (44870) *(G-13095)*
Thermoid, Dublin Also Called: Hbd/Thermoid Inc *(G-6892)*
Thermoplastic Accessories Corp 614 771-4777
  3949 Lyman Dr Hilliard (43026) *(G-8448)*
Thermoprene Inc 440 543-8660
  5718 Transportation Blvd Cleveland (44125) *(G-4793)*
Thermoseal Inc (PA) 937 498-2222
  2350 Campbell Rd Sidney (45365) *(G-13292)*
Thermotion Corp 440 639-8325
  6520 Hopkins Rd Mentor (44060) *(G-10576)*
Thermotion-Madison, Mentor Also Called: Thermotion Corp *(G-10576)*
Thermtrol, North Canton Also Called: Thermtrol Corporation *(G-11765)*
Thermtrol Corporation 330 497-4148
  8914 Pleasantwood Ave Nw North Canton (44720) *(G-11765)*
Thieman Quality Metal Fab Inc 419 629-2612
  05140 Dicke Rd New Bremen (45869) *(G-11409)*
Thieman Tailgates Inc 419 586-7727
  600 E Wayne St Celina (45822) *(G-2353)*
Thinkcsc, Worthington Also Called: Ideal Integrations LLC *(G-16197)*
Third Eye Brewing Company, Cincinnati Also Called: BT 4 LLC *(G-2692)*

Third Millennium Materials LLC..740 947-1023
974 Prosperity Rd Waverly (45690) *(G-15291)*

Third Salvo Company..740 818-9669
16355 Tick Ridge Rd Amesville (45711) *(G-472)*

Thirion Brothers Eqp Co LLC..440 357-8004
340 W Prospect St Painesville (44077) *(G-12271)*

This Is L Inc..415 630-5172
1100 Sycamore St Ste 300 Cincinnati (45202) *(G-3452)*

Thk Manufacturing America Inc...740 928-1415
471 N High St Hebron (43025) *(G-8365)*

Thogus Products Company..440 933-8850
33490 Pin Oak Pkwy Avon Lake (44012) *(G-825)*

Thomas Cabinet Shop Inc..937 847-8239
321 Gargrave Rd Dayton (45449) *(G-6621)*

Thomas Creative Apparel Inc...419 929-1506
1 Harmony Pl New London (44851) *(G-11470)*

Thomas D Epperson..937 855-3300
7440 Weaver Rd Germantown (45327) *(G-7954)*

Thomas Do-It Center Inc (PA)..740 446-2002
176 Mccormick Rd Gallipolis (45631) *(G-7903)*

Thomas J Weaver Inc (PA)..740 622-2040
1501 Kenilworth Ave Coshocton (43812) *(G-5998)*

Thomas Processing Company, Warren *Also Called: Thomas Steel Strip Corporation* *(G-15210)*

Thomas Products Co Inc (PA)..513 756-9009
3625 Spring Grove Ave Cincinnati (45223) *(G-3453)*

Thomas Rental, Gallipolis *Also Called: Thomas Do-It Center Inc (G-7903)*

Thomas Steel Inc..419 483-7540
305 Elm St Bellevue (44811) *(G-1238)*

Thomas Steel Strip Corporation (HQ)..................................330 841-6429
2518 W Market St Warren (44485) *(G-15210)*

Thomas Tool & Mold Company..614 890-4978
271 Broad St Westerville (43081) *(G-15722)*

Thompson Aluminum Casting Co...216 206-2781
5161 Canal Rd Cleveland (44125) *(G-4794)*

Thompson Bros Mining Co...330 549-3979
3379 E Garfield Rd New Springfield (44443) *(G-11542)*

Thompson Brothers Mining, New Springfield *Also Called: Thompson Bros Mining Co* *(G-11542)*

Thompson Castings, Cleveland *Also Called: Thompson Aluminum Casting Co (G-4794)*

Thomson Higher Education, Mason *Also Called: Cengage Learning Inc (G-9972)*

Thor Industries Inc..937 596-6111
419 W Pike St Jackson Center (45334) *(G-8739)*

Thornton Powder Coatings Inc...419 522-7183
2300 N Main St Mansfield (44903) *(G-9727)*

Thorwald Holdings Inc...740 756-9271
866 Mill Park Dr Lancaster (43130) *(G-9044)*

Thorworks Industries Inc (PA)..419 626-4375
2520 Campbell St Sandusky (44870) *(G-13096)*

Those Chrcters From Clvland LL..216 252-7300
1 American Rd Cleveland (44144) *(G-4795)*

Thread Works Custom Embroidery.......................................937 478-5231
2630 Colonel Glenn Hwy Beavercreek (45324) *(G-1066)*

Thread Wrks EMB Screenprinting, Beavercreek *Also Called: Thread Works Custom Embroidery (G-1066)*

Threat Extinguisher LLC..614 882-2959
8100 Maxtown Rd Westerville (43082) *(G-15682)*

Three Bond International Inc...937 610-3000
101 Daruma Pkwy Dayton (45439) *(G-6622)*

Three Bond International Inc (DH)......................................513 779-7300
6184 Schumacher Park Dr West Chester (45069) *(G-15515)*

Thrift Tool Inc...937 275-3600
5916 Milo Rd Dayton (45414) *(G-6623)*

Tht Presses, Dayton *Also Called: THT Presses Inc (G-6624)*

THT Presses Inc..937 898-2012
7475 Webster St Dayton (45414) *(G-6624)*

Thurns Bakery & Deli..614 221-9246
541 S 3rd St Columbus (43215) *(G-5825)*

Thycurb, Akron *Also Called: Burt Manufacturing Company Inc (G-97)*

Thyme Inc..484 872-8430
3245 Pickle Rd Akron (44312) *(G-357)*

Thyssenkrupp Bilstein Amer Inc (HQ)..................................513 881-7600
8685 Bilstein Blvd Hamilton (45015) *(G-8249)*

Thyssenkrupp Materials NA Inc...216 883-8100
6050 Oak Tree Blvd Ste 110 Independence (44131) *(G-8687)*

Thyssnkrupp Rothe Erde USA Inc (DH)................................330 562-4000
1400 S Chillicothe Rd Aurora (44202) *(G-736)*

Ti Inc...419 332-8484
2107 Hayes Ave Fremont (43420) *(G-7815)*

TI Group Auto Systems LLC..740 929-2049
3600 Hebron Rd Hebron (43025) *(G-8366)*

TI Marie Candle Company LLC..513 746-7798
311 Elm St Ste 270 Cincinnati (45202) *(G-3454)*

Tiama Americas Inc..269 274-3107
6500 Weatherfield Ct Maumee (43537) *(G-10240)*

Tiba LLC (PA)...614 328-2040
2228 Citygate Dr Columbus (43219) *(G-5826)*

Tierra-Derco International LLC..419 929-2240
40 S Main St New London (44851) *(G-11471)*

Tiffin Candle Co Ltd..567 268-9015
17 Lelar St Tiffin (44883) *(G-14108)*

Tiffin Foundry & Machine Inc..419 447-3991
423 W Adams St Tiffin (44883) *(G-14109)*

Tiffin Metal Products Co (PA)..419 447-8414
450 Wall St Tiffin (44883) *(G-14110)*

Tiffin Paper Company (PA)..419 447-2121
401 Wall St Tiffin (44883) *(G-14111)*

Tiffin Scenic Studios Inc (PA)..800 445-1546
146 Riverside Dr Tiffin (44883) *(G-14112)*

Tiger Cat Furniture...330 220-7232
294 Marks Rd Brunswick (44212) *(G-1794)*

Tiger General LLC..330 239-4949
6867 Wooster Pike Medina (44256) *(G-10387)*

Tiger Inds Oil & Gas Lsg LLC..330 533-1776
8050 Camden Way Canfield (44406) *(G-2021)*

Tiger Lebanese Bakery, Toledo *Also Called: Investors United Inc (G-14336)*

Tiger Sand & Gravel LLC..330 833-6325
411 Oberlin Ave Sw Massillon (44647) *(G-10150)*

Tiger Wood Co Ltd..330 893-2744
4112 State Route 557 Millersburg (44654) *(G-10999)*

Tigerpoly Manufacturing Inc..614 871-0045
6231 Enterprise Pkwy Grove City (43123) *(G-8122)*

Tii Treeman Industries, Boardman *Also Called: Treemen Industries Inc (G-1519)*

Tilden Mining Company LC (HQ)...216 694-5700
200 Public Sq Ste 3300 Cleveland (44114) *(G-4796)*

Tiller Foods, Dayton *Also Called: Instantwhip-Dayton Inc (G-6384)*

Tiller Foods, Dayton *Also Called: Instantwhip-Dayton Inc (G-6385)*

Tilt 15 Inc..330 239-4192
1440 Wolf Creek Trl Sharon Center (44274) *(G-13169)*

Tilt-Or-Lift Inc (PA)...419 893-6944
124 E Dudley St Maumee (43537) *(G-10241)*

Tim L Humbert...330 497-4944
6535 Promler St Nw Canton (44720) *(G-2245)*

Timac Manufacturing Company..937 372-3305
825 Bellbrook Ave Xenia (45385) *(G-16275)*

Timber Framing LLC...330 749-7837
10864 Ely Rd Orrville (44667) *(G-12159)*

Timberlake Automation Inc..330 523-5300
3778 Timberlake Dr Richfield (44286) *(G-12801)*

Timbertech, Wilmington *Also Called: Cpg International LLC (G-16047)*

Timbertech, Wilmington *Also Called: Timbertech Limited (G-16059)*

Timbertech Limited...937 655-8766
894 Prairie Rd Wilmington (45177) *(G-16059)*

Timco Inc...740 685-2594
57051 Marietta Rd Byesville (43723) *(G-1900)*

Timco Rubber Products Inc (PA)...216 267-6242
125 Blaze Industrial Pkwy Berea (44017) *(G-1296)*

Timekap Inc...330 747-2122
2315 Belmont Ave Youngstown (44505) *(G-16455)*

Timekap Indus Sls Svc & Mch, Youngstown *Also Called: Timekap Inc (G-16455)*

Timekeeping Systems Inc..216 595-0890
30700 Bainbridge Rd Ste H Solon (44139) *(G-13439)*

Times Reporter — ALPHABETIC SECTION

Times Reporter, New Philadelphia *Also Called:* Mansfield Journal Co **(G-11513)**

Times Reporter/Midwest Offset, New Philadelphia *Also Called:* Copley Ohio Newspapers Inc **(G-11493)**

Timet Toronto, Toronto *Also Called:* Titanium Metals Corporation **(G-14535)**

TIMKEN, North Canton *Also Called:* Timken Company **(G-11766)**

Timken Company 614 836-3337
3782 Potomac St Groveport (43125) **(G-8162)**

Timken Company (PA) 234 262-3000
4500 Mount Pleasant St Nw North Canton (44720) **(G-11766)**

Timken Newco I LLC 234 262-3000
4500 Mount Pleasant St Nw North Canton (44720) **(G-11767)**

Timken Receivables Corporation 234 262-3000
4500 Mount Pleasant St Nw North Canton (44720) **(G-11768)**

Timkensteel Fircrest Stl Plant, Canton *Also Called:* Metallus Inc **(G-2163)**

Timkensteel Material Svcs LLC 281 449-0319
1835 Dueber Ave Sw Canton (44706) **(G-2246)**

Timmys Sandwich Shop 419 350-8267
5426 Cresthaven Ln Toledo (43614) **(G-14486)**

Timothy Whatman 419 883-2443
6617 Stoffer Rd Bellville (44813) **(G-1248)**

Tin Wizard Heating & Coolg Inc 330 467-9826
8853 Robinwood Ter Macedonia (44056) **(G-9584)**

Tinker Omega Sinto LLC 937 322-2272
2424 Columbus Rd Springfield (45503) **(G-13648)**

Tinnerman Palnut Engineered PR 330 220-5100
1060 W 130th St Brunswick (44212) **(G-1795)**

Tiny Foot Prnts Child Enrchmen, Cleveland *Also Called:* Tiny Footprints Daycare LLC **(G-4797)**

Tiny Footprints Daycare LLC 216 938-7306
1367 W 65th St Cleveland (44102) **(G-4797)**

Tiny Lion Music Groups 419 874-7353
144 E 5th St Perrysburg (43551) **(G-12435)**

Tinycircuits 330 329-5753
540 S Main St Akron (44311) **(G-358)**

Tip Products Inc 216 252-2535
106 Industrial Dr New London (44851) **(G-11472)**

Tipco Punch Inc 513 874-9140
6 Rowe Ct Hamilton (45015) **(G-8250)**

Tipp Machine & Tool Inc 937 890-8428
4201 Little York Rd Dayton (45414) **(G-6625)**

Tipton Environmental Intl Inc 513 735-2777
4446 State Route 132 Batavia (45103) **(G-953)**

Tires Plus 7061 .... 513 851-1900
11994 Chase Plz Cincinnati (45240) **(G-3455)**

Tisch Environmental Inc (PA) 513 467-9000
145 S Miami Ave Cleves (45002) **(G-4967)**

Titan Tire Corporation 419 633-4221
927 S Union St Bryan (43506) **(G-1840)**

Titan Tire Corporation Bryan 419 633-4224
927 S Union St Bryan (43506) **(G-1841)**

Titan Tire Corporation Bryan, Bryan *Also Called:* Titan Tire Corporation **(G-1840)**

Titanium Contractors Ltd 513 256-2152
9400 Reading Rd Cincinnati (45215) **(G-3456)**

Titanium Metals Corporation 740 537-1571
100 Titanium Way Toronto (43964) **(G-14535)**

Titans Packaging LLC 513 449-0014
33 Circle Freeway Dr West Chester (45246) **(G-15597)**

TJ Clark International LLC 614 388-8869
320 London Rd Ste 608 Delaware (43015) **(G-6755)**

Tj Metzgers Inc 419 861-8611
207 Arco Dr Toledo (43607) **(G-14487)**

TJ Oil & Gas Inc 740 623-0190
27353 State Route 621 Fresno (43824) **(G-7826)**

Tjar Innovations LLC 937 347-1999
1004 Cincinnati Ave Xenia (45385) **(G-16276)**

Tk America, West Chester *Also Called:* Toyobo Kureha America Co Ltd **(G-15517)**

Tk Gas Services Inc 740 826-0303
2303 John Glenn Hwy New Concord (43762) **(G-11434)**

Tkf Conveyor Systems LLC 513 621-5260
5298 River Rd Cincinnati (45233) **(G-3457)**

Tkm Print Solutions Inc 330 237-4029
3455 Forest Lake Dr Uniontown (44685) **(G-14795)**

Tkn Oilfield Services LLC 740 516-2583
108 Woodcrest Dr Marietta (45750) **(G-9837)**

Tko Mfg Services Inc 937 299-1637
2360 W Dorothy Ln Ste 111 Moraine (45439) **(G-1215)**

TL Industries Inc (PA) 419 666-8144
28271 Cedar Park Blvd Ste 8 Perrysburg (43551) **(G-12436)**

TLC Products, Westlake *Also Called:* TLC Products Inc **(G-15797)**

TLC Products Inc 216 472-3030
26100 1st St Westlake (44145) **(G-15797)**

Tlg Cochran Inc (PA) 440 914-1122
2026 Summit Commerce Park Twinsburg (44087) **(G-14744)**

Tlg Laporte Inc (PA) 440 914-1122
2026 Summit Commerce Park Twinsburg (44087) **(G-14745)**

Tlt-Babcock Inc 330 867-8540
260 Springside Dr Akron (44333) **(G-359)**

Tlt-Turbo Inc 330 776-5115
2693 Wingate Ave Akron (44314) **(G-360)**

Tm Machine & Tool Inc 419 478-0310
521 Mel Simon Dr Toledo (43612) **(G-14488)**

Tmarzetti Company (HQ) 614 846-2232
380 Polaris Pkwy Ste 400 Westerville (43082) **(G-15683)**

Tmd, Toledo *Also Called:* Toledo Molding & Die LLC **(G-14499)**

Tmd Inc 419 476-4581
4 E Laskey Rd Toledo (43612) **(G-14489)**

Tmd Wek North LLC 440 576-6940
1085 Jefferson Eagleville Rd Jefferson (44047) **(G-8761)**

Tmg Performance Products LLC 440 891-0999
140 Blaze Industrial Pkwy Berea (44017) **(G-1292)**

TMI, Cincinnati *Also Called:* Win Plastic Extrusions LLC **(G-3521)**

Tmi Inc 330 270-9780
6475 Victoria East Rd Youngstown (44515) **(G-1456)**

Tmk Farm Service, Sugarcreek *Also Called:* Mullet Enterprises Inc **(G-13932)**

Tmm, Waverly *Also Called:* Third Millennium Materials LLC **(G-15291)**

Tms International LLC 216 441-9702
4300 E 49th St Cleveland (44125) **(G-4798)**

Tms International LLC 513 425-6462
1801 Crawford St Middletown (45044) **(G-10863)**

Tms International LLC 513 422-4572
3018 Oxford State Rd Middletown (45044) **(G-10864)**

Tms International Corp 513 422-9497
2601 S Verity Pkwy Bldg 3 Middletown (45044) **(G-10865)**

Tmsi, North Canton *Also Called:* Tmsi LLC **(G-11769)**

Tmsi LLC 888 867-4872
8817 Pleasantwood Ave Nw North Canton (44720) **(G-11769)**

Tmt Inc 419 592-1041
655 D St Perrysburg (43551) **(G-12437)**

Tmt Logistics, Perrysburg *Also Called:* Tmt Inc **(G-12437)**

Tmw Engineering Services LLC 440 582-4700
8536 W 130th St Strongsville (44136) **(G-13890)**

Tmw Racks, Strongsville *Also Called:* Tmw Engineering Services LLC **(G-13890)**

Tnemec Co Inc 614 850-8160
3974 Brown Park Dr Ste A Hilliard (43026) **(G-8419)**

TNT Solid Solutions LLC 419 262-6228
6120 N Detroit Ave Toledo (43612) **(G-14490)**

To Scale Software LLC 513 253-0053
6398 Thornberry Ct Mason (45040) **(G-10066)**

TOA Technologies Inc (PA) 216 925-5950
3333 Richmond Rd Ste 420 Beachwood (44122) **(G-1028)**

Toagosei America Inc 614 718-3855
1450 W Main St West Jefferson (43162) **(G-1565)**

Toast With Cake LLC 937 554-5900
9231 Towering Pine Dr Apt L Miamisburg (45342) **(G-10695)**

Toastmasters International 937 429-2680
1854 Redleaf Ct Dayton (45432) **(G-6174)**

Tobacco Company, Cleveland *Also Called:* Memphis Smokehouse Inc **(G-4393)**

Tobal Products, Columbus *Also Called:* Abbott Laboratories **(G-5087)**

Tod Thin Brushes Inc 440 576-6859
1152 State Route 46 N Jefferson (44047) **(G-8762)**

Todco 740 223-2542
1295 E Fairground Rd Marion (43302) **(G-9886)**

ALPHABETIC SECTION — Tooling Connection Inc

Todco, Upper Sandusky *Also Called: Overhead Door Corporation* **(G-14820)**

Todd Industries Inc.. 440 439-2900
7300 Northfield Rd Ste 1 Cleveland (44146) **(G-4799)**

Todd Peak Woodwork LLC....................................... 513 560-6760
208 Saddle Creek Ln Maineville (45039) **(G-9602)**

Toft Dairy Inc... 419 625-4376
3717 Venice Rd Sandusky (44870) **(G-13097)**

Toga-Pak Inc.. 937 294-7311
2208 Sandridge Dr Dayton (45439) **(G-6626)**

Tok Dawgs Chicken LLC... 614 813-2698
1743 Quigley Rd Columbus (43227) **(G-5827)**

Toku America Inc... 440 954-9923
3900 Ben Hur Ave Ste 3 Willoughby (44094) **(G-16006)**

Tolco, Toledo *Also Called: Tolco Corporation* **(G-14491)**

Tolco Corporation (PA).. 419 241-1113
1920 Linwood Ave Toledo (43604) **(G-14491)**

Toledo Alfalfa Mills Inc... 419 836-3705
861 S Stadium Rd Oregon (43616) **(G-12112)**

Toledo Blade Company.. 419 724-6000
541 N Superior St Toledo (43660) **(G-14492)**

Toledo Business Journals, Toledo *Also Called: Telex Communications Inc* **(G-14482)**

Toledo City Paper, Toledo *Also Called: Adams Street Publishing Co Inc* **(G-14177)**

Toledo Controls.. 419 474-2537
3550 Maxwell Rd Toledo (43606) **(G-14493)**

Toledo Cut Stone Inc.. 419 531-1623
4011 South Ave Toledo (43615) **(G-14494)**

Toledo Cutting Tools, Perrysburg *Also Called: Imco Carbide Tool Inc* **(G-12390)**

Toledo Deburring Co, Northwood *Also Called: Toledo Metal Finishing Inc* **(G-11929)**

Toledo Division, Perrysburg *Also Called: Terex Utilities Inc* **(G-12434)**

Toledo Driveline, Toledo *Also Called: Dana Light Axle Mfg LLC* **(G-14260)**

Toledo Electromotive Inc.. 419 874-7751
28765 White Rd Perrysburg (43551) **(G-12438)**

Toledo Engineering Co Inc (PA)................................ 419 537-9711
3400 Executive Pkwy Toledo (43606) **(G-14495)**

Toledo Express, Swanton *Also Called: Toledo Jet Center LLC* **(G-13985)**

Toledo Fiber Products Corp...................................... 419 720-0303
1245 E Manhattan Blvd Toledo (43608) **(G-14496)**

Toledo Grmtor Blffton Mtr Wrks, Sylvania *Also Called: Tgm Holdings Company* **(G-14018)**

Toledo Integrated Systems, Maumee *Also Called: Toledo Transducers Inc* **(G-10242)**

Toledo Jet Center LLC (PA)...................................... 419 866-9050
11591 W Airport Service Rd Swanton (43558) **(G-13985)**

Toledo Machining Inc... 419 343-7738
8261 W Bancroft St Toledo (43617) **(G-14497)**

Toledo Metal Finishing Inc....................................... 419 661-1422
7880 Caple Blvd Northwood (43619) **(G-11929)**

Toledo Metal Spinning Company.............................. 419 535-5931
1819 Clinton St Toledo (43607) **(G-14498)**

Toledo Molding & Die LLC....................................... 419 354-6050
515 E Gypsy Lane Rd Bowling Green (43402) **(G-1592)**

Toledo Molding & Die LLC....................................... 419 692-6022
900 Gressel Dr Delphos (45833) **(G-6772)**

Toledo Molding & Die LLC....................................... 419 692-6022
24086 State Route 697 Delphos (45833) **(G-6773)**

Toledo Molding & Die LLC....................................... 419 443-9031
1441 Maule Rd Tiffin (44883) **(G-14113)**

Toledo Molding & Die LLC (DH)............................... 419 470-3950
1429 Coining Dr Toledo (43612) **(G-14499)**

Toledo Molding & Die LLC....................................... 419 476-0581
4 E Laskey Rd Toledo (43612) **(G-14500)**

Toledo Optical, Toledo *Also Called: Toledo Optical Laboratory Inc* **(G-14501)**

Toledo Optical Laboratory Inc.................................. 419 248-3384
1201 Jefferson Ave Toledo (43604) **(G-14501)**

Toledo Precision Machining LLC............................... 419 724-3010
5222 Tractor Rd Ste H Toledo (43612) **(G-14502)**

Toledo Pro Fiberglass Inc.. 419 241-9390
210 Wade St Toledo (43604) **(G-14503)**

Toledo Scales & Systems, Worthington *Also Called: Mettler-Toledo LLC* **(G-16202)**

Toledo Sign Company Inc (PA)................................. 419 244-4444
2021 Adams St Toledo (43604) **(G-14504)**

Toledo Solar Inc.. 567 202-4145
1775 Progress Dr Perrysburg (43551) **(G-12439)**

Toledo Spirits Company LLC.................................... 419 704-3705
1301 N Summit St Toledo (43604) **(G-14505)**

Toledo Tarp Service Inc... 419 837-5098
3273 Genoa Rd Perrysburg (43551) **(G-12440)**

Toledo Ticket Company... 419 476-5424
3963 Catawba St Toledo (43612) **(G-14506)**

Toledo Tool & Die, Toledo *Also Called: Toledo Tool and Die Co Inc* **(G-14507)**

Toledo Tool and Die Co Inc (PA).............................. 419 476-4422
105 W Alexis Rd Toledo (43612) **(G-14507)**

Toledo Tool and Die Co Inc..................................... 419 266-8458
4100 Bennett Rd Toledo (43612) **(G-14508)**

Toledo Transducers Inc... 419 724-4170
1345 Ford St Maumee (43537) **(G-10242)**

Toledo Window & Awning Inc................................. 419 474-3396
3035 W Sylvania Ave Toledo (43613) **(G-14509)**

Toli Vault.. 866 998-8654
2035 Crocker Rd Ste 103 Westlake (44145) **(G-15798)**

Tolloti Pipe LLC.. 330 364-6627
102 Barnhill Rd Se New Philadelphia (44663) **(G-11529)**

Tolloti Plastic Pipe Inc (PA)..................................... 330 364-6627
102 Barnhill Rd Se New Philadelphia (44663) **(G-11530)**

Tolson Pallet Mfg Inc.. 937 787-3511
10240 State Rte 122 Gratis (45330) **(G-8023)**

Tom Barbour Auto Parts Inc (PA)............................ 740 354-4654
915 11th St Portsmouth (45662) **(G-12659)**

Tom Richards Inc (PA).. 440 974-1300
38809 Mentor Ave Willoughby (44094) **(G-16007)**

Tom Smith Industries Inc.. 937 832-1555
500 Smith Dr Englewood (45315) **(G-7245)**

Tom Thumb Clip Co Inc.. 440 953-9606
36300 Lakeland Blvd Unit 2 Willoughby (44095) **(G-16008)**

Tomahawk Entrmt Group LLC................................. 216 505-0548
26870 Drakefield Ave Euclid (44132) **(G-7302)**

Tomahawk Printing Inc... 419 335-3161
229 N Fulton St Wauseon (43567) **(G-15274)**

Tomahawk Tool Supply... 419 485-8737
1604 Magda Dr Montpelier (43543) **(G-11143)**

Tomak Precision, Lebanon *Also Called: Aws Industries Inc* **(G-9063)**

Tomco Tool Inc... 937 322-5768
203 S Wittenberg Ave Springfield (45506) **(G-13649)**

Tomlinson Industries, Chagrin Falls *Also Called: Meyer Company* **(G-2382)**

Tomlinson Industries LLC.. 216 587-3400
4350 Renaissance Pkwy Ste A Cleveland (44128) **(G-4800)**

Tomson Steel Company... 513 420-8600
1400 Made Dr Middletown (45044) **(G-10866)**

Toney Tool, Dayton *Also Called: Toney Tool Manufacturing Inc* **(G-6627)**

Toney Tool Manufacturing Inc................................. 937 890-8535
3488 Stop 8 Rd Dayton (45414) **(G-6627)**

Tonys Wldg & Fabrication LLC................................. 740 333-4000
2305 Robinson Rd Se Wshngtn Ct Hs (43160) **(G-16242)**

Tool and Die Systems.. 440 327-5800
38900 Taylor Pkwy Elyria (44035) **(G-7212)**

Tool and Die Welding.. 513 265-3095
6831 Franklin Madison Rd Middletown (45042) **(G-10867)**

Tool Systems Incorporated...................................... 440 461-6363
71 Alpha Park Cleveland (44143) **(G-4801)**

Tool Tech LLC... 614 893-5876
4901 Urbana Rd Springfield (45502) **(G-13650)**

Tool Technologies Van Dyke.................................... 937 349-4900
639 Clymer Rd Marysville (43040) **(G-9942)**

Toolbold Corporation... 440 543-1660
5330 Commerce Pkwy W Cleveland (44130) **(G-4802)**

Toolbold Corporation (PA)....................................... 216 676-9840
5330 Commerce Pkwy W Cleveland (44130) **(G-4803)**

Toolcomp, Toledo *Also Called: Tooling & Components Corp* **(G-14510)**

Toolcraft Products Inc... 937 223-8271
1265 Mccook Ave Dayton (45404) **(G-6628)**

Tooling & Components Corp................................... 419 478-9122
5261 Tractor Rd Toledo (43612) **(G-14510)**

Tooling Components Division, Cleveland *Also Called: Jergens Inc* **(G-4253)**

Tooling Connection Inc.. 419 594-3339
State Rte 66 N Ste 12603 Oakwood (45873) **(G-12034)**

Tooling Tech Holdings LLC (HQ)..937 295-3672
100 Enterprise Dr Fort Loramie (45845) *(G-7612)*

Tooling Zone Inc..937 550-4180
285 S Pioneer Blvd Springboro (45066) *(G-13523)*

Toolrite Manufacturing Inc...937 278-1962
2608 Nordic Rd Dayton (45414) *(G-6629)*

Tooltex Inc..614 539-3222
6497 Seeds Rd Grove City (43123) *(G-8123)*

Top Cat Air Tools, Willoughby Also Called: T C Service Co *(G-16001)*

Top Knotch Products Inc..419 543-2266
819 Colonel Dr Cleveland (44109) *(G-4804)*

Top Network, Columbus Also Called: Essilor Laboratories Amer Inc *(G-5361)*

Top Shelf Embroidery LLC..440 209-8566
9254 Mentor Ave Mentor (44060) *(G-10577)*

Top Shot Ammunition, Akron Also Called: TS Sales LLC *(G-365)*

Top Tool & Die Inc..216 267-5878
15500 Brookpark Rd Cleveland (44135) *(G-4805)*

Tope Printing Inc...330 674-4993
1056 S Washington St Millersburg (44654) *(G-11000)*

Topkote Inc...440 428-0525
404 N Lake St Madison (44057) *(G-9594)*

Topps Products Inc..913 685-2500
3201 E 66th St Cleveland (44127) *(G-4806)*

Torax Medical Inc..651 361-8900
4545 Creek Rd Blue Ash (45242) *(G-1482)*

Torbeck Industries, Harrison Also Called: R L Torbeck Industries Inc *(G-8289)*

Torbot Group Inc...419 724-1475
3461 Curtice Rd Northwood (43619) *(G-11930)*

Torque 2020 CMA Acqisition LLC (PA)................................330 874-2900
10896 Industrial Pkwy Nw Bolivar (44612) *(G-1539)*

Torque Transmission, Fairport Harbor Also Called: Rampe Manufacturing Company *(G-7458)*

Torrmetal LLC..216 671-1616
12125 Bennington Ave Cleveland (44135) *(G-4807)*

Torrmetal Corporation..216 671-1616
12125 Bennington Ave Cleveland (44135) *(G-4808)*

Torsion Control Products Inc..248 537-1900
1441 Wolf Creek Trl Wadsworth (44281) *(G-15070)*

Tortilla Factory, Toledo Also Called: La Perla Inc *(G-14356)*

Tortillas La Reyna LLC...630 247-9453
2171 E Dublin Granville Rd Columbus (43229) *(G-5828)*

Tortilleria La Bamba LLC...216 515-1600
12119 Bennington Ave Cleveland (44135) *(G-4809)*

Tosoh America Inc (HQ)...614 539-8622
3600 Gantz Rd Grove City (43123) *(G-8124)*

Tosoh SMD Inc (DH)...614 875-7912
3600 Gantz Rd Grove City (43123) *(G-8125)*

Total Automation, Columbia Station Also Called: Columbia Stamping Inc *(G-5010)*

Total Baking Solutions LLC
474 S Nelson Ave Wilmington (45177) *(G-16060)*

Total Call Center Solutions..330 869-9844
1014 Margate Dr Ste 200 Akron (44313) *(G-361)*

Total Education Solutions Inc...330 668-4041
3428 W Market St Fairlawn (44333) *(G-7453)*

Total Engine Airflow..330 634-2155
285 West Ave Tallmadge (44278) *(G-14052)*

Total Life Safety LLC..866 955-2318
6228 Centre Park Dr Ste C West Chester (45069) *(G-15516)*

Total Manufacturing Co Inc..440 205-9700
7777 Saint Clair Ave Mentor (44060) *(G-10578)*

Total Molding Solutions Inc...517 424-5900
3315 Centennial Rd Ste J Sylvania (43560) *(G-14019)*

Total Plastics Resources LLC...440 891-1140
17851 Englewood Dr Ste A Cleveland (44130) *(G-4810)*

Total Quality Machining Inc...937 746-7765
10 Shotwell Dr Franklin (45005) *(G-7706)*

Total Repair Express Mich LLC...248 690-9410
4575 Hudson Dr Stow (44224) *(G-13731)*

Total Tennis Inc...614 488-5004
1733 Cardiff Rd Columbus (43221) *(G-5829)*

Total Tennis Inc...614 504-7446
321 W Bigelow Ave Plain City (43064) *(G-12595)*

Total Touch LLC..800 726-2117
250 W Huron Rd Ste 400 Cleveland (44113) *(G-4411)*

Total Water Solutions LLC..234 567-5912
41562 Lodge Rd Leetonia (44431) *(G-9131)*

Totally Promotional, Coldwater Also Called: Casad Company Inc *(G-4984)*

Totes Isotoner Corporation (HQ)......................................513 682-8200
9655 International Blvd West Chester (45246) *(G-15598)*

Totes Isotoner Holdings Corp (PA)....................................513 682-8200
9655 International Blvd West Chester (45246) *(G-15599)*

Toth Mold & Die Inc..440 232-8530
380 Solon Rd Ste 6 Bedford (44146) *(G-1158)*

Touch Bionics Inc (DH)..800 233-6263
6640 Riverside Dr Dublin (43017) *(G-6953)*

Touch Print Solution, Cincinnati Also Called: Onetouchpoint East Corp *(G-3225)*

Touchmark, Dublin Also Called: Advanced Prgrm Resources Inc *(G-6857)*

Tow Path Ready Mix, Jackson Also Called: D G M Inc *(G-8713)*

Tower Atmtive Oprtons USA I LL......................................419 483-1500
630 Southwest St Bellevue (44811) *(G-1239)*

Tower Atmtive Oprtons USA I LL......................................419 358-8966
18717 County Road 15 Bluffton (45817) *(G-1508)*

Tower Automotive, Bluffton Also Called: Tower Atmtive Oprtons USA I LL *(G-1508)*

Tower Countertops, Massillon Also Called: Tower Industries Ltd *(G-10151)*

Tower Industries Ltd...330 837-2216
2101 9th St Sw Massillon (44647) *(G-10151)*

Tower Press Development..216 241-4069
3030 E 63rd St Cleveland (44127) *(G-4812)*

Town Cntry Technical Svcs Inc...614 866-7700
6200 Eastgreen Blvd Reynoldsburg (43068) *(G-2775)*

Toxco Inc..740 653-6290
265 Quarry Rd Se Lancaster (43130) *(G-9045)*

Toyo Seiki Usa Inc..513 546-9657
11130 Luschek Dr Blue Ash (45241) *(G-1483)*

Toyobo Kureha America Co Ltd..513 771-6788
4591 Brate Dr West Chester (45011) *(G-15517)*

Tpam Inc...567 315-8694
5915 Jason St Toledo (43611) *(G-14511)*

TPC Food Service, Tiffin Also Called: Tiffin Paper Company *(G-14111)*

Tpf Inc..513 761-9968
313 S Wayne Ave Cincinnati (45215) *(G-3458)*

Tpl Holdings LLC...800 475-4030
3380 Gilchrist Rd Mogadore (44260) *(G-11088)*

Tpo Hess Holdings Inc...815 334-6140
3765 Sunnybrook Rd Kent (44240) *(G-8876)*

Tpr, Hinckley Also Called: Tarantula Performance Racg LLC *(G-8477)*

Tq Manufacturing Company Inc...440 255-9000
7345 Production Dr Mentor (44060) *(G-10579)*

Tr Boes Holdings Inc..419 595-2255
14 N Perry St New Riegel (44853) *(G-11538)*

Tracer Specialties Inc..216 696-2363
1842 Columbus Rd Cleveland (44113) *(G-4813)*

Tracewell Systems Inc (PA)...614 846-6175
567 Enterprise Dr Lewis Center (43035) *(G-9182)*

Tracker Management Systems...800 445-2438
10091 Brecksville Rd Brecksville (44141) *(G-1636)*

Tractor Supply Company..740 963-8023
11309 Broad St Sw Pataskala (43062) *(G-12319)*

Trademark Designs Inc..419 628-3897
17 Jackson St Minster (45865) *(G-11063)*

Tradewinds Prin Twear..740 214-5005
35 E Athens Rd Roseville (43777) *(G-12860)*

Trading Corp of America, Columbus Also Called: Marfo Company *(G-5541)*

Trading Post...740 922-1199
202 N Water St Uhrichsville (44683) *(G-14771)*

Tradye Machine & Tool Inc..740 625-7550
3116a Wilson Rd Centerburg (43011) *(G-2358)*

Traffic Cntrl Sgnls Signs & MA...740 670-7763
1195 E Main St Newark (43055) *(G-11609)*

Traffic Detectors & Signs, Youngstown Also Called: Traffic Detectors & Signs Inc *(G-16457)*

Traffic Detectors & Signs Inc..330 707-9060
7521 Forest Hill Ave Youngstown (44514) *(G-16457)*

ALPHABETIC SECTION — Tremco Cpg Inc

Traffic Engineering Department, Canton *Also Called: City of Canton (G-2075)*
Traichal Construction Company (PA) 800 255-3667
  332 Plant St Niles (44446) *(G-11689)*
Trail Cabinet 330 893-3791
  2270 Township Road 415 Dundee (44624) *(G-6969)*
Trail Mix 330 657-2277
  1565 Boston Mills Rd W Peninsula (44264) *(G-12343)*
Trail Sprayer & Service LLC 330 720-2966
  4211 Karg Industrial Pkwy Kent (44240) *(G-8877)*
Trailer Component Mfg Inc 440 255-2888
  8120 Tyler Blvd Mentor (44060) *(G-10580)*
Trailer One Inc 330 723-7474
  1030 W Liberty St Medina (44256) *(G-10388)*
Trailstar, Alliance *Also Called: Trailstar International Inc (G-433)*
Trailstar International Inc (PA) 330 821-9900
  20700 Harrisburg Westville Rd Alliance (44601) *(G-433)*
Trailway II 330 893-9195
  2261 County Road 168 Dundee (44624) *(G-6970)*
Tramonte & Sons LLC 513 770-5501
  3850 Welden Dr Lebanon (45036) *(G-9114)*
Trane, Cincinnati *Also Called: Trane US Inc (G-3460)*
Trane, Groveport *Also Called: Trane US Inc (G-8163)*
Trane Cleveland, Cleveland *Also Called: Trane Inc (G-4814)*
Trane Company 419 491-2278
  1001 Hamilton Dr Holland (43528) *(G-8534)*
Trane Inc 440 946-7823
  9555 Rockside Rd Ste 350 Cleveland (44125) *(G-4814)*
Trane National Account Service, Columbus *Also Called: Trane US Inc (G-5831)*
Trane Technologies Company LLC 419 633-6800
  209 N Main St Bryan (43506) *(G-1842)*
Trane Technologies Company LLC 419 636-4242
  1 Aro Ctr Bryan (43506) *(G-1843)*
Trane Technologies Company LLC 513 459-4580
  10300 Springfield Pike Cincinnati (45215) *(G-3459)*
Trane US Inc 513 771-8884
  10300 Springfield Pike Cincinnati (45215) *(G-3460)*
Trane US Inc 614 473-3131
  2300 Citygate Dr Ste 100 Columbus (43219) *(G-5830)*
Trane US Inc 614 473-8701
  2300 Citygate Dr Ste 250 Columbus (43219) *(G-5831)*
Trane US Inc 614 497-6300
  6600 Port Rd Ste 200 Groveport (43125) *(G-8163)*
Tranquility, Bowling Green *Also Called: Principle Business Entps Inc (G-1586)*
Trans Ash Inc 859 341-1528
  360 S Wayne Ave Cincinnati (45215) *(G-3461)*
Trans-Acc Inc (PA) 513 793-6410
  11167 Deerfield Rd Blue Ash (45242) *(G-1484)*
Trans-Foam Inc 330 630-9444
  281 Southwest Ave Tallmadge (44278) *(G-14053)*
Transcendia Inc 740 929-5100
  3700 Hebron Rd Hebron (43025) *(G-8367)*
Transcendia Inc 440 638-2000
  22889 Lunn Rd Strongsville (44149) *(G-13891)*
Transco Railway Products 419 562-1031
  820 Hopley Ave Bucyrus (44820) *(G-1869)*
Transco Railway Products Inc 330 872-0934
  2310 S Center St Newton Falls (44444) *(G-11659)*
Transdigm, Cleveland *Also Called: Transdigm Group Incorporated (G-4817)*
Transdigm Inc 216 291-6025
  4223 Monticello Blvd Cleveland (44121) *(G-4815)*
Transdigm Inc (HQ) 216 706-2960
  1350 Euclid Ave Cleveland (44115) *(G-4816)*
Transdigm Inc 330 676-7147
  2146 State Route 59 Kent (44240) *(G-8878)*
Transdigm Inc 440 352-6182
  313 Gillett St Painesville (44077) *(G-12272)*
Transdigm Group Incorporated (PA) 216 706-2960
  1301 E 9th St Ste 3000 Cleveland (44114) *(G-4817)*
Transducers Direct, Cincinnati *Also Called: Transducers Direct Llc (G-3462)*
Transducers Direct Llc 513 247-0601
  12115 Ellington Ct Cincinnati (45249) *(G-3462)*

Transfer Express Inc 440 918-1900
  7650 Tyler Blvd Mentor (44060) *(G-10581)*
Transformer Associates Limited 330 430-0750
  831 Market Ave N Canton (44702) *(G-2247)*
Transit Fittings N Amer Inc 330 797-2516
  295 S Meridian Rd Youngstown (44509) *(G-16458)*
Transit Sittings of NA 330 797-2516
  295 S Meridian Rd Youngstown (44509) *(G-16459)*
Transmet Corporation 614 276-5522
  4290 Perimeter Dr Columbus (43228) *(G-5832)*
Transportation Group, Mantua *Also Called: Mantaline Corporation (G-9739)*
Transtar Holding Company (PA) 800 359-3339
  7350 Young Dr Walton Hills (44146) *(G-15103)*
Transtechbio Inc 734 994-4728
  2071 Midway Dr Twinsburg (44087) *(G-14746)*
Transue & Williams Stampg Corp 330 821-5777
  207 N Four Mile Run Rd Austintown (44515) *(G-756)*
Tranzonic Companies 440 446-0643
  26301 Curtiss Wright Pkwy Ste 200 Cleveland (44143) *(G-4818)*
Tranzonic Companies 216 535-4300
  26301 Curtiss Wright Pkwy Ste 200 Richmond Heights (44143) *(G-12811)*
Tranzonic Companies, Richmond Heights *Also Called: Tz Acquisition Corp (G-12812)*
Trapeze Software Group Inc 905 629-8727
  23215 Commerce Park Ste 200 Beachwood (44122) *(G-1029)*
Travelers Custom Case Inc 216 621-8447
  7444 Tyler Blvd Ste C Mentor (44060) *(G-10582)*
Travelers Vacation Guide 440 582-4949
  10143 Royalton Rd North Royalton (44133) *(G-11898)*
Traveling Recycle WD Pdts Inc 419 968-2649
  19590 Bellis Rd Middle Point (45863) *(G-10713)*
Travis Cochran 740 294-2368
  13065 Hamby Hill Rd Frazeysburg (43822) *(G-7716)*
Travis Products Mfg Inc 234 759-3741
  80 Eastgate Dr North Lima (44452) *(G-11815)*
Traxium LLC 330 572-8200
  4246 Hudson Dr Stow (44224) *(G-13732)*
Traxler Printing 614 593-1270
  310 W Pacemont Rd Apt A Columbus (43202) *(G-5833)*
Traxler Tees LLC 614 593-1270
  3029 Silver Dr Columbus (43224) *(G-5834)*
Traxx North America Inc 513 554-4700
  10810 Kenwood Rd Blue Ash (45242) *(G-1485)*
Treadway Manufacturing LLC 937 266-3423
  8800 Frederick Pike Dayton (45414) *(G-6630)*
Treality Svs LLC (PA) 937 372-7579
  600 Bellbrook Ave Xenia (45385) *(G-16277)*
Trebnick Systems Inc 937 743-1550
  215 S Pioneer Blvd Springboro (45066) *(G-13524)*
Trebnick Tags and Labels, Springboro *Also Called: Trebnick Systems Inc (G-13524)*
Trec Industries Inc 216 741-4114
  4713 Spring Rd Cleveland (44131) *(G-4819)*
Tree Free Resources LLC 740 751-4844
  175 Park Blvd Marion (43302) *(G-9887)*
Treefrogg Specialties Inc 513 212-3581
  1786 Craver Rd Batavia (45103) *(G-954)*
Treehouse Private Brands Inc 740 654-8880
  3775 Lancaster New Lexington Rd Se Lancaster (43130) *(G-9046)*
Treehouse Private Brands Inc 740 654-8880
  276 Bremen Rd Lancaster (43130) *(G-9047)*
Treemen Industries Inc 330 965-3777
  691 Mcclurg Rd Boardman (44512) *(G-1519)*
Trek Diagnostics Inc 440 808-0000
  982 Keynote Cir Brooklyn Heights (44131) *(G-1702)*
Trellborg Sling Prfiles US Inc 330 995-9725
  285 Lena Dr Aurora (44202) *(G-737)*
Trellborg Whl Systems Amrcas I, Akron *Also Called: Yokohama Tws North America Inc (G-379)*
Trelleborg, Aurora *Also Called: Trellborg Sling Prfiles US Inc (G-737)*
Tremcar USA Inc 330 878-7708
  436 12th St Ne Strasburg (44680) *(G-13750)*
Tremco Cpg Inc 419 289-2050
  1451 Jacobson Ave Ashland (44805) *(G-618)*

ALPHABETIC SECTION

Tremco Cpg Inc 216 514-7783
23150 Commerce Park Beachwood (44122) *(G-1030)*

Tremco Incorporated (HQ) 3735 Green Rd Beachwood (44122) *(G-1031)*

Tremont Electric Incorporated 888 214-3137
2112 W 7th St Cleveland (44113) *(G-4820)*

Trenchless Rsrces Globl Hldngs 419 419-6498
420 Industrial Pkwy Bowling Green (43402) *(G-1593)*

Trent Manufacturing Company 216 391-1551
7310 Corporate Blvd Mentor (44060) *(G-10583)*

Tresslers Plumbing LLC 419 784-2142
9170 State Route 15 Defiance (43512) *(G-6697)*

Treved Exteriors 513 771-3888
10235 Spartan Dr Ste T Cincinnati (45215) *(G-3463)*

Trevor Clatterbuck 330 359-2129
927 Us Route 62 Wilmot (44689) *(G-16070)*

Trewbric III Inc 614 444-2184
1701 Moler Rd Columbus (43207) *(G-5835)*

Trexler Rubber Co Inc (PA) 330 296-9677
503 N Diamond St Ravenna (44266) *(G-12739)*

Trey Corrugated Inc 513 942-4800
9048 Port Union Rialto Rd West Chester (45069) *(G-15518)*

Trg United, Columbus *Also Called: Russell Group United LLC (G-5734)*

Tri - Flex of Ohio Inc (PA) 330 705-7084
2701 Applegrove St Nw North Canton (44720) *(G-11770)*

Tri Cast Limited Partnership 330 733-8718
2128 Killian Rd Akron (44312) *(G-362)*

Tri County Concrete Inc 330 425-4464
10155 Royalton Rd Cleveland (44133) *(G-4821)*

Tri County Concrete Inc (PA) 330 425-4464
9423 Darrow Rd Twinsburg (44087) *(G-14747)*

Tri County Door Service Inc 216 531-2245
21701 Tungsten Rd Euclid (44117) *(G-7303)*

Tri County Eggs, Versailles *Also Called: Weaver Bros Inc (G-14992)*

Tri County Locksmith, Cincinnati *Also Called: AB Bonded Locksmiths Inc (G-2589)*

Tri County Ready Mixed Con Co, Cleveland *Also Called: Tri County Concrete Inc (G-4821)*

Tri County Tarp LLC (PA) 419 288-3350
13100 Us Highway 23 Gibsonburg (43431) *(G-7956)*

Tri State Corebuyers LLC 513 288-8063
1427 Glenwood Ct Amelia (45102) *(G-468)*

Tri State Dairy LLC (PA) 330 897-5555
9946 Fiat Rd Sw Baltic (43804) *(G-842)*

Tri State Dairy LLC 419 542-8788
210 Wendell Ave Hicksville (43526) *(G-8381)*

Tri State Equipment Company 513 738-7227
5009 Cincinnati-Brookville Rd Shandon (45063) *(G-13161)*

Tri State Media LLC 513 933-0101
325 Davids Dr Wilmington (45177) *(G-16061)*

Tri State Pallet Inc (PA) 937 746-8702
8401 Claude Thomas Rd Franklin (45005) *(G-7707)*

Tri-America Contractors, Wheelersburg *Also Called: Tri-America Contractors Inc (G-15811)*

Tri-America Contractors Inc (PA) 740 574-0148
1664 State Route 522 Wheelersburg (45694) *(G-15810)*

Tri-America Contractors Inc 740 574-0148
1664 State Route 522 Wheelersburg (45694) *(G-15811)*

Tri-Cast Inc (PA) 330 733-8718
2128 Killian Rd Akron (44312) *(G-363)*

Tri-County Block and Brick Inc 419 826-7060
1628 Us Highway 20a Swanton (43558) *(G-13986)*

Tri-Craft Inc 440 826-1050
17941 Englewood Dr Cleveland (44130) *(G-4822)*

Tri-Fab Inc 330 337-3425
10372 W South Range Rd Salem (44460) *(G-13034)*

Tri-K Enterprises Inc 330 832-7380
935 Mckinley Ave Sw Canton (44707) *(G-2248)*

Tri-M Block and Supply Inc 330 264-8771
111 Stow Ave Ste 100 Cuyahoga Falls (44221) *(G-6122)*

Tri-Mac Mfg & Serv, Hamilton *Also Called: Tri-Mac Mfg & Svcs Co (G-8251)*

Tri-Mac Mfg & Svcs Co 513 896-4445
860 Belle Ave Hamilton (45015) *(G-8251)*

Tri-R Dies, Youngstown *Also Called: Mordies Inc (G-16402)*

Tri-R Tooling Inc 419 522-8665
220 Piper Rd Mansfield (44905) *(G-9728)*

Tri-State Archtctural Panl Sls, Toledo *Also Called: Toledo Cut Stone Inc (G-14494)*

Tri-State Asphalt Co, Rayland *Also Called: Shelly and Sands Inc (G-12745)*

Tri-State Beef Co Inc 513 579-1722
2124 Baymiller St Cincinnati (45214) *(G-3464)*

Tri-State Fabricators Inc 513 752-5005
1146 Ferris Rd Amelia (45102) *(G-469)*

Tri-State Hobbies Raceway LLC 513 889-3954
3379 Dixie Hwy Hamilton (45015) *(G-8252)*

Tri-State Jet Mfg LLC 513 896-4538
1480 Beissinger Rd Hamilton (45013) *(G-8253)*

Tri-State Kitchens LLC 740 574-6727
663 Kittle Rd Wheelersburg (45694) *(G-15812)*

Tri-State Paper Inc 937 885-3365
9000 Kenrick Rd Dayton (45458) *(G-6631)*

Tri-State Plating & Polishing 304 529-2579
187 Township Road 1204 Proctorville (45669) *(G-12688)*

Tri-State Printing, Steubenville *Also Called: Tri-State Publishing Company (G-13679)*

Tri-State Publishing Company (PA) 740 283-3686
157 N 3rd St Steubenville (43952) *(G-13679)*

Tri-State Supply Co Inc 614 272-6767
3840 Fisher Rd Columbus (43228) *(G-5836)*

Tri-State Wilbert Vault Co, Ironton *Also Called: Allen Enterprises Inc (G-8694)*

Tri-Tech, Baltimore *Also Called: Tri-Tech Led Systems LLC (G-848)*

Tri-Tech Laboratories Inc 740 927-2817
8825 Smiths Mill Rd N Johnstown (43031) *(G-8180)*

Tri-Tech Laboratories LLC 614 656-1130
8825 Smiths Mill Rd New Albany (43054) *(G-11791)*

Tri-Tech Laboratories LLC (PA) 434 845-7073
4400 S Hamilton Rd Groveport (43125) *(G-8160)*

Tri-Tech Laboratories LLC 434 845-7073
8825 Smiths Mill Rd N Johnstown (43031) *(G-8181)*

Tri-Tech Led Systems LLC 614 593-2868
600 W Market St Baltimore (43105) *(G-848)*

Tri-W Group Inc 614 228-5000
835 Goodale Blvd Columbus (43212) *(G-5837)*

Tri-Weld Inc 216 281-6009
4411 Detroit Ave Cleveland (44113) *(G-4823)*

Triad Capital Group LLC 440 236-6677
13676 Station Rd Columbia Station (44028) *(G-5023)*

Triad Energy Corporation 740 374-2940
125 Putnam St Marietta (45750) *(G-9838)*

Triad Governmental Systems 937 376-5446
358 S Monroe St Xenia (45385) *(G-16278)*

Triad Hunter LLC (DH) 740 374-2940
125 Putnam St Ste 100 Marietta (45750) *(G-9839)*

Triad Metal Products Company 216 676-6505
12990 Snow Rd Chagrin Falls (44023) *(G-240)*

Triage Ortho Group 937 653-6431
132 Lafayette Ave Urbana (43078) *(G-14848)*

Triangle Machine Products Co 216 524-5872
6055 Hillcrest Dr Cleveland (44125) *(G-4824)*

Triangle Precision Industries 937 299-6776
1650 Delco Park Dr Dayton (45420) *(G-6632)*

Triangle Sign Co LLC 513 266-1009
221 N B St Hamilton (45013) *(G-8254)*

Tribco Incorporated 216 486-2000
18901 Cranwood Pkwy Cleveland (44128) *(G-4825)*

TRIBORO QUILT MANUFACTURING CORPORATION, Vandalia *Also Called: Triboro Quilt Mfg Corp (G-14962)*

Triboro Quilt Mfg Corp 937 222-2132
303 Corporate Center Dr Ste 108 Vandalia (45377) *(G-14962)*

Tribotech Composites Inc 216 901-1300
7800 Exchange St Cleveland (44125) *(G-4826)*

Tribune , The, Jefferson *Also Called: The Gazette Printing Co Inc (G-8760)*

Tribune Printing Inc 419 542-7764
147 E High St Hicksville (43526) *(G-8382)*

Tribune Shopping News, The, New Lexington *Also Called: Perry County Tribune (G-11455)*

Trico, Cleveland *Also Called: Trico Products Corporation (G-4829)*

Trico Enterprises LLC 216 970-9984
17717 Hilliard Rd Lakewood (44107) *(G-8983)*

Trico Holding Corporation (DH) 216 589-0198
127 Public Sq Ste 5110 Cleveland (44114) *(G-4827)*

Trico Machine Products Corp..216 662-4194
5081 Corbin Dr Cleveland (44128) *(G-4828)*

Trico Products Corporation (DH)..248 371-1700
127 Public Sq Cleveland (44114) *(G-4829)*

Tricor Industrial Inc (PA)...330 264-3299
3225 W Old Lincoln Way Wooster (44691) *(G-16178)*

Tricor Metals, Wooster Also Called: Tricor Industrial Inc *(G-16178)*

Tridelta Industries Inc (PA)..440 255-1080
7333 Corporate Blvd Mentor (44060) *(G-10584)*

Trifecta Tool and Engrg LLC..937 291-0933
4648 Gateway Cir Dayton (45440) *(G-6633)*

Trillium Health Care Products...513 242-2227
5177 Spring Grove Ave Cincinnati (45217) *(G-3465)*

Trilogy Plastics, Alliance Also Called: Myers Industries Inc *(G-417)*

Trilogy Plastics, Alliance Also Called: Trilogy Plastics Alliance Inc *(G-434)*

Trilogy Plastics Alliance Inc..330 821-4700
2290 W Main St Alliance (44601) *(G-434)*

Trim Parts Inc..513 934-0815
2175 Deerfield Rd Lebanon (45036) *(G-9115)*

Trim Systems Operating Corp...740 772-5998
75 Chamber Dr Chillicothe (45601) *(G-2539)*

Trim Systems Operating Corp (HQ)....................................614 289-5360
7800 Walton Pkwy New Albany (43054) *(G-11392)*

Trim Tool & Machine Inc..216 889-1916
3431 Service Rd Cleveland (44111) *(G-4830)*

Trimble Engineering & Cnstr, Tipp City Also Called: Trimble Inc *(G-14160)*

Trimble Inc...937 233-8921
5475 Kellenburger Rd Dayton (45424) *(G-6634)*

Trimble Inc...937 233-8921
4450 Gibson Dr Tipp City (45371) *(G-14160)*

Trimble Trnsp Entp Sltions Inc (HQ)...................................216 831-6606
6085 Parkland Blvd Mayfield Heights (44124) *(G-10255)*

Trimco...614 679-3931
7265 Park Bend Dr Westerville (43082) *(G-15684)*

Trimline Die Corporation...440 355-6900
421 Commerce Dr E Lagrange (44050) *(G-8956)*

Trimold LLC..740 474-7591
200 Pittsburg Rd Circleville (43113) *(G-3559)*

Trimtec Systems Ltd...614 820-0340
2455 Harrisburg Pike Grove City (43123) *(G-8126)*

Trinel Inc..216 265-9190
5251 W 137th St Cleveland (44142) *(G-4831)*

Trinity Midwest Aviation LLC..513 583-0519
8123 S State Route 48 Maineville (45039) *(G-9603)*

Trinity Specialty Compounding Inc....................................419 924-9090
600 Oak St West Unity (43570) *(G-15644)*

Trinity Water Solutions LLC..740 318-0585
17226 Industrial Hwy Caldwell (43724) *(G-1914)*

Trionix Research Lab Inc..330 425-9055
8037 Bavaria Rd Twinsburg (44087) *(G-14748)*

Trip Transport LLC..773 969-1402
2905 Sunbury Sq Columbus (43219) *(G-5838)*

Triple A Builders Inc...216 249-0327
540 E 105th St Cleveland (44108) *(G-4832)*

Triple Arrow Industries Inc...614 437-5588
13311 Industrial Pkwy Marysville (43040) *(G-9943)*

Triple Diamond Plastics, Liberty Center Also Called: Triple Diamond Plastics LLC *(G-9204)*

Triple Diamond Plastics LLC...419 533-0085
405 N Pleasantview Dr Liberty Center (43532) *(G-9204)*

Triple J Oilfield Services LLC..740 609-3050
54382 National Rd Bridgeport (43912) *(G-1650)*

Triplett Bluffton Corporation...419 358-8750
1 Triplett Dr Bluffton (45817) *(G-1509)*

Tristan Rubber Molding Inc (PA)..330 499-4055
7255 Whipple Ave Nw North Canton (44720) *(G-11771)*

Tristate Steel Contractors LLC...513 648-9000
2508 Civic Center Dr Ste A Cincinnati (45231) *(G-3466)*

Triton Duro Werks Inc...216 267-1117
12200 Sprecher Ave Cleveland (44135) *(G-4833)*

Triumph Signs & Consulting Inc..513 576-8090
480 Milford Pkwy Milford (45150) *(G-10926)*

Triumph Thermal Systems LLC (HQ)..................................419 273-2511
200 Railroad St Forest (45843) *(G-7593)*

Triumphant Enterprises Inc..513 617-1668
7096 Hill Station Rd Goshen (45122) *(G-7995)*

Trivium Alum Packg USA Corp (DH)...................................330 744-9505
1 Performance Pl Youngstown (44502) *(G-16460)*

TRM Manufacturing Inc..330 769-2600
601 Munroe Falls Ave Cuyahoga Falls (44221) *(G-6123)*

Trogdan Publishing...614 880-0178
1635 Strathshire Hall Pl Powell (43065) *(G-12683)*

Trogdon Publishing Inc...330 721-7678
5164 Normandy Park Dr Ste 100 Medina (44256) *(G-10389)*

Tronair Inc (DH)...419 866-6301
1 Air Cargo Pkwy E Swanton (43558) *(G-13987)*

Trophy Nut Co (PA)...937 667-8478
320 N 2nd St Tipp City (45371) *(G-14161)*

Trophy Nut Co...937 669-5513
1567 Harmony Dr Tipp City (45371) *(G-14162)*

Trophy Sports Center LLC..937 376-2311
26 Kinsey Rd Xenia (45385) *(G-16279)*

Trophy's Unlimited, Wheelersburg Also Called: Greg Blume *(G-15809)*

Tropical Nut & Fruit, Urbancrest Also Called: Hayden Valley Foods Inc *(G-14853)*

Trotwood Corporation...937 854-3047
11 N Broadway St Trotwood (45426) *(G-14547)*

Troy, Burton Also Called: Troy Manufacturing Co *(G-1888)*

Troy Chemical, Burton Also Called: Troy Chemical Industries Inc *(G-1887)*

Troy Chemical Industries Inc (PA).....................................440 834-4408
17040 Rapids Rd Burton (44021) *(G-1887)*

Troy Engnred Cmpnnts Assmblies....................................937 335-8070
4900 Webster St Dayton (45414) *(G-6635)*

Troy Filters Ltd..614 777-8222
1680 Westbelt Dr Columbus (43228) *(G-5839)*

Troy Innovative Instrs Inc...440 834-9567
15111 White Rd Middlefield (44062) *(G-10792)*

Troy Manufacturing Co...440 834-8262
17090 Rapids Rd Burton (44021) *(G-1888)*

Troy Precision Carbide, Burton Also Called: Troy Precision Carbide Die Inc *(G-1889)*

Troy Precision Carbide Die Inc...440 834-4477
17720 Claridon Troy Rd Burton (44021) *(G-1889)*

Troy Sand and Gravel, Troy Also Called: Marietta Martin Materials Inc *(G-14596)*

Troy Valley Petroleum...937 604-0012
201 Valley St Dayton (45404) *(G-6636)*

Troy Water Treatment Plant, Troy Also Called: City of Troy *(G-14555)*

Troyer Cheese, Inc., Millersburg Also Called: Cheese Holdings Inc *(G-10951)*

Troyer Manufacturing, Millersburg Also Called: Lipari Foods Operating Co LLC *(G-10973)*

Troyer Manufacturing, Millersburg Also Called: Lipari Foods Operating Co LLC *(G-10974)*

Troyers Cabinet Shop Ltd...937 464-7702
9442 County Road 101 Belle Center (43310) *(G-1198)*

Troyers Pallet Shop..330 897-1038
31052 Township Road 227 Fresno (43824) *(G-7827)*

Troyers Trail Bologna Inc..330 893-2414
6552 State Route 515 Dundee (44624) *(G-6971)*

Troyke Manufacturing Company..513 769-4242
11294 Orchard St Cincinnati (45241) *(G-3467)*

Troymill Lumber Company..440 632-6353
7000 Granger Rd Ste 1 Independence (44131) *(G-8688)*

Troymill Manufacturing Inc (PA)..440 632-5580
17055 Kinsman Rd Middlefield (44062) *(G-10793)*

Troymill Wood Products, Middlefield Also Called: Troymill Manufacturing Inc *(G-10793)*

Troyridge Mfg..330 893-7516
3998 County Road 168 Millersburg (44654) *(G-11001)*

Tru Comfort Mattress..614 595-8600
8994 Mediterra Pl Dublin (43016) *(G-6954)*

Tru Form Metal Products Inc..216 252-3700
12305 Grimsby Ave Cleveland (44135) *(G-4834)*

Tru-Bore Machine Co Inc..330 928-6215
1220 Orlen Ave Cuyahoga Falls (44221) *(G-6124)*

Tru-Cal Inc (PA)...419 202-1296
11001 Us Highway 250 N Unit 12b Milan (44846) *(G-10888)*

Tru-Fab Inc..937 435-1733
2225 Lyons Rd Miamisburg (45342) *(G-10696)*

Tru-Fab Technology Inc 440 954-9760
  34820 Lakeland Blvd Willoughby (44095) *(G-16009)*

Tru-Form Steel & Wire Inc 765 348-5001
  5509 Telegraph Rd Toledo (43612) *(G-14512)*

Tru-Tex International Corp 513 825-8844
  11050 Southland Rd Cincinnati (45240) *(G-3468)*

Tru-Weld Stud Welding Div, Medina Also Called: Tfp Corporation *(G-10384)*

Truax Printing Inc 419 994-4166
  425 E Haskell St Loudonville (44842) *(G-9452)*

Trucast Inc 440 942-4923
  4382 Hamann Pkwy Willoughby (44094) *(G-16010)*

Truck Cab Manufacturers Inc (PA) 513 922-1300
  2420 Anderson Ferry Rd Cincinnati (45238) *(G-3469)*

Truck Fax Inc 216 921-8866
  17700 S Woodland Rd Cleveland (44120) *(G-4835)*

Truck Stop Embroidery 419 257-2860
  12906 Deshler Rd North Baltimore (45872) *(G-11702)*

Trucut Incorporated (PA) 330 938-9806
  1145 Allied Dr Sebring (44672) *(G-13127)*

True Dinero Records & Tech LLC 513 428-4610
  2611 Kemper Ln Uppr Level1 Cincinnati (45206) *(G-3470)*

True Industries Inc 330 296-4342
  666 Pratt St Ravenna (44266) *(G-12740)*

True Step LLC 513 933-0933
  1105 S Us Route 42 Lebanon (45036) *(G-9116)*

True Value, North Baltimore Also Called: Mid-Wood Inc *(G-11696)*

True Value, Woodsfield Also Called: Woodsfeld True Vlue HM Ctr Inc *(G-16090)*

True Vision 740 277-7550
  1726 E Main St Lancaster (43130) *(G-9048)*

Truechoicepack Corp 937 630-3832
  9565 Cincinnati Columbus Rd West Chester (45069) *(G-15519)*

Truex Tool & Die Div, Youngstown Also Called: Jamen Tool & Die Co *(G-16381)*

Trufast, Bryan Also Called: Altenloh Brinck & Co US Inc *(G-1806)*

Truflex Rubber Products Co 740 967-9015
  200 E Coshocton St Johnstown (43031) *(G-8782)*

Trulil Inc 937 652-1242
  625 S Edgewood Ave Urbana (43078) *(G-14849)*

Truline Industries Inc 440 729-0140
  1400 Silver St Wickliffe (44092) *(G-15855)*

Trulite GL Alum Solutions LLC 740 929-2443
  160 N High St Hebron (43025) *(G-8368)*

Trulou Holdings Inc 513 347-0100
  5311 Robert Ave Ste A Cincinnati (45248) *(G-3471)*

Trumbull Asphalt, Toledo Also Called: Owens Corning Roofg & Asp LLC *(G-14423)*

Trumbull Cement Products Co 330 372-4342
  2185 Larchmont Ave Ne Warren (44483) *(G-15211)*

Trumbull County Hardwoods 440 632-0555
  9446 Bundysburg Rd Middlefield (44062) *(G-10794)*

Trumbull Manufacturing 330 270-7888
  3850 Hendricks Rd Youngstown (44515) *(G-16461)*

Trumbull Mobile Meals 330 394-2538
  323 E Market St Warren (44481) *(G-15212)*

Trupoint Products LLC 330 204-3302
  Uknown Sugarcreek (44681) *(G-13945)*

Truseal Technologies Inc (HQ) 216 910-1500
  388 S Main St Ste 700 Akron (44311) *(G-364)*

Truss Worx LLC 419 363-2100
  12412 Frysinger Rd Rockford (45882) *(G-12834)*

Trusscore USA Inc 888 418-4679
  6161 Ventnor Ave Dayton (45414) *(G-6637)*

Trust Manufacturing LLC (PA) 216 531-8787
  20080 Saint Clair Ave Euclid (44117) *(G-7304)*

Trust Technologies, Cleveland Also Called: Kilroy Company *(G-4289)*

Trutech Cabinetry LLC 614 338-0680
  2121 S James Rd Columbus (43232) *(G-5840)*

Trv Incorporated 440 951-7722
  4860 E 345th St Willoughby (44094) *(G-16011)*

TS Oak Inc 513 252-7241
  544 Mitchell Way Ct Cincinnati (45238) *(G-3472)*

TS Sales LLC 727 804-8060
  847 Pier Dr Akron (44307) *(G-365)*

TS Tech Americas Inc (HQ) 614 575-4100
  8458 E Broad St Reynoldsburg (43068) *(G-12776)*

TS Tech Co Ltd (PA) 740 420-5617
  200 Pittsburgh Rd Circleville (43113) *(G-3560)*

TS Tech USA Corporation (DH) 614 577-1088
  8400 E Broad St Reynoldsburg (43068) *(G-12777)*

TS Trim Industries Inc (DH) 614 837-4114
  6380 Canal St Canal Winchester (43110) *(G-1993)*

TS USA 937 323-2556
  2015 Progress Rd Springfield (45505) *(G-13651)*

Tsjmedia, Blue Ash Also Called: Gate West Coast Ventures LLC *(G-1397)*

Tsk America Co Ltd 513 942-4002
  9668 Inter Ocean Dr West Chester (45246) *(G-15600)*

Tsp Inc 513 732-8900
  2009 Glenn Pkwy Batavia (45103) *(G-955)*

TSR Machinery Services Inc 513 874-9697
  100 Security Dr Fairfield (45014) *(G-7420)*

TSS Acquisition Company 513 772-7000
  1201 Hill Smith Dr Cincinnati (45215) *(G-3473)*

TSS Technologies, West Chester Also Called: Cbn Westside Holdings Inc *(G-15386)*

TSS Technologies, West Chester Also Called: Cbn Westside Technologies Inc *(G-15387)*

Tsw Industries Inc 440 572-7200
  14960 Foltz Pkwy Strongsville (44149) *(G-13892)*

TT Electronics IMS, Perry Also Called: TT Electronics Integrated Manufacturing Services Inc *(G-12357)*

TT Electronics Integrated Manufacturing Services Inc 440 352-8961
  3700 Lane Rd Ext Perry (44081) *(G-12357)*

TTI Sports Equipment, Columbus Also Called: Total Tennis Inc *(G-5829)*

Ttm, North Jackson Also Called: Cleveland Coretec Inc *(G-11781)*

Ttm Technologies, North Jackson Also Called: Ttm Technologies North America LLC *(G-11793)*

Ttm Technologies Inc 330 538-3900
  12080 Debartolo Dr North Jackson (44451) *(G-11792)*

Ttm Technologies North America LLC 330 572-3400
  12080 Debartolo Dr North Jackson (44451) *(G-11793)*

Ttr Manufacturing LLC 440 366-5005
  740 Sugar Ln Elyria (44035) *(G-7213)*

Tubar Eureka Industrial Group, Canton Also Called: Uhrden Inc *(G-2249)*

Tube Fittings Division, Columbus Also Called: Parker-Hannifin Corporation *(G-5656)*

Tubetech Inc (PA) 330 426-9476
  900 E Taggart St East Palestine (44413) *(G-7011)*

Tubetech North America, East Palestine Also Called: Tubetech Inc *(G-7011)*

Tuboscope, Youngstown Also Called: Varco LP *(G-16468)*

Tubular Techniques Inc 614 529-4130
  3025 Scioto Darby Executive Ct Hilliard (43026) *(G-8450)*

Tucker Printers Inc 585 359-3030
  8740 Global Way West Chester (45069) *(G-15520)*

Tuf-N-Lite, Liberty Twp Also Called: Feather Lite Innovations Inc *(G-9215)*

Tuf-N-Lite, Springboro Also Called: Feather Lite Innovations Inc *(G-13501)*

Tuf-N-Lite LLC 513 472-8400
  7649 Keister Rd Middletown (45042) *(G-10868)*

Tuf-Tug Inc 937 299-1213
  3434 Encrete Ln Moraine (45439) *(G-11216)*

Tuffco Sand and Gravel Inc 614 873-3977
  8195 Old State Route 161 Plain City (43064) *(G-12596)*

Tuffy Manufacturing 330 940-2356
  140 Ascot Pkwy Cuyahoga Falls (44223) *(G-6125)*

Tuffy Pad Company 330 688-0043
  454 Seasons Rd Stow (44224) *(G-13733)*

Tugz International LLC 216 621-4854
  4500 Division Ave Cleveland (44102) *(G-4836)*

Tulkoff Food Products Ohio LLC 410 864-0523
  3015 E Kemper Rd Cincinnati (45241) *(G-3474)*

Tulua Nutrition 419 764-0664
  11580 County Road L Wauseon (43567) *(G-15275)*

Tune Town, Sandusky Also Called: Tune Town Car Audio *(G-13098)*

Tune Town Car Audio 419 627-1100
  2345 E Perkins Ave Sandusky (44870) *(G-13098)*

Tungsten and Capital, Solon Also Called: Bowes Manufacturing Inc *(G-13321)*

Turbine Eng Cmpnents Tech Corp 216 692-5200
  23555 Euclid Ave Cleveland (44117) *(G-4837)*

ALPHABETIC SECTION — Ugly Bunny Winery LLC

Turbine Standard Ltd (PA)..419 865-0355
1750 Eber Rd Ste A Holland (43528) *(G-8535)*

Turf Care Supply LLC (PA)..877 220-1014
50 Pearl Rd Ste 200 Brunswick (44212) *(G-1796)*

Turfware Manufacturing Inc...330 688-8500
1337 Commerce Dr Ste 4 Stow (44224) *(G-13734)*

Turkeyfoot Printing, Napoleon *Also Called: Mustang Printing (G-11325)*

Turn & Earn Corporation..516 761-0236
445 Havendale Dr Westerville (43082) *(G-15685)*

Turn-All Machine & Gear Co..937 342-8710
5499 Tremont Ln Springfield (45502) *(G-13652)*

Turn-Key Industrial Svcs LLC...614 274-1128
4512 Harrisburg Pike Grove City (43123) *(G-8127)*

Turn-Key Tunneling Inc..614 275-4832
1247 Stimmel Rd Columbus (43223) *(G-5841)*

Turner Concrete Products..419 662-9007
2121 Tracy Rd Northwood (43619) *(G-11931)*

Turner Machine Co...330 332-5821
1433 Salem Pkwy Salem (44460) *(G-13035)*

Turner Vault Co..419 537-1133
2121 Tracy Rd Northwood (43619) *(G-11932)*

Turning Technologies LLC (PA)...330 746-3015
6000 Mahoning Ave Youngstown (44515) *(G-16462)*

Turnwood Industry Inc...330 278-2421
365 State Rd Hinckley (44233) *(G-8478)*

TURTLE PLASTICS, Lorain *Also Called: Cleveland Reclaim Inds Inc (G-9407)*

Turtlecreek Township...513 932-4080
670 N State Route 123 Lebanon (45036) *(G-9117)*

Tuscarora Wood Midwest LLC..937 603-8882
6506 W Us Route 36 Covington (45318) *(G-6032)*

Tusco Display, Gnadenhutten *Also Called: Tusco Limited Partnership (G-7991)*

Tusco Hardwoods LLC..330 852-4281
10887 Gerber Valley Rd Nw Sugarcreek (44681) *(G-13946)*

Tusco Limited Partnership..740 254-4343
239 S Chestnut St Gnadenhutten (44629) *(G-7991)*

Tvh Parts Co...877 755-7311
8756 Global Way West Chester (45069) *(G-15521)*

Tvone Ncsa..859 282-7303
621 Wilmer Ave Cincinnati (45226) *(G-3475)*

Tvone Ncsa - N Centl & S Amer, Cincinnati *Also Called: Tvone Ncsa (G-3475)*

TW Manufacturing Co..440 439-3243
6065 Parkland Blvd Cleveland (44124) *(G-4838)*

Twb Company LLC..330 558-2026
5569 Innovation Dr Valley City (44280) *(G-14899)*

Twenty One Barrels Ltd..937 467-4498
9717 Horatio Harris Creek Rd Bradford (45308) *(G-1602)*

Twin Cities Concrete Co..330 627-2158
1031 Kensington Rd Ne Carrollton (44615) *(G-2316)*

Twin Cities Concrete Co (DH)...330 343-4491
141 S Tuscarawas Ave Dover (44622) *(G-6848)*

Twin Creek Mfg LLC..937 634-3470
8111 Lantis Geeting Rd Camden (45311) *(G-1964)*

Twin Point Inc (PA)..419 923-7525
11955 County Road 10-2 Delta (43515) *(G-6791)*

Twin Rivers Technologies Mfg, Painesville *Also Called: Twin Rvers Tech - Pnsville LLC (G-12273)*

Twin Rvers Tech - Pnsville LLC..440 350-6300
679 Hardy Rd Painesville (44077) *(G-12273)*

Twin Sisters Productions LLC..330 631-0361
4710 Hudson Dr Stow (44224) *(G-13735)*

Twin Valley Metalcraft, West Alexandria *Also Called: Twin Valley Metalcraft Asm LLC (G-15345)*

Twin Valley Metalcraft Asm LLC......................................937 787-4634
4739 Enterprise Rd West Alexandria (45381) *(G-15345)*

Twin Valley Mold & Tool LLC..937 962-1403
8725 Verona Rd Lewisburg (45338) *(G-9193)*

Twin Ventures Inc..330 405-3838
2457 Edison Blvd Twinsburg (44087) *(G-14749)*

Twinsource LLC...440 248-6800
32333 Aurora Rd Ste 50 Solon (44139) *(G-13440)*

Twist Inc (PA)...937 675-9581
47 S Limestone St Jamestown (45335) *(G-8742)*

Twist Inc...937 675-9581
5100 Waynesville Jamestown (45335) *(G-8743)*

Twister Displays, East Liverpool *Also Called: Delta Manufacturing Inc (G-6994)*

Twisty Treat LLC..419 873-8033
750 W Boundary St Perrysburg (43551) *(G-12441)*

Twm LLC..419 562-9622
314 N Sandusky Ave Bucyrus (44820) *(G-1870)*

Two Grndmthers Gourmet Kit LLC...................................614 746-0888
9127 Firstgate Dr Reynoldsburg (43068) *(G-12778)*

Twr Services LLC..513 604-4796
871 Meadow Ridge Dr Cincinnati (45245) *(G-2575)*

Tyco Fire Products LP...216 265-0505
5565 Venture Dr Ste A Cleveland (44130) *(G-4839)*

Tyco Fire Protection Products, Cleveland *Also Called: Tyco Fire Products LP (G-4839)*

Tyjen..740 797-4064
8 Slater Dr The Plains (45780) *(G-14059)*

Tykma Inc...877 318-9562
370 Gateway Dr Chillicothe (45601) *(G-2540)*

Tykma Electrox, Chillicothe *Also Called: Tykma Inc (G-2540)*

Tyler Elevator Products, Twinsburg *Also Called: Wittur Usa Inc (G-14756)*

Tyler Haver Inc (DH)..440 974-1047
8570 Tyler Blvd Mentor (44060) *(G-10585)*

Tyler Industries Inc..440 578-1104
7471 Tyler Blvd Ste C Mentor (44060) *(G-10586)*

Tyler Technologies Inc..800 800-2581
1 Tyler Way Moraine (45439) *(G-11217)*

Tylok International Inc..216 261-7310
1061 E 260th St Cleveland (44132) *(G-4840)*

Tymex Plastics Inc...216 429-8950
5300 Harvard Ave Cleveland (44105) *(G-4841)*

Tymoca Partners LLC..440 946-4327
33220 Lakeland Blvd Eastlake (44095) *(G-7052)*

Tyson, West Chester *Also Called: Advancepierre Foods Inc (G-15531)*

Tz Acquisition Corp...216 535-4300
26301 Curtiss Wright Pkwy 2nd Fl Richmond Heights (44143) *(G-12812)*

U D F, Cincinnati *Also Called: United Dairy Farmers Inc (G-3479)*

U M D, Fredericktown *Also Called: Umd Automated Systems Inc (G-7756)*

U P I, Cleveland *Also Called: Urethane Polymers Intl (G-4855)*

U S Alloy Die Corp...216 749-9700
4007 Brookpark Rd Cleveland (44134) *(G-4842)*

U S Army Corps of Engineers..740 537-2571
29501 State Rte 7 Toronto (43964) *(G-14536)*

U S Chemical & Plastics...330 830-6000
600 Nova Dr Se Massillon (44646) *(G-10152)*

U S Chrome Corporation Ohio...877 872-7716
107 Westboro St Dayton (45417) *(G-6638)*

U S Development Corp..330 673-6900
900 W Main St Kent (44240) *(G-8879)*

U S Hair Inc..614 235-5190
3727 E Broad St Columbus (43213) *(G-5842)*

U S M, Wickliffe *Also Called: Usm Precision Products Inc (G-15858)*

U S Molding Machinery Co Inc...440 918-1701
38294 Pelton Rd Willoughby (44094) *(G-16012)*

U S Weatherford L P..330 746-2502
1100 Performance Pl Youngstown (44502) *(G-16463)*

U.S. Bridge, Cambridge *Also Called: Ohio Bridge Corporation (G-1945)*

UAS, Blue Ash *Also Called: United Air Specialists Inc (G-1486)*

Uc Trailer Co., Sunbury *Also Called: Universal Composite LLC (G-13965)*

UCAR Carbon, Brooklyn Heights *Also Called: Graftech Intl Holdings Inc (G-1692)*

UCI, Toledo *Also Called: United Components LLC (G-14513)*

UCI Controls Inc (PA)..216 398-0330
1111 Brookpark Rd Cleveland (44109) *(G-4843)*

UCI International LLC (DH)...330 899-0340
2100 International Pkwy North Canton (44720) *(G-11772)*

Udderly Smooth, Salem *Also Called: Redex Industries Inc (G-13026)*

Udecx LLC..877 698-3329
320 N 4th St Tipp City (45371) *(G-14163)*

UGL Inc...630 250-1600
3118 Transportation Rd Dayton (45404) *(G-6639)*

Ugly Bunny Winery LLC..330 988-9057
16104 State Route 39 Loudonville (44842) *(G-9453)*

UGN Inc
 201 Exploration Dr Lebanon (45036) *(G-9118)* 513 360-3500

Uhrden Inc 330 456-0031
 700 Tuscarawas St W Canton (44702) *(G-2249)*

Uhrichsville Carbide Inc 740 922-9197
 410 N Water St Uhrichsville (44683) *(G-14772)*

UIC West Chester Plant, West Chester *Also Called: Usui International Corporation (G-15523)*

Ulterior Products LLC 614 441-9465
 3142 N Section Line Rd Radnor (43066) *(G-12696)*

Ultimate Chem Solutions Inc 440 998-6751
 1800 E 21st St Ashtabula (44004) *(G-662)*

Ultimate Printing Co Inc 330 847-2941
 6090 Mahoning Ave Nw Ste C Warren (44481) *(G-15213)*

Ultimate Rb Inc (DH) 419 692-3000
 1430 N Main St Delphos (45833) *(G-6774)*

Ultimate Systems Ltd 419 692-3005
 1430 N Main St Delphos (45833) *(G-6775)*

Ultium Cells LLC (PA) 586 295-5429
 7400 Tod Ave Sw Warren (44481) *(G-15214)*

Ultra Machine Inc 440 323-7632
 530 Lowell St Elyria (44035) *(G-7214)*

Ultra Punch, Dayton *Also Called: Stolle Machinery Company LLC (G-6596)*

Ultra Tech International Inc 440 974-8999
 7278 Justin Way Mentor (44060) *(G-10587)*

Ultra Tech Machinery Inc 330 929-5544
 297 Ascot Pkwy Cuyahoga Falls (44223) *(G-6126)*

Ultra-Met, Urbana *Also Called: Ultra-Met Company (G-14850)*

Ultra-Met Company 937 653-7133
 720 N Main St Urbana (43078) *(G-14850)*

Ultra-Met Company 937 653-7133
 120 Fyffe St Urbana (43078) *(G-14851)*

Ultrabilt Play Systems Nova Lt 234 248-4414
 437 Northvale Dr Chippewa Lake (44215) *(G-2543)*

Ultrabuilt Play Systems Inc 419 652-2294
 1114 Us Highway 224 Nova (44859) *(G-12005)*

Ultraedit Inc 216 464-7465
 5559 Eureka Dr Ste B Hamilton (45011) *(G-8255)*

Ultratech Polymers Inc 330 945-9410
 280 Ascot Pkwy Cuyahoga Falls (44223) *(G-6127)*

Umd Automated Systems Inc 740 694-8614
 9855 Salem Rd Fredericktown (43019) *(G-7756)*

Umd Contractors Inc 740 694-8614
 9855 Salem Rd Fredericktown (43019) *(G-7757)*

Uncle Jays Cakes LLC 513 882-3433
 2516 Clifton Ave Cincinnati (45219) *(G-3476)*

Under Hill Water Well 740 852-0858
 1789 Itawamba Trl London (43140) *(G-9396)*

Under Pressure Systems Inc 330 602-4466
 322 North Ave Ne New Philadelphia (44663) *(G-11531)*

Underground Eyes II LLC 352 601-1446
 2828 Ritchey Rd Heath (43056) *(G-8332)*

Underground Sports Shop Inc 513 751-1662
 1233 Findlay St Ste Frnt Cincinnati (45214) *(G-3477)*

Unger Kosher Bakery Inc 216 321-7176
 1831 S Taylor Rd Cleveland Heights (44118) *(G-4944)*

Ungers Bakery, Cleveland Heights *Also Called: Unger Kosher Bakery Inc (G-4944)*

UNI-Facs, Columbus *Also Called: Universal Fabg Cnstr Svcs Inc (G-5845)*

Unibat, Cleveland *Also Called: Cleanlife Energy LLC (G-3827)*

Unibilt Industries Inc 937 890-7570
 8005 Johnson Station Rd Vandalia (45377) *(G-14963)*

Unifi LLC 614 288-9217
 341 Cheyenne Way Reynoldsburg (43068) *(G-12779)*

Unified Scrning Crshing - OH I 937 836-3201
 200 Cass Dr Englewood (45315) *(G-7246)*

Unifin Chesapeake, Salem *Also Called: Cardinal Pumps Exchangers Inc (G-12981)*

Unifrax Sebring S Operations, Sebring *Also Called: Refractory Specialties Inc (G-13125)*

Uniloy Century LLC 419 332-2693
 215 N Stone St Fremont (43420) *(G-7816)*

Uniloy Milacron Inc 513 487-5000
 4165 Half Acre Rd Batavia (45103) *(G-956)*

Uninterrupted LLC 216 771-2323
 3800 Embassy Pkwy Ste 360 Akron (44333) *(G-366)*

Union America, Cincinnati *Also Called: United Precision Services Inc (G-3481)*

Union Camp Corp 330 343-7701
 875 Harger St Dover (44622) *(G-6849)*

Union Carbide Corporation 216 529-3784
 11709 Madison Ave Cleveland (44107) *(G-4844)*

Union Fabricating and Mch Co 419 626-5963
 3427 Venice Rd Sandusky (44870) *(G-13099)*

Union Gospel Press Division, Middleburg Heights *Also Called: Incorprted Trstees of The Gspl (G-10721)*

Union Metal Corporation 330 456-7653
 1432 Maple Ave Ne Canton (44705) *(G-2250)*

Union Metal Industries Corp 330 456-7653
 1432 Maple Ave Ne Canton (44705) *(G-2251)*

Union Rome Sewer System, Chesapeake *Also Called: Aqua Ohio Inc (G-2472)*

Uniontown Septic Tanks Inc 330 699-3386
 2781 Raber Rd Uniontown (44685) *(G-14796)*

Uniontown Stone 740 968-4313
 72607 Gun Club Rd Flushing (43977) *(G-7588)*

Unipac Inc 740 929-2000
 2109 National Rd Sw Hebron (43025) *(G-8369)*

Uniqative LLC 800 337-2870
 5834 Monroe St Ste A-18 Sylvania (43560) *(G-14020)*

Unique Awards & Signs, Saint Marys *Also Called: Behrco Inc (G-12945)*

UNIQUE EXPRESSIONS, Gallipolis *Also Called: Riverview Productions Inc (G-7900)*

Unique Fabrications Inc 419 355-1700
 2520 Hayes Ave Fremont (43420) *(G-7817)*

Unique Packaging & Printing 440 785-6730
 9086 Goldfinch Ct Mentor (44060) *(G-10588)*

Unique Solutions, Newark *Also Called: Holophane Corporation (G-11579)*

Unisand Incorporated 330 722-0222
 1097 Industrial Pkwy Medina (44256) *(G-10390)*

Unison Industries LLC 937 426-0621
 2070 Heller Rd Alpha (45301) *(G-439)*

Unison Industries LLC 904 667-9904
 2455 Dayton Xenia Rd Dayton (45434) *(G-6175)*

Unison UCI Inc
 1111 Brookpark Rd Cleveland (44109) *(G-4845)*

Unisport Inc 419 529-4727
 2254 Stumbo Rd Ontario (44906) *(G-12096)*

Unit Sets Inc 937 840-6123
 835 S High St Hillsboro (45133) *(G-8468)*

United - Maier Signs Inc 513 681-6600
 1030 Straight St Cincinnati (45214) *(G-3478)*

United Abrasives & Welding LLC 304 996-1490
 2751 Wisemill Cir Ne Canton (44721) *(G-2252)*

United Air Specialists Inc 513 891-0400
 4440 Creek Rd Blue Ash (45242) *(G-1486)*

United Buff and Supply Co Inc 419 738-2417
 2 E Harrison St Wapakoneta (45895) *(G-15131)*

United Candle Company LLC 740 872-3248
 102 N Sundale Rd Norwich (43767) *(G-11993)*

United Chart Processors Inc 740 373-5801
 1461 Masonic Park Rd Marietta (45750) *(G-9840)*

United Components LLC (DH) 330 899-0340
 6056 Deer Park Ct Toledo (43614) *(G-14513)*

United Dairy Inc 740 373-4121
 1701 Greene St Marietta (45750) *(G-9841)*

United Dairy Inc (PA) 740 633-1451
 300 N 5th St Martins Ferry (43935) *(G-9900)*

United Dairy Company, Martins Ferry *Also Called: United Dairy Inc (G-9900)*

United Dairy Farmers Inc (PA) 513 396-8700
 3955 Montgomery Rd Cincinnati (45212) *(G-3479)*

United Dental Laboratories (PA) 330 253-1810
 261 South Ave Tallmadge (44278) *(G-14054)*

United Die & Mfg Sales Co 330 938-6141
 100 S 17th St Sebring (44672) *(G-13128)*

United Engineering & Fndry Co 330 456-2761
 1400 Grace Ave Ne Canton (44705) *(G-2253)*

United Engraving, Cincinnati *Also Called: Wood Graphics Inc (G-3525)*

United Envelope LLC 513 542-4700
 4890 Spring Grove Ave Cincinnati (45232) *(G-3480)*

ALPHABETIC SECTION — Universal Polymer & Rubber Ltd

United Extrusion Dies Inc 330 533-2915
  5171 W Western Reserve Rd Canfield (44406) *(G-2022)*

United Feed Screws Ltd 330 798-5532
  487 Wellington Ave Akron (44305) *(G-367)*

United Finshg & Die Cutng Inc 216 881-0239
  3875 King Ave Cleveland (44114) *(G-4846)*

United Grinding and Machine Co 330 453-7402
  2315 Ellis Ave Ne Canton (44705) *(G-2254)*

United Group Services Inc (PA) 800 633-9690
  9740 Near Dr West Chester (45246) *(G-15601)*

United Hardwoods Ltd 330 878-9510
  5508 Hilltop Dr Nw Strasburg (44680) *(G-13751)*

United Hydraulics 440 585-0906
  29627 Lakeland Blvd Wickliffe (44092) *(G-15856)*

United Ignition Wire Corp 216 898-1112
  15620 Industrial Pkwy Cleveland (44135) *(G-4847)*

United Initiators Inc (HQ) 440 323-3112
  555 Garden St Elyria (44035) *(G-7215)*

United Machine and Tool Inc 440 946-7677
  1956 E 337th St Eastlake (44095) *(G-7053)*

United McGill Corporation (HQ) 614 829-1200
  1 Mission Park Groveport (43125) *(G-8165)*

United McGill Corporation 614 920-1267
  122 E Columbus St Lithopolis (43136) *(G-9331)*

United Medical Supply Company 866 678-8633
  2948 Nationwide Pkwy Brunswick (44212) *(G-1797)*

United Metal Fabricators Inc 216 662-2000
  14301 Industrial Ave S Maple Heights (44137) *(G-9763)*

United Packaging Supply Co Div, Bedford Also Called: Overseas Packing LLC *(G-1148)*

United Plastic Film, Cleveland Also Called: A Aabaco Plastics Inc *(G-3577)*

United Precast Inc 740 393-1121
  400 Howard St Mount Vernon (43050) *(G-11298)*

United Precision Services Inc 513 851-6900
  11183 Southland Rd Cincinnati (45240) *(G-3481)*

United Refractories Inc 330 372-3716
  1929 Larchmont Ave Ne Warren (44483) *(G-15215)*

United Roller Co LLC 440 564-9698
  14910 Cross Creek Pkwy Newbury (44065) *(G-11638)*

United Rolls Inc (DH) 330 456-2761
  1400 Grace Ave Ne Canton (44705) *(G-2255)*

United Rotary Brush Inc 937 644-3515
  8150 Business Way Plain City (43064) *(G-12597)*

United Seal Company, Columbus Also Called: United Security Seals Inc *(G-5843)*

United Security Seals Inc (PA) 614 443-7633
  2000 Fairwood Ave Columbus (43207) *(G-5843)*

United Sport Apparel 330 722-0818
  229 Harding St Ste B Medina (44256) *(G-10391)*

United States Controls 330 758-1147
  8511 Foxwood Ct Youngstown (44514) *(G-16464)*

United States Controls, Poland Also Called: US Controls Acquisition Ltd *(G-12612)*

United States Drill Head Co 513 941-0300
  5298 River Rd Cincinnati (45233) *(G-3482)*

United States Gypsum Company 419 734-3161
  121 S Lake St Gypsum (43433) *(G-8171)*

United States Plastic Corp 419 228-2242
  1390 Neubrecht Rd Lima (45801) *(G-9299)*

United Sttes Endscopy Group In (DH) 440 639-4494
  5976 Heisley Rd Mentor (44060) *(G-10589)*

United Surface Finishing Inc 330 453-2786
  2202 Gilbert Ave Ne Canton (44705) *(G-2256)*

United Titanium, Wooster Also Called: United Titanium Inc *(G-16179)*

United Titanium Inc (PA) 330 264-2111
  3450 Old Airport Rd Wooster (44691) *(G-16179)*

United Tool and Machine Inc 937 843-5603
  490 N Main St Lakeview (43331) *(G-8961)*

United Tool Supply Inc 513 752-6000
  851 Ohio Pike Ste 101 Cincinnati (45245) *(G-2576)*

United Trade Printers LLC 614 326-4829
  94 N High St Ste 290 Dublin (43017) *(G-6955)*

United Tube Corporation 330 725-4196
  960 Lake Rd Medina (44256) *(G-10392)*

United Wheel and Hub LLC 419 483-2639
  214 Marshall Ave Sandusky (44870) *(G-13100)*

Unitrex Ltd 216 831-1900
  5060 Taylor Dr Ste D Bedford Heights (44128) *(G-1180)*

Unitus, Solon Also Called: Sensical Inc *(G-13420)*

Unity Enterprises Inc 614 231-1370
  3757 Courtright Ct Columbus (43227) *(G-5844)*

Unity Tube Inc 330 426-4282
  1862 State Route 165 East Palestine (44413) *(G-7012)*

Univar Solutions USA LLC 800 531-7106
  6000 Parkwood Pl Dublin (43016) *(G-6956)*

Univar Solutions USA LLC 513 714-5264
  4600 Dues Dr West Chester (45246) *(G-15602)*

Universal Auto Filter LLC 216 589-0198
  127 Public Sq Ste 5110 Cleveland (44114) *(G-4848)*

Universal Black Oxiding, Aurora Also Called: Universal Heat Treating Inc *(G-738)*

Universal Cargo, Cleveland Also Called: Acme Lifting Products Inc *(G-3591)*

Universal Ch Directories LLC 419 522-5011
  1150 National Pkwy Mansfield (44906) *(G-9729)*

Universal Clay Products, Sandusky Also Called: Ethima Inc *(G-13057)*

Universal Coatings Division, Twinsburg Also Called: Universal Rack & Eqp Co Inc *(G-14751)*

Universal Composite LLC 614 507-1646
  200 Kintner Pkwy Sunbury (43074) *(G-13965)*

Universal Creative Concepts, North Royalton Also Called: Universal North Inc *(G-11899)*

Universal Drect Flfllment Corp 330 650-5000
  5581 Hudson Industrial Pkwy Hudson (44236) *(G-8617)*

Universal Dsign Fbrication LLC 419 202-5269
  7319 Portland Rd Sandusky (44870) *(G-13101)*

Universal Electronics Inc 330 487-1110
  1864 Enterprise Pkwy Ste B Twinsburg (44087) *(G-14750)*

Universal Fabg Cnstr Svcs Inc 614 274-1128
  1241 Mckinley Ave Columbus (43222) *(G-5845)*

Universal Forest Products, Dayton Also Called: Idx Dayton LLC *(G-6379)*

Universal Grinding Corporation 216 631-9410
  1234 West 78th St Cleveland (44102) *(G-4849)*

Universal Heat Treating Inc 216 641-2000
  60 Samantha Dr Aurora (44202) *(G-738)*

Universal Hydraulik USA Corp 419 873-6340
  25651 Fort Meigs Rd Perrysburg (43551) *(G-12442)*

Universal Industrial Pdts Inc 419 737-9584
  1 Coreway Dr Pioneer (43554) *(G-12500)*

Universal J&Z Machine LLC 216 486-2220
  4781 E 355th St Willoughby (44094) *(G-16013)*

Universal Lettering Inc 419 238-9320
  1197 Grill Rd # B Van Wert (45891) *(G-14929)*

Universal Lettering Company, Van Wert Also Called: Universal Lettering Inc *(G-14929)*

Universal Manufacturing 816 396-0101
  9900 Clinton Rd Cleveland (44144) *(G-4850)*

Universal Metal Products Inc 419 287-3223
  850 W Front St Pemberville (43450) *(G-12336)*

Universal Metal Products Inc (PA) 440 943-3040
  29980 Lakeland Blvd Wickliffe (44092) *(G-15857)*

Universal Metals Cutting Inc 330 580-5192
  2656 Harrison Ave Sw Canton (44706) *(G-2257)*

Universal North Inc 440 230-1366
  10143 Royalton Rd Ste E North Royalton (44133) *(G-11899)*

Universal Oil Inc 216 771-4300
  265 Jefferson Ave Cleveland (44113) *(G-4851)*

Universal Packg Systems Inc 513 732-2000
  5055 State Route 276 Batavia (45103) *(G-957)*

Universal Packg Systems Inc 513 735-4777
  5069 State Route 276 Batavia (45103) *(G-958)*

Universal Packg Systems Inc 513 674-9400
  470 Northland Blvd Cincinnati (45240) *(G-3483)*

Universal Pallets Inc 614 444-1095
  611 Marion Rd Columbus (43207) *(G-5846)*

Universal Plastics, North Canton Also Called: UPL International Inc *(G-11773)*

Universal Polymer & Rubber Ltd (PA) 440 632-1691
  15730 Madison Rd Middlefield (44062) *(G-10795)*

Universal Polymer & Rubber Ltd 330 633-1666
  165 Northeast Ave Tallmadge (44278) *(G-14055)*

Universal Production Corp. 740 522-1147
1776 Tamarack Rd Newark (43055) *(G-11610)*

Universal Rack & Eqp Co Inc 330 963-6776
8511 Tower Dr Twinsburg (44087) *(G-14751)*

Universal Rubber & Plastics, Tallmadge Also Called: Universal Polymer & Rubber Ltd *(G-14055)*

Universal Scientific Inc 440 428-1777
6210 Campbell Dr Madison (44057) *(G-9595)*

Universal Screen Arts Inc (PA) 330 650-5000
5581 Hudson Industrial Pkwy Hudson (44236) *(G-8618)*

Universal Steel Company 216 883-4972
6600 Grant Ave Cleveland (44105) *(G-4852)*

Universal Tool Co, Dayton Also Called: Precision Machining Services *(G-6513)*

Universal Tool Technology LLC 937 222-4608
3488 Stop 8 Rd Dayton (45414) *(G-6640)*

Universal Urethane Pdts Inc 419 693-7400
410 1st St Toledo (43605) *(G-14514)*

Universal Veneer Mill Corp 740 522-1147
1776 Tamarack Rd Newark (43055) *(G-11611)*

Universal Veneer Sales Corp (PA) 740 522-1147
1776 Tamarack Rd Newark (43055) *(G-11612)*

Universal Well Services Inc 814 333-2656
11 S Washington St Millersburg (44654) *(G-11002)*

University Hring Aid Assctions, Cincinnati Also Called: Communications Aid Inc *(G-2783)*

University of Toledo 419 530-2311
2801 W Bancroft St Toledo (43606) *(G-14515)*

University Sports Publications 614 291-6416
1265 Indianola Ave Columbus (43201) *(G-5847)*

Uniwall Mfg Co (HQ) 330 875-1444
3750 Beck Ave Louisville (44641) *(G-9472)*

Unlimited Energy Services LLC 304 517-7097
19371 State Route 60 Beverly (45715) *(G-1322)*

Unlimited Machine and Tool LLC 419 269-1730
5139 Tractor Rd Ste C Toledo (43612) *(G-14516)*

Unlimted Rcovery Solutions LLC 419 868-4888
2701 S Eberd Rd Ste B Wauseon (43567) *(G-15276)*

Unverferth, Kalida Also Called: Unverferth Mfg Co Inc *(G-8787)*

Unverferth Mfg Co Inc (PA) 419 532-3121
601 S Broad St Kalida (45853) *(G-8787)*

UPA Technology Inc 513 755-1380
8963 Cincinnati Columbus Rd West Chester (45069) *(G-15522)*

Updike Supply Company 937 482-4000
8241 Expansion Way Huber Heights (45424) *(G-8580)*

UPL International Inc 330 433-2860
7661 Freedom Ave Nw North Canton (44720) *(G-11773)*

Upper Arlington Crew Inc 614 485-0089
5257 Sinclair Rd Columbus (43229) *(G-5848)*

Upper State Fuel Inc 419 843-5931
2433 Wimbledon Park Blvd Toledo (43617) *(G-14517)*

Upright Press LLC 614 619-7337
2060 S High St Columbus (43207) *(G-5849)*

Upright Steel LLC 216 923-0852
1335 E 171st St Cleveland (44110) *(G-4853)*

Upright Steel Fabricators LLC 216 923-0852
1335 E 171st St Cleveland (44110) *(G-4854)*

Uprising Food Inc 513 313-1087
4200 Plainville Rd Cincinnati (45227) *(G-3484)*

UPS, Ashland Also Called: UPS Store *(G-619)*

UPS Store 419 289-6688
1130 E Main St Ashland (44805) *(G-619)*

UPS Store 7395, Cincinnati Also Called: Cree Logistics LLC *(G-2802)*

Upshift, Cincinnati Also Called: Upshift Work LLC *(G-3485)*

Upshift Work LLC 513 813-5695
2300 Montana Ave Ste 301 Cincinnati (45211) *(G-3485)*

Urban Hershberger 330 763-0407
8260 Township Road 652 Millersburg (44654) *(G-11003)*

Urban Industries, Galion Also Called: Urban Industries of Ohio Inc *(G-7886)*

Urban Industries of Ohio Inc 419 468-3578
525 King Ave Galion (44833) *(G-7886)*

Urban Pine Winery, Maumee Also Called: McAlear Winery LLC *(G-10219)*

Urbn Timber LLC 614 981-3043
29 Kingston Ave Columbus (43207) *(G-5850)*

Urc, Chagrin Falls Also Called: Utility Relay Co Ltd *(G-2431)*

Urethane Polymers Intl (HQ) 216 430-3655
3800 E 91st St Cleveland (44105) *(G-4855)*

US Aeroteam Inc 937 458-0344
2601 W Stroop Rd Ste 60 Dayton (45439) *(G-6641)*

US Coexcell Inc 419 897-9110
640 Mingo Dr Maumee (43537) *(G-10243)*

US Controls Acquisition Ltd 330 758-1147
8511 Foxwood Ct Poland (44514) *(G-12612)*

US Cotton LLC 216 676-6400
15501 Industrial Pkwy Cleveland (44135) *(G-4856)*

US Endoscopy, Mentor Also Called: United Sttes Endscopy Group In *(G-10589)*

US Filter, Pickerington Also Called: Evoqua Water Technologies LLC *(G-12461)*

US Fittings Inc 234 212-9420
2182 E Aurora Rd Twinsburg (44087) *(G-14752)*

US Footwear Holdings LLC 740 753-9100
39 E Canal St Nelsonville (45764) *(G-11360)*

US Group, East Palestine Also Called: E R Advanced Ceramics Inc *(G-7004)*

US Kondo Corporation 937 916-3045
233 1st St Piqua (45356) *(G-12557)*

US Lighting Group Inc 216 896-7000
1148 E 222nd St Euclid (44117) *(G-7305)*

US Metalcraft Inc 419 692-4962
101 S Franklin St Delphos (45833) *(G-6776)*

US Refractory Products LLC 440 386-4580
7660 Race Rd North Ridgeville (44039) *(G-11862)*

US Technology Corporation 330 455-1181
4200 Munson St Nw Canton (44718) *(G-2258)*

US Technology Media Inc 330 874-3094
509 Water St Sw Bolivar (44612) *(G-1540)*

US Tsubaki Power Transm LLC 419 626-4560
1010 Edgewater Ave Sandusky (44870) *(G-1312)*

US Tubular Products Inc 330 832-1734
14852 Lincoln Way W North Lawrence (44666) *(G-11800)*

US Water Company LLC 740 453-0604
1115 Newark Rd Zanesville (43701) *(G-16567)*

US Welding Training LLC 440 669-9380
518 5th St Fairport Harbor (44077) *(G-7459)*

US Yachiyo Inc 740 375-4687
1177 Kellogg Pkwy Marion (43302) *(G-9888)*

USA Instruments Inc 330 562-1000
1515 Danner Dr Aurora (44202) *(G-739)*

USA Quickprint Inc (PA) 330 455-5119
409 3rd St Sw Canton (44702) *(G-2259)*

USA Rolls, Canfield Also Called: Alstart Enterprises LLC *(G-1998)*

Usalco, Fairfield Also Called: Usalco Michigan City Plant LLC *(G-7422)*

Usalco Fairfield Plant LLC 513 737-7100
3700 Dixie Hwy Fairfield (45014) *(G-7421)*

Usalco Michigan City Plant LLC 513 737-7100
3700 Dixie Hwy Fairfield (45014) *(G-7422)*

USB Corporation 216 765-5000
26111 Miles Rd Cleveland (44128) *(G-4857)*

User Friendly Phone Book LLC 216 674-6500
2 Summit Park Dr Ste 105 Independence (44131) *(G-8689)*

Usm Precision Products Inc 440 975-8600
1340 Lloyd Rd Ste D Wickliffe (44092) *(G-15855)*

Ustek Incorporated 614 538-8000
4663 Executive Dr Ste 3 Columbus (43220) *(G-5851)*

Usui International Corporation 513 448-0410
88 Partnership Way Sharonville (45241) *(G-13134)*

Usui International Corporation 734 354-3626
8748 Jacquemin Dr Ste 100 West Chester (45069) *(G-15523)*

Utahamerican Energy Inc 435 888-4000
153 Highway 7 S Powhatan Point (43942) *(G-12385)*

Utica East Ohio Midstream LLC 740 431-4168
8349 Azalea Rd Sw Dennison (44621) *(G-6796)*

Utica East Ohio Midstream LLC 740 945-2226
117 Fowler Ave Scio (43988) *(G-13113)*

Utilco Div, Cincinnati Also Called: Ilsco LLC *(G-2317)*

Utility Relay Co Ltd 440 708-1000
10100 Queens Way Chagrin Falls (44023) *(G-2431)*

ALPHABETIC SECTION

Utility Wire Products Inc 216 441-2180
3302 E 87th St Cleveland (44127) *(G-4858)*

Uvonics Co 614 458-1163
1078 Goodale Blvd Columbus (43212) *(G-5852)*

V & A Process Inc 440 288-8137
2345 E 28th St Lorain (44055) *(G-9442)*

V & C Enterprises Co 614 221-1412
41 S Grant Ave Columbus (43215) *(G-5853)*

V & M Star LP 330 742-6300
2669 Martin Luther King Jr Blvd Youngstown (44510) *(G-16465)*

V & S Schuler Engineering Inc (DH) 330 452-5200
2240 Allen Ave Se Canton (44707) *(G-2260)*

V & S Schuler Engineering Inc 330 452-5200
15175 Kinsman Rd Middlefield (44062) *(G-10796)*

V H Cooper & Co Inc (HQ) 419 375-4116
2321 State Route 49 Fort Recovery (45846) *(G-7626)*

V H Cooper & Co Inc 419 678-4853
1 Cooper Farm Dr Saint Henry (45883) *(G-12940)*

V H Cooper & Co Inc 419 678-4853
1 Cooper Farm Dr Saint Henry (45883) *(G-12941)*

V K C Inc 440 951-9634
7667 Jenther Dr Mentor (44060) *(G-10590)*

V Metro, Fairborn *Also Called: Vmetro Inc (G-7326)*

V P, Newton Falls *Also Called: Venture Plastics Inc (G-11660)*

V S I, Massillon *Also Called: Vehicle Systems Inc (G-10153)*

V-I-S-c-e-r-o-t-o-n-i-c Inc 330 690-3355
118 W Market St Akron (44303) *(G-368)*

VA Technology, Solon *Also Called: Versatile Automation Tech Ltd (G-13442)*

Vacono America LLC 216 938-7428
1163 E 40th St Ste 301 Cleveland (44114) *(G-4859)*

Vacuform Inc 330 938-9674
500 Courtney Rd Sebring (44672) *(G-13129)*

Vacuum Electric Switch Co Inc (PA) 330 374-5156
3900 Mogadore Industrial Pkwy Mogadore (44260) *(G-11089)*

Vadose Syn Fuels Inc 330 564-0545
323 S Main St Munroe Falls (44262) *(G-11307)*

Vail Rubber Works Inc 513 705-2060
605 Clark St Middletown (45042) *(G-10869)*

Val Casting Inc 419 562-2499
108 E Rensselaer St Bucyrus (44820) *(G-1871)*

Val Products, Coldwater *Also Called: Val-Co Pax Inc (G-5003)*

Val-Co Pax Inc (DH) 717 354-4586
210 E Main St Coldwater (45828) *(G-5003)*

Val-Con Inc 440 357-1898
7201 Hermitage Rd Concord Township (44077) *(G-5913)*

Valco Cincinnati Inc (PA) 513 874-6550
411 Circle Freeway Dr West Chester (45246) *(G-15603)*

Valco Division, North Royalton *Also Called: Valley Tool & Die Inc (G-11900)*

Valco Industries LLC 937 399-7400
625 Burt St Springfield (45505) *(G-13653)*

Valco Melton, West Chester *Also Called: Valco Cincinnati Inc (G-15603)*

Valco Melton Inc 513 874-6550
497 Circle Freeway Dr Ste 490 West Chester (45246) *(G-15604)*

Valen Foundry Inc 724 712-3500
7259 Leemel Dr West Chester (45069) *(G-15524)*

Valensil Technologies LLC 440 937-8181
34910 Commerce Way Avon (44011) *(G-790)*

Valentine Research Inc 513 984-8900
10280 Alliance Rd Blue Ash (45242) *(G-1487)*

Valgroup LLC 419 423-6500
3441 N Main St Findlay (45840) *(G-7576)*

Valgroup North America Inc (PA) 419 423-6500
3441 N Main St Findlay (45840) *(G-7577)*

Valley, Toronto *Also Called: Valley Converting Co Inc (G-14537)*

Valley Asphalt Corporation (HQ) 513 771-0820
11641 Mosteller Rd Cincinnati (45241) *(G-3486)*

Valley Asphalt Corporation 513 381-0652
4850 Stubbs Mills Rd Morrow (45152) *(G-11226)*

Valley Concrete, Carrollton *Also Called: Ernst Enterprises Inc (G-2306)*

Valley Concrete Division, Fairborn *Also Called: Ernst Enterprises Inc (G-7313)*

Valley Containers Inc 330 544-2244
3515 Union St Mineral Ridge (44440) *(G-11024)*

Valley Converting Co Inc (PA) 740 537-2152
405 Daniels St Toronto (43964) *(G-14537)*

Valley Electric Company 419 332-6405
432 N Wood St Fremont (43420) *(G-7818)*

Valley Machine Tool Inc 513 899-2737
9773 Morrow Cozaddale Rd Morrow (45152) *(G-11227)*

Valley Mining Inc 740 922-3942
4412 Pleasant Valley Rd Se Dennison (44621) *(G-6797)*

Valley Plastics Company Inc 419 666-2349
399 Phillips Ave Toledo (43612) *(G-14518)*

Valley Tool & Die Inc 440 237-0160
10020 York Theta Dr North Royalton (44133) *(G-11900)*

Valley Trailers, Leesburg *Also Called: Creative Fab & Welding LLC (G-9123)*

Valley View Pallets LLC 740 599-0010
22414 Hostetler Rd Danville (43014) *(G-6149)*

Valley View Pallets Partners, Danville *Also Called: Valley View Pallets LLC (G-6149)*

Valley Vitamins II Inc 330 533-0051
4449 Easton Way Fl 2 Columbus (43219) *(G-5854)*

Valleyview Wood Turning Co, Millersburg *Also Called: Urban Hershberger (G-11003)*

Vallourec Star LP 330 742-6227
706 S State St Girard (44420) *(G-7976)*

Vallourec Star LP (HQ) 330 742-6300
2669 Martin Luther King Jr Blvd Youngstown (44510) *(G-16466)*

Valmac Industries Inc 937 890-5558
825 Scholz Dr Vandalia (45377) *(G-14964)*

Valspar, Medina *Also Called: Plasti-Kote Co Inc (G-10363)*

Valtris, Independence *Also Called: Polymer Additives Holdings Inc (G-8680)*

Valtris Specialty Chemicals 216 875-7200
7050 Krick Rd Walton Hills (44146) *(G-15104)*

Valtronic Technology Inc 440 349-1239
29200 Fountain Pkwy Solon (44139) *(G-13441)*

Value Added Packaging Inc 937 832-9595
44 Lau Pkwy Englewood (45315) *(G-7247)*

Value-Rooter, Elyria *Also Called: Personal Plumber Service Corp (G-7195)*

Valued Relationships Inc 800 860-4230
1400 Commerce Center Dr Ste B Franklin (45005) *(G-7708)*

Valutex Reinforcements Inc 800 251-2507
2302 Kenskill Ave Wshngtn Ct Hs (43160) *(G-16243)*

Valv-Trol LLC 330 686-2800
1340 Commerce Dr Stow (44224) *(G-13736)*

Valve Related Controls Inc 513 677-8724
143 Commerce Dr Loveland (45140) *(G-9507)*

Valvsys LLC 513 870-1234
2 Rowe Ct Hamilton (45015) *(G-8256)*

Vam Usa Llc 330 742-3130
1053 Ohio Works Dr Youngstown (44510) *(G-16467)*

Van Dyke Custom Iron Inc 614 860-9300
700 Janice Ln Pickerington (43147) *(G-12472)*

Van Engineering Co, Cincinnati *Also Called: R Vandewalle Inc (G-3322)*

Van Orders Pallet Company Inc 419 875-6932
5188 County Road 424 Liberty Center (43532) *(G-9205)*

Van Tilburg Farms Inc 419 586-3077
8398 Celina Mendon Rd Celina (45822) *(G-2354)*

Van Wert Division, Van Wert *Also Called: Tecumseh Packg Solutions Inc (G-14927)*

Van Wert Machine Inc 419 692-6836
210 E Cleveland St Delphos (45833) *(G-6777)*

Van Wert Pallets LLC 419 203-1823
9042 John Brown Rd Van Wert (45891) *(G-14930)*

Van-Griner LLC 419 733-7951
1009 Delta Ave Cincinnati (45208) *(G-3487)*

Van-Griner LLC 419 733-7951
1 Executive Pkwy Minster (45865) *(G-11064)*

Vanamatic Company 419 692-6085
701 Ambrose Dr Delphos (45833) *(G-6778)*

Vandalia Massage Therapy 937 890-8660
147 W National Rd Vandalia (45377) *(G-14965)*

Vandalia Sportswear LLC 937 264-3204
515 S Dixie Dr Vandalia (45377) *(G-14966)*

Vandava Inc 614 277-8003
4094 Broadway Grove City (43123) *(G-8128)*

Vanex Tube Corporation... 330 544-9500
  301 Mckees Ln Ste 2 Niles (44446) **(G-11690)**
Vanguard Paints and Finishes Inc............................... 740 373-5261
  1409 Greene St Marietta (45750) **(G-9842)**
Vanner, Hilliard Also Called: Vanner Holdings Inc **(G-8451)**
Vanner Holdings Inc.. 614 771-2718
  4282 Reynolds Dr Hilliard (43026) **(G-8451)**
Vanscoyk Sheet Metal Corp...................................... 937 845-0581
  475 Quick Rd New Carlisle (45344) **(G-11429)**
Vantage Spclty Ingredients Inc................................. 937 264-1222
  707 Harco Dr Englewood (45315) **(G-7248)**
Vantilburg Farms, Celina Also Called: Van Tilburg Farms Inc **(G-2354)**
Vapor Pin Enterprises Inc.. 614 504-6915
  7750 Corporate Blvd Plain City (43064) **(G-12598)**
Varbros LLC (PA)... 216 267-5200
  16025 Brookpark Rd Cleveland (44142) **(G-4860)**
Varco LP.. 330 746-2922
  2669 Martin Luther King Jr Blvd Youngstown (44510) **(G-16468)**
Vari-Wall Tube Specialists Inc.................................... 330 482-0000
  1350 Wardingsley Ave Columbiana (44408) **(G-5053)**
Variety Glass Inc.. 740 432-3643
  201 Foster Ave Cambridge (43725) **(G-1959)**
Varland Metal Service Inc.. 513 861-0555
  3231 Fredonia Ave Cincinnati (45229) **(G-3488)**
Varland Plating Company, Cincinnati Also Called: Varland Metal Service Inc **(G-3488)**
Varmland Inc.. 216 741-1510
  1200 Brookpark Rd Cleveland (44109) **(G-4861)**
Ve Global Vending Inc.. 216 785-2611
  8700 Brookpark Rd Cleveland (44129) **(G-4862)**
Vector Electromagnetics LLC..................................... 937 478-5904
  1245 Airport Rd Wilmington (45177) **(G-16062)**
Vector International Corp... 440 942-2002
  7404 Tyler Blvd Mentor (44060) **(G-10591)**
Vector Mechanical LLC... 216 337-4042
  10917 Dale Ave Cleveland (44111) **(G-4863)**
Vector Screenprinting & EMB, Mentor Also Called: Vector International Corp **(G-10591)**
Vectra Inc.. 614 351-6868
  3950 Business Park Dr Columbus (43204) **(G-5855)**
Vectra Visual, Columbus Also Called: Vectra Inc **(G-5855)**
Vectron Inc.. 440 323-3369
  201 Perry Ct Elyria (44035) **(G-7216)**
Vedda Printing, Cleveland Also Called: Phil Vedda & Sons Inc **(G-4546)**
Veeam Government Solutions LLC............................ 614 339-8200
  8800 Lyra Dr Ste 350 Columbus (43240) **(G-5071)**
Veeam Software Corporation (PA)........................... 614 339-8200
  8800 Lyra Dr Ste 350 Columbus (43240) **(G-5072)**
Veepak OH LLC... 740 927-9002
  9040 Smiths Mill Rd New Albany (43054) **(G-11393)**
Vega Americas Inc (HQ)... 513 272-0131
  3877 Mason Research Pkwy Lebanon (45036) **(G-9119)**
Vegv, Cleveland Also Called: Ve Global Vending Inc **(G-4862)**
Vehicle Systems Inc... 330 854-0535
  7130 Lutz Ave Nw Massillon (44646) **(G-10153)**
Vehtek Systems Inc... 419 373-8741
  2125 Wood Bridge Blvd Bowling Green (43402) **(G-1594)**
Veitsch-Radex America LLC...................................... 717 793-7122
  4741 Kister Ct Ashtabula (44004) **(G-663)**
Velocity Concept Dev Group LLC.............................. 740 685-2637
  8824 Clay Pike Byesville (43723) **(G-1901)**
Velocity Concept Dev Group LLC (PA)...................... 513 204-2100
  4393 Digital Way Mason (45040) **(G-10067)**
Velocys Inc.. 614 733-3300
  8520 Warner Rd Plain City (43064) **(G-12599)**
Velvet Ice Cream Company...................................... 419 562-2009
  1233 Whetstone St Bucyrus (44820) **(G-1872)**
Velvet Ice Cream Company (PA).............................. 740 892-3921
  11324 Mount Vernon Rd Utica (43080) **(G-14859)**
Velvetflow, Hannibal Also Called: Ormet Primary Aluminum Corp **(G-8262)**
Venco Manufacturing Inc... 513 772-8448
  12110 Best Pl Cincinnati (45241) **(G-3489)**
Venco Venturo Industries LLC (PA)........................... 513 772-8448
  12110 Best Pl Cincinnati (45241) **(G-3490)**

Venco/Venturo Div, Cincinnati Also Called: Venco Venturo Industries LLC **(G-3490)**
Vengeance Is Mine LLC.. 614 670-4745
  4612 Sawmill Rd Columbus (43220) **(G-5856)**
Ventari Corporation... 937 278-4269
  8641 Washington Church Rd Miamisburg (45342) **(G-10697)**
Ventco Inc... 440 834-8888
  66 Windward Way Chagrin Falls (44023) **(G-2432)**
Venti-Now... 513 334-3375
  9891 Montgomery Rd Ste 302 Montgomery (45242) **(G-11132)**
Ventilation Systems Jsc... 513 348-3853
  400 Murray Rd Cincinnati (45217) **(G-3491)**
Ventra Sandusky LLC... 419 627-3600
  3020 Tiffin Ave Sandusky (44870) **(G-13103)**
Vents - US, Cincinnati Also Called: Ventilation Systems Jsc **(G-3491)**
Vents US, Cincinnati Also Called: Bodor Vents Inc **(G-2674)**
Venture, Dayton Also Called: Venture Mfg Co **(G-6642)**
Venture Medical, Plain City Also Called: Bahler Medical Inc **(G-12564)**
Venture Mfg Co... 937 233-8792
  3636 Dayton Park Dr Dayton (45414) **(G-6642)**
Venture Packaging Inc... 419 465-2534
  311 Monroe St Monroeville (44847) **(G-11127)**
Venture Packaging Midwest Inc................................ 419 465-2534
  311 Monroe St Monroeville (44847) **(G-11128)**
Venture Plastics Inc (PA)... 330 872-5774
  4000 Warren Rd Newton Falls (44444) **(G-11660)**
Venture Products Inc... 330 683-0075
  500 Venture Dr Orrville (44667) **(G-12160)**
Venturo Manufacturing Inc...................................... 513 772-8448
  12110 Best Pl Cincinnati (45241) **(G-3492)**
Venu On 3rd... 937 222-2891
  905 E 3rd St Dayton (45402) **(G-6643)**
Venue Lifestyle & Event Guide.................................. 513 405-6822
  11959 Tramway Dr Cincinnati (45241) **(G-3493)**
Veolia Wts Systems Usa Inc.................................... 513 794-1010
  11799 Enterprise Dr Cincinnati (45241) **(G-3494)**
Veolia Wts Systems Usa Inc.................................... 330 929-1639
  887 Hampshire Rd Ste I Stow (44224) **(G-13737)**
Veoneer Brake Systems LLC..................................... 419 425-6725
  2001 Industrial Dr Findlay (45840) **(G-7578)**
Ver Mich Ltd... 330 493-7330
  4210 Cleveland Ave Nw Canton (44709) **(G-2267)**
Ver-Mac Industries Inc... 740 397-6511
  100 Progress Dr Mount Vernon (43050) **(G-11299)**
Verantis Corporation (PA)....................................... 440 243-0700
  7251 Engle Rd Ste 300 Middleburg Heights (44130) **(G-10728)**
Verdin Company, Cincinnati Also Called: I T Verdin Co **(G-3015)**
Verdin Organ Division... 513 502-2333
  1118 Pendleton St Ste 410 Cincinnati (45202) **(G-3495)**
Verhoff Alfalfa Mills Inc (PA).................................... 419 523-4767
  1188 Sugar Mill Dr Ottawa (45875) **(G-12195)**
Verhoff Machine & Welding Inc................................ 419 596-3202
  7300 Road 18 Continental (45831) **(G-5939)**
Veriano Fine Foods Spirits Ltd.................................. 614 745-7705
  5175 Zarley St Ste A New Albany (43054) **(G-11394)**
Verifone Inc... 800 837-4366
  855 Grandview Ave Ste 110 Columbus (43215) **(G-5857)**
Veritiv... 614 323-3335
  2344 Limestone Way Columbus (43228) **(G-5858)**
Verizon Business, Kenton Also Called: Mci Inc **(G-8889)**
Vermilion Custom Canvas Inc................................... 440 963-5483
  4523 Liberty Ave Vermilion (44089) **(G-14974)**
Vermilion Valley Vineyards LLC................................ 440 935-1363
  29457 Hummingbird Cir Westlake (44145) **(G-15199)**
Vernay Manufacturing Inc (HQ)............................... 937 767-7261
  120 E South College St Yellow Springs (45387) **(G-16286)**
Verona Agriculture Center, Verona Also Called: Keystone Cooperative Inc **(G-14975)**
Versa Tech Technologies, Apple Creek Also Called: Versi-Tech Incorporated **(G-512)**
Versa-Pak Ltd.. 419 586-5466
  500 Staeger Rd Celina (45822) **(G-2355)**
Versailles Building Supply.. 937 526-3238
  741 N Center St Versailles (45380) **(G-14990)**

ALPHABETIC SECTION

Versalift East Inc.. 610 866-1400
   4884 Corporate St Sw Canton (44706) *(G-2262)*

VERSALIFT EAST, INC., Canton Also Called: Versalift East Inc *(G-2262)*

Versatile Automation Tech Corp.............................. 330 220-2600
   2853 Westway Dr Brunswick (44212) *(G-1798)*

Versatile Automation Tech Ltd................................ 440 589-6700
   30355 Solon Industrial Pkwy Solon (44139) *(G-13442)*

Versatile Machine... 330 618-9895
   402 Commerce St Tallmadge (44278) *(G-14056)*

Versi-Tech Incorporated... 586 944-2230
   32 Hunter St Apple Creek (44606) *(G-512)*

Versitec Manufacturing Inc..................................... 440 354-4283
   152 Elevator Ave Painesville (44077) *(G-12274)*

Versitech Mold Div, Akron Also Called: Saehwa IMC Na Inc *(G-323)*

Verso Paper, West Chester Also Called: Billerud Americas Corporation *(G-15379)*

Verso Paper Inc.. 901 369-4100
   8540 Gander Creek Dr Miamisburg (45342) *(G-10698)*

Verso Quinnesec Rep LLC (DH)............................... 901 369-4100
   8540 Gander Creek Dr Miamisburg (45342) *(G-10699)*

Verstrete In Mold Lbels USA In.............................. 513 943-0080
   4101 Founders Blvd Batavia (45103) *(G-959)*

Vertex Inc... 330 628-6230
   3956 Mogadore Industrial Pkwy Mogadore (44260) *(G-11090)*

Vertical Data LLC... 330 289-0313
   2169 Chuckery Ln Akron (44333) *(G-369)*

Vertiflo Pump Company... 513 530-0888
   7807 Redsky Dr Cincinnati (45249) *(G-3496)*

Vertiv, Ironton Also Called: Vertiv Corporation *(G-8705)*

Vertiv, Lorain Also Called: Vertiv Energy Systems Inc *(G-9443)*

Vertiv Co., Westerville Also Called: Vertiv Group Corporation *(G-15687)*

Vertiv Corporation.. 614 491-9286
   5350 Centerpoint Pkwy Groveport (43125) *(G-8166)*

Vertiv Corporation.. 740 547-5100
   3040 S 9th St Ironton (45638) *(G-8705)*

Vertiv Corporation.. 614 888-0246
   1595 London Groveport Rd Lockbourne (43137) *(G-9341)*

Vertiv Corporation (DH).. 614 888-0246
   505 N Cleveland Ave Westerville (43082) *(G-15686)*

Vertiv Energy Systems Inc...................................... 440 288-1122
   1510 Kansas Ave Lorain (44052) *(G-9443)*

Vertiv Group Corporation.. 440 460-3600
   5900 Landerbrook Dr Ste 300 Cleveland (44124) *(G-4864)*

Vertiv Group Corporation.. 440 288-1122
   1510 Kansas Ave Lorain (44052) *(G-9444)*

Vertiv Group Corporation (DH).............................. 614 888-0246
   505 N Cleveland Ave Westerville (43082) *(G-15687)*

Vertiv Holdings Co (PA)... 614 888-0246
   505 N Cleveland Ave Westerville (43082) *(G-15688)*

Vertiv JV Holdings LLC... 614 888-0246
   1050 Dearborn Dr Columbus (43085) *(G-5859)*

Vesco LLC.. 330 374-5156
   3900 Mogadore Industrial Pkwy Mogadore (44260) *(G-11091)*

Vesco Medical LLC... 614 914-5991
   60 Collegeview Rd Ste 144 Westerville (43081) *(G-15723)*

Vesi, Cincinnati Also Called: Vesi Incorporated *(G-3497)*

Vesi Incorporated.. 513 563-6002
   7289 Kirkridge Dr Cincinnati (45233) *(G-3497)*

Vestcom Retail Solutions, Lewis Center Also Called: Electronic Imaging Svcs Inc *(G-9159)*

Veterans Representative Co LLC............................ 330 779-0768
   1584 Tamarisk Trl Youngstown (44514) *(G-16469)*

Veterans Steel Inc.. 216 938-7476
   900 E 69th St Cleveland (44103) *(G-4865)*

Vetgraft LLC.. 614 203-0603
   7590 Brandon Rd New Albany (43054) *(G-11395)*

Vexos Inc.. 440 284-2500
   110 Commerce Dr Lagrange (44050) *(G-8957)*

Vexos Electronic Mfg Svcs, Lagrange Also Called: Vexos Inc *(G-8957)*

Vgs Inc... 216 431-7800
   2239 E 55th St Cleveland (44103) *(G-4866)*

Vgu Industries Inc.. 216 676-9203
   4747 Manufacturing Ave Cleveland (44135) *(G-4867)*

Viavi Solutions Inc... 316 522-4981
   8740 Orion Pl Ste 100 Columbus (43240) *(G-5073)*

Vib-ISO, Wooster Also Called: Vib-Iso LLC *(G-16180)*

Vib-Iso LLC.. 800 735-9645
   449 Freedlander Rd Wooster (44691) *(G-16180)*

Vibra Finish Co... 513 870-6300
   8411 Seward Rd Fairfield (45011) *(G-7423)*

Vibrantz Color Solutions Inc (DH).......................... 440 997-5137
   2600 Michigan Ave Ashtabula (44004) *(G-664)*

Vibrantz Corporation.. 216 875-6213
   4150 E 56th St Cleveland (44105) *(G-4868)*

Vibrantz Corporation.. 724 207-2152
   4150 E 56th St Cleveland (44105) *(G-4869)*

Vibrantz Corporation.. 442 224-6100
   6060 Parkland Blvd Ste 250 Cleveland (44124) *(G-4870)*

Vibrantz Corporation.. 216 875-5600
   6060 Parkland Blvd Cleveland (44124) *(G-4871)*

Vibrantz Corporation (DH)...................................... 216 875-5600
   6060 Parkland Blvd Ste 250 Mayfield Heights (44124) *(G-10256)*

Vibrantz Technologies Inc....................................... 330 765-4378
   1560 N Main St Orrville (44667) *(G-12161)*

Vibrodyne Division, Moraine Also Called: Tailored Systems Inc *(G-11213)*

Vibronic... 937 274-1114
   5208 Wadsworth Rd Dayton (45414) *(G-6644)*

Vic Maroscher.. 330 332-4958
   36135 Salem Grange Rd Salem (44460) *(G-13036)*

Vicart Prcsion Fabricators Inc................................ 614 771-0080
   4101 Leap Rd Hilliard (43026) *(G-8452)*

Vicas Manufacturing Co Inc.................................... 513 791-7741
   8407 Monroe Ave Cincinnati (45236) *(G-3498)*

Vickers International Inc.. 419 867-2200
   3000 Strayer Rd Maumee (43537) *(G-10244)*

Vicon Fabricating Company Ltd.............................. 440 205-6700
   7200 Justin Way Mentor (44060) *(G-10592)*

Vics Turning Coinc.. 216 531-5016
   16911 Saint Clair Ave Cleveland (44110) *(G-4872)*

Victaulic.. 513 479-1764
   3605 Springlake Cir Loveland (45140) *(G-9508)*

Victor, Cincinnati Also Called: Vy Inc *(G-3505)*

Victor McKenzie Drlg Co Inc.................................. 740 453-0834
   3596 Maple Ave Ste A Zanesville (43701) *(G-16568)*

Victor Organ Company.. 330 792-1321
   5340 Mahoning Ave Youngstown (44515) *(G-16470)*

Victorias Secret Service Co, Reynoldsburg Also Called: Vs Service Company LLC *(G-12780)*

Victory Direct LLC.. 614 626-0000
   750 Cross Pointe Rd Ste M Gahanna (43230) *(G-7852)*

Victory Postcards Inc... 614 764-8975
   6129 Balmoral Dr Dublin (43017) *(G-6957)*

Victory Postcards & Souvenirs, Dublin Also Called: Victory Postcards Inc *(G-6957)*

Victory White Metal Company................................ 216 641-2575
   7930 Jones Rd Cleveland (44105) *(G-4873)*

Victory White Metal Company (PA)....................... 216 271-1400
   6100 Roland Ave Cleveland (44127) *(G-4874)*

Victory White Metal Company................................ 216 271-1400
   3027 E 55th St Cleveland (44127) *(G-4875)*

Video Products Inc... 330 562-2622
   1275 Danner Dr Aurora (44202) *(G-740)*

Viewpoint Graphic Design....................................... 419 447-6073
   132 S Washington St Tiffin (44883) *(G-14114)*

Viewray Inc (PA).. 440 703-3210
   2 Thermo Fisher Way Oakwood Village (44146) *(G-12045)*

Viewray Technologies Inc (HQ)............................. 440 703-3210
   2 Thermo Fisher Way Oakwood Village (44146) *(G-12046)*

Viking Fabricators Inc.. 740 374-5246
   2021 Hanna Rd Marietta (45750) *(G-9843)*

Viking Forge LLC... 330 562-3366
   4500 Crane Centre Dr Streetsboro (44241) *(G-13797)*

Viking Paper, Toledo Also Called: Tex-Tyler Corporation *(G-14484)*

Viking Paper Company (PA)................................... 419 729-4951
   5148 Stickney Ave Toledo (43612) *(G-14519)*

Viking Well Service Inc.. 681 205-1999
   64201 Wintergreen Rd Lore City (43755) *(G-9447)*

Village Cabinet Shop Inc 704 966-0801
  1820 Loisview Ln Cincinnati (45255) *(G-3499)*
Village of Ansonia 937 337-5741
  700 W Canal St Greenville (45331) *(G-8063)*
Village of Grafton 440 926-2075
  1013 Chestnut St Grafton (44044) *(G-8006)*
Village Plastics Co 330 753-0100
  23610 Saint Clair Ave Euclid (44117) *(G-7306)*
Village Reporter 419 485-4851
  115 Broad St Montpelier (43543) *(G-11144)*
Village Woodworking 740 326-4461
  8033 Ridge Rd Fredericktown (43019) *(G-7758)*
Vincent Rx LLC 740 678-2384
  8465 State Route 339 Vincent (45784) *(G-15010)*
Vindicator 330 841-1600
  240 Franklin St Se Warren (44483) *(G-15216)*
Vindy.com., Youngstown *Also Called: The Vindicator Printing Company (G-16454)*
Vino Bellissimo 419 296-4267
  2412 Cable Ct Lima (45805) *(G-9300)*
Vino Di Piccin LLC 740 738-0261
  55155 National Rd Lansing (43934) *(G-9050)*
Vinoklet Winery Inc 513 385-9309
  11069 Colerain Rd Cincinnati (45252) *(G-3500)*
Vintage Automotive Elc Inc 419 472-9349
  3335 Mcgregor Ln Toledo (43623) *(G-14520)*
Vintage Heating and Air, Toledo *Also Called: Vintage Automotive Elc Inc (G-14520)*
Vintage Wine Distributor Inc 513 443-4300
  9422 Meridian Way West Chester (45069) *(G-15525)*
Vinyl Design Corporation 419 283-4009
  7856 Hill Ave Holland (43528) *(G-8536)*
Vinyl Graphics, Cleveland *Also Called: Vgu Industries Inc (G-4867)*
Vinyl Mng Llc DBA Vinylone 440 261-5799
  8001 Krueger Ave Cleveland (44105) *(G-4876)*
Vinyl Profiles Acquisition LLC 330 538-0660
  11675 Mahoning Ave North Jackson (44451) *(G-11794)*
Vinyl Tool & Die Company 330 782-0254
  1144 Meadowbrook Ave Youngstown (44512) *(G-16471)*
Vinyltech Inc 330 538-0369
  11635 Mahoning Ave North Jackson (44451) *(G-11795)*
Vinylume Products Inc 330 799-2000
  3745 Hendricks Rd Youngstown (44515) *(G-16472)*
Viper Acquisition I Inc (DH) 216 589-0198
  127 Public Sq Ste 5300 Cleveland (44114) *(G-4877)*
Viral Antigens, Cincinnati *Also Called: Meridian Life Science Inc (G-3150)*
Virginia Air Distributors Inc 614 262-1129
  2821 Silver Dr Columbus (43211) *(G-5860)*
Virtual Hold Tech Slutions LLC (DH) 330 670-2200
  3875 Embassy Pkwy Ste 350 Akron (44333) *(G-370)*
Virtus Stunts LLC 440 543-0472
  16320 Snyder Rd Chagrin Falls (44023) *(G-2433)*
Visi-Trak Worldwide LLC (PA) 216 524-2363
  8400 Sweet Valley Dr Ste 406 Cleveland (44125) *(G-4878)*
Vision Color LLC 419 924-9450
  214 S Defiance St West Unity (43570) *(G-15645)*
Vision Graphix Inc 440 835-6540
  29275 Clemens Rd Westlake (44145) *(G-15800)*
Vision Manufacturing Inc 937 332-1801
  513 Garfield Ave Troy (45373) *(G-14615)*
Vision Press Inc 440 357-6362
  1634 W Jackson St Painesville (44077) *(G-12275)*
Vision Projects Inc 937 667-8648
  1350 Commerce Park Dr. Tipp City (45371) *(G-14164)*
Vision Quest, Elmore *Also Called: Alvin L Roepke (G-7099)*
Visionmark Nameplate Co LLC 419 977-3131
  100 White Mountain Dr New Bremen (45869) *(G-11410)*
Vista Community Church 614 718-2294
  8500 Memorial Dr Ste C Plain City (43064) *(G-12600)*
Vista Creations LLC 440 954-9191
  7896 Tyler Blvd Mentor (44060) *(G-10593)*
Vistech, Fairfield *Also Called: Vistech Mfg Solutions LLC (G-7424)*
Vistech Mfg Solutions LLC 513 860-1408
  4274 Thunderbird Ln Fairfield (45014) *(G-7424)*

Vistech Mfg Solutions LLC 513 933-9300
  265 S West St Lebanon (45036) *(G-9120)*
Visual Art Graphic Services 330 274-2775
  5244 Goodell Rd Mantua (44255) *(G-9745)*
Visual Marking Systems Inc (PA) 330 425-7100
  2097 E Aurora Rd Twinsburg (44087) *(G-14753)*
Vita-Mix Manufacturing Corporation (PA) 440 235-4840
  8615 Usher Rd Olmsted Falls (44138) *(G-12083)*
Vitakraft Sun Seed Inc 419 832-1641
  20584 Long Judson Rd Weston (43569) *(G-1580)*
Vital & Fhr North America LLC 650 405-9975
  1201 Brim Rd Bowling Green (43402) *(G-1595)*
Vitamix, Olmsted Falls *Also Called: Vita-Mix Manufacturing Corporation (G-12083)*
Vitatoe Industries Inc (PA) 740 773-2425
  100 Chamber Dr Chillicothe (45601) *(G-2541)*
Vitec Inc 216 464-4670
  26901 Cannon Rd Bedford (44146) *(G-1159)*
Vitex Corporation 216 883-0920
  2960 Broadway Ave Cleveland (44115) *(G-4879)*
Vivid Graphix, Bellaire *Also Called: Charles Wisveri (G-1184)*
Vivo Brothers LLC 330 629-8686
  1387 Columbiana Lisbon Rd Columbiana (44408) *(G-5054)*
Vmaxx Inc 419 738-4044
  323 Commerce Rd Wapakoneta (45895) *(G-1512)*
Vmetro Inc (DH) 281 584-0728
  2600 Paramount Pl Ste 200 Fairborn (45324) *(G-326)*
Vmi Americas Inc (HQ) 330 929-6800
  4670 Allen Rd Stow (44224) *(G-13738)*
Vmi Liquidating Inc 937 492-3100
  2309 Industrial Dr Sidney (45365) *(G-13293)*
Vndly LLC 513 572-2500
  4900 Parkway Dr Ste 125 Mason (45040) *(G-10058)*
Vnl Molding Ltd 330 220-5951
  669 Marguerite Way Brunswick (44212) *(G-1799)*
Vocational Services Inc 216 431-8085
  2239 E 55th St Cleveland (44103) *(G-4880)*
Voice Products Inc 216 360-0433
  23715 Mercantile Rd Ste A200 Cleveland (44122) *(G-4881)*
Voigt & Schweitzer LLC (HQ) 614 449-8281
  987 Buckeye Park Rd Columbus (43207) *(G-586)*
Voisard Manufacturing Inc 419 896-3191
  60 Scott St Shiloh (44878) *(G-13207)*
Volant Performance, Berea *Also Called: Tmg Performance Products LLC (G-1297)*
Volens LLC 216 544-1200
  480 Highland Rd E Macedonia (44056) *(G-9585)*
Volk Corporation 513 621-1052
  635 Main St Ste 1 Cincinnati (45202) *(G-3501)*
Volk Optical, Mentor *Also Called: Volk Optical Inc (G-10594)*
Volk Optical Inc 440 942-6161
  7893 Enterprise Dr Mentor (44060) *(G-10594)*
Volpe Millwork Inc 216 581-0200
  4500 Lee Rd Cleveland (44128) *(G-4882)*
Von Roll Isola, Cleveland *Also Called: Von Roll Usa Inc (G-4883)*
Von Roll Usa Inc 216 433-7474
  4853 W 130th St Cleveland (44135) *(G-4883)*
Voo Doo Industries LLC 440 653-5333
  33640 Pin Oak Pkwy Ste 4 Avon Lake (44012) *(G-826)*
Vores Steve Welding & Steel, Fort Recovery *Also Called: Steve Vore Welding and Steel (G-7624)*
Vortec and Paxton Products 513 891-7474
  10125 Carver Rd Blue Ash (45242) *(G-1488)*
Vortec Corporation
  10125 Carver Rd Blue Ash (45242) *(G-1489)*
Vortec-An Illinois TI Works Co, Blue Ash *Also Called: Vortec Corporation (G-1489)*
Vorti-Siv, Salem *Also Called: Mm Industries Inc (G-13019)*
Voss Industries LLC 216 771-7655
  1000 W Bagley Rd Berea (44017) *(G-1298)*
Voss Industries LLC (DH) 216 771-7655
  2168 W 25th St Cleveland (44113) *(G-4884)*
Voyale Minority Enterprise LLC 216 271-3661
  5855 Grant Ave Cleveland (44105) *(G-4885)*

ALPHABETIC SECTION

Voyant Beauty, New Albany *Also Called: Veepak OH LLC* **(G-11393)**

VPI, Aurora *Also Called: Video Products Inc* **(G-740)**

Vpi LLC 330 549-0195
14101 Market St Columbiana (44408) **(G-5055)**

Vpp Industries Inc 937 526-3775
960 E Main St Versailles (45380) **(G-14991)**

Vr Assets LLC 440 600-2963
5265 Naiman Pkwy Ste J Solon (44139) **(G-13443)**

Vrc, Loveland *Also Called: Valve Related Controls Inc* **(G-9507)**

Vrc Inc 440 243-6666
696 W Bagley Rd Berea (44017) **(G-1299)**

Vrc Manufacturers, Berea *Also Called: Vrc Inc* **(G-1299)**

Vs Service Company LLC 614 415-2348
4 Limited Pkwy E Reynoldsburg (43068) **(G-12780)**

Vscorp LLC 937 305-3562
4754 Us Route 40 Tipp City (45371) **(G-14165)**

Vsp Lab Columbus 614 409-8900
2605 Rohr Rd Lockbourne (43137) **(G-9342)**

VT Industries LLC 614 804-6904
1999 Friston Blvd Hilliard (43026) **(G-8453)**

Vtd Systems Inc 440 323-4122
7600 W River Rd S Elyria (44035) **(G-7217)**

Vts Co Ltd 419 273-4010
607 E Lima St Forest (45843) **(G-7594)**

Vulcan Corporation 513 621-2850
708 Walnut St Cincinnati (45202) **(G-3502)**

Vulcan International Corp 513 621-2850
30 Garfield Pl Ste 1000 Cincinnati (45202) **(G-3503)**

Vulcan Machinery Corporation 330 376-6025
20 N Case Ave Akron (44305) **(G-371)**

Vulcan Products Co Inc 419 468-1039
208 S Washington St Galion (44833) **(G-7887)**

Vulcraft, Beavercreek *Also Called: Nucor Corporation* **(G-1057)**

Vulkor, Warren *Also Called: Therm-O-Link Inc* **(G-15209)**

Vulkor Incorporated (PA) 330 393-7600
621 Dana St Ne Ste V Warren (44483) **(G-15217)**

Vurvey Labs Inc 513 379-3595
1008 Race St Ste 4 Cincinnati (45202) **(G-3504)**

Vwm Republic Metals, Cleveland *Also Called: Victory White Metal Company* **(G-4873)**

Vwm-Republic Inc 216 641-2575
7930 Jones Rd Cleveland (44105) **(G-4886)**

VWR Chemicals LLC (DH) 800 448-4442
28600 Fountain Pkwy Solon (44139) **(G-13444)**

VWR Part of Avantor (DH) 440 349-1199
28600 Fountain Pkwy Solon (44139) **(G-13445)**

Vy Inc 513 421-8100
3307 Clifton Ave Ste 2 Cincinnati (45220) **(G-3505)**

Vya Inc 513 772-5400
1325 Glendale Milford Rd Cincinnati (45215) **(G-3506)**

Vylon Pipe, Bowling Green *Also Called: Trenchless Rsrces Globl Hldngs* **(G-1593)**

Vyral LLC 937 993-7765
2078 E Dorothy Ln Dayton (45420) **(G-6645)**

W & W Automotive, Beavercreek Township *Also Called: W&W Automotive & Towing Inc* **(G-1095)**

W A S P Inc 740 439-2398
59100 Claysville Rd Cambridge (43725) **(G-1960)**

W B, Marion *Also Called: Wilson Bohannan Company* **(G-9891)**

W B Becherer Inc 330 758-6616
7905 Southern Blvd Youngstown (44512) **(G-16473)**

W C Bunting Co Inc 330 385-2050
1425 Globe St East Liverpool (43920) **(G-7002)**

W C Heller & Co Inc 419 485-3176
201 W Wabash St Montpelier (43543) **(G-11145)**

W C R, Fairborn *Also Called: Wcr Incorporated* **(G-7327)**

W E Lott Company 419 563-9400
1432 Isaac Beal Rd Bucyrus (44820) **(G-1873)**

W G Lockhart Construction Co 330 745-6520
800 W Waterloo Rd Akron (44314) **(G-372)**

W H Patten Drilling Co Inc 330 674-3046
6336 County Road 207 Millersburg (44654) **(G-11004)**

W J Egli Company Inc (PA) 330 823-3666
205 E Columbia St Alliance (44601) **(G-435)**

W M Dauch Concrete Inc 419 562-6917
900 Nevada Rd Bucyrus (44820) **(G-1874)**

W of Ohio Inc (PA) 614 873-4664
225 Guy St Plain City (43064) **(G-12601)**

W P Brown Enterprises Inc 740 685-2594
57051 Marietta Rd Byesville (43723) **(G-1902)**

W Pole Contracting Inc 330 325-7177
4188 State Route 14 Ravenna (44266) **(G-12741)**

W R G Inc 216 351-8494
631 Parkside Dr Avon Lake (44012) **(G-827)**

W S Tyler, Mentor *Also Called: Tyler Haver Inc* **(G-10585)**

W W Cross Industries Inc 330 588-8400
2510 Allen Ave Se Canton (44707) **(G-2263)**

W W Williams Company LLC (DH) 614 228-5000
400 Metro Pl N Dublin (43017) **(G-6958)**

W.britain Model Figures, Chillicothe *Also Called: On The Mantle LLC* **(G-2521)**

W.T.nickell Co., Batavia *Also Called: D&D Design Concepts Inc* **(G-919)**

W/S Packaging Group Inc 513 459-8800
7400 Industrial Row Dr Mason (45040) **(G-10069)**

W&W Automotive & Towing Inc 937 429-1699
680 Orchard Ln Beavercreek Township (45434) **(G-1095)**

W&W Rock Sand and Gravel 513 266-3708
1451 Maple Grove Rd Williamsburg (45176) **(G-15867)**

W3 Ultrasonics LLC 330 284-3667
5288 Huckleberry St Nw North Canton (44720) **(G-11774)**

WA Hammond Drierite Co Ltd 937 376-2927
138 Dayton Ave Xenia (45385) **(G-16280)**

Wabash National Corporation 419 434-9409
2000 Fostoria Ave Findlay (45840) **(G-7579)**

Wabtec Corporation 216 362-7500
4677 Manufacturing Ave Cleveland (44135) **(G-4887)**

Wabtec Global Services, Mansfield *Also Called: Westinghouse A Brake Tech Corp* **(G-9733)**

Wabush Mnes Clffs Min Mnging A 216 694-5700
200 Public Sq Ste 3300 Cleveland (44114) **(G-4888)**

Wacker Chemical Corporation 330 899-0847
2215 International Pkwy Canton (44720) **(G-2264)**

Wacker Sign, Massillon *Also Called: Mel Wacker Signs Inc* **(G-10126)**

Waco Scaffolding & Equipment Inc 216 749-8900
4545 Spring Rd Cleveland (44131) **(G-4889)**

Waddell A Div GMI Companies, Greenfield *Also Called: GMI Companies Inc* **(G-8030)**

Wade Dynamics Inc 216 431-8484
1411 E 39th St Cleveland (44114) **(G-4890)**

Wagner Farms Sawmill Ltd Lblty 419 653-4126
13201 Road X Leipsic (45856) **(G-9141)**

Wagner Machine Inc 330 706-0700
5151 Wooster Rd W Norton (44203) **(G-11951)**

Wagner Quarries Company 419 625-8141
4203 Milan Rd Sandusky (44870) **(G-13104)**

Wagner Rustproofing Co Inc 216 361-4930
7708 Quincy Ave Cleveland (44104) **(G-4891)**

Wahl, Fremont *Also Called: Wahl Refractory Solutions LLC* **(G-7819)**

Wahl Refractory Solutions LLC (PA) 419 334-2658
767 S State Route 19 Fremont (43420) **(G-7819)**

Waibel Electric Co Inc 740 964-2956
133 Humphries Dr Etna (43068) **(G-7253)**

Wal Plax, Bedford *Also Called: Walton Plastics Inc* **(G-1160)**

Wal-Bon of Ohio Inc (PA) 740 423-6351
210 Main St Belpre (45714) **(G-1261)**

Wal-Bon of Ohio Inc 740 423-8178
708 Main St Belpre (45714) **(G-1262)**

Walbridge Coatings, Walbridge *Also Called: Material Sciences Corporation* **(G-15084)**

Walbridge Coatings, Walbridge *Also Called: MSC Walbridge Coatings Inc* **(G-15085)**

Walden Industries Inc 740 633-5971
101 Walden Ave Tiltonsville (43963) **(G-14117)**

Waldorf Marking Devices, New London *Also Called: Monode Marking Products Inc* **(G-11464)**

Walest Incorporated 216 362-8110
306 Aynesly Way Brunswick (44212) **(G-1800)**

Walker National Inc 614 492-1614
2195 Wright Brothers Ave Columbus (43217) **(G-5862)**

Walker Printing Co., Mentor Also Called: Jack Walker Printing Co (G-10481)

Walker Tool & Machine Company 419 661-8000
7700 Ponderosa Rd Perrysburg (43551) **(G-12443)**

Wall Colmonoy Corporation 513 842-4200
940 Redna Ter Cincinnati (45215) **(G-3507)**

Wall Polishing LLC 937 698-1330
1953 S State Route 48 Ludlow Falls (45339) **(G-9530)**

Wall Technology Inc 715 532-5548
1 Owens Corning Pkwy Toledo (43659) **(G-14521)**

Wallace Forge Company 330 488-1203
3700 Georgetown Rd Ne Canton (44704) **(G-2265)**

Waller Brothers Stone Company 740 858-1948
744 Mcdermott Rushtown Rd Mc Dermott (45652) **(G-10275)**

Walleye Investments Ltd 440 564-7210
6750 Arnold Miller Pkwy Solon (44139) **(G-13446)**

Wallover Enterprises Inc (DH) 440 238-9250
21845 Drake Rd Strongsville (44149) **(G-13893)**

Wallover Oil Company Inc (DH) 440 238-9250
21845 Drake Rd Strongsville (44149) **(G-13894)**

Wallover Oil Hamilton Inc 513 896-6692
1000 Forest Ave Hamilton (45015) **(G-8257)**

Wallsseye Concrete Corp (PA) 440 235-1800
26000 Sprague Rd Cleveland (44138) **(G-4892)**

Walnut Creek Chocolate Co Inc (PA) 330 893-2995
4917 State Rte 515 Walnut Creek (44687) **(G-15096)**

Walnut Creek Lumber Co Ltd 330 852-4559
10433 Pleasant Hill Rd Nw Dundee (44624) **(G-6972)**

Walnut Creek Planing Ltd 330 893-3244
5778 State Route 515 Millersburg (44654) **(G-11005)**

Walsh Manufacturing, Cleveland Also Called: Herman Manufacturing LLC (G-4185)

Waltco Lift Corp (DH) 330 633-9191
1777 Miller Pkwy Streetsboro (44241) **(G-13798)**

Waltek & Company, Cincinnati Also Called: Wt Acquisition Company Ltd (G-3528)

Walter F Stephens Jr Inc 937 746-0521
415 South Ave Franklin (45005) **(G-7709)**

Walter Grinders Inc 937 859-1975
510 Earl Blvd Miamisburg (45342) **(G-10700)**

Walter H Drane Co Inc 216 514-1022
23811 Chagrin Blvd Ste 344 Beachwood (44122) **(G-1032)**

Walter North 937 204-6050
900 Pimlico Dr Apt 2a Dayton (45459) **(G-6646)**

Walters Buildings, Urbana Also Called: Jack Walters & Sons Corp (G-14840)

Walther EMC, Franklin Also Called: Walther Engrg & Mfg Co Inc (G-7710)

Walther Engrg & Mfg Co Inc 937 743-8125
3501 Shotwell Dr Franklin (45005) **(G-7710)**

Walton Hills, Walton Hills Also Called: Controllix Corporation (G-15097)

Walton Plastics Inc 440 786-7711
20493 Hannan Pkwy Bedford (44146) **(G-1160)**

Wan Dynamics Inc 877 400-9490
303 N Court St Unit 1758 Medina (44258) **(G-10393)**

Wannemacher Enterprises Inc 419 771-1101
422 W Guthrie Dr Upper Sandusky (43351) **(G-14824)**

Wannemacher Packaging, Upper Sandusky Also Called: Wannemacher Enterprises Inc (G-14824)

Wanner Metal Worx Inc 740 369-4034
525 London Rd Delaware (43015) **(G-6756)**

Wapakoneta Plant, Wapakoneta Also Called: General Aluminum Mfg Company (G-15115)

Wappoo Wood Products Inc 937 492-1166
12877 Kirkwood Rd Sidney (45365) **(G-13294)**

Ward Construction Co (PA) 419 943-2450
385 Oak St Leipsic (45856) **(G-9142)**

Ward Engineering Inc 614 442-8063
2041 Arlingate Ln Columbus (43228) **(G-5863)**

Ward Industrial Services Inc 877 459-9272
1040 Industrial Pkwy N Brunswick (44212) **(G-1801)**

Ward/Kraft Forms of Ohio Inc 740 694-0015
700 Salem Ave Ext Fredericktown (43019) **(G-7759)**

Warehouse, Mansfield Also Called: Gorman-Rupp Company (G-9662)

Warehouse, Painesville Also Called: De Nora Tech LLC (G-12227)

Warfighter Fcsed Logistics Inc 740 513-4692
8800 Global Way Ste 100a West Chester (45069) **(G-15526)**

Warmus and Associates Inc 330 659-4440
2324 N Cleveland Massillon Rd Bath (44210) **(G-962)**

Warner Fabricating Inc 330 848-3191
7812 Hartman Rd Wadsworth (44281) **(G-15071)**

Warren Castings Inc 216 883-2520
2934 E 55th St Cleveland (44127) **(G-4893)**

Warren Concrete and Supply Co 330 393-1581
1113 Parkman Rd Nw Warren (44485) **(G-15218)**

Warren Door, Niles Also Called: Traichal Construction Company (G-11689)

Warren Drilling Co Inc 740 783-2775
305 Smithson St Dexter City (45727) **(G-6803)**

Warren Fabricating Corporation (PA) 330 534-5017
7845 Chestnut Ridge Rd Hubbard (44425) **(G-8572)**

Warren Metal Lithography, Warren Also Called: Tecnocap LLC (G-15208)

Warren Printing & Off Pdts Inc 419 523-3635
250 E Main St Ottawa (45875) **(G-12196)**

Warren Rupp Inc 419 524-8388
800 N Main St Mansfield (44902) **(G-9730)**

Warren Screw Machine Inc 330 609-6020
3869 Niles Rd Se Warren (44484) **(G-15219)**

Warren Steel Holdings LLC 330 847-0487
4000 Mahoning Ave Nw Warren (44483) **(G-15220)**

Warren Steel Specialties Corp 330 399-8360
1309 Niles Rd Se Warren (44484) **(G-15221)**

Warren Trucking, Dexter City Also Called: Warren Drilling Co Inc (G-6803)

Warren Welding and Fabrication, Lebanon Also Called: Kirbys Auto and Truck Repr Inc (G-9093)

Warrior Imports Inc 954 935-5536
112 S Meridian Rd Youngstown (44509) **(G-1647)**

Warther Cutlery, Dover Also Called: E Warther & Sons Inc (G-6823)

Warthman Drilling Inc 740 746-9950
7525 Lancaster Logan Rd Sugar Grove (43155) **(G-13917)**

Warwick Products Company 216 334-1200
5350 Tradex Pkwy Cleveland (44102) **(G-4894)**

Wasca LLC 937 723-9031
750 Rosedale Dr Dayton (45402) **(G-6647)**

Washing Systems LLC (HQ) 800 272-1974
167 Commerce Dr Loveland (45140) **(G-9509)**

Washington County Coal Company 740 338-3100
46226 National Rd Saint Clairsville (43950) **(G-12928)**

Washington Crt Hse Converting, Wshngtn Ct Hs Also Called: Weyerhaeuser Company (G-16246)

Washington Group, Oregon Also Called: Aecom Energy & Cnstr Inc (G-12101)

Washington Products Inc (PA) 330 837-5101
1875 Harsh Ave Se Ste 1 Massillon (44646) **(G-10154)**

Washita Valley Enterprises Inc 330 510-1568
3707 Tulane Ave Bldg 9 Louisville (44641) **(G-9413)**

Wasserstrom Co 614 737-8568
1641 Harmon Ave Columbus (43223) **(G-5864)**

Wasserstrom Company (PA) 614 228-6525
4500 E Broad St Columbus (43213) **(G-5865)**

Wasserstrom Marketing Division, Columbus Also Called: N Wasserstrom & Sons Inc (G-5588)

Waste King, North Olmsted Also Called: Anaheim Manufacturing Company (G-11817)

Waste Parchment Inc 330 674-6868
4510 Township Road 307 Millersburg (44654) **(G-11006)**

Waste Water Plant, The, Ravenna Also Called: City of Ravenna (G-12710)

Waste Water Treatment Plant, Madison Also Called: County of Lake (G-9591)

Watch-Us Inc 513 829-8870
4450 Dixie Hwy Fairfield (45014) **(G-7425)**

Water & Sewer, Chardon Also Called: City of Chardon (G-2446)

Water & Waste Water Dept., Mount Vernon Also Called: City of Mount Vernon (G-11268)

Water & Waste Water Eqp Co 440 542-0972
32100 Solon Rd Ste 101a Solon (44139) **(G-13447)**

Water Drop Media Inc 234 600-5817
289 Youngstown Kingsville Rd Se Vienna (44473) **(G-15005)**

Water Star Inc 440 996-0800
7590 Discovery Ln Concord Township (44077) **(G-5914)**

Water Treatment, Middletown Also Called: City of Middletown (G-10807)

Waterco of The Central States 937 294-0375
3215 Homeward Way Fairfield (45014) **(G-7426)**

ALPHABETIC SECTION

Waterford Tank Fabrication Ltd..740 984-4100
203 State Route 83 Beverly (45715) *(G-1323)*

Waterloo Coal Company Inc (PA)...740 286-0004
235 E Main St Jackson (45640) *(G-8727)*

Waterloo Industries Inc..800 833-8851
12487 Plaza Dr Cleveland (44130) *(G-4895)*

Waterlox Coatings Corporation..216 641-4877
9808 Meech Ave Cleveland (44105) *(G-4896)*

Wateropolis Corp...440 564-5061
12361 Kinsman Rd Newbury (44065) *(G-11639)*

Waterpro..330 372-3565
2926 Commonwealth Ave Ne Warren (44483) *(G-15222)*

Watershed Distillery LLC..614 357-1936
1145 Chesapeake Ave Ste D Columbus (43212) *(G-5866)*

Watershed Mangement LLC...740 852-5607
10460 State Route 56 Se Mount Sterling (43143) *(G-11258)*

Watersource LLC...419 747-9552
1225 W Longview Ave Mansfield (44906) *(G-9731)*

Waterville Sheet Metal Company..419 878-5050
1210 Waterville Monclova Rd Waterville (43566) *(G-15255)*

Watkins Printing Company..614 297-8270
1401 E 17th Ave Columbus (43211) *(G-5867)*

Watson Gravel Inc (PA)..513 863-0070
2728 Hamilton Cleves Rd Hamilton (45013) *(G-8258)*

Watson Gravel Inc..513 422-3781
2100 S Main St Middletown (45044) *(G-10870)*

Watson Haran & Company Inc..937 436-1414
1500 Yankee Park Pl Dayton (45458) *(G-6648)*

Watson Wood Works..513 233-5321
2765 Frazee Rd Somerville (45064) *(G-13453)*

Watson's, Cincinnati *Also Called: Entertrainment Junction (G-2876)*

Watt Printers, Olmsted Falls *Also Called: Gergel-Kellem Company Inc (G-12080)*

Watteredge, Avon Lake *Also Called: Watteredge LLC (G-828)*

Watteredge LLC (DH)..440 933-6110
567 Miller Rd Avon Lake (44012) *(G-828)*

Watters Manufacturing Co Inc..216 281-8600
1931 W 47th St Cleveland (44102) *(G-4897)*

Watts Antenna Company...740 797-9380
70 N Plains Rd Ste H The Plains (45780) *(G-14060)*

Watts Water..614 491-5143
6201 Green Pointe Dr S Groveport (43125) *(G-8167)*

Waugs Inc...440 315-4851
956 State Route 302 Ashland (44805) *(G-620)*

Wausau Mosinee Paper, Middletown *Also Called: Wausau Paper Corp (G-10871)*

Wausau Paper Corp...513 217-3623
700 Columbia Ave Middletown (45042) *(G-10871)*

Wauseon Machine & Mfg Inc, Wauseon *Also Called: Cornerstone Wauseon Inc (G-15259)*

Waveflex Inc..740 513-1334
5480 Roesland Dr Galena (43021) *(G-7856)*

Wavy Ticket LLC...513 827-0886
3748 State Line Rd Okeana (45053) *(G-12068)*

Waxco International Inc..937 746-4845
727 Dayton Oxford Rd Miamisburg (45342) *(G-10701)*

Waxman Industries Inc (PA)..440 439-1830
24460 Aurora Rd Bedford Heights (44146) *(G-1181)*

Waygate Technologies Usa LP..866 243-2638
1 Neumann Way Cincinnati (45215) *(G-3508)*

Waylens Inc...513 445-8684
108 W Main St Ste 1 Mason (45040) *(G-10070)*

Wayne - Dalton Plastics, Conneaut *Also Called: Overhead Door Corporation (G-5929)*

Wayne - Dalton Rolling Doors, Dalton *Also Called: Hrh Door Corp (G-6132)*

Wayne A Whaley...330 525-7779
4466 12th St Homeworth (44634) *(G-8556)*

Wayne Builders Supply, Greenville *Also Called: St Henry Tile Co Inc (G-8061)*

Wayne Concrete Company LLC...937 545-9919
223 Western Dr Medway (45341) *(G-10400)*

Wayne County Rubber Inc...330 264-5553
1205 E Bowman St Wooster (44691) *(G-16181)*

Wayne Manufacturing, Zanesville *Also Called: New Wayne Inc (G-16549)*

Wayne Morgan Corp...419 222-4181
895 Shawnee Rd Lima (45805) *(G-9301)*

Wayne Tire Service, Homeworth *Also Called: Wayne A Whaley (G-8556)*

Wayne Water Systems, Harrison *Also Called: Wayne/Scott Fetzer Company (G-8296)*

Wayne/Scott Fetzer Company...800 237-0987
101 Production Dr Harrison (45030) *(G-8296)*

Waynedale Truss and Panel Co..330 698-7373
8971 Dover Rd Apple Creek (44606) *(G-513)*

Waynedale Truss and Panel Co..330 683-4471
93 Lake Dr Dalton (44618) *(G-6144)*

Ways Cstm Wldg & Fabrication...440 354-1350
1580 N Ridge Rd Painesville (44077) *(G-12276)*

Waytek Corporation..937 743-6142
400 Shotwell Dr Franklin (45005) *(G-7711)*

Wb Industries Inc...440 708-0309
16461 Messenger Rd. Burton (44021) *(G-1890)*

Wccv Floor Coverings LLC (PA)..330 688-0114
4535 State Rd Peninsula (44264) *(G-12344)*

Wch Molding LLC...740 335-6320
1850 Lowes Blvd Wshngtn Ct Hs (43160) *(G-16244)*

Wcm Holdings Inc..513 705-2100
11500 Canal Rd Cincinnati (45241) *(G-3509)*

Wcr Incorporated (PA)...937 223-0703
2377 Commerce Center Blvd Ste B Fairborn (45324) *(G-7327)*

Wcr Incorporated...740 333-3448
809 Delaware St Wshngtn Ct Hs (43160) *(G-16245)*

WD Pumpco LLC..740 454-2576
620 Marietta St Zanesville (43701) *(G-16569)*

Wdi Group Inc...216 251-5509
4031 W 150th St Cleveland (44135) *(G-4898)*

Wear Technology, Batavia *Also Called: Milacron Marketing Company LLC (G-936)*

Weastec Incorporated (HQ)...937 393-6800
1600 N High St Hillsboro (45133) *(G-8469)*

Weather King Heating & AC...330 908-0281
51 Meadow Ln Ste E Northfield (44067) *(G-11914)*

Weatherchem Corporation...330 425-4206
2222 Highland Rd Twinsburg (44087) *(G-14754)*

Weaver Barns Ltd..330 852-2103
1696 State Route 39 Sugarcreek (44681) *(G-13947)*

Weaver Bros Inc (PA)...937 526-3907
895 E Main St Versailles (45380) *(G-14992)*

Weaver Craft of Sugarcreek, Sugarcreek *Also Called: Weavers Furniture Ltd (G-13948)*

Weaver Fab & Finishing, Akron *Also Called: Bogie Industries Inc Ltd (G-89)*

Weaver Industries Propak...330 475-8160
480 Baltimore Ave Akron (44306) *(G-373)*

Weaver Leather LLC (HQ)..330 674-7548
7540 County Road 201 Millersburg (44654) *(G-11007)*

Weaver Lumber Co..330 359-5091
1925 Us Route 62 Wilmot (44689) *(G-16071)*

Weaver Propack - Marc Drive..330 379-3660
129 Marc Dr Cuyahoga Falls (44223) *(G-6128)*

Weaver Screen Print LLC...440 725-0116
9450 Metcalf Rd Willoughby (44094) *(G-16014)*

Weaver Woodcraft L L C..330 695-2150
9652 Harrison Rd Apple Creek (44606) *(G-514)*

Weavers Furniture Ltd...330 852-2701
7011 Old Route 39 Nw Sugarcreek (44681) *(G-13948)*

Weber Ready Mix Inc...419 394-9097
16672 County Road 66a Saint Marys (45885) *(G-12969)*

Weber Sand & Gravel Inc..419 636-7920
14586 Us Highway 127 Ew Bryan (43506) *(G-1844)*

Weber Sand & Gravel Inc..419 298-2388
2702 County Road 3b Edgerton (43517) *(G-7083)*

Webers Body & Frame Inc...937 839-5946
2017 State Route 503 N West Alexandria (45381) *(G-15346)*

Webster Industries Inc (PA)..419 447-8232
325 Hall St Tiffin (44883) *(G-14115)*

Webster Manufacturing Company, Tiffin *Also Called: Webster Industries Inc (G-14115)*

Wecall Inc..440 437-8202
510 Center St Chardon (44024) *(G-2470)*

Wecan Fabricators LLC...740 667-0731
49425 E Park Dr Tuppers Plains (45783) *(G-14619)*

Wedco LLC..513 309-0781
716 N High St Mount Orab (45154) *(G-11247)*

(PA)=Parent Co (HQ)=Headquarters (DH)=Div Headquarters

Wedge Products Inc

ALPHABETIC SECTION

Wedge Products Inc.. 330 405-4477
  2181 Enterprise Pkwy Twinsburg (44087) *(G-14755)*
Wedgewood Connect Ohio LLC.................................. 800 331-8272
  2364 Blizzard Ln Albany (45710) *(G-382)*
Wedgeworks Mch TI Boring Inc................................... 216 441-1200
  3169 E 80th St Cleveland (44104) *(G-4899)*
Wedron Silica LLC... 815 433-2449
  3 Summit Park Dr Ste 700 Independence (44131) *(G-8690)*
Weekend Learning Publs LLC..................................... 614 336-7711
  5584 Boulder Crest St Columbus (43235) *(G-5868)*
Weidmann, Cleveland *Also Called: Weidmann Electrical Tech Inc (G-4900)*
Weidmann Electrical Tech Inc..................................... 937 508-2112
  1300 E 9th St Cleveland (44114) *(G-4900)*
Weighing Division, Columbus *Also Called: Interface Logic Systems Inc (G-5472)*
Weirton Daily Times, The, Steubenville *Also Called: Ogden Newspapers Inc (G-13674)*
Weiskopf Industries Corp... 440 442-4400
  54 Alpha Park Cleveland (44143) *(G-4901)*
Weiss Industries Inc.. 419 526-2480
  2480 N Main St Mansfield (44903) *(G-9732)*
Weiss Metallurgical Services, Mansfield *Also Called: Weiss Industries Inc (G-9732)*
Wek Industries, Jefferson *Also Called: Tmd Wek North LLC (G-8761)*
Wek Industries, Inc., Akron *Also Called: WI Inc (G-375)*
Welage Corporation... 513 681-2300
  7712 Reinhold Dr Cincinnati (45237) *(G-3510)*
Welch Foods, Cincinnati *Also Called: Welch Foods Inc A Cooperative (G-3511)*
Welch Foods Inc A Cooperative................................... 513 632-5610
  720 E Pete Rose Way Cincinnati (45202) *(G-3511)*
Welch Holdings Inc... 513 353-3220
  8953 E Miami River Rd Cincinnati (45247) *(G-3512)*
Welch Packaging Columbus, Columbus *Also Called: Welch Packaging Group Inc (G-5869)*
Welch Packaging Group Inc.. 614 870-2000
  4700 Alkire Rd Columbus (43228) *(G-5869)*
Welch Publishing Co (PA)... 419 874-2528
  117 E 2nd St Perrysburg (43551) *(G-12444)*
Welch Publishing Co... 419 666-5344
  215 Osborne St Rossford (43460) *(G-12873)*
Welch Sand & Gravel Inc.. 513 353-3220
  8953 E Miami River Rd Cincinnati (45247) *(G-3513)*
Weld Tech LLC... 419 357-3214
  12316 Berlin Rd Berlin Heights (44814) *(G-1317)*
Weld-Action Company Inc... 330 372-1063
  2100 N River Rd Ne Warren (44483) *(G-15223)*
Weldco Inc.. 513 744-9353
  2121 Spring Grove Ave Cincinnati (45214) *(G-3514)*
Weldcraft Products Co, Tipp City *Also Called: Wpc Successor Inc (G-14167)*
Welded Ring Products Co (PA)................................... 216 961-3800
  2180 W 114th St Cleveland (44102) *(G-4902)*
Welded Tubes, Orwell *Also Called: Lock Joint Tube Ohio LLC (G-12167)*
Welded Tubes, Inc., Orwell *Also Called: Lsp Tubes Inc (G-12168)*
Welders Supply Inc... 216 267-4470
  5575 Engle Rd Brookpark (44142) *(G-1727)*
Welders Supply Inc (HQ)... 216 241-1696
  2020 Train Ave Cleveland (44113) *(G-4903)*
Welding Consultants Inc... 614 258-7018
  889 N 22nd St Columbus (43219) *(G-5870)*
Welding Consultants LLC.. 614 258-7018
  889 N 22nd St Columbus (43219) *(G-5871)*
Welding Improvement Company................................. 330 424-9666
  10070 Stookesberry Rd Lisbon (44432) *(G-9327)*
Weldments Inc... 937 235-9261
  167 Heid Ave Dayton (45404) *(G-6649)*
Weldon Ice Cream Company....................................... 740 467-2400
  2887 Canal Dr Millersport (43046) *(G-11015)*
Weldon Pump, Cleveland *Also Called: Bergstrom Company Ltd Partnr (G-3730)*
Weldon Pump, Oakwood Village *Also Called: Weldon Pump LLC (G-12047)*
Weldon Pump LLC... 440 232-2282
  640 Golden Oak Pkwy Oakwood Village (44146) *(G-12047)*
Weldon Technologies, Columbus *Also Called: Akron Brass Company (G-5109)*
Well Service Group Inc... 330 308-0880
  1490 Truss Rd Sw New Philadelphia (44663) *(G-11532)*

Wellex AMG... 513 734-1700
  3214 Marshall Dr Amelia (45102) *(G-470)*
Wellex Manufacturing Inc.. 513 734-1700
  3214 Marshall Dr Amelia (45102) *(G-471)*
Wellington Die Division, Valley City *Also Called: Ehl Liquidation Sectional Co (G-14897)*
Wellington Stamping, Valley City *Also Called: Sh Liquidation Stamping Inc (G-14898)*
Wellman Container Corporation.................................. 513 860-3040
  412 S Cooper Ave Cincinnati (45215) *(G-3515)*
Wellman Friction Products, Solon *Also Called: S Wellman Corp (G-13421)*
Wellnitz, Columbus *Also Called: Hazelbaker Industries Ltd (G-5424)*
Wellpoint... 614 771-9600
  6740 N High St Worthington (43085) *(G-16217)*
Wells Group LLC... 740 532-9240
  487 Gallia Pike Ironton (45638) *(G-8706)*
Wells Inc.. 419 457-2611
  8176 Us Highway 23 Risingsun (43457) *(G-1282)*
Wells Manufacturing Llc.. 937 987-2481
  280 W Main St New Vienna (45159) *(G-11544)*
Wellston Aerosol Mfg Co... 740 384-2320
  105 W A St Wellston (45692) *(G-15333)*
Welser Profile North Amer LLC (DH)........................... 330 225-2500
  615 Liverpool Dr Valley City (44280) *(G-14900)*
Wengerd Wood Inc... 330 359-4300
  1760 County Road 200 Dundee (44624) *(G-697)*
Wengerds Welding & Repair LLC................................ 740 599-9071
  21701 Pealer Mill Rd Butler (44822) *(G-1891)*
Wenrick Machine, Tipp City *Also Called: Wenrick Machine and Tool Corp (G-14166)*
Wenrick Machine and Tool Corp................................. 937 667-7307
  4685 Us Route 40 Tipp City (45371) *(G-14166)*
Wentworth Mold Inc Electra.. 937 898-8460
  852 Scholz Dr Vandalia (45377) *(G-14967)*
Wentworth Solutions... 440 212-7696
  1265 Ridge Rd Hinckley (44233) *(G-8479)*
Weprintquick.com, Cleveland *Also Called: Eveready Printing Inc (G-4038)*
Werk Brau.. 419 421-4703
  4000 Fostoria Ave Findlay (45840) *(G-7580)*
Werk Brau Co, Findlay *Also Called: Werk Brau (G-7580)*
Werk-Brau, Findlay *Also Called: Werk-Brau Company (G-7581)*
Werk-Brau Company (HQ).. 419 422-2912
  2800 Fostoria Ave Findlay (45840) *(G-7581)*
Werk-Brau Company.. 419 422-2912
  616 N Blanchard St Findlay (45840) *(G-7582)*
Werks Kraft Engineering LLC...................................... 330 721-7374
  935 Heritage Dr Medina (44256) *(G-10394)*
Werling and Sons Inc.. 937 338-3281
  100 Plum St Burkettsville (45310) *(G-1879)*
Werlor Inc.. 419 784-4285
  1420 Ralston Ave Defiance (43512) *(G-6698)*
Werlor Waste Control, Defiance *Also Called: Werlor Inc (G-6698)*
Werner G Smith Inc... 216 861-3676
  1730 Train Ave Cleveland (44113) *(G-4904)*
Wernet Inc.. 330 452-2200
  606 Cherry Ave Ne Canton (44702) *(G-2266)*
Wernke Wldg & Stl Erection Co................................... 513 353-4173
  3150 State Line Rd North Bend (45052) *(G-1170)*
Wernli Realty Corporation... 937 258-7878
  1300 Grange Hall Rd Beavercreek (45430) *(G-183)*
Wes-Garde Components Group Inc............................ 614 885-0319
  300 Enterprise Dr Westerville (43081) *(G-15724)*
Weschler Instruments, Strongsville *Also Called: Hughes Corporation (G-13842)*
Wesco Distribution, Northwood *Also Called: Wesco Distribution Inc (G-11933)*
Wesco Distribution Inc.. 419 666-1670
  6519 Fairfield Dr Northwood (43619) *(G-11933)*
Wesco Machine Inc... 330 688-6973
  2304 Roberts Journey Ravenna (44266) *(G-1272)*
West & Barker Inc... 330 652-9923
  950 Summit Ave Niles (44446) *(G-11691)*
West 6th Products Company (PA)............................... 330 467-7446
  60 Meadow Ln Northfield (44067) *(G-11915)*
West Bend Printing & Pubg Inc................................... 419 258-2000
  101 N Main St Antwerp (45813) *(G-494)*

ALPHABETIC SECTION — Whemco

West Carrollton Converting Inc 937 859-3621
   400 E Dixie Dr West Carrollton (45449) *(G-15357)*

West Carrollton Mfg Fcilty, West Carrollton *Also Called: Domtar Corporation (G-15352)*

West Chester Holdings LLC 513 705-2100
   11500 Canal Rd Cincinnati (45241) *(G-3516)*

West Chester Protective Gear, Cincinnati *Also Called: West Chester Holdings LLC (G-3516)*

West Crrllton Prchment Cnvrtin 513 594-3341
   400 E Dixie Dr West Carrollton (45449) *(G-15358)*

West Equipment Company Inc (PA) 419 698-1601
   1545 E Broadway St Toledo (43605) *(G-14522)*

West Liberty Commons, Medina *Also Called: Al Root Company (G-10291)*

West Ohio Tool Co 937 842-6688
   7311 World Class Dr Russells Point (43348) *(G-12879)*

West Reserve Controls, Akron *Also Called: Summit Design and Tech Inc (G-339)*

West Side Leader, Fairlawn *Also Called: Leader Publications Inc (G-7443)*

West-Camp Press Inc 216 426-2660
   1538 E 41st St Cleveland (44103) *(G-4905)*

West-Camp Press Inc 614 895-0233
   5178 Sinclair Rd Columbus (43229) *(G-5872)*

West-Camp Press Inc (PA) 614 882-2378
   39 Collegeview Rd Westerville (43081) *(G-15725)*

West-Ward Columbus Inc 614 276-4000
   1809 Wilson Rd Columbus (43228) *(G-5873)*

Westar Plastics, Bryan *Also Called: Westar Plastics Llc (G-1845)*

Westar Plastics Llc 419 636-1333
   4271 County Road 15d Bryan (43506) *(G-1845)*

Westbrook Manufacturing, Dayton *Also Called: Westbrook Mfg Inc (G-6650)*

Westbrook Mfg Inc 937 254-2004
   600 N Irwin St Dayton (45403) *(G-6650)*

Westcott Woodworks HM Svcs LLC 419 706-2250
   21 N Hester St Norwalk (44857) *(G-11990)*

Westerman Inc (PA) 800 338-8265
   245 N Broad St Bremen (43107) *(G-1640)*

Western & Southern Lf Insur Co (DH) 513 629-1800
   400 Broadway St Stop G Cincinnati (45202) *(G-3517)*

Western Branch Diesel LLC 330 454-8800
   1616 Metric Ave Sw Canton (44706) *(G-2267)*

Western Cutterheads LLC 270 665-5302
   4041 Township Road 606 Fredericksburg (44627) *(G-7734)*

Western Enterprises, Westlake *Also Called: Western/Scott Fetzer Company (G-15802)*

Western Kentucky Coal Co LLC 740 338-3334
   46226 National Rd Saint Clairsville (43950) *(G-12929)*

Western KY Cnsld Resources LLC (DH) 740 338-3100
   46226 National Rd Saint Clairsville (43950) *(G-12930)*

Western KY Coal Resources LLC (DH) 740 338-3100
   46226 National Rd Saint Clairsville (43950) *(G-12931)*

Western KY Resources Fing LLC (DH) 740 338-3100
   46226 National Rd Saint Clairsville (43950) *(G-12932)*

Western Ohio Cut Stone Ltd 937 492-4722
   1130 Dingman Slagle Rd Sidney (45365) *(G-13295)*

Western Ohio Graphics 937 335-8769
   402 E Main St Troy (45373) *(G-14616)*

Western Ohio Graphics, Troy *Also Called: Painted Hill Inv Group Inc (G-14600)*

Western Reserve Distillers LLC 330 780-9599
   14221 Madison Ave Lakewood (44107) *(G-8984)*

Western Reserve Lubricants 440 951-5700
   13981 Leroy Center Rd Painesville (44077) *(G-12277)*

Western Reserve Sleeve Inc 440 238-8850
   22360 Royalton Rd Strongsville (44149) *(G-13895)*

Western Reserve Wire Products, Twinsburg *Also Called: Wrwp LLC (G-14759)*

Western Roto Engravers Inc 330 336-7636
   668 Seville Rd Wadsworth (44281) *(G-15072)*

Western States Envelope Co 419 666-7480
   6859 Commodore Dr Walbridge (43465) *(G-15088)*

Western States Envelope Label, Walbridge *Also Called: Western States Envelope Co (G-15088)*

Western-Southern Life, Cincinnati *Also Called: Western & Southern Lf Insur Co (G-3517)*

Western/Scott Fetzer Company (HQ) 440 892-3000
   28800 Clemens Rd Westlake (44145) *(G-15801)*

Western/Scott Fetzer Company 440 871-2160
   875 Bassett Rd Westlake (44145) *(G-15802)*

Westerville Endoscopy Ctr LLC 614 568-1666
   300 Polaris Pkwy Ste 1500 Westerville (43082) *(G-15689)*

Westfield Steel Inc 937 322-2414
   1120 S Burnett Rd Springfield (45505) *(G-13654)*

Westinghouse A Brake Tech Corp 419 526-5323
   472 Rembrandt St Mansfield (44902) *(G-9733)*

Westlake Corporation 614 986-2497
   180 E Broad St Columbus (43215) *(G-5874)*

Westlake Dimex LLC 740 374-3100
   28305 State Route 7 Marietta (45750) *(G-9844)*

Westlake Epoxy, Columbus *Also Called: Westlake Corporation (G-5874)*

Westlake Tool & Die Mfg Co 440 934-5305
   1280 Moore Rd Avon (44011) *(G-791)*

Westmont Inc 330 862-3080
   3035 Union Ave Ne Minerva (44657) *(G-11042)*

Westmoreland Resources Gp LLC 740 622-6302
   544 Chestnut St Coshocton (43812) *(G-5999)*

Weston Brands Inc 800 814-4895
   7575 E Pleasant Valley Rd Ste 100 Independence (44131) *(G-8691)*

Westrock Commercial LLC 419 476-9101
   1635 Coining Dr Toledo (43612) *(G-14523)*

Westrock Mwv LLC 937 495-6323
   10 W 2nd St Dayton (45402) *(G-6651)*

Westrock Rkt LLC 513 860-5546
   9245 Meridian Way West Chester (45069) *(G-15527)*

Westshore Metal Finishing LLC 440 892-0774
   26891 Kenley Ct Westlake (44145) *(G-15803)*

Westview Concrete Corp 440 458-5800
   40105 Butternut Ridge Rd Elyria (44035) *(G-7218)*

Westview Concrete Corp (PA) 440 235-1800
   26000 Sprague Rd Olmsted Falls (44138) *(G-12084)*

Westwood Fbrction Shtmetal Inc 937 837-0494
   1752 Stanley Ave Dayton (45404) *(G-6652)*

Westwood Finishing Company 937 837-1488
   5881 Wolf Creek Pike Dayton (45426) *(G-6653)*

Wetsu Group Inc 937 324-9353
   125 W North St Springfield (45504) *(G-13655)*

Wettle Corp 419 865-6923
   952 Holland Park Blvd Holland (43528) *(G-8537)*

Weybridge LLC 440 951-5500
   4530 Hamann Pkwy Willoughby (44094) *(G-16015)*

Weyerhaeuser Co Containeerboar 740 397-5215
   8800 Granville Rd Mount Vernon (43050) *(G-11300)*

Weyerhaeuser Company 740 335-4480
   1803 Lowes Blvd Wshngtn Ct Hs (43160) *(G-16246)*

Wfs Filter Co, Cleveland *Also Called: Micropure Filtration Inc (G-4402)*

Wfsr Holdings LLC 877 735-4966
   220 E Monument Ave Dayton (45402) *(G-6654)*

What On Earth, Hudson *Also Called: Universal Screen Arts Inc (G-8618)*

Whatifsportscom Inc 513 333-0313
   10200 Alliance Rd Ste 301 Blue Ash (45242) *(G-1490)*

Wheat Ridge Pallet & Lumber, Peebles *Also Called: Schrock John (G-12332)*

Wheatland Tube LLC 724 342-6851
   1800 Hunter Ave Niles (44446) *(G-11692)*

Wheatland Tube LLC 330 372-6611
   901 Dietz Rd Ne Warren (44483) *(G-15224)*

Wheatland Tube Company, Cambridge *Also Called: Zekelman Industries Inc (G-1961)*

Wheatland Tube Company, Niles *Also Called: Wheatland Tube LLC (G-11692)*

Wheatland Tube Company, Warren *Also Called: Wheatland Tube LLC (G-15224)*

Wheel Group Holdings LLC 614 253-6247
   2901 E 4th Ave Ste 3 Columbus (43219) *(G-5875)*

Wheel One, Columbus *Also Called: Wheel Group Holdings LLC (G-5875)*

Wheeler Manufacturing, Ashtabula *Also Called: Rex International USA Inc (G-659)*

Wheeling Coffee & Spice Co 304 232-0141
   117 Pinecrest Dr Saint Clairsville (43950) *(G-12933)*

Wheelskins Inc 800 755-2128
   10589 Kings Way North Royalton (44133) *(G-11901)*

Whelco Industrial Ltd 419 385-4627
   28210 Cedar Park Blvd Perrysburg (43551) *(G-12445)*

Whemco, Canton *Also Called: United Rolls Inc (G-2255)*

Whemco

ALPHABETIC SECTION

Whemco, Lima *Also Called: Whemco-Ohio Foundry Inc (G-9302)*

Whemco-Ohio Foundry Inc.. 419 222-2111
1600 Mcclain Rd Lima (45804) *(G-9302)*

Whempys Corp.. 614 888-6670
6969 Worthington Galena Rd Ste P Worthington (43085) *(G-16218)*

Whip Guide Co.. 440 543-5151
16829 Park Circle Dr Chagrin Falls (44023) *(G-2434)*

Whirlaway Corporation... 440 647-4711
125 Bennett St Wellington (44090) *(G-15323)*

Whirlaway Corporation... 440 647-4711
125 Bennett St Wellington (44090) *(G-15324)*

Whirlaway Corporation (HQ).. 440 647-4711
720 Shiloh Ave Wellington (44090) *(G-15325)*

Whirlpool, Clyde *Also Called: Whirlpool Corporation (G-4979)*

Whirlpool, Clyde *Also Called: Whirlpool Corporation (G-4980)*

Whirlpool, Lockbourne *Also Called: Whirlpool Corporation (G-9343)*

Whirlpool Corporation... 419 547-7711
119 Birdseye St Clyde (43410) *(G-4979)*

Whirlpool Corporation... 419 547-2610
1081 W Mcpherson Hwy Clyde (43410) *(G-4980)*

Whirlpool Corporation... 419 423-8123
4901 N Main St Findlay (45840) *(G-7583)*

Whirlpool Corporation... 937 548-4126
1701 Kitchen Aid Way Greenville (45331) *(G-8064)*

Whirlpool Corporation... 614 409-4340
6241 Shook Rd Lockbourne (43137) *(G-9343)*

Whirlpool Corporation... 740 383-7122
1300 Marion Agosta Rd Marion (43302) *(G-9889)*

Whitacre Engineering Company (PA).............................. 330 455-8505
4645 Rebar Ave Ne Canton (44705) *(G-2268)*

Whitacre Enterprises Inc.. 740 934-2331
35651 State Route 537 Graysville (45734) *(G-8024)*

Whitacre Greer Company (PA).. 330 823-1610
1400 S Mahoning Ave Alliance (44601) *(G-436)*

Whitaker Finishing LLC... 419 666-7746
2707 Tracy Rd Northwood (43619) *(G-11934)*

Whitcraft Cleveland, Cleveland *Also Called: Turbine Eng Cmpnents Tech Corp (G-4837)*

White Castle, Columbus *Also Called: White Castle System Inc (G-5876)*

White Castle System Inc.. 513 563-2290
3126 Exon Ave Cincinnati (45241) *(G-3518)*

White Castle System Inc (PA)... 614 228-5781
555 Edgar Waldo Way Columbus (43215) *(G-5876)*

White Feather Foods Inc.. 419 738-8975
13845 Cemetery Rd Wapakoneta (45895) *(G-15133)*

White Gravel Mines Productions...................................... 740 776-0510
1160 Simon Miller Rd Portsmouth (45662) *(G-12660)*

White Industrial Tool Inc... 330 773-6889
102 W Wilbeth Rd Akron (44301) *(G-374)*

White Jewelers Inc... 330 264-3324
516 N Bever St Apt 1 Wooster (44691) *(G-16182)*

White Machine Inc... 440 237-3282
9621 York Alpha Dr Side North Royalton (44133) *(G-11902)*

White Machine & Mfg Co (PA)... 740 453-5451
120 Graham St Zanesville (43701) *(G-16570)*

White Mule Company... 740 382-9008
2420 W 4th St Ontario (44906) *(G-12097)*

White Oak Pharmacy, Vincent *Also Called: Vincent Rx LLC (G-15010)*

White Tiger Inc.. 740 852-4873
131 S Oak St London (43140) *(G-9397)*

White Tiger Graphics, London *Also Called: White Tiger Inc (G-9397)*

White Tool, Akron *Also Called: White Industrial Tool Inc (G-374)*

White Water Forest, Batavia *Also Called: Whitewater Forest Products LLC (G-960)*

Whitebrook Inc.. 330 575-7405
1824 Whipple Ave Nw Canton (44708) *(G-2269)*

Whitefeather Foods, Wapakoneta *Also Called: White Feather Foods Inc (G-15133)*

Whiteford Industries Inc... 419 381-1155
3323 South Ave Toledo (43609) *(G-14524)*

Whitehouse Bros Inc... 513 621-2259
4393 Creek Rd Blue Ash (45241) *(G-1491)*

Whiterock Pigments Inc... 216 391-7765
1768 E 25th St Cleveland (44114) *(G-4906)*

Whites Logging & Land Clearin....................................... 419 921-9878
197 Taylor St Fredericktown (43019) *(G-7760)*

Whiteside Manufacturing Co... 740 363-1179
309 Hayes St Delaware (43015) *(G-6757)*

Whitewater Forest Products LLC..................................... 513 724-0157
1970 Clark Ln Batavia (45103) *(G-960)*

Whitewater Processing LLC... 513 367-4133
10964 Campbell Rd Harrison (45030) *(G-8297)*

Whitman Corporation.. 513 541-3223
2530 Joyce Ln Okeana (45053) *(G-12069)*

Whitmer Woodworks Inc.. 614 873-1196
8490 Carters Mill Rd Plain City (43064) *(G-1260)*

Whitmore Productions Inc... 216 752-3960
20209 Harvard Ave Warrensville Heights (44122) *(G-15231)*

Whitmore's Bbq, Warrensville Heights *Also Called: Whitmore Productions Inc (G-15231)*

Whitney Stained GL Studio Inc.. 216 348-1616
5939 Broadway Ave Cleveland (44127) *(G-4907)*

Whits Frozen Custard.. 740 965-1427
101 W Cherry St Unit A Sunbury (43074) *(G-1396)*

Whitt Machine Inc.. 513 423-7624
806 Central Ave Middletown (45044) *(G-10872)*

Whole Shop Inc.. 330 630-5305
181 S Thomas Rd Tallmadge (44278) *(G-14057)*

Wholecycle Inc... 330 929-8123
100 Cuyahoga Falls Industrial Pkwy Peninsula (44264) *(G-12345)*

Wholesale, Cincinnati *Also Called: Hen of Woods LLC (G-2993)*

Wholesale and Manufacturer, Toledo *Also Called: Estone Group LLC (G-14280)*

Wholesale Bait Co Inc... 513 863-2380
2619 Bobmeyer Rd Fairfield (45014) *(G-7427)*

Wholesale Channel Letters.. 440 256-3200
8603 Euclid Chardon Rd Kirtland (44094) *(G-8942)*

Wholesale Imprints Inc... 440 224-3527
6259 Hewitt Lane North Kingsville (44068) *(G-11797)*

Wholesome Valley Farm, Wilmot *Also Called: Trevor Clatterbuck (G-16070)*

WI Inc... 440 576-6940
1293 S Main St Akron (44301) *(G-375)*

Wicked Premiums LLC.. 216 364-0322
8748 Brecksville Rd Ste 224 Brecksville (44141) *(G-1637)*

Wicom Services, Lisbon *Also Called: Welding Improvement Company (G-9327)*

Wieland, Archbold *Also Called: Sauder Manufacturing Co (G-544)*

Wieland Metal Svcs Foils LLC.. 330 823-1700
2081 Mccrea St Alliance (44601) *(G-437)*

Wiholi Inc.. 440 543-8233
17050 Munn Rd Chagrin Falls (44023) *(G-2435)*

WIKA Sensor Technlgy LP.. 614 430-0683
6957 Green Meadows Dr Lewis Center (43035) *(G-9183)*

Wikoff Color Corporation... 513 423-0727
1392 Oxford State Rd Middletown (45044) *(G-10873)*

Wil-Mark Froyo LLC... 330 421-6043
124 Joshua Dr Rittman (44270) *(G-12829)*

Wilcox Awning & Sign, Perrysburg *Also Called: Toledo Tarp Service Inc (G-12440)*

Wilcoxon, James H Jr, Columbus *Also Called: Johnsons Real Ice Cream LLC (G-5500)*

Wild Berry Incense Inc... 513 523-8583
5475 College Corner Pike Oxford (45056) *(G-12214)*

Wild Berry Incense Factory, Oxford *Also Called: Wild Berry Incense Inc (G-12214)*

Wild Fire Systems.. 440 442-8999
535 Ransome Rd Cleveland (44143) *(G-4908)*

Wild Ohio Brewing Company... 614 262-0000
2025 S High St Columbus (43207) *(G-5877)*

Wildcat Creek Farms Inc.. 419 263-2549
4633 Road 94 Payne (45880) *(G-12324)*

Wildcat Creek Popcorn, Payne *Also Called: Wildcat Creek Farms Inc (G-12324)*

Wiley Companies (PA).. 740 622-0755
545 Walnut St Coshocton (43812) *(G-6000)*

Wiley Organics Inc.. 740 622-0755
1245 S 6th St Coshocton (43812) *(G-6001)*

Wileys Finest LLC (PA)... 740 622-1072
545 Walnut St Ste B Coshocton (43812) *(G-6002)*

Will-Burt Company... 330 682-7015
312 Collins Blvd Orrville (44667) *(G-12162)*

ALPHABETIC SECTION — WIRE PRODUCTS COMPANY, INC.

Will-Burt Company (PA) 330 682-7015
   401 Collins Blvd Orrville (44667) *(G-12163)*

Willard Machine & Welding Inc 330 467-0642
   556 Highland Rd E Ste 3 Macedonia (44056) *(G-9586)*

William Dauch Concrete Company 419 562-6917
   900 Nevada Wynford Rd Bucyrus (44820) *(G-1875)*

William Dauch Concrete Company (PA) 419 668-4458
   84 Cleveland Rd Norwalk (44857) *(G-11991)*

William Exline Inc 216 941-0800
   12301 Bennington Ave Cleveland (44135) *(G-4909)*

William J Bergen & Co 440 248-6132
   32520 Arthur Rd Solon (44139) *(G-13448)*

William Niccum 330 415-0154
   11882 Sandyville Ave Se East Sparta (44626) *(G-7015)*

William Oeder Ready Mix Inc 513 899-3901
   8807 State Route 134 Martinsville (45146) *(G-9903)*

William Powell Company (PA) 513 852-2000
   3261 Spring Grove Ave Cincinnati (45225) *(G-3519)*

William R Hague Inc 614 836-2115
   4343 S Hamilton Rd Groveport (43125) *(G-8168)*

William S Miller Inc 330 223-1794
   11250 Montgomery Rd Kensington (44427) *(G-8791)*

Williams Concrete Inc 419 893-3251
   1350 Ford St Maumee (43537) *(G-10245)*

Williams Grgory Martin Fnrl HM, Steubenville *Also Called: Martin M Hardin (G-13671)*

Williams Leather Products Inc 740 223-1604
   1476 Likens Rd Ste 104 Marion (43302) *(G-9890)*

Williams Partners LP 330 414-6201
   7235 Whipple Ave Nw North Canton (44720) *(G-11775)*

Williams Pork Co Op 419 682-9022
   18487 County Road F Stryker (43557) *(G-13914)*

Williams Scotsman Inc 614 449-8675
   871 Buckeye Park Rd Columbus (43207) *(G-5878)*

Williams Steel Rule Die Co 216 431-3232
   1633 E 40th St Cleveland (44103) *(G-4910)*

Williamson Safe Inc 937 393-9919
   5631 State Route 73 Hillsboro (45133) *(G-8470)*

Willis Cnc 440 926-0434
   1008 Commerce Dr Grafton (44044) *(G-8007)*

Willis Music Company 513 671-3288
   11700 Princeton Pike Unit E209 Cincinnati (45246) *(G-3520)*

Willison Wred Den Incorporate 440 236-9693
   27852 Royalton Rd Columbia Station (44028) *(G-5024)*

Willoughby Brewing Company LLC 440 975-0202
   4057 Erie St Willoughby (44094) *(G-16016)*

Willoughby Printing Co Inc 440 946-0800
   37946 Elm St Willoughby (44094) *(G-16017)*

Willow Hill Industries LLC 440 942-3003
   37611 Euclid Ave Willoughby (44094) *(G-16018)*

Willow Tool & Machining Ltd 440 572-2288
   15110 Foltz Pkwy Ste 1 Strongsville (44149) *(G-13896)*

Willowwood Global LLC 740 869-3377
   15441 Scioto Darby Rd Mount Sterling (43143) *(G-11259)*

Wilmington Forest Products 937 382-7813
   5562 S Us Highway 68 Wilmington (45177) *(G-16063)*

Wilmington Prcsion McHning Inc 937 382-3700
   397 Starbuck Rd Wilmington (45177) *(G-16064)*

Wilmington Precision Machining, Wilmington *Also Called: Wilmington Prcsion McHning Inc (G-16064)*

Wilson Blacktop Corp 740 635-3566
   915 Carlisle St Rear Martins Ferry (43935) *(G-9901)*

Wilson Bohannan Company 740 382-3639
   621 Buckeye St Marion (43302) *(G-9891)*

Wilson Cabinet Co 330 276-8711
   Straits Industrial Park Killbuck (44637) *(G-8925)*

Wilson Custom Woodworking Inc 513 233-5613
   1594 Saint John Pl Kings Mills (45034) *(G-8930)*

Wilson Optical Labs Inc 440 357-7000
   9450 Pineneedle Dr Mentor (44060) *(G-10595)*

Wilson Seat Company 513 732-2460
   199 Foundry Ave Batavia (45103) *(G-961)*

Wilson Specialties, North Jackson *Also Called: Canfield Manufacturing Co Inc (G-11780)*

Wilson Sporting Goods Co 419 634-9901
   217 Liberty St Ada (45810) *(G-6)*

Wilson's, Killbuck *Also Called: Wilsons Country Creations Inc (G-8926)*

Wilsons Country Creations Inc 330 377-4190
   13248 County Road 6 Killbuck (44637) *(G-8926)*

Win Cd Inc 330 929-1999
   3333 Win St Cuyahoga Falls (44223) *(G-6129)*

Win Plastic Extrusions LLC 330 929-1999
   11502 Century Blvd Cincinnati (45246) *(G-3521)*

Win Plex, Cuyahoga Falls *Also Called: Win Cd Inc (G-6129)*

Winans Chocolate and Coffee, Piqua *Also Called: Piqua Chocolate Company Inc (G-12544)*

Winco Industries, Inc., Tipp City *Also Called: Sp3 Winco LLC (G-14157)*

Windsor Airmotive, West Chester *Also Called: Barnes Group Inc (G-15374)*

Windsor Mill Lumber LLC 440 272-5930
   8506 Bundysburg Rd Middlefield (44062) *(G-10797)*

Windsor Mold USA Inc (DH) 419 483-0653
   560 Goodrich Rd Bellevue (44811) *(G-1240)*

Windsor Tool Inc 216 671-1900
   10714 Bellaire Rd Cleveland (44111) *(G-4911)*

Windsor Wire 662 634-5908
   8300 Dow Cir Ste 600 Strongsville (44136) *(G-13897)*

Windy Hills Woodworking 419 892-3389
   1761 Leiter Rd Lucas (44843) *(G-9520)*

Windy Knoll Woodworking LLC 440 636-5092
   15919 Mayfield Rd Huntsburg (44046) *(G-8621)*

Wine Cellar Innovations LLC 513 321-3733
   4575 Eastern Ave Cincinnati (45226) *(G-3522)*

Wine Mill 234 571-2594
   4964 Akron Cleveland Rd Peninsula (44264) *(G-12346)*

Winery At Spring Hill Inc 440 466-0626
   6062 S Ridge Rd W Geneva (44041) *(G-7946)*

Winery At Wilcox Inc 937 526-3232
   6572 State Route 47 Versailles (45380) *(G-14993)*

Winery At Wolf Creek 330 666-9285
   2637 S Cleveland Massillon Rd Barberton (44203) *(G-900)*

Winesburg Hardwood Lbr Co LLC 330 893-2705
   2871 Us Route 62 Dundee (44624) *(G-6974)*

Winesburg Meats Inc 330 359-5092
   2181 Us Rte 62 Winesburg (44690) *(G-16083)*

Wings N Wheels 419 586-6531
   1217 Brooke Ave Celina (45822) *(G-2356)*

Winkle Industries Inc 330 823-9730
   2080 W Main St Alliance (44601) *(G-438)*

Winkler Co Inc 937 294-2662
   435 Patterson Rd Dayton (45419) *(G-6655)*

Winner Corporation (PA) 419 582-4321
   8544 State Route 705 Yorkshire (45388) *(G-16293)*

Winner's Meat Service, Yorkshire *Also Called: Winner Corporation (G-16293)*

Winston Heat Treating Inc 937 226-0110
   711 E 2nd St Dayton (45402) *(G-6656)*

Winston Oil Co Inc 740 373-9664
   1 Court House Ln Ste 3 Marietta (45750) *(G-9845)*

Winter Equipment Company Incorporated 440 946-8377
   1900 Joseph Lloyd Pkwy Willoughby (44094) *(G-16019)*

Winters Concrete, Jackson *Also Called: Winters Products Inc (G-8728)*

Winters Products Inc 740 286-4149
   109 Athens St Jackson (45640) *(G-8728)*

Winzeler Couplings & Mtls LLC 419 485-3147
   910 E Main St Montpelier (43543) *(G-11146)*

Winzeler Stamping Co (HQ) 419 485-3147
   129 W Wabash St Montpelier (43543) *(G-11147)*

Wipe Out Enterprises Inc 937 497-9473
   6523 Dawson Rd Sidney (45365) *(G-13296)*

Wire Lab Company, Cleveland *Also Called: Omni Technical Products Inc (G-4504)*

Wire Products Company Inc 216 267-0777
   14700 Industrial Pkwy Cleveland (44135) *(G-4912)*

Wire Products Company LLC (PA) 216 267-0777
   14601 Industrial Pkwy Cleveland (44135) *(G-4913)*

WIRE PRODUCTS COMPANY, INC., Cleveland *Also Called: Wire Products Company Inc (G-4912)*

Wire Shop Inc — ALPHABETIC SECTION

Wire Shop Inc 440 354-6842
5959 Pinecone Dr Mentor (44060) *(G-10596)*

Wireless Retail LLC 614 657-5182
6750 Commerce Court Dr Blacklick (43004) *(G-1345)*

Wiremax A Heico Company, Toledo *Also Called: Connectronics Corp (G-14250)*

Wiremax Ltd 419 531-9500
705 Wamba Ave Toledo (43607) *(G-14525)*

Wis 1985 Inc 423 581-4916
1347 E 4th St Dayton (45402) *(G-6657)*

Wisco Products Incorporated 937 228-2101
109 Commercial St Dayton (45402) *(G-6658)*

Wisconsin Indus Sand Co LLC 715 235-0942
3 Summit Park Dr Ste 700 Independence (44131) *(G-8692)*

Wise Edge LLC 330 208-0889
981 Home Ave Akron (44310) *(G-376)*

Wiseco, Mentor *Also Called: Race Winning Brands Inc (G-10544)*

Wiseman Bros Fabg & Stl Ltd 740 988-5121
2598 Glade Rd Beaver (45613) *(G-1036)*

Wismar Prcsion Toling Prod Inc 440 296-0487
7505 Tyler Blvd Ste 2 Mentor (44060) *(G-10597)*

Witt Enterprises Inc 440 992-8333
2024 Aetna Rd Ashtabula (44004) *(G-665)*

Witt Industries Inc (HQ) 513 871-5700
4600 N Mason Montgomery Rd Mason (45040) *(G-10071)*

Witt Products, Mason *Also Called: Witt Industries Inc (G-10071)*

Wittrock Wdwkg & Mfg Co Inc 513 891-5800
4201 Malsbary Rd Blue Ash (45242) *(G-1492)*

Wittur Usa Inc 216 524-0100
7852 Bavaria Rd Twinsburg (44087) *(G-14756)*

Wiwa LLC 419 757-0141
107 N Main St Alger (45812) *(G-384)*

Wiwa LP 419 757-0141
107 N Main St Alger (45812) *(G-385)*

Wjf Enterprises LLC 513 871-7320
1347 Custer Ave Cincinnati (45208) *(G-3523)*

Wls Stamping & Fabricating, Cleveland *Also Called: WLS Stamping Co (G-4914)*

WLS Stamping Co (PA) 216 271-5100
3292 E 80th St Cleveland (44104) *(G-4914)*

Wm Lang & Sons Company 513 541-3304
3280 Beekman St Cincinnati (45223) *(G-3524)*

Wm Plotz Machine and Forge Co 216 861-0441
2514 Center St Cleveland (44113) *(G-4915)*

Wmg Wood More 440 350-3970
51 Johnnycake Ridge Rd Painesville (44077) *(G-12278)*

Woco, Strongsville *Also Called: Wallover Oil Company Inc (G-13894)*

Wodin Inc 440 439-4222
5441 Perkins Rd Cleveland (44146) *(G-4916)*

Woeber Mustard Mfg Co 937 323-6281
1966 Commerce Cir Springfield (45504) *(G-13656)*

Wogen Resources America LLC 216 272-0062
6980 Country View Dr Valley City (44280) *(G-14901)*

Wolf Composite Solutions 614 219-6990
3991 Fondorf Dr Columbus (43228) *(G-5879)*

Wolf G T Awning & Tent Co 937 548-4161
3352 State Route 571 Greenville (45331) *(G-8065)*

Wolf Machine Company (PA) 513 791-5194
5570 Creek Rd Blue Ash (45242) *(G-1493)*

Wolf Metals Inc 614 461-6361
1625 W Mound St Columbus (43223) *(G-5880)*

Wolfe Grinding Inc 330 929-6677
4582 Allen Rd Stow (44224) *(G-13739)*

Wolff Bros Supply Inc 440 327-1650
38777 Taylor Industrial Pkwy North Ridgeville (44035) *(G-11864)*

Wolff Tool & Mfg Company Inc 440 933-7797
139 Lear Rd Avon Lake (44012) *(G-829)*

Wolford Industrial Park 216 281-3980
9801 Walford Ave Cleveland (44102) *(G-4917)*

Wolters Kluwer Clinical Drug Information Inc 330 650-6506
1100 Terex Rd Hudson (44236) *(G-8619)*

Wonder Machine Services Inc 440 937-7500
35340 Avon Commerce Pkwy Avon (44011) *(G-792)*

Wonder-Shirts Inc 917 679-2336
7695 Crawley Dr Dublin (43017) *(G-6959)*

Wonderly Trucking & Excvtg LLC 419 837-6294
3939 Fremont Pike Perrysburg (43551) *(G-1244)*

Wood County Ohio 419 353-1227
991 S Main St Bowling Green (43402) *(G-1596)*

Wood Duck Enterprises Ltd 937 776-0606
2225 La Grange Rd Beavercreek (45431) *(G-107)*

Wood Graphics Inc (PA) 513 771-6300
8075 Reading Rd Ste 301 Cincinnati (45237) *(G-3525)*

Wood Recovery, Newark *Also Called: Hope Timber & Marketing Group (G-11580)*

Wood Working, Troy *Also Called: Stull Woodworks Inc (G-14614)*

Wood-Sebring Corporation 216 267-3191
13800 Enterprise Ave Cleveland (44135) *(G-4918)*

Woodbine Products Company 330 725-0165
915 W Smith Rd Medina (44256) *(G-10395)*

Woodbridge, Fremont *Also Called: Woodbridge Group (G-7820)*

Woodbridge Englewood Inc 937 540-9889
300 Lau Pkwy Englewood (45315) *(G-7249)*

Woodbridge Group 419 334-3666
827 Graham Dr Fremont (43420) *(G-7820)*

Woodburn Press Ltd 937 293-9245
405 Littell Ave Dayton (45419) *(G-6659)*

Woodco US, Waverly *Also Called: Clarksville Stave & Veneer Co (G-15279)*

Woodcraft 419 389-0560
5311 Airport Hwy Toledo (43615) *(G-14526)*

Woodcraft, Dayton *Also Called: Ryanworks Inc (G-6555)*

Woodcraft Industries Inc 440 632-9655
15351 S State Ave Middlefield (44062) *(G-10798)*

Woodcraft Industries Inc 440 437-7811
131 Grand Valley Ave Orwell (44076) *(G-12171)*

WOODCRAFT INDUSTRIES, INC., Middlefield *Also Called: Woodcraft Industries Inc (G-10798)*

WOODCRAFT INDUSTRIES, INC., Orwell *Also Called: Woodcraft Industries Inc (G-12171)*

Wooden Horse 740 503-5243
204 N Main St Baltimore (43105) *(G-849)*

Woodford Logistics 513 417-8453
15 Sprague Rd South Charleston (45368) *(G-1355)*

Woodgrain Enterprises LLC 216 854-8151
3755 E 154th St Cleveland (44128) *(G-4919)*

Woodhill Plating Works Company 216 883-1344
9114 Reno Ave Cleveland (44105) *(G-4920)*

Woodland Cellars LLC 330 240-4883
212 N Main St Hubbard (44425) *(G-8573)*

Woodlawn Rubber Co 513 489-1718
11268 Williamson Rd Blue Ash (45241) *(G-1494)*

Woodman Agitator Inc 440 937-9865
1404 Lear Industrial Pkwy Avon (44011) *(G-793)*

Woodrow Manufacturing Co 937 399-9333
4300 River Rd Springfield (45502) *(G-13657)*

Woodsage Industries LLC 419 866-8000
7400 Airport Hwy Holland (43528) *(G-8538)*

Woodsage LLC 419 866-8000
7400 Airport Hwy Holland (43528) *(G-8539)*

Woodsfeld True Vlue HM Ctr Inc 740 472-1651
218 State Rte 78 Woodsfield (43793) *(G-16090)*

Woodsmiths Design & Mfg, Bowerston *Also Called: Novo Manufacturing LLC (G-1546)*

Woodstock Products Inc 216 641-3811
2914 Broadway Ave Cleveland (44115) *(G-4921)*

Woodworking Shop LLC 513 330-9663
1195 Mound Rd Miamisburg (45342) *(G-10702)*

Woodworks Design 440 693-4414
9005 N Girdle Rd Middlefield (44062) *(G-10799)*

Woodworks Unlimited 740 574-0500
330 Lambro Ln Franklin Furnace (45629) *(G-773)*

Woodworks Zanesville 740 624-3396
7079 County Road 121 Mount Gilead (43338) *(G-11236)*

Wooldridge Lumber Co 740 289-4912
3264 Laurel Ridge Rd Piketon (45661) *(G-1248)*

Wooster Abruzzi Company (PA) 330 345-3968
3310 Columbus Rd Wooster (44691) *(G-16183)*

ALPHABETIC SECTION

Wooster Book Company, The, Wooster *Also Called: Ketman Corporation (G-16142)*

Wooster Brush Company 440 322-8081
870 Infirmary Rd Elyria (44035) *(G-7219)*

Wooster Daily Record Inc LLC (HQ) 330 264-1125
212 E Liberty St Wooster (44691) *(G-16184)*

Wooster Printing & Litho Inc
1345 W Old Lincoln Way Wooster (44691) *(G-16185)*

Wooster Products Inc (PA) 330 264-2844
1000 Spruce St Wooster (44691) *(G-16186)*

Wooster Products Inc 330 264-2854
1000 Spruce St Wooster (44691) *(G-16187)*

Worker Automation Inc 937 473-2111
953 Belfast Dr Dayton (45440) *(G-6660)*

Workflowone LLC 877 735-4966
220 E Monument Ave Dayton (45402) *(G-6661)*

Workhorse, Sharonville *Also Called: Workhorse Group Inc (G-13175)*

Workhorse Group Inc (PA) 888 646-5205
3600 Park 42 Dr Ste 160e Sharonville (45241) *(G-13175)*

Workhorse Technologies Inc 888 646-5205
3600 Park 42 Dr Ste 160 Sharonville (45241) *(G-13176)*

Workman Electronic Pdts Inc 419 923-7525
11955 County Road 10-2 Delta (43515) *(G-6792)*

Workman Electronics, Delta *Also Called: Twin Point Inc (G-6791)*

Works In Progress Inc (PA) 802 658-3797
3825 Edwards Rd Ste 800 Cincinnati (45209) *(G-3526)*

Workstream Inc (HQ) 513 870-4400
3158 Production Dr Fairfield (45014) *(G-7428)*

World Class Carriages LLC 330 857-7811
5090 Mount Eaton Rd S Dalton (44618) *(G-6145)*

World Class Plastics Inc 937 843-3003
7695 State Route 708 Russells Point (43348) *(G-12880)*

World Connections Corps 419 363-2681
10803 Erastus Durbin Rd Rockford (45882) *(G-12835)*

World Digital Imaging, Beavercreek *Also Called: Program Managers Inc (G-1078)*

World Harvest Church Inc (PA) 614 837-1990
4595 Gender Rd Canal Winchester (43110) *(G-1994)*

World Journal 216 458-0988
1735 E 36th St Cleveland (44114) *(G-4922)*

World Resource Solutons Corp 614 733-3737
8485 Estates Ct Plain City (43064) *(G-12603)*

World Wide Recyclers Inc 614 554-3296
3755 S High St Columbus (43207) *(G-5881)*

Worldclass Processing Corp
1400 Enterprise Pkwy Twinsburg (44087) *(G-14757)*

Worldmark, Strongsville *Also Called: Donprint Inc (G-13828)*

Worldwide Graphics and Sign, Blue Ash *Also Called: Beebe Worldwide Graphics Sign (G-1367)*

Wornick Company, The, West Chester *Also Called: Baxters North America Inc (G-15540)*

Wornick Foods, Blue Ash *Also Called: Baxters North America Inc (G-1366)*

Wornick Foods, Cincinnati *Also Called: Baxters North America Inc (G-2661)*

Wornick Holding Company Inc 513 794-9800
4700 Creek Rd Blue Ash (45242) *(G-1495)*

Worthignton Products Inc 330 452-7400
1520 Wood Ave Se East Canton (44730) *(G-6982)*

Worthington, Beachwood *Also Called: RSI Company (G-1020)*

Worthington, Worthington *Also Called: Worthington Enterprises Inc (G-16220)*

Worthington Cylinder, Worthington *Also Called: Worthington Cylinder Corp (G-16219)*

Worthington Cylinder Corp 740 569-4143
245 N Broad St Bremen (43107) *(G-1641)*

Worthington Cylinder Corp 614 438-7900
1085 Dearborn Dr Columbus (43085) *(G-5882)*

Worthington Cylinder Corp 440 576-5847
863 State Route 307 E Jefferson (44047) *(G-8763)*

Worthington Cylinder Corp 614 840-3800
333 Maxtown Rd Westerville (43082) *(G-15690)*

Worthington Cylinder Corp 330 262-1762
899 Venture Blvd Wooster (44691) *(G-16188)*

Worthington Cylinder Corp (HQ) 614 840-3210
200 W Old Wilson Bridge Rd Worthington (43085) *(G-16219)*

Worthington Energy Innovations, Fremont *Also Called: Professional Supply Inc (G-7803)*

Worthington Enterprises Inc 513 539-9291
350 Lawton Ave Monroe (45050) *(G-11121)*

Worthington Enterprises Inc (PA) 614 438-3210
200 W Old Wilson Bridge Rd Worthington (43085) *(G-16220)*

Worthington Foods Inc 740 453-5501
1675 Fairview Rd Zanesville (43701) *(G-16571)*

Worthington Industries, Cleveland *Also Called: Worthington Mid-Rise Cnstr Inc (G-4923)*

Worthington Industries Inc 614 438-3028
1055 Dearborn Dr Columbus (43085) *(G-5883)*

Worthington Industries Inc 614 438-3190
1127 Dearborn Dr Columbus (43085) *(G-5884)*

Worthington Industries Inc 614 438-3113
1818 West Case Rd # 101 Columbus (43235) *(G-5885)*

Worthington Industries Lsg LLC 614 438-3210
200 W Old Wilson Bridge Rd Worthington (43085) *(G-16221)*

WORTHINGTON INDUSTRIES, INC., Columbus *Also Called: Worthington Industries Inc (G-5885)*

Worthington Mid-Rise Cnstr Inc (HQ) 216 472-1511
3100 E 45th St Ste 400 Cleveland (44127) *(G-4923)*

Worthington Military Cnstr Inc 615 599-6446
200 W Old Wilson Bridge Rd Worthington (43085) *(G-16222)*

Worthington Services LLC 937 848-2164
3157 Sears Rd Spring Valley (45370) *(G-13492)*

Worthington Steel, Worthington *Also Called: Worthington Steel Company (G-16223)*

Worthington Steel Company (PA) 800 944-2255
100 W Old Wilson Bridge Rd Worthington (43085) *(G-16223)*

Worthington Steel Div, Columbus *Also Called: Worthington Industries Inc (G-5884)*

Worthngton Smuel Coil Proc LLC (HQ) 330 963-3777
1400 Enterprise Pkwy Twinsburg (44087) *(G-14758)*

Worthngton Stelpac Systems LLC (HQ) 614 438-3205
1205 Dearborn Dr Columbus (43085) *(G-5886)*

Worthngton Stl Mexico SA De Cv 800 944-2255
200 W Old Wilson Bridge Rd Worthington (43085) *(G-16224)*

Wp Cpp Holdings LLC (DH) 216 453-4800
1621 Euclid Ave Ste 1850 Cleveland (44115) *(G-4924)*

Wpc Successor Inc 937 233-6141
6555 Oh 202 Tipp City (45371) *(G-14167)*

Wrap-Tite, Solon *Also Called: B D G Wrap-Tite Inc (G-13315)*

Wray Precision Products Inc 513 228-5000
3650 Turtlecreek Rd Lebanon (45036) *(G-9121)*

Wrayco Industries Inc 330 688-5617
858 Seasons Rd Stow (44224) *(G-13740)*

Wrayco Manufacturing In 330 688-5617
5010 Hudson Dr Stow (44224) *(G-13741)*

Wrc, Akron *Also Called: Wrc Holdings Inc (G-377)*

Wrc Holdings Inc 330 733-6662
1485 Exeter Rd Akron (44306) *(G-377)*

Wre Color Tech, Wadsworth *Also Called: Western Roto Engravers Inc (G-15072)*

Wrena LLC 937 667-4403
265 Lightner Rd Tipp City (45371) *(G-14168)*

Wright Brothers Inc (PA) 513 731-2222
1930 Losantiville Ave Cincinnati (45237) *(G-3527)*

Wright Enrichment Incorporated 337 783-3096
8000 Memorial Dr Plain City (43064) *(G-12604)*

Wright Group, The, Plain City *Also Called: Wright Enrichment Incorporated (G-12604)*

Wright Tool Company 330 848-0600
1 Wright Pl Barberton (44203) *(G-901)*

Wrights Well Service LLC 740 380-9602
37940 Scout Rd Logan (43138) *(G-9378)*

Wrong Turn Fabrication LLC 330 802-8686
2792 Hartville Rd Rootstown (44272) *(G-12858)*

Wrwp, Twinsburg *Also Called: C C M Wire Inc (G-14638)*

Wrwp LLC 330 425-3421
1920 Case Pkwy S Twinsburg (44087) *(G-14759)*

Ws Thermal Process Tech Inc 440 385-6829
8301 W Erie Ave Lorain (44053) *(G-9445)*

WS Tyler Screening Inc 440 974-1047
8570 Tyler Blvd Mentor (44060) *(G-10598)*

Wsny FM, Columbus *Also Called: Franklin Communications Inc (G-5386)*

Wt Acquisition Company Ltd 513 577-7980
2130 Waycross Rd Cincinnati (45240) *(G-3528)*

Wtd Real Estate Inc 440 934-5305
1280 Moore Rd Avon (44011) *(G-794)*

Wulco Inc (PA) 513 679-2600
6899 Steger Dr Ste A Cincinnati (45237) *(G-3529)*

Wulco Inc 513 679-2600
6900 Steger Dr Cincinnati (45237) *(G-3530)*

Wulco Inc 513 379-6115
1010 Eaton Ave Ste B # B Hamilton (45013) *(G-8259)*

Wurms Woodworking Company 419 492-2184
725 W Mansfield St New Washington (44854) *(G-11552)*

Wurtec Incorporated 419 726-1066
800 Seneca St Toledo (43608) *(G-14527)*

Wurtec Manufacturing Service 419 726-1066
6200 Brent Dr Toledo (43611) *(G-14528)*

Wurth Elecktronik, Miamisburg *Also Called: Wurth Electronics Ics Inc (G-10703)*

Wurth Electronics Ics Inc 937 415-7700
1982 Byers Rd Miamisburg (45342) *(G-10703)*

WV CHS Pharmacy Services LLC 844 595-4652
10123 Alliance Rd Ste 320 Blue Ash (45242) *(G-1496)*

Www.slidepartsexpress.com, Willoughby *Also Called: Quality Specialists Inc (G-15979)*

Wyandot Dolomite Inc 419 396-7641
1794 County Highway 99 Carey (43316) *(G-2286)*

Wyandot Snacks, Marion *Also Called: Wyandot Usa LLC (G-9892)*

Wyandot Usa LLC (PA) 740 383-4031
135 Wyandot Ave Marion (43302) *(G-9892)*

Wyandotte Winery LLC 614 357-7522
4640 Wyandotte Dr Columbus (43230) *(G-5887)*

Wyatt Industries LLC 330 954-1790
1790 Miller Pkwy Streetsboro (44241) *(G-13799)*

Wyatt Specialties Inc 614 989-5362
4761 State Route 361 Circleville (43113) *(G-3561)*

Wyman Gordon, Cleveland *Also Called: Wyman-Gordon Company (G-4925)*

Wyman Woodworking 614 338-0615
389 Robinwood Ave Columbus (43213) *(G-5888)*

Wyman-Gordon Company 216 341-0085
3097 E 61st St Cleveland (44127) *(G-4925)*

Wyoming Casing Service Inc 330 479-8785
1414 Raff Rd Sw Canton (44710) *(G-2270)*

Wyse Industrial Carts Inc 419 923-7353
10510 County Road 12 Wauseon (43567) *(G-15277)*

Wysong Gravel Co Inc 937 452-1523
120 Camden College Corner Rd Camden (45311) *(G-1965)*

Wysong Gravel Co Inc (PA) 937 456-4539
2332 State Route 503 N West Alexandria (45381) *(G-15347)*

Wysong Gravel Co Inc 937 839-5497
2032 State Route 503 N West Alexandria (45381) *(G-15348)*

X L Sand and Gravel Co 330 426-9876
9289 Jackman Rd Negley (44441) *(G-11355)*

X M C, Sylvania *Also Called: Don-Ell Corporation (G-13994)*

X M C Division, Sylvania *Also Called: Don-Ell Corporation (G-13993)*

X-Mil Inc 937 444-1323
220 Homan Way Mount Orab (45154) *(G-11248)*

X-Press Tool Inc 330 225-8748
2845 Interstate Pkwy Brunswick (44212) *(G-1802)*

X-Treme Finishes Inc 330 474-0614
4821 Brookhaven Dr North Royalton (44133) *(G-11903)*

X44 Corp 330 657-2335
1601 Mill St W Peninsula (44264) *(G-12347)*

Xact Spec Industries LLC (PA) 440 543-8157
16959 Munn Rd Chagrin Falls (44023) *(G-2436)*

Xact Spec Industries LLC 440 543-8157
16959 Munn Rd Chagrin Falls (44023) *(G-2437)*

Xaloy LLC (PA) 330 726-4000
375 Victoria Rd Ste 1 Austintown (44515) *(G-757)*

Xapc Co 216 362-4100
15583 Brookpark Rd Cleveland (44142) *(G-4926)*

XCEL Mold and Machine Inc 330 499-8450
7661 Freedom Ave Nw Canton (44720) *(G-2271)*

Xcellence Publications Inc 216 326-1891
860 Eddy Rd Cleveland (44108) *(G-4927)*

Xcite Systems Corporation 513 965-0300
675 Cincinnati Batavia Pike Cincinnati (45245) *(G-2577)*

Xenia City Water Treatment Div, Xenia *Also Called: City of Xenia (G-16256)*

Xenia Daily Gazette 937 372-4444
1836 W Park Sq Xenia (45385) *(G-16281)*

Xerion Advanced Battery Corp 720 229-0697
3100 Research Blvd Ste 320 Kettering (45420) *(G-8911)*

Xomox Corporation 513 745-6000
4477 Malsbary Rd Blue Ash (45242) *(G-1497)*

Xomox Corporation 936 271-6500
4444 Cooper Rd Cincinnati (45242) *(G-3531)*

Xomox Pft Corp 936 271-6500
4444 Cooper Rd Cincinnati (45242) *(G-3532)*

Xorb Corporation 419 354-6021
455 W Woodland Cir Bowling Green (43402) *(G-597)*

Xpansion Instrument LLC 330 618-0062
1425 Glenoak Dr Tallmadge (44278) *(G-14058)*

Xperion E & E USA LLC 740 788-9560
1475 James Pkwy Heath (43056) *(G-8333)*

Xponet Inc 440 354-6617
20 Elberta Rd Painesville (44077) *(G-12279)*

XS Smith Inc (PA) 252 940-5060
5513 Vine St Ste 1 Cincinnati (45217) *(G-3533)*

Xt Innovations Ltd 419 562-1989
4799 Stetzer Rd Bucyrus (44820) *(G-1876)*

Xtek Inc (PA) 513 733-7800
11451 Reading Rd Cincinnati (45241) *(G-3534)*

Xto Energy, Bellaire *Also Called: Xto Energy Inc (G-1190)*

Xto Energy Inc 740 671-9901
2358 W 23rd St Bellaire (43906) *(G-1190)*

Xtreme Outdoors LLC 330 731-4137
1519 Boettler Rd Ste A Uniontown (44685) *(G-1797)*

Xunlight Corporation 419 469-8600
3145 Nebraska Ave Toledo (43607) *(G-14529)*

Xylem Inc 937 767-7241
1700 Brannum Ln Ste 1725 Yellow Springs (45387) *(G-16287)*

Xylem Ysi, A Xylem Brand, Yellow Springs *Also Called: Ysi Environmental Inc (G-16291)*

Y & T Woodcraft Inc 330 464-3432
10861 Lautenschlager Rd Apple Creek (44606) *(G-515)*

Y City Recycling LLC 740 452-2500
4005 All American Way Zanesville (43701) *(G-1572)*

Y&B Logging 440 437-1053
3647 Montgomery Rd Orwell (44076) *(G-12172)*

Yachiyo Manufacturing America, Columbus *Also Called: Yachiyo of America Inc (G-5889)*

Yachiyo of America Inc (DH) 614 876-3220
2285 Walcutt Rd Columbus (43228) *(G-5889)*

Yakpads Inc 419 357-5684
3504 Hull Rd Huron (44839) *(G-8646)*

Yamada North America Inc 937 462-7111
9000 Columbus Cincinnati Rd South Charleston (45368) *(G-13456)*

Yanfeng US Auto Intr Systems I 419 636-4211
918 S Union St Bryan (43506) *(G-1846)*

Yanfeng US Auto Intr Systems I 419 633-1873
918 S Union St Bryan (43506) *(G-1847)*

Yanfeng US Auto Intr Systems I 616 834-9422
715 E South St Bryan (43506) *(G-1848)*

Yanfeng US Auto Intr Systems I 419 662-4905
7560 Arbor Dr Northwood (43619) *(G-11935)*

YANFENG US AUTOMOTIVE INTERIOR SYSTEMS I LLC, Bryan *Also Called: Yanfeng US Auto Intr Systems I (G-1847)*

YANFENG US AUTOMOTIVE INTERIOR SYSTEMS I LLC, Bryan *Also Called: Yanfeng US Auto Intr Systems I (G-1848)*

YANFENG US AUTOMOTIVE INTERIOR SYSTEMS II LLC, Bryan *Also Called: Yanfeng US Auto Intr Systems I (G-1846)*

Yanke Bionics Inc (PA) 330 762-6411
303 W Exchange St Akron (44302) *(G-378)*

Yankee Candle Company Inc 413 712-9416
175 Heritage Dr Etna (43062) *(G-7257)*

Yankee Wire Cloth Products Inc 740 545-9129
221 W Main St West Lafayette (43845) *(G-1562)*

YAR Corporation 330 652-1222
406 S Main St Niles (44446) *(G-11693)*

Yarder Manufacturing Company (PA) 419 476-3933
722 Phillips Ave Toledo (43612) *(G-14530)*

ALPHABETIC SECTION — Z Line Kitchen and Bath

Yaskawa America Inc.. 937 847-6200
100 Automation Way Miamisburg (45342) *(G-10704)*

Yaskawa America Inc.. 937 440-2600
1050 S Dorset Rd Troy (45373) *(G-14617)*

Yaya's, Kent *Also Called: Mark Grzianis St Treats Ex Inc (G-8832)*

Ye Olde Mille Shoppe, Utica *Also Called: Velvet Ice Cream Company (G-14859)*

Yellow Creek Casting Co Inc.. 330 532-4608
18141 Fife Coal Rd Wellsville (43968) *(G-15338)*

Yellow Creek Industries.. 330 757-1065
64 Poland Mnr Youngstown (44514) *(G-16475)*

Yellow Springs International, Yellow Springs *Also Called: Ysi Incorporated (G-16292)*

Yellow Springs News Inc.. 937 767-7373
253 And A Half Xenia Ave Yellow Springs (45387) *(G-16288)*

Yellow Springs Pottery LLC... 937 767-1666
222 Xenia Ave Ste 1 Yellow Springs (45387) *(G-16289)*

Yes Mfg LLC... 614 296-3553
8919 Whitney Dr Lewis Center (43035) *(G-9184)*

Yesco Sign & Lighting Service.. 419 407-6581
5924 American Rd E Toledo (43612) *(G-14531)*

Yespress Graphics LLC.. 614 899-1403
515 S State St Westerville (43081) *(G-15726)*

Yipes Stripes, Englewood *Also Called: TCS Schindler & Co LLC (G-7243)*

Yizumi-HPM Corporation.. 740 382-5600
3424 State Rt 309 Iberia (43325) *(G-8649)*

YKK AP America Inc... 513 942-7200
8748 Jacquemin Dr Ste 400 West Chester (45069) *(G-15528)*

YKK USA, West Chester *Also Called: YKK AP America Inc (G-15528)*

Ylt Red Cleveland LLC.. 216 664-0941
417 Prospect Ave E Cleveland (44115) *(G-4928)*

Yockey Group Inc... 513 860-9053
9053 Le Saint Dr West Chester (45014) *(G-15529)*

Yoder Industries Inc (PA)... 937 278-5769
2520 Needmore Rd Dayton (45414) *(G-6662)*

Yoder Lumber Co Inc (PA)... 330 893-3121
4515 Township Road 367 Millersburg (44654) *(G-11008)*

Yoder Lumber Co Inc... 330 674-1435
7100 County Road 407 Millersburg (44654) *(G-11009)*

Yoder Lumber Co Inc... 330 893-3131
3799 County Road 70 Sugarcreek (44681) *(G-13949)*

Yoder Manufacturing... 740 504-5028
7679 Flack Rd Howard (43028) *(G-8560)*

Yoder Window & Siding Ltd (PA)... 330 695-6960
7846 Harrison Rd Fredericksburg (44627) *(G-7735)*

Yoder Window and Siding, Fredericksburg *Also Called: Yoder Window & Siding Ltd (G-7735)*

Yoder Woodworking.. 740 399-9400
21198 Swendal Rd Butler (44822) *(G-1892)*

Yoder's Cider Barn, Gambier *Also Called: Yoders Fine Foods LLC (G-7910)*

Yoders Fine Foods LLC... 740 668-4961
3361 Martinsburg Rd Gambier (43022) *(G-7910)*

Yoders Produce Inc.. 330 695-5900
9599 S Apple Creek Rd Fredericksburg (44627) *(G-7736)*

Yokohama Inds Amricas Ohio Inc... 440 352-3321
474 Newell St Painesville (44077) *(G-12280)*

Yokohama Tire Corporation... 440 352-3321
474 Newell St Painesville (44077) *(G-12281)*

Yokohama Tws North America Inc (DH)............................. 866 633-8473
1501 Exeter Rd Akron (44306) *(G-379)*

Yonezawa Usa Inc.. 614 799-2210
7920 Corporate Blvd Ste A Plain City (43064) *(G-12605)*

Yonghe Precision Castings Ohio... 330 447-6685
1810 Eber Rd Holland (43528) *(G-8540)*

Yost Labs Inc.. 740 876-4936
630 2nd St Portsmouth (45662) *(G-12661)*

Yost Superior Co.. 937 323-7591
300 S Center St Ste 1 Springfield (45506) *(G-13658)*

Yotec, South Charleston *Also Called: Yamada North America Inc (G-13456)*

Young & Bertke Air Systems Co., Cincinnati *Also Called: Rmt Acquisition Inc (G-3347)*

Young Regulator Company Inc... 440 232-9452
7100 Krick Rd Ste A Bedford (44146) *(G-1161)*

Youngs Jersey Dairy Inc.. 937 325-0629
6880 Springfield Xenia Rd Yellow Springs (45387) *(G-16290)*

Youngs Locker Serv & Meat Proc, Danville *Also Called: Youngs Locker Service Inc (G-6150)*

Youngs Locker Service Inc.. 740 599-6833
16201 Nashville Rd Danville (43014) *(G-6150)*

Youngs Publishing Inc... 937 259-6575
4130 Linden Ave Ste 150 Dayton (45432) *(G-6176)*

Youngs Sand & Gravel Co Inc.. 419 994-3040
689 State Route 39 Loudonville (44842) *(G-9454)*

Youngs Sealcoating LLC.. 330 591-5446
2445 Station Rd Medina (44256) *(G-10396)*

Youngstown ARC Engraving Co.. 330 793-2471
380 Victoria Rd Youngstown (44515) *(G-16476)*

Youngstown Belt Railroad Co.. 740 622-8092
123 Division Street Ext Youngstown (44510) *(G-16477)*

Youngstown Bending Rolling.. 330 799-2227
3710 Hendricks Rd Bldg 2b Youngstown (44515) *(G-16478)*

Youngstown Bending Rolling Inc... 330 898-3878
1052 Mahoning Ave Nw Warren (44483) *(G-15225)*

Youngstown Bolt & Supply Co... 330 799-3201
340 N Meridian Rd Youngstown (44509) *(G-16479)*

Youngstown Burial Vault Co.. 330 782-0015
316 Forsythe Ave Girard (44420) *(G-7977)*

Youngstown Curve Form Inc.. 330 744-3028
1102 Rigby St Youngstown (44506) *(G-16480)*

Youngstown Fence Incorporated.. 330 788-8110
235 E Indianola Ave Youngstown (44507) *(G-16481)*

Youngstown Hard Chrome Pltg Gr....................................... 330 758-9721
8451 Southern Blvd Youngstown (44512) *(G-16482)*

Youngstown Heat Trting Ntrding... 330 788-3025
1118 Meadowbrook Ave Youngstown (44512) *(G-16483)*

Youngstown Letter Shop Inc.. 330 793-4935
3650 Connecticut Ave Youngstown (44515) *(G-16484)*

Youngstown Lithographing Co, Youngstown *Also Called: Youngstown ARC Engraving Co (G-16476)*

Youngstown Metal Fabricating, Youngstown *Also Called: M F Y Inc (G-16391)*

Youngstown Plastic Tooling (PA).. 330 782-7222
1209 Velma Ct Youngstown (44512) *(G-16485)*

Youngstown Pre-Press Inc.. 330 793-3690
3691 Leharps Dr Youngstown (44515) *(G-16486)*

Youngstown Rubber Products, Youngstown *Also Called: Mid-State Sales Inc (G-16400)*

Youngstown Shade & Alum LLC... 330 782-2373
3335 South Ave Youngstown (44502) *(G-16487)*

Youngstown Specialty Mtls Inc.. 330 259-1110
571 Andrews Ave Youngstown (44505) *(G-16488)*

Youngstown Tool & Die Company... 330 747-4464
2572 Salt Springs Rd Youngstown (44509) *(G-16489)*

Youngstown Tube Co... 330 743-7414
401 Andrews Ave Youngstown (44505) *(G-16490)*

Youngstown-Kenworth Inc (PA).. 330 534-9761
7255 Hubbard Masury Rd Hubbard (44425) *(G-8574)*

Your Carpenter Inc... 216 621-2166
2403 Saint Clair Ave Ne Cleveland (44114) *(G-4929)*

Ysd Industries Inc... 330 792-6521
3710 Hendricks Rd Youngstown (44515) *(G-16491)*

Ysi, Yellow Springs *Also Called: Xylem Inc (G-16287)*

Ysi Environmental Inc... 937 767-7241
1725 Brannum Ln Yellow Springs (45387) *(G-16291)*

Ysi Incorporated (HQ).. 937 767-7241
1700 Brannum Ln # 1725 Yellow Springs (45387) *(G-16292)*

Ysk Corporation... 740 774-7315
1 Colomet Rd Chillicothe (45601) *(G-2542)*

Yugo Mold Inc.. 330 606-0710
1733 Wadsworth Rd Akron (44320) *(G-380)*

Yukon Industries Inc... 440 478-4174
7665 Mentor Ave Ste 113 Mentor (44060) *(G-10599)*

Yusa Corporation (HQ).. 740 335-0335
151 Jamison Rd. Sw Washington Court Hou (43160) *(G-15234)*

Yutzy Woodworking Ltd... 330 359-6166
2441 Us Route 62 Dundee (44624) *(G-6975)*

Yz Enterprises Inc... 419 893-8777
1930 Indian Wood Cir Ste 100 Maumee (43537) *(G-10246)*

Z Line Kitchen and Bath, Marysville *Also Called: Z Line Kitchen and Bath LLC (G-9944)*

ALPHABETIC SECTION

Z Line Kitchen and Bath LLC (PA) 614 777-5004
  916 Delaware Ave Marysville (43040) **(G-9944)**

Z M O Company (PA) 614 875-0230
  2140 Eakin Rd Columbus (43223) **(G-5890)**

Z M O Oil, Columbus *Also Called: Z M O Company* **(G-5890)**

Z-Kan Metal Products LLC 330 695-2397
  8724 County Road 235 Fredericksburg (44627) **(G-7737)**

Zaclon LLC 216 271-1601
  2981 Independence Rd Cleveland (44115) **(G-4930)**

Zaenkert Surveying Essentials 513 738-2917
  7461a Cincinnati Brookville Rd Okeana (45053) **(G-12070)**

Zagar Inc 216 731-0500
  24000 Lakeland Blvd Cleveland (44132) **(G-4931)**

Zane Petroleum Inc 740 454-8779
  575 S 3rd St Columbus (43215) **(G-5891)**

Zaner-Bloser Inc (HQ) 614 486-0221
  1400 Goodale Blvd Ste 200 Columbus (43212) **(G-5892)**

Zanesville Fabricators Inc 740 452-2439
  2981 E Military Rd Zanesville (43701) **(G-16573)**

Zanesville Pallet Co Inc 740 454-3700
  2235 Licking Rd Zanesville (43701) **(G-16574)**

Zarbana Alum Extrusions LLC 330 482-5092
  41738 Esterly Dr Columbiana (44408) **(G-5056)**

Zarbana Industries Inc 330 482-5092
  41738 Esterly Dr Columbiana (44408) **(G-5057)**

Zaytran Inc 440 324-2814
  41535 Schadden Rd Elyria (44035) **(G-7220)**

Zebco Industries Inc 740 654-4510
  211 N Columbus St Lancaster (43130) **(G-9049)**

Zebec of North America Inc 513 829-5533
  210 Donald Dr Fairfield (45014) **(G-7429)**

Zed Digital, Columbus *Also Called: IPA Ltd* **(G-5479)**

Zed Industries Inc 937 667-8407
  3580 Lightner Rd Vandalia (45377) **(G-14968)**

Zeda Inc 513 966-4633
  11560 Goldcoast Dr Cincinnati (45249) **(G-3535)**

Zehrco-Giancola Composites Inc (PA) 440 994-6317
  1501 W 47th St Ashtabula (44004) **(G-666)**

Zeiger Industries Inc 330 484-4413
  4704 Wiseland Ave Se Canton (44707) **(G-2272)**

Zekelman Industries Inc 216 910-3700
  3201 Entp Pkwy Ste 150 Beachwood (44122) **(G-1033)**

Zekelman Industries Inc 740 432-2146
  9208 Jeffrey Dr Cambridge (43725) **(G-1961)**

Zelaya Stoneworks LLC 513 777-8030
  7590 Wyandot Ln Ste 1 Liberty Township (45044) **(G-9211)**

Zen Industries Inc 216 432-3240
  6200 Harvard Ave Cleveland (44105) **(G-4932)**

Zena Baby Soap Company 216 317-6433
  6651 Hedgeline Dr Bedford Heights (44146) **(G-1182)**

Zenex International 440 232-4155
  7777 First Pl Bedford (44146) **(G-1162)**

Zenni USA LLC 614 439-9850
  4531 Industrial Center Dr Obetz (43207) **(G-12065)**

Zephyr Industries Inc 419 281-4485
  600 Township Road 1500 Ashland (44805) **(G-621)**

Zephyr Solutions LLC 440 937-9993
  1050 Lear Industrial Pkwy Bldg 1 Avon (44011) **(G-795)**

Zeres Inc 419 354-5555
  2018 Clearwater Cir Bowling Green (43402) **(G-1598)**

Zero-D Products Inc 440 942-5005
  37939 Stevens Blvd Willoughby (44094) **(G-16020)**

ZF Active Safety & Elec US LLC 216 750-2400
  8333 Rockside Rd Cleveland (44125) **(G-4933)**

ZF Active Safety & Elec US LLC 419 726-5599
  5915 Jason St Toledo (43611) **(G-14532)**

ZF Active Safety US Inc 419 237-2511
  705 N Fayette St Fayette (43521) **(G-7463)**

ZF Active Safety US Inc 734 812-6979
  1750 Production Dr Findlay (45840) **(G-7584)**

Zide Screen Printing, Marietta *Also Called: Zide Sport Shop of Ohio Inc* **(G-9846)**

Zide Sport Shop of Ohio Inc 740 373-8199
  118 Industry Rd Marietta (45750) **(G-9846)**

Zidian Management Corp (PA) 330 743-6050
  574 Mcclurg Rd Boardman (44512) **(G-1520)**

Zidian Manufacturing Inc 330 965-8455
  500 Mcclurg Rd Boardman (44512) **(G-1521)**

Zidian Specialty Foods, Youngstown *Also Called: John Zidian Company* **(G-16384)**

Zie Bart Rhino Linings Toledo 419 841-2886
  3343 N Holland Sylvania Rd Toledo (43615) **(G-1533)**

Ziegler Oil Co, Dover *Also Called: Ziegler Tire and Supply Co* **(G-6850)**

Ziegler Tire and Supply Co 330 434-7126
  547 Wolf Ledges Pkwy Akron (44311) **(G-381)**

Ziegler Tire and Supply Co 330 477-3463
  4300 Tuscarawas St W Canton (44708) **(G-2273)**

Ziegler Tire and Supply Co 330 343-7739
  411 Commercial Pkwy Dover (44622) **(G-6850)**

Ziegler Tire Oil, Akron *Also Called: Ziegler Tire and Supply Co* **(G-381)**

Zilla 614 763-5311
  6728 Liggett Rd Ste 110 Dublin (43016) **(G-6960)**

Zimcom Internet Solutions, Cincinnati *Also Called: One Cloud Services LLC* **(G-3223)**

Zimmer Enterprises Inc (PA) 937 428-1057
  911 Senate Dr Dayton (45459) **(G-6663)**

Zimmer Orthopaedic Surgical, Dover *Also Called: Zimmer Surgical Inc* **(G-6851)**

Zimmer Surgical Inc 800 321-5533
  200 W Ohio Ave Dover (44622) **(G-6851)**

Zimmerman Steel & Sup Co LLC 330 828-1010
  18543 Davis Rd Dalton (44618) **(G-6146)**

Zing Pac Inc 440 248-7997
  30300 Solon Industrial Pkwy Cleveland (44139) **(G-4934)**

Zinkan Enterprises Inc (PA) 330 487-1500
  1919 Case Pkwy Twinsburg (44087) **(G-14760)**

Zion Industries Inc (PA) 330 225-3246
  6229 Grafton Rd Valley City (44280) **(G-14902)**

Zip Center, The-Division, Marietta *Also Called: Richardson Printing Corp* **(G-9820)**

Zip Publishing 614 485-0721
  1091 W 1st Ave Columbus (43212) **(G-5893)**

Zippitycom Print LLC 216 438-0001
  1600 E 23rd St Cleveland (44114) **(G-4935)**

Zipscene, Cincinnati *Also Called: Zipscene LLC* **(G-3536)**

Zipscene LLC 513 201-5174
  615 Main St Fl 5 Cincinnati (45202) **(G-3536)**

Zircoa Inc (PA) 440 248-0500
  31501 Solon Rd Cleveland (44139) **(G-4936)**

Zoia, Cleveland *Also Called: Artistic Metal Spinning Inc* **(G-3682)**

Zomir LLC 513 771-1516
  895 Glendale Milford Rd Cincinnati (45215) **(G-1537)**

Zook Enterprises LLC (PA) 440 543-1010
  16809 Park Circle Dr Chagrin Falls (44023) **(G-2138)**

Zorich Industries Inc 330 482-9803
  1400 Wardingsley Ave Columbiana (44408) **(G-1058)**

ZS Cream & Bean LLC 440 652-6369
  2706 Boston Rd Hinckley (44233) **(G-8480)**

Zshot Inc 800 385-8581
  6155 Huntley Rd Ste D Columbus (43229) **(G-5394)**

Zsi Manufacturing Inc 440 266-0701
  8059 Crile Rd Concord Township (44077) **(G-5595)**

Zts Inc 513 271-2557
  5628 Wooster Pike Cincinnati (45227) **(G-3538)**

Zullix LLC 440 536-9300
  18500 Lake Rd Rocky River (44116) **(G-12846)**

Zurn Industries LLC 814 455-0921
  4501 Sutphen Ct Hilliard (43026) **(G-8454)**

Zygo Inc 513 281-0888
  2832 Jefferson Ave Cincinnati (45219) **(G-3539)**

Zyvex Performance Mtls Inc (HQ) 614 481-2222
  1255 Kinnear Rd Ste 100 Columbus (43212) **(G-5895)**

Zyvex Technologies, Columbus *Also Called: Zyvex Performance Mtls Inc* **(G-5895)**

PRODUCT INDEX

- Product categories are listed in alphabetical order.

A

ABRASIVES
ABRASIVES: Coated
ACCELERATION INDICATORS & SYSTEM COMPONENTS: Aerospace
ACIDS
ACIDS: Hydrochloric
ACIDS: Inorganic
ACIDS: Sulfuric, Oleum
ACOUSTICAL BOARD & TILE
ACRYLIC RESINS
ACTUATORS: Indl, NEC
ADAPTERS: Well
ADDITIVE BASED PLASTIC MATERIALS: Plasticizers
ADDRESSING SVCS
ADHESIVES
ADHESIVES & SEALANTS
ADHESIVES & SEALANTS WHOLESALERS
ADHESIVES: Adhesives, plastic
ADHESIVES: Epoxy
ADVERTISING AGENCIES
ADVERTISING AGENCIES: Consultants
ADVERTISING DISPLAY PRDTS
ADVERTISING REPRESENTATIVES: Electronic Media
ADVERTISING REPRESENTATIVES: Newspaper
ADVERTISING SPECIALTIES, WHOLESALE
ADVERTISING SVCS: Direct Mail
ADVERTISING SVCS: Display
ADVERTISING SVCS: Outdoor
ADVERTISING SVCS: Sample Distribution
AERIAL WORK PLATFORMS
AEROSOLS
AGRICULTURAL EQPT: Barn Cleaners
AGRICULTURAL EQPT: BARN, SILO, POULTRY, DAIRY/LIVESTOCK MACH
AGRICULTURAL EQPT: Elevators, Farm
AGRICULTURAL EQPT: Fertilizing Machinery
AGRICULTURAL EQPT: Grounds Mowing Eqpt
AGRICULTURAL EQPT: Tractors, Farm
AGRICULTURAL EQPT: Turf & Grounds Eqpt
AGRICULTURAL MACHINERY & EQPT: Wholesalers
AIR CLEANING SYSTEMS
AIR CONDITIONERS: Motor Vehicle
AIR CONDITIONING & VENTILATION EQPT & SPLYS: Wholesales
AIR CONDITIONING EQPT
AIR CONDITIONING REPAIR SVCS
AIR CONDITIONING UNITS: Complete, Domestic Or Indl
AIR DUCT CLEANING SVCS
AIR MATTRESSES: Plastic
AIR PURIFICATION EQPT
AIRCRAFT & AEROSPACE FLIGHT INSTRUMENTS & GUIDANCE SYSTEMS
AIRCRAFT & HEAVY EQPT REPAIR SVCS
AIRCRAFT ASSEMBLY PLANTS
AIRCRAFT CONTROL SYSTEMS:
AIRCRAFT ELECTRICAL EQPT REPAIR SVCS
AIRCRAFT ENGINES & ENGINE PARTS: Airfoils
AIRCRAFT ENGINES & ENGINE PARTS: Nonelectric Starters
AIRCRAFT ENGINES & ENGINE PARTS: Pumps
AIRCRAFT ENGINES & ENGINE PARTS: Research & Development, Mfr
AIRCRAFT ENGINES & PARTS
AIRCRAFT EQPT & SPLYS WHOLESALERS
AIRCRAFT MAINTENANCE & REPAIR SVCS
AIRCRAFT PARTS & AUXILIARY EQPT: Assys, Subassemblies/Parts
AIRCRAFT PARTS & AUXILIARY EQPT: Body & Wing Assys & Parts
AIRCRAFT PARTS & AUXILIARY EQPT: Body Assemblies & Parts
AIRCRAFT PARTS & AUXILIARY EQPT: Brakes
AIRCRAFT PARTS & AUXILIARY EQPT: Landing Assemblies & Brakes
AIRCRAFT PARTS & AUXILIARY EQPT: Lighting/Landing Gear Assy
AIRCRAFT PARTS & AUXILIARY EQPT: Military Eqpt & Armament
AIRCRAFT PARTS & AUXILIARY EQPT: Research & Development, Mfr
AIRCRAFT PARTS & AUXILIARY EQPT: Tanks, Fuel
AIRCRAFT PARTS & EQPT, NEC
AIRCRAFT PARTS WHOLESALERS
AIRCRAFT PROPELLERS & PARTS
AIRCRAFT SERVICING & REPAIRING
AIRCRAFT TURBINES
AIRCRAFT WHEELS
AIRCRAFT: Airplanes, Fixed Or Rotary Wing
AIRCRAFT: Motorized
AIRCRAFT: Research & Development, Manufacturer
AIRPORTS, FLYING FIELDS & SVCS
ALARMS: Fire
ALCOHOL, GRAIN: For Medicinal Purposes
ALCOHOL: Ethyl & Ethanol
ALKALIES & CHLORINE
ALLOYS: Additive, Exc Copper Or Made In Blast Furnaces
ALTERNATORS & GENERATORS: Battery Charging
ALTERNATORS: Automotive
ALUMINUM
ALUMINUM PRDTS
ALUMINUM: Coil & Sheet
ALUMINUM: Ingots & Slabs
ALUMINUM: Pigs
ALUMINUM: Rolling & Drawing
AMMUNITION
AMMUNITION: Arming & Fusing Devices
AMMUNITION: Shot, Steel
AMMUNITION: Small Arms
AMPLIFIERS
AMUSEMENT & RECREATION SVCS: Exhibition Operation
AMUSEMENT & RECREATION SVCS: Exposition Operation
AMUSEMENT & RECREATION SVCS: Golf Club, Membership
AMUSEMENT & RECREATION SVCS: Physical Fitness Instruction
AMUSEMENT PARK DEVICES & RIDES
ANALYZERS: Network
ANESTHESIA EQPT
ANIMAL FEED & SUPPLEMENTS: Livestock & Poultry
ANIMAL FEED: Wholesalers
ANIMAL FOOD & SUPPLEMENTS: Bird Food, Prepared
ANIMAL FOOD & SUPPLEMENTS: Cat
ANIMAL FOOD & SUPPLEMENTS: Dog
ANIMAL FOOD & SUPPLEMENTS: Dog & Cat
ANIMAL FOOD & SUPPLEMENTS: Feed Premixes
ANIMAL FOOD & SUPPLEMENTS: Feed Supplements
ANIMAL FOOD & SUPPLEMENTS: Livestock
ANIMAL FOOD & SUPPLEMENTS: Pet, Exc Dog & Cat, Canned
ANIMAL FOOD & SUPPLEMENTS: Pet, Exc Dog & Cat, Dry
ANIMAL FOOD & SUPPLEMENTS: Poultry
ANIMAL FOOD/SUPPLEMENTS: Feeds Fm Meat/Meat/Veg Combnd Meals
ANNEALING: Metal
ANODIZING EQPT
ANODIZING SVC
ANTENNA REPAIR & INSTALLATION SVCS
ANTENNAS: Radar Or Communications
ANTENNAS: Receiving
ANTIBIOTICS
ANTIFREEZE
ANTIQUE REPAIR & RESTORATION SVCS, EXC FURNITURE & AUTOS
APPAREL ACCESS STORES
APPAREL DESIGNERS: Commercial
APPLIANCE PARTS: Porcelain Enameled
APPLIANCES, HOUSEHOLD OR COIN OPERATED: Laundry Dryers
APPLIANCES, HOUSEHOLD: Kitchen, Major, Exc Refrigs & Stoves
APPLIANCES, HOUSEHOLD: Laundry Machines, Incl CoinOperated
APPLIANCES, HOUSEHOLD: Refrigs, Mechanical & Absorption
APPLIANCES: Household, Refrigerators & Freezers
APPLIANCES: Major, Cooking
APPLIANCES: Small, Electric
APPLICATIONS SOFTWARE PROGRAMMING
APPRAISAL SVCS, EXC REAL ESTATE
APRONS: Rubber, Vulcanized Or Rubberized Fabric
AQUARIUMS & ACCESS: Plastic
ARCHITECTURAL SVCS
ARMATURE REPAIRING & REWINDING SVC
ART DEALERS & GALLERIES
ART MARBLE: Concrete
ARTISTS' MATERIALS: Brushes, Air
ARTS & CRAFTS SCHOOL
ASBESTOS PRDTS: Roofing, Felt Roll
ASBESTOS PRODUCTS
ASPHALT & ASPHALT PRDTS
ASPHALT COATINGS & SEALERS
ASPHALT MIXTURES WHOLESALERS
ASPHALT PLANTS INCLUDING GRAVEL MIX TYPE
ASSEMBLING SVC: Plumbing Fixture Fittings, Plastic
ASSOCIATION FOR THE HANDICAPPED
ASSOCIATIONS: Business
ASSOCIATIONS: Real Estate Management
ASSOCIATIONS: Scientists'
ASSOCIATIONS: Trade
ATOMIZERS
AUDIO & VIDEO EQPT, EXC COMMERCIAL
AUDIO COMPONENTS
AUDIO ELECTRONIC SYSTEMS
AUTO & HOME SUPPLY STORES: Auto & Truck Eqpt & Parts
AUTO & HOME SUPPLY STORES: Automotive Access
AUTO & HOME SUPPLY STORES: Automotive parts
AUTO & HOME SUPPLY STORES: Batteries, Automotive & Truck
AUTO & HOME SUPPLY STORES: Trailer Hitches, Automotive
AUTO & HOME SUPPLY STORES: Truck Eqpt & Parts
AUTO SPLYS & PARTS, NEW, WHSLE: Exhaust Sys, Mufflers, Etc
AUTOMATIC REGULATING CONTROL: Building Svcs Monitoring, Auto
AUTOMATIC REGULATING CONTROLS: AC & Refrigeration
AUTOMATIC REGULATING CONTROLS: Appliance, Exc AirCond/Refr
AUTOMATIC REGULATING CONTROLS: Hardware, Environmental Reg
AUTOMATIC REGULATING CTRLS: Damper, Pneumatic Or Electric
AUTOMATIC TELLER MACHINES
AUTOMOBILE FINANCE LEASING
AUTOMOBILES & OTHER MOTOR VEHICLES WHOLESALERS
AUTOMOBILES: Wholesalers
AUTOMOTIVE & TRUCK GENERAL REPAIR SVC
AUTOMOTIVE BODY SHOP
AUTOMOTIVE BODY, PAINT & INTERIOR REPAIR & MAINTENANCE SVC
AUTOMOTIVE CUSTOMIZING SVCS, NONFACTORY BASIS
AUTOMOTIVE GLASS REPLACEMENT SHOPS
AUTOMOTIVE PAINT SHOP
AUTOMOTIVE PARTS, ACCESS & SPLYS
AUTOMOTIVE PARTS: Plastic
AUTOMOTIVE PRDTS: Rubber
AUTOMOTIVE RADIATOR REPAIR SHOPS
AUTOMOTIVE REPAIR SHOPS: Diesel Engine Repair
AUTOMOTIVE REPAIR SHOPS: Electrical Svcs
AUTOMOTIVE REPAIR SHOPS: Engine Rebuilding
AUTOMOTIVE REPAIR SHOPS: Engine Repair
AUTOMOTIVE REPAIR SHOPS: Machine Shop
AUTOMOTIVE REPAIR SHOPS: Muffler Shop, Sale/Rpr/Installation
AUTOMOTIVE REPAIR SHOPS: Rebuilding & Retreading Tires
AUTOMOTIVE REPAIR SHOPS: Tire Recapping
AUTOMOTIVE REPAIR SHOPS: Tire Repair Shop

PRODUCT INDEX

AUTOMOTIVE REPAIR SHOPS: Trailer Repair
AUTOMOTIVE REPAIR SHOPS: Truck Engine Repair, Exc Indl
AUTOMOTIVE REPAIR SVC
AUTOMOTIVE SPLYS & PARTS, NEW, WHOL: Auto Servicing Eqpt
AUTOMOTIVE SPLYS & PARTS, NEW, WHOLESALE: Clutches
AUTOMOTIVE SPLYS & PARTS, NEW, WHOLESALE: Engines/Eng Parts
AUTOMOTIVE SPLYS & PARTS, NEW, WHOLESALE: Filters, Air & Oil
AUTOMOTIVE SPLYS & PARTS, NEW, WHOLESALE: Splys
AUTOMOTIVE SPLYS & PARTS, NEW, WHOLESALE: Stampings
AUTOMOTIVE SPLYS & PARTS, NEW, WHOLESALE: Tools & Eqpt
AUTOMOTIVE SPLYS & PARTS, NEW, WHOLESALE: Trailer Parts
AUTOMOTIVE SPLYS & PARTS, NEW, WHOLESALE: Wheels
AUTOMOTIVE SPLYS & PARTS, WHOLESALE, NEC
AUTOMOTIVE SPLYS/PART, NEW, WHOL: Spring, Shock Absorb/Strut
AUTOMOTIVE SVCS, EXC REPAIR & CARWASHES: Trailer Maintenance
AUTOMOTIVE SVCS, EXC RPR/CARWASHES: High Perf Auto Rpr/Svc
AUTOMOTIVE TRANSMISSION REPAIR SVC
AUTOMOTIVE WELDING SVCS
AUTOMOTIVE: Bodies
AUTOMOTIVE: Seat Frames, Metal
AUTOMOTIVE: Seating
AUTOTRANSFORMERS: Electric
AVIATION SCHOOL
AWNINGS & CANOPIES: Awnings, Fabric, From Purchased Matls
AWNINGS: Fiberglass
AWNINGS: Metal
AXLES

B

BACKHOES
BADGES: Identification & Insignia
BAGS & CONTAINERS: Textile, Exc Sleeping
BAGS & SACKS: Shipping & Shopping
BAGS: Canvas
BAGS: Cellophane
BAGS: Duffle, Canvas, Made From Purchased Materials
BAGS: Food Storage & Frozen Food, Plastic
BAGS: Food Storage & Trash, Plastic
BAGS: Paper
BAGS: Paper, Made From Purchased Materials
BAGS: Plastic
BAGS: Plastic & Pliofilm
BAGS: Plastic, Made From Purchased Materials
BAGS: Rubber Or Rubberized Fabric
BAGS: Shipping
BAGS: Shopping, Made From Purchased Materials
BAGS: Textile
BAKERIES, COMMERCIAL: On Premises Baking Only
BAKERIES: On Premises Baking & Consumption
BAKERY MACHINERY
BAKERY PRDTS: Bakery Prdts, Partially Cooked, Exc frozen
BAKERY PRDTS: Biscuits, Dry
BAKERY PRDTS: Bread, All Types, Fresh Or Frozen
BAKERY PRDTS: Buns, Bread Type, Fresh Or Frozen
BAKERY PRDTS: Cakes, Bakery, Exc Frozen
BAKERY PRDTS: Cakes, Bakery, Frozen
BAKERY PRDTS: Cones, Ice Cream
BAKERY PRDTS: Cookies
BAKERY PRDTS: Cookies & crackers
BAKERY PRDTS: Doughnuts, Exc Frozen
BAKERY PRDTS: Dry
BAKERY PRDTS: Frozen
BAKERY PRDTS: Pastries, Exc Frozen
BAKERY PRDTS: Pies, Bakery, Frozen
BAKERY PRDTS: Pies, Exc Frozen
BAKERY PRDTS: Pretzels
BAKERY PRDTS: Rice Cakes
BAKERY PRDTS: Wholesalers
BAKERY: Wholesale Or Wholesale & Retail Combined
BALLOONS: Toy & Advertising, Rubber

BANNERS: Fabric
BANQUET HALL FACILITIES
BAR
BAR FIXTURES: Wood
BAR JOISTS & CONCRETE REINFORCING BARS: Fabricated
BARBECUE EQPT
BARGES BUILDING & REPAIR
BARRICADES: Metal
BARS & BAR SHAPES: Copper & Copper Alloy
BARS & BAR SHAPES: Steel, Hot-Rolled
BARS, COLD FINISHED: Steel, From Purchased Hot-Rolled
BARS: Concrete Reinforcing, Fabricated Steel
BARS: Iron, Made In Steel Mills
BASEMENT WINDOW AREAWAYS: Concrete
BASKETS: Steel Wire
BATH SALTS
BATHROOM ACCESS & FITTINGS: Vitreous China & Earthenware
BATHROOM FIXTURES: Plastic
BATTERIES, EXC AUTOMOTIVE: Wholesalers
BATTERIES: Alkaline, Cell Storage
BATTERIES: Lead Acid, Storage
BATTERIES: Rechargeable
BATTERIES: Storage
BATTERIES: Wet
BATTERY CASES: Plastic Or Plastics Combination
BATTERY CHARGERS
BATTERY CHARGERS: Storage, Motor & Engine Generator Type
BEARINGS & PARTS Ball
BEARINGS: Ball & Roller
BEARINGS: Railroad Car Journal
BEARINGS: Roller & Parts
BEAUTY & BARBER SHOP EQPT
BEAUTY & BARBER SHOP EQPT & SPLYS WHOLESALERS
BEAUTY SALONS
BEDDING & BEDSPRINGS STORES
BEDDING, BEDSPREADS, BLANKETS & SHEETS
BEDS: Institutional
BEDSPREADS, COTTON
BEER & ALE WHOLESALERS
BEER, WINE & LIQUOR STORES: Beer, Packaged
BELLOWS
BELTING: Rubber
BELTS: Conveyor, Made From Purchased Wire
BERYLLIUM
BEVERAGE BASES & SYRUPS
BEVERAGE PRDTS: Brewers' Grain
BEVERAGE PRDTS: Malt, Barley
BEVERAGES, ALCOHOLIC: Ale
BEVERAGES, ALCOHOLIC: Applejack
BEVERAGES, ALCOHOLIC: Beer & Ale
BEVERAGES, ALCOHOLIC: Bourbon Whiskey
BEVERAGES, ALCOHOLIC: Distilled Liquors
BEVERAGES, ALCOHOLIC: Near Beer
BEVERAGES, ALCOHOLIC: Wines
BEVERAGES, MALT
BEVERAGES, NONALCOHOLIC: Bottled & canned soft drinks
BEVERAGES, NONALCOHOLIC: Carbonated
BEVERAGES, NONALCOHOLIC: Carbonated, Canned & Bottled, Etc
BEVERAGES, NONALCOHOLIC: Flavoring extracts & syrups, nec
BEVERAGES, NONALCOHOLIC: Fruit Drnks, Under 100% Juice, Can
BEVERAGES, NONALCOHOLIC: Soft Drinks, Canned & Bottled, Etc
BEVERAGES, NONALCOHOLIC: Tea, Iced, Bottled & Canned, Etc
BEVERAGES, WINE & DISTILLED ALCOHOLIC, WHOLESALE: Liquor
BEVERAGES, WINE & DISTILLED ALCOHOLIC, WHOLESALE: Wine
BICYCLES, PARTS & ACCESS
BILLING & BOOKKEEPING SVCS
BINDING SVC: Books & Manuals
BINDING SVC: Pamphlets
BINDING SVC: Trade
BINDINGS: Bias, Made From Purchased Materials
BIOLOGICAL PRDTS: Blood Derivatives
BIOLOGICAL PRDTS: Exc Diagnostic

BIOLOGICAL PRDTS: Vaccines & Immunizing
BIOLOGICAL PRDTS: Veterinary
BLACKBOARDS & CHALKBOARDS
BLADES: Knife
BLADES: Saw, Hand Or Power
BLANKBOOKS & LOOSELEAF BINDERS
BLANKBOOKS: Albums, Record
BLANKBOOKS: Passbooks, Bank, Etc
BLANKETS & BLANKETING, COTTON
BLAST FURNACE & RELATED PRDTS
BLASTING SVC: Sand, Metal Parts
BLINDS & SHADES: Vertical
BLINDS : Window
BLOCKS & BRICKS: Concrete
BLOCKS: Landscape Or Retaining Wall, Concrete
BLOCKS: Paving
BLOCKS: Paving, Concrete
BLOCKS: Paving, Cut Stone
BLOCKS: Standard, Concrete Or Cinder
BLOOD BANK
BLOWERS & FANS
BLOWERS & FANS
BLUEPRINTING SVCS
BOAT & BARGE COMPONENTS: Metal, Prefabricated
BOAT BUILDING & REPAIR
BOAT BUILDING & REPAIRING: Motorized
BOAT DEALERS
BOAT DEALERS: Marine Splys & Eqpt
BOAT REPAIR SVCS
BOATS & OTHER MARINE EQPT: Plastic
BODIES: Truck & Bus
BODY PARTS: Automobile, Stamped Metal
BOILER & HEATING REPAIR SVCS
BOILERS: Low Pressure Heating, Steam Or Hot Water
BOLTS: Metal
BOOK STORES
BOOK STORES: Children's
BOOKS, WHOLESALE
BOTTLED GAS DEALERS: Propane
BOTTLES: Plastic
BOWLING CENTERS
BOWLING EQPT & SPLYS
BOXES & CRATES: Rectangular, Wood
BOXES & SHOOK: Nailed Wood
BOXES: Corrugated
BOXES: Filing, Paperboard Made From Purchased Materials
BOXES: Packing & Shipping, Metal
BOXES: Paperboard, Folding
BOXES: Paperboard, Set-Up
BOXES: Plastic
BOXES: Wooden
BRAKES & BRAKE PARTS
BRAKES: Bicycle, Friction Clutch & Other
BRAKES: Metal Forming
BRASS & BRONZE PRDTS: Die-casted
BRASS FOUNDRY, NEC
BRAZING SVCS
BRAZING: Metal
BRICK, STONE & RELATED PRDTS WHOLESALERS
BRICKS & BLOCKS: Structural
BRICKS : Ceramic Glazed, Clay
BRICKS : Flooring, Clay
BRICKS : Paving, Clay
BRICKS: Clay
BRIDGE COMPONENTS: Bridge sections, prefabricated, highway
BROACHING MACHINES
BROADCASTING & COMMS EQPT: Antennas, Transmitting/Comms
BROADCASTING & COMMS EQPT: Rcvr-Transmitter Unt, Transceiver
BROADCASTING & COMMUNICATIONS EQPT: Light Comms Eqp
BROKERS' SVCS
BROKERS: Food
BROKERS: Log & Lumber
BROKERS: Printing
BRONZE FOUNDRY, NEC
BRONZE ROLLING & DRAWING
BROOMS
BROOMS & BRUSHES
BROOMS & BRUSHES: Household Or Indl
BROOMS & BRUSHES: Paint & Varnish

2024 Harris Ohio Industrial Directory

PRODUCT INDEX

BROOMS & BRUSHES: Street Sweeping, Hand Or Machine
BUCKETS: Plastic
BUILDING & OFFICE CLEANING SVCS
BUILDING & STRUCTURAL WOOD MEMBERS
BUILDING CLEANING & MAINTENANCE SVCS
BUILDING COMPONENTS: Structural Steel
BUILDING MAINTENANCE SVCS, EXC REPAIRS
BUILDING PRDTS & MATERIALS DEALERS
BUILDING PRDTS: Concrete
BUILDING PRDTS: Stone
BUILDING SCALES MODELS
BUILDINGS & COMPONENTS: Prefabricated Metal
BUILDINGS: Mobile, For Commercial Use
BUILDINGS: Portable
BUILDINGS: Prefabricated, Metal
BUILDINGS: Prefabricated, Wood
BULLETIN BOARDS: Wood
BULLETPROOF VESTS
BUMPERS: Motor Vehicle
BUOYS: Plastic
BURIAL VAULTS: Concrete Or Precast Terrazzo
BURNERS: Gas, Indl
BURNERS: Oil, Domestic Or Indl
BUS BARS: Electrical
BUSHINGS & BEARINGS
BUSHINGS & BEARINGS: Brass, Exc Machined
BUSINESS ACTIVITIES: Non-Commercial Site
BUSINESS FORMS WHOLESALERS
BUSINESS FORMS: Printed, Continuous
BUSINESS FORMS: Printed, Manifold
BUSINESS MACHINE REPAIR, ELECTRIC
BUSINESS TRAINING SVCS
BUTTER WHOLESALERS
BUTTONS

C

CABINETS & CASES: Show, Display & Storage, Exc Wood
CABINETS: Bathroom Vanities, Wood
CABINETS: Entertainment
CABINETS: Entertainment Units, Household, Wood
CABINETS: Factory
CABINETS: Kitchen, Metal
CABINETS: Kitchen, Wood
CABINETS: Office, Wood
CABINETS: Show, Display, Etc, Wood, Exc Refrigerated
CABLE & OTHER PAY TELEVISION DISTRIBUTION
CABLE TELEVISION
CABLE: Fiber
CABLE: Fiber Optic
CABLE: Noninsulated
CABLE: Ropes & Fiber
CABLE: Steel, Insulated Or Armored
CABS: Indl Trucks & Tractors
CAFES
CAFETERIAS
CALCULATING & ACCOUNTING EQPT
CALIBRATING SVCS, NEC
CAMSHAFTS
CANDLES
CANDY & CONFECTIONS: Cake Ornaments
CANDY & CONFECTIONS: Candy Bars, Including Chocolate Covered
CANDY & CONFECTIONS: Chocolate Candy, Exc Solid Chocolate
CANDY & CONFECTIONS: Popcorn Balls/Other Trtd Popcorn Prdts
CANDY, NUT & CONFECTIONERY STORES: Candy
CANDY: Chocolate From Cacao Beans
CANNED SPECIALTIES
CANS: Aluminum
CANS: Metal
CANS: Tin
CANVAS PRDTS
CANVAS PRDTS: Convertible Tops, Car/Boat, Fm Purchased Mtrl
CAPACITORS: NEC
CAPS & PLUGS: Electric, Attachment
CAPS: Plastic
CAR WASH EQPT
CAR WASH EQPT & SPLYS WHOLESALERS
CARBON & GRAPHITE PRDTS, NEC
CARBON BLACK
CARBON PAPER & INKED RIBBONS
CARDIOVASCULAR SYSTEM DRUGS, EXC DIAGNOSTIC
CARDS: Beveled
CARDS: Color
CARDS: Greeting
CARDS: Identification
CARPET & UPHOLSTERY CLEANING SVCS
CARPET & UPHOLSTERY CLEANING SVCS: Carpet/Furniture, On Loc
CARPETS & RUGS: Tufted
CARPETS, RUGS & FLOOR COVERING
CARRIERS: Infant, Textile
CARS: Electric
CARTONS: Egg, Molded Pulp, Made From Purchased Materials
CARTS: Grocery
CASES: Carrying
CASES: Carrying, Clothing & Apparel
CASES: Plastic
CASKETS & ACCESS
CAST STONE: Concrete
CASTINGS GRINDING: For The Trade
CASTINGS: Aerospace Investment, Ferrous
CASTINGS: Aerospace, Aluminum
CASTINGS: Aerospace, Nonferrous, Exc Aluminum
CASTINGS: Aluminum
CASTINGS: Brass, NEC, Exc Die
CASTINGS: Bronze, NEC, Exc Die
CASTINGS: Commercial Investment, Ferrous
CASTINGS: Die, Aluminum
CASTINGS: Die, Magnesium & Magnesium-Base Alloy
CASTINGS: Die, Nonferrous
CASTINGS: Ductile
CASTINGS: Gray Iron
CASTINGS: Lead
CASTINGS: Machinery, Aluminum
CASTINGS: Machinery, Nonferrous, Exc Die or Aluminum Copper
CASTINGS: Magnesium
CASTINGS: Precision
CASTINGS: Steel
CASTINGS: Titanium
CATALOG & MAIL-ORDER HOUSES
CATALYSTS: Chemical
CATAPULTS
CATERERS
CATTLE WHOLESALERS
CAULKING COMPOUNDS
CEILING SYSTEMS: Luminous, Commercial
CELLULOSE DERIVATIVE MATERIALS
CEMENT & CONCRETE RELATED PRDTS & EQPT: Bituminous
CEMENT ROCK: Crushed & Broken
CEMENT, EXC LINOLEUM & TILE
CEMENT: Hydraulic
CEMENT: Masonry
CEMENT: Natural
CEMENT: Portland
CERAMIC FIBER
CHARCOAL
CHARCOAL: Activated
CHASSIS: Motor Vehicle
CHEESE WHOLESALERS
CHEMICAL CLEANING SVCS
CHEMICAL ELEMENTS
CHEMICAL PROCESSING MACHINERY & EQPT
CHEMICALS & ALLIED PRDTS WHOLESALERS, NEC
CHEMICALS & ALLIED PRDTS, WHOLESALE: Chemical Additives
CHEMICALS & ALLIED PRDTS, WHOLESALE: Chemicals, Indl
CHEMICALS & ALLIED PRDTS, WHOLESALE: Chemicals, Indl & Heavy
CHEMICALS & ALLIED PRDTS, WHOLESALE: Detergent/Soap
CHEMICALS & ALLIED PRDTS, WHOLESALE: Detergents
CHEMICALS & ALLIED PRDTS, WHOLESALE: Oxygen
CHEMICALS & ALLIED PRDTS, WHOLESALE: Plastics Film
CHEMICALS & ALLIED PRDTS, WHOLESALE: Plastics Materials, NEC
CHEMICALS & ALLIED PRDTS, WHOLESALE: Plastics Prdts, NEC
CHEMICALS & ALLIED PRDTS, WHOLESALE: Plastics Sheets & Rods
CHEMICALS & ALLIED PRDTS, WHOLESALE: Resins
CHEMICALS & ALLIED PRDTS, WHOLESALE: Resins, Plastics
CHEMICALS & ALLIED PRDTS, WHOLESALE: Rubber, Synthetic
CHEMICALS & ALLIED PRDTS, WHOLESALE: Spec Clean/Sanitation
CHEMICALS & ALLIED PRDTS, WHOLESALE: Syn Resin, Rub/Plastic
CHEMICALS & OTHER PRDTS DERIVED FROM COKING
CHEMICALS, AGRICULTURE: Wholesalers
CHEMICALS: Agricultural
CHEMICALS: Alkalies
CHEMICALS: Aluminum Compounds
CHEMICALS: Aluminum Sulfate
CHEMICALS: Anhydrous Ammonia
CHEMICALS: Bleaching Powder, Lime Bleaching Compounds
CHEMICALS: Bromine, Elemental
CHEMICALS: Caustic Potash & Potassium Hydroxide
CHEMICALS: Caustic Soda
CHEMICALS: Fire Retardant
CHEMICALS: High Purity Grade, Organic
CHEMICALS: High Purity, Refined From Technical Grade
CHEMICALS: Inorganic, NEC
CHEMICALS: Lithium Compounds, Inorganic
CHEMICALS: Medicinal
CHEMICALS: Medicinal, Organic, Uncompounded, Bulk
CHEMICALS: NEC
CHEMICALS: Phenol
CHEMICALS: Phosphates, Defluorinated/Ammoniated, Exc Fertlr
CHEMICALS: Reagent Grade, Refined From Technical Grade
CHEMICALS: Silica Compounds
CHEMICALS: Sodium Bicarbonate
CHEMICALS: Water Treatment
CHICKEN SLAUGHTERING & PROCESSING
CHILD DAY CARE SVCS
CHILD RESTRAINT SEATS, AUTOMOTIVE, WHOLESALE
CHILDREN'S & INFANTS' CLOTHING STORES
CHILDREN'S WEAR STORES
CHOCOLATE, EXC CANDY FROM BEANS: Chips, Powder, Block, Syrup
CHOCOLATE, EXC CANDY FROM PURCH CHOC: Chips, Powder, Block
CHUCKS
CHURCHES
CIGARETTE & CIGAR PRDTS & ACCESS
CIGARETTE LIGHTERS
CIRCUIT BOARD REPAIR SVCS
CIRCUIT BOARDS: Wiring
CIRCUITS: Electronic
CLAMPS & COUPLINGS: Hose
CLAMPS: Metal
CLEANING EQPT: Commercial
CLEANING EQPT: Floor Washing & Polishing, Commercial
CLEANING OR POLISHING PREPARATIONS, NEC
CLEANING PRDTS: Automobile Polish
CLEANING PRDTS: Bleaches, Household, Dry Or Liquid
CLEANING PRDTS: Degreasing Solvent
CLEANING PRDTS: Deodorants, Nonpersonal
CLEANING PRDTS: Drain Pipe Solvents Or Cleaners
CLEANING PRDTS: Laundry Preparations
CLEANING PRDTS: Sanitation Preparations
CLEANING PRDTS: Sanitation Preps, Disinfectants/Deodorants
CLEANING PRDTS: Specialty
CLEANING PRDTS: Stain Removers
CLEANING SVCS: Industrial Or Commercial
CLIPS & FASTENERS, MADE FROM PURCHASED WIRE
CLOSURES: Closures, Stamped Metal
CLOSURES: Plastic
CLOTHING & ACCESS, WOMEN, CHILDREN & INFANT, WHOL: Uniforms
CLOTHING & ACCESS: Costumes, Theatrical
CLOTHING & ACCESS: Men's Miscellaneous Access
CLOTHING & APPAREL STORES: Custom
CLOTHING & FURNISHINGS, MEN'S & BOYS', WHOLESALE: Uniforms
CLOTHING & FURNISHINGS, MENS & BOYS, WHOLESALE: Apprl Belts
CLOTHING ACCESS STORES: Umbrellas
CLOTHING STORES: T-Shirts, Printed, Custom
CLOTHING STORES: Uniforms & Work

PRODUCT INDEX

CLOTHING STORES: Unisex
CLOTHING STORES: Work
CLOTHING/ACCESS, WOMEN, CHILDREN/INFANT, WHOL: Apparel Belt
CLOTHING/ACCESS, WOMEN, CHILDREN/INFANT, WHOL: Hosp Gowns
CLOTHING: Access, Women's & Misses'
CLOTHING: Aprons, Exc Rubber/Plastic, Women, Misses, Junior
CLOTHING: Aprons, Harness
CLOTHING: Athletic & Sportswear, Men's & Boys'
CLOTHING: Athletic & Sportswear, Women's & Girls'
CLOTHING: Blouses, Women's & Girls'
CLOTHING: Blouses, Womens & Juniors, From Purchased Mtrls
CLOTHING: Bridal Gowns
CLOTHING: Caps, Baseball
CLOTHING: Children's, Girls'
CLOTHING: Coats & Suits, Men's & Boys'
CLOTHING: Costumes
CLOTHING: Disposable
CLOTHING: Dresses
CLOTHING: Hospital, Men's
CLOTHING: Jerseys, Knit
CLOTHING: Men's & boy's underwear & nightwear
CLOTHING: Mens & Boys Jackets, Sport, Suede, Leatherette
CLOTHING: Neckwear
CLOTHING: Outerwear, Lthr, Wool/Down-Filled, Men, Youth/Boy
CLOTHING: Outerwear, Women's & Misses' NEC
CLOTHING: Robes & Dressing Gowns
CLOTHING: Shirts, Dress, Men's & Boys'
CLOTHING: Socks
CLOTHING: Sweaters & Sweater Coats, Knit
CLOTHING: Sweatshirts & T-Shirts, Men's & Boys'
CLOTHING: T-Shirts & Tops, Knit
CLOTHING: Underwear, Women's & Children's
CLOTHING: Uniforms & Vestments
CLOTHING: Uniforms, Ex Athletic, Women's, Misses' & Juniors'
CLOTHING: Uniforms, Firemen's, From Purchased Materials
CLOTHING: Uniforms, Men's & Boys'
CLOTHING: Uniforms, Military, Men/Youth, Purchased Materials
CLOTHING: Uniforms, Work
CLOTHING: Waterproof Outerwear
CLOTHING: Work Apparel, Exc Uniforms
CLOTHING: Work, Men's
CLOTHING: Work, Waterproof, Exc Raincoats
CLUTCHES, EXC VEHICULAR
COAL & OTHER MINERALS & ORES WHOLESALERS
COAL MINING SERVICES
COAL MINING: Anthracite
COAL MINING: Bituminous & Lignite Surface
COAL MINING: Bituminous Coal & Lignite-Surface Mining
COAL MINING: Bituminous, Strip
COAL MINING: Bituminous, Surface, NEC
COAL MINING: Lignite, Surface, NEC
COAL PREPARATION PLANT: Bituminous or Lignite
COAL TAR CRUDES: Derived From Chemical Recovery Coke Oven
COATED OR PLATED PRDTS
COATING COMPOUNDS: Tar
COATING SVC: Metals, With Plastic Or Resins
COATINGS: Epoxy
COATINGS: Polyurethane
COILS & TRANSFORMERS
COILS, WIRE: Aluminum, Made In Rolling Mills
COILS: Electric Motors Or Generators
COILS: Pipe
COLOR LAKES OR TONERS
COLOR PIGMENTS
COLORS: Pigments, Inorganic
COMBINED ELEMENTARY & SECONDARY SCHOOLS, PUBLIC
COMMERCIAL & OFFICE BUILDINGS RENOVATION & REPAIR
COMMERCIAL ART & GRAPHIC DESIGN SVCS
COMMERCIAL ART & ILLUSTRATION SVCS
COMMERCIAL CONTAINERS WHOLESALERS
COMMERCIAL EQPT WHOLESALERS, NEC
COMMERCIAL EQPT, WHOLESALE: Display Eqpt, Exc Refrigerated
COMMERCIAL EQPT, WHOLESALE: Restaurant, NEC
COMMERCIAL EQPT, WHOLESALE: Store Fixtures & Display Eqpt
COMMERCIAL PHOTOGRAPHIC STUDIO
COMMERCIAL PRINTING & NEWSPAPER PUBLISHING
COMMON SAND MINING
COMMUNICATIONS EQPT WHOLESALERS
COMMUNICATIONS SVCS: Data
COMMUNICATIONS SVCS: Internet Connectivity Svcs
COMMUNICATIONS SVCS: Online Svc Providers
COMMUNICATIONS SVCS: Telephone, Local & Long Distance
COMMUTATORS: Electronic
COMPACT LASER DISCS: Prerecorded
COMPOSITION STONE: Plastic
COMPOST
COMPRESSORS: Air & Gas
COMPRESSORS: Air & Gas, Including Vacuum Pumps
COMPRESSORS: Refrigeration & Air Conditioning Eqpt
COMPUTER & COMPUTER SOFTWARE STORES
COMPUTER & COMPUTER SOFTWARE STORES: Software & Access
COMPUTER & COMPUTER SOFTWARE STORES: Software, Bus/Non-Game
COMPUTER & COMPUTER SOFTWARE STORES: Software, Computer Game
COMPUTER & OFFICE MACHINE MAINTENANCE & REPAIR
COMPUTER FACILITIES MANAGEMENT SVCS
COMPUTER FORMS
COMPUTER GRAPHICS SVCS
COMPUTER PERIPHERAL EQPT REPAIR & MAINTENANCE
COMPUTER PERIPHERAL EQPT, NEC
COMPUTER PERIPHERAL EQPT, WHOLESALE
COMPUTER PERIPHERAL EQPT: Input Or Output
COMPUTER PROCESSING SVCS
COMPUTER PROGRAMMING SVCS: Custom
COMPUTER RELATED MAINTENANCE SVCS
COMPUTER SERVICE BUREAU
COMPUTER SOFTWARE DEVELOPMENT
COMPUTER SOFTWARE DEVELOPMENT & APPLICATIONS
COMPUTER SOFTWARE SYSTEMS ANALYSIS & DESIGN: Custom
COMPUTER STORAGE DEVICES, NEC
COMPUTER STORAGE UNITS: Auxiliary
COMPUTER SYSTEM SELLING SVCS
COMPUTER SYSTEMS ANALYSIS & DESIGN
COMPUTER TERMINALS
COMPUTER TIME-SHARING
COMPUTERS, NEC
COMPUTERS, PERIPHERALS & SOFTWARE, WHOLESALE: Printers
COMPUTERS, PERIPHERALS & SOFTWARE, WHOLESALE: Software
COMPUTERS: Mainframe
COMPUTERS: Personal
CONCENTRATES, DRINK
CONCENTRATES, FLAVORING, EXC DRINK
CONCRETE BUILDING PRDTS WHOLESALERS
CONCRETE CURING & HARDENING COMPOUNDS
CONCRETE PLANTS
CONCRETE PRDTS
CONCRETE PRDTS, PRECAST, NEC
CONCRETE: Asphaltic, Not From Refineries
CONCRETE: Bituminous
CONCRETE: Dry Mixture
CONCRETE: Ready-Mixed
CONDENSERS: Heat Transfer Eqpt, Evaporative
CONDENSERS: Refrigeration
CONDUITS & FITTINGS: Electric
CONNECTORS: Cord, Electric
CONNECTORS: Electronic
CONSTRUCTION & MINING MACHINERY WHOLESALERS
CONSTRUCTION EQPT REPAIR SVCS
CONSTRUCTION EQPT: Attachments, Snow Plow
CONSTRUCTION EQPT: Roofing Eqpt
CONSTRUCTION MATERIALS, WHOLESALE: Architectural Metalwork
CONSTRUCTION MATERIALS, WHOLESALE: Awnings
CONSTRUCTION MATERIALS, WHOLESALE: Brick, Exc Refractory
CONSTRUCTION MATERIALS, WHOLESALE: Building Stone
CONSTRUCTION MATERIALS, WHOLESALE: Building Stone, Marble
CONSTRUCTION MATERIALS, WHOLESALE: Building, Exterior
CONSTRUCTION MATERIALS, WHOLESALE: Building, Interior
CONSTRUCTION MATERIALS, WHOLESALE: Cement
CONSTRUCTION MATERIALS, WHOLESALE: Door Frames
CONSTRUCTION MATERIALS, WHOLESALE: Doors, Garage
CONSTRUCTION MATERIALS, WHOLESALE: Doors, Sliding
CONSTRUCTION MATERIALS, WHOLESALE: Glass
CONSTRUCTION MATERIALS, WHOLESALE: Gravel
CONSTRUCTION MATERIALS, WHOLESALE: Limestone
CONSTRUCTION MATERIALS, WHOLESALE: Masons' Materials
CONSTRUCTION MATERIALS, WHOLESALE: Molding, All Materials
CONSTRUCTION MATERIALS, WHOLESALE: Pallets, Wood
CONSTRUCTION MATERIALS, WHOLESALE: Particleboard
CONSTRUCTION MATERIALS, WHOLESALE: Paving Materials
CONSTRUCTION MATERIALS, WHOLESALE: Prefabricated Structures
CONSTRUCTION MATERIALS, WHOLESALE: Roofing & Siding Materia
CONSTRUCTION MATERIALS, WHOLESALE: Sand
CONSTRUCTION MATERIALS, WHOLESALE: Septic Tanks
CONSTRUCTION MATERIALS, WHOLESALE: Sewer Pipe, Clay
CONSTRUCTION MATERIALS, WHOLESALE: Siding, Exc Wood
CONSTRUCTION MATERIALS, WHOLESALE: Stone, Crushed Or Broken
CONSTRUCTION MATERIALS, WHOLESALE: Windows
CONSTRUCTION SAND MINING
CONSTRUCTION: Athletic & Recreation Facilities
CONSTRUCTION: Bridge
CONSTRUCTION: Commercial & Office Building, New
CONSTRUCTION: Drainage System
CONSTRUCTION: Food Prdts Manufacturing or Packing Plant
CONSTRUCTION: Foundation & Retaining Wall
CONSTRUCTION: Heavy Highway & Street
CONSTRUCTION: Indl Buildings, New, NEC
CONSTRUCTION: Indl Plant
CONSTRUCTION: Land Preparation
CONSTRUCTION: Pipeline, NEC
CONSTRUCTION: Power Plant
CONSTRUCTION: Residential, Nec
CONSTRUCTION: Scaffolding
CONSTRUCTION: Sewer Line
CONSTRUCTION: Single-Family Housing
CONSTRUCTION: Single-family Housing, New
CONSTRUCTION: Street Sign Installation & Mntnce
CONSTRUCTION: Swimming Pools
CONSTRUCTION: Waste Water & Sewage Treatment Plant
CONSULTING SVC: Business, NEC
CONSULTING SVC: Financial Management
CONSULTING SVC: Human Resource
CONSULTING SVC: Management
CONSULTING SVCS, BUSINESS: Communications
CONSULTING SVCS, BUSINESS: Energy Conservation
CONSULTING SVCS, BUSINESS: Environmental
CONSULTING SVCS, BUSINESS: Safety Training Svcs
CONSULTING SVCS, BUSINESS: Sys Engnrg, Exc Computer/ Fr
CONSULTING SVCS, BUSINESS: Systems Analysis & Engineering
CONSULTING SVCS, BUSINESS: Systems Analysis Or Design
CONSULTING SVCS: Scientific
CONTACT LENSES
CONTAINERS, GLASS: Food
CONTAINERS, GLASS: Water Bottles
CONTAINERS: Cargo, Wood & Metal Combination
CONTAINERS: Food & Beverage
CONTAINERS: Food, Folding, Made From Purchased Materials
CONTAINERS: Food, Liquid Tight, Including Milk
CONTAINERS: Food, Metal
CONTAINERS: Glass
CONTAINERS: Ice Cream, Made From Purchased Materials
CONTAINERS: Laminated Phenolic & Vulcanized Fiber

PRODUCT INDEX

CONTAINERS: Metal
CONTAINERS: Plastic
CONTAINERS: Sanitary, Food
CONTAINERS: Shipping, Bombs, Metal Plate
CONTAINERS: Wood
CONTAINMENT VESSELS: Reactor, Metal Plate
CONTRACTOR: Rigging & Scaffolding
CONTRACTORS: Acoustical & Insulation Work
CONTRACTORS: Asbestos Removal & Encapsulation
CONTRACTORS: Boiler Maintenance Contractor
CONTRACTORS: Building Site Preparation
CONTRACTORS: Carpentry Work
CONTRACTORS: Carpentry, Cabinet & Finish Work
CONTRACTORS: Closet Organizers, Installation & Design
CONTRACTORS: Coating, Caulking & Weather, Water & Fire
CONTRACTORS: Commercial & Office Building
CONTRACTORS: Communications Svcs
CONTRACTORS: Computerized Controls Installation
CONTRACTORS: Concrete Block Masonry Laying
CONTRACTORS: Concrete Reinforcement Placing
CONTRACTORS: Core Drilling & Cutting
CONTRACTORS: Corrosion Control Installation
CONTRACTORS: Decontamination Svcs
CONTRACTORS: Directional Oil & Gas Well Drilling Svc
CONTRACTORS: Electric Power Systems
CONTRACTORS: Electronic Controls Installation
CONTRACTORS: Energy Management Control
CONTRACTORS: Erection & Dismantling, Poured Concrete Forms
CONTRACTORS: Fence Construction
CONTRACTORS: Floor Laying & Other Floor Work
CONTRACTORS: Foundation & Footing
CONTRACTORS: Gas Field Svcs, NEC
CONTRACTORS: General Electric
CONTRACTORS: Glass Tinting, Architectural & Automotive
CONTRACTORS: Heating & Air Conditioning
CONTRACTORS: Heating Systems Repair & Maintenance Svc
CONTRACTORS: Highway & Street Construction, General
CONTRACTORS: Highway & Street Paving
CONTRACTORS: Hydraulic Eqpt Installation & Svcs
CONTRACTORS: Machine Rigging & Moving
CONTRACTORS: Machinery Installation
CONTRACTORS: Marble Installation, Interior
CONTRACTORS: Masonry & Stonework
CONTRACTORS: Office Furniture Installation
CONTRACTORS: Oil & Gas Building, Repairing & Dismantling Svc
CONTRACTORS: Oil & Gas Field Geological Exploration Svcs
CONTRACTORS: Oil & Gas Field Geophysical Exploration Svcs
CONTRACTORS: Oil & Gas Field Tools Fishing Svcs
CONTRACTORS: Oil & Gas Well Plugging & Abandoning Svcs
CONTRACTORS: Oil & Gas Well Redrilling
CONTRACTORS: Oil & Gas Wells Pumping Svcs
CONTRACTORS: Oil & Gas Wells Svcs
CONTRACTORS: Oil Field Haulage Svcs
CONTRACTORS: Oil Field Mud Drilling Svcs
CONTRACTORS: Oil Field Pipe Testing Svcs
CONTRACTORS: Ornamental Metal Work
CONTRACTORS: Painting, Commercial
CONTRACTORS: Painting, Commercial, Exterior
CONTRACTORS: Painting, Indl
CONTRACTORS: Petroleum Storage Tanks, Pumping & Draining
CONTRACTORS: Plumbing
CONTRACTORS: Pollution Control Eqpt Installation
CONTRACTORS: Power Generating Eqpt Installation
CONTRACTORS: Prefabricated Window & Door Installation
CONTRACTORS: Process Piping
CONTRACTORS: Refractory or Acid Brick Masonry
CONTRACTORS: Roustabout Svcs
CONTRACTORS: Septic System
CONTRACTORS: Sheet Metal Work, NEC
CONTRACTORS: Siding
CONTRACTORS: Skylight Installation
CONTRACTORS: Structural Iron Work, Structural
CONTRACTORS: Structural Steel Erection
CONTRACTORS: Tile Installation, Ceramic
CONTRACTORS: Underground Utilities
CONTRACTORS: Ventilation & Duct Work
CONTRACTORS: Warm Air Heating & Air Conditioning
CONTRACTORS: Water Well Drilling
CONTRACTORS: Well Logging Svcs
CONTRACTORS: Windows & Doors
CONTRACTORS: Wood Floor Installation & Refinishing
CONTRACTORS: Wrecking & Demolition
CONTROL EQPT: Electric
CONTROL EQPT: Electric Buses & Locomotives
CONTROL EQPT: Noise
CONTROLS & ACCESS: Indl, Electric
CONTROLS & ACCESS: Motor
CONTROLS: Automatic Temperature
CONTROLS: Electric Motor
CONTROLS: Environmental
CONTROLS: Hydronic
CONTROLS: Thermostats, Built-in
CONVENIENCE STORES
CONVEYOR SYSTEMS
CONVEYOR SYSTEMS: Belt, General Indl Use
CONVEYOR SYSTEMS: Bucket Type
CONVEYOR SYSTEMS: Bulk Handling
CONVEYOR SYSTEMS: Pneumatic Tube
CONVEYOR SYSTEMS: Robotic
CONVEYORS & CONVEYING EQPT
COOKING & FOODWARMING EQPT: Commercial
COOKING EQPT, HOUSEHOLD: Ranges, Gas
COOLING TOWERS: Metal
COPPER: Rolling & Drawing
CORD & TWINE
CORRECTION FLUID
CORRUGATING MACHINES
COSMETIC PREPARATIONS
COSMETICS & TOILETRIES
COSMETOLOGY & PERSONAL HYGIENE SALONS
COUNTER & SINK TOPS
COUNTERS OR COUNTER DISPLAY CASES, EXC WOOD
COUNTERS OR COUNTER DISPLAY CASES, WOOD
COUNTING DEVICES: Controls, Revolution & Timing
COUNTING DEVICES: Tachometer, Centrifugal
COUPLINGS: Hose & Tube, Hydraulic Or Pneumatic
COUPLINGS: Pipe
COUPLINGS: Shaft
COVERS: Automobile Seat
CRANE & AERIAL LIFT SVCS
CRANES & MONORAIL SYSTEMS
CRANES: Indl Plant
CRANES: Indl Truck
CRANES: Overhead
CROWNS & CLOSURES
CRUDE PETROLEUM & NATURAL GAS PRODUCTION
CRUDE PETROLEUM PRODUCTION
CRYOGENIC COOLING DEVICES: Infrared Detectors, Masers
CULVERTS: Sheet Metal
CUPS: Paper, Made From Purchased Materials
CURBING: Granite Or Stone
CURTAINS: Window, From Purchased Materials
CUSHIONS & PILLOWS
CUSHIONS & PILLOWS: Bed, From Purchased Materials
CUSHIONS: Carpet & Rug, Foamed Plastics
CUSTOM COMPOUNDING OF RUBBER MATERIALS
CUT STONE & STONE PRODUCTS
CUTLERY
CYCLIC CRUDES & INTERMEDIATES
CYLINDER & ACTUATORS: Fluid Power
CYLINDERS: Pressure
CYLINDERS: Pump

D

DAIRY PRDTS STORE: Butter
DAIRY PRDTS STORE: Cheese
DAIRY PRDTS STORE: Ice Cream, Packaged
DAIRY PRDTS STORES
DAIRY PRDTS: Butter
DAIRY PRDTS: Canned Milk, Whole
DAIRY PRDTS: Cheese
DAIRY PRDTS: Cheese, Cottage
DAIRY PRDTS: Condensed Milk
DAIRY PRDTS: Cream Substitutes
DAIRY PRDTS: Dietary Supplements, Dairy & Non-Dairy Based
DAIRY PRDTS: Evaporated Milk
DAIRY PRDTS: Ice Cream & Ice Milk
DAIRY PRDTS: Ice Cream, Bulk
DAIRY PRDTS: Ice Cream, Packaged, Molded, On Sticks, Etc.
DAIRY PRDTS: Milk, Condensed & Evaporated
DAIRY PRDTS: Milk, Fluid
DAIRY PRDTS: Natural Cheese
DAIRY PRDTS: Powdered Milk
DAIRY PRDTS: Processed Cheese
DAIRY PRDTS: Whipped Topping, Exc Frozen Or Dry Mix
DATA PROCESSING & PREPARATION SVCS
DATA PROCESSING SVCS
DECORATIVE WOOD & WOODWORK
DEFENSE SYSTEMS & EQPT
DEGREASING MACHINES
DENTAL EQPT & SPLYS
DENTAL EQPT & SPLYS WHOLESALERS
DENTAL EQPT & SPLYS: Impression Materials
DENTAL EQPT & SPLYS: Orthodontic Appliances
DEODORANTS: Personal
DEPARTMENT STORES
DEPARTMENT STORES: Army-Navy Goods
DEPARTMENT STORES: Country General
DEPILATORIES, COSMETIC
DERMATOLOGICALS
DESIGN SVCS, NEC
DESIGN SVCS: Commercial & Indl
DESIGN SVCS: Computer Integrated Systems
DETECTION APPARATUS: Electronic/Magnetic Field, Light/Heat
DETECTION EQPT: Magnetic Field
DIAGNOSTIC SUBSTANCES
DIAGNOSTIC SUBSTANCES OR AGENTS: Radioactive
DIAGNOSTIC SUBSTANCES OR AGENTS: Veterinary
DIE CUTTING SVC: Paper
DIE SETS: Presses, Metal Stamping
DIES & TOOLS: Special
DIES: Cutting, Exc Metal
DIES: Extrusion
DIES: Paper Cutting
DIES: Plastic Forming
DIES: Steel Rule
DIODES: Light Emitting
DIODES: Solid State, Germanium, Silicon, Etc
DIRECT SELLING ESTABLISHMENTS: Food Svcs
DISCS & TAPE: Optical, Blank
DISPLAY FIXTURES: Wood
DISPLAY ITEMS: Corrugated, Made From Purchased Materials
DISPLAY ITEMS: Solid Fiber, Made From Purchased Materials
DISTRIBUTORS: Motor Vehicle Engine
DOCK EQPT & SPLYS, INDL
DOLOMITE: Crushed & Broken
DOOR FRAMES: Wood
DOOR MATS: Rubber
DOORS & WINDOWS: Screen & Storm
DOORS & WINDOWS: Storm, Metal
DOORS: Combination Screen & Storm, Wood
DOORS: Fiberglass
DOORS: Folding, Plastic Or Plastic Coated Fabric
DOORS: Garage, Overhead, Metal
DOORS: Garage, Overhead, Wood
DOORS: Glass
DRAPERIES & CURTAINS
DRAPERIES: Plastic & Textile, From Purchased Materials
DRAPERY & UPHOLSTERY STORES: Draperies
DRILL BITS
DRILLING MACHINERY & EQPT: Oil & Gas
DRILLS & DRILLING EQPT: Mining
DRINK MIXES, NONALCOHOLIC: Cocktail
DRINKING FOUNTAINS: Metal, Nonrefrigerated
DRINKING PLACES: Bars & Lounges
DRINKING PLACES: Beer Garden
DRINKING WATER COOLERS WHOLESALERS: Mechanical
DRUG STORES
DRUGS & DRUG PROPRIETARIES, WHOLESALE
DRUGS & DRUG PROPRIETARIES, WHOLESALE: Patent Medicines
DRUGS & DRUG PROPRIETARIES, WHOLESALE: Pharmaceuticals
DRUGS & DRUG PROPRIETARIES, WHOLESALE: Vitamins & Minerals
DRUMS: Fiber
DRUMS: Shipping, Metal

PRODUCT INDEX

DUCTS: Sheet Metal
DUMPSTERS: Garbage
DUST OR FUME COLLECTING EQPT: Indl
DYES & PIGMENTS: Organic
DYES OR COLORS: Food, Synthetic

E

EATING PLACES
EDUCATIONAL SVCS
ELECTRIC MOTOR REPAIR SVCS
ELECTRIC SERVICES
ELECTRICAL APPARATUS & EQPT WHOLESALERS
ELECTRICAL DEVICE PARTS: Porcelain, Molded
ELECTRICAL DISCHARGE MACHINING, EDM
ELECTRICAL EQPT REPAIR SVCS
ELECTRICAL EQPT: Automotive, NEC
ELECTRICAL GOODS, WHOLESALE: Boxes & Fittings
ELECTRICAL GOODS, WHOLESALE: Cable Conduit
ELECTRICAL GOODS, WHOLESALE: Electronic Parts
ELECTRICAL GOODS, WHOLESALE: Fittings & Construction Mat
ELECTRICAL GOODS, WHOLESALE: Generators
ELECTRICAL GOODS, WHOLESALE: Household Appliances, NEC
ELECTRICAL GOODS, WHOLESALE: Light Bulbs & Related Splys
ELECTRICAL GOODS, WHOLESALE: Lighting Fittings & Access
ELECTRICAL GOODS, WHOLESALE: Modems, Computer
ELECTRICAL GOODS, WHOLESALE: Security Control Eqpt & Systems
ELECTRICAL GOODS, WHOLESALE: Switches, Exc Electronic, NEC
ELECTRICAL GOODS, WHOLESALE: Telephone Eqpt
ELECTRICAL GOODS, WHOLESALE: Wire & Cable
ELECTRICAL MEASURING INSTRUMENT REPAIR & CALIBRATION SVCS
ELECTRICAL SPLYS
ELECTRICAL SUPPLIES: Porcelain
ELECTRODES: Thermal & Electrolytic
ELECTROMEDICAL EQPT
ELECTROMEDICAL EQPT WHOLESALERS
ELECTROMETALLURGICAL PRDTS
ELECTRONIC DEVICES: Solid State, NEC
ELECTRONIC EQPT REPAIR SVCS
ELECTRONIC LOADS & POWER SPLYS
ELECTRONIC PARTS & EQPT WHOLESALERS
ELECTRONIC SHOPPING
ELECTRONIC TRAINING DEVICES
ELECTROPLATING & PLATING SVC
ELEVATORS & EQPT
ELEVATORS WHOLESALERS
ELEVATORS: Installation & Conversion
EMBLEMS: Embroidered
EMBROIDERY ADVERTISING SVCS
EMERGENCY ALARMS
ENAMELS
ENCLOSURES: Electronic
ENCLOSURES: Screen
ENCODERS: Digital
ENGINE REBUILDING: Diesel
ENGINEERING SVCS
ENGINEERING SVCS: Acoustical
ENGINEERING SVCS: Building Construction
ENGINEERING SVCS: Chemical
ENGINEERING SVCS: Civil
ENGINEERING SVCS: Construction & Civil
ENGINEERING SVCS: Electrical Or Electronic
ENGINEERING SVCS: Machine Tool Design
ENGINEERING SVCS: Mechanical
ENGINES: Diesel & Semi-Diesel Or Duel Fuel
ENGINES: Gasoline, NEC
ENGINES: Internal Combustion, NEC
ENGINES: Jet Propulsion
ENGINES: Marine
ENGRAVING SVC, NEC
ENGRAVING SVCS
ENVELOPES
ENVELOPES WHOLESALERS
ENZYMES
EPOXY RESINS
EQUIPMENT: Rental & Leasing, NEC
ETCHING & ENGRAVING SVC

ETHYLENE
ETHYLENE-PROPYLENE RUBBERS: EPDM Polymers
EXHAUST HOOD OR FAN CLEANING SVCS
EXHAUST SYSTEMS: Eqpt & Parts
EXPLOSIVES
EXPLOSIVES, FUSES & DETONATORS: Primary explosives
EXTENSION CORDS
EXTRACTS, FLAVORING

F

FABRIC STORES
FABRICS & CLOTHING: Rubber Coated
FABRICS: Apparel & Outerwear, Cotton
FABRICS: Automotive, From Manmade Fiber
FABRICS: Cotton, Narrow
FABRICS: Decorative Trim & Specialty, Including Twist Weave
FABRICS: Denims
FABRICS: Fiberglass, Broadwoven
FABRICS: Glass & Fiberglass, Broadwoven
FABRICS: Nonwoven
FABRICS: Nylon, Broadwoven
FABRICS: Resin Or Plastic Coated
FABRICS: Rubber & Elastic Yarns & Fabrics
FABRICS: Scrub Cloths
FABRICS: Shirting, Cotton
FABRICS: Shoe Laces, Exc Leather
FABRICS: Umbrella Cloth, Cotton
FABRICS: Upholstery, Wool
FACILITIES SUPPORT SVCS
FAMILY CLOTHING STORES
FANS, BLOWING: Indl Or Commercial
FANS, EXHAUST: Indl Or Commercial
FANS, VENTILATING: Indl Or Commercial
FANS: Ceiling
FARM & GARDEN MACHINERY WHOLESALERS
FARM MACHINERY REPAIR SVCS
FARM SPLYS WHOLESALERS
FARM SPLYS, WHOLESALE: Feed
FARM SPLYS, WHOLESALE: Fertilizers & Agricultural Chemicals
FASTENERS WHOLESALERS
FASTENERS: Metal
FASTENERS: Metal
FAUCETS & SPIGOTS: Metal & Plastic
FEATHERS & FEATHER PRODUCTS
FENCE POSTS: Iron & Steel
FENCES OR POSTS: Ornamental Iron Or Steel
FENCING MATERIALS: Docks & Other Outdoor Prdts, Wood
FENCING MATERIALS: Wood
FENCING: Chain Link
FERROALLOYS
FERROMANGANESE, NOT MADE IN BLAST FURNACES
FERROSILICON, EXC MADE IN BLAST FURNACES
FERROUS METALS: Reclaimed From Clay
FERTILIZER, AGRICULTURAL: Wholesalers
FERTILIZERS: Nitrogen Solutions
FERTILIZERS: Nitrogenous
FERTILIZERS: Phosphatic
FIBER & FIBER PRDTS: Elastomeric
FIBER & FIBER PRDTS: Protein
FIBER OPTICS
FIBERS: Carbon & Graphite
FILM BASE: Cellulose Acetate Or Nitrocellulose Plastics
FILTERS
FILTERS & SOFTENERS: Water, Household
FILTERS & STRAINERS: Pipeline
FILTERS: Air
FILTERS: Air Intake, Internal Combustion Engine, Exc Auto
FILTERS: General Line, Indl
FILTERS: Oil, Internal Combustion Engine, Exc Auto
FILTRATION DEVICES: Electronic
FINANCIAL SVCS
FINISHING AGENTS
FIRE ARMS, SMALL: Guns Or Gun Parts, 30 mm & Below
FIRE ARMS, SMALL: Rifles Or Rifle Parts, 30 mm & below
FIRE CONTROL EQPT REPAIR SVCS, MILITARY
FIRE CONTROL OR BOMBING EQPT: Electronic
FIRE DETECTION SYSTEMS
FIRE EXTINGUISHERS, WHOLESALE
FIRE EXTINGUISHERS: Portable
FIRE OR BURGLARY RESISTIVE PRDTS
FIREFIGHTING APPARATUS
FIREPLACE EQPT & ACCESS

FIREWORKS
FIRST AID SPLYS, WHOLESALE
FISH & SEAFOOD WHOLESALERS
FISH FOOD
FITTINGS & ASSEMBLIES: Hose & Tube, Hydraulic Or Pneumatic
FITTINGS: Pipe
FITTINGS: Pipe Fabricated
FIXTURES & EQPT: Kitchen, Metal, Exc Cast Aluminum
FIXTURES & EQPT: Kitchen, Porcelain Enameled
FIXTURES: Cut Stone
FLAGS: Fabric
FLAGSTONES
FLAT GLASS: Construction
FLAT GLASS: Float
FLAT GLASS: Fixture
FLAT GLASS: Plate, Polished & Rough
FLAT GLASS: Window, Clear & Colored
FLAVORS OR FLAVORING MATERIALS: Synthetic
FLIGHT RECORDERS
FLOOR COVERING STORES
FLOOR COVERING STORES: Carpets
FLOOR COVERINGS WHOLESALERS
FLOOR COVERINGS: Aircraft & Automobile
FLOOR COVERINGS: Rubber
FLOORING & SIDING: Metal
FLOORING: Hardwood
FLOORING: Rubber
FLORIST: Flowers, Fresh
FLOWERS, FRESH, WHOLESALE
FLUID METERS & COUNTING DEVICES
FLUID POWER PUMPS & MOTORS
FLUID POWER VALVES & HOSE FITTINGS
FOAM RUBBER
FOAMS & RUBBER, WHOLESALE
FOIL & LEAF: Metal
FOIL: Laminated To Paper Or Other Materials
FOOD PRDTS, BREAKFAST: Cereal, Oatmeal
FOOD PRDTS, BREAKFAST: Cereal, Wheat Flakes
FOOD PRDTS, CANNED OR FRESH PACK: Fruit Juices
FOOD PRDTS, CANNED: Baby Food
FOOD PRDTS, CANNED: Barbecue Sauce
FOOD PRDTS, CANNED: Beans & Bean Sprouts
FOOD PRDTS, CANNED: Fruit Juices, Fresh
FOOD PRDTS, CANNED: Fruits
FOOD PRDTS, CANNED: Fruits
FOOD PRDTS, CANNED: Jams, Including Imitation
FOOD PRDTS, CANNED: Jams, Jellies & Preserves
FOOD PRDTS, CANNED: Jellies, Edible, Including Imitation
FOOD PRDTS, CANNED: Puddings, Exc Meat
FOOD PRDTS, CANNED: Spaghetti & Other Pasta Sauce
FOOD PRDTS, CANNED: Tomato Sauce.
FOOD PRDTS, CANNED: Vegetables
FOOD PRDTS, CONFECTIONERY, WHOLESALE: Candy
FOOD PRDTS, CONFECTIONERY, WHOLESALE: Pretzels
FOOD PRDTS, CONFECTIONERY, WHOLESALE: Snack Foods
FOOD PRDTS, FISH & SEAFOOD: Fish, Fresh, Prepared
FOOD PRDTS, FROZEN: Ethnic Foods, NEC
FOOD PRDTS, FROZEN: Fruit Juice, Concentrates
FOOD PRDTS, FROZEN: Fruit Juices
FOOD PRDTS, FROZEN: Fruits
FOOD PRDTS, FROZEN: Fruits & Vegetables
FOOD PRDTS, FROZEN: Fruits, Juices & Vegetables
FOOD PRDTS, WHOLESALE: Baking Splys
FOOD PRDTS, WHOLESALE: Beverages, Exc Coffee & Tea
FOOD PRDTS, WHOLESALE: Chocolate
FOOD PRDTS, WHOLESALE: Coffee, Green Or Roasted
FOOD PRDTS, WHOLESALE: Condiments
FOOD PRDTS, WHOLESALE: Cookies
FOOD PRDTS, WHOLESALE: Dried or Canned Foods
FOOD PRDTS, WHOLESALE: Grain Elevators
FOOD PRDTS, WHOLESALE: Grains
FOOD PRDTS, WHOLESALE: Juices
FOOD PRDTS, WHOLESALE: Salt, Edible
FOOD PRDTS, WHOLESALE: Specialty
FOOD PRDTS, WHOLESALE: Water, Distilled
FOOD PRDTS: Animal & marine fats & oils
FOOD PRDTS: Bread Crumbs, Exc Made In Bakeries
FOOD PRDTS: Chicken, Processed, Cooked
FOOD PRDTS: Chicken, Processed, Fresh
FOOD PRDTS: Chocolate Bars, Solid
FOOD PRDTS: Cocoa, Powdered

PRODUCT INDEX

FOOD PRDTS: Coffee
FOOD PRDTS: Coffee Extracts
FOOD PRDTS: Corn Oil Prdts
FOOD PRDTS: Dips, Exc Cheese & Sour Cream Based
FOOD PRDTS: Dough, Pizza, Prepared
FOOD PRDTS: Doughs, Frozen Or Refrig From Purchased Flour
FOOD PRDTS: Dressings, Salad, Raw & Cooked Exc Dry Mixes
FOOD PRDTS: Dried & Dehydrated Fruits, Vegetables & Soup Mix
FOOD PRDTS: Edible fats & oils
FOOD PRDTS: Emulsifiers
FOOD PRDTS: Flour
FOOD PRDTS: Flour & Other Grain Mill Products
FOOD PRDTS: Flour Mixes & Doughs
FOOD PRDTS: Flour, Blended From Purchased Flour
FOOD PRDTS: Flours & Flour Mixes, From Purchased Flour
FOOD PRDTS: Fruit Pops, Frozen
FOOD PRDTS: Fruits & Vegetables, Pickled
FOOD PRDTS: Ice, Cubes
FOOD PRDTS: Mixes, Cake, From Purchased Flour
FOOD PRDTS: Mixes, Flour
FOOD PRDTS: Mixes, Sauces, Dry
FOOD PRDTS: Mustard, Prepared
FOOD PRDTS: Oils & Fats, Animal
FOOD PRDTS: Olive Oil
FOOD PRDTS: Pasta, Uncooked, Packaged With Other Ingredients
FOOD PRDTS: Peanut Butter
FOOD PRDTS: Pizza Doughs From Purchased Flour
FOOD PRDTS: Pork Rinds
FOOD PRDTS: Potato Chips & Other Potato-Based Snacks
FOOD PRDTS: Poultry, Processed, Frozen
FOOD PRDTS: Raw cane sugar
FOOD PRDTS: Salad Oils, Refined Vegetable, Exc Corn
FOOD PRDTS: Sandwiches
FOOD PRDTS: Seasonings & Spices
FOOD PRDTS: Shortening & Solid Edible Fats
FOOD PRDTS: Starch, Corn
FOOD PRDTS: Sugar
FOOD PRDTS: Sugar, Beet
FOOD PRDTS: Syrup, Maple
FOOD PRDTS: Syrups
FOOD PRDTS: Tofu, Exc Frozen Desserts
FOOD PRDTS: Turkey, Slaughtered & Dressed
FOOD PRODUCTS MACHINERY
FOOD STORES: Convenience, Chain
FOOD STORES: Convenience, Independent
FOOD STORES: Delicatessen
FOOD STORES: Grocery, Independent
FOOD STORES: Supermarkets, Chain
FOOTWEAR, WHOLESALE: Shoes
FOOTWEAR: Cut Stock
FORESTRY RELATED EQPT
FORGINGS: Aircraft, Ferrous
FORGINGS: Aluminum
FORGINGS: Automotive & Internal Combustion Engine
FORGINGS: Construction Or Mining Eqpt, Ferrous
FORGINGS: Iron & Steel
FORGINGS: Machinery, Ferrous
FORGINGS: Machinery, Nonferrous
FORGINGS: Metal , Ornamental, Ferrous
FORGINGS: Nonferrous
FORGINGS: Nuclear Power Plant, Ferrous
FORGINGS: Plumbing Fixture, Nonferrous
FORMS: Concrete, Sheet Metal
FOUNDRIES: Aluminum
FOUNDRIES: Gray & Ductile Iron
FOUNDRIES: Iron
FOUNDRIES: Nonferrous
FOUNDRIES: Steel
FOUNDRIES: Steel Investment
FOUNDRY MACHINERY & EQPT
FOUNTAINS: Concrete
FRACTIONATION PRDTS OF CRUDE PETROLEUM, HYDROCARBONS, NEC
FRANCHISES, SELLING OR LICENSING
FREIGHT FORWARDING ARRANGEMENTS
FRICTION MATERIAL, MADE FROM POWDERED METAL
FRUIT STANDS OR MARKETS
FRUITS & VEGETABLES WHOLESALERS: Fresh
FUEL ADDITIVES

FUEL CELLS: Solid State
FUEL DEALERS: Coal
FUEL OIL DEALERS
FUEL TREATING
FUELS: Diesel
FUNGICIDES OR HERBICIDES
FURNACES & OVENS: Indl
FURNACES: Indl, Electric
FURNACES: Indl, Electric
FURNACES: Warm Air, Electric
FURNITURE PARTS: Metal
FURNITURE REFINISHING SVCS
FURNITURE REPAIR & MAINTENANCE SVCS
FURNITURE STOCK & PARTS: Hardwood
FURNITURE STORES
FURNITURE WHOLESALERS
FURNITURE, HOUSEHOLD: Wholesalers
FURNITURE, MATTRESSES: Wholesalers
FURNITURE, OFFICE: Wholesalers
FURNITURE, WHOLESALE: Chairs
FURNITURE, WHOLESALE: Lockers
FURNITURE, WHOLESALE: Racks
FURNITURE, WHOLESALE: Shelving
FURNITURE: Bedroom, Wood
FURNITURE: Beds, Household, Incl Folding & Cabinet, Metal
FURNITURE: Cabinets & Filing Drawers, Office, Exc Wood
FURNITURE: Chairs, Household Upholstered
FURNITURE: Chairs, Household Wood
FURNITURE: Chairs, Office Wood
FURNITURE: Church
FURNITURE: Console Tables, Wood
FURNITURE: Fiberglass & Plastic
FURNITURE: Hotel
FURNITURE: Household, Metal
FURNITURE: Household, Upholstered, Exc Wood Or Metal
FURNITURE: Juvenile, Metal
FURNITURE: Lawn & Garden, Metal
FURNITURE: Lawn, Exc Wood, Metal, Stone Or Concrete
FURNITURE: Living Room, Upholstered On Wood Frames
FURNITURE: Mattresses & Foundations
FURNITURE: Mattresses, Box & Bedsprings
FURNITURE: Mattresses, Innerspring Or Box Spring
FURNITURE: Office, Exc Wood
FURNITURE: Office, Wood
FURNITURE: Play Pens, Children's, Wood
FURNITURE: School
FURNITURE: Table Tops, Marble
FURNITURE: Upholstered
FURNITURE: Vehicle
FUSE MOUNTINGS: Electric Power
FUSES & FUSE EQPT

G

GAMES & TOYS: Board Games, Children's & Adults'
GAMES & TOYS: Child Restraint Seats, Automotive
GAMES & TOYS: Craft & Hobby Kits & Sets
GARBAGE CONTAINERS: Plastic
GARBAGE DISPOSERS & COMPACTORS: Commercial
GAS & OIL FIELD EXPLORATION SVCS
GAS & OIL FIELD SVCS, NEC
GAS FIELD MACHINERY & EQPT
GASES & LIQUIFIED PETROLEUM GASES
GASES: Acetylene
GASES: Carbon Dioxide
GASES: Indl
GASES: Nitrogen
GASES: Oxygen
GASKET MATERIALS
GASKETS
GASKETS & SEALING DEVICES
GASOLINE FILLING STATIONS
GASOLINE WHOLESALERS
GEARS
GEARS & GEAR UNITS: Reduction, Exc Auto
GEARS: Power Transmission, Exc Auto
GENERATING APPARATUS & PARTS: Electrical
GENERATION EQPT: Electronic
GENERATORS SETS: Steam
GENERATORS: Electrochemical, Fuel Cell
GENERATORS: Gas
GIFT SHOP
GIFT WRAP: Paper, Made From Purchased Materials
GIFT, NOVELTY & SOUVENIR STORES: Gifts & Novelties

GIFTS & NOVELTIES: Wholesalers
GLASS & GLASS CERAMIC PRDTS, PRESSED OR BLOWN: Tableware
GLASS PRDTS, FROM PURCHASED GLASS: Glassware
GLASS PRDTS, FROM PURCHASED GLASS: Insulating
GLASS PRDTS, FROM PURCHASED GLASS: Mirrored
GLASS PRDTS, FROM PURCHASED GLASS: Sheet, Bent
GLASS PRDTS, FROM PURCHASED GLASS: Windshields
GLASS PRDTS, FROM PURCHD GLASS: Strengthened Or Reinforced
GLASS PRDTS, PRESSED OR BLOWN: Furnishings & Access
GLASS PRDTS, PRESSED OR BLOWN: Glass Fibers, Textile
GLASS PRDTS, PRESSED OR BLOWN: Glassware, Art Or Decorative
GLASS PRDTS, PRESSED OR BLOWN: Scientific Glassware
GLASS PRDTS, PRESSED OR BLOWN: Tubing
GLASS PRDTS, PRESSED OR BLOWN: Yarn, Fiberglass
GLASS, AUTOMOTIVE: Wholesalers
GLASS: Fiber
GLASS: Flat
GLASS: Pressed & Blown, NEC
GLASS: Tempered
GLASSWARE WHOLESALERS
GLOVES: Safety
GLOVES: Work
GLOVES: Woven Or Knit, From Purchased Materials
GLYCOL ETHERS
GOLF COURSES: Public
GOLF DRIVING RANGES
GOLF EQPT
GOURMET FOOD STORES
GOVERNMENT, GENERAL: Administration
GRADING SVCS
GRANITE: Crushed & Broken
GRANITE: Cut & Shaped
GRAPHIC ARTS & RELATED DESIGN SVCS
GRAPHITE MINING SVCS
GRATINGS: Open Steel Flooring
GRAVE VAULTS, METAL
GRAVEL MINING
GREASES: Lubricating
GREENHOUSES: Prefabricated Metal
GRINDING SVC: Precision, Commercial Or Indl
GROCERIES, GENERAL LINE WHOLESALERS
GUIDED MISSILES & SPACE VEHICLES
GUM & WOOD CHEMICALS
GUTTERS: Sheet Metal
GYPSUM PRDTS
GYROSCOPES

H

HAIR & HAIR BASED PRDTS
HAIR CARE PRDTS
HAND TOOLS, NEC: Wholesalers
HANDBAGS
HANDBAGS: Women's
HARD RUBBER PRDTS, NEC
HARDWARE
HARDWARE & BUILDING PRDTS: Plastic
HARDWARE & EQPT: Stage, Exc Lighting
HARDWARE STORES
HARDWARE STORES: Pumps & Pumping Eqpt
HARDWARE STORES: Tools
HARDWARE WHOLESALERS
HARDWARE, WHOLESALE: Bolts
HARDWARE, WHOLESALE: Builders', NEC
HARDWARE, WHOLESALE: Nuts
HARDWARE, WHOLESALE: Power Tools & Access
HARDWARE, WHOLESALE: Screws
HARDWARE: Aircraft
HARDWARE: Aircraft & Marine, Incl Pulleys & Similar Items
HARDWARE: Builders'
HARDWARE: Casket
HARDWARE: Furniture, Builders' & Other Household
HARDWARE: Rubber
HARNESS ASSEMBLIES: Cable & Wire
HARNESS WIRING SETS: Internal Combustion Engines
HEARING AIDS
HEAT EMISSION OPERATING APPARATUS
HEAT EXCHANGERS: After Or Inter Coolers Or Condensers, Etc
HEAT TREATING: Metal

PRODUCT INDEX

HEATERS: Swimming Pool, Electric
HEATING & AIR CONDITIONING UNITS, COMBINATION
HEATING APPARATUS: Steam
HEATING EQPT: Complete
HEATING EQPT: Induction
HEATING UNITS & DEVICES: Indl, Electric
HEAVY DISTILLATES
HELMETS: Steel
HELP SUPPLY SERVICES
HOBBY, TOY & GAME STORES: Ceramics Splys
HOBBY, TOY & GAME STORES: Toys & Games
HOISTING SLINGS
HOISTS
HOLDING COMPANIES: Investment, Exc Banks
HOLDING COMPANIES: Personal, Exc Banks
HOME FOR THE MENTALLY HANDICAPPED
HOMEFURNISHING STORES: Beddings & Linens
HOMEFURNISHING STORES: Brushes
HOMEFURNISHING STORES: Cutlery
HOMEFURNISHING STORES: Pottery
HOMEFURNISHINGS, WHOLESALE: Blinds, Vertical
HOMEFURNISHINGS, WHOLESALE: Decorating Splys
HOMEFURNISHINGS, WHOLESALE: Draperies
HOMEFURNISHINGS, WHOLESALE: Grills, Barbecue
HOMEFURNISHINGS, WHOLESALE: Kitchenware
HOMES: Log Cabins
HONING & LAPPING MACHINES
HOODS: Range, Sheet Metal
HORSESHOES
HOSE: Automobile, Rubber
HOSE: Flexible Metal
HOSE: Plastic
HOSE: Rubber
HOSPITALS: Medical & Surgical
HOTELS & MOTELS
HOUSEHOLD ARTICLES, EXC KITCHEN: Pottery
HOUSEHOLD ARTICLES: Metal
HOUSEHOLD FURNISHINGS, NEC
HOUSEWARES, ELECTRIC: Air Purifiers, Portable
HOUSEWARES, ELECTRIC: Cooking Appliances
HOUSEWARES, ELECTRIC: Fans, Exhaust & Ventilating
HOUSEWARES: Food Dishes & Utensils, Pressed & Molded Pulp
HUMIDIFIERS & DEHUMIDIFIERS
HYDRAULIC EQPT REPAIR SVC

I

ICE
ICE CREAM & ICES WHOLESALERS
IDENTIFICATION TAGS, EXC PAPER
IGNITION APPARATUS & DISTRIBUTORS
IGNITION SYSTEMS: High Frequency
INCINERATORS
INCUBATORS & BROODERS: Farm
INDL & PERSONAL SVC PAPER WHOLESALERS
INDL & PERSONAL SVC PAPER, WHOLESALE: Boxes & Containers
INDL & PERSONAL SVC PAPER, WHOLESALE: Shipping Splys
INDL CONTRACTORS: Exhibit Construction
INDL DIAMONDS WHOLESALERS
INDL EQPT SVCS
INDL GASES WHOLESALERS
INDL HELP SVCS
INDL MACHINERY & EQPT WHOLESALERS
INDL PATTERNS: Foundry Cores
INDL PATTERNS: Foundry Patternmaking
INDL PROCESS INSTRUMENTS: Chromatographs
INDL PROCESS INSTRUMENTS: Control
INDL SPLYS WHOLESALERS
INDL SPLYS, WHOLESALE: Abrasives
INDL SPLYS, WHOLESALE: Adhesives, Tape & Plasters
INDL SPLYS, WHOLESALE: Bearings
INDL SPLYS, WHOLESALE: Bins & Containers, Storage
INDL SPLYS, WHOLESALE: Drums, New Or Reconditioned
INDL SPLYS, WHOLESALE: Gaskets & Seals
INDL SPLYS, WHOLESALE: Gears
INDL SPLYS, WHOLESALE: Glass Bottles
INDL SPLYS, WHOLESALE: Power Transmission, Eqpt & Apparatus
INDL SPLYS, WHOLESALE: Rubber Goods, Mechanical
INDL SPLYS, WHOLESALE: Seals
INDL SPLYS, WHOLESALE: Tools

INDL SPLYS, WHOLESALE: Valves & Fittings
INDUSTRIAL & COMMERCIAL EQPT INSPECTION SVCS
INFORMATION RETRIEVAL SERVICES
INFRARED OBJECT DETECTION EQPT
INGOT, EXTRUSION: Extrusion ingot, aluminum: rolling mills
INGOT: Aluminum
INK OR WRITING FLUIDS
INK: Gravure
INK: Printing
INSECTICIDES
INSECTICIDES & PESTICIDES
INSPECTION & TESTING SVCS
INSTRUMENTS & METERS: Measuring, Electric
INSTRUMENTS, LABORATORY: Analyzers, Automatic Chemical
INSTRUMENTS, LABORATORY: Spectrometers
INSTRUMENTS, MEASURING & CNTRL: Geophysical & Meteorological
INSTRUMENTS, MEASURING & CNTRL: Radiation & Testing, Nuclear
INSTRUMENTS, MEASURING & CNTRLG: Aircraft & Motor Vehicle
INSTRUMENTS, MEASURING & CNTRLNG: Nuclear Instrument Modules
INSTRUMENTS, MEASURING & CONTROLLING: Cable Testing
INSTRUMENTS, MEASURING & CONTROLLING: Magnetometers
INSTRUMENTS, MEASURING & CONTROLLING: Ultrasonic Testing
INSTRUMENTS, OPTICAL: Mirrors
INSTRUMENTS, OPTICAL: Test & Inspection
INSTRUMENTS, SURGICAL & MED: Needles & Syringes, Hypodermic
INSTRUMENTS, SURGICAL & MEDICAL: Blood & Bone Work
INSTRUMENTS, SURGICAL & MEDICAL: Inhalation Therapy
INSTRUMENTS, SURGICAL & MEDICAL: IV Transfusion
INSTRUMENTS, SURGICAL & MEDICAL: Operating Tables
INSTRUMENTS, SURGICAL/MED: Microsurgical, Exc Electromedical
INSTRUMENTS: Analytical
INSTRUMENTS: Combustion Control, Indl
INSTRUMENTS: Electrocardiographs
INSTRUMENTS: Endoscopic Eqpt, Electromedical
INSTRUMENTS: Flow, Indl Process
INSTRUMENTS: Indl Process Control
INSTRUMENTS: Infrared, Indl Process
INSTRUMENTS: Laser, Scientific & Engineering
INSTRUMENTS: Liquid Level, Indl Process
INSTRUMENTS: Measurement, Indl Process
INSTRUMENTS: Measuring, Electrical Energy
INSTRUMENTS: Measuring, Electrical Power
INSTRUMENTS: Medical & Surgical
INSTRUMENTS: Particle Size Analyzers
INSTRUMENTS: Pressure Measurement, Indl
INSTRUMENTS: Radio Frequency Measuring
INSTRUMENTS: Signal Generators & Averagers
INSTRUMENTS: Temperature Measurement, Indl
INSTRUMENTS: Test, Electrical, Engine
INSTRUMENTS: Test, Electronic & Electric Measurement
INSULATION & ROOFING MATERIALS: Wood, Reconstituted
INSULATION MATERIALS WHOLESALERS
INSULATION: Fiberglass
INSULATORS & INSULATION MATERIALS: Electrical
INSULATORS, PORCELAIN: Electrical
INSURANCE BROKERS, NEC
INSURANCE CARRIERS: Life
INSURANCE CLAIM PROCESSING, EXC MEDICAL
INSURANCE: Agents, Brokers & Service
INTEGRATED CIRCUITS, SEMICONDUCTOR NETWORKS, ETC
INTERIOR DESIGN SVCS, NEC
INTRAVENOUS SOLUTIONS
INVERTERS: Nonrotating Electrical
INVESTMENT ADVISORY SVCS
INVESTMENT FIRM: General Brokerage
INVESTORS, NEC
IRON & STEEL PRDTS: Hot-Rolled
IRON ORE MINING
IRON ORES

J

JACKS: Hydraulic
JEWELERS' FINDINGS & MATERIALS
JEWELRY & PRECIOUS STONES WHOLESALERS
JEWELRY REPAIR SVCS
JEWELRY STORES
JEWELRY STORES: Precious Stones & Precious Metals
JEWELRY STORES: Silverware
JEWELRY, PRECIOUS METAL: Settings & Mountings
JEWELRY, WHOLESALE
JEWELRY: Precious Metal
JIGS & FIXTURES
JOB PRINTING & NEWSPAPER PUBLISHING COMBINED
JOINTS: Expansion, Pipe
JOINTS: Swivel & Universal, Exc Aircraft & Auto
JOISTS: Long-Span Series, Open Web Steel

K

KILNS & FURNACES: Ceramic
KITCHEN CABINETS WHOLESALERS
KITCHEN UTENSILS: Food Handling & Processing Prdts, Wood
KITCHENWARE STORES
KITCHENWARE: Plastic
KITS: Plastic
KNIVES: Agricultural Or Indl

L

LABELS: Paper, Made From Purchased Materials
LABELS: Woven
LABORATORIES, TESTING: Food
LABORATORIES, TESTING: Metallurgical
LABORATORIES, TESTING: Pollution
LABORATORIES, TESTING: Product Testing
LABORATORIES, TESTING: Product Testing, Safety/Performance
LABORATORIES: Biological Research
LABORATORIES: Biotechnology
LABORATORIES: Commercial Nonphysical Research
LABORATORIES: Dental, Crown & Bridge Production
LABORATORIES: Electronic Research
LABORATORIES: Medical
LABORATORIES: Noncommercial Research
LABORATORIES: Physical Research, Commercial
LABORATORIES: Testing
LABORATORIES: Testing
LABORATORY APPARATUS & FURNITURE
LABORATORY APPARATUS, EXC HEATING & MEASURING
LABORATORY APPARATUS: Freezers
LABORATORY APPARATUS: Pipettes, Hemocytometer
LABORATORY CHEMICALS: Organic
LABORATORY EQPT, EXC MEDICAL: Wholesalers
LABORATORY EQPT: Chemical
LABORATORY EQPT: Clinical Instruments Exc Medical
LABORATORY EQPT: Incubators
LABORATORY EQPT: Measuring
LABORATORY EQPT: Sterilizers
LABORATORY INSTRUMENT REPAIR SVCS
LADDERS: Metal
LADLES: Metal Plate
LAMINATED PLASTICS: Plate, Sheet, Rod & Tubes
LAMINATING SVCS
LAMP & LIGHT BULBS & TUBES
LAMP BULBS & TUBES/PARTS, ELECTRIC: Generalized Applications
LAMP SHADES: Glass
LAMPS: Fluorescent
LAMPS: Table, Residential
LAND SUBDIVISION & DEVELOPMENT
LASER SYSTEMS & EQPT
LASERS: Welding, Drilling & Cutting Eqpt
LATEX: Foamed
LATH: Expanded Metal
LAUNDRY EQPT: Commercial
LAUNDRY EQPT: Household
LAWN & GARDEN EQPT
LAWN & GARDEN EQPT: Grass Catchers, Lawn Mower
LAWN & GARDEN EQPT: Lawnmowers, Residential, Hand Or Power
LAWN & GARDEN EQPT: Rototillers
LAWN & GARDEN EQPT: Tractors & Eqpt
LEAD & ZINC ORES
LEAD PENCILS & ART GOODS
LEASING & RENTAL SVCS: Cranes & Aerial Lift Eqpt

PRODUCT INDEX

LEASING & RENTAL SVCS: Oil Field Eqpt
LEASING & RENTAL SVCS: Oil Well Drilling
LEASING & RENTAL: Construction & Mining Eqpt
LEASING & RENTAL: Medical Machinery & Eqpt
LEASING & RENTAL: Trucks, Indl
LEASING & RENTAL: Trucks, Without Drivers
LEATHER & CUT STOCK WHOLESALERS
LEATHER GOODS, EXC FOOTWEAR, GLOVES, LUGGAGE/ BELTING, WHOL
LEATHER GOODS: Garments
LEATHER GOODS: Holsters
LEATHER GOODS: Personal
LEATHER GOODS: Wallets
LEATHER TANNING & FINISHING
LEGAL OFFICES & SVCS
LEGAL SVCS: General Practice Attorney or Lawyer
LICENSE TAGS: Automobile, Stamped Metal
LIGHTING EQPT: Area & Sports Luminaries
LIGHTING EQPT: Flashlights
LIGHTING EQPT: Motor Vehicle
LIGHTING EQPT: Motor Vehicle, Headlights
LIGHTING EQPT: Motor Vehicle, NEC
LIGHTING EQPT: Outdoor
LIGHTING FIXTURES WHOLESALERS
LIGHTING FIXTURES, NEC
LIGHTING FIXTURES: Decorative Area
LIGHTING FIXTURES: Fluorescent, Commercial
LIGHTING FIXTURES: Indl & Commercial
LIGHTING FIXTURES: Motor Vehicle
LIGHTING FIXTURES: Ornamental, Commercial
LIGHTING FIXTURES: Public
LIGHTING FIXTURES: Residential, Electric
LIGHTING FIXTURES: Street
LIME
LIME ROCK: Ground
LIMESTONE: Crushed & Broken
LIMESTONE: Cut & Shaped
LIMESTONE: Dimension
LIMESTONE: Ground
LINENS & TOWELS WHOLESALERS
LINERS & COVERS: Fabric
LINERS & LINING
LININGS: Fabric, Apparel & Other, Exc Millinery
LIQUEFIED PETROLEUM GAS DEALERS
LIQUEFIED PETROLEUM GAS WHOLESALERS
LIQUID CRYSTAL DISPLAYS
LITHOGRAPHIC PLATES
LIVESTOCK WHOLESALERS, NEC
LOADS: Electronic
LOCKERS
LOCKSMITHS
LOCOMOTIVES & PARTS
LOGGING
LOGGING CAMPS & CONTRACTORS
LOGGING: Timber, Cut At Logging Camp
LOGGING: Wooden Logs
LOGS: Gas, Fireplace
LOTIONS OR CREAMS: Face
LUBRICANTS: Corrosion Preventive
LUBRICATING EQPT: Indl
LUBRICATING OIL & GREASE WHOLESALERS
LUBRICATION SYSTEMS & EQPT
LUGGAGE & BRIEFCASES
LUGGAGE & LEATHER GOODS STORES
LUGGAGE: Traveling Bags
LUMBER & BLDG MATLS DEALER, RET: Garage Doors, Sell/ Install
LUMBER & BLDG MATRLS DEALERS, RET: Bath Fixtures, Eqpt/Sply
LUMBER & BLDG MATRLS DEALERS, RETAIL: Doors, Wood/Metal
LUMBER & BLDG MTRLS DEALERS, RET: Planing Mill Prdts/ Lumber
LUMBER & BUILDING MATERIALS DEALER, RET: Door & Window Prdts
LUMBER & BUILDING MATERIALS DEALER, RET: Masonry Matls/Splys
LUMBER & BUILDING MATERIALS DEALERS, RET: Solar Heating Eqpt
LUMBER & BUILDING MATERIALS DEALERS, RETAIL: Brick
LUMBER & BUILDING MATERIALS DEALERS, RETAIL: Cement
LUMBER & BUILDING MATERIALS DEALERS, RETAIL: Modular Homes
LUMBER & BUILDING MATERIALS DEALERS, RETAIL: Tile, Ceramic
LUMBER & BUILDING MATERIALS RET DEALERS: Millwork & Lumber
LUMBER & BUILDING MATLS DEALERS, RET: Concrete/ Cinder Block
LUMBER: Dimension, Hardwood
LUMBER: Fiberboard
LUMBER: Flooring, Dressed, Softwood
LUMBER: Hardwood Dimension
LUMBER: Hardwood Dimension & Flooring Mills
LUMBER: Kiln Dried
LUMBER: Plywood, Hardwood
LUMBER: Plywood, Prefinished, Hardwood
LUMBER: Plywood, Softwood
LUMBER: Treated
LUMBER: Veneer, Softwood

M

MACHINE PARTS: Stamped Or Pressed Metal
MACHINE TOOL ACCESS: Drill Bushings, Drilling Jig
MACHINE TOOL ACCESS: Drills
MACHINE TOOL ACCESS: Tools & Access
MACHINE TOOL ATTACHMENTS & ACCESS
MACHINE TOOLS & ACCESS
MACHINE TOOLS, METAL CUTTING: Drilling
MACHINE TOOLS, METAL CUTTING: Drilling & Boring
MACHINE TOOLS, METAL CUTTING: Exotic, Including Explosive
MACHINE TOOLS, METAL CUTTING: Home Workshop
MACHINE TOOLS, METAL CUTTING: Numerically Controlled
MACHINE TOOLS, METAL CUTTING: Pipe Cutting & Threading
MACHINE TOOLS, METAL CUTTING: Plasma Process
MACHINE TOOLS, METAL CUTTING: Tool Replacement & Rpr Parts
MACHINE TOOLS, METAL CUTTING: Vertical Turning & Boring
MACHINE TOOLS, METAL FORMING: Bending
MACHINE TOOLS, METAL FORMING: Die Casting & Extruding
MACHINE TOOLS, METAL FORMING: Magnetic Forming
MACHINE TOOLS, METAL FORMING: Marking
MACHINE TOOLS, METAL FORMING: Mechanical, Pneumatic Or Hyd
MACHINE TOOLS, METAL FORMING: Pressing
MACHINE TOOLS, METAL FORMING: Rebuilt
MACHINE TOOLS: Metal Cutting
MACHINE TOOLS: Metal Forming
MACHINERY & EQPT FINANCE LEASING
MACHINERY & EQPT, AGRICULTURAL, WHOLESALE: Lawn & Garden
MACHINERY & EQPT, INDL, WHOLESALE: Chemical Process
MACHINERY & EQPT, INDL, WHOLESALE: Conveyor Systems
MACHINERY & EQPT, INDL, WHOLESALE: Cranes
MACHINERY & EQPT, INDL, WHOLESALE: Engines & Parts, Diesel
MACHINERY & EQPT, INDL, WHOLESALE: Engs & Parts, Air-Cooled
MACHINERY & EQPT, INDL, WHOLESALE: Engs/ Transportation Eqpt
MACHINERY & EQPT, INDL, WHOLESALE: Fans
MACHINERY & EQPT, INDL, WHOLESALE: Food Product Manufacturng
MACHINERY & EQPT, INDL, WHOLESALE: Heat Exchange
MACHINERY & EQPT, INDL, WHOLESALE: Hydraulic Systems
MACHINERY & EQPT, INDL, WHOLESALE: Indl Machine Parts
MACHINERY & EQPT, INDL, WHOLESALE: Instruments & Cntrl Eqpt
MACHINERY & EQPT, INDL, WHOLESALE: Lift Trucks & Parts
MACHINERY & EQPT, INDL, WHOLESALE: Machine Tools & Access
MACHINERY & EQPT, INDL, WHOLESALE: Packaging
MACHINERY & EQPT, INDL, WHOLESALE: Paint Spray
MACHINERY & EQPT, INDL, WHOLESALE: Paper Manufacturing
MACHINERY & EQPT, INDL, WHOLESALE: Petroleum Industry
MACHINERY & EQPT, INDL, WHOLESALE: Processing & Packaging
MACHINERY & EQPT, INDL, WHOLESALE: Pulp Manufacturing, Wood
MACHINERY & EQPT, INDL, WHOLESALE: Recycling
MACHINERY & EQPT, INDL, WHOLESALE: Safety Eqpt
MACHINERY & EQPT, INDL, WHOLESALE: Trailers, Indl
MACHINERY & EQPT, INDL, WHOLESALE: Water Pumps
MACHINERY & EQPT, WHOLESALE: Construction, General
MACHINERY & EQPT, WHOLESALE: Oil Field Eqpt
MACHINERY & EQPT, WHOLESALE: Road Construction & Maintenance
MACHINERY & EQPT: Electroplating
MACHINERY & EQPT: Farm
MACHINERY & EQPT: Liquid Automation
MACHINERY, CALCULATING: Calculators & Adding
MACHINERY, EQPT & SUPPLIES: Parking Facility
MACHINERY, FOOD PRDTS: Beverage
MACHINERY, FOOD PRDTS: Cutting, Chopping, Grinding, Mixing
MACHINERY, FOOD PRDTS: Food Processing, Smokers
MACHINERY, FOOD PRDTS: Oilseed Crushing & Extracting
MACHINERY, FOOD PRDTS: Ovens, Bakery
MACHINERY, FOOD PRDTS: Processing, Poultry
MACHINERY, METALWORKING: Coiling
MACHINERY, OFFICE: Paper Handling
MACHINERY, PACKAGING: Canning, Food
MACHINERY, PACKAGING: Packing & Wrapping
MACHINERY, PACKAGING: Vacuum
MACHINERY, PAPER INDUSTRY: Converting, Die Cutting & Stampng
MACHINERY, PAPER INDUSTRY: Paper Mill, Plating, Etc
MACHINERY, PAPER INDUSTRY: Pulp Mill
MACHINERY, PRINTING TRADES: Plates
MACHINERY, SEWING: Sewing & Hat & Zipper Making
MACHINERY, TEXTILE: Printing
MACHINERY: Ammunition & Explosives Loading
MACHINERY: Automotive Related
MACHINERY: Concrete Prdts
MACHINERY: Construction
MACHINERY: Cryogenic, Industrial
MACHINERY: Custom
MACHINERY: Electronic Component Making
MACHINERY: Gas Separators
MACHINERY: Ice Cream
MACHINERY: Metalworking
MACHINERY: Mining
MACHINERY: Pack-Up Assemblies, Wheel Overhaul
MACHINERY: Packaging
MACHINERY: Paint Making
MACHINERY: Plastic Working
MACHINERY: Printing Presses
MACHINERY: Recycling
MACHINERY: Road Construction & Maintenance
MACHINERY: Robots, Molding & Forming Plastics
MACHINERY: Rubber Working
MACHINERY: Screening Eqpt, Electric
MACHINERY: Semiconductor Manufacturing
MACHINERY: Separation Eqpt, Magnetic
MACHINERY: Sifting & Screening
MACHINERY: Textile
MACHINERY: Tire Retreading
MACHINERY: Wire Drawing
MACHINERY: Woodworking
MACHINISTS' TOOLS & MACHINES: Measuring, Metalworking Type
MACHINISTS' TOOLS: Measuring, Precision
MACHINISTS' TOOLS: Precision
MACHINISTS' TOOLS: Scales, Measuring, Precision
MAGNESIUM
MAGNESIUM
MAGNETIC INK & OPTICAL SCANNING EQPT
MAGNETS: Permanent
MAIL-ORDER HOUSE, NEC
MAIL-ORDER HOUSES: Educational Splys & Eqpt
MAILING & MESSENGER SVCS
MAILING LIST: Compilers
MAILING SVCS, NEC
MANAGEMENT CONSULTING SVCS: Automation & Robotics
MANAGEMENT CONSULTING SVCS: Business

PRODUCT INDEX

MANAGEMENT CONSULTING SVCS: Business Planning & Organizing
MANAGEMENT CONSULTING SVCS: Construction Project
MANAGEMENT CONSULTING SVCS: Corporation Organizing
MANAGEMENT CONSULTING SVCS: Distribution Channels
MANAGEMENT CONSULTING SVCS: General
MANAGEMENT CONSULTING SVCS: Hospital & Health
MANAGEMENT CONSULTING SVCS: Industrial
MANAGEMENT CONSULTING SVCS: Industry Specialist
MANAGEMENT CONSULTING SVCS: Information Systems
MANAGEMENT CONSULTING SVCS: Training & Development
MANAGEMENT CONSULTING SVCS: Transportation
MANAGEMENT SERVICES
MANAGEMENT SVCS: Administrative
MANAGEMENT SVCS: Business
MANAGEMENT SVCS: Construction
MANPOWER POOLS
MANUFACTURING INDUSTRIES, NEC
MARBLE, BUILDING: Cut & Shaped
MARINE CARGO HANDLING SVCS
MARINE HARDWARE
MARINE SPLYS WHOLESALERS
MARKETS: Meat & fish
MARKING DEVICES
MARKING DEVICES: Canceling Stamps, Hand, Rubber Or Metal
MARKING DEVICES: Embossing Seals & Hand Stamps
MARKING DEVICES: Embossing Seals, Corporate & Official
MATS OR MATTING, NEC: Rubber
MATS, MATTING & PADS: Nonwoven
MEAT MARKETS
MEAT PRDTS: Bacon, Side & Sliced, From Purchased Meat
MEAT PRDTS: Boxed Beef, From Slaughtered Meat
MEAT PRDTS: Cooked Meats, From Purchased Meat
MEAT PRDTS: Frozen
MEAT PRDTS: Luncheon Meat, From Purchased Meat
MEAT PRDTS: Prepared Beef Prdts From Purchased Beef
MEAT PRDTS: Sausages & Related Prdts, From Purchased Meat
MEAT PRDTS: Sausages, From Purchased Meat
MEAT PRDTS: Snack Sticks, Incl Jerky, From Purchased Meat
MEDIA: Magnetic & Optical Recording
MEDICAL & HOSPITAL EQPT WHOLESALERS
MEDICAL & SURGICAL SPLYS: Bandages & Dressings
MEDICAL & SURGICAL SPLYS: Braces, Elastic
MEDICAL & SURGICAL SPLYS: Braces, Orthopedic
MEDICAL & SURGICAL SPLYS: Clothing, Fire Resistant & Protect
MEDICAL & SURGICAL SPLYS: Foot Appliances, Orthopedic
MEDICAL & SURGICAL SPLYS: Grafts, Artificial
MEDICAL & SURGICAL SPLYS: Limbs, Artificial
MEDICAL & SURGICAL SPLYS: Orthopedic Appliances
MEDICAL & SURGICAL SPLYS: Personal Safety Eqpt
MEDICAL & SURGICAL SPLYS: Prosthetic Appliances
MEDICAL & SURGICAL SPLYS: Splints, Pneumatic & Wood
MEDICAL & SURGICAL SPLYS: Stretchers
MEDICAL EQPT REPAIR SVCS, NON-ELECTRIC
MEDICAL EQPT: Diagnostic
MEDICAL EQPT: Electromedical Apparatus
MEDICAL EQPT: Sterilizers
MEDICAL EQPT: Ultrasonic Scanning Devices
MEDICAL EQPT: X-Ray Apparatus & Tubes, Radiographic
MEDICAL INSURANCE CLAIM PROCESSING: Contract Or Fee Basis
MEDICAL SUNDRIES: Rubber
MEDICAL, DENTAL & HOSP EQPT, WHOLESALE: X-ray Film & Splys
MEDICAL, DENTAL & HOSPITAL EQPT, WHOL: Hospital Eqpt & Splys
MEDICAL, DENTAL & HOSPITAL EQPT, WHOL: Surgical Eqpt & Splys
MELAMINE RESINS: Melamine-Formaldehyde
MEMBERSHIP ORGANIZATIONS, NEC: Personal Interest
MEN'S & BOYS' CLOTHING ACCESS STORES
MEN'S & BOYS' CLOTHING STORES
MEN'S & BOYS' CLOTHING WHOLESALERS, NEC
METAL & STEEL PRDTS: Abrasive
METAL COMPONENTS: Prefabricated
METAL DETECTORS
METAL FABRICATORS: Plate
METAL FINISHING SVCS
METAL MINING SVCS
METAL SERVICE CENTERS & OFFICES
METAL STAMPING, FOR THE TRADE
METAL STAMPINGS: Perforated
METAL TREATING COMPOUNDS
METAL, TITANIUM: Sponge & Granules
METAL: Battery
METALS SVC CENTERS & WHOLESALERS: Cable, Wire
METALS SVC CENTERS & WHOLESALERS: Ferrous Metals
METALS SVC CENTERS & WHOLESALERS: Flat Prdts, Iron Or Steel
METALS SVC CENTERS & WHOLESALERS: Pipe & Tubing, Steel
METALS SVC CENTERS & WHOLESALERS: Sheets, Metal
METALS SVC CENTERS & WHOLESALERS: Steel
METALS SVC CENTERS & WHOLESALERS: Tubing, Metal
METALS: Precious NEC
METALS: Precious, Secondary
METALS: Primary Nonferrous, NEC
METALWORK: Miscellaneous
METALWORK: Ornamental
METALWORKING MACHINERY WHOLESALERS
METERING DEVICES: Flow Meters, Impeller & Counter Driven
METERING DEVICES: Water Quality Monitoring & Control Systems
METERS: Pyrometers, Indl Process
MICROPHONES
MICROPROCESSORS
MICROWAVE COMPONENTS
MILITARY INSIGNIA
MILL PRDTS: Structural & Rail
MILLWORK
MINE & QUARRY SVCS: Nonmetallic Minerals
MINE DEVELOPMENT SVCS: Nonmetallic Minerals
MINE PREPARATION SVCS
MINERAL WOOL
MINERAL WOOL INSULATION PRDTS
MINERALS: Ground Or Otherwise Treated
MINERALS: Ground or Treated
MINIATURES
MINING EXPLORATION & DEVELOPMENT SVCS
MINING MACHINERY & EQPT WHOLESALERS
MIXTURES & BLOCKS: Asphalt Paving
MOBILE COMMUNICATIONS EQPT
MOBILE HOMES
MOBILE HOMES, EXC RECREATIONAL
MOBILE HOMES: Personal Or Private Use
MODELS: General, Exc Toy
MODULES: Computer Logic
MOLDED RUBBER PRDTS
MOLDING COMPOUNDS
MOLDINGS & TRIM: Metal, Exc Automobile
MOLDINGS & TRIM: Wood
MOLDINGS OR TRIM: Automobile, Stamped Metal
MOLDS: Gray, Ingot, Cast Iron
MOLDS: Indl
MOLYBDENUM SILICON, EXC MADE IN BLAST FURNACES
MOPS: Floor & Dust
MORTAR: High Temperature, Nonclay
MOTOR & GENERATOR PARTS: Electric
MOTOR CONTROL CENTERS
MOTOR HOMES
MOTOR SCOOTERS & PARTS
MOTOR VEHICLE ASSEMBLY, COMPLETE: Ambulances
MOTOR VEHICLE ASSEMBLY, COMPLETE: Buses, All Types
MOTOR VEHICLE ASSEMBLY, COMPLETE: Fire Department Vehicles
MOTOR VEHICLE ASSEMBLY, COMPLETE: Military Motor Vehicle
MOTOR VEHICLE ASSEMBLY, COMPLETE: Wreckers, Tow Truck
MOTOR VEHICLE DEALERS: Automobiles, New & Used
MOTOR VEHICLE DEALERS: Vans, New & Used
MOTOR VEHICLE PARTS & ACCESS: Acceleration Eqpt
MOTOR VEHICLE PARTS & ACCESS: Air Conditioner Parts
MOTOR VEHICLE PARTS & ACCESS: Ball Joints
MOTOR VEHICLE PARTS & ACCESS: Bearings
MOTOR VEHICLE PARTS & ACCESS: Body Components & Frames
MOTOR VEHICLE PARTS & ACCESS: Brakes, Air
MOTOR VEHICLE PARTS & ACCESS: Clutches
MOTOR VEHICLE PARTS & ACCESS: Connecting Rods
MOTOR VEHICLE PARTS & ACCESS: Electrical Eqpt
MOTOR VEHICLE PARTS & ACCESS: Engines & Parts
MOTOR VEHICLE PARTS & ACCESS: Fuel Pumps
MOTOR VEHICLE PARTS & ACCESS: Fuel Systems & Parts
MOTOR VEHICLE PARTS & ACCESS: Gas Tanks
MOTOR VEHICLE PARTS & ACCESS: Gears
MOTOR VEHICLE PARTS & ACCESS: Heaters
MOTOR VEHICLE PARTS & ACCESS: Instrument Board Assemblies
MOTOR VEHICLE PARTS & ACCESS: Lubrication Systems & Parts
MOTOR VEHICLE PARTS & ACCESS: Mufflers, Exhaust
MOTOR VEHICLE PARTS & ACCESS: Oil Strainers
MOTOR VEHICLE PARTS & ACCESS: Power Steering Eqpt
MOTOR VEHICLE PARTS & ACCESS: Propane Conversion Eqpt
MOTOR VEHICLE PARTS & ACCESS: Pumps, Hydraulic Fluid Power
MOTOR VEHICLE PARTS & ACCESS: Rear Axel Housings
MOTOR VEHICLE PARTS & ACCESS: Sanders, Safety
MOTOR VEHICLE PARTS & ACCESS: Tire Valve Cores
MOTOR VEHICLE PARTS & ACCESS: Trailer Hitches
MOTOR VEHICLE PARTS & ACCESS: Transmission Housings Or Parts
MOTOR VEHICLE PARTS & ACCESS: Transmissions
MOTOR VEHICLE PARTS & ACCESS: Water Pumps
MOTOR VEHICLE PARTS & ACCESS: Wiring Harness Sets
MOTOR VEHICLE SPLYS & PARTS WHOLESALERS: New
MOTOR VEHICLE SPLYS & PARTS WHOLESALERS: Used
MOTOR VEHICLE: Radiators
MOTOR VEHICLE: Shock Absorbers
MOTOR VEHICLE: Wheels
MOTOR VEHICLES & CAR BODIES
MOTOR VEHICLES, WHOLESALE: Fire Trucks
MOTOR VEHICLES, WHOLESALE: Truck tractors
MOTOR VEHICLES, WHOLESALE: Trucks, commercial
MOTORCYCLE ACCESS
MOTORCYCLE PARTS: Wholesalers
MOTORCYCLES & RELATED PARTS
MOTORS: Electric
MOTORS: Generators
MOTORS: Pneumatic
MOUTHWASHES
MULTIPLEXERS: Telephone & Telegraph
MUSICAL INSTRUMENTS & ACCESS: Carrying Cases
MUSICAL INSTRUMENTS & ACCESS: NEC
MUSICAL INSTRUMENTS & PARTS: Percussion
MUSICAL INSTRUMENTS WHOLESALERS
MUSICAL INSTRUMENTS: Guitars & Parts, Electric & Acoustic

N

NAME PLATES: Engraved Or Etched
NATURAL GAS DISTRIBUTION TO CONSUMERS
NATURAL GAS LIQUIDS PRODUCTION
NATURAL GAS PRODUCTION
NATURAL GAS TRANSMISSION
NATURAL GAS TRANSMISSION & DISTRIBUTION
NATURAL GASOLINE PRODUCTION
NATURAL PROPANE PRODUCTION
NAVIGATIONAL SYSTEMS & INSTRUMENTS
NETS: Launderers & Dyers
NEW & USED CAR DEALERS
NEWS SYNDICATES
NICKEL
NONCURRENT CARRYING WIRING DEVICES
NONFERROUS: Rolling & Drawing, NEC
NOTEBOOKS, MADE FROM PURCHASED MATERIALS
NOVELTIES
NOVELTIES: Plastic
NOZZLES: Fire Fighting
NOZZLES: Spray, Aerosol, Paint Or Insecticide
NUCLEAR SHIELDING: Metal Plate
NURSERIES & LAWN & GARDEN SPLY STORES, RETAIL: Fertilizer
NURSING CARE FACILITIES: Skilled
NUTS: Metal
NYLON FIBERS

O

OFFICE EQPT WHOLESALERS
OFFICE EQPT, WHOLESALE: Photocopy Machines

PRODUCT INDEX

OFFICE FURNITURE REPAIR & MAINTENANCE SVCS
OFFICE SPLY & STATIONERY STORES: Office Forms & Splys
OFFICE SPLYS, NEC, WHOLESALE
OIL & GAS FIELD EQPT: Drill Rigs
OIL & GAS FIELD MACHINERY
OIL FIELD MACHINERY & EQPT
OIL FIELD SVCS, NEC
OIL TREATING COMPOUNDS
OILS & ESSENTIAL OILS
OILS: Cutting
OILS: Lubricating
OILS: Mineral, Natural
OLEFINS
OPERATOR TRAINING, COMPUTER
OPHTHALMIC GOODS
OPHTHALMIC GOODS WHOLESALERS
OPHTHALMIC GOODS: Frames & Parts, Eyeglass & Spectacle
OPHTHALMIC GOODS: Frames, Lenses & Parts, Eyeglasses
OPHTHALMIC GOODS: Lenses, Ophthalmic
OPTICAL GOODS STORES
OPTICAL INSTRUMENTS & APPARATUS
OPTICAL INSTRUMENTS & LENSES
OPTICAL ISOLATORS
ORGANIZATIONS: Medical Research
ORGANIZATIONS: Physical Research, Noncommercial
ORGANIZATIONS: Religious
ORNAMENTS: Christmas Tree, Exc Electrical & Glass
OVENS: Laboratory

P

PACKAGE DESIGN SVCS
PACKAGING & LABELING SVCS
PACKAGING MATERIALS, WHOLESALE
PACKAGING MATERIALS: Paper
PACKAGING MATERIALS: Paper, Coated Or Laminated
PACKAGING MATERIALS: Plastic Film, Coated Or Laminated
PACKAGING: Blister Or Bubble Formed, Plastic
PACKING & CRATING SVC
PADDING: Foamed Plastics
PAINTS & ADDITIVES
PAINTS & ALLIED PRODUCTS
PAINTS, VARNISHES & SPLYS WHOLESALERS
PAINTS, VARNISHES & SPLYS, WHOLESALE: Paints
PAINTS: Oil Or Alkyd Vehicle Or Water Thinned
PALLET REPAIR SVCS
PALLETIZERS & DEPALLETIZERS
PALLETS & SKIDS: Wood
PALLETS: Plastic
PALLETS: Wood & Metal Combination
PANEL & DISTRIBUTION BOARDS & OTHER RELATED APPARATUS
PANEL & DISTRIBUTION BOARDS: Electric
PANELS: Building, Plastic, NEC
PAPER & BOARD: Die-cut
PAPER & PAPER PRDTS: Crepe, Made From Purchased Materials
PAPER PRDTS: Infant & Baby Prdts
PAPER PRDTS: Molded Pulp Prdts
PAPER PRDTS: Napkins, Sanitary, Made From Purchased Material
PAPER PRDTS: Sanitary
PAPER PRDTS: Tampons, Sanitary, Made From Purchased Material
PAPER, WHOLESALE: Printing
PAPER: Adhesive
PAPER: Book
PAPER: Building, Insulating & Packaging
PAPER: Cardboard
PAPER: Cloth, Lined, Made From Purchased Materials
PAPER: Coated & Laminated, NEC
PAPER: Coated, Exc Photographic, Carbon Or Abrasive
PAPER: Fine
PAPER: Newsprint
PAPER: Packaging
PAPER: Specialty
PAPER: Specialty Or Chemically Treated
PAPER: Tissue
PAPER: Wrapping & Packaging
PAPERBOARD PRDTS: Folding Boxboard
PAPERBOARD PRDTS: Packaging Board
PARTICLEBOARD: Laminated, Plastic

PARTITIONS & FIXTURES: Except Wood
PARTITIONS: Solid Fiber, Made From Purchased Materials
PARTITIONS: Wood & Fixtures
PARTS: Metal
PATIENT MONITORING EQPT WHOLESALERS
PATTERNS: Indl
PAVERS
PAVING MIXTURES
PAYROLL SVCS
PENCILS & PENS WHOLESALERS
PERFUME: Perfumes, Natural Or Synthetic
PERFUMES
PERISCOPES
PEST CONTROL IN STRUCTURES SVCS
PEST CONTROL SVCS
PESTICIDES
PET SPLYS
PETROLEUM & PETROLEUM PRDTS, WHOLESALE: Bulk Stations
PHARMACEUTICAL PREPARATIONS: Adrenal
PHARMACEUTICAL PREPARATIONS: Druggists' Preparations
PHARMACEUTICAL PREPARATIONS: Pills
PHARMACEUTICAL PREPARATIONS: Proprietary Drug
PHARMACEUTICAL PREPARATIONS: Solutions
PHARMACEUTICALS
PHOSPHATES
PHOTOCOPY MACHINES
PHOTOCOPYING & DUPLICATING SVCS
PHOTOGRAPHIC EQPT & SPLYS
PHOTOGRAPHIC EQPT & SPLYS WHOLESALERS
PHOTOGRAPHIC EQPT & SPLYS: Film, Sensitized
PHOTOGRAPHIC EQPT & SPLYS: Graphic Arts Plates, Sensitized
PHOTOGRAPHIC EQPT & SPLYS: Printing Eqpt
PHOTOGRAPHY SVCS: Commercial
PHYSICIANS' OFFICES & CLINICS: Medical doctors
PICTURE FRAMES: Metal
PICTURE FRAMES: Wood
PICTURE FRAMING SVCS, CUSTOM
PIECE GOODS & NOTIONS WHOLESALERS
PIECE GOODS, NOTIONS/DRY GOODS, WHOL: Fabrics, Synthetic
PIGMENTS, INORGANIC: Metallic & Mineral, NEC
PILOT SVCS: Aviation
PINS
PINS: Dowel
PIPE & FITTINGS: Cast Iron
PIPE & TUBES: Seamless
PIPE FITTINGS: Plastic
PIPE SECTIONS, FABRICATED FROM PURCHASED PIPE
PIPE, CYLINDER: Concrete, Prestressed Or Pretensioned
PIPE, SEWER: Concrete
PIPE: Concrete
PIPE: Plastic
PIPE: Sheet Metal
PIPELINES: Natural Gas
PIPES & TUBES
PIPES & TUBES: Steel
PIPES & TUBES: Welded
PIPES: Steel & Iron
PISTONS & PISTON RINGS
PLACER GOLD MINING
PLAQUES: Picture, Laminated
PLASTICIZERS, ORGANIC: Cyclic & Acyclic
PLASTICS FILM & SHEET
PLASTICS FILM & SHEET: Polyethylene
PLASTICS FILM & SHEET: Polypropylene
PLASTICS FILM & SHEET: Polyvinyl
PLASTICS FILM & SHEET: Vinyl
PLASTICS FINISHED PRDTS: Laminated
PLASTICS MATERIAL & RESINS
PLASTICS MATERIALS, BASIC FORMS & SHAPES WHOLESALERS
PLASTICS PROCESSING
PLASTICS SHEET: Packing Materials
PLASTICS: Blow Molded
PLASTICS: Extruded
PLASTICS: Finished Injection Molded
PLASTICS: Molded
PLASTICS: Polystyrene Foam
PLASTICS: Thermoformed
PLATE WORK: Metalworking Trade

PLATES: Steel
PLATING & POLISHING SVC
PLATING COMPOUNDS
PLATING SVC: Chromium, Metals Or Formed Prdts
PLAYGROUND EQPT
PLEATING & STITCHING FOR THE TRADE: Decorative & Novelty
PLEATING & STITCHING SVC
PLUMBING FIXTURES
PLUMBING FIXTURES: Plastic
PLUMBING FIXTURES: Vitreous
PLUMBING FIXTURES: Vitreous China
POINT OF SALE DEVICES
POLE LINE HARDWARE
POLISHING SVC: Metals Or Formed Prdts
POLYESTERS
POLYETHYLENE RESINS
POLYMETHYL METHACRYLATE RESINS: Plexiglas
POLYSTYRENE RESINS
POLYTETRAFLUOROETHYLENE RESINS
POLYURETHANE RESINS
POLYVINYL CHLORIDE RESINS
POULTRY & POULTRY PRDTS WHOLESALERS
POULTRY & SMALL GAME SLAUGHTERING & PROCESSING
POULTRY SLAUGHTERING & PROCESSING
POWDER: Iron
POWDER: Metal
POWER GENERATORS
POWER SPLY CONVERTERS: Static, Electronic Applications
POWER SUPPLIES: All Types, Static
POWER SWITCHING EQPT
PRECAST TERRAZZO OR CONCRETE PRDTS
PRECIPITATORS: Electrostatic
PRESTRESSED CONCRETE PRDTS
PRIMARY FINISHED OR SEMIFINISHED SHAPES
PRIMARY ROLLING MILL EQPT
PRINT CARTRIDGES: Laser & Other Computer Printers
PRINTED CIRCUIT BOARDS
PRINTERS & PLOTTERS
PRINTERS' SVCS: Folding, Collating, Etc
PRINTERS: Computer
PRINTERS: Magnetic Ink, Bar Code
PRINTING & BINDING: Books
PRINTING & EMBOSSING: Plastic Fabric Articles
PRINTING & ENGRAVING: Card, Exc Greeting
PRINTING & ENGRAVING: Financial Notes & Certificates
PRINTING & STAMPING: Fabric Articles
PRINTING & WRITING PAPER WHOLESALERS
PRINTING MACHINERY
PRINTING, COMMERCIAL: Bags, Plastic, NEC
PRINTING, COMMERCIAL: Business Forms, NEC
PRINTING, COMMERCIAL: Calendars, NEC
PRINTING, COMMERCIAL: Decals, NEC
PRINTING, COMMERCIAL: Envelopes, NEC
PRINTING, COMMERCIAL: Imprinting
PRINTING, COMMERCIAL: Labels & Seals, NEC
PRINTING, COMMERCIAL: Letterpress & Screen
PRINTING, COMMERCIAL: Literature, Advertising, NEC
PRINTING, COMMERCIAL: Magazines, NEC
PRINTING, COMMERCIAL: Periodicals, NEC
PRINTING, COMMERCIAL: Promotional
PRINTING, COMMERCIAL: Screen
PRINTING, COMMERCIAL: Stationery, NEC
PRINTING, LITHOGRAPHIC: Calendars
PRINTING, LITHOGRAPHIC: Circulars
PRINTING, LITHOGRAPHIC: Color
PRINTING, LITHOGRAPHIC: Forms, Business
PRINTING, LITHOGRAPHIC: Offset & photolithographic printing
PRINTING, LITHOGRAPHIC: Posters
PRINTING, LITHOGRAPHIC: Tags
PRINTING, LITHOGRAPHIC: Tickets
PRINTING: Books
PRINTING: Books
PRINTING: Commercial, NEC
PRINTING: Flexographic
PRINTING: Gravure, Forms, Business
PRINTING: Gravure, Labels
PRINTING: Gravure, Rotogravure
PRINTING: Laser
PRINTING: Letterpress
PRINTING: Lithographic

PRODUCT INDEX

PRINTING: Offset
PRINTING: Photo-Offset
PRINTING: Photolithographic
PRINTING: Rotogravure
PRINTING: Screen, Broadwoven Fabrics, Cotton
PRINTING: Screen, Fabric
PRINTING: Screen, Manmade Fiber & Silk, Broadwoven Fabric
PRINTING: Thermography
PROFESSIONAL EQPT & SPLYS, WHOLESALE: Analytical Instruments
PROFESSIONAL EQPT & SPLYS, WHOLESALE: Engineers', NEC
PROFESSIONAL EQPT & SPLYS, WHOLESALE: Optical Goods
PROFESSIONAL INSTRUMENT REPAIR SVCS
PROFILE SHAPES: Unsupported Plastics
PROTECTION EQPT: Lightning
PROTECTIVE FOOTWEAR: Rubber Or Plastic
PUBLIC RELATIONS & PUBLICITY SVCS
PUBLISHERS: Music Book & Sheet Music
PUBLISHERS: Music, Sheet
PUBLISHERS: Sheet Music
PUBLISHERS: Telephone & Other Directory
PUBLISHING & BROADCASTING: Internet Only
PUBLISHING & PRINTING: Art Copy
PUBLISHING & PRINTING: Book Music
PUBLISHING & PRINTING: Books
PUBLISHING & PRINTING: Directories, NEC
PUBLISHING & PRINTING: Directories, Telephone
PUBLISHING & PRINTING: Guides
PUBLISHING & PRINTING: Magazines: publishing & printing
PUBLISHING & PRINTING: Newsletters, Business Svc
PUBLISHING & PRINTING: Newspapers
PUBLISHING & PRINTING: Pamphlets
PUBLISHING & PRINTING: Textbooks
PUBLISHING & PRINTING: Trade Journals
PULLEYS: Metal
PULLEYS: Power Transmission
PULP MILLS
PULP MILLS: Mechanical & Recycling Processing
PUMPS & PARTS: Indl
PUMPS & PUMPING EQPT REPAIR SVCS
PUMPS & PUMPING EQPT WHOLESALERS
PUMPS: Domestic, Water Or Sump
PUMPS: Fluid Power
PUMPS: Gasoline, Measuring Or Dispensing
PUMPS: Hydraulic Power Transfer
PUMPS: Measuring & Dispensing
PUMPS: Oil Well & Field
PUMPS: Oil, Measuring Or Dispensing
PUNCHES: Forming & Stamping
PURIFICATION & DUST COLLECTION EQPT

R

RACEWAYS
RADAR SYSTEMS & EQPT
RADIO & TELEVISION COMMUNICATIONS EQUIPMENT
RADIO BROADCASTING & COMMUNICATIONS EQPT
RADIO BROADCASTING STATIONS
RADIO COMMUNICATIONS: Airborne Eqpt
RADIO COMMUNICATIONS: Carrier Eqpt
RADIO, TV & CONSUMER ELEC STORES: High Fidelity Stereo Eqpt
RADIO, TV/CONSUMER ELEC STORES: Antennas, Satellite Dish
RAILINGS: Prefabricated, Metal
RAILINGS: Wood
RAILROAD CAR REPAIR SVCS
RAILROAD EQPT
RAILROAD EQPT & SPLYS WHOLESALERS
RAILROAD EQPT: Brakes, Air & Vacuum
RAILROAD MAINTENANCE & REPAIR SVCS
RAILROAD RELATED EQPT
RAMPS: Prefabricated Metal
RAZORS, RAZOR BLADES
RAZORS: Electric
REAL ESTATE AGENCIES & BROKERS
REAL ESTATE AGENTS & MANAGERS
REAL ESTATE INVESTMENT TRUSTS
RECEIVERS: Radio Communications
RECORDS & TAPES: Prerecorded
RECOVERY SVC: Iron Ore, From Open Hearth Slag

RECREATIONAL VEHICLE PARTS & ACCESS STORES
REFINERS & SMELTERS: Copper
REFINERS & SMELTERS: Silicon, Primary, Over 99% Pure
REFINING: Petroleum
REFRACTORIES: Brick
REFRACTORIES: Cement
REFRACTORIES: Clay
REFRACTORIES: Foundry, Clay
REFRACTORIES: Graphite, Carbon Or Ceramic Bond
REFRACTORIES: Nonclay
REFRACTORIES: Tile & Brick, Exc Plastic
REFRIGERATION & HEATING EQUIPMENT
REFRIGERATION EQPT & SPLYS WHOLESALERS
REFRIGERATION EQPT: Complete
REFRIGERATION REPAIR SVCS
REFRIGERATION SVC & REPAIR
REFUSE SYSTEMS
REGISTERS: Air, Metal
REGULATORS: Power
REHABILITATION SVCS
RELAYS & SWITCHES: Indl, Electric
RELAYS: Control Circuit, Ind
RELIGIOUS SPLYS WHOLESALERS
REMOVERS & CLEANERS
REMOVERS: Paint
RENTAL SVCS: Costume
RENTAL SVCS: Eqpt, Theatrical
RENTAL SVCS: Sign
RENTAL SVCS: Sound & Lighting Eqpt
RENTAL SVCS: Tent & Tarpaulin
RENTAL SVCS: Vending Machine
RENTAL SVCS: Work Zone Traffic Eqpt, Flags, Cones, Etc
RENTAL: Portable Toilet
RENTAL: Video Tape & Disc
RESEARCH & DEVELOPMENT SVCS, COMMERCIAL: Engineering Lab
RESEARCH, DEVELOPMENT & TESTING SVCS, COMM: Agricultural
RESEARCH, DEVELOPMENT & TESTING SVCS, COMMERCIAL: Energy
RESEARCH, DEVELOPMENT & TESTING SVCS, COMMERCIAL: Medical
RESEARCH, DEVELOPMENT & TESTING SVCS, COMMERCIAL: Physical
RESINS: Custom Compound Purchased
RESISTORS & RESISTOR UNITS
RESPIRATORS
RESTAURANT EQPT: Carts
RESTAURANT EQPT: Sheet Metal
RESTAURANTS:Full Svc, American
RETAIL BAKERY: Bread
RETAIL BAKERY: Cakes
RETAIL BAKERY: Cookies
RETAIL BAKERY: Doughnuts
RETAIL BAKERY: Pastries
RETAIL BAKERY: Pretzels
RETAIL STORES: Alcoholic Beverage Making Eqpt & Splys
RETAIL STORES: Audio-Visual Eqpt & Splys
RETAIL STORES: Batteries, Non-Automotive
RETAIL STORES: Business Machines & Eqpt
RETAIL STORES: Cake Decorating Splys
RETAIL STORES: Christmas Lights & Decorations
RETAIL STORES: Cleaning Eqpt & Splys
RETAIL STORES: Communication Eqpt
RETAIL STORES: Concrete Prdts, Precast
RETAIL STORES: Cosmetics
RETAIL STORES: Educational Aids & Electronic Training Mat
RETAIL STORES: Electronic Parts & Eqpt
RETAIL STORES: Flags
RETAIL STORES: Hair Care Prdts
RETAIL STORES: Ice
RETAIL STORES: Medical Apparatus & Splys
RETAIL STORES: Orthopedic & Prosthesis Applications
RETAIL STORES: Pet Splys
RETAIL STORES: Religious Goods
RETAIL STORES: Safety Splys & Eqpt
RETAIL STORES: Swimming Pools, Above Ground
RETAIL STORES: Telephone & Communication Eqpt
RETAIL STORES: Tents
RETAIL STORES: Water Purification Eqpt
RETAIL STORES: Welding Splys
REUPHOLSTERY & FURNITURE REPAIR
RIBBONS & BOWS

RIVETS: Metal
ROAD CONSTRUCTION EQUIPMENT WHOLESALERS
ROBOTS: Assembly Line
ROBOTS: Indl Spraying, Painting, Etc
RODS: Rolled, Aluminum
RODS: Steel & Iron, Made In Steel Mills
ROLL FORMED SHAPES: Custom
ROLLING MILL EQPT: Finishing
ROLLING MILL MACHINERY
ROLLING MILL ROLLS: Cast Steel
ROLLS: Rubber Solid Or Covered
ROOFING MATERIALS: Asphalt
ROOFING MEMBRANE: Rubber
RUBBER BANDS
RUBBER PRDTS: Appliance, Mechanical
RUBBER PRDTS: Automotive, Mechanical
RUBBER PRDTS: Medical & Surgical Tubing, Extrudd & Lathe-Cut
RUBBER PRDTS: Oil & Gas Field Machinery, Mechanical
RUBBER PRDTS: Silicone
RUBBER PRDTS: Sponge
RUBBER STRUCTURES: Air-Supported

S

SAFE DEPOSIT BOXES
SAFES & VAULTS: Metal
SAFETY EQPT & SPLYS WHOLESALERS
SAFETY INSPECTION SVCS
SALT
SAND & GRAVEL
SAND LIME PRDTS
SAND MINING
SANDBLASTING EQPT
SANITARY SVC, NEC
SANITARY SVCS: Liquid Waste Collection & Disposal
SANITARY SVCS: Refuse Collection & Disposal Svcs
SANITARY SVCS: Waste Materials, Recycling
SASHES: Door Or Window, Metal
SATELLITES: Communications
SAW BLADES
SAWDUST & SHAVINGS
SCAFFOLDS: Mobile Or Stationary, Metal
SCALES & BALANCES, EXC LABORATORY
SCALES: Indl
SCIENTIFIC EQPT REPAIR SVCS
SCIENTIFIC INSTRUMENTS WHOLESALERS
SCRAP & WASTE MATERIALS, WHOLESALE: Ferrous Metal
SCRAP & WASTE MATERIALS, WHOLESALE: Metal
SCRAP & WASTE MATERIALS, WHOLESALE: Nonferrous Metals Scrap
SCRAP & WASTE MATERIALS, WHOLESALE: Paper
SCRAP STEEL CUTTING
SCREENS: Projection
SCREENS: Window, Metal
SCREENS: Woven Wire
SCREW MACHINE PRDTS
SCREWS: Metal
SEALANTS
SEALING COMPOUNDS: Sealing, synthetic rubber or plastic
SEALS: Hermetic
SEARCH & NAVIGATION SYSTEMS
SEATING: Stadium
SECURITY CONTROL EQPT & SYSTEMS
SECURITY DEVICES
SECURITY SYSTEMS SERVICES
SEMICONDUCTOR CIRCUIT NETWORKS
SEMICONDUCTORS & RELATED DEVICES
SENSORS: Temperature, Exc Indl Process
SEPARATORS: Metal Plate
SEPTIC TANKS: Concrete
SEPTIC TANKS: Plastic
SEWAGE & WATER TREATMENT EQPT
SEWER CLEANING EQPT: Power
SHADES: Window
SHAPES & PILINGS, STRUCTURAL: Steel
SHAPES: Extruded, Aluminum, NEC
SHAVING PREPARATIONS
SHEET METAL SPECIALTIES, EXC STAMPED
SHEETS: Hard Rubber
SHELVING, MADE FROM PURCHASED WIRE
SHIMS: Metal
SHOE STORES: Boots, Men's
SHOE STORES: Men's

PRODUCT INDEX

SHOES: Men's
SHOES: Men's, Work
SHOES: Plastic Or Rubber
SHOES: Women's
SHOES: Women's, Dress
SHOT PEENING SVC
SHOWCASES & DISPLAY FIXTURES: Office & Store
SHOWER STALLS: Plastic & Fiberglass
SHREDDERS: Indl & Commercial
SHUTTERS, DOOR & WINDOW: Metal
SHUTTERS, DOOR & WINDOW: Plastic
SIDING MATERIALS
SIDING: Plastic
SIDING: Precast Stone
SIDING: Sheet Metal
SIGN PAINTING & LETTERING SHOP
SIGNALS: Traffic Control, Electric
SIGNS & ADVERTISING SPECIALTIES
SIGNS & ADVERTISING SPECIALTIES: Artwork, Advertising
SIGNS & ADVERTISING SPECIALTIES: Displays, Paint Process
SIGNS & ADVERTISING SPECIALTIES: Letters For Signs, Metal
SIGNS & ADVERTISING SPECIALTIES: Novelties
SIGNS & ADVERTISING SPECIALTIES: Scoreboards, Electric
SIGNS, ELECTRICAL: Wholesalers
SIGNS, EXC ELECTRIC, WHOLESALE
SIGNS: Electrical
SIGNS: Neon
SILICA MINING
SILICON WAFERS: Chemically Doped
SILICON: Pure
SILICONE RESINS
SILICONES
SILK SCREEN DESIGN SVCS
SILVERWARE & PLATED WARE
SIMULATORS: Flight
SINTER: Iron
SLAG: Crushed Or Ground
SMOKE DETECTORS
SOFT DRINKS WHOLESALERS
SOFTWARE PUBLISHERS: Home Entertainment
SOFTWARE PUBLISHERS: Operating Systems
SOLAR CELLS
SOLAR HEATING EQPT
SOLES, BOOT OR SHOE: Rubber, Composition Or Fiber
SOLID CONTAINING UNITS: Concrete
SOLVENTS
SOLVENTS: Organic
SONAR SYSTEMS & EQPT
SOUND EFFECTS & MUSIC PRODUCTION: Motion Picture
SOUND EQPT: Electric
SPEAKER SYSTEMS
SPECIALTY FOOD STORES: Coffee
SPECIALTY FOOD STORES: Eggs & Poultry
SPECIALTY FOOD STORES: Health & Dietetic Food
SPORTING & ATHLETIC GOODS: Basketball Eqpt & Splys, NEC
SPORTING & ATHLETIC GOODS: Camping Eqpt & Splys
SPORTING & ATHLETIC GOODS: Cases, Gun & Rod
SPORTING & ATHLETIC GOODS: Fishing Eqpt
SPORTING & ATHLETIC GOODS: Hunting Eqpt
SPORTING & ATHLETIC GOODS: Shafts, Golf Club
SPORTING & ATHLETIC GOODS: Team Sports Eqpt
SPORTING & ATHLETIC GOODS: Water Sports Eqpt
SPORTING & RECREATIONAL GOODS, WHOLESALE: Athletic Goods
SPORTING & RECREATIONAL GOODS, WHOLESALE: Boat Access & Part
SPORTING GOODS STORES: Firearms
SPORTING GOODS STORES: Playground Eqpt
SPORTS APPAREL STORES
SPRINGS: Clock, Precision
SPRINGS: Coiled Flat
SPRINGS: Leaf, Automobile, Locomotive, Etc
SPRINGS: Mechanical, Precision
SPRINGS: Precision
SPRINGS: Steel
SPRINGS: Torsion Bar
SPRINGS: Wire
SPROCKETS: Power Transmission
STAINLESS STEEL

STAIRCASES & STAIRS, WOOD
STAMPINGS: Automotive
STAMPINGS: Metal
STAPLES: Steel, Wire Or Cut
STATIONERY & OFFICE SPLYS WHOLESALERS
STATIONERY: Made From Purchased Materials
STATUARY & OTHER DECORATIVE PRDTS: Nonmetallic
STEEL & ALLOYS: Tool & Die
STEEL, COLD-ROLLED: Flat Bright, From Purchased HotRolled
STEEL, COLD-ROLLED: Sheet Or Strip, From Own HotRolled
STEEL, COLD-ROLLED: Strip NEC, From Purchased HotRolled
STEEL, COLD-ROLLED: Strip Or Wire
STEEL, HOT-ROLLED: Sheet Or Strip
STOCK SHAPES: Plastic
STONE: Dimension, NEC
STONE: Quarrying & Processing, Own Stone Prdts
STONEWARE PRDTS: Pottery
STORE FIXTURES: Exc Wood
STORE FIXTURES: Wood
STORES: Auto & Home Supply
STRAINERS: Line, Piping Systems
STRAWS: Drinking, Made From Purchased Materials
STRUCTURAL SUPPORT & BUILDING MATERIAL: Concrete
STUDS & JOISTS: Sheet Metal
SUNDRIES & RELATED PRDTS: Medical & Laboratory, Rubber
SURFACE ACTIVE AGENTS
SURGICAL APPLIANCES & SPLYS
SURGICAL APPLIANCES & SPLYS
SURGICAL IMPLANTS
SURGICAL INSTRUMENT REPAIR SVCS
SURVEYING INSTRUMENTS WHOLESALERS
SUSPENSION SYSTEMS: Acoustical, Metal
SVC ESTABLISHMENT EQPT, WHOLESALE: Firefighting Eqpt
SVC ESTABLISHMENT EQPT, WHOLESALE: Laundry Eqpt & Splys
SVC ESTABLISHMENT EQPT, WHOLESALE: Restaurant Splys
SWEEPING COMPOUNDS
SWIMMING POOL EQPT: Filters & Water Conditioning Systems
SWIMMING POOLS, EQPT & SPLYS: Wholesalers
SWITCHBOARDS & PARTS: Power
SWITCHES: Electric Power
SWITCHES: Electronic
SWITCHES: Electronic Applications
SWITCHES: Time, Electrical Switchgear Apparatus
SWITCHGEAR & SWITCHBOARD APPARATUS
SWITCHGEAR & SWITCHGEAR ACCESS, NEC
SYNTHETIC RESIN FINISHED PRDTS, NEC
SYRUPS, DRINK
SYSTEMS ENGINEERING: Computer Related
SYSTEMS INTEGRATION SVCS
SYSTEMS INTEGRATION SVCS: Local Area Network
SYSTEMS SOFTWARE DEVELOPMENT SVCS

T

TABLE OR COUNTERTOPS, PLASTIC LAMINATED
TABLEWARE: Vitreous China
TAGS & LABELS: Paper
TANK REPAIR & CLEANING SVCS
TANK REPAIR SVCS
TANK TOWERS: Metal Plate
TANKS & OTHER TRACKED VEHICLE CMPNTS
TANKS: Concrete
TANKS: Cryogenic, Metal
TANKS: For Tank Trucks, Metal Plate
TANKS: Fuel, Including Oil & Gas, Metal Plate
TANKS: Lined, Metal
TANKS: Military, Including Factory Rebuilding
TANKS: Plastic & Fiberglass
TANKS: Standard Or Custom Fabricated, Metal Plate
TANKS: Storage, Farm, Metal Plate
TAPE DRIVES
TAPES: Coated Fiberglass, Pipe Sealing Or Insulating
TAPES: Pressure Sensitive
TAPES: Pressure Sensitive, Rubber
TARGET DRONES
TARPAULINS
TARPAULINS, WHOLESALE

TECHNICAL MANUAL PREPARATION SVCS
TELECOMMUNICATION EQPT REPAIR SVCS, EXC TELEPHONES
TELEMETERING EQPT
TELEPHONE BOOTHS, EXC WOOD
TELEPHONE EQPT: Modems
TELEPHONE EQPT: NEC
TELEPHONE STATION EQPT & PARTS: Wire
TELEPHONE SVCS
TELEVISION BROADCASTING & COMMUNICATIONS EQPT
TELEVISION BROADCASTING STATIONS
TELEVISION: Closed Circuit Eqpt
TELEVISION: Monitors
TEMPORARY HELP SVCS
TERMINAL BOARDS
TESTERS: Battery
TESTERS: Physical Property
TESTING SVCS
TEXTILE DESIGNERS
TEXTILE FINISHING: Napping, Manmade Fiber & Silk, Broadwoven
TEXTILES: Linen Fabrics
THEATRICAL PRODUCTION SVCS
THEATRICAL SCENERY
THERMISTORS, EXC TEMPERATURE SENSORS
THERMOCOUPLES
THERMOPLASTIC MATERIALS
THERMOSETTING MATERIALS
TILE: Brick & Structural, Clay
TILE: Clay, Drain & Structural
TILE: Wall & Floor, Ceramic
TIN
TIRE & INNER TUBE MATERIALS & RELATED PRDTS
TIRE & TUBE REPAIR MATERIALS, WHOLESALE
TIRE CORD & FABRIC
TIRE SUNDRIES OR REPAIR MATERIALS: Rubber
TIRES & INNER TUBES
TIRES & TUBES WHOLESALERS
TIRES & TUBES, WHOLESALE: Automotive
TOBACCO & TOBACCO PRDTS WHOLESALERS
TOBACCO: Chewing & Snuff
TOBACCO: Cigarettes
TOBACCO: Smoking
TOILET PREPARATIONS
TOILETRIES, WHOLESALE: Hair Preparations
TOILETRIES, WHOLESALE: Perfumes
TOILETRIES, WHOLESALE: Toiletries
TOILETS: Portable Chemical, Plastics
TOOL & DIE STEEL
TOOLS: Hand, Mechanics
TOWELS: Fabric & Nonwoven, Made From Purchased Materials
TOWELS: Paper
TOWERS, SECTIONS: Transmission, Radio & Television
TOWING SVCS: Marine
TOYS & HOBBY GOODS & SPLYS, WHOLESALE: Toys & Games
TOYS & HOBBY GOODS & SPLYS, WHOLESALE: Toys, NEC
TOYS: Rubber
TRADE SHOW ARRANGEMENT SVCS
TRAILERS & PARTS: Boat
TRAILERS & TRAILER EQPT
TRAILERS: Semitrailers, Missile Transportation
TRAILERS: Semitrailers, Truck Tractors
TRANSDUCERS: Electrical Properties
TRANSDUCERS: Pressure
TRANSFORMERS: Distribution
TRANSFORMERS: Distribution, Electric
TRANSFORMERS: Instrument
TRANSFORMERS: Specialty
TRANSFORMERS: Voltage Regulating
TRANSMISSIONS: Motor Vehicle
TRANSPORTATION EQPT & SPLYS WHOLESALERS, NEC
TRANSPORTATION SVCS, AIR, NONSCHEDULED: Air Cargo Carriers
TRAVEL TRAILERS & CAMPERS
TROPHIES, NEC
TROPHIES, WHOLESALE
TROPHIES: Metal, Exc Silver
TRUCK & BUS BODIES: Bus Bodies
TRUCK & BUS BODIES: Car Carrier
TRUCK & BUS BODIES: Cement Mixer

PRODUCT INDEX

TRUCK & BUS BODIES: Motor Vehicle, Specialty
TRUCK & BUS BODIES: Truck Beds
TRUCK & BUS BODIES: Utility Truck
TRUCK BODIES: Body Parts
TRUCK BODY SHOP
TRUCK GENERAL REPAIR SVC
TRUCK PARTS & ACCESSORIES: Wholesalers
TRUCKING & HAULING SVCS: Contract Basis
TRUCKING & HAULING SVCS: Lumber & Log, Local
TRUCKING & HAULING SVCS: Machinery, Heavy
TRUCKING: Except Local
TRUCKING: Local, With Storage
TRUCKING: Local, Without Storage
TRUCKS & TRACTORS: Industrial
TRUCKS: Forklift
TRUCKS: Indl
TRUSSES & FRAMING: Prefabricated Metal
TRUSSES: Wood, Floor
TUBES: Paper
TUBES: Steel & Iron
TUBES: Wrought, Welded Or Lock Joint
TUBING: Copper
TUBING: Flexible, Metallic
TUBING: Glass
TUBING: Rubber
TUGBOAT SVCS
TURBINES & TURBINE GENERATOR SETS
TURBINES: Gas, Mechanical Drive
TURBINES: Hydraulic, Complete
TURBINES: Steam
TYPESETTING SVC
TYPESETTING SVC: Computer

U

UNDERGROUND GOLD MINING
UNIFORM SPLY SVCS: Indl
UNIFORM STORES
UNSUPPORTED PLASTICS: Floor Or Wall Covering
UPHOLSTERY WORK SVCS
USED CAR DEALERS
UTENSILS: Cast Aluminum, Cooking Or Kitchen
UTILITY TRAILER DEALERS

V

VACUUM CLEANERS: Indl Type
VALUE-ADDED RESELLERS: Computer Systems
VALVES
VALVES & PARTS: Gas, Indl
VALVES & PIPE FITTINGS
VALVES & REGULATORS: Pressure, Indl
VALVES: Aerosol, Metal
VALVES: Aircraft, Control, Hydraulic & Pneumatic
VALVES: Aircraft, Fluid Power
VALVES: Aircraft, Hydraulic
VALVES: Control, Automatic
VALVES: Electrohydraulic Servo, Metal
VALVES: Fluid Power, Control, Hydraulic & pneumatic
VALVES: Gas Cylinder, Compressed
VALVES: Indl
VALVES: Plumbing & Heating
VALVES: Regulating & Control, Automatic
VALVES: Regulating, Process Control
VAN CONVERSIONS
VARNISHES, NEC
VAULTS & SAFES WHOLESALERS
VEHICLES: Recreational
VENDING MACHINE REPAIR SVCS

VENDING MACHINES & PARTS
VENTILATING EQPT: Metal
VENTILATING EQPT: Sheet Metal
VENTURE CAPITAL COMPANIES
VETERINARY PHARMACEUTICAL PREPARATIONS
VIDEO TAPE PRODUCTION SVCS
VIDEO TAPE WHOLESALERS, RECORDED
VIDEO TRIGGERS: Remote Control TV Devices
VINYL RESINS, NEC
VISUAL COMMUNICATIONS SYSTEMS
VITAMINS: Natural Or Synthetic, Uncompounded, Bulk
VOCATIONAL REHABILITATION AGENCY
VOCATIONAL TRAINING AGENCY

W

WALL COVERINGS WHOLESALERS
WALL COVERINGS: Rubber
WALLPAPER & WALL COVERINGS
WALLPAPER: Made From Purchased Paper
WALLS: Curtain, Metal
WAREHOUSING & STORAGE FACILITIES, NEC
WAREHOUSING & STORAGE, REFRIGERATED: Cold Storage Or Refrig
WAREHOUSING & STORAGE, REFRIGERATED: Frozen Or Refrig Goods
WAREHOUSING & STORAGE: General
WAREHOUSING & STORAGE: Refrigerated
WAREHOUSING & STORAGE: Self Storage
WARM AIR HEATING/AC EQPT/SPLYS, WHOL Warm Air Htg Eqpt/Splys
WASHERS
WASHERS: Metal
WATCH & CLOCK STORES
WATCH REPAIR SVCS
WATER HEATERS
WATER PURIFICATION EQPT: Household
WATER SOFTENING WHOLESALERS
WATER SUPPLY
WATER TREATMENT EQPT: Indl
WATER: Distilled
WATER: Pasteurized, Canned & Bottled, Etc
WATERPROOFING COMPOUNDS
WAXES: Petroleum, Not Produced In Petroleum Refineries
WEATHER STRIP: Sponge Rubber
WEATHER STRIPS: Metal
WEIGHING MACHINERY & APPARATUS
WELDING & CUTTING APPARATUS & ACCESS, NEC
WELDING EQPT
WELDING EQPT & SPLYS WHOLESALERS
WELDING EQPT & SPLYS: Gas
WELDING EQPT & SPLYS: Generators, Arc Welding, AC & DC
WELDING EQPT REPAIR SVCS
WELDING EQPT: Electric
WELDING EQPT: Electrical
WELDING MACHINES & EQPT: Ultrasonic
WELDING REPAIR SVC
WELDING SPLYS, EXC GASES: Wholesalers
WELDING TIPS: Heat Resistant, Metal
WELDMENTS
WET CORN MILLING
WHEELCHAIR LIFTS
WHEELCHAIRS
WHEELS & PARTS
WHEELS, GRINDING: Artificial
WHEELS: Abrasive
WHEELS: Disc, Wheelbarrow, Stroller, Etc, Stamped Metal

WHEELS: Iron & Steel, Locomotive & Car
WHEELS: Railroad Car, Cast Steel
WHITING MINING: Crushed & Broken
WINCHES
WINDINGS: Coil Electronic
WINDMILLS: Electric Power Generation
WINDOW & DOOR FRAMES
WINDOW FRAMES & SASHES: Plastic
WINDOW FRAMES, MOLDING & TRIM: Vinyl
WINDOW SCREENING: Plastic
WINDOWS: Louver, Glass, Wood Framed
WINDOWS: Wood
WINDSHIELD WIPER SYSTEMS
WINDSHIELDS: Plastic
WIRE
WIRE & CABLE: Aluminum
WIRE & CABLE: Nonferrous, Building
WIRE & WIRE PRDTS
WIRE CLOTH & WOVEN WIRE PRDTS, MADE FROM PURCHASED
WIRE FABRIC: Welded Steel
WIRE MATERIALS: Aluminum
WIRE MATERIALS: Copper
WIRE MATERIALS: Steel
WIRE PRDTS: Ferrous Or Iron, Made In Wiredrawing Plants
WIRE PRDTS: Steel & Iron
WIRE WINDING OF PURCHASED WIRE
WIRE, FLAT: Strip, Cold-Rolled, Exc From Hot-Rolled Mills
WIRE: Communication
WIRE: Magnet
WIRE: Mesh
WIRE: Nonferrous
WIRE: Steel, Insulated Or Armored
WIRE: Wire, Ferrous Or Iron
WIRING DEVICES WHOLESALERS
WOMEN'S & CHILDREN'S CLOTHING WHOLESALERS, NEC
WOMEN'S & GIRLS' SPORTSWEAR WHOLESALERS
WOMEN'S CLOTHING STORES
WOOD & WOOD BY-PRDTS, WHOLESALE
WOOD CHIPS PRODUCED AT THE MILL
WOOD FENCING WHOLESALERS
WOOD PRDTS: Laundry
WOOD PRDTS: Moldings, Unfinished & Prefinished
WOOD PRDTS: Mulch Or Sawdust
WOOD PRDTS: Mulch, Wood & Bark
WOOD PRDTS: Novelties, Fiber
WOOD PRDTS: Outdoor, Structural
WOOD PRDTS: Plugs
WOOD PRDTS: Signboards
WOOD PRDTS: Trophy Bases
WOOD TREATING: Millwork
WOOD TREATING: Structural Lumber & Timber
WOOD TREATING: Wood Prdts, Creosoted
WOODWORK & TRIM: Exterior & Ornamental
WOODWORK & TRIM: Interior & Ornamental
WOODWORK: Interior & Ornamental, NEC
WORK EXPERIENCE CENTER
WOVEN WIRE PRDTS, NEC
WRENCHES

X

X-RAY EQPT & TUBES
X-RAY EQPT REPAIR SVCS

Y

YARN & YARN SPINNING

PRODUCT SECTION

Product category — **BOXES:** Folding
City — Edgar & Son Paperboard ....G..999 999-9999
  Yourtown *(G-47)*
Ready Box Co ....E..999 999-9999
  Anytown *(G-1723)*

Indicates approximate employment figure
A = over 500 employees, B = 251-500
C = 101-250, D = 51-100, E = 20-50
F = 10-19, G = 1-9

Business phone

Geographic Section entry number where full company information appears

See footnotes for symbols and codes identification.
- Refer to the Industrial Product Index preceding this section to locate product headings.

ABRASIVES

Abrasive Products.................G..... 513 502-9150
  Cincinnati *(G-2593)*
Abrasive Source Inc..............F..... 937 526-9753
  Russia *(G-12882)*
Abrasive Supply Company Inc......F..... 330 894-2818
  Minerva *(G-11025)*
Abrasive Technology Lapidary......E..... 740 548-4855
  Lewis Center *(G-9145)*
Alb Tyler Holdings Inc...........G..... 440 946-7171
  Mentor *(G-10410)*
Ali Industries LLC...............B..... 937 878-3946
  Fairborn *(G-7308)*
Alliance Abrasives LLC...........F..... 330 823-7957
  Alliance *(G-390)*
Belanger Inc.....................D..... 517 870-3206
  West Chester *(G-15375)*
Buffalo Abrasives Inc............E..... 614 891-6450
  Westerville *(G-15695)*
Diamond Innovations Inc..........B..... 614 438-2000
  Columbus *(G-5326)*
Even Cut Abrasive Company........F..... 216 881-9595
  Cleveland *(G-4037)*
Hec Investments Inc..............C..... 937 278-9123
  Dayton *(G-6367)*
Jason Incorporated...............C..... 513 860-3400
  Hamilton *(G-8224)*
Lawrence Industries Inc..........E..... 216 518-7000
  Cleveland *(G-4318)*
Mill-Rose Company................C..... 440 255-9171
  Mentor *(G-10505)*
National Lime and Stone Co.......E..... 419 396-7671
  Carey *(G-2281)*
Sure-Foot Industries Corp........F..... 440 234-4446
  Cleveland *(G-4756)*
US Technology Corporation........E..... 330 455-1181
  Canton *(G-2258)*
US Technology Media Inc..........F..... 330 874-3094
  Bolivar *(G-1540)*
Vibra Finish Co..................E..... 513 870-6300
  Fairfield *(G-7423)*

ABRASIVES: Coated

Nanolap Technologies LLC.........F..... 877 658-4949
  Englewood *(G-7237)*
Premier Coatings Ltd.............F..... 513 942-1070
  West Chester *(G-15484)*

ACCELERATION INDICATORS & SYSTEM COMPONENTS: Aerospace

Midwest Precision Holdings Inc...F..... 440 497-4086
  Eastlake *(G-7040)*

Nhvs International Inc...........B..... 440 527-8610
  Mentor *(G-10509)*

ACIDS

Emery Oleochemicals LLC..........E..... 513 762-2500
  Cincinnati *(G-2866)*

ACIDS: Hydrochloric

Jones-Hamilton Co................D..... 419 666-9838
  Walbridge *(G-15083)*

ACIDS: Inorganic

Capital Resin Corporation........D..... 614 445-7177
  Columbus *(G-5233)*
Detrex Corporation...............F..... 216 749-2605
  Cleveland *(G-3954)*

ACIDS: Sulfuric, Oleum

Marsulex Inc.....................E..... 419 698-8181
  Oregon *(G-12107)*

ACOUSTICAL BOARD & TILE

Essi Acoustical Products.........F..... 216 251-7888
  Cleveland *(G-4030)*
Mpc Inc..........................E..... 440 835-1405
  Cleveland *(G-4424)*

ACRYLIC RESINS

Capital Resin Corporation........D..... 614 445-7177
  Columbus *(G-5233)*
Plaskolite LLC...................E..... 614 294-3281
  Columbus *(G-5677)*
Plaskolite LLC...................C..... 740 450-1109
  Zanesville *(G-16556)*

ACTUATORS: Indl, NEC

Automation Technology Inc........E..... 937 233-6084
  Dayton *(G-6219)*
Moog Inc.........................E..... 330 682-0010
  Orrville *(G-12138)*
Norgren Inc......................C..... 937 833-4033
  Brookville *(G-1742)*
SMC Corporation of America.......F..... 330 659-2006
  Richfield *(G-12798)*
Thermotion Corp..................F..... 440 639-8325
  Mentor *(G-10576)*
Venture Mfg Co...................E..... 937 233-8792
  Dayton *(G-6642)*

ADAPTERS: Well

Wells Inc........................F..... 419 457-2611
  Risingsun *(G-12820)*

ADDITIVE BASED PLASTIC MATERIALS: Plasticizers

Jaco Products LLC................G..... 614 219-1670
  Hilliard *(G-8415)*
Mum Industries Inc...............D..... 440 269-4966
  Mentor *(G-10508)*
Nanofiber Solutions LLC..........F..... 614 319-3075
  Dublin *(G-6913)*

ADDRESSING SVCS

Cleveland Letter Service Inc.....G..... 216 781-8300
  Chagrin Falls *(G-2371)*
Franklin Printing Company........F..... 740 452-6375
  Zanesville *(G-16533)*
Gerald L Herrmann Company Inc....F..... 513 661-1818
  Cincinnati *(G-2949)*
Hecks Direct Mail Prtg Svc Inc...F..... 419 697-3505
  Toledo *(G-14315)*

ADHESIVES

Adchem Adhesives Inc.............F..... 440 526-1976
  Cleveland *(G-3597)*
Adherex Group....................F..... 201 440-3806
  Cleveland *(G-3600)*
Adhesives Lab USA North LLC......F..... 567 825-2004
  Lima *(G-9217)*
Akron Coating Adhesives Co Inc...F..... 330 724-4716
  Akron *(G-30)*
Akzo Nobel Paints LLC............A..... 440 297-8000
  Strongsville *(G-13803)*
Certon Technologies Inc..........F..... 440 786-7185
  Bedford *(G-1111)*
Chemspec Usa Inc.................D..... 330 669-8512
  Orrville *(G-12121)*
Choice Brands Adhesives Ltd......E..... 800 330-5566
  Cincinnati *(G-2733)*
Conversion Tech Intl Inc.........E..... 419 924-5566
  West Unity *(G-15638)*
CP Industries Inc................F..... 740 763-2886
  Newark *(G-11573)*
Edge Adhesives Inc...............E..... 614 875-6343
  Grove City *(G-8090)*
Entrochem Inc....................F..... 614 946-7602
  Columbus *(G-5356)*
Evans Adhesive Corporation.......E..... 614 451-2665
  Columbus *(G-5362)*
Evans Adhesive Corporation Ltd...E..... 614 451-2665
  Columbus *(G-5363)*
Franklin International Inc.......B..... 614 443-0241
  Columbus *(G-5387)*
Har Equipment Sales Inc..........F..... 440 786-7189
  Bedford *(G-1123)*

ADHESIVES

PRODUCT SECTION

HB Fuller Company .... E 513 719-3600
  Blue Ash *(G-1404)*
HB Fuller Company .... F 513 719-3600
  Blue Ash *(G-1405)*
HB Fuller Company .... G 440 708-1212
  Chagrin Falls *(G-2399)*
Henkel US Operations Corp .... E 513 830-0260
  Cincinnati *(G-2994)*
Henkel US Operations Corp .... C 216 475-3600
  Cleveland *(G-4180)*
Henkel US Operations Corp .... C 440 255-8900
  Mentor *(G-10469)*
Mitsubishi Chemical Amer Inc .... D 419 483-2931
  Bellevue *(G-1230)*
Morgan Adhesives Company LLC .... B 330 688-1111
  Stow *(G-13709)*
Nagase Chemtex America LLC .... E 740 362-4444
  Delaware *(G-6739)*
Paramelt Argueso Kindt Inc .... G 216 252-4122
  Cleveland *(G-4521)*
Premier Building Solutions LLC .... E 330 244-2907
  Massillon *(G-10136)*
Royal Adhesives .... G 440 708-1212
  Chagrin Falls *(G-2420)*
RPM Consumer Holding Company .... E 330 273-5090
  Medina *(G-10371)*
Rubex Inc .... G 614 875-6343
  Grove City *(G-8118)*
Shelli R McMurray .... E 614 275-4381
  Columbus *(G-5761)*
Spectra Group Limited Inc .... G 419 837-9783
  Millbury *(G-10936)*
Sunstar Engrg Americas Inc .... E 937 746-8575
  Springboro *(G-13520)*
Synthomer USA LLC .... E 678 400-6655
  Beachwood *(G-1026)*
Technicote Inc .... E 330 928-1476
  Cuyahoga Falls *(G-6121)*
Techno Adhesives Co .... G 513 771-1584
  Cincinnati *(G-3443)*
Three Bond International Inc .... E 937 610-3000
  Dayton *(G-6622)*
Three Bond International Inc .... D 513 779-7300
  West Chester *(G-15515)*
Toagosei America Inc .... D 614 718-3855
  West Jefferson *(G-15615)*

ADHESIVES & SEALANTS

Akron Paint & Varnish Inc .... D 330 773-8911
  Akron *(G-38)*
Alpha Coatings Inc .... E 419 435-5111
  Fostoria *(G-7627)*
Arclin USA LLC .... G 419 726-5013
  Toledo *(G-14198)*
Avery Dennison Corporation .... B 440 358-2564
  Painesville *(G-12218)*
Bostik Inc .... E 419 289-9588
  Ashland *(G-559)*
Bostik Inc .... E 614 232-8510
  Columbus *(G-5205)*
Brewer Company .... G 513 576-6300
  Cincinnati *(G-2681)*
Cardinal Rubber Company .... E 330 745-2191
  Barberton *(G-864)*
Chemspec Ltd .... F 330 364-4422
  New Philadelphia *(G-11492)*
Chemspec Ltd .... E 330 896-0355
  Canton *(G-2073)*
Cincinnati Assn For The Blind .... C 513 221-8558
  Cincinnati *(G-2740)*
Consolidated Coatings Corp .... A 216 514-7596
  Cleveland *(G-3898)*

Ddp Specialty Electronic MA .... C 937 839-4612
  West Alexandria *(G-15341)*
Elmers Products Inc .... D 614 225-4000
  Columbus *(G-5349)*
Engineered Conductive Mtl LLC .... G 740 362-4444
  Delaware *(G-6720)*
Foam Seal Inc .... C 216 881-8111
  Cleveland *(G-4074)*
Gdc Inc .... F 574 533-3128
  Wooster *(G-16123)*
Glenrock Company .... G 513 489-6710
  Blue Ash *(G-1398)*
Gold Key Processing Inc .... C 440 632-0901
  Middlefield *(G-10752)*
HB Fuller Company .... G 833 672-1482
  Bellevue *(G-1227)*
Henkel US Operations Corp .... D 440 250-7700
  Westlake *(G-15755)*
Hexpol Compounding LLC .... C 440 834-4644
  Burton *(G-1880)*
Hoover & Wells Inc .... C 419 691-9220
  Toledo *(G-14319)*
Illinois Tool Works Inc .... C 513 489-7600
  Blue Ash *(G-1408)*
Illinois Tool Works Inc .... D 440 914-3100
  Solon *(G-13366)*
J C Whitlam Manufacturing Co .... C 330 334-2524
  Wadsworth *(G-15037)*
Laird Technologies Inc .... D 216 939-2300
  Cleveland *(G-4305)*
Laminate Technologies Inc .... D 800 231-2523
  Tiffin *(G-1880)*
Laurenco Systems of Ohio LLC .... G
  Leavittsburg *(G-9058)*
Lubrizol Global Management Inc .... F 216 447-5000
  Cleveland *(G-4339)*
M Argueso & Co Inc .... C 216 252-4122
  Cleveland *(G-4344)*
Mactac Americas LLC .... E 800 762-2822
  Stow *(G-13707)*
Merryweather Foam Inc .... E 330 753-0353
  Barberton *(G-882)*
Millennium Adhesive Pdts LLC .... F 440 708-1212
  Chagrin Falls *(G-2383)*
Neyra Interstate Inc .... E 513 733-1000
  Cincinnati *(G-3196)*
Pmbp Legacy Co Inc .... E 330 253-8148
  Akron *(G-278)*
Polymerics Inc .... E 330 928-2210
  Cuyahoga Falls *(G-6110)*
PPG Architectural Coatings LLC .... D 440 297-8000
  Strongsville *(G-13866)*
Priest Services Inc .... G 440 333-1123
  Mayfield Heights *(G-10254)*
Republic Powdered Metals Inc .... D 330 225-3192
  Medina *(G-10370)*
RPM International Inc .... D 330 273-5090
  Medina *(G-10372)*
Ruscoe Company .... E 330 253-8148
  Akron *(G-314)*
Sem-Com Company Inc .... G 419 537-8813
  Toledo *(G-14466)*
Sherwin-Williams Company .... C 330 830-6000
  Massillon *(G-10144)*
Shincor Silicones Inc .... E 330 630-9460
  Akron *(G-329)*
Signature Flexible Packg LLC .... F 614 252-2121
  Columbus *(G-5769)*
Silicone Solutions Inc .... F 330 920-3125
  Cuyahoga Falls *(G-6117)*
Simona Boltaron Inc .... D 740 498-5900
  Newcomerstown *(G-11651)*

Sirrus Inc .... E 513 448-0308
  Loveland *(G-9506)*
Sonoco Products Company .... D 937 429-0040
  Beavercreek Township *(G-1094)*
Sportsmaster .... G 440 257-3900
  Mentor *(G-10559)*
Thermagon Inc .... D 216 939-2300
  Cleveland *(G-791)*
Thorworks Industries Inc .... E 419 626-4375
  Sandusky *(G-3096)*
Tremco Cpg Inc .... E 419 289-2050
  Ashland *(G-638)*
United McGill Corporation .... E 614 829-1200
  Groveport *(G-3165)*
Valco Cincinnati Inc .... C 513 874-6550
  West Chester *(G-15603)*
Waytek Corporation .... E 937 743-6142
  Franklin *(G-7711)*

ADHESIVES & SEALANTS WHOLESALERS

Brewpro Inc .... G 513 577-7200
  Cincinnati *(G-2682)*
Consolidated Coatings Corp .... A 216 514-7596
  Cleveland *(G-3898)*
National Polymer Inc .... F 440 708-1245
  Chagrin Falls *(G-2409)*
Novagard Solutions Inc .... C 216 881-8111
  Cleveland *(G-4483)*

ADHESIVES: Adhesives, plastic

Durez Corporation .... E 567 295-6400
  Kenton *(G-8982)*
National Polymer Inc .... F 440 708-1245
  Chagrin Falls *(G-2409)*

ADHESIVES: Epoxy

Nanosperse LLC .... G 937 296-5030
  Kettering *(G-8908)*
Renegade Materials Corporation .... D 937 350-5274
  Miamisburg *(G-10675)*
Summitville Tiles Inc .... E 330 868-6463
  Minerva *(G-11040)*

ADVERTISING AGENCIES

Aardvark Screen Prtg & EMB LLC .... F 419 354-6686
  Bowling Green *(G-1548)*
Advertising Joe LLC Mean .... G 440 247-8200
  Chagrin Falls *(G-2367)*
Black River Group Inc .... E 419 524-6699
  Mansfield *(G-9628)*
Buckeye Business Forms Inc .... E 614 882-1890
  Westerville *(G-15649)*
Dee Printing Inc .... F 614 777-8700
  Columbus *(G-5322)*
Mark Advertising Agency Inc .... F 419 626-9000
  Sandusky *(G-13079)*
Propress Inc .... F 216 631-8200
  Cleveland *(G-4593)*

ADVERTISING AGENCIES: Consultants

Airmate Co Inc .... D 419 636-3184
  Bryan *(G-803)*
Just Business Inc .... F 866 577-3303
  Dayton *(G-6395)*
Kyle Media Inc .... G 877 775-2538
  Toledo *(G-14355)*

ADVERTISING DISPLAY PRDTS

Aster Industries Inc .... E 330 762-7965
  Akron *(G-56)*
Edi Custom Interiors Inc .... F 513 829-3895
  Fairfield *(G-7355)*

PRODUCT SECTION — AIR CONDITIONERS: Motor Vehicle

Indispenser Ltd.. E 419 625-5763
Sandusky (G-13065)

On Display Ltd....................................... E 513 841-1600
Batavia (G-941)

ADVERTISING REPRESENTATIVES: Electronic Media

Retain Loyalty LLC................................ G 330 830-0839
Massillon (G-10139)

ADVERTISING REPRESENTATIVES: Newspaper

American City Bus Journals Inc........... B 937 528-4400
Dayton (G-6199)

Copley Ohio Newspapers Inc................ C 330 364-5577
New Philadelphia (G-11493)

Gazette Publishing Company................. D 419 335-2010
Napoleon (G-11314)

News Watchman & Paper........................ F 740 947-2149
Waverly (G-15288)

Ohio Newspaper Services Inc................ G 614 486-6477
Columbus (G-5623)

Progressor Times..................................... G 419 396-7567
Carey (G-2283)

ADVERTISING SPECIALTIES, WHOLESALE

Ace Plastics Company............................. G 330 928-7720
Stow (G-13680)

American Business Forms Inc............... E 513 312-2522
West Chester (G-15535)

Associated Premium Corporation......... E 513 679-4444
Cincinnati (G-2637)

Auto Dealer Designs Inc........................ E 330 374-7666
Akron (G-70)

Baker Plastics Inc................................... G 330 743-3142
Youngstown (G-16317)

Benchmark Prints..................................... F 419 332-7640
Fremont (G-7766)

Bottomline Ink Corporation................... E 419 897-8000
Perrysburg (G-12364)

Cal Sales Embroidery.............................. G 440 236-3820
Columbia Station (G-5007)

Capehart Enterprises LLC..................... F 614 769-7746
Columbus (G-5230)

Charizma Corp... G 216 621-2220
Cleveland (G-3807)

Custom Sportswear Imprints LLC........ G 330 335-8326
Wadsworth (G-15024)

Flashions Sportswear Ltd..................... G 937 323-5885
Springfield (G-13565)

Gary Lawrence Enterprises Inc............ G 330 833-7181
Massillon (G-10099)

Gq Business Products Inc..................... G 513 792-4750
Loveland (G-9482)

Identity Group LLC................................ G 614 337-6167
Westerville (G-15658)

Marathon Mfg & Sup Co......................... F 330 343-2656
New Philadelphia (G-11514)

Mr Emblem Inc.. G 419 697-1888
Oregon (G-12108)

Novelty Advertising Co Inc.................... E 740 622-3113
Coshocton (G-5988)

Ohio State Institute Fin Inc................... G 614 861-8811
Reynoldsburg (G-12770)

Peter Graham Dunn Inc........................... E 330 816-0035
Dalton (G-6139)

PS Superior Inc....................................... E 216 587-1000
Cleveland (G-4596)

Publishing Group Ltd.............................. F 614 572-1240
Columbus (G-5697)

Randd Assoc Prtg & Promotions............ G 937 294-1874
Dayton (G-6541)

Screen Works Inc.................................... E 937 264-9111
Dayton (G-6564)

Sew & Sew Embroidery Inc.................... F 330 676-1600
Kent (G-8863)

Shamrock Companies Inc........................ D 440 899-9510
Westlake (G-15786)

Solar Arts Graphic Designs.................... G 330 744-0535
Youngstown (G-16441)

Solo Vino Imports Ltd............................ G 440 714-9591
Vermilion (G-14973)

T & L Custom Screening Inc.................. G 937 237-3121
Dayton (G-6605)

Traichal Construction Company............. E 800 255-3667
Niles (G-11689)

Underground Sports Shop Inc................ F 513 751-1662
Cincinnati (G-3477)

White Tiger Inc....................................... F 740 852-4873
London (G-9397)

ADVERTISING SVCS: Direct Mail

Amsive OH LLC....................................... D 937 885-8000
Miamisburg (G-10611)

Angstrom Graphics Inc Midwest............ C 216 271-5300
Cleveland (G-3669)

Baesman Group Inc................................. D 614 771-2300
Hilliard (G-8402)

Consolidated Graphics Group Inc.......... C 216 881-9191
Cleveland (G-3896)

Digital Color Intl LLC............................ F
Akron (G-130)

Hecks Direct Mail & Prtg Svc................ E 419 661-6028
Toledo (G-14314)

Laipplys Prtg Mktg Sltions Inc.............. G 740 387-9282
Marion (G-9859)

Malik Media LLC..................................... F 614 933-0328
New Albany (G-11383)

Network Printing & Graphics................. F 614 230-2084
Columbus (G-5593)

Quez Media Marketing Inc..................... F 216 910-0202
Independence (G-8683)

Retain Loyalty LLC................................ G 330 830-0839
Massillon (G-10139)

Traxium LLC.. E 330 572-8200
Stow (G-13732)

ADVERTISING SVCS: Display

Cgs Imaging Inc....................................... F 419 897-3000
Holland (G-8497)

Design Masters Inc.................................. G 513 772-7175
Cincinnati (G-2826)

Digital Color Intl LLC............................ F
Akron (G-130)

Display Dynamics Inc.............................. E 937 832-2830
Englewood (G-7229)

Kyle Media Inc... G 877 775-2538
Toledo (G-14355)

Performance Packaging Inc.................... F 419 478-8805
Toledo (G-14433)

ADVERTISING SVCS: Outdoor

Ike Smart City... E 614 294-4898
Columbus (G-5453)

Kessler Sign Company............................ E 740 453-0668
Zanesville (G-16542)

Ohio Shelterall Inc.................................. F 614 882-1110
Westerville (G-15717)

Orange Barrel Media LLC...................... D 614 294-4898
Columbus (G-5643)

ADVERTISING SVCS: Sample Distribution

Aztech Printing & Promotions................ G 937 339-0100
Troy (G-14551)

AERIAL WORK PLATFORMS

G & T Manufacturing Co......................... F 440 639-7777
Mentor (G-10462)

Haulotte US Inc....................................... F 419 445-8915
Archbold (G-531)

AEROSOLS

Wellston Aerosol Mfg Co........................ F 740 384-2320
Wellston (G-15333)

Zenex International.................................. F 440 232-4155
Bedford (G-1162)

AGRICULTURAL EQPT: Barn Cleaners

Barn Small Engine Repa......................... G 419 583-6595
Wauseon (G-15257)

AGRICULTURAL EQPT: BARN, SILO, POULTRY, DAIRY/LIVESTOCK MACH

Fort Recovery Equipment Inc................. F 419 375-1006
Fort Recovery (G-7615)

Stein-Way Equipment.............................. G 330 857-8700
Apple Creek (G-511)

AGRICULTURAL EQPT: Elevators, Farm

Afs Technology LLC................................ F 937 545-0627
Dayton (G-6190)

Gerald Grain Center Inc......................... E 419 445-2451
Archbold (G-529)

Sweet Manufacturing Company.............. E 937 325-1511
Springfield (G-13641)

AGRICULTURAL EQPT: Fertilizing Machinery

Shearer Farm Inc..................................... C 330 345-9023
Wooster (G-16171)

AGRICULTURAL EQPT: Grounds Mowing Eqpt

TD Landscape Inc................................... F 740 694-0244
Fredericktown (G-7754)

AGRICULTURAL EQPT: Tractors, Farm

Miners Tractor Sales Inc........................ F 330 325-9914
Rootstown (G-12854)

AGRICULTURAL EQPT: Turf & Grounds Eqpt

Randall Richard & Moore LLC.............. E 330 455-8873
Canton (G-2210)

Rhinestahl Corporation............................ D 513 489-1317
Mason (G-10048)

AGRICULTURAL MACHINERY & EQPT: Wholesalers

Bortnick Tractor Sales Inc..................... F 330 924-2555
Cortland (G-5960)

Buckeye Companies.................................. E 740 452-3641
Zanesville (G-16513)

S I Distributing Inc................................ F 419 647-4909
Spencerville (G-13489)

AIR CLEANING SYSTEMS

H-P Products Inc..................................... C 330 875-5556
Louisville (G-9459)

United Air Specialists Inc...................... C 513 891-0400
Blue Ash (G-1486)

AIR CONDITIONERS: Motor Vehicle

Jbar A/C Inc .... E 216 447-4294
  Cleveland *(G-4252)*

AIR CONDITIONING & VENTILATION EQPT & SPLYS: Wholesales

Weather King Heating & AC .... G 330 908-0281
  Northfield *(G-11914)*

AIR CONDITIONING EQPT

Duro Dyne Midwest Corp .... C 513 870-6000
  Hamilton *(G-8201)*
Hydro-Thrift Corporation .... E 330 837-5141
  Massillon *(G-10110)*
J D Indoor Comfort Inc .... F 440 949-8758
  Sheffield Village *(G-13184)*
Snap Rite Manufacturing Inc .... E 910 897-4080
  Cleveland *(G-4709)*
Vertiv Corporation .... G 614 888-0246
  Lockbourne *(G-9341)*
Vertiv Corporation .... A 614 888-0246
  Westerville *(G-15686)*

AIR CONDITIONING REPAIR SVCS

Air-Rite Inc .... E 216 228-8200
  Cleveland *(G-3617)*
Weather King Heating & AC .... G 330 908-0281
  Northfield *(G-11914)*

AIR CONDITIONING UNITS: Complete, Domestic Or Indl

Air Enterprises Inc .... A 330 794-9770
  Akron *(G-24)*
Ecu Corporation .... F 513 898-9294
  Cincinnati *(G-2859)*
Fred D Pfening Company .... E 614 294-5361
  Columbus *(G-5389)*
Hdt Ep Inc .... C 216 438-6111
  Solon *(G-13359)*
Hdt Expeditionary Systems Inc .... F 440 466-6640
  Geneva *(G-7938)*
Lintern Corporation .... E 440 255-9333
  Mentor *(G-10494)*
Taylor & Moore Co .... E 513 733-5530
  Cincinnati *(G-3442)*
Vertiv Group Corporation .... A 614 888-0246
  Westerville *(G-15687)*
Vertiv JV Holdings LLC .... A 614 888-0246
  Columbus *(G-5859)*
Whirlpool Corporation .... F 614 409-4340
  Lockbourne *(G-9343)*

AIR DUCT CLEANING SVCS

Indoor Envmtl Specialists Inc .... E 937 433-5202
  Dayton *(G-6381)*

AIR MATTRESSES: Plastic

Fiber -Tech Industries Inc .... D 740 335-9400
  Wshngtn Ct Hs *(G-16231)*
Kmak Group LLC .... F 937 308-1023
  London *(G-9390)*

AIR PURIFICATION EQPT

Airecon Manufacturing Corp .... E 513 561-5522
  Cincinnati *(G-2604)*
Allied Separation Tech Inc .... F 704 736-0420
  Twinsburg *(G-14629)*
Extreme Microbial Tech LLC .... E 844 885-0088
  Moraine *(G-11179)*

Guardian Technologies LLC .... E 866 603-5900
  Euclid *(G-7270)*
Indoor Envmtl Specialists Inc .... E 937 433-5202
  Dayton *(G-6381)*
Met-Pro Technologies LLC .... F 513 458-2600
  Cincinnati *(G-3153)*

AIRCRAFT & AEROSPACE FLIGHT INSTRUMENTS & GUIDANCE SYSTEMS

General Electric Company .... A 617 443-3000
  Cincinnati *(G-2942)*
Landrum Brown Wrldwide Svcs LL ..... F 513 530-5333
  Blue Ash *(G-1418)*
Ryse Aero Holdco Inc .... E 513 318-9907
  Mason *(G-10051)*
Tri-State Jet Mfg LLC .... G 513 896-4538
  Hamilton *(G-8253)*

AIRCRAFT & HEAVY EQPT REPAIR SVCS

Apph Wichita Inc .... E 316 943-5752
  Strongsville *(G-13808)*
Grimes Aerospace Company .... D 937 484-2001
  Urbana *(G-14832)*
K & J Machine Inc .... F 740 425-3282
  Barnesville *(G-903)*
McNational Inc .... D 740 377-4391
  South Point *(G-13471)*
Ohio Machinery Co .... C 440 526-6200
  Broadview Heights *(G-1665)*
Pas Technologies Inc .... D 937 840-1053
  Hillsboro *(G-8464)*
Tri State Equipment Company .... G 513 738-7227
  Shandon *(G-13161)*

AIRCRAFT ASSEMBLY PLANTS

Avari Aero LLC .... G 513 828-0860
  Cincinnati *(G-2646)*
Executive Wings Inc .... G 440 254-1812
  Painesville *(G-12234)*
Goodrich Corporation .... A 937 339-3811
  Troy *(G-14574)*
Hii Mission Technologies Corp .... G 937 426-3421
  Beavercreek *(G-1074)*
K&M Aviation LLC .... D 216 261-9000
  Cleveland *(G-4270)*
Nextant Aerospace LLC .... E 216 898-4800
  Cleveland *(G-4456)*
Nextant Aircraft LLC .... G 216 261-9000
  Cleveland *(G-4457)*
Ruhe Sales Inc .... F 419 943-3357
  Leipsic *(G-9140)*
Sea Air Space McHning Mlding L ...... F 440 248-3025
  Streetsboro *(G-13791)*
Snow Aviation Intl Inc .... E 614 588-2452
  Gahanna *(G-7849)*
Star Jet LLC .... E 614 338-4379
  Columbus *(G-5789)*
Tessec Manufacturing Svcs LLC .... E 937 985-3552
  Dayton *(G-6616)*
Textron Aviation Inc .... G 330 286-3043
  Canfield *(G-2020)*
Theiss Uav Solutions LLC .... G 330 584-2070
  North Benton *(G-11711)*
Toledo Jet Center LLC .... G 419 866-9050
  Swanton *(G-13985)*

AIRCRAFT CONTROL SYSTEMS:

Esterline Technologies Corp .... E 216 706-2960
  Cleveland *(G-4031)*

AIRCRAFT ELECTRICAL EQPT REPAIR SVCS

General Electric Company .... E 513 977-1500
  Cincinnati *(G-2943)*
Spirit Avionics Ltd .... F 614 237-4271
  Columbus *(G-5786)*

AIRCRAFT ENGINES & ENGINE PARTS: Airfoils

PCC Airfoils LLC .... C 440 255-9770
  Mentor *(G-10521)*
Turbine Eng Cmpnents Tech Corp ..... B 216 692-5200
  Cleveland *(G-4837)*

AIRCRAFT ENGINES & ENGINE PARTS: Nonelectric Starters

Dreison International Inc .... C 216 362-0755
  Cleveland *(G-3972)*

AIRCRAFT ENGINES & ENGINE PARTS: Pumps

At Holdings Corporation .... A 216 692-6000
  Cleveland *(G-3694)*
Eaton Industrial Corporation .... B 216 523-4205
  Cleveland *(G-3998)*

AIRCRAFT ENGINES & ENGINE PARTS: Research & Development, Mfr

Defense Research Assoc Inc .... E 937 431-1644
  Dayton *(G-658)*

AIRCRAFT ENGINES & PARTS

Advanced Ground Systems .... F 513 402-7226
  Cincinnati *(G-2598)*
Aero Jet Wash Llc .... F 866 381-7955
  Dayton *(G-186)*
American Aero Components Llc .... G 937 367-5068
  Dayton *(G-197)*
Avidyne .... G 800 284-3963
  Dublin *(G-665)*
Avion Tool Corporation .... F 937 278-0779
  Dayton *(G-220)*
Barnes Group Inc .... F 513 779-6888
  West Chester *(G-15374)*
CFM International Inc .... F 513 563-4180
  Cincinnati *(G-2721)*
CFM International Inc .... F 513 563-4180
  Cincinnati *(G-2722)*
CFM International Inc .... E 513 552-2787
  West Chester *(G-15389)*
Drt Aerospace LLC .... E 937 492-6121
  Sidney *(G-3242)*
Enjet Aero Dayton Inc .... E 937 878-3800
  Huber Heights *(G-8576)*
Ferrotherm Corporation .... C 216 883-9350
  Cleveland *(G-4058)*
GE Military Systems .... D 513 243-2000
  Cincinnati *(G-2938)*
General Electric Company .... E 513 948-4170
  Cincinnati *(G-2941)*
Golden Eagle Aviation LLC .... G 937 308-4709
  Sidney *(G-13251)*
Heico Aerospace Parts Corp .... B 954 987-6101
  Highland Heights *(G-8388)*
Henry Tool Inc .... G 216 291-1011
  Cleveland *(G-4182)*
Hi-Tek Manufacturing Inc .... C 513 459-1094
  Mason *(G-10001)*

PRODUCT SECTION

AIRCRAFT PARTS & EQPT, NEC

Honeywell International I............... F 513 282-5519
  Mason *(G-10002)*

Honeywell International Inc............. G 513 745-7200
  Cincinnati *(G-3007)*

Honeywell International Inc............. E 440 329-9000
  Elyria *(G-7157)*

Honeywell Lebow Products............. C 614 850-5000
  Columbus *(G-5445)*

Lsp Technologies Inc...................... E 614 718-3000
  Dublin *(G-6907)*

Magellan Arospc Middletown Inc...... D 513 422-2751
  Middletown *(G-10839)*

Meyer Tool Inc................................ A 513 681-7362
  Cincinnati *(G-3160)*

Miba Bearings US LLC.................... B 740 962-4242
  Mcconnelsville *(G-10282)*

Optical Display Engrg Inc................ F 440 995-6555
  Highland Heights *(G-8390)*

Otto Konigslow Mfg Co.................... F 216 851-7900
  Cleveland *(G-4513)*

Pako Inc... C 440 946-8030
  Mentor *(G-10519)*

Parker-Hannifin Corporation............. C 440 284-6277
  Elyria *(G-7192)*

Pas Technologies Inc...................... D 937 840-1053
  Hillsboro *(G-8464)*

Precision Castparts Corp................. F 440 350-6150
  Painesville *(G-12258)*

Sifco Industries Inc........................ C 216 881-8600
  Cleveland *(G-4700)*

Snow Aviation Intl Inc..................... E 614 588-2452
  Gahanna *(G-7849)*

Spirit Avionics Ltd.......................... F 614 237-4271
  Columbus *(G-5786)*

Superalloy Mfg Solutions Corp........ C 513 489-9800
  Blue Ash *(G-1473)*

Tessec LLC.................................... D 937 576-0010
  Dayton *(G-6615)*

Turbine Standard Ltd...................... G 419 865-0355
  Holland *(G-8535)*

Welded Ring Products Co................ D 216 961-3800
  Cleveland *(G-4902)*

AIRCRAFT EQPT & SPLYS WHOLESALERS

17111 Waterview Pkwy LLC............. F 216 706-2960
  Cleveland *(G-3569)*

Cleveland Wheels........................... G 440 937-6211
  Avon *(G-767)*

Transdigm Group Incorporated........ B 216 706-2960
  Cleveland *(G-4817)*

AIRCRAFT MAINTENANCE & REPAIR SVCS

General Electric Company................ A 617 443-3000
  Cincinnati *(G-2942)*

Malta Dynamics LLC....................... F 740 749-3512
  Waterford *(G-15238)*

Toledo Jet Center LLC..................... G 419 866-9050
  Swanton *(G-13985)*

AIRCRAFT PARTS & AUXILIARY EQPT: Assys, Subassemblies/Parts

Ctl-Aerospace Inc........................... C 513 874-7900
  West Chester *(G-15547)*

Electronic Concepts Engrg Inc......... F 419 861-9000
  Holland *(G-8509)*

Esterline Technologies Corp............ E 216 706-2960
  Cleveland *(G-4031)*

Master Swaging Inc......................... G 937 596-6171
  Jackson Center *(G-8735)*

Parker-Hannifin Corporation............. C 440 284-6277
  Elyria *(G-7192)*

Snow Aviation Intl Inc..................... E 614 588-2452
  Gahanna *(G-7849)*

AIRCRAFT PARTS & AUXILIARY EQPT: Body & Wing Assys & Parts

Achilles Aerospace Pdts Inc............ E 330 425-8444
  Twinsburg *(G-14623)*

Columbus Jack Corporation............. E 614 443-7492
  Swanton *(G-13971)*

GSE Production and Support LLC..... F 419 866-6301
  Swanton *(G-13975)*

Industrial Mfg Co LLC..................... F 440 838-4700
  Brecksville *(G-1621)*

AIRCRAFT PARTS & AUXILIARY EQPT: Body Assemblies & Parts

Magellan Arospc Middletown Inc...... D 513 422-2751
  Middletown *(G-10839)*

Pacific Piston Ring Co Inc............... E 513 387-6100
  Blue Ash *(G-1449)*

AIRCRAFT PARTS & AUXILIARY EQPT: Brakes

Meggitt Arcft Brking Systems C....... A 330 796-4400
  Akron *(G-243)*

AIRCRAFT PARTS & AUXILIARY EQPT: Landing Assemblies & Brakes

Friction Products Co....................... B 330 725-4941
  Medina *(G-10328)*

Goodrich Corporation...................... A 937 339-3811
  Troy *(G-14574)*

AIRCRAFT PARTS & AUXILIARY EQPT: Lighting/Landing Gear Assy

Hdi Landing Gear USA Inc............... E 937 325-1586
  Strongsville *(G-13840)*

Hdi Landing Gear USA Inc............... D 937 325-1586
  Springfield *(G-13572)*

AIRCRAFT PARTS & AUXILIARY EQPT: Military Eqpt & Armament

Dircksen and Associates Inc........... G 614 238-0413
  Columbus *(G-5327)*

Test-Fuchs Corporation................... G 440 708-3505
  Brecksville *(G-1635)*

AIRCRAFT PARTS & AUXILIARY EQPT: Research & Development, Mfr

Drt Aerospace LLC.......................... E 937 492-6121
  Sidney *(G-13242)*

Long-Lok LLC.................................. E 336 343-7319
  Cincinnati *(G-3111)*

Weldon Pump LLC........................... E 440 232-2282
  Oakwood Village *(G-12047)*

AIRCRAFT PARTS & AUXILIARY EQPT: Tanks, Fuel

Bosserman Aviation Equipment Inc... E 419 722-2879
  Carey *(G-2277)*

AIRCRAFT PARTS & EQPT, NEC

17111 Waterview Pkwy LLC............. F 216 706-2960
  Cleveland *(G-3569)*

Advanced Fuel Systems Inc............. G 614 252-8422
  Columbus *(G-5103)*

Aero Tech Tool & Mold Inc.............. G 440 942-3327
  Mentor *(G-10406)*

Aerospace LLC................................ F 937 561-1104
  Moraine *(G-11153)*

Aerospace Maint Solutions LLC....... E 440 729-7703
  Solon *(G-13307)*

Aim International............................ G 513 831-2938
  Miamiville *(G-10710)*

Aircraft Ground Services................. G 419 356-5027
  Monclova *(G-11092)*

Allen Aircraft Products Inc.............. E 330 296-9621
  Ravenna *(G-12702)*

Allen Aircraft Products Inc.............. D 330 296-9621
  Ravenna *(G-12704)*

American Aero Components Llc....... G 937 367-5068
  Dayton *(G-6197)*

Apph Wichita Inc............................ E 316 943-5752
  Strongsville *(G-13808)*

Arctos Mission Solutions LLC......... E 813 609-5591
  Beavercreek *(G-1040)*

At Holdings Corporation.................. A 216 692-6000
  Cleveland *(G-3694)*

Auto-Valve Inc................................. E 937 854-3037
  Dayton *(G-6217)*

Aviation Cmpnent Solutions Inc....... F 440 295-6590
  Richmond Heights *(G-12805)*

Avtron Aerospace Inc...................... C 216 750-5152
  Cleveland *(G-3709)*

Aws Industries Inc.......................... E 513 932-7941
  Lebanon *(G-9063)*

Barnes Group Inc............................ E 513 779-6888
  West Chester *(G-15373)*

Composite Solutions LLC................ G 513 321-7337
  Cincinnati *(G-2785)*

Ctl-Aerospace Inc........................... E 513 874-7900
  West Chester *(G-15546)*

Danfoss Power Solutions II LLC....... G 419 238-1190
  Van Wert *(G-14913)*

Drt Holdings Inc............................. D 937 298-7391
  Dayton *(G-6305)*

Dukes Aerospace Inc...................... D 818 998-9811
  Painesville *(G-12229)*

Eaton Aeroquip LLC......................... C 440 523-5000
  Cleveland *(G-3991)*

Eaton Industrial Corporation............ C 216 692-5456
  Cleveland *(G-3997)*

Eaton Industrial Corporation............ B 216 523-4205
  Cleveland *(G-3998)*

Enjet Aero LLC................................ F 937 878-3800
  Huber Heights *(G-8575)*

Enjet Aero Dayton Inc..................... E 937 878-3800
  Huber Heights *(G-8576)*

Eti Tech LLC................................... F 937 832-4200
  Kettering *(G-8907)*

Exito Manufacturing LLC................. G 937 291-9871
  Beavercreek *(G-1073)*

Federal Equipment Company........... D 513 621-5260
  Cincinnati *(G-2899)*

Ferco Tech LLC............................... C 937 746-6696
  Franklin *(G-7674)*

Field Aviation Inc........................... E 513 792-2282
  Cincinnati *(G-2903)*

GE Aviation Systems LLC................ B 937 898-5881
  Vandalia *(G-14940)*

GE Engine Services LLC.................. B 513 977-1500
  Cincinnati *(G-2936)*

General Dynamics-Ots Inc............... C 937 746-8500
  Springboro *(G-13502)*

General Electric Company............... E 513 977-1500
  Cincinnati *(G-2943)*

Goodrich Aerospace........................ G 704 423-7000
  Uniontown *(G-14784)*

Goodrich Corporation...................... G 330 374-2358
  North Canton *(G-11732)*

Employee Codes: A=Over 500 employees, B=251-500
C=101-250, D=51-100, E=20-50, F=10-19, G=1-9

AIRCRAFT PARTS & EQPT, NEC

Goodrich Corporation .... F 216 429-4378
  Troy (G-14575)
Grimes Aerospace Company .... D 937 484-2000
  Urbana (G-14831)
Grimes Aerospace Company .... A 937 484-2000
  Urbana (G-14830)
Heller Machine Products Inc .... G 216 281-2951
  Cleveland (G-4179)
Heroux-Devtek Inc .... F 937 325-1586
  Springfield (G-13575)
Hydro-Aire Inc .... C 440 323-3211
  Elyria (G-7158)
Hydro-Aire Aerospace Corp .... C 440 323-3211
  Elyria (G-7159)
Hyfast Aerospace LLC .... G 216 712-4158
  Parma (G-12291)
JCB Arrowhead Products Inc .... G 440 546-4288
  Brecksville (G-1623)
Kbr Inc .... F 937 320-2731
  Dayton (G-6397)
Kelly Arspc Thrmal Systems LLC .... E 440 951-4744
  Willoughby (G-15938)
Lincoln Electric Automtn Inc .... B 937 295-2120
  Fort Loramie (G-7603)
Lkd Aerospace Holdings Inc .... F 216 262-8481
  Cleveland (G-4333)
Logan Machine Company .... D 330 633-6163
  Akron (G-223)
Malabar .... E 419 866-6301
  Swanton (G-13978)
Mar-Con Tool Company .... E 937 299-2244
  Moraine (G-11191)
Maverick Molding Co .... F 513 387-6100
  Blue Ash (G-1431)
McKechnie Arospc Holdings Inc .... E 216 706-2960
  Cleveland (G-4381)
Meggitt Polymers & Composites .... F 513 851-5550
  Cincinnati (G-3144)
Meggitt Rockmart Inc .... E 770 684-7855
  Akron (G-244)
Microweld Engineering Inc .... G 614 847-9410
  Worthington (G-16204)
Middleton Enterprises Inc .... G 614 885-2514
  Worthington (G-16205)
Midwest Aircraft Products Co .... F 419 884-2164
  Mansfield (G-9692)
Pako Inc .... C 440 946-8030
  Mentor (G-10519)
PCC Airfoils LLC .... B 740 982-6025
  Crooksville (G-6048)
Skidmore-Wilhelm Mfg Company .... F 216 481-4774
  Solon (G-13422)
Starwin Industries LLC .... E 937 293-8568
  Dayton (G-6591)
Summit Aerospace Product Corp .... G 440 652-6829
  Brecksville (G-1631)
Summit Avionics Inc .... F 330 425-1440
  Twinsburg (G-14739)
Taylor Manufacturing Co Inc .... F 937 322-8622
  Springfield (G-13643)
Tessec Technology Services LLC .... E 513 240-5601
  Dayton (G-6617)
Tracewell Systems Inc .... D 614 846-6175
  Lewis Center (G-9182)
Transdigm Group Incorporated .... B 216 706-2960
  Cleveland (G-4817)
Trinity Midwest Aviation LLC .... G 513 583-0519
  Maineville (G-9603)
Triumph Thermal Systems LLC .... D 419 273-2511
  Forest (G-7593)
Tronair Inc .... C 419 866-6301
  Swanton (G-13987)

Truline Industries Inc .... D 440 729-0140
  Wickliffe (G-15855)
Turbine Eng Cmpnents Tech Corp ..... B 216 692-5200
  Cleveland (G-4837)
Unison Industries LLC .... B 904 667-9904
  Dayton (G-6175)
US Aeroteam Inc .... E 937 458-0344
  Dayton (G-6641)
US Technology Corporation .... E 330 455-1181
  Canton (G-2258)
White Machine Inc .... G 440 237-3282
  North Royalton (G-11902)

AIRCRAFT PARTS WHOLESALERS

Grimes Aerospace Company .... D 937 484-2001
  Urbana (G-14832)

AIRCRAFT PROPELLERS & PARTS

Hartzell Propeller Inc .... B 937 778-4200
  Piqua (G-12523)
Spectrum Textiles Inc .... F 513 933-8346
  Lebanon (G-9111)

AIRCRAFT SERVICING & REPAIRING

Spirit Avionics Ltd .... F 614 237-4271
  Columbus (G-5786)
Unison Industries LLC .... B 904 667-9904
  Dayton (G-6175)

AIRCRAFT TURBINES

Honeywell International Inc .... F 216 459-6048
  Brookpark (G-1718)
Wp Cpp Holdings LLC .... G 216 453-4800
  Cleveland (G-4924)

AIRCRAFT WHEELS

Aircraft Wheel & Brake LLC .... D 440 937-6211
  Avon (G-762)
Jay-Em Aerospace Corporation .... E 330 923-0333
  Cuyahoga Falls (G-6092)
Parker-Hannifin Corporation .... C 440 937-6211
  Avon (G-782)

AIRCRAFT: Airplanes, Fixed Or Rotary Wing

Boeing Company .... E 740 788-4000
  Heath (G-8318)
Pacer Flight LLC .... G 419 433-5562
  Huron (G-8644)
Steel Aviation Aircraft Sales .... G 937 332-7587
  Casstown (G-2317)

AIRCRAFT: Motorized

Tessec LLC .... D 937 576-0010
  Dayton (G-6615)

AIRCRAFT: Research & Development, Manufacturer

Aerovation Tech Holdings LLC .... G 567 208-5525
  Forest (G-7589)

AIRPORTS, FLYING FIELDS & SVCS

Grand Aire Inc .... E 419 861-6700
  Swanton (G-13974)
Ruhe Sales Inc .... F 419 943-3357
  Leipsic (G-9140)

ALARMS: Fire

Honeywell International Inc .... A 937 484-2000
  Urbana (G-14835)

ALCOHOL, GRAIN: For Medicinal Purposes

Kdc US Holdings Inc .... F 434 845-7073
  Groveport (G-8748)
Tri-Tech Laboratories LLC .... G 434 845-7073
  Groveport (G-8164)

ALCOHOL: Ethyl & Ethanol

Andersons Mrathon Holdings LLC ...... E 937 316-3700
  Greenville (G-8036)
Coshocton Ethanol LLC .... F 740 623-3046
  Coshocton (G-5976)
Guardian Energy Holdings LLC .... C 567 940-9500
  Lima (G-9247)
Guardian Lima LLC .... E 567 940-9500
  Lima (G-9248)
Poet Biorefining - Leipsic LLC .... E 419 943-7447
  Leipsic (G-9135)
Poet Biorefining Marion LLC .... E 740 383-4400
  Marion (G-9873)
Poet Biorefining - Fostoria LLC .... E 419 436-0954
  Fostoria (G-7650)
The Andersons Clymers Ethanol LLC .... E 574 722-2627
  Maumee (G-10239)

ALKALIES & CHLORINE

Albemarle Amendments LLC .... E 330 425-2354
  Twinsburg (G-14627)
Eltech Systems Corporation .... G 440 285-0380
  Concord Township (G-5906)
GFS Chemicals Inc .... E 740 881-5501
  Powell (G-12574)
National Colloid Company .... E 740 282-1171
  Steubenville (G-13673)
National Lime and Stone Co .... E 419 396-7671
  Carey (G-2231)
Occidental Chemical Corp .... E 513 242-2900
  Cincinnati (C-3211)

ALLOYS: Additive, Exc Copper Or Made In Blast Furnaces

GE Aviation Systems LLC .... E 620 218-5237
  Springdale (G-13525)
GE Aviation Systems LLC .... F 513 889-5150
  West Chester (G-15437)
Morris Technologies Inc .... E 513 733-1611
  Cincinnati (G-3174)
Theken Port Park LLC .... D 330 733-7600
  Akron (G-354)

ALTERNATORS & GENERATORS: Battery Charging

Asidaco LLC .... G 800 204-1544
  Dayton (G-5215)
Rv Mobile Power LLC .... G 855 427-7978
  Columbus (G-5735)

ALTERNATORS: Automotive

Cuyahoga Febuilders Inc .... G 216 635-0659
  Cleveland (G-3931)
Hitachi Astemo Americas Inc .... B 740 965-1133
  Sunbury (G-13955)
M W Solutions LLC .... F 419 782-1611
  Defiance (G-6689)

ALUMINUM

Alcan Primary Products Corp .... A
  Independence (G-8653)
Kaiser Aluminum Fab Pdts LLC .... C 740 522-1151
  Heath (G-8323)
Ormet Corporation .... A 740 483-1381
  Hannibal (G-8261)

PRODUCT SECTION

ANIMAL FEED & SUPPLEMENTS: Livestock & Poultry

P&The Mfg Acquisition LLC.................. D 937 492-4134
  Sidney *(G-13269)*

ALUMINUM PRDTS

Accu-Tek Tool & Die Inc...................... G 330 726-1946
  Salem *(G-12975)*
Alanod Westlake Metal Ind Inc............ E 440 327-8184
  North Ridgeville *(G-11826)*
Allite Inc... G 937 200-0831
  Miamisburg *(G-10610)*
Alufab Inc.. G 513 528-7281
  Cincinnati *(G-2551)*
Aluminum Extruded Shapes Inc........... C 513 563-2205
  Cincinnati *(G-2613)*
American Aluminum Extrusions........... C 330 458-0300
  Canton *(G-2035)*
AMG Aluminum North America LLC....... F 659 348-3620
  Cambridge *(G-1920)*
Arem Co.. F 440 974-6740
  Mentor *(G-10423)*
Astro Aluminum Enterprises Inc.......... E 330 755-1414
  Struthers *(G-13900)*
Astro Shapes....................................... G 330 755-1414
  Youngstown *(G-16314)*
Astro Shapes LLC................................ B 330 755-1414
  Struthers *(G-13901)*
Astro-Coatings Inc............................... E 330 755-1414
  Struthers *(G-13902)*
Bidwell Family Corporation.................. C 513 988-6351
  Trenton *(G-14540)*
BRT Extrusions Inc.............................. C 330 544-0177
  Niles *(G-11662)*
Central Aluminum Company LLC........ E 614 491-5700
  Obetz *(G-12057)*
Da Investments Inc.............................. D 330 781-6100
  Youngstown *(G-16346)*
Extrudex Aluminum Inc........................ C 330 538-4444
  North Jackson *(G-11783)*
Fom USA Incorporated......................... G 234 248-4400
  Medina *(G-10325)*
H-P Products Inc.................................. C 330 875-5556
  Louisville *(G-9459)*
Hydro Aluminum Fayetteville................ F 937 492-9194
  Sidney *(G-13254)*
Industrial Mold Inc............................... E 330 425-7374
  Twinsburg *(G-14676)*
Isaiah Industries Inc............................. D 937 773-9840
  Piqua *(G-12527)*
Knoble Glass & Metal Inc..................... G 513 753-1246
  Cincinnati *(G-3084)*
L & L Ornamental Iron Co.................... E 513 353-1930
  Cleves *(G-4958)*
Langstons Ultmate Clg Svcs Inc.......... F 330 298-9150
  Ravenna *(G-12722)*
M-D Building Products Inc................... F 513 539-2255
  Middletown *(G-10837)*
McKnight Industries Inc........................ E 937 592-9010
  Bellefontaine *(G-1216)*
National Metal Shapes Inc................... E 740 363-9559
  Delaware *(G-6741)*
Orrvilon Inc.. C 330 684-9400
  Orrville *(G-12145)*
Owens Corning Sales LLC................... F 740 983-1300
  Ashville *(G-671)*
Pennex Aluminum Company LLC........ D 330 427-6704
  Leetonia *(G-9129)*
Star Extruded Shapes Inc.................... B 330 533-9863
  Canfield *(G-2018)*
Star Fab Inc.. E 330 482-1601
  Columbiana *(G-5052)*
Star Fab Inc.. C 330 533-9863
  Canfield *(G-2019)*

T & D Fabricating Inc........................... E 440 951-5646
  Eastlake *(G-7051)*
Tecnocap LLC..................................... C 330 392-7222
  Warren *(G-15208)*
Tri County Tarp LLC............................ E 419 288-3350
  Gibsonburg *(G-7956)*
Trivium Alum Packg USA Corp............ E 330 744-9505
  Youngstown *(G-16460)*
Urban Industries of Ohio Inc................ E 419 468-3578
  Galion *(G-7886)*
Youngstown Tool & Die Company........ D 330 747-4464
  Youngstown *(G-16489)*
Zarbana Alum Extrusions LLC............. E 330 482-5092
  Columbiana *(G-5056)*
Zarbana Industries Inc......................... E 330 482-5092
  Columbiana *(G-5057)*

ALUMINUM: Coil & Sheet

Monarch Steel Company Inc................ E 216 587-8000
  Cleveland *(G-4420)*

ALUMINUM: Ingots & Slabs

Homan Metals LLC.............................. G 513 721-5010
  Cincinnati *(G-3004)*
Ormet Primary Aluminum Corp............ A 740 483-1381
  Hannibal *(G-8262)*

ALUMINUM: Pigs

Real Alloy Specialty Pdts LLC............. A 216 755-8836
  Beachwood *(G-1014)*
Real Alloy Specification LLC............... D 216 755-8900
  Beachwood *(G-1016)*

ALUMINUM: Rolling & Drawing

Aleris Rm Inc...................................... A 216 910-3400
  Beachwood *(G-973)*
Eastman Kodak Company.................... E 937 259-3000
  Dayton *(G-6311)*
Howmet Aerospace Inc........................ E 330 544-7633
  Niles *(G-11671)*
Novelis Alr Aluminum LLC................... A 216 910-3400
  Beachwood *(G-1004)*
Novelis Alr Rolled Pdts LLC................. A 740 983-2571
  Ashville *(G-669)*
Novelis Alr Rolled Pdts LLC................. E 216 910-3400
  Beachwood *(G-1005)*
Novelis Corporation............................. D 330 841-3456
  Warren *(G-15193)*
Real Alloy Specialty Pdts LLC............. E 440 322-0072
  Elyria *(G-7199)*
Real Alloy Specialty Pdts LLC............. C 216 755-8836
  Beachwood *(G-1015)*

AMMUNITION

Reloading Supplies Corp...................... G 440 228-0367
  Ashtabula *(G-658)*

AMMUNITION: Arming & Fusing Devices

L3harris Fzing Ord Systems Inc........... A 513 943-2000
  Cincinnati *(G-2570)*

AMMUNITION: Shot, Steel

Premier Shot Company........................ G 330 405-0583
  Twinsburg *(G-14717)*

AMMUNITION: Small Arms

Ares Inc.. D 419 635-2175
  Port Clinton *(G-12615)*
BTR Enterprises LLC........................... G 740 975-2526
  Newark *(G-11568)*
Galion LLC.. C 419 468-5214
  Galion *(G-7875)*

R & S Monitions Inc............................. G 614 846-0597
  Columbus *(G-5706)*

AMPLIFIERS

Dare Electronics Inc............................ E 937 335-0031
  Troy *(G-14559)*
Dr Z Amps Inc..................................... F 216 475-1444
  Maple Heights *(G-9751)*

AMUSEMENT & RECREATION SVCS: Exhibition Operation

Asm International................................ D 440 338-5151
  Novelty *(G-12007)*

AMUSEMENT & RECREATION SVCS: Exposition Operation

Park Corporation................................. B 216 267-4870
  Medina *(G-10362)*

AMUSEMENT & RECREATION SVCS: Golf Club, Membership

Hilltop Recreation Inc.......................... F 937 549-2904
  Manchester *(G-9619)*

AMUSEMENT & RECREATION SVCS: Physical Fitness Instruction

Building Block Performance LLC.......... G 614 918-7476
  Plain City *(G-12568)*

AMUSEMENT PARK DEVICES & RIDES

Advanced Indus Machining Inc............. F 614 596-4183
  Powell *(G-12662)*
ARM (usa) Inc..................................... E 740 264-6599
  Wintersville *(G-16085)*
Cutting Dynamics Inc........................... D 440 249-4666
  Avon *(G-770)*
Delta Manufacturing Inc....................... F 330 386-1270
  East Liverpool *(G-6994)*
Hearn Plating Co Ltd.......................... F 419 473-9773
  Toledo *(G-14313)*
OReilly Precision Pdts Inc.................... E 937 526-4677
  Russia *(G-12886)*
Wavy Ticket LLC.................................. E 513 827-0886
  Okeana *(G-12068)*

ANALYZERS: Network

Community Care Network Inc............. E 216 671-0977
  Cleveland *(G-3890)*

ANESTHESIA EQPT

Lababidi Enterprises Inc...................... G 330 733-2907
  Akron *(G-214)*

ANIMAL FEED & SUPPLEMENTS: Livestock & Poultry

Archer-Daniels-Midland Company......... G 330 852-3025
  Sugarcreek *(G-13918)*
Archer-Daniels-Midland Company......... G 419 705-3292
  Toledo *(G-14197)*
Cargill Incorporated............................. C 330 745-0031
  Akron *(G-100)*
Cargill Incorporated............................. C 216 651-7200
  Cleveland *(G-3792)*
Cargill Incorporated............................. E 419 394-3374
  Saint Marys *(G-12949)*
Cargill Incorporated............................. F 937 497-4848
  Sidney *(G-13230)*
Cooper Hatchery Inc............................ C 419 594-3325
  Oakwood *(G-12030)*

Employee Codes: A=Over 500 employees, B=251-500
C=101-250, D=51-100, E=20-50, F=10-19, G=1-9

ANIMAL FEED & SUPPLEMENTS: Livestock & Poultry

Csa Nutrition Services Inc............... E 800 257-3788
　Brookville *(G-1731)*
Granville Milling Co........................... G 740 345-1305
　Newark *(G-11578)*
Hamlet Protein Inc............................ E 567 525-5627
　Findlay *(G-7518)*
Hartz Mountain Corporation.............. D 513 877-2131
　Pleasant Plain *(G-12607)*
Legacy Farmers Cooperative............. F 419 423-2611
　Findlay *(G-7528)*
Magnus International Group Inc........ G 216 592-8355
　Painesville *(G-12248)*
Mid-Wood Inc.................................. F 419 257-3331
　North Baltimore *(G-11696)*
Occidental Chemical Corp................. E 513 242-2900
　Cincinnati *(G-3211)*
Ohio Blenders Inc............................ F 419 726-2655
　Toledo *(G-14407)*
Pettisville Grain Co........................... E 419 446-2547
　Pettisville *(G-12452)*
Premier Feeds LLC........................... G 937 584-2411
　Sabina *(G-12891)*
Premier Grain LLC........................... G 937 584-6552
　Sabina *(G-12892)*
Pro-Pet LLC..................................... D 419 394-3374
　Saint Marys *(G-12964)*
Provimi North America Inc................ E 937 770-2400
　Lewisburg *(G-9191)*
Provimi North America Inc................ F 937 770-2400
　Lewisburg *(G-9192)*
Provimi North America Inc................ B 937 770-2400
　Lewisburg *(G-9190)*
Purina Mills LLC............................... E 330 682-1951
　Orrville *(G-12146)*
Quality Liquid Feeds Inc................... F 330 532-4635
　Wellsville *(G-15336)*
Rek Associates LLC........................ F 419 294-3838
　Upper Sandusky *(G-14822)*
The F L Emmert Co Inc.................... F 513 721-5808
　Cincinnati *(G-3448)*
The Mennel Milling Company............ E 419 435-8151
　Fostoria *(G-7656)*

ANIMAL FEED: Wholesalers

Gerald Grain Center Inc................... E 419 445-2451
　Archbold *(G-529)*
Granville Milling Co........................... G 740 345-1305
　Newark *(G-11578)*
Land OLakes Inc.............................. E 330 879-2158
　Massillon *(G-10119)*
Provimi North America Inc................ B 937 770-2400
　Lewisburg *(G-9190)*
Ridley USA Inc................................. F 800 837-8222
　Botkins *(G-1543)*

ANIMAL FOOD & SUPPLEMENTS: Bird Food, Prepared

Centerra Co-Op................................ E 419 281-2153
　Ashland *(G-562)*
Four Natures Keepers Inc................. F 740 363-8007
　Delaware *(G-6722)*
Natures Way Bird Products LLC........ E 440 554-6166
　Chagrin Falls *(G-2410)*
Stony Hill Mixing Ltd....................... G 330 674-0814
　Millersburg *(G-10995)*
Vitakraft Sun Seed Inc..................... D 419 832-1641
　Weston *(G-15807)*

ANIMAL FOOD & SUPPLEMENTS: Cat

Hartz Mountain Corporation.............. D 513 877-2131
　Pleasant Plain *(G-12607)*
Pro-Pet LLC..................................... D 419 394-3374
　Saint Marys *(G-12964)*

ANIMAL FOOD & SUPPLEMENTS: Dog

Bil-Jac Foods Inc.............................. E 330 722-7888
　Medina *(G-10301)*
Bravo LLC.. F 866 922-9222
　Moraine *(G-11163)*
Foster Canning Inc........................... E 419 841-6755
　Toledo *(G-14293)*
G & C Raw LLC................................ G 937 827-0010
　Versailles *(G-14980)*
JM Smucker LLC.............................. D 330 682-3000
　Orrville *(G-12132)*
Mars Petcare Us Inc......................... F 419 943-4280
　Leipsic *(G-9133)*
Milos Kitchen LLC............................ G 330 682-3000
　Orrville *(G-12136)*
Ohio Pet Foods Inc.......................... E 330 424-1431
　Lisbon *(G-9323)*
Petrition LLC.................................... G 717 572-5665
　Lodi *(G-9354)*

ANIMAL FOOD & SUPPLEMENTS: Dog & Cat

Cargill Incorporated.......................... E 419 394-3374
　Saint Marys *(G-12949)*
Kelly Foods Corporation.................... E 330 722-8855
　Medina *(G-10342)*
Land OLakes Inc.............................. E 330 879-2158
　Massillon *(G-10119)*
Nestle Purina Petcare Company........ D 740 454-8575
　Zanesville *(G-16548)*
Ohio Blenders Inc............................ F 419 726-2655
　Toledo *(G-14407)*
Vitakraft Sun Seed Inc..................... D 419 832-1641
　Weston *(G-15807)*

ANIMAL FOOD & SUPPLEMENTS: Feed Premixes

Rowe Premix Inc.............................. E 937 678-9015
　West Manchester *(G-15624)*

ANIMAL FOOD & SUPPLEMENTS: Feed Supplements

Direct Action Co Inc......................... F 330 364-3219
　Dover *(G-6815)*

ANIMAL FOOD & SUPPLEMENTS: Livestock

Gerber & Sons Inc............................ E 330 897-6201
　Baltic *(G-837)*
Hanby Farms Inc.............................. E 740 763-3554
　Nashport *(G-11337)*
Kalmbach Feeds Inc......................... C 419 294-3838
　Upper Sandusky *(G-14811)*
L E Sommer Kidron Inc..................... G 330 857-2031
　Apple Creek *(G-503)*
Land OLakes Inc.............................. E 330 879-2158
　Massillon *(G-10119)*
Republic Mills Inc............................. E 419 758-3511
　Okolona *(G-12071)*
Ridley USA Inc................................. F 800 837-8222
　Botkins *(G-1543)*
Spencer Feed & Supply LLC............. F 330 648-2111
　Spencer *(G-13483)*

ANIMAL FOOD & SUPPLEMENTS: Pet, Exc Dog & Cat, Canned

Brightpet Nutrition Group LLC........... E 330 424-1431
　Lisbon *(G-9308)*

ANIMAL FOOD & SUPPLEMENTS: Pet, Exc Dog & Cat, Dry

Kelly Foods Corporation.................... E 330 722-8855
　Medina *(G-10342)*

ANIMAL FOOD & SUPPLEMENTS: Poultry

Cooper Farms Inc............................. D 419 375-4116
　Fort Recovery *(G-7614)*
Nature Pure LLC.............................. F 937 358-2364
　Raymond *(G-12746)*

ANIMAL FOOD/SUPPLEMENTS: Feeds Fm Meat/Meat/Veg Combnd Meals

G A Wintzer and Son Company......... D 419 739-4913
　Wapakoneta *(G-15113)*
G A Wintzer and Son Company......... F 419 739-4900
　Wapakoneta *(G-15112)*

ANNEALING: Metal

Atmosphere Annealing LLC............... D 330 478-0314
　Kenton *(G-8880)*
FB Acquisition LLC........................... E 513 459-7782
　Lebanon *(G-9074)*
Northlake Steel Corporation.............. D 330 220-7717
　Valley City *(G-14887)*
Ohio Coatings Company................... D 740 859-5500
　Yorkville *(G-16294)*
Pro-TEC Coating Company LLC........ D 419 943-1100
　Leipsic *(G-9139)*
Youngstown Heat Trting Ntrding........ G 330 788-3025
　Youngstown *(G-16483)*

ANODIZING EQPT

Singleton Corporation....................... F 216 651-7800
　Cleveland *(G-4703)*

ANODIZING SVC

Allen Aircraft Products Inc................ D 330 296-9621
　Ravenna *(G-12704)*
Amac Enterprises Inc....................... F 216 362-1880
　Cleveland *(G-3645)*
Anomatic Corporation....................... B 740 522-2203
　Newark *(G-11564)*
Anomatic Corporation....................... E 740 522-2203
　New Albany *(G-11366)*
Commercial Anodizing Co................. E 440 942-8384
　Willoughby *(G-15900)*
Luke Engineering & Mfg Corp........... E 330 335-1501
　Wadsworth *(G-15043)*
Russell Products Co Inc.................... F 330 535-9246
　Akron *(G-316)*
Russell Products Co Inc.................... F 330 535-9246
　Akron *(G-317)*
Sifco Industries Inc.......................... C 216 881-8600
　Cleveland *(G-4700)*

ANTENNA REPAIR & INSTALLATION SVCS

Central USA Wireless LLC................ F 513 469-1500
　Cincinnati *(G-2719)*
Dss Installations Ltd........................ F 513 761-7000
　Cincinnati *(G-2842)*

ANTENNAS: Radar Or Communications

Circle Prime Manufacturing............... E 330 923-0019
　Cuyahoga Falls *(G-6074)*
Editencom Ltd.................................. E 419 865-5877
　Holland *(G-8508)*
Quasonix Inc.................................... E 513 942-1287
　West Chester *(G-15491)*

PRODUCT SECTION

ASPHALT & ASPHALT PRDTS

ANTENNAS: Receiving
Gem City Engineering Co .... C 937 223-5544
   Dayton *(G-6348)*
Sinbon Usa LLC .... E 937 667-8999
   Tipp City *(G-14154)*

ANTIBIOTICS
Pfizer Inc .... F 937 746-3603
   Franklin *(G-7691)*

ANTIFREEZE
BASF Corporation .... D 614 662-5682
   Columbus *(G-5176)*
Kost Usa Inc .... E 513 583-7070
   Cincinnati *(G-3088)*

ANTIQUE REPAIR & RESTORATION SVCS, EXC FURNITURE & AUTOS
Midwest Rlwy Prsrvtion Soc Inc .... G 216 781-3629
   Cleveland *(G-4412)*

APPAREL ACCESS STORES
Trophy Sports Center LLC .... F 937 376-2311
   Xenia *(G-16279)*

APPAREL DESIGNERS: Commercial
Struggle Grind Success LLC .... G 330 834-6738
   Boardman *(G-1518)*

APPLIANCE PARTS: Porcelain Enameled
Destiny Manufacturing Inc .... E 330 273-9000
   Brunswick *(G-1757)*
Whirlaway Corporation .... C 440 647-4711
   Wellington *(G-15325)*

APPLIANCES, HOUSEHOLD OR COIN OPERATED: Laundry Dryers
Whirlpool Corporation .... E 740 383-7122
   Marion *(G-9889)*

APPLIANCES, HOUSEHOLD: Kitchen, Major, Exc Refrigs & Stoves
ABC Appliance Inc .... E 419 693-4414
   Oregon *(G-12099)*
New Path International LLC .... E 614 410-3974
   Powell *(G-12679)*
Robura Inc .... D 800 438-5346
   Dalton *(G-6141)*
Sandco Industries .... E 419 547-3273
   Clyde *(G-4978)*

APPLIANCES, HOUSEHOLD: Laundry Machines, Incl CoinOperated
Whirlpool Corporation .... F 614 409-4340
   Lockbourne *(G-9343)*

APPLIANCES, HOUSEHOLD: Refrigs, Mechanical & Absorption
Norcold LLC .... G 800 543-1219
   Sidney *(G-13268)*
Whirlpool Corporation .... F 614 409-4340
   Lockbourne *(G-9343)*

APPLIANCES: Household, Refrigerators & Freezers
Dover Corporation .... D 513 870-3206
   West Chester *(G-15415)*

Whirlpool Corporation .... D 419 423-8123
   Findlay *(G-7583)*
Whirlpool Corporation .... E 740 383-7122
   Marion *(G-9889)*

APPLIANCES: Major, Cooking
Garland Commercial Industries LLC .... E 800 338-2204
   Cleveland *(G-4103)*
Nacco Industries Inc .... E 440 229-5151
   Cleveland *(G-4434)*
Royalton Foodservice Eqp Co .... F 440 237-0806
   North Royalton *(G-11894)*

APPLIANCES: Small, Electric
Ces Nationwide .... G 937 322-0771
   Springfield *(G-13543)*
Cleveland Range LLC .... C 216 481-4900
   Cleveland *(G-3852)*
Dyoung Enterprise Inc .... C 440 918-0505
   Willoughby *(G-15913)*
Glo-Quartz Electric Htr Co Inc .... E 440 255-9701
   Mentor *(G-10464)*
Johnson Bros Rubber Co Inc .... E 419 752-4814
   Greenwich *(G-8067)*
Nutone Inc .... A 888 336-3948
   Blue Ash *(G-1444)*
Qualtek Electronics Corp .... C 440 951-3300
   Mentor *(G-10541)*
Vita-Mix Manufacturing Corporation .... C 440 235-4840
   Olmsted Falls *(G-12083)*

APPLICATIONS SOFTWARE PROGRAMMING
Analytica Usa Inc .... F 513 348-2333
   Dayton *(G-6206)*
Cerkl Incorporated .... D 513 813-8425
   Blue Ash *(G-1378)*
Foundation Software LLC .... B 330 220-8383
   Strongsville *(G-13834)*
NCR Technology Center .... G 937 445-1936
   Dayton *(G-6466)*
Profound Logic Software Inc .... E 937 439-7925
   Dayton *(G-6532)*
Pwi Inc .... G 732 212-8110
   New Albany *(G-11389)*
Qxsoft LLC .... G 740 777-9609
   Lewis Center *(G-9177)*

APPRAISAL SVCS, EXC REAL ESTATE
Amos Media Company .... C 937 638-0967
   Sidney *(G-13221)*
Pughs Designer Jewelers Inc .... G 740 344-9259
   Newark *(G-11603)*

APRONS: Rubber, Vulcanized Or Rubberized Fabric
Leisure Time Pdts Design Corp .... G 440 934-1032
   Avon *(G-779)*

AQUARIUMS & ACCESS: Plastic
Th Plastics Inc .... D 419 425-5825
   Findlay *(G-7574)*

ARCHITECTURAL SVCS
Ceso Inc .... E 937 435-8584
   Miamisburg *(G-10626)*
Dlz Ohio Inc .... C 614 888-0040
   Columbus *(G-5332)*
Garland Industries Inc .... G 216 641-7500
   Cleveland *(G-4104)*
Garland/Dbs Inc .... C 216 641-7500
   Cleveland *(G-4105)*

Golden Angle Archtctral Group .... G 614 531-7932
   Columbus *(G-5406)*

ARMATURE REPAIRING & REWINDING SVC
City Machine Technologies Inc .... F 330 747-2639
   Youngstown *(G-16336)*
Horner Industrial Services Inc .... G 513 874-8722
   West Chester *(G-15562)*
Kcn Technologies LLC .... G 440 439-4219
   Bedford *(G-1131)*
Rel Enterprises Inc .... E 216 741-1700
   Brooklyn Heights *(G-1698)*
Yaskawa America Inc .... C 937 847-6200
   Miamisburg *(G-10704)*

ART DEALERS & GALLERIES
Fenwick Gallery of Fine Arts .... G 419 475-1651
   Toledo *(G-14286)*
Lazars Art Gllery Crtive Frmng .... G 330 477-8351
   Canton *(G-2144)*

ART MARBLE: Concrete
Agean Marble Manufacturing .... F 513 874-1475
   West Chester *(G-15533)*
Artistic Rock LLC .... G 216 291-8856
   Cleveland *(G-3683)*

ARTISTS' MATERIALS: Brushes, Air
Airbrush Sugar Shack Inc .... G 614 735-4988
   Columbus *(G-5108)*
RPM Consumer Holding Company ..... E 330 273-5090
   Medina *(G-10371)*

ARTS & CRAFTS SCHOOL
Studio Arts and Glass Inc .... F 330 494-9779
   Canton *(G-2237)*
Wooden Horse .... G 740 503-5243
   Baltimore *(G-849)*

ASBESTOS PRDTS: Roofing, Felt Roll
American Way Exteriors LLC .... G 937 221-8860
   Dayton *(G-6204)*

ASBESTOS PRODUCTS
Owens Corning .... A 419 248-8000
   Toledo *(G-14421)*
Owens Crning Tchncal Fbrics LL .... E 419 248-5535
   Toledo *(G-14425)*

ASPHALT & ASPHALT PRDTS
Central Allied Enterprises Inc .... E 330 477-6751
   Canton *(G-2071)*
Central Oil Asphalt Corp .... G 614 224-8111
   Columbus *(G-5242)*
Gerken Materials Inc .... E 419 533-2421
   Napoleon *(G-11315)*
Heidelberg Mtls Mdwest Agg Inc .... G 419 878-2006
   Waterville *(G-15245)*
Heritage Group Inc .... A 330 875-5566
   Louisville *(G-9460)*
Kokosing Materials Inc .... F 740 694-5872
   Fredericktown *(G-7750)*
Kokosing Materials Inc .... F 419 522-2715
   Mansfield *(G-9677)*
Kokosing Materials Inc .... F 740 745-3341
   Saint Louisville *(G-12943)*
Kokosing Materials Inc .... E 614 491-1199
   Columbus *(G-5513)*
Kokosing Materials Inc .... F 740 694-9585
   Fredericktown *(G-7751)*
Koski Construction Co .... G 440 997-5337
   Ashtabula *(G-644)*

Employee Codes: A=Over 500 employees, B=251-500
C=101-250, D=51-100, E=20-50, F=10-19, G=1-9

ASPHALT & ASPHALT PRDTS

M & B Asphalt Company Inc .... F 419 992-4235
  Tiffin *(G-14091)*

Maintenance + Inc .... F 330 264-6262
  Wooster *(G-16149)*

Morrow Gravel Company Inc .... E 513 771-0820
  Cincinnati *(G-3175)*

Mt Pleasant Blacktopping Inc .... G 513 874-3777
  Fairfield *(G-7385)*

Nes Corp .... E 440 834-0438
  Hiram *(G-8487)*

S E Johnson Companies Inc .... E 419 893-8731
  Maumee *(G-10228)*

Seneca Petroleum Co Inc .... F 419 691-3581
  Toledo *(G-14468)*

Shelly and Sands Inc .... F 740 453-0721
  Zanesville *(G-16562)*

Shelly Materials Inc .... E 740 666-5841
  Ostrander *(G-12176)*

Stoneco Inc .... E 419 422-8854
  Findlay *(G-7569)*

Valley Asphalt Corporation .... E 513 771-0820
  Cincinnati *(G-3486)*

Wilson Blacktop Corp .... F 740 635-3566
  Martins Ferry *(G-9901)*

Wyandot Dolomite Inc .... E 419 396-7641
  Carey *(G-2286)*

ASPHALT COATINGS & SEALERS

All Seal .... G 740 852-2628
  London *(G-9380)*

Aluminum Coating Manufacturers .... F 216 341-2000
  Cleveland *(G-3644)*

Atlas Roofing Corporation .... C 937 746-9941
  Franklin *(G-7663)*

Blackfish Sealcoating LLC .... G 419 647-4010
  Spencerville *(G-13485)*

Broke Boys Sealcoating LLC .... G 614 477-0322
  Mount Sterling *(G-11254)*

Century Industries Corporation .... E 330 457-2367
  New Waterford *(G-11556)*

Hy-Grade Corporation .... E 216 341-7711
  Cleveland *(G-4210)*

Hyload Inc .... G 330 336-6604
  Seville *(G-13142)*

Isaiah Industries Inc .... D 937 773-9840
  Piqua *(G-12527)*

Kettering Roofing & Shtmtl Inc .... F 513 281-6413
  Cincinnati *(G-3075)*

M & B Asphalt Company Inc .... F 419 992-4235
  Tiffin *(G-14091)*

Metal Sales Manufacturing Corp .... F 440 319-3779
  Jefferson *(G-8753)*

Mfm Building Products Corp .... E 740 622-2645
  Coshocton *(G-5984)*

National Tool & Equipment Inc .... F 330 629-8665
  Youngstown *(G-16403)*

Owens Corning Sales LLC .... A 419 248-8000
  Toledo *(G-14424)*

Pioneer Manufacturing Inc .... D 216 671-5500
  Cleveland *(G-4555)*

Roof Maxx Technologies LLC .... C 855 766-3629
  Westerville *(G-15676)*

Simon Roofing and Shtmtl Corp .... C 330 629-7392
  Youngstown *(G-16439)*

Sr Products .... F 330 998-6500
  Macedonia *(G-9576)*

State Industrial Products Corp .... B 877 747-6986
  Cleveland *(G-4731)*

Terry Asphalt Materials Inc .... E 513 874-6192
  Hamilton *(G-8247)*

Thorworks Industries Inc .... C 419 626-4375
  Sandusky *(G-13096)*

Transtar Holding Company .... G 800 359-3339
  Walton Hills *(G-15103)*

Youngs Sealcoating LLC .... G 330 591-5446
  Medina *(G-10396)*

ASPHALT MIXTURES WHOLESALERS

Hy-Grade Corporation .... E 216 341-7711
  Cleveland *(G-4210)*

Russell Standard Corporation .... E 330 733-9400
  Akron *(G-318)*

ASPHALT PLANTS INCLUDING GRAVEL MIX TYPE

Geauga Highway Co .... F 440 834-4580
  Hiram *(G-8484)*

ASSEMBLING SVC: Plumbing Fixture Fittings, Plastic

Langenau Manufacturing Company .... E 216 651-3400
  Cleveland *(G-4310)*

ASSOCIATION FOR THE HANDICAPPED

Cincinnati Assn For The Blind .... C 513 221-8558
  Cincinnati *(G-2740)*

ASSOCIATIONS: Business

Hirzel Canning Company .... E 419 693-0531
  Northwood *(G-11919)*

Interstate Contractors LLC .... E 513 372-5393
  Mason *(G-10013)*

ASSOCIATIONS: Real Estate Management

Elite Property Group LLC .... F 216 356-7469
  Elyria *(G-7139)*

Nesco Inc .... E 440 461-6000
  Cleveland *(G-4448)*

ASSOCIATIONS: Scientists'

American Ceramic Society .... E 614 890-4700
  Westerville *(G-15647)*

ASSOCIATIONS: Trade

Precision Metalforming Assn .... E 216 901-8800
  Independence *(G-8681)*

ATOMIZERS

Automtive Rfnish Clor Sltons I .... E 330 461-6067
  Medina *(G-10298)*

Henry-Griffitts Limited .... G 419 482-9095
  Maumee *(G-10206)*

Jrb Industries LLC .... E 567 825-7022
  Greenville *(G-8048)*

Triboro Quilt Mfg Corp .... F 937 222-2132
  Vandalia *(G-14962)*

Truck Fax Inc .... G 216 921-8866
  Cleveland *(G-4835)*

Velocity Concept Dev Group LLC .... G 513 204-2100
  Mason *(G-10067)*

Woodsage Industries LLC .... F 419 866-8000
  Holland *(G-8538)*

Zorich Industries Inc .... G 330 482-9803
  Columbiana *(G-5058)*

AUDIO & VIDEO EQPT, EXC COMMERCIAL

Eprad Inc .... G 419 666-3266
  Perrysburg *(G-12379)*

Fellhauer Mechanical Systems .... E 419 734-3674
  Port Clinton *(G-12617)*

Floyd Bell Inc .... D 614 294-4000
  Columbus *(G-5381)*

Mitsubishi Elc Auto Amer Inc .... B 513 573-6614
  Mason *(G-10030)*

Ohio Hd Video .... F 614 656-1162
  New Albany *(G-11387)*

Pioneer Automotive Tech Inc .... C 937 746-2293
  Miamisburg *(G-10670)*

Tech Products Corporation .... F 937 438-1100
  Miamisburg *(G-10690)*

Technicolor Usa Inc .... A 614 474-8821
  Circleville *(G-557)*

Tune Town Car Audio .... G 419 627-1100
  Sandusky *(G-3098)*

AUDIO COMPONENTS

Avtek International Inc .... G 330 633-7500
  Tallmadge *(G-14023)*

China Enterprises Inc .... F 419 885-1485
  Toledo *(G-14238)*

AUDIO ELECTRONIC SYSTEMS

5 Core Inc .... F 951 386-6372
  Bellefontaine *(G-1199)*

Andersound PA Service .... G 216 401-4631
  Cleveland *(G-3667)*

Db Unlimited LLC .... F 937 401-2602
  Dayton *(G-6293)*

Pro Audio .... G 513 752-7500
  Cincinnati *(G-2572)*

AUTO & HOME SUPPLY STORES: Auto & Truck Eqpt & Parts

Abutilon Company Inc .... F 419 536-6123
  Toledo *(G-14175)*

Horizon Global Corporation .... E 734 656-3000
  Cleveland *(G-4200)*

Ohio Truck Equipment LLC .... F 740 830-6488
  Mount Vernon *(G-11283)*

Tbone Sales LLC .... F 330 897-6131
  Baltic *(G-841)*

AUTO & HOME SUPPLY STORES: Automotive Access

Bucyrus Precision Tech Inc .... C 419 563-9950
  Bucyrus *(G-1852)*

Cequent Consumer Products Inc .... D 440 498-0001
  Solon *(G-1327)*

Epix Tube Co Inc .... F 937 529-4858
  Dayton *(G-6321)*

Front Pocket Innovations LLC .... G 330 441-2365
  Wadsworth *(G-15031)*

Steves Vans ACC Unlimited LLC .... G 740 374-3154
  Marietta *(G-9832)*

Superior Production LLC .... C 614 444-2181
  Columbus *(G-5800)*

AUTO & HOME SUPPLY STORES: Automotive parts

American Cold Forge LLC .... E 419 836-1062
  Northwood *(G-11917)*

K-M-S Industries Inc .... F 440 243-6680
  Brookpark *(G-1720)*

M Technologies Inc .... F 330 477-9009
  Canton *(G-2151)*

Mader Automotive Center Inc .... F 937 339-2681
  Troy *(G-14595)*

Mark Knupp Muffler & Tire Inc .... E 937 773-1334
  Piqua *(G-12535)*

Ohio Auto Supply Company .... F 330 454-5105
  Canton *(G-2182)*

PRODUCT SECTION

AUTOMOTIVE PARTS, ACCESS & SPLYS

Rust Belt Broncos LLC.................................. E 330 533-0048
Canfield *(G-2017)*

Tom Barbour Auto Parts Inc.................... F 740 354-4654
Portsmouth *(G-12659)*

AUTO & HOME SUPPLY STORES: Batteries, Automotive & Truck

Battery Unlimited.. G 740 452-5030
Zanesville *(G-16506)*

J & J Tire & Alignment............................... G 330 424-5200
Lisbon *(G-9316)*

AUTO & HOME SUPPLY STORES: Trailer Hitches, Automotive

Overhead Door of Pike County................ G 740 289-3925
Piketon *(G-12481)*

AUTO & HOME SUPPLY STORES: Truck Eqpt & Parts

Ace Truck Equipment Co.......................... E 740 453-0551
Zanesville *(G-16494)*

Crown Equipment Corporation................ A 419 629-2311
New Bremen *(G-11400)*

Galion-Godwin Truck Bdy Co LLC........... F 330 359-5495
Dundee *(G-6965)*

H & H Truck Parts LLC............................. E 216 642-4540
Cleveland *(G-4160)*

Kaffenbarger Truck Eqp Co....................... E 513 772-6800
Cincinnati *(G-3056)*

Martin Diesel Inc...................................... E 419 782-9911
Defiance *(G-6691)*

Perkins Motor Service Ltd........................ F 440 277-1256
Lorain *(G-9430)*

River City Body Company......................... F 513 772-9317
Cincinnati *(G-3343)*

Western Branch Diesel LLC..................... F 330 454-8800
Canton *(G-2267)*

X-Treme Finishes Inc............................... F 330 474-0614
North Royalton *(G-11903)*

AUTO SPLYS & PARTS, NEW, WHSLE: Exhaust Sys, Mufflers, Etc

Dreison International Inc......................... C 216 362-0755
Cleveland *(G-3972)*

AUTOMATIC REGULATING CONTROL: Building Svcs Monitoring, Auto

Evokes LLC... E 513 947-8433
Mason *(G-9992)*

AUTOMATIC REGULATING CONTROLS: AC & Refrigeration

Air Enterprises Inc.................................... A 330 794-9770
Akron *(G-24)*

Young Regulator Company Inc................. E 440 232-9452
Bedford *(G-1161)*

AUTOMATIC REGULATING CONTROLS: Appliance, Exc AirCond/Refr

K Davis Inc... G 419 307-7051
Fremont *(G-7791)*

Melink Corporation................................... D 513 685-0958
Milford *(G-10913)*

Portage Electric Products Inc................... C 330 499-2727
North Canton *(G-11752)*

AUTOMATIC REGULATING CONTROLS: Hardware, Environmental Reg

Ecopro Solutions LLC............................... E 216 232-4040
Independence *(G-8665)*

Mestek Inc.. F 419 288-2703
Bradner *(G-1603)*

West 6th Products Company.................... D 330 467-7446
Northfield *(G-11915)*

AUTOMATIC REGULATING CTRLS: Damper, Pneumatic Or Electric

Mader Machine Co Inc............................. E 440 355-4505
Lagrange *(G-8951)*

Tlt-Babcock Inc... D 330 867-8540
Akron *(G-359)*

AUTOMATIC TELLER MACHINES

Atm Nerds LLC... F 614 983-3056
Columbus *(G-5164)*

Diebold Nixdorf Incorporated.................. D 330 490-4000
Canton *(G-2092)*

Diebold Nixdorf Incorporated.................. D 740 928-0200
Hebron *(G-8338)*

Diebold Nixdorf Incorporated.................. A 330 490-4000
North Canton *(G-11722)*

Ginko Voting Systems LLC...................... E 937 291-4060
Dayton *(G-6352)*

Glenn Michael Brick................................ F 740 391-5735
Flushing *(G-7587)*

Testlink Usa Inc....................................... E 513 272-1081
Cincinnati *(G-3445)*

AUTOMOBILE FINANCE LEASING

Momentum Fleet MGT Group Inc............ D 440 759-2219
Westlake *(G-15765)*

AUTOMOBILES & OTHER MOTOR VEHICLES WHOLESALERS

Btw LLC.. G 419 382-4443
Toledo *(G-14223)*

Doug Marine Motors Inc.......................... E 740 335-3700
Wshngtn Ct Hs *(G-16230)*

Interstate Truckway Inc........................... F 614 771-1220
Columbus *(G-5477)*

AUTOMOBILES: Wholesalers

Tpam Inc.. E 567 315-8694
Toledo *(G-14511)*

AUTOMOTIVE & TRUCK GENERAL REPAIR SVC

Abutilon Company Inc............................. F 419 536-6123
Toledo *(G-14175)*

Automtive Rfnish Clor Sltons I................ E 330 461-6067
Medina *(G-10298)*

Bob Sumerel Tire Co Inc......................... F 330 769-9092
Seville *(G-13140)*

Bridgestone Ret Operations LLC............. F 440 299-6126
Mentor *(G-10431)*

Bridgestone Ret Operations LLC............. G 419 625-6571
Sandusky *(G-13045)*

Doug Marine Motors Inc.......................... E 740 335-3700
Wshngtn Ct Hs *(G-16230)*

Firestone Complete Auto Care................ G 937 528-2496
Centerville *(G-2362)*

Goodyear Tire & Rubber Company.......... A 330 796-2121
Akron *(G-171)*

Grismer Tire Company............................ E 937 643-2526
Centerville *(G-2363)*

Hutter Racing Engines Ltd...................... F 440 285-2175
Chardon *(G-2453)*

J & J Tire & Alignment............................ G 330 424-5200
Lisbon *(G-9316)*

Kirbys Auto and Truck Repr Inc.............. G 513 934-3999
Lebanon *(G-9093)*

Nice Body Automotive LLC..................... G 440 752-5568
Elyria *(G-7185)*

Ohio Trailer Inc....................................... F 330 392-4444
Warren *(G-15196)*

Pattons Trck & Hvy Eqp Svc Inc............. E 740 385-4067
Logan *(G-9373)*

Sammy S Auto Detail.............................. F 614 263-2728
Columbus *(G-5743)*

Youngstown-Kenworth Inc...................... F 330 534-9761
Hubbard *(G-8574)*

AUTOMOTIVE BODY SHOP

ABRA Auto Body & Glass LP.................. G 513 247-3400
Cincinnati *(G-2592)*

ABRA Auto Body & Glass LP.................. G 513 367-9200
Harrison *(G-8263)*

ABRA Auto Body & Glass LP.................. F 513 755-7709
West Chester *(G-15359)*

Chardon Square Auto & Body Inc........... F 440 286-7600
Chardon *(G-2444)*

Obs Inc... F 330 453-3725
Canton *(G-2180)*

W&W Automotive & Towing Inc............. F 937 429-1699
Beavercreek Township *(G-1095)*

Webers Body & Frame Inc...................... G 937 839-5946
West Alexandria *(G-15346)*

AUTOMOTIVE BODY, PAINT & INTERIOR REPAIR & MAINTENANCE SVC

Bobbart Industries Inc............................ E 419 350-5477
Sylvania *(G-13991)*

Willard Machine & Welding Inc.............. F 330 467-0642
Macedonia *(G-9586)*

AUTOMOTIVE CUSTOMIZING SVCS, NONFACTORY BASIS

Afg Industries Inc.................................... D 614 322-4580
Grove City *(G-8074)*

AUTOMOTIVE GLASS REPLACEMENT SHOPS

A Service Glass Inc................................. E 937 426-4920
Beavercreek *(G-1038)*

J W Goss Company.................................. F 330 395-0739
Warren *(G-15179)*

Keystone Auto Glass Inc......................... D 419 509-0497
Maumee *(G-10211)*

Safelite Group Inc................................... A 614 210-9000
Columbus *(G-5740)*

Support Svc LLC..................................... G 419 617-0660
Lexington *(G-9203)*

Webers Body & Frame Inc...................... G 937 839-5946
West Alexandria *(G-15346)*

AUTOMOTIVE PAINT SHOP

Michael W Newton................................... G 740 352-9334
Lucasville *(G-9525)*

Newbury Sndblst & Pntg Inc................... G 440 564-7204
Newbury *(G-11631)*

Precision Coatings Systems.................... E 937 642-4727
Marysville *(G-9931)*

AUTOMOTIVE PARTS, ACCESS & SPLYS

Employee Codes: A=Over 500 employees, B=251-500
C=101-250, D=51-100, E=20-50, F=10-19, G=1-9

AUTOMOTIVE PARTS, ACCESS & SPLYS — PRODUCT SECTION

ABC Technologies Dlhb Inc .... B 330 478-2503
   Canton *(G-2026)*
Accel Performance Group LLC .... C 216 658-6413
   Independence *(G-8651)*
Ach LLC .... G 419 621-5748
   Sandusky *(G-13040)*
Ad Industries Inc .... A 303 744-1911
   Dayton *(G-6183)*
Adient US LLC .... C 937 981-2176
   Greenfield *(G-8026)*
Adient US LLC .... C 419 662-4900
   Northwood *(G-11916)*
Adient US LLC .... D 419 394-7800
   Saint Marys *(G-12944)*
Airstream Inc .... B 937 596-6111
   Jackson Center *(G-8729)*
Airtex Industries LLC .... B 330 899-0340
   Toledo *(G-14181)*
American Axle & Mfg Inc .... E 330 863-7500
   Malvern *(G-9608)*
American Axle & Mfg Inc .... D 330 486-3200
   Twinsburg *(G-14630)*
American Manufacturing & Eqp .... G 513 829-2248
   Fairfield *(G-7335)*
Amsoil Inc .... G 614 274-9851
   Urbancrest *(G-14852)*
Amsted Industries Incorporated .... D 614 836-2323
   Groveport *(G-8129)*
Aptiv Services Us LLC .... C 330 367-6000
   Vienna *(G-14994)*
Aptiv Services Us LLC .... B 330 505-3150
   Warren *(G-15143)*
Arlington Rack & Packaging Co .... F 419 476-4700
   Toledo *(G-14199)*
Atc Lighting & Plastics Inc .... C 440 466-7670
   Andover *(G-485)*
Atwood Mobile Products LLC .... D 419 258-5531
   Antwerp *(G-492)*
Auria Fremont LLC .... B 419 332-1587
   Fremont *(G-7764)*
Auria Holmesville LLC .... B 330 279-4505
   Holmesville *(G-8542)*
Auria Sidney LLC .... B 937 492-1225
   Sidney *(G-13224)*
Austin Parts & Service .... G 330 253-7791
   Akron *(G-69)*
Autoneum North America Inc .... D 419 690-8924
   Oregon *(G-12102)*
Autoneum North America Inc .... B 419 693-0511
   Oregon *(G-12103)*
B A Malcuit Racing Inc .... G 330 878-7111
   Strasburg *(G-13743)*
B&C Machine Co LLC .... E 330 745-4013
   Barberton *(G-859)*
Beach Manufacturing Co .... C 937 882-6372
   Donnelsville *(G-6806)*
Beijing West Industries .... F 937 455-5281
   Dayton *(G-6225)*
Bobbart Industries Inc .... E 419 350-5477
   Sylvania *(G-13991)*
Boler Company .... C 330 445-6728
   Canton *(G-2049)*
Bores Manufacturing Inc .... F 419 465-2606
   Monroeville *(G-11123)*
Bowden Manufacturing Corp .... E 440 946-1770
   Willoughby *(G-15891)*
Buyers Products Company .... C 440 974-8888
   Mentor *(G-10435)*
Bwi Chassis Dynamics NA Inc .... F 937 455-5100
   Kettering *(G-8902)*
Bwi North America Inc .... B 937 455-5190
   Kettering *(G-8903)*

Bwi North America Inc .... E 937 253-1130
   Kettering *(G-8904)*
C&C Indy Cylinder Head LLC .... G 937 708-8563
   Xenia *(G-16254)*
Cequent Consumer Products Inc .... D 440 498-0001
   Solon *(G-13327)*
Champion Spark Plug Cmbrdge Pl .... G 740 432-2393
   Cambridge *(G-1928)*
Champion Spark Plug Company .... D 419 535-2567
   Toledo *(G-14232)*
Cleveland Ignition Co Inc .... G 440 439-3688
   Cleveland *(G-3842)*
CMI Holding Company Crawford .... D 419 468-9122
   Galion *(G-7866)*
Crown Div of Allen Gr .... G 330 263-4919
   Wooster *(G-16111)*
Cummins Filtration Inc C
   Findlay *(G-7500)*
Cummins Inc .... E 614 604-6004
   Grove City *(G-8085)*
Custom Floaters LLC .... F 216 536-8979
   Brookpark *(G-1710)*
Cvg National Seating Co LLC .... F 219 872-7295
   New Albany *(G-11377)*
Cwd LLC .... E 310 218-1082
   Cleveland *(G-3933)*
D-Terra Solutions LLC .... G 614 450-1040
   Powell *(G-12670)*
Daido Metal Bellefontaine LLC .... D 937 592-5010
   Bellefontaine *(G-1205)*
Dana .... E 419 887-3000
   Toledo *(G-14259)*
Dana Auto Systems Group LLC .... E 419 887-3000
   Maumee *(G-10176)*
Dana Automotive Mfg Inc .... D 419 887-3000
   Maumee *(G-10177)*
Dana Brazil Holdings I LLC .... G 419 887-3000
   Maumee *(G-10178)*
Dana Commercial Vhcl Pdts LLC .... C 419 887-3000
   Maumee *(G-10179)*
Dana Driveshaft Mfg LLC .... G 419 887-3000
   Maumee *(G-10180)*
Dana Driveshaft Products LLC .... E 419 887-3000
   Maumee *(G-10181)*
Dana Global Products Inc .... E 419 887-3000
   Maumee *(G-10182)*
Dana Heavy Vehicle Systems .... D 419 866-3900
   Holland *(G-8502)*
Dana Hvy Vhcl Systems Group LL .... E 419 887-3000
   Maumee *(G-10183)*
Dana Incorporated .... A 419 887-3000
   Maumee *(G-10184)*
Dana Light Axle Mfg LLC .... B 419 887-3000
   Toledo *(G-14260)*
Dana Light Axle Mfg LLC .... G 419 346-4528
   Maumee *(G-10185)*
Dana Limited .... D 419 866-7253
   Holland *(G-8503)*
Dana Limited .... E 419 887-3000
   Maumee *(G-10187)*
Dana Limited .... F 419 887-3000
   Maumee *(G-10188)*
Dana Limited .... D 419 482-2000
   Maumee *(G-10189)*
Dana Limited .... B 419 887-3000
   Maumee *(G-10186)*
Dana Off Highway Products LLC .... D 614 864-1116
   Blacklick *(G-1334)*
Dana Off Highway Products LLC .... E 419 887-3000
   Maumee *(G-10190)*
Dana Sac USA Inc .... E 419 887-3550
   Maumee *(G-10191)*

Dana Sealing Manufacturing LLC .... D
   Maumee *(G-10192)*
Dana Sealing Products LLC .... F 419 887-3000
   Maumee *(G-10193)*
Dana Structural Mfg LLC .... C 419 887-3000
   Maumee *(G-10194)*
Dana Structural Products LLC .... E 419 887-3000
   Maumee *(G-10195)*
Dana Thermal Products LLC .... E 419 887-3000
   Maumee *(G-10196)*
Dana World Trade Corporation .... F 419 887-3000
   Maumee *(G-10197)*
Davis Cummins Inc .... G 614 309-6077
   Columbus *(G-4317)*
Dayton Clutch & Joint Inc .... F 937 236-9770
   Dayton *(G-6226)*
Dcm Manufacturing Inc .... E 216 265-8006
   Cleveland *(G-3948)*
Doug Marine Motors Inc .... E 740 335-3700
   Wshngtn Ct H *(G-16230)*
Driveline 1 Inc .... C 614 279-7734
   Columbus *(G-5336)*
Dusty Ductz LLC .... G 317 462-9622
   Lebanon *(G-8970)*
Ebco Inc .... E 330 562-8265
   Streetsboro *(G-13769)*
Ebog Legacy Inc .... D 330 239-4933
   Sharon Center *(G-13166)*
Edgerton Forge Inc .... D 419 298-2333
   Edgerton *(G-7074)*
Egr Products Company Inc .... F 330 833-6554
   Dalton *(G-6131)*
Ernie Green Industries Inc .... E 740 420-5252
   Circleville *(G-3550)*
Exito Manufacturing LLC .... G 937 291-9871
   Beavercreek *(G-1073)*
Falls Stamping & Welding Co .... C 330 928-1191
   Cuyahoga Falls *(G-6083)*
Farin Industries Inc .... F 440 275-2755
   Austinburg *(G-746)*
Flex Technologies Inc .... D 330 359-5415
   Mount Eaton *(G-11230)*
Florida Production Engrg Inc .... D 937 996-4361
   New Madison *(G-11474)*
Force Control Industries Inc .... E 513 868-0900
   Fairfield *(G-7363)*
Ford Motor Company .... D 216 676-7918
   Brookpark *(G-1715)*
Fram Group .... G 479 271-7934
   Cleveland *(G-4089)*
Fram Group Operations LLC .... E 419 436-5827
   Fostoria *(G-7637)*
Fremont Plastic Products Inc .... C 419 332-6407
   Fremont *(G-7783)*
Freudenberg-Nok Sealing Tech .... F 877 331-8427
   Milan *(G-10883)*
Ftech R&D North America Inc .... E 937 339-2777
   Troy *(G-14572)*
Fuserashi Intl Tech Inc .... E 330 273-0140
   Valley City *(G-14870)*
General Aluminum Mfg Company .... C 419 739-9300
   Wapakoneta *(G-15115)*
General Metals Powder Co LLC .... E 330 633-1226
   Akron *(G-66)*
General Motors LLC .... A 216 265-5000
   Cleveland *(G-4116)*
General Motors LLC .... C 330 824-5840
   Warren *(G-15173)*
GKN Driveline North Amer Inc .... D 419 354-3955
   Bowling Green *(G-1568)*
God Speed Turbo Innovations .... G 513 307-5584
   West Chester *(G-15443)*

PRODUCT SECTION

AUTOMOTIVE PARTS, ACCESS & SPLYS

Gra-Mag Truck Intr Systems LLC............ E 740 490-1000
London *(G-9388)*

Grand-Rock Company Inc...................... E 440 639-2000
Painesville *(G-12240)*

Green Rdced Emssons Netwrk LLC....... G 330 340-0941
Strasburg *(G-13746)*

Green Tokai Co Ltd................................ C 937 237-1630
Dayton *(G-6362)*

Hall-Toledo Inc..................................... F 419 893-4334
Maumee *(G-10203)*

Hendrickson.. F 740 678-8033
Vincent *(G-15008)*

Hendrickson International Corp.............. D 740 929-5600
Hebron *(G-8343)*

Hendrickson Usa LLC............................ C 330 456-7288
Canton *(G-2124)*

Hendrickson Usa LLC............................ B 740 929-5600
Hebron *(G-8344)*

Hendrickson Usa LLC............................ D 630 910-2800
North Canton *(G-11737)*

Hfi LLC.. B 614 491-0700
Canal Winchester *(G-1987)*

Hi-Tek Manufacturing Inc...................... C 513 459-1094
Mason *(G-10001)*

Hilite Intl... G 216 641-9632
Cleveland *(G-4189)*

Hirschvogel Incorporated....................... B 614 445-6060
Columbus *(G-5441)*

Honda Dev & Mfg Amer LLC................ A 937 843-5555
Russells Point *(G-12876)*

Igw USA.. F 740 588-1722
Zanesville *(G-16539)*

Illinois Tool Works Inc........................... C 513 489-7600
Blue Ash *(G-1408)*

Illinois Tool Works Inc........................... E 262 248-8277
Bryan *(G-1821)*

Imasen Bucyrus Technology Inc............. C 419 563-9590
Bucyrus *(G-1862)*

Industry Products Co............................. B 937 778-0585
Piqua *(G-12526)*

Interntnal Auto Cmpnnts Group............. E 419 335-1000
Wauseon *(G-15264)*

Interntnal Auto Cmpnnts Group............. A 419 433-5653
Wauseon *(G-15265)*

Inteva Products LLC.............................. C 937 280-8500
Vandalia *(G-14945)*

Johnson Controls Inc............................. E 414 524-1200
Saint Marys *(G-12954)*

Joseph Industries Inc............................. D 330 528-0091
Streetsboro *(G-13776)*

Julie Maynard Inc................................... F 937 443-0408
Dayton *(G-6394)*

K Wm Beach Mfg Co Inc....................... F 937 399-3838
Springfield *(G-13586)*

Kalida Manufacturing Inc....................... C 419 532-2026
Kalida *(G-8785)*

Kasai North America Inc....................... E 614 356-1494
Dublin *(G-6903)*

Kasai North America Inc....................... C 419 209-0399
Upper Sandusky *(G-14812)*

Kenley Enterprises LLC........................ F 419 630-0921
Bryan *(G-1824)*

Keystone Auto Glass Inc....................... D 419 509-0497
Maumee *(G-10211)*

KG Medina LLC.................................... E 256 330-4273
Medina *(G-10343)*

Kic Ltd.. G 614 775-9570
Gahanna *(G-7841)*

Kilar Manufacturing Inc......................... F 330 534-8961
Hubbard *(G-8567)*

Knippen Chrysler Ddge Jeep Inc............ E 419 695-4976
Delphos *(G-6767)*

Kongsberg Actation Systems LLC......... E 440 639-8778
Grand River *(G-8012)*

Kth Parts Industries Inc........................ A 937 663-5941
Saint Paris *(G-12973)*

Ktri Holdings Inc................................... F 216 400-9308
Cleveland *(G-4301)*

KWD Automotive Inc............................ G 419 344-8232
Whitehouse *(G-15820)*

Lacal Equipment Inc.............................. E 937 596-6106
Jackson Center *(G-8734)*

Leadec Corp.. E 513 731-3590
Blue Ash *(G-1420)*

Lear Corporation................................... C 740 928-4358
Hebron *(G-8347)*

Lear Corporation................................... E 419 335-6010
Wauseon *(G-15267)*

Linde Hydraulics Corporation................. E 330 533-6801
Canfield *(G-2009)*

Ltf Acquisition LLC............................... E 330 533-0111
Canfield *(G-2010)*

Maags Automotive & Mch Inc................ G 419 626-1539
Sandusky *(G-13076)*

Magna International Amer Inc............... C 330 824-3101
Sheffield Village *(G-13185)*

Magna International Amer Inc............... D 419 410-4780
Swanton *(G-13977)*

Magnaco Industries Inc......................... E 216 961-3636
Lodi *(G-9353)*

Mahle Behr Dayton LLC........................ A 937 356-2001
Vandalia *(G-14948)*

Mahle Behr Dayton LLC........................ D 937 369-2900
Dayton *(G-6424)*

Mahle Behr USA Inc.............................. C 937 356-2001
Vandalia *(G-14949)*

Mahle Industries Incorporated............... E 937 890-2739
Dayton *(G-6426)*

Maxion Wheels Sedalia LLC.................. A 330 794-2300
Akron *(G-239)*

Milark Industries Inc............................. D 419 524-7627
Mansfield *(G-9693)*

Milark Industries Inc............................. D 419 524-7627
Mansfield *(G-9694)*

Millat Industries Corp........................... F 937 535-1500
Dayton *(G-6450)*

Millat Industries Corp........................... D 937 434-6666
Dayton *(G-6449)*

Mitec Powertrain Inc............................. C 567 525-5606
Findlay *(G-7538)*

Mitsubishi Elc Auto Amer Inc................ B 513 573-6614
Mason *(G-10030)*

Monarch Plastic Inc.............................. F 330 683-0822
Orrville *(G-12137)*

Namoh Ohio Holdings Inc..................... E
Norwood *(G-11996)*

Nanogate North America LLC................ B 419 522-7745
Mansfield *(G-9701)*

Nebraska Industries Corp...................... F 419 335-6010
Wauseon *(G-15270)*

Newburgh Crankshaft Inc...................... G 440 502-6998
Cleveland *(G-4455)*

Nitto Inc... F 937 773-4820
Piqua *(G-12539)*

Nitto Inc... F 937 773-4820
Piqua *(G-12540)*

Norlake Manufacturing Company........... D 440 353-3200
North Ridgeville *(G-11851)*

Norplas Industries Inc........................... B 419 662-3200
Northwood *(G-11922)*

North Coast Exotics Inc........................ G 216 651-5512
Cleveland *(G-4468)*

Northern Stamping Co........................... F 216 642-8081
Cleveland *(G-4479)*

Norton Manufacturing Co Inc................. F 419 435-0411
Fostoria *(G-7648)*

O D L LLC... G 419 833-2533
Bowling Green *(G-1579)*

Ohio Auto Supply Company................... F 330 454-5105
Canton *(G-2182)*

Ohta Press US Inc................................ F 937 374-3382
Xenia *(G-16271)*

Pacific Manufacturing Ohio Inc.............. B 513 860-3900
Fairfield *(G-7390)*

Pako Inc... C 440 946-8030
Mentor *(G-10519)*

Parker-Hannifin Corporation.................. B 440 943-5700
Wickliffe *(G-15846)*

Performance Motorsports Inc................ F 440 951-6600
Mentor *(G-10522)*

Pioneer Automotive Tech Inc................. C 937 746-2293
Miamisburg *(G-10670)*

Piston Automotive LLC......................... A 419 464-0250
Toledo *(G-14437)*

Powers and Sons LLC............................ C 419 485-3151
Montpelier *(G-11140)*

Quality Reproductions Inc..................... G 330 335-5000
Wadsworth *(G-15058)*

Race Winning Brands Inc...................... B 440 951-6600
Mentor *(G-10544)*

Radar Love Co...................................... E 419 951-4750
Findlay *(G-7555)*

Ramco Specialties Inc.......................... D 330 653-5135
Hudson *(G-8609)*

Reactive Resin Products Co.................. E 419 666-6119
Perrysburg *(G-12423)*

Restortion Parts Unlimited Inc.............. F 513 934-0815
Lebanon *(G-9108)*

Resz Fabrication Inc............................. G 440 207-0044
Eastlake *(G-7047)*

Rubber Duck 4x4 Inc............................ G 513 889-1735
Hamilton *(G-8239)*

Saia-Burgess Lcc.................................. D 937 898-3621
Vandalia *(G-14958)*

Sanoh America Inc................................ D 419 425-2600
Findlay *(G-7558)*

Schaeffler Transm Systems LLC........... A 330 202-6212
Wooster *(G-16166)*

Schaeffler Transm Systems LLC........... E 330 264-4383
Wooster *(G-16167)*

Schott Metal Products Company........... E 330 773-7873
Akron *(G-326)*

Seabiscuit Motorsports Inc................... B 440 951-6600
Mentor *(G-10551)*

Sew-Eurodrive Inc................................ D 937 335-0036
Troy *(G-14609)*

Sfs Group Usa Inc................................ C 330 239-7100
Medina *(G-10375)*

Sfs Intec Inc.. E 330 239-7100
Medina *(G-10376)*

Solo Dyna Systems Ltd........................ G 440 871-7112
Bay Village *(G-967)*

Speedline North America Inc................ G 937 291-7000
Dayton *(G-6584)*

Steck Manufacturing Co LLC................ F 937 222-0062
Dayton *(G-6594)*

Steere Enterprises Inc.......................... D 330 633-4926
Tallmadge *(G-14049)*

Sumiriko Ohio Inc................................. E 419 358-2121
Bluffton *(G-1507)*

Superior Trim Holdings Limited............. G 419 425-5555
Findlay *(G-7572)*

Sutphen Corporation............................. E 937 969-8851
Springfield *(G-13640)*

Teijin Automotive Tech Inc................... B 419 396-1980
Carey *(G-2285)*

Employee Codes: A=Over 500 employees, B=251-500
C=101-250, D=51-100, E=20-50, F=10-19, G=1-9

2024 Harris Ohio Industrial Directory

AUTOMOTIVE PARTS, ACCESS & SPLYS — PRODUCT SECTION

Teijin Automotive Tech Inc .... B 419 257-2231
 North Baltimore (G-11700)
Teijin Automotive Tech Inc .... B 419 238-4628
 Van Wert (G-14928)
Tenneco Inc .... F 419 499-2541
 Milan (G-10887)
Tetra Mold & Tool Inc .... E 937 845-1651
 New Carlisle (G-11428)
Tfo Tech Co Ltd .... C 740 426-6381
 Jeffersonville (G-8766)
TI Group Auto Systems LLC .... E 740 929-2049
 Hebron (G-8366)
Tigerpoly Manufacturing Inc .... B 614 871-0045
 Grove City (G-8122)
Tko Mfg Services Inc .... E 937 299-1637
 Moraine (G-11215)
Toledo Molding & Die LLC .... C 419 692-6022
 Delphos (G-6772)
Toledo Molding & Die LLC .... B 419 692-6022
 Delphos (G-6773)
Toledo Pro Fiberglass Inc .... G 419 241-9390
 Toledo (G-14503)
Tom Smith Industries Inc .... D 937 832-1555
 Englewood (G-7245)
Total Engine Airflow .... G 330 634-2155
 Tallmadge (G-14052)
Tower Atmtive Oprtons USA I LL .... C 419 483-1500
 Bellevue (G-1239)
Trailer Component Mfg Inc .... E 440 255-2888
 Mentor (G-10580)
Tri State Corebuyers LLC .... F 513 288-8063
 Amelia (G-468)
Tri-Mac Mfg & Svcs Co .... F 513 896-4445
 Hamilton (G-8251)
Trico Holding Corporation .... G 216 589-0198
 Cleveland (G-4827)
Trim Parts Inc .... E 513 934-0815
 Lebanon (G-9115)
Trim Systems Operating Corp .... D 614 289-5360
 New Albany (G-11392)
TS Trim Industries Inc .... B 614 837-4114
 Canal Winchester (G-1993)
UCI International LLC .... E 330 899-0340
 North Canton (G-11772)
UGN Inc .... C 513 360-3500
 Lebanon (G-9118)
Unison Industries LLC .... B 904 667-9904
 Dayton (G-6175)
United Components LLC .... E 330 899-0340
 Toledo (G-14513)
Universal Auto Filter LLC .... G 216 589-0198
 Cleveland (G-4848)
US Kondo Corporation .... F 937 916-3045
 Piqua (G-12557)
US Tsubaki Power Transm LLC .... C 419 626-4560
 Sandusky (G-13102)
Usui International Corporation .... D 734 354-3626
 West Chester (G-15523)
Varbros LLC .... E 216 267-5200
 Cleveland (G-4860)
Vari-Wall Tube Specialists Inc .... D 330 482-0000
 Columbiana (G-5053)
Venco Manufacturing Inc .... F 513 772-8448
 Cincinnati (G-3489)
Venco Venturo Industries LLC .... E 513 772-8448
 Cincinnati (G-3490)
Ventra Sandusky LLC .... B 419 627-3500
 Sandusky (G-13103)
Walther Engrg & Mfg Co Inc .... E 937 743-8125
 Franklin (G-7710)
West & Barker Inc .... E 330 652-9923
 Niles (G-11691)

Westbrook Mfg Inc .... B 937 254-2004
 Dayton (G-6650)
Western Branch Diesel LLC .... F 330 454-8800
 Canton (G-2267)
Wheelskins Inc .... G 800 755-2128
 North Royalton (G-11901)
Whirlaway Corporation .... D 440 647-4711
 Wellington (G-15323)
Whirlaway Corporation .... D 440 647-4711
 Wellington (G-15324)
Winzeler Stamping Co .... E 419 485-3147
 Montpelier (G-11147)
Woodbridge Group .... C 419 334-3666
 Fremont (G-7820)
Workhorse Group Inc .... D 888 646-5205
 Sharonville (G-13175)
Workhorse Technologies Inc .... E 888 646-5205
 Sharonville (G-13176)
Yanfeng US Auto Intr Systems I .... D 419 633-1873
 Bryan (G-1847)
Yanfeng US Auto Intr Systems I .... B 419 834-9422
 Bryan (G-1848)
ZF Active Safety & Elec US LLC .... C 216 750-2400
 Cleveland (G-4933)
ZF Active Safety & Elec US LLC .... E 419 726-5599
 Toledo (G-14532)
ZF Active Safety US Inc .... F 419 237-2511
 Fayette (G-7463)

AUTOMOTIVE PARTS: Plastic

Cpp Group Holdings LLC .... E 216 453-4800
 Cleveland (G-3912)
Daddy Katz LLC .... G 937 296-0347
 Moraine (G-11168)
Fpe Inc .... C 740 420-5252
 Circleville (G-3552)
Greenville Techniology Inc .... G 937 642-6744
 Marysville (G-9912)
M W Solutions LLC .... F 419 782-1611
 Defiance (G-6689)
Marsh Composites LLC .... G 937 350-1214
 Dayton (G-6169)
Molten North America Corp .... C 419 425-2700
 Findlay (G-7539)
Mos International Inc .... F 330 329-0905
 Stow (G-13710)
National Fleet Svcs Ohio LLC .... F 440 930-5177
 Avon Lake (G-818)
Nifco America Corporation .... C 614 836-3808
 Canal Winchester (G-1990)
Nifco America Corporation .... C 614 836-8691
 Groveport (G-8155)
Nifco America Corporation .... B 614 920-6800
 Canal Winchester (G-1989)
Polyfill LLC .... E 937 493-0041
 Sidney (G-13272)
Precision Engineered Plas Inc .... E 216 334-1105
 Cleveland (G-4574)
Precision Mfg & Assembly LLC .... D 937 252-3507
 Dayton (G-6515)
Reinalt-Thomas Corporation .... G 330 863-1936
 Carrollton (G-2314)
Toledo Molding & Die LLC .... B 419 443-9031
 Tiffin (G-14113)
Trifecta Tool and Engrg LLC .... G 937 291-0933
 Dayton (G-6633)
Woodbridge Englewood Inc .... E 937 540-9889
 Englewood (G-7249)
Xaloy LLC .... C 330 726-4000
 Austintown (G-757)

AUTOMOTIVE PRDTS: Rubber

Green Tokai Co Ltd .... A 937 833-5444
 Brookville (G-1438)
Kn Rubber LLC .... C 419 739-4200
 Wapakoneta (G-15121)
Myers Industries Inc .... D 330 336-6621
 Wadsworth (G-15047)
Myers Industries Inc .... E 330 253-5592
 Akron (G-2607)
S P E Inc .... E 330 733-0101
 Mogadore (G-1082)
Seal Div Natl .... E 419 238-0030
 Van Wert (G-1926)
Soffseal Inc .... E 513 934-0815
 Cincinnati (G-4400)

AUTOMOTIVE RADIATOR REPAIR SHOPS

Albright Radiator Inc .... G 330 264-8886
 Wooster (G-1100)
Brock RAD Wlg Fabrication Inc .... G 740 773-2540
 Chillicothe (G-2496)
Cincinnati Radiator Inc .... F 513 874-5555
 Hamilton (G-193)
Friess Welding Inc .... G 330 644-8160
 Coventry Township (G-6009)
Perkins Motor Service Ltd .... F 440 277-1256
 Lorain (G-9440)

AUTOMOTIVE REPAIR SHOPS: Diesel Engine Repair

Power Acquisition LLC .... D 614 228-5000
 Dublin (G-6525)
Tri-W Group Inc .... A 614 228-5000
 Columbus (G-5837)
W W Williams Company LLC .... D 614 228-5000
 Dublin (G-6558)

AUTOMOTIVE REPAIR SHOPS: Electrical Svcs

Entratech Systems LLC .... G 419 433-7683
 Sandusky (G-13055)
Miscor Group Ltd .... B 330 830-3500
 Massillon (G-10129)
Vintage Automotive Elc Inc .... F 419 472-9349
 Toledo (G-4520)

AUTOMOTIVE REPAIR SHOPS: Engine Rebuilding

Maags Automotive & Mch Inc .... G 419 626-1539
 Sandusky (G-13076)

AUTOMOTIVE REPAIR SHOPS: Engine Repair

Heisley Tire & Brake Inc .... F 440 357-9797
 Mentor (G-10468)

AUTOMOTIVE REPAIR SHOPS: Machine Shop

Mc Machine Llc .... E 216 398-3666
 Cleveland (G-4378)
RL Best Company .... E 330 758-8601
 Boardman (G-1517)
Tuf-Tug Inc .... F 937 299-1213
 Moraine (G-11216)

AUTOMOTIVE REPAIR SHOPS: Muffler Shop, Sale/Rpr/Installation

PRODUCT SECTION — AUTOMOTIVE SPLYS & PARTS, NEW, WHOLESALE: Trailer Parts

Mark Knupp Muffler & Tire Inc............ E 937 773-1334
  Piqua (G-12535)

AUTOMOTIVE REPAIR SHOPS: Rebuilding & Retreading Tires

Bell Tire Co.. F 440 234-8022
  Olmsted Falls (G-12076)
Bridgestone Ret Operations LLC........... G 740 592-3075
  Athens (G-677)
Bridgestone Ret Operations LLC........... G 330 454-9478
  Canton (G-2053)
Bridgestone Ret Operations LLC........... G 440 461-4747
  Cleveland (G-3757)
Bridgestone Ret Operations LLC........... G 216 229-2550
  Cleveland (G-3758)
Bridgestone Ret Operations LLC........... G 216 382-8970
  Cleveland (G-3759)
Bridgestone Ret Operations LLC........... F 614 864-3350
  Columbus (G-5214)
Bridgestone Ret Operations LLC........... F 614 491-8062
  Columbus (G-5215)
Bridgestone Ret Operations LLC........... G 614 224-4221
  Columbus (G-5216)
Bridgestone Ret Operations LLC........... G 440 324-3327
  Elyria (G-7117)
Bridgestone Ret Operations LLC........... G 440 365-8308
  Elyria (G-7118)
Bridgestone Ret Operations LLC........... G 937 548-1197
  Greenville (G-8039)
Bridgestone Ret Operations LLC........... G 513 868-7399
  Hamilton (G-8186)
Bridgestone Ret Operations LLC........... G 330 673-1700
  Kent (G-8803)
Bridgestone Ret Operations LLC........... G 614 861-7994
  Reynoldsburg (G-12756)
Bridgestone Ret Operations LLC........... G 330 758-0921
  Youngstown (G-16325)
Bridgestone Ret Operations LLC........... G 330 759-3697
  Youngstown (G-16326)
Grismer Tire Company........................... E 937 643-2526
  Centerville (G-2363)
Heartland Retreaders Inc...................... F 740 472-0558
  Woodsfield (G-16087)
K S Bandag Inc...................................... E 330 264-9237
  Wooster (G-16139)
Premier Bandag Inc.............................. F 513 248-8850
  Milford (G-10918)
Ziegler Tire and Supply Co.................... E 330 343-7739
  Dover (G-6850)

AUTOMOTIVE REPAIR SHOPS: Tire Recapping

Best One Tire & Svc Lima Inc................ G 419 425-3322
  Findlay (G-7484)
Best One Tire & Svc Lima Inc................ E 419 229-2380
  Lima (G-9223)
Central Ohio Bandag LP........................ F 740 454-9728
  Zanesville (G-16520)
Custom Recapping Inc.......................... G 937 324-4331
  Springfield (G-13550)
JTL Enterprises LLC.............................. E 937 890-8189
  Dayton (G-6392)
Mitchell Bros Tire Rtread Svc................ G 740 353-1551
  Portsmouth (G-12649)
Skinner Firestone Inc........................... F 740 984-4247
  Beverly (G-1321)

AUTOMOTIVE REPAIR SHOPS: Tire Repair Shop

AB Tire & Repair.................................... G 440 543-2929
  Chagrin Falls (G-2386)
Associates Tire and Svc Inc................... F 937 436-4692
  Centerville (G-2359)
Big Oki LLC... E 513 874-1111
  Fairfield (G-7338)
Bob Sumerel Tire Company Inc............. G 740 927-2811
  Reynoldsburg (G-12755)
Bridgestone Ret Operations LLC........... G 440 842-3200
  Cleveland (G-3756)
Bridgestone Ret Operations LLC........... F 740 397-5601
  Mount Vernon (G-11265)
Colyer C & Sons Truck Service.............. G 513 563-0663
  Cincinnati (G-2781)
Exit 11 Truck Tire Service..................... G 330 659-6372
  Richfield (G-12786)
Fleet Relief Company............................ G 419 525-2625
  Mansfield (G-9657)
Forklift Tire East Mich Inc..................... F 586 771-1330
  Toledo (G-14292)
Goodyear Tire & Rubber Company........ G 330 966-1274
  Canton (G-2116)
Goodyear Tire & Rubber Company........ G 330 759-9343
  Youngstown (G-16371)
Gt Tire Service Inc............................... G 740 927-7226
  Pataskala (G-12298)
Heisley Tire & Brake Inc....................... F 440 357-9797
  Mentor (G-10468)
L & O Tire Service Inc.......................... G 937 394-8462
  Anna (G-490)
Mark Knupp Muffler & Tire Inc.............. E 937 773-1334
  Piqua (G-12535)
North Coast Tire Co Inc....................... G 216 447-1690
  Cleveland (G-4473)
Ntb National Tire and Battery............... G 614 870-8945
  Columbus (G-5606)
Paul Shovlin... G 330 757-0032
  Youngstown (G-16416)
Philip Radke.. G 614 475-6788
  Columbus (G-5673)
Swiss Valley Tire LLC........................... G 330 231-6187
  Wilmot (G-16069)
Wayne A Whaley.................................. G 330 525-7779
  Homeworth (G-8556)
Ziegler Tire and Supply Co.................... G 330 434-7126
  Akron (G-381)

AUTOMOTIVE REPAIR SHOPS: Trailer Repair

J & L Body Inc..................................... F 216 661-2323
  Brooklyn Heights (G-1693)
M & W Trailers Inc............................... F 419 453-3331
  Ottoville (G-12201)
Mac Trailer Manufacturing Inc............. A 800 795-8454
  Alliance (G-411)
Nelson Manufacturing Company........... D 419 523-5321
  Ottawa (G-12185)

AUTOMOTIVE REPAIR SHOPS: Truck Engine Repair, Exc Indl

Carl E Oeder Sons Sand & Grav............ F 513 494-1555
  Lebanon (G-9066)
Fleetpride Inc...................................... E 740 282-2711
  Steubenville (G-13667)
Kaffenbarger Truck Eqp Co.................. E 513 772-6800
  Cincinnati (G-3056)
Kinstle Truck & Auto Svc Inc................ F 419 738-7493
  Wapakoneta (G-15120)
Sutphen Towers Inc............................. D 614 876-1262
  Hilliard (G-8444)

AUTOMOTIVE REPAIR SVC

East Manufacturing Corporation........... B 330 325-9921
  Randolph (G-12697)
Goodyear Tire & Rubber Company........ A 330 796-2121
  Akron (G-171)
J & J Tire & Alignment......................... G 330 424-5200
  Lisbon (G-9316)
Jordon Auto Service & Tire Inc............. G 216 214-6528
  Cleveland (G-4259)
Maags Automotive & Mch Inc............... G 419 626-1539
  Sandusky (G-13076)
Midwest Muffler Pros & More............... G 937 293-2450
  Moraine (G-11195)
Mikes Transm & Auto Svc LLC............. F 330 799-8266
  Youngstown (G-16401)

AUTOMOTIVE SPLYS & PARTS, NEW, WHOL: Auto Servicing Eqpt

D & J Electric Motor Repair Co............. F 330 336-4343
  Wadsworth (G-15025)
Tuffy Manufacturing............................. F 330 940-2356
  Cuyahoga Falls (G-6125)

AUTOMOTIVE SPLYS & PARTS, NEW, WHOLESALE: Clutches

All Wright Enterprises LLC................... G 440 259-5656
  Perry (G-12349)

AUTOMOTIVE SPLYS & PARTS, NEW, WHOLESALE: Engines/Eng Parts

Interstate Diesel Service Inc................. C 216 881-0015
  Cleveland (G-4233)
Mahle Behr Mt Sterling Inc................... B 740 869-3333
  Mount Sterling (G-11256)
Ultra-Met Company............................. F 937 653-7133
  Urbana (G-14851)

AUTOMOTIVE SPLYS & PARTS, NEW, WHOLESALE: Filters, Air & Oil

OSI Environmental LLC......................... E 440 237-4600
  North Royalton (G-11890)

AUTOMOTIVE SPLYS & PARTS, NEW, WHOLESALE: Splys

Autobody Supply Company Inc............. D 614 228-4328
  Columbus (G-5166)
Finale Products Inc.............................. G 419 874-2662
  Perrysburg (G-12381)
Finishmaster Inc.................................. F 614 228-4328
  Groveport (G-8139)

AUTOMOTIVE SPLYS & PARTS, NEW, WHOLESALE: Stampings

Namoh Ohio Holdings Inc..................... E
  Norwood (G-11996)
T A Bacon Co....................................... E 216 851-1404
  Chesterland (G-2489)

AUTOMOTIVE SPLYS & PARTS, NEW, WHOLESALE: Tools & Eqpt

Cedar Elec Holdings Corp.................... D 773 804-6288
  West Chester (G-15388)
Matco Tools Corporation...................... B 330 929-4949
  Stow (G-13708)
Myers Industries Inc............................ E 330 253-5592
  Akron (G-260)

Employee Codes: A=Over 500 employees, B=251-500
C=101-250, D=51-100, E=20-50, F=10-19, G=1-9

AUTOMOTIVE SPLYS & PARTS, NEW, WHOLESALE: Trailer Parts

AUTOMOTIVE SPLYS & PARTS, NEW, WHOLESALE: Trailer Parts

Frontier Tank Center Inc .... F 330 659-3888
  Richfield *(G-12788)*
Ohio Trailer Supply Inc .... G 614 471-9121
  Columbus *(G-5629)*

AUTOMOTIVE SPLYS & PARTS, NEW, WHOLESALE: Wheels

Starr Wheel Group Inc .... F 954 935-5536
  Warren *(G-15206)*
The Hamilton Caster & Mfg Company ... D 513 863-3300
  Hamilton *(G-8248)*
United Wheel and Hub LLC .... G 419 483-2639
  Sandusky *(G-13100)*
Wings N Wheels .... G 419 586-6531
  Celina *(G-2356)*

AUTOMOTIVE SPLYS & PARTS, WHOLESALE, NEC

Accel Performance Group LLC .... C 216 658-6413
  Independence *(G-8651)*
Alegre Inc .... F 937 885-6786
  Miamisburg *(G-10609)*
Bendix Coml Vhcl Systems LLC .... B 440 329-9000
  Avon *(G-763)*
Brookville Roadster Inc .... F 937 833-4605
  Brookville *(G-1730)*
D-G Custom Chrome LLC .... G 513 531-1881
  Cincinnati *(G-2815)*
Gmelectric Inc .... G 330 477-3392
  Canton *(G-2114)*
Hite Parts Exchange Inc .... F 614 272-5115
  Columbus *(G-5442)*
Mader Automotive Center Inc .... G 937 339-2681
  Troy *(G-14595)*
Martin Diesel Inc .... E 419 782-9911
  Defiance *(G-6691)*
Ohashi Technica USA Inc .... E 740 965-5115
  Sunbury *(G-13960)*
Ohio Auto Supply Company .... F 330 454-5105
  Canton *(G-2182)*
Pioneer Automotive Tech Inc .... C 937 746-2293
  Miamisburg *(G-10670)*
Qualitor Subsidiary H Inc .... C 419 562-7987
  Bucyrus *(G-1865)*
Sims Bros Inc .... D 740 387-9041
  Marion *(G-9883)*
TS Trim Industries Inc .... B 614 837-4114
  Canal Winchester *(G-1993)*
Vintage Automotive Elc Inc .... F 419 472-9349
  Toledo *(G-14520)*
Wis 1985 Inc .... F 423 581-4916
  Dayton *(G-6657)*

AUTOMOTIVE SPLYS/PART, NEW, WHOL: Spring, Shock Absorb/Strut

Thyssenkrupp Bilstein Amer Inc .... C 513 881-7600
  Hamilton *(G-8249)*

AUTOMOTIVE SVCS, EXC REPAIR & CARWASHES: Trailer Maintenance

J & L Body Inc .... F 216 661-2323
  Brooklyn Heights *(G-1693)*

AUTOMOTIVE SVCS, EXC RPR/CARWASHES: High Perf Auto Rpr/Svc

Mikes Transm & Auto Svc LLC .... F 330 799-8266
  Youngstown *(G-16401)*

AUTOMOTIVE TRANSMISSION REPAIR SVC

Bob Sumerel Tire Co Inc .... F 330 769-9092
  Seville *(G-13140)*
Bob Sumerel Tire Company .... G 330 262-1220
  Wooster *(G-16105)*
Mikes Transm & Auto Svc LLC .... F 330 799-8266
  Youngstown *(G-16401)*
Power Acquisition LLC .... D 614 228-5000
  Dublin *(G-6925)*
Rumpke Transportation Co LLC .... F 513 851-0122
  Cincinnati *(G-3355)*
Tri-W Group Inc .... A 614 228-5000
  Columbus *(G-5837)*
W W Williams Company LLC .... D 614 228-5000
  Dublin *(G-6958)*

AUTOMOTIVE WELDING SVCS

Brock RAD Wldg Fabrication Inc .... G 740 773-2540
  Chillicothe *(G-2496)*
Brown Industrial Inc .... E 937 693-3838
  Botkins *(G-1542)*
Industry Products Co .... B 937 778-0585
  Piqua *(G-12526)*
McGregor Mtal Leffel Works LLC .... D 937 325-5561
  Springfield *(G-13603)*
Perkins Motor Service Ltd .... F 440 277-1256
  Lorain *(G-9430)*
Process Eqp Co Wldg Svcs LLC .... G 937 667-4451
  Tipp City *(G-14149)*
R K Industries Inc .... D 419 523-5001
  Ottawa *(G-12190)*
Turn-Key Industrial Svcs LLC .... D 614 274-1128
  Grove City *(G-8127)*

AUTOMOTIVE: Bodies

Monarch Plastic Inc .... F 330 683-0822
  Orrville *(G-12137)*
Scottrods LLC .... G 419 499-2705
  Monroeville *(G-11125)*

AUTOMOTIVE: Seat Frames, Metal

Camaco LLC .... A 440 288-4444
  Lorain *(G-9405)*
Jay Mid-South LLC .... E 256 439-6600
  Mansfield *(G-9672)*
Pfi USA .... F 937 547-0413
  Greenville *(G-8055)*

AUTOMOTIVE: Seating

Clarios LLC .... D 419 636-4211
  Bryan *(G-1814)*
Clarios LLC .... E 440 205-7221
  Mentor *(G-10438)*
Commercial Vehicle Group Inc .... B 614 289-5360
  New Albany *(G-11374)*
Evenflo Company Inc .... E 937 415-3300
  Miamisburg *(G-10638)*
Group Endeavor LLC .... D 234 571-5096
  Akron *(G-174)*
Jay Industries Inc .... A 419 747-4161
  Mansfield *(G-9671)*
Johnson Controls Inc .... E 216 587-0100
  Brecksville *(G-1624)*
Johnson Controls Inc .... D 513 489-0950
  Cincinnati *(G-3048)*
Johnson Controls Inc .... F 513 671-6338
  Cincinnati *(G-3049)*
Johnson Controls Inc .... D 614 895-6600
  Westerville *(G-15712)*
Johnson Controls Inc .... E 330 270-4385
  Youngstown *(G-16385)*
Magna International Amer Inc .... C 330 824-3101
  Sheffield Village *(G-13185)*
Setex Inc .... B 419 394-7800
  Saint Marys *(G-12967)*

AUTOTRANSFORMERS: Electric

SGB Usa Inc .... G 330 472-1187
  Tallmadge *(G-4046)*

AVIATION SCHOOL

Flightsafety International Inc .... C 614 324-3500
  Columbus *(G-380)*

AWNINGS & CANOPIES: Awnings, Fabric, From Purchased Matls

ABC Signs Inc .... F 513 241-8884
  Cincinnati *(G-2590)*
Awning Fabricaters Inc .... G 216 476-4888
  Cleveland *(G-3712)*
Canvas Specialty Mfg Co .... G 216 881-0647
  Cleveland *(G-3785)*
Capital City Awning Company .... E 614 221-5404
  Columbus *(G-5231)*
Fabric Forms Inc .... E 513 281-6300
  Cincinnati *(G-2893)*
Glawe Manufacturing Co Inc .... G 937 754-0064
  Fairborn *(G-317)*
Main Awning & Tent Inc .... G 513 621-6947
  Cincinnati *(G-3127)*
Ohio Awning & Manufacturing Co .... E 216 861-2400
  Cleveland *(G-4494)*
ONeals Tarpaulin & Awning Co .... F 330 788-6504
  Youngstown *(G-16406)*
Queen City Awning & Tent Co .... E 513 530-9660
  Cincinnati *(G-3315)*
Schaaf Co Inc .... G 513 241-7044
  Cincinnati *(G-3367)*
South Akron Awning Co .... F 330 848-7611
  Akron *(G-313)*
Tarped Out Inc .... E 330 325-7722
  Ravenna *(G-12738)*

AWNINGS: Fiberglass

PCR Restorations Inc .... F 419 747-7957
  Mansfield *(G-9709)*
Superior Fibers Inc .... B 740 394-2491
  Shawnee *(G-13177)*

AWNINGS: Metal

Alumetal Manufacturing Company .... E 419 268-2311
  Coldwater *(G-4981)*
Crest Products Inc .... F 440 942-5770
  Mentor *(G-10446)*
General Awning Company Inc .... F 216 749-0110
  Cleveland *(G-4111)*
Joyce Manufacturing Co .... D 440 239-9100
  Berea *(G-286)*
Toledo Window & Awning Inc .... F 419 474-3396
  Toledo *(G-14509)*
Youngstown Shade & Alum LLC .... G 330 782-2373
  Youngstown *(G-16487)*

AXLES

Alta Mira Corporation .... D 330 648-2461
  Spencer *(G-13479)*
Meritor Inc .... C 740 348-3270
  Granville *(G-8020)*
Schafer Driveline LLC .... F 740 694-2055
  Fredericktown *(G-7753)*

PRODUCT SECTION — BAKERIES, COMMERCIAL: On Premises Baking Only

Spencer Manufacturing Company Inc .... D 330 648-2461
  Spencer *(G-13484)*

BACKHOES
Donald E Dornon .... G 740 926-9144
  Beallsville *(G-1034)*

BADGES: Identification & Insignia
Identiphoto Co Ltd .... F 440 306-9000
  Willoughby *(G-15930)*

BAGS & CONTAINERS: Textile, Exc Sleeping
Baggallini Inc .... F 800 448-8753
  Pickerington *(G-12456)*

BAGS & SACKS: Shipping & Shopping
Pantrybag .... F 614 927-8744
  Columbus *(G-5654)*

BAGS: Canvas
American Made Bags LLC .... F 330 475-1385
  Akron *(G-59)*
Capital City Awning Company .... E 614 221-5404
  Columbus *(G-5231)*

BAGS: Cellophane
Buckeye Boxes Inc .... D 614 274-8484
  Columbus *(G-5219)*

BAGS: Duffle, Canvas, Made From Purchased Materials
R J Manray Inc .... G 330 559-6716
  Canfield *(G-2015)*

BAGS: Food Storage & Frozen Food, Plastic
Global Plastic Tech Inc .... G 440 879-6045
  Lorain *(G-9412)*

BAGS: Food Storage & Trash, Plastic
American Plastics LLC .... C 419 423-1213
  Findlay *(G-7476)*

BAGS: Paper
A To Z Paper Box Company .... G 330 325-8722
  Rootstown *(G-12850)*
Dazpak Flexible Packaging Corp .... C 614 252-2121
  Columbus *(G-5318)*
Ray C Sprosty Bag Co Inc .... F 330 669-0045
  Smithville *(G-13301)*
Ricking Holding Co .... E 513 825-3551
  Cleveland *(G-4633)*

BAGS: Paper, Made From Purchased Materials
Ecopac LLC .... G 732 715-0236
  Cincinnati *(G-2858)*
Greif Inc .... E 740 657-6500
  Delaware *(G-6725)*
Greif Inc .... E 740 549-6000
  Delaware *(G-6724)*

BAGS: Plastic
Automated Packg Systems Inc .... E 330 342-2000
  Bedford *(G-1103)*
Automated Packg Systems Inc .... C 216 663-2000
  Cleveland *(G-3702)*
Buckeye Packaging Co Inc .... D 330 935-0301
  Alliance *(G-396)*
Command Plastic Corporation .... F 800 321-8001
  Bedford *(G-1112)*

Flavorseal LLC .... D 440 937-3900
  Avon *(G-774)*
Hood Packaging Corporation .... C 937 382-6681
  Wilmington *(G-16053)*
Kennedy Group Incorporated .... D 440 951-7660
  Willoughby *(G-15939)*
Noramco Inc .... D 216 531-3400
  Euclid *(G-7288)*
Packaging Materials Inc .... E 740 432-6337
  Cambridge *(G-1946)*
Pitt Plastics Inc .... D 614 868-8660
  Columbus *(G-5675)*
Safeway Packaging Inc .... E 419 629-3200
  New Bremen *(G-11408)*
Signature Flexible Packg LLC .... F 614 252-2121
  Columbus *(G-5769)*

BAGS: Plastic & Pliofilm
Charter Nex Films - Delaware Oh Inc .... E 740 369-2770
  Delaware *(G-6708)*
Engineered Films Division Inc .... D 419 884-8150
  Lexington *(G-9201)*
General Films Inc .... D 888 436-3456
  Covington *(G-6023)*
North American Plas Chem Inc .... E 216 531-3400
  Euclid *(G-7290)*

BAGS: Plastic, Made From Purchased Materials
Ampac Holdings LLC .... A 513 671-1777
  Cincinnati *(G-2622)*
B K Plastics Inc .... G 937 473-2087
  Covington *(G-6019)*
Cpg - Ohio LLC .... D 513 825-4800
  Cincinnati *(G-2800)*
Crayex Corporation .... D 937 773-7000
  Piqua *(G-12511)*
Custom Poly Bag LLC .... D 330 935-2408
  Alliance *(G-399)*
Dazpak Flexible Packaging Corp .... C 614 252-2121
  Columbus *(G-5318)*
Liqui-Box Corporation .... E 419 289-9696
  Ashland *(G-589)*

BAGS: Rubber Or Rubberized Fabric
Midwestern Bag Co Inc .... G 419 241-3112
  Toledo *(G-14386)*
Timco Rubber Products Inc .... E 216 267-6242
  Berea *(G-1296)*

BAGS: Shipping
Hood Packaging Corporation .... C 937 382-6681
  Wilmington *(G-16053)*

BAGS: Shopping, Made From Purchased Materials
Ampac Holdings LLC .... A 513 671-1777
  Cincinnati *(G-2622)*

BAGS: Textile
Baggallini Inc .... F 800 448-8753
  Pickerington *(G-12456)*

BAKERIES, COMMERCIAL: On Premises Baking Only
614 Cupcakes LLC .... G 614 245-8800
  New Albany *(G-11363)*
Amish Door Inc .... C 330 359-5464
  Wilmot *(G-16065)*

Arlington Valley Farms LLC .... E 216 426-5000
  Hudson *(G-8586)*
Blf Enterprises Inc .... F 937 642-6425
  Westerville *(G-15694)*
Bread Kneads Inc .... G 419 422-3863
  Findlay *(G-7486)*
Breaking Bread Pizza Company .... G 614 754-4777
  Columbus *(G-5059)*
Buns of Delaware Inc .... E 740 363-2867
  Delaware *(G-6706)*
Chestnut Land Company .... G 330 652-1939
  Niles *(G-11663)*
Cincy Cupcakes LLC .... F 513 985-4440
  Cincinnati *(G-2764)*
DC Orrville Inc .... F 330 683-0646
  Orrville *(G-12123)*
Flowers Baking Co Ohio LLC .... E 937 260-4412
  Dayton *(G-6336)*
Flowers Baking Co Ohio LLC .... E 419 269-9202
  Toledo *(G-14290)*
Fragapane Bakeries Inc .... G 440 779-6050
  North Olmsted *(G-11823)*
Gardner Pie Company .... C 330 245-2030
  Coventry Township *(G-6010)*
Garys Chesecakes Fine Desserts ...... G 513 574-1700
  Cincinnati *(G-2932)*
Graeters Ice Cream Company .... D 513 721-3323
  Cincinnati *(G-2968)*
Harvest Commissary LLC .... E 513 706-1951
  Granville *(G-8017)*
Heinens Inc .... C 330 562-5297
  Aurora *(G-718)*
Hot Mama Foods Inc .... F 419 474-3402
  Toledo *(G-14321)*
Interbake Foods LLC .... D 614 294-4931
  Columbus *(G-5471)*
Kellanova .... B 513 271-3500
  Cincinnati *(G-3072)*
Kennedys Bakery Inc .... F 740 432-2301
  Cambridge *(G-1938)*
Klosterman Baking Co LLC .... D 513 242-5667
  Cincinnati *(G-3081)*
Main Street Gourmet LLC .... C 330 929-0000
  Cuyahoga Falls *(G-6101)*
Meeks Pastry Shop .... G 419 782-4871
  Defiance *(G-6692)*
Morgan4140 LLC .... F 513 873-1426
  Cincinnati *(G-3173)*
Mustard Seed Health Fd Mkt Inc .... E 440 519-3663
  Solon *(G-13394)*
Osmans Pies Inc .... E 330 607-9083
  Stow *(G-13716)*
Pesce Bakery Company Ltd .... G 330 746-6537
  Youngstown *(G-16417)*
Pf Management Inc .... G 513 874-8741
  West Chester *(G-15575)*
Pierre Holding Corp .... G 513 874-8741
  West Chester *(G-15576)*
Pretzelhaus Bakery LLC .... G 513 906-2017
  West Chester *(G-15485)*
Quality Bakery Company Inc .... C 614 224-1424
  Columbus *(G-5702)*
Rich Products Corporation .... C 614 771-1117
  Hilliard *(G-8436)*
Riesbeck Food Markets Inc .... C 740 695-3401
  Saint Clairsville *(G-12921)*
Schulers Bakery Inc .... E 937 323-4154
  Springfield *(G-13630)*
Schwebel Baking Company .... G 330 783-2860
  Hebron *(G-8361)*
Schwebel Baking Company .... G 330 926-9410
  North Canton *(G-11758)*

Employee Codes: A=Over 500 employees, B=251-500
C=101-250, D=51-100, E=20-50, F=10-19, G=1-9

BAKERIES, COMMERCIAL: On Premises Baking Only

Schwebel Baking Company .... G 330 783-2860
 Youngstown (G-16434)
Schwebel Baking Company .... B 330 783-2860
 Youngstown (G-16433)
Servatii Inc .... G 513 271-5040
 Cincinnati (G-3383)
Thurns Bakery & Deli .... F 614 221-9246
 Columbus (G-5825)
Unger Kosher Bakery Inc .... F 216 321-7176
 Cleveland Heights (G-4944)
Uprising Food Inc .... G 513 313-1087
 Cincinnati (G-3484)
White Castle System Inc .... B 614 228-5781
 Columbus (G-5876)

BAKERIES: On Premises Baking & Consumption

Alfred Nickles Bakery Inc .... E 740 453-6522
 Zanesville (G-16498)
Buns of Delaware Inc .... E 740 363-2867
 Delaware (G-6706)
Crumbs Inc .... F 740 592-3803
 Athens (G-680)
Fragapane Bakeries Inc .... G 440 779-6050
 North Olmsted (G-11823)
Giminetti Baking Company .... F 513 751-7655
 Cincinnati (G-2951)
Minus G LLC .... G 440 817-0338
 Newbury (G-11630)
Osmans Pies Inc .... E 330 607-9083
 Stow (G-13716)
Pepperidge Farm Incorporated .... G 419 933-2611
 Willard (G-15863)
Thurns Bakery & Deli .... F 614 221-9246
 Columbus (G-5825)

BAKERY MACHINERY

Coperion Food Equipment LLC .... E 937 492-4158
 Sidney (G-13239)
Fred D Pfening Company .... G 614 294-5361
 Columbus (G-5388)
Ingredient Masters Inc .... G 513 231-7432
 Batavia (G-926)
Magna Machine Co .... C 513 851-6900
 Cincinnati (G-3125)
Peerless Foods Inc .... D 937 492-4158
 Sidney (G-13270)
the Perfect Score Company .... F 440 439-9320
 Bedford Heights (G-1179)

BAKERY PRDTS: Bakery Prdts, Partially Cooked, Exc frozen

Suelos Sweetz LLC .... G 440 478-1301
 Willowick (G-16036)
Toast With Cake LLC .... G 937 554-5900
 Miamisburg (G-10695)

BAKERY PRDTS: Biscuits, Dry

Consolidated Biscuit Company .... F 419 293-2911
 Mc Comb (G-10268)
Kellanova .... B 513 271-3500
 Cincinnati (G-3072)

BAKERY PRDTS: Bread, All Types, Fresh Or Frozen

Brooks Pastries Inc .... G 614 274-4880
 Plain City (G-12567)
New York Frozen Foods Inc .... B 216 292-5655
 Bedford (G-1144)

Orlando Baking Company .... B 216 361-1872
 Cleveland (G-4509)

BAKERY PRDTS: Buns, Bread Type, Fresh Or Frozen

B & J Baking Company .... F 513 541-2386
 Cincinnati (G-2649)
New Horizons Baking Co LLC .... C 419 668-8226
 Norwalk (G-11980)
New York Frozen Foods Inc .... E 626 338-3000
 Westerville (G-15670)

BAKERY PRDTS: Cakes, Bakery, Exc Frozen

Beckers Bake Shop Inc .... G 216 752-4161
 Broadview Heights (G-1655)
Cake House Cleveland LLC .... F 216 870-4659
 Cleveland (G-3782)
Uncle Jays Cakes LLC .... G 513 882-3433
 Cincinnati (G-3476)

BAKERY PRDTS: Cakes, Bakery, Frozen

Kissicakes-N-Sweets LLC .... G 614 940-2779
 Columbus (G-5511)

BAKERY PRDTS: Cones, Ice Cream

Frischco Inc .... F 740 363-7537
 Delaware (G-6723)
Norse Dairy Systems LP .... B 614 294-4931
 Columbus (G-5601)

BAKERY PRDTS: Cookies

Beckers Bake Shop Inc .... G 216 752-4161
 Broadview Heights (G-1655)
Cleveland Bean Sprout Inc .... F 216 881-2112
 Cleveland (G-3832)
Great American Cookie Company .... F 419 474-9417
 Toledo (G-14302)
Hearthside Food Solutions LLC .... A 419 293-2911
 Mc Comb (G-10270)
Interbake Foods LLC .... D 614 294-4931
 Columbus (G-5471)
Keebler Company .... D 513 271-3500
 Cincinnati (G-3071)
Pepperidge Farm Incorporated .... G 419 933-2611
 Willard (G-15863)
Yz Enterprises Inc .... E 419 893-8777
 Maumee (G-10246)

BAKERY PRDTS: Cookies & crackers

Blf Enterprises Inc .... F 937 642-6425
 Westerville (G-15694)
Cheryl & Co .... F 614 776-1500
 Obetz (G-12058)
Cookie Bouquets Inc .... G 614 888-2171
 Columbus (G-5293)
Kennedys Bakery Inc .... F 740 432-2301
 Cambridge (G-1938)
Main Street Gourmet LLC .... C 330 929-0000
 Cuyahoga Falls (G-6101)
Norcia Bakery .... F 330 454-1077
 Canton (G-2174)
Osmans Pies Inc .... E 330 607-9083
 Stow (G-13716)
Rudys Strudel Shop .... G 440 886-4430
 Cleveland (G-4662)
Schulers Bakery Inc .... E 937 323-4154
 Springfield (G-13630)

BAKERY PRDTS: Doughnuts, Exc Frozen

Crispie Creme Chillicothe Inc .... G 740 774-3770
 Chillicothe (G-2500)

Dandi Enterprises Inc .... F 419 516-9070
 Solon (G-13330)
Donut Place Kings Inc .... G 937 829-9725
 Dayton (G-6300)
Mary Ann Donut Shoppe Inc .... G 330 478-1655
 Canton (G-2152)
McHappys Donuts of Parkersburg .... D 740 593-8744
 Athens (G-687)
Wal-Bon of Ohio Inc .... F 740 423-8178
 Belpre (G-1262)

BAKERY PRDTS: Dry

Cerelia USA Corp .... E 614 471-9994
 Columbus (G-3243)
Good Fortunes Inc .... G 440 942-2888
 Willoughby (G-15926)

BAKERY PRDTS: Frozen

Big Mouth Egg Rolls LLC .... F 614 404-3607
 Columbus (G-5186)
Main Street Gourmet LLC .... C 330 929-0000
 Cuyahoga Falls (G-6101)
Pepperidge Farm Incorporated .... G 419 933-2611
 Willard (G-15863)

BAKERY PRDTS: Pastries, Exc Frozen

Krispy Kreme Doughnut Corp .... E 614 798-0812
 Columbus (G-5515)
Krispy Kreme Doughnut Corp .... D 614 876-0058
 Columbus (G-5516)

BAKERY PRDTS: Pies, Bakery, Frozen

Gardner Pie Company .... C 330 245-2030
 Coventry Township (G-6010)

BAKERY PRDTS: Pies, Exc Frozen

K & B Acquisitions Inc .... F 937 253-1163
 Dayton (G-696)
Papa Joes Pies Inc .... F 440 960-7437
 Amherst (G-481)

BAKERY PRDTS: Pretzels

Ditsch Usa LLC .... E 513 782-8888
 Cincinnati (G-2830)

BAKERY PRDTS: Rice Cakes

Basic Grain Products Inc .... D 419 678-2304
 Coldwater (G-4982)

BAKERY PRDTS: Wholesalers

Busken Bakery Inc .... D 513 871-2114
 Cincinnati (G-2695)
Ditsch Usa LLC .... E 513 782-8888
 Cincinnati (G-2830)
Food Plant Engineering LLC .... F 513 618-3165
 Blue Ash (G-1396)
Klosterman Baking Co LLC .... D 513 242-5667
 Cincinnati (G-3081)
Osmans Pies Inc .... E 330 607-9083
 Stow (G-13716)
Thurns Bakery & Deli .... F 614 221-9246
 Columbus (G-5825)
Unger Kosher Bakery Inc .... F 216 321-7176
 Cleveland Heights (G-4944)

BAKERY Wholesale Or Wholesale & Retail Combined

Alfred Nickles Bakery Inc .... E 740 453-6522
 Zanesville (G-16498)
Bimbo Bkries USA Clvland Hts D .... G 216 641-5700
 Cleveland (G-3737)

PRODUCT SECTION — BATTERIES: Storage

Bimbo Qsr Us LLC .... G 740 562-4188
　Zanesville (G-16509)
Calvary Christian Ch of Ohio .... F 740 828-9000
　Frazeysburg (G-7714)
Country Crust Bakery .... G 888 860-2940
　Bainbridge (G-830)
Crumbs Inc. .... F 740 592-3803
　Athens (G-680)
DUrso Bakery Inc .... F 330 652-4741
　Niles (G-11667)
Evans Bakery Inc .... G 937 228-4151
　Dayton (G-6326)
Gawa Traders Wholesale & Dist. ...... E 614 697-1440
　Columbus (G-5396)
Gibson Bros Inc .... F 440 774-2401
　Oberlin (G-12051)
Giminetti Baking Company .... F 513 751-7655
　Cincinnati (G-2951)
Home Bakery .... F 419 678-3018
　Coldwater (G-4993)
Imeldas Baking Company LLC .... G 937 484-5405
　Urbana (G-14837)
Killer Brownie Ltd .... D 937 535-5690
　Miamisburg (G-10651)
Klosterman Baking Co .... F 513 398-2707
　Mason (G-10017)
Klosterman Baking Co LLC .... E 513 242-1004
　Cincinnati (G-3082)
McL Inc. .... E 614 861-6259
　Columbus (G-5554)
Norcia Bakery .... F 330 454-1077
　Canton (G-2174)
Rudys Strudel Shop .... G 440 886-4430
　Cleveland (G-4662)
Scheiders Foods LLC .... F 740 404-6641
　Mount Perry (G-11252)
Schwebel Baking Company .... G 440 846-1921
　Strongsville (G-13875)
Skyliner .... G 740 738-0874
　Bridgeport (G-1649)
Studgionsgroup LLC .... E 216 804-1561
　Cleveland (G-4743)
Sweet Persuasions LLC .... G 614 216-9052
　Pickerington (G-12471)
Wal-Bon of Ohio Inc .... F 740 423-6351
　Belpre (G-1261)

BALLOONS: Toy & Advertising, Rubber

MCR of Norwalk Inc .... E 419 668-8261
　Norwalk (G-11979)
Perfect Products Company .... E
　Malvern (G-9614)
Scherba Industries Inc .... D 330 273-3200
　Brunswick (G-1790)

BANNERS: Fabric

Party Animal Inc. .... F 440 471-1030
　Westlake (G-15771)

BANQUET HALL FACILITIES

Buns of Delaware Inc. .... E 740 363-2867
　Delaware (G-6706)
Mustard Seed Health Fd Mkt Inc .... E 440 519-3663
　Solon (G-13394)
Vulcan Machinery Corporation .... E 330 376-6025
　Akron (G-371)

BAR

Bajio Brewing Company LLC .... G 419 410-8275
　Toledo (G-14205)
Great Lakes Brewing Co .... C 216 771-4404
　Cleveland (G-4142)

BAR FIXTURES: Wood

Ingle-Barr Inc .... D 740 702-6117
　Chillicothe (G-2513)

BAR JOISTS & CONCRETE REINFORCING BARS: Fabricated

Foundation Systems Anchors Inc. ... F 330 454-1700
　Canton (G-2104)
Worthington Enterprises Inc .... C 614 438-3210
　Worthington (G-16220)

BARBECUE EQPT

Gosun Inc. .... F 888 868-6154
　Cincinnati (G-2966)

BARGES BUILDING & REPAIR

McGinnis Inc. .... C 740 377-4391
　South Point (G-13470)
McNational Inc. .... D 740 377-4391
　South Point (G-13471)
O-Kan Marine Repair Inc .... E 740 446-4686
　Gallipolis (G-7897)
Superior Marine Ways Inc .... C 740 894-6224
　Proctorville (G-12687)

BARRICADES: Metal

Df Supply Inc. .... E 330 650-9226
　Twinsburg (G-14650)

BARS & BAR SHAPES: Copper & Copper Alloy

Avtron Aerospace Inc .... C 216 750-5152
　Cleveland (G-3709)

BARS & BAR SHAPES: Steel, Hot-Rolled

McDonald Steel Corporation .... D 330 530-9118
　Mc Donald (G-10279)

BARS, COLD FINISHED: Steel, From Purchased Hot-Rolled

Telling Industries LLC .... E 740 435-8900
　Cambridge (G-1958)
Telling Industries LLC .... F 440 974-3370
　Willoughby (G-16004)

BARS: Concrete Reinforcing, Fabricated Steel

Action Group Inc. .... D 614 868-8868
　Blacklick (G-1330)
Akron Rebar Co. .... E
　Akron (G-42)
Austintown Metal Works Inc .... F 330 259-4673
　Youngstown (G-16315)
Barsplice Products Inc .... E 937 275-8700
　Dayton (G-6223)
Bridge Components Incorporated ... G 614 873-0777
　Columbus (G-5212)
Gateway Con Forming Svcs Inc ..... D 513 353-2000
　Miamitown (G-10708)
Industrial Millwright Svcs LLC .... E 419 523-9147
　Ottawa (G-12181)
Mound Steel Corp. .... F 937 748-2937
　Springboro (G-13510)
Ohio Bridge Corporation .... C 740 432-6334
　Cambridge (G-1945)
Sky Climber Fabricating LLC .... F 740 990-9430
　Delaware (G-6750)
Smith Brothers Erection Inc .... G 740 373-3575
　Marietta (G-9826)

Steel Structures of Ohio LLC .... F 330 374-9900
　Akron (G-337)
Veterans Steel Inc .... F 216 938-7476
　Cleveland (G-4865)

BARS: Iron, Made In Steel Mills

Republic Engineered Products .... F 440 277-2000
　Lorain (G-9434)
Republic Steel .... F 330 438-5435
　Canton (G-2214)

BASEMENT WINDOW AREAWAYS: Concrete

Bilco Company .... E 740 455-9020
　Zanesville (G-16508)

BASKETS: Steel Wire

Cherokee Manufacturing LLC .... F 800 777-5030
　Perry (G-12350)

BATH SALTS

Midwest Bath Salt Company LLC ... G 513 770-9177
　Mason (G-10029)

BATHROOM ACCESS & FITTINGS: Vitreous China & Earthenware

Crane Plumbing LLC .... A 419 522-4211
　Mansfield (G-9642)

BATHROOM FIXTURES: Plastic

American Platinum Door LLC .... G 440 497-6213
　Solon (G-13312)
Marble Arch Products Inc .... G 937 746-8388
　Franklin (G-7685)

BATTERIES, EXC AUTOMOTIVE: Wholesalers

Ametek Inc. .... F 937 440-0800
　Troy (G-14550)
Battery Unlimited .... G 740 452-5030
　Zanesville (G-16506)
D C Systems Inc .... F 330 273-3030
　Brunswick (G-1756)
One Wish LLC .... F 800 505-6883
　Bedford (G-1147)

BATTERIES: Alkaline, Cell Storage

Energizer Manufacturing Inc .... G
　Westlake (G-15749)
Transdigm Inc. .... F 216 291-6025
　Cleveland (G-4815)

BATTERIES: Lead Acid, Storage

All Power Battery Inc .... G 330 453-5236
　Canton (G-2033)
Enersys .... C 216 252-4242
　Cleveland (G-4017)

BATTERIES: Rechargeable

Cirba Solutions Us Inc .... D 740 653-6290
　Lancaster (G-9001)
Clarios LLC .... A 419 865-0542
　Holland (G-8498)
Graywacke Inc. .... F 419 884-7014
　Mansfield (G-9664)
Millertech Energy Solutions .... F 855 629-5484
　West Farmington (G-15606)
Toxco Inc. .... E 740 653-6290
　Lancaster (G-9045)
Xerion Advanced Battery Corp .... F 720 229-0697
　Kettering (G-8911)

Employee Codes: A=Over 500 employees, B=251-500
C=101-250, D=51-100, E=20-50, F=10-19, G=1-9

BATTERIES: Storage

BATTERIES: Storage
Acculon Energy Inc................................F 614 259-7792
Columbus (G-5094)

Crown Battery Manufacturing Co............G 330 425-3308
Twinsburg (G-14646)

Crown Battery Manufacturing Co............B 419 334-7181
Fremont (G-7773)

Energizer Battery Inc............................E 440 835-7500
Westlake (G-15748)

Glx Power Systems Inc..........................G 440 338-6526
Chagrin Falls (G-2378)

Lithchem Intl Toxco Inc..........................F 740 653-6290
Lancaster (G-9022)

Reliant Worth Corp................................G 440 232-1422
Bedford (G-1152)

Spectrum Brands Inc............................G 567 998-7930
Vandalia (G-14961)

BATTERIES: Wet
Glx Power Systems Inc..........................G 440 338-6526
Chagrin Falls (G-2378)

Inventus Power (ohio) Inc......................F 614 351-2191
Dublin (G-6901)

BATTERY CASES: Plastic Or Plastics Combination
Rjf International Corporation..................A 330 668-2069
Fairlawn (G-7447)

BATTERY CHARGERS
Asg Division Jergens Inc........................E 888 486-6163
Cleveland (G-3688)

Brookwood Group Inc............................F 513 791-3030
Cincinnati (G-2691)

D C Systems Inc..................................F 330 273-3030
Brunswick (G-1756)

Exide Technologies LLC........................G 614 863-3866
Gahanna (G-7835)

Noco Company....................................D 216 464-8131
Solon (G-13399)

TL Industries Inc..................................C 419 666-8144
Perrysburg (G-12436)

BATTERY CHARGERS: Storage, Motor & Engine Generator Type
Brinkley Technology Group LLC..............F 330 830-2498
Massillon (G-10079)

One Three Energy Inc..........................F 513 996-6973
Cincinnati (G-3224)

BEARINGS & PARTS Ball
Bearings Manufacturing Company..........F 440 846-5517
Strongsville (G-13815)

Jay Dee Service Corporation..................G 330 425-1546
Macedonia (G-9558)

Kaydon Corporation..............................D 231 755-3741
Avon (G-777)

Miller Bearing Company Inc..................E 330 678-8844
Kent (G-8837)

Nn Inc..E 440 647-4711
Wellington (G-15318)

Thyssenkrupp Rothe Erde USA Inc..........C 330 562-4000
Aurora (G-736)

Tsk America Co Ltd..............................F 513 942-4002
West Chester (G-15600)

BEARINGS: Ball & Roller
Ggb US Holdco LLC..............................F 234 262-3000
North Canton (G-11730)

Gt Technologies Inc..............................D 419 782-8955
Defiance (G-6680)

Schaeffler Group USA Inc......................E 800 274-5001
Valley City (G-14889)

Timken Company..................................F 614 836-3337
Groveport (G-8162)

Timken Company..................................A 234 262-3000
North Canton (G-11766)

Timken Newco I LLC............................E 234 262-3000
North Canton (G-11767)

BEARINGS: Railroad Car Journal
Rail Bearing Service LLC......................B 234 262-3000
North Canton (G-11756)

BEARINGS: Roller & Parts
HMS Industries LLC............................F 440 899-0001
Westlake (G-15756)

BEAUTY & BARBER SHOP EQPT
Aluminum Line Products Company..........D 440 835-8880
Westlake (G-15729)

Carroll Hills Industries..........................F 330 627-5524
Carrollton (G-2304)

Clarity Retail Services LLC..................D 513 800-9369
West Chester (G-15395)

Clearsonic Manufacturing Inc................G 828 772-9809
Akron (G-113)

Country Clippins LLC..........................G 740 472-5228
Woodsfield (G-16086)

Dayton Armor LLC..............................G 937 723-8675
Moraine (G-11170)

Downing Enterprises Inc......................G 330 666-3888
Copley (G-5948)

Duraflow Industries Inc........................G 440 965-5047
Wakeman (G-15074)

Elite Manufacturing Inds LLC................G 440 934-0920
Avon (G-773)

Excalibur Barber LLC..........................F 330 729-9006
Boardman (G-1512)

Firelands Manufacturing LLC................G 419 687-8237
Plymouth (G-12608)

Foundation Industries Inc....................E 330 564-1250
Akron (G-157)

GKN Driveline Bowl Green Inc..............E 419 373-7700
Bowling Green (G-1567)

Ideal Image Inc..................................D 937 832-1660
Englewood (G-7233)

K K Tool Co..E 937 325-1373
Springfield (G-13585)

Lincoln Manufacturing Inc....................F 330 878-7772
Strasburg (G-13749)

Pacific Manufacturing Ohio Inc..............E 513 860-3900
Fairfield (G-7391)

Production TI Co Cleveland Inc..............F 330 425-4466
Twinsburg (G-14719)

Quick Tech Business Forms Inc............F 937 743-5952
Springboro (G-13517)

RB Sigma LLC....................................D 440 290-0577
Mentor (G-10545)

Rowend Industries Inc........................G 419 333-8300
Fremont (G-7806)

Schreiner Manufacturing LLC................G 419 937-0300
New Riegel (G-11537)

T J Davies Company Inc......................G 440 248-5510
Mantua (G-9744)

Tango Echo Bravo Mfg Inc....................G 440 353-2605
North Ridgeville (G-11861)

TLC Products Inc................................F 216 472-3030
Westlake (G-15797)

Vistech Mfg Solutions LLC....................F 513 860-1408
Fairfield (G-7424)

BEAUTY & BARBER SHOP EQPT & SPLYS WHOLESALERS
Beaute Asylum LLC..............................F 419 377-9933
Toledo (G-1423)

Excalibur Barber LLC..........................F 330 729-9006
Boardman (G-1512)

BEAUTY SALONS
James C Robinson..............................G 513 969-7482
Cincinnati (G-336)

Ransome AC LLC................................G 234 205-6907
Akron (G-297)

BEDDING & BEDSPRINGS STORES
Ahmf Inc..E 614 921-1223
Columbus (G-107)

BEDDING, BEDSPREADS, BLANKETS & SHEETS
Fluvitex USA Inc..................................C 614 610-1199
Groveport (G-141)

Sewline Products Inc..........................G 419 929-1114
New London (G-11469)

BEDS: Institutional
Belmont Community Hospital................E 740 671-1216
Bellaire (G-1173)

BEDSPREADS, COTTON
Sk Textile Inc......................................C 800 888-9112
Cincinnati (G-396)

BEER & ALE WHOLESALERS
Frontwaters Rest & Brewing Co............G 419 798-8058
Marblehead (G-9765)

Wild Ohio Brewing Company..................G 614 262-0000
Columbus (G-5877)

BEER, WINE & LIQUOR STORES: Beer, Packaged
Currier Richard & James......................G 440 988-4132
Amherst (G-74)

Millersburg Ice Company......................E 330 674-3016
Millersburg (G-10983)

BELLOWS
Alloy Precision Tech Inc......................D 440 266-7700
Mentor (G-10412)

International Bellows............................F 937 294-6261
Englewood (G-7234)

BELTING: Rubber
Fenner Dunlop (toledo) LLC..................D 419 531-5300
Toledo (G-1285)

Novex Operating Company LLC............F 330 335-2371
Wadsworth (G-15049)

BELTS: Conveyor, Made From Purchased Wire
Akron Belting & Supply Company..........G 330 633-8212
Akron (G-27)

May Conveyor Inc................................F 440 237-8012
North Royalton (G-11885)

BERYLLIUM
Materion Brush Inc..............................A 419 862-2745
Elmore (G-703)

Materion Brush Inc..............................D 216 486-4200
Mayfield Heights (G-10250)

PRODUCT SECTION

BEVERAGES, ALCOHOLIC: Wines

Materion Corporation................................ C 216 486-4200
  Mayfield Heights *(G-10251)*

BEVERAGE BASES & SYRUPS

Hen of Woods LLC................................... G 513 954-8871
  Cincinnati *(G-2993)*

J M Smucker Company............................. A 330 682-3000
  Orrville *(G-12129)*

Mapledale Farm Inc................................. F 440 286-3389
  Chardon *(G-2458)*

Nu Pet Company....................................... F 330 682-3000
  Orrville *(G-12142)*

BEVERAGE PRDTS: Brewers' Grain

Hansa Brewery LLC................................... G 216 631-6585
  Cleveland *(G-4169)*

Wedco LLC.. G 513 309-0781
  Mount Orab *(G-11247)*

BEVERAGE PRDTS: Malt, Barley

Ohio Crafted Malt House LLC................... F 614 961-7805
  New Albany *(G-11386)*

BEVERAGES, ALCOHOLIC: Ale

Wild Ohio Brewing Company.................... G 614 262-0000
  Columbus *(G-5877)*

BEVERAGES, ALCOHOLIC: Applejack

Toledo Spirits Company LLC.................... F 419 704-3705
  Toledo *(G-14505)*

BEVERAGES, ALCOHOLIC: Beer

Anheuser-Busch LLC................................ D 330 438-2036
  Canton *(G-2037)*

Anheuser-Busch LLC................................ B 614 847-6213
  Columbus *(G-5146)*

Artisan Ales LLC....................................... E 216 544-8703
  Cleveland *(G-3679)*

Branch & Bone Artisan Ales LLC............. F 937 723-7608
  Dayton *(G-6235)*

Brew Kettle Inc... F 440 234-8788
  Strongsville *(G-13817)*

Brewdog Brewing Company LLC............. F 614 908-3051
  Canal Winchester *(G-1981)*

Brewery Real Estate Partnr..................... G 614 224-9023
  Columbus *(G-5210)*

Bummin Beaver Brewery LLC.................. G 440 543-9900
  Chagrin Falls *(G-2390)*

Cincinnati Beverage Company................ E 513 904-8910
  Cincinnati *(G-2741)*

Cineen Inc.. G 440 236-3658
  Columbia Station *(G-5009)*

Dayton Heidelberg Distrg Co................... C 440 989-1027
  Lorain *(G-9410)*

District Brewing Company Inc................ E 614 224-3626
  Columbus *(G-5331)*

Fifty West Brewing Company LLC........... E 740 775-2337
  Chillicothe *(G-2502)*

Frontwaters Rest & Brewing Co.............. G 419 798-8058
  Marblehead *(G-9765)*

Great Lakes Brewing Co........................... C 216 771-4404
  Cleveland *(G-4142)*

Lock 27 Brewing LLC............................... F 937 433-2739
  Dayton *(G-6414)*

Mansfield Brew Works LLC..................... F 419 631-3153
  Mansfield *(G-9684)*

Miiler Brewing Company.......................... E 513 896-9200
  Trenton *(G-14541)*

Modern Methods Brewing Co LLC........... G 330 506-4613
  Warren *(G-15191)*

Molson Coors Bev Co USA LLC................ D 513 896-9200
  Trenton *(G-14542)*

Phunkenship - Platform Beer Co............. F 216 417-7743
  Cleveland *(G-4549)*

Samuel Adams Brewery Company Ltd.. D 513 412-3200
  Cincinnati *(G-3361)*

Snyder Intl Brewing Group LLC............... E 216 619-7424
  Cleveland *(G-4711)*

South Side Drive Thru............................. G 937 295-2927
  Fort Loramie *(G-7610)*

Willoughby Brewing Company LLC......... F 440 975-0202
  Willoughby *(G-16016)*

BEVERAGES, ALCOHOLIC: Beer & Ale

2 Tones Brewing Co................................. G 740 412-0845
  Columbus *(G-5075)*

Bajio Brewing Company LLC................... G 419 410-8275
  Toledo *(G-14205)*

Brew Cleveland LLC................................ F 440 455-9218
  North Olmsted *(G-11820)*

Brew Kettle Strongsville LLC.................. F 440 915-7074
  Medina *(G-10307)*

Brewpub Restaurant Corporation............ E 614 228-2537
  Columbus *(G-5211)*

Columbus Kombucha Company LLC....... G 614 262-0000
  Columbus *(G-5270)*

Dswdwk LLC.. G 513 853-5021
  Cincinnati *(G-2843)*

Great Lakes Brewing Co........................... E 216 771-4404
  Cleveland *(G-4141)*

Great Lakes Brewing Co........................... E 216 771-4404
  Strongsville *(G-13836)*

Lock 15 Brewing Company LLC.............. E 234 900-8277
  Akron *(G-221)*

Moeller Brew Barn LLC........................... G 937 400-8628
  Dayton *(G-6455)*

Moeller Brew Barn LLC........................... G 937 400-8626
  Monroe *(G-11116)*

Moeller Brew Barn LLC........................... G 419 925-3005
  Maria Stein *(G-9772)*

Municipal Brew Works LLC..................... G 513 889-8369
  Hamilton *(G-8230)*

Nine Giant Brewing LLC.......................... G 510 220-5104
  Cincinnati *(G-3199)*

Noble Beast Brewing LLC........................ G 570 809-6405
  Cleveland *(G-4461)*

Rhinegeist Holding Company Inc............ F 513 381-1367
  Cincinnati *(G-3336)*

Rocky River Brewing Co.......................... F 440 895-2739
  Rocky River *(G-12842)*

Royal Docks Brewing Co LLC.................. D 330 353-9103
  Massillon *(G-10140)*

TS Oak Inc... G 513 252-7241
  Cincinnati *(G-3472)*

BEVERAGES, ALCOHOLIC: Bourbon Whiskey

Brain Brew Ventures 30 Inc.................... F 513 310-6374
  Newtown *(G-11661)*

Luxco Inc.. G 216 671-6300
  Cleveland *(G-4341)*

BEVERAGES, ALCOHOLIC: Distilled Liquors

Karrikin Spirits Company LLC................. F 513 561-5000
  Cincinnati *(G-3064)*

March First Manufacturing LLC.............. G 513 266-3076
  Cincinnati *(G-3130)*

Paramount Distillers Inc......................... B 216 671-6300
  Cleveland *(G-4522)*

Veriano Fine Foods Spirits Ltd................ F 614 745-7705
  New Albany *(G-11394)*

Watershed Distillery LLC........................ E 614 357-1936
  Columbus *(G-5866)*

Western Reserve Distillers LLC.............. G 330 780-9599
  Lakewood *(G-8984)*

BEVERAGES, ALCOHOLIC: Near Beer

Georgetown Vineyards Inc...................... E 740 435-3222
  Cambridge *(G-1936)*

Green Room Brewing LLC....................... G 614 421-2337
  Columbus *(G-5412)*

Platform Beers LLC................................. F 440 539-3245
  Cleveland *(G-4561)*

BEVERAGES, ALCOHOLIC: Wines

Amani Vines LLC..................................... F 440 335-5432
  Cleveland *(G-3646)*

Barrel Run Crssing Wnery Vnyrd............. G 330 325-1075
  Rootstown *(G-12851)*

Biscotti Winery LLC................................ F 440 466-1248
  Geneva *(G-7933)*

Breitenbach Wine Cellars Inc................. G 330 343-3603
  Dover *(G-6810)*

Buckeye Lake Winery............................. E 614 439-7576
  Thornville *(G-14065)*

Camelot Cellars Winery........................... F 614 441-8860
  Plain City *(G-12570)*

Casa Di Vino Winery and....................... G 440 494-7878
  Wickliffe *(G-15826)*

Chalet Debonne Vineyards Inc................ F 440 466-3485
  Madison *(G-9588)*

Cyrpress Wine Cellars............................ G 419 295-2124
  Mansfield *(G-9644)*

Delaware City Vineyard.......................... G 740 362-6383
  Delaware *(G-6712)*

Diletto Winery LLC.................................. F 440 991-6217
  Youngstown *(G-16349)*

Drake Brothers Ltd................................. G 415 819-4941
  Columbus *(G-5335)*

E & J Gallo Winery.................................. E 513 381-4050
  Cincinnati *(G-2847)*

Ferrante Wine Farm Inc......................... E 440 466-8466
  Geneva *(G-7936)*

Five Vines Winery LLC............................ G 419 657-2675
  Wapakoneta *(G-15111)*

Gillig Custom Winery Inc....................... G 419 202-6057
  Findlay *(G-7513)*

Glenn Ravens Winery............................. F 740 545-1000
  West Lafayette *(G-15617)*

Happy Grape LLC.................................... G 419 884-9463
  Mansfield *(G-9666)*

High Low Winery..................................... G 844 466-4456
  Akron *(G-184)*

Hillside Winery.. G 419 456-3108
  Gilboa *(G-7957)*

Indian Bear Winery Ltd.......................... G 740 507-3322
  Walhonding *(G-15093)*

J E Nicolozakes Co.................................. G 740 310-1606
  Cambridge *(G-1937)*

John Christ Winery Inc........................... G 440 933-9672
  Avon Lake *(G-813)*

Kelleys Island Winery Inc....................... G 419 746-2678
  Kelleys Island *(G-8788)*

Klingshirn Winery Inc............................. G 440 933-6666
  Avon Lake *(G-814)*

Laurentia Winery.................................... F 440 296-9170
  Madison *(G-9593)*

Lonz Winery... F 419 625-5474
  Sandusky *(G-13075)*

Losantiville Winery LLC.......................... G 513 918-3015
  Cincinnati *(G-3114)*

Mastropietro Winery Inc........................ G 330 547-2151
  Berlin Center *(G-1309)*

Matus Winery Inc................................... G 440 774-9463
  Wakeman *(G-15077)*

Employee Codes: A=Over 500 employees, B=251-500
C=101-250, D=51-100, E=20-50, F=10-19, G=1-9

BEVERAGES, ALCOHOLIC: Wines

McAlear Winery LLC .... G 567 703-1281
  Maumee *(G-10219)*
Meiers Wine Cellars Inc .... E 513 891-2900
  Cincinnati *(G-3146)*
Milo Family Vineyards Ltd .... G 440 922-0190
  Brecksville *(G-1627)*
Moyer Vineyards Inc .... F 937 549-2957
  Mount Orab *(G-11243)*
Old Mason Winery Inc .... G 937 698-1122
  West Milton *(G-15630)*
Old Mill Winery Inc .... G 440 466-5560
  Geneva *(G-7944)*
Paramount Distillers Inc .... B 216 671-6300
  Cleveland *(G-4522)*
Perennial Vineyards LLC .... F 330 832-3677
  Navarre *(G-11349)*
Pleasant Hill Vineyards LLC .... G 740 502-3567
  Athens *(G-691)*
Quinami LLC .... G 419 797-4445
  Port Clinton *(G-12626)*
R & T Estate LLC .... F 216 862-0822
  Cleveland *(G-4611)*
Revel Otr Urban Winery .... G 513 929-4263
  Cincinnati *(G-3333)*
Sandra Weddington .... F 740 417-4286
  Delaware *(G-6749)*
Sapphire Creek Wnery Grdns LLC .... F 440 543-7777
  Chagrin Falls *(G-2422)*
Sarahs Vineyard Inc .... G 330 929-8057
  Cuyahoga Falls *(G-6116)*
Shawne Springs Winery .... G 740 623-0744
  Coshocton *(G-5996)*
Solo Vino Imports Ltd .... G 440 714-9591
  Vermilion *(G-14973)*
Swiss Heritage Winery .... G 330 343-4108
  Dover *(G-6846)*
Tramonte & Sons LLC .... F 513 770-5501
  Lebanon *(G-9114)*
Twenty One Barrels Ltd .... G 937 467-4498
  Bradford *(G-1602)*
Ugly Bunny Winery LLC .... F 330 988-9057
  Loudonville *(G-9453)*
Vermilion Valley Vineyards LLC .... G 440 935-1363
  Westlake *(G-15799)*
Vino Bellissimo .... G 419 296-4267
  Lima *(G-9300)*
Vinoklet Winery Inc .... E 513 385-9309
  Cincinnati *(G-3500)*
Vintage Wine Distributor Inc .... F 513 443-4300
  West Chester *(G-15525)*
Vpl LLC .... G 330 549-0195
  Columbiana *(G-5055)*
Wine Mill .... G 234 571-2594
  Peninsula *(G-12346)*
Winery At Spring Hill Inc .... G 440 466-0626
  Geneva *(G-7946)*
Winery At Wilcox Inc .... G 937 526-3232
  Versailles *(G-14993)*
Winery At Wolf Creek .... F 330 666-9285
  Barberton *(G-900)*
Woodland Cellars LLC .... G 330 240-4883
  Hubbard *(G-8573)*
Wyandotte Winery LLC .... G 614 357-7522
  Columbus *(G-5887)*

BEVERAGES, MALT

BT 4 LLC .... G 513 771-2739
  Cincinnati *(G-2692)*

BEVERAGES, NONALCOHOLIC: Bottled & canned soft drinks

Abbott Laboratories .... A 614 624-3191
  Columbus *(G-5085)*
Akron Coca-Cola Bottling Co .... A 330 784-2653
  Akron *(G-31)*
Belton Foods LLC .... E 937 890-7768
  Dayton *(G-6226)*
Borden Dairy Co Cincinnati LLC .... E 513 948-8811
  Cleveland *(G-3748)*
Cadbury Schweppes Bottling .... G 614 238-0469
  Columbus *(G-5225)*
Central Coca-Cola Btlg Co Inc .... E 330 875-1487
  Akron *(G-105)*
Central Coca-Cola Btlg Co Inc .... E 740 474-2180
  Circleville *(G-3543)*
Central Coca-Cola Btlg Co Inc .... C 614 863-7200
  Columbus *(G-5241)*
Central Coca-Cola Btlg Co Inc .... E 440 324-3335
  Elyria *(G-7125)*
Central Coca-Cola Btlg Co Inc .... D 419 522-2653
  Mansfield *(G-9637)*
Central Coca-Cola Btlg Co Inc .... C 419 476-6622
  Toledo *(G-14230)*
Central Coca-Cola Btlg Co Inc .... B 330 425-4401
  Twinsburg *(G-14641)*
Central Coca-Cola Btlg Co Inc .... E 440 269-1433
  Willoughby *(G-15898)*
Central Coca-Cola Btlg Co Inc .... E 330 783-1982
  Youngstown *(G-16333)*
Central Coca-Cola Btlg Co Inc .... E 740 452-3608
  Zanesville *(G-16519)*
Cleveland Coca-Cola Btlg Inc .... C 216 690-2653
  Bedford Heights *(G-1167)*
Coca Cola .... G 513 898-7709
  West Chester *(G-15399)*
Coca Cola Offices .... G 678 327-8959
  Cincinnati *(G-2779)*
Coca-Cola .... G 937 446-4644
  Sardinia *(G-13106)*
Coca-Cola Company .... E 614 491-6305
  Columbus *(G-5259)*
Coca-Cola Consolidated Inc .... A 513 527-6600
  Cincinnati *(G-2780)*
Coca-Cola Consolidated Inc .... B 937 878-5000
  Dayton *(G-6257)*
Coca-Cola Consolidated Inc .... A 419 422-3743
  Lima *(G-9228)*
Coca-Cola Consolidated Inc .... C 740 353-3133
  Portsmouth *(G-12642)*
Currier Richard & James .... G 440 988-4132
  Amherst *(G-474)*
Fbg Bottling Group LLC .... F 614 580-7063
  Columbus *(G-5371)*
Gordon Brothers Btlg Group Inc .... G 330 337-8754
  Salem *(G-12997)*
Hornell Brewing Co Inc .... G 516 812-0384
  Cincinnati *(G-3009)*
Meiers Wine Cellars Inc .... E 513 891-2900
  Cincinnati *(G-3146)*
Niagara Bottling LLC .... G 614 751-7420
  Gahanna *(G-7846)*
Pepsi-Cola Metro Btlg Co Inc .... C 330 425-8236
  Twinsburg *(G-14711)*
Smucker International Inc .... E 330 682-3000
  Orrville *(G-12154)*
Smucker Natural Foods Inc .... A 330 682-3000
  Orrville *(G-12156)*

BEVERAGES, NONALCOHOLIC: Carbonated

Central Investment LLC .... F 513 563-4700
  Cincinnati *(G-2716)*
Consolidated Bottling Company .... C 419 227-3541
  Lima *(G-9229)*

G & J Pepsi-Cola Bottlers Inc .... E 740 593-3366
  Athens *(G-683)*
G & J Pepsi-Cola Bottlers Inc .... E 740 774-2148
  Chillicothe *(G-2504)*
G & J Pepsi-Cola Bottlers Inc .... E 866 647-2734
  Columbus *(G-5393)*
G & J Pepsi-Cola Bottlers Inc .... A 614 253-8771
  Columbus *(G-5294)*
G & J Pepsi-Cola Bottlers Inc .... B 740 354-9191
  Franklin Furnace *(G-7712)*
G & J Pepsi-Cola Bottlers Inc .... D 513 896-3700
  Hamilton *(G-8210)*
G & J Pepsi-Cola Bottlers Inc .... E 740 354-9191
  Zanesville *(G-16534)*
G & J Pepsi-Cola Bottlers Inc .... F 513 785-6060
  Cincinnati *(G-2524)*
P-Americas LLC .... B 513 948-5100
  Cincinnati *(G-3333)*
Pepsi-Cola Metro Btlg Co Inc .... F 614 261-8193
  Columbus *(G-5068)*
Pepsi-Cola Metro Btlg Co Inc .... C 440 323-5524
  Elyria *(G-7193)*
Pepsi-Cola Metro Btlg Co Inc .... G 937 328-6750
  Springfield *(G-1618)*
Pepsi-Cola Metro Btlg Co Inc .... D 419 534-2186
  Toledo *(G-14432)*
Pepsi-Cola Metro Btlg Co Inc .... F 330 963-5300
  Twinsburg *(G-14712)*
Pepsico .... G 513 229-3046
  Mason *(G-10035)*

BEVERAGES, NONALCOHOLIC: Carbonated, Canned & Bottled, Etc

Gehm & Sons Limited .... G 330 724-8423
  Akron *(G-164)*
L & J Drive Thru LLC .... G 330 767-2185
  Brewster *(G-1641)*
Smithfoods Orrville Inc .... C 330 683-8710
  Orrville *(G-12152)*

BEVERAGES, NONALCOHOLIC: Flavoring extracts & syrups, nec

Abbott Laboratories .... A 614 624-3191
  Columbus *(G-5085)*
Agrana Fruit Us Inc .... C 937 693-3821
  Anna *(G-488)*
Agrana Fruit Us Inc .... E 440 546-1199
  Brecksville *(G-1625)*
Cargill Incorporated .... E 937 236-1971
  Dayton *(G-6246)*
Flavor Systems Intl Inc .... E 513 870-4900
  Cincinnati *(G-2907)*
Givaudan Flavors Corporation .... G 513 786-0124
  Cincinnati *(G-2954)*
Givaudan Flavors Corporation .... E 513 948-8000
  Cincinnati *(G-2955)*
Givaudan Flavors Corporation .... C 513 948-8000
  Cincinnati *(G-2955)*
Givaudan Fragrances Corp .... E 513 948-3428
  Cincinnati *(G-2957)*
Hydralyte LLC .... G 844 301-2109
  Solon *(G-13365)*
Joseph Adams Corp .... F 330 225-9125
  Valley City *(G-14874)*
Mane Inc .... C 513 248-9876
  Cincinnati *(G-3120)*
Phillips Syrup LLC .... F 440 835-8001
  Westlake *(G-15774)*
Primary Pdts Ingrdts Amrcas L .... D 937 236-5906
  Dayton *(G-6520)*

PRODUCT SECTION — BINDING SVC: Books & Manuals

BEVERAGES, NONALCOHOLIC: Fruit Drnks, Under 100% Juice, Can

Company	Code	Phone
Beverages Holdings LLC	A	513 483-3300
Blue Ash *(G-1369)*		
Country Pure Foods Inc	C	330 753-2293
Akron *(G-116)*		
Life Support Development Ltd	G	614 221-1765
Columbus *(G-5525)*		
Ohio Beverage Systems Inc	F	216 475-3900
Cleveland *(G-4495)*		
Ohio Pure Foods Inc	D	330 753-2293
Akron *(G-271)*		

BEVERAGES, NONALCOHOLIC: Soft Drinks, Canned & Bottled, Etc

Company	Code	Phone
American Bottling Company	E	330 733-3830
Akron *(G-58)*		
American Bottling Company	D	513 381-4891
Cincinnati *(G-2615)*		
American Bottling Company	D	513 242-5151
Cincinnati *(G-2616)*		
American Bottling Company	D	614 237-4201
Columbus *(G-5120)*		
American Bottling Company	C	614 237-4201
Columbus *(G-5121)*		
American Bottling Company	D	937 236-0333
Dayton *(G-6198)*		
American Bottling Company	D	419 229-7777
Lima *(G-9220)*		
American Bottling Company	D	740 423-9230
Little Hocking *(G-9333)*		
American Bottling Company	E	740 922-5253
Midvale *(G-10874)*		
American Bottling Company	D	740 377-4371
South Point *(G-13465)*		
American Bottling Company	D	419 535-0777
Toledo *(G-14186)*		
Dr Pepper Bottlers Associates	G	330 746-7651
Youngstown *(G-16351)*		
Dr Pepper Bottling Company	G	740 452-2721
Zanesville *(G-16528)*		
Dr Pepper Snapple Group	F	419 223-0072
Lima *(G-9237)*		
Dr Pepper/Seven Up Inc	F	513 875-2466
Fayetteville *(G-7465)*		
Dr Pepper/Seven Up Inc	F	419 229-7777
Lima *(G-9238)*		
Gem Beverages Inc	F	740 384-2411
Wellston *(G-15327)*		
Keurig Dr Pepper Inc	D	614 237-4201
Columbus *(G-5509)*		
National Beverage Corp	G	614 491-5415
Obetz *(G-12063)*		
Pepsi-Cola Metro Btlg Co Inc	E	937 461-4664
Dayton *(G-6501)*		
Shasta Beverages	G	614 409-2965
Groveport *(G-8159)*		
Shasta Beverages Inc	D	614 491-5415
Obetz *(G-12064)*		

BEVERAGES, NONALCOHOLIC: Tea, Iced, Bottled & Canned, Etc

Company	Code	Phone
Ohio Eagle Distributing LLC	E	513 539-8483
West Chester *(G-15469)*		

BEVERAGES, WINE & DISTILLED ALCOHOLIC, WHOLESALE: Liquor

Company	Code	Phone
Blue Collar M LLC	F	216 209-5666
Solon *(G-13320)*		
Veriano Fine Foods Spirits Ltd	F	614 745-7705
New Albany *(G-11394)*		

BEVERAGES, WINE & DISTILLED ALCOHOLIC, WHOLESALE: Wine

Company	Code	Phone
Old Firehouse Winery Inc	E	440 466-9300
Geneva *(G-7943)*		
Paramount Distillers Inc	B	216 671-6300
Cleveland *(G-4522)*		
Sandra Weddington	F	740 417-4286
Delaware *(G-6749)*		
Watershed Distillery LLC	E	614 357-1936
Columbus *(G-5866)*		
Wedco LLC	G	513 309-0781
Mount Orab *(G-11247)*		

BICYCLES, PARTS & ACCESS

Company	Code	Phone
Safe Haven Brands LLC	F	937 550-9407
Springboro *(G-13519)*		

BILLING & BOOKKEEPING SVCS

Company	Code	Phone
Michele Caldwell	G	937 505-7744
Dayton *(G-6442)*		
Steward Edge Bus Solutions	F	614 826-5305
Columbus *(G-5795)*		

BINDING SVC: Books & Manuals

Company	Code	Phone
A-A Blueprint Co Inc	E	330 794-8803
Akron *(G-11)*		
AAA Laminating and Bindery Inc	G	513 860-2680
Fairfield *(G-7329)*		
Activities Press Inc	E	440 953-1200
Mentor *(G-10404)*		
AGS Custom Graphics Inc	D	330 963-7770
Macedonia *(G-9534)*		
Allen Graphics Inc	G	440 349-4100
Solon *(G-13308)*		
American Printing & Lithog Co	F	513 867-0602
Hamilton *(G-8177)*		
Anderson Graphics Inc	E	330 745-2165
Barberton *(G-855)*		
Andrin Enterprises Inc	F	937 276-7794
Moraine *(G-11157)*		
Baesman Group Inc	D	614 771-2300
Hilliard *(G-8402)*		
Barnhart Printing Corp	F	330 456-2279
Canton *(G-2044)*		
Bindery & Spc Pressworks Inc	D	614 873-4623
Plain City *(G-12566)*		
Bindusa	F	513 247-3000
Blue Ash *(G-1370)*		
Black River Group Inc	E	419 524-6699
Mansfield *(G-9628)*		
Bookfactory LLC	E	937 226-7100
Dayton *(G-6234)*		
Boundless Cmnty Pathways Inc	A	937 461-0034
West Carrollton *(G-15351)*		
Century Graphics Inc	F	614 895-7698
Westerville *(G-15651)*		
Cincinnati Bindery & Packg Inc	G	859 816-0282
Cincinnati *(G-2742)*		
Classic Laminations Inc	E	440 735-1333
Oakwood Village *(G-12037)*		
Cleveland Letter Service Inc	G	216 781-8300
Chagrin Falls *(G-2371)*		
Consolidated Graphics Group Inc	C	216 881-9191
Cleveland *(G-3896)*		
Copley Ohio Newspapers Inc	C	330 364-5577
New Philadelphia *(G-11493)*		
COS Blueprint Inc	E	330 376-0022
Akron *(G-115)*		
Cox Printing Company	G	937 382-2312
Wilmington *(G-16046)*		
Davis Printing Company	E	330 745-3113
Barberton *(G-866)*		
Dayton Bindery Service Inc	E	937 235-3111
Dayton *(G-6274)*		
Dayton Legal Blank Inc	F	937 435-4405
Dayton *(G-6281)*		
Eugene Stewart	G	937 898-1117
Dayton *(G-6325)*		
Folks Creative Printers Inc	F	740 383-6326
Marion *(G-9852)*		
Franklin Printing Company	F	740 452-6375
Zanesville *(G-16533)*		
Gli Holdings Inc	D	216 651-1500
Stow *(G-13701)*		
Greg Blume	G	740 574-2308
Wheelersburg *(G-15809)*		
Harris Paper Crafts Inc	F	614 299-2141
Columbus *(G-5421)*		
Hecks Direct Mail Prtg Svc Inc	F	419 697-3505
Toledo *(G-14315)*		
Hf Group LLC	C	440 729-9411
Chesterland *(G-2482)*		
HP Industries Inc	E	419 478-0695
Toledo *(G-14322)*		
Innomark Communications LLC	C	937 454-5555
Miamisburg *(G-10648)*		
Jack Walker Printing Co	F	440 352-4222
Mentor *(G-10481)*		
Kehl-Kolor Inc	E	419 281-3107
Ashland *(G-585)*		
Kenwel Printers Inc	E	614 261-1011
Columbus *(G-5508)*		
Kevin K Tidd	G	419 885-5603
Sylvania *(G-14003)*		
Keystone Press Inc	G	419 243-7326
Toledo *(G-14347)*		
Krieg Rev 2 Inc	E	513 542-1522
Cincinnati *(G-3090)*		
Laipplys Prtg Mktg Sltions Inc	G	740 387-9282
Marion *(G-9859)*		
Lam Pro Inc	F	216 426-0661
Cleveland *(G-4308)*		
Lee Corporation	G	513 771-3602
Cincinnati *(G-3099)*		
Lilienthal/Southeastern Inc	G	740 439-1640
Cambridge *(G-1940)*		
Liturgical Publications Inc	D	216 325-6825
Cleveland *(G-4332)*		
Mmp Printing Inc	E	513 381-0990
Cincinnati *(G-3168)*		
Multi-Craft Litho Inc	E	859 581-2754
Blue Ash *(G-1442)*		
Network Printing & Graphics	F	614 230-2084
Columbus *(G-5593)*		
North End Press Incorporated	F	740 653-6514
Lancaster *(G-9030)*		
Ohio Laminating & Binding Inc	F	614 771-4868
Hilliard *(G-8426)*		
Old Trail Printing Company	C	614 443-4852
Columbus *(G-5636)*		
Onetouchpoint East Corp	D	513 421-1600
Cincinnati *(G-3225)*		
Orange Blossom Press Inc	G	216 781-8655
Willoughby *(G-15966)*		
Painesville Publishing Inc	G	440 354-4142
Austinburg *(G-748)*		
Penguin Enterprises Inc	E	440 899-5112
Westlake *(G-15773)*		
Prime Printing Inc	E	937 438-3707
Dayton *(G-6522)*		

Employee Codes: A=Over 500 employees, B=251-500
C=101-250, D=51-100, E=20-50, F=10-19, G=1-9

BINDING SVC: Books & Manuals

Print-Digital Incorporated.................. G 330 686-5945
  Stow (G-13718)
Prodigy Print Inc................................ F
  Dayton (G-6528)
Promatch Solutions LLC................. F 877 299-0185
  Moraine (G-11205)
Quick Tab II Inc.................................. D 419 448-6622
  Tiffin (G-14101)
Repro Acquisition Company LLC...... F 216 738-3800
  Cleveland (G-4626)
Robin Enterprises Company.............. C 614 891-0250
  Westerville (G-15719)
RT Industries Inc............................... G 937 335-5784
  Troy (G-14606)
Standard Printing Co of Canton........ D 330 453-8247
  Canton (G-2230)
Star Printing Company Inc................ E 330 376-0514
  Akron (G-336)
Suburban Press Incorporated............ E 216 961-0766
  Cleveland (G-4744)
The D B Hess Company.................... E 330 678-5868
  Kent (G-8874)
Tj Metzgers Inc................................. D 419 861-8611
  Toledo (G-14487)
Traxium LLC...................................... E 330 572-8200
  Stow (G-13732)
Watkins Printing Company................. E 614 297-8270
  Columbus (G-5867)
West-Camp Press Inc....................... D 614 882-2378
  Westerville (G-15725)
Wfsr Holdings LLC............................. A 877 735-4966
  Dayton (G-6654)
Youngstown ARC Engraving Co........ G 330 793-2471
  Youngstown (G-16476)

BINDING SVC: Pamphlets

Macke Brothers Inc.......................... E 513 771-7500
  Cincinnati (G-3123)

BINDING SVC: Trade

Bip Printing Solutions LLC................ F 216 832-5673
  Beachwood (G-974)

BINDINGS: Bias, Made From Purchased Materials

National Bias Fabric Co.................... F 216 361-0530
  Cleveland (G-4435)

BIOLOGICAL PRDTS: Blood Derivatives

Transtechbio Inc................................ G 734 994-4728
  Twinsburg (G-14746)

BIOLOGICAL PRDTS: Exc Diagnostic

ABI Inc... F 800 847-8950
  Cleveland (G-3587)
Algix LLC... G 706 207-3425
  Stow (G-13683)
Bio-Blood Components Inc................ C 614 294-3183
  Columbus (G-5189)
Copernicus Therapeutics Inc............. F 216 231-0227
  Cleveland (G-3904)
EMD Millipore Corporation................ E 513 631-0445
  Norwood (G-11995)
Ferro Corporation.............................. D 216 577-7144
  Bedford (G-1121)
Forge Biologics Inc........................... G 216 401-7611
  Grove City (G-8094)
Jsh International LLC......................... G 330 734-0251
  Akron (G-200)
PEC Biofuels LLC.............................. G 419 542-8210
  Hicksville (G-8378)

Protein Technologies Ltd................... G 513 769-0840
  Cincinnati (G-3307)
Revvity Health Sciences Inc............. E 330 825-4525
  Akron (G-303)

BIOLOGICAL PRDTS: Vaccines & Immunizing

Decaria Brothers Inc........................ G 330 385-0825
  East Liverpool (G-6993)

BIOLOGICAL PRDTS: Veterinary

No Rinse Laboratories LLC............ G 937 746-7357
  Springboro (G-13512)

BLACKBOARDS & CHALKBOARDS

GMI Companies Inc.......................... G 937 981-0244
  Greenfield (G-8029)
GMI Companies Inc.......................... G 513 932-3445
  Lebanon (G-9084)
GMI Companies Inc.......................... C 513 932-3445
  Lebanon (G-9083)
Marsh Industries Inc......................... D 800 426-4244
  New Philadelphia (G-11516)
Tri-State Supply Co Inc.................... F 614 272-6767
  Columbus (G-5836)

BLADES: Knife

Advetech Inc..................................... E 330 533-2227
  Canfield (G-1995)
American Quicksilver Company........ G 513 871-4517
  Cincinnati (G-2620)
Busse Knife Co.................................. F 419 923-6471
  Wauseon (G-15258)

BLADES: Saw, Hand Or Power

M K Morse Company......................... B 330 453-8187
  Canton (G-2149)
Peerless Saw Company..................... E 614 836-5790
  Groveport (G-8157)

BLANKBOOKS & LOOSELEAF BINDERS

Deluxe Corporation............................ D 330 342-1500
  Streetsboro (G-13766)
Dupli-Systems Inc.............................. C 440 234-9415
  Strongsville (G-13830)
Quick Tech Graphics Inc.................... E 937 743-5952
  Springboro (G-13518)

BLANKBOOKS: Albums, Record

Live Off Loyalty Inc........................... G 513 413-2401
  Cincinnati (G-3109)

BLANKBOOKS: Passbooks, Bank, Etc

William Exline Inc.............................. E 216 941-0800
  Cleveland (G-4909)

BLANKETS & BLANKETING, COTTON

R J Manray Inc.................................. G 330 559-6716
  Canfield (G-2015)

BLAST FURNACE & RELATED PRDTS

Custom Blast & Coat Inc................... G 419 225-6024
  Lima (G-9233)
Rmi Titanium Company LLC............ C 330 471-1844
  Canton (G-2216)

BLASTING SVC: Sand, Metal Parts

American Indus Maintenance............ G 937 254-3400
  Dayton (G-6201)
Badboy Blasters Incorporated........... F 330 454-2699
  Canton (G-2042)

Boville Indus Coatings Inc................ E 330 669-8558
  Smithville (G-13298)
Derrick Company Inc....................... E 513 321-8122
  Cincinnati (G-2825)
Industrial Mill Maintenance................ E 330 746-1155
  Youngstown (G-16379)
Newbury Sndblst & Pntg Inc............. G 440 564-7204
  Newbury (G-11631)
Newsome & Work Metalizing Co...... G 330 376-7144
  Akron (G-263)
Pki Inc... F 513 832-8749
  Cincinnati (G-3259)
Witt Enterprises Inc........................... E 440 992-8333
  Ashtabula (G-665)

BLINDS & SHADES: Vertical

11 92 Holdings LLC............................ F 216 920-7790
  Chagrin Falls (G-2366)
Blind Factory Showroom.................... F 614 771-6549
  Hilliard (G-8405)

BLINDS : Window

Black Gate Blinds LLC....................... G 937 402-6158
  Peebles (G-12325)
Designer Window Treatments Inc..... G 419 822-4967
  Delta (G-6782)
Golden Drapery Supply Inc............... E 216 351-3283
  Cleveland (G-4133)
Keys Cheesecakes and Pies LLC.... G 513 356-1221
  West Chester (G-15454)
Mag Resources LLC......................... F 330 294-0494
  Barberton (G-878)
Rustic Cheesecake LLC.................... G 419 680-6156
  Fremont (G-7807)

BLOCKS & BRICKS: Concrete

Charles Svec Inc................................ E 216 662-5200
  Maple Heights (G-9748)
Midwest Specialties Inc..................... F 800 837-2503
  Wapakoneta (G-15127)
Northfield Block Co............................ G 513 242-3644
  Cincinnati (G-3204)
Oberfields LLC................................... E 614 252-0955
  Columbus (G-5610)
R W Sidley Incorporated.................... G 440 564-2221
  Newbury (G-11635)
RE Connors Construction Ltd........... G 740 644-0261
  Thornville (G-14058)
S & S Aggregates Inc........................ F 740 453-0721
  Zanesville (G-16561)
Stocker Concrete Company.............. F 740 254-4626
  Gnadenhutten (G-7989)
The Ideal Builders Supply & Fuel Co Inc F 216 741-1600
  Cleveland (G-4787)
Tri-M Block and Supply Inc.............. G 330 264-8771
  Cuyahoga Falls (G-6122)
Triple A Builders Inc.......................... G 216 249-0327
  Cleveland (G-4832)
William Dauch Concrete Company... F 419 668-4458
  Norwalk (G-11991)

BLOCKS: Landscape Or Retaining Wall, Concrete

Benchmark Land Management LLC... G 513 310-7850
  West Chester (G-15376)
Fine Line Excvtg & Ldscpg LLC....... G 330 541-0590
  Ravenna (G-12715)
Green Impressions LLC.................... D 440 240-8508
  Sheffield Village (G-13182)
Green Vision Materials Inc............... F 440 564-5500
  Newbury (G-11625)

PRODUCT SECTION

BOAT DEALERS: Marine Splys & Eqpt

Meridienne International Inc................ G 330 274-8317
  Aurora *(G-725)*

Ready Field Solutions LLC.................... F 330 562-0550
  Streetsboro *(G-13788)*

Ssr Community Dev Group LLC............ G 216 466-2674
  Cleveland *(G-4724)*

BLOCKS: Paving

LA Rose Paving Co.................................. G 440 632-0330
  Middlefield *(G-10763)*

BLOCKS: Paving, Concrete

E C S Corp... G 440 323-1707
  Elyria *(G-7136)*

BLOCKS: Paving, Cut Stone

Rock Solid Cut Stone & Sup Inc............. G 330 877-2775
  Hartville *(G-8305)*

BLOCKS: Standard, Concrete Or Cinder

American Concrete Products Inc............ F 937 224-1433
  Dayton *(G-6200)*

Beazer East Inc...................................... F 740 474-3169
  Circleville *(G-3542)*

Cantelli Block and Brick Inc................... E 419 433-0102
  Sandusky *(G-13048)*

Cement Products Inc.............................. E 419 524-4342
  Mansfield *(G-9636)*

Dearth Resources Inc............................. G 937 663-4171
  Springfield *(G-13552)*

Dearth Resources Inc............................. G 937 325-0651
  Springfield *(G-13551)*

Hazelbaker Industries Ltd....................... F
  Columbus *(G-5424)*

J P Sand & Gravel Company.................. F 614 497-0083
  Lockbourne *(G-9337)*

Koltcz Concrete Block Co....................... E 440 232-3630
  Bedford *(G-1132)*

National Lime and Stone Co................... F 614 497-0083
  Lockbourne *(G-9340)*

Osborne Inc.. E 440 942-7000
  Mentor *(G-10517)*

Portsmouth Block Inc............................. E 740 353-4113
  Portsmouth *(G-12653)*

Prairie Builders Supply Inc.................... G 419 332-7546
  Fremont *(G-7802)*

Quality Block & Supply Inc.................... E 330 364-4411
  Mount Eaton *(G-11231)*

Reading Rock Incorporated.................... C 513 874-2345
  West Chester *(G-15580)*

Snyder Concrete Products Inc............... G 937 224-1433
  Dayton *(G-6577)*

Snyder Concrete Products Inc............... G 937 885-5176
  Moraine *(G-11211)*

St Henry Tile Co Inc.............................. G 937 548-1101
  Greenville *(G-8061)*

St Henry Tile Co Inc.............................. E 419 678-4841
  Saint Henry *(G-12938)*

Stiger Pre Cast Inc................................. G 740 482-2313
  Nevada *(G-11362)*

Stocker Sand & Gravel Co...................... F 740 254-4635
  Gnadenhutten *(G-7990)*

Tri-County Block and Brick Inc............... E 419 826-7060
  Swanton *(G-13986)*

Trumbull Cement Products Co............... G 330 372-4342
  Warren *(G-15211)*

Tyjen Inc.. G 740 797-4064
  The Plains *(G-14059)*

BLOOD BANK

Bio-Blood Components Inc..................... C 614 294-3183
  Columbus *(G-5189)*

BLOWERS & FANS

A A S Amels Sheet Meta L Inc................ F 330 793-9326
  Youngstown *(G-16297)*

Air Enterprises Inc................................. A 330 794-9770
  Akron *(G-24)*

Air-Rite Inc.. E 216 228-8200
  Cleveland *(G-3617)*

American Manufacturing & Eqp.............. G 513 829-2248
  Fairfield *(G-7335)*

Atmos360 Inc... E 513 772-4777
  West Chester *(G-15539)*

Beckett Air Incorporated........................ D 440 327-9999
  North Ridgeville *(G-11829)*

Bry-Air Inc... E 740 965-2974
  Sunbury *(G-13951)*

Burt Manufacturing Company Inc........... E 330 762-0061
  Akron *(G-97)*

Cardinal Air Design LLC......................... G 440 638-4717
  North Royalton *(G-11869)*

Famous Industries Inc............................ F 740 685-2592
  Byesville *(G-1896)*

Flex Technologies Inc............................. D 330 359-5415
  Mount Eaton *(G-11230)*

FM AF LLC.. C 866 771-6266
  Fairfield *(G-7362)*

Howden North America Inc.................... C 513 874-2400
  Fairfield *(G-7369)*

Howden North America Inc.................... F 330 721-7374
  Medina *(G-10334)*

Illinois Tool Works Inc............................ E 262 248-8277
  Bryan *(G-1821)*

Kirk Williams Company Inc..................... D 614 875-9023
  Grove City *(G-8100)*

Langdon Inc... E 513 733-5955
  Cincinnati *(G-3095)*

Mestek Inc... F 419 288-2703
  Bradner *(G-1603)*

Midwestern Industries Inc..................... D 330 837-4203
  Massillon *(G-10127)*

Nupro Company..................................... D 440 951-9729
  Willoughby *(G-15962)*

Ohio Blow Pipe Company....................... E 216 681-7379
  Cleveland *(G-4496)*

OSI Environmental LLC........................... E 440 237-4600
  North Royalton *(G-11890)*

Plas-Tanks Industries Inc....................... E 513 942-3800
  Hamilton *(G-8235)*

Qualtek Electronics Corp........................ C 440 951-3300
  Mentor *(G-10541)*

Quickdraft Inc.. E 330 477-4574
  Canton *(G-2206)*

Rmt Acquisition Inc................................ E 513 241-5566
  Cincinnati *(G-3347)*

Selas Heat Technology Co LLC............... E 800 523-6500
  Streetsboro *(G-13792)*

Starr Fabricating Inc............................. D 330 394-9891
  Vienna *(G-15004)*

Stelter and Brinck Inc............................ E 513 367-9300
  Harrison *(G-8293)*

Thermo Vent Manufacturing Inc............. F 330 239-0239
  Medina *(G-10386)*

Tisch Environmental Inc........................ E 513 467-9000
  Cleves *(G-4967)*

Tosoh America Inc.................................. B 614 539-8622
  Grove City *(G-8124)*

Windsor Wire.. G 662 634-5908
  Strongsville *(G-13897)*

Americraft Mfg Co Inc............................ F 513 489-1047
  Cincinnati *(G-2621)*

Buckeye BOP LLC................................... G 740 498-9898
  Newcomerstown *(G-11643)*

Hartzell Fan Inc..................................... C 937 773-7411
  Piqua *(G-12520)*

Shupert Manufacturing Inc.................... F 937 859-7492
  Miamisburg *(G-10682)*

Tlt-Babcock Inc...................................... D 330 867-8540
  Akron *(G-359)*

Verantis Corporation.............................. E 440 243-0700
  Middleburg Heights *(G-10728)*

Vortec and Paxton Products................... F 513 891-7474
  Blue Ash *(G-1488)*

BLUEPRINTING SVCS

Northeast Blueprint and Sup Co............. G 216 261-7500
  Cleveland *(G-4475)*

Queen City Reprographics...................... C 513 326-2300
  Cincinnati *(G-3319)*

Robert Becker Impressions Inc.............. F 419 385-5303
  Toledo *(G-14456)*

BOAT & BARGE COMPONENTS: Metal, Prefabricated

PC Campana Inc..................................... E 800 321-0151
  Lorain *(G-9429)*

BOAT BUILDING & REPAIR

Allmand Boats LLC.................................. G 513 805-4673
  Hamilton *(G-8176)*

Ceasars Creek Marine............................. G 513 897-2912
  Loveland *(G-9477)*

Checkmate Marine Inc............................ F 419 562-3881
  Bucyrus *(G-1853)*

Don Wartko Construction Co.................. D 330 673-5252
  Kent *(G-8810)*

Fife Services LLC.................................... G 614 829-6285
  Ravenna *(G-12714)*

G M Greco Inc.. G 614 822-0522
  Dublin *(G-6884)*

Hesseling & Sons LLC............................. G 419 642-0013
  Lima *(G-9251)*

Mariners Landing Inc............................. F 513 941-3625
  Cincinnati *(G-3131)*

O-Kan Marine Repair Inc........................ E 740 446-4686
  Gallipolis *(G-7897)*

Racelite Southcoast Inc.......................... F 216 581-4600
  Maple Heights *(G-9759)*

Samkat Enterprises Inc.......................... G 937 398-6704
  Medway *(G-10399)*

Screaming Eagle Boats........................... G 937 292-7674
  Bellefontaine *(G-1218)*

Spectre Powerboats LLC......................... G 937 292-7674
  Bellefontaine *(G-1220)*

Tugz International LLC........................... F 216 621-4854
  Cleveland *(G-4836)*

Underground Eyes II LLC....................... G 352 601-1446
  Heath *(G-8332)*

W of Ohio Inc... G 614 873-4664
  Plain City *(G-12601)*

BOAT BUILDING & REPAIRING: Motorized

Nauticus Inc... G 440 746-1290
  Brecksville *(G-1629)*

BOAT DEALERS

Ceasars Creek Marine............................. G 513 897-2912
  Loveland *(G-9477)*

Dynamic Plastics Inc.............................. G 937 437-7261
  New Paris *(G-11481)*

Mariners Landing Inc............................. F 513 941-3625
  Cincinnati *(G-3131)*

BOAT DEALERS: Marine Splys & Eqpt

Employee Codes: A=Over 500 employees, B=251-500
C=101-250, D=51-100, E=20-50, F=10-19, G=1-9

BOAT DEALERS: Marine Splys & Eqpt

Hydromotive Engineering Co .... G 330 425-4266
 Twinsburg *(G-14673)*
Sailors Tailor Inc .... F 937 862-7781
 Spring Valley *(G-13491)*

BOAT REPAIR SVCS

Superior Marine Ways Inc .... C 740 894-6224
 Proctorville *(G-12687)*

BOATS & OTHER MARINE EQPT: Plastic

Boat Decor LLC .... G 216 831-1889
 Beachwood *(G-975)*

BODIES: Truck & Bus

Abutilon Company Inc .... F 419 536-6123
 Toledo *(G-14175)*
Ace Truck Equipment Co .... E 740 453-0551
 Zanesville *(G-16494)*
Airstream Inc .... B 937 596-6111
 Jackson Center *(G-8729)*
Atc Lighting & Plastics Inc .... C 440 466-7670
 Andover *(G-485)*
Bores Manufacturing Inc .... F 419 465-2606
 Monroeville *(G-11123)*
Cascade Corporation .... D 937 327-0300
 Springfield *(G-13541)*
Field Gymmy Inc .... G 419 538-6511
 Glandorf *(G-7978)*
Hendrickson International Corp .... D 740 929-5600
 Hebron *(G-8343)*
Joseph Industries Inc .... D 330 528-0091
 Streetsboro *(G-13776)*
King Kutter II Inc .... E 740 446-0351
 Gallipolis *(G-7896)*
Kuka Tledo Prdction Oprtons LL ...... C 419 727-5500
 Toledo *(G-14353)*
Martin Sheet Metal Inc .... E 216 377-8200
 Cleveland *(G-4362)*
Meritor Inc .... C 740 348-3270
 Granville *(G-8020)*
Paccar Inc .... D 740 774-5111
 Chillicothe *(G-2522)*
Radar Love Co .... E 419 951-4750
 Findlay *(G-7555)*
Skymark Refuelers LLC .... D 419 957-1709
 Findlay *(G-7562)*
Tarpstop LLC .... F 419 873-7867
 Perrysburg *(G-12428)*
Vitatoe Industries Inc .... E 740 773-2425
 Chillicothe *(G-2541)*
Wallace Forge Company .... D 330 488-1203
 Canton *(G-2265)*
Youngstown-Kenworth Inc .... F 330 534-9761
 Hubbard *(G-8574)*

BODY PARTS: Automobile, Stamped Metal

Antique Auto Sheet Metal Inc .... F 937 833-4422
 Brookville *(G-1729)*
Aptiv Services Us LLC .... A 330 373-3568
 Warren *(G-15144)*
Artiflex Manufacturing Inc .... B 330 262-2015
 Wooster *(G-16101)*
Autotx Inc .... G 216 510-6666
 Cleveland *(G-3706)*
Buyers Products Company .... B 440 974-8888
 Mentor *(G-10434)*
Clevelnd-Clffs Tling Stmping H .... F 519 969-4632
 West Chester *(G-15397)*
Clevelnd-Clffs Toling Stamping .... C 216 694-5700
 West Chester *(G-15398)*
Custom Floaters LLC .... G 216 337-9118
 Brookpark *(G-1709)*

Decoma Systems Integration Gro ..... D 419 324-3387
 Toledo *(G-14263)*
General Motors LLC .... A 216 265-5000
 Cleveland *(G-4116)*
Matsu Ohio Inc .... C 419 298-2394
 Edgerton *(G-7077)*
Murotech Ohio Corporation .... C 419 394-6529
 Saint Marys *(G-12958)*
Trellborg Sling Prfiles US Inc .... C 330 995-9725
 Aurora *(G-737)*
Valco Industries LLC .... E 937 399-7400
 Springfield *(G-13653)*
Vehtek Systems Inc .... A 419 373-8741
 Bowling Green *(G-1594)*
Wrena LLC .... E 937 667-4403
 Tipp City *(G-14168)*

BOILER & HEATING REPAIR SVCS

Air-Rite Inc .... E 216 228-8200
 Cleveland *(G-3617)*
Babcock & Wilcox Company .... A 330 753-4511
 Akron *(G-73)*
Nbw Inc .... E 216 377-1700
 Cleveland *(G-4442)*
Weather King Heating & AC .... G 330 908-0281
 Northfield *(G-11914)*

BOILERS: Low-Pressure Heating, Steam Or Hot Water

Nbbi .... G 614 888-8320
 Columbus *(G-5591)*
Weather King Heating & AC .... G 330 908-0281
 Northfield *(G-11914)*

BOLTS: Metal

Airfasco Inc .... E 330 430-6190
 Canton *(G-2029)*
Auto Bolt Company .... D 216 881-3913
 Cleveland *(G-3700)*
Bowes Manufacturing Inc .... E 216 378-2110
 Solon *(G-13321)*
Cold Headed Fas Assemblies Inc ...... F 330 833-0800
 Massillon *(G-10085)*
Consolidated Metal Pdts Inc .... D 513 251-2624
 Cincinnati *(G-2788)*
Curtiss-Wright Flow Ctrl Corp .... D 216 267-3200
 Cleveland *(G-3922)*
Gray America Corp .... E 937 293-9313
 Moraine *(G-11182)*
Iwata Bolt USA Inc .... F 513 942-5050
 Fairfield *(G-7374)*
Jacodar Inc .... F 330 832-9557
 Massillon *(G-10113)*
Jacodar Fsa LLC .... E 330 454-1832
 Canton *(G-2134)*
Keystone Bolt & Nut Company .... D 216 524-9626
 Cleveland *(G-4285)*
Matdan Corporation .... E 513 794-0500
 Blue Ash *(G-1429)*
Mid-West Fabricating Co .... E 740 277-7021
 Lancaster *(G-9024)*
Nova Machine Products Inc .... C 216 267-3200
 Middleburg Heights *(G-10724)*
Qrp Inc .... D 910 371-0700
 Berea *(G-1291)*
Rs Manufacturing Inc .... F 440 946-8002
 Mentor *(G-10549)*
Stelfast LLC .... E 440 879-0077
 Strongsville *(G-13886)*

BOOK STORES

Bookfactory LLC .... E 937 226-7100
 Dayton *(G-623)*

BOOK STORES: Children's

Auguste Moone Enterprises Ltd .... E 216 333-9248
 Cleveland Heights *(G-4937)*

BOOKS, WHOLESALE

CSS Publishing Company .... E 419 227-1818
 Lima *(G-9232)*
Hubbard Company .... E 419 784-4455
 Defiance *(G-6612)*
Zaner-Bloser Inc .... C 614 486-0221
 Columbus *(G-5592)*

BOTTLED GAS DEALERS: Propane

Brightstar Propane & Fuels .... F 614 891-8395
 Westerville *(G-5648)*
Jomac Ltd .... E 330 627-7727
 Carrollton *(G-2311)*
Ngo Development Corporation .... B 740 622-9560
 Coshocton *(G-5787)*
Welders Supply Inc .... E 216 267-4470
 Brookpark *(G-1727)*

BOTTLES: Plastic

Al Root Company .... G 330 725-6677
 Medina *(G-1025)*
Al Root Company .... C 330 723-4359
 Medina *(G-1025)*
Alpha Packaging Holdings Inc .... B 216 252-5595
 Cleveland *(G-3618)*
Ark Operations Inc .... G 419 871-1186
 Dayton *(G-6213)*
Eco-Groupe Inc .... F 937 898-2603
 Dayton *(G-6312)*
Encon Inc .... C 937 898-2603
 Dayton *(G-6320)*
Graham Packaging Pet Tech Inc ...... E 419 334-4197
 Fremont *(G-7782)*
Graham Packg Plastic Pdts Inc .... C 419 421-8037
 Findlay *(G-7515)*
Novatex North America Inc .... D 419 282-4264
 Ashland *(G-595)*
PC Molding LLC .... G 614 873-7712
 Plain City *(G-12510)*
Phoenix Technologies Intl LLC .... E 419 353-7738
 Bowling Green *(G-1583)*
Plastipak Packaging Inc .... C 740 928-4435
 Hebron *(G-8356)*
Plastipak Packaging Inc .... B 937 596-6142
 Jackson Center *(G-8736)*
Rexam PLC .... F 330 893-2451
 Millersburg *(G-10290)*
Ring Container Tech LLC .... D 937 492-0961
 Sidney *(G-13277)*
Silly Brandz Global LLC .... D 419 697-8324
 Toledo *(G-14473)*
Southeastern Container Inc .... D 419 352-6300
 Bowling Green *(G-1589)*

BOWLING CENTERS

Greater Cincinnati Bowl Assn .... E 513 761-7387
 Cincinnati *(G-2970)*

BOWLING EQPT & SPLYS

Done-Rite Bowling Service Co .... E 440 232-3280
 Bedford *(G-1118)*
H & S Distributing Inc .... G 800 336-7784
 North Ridgeville *(G-11843)*

PRODUCT SECTION

BOXES: Filing, Paperboard Made From Purchased Materials

BOXES & CRATES: Rectangular, Wood

Company	Emp	Phone
Cassis Packaging Co. Dayton (G-6249)	F	937 223-8868
Cima Inc. Hamilton (G-8192)	G	513 382-8976
Custom Built Crates Inc. Milford (G-10904)	E	
J & L Wood Products Inc. Tipp City (G-14139)	E	937 667-4064
Schaefer Box & Pallet Co. Hamilton (G-8241)	E	513 738-2500
Silvesco Inc. Marietta (G-9824)	F	740 373-6661
Terry Lumber and Supply Co. Peninsula (G-12342)	F	330 659-6800

BOXES & SHOOK: Nailed Wood

Company	Emp	Phone
Caravan Packaging Inc. Cleveland (G-3790)	G	440 243-4100
Cassady Woodworks Inc. Dayton (G-6155)	E	937 256-7948
Clark Rm Inc. Findlay (G-7494)	F	419 425-9889
Hann Manufacturing Inc. Mcconnelsville (G-10281)	E	740 962-3752
Hines Builders Inc. Troy (G-14577)	F	937 335-4586
J & L Wood Products Inc. Tipp City (G-14139)	E	937 667-4064
Kennedy Group Incorporated Willoughby (G-15939)	D	440 951-7660
Lima Pallet Company Inc. Lima (G-9262)	E	419 229-5736
Quadco Rehabilitation Ctr Inc. Stryker (G-13912)	B	419 682-1011
Schaefer Box & Pallet Co. Hamilton (G-8241)	E	513 738-2500
Van Orders Pallet Company Inc. Liberty Center (G-9205)	F	419 875-6932

BOXES: Corrugated

Company	Emp	Phone
A-Kobak Container Company Inc. Hinckley (G-8471)	F	330 225-7791
Action Specialty Packaging LLC West Chester (G-15530)	G	
Adapt-A-Pak Inc. Fairborn (G-7307)	E	937 845-0386
Akers Packaging Service Inc. Middletown (G-10802)	C	513 422-6312
Akers Packaging Solutions Inc. Middletown (G-10803)	D	513 422-6312
American Corrugated Products Inc. Columbus (G-5124)	C	614 870-2000
American Made Corrugated Packg. Greenfield (G-8027)	F	937 981-2111
Archbold Container Corp. Archbold (G-522)	C	800 446-2520
Argrov Box Co. Dayton (G-6212)	F	937 898-1700
B & B Box Company Inc. Perrysburg (G-12363)	F	419 872-5600
BDS Packaging Inc. Moraine (G-11161)	F	937 643-0530
Billerud Americas Corporation West Chester (G-15379)	D	901 369-4105
Brimar Packaging Inc. Avon (G-764)	E	440 934-3080
Buckeye Boxes Inc. Columbus (G-5219)	D	614 274-8484
Buckeye Corrugated Inc. Wooster (G-16107)	D	330 264-6336
Buckeye Corrugated Inc. Fairlawn (G-7434)	G	330 576-0590
Cambridge Packaging Inc. Cambridge (G-1925)	E	740 432-3351
Cameron Packaging Inc. Lima (G-9227)	G	419 222-9404
Chillicothe Packaging Corp. Chillicothe (G-2497)	E	740 773-5800
Clecorr Inc. Cleveland (G-3829)	E	216 961-5500
Corpad Company Inc. Mansfield (G-9641)	D	419 522-7818
Creative Packaging LLC Zanesville (G-16524)	E	740 452-8497
Family Packaging Inc. Springfield (G-13563)	G	937 325-4106
Folding Carton Service Inc. Ashland (G-573)	F	419 281-4099
Gatton Packaging Inc. Bellville (G-1242)	E	419 886-2577
Georgia-Pacific LLC Circleville (G-3553)	C	740 477-3347
Georgia-Pacific Pcpi Inc. Lebanon (G-9081)	D	513 932-9855
Graphic Paper Products Corp. Springfield (G-13570)	D	937 325-5503
Green Bay Packaging Inc. Fremont (G-7789)	C	419 332-5593
Green Bay Packaging Inc. Lebanon (G-9087)	D	513 489-8700
Greif Inc. Delaware (G-6725)	E	740 657-6500
Greif Inc. Delaware (G-6724)	E	740 549-6000
International Paper Company Delaware (G-6732)	C	740 369-7691
International Paper Company Streetsboro (G-13775)	E	330 626-7300
International Paper Company Wooster (G-16133)	D	330 264-1322
Jamestown Cont Cleveland Inc. Cleveland (G-4250)	B	216 831-3700
Jeff Lori Jed Holdings Inc. Middletown (G-10833)	E	513 423-0319
Jet Container Company Columbus (G-5494)	D	614 444-2133
Larsen Packaging Products Inc. Marysville (G-9923)	F	937 644-5511
Lewisburg Container Company Lewisburg (G-9187)	C	937 962-2681
Marshalltown Packaging Inc. Columbus (G-5543)	G	641 753-5272
McKinley Packaging Company Maple Heights (G-9755)	F	216 663-3344
Menasha Packaging Company LLC West Jefferson (G-15613)	E	614 202-4084
Metro Containers Inc. Cincinnati (G-3158)	D	513 351-6800
Miami Vly Packg Solutions Inc. Dayton (G-6441)	F	937 224-1800
Midwest Box Company Cleveland (G-4409)	E	216 281-9021
Midwest Container Corporation Lebanon (G-9097)	E	513 870-3000
Mount Vernon Packaging Inc. Mount Vernon (G-11280)	F	740 397-3221
Northeast Box Company Ashtabula (G-653)	D	440 992-5500
Novolex Holdings Inc. Franklin (G-7690)	B	937 746-1933
Omer J Smith Inc. West Chester (G-15470)	E	513 921-4717
Packaging Corporation America Ashland (G-597)	C	419 282-5809
Packaging Corporation America Coventry Township (G-6015)	D	330 644-9542
Packaging Corporation America Middletown (G-10848)	D	513 424-3542
Packaging Corporation America Newark (G-11601)	C	740 344-1126
Piqua Paper Box Company Piqua (G-12548)	E	937 773-0313
Pjs Corrugated Inc. Swanton (G-13980)	F	419 644-3383
Pratt (jet Corr) Inc. Springfield (G-13621)	A	937 390-7100
Pratt Industries Inc. Dayton (G-6509)	F	513 262-6253
Pro-Pak Industries Inc. Maumee (G-10225)	C	419 729-0751
Protective Packg Solutions LLC Cincinnati (G-3306)	E	513 769-5777
Raymar Holdings Corporation Columbus (G-5712)	E	614 497-3033
Riverview Packaging Inc. Franklin (G-7698)	E	937 743-9530
Safeway Packaging Inc. New Bremen (G-11408)	E	419 629-3200
Schwarz Partners Packaging LLC Marion (G-9879)	D	740 387-3700
Schwarz Partners Packaging LLC Sidney (G-13283)	F	317 290-1140
Skybox Packaging LLC Mansfield (G-9719)	C	419 525-7209
Smith-Lustig Paper Box Mfg Co. Bedford (G-1155)	F	216 621-0453
Sobel Corrugated Containers Inc. Cleveland (G-4712)	C	216 475-2100
Square One Solutions LLC Findlay (G-7567)	F	419 425-5445
Summit Container Corporation West Chester (G-15511)	F	719 481-8400
Tavens Container Inc. Bedford (G-1156)	D	216 883-3333
Tecumseh Packg Solutions Inc. Van Wert (G-14927)	F	419 238-1122
Temple Inland Middletown (G-10862)	G	513 425-0830
The Mead Corporation Dayton (G-6619)	B	937 495-6323
Trey Corrugated Inc. West Chester (G-15518)	C	513 942-4800
Tri-State Paper Inc. Dayton (G-6631)	F	937 885-3365
Unipac Inc. Hebron (G-8369)	E	740 929-2000
Valley Containers Inc. Mineral Ridge (G-11024)	F	330 544-2244
Value Added Packaging Inc. Englewood (G-7247)	F	937 832-9595
Viking Paper Company Toledo (G-14519)	E	419 729-4951
Wellman Container Corporation Cincinnati (G-3515)	E	513 860-3040
Westrock Rkt LLC West Chester (G-15527)	D	513 860-5546
Weyerhaeuser Co Containeerboar Mount Vernon (G-11300)	F	740 397-5215
Weyerhaeuser Company Wshngtn Ct Hs (G-16246)	G	740 335-4480
Wolford Industrial Park Cleveland (G-4917)	G	216 281-3980

Employee Codes: A=Over 500 employees, B=251-500, C=101-250, D=51-100, E=20-50, F=10-19, G=1-9

BOXES: Filing, Paperboard Made From Purchased Materials

A To Z Paper Box Company .... G 330 325-8722
Rootstown *(G-12850)*

BOXES: Packing & Shipping, Metal

Karyall-Telday Inc .... F 216 281-4063
Cleveland *(G-4274)*

Yarder Manufacturing Company .... E 419 476-3933
Toledo *(G-14530)*

BOXES: Paperboard, Folding

American Corrugated Products Inc .... C 614 870-2000
Columbus *(G-5124)*

Americraft Carton Inc .... G 419 668-1006
Norwalk *(G-11954)*

Boxit Corporation .... D 216 416-9475
Cleveland *(G-3751)*

Boxit Corporation .... F 216 631-6900
Cleveland *(G-3750)*

Brimar Packaging Inc .... E 440 934-3080
Avon *(G-764)*

Cardpak Incorporated .... C 440 542-3100
Solon *(G-13326)*

Chilcote Company .... C 216 781-6000
Cleveland *(G-3819)*

Gpi Ohio LLC .... F 605 332-6721
Groveport *(G-8145)*

Graphic Packaging Intl LLC .... C 513 424-4200
Middletown *(G-10828)*

Graphic Packaging Intl LLC .... C 440 248-4370
Solon *(G-13357)*

Jefferson Smurfit Corporation .... G 440 248-4370
Solon *(G-13369)*

Oak Hills Carton Co .... E 513 948-4200
Cincinnati *(G-3210)*

R R Donnelley & Sons Company .... E 513 870-4040
West Chester *(G-15495)*

Saica Pack US LLC .... E 513 399-5602
Hamilton *(G-8240)*

Sandusky Packaging Corporation .... E 419 626-8520
Sandusky *(G-13092)*

Shelby Company .... E 440 871-9901
Westlake *(G-15787)*

The Apex Paper Box Company .... G 216 631-4000
Cleveland *(G-4778)*

Unipac Inc .... E 740 929-2000
Hebron *(G-8369)*

BOXES: Paperboard, Set-Up

Boxit Corporation .... D 216 416-9475
Cleveland *(G-3751)*

Boxit Corporation .... F 216 631-6900
Cleveland *(G-3750)*

Brimar Packaging Inc .... E 440 934-3080
Avon *(G-764)*

Chilcote Company .... C 216 781-6000
Cleveland *(G-3819)*

Clarke-Boxit Corporation .... E 716 487-1950
Cleveland *(G-3825)*

Graphic Paper Products Corp .... D 937 325-5503
Springfield *(G-13570)*

Sandusky Packaging Corporation .... E 419 626-8520
Sandusky *(G-13092)*

The Apex Paper Box Company .... G 216 631-4000
Cleveland *(G-4778)*

BOXES: Plastic

Triple Diamond Plastics LLC .... D 419 533-0085
Liberty Center *(G-9204)*

BOXES: Wooden

Aslan Worldwide .... F 513 671-0671
West Chester *(G-15370)*

Buckeye Diamond Logistics Inc .... C 937 462-8361
South Charleston *(G-13454)*

Built-Rite Box & Crate Inc .... E 330 263-0936
Wooster *(G-16109)*

Cedar Craft Products Inc .... F 614 759-1600
Blacklick *(G-1333)*

Damar Products Inc .... F 937 492-9023
Sidney *(G-13240)*

Forest City Companies Inc .... E 216 586-5279
Cleveland *(G-4081)*

Lalac One LLC .... E 216 432-4422
Cleveland *(G-4307)*

Ohio Box & Crate Inc .... F 440 526-3133
Burton *(G-1885)*

Sterling Industries Inc .... F 419 523-3788
Ottawa *(G-12193)*

Thomas J Weaver Inc .... F 740 622-2040
Coshocton *(G-5998)*

Traveling Recycle WD Pdts Inc .... F 419 968-2649
Middle Point *(G-10713)*

BRAKES & BRAKE PARTS

Advics Manufacturing Ohio Inc .... A 513 932-7878
Lebanon *(G-9060)*

Bendix Coml Vhcl Systems LLC .... B 440 329-9000
Avon *(G-763)*

Bpi Ec LLC .... G 216 589-0198
Cleveland *(G-3752)*

Brake Parts Inc China LLC .... G 216 589-0198
Cleveland *(G-3753)*

Buckeye Brake Mfg Inc .... F 740 782-1379
Morristown *(G-11222)*

Cmbf Products Inc .... B 440 528-4000
Solon *(G-13330)*

Cooper-Standard Automotive Inc .... D 740 342-3523
New Lexington *(G-11451)*

Friction Products Co .... B 330 725-4941
Medina *(G-10328)*

Harco Manufacturing Group LLC .... C 937 528-5000
Moraine *(G-11184)*

Harco Manufacturing Group LLC .... C 937 528-5000
Moraine *(G-11183)*

Hitachi Astemo Americas Inc .... C 419 425-1259
Findlay *(G-7523)*

Kerr Friction Products Inc .... F 330 455-3983
Canton *(G-2138)*

Knott Brake Company 800 566-8887
Lodi *(G-9352)*

Lucas Sumitomo Brakes Inc .... E 513 934-0024
Lebanon *(G-9094)*

Qualitor Subsidiary H Inc .... F 419 562-7987
Bucyrus *(G-1865)*

Vehicle Systems Inc .... G 330 854-0535
Massillon *(G-10153)*

Veoneer Brake Systems LLC .... B 419 425-6725
Findlay *(G-7578)*

Whirlaway Corporation .... C 440 647-4711
Wellington *(G-15325)*

BRAKES: Bicycle, Friction Clutch & Other

Cmbf Products Inc .... C 440 528-4000
Medina *(G-10310)*

BRAKES: Metal Forming

Eaton Corporation .... C 216 281-2211
Cleveland *(G-3992)*

Ebog Legacy Inc .... D 330 239-4933
Sharon Center *(G-13166)*

Pioneer Solutions LLC .... E 216 383-3400
Euclid *(G-7292)*

BRASS & BRONZE PRDTS: Die-casted

American De Rosa Lamparts LLC .... D
Cuyahoga Falls *(G-6063)*

Hamilton Brass & Alum Castings .... E
Hamilton *(G-8216)*

Model Pattern & Foundry Co .... F 513 542-2322
Cincinnati *(G-3169)*

The Kindt-Collins Company LLC .... D 216 252-4122
Cleveland *(G-4788)*

BRASS FOUNDRY, NEC

Brost Foundry Company .... E 419 522-1133
Mansfield *(G-9632)*

Bunting Bearings LLC .... D 419 866-7000
Holland *(G-8495)*

Maass Midwest Mfg Inc .... G 419 894-6424
Arcadia *(G-516)*

Non-Ferrous Casting Company .... G 937 228-1162
Dayton *(G-6473)*

BRAZING SVCS

CRA Welding LLC .... G 330 317-2007
Fredericksburg *(G-7721)*

Paulo Products Company .... E 440 942-0153
Willoughby *(G-15969)*

Prince & Izant LLC .... E 216 362-7000
Cleveland *(G-4587)*

BRAZING: Metal

American Metal Treating Co .... E 216 431-4492
Cleveland *(G-3654)*

Fbf Limited .... E 513 541-6300
Cincinnati *(G-2898)*

HI Tecmetal Group Inc .... E 216 881-8100
Wickliffe *(G-15835)*

Kando of Cincinnati Inc .... E 513 459-7782
Lebanon *(G-9092)*

Ohio Flame Hardening Company .... E 513 336-6160
Cincinnati *(G-3214)*

Surface Enhancement Tech LLC .... F 513 561-1520
Cincinnati *(G-3435)*

Zion Industries Inc .... D 330 225-3246
Valley City *(G-14902)*

BRICK, STONE & RELATED PRDTS WHOLESALERS

Collinwood Shale Brick Sup Co .... E 216 587-2700
Cleveland *(G-3882)*

Exhibit Concepts Inc .... D 937 890-7000
Vandalia *(G-14939)*

Grafton Ready Mix Concret Inc .... C 440 926-2911
Grafton *(G-8001)*

Kuhlman Corporation .... E 419 897-6000
Maumee *(G-10213)*

Lancaster W Side Coal Co Inc .... F 740 862-4713
Lancaster *(G-9021)*

Modern Builders Supply Inc .... E 419 526-0002
Mansfield *(G-9698)*

Modern Builders Supply Inc .... C 419 241-3961
Toledo *(G-14389)*

R W Sidley Incorporated .... G 330 793-7374
Youngstown *(G-16426)*

Stamm Contracting Company Inc .... E 330 274-8230
Mantua *(G-9743)*

Trumbull Cement Products Co .... G 330 372-4342
Warren *(G-15211)*

Warren Concrete and Supply Co .... E 330 393-1581
Warren *(G-15218)*

PRODUCT SECTION

BUILDING COMPONENTS: Structural Steel

William Dauch Concrete Company......... F 419 668-4458
  Norwalk *(G-11991)*

BRICKS & BLOCKS: Structural

Belden Brick Company LLC..................... E 330 456-0031
  Sugarcreek *(G-13919)*
Belden Brick Company LLC..................... E 330 265-2030
  Sugarcreek *(G-13920)*
Glen-Gery Corporation............................. E 419 468-5002
  Iberia *(G-8648)*
The Belden Brick Company LLC............. E 330 456-0031
  Canton *(G-2243)*

BRICKS : Ceramic Glazed, Clay

Afc Company.. F 330 533-5581
  Canfield *(G-1997)*
Nutro Inc... E 440 572-3800
  Strongsville *(G-13861)*

BRICKS : Flooring, Clay

Kona Blackbird Inc.................................. E 440 285-3189
  Chardon *(G-2455)*

BRICKS : Paving, Clay

Whitacre Greer Company......................... E 330 823-1610
  Alliance *(G-436)*

BRICKS: Clay

Bowerston Shale Company...................... C 740 763-3921
  Newark *(G-11567)*
Bowerston Shale Company...................... E 740 269-2921
  Bowerston *(G-1544)*
Glen-Gery Corporation............................. D 419 845-3321
  Caledonia *(G-1915)*

BRIDGE COMPONENTS: Bridge sections, prefabricated, highway

DS Techstar Inc....................................... G 419 424-0888
  Findlay *(G-7503)*

BROACHING MACHINES

Ohio Broach & Machine Company........... E 440 946-1040
  Willoughby *(G-15963)*

BROADCASTING & COMMS EQPT: Antennas, Transmitting/Comms

AG Antenna Group LLC.......................... G 513 289-6521
  Cincinnati *(G-2601)*
Central USA Wireless LLC..................... F 513 469-1500
  Cincinnati *(G-2719)*
Electro-Magwave Inc.............................. G 216 453-1160
  Cleveland *(G-4004)*
Tencom Ltd.. E 419 865-5877
  Holland *(G-8533)*
Watts Antenna Company......................... G 740 797-9380
  The Plains *(G-14060)*

BROADCASTING & COMMS EQPT: Rcvr-Transmitter Unt, Transceiver

Control Industries Inc.............................. G 937 653-7694
  Findlay *(G-7496)*

BROADCASTING & COMMUNICATIONS EQPT: Light Comms Eqpt

Armada Power LLC................................. G 614 721-4844
  Columbus *(G-5154)*
LSI Industries Inc.................................... B 513 793-3200
  Cincinnati *(G-3115)*

BROKERS' SVCS

Shamrock Companies Inc....................... D 440 899-9510
  Westlake *(G-15786)*

BROKERS: Food

Comber Holdings Inc............................... E 216 961-8600
  Cleveland *(G-3886)*

BROKERS: Log & Lumber

Dale R Adkins... G 740 682-7312
  Oak Hill *(G-12017)*
Hochstetler Milling LLC.......................... E 419 368-0004
  Loudonville *(G-9449)*
Southwood Pallet LLC........................... D 330 682-3747
  Orrville *(G-12158)*

BROKERS: Printing

Depot Direct Inc...................................... E 419 661-1233
  Perrysburg *(G-12375)*

BRONZE FOUNDRY, NEC

Advance Bronzehubco Div...................... E 304 232-4414
  Lodi *(G-9346)*
Foundry Artists Inc................................. G 216 391-9030
  Cleveland *(G-4086)*
Meierjohan-Wengler Inc......................... D 513 771-6074
  Cincinnati *(G-3145)*

BRONZE ROLLING & DRAWING

Jj Seville LLC.. F 330 769-2071
  Seville *(G-13144)*

BROOMS

Delaware Paint Company Ltd.................. F 740 368-9981
  Plain City *(G-12574)*

BROOMS & BRUSHES

Deco Tools Inc.. E 419 476-9321
  Toledo *(G-14262)*
Designetics Inc....................................... D 419 866-0700
  Holland *(G-8504)*
Fimm USA Inc... F 614 568-4874
  Lancaster *(G-9016)*
Mill Rose Laboratories Inc..................... E 440 974-6730
  Mentor *(G-10504)*
Stephen M Trudick.................................. E 440 834-1891
  Burton *(G-1886)*
Unique Packaging & Printing.................. F 440 785-6730
  Mentor *(G-10588)*

BROOMS & BRUSHES: Household Or Indl

Brushes Inc... E 216 267-8084
  Cleveland *(G-3766)*
Ekco Cleaning Inc................................... C 513 733-8882
  Cincinnati *(G-2860)*
Malish Corporation.................................. D 440 951-5356
  Mentor *(G-10499)*
Mill-Rose Company................................. C 440 255-9171
  Mentor *(G-10505)*
Precision Brush Co................................. F 440 542-9600
  Solon *(G-13407)*
Spiral Brushes Inc.................................. E 330 686-2861
  Stow *(G-13725)*
Tod Thin Brushes Inc............................. F 440 576-6859
  Jefferson *(G-8762)*
Trent Manufacturing Company................ G 216 391-1551
  Mentor *(G-10583)*
United Rotary Brush Inc......................... E 937 644-3515
  Plain City *(G-12597)*

BROOMS & BRUSHES: Paint & Varnish

D A L E S Corporation............................. G 419 255-5335
  Toledo *(G-14257)*
The Wooster Brush Company.................. C 330 264-4440
  Wooster *(G-16177)*
Wooster Brush Company......................... G 440 322-8081
  Elyria *(G-7219)*

BROOMS & BRUSHES: Street Sweeping, Hand Or Machine

Public Works Dept Street Div.................. G 740 283-6013
  Steubenville *(G-13675)*

BUCKETS: Plastic

Graham Packaging Pet Tech Inc............. E 513 398-5000
  Mason *(G-9998)*
Impact Products LLC.............................. D 419 841-2891
  Toledo *(G-14328)*

BUILDING & OFFICE CLEANING SVCS

High-TEC Industrial Services.................. D 937 667-1772
  Tipp City *(G-14137)*
Image By J & K LLC................................ F 888 667-6929
  Maumee *(G-10207)*

BUILDING & STRUCTURAL WOOD MEMBERS

Carter-Jones Lumber Company............... F 330 674-9060
  Millersburg *(G-10950)*
Holmes Lumber & Bldg Ctr Inc............... E 330 479-8314
  Canton *(G-2125)*
Holmes Lumber & Bldg Ctr Inc............... C 330 674-9060
  Millersburg *(G-10967)*
Laminate Technologies Inc..................... D 800 231-2523
  Tiffin *(G-14090)*
Socar of Ohio Inc.................................... D 419 596-3100
  Continental *(G-5938)*

BUILDING CLEANING & MAINTENANCE SVCS

All Pack Services LLC............................ G 614 935-0964
  Grove City *(G-8076)*
Contract Lumber Inc............................... F 614 751-1109
  Columbus *(G-5289)*
Green Impressions LLC......................... D 440 240-8508
  Sheffield Village *(G-13182)*
Omnipresence Cleaning LLC.................. F 937 250-4749
  Dayton *(G-6491)*
Phase II Enterprises Inc......................... G 330 484-2113
  Canton *(G-2196)*
Richland Newhope Inds Inc.................... C 419 774-4400
  Mansfield *(G-9712)*
Sand PROperties&landscaping............... G 440 360-7386
  Westlake *(G-15781)*

BUILDING COMPONENTS: Structural Steel

Applied Engneered Surfaces Inc............. E 440 366-0440
  Elyria *(G-7111)*
Boardman Steel Inc................................ D 330 758-0951
  Columbiana *(G-5028)*
Dietrich Industries Inc............................ C 330 372-4014
  Warren *(G-15161)*
Fabx LLC... F 614 565-5835
  Columbus *(G-5369)*
Frederick Steel Company LLC................ D 513 821-6400
  Cincinnati *(G-2922)*
J A McMahon Incorporated.................... E 330 652-2588
  Niles *(G-11674)*

Employee Codes: A=Over 500 employees, B=251-500
C=101-250, D=51-100, E=20-50, F=10-19, G=1-9

BUILDING COMPONENTS: Structural Steel

JJ&pl Services-Consulting LLC .... E 330 923-5783
  Cuyahoga Falls *(G-6093)*
Judo Steel Company Inc .... F
  Dayton *(G-6393)*
Kirwan Industries Inc .... G 513 333-0766
  Cincinnati *(G-3079)*
Lake Building Products Inc .... E 216 486-1500
  Cleveland *(G-4306)*
Lake Building Products Ltd .... F 216 486-1500
  Euclid *(G-7281)*
Louis Arthur Steel Company .... G 440 997-5545
  Geneva *(G-7941)*
M & M Fabrication Inc .... F 740 779-3071
  Chillicothe *(G-2515)*
Mad River Steel Ltd .... G 937 845-4046
  New Carlisle *(G-11420)*
Mc Elwain Industries Inc .... E 419 532-3126
  Ottawa *(G-12184)*
Mound Technologies Inc .... E 937 748-2937
  Springboro *(G-13511)*
Niles Building Products Company .... F 330 544-0880
  Niles *(G-11677)*
R L Waller Construction Inc .... F 740 772-6185
  Chillicothe *(G-2531)*
Rol- Fab Inc .... E 216 662-2500
  Cleveland *(G-4646)*
Thomas Steel Inc .... E 419 483-7540
  Bellevue *(G-1238)*
Turn-Key Industrial Svcs LLC .... D 614 274-1128
  Grove City *(G-8127)*
Unique Fabrications Inc .... F 419 355-1700
  Fremont *(G-7817)*
Universal Fabg Cnstr Svcs Inc .... E 614 274-1128
  Columbus *(G-5845)*
Waterford Tank Fabrication Ltd .... D 740 984-4100
  Beverly *(G-1323)*
Wernli Realty Corporation .... F 937 258-7878
  Beavercreek *(G-1083)*
Wm Lang & Sons Company .... F 513 541-3304
  Cincinnati *(G-3524)*

BUILDING MAINTENANCE SVCS, EXC REPAIRS

Lima Sheet Metal Machine & Mfg .... E 419 229-1161
  Lima *(G-9264)*

BUILDING PRDTS & MATERIALS DEALERS

Adams Brothers Inc .... F 740 819-0323
  Zanesville *(G-16496)*
Building Concepts Inc .... F 419 298-2371
  Edgerton *(G-7072)*
Carter-Jones Lumber Company .... F 330 674-9060
  Millersburg *(G-10950)*
Consumeracq Inc .... E 440 277-9305
  Lorain *(G-9408)*
Consumers Builders Supply Co .... E 440 277-9306
  Lorain *(G-9409)*
Contract Lumber Inc .... F 614 751-1109
  Columbus *(G-5289)*
Counter Concepts Inc .... F 330 848-4848
  Doylestown *(G-6853)*
Dearth Resources Inc .... G 937 325-0651
  Springfield *(G-13551)*
Dowel Yoder & Molding .... G 330 231-2962
  Fredericksburg *(G-7723)*
E P Gerber & Sons Inc .... D 330 857-2021
  Kidron *(G-8913)*
Great Lakes Window Inc .... A 419 666-5555
  Walbridge *(G-15202)*
Higgins Construction & Supply Co Inc .. F 937 364-2331
  Hillsboro *(G-8458)*
Holmes Lumber & Bldg Ctr Inc .... E 330 479-8314
  Canton *(G-2125)*
Holmes Lumber & Bldg Ctr Inc .... C 330 674-9060
  Millersburg *(G-10967)*
Holmes Panel LLC .... G 330 897-5040
  Baltic *(G-838)*
Judy Mills Company Inc .... E 513 271-4241
  Cincinnati *(G-3053)*
K M B Inc .... E 330 889-3451
  Bristolville *(G-1652)*
Khempco Bldg Sup Co Ltd Partnr .... D 740 549-0465
  Delaware *(G-6733)*
Lancaster W Side Coal Co Inc .... F 740 862-4713
  Lancaster *(G-9021)*
Lang Stone Company Inc .... E 614 235-4099
  Columbus *(G-5520)*
Menard Inc .... C 513 583-1444
  Loveland *(G-9496)*
Osborne Inc .... E 440 942-7000
  Mentor *(G-10517)*
Portsmouth Block Inc .... E 740 353-4113
  Portsmouth *(G-12653)*
Stamm Contracting Company Inc .... E 330 274-8230
  Mantua *(G-9743)*
Stiber Fabricating Inc .... F 216 771-7210
  Cleveland *(G-4735)*
T C Redi Mix Youngstown Inc .... E 330 755-2143
  Youngstown *(G-16450)*
Terry Lumber and Supply Co .... F 330 659-6800
  Peninsula *(G-12342)*
The F A Requarth Company .... E 937 224-1141
  Dayton *(G-6618)*
Tri-County Block and Brick Inc .... F 419 826-7060
  Swanton *(G-13986)*
Trumbull Cement Products Co .... G 330 372-4342
  Warren *(G-15211)*
Warren Concrete and Supply Co .... E 330 393-1581
  Warren *(G-15218)*
Wmg Wood More .... F 440 350-3970
  Painesville *(G-12278)*
Zaenkert Surveying Essentials .... G 513 738-2917
  Okeana *(G-12070)*

BUILDING PRDTS: Concrete

Olde Wood Ltd .... E 330 866-1441
  Magnolia *(G-9596)*
One Wish LLC .... F 800 505-6883
  Bedford *(G-1147)*
Quanex Building Products Corp .... F 360 345-1241
  Akron *(G-290)*
Tamarron Technology Inc .... F 800 277-3207
  Cincinnati *(G-3440)*

BUILDING PRDTS: Stone

Jalco Industries Inc .... F 740 286-3808
  Jackson *(G-8717)*
Toledo Cut Stone Inc .... F 419 531-1623
  Toledo *(G-14494)*

BUILDING SCALES MODELS

3-D Technical Services Company .... E 937 746-2901
  Franklin *(G-7659)*

BUILDINGS & COMPONENTS: Prefabricated Metal

American Ramp Systems .... G 440 336-4988
  North Olmsted *(G-11816)*
Benchmark Archtectural Systems .... E 614 444-0110
  Columbus *(G-5182)*
Benko Products Inc .... E 440 934-2180
  Sheffield Village *(G-13181)*
Cdc Fab Co .... F 419 866-7705
  Maumee *(G-10474)*
Connect Housing Blocks LLC .... E 614 503-4344
  Columbus *(G-5286)*
Consoldted Anlycal Systems In .... F 513 542-1200
  Cincinnati *(G-2387)*
Hoge Lumber Company .... E 419 753-2263
  New Knoxville *(G-11447)*
Lab-Pro Inc .... G 937 434-9600
  Miamisburg *(G-10653)*
Morton Buildings Inc .... E 419 399-4549
  Kenton *(G-8893)*
ONeals Tarpaulin & Awning Co .... F 330 788-6504
  Youngstown *(G-16406)*
R L Torbeck Industries Inc .... F 513 367-0080
  Harrison *(G-8259)*
Rebsco Inc .... F 937 548-2246
  Greenville *(G-8657)*
Reliable Metal Buildings LLC .... G 419 737-1300
  Pioneer *(G-12459)*
Sheds Direct Inc .... G 330 674-3001
  Millersburg *(G-17993)*
Sheltervision LLC .... F 419 852-7788
  Minster *(G-11060)*
Skyline Corporation .... C 330 852-2483
  Sugarcreek *(G-13938)*

BUILDINGS: Mobile, For Commercial Use

Muster Rdu Inc .... G 614 537-5440
  Lancaster *(G-9046)*

BUILDINGS: Portable

Affordable Barn Co Ltd .... F 330 674-3001
  Millersburg *(G-1938)*
Golden Giant Inc .... E 419 674-4038
  Kenton *(G-8883)*
Jack Walters & Sons Corp .... E 937 653-8986
  Urbana *(G-14840)*
Morton Buildings Inc .... E 330 345-6188
  Wooster *(G-16155)*
Williams Scotsman Inc .... D 614 449-8675
  Columbus *(G-5883)*

BUILDINGS: Prefabricated, Metal

Cornerstone Bldg Brands Inc .... C 937 584-3300
  Middletown *(G-1813)*
Enclosure Supplies LLC .... E 513 782-3900
  Cincinnati *(G-2865)*
Great Day Improvements LLC .... B 267 223-1289
  Macedonia *(G-955)*
Joyce Manufacturing Co .... D 440 239-9100
  Berea *(G-1286)*
Pei Liquidation Company .... C 330 467-4267
  Macedonia *(G-954)*
Rayhaven Group Inc .... G 330 659-3183
  Richfield *(G-12790)*
Republic Technology Corp .... F 216 622-5000
  Cleveland *(G-4627)*

BUILDINGS: Prefabricated, Wood

Beachy Barns Ltd .... F 614 873-4193
  Plain City *(G-1256)*
Cooper Enterprise Inc .... D 419 347-5232
  Shelby *(G-13193)*
Fifth Avenue Lumber Co .... E 614 833-6655
  Canal Winchester *(G-1986)*
J Aaron Weaver .... G 440 474-9185
  Rome *(G-12848)*
Morton Buildings Inc .... E 419 675-2311
  Kenton *(G-8894)*
Patio Enclosures .... F 513 733-4646
  Cincinnati *(G-3236)*

PRODUCT SECTION

BUSINESS FORMS: Printed, Manifold

Rona Enterprises Inc .... G 740 927-9971
  Pataskala *(G-12306)*

Skyline Corporation .... C 330 852-2483
  Sugarcreek *(G-13938)*

Vinyl Design Corporation .... E 419 283-4009
  Holland *(G-8536)*

BULLETIN BOARDS: Wood

GMI Companies Inc .... G 513 932-3445
  Lebanon *(G-9084)*

GMI Companies Inc .... C 513 932-3445
  Lebanon *(G-9083)*

Marsh Industries Inc .... D 800 426-4244
  New Philadelphia *(G-11516)*

Tri-State Supply Co Inc .... F 614 272-6767
  Columbus *(G-5836)*

BULLETPROOF VESTS

Forceone LLC .... F 513 939-1018
  Hebron *(G-8342)*

BUMPERS: Motor Vehicle

Superior Production LLC .... C 614 444-2181
  Columbus *(G-5800)*

BUOYS: Plastic

Worthignton Products Inc .... G 330 452-7400
  East Canton *(G-6982)*

BURIAL VAULTS: Concrete Or Precast Terrazzo

Akron Vault Company Inc .... E 330 784-5475
  Akron *(G-48)*

Alexander Wilbert Vault Co .... G 419 468-3477
  Galion *(G-7859)*

Baumgardner Products Co .... G 330 376-2466
  Akron *(G-78)*

Bell Vault and Monu Works Inc .... E 937 866-2444
  Miamisburg *(G-10615)*

Fithian-Wilbert Burial Vlt Co .... F 330 758-2327
  Youngstown *(G-16357)*

Galena Vault Ltd .... G 740 965-2200
  Galena *(G-7854)*

Landon Vault Company .... E 614 443-5505
  Columbus *(G-5519)*

Mack Industries .... E 419 353-7081
  Bowling Green *(G-1572)*

Mack Industries Inc .... G 740 393-1121
  Mount Vernon *(G-11277)*

National Con Burial Vlt Assn .... G 407 788-1996
  Dayton *(G-6463)*

Neher Burial Vault Company .... E 937 399-4494
  Springfield *(G-13612)*

Paws & Remember NW Ohio LLC .... G 419 662-9000
  Northwood *(G-11925)*

Seislove Vault & Septic Tanks .... G 419 447-5473
  Tiffin *(G-14103)*

Southern Ohio Vault Co Inc .... G 740 456-5898
  Portsmouth *(G-12657)*

Stuart Burial Vault Co Inc .... E 740 569-4158
  Bremen *(G-1639)*

Toli Vault .... G 866 998-8654
  Westlake *(G-15798)*

Turner Vault Co .... E 419 537-1133
  Northwood *(G-11932)*

Youngstown Burial Vault Co .... G 330 782-0015
  Girard *(G-7977)*

BURNERS: Gas, Indl

Ws Thermal Process Tech Inc .... G 440 385-6829
  Lorain *(G-9445)*

BURNERS: Oil, Domestic Or Indl

Es Thermal Inc .... E 440 323-3291
  Berea *(G-1277)*

RW Beckett Corporation .... C 440 327-1060
  North Ridgeville *(G-11860)*

BUS BARS: Electrical

Crown Electric Engrg & Mfg LLC .... E 513 539-7394
  Middletown *(G-10816)*

Reliable Hermetic Seals LLC .... F 888 747-3250
  Beavercreek *(G-1060)*

Schneider Electric Usa Inc .... D 513 777-4445
  West Chester *(G-15506)*

BUSHINGS & BEARINGS

Advance Bronze Inc .... F 330 948-1231
  Lodi *(G-9345)*

Climax Metal Products Company .... D 440 943-8898
  Mentor *(G-10440)*

Dupont Specialty Pdts USA LLC .... C 216 901-3600
  Cleveland *(G-3978)*

McNeil Industries Inc .... E 440 951-7756
  Painesville *(G-12251)*

S C Industries Inc .... E 216 732-9000
  Euclid *(G-7300)*

BUSHINGS & BEARINGS: Brass, Exc Machined

Johnson Metall Inc .... D 440 245-6826
  Lorain *(G-9415)*

BUSINESS ACTIVITIES: Non-Commercial Site

As Clean As It Gets Off Brkroo .... E 216 256-1143
  South Euclid *(G-13459)*

Atlantic Welding LLC .... F 937 570-5094
  Piqua *(G-12505)*

Bridgits Bath LLC .... G 937 259-1960
  Dayton *(G-6236)*

Coffing Corporation .... E 513 919-2813
  Liberty Twp *(G-9212)*

Custom Information Systems Inc .... F 614 875-2245
  Grove City *(G-8086)*

Facility Service Pros LLC .... G 419 577-6123
  Collins *(G-5004)*

Flexsys Inc .... B 212 605-6000
  Akron *(G-156)*

Geauga Highway Co .... F 440 834-4580
  Hiram *(G-8484)*

Groundhogs 2000 LLC .... G 440 653-1647
  Bedford *(G-1122)*

Hands On International LLC .... G 513 502-9000
  West Chester *(G-15560)*

Health Nuts Media LLC .... B 818 802-5222
  Cleveland *(G-4175)*

Ineos ABS (usa) LLC .... C 513 467-2400
  Addyston *(G-8)*

Jnp Group LLC .... F 800 735-9645
  Wooster *(G-16137)*

Joseph G Pappas .... G 330 383-2917
  East Liverpool *(G-6995)*

Liminal Esports LLC .... G 440 423-5856
  Gates Mills *(G-7928)*

Link To Success Inc .... G 888 959-4203
  Norwalk *(G-11978)*

Mark Grzianis St Treats Ex Inc .... F 330 414-6266
  Kent *(G-8832)*

Mettler Footwear Inc .... G 330 703-0079
  Hudson *(G-8605)*

Millers Aplus Cmpt Svcs LLC .... F 330 620-5288
  Akron *(G-250)*

Natures Health Food LLC .... F 419 260-9265
  Mount Victory *(G-11301)*

North Shore Printing LLC .... G 740 876-9066
  Portsmouth *(G-12651)*

Park Press Direct .... G 419 626-4426
  Sandusky *(G-13086)*

Prospect Rock LLC .... F 740 512-0542
  Saint Clairsville *(G-12919)*

Pur Hair Extensions LLC .... G 330 786-5772
  Akron *(G-287)*

R & H Enterprises Llc .... G 216 702-4449
  Richmond Heights *(G-12810)*

RE Connors Construction Ltd .... G 740 644-0261
  Thornville *(G-14068)*

Red Barakuda LLC .... G 614 596-5432
  Columbus *(G-5715)*

Rock Iron Corporation .... F 419 529-9411
  Crestline *(G-6037)*

Scottrods LLC .... G 419 499-2705
  Monroeville *(G-11125)*

Shousha Trucking LLC .... G 937 270-4471
  Dayton *(G-6571)*

Simply Unique Snacks LLC .... G 513 223-7736
  Cincinnati *(G-3394)*

Standard Wellness Company LLC .... C 330 931-1037
  Cleveland *(G-4729)*

TI Marie Candle Company LLC .... F 513 746-7798
  Cincinnati *(G-3454)*

Valley View Pallets LLC .... G 740 599-0010
  Danville *(G-6149)*

BUSINESS FORMS WHOLESALERS

American Business Forms Inc .... E 513 312-2522
  West Chester *(G-15535)*

Anthony Business Forms Inc .... G 937 253-0072
  Dayton *(G-6153)*

Bay Business Forms Inc .... E 937 322-3000
  Springfield *(G-13539)*

Bloch Printing Company .... G 330 576-6760
  Copley *(G-5945)*

GBS Corp .... C 330 494-5330
  North Canton *(G-11729)*

Gq Business Products Inc .... G 513 792-4750
  Loveland *(G-9482)*

Highland Computer Forms Inc .... D 937 393-4215
  Hillsboro *(G-8459)*

Optimum System Products Inc .... E 614 885-4464
  Westerville *(G-15718)*

Shamrock Companies Inc .... D 440 899-9510
  Westlake *(G-15786)*

William J Bergen & Co .... G 440 248-6132
  Solon *(G-13448)*

BUSINESS FORMS: Printed, Continuous

Rotary Forms Press Inc .... E 937 393-3426
  Hillsboro *(G-8465)*

BUSINESS FORMS: Printed, Manifold

Anderson Graphics Inc .... E 330 745-2165
  Barberton *(G-855)*

Anthony Business Forms Inc .... G 937 253-0072
  Dayton *(G-6153)*

Custom Products Corporation .... D 440 528-7100
  Solon *(G-13334)*

Dupli-Systems Inc .... C 440 234-9415
  Strongsville *(G-13830)*

Eleet Cryogenics Inc .... E 330 874-4009
  Bolivar *(G-1524)*

GBS Corp .... C 330 863-1828
  Malvern *(G-9612)*

BUSINESS FORMS: Printed, Manifold

GBS Corp .... C 330 494-5330
North Canton *(G-11729)*

Geygan Enterprises Inc .... F 513 932-4222
Lebanon *(G-9082)*

Glatfelter Corporation .... G 419 333-6700
Fremont *(G-7787)*

Kroy LLC .... C 216 426-5600
Cleveland *(G-4299)*

Plastilene Inc .... E 614 592-8699
Wshngtn Ct Hs *(G-16236)*

Print-Digital Incorporated .... G 330 686-5945
Stow *(G-13718)*

Quick Tech Graphics Inc .... E 937 743-5952
Springboro *(G-13518)*

Reynolds and Reynolds Company .... F 419 584-7000
Celina *(G-2346)*

S F Mock & Associates LLC .... F 937 438-0196
Dayton *(G-6556)*

Shawnee Systems Inc .... D 513 561-9932
Cincinnati *(G-3387)*

SRC Liquidation LLC .... G 937 221-1000
Dayton *(G-6586)*

Taylor Communications Inc .... E 937 221-1000
Dayton *(G-6609)*

Taylor Communications Inc .... F 732 356-0081
Dayton *(G-6610)*

Taylor Communications Inc .... F 937 221-3347
Grove City *(G-8121)*

Taylor Communications Inc .... F 216 265-1800
Richfield *(G-12800)*

Thomas Products Co Inc .... E 513 756-9009
Cincinnati *(G-3453)*

Wfsr Holdings LLC .... A 877 735-4966
Dayton *(G-6654)*

BUSINESS MACHINE REPAIR, ELECTRIC

Queen City Office Machine .... F 513 251-7200
Cincinnati *(G-3317)*

BUSINESS TRAINING SVCS

Pakra LLC .... F 614 477-6965
Columbus *(G-5651)*

BUTTER WHOLESALERS

Frank L Harter & Son Inc .... G 513 574-1330
Cincinnati *(G-2920)*

BUTTONS

Purebuttonscom LLC .... F 330 721-1600
Medina *(G-10367)*

CABINETS & CASES: Show, Display & Storage, Exc Wood

D Lewis Inc .... G 740 695-2615
Saint Clairsville *(G-12901)*

GMR Furniture Services Ltd .... G 216 244-5072
Cleveland *(G-4130)*

Metal Fabricating Corporation .... D 216 631-8121
Cleveland *(G-4396)*

Paul Yoder .... G 740 439-5811
Senecaville *(G-13130)*

CABINETS: Bathroom Vanities, Wood

Bison Builders LLC .... F 614 636-0365
Columbus *(G-5191)*

East Oberlin Cabinets LLC .... G 440 775-1166
Oberlin *(G-12050)*

Hampshire Co .... F 937 773-3493
Piqua *(G-12518)*

Profiles In Design Inc .... F 513 751-2212
Cincinnati *(G-3302)*

S & G Manufacturing Group LLC .... C 614 529-0100
Hilliard *(G-8437)*

Wilson Cabinet Co .... G 330 276-8711
Killbuck *(G-8925)*

CABINETS: Entertainment

Innerwood & Company .... F 513 677-2229
Loveland *(G-9486)*

Kraftmaid Trucking Inc .... D 440 632-2531
Middlefield *(G-10762)*

CABINETS: Entertainment Units, Household, Wood

Progressive Furniture Inc .... E 419 446-4500
Archbold *(G-542)*

CABINETS: Factory

Bolons Custom Kitchens Inc .... G 330 499-0092
Canton *(G-2050)*

Custom Surroundings Inc .... F 913 839-0100
Valley City *(G-14868)*

Home Idea Center Inc .... F 419 375-4951
Fort Recovery *(G-7619)*

Kinnemyers Cornerstone Cab Inc .... G 513 353-3030
Cleves *(G-4957)*

Mro Built LLC .... D 330 526-0555
North Canton *(G-11746)*

Vivo Brothers LLC .... F 330 629-8686
Columbiana *(G-5054)*

Woodworking Shop LLC .... F 513 330-9663
Miamisburg *(G-10702)*

CABINETS: Kitchen, Metal

C-Link Enterprises LLC .... F 937 222-2829
Dayton *(G-6244)*

CABINETS: Kitchen, Wood

4-B Wood Specialties Inc .... F 330 769-2188
Seville *(G-13133)*

A & J Woodworking Inc .... G 419 695-5655
Delphos *(G-6759)*

A-Display Service Corp .... F 614 469-1230
Columbus *(G-5082)*

Affordable Cabinet Doors .... G 513 734-9663
Bethel *(G-1318)*

Agean Marble Manufacturing .... F 513 874-1475
West Chester *(G-15533)*

Ailes Millwork Inc .... E 330 678-4300
Kent *(G-8796)*

Al-Co Products Inc .... G 419 399-3867
Latty *(G-9053)*

Alpine Cabinets .... F 330 359-5724
Dundee *(G-6962)*

American Wood Reface Inc .... G 440 944-3750
Medina *(G-10294)*

Anthony Flottemesch & Son Inc .... F 513 561-1212
Cincinnati *(G-2628)*

Approved Plumbing Co .... F 216 663-5063
Cleveland *(G-3671)*

As America Inc .... E 419 522-4211
Mansfield *(G-9626)*

Benchmark-Cabinets LLC .... G 740 694-1144
Fredericktown *(G-7739)*

Bestwood Cabinetry LLC .... G 937 661-9621
Xenia *(G-16252)*

Bruewer Woodwork Mfg Co .... D 513 353-3505
Cleves *(G-4946)*

Cabinet and Granite Depot LLC .... F 513 874-2100
West Chester *(G-15383)*

Cabinet Concepts Inc .... G 440 232-4644
Oakwood Village *(G-12036)*

Cabinet Creat B Lillibridge .... F 419 476-6838
Toledo *(G-14225)*

Cabinet Shop .... G 614 885-9676
Columbus *(G-5061)*

Cabinet Specialties Inc .... G 330 695-3463
Fredericksburg *(G-7718)*

Cabinetworks Group Mich LLC .... E 440 247-3091
Chagrin Falls *(G-2368)*

Cabinetworks Group Mich LLC .... C 440 632-2547
Middlefield *(G-10737)*

Cabintwrks Group Mddlfield LLC .... A 888 562-7744
Middlefield *(G-10738)*

Carter-Jones Lumber Company .... F 330 674-9060
Millersburg *(G-10950)*

Cass Woodworking Inc .... F 800 589-8841
Galion *(G-7864)*

Cedee Cedar Inc .... F 740 363-3148
Delaware *(G-6707)*

Clancys Cabinet LLC .... G 419 445-4455
Archbold *(G-520)*

Clark Son Actn Liquidation Inc .... G 330 866-9330
East Sparta *(G-7013)*

Cleveland Cabinets LLC .... G 216 459-7676
Cleveland *(G-3534)*

Climate Pros LLC .... D 216 881-5200
Cleveland *(G-3578)*

Climate Pros LLC .... D 330 744-2732
Youngstown *(G-6340)*

Colby Woodworking Inc .... E 937 224-7676
Dayton *(G-6258)*

Colonial Cabinets Inc .... G 440 355-9663
Lagrange *(G-8916)*

Counter-Advice Inc .... F 937 291-1600
Franklin *(G-7668)*

Countryside Cabinets .... G 740 397-6488
Fredericktown *(G-7742)*

Creative Cabinets Ltd .... F 740 689-0603
Lancaster *(G-9074)*

Creative Edge Cbnets Wdwkg LLC ...... G 419 453-3416
Ottoville *(G-12153)*

Crowes Cabinets Inc .... E 330 729-9911
Youngstown *(G-6343)*

Custom Woodworking Inc .... G 419 456-3330
Ottawa *(G-12177)*

D Lewis Inc .... G 740 695-2615
Saint Clairsville *(G-12901)*

Dgl Woodworking Inc .... F 937 837-7091
Dayton *(G-6298)*

Distinctive Surfaces LLC .... F 614 431-0898
Columbus *(G-5330)*

Dover Cabinet Industries Inc .... F 330 343-9074
Dover *(G-6817)*

Dutch Valley Woodworking Inc .... F 330 852-4319
Sugarcreek *(G-13923)*

E J Skok Industries .... E 216 292-7533
Bedford *(G-1119)*

Fairfield Wood Works Ltd .... G 740 689-1953
Lancaster *(G-9075)*

Fdi Cabinetry LLC .... G 513 353-4500
Cleves *(G-4952)*

Forum III Inc .... G 513 961-5123
Cincinnati *(G-2917)*

Franklin Cabinet Company Inc .... E 937 743-9606
Franklin *(G-7676)*

Gillard Construction Inc .... F 740 376-9744
Marietta *(G-9795)*

Gross & Sons Custom Millwork .... G 419 227-0214
Lima *(G-9246)*

Holmes Lumber & Bldg Ctr Inc .... E 330 479-8314
Canton *(G-2125)*

Holmes Lumber & Bldg Ctr Inc .... C 330 674-9060
Millersburg *(G-10957)*

| PRODUCT SECTION | | CABLE: Ropes & Fiber |

Idx Corporation.................................... C 937 401-3225
   Dayton *(G-6378)*

J & K Cabinetry Inc............................. F 513 860-3461
   West Chester *(G-15450)*

Jacob & Levis Ltd............................... G 330 852-7600
   Sugarcreek *(G-13926)*

Johannings Inc.................................... G 330 875-1706
   Louisville *(G-9463)*

JP Cabinets LLC................................ G 440 232-9780
   Cleveland *(G-4264)*

Kellogg Cabinets Inc........................... G 614 833-9596
   Canal Winchester *(G-1988)*

Kinnemyers Cornerstone Cab Inc....... G 513 353-3030
   Cleves *(G-4957)*

Kinsella Manufacturing Co Inc............ F 513 561-5285
   Cincinnati *(G-3077)*

Kitchen Designs Plus Inc.................... E 419 536-6605
   Toledo *(G-14348)*

Kitchens By Java................................. G 419 621-7677
   Sandusky *(G-13071)*

Kitchens By Rutenschroer Inc............ G 513 251-8333
   Cincinnati *(G-3080)*

Knapke Cabinets Inc............................ E 937 335-8383
   Troy *(G-14592)*

Knapke Custom Cabinetry Ltd............. G 937 459-8866
   Versailles *(G-14985)*

Kreager Co LLC.................................. G 740 345-1605
   Newark *(G-11585)*

Laminated Concepts Inc...................... F 216 475-4141
   Maple Heights *(G-9753)*

Larsen Cusotm Cabinetry................... G 614 282-3929
   Columbus *(G-5522)*

Leiden Cabinet Co............................... G 330 425-8555
   Twinsburg *(G-14686)*

Lily Ann Cabinets................................. G 419 360-2455
   Toledo *(G-14367)*

Lima Millwork Inc................................ F 419 331-3303
   Elida *(G-7094)*

Mac Lean J S Co.................................. E 614 878-5454
   Columbus *(G-5538)*

Mammana Custom Woodworking Inc.... E 216 581-9059
   Maple Heights *(G-9754)*

Marsh Industries Inc............................. E 330 308-8667
   New Philadelphia *(G-11515)*

Marzano Inc.. G 216 459-2051
   Cleveland *(G-4364)*

Masterbrand Cabinets LLC................... B 812 482-2527
   Beachwood *(G-999)*

Miami Vly Counters & Spc Inc............. G 937 865-0562
   Miamisburg *(G-10658)*

Midwest Woodworking Co Inc............. F 513 631-6684
   Cincinnati *(G-3164)*

Miller Cabinet Ltd................................. F 614 873-4221
   Plain City *(G-12586)*

Mills Pride Premier Inc........................ G 740 941-1300
   Waverly *(G-15285)*

Mock Woodworking Company LLC..... E 740 452-2701
   Zanesville *(G-16546)*

Modern Designs Inc............................ G 330 644-1771
   Green *(G-8025)*

Mro Built LLC....................................... D 330 526-0555
   North Canton *(G-11746)*

Nicklaus Group LLC............................ F 740 277-5700
   Lancaster *(G-9029)*

Northeast Cabinet Co LLC................. G 614 759-0800
   Columbus *(G-5603)*

Ohio River Valley Cabinet................... G 740 975-8846
   Newark *(G-11599)*

Online Mega Sellers Corp................... G 888 384-6468
   Toledo *(G-14415)*

Phelps Creek Wood Works Llc.......... G 440 693-4314
   Middlefield *(G-10780)*

Pro Choice Cabinetry LLC................... G 937 313-9297
   Dayton *(G-6525)*

Red Barn Cabinet Co.......................... G 937 884-9800
   Arcanum *(G-519)*

Reserve Millwork LLC......................... E 216 531-6982
   Bedford *(G-1153)*

Rheaco Builders Inc............................ G 330 425-3090
   Twinsburg *(G-14725)*

Riceland Cabinet Inc........................... D 330 601-1071
   Wooster *(G-16163)*

Riceland Cabinet Corporation.............. F 330 601-1071
   Wooster *(G-16164)*

Richard Benhase & Assoc Inc............. G 513 772-1896
   Cincinnati *(G-3338)*

River East Custom Cabinets................ E 419 244-3226
   Toledo *(G-14452)*

Riverside Cnstr Svcs Inc..................... E 513 723-0900
   Cincinnati *(G-3344)*

Roettger Hardwood Inc....................... F 937 693-6811
   Kettlersville *(G-8912)*

Royal Cabinet Design Co Inc............... F 216 267-5330
   Cleveland *(G-4656)*

Salem Mill & Cabinet Co...................... G 330 337-9568
   Salem *(G-13028)*

Signature Cabinetry Inc....................... G 614 252-2227
   Columbus *(G-5768)*

Snows Wood Shop Inc........................ E 419 836-3805
   Oregon *(G-12111)*

Springhill Dimensions.......................... E 330 317-1926
   Dalton *(G-6143)*

Supply One Corporation...................... F 937 297-1111
   Bellbrook *(G-1194)*

Surface Enterprises Inc....................... G 419 476-5670
   Toledo *(G-14479)*

TDS Custom Cabinets LLC................. G 614 517-2220
   Columbus *(G-5814)*

The Hattenbach Company.................... D 216 881-5200
   Cleveland *(G-4785)*

Thomas Cabinet Shop Inc................... F 937 847-8239
   Dayton *(G-6621)*

Tiffin Metal Products Co...................... C 419 447-8414
   Tiffin *(G-14110)*

Trail Cabinet.. G 330 893-3791
   Dundee *(G-6969)*

Tri-State Kitchens LLC........................ G 740 574-6727
   Wheelersburg *(G-15812)*

Troyers Cabinet Shop Ltd.................... F 937 464-7702
   Belle Center *(G-1198)*

Trutech Cabinetry LLC........................ G 614 338-0680
   Columbus *(G-5840)*

Turnwood Industry Inc......................... G 330 278-2421
   Hinckley *(G-8478)*

Woodcraft Industries Inc...................... D 440 632-9655
   Middlefield *(G-10798)*

Woodcraft Industries Inc...................... C 440 437-7811
   Orwell *(G-12171)*

Wurms Woodworking Company........... E 419 492-2184
   New Washington *(G-11552)*

X44 Corp.. F 330 657-2335
   Peninsula *(G-12347)*

CABINETS: Office, Wood

Custom Millcraft Corp.......................... E 513 874-7080
   West Chester *(G-15410)*

East Woodworking Company............... E 216 791-5950
   Cleveland *(G-3990)*

Geograph Industries Inc...................... E 513 202-9200
   Harrison *(G-8276)*

Hoge Lumber Company........................ E 419 753-2263
   New Knoxville *(G-11447)*

Interior Products Co Inc...................... E 216 641-1919
   Cleveland *(G-4232)*

Mel Heitkamp Builders Ltd.................. G 419 375-0405
   Fort Recovery *(G-7623)*

Richard Benhase & Assoc Inc............. G 513 772-1896
   Cincinnati *(G-3338)*

Specialty Svcs Cabinetry Inc................ G 614 421-1599
   Columbus *(G-5784)*

CABINETS: Show, Display, Etc, Wood, Exc Refrigerated

A J Construction Co............................ G 330 539-9544
   Girard *(G-7958)*

Amtekco Industries LLC..................... D 614 228-6590
   Columbus *(G-5136)*

Case Crafters Inc................................ G 937 667-9473
   Tipp City *(G-14127)*

Climate Pros LLC................................ D 216 881-5200
   Cleveland *(G-3878)*

Climate Pros LLC................................ D 330 744-2732
   Youngstown *(G-16340)*

Custom Design Cabinets & Tops......... G 440 639-9900
   Painesville *(G-12225)*

Designer Cntemporary Laminates....... G 440 946-8207
   Painesville *(G-12228)*

Gary L Gast... G 419 626-5915
   Sandusky *(G-13059)*

Kellogg Cabinets Inc........................... G 614 833-9596
   Canal Winchester *(G-1988)*

Miller Cabinet Ltd................................. F 614 873-4221
   Plain City *(G-12586)*

Rinos Woodworking Shop Inc............. F 440 946-1718
   Willoughby *(G-15984)*

Robertson Cabinets Inc....................... F 937 698-3755
   West Milton *(G-15631)*

The Hattenbach Company.................... D 216 881-5200
   Cleveland *(G-4785)*

Village Cabinet Shop Inc..................... G 704 966-0801
   Cincinnati *(G-3499)*

CABLE & OTHER PAY TELEVISION DISTRIBUTION

Ohio News Network............................. E 614 460-3700
   Columbus *(G-5622)*

CABLE TELEVISION

Block Communications Inc................. F 419 724-6212
   Toledo *(G-14214)*

CABLE: Fiber

Connect Television.............................. G 614 876-4402
   Hilliard *(G-8409)*

Core Optix Inc..................................... F 855 267-3678
   Cincinnati *(G-2796)*

Katimex USA Inc.................................. G 440 338-3500
   Chagrin Falls *(G-2381)*

CABLE: Fiber Optic

Cbst Acquisition LLC........................... D 513 361-9600
   Cincinnati *(G-2711)*

Core Optix Inc..................................... F 855 267-3678
   Cincinnati *(G-2796)*

CABLE: Noninsulated

Assembly Specialty Pdts Inc................ E 216 676-5600
   Cleveland *(G-3693)*

Microplex Inc....................................... E 330 498-0600
   North Canton *(G-11743)*

CABLE: Ropes & Fiber

Atwood Rope Manufacturing Inc.......... E 614 920-0534
   Canal Winchester *(G-1979)*

CABLE: Ropes & Fiber

Atwood Rope Manufacturing Inc............... G 614 920-0534
Millersport (G-11010)
Automted Cmpnent Spcalists LLC........... E 513 335-4285
Cincinnati (G-2645)
Radix Wire & Cable LLC......................... D 216 731-9191
Solon (G-13410)

CABLE: Steel, Insulated Or Armored

Heilind Electronics Inc............................. E 440 473-9600
Cleveland (G-4177)
Torque 2020 CMA Acqisition LLC............ C 330 874-2900
Bolivar (G-1539)

CABS: Indl Trucks & Tractors

Martin Sheet Metal Inc............................. E 216 377-8200
Cleveland (G-4362)

CAFES

R & T Estate LLC..................................... F 216 862-0822
Cleveland (G-4611)
Shawadi LLC.. E 614 839-0698
Westerville (G-15720)

CAFETERIAS

Mark Grzianis St Treats Ex Inc................ F 330 414-6266
Kent (G-8832)

CALCULATING & ACCOUNTING EQPT

Diebold Nixdorf Incorporated................... E 336 662-1115
North Canton (G-11721)
Thyme Inc... F 484 872-8430
Akron (G-357)

CALIBRATING SVCS, NEC

Mjcj Holdings Inc..................................... G 937 885-0800
Miamisburg (G-10663)

CAMSHAFTS

Park-Ohio Industries Inc.......................... C 216 341-2300
Newburgh Heights (G-11620)

CANDLES

212 Scent Studio LLC............................. G 614 906-3673
Columbus (G-5076)
Al Root Company.................................... G 330 725-6677
Medina (G-10290)
Al Root Company.................................... C 330 723-4359
Medina (G-10291)
Alene Candles Midwest LLC................... F 614 933-4005
New Albany (G-11364)
Ambrosia Inc... G 419 825-3896
Swanton (G-13967)
Candle Coach... G 330 455-4444
Canton (G-2059)
Candle-Lite Company LLC..................... G 513 662-8616
Cincinnati (G-2699)
Candle-Lite Company LLC..................... D 937 780-2563
Leesburg (G-9122)
Cleveland Plant and Flower Co.............. G 614 478-9900
Columbus (G-5253)
Connies Candles.................................... G 740 574-1224
Wheelersburg (G-15808)
Coopers Mill Incorporated...................... C 419 562-2878
Bucyrus (G-1855)
Fallen Oak Candles Inc.......................... G 419 204-8162
Celina (G-2332)
Friendly Candle LLC.............................. G 740 683-0312
Columbus (G-5390)
Gorant Chocolatier LLC......................... C 330 726-8821
Boardman (G-1513)
Hyggelight LLC....................................... G 419 309-6321
Toledo (G-14323)

Inez Essentials LLC................................ F 216 701-8360
Maple Heights (G-9752)
Lumi-Lite Candle Company.................... D 740 872-3248
Norwich (G-11992)
Manitou Candle Co LLC........................ G 513 429-5254
Cincinnati (G-3129)
R&R Candles LLC.................................. G 614 600-7729
Columbus (G-5708)
Saint Johnsbury Perfect Scents.............. G 330 846-0175
New Waterford (G-11559)
TI Marie Candle Company LLC.............. F 513 746-7798
Cincinnati (G-3454)
Tiffin Candle Co Ltd............................... G 567 268-9015
Tiffin (G-14108)
United Candle Company LLC................. G 740 872-3248
Norwich (G-11993)
Yankee Candle Company Inc................. G 413 712-9416
Etna (G-7257)

CANDY & CONFECTIONS: Cake Ornaments

Decko Products Inc................................ D 419 626-5757
Sandusky (G-13050)

CANDY & CONFECTIONS: Candy Bars, Including Chocolate Covered

Barfections LLC..................................... F 330 759-3100
Girard (G-7962)
Malleys Candies Inc.............................. D 216 362-8700
Cleveland (G-4353)
Maries Candies LLC.............................. F 937 465-3061
West Liberty (G-15623)

CANDY & CONFECTIONS: Chocolate Candy, Exc Solid Chocolate

Executive Sweets East Inc..................... G 440 359-9866
Oakwood Village (G-12038)
International Confections C................... C 800 288-8002
Columbus (G-5474)
Suzin L Chocolatiers.............................. G 440 323-3372
Elyria (G-7208)

CANDY & CONFECTIONS: Popcorn Balls/ Other Trtd Popcorn Prdts

Crawford Acquisition Corp...................... G 216 486-0702
Cleveland (G-3915)
Humphrey Popcorn Company................. F 216 662-6629
Strongsville (G-13843)
Jml Holdings Inc.................................... E 419 866-7500
Holland (G-8515)

CANDY, NUT & CONFECTIONERY STORES: Candy

Brandts Candies Inc.............................. G 440 942-1016
Willoughby (G-15892)
Fannie May Confections Inc.................. A 330 494-0833
North Canton (G-11726)
Fawn Confectionery Inc........................ F 513 574-9612
Cincinnati (G-2897)
Gorant Chocolatier LLC........................ C 330 726-8821
Boardman (G-1513)
Harry London Candies Inc.................... E 330 494-0833
North Canton (G-11736)
Hartville Chocolates Inc........................ F 330 877-1999
Hartville (G-8300)
Island Delights Inc............................... G 866 887-4100
Seville (G-13143)
Linneas Candy Supplies Inc.................. E 330 678-7112
Kent (G-8828)
Malleys Candies Inc.............................. D 216 362-8700
Cleveland (G-4353)

Maries Candies LLC.............................. F 937 465-3061
West Liberty (G-15623)
Piqua Chocolate Company Inc.............. G 937 773-1981
Piqua (G-1254)
Robert E McGrath Inc.......................... F 440 572-7747
Strongsville (G-3872)
Suzin L Chocolatiers............................. G 440 323-3372
Elyria (G-7208)
Sweeties Olympia Treats LLC............... F 440 572-7747
Strongsville (G-3888)
Walnut Creek Chocolate Co Inc............ E 330 893-2995
Walnut Creek (G-15096)

CANDY: Chocolate From Cacao Beans

American Confections Co LLC............... G 614 888-8838
Coventry Township (G-6006)
Giannios Candy Co Inc......................... E 330 755-7000
Struthers (G-13304)
L C F Inc... G 330 877-3322
Hartville (G-8300)
Walnut Creek Chocolate Co Inc............ E 330 893-2995
Walnut Creek (G-15096)

CANNED SPECIALTIES

Abbott Laboratories.............................. A 614 624-3191
Columbus (G-5035)
Baxters North America Inc................... E 513 552-7463
Blue Ash (G-1361)
Baxters North America Inc................... C 513 552-7400
Blue Ash (G-1365)
Bittersweet Inc..................................... D 419 875-6986
Whitehouse (G-5816)
Calm Distributors LLC.......................... G 614 678-5554
Columbus (G-5208)
Hayden Valley Foods Inc..................... D 614 539-7233
Urbancrest (G-1553)
Heritage Cooperative Inc..................... F 740 828-2215
Nashport (G-11318)
JES Foods/Celina Inc........................... C 419 586-7446
Celina (G-2339)
L J Minor Corp...................................... F 216 861-8350
Cleveland (G-4302)
Oasis Mditerranean Cuisine Inc............ E 419 269-1459
Toledo (G-14402)
Robert Rothschild Farm LLC................ F 855 969-8050
West Chester (G-15501)
Skyline Cem Holdings LLC................... C 513 874-1188
Fairfield (G-7408)
Trevor Clatterbuck............................... G 330 359-2129
Wilmot (G-16070)
Wornick Holding Company Inc............. E 513 794-9800
Blue Ash (G-1495)

CANS: Aluminum

Crown Cork & Seal Usa Inc.................. B 330 833-1011
Massillon (G-10025)
Trivium Alum Packg USA Corp............. E 330 744-9505
Youngstown (G-1460)

CANS: Metal

Anchor Hocking LLC............................ A 740 687-2500
Columbus (G-5130)
Ball Corporation.................................... D 614 771-9112
Columbus (G-5170)
Bway Corporation................................. E 513 388-2200
Cincinnati (G-2692)
Cardinal Welding Inc............................ G 330 426-2404
East Palestine (G-7003)
Cleveland Steel Container Corp........... E 330 656-5600
Streetsboro (G-13362)
Crown Cork & Seal Usa Inc................. D 740 681-3000
Lancaster (G-9006)

PRODUCT SECTION CARPETS & RUGS: Tufted

Crown Cork & Seal Usa Inc .... D 740 681-6593
  Lancaster *(G-9007)*
Crown Cork & Seal Usa Inc .... C 937 299-2027
  Moraine *(G-11167)*
Crown Cork & Seal Usa Inc .... C 419 727-8201
  Toledo *(G-14253)*
Drt Holdings LLC .... F 937 297-6676
  West Chester *(G-15417)*
Eisenhauer Mfg Co LLC .... D 419 238-0081
  Van Wert *(G-14915)*
Encore Industries Inc .... C 419 626-8000
  Sandusky *(G-13053)*
Ghp II LLC .... C 740 687-2500
  Lancaster *(G-9017)*
Industrial Container Svcs LLC .... E 614 864-1900
  Blacklick *(G-1338)*
Industrial Container Svcs LLC .... E 513 921-8811
  Cincinnati *(G-3021)*
Organized Living Inc .... E 513 489-9300
  Cincinnati *(G-3230)*
Packaging Specialties Inc .... E 330 723-6000
  Medina *(G-10361)*
Winzeler Stamping Co .... E 419 485-3147
  Montpelier *(G-11147)*
Witt Industries Inc .... D 513 871-5700
  Mason *(G-10071)*

CANS: Tin

Independent Can Company .... F 440 593-5300
  Conneaut *(G-5921)*
Stolle Machinery Company LLC .... D 330 244-0555
  Canton *(G-2236)*

CANVAS PRDTS

Advantage Tent Fittings Inc .... F 740 773-3015
  Chillicothe *(G-2491)*
Chalfant Sew Fabricators Inc .... E 216 521-7922
  Cleveland *(G-3805)*
Cleveland Canvas Goods Mfg Co .... E 216 361-4567
  Cleveland *(G-3835)*
Columbus Canvas Products Inc .... F 614 375-1397
  Columbus *(G-5263)*
DCW Acquisition Inc .... E 216 451-0666
  Cleveland *(G-3949)*
Delphos Tent and Awning Inc .... F 419 692-5776
  Delphos *(G-6762)*
Electra Tarp Inc .... F 330 477-7168
  Canton *(G-2095)*
Forest City Companies Inc .... E 216 586-5279
  Cleveland *(G-4081)*
Galion Canvas Products .... G 419 468-5333
  Galion *(G-7876)*
National Bias Fabric Co .... F 216 361-0530
  Cleveland *(G-4435)*
Samsel Rope & Marine Supply Co ...... E 216 241-0333
  Cleveland *(G-4670)*
Scherba Industries Inc .... D 330 273-3200
  Brunswick *(G-1790)*
Wolf G T Awning & Tent Co .... F 937 548-4161
  Greenville *(G-8065)*
Youngstown Shade & Alum LLC .... G 330 782-2373
  Youngstown *(G-16487)*

CANVAS PRDTS: Convertible Tops, Car/ Boat, Fm Purchased Mtrl

American Canvas Products Inc .... F 419 382-8450
  Toledo *(G-14187)*
Griffin Fisher Co Inc .... G 513 961-2110
  Cincinnati *(G-2973)*

CAPACITORS: NEC

CPI Group Limited .... F 216 525-0046
  Cleveland *(G-3911)*
Oren Elliot Products LLC .... E 419 298-0015
  Edgerton *(G-7079)*
Soemhejee Inc .... E 419 298-2306
  Edgerton *(G-7080)*
Standex International Corp .... D 513 533-7171
  Fairfield *(G-7412)*

CAPS & PLUGS: Electric, Attachment

Knappco Corporation .... C 513 870-3100
  West Chester *(G-15455)*

CAPS: Plastic

Bprex Halthcare Brookville Inc .... C 847 541-9700
  Perrysburg *(G-12365)*
Electro-Cap International Inc .... F 937 456-6099
  Eaton *(G-7058)*
Wisco Products Incorporated .... E 937 228-2101
  Dayton *(G-6658)*

CAR WASH EQPT

Giant Industries Inc .... E 419 531-4600
  Toledo *(G-14300)*
Legends Auto Spa LLC .... G 216 333-8030
  Bedford *(G-1133)*
National Pride Equipment Inc .... G 419 289-2886
  Mansfield *(G-9703)*
Route 62 .... G 740 548-5418
  Johnstown *(G-8777)*
Russ Jr Enterprises Inc .... F 440 237-4642
  North Royalton *(G-11895)*
Sammy S Auto Detail .... F 614 263-2728
  Columbus *(G-5743)*
Wb Industries Inc .... G 440 708-0309
  Burton *(G-1890)*

CAR WASH EQPT & SPLYS WHOLESALERS

National Pride Equipment Inc .... G 419 289-2886
  Mansfield *(G-9703)*
Service Station Equipment Co .... G 216 431-6100
  Cleveland *(G-4686)*

CARBON & GRAPHITE PRDTS, NEC

Active Chemical Systems Inc .... F 440 543-7755
  Chagrin Falls *(G-2388)*
American Spring Wire Corp .... C 216 292-4620
  Bedford Heights *(G-1163)*
Applied Sciences Inc .... F 937 766-2020
  Cedarville *(G-2322)*
GE Aviation Systems LLC .... B 937 898-5881
  Vandalia *(G-14941)*
Ges Graphite Inc .... E 216 658-6660
  Parma *(G-12290)*
Graftech Holdings Inc .... D 216 676-2000
  Independence *(G-8669)*
Graftech International Ltd .... D 216 676-2000
  Brooklyn Heights *(G-1691)*
Graftech Intl Trdg Inc .... E 216 676-2000
  Cleveland *(G-4136)*
Graftech NY Inc .... F 216 676-2000
  Cleveland *(G-4137)*
Metaullics Systems LP .... C 509 926-6212
  Solon *(G-13387)*
Mill-Rose Company .... C 440 255-9171
  Mentor *(G-10505)*
Morgan Advanced Materials .... C 419 435-8182
  Fostoria *(G-7645)*
Morgan AM&t .... G 419 435-8182
  Fostoria *(G-7646)*
Ocsial LLC .... F 415 906-5271
  Gahanna *(G-7847)*

Ohio Carbon Blank Inc .... E 440 953-9302
  Willoughby *(G-15964)*
Randall Bearings Inc .... F 419 678-2486
  Coldwater *(G-5000)*
Randall Bearings Inc .... D 419 223-1075
  Lima *(G-9282)*
Sentinel Management Inc .... E 440 821-7372
  Lorain *(G-9437)*
Zyvex Performance Mtls Inc .... G 614 481-2222
  Columbus *(G-5895)*

CARBON BLACK

Chromascape LLC .... E 330 998-7574
  Independence *(G-8658)*
Jacobi Carbons Inc .... D 215 546-3900
  Columbus *(G-5485)*

CARBON PAPER & INKED RIBBONS

Kroy LLC .... C 216 426-5600
  Cleveland *(G-4299)*
Pubco Corporation .... D 216 881-5300
  Cleveland *(G-4597)*

CARDIOVASCULAR SYSTEM DRUGS, EXC DIAGNOSTIC

Pfizer Inc .... F 937 746-3603
  Franklin *(G-7691)*

CARDS: Beveled

Cott Systems Inc .... D 614 847-4405
  Columbus *(G-5299)*

CARDS: Color

Dorn Color LLC .... C 216 634-2252
  Cleveland *(G-3969)*
Golf Marketing Group Inc .... G 330 963-5155
  Twinsburg *(G-14669)*

CARDS: Greeting

American Greetings Corporation .... A 216 252-7300
  Cleveland *(G-3652)*
Naptime Productions LLC .... G 419 662-9521
  Rossford *(G-12868)*
Papyrus-Recycled Greetings Inc .... D 773 348-6410
  Westlake *(G-15770)*
Plus Mark LLC .... D 216 252-6770
  Cleveland *(G-4562)*
Those Chrcters From Clvland LL .... F 216 252-7300
  Cleveland *(G-4795)*

CARDS: Identification

Griffin Technology Inc .... C 585 924-7121
  Hudson *(G-8594)*
Octsys Security Corp .... G 614 470-4510
  Columbus *(G-5611)*
Plasticards Inc .... E 330 896-5555
  Uniontown *(G-14791)*

CARPET & UPHOLSTERY CLEANING SVCS

Image By J & K LLC .... F 888 667-6929
  Maumee *(G-10207)*

CARPET & UPHOLSTERY CLEANING SVCS: Carpet/Furniture, On Loc

Shaheen Oriental Rug Co Inc .... F 330 493-9000
  Canton *(G-2222)*
Stanley Steemer Intl Inc .... C 614 764-2007
  Dublin *(G-6945)*

CARPETS & RUGS: Tufted

CARPETS & RUGS: Tufted

Columbus Public School Dst .... F 614 365-6517
  Columbus (G-5275)
Mohawk Industries Inc .... F 800 837-3812
  Grove City (G-8108)

CARPETS, RUGS & FLOOR COVERING

3359 Kingston LLC .... G 614 871-8989
  Grove City (G-8071)
4blar LLC .... G 513 576-0441
  Milford (G-10889)
Alliance Carpet Cushion Co .... E 740 966-5001
  Johnstown (G-8768)
Boardman Molded Products Inc .... D 330 788-2400
  Youngstown (G-16322)
Ccp Industries Inc .... B 216 535-4227
  Richmond Heights (G-12807)
David Moore .... G 614 836-9331
  Groveport (G-8137)
Dribble Creek Inc .... F 440 439-8650
  Twinsburg (G-14654)
Johns Manville Corporation .... D 419 878-8111
  Waterville (G-15246)
Jpc Llc .... G 513 310-1608
  Mason (G-10015)
Mat Basics Incorporated .... G 513 793-0313
  Blue Ash (G-1428)
Mohawk 11 Inc .... G 614 771-0327
  Hilliard (G-8420)
Shaw Industries Inc .... A 513 942-3692
  Fairfield (G-7407)
Xt Innovations Ltd .... G 419 562-1989
  Bucyrus (G-1876)

CARRIERS: Infant, Textile

Sewline Products Inc .... G 419 929-1114
  New London (G-11469)

CARS: Electric

Mobile Solutions LLC .... F 614 286-3944
  Columbus (G-5575)

CARTONS: Egg, Molded Pulp, Made From Purchased Materials

Tekni-Plex Inc .... E 419 491-2399
  Holland (G-8532)

CARTS: Grocery

Saraga Northern Lights LLC .... F 614 928-3100
  Columbus (G-5747)

CASES: Carrying

Clipper Products Inc .... G 513 688-7300
  Cincinnati (G-2555)
Professional Case Inc .... F 513 682-2520
  West Chester (G-15578)
Travelers Custom Case Inc .... F 216 621-8447
  Mentor (G-10582)
Whitman Corporation .... G 513 541-3223
  Okeana (G-12069)

CASES: Carrying, Clothing & Apparel

Made Men Circle LLC .... G 216 501-0414
  Cleveland Heights (G-4940)
Northhill T-Shirt Print Dsign .... G 330 208-0338
  Akron (G-268)
T & CS Repairs & Retail LLC .... E 704 964-7325
  Akron (G-344)

CASES: Plastic

Aerocase Incorporated .... F 440 617-9294
  Westlake (G-15728)

M T M Molded Products Company .... E 937 890-7461
  Dayton (G-6418)
Warwick Products Company .... E 216 334-1200
  Cleveland (G-4894)

CASKETS & ACCESS

Case Ohio Burial Co .... F 440 779-1992
  Cleveland (G-3797)

CAST STONE: Concrete

Fibreboard Corporation .... C 419 248-8000
  Toledo (G-14287)

CASTINGS GRINDING: For The Trade

Cincinnati Grinding Technologies Inc .... G 866 983-1097
  Fairfield (G-7347)
Micro Lapping & Grinding Co .... F 216 267-6500
  Cleveland (G-4401)
P & L Heat Trting Grinding Inc .... E 330 746-1339
  Youngstown (G-16408)
Trinel Inc .... F 216 265-9190
  Cleveland (G-4831)
Wise Edge LLC .... G 330 208-0889
  Akron (G-376)
Youngstown Hard Chrome Pltg Gr .... E 330 758-9721
  Youngstown (G-16482)

CASTINGS: Aerospace Investment, Ferrous

Aeropact Manufacturing LLC .... F 419 373-1711
  Bowling Green (G-1551)
Bescast Inc .... C 440 946-5300
  Willoughby (G-15889)
Consolidated Foundries Inc .... C 909 595-2252
  Cleveland (G-3899)
General Aluminum Mfg Company .... E 419 739-9300
  Wapakoneta (G-15115)

CASTINGS: Aerospace, Aluminum

Howmet Aluminum Casting Inc .... E 216 641-4340
  Newburgh Heights (G-11616)
Htci Co .... F 937 845-1204
  New Carlisle (G-11417)
Mpe Aeroengines Inc .... E 937 878-3800
  Huber Heights (G-8578)
Ransom & Randolph LLC .... G 419 865-9497
  Maumee (G-10227)
T W Corporation .... F 440 461-3234
  Akron (G-346)
Tessec LLC .... D 937 576-0010
  Dayton (G-6615)

CASTINGS: Aerospace, Nonferrous, Exc Aluminum

Hydro-Aire Aerospace Corp .... C 440 323-3211
  Elyria (G-7159)
Microweld Engineering Inc .... G 614 847-9410
  Worthington (G-16204)
Voss Industries LLC .... C 216 771-7655
  Cleveland (G-4884)

CASTINGS: Aluminum

Boscott Metals Inc .... E 937 448-2018
  Bradford (G-1599)
Brost Foundry Company .... E 216 641-1131
  Cleveland (G-3763)
Cast Metals Technology Inc .... E 937 968-5460
  Union City (G-14777)
Castek Inc .... E 440 365-2333
  Elyria (G-7124)
General Aluminum Mfg Company .... B 440 593-6225
  Conneaut (G-5918)

General Aluminum Mfg Company .... E 330 297-1020
  Ravenna (G-12717)
General Aluminum Mfg LLC .... C 330 297-1225
  Ravenna (G-12718)
General Motors LLC .... B 419 782-7010
  Defiance (G-6678)
Iabf Inc .... G 614 279-4498
  Columbus (G-5251)
Jrm 2 Company .... D 513 554-1700
  Cincinnati (G-3652)
Morris Bean & Company .... C 937 767-7301
  Yellow Springs (G-16285)
Multi Cast LLC .... E 419 335-0010
  Wauseon (G-15269)
New Mansfield Brass & Alum Co .... F 419 492-2166
  New Washington (G-11549)
P C M Co .... E 330 336-8040
  Wadsworth (G-15050)
Piqua Emery Cutter & Fndry Co .... D 937 773-4134
  Piqua (G-12545)
Pride Cast Metals Inc .... D 513 541-1295
  Cincinnati (G-3274)
Reliable Castings Corporation .... D
  Cincinnati (G-3331)
Ross Aluminum Castings LLC .... C 937 492-4134
  Sidney (G-13272)
Rotocast Technologies Inc .... E 330 798-9091
  Akron (G-310)
Specialized Castings Ltd .... F 937 669-5620
  Greenville (G-8050)
US Metalcraft Inc .... E 419 692-4962
  Delphos (G-6770)

CASTINGS: Brass, NEC, Exc Die

Accurate Products Company .... G 740 498-7202
  Newcomerstown (G-11641)

CASTINGS: Bronze, NEC, Exc Die

Albco Foundry Inc .... E 330 424-7716
  Lisbon (G-9307)
Brost Foundry Company .... E 216 641-1131
  Cleveland (G-3763)
Oakes Foundry Inc .... E 330 372-4010
  Warren (G-15194)
Piqua Emery Cutter & Fndry Co .... D 937 773-4134
  Piqua (G-12545)
Pride Cast Metals Inc .... D 513 541-1295
  Cincinnati (G-3274)

CASTINGS: Commercial Investment, Ferrous

B W Grinding Co .... E 419 923-1376
  Lyons (G-9531)
Cmt Imports Inc .... G 513 615-1851
  Cincinnati (G-2777)
Dd Foundry Inc .... F 216 362-4100
  Brookpark (G-1712)
Rimer Enterprises Inc .... E 419 878-8156
  Waterville (G-15251)

CASTINGS: Die, Aluminum

Accro-Cast Corporation .... E 937 228-0497
  Dayton (G-6179)
Ahresty Wilmington Corporation .... B 937 382-6112
  Wilmington (G-16238)
Akron Foundry Co .... C 330 745-3101
  Akron (G-33)
American Light Metals LLC .... C 330 908-3065
  Macedonia (G-955)
Apex Aluminum Die Cast Co Inc .... E 937 773-0432
  Piqua (G-12503)
Cmt Imports Inc .... G 513 615-1851
  Cincinnati (G-2777)

PRODUCT SECTION

CASTINGS: Steel

CSM Horvath Ledgebrook Inc............ G 419 522-1133
  Mansfield *(G-9643)*

Destin Die Casting LLC...................... E 937 347-1111
  Xenia *(G-16259)*

Edc Liquidating Inc................................ C 330 467-0750
  Macedonia *(G-9548)*

Fort Recovery Industries Inc............ C 419 375-4121
  Fort Recovery *(G-7617)*

General Aluminum Mfg Company......... C 419 739-9300
  Wapakoneta *(G-15115)*

General Die Casters Inc...................... D 330 467-6700
  Northfield *(G-11906)*

General Die Casters Inc...................... E 330 678-2528
  Twinsburg *(G-14667)*

Krengel Equipment LLC........................ C 440 946-3570
  Eastlake *(G-7037)*

Matalco (us) Inc.................................... E 234 806-0600
  Warren *(G-15189)*

Matalco Inc... D 330 452-4760
  Canton *(G-2153)*

Model Pattern & Foundry Co................ F 513 542-2322
  Cincinnati *(G-3169)*

Ohio Aluminum Industries Inc............ C 216 641-8865
  Cleveland *(G-4493)*

Ohio Decorative Products LLC............ C 419 647-9033
  Spencerville *(G-13487)*

Omni USA Inc.. E 330 830-5500
  Massillon *(G-10132)*

Park-Ohio Holdings Corp...................... F 440 947-2000
  Cleveland *(G-4524)*

Park-Ohio Industries Inc...................... C 440 947-2000
  Cleveland *(G-4525)*

Plaster Process Castings Co................ E 216 663-1814
  Cleveland *(G-4559)*

Ramco Electric Motors Inc.................. D 937 548-2525
  Greenville *(G-8056)*

Ravana Industries Inc......................... G 330 536-4015
  Lowellville *(G-9518)*

Reliable Castings Corporation............ D 937 497-5217
  Sidney *(G-13275)*

Ross Casting & Innovation LLC............ B 937 497-4500
  Sidney *(G-13280)*

Seilkop Industries Inc........................... F 513 679-5680
  Cincinnati *(G-3376)*

Seilkop Industries Inc........................... E 513 761-1035
  Cincinnati *(G-3377)*

Seyekcub Inc... G 330 324-1394
  Uhrichsville *(G-14769)*

SRS Die Casting Holdings LLC............ E 330 467-0750
  Macedonia *(G-9577)*

SRS Light Metals Inc............................ F 330 467-0750
  Macedonia *(G-9578)*

The Basic Aluminum Castings Co........ D 216 481-5606
  Cleveland *(G-4779)*

The Kindt-Collins Company LLC........... D 216 252-4122
  Cleveland *(G-4788)*

Thompson Aluminum Casting Co......... D 216 206-2781
  Cleveland *(G-4794)*

United States Drill Head Co................. E 513 941-0300
  Cincinnati *(G-3482)*

W E Lott Company................................ F 419 563-9400
  Bucyrus *(G-1873)*

Yoder Industries Inc............................. C 937 278-5769
  Dayton *(G-6662)*

CASTINGS: Die, Magnesium & Magnesium-Base Alloy

Thompson Aluminum Casting Co......... D 216 206-2781
  Cleveland *(G-4794)*

CASTINGS: Die, Nonferrous

Dd Foundry Inc...................................... F 216 362-4100
  Brookpark *(G-1712)*

Empire Brass Co.................................... G 216 431-6565
  Cleveland *(G-4012)*

M & M Dies Inc...................................... G 216 883-6628
  Cleveland *(G-4342)*

Martina Metal LLC................................. E 614 291-9700
  Columbus *(G-5544)*

Oakwood Industries Inc....................... D 440 232-8700
  Bedford *(G-1146)*

Support Svc LLC.................................... G 419 617-0660
  Lexington *(G-9203)*

Yoder Industries Inc............................. C 937 278-5769
  Dayton *(G-6662)*

CASTINGS: Ductile

Cmt Imports Inc.................................... G 513 615-1851
  Cincinnati *(G-2777)*

Sancast Inc... E 740 622-8660
  Coshocton *(G-5995)*

CASTINGS: Gray Iron

A C Williams Co Inc.............................. E 330 296-6110
  Ravenna *(G-12699)*

Barberton Steel Industries Inc............ E 330 745-6837
  Barberton *(G-861)*

Blanchester Foundry Co Inc................. F
  Blanchester *(G-1348)*

Brittany Stamping LLC.......................... A 216 267-0850
  Cleveland *(G-3760)*

Cast Metals Incorporated.................... F 419 278-2010
  Deshler *(G-6799)*

Cast-Fab Technologies Inc.................. C 513 758-1000
  Cincinnati *(G-2707)*

Casting Solutions LLC.......................... C 740 452-9371
  Zanesville *(G-16518)*

Castings Usa Inc.................................. G 330 339-3611
  New Philadelphia *(G-11491)*

Chris Erhart Foundry & Mch Co............ E 513 421-6550
  Cincinnati *(G-2734)*

Col-Pump Company Inc........................ D 330 482-1029
  Columbiana *(G-5033)*

Columbiana Foundry Company............ C 330 482-3336
  Columbiana *(G-5034)*

Domestic Casting Company LLC......... F 717 532-6615
  Delaware *(G-6718)*

Ej Usa Inc... F 216 692-3001
  South Euclid *(G-13460)*

Elyria Foundry Company LLC.............. D 440 322-4657
  Elyria *(G-7141)*

Foote Foundry LLC................................ E 740 694-1595
  Fredericktown *(G-7746)*

General Motors LLC............................. B 419 782-7010
  Defiance *(G-6678)*

Liberty Casting Company LLC............. D 740 363-1941
  Delaware *(G-6735)*

Miami-Cast Inc..................................... F 937 866-2951
  Miamisburg *(G-10659)*

Old Smo Inc... C 419 394-3346
  Saint Marys *(G-12961)*

OS Kelly Corporation............................ E 937 322-4921
  Springfield *(G-13614)*

Osco Industries Inc.............................. D 740 286-5004
  Jackson *(G-8720)*

Osco Industries Inc.............................. B 740 354-3183
  Portsmouth *(G-12652)*

Pioneer City Casting Company........... E 740 423-7533
  Belpre *(G-1260)*

Piqua Champion Foundry Inc............... D
  Piqua *(G-12543)*

Quality Castings Company.................. B 330 682-6010
  Orrville *(G-12147)*

T & B Foundry Company....................... E 216 391-4200
  Cleveland *(G-4764)*

Tri Cast Limited Partnership.............. E 330 733-8718
  Akron *(G-362)*

Tri-Cast Inc... E 330 733-8718
  Akron *(G-363)*

Whemco-Ohio Foundry Inc.................. C 419 222-2111
  Lima *(G-9302)*

Yellow Creek Casting Co Inc................ F 330 532-4608
  Wellsville *(G-15338)*

CASTINGS: Lead

Cpp-Cleveland Inc................................ C 440 953-0053
  Eastlake *(G-7024)*

Cpp-Cleveland Inc................................ D 216 453-4800
  Cleveland *(G-3913)*

CASTINGS: Machinery, Aluminum

Enprotech Industrial Tech LLC........... E 216 883-3220
  Cleveland *(G-4019)*

General Precision Corporation........... G 440 951-9380
  Willoughby *(G-15925)*

Nelson Aluminum Foundry Inc........... G 440 543-1941
  Chagrin Falls *(G-2411)*

Tri - Flex of Ohio Inc............................. G 330 705-7084
  North Canton *(G-11770)*

Zephyr Industries Inc.......................... G 419 281-4485
  Ashland *(G-621)*

CASTINGS: Machinery, Nonferrous, Exc Die or Aluminum Copper

Rossborough Supply Co....................... F 216 941-6115
  Cleveland *(G-4652)*

CASTINGS: Magnesium

A C Williams Co Inc.............................. E 330 296-6110
  Ravenna *(G-12699)*

Garfield Alloys Inc............................... F 216 587-4843
  Cleveland *(G-4101)*

Thompson Aluminum Casting Co......... D 216 206-2781
  Cleveland *(G-4794)*

CASTINGS: Precision

Akron Foundry Co................................ C 330 745-3101
  Akron *(G-33)*

Consoldted Precision Pdts Corp........... B 440 953-0053
  Eastlake *(G-7023)*

Esco Turbine Technologies -............... C 440 953-0053
  Eastlake *(G-7031)*

McM Precision Castings Inc................ E 419 669-3226
  Weston *(G-15806)*

PCC Airfoils LLC................................... C 216 692-7900
  Cleveland *(G-4537)*

PCC Airfoils LLC................................... B 740 982-6025
  Crooksville *(G-6048)*

PCC Airfoils LLC................................... B 440 585-8247
  Eastlake *(G-7044)*

PCC Airfoils LLC................................... C 440 255-9770
  Mentor *(G-10521)*

Sam Americas Inc................................ E 330 628-1118
  Mogadore *(G-11083)*

Sandusky International Inc.................. C 419 626-5340
  Sandusky *(G-13090)*

Warren Castings Inc............................ E 216 883-2520
  Cleveland *(G-4893)*

CASTINGS: Steel

Alcon Industries Inc............................. D 216 961-1100
  Cleveland *(G-3625)*

Coronado Steel Co................................ E 330 744-1143
  Youngstown *(G-16341)*

Employee Codes: A=Over 500 employees, B=251-500
C=101-250, D=51-100, E=20-50, F=10-19, G=1-9

CASTINGS: Steel

Jrm 2 Company .... D 513 554-1700
Cincinnati *(G-3052)*

Precision Polymer Casting LLC .... G 440 343-0461
Moreland Hills *(G-11220)*

Rampp Company .... E 740 373-7886
Marietta *(G-9819)*

Sandusky International Inc .... C 419 626-5340
Sandusky *(G-13090)*

Worthington Enterprises Inc .... C 614 438-3210
Worthington *(G-16220)*

CASTINGS: Titanium

Rmi Titanium Company LLC .... G 330 652-9955
Niles *(G-11685)*

Rmi Titanium Company LLC .... E 330 652-9952
Niles *(G-11684)*

Rti International Metals Inc .... A
Niles *(G-11687)*

Tailwind Technologies Inc .... A 937 778-4200
Piqua *(G-12555)*

Titanium Contractors Ltd .... G 513 256-2152
Cincinnati *(G-3456)*

Water Star Inc .... F 440 996-0800
Concord Township *(G-5914)*

CATALOG & MAIL-ORDER HOUSES

Hen of Woods LLC .... G 513 954-8871
Cincinnati *(G-2993)*

Universal Drect Flfllment Corp .... C 330 650-5000
Hudson *(G-8617)*

Universal Screen Arts Inc .... E 330 650-5000
Hudson *(G-8618)*

CATALYSTS: Chemical

BASF Catalysts LLC .... C 216 360-5005
Cleveland *(G-3723)*

BASF Catalysts LLC .... C 440 322-3741
Elyria *(G-7115)*

BLaster Holdings LLC .... G 216 901-5800
Cleveland *(G-3741)*

BLaster LLC .... E 216 901-5800
Cleveland *(G-3742)*

Chemspec Usa Inc .... D 330 669-8512
Orrville *(G-12121)*

Christy Catalytics LLC .... G 740 982-1302
Crooksville *(G-6045)*

Essential Elements Usa LLC .... E 513 482-5700
Cincinnati *(G-2884)*

United Initiators Inc .... D 440 323-3112
Elyria *(G-7215)*

CATAPULTS

Universal Fabg Cnstr Svcs Inc .... E 614 274-1128
Columbus *(G-5845)*

CATERERS

Kenyetta Bagby Enterprise LLC .... F 614 584-3426
Reynoldsburg *(G-12768)*

Mustard Seed Health Fd Mkt Inc .... E 440 519-3663
Solon *(G-13394)*

CATTLE WHOLESALERS

Gardner Lumber Company Inc .... F 740 254-4664
Tippecanoe *(G-14170)*

CAULKING COMPOUNDS

Dap Products Inc .... D 937 667-4461
Tipp City *(G-14231)*

CEILING SYSTEMS: Luminous, Commercial

Eaton Electric Holdings LLC .... B 440 523-5000
Cleveland *(G-3995)*

Nordic Light America Inc .... F 614 981-9497
Canal Winchester *(G-1991)*

Norton Industries Inc .... E 888 357-2345
Lakewood *(G-8980)*

CELLULOSE DERIVATIVE MATERIALS

Advanced Fiber LLC .... E 419 562-1337
Bucyrus *(G-1849)*

Oak View Enterprises Inc .... E 513 860-4446
Bucyrus *(G-1864)*

CEMENT & CONCRETE RELATED PRDTS & EQPT: Bituminous

Mesa Industries Inc .... F 513 999-9781
Cincinnati *(G-3152)*

Mesa Industries Inc .... E 513 321-2950
Cincinnati *(G-3151)*

CEMENT ROCK: Crushed & Broken

R W Sidley Incorporated .... F 440 352-9343
Painesville *(G-12261)*

CEMENT, EXC LINOLEUM & TILE

Hartline Products Coinc .... G 216 851-7189
Cleveland *(G-4171)*

CEMENT: Hydraulic

Hartline Products Coinc .... G 216 851-7189
Cleveland *(G-4171)*

Holcim (us) Inc .... E 216 781-9330
Cleveland *(G-4194)*

Holcim (us) Inc .... C 419 399-4861
Paulding *(G-12314)*

Holcim Quarries Ny Inc .... E 216 566-0545
Cleveland *(G-4195)*

Huron Cement Products Company ..... E 419 433-4161
Huron *(G-8633)*

Lafarge Holcim .... G 419 798-4866
Lakeside Marblehead *(G-8960)*

Lone Star Industries Inc .... F 513 467-0430
Cincinnati *(G-3110)*

Quikrete Companies LLC .... E 614 885-4406
Columbus *(G-5704)*

Quikrete Companies LLC .... E 330 296-6080
Ravenna *(G-12729)*

Quikrete Companies LLC .... F 419 241-1148
Toledo *(G-14445)*

Skyway Cement Company LLC .... E 513 478-0034
Fairfield *(G-7409)*

CEMENT: Masonry

Kona Blackbird Inc .... E 440 285-3189
Chardon *(G-2455)*

CEMENT: Natural

Fairborn Cement Company LLC .... C 937 879-8393
Xenia *(G-16261)*

CEMENT: Portland

A & A Quality Paving & Cem LLC .... G 440 886-9595
Cleveland *(G-3574)*

Lehigh Portland Cement .... E 513 769-3666
Cincinnati *(G-3100)*

Wallseye Concrete Corp .... F 440 235-1800
Cleveland *(G-4892)*

CERAMIC FIBER

Astro Met Inc .... F 513 772-1242
Cincinnati *(G-2638)*

Maverick Corporation .... F 513 469-9919
Blue Ash *(G-1430)*

CHARCOAL

Nucon International Inc .... F 614 846-5710
Columbus *(G-5307)*

CHARCOAL: Activated

Calgon Carbon Corporation .... E 614 258-9501
Columbus *(G-5326)*

CHASSIS: Motor Vehicle

Custom Chassis Inc .... G 440 839-5574
Wakeman *(G-13073)*

Falls Stamping & Welding Co .... C 330 928-1191
Cuyahoga Falls *(G-6083)*

Jefferson Industries Corp .... C 614 879-5300
West Jefferson *(G-15610)*

Ohio Module Manufacturing C .... A 419 729-6700
Toledo *(G-14403)*

Sutphen Corporation .... E 937 969-8851
Springfield *(G-13640)*

W&W Automotive & Towing Inc .... E 937 429-1699
Beavercreek Township *(G-1095)*

CHEESE WHOLESALERS

Bunker Hill Cheese Co Inc .... D 330 893-2131
Millersburg *(G-1949)*

Food Plant Engineering LLC .... F 513 618-3165
Blue Ash *(G-1355)*

Grays Orange Barn Inc .... G 419 568-2718
Wapakoneta *(G-5116)*

Guggisberg Cheese Inc .... E 330 893-2550
Millersburg *(G-1956)*

CHEMICAL CLEANING SVCS

Bleachtech LLC .... E 216 921-1980
Seville *(G-13139)*

Chemical Solvents Inc .... E 216 741-9310
Cleveland *(G-3806)*

CHEMICAL ELEMENTS

Element 41 Inc .... F 440 579-5531
Painesville *(G-12232)*

Element 41 Inc .... G 216 410-5646
Chardon *(G-2450)*

Elements Hr Inc .... G 614 488-6944
Columbus *(G-5343)*

Four Elements Inc .... G 330 591-4505
Medina *(G-10327)*

Perstorp Polyols Inc .... C 419 729-5448
Toledo *(G-14434)*

CHEMICAL PROCESSING MACHINERY & EQPT

Aquila Pharmatech LLC .... G 419 386-2527
Waterville *(G-15259)*

Chemineer Inc .... C 937 454-3200
Dayton *(G-6254)*

Guild Associates Inc .... G 843 573-0095
Dublin *(G-6889)*

Guild Associates Inc .... D 614 798-8215
Dublin *(G-6888)*

Hydro Systems Company .... E 513 271-8800
West Chester *(G-5447)*

CHEMICALS & ALLIED PRDTS WHOLESALERS, NEC

AIN Industries Inc .... G 440 781-0950
Cleveland *(G-3614)*

Aquablue Incorporated .... G 330 343-0220
New Philadelphia *(G-11484)*

PRODUCT SECTION

CHEMICALS: Alkalies

Ashland Chemco Inc .... C 614 790-3333
  Columbus *(G-5156)*
Bleachtech LLC .... E 216 921-1980
  Seville *(G-13139)*
Calvary Industries Inc .... E 513 874-1113
  Fairfield *(G-7342)*
Chem-Sales Inc .... F
  Toledo *(G-14235)*
Chemmasters Inc .... E 440 428-2105
  Madison *(G-9589)*
Corrugated Chemicals Inc .... G 513 561-7773
  Cincinnati *(G-2798)*
Dover Chemical Corporation .... C 330 343-7711
  Dover *(G-6818)*
Finale Products Inc .... G 419 874-2662
  Perrysburg *(G-12381)*
Formlabs Ohio Inc .... E 419 837-9783
  Millbury *(G-10932)*
Hickman Williams & Company .... F 513 621-1946
  Cincinnati *(G-2998)*
Imcd Us LLC .... E 216 228-8900
  Westlake *(G-15760)*
Knight Material Tech LLC .... D 330 488-1651
  East Canton *(G-6979)*
Maroon Intrmdiate Holdings LLC .... G 440 937-1000
  Avon *(G-781)*
Netherland Rubber Company .... F 513 733-0883
  Cincinnati *(G-3187)*
Polymer Additives Holdings Inc .... C 216 875-7200
  Independence *(G-8680)*
PVS Chemical Solutions Inc .... F 330 666-0888
  Copley *(G-5955)*
Quality Borate Co LLC .... F 216 896-1949
  Cleveland *(G-4604)*
Sigma-Aldrich Corporation .... D 216 206-5424
  Cleveland *(G-4701)*
Toagosei America Inc .... D 614 718-3855
  West Jefferson *(G-15615)*
Tricor Industrial Inc .... D 330 264-3299
  Wooster *(G-16178)*

CHEMICALS & ALLIED PRDTS, WHOLESALE: Chemical Additives

Chemcore Inc .... F 937 228-6118
  Dayton *(G-6253)*

CHEMICALS & ALLIED PRDTS, WHOLESALE: Chemicals, Indl

Polar Inc .... F 937 297-0911
  Moraine *(G-11201)*
Rhein Chemie Corporation .... C 440 279-2367
  Chardon *(G-2465)*
Tembec Btlsr Inc .... E 419 244-5856
  Toledo *(G-14483)*
Tosoh America Inc .... B 614 539-8622
  Grove City *(G-8124)*
Univar Solutions USA LLC .... F 800 531-7106
  Dublin *(G-6956)*
Univar Solutions USA LLC .... F 513 714-5264
  West Chester *(G-15602)*

CHEMICALS & ALLIED PRDTS, WHOLESALE: Chemicals, Indl & Heavy

Environmental Chemical Corp .... F 330 453-5200
  Uniontown *(G-14782)*
Hexion Inc .... C 888 443-9466
  Columbus *(G-5428)*

CHEMICALS & ALLIED PRDTS, WHOLESALE: Detergent/Soap

Chemical Solvents Inc .... E 216 741-9310
  Cleveland *(G-3816)*
Love Laugh & Laundry .... G 567 377-1951
  Toledo *(G-14370)*

CHEMICALS & ALLIED PRDTS, WHOLESALE: Detergents

Cleaning Lady Inc .... G 419 589-5566
  Mansfield *(G-9638)*
Washing Systems LLC .... C 800 272-1974
  Loveland *(G-9509)*

CHEMICALS & ALLIED PRDTS, WHOLESALE: Oxygen

Jerrys Welding Supply Inc .... G 937 364-1500
  Hillsboro *(G-8460)*

CHEMICALS & ALLIED PRDTS, WHOLESALE: Plastics Film

Cleveland Supplyone Inc .... E 216 514-7000
  Cleveland *(G-3857)*

CHEMICALS & ALLIED PRDTS, WHOLESALE: Plastics Materials, NEC

Alro Steel Corporation .... E 614 878-7271
  Columbus *(G-5116)*
Alro Steel Corporation .... D 419 720-5300
  Toledo *(G-14184)*
Plastics Family Holdings Inc .... F 614 272-0777
  Columbus *(G-5680)*
Plastics R Unique Inc .... E 330 334-4820
  Wadsworth *(G-15053)*

CHEMICALS & ALLIED PRDTS, WHOLESALE: Plastics Prdts, NEC

Carney Plastics Inc .... G 330 746-8273
  Youngstown *(G-16331)*
Polymer Packaging Inc .... D 330 832-2000
  North Canton *(G-11751)*
Queen City Polymers Inc .... E 513 779-0990
  West Chester *(G-15492)*
Tahoma Enterprises Inc .... D 330 745-9016
  Barberton *(G-897)*
Tahoma Rubber & Plastics Inc .... D 330 745-9016
  Barberton *(G-898)*
UPL International Inc .... E 330 433-2860
  North Canton *(G-11773)*

CHEMICALS & ALLIED PRDTS, WHOLESALE: Plastics Sheets & Rods

HP Manufacturing Company Inc .... D 216 361-6500
  Cleveland *(G-4204)*
Total Plastics Resources LLC .... G 440 891-1140
  Cleveland *(G-4810)*

CHEMICALS & ALLIED PRDTS, WHOLESALE: Resins

Avient Corporation .... D 440 930-1000
  Avon Lake *(G-797)*
Epsilyte Holdings LLC .... D 937 778-9500
  Piqua *(G-12515)*
Hexpol Compounding LLC .... C 440 834-4664
  Burton *(G-1880)*

CHEMICALS & ALLIED PRDTS, WHOLESALE: Resins, Plastics

Network Polymers Inc .... E 330 773-2700
  Akron *(G-261)*

CHEMICALS & ALLIED PRDTS, WHOLESALE: Rubber, Synthetic

Goldsmith & Eggleton Inc .... F 330 336-6616
  Wadsworth *(G-15032)*
Goldsmith & Eggleton LLC .... F 203 855-6000
  Wadsworth *(G-15033)*
Mantaline Corporation .... G 330 274-2264
  Mantua *(G-9739)*

CHEMICALS & ALLIED PRDTS, WHOLESALE: Spec Clean/Sanitation

Ccp Industries Inc .... B 216 535-4227
  Richmond Heights *(G-12807)*

CHEMICALS & ALLIED PRDTS, WHOLESALE: Syn Resin, Rub/Plastic

Akrochem Corporation .... D 330 535-2100
  Akron *(G-26)*
Flex Technologies Inc .... D 330 897-6311
  Baltic *(G-836)*
Kraton Polymers US LLC .... B 740 423-7571
  Belpre *(G-1257)*
Phoenix Technologies Intl LLC .... E 419 353-7738
  Bowling Green *(G-1583)*

CHEMICALS & OTHER PRDTS DERIVED FROM COKING

Acadia Scientific LLC .... G 267 980-1644
  Perrysburg *(G-12358)*
FBC Chemical Corporation .... E 216 341-2000
  Cleveland *(G-4051)*
Geauga Coatings LLC .... G 440 221-7286
  Chardon *(G-2451)*
Worthington Steel Company .... B 800 944-2255
  Worthington *(G-16223)*

CHEMICALS, AGRICULTURE: Wholesalers

Helena Agri-Enterprises LLC .... G 614 275-4200
  Columbus *(G-5426)*
Imcd Us LLC .... E 216 228-8900
  Westlake *(G-15760)*
Keystone Cooperative Inc .... G 937 884-5526
  Verona *(G-14975)*

CHEMICALS: Agricultural

BASF Corporation .... D 614 662-5682
  Columbus *(G-5176)*
Damon Industries Inc .... D 330 821-5310
  Alliance *(G-400)*
Dupont .... G 740 412-9752
  Orient *(G-12114)*
Hawthorne Hydroponics LLC .... F 888 478-6544
  Marysville *(G-9914)*
Keystone Cooperative Inc .... G 937 884-5526
  Verona *(G-14975)*
Monsanto Company .... F 937 548-7858
  Greenville *(G-8052)*
Quality Borate Co LLC .... F 216 896-1949
  Cleveland *(G-4604)*
TLC Products Inc .... F 216 472-3030
  Westlake *(G-15797)*

CHEMICALS: Alkalies

Employee Codes: A=Over 500 employees, B=251-500
C=101-250, D=51-100, E=20-50, F=10-19, G=1-9

CHEMICALS: Aluminum Compounds

Valvsys LLC................................. G 513 870-1234
  Hamilton *(G-8256)*

CHEMICALS: Aluminum Compounds

Gayston Corporation...................... C 937 743-6050
  Miamisburg *(G-10640)*

CHEMICALS: Aluminum Sulfate

Chemtrade Chemicals US LLC........... G 419 255-0193
  Toledo *(G-14237)*

CHEMICALS: Anhydrous Ammonia

CF Industries Inc............................ C 330 385-5424
  East Liverpool *(G-6990)*
Talus Renewables Inc..................... E 650 248-5374
  Cleveland Heights *(G-4943)*

CHEMICALS: Bleaching Powder, Lime Bleaching Compounds

Bleachtech LLC............................. E 216 921-1980
  Seville *(G-13139)*

CHEMICALS: Bromine, Elemental

Albemarle Amendments LLC............ E 330 425-2354
  Twinsburg *(G-14627)*

CHEMICALS: Caustic Potash & Potassium Hydroxide

INEOS KOH INC............................ C 440 997-5221
  Ashtabula *(G-639)*

CHEMICALS: Caustic Soda

National Colloid Company................ E 740 282-1171
  Steubenville *(G-13673)*

CHEMICALS: Fire Retardant

No Burn Inc.................................. G 330 336-1500
  Wadsworth *(G-15048)*
No Burn North America Inc.............. F 419 841-6055
  Toledo *(G-14397)*
Pyro-Chem Corporation................... F 740 377-2244
  South Point *(G-13474)*

CHEMICALS: High Purity Grade, Organic

Ronald T Dodge Co........................ F 937 439-4497
  Dayton *(G-6552)*

CHEMICALS: High Purity, Refined From Technical Grade

Arboris LLC.................................. E 740 522-9350
  Newark *(G-11565)*
Helena Agri-Enterprises LLC............ G 614 275-4200
  Columbus *(G-5426)*
Helena Agri-Enterprises LLC............ G 419 596-3806
  Continental *(G-5937)*
Heraeus Epurio LLC....................... E 937 264-1000
  Vandalia *(G-14942)*
Pureti Group LLC........................... F 513 708-3631
  Blue Ash *(G-1458)*

CHEMICALS: Inorganic, NEC

5th Element Fitness LLC................. G 614 537-6038
  Columbus *(G-5078)*
Airgas Usa LLC............................ G 937 222-8312
  Moraine *(G-11154)*
Airgas Usa LLC............................ G 440 232-6397
  Twinsburg *(G-14625)*
Akron Dispersions Inc.................... E 330 666-0045
  Copley *(G-5942)*

Alchem Corporation....................... G 330 725-2436
  Medina *(G-10292)*
Alfrebro LLC................................. F 513 539-7373
  Monroe *(G-11093)*
Alpha Zeta Holdings Inc.................. G 216 271-1601
  Cleveland *(G-3640)*
Aluchem Inc................................. E 513 733-8519
  Cincinnati *(G-2612)*
Aluchem of Jackson Inc.................. E 740 286-2455
  Jackson *(G-8708)*
Americhem Inc.............................. D 330 929-4213
  Cuyahoga Falls *(G-6064)*
BASF Corporation.......................... D 614 662-5682
  Columbus *(G-5176)*
Bio-Systems Corporation................. E 608 365-9550
  Bowling Green *(G-1555)*
Bond Chemicals Inc....................... F 330 725-5935
  Medina *(G-10303)*
Borchers Americas Inc................... D 440 899-2950
  Westlake *(G-15741)*
Calvary Industries Inc.................... E 513 874-1113
  Fairfield *(G-7342)*
Chem Technologies Ltd.................. D 440 632-9311
  Middlefield *(G-10740)*
Chemtrade Logistics Inc.................. E 216 566-8070
  Cleveland *(G-3817)*
Chemtrade Refinery Svcs Inc........... F 419 641-4151
  Cairo *(G-1905)*
Cil Isotope Separations LLC............ F 937 376-5413
  Xenia *(G-16255)*
Cirba Solutions Us Inc.................... E 740 653-6290
  Lancaster *(G-9000)*
Coolant Control Inc....................... E 513 471-8770
  Cincinnati *(G-2795)*
Current Lighting Solutions LLC......... B 216 462-4700
  Beachwood *(G-982)*
Db Parent Inc............................... G 513 475-3265
  Cincinnati *(G-2821)*
Diverseylever Inc........................... G 513 554-4200
  Cincinnati *(G-2831)*
Diversified Brands......................... G 216 595-8777
  Bedford *(G-1117)*
Dover Chemical Corporation............ C 330 343-7711
  Dover *(G-6818)*
Dupont Electronic Polymers LP........ D 937 268-3411
  Dayton *(G-6308)*
Eagle Chemicals Inc....................... F 513 868-9662
  Hamilton *(G-8204)*
Elco Corporation........................... E 440 997-6131
  Ashtabula *(G-631)*
Eliokem Inc.................................. D 330 734-1100
  Fairlawn *(G-7438)*
Engelhard Corp............................. G 440 322-3741
  Elyria *(G-7149)*
Evonik Corporation........................ D 513 554-8969
  Cincinnati *(G-2889)*
Ferro Corporation.......................... D 216 577-7144
  Bedford *(G-1121)*
Ferroglobe USA Mtllurgical Inc........ C 740 984-2361
  Waterford *(G-15236)*
Flexsys Inc.................................. B 212 605-6000
  Akron *(G-156)*
General Electric Company............... E 216 268-3846
  Cleveland *(G-4114)*
GFS Chemicals Inc........................ E 614 351-5347
  Columbus *(G-5402)*
Hilltop Energy Inc.......................... F 330 859-2108
  Mineral City *(G-11018)*
Illinois Tool Works Inc.................... D 440 914-3100
  Solon *(G-13366)*
Ineos Pigments Asu LLC................ E 440 994-1999
  Ashtabula *(G-640)*

Ineos Pigments Usa Inc.................. C 440 994-1400
  Ashtabula *(G-641)*
Intrepid Co................................... G 440 355-6089
  Lagrange *(G-8949)*
J R M Chemical Inc....................... F 216 475-8488
  Cleveland *(G-4245)*
Jmp Industries.............................. G 216 749-6030
  Cleveland *(G-4257)*
Kerry Flavor Systems Us LLC........... F 513 539-7373
  Monroe *(G-11113)*
Kingscote Chemicals Inc................. G 330 523-5300
  Richfield *(G-12290)*
Littlern Corporation........................ G 330 848-8847
  Fairlawn *(G-7444)*
Malco Products Inc....................... C 330 753-0361
  Barberton *(G-872)*
McGean-Rohco Inc........................ F 216 441-4900
  Newburgh Heights *(G-11618)*
McGean-Rohco Inc........................ D 216 441-4900
  Newburgh Heights *(G-11619)*
Nachurs Alpine Solutions LLC.......... E 740 382-5701
  Marion *(G-9864)*
National Colloid Company................ E 740 282-1171
  Steubenville *(G-13673)*
Norlab Inc.................................... F 440 282-5265
  Lorain *(G-9426)*
Nutrien AG Solutions Inc................ G 513 941-4100
  North Bend *(G-11705)*
Occidental Chemical Corp............... E 513 242-2900
  Cincinnati *(G-3211)*
Occidental Chemical Durez............. F 419 675-1310
  Kenton *(G-8895)*
Om Group Inc............................... E 216 781-0083
  Cleveland *(G-4521)*
Omnova Wallcovering USA Inc........ D 216 682-7000
  Beachwood *(G-1008)*
P Q Corp..................................... G 216 621-0840
  Cleveland *(G-4556)*
PMC Specialties Group Inc.............. F 513 242-3300
  Cincinnati *(G-3253)*
PMC Specialties Group Inc.............. E 513 242-3300
  Cincinnati *(G-3252)*
Polymerics Inc.............................. E 330 928-2210
  Cuyahoga Falls *(G-6110)*
Primary Pdts Ingrdnts Amrcas L....... D 937 236-5906
  Dayton *(G-6520)*
Quanta International LLC................ F 513 354-3639
  Cincinnati *(G-3333)*
Saint-Gobain Ceramics Plas Inc........ C 330 673-5860
  Stow *(G-13721)*
Shepherd Widnes Ltd..................... D 513 731-1110
  Norwood *(G-11929)*
Synthomer Inc.............................. F 330 734-1237
  Akron *(G-342)*
Synthomer Inc.............................. C 216 682-7000
  Beachwood *(G-1025)*
Union Camp Corp.......................... G 330 343-7701
  Dover *(G-6849)*
Univar Solutions USA LLC............... F 513 714-5264
  West Chester *(G-15602)*
Usalco Michigan City Plant LLC....... F 513 737-7100
  Fairfield *(G-7422)*
Vibrantz Corporation...................... F 442 224-6100
  Cleveland *(G-4872)*
VWR Chemicals LLC...................... E 800 448-4442
  Solon *(G-13444)*
WA Hammond Drierite Co Ltd......... E 937 376-2927
  Xenia *(G-16280)*
Zaclon LLC.................................. E 216 271-1601
  Cleveland *(G-4937)*

CHEMICALS: Lithium Compounds, Inorganic

Lithium Innovations Co LLC .... G 419 725-3525
Toledo *(G-14369)*

CHEMICALS: Medicinal

Pharmacia Hepar LLC .... E 937 746-3603
Franklin *(G-7692)*

CHEMICALS: Medicinal, Organic, Uncompounded, Bulk

Nutritional Medicinals LLC .... F 937 433-4673
West Chester *(G-15467)*

CHEMICALS: NEC

Addivant .... G 440 352-1719
Concord Township *(G-5900)*
Akron Dispersions Inc .... E 330 666-0045
Copley *(G-5942)*
Albemarle Amendments LLC .... E 330 425-2354
Twinsburg *(G-14627)*
Aldrich Chemical .... D 937 859-1808
Miamisburg *(G-10608)*
Alterra Energy LLC .... G 800 569-6061
Akron *(G-56)*
Aps-Materials Inc .... D 937 278-6547
Dayton *(G-6210)*
Ashland Chemco Inc .... F 216 961-4690
Cleveland *(G-3689)*
Ashland Chemco Inc .... C 614 790-3333
Columbus *(G-5156)*
Ashland Spcalty Ingredients GP .... C 614 529-3311
Columbus *(G-5157)*
ASK Chemicals LLC .... B 800 848-7485
Dublin *(G-6863)*
Ask Chemicals LP .... G 614 763-0248
Columbus *(G-5159)*
Attia Applied Sciences Inc .... G 740 369-1891
Delaware *(G-6704)*
Bernard Laboratories Inc .... E 513 681-7373
Cincinnati *(G-2666)*
Bird Control International .... F 330 425-2377
Twinsburg *(G-14637)*
BLaster LLC .... E 216 901-5800
Cleveland *(G-3742)*
Bond Distributing LLC .... G 440 461-7920
Eastlake *(G-7022)*
Borchers Americas Inc .... D 440 899-2950
Westlake *(G-15741)*
Buckeye Fabric Finishers Inc .... F 740 622-3251
Coshocton *(G-5975)*
Cargill Incorporated .... F 513 941-7400
Cincinnati *(G-2702)*
Cargill Incorporated .... C 216 651-7200
Cleveland *(G-3792)*
Cfo Ntic .... G 216 450-5700
Beachwood *(G-976)*
Chem Technologies Ltd .... D 440 632-9311
Middlefield *(G-10740)*
Chemical Methods Incorporated .... E 216 476-8400
Brunswick *(G-1751)*
Chemstation International Inc .... E 937 294-8265
Moraine *(G-11166)*
Cinchempro Inc .... C 513 724-6111
Batavia *(G-914)*
Cincinnati - Vulcan Company .... D 513 242-5300
Cincinnati *(G-2736)*
Coolant Control Inc .... E 513 471-8770
Cincinnati *(G-2795)*
CP Chemicals Group LP .... F 440 833-3000
Wickliffe *(G-15829)*

Cresset Chemical Co Inc .... F 419 669-2041
Weston *(G-15805)*
Cresset Chemical Co Inc .... F 419 669-2041
Weston *(G-15804)*
Dayton Superior Corporation .... C 937 866-0711
Miamisburg *(G-10633)*
Dover Chemical Corporation .... C 330 343-7711
Dover *(G-6818)*
Elco Corporation .... E 440 997-6131
Ashtabula *(G-631)*
EMD Millipore Corporation .... C 513 631-0445
Norwood *(G-11995)*
Ensign Product Company Inc .... G 216 341-5911
Cleveland *(G-4020)*
Enviri Corporation .... F 330 372-1781
Warren *(G-15168)*
Environmental Chemical Corp .... F 330 453-5200
Uniontown *(G-14782)*
ESP Akron Sub LLC .... D 330 374-2242
Akron *(G-144)*
Essential Elements Usa LLC .... E 513 482-5700
Cincinnati *(G-2884)*
Etna Products Incorporated .... E 440 543-9845
Chagrin Falls *(G-2395)*
Euclid Chemical Company .... E 800 321-7628
Cleveland *(G-4032)*
Flexsys America LP .... D 330 666-4111
Akron *(G-155)*
Formlabs Ohio Inc .... E 419 837-9783
Millbury *(G-10932)*
Fuchs Lubricants Co .... E 330 963-0400
Twinsburg *(G-14663)*
Fusion Ceramics Inc .... E 330 627-5821
Carrollton *(G-2307)*
Fusion Incorporated .... D 440 946-3300
Willoughby *(G-15922)*
Galapagos Inc .... E 937 890-3068
Dayton *(G-6344)*
General Electric Company .... E 216 268-3846
Cleveland *(G-4114)*
GFS Chemicals Inc .... D 614 224-5345
Columbus *(G-5403)*
GFS Chemicals Inc .... E 740 881-5501
Powell *(G-12674)*
H&G Legacy Co .... F 513 921-1075
Cincinnati *(G-2982)*
Hexion LLC .... D 614 225-4000
Columbus *(G-5429)*
Hexpol Compounding LLC .... C 440 834-4644
Burton *(G-1880)*
Howard Industries Inc .... F 614 444-9900
Columbus *(G-5447)*
Hunt Imaging LLC .... E 440 826-0433
Berea *(G-1283)*
Huntsman Corporation .... D 330 374-2418
Akron *(G-187)*
Illinois Tool Works Inc .... D 440 914-3100
Solon *(G-13366)*
Innovative Food Processors Inc .... G 507 334-2730
Defiance *(G-6683)*
Intercontinental Chemical Corp .... E 513 541-7100
Cincinnati *(G-3026)*
Italmatch Sc LLC .... F 216 749-2605
Cleveland *(G-4239)*
J C Whitlam Manufacturing Co .... E 330 334-2524
Wadsworth *(G-15037)*
Leonhardt Plating Company .... F 513 242-1410
Cincinnati *(G-3102)*
Liquid Development Company .... G 216 641-9366
Independence *(G-8671)*
Lubrizol Advanced Mtls Inc .... F 216 447-5000
Brecksville *(G-1625)*

Lubrizol Corporation .... F 216 447-5447
Brecksville *(G-1626)*
Lubrizol Global Management Inc .... E 440 933-0400
Avon Lake *(G-815)*
Lubrizol Global Management Inc .... F 216 447-5000
Cleveland *(G-4339)*
Lubrizol Holdings LLC .... F 440 943-4200
Wickliffe *(G-15838)*
Malco Products Inc .... C 330 753-0361
Barberton *(G-879)*
Master Chemical Corporation .... D 419 874-7902
Perrysburg *(G-12399)*
McGean-Rohco Inc .... F 216 441-4900
Newburgh Heights *(G-11618)*
McGean-Rohco Inc .... D 216 441-4900
Newburgh Heights *(G-11619)*
Midwest Glycol Services LLC .... E 419 946-3326
Marion *(G-9862)*
Monarch Engraving Inc .... F 440 638-1500
Strongsville *(G-13857)*
Morgan Advanced Ceramics Inc .... E 330 405-1033
Twinsburg *(G-14700)*
Morton Salt Inc .... C 330 925-3015
Rittman *(G-12825)*
National Colloid Company .... E 740 282-1171
Steubenville *(G-13673)*
Noco Company .... D 216 464-8131
Solon *(G-13399)*
Nof Metal Coatings N Amer Inc .... E 440 285-2231
Chardon *(G-2459)*
Noveon Fcc Inc .... E 440 943-4200
Wickliffe *(G-15841)*
Ohio Aluminum Chemicals LLC .... G 513 860-3842
West Chester *(G-15468)*
Parker Trutec Incorporated .... D 937 653-8500
Urbana *(G-14846)*
Pchem LLC .... G 419 699-1582
Northwood *(G-11926)*
Polymer Additives Holdings Inc .... C 216 875-7200
Independence *(G-8680)*
Polymerics Inc .... E 330 677-1131
Kent *(G-8845)*
PPG Architectural Coatings LLC .... D 440 297-8000
Strongsville *(G-13866)*
Premier Chemicals .... G 440 234-4600
Cleveland *(G-4579)*
Premier Ink Systems Inc .... F 513 367-2300
Harrison *(G-8286)*
Primary Pdts Ingrdnts Amrcas L .... D 937 236-5906
Dayton *(G-6520)*
Proklean Services LLC .... E 330 273-0122
Brunswick *(G-1783)*
Quaker Chemical Corporation .... E 513 422-9600
Middletown *(G-10853)*
Quikrete Companies LLC .... E 614 885-4406
Columbus *(G-5704)*
Railtech Matweld Inc .... E 419 592-5050
Napoleon *(G-11332)*
Ravago Chemical Dist Inc .... E 330 920-8023
Twinsburg *(G-14723)*
Research Organics LLC .... D 216 883-8025
Cleveland *(G-4628)*
Rhenium Alloys Inc .... E 440 365-7388
North Ridgeville *(G-11858)*
Rozzi Company Inc .... F 513 683-0620
Martinsville *(G-9902)*
Sigma-Aldrich Corporation .... D 216 206-5424
Cleveland *(G-4701)*
Signet Enterprises LLC .... E 330 762-9102
Akron *(G-331)*
State Industrial Products Corp .... B 877 747-6986
Cleveland *(G-4731)*

CHEMICALS: NEC

Summitville Tiles Inc .... E 330 868-6463
Minerva (G-11040)

Teknol Inc .... D 937 264-0190
Dayton (G-6613)

The Lubrizol Corporation .... C 440 357-7064
Painesville (G-12270)

U S Chemical & Plastics .... G 330 830-6000
Massillon (G-10152)

Univar Solutions USA LLC .... F 513 714-5264
West Chester (G-15602)

Valtris Specialty Chemicals .... F 216 875-7200
Walton Hills (G-15104)

Vibrantz Corporation .... E 216 875-5600
Cleveland (G-4871)

Zinkan Enterprises Inc .... F 330 487-1500
Twinsburg (G-14760)

CHEMICALS: Phenol

Altivia Petrochemicals LLC .... E 740 532-3420
Haverhill (G-8308)

CHEMICALS: Phosphates, Defluorinated/ Ammoniated, Exc Fertlr

Pcs Phosphate Company Inc .... C 513 738-1261
Harrison (G-8283)

CHEMICALS: Reagent Grade, Refined From Technical Grade

GFS Chemicals Inc .... D 614 224-5345
Columbus (G-5403)

GFS Chemicals Inc .... E 740 881-5501
Powell (G-12674)

CHEMICALS: Silica Compounds

Wisconsin Indus Sand Co LLC .... E 715 235-0942
Independence (G-8692)

CHEMICALS: Sodium Bicarbonate

Church & Dwight Co Inc .... F 740 852-3621
London (G-9384)

Church & Dwight Co Inc .... F 419 992-4244
Old Fort (G-12072)

CHEMICALS: Water Treatment

AP Tech Group Inc .... F 513 761-8111
West Chester (G-15366)

Applied Specialties Inc .... E 440 933-9442
Avon Lake (G-796)

Aqua Science Inc .... E 614 252-5000
Columbus (G-5151)

Aquablue Incorporated .... G 330 343-0220
New Philadelphia (G-11484)

Bond Chemicals Inc .... F 330 725-5935
Medina (G-10303)

City of Mount Vernon .... G 740 393-9508
Mount Vernon (G-11268)

Damon Industries Inc .... D 330 821-5310
Alliance (G-400)

Ques Industries Inc .... F 216 267-8989
Cleveland (G-4610)

US Water Company LLC .... G 740 453-0604
Zanesville (G-16567)

Usalco Fairfield Plant LLC .... E 513 737-7100
Fairfield (G-7421)

CHICKEN SLAUGHTERING & PROCESSING

Pf Management Inc .... G 513 874-8741
West Chester (G-15575)

Pierre Holding Corp .... G 513 874-8741
West Chester (G-15576)

V H Cooper & Co Inc .... C 419 375-4116
Fort Recovery (G-7626)

CHILD DAY CARE SVCS

Learn21 A Flxble Lrng Cllbrtiv .... F 513 402-2121
Blue Ash (G-1421)

CHILD RESTRAINT SEATS, AUTOMOTIVE, WHOLESALE

Recaro Child Safety LLC .... G 248 904-1570
Cincinnati (G-3326)

TS Tech Americas Inc .... B 614 575-4100
Reynoldsburg (G-12776)

CHILDREN'S & INFANTS' CLOTHING STORES

Fancy ME Boutique LLC .... G 419 357-8927
Sandusky (G-13058)

CHILDREN'S WEAR STORES

Love Laugh & Laundry .... G 567 377-1951
Toledo (G-14370)

CHOCOLATE, EXC CANDY FROM BEANS: Chips, Powder, Block, Syrup

72 Chocolate LLC .... G 216 672-6040
Cleveland (G-3573)

Anthony-Thomas Candy Company .... C 614 274-8405
Columbus (G-5147)

Brandts Candies Inc .... G 440 942-1016
Willoughby (G-15892)

Brantley Partners IV LP .... G 216 464-8400
Cleveland (G-3754)

Cheryl & Co .... F 614 776-1500
Obetz (G-12058)

Chocolate Ecstasy Inc .... G 330 434-4199
Akron (G-108)

Chocolate Pig Inc .... G 440 461-4511
Cleveland (G-3820)

Dietsch Brothers Incorporated .... E 419 422-4474
Findlay (G-7501)

Executive Sweets East Inc .... G 440 359-9866
Oakwood Village (G-12038)

Fawn Confectionery Inc .... F 513 574-9612
Cincinnati (G-2897)

Gorant Chocolatier LLC .... C 330 726-8821
Boardman (G-1513)

Graeters Ice Cream Company .... D 513 721-3323
Cincinnati (G-2968)

Harry London Candies Inc .... E 330 494-0833
North Canton (G-11736)

Lil Turtles .... G 330 897-6400
Baltic (G-839)

Linneas Candy Supplies Inc .... E 330 678-7112
Kent (G-8828)

Malleys Candies Inc .... D 216 362-8700
Cleveland (G-4353)

Milk Hney Cndy Soda Shoppe LLC .... F 330 492-5884
Canton (G-2165)

Robert E McGrath Inc .... F 440 572-7747
Strongsville (G-13872)

Sweeties Olympia Treats LLC .... F 440 572-7747
Strongsville (G-13888)

CHOCOLATE, EXC CANDY FROM PURCH CHOC: Chips, Powder, Block

Golden Turtle Chocolate Fctry .... G 513 932-1990
Lebanon (G-9085)

Hartville Chocolates Inc .... F 330 877-1999
Hartville (G-8300)

CHUCKS

Flex-E-On Inc .... F 330 928-4496
Cuyahoga Falls (G-6084)

Hammill Manufacturing Co .... D 419 476-0789
Maumee (G-10204)

Jerry Tools Inc .... F 513 242-3211
Cincinnati (G-301)

Shook Manufactured Pdts Inc .... G 440 247-9130
Chagrin Falls (G-2385)

Shook Manufactured Pdts Inc .... G 330 848-9780
Akron (G-330)

CHURCHES

Christian Missionary Alliance .... C 380 208-6200
Reynoldsburg (G-12758)

CIGARETTE & CIGAR PRDTS & ACCESS

Gumbys LLC .... F 740 671-0818
Bellaire (G-1187)

Twm LLC .... G 419 562-9622
Bucyrus (G-1872)

CIGARETTE LIGHTERS

Hunters Manufacturing Co Inc .... E 330 628-9245
Mogadore (G-1175)

CIRCUIT BOARD REPAIR SVCS

Mid-Ohio Electric Co .... E 614 274-8000
Columbus (G-5553)

CIRCUIT BOARDS: Wiring

Parlex USA LLC .... E 937 898-3621
Vandalia (G-14915)

R-K Electronics Inc .... F 513 204-6060
Mason (G-10046)

CIRCUITS: Electronic

Accurate Electronics Inc .... C 330 682-7015
Orrville (G-12116)

Alphabet Inc .... D 330 856-3366
Warren (G-15130)

Astro Industries Inc .... E 937 429-5900
Beavercreek (G-041)

B5 Systems Inc .... G 937 372-4768
Xenia (G-16249)

C DI Services LLC .... G 440 354-1433
Painesville (G-12220)

C E Electronics Inc .... D 419 636-6705
Bryan (G-1813)

Captor Corporation .... D 937 667-8484
Tipp City (G-14125)

CCS International Circuits LLC .... G 440 563-3462
Roaming Shores (G-12830)

CEC Electronics Corp .... G 330 916-8100
Akron (G-102)

Channel Products Inc .... D 440 423-0113
Solon (G-13328)

Cutting Edge Technologies Inc .... F 216 574-4759
Cleveland (G-3920)

Dynalab Ems Inc .... D 614 866-9999
Reynoldsburg (G-2762)

Dynalab Ff Inc .... D 614 866-9999
Reynoldsburg (G-2763)

Electro-Line Inc .... F 937 461-5683
Dayton (G-6315)

Electronauts LLC .... F 859 261-3600
Cincinnati (G-2862)

Eti Tech LLC .... F 937 832-4200
Kettering (G-8907)

Great Lakes Glassworks Inc .... G 440 358-0460
Painesville (G-12221)

PRODUCT SECTION

CLEANING PRDTS: Specialty

Inservco Inc.. D 847 855-9600
  Lagrange *(G-8948)*
Laird Technologies Inc......................... F 330 434-7929
  Akron *(G-215)*
Lintech Electronics LLC....................... F 513 528-6190
  Cincinnati *(G-2571)*
Mjo Industries Inc................................ D 800 590-4055
  Huber Heights *(G-8577)*
Niktec Inc... G 513 282-3747
  Franklin *(G-7689)*
Parker-Hannifin Corporation................ F 937 644-3915
  Marysville *(G-9930)*
Performance Electronics Ltd............... G 513 777-5233
  Cincinnati *(G-3247)*
Precision Manufacturing Co Inc........... D 937 236-2170
  Dayton *(G-6514)*
Qlog Corp.. G 513 874-1211
  Hamilton *(G-8238)*
Rct Industries Inc................................ F 937 602-1100
  Dayton *(G-6543)*
Rpa Electronic Distrs Inc..................... F 937 223-7001
  Dayton *(G-6553)*
Sentrilock LLC..................................... C 513 618-5800
  West Chester *(G-15507)*
Shiloh Industries Inc............................ F 937 236-5100
  Dayton *(G-6569)*
Sovereign Circuits Inc......................... G 330 538-3900
  North Jackson *(G-11790)*
Spectron Inc.. G 937 461-5590
  Dayton *(G-6583)*
Staci Holdings Inc................................ G 440 284-2500
  Lagrange *(G-8955)*
The W L Jenkins Company.................. F 330 477-3407
  Canton *(G-2244)*
Tinycircuits... G 330 329-5753
  Akron *(G-358)*
Twin Point Inc..................................... G 419 923-7525
  Delta *(G-6791)*
US Lighting Group Inc......................... E 216 896-7000
  Euclid *(G-7305)*
Valley Electric Company..................... G 419 332-6405
  Fremont *(G-7818)*
Workman Electronic Pdts Inc.............. G 419 923-7525
  Delta *(G-6792)*

CLAMPS & COUPLINGS: Hose

Bowes Manufacturing Inc..................... E 216 378-2110
  Solon *(G-13321)*
Eaton Aeroquip LLC............................. C 440 523-5000
  Cleveland *(G-3991)*
Eaton Corporation............................... A 419 238-1190
  Van Wert *(G-14914)*
Voss Industries LLC............................. C 216 771-7655
  Cleveland *(G-4884)*
Winzeler Stamping Co......................... E 419 485-3147
  Montpelier *(G-11147)*

CLAMPS: Metal

Case Maul Clamps Inc......................... F 419 668-6563
  Norwalk *(G-11958)*
Clampco Products Inc......................... C 330 336-8857
  Wadsworth *(G-15023)*
Etl Performance Products Inc............. G 234 575-7226
  Salem *(G-12992)*
Herman Machine Inc........................... F 330 633-3261
  Tallmadge *(G-14032)*
Ottawa Products Co............................ F 419 836-5415
  Curtice *(G-6057)*

CLEANING EQPT: Commercial

As Clean As It Gets Off Brkroo............. E 216 256-1143
  South Euclid *(G-13459)*

Cold Jet International LLC................... D 513 831-3211
  Loveland *(G-9478)*
Detrex Corporation............................. F 216 749-2605
  Cleveland *(G-3954)*
Evers Enterprises Inc......................... G 513 541-7200
  Cincinnati *(G-2886)*
High-TEC Industrial Services.............. D 937 667-1772
  Tipp City *(G-14137)*
Holdren Brothers Inc.......................... F 937 465-7050
  West Liberty *(G-15622)*
Kaivac Inc... D 513 887-4600
  Hamilton *(G-8225)*
Kellermyer Bergensons Svcs LLC....... F 419 867-4300
  Maumee *(G-10210)*
MPW Industrial Svcs Group Inc.......... B 740 927-8790
  Hebron *(G-8350)*
Squeaky Clean Cincinnati Inc............. F 513 729-2712
  Cincinnati *(G-3412)*
W3 Ultrasonics LLC............................. G 330 284-3667
  North Canton *(G-11774)*

CLEANING EQPT: Floor Washing & Polishing, Commercial

Diversey Taski Inc.............................. E 419 531-2121
  Toledo *(G-14269)*
Image By J & K LLC............................ F 888 667-6929
  Maumee *(G-10207)*
MJB Toledo Inc................................... D 419 531-2121
  Toledo *(G-14387)*
Powerbuff Inc...................................... F 419 241-2156
  Toledo *(G-14441)*

CLEANING OR POLISHING PREPARATIONS, NEC

Aromair Fine Fragrance Company....... B 614 984-2900
  New Albany *(G-11368)*
Canberra Corporation......................... C 419 724-4300
  Toledo *(G-14226)*
Chemical Methods Incorporated........ E 216 476-8400
  Brunswick *(G-1751)*
Chempace Corporation....................... F 419 535-0101
  Toledo *(G-14236)*
Chemstation International Inc............ E 937 294-8265
  Moraine *(G-11166)*
Damon Industries Inc......................... D 330 821-5310
  Alliance *(G-400)*
Emes Supply LLC............................... G 216 400-8025
  Willowick *(G-16031)*
Kleen Test Products Corp................... B 330 878-5586
  Strasburg *(G-13747)*
Kona Blackbird Inc.............................. E 440 285-3189
  Chardon *(G-2455)*
Ohio Auto Supply Company................ F 330 454-5105
  Canton *(G-2182)*
Paro Services Co................................ F 330 467-1300
  Twinsburg *(G-14707)*
Ventco Inc... F 440 834-8888
  Chagrin Falls *(G-2432)*
Vitex Corporation............................... F 216 883-0920
  Cleveland *(G-4879)*
Woodbine Products Company............ F 330 725-0165
  Medina *(G-10395)*

CLEANING PRDTS: Automobile Polish

BLaster Holdings LLC......................... G 216 901-5800
  Cleveland *(G-3741)*
BLaster LLC.. E 216 901-5800
  Cleveland *(G-3742)*
Custom Chemical Packaging LLC....... G 330 331-7416
  Medina *(G-10316)*

James C Robinson............................... G 513 969-7482
  Cincinnati *(G-3036)*
Jax Wax Inc... F 614 476-6769
  Columbus *(G-5489)*

CLEANING PRDTS: Bleaches, Household, Dry Or Liquid

K-O-K Products Inc............................. F 740 548-0526
  Galena *(G-7855)*

CLEANING PRDTS: Degreasing Solvent

Pneumatic Specialties Inc................... G 440 729-4400
  Chesterland *(G-2488)*

CLEANING PRDTS: Deodorants, Nonpersonal

Fresh Products LLC............................. D 419 531-9741
  Perrysburg *(G-12384)*
Nilodor Inc.. E 800 443-4321
  Bolivar *(G-1530)*

CLEANING PRDTS: Drain Pipe Solvents Or Cleaners

Personal Plumber Service Corp........... F 440 324-4321
  Elyria *(G-7195)*

CLEANING PRDTS: Laundry Preparations

Procter & Gamble Far East Inc............ C 513 983-1100
  Cincinnati *(G-3295)*

CLEANING PRDTS: Sanitation Preparations

New Waste Concepts Inc..................... F 877 736-6924
  Perrysburg *(G-12402)*

CLEANING PRDTS: Sanitation Preps, Disinfectants/Deodorants

D & J Distributing & Mfg..................... E 419 865-2552
  Holland *(G-8501)*
Ecolab Inc... G 513 932-0830
  Lebanon *(G-9072)*
Lucas Specialty Products LLC............. G 419 290-6168
  Toledo *(G-14373)*
R&R Sanitation.................................... F 419 561-8090
  Crestline *(G-6036)*
Tranzonic Companies.......................... C 440 446-0643
  Cleveland *(G-4818)*
Tz Acquisition Corp............................ E 216 535-4300
  Richmond Heights *(G-12812)*

CLEANING PRDTS: Specialty

Carbonklean Llc.................................. G 614 980-9515
  Powell *(G-12666)*
Kinzua Environmental Inc................... E 216 881-4040
  Cleveland *(G-4292)*
Orchem Corporation........................... E 513 874-9700
  Dayton *(G-6493)*
Procter & Gamble Company................ D 513 983-1100
  Cincinnati *(G-3281)*
Procter & Gamble Company................ F 513 266-4375
  Cincinnati *(G-3282)*
Procter & Gamble Company................ G 513 871-7557
  Cincinnati *(G-3283)*
Procter & Gamble Company................ F 513 482-6789
  Cincinnati *(G-3286)*
Procter & Gamble Company................ C 513 983-3000
  Cincinnati *(G-3288)*
Procter & Gamble Company................ E 513 627-7115
  Cincinnati *(G-3289)*
Procter & Gamble Company................ F 513 945-0340
  Cincinnati *(G-3292)*

Employee Codes: A=Over 500 employees, B=251-500
C=101-250, D=51-100, E=20-50, F=10-19, G=1-9

CLEANING PRDTS: Specialty

Procter & Gamble Company............... D 513 622-1000
  Mason (G-10043)
Procter & Gamble Company............... C 513 634-9600
  West Chester (G-15486)
Procter & Gamble Company............... C 513 634-9110
  West Chester (G-15487)
Procter & Gamble Company............... A 513 983-1100
  Cincinnati (G-3280)
Procter & Gamble Mexico Inc............. ..... 513 983-1100
  Cincinnati (G-3297)
Republic Powdered Metals Inc........... D 330 225-3192
  Medina (G-10370)
Rose Products and Services Inc......... F 614 443-7647
  Columbus (G-5731)
RPM International Inc..................... D 330 273-5090
  Medina (G-10372)

CLEANING PRDTS: Stain Removers

Sherwin-Williams Company................ C 330 830-6000
  Massillon (G-10144)

CLEANING SVCS: Industrial Or Commercial

MPW Industrial Svcs Group Inc.......... B 740 927-8790
  Hebron (G-8350)
Omega Cementing Co...................... G 330 695-7147
  Apple Creek (G-508)
Paro Services Co............................ F 330 467-1300
  Twinsburg (G-14707)

CLIPS & FASTENERS, MADE FROM PURCHASED WIRE

Pennant Inc................................... E 937 584-5411
  Columbus (G-5666)
Stud Welding Associates Inc............. D 440 783-3160
  Strongsville (G-13887)
Tom Thumb Clip Co Inc................... F 440 953-9606
  Willoughby (G-16008)

CLOSURES: Closures, Stamped Metal

Crown Cork & Seal Usa Inc............... D 740 681-3000
  Lancaster (G-9006)
Winzeler Couplings & Mtls LLC.......... D 419 485-3147
  Montpelier (G-11146)

CLOSURES: Plastic

Crown Cork & Seal Usa Inc............... D 740 681-3000
  Lancaster (G-9006)
Mold-Rite Plastics LLC..................... C 330 405-7739
  Twinsburg (G-14698)

CLOTHING & ACCESS, WOMEN, CHILDREN & INFANT, WHOL: Uniforms

Cintas Sales Corporation.................. B 513 459-1200
  Cincinnati (G-2771)
Digitek Corp.................................. F 513 794-3190
  Mason (G-9984)

CLOTHING & ACCESS: Costumes, Theatrical

Costume Specialists Inc................... E 614 464-2115
  Columbus (G-5298)
Schenz Theatrical Supply Inc............ F 513 542-6100
  Cincinnati (G-3369)
Snaps Inc..................................... G 419 477-5100
  Mount Cory (G-11228)

CLOTHING & ACCESS: Men's Miscellaneous Access

MA Workwear LLC.......................... G 800 459-4405
  Akron (G-233)

Rocky Brands Inc........................... B 740 753-9100
  Nelsonville (G-11359)
Salindia LLC.................................. G 614 501-4799
  Columbus (G-5742)
Status Mens Accessories.................. G 440 786-9394
  Oakwood Village (G-12042)

CLOTHING & APPAREL STORES: Custom

Charles Wisvari............................. G 740 671-9960
  Bellaire (G-1184)

CLOTHING & FURNISHINGS, MEN'S & BOYS', WHOLESALE: Uniforms

Cintas Sales Corporation.................. B 513 459-1200
  Cincinnati (G-2771)
Digitek Corp.................................. F 513 794-3190
  Mason (G-9984)
Identity Group LLC......................... G 614 337-6167
  Westerville (G-15658)
Walter F Stephens Jr Inc.................. E 937 746-0521
  Franklin (G-7709)

CLOTHING & FURNISHINGS, MENS & BOYS, WHOLESALE: Apprl Belts

Rbr Enterprises LLC........................ F 866 437-9327
  Brecksville (G-1630)

CLOTHING ACCESS STORES: Umbrellas

Totes Isotoner Corporation............... D 513 682-8200
  West Chester (G-15598)
Totes Isotoner Holdings Corp............ C 513 682-8200
  West Chester (G-15599)

CLOTHING STORES: T-Shirts, Printed, Custom

Impact Printing and Design LLC......... F 833 522-6200
  Columbus (G-5456)
Vandalia Sportswear LLC.................. G 937 264-3204
  Vandalia (G-14966)

CLOTHING STORES: Uniforms & Work

Appleheart Inc............................... G 937 384-0430
  Miamisburg (G-10612)
Markt LLC..................................... G 740 397-5900
  Mount Vernon (G-11278)
Rbr Enterprises LLC........................ F 866 437-9327
  Brecksville (G-1630)

CLOTHING STORES: Unisex

Chris Stepp.................................. G 513 248-0822
  Milford (G-10898)
Ohio Mills Corporation..................... G 216 431-3979
  Cleveland (G-4499)

CLOTHING STORES: Work

Karl Kuemmerling Inc...................... F
  Massillon (G-10114)

CLOTHING/ACCESS, WOMEN, CHILDREN/ INFANT, WHOL: Apparel Belt

Rbr Enterprises LLC........................ F 866 437-9327
  Brecksville (G-1630)

CLOTHING/ACCESS, WOMEN, CHILDREN/ INFANT, WHOL: Hosp Gowns

Philips Med Systems Clvland In......... B 440 483-3000
  Cleveland (G-4547)

CLOTHING: Access, Women's & Misses'

Blingflingforever LLC....................... G 216 215-6955
  Mentor On The Lake (G-10601)
Knh Industries Inc........................... F 330 510-8390
  Stow (G-13704)
Knh Industries Inc........................... G 330 235-1235
  Stow (G-13703)
Lettermans LLC............................. G 330 345-2628
  Wooster (G-16145)
Rocky Brands Inc........................... B 740 753-9100
  Nelsonville (G-11359)

CLOTHING: Aprons, Exc Rubber/Plastic, Women, Misses, Junior

Carrera Holdings Inc....................... E 216 687-1311
  Cleveland (G-3725)
Geauga Group LLC......................... G 440 543-8797
  Chagrin Falls (G-2397)

CLOTHING: Aprons, Harness

Seven Mile Creek Corporation............ G 937 456-3320
  Eaton (G-7069)
Watershed Mangement LLC.............. F 740 852-5607
  Mount Sterling (G-11258)

CLOTHING: Athletic & Sportswear, Men's & Boys'

Augusta Sportswear Inc................... G 937 497-7575
  Sidney (G-13223)
Kam Manufacturing Inc.................... C 419 238-6037
  Van Wert (G-14919)
Lettermans LLC............................. G 330 345-2628
  Wooster (G-16145)
Rocky Brands Inc........................... B 740 753-9100
  Nelsonville (G-11359)
Vesi Incorporated........................... E 513 563-6002
  Cincinnati (G-3457)

CLOTHING: Athletic & Sportswear, Women's & Girls'

Bodied Beauties LLC....................... G 216 971-1155
  Richmond Heights (G-12806)
Columbus Apparel Studio LLC........... F 614 706-7292
  Columbus (G-5261)
Fluff Boutique............................... G 513 227-6614
  Cincinnati (G-2971)

CLOTHING: Blouses, Women's & Girls'

Columbus Apparel Studio LLC........... F 614 706-7292
  Columbus (G-5261)
Kam Manufacturing Inc.................... C 419 238-6037
  Van Wert (G-14919)
Love Laugh & Laundry.................... G 567 377-1951
  Toledo (G-14370)
Rocky Brands Inc........................... B 740 753-9100
  Nelsonville (G-11359)

CLOTHING: Blouses, Womens & Juniors, From Purchased Mtrls

J C L S Enterprises LLC................... G 740 472-0314
  Woodsfield (G-16088)

CLOTHING: Bridal Gowns

Renee Grace LLC............................ G 513 399-5616
  Cincinnati (G-3332)
Surili Couture LLC........................... F 440 600-1456
  Westlake (G-15754)

CLOTHING: Caps, Baseball

Barbs Graffiti Inc............................ E 216 881-5550
  Cleveland (G-3719)

PRODUCT SECTION — COAL MINING SERVICES

CLOTHING: Children's, Girls'
Emblem Athletic LLC.................................. G 614 743-6955
Powell (G-12671)

CLOTHING: Coats & Suits, Men's & Boys'
Bea-Ecc Apparels Inc................................. G 216 650-6336
Cleveland (G-3726)

CLOTHING: Costumes
Akron Design & Costume LLC................... G 330 644-0425
Coventry Township (G-6004)
Deborah Meredith.. G 330 644-0425
Coventry Township (G-6008)

CLOTHING: Disposable
Direct Disposables LLC............................. G 440 717-3335
Brecksville (G-1613)
Rich Industries Inc..................................... E 330 339-4113
New Philadelphia (G-11526)

CLOTHING: Dresses
Purple Orchid Boutique LLC..................... G 614 554-7686
Columbus (G-5698)

CLOTHING: Hospital, Men's
Angels Uniform & Print Sp LLC................. G 330 707-6506
Youngstown (G-16313)
Model Medical LLC.................................... F 216 972-0573
Shaker Heights (G-13156)

CLOTHING: Jerseys, Knit
Spalding.. F 440 286-5717
Chardon (G-2469)

CLOTHING: Men's & boy's underwear & nightwear
Tranzonic Companies................................ D 216 535-4300
Richmond Heights (G-12811)

CLOTHING: Mens & Boys Jackets, Sport, Suede, Leatherette
Neff Motivation Inc..................................... C 937 548-3194
Greenville (G-8203)

CLOTHING: Neckwear
Outfit Good LLC... G 419 565-3770
Columbus (G-5647)

CLOTHING: Outerwear, Lthr, Wool/Down-Filled, Men, Youth/Boy
Holloway Sportswear Inc........................... D 937 497-7575
Sidney (G-13253)
Universal Lettering Inc............................... F 419 238-9320
Van Wert (G-14929)

CLOTHING: Outerwear, Women's & Misses' NEC
Barton-Carey Medical Pdts Inc................. E 419 887-1285
Maumee (G-10169)
Holloway Sportswear Inc........................... D 937 497-7575
Sidney (G-13253)
Kip-Craft Incorporated............................... D 216 898-5500
Cleveland (G-4293)
The Fechheimer Brothers Co.................... C 513 793-5400
Blue Ash (G-1480)

CLOTHING: Robes & Dressing Gowns
Thomas Creative Apparel Inc................... F 419 929-1506
New London (G-11470)

CLOTHING: Shirts, Dress, Men's & Boys'
Columbus Apparel Studio LLC.................. F 614 706-7292
Columbus (G-5261)

CLOTHING: Socks
Broken Spinning Wheel............................. G 419 825-1609
Swanton (G-13970)
Hype Socks LLC.. F 855 497-3769
Columbus (G-5448)
Rock Em Sock Em Retro LLC................... G 419 575-9309
Walbridge (G-15087)

CLOTHING: Sweaters & Sweater Coats, Knit
Fine Points Inc... F 216 229-6644
Cleveland (G-4060)

CLOTHING: Sweatshirts & T-Shirts, Men's & Boys'
J C L S Enterprises LLC............................ G 740 472-0314
Woodsfield (G-16088)

CLOTHING: T-Shirts & Tops, Knit
Digitek Corp... F 513 794-3190
Mason (G-9984)
E Retailing Associates LLC....................... D 614 300-5785
Columbus (G-5339)
Pjs Wholesale Inc...................................... G 614 402-9363
Columbus (G-5676)
Wonder-Shirts Inc...................................... G 917 679-2336
Dublin (G-6959)

CLOTHING: Underwear, Women's & Children's
Tranzonic Companies................................ D 216 535-4300
Richmond Heights (G-12811)
Vs Service Company LLC......................... A 614 415-2348
Reynoldsburg (G-12780)

CLOTHING: Uniforms & Vestments
Fire-Dex LLC... D 330 723-0000
Medina (G-10324)
Walter F Stephens Jr Inc........................... E 937 746-0521
Franklin (G-7709)

CLOTHING: Uniforms, Ex Athletic, Women's, Misses' & Juniors'
Cintas Corporation..................................... D 513 631-5750
Cincinnati (G-2770)
Cintas Corporation..................................... A 513 459-1200
Cincinnati (G-2769)
Cintas Corporation No 2............................ D 330 966-7800
Canton (G-2074)

CLOTHING: Uniforms, Firemen's, From Purchased Materials
Lion Apparel Inc.. C 937 898-1949
Dayton (G-6408)
Lion Apparel Inc.. D 937 898-1949
Dayton (G-6409)
Lion First Responder Ppe Inc................... D 937 898-1949
Dayton (G-6410)
Lion Group Inc... D 937 898-1949
Dayton (G-6411)

CLOTHING: Uniforms, Men's & Boys'
Empirical Manufacturing Co Inc................ E 513 948-1616
Cincinnati (G-2867)
The Fechheimer Brothers Co.................... C 513 793-5400
Blue Ash (G-1480)

CLOTHING: Uniforms, Military, Men/Youth, Purchased Materials
Vgs Inc... C 216 431-7800
Cleveland (G-4866)

CLOTHING: Uniforms, Work
Cintas Corporation..................................... D 513 631-5750
Cincinnati (G-2770)
Cintas Corporation..................................... A 513 459-1200
Cincinnati (G-2769)
Cintas Corporation No 2............................ D 330 966-7800
Canton (G-2074)
Cintas Sales Corporation.......................... B 513 459-1200
Cincinnati (G-2771)
School Uniforms and More Inc................. G 216 365-1957
Cleveland (G-4674)
Vgs Inc... C 216 431-7800
Cleveland (G-4866)

CLOTHING: Waterproof Outerwear
Totes Isotoner Corporation........................ D 513 682-8200
West Chester (G-15598)

CLOTHING: Work Apparel, Exc Uniforms
Hands On International LLC..................... G 513 502-9000
West Chester (G-15560)

CLOTHING: Work, Men's
Hands On International LLC..................... G 513 502-9000
West Chester (G-15560)

CLOTHING: Work, Waterproof, Exc Raincoats
Linsalata Cpitl Prtners Fund I.................... G 440 684-1400
Cleveland (G-4330)
Tranzonic Companies................................ C 440 446-0643
Cleveland (G-4818)
Tz Acquisition Corp.................................... E 216 535-4300
Richmond Heights (G-12812)

CLUTCHES, EXC VEHICULAR
Eaton Corporation...................................... C 216 281-2211
Cleveland (G-3992)
Ebog Legacy Inc.. D 330 239-4933
Sharon Center (G-13166)
Force Control Industries Inc...................... E 513 868-0900
Fairfield (G-7363)
Logan Clutch Corporation......................... E 440 808-4258
Cleveland (G-4334)
NIDEC MINSTER CORPORATION........... B 419 628-2331
Minster (G-11057)

COAL & OTHER MINERALS & ORES WHOLESALERS
B & S Transport Inc................................... G 330 767-4319
Navarre (G-11340)
Graphel Corporation.................................. C 513 779-6166
West Chester (G-15444)
Hickman Williams & Company.................. F 513 621-1946
Cincinnati (G-2998)
Tosoh America Inc.................................... B 614 539-8622
Grove City (G-8124)

COAL MINING SERVICES
American Cnsld Ntral Rsrces In................ E 740 338-3100
Saint Clairsville (G-12894)
American Coal Company.......................... F 740 338-3334
Saint Clairsville (G-12895)
Appalachian Fuels LLC............................. C 606 928-0460
Dublin (G-6862)
Coal Services Inc...................................... B 740 795-5220
Powhatan Point (G-12684)

COAL MINING SERVICES

Crimson Oak Grove Rsources LLC............ F 740 338-3100
　Saint Clairsville (G-12900)
Emery Cnty Coal Resources Inc............... G 740 338-3100
　Saint Clairsville (G-12902)
Global Coal Sales Group LLC................. G 614 221-0101
　Dublin (G-6886)
Ohio Valley Coal Company........................ B 740 926-1351
　Saint Clairsville (G-12918)
Peabody Coal Company............................. E 740 450-2420
　Zanesville (G-16554)
Rosebud Mining Company......................... D 740 658-4217
　Freeport (G-7761)
Suncoke Energy Inc................................... E 513 727-5571
　Middletown (G-10860)
Terradyn Corporation................................ F 614 805-0897
　Dublin (G-6951)
Western KY Cnsld Resources LLC............ G 740 338-3100
　Saint Clairsville (G-12930)
Western KY Resources Fing LLC.............. G 740 338-3100
　Saint Clairsville (G-12932)

COAL MINING: Anthracite

Coal Services Inc..................................... B 740 795-5220
　Powhatan Point (G-12684)

COAL MINING: Bituminous & Lignite Surface

Commercial Minerals Inc............................ G 330 549-2165
　North Lima (G-11803)
Ivi Mining Group Ltd.................................. G 740 418-7745
　Vinton (G-15011)
J & D Mining Inc....................................... E 330 339-4935
　New Philadelphia (G-11506)
McElroy Coal Company............................. F 724 485-4000
　Saint Clairsville (G-12911)
Murray American Energy Inc..................... C 740 338-3100
　Saint Clairsville (G-12915)
PM Coal Company LLC............................ G 440 256-7624
　Willoughby (G-15971)
Symmes Creek Mining LLC....................... G 740 353-1509
　Portsmouth (G-12658)
Washington County Coal Company........... G 740 338-3100
　Saint Clairsville (G-12928)

COAL MINING: Bituminous Coal & Lignite-Surface Mining

Anthony Mining Co Inc.............................. G 740 282-5301
　Wintersville (G-16084)
Buckingham Coal Company LLC............... D
　Zanesville (G-16515)
Coal Resources Inc.................................. E 216 765-1240
　Saint Clairsville (G-12899)
Coal Services Inc..................................... B 740 795-5220
　Powhatan Point (G-12684)
D & D Mining Co Inc................................. F 330 549-3127
　New Springfield (G-11540)
Franklin County Coal Company................. G 740 338-3100
　Saint Clairsville (G-12905)
Harrison County Coal Company................ F 740 338-3100
　Saint Clairsville (G-12906)
Kimble Company....................................... C 330 343-1226
　Dover (G-6830)
L & M Mineral Co...................................... G 330 852-3696
　Sugarcreek (G-13927)
Meigs County Coal Company.................... B 740 338-3100
　Saint Clairsville (G-12912)
Muhlenberg County Coal Co LLC.............. D 740 338-3100
　Saint Clairsville (G-12914)
Oxford Mining Company Inc...................... C 740 588-0190
　Zanesville (G-16552)
Oxford Mining Company Inc...................... G 740 622-3100
　Coshocton (G-5991)

Oxford Mining Company LLC.................... F 740 622-6302
　Coshocton (G-5992)
Rosebud Mining Company........................ D 740 768-2275
　Bergholz (G-1301)
Straight Creek Bushman LLC................... G 513 732-1698
　Batavia (G-950)
Subtropolis Mining Co............................... E 330 549-2165
　Petersburg (G-12450)
Westmoreland Resources Gp LLC............ D 740 622-6302
　Coshocton (G-5999)

COAL MINING: Bituminous, Strip

B&N Coal Inc.. E 740 783-3575
　Dexter City (G-6802)
Holmes Limestone Co............................... G 330 893-2721
　Berlin (G-1307)
Oxford Mining Company - KY LLC............ E 740 622-6302
　Coshocton (G-5993)
Thompson Bros Mining Co........................ F 330 549-3979
　New Springfield (G-11542)
Waterloo Coal Company Inc...................... D 740 286-0004
　Jackson (G-8727)

COAL MINING: Bituminous, Surface, NEC

Marietta Coal Co...................................... E 740 695-2197
　Saint Clairsville (G-12908)
Rayle Coal Co.. F 740 695-2197
　Saint Clairsville (G-12920)

COAL MINING: Lignite, Surface, NEC

Nacco Industries Inc................................. E 440 229-5151
　Cleveland (G-4434)

COAL PREPARATION PLANT: Bituminous or Lignite

Cliffs Logan County Coal LLC................... C 216 694-5700
　Cleveland (G-3871)

COAL TAR CRUDES: Derived From Chemical Recovery Coke Oven

Marion County Coal Company................... D 740 338-3100
　Saint Clairsville (G-12910)

COATED OR PLATED PRDTS

Ohio Coatings Company............................ D 740 859-5500
　Yorkville (G-16294)

COATING COMPOUNDS: Tar

Brewer Company...................................... G 513 576-6300
　Cincinnati (G-2681)
Brewer Company...................................... G 800 394-0017
　Milford (G-10896)
Dnd Emulsions Inc.................................... F 419 525-4988
　Mansfield (G-9646)
Neyra Interstate Inc.................................. E 513 733-1000
　Cincinnati (G-3196)

COATING SVC: Metals, With Plastic Or Resins

Corrotec Inc... E 937 325-3585
　Springfield (G-13547)
Gem Coatings Ltd.................................... F 740 589-2998
　Athens (G-684)
Godfrey & Wing Inc.................................. E 330 562-1440
　Aurora (G-716)
Harwood Entp Holdings Inc...................... F 330 923-3256
　Cuyahoga Falls (G-6090)
Perfection Finishers Inc........................... E 419 337-8015
　Wauseon (G-15272)

PRODUCT SECTION

Rack Processing Company Inc................ E 937 294-1911
　Moraine (G-1127)
Reliable Coating Svc Co Inc.................... G 513 217-4680
　Middletown (G-3855)
Techneglas LLC....................................... F 419 873-2000
　Perrysburg (G-12432)
Universal Rack & Eqp Co Inc................... D 330 963-6776
　Twinsburg (G-1751)

COATINGS: Epoxy

CPI Industrial Co...................................... E 614 445-0800
　Mount Sterling (G-11255)
Epoxy Systems Elstg Cating Inc.............. F 513 924-1800
　Cleves (G-4950)
Master Builders LLC................................ E 800 228-3318
　Beachwood (G-398)
Nanosperse LLC...................................... G 937 296-5030
　Kettering (G-8908)
Postle Industries Inc................................ E 216 265-9000
　Cleveland (G-465)
Quality Durable Indus Floors................... F 937 696-2833
　Farmersville (G-7460)
The Garland Company Inc....................... D 216 641-7500
　Cleveland (G-483)
X-Treme Finishes Inc.............................. F 330 474-0614
　North Royalton (G-11903)

COATINGS: Polyurethane

Trexler Rubber Co Inc............................. E 330 296-9677
　Ravenna (G-1739)

COILS & TRANSFORMERS

Barnes International LLC......................... E 419 352-7501
　Bowling Green (G-1552)
Custom Coil & Transformer Co................ G 740 452-5211
　Zanesville (G-6525)
Duca Manufacturing & Consulting Inc...... E 330 758-0828
　Youngstown (G-16352)
Electromotive Inc..................................... E 330 688-6494
　Stow (G-1369)
Industrial Quartz Corporation.................... E 440 942-0909
　Mentor (G-1071)
Kurz-Kasch Inc.. E 740 498-8343
　Newcomerstown (G-11647)
Npas Inc... F 614 595-6916
　Mansfield (G-706)
PCC Airfoils LLC...................................... C 216 692-7900
　Cleveland (G-1537)
Rapid Mr International LLC....................... G 614 486-6300
　Columbus (G-5711)
Schneider Electric Usa Inc....................... B 513 523-4171
　Oxford (G-1213)
Staco Energy Products Co....................... G 937 253-1191
　Miamisburg (G-10685)
Swiger Coil Systems Ltd.......................... E 216 362-7500
　Cleveland (G-4760)
USA Instruments Inc................................ C 330 562-1000
　Aurora (G-737)
Wabtec Corporation................................. F 216 362-7500
　Cleveland (G-4887)

COILS, WIRE: Aluminum, Made In Rolling Mills

Amh Holdings Inc..................................... B 330 929-1811
　Cuyahoga Falls (G-6066)

COILS: Electric Motors Or Generators

Custom Coil & Transformer Co................ G 740 452-5211
　Zanesville (G-16525)

COILS: Pipe

PRODUCT SECTION — COMMERCIAL PRINTING & NEWSPAPER PUBLISHING

Industrial Power Systems Inc............. B 419 531-3121
  Rossford *(G-12867)*

COLOR LAKES OR TONERS

Vibrantz Corporation............................. C 216 875-6213
  Cleveland *(G-4868)*

COLOR PIGMENTS

American Colors Inc.............................. E 419 621-4000
  Sandusky *(G-13043)*
Chromascape LLC................................. E 330 998-7574
  Independence *(G-8658)*
Ferro International Svcs Inc................... G 216 875-5600
  Mayfield Heights *(G-10248)*
General Color Investments Inc............... D 330 868-4161
  Minerva *(G-11031)*
Gsdi Specialty Dispersions Inc................ E 330 848-9200
  Massillon *(G-10103)*
McCann Color Inc................................... E 330 498-4840
  Canton *(G-2156)*
Vibrantz Corporation............................. E 724 207-2152
  Cleveland *(G-4869)*
Vibrantz Corporation............................. D 216 875-5600
  Mayfield Heights *(G-10256)*

COLORS: Pigments, Inorganic

Americhem Inc....................................... E 330 926-3185
  Cuyahoga Falls *(G-6065)*
Americhem Inc....................................... D 330 929-4213
  Cuyahoga Falls *(G-6064)*
Ampacet Corporation............................. D 740 929-5521
  Newark *(G-11561)*
Arconic... E 330 471-1844
  Canton *(G-2039)*
Avient Corporation................................ E 419 668-4844
  Norwalk *(G-11955)*
Colormatrix Corporation........................ C 216 622-0100
  Berea *(G-1272)*
Day-Glo Color Corp................................ F 216 391-7070
  Cleveland *(G-3945)*
Day-Glo Color Corp................................ F 216 391-7070
  Twinsburg *(G-14647)*
Day-Glo Color Corp................................ C 216 391-7070
  Cleveland *(G-3944)*
Degussa Incorporated........................... G 513 733-5111
  Cincinnati *(G-2823)*
Eckart America Corporation.................. D 440 954-7600
  Painesville *(G-12231)*
Kish Company Inc................................. F 440 205-9970
  Mentor *(G-10487)*
Lancer Dispersions Inc.......................... D
  Akron *(G-216)*
Leonhardt Plating Company.................. F 513 242-1410
  Cincinnati *(G-3102)*
Lyondllbsell Advnced Plymers I............ E 419 682-3311
  Stryker *(G-13910)*
Mason Color Works Inc......................... F 330 385-4400
  East Liverpool *(G-6998)*
PMC Specialties Group Inc................... F 513 242-3300
  Cincinnati *(G-3263)*
PMC Specialties Group Inc................... E 513 242-3300
  Cincinnati *(G-3262)*
Revlis Corporation................................. F 330 535-2108
  Barberton *(G-893)*
Sun Chemical Corporation.................... C 513 681-5950
  Cincinnati *(G-3431)*
The Shepherd Color Company.............. F 513 874-0714
  West Chester *(G-15596)*
Thorworks Industries Inc...................... C 419 626-4375
  Sandusky *(G-13096)*
Vibrantz Color Solutions Inc................. C 440 997-5137
  Ashtabula *(G-664)*

COMBINED ELEMENTARY & SECONDARY SCHOOLS, PUBLIC

Butler Tech.. E 513 867-1028
  Fairfield Township *(G-7430)*

COMMERCIAL & OFFICE BUILDINGS RENOVATION & REPAIR

Facility Service Pros LLC....................... G 419 577-6123
  Collins *(G-5004)*
Thomas Cabinet Shop Inc..................... F 937 847-8239
  Dayton *(G-6621)*
Youngstown Shade & Alum LLC............ G 330 782-2373
  Youngstown *(G-16487)*

COMMERCIAL ART & GRAPHIC DESIGN SVCS

Clarity Retail Services LLC.................... D 513 800-9369
  West Chester *(G-15395)*
Converters/Prepress Inc....................... F 937 743-0935
  Carlisle *(G-2287)*
Enlarging Arts Inc.................................. G 330 434-3433
  Akron *(G-142)*
Fx Digital Media Inc.............................. F 216 241-4040
  Cleveland *(G-4095)*
General Theming Contrs LLC................ C 614 252-6342
  Columbus *(G-5397)*
Malik Media LLC................................... F 614 933-0328
  New Albany *(G-11383)*
Midwest Menu Mate Inc....................... F 740 323-2599
  Newark *(G-11592)*
Morse Enterprises Inc........................... G 513 229-3600
  Mason *(G-10031)*
Painted Hill Inv Group Inc..................... F 937 339-1756
  Troy *(G-14600)*
Quez Media Marketing Inc.................... F 216 910-0202
  Independence *(G-8683)*
Sylvan Studios Inc................................ G 419 882-3423
  Sylvania *(G-14016)*
The Photo-Type Engraving Company.... D 513 281-0999
  Cincinnati *(G-3450)*
True Dinero Records & Tech LLC.......... G 513 428-4610
  Cincinnati *(G-3470)*
Visual Art Graphic Services.................. G 330 274-2775
  Mantua *(G-9745)*
Western Ohio Graphics......................... F 937 335-8769
  Troy *(G-14616)*

COMMERCIAL ART & ILLUSTRATION SVCS

ONeil & Associates Inc.......................... C 937 865-0800
  Miamisburg *(G-10669)*

COMMERCIAL CONTAINERS WHOLESALERS

Brimar Packaging Inc............................ E 440 934-3080
  Avon *(G-764)*
Kaufman Container Company............... C 216 898-2000
  Cleveland *(G-4276)*

COMMERCIAL EQPT WHOLESALERS, NEC

Active Aeration Systems Inc................. G 614 873-3626
  Plain City *(G-12559)*
Cummins - Allison Corp........................ G 513 469-2924
  Blue Ash *(G-1384)*
Cummins - Allison Corp........................ G 440 824-5050
  Cleveland *(G-3919)*
General Data Company Inc................... B 513 752-7978
  Cincinnati *(G-2561)*
National Pride Equipment Inc............... G 419 289-2886
  Mansfield *(G-9703)*
Rayhaven Group Inc............................. G 330 659-3183
  Richfield *(G-12795)*

COMMERCIAL EQPT, WHOLESALE: Display Eqpt, Exc Refrigerated

Abstract Displays Inc............................ F 513 985-9700
  Blue Ash *(G-1356)*
Ternion Inc.. E 216 642-6180
  Cleveland *(G-4777)*

COMMERCIAL EQPT, WHOLESALE: Restaurant, NEC

Harry C Lobalzo & Sons Inc.................. E 330 666-6758
  Akron *(G-180)*
ITW Food Equipment Group LLC........... A 937 332-2396
  Troy *(G-14589)*
N Wasserstrom & Sons Inc................... C 614 228-5550
  Columbus *(G-5588)*

COMMERCIAL EQPT, WHOLESALE: Store Fixtures & Display Eqpt

Baker Plastics Inc................................. G 330 743-3142
  Youngstown *(G-16317)*

COMMERCIAL PHOTOGRAPHIC STUDIO

Eclipse 3d/Pi LLC.................................. E 614 626-8536
  Columbus *(G-5343)*

COMMERCIAL PRINTING & NEWSPAPER PUBLISHING

Belem Group LLC.................................. G 614 604-6870
  Columbus *(G-5181)*
Carrollton Publishing Company............ F 330 627-5591
  Carrollton *(G-2305)*
Copley Ohio Newspapers Inc................ C 330 364-5577
  New Philadelphia *(G-11493)*
Copley Ohio Newspapers Inc................ D 585 598-0030
  Canton *(G-2081)*
Daily Chief Union.................................. F 419 294-2331
  Upper Sandusky *(G-14806)*
Defiance Publishing Co Ltd................... A 419 784-5441
  Defiance *(G-6677)*
Delaware Gazette Company.................. E 740 363-1161
  Delaware *(G-6714)*
Digicom Inc... F 216 642-3838
  Brooklyn Heights *(G-1690)*
Hamilton Journal News Inc................... E 513 863-8200
  Liberty Township *(G-9208)*
Herald Reflector Inc.............................. E 419 668-3771
  Norwalk *(G-11974)*
Horizon Ohio Publications Inc............... D 419 738-2128
  Wapakoneta *(G-15117)*
Horizon Ohio Publications Inc............... F 419 394-7414
  Saint Marys *(G-12953)*
Hubbard Publishing Co......................... E 937 592-3060
  Bellefontaine *(G-1212)*
King Media Enterprises Inc................... E 216 588-6700
  Cleveland *(G-4290)*
Kml Acquisitions Ltd............................. G 614 732-9777
  Plain City *(G-12582)*
Kroner Publications Inc........................ E 330 544-5500
  Niles *(G-11675)*
Ohio Newspapers Inc............................ A 937 225-2000
  Dayton *(G-6490)*
Progrssive Communications Corp......... D 740 397-5333
  Mount Vernon *(G-11290)*
Record Herald Publishing Co................ E 717 762-2151
  Cincinnati *(G-3327)*
Register Herald Office........................... F 937 456-5553
  Eaton *(G-7068)*

Employee Codes: A=Over 500 employees, B=251-500
C=101-250, D=51-100, E=20-50, F=10-19, G=1-9

COMMERCIAL PRINTING & NEWSPAPER PUBLISHING — PRODUCT SECTION

Samuel L Peters LLC .... G 513 745-1500
  Blue Ash *(G-1463)*
Sentinel Daily .... F 740 992-2155
  Gallipolis *(G-7902)*
Standard Printing Co Inc .... E 419 586-2371
  Celina *(G-2350)*
Toledo Blade Company .... B 419 724-6000
  Toledo *(G-14492)*
Wooster Daily Record Inc LLC .... C 330 264-1125
  Wooster *(G-16184)*

COMMON SAND MINING

Demilta Sand and Gravel Inc .... E 440 942-2015
  Willoughby *(G-15907)*
Demmy Sand and Gravel LLC .... E
  Springfield *(G-13554)*
Kirby and Sons Inc .... F 419 927-2260
  Upper Sandusky *(G-14813)*
Nelson Sand & Gravel Inc .... F 440 224-0198
  Kingsville *(G-8933)*
Stocker Sand & Gravel Co .... F 740 254-4635
  Gnadenhutten *(G-7990)*
Weber Sand & Gravel Inc .... G 419 298-2388
  Edgerton *(G-7083)*
Welch Holdings Inc .... E 513 353-3220
  Cincinnati *(G-3512)*
X L Sand and Gravel Co .... E 330 426-9876
  Negley *(G-11355)*

COMMUNICATIONS EQPT WHOLESALERS

Cattron Holdings Inc .... E 234 806-0018
  Warren *(G-15150)*
Cota International Inc .... F 937 526-5520
  Versailles *(G-14978)*
Quasonix Inc .... E 513 942-1287
  West Chester *(G-15491)*
Ray Communications Inc .... G 330 686-0226
  Stow *(G-13720)*
Securcom Inc .... E 419 628-1049
  Minster *(G-11060)*

COMMUNICATIONS SVCS: Data

Springdot Inc .... D 513 542-4000
  Cincinnati *(G-3411)*
Water Drop Media Inc .... G 234 600-5817
  Vienna *(G-15005)*

COMMUNICATIONS SVCS: Internet Connectivity Svcs

Great Lakes Telcom Ltd .... E 330 629-8848
  Youngstown *(G-16373)*
Revolution Group Inc .... D 614 212-1111
  Westerville *(G-15675)*

COMMUNICATIONS SVCS: Online Svc Providers

F+w Media Inc .... A 513 531-2690
  Blue Ash *(G-1393)*

COMMUNICATIONS SVCS: Telephone, Local & Long Distance

Airwave Communications Cons .... G 419 331-1526
  Lima *(G-9218)*
AT&T Corp .... G 513 792-9300
  Cincinnati *(G-2639)*

COMMUTATORS: Electronic

Ra Consultants LLC .... E 513 469-6600
  Blue Ash *(G-1459)*

COMPACT LASER DISCS: Prerecorded

Jk Digital Publishing LLC .... F 937 299-1985
  Springboro *(G-13506)*

COMPOSITION STONE: Plastic

Rsl LLC .... E 330 392-8900
  Warren *(G-15203)*
Silver Line Building Pdts LLC .... A 740 382-5595
  Marion *(G-9881)*

COMPOST

Hyponex Corporation .... C 330 262-1300
  Shreve *(G-13209)*
Kurtz Bros Compost Services .... F 330 864-2621
  Akron *(G-213)*
Midwest Compost Inc .... F 419 547-7979
  Clyde *(G-4974)*
Opal Diamond LLC .... G 330 653-5876
  Rocky River *(G-12839)*
Price Farms Organics Ltd .... F 740 369-1000
  Delaware *(G-6745)*
Van Tilburg Farms Inc .... F 419 586-3077
  Celina *(G-2354)*
Werlor Inc .... E 419 784-4285
  Defiance *(G-6698)*

COMPRESSORS: Air & Gas

Airtech .... G 419 269-1000
  Walbridge *(G-15078)*
Airtx International Ltd .... F 513 631-0660
  Cincinnati *(G-2605)*
Ariel Corporation .... F 740 397-0311
  Mount Vernon *(G-11263)*
Eaton Comprsr Fabrication Inc .... E 877 283-7614
  Englewood *(G-7230)*
Edwards Vacuum LLC .... G 440 248-4453
  Solon *(G-13340)*
Ernest Industries Inc .... F 937 325-9851
  Springfield *(G-13559)*
Field Gymmy Inc .... G 419 538-6511
  Glandorf *(G-7978)*
G Denver and Co LLC .... E 937 498-2555
  Sidney *(G-13250)*
General Fabrications Corp .... E 419 625-6055
  Sandusky *(G-13061)*
Ingersoll Rand .... F 440 277-7100
  Lorain *(G-9414)*
Kingsly Compression Inc .... G 740 439-0772
  Cambridge *(G-1939)*
Lsq Manufacturing Inc .... F 330 725-4905
  Medina *(G-10345)*
National Compressor Svcs LLC .... E 419 868-4980
  Holland *(G-8519)*
Nordson Corporation .... B 440 985-4496
  Amherst *(G-478)*
Nordson Medical Corporation .... D 440 892-1580
  Westlake *(G-15769)*
Powerex-Iwata Air Tech Inc .... D 888 769-7979
  Harrison *(G-8284)*
Transdigm Inc .... F 216 291-6025
  Cleveland *(G-4815)*

COMPRESSORS: Air & Gas, Including Vacuum Pumps

Aci Services Inc .... E 740 435-0240
  Cambridge *(G-1918)*
Airbase Industries LLC .... F 937 540-1140
  Englewood *(G-7222)*
Ariel Corporation .... D 330 896-2660
  Akron *(G-64)*

Ariel Corporation .... C 740 397-0311
  Mount Vernon *(G-11264)*
Autobody Supply Company Inc .... D 614 228-4328
  Columbus *(G-5156)*
Ch Transition Company LLC .... C 800 543-6400
  Cincinnati *(G-2714)*
Finishmaster Inc .... F 614 228-4328
  Groveport *(G-8199)*
Potemkin Industries Inc .... F 740 397-4888
  Mount Vernon *(G-11288)*

COMPRESSORS: Refrigeration & Air Conditioning Eqpt

Copeland LP .... A 937 498-3011
  Sidney *(G-1325)*
Hanon Systems Usa LLC .... C 313 920-0583
  Carey *(G-2279)*

COMPUTER & COMPUTER SOFTWARE STORES

Copier Resources Inc .... G 614 268-1100
  Columbus *(G-295)*
Gordons Graphics Inc .... G 330 863-2322
  Malvern *(G-9663)*
Journey Systems LLC .... F 513 831-6200
  Milford *(G-10962)*

COMPUTER & COMPUTER SOFTWARE STORES: Software & Access

Lantek Systems Inc .... G 877 805-1028
  Mason *(G-10010)*

COMPUTER & COMPUTER SOFTWARE STORES: Software, Bus/Non-Game

RB Sigma LLC .... D 440 290-0577
  Mentor *(G-10045)*
Retalix Inc .... E 937 384-2277
  Miamisburg *(G-10676)*

COMPUTER & COMPUTER SOFTWARE STORES: Software, Computer Game

Thyme Inc .... F 484 872-8430
  Akron *(G-357)*

COMPUTER & OFFICE MACHINE MAINTENANCE & REPAIR

Eaj Services LLC .... F 513 792-3400
  Blue Ash *(G-1387)*
Government Acquisitions Inc .... E 513 721-8700
  Cincinnati *(G-2967)*
Magnum Computers Inc .... F 216 781-1757
  Cleveland *(G-4351)*
Pinnacle Data Systems Inc .... C 614 748-1150
  Groveport *(G-8158)*
Programmable Control Svc Inc .... G 740 927-0744
  Pataskala *(G-12304)*
Vr Assets LLC .... G 440 600-2963
  Solon *(G-13743)*

COMPUTER FACILITIES MANAGEMENT SVCS

Park Place Technologies LLC .... C 877 778-8707
  Cleveland *(G-4523)*

COMPUTER FORMS

R R Donnelley & Sons Company .... D 440 774-2101
  Oberlin *(G-12055)*

PRODUCT SECTION — COMPUTER SOFTWARE DEVELOPMENT & APPLICATIONS

COMPUTER GRAPHICS SVCS

Great Lakes Publishing Company........... D 216 771-2833
  Cleveland *(G-4146)*

IPA Ltd... F 614 523-3974
  Columbus *(G-5479)*

Quez Media Marketing Inc........................ F 216 910-0202
  Independence *(G-8683)*

COMPUTER PERIPHERAL EQPT REPAIR & MAINTENANCE

Park Place Technologies LLC................. C 877 778-8707
  Cleveland *(G-4523)*

Smartronix Inc... F 216 378-3300
  Northfield *(G-11910)*

COMPUTER PERIPHERAL EQPT, NEC

Airwave Communications Cons.............. G 419 331-1526
  Lima *(G-9218)*

AT&T Corp... G 513 792-9300
  Cincinnati *(G-2639)*

Black Box Corporation............................... F 800 676-8850
  Brecksville *(G-1609)*

Black Box Corporation............................... G 800 837-7777
  Dublin *(G-6868)*

Black Box Corporation............................... G 855 324-9909
  Westlake *(G-15738)*

Contact Control Interfaces LLC.............. E 609 333-3264
  Cincinnati *(G-2789)*

Data Processing Sciences Corporation. D 513 791-7100
  Cincinnati *(G-2820)*

Dataq Instruments Inc.............................. E 330 668-1444
  Akron *(G-123)*

Ds World LLC... G 925 200-4985
  West Chester *(G-15418)*

Eastman Kodak Company........................ E 937 259-3000
  Dayton *(G-6311)*

Embedded Planet Inc................................ F 216 245-4180
  Solon *(G-13342)*

Gleason Metrology Systems Corp.......... E 937 384-8901
  Dayton *(G-6353)*

Government Acquisitions Inc................. E 513 721-8700
  Cincinnati *(G-2967)*

Grimes Aerospace Company.................. A 937 484-2000
  Urbana *(G-14830)*

Honeywell International Inc..................... E 513 874-5882
  West Chester *(G-15446)*

Interactive Products Corp......................... G 513 313-3397
  Monroe *(G-11111)*

Kern Inc... C 440 930-7315
  Cleveland *(G-4284)*

Phase Array Company LLC...................... G 513 785-0801
  West Chester *(G-15475)*

Qualtek Electronics Corp........................... C 440 951-3300
  Mentor *(G-10541)*

Scriptel Corporation................................... F 877 848-6824
  Columbus *(G-5756)*

Sierra Nevada Corporation....................... C 937 431-2400
  Beavercreek *(G-1062)*

Signature Technologies Inc...................... E 937 859-6323
  Miamisburg *(G-10683)*

Stellar Systems Inc.................................... G 513 921-8748
  Cincinnati *(G-3421)*

Superior Label Systems Inc..................... B 513 336-0825
  Mason *(G-10061)*

Sutter Llc... F 513 891-2261
  Blue Ash *(G-1476)*

Systemax Manufacturing Inc................... D 937 368-2300
  Dayton *(G-6604)*

Tech Pro Inc... G 330 923-3546
  Akron *(G-350)*

Timekeeping Systems Inc........................ F 216 595-0890
  Solon *(G-13439)*

Treality Svs LLC.. E 937 372-7579
  Xenia *(G-16277)*

Uvonics Co.. F 614 458-1163
  Columbus *(G-5852)*

Video Products Inc..................................... D 330 562-2622
  Aurora *(G-740)*

Vmetro Inc.. D 281 584-0728
  Fairborn *(G-7326)*

Vyral LLC... F 937 993-7765
  Dayton *(G-6645)*

Xponet Inc... E 440 354-6617
  Painesville *(G-12279)*

Yonezawa Usa Inc..................................... F 614 799-2210
  Plain City *(G-12605)*

COMPUTER PERIPHERAL EQPT, WHOLESALE

Black Box Corporation............................... G 855 324-9909
  Westlake *(G-15738)*

Legrand North America LLC................... B 937 224-0639
  Dayton *(G-6403)*

Microplex Inc... E 330 498-0600
  North Canton *(G-11743)*

Systemax Manufacturing Inc................... D 937 368-2300
  Dayton *(G-6604)*

COMPUTER PERIPHERAL EQPT: Input Or Output

New Dawn Labs LLC.................................. F 203 675-5644
  Union *(G-14773)*

COMPUTER PROCESSING SVCS

Sightgain Inc.. F 202 494-9317
  Mason *(G-10056)*

COMPUTER PROGRAMMING SVCS: Custom

Corporate Elevator LLC............................. G 614 288-1847
  Columbus *(G-5297)*

Jasstek Inc.. F 614 808-3600
  Dublin *(G-6902)*

Teachers Publishing Group...................... F 614 486-0631
  Hilliard *(G-8445)*

Timekeeping Systems Inc........................ F 216 595-0890
  Solon *(G-13439)*

COMPUTER RELATED MAINTENANCE SVCS

Freedom Usa Inc... E 216 503-6374
  Twinsburg *(G-14662)*

NCR Technology Center........................... G 937 445-1936
  Dayton *(G-6466)*

Proficient Info Tech Inc............................. F 937 470-1300
  Dayton *(G-6531)*

Syntec LLC... F 440 229-6262
  Rocky River *(G-12845)*

Wolters Kluwer Clinical Dru..................... D 330 650-8506
  Hudson *(G-8619)*

COMPUTER SERVICE BUREAU

CD Solutions Inc... G 937 676-2376
  Pleasant Hill *(G-12606)*

COMPUTER SOFTWARE DEVELOPMENT

Brainmaster Technologies Inc................. G 440 232-6000
  Bedford *(G-1107)*

Computer Allied Technology Co.............. G 614 457-2292
  Columbus *(G-5284)*

Eci Macola/Max LLC.................................. C 978 539-6186
  Dublin *(G-6883)*

Electronic Concepts Engrg Inc................ F 419 861-9000
  Holland *(G-8509)*

Embedded Planet Inc................................ F 216 245-4180
  Solon *(G-13342)*

Fscreations Corporation............................ D 330 746-3015
  Youngstown *(G-16360)*

Ganymede Technologies Corp................ G 419 562-5522
  Bucyrus *(G-1860)*

Global Realms LLC..................................... G 614 828-7284
  Gahanna *(G-7836)*

H Mack Charles & Associates Inc.......... E 513 791-4456
  Blue Ash *(G-1402)*

Intelligrated Systems Inc.......................... A 866 936-7300
  Mason *(G-10010)*

Intelligrated Systems LLC........................ A 513 701-7300
  Mason *(G-10011)*

IPA Ltd... F 614 523-3974
  Columbus *(G-5479)*

Keithley Instruments LLC......................... C 440 248-0400
  Solon *(G-13377)*

Leidos Inc... D 937 656-8433
  Beavercreek *(G-1055)*

Link Systems Inc.. F 800 321-8770
  Solon *(G-13381)*

Masterbrand Cabinets LLC....................... B 812 482-2527
  Beachwood *(G-999)*

Navistone Inc... E 844 677-3667
  Cincinnati *(G-3184)*

Qc Software LLC... E 513 469-1424
  Cincinnati *(G-3308)*

Sanctuary Software Studio Inc............... E 330 666-9690
  Fairlawn *(G-7448)*

Santec Resources Inc................................ F 614 664-9540
  Columbus *(G-5746)*

Stellar Systems Inc.................................... G 513 921-8748
  Cincinnati *(G-3421)*

Tech4imaging LLC...................................... F 614 214-2655
  Columbus *(G-5817)*

Thyme Inc... F 484 872-8430
  Akron *(G-357)*

Triad Governmental Systems.................. E 937 376-5446
  Xenia *(G-16278)*

Truck Fax Inc... G 216 921-8866
  Cleveland *(G-4835)*

Virtual Hold Tech Slutions LLC............... E 330 670-2200
  Akron *(G-370)*

COMPUTER SOFTWARE DEVELOPMENT & APPLICATIONS

Chatterbox Sports LLC............................. F 513 545-4754
  Hamilton *(G-8190)*

Cott Systems Inc.. D 614 847-4405
  Columbus *(G-5299)*

Deemsys Inc... D 614 322-9928
  Gahanna *(G-7833)*

Forcam Inc.. F 513 878-2780
  Cincinnati *(G-2914)*

Generic Systems Inc.................................. F 419 841-8460
  Holland *(G-8510)*

Hab Inc.. E 608 785-7650
  Solon *(G-13358)*

Lantek Systems Inc................................... G 877 805-1028
  Mason *(G-10020)*

Miles Midprint Inc....................................... F 216 860-4770
  Cleveland *(G-4413)*

Rockhead Group Usa LLC....................... G 216 310-1569
  Beachwood *(G-1019)*

Sest Inc... F 440 777-9777
  Westlake *(G-15785)*

Signalysis Inc... F 513 528-6164
  Cincinnati *(G-3392)*

Employee Codes: A=Over 500 employees, B=251-500
C=101-250, D=51-100, E=20-50, F=10-19, G=1-9

COMPUTER SOFTWARE SYSTEMS ANALYSIS & DESIGN: Custom

Simplevms LLC .... F 888 255-8918
 Cincinnati (G-3393)

COMPUTER SOFTWARE SYSTEMS ANALYSIS & DESIGN: Custom

Airwave Communications Cons .... G 419 331-1526
 Lima (G-9218)
American Power LLC .... F 937 235-0418
 Dayton (G-6202)
Armada Power LLC .... G 614 721-4844
 Columbus (G-5154)
Associated Software Cons Inc .... F 440 826-1010
 Lakewood (G-8966)
Atr Distributing Company .... G 513 353-1800
 Cincinnati (G-2641)
Empyracom Inc .... F 330 744-5570
 Boardman (G-1511)
Facts Inc .... E 330 928-2332
 Cuyahoga Falls (G-6082)
Online Mega Sellers Corp .... G 888 384-6468
 Toledo (G-14415)
Quez Media Marketing Inc .... F 216 910-0202
 Independence (G-8683)
Sightgain Inc .... F 202 494-9317
 Mason (G-10056)
Soaring Software Solutions Inc ...... F 419 442-7676
 Swanton (G-13982)
Steward Edge Bus Solutions .... F 614 826-5305
 Columbus (G-5795)

COMPUTER STORAGE DEVICES, NEC

1 Emc LLC .... G 216 990-2586
 Findlay (G-7469)
Capsa Solutions LLC .... D 800 437-6633
 Canal Winchester (G-1983)
Freedom Usa Inc .... E 216 503-6374
 Twinsburg (G-14662)
Gemco Pacific Energy LLC .... F 216 937-1371
 Cleveland (G-4110)
Magnext Ltd .... F 614 433-0011
 Columbus (G-5539)
Park Place Technologies LLC .... C 877 778-8707
 Cleveland (G-4523)
Quantum .... F 740 328-2548
 Newark (G-11604)
Quantum Commerce LLC .... G 513 777-0737
 West Chester (G-15490)
Quantum Integration Llc .... G 330 609-0355
 Cortland (G-5967)
Quantum Solutions Group .... G 614 442-0664
 Columbus (G-5703)
Solsys Inc .... G 419 886-4683
 Mansfield (G-9720)
Town Cntry Technical Svcs Inc ...... F 614 866-7700
 Reynoldsburg (G-12775)
Tracewell Systems Inc .... D 614 846-6175
 Lewis Center (G-9182)

COMPUTER STORAGE UNITS: Auxiliary

Pinnacle Data Systems Inc .... C 614 748-1150
 Groveport (G-8158)

COMPUTER SYSTEM SELLING SVCS

Lantek Systems Inc .... G 877 805-1028
 Mason (G-10020)
R & L Software LLC .... G 513 847-4922
 Monroe (G-11118)

COMPUTER SYSTEMS ANALYSIS & DESIGN

David Chojnacki .... E 303 905-1918
 Westerville (G-15699)

Sightgain Inc .... F 202 494-9317
 Mason (G-10056)

COMPUTER TERMINALS

Fivepoint LLC .... F 937 374-3193
 Xenia (G-16262)
Freedom Usa Inc .... E 216 503-6374
 Twinsburg (G-14662)
Pinnacle Data Systems Inc .... C 614 748-1150
 Groveport (G-8158)
Td Synnex Corporation .... E 614 669-6889
 Groveport (G-8161)

COMPUTER TIME-SHARING

Miami Valley Eductl Cmpt Assn ..... F 937 767-1468
 Yellow Springs (G-16284)

COMPUTERS, NEC

Apple & Apple LLC .... F 740 972-2209
 Lewis Center (G-9150)
Apple of His Eye Inc .... G 513 521-0655
 Cincinnati (G-2630)
AT&T Corp .... G 513 792-9300
 Cincinnati (G-2639)
Cardinal Health Tech LLC .... E 614 757-5000
 Dublin (G-6874)
Dapsco .... F 937 294-5331
 Moraine (G-11169)
Delohio Tech .... G 740 816-5628
 Delaware (G-6715)
Eaj Services LLC .... F 513 792-3400
 Blue Ash (G-1387)
General Dynmics Mssion Systems ... G 937 723-2001
 Dayton (G-6350)
Global Realms LLC .... G 614 828-7284
 Gahanna (G-7836)
Grimes Aerospace Company .... A 937 484-2000
 Urbana (G-14830)
Interntnal Pdts Srcing Group I .... C 614 334-1500
 Columbus (G-5475)
Journey Systems LLC .... F 513 831-6200
 Milford (G-10912)
Magnum Computers Inc .... F 216 781-1757
 Cleveland (G-4351)
Park Place Technologies LLC .... C 877 778-8707
 Cleveland (G-4523)
Powersonic Industries LLC .... E 513 429-2329
 West Chester (G-15577)
Predicor LLC .... G 419 460-1831
 Cleveland (G-4578)
Smartronix Inc .... F 216 378-3300
 Northfield (G-11910)
Systemax Manufacturing Inc .... D 937 368-2300
 Dayton (G-6604)
Teradata Operations Inc .... B 937 866-0032
 Miamisburg (G-10693)
Town Cntry Technical Svcs Inc ...... F 614 866-7700
 Reynoldsburg (G-12775)
Tracewell Systems Inc .... D 614 846-6175
 Lewis Center (G-9182)
Vr Assets LLC .... G 440 600-2963
 Solon (G-13443)
Walter North .... F 937 204-6050
 Dayton (G-6646)

COMPUTERS, PERIPHERALS & SOFTWARE, WHOLESALE: Printers

Printer Components Inc .... G 585 924-5190
 Fairfield (G-7397)

COMPUTERS PERIPHERALS & SOFTWARE, WHOLESALE Software

Eci Macola/Max LLC .... C 978 539-6186
 Dublin (G-6883)
GBS Corp .... C 330 494-5330
 North Canton (G-11729)
Government Acquisitions Inc .... E 513 721-8700
 Cincinnati (G-2957)
Miles Midprint Inc .... F 216 860-4770
 Cleveland (G-4413)
Software Solutions Inc .... E 513 932-6667
 Dayton (G-6578)

COMPUTERS Mainframe

Griffin Technology Inc .... C 585 924-7121
 Hudson (G-8594)

COMPUTERS Personal

Accurate Insullation LLC .... F 302 241-0940
 Columbus (G-5095)
Dell Inc .... F 614 491-4603
 Lockbourne (G-1334)
Eaton Corporation .... B 440 523-5000
 Cleveland (G-3394)
Inns Holdings Ltd .... F 740 345-3700
 Newark (G-11554)
Lorain Apples .... G 440 282-4471
 Lorain (G-9420)

CONCENTRATES, DRINK

Belton Foods LLC .... E 937 890-7768
 Dayton (G-6222)
Inter American Products Inc .... D 800 645-2233
 Cincinnati (G-3025)

CONCENTRATES, FLAVORING, EXC DRINK

Flavor Producers LLC .... E 513 771-0777
 Cincinnati (G-2906)
Wiley Companies .... C 740 622-0755
 Coshocton (G-2000)
Wiley Organics Inc .... C 740 622-0755
 Coshocton (G-2001)

CONCRETE BUILDING PRDTS WHOLESALERS

Jalco Industries Inc .... F 740 286-3808
 Jackson (G-8727)
Michaels Pre-Cast Con Pdts .... F 513 683-1292
 Loveland (G-9407)
Moritz Materials Inc .... E 419 281-0575
 Ashland (G-593)
Stocker Concrete Company .... F 740 254-4626
 Gnadenhutten (G-7989)
Tamarron Technology Inc .... F 800 277-3207
 Cincinnati (G-3240)

CONCRETE CURING & HARDENING COMPOUNDS

Blackthorn LLC .... F 937 836-9296
 Clayton (G-3564)
Bomat Inc .... G 216 692-8382
 Cleveland (G-746)
Chemmasters Inc .... E 440 428-2105
 Madison (G-959)
Master Bldrs Slons Admxtres U ..... E 216 839-7500
 Beachwood (G-997)
Master Builders LLC .... E 800 228-3318
 Beachwood (G-998)

Tuf-N-Lite LLC................................. F 513 472-8400
  Middletown (G-10868)

CONCRETE PLANTS

McNeilus Truck and Mfg Inc................ E 513 874-2022
  Fairfield (G-7382)

CONCRETE PRDTS

American Spring Wire Corp................. C 216 292-4620
  Bedford Heights (G-1163)
Baxter Burial Vault Svc Inc................. F 513 641-1010
  Cincinnati (G-2660)
Carruth Studio Inc............................ F 419 878-3060
  Waterville (G-15240)
Cement Products Inc......................... E 419 524-4342
  Mansfield (G-9636)
Charles Svec Inc.............................. E 216 662-5200
  Maple Heights (G-9748)
Concrete Material Supply LLC............ F 419 261-6404
  Woodville (G-16092)
Contech Bridge Solutions LLC............ G 937 878-2170
  Dayton (G-6263)
DCA Construction Products LLC......... E 330 527-4308
  Garrettsville (G-7912)
Dm2018 LLC................................... F 513 893-5483
  Liberty Twp (G-9214)
Euclid Chemical Company................. E 800 321-7628
  Cleveland (G-4032)
Forterra Pipe & Precast LLC.............. F 614 445-3830
  Columbus (G-5382)
Growco Inc..................................... F 419 886-4628
  Mansfield (G-9665)
Hazelbaker Industries Ltd................... F
  Columbus (G-5424)
Hilltop Basic Resources Inc................ D 513 621-1500
  Cincinnati (G-3000)
Huron Cement Products Company....... E 419 433-4161
  Huron (G-8633)
Jerry Offenberger Cnstr LLC.............. G 740 374-2578
  Marietta (G-9803)
K M B Inc....................................... E 330 889-3451
  Bristolville (G-1652)
Lang Stone Company Inc.................. E 614 235-4099
  Columbus (G-5520)
Ludowici Roof Tile Inc...................... D 740 342-1995
  New Lexington (G-11454)
Mack Industries PA Inc..................... D 330 638-7680
  Vienna (G-15000)
Michaels Pre-Cast Con Pdts............... F 513 683-1292
  Loveland (G-9497)
Northfield....................................... G 440 949-1815
  Sheffield Village (G-13186)
Oberfields LLC................................ E 614 252-0955
  Columbus (G-5610)
Occv1 Inc....................................... G 419 248-8000
  Toledo (G-14404)
OK Brugmann Jr & Sons Inc.............. F 330 274-2106
  Mantua (G-9741)
Oldcastle Infrastructure Inc................ E 419 592-2309
  Napoleon (G-11329)
Orrville Trucking & Grading Co........... E 330 682-4010
  Orrville (G-12144)
Pawnee Maintenance Inc................... F 740 373-6861
  Marietta (G-9815)
Premiere Con Solutions LLC............... F 419 737-9808
  Pioneer (G-12496)
Prestress Services Inds LLC............... C 859 299-0461
  Grove City (G-8116)
R W Sidley Incorporated.................... G 440 564-2221
  Newbury (G-11635)
R W Sidley Incorporated.................... C 440 298-3452
  Thompson (G-14062)

Rocla Concrete Tie Inc...................... E 740 776-3238
  Portsmouth (G-12654)
Russell Cast Stone Inc...................... D 856 753-4000
  West Chester (G-15582)
S & S Aggregates Inc........................ F 740 453-0721
  Zanesville (G-16561)
Snyder Concrete Products Inc............ E 937 885-5176
  Moraine (G-11211)
Tri County Concrete Inc.................... F 330 425-4464
  Twinsburg (G-14747)
William Dauch Concrete Company....... F 419 668-4458
  Norwalk (G-11991)
Wilsons Country Creations Inc............ F 330 377-4190
  Killbuck (G-8926)
Wyandot Dolomite Inc....................... F 419 396-7641
  Carey (G-2286)

CONCRETE PRDTS, PRECAST, NEC

A L D Precast Corp........................... G 614 449-3366
  Columbus (G-5080)
Aco Inc.. E 440 639-7230
  Mentor (G-10403)
Carey Precast Concrete Company....... G 419 396-7142
  Carey (G-2278)
Cox Inc.. G 740 858-4400
  Lucasville (G-9521)
E Pompili Sons Inc........................... E 216 581-8080
  Cleveland (G-3985)
Eldorado Stone LLC.......................... E 330 698-3931
  Apple Creek (G-498)
Fin Pan Inc..................................... F 513 870-9200
  Hamilton (G-8208)
Mack Concrete Industries Inc............. F 330 483-3111
  Valley City (G-14877)
Mack Industries PA Inc..................... D 330 483-3111
  Valley City (G-14878)
McGill Septic Tank Co....................... E 330 876-2171
  Kinsman (G-8936)
North American Cast Stone Inc........... F 440 286-1999
  Chardon (G-2460)
Norwalk Concrete Inds Inc................. E 419 668-8167
  Norwalk (G-11982)
Oberfields LLC................................ E 740 369-7644
  Sunbury (G-13959)
Oberfields LLC................................ E 740 369-7644
  Delaware (G-6742)
Oldcastle Apg Midwest Inc................ E 440 949-1815
  Sheffield Village (G-13187)
Premere Precast Products.................. G 740 533-3333
  Ironton (G-8700)
Spoerr Precast Concrete Inc.............. F 419 625-9132
  Sandusky (G-13094)
St Henry Tile Co Inc......................... G 937 548-1101
  Greenville (G-8061)
Uniontown Septic Tanks Inc............... F 330 699-3386
  Uniontown (G-14796)
United Precast Inc............................ C 740 393-1121
  Mount Vernon (G-11298)
United Refractories Inc..................... E 330 372-3716
  Warren (G-15215)

CONCRETE: Asphaltic, Not From Refineries

Shelly Materials Inc.......................... D 740 246-6315
  Thornville (G-14072)

CONCRETE: Bituminous

Russell Standard Corporation.............. G 330 733-9400
  Akron (G-318)

CONCRETE: Dry Mixture

Quikrete Companies LLC................... E 614 885-4406
  Columbus (G-5704)

Quikrete Companies LLC................... E 513 367-6135
  Harrison (G-8288)
Quikrete Companies LLC................... E 330 296-6080
  Ravenna (G-12729)
Quikrete Companies LLC................... F 419 241-1148
  Toledo (G-14445)
Smith Concrete Co........................... E 740 373-7441
  Dover (G-6843)

CONCRETE: Ready-Mixed

Ace Ready Mix Concrete Co Inc.......... F 330 745-8125
  Norton (G-11937)
Adams Bros Concrete Pdts Ltd........... F 740 452-7566
  Zanesville (G-16495)
Adams Brothers Inc.......................... F 740 819-0323
  Zanesville (G-16496)
AK Ready Mix LLC........................... G 740 286-8900
  Jackson (G-8707)
Alexis Concrete Enterprise Inc............ F 440 366-0031
  Elyria (G-7106)
All Ohio Ready Mix Concrete............. G 419 841-3838
  Perrysburg (G-12360)
Allega Concrete Corp........................ E 216 447-0814
  Richfield (G-12781)
Alliance Redi-Mix Inc........................ F 330 821-9244
  Alliance (G-394)
Anderson Concrete Corp.................... C 614 443-0123
  Columbus (G-5144)
ASAP Ready Mix Inc......................... G 513 797-1774
  Amelia (G-453)
Associated Associates Inc.................. E 330 626-3300
  Mantua (G-9734)
Baird Concrete Products Inc............... F 740 623-8600
  Coshocton (G-5972)
Baker-Shindler Contracting Co............ E 419 782-5080
  Defiance (G-6671)
Barrett Paving Materials Inc............... F 937 293-9033
  Moraine (G-11159)
Beazer East Inc............................... F 740 474-3169
  Circleville (G-3542)
Beazer East Inc............................... E 937 364-2311
  Hillsboro (G-8455)
Beazer East Inc............................... F 740 947-4677
  Waverly (G-15278)
Bhi Transition Inc............................ E 937 663-4152
  Saint Paris (G-12971)
Brock Corporation............................ G 440 235-1806
  Olmsted Falls (G-12078)
Buckeye Ready Mix Concrete.............. G 330 798-5511
  Akron (G-94)
Buckeye Ready-Mix LLC.................... F 740 967-4801
  Johnstown (G-8770)
Buckeye Ready-Mix LLC.................... G 614 879-6316
  West Jefferson (G-15608)
Buckeye Ready-Mix LLC.................... E 740 654-4423
  Lancaster (G-8995)
Buckeye Ready-Mix LLC.................... E 937 642-2951
  Marysville (G-9905)
Buckeye Ready-Mix LLC.................... E 614 575-2132
  Reynoldsburg (G-12757)
C F Poeppelman Inc.......................... E 937 448-2191
  Bradford (G-1600)
Caldwell Lumber & Supply Co............. E 740 732-2306
  Caldwell (G-1908)
Camden Ready Mix Co....................... G 937 456-4539
  Camden (G-1962)
Car Bros Inc.................................... F 440 232-1840
  Bedford (G-1109)
Carr Bros Inc................................... F 440 232-3700
  Bedford (G-1110)
Carr Bros Bldrs Sup & Coal Co............ E 440 232-3700
  Cleveland (G-3794)

CONCRETE: Ready-Mixed

Cashen Ready Mix .... G 440 354-3227
  Painesville *(G-12222)*

Castalia Trenching & Rdymx LLC .... F 419 684-5502
  Castalia *(G-2319)*

Castalia Trenching & Ready Mix .... F 419 684-5502
  Castalia *(G-2320)*

Cemco Construction Corporation .... G 440 567-7708
  Concord Township *(G-5903)*

Cement Products Inc .... E 419 524-4342
  Mansfield *(G-9636)*

Cemex Cement Inc .... C 937 873-9858
  Fairborn *(G-7311)*

Cemex Materials LLC .... C 330 654-2501
  Diamond *(G-6804)*

Center Concrete Inc .... G 419 782-2495
  Defiance *(G-6673)*

Center Concrete Inc .... F 800 453-4224
  Edgerton *(G-7073)*

Central Ready Mix LLC .... E 513 402-5001
  Cincinnati *(G-2717)*

Central Ready-Mix of Ohio LLC .... G 614 252-3452
  Cincinnati *(G-2718)*

Cioffi Holdings LLC .... F 330 794-9448
  Akron *(G-111)*

City Concrete LLc .... F 330 743-2825
  Youngstown *(G-16335)*

Citywide Materials Inc .... E 513 533-1111
  Cincinnati *(G-2772)*

Collinwood Shale Brick Sup Co .... E 216 587-2700
  Cleveland *(G-3882)*

Consumeracq Inc .... E 440 277-9305
  Lorain *(G-9408)*

Consumers Builders Supply Co .... E 440 277-9306
  Lorain *(G-9409)*

D G M Inc .... F 740 286-2131
  Jackson *(G-8713)*

D W Dickey and Son Inc .... C 330 424-1441
  Lisbon *(G-9311)*

Dan K Williams Inc .... E 419 893-3251
  Maumee *(G-10175)*

Dearth Resources Inc .... F 937 663-4171
  Springfield *(G-13552)*

Dearth Resources Inc .... G 937 325-0651
  Springfield *(G-13551)*

Deco Crete Supply .... G 614 372-5142
  Columbus *(G-5321)*

Diano Construction and Sup Co .... F 330 456-7229
  Canton *(G-2091)*

Diversified Ready Mix Ltd .... G 330 628-3555
  Tallmadge *(G-14028)*

Eagle Specialty Materials LLC .... G 216 401-6075
  Columbus *(G-5341)*

Ellis Brothers Inc Upg .... G 740 397-9191
  Mount Vernon *(G-11272)*

Elyria Concrete Inc .... F 440 322-2750
  Elyria *(G-7140)*

Ernst Enterprises Inc .... E 937 848-6811
  Bellbrook *(G-1192)*

Ernst Enterprises Inc .... F 937 866-9441
  Carrollton *(G-2306)*

Ernst Enterprises Inc .... F 513 367-1939
  Cleves *(G-4951)*

Ernst Enterprises Inc .... E 614 443-9456
  Columbus *(G-5358)*

Ernst Enterprises Inc .... F 614 308-0063
  Columbus *(G-5359)*

Ernst Enterprises Inc .... E 937 878-9378
  Fairborn *(G-7313)*

Ernst Enterprises Inc .... F 513 874-8300
  Lebanon *(G-9073)*

Ernst Enterprises Inc .... F 513 422-3651
  Middletown *(G-10821)*

Ernst Enterprises Inc .... F 937 339-6249
  Troy *(G-14565)*

Ernst Enterprises Inc .... E 937 233-5555
  Dayton *(G-6322)*

Fairborn Cement Plant .... F 937 879-8466
  Fairborn *(G-7314)*

G Big Inc .... E 740 867-5758
  Chesapeake *(G-2473)*

Geauga Concrete Inc .... F 440 338-4915
  Newbury *(G-11624)*

Grafton Ready Mix Concret Inc .... C 440 926-2911
  Grafton *(G-8001)*

Heidelberg Materials Us Inc .... E 937 587-2671
  Peebles *(G-12327)*

Heidelberg Materials Us Inc .... E 937 442-6009
  Winchester *(G-16073)*

Heidelberg Mtls US Cem LLC .... F 330 499-9100
  Middlebranch *(G-10714)*

Heidelberg Mtls US Cem LLC .... F 972 653-5500
  Sylvania *(G-13998)*

Hilltop Basic Resources Inc .... F 937 795-2020
  Aberdeen *(G-1)*

Hilltop Basic Resources Inc .... F 513 242-8400
  Cincinnati *(G-2999)*

Hilltop Basic Resources Inc .... D 513 621-1500
  Cincinnati *(G-3000)*

Hilltop Big Bend Quarry LLC .... E 513 651-5000
  Cincinnati *(G-3001)*

Hocking Valley Concrete Inc .... G 740 592-5335
  Athens *(G-686)*

Hocking Valley Concrete Inc .... G 740 342-1948
  New Lexington *(G-11452)*

Hocking Valley Concrete Inc .... F 740 385-2165
  Logan *(G-9365)*

Hull Ready Mix Concrete Inc .... F 419 625-8070
  Sandusky *(G-13064)*

Huron Cement Products Company .... E 419 433-4161
  Huron *(G-8633)*

Huth Ready Mix & Supply Co .... E 330 833-4191
  Massillon *(G-10108)*

IMI-Irving Materials Inc .... G 513 844-8444
  Hamilton *(G-8219)*

Integrated Resources Inc .... E 419 885-7122
  Sylvania *(G-14002)*

Ioppolo Concrete Corporation .... E 440 439-6606
  Bedford *(G-1130)*

Irving Materials Inc .... G 513 769-3666
  Cincinnati *(G-3032)*

Irving Materials Inc .... F 513 844-8444
  Hamilton *(G-8222)*

K & L Ready Mix Inc .... F 419 293-2937
  Mc Comb *(G-10271)*

K & L Ready Mix Inc .... F 419 523-4376
  Ottawa *(G-12183)*

K M B Inc .... E 330 889-3451
  Bristolville *(G-1652)*

Kuhlman Corporation .... E 330 724-9900
  Coventry Township *(G-6012)*

Kuhlman Corporation .... F 419 321-1670
  Toledo *(G-14351)*

Kuhlman Corporation .... E 419 897-6000
  Maumee *(G-10213)*

Lancaster W Side Coal Co Inc .... F 740 862-4713
  Lancaster *(G-9021)*

Lexington Concrete & Sup Inc .... G 419 529-3232
  Mansfield *(G-9679)*

M & B Asphalt Company Inc .... G 419 992-4236
  Old Fort *(G-12073)*

M & R Redi Mix Inc .... E 419 445-7771
  Pettisville *(G-12451)*

Mack Concrete Industries Inc .... E 330 784-7008
  Akron *(G-234)*

Market Ready .... G 513 289-9231
  Maineville *(G-9671)*

McClelland Inc .... F 740 452-3036
  Zanesville *(G-16544)*

McConnell Ready Mix .... G 440 458-4325
  Elyria *(G-7179)*

McGovney Ready Mix Inc .... E 740 353-4111
  Portsmouth *(G-12648)*

Medina Supply Company .... G 330 425-0752
  Twinsburg *(G-14694)*

Medina Supply Company .... E 330 723-3681
  Medina *(G-10352)*

Mini Mix Inc .... G 513 353-3811
  Cleves *(G-4960)*

Mix Marketing L C .... G 614 791-0489
  Dublin *(G-6911)*

Moritz Concrete Inc .... E 419 529-3232
  Mansfield *(G-9639)*

Moritz Materials Inc .... E 419 281-0575
  Ashland *(G-593)*

Moritz Ready Mix Inc .... F 419 253-0001
  Marengo *(G-9759)*

National Lime and Stone Co .... F 419 423-3400
  Findlay *(G-7540)*

OK Brugmann J & Sons Inc .... F 330 274-2106
  Mantua *(G-9741)*

Olen Corporation .... F 419 294-2611
  Upper Sandusky *(G-14819)*

Orrville Trucking & Grading Co .... E 330 682-4010
  Orrville *(G-12174)*

Osborne Inc .... F 440 232-1440
  Cleveland *(G-3510)*

Osborne Inc .... F 440 942-7000
  Mentor *(G-10517)*

Osborne Co .... F 440 942-7000
  Mentor *(G-10518)*

Pahl Ready Mix Concrete Inc .... F 419 636-4238
  Bryan *(G-1833)*

Palmer Bros Transit Mix Con .... F 419 332-6363
  Fremont *(G-7200)*

Palmer Bros Transit Mix Con .... F 419 686-2366
  Portage *(G-12636)*

Palmer Bros Transit Mix Con .... G 419 447-2018
  Tiffin *(G-14094)*

Palmer Bros Transit Mix Con .... F 419 352-4681
  Bowling Green *(G-1582)*

Paul H Rohe Company Inc .... G 513 326-6789
  Cincinnati *(G-3240)*

Paul R Lipp & Son Inc .... F 330 227-9614
  Rogers *(G-12947)*

Phillips Ready Mix Co .... E 937 426-5151
  Beavercreek Township *(G-1090)*

Placecrete Inc .... F 937 298-2121
  Moraine *(G-11200)*

Pleasant Valley Ready Mix Inc .... F 330 852-2613
  Sugarcreek *(G-13934)*

Quality Block & Supply Inc .... E 330 364-4411
  Mount Eaton *(G-11231)*

Quality Ready Mix Inc .... F 419 394-8870
  Saint Marys *(G-12965)*

Quikrete Companies LLC .... E 513 367-6135
  Harrison *(G-2288)*

Quikrete Companies LLC .... E 330 296-6080
  Ravenna *(G-12729)*

R W Sidley Inc .... E 440 224-2664
  Kingsville *(G-8934)*

R W Sidley Incorporated .... G 330 499-5616
  Canton *(G-2209)*

R W Sidley Incorporated .... G 440 564-2221
  Newbury *(G-11635)*

R W Sidley Incorporated .... E 440 298-3232
  Thompson *(G-14063)*

CONSTRUCTION MATERIALS, WHOLESALE: Brick, Exc Refractory

R W Sidley Incorporated............................ G 330 392-2721
   Warren *(G-15201)*

R W Sidley Incorporated............................ G 330 793-7374
   Youngstown *(G-16426)*

Reliable Ready Mix Co............................... E 330 453-8266
   Canton *(G-2212)*

Rockport Ready Mix Inc............................. E 216 432-9465
   Cleveland *(G-4642)*

Ross-Co Redi-Mix Co Inc........................... F 740 775-4466
   Chillicothe *(G-2533)*

S J Roth Enterprises Inc............................ D 513 543-1140
   Cincinnati *(G-3358)*

Sakrete Inc.. E 513 242-3644
   Cincinnati *(G-3359)*

Sardinia Concrete Company..................... E 513 248-0090
   Milford *(G-10921)*

Sardinia Ready Mix Inc.............................. E 937 446-2523
   Sardinia *(G-13108)*

Schwab Industries Inc............................... F 330 364-4411
   Dover *(G-6842)*

Scioto Ready Mix LLC................................ D 740 924-9273
   Pataskala *(G-12308)*

Scsrm Concrete Company Ltd.................. F 937 533-1001
   Sidney *(G-13284)*

Shelly Materials Inc................................... E 740 775-4567
   Chillicothe *(G-2534)*

Shelly Materials Inc................................... E 614 871-6704
   Grove City *(G-8119)*

Shelly Materials Inc................................... F 330 723-3681
   Medina *(G-10377)*

Shelly Materials Inc................................... G 937 325-7386
   Springfield *(G-13631)*

Shelly Materials Inc................................... F 330 963-5180
   Twinsburg *(G-14735)*

Show Ready Professionals....................... G 614 817-5849
   Columbus *(G-5766)*

Sidwell Materials Inc.................................. F 740 968-4313
   Saint Clairsville *(G-12923)*

Small Sand & Gravel Inc............................ E 740 427-3130
   Gambier *(G-7907)*

Smalls Inc.. F 740 427-3633
   Gambier *(G-7909)*

Smith Concrete... F 740 439-7714
   Cambridge *(G-1952)*

Smith Concrete Co..................................... G 740 593-5633
   Athens *(G-697)*

Smith Concrete Co..................................... E 740 373-7441
   Dover *(G-6843)*

Smyrna Ready Mix Concrete LLC............ E 937 855-0410
   Germantown *(G-7952)*

Smyrna Ready Mix Concrete LLC............ D 937 773-0841
   Piqua *(G-12554)*

Smyrna Ready Mix Concrete LLC............ D 937 698-7229
   Vandalia *(G-14960)*

Spurlino Materials LLC.............................. G 513 202-1111
   Cleves *(G-4964)*

Spurlino Materials LLC.............................. E 513 705-0111
   Middletown *(G-10858)*

St Henry Tile Co Inc................................... E 419 678-4841
   Saint Henry *(G-12938)*

Stamm Contracting Company Inc............ E 330 274-8230
   Mantua *(G-9743)*

Stocker Concrete Company..................... F 740 254-4626
   Gnadenhutten *(G-7989)*

T C Redi Mix Youngstown Inc................... G 330 755-2143
   Youngstown *(G-16450)*

Tech Ready Mix Inc................................... E 216 361-5000
   Cleveland *(G-4772)*

Terminal Ready-Mix Inc............................ E 440 288-0181
   Lorain *(G-9141)*

The National Lime and Stone Company. E 419 422-4341
   Findlay *(G-7575)*

Trail Mix... G 330 657-2277
   Peninsula *(G-12343)*

Tri County Concrete Inc............................. F 330 425-4464
   Cleveland *(G-4821)*

Tri County Concrete Inc............................. F 330 425-4464
   Twinsburg *(G-14747)*

Turner Concrete Products........................ F 419 662-9007
   Northwood *(G-11931)*

Twin Cities Concrete Co........................... B 330 627-2158
   Carrollton *(G-2316)*

Twin Cities Concrete Co........................... F 330 343-4491
   Dover *(G-6848)*

W G Lockhart Construction Co................ E 330 745-6520
   Akron *(G-372)*

W M Dauch Concrete Inc.......................... G 419 562-6917
   Bucyrus *(G-1874)*

Walden Industries Inc............................... E 740 633-5971
   Tiltonsville *(G-14117)*

Warren Concrete and Supply Co............. E 330 393-1581
   Warren *(G-15218)*

Weber Ready Mix Inc................................ E 419 394-9097
   Saint Marys *(G-12969)*

Wells Group LLC.. F 740 532-9240
   Ironton *(G-8706)*

Westview Concrete Corp........................... F 440 458-5800
   Elyria *(G-7218)*

Westview Concrete Corp........................... F 440 235-1800
   Olmsted Falls *(G-12084)*

William Dauch Concrete Company......... F 419 562-6917
   Bucyrus *(G-1875)*

William Dauch Concrete Company......... F 419 668-4458
   Norwalk *(G-11991)*

William Oeder Ready Mix Inc................... E 513 899-3901
   Martinsville *(G-9903)*

Williams Concrete Inc................................ E 419 893-3251
   Maumee *(G-10245)*

Winters Products Inc................................. F 740 286-4149
   Jackson *(G-8728)*

CONDENSERS: Heat Transfer Eqpt, Evaporative

Hydro-Dyne Inc.. E 330 832-5076
   Massillon *(G-10109)*

Lfg Specialties LLC................................... E 419 424-4999
   Findlay *(G-7529)*

CONDENSERS: Refrigeration

Copeland LP... C 937 498-3011
   Sidney *(G-13236)*

Copeland LP... C 937 498-3587
   Sidney *(G-13237)*

CONDUITS & FITTINGS: Electric

Allied Tube & Conduit Corp...................... F 740 928-1018
   Hebron *(G-8335)*

Lagonda Investments III Inc..................... F 937 325-7305
   Springfield *(G-13594)*

Madison Electric Products Inc................. E 216 391-7776
   Solon *(G-13382)*

Saylor Products Corporation.................... F 419 832-2125
   Grand Rapids *(G-8010)*

CONNECTORS: Cord, Electric

Tip Products Inc... E 216 252-2535
   New London *(G-11472)*

CONNECTORS: Electronic

Mjo Industries Inc...................................... D 800 590-4055
   Huber Heights *(G-8577)*

CONSTRUCTION & MINING MACHINERY WHOLESALERS

Advanced Specialty Products.................. G 419 882-6528
   Bowling Green *(G-1550)*

Columbus Pipe and Equipment Co......... F 614 444-7871
   Columbus *(G-5273)*

Great Lakes Power Service Co................ G 440 259-0025
   Perry *(G-12351)*

JD Power Systems LLC............................ F 614 317-9394
   Hilliard *(G-8416)*

Koenig Equipment Inc.............................. F 937 653-5281
   Urbana *(G-14842)*

La Mfg Inc... G 513 577-7200
   Cincinnati *(G-3094)*

Mesa Industries Inc................................... E 513 321-2950
   Cincinnati *(G-3151)*

Murphy Tractor & Eqp Co Inc................... G 330 220-4999
   Brunswick *(G-1774)*

Murphy Tractor & Eqp Co Inc................... G 330 477-9304
   Canton *(G-2169)*

Murphy Tractor & Eqp Co Inc................... G 614 876-1141
   Columbus *(G-5585)*

Murphy Tractor & Eqp Co Inc................... G 419 221-3666
   Lima *(G-9272)*

Murphy Tractor & Eqp Co Inc................... G 937 898-4198
   Vandalia *(G-14954)*

Shearer Farm Inc....................................... C 330 345-9023
   Wooster *(G-16171)*

Simpson Strong-Tie Company Inc........... C 614 876-8060
   Columbus *(G-5773)*

The Wagner-Smith Company................... B 866 338-0398
   Moraine *(G-11214)*

CONSTRUCTION EQPT REPAIR SVCS

West Equipment Company Inc................ G 419 698-1601
   Toledo *(G-14522)*

CONSTRUCTION EQPT: Attachments, Snow Plow

H Y O Inc... E 614 488-2861
   Columbus *(G-5414)*

Ironhawk Industrial Dist LLC.................... G 216 502-3700
   Euclid *(G-7276)*

Snow Dragon LLC...................................... F 440 295-0238
   Cleveland *(G-4710)*

Winter Equipment Company In................ E 440 946-8377
   Willoughby *(G-16019)*

CONSTRUCTION EQPT: Roofing Eqpt

A JC Inc... F 800 428-2438
   Hudson *(G-8581)*

Dimensional Metals Inc............................. E 740 927-3633
   Reynoldsburg *(G-12761)*

CONSTRUCTION MATERIALS, WHOLESALE: Architectural Metalwork

Charles Mfg Co.. F 330 395-3490
   Warren *(G-15153)*

CONSTRUCTION MATERIALS, WHOLESALE: Awnings

PCR Restorations Inc................................ F 419 747-7957
   Mansfield *(G-9709)*

CONSTRUCTION MATERIALS, WHOLESALE: Brick, Exc Refractory

Snyder Concrete Products Inc................. G 937 224-1433
   Dayton *(G-6577)*

CONSTRUCTION MATERIALS, WHOLESALE: Brick, Exc Refractory

Snyder Concrete Products Inc............. E 937 885-5176
  Moraine *(G-11211)*

The Ideal Builders Supply & Fuel Co Inc F 216 741-1600
  Cleveland *(G-4787)*

CONSTRUCTION MATERIALS, WHOLESALE: Building Stone

Toledo Cut Stone Inc........................... F 419 531-1623
  Toledo *(G-14494)*

CONSTRUCTION MATERIALS, WHOLESALE: Building Stone, Marble

Castelli Marble LLC............................. G 216 361-1222
  Cleveland *(G-3799)*

Helmart Company Inc........................... G 513 941-3095
  Cincinnati *(G-2992)*

CONSTRUCTION MATERIALS, WHOLESALE: Building, Exterior

Francis-Schulze Co............................. E 937 295-3941
  Russia *(G-12884)*

Higgins Construction & Supply Co Inc.. F 937 364-2331
  Hillsboro *(G-8458)*

Orrville Trucking & Grading Co............. E 330 682-4010
  Orrville *(G-12144)*

CONSTRUCTION MATERIALS, WHOLESALE: Building, Interior

Youngstown Curve Form Inc................. F 330 744-3028
  Youngstown *(G-16480)*

CONSTRUCTION MATERIALS, WHOLESALE: Cement

Huron Cement Products Company......... E 419 433-4161
  Huron *(G-8633)*

CONSTRUCTION MATERIALS, WHOLESALE: Door Frames

Provia Holdings Inc............................ C 330 852-4711
  Sugarcreek *(G-13935)*

CONSTRUCTION MATERIALS, WHOLESALE: Doors, Garage

Alumo Extrusions and Mfg Co.............. E 330 779-3333
  Youngstown *(G-16308)*

CONSTRUCTION MATERIALS, WHOLESALE: Doors, Sliding

Alumo Extrusions and Mfg Co.............. E 330 779-3333
  Youngstown *(G-16308)*

CONSTRUCTION MATERIALS, WHOLESALE: Glass

A Service Glass Inc............................. E 937 426-4920
  Beavercreek *(G-1038)*

Dale Kestler....................................... G 513 871-9000
  Cincinnati *(G-2817)*

Machined Glass Specialist Inc............. F 937 743-6166
  Springboro *(G-13509)*

CONSTRUCTION MATERIALS, WHOLESALE: Gravel

Hilltop Basic Resources Inc.................. F 937 859-3616
  Miamisburg *(G-10646)*

CONSTRUCTION MATERIALS, WHOLESALE: Limestone

Pinney Dock & Transport LLC............... D 440 964-7186
  Ashtabula *(G-655)*

R W Sidley Incorporated..................... C 440 298-3232
  Thompson *(G-14062)*

CONSTRUCTION MATERIALS, WHOLESALE: Masons' Materials

Koltcz Concrete Block Co..................... E 440 232-3630
  Bedford *(G-1132)*

CONSTRUCTION MATERIALS, WHOLESALE: Molding, All Materials

Architctral Mllwk Cbinetry Inc.............. G 440 708-0086
  Chagrin Falls *(G-2389)*

Toledo Molding & Die LLC................... B 419 692-6022
  Delphos *(G-6773)*

CONSTRUCTION MATERIALS, WHOLESALE: Pallets, Wood

Component Solutions Group Inc............ F 937 434-8100
  Dayton *(G-6261)*

Universal Pallets Inc........................... E 614 444-1095
  Columbus *(G-5846)*

CONSTRUCTION MATERIALS, WHOLESALE: Particleboard

Litco International Inc........................ D 330 539-5433
  Vienna *(G-14999)*

CONSTRUCTION MATERIALS, WHOLESALE: Paving Materials

The D S Brown Company..................... C 419 257-3561
  North Baltimore *(G-11701)*

CONSTRUCTION MATERIALS, WHOLESALE: Prefabricated Structures

Morton Buildings Inc........................... E 419 675-2311
  Kenton *(G-8894)*

Morton Buildings Inc........................... E 330 345-6188
  Wooster *(G-16153)*

Patio Enclosures................................ F 513 733-4646
  Cincinnati *(G-3236)*

Will-Burt Company............................. F 330 682-7015
  Orrville *(G-12162)*

Will-Burt Company............................. C 330 682-7015
  Orrville *(G-12163)*

CONSTRUCTION MATERIALS, WHOLESALE: Roofing & Siding Material

Associated Materials LLC.................... A 330 929-1811
  Cuyahoga Falls *(G-6069)*

Associated Materials Group Inc............ C 330 929-1811
  Cuyahoga Falls *(G-6070)*

Associated Mtls Holdings LLC.............. A 330 929-1811
  Cuyahoga Falls *(G-6071)*

CONSTRUCTION MATERIALS, WHOLESALE: Sand

Phoenix Asphalt Company Inc.............. G 330 339-4935
  Magnolia *(G-9597)*

CONSTRUCTION MATERIALS, WHOLESALE: Septic Tanks

Active Aeration Systems Inc................ G 614 873-3626
  Plain City *(G-1259)*

Allen Enterprises Inc........................... E 740 532-5913
  Ironton *(G-8694)*

CONSTRUCTION MATERIALS, WHOLESALE: Sewer Pipe, Clay

Sewer Rodding Equipment Co.............. C 419 991-2065
  Lima *(G-9288)*

CONSTRUCTION MATERIALS, WHOLESALE: Siding, Exc Wood

Alside Inc... D 419 865-0934
  Maumee *(G-1051)*

Vinyl Design Corporation..................... E 419 283-4009
  Holland *(G-8530)*

CONSTRUCTION MATERIALS, WHOLESALE: Stone, Crushed Or Broken

Olen Corporation................................ F 419 294-2611
  Upper Sandusky *(G-14819)*

Palmer Bros Transit Mix Con................ F 419 686-2366
  Portage *(G-12606)*

Ridge Township Stone Quarry.............. G 419 968-2222
  Van Wert *(G-14925)*

Stoneco Inc....................................... E 419 893-7645
  Maumee *(G-10736)*

CONSTRUCTION MATERIALS, WHOLESALE: Windows

Associated Materials LLC.................... A 330 929-1811
  Cuyahoga Falls *(G-6069)*

Associated Materials Group Inc............ C 330 929-1811
  Cuyahoga Falls *(G-6070)*

Associated Mtls Holdings LLC.............. A 330 929-1811
  Cuyahoga Falls *(G-6071)*

Blockamerica Corporation................... G 614 274-0700
  Columbus *(G-201)*

Champion Win Co Cleveland LLC......... F 440 899-2562
  Macedonia *(G-9541)*

Roofing Annex LLC............................. G 513 942-0555
  West Chester *(G-15581)*

CONSTRUCTION SAND MINING

Arden J Neer Sr................................. F 937 585-6733
  Bellefontaine *(G-1200)*

Hocking Valley Concrete Inc................ F 740 385-2165
  Logan *(G-9365)*

Hugo Sand Company.......................... G 216 570-1212
  Kent *(G-8818)*

J P Sand & Gravel Company................ F 614 497-0083
  Lockbourne *(G-9337)*

Lakeside Sand & Gravel Inc................. E 330 274-2569
  Mantua *(G-9338)*

Masons Sand and Gravel Co................ G 614 491-3611
  Obetz *(G-12652)*

Mechanicsburg Sand & Gravel............. F 937 834-2606
  Mechanicsburg *(G-10286)*

Morrow Gravel Company Inc............... E 513 771-0820
  Cincinnati *(G-3175)*

National Lime and Stone Co................ F 614 497-0083
  Lockbourne *(G-9340)*

Oscar Brugmann Sand & Gravel........... E 330 274-8224
  Mantua *(G-9342)*

S & S Aggregates Inc......................... B 419 938-5604
  Perrysville *(G-12448)*

Seville Sand & Gravel Inc.................... E 330 948-0168
  Strongsville *(G-13877)*

Shelly and Sands Inc.......................... F 740 453-0721
  Zanesville *(G-16562)*

PRODUCT SECTION

CONSTRUCTION: Athletic & Recreation Facilities

MGM Construction Inc.................................. F 440 234-7660
  Berea *(G-1288)*

CONSTRUCTION: Bridge

Ohio Bridge Corporation............................. C 740 432-6334
  Cambridge *(G-1945)*
S E Johnson Companies Inc..................... E 419 893-8731
  Maumee *(G-10228)*

CONSTRUCTION: Commercial & Office Building, New

Fleming Construction Co.............................. F 740 494-2177
  Prospect *(G-12689)*
Ingle-Barr Inc... D 740 702-6117
  Chillicothe *(G-2513)*
Rebsco Inc.. F 937 548-2246
  Greenville *(G-8057)*
Scs Construction Services Inc.................... E 513 929-0260
  Cincinnati *(G-3371)*
The Galehouse Companies Inc................. E 330 658-2023
  Doylestown *(G-6854)*
Thomas J Weaver Inc.................................. F 740 622-2040
  Coshocton *(G-5998)*

CONSTRUCTION: Drainage System

Fine Line Excvtg & Ldscpg LLC................. G 330 541-0590
  Ravenna *(G-12715)*

CONSTRUCTION: Food Prdts Manufacturing or Packing Plant

Iron Bean Inc... F 518 641-9917
  Perrysburg *(G-12393)*
Milos Whole World Gourmet LLC............. G 740 589-6456
  Nelsonville *(G-11358)*

CONSTRUCTION: Foundation & Retaining Wall

Third Salvo Company................................. G 740 818-9669
  Amesville *(G-472)*

CONSTRUCTION: Heavy Highway & Street

Central Allied Enterprises Inc.................... E 330 477-6751
  Canton *(G-2071)*
Hull Ready Mix Concrete Inc..................... F 419 625-8070
  Sandusky *(G-13064)*
Seneca Petroleum Co Inc.......................... F 419 691-3581
  Toledo *(G-14467)*
Smalls Asphalt Paving Inc.......................... F 740 427-4096
  Gambier *(G-7908)*
W G Lockhart Construction Co................. E 330 745-6520
  Akron *(G-372)*

CONSTRUCTION: Indl Buildings, New, NEC

Baker-Shindler Contracting Co................. E 419 782-5080
  Defiance *(G-6671)*
Fleming Construction Co............................ F 740 494-2177
  Prospect *(G-12689)*
Hines Builders Inc....................................... F 937 335-4586
  Troy *(G-14577)*
Thomas J Weaver Inc................................. F 740 622-2040
  Coshocton *(G-5998)*

CONSTRUCTION: Indl Plant

Advanced Indus Machining Inc................. F 614 596-4183
  Powell *(G-12662)*
Babcock & Wilcox Company..................... A 330 753-4511
  Akron *(G-73)*

Htec Systems Inc... F 937 438-3010
  Dayton *(G-6376)*
Tri-America Contractors Inc...................... E 740 574-0148
  Wheelersburg *(G-15810)*

CONSTRUCTION: Land Preparation

Valley Mining Inc... C 740 922-3942
  Dennison *(G-6797)*

CONSTRUCTION: Pipeline, NEC

Eastern Automated Piping......................... G 740 535-8184
  Mingo Junction *(G-11044)*
Sterling Process Equipment .... E 614 868-5151
  Columbus *(G-5794)*

CONSTRUCTION: Power Plant

Enerfab LLC... B 513 641-0500
  Cincinnati *(G-2872)*
Siemens Energy Inc.................................... E 740 393-8897
  Mount Vernon *(G-11295)*

CONSTRUCTION: Residential, Nec

American Egle Prprty Prsrvtion.................. G 855 440-6938
  North Ridgeville *(G-11828)*
Artisan Constructors LLC............................ E 216 800-7641
  Cleveland *(G-3680)*
Dunn Industrial Services............................. G 513 738-4999
  Hamilton *(G-8200)*

CONSTRUCTION: Scaffolding

Waco Scaffolding & Equipment Inc.......... A 216 749-8900
  Cleveland *(G-4889)*

CONSTRUCTION: Sewer Line

Fleming Construction Co............................ F 740 494-2177
  Prospect *(G-12689)*
Mt Pleasant Blacktopping Inc.................... G 513 874-3777
  Fairfield *(G-7385)*

CONSTRUCTION: Single-Family Housing

Building Concepts Inc................................. F 419 298-2371
  Edgerton *(G-7072)*
Cirigliano Enterprises LLC.......................... G 567 525-4571
  Findlay *(G-7492)*
Manufactured Housing Entps Inc............. E 419 636-4511
  Bryan *(G-1827)*
Plumb Builders Inc...................................... F 937 293-1111
  Dayton *(G-6508)*
Third Salvo Company................................. G 740 818-9669
  Amesville *(G-472)*

CONSTRUCTION: Single-family Housing, New

Al Yoder Construction Co........................... G 330 359-5726
  Millersburg *(G-10939)*
Hoge Lumber Company............................. E 419 753-2263
  New Knoxville *(G-11447)*
The Galehouse Companies Inc................. E 330 658-2023
  Doylestown *(G-6854)*
Thomas J Weaver Inc................................. F 740 622-2040
  Coshocton *(G-5998)*

CONSTRUCTION: Street Sign Installation & Mntnce

A & A Safety Inc.. F 937 567-9781
  Beavercreek *(G-1068)*
A & A Safety Inc.. E 513 943-6100
  Amelia *(G-447)*

CONSTRUCTION: Swimming Pools

Imperial On-Pece Fibrgls Pools................ F 740 747-2971
  Ashley *(G-622)*

CONSTRUCTION: Waste Water & Sewage Treatment Plant

Artesian of Pioneer Inc............................... F 419 737-2352
  Pioneer *(G-12490)*

CONSULTING SVC: Business, NEC

Apex Control Systems Inc.......................... D 330 938-2588
  Sebring *(G-13117)*
D M L Steel Tech... G 513 737-9911
  Liberty Twp *(G-9213)*
Deemsys Inc... D 614 322-9928
  Gahanna *(G-7833)*
E Retailing Associates LLC........................ D 614 300-5785
  Columbus *(G-5339)*
Estone Group LLC...................................... E 888 653-2246
  Toledo *(G-14280)*
Ktsdi LLC.. G 330 783-2000
  North Lima *(G-11808)*
Lake Publishing Inc.................................... G 440 299-8500
  Mentor *(G-10490)*
Magnum Computers Inc............................ F 216 781-1757
  Cleveland *(G-4351)*
Optum Infusion Svcs 550 LLC................... D 866 442-4679
  Cincinnati *(G-3227)*
Ream and Haager Laboratory Inc........... F 330 343-3711
  Dover *(G-6840)*
Russell Group United LLC......................... F 614 353-6853
  Columbus *(G-5734)*
Simplevms LLC.. F 888 255-8918
  Cincinnati *(G-3393)*
Sutter Llc.. F 513 891-2261
  Blue Ash *(G-1476)*

CONSULTING SVC: Financial Management

Dco LLC... E 419 931-9086
  Perrysburg *(G-12373)*
Jmac Inc.. E 614 436-2418
  Columbus *(G-5498)*

CONSULTING SVC: Human Resource

Delphia Consulting LLC.............................. E 614 421-2000
  Columbus *(G-5325)*
Organalytix LLC... G 908 938-6711
  West Chester *(G-15473)*
Paycor Hcm Inc.. F 800 381-0053
  Cincinnati *(G-3243)*
Simplevms LLC.. F 888 255-8918
  Cincinnati *(G-3393)*

CONSULTING SVC: Management

Advanced Prgrm Resources Inc............... E 614 761-9994
  Dublin *(G-6857)*
American Egle Prprty Prsrvtion.................. G 855 440-6938
  North Ridgeville *(G-11828)*
Amerihua Intl Entps Inc.............................. G 740 549-0300
  Lewis Center *(G-9148)*
Dms Inc... C 440 951-9838
  Willoughby *(G-15910)*
EP Ferris & Associates Inc......................... E 614 299-2999
  Columbus *(G-5357)*
Equip Business Solutions Co..................... G 614 854-9755
  Jackson *(G-8715)*
Link To Success Inc.................................... G 888 959-4203
  Norwalk *(G-11978)*
Michele Caldwell....................................... G 937 505-7744
  Dayton *(G-6442)*
Pakra LLC... F 614 477-6965
  Columbus *(G-5651)*

Employee Codes: A=Over 500 employees, B=251-500
C=101-250, D=51-100, E=20-50, F=10-19, G=1-9

CONSULTING SVC: Management

Quality Solutions Inc .... E 440 933-9946
  Cleveland (G-4608)
Russell Group United LLC .... F 614 353-6853
  Columbus (G-5734)
Santec Resources Inc .... F 614 664-9540
  Columbus (G-5746)
SSP Industrial Group Inc .... G 330 665-2900
  Fairlawn (G-7452)
Vehicle Systems Inc .... G 330 854-0535
  Massillon (G-10153)
Welding Consultants Inc .... G 614 258-7018
  Columbus (G-5870)

CONSULTING SVCS, BUSINESS: Communications

Telex Communications Inc .... G 419 865-0972
  Toledo (G-14482)

CONSULTING SVCS, BUSINESS: Energy Conservation

Aeroseal LLC .... E 937 428-9300
  Dayton (G-6187)
Aeroseal LLC .... E 937 428-9300
  Miamisburg (G-10607)
Melink Corporation .... D 513 685-0958
  Milford (G-10913)

CONSULTING SVCS, BUSINESS: Environmental

Radon Eliminator LLC .... F 330 844-0703
  North Canton (G-11755)

CONSULTING SVCS, BUSINESS: Safety Training Svcs

Nkh-Safety Inc .... F 513 771-3839
  Cincinnati (G-3200)

CONSULTING SVCS, BUSINESS: Sys Engnrg, Exc Computer/ Prof

Jasstek Inc .... F 614 808-3600
  Dublin (G-6902)
Millers Aplus Cmpt Svcs LLC .... F 330 620-5288
  Akron (G-250)
Tangible Solutions Inc .... E 937 912-4603
  Fairborn (G-7324)

CONSULTING SVCS, BUSINESS: Systems Analysis & Engineering

Defense Research Assoc Inc .... E 937 431-1644
  Dayton (G-6158)
Great Lakes Mfg Group Ltd .... G 440 391-8266
  Rocky River (G-12838)
Interactive Engineering Corp .... E 330 239-6888
  Medina (G-10337)
Sentek Corporation .... G 614 586-1123
  Columbus (G-5759)
Tekworx LLC .... F 513 533-4777
  Blue Ash (G-1479)

CONSULTING SVCS, BUSINESS: Systems Analysis Or Design

Architctral Identification Inc .... F 614 868-8400
  Gahanna (G-7830)
Qlog Corp .... G 513 874-1211
  Hamilton (G-8238)

CONSULTING SVCS: Scientific

Advanced Green Tech Inc .... G 614 397-8130
  Plain City (G-12560)
Mrl Materials Resources LLC .... E 937 531-6657
  Xenia (G-16269)

CONTACT LENSES

Albright Albright & Schn .... F 614 825-4829
  Worthington (G-16189)
Diversified Ophthalmics Inc .... E 803 783-3454
  Cincinnati (G-2832)

CONTAINERS, GLASS: Food

Bprex Plastic Packaging Inc .... F 419 247-5000
  Toledo (G-14218)

CONTAINERS, GLASS: Water Bottles

Waterco of The Central States .... E 937 294-0375
  Fairfield (G-7426)

CONTAINERS: Cargo, Wood & Metal Combination

Schutz Container Systems Inc .... D 419 872-2477
  Perrysburg (G-12425)

CONTAINERS: Food & Beverage

Ball Arosol Specialty Cont Inc .... E 330 534-1903
  Hubbard (G-8561)
Ball Corporation .... E 419 423-3071
  Findlay (G-7480)
Ball Corporation .... F 330 244-2313
  North Canton (G-11716)
Broodle Brands LLC .... G 855 276-6353
  Cincinnati (G-2690)
Envases Media Inc .... E 419 636-5461
  Bryan (G-1817)
SSP Industrial Group Inc .... G 330 665-2900
  Fairlawn (G-7452)

CONTAINERS: Food, Folding, Made From Purchased Materials

Graphic Packaging Intl LLC .... E 419 668-1006
  Norwalk (G-11970)

CONTAINERS: Food, Liquid Tight, Including Milk

Billerud Americas Corporation .... D 901 369-4105
  West Chester (G-15379)
Island Aseptics LLC .... C 740 685-2548
  Byesville (G-1898)
Kerry Inc .... E 760 685-2548
  Byesville (G-1899)
Ohio State Plastics .... D 614 299-5618
  Columbus (G-5627)

CONTAINERS: Food, Metal

G W Cobb Co .... F 216 341-0100
  Cleveland (G-4099)

CONTAINERS: Glass

Anchor Glass Container Corp .... D 740 452-2743
  Zanesville (G-16500)
Anchor Hocking LLC .... A 740 687-2500
  Columbus (G-5139)
Chantilly Development Corp .... E 419 243-8109
  Toledo (G-14233)
Ghp II LLC .... C 740 687-2500
  Lancaster (G-9017)
O-I Glass Inc .... C 567 336-5000
  Perrysburg (G-12405)

PRODUCT SECTION

Oi California Containers Inc .... F 567 336-5000
  Perrysburg (G-12410)
Oi Castalia STS Inc .... E 419 247-5000
  Toledo (G-14411)
Owens-Brockway Glass Cont Inc .... E 740 455-4516
  Zanesville (G-16451)
Owens-Brockway Glass Cont Inc .... C 567 336-8449
  Perrysburg (G-12414)
Owens-Illinois General Inc .... A 567 336-5000
  Perrysburg (G-12415)
Owens-Illinois Group Inc .... D 567 336-5000
  Perrysburg (G-12416)
Owens-Illinois Inc .... A 567 336-5000
  Perrysburg (G-12417)
Paddock Enterprises LLC .... E 567 336-5000
  Perrysburg (G-12418)
Pyromatics Corp .... F 440 352-3500
  Mentor (G-10537)
Tiama Americas Inc .... E 269 274-3107
  Maumee (G-10210)

CONTAINERS: Ice Cream, Made From Purchased Materials

Huhtamaki Inc .... C 513 201-1525
  Batavia (G-925)
Huhtamaki Inc .... D 937 746-9700
  Franklin (G-7681)
Norse Dairy Systems LP .... B 614 294-4931
  Columbus (G-5401)

CONTAINERS: Laminated Phenolic & Vulcanized Fiber

Polystar Inc .... F 330 963-5100
  Stow (G-13717)

CONTAINERS: Metal

G P Manufacturing Inc .... G 937 544-3190
  Peebles (G-12226)
Premier Container Inc .... E 800 230-7132
  Cleveland (G-4480)
Shanafelt Manufacturing Co .... E 330 455-0315
  Canton (G-2221)

CONTAINERS: Plastic

Alpla Inc .... F 419 991-9484
  Lima (G-9304)
Amcor Rigid Packaging Usa LLC .... G 419 483-4343
  Bellevue (G-1221)
Axium Packaging LLC .... A 614 706-5955
  New Albany (G-11369)
Bakelite N Sumitomo Amer Inc .... E 419 675-1282
  Kenton (G-8881)
Bprex Plastic Packaging Inc .... F 419 247-5000
  Toledo (G-14219)
Cell-O-Core Co .... F 800 239-4370
  Wadsworth (G-15022)
Century Container LLC .... E 330 457-2367
  Columbiana (G-5031)
Century Container LLC .... F 330 457-2367
  New Waterford (G-11554)
Century Container Corporation .... C 330 457-2367
  New Waterford (G-11555)
Composite Technologies Co LLC .... D 937 228-2880
  Dayton (G-6262)
Dadco Inc .... F 513 489-2244
  Cincinnati (G-316)
Dester Corporation .... F 419 362-8020
  Lima (G-9236)
Dester Corporation .... F 419 362-8020
  Lima (G-9235)

PRODUCT SECTION

CONTRACTORS: Commercial & Office Building

Dometic Sanitation Corporation............ E 330 439-5550
  Big Prairie (G-1328)
Eaton Corporation.................................. E 330 274-0743
  Aurora (G-712)
Ebco Inc... E 330 562-8265
  Streetsboro (G-13769)
Eliason Corporation................................ E 800 828-3655
  West Chester (G-15550)
Encon Inc.. C 937 898-2603
  Dayton (G-6320)
Enpac LLC... D 440 975-0070
  Eastlake (G-7028)
Environmental Sampling Sup Inc............ D 330 497-9396
  North Canton (G-11725)
Fields Process Technology Inc............... G 216 781-4787
  Cleveland (G-4059)
Flambeau Inc.. D 440 632-6131
  Middlefield (G-10750)
G3 Packaging LLC................................... G 334 799-0015
  Monroe (G-11107)
Genpak LLC.. E 614 276-5156
  Columbus (G-5399)
Graham Packaging Pet Tech Inc............. E 419 334-4197
  Fremont (G-7788)
Greif Inc.. E 740 657-6500
  Delaware (G-6725)
Greif Inc.. E 740 549-6000
  Delaware (G-6724)
Hamilton Custom Molding Inc................. G 513 844-6463
  Hamilton (G-8217)
Hanlon Composites LLC......................... E 216 261-7056
  Euclid (G-7272)
Hendrickson International Corp.............. D 740 929-5600
  Hebron (G-8343)
HP Liquidating Inc.................................. D 614 861-1791
  Blacklick (G-1337)
Iml Containers Ohio Inc.......................... F 330 754-1066
  Canton (G-2129)
Kennedy Group Incorporated.................. D 440 951-7660
  Willoughby (G-15939)
Kreate Extrusion LLC............................. G 419 683-4057
  Findlay (G-7527)
Landmark Plastic Corporation................ C 330 785-2200
  Akron (G-217)
Molded Fiber Glass Companies.............. E 440 994-5100
  Ashtabula (G-652)
Oneida Consumer LLC........................... F 740 687-2500
  Columbus (G-5641)
Patrick Products Inc............................... C 419 943-4137
  Leipsic (G-9134)
Plastics R Unique Inc............................. E 330 334-4820
  Wadsworth (G-15053)
Plastipak Packaging Inc......................... C 740 928-4435
  Hebron (G-8356)
Polyflex LLC.. F 440 946-0758
  Willoughby (G-15975)
Polymer & Steel Tech Inc....................... E 440 510-0108
  Eastlake (G-7045)
Premium Balloon ACC Inc....................... E 330 239-4547
  Wadsworth (G-15054)
Resource Mtl Hdlg & Recycl Inc............. E 440 834-0727
  Middlefield (G-10784)
S Toys Holdings LLC............................... A 330 656-0440
  Streetsboro (G-13789)
Shirley KS Storage Trays LLC................ G 740 868-8140
  Zanesville (G-16564)
Silgan Plastics LLC................................. C 419 523-3737
  Ottawa (G-12191)
Soterra LLC... G 740 549-6072
  Delaware (G-6752)
Southeastern Container Inc.................... G 419 352-6500
  Bowling Green (G-1589)

Spartech LLC... C 937 548-1395
  Greenville (G-8059)
Tbk Holdings LLC.................................... G 313 584-0400
  Perrysburg (G-12429)
US Coexcell Inc....................................... E 419 897-9110
  Maumee (G-10243)

CONTAINERS: Sanitary, Food

Champion International........................... G 440 235-7200
  Olmsted Falls (G-12079)
Duracorp LLC.. D 740 549-3336
  Lewis Center (G-9158)
Novolex Holdings Inc............................. B 937 746-1933
  Franklin (G-7690)
Sonoco Products Company..................... E 513 870-3985
  West Chester (G-15588)
The Mead Corporation............................ B 937 495-6323
  Dayton (G-6619)
Washington Products Inc........................ F 330 837-5101
  Massillon (G-10154)

CONTAINERS: Shipping, Bombs, Metal Plate

Industrial Repair and Mfg....................... E 419 822-4232
  Delta (G-6787)

CONTAINERS: Wood

Brimar Packaging Inc.............................. E 440 934-3080
  Avon (G-764)
Brown-Forman Corporation.................... F 740 384-3027
  Wellston (G-15326)
Cima Inc.. E 513 382-8976
  Hamilton (G-8191)
Clark Rm Inc... F 419 425-9889
  Findlay (G-7494)
Denoon Lumber Company LLC............... D 740 768-2220
  Bergholz (G-1300)
Haessly Lumber Sales Co...................... D 740 373-6681
  Marietta (G-9798)
Hinchcliff Lumber Company................... D 440 238-5200
  Strongsville (G-13841)
Joe Gonda Company Incorporated......... G 440 458-6000
  Grafton (G-8003)
Overseas Packing LLC............................ E 440 232-2917
  Bedford (G-1148)
T & D Thompson Inc............................... E 740 332-8515
  Laurelville (G-9056)
Traveling Recycle WD Pdts Inc.............. F 419 968-2649
  Middle Point (G-10713)
Wellman Container Corporation............. E 513 860-3040
  Cincinnati (G-3515)

CONTAINMENT VESSELS: Reactor, Metal Plate

FSRc Tanks Inc....................................... E 234 221-2015
  Bolivar (G-1525)

CONTRACTOR: Rigging & Scaffolding

Janson Industries................................... D 330 455-7029
  Canton (G-2135)

CONTRACTORS: Acoustical & Insulation Work

Holland Assocts LLC DBA Archou......... F 513 891-0006
  Cincinnati (G-3003)
One Wish LLC... F 800 505-6883
  Bedford (G-1147)

CONTRACTORS: Asbestos Removal & Encapsulation

American Way Exteriors LLC.................. G 937 221-8860
  Dayton (G-6204)

CONTRACTORS: Boiler Maintenance Contractor

Holgate Metal Fab Inc............................. F 419 599-2000
  Napoleon (G-11319)
Prout Boiler Htg & Wldg Inc................... E 330 744-0293
  Youngstown (G-16423)

CONTRACTORS: Building Site Preparation

Barrett Paving Materials Inc.................. E 973 533-1001
  Hamilton (G-8183)
Ohio Luxury Bulders LLC....................... G 330 881-0073
  Austintown (G-753)

CONTRACTORS: Carpentry Work

Acme Home Improvement Co Inc............ F 614 252-2129
  Columbus (G-5098)
AK Fabrication Inc.................................. F 330 458-1037
  Canton (G-2032)
Finelli Ornamental Iron Co..................... E 440 248-0050
  Cleveland (G-4061)
Joseph Sabatino.................................... G 330 332-5879
  Salem (G-13007)
Millwood Wholesale Inc......................... F 330 359-6109
  Dundee (G-6968)
Overhead Door of Pike County............... G 740 289-3925
  Piketon (G-12481)
Premier Construction Company............. F 513 874-2611
  Fairfield (G-7395)
Riverside Cnstr Svcs Inc........................ E 513 723-0900
  Cincinnati (G-3344)
Tri County Door Service Inc.................. F 216 531-2245
  Euclid (G-7303)
Triple A Builders Inc.............................. G 216 249-0327
  Cleveland (G-4832)

CONTRACTORS: Carpentry, Cabinet & Finish Work

Architctral Mllwk Cbinetry Inc............... G 440 708-0086
  Chagrin Falls (G-2389)
Case Crafters Inc................................... G 937 667-9473
  Tipp City (G-14127)
Dgl Woodworking Inc.............................. F 937 837-7091
  Dayton (G-6298)
Display Dynamics Inc............................. E 937 832-2830
  Englewood (G-7229)
Snows Wood Shop Inc........................... E 419 836-3805
  Oregon (G-12111)

CONTRACTORS: Closet Organizers, Installation & Design

Ptmj Enterprises Inc.............................. D 440 543-8000
  Solon (G-13408)

CONTRACTORS: Coating, Caulking & Weather, Water & Fire

Akay Holdings Inc.................................. E 330 753-8458
  Barberton (G-852)
Sika Mbcc US LLC.................................. A 216 839-7500
  Beachwood (G-1024)

CONTRACTORS: Commercial & Office Building

Bent Wood Solutions LLC...................... G 330 674-1454
  Millersburg (G-10943)
Brenmar Construction Inc..................... D 740 286-2151
  Jackson (G-8711)

CONTRACTORS: Commercial & Office Building

Commercial Cnstr Group LLC.................. G 513 722-1357
Milford *(G-10902)*

MGM Construction Inc.......................... F 440 234-7660
Berea *(G-1288)*

Stamm Contracting Company Inc........... E 330 274-8230
Mantua *(G-9743)*

CONTRACTORS: Communications Svcs

Gatesair Inc.. D 513 459-3400
Mason *(G-9995)*

Legrand North America LLC.................. B 937 224-0639
Dayton *(G-6403)*

Vertiv Group Corporation....................... G 440 460-3600
Cleveland *(G-4864)*

CONTRACTORS: Computerized Controls Installation

Computer Enterprise Inc........................ G 216 228-7156
Lakewood *(G-8972)*

CONTRACTORS: Concrete Block Masonry Laying

G L Pierce Inc...................................... G 513 772-7202
Cincinnati *(G-2927)*

North Central Con Designs Inc.............. G 419 606-1908
Wooster *(G-16155)*

CONTRACTORS: Concrete Reinforcement Placing

Upright Steel LLC................................ E 216 923-0852
Cleveland *(G-4853)*

CONTRACTORS: Core Drilling & Cutting

Barr Engineering Incorporated............... E 614 714-0299
Columbus *(G-5175)*

CONTRACTORS: Corrosion Control Installation

Mesocoat Inc.. F 216 453-0866
Euclid *(G-7286)*

CONTRACTORS: Decontamination Svcs

Extreme Microbial Tech LLC.................. E 844 885-0088
Moraine *(G-11179)*

CONTRACTORS: Directional Oil & Gas Well Drilling Svc

Brendel Producing Company................. G 330 854-4151
Canton *(G-2052)*

Clearpath Utility Solutions LLC.............. F 740 661-4240
Zanesville *(G-16521)*

Directional One Svcs Inc USA............... G 740 371-5031
Marietta *(G-9788)*

Groundhogs 2000 LLC.......................... G 440 653-1647
Bedford *(G-1122)*

Ngo Development Corporation.............. E 740 344-3790
Newark *(G-11598)*

Temple Oil and Gas LLC....................... G 740 452-7878
Crooksville *(G-6050)*

Warren Drilling Co Inc......................... C 740 783-2775
Dexter City *(G-6803)*

CONTRACTORS: Electric Power Systems

Asg Division Jergens Inc...................... E 888 486-6163
Cleveland *(G-3688)*

Asidaco LLC... G 800 204-1544
Dayton *(G-6215)*

CONTRACTORS: Electronic Controls Installation

Controls Inc... E 330 239-4345
Medina *(G-10312)*

Industrial Electronic Service................. F 937 746-9750
Carlisle *(G-2288)*

Safe-Grain Inc..................................... G 513 398-2500
Loveland *(G-9503)*

CONTRACTORS: Energy Management Control

Siemens Energy Inc............................. E 740 393-8897
Mount Vernon *(G-11295)*

Tekworx LLC....................................... F 513 533-4777
Blue Ash *(G-1479)*

CONTRACTORS: Erection & Dismantling, Poured Concrete Forms

R W Sidley Incorporated....................... C 440 298-3232
Thompson *(G-14062)*

CONTRACTORS: Fence Construction

Connaughton Wldg & Fence LLC........... G 513 867-0230
Hamilton *(G-8195)*

Cuyahoga Fence LLC........................... F 216 830-2200
Cleveland *(G-3930)*

Double D D Mtls Instlltion Inc............... G 937 898-2534
Dayton *(G-6302)*

Fence One Inc..................................... F 216 441-2600
Cleveland *(G-4056)*

Security Fence Group Inc.................... E 513 681-3700
Cincinnati *(G-3374)*

Youngstown Fence Incorporated........... G 330 788-8110
Youngstown *(G-16481)*

CONTRACTORS: Floor Laying & Other Floor Work

Done-Rite Bowling Service Co............... E 440 232-3280
Bedford *(G-1118)*

Tremco Incorporated............................ B
Beachwood *(G-1031)*

Triple A Builders Inc........................... G 216 249-0327
Cleveland *(G-4832)*

CONTRACTORS: Foundation & Footing

Gateway Con Forming Svcs Inc............. D 513 353-2000
Miamitown *(G-10708)*

CONTRACTORS: Gas Field Svcs, NEC

Critical Ctrl Enrgy Svcs Inc................... F 330 539-4267
Girard *(G-7966)*

Stingray Pressure Pumping LLC............ D 405 648-4177
Belmont *(G-1249)*

CONTRACTORS: General Electric

D & E Electric Inc................................ G 513 738-1172
Okeana *(G-12067)*

D & J Electric Motor Repair Co............. F 330 336-4343
Wadsworth *(G-15025)*

Darana Hybrid Inc............................... D 513 860-4490
Hamilton *(G-8199)*

Helios Quartz America Inc.................... G 419 882-3377
Sylvania *(G-13999)*

Industrial Power Systems Inc................ B 419 531-3121
Rossford *(G-12867)*

Instrmntation Ctrl Systems Inc.............. E 513 662-2600
Cincinnati *(G-3024)*

JC Electric Llc..................................... F 330 760-2915
Garrettsville *(G-7917)*

PRODUCT SECTION

Jeff Bonham Electric Inc...................... E 937 233-7662
Dayton *(G-6388)*

Magnum Computers Inc....................... F 216 781-1757
Cleveland *(G-4351)*

Mikes Transm & Auto Svc LLC............. F 330 799-8266
Youngstown *(G-6401)*

P S C Inc... E 216 531-3375
Cleveland *(G-4577)*

Security Fence Group Inc.................... E 513 681-3700
Cincinnati *(G-3374)*

Tcb Automation LLC............................ F 330 556-6444
Dover *(G-6847)*

The Wagner-Smith Company................ B 866 338-0398
Moraine *(G-11274)*

Valley Electric Company....................... G 419 332-6405
Fremont *(G-7875)*

Waibel Electric Co Inc......................... F 740 964-2956
Etna *(G-7253)*

CONTRACTORS: Glass Tinting, Architectural & Automotive

Afg Industries Inc............................... D 614 322-4580
Grove City *(G-8874)*

CONTRACTORS: Heating & Air Conditioning

Air-Tech Mechanical Inc....................... F 419 292-0074
Toledo *(G-1418)*

Hess Advanced Solutions Llc................ G 937 829-4794
Dayton *(G-6368)*

Northeastern Rfrgn Corp..................... E 440 942-7676
Willoughby *(G-5960)*

CONTRACTORS: Heating Systems Repair & Maintenance Svc

Whempys Corp..................................... G 614 888-6670
Worthington *(G-16218)*

CONTRACTORS: Highway & Street Construction General

John R Jurgensen Co........................... B 513 771-0820
Cincinnati *(G-3014)*

Kenmore Construction Co Inc............... D 330 832-8888
Massillon *(G-10716)*

S E Johnson Companies Inc................. E 419 893-8731
Maumee *(G-10728)*

Valley Asphalt Corporation.................. E 513 771-0820
Cincinnati *(G-3036)*

Ward Construction Co......................... F 419 943-2450
Leipsic *(G-9142)*

CONTRACTORS: Highway & Street Paving

Barrett Paving Materials Inc................. E 973 533-1001
Hamilton *(G-813)*

Gerken Materials Inc............................ E 419 533-2421
Napoleon *(G-1215)*

M & B Asphalt Company Inc................. F 419 992-4235
Tiffin *(G-14091)*

Terminal Ready-Mix Inc....................... E 440 288-0181
Lorain *(G-9441)*

Wilson Blacktop Corp........................... F 740 635-3566
Martins Ferry *(G-9901)*

CONTRACTORS: Hydraulic Eqpt Installation & Svcs

Kcn Technologies LLC.......................... G 440 439-4219
Bedford *(G-1130)*

CONTRACTORS: Machine Rigging & Moving

Atlas Industrial Contrs LLC.................. B 614 841-4500
Columbus *(G-5063)*

CONTRACTORS: Machinery Installation

Chagrin Vly Stl Erectors Inc........................ F 440 975-1356
  Willoughby Hills *(G-16023)*

Expert Crane Inc....................................... E 216 451-9900
  Wellington *(G-15307)*
Intertec Corporation.................................. F 419 537-9711
  Toledo *(G-14335)*
Spallinger Millwright Svc Co...................... E 419 225-5830
  Lima *(G-9291)*

CONTRACTORS: Marble Installation, Interior

Cutting Edge Countertops Inc.................... E 419 873-9500
  Perrysburg *(G-12372)*
Distinctive Marble & Gran Inc.................... F 614 760-0003
  Plain City *(G-12575)*

CONTRACTORS: Masonry & Stonework

Albert Freytag Inc...................................... E 419 628-2018
  Minster *(G-11047)*
North Hill Marble & Granite Co................... F 330 253-2179
  Akron *(G-267)*
Pioneer Cldding Glzing Systems................ E 216 816-4242
  Cleveland *(G-4554)*
Rmi Titanium Company LLC...................... E 330 652-9952
  Niles *(G-11684)*

CONTRACTORS: Office Furniture Installation

National Electro-Coatings Inc..................... D 216 898-0080
  Cleveland *(G-4436)*

CONTRACTORS: Oil & Gas Building, Repairing & Dismantling Svc

Dow Cameron Oil & Gas LLC..................... G 740 452-1568
  Zanesville *(G-16527)*
Formation Cementing Inc.......................... G 740 453-6926
  Zanesville *(G-16532)*
J-Well Service Inc..................................... G 330 824-2718
  Warren *(G-15180)*
Ralph Robinson Inc................................... G 740 385-2747
  Logan *(G-9375)*

CONTRACTORS: Oil & Gas Field Geological Exploration Svcs

David R Hill Inc... G 740 685-5168
  Byesville *(G-1893)*
New World Energy Resources................... F 740 344-4087
  Newark *(G-11597)*

CONTRACTORS: Oil & Gas Field Geophysical Exploration Svcs

Dlz Ohio Inc... C 614 888-0040
  Columbus *(G-5332)*
Hocking Hlls Enrgy Well Svcs L.................. G 740 385-6690
  Logan *(G-9364)*

CONTRACTORS: Oil & Gas Field Tools Fishing Svcs

Klx Energy Services LLC............................ E 740 922-1155
  Midvale *(G-10880)*

CONTRACTORS: Oil & Gas Well Plugging & Abandoning Svcs

Omega Cementing Co............................... G 330 695-7147
  Apple Creek *(G-508)*

CONTRACTORS: Oil & Gas Well Redrilling

Decker Drilling Inc..................................... F 740 749-3939
  Vincent *(G-15007)*

CONTRACTORS: Oil & Gas Wells Pumping Svcs

Lld Gas & Oil Corp.................................... G 330 364-6331
  Dover *(G-6832)*
Ottawa Oil Co Inc...................................... F 419 425-3301
  Findlay *(G-7548)*
Performance Technologies LLC................. D 330 875-1216
  Louisville *(G-9468)*

CONTRACTORS: Oil & Gas Wells Svcs

Bakerwell Inc... E 330 276-2161
  Killbuck *(G-8916)*
Wrights Well Service LLC.......................... G 740 380-9602
  Logan *(G-9378)*

CONTRACTORS: Oil Field Haulage Svcs

Fishburn Tank Truck Service...................... F 419 253-6031
  Marengo *(G-9767)*

CONTRACTORS: Oil Field Mud Drilling Svcs

Kelchner Inc.. C 937 704-9890
  Springboro *(G-13508)*

CONTRACTORS: Oil Field Pipe Testing Svcs

Leak Finder Inc... G 440 735-0130
  Hudson *(G-8602)*
Ream and Haager Laboratory Inc.............. F 330 343-3711
  Dover *(G-6840)*

CONTRACTORS: Ornamental Metal Work

Custom Way Welding Inc........................... F 937 845-9469
  New Carlisle *(G-11414)*
Spradlin Bros Welding Co......................... F 800 219-2182
  Springfield *(G-13634)*
Stuart-Dean Co Inc................................... G 412 765-2752
  Cleveland *(G-4742)*

CONTRACTORS: Painting, Commercial

Mes Painting and Graphics Ltd.................. E 614 496-1696
  Westerville *(G-15715)*
Napoleon Machine LLC............................. E 419 591-7010
  Napoleon *(G-11327)*

CONTRACTORS: Painting, Commercial, Exterior

Ohio Building Restoration Inc.................... E 419 244-7372
  Toledo *(G-14408)*

CONTRACTORS: Painting, Indl

A1 Industrial Painting Inc........................... E 330 750-9441
  Youngstown *(G-16298)*
Banks Manufacturing Company................. F 440 458-8661
  Grafton *(G-7997)*
Industrial Mill Maintenance........................ E 330 746-1155
  Youngstown *(G-16379)*
Js Fabrications Inc.................................... G 419 333-0323
  Fremont *(G-7790)*
Kars Ohio LLC.. G 614 655-1099
  Pataskala *(G-12300)*
Semper Quality Industry Inc...................... G 440 352-8111
  Mentor *(G-10552)*

CONTRACTORS: Petroleum Storage Tanks, Pumping & Draining

Envirnmntal Cmpliance Tech LLC............. F 216 634-0400
  North Royalton *(G-11874)*

CONTRACTORS: Plumbing

Approved Plumbing Co.............................. F 216 663-5063
  Cleveland *(G-3671)*
GM Mechanical Inc.................................... D 937 473-3006
  Covington *(G-6024)*
Personal Plumber Service Corp................. F 440 324-4321
  Elyria *(G-7195)*
Pioneer Pipe Inc.. A 740 376-2400
  Marietta *(G-9817)*

CONTRACTORS: Pollution Control Eqpt Installation

Cleveland Roll Forming Envi..................... F 440 899-3888
  Westlake *(G-15744)*
L Haberny Co Inc...................................... F 440 543-5999
  Chagrin Falls *(G-2404)*
McGill Airclean LLC.................................. D 614 829-1200
  Columbus *(G-5550)*

CONTRACTORS: Power Generating Eqpt Installation

Clopay Corporation................................... C 800 282-2260
  Mason *(G-9979)*

CONTRACTORS: Prefabricated Window & Door Installation

Alside Inc.. D 419 865-0934
  Maumee *(G-10161)*
Cabinet Restylers Inc................................ D 419 281-8449
  Ashland *(G-561)*
General Awning Company Inc................... F 216 749-0110
  Cleveland *(G-4111)*
Midwest Curtainwalls Inc........................... D 216 641-7900
  Cleveland *(G-4410)*
Yoder Window & Siding Ltd...................... F 330 695-6960
  Fredericksburg *(G-7735)*

CONTRACTORS: Process Piping

United Group Services Inc........................ C 800 633-9690
  West Chester *(G-15601)*

CONTRACTORS: Refractory or Acid Brick Masonry

The Schaefer Group Inc............................ E 937 253-3342
  Beavercreek *(G-1082)*

CONTRACTORS: Roustabout Svcs

Prospect Rock LLC................................... F 740 512-0542
  Saint Clairsville *(G-12919)*
Ruscilli Real Estate Services..................... F 614 923-6400
  Dublin *(G-6932)*

CONTRACTORS: Septic System

Accurate Mechanical Inc........................... D 740 681-1332
  Lancaster *(G-8985)*
Mack Industries.. E 419 353-7081
  Bowling Green *(G-1572)*

CONTRACTORS: Sheet Metal Work, NEC

All-Type Welding & Fabrication.................. E 440 439-3990
  Cleveland *(G-3635)*
Anchor Metal Processing Inc..................... F 216 362-6463
  Cleveland *(G-3662)*
Anchor Metal Processing Inc..................... E 216 362-1850
  Cleveland *(G-3663)*
Avon Lake Sheet Metal Co........................ E 440 933-3505
  Avon Lake *(G-800)*
Budde Sheet Metal Works Inc................... E 937 224-0868
  Dayton *(G-6241)*
Cmt Machining & Fabg LLC...................... F 937 652-3740
  Urbana *(G-14827)*

CONTRACTORS: Sheet Metal Work, NEC

Defabco Inc... D 614 231-2700
  Columbus (G-5323)
Dimensional Metals Inc..................... E 740 927-3633
  Reynoldsburg (G-12761)
Ducts Inc... F 216 391-2400
  Cleveland (G-3977)
Everyday Technologies Inc................ F 937 497-7774
  Sidney (G-13247)
Franck and Fric Incorporated............ D 216 524-4451
  Cleveland (G-4090)
Holgate Metal Fab Inc....................... F 419 599-2000
  Napoleon (G-11319)
Jim Nier Construction Inc.................. E 740 289-3925
  Piketon (G-12477)
Kettering Roofing & Shtmtl Inc.......... F 513 281-6413
  Cincinnati (G-3075)
Kirk & Blum Manufacturing Co.......... C 513 458-2600
  Cincinnati (G-3078)
Martina Metal LLC............................. E 614 291-9700
  Columbus (G-5544)
Precision Impacts LLC...................... D 937 530-8254
  Miamisburg (G-10671)
Rmt Acquisition Inc........................... E 513 241-5566
  Cincinnati (G-3347)
Seneca Sheet Metal Company.......... F 419 447-8434
  Tiffin (G-14105)

CONTRACTORS: Siding

Cardinal Builders Inc......................... E 614 237-1000
  Columbus (G-5236)
Champion Opco LLC......................... B 513 327-7338
  Cincinnati (G-2725)
General Awning Company Inc........... F 216 749-0110
  Cleveland (G-4111)
Waxco International Inc.................... F 937 746-4845
  Miamisburg (G-10701)

CONTRACTORS: Skylight Installation

Scs Construction Services Inc........... E 513 929-0260
  Cincinnati (G-3371)

CONTRACTORS: Structural Iron Work, Structural

Wernke Wldg & Stl Erection Co......... F 513 353-4173
  North Bend (G-11708)
White Mule Company......................... E 740 382-9008
  Ontario (G-12097)

CONTRACTORS: Structural Steel Erection

Affiliated Metal Industries Inc............ F 440 235-3345
  Olmsted Falls (G-12075)
Atlantic Welding LLC......................... F 937 570-5094
  Piqua (G-12505)
Chagrin Vly Stl Erectors Inc............... F 440 975-1556
  Willoughby Hills (G-16023)
Chc Fabricating Corp......................... D 513 821-7757
  Cincinnati (G-2729)
Concord Fabricators Inc.................... E 614 875-2500
  Grove City (G-8083)
Evers Welding Co Inc........................ F 513 385-7352
  Cincinnati (G-2887)
Frederick Steel Company LLC.......... D 513 821-6400
  Cincinnati (G-2922)
G & P Construction LLC.................... E 855 494-4830
  North Royalton (G-11875)
Lake Building Products Inc................ E 216 486-1500
  Cleveland (G-4306)
Marysville Steel Inc........................... E 937 642-5971
  Marysville (G-9927)
Mound Technologies Inc................... F 937 748-2937
  Springboro (G-13511)

Pro-Fab Inc.. E 330 644-0044
  Akron (G-284)
Rex Welding Inc................................ F 740 387-1650
  Marion (G-9875)
Rittman Inc.. D 330 927-6855
  Rittman (G-12827)
Smith Brothers Erection Inc............... G 740 373-3575
  Marietta (G-9826)

CONTRACTORS: Tile Installation, Ceramic

Prints & Paints Flr Cvg Co Inc........... E 419 462-5663
  Galion (G-7883)

CONTRACTORS: Underground Utilities

Great Lakes Crushing Ltd................. D 440 944-5500
  Wickliffe (G-15833)

CONTRACTORS: Ventilation & Duct Work

A A S Amels Sheet Meta L Inc......... F 330 793-9326
  Youngstown (G-16297)
Franck and Fric Incorporated............ D 216 524-4451
  Cleveland (G-4090)
Jacobs Mechanical Co...................... C 513 681-6800
  Cincinnati (G-3033)

CONTRACTORS: Warm Air Heating & Air Conditioning

Controls and Sheet Metal Inc............ E 513 721-3610
  Cincinnati (G-2793)
Daikin Applied Americas Inc............. G 614 351-9862
  Westerville (G-15697)
Glt Inc... F 937 237-0055
  Dayton (G-6358)
Style Crest Enterprises Inc............... D 419 355-8586
  Fremont (G-7811)
Yanfeng US Auto Intr Systems I....... E 419 662-4905
  Northwood (G-11935)

CONTRACTORS: Water Well Drilling

Stoepfel Drilling Co........................... G 419 532-3307
  Ottawa (G-12194)

CONTRACTORS: Well Logging Svcs

Oaktree Wireline LLC....................... G 330 352-7250
  New Philadelphia (G-11520)

CONTRACTORS: Windows & Doors

Artisan Constructors LLC.................. E 216 800-7641
  Cleveland (G-3680)
Golden Angle Archtctral Group......... G 614 531-7932
  Columbus (G-5406)
Seemray LLC.................................... E 440 536-8705
  Cleveland (G-4685)
Traichal Construction Company........ E 800 255-3667
  Niles (G-11689)

CONTRACTORS: Wood Floor Installation & Refinishing

Hoover & Wells Inc........................... C 419 691-9220
  Toledo (G-14319)

CONTRACTORS: Wrecking & Demolition

Allgeier & Son Inc............................. F 513 574-3735
  Cincinnati (G-2611)
Rnw Holdings Inc.............................. E 330 792-0600
  Youngstown (G-16429)

CONTROL EQPT: Electric

Cincinnati Ctrl Dynamics Inc............. G 513 242-7300
  Cincinnati (G-2746)

Controls Inc....................................... E 330 239-4345
  Medina (G-10317)
Davis Technologies Inc..................... F 330 823-2544
  Alliance (G-401)
Machine Drive Company................... D 513 793-7077
  Cincinnati (G-3172)
R-K Electronics Inc........................... F 513 204-6060
  Mason (G-10040)
Rockwell Automation Inc................... B 330 425-3211
  Twinsburg (G-1427)
Spang & Company............................ E 440 350-6108
  Mentor (G-1055)
Superb Industries Inc........................ D 330 852-0500
  Sugarcreek (G-13943)
Uvonics Co.. F 614 458-1163
  Columbus (G-5852)

CONTROL EQPT: Electric Buses & Locomotives

Precision Design Inc......................... G 419 289-1553
  Ashland (G-605)

CONTROL EQPT: Noise

Acon Inc.. G 513 276-2111
  Tipp City (G-14121)
Keene Building Products Co............. D 440 605-1020
  Cleveland (G-4279)
Kinetics Noise Control Inc................. C 614 889-0480
  Dublin (G-6905)
Seneca Environmental Products Inc. E 419 447-1282
  Tiffin (G-14104)
Tech Products Corporation............... F 937 438-1100
  Miamisburg (G-10690)

CONTROLS & ACCESS: Indl, Electric

Apex Control Systems Inc................. D 330 938-2588
  Sebring (G-13117)
Avtron Holdings LLC......................... E 216 642-1230
  Cleveland (G-3710)
Corrotec Inc....................................... E 937 325-3585
  Springfield (G-1547)
Filnor Inc... F 330 821-8731
  Alliance (G-403)
Miami Control Systems Inc............... G 937 233-8146
  Dayton (G-6438)
PMC Systems Limited....................... E 330 538-2268
  North Jackson (G-11789)
Rockwell Automation Inc................... D 440 646-5000
  Cleveland (G-4644)
Tekworx LLC..................................... F 513 533-4777
  Blue Ash (G-14129)

CONTROLS & ACCESS: Motor

Eaton Corporation............................. B 440 523-5000
  Cleveland (G-3994)
Eaton Electrical................................. F 787 257-4470
  Cleveland (G-3996)
Standex Electronics Inc..................... D 513 871-3777
  Fairfield (G-7417)

CONTROLS: Automatic Temperature

Acutemp Thermal Systems............... F 937 312-0114
  Moraine (G-11112)
Building Ctrl Integrators LLC............. G 513 247-6154
  Cincinnati (G-2694)
Building Ctrl Integrators LLC............. G 513 860-9600
  West Chester (G-15542)
Building Ctrl Integrators LLC............. E 614 334-3300
  Powell (G-12667)
Energy & Ctrl Integrators Inc............. G 419 222-0025
  Lima (G-9240)

PRODUCT SECTION

CONVEYORS & CONVEYING EQPT

Ignio Systems LLC.................................. G 419 708-0503
 Toledo *(G-14326)*

CONTROLS: Electric Motor

Ignio Systems LLC.................................. G 419 708-0503
 Toledo *(G-14326)*

Toledo Electromotive Inc.......................... G 419 874-7751
 Perrysburg *(G-12438)*

TT Electronics Integrated M..................... B 440 352-8961
 Perry *(G-12357)*

CONTROLS: Environmental

Ademco Inc.. G 440 439-7002
 Bedford *(G-1098)*

Ademco Inc.. F 513 772-1851
 Blue Ash *(G-1358)*

Alan Manufacturing Inc............................ E 330 262-1555
 Wooster *(G-16099)*

Babcock & Wilcox Company.................... A 330 753-4511
 Akron *(G-73)*

Bry-Air Inc... E 740 965-2974
 Sunbury *(G-13951)*

Cincinnati Air Conditioning Co................. D 513 721-5622
 Cincinnati *(G-2739)*

Columbus Controls Inc............................ E 614 882-9029
 Columbus *(G-5264)*

Doan/Pyramid Solutions LLC.................. D 216 587-9510
 Cleveland *(G-3965)*

Dyoung Enterprise Inc............................. C 440 918-0505
 Willoughby *(G-15913)*

Envirnment Ctrl Sthwest Ohio I............... E 937 669-9900
 Tipp City *(G-14134)*

Future Controls Corporation..................... E 440 275-3191
 Austinburg *(G-747)*

Helm Instrument Company Inc............... E 419 893-4356
 Maumee *(G-10205)*

Honeywell International Inc..................... A 937 484-2000
 Urbana *(G-14835)*

Hunter Defense Tech Inc......................... E 216 438-6111
 Solon *(G-13363)*

Integrated Development & Mfg................ F 440 543-2423
 Chagrin Falls *(G-2403)*

Integrated Development & Mfg................ F 440 247-5100
 Chagrin Falls *(G-2380)*

Karman Rubber Company....................... D 330 864-2161
 Akron *(G-201)*

Logisync Corporation................................ F 440 937-0388
 Avon *(G-780)*

Parker-Hannifin Corporation.................... G 216 433-1795
 Cleveland *(G-4531)*

Pepperl + Fuchs Inc................................ C 330 425-3555
 Twinsburg *(G-14709)*

Pepperl + Fuchs Entps Inc..................... F 330 425-3555
 Twinsburg *(G-14710)*

Ruskin Manufacturing............................... G 937 476-6500
 Dayton *(G-6172)*

Sje Rhombus Controls............................. G 419 281-5767
 Ashland *(G-614)*

Skuttle Mfg Co... F 740 373-9169
 Marietta *(G-9825)*

Tridelta Industries Inc.............................. G 440 255-1080
 Mentor *(G-10584)*

Ventra Sandusky LLC............................. B 419 627-3600
 Sandusky *(G-13103)*

Vib-Iso LLC.. F 800 735-9645
 Wooster *(G-16180)*

Vortec Corporation................................... E
 Blue Ash *(G-1489)*

CONTROLS: Hydronic

Certified Labs & Service Inc................... G 419 289-7462
 Ashland *(G-563)*

CONTROLS: Thermostats, Built-in

Therm-O-Disc Incorporated..................... A 419 525-8500
 Westerville *(G-15681)*

CONVENIENCE STORES

Tbone Sales LLC..................................... F 330 897-6131
 Baltic *(G-841)*

CONVEYOR SYSTEMS

2e Associates Inc.................................... E 440 975-9955
 Willoughby *(G-15871)*

Hostar International Inc........................... F 440 564-5362
 Solon *(G-13362)*

Ulterior Products LLC.............................. G 614 441-9465
 Radnor *(G-12696)*

CONVEYOR SYSTEMS: Belt, General Indl Use

Allgaier Process Technology.................... G 513 402-2566
 West Chester *(G-15363)*

Blair Rubber Company............................ D 330 769-5583
 Seville *(G-13137)*

Conveyor Solutions LLC......................... F 513 367-4845
 Cleves *(G-4948)*

Manufacturers Equipment Co.................. F 513 424-3573
 Middletown *(G-10841)*

Mayfran International Inc........................ E 440 461-4100
 Cleveland *(G-4373)*

Mfh Partners Inc...................................... B 440 461-4100
 Cleveland *(G-4398)*

Midwest Conveyor Products Inc............. E 419 281-1235
 Ashland *(G-592)*

CONVEYOR SYSTEMS: Bucket Type

Fenner Dunlop Port Clinton LLC............ C 419 635-2191
 Port Clinton *(G-12618)*

Joy Global Underground Min LLC.......... E 440 248-7970
 Cleveland *(G-4262)*

CONVEYOR SYSTEMS: Bulk Handling

Air Technical Industries Inc.................... E 440 951-5191
 Mentor *(G-10409)*

Bulk Handling Equipment Co.................. G 330 468-5703
 Northfield *(G-11904)*

Lewco Inc... C 419 625-4014
 Sandusky *(G-13074)*

Webster Industries Inc............................ B 419 447-8232
 Tiffin *(G-14115)*

CONVEYOR SYSTEMS: Pneumatic Tube

American Solving Inc............................... G 440 234-7373
 Brookpark *(G-1703)*

Fred D Pfening Company........................ E 614 294-5361
 Columbus *(G-5389)*

Schenck Process LLC............................. F 513 576-9200
 Solon *(G-13419)*

CONVEYOR SYSTEMS: Robotic

Automation Systems Design Inc............. E 937 387-0351
 Dayton *(G-6218)*

Grob Systems Inc.................................... A 419 358-9015
 Bluffton *(G-1504)*

Imperial Conveying Systems LLC........... F 330 491-3200
 Canton *(G-2130)*

CONVEYORS & CONVEYING EQPT

Ad Industries Inc...................................... A 303 744-1911
 Dayton *(G-6183)*

Advanced Equipment Systems LLC........ G 216 289-6505
 Euclid *(G-7258)*

Alan Bortree... G 937 585-6962
 De Graff *(G-6664)*

Alba Manufacturing Inc........................... D 513 874-0551
 Fairfield *(G-7332)*

Allied Consolidated Inds Inc................... C 330 744-0808
 Youngstown *(G-16307)*

Allied Fabricating & Wldg Co................. E 614 751-6664
 Columbus *(G-5113)*

Ambaflex Inc.. E 330 478-1858
 Canton *(G-2034)*

Barth Industries Co LLC......................... E 216 267-1950
 Cleveland *(G-3722)*

Bobco Enterprises Inc............................. F 419 867-3560
 Toledo *(G-14215)*

Bry-Air Inc... E 740 965-2974
 Sunbury *(G-13951)*

C A Litzler Co Inc................................... E 216 267-8020
 Cleveland *(G-3778)*

Cincinnati Mine Machinery Co................ D 513 522-7777
 Cincinnati *(G-2755)*

Coating Systems Group Inc.................... F 440 816-9306
 Middleburg Heights *(G-10717)*

Con-Belt Inc... F 330 273-2003
 Valley City *(G-14865)*

Conveyor Metal Works Inc..................... E 740 477-8700
 Frankfort *(G-7657)*

Conveyor Technologies Ltd.................... G 513 248-0663
 Milford *(G-10903)*

Daifuku America Corporation................. C 614 863-1888
 Reynoldsburg *(G-12760)*

Decision Systems Inc.............................. F 330 456-7600
 Canton *(G-2090)*

Defabco Inc.. D 614 231-2700
 Columbus *(G-5323)*

Dematic Corp... D 440 526-2770
 Brecksville *(G-1612)*

Dillin Engineered Systems Corp............. E 419 666-6789
 Perrysburg *(G-12376)*

Dover Conveyor Inc................................. E 740 922-9390
 Midvale *(G-10876)*

Duplex Mill & Manufacturing Co............. E 937 325-5555
 Springfield *(G-13557)*

Eagle Crusher Co Inc.............................. D 419 468-2288
 Galion *(G-7872)*

Enviri Corporation.................................... F 740 387-1150
 Marion *(G-9851)*

ES Industries Inc..................................... F 419 643-2625
 Lima *(G-9242)*

Esco Turbine Tech Cleveland................. F 440 953-0053
 Eastlake *(G-7030)*

Fabacraft Inc.. E 513 677-0500
 Maineville *(G-9600)*

Fabco Inc.. E 419 422-4533
 Findlay *(G-7504)*

Falcon Industries Inc............................... E 330 723-0099
 Medina *(G-10322)*

Federal Equipment Company.................. D 513 621-5260
 Cincinnati *(G-2899)*

Feedall Inc.. F 440 942-8100
 Willoughby *(G-15920)*

Fki Logistex Automation Inc.................... A 513 881-5251
 West Chester *(G-15554)*

Formtek Inc.. D 216 292-4460
 Cleveland *(G-4084)*

Glassline Corporation.............................. E 419 666-9712
 Perrysburg *(G-12385)*

Global TBM Company............................. C 440 248-3303
 Solon *(G-13355)*

Gray-Eering Ltd....................................... G 740 498-8816
 Tippecanoe *(G-14171)*

Hawthorne-Seving Inc............................. E 419 643-5531
 Cridersville *(G-6041)*

Employee Codes: A=Over 500 employees, B=251-500
C=101-250, D=51-100, E=20-50, F=10-19, G=1-9

CONVEYORS & CONVEYING EQPT

Ibiza Holdings Inc .... G 513 701-7300
　Mason (G-10004)
Innovative Controls Corp .... E 419 691-6684
　Toledo (G-14333)
Ins Robotics Inc .... G 888 293-5325
　Hilliard (G-8414)
Intelligrated Inc .... A 513 874-0788
　West Chester (G-15565)
Intelligrated Inc .... E 866 936-7300
　Mason (G-10007)
Intelligrated Headquarters LLC .... E 866 936-7300
　Mason (G-10008)
Intelligrated Products LLC .... E 740 490-0300
　London (G-9389)
Intelligrated Sub Holdings Inc .... D 513 701-7300
　Mason (G-10009)
Intelligrated Systems Inc .... C 513 881-5136
　West Chester (G-15448)
Intelligrated Systems Inc .... A 866 936-7300
　Mason (G-10010)
Intelligrated Systems LLC .... A 513 701-7300
　Mason (G-10011)
Intelligrated Systems Ohio LLC .... G 513 682-6600
　West Chester (G-15566)
Intelligrated Systems Ohio LLC .... A 513 701-7300
　Mason (G-10012)
Kleenline LLC .... F 800 259-5973
　Loveland (G-9489)
Kolinahr Systems Inc .... F 513 745-9401
　Blue Ash (G-1417)
Laser Automation Inc .... F 440 543-9291
　Chagrin Falls (G-2405)
Logitech Inc .... E 614 871-2822
　Grove City (G-8102)
Material Holdings Inc .... E 513 583-5500
　Loveland (G-9494)
Met Fab Fabrication and Mch .... G 513 724-3715
　Batavia (G-933)
Miller Products Inc .... E 330 308-5934
　New Philadelphia (G-11518)
Mulhern Belting Inc .... E 201 337-5700
　Fairfield (G-7386)
Nesco Inc .... E 440 461-6000
　Cleveland (G-4448)
Ocs Intellitrak Inc .... F 513 742-5600
　Fairfield (G-7388)
Ohio Magnetics Inc .... E 216 662-8484
　Maple Heights (G-9756)
Opw Engineered Systems Inc .... E 888 771-9438
　West Chester (G-15471)
PB Fbrction Mech Contrs Corp .... E 419 478-4869
　Toledo (G-14429)
Pfpc Enterprises Inc .... F 513 941-6200
　Cincinnati (G-3253)
Pneumatic Scale Corporation .... C 330 923-0491
　Cuyahoga Falls (G-6109)
Pomacon Inc .... F 330 273-1576
　Brunswick (G-1781)
Pro Mach Inc .... D 513 771-7374
　Cincinnati (G-3278)
Quickdraft Inc .... E 330 477-4574
　Canton (G-2206)
Richmond Machine Co .... E 419 485-5740
　Montpelier (G-11142)
Rolcon Inc .... F 513 821-7259
　Cincinnati (G-3349)
Sandusky Fabricating & Sls Inc .... E 419 626-4465
　Sandusky (G-13089)
Sparks Belting Company Inc .... G 216 398-7774
　Cleveland (G-4719)
Spirex Corporation .... C 330 726-1166
　Youngstown (G-16268)

Stacy Equipment Co .... G 419 447-6903
　Tiffin (G-14106)
Stock Equipment Company Inc .... C 440 543-6000
　Chagrin Falls (G-2424)
Stock Fairfield Corporation .... C 440 543-6000
　Solon (G-13425)
Sweet Manufacturing Company .... E 937 325-1511
　Springfield (G-13641)
Tkf Conveyor Systems LLC .... C 513 621-5260
　Cincinnati (G-3457)
Uhrden Inc .... E 330 456-0031
　Canton (G-2249)
Werks Kraft Engineering LLC .... E 330 721-7374
　Medina (G-10394)

COOKING & FOODWARMING EQPT: Commercial

Belanger Inc .... D 517 870-3206
　West Chester (G-15375)
Cleveland Range LLC .... C 216 481-4900
　Cleveland (G-3852)
Lima Sheet Metal Machine & Mfg .... E 419 229-1161
　Lima (G-9264)
Siebtechnik Tema Inc .... E 513 489-7811
　Cincinnati (G-3390)
Stellar Process Inc .... F 866 777-4725
　Twinsburg (G-14737)

COOKING EQPT, HOUSEHOLD: Ranges, Gas

Z Line Kitchen and Bath LLC .... G 614 777-5004
　Marysville (G-9944)

COOLING TOWERS: Metal

Air-Tech Mechanical Inc .... F 419 292-0074
　Toledo (G-14180)

COPPER: Rolling & Drawing

Production Tube Cutting Inc .... E 937 254-6138
　Dayton (G-6530)
T & D Fabricating Inc .... E 440 951-5646
　Eastlake (G-7051)

CORD & TWINE

International Jump Rope Union .... G 937 409-1006
　Springboro (G-13505)

CORRECTION FLUID

Milacron LLC .... E 513 487-5000
　Blue Ash (G-1439)

CORRUGATING MACHINES

Rebiltco Inc .... G 513 424-2024
　Middletown (G-10854)

COSMETIC PREPARATIONS

AA Hand Sanitizer .... G 513 506-7575
　Cincinnati (G-2587)
B & P Company Inc .... G 937 298-0265
　Dayton (G-6221)
Bonne Bell Inc .... C 440 835-2440
　Westlake (G-15739)
Bonne Bell LLC .... C 440 835-2440
　Westlake (G-15740)
KAO Brands Company .... G 513 977-2931
　Cincinnati (G-3061)
KAO USA Inc .... F 513 629-5210
　Cincinnati (G-3063)
KAO USA Inc .... B 513 421-1400
　Cincinnati (G-3062)
Kdc One .... G 614 984-2871
　New Albany (G-11382)

Kdc US Holdings Inc .... F 434 845-7073
　Groveport (G-8138)
Merle Norman Cosmetics Inc .... E 419 282-0630
　Mansfield (G-9650)
Natural Essentials Inc .... C 330 562-8022
　Streetsboro (G-12781)
Olay LLC .... C 787 535-2191
　Blue Ash (G-1445)
Tri-Tech Laboratories LLC .... C 614 656-1130
　New Albany (G-11391)
Universal Packg Systems Inc .... C 513 732-2000
　Batavia (G-957)
Universal Packg Systems Inc .... C 513 735-4777
　Batavia (G-958)
Universal Packg Systems Inc .... C 513 674-9400
　Cincinnati (G-3453)
Veepak OH LLC .... F 740 927-9002
　New Albany (G-11393)

COSMETICS & TOILETRIES

Abitec Corporation .... E 614 429-6464
　Columbus (G-5620)
Bath & Body Works LLC .... B 614 856-6000
　Reynoldsburg (G-12753)
Brand5 LLC .... F 614 920-9254
　Pickerington (G-12457)
Cameo Inc .... G 419 661-9611
　Perrysburg (G-12367)
Colgate-Palmolive Company .... C 212 310-2000
　Cambridge (G-1929)
French Transit LLC .... G 650 431-3959
　Mason (G-9994)
Gojo Industries Inc .... C 330 255-6000
　Akron (G-170)
High Ridge Brands Co .... G 614 497-1660
　Columbus (G-5633)
Interco Division 0 Ohio Inc .... G 614 875-2959
　Grove City (G-8099)
Kathleen Williams .... G 740 360-3515
　Marion (G-9852)
Luminex HM Dcor Frgrnce Hldg C .... B 513 563-1113
　Blue Ash (G-1447)
Meridian Industries Inc .... E 330 359-5809
　Beach City (G-168)
My Soaps LLC .... G 614 832-4634
　Johnstown (G-9775)
Natural Essentials Inc .... F 330 562-8022
　Aurora (G-726)
Nehemiah Manufacturing Co LLC .... D 513 351-5700
　Cincinnati (G-3185)
Primal Life Organics LLC .... E 800 260-4946
　Copley (G-595)
Procter & Gamble Mexico Inc .... G 513 983-1100
　Cincinnati (G-3297)
Procter & Gamble Mfg Co .... C 419 226-5500
　Lima (G-9278)
Sysco Guest Supply LLC .... E 440 960-2515
　Lorain (G-9440)
Tri-Tech Laboratories LLC .... G 434 845-7073
　Groveport (G-8164)
US Cotton LLC .... D 216 676-6400
　Cleveland (G-4356)
Woodbine Products Company .... F 330 725-0165
　Medina (G-10395)
Zena Baby Soap Company .... G 216 317-6433
　Bedford Heights (G-1182)

COSMETOLOGY & PERSONAL HYGIENE SALONS

Pur Hair Extensions LLC .... G 330 786-5772
　Akron (G-287)

COUNTER & SINK TOPS

3jd Inc..................................F 513 324-9655
  Moraine *(G-11151)*
Benchmark-Cabinets LLC..................G 740 694-1144
  Fredericktown *(G-7739)*
Cameo Countertops Inc..................E 419 865-6371
  Holland *(G-8496)*
Countertop Sales..................F 614 626-4476
  Columbus *(G-5300)*
Crafted Surface and Stone LLC..................E 440 658-3799
  Chagrin Falls *(G-2391)*
Formica Corporation..................E 513 786-3400
  Cincinnati *(G-2916)*
Gross & Sons Custom Millwork..................G 419 227-0214
  Lima *(G-9246)*
Zanesville Fabricators Inc..................G 740 452-2439
  Zanesville *(G-16573)*

COUNTERS OR COUNTER DISPLAY CASES, EXC WOOD

Formatech Inc..................E 330 273-2800
  Brunswick *(G-1760)*
Stiber Fabricating Inc..................F 216 771-7210
  Cleveland *(G-4735)*

COUNTERS OR COUNTER DISPLAY CASES, WOOD

Counter Concepts Inc..................F 330 848-4848
  Doylestown *(G-6853)*
Formatech Inc..................E 330 273-2800
  Brunswick *(G-1760)*
Kinsella Manufacturing Co Inc..................F 513 561-5285
  Cincinnati *(G-3077)*

COUNTING DEVICES: Controls, Revolution & Timing

L3harris Electrodynamics Inc..................C 847 259-0740
  Cincinnati *(G-2569)*
Thermo Gamma-Metrics LLC..................E 858 450-9811
  Bedford *(G-1157)*

COUNTING DEVICES: Tachometer, Centrifugal

Lake Shore Cryotronics Inc..................D 614 891-2243
  Westerville *(G-15662)*

COUPLINGS: Hose & Tube, Hydraulic Or Pneumatic

Custom Cltch Jint Hydrlics Inc..................F 216 431-1630
  Cleveland *(G-3923)*
Dyna-Flex Inc..................F 440 946-9424
  Painesville *(G-12230)*

COUPLINGS: Pipe

B S F Inc..................F 937 890-6121
  Tipp City *(G-14123)*
B S F Inc..................F 937 890-6121
  Dayton *(G-6222)*

COUPLINGS: Shaft

B S F Inc..................F 937 890-6121
  Tipp City *(G-14123)*
B S F Inc..................F 937 890-6121
  Dayton *(G-6222)*
Bowes Manufacturing Inc..................E 216 378-2110
  Solon *(G-13321)*
Climax Metal Products Company..................D 440 943-8898
  Mentor *(G-10440)*

COVERS: Automobile Seat

Besi Manufacturing Inc..................G 513 874-1460
  West Chester *(G-15377)*
Besi Manufacturing Inc..................E 513 874-0232
  West Chester *(G-15378)*
Griffin Fisher Co Inc..................G 513 961-2110
  Cincinnati *(G-2973)*

CRANE & AERIAL LIFT SVCS

IBI Brake Products Inc..................G 440 543-7962
  Chagrin Falls *(G-2402)*
Konecranes Inc..................F 440 461-8400
  Broadview Heights *(G-1660)*
Pollock Research & Design Inc..................E 330 332-3300
  Salem *(G-13023)*
Rex Welding Inc..................F 740 387-1650
  Marion *(G-9875)*

CRANES & MONORAIL SYSTEMS

Crane 1 Services Inc..................E 937 704-9900
  West Chester *(G-15408)*
Emh Inc..................D 330 220-8600
  Valley City *(G-14869)*

CRANES: Indl Plant

Demag Cranes & Components Corp..................C 440 248-2400
  Solon *(G-13337)*
Hiab USA Inc..................D 419 482-6000
  Perrysburg *(G-12388)*
Kci Holding USA Inc..................F 937 525-5533
  Springfield *(G-13587)*
Konecranes Inc..................F 937 328-5100
  Springfield *(G-13589)*
Konecranes Inc..................B 937 525-5533
  Springfield *(G-13590)*
Radocy Inc..................F 419 666-4400
  Rossford *(G-12870)*

CRANES: Indl Truck

Hoist Equipment Co Inc..................E 440 232-0300
  Bedford Heights *(G-1174)*
Skylift Inc..................D 440 960-2100
  Lorain *(G-9438)*
Venturo Manufacturing Inc..................F 513 772-8448
  Cincinnati *(G-3492)*

CRANES: Overhead

ACC Automation Co Inc..................E 330 928-3821
  Akron *(G-14)*
Altec Industries Inc..................E 205 408-2341
  Cuyahoga Falls *(G-6062)*
Morgan Engineering Systems Inc..................E 330 821-4721
  Alliance *(G-414)*
Morgan Engineering Systems Inc..................E 330 823-6130
  Alliance *(G-415)*
Rnm Holdings Inc..................F 614 444-5556
  Columbus *(G-5726)*

CROWNS & CLOSURES

Boardman Molded Products Inc..................D 330 788-2400
  Youngstown *(G-16322)*
Eisenhauer Mfg Co LLC..................D 419 238-0081
  Van Wert *(G-14915)*

CRUDE PETROLEUM & NATURAL GAS PRODUCTION

Bijoe Development Inc..................E 330 674-5981
  Millersburg *(G-10946)*
Exco Resources LLC..................F 740 254-4061
  Tippecanoe *(G-14169)*
John D Oil and Gas Company..................G 440 255-6325
  Mentor *(G-10484)*
Kenoil Inc..................G 330 262-1144
  Wooster *(G-16141)*
Pin Oak Energy Partners LLC..................F 888 748-0763
  Akron *(G-275)*

CRUDE PETROLEUM PRODUCTION

Apache Acquisitions LLC..................G 419 782-8003
  Defiance *(G-6669)*
Bakerwell Inc..................E 330 276-2161
  Killbuck *(G-8916)*
Buckeye Oil Producing Co..................F 330 264-8847
  Wooster *(G-16108)*
Cameron Drilling Co Inc..................F 740 453-3300
  Zanesville *(G-16516)*
Cgas Exploration Inc..................G 614 436-4631
  Worthington *(G-16190)*
Cgas Inc..................F 614 975-4697
  Worthington *(G-16191)*
Derrick Petroleum Inc..................G 740 668-5711
  Bladensburg *(G-1346)*
Devco Oil Inc..................F 740 439-3833
  Cambridge *(G-1932)*
Dome Drilling Company..................G 440 892-9434
  Westlake *(G-15746)*
Elkhead Gas & Oil Co..................G 740 763-3966
  Newark *(G-11574)*
Exco Resources (pa) LLC..................F 740 796-5231
  Adamsville *(G-7)*
Franklin Gas & Oil Company LLC..................G 330 264-8739
  Wooster *(G-16120)*
Green Energy Inc..................G 330 262-5112
  Wooster *(G-16125)*
Henthorne Jr Jay Mary Beth..................G 330 264-1049
  Wooster *(G-16130)*
Knight Material Tech LLC..................D 330 488-1651
  East Canton *(G-6979)*
Marietta Resources Corporation..................F 740 373-6305
  Marietta *(G-9806)*
Robert Barr..................G 740 826-7325
  New Concord *(G-11433)*
Tatum Petroleum Corporation..................F 740 819-6810
  Worthington *(G-16214)*
Triad Hunter LLC..................F 740 374-2940
  Marietta *(G-9839)*
W H Patten Drilling Co Inc..................G 330 674-3046
  Millersburg *(G-11004)*
W P Brown Enterprises Inc..................G 740 685-2594
  Byesville *(G-1902)*
William S Miller Inc..................G 330 223-1794
  Kensington *(G-8791)*
Xto Energy Inc..................G 740 671-9901
  Bellaire *(G-1190)*

CRYOGENIC COOLING DEVICES: Infrared Detectors, Masers

Advanced Cryogenic Entps LLC..................G 330 922-0750
  Akron *(G-22)*
Drivetrain USA Inc..................F 614 733-0940
  Plain City *(G-12576)*
Lake Shore Cryotronics Inc..................D 614 891-2243
  Westerville *(G-15662)*

CULVERTS: Sheet Metal

Contech Engnered Solutions Inc..................E 513 645-7000
  West Chester *(G-15402)*
Edwards Sheet Metal Works Inc..................E 740 694-0010
  Fredericktown *(G-7745)*

CUPS: Paper, Made From Purchased Materials

American Greetings Corporation .... A 216 252-7300
Cleveland (G-3652)

Graphic Packaging Intl LLC .... B 419 673-0711
Kenton (G-8884)

Ricking Holding Co .... E 513 825-3551
Cleveland (G-4633)

CURBING: Granite Or Stone

Distinctive Marble & Gran Inc .... F 614 760-0003
Plain City (G-12575)

Granex Industries Inc .... F 440 248-4915
Solon (G-13356)

CURTAINS: Window, From Purchased Materials

Style-Line Incorporated .... E 614 291-0600
Columbus (G-5796)

CUSHIONS & PILLOWS

Dorex LLC .... G 216 271-7064
Newburgh Heights (G-11613)

Easy Way Leisure Company LLC .... E 513 731-5640
Cincinnati (G-2855)

Greendale Home Fashions LLC .... D 859 916-5475
Cincinnati (G-2971)

CUSHIONS & PILLOWS: Bed, From Purchased Materials

Brentwood Originals Inc .... C 330 793-2255
Youngstown (G-16324)

Down-Lite International Inc .... C 513 229-3696
Mason (G-9985)

Downhome Inc .... E 513 921-3373
Cincinnati (G-2839)

Downhome Inc .... E 513 921-3373
Cincinnati (G-2840)

CUSHIONS: Carpet & Rug, Foamed Plastics

Johnsonite Inc .... B 440 632-3441
Middlefield (G-10761)

Scottdel Cushion Inc .... E 419 825-0432
Swanton (G-13981)

Solo Products Inc .... F 513 321-7884
Cincinnati (G-3402)

CUSTOM COMPOUNDING OF RUBBER MATERIALS

Bdu Holdings Inc .... F 330 374-1810
Akron (G-80)

Dnh Mixing Inc .... E 330 296-6327
Mogadore (G-11069)

Gen-Rubber LLC .... G 440 655-3643
Galion (G-7877)

Killian Latex Inc .... F 330 644-6746
Akron (G-207)

Kiltex Corporation .... F 330 644-6746
Akron (G-208)

Polymerics Inc .... E 330 928-2210
Cuyahoga Falls (G-6110)

Prcc Holdings Inc .... C 330 798-4790
Copley (G-5953)

Preferred Compounding Corp .... C 330 798-4790
Barberton (G-892)

Wayne County Rubber Inc .... E 330 264-5553
Wooster (G-16181)

CUT STONE & STONE PRODUCTS

Agean Marble Manufacturing .... F 513 874-1475
West Chester (G-15533)

As America Inc .... E 419 522-4211
Mansfield (G-9626)

Bell Vault and Monu Works Inc .... E 937 866-2444
Miamisburg (G-10615)

Blu Bird LLC .... F 513 271-5646
Cincinnati (G-2672)

Blu Bird LLC .... G 614 276-3585
Columbus (G-5202)

Castelli Marble LLC .... G 216 361-1222
Cleveland (G-3799)

Classic Stone Company Inc .... F 614 833-3946
Columbus (G-5252)

Dutch Quality Stone Inc .... D 877 359-7866
Mount Eaton (G-11229)

Jack Huffman .... G 740 384-5178
Wellston (G-15329)

Kellstone Inc .... E 419 746-2396
Kelleys Island (G-8789)

Lang Stone Company Inc .... E 614 235-4099
Columbus (G-5520)

Lima Millwork Inc .... F 419 331-3303
Elida (G-7094)

Marsh Industries Inc .... E 330 308-8667
New Philadelphia (G-11515)

Maumee Valley Memorials Inc .... F 419 878-9030
Waterville (G-15250)

Medina Supply Company .... E 330 723-3681
Medina (G-10352)

Melvin Stone Co LLC .... F 513 771-0820
Cincinnati (G-3147)

National Lime and Stone Co .... E 419 562-0771
Bucyrus (G-1863)

National Lime and Stone Co .... E 419 396-7671
Carey (G-2281)

North Hill Marble & Granite Co .... F 330 253-2179
Akron (G-267)

Pavestone LLC .... D 513 474-3783
Cincinnati (G-3242)

Riceland Cabinet Inc .... D 330 601-1071
Wooster (G-16163)

Shelly Materials Inc .... G 937 358-2224
West Mansfield (G-15628)

Sims-Lohman Inc .... D 440 799-8285
Brooklyn Heights (G-1701)

Solid Surface Concepts Inc .... E 513 948-8677
Cincinnati (G-3401)

Studio Vertu Inc .... G 513 241-9038
Cincinnati (G-3426)

Take It For Granite LLC .... F 513 735-0555
Cincinnati (G-2574)

Transtar Holding Company .... G 800 359-3339
Walton Hills (G-15103)

Western Ohio Cut Stone Ltd .... F 937 492-4722
Sidney (G-13295)

CUTLERY

American Punch Co .... E 216 731-4501
Euclid (G-7262)

Crescent Manufacturing Company .... D 419 332-6484
Fremont (G-7772)

Edgewell Per Care Brands LLC .... F 330 527-2191
Garrettsville (G-7914)

G & S Metal Products Co Inc .... C 216 441-0700
Cleveland (G-4096)

General Cutlery Inc .... F 419 332-2316
Fremont (G-7786)

Libbey Glass LLC .... C 419 727-2211
Toledo (G-14365)

Madison Property Holdings Inc .... E 800 215-3210
Cincinnati (G-3174)

Npk Construction Equipment Inc .... D 440 232-7900
Bedford (G-1145)

CYCLIC CRUDES & INTERMEDIATES

Color Products Inc .... G 513 860-2749
Hamilton (G-8194)

Ferro Corporation .... E 330 682-8015
Orrville (G-1212)

Marathon Petroleum Company LP .... F 419 422-2121
Findlay (G-7532)

Neyra Interstate Inc .... E 513 733-1000
Cincinnati (G-3176)

Polymerics Inc .... E 330 928-2210
Cuyahoga Falls (G-6110)

Standridge Color Corporation .... F 770 464-3362
Defiance (G-6655)

Sun Chemical Corporation .... D 513 753-9550
Amelia (G-467)

Sun Chemical Corporation .... C 513 681-5950
Cincinnati (G-3411)

CYLINDER & ACTUATORS: Fluid Power

Cascade Corporation .... D 937 327-0300
Springfield (G-1541)

Control Line Equipment Inc .... F 216 433-7766
Cleveland (G-3503)

Custom Hoists Inc .... C 419 368-4721
Ashland (G-570)

Cylinders and Valves Inc .... G 440 238-7343
Strongsville (G-3826)

Eaton Aeroquip LLC .... A 419 891-7775
Maumee (G-10201)

Eaton Leasing Corporation .... B 216 382-2292
Beachwood (G-86)

Hydraulic Parts Store Inc .... E 330 364-6667
New Philadelphia (G-11505)

Hydraulic Specialists Inc .... F 740 922-3343
Midvale (G-1083)

Ic-Fluid Power Inc .... F 419 661-8811
Rossford (G-12256)

North Coast Instruments Inc .... G 216 251-2353
Cleveland (G-4459)

Parker-Hannifin Corporation .... E 330 336-3511
Wadsworth (G-5051)

Parker-Hannifin Corporation .... A 216 896-3000
Cleveland (G-4532)

Robeck Fluid Power Co .... D 330 562-1140
Aurora (G-734)

Sebring Fluid Power Corp .... G 330 938-9984
Sebring (G-13136)

Skidmore-Wilhelm Mfg Company .... F 216 481-4774
Solon (G-13422)

Steel Eqp Specialists Inc .... D 330 823-8260
Alliance (G-427)

Suburban Manufacturing Co .... D 440 953-2024
Eastlake (G-705)

Swagelok Company .... D 440 349-5934
Solon (G-13431)

Xomox Pft Corp .... B 936 271-6500
Cincinnati (G-3532)

CYLINDERS: Pressure

Gayston Corporation .... C 937 743-6050
Miamisburg (G-0640)

Hutnik Company .... G 330 336-9700
Wadsworth (G-5035)

Toledo Metal Spinning Company .... E 419 535-5931
Toledo (G-1449)

Worthington Cylinder Corp .... D 740 569-4143
Bremen (G-1640)

PRODUCT SECTION

DAIRY PRDTS: Natural Cheese

Worthington Cylinder Corp..................... C 614 438-7900
  Columbus *(G-5882)*
Worthington Cylinder Corp..................... C 614 840-3800
  Westerville *(G-15690)*
Worthington Cylinder Corp..................... E 330 262-1762
  Wooster *(G-16188)*
Worthington Cylinder Corp..................... C 614 840-3210
  Worthington *(G-16219)*

CYLINDERS: Pump

Custom Cltch Jint Hydrlics Inc................. F 216 431-1630
  Cleveland *(G-3923)*
Eric Allshouse LLC............................. G 330 533-4258
  Canfield *(G-2005)*
Rolcon Inc..................................... F 513 821-7259
  Cincinnati *(G-3349)*

DAIRY PRDTS STORE: Butter

Nosh Butters LLC............................... G 773 710-0668
  Cleveland *(G-4482)*

DAIRY PRDTS STORE: Cheese

Cheese Holdings Inc............................ E 330 893-2479
  Millersburg *(G-10951)*
Grays Orange Barn Inc.......................... G 419 568-2718
  Wapakoneta *(G-15116)*
Great Lakes Cheese Co Inc...................... B 440 834-2500
  Hiram *(G-8485)*
Lori Holding Co................................ E 740 342-3230
  New Lexington *(G-11453)*

DAIRY PRDTS STORE: Ice Cream, Packaged

Jenis Splendid Ice Creams LLC.................. E 614 488-3224
  Columbus *(G-5492)*
Malleys Candies Inc............................ D 216 362-8700
  Cleveland *(G-4353)*
Milk Hney Cndy Soda Shoppe LLC................. F 330 492-5884
  Canton *(G-2165)*

DAIRY PRDTS STORES

Hans Rothenbuhler & Son Inc.................... E 440 632-6000
  Middlefield *(G-10753)*
United Dairy Inc............................... B 740 373-4121
  Marietta *(G-9841)*
United Dairy Farmers Inc....................... C 513 396-8700
  Cincinnati *(G-3479)*
Youngs Jersey Dairy Inc........................ B 937 325-0629
  Yellow Springs *(G-16290)*

DAIRY PRDTS: Butter

Black Radish Creamery Ltd...................... G 614 517-9520
  Columbus *(G-5197)*
Butt Kickn Creamery Inc........................ G 419 482-6610
  Perrysburg *(G-12366)*
California Creamery Operators.................. G 440 264-5351
  Solon *(G-13325)*
Dairy Farmers America Inc...................... E 330 670-7800
  Medina *(G-10317)*
Heavenly Creamery Inc.......................... G 440 593-6080
  Conneaut *(G-5920)*
Minerva Dairy Inc.............................. D 330 868-4196
  Minerva *(G-11035)*
New Dairy Cincinnati LLC....................... D 214 258-1200
  Cincinnati *(G-3188)*
New Dairy Ohio LLC............................. D 214 258-1200
  Cleveland *(G-4453)*

DAIRY PRDTS: Canned Milk, Whole

J M Smucker Company............................ A 330 682-3000
  Orrville *(G-12129)*
Nu Pet Company................................. F 330 682-3000
  Orrville *(G-12142)*

DAIRY PRDTS: Cheese

Amish Wedding Foods Inc........................ E 330 674-9199
  Millersburg *(G-10941)*
Dairy Farmers America Inc...................... E 330 670-7800
  Medina *(G-10317)*
Lake Erie Frozen Foods Mfg Co.................. D 419 289-9204
  Ashland *(G-588)*
Lakeview Farms LLC............................. C 419 695-9925
  Delphos *(G-6769)*
Land OLakes Inc................................ D 330 678-1578
  Kent *(G-8827)*
Lipari Foods Operating Co LLC.................. E 330 893-2479
  Millersburg *(G-10973)*
Lipari Foods Operating Co LLC.................. E 330 674-9199
  Millersburg *(G-10974)*
Tri State Dairy LLC............................ G 330 897-5555
  Baltic *(G-842)*

DAIRY PRDTS: Cheese, Cottage

United Dairy Inc............................... B 740 373-4121
  Marietta *(G-9841)*

DAIRY PRDTS: Condensed Milk

Eagle Family Foods Group LLC................... E 330 382-3725
  Cleveland *(G-3987)*

DAIRY PRDTS: Cream Substitutes

Instantwhip-Dayton Inc......................... G 937 435-4371
  Dayton *(G-6385)*
Instantwhip-Dayton Inc......................... G 937 235-5930
  Dayton *(G-6384)*

DAIRY PRDTS: Dietary Supplements, Dairy & Non-Dairy Based

Ai Life LLC.................................... F 513 605-1079
  Mason *(G-9947)*
All-In Nutritionals LLC........................ G 888 400-0333
  Springfield *(G-13530)*
Cbd Relieve ME Inc............................. G 216 544-1696
  Euclid *(G-7265)*
Freedom Health LLC............................. E 330 562-0888
  Aurora *(G-715)*
Heart Healthy Homes Corp....................... G 216 521-6029
  Lakewood *(G-8976)*
Infinit Nutrition LLC.......................... F 513 791-3500
  Blue Ash *(G-1409)*
Innovated Health LLC........................... G 330 858-0651
  Cuyahoga Falls *(G-6091)*
Instantwhip-Columbus Inc....................... E 614 871-9447
  Grove City *(G-8098)*
Lifestyle Nutraceuticals Ltd................... G 513 376-7218
  Cincinnati *(G-3105)*
Muscle Feast LLC............................... F 740 877-8808
  Nashport *(G-11339)*
Wileys Finest LLC.............................. C 740 622-1072
  Coshocton *(G-6002)*

DAIRY PRDTS: Evaporated Milk

Nestle Usa Inc................................. A 440 349-5757
  Solon *(G-13397)*
Nestle Usa Inc................................. B 440 264-6600
  Solon *(G-13398)*

DAIRY PRDTS: Ice Cream & Ice Milk

Cfgsc LLC...................................... G 513 772-5920
  Cincinnati *(G-2720)*
Double Dippin Inc.............................. G 937 847-2572
  Miamisburg *(G-10636)*
Gibson Bros Inc................................ F 440 774-2401
  Oberlin *(G-12051)*
International Brand Services................... G 513 376-8209
  Cincinnati *(G-3028)*
Malleys Candies Inc............................ D 216 362-8700
  Cleveland *(G-4353)*
Toft Dairy Inc................................. D 419 625-4376
  Sandusky *(G-13097)*
United Dairy Farmers Inc....................... C 513 396-8700
  Cincinnati *(G-3479)*

DAIRY PRDTS: Ice Cream, Bulk

Country Parlour Ice Cream Co................... F 440 237-4040
  Cleveland *(G-3908)*
Dairy Shed..................................... G 937 848-3504
  Bellbrook *(G-1191)*
Fritzie Freeze Inc............................. G 419 727-0818
  Toledo *(G-14294)*
United Dairy Inc............................... C 740 633-1451
  Martins Ferry *(G-9900)*
Velvet Ice Cream Company....................... D 740 892-3921
  Utica *(G-14859)*
Weldon Ice Cream Company....................... G 740 467-2400
  Millersport *(G-11015)*
Whits Frozen Custard........................... G 740 965-1427
  Sunbury *(G-13966)*
ZS Cream & Bean LLC............................ G 440 652-6369
  Hinckley *(G-8480)*

DAIRY PRDTS: Ice Cream, Packaged, Molded, On Sticks, Etc.

Cygnus Home Service LLC........................ E 419 222-9977
  Lima *(G-9234)*
Graeters Ice Cream Company..................... D 513 721-3323
  Cincinnati *(G-2968)*
United Dairy Inc............................... B 740 373-4121
  Marietta *(G-9841)*

DAIRY PRDTS: Milk, Condensed & Evaporated

Hans Rothenbuhler & Son Inc.................... E 440 632-6000
  Middlefield *(G-10753)*
Ingredia Inc................................... E 419 738-4060
  Wapakoneta *(G-15118)*
Minerva Dairy Inc.............................. D 330 868-4196
  Minerva *(G-11035)*
Nestle Usa Inc................................. D 216 861-8350
  Cleveland *(G-4450)*
New Diry Cincinnati Trnspt LLC................. D 214 258-1200
  Cincinnati *(G-3189)*
Rich Products Corporation...................... C 614 771-1117
  Hilliard *(G-8436)*

DAIRY PRDTS: Milk, Fluid

Consun Food Industries Inc..................... F 440 322-6301
  Elyria *(G-7128)*
Dairy Farmers America Inc...................... E 330 670-7800
  Medina *(G-10317)*
Dfa Dairy Brands Ice Cream LLC................. B 419 473-9621
  Toledo *(G-14267)*
Green Field Farms Co-Op........................ G 330 263-0246
  Wooster *(G-16126)*
Instantwhip Foods Inc.......................... F 614 488-2536
  Columbus *(G-5464)*
Reiter Dairy LLC Dean Foods.................... G 937 323-5777
  Springfield *(G-13626)*
Smithfoods Inc................................. E 330 683-8710
  Orrville *(G-12151)*
Snowville Creamery LLC......................... E 740 698-2301
  Pomeroy *(G-12614)*
Superior Dairy Inc............................. C 330 477-4515
  Canton *(G-2239)*

DAIRY PRDTS: Natural Cheese

9444 Ohio Holding Co .... E 330 359-6291
  Winesburg (G-16077)
A&M Cheese Co .... D 419 476-8369
  Toledo (G-14173)
Brewster Cheese Company .... C 330 767-3492
  Brewster (G-1642)
Bunker Hill Cheese Co Inc .... D 330 893-2131
  Millersburg (G-10949)
Great Lakes Cheese Co Inc .... B 440 834-2500
  Hiram (G-8485)
Guggisberg Cheese Inc .... E 330 893-2550
  Millersburg (G-10956)
Hans Rothenbuhler & Son Inc .... E 440 632-6000
  Middlefield (G-10753)
Holmes Cheese Co .... E 330 674-6451
  Millersburg (G-10964)
Kathys Krafts and Kollectibles .... G 423 787-3709
  Medina (G-10341)
Krafts Exotika LLC .... G 216 563-1178
  Cleveland (G-4298)
Miceli Dairy Products Co .... D 216 791-6222
  Cleveland (G-4400)
Middlfeld Original Cheese Coop .... F 440 632-5567
  Middlefield (G-10768)
Pearl Valley Cheese Inc .... E 740 545-6002
  Fresno (G-7823)
Rothenbhler Whey Ingrdents Inc .... F 440 632-0157
  Middlefield (G-10785)
Rothenbuhler Cheese Chalet LLC .... F 800 327-9477
  Middlefield (G-10786)
Rothenbuhler Holding Company .... E 440 632-6000
  Middlefield (G-10787)
Tri State Dairy LLC .... G 419 542-8788
  Hicksville (G-8381)

DAIRY PRDTS: Powdered Milk

Stolle Milk Biologics Inc .... F 513 489-7997
  West Chester (G-15591)

DAIRY PRDTS: Processed Cheese

Alpine Dairy LLC .... E 330 359-6291
  Dundee (G-6963)
Inter American Products Inc .... D 800 645-2233
  Cincinnati (G-3025)
Minerva Dairy Inc .... D 330 868-4196
  Minerva (G-11035)

DAIRY PRDTS: Whipped Topping, Exc Frozen Or Dry Mix

Instantwhip Connecticut Inc .... F 614 488-2536
  Columbus (G-5463)
Instantwhip Products Co PA .... F 614 488-2536
  Columbus (G-5465)
Instantwhip-Buffalo Inc .... F 614 488-2536
  Columbus (G-5466)
Instantwhip-Columbus Inc .... E 614 871-9447
  Grove City (G-8098)
Instantwhip-Syracuse Inc .... F 614 488-2536
  Columbus (G-5468)
Louis Instantwhip-St Inc .... F 614 488-2536
  Columbus (G-5535)
Peak Foods Llc .... D 937 440-0707
  Troy (G-14601)
Philadelphia Instantwhip Inc .... F 614 488-2536
  Columbus (G-5672)

DATA PROCESSING & PREPARATION SVCS

Datatrak International Inc .... E 440 443-0082
  Beachwood (G-983)
Gracie Plum Investments Inc .... E 740 355-9029
  Portsmouth (G-12645)
ITM Marketing Inc .... C 740 295-3575
  Coshocton (G-5981)
NCR Technology Center .... G 937 445-1936
  Dayton (G-6466)
Northrop Grmmn Spce & Mssn Sys .... D 937 259-4956
  Dayton (G-6474)
Sarcom Inc .... A 614 854-1300
  Lewis Center (G-9180)
SC Strategic Solutions LLC .... C 567 424-6054
  Norwalk (G-11988)

DATA PROCESSING SVCS

Aero Fulfillment Services Corp .... D 800 225-7145
  Mason (G-9945)
Amsive OH LLC .... D 937 885-8000
  Miamisburg (G-10611)
Cpmm Services Group Inc .... E 614 447-0165
  Columbus (G-5304)
Vndly LLC .... E 513 572-2500
  Mason (G-10068)

DECORATIVE WOOD & WOODWORK

77 Coach Supply Ltd .... G 330 674-1454
  Millersburg (G-10937)
Barkman Products LLC .... G 330 893-2520
  Millersburg (G-10942)
Brown Wood Products Company .... G 330 339-8000
  New Philadelphia (G-11488)
CM Paula Company .... E 513 759-7473
  Mason (G-9980)
Hardwood Solutions .... G 330 359-5755
  Wilmot (G-16068)
Hardwood Store Inc .... G 937 864-2899
  Enon (G-7250)
Insta Plak Inc .... F 419 537-1555
  Toledo (G-14334)
J R Custom Unlimited Inc .... F 513 894-9800
  Hamilton (G-8223)
Jakes Woodshop .... G 937 672-4964
  Waynesville (G-15297)
Mark Andronis .... G 740 259-5613
  Lucasville (G-9524)
Miami Valley Spray Foam LLC .... G 419 295-6536
  Lewisburg (G-9188)
Miller Manufacturing Inc .... E 330 852-0689
  Sugarcreek (G-13931)
Newbury Woodworks .... G 440 564-5273
  Newbury (G-11632)
P & T Millwork Inc .... F 440 543-2151
  Chagrin Falls (G-2412)
Peters Family Enterprises Inc .... G 419 339-0555
  Elida (G-7096)
Ryanworks Inc .... F 937 438-1282
  Dayton (G-6555)
Steeles 5 Acre Mill Inc .... G 419 542-9363
  Hicksville (G-8380)
Walnut Creek Planing Ltd .... D 330 893-3244
  Millersburg (G-11005)

DEFENSE SYSTEMS & EQPT

Alternate Defense LLC .... G 216 225-5889
  Maple Heights (G-9746)
Defense Surplus LLC .... G 419 460-9906
  Maumee (G-10198)
IMT Defense Corp .... G 614 891-8812
  Westerville (G-15659)
Mrl Materials Resources LLC .... G 937 531-6657
  Xenia (G-16269)
Ohio Defense Services Inc .... G 937 608-2371
  Dayton (G-6487)
On Guard Defense LLC .... G 740 596-1984
  New Plymouth (G-11533)
Personal Defense & Tactics LLC .... G 513 571-7163
  Middletown (G-1?849)
Raven Personal Defense Systems .... G 419 631-0573
  Ontario (G-12093)
Transdigm Inc .... G 216 706-2960
  Cleveland (G-4846)
Vector Electromagnetics LLC .... F 937 478-5904
  Wilmington (G-16062)

DEGREASING MACHINES

Auto-Tap Inc .... G 216 671-1043
  Cleveland (G-3771)
Crowne Group LLC .... F 216 589-0198
  Cleveland (G-3977)

DENTAL EQPT & SPLYS

Boxout LLC .... C 833 462-7746
  Hudson (G-8587)
Dental Ceramics Inc .... E 330 523-5240
  Richfield (G-12735)
Midmark Corporation .... G 937 526-3662
  Versailles (G-14986)
Midmark Corporation .... A 937 528-7500
  Miamisburg (G-10661)
Palm Plastics Ltd .... G 561 776-6700
  Bowling Green (G-1581)
Precision Swiss LLC .... G 513 716-7000
  Cincinnati (G-3771)
Sentage Corporation .... G 419 842-6730
  Sylvania (G-14013)
United Dental Laboratories .... E 330 253-1810
  Tallmadge (G-15054)

DENTAL EQPT & SPLYS WHOLESALERS

Dentronix Inc .... D 330 916-7300
  Cuyahoga Falls (G-6080)

DENTAL EQPT & SPLYS: Impression Materials

Dentsply Sirona Inc .... E 419 865-9497
  Maumee (G-10700)

DENTAL EQPT & SPLYS: Orthodontic Appliances

Dentronix Inc .... D 330 916-7300
  Cuyahoga Falls (G-6080)

DEODORANTS: Personal

Dover Wipes Company .... D 513 983-1100
  Cincinnati (G-238)
Procter & Gamble Company .... E 513 626-2500
  Blue Ash (G-157)
Procter & Gamble Company .... D 513 983-1100
  Cincinnati (G-281)
Procter & Gamble Company .... F 513 266-4375
  Cincinnati (G-282)
Procter & Gamble Company .... G 513 871-7557
  Cincinnati (G-283)
Procter & Gamble Company .... E 513 983-1100
  Cincinnati (G-284)
Procter & Gamble Company .... F 513 634-2070
  Cincinnati (G-285)
Procter & Gamble Company .... F 513 482-6789
  Cincinnati (G-286)
Procter & Gamble Company .... F 513 634-5069
  Cincinnati (G-287)
Procter & Gamble Company .... C 513 983-3000
  Cincinnati (G-288)

PRODUCT SECTION

DIES & TOOLS: Special

Procter & Gamble Company.................... E 513 627-7115
  Cincinnati *(G-3289)*
Procter & Gamble Company.................... G 513 658-9853
  Cincinnati *(G-3290)*
Procter & Gamble Company.................... B 513 983-1100
  Cincinnati *(G-3291)*
Procter & Gamble Company.................... F 513 945-0340
  Cincinnati *(G-3292)*
Procter & Gamble Company.................... E 513 242-5752
  Cincinnati *(G-3293)*
Procter & Gamble Company.................... D 513 622-1000
  Mason *(G-10043)*
Procter & Gamble Company.................... C 513 634-9600
  West Chester *(G-15486)*
Procter & Gamble Company.................... C 513 634-9110
  West Chester *(G-15487)*

DEPARTMENT STORES

Siemens Industry Inc........................... E 513 576-2088
  Milford *(G-10922)*

DEPARTMENT STORES: Army-Navy Goods

Raven Concealment Systems LLC........... E 440 508-9000
  North Ridgeville *(G-11856)*

DEPARTMENT STORES: Country General

Crownplace Brands Ltd......................... G 888 332-5534
  Apple Creek *(G-497)*
John Purdum.. G 513 897-9686
  Waynesville *(G-15298)*

DEPILATORIES, COSMETIC

Cosmetic Technologies LLC................... G 614 656-1130
  New Albany *(G-11375)*
Scarlett Kitty LLC................................. F 678 438-3796
  Dayton *(G-6559)*

DERMATOLOGICALS

Ohio Dermatological Assn..................... G 330 465-8281
  Dalton *(G-6137)*

DESIGN SVCS, NEC

Bollin & Sons Inc.................................. E 419 693-6573
  Toledo *(G-14216)*
Controls Inc.. E 330 239-4345
  Medina *(G-10312)*
Gencraft Designs LLC........................... E 330 359-6251
  Navarre *(G-11342)*
Htec Systems Inc.................................. F 937 438-3010
  Dayton *(G-6376)*
IEC Infrared Systems LLC..................... E 440 234-8000
  Middleburg Heights *(G-10720)*
Impact Printing and Design LLC............ F 833 522-6200
  Columbus *(G-5456)*
Signs Unlmted The Grphic Advnt........... G 614 836-7446
  Logan *(G-9376)*
Universal Dsign Fbrication LLC.............. F 419 202-5269
  Sandusky *(G-13101)*

DESIGN SVCS: Commercial & Indl

Acreo Inc.. G 513 734-3327
  Amelia *(G-448)*
Electrovations Inc................................. E 330 274-3558
  Solon *(G-13341)*
Hutnik Company................................... G 330 336-9700
  Wadsworth *(G-15035)*
Ies Systems Inc.................................... E 330 533-6683
  Canfield *(G-2008)*
New Path International LLC.................. E 614 410-3974
  Powell *(G-12679)*
R and J Corporation............................. E 440 871-6009
  Westlake *(G-15777)*

R J K Enterprises Inc............................ F 440 257-6018
  Mentor *(G-10542)*
Tugz International LLC......................... F 216 621-4854
  Cleveland *(G-4836)*
Ultra Tech Machinery Inc...................... E 330 929-5544
  Cuyahoga Falls *(G-6126)*

DESIGN SVCS: Computer Integrated Systems

Aclara Technologies LLC....................... C 440 528-7200
  Solon *(G-13305)*
Applied Experience LLC........................ G 614 943-2970
  Plain City *(G-12562)*
Bcs Technologies Ltd........................... F 513 829-4577
  Fairfield *(G-7337)*
Cott Systems Inc.................................. D 614 847-4405
  Columbus *(G-5299)*
Eaj Services LLC................................... F 513 792-3400
  Blue Ash *(G-1387)*
Electronic Concepts Engrg Inc............... F 419 861-9000
  Holland *(G-8509)*
IPA Ltd... F 614 523-3974
  Columbus *(G-5479)*
Logisync Corporation............................ F 440 937-0388
  Avon *(G-780)*
M T Systems Inc................................... G 330 453-4646
  Canton *(G-2150)*
Matrix Management Solutions............... E 330 470-3700
  Canton *(G-2154)*
Northrop Grmman Tchncal Svcs I......... D 937 320-3100
  Beavercreek Township *(G-1086)*
Sarcom Inc... A 614 854-1300
  Lewis Center *(G-9180)*
Sentient Studios Ltd............................. E 330 204-8636
  Fairlawn *(G-7449)*
Sgi Matrix LLC...................................... D 937 438-9033
  Miamisburg *(G-10681)*
Software Solutions Inc......................... E 513 932-6667
  Dayton *(G-6578)*
Syntec LLC... F 440 229-6262
  Rocky River *(G-12845)*
Tata America Intl Corp.......................... B 513 677-6500
  Milford *(G-10925)*
Thyme Inc.. F 484 872-8430
  Akron *(G-357)*
Worker Automation Inc......................... G 937 473-2111
  Dayton *(G-6660)*

DETECTION APPARATUS: Electronic/Magnetic Field, Light/Heat

L3harris Cincinnati Elec Corp................ A 513 573-6100
  Mason *(G-10019)*

DETECTION EQPT: Magnetic Field

Ceia Usa Ltd.. D 330 310-4741
  Hudson *(G-8588)*
HBD Industries Inc............................... E 614 526-7000
  Dublin *(G-6891)*

DIAGNOSTIC SUBSTANCES

Diagnostic Hybrids Inc.......................... C 740 593-1784
  Athens *(G-681)*
GE Healthcare Inc................................. F 513 241-5955
  Cincinnati *(G-2937)*
Meridian Bioscience Inc........................ C 513 271-3700
  Cincinnati *(G-3149)*
Nanofiber Solutions LLC....................... F 614 319-3075
  Dublin *(G-6913)*
Navidea Biopharmaceuticals Inc........... G 614 793-7500
  Dublin *(G-6915)*

Quest Diagnostics Incorporated............ G 513 229-5500
  Mason *(G-10045)*
Quidel Corporation............................... D 858 552-1100
  Athens *(G-694)*
Quidel Corporation............................... E 740 589-3300
  Athens *(G-695)*
Revvity Health Sciences Inc.................. E 330 825-4525
  Akron *(G-303)*
Thermo Fisher Scientific Inc.................. E 800 871-8909
  Oakwood Village *(G-12044)*

DIAGNOSTIC SUBSTANCES OR AGENTS: Radioactive

Cardinal Health 414 LLC....................... G 513 759-1900
  West Chester *(G-15384)*
Cardinal Health 414 LLC....................... C 614 757-5000
  Dublin *(G-6873)*
Petnet Solutions Inc............................. G 865 218-2000
  Cincinnati *(G-3252)*
Petnet Solutions Cleveland LLC............ F 865 218-2000
  Cleveland *(G-4543)*
USB Corporation................................... D 216 765-5000
  Cleveland *(G-4857)*

DIAGNOSTIC SUBSTANCES OR AGENTS: Veterinary

Cleveland AEC West LLC....................... G 216 362-6000
  Cleveland *(G-3831)*
Meridian Life Science Inc...................... F 513 271-3700
  Cincinnati *(G-3150)*
Vetgraft LLC... G 614 203-0603
  New Albany *(G-11395)*

DIE CUTTING SVC: Paper

Forest Converting Co Inc...................... G 513 631-4190
  Cincinnati *(G-2915)*
P & R Specialty Inc.............................. E 937 773-0263
  Piqua *(G-12541)*
Williams Steel Rule Die Co.................... F 216 431-3232
  Cleveland *(G-4910)*

DIE SETS: Presses, Metal Stamping

Brassgate Industries Inc....................... F 937 339-2192
  Troy *(G-14552)*
Centaur Tool & Die Inc......................... E 419 352-7704
  Bowling Green *(G-1557)*
Columbia Stamping Inc......................... E 440 236-6677
  Columbia Station *(G-5010)*
Kurtz Tool & Die Co Inc........................ G 330 755-7723
  Struthers *(G-13905)*
McAfee Tool & Die Inc........................... E 330 896-9555
  Uniontown *(G-14787)*
Rock Iron Corporation........................... F 419 529-9411
  Crestline *(G-6037)*
Toolcraft Products Inc.......................... E 937 223-8271
  Dayton *(G-6628)*

DIES & TOOLS: Special

A & B Tool & Manufacturing.................. G 419 382-0215
  Toledo *(G-14172)*
Accu-Rite Tool & Die Co Corp............... G 330 497-9959
  Canton *(G-2027)*
Accu-Tek Tool & Die Inc....................... G 330 726-1946
  Salem *(G-12975)*
Accu-Tool Inc....................................... G 937 667-5878
  Tipp City *(G-14120)*
Ace American Wire Die Co.................... F 330 425-7269
  Twinsburg *(G-14622)*
Acro Tool & Die Company..................... E 330 773-5173
  Akron *(G-17)*

Employee Codes: A=Over 500 employees, B=251-500
C=101-250, D=51-100, E=20-50, F=10-19, G=1-9

DIES & TOOLS: Special — PRODUCT SECTION

Adept Manufacturing Corp............... F 937 222-7110
  Dayton (G-6185)
Afc Tool Co Inc................................... E 937 275-8700
  Dayton (G-6189)
Allied Tool & Die Inc.......................... F 216 941-6196
  Cleveland (G-3637)
Alpha Tool & Mold Inc....................... F 440 473-2343
  Cleveland (G-3639)
Alpine Gage Inc.................................. G 937 669-8665
  Tipp City (G-14122)
Amcraft Inc... G 419 729-7900
  Toledo (G-14185)
Antwerp Tool & Die Inc..................... F 419 258-5271
  Antwerp (G-491)
Apollo Products Inc........................... F 440 269-8551
  Willoughby (G-15880)
Arnett Tool Inc.................................... G 937 437-0361
  New Paris (G-11480)
Artisan Tool & Die Corp.................... D 216 883-2769
  Cleveland (G-3681)
Atama Tech LLC................................ G 614 763-0499
  Powell (G-12663)
Athens Mold and Machine Inc......... D 740 593-6613
  Athens (G-675)
Automation Tool & Die Inc............... G 330 558-8128
  Brunswick (G-1749)
Automation Tool & Die Inc............... D 330 225-8336
  Valley City (G-14862)
B-K Tool & Design Inc...................... D 419 532-3890
  Kalida (G-8784)
Banco Die Inc..................................... F 330 821-8511
  Alliance (G-395)
Banner Metals Group Inc.................. E 614 291-3105
  Columbus (G-5174)
Bk Tool Company Inc........................ F 513 870-9622
  Fairfield (G-7339)
Bollinger Tool & Die Inc.................... F 419 866-5180
  Holland (G-8494)
Brothers Tool and Mfg Ltd................ F 513 353-9700
  Miamitown (G-10706)
Brw Tool Inc....................................... F 419 394-3371
  Saint Marys (G-12948)
Bryan Die-Cast Products Ltd............ G 419 252-6208
  Toledo (G-14222)
Capital Precision Machine & Tl....... G 937 258-1176
  Dayton (G-6154)
Capital Tool Company....................... E 216 661-5750
  Cleveland (G-3787)
Chippewa Tool and Mfg Co............. F 419 849-2790
  Woodville (G-16091)
Cleveland Metal Processing Inc...... C 440 243-3404
  Cleveland (G-3848)
Cleveland Roll Forming Co.............. G 216 281-0202
  Cleveland (G-3854)
Clyde Tool & Die Inc......................... F 419 547-9574
  Clyde (G-4971)
Coach Tool & Die LLC...................... G 937 890-4716
  Springboro (G-13498)
Coldwater Machine Company LLC.. C 419 678-4877
  Coldwater (G-4985)
Cole Tool & Die Company................ E 419 522-1272
  Ontario (G-12090)
Colonial Machine Company Inc...... D 330 673-5859
  Kent (G-8804)
Compco Quaker Mfg Inc.................. E 330 482-0200
  Salem (G-12986)
Condor Tool & Die Inc...................... E 216 671-6000
  Cleveland (G-3895)
Contour Tool Inc................................ E 440 365-7333
  North Ridgeville (G-11836)
Cornerstone Manufacturing Inc...... G 937 456-5930
  Eaton (G-7057)

Custom Machine Inc........................ E 419 986-5122
  Tiffin (G-14082)
D A Fitzgerald Co Inc....................... G 937 548-0511
  Greenville (G-8044)
Darke Precision Inc.......................... F 937 548-2232
  Piqua (G-12512)
Dayton Progress Intl Corp............... D 937 859-5111
  Dayton (G-6289)
DC Legacy Corp................................ E 330 896-4220
  Akron (G-125)
Defiance Metal Products Co........... B 419 784-5332
  Defiance (G-6676)
Die-Mension Corporation................ F 330 273-5872
  Brunswick (G-1758)
Direct Wire Service LLP................... G 937 526-4447
  Versailles (G-14979)
Diversified Mold Castings LLC....... E 216 663-1814
  Cleveland (G-3964)
DMG Tool & Die LLC........................ G 937 407-0810
  Bellefontaine (G-1207)
Dove Die and Stamping Company.. E 216 267-3720
  Cleveland (G-3970)
Drt Mfg Co LLC.................................. D 937 297-6670
  Dayton (G-6307)
Duco Tool & Die Inc.......................... F 419 628-2031
  Minster (G-11050)
Duncan Tool Inc................................ F 937 667-9364
  Tipp City (G-14132)
Dyco Manufacturing Inc.................. F 419 485-5525
  Montpelier (G-11137)
Dynamic Dies Inc............................. E 513 705-9524
  Middletown (G-10819)
Dynamic Dies Inc............................. E 419 865-0249
  Holland (G-8507)
Dynamic Tool & Mold Inc................ G 440 237-8665
  Cleveland (G-3982)
E D M Fastar Inc............................... G 216 676-0100
  Cleveland (G-3984)
Eagle Precision Products LLC....... G 440 582-9393
  North Royalton (G-11873)
Edfa LLC... G 937 222-1415
  Dayton (G-6313)
Estee 2 Inc.. E 937 224-7853
  Dayton (G-6323)
Euclid Design and Mfg Inc.............. F 440 942-0066
  Willoughby (G-15918)
Exco Engineering USA Inc.............. E 419 726-1595
  Toledo (G-14281)
F & G Tool and Die Co..................... E 937 294-1405
  Moraine (G-11180)
Fabrication Shop Inc....................... F 419 435-7934
  Fostoria (G-7631)
Faith Tool & Manufacturing............. G 440 951-5934
  Willoughby (G-15919)
Falls Tool and Die Inc..................... G 330 633-4884
  Akron (G-149)
Faull & Son LLC................................ G 330 652-4341
  Niles (G-11668)
Fc Industries Inc.............................. E 937 275-8700
  Dayton (G-6330)
Feller Tool Co.................................... F 440 324-6277
  Elyria (G-7151)
First Machine & Tool Corp.............. F 440 269-8644
  Willoughby (G-15921)
Fremar Industries Inc...................... G 330 220-3700
  Brunswick (G-1761)
G & S Custom Tooling LLC............ G 419 286-2888
  Fort Jennings (G-7595)
Gasdorf Tool and Mch Co Inc......... E 419 227-0103
  Lima (G-9244)
Gem City Engineering Co............... C 937 223-5544
  Dayton (G-6348)

General Tool Company..................... C 513 733-5500
  Cincinnati (G-2945)
Gentzler Tool & Die Corp................. E 330 896-1941
  Akron (G-168)
Gokoh Corporation........................... F 937 339-4977
  Troy (G-14573)
Greenfield Die & Mfg Corp.............. D 734 454-4000
  Valley City (G-14371)
H Machining Inc................................ F 419 636-6890
  Bryan (G-1820)
Hamilton Mold & Machine Co......... E 216 732-8200
  Cleveland (G-4157)
Hardin Creek Machine & Tl Inc....... F 419 678-4913
  Coldwater (G-4991)
Hedges Selective Tl & Prod Inc...... F 419 478-8670
  Toledo (G-14310)
Herd Manufacturing Inc................... E 216 651-4221
  Cleveland (G-4184)
Hi-Tech Wire Inc............................... D 419 678-8376
  Saint Henry (G-2935)
Hocker Tool and Die Inc.................. E 937 274-3443
  Dayton (G-6370)
Hofacker Prcsion Machining LLC.. F 937 832-7712
  Clayton (G-3560)
Holland Engraving Company.......... E 419 865-2765
  Toledo (G-14312)
Honda Engineering North America LLC. B 937 642-5000
  Marysville (G-9018)
Horizon Industries Corporation...... G 937 323-0801
  Springfield (G-13578)
Ibycorp.. G 330 425-8226
  Twinsburg (G-1674)
Impact Industries Inc....................... E 440 327-2360
  North Ridgeville (G-11845)
Imperial Die & Mfg Co...................... F 440 268-9080
  Strongsville (G-13844)
Independent Stamping Inc.............. E 216 251-3500
  Cleveland (G-4223)
Innovative Tool & Die Inc................ G 419 599-0492
  Napoleon (G-1320)
Intelitool Mfg Svcs Inc.................... G 440 953-1071
  Willoughby (G-15933)
Ishmael Precision Tool Corp.......... E 937 335-8070
  Troy (G-14585)
J & J Tool & Die Inc......................... G 330 343-4721
  Dover (G-6820)
J Tek Tool & Mold Inc...................... F 419 547-9476
  Clyde (G-4973)
J W Harwood Co.............................. F 216 531-6230
  Cleveland (G-4247)
Jena Tool Inc.................................... G 937 296-1122
  Moraine (G-11187)
Johnston Mfg Co Inc....................... G 440 269-1420
  Mentor (G-10485)
K & L Tool Inc................................... E 419 258-2086
  Antwerp (G-493)
K B Machine & Tool Inc................... G 937 773-1624
  Piqua (G-12551)
Kalt Manufacturing Company......... D 440 327-2102
  North Ridgeville (G-11848)
Ken Forging Inc................................ C 440 993-8091
  Jefferson (G-8749)
Kent Mold and Manufacturing Co.. E 330 673-3469
  Kent (G-8825)
Kiffer Industries Inc......................... E 216 267-1818
  Cleveland (G-4288)
Knowlton Manufacturing Co Inc.... F 513 631-7353
  Cincinnati (G-3085)
Kramer & Kieffer Inc........................ G 330 336-8742
  Wadsworth (G-15041)
La Ganke & Sons Stamping Co...... F 216 451-0278
  Columbia Station (G-5013)

2024 Harris Ohio Industrial Directory

(G-000) Company's Geographic Section entry number

PRODUCT SECTION
DIES & TOOLS: Special

Lako Tool & Manufacturing Inc............ F 419 662-5256
 Perrysburg *(G-12396)*

Laspina Tool and Die Inc.................... F 330 923-9996
 Stow *(G-13705)*

Lincoln Electric Automtn Inc................ C 419 678-4877
 Coldwater *(G-4996)*

Lowry Tool & Die Inc........................... F 330 332-1722
 Salem *(G-13012)*

Lrb Tool & Die Ltd.............................. F 330 898-5783
 Warren *(G-15186)*

Lukens Inc... D 937 440-2500
 Troy *(G-14594)*

Lunar Tool & Mold Inc......................... E 440 237-2141
 North Royalton *(G-11884)*

M & M Dies Inc.................................. G 216 883-6628
 Cleveland *(G-4342)*

Machine Tek Systems Inc................... E 330 527-4450
 Garrettsville *(G-7921)*

Machine Tool Design & Fab LLC......... F 419 435-7676
 Fostoria *(G-7641)*

Magnum Tool Corp............................. F 937 228-0900
 Dayton *(G-6422)*

Mahoning Valley Tool & Mch LLC........ F 330 482-0870
 Columbiana *(G-5044)*

Manufacturers Service Inc.................. E 216 267-3771
 Cleveland *(G-4355)*

Mar-Metal Mfg Inc.............................. E 419 447-1102
 Upper Sandusky *(G-14815)*

Mar-Vel Tool Co.................................. F 937 223-2137
 Dayton *(G-6429)*

Master Craft Products Inc................... F 216 281-5910
 Cleveland *(G-4366)*

Match Mold & Machine Inc................. F 330 830-5503
 Massillon *(G-10124)*

May Industries of Ohio Inc.................. E 440 237-8012
 North Royalton *(G-11886)*

Mdf Tool Corporation.......................... F 440 237-2277
 North Royalton *(G-11887)*

Midwest Tool & Engineering Co........... E
 Dayton *(G-6445)*

Mold Shop Inc.................................... F 419 829-2041
 Sylvania *(G-14005)*

Moldmakers Inc.................................. F 419 673-0902
 Kenton *(G-8892)*

Monarch Products Co......................... F 330 868-7717
 Minerva *(G-11037)*

Mt Vernon Mold Works Inc.................. E 618 242-6040
 Akron *(G-255)*

Mtd Holdings Inc................................ B 330 225-2600
 Valley City *(G-14882)*

National Roller Die Inc........................ F 440 951-3850
 Willoughby *(G-15956)*

Nelson Tool Corporation..................... F 740 965-1894
 Sunbury *(G-13958)*

New Bremen Machine & Tool Co.......... E 419 629-3295
 New Bremen *(G-11405)*

New Die Inc....................................... E 419 726-7581
 Toledo *(G-14396)*

Noble Tool Corp.................................. F 937 461-4040
 Dayton *(G-6472)*

Ohio Custom Dies LLC....................... F 330 538-3396
 North Jackson *(G-11787)*

Ohio Specialty Dies LLC..................... F 330 538-3396
 North Jackson *(G-11788)*

Omni Manufacturing Inc..................... F 419 394-7424
 Saint Marys *(G-12963)*

Omni Manufacturing Inc..................... D 419 394-7424
 Saint Marys *(G-12962)*

PA MA Inc.. G 440 846-3799
 Strongsville *(G-13864)*

Palisin & Associates Inc..................... E 216 252-3470
 Cleveland *(G-4520)*

Phillips Mch & Stamping Corp............. G 330 882-6714
 New Franklin *(G-11441)*

Phoenix Tool Company........................ G 330 372-4627
 Warren *(G-15198)*

Pier Tool & Die Inc.............................. E 440 236-3188
 Columbia Station *(G-5017)*

Porter Precision Products Co.............. D 513 385-1569
 Cincinnati *(G-3265)*

Precision Details Inc.......................... F 937 596-0068
 Jackson Center *(G-8737)*

Precision Die & Stamping Inc.............. G 513 942-8220
 West Chester *(G-15483)*

Precision Die Masters Inc................... F 440 255-1204
 Mentor *(G-10529)*

Pro-Tech Manufacturing Inc................ F 937 444-6484
 Mount Orab *(G-11246)*

Progage Inc....................................... F 440 951-4477
 Mentor *(G-10536)*

Progress Tool & Stamping Inc............. E 419 628-2384
 Minster *(G-11059)*

Project Engineering Company.............. F 937 743-9114
 Germantown *(G-7951)*

PSK Steel Corp................................... E 330 759-1251
 Hubbard *(G-8570)*

Pyramid Mold & Machine Co Inc.......... F 330 673-5200
 Kent *(G-8850)*

Quaker Mfg Corp................................. C 330 332-4631
 Salem *(G-13024)*

Quality Specialists Inc....................... G 440 946-9129
 Willoughby *(G-15979)*

Queen City Tool Works Inc.................. G 513 874-0111
 Fairfield *(G-7401)*

Quicksilver Die Casting Svc................ F 330 757-1160
 Youngstown *(G-16424)*

R M Tool & Die Inc.............................. F 440 238-6459
 Strongsville *(G-13870)*

Ram Tool Inc...................................... F 937 277-0717
 Dayton *(G-6539)*

Raymath Company.............................. C 937 335-1860
 Troy *(G-14604)*

Reserve Industries Inc........................ G 440 871-2796
 Bay Village *(G-966)*

Rockstedt Tool & Die Inc..................... F 330 273-9000
 Brunswick *(G-1788)*

Roman Tool & Die............................... G 440 503-5271
 Strongsville *(G-13873)*

Ronlen Industries Inc......................... E 330 273-6468
 Brunswick *(G-1789)*

Roto-Die Company Inc........................ G 513 942-3500
 West Chester *(G-15503)*

RPM Carbide Die Inc.......................... F 419 894-6426
 Arcadia *(G-517)*

Saint-Gobain Ceramics Plas Inc.......... C 330 673-5860
 Stow *(G-13721)*

Schmitmeyer Inc................................ G 937 295-2091
 Fort Loramie *(G-7607)*

Seilkop Industries Inc........................ E 513 761-1035
 Cincinnati *(G-3377)*

Select Industries Corporation.............. C 937 233-9191
 Dayton *(G-6567)*

Self Made Holdings LLC..................... E 330 477-1052
 Canton *(G-2220)*

Shalix Inc.. F 216 941-3546
 Cleveland *(G-4687)*

Shl Liquidation Industries Inc............. B 248 299-7500
 Valley City *(G-14893)*

Shl Liquidation Sectional Co............... B 330 558-2600
 Valley City *(G-14897)*

Sk Mold & Tool Inc.............................. E 937 339-0299
 Troy *(G-14610)*

Sk Mold & Tool Inc.............................. E 937 339-0299
 Tipp City *(G-14155)*

Skrl Die Casting Inc........................... E 440 946-7200
 Willoughby *(G-15993)*

Sluterbeck Tool & Die Co Inc............... F 937 836-5736
 Clayton *(G-3568)*

Smithville Mfg Co............................... F 330 345-5818
 Wooster *(G-16173)*

Stanco Precision Mfg Inc.................... G 937 274-1785
 Dayton *(G-6589)*

Standard Engineering Group Inc.......... G 330 494-4300
 North Canton *(G-11762)*

Summit Tool Company........................ D 330 535-7177
 Akron *(G-341)*

Superior Die...................................... G 937 225-6369
 Dayton *(G-6598)*

Superior Production LLC..................... C 614 444-2181
 Columbus *(G-5800)*

Sure Tool & Manufacturing Co............. E 937 253-9111
 Dayton *(G-6602)*

Sutterlin Machine & Tl Co Inc.............. F 440 357-0817
 Mentor *(G-10571)*

Symbol Tool & Die Inc......................... G 440 582-5989
 North Royalton *(G-11897)*

Taft Tool & Production Co................... F 419 385-2576
 Toledo *(G-14481)*

Taylor Tool & Die Inc........................... G 937 845-1491
 New Carlisle *(G-11427)*

Tech Industries Inc............................. F 216 861-7337
 Cleveland *(G-4771)*

Tech Mold and Tool Co........................ G 937 667-8851
 Tipp City *(G-14159)*

Technical Tool & Gauge Inc................. E 330 273-1778
 Brunswick *(G-1793)*

The Kordenbrock Tool and Die Co........ F 513 326-4390
 Cincinnati *(G-3449)*

The Louis G Freeman Company LLC... D 419 334-9709
 Fremont *(G-7813)*

The Vulcan Tool Company.................... G 937 253-6194
 Dayton *(G-6620)*

Tipco Punch Inc.................................. E 513 874-9140
 Hamilton *(G-8250)*

Tipp Machine & Tool Inc...................... C 937 890-8428
 Dayton *(G-6625)*

Tm Machine & Tool Inc........................ G 419 478-0310
 Toledo *(G-14488)*

Tomahawk Tool Supply........................ G 419 485-8737
 Montpelier *(G-11143)*

Toney Tool Manufacturing Inc.............. E 937 890-8535
 Dayton *(G-6627)*

Tooling Connection Inc....................... G 419 594-3339
 Oakwood *(G-12034)*

Tooling Zone Inc................................. E 937 550-4180
 Springboro *(G-13523)*

Toolrite Manufacturing Inc.................. F 937 278-1962
 Dayton *(G-6629)*

Top Tool & Die Inc.............................. F 216 267-5878
 Cleveland *(G-4805)*

Tradye Machine & Tool Inc.................. G 740 625-7550
 Centerburg *(G-2358)*

Trim Tool & Machine Inc..................... E 216 889-1916
 Cleveland *(G-4830)*

Trimline Die Corporation..................... E 440 355-6900
 Lagrange *(G-8956)*

Troy Precision Carbide Die Inc............ F 440 834-4477
 Burton *(G-1889)*

Trucut Incorporated............................ D 330 938-9806
 Sebring *(G-13127)*

True Industries Inc............................. E 330 296-4342
 Ravenna *(G-12740)*

U S Alloy Die Corp.............................. F 216 749-9700
 Cleveland *(G-4842)*

United Extrusion Dies Inc.................... F 330 533-2915
 Canfield *(G-2022)*

Employee Codes: A=Over 500 employees, B=251-500
C=101-250, D=51-100, E=20-50, F=10-19, G=1-9

DIES & TOOLS: Special

United Finshg & Die Cutng Inc............ F 216 881-0239
  Cleveland *(G-4846)*
Universal Tool Technology LLC............ F 937 222-4608
  Dayton *(G-6640)*
Unlimited Machine and Tool LLC.......... F 419 269-1730
  Toledo *(G-14516)*
Valley Tool & Die Inc.......................... D 440 237-0160
  North Royalton *(G-11900)*
Van Wert Machine Inc........................ F 419 692-6836
  Delphos *(G-6777)*
Walest Incorporated........................... G 216 362-8110
  Brunswick *(G-1800)*
Walker Tool & Machine Company......... F 419 661-8000
  Perrysburg *(G-12443)*
Weiss Industries Inc........................... F 419 526-2480
  Mansfield *(G-9732)*
Wilmington Prcsion McHning Inc.......... E 937 382-3700
  Wilmington *(G-16064)*
Windsor Tool Inc................................ F 216 671-1900
  Cleveland *(G-4911)*
Wire Shop Inc.................................... F 440 354-6842
  Mentor *(G-10596)*
WLS Stamping Co.............................. D 216 271-5100
  Cleveland *(G-4914)*
Worthington Industries Inc.................. E 614 438-3028
  Columbus *(G-5883)*
Wrena LLC.. E 937 667-4403
  Tipp City *(G-14168)*
Youngstown Tool & Die Company........ D 330 747-4464
  Youngstown *(G-16489)*

DIES: Cutting, Exc Metal

D & M Saw & Tool Inc......................... G 513 871-5433
  Cincinnati *(G-2811)*

DIES: Extrusion

Amex Dies Inc................................... F 330 545-9766
  Girard *(G-7961)*
B V Mfg Inc....................................... F 330 549-5331
  New Springfield *(G-11539)*
Diamond America Corporation............. E 330 762-9269
  Akron *(G-126)*
Jamen Tool & Die Co.......................... F 330 788-6521
  Youngstown *(G-16381)*
Mordies Inc....................................... E 330 758-8050
  Youngstown *(G-16402)*
Village Plastics Co.............................. G 330 753-0100
  Euclid *(G-7306)*
Vinyl Tool & Die Company................... F 330 782-0254
  Youngstown *(G-16471)*

DIES: Paper Cutting

Williams Steel Rule Die Co.................. F 216 431-3232
  Cleveland *(G-4910)*

DIES: Plastic Forming

National Pattern Mfgco....................... F 330 682-6871
  Orrville *(G-12140)*
Progrssive Molding Bolivar Inc............. E 330 874-3000
  Bolivar *(G-1534)*

DIES: Steel Rule

Aukerman J F Steel Rule Die............... G 937 456-4498
  Eaton *(G-7054)*
Csw Inc... E 413 589-1311
  Sylvania *(G-13992)*
Customformed Products Inc................ F 937 388-0480
  Miamisburg *(G-10631)*
Die Guys Inc...................................... F 330 239-3437
  Medina *(G-10318)*
Hedalloy Die Corporation.................... F 216 341-3768
  Cleveland *(G-4176)*

Lorain Rled Die Pdts Indus Sup............ G 440 281-8607
  North Ridgeville *(G-11849)*
Loroco Industries Inc.......................... D 513 891-9544
  Cincinnati *(G-3113)*

DIODES: Light Emitting

Bestlight Led Corporation................... G 440 205-1552
  Mentor *(G-10430)*
Ceso Inc... E 937 435-8584
  Miamisburg *(G-10626)*
Cks Solution Incorporated................... E 513 947-1277
  Fairfield *(G-7348)*
Energy Focus Inc............................... F 440 715-1300
  Solon *(G-13343)*
Hawthorne Hydroponics LLC............... F 888 478-6544
  Marysville *(G-9914)*
Refocus Holdings Inc.......................... F 216 751-8384
  Cleveland *(G-4622)*
Tri-Tech Led Systems LLC.................. G 614 593-2868
  Baltimore *(G-848)*

DIODES: Solid State, Germanium, Silicon, Etc

Measurement Specialties Inc............... E 937 427-1231
  Dayton *(G-6433)*

DIRECT SELLING ESTABLISHMENTS: Food Svcs

Cygnus Home Service LLC................. E 419 222-9977
  Lima *(G-9234)*

DISCS & TAPE: Optical, Blank

Folio Photonics Inc............................. F 440 420-4500
  Solon *(G-13352)*

DISPLAY FIXTURES: Wood

A G Industries Inc.............................. D 216 252-7300
  Cleveland *(G-3580)*
Cassady Woodworks Inc..................... E 937 256-7948
  Dayton *(G-6155)*
Couch Business Development Inc......... F 937 253-1099
  Dayton *(G-6264)*
Gabriel Logan LLC.............................. D 740 380-6809
  Groveport *(G-8144)*
Kdm Signs Inc.................................... F 513 769-3900
  Cincinnati *(G-3070)*
Midwest Woodworking Co Inc.............. F 513 631-6684
  Cincinnati *(G-3164)*
Murray Display Fixtures Ltd................ F 614 875-1594
  Grove City *(G-8109)*
Ohio Woodworking Co Inc................... E 513 631-0870
  Cincinnati *(G-3219)*
Ptmj Enterprises Inc.......................... D 440 543-8000
  Solon *(G-13408)*
Scenic Solutions Ltd Lblty Co............... G 937 866-5062
  Dayton *(G-6560)*
Ultrabuilt Play Systems Inc................. F 419 652-2294
  Nova *(G-12005)*
W J Egli Company Inc........................ F 330 823-3666
  Alliance *(G-435)*

DISPLAY ITEMS: Corrugated, Made From Purchased Materials

Shelby Company................................ E 440 871-9901
  Westlake *(G-15787)*

DISPLAY ITEMS: Solid Fiber, Made From Purchased Materials

Digital Color Intl LLC.......................... F
  Akron *(G-130)*

DISTRIBUTORS: Motor Vehicle Engine

Brinkley Technology Group LLC........... F 330 830-2498
  Massillon *(G-10079)*
Legacy Supplies Inc............................ F 330 405-4565
  Twinsburg *(G-14685)*
Power Acquisition LLC........................ D 614 228-5000
  Dublin *(G-6925)*
Thirion Brothers Eqp Co LLC............... G 440 357-8004
  Painesville *(G-12271)*
Tri-W Group Inc.................................. A 614 228-5000
  Columbus *(G-5837)*
W W Williams Company LLC............... D 614 228-5000
  Dublin *(G-6958)*
Weldon Pump LLC.............................. E 440 232-2282
  Oakwood Village *(G-12047)*

DOCK EQPT & SPLYS, INDL

Rbs Manufacturing Inc........................ E 330 426-9486
  East Palestine *(G-7007)*
Tmt Inc... F 419 592-1041
  Perrysburg *(G-12437)*
Ward Industrial Services Inc................ G 877 459-9272
  Brunswick *(G-1801)*

DOLOMITE: Crushed & Broken

Drummond Dolomite Inc...................... F 440 942-7000
  Mentor *(G-10449)*

DOOR FRAMES: Wood

All Pro Ovrhd Door Systems LLC.......... G 614 444-3667
  Columbus *(G-5111)*
Framework Industries LLC................... G 234 759-2080
  North Lima *(G-11805)*
Rsl LLC... E 330 392-8900
  Warren *(G-15203)*

DOOR MATS: Rubber

Ultimate Systems Ltd.......................... E 419 692-3005
  Delphos *(G-6775)*

DOORS & WINDOWS: Screen & Storm

Duo-Corp... F 330 549-2149
  North Lima *(G-11804)*
Euclid Jalousies Inc............................ G 440 953-1112
  Cleveland *(G-4034)*
Quanex Screens LLC........................... E 419 662-5001
  Perrysburg *(G-12422)*

DOORS & WINDOWS: Storm, Metal

Champion Opco LLC........................... B 513 327-7338
  Cincinnati *(G-2725)*
Champion Win Co Cleveland LLC......... F 440 899-2562
  Macedonia *(G-9541)*

DOORS: Combination Screen & Storm, Wood

R C Moore Lumber Co......................... F 740 732-4950
  Caldwell *(G-1912)*

DOORS: Fiberglass

Schmidt Progressive LLC.................... E 513 934-2600
  Lebanon *(G-9110)*
Toledo Pro Fiberglass Inc.................... G 419 241-9390
  Toledo *(G-14503)*

DOORS: Folding, Plastic Or Plastic Coated Fabric

Alumo Extrusions and Mfg Co.............. E 330 779-3333
  Youngstown *(G-16308)*
Modern Builders Supply Inc................. E 419 526-0002
  Mansfield *(G-9698)*

PRODUCT SECTION — DUCTS: Sheet Metal

National Access Design LLC .... F 513 351-3400
Cincinnati (G-3179)

Pease Industies Inc .... D 513 870-3600
Fairfield (G-7393)

DOORS: Garage, Overhead, Metal

Anderson Door Co .... F 216 475-5700
Cleveland (G-3666)

Clopay Corporation .... C 800 282-2260
Mason (G-9979)

Division Overhead Door Inc .... F 513 872-0888
Cincinnati (G-2834)

Haas Door Company .... C 419 337-9900
Wauseon (G-15262)

Hrh Door Corp .... E 513 674-9300
Cincinnati (G-3011)

Hrh Door Corp .... E 330 828-2291
Dalton (G-6132)

Hrh Door Corp .... A 850 208-3400
Mount Hope (G-11238)

Overhead Door Corporation .... D 740 383-6376
Marion (G-9870)

Overhead Door Corporation .... F 419 294-3874
Upper Sandusky (G-14820)

Overhead Door of Pike County .... G 740 289-3925
Piketon (G-12481)

Tri County Door Service Inc .... F 216 531-2245
Euclid (G-7303)

DOORS: Garage, Overhead, Wood

Anderson Door Co .... F 216 475-5700
Cleveland (G-3666)

Clopay Building Pdts Co Inc .... E 513 770-4800
Mason (G-9978)

Clopay Corporation .... C 800 282-2260
Mason (G-9979)

Division Overhead Door Inc .... F 513 872-0888
Cincinnati (G-2834)

Hrh Door Corp .... E 513 674-9300
Cincinnati (G-3011)

Hrh Door Corp .... A 850 208-3400
Mount Hope (G-11238)

DOORS: Glass

A Service Glass Inc .... E 937 426-4920
Beavercreek (G-1038)

Basco Manufacturing Company .... C 513 573-1900
Mason (G-9957)

Scs Construction Services Inc .... E 513 929-0260
Cincinnati (G-3371)

DRAPERIES & CURTAINS

Accent Drapery Co Inc .... E 614 488-0741
Columbus (G-5092)

Ikiriska LLC .... F 614 389-8994
Powell (G-12675)

Janson Industries .... D 330 455-7029
Canton (G-2135)

Sk Textile Inc .... C 800 888-9112
Cincinnati (G-3396)

STI Liquidation Inc .... E 614 733-0099
Plain City (G-12592)

Vocational Services Inc .... E 216 431-8085
Cleveland (G-4880)

DRAPERIES: Plastic & Textile, From Purchased Materials

Drapery Stitch of Delphos .... F 419 692-3921
Delphos (G-6763)

Drapery Sttch - Cincinnati Inc .... F 513 561-2443
Cincinnati (G-2841)

Elden Draperies of Toledo Inc .... F 419 535-1909
Toledo (G-14272)

Tiffin Scenic Studios Inc .... E 800 445-1546
Tiffin (G-14112)

DRAPERY & UPHOLSTERY STORES: Draperies

Accent Drapery Co Inc .... E 614 488-0741
Columbus (G-5092)

Elden Draperies of Toledo Inc .... F 419 535-1909
Toledo (G-14272)

Nancys Draperies Inc .... G 330 855-7751
Marshallville (G-9894)

DRILL BITS

Arch Cutng Tls Cincinnati LLC .... F 513 851-6363
West Chester (G-15538)

DRILLING MACHINERY & EQPT: Oil & Gas

Buckeye Oil Equipment Co .... F 937 387-0671
Dayton (G-6239)

Rmi Titanium Company LLC .... E 330 652-9952
Niles (G-11684)

Stonebridge Oilfield Svcs LLC .... G 740 373-6134
Marietta (G-9833)

Tiger General LLC .... F 330 239-4949
Medina (G-10387)

DRILLS & DRILLING EQPT: Mining

Davey Kent Inc .... E 330 673-5400
Kent (G-8807)

DRINK MIXES, NONALCOHOLIC: Cocktail

Gwj Liquidation Inc .... F 216 475-5770
Cleveland (G-4158)

DRINKING FOUNTAINS: Metal, Nonrefrigerated

Lvd Acquisition LLC .... D 614 861-1350
Columbus (G-5537)

DRINKING PLACES: Bars & Lounges

Brewdog Brewing Company LLC .... F 614 908-3051
Canal Winchester (G-1981)

District Brewing Company Inc .... E 614 224-3626
Columbus (G-5331)

Green Room Brewing LLC .... G 614 421-2337
Columbus (G-5412)

Lock 15 Brewing Company LLC .... E 234 900-8277
Akron (G-221)

Mansfield Brew Works LLC .... F 419 631-3153
Mansfield (G-9684)

DRINKING PLACES: Beer Garden

Lock 27 Brewing LLC .... F 937 433-2739
Dayton (G-6414)

DRINKING WATER COOLERS WHOLESALERS: Mechanical

Lvd Acquisition LLC .... D 614 861-1350
Columbus (G-5537)

DRUG STORES

Omnicare Phrm of Midwest LLC .... D 513 719-2600
Cincinnati (G-3222)

DRUGS & DRUG PROPRIETARIES, WHOLESALE

Buderer Drug Company Inc .... E 419 627-2800
Sandusky (G-13046)

Omnicare Phrm of Midwest LLC .... D 513 719-2600
Cincinnati (G-3222)

DRUGS & DRUG PROPRIETARIES, WHOLESALE: Patent Medicines

Teva Womens Health LLC .... C 513 731-9900
Cincinnati (G-3446)

DRUGS & DRUG PROPRIETARIES, WHOLESALE: Pharmaceuticals

American Regent Inc .... D 614 436-2222
Hilliard (G-8397)

Cardinal Health Inc .... E 614 553-3830
Dublin (G-6871)

Cardinal Health Inc .... G 614 757-2863
Lewis Center (G-9155)

Cardinal Health Inc .... A 614 757-5000
Dublin (G-6872)

Optum Infusion Svcs 550 LLC .... D 866 442-4679
Cincinnati (G-3227)

River City Pharma .... F 513 870-1680
Fairfield (G-7403)

DRUGS & DRUG PROPRIETARIES, WHOLESALE: Vitamins & Minerals

Boxout LLC .... C 833 462-7746
Hudson (G-8587)

Direct Action Co Inc .... F 330 364-3219
Dover (G-6815)

DRUMS: Fiber

Greif Inc .... E 740 657-6500
Delaware (G-6725)

Greif Inc .... E 419 238-0565
Van Wert (G-14917)

DRUMS: Shipping, Metal

Drum Parts Inc .... F 216 271-0702
Cleveland (G-3974)

Greif Inc .... E 740 657-6500
Delaware (G-6725)

Greif Inc .... E 740 549-6000
Delaware (G-6724)

Mauser Usa LLC .... D 513 398-1300
Mason (G-10026)

North Coast Container LLC .... E 216 441-6214
Cleveland (G-4466)

DUCTS: Sheet Metal

Controls and Sheet Metal Inc .... E 513 721-3610
Cincinnati (G-2793)

Eastern Sheet Metal Inc .... D 513 793-3440
Blue Ash (G-1388)

Kerber Sheetmetal Works Inc .... F 937 339-6366
Troy (G-14591)

Langdon Inc .... E 513 733-5955
Cincinnati (G-3095)

Lukjan Metal Products Inc .... C 440 599-8127
Conneaut (G-5926)

McGill Airflow LLC .... D 614 829-1200
Columbus (G-5551)

McGill Corporation .... F 614 829-1200
Groveport (G-8153)

Precision Duct Fabrication LLC .... F 614 580-9385
Columbus (G-5686)

R G Smith Company .... D 330 456-3415
Canton (G-2207)

Technibus Inc .... D 330 479-4202
Canton (G-2241)

DUMPSTERS: Garbage

United McGill Corporation............................ E 614 829-1200
Groveport (G-8165)

DUMPSTERS: Garbage

Budget Dumpsters.. G 419 690-9896
Curtice (G-6056)

E-Pak Manufacturing LLC........................... D 330 264-0825
Wooster (G-16115)

Giuseppes Concessions LLC....................... F 614 554-2551
Marengo (G-9768)

North Coast Dumpster Svcs LLC.................. G 216 644-5647
Cleveland (G-4467)

DUST OR FUME COLLECTING EQPT: Indl

Envirofab Inc.. F 216 651-1767
Cleveland (G-4023)

Herman Manufacturing LLC......................... F 216 251-6400
Cleveland (G-4185)

Schenck Process LLC................................. F 513 576-9200
Solon (G-13419)

Sly Inc.. E 800 334-2957
Strongsville (G-13881)

DYES & PIGMENTS: Organic

Accel Corporation...................................... G 440 327-7418
Avon (G-760)

Avient Corporation..................................... E 419 668-4844
Norwalk (G-11955)

Colormatrix Corporation.............................. C 216 622-0100
Berea (G-1272)

Hexpol Compounding LLC........................... C 440 834-4644
Burton (G-1880)

Republic Powdered Metals Inc..................... D 330 225-3192
Medina (G-10370)

Revlis Corporation..................................... E 330 535-2100
Akron (G-302)

RPM International Inc................................. D 330 273-5090
Medina (G-10372)

Sun Chemical Corporation........................... E 513 830-8667
Cincinnati (G-3430)

DYES OR COLORS: Food, Synthetic

Berghausen Corporation.............................. E 513 591-4491
Cincinnati (G-2665)

EATING PLACES

Breitenbach Wine Cellars Inc....................... G 330 343-3603
Dover (G-6810)

Buns of Delaware Inc.................................. E 740 363-2867
Delaware (G-6706)

Chestnut Land Company............................. G 330 652-1939
Niles (G-11663)

Christopher Sweeney.................................. G 513 276-4350
Troy (G-14554)

Ferrante Wine Farm Inc.............................. E 440 466-8466
Geneva (G-7936)

Grace Juice Company LLC........................... F 614 398-6879
Westerville (G-15707)

Guggisberg Cheese Inc............................... E 330 893-2550
Millersburg (G-10956)

John Purdum... G 513 897-9686
Waynesville (G-15298)

Karrikin Spirits Company LLC....................... F 513 561-5000
Cincinnati (G-3064)

McDonalds.. F 513 336-0820
Mason (G-10028)

Paramount Distillers Inc.............................. B 216 671-6300
Cleveland (G-4522)

Rocky River Brewing Co.............................. F 440 895-2739
Rocky River (G-12842)

Willoughby Brewing Company LLC................ F 440 975-0202
Willoughby (G-16016)

EDUCATIONAL SVCS

Auguste Moone Enterprises Ltd.................... E 216 333-9248
Cleveland Heights (G-4937)

Dietrich Von Hldbrand Lgacy PR.................... G 703 496-7821
Steubenville (G-13666)

Health Sense Inc....................................... G 440 354-8057
Painesville (G-12244)

Tangible Solutions Inc................................ E 937 912-4603
Fairborn (G-7324)

ELECTRIC MOTOR REPAIR SVCS

3-D Service Ltd... C 330 830-3500
Massillon (G-10072)

Als High Tech Inc....................................... F 440 232-7090
Bedford (G-1099)

Bennett Electric Inc.................................... F 800 874-5405
Norwalk (G-11956)

Big River Electric Inc.................................. G 740 446-4360
Gallipolis (G-7889)

Bornhorst Motor Service Inc......................... G 937 773-0426
Piqua (G-12507)

Clark-Fowler Enterprises Inc........................ E 330 262-0906
Wooster (G-16110)

D & J Electric Motor Repair Co..................... F 330 336-4343
Wadsworth (G-15025)

E M Service Inc... F 440 323-3260
Elyria (G-7137)

E-Z Electric Motor Svc Corp......................... E 216 581-8820
Cleveland (G-3986)

Fenton Bros Electric Co............................... E 330 343-0093
New Philadelphia (G-11501)

Hackworth Electric Motors Inc...................... G 330 345-6049
Wooster (G-16128)

Hannon Company....................................... F 330 343-7758
Dover (G-6826)

Hannon Company....................................... F 740 453-0527
Zanesville (G-16536)

Hennings Quality Service Inc........................ F 216 941-9120
Cleveland (G-4181)

Horner Industrial Services Inc...................... F 937 390-6667
Springfield (G-13579)

Integrated Power Services LLC..................... D 216 433-7808
Cleveland (G-4231)

Integrated Power Services LLC..................... E 513 863-8816
Hamilton (G-8221)

Kiemle-Hankins Company............................ E 419 661-2430
Perrysburg (G-12395)

Lemsco Inc... G 419 242-4005
Toledo (G-14363)

Lima Armature Works Inc............................ G 419 222-4010
Lima (G-9261)

Mader Elc Mtr Pwr Trnsmssons L.................. G 937 325-5576
Springfield (G-13599)

Magnetech Industrial Svcs Inc...................... D 330 830-3500
Massillon (G-10121)

Masteller Electric Motor Svc......................... G 937 492-8500
Sidney (G-13262)

Matlock Electric Co Inc............................... E 513 731-9600
Cincinnati (G-3134)

Mid-Ohio Electric Co.................................. E 614 274-8000
Columbus (G-5563)

National Electric Coil Inc............................. B 614 488-1151
Columbus (G-5589)

Ohio Electric Motor Service Center Inc.......... F 614 444-1451
Columbus (G-5617)

Ohio Electric Motor Svc LLC......................... F 614 444-1451
Columbus (G-5618)

Phillips Electric Co..................................... F 216 361-0014
Cleveland (G-4548)

Shoemaker Electric Company....................... E 614 294-5626
Columbus (G-5764)

Whelco Industrial Ltd.................................. D 419 385-4627
Perrysburg (G-12445)

ELECTRIC SERVICES

National Gas & Oil Corporation..................... E 740 344-2102
Newark (G-1155)

ELECTRICAL APPARATUS & EQPT WHOLESALERS

Acorn Technology Corporation...................... E 216 663-1244
Shaker Heights (G-13149)

Ademco Inc.. G 440 439-7002
Bedford (G-1098)

Allen Fields Assoc Inc................................. E 513 228-1010
Lebanon (G-906)

Als High Tech Inc....................................... F 440 232-7090
Bedford (G-1099)

Best Lighting Products Inc........................... D 740 964-1198
Etna (G-7254)

Black Box Corporation................................ G 855 324-9909
Westlake (G-15338)

C & S Industrial Ltd................................... G 440 327-2360
North Ridgeville (G-11835)

Controllix Corporation................................ F 440 232-8757
Walton Hills (G-5097)

Filnor Inc... F 330 821-8731
Alliance (G-403)

Hughes Corporation.................................... E 440 238-2550
Strongsville (G-7842)

Industrial Power Systems Inc....................... B 419 531-3121
Rossford (G-12657)

Kirk Key Interlock Company LLC................... E 330 833-8223
North Canton (G-11740)

LSI Lightron Inc... A 845 562-5500
Blue Ash (G-1425)

Machine Drive Company.............................. D 513 793-7077
Cincinnati (G-3112)

Peak Electric Inc....................................... F 419 726-4848
Toledo (G-14430)

Powell Electrical Systems Inc....................... D 330 966-1750
North Canton (G-11753)

Schneider Electric Usa Inc........................... D 513 777-4445
West Chester (G-15506)

Sieb & Meyer America Inc........................... F 513 563-0860
West Chester (G-15585)

Specialty Switch Company LLC..................... F 330 427-3000
Youngstown (G-5444)

Tesa Inc.. G 614 847-8200
Lewis Center (G-181)

Warmus and Associates Inc......................... F 330 659-4440
Bath (G-962)

ELECTRICAL DEVICE PARTS: Porcelain, Molded

Materion Brush Inc.................................... D 216 486-4200
Mayfield Heights (G-10250)

ELECTRICAL DISCHARGE MACHINING, EDM

Detroit Diesl Specialty TI Inc....................... C 740 435-4452
Byesville (G-189)

Morris Technologies Inc.............................. E 513 733-1611
Cincinnati (G-3174)

Skinner Machining Co................................. G 216 486-6636
Willoughby (G-15792)

The Kordenbrock Tool and Die Co................. F 513 326-4390
Cincinnati (G-344)

U S Alloy Die Corp..................................... F 216 749-9700
Cleveland (G-484)

ELECTRICAL EQPT REPAIR SVCS

PRODUCT SECTION — ELECTROMEDICAL EQPT

D & J Electric Motor Repair Co .... F 330 336-4343
  Wadsworth *(G-15025)*

Kiemle-Hankins Company .... E 419 661-2430
  Perrysburg *(G-12395)*

Miscor Group Ltd .... B 330 830-3500
  Massillon *(G-10129)*

ELECTRICAL EQPT: Automotive, NEC

Commercial Vehicle Group Inc .... B 614 289-5360
  New Albany *(G-11374)*

Electra Sound Inc .... D 216 433-9600
  Avon Lake *(G-805)*

Stanley Electric US Co Inc .... D 740 852-5200
  London *(G-9394)*

ELECTRICAL GOODS, WHOLESALE: Boxes & Fittings

Akron Foundry Co .... C 330 745-3101
  Akron *(G-33)*

Ignio Systems LLC .... G 419 708-0503
  Toledo *(G-14326)*

Osburn Associates Inc .... F 740 385-5732
  Logan *(G-9372)*

ELECTRICAL GOODS, WHOLESALE: Cable Conduit

Legrand North America LLC .... B 937 224-0639
  Dayton *(G-6403)*

ELECTRICAL GOODS, WHOLESALE: Electronic Parts

Heilind Electronics Inc .... E 440 473-9600
  Cleveland *(G-4177)*

Kontron America Incorporated .... G 937 324-2420
  Springfield *(G-13591)*

Pemro Corporation .... F 800 440-5441
  Cleveland *(G-4540)*

Rixan Associates Inc .... E 937 438-3005
  Dayton *(G-6550)*

Rpa Electronic Distrs Inc .... G 937 223-7001
  Dayton *(G-6553)*

Wes-Garde Components Group Inc ...... G 614 885-0319
  Westerville *(G-15724)*

Wurth Electronics Ics Inc .... E 937 415-7700
  Miamisburg *(G-10703)*

ELECTRICAL GOODS, WHOLESALE: Fittings & Construction Mat

Schneider Electric Usa Inc .... B 513 523-4171
  Oxford *(G-12213)*

ELECTRICAL GOODS, WHOLESALE: Generators

Rv Mobile Power LLC .... G 855 427-7978
  Columbus *(G-5735)*

Western Branch Diesel LLC .... F 330 454-8800
  Canton *(G-2267)*

ELECTRICAL GOODS, WHOLESALE: Household Appliances, NEC

World Wide Recyclers Inc .... G 614 554-3296
  Columbus *(G-5881)*

ELECTRICAL GOODS, WHOLESALE: Light Bulbs & Related Splys

Daycoa Inc .... F 937 849-1315
  Medway *(G-10397)*

ELECTRICAL GOODS, WHOLESALE: Lighting Fittings & Access

Current Elec & Enrgy Solutions .... G 513 575-4600
  Loveland *(G-9479)*

ELECTRICAL GOODS, WHOLESALE: Modems, Computer

Black Box Corporation .... G 855 324-9909
  Westlake *(G-15738)*

ELECTRICAL GOODS, WHOLESALE: Security Control Eqpt & Systems

H2flow Controls Inc .... G 419 841-7774
  Toledo *(G-14307)*

Mace Personal Def & SEC Inc .... E 440 424-5321
  Cleveland *(G-4348)*

Sage Integration Holdings LLC .... E 330 733-8183
  Kent *(G-8857)*

ELECTRICAL GOODS, WHOLESALE: Switches, Exc Electronic, NEC

Wes-Garde Components Group Inc ...... G 614 885-0319
  Westerville *(G-15724)*

ELECTRICAL GOODS, WHOLESALE: Telephone Eqpt

ABC Appliance Inc .... E 419 693-4414
  Oregon *(G-12099)*

Cbst Acquisition LLC .... D 513 361-9600
  Cincinnati *(G-2711)*

Famous Industries Inc .... E 330 535-1811
  Akron *(G-150)*

Floyd Bell Inc .... D 614 294-4000
  Columbus *(G-5381)*

Pro Oncall Technologies LLC .... F 614 761-1400
  Dublin *(G-6927)*

ELECTRICAL GOODS, WHOLESALE: Wire & Cable

Associated Mtls Holdings LLC .... A 330 929-1811
  Cuyahoga Falls *(G-6071)*

Mjo Industries Inc .... D 800 590-4055
  Huber Heights *(G-8577)*

Multilink Inc .... C 440 366-6966
  Elyria *(G-7183)*

Noco Company .... D 216 464-8131
  Solon *(G-13399)*

Scott Fetzer Company .... C 216 267-9000
  Cleveland *(G-4678)*

Sumitomo Elc Wirg Systems Inc .... E 937 642-7579
  Marysville *(G-9941)*

ELECTRICAL MEASURING INSTRUMENT REPAIR & CALIBRATION SVCS

Instrmntation Ctrl Systems Inc .... E 513 662-2600
  Cincinnati *(G-3024)*

Interface Logic Systems Inc .... G 614 236-8388
  Columbus *(G-5472)*

Tegam Inc .... E 440 466-6100
  Geneva *(G-7945)*

ELECTRICAL SPLYS

Accurate Mechanical Inc .... D 740 681-1332
  Lancaster *(G-8985)*

Ces Nationwide .... G 937 322-0771
  Springfield *(G-13543)*

Fenton Bros Electric Co .... E 330 343-0093
  New Philadelphia *(G-11501)*

ELECTRICAL SUPPLIES: Porcelain

Akron Porcelain & Plastics Co .... C 330 745-2159
  Akron *(G-41)*

CAM-Lem Inc .... G 216 391-7750
  Cleveland *(G-3783)*

Channel Products Inc .... D 440 423-0113
  Solon *(G-13328)*

Electrodyne Company Inc .... F 513 732-2822
  Batavia *(G-921)*

Fram Group Operations LLC .... E 419 436-5827
  Fostoria *(G-7637)*

Petro Ware Inc .... E 740 982-1302
  Crooksville *(G-6049)*

Vibrantz Corporation .... C 216 875-6213
  Cleveland *(G-4868)*

Weldco Inc .... E 513 744-9353
  Cincinnati *(G-3514)*

ELECTRODES: Thermal & Electrolytic

De Nora Tech LLC .... D 440 710-5334
  Concord Township *(G-5905)*

Graftech Intl Holdings Inc .... C 216 676-2000
  Brooklyn Heights *(G-1692)*

Graphel Corporation .... C 513 779-6166
  West Chester *(G-15444)*

Graphite Sales Inc .... F 419 652-3388
  Nova *(G-12003)*

Neograf Solutions LLC .... C 216 529-3777
  Lakewood *(G-8979)*

Sangraf International Inc .... E 216 543-3288
  Westlake *(G-15782)*

Sherbrooke Corporation .... E 440 942-3520
  Willoughby *(G-15990)*

ELECTROMEDICAL EQPT

Brainmaster Technologies Inc .... G 440 232-6000
  Bedford *(G-1107)*

Cardiac Analytics LLC .... F 614 314-1332
  Powell *(G-12667)*

Checkpoint Surgical Inc .... D 216 378-9107
  Independence *(G-8657)*

Ctl Analyzers LLC .... E 216 791-5084
  Shaker Heights *(G-13153)*

Deep Brain Innovations LLC .... F 216 378-9106
  Beachwood *(G-984)*

Eoi Inc .... F 740 201-3300
  Lewis Center *(G-9160)*

Gyrus Acmi LP .... C 419 668-8201
  Norwalk *(G-11971)*

Lumitex Inc .... D 440 243-8401
  Strongsville *(G-13852)*

Mrpicker .... G 440 354-6497
  Cleveland *(G-4429)*

Ndi Medical LLC .... F 216 378-9106
  Cleveland *(G-4443)*

Neuros Medical Inc .... G 440 951-2565
  Willoughby Hills *(G-16026)*

Nkh-Safety Inc .... F 513 771-3839
  Cincinnati *(G-3200)*

Pemco Inc .... E 216 524-2990
  Cleveland *(G-4539)*

Rapiscan Systems High Enrgy In .... E 937 879-4200
  Fairborn *(G-7321)*

Respironics Novametrix LLC .... A 800 345-6443
  Columbus *(G-5719)*

Sonosite Inc .... G 425 951-1200
  Hamilton *(G-8244)*

Viewray Inc .... D 440 703-3210
  Oakwood Village *(G-12045)*

ELECTROMEDICAL EQPT

Viewray Technologies Inc .... F 440 703-3210
  Oakwood Village (G-12046)

ELECTROMEDICAL EQPT WHOLESALERS

Relevium Labs Inc .... G 614 568-7000
  Oxford (G-12212)
Smiths Medical Pm Inc .... F 614 210-7300
  Dublin (G-6940)

ELECTROMETALLURGICAL PRDTS

Rhenium Alloys Inc .... E 440 365-7388
  North Ridgeville (G-11858)

ELECTRONIC DEVICES: Solid State, NEC

Burke Products Inc .... E 937 372-3516
  Xenia (G-16253)
D F Electronics Inc .... D 513 772-7792
  Cincinnati (G-2813)
Dan-Mar Company Inc .... E 419 660-8830
  Norwalk (G-11961)

ELECTRONIC EQPT REPAIR SVCS

Bentronix Corp .... G 440 632-0606
  Middlefield (G-10734)
Electric Service Co Inc .... E 513 271-6387
  Cincinnati (G-2861)
Sasha Electronics Inc .... F 419 662-8100
  Rossford (G-12872)
Vacuum Electric Switch Co Inc .... F 330 374-5156
  Mogadore (G-11089)
Vertiv Corporation .... G 614 888-0246
  Lockbourne (G-9341)
Vertiv Corporation .... A 614 888-0246
  Westerville (G-15686)

ELECTRONIC LOADS & POWER SPLYS

Vertiv Holdings Co .... D 614 888-0246
  Westerville (G-15688)

ELECTRONIC PARTS & EQPT WHOLESALERS

Cartessa Corp .... F 513 738-4477
  Shandon (G-13159)
Certified Comparator Products .... G 937 426-9677
  Beavercreek (G-1072)
Electro-Line Inc .... F 937 461-5683
  Dayton (G-6315)
Pepperl + Fuchs Inc .... C 330 425-3555
  Twinsburg (G-14709)
Pepperl + Fuchs Entps Inc .... F 330 425-3555
  Twinsburg (G-14710)
Premier Farnell Holding Inc .... E 330 523-4273
  Richfield (G-12794)
Projects Unlimited Inc .... C 937 918-2200
  Dayton (G-6534)
Spirit Avionics Ltd .... F 614 237-4271
  Columbus (G-5786)
Standex Electronics Inc .... D 513 871-3777
  Fairfield (G-7411)
Vmetro Inc .... D 281 584-0728
  Fairborn (G-7326)

ELECTRONIC SHOPPING

E Retailing Associates LLC .... D 614 300-5785
  Columbus (G-5339)
Jfab LLC .... G 740 572-0227
  Jeffersonville (G-8764)

ELECTRONIC TRAINING DEVICES

Ahkeo Labs LLC .... G 216 406-1919
  Mayfield Village (G-10258)

E-Beam Services Inc .... E 513 933-0031
  Lebanon (G-9071)

ELECTROPLATING & PLATING SVC

Cleveland LLC .... F 216 249-3098
  Cleveland (G-3845)
Krendl Rack Co Inc .... G 419 667-4800
  Venedocia (G-14970)
Twist Inc .... C 937 675-9581
  Jamestown (G-8742)
Worthington Steel Company .... B 800 944-2255
  Worthington (G-16223)

ELEVATORS & EQPT

Adams Elevator Equipment Co .... D 847 581-2900
  Holland (G-8492)
Avt Beckett Elevators USA Inc .... G 844 360-0288
  Logan (G-9359)
Canton Elevator Inc .... D 330 833-3600
  North Canton (G-11719)
Cleveland Elevator Inc .... G 216 924-0505
  Cuyahoga Falls (G-6075)
Elevator Cncepts By Wurtec LLC ...... F 734 246-4700
  Toledo (G-14275)
Gray-Eering Ltd .... G 740 498-8816
  Tippecanoe (G-14171)
Otis Elevator Company .... E 216 573-2333
  Cleveland (G-4512)
Schindler Elevator Corporation .... F 419 861-5900
  Holland (G-8529)
Schindler Elevator Corporation .... C 937 492-3186
  Sidney (G-13281)
Sweet Manufacturing Company .... E 937 325-1511
  Springfield (G-13641)
Wittur Usa Inc .... E 216 524-0100
  Twinsburg (G-14756)

ELEVATORS WHOLESALERS

Otis Elevator Company .... E 216 573-2333
  Cleveland (G-4512)

ELEVATORS: Installation & Conversion

Otis Elevator Company .... E 216 573-2333
  Cleveland (G-4512)

EMBLEMS: Embroidered

Atlantis Sportswear Inc .... E 937 773-0680
  Piqua (G-12506)
Craco Embroidery Inc .... G 513 563-6999
  Cincinnati (G-2801)
Novak J F Manufacturing Co LLC ..... G 216 741-5112
  Cleveland (G-4484)
R J Manray Inc .... G 330 559-6716
  Canfield (G-2015)
Randy Gray .... G 513 533-3200
  Cincinnati (G-3324)
Sportsco Imprinting .... G 513 641-5111
  Cincinnati (G-3409)

EMBROIDERY ADVERTISING SVCS

City Apparel Inc .... F 419 434-1155
  Findlay (G-7493)
Custom Sportswear Imprints LLC ..... G 330 335-8326
  Wadsworth (G-15024)
Screen Works Inc .... E 937 264-9111
  Dayton (G-6564)
Underground Sports Shop Inc .... F 513 751-1662
  Cincinnati (G-3477)

EMERGENCY ALARMS

Ademco Inc .... G 440 439-7002
  Bedford (G-1098)

PRODUCT SECTION

Ademco Inc .... F 513 772-1851
  Blue Ash (G-1357)
Floyd Bell Inc .... D 614 294-4000
  Columbus (G-5371)
Status Solutions LLC .... D 434 296-1789
  Westerville (G-15680)

ENAMELS

J C Whitlam Manufacturing Co .... E 330 334-2524
  Wadsworth (G-17037)
North Shore Strapping Company ..... E 216 661-5200
  Brooklyn Heights (G-1696)
RPM Consumer Holding Company ... E 330 273-5090
  Medina (G-10377)

ENCLOSURES: Electronic

American Rugged Enclosures Inc ..... F 513 942-3004
  Hamilton (G-8177)
Ecp Corporation .... E 440 934-0444
  Avon (G-771)
Nn Metal Stampings LLC .... E 419 737-2311
  Pioneer (G-1245)

ENCLOSURES: Screen

Patton Aluminum Products Inc .... F 937 845-9404
  New Carlisle (G-1424)

ENCODERS: Digital

Garage Scenes Ltd .... F 614 407-6094
  Westerville (G-5657)
Liquid Image Com America .... G 216 458-9800
  Cleveland (G-431)

ENGINE REBUILDING: Diesel

Chemequip Sales Inc .... E 330 724-8300
  Coventry Township (G-6007)
Detroit Desl Rmnfctrng-Ast Inc .... B 740 439-7701
  Byesville (G-1834)
Detroit Desl Rmnufacturing LLC .... C 740 439-7701
  Cambridge (G-931)
General Engine Products LLC .... D 937 704-0160
  Franklin (G-7677)
Jatrodiesel Inc .... F
  Miamisburg (G-10649)
Maags Automotive & Mch Inc .... G 419 626-1539
  Sandusky (G-1976)
Performance Diesel Inc .... F 740 392-3693
  Mount Vernon (G-11287)

ENGINEERING SVCS

A+ Engineering Fabrication Inc .... F 419 832-0748
  Grand Rapids (G-8008)
Alfons Haar Inc .... E 937 560-2031
  Springboro (G-3495)
Applied Experience LLC .... G 614 943-2970
  Plain City (G-12562)
Automted Cmpnt Spcalists LLC .... E 513 335-4285
  Cincinnati (G-245)
B&N Coal Inc .... E 740 783-3575
  Dexter City (G-802)
Babcock & Wilcox Holdings Inc .... A 704 625-4900
  Akron (G-75)
Bender Engineering Company .... G 330 938-2355
  Beloit (G-1250)
Beringer Plating Inc .... G 330 633-8409
  Akron (G-82)
Circle Prime Manufacturing .... E 330 923-0019
  Cuyahoga Falls (G-6074)
Clarkwestern Dietrich Building .... E 330 372-5564
  Warren (G-15174)
Clarkwestern Dtrch Bldg System ..... C 513 870-1100
  West Chester (G-15396)

Cleveland Roll Forming Envi............ F 440 899-3888
  Westlake *(G-15744)*
Coal Services Inc................................... B 740 795-5220
  Powhatan Point *(G-12684)*
Coating Systems Group Inc................. F 440 816-9306
  Middleburg Heights *(G-10717)*
Comtec Incorporated............................. F 330 425-8102
  Twinsburg *(G-14644)*
Control Electric Co................................. E 216 671-8010
  Columbia Station *(G-5011)*
Corrpro Companies Inc......................... E 330 725-6681
  Medina *(G-10314)*
Custom Craft Controls Inc.................... F 330 630-9599
  Akron *(G-120)*
DA Precision Products Inc.................... F 513 459-1113
  West Chester *(G-15411)*
Decision Systems Inc............................ F 330 456-7600
  Canton *(G-2090)*
Dms Inc... C 440 951-9838
  Willoughby *(G-15910)*
Donald E Didion II................................. E 419 483-2226
  Bellevue *(G-1226)*
Enprotech Industrial Tech LLC............. E 216 883-3220
  Cleveland *(G-4019)*
Eti Tech LLC... F 937 832-4200
  Kettering *(G-8907)*
Fishel Company..................................... C 614 850-4400
  Columbus *(G-5377)*
Frost Engineering Inc............................ E 513 541-6330
  Cincinnati *(G-2923)*
General Precision Corporation.............. G 440 951-9380
  Willoughby *(G-15925)*
Hii Mission Technologies Corp............. G 937 426-3421
  Beavercreek *(G-1074)*
Hunter Defense Tech Inc...................... E 216 438-6111
  Solon *(G-13363)*
Hydro-Dyne Inc....................................... E 330 832-5076
  Massillon *(G-10109)*
Imax Industries Inc................................ F 440 639-0242
  Painesville *(G-12246)*
Innovative Controls Corp...................... E 419 691-6684
  Toledo *(G-14333)*
Integris Composites Inc........................ D 740 928-0326
  Hebron *(G-8345)*
Jotco Inc... G 513 721-4943
  Mansfield *(G-9675)*
Matrix Research Inc.............................. D 937 427-8433
  Beavercreek *(G-1075)*
Mendenhall Technical Services Inc..... E 513 860-1280
  Fairfield *(G-7383)*
Micro Industries Corporation................ D 740 548-7878
  Westerville *(G-15716)*
Mrl Materials Resources LLC............... F 937 531-6657
  Xenia *(G-16269)*
Nesco Inc... E 440 461-6000
  Cleveland *(G-4448)*
New Path International LLC................. E 614 410-3974
  Powell *(G-12679)*
Northrop Grmman Tchncal Svcs I....... D 937 320-3100
  Beavercreek Township *(G-1086)*
Ohio Blow Pipe Company..................... E 216 681-7379
  Cleveland *(G-4496)*
Plate-All Metal Company Inc................ G 330 633-6166
  Akron *(G-277)*
Providence REES Inc............................ F 614 833-6231
  Columbus *(G-5696)*
Quality Plating Co.................................. G 216 361-0151
  Cleveland *(G-4607)*
RAD-Con Inc.. E 440 871-5720
  Lakewood *(G-8981)*
Rolls-Royce Energy Systems Inc......... A 703 834-1700
  Mount Vernon *(G-11292)*

Sgi Matrix LLC....................................... D 937 438-9033
  Miamisburg *(G-10681)*
Star Distribution and Mfg LLC.............. E 513 860-3573
  West Chester *(G-15590)*
Sunpower Inc... D 740 594-2221
  Athens *(G-699)*
Support Svc LLC................................... F 419 617-0660
  Lexington *(G-9203)*
Systech Handling Inc............................ F 419 445-8226
  Archbold *(G-547)*
Tangent Company LLC......................... G 440 543-2775
  Chagrin Falls *(G-2427)*
Tangible Solutions Inc.......................... E 937 912-4603
  Fairborn *(G-7324)*
Tfi Manufacturing LLC.......................... G 440 290-9411
  Mentor *(G-10575)*
Thermal Treatment Center Inc............. E 216 881-8100
  Wickliffe *(G-15854)*
Timekeeping Systems Inc..................... F 216 595-0890
  Solon *(G-13439)*
Torsion Control Products Inc............... F 248 537-1900
  Wadsworth *(G-15070)*
U S Army Corps of Engineers............... G 740 537-2571
  Toronto *(G-14536)*
Uvonics Co... E 614 458-1163
  Columbus *(G-5852)*
Welding Consultants Inc....................... E 614 258-7018
  Columbus *(G-5870)*
Werks Kraft Engineering LLC.............. E 330 721-7374
  Medina *(G-10394)*
Xaloy LLC... C 330 726-4000
  Austintown *(G-757)*
Xcite Systems Corporation................... E 513 965-0300
  Cincinnati *(G-2577)*

ENGINEERING SVCS: Acoustical

Straight 72 Inc...................................... D 740 943-5730
  Marysville *(G-9940)*

ENGINEERING SVCS: Building Construction

Owens Corning Sales LLC................... F 330 633-6735
  Tallmadge *(G-14042)*

ENGINEERING SVCS: Chemical

Hexion Inc.. C 888 443-9466
  Columbus *(G-5428)*

ENGINEERING SVCS: Civil

Barr Engineering Incorporated............. E 614 714-0299
  Columbus *(G-5175)*
Ceso Inc... E 937 435-8584
  Miamisburg *(G-10626)*
Ever Secure SEC Systems Inc............ F 937 369-8294
  Dayton *(G-6327)*
Pollock Research & Design Inc........... E 330 332-3300
  Salem *(G-13023)*
Ra Consultants LLC.............................. E 513 469-6600
  Blue Ash *(G-1459)*

ENGINEERING SVCS: Construction & Civil

EP Ferris & Associates Inc.................. E 614 299-2999
  Columbus *(G-5357)*

ENGINEERING SVCS: Electrical Or Electronic

American Controls Inc.......................... E 440 944-9735
  Wickliffe *(G-15824)*
CPI Group Limited................................ F 216 525-0046
  Cleveland *(G-3911)*
Davis Technologies Inc........................ F 330 823-2544
  Alliance *(G-401)*

Electrovations Inc................................. G 330 274-3558
  Solon *(G-13341)*
Field Apparatus Service & Tstg.......... G 513 353-9399
  Cincinnati *(G-2902)*
L-3 Cmmncations Nova Engrg Inc...... C 877 282-1168
  Mason *(G-10018)*
Lintech Electronics LLC....................... F 513 528-6190
  Cincinnati *(G-2571)*
Mid-Ohio Electric Co............................ E 614 274-8000
  Columbus *(G-5563)*
New Dawn Labs LLC............................ F 203 675-5644
  Union *(G-14773)*
PMC Systems Limited.......................... E 330 538-2268
  North Jackson *(G-11789)*
Stock Fairfield Corporation.................. C 440 543-6000
  Solon *(G-13425)*
TL Industries Inc.................................. C 419 666-8144
  Perrysburg *(G-12436)*
Vector Electromagnetics LLC.............. F 937 478-5904
  Wilmington *(G-16062)*

ENGINEERING SVCS: Machine Tool Design

Hahn Automation Group Us Inc.......... D 937 886-3232
  Miamisburg *(G-10641)*
Jet Di Inc... G 330 607-7913
  Brunswick *(G-1772)*
Mound Manufacturing Center Inc....... F 937 236-8387
  Dayton *(G-6459)*
Youngstown Plastic Tooling................. F 330 782-7222
  Youngstown *(G-16485)*

ENGINEERING SVCS: Mechanical

Cbn Westside Technologies Inc......... B 513 772-7000
  West Chester *(G-15387)*
Dillin Engineered Systems Corp......... E 419 666-6789
  Perrysburg *(G-12376)*
Genius Solutions Engrg Co................. E 419 794-9914
  Maumee *(G-10202)*
Genpact LLC.. E 513 763-7660
  Cincinnati *(G-2947)*
Johnson Mfg Systems LLC.................. F 937 866-4744
  Miamisburg *(G-10650)*
Morris Technologies Inc...................... E 513 733-1611
  Cincinnati *(G-3174)*
Performnce Plymr Solutions Inc......... F 937 298-3713
  Moraine *(G-11196)*
Projects Designed & Built.................... E 419 726-7400
  Toledo *(G-14443)*
Qcsm LLC... G 216 650-8731
  Cleveland *(G-4602)*
Systems Kit LLC MB.............................. E 330 945-4500
  Akron *(G-343)*

ENGINES: Diesel & Semi-Diesel Or Duel Fuel

Clarke Fire Prtection Pdts Inc............. E 513 771-2200
  West Chester *(G-15545)*
Miscor Group Ltd.................................. B 330 830-3500
  Massillon *(G-10129)*

ENGINES: Gasoline, NEC

Miba Bearings US LLC......................... B 740 962-4242
  Mcconnelsville *(G-10282)*

ENGINES: Internal Combustion, NEC

B A Malcuit Racing Inc......................... G 330 878-7111
  Strasburg *(G-13743)*
Bowden Manufacturing Corp............... E 440 946-1770
  Willoughby *(G-15891)*
Cummins - Allison Corp....................... G 513 469-2924
  Blue Ash *(G-1384)*
Cummins - Allison Corp....................... G 440 824-5050
  Cleveland *(G-3919)*

Employee Codes: A=Over 500 employees, B=251-500
C=101-250, D=51-100, E=20-50, F=10-19, G=1-9

ENGINES: Internal Combustion, NEC

Cummins Inc .... E 614 604-6004
  Grove City (G-8085)
Ford Motor Company .... A 419 226-7000
  Lima (G-9243)
Precision Castparts Corp .... F 440 350-6150
  Painesville (G-12258)
Precision Engneered Components .... F 614 436-0392
  Worthington (G-16207)
Western Branch Diesel LLC .... F 330 454-8800
  Canton (G-2267)

ENGINES: Jet Propulsion

Enjet Aero Dayton Inc .... E 937 878-3800
  Huber Heights (G-8576)
GE Rolls Royce Fighter .... F 513 243-2787
  Cincinnati (G-2939)
General Electric Company .... A 617 443-3000
  Cincinnati (G-2942)

ENGINES: Marine

Performance Research Inc .... E 614 475-8300
  Columbus (G-5670)

ENGRAVING SVC, NEC

Gordons Graphics Inc .... G 330 863-2322
  Malvern (G-9613)
Handcrafted Jewelry Inc .... G 330 650-9011
  Hudson (G-8595)
Irwin Engraving & Printing Co .... G 216 391-7300
  Cleveland (G-4238)
Sams Graphic Industries .... F 330 821-4710
  Alliance (G-422)

ENGRAVING SVCS

Engravers Gallery & Sign Co .... G 330 830-1271
  Massillon (G-10094)
Genius Solutions Engrg Co .... E 419 794-9914
  Maumee (G-10202)
Hafners Hrdwood Connection LLC .... G 419 726-4828
  Toledo (G-14309)
Professional Award Service .... G 513 389-3600
  Cincinnati (G-3301)
Queen City Spirit LLC .... F 513 533-2662
  Cincinnati (G-3320)
Ryder Engraving Inc .... G 740 927-7193
  Pataskala (G-12307)

ENVELOPES

Access Envelope Inc .... F 513 889-0888
  Middletown (G-10801)
American Paper Group Inc .... B 330 758-4545
  Youngstown (G-16309)
Ampac Holdings LLC .... A 513 671-1777
  Cincinnati (G-2622)
Church Budget Monthly Inc .... G 330 337-1122
  Salem (G-12983)
Church-Budget Envelope Company .... E 800 446-9780
  Salem (G-12984)
E-1 (2012) Holdings Inc .... C 330 482-3900
  Columbiana (G-5037)
Envelope 1 Inc .... D 330 482-3900
  Columbiana (G-5038)
Envelope Mart of Ohio Inc .... F 440 365-8177
  Elyria (G-7150)
Jbm Packaging Company .... C 513 933-8333
  Lebanon (G-9090)
Keene Building Products Co .... D 440 605-1020
  Cleveland (G-4279)
Ohio Envelope Manufacturing Co .... E 216 267-2920
  Cleveland (G-4497)
Pac Worldwide Corporation .... E 800 535-0039
  Monroe (G-11117)
Quality Envelope Inc .... G 513 942-7578
  West Chester (G-15579)
SRC Liquidation LLC .... A 937 221-1000
  Dayton (G-6586)
United Envelope LLC .... B 513 542-4700
  Cincinnati (G-3480)
Western States Envelope Co .... E 419 666-7480
  Walbridge (G-15088)

ENVELOPES WHOLESALERS

Envelope Mart of Ohio Inc .... F 440 365-8177
  Elyria (G-7150)
Jbm Packaging Company .... C 513 933-8333
  Lebanon (G-9090)
Pac Worldwide Corporation .... E 800 535-0039
  Monroe (G-11117)
Western States Envelope Co .... E 419 666-7480
  Walbridge (G-15088)

ENZYMES

Biowish Technologies Inc .... G 312 572-6700
  Cincinnati (G-2669)
Mp Biomedicals LLC .... C 440 337-1200
  Solon (G-13393)
Oxyrase Inc .... F 419 589-8800
  Ontario (G-12093)

EPOXY RESINS

General Polymers .... F 330 896-7126
  Akron (G-167)
Hexion Inc .... C 888 443-9466
  Columbus (G-5428)
Key Resin Company .... F 513 943-4225
  Batavia (G-927)
Lattice Composites LLC .... B 440 543-7526
  Chagrin Falls (G-2406)
Nanosperse LLC .... G 937 296-5030
  Kettering (G-8908)
Renegade Materials Corporation .... D 937 350-5274
  Miamisburg (G-10675)
Westlake Corporation .... E 614 986-2497
  Columbus (G-5874)

EQUIPMENT: Rental & Leasing, NEC

Brinkman LLC .... F 419 204-5934
  Lima (G-9225)
Cattron Holdings Inc .... E 234 806-0018
  Warren (G-15150)
De Nora Tech LLC .... D 440 710-5334
  Concord Township (G-5905)
Dearing Compressor and Pump .... E 330 783-2258
  Youngstown (G-16348)
Eaton Leasing Corporation .... B 216 382-2292
  Beachwood (G-986)
Elliott Tool Technologies Ltd .... D 937 253-6133
  Dayton (G-6318)
Glawe Manufacturing Co Inc .... F 937 754-0064
  Fairborn (G-7317)
Great Lakes Crushing Ltd .... D 440 944-5500
  Wickliffe (G-15833)
Hansen Scaffolding LLC .... F 513 574-9000
  West Chester (G-15561)
Higgins Construction & Supply Co Inc ...... F 937 364-2331
  Hillsboro (G-8458)
Powerclean Equipment Company .... F 513 202-0001
  Cleves (G-4963)
Rambasek Realty Inc .... F 937 228-1189
  Dayton (G-6540)
Thomas Do-It Center Inc .... E 740 446-2002
  Gallipolis (G-7903)
Trailer One Inc .... F 330 723-7474
  Medina (G-10388)
Tri State Equipment Company .... G 513 738-7227
  Shandon (G-13151)
Waco Scaffolding & Equipment Inc .... A 216 749-8900
  Cleveland (G-4859)
West Equipment Company Inc .... G 419 698-1601
  Toledo (G-14522)
Williams Scotsman Inc .... D 614 449-8675
  Columbus (G-5878)

ETCHING & ENGRAVING SVC

Canton Galvanizing LLC .... E 330 685-9060
  Canton (G-2063)
Centria Inc .... G 740 432-7351
  Cambridge (G-1127)
Cubbison Company .... D 330 793-2481
  Youngstown (G-6344)
Doak Laser .... G 740 374-0090
  Marietta (G-9790)
Etchworks .... G 330 274-8345
  Mantua (G-9736)
Hadronics Inc .... D 513 321-9350
  Cincinnati (G-2953)
Old World Stones .... G 330 299-1128
  Litchfield (G-9327)
Schnipke Engraving Co Inc .... C 419 453-3376
  Ottoville (G-12204)
Scioto Industrial Coatings Inc .... G 740 352-1011
  Minford (G-11045)
Sterling Coating .... G 513 942-4900
  West Chester (G-15510)
Worldclass Processing Corp .... E
  Twinsburg (G-14457)
X-Treme Finishes Inc .... F 330 474-0614
  North Royalton (G-11903)

ETHYLENE

Geon Company .... A 216 447-6000
  Cleveland (G-4131)

ETHYLENE-PROPYLENE RUBBERS: EPDM Polymers

Allied Polymers .... G 330 975-4200
  Seville (G-13134)
Canton OH Rubber Speclty Prods .... G 330 454-3847
  Canton (G-2065)
Geon Performance Solutions LLC .... F 800 438-4366
  Westlake (G-15774)
Great Lakes Polymer Proc Inc .... F 313 655-4024
  Akron (G-173)
Innoplast Inc .... F 440 543-8660
  Cleveland (G-4227)
Key Resin Company .... F 513 943-4225
  Batavia (G-927)
Mexichem Specialty Resins Inc .... E 440 930-1435
  Avon Lake (G-817)
Polyshield Corporation .... F 614 755-7674
  Pickerington (G-12466)
Protective Industrial Polymers .... F 440 327-0015
  North Ridgeville (G-11854)
Recycled Polymer Solutions LLC .... G 937 821-4020
  Lima (G-9283)
Toyo Seiki Usa Inc .... F 513 546-9657
  Blue Ash (G-148)

EXHAUST HOOD OR FAN CLEANING SVCS

Link To Success Inc .... G 888 959-4203
  Norwalk (G-11970)

EXHAUST SYSTEMS: Eqpt & Parts

Cardington Yutaka Tech Inc .... A 419 864-8777
  Cardington (G-2274)

PRODUCT SECTION

FARM & GARDEN MACHINERY WHOLESALERS

Dbw Fiber Corporation....................... D
  Wooster (G-16113)
Emssons Faurecia Ctrl Systems............ B 937 743-0551
  Franklin (G-7672)
Faurecia Exhaust Systems Inc............. B 937 339-0551
  Troy (G-14568)
Tmg Performance Products LLC........... D 440 891-0999
  Berea (G-1297)

EXPLOSIVES

Austin Powder Company....................... G 419 299-3347
  Findlay (G-7478)
Austin Powder Company....................... C 740 596-5286
  Mc Arthur (G-10262)
Austin Powder Company....................... G 740 968-1555
  Saint Clairsville (G-12896)
Austin Powder Company....................... D 216 464-2400
  Cleveland (G-3698)
Austin Powder Holdings Company........ D 216 464-2400
  Cleveland (G-3699)
Hilltop Energy Inc............................... F 330 859-2108
  Mineral City (G-11018)

EXPLOSIVES, FUSES & DETONATORS: Primary explosives

Sloat Inc.. G 440 951-9554
  Willoughby (G-15995)

EXTENSION CORDS

Rah Investment Holding Inc................. D 330 832-8124
  Massillon (G-10138)

EXTRACTS, FLAVORING

Berghausen Corporation....................... E 513 591-4491
  Cincinnati (G-2665)
Frutarom USA Inc............................... C 513 870-4900
  West Chester (G-15556)
Mane Inc... D 513 248-9876
  Lebanon (G-9096)

FABRIC STORES

Fabric Square Shop............................. G 330 752-3044
  Stow (G-13696)

FABRICS & CLOTHING: Rubber Coated

Ansell Healthcare Products LLC............ E 740 622-4311
  Coshocton (G-5970)

FABRICS: Apparel & Outerwear, Cotton

Fabric Square Shop............................. G 330 752-3044
  Stow (G-13696)
Heritage Hill LLC................................. G 513 237-0240
  Blue Ash (G-1407)
Roach Studios LLC.............................. F 614 725-1405
  Columbus (G-5727)
Struggle Grind Success LLC................. G 330 834-6738
  Boardman (G-1518)
Trophy Sports Center LLC................... F 937 376-2311
  Xenia (G-16279)
Wonder-Shirts Inc................................ G 917 679-2336
  Dublin (G-6959)

FABRICS: Automotive, From Manmade Fiber

Marsh Composites LLC........................ G 937 350-1214
  Dayton (G-6169)

FABRICS: Cotton, Narrow

US Cotton LLC................................... D 216 676-0400
  Cleveland (G-4856)

FABRICS: Decorative Trim & Specialty, Including Twist Weave

Stitches Usa LLC................................ F 330 852-0500
  Walnut Creek (G-15095)
Synthomer Inc.................................... C 216 682-7000
  Beachwood (G-1025)

FABRICS: Denims

Denim6729 Inc.................................... G 216 854-3634
  Cleveland (G-3951)
Noble Denim Workshop....................... G 513 560-5640
  Cincinnati (G-3202)

FABRICS: Fiberglass, Broadwoven

Schmelzer Industries Inc..................... E 740 743-2866
  Somerset (G-13450)

FABRICS: Glass & Fiberglass, Broadwoven

Architectural Fiberglass Inc................. E 216 641-8300
  Cleveland (G-3673)
Valutex Reinforcements Inc................. E 800 251-2507
  Wshngtn Ct Hs (G-16243)

FABRICS: Nonwoven

Amantea Nonwovens LLC..................... F 513 842-6600
  Cincinnati (G-2614)
Autoneum North America Inc.............. B 419 693-0511
  Oregon (G-12103)
Ccp Industries Inc.............................. B 216 535-4227
  Richmond Heights (G-12807)
Toyobo Kureha America Co Ltd........... G 513 771-6788
  West Chester (G-15517)

FABRICS: Nylon, Broadwoven

Seaman Corporation............................ C 330 262-1111
  Wooster (G-16170)

FABRICS: Resin Or Plastic Coated

Biothane Coated Webbing Corp............ E 440 327-0485
  North Ridgeville (G-11832)
Diamond Polymers Incorporated.......... D 330 773-2700
  Akron (G-128)
Duracote Corporation......................... E 330 296-9600
  Ravenna (G-12712)
Durez Corporation.............................. E 567 295-6400
  Kenton (G-8882)
Schneller LLC.................................... G 330 676-7183
  Kent (G-8858)

FABRICS: Rubber & Elastic Yarns & Fabrics

CT Specialty Polymers Ltd................... G 440 632-9311
  Middlefield (G-10744)
Murrubber Technologies Inc................. G 330 688-4881
  Stow (G-13711)

FABRICS: Scrub Cloths

Akron Cotton Products Inc................. G 330 434-7171
  Akron (G-32)
Canton Sterilized Wiping Cloth............ G 330 455-5179
  Canton (G-2068)
Linsalata Cpitl Prtners Fund I............. G 440 684-1400
  Cleveland (G-4330)
Tranzonic Companies.......................... C 440 446-0643
  Cleveland (G-4818)
Tz Acquisition Corp........................... E 216 535-4300
  Richmond Heights (G-12812)

FABRICS: Shirting, Cotton

Kdae Inc... G 844 543-8339
  Lewis Center (G-9167)

FABRICS: Shoe Laces, Exc Leather

Mitchellace Inc................................... D 740 354-2813
  Portsmouth (G-12650)
Sole Choice Inc.................................. E 740 354-2813
  Portsmouth (G-12656)

FABRICS: Umbrella Cloth, Cotton

Totes Isotoner Holdings Corp.............. C 513 682-8200
  West Chester (G-15599)

FABRICS: Upholstery, Wool

Midwest Composites LLC..................... F 419 738-2431
  Wapakoneta (G-15123)

FACILITIES SUPPORT SVCS

Facility Service Pros LLC.................... G 419 577-6123
  Collins (G-5004)
MPW Industrial Svcs Group Inc........... B 740 927-8790
  Hebron (G-8350)
Taylor Communications Inc.................. E 937 221-1000
  Dayton (G-6609)

FAMILY CLOTHING STORES

Fancy ME Boutique LLC....................... G 419 357-8927
  Sandusky (G-13058)

FANS, BLOWING: Indl Or Commercial

Cincinnati Fan & Ventilator................. D 513 573-0600
  Mason (G-9974)
Howden North America Inc.................. E 330 867-8540
  Medina (G-10335)

FANS, EXHAUST: Indl Or Commercial

American Fan Company....................... C 513 874-2400
  Fairfield (G-7333)
ARI Phoenix Inc.................................. E 513 229-3750
  Sharonville (G-13170)
Criticalaire LLC.................................. E 513 475-3800
  Westerville (G-15652)
Howden USA Company......................... E 513 874-2400
  Fairfield (G-7370)
Multi-Wing America Inc...................... E 440 834-9400
  Middlefield (G-10772)

FANS, VENTILATING: Indl Or Commercial

Ad Industries Inc............................... A 303 744-1911
  Dayton (G-6183)
Duro Dyne Midwest Corp.................... C 513 870-6000
  Hamilton (G-8201)
Humongous Holdings Llc..................... F 216 663-8830
  Cleveland (G-4208)
Lau Holdings LLC............................... E 937 476-6500
  Dayton (G-6166)
Lau Holdings LLC............................... D 216 486-4000
  Cleveland (G-4316)
Lau Industries Inc.............................. A 216 894-3903
  Dayton (G-6167)
Tlt-Turbo Inc.................................... G 330 776-5115
  Akron (G-360)
Vector Mechanical LLC........................ G 216 337-4042
  Cleveland (G-4863)

FANS: Ceiling

Acorn Technology Corporation............ E 216 663-1244
  Shaker Heights (G-13149)
Hinkley Lighting Inc........................... E 440 653-5500
  Avon Lake (G-812)

FARM & GARDEN MACHINERY WHOLESALERS

Employee Codes: A=Over 500 employees, B=251-500
C=101-250, D=51-100, E=20-50, F=10-19, G=1-9

2024 Harris Ohio Industrial Directory

FARM & GARDEN MACHINERY WHOLESALERS

All Power Equipment LLC.................... F 740 593-3279
  Athens *(G-674)*
J L Wannemacher Sls Svc Inc.............. F 419 453-3445
  Ottoville *(G-12200)*
Smg Growing Media Inc................... F 937 644-0011
  Marysville *(G-9938)*

FARM MACHINERY REPAIR SVCS

J L Wannemacher Sls Svc Inc.............. F 419 453-3445
  Ottoville *(G-12200)*

FARM SPLYS WHOLESALERS

Andersons Inc.................................. G 419 536-0460
  Toledo *(G-14194)*
Andersons Inc.................................. C 419 893-5050
  Maumee *(G-10165)*
Countyline Co-Op Inc...................... F 419 287-3241
  Pemberville *(G-12334)*
Darling Ingredients Inc..................... G 216 651-9300
  Cleveland *(G-3940)*
Green Field Farms Co-Op................. G 330 263-0246
  Wooster *(G-16126)*
Legacy Farmers Cooperative............. F 419 423-2611
  Findlay *(G-7528)*
Minster Farmers Coop Exch.............. D 419 628-4705
  Minster *(G-11056)*
Phillips Ready Mix Co...................... E 937 426-5151
  Beavercreek Township *(G-1090)*

FARM SPLYS, WHOLESALE: Feed

Cooper Farms Inc............................. D 419 375-4116
  Fort Recovery *(G-7614)*
K M B Inc.. E 330 889-3451
  Bristolville *(G-1652)*
Keynes Bros Inc............................... D 740 385-6824
  Logan *(G-9366)*
Mennel Milling Company................... E 740 385-6824
  Logan *(G-9371)*
Republic Mills Inc............................ E 419 758-3511
  Okolona *(G-12071)*
Stony Hill Mixing Ltd....................... G 330 674-0814
  Millersburg *(G-10995)*
Sunrise Cooperative Inc.................... G 419 628-4705
  Minster *(G-11062)*

FARM SPLYS, WHOLESALE: Fertilizers & Agricultural Chemicals

Helena Agri-Enterprises LLC............. G 419 596-3806
  Continental *(G-5937)*
Nutrien AG Solutions Inc.................. G 614 873-4253
  Milford Center *(G-10929)*

FASTENERS WHOLESALERS

Aspen Fasteners USA....................... G 800 479-0056
  Cleveland *(G-3692)*
Bamal Corp..................................... G 937 492-9484
  Sidney *(G-13225)*
Beckett-Greenhill LLC...................... F 216 861-5730
  Cleveland *(G-3728)*
Cardinal Fstener Specialty Inc........... E 216 831-3800
  Bedford Heights *(G-1166)*
Dimcogray Corporation..................... D 937 433-7600
  Centerville *(G-2361)*
Dubose Nat Enrgy Fas McHned PR... F 216 362-1700
  Middleburg Heights *(G-10718)*
Efg Holdings Inc.............................. A 440 325-4337
  Berea *(G-1275)*
Erico International Corp................... B 440 248-0100
  Solon *(G-13345)*
ET&f Fastening Systems Inc............. F 800 248-2376
  Solon *(G-13346)*

Global Specialties Inc...................... G 800 338-0814
  Brunswick *(G-1765)*
Master Bolt LLC.............................. E 440 323-5529
  Elyria *(G-7178)*
Midwest Motor Supply Co................. C 800 233-1294
  Columbus *(G-5565)*
Ohashi Technica USA Mfg Inc........... F 740 965-9002
  Sunbury *(G-13961)*
Ramco Specialties Inc...................... D 330 653-5135
  Hudson *(G-8609)*
Stanley Engineered Fasten................ F 440 657-3537
  Elyria *(G-7205)*
Stelfast LLC.................................... E 440 879-0077
  Strongsville *(G-13886)*
Tfp Corporation............................... E 330 725-7741
  Medina *(G-10384)*
W W Cross Industries Inc................. F 330 588-8400
  Canton *(G-2263)*
Wodin Inc....................................... E 440 439-4222
  Cleveland *(G-4916)*
Youngstown Bolt & Supply Co........... G 330 799-3201
  Youngstown *(G-16479)*

FASTENERS: Metal

Contitech Usa Inc............................ D 937 644-8900
  Marysville *(G-9906)*
Midwest Motor Supply Co................. C 800 233-1294
  Columbus *(G-5565)*
Seaway Bolt And Specials Company... D 440 236-5015
  Columbia Station *(G-5021)*
Valen Foundry Inc........................... F 724 712-3500
  West Chester *(G-15524)*
Wecall Inc...................................... G 440 437-8202
  Chardon *(G-2470)*

FAUCETS & SPIGOTS: Metal & Plastic

Toolbold Corporation........................ F 440 543-1660
  Cleveland *(G-4802)*

FEATHERS & FEATHER PRODUCTS

Ohio Feather Company Inc................ G 513 921-3373
  Cincinnati *(G-3213)*

FENCE POSTS: Iron & Steel

Msls Group LLC.............................. E 330 723-4431
  Medina *(G-10355)*

FENCES OR POSTS: Ornamental Iron Or Steel

Akron Products Company.................. D 330 576-1750
  Wadsworth *(G-15016)*
Randy Lewis Inc.............................. F 330 784-0456
  Akron *(G-296)*

FENCING MATERIALS: Docks & Other Outdoor Prdts, Wood

Juno Enterprises LLC....................... G 419 448-9350
  New Riegel *(G-11536)*

FENCING MATERIALS: Wood

Kalinich Fence Company Inc............. F 440 238-6127
  Strongsville *(G-13848)*
Randy Lewis Inc.............................. F 330 784-0456
  Akron *(G-296)*
Youngstown Fence Incorporated........ G 330 788-8110
  Youngstown *(G-16481)*

FENCING: Chain Link

Randy Lewis Inc.............................. F 330 784-0456
  Akron *(G-296)*

Richards Whl Fence Co Inc............... E 330 773-0423
  Akron *(G-304)*

FERROALLOYS

ERAMET MARIETTA INC................... C 740 374-1000
  Marietta *(G-9792)*
International Metal Supply LLC......... G 330 764-1004
  Medina *(G-10330)*

FERROMANGANESE, NOT MADE IN BLAST FURNACES

Real Alloy Specialty Pdts LLC........... A 216 755-8836
  Beachwood *(G-1714)*
Real Alloy Specification LLC............. D 216 755-8900
  Beachwood *(G-1716)*

FERROSILICON, EXC MADE IN BLAST FURNACES

Ferroglobe USA Mtllurgical Inc.......... C 740 984-2361
  Waterford *(G-15536)*

FERROUS METALS: Reclaimed From Clay

A-Gas US Holdings Inc..................... F 419 867-8990
  Bowling Green *(G-1547)*

FERTILIZER, AGRICULTURAL: Wholesalers

Hanby Farms Inc............................. E 740 763-3554
  Nashport *(G-11317)*
Ohigro Inc...................................... E 740 726-2429
  Waldo *(G-15090)*

FERTILIZERS: Nitrogen Solutions

Pcs Nitrogen Inc.............................. F 419 226-1200
  Lima *(G-9275)*

FERTILIZERS: Nitrogenous

Agrium Advanced Tech US Inc........... G 614 276-5103
  Columbus *(G-5176)*
Hawthorne Collective Inc.................. E 937 644-0011
  Columbus *(G-5423)*
Keystone Cooperative Inc................. G 937 884-5526
  Verona *(G-14979)*
Nutrien AG Solutions Inc.................. G 513 941-4100
  North Bend *(G-11705)*
Pcs Nitrogen Ohio LP....................... D 419 879-8989
  Lima *(G-9276)*
R & J AG Manufacturing Inc............. F 419 962-4707
  Ashland *(G-608)*
Royster-Clark Inc............................ G 513 941-4100
  North Bend *(G-11706)*
Scotts Miracle-Gro Company............. B 937 644-0011
  Marysville *(G-9915)*
Smgm LLC...................................... E 937 644-0011
  Marysville *(G-9929)*
Synagro Midwest Inc........................ F 937 384-0669
  Miamisburg *(G-11687)*
Turf Care Supply LLC....................... D 877 220-1014
  Brunswick *(G-1776)*

FERTILIZERS: Phosphatic

Andersons Inc.................................. G 419 536-0460
  Toledo *(G-14194)*
Andersons Inc.................................. C 419 893-5050
  Maumee *(G-10165)*
Occidental Chemical Corp................. E 513 242-2900
  Cincinnati *(G-3271)*

FIBER & FIBER PRDTS: Elastomeric

Bridge Components Incorporated....... G 614 873-0777
  Columbus *(G-5212)*

FIBER & FIBER PRDTS: Protein

Matrix Meats Inc......................................F.....614 602-1846
 Dublin *(G-6908)*

FIBER OPTICS

Nextgen Fiber Optics LLC...................G.....513 549-4691
 Cincinnati *(G-3194)*
Sem-Com Company Inc.......................G.....419 537-8813
 Toledo *(G-14466)*

FIBERS: Carbon & Graphite

Ges AGM...E.....216 658-6528
 Cleveland *(G-4123)*
Wolf Composite Solutions....................F.....614 219-6990
 Columbus *(G-5879)*
Xperion E & E USA LLC.......................E.....740 788-9560
 Heath *(G-8333)*

FILM BASE: Cellulose Acetate Or Nitrocellulose Plastics

American Insulation Tech LLC.............F.....513 733-4248
 Milford *(G-10892)*
Simona Boltaron Inc.............................D.....740 498-5900
 Newcomerstown *(G-11651)*

FILTERS

Abanaki Corporation..............................F.....440 543-7400
 Chagrin Falls *(G-2387)*
Allied Separation Tech Inc....................E.....704 732-8034
 Twinsburg *(G-14628)*
Columbus Industries Inc......................D.....740 983-2552
 Ashville *(G-667)*
Columbus Industries One LLC............F.....740 983-2552
 Ashville *(G-668)*
Cummins Filtration Inc..........................C
 Findlay *(G-7500)*
Ddp Specialty Electronic MA................C.....937 839-4612
 West Alexandria *(G-15341)*
E R Advanced Ceramics Inc................E.....330 426-9343
 East Palestine *(G-7004)*
Evoqua Water Technologies LLC........G.....614 861-5440
 Pickerington *(G-12461)*
Filter Technology Inc............................G.....614 921-9801
 Baltimore *(G-844)*
Hdt Expeditionary Systems Inc............F.....216 438-6111
 Solon *(G-13360)*
Hdt Tactical Systems Inc......................C.....216 438-6111
 Solon *(G-13361)*
Hunter Defense Tech Inc......................F.....216 438-6111
 Solon *(G-13363)*
Joyce/Dayton Corp................................E.....937 294-6261
 Dayton *(G-6391)*
OSI Environmental LLC........................E.....440 237-4600
 North Royalton *(G-11890)*
Raymond W Reisiger............................G.....740 400-4090
 Baltimore *(G-846)*
Swift Filters Inc.....................................E.....440 735-0995
 Oakwood Village *(G-12043)*

FILTERS & SOFTENERS: Water, Household

Amsoil Inc..G.....614 274-9851
 Urbancrest *(G-14852)*
Enting Water Conditioning Inc.............E.....937 294-5100
 Moraine *(G-11175)*
Monarch Water Systems Inc................F.....937 426-5773
 Beavercreek *(G-1056)*
New Aqua LLC......................................G.....614 265-9000
 Columbus *(G-5594)*
Obic LLC..G.....419 633-3147
 Bryan *(G-1832)*

United McGill Corporation....................F.....614 920-1267
 Lithopolis *(G-9331)*
William R Hague Inc.............................D.....614 836-2115
 Groveport *(G-8168)*

FILTERS & STRAINERS: Pipeline

Hellan Strainer Company.....................G.....216 206-4200
 Cleveland *(G-4178)*

FILTERS: Air

Cincinnati A Flter Sls Svc Inc...............E.....513 242-3400
 Cincinnati *(G-2737)*
Swift Filters Inc.....................................E.....440 735-0995
 Oakwood Village *(G-12043)*

FILTERS: Air Intake, Internal Combustion Engine, Exc Auto

Androm Industries Inc..........................G.....614 408-9067
 Newark *(G-11563)*
Metalctting Spclists Group Ltd............G.....330 962-4980
 Akron *(G-245)*
Plas-Mac Corp......................................D.....440 349-3222
 Solon *(G-13405)*

FILTERS: General Line, Indl

1200 Feet Limited.................................G.....419 827-6061
 Lakeville *(G-8962)*
Falls Filtration Tech Inc........................E.....330 928-4100
 Stow *(G-13697)*
Gvs Filtration Inc..................................B.....419 423-9040
 Findlay *(G-7517)*
Kavon Filter Products Co.....................F.....732 938-3135
 Cleveland *(G-4277)*
Metaullics Systems LP.........................C.....509 926-6212
 Solon *(G-13587)*
Midwest Filtration LLC.........................D.....513 874-6510
 West Chester *(G-15572)*
Nupro Company....................................D.....440 951-9729
 Willoughby *(G-15962)*
Petro Ware Inc......................................E.....740 982-1302
 Crooksville *(G-6049)*
S A Langmack Company.....................F.....216 541-0500
 Cleveland *(G-4666)*

FILTERS: Oil, Internal Combustion Engine, Exc Auto

Brinkley Technology Group LLC..........F.....330 830-2498
 Massillon *(G-10079)*

FILTRATION DEVICES: Electronic

Contech Strmwter Solutions LLC........G.....513 645-7000
 West Chester *(G-15404)*
Fontaine Pieciak Engrg Inc..................E.....413 592-2273
 Twinsburg *(G-14661)*
Illinois Tool Works Inc..........................E.....262 248-8277
 Bryan *(G-1821)*
Micropure Filtration Inc........................E.....952 472-2323
 Cleveland *(G-4402)*
Nu Stream Filtration Inc.......................F.....937 949-3174
 Dayton *(G-6482)*

FINANCIAL SVCS

Dollars N Cent Inc................................F.....971 381-0406
 Cleveland *(G-3966)*

FINISHING AGENTS

Pilot Chemical Company Ohio.............E.....513 326-0600
 West Chester *(G-15476)*

FIRE ARMS, SMALL: Guns Or Gun Parts, 30 mm & Below

Highpoint Firearms...............................E.....419 747-9444
 Mansfield *(G-9668)*
Ohio Ordnance Works Inc...................E.....440 285-3481
 Chardon *(G-2461)*
Stealth Arms LLC................................G.....419 925-7005
 Celina *(G-2351)*
TS Sales LLC.......................................F.....727 804-8060
 Akron *(G-365)*

FIRE ARMS, SMALL: Rifles Or Rifle Parts, 30 mm & below

Kelblys Rifle Range Inc.......................G.....330 683-4674
 North Lawrence *(G-11798)*
Zshot Inc...G.....800 385-8581
 Columbus *(G-5894)*

FIRE CONTROL EQPT REPAIR SVCS, MILITARY

Fire Foe Corp..E.....330 759-9834
 Girard *(G-7968)*

FIRE CONTROL OR BOMBING EQPT: Electronic

Fire-End & Croker Corp.......................E.....513 870-0517
 West Chester *(G-15553)*
Highcom Global Security Inc...............G.....727 592-9400
 Columbus *(G-5434)*

FIRE DETECTION SYSTEMS

Total Life Safety LLC...........................F.....866 955-2318
 West Chester *(G-15516)*

FIRE EXTINGUISHERS, WHOLESALE

A-Gas US Holdings Inc........................F.....419 867-8990
 Bowling Green *(G-1547)*
Fire Safety Services Inc.......................F.....937 686-2000
 Huntsville *(G-8623)*

FIRE EXTINGUISHERS: Portable

Fire Safety Services Inc.......................F.....937 686-2000
 Huntsville *(G-8623)*
Threat Extinguisher LLC......................G.....614 882-2959
 Westerville *(G-15682)*

FIRE OR BURGLARY RESISTIVE PRDTS

Alchemical Transmutation Corp...........G.....216 313-8674
 Cleveland *(G-3623)*
All Ohio Welding Inc............................G.....937 663-7116
 Saint Paris *(G-12970)*
Central Machinery Company LLC.......F.....740 387-1289
 Marion *(G-9849)*
Donald E Didion II................................E.....419 483-2226
 Bellevue *(G-1226)*
Fabricating Solutions Inc.....................F.....330 486-0998
 Twinsburg *(G-14658)*
Hamilton Products Group Inc..............E.....800 876-6066
 Milford *(G-10908)*
MAK Fabricating Inc............................F.....330 747-0040
 Youngstown *(G-16395)*
Mast Farm Service Ltd........................F.....330 893-2972
 Walnut Creek *(G-15094)*
Master Magnetics Inc..........................F.....740 373-0909
 Marietta *(G-9807)*
Penny Fab LLC....................................F.....740 967-3669
 Columbus *(G-5667)*
Quest Technologies Inc.......................F.....937 743-1200
 Franklin *(G-7696)*

FIREFIGHTING APPARATUS
Johnsons Fire Equipment Co............... F 740 357-4916
  Wellston (G-15330)

FIREPLACE EQPT & ACCESS
Thermo-Rite Mfg Company............... E 330 633-8680
  Akron (G-356)

FIREWORKS
Phantom Fireworks Wstn Reg LLC....... F 330 746-1064
  Youngstown (G-16418)
Rozzi Company Inc............................ E 513 683-0620
  Loveland (G-9502)

FIRST AID SPLYS, WHOLESALE
Eleven 10 LLC.................................... F 888 216-4049
  Westlake (G-15747)

FISH & SEAFOOD WHOLESALERS
Alsatian Llc....................................... G 330 661-0600
  Medina (G-10293)

FISH FOOD
Alsatian Llc....................................... G 330 661-0600
  Medina (G-10293)

FITTINGS & ASSEMBLIES: Hose & Tube, Hydraulic Or Pneumatic
Ace Manufacturing Company............ E 513 541-2490
  West Chester (G-15360)
Danfoss Power Solutions II LLC........ G 419 238-1190
  Van Wert (G-14913)
Eaton Aeroquip LLC.......................... C 440 523-5000
  Cleveland (G-3991)
Hombre Capital Inc........................... F 440 838-5335
  Brecksville (G-1620)
Industrial Connections Inc................. G 330 274-2155
  Mantua (G-9737)
Mid-State Sales Inc........................... G 330 744-2158
  Youngstown (G-16400)
Mid-State Sales Inc........................... D 614 864-1811
  Columbus (G-5564)
Netherland Rubber Company............ F 513 733-0883
  Cincinnati (G-3187)
Ohio Hydraulics Inc........................... E 513 771-2590
  Cincinnati (G-3215)
Omega 1 Inc..................................... F 216 663-8424
  Willoughby (G-15965)
State Metal Hose Inc......................... G 614 527-4700
  Hilliard (G-8443)
Tylok International Inc....................... D 216 261-7310
  Cleveland (G-4840)
US Controls Acquisition Ltd.............. G 330 758-1147
  Poland (G-12612)

FITTINGS: Pipe
Adaptall America Inc........................ F 330 425-4114
  Twinsburg (G-14624)
Amaltech Inc..................................... G 440 248-7500
  Solon (G-13311)
Campion Pipe Fitting......................... G 740 627-1125
  Steubenville (G-13664)
Drainage Pipe & Fittings LLC............ G 419 538-6337
  Ottawa (G-12179)
General Plug and Mfg Co.................. C 440 926-2411
  Grafton (G-8000)
Greater Cleve Pipe Ftting Fund......... F 216 524-8334
  Cleveland (G-4148)
Mid-State Sales Inc........................... D 614 864-1811
  Columbus (G-5564)

Parker-Hannifin Corporation.............. C 614 279-7070
  Columbus (G-5656)
Parker-Hannifin Corporation.............. D 937 456-5571
  Eaton (G-7067)
Richards Industrials Inc..................... D 513 533-5600
  Cincinnati (G-3339)
SSP Fittings Corp.............................. D 330 425-4250
  Twinsburg (G-14736)
Swagelok Company........................... E 440 473-1050
  Cleveland (G-4758)
Swagelok Company........................... E 440 349-5652
  Solon (G-13429)
Swagelok Company........................... E 440 349-5836
  Solon (G-13430)
Swagelok Company........................... A 440 248-4600
  Solon (G-13428)
TCH Industries Incorporated............. F 330 487-5155
  Twinsburg (G-14741)
US Fittings Inc.................................. F 234 212-9420
  Twinsburg (G-14752)

FITTINGS: Pipe, Fabricated
Phoenix Forge Group LLC................. C 800 848-6125
  West Jefferson (G-15614)
Pipe Line Development Company...... D 440 871-5700
  Strongsville (G-13865)
Pipe Products Inc.............................. C 513 587-7532
  West Chester (G-15480)

FIXTURES & EQPT: Kitchen, Metal, Exc Cast Aluminum
Amtekco Industries LLC.................... D 614 228-6590
  Columbus (G-5136)
Washington Products Inc.................. F 330 837-5101
  Massillon (G-10154)
Wasserstrom Co................................ G 614 737-8568
  Columbus (G-5864)

FIXTURES & EQPT: Kitchen, Porcelain Enameled
Anchor Hocking Holdings Inc............ A 740 687-2500
  Columbus (G-5141)

FIXTURES: Cut Stone
Rainbow Cultured Marble.................. F 330 225-3400
  Brunswick (G-1786)

FLAGS: Fabric
Annin & Co Inc.................................. C 740 622-4447
  Coshocton (G-5968)
Flag Lady Inc.................................... G 614 263-1776
  Columbus (G-5378)

FLAGSTONES
9729 Flagstone Way LLC.................. G 513 239-1950
  Milford (G-10890)

FLAT GLASS: Construction
Imaging Sciences LLC....................... G 440 975-9640
  Willoughby (G-15931)
Kaaa/Hamilton Enterprises Inc.......... E 513 874-5874
  Fairfield (G-7377)
Pilkington North America Inc............ C 419 247-3731
  Urbancrest (G-14854)
Pilkington North America Inc............ C 419 247-3731
  Toledo (G-14436)
S R Door Inc..................................... D 740 927-3558
  Hebron (G-8360)
Wt Acquisition Company Ltd............. E 513 577-7980
  Cincinnati (G-3528)

FLAT GLASS: Float
Pilkington North America Inc............ B 419 247-3211
  Rossford (G-1289)

FLAT GLASS: Picture
Knight Industries Corp...................... F 419 478-8550
  Toledo (G-14349)

FLAT GLASS: Plate, Polished & Rough
Guardian Fabrication LLC.................. C 419 855-7706
  Millbury (G-1093)

FLAT GLASS: Window, Clear & Colored
Sonalysts Inc.................................... E 937 429-9711
  Beavercreek (G-1064)

FLAVORS OR FLAVORING MATERIALS: Synthetic
Frutarom USA Holding Inc................ G 201 861-9500
  West Chester (G-15555)
Givaudan Flavors Corporation........... F 513 948-3428
  Cincinnati (G-253)
Givaudan Flavors Corporation........... G 513 786-0124
  Cincinnati (G-254)
Givaudan Flavors Corporation........... C 513 948-8000
  Cincinnati (G-255)
Givaudan Fragrances Corp................ E 513 948-3428
  Cincinnati (G-257)
Kerry Flavor Systems Us LLC........... C 513 539-7373
  Monroe (G-1113)

FLIGHT RECORDERS
L3harris Electrodynamics Inc............ C 847 259-0740
  Cincinnati (G-269)

FLOOR COVERING STORES
Armstrong World Industries Inc........ E 614 771-9307
  Hilliard (G-8393)
Hardwood Lumber Company Inc....... F 440 834-1891
  Middlefield (G-10754)
Wccv Floor Coverings LLC................ F 330 688-0114
  Peninsula (G-12344)

FLOOR COVERING STORES: Carpets
Prints & Paints Flr Cvg Co Inc........... E 419 462-5663
  Galion (G-7883)
Shaheen Oriental Rug Co Inc............ F 330 493-9000
  Canton (G-2222)
Stanley Steemer Intl Inc.................... C 614 764-2007
  Dublin (G-6949)

FLOOR COVERINGS WHOLESALERS
Pfpc Enterprise Inc........................... F 513 941-6200
  Cincinnati (G-253)

FLOOR COVERINGS: Aircraft & Automobile
Angstrom Fiber Englewood LLC........ E 734 756-1164
  Englewood (G-7223)

FLOOR COVERINGS: Rubber
Dandy Products Inc........................... G 513 625-3000
  Goshen (G-792)
Delphos Rubber Company................. E 419 692-3000
  Delphos (G-6751)
Johnsonite Inc................................... B 440 543-8916
  Solon (G-13370)
Mameco International Inc.................. D 216 752-4400
  Cleveland (G-354)

FLOORING & SIDING: Metal

PRODUCT SECTION

FOOD PRDTS, CANNED OR FRESH PACK: Fruit Juices

Higgins Construction & Supply Co Inc.. F 937 364-2331
  Hillsboro *(G-8458)*

FLOORING: Hardwood

Prestige Enterprise Intl Inc................... D 513 469-6044
  Blue Ash *(G-1456)*
Robbins Inc.. E 513 871-8988
  Cincinnati *(G-3348)*
Timothy Whatman................................. E 419 883-2443
  Bellville *(G-1248)*

FLOORING: Rubber

Roppe Corporation................................ B 419 435-8546
  Fostoria *(G-7651)*
Tarkett Inc... E 440 543-8916
  Chagrin Falls *(G-2428)*
Tarkett Inc... D 800 899-8916
  Solon *(G-13433)*

FLORIST: Flowers, Fresh

Cleveland Plant and Flower Co............. G 614 478-9900
  Columbus *(G-5253)*

FLOWERS, FRESH, WHOLESALE

Cleveland Plant and Flower Co............. G 614 478-9900
  Columbus *(G-5253)*

FLUID METERS & COUNTING DEVICES

Aqua Technology Group LLC................ G 513 298-1183
  West Chester *(G-15367)*
Exact Equipment Corporation............... F 215 295-2000
  Columbus *(G-5062)*
Reliable Manufacturing LLC.................. E 740 756-9373
  Carroll *(G-2301)*
Triplett Bluffton Corporation.................. G 419 358-8750
  Bluffton *(G-1509)*

FLUID POWER PUMPS & MOTORS

Aerocontrolex Group Inc....................... D 216 291-6025
  South Euclid *(G-13457)*
Anchor Flange Company....................... D 513 527-3512
  Cincinnati *(G-2626)*
Apph Wichita Inc.................................. E 316 943-5752
  Strongsville *(G-13808)*
Bergstrom Company Ltd Partnr............. E 440 232-2282
  Cleveland *(G-3730)*
Eaton Aeroquip LLC.............................. A 419 891-7775
  Maumee *(G-10201)*
Eaton Leasing Corporation................... B 216 382-2292
  Beachwood *(G-986)*
Emerson Process Management............. C 419 529-4311
  Ontario *(G-12091)*
Fluid Power Solutions LLC................... G 614 777-8954
  Hilliard *(G-8412)*
Force Control Industries Inc................. E 513 868-0900
  Fairfield *(G-7363)*
Furukawa Rock Drill USA Co Ltd........... F 330 673-5826
  Kent *(G-8816)*
Giant Industries Inc.............................. E 419 531-4600
  Toledo *(G-14300)*
Gorman-Rupp Company........................ C 419 755-1011
  Mansfield *(G-9663)*
H Y O Inc.. E 614 488-2861
  Columbus *(G-5414)*
Hite Parts Exchange Inc....................... F 614 272-5115
  Columbus *(G-5442)*
Hy-Production Inc................................. C 330 273-2400
  Valley City *(G-14873)*
Hydraulic Parts Store Inc..................... E 330 364-6667
  New Philadelphia *(G-11505)*
Midwest Tool & Engineering Co............. E
  Dayton *(G-6445)*

Parker Hannifin Partner B LLC.............. E 216 896-3000
  Cleveland *(G-4528)*
Parker Royalty Partnership................... E 216 896-3000
  Cleveland *(G-4529)*
Parker-Hannifin Corporation................. G 330 261-1618
  Berlin Center *(G-1311)*
Parker-Hannifin Corporation................. C 419 644-4311
  Metamora *(G-10603)*
Permco Inc.. C 330 626-2801
  Streetsboro *(G-13783)*
Pfpc Enterprises Inc............................. F 513 941-6200
  Cincinnati *(G-3253)*
Quad Fluid Dynamics Inc...................... G 330 220-3005
  Brunswick *(G-1785)*
Radocy Inc.. F 419 666-4400
  Rossford *(G-12870)*
Robeck Fluid Power Co......................... D 330 562-1140
  Aurora *(G-734)*
Semtorq Inc.. F 330 487-0600
  Twinsburg *(G-14734)*
Starkey Machinery Inc.......................... E 419 468-2560
  Galion *(G-7885)*
Sunset Industries Inc........................... E 440 306-8284
  Mentor *(G-10570)*
Swagelok Company................................ E 440 349-5836
  Solon *(G-13430)*
Trane Technologies Company LLC........ E 419 633-6800
  Bryan *(G-1842)*

FLUID POWER VALVES & HOSE FITTINGS

Alkon Corporation................................. D 419 355-9111
  Fremont *(G-7762)*
Amfm Inc... F 440 953-4545
  Willoughby *(G-15877)*
Cho Bedford Inc................................... D 330 343-8896
  Dover *(G-6811)*
Dixon Valve & Coupling Co LLC............ F 330 425-3000
  Twinsburg *(G-14652)*
Eaton Aeroquip LLC.............................. A 419 891-7775
  Maumee *(G-10201)*
Freudenberg-Nok General Partnr.......... C 419 427-5221
  Findlay *(G-7511)*
Hydac Technology Corp........................ F 610 266-0100
  Wooster *(G-16131)*
Hydraulic Parts Store Inc..................... E 330 364-6667
  New Philadelphia *(G-11505)*
Ic-Fluid Power Inc................................ F 419 661-8811
  Rossford *(G-12866)*
Kirtland Capital Partners LP................ E 216 593-0100
  Beachwood *(G-993)*
Parker-Hannifin Corporation................. D 937 456-5571
  Eaton *(G-7067)*
Parker-Hannifin Corporation................. B 440 943-5700
  Wickliffe *(G-15846)*
Pima Valve LLC.................................... D 330 337-9535
  Salem *(G-13022)*
Precision Engneered Components........ F 614 436-0392
  Worthington *(G-16207)*
Pressure Connections Corp.................. D 614 863-6930
  Columbus *(G-5689)*
Quality Machining and Mfg Inc............. F 419 899-2543
  Sherwood *(G-13202)*
SSP Fittings Corp................................. D 330 425-4250
  Twinsburg *(G-14736)*
Superior Holding LLC........................... E 216 651-9400
  Cleveland *(G-4748)*
Superior Products LLC......................... E 216 651-9400
  Cleveland *(G-4751)*
Swagelok Company................................ E 440 349-5836
  Solon *(G-13430)*
Thogus Products Company................... D 440 933-8850
  Avon Lake *(G-825)*

Transdigm Inc....................................... F 216 291-6025
  Cleveland *(G-4815)*
United States Controls......................... G 330 758-1147
  Youngstown *(G-16464)*
Zaytran Inc... E 440 324-2814
  Elyria *(G-7220)*

FOAM RUBBER

Archem America Inc.............................. F 419 294-6304
  Upper Sandusky *(G-14803)*
ISO Technologies Inc............................ F 740 928-0084
  Hebron *(G-8346)*
Ohio Foam Corporation......................... G 614 252-4877
  Columbus *(G-5619)*
Ohio Foam Corporation......................... F 419 492-2151
  New Washington *(G-11550)*
Ohio Foam Corporation......................... E 330 799-4553
  Youngstown *(G-16405)*
Pfp Holdings LLC.................................. A 419 647-4191
  Spencerville *(G-13488)*
Precision Fab Products Inc.................. G 937 526-5681
  Versailles *(G-14988)*

FOAMS & RUBBER, WHOLESALE

Acor Orthopaedic LLC........................... E 216 662-4500
  Cleveland *(G-3594)*
Global Manufacturing Solutions............ F 937 236-8315
  Dayton *(G-6355)*
Johnson Bros Rubber Co Inc................ E 419 752-4814
  Greenwich *(G-8067)*
Johnson Bros Rubber Co....................... D 419 853-4122
  West Salem *(G-15634)*
Tahoma Enterprises Inc........................ D 330 745-9016
  Barberton *(G-897)*
Tahoma Rubber & Plastics Inc............. D 330 745-9016
  Barberton *(G-898)*

FOIL & LEAF: Metal

Avery Dennison Corporation................. D 440 639-3900
  Mentor *(G-10427)*
Avery Dennison Corporation................. B 440 534-6000
  Mentor *(G-10426)*
CCL Label Inc....................................... D 216 676-2703
  Cleveland *(G-3801)*
CCL Label Inc....................................... D 440 878-7000
  Strongsville *(G-13819)*
Compco Quaker Mfg Inc........................ E 330 482-0200
  Salem *(G-12986)*
Quaker Mfg Corp................................... C 330 332-4631
  Salem *(G-13024)*
Wieland Metal Svcs Foils LLC............... D 330 823-1700
  Alliance *(G-437)*

FOIL: Laminated To Paper Or Other Materials

Foil Tapes LLC..................................... G 216 255-6655
  Cleveland *(G-4076)*

FOOD PRDTS, BREAKFAST: Cereal, Oatmeal

Niese Farms... G 419 347-1204
  Crestline *(G-6035)*

FOOD PRDTS, BREAKFAST: Cereal, Wheat Flakes

General Mills Inc.................................. F 419 269-3100
  Toledo *(G-14299)*

FOOD PRDTS, CANNED OR FRESH PACK: Fruit Juices

Fremont Company................................. E 419 363-2924
  Rockford *(G-12833)*

FOOD PRDTS, CANNED: Baby Food

Refresco Us Inc .... C 937 790-1400
  Carlisle (G-2293)

FOOD PRDTS, CANNED: Baby Food

Baxters North America Inc .... E 513 552-7728
  Blue Ash (G-1366)
Baxters North America Inc .... E 513 552-7718
  West Chester (G-15540)
Baxters North America Inc .... E 513 552-7485
  Cincinnati (G-2661)

FOOD PRDTS, CANNED: Barbecue Sauce

Dominion Liquid Tech LLC .... E 513 272-2824
  Cincinnati (G-2836)

FOOD PRDTS, CANNED: Beans & Bean Sprouts

B&G Foods Inc .... E 513 482-8226
  Cincinnati (G-2653)

FOOD PRDTS, CANNED: Fruit Juices, Fresh

Country Pure Foods Inc .... C 330 753-2293
  Akron (G-116)
Gwj Liquidation Inc .... F 216 475-5770
  Cleveland (G-4158)
Meiers Wine Cellars Inc .... E 513 891-2900
  Cincinnati (G-3146)
Ohio Pure Foods Inc .... D 330 753-2293
  Akron (G-271)

FOOD PRDTS, CANNED: Fruits

B&G Foods Inc .... E 513 482-8226
  Cincinnati (G-2653)
Dutch Country Kettles Ltd .... G 937 780-6718
  Leesburg (G-9124)
Fry Foods Inc .... E 419 448-0831
  Tiffin (G-14087)
J M Smucker Flight Dept .... G 330 497-0073
  North Canton (G-11739)
JES Foods Inc .... F 216 883-8987
  Medina (G-10339)
JES Foods/Celina Inc .... F 419 586-7446
  Celina (G-2339)
Milos Whole World Gourmet LLC .... G 740 589-6456
  Nelsonville (G-11358)
Pillsbury Company LLC .... E 419 845-3751
  Caledonia (G-1917)
Pillsbury Company LLC .... D 740 286-2170
  Wellston (G-15331)
Robert Rothschild Farm LLC .... F 855 969-8050
  West Chester (G-15501)
Rosebuds Ranch and Garden LLC ..... F 937 214-1801
  Covington (G-6031)
Smucker International Inc .... E 330 682-3000
  Orrville (G-12154)
The Fremont Kraut Company .... E 419 332-6481
  Fremont (G-7812)
Trevor Clatterbuck .... G 330 359-2129
  Wilmot (G-16070)
Two Grndmthers Gourmet Kit LLC ..... G 614 746-0888
  Reynoldsburg (G-12778)
Welch Foods Inc A Cooperative .... D 513 632-5610
  Cincinnati (G-3511)
Clovervale Farms LLC .... D 440 960-0146
  Amherst (G-473)

FOOD PRDTS, CANNED: Jams, Including Imitation

Yoders Fine Foods LLC .... F 740 668-4961
  Gambier (G-7910)

FOOD PRDTS, CANNED: Jams, Jellies & Preserves

Coopers Mill Inc .... F 419 562-4215
  Bucyrus (G-1854)
J M Smucker Company .... A 330 682-3000
  Orrville (G-12129)
Nu Pet Company .... F 330 682-3000
  Orrville (G-12142)
Smucker Foodservice Inc .... F 877 858-3855
  Orrville (G-12153)
Smucker Manufacturing Inc .... F 888 550-9555
  Orrville (G-12155)
Smucker Retail Foods Inc .... F 330 682-3000
  Orrville (G-12157)

FOOD PRDTS, CANNED: Jellies, Edible, Including Imitation

Inter American Products Inc .... D 800 645-2233
  Cincinnati (G-3025)

FOOD PRDTS, CANNED: Puddings, Exc Meat

Clovervale Farms LLC .... D 440 960-0146
  Amherst (G-473)

FOOD PRDTS, CANNED: Spaghetti & Other Pasta Sauce

Annarino Foods Ltd .... F 937 274-3663
  Dayton (G-6207)
Bellisio Foods Inc .... C 740 286-5505
  Jackson (G-8710)
RC Industries Inc .... E 330 879-5486
  Navarre (G-11352)

FOOD PRDTS, CANNED: Tomato Sauce

Kraft Heinz Company .... A 330 837-8331
  Massillon (G-10118)

FOOD PRDTS, CANNED: Vegetables

Bfc Inc .... E 330 364-6645
  Dover (G-6809)

FOOD PRDTS, CONFECTIONERY, WHOLESALE: Candy

Bendon Inc .... D 419 207-3600
  Ashland (G-556)
Gorant Chocolatier LLC .... C 330 726-8821
  Boardman (G-1513)
International Leisure Activities Inc .... G
  Springfield (G-13582)
Robert E McGrath Inc .... F 440 572-7747
  Strongsville (G-13872)
Sweeties Olympia Treats LLC .... F 440 572-7747
  Strongsville (G-13888)

FOOD PRDTS, CONFECTIONERY, WHOLESALE: Pretzels

Mike-Sells West Virginia Inc .... D 937 228-9400
  Dayton (G-6448)

FOOD PRDTS, CONFECTIONERY, WHOLESALE: Snack Foods

Hen of Woods LLC .... G 513 954-8871
  Cincinnati (G-2993)
Mike-Sells Potato Chip Co .... E 937 228-9400
  Dayton (G-6447)
Shearers Foods LLC .... A 800 428-6843
  Massillon (G-10142)

FOOD PRDTS, FISH & SEAFOOD: Fish, Fresh, Prepared

Pacific Atlantic Povs Inc .... G 330 467-0150
  Northfield (G-1109)

FOOD PRDTS, FROZEN: Ethnic Foods, NEC

Lopaus Point LLC .... F 614 302-7242
  Groveport (G-8152)
Sunrise Foods Inc .... E 614 276-2880
  Columbus (G-5708)

FOOD PRDTS, FROZEN: Fruit Juice, Concentrates

Beverages Holdings LLC .... A 513 483-3300
  Blue Ash (G-139)
Country Pure Foods Inc .... C 330 753-2293
  Akron (G-116)
Cygnus Home Service LLC .... E 419 222-9977
  Lima (G-9234)

FOOD PRDTS, FROZEN: Fruit Juices

Simply Unique Snacks LLC .... G 513 223-7736
  Cincinnati (G-3304)

FOOD PRDTS, FROZEN: Fruits

National Frt Vgtble Tech Corp .... E 740 400-4055
  Columbus (G-5090)

FOOD PRDTS, FROZEN: Fruits & Vegetables

Heinz Foreign Investment Co .... F 330 837-8331
  Massillon (G-1005)
HJ Heinz Company LP .... D 330 837-8331
  Massillon (G-1007)

FOOD PRDTS, FROZEN: Fruits, Juices & Vegetables

Buckeye Smoothies LLC .... G 740 589-2900
  Athens (G-678)
Creek Smoothie LLC .... G 937 429-1519
  Beavercreek (G-1044)
Nestle Prepared Foods Company .... B 440 349-5757
  Solon (G-13393)
Ohios Best Juice Company LLC .... F 440 258-0834
  Reynoldsburg (G-12771)

FOOD PRDTS, WHOLESALE: Baking Splys

Cassanos Inc .... E 937 294-8400
  Dayton (G-624)

FOOD PRDTS, WHOLESALE: Beverages, Exc Coffee & Tea

G & J Pepsi-Cola Bottlers Inc .... E 740 593-3366
  Athens (G-683)

FOOD PRDTS, WHOLESALE: Chocolate

Walnut Creek Chocolate Co Inc .... E 330 893-2995
  Walnut Creek (G-15096)

FOOD PRDTS, WHOLESALE: Coffee, Green Or Roasted

Iron Bean Inc .... F 518 641-9917
  Perrysburg (G-2393)
Ohio Coffee Collaborative Ltd .... F 614 564-9852
  Columbus (G-513)

FOOD PRDTS, WHOLESALE: Condiments

Kerry Inc .... E 760 685-2548
  Byesville (G-199)

PRODUCT SECTION

FOOD PRDTS: Flour & Other Grain Mill Products

FOOD PRDTS, WHOLESALE: Cookies
Bendon Inc..D..... 419 207-3600
  Ashland (G-556)

FOOD PRDTS, WHOLESALE: Dried or Canned Foods
James C Robinson..............................G..... 513 969-7482
  Cincinnati (G-3036)
Tarrier Foods Corp..............................E..... 614 876-8594
  Columbus (G-5810)

FOOD PRDTS, WHOLESALE: Grain Elevators
Fort Recovery Equity Inc....................E..... 419 375-4119
  Fort Recovery (G-7616)
Keystone Cooperative Inc..................G..... 937 884-5526
  Verona (G-14975)
Minster Farmers Coop Exch................D..... 419 628-4705
  Minster (G-11056)
Mullet Enterprises Inc.........................G..... 330 852-4681
  Sugarcreek (G-13932)
Pettisville Grain Co..............................E..... 419 446-2547
  Pettisville (G-12452)
Sunrise Cooperative Inc....................G..... 419 628-4705
  Minster (G-11062)

FOOD PRDTS, WHOLESALE: Grains
Andersons Inc......................................G..... 419 536-0460
  Toledo (G-14194)
Andersons Inc......................................C..... 419 893-5050
  Maumee (G-10165)
Cooper Hatchery Inc...........................C..... 419 594-3325
  Oakwood (G-12030)
Countyline Co-Op Inc..........................F..... 419 287-3241
  Pemberville (G-12334)
Legacy Farmers Cooperative.............F..... 419 423-2611
  Findlay (G-7528)
Mid-Wood Inc.......................................F..... 419 257-3331
  North Baltimore (G-11696)
Premier Feeds LLC.............................G..... 937 584-2411
  Sabina (G-12891)
Simmons Feed & Supply LLC............E..... 800 754-1228
  Salem (G-13031)
Van Tilburg Farms Inc.........................F..... 419 586-3077
  Celina (G-2354)

FOOD PRDTS, WHOLESALE: Juices
Grace Juice Company LLC.................F..... 614 398-6879
  Westerville (G-15707)

FOOD PRDTS, WHOLESALE: Salt, Edible
Morton Salt Inc....................................C..... 330 925-3015
  Rittman (G-12825)

FOOD PRDTS, WHOLESALE: Specialty
Amerihua Intl Entps Inc.......................G..... 740 549-0300
  Lewis Center (G-9148)
Cheese Holdings Inc...........................E..... 330 893-2479
  Millersburg (G-10951)
JM Smucker LLC.................................D..... 330 682-3000
  Orrville (G-12132)

FOOD PRDTS, WHOLESALE: Water, Distilled
Distillata Company..............................D..... 216 771-2900
  Cleveland (G-3962)
Rambasek Realty Inc..........................F..... 937 228-1189
  Dayton (G-6540)

FOOD PRDTS: Animal & marine fats & oils
Archer-Daniels-Midland Company......E..... 419 435-6633
  Fostoria (G-7628)

Cargill Incorporated............................D..... 937 498-4555
  Sidney (G-13231)
Darling Ingredients Inc........................G..... 972 717-0300
  Cincinnati (G-2819)
Darling Ingredients Inc........................G..... 216 651-9300
  Cleveland (G-3940)
Darling Ingredients Inc........................G..... 216 351-3440
  Cleveland (G-3941)
Fiske Brothers Refining Co.................D..... 419 691-2491
  Toledo (G-14289)
Griffin Industries LLC..........................F..... 513 549-0041
  Blue Ash (G-1400)
Holmes By-Products Co Inc...............E..... 330 893-2322
  Millersburg (G-10963)
Werner G Smith Inc.............................F..... 216 861-3676
  Cleveland (G-4904)

FOOD PRDTS: Bread Crumbs, Exc Made In Bakeries
Pepperidge Farm Incorporated...........G..... 419 933-2611
  Willard (G-15863)

FOOD PRDTS: Chicken, Processed, Cooked
Roots Poultry Inc................................F..... 419 332-0041
  Fremont (G-7805)

FOOD PRDTS: Chicken, Processed, Fresh
Gerber Farm Division Inc....................F..... 800 362-7381
  Orrville (G-12126)
Rcf Kitchens Indiana LLC...................G..... 765 478-6600
  Beavercreek (G-1079)

FOOD PRDTS: Chocolate Bars, Solid
Fannie May Confections Inc...............A..... 330 494-0833
  North Canton (G-11726)

FOOD PRDTS: Cocoa, Powdered
Benjamin P Forbes Company.............F..... 440 838-4400
  Broadview Heights (G-1656)

FOOD PRDTS: Coffee
Altraserv LLC......................................G..... 614 889-2500
  Plain City (G-12561)
Hinterland Cof Strategies LLC............G..... 440 829-5604
  Cleveland (G-4190)
Inter American Products Inc..............D..... 800 645-2233
  Cincinnati (G-3025)
Iron Bean Inc......................................F..... 518 641-9917
  Perrysburg (G-12393)
Mc Concepts Llc.................................G..... 330 933-6402
  Canton (G-2155)
Nutz4coffee Ltd...................................G..... 216 236-5292
  Cleveland (G-4488)
Ohio Coffee Collaborative Ltd............F..... 614 564-9852
  Columbus (G-5613)
Rosebuds Ranch and Garden LLC....F..... 937 214-1801
  Covington (G-6031)

FOOD PRDTS: Coffee Extracts
Queen Beanery Coffeehouse LLC......G..... 937 798-4023
  Peebles (G-12330)

FOOD PRDTS: Corn Oil Prdts
Poet Biorefining Marion LLC..............E..... 740 383-4400
  Marion (G-9873)

FOOD PRDTS: Dips, Exc Cheese & Sour Cream Based
Gomez Salsa LLC...............................E..... 513 314-1978
  Cincinnati (G-2965)

Lakeview Farms LLC..........................C..... 419 695-9925
  Delphos (G-6769)
Oasis Mditerranean Cuisine Inc.........E..... 419 269-1459
  Toledo (G-14402)
Salsa Rica II LLC................................G..... 740 616-9918
  Hilliard (G-8438)

FOOD PRDTS: Dough, Pizza, Prepared
Crestar Crusts Inc..............................E..... 740 335-4813
  Wshngtn Ct Hs (G-16228)

FOOD PRDTS: Doughs, Frozen Or Refrig From Purchased Flour
Mid American Ventures Inc................F..... 216 524-0974
  Cleveland (G-4405)

FOOD PRDTS: Dressings, Salad, Raw & Cooked Exc Dry Mixes
Annarino Foods Ltd............................F..... 937 274-3663
  Dayton (G-6207)
Consumer Guild Foods Inc................F..... 419 726-3406
  Toledo (G-14251)
Lancaster Colony Corporation...........F..... 614 792-9774
  Dublin (G-6906)
Lancaster Colony Corporation...........E..... 614 224-7141
  Westerville (G-15663)
Lancaster Glass Corporation.............E..... 614 224-7141
  Westerville (G-15664)
Lbzb Restaurants Inc.........................F..... 567 413-4700
  Bowling Green (G-1570)
Mark Grzianis St Treats Ex Inc..........F..... 330 414-6266
  Kent (G-8832)
Tmarzetti Company.............................C..... 614 846-2232
  Westerville (G-15683)
Tulkoff Food Products Ohio LLC........G..... 410 864-0523
  Cincinnati (G-3474)

FOOD PRDTS: Dried & Dehydrated Fruits, Vegetables & Soup Mix
Appalachia Freeze Dry Co LLC..........F..... 740 412-0169
  Richmond Dale (G-12804)
Hayden Valley Foods Inc...................D..... 614 539-7233
  Urbancrest (G-14853)
Hirzel Canning Company....................E..... 419 693-0531
  Northwood (G-11919)

FOOD PRDTS: Edible fats & oils
Cincinnati Biorefining Corp................F..... 513 482-8800
  Cincinnati (G-2743)
Cincinnati Renewable Fuels LLC.......D..... 513 482-8800
  Cincinnati (G-2759)
Wileys Finest LLC...............................C..... 740 622-1072
  Coshocton (G-6002)

FOOD PRDTS: Emulsifiers
Generations Ace Inc...........................G..... 440 835-4872
  Bay Village (G-965)
Lasenor Usa LLC................................F..... 800 754-1228
  Salem (G-13010)

FOOD PRDTS: Flour
Mennel Milling Company....................G..... 419 294-2337
  Upper Sandusky (G-14816)
The Mennel Milling Company.............E..... 419 435-8151
  Fostoria (G-7656)

FOOD PRDTS: Flour & Other Grain Mill Products
Archer-Daniels-Midland Company......E..... 419 435-6633
  Fostoria (G-7628)

Employee Codes: A=Over 500 employees, B=251-500
C=101-250, D=51-100, E=20-50, F=10-19, G=1-9

FOOD PRDTS: Flour & Other Grain Mill Products

Archer-Daniels-Midland Company...... G 419 705-3292
  Toledo (G-14197)
Bunge North America East LLC.......... G 419 483-5340
  Bellevue (G-1224)
Cargill Incorporated........................... E 937 236-1971
  Dayton (G-6246)
Countyline Co-Op Inc........................ F 419 287-3241
  Pemberville (G-12334)
I Dream of Cakes.............................. G 937 533-6024
  Eaton (G-7061)
Legacy Farmers Cooperative.............. F 419 423-2611
  Findlay (G-7528)
Mennel Milling Company.................... D 419 436-5130
  Fostoria (G-7644)
Minster Farmers Coop Exch............... D 419 628-4705
  Minster (G-11056)
Mullet Enterprises Inc....................... G 330 852-4681
  Sugarcreek (G-13932)
Pettisville Grain Co........................... E 419 446-2547
  Pettisville (G-12452)
Pillsbury Company LLC..................... E 419 845-3751
  Caledonia (G-1917)
Pillsbury Company LLC..................... D 740 286-2170
  Wellston (G-15331)
Premier Feeds LLC.......................... G 937 584-2411
  Sabina (G-12891)
Sunrise Cooperative Inc.................... G 419 628-4705
  Minster (G-11062)

FOOD PRDTS: Flour Mixes & Doughs

Abitec Corporation............................ E 614 429-6464
  Columbus (G-5090)
Athens Foods Inc............................. C 216 676-8500
  Cleveland (G-3697)
Minus G LLC.................................... G 440 817-0338
  Newbury (G-11630)
Rich Products Corporation................. C 614 771-1117
  Hilliard (G-8436)

FOOD PRDTS: Flour, Blended From Purchased Flour

Busken Bakery Inc........................... D 513 871-2114
  Cincinnati (G-2695)
Fleetchem LLC................................. F 513 539-1111
  Monroe (G-11106)

FOOD PRDTS: Flours & Flour Mixes, From Purchased Flour

Bakemark USA LLC........................... F 440 323-5100
  Elyria (G-7114)

FOOD PRDTS: Fruit Pops, Frozen

Streetpops Inc................................. G 513 446-7505
  Cincinnati (G-3424)

FOOD PRDTS: Fruits & Vegetables, Pickled

Cle Pickles Inc................................. G 440 473-3740
  Cleveland (G-3826)
Kaiser Pickles LLC............................ F 513 621-2053
  Cincinnati (G-3060)
Kaiser Pickles LLC............................ G 513 621-2053
  Cincinnati (G-3059)

FOOD PRDTS: Ice, Cubes

Home City Ice Company.................... G 513 851-4040
  Cincinnati (G-3005)
Zygo Inc.. G 513 281-0888
  Cincinnati (G-3539)

FOOD PRDTS: Mixes, Cake, From Purchased Flour

Procter & Gamble Mfg Co.................. F 513 983-1100
  Cincinnati (G-3298)

FOOD PRDTS: Mixes, Flour

1-2-3 Gluten Free Inc........................ G 216 378-9233
  Chagrin Falls (G-2365)

FOOD PRDTS: Mixes, Sauces, Dry

Whitmore Productions Inc.................. F 216 752-3960
  Warrensville Heights (G-15231)

FOOD PRDTS: Mustard, Prepared

Woeber Mustard Mfg Co.................... C 937 323-6281
  Springfield (G-13656)

FOOD PRDTS: Oils & Fats, Animal

Wileys Finest LLC............................. C 740 622-1072
  Coshocton (G-6002)

FOOD PRDTS: Olive Oil

Liquid Manufacturing Solutions........... E 937 401-0821
  Franklin (G-7684)
Olive Romanum Oil Inc...................... G 330 554-4102
  Kent (G-8840)
Spicy Olive LLC................................ F 513 376-9061
  Montgomery (G-11131)
Spicy Olive LLC................................ G 513 847-4397
  West Chester (G-15509)

FOOD PRDTS: Pasta, Uncooked, Packaged With Other Ingredients

Food Designs Inc.............................. F 216 651-9221
  Cleveland (G-4078)

FOOD PRDTS: Peanut Butter

Krema Group Inc.............................. F 614 889-4824
  Plain City (G-12584)
Procter & Gamble Mfg Co.................. F 513 983-1100
  Cincinnati (G-3298)

FOOD PRDTS: Pizza Doughs From Purchased Flour

B & D Commissarys LLC.................... G 740 743-3890
  Mount Perry (G-11249)
Cassanos Inc.................................... E 937 294-8400
  Dayton (G-6248)

FOOD PRDTS: Pork Rinds

Evans Food Group Ltd....................... F 626 636-8110
  Portsmouth (G-12643)
Evans Food Group Ltd....................... G 740 285-3078
  Portsmouth (G-12644)
Rudolph Foods Company Inc............. C 909 383-7463
  Lima (G-9287)
White Feather Foods Inc.................... F 419 738-8975
  Wapakoneta (G-15133)

FOOD PRDTS: Potato Chips & Other Potato-Based Snacks

Advanced Green Tech Inc.................. G 614 397-8130
  Plain City (G-12560)
Ballreich Bros Inc.............................. C 419 447-1814
  Tiffin (G-14078)
Conns Potato Chip Co Inc.................. E 740 452-4615
  Zanesville (G-16523)
Frito-Lay North America Inc............... D 330 477-7009
  Canton (G-2106)
Grippo Potato Chip Co Inc................. E 513 923-1900
  Cincinnati (G-2915)
Herr Foods Incorporated.................... E 740 773-8282
  Chillicothe (G-2519)
Herr Foods Incorporated.................... F 800 344-3777
  Chillicothe (G-2520)
Jones Potato Chip Co........................ E 419 529-9424
  Mansfield (G-9614)
Mike-Sells Potato Chip Co.................. E 937 228-9400
  Dayton (G-6447)
Mike-Sells West Virginia Inc............... D 937 228-9400
  Dayton (G-6448)
Mumfords Potato Chips & Deli............ G 937 653-3491
  Urbana (G-14842)

FOOD PRDTS: Poultry, Processed, Frozen

Martin-Brower Company LLC.............. C 513 773-2301
  West Chester (G-15462)

FOOD PRDTS: Raw cane sugar

Derma Glow Med Spa Corp................ G 440 641-1406
  Cleveland (G-3513)

FOOD PRDTS: Salad Oils, Refined Vegetable, Exc Corn

Inter American Products Inc............... D 800 645-2233
  Cincinnati (G-3015)

FOOD PRDTS: Sandwiches

Advancpierre Foods Holdings Inc........ D 513 428-5699
  West Chester (G-15532)
Caruso Foods LLC............................. D 513 860-9200
  Cincinnati (G-2715)
White Castle System Inc.................... E 513 563-2290
  Cincinnati (G-3518)

FOOD PRDTS: Seasonings & Spices

Alimento Ventures Inc....................... G 855 510-2866
  Blue Ash (G-1317)
Hen of Woods LLC............................. G 513 954-8871
  Cincinnati (G-2913)
National Foods Packaging Inc............. E 216 622-2740
  Cleveland (G-4417)
Rosebuds Ranch and Garden LLC....... F 937 214-1801
  Covington (G-6011)
Savor Seasoning LLC........................ F 513 732-2333
  Batavia (G-947)

FOOD PRDTS: Shortening & Solid Edible Fats

Procter & Gamble Mfg Co.................. F 513 983-1100
  Cincinnati (G-3218)

FOOD PRDTS: Starch, Corn

Cargill Incorporated........................... E 937 236-1971
  Dayton (G-6246)

FOOD PRDTS: Sugar

Domino Foods In............................... C 216 432-3222
  Cleveland (G-3918)

FOOD PRDTS: Sugar, Beet

Michigan Sugar Company................... F 419 332-9931
  Fremont (G-7793)

FOOD PRDTS: Syrup, Maple

Natures Health Food LLC................... F 419 260-9265
  Mount Victory (G-11301)

FOOD PRDTS: Syrups

B&G Foods Inc .... E 513 482-8226
  Cincinnati *(G-2653)*
J M Smucker Company .... A 330 682-3000
  Orrville *(G-12129)*
Nu Pet Company .... F 330 682-3000
  Orrville *(G-12142)*
Smartsoda Holdings Inc .... E 888 998-9668
  Cleveland *(G-4708)*
Smucker International Inc .... E 330 682-3000
  Orrville *(G-12154)*

FOOD PRDTS: Tofu, Exc Frozen Desserts

Foodies Vegan Ltd .... F 513 487-3037
  Cincinnati *(G-2913)*

FOOD PRDTS: Turkey, Slaughtered & Dressed

Whitewater Processing LLC .... D 513 367-4133
  Harrison *(G-8297)*

FOOD PRODUCTS MACHINERY

Abj Equipfix LLC .... E 419 684-5236
  Castalia *(G-2318)*
Acreo Inc .... G 513 734-3327
  Amelia *(G-448)*
American Pan Company .... C 937 652-3232
  Urbana *(G-14825)*
Binos Inc .... G 330 938-0888
  Sebring *(G-13118)*
Biro Manufacturing Company .... F 419 798-4451
  North Canton *(G-11717)*
Chemineer Inc .... C 937 454-3200
  Dayton *(G-6254)*
Christy Machine Company .... F 419 332-6451
  Fremont *(G-7771)*
Cleveland Range LLC .... C 216 481-4900
  Cleveland *(G-3852)*
Crescent Metal Products Inc .... C 440 350-1100
  Mentor *(G-10445)*
Edge Exponential LLC .... F 614 226-4421
  Columbus *(G-5346)*
ES Industries Inc .... F 419 643-2625
  Lima *(G-9242)*
G & S Metal Products Co Inc .... C 216 441-0700
  Cleveland *(G-4096)*
G F Frank and Sons Inc .... F 513 870-9075
  West Chester *(G-15433)*
Gold Medal Products Co .... B 513 769-7676
  Cincinnati *(G-2962)*
Harry C Lobalzo & Sons Inc .... E 330 666-6758
  Akron *(G-180)*
Hawthorne-Seving Inc .... E 419 643-5531
  Cridersville *(G-6041)*
Hobart LLC .... E 937 332-2797
  Piqua *(G-12525)*
Hobart LLC .... E 937 332-3000
  Troy *(G-14581)*
Hobart LLC .... D 937 332-3000
  Troy *(G-14582)*
Innovative Controls Corp .... E 419 691-6684
  Toledo *(G-14333)*
ITW Food Equipment Group LLC .... A 937 332-2396
  Troy *(G-14589)*
JE Grote Company Inc .... D 614 868-8414
  Columbus *(G-5491)*
John Bean Technologies Corp .... B 419 626-0304
  Sandusky *(G-13070)*
Lima Sheet Metal Machine & Mfg .... E 419 229-1161
  Lima *(G-9264)*
Martin Mohr .... F 740 727-2233
  New Boston *(G-11397)*

Maverick Innvtive Slutions LLC .... D 419 281-7944
  Ashland *(G-590)*
Meyer Company .... C 216 587-3400
  Chagrin Falls *(G-2382)*
N Wasserstrom & Sons Inc .... C 614 228-5550
  Columbus *(G-5588)*
National Oilwell Varco LP .... D 937 454-4660
  Dayton *(G-6464)*
Nemco Food Equipment Ltd .... D 419 542-7751
  Hicksville *(G-8376)*
Norse Dairy Systems Inc .... C 614 294-4931
  Columbus *(G-5600)*
Peerless Stove & Mfg Co .... F 419 625-4514
  Sandusky *(G-13087)*
Premier Industries Inc .... E 513 271-2550
  Cincinnati *(G-3272)*
R and J Corporation .... E 440 871-6009
  Westlake *(G-15777)*
Royalton Foodservice Eqp Co .... F 440 237-0806
  North Royalton *(G-11894)*
RS Industries Inc .... G 216 351-8200
  Brooklyn Heights *(G-1699)*
Sarka Bros Machining Inc .... G 419 532-2393
  Kalida *(G-8786)*
Sidney Manufacturing Company .... E 937 492-4154
  Sidney *(G-13288)*
Siebtechnik Tema Inc .... E 513 489-7811
  Cincinnati *(G-3390)*
Sir Steak Machinery Inc .... E 419 526-9181
  Mansfield *(G-9718)*
Sterling Process Equipment .... E 614 868-5151
  Columbus *(G-5794)*
Tomlinson Industries LLC .... C 216 587-3400
  Cleveland *(G-4800)*
Wolf Machine Company .... E 513 791-5194
  Blue Ash *(G-1493)*

FOOD STORES: Convenience, Chain

United Dairy Farmers Inc .... C 513 396-8700
  Cincinnati *(G-3479)*

FOOD STORES: Convenience, Independent

Whitacre Enterprises Inc .... E 740 934-2331
  Graysville *(G-8024)*

FOOD STORES: Delicatessen

Baltic Country Meats .... G 330 897-7025
  Baltic *(G-834)*
Bread Kneads Inc .... G 419 422-3863
  Findlay *(G-7486)*
Fragapane Bakeries Inc .... G 440 779-6050
  North Olmsted *(G-11823)*
Investors United Inc .... F 419 473-8942
  Toledo *(G-14336)*
Mumfords Potato Chips & Deli .... G 937 653-3491
  Urbana *(G-14844)*
Zygo Inc .... G 513 281-0888
  Cincinnati *(G-3539)*

FOOD STORES: Grocery, Independent

Brinkman Turkey Farms Inc .... F 419 365-5127
  Findlay *(G-7487)*
C J Kraft Enterprises Inc .... G 740 653-9606
  Lancaster *(G-8997)*
Dioguardis Italian Foods Inc .... F 330 492-3777
  Canton *(G-2093)*
Gibson Bros Inc .... F 440 774-2401
  Oberlin *(G-12051)*
Lariccias Italian Foods Inc .... F 330 729-0222
  Youngstown *(G-16388)*
Troyers Trail Bologna Inc .... F 330 893-2414
  Dundee *(G-6971)*

Unger Kosher Bakery Inc .... F 216 321-7176
  Cleveland Heights *(G-4944)*

FOOD STORES: Supermarkets, Chain

Heinens Inc .... C 330 562-5297
  Aurora *(G-718)*
Riesbeck Food Markets Inc .... C 740 695-3401
  Saint Clairsville *(G-12921)*

FOOTWEAR, WHOLESALE: Shoes

Careismatic Brands LLC .... G 561 843-8727
  Groveport *(G-8135)*
Georgia-Boot Inc .... D 740 753-1951
  Nelsonville *(G-11356)*

FOOTWEAR: Cut Stock

Remington Products Company .... D 330 335-1571
  Upper Arlington *(G-14802)*

FORESTRY RELATED EQPT

Jrb Family Holdings Inc C
  Wooster *(G-16138)*
Morbark LLC .... C 330 264-8699
  Wooster *(G-16152)*

FORGINGS: Aircraft, Ferrous

Sifco Industries Inc .... C 216 881-8600
  Cleveland *(G-4700)*

FORGINGS: Aluminum

Howmet Aerospace Inc .... A 216 641-3600
  Newburgh Heights *(G-11615)*
Howmet Aerospace Inc .... E 330 544-7633
  Niles *(G-11671)*

FORGINGS: Automotive & Internal Combustion Engine

American Cold Forge LLC .... E 419 836-1062
  Northwood *(G-11917)*
Presrite Corporation .... B 216 441-5990
  Cleveland *(G-4584)*
R E H Inc .... G 330 876-2775
  Kinsman *(G-8937)*

FORGINGS: Construction Or Mining Eqpt, Ferrous

Dayton Superior Corporation .... C 937 866-0711
  Miamisburg *(G-10633)*
Pumpco Concrete Pumping LLC .... F 740 809-1473
  Johnstown *(G-8776)*
Rudd Equipment Company Inc .... D 513 321-7833
  Cincinnati *(G-3354)*

FORGINGS: Iron & Steel

Forge Products Corporation .... E 216 231-2600
  Cleveland *(G-4083)*
Lynx Precision Products Corp .... F 866 305-9012
  Mason *(G-10023)*
S&V Industries Inc .... E 330 666-1986
  Medina *(G-10373)*

FORGINGS: Machinery, Ferrous

Dayton Forging Heat Treating .... D 937 253-4126
  Dayton *(G-6278)*
Wodin Inc .... E 440 439-4222
  Cleveland *(G-4916)*

FORGINGS: Machinery, Nonferrous

Mp Technologies Inc .... F 440 838-4466
  Ashland *(G-594)*

FORGINGS: Metal, Ornamental, Ferrous

Alliance Forging Group LLC .... G 330 680-4861
  Akron *(G-55)*

FORGINGS: Nonferrous

Canton Drop Forge Inc .... B 330 477-4511
  Canton *(G-2061)*
Colfor Manufacturing Inc .... B 330 470-6207
  Malvern *(G-9610)*
Edward W Daniel LLC .... E 440 647-1960
  Wellington *(G-15306)*
Forge Products Corporation .... E 216 231-2600
  Cleveland *(G-4083)*
Thyssnkrupp Rothe Erde USA Inc .... C 330 562-4000
  Aurora *(G-736)*
Turbine Eng Cmpnents Tech Corp ...... B 216 692-5200
  Cleveland *(G-4837)*
Wallace Forge Company .... D 330 488-1203
  Canton *(G-2265)*
Wodin Inc .... E 440 439-4222
  Cleveland *(G-4916)*

FORGINGS: Nuclear Power Plant, Ferrous

Advanced FME Products Inc .... F 440 953-0700
  Mentor *(G-10405)*

FORGINGS: Plumbing Fixture, Nonferrous

Guarantee Specialties Inc .... D 216 451-9744
  Strongsville *(G-13838)*
Mansfield Plumbing Pdts LLC .... A 419 938-5211
  Perrysville *(G-12447)*

FORMS: Concrete, Sheet Metal

C L W Inc .... G 740 374-8443
  Marietta *(G-9780)*
Efco Corp .... G 614 876-1226
  Columbus *(G-5347)*
Feather Lite Innovations Inc .... F 513 893-5483
  Liberty Twp *(G-9215)*
Feather Lite Innovations Inc .... E 937 743-9008
  Springboro *(G-13501)*

FOUNDRIES: Aluminum

Acuity Brands Lighting Inc .... D 740 349-4343
  Newark *(G-11560)*
Air Craft Wheels LLC .... G 440 937-7903
  Ravenna *(G-12701)*
Akron Foundry Co .... C 330 745-3101
  Akron *(G-33)*
Aluminum Line Products Company ...... D 440 835-8880
  Westlake *(G-15729)*
AMG Aluminum North America LLC ..... F 659 348-3620
  Cambridge *(G-1920)*
Aztec Manufacturing Inc .... E 330 783-9747
  Youngstown *(G-16316)*
C M M S - Re LLC .... F 513 489-5111
  Blue Ash *(G-1375)*
Consoldted Precision Pdts Corp .... C 216 453-4800
  Cleveland *(G-3897)*
Dd Foundry Inc .... F 216 362-4100
  Brookpark *(G-1712)*
Durivage Pattern and Mfg Inc .... E 419 836-8655
  Williston *(G-15870)*
Francis Manufacturing Company .... C 937 526-4551
  Russia *(G-12883)*
General Die Casters Inc .... E 330 678-2528
  Twinsburg *(G-14667)*
Lite Metals Company .... E 330 296-6110
  Ravenna *(G-12724)*
Mansfield Brass & Aluminum .... D 419 492-2154
  New Washington *(G-11548)*
Miba Bearings US LLC .... B 740 962-4242
  Mcconnelsville *(G-10282)*
Miller Castings Inc .... D 330 482-2923
  Columbiana *(G-5045)*
Model Pattern & Foundry Co .... F 513 542-2322
  Cincinnati *(G-3169)*
Reliable Castings Corporation .... D 937 497-5217
  Sidney *(G-13275)*
Seilkop Industries Inc .... F 513 679-5680
  Cincinnati *(G-3376)*
Skuld LLC .... G 330 423-7339
  Springfield *(G-13633)*
Stripmatic Products Inc .... E 216 241-7143
  Cleveland *(G-4740)*
Thompson Aluminum Casting Co .... D 216 206-2781
  Cleveland *(G-4794)*
Yoder Industries Inc .... C 937 278-5769
  Dayton *(G-6662)*

FOUNDRIES: Gray & Ductile Iron

Akron Gear & Engineering Inc .... E 330 773-6608
  Akron *(G-34)*
Arcelrmttal Tblar Pdts Shlby L .... A 419 347-2424
  Shelby *(G-13191)*
Castco Inc .... F 440 365-2333
  Elyria *(G-7123)*
D Picking & Co .... G 419 562-6891
  Bucyrus *(G-1856)*
Dd Foundry Inc .... F 216 362-4100
  Brookpark *(G-1712)*
Ford Motor Company .... D 216 676-7918
  Brookpark *(G-1715)*
Hamilton Brass & Alum Castings .... E
  Hamilton *(G-8216)*
Hobart LLC .... E 937 332-2797
  Piqua *(G-12525)*
Hobart LLC .... E 937 332-3000
  Troy *(G-14581)*
Hobart LLC .... D 937 332-3000
  Troy *(G-14582)*
Howmet Aerospace Inc .... A 216 641-3600
  Newburgh Heights *(G-11615)*
Korff Holdings LLC .... C 330 332-1566
  Salem *(G-13008)*
Old Smo Inc .... G 419 394-3346
  Saint Marys *(G-12960)*
Skuld LLC .... G 330 423-7339
  Springfield *(G-13633)*
Thyssnkrupp Rothe Erde USA Inc .... C 330 562-4000
  Aurora *(G-736)*
Tiffin Foundry & Machine Inc .... E 419 447-3991
  Tiffin *(G-14109)*
Vanex Tube Corporation .... D 330 544-9500
  Niles *(G-11690)*
W E Lott Company .... F 419 563-9400
  Bucyrus *(G-1873)*
Wallace Forge Company .... D 330 488-1203
  Canton *(G-2265)*

FOUNDRIES: Iron

Cast-Fab Technologies Inc .... C 513 758-1000
  Cincinnati *(G-2707)*
Ej Usa Inc .... F 216 692-3001
  South Euclid *(G-13460)*
Ellwood Engineered Castings Co .... C 330 568-3000
  Hubbard *(G-8563)*
General Aluminum Mfg Company .... C 419 739-9300
  Wapakoneta *(G-15115)*
General Motors LLC .... B 419 782-7010
  Defiance *(G-6678)*
Kenton Iron Products Inc .... E 419 674-4178
  Kenton *(G-8886)*
Old Smo Inc .... C 419 394-3346
  Saint Marys *(G-12961)*
Osco Industries Inc .... D 740 286-5004
  Jackson *(G-8720)*
Pioneer City Casting Company .... E 740 423-7533
  Belpre *(G-1260)*
Sancast Inc .... E 740 622-8660
  Coshocton *(G-5995)*
T & B Foundry Company .... E 216 391-4200
  Cleveland *(G-4774)*
Tiffin Foundry & Machine Inc .... E 419 447-3991
  Tiffin *(G-14109)*
W E Lott Company .... F 419 563-9400
  Bucyrus *(G-1873)*
Whemco-Ohio Foundry Inc .... C 419 222-2111
  Lima *(G-9302)*
Yellow Creek Casting Co Inc .... F 330 532-4608
  Wellsville *(G-15338)*

FOUNDRIES: Nonferrous

Air Craft Wheels LLC .... G 440 937-7903
  Ravenna *(G-12701)*
Alcon Industries Inc .... D 216 961-1100
  Cleveland *(G-3695)*
Apex Aluminum Die Cast Co Inc .... E 937 773-0432
  Piqua *(G-12503)*
Brost Foundry Company .... E 216 641-1131
  Cleveland *(G-3773)*
Bunting Bearings LLC .... E 419 522-3323
  Mansfield *(G-9664)*
Catania Medallic Specialty Inc .... E 440 933-9595
  Avon Lake *(G-801)*
Columbiana Foundry Company .... C 330 482-3336
  Columbiana *(G-2034)*
Curtiss-Wright Flow Ctrl Corp .... D 216 267-3200
  Cleveland *(G-3592)*
Dd Foundry Inc .... F 216 362-4100
  Brookpark *(G-1712)*
Dmk Industries Inc .... F 513 727-4549
  Middletown *(G-1818)*
Durivage Pattern and Mfg Inc .... E 419 836-8655
  Williston *(G-15870)*
Ecm Industries LLC .... E 513 533-6242
  Cincinnati *(G-2807)*
Ellwood Engineered Castings Co .... C 330 568-3000
  Hubbard *(G-8560)*
Elyria Foundry Company LLC .... D 440 322-4657
  Elyria *(G-7141)*
Francis Manufacturing Company .... C 937 526-4551
  Russia *(G-12883)*
Frohn North America Inc .... G 770 819-0089
  Bedford Heights *(G-1173)*
General Aluminum Mfg Company .... B 440 593-6225
  Conneaut *(G-5948)*
General Aluminum Mfg Company .... E 330 297-1020
  Ravenna *(G-12717)*
General Aluminum Mfg LLC .... C 330 297-1225
  Ravenna *(G-12718)*
General Die Casters Inc .... E 330 678-2528
  Twinsburg *(G-14667)*
General Motors LLC .... B 419 782-7010
  Defiance *(G-6678)*
Harbor Castings Inc .... E 330 499-7178
  Cuyahoga Falls *(G-6089)*
Iabf Inc .... G 614 279-4498
  Columbus *(G-5951)*
Ilsco LLC .... C 513 533-6200
  Cincinnati *(G-3017)*
Jrm 2 Company .... D 513 554-1700
  Cincinnati *(G-3062)*
Kse Manufacturing .... F 937 409-9831
  Sidney *(G-13257)*

PRODUCT SECTION

FUELS: Diesel

Lite Metals Company .... E 330 296-6110
  Ravenna *(G-12724)*

Materion Brush Inc .... A 419 862-2745
  Elmore *(G-7103)*

Morris Bean & Company .... C 937 767-7301
  Yellow Springs *(G-16285)*

Nelson Aluminum Foundry Inc .... G 440 543-1941
  Chagrin Falls *(G-2411)*

Nova Machine Products Inc .... C 216 267-3200
  Middleburg Heights *(G-10724)*

Old Smo Inc .... C 419 394-3346
  Saint Marys *(G-12961)*

PCC Airfoils LLC .... E 216 831-3590
  Cleveland *(G-4536)*

PCC Airfoils LLC .... F 216 766-6206
  Beachwood *(G-1009)*

PCC Airfoils LLC .... C 330 868-6441
  Minerva *(G-11038)*

PCC Airfoils LLC .... D 440 350-6150
  Painesville *(G-12256)*

Piqua Emery Cutter & Fndry Co .... D 937 773-4134
  Piqua *(G-12545)*

Precision Castparts Corp .... F 440 350-6150
  Painesville *(G-12258)*

Reliable Castings Corporation .... D 937 497-5217
  Sidney *(G-13275)*

Ross Aluminum Castings LLC .... C 937 492-4134
  Sidney *(G-13279)*

Seaport Mold & Casting Company .... E 419 243-1422
  Toledo *(G-14464)*

Seilkop Industries Inc .... F 513 679-5680
  Cincinnati *(G-3376)*

T & B Foundry Company .... E 216 391-4200
  Cleveland *(G-4764)*

Technology House Ltd .... G 440 248-3025
  Streetsboro *(G-13795)*

Telcon LLC .... D 330 562-5566
  Streetsboro *(G-13796)*

Yoder Industries Inc .... C 937 278-5769
  Dayton *(G-6662)*

FOUNDRIES: Steel

Brost Foundry Company .... E 216 641-1131
  Cleveland *(G-3763)*

Castings Usa Inc .... G 330 339-3611
  New Philadelphia *(G-11491)*

Columbiana Foundry Company .... C 330 482-3336
  Columbiana *(G-5034)*

Columbus Steel Castings Co .... A 614 444-2121
  Columbus *(G-5278)*

Dd Foundry Inc .... F 216 362-4100
  Brookpark *(G-1712)*

Durivage Pattern and Mfg Inc .... E 419 836-8655
  Williston *(G-15870)*

Elyria Foundry Company LLC .... D 440 322-4657
  Elyria *(G-7141)*

Evertz Technology Svc USA Inc .... F 513 422-8400
  Middletown *(G-10824)*

Harbor Castings Inc .... E 330 499-7178
  Cuyahoga Falls *(G-6089)*

Jmac Inc .... E 614 436-2418
  Columbus *(G-5498)*

Korff Holdings LLC .... C 330 332-1566
  Salem *(G-13008)*

Lakeway Mfg Inc .... E 419 433-3030
  Huron *(G-8637)*

Premier Inv Cast Group LLC .... E 937 299-7333
  Moraine *(G-11202)*

Shl Liquidation Medina Inc C
  Valley City *(G-14895)*

Tiffin Foundry & Machine Inc .... E 419 447-3991
  Tiffin *(G-14109)*

W E Lott Company .... F 419 563-9400
  Bucyrus *(G-1873)*

Whemco-Ohio Foundry Inc .... C 419 222-2111
  Lima *(G-9302)*

Worthington Enterprises Inc .... D 513 539-9291
  Monroe *(G-11121)*

Worthngton Stelpac Systems LLC .... C 614 438-3205
  Columbus *(G-5886)*

FOUNDRIES: Steel Investment

Brost Foundry Company .... E 216 641-1131
  Cleveland *(G-3763)*

Castalloy Inc .... D 216 961-7990
  Cleveland *(G-3798)*

Consoldted Precision Pdts Corp .... C 216 453-4800
  Cleveland *(G-3897)*

Harbor Castings Inc .... E 330 499-7178
  Cuyahoga Falls *(G-6089)*

Mercury Machine Co .... D 440 349-3222
  Solon *(G-13386)*

Mold Masters Intl LLC .... C 440 953-0220
  Eastlake *(G-7042)*

P-Mac Ltd .... G 419 235-2245
  Bowling Green *(G-1580)*

PCC Airfoils LLC .... C 440 255-9770
  Mentor *(G-10521)*

PCC Airfoils LLC .... C 330 868-6441
  Minerva *(G-11038)*

Precision Castparts Corp .... F 440 350-6150
  Painesville *(G-12258)*

Skuld LLC .... G 330 423-7339
  Springfield *(G-13633)*

Steel Ceilings Inc .... E 740 967-1063
  Johnstown *(G-8778)*

W E Lott Company .... F 419 563-9400
  Bucyrus *(G-1873)*

Xapc Co .... C 216 362-4100
  Cleveland *(G-4926)*

FOUNDRY MACHINERY & EQPT

A & B Foundry LLC .... F 937 412-1900
  Tipp City *(G-14118)*

Empire Systems Inc .... F 440 653-9300
  Avon Lake *(G-806)*

Equipment Mfrs Intl Inc .... E 216 651-6700
  Cleveland *(G-4026)*

Exomet Inc .... E 440 593-1161
  Conneaut *(G-5917)*

Fremont Flask Co .... F 419 332-2231
  Fremont *(G-7782)*

Gokoh Corporation .... F 937 339-4977
  Troy *(G-14573)*

FOUNTAINS: Concrete

Fountain Specialists Inc .... G 513 831-5717
  Milford *(G-10906)*

FRACTIONATION PRDTS OF CRUDE PETROLEUM, HYDROCARBONS, NEC

Enrevo Pyro LLC .... G 203 517-5002
  Brookfield *(G-1669)*

FRANCHISES, SELLING OR LICENSING

Cassanos Inc .... E 937 294-8400
  Dayton *(G-6248)*

Chemstation International Inc .... E 937 294-8265
  Moraine *(G-11166)*

Gold Star Chili Inc .... E 513 231-4541
  Cincinnati *(G-2963)*

Instantwhip Foods Inc .... F 614 488-2536
  Columbus *(G-5464)*

R&D Marketing Group Inc .... G 216 398-9100
  Brooklyn Heights *(G-1697)*

Skyline Cem Holdings LLC .... C 513 874-1188
  Fairfield *(G-7408)*

Stanley Steemer Intl Inc .... C 614 764-2007
  Dublin *(G-6945)*

The Cornwell Quality Tools Company .... D 330 336-3506
  Wadsworth *(G-15069)*

FREIGHT FORWARDING ARRANGEMENTS

Tgs International Inc .... E 330 893-4828
  Millersburg *(G-10997)*

FRICTION MATERIAL, MADE FROM POWDERED METAL

Addup Inc .... E 513 745-4510
  Blue Ash *(G-1357)*

General Metals Powder Co LLC .... E 330 633-1226
  Akron *(G-166)*

Lewark Metal Spinning Inc .... E 937 275-3303
  Dayton *(G-6406)*

Miscellnous Mtals Fbrction Inc .... F 740 779-3071
  Chillicothe *(G-2519)*

Rmi Titanium Company LLC .... C 330 455-4010
  Canton *(G-2218)*

SK Wellman Corp .... C 440 528-4000
  Solon *(G-13421)*

Tribco Incorporated .... E 216 486-2000
  Cleveland *(G-4825)*

FRUIT STANDS OR MARKETS

Coopers Mill Inc .... F 419 562-4215
  Bucyrus *(G-1854)*

Grays Orange Barn Inc .... G 419 568-2718
  Wapakoneta *(G-15116)*

FRUITS & VEGETABLES WHOLESALERS: Fresh

Chefs Garden Inc .... C 419 433-4947
  Huron *(G-8630)*

Frank L Harter & Son Inc .... G 513 574-1330
  Cincinnati *(G-2920)*

Produce Packaging Inc .... C 216 391-6129
  Willoughby Hills *(G-16027)*

FUEL ADDITIVES

BLaster Holdings LLC .... G 216 901-5800
  Cleveland *(G-3741)*

BLaster LLC .... E 216 901-5800
  Cleveland *(G-3742)*

FUEL CELLS: Solid State

Plug Power Inc .... G 518 605-5703
  West Carrollton *(G-15356)*

FUEL DEALERS: Coal

Cliffs Logan County Coal LLC .... C 216 694-5700
  Cleveland *(G-3871)*

FUEL OIL DEALERS

Centerra Co-Op .... E 419 281-2153
  Ashland *(G-562)*

Cincinnati - Vulcan Company .... D 513 242-5300
  Cincinnati *(G-2736)*

FUEL TREATING

Opw Fueling Components Inc .... D 800 422-2525
  West Chester *(G-15472)*

FUELS: Diesel

FUELS: Diesel

Federal Parkway Diesel Co LLC .... G 614 571-0488
  Columbus (G-5374)
PEC Biofuels LLC .... G 419 542-8210
  Hicksville (G-8378)

FUNGICIDES OR HERBICIDES

Scotts Company LLC .... C 937 644-0011
  Marysville (G-9934)
Scotts Miracle-Gro Company .... E 937 578-5065
  Marysville (G-9936)

FURNACES & OVENS: Indl

A Jacks Manufacturing Co .... E 216 531-1010
  Cleveland (G-3581)
Abp Induction LLC .... F 262 878-6390
  Massillon (G-10075)
Armature Coil Equipment Inc .... F 216 267-6366
  Strongsville (G-13809)
Benko Products Inc .... E 440 934-2180
  Sheffield Village (G-13181)
C A Litzler Co Inc .... E 216 267-8020
  Cleveland (G-3778)
CA Litzler Holding Company .... D 216 267-8020
  Cleveland (G-3780)
Crescent Metal Products Inc .... C 440 350-1100
  Mentor (G-10445)
Custom Services and Designs .... G 937 866-7636
  Miamisburg (G-10630)
Delta H Technologies LLC .... G 740 756-7676
  Carroll (G-2296)
Duca Mfg & Consulting Inc .... G 330 726-7175
  Youngstown (G-16353)
Ebner Furnaces Inc .... D 330 335-2311
  Wadsworth (G-15028)
Garland Commercial Industries LLC ...... E 800 338-2204
  Cleveland (G-4103)
Hannon Company .... D 330 456-4728
  Canton (G-2121)
I Cerco Inc .... C 740 982-2050
  Crooksville (G-6047)
Kaufman Engineered Systems Inc .... D 419 878-9727
  Waterville (G-15248)
L Haberny Co Inc .... F 440 543-5999
  Chagrin Falls (G-2404)
Lakeway Mfg Inc .... E 419 433-3030
  Huron (G-8637)
Lewco Inc .... C 419 625-4014
  Sandusky (G-13074)
Micropyretics Heaters Intl Inc .... E 513 772-0404
  Cincinnati (G-3162)
Pillar Induction .... F 262 317-5300
  Warren (G-15199)
RAD-Con Inc .... E 440 871-5720
  Lakewood (G-8981)
Resilience Fund III LP .... E 216 292-0200
  Cleveland (G-4629)
Selas Heat Technology Co LLC .... E 800 523-6500
  Streetsboro (G-13792)
Sentro Tech Corporation .... G 440 260-0364
  Strongsville (G-13876)
Stelter and Brinck Inc .... E 513 367-9300
  Harrison (G-8293)
Strohecker Incorporated .... E 330 426-9496
  East Palestine (G-7009)
Surface Combustion Inc .... D 419 891-7150
  Maumee (G-10238)
T E Q HI Inc .... F 877 448-3701
  Columbus (G-5805)
T J F Inc .... F 419 878-4400
  Waterville (G-15253)
United McGill Corporation .... E 614 829-1200
  Groveport (G-8165)

FURNACES: Indl, Electric

Ajax Tocco Magnethermic Corp .... C 800 547-1527
  Warren (G-15135)
CMI Industry Americas Inc .... D 330 332-4661
  Salem (G-12985)
Duca Manufacturing & Consulting Inc ... E 330 758-0828
  Youngstown (G-16352)
The Schaefer Group Inc .... E 937 253-3342
  Beavercreek (G-1082)
Ajax Tocco Magnethermic Corp .... C 800 547-1527
  Warren (G-15135)

FURNACES: Warm Air, Electric

Columbus Heating & Vent Co .... C 614 274-1177
  Columbus (G-5265)

FURNITURE PARTS: Metal

Mansfield Engineered Components LLC . C 419 524-1331
  Mansfield (G-9685)
McNeil Group Inc .... E 614 298-0300
  Columbus (G-5556)
Pucel Enterprises Inc .... D 216 881-4604
  Cleveland (G-4598)
Pucel Enterprises Inc .... G 800 336-4986
  Cleveland (G-4599)

FURNITURE REFINISHING SVCS

Mielke Furniture Repair Inc .... G 419 625-4572
  Sandusky (G-13082)
Soft Touch Wood LLC .... E 330 545-4204
  Girard (G-7975)

FURNITURE REPAIR & MAINTENANCE SVCS

Furniture Concepts Inc .... F 216 292-9100
  Cleveland (G-4093)

FURNITURE STOCK & PARTS: Hardwood

Ogonek Custom Hardwood Inc .... G 833 718-2531
  Barberton (G-885)
Regency Seating Inc .... E 330 848-3700
  Akron (G-300)

FURNITURE STORES

Archbold Furniture Co .... E 567 444-4666
  Archbold (G-523)
Bruening Glass Works Inc .... G 440 333-4768
  Cleveland (G-3765)
Chagrin Valley Custom Furn LLC .... G 440 591-5511
  Warrensville Heights (G-15227)
Coconis Furniture Inc .... E 740 452-1231
  South Zanesville (G-13477)
Eoi Inc .... F 740 201-3300
  Lewis Center (G-9160)
Fortner Upholstering Inc .... F 614 475-8282
  Columbus (G-5384)
Furniture By Otmar Inc .... E 937 435-2039
  Dayton (G-6342)
Hallmark Industries Inc .... E 937 864-7378
  Springfield (G-13571)
Hilltop Glass & Mirror LLC .... G 513 931-3688
  Cincinnati (G-3002)
Home Stor & Off Solutions Inc .... E 216 362-4660
  Cleveland (G-4199)
Ohio Table Pad Company .... F 419 872-6400
  Perrysburg (G-12407)
Precision Fab Products Inc .... G 937 526-5681
  Versailles (G-14988)
Sailors Tailor Inc .... F 937 862-7781
  Spring Valley (G-13491)

FURNITURE WHOLESALERS

Fabcor Inc .... F 419 628-4428
  Minster (G-1105)
Friends Service Co Inc .... F 800 427-1704
  Dayton (G-6339)
Friends Service Co Inc .... D 419 427-1704
  Findlay (G-7512)
Sauder Woodworking Co .... F 419 446-2711
  Archbold (G-545)
Urbn Timber LLC .... G 614 981-3043
  Columbus (G-5860)

FURNITURE, HOUSEHOLD: Wholesalers

Sauder Woodworking Co .... A 419 446-2711
  Archbold (G-546)

FURNITURE, MATTRESSES: Wholesalers

Ahmf Inc .... E 614 921-1223
  Columbus (G-5197)
Bailey & Jensen Inc .... G 937 272-1784
  Centerville (G-2350)

FURNITURE, OFFICE: Wholesalers

Furniture Concepts Inc .... F 216 292-9100
  Cleveland (G-4093)
Wasserstrom Company .... B 614 228-6525
  Columbus (G-5865)

FURNITURE, WHOLESALE: Chairs

Millwood Wholesale Inc .... F 330 359-6109
  Dundee (G-6968)

FURNITURE, WHOLESALE: Lockers

American Platinum Door LLC .... G 440 497-6213
  Solon (G-13312)

FURNITURE, WHOLESALE: Racks

KMC Holdings LLC .... C 419 238-2442
  Van Wert (G-14500)
Partitions Plus Incorporated .... E 419 422-2600
  Findlay (G-7550)

FURNITURE, WHOLESALE: Shelving

G & P Construction LLC .... E 855 494-4830
  North Royalton (G-11875)

FURNITURE: Bedroom, Wood

Andal Woodworking .... F 330 897-8059
  Baltic (G-833)

FURNITURE: Beds, Household, Incl Folding & Cabinet, Metal

Invacare Corporation .... G 800 333-6900
  Elyria (G-7166)
Invacare Corporation .... A 440 329-6000
  Elyria (G-7164)
Invacare Holdings Corporation .... C 440 329-6000
  Elyria (G-7169)

FURNITURE: Cabinets & Filing Drawers, Office, Exc Wood

East Woodworking Company .... G 216 791-5950
  Cleveland (G-3950)
Jsc Employee Leasing Corp .... D 330 773-8971
  Akron (G-199)

FURNITURE: Chairs, Household Upholstered

Buckeye Seating LLC .... F 330 893-7700
  Millersburg (G-1047)

FURNITURE: Chairs, Household Wood

PRODUCT SECTION

FURNITURE: Office, Exc Wood

Anthony Flottemesch & Son Inc.............. F 513 561-1212
  Cincinnati *(G-2628)*
Artistic Finishes Inc................................. F 440 951-7850
  Willoughby *(G-15886)*
Basic Cases Inc..................................... G 216 662-3900
  Cleveland *(G-3724)*
Berlin Gardens Gazebos Ltd................... F 330 893-3411
  Berlin *(G-1303)*
Cabintwrks Group Mddlfield LLC............. A 888 562-7744
  Middlefield *(G-10738)*
Carlisle Oak.. G 330 852-8734
  Sugarcreek *(G-13921)*
Criswell Furniture LLC............................ F 330 695-2082
  Fredericksburg *(G-7722)*
Custom Surfaces Inc.............................. G 440 439-2310
  Bedford *(G-1114)*
Diversified Products & Svcs.................... F 740 393-6202
  Mount Vernon *(G-11270)*
Dutch Heritage Woodcraft....................... F 330 893-2211
  Berlin *(G-1306)*
Fountain Nook Woodcraft........................ G 330 473-2162
  Apple Creek *(G-500)*
Furniture By Otmar Inc............................ F 937 435-2039
  Dayton *(G-6342)*
Gasser Chair Co Inc................................ D 330 759-2234
  Youngstown *(G-16363)*
Gencraft Designs LLC............................. E 330 359-6251
  Navarre *(G-11342)*
Grabo Interiors Inc.................................. G 216 391-6977
  Cleveland *(G-4134)*
Greenway Home Products Inc................. F
  Perrysburg *(G-12387)*
Hardwood Lumber Company Inc.............. F 440 834-1891
  Middlefield *(G-10754)*
Hochstetler Wood Ltd............................. G 330 893-1601
  Millersburg *(G-10962)*
Holmes Panel LLC.................................. G 330 897-5040
  Baltic *(G-838)*
Hopewood Inc.. G 330 359-5656
  Millersburg *(G-10969)*
Idx Corporation....................................... C 937 401-3225
  Dayton *(G-6378)*
Integral Design Inc.................................. F 216 524-0555
  Cleveland *(G-4230)*
James L Deckebach LLC......................... F 513 321-3733
  Cincinnati *(G-3037)*
Jeffco Sheltered Workshop..................... F 740 264-4608
  Steubenville *(G-13669)*
Kitchens By Rutenschroer Inc................. G 513 251-8333
  Cincinnati *(G-3080)*
Lauber Manufacturing Co....................... G 419 446-2450
  Archbold *(G-533)*
Lima Millwork Inc................................... F 419 331-3303
  Elida *(G-7094)*
Mamabees HM Gds Lifestyle LLC............ G 419 277-2914
  Fostoria *(G-7642)*
Michaels Pre-Cast Con Pdts.................... F 513 683-1292
  Loveland *(G-9497)*
Mielke Furniture Repair Inc..................... G 419 625-4572
  Sandusky *(G-13082)*
Miller Cabinet Ltd................................... F 614 873-4221
  Plain City *(G-12586)*
N Wasserstrom & Sons Inc...................... G 614 737-5410
  Columbus *(G-5587)*
Pedagogy Furniture................................. G 888 394-8484
  Chardon *(G-2463)*
Penwood Mfg.. G 330 359-5600
  Fresno *(G-7824)*
R A Hamed International Inc.................... F 330 247-0190
  Twinsburg *(G-14722)*
Richard Benhase & Assoc Inc................. G 513 772-1896
  Cincinnati *(G-3338)*

Rnr Enterprises LLC............................... F 330 852-3022
  Sugarcreek *(G-13936)*
Specialty Svcs Cabinetry Inc................... G 614 421-1599
  Columbus *(G-5784)*
Stark Truss Company Inc........................ E 330 478-2100
  Canton *(G-2233)*
Stark Truss Company Inc........................ D 419 298-3777
  Edgerton *(G-7082)*
Tappan Chairs LLC................................ G 800 840-9121
  Blue Ash *(G-1477)*
Textiles Inc.. G 614 529-8642
  Hilliard *(G-8446)*
Textiles Inc.. G 740 852-0782
  London *(G-9395)*
Vocational Services Inc.......................... E 216 431-8085
  Cleveland *(G-4880)*
Waller Brothers Stone Company.............. E 740 858-1948
  Mc Dermott *(G-10275)*
Weaver Woodcraft L L C.......................... G 330 695-2150
  Apple Creek *(G-514)*
Wine Cellar Innovations LLC................... C 513 321-3733
  Cincinnati *(G-3522)*
Woodcraft... G 419 389-0560
  Toledo *(G-14526)*
Woodworking Shop LLC.......................... F 513 330-9663
  Miamisburg *(G-10702)*

FURNITURE: Chairs, Office Wood

Buckeye Seating LLC............................. F 330 893-7700
  Millersburg *(G-10947)*
Buzz Seating Inc.................................... G 877 263-5737
  West Chester *(G-15543)*
Gasser Chair Co Inc................................ E 330 534-2234
  Youngstown *(G-16362)*

FURNITURE: Church

Sauder Manufacturing Co....................... C 419 445-7670
  Archbold *(G-544)*

FURNITURE: Console Tables, Wood

Dorel Home Furnishings Inc.................... D 419 447-7448
  Tiffin *(G-14083)*

FURNITURE: Fiberglass & Plastic

Evenflo Company Inc.............................. D 937 773-3971
  Troy *(G-14566)*
Office Magic Inc..................................... F 510 782-6100
  Medina *(G-10357)*
Owens Corning....................................... A 419 248-8000
  Toledo *(G-14421)*
Sauder Woodworking Co......................... F 419 446-2711
  Archbold *(G-545)*

FURNITURE: Hotel

Textiles Inc.. G 614 529-8642
  Hilliard *(G-8446)*

FURNITURE: Household, Metal

Bailey & Jensen Inc................................ G 937 272-1784
  Centerville *(G-2360)*
Metal Fabricating Corporation.................. D 216 631-8121
  Cleveland *(G-4396)*

FURNITURE: Household, Upholstered, Exc Wood Or Metal

Bulk Carrier Trnsp Eqp Co....................... E 330 339-3333
  New Philadelphia *(G-11489)*
John Purdum.. G 513 897-9686
  Waynesville *(G-15298)*
Kitchens By Rutenschroer Inc................. G 513 251-8333
  Cincinnati *(G-3080)*

Sailors Tailor Inc.................................... F 937 862-7781
  Spring Valley *(G-13491)*

FURNITURE: Juvenile, Metal

Angels Landing Inc................................. G 513 687-3681
  Moraine *(G-11158)*

FURNITURE: Lawn & Garden, Metal

Sunnest Service LLC.............................. E 740 283-2815
  Steubenville *(G-13678)*

FURNITURE: Lawn, Exc Wood, Metal, Stone Or Concrete

Hershy Way Ltd...................................... G 330 893-2809
  Millersburg *(G-10958)*

FURNITURE: Living Room, Upholstered On Wood Frames

Hallmark Industries Inc........................... E 937 864-7378
  Springfield *(G-13571)*
Morris Furniture Co Inc........................... C 937 874-7100
  Fairborn *(G-7320)*

FURNITURE: Mattresses & Foundations

Ahmf Inc.. E 614 921-1223
  Columbus *(G-5107)*
Homecare Mattress Inc.......................... F 937 746-2556
  Franklin *(G-7680)*
Tru Comfort Mattress.............................. G 614 595-8600
  Dublin *(G-6954)*
Walter F Stephens Jr Inc......................... F 937 746-0521
  Franklin *(G-7709)*

FURNITURE: Mattresses, Box & Bedsprings

Banner Mattress Co Inc........................... D 419 324-7181
  Toledo *(G-14206)*
Coconis Furniture Inc............................. E 740 452-1231
  South Zanesville *(G-13477)*
HSP Bedding Solutions LLC................... E 440 437-4425
  Orwell *(G-12165)*
Midwest Quality Bedding Inc................... E 614 504-5971
  Columbus *(G-5566)*
Solstice Sleep Products Inc.................... E 614 279-8850
  Columbus *(G-5777)*
V-I-S-c-e-r-o-t-o-n-i-c Inc........................ D 330 690-3355
  Akron *(G-368)*

FURNITURE: Mattresses, Innerspring Or Box Spring

Quilting Inc.. D 614 504-5971
  Plain City *(G-12591)*
Sealy Mattress Mfg Co LLC..................... F 800 697-3259
  Medina *(G-10374)*

FURNITURE: Office, Exc Wood

Americas Mdular Off Specialist................ G 614 277-0216
  Grove City *(G-8078)*
Axess International LLC.......................... G 330 460-4840
  Brunswick *(G-1750)*
Casco Mfg Solutions Inc......................... D 513 681-0003
  Cincinnati *(G-2706)*
Custom Craft Collection Inc..................... F 440 998-3000
  Ashtabula *(G-630)*
Custom Millcraft Corp............................. E 513 874-7080
  West Chester *(G-15410)*
Ergo Desktop LLC.................................. E 567 890-3746
  Celina *(G-2331)*
Frontier Signs & Displays Inc.................. G 513 367-0813
  Harrison *(G-8275)*

Employee Codes: A=Over 500 employees, B=251-500
C=101-250, D=51-100, E=20-50, F=10-19, G=1-9

FURNITURE: Office, Exc Wood

Furniture Concepts Inc .... F 216 292-9100
Cleveland (G-4093)

Gasser Chair Co Inc .... D 330 759-2234
Youngstown (G-16363)

Infinium Wall Systems Inc .... E 440 572-5000
Strongsville (G-13845)

M/W International Inc .... F 440 526-6900
Lorain (G-9423)

Marsh Industries Inc .... E 330 308-8667
New Philadelphia (G-11515)

Metal Fabricating Corporation .... D 216 631-8121
Cleveland (G-4396)

National Electro-Coatings Inc .... D 216 898-0080
Cleveland (G-4436)

Pucel Enterprises Inc .... D 216 881-4604
Cleveland (G-4598)

Recycled Systems Furniture Inc .... E 614 880-9110
Worthington (G-16210)

Senator International Inc .... E 419 887-5806
Maumee (G-10229)

Starr Fabricating Inc .... D 330 394-9891
Vienna (G-15004)

Tiffin Metal Products Co .... C 419 447-8414
Tiffin (G-14110)

FURNITURE: Office, Wood

Basic Cases Inc .... G 216 662-3900
Cleveland (G-3724)

Crow Works LLC .... E 888 811-2769
Killbuck (G-8918)

Dvuv LLC .... E 216 741-5511
Cleveland (G-3981)

Frontier Signs & Displays Inc .... G 513 367-0813
Harrison (G-8275)

Gasser Chair Co Inc .... D 330 759-2234
Youngstown (G-16363)

Idx Corporation .... C 937 401-3225
Dayton (G-6378)

Lima Millwork Inc .... F 419 331-3303
Elida (G-7094)

Miller Cabinet Ltd .... F 614 873-4221
Plain City (G-12586)

Sauder Manufacturing Co .... D 419 682-3061
Stryker (G-13913)

Senator International Inc .... E 419 887-5806
Maumee (G-10229)

Symatic Inc .... F 330 225-1510
Medina (G-10381)

Tiffin Metal Products Co .... C 419 447-8414
Tiffin (G-14110)

FURNITURE: Play Pens, Children's, Wood

Western & Southern Lf Insur Co .... A 513 629-1800
Cincinnati (G-3517)

FURNITURE: School

Shiffler Equipment Sales Inc .... E 440 285-9175
Chardon (G-2467)

W C Heller & Co Inc .... F 419 485-3176
Montpelier (G-11145)

FURNITURE: Table Tops, Marble

Accent Manufacturing Inc .... F 330 724-7704
Norton (G-11936)

FURNITURE: Upholstered

Custom Craft Collection Inc .... F 440 998-3000
Ashtabula (G-630)

Fortner Upholstering Inc .... F 614 475-8282
Columbus (G-5384)

Franklin Cabinet Company Inc .... E 937 743-9606
Franklin (G-7676)

Hopewood Inc .... G 330 359-5656
Millersburg (G-10969)

Njm Furniture Outlet Inc .... F 330 893-3514
Millersburg (G-10987)

Robert Mayo Industries .... G 330 426-2587
East Palestine (G-7008)

Sauder Woodworking Co .... A 419 446-2711
Archbold (G-546)

Weavers Furniture Ltd .... F 330 852-2701
Sugarcreek (G-13948)

Y & T Woodcraft Inc .... G 330 464-3432
Apple Creek (G-515)

FURNITURE: Vehicle

Wurms Woodworking Company .... E 419 492-2184
New Washington (G-11552)

FUSE MOUNTINGS: Electric Power

Regal Beloit America Inc .... C 419 352-8441
Bowling Green (G-1588)

FUSES & FUSE EQPT

Marathon Special Products Corp .... C 419 352-8441
Bowling Green (G-1573)

GAMES & TOYS: Board Games, Children's & Adults'

Late For Sky Production Co .... E 513 531-4400
Cincinnati (G-3096)

GAMES & TOYS: Child Restraint Seats, Automotive

Evenflo Company Inc .... D 937 773-3971
Troy (G-14566)

Recaro Child Safety LLC .... G 248 904-1570
Cincinnati (G-3326)

Rocky Hinge Inc .... G 330 539-6296
Girard (G-7974)

GAMES & TOYS: Craft & Hobby Kits & Sets

Michaels Stores Inc .... F 330 505-1168
Niles (G-11676)

GARBAGE CONTAINERS: Plastic

1 888 U Pitch It .... G 440 796-9028
Mentor (G-10401)

MCS Midwest LLC .... G 513 217-0805
Franklin (G-7686)

GARBAGE DISPOSERS & COMPACTORS: Commercial

City of Ashland .... G 419 289-8728
Ashland (G-565)

Knight Manufacturing Co Inc .... G 740 676-5516
Shadyside (G-13146)

GAS & OIL FIELD EXPLORATION SVCS

AB Resources LLC .... E 440 922-1098
Brecksville (G-1604)

Access Midstream .... G 330 679-2019
Salineville (G-13037)

Antero Resources Corporation .... E 303 357-7310
Caldwell (G-1906)

Antero Resources Corporation .... D 740 760-1000
Marietta (G-9775)

Artex Energy Group LLC .... G 740 373-3313
Marietta (G-9776)

Atlas America Inc .... F 330 339-3155
New Philadelphia (G-11485)

BD Oil Gathering Corp .... E 740 374-9355
Marietta (G-9777)

Beck Energy Corporation .... E 330 297-6891
Ravenna (G-1276)

Blue Racer Midstream LLC .... D 740 630-7556
Cambridge (G-1523)

Canton Oil Well Service Inc .... G 330 494-1221
Canton (G-2066)

Cardinal Operating Company .... G 614 846-5757
Columbus (G-5238)

Cgas Exploration Inc .... G 614 436-4631
Worthington (G-6190)

Diversified Production LLC .... C 740 373-8771
Marietta (G-9782)

Dome Drilling Company .... G 440 892-9434
Westlake (G-1546)

Elkhead Gas & Oil Co .... G 740 763-3966
Newark (G-1154)

Empress Royalty Ltd .... G 614 943-1903
Columbus (G-5252)

Equitrans Midstream Corpo .... G 304 626-7934
Saint Clairsville (G-12903)

Everflow Eastern Partners LP .... G 330 533-2692
Canfield (G-2015)

Fioritto of Wooster LLC .... G 330 466-3776
Wooster (G-16719)

G&O Resources Ltd .... F 330 253-2525
Akron (G-159)

Gonzoil Inc .... G 330 497-5888
Canton (G-2113)

Hess Corporation .... G 740 266-7835
Steubenville (G-13668)

Hilcorp Energy Co .... G 330 536-6406
Lowellville (G-516)

Hilcorp Energy Co .... G 330 532-9300
Wellsville (G-1335)

Hunter Eureka Pipeline LLC .... E 740 374-2940
Marietta (G-9840)

Husky Marketing and Supply Co .... E 614 210-2300
Dublin (G-6894)

John D Oil and Gas Company .... G 440 255-6325
Mentor (G-10414)

K Petroleum Inc .... F 614 532-5420
Gahanna (G-7239)

Knox Energy In .... F 740 927-6731
Pataskala (G-12301)

Knox Energy Inc .... G 614 885-4828
Columbus (G-512)

Lake Region Oil Inc .... G 330 828-8420
Dalton (G-6134)

M3 Midstream LLC .... E 330 223-2220
Kensington (G-3790)

M3 Midstream LLC .... E 330 679-5580
Salineville (G-13039)

M3 Midstream LLC .... E 740 945-1170
Scio (G-13111)

Miller Energy LLC .... C 614 367-1812
Columbus (G-570)

Mori Shuji .... G 614 459-1296
Columbus (G-580)

N & G Takhar Oil LLC .... G 937 604-0012
Tipp City (G-1144)

Ngo Development Corporation .... B 740 622-9560
Coshocton (G-5987)

Northwood Energy Corporation .... E 614 457-1024
Columbus (G-604)

Precision Geophysical Inc .... E 330 674-2198
Millersburg (G-10989)

Prominence Energy Corporation .... G 513 818-8329
Cincinnati (G-304)

Quantum Energy LLC .... F 440 285-7381
Chardon (G-2264)

PRODUCT SECTION — GASKETS

Reserve Energy Exploration Co............... G 440 543-0770
  Chagrin Falls *(G-2419)*
Resource America Inc......................... G 330 896-8510
  Uniontown *(G-14792)*
Sadaf Oil & Gas Inc........................... G 330 448-6631
  Brookfield *(G-1673)*
Santec Resources Inc......................... F 614 664-9540
  Columbus *(G-5746)*
Second Oil Ltd................................ G 419 830-4688
  Mc Clure *(G-10267)*
Silcor Oilfield Services Inc.................. F 330 448-8500
  Brookfield *(G-1674)*
St Paul Park Refining Co...................... G 419 422-2121
  Findlay *(G-7568)*
Stevens Oil & Gas LLC......................... G 740 374-4542
  Marietta *(G-9831)*
T-N-T Rgulatory Compliance Inc................ G 513 442-2464
  Cincinnati *(G-3438)*
Tgs Systems LLC............................... G 614 431-6927
  Columbus *(G-5819)*
Triad Energy Corporation...................... F 740 374-2940
  Marietta *(G-9838)*
Unlimited Energy Services LLC................. F 304 517-7097
  Beverly *(G-1322)*
Utica East Ohio Midstream LLC................. B 740 431-4168
  Dennison *(G-6796)*
Utica East Ohio Midstream LLC................. G 740 945-2226
  Scio *(G-13113)*
Whitacre Enterprises Inc...................... E 740 934-2331
  Graysville *(G-8024)*
Zane Petroleum Inc............................ F 740 454-8779
  Columbus *(G-5891)*

GAS & OIL FIELD SVCS, NEC

Adapt Oil..................................... G 330 658-1482
  Doylestown *(G-6852)*
Aim Services Company.......................... F 800 321-9038
  Girard *(G-7959)*
Aj Enterprise LLC............................. F 740 231-2205
  Zanesville *(G-16497)*
Joseph G Pappas............................... G 330 383-2917
  East Liverpool *(G-6995)*
Killbuck Oil and Gas LLC...................... G 330 447-8423
  Akron *(G-206)*

GAS FIELD MACHINERY & EQPT

Jet Rubber Company............................ E 330 325-1821
  Rootstown *(G-12853)*

GASES & LIQUIFIED PETROLEUM GASES

Simco Gas Ohio 2005 Partne.................... F 330 799-2268
  Youngstown *(G-16438)*

GASES: Acetylene

Delille Oxygen Company........................ E 614 444-1177
  Columbus *(G-5324)*

GASES: Carbon Dioxide

Linde Gas & Equipment Inc..................... G 513 821-2192
  Cincinnati *(G-3107)*

GASES: Indl

Airgas Usa LLC................................ G 937 222-8312
  Moraine *(G-11154)*
Airgas Usa LLC................................ G 440 232-6397
  Twinsburg *(G-14625)*
Atlantic Welding LLC.......................... F 937 570-5094
  Piqua *(G-12505)*
Delille Oxygen Company........................ G 937 325-9595
  Springfield *(G-13553)*
Endurance Manufacturing Inc................... F 330 628-2600
  Akron *(G-139)*
Invacare Corporation.......................... G 800 333-6900
  Elyria *(G-7166)*
Invacare Corporation.......................... A 440 329-6000
  Elyria *(G-7164)*
Linde Gas & Equipment Inc..................... E 614 443-7687
  Columbus *(G-5529)*
Linde Gas & Equipment Inc..................... E 419 729-7732
  Toledo *(G-14368)*
Linde Gas & Equipment Inc..................... G 440 944-8844
  Wickliffe *(G-15837)*
Linde Gas USA LLC............................. F 330 425-3989
  Twinsburg *(G-14689)*
Linde Inc..................................... G 330 825-4449
  Barberton *(G-877)*
Linde Inc..................................... F 440 237-8690
  Cleveland *(G-4327)*
Linde Inc..................................... F 419 698-8005
  Oregon *(G-12106)*
Messer LLC.................................... F 419 822-3909
  Delta *(G-6788)*
Messer LLC.................................... G 614 539-2259
  Grove City *(G-8105)*
Messer LLC.................................... F 419 227-9585
  Lima *(G-9268)*
Messer LLC.................................... F 330 608-3008
  Uniontown *(G-14788)*
National Gas & Oil Corporation................ E 740 344-2102
  Newark *(G-11596)*
Plasti-Kote Co Inc............................ C 330 725-4511
  Medina *(G-10363)*
Reliable Mfg Co LLC........................... G 740 756-9373
  Carroll *(G-2302)*
Wright Brothers Inc........................... F 513 731-2222
  Cincinnati *(G-3527)*
Zephyr Solutions LLC.......................... F 440 937-9993
  Avon *(G-795)*

GASES: Nitrogen

Linde Gas & Equipment Inc..................... G 614 846-7048
  Columbus *(G-5528)*
Matheson Tri-Gas Inc.......................... E 419 865-8881
  Holland *(G-8518)*
Matheson Tri-Gas Inc.......................... E 513 727-9638
  Middletown *(G-10842)*
Messer LLC.................................... F 419 221-5043
  Lima *(G-9269)*
Messer LLC.................................... F 513 831-4742
  Miamiville *(G-10712)*
Messer LLC.................................... G 330 394-4541
  Warren *(G-15190)*
Ohio Nitrogen LLC............................. G 216 839-5485
  Beachwood *(G-1006)*
Osair Inc..................................... G 440 974-6500
  Mentor *(G-10516)*

GASES: Oxygen

Airgas Usa LLC................................ E 330 454-1330
  Canton *(G-2031)*
Linde Inc..................................... F 440 994-1000
  Ashtabula *(G-646)*
Messer LLC.................................... E 216 533-7256
  Cleveland *(G-4395)*
Welders Supply Inc............................ F 216 241-1696
  Cleveland *(G-4903)*
Western/Scott Fetzer Company.................. E 440 892-3000
  Westlake *(G-15801)*

GASKET MATERIALS

Flow Dry Technology Inc....................... C 937 833-2161
  Brookville *(G-1736)*
Forest City Technologies Inc.................. C 440 647-2115
  Wellington *(G-15310)*
Forest City Technologies Inc.................. D 440 647-2115
  Wellington *(G-15311)*
Thermoseal Inc................................ G 937 498-2222
  Sidney *(G-13292)*

GASKETS

Akalina Associates Inc........................ C 440 992-2195
  Ashtabula *(G-626)*
Akron Gasket & Packg Entps Inc................ F 330 633-3742
  Tallmadge *(G-14021)*
Blackthorn LLC................................ F 937 836-9296
  Clayton *(G-3564)*
Cgs Liquidation Company LLC................... F 614 878-6041
  Columbus *(G-5246)*
Cincinnati Gasket Pkg Mfg Inc................. E 513 761-3458
  Cincinnati *(G-2749)*
Durox Company................................. D 440 238-5350
  Strongsville *(G-13831)*
Epg Inc....................................... D 330 995-5125
  Aurora *(G-714)*
Epg Inc....................................... F 330 995-9725
  Streetsboro *(G-13770)*
Espi Enterprises Inc.......................... G 440 543-8108
  Chagrin Falls *(G-2394)*
Forest City Technologies Inc.................. B 440 647-2115
  Wellington *(G-15312)*
Fouty & Company Inc........................... E 419 693-0017
  Oregon *(G-12105)*
Freudenberg-Nok General Partnr................ C 419 427-5221
  Findlay *(G-7511)*
G-M-I Inc..................................... G 440 953-8811
  Willoughby *(G-15923)*
Gasko Fabricated Products LLC................. E 330 239-1781
  Medina *(G-10330)*
Grand River Rubber & Plasti................... C 440 998-2900
  Ashtabula *(G-635)*
Green Technologies Ohio LLC................... G 330 630-3350
  Tallmadge *(G-14031)*
Industry Products Co.......................... B 937 778-0585
  Piqua *(G-12526)*
Ishikawa Gasket America Inc................... F 419 353-7300
  Maumee *(G-10208)*
James K Green Enterprises Inc................. G 614 878-6041
  Columbus *(G-5487)*
Jbc Technologies Inc.......................... D 440 327-4522
  North Ridgeville *(G-11847)*
K Wm Beach Mfg Co Inc......................... C 937 399-3838
  Springfield *(G-13586)*
Klinger Agency Inc............................ G 419 893-9759
  Maumee *(G-10212)*
May Lin Silicone Products Inc................. G 330 825-9091
  Barberton *(G-880)*
Mechanical Rubber Ohio LLC.................... E 845 986-2271
  Strongsville *(G-13853)*
Miles Rubber & Packing Company................ E 330 425-3888
  Twinsburg *(G-14697)*
Netherland Rubber Company..................... F 513 733-0883
  Cincinnati *(G-3187)*
Newman Diaphragms LLC......................... E 513 932-7379
  Lebanon *(G-9098)*
Newman International Inc...................... F 513 932-7379
  Lebanon *(G-9099)*
Newman Sanitary Gasket Company................ E 513 932-7379
  Lebanon *(G-9100)*
Ohio Gasket and Shim Co Inc................... E 330 630-0626
  Akron *(G-270)*
P & R Specialty Inc........................... E 937 773-0263
  Piqua *(G-12541)*
Paul J Tatulinski Ltd......................... F 330 584-8251
  North Benton *(G-11710)*
Phoenix Associates............................ E 440 543-9701
  Chagrin Falls *(G-2416)*

GASKETS

Sur-Seal LLC... C 513 574-8500
Cincinnati (G-3434)

GASKETS & SEALING DEVICES

Dana Limited... B 419 887-3000
Maumee (G-10186)

Forest City Technologies Inc................ C 440 647-2115
Wellington (G-15309)

Seal Master Corporation........................ E 330 673-8410
Kent (G-8861)

Superior Plastics Intl Inc........................ G 419 424-3113
Findlay (G-7571)

GASOLINE FILLING STATIONS

Calvary Christian Ch of Ohio................ F 740 828-9000
Frazeysburg (G-7714)

Shelly and Sands Inc............................ F 740 453-0721
Zanesville (G-16562)

Tbone Sales LLC................................... F 330 897-6131
Baltic (G-841)

United Dairy Farmers Inc...................... C 513 396-8700
Cincinnati (G-3479)

GASOLINE WHOLESALERS

Marathon Petroleum Company LP......... F 419 422-2121
Findlay (G-7532)

Marathon Petroleum Corporation.......... A 419 422-2121
Findlay (G-7533)

Mplx Terminals LLC............................... D 330 479-5539
Canton (G-2167)

GEARS

Cincinnati Gearing Systems Inc............ E 513 527-8634
Cincinnati (G-2750)

Gear Company of America Inc............. D 216 671-5400
Cleveland (G-4107)

Landerwood Industries Inc................... E 440 233-4234
Willoughby (G-15944)

GEARS & GEAR UNITS: Reduction, Exc Auto

Hefty Hoist Inc...................................... E 740 467-2515
Millersport (G-11012)

GEARS: Power Transmission, Exc Auto

Akron Gear & Engineering Inc............. E 330 773-6608
Akron (G-34)

B & B Gear and Machine Co Inc.......... E 937 687-1771
New Lebanon (G-11448)

Cage Gear & Machine LLC................... E 330 452-1532
Canton (G-2057)

Canton Gear Mfg Designing Inc........... F 330 455-2771
Canton (G-2064)

Dayton Gear and Tool Co..................... E 937 866-4327
Dayton (G-6279)

Forge Industries Inc............................. A 330 960-2468
Youngstown (G-16359)

Gear Company of America Inc............. D 216 671-5400
Cleveland (G-4107)

Geartec Inc... E 440 953-3900
Willoughby (G-15924)

Geneva Gear & Machine Inc................ F 937 866-0318
Dayton (G-6351)

Horsburgh & Scott Co........................... C 216 431-3900
Cleveland (G-4202)

Jonmar Gear and Machine Inc............. G 330 854-6500
Canal Fulton (G-1971)

Linde Hydraulics Corporation............... E 330 533-6801
Canfield (G-2009)

Little Mountain Precision LLC............... F 440 290-2903
Mentor (G-10495)

Petro Gear Corporation......................... F 216 431-2820
Cleveland (G-4544)

Robertson Manufacturing Co................ F 216 531-8222
Concord Township (G-5912)

Sew-Eurodrive Inc................................ D 937 335-0036
Troy (G-14609)

Stahl Gear & Machine Co..................... E 216 431-2820
Cleveland (G-4725)

Tgm Holdings Company........................ E 419 885-3769
Sylvania (G-14018)

Timken Newco I LLC............................. E 234 262-3000
North Canton (G-11767)

GENERATING APPARATUS & PARTS: Electrical

Turtlecreek Township............................ F 513 932-4080
Lebanon (G-9117)

GENERATION EQPT: Electronic

Caudabe LLC.. G 513 501-9799
Blue Ash (G-1376)

Energy Technologies Inc....................... D 419 522-4444
Mansfield (G-9653)

Erico Products Inc................................ B 440 248-0100
Cleveland (G-4027)

Eti Tech LLC... F 937 832-4200
Kettering (G-8907)

Lubrizol Global Management Inc.......... F 216 447-5000
Cleveland (G-4339)

Proteus Electronics Inc......................... G 419 886-2296
Bellville (G-1247)

Sarica Manufacturing Company............ E 937 484-4030
Urbana (G-14847)

Spirit Avionics Ltd................................. F 614 237-4271
Columbus (G-5786)

Superior Packaging.............................. F 419 380-3335
Toledo (G-14478)

Tecmark Corporation............................ D 440 205-7600
Mentor (G-10573)

GENERATORS SETS: Steam

Wayne Morgan Corp.............................. G 419 222-4181
Lima (G-9301)

GENERATORS: Electrochemical, Fuel Cell

Plug Power Inc...................................... G 518 605-5703
West Carrollton (G-15356)

GENERATORS: Gas

Rexarc International Inc....................... E 937 839-4604
West Alexandria (G-15344)

Rti Remmele Engineering Inc.............. D 651 635-4179
Cleveland (G-4660)

GIFT SHOP

Amish Door Inc..................................... C 330 359-5464
Wilmot (G-16065)

Crownplace Brands Ltd....................... G 888 332-5534
Apple Creek (G-497)

Down Home.. G 740 393-1186
Mount Vernon (G-11271)

E Warther & Sons Inc........................... F 330 343-7513
Dover (G-6823)

Handcrafted Jewelry Inc...................... G 330 650-9011
Hudson (G-8595)

R J Manray Inc..................................... G 330 559-6716
Canfield (G-2015)

S-P Company Inc.................................. D 330 782-5651
Columbiana (G-5050)

Scholz & Ey Engravers Inc................... F 614 444-8052
Columbus (G-5752)

Shops By Todd Inc................................ G 937 458-3192
Beavercreek (G-1061)

Suzin L Chocolatiers.............................. G 440 323-3372
Elyria (G-7208)

Velvet Ice Cream Company................... D 740 892-3921
Utica (G-14859)

Youngs Jersey Dairy Inc....................... B 937 325-0629
Yellow Springs (G-16290)

GIFT WRAP: Paper, Made From Purchased Materials

American Greetings Corporation........... A 216 252-7300
Cleveland (G-362)

GIFT, NOVELTY & SOUVENIR STORES: Gifts & Novelties

City Apparel Inc.................................... F 419 434-1155
Findlay (G-7493)

Global Manufacturing Solutions........... F 937 236-8315
Dayton (G-6355)

Golden Turtle Chocolate Fctry.............. G 513 932-1990
Lebanon (G-9005)

GIFTS & NOVELTIES: Wholesalers

Papyrus-Recycled Greetings Inc........... D 773 348-6410
Westlake (G-15570)

Scholz & Ey Engravers Inc................... F 614 444-8052
Columbus (G-5752)

GLASS & GLASS CERAMIC PRDTS, PRESSED OR BLOWN: Tableware

Anchor Hocking LLC............................. A 740 687-2500
Columbus (G-539)

Ghp II LLC... C 740 687-2500
Lancaster (G-9017)

Libbey Glass LLC.................................. C 419 727-2211
Toledo (G-14367)

Libbey Glass LLC.................................. C 419 325-2100
Toledo (G-14368)

GLASS PRDTS, FROM PURCHASED GLASS: Glassware

Mosser Glass Inc................................... E 740 439-1827
Cambridge (G-1344)

GLASS PRDTS, FROM PURCHASED GLASS: Insulating

Intigral Inc... G 440 439-0980
Youngstown (G-16380)

Intigral Inc... C 440 439-0980
Walton Hills (G-5099)

GLASS PRDTS, FROM PURCHASED GLASS: Mirrored

Bruening Glass Works Inc..................... G 440 333-4768
Cleveland (G-365)

Chantilly Development Corp................. E 419 243-8109
Toledo (G-1423)

GLASS PRDTS, FROM PURCHASED GLASS: Sheet, Bent

Glasstech Inc.. C 419 661-9500
Perrysburg (G-2386)

GLASS PRDTS, FROM PURCHASED GLASS: Windshields

Aag Glass LLC...................................... E 513 286-8268
Batavia (G-907)

Safelite Group Inc................................. A 614 210-9000
Columbus (G-540)

GLASS PRDTS, FROM PURCHD GLASS: Strengthened Or Reinforced

Glass Surface Systems Inc.................. D 330 745-8500
Barberton *(G-870)*

Kimmatt Corp.................................... G 937 228-3811
West Alexandria *(G-15342)*

GLASS PRDTS, PRESSED OR BLOWN: Furnishings & Access

Libbey Inc.. C 419 325-2100
Toledo *(G-14366)*

GLASS PRDTS, PRESSED OR BLOWN: Glass Fibers, Textile

Knoble Glass & Metal Inc.................. G 513 753-1246
Cincinnati *(G-3084)*

Owens Corning Ht Inc...................... E 419 248-8000
Toledo *(G-14422)*

Owens Corning Sales LLC................ A 419 248-8000
Toledo *(G-14424)*

GLASS PRDTS, PRESSED OR BLOWN: Glassware, Art Or Decorative

Anchor Hocking Consmr GL Corp...... G 740 653-2527
Lancaster *(G-8987)*

Modern China Company Inc............. E 330 938-6104
Sebring *(G-13123)*

GLASS PRDTS, PRESSED OR BLOWN: Scientific Glassware

Technical Glass Products Inc........... F 425 396-8420
Perrysburg *(G-12433)*

Variety Glass Inc............................. F 740 432-3643
Cambridge *(G-1959)*

GLASS PRDTS, PRESSED OR BLOWN: Tubing

M R Echo-E Inc................................ F 937 322-4972
Springfield *(G-13597)*

GLASS PRDTS, PRESSED OR BLOWN: Yarn, Fiberglass

Integris Composites Inc................... D 740 928-0326
Hebron *(G-8345)*

GLASS, AUTOMOTIVE: Wholesalers

Fuyao Glass America Inc................. F 937 496-5777
Dayton *(G-6343)*

GLASS: Fiber

Dal-Little Fabricating Inc................. G 216 883-3323
Cleveland *(G-3938)*

Industrial Fiberglass Spc Inc............ E 937 222-9000
Dayton *(G-6382)*

Mfg Composite Systems Company... B 440 997-5851
Ashtabula *(G-648)*

Midwest Composites LLC................. F 419 738-2431
Wapakoneta *(G-15123)*

Scottrods LLC................................. G 419 499-2705
Monroeville *(G-11125)*

GLASS: Flat

Custom Glass Solutions LLC............ E 248 340-1800
Worthington *(G-16192)*

K A Ventures Inc............................. F 513 860-3340
West Chester *(G-15451)*

Nsg Glass North America Inc.......... C 734 755-5816
Luckey *(G-9527)*

Nsg Glass North America Inc.......... E 419 247-4800
Toledo *(G-14400)*

Pilkington Holdings Inc.................... B
Toledo *(G-14435)*

Pilkington North America Inc.......... C 800 547-9280
Northwood *(G-11927)*

Rsl LLC... E 330 392-8900
Warren *(G-15203)*

Schodorf Truck Body & Eqp Co........ E 614 228-6793
Columbus *(G-5751)*

Taylor Products Inc......................... E 419 263-2313
Payne *(G-12323)*

Vinylume Products Inc.................... E 330 799-2000
Youngstown *(G-16472)*

GLASS: Pressed & Blown, NEC

Anchor Hocking Corporation............ F 614 633-4247
Columbus *(G-5140)*

Anchor Hocking Glass Corp PA....... G 740 681-6275
Lancaster *(G-8989)*

Anderson Glass Co Inc.................... E 614 476-4877
Columbus *(G-5145)*

General Electric Company............... E 740 385-2114
Logan *(G-9363)*

General Electric Company............... E 330 373-1400
Warren *(G-15172)*

Hilltop Glass & Mirror LLC.............. G 513 931-3688
Cincinnati *(G-3002)*

Interntnal Auto Cmpnnts Group...... A 419 433-5653
Wauseon *(G-15265)*

Jack Pine Studio LLC...................... G 740 332-2223
Laurelville *(G-9055)*

Johns Manville Corporation............. D 419 878-8111
Waterville *(G-15246)*

Pittsburg Corning Corp Di............... G 724 327-6100
Toledo *(G-14438)*

Pittsburgh Corning LLC................... B 724 327-6100
Toledo *(G-14439)*

Rocket Ventures LLC....................... G 419 530-6083
Toledo *(G-14457)*

Technical Glass Products Inc........... F 440 639-6399
Painesville *(G-12267)*

Wilson Optical Labs Inc................... E 440 357-7000
Mentor *(G-10595)*

GLASS: Tempered

Cardinal CT Company...................... E 740 892-2324
Utica *(G-14857)*

Cardinal Glass Industries Inc........... E 740 892-2324
Utica *(G-14858)*

Glasstech Inc.................................. C 419 661-9500
Perrysburg *(G-12386)*

Machined Glass Specialist Inc......... F 937 743-6166
Springboro *(G-13509)*

Trulite GL Alum Solutions LLC......... E 740 929-2443
Hebron *(G-8368)*

GLASSWARE WHOLESALERS

Anchor Hocking Glass Company...... G 740 681-6025
Lancaster *(G-8988)*

GLOVES: Safety

Ansell Healthcare Products LLC....... C 740 622-4369
Coshocton *(G-5969)*

Ansell Healthcare Products LLC....... E 740 622-4311
Coshocton *(G-5970)*

Enespro LLC.................................... G 630 332-2801
Cleveland *(G-4018)*

National Safety Apparel Inc............. D 216 941-1111
Cleveland *(G-4440)*

GLOVES: Work

Wcm Holdings Inc........................... C 513 705-2100
Cincinnati *(G-3509)*

West Chester Holdings LLC............. C 513 705-2100
Cincinnati *(G-3516)*

GLOVES: Woven Or Knit, From Purchased Materials

Totes Isotoner Holdings Corp.......... C 513 682-8200
West Chester *(G-15599)*

GLYCOL ETHERS

Catexel Nease LLC.......................... D 513 738-1255
Harrison *(G-8267)*

GOLF COURSES: Public

McClelland Inc................................ E 740 452-3036
Zanesville *(G-16544)*

GOLF DRIVING RANGES

Mudbrook Golf Ctr At Thndrbird..... G 419 433-2945
Huron *(G-8640)*

GOLF EQPT

Dayton Stencil Works Company...... F 937 223-3233
Dayton *(G-6290)*

EJ Weber Ltd.................................. G 513 759-0103
West Chester *(G-15424)*

Golf Galaxy Golfworks Inc.............. C 740 328-4193
Newark *(G-11577)*

Grip Spritz LLC............................... G 440 888-7022
Cleveland *(G-4150)*

Sunset Golf LLC.............................. G 419 994-5563
Tallmadge *(G-14051)*

GOURMET FOOD STORES

Mustard Seed Health Fd Mkt Inc..... E 440 519-3663
Solon *(G-13394)*

GOVERNMENT, GENERAL: Administration

City of Cleveland............................ E 216 664-3013
Cleveland *(G-3822)*

Turtlecreek Township...................... F 513 932-4080
Lebanon *(G-9117)*

GRADING SVCS

Great Lakes Crushing Ltd................ D 440 944-5500
Wickliffe *(G-15833)*

GRANITE: Crushed & Broken

Bradley Stone Industries LLC.......... F 440 519-3277
Solon *(G-13323)*

Martin Marietta Materials Inc.......... G 513 701-1140
West Chester *(G-15461)*

The National Lime and Stone Company. E 419 422-4341
Findlay *(G-7575)*

GRANITE: Cut & Shaped

Creative Countertops Ohio Inc........ F 937 540-9450
Englewood *(G-7226)*

Cutting Edge Countertops Inc......... E 419 873-9500
Perrysburg *(G-12372)*

Quarrymasters Inc.......................... G 330 612-0474
Akron *(G-292)*

Zelaya Stoneworks LLC................... F 513 777-8030
Liberty Township *(G-9211)*

GRAPHIC ARTS & RELATED DESIGN SVCS

Abstract Displays Inc...................... F 513 985-9700
Blue Ash *(G-1356)*

GRAPHIC ARTS & RELATED DESIGN SVCS

Academy Graphic Comm Inc.................. E 216 661-2550
  Cleveland (G-3589)
Alonovus Corp.. E 330 674-2300
  Millersburg (G-10940)
Art-American Printing Plates................. F 216 241-4420
  Cleveland (G-3678)
Container Graphics Corp........................ E 419 531-5133
  Toledo (G-14252)
Coyne Graphic Finishing Inc................. E 740 397-6232
  Mount Vernon (G-11269)
Envoi Design Inc..................................... G 513 651-4229
  Cincinnati (G-2877)
Great Lakes Graphics Inc...................... F 216 391-0077
  Cleveland (G-4144)
Insignia Signs Inc................................... G 937 866-2341
  Moraine (G-11186)
Laipplys Prtg Mktg Sltions Inc............... G 740 387-9282
  Marion (G-9859)
ML Advertising & Design LLC................ G 419 447-6523
  Tiffin (G-14094)
Mueller Art Cover & Binding Co............ E 440 238-3303
  Strongsville (G-13858)
Perrons Printing Company..................... F 440 236-8870
  Columbia Station (G-5016)
Phantasm Dsgns Sprtsn More Ltd........ G 419 538-6737
  Ottawa (G-12188)
Rba Inc... G 330 336-6700
  Wadsworth (G-15062)
Sanger & EBY Design LLC.................... F 513 784-9046
  Cincinnati (G-3362)
Schuerholz Inc... G 937 294-5218
  Dayton (G-6561)
White Tiger Inc.. F 740 852-4873
  London (G-9397)
Youngstown Pre-Press Inc..................... F 330 793-3690
  Youngstown (G-16486)

GRAPHITE MINING SVCS

Graftech Holdings Inc............................. D 216 676-2000
  Independence (G-8669)

GRATINGS: Open Steel Flooring

Ohio Gratings Inc.................................... B 800 321-9800
  Canton (G-2184)

GRAVE VAULTS, METAL

American Steel Grave Vault Co.............. F 419 468-6715
  Galion (G-7860)

GRAVEL MINING

Beck Sand & Gravel Inc......................... G 330 626-3863
  Ravenna (G-12707)
Fleming Construction Co........................ F 740 494-2177
  Prospect (G-12689)
Fouremans Sand & Gravel Inc............... G 937 547-1005
  Greenville (G-8045)
John L Garber Materials Corp................ F 419 884-1567
  Mansfield (G-9673)
Kipps Gravel Company Inc..................... G 513 732-1024
  Kingston (G-8931)
Oster Sand and Gravel Inc..................... G 330 494-5472
  Canton (G-2189)
Stansley Mineral Resources Inc............ E 419 843-2813
  Sylvania (G-14015)
Watson Gravel Inc................................... G 513 422-3781
  Middletown (G-10870)
Watson Gravel Inc................................... E 513 863-0070
  Hamilton (G-8258)
Weber Sand & Gravel Inc....................... G 419 636-7920
  Bryan (G-1844)
Wysong Gravel Co Inc............................ G 937 452-1523
  Camden (G-1965)

Wysong Gravel Co Inc............................ G 937 839-5497
  West Alexandria (G-15348)
Wysong Gravel Co Inc............................ F 937 456-4539
  West Alexandria (G-15347)

GREASES: Lubricating

Foam Seal Inc.. C 216 881-8111
  Cleveland (G-4074)

GREENHOUSES: Prefabricated Metal

Cropking Incorporated............................ F 330 302-4203
  Lodi (G-9349)
Ludy Greenhouse Mfg Corp.................. D 800 255-5839
  New Madison (G-11475)
Prospiant Inc... E 513 242-0310
  Cincinnati (G-3305)
Rough Brothers Mfg Inc......................... D 513 242-0310
  Cincinnati (G-3352)
Superior Structures Inc.......................... F 513 942-5954
  Harrison (G-8295)
XS Smith Inc.. E 252 940-5060
  Cincinnati (G-3533)

GRINDING SVC: Precision, Commercial Or Indl

Advanced Cryogenic Entps LLC............ G 330 922-0750
  Akron (G-22)
Afc Company... F 330 533-5581
  Canfield (G-1997)
G H Cutter Services Inc.......................... G 419 476-0476
  Toledo (G-14296)
Herman Machine Inc............................... F 330 633-3261
  Tallmadge (G-14032)
Micro Products Co Inc............................ E 440 943-0258
  Willoughby Hills (G-16025)
P & L Precision Grinding Llc.................. F 330 746-8081
  Youngstown (G-16410)
S C Industries Inc................................... E 216 732-9000
  Euclid (G-7300)
Sandwisch Enterprises Inc..................... G 419 944-6446
  Toledo (G-14462)
Tipp Machine & Tool Inc......................... C 937 890-8428
  Dayton (G-6625)

GROCERIES, GENERAL LINE WHOLESALERS

Brantley Partners IV LP.......................... G 216 464-8400
  Cleveland (G-3754)
La Perla Inc... G 419 534-2074
  Toledo (G-14356)
R S Hanline and Co Inc.......................... C 419 347-8077
  Shelby (G-13199)
Ricking Holding Co................................. E 513 825-3551
  Cleveland (G-4633)
The Ellenbee-Leggett Company Inc...... C 513 874-3200
  Fairfield (G-7417)

GUIDED MISSILES & SPACE VEHICLES

Tessec Manufacturing Svcs LLC........... E 937 985-3552
  Dayton (G-6616)

GUM & WOOD CHEMICALS

Damon Industries Inc.............................. D 330 821-5310
  Alliance (G-400)
PPG Architectural Coatings LLC........... D 440 297-8000
  Strongsville (G-13866)

GUTTERS: Sheet Metal

Gutter Logic Charlotte LLC.................... G 833 714-5970
  North Canton (G-11734)

Matteo Aluminum Inc.............................. E 440 585-5213
  Wickliffe (G-1583)
Roofing Annex LLC................................. G 513 942-0555
  West Chester (G-15581)

GYPSUM PRDTS

Caraustar Industries Inc......................... E 330 665-7700
  Copley (G-5946)
Ernst Enterprises Inc.............................. E 419 222-2015
  Lima (G-9241)
Mineral Processing Company................ G 419 396-3501
  Carey (G-2280)
Owens Corning Sales LLC..................... C 330 634-0460
  Tallmadge (G-1041)
Priest Services Inc.................................. G 440 333-1123
  Mayfield Heights (G-10254)
United States Gypsum Company........... B 419 734-3161
  Gypsum (G-811)
Wall Technology Inc................................ F 715 532-5548
  Toledo (G-1452)

GYROSCOPES

Atlantic Inertial Systems Inc................... C 740 788-3800
  Heath (G-8317)

HAIR & HAIR BASED PRDTS

Aajaj Hair Company LLC........................ F 216 309-0816
  Cleveland (G-584)
Ariezhair Collection LLC........................ F 614 964-5748
  Columbus (G-153)
Crownme Coil Care LLC........................ F 937 797-2070
  Trotwood (G-4543)
Pur Hair Extensions LLC........................ G 330 786-5772
  Akron (G-287)
U S Hair Inc... G 614 235-5190
  Columbus (G-5842)

HAIR CARE PRDTS

John Frieda Prof Hair Care Inc.............. E 800 521-3189
  Cincinnati (G-3043)
Mantra Haircare LLC.............................. F 440 526-3304
  Broadview Heights (G-1661)
Natural Beauty Products Inc.................. F 513 420-9400
  Middletown (G-10847)
Pfizer Inc.. F 937 746-3603
  Franklin (G-691)
Procter & Gamble Company.................. A 513 983-1100
  Cincinnati (G-3280)

HAND TOOLS, NEC: Wholesalers

Elliott Tool Technologies Ltd.................. D 937 253-6133
  Dayton (G-318)
National Tool & Equipment Inc.............. F 330 629-8665
  Youngstown (G-16403)
Norbar Torque Tools Inc......................... F 440 953-1175
  Willoughby (G-15959)

HANDBAGS

Judith Leiber LLC.................................... E 614 449-4217
  Columbus (G-5501)
Ravenworks Deer Skin............................ G 937 354-5151
  Mount Victory (G-11302)

HANDBAGS: Women's

Hugo Bosca Company Inc..................... F 937 323-5523
  Springfield (G-13581)

HARD RUBBER PRDTS, NEC

International Automotive Compo........... F 330 279-6557
  Holmesville (G-8549)

PRODUCT SECTION — HARDWARE STORES

HARDWARE

Company	Code	Phone
A JC Inc. Hudson *(G-8581)*	F	800 428-2438
AB Bonded Locksmiths Inc. Cincinnati *(G-2589)*	G	513 531-7334
Action Coupling & Eqp Inc. Holmesville *(G-8541)*	D	330 279-4242
Aluminum Bearing Co of America. Cleveland *(G-3643)*	G	216 267-8560
Ampex Metal Products Company. Brookpark *(G-1704)*	D	216 267-9242
Annin & Co Inc. Coshocton *(G-5968)*	C	740 622-4447
Arnco Corporation. Elyria *(G-7112)*	D	800 847-7661
Boardman Molded Products Inc. Youngstown *(G-16322)*	D	330 788-2400
Chantilly Development Corp. Toledo *(G-14233)*	E	419 243-8109
Conform Automotive LLC. Sidney *(G-13233)*	B	937 492-2708
Curtiss-Wright Flow Ctrl Corp. Cleveland *(G-3922)*	D	216 267-3200
Custom Metal Works Inc. Norwalk *(G-11959)*	F	419 668-7831
Dayton Superior Corporation. Rushsylvania *(G-12874)*	F	937 682-4015
Desco Corporation. New Albany *(G-11378)*	G	614 888-8855
Die Co Inc. Eastlake *(G-7025)*	E	440 942-8856
Eaton Corporation. Aurora *(G-712)*	E	330 274-0743
Edward W Daniel LLC. Wellington *(G-15306)*	E	440 647-1960
Elster Perfection Corporation. Geneva *(G-7935)*	D	440 428-1171
Faull & Son LLC. Niles *(G-11668)*	F	330 652-4341
Federal Equipment Company. Cincinnati *(G-2899)*	D	513 621-5260
Feitl Manufacturing Co Inc. Macedonia *(G-9550)*	E	330 405-6600
First Francis Company Inc. Painesville *(G-12237)*	E	440 352-8927
Flex-Strut Inc. Warren *(G-15170)*	D	330 372-9999
Florida Production Engrg Inc. New Madison *(G-11474)*	D	937 996-4361
Fort Recovery Industries Inc. Fort Recovery *(G-7617)*	C	419 375-4121
Gateway Con Forming Svcs Inc. Miamitown *(G-10708)*	D	513 353-2000
Group Industries Inc. Cleveland *(G-4152)*	E	216 271-0702
Hbd/Thermoid Inc. Bellefontaine *(G-1210)*	C	937 593-5010
Hbd/Thermoid Inc. Dublin *(G-6892)*	D	614 526-7000
Hdt Expeditionary Systems Inc. Cincinnati *(G-2564)*	F	513 943-1111
Heller Machine Products Inc. Cleveland *(G-4179)*	G	216 281-2951
Hey 9 Inc. Willoughby *(G-15928)*	G	919 259-2884
Hfi LLC. Canal Winchester *(G-1987)*	B	614 491-0500
Interntnal Auto Cmpnnts Group. Wauseon *(G-15265)*	A	419 433-5653
Kasai North America Inc. Dublin *(G-6903)*	E	614 356-1494
L & W Inc. Avon *(G-778)*	E	734 397-6300
Linear It Solutions LLC. Marysville *(G-9924)*	F	614 306-0761
Matdan Corporation. Blue Ash *(G-1429)*	E	513 794-0500
McGregor Mtal Yllow Sprng Wrks. Springfield *(G-13604)*	D	937 325-5561
Meese Inc. Ashtabula *(G-647)*	F	440 998-1202
Midlake Products & Mfg Co. Louisville *(G-9464)*	D	330 875-4202
Miller Studio Inc. New Philadelphia *(G-11519)*	E	330 339-1100
Netherland Rubber Company. Cincinnati *(G-3187)*	F	513 733-0883
Nova Machine Products Inc. Middleburg Heights *(G-10724)*	C	216 267-3200
Ohio Hydraulics Inc. Cincinnati *(G-3215)*	E	513 771-2590
Parker-Hannifin Corporation. Wickliffe *(G-15845)*	G	704 637-1190
Peterson American Corporation. Holland *(G-8523)*	E	419 867-8711
Pure Safety Group Inc. Worthington *(G-16208)*	F	614 436-0700
Qualitor Subsidiary H Inc. Bucyrus *(G-1865)*	C	419 562-7987
R & R Tool Inc. Blanchester *(G-1352)*	E	937 783-8665
S & K Products Company. Celina *(G-2347)*	E	419 268-2244
S Lehman Central Warehouse. Dalton *(G-6142)*	G	330 828-8828
Samsel Rope & Marine Supply Co. Cleveland *(G-4670)*	E	216 241-0333
Sarasota Quality Products. Westlake *(G-15783)*	G	440 899-9820
Sheet Metal Products Co Inc. Mentor *(G-10554)*	E	440 392-9000
Summers Acquisition Corp. Cleveland *(G-4745)*	E	216 941-7700
Superior Metal Products Inc. Lima *(G-9294)*	E	419 228-1145
Te-Co Manufacturing LLC. Englewood *(G-7244)*	D	937 836-0961
Technoform GL Insul N Amer Inc. Twinsburg *(G-14742)*	E	330 487-6600
Texmaster Tools Inc. Fredericktown *(G-7755)*	F	740 965-8778
Trim Parts Inc. Lebanon *(G-9115)*	E	513 934-0815
United Die & Mfg Sales Co. Sebring *(G-13128)*	E	330 938-6141
Universal Industrial Pdts Inc. Pioneer *(G-12500)*	F	419 737-9584
Verhoff Machine & Welding Inc. Continental *(G-5939)*	E	419 596-3202
Voss Industries LLC. Berea *(G-1298)*	E	216 771-7655
Washington Products Inc. Massillon *(G-10154)*	F	330 837-5101
Whiteside Manufacturing Co. Delaware *(G-6757)*	E	740 363-1179

HARDWARE & BUILDING PRDTS: Plastic

Company	Code	Phone
Associated Materials LLC. Cuyahoga Falls *(G-6069)*	A	330 929-1811
Associated Materials Group Inc. Cuyahoga Falls *(G-6070)*	C	330 929-1811
Axion International Inc. Zanesville *(G-16502)*	G	740 452-2500
Blackthorn LLC. Clayton *(G-3564)*	F	937 836-9296
Calorplast USA LLC. Milford *(G-10897)*	G	513 576-6333
Cosmo Plastics Company. Cleveland *(G-3907)*	C	440 498-7500
Cpg International LLC. Wilmington *(G-16047)*	B	937 655-8766
Dayton Superior Corporation. Miamisburg *(G-10633)*	C	937 866-0711
Deflecto LLC. Dover *(G-6814)*	C	330 602-0840
Fox Lite Inc. Fairborn *(G-7315)*	E	937 864-1966
Gorell Enterprises Inc. Streetsboro *(G-13772)*	B	724 465-1800
Harbor Industrial Corp. Conneaut *(G-5919)*	F	440 599-8366
MTI Acquisition LLC. Hebron *(G-8351)*	F	740 929-2065
Pro-TEC Industries Inc. Avon *(G-783)*	G	440 937-4142
Stonyridge Inc. New Carlisle *(G-11426)*	F	937 845-9482
Style Crest Enterprises Inc. Fremont *(G-7811)*	D	419 355-8586
Timbertech Limited. Wilmington *(G-16059)*	B	937 655-8766
Trusscore USA Inc. Dayton *(G-6637)*	E	888 418-4679
West & Barker Inc. Niles *(G-11691)*	E	330 652-9923
Westlake Dimex LLC. Marietta *(G-9844)*	C	740 374-3100

HARDWARE & EQPT: Stage, Exc Lighting

Company	Code	Phone
Beck Studios Inc. Milford *(G-10895)*	E	513 831-6650
Janson Industries. Canton *(G-2135)*	D	330 455-7029
Millers Aplus Cmpt Svcs LLC. Akron *(G-250)*	F	330 620-5288
Pwa Great Northern Corp Ctr LP. North Olmsted *(G-11825)*	G	412 415-1177
Tiffin Scenic Studios Inc. Tiffin *(G-14112)*	E	800 445-1546

HARDWARE STORES

Company	Code	Phone
Caldwell Lumber & Supply Co. Caldwell *(G-1908)*	E	740 732-2306
E P Gerber & Sons Inc. Kidron *(G-8913)*	D	330 857-2021
Hyde Park Lumber Company. Cincinnati *(G-3013)*	E	513 271-1500
Judy Mills Company Inc. Cincinnati *(G-3053)*	E	513 271-4241
Lochard Inc. Sidney *(G-13261)*	D	937 492-8811
Matco Tools Corporation. Stow *(G-13708)*	B	330 929-4949
Mid-Wood Inc. North Baltimore *(G-11696)*	F	419 257-3331
Rocky Hinge Inc. Girard *(G-7974)*	G	330 539-6296
S Lehman Central Warehouse. Dalton *(G-6142)*	G	330 828-8828
Spencer Feed & Supply LLC. Spencer *(G-13483)*	F	330 648-2111
Terry Lumber and Supply Co. Peninsula *(G-12342)*	F	330 659-6800
Thomas Do-It Center Inc. Gallipolis *(G-7903)*	E	740 446-2002

Employee Codes: A=Over 500 employees, B=251-500
C=101-250, D=51-100, E=20-50, F=10-19, G=1-9

2024 Harris Ohio Industrial Directory

HARDWARE STORES

PRODUCT SECTION

Woodsfeld True Vlue HM Ctr Inc............ E 740 472-1651
  Woodsfield (G-16090)

HARDWARE STORES: Pumps & Pumping Eqpt

Fountain Specialists Inc..................... G 513 831-5717
  Milford (G-10906)
Graco Ohio Inc.................................. D 330 494-1313
  North Canton (G-11733)
Oase North America Inc..................... G 800 365-3880
  Aurora (G-728)

HARDWARE STORES: Tools

Cammel Saw Company........................ F 330 477-3764
  Canton (G-2058)
Gordon Tool Inc................................. F 419 263-3151
  Payne (G-12321)
National Tool & Equipment Inc............. F 330 629-8665
  Youngstown (G-16403)
Simonds International LLC.................. G 978 424-0100
  Kimbolton (G-8928)
Stanley Industrial & Auto LLC.............. C 614 755-7089
  Dublin (G-6943)
Stanley Industrial & Auto LLC.............. D 614 755-7000
  Dublin (G-6944)

HARDWARE WHOLESALERS

Atlas Bolt & Screw Company LLC......... C 419 289-6171
  Ashland (G-554)
Barnes Group Inc............................... C 419 891-9292
  Maumee (G-10168)
Diy Holster LLC.................................. G 419 921-2168
  Elyria (G-7132)
DL Schwartz Co LLC........................... G 260 692-1464
  Hicksville (G-8373)
F & M Mafco Inc................................. C 513 367-2151
  Harrison (G-8273)
G & S Metal Products Co Inc............... C 216 441-0700
  Cleveland (G-4096)
Khempco Bldg Sup Co Ltd Partnr......... D 740 549-0465
  Delaware (G-6733)
Matco Tools Corporation..................... B 330 929-4949
  Stow (G-13708)
Ohashi Technica USA Inc.................... E 740 965-5115
  Sunbury (G-13960)
Paulin Industries Inc.......................... E 216 433-7633
  Parma (G-12293)
Shook Manufactured Pdts Inc.............. G 330 848-9780
  Akron (G-330)
Specialty Hardware Inc...................... E 216 291-1160
  Cleveland (G-4720)
Superior Caster Inc........................... F 513 539-8980
  Middletown (G-10861)
Texmaster Tools Inc........................... F 740 965-8778
  Fredericktown (G-7755)
Twin Ventures Inc.............................. F 330 405-3838
  Twinsburg (G-14749)
Waxman Industries Inc....................... C 440 439-1830
  Bedford Heights (G-1181)

HARDWARE, WHOLESALE: Bolts

Akko Fastener Inc.............................. F 513 489-8300
  Middletown (G-10804)

HARDWARE, WHOLESALE: Builders', NEC

L E Smith Company............................ D 419 636-4555
  Bryan (G-1825)
Twin Cities Concrete Co...................... F 330 343-4491
  Dover (G-6848)

HARDWARE, WHOLESALE: Nuts

Facil North America Inc...................... C 330 487-2500
  Twinsburg (G-14659)

HARDWARE, WHOLESALE: Power Tools & Access

Noco Company................................... D 216 464-8131
  Solon (G-13399)

HARDWARE, WHOLESALE: Screws

Maumee Machine & Tool Corp.............. E 419 385-2501
  Toledo (G-14379)

HARDWARE: Aircraft

Esterline Technologies Corp................. E 216 706-2960
  Cleveland (G-4031)
Tessec LLC....................................... D 937 576-0010
  Dayton (G-6615)
Twin Valley Metalcraft Asm LLC........... G 937 787-4634
  West Alexandria (G-15345)

HARDWARE: Aircraft & Marine, Incl Pulleys & Similar Items

Acorn Technology Corporation.............. E 216 663-1244
  Shaker Heights (G-13149)

HARDWARE: Builders'

Arrow Tru-Line Inc............................. G 419 636-7013
  Bryan (G-1808)
Cleveland Steel Specialty Co................ E 216 464-9400
  Bedford Heights (G-1168)
Leetonia Tool Company....................... F 330 427-6944
  Leetonia (G-9127)
Napoleon Spring Works Inc................. C 419 445-1010
  Archbold (G-537)

HARDWARE: Casket

Langenau Manufacturing Company........ E 216 651-3400
  Cleveland (G-4310)

HARDWARE: Furniture, Builders' & Other Household

Dudick Inc.. E 330 562-1970
  Streetsboro (G-13768)
Fortner Upholstering Inc..................... F 614 475-8282
  Columbus (G-5384)
Master Mfg Co Inc............................. E 216 641-0500
  Cleveland (G-4367)

HARDWARE: Rubber

Reynolds Industries Inc...................... G 330 889-9466
  West Farmington (G-15607)

HARNESS ASSEMBLIES: Cable & Wire

American Advnced Assmblies LLC......... E 937 339-6267
  Troy (G-14549)
Ankim Enterprises Incorporated............ F 937 599-1121
  Sidney (G-13222)
C C M Wire Inc.................................. E 330 425-3421
  Twinsburg (G-14638)
Co-Ax Technology Inc......................... C 440 914-9200
  Solon (G-13332)
Connective Design Incorporated........... F 937 746-8252
  Miamisburg (G-10628)
D H S LLC... F 937 599-2485
  Bellefontaine (G-1204)
Deca Mfg Co..................................... F 419 884-0071
  Mansfield (G-9645)
Dynalab Inc...................................... D 614 866-9999
  Reynoldsburg (G-12764)
Ewh Spectrum LLC............................. D 937 593-8010
  Bellefontaine (G-1208)
Gmelectric Inc................................... G 330 477-3392
  Canton (G-2114)
L & J Cable Inc.................................. E 937 526-9445
  Russia (G-12865)
La Grange Elec Assemblies Co............. E 440 355-5388
  Lagrange (G-8650)
Malabar Properties LLC...................... F 419 884-0071
  Mansfield (G-9682)
Mega Techway Inc............................. C 440 605-0700
  Cleveland (G-4391)
Microplex Inc.................................... E 330 498-0600
  North Canton (G-11743)
MJM Industries Inc............................ C 440 350-1230
  Fairport Harbo (G-7456)
Mueller Electric Company Inc.............. F 614 888-8855
  New Albany (G-11384)
Nimers & Wood II Inc......................... C 937 454-0722
  Vandalia (G-1955)
Nyle LLC.. F 888 235-2097
  Springboro (G-13513)
Ogc Industries Inc............................. F 330 456-1500
  Canton (G-2131)
Ohio Wire Harness LLC....................... F 937 292-7355
  Bellefontaine (G-1217)
Projects Unlimited Inc........................ C 937 918-2200
  Dayton (G-6534)
RTD Electronics Inc............................ F 330 487-0716
  Twinsburg (G-14729)
Russell Group United LLC................... F 614 353-6853
  Columbus (G-5734)
Thermtrol Corporation........................ A 330 497-4148
  North Canton (G-11765)
Westbrook Mfg Inc............................. B 937 254-2004
  Dayton (G-6650)
Wetsu Group Inc................................ F 937 324-9353
  Springfield (G-13655)

HARNESS WIRING SETS: Internal Combustion Engines

Electripack Inc.................................. E 937 433-2602
  Moraine (G-11174)
Mueller Electric Company Inc.............. E 216 771-5225
  Akron (G-256)

HEARING AIDS

Communications Aid Inc..................... F 513 475-8453
  Cincinnati (G-2783)
Hearingaid Medina Service.................. G 330 725-1060
  Medina (G-10332)
Soundtrace Inc.................................. G 513 278-5288
  Mason (G-10057)

HEAT EMISSION OPERATING APPARATUS

Hanon Systems Usa LLC..................... C 313 920-0583
  Carey (G-2279)

HEAT EXCHANGERS: After Or Inter Coolers Or Condensers, Etc

Ohio Heat Transfer Ltd....................... F 740 695-0635
  Saint Clairsville (G-12917)
Universal Hydraulik USA Corp.............. G 419 873-6340
  Perrysburg (G-12442)

HEAT TREATING: Metal

Akron Steel Treating Co...................... E 330 773-8211
  Akron (G-45)
Al Fe Heat Treating-Ohio Inc............... E 330 336-0211
  Wadsworth (G-15017)

| PRODUCT SECTION | | HELP SUPPLY SERVICES |

Al-Fe Heat Treating LLC.................................... F 419 782-7200
  Defiance *(G-6668)*
Alternative Flash Inc..................................... F 330 334-6111
  Wadsworth *(G-15018)*
AM Castle & Co... F 330 425-7000
  Bedford *(G-1100)*
Amac Enterprises Inc..................................... C 216 362-1880
  Parma *(G-12286)*
American Quality Stripping Inc........................ E 419 625-6288
  Sandusky *(G-13044)*
American Steel Treating Inc............................ D 419 874-2044
  Perrysburg *(G-12361)*
ATI Flat Rlled Pdts Hldngs LLC........................ F 330 875-2244
  Louisville *(G-9455)*
B&C Machine Co LLC..................................... E 330 745-4013
  Barberton *(G-859)*
Bekaert Corporation....................................... E 330 683-5060
  Orrville *(G-12119)*
Berkshire Road Holdings Inc........................... F 216 883-4200
  Cleveland *(G-3731)*
Bob Lanes Welding Inc.................................. F 740 373-3567
  Marietta *(G-9779)*
Bodycote Imt Inc... F 740 852-5000
  London *(G-9382)*
Bodycote Srfc Tech Prperty LLC....................... C 513 770-4900
  Mason *(G-9961)*
Bodycote Srfc Tech Wrtburg Inc...................... E 513 770-4900
  Mason *(G-9962)*
Bodycote Surfc Tech Mexico LLC..................... C 513 770-4900
  Mason *(G-9965)*
Bodycote Thermal Proc Inc.............................. E 513 921-2300
  Cincinnati *(G-2675)*
Bodycote Thermal Proc Inc.............................. E 440 473-2020
  Cleveland *(G-3744)*
Bodycote Thermal Proc Inc.............................. G 740 852-4955
  London *(G-9383)*
Bolttech Mannings Inc................................... G 614 836-0021
  Groveport *(G-8133)*
Bowdil Company... F 800 356-8663
  Canton *(G-2051)*
Carpe Diem Industries LLC............................. D 419 358-0129
  Bluffton *(G-1502)*
Carpe Diem Industries LLC............................. D 419 659-5639
  Columbus Grove *(G-5897)*
Certified Heat Treating Inc............................. F 937 866-0245
  Dayton *(G-6250)*
Cincinnati Gearing Systems Inc....................... D 513 527-8600
  Cincinnati *(G-2751)*
Cincinnati Stl Treating Co LLC........................ E 513 271-3173
  Cincinnati *(G-2762)*
Cleveland-Cliffs Columbus LLC....................... D 614 492-6800
  Richfield *(G-12784)*
Clifton Steel Company................................... D 216 662-6111
  Maple Heights *(G-9749)*
Dayton Forging Heat Treating.......................... D 937 253-4126
  Dayton *(G-6278)*
Derrick Company Inc..................................... E 513 321-8122
  Cincinnati *(G-2825)*
Detroit Flame Hardening Co........................... F 513 942-1400
  Fairfield *(G-7352)*
Dewitt Inc.. G 216 662-0800
  Maple Heights *(G-9750)*
Die Co Inc.. E 440 942-8856
  Eastlake *(G-7025)*
Dowa Tht America Inc................................... E 419 354-4144
  Bowling Green *(G-1564)*
Erie Steel Ltd... E 419 478-3743
  Toledo *(G-14279)*
Euclid Heat Treating Co................................. D 216 481-8444
  Euclid *(G-7269)*
Flynn Inc.. E 419 478-3743
  Toledo *(G-14291)*

Fusion Incorporated...................................... D 440 946-3300
  Willoughby *(G-15922)*
General Steel Corporation.............................. F 216 883-4200
  Cleveland *(G-4118)*
Gerdau McSteel Atmsphere Annli................... E 330 478-0314
  Canton *(G-2112)*
Gt Technologies Inc...................................... D 419 782-8955
  Defiance *(G-6680)*
H & M Metal Processing Co........................... E 330 745-3075
  Akron *(G-176)*
Heat Treating Inc.. E 937 325-3121
  Springfield *(G-13573)*
Heat Treating Equipment Inc.......................... E 740 549-3700
  Lewis Center *(G-9162)*
Heat Treating Inc.. F 614 759-9963
  Gahanna *(G-7837)*
Heat Treating Technologies............................ E 419 224-8324
  Lima *(G-9249)*
Induction Management Svcs LLC.................... G 440 947-2000
  Warren *(G-15178)*
Kowalski Heat Treating Co............................. F 216 631-4411
  Cleveland *(G-4297)*
Lapham-Hickey Steel Corp............................. E 614 443-4881
  Columbus *(G-5521)*
Lapham-Hickey Steel Corp............................. F 419 399-4803
  Paulding *(G-12317)*
McOn Inds Inc.. E 937 294-2681
  Moraine *(G-11192)*
Metallurgical Service Inc................................ F 937 294-2681
  Moraine *(G-11193)*
Moore Mc Millen Holdings............................. E 330 745-3075
  Cuyahoga Falls *(G-6105)*
Neturen America Corporation........................ F 513 863-1900
  Hamilton *(G-8231)*
Northwind Industries Inc............................... E 216 433-0666
  Cleveland *(G-4481)*
Ohio Metallurgical Service Inc........................ D 440 365-4104
  Elyria *(G-7190)*
Ohio Vertical Heat Treat Inc........................... D 330 456-7176
  Canton *(G-2187)*
Oliver Steel Plate Co...................................... D 330 425-7000
  Twinsburg *(G-14704)*
P & L Heat Trting Grinding Inc........................ E 330 746-1339
  Youngstown *(G-16408)*
P & L Precision Grinding Llc........................... F 330 746-8081
  Youngstown *(G-16410)*
Parker Trutec Incorporated............................ D 937 323-8833
  Springfield *(G-13615)*
Precision Powder Coating Inc......................... E 330 478-0741
  Canton *(G-2199)*
Pressure Technology Ohio Inc........................ E 215 628-1975
  Concord Township *(G-5910)*
Pride Investments LLC................................... F 937 461-1121
  Dayton *(G-6519)*
Ridge Machine & Welding Co........................ G 740 537-2821
  Toronto *(G-14534)*
Ropama Inc... F 440 358-1304
  Painesville *(G-12262)*
Team Inc... F 614 263-1808
  Columbus *(G-5815)*
Techniques Surfaces Usa Inc......................... G 937 323-2556
  Springfield *(G-13644)*
Thermal Solutions Inc................................... G 614 263-1808
  Columbus *(G-5824)*
Thermal Treatment Center Inc....................... E 216 881-8100
  Wickliffe *(G-15854)*
Universal Heat Treating Inc............................ E 216 641-2000
  Aurora *(G-738)*
Vicon Fabricating Company Ltd...................... E 440 205-6700
  Mentor *(G-10592)*
Weiss Industries Inc...................................... E 419 526-2480
  Mansfield *(G-9732)*

Winston Heat Treating Inc............................. E 937 226-0110
  Dayton *(G-6656)*
Worthngton Smuel Coil Proc LLC................... E 330 963-3777
  Twinsburg *(G-14758)*
Xtek Inc.. B 513 733-7800
  Cincinnati *(G-3534)*

HEATERS: Swimming Pool, Electric

Aquapro Systems LLC................................... F 877 278-2797
  Oakwood *(G-12026)*
Siemens Industry Inc.................................... E 513 576-2088
  Milford *(G-10922)*

HEATING & AIR CONDITIONING UNITS, COMBINATION

Crawford Ae LLC.. D 330 794-9770
  Akron *(G-117)*
Famous Realty Cleveland Inc......................... F 740 685-2533
  Byesville *(G-1897)*
Insource Tech Inc... F 419 399-3600
  Paulding *(G-12316)*
J&I Duct Fab LLC.. F 937 473-2121
  Covington *(G-6026)*

HEATING APPARATUS: Steam

Grid Industrial Heating Inc............................. G 330 332-9931
  Salem *(G-12998)*

HEATING EQPT: Complete

Chilltex LLC.. G 937 710-3308
  Anna *(G-489)*
Hatfield Industries LLC.................................. G 513 225-0456
  West Chester *(G-15445)*
Sticker Corporation...................................... F 440 946-2100
  Willoughby *(G-15998)*
Trane Company... F 419 491-2278
  Holland *(G-8534)*
Yukon Industries Inc..................................... E 440 478-4174
  Mentor *(G-10599)*

HEATING EQPT: Induction

Induction Tooling Inc.................................... F 440 237-0711
  North Royalton *(G-11879)*
Magneforce Inc.. F 330 856-9300
  Warren *(G-15188)*
Park-Ohio Holdings Corp............................... F 440 947-2000
  Cleveland *(G-4524)*
Park-Ohio Industries Inc................................ C 440 947-2000
  Cleveland *(G-4525)*
Taylor - Winfield Corporation......................... C 330 259-8500
  Hubbard *(G-8571)*

HEATING UNITS & DEVICES: Indl, Electric

Furnace Technologies Inc.............................. F 419 878-2100
  Waterville *(G-15244)*
Glo-Quartz Electric Htr Co Inc........................ E 440 255-9701
  Mentor *(G-10464)*
Heat Sensor Technologie LLC........................ D 513 228-0481
  Lebanon *(G-9088)*
Lanly Company.. E 216 731-1115
  Cleveland *(G-4312)*
Thermo Systems Technology Inc.................... F 216 292-8250
  Cleveland *(G-4792)*

HEAVY DISTILLATES

Ineos Neal LLC... E 610 790-3333
  Dublin *(G-6896)*

HELMETS: Steel

Armorsource LLC... E 740 928-0070
  Hebron *(G-8336)*

Employee Codes: A=Over 500 employees, B=251-500
C=101-250, D=51-100, E=20-50, F=10-19, G=1-9

HELP SUPPLY SERVICES

HELP SUPPLY SERVICES
Fluff Boutique .... G 513 227-6614
  Cincinnati *(G-2911)*
Industrial Repair and Mfg .... F 419 822-0314
  Delta *(G-6786)*

HOBBY, TOY & GAME STORES: Ceramics Splys
Elite Ceramics and Metals LLC .... G 330 787-2777
  Warren *(G-15166)*

HOBBY, TOY & GAME STORES: Toys & Games
Anime Palace .... G 408 858-1918
  Lewis Center *(G-9149)*
Intrism Inc .... F 614 733-9304
  Worthington *(G-16199)*
Ohio Art Company .... D 419 636-3141
  Bryan *(G-1833)*

HOISTING SLINGS
Acme Lifting Products Inc .... G 440 838-4430
  Cleveland *(G-3591)*

HOISTS
ARI Phoenix Inc .... E 513 229-3750
  Sharonville *(G-13170)*
Drc Acquisition Inc .... E 330 656-1600
  Streetsboro *(G-13767)*
Hoist Equipment Co Inc .... E 440 232-0300
  Bedford Heights *(G-1174)*
Lift-Tech International Inc .... B 330 424-7248
  Salem *(G-13011)*

HOLDING COMPANIES: Investment, Exc Banks
Akron Brass Holding Corp .... E 330 264-5678
  Wooster *(G-16098)*
Ampac Holdings LLC .... A 513 671-1777
  Cincinnati *(G-2622)*
Armor Consolidated Inc .... A 513 923-5260
  Mason *(G-9952)*
Cpp Group Holdings LLC .... E 216 453-4800
  Cleveland *(G-3912)*
Crane Carrier Holdings LLC .... C 918 286-2889
  New Philadelphia *(G-11496)*
Drt Holdings Inc .... D 937 298-7391
  Dayton *(G-6305)*
Elite Property Group LLC .... F 216 356-7469
  Elyria *(G-7139)*
Hexion Topco LLC .... D 614 225-4000
  Columbus *(G-5430)*
Hexpol Holding Inc .... F 440 834-4644
  Burton *(G-1882)*
Lion Group Inc .... D 937 898-1949
  Dayton *(G-6411)*
Norse Dairy Systems Inc .... C 614 294-4931
  Columbus *(G-5600)*
Vertiv JV Holdings LLC .... A 614 888-0246
  Columbus *(G-5859)*

HOLDING COMPANIES: Personal, Exc Banks
Hartzell Industries Inc .... F 937 773-6295
  Piqua *(G-12522)*

HOME FOR THE MENTALLY HANDICAPPED
Bittersweet Inc .... D 419 875-6986
  Whitehouse *(G-15816)*

RT Industries Inc .... G 937 335-5784
  Troy *(G-14606)*

HOMEFURNISHING STORES: Beddings & Linens
Morris Furniture Co Inc .... C 937 874-7100
  Fairborn *(G-7320)*

HOMEFURNISHING STORES: Brushes
Buckeye BOP LLC .... G 740 498-9898
  Newcomerstown *(G-11643)*

HOMEFURNISHING STORES: Cutlery
Handy Twine Knife Co .... G 419 294-3424
  Upper Sandusky *(G-14810)*

HOMEFURNISHING STORES: Pottery
All Fired Up Pnt Your Own Pot .... G 330 865-5858
  Copley *(G-5943)*

HOMEFURNISHINGS, WHOLESALE: Blinds, Vertical
Blind Factory Showroom .... F 614 771-6549
  Hilliard *(G-8405)*
Custom Blind Corporation .... F 937 643-2907
  Dayton *(G-6270)*

HOMEFURNISHINGS, WHOLESALE: Decorating Splys
Rhc Inc .... E 330 874-3750
  Bolivar *(G-1536)*

HOMEFURNISHINGS, WHOLESALE: Draperies
Accent Drapery Co Inc .... E 614 488-0741
  Columbus *(G-5092)*
Inside Outfitters Inc .... E 614 798-3500
  Lewis Center *(G-9165)*
Lumenomics Inc .... E 614 798-3500
  Lewis Center *(G-9170)*

HOMEFURNISHINGS, WHOLESALE: Grills, Barbecue
S I Distributing Inc .... F 419 647-4909
  Spencerville *(G-13489)*

HOMEFURNISHINGS, WHOLESALE: Kitchenware
G & S Metal Products Co Inc .... C 216 441-0700
  Cleveland *(G-4096)*
Walter F Stephens Jr Inc .... E 937 746-0521
  Franklin *(G-7709)*

HOMES: Log Cabins
Al Yoder Construction Co .... G 330 359-5726
  Millersburg *(G-10939)*
Gillard Construction Inc .... F 740 376-9744
  Marietta *(G-9795)*
Hochstetler Milling LLC .... E 419 368-0004
  Loudonville *(G-9449)*

HONING & LAPPING MACHINES
Diversified Honing Inc .... G 330 874-4663
  Bolivar *(G-1523)*

HOODS: Range, Sheet Metal
Z Line Kitchen and Bath LLC .... G 614 777-5004
  Marysville *(G-9944)*

HORSESHOES
Horseshoe Express Inc .... G 330 692-1209
  Canfield *(G-2007)*

HOSE: Automobile, Rubber
Cooper-Standard Automotive Inc .... D 419 352-3533
  Bowling Green *(G-1562)*
Mm Outsourcing LLC .... F 937 661-4300
  Leesburg *(G-9126)*
Myers Industries Inc .... D 330 336-6621
  Wadsworth *(G-5047)*
Myers Industries Inc .... E 330 253-5592
  Akron *(G-260)*
Sumiriko Ohio Inc .... E 419 358-2121
  Bluffton *(G-1507)*

HOSE: Flexible Metal
Ace Manufacturing Company .... E 513 541-2490
  West Chester *(G-15360)*
Federal Hose Manufacturing LLC .... E 800 346-4673
  Cleveland *(G-4054)*
First Francis Company Inc .... E 440 352-8927
  Painesville *(G-12237)*
Hose Master LLC .... B 216 481-2020
  Cleveland *(G-4203)*

HOSE: Plastic
Kentak Products Company .... D 330 386-3700
  East Liverpool *(G-6996)*
Kentak Products Company .... E 330 382-2000
  East Liverpool *(G-6997)*

HOSE: Rubber
Danfoss Power Solutions II LLC .... G 419 238-1190
  Van Wert *(G-14513)*
Eaton Aeroquip LLC .... A 419 891-7775
  Maumee *(G-10271)*
Eaton Aeroquip LLC .... C 440 523-5000
  Cleveland *(G-3991)*
Eaton Corporation .... A 419 238-1190
  Van Wert *(G-14514)*
HBD Industries Inc .... E 614 526-7000
  Dublin *(G-6891)*
Parker-Hannifin Corporation .... G 704 637-1190
  Wickliffe *(G-15865)*

HOSPITALS: Medical & Surgical
Dan Allen Surgical LLC .... F 800 261-9953
  Newbury *(G-11622)*
Optoquest Corporation .... F 216 445-3637
  Cleveland *(G-4597)*

HOTELS & MOTELS
Amish Door Inc .... C 330 359-5464
  Wilmot *(G-16065)*
John Purdum .... G 513 897-9686
  Waynesville *(G-15298)*

HOUSEHOLD ARTICLES, EXC KITCHEN: Pottery
Bodycote Imt Inc .... F 740 852-5000
  London *(G-9382)*

HOUSEHOLD ARTICLES: Metal
R L Torbeck Industries Inc .... E 513 367-0080
  Harrison *(G-8289)*
Voyale Minority Enterprise LLC .... E 216 271-3661
  Cleveland *(G-4865)*

HOUSEHOLD FURNISHINGS, NEC

PRODUCT SECTION — INDL MACHINERY & EQPT WHOLESALERS

Casco Mfg Solutions Inc .... D 513 681-0003
  Cincinnati (G-2706)
Ccp Industries Inc .... B 216 535-4227
  Richmond Heights (G-12807)
Columbus Canvas Products Inc .... F 614 375-1397
  Columbus (G-5263)
DCW Acquisition Inc .... E 216 451-0666
  Cleveland (G-3949)
Master Mfg Co Inc .... E 216 641-0500
  Cleveland (G-4367)
Nestaway LLC .... D 216 587-1500
  Cleveland (G-4449)
Ohio Table Pad Company .... F 419 872-6400
  Perrysburg (G-12407)
STI Liquidation Inc .... E 614 733-0099
  Plain City (G-12592)

HOUSEWARES, ELECTRIC: Air Purifiers, Portable

Hmi Industries Inc .... E 440 846-7800
  Brooklyn (G-1678)

HOUSEWARES, ELECTRIC: Cooking Appliances

Nacco Industries Inc .... E 440 229-5151
  Cleveland (G-4434)
Whirlpool Corporation .... D 937 548-4126
  Greenville (G-8064)

HOUSEWARES, ELECTRIC: Fans, Exhaust & Ventilating

Ad Industries Inc .... A 303 744-1911
  Dayton (G-6183)
Ventilation Systems Jsc .... F 513 348-3853
  Cincinnati (G-3491)

HOUSEWARES: Food Dishes & Utensils, Pressed & Molded Pulp

Pressed Paperboard Tech LLC .... C 419 423-4030
  Findlay (G-7552)

HUMIDIFIERS & DEHUMIDIFIERS

Guardian Technologies LLC .... E 866 603-5900
  Euclid (G-7270)

HYDRAULIC EQPT REPAIR SVC

American Hydraulic Svcs Inc .... E 606 739-8680
  Ironton (G-8695)
Fluid System Service Inc .... G 216 651-2450
  Cleveland (G-4072)
Hunger Hydraulics CC Ltd .... F 419 666-4510
  Rossford (G-12865)
Hunter Hydraulics Inc .... G 330 455-3983
  Canton (G-2126)
Hydraulic Specialists Inc .... F 740 922-3343
  Midvale (G-10879)
Ic-Fluid Power Inc .... F 419 661-8811
  Rossford (G-12866)
Perkins Motor Service Ltd .... F 440 277-1456
  Lorain (G-9430)
Quad Fluid Dynamics Inc .... F 330 220-3005
  Brunswick (G-1785)

ICE

Haller Enterprises Inc .... F 330 733-9693
  Akron (G-177)
Home City Ice Company .... G 937 461-6028
  Dayton (G-6371)
Home City Ice Company .... F 419 562-4953
  Delaware (G-6731)
Home City Ice Company .... F 614 836-2877
  Groveport (G-8146)
Home City Ice Company .... F 513 353-9346
  Harrison (G-8279)
Home City Ice Company .... G 513 598-3000
  Olmsted Twp (G-12087)
Lori Holding Co .... E 740 342-3230
  New Lexington (G-11453)
Millersburg Ice Company .... E 330 674-3016
  Millersburg (G-10983)
Velvet Ice Cream Company .... E 419 562-2009
  Bucyrus (G-1872)

ICE CREAM & ICES WHOLESALERS

United Dairy Farmers Inc .... C 513 396-8700
  Cincinnati (G-3479)
Velvet Ice Cream Company .... E 419 562-2009
  Bucyrus (G-1872)

IDENTIFICATION TAGS, EXC PAPER

Silly Brandz Global LLC .... D 419 697-8324
  Toledo (G-14473)

IGNITION APPARATUS & DISTRIBUTORS

Lake Erie Interlock Inc .... G 440 918-9898
  Willoughby (G-15943)

IGNITION SYSTEMS: High Frequency

Altronic LLC .... C 330 545-9768
  Girard (G-7960)

INCINERATORS

Novagard Solutions Inc .... C 216 881-8111
  Cleveland (G-4483)

INCUBATORS & BROODERS: Farm

Chick Master Incubator Company .... D 330 722-5591
  Medina (G-10308)

INDL & PERSONAL SVC PAPER WHOLESALERS

Buckeye Paper Co Inc .... E 330 477-5925
  Canton (G-2054)
CJ Dannemiller Co .... E 330 825-7808
  Norton (G-11939)
Cleveland Supplyone Inc .... E 216 514-7000
  Cleveland (G-3857)
Gt Industrial Supply Inc .... F 513 771-7000
  Cincinnati (G-2976)
Gvs Industries Inc .... G 513 851-3606
  Hamilton (G-8214)
Millcraft Group LLC .... D 216 441-5500
  Independence (G-8675)
Putnam Plastics Inc .... G 937 866-6261
  Dayton (G-6535)
Zebco Industries Inc .... F 740 654-4510
  Lancaster (G-9049)

INDL & PERSONAL SVC PAPER, WHOLESALE: Boxes & Containers

Argrov Box Co .... F 937 898-1700
  Dayton (G-6212)
Deufol Worldwide Packaging LLC .... E 440 232-1900
  Bedford (G-1116)

INDL & PERSONAL SVC PAPER, WHOLESALE: Shipping Splys

Adapt-A-Pak Inc .... E 937 845-0386
  Fairborn (G-7307)

Systems Pack Inc .... E 330 467-5729
  Macedonia (G-9583)

INDL CONTRACTORS: Exhibit Construction

Abstract Displays Inc .... F 513 985-9700
  Blue Ash (G-1356)
Benchmark Craftsman Inc .... E 866 313-4700
  Seville (G-13135)
Display Dynamics Inc .... E 937 832-2830
  Englewood (G-7229)
Exhibit Concepts Inc .... D 937 890-7000
  Vandalia (G-14939)

INDL DIAMONDS WHOLESALERS

Chardon Tool & Supply Co Inc .... E 440 286-6440
  Chardon (G-2445)

INDL EQPT SVCS

3-D Service Ltd .... C 330 830-3500
  Massillon (G-10072)
Commercial Electric Pdts Corp .... E 216 241-2886
  Cleveland (G-3889)
Forge Industries Inc .... A 330 960-2468
  Youngstown (G-16359)
Graphic Systems Services Inc .... E 937 746-0708
  Springboro (G-13503)
Grob Systems Inc .... A 419 358-9015
  Bluffton (G-1504)
L M Equipment & Design Inc .... F 330 332-9951
  Salem (G-13009)
Lubrisource Inc .... F 937 432-9292
  Middletown (G-10836)
Mesocoat Inc .... F 216 453-0866
  Euclid (G-7286)
Miami Valley Punch & Mfg .... F 937 237-0533
  Dayton (G-6440)
Northwood Industries Inc .... F 419 666-2100
  Perrysburg (G-12404)
Obr Cooling Towers Inc .... E 419 243-3443
  Northwood (G-11924)
Quintus Technologies LLC .... E 614 891-2732
  Lewis Center (G-9176)
Slater Road Mills Inc .... E 330 332-9951
  Salem (G-13032)
T E Brown LLC .... F 937 223-2241
  Dayton (G-6607)
U S Molding Machinery Co Inc .... E 440 918-1701
  Willoughby (G-16012)
Walker National Inc .... E 614 492-1614
  Columbus (G-5862)

INDL GASES WHOLESALERS

Airgas Usa LLC .... G 937 222-8312
  Moraine (G-11154)
Airgas Usa LLC .... G 440 232-6397
  Twinsburg (G-14625)

INDL HELP SVCS

Aqua Technology Group LLC .... G 513 298-1183
  West Chester (G-15367)

INDL MACHINERY & EQPT WHOLESALERS

2e Associates Inc .... E 440 975-9955
  Willoughby (G-15871)
Addition Manufacturing Tech .... C 513 228-7000
  Lebanon (G-9059)
Aerocontrolex Group Inc .... D 216 291-6025
  South Euclid (G-13457)
Alkon Corporation .... E 614 799-6650
  Dublin (G-6858)
Alkon Corporation .... D 419 355-9111
  Fremont (G-7762)

Employee Codes: A=Over 500 employees, B=251-500
C=101-250, D=51-100, E=20-50, F=10-19, G=1-9

INDL MACHINERY & EQPT WHOLESALERS

Ats Systems Oregon Inc.............................. C 541 738-9122
  Lewis Center (G-9152)
Avure Autoclave Systems Inc..................... F 614 891-2732
  Columbus (G-5167)
Bionix Safety Technologies Ltd.................. E 419 727-0552
  Maumee (G-10172)
Brown Industrial Inc................................... E 937 693-3838
  Botkins (G-1542)
Contitech Usa Inc...................................... D 937 644-8900
  Marysville (G-9906)
Cortest Inc... F 440 942-1235
  Willoughby (G-15903)
Country Sales & Service LLC..................... F 330 683-2500
  Orrville (G-12122)
Ctm Integration Incorporated..................... E 330 332-1800
  Salem (G-12988)
Dengensha America Corporation................ F 440 439-8081
  Bedford (G-1115)
Dura Magnetics Inc.................................... F 419 882-0591
  Sylvania (G-13995)
Eltool Corporation...................................... G 513 723-1772
  Mansfield (G-9652)
EMI Corp... D 937 596-5511
  Jackson Center (G-8733)
Equipment Guys Inc................................... F 614 871-9220
  Newark (G-11575)
Equipment Mfrs Intl Inc.............................. E 216 651-6700
  Cleveland (G-4026)
Exomet Inc... E 440 593-1161
  Conneaut (G-5917)
Freeman Manufacturing & Sup Co.............. E 440 934-1902
  Avon (G-775)
G & P Construction LLC............................. E 855 494-4830
  North Royalton (G-11875)
G W Cobb Co... F 216 341-0100
  Cleveland (G-4099)
Ged Holdings Inc....................................... F 330 963-5401
  Twinsburg (G-14666)
Glavin Industries Inc.................................. F 440 349-0049
  Solon (G-13353)
Gokoh Corporation..................................... F 937 339-4977
  Troy (G-14573)
Grand Harbor Yacht Sales & Svc................ G 440 442-2919
  Cleveland (G-4139)
Grenga Machine & Welding....................... F 330 743-1113
  Youngstown (G-16374)
Hannon Company....................................... D 330 456-4728
  Canton (G-2121)
Hendrickson International Corp.................. D 740 929-5600
  Hebron (G-8343)
Hickman Williams & Company................... F 513 621-1946
  Cincinnati (G-2998)
Hydrotech Inc... D 888 651-5712
  West Chester (G-15563)
IBI Brake Products Inc............................... G 440 543-7962
  Chagrin Falls (G-2402)
Intelligrated Inc.. A 513 874-0788
  West Chester (G-15565)
Intelligrated Systems Inc........................... A 866 936-7300
  Mason (G-10010)
Intelligrated Systems Ohio LLC................. A 513 701-7300
  Mason (G-10012)
J McCaman Enterprises Inc........................ G 330 825-2401
  New Franklin (G-11437)
Jed Industries Inc...................................... F 440 639-9973
  Grand River (G-8011)
JPS Technologies Inc................................. F 513 984-6400
  Blue Ash (G-1415)
JPS Technologies Inc................................. F 513 984-6400
  Blue Ash (G-1414)
Jsh International LLC................................. G 330 734-0251
  Akron (G-200)

Kinetics Noise Control Inc.......................... C 614 889-0480
  Dublin (G-6905)
Kolinahr Systems Inc................................. F 513 745-9401
  Blue Ash (G-1417)
Kyocera SGS Precision Tls Inc.................... E 330 688-6667
  Cuyahoga Falls (G-6098)
Linden-Two Inc.. E 330 928-4064
  Cuyahoga Falls (G-6100)
M & S Equipment Leasing Co..................... F 216 662-8800
  Cleveland (G-4343)
Mfh Partners Inc.. B 440 461-4100
  Cleveland (G-4398)
Minerva Welding and Fabg Inc................... E 330 868-7731
  Minerva (G-11036)
Monaghan & Associates Inc....................... F 937 253-7706
  Dayton (G-6456)
Multi Products Company............................ E 330 674-5981
  Millersburg (G-10986)
Neil R Scholl Inc.. F 740 653-6593
  Lancaster (G-9027)
Off Contact Inc.. F 419 255-5546
  Toledo (G-14406)
Park Corporation.. B 216 267-4870
  Medina (G-10362)
Pfpc Enterprises Inc................................... F 513 941-6200
  Cincinnati (G-3253)
Pines Manufacturing Inc............................ E 440 835-5553
  Westlake (G-15775)
Plastic Process Equipment Inc................... E 216 367-7000
  Macedonia (G-9566)
Progressive Mfg Co Inc.............................. G 330 784-4717
  Akron (G-286)
Reduction Engineering Inc......................... E 330 677-2225
  Kent (G-8852)
Rubber City Machinery Corp...................... E 330 434-3500
  Akron (G-312)
Samuel Son & Co (usa) Inc........................ D 740 522-2500
  Heath (G-8331)
Sequa Can Machinery Inc.......................... E 330 493-0444
  Canton (G-2221)
Stanley Bittinger.. G 740 942-4302
  Cadiz (G-1904)
Starkey Machinery Inc............................... E 419 468-2560
  Galion (G-7885)
Super Systems Inc..................................... E 513 772-0060
  Cincinnati (G-3432)
Tilt-Or-Lift Inc.. G 419 893-6944
  Maumee (G-10241)
Tooltex Inc... F 614 539-3222
  Grove City (G-8123)
Tri State Equipment Company................... G 513 738-7227
  Shandon (G-13161)
United Hydraulics...................................... G 440 585-0906
  Wickliffe (G-15856)
Valv-Trol LLC... F 330 686-2800
  Stow (G-13736)
Valve Related Controls Inc......................... F 513 677-8724
  Loveland (G-9507)
Venturo Manufacturing Inc........................ F 513 772-8448
  Cincinnati (G-3492)

INDL PATTERNS: Foundry Cores

Founders Service & Mfg Inc....................... G 330 584-7759
  Deerfield (G-6666)
Humtown Pattern Company....................... D 330 482-5555
  Columbiana (G-5041)
PCC Airfoils LLC.. C 216 692-7900
  Cleveland (G-4537)
Sinel Company Inc..................................... F 937 433-4772
  Dayton (G-6576)
TW Manufacturing Co................................ E 440 439-3243
  Cleveland (G-4838)

PRODUCT SECTION

INDL PATTERNS: Foundry Patternmaking

Accuform Manufacturing Inc...................... E 330 797-9291
  Youngstown (G-16300)
Cincinnati Pattern Company....................... E 513 241-9872
  Cincinnati (G-2257)
National Pattern Mfgco.............................. F 330 682-6871
  Orrville (G-1214)
Plas-Mac Corp... D 440 349-3222
  Solon (G-13405)
Seilkop Industries Inc................................ F 513 679-5680
  Cincinnati (G-3376)

INDL PROCESS INSTRUMENTS: Chromatographs

Consoldted Anlycal Systems In.................. F 513 542-1200
  Cincinnati (G-2237)

INDL PROCESS INSTRUMENTS: Control

Bay Controls LLC....................................... E 419 891-4390
  Maumee (G-10170)
Dalton Corporation.................................... G 419 682-6328
  Stryker (G-1390)
Gc Controls Inc.. G 440 779-4777
  Westlake (G-15552)

INDL SPLYS WHOLESALERS

Alb Tyler Holdings Inc................................ G 440 946-7171
  Mentor (G-10410)
Alkon Corporation...................................... E 614 799-6650
  Dublin (G-6858)
All Ohio Threaded Rod Co Inc.................... E 216 426-1800
  Cleveland (G-3622)
Allied Shipping and Packagi...................... F 937 222-7422
  Moraine (G-1115)
Alro Steel Corporation............................... E 614 878-7271
  Columbus (G-516)
Alro Steel Corporation............................... D 419 720-5300
  Toledo (G-14184)
Anchor Flange Company............................ D 513 527-3512
  Cincinnati (G-2656)
Aqua Technology Group LLC..................... G 513 298-1183
  West Chester (G-15367)
Ci Disposition Co...................................... D 216 587-5200
  Brooklyn Heights (G-1687)
Cmt Machining & Fabg LLC....................... F 937 652-3740
  Urbana (G-14827)
Cornwell Quality Tools Company............... D 330 628-2627
  Mogadore (G-11168)
Dayton Stencil Works Company................. F 937 223-3233
  Dayton (G-6290)
Dearing Compressor and Pump................. E 330 783-2258
  Youngstown (G-15348)
Dynatech Systems Inc............................... F 440 365-1774
  Elyria (G-7135)
Eagle Industrial Truck Mfg LLC................. E 419 866-6301
  Swanton (G-1393)
Edward W Daniel LLC................................ E 440 647-1960
  Wellington (G-15506)
Fcx Performance Inc.................................. E 614 253-1996
  Columbus (G-533)
Ges Graphite Inc....................................... E 216 658-6660
  Parma (G-12290)
Gokoh Corporation..................................... F 937 339-4977
  Troy (G-14573)
H3d Tool Corporation................................ E 740 498-5181
  Newcomerstown (G-11644)
HMS Industries LLC................................... F 440 899-0001
  Westlake (G-15755)
Indelco Custom Products Inc..................... E 216 797-7300
  Euclid (G-7274)

2024 Harris Ohio Industrial Directory

(G-0000) Company's Geographic Section entry number

PRODUCT SECTION — INDL SPLYS, WHOLESALE: Rubber Goods, Mechanical

Company	Code	Phone
Industrial Mold Inc	E	330 425-7374
Twinsburg (G-14676)		
Japo Inc	E	614 263-2850
Columbus (G-5488)		
Lawrence Industries Inc	E	216 518-7000
Cleveland (G-4318)		
Logan Clutch Corporation	E	440 808-4258
Cleveland (G-4334)		
Lynk Packaging Inc	E	330 562-8080
Aurora (G-723)		
Maintenance Repair Supply Inc	F	740 922-3006
Midvale (G-10881)		
McWane Inc	B	740 622-6651
Coshocton (G-5983)		
Metzger Machine Co	F	513 241-3360
Cincinnati (G-3159)		
Mill-Rose Company	C	440 255-9171
Mentor (G-10505)		
Newact Inc	F	513 321-5177
Batavia (G-940)		
Orbytel Print and Packg Inc	G	216 267-8734
Cleveland (G-4508)		
Plastic Process Equipment Inc	E	216 367-7000
Macedonia (G-9566)		
Pressure Connections Corp	D	614 863-6930
Columbus (G-5689)		
Samsel Rope & Marine Supply Co	E	216 241-0333
Cleveland (G-4670)		
Samuel Son & Co (usa) Inc	D	740 522-2500
Heath (G-8331)		
Service Spring Corp	G	419 867-0212
Maumee (G-10230)		
SSP Fittings Corp	D	330 425-4250
Twinsburg (G-14736)		
Steam Trbine Altrntive Rsrces	E	740 387-5535
Marion (G-9884)		
Superior Holding LLC	E	216 651-9400
Cleveland (G-4748)		
The Cornwell Quality Tools Company	D	330 336-3506
Wadsworth (G-15069)		
The Kindt-Collins Company LLC	D	216 252-4122
Cleveland (G-4788)		
Tlg Cochran Inc	E	440 914-1122
Twinsburg (G-14744)		
Toledo Tarp Service Inc	E	419 837-5098
Perrysburg (G-12440)		
United Tool Supply Inc	G	513 752-6000
Cincinnati (G-2576)		
Watteredge LLC	D	440 933-6110
Avon Lake (G-828)		
Wesco Distribution Inc	F	419 666-1670
Northwood (G-11933)		
Wulco Inc	D	513 379-6115
Hamilton (G-8259)		
Wulco Inc	D	513 679-2600
Cincinnati (G-3529)		

INDL SPLYS, WHOLESALE: Abrasives

Company	Code	Phone
Cincinnati Abrasive Supply Co	G	513 941-8866
Cincinnati (G-2738)		
Hickman Williams & Company	F	513 621-1946
Cincinnati (G-2998)		

INDL SPLYS, WHOLESALE: Adhesives, Tape & Plasters

Company	Code	Phone
Strata-Tac Inc	F	630 879-9388
Troy (G-14613)		

INDL SPLYS, WHOLESALE: Bearings

Company	Code	Phone
Forge Industries Inc	A	330 960-2468
Youngstown (G-16359)		
Miba Bearings US LLC	B	740 962-4242
Mcconnelsville (G-10282)		

INDL SPLYS, WHOLESALE: Bins & Containers, Storage

Company	Code	Phone
Creative Plastic Concepts LLC	F	419 927-9588
Sycamore (G-13988)		
Dadco Inc	F	513 489-2244
Cincinnati (G-2816)		
Modroto	G	440 998-1202
Ashtabula (G-649)		

INDL SPLYS, WHOLESALE: Drums, New Or Reconditioned

Company	Code	Phone
Horwitz & Pintis Co	F	419 666-2220
Toledo (G-14320)		

INDL SPLYS, WHOLESALE: Gaskets & Seals

Company	Code	Phone
North Coast Seal Incorporated	F	216 898-5000
Brookpark (G-1722)		

INDL SPLYS, WHOLESALE: Gears

Company	Code	Phone
Ig Watteeuw Usa LLC	F	740 588-1722
Zanesville (G-16538)		

INDL SPLYS, WHOLESALE: Glass Bottles

Company	Code	Phone
Cleveland Supplyone Inc	E	216 514-7000
Cleveland (G-3857)		

INDL SPLYS, WHOLESALE: Power Transmission, Eqpt & Apparatus

Company	Code	Phone
Commercial Electric Pdts Corp	E	216 241-2886
Cleveland (G-3889)		
Great Lakes Power Products Inc	D	440 951-5111
Mentor (G-10465)		

INDL SPLYS, WHOLESALE: Rubber Goods, Mechanical

Company	Code	Phone
Akalina Associates Inc	C	440 992-2195
Ashtabula (G-626)		
Alloy Extrusion Company	E	330 677-4946
Kent (G-8798)		
Alternative Flash Inc	F	330 334-6111
Wadsworth (G-15018)		
American Pro-Mold Inc	F	330 336-4111
Wadsworth (G-15019)		
ARC Rubber Inc	F	440 466-4555
Geneva (G-7931)		
Brp Manufacturing Company	E	800 858-0482
Lima (G-9226)		
C & M Rubber Co Inc	F	937 299-2782
Dayton (G-6242)		
Chardon Custom Polymers LLC	F	440 285-2161
Chardon (G-2442)		
Clark Rubber & Plastic Company	C	440 255-9793
Mentor (G-10439)		
Colonial Rubber Company	E	330 296-2831
Ravenna (G-12711)		
Contitech North America Inc	F	330 664-7180
Fairlawn (G-7435)		
Datwyler Sling Sltions USA Inc	D	937 387-2800
Vandalia (G-14937)		
Dayton Molded Urethanes LLC	E	937 279-1910
Dayton (G-6284)		
Duramax Global Corp	F	440 834-5400
Hiram (G-8482)		
Dybrook Products Inc	E	330 392-7665
Warren (G-15165)		
Epg Inc	D	330 995-5125
Aurora (G-714)		
Epg Inc	F	330 995-9725
Streetsboro (G-13770)		
Extruded Slcone Pdts Gskets In	E	330 733-0101
Mogadore (G-11072)		
Frankes Wood Products LLC	E	937 642-0706
Marysville (G-9910)		
Harwood Entp Holdings Inc	F	330 923-3256
Cuyahoga Falls (G-6090)		
Hygenic Company LLC	B	330 633-8460
Akron (G-188)		
Ier Fujikura Inc	C	330 425-7121
Macedonia (G-9556)		
Jakmar Incorporated	F	513 631-4303
Cincinnati (G-3034)		
Johnson Bros Rubber Co	D	419 853-4122
West Salem (G-15634)		
Karman Rubber Company	D	330 864-2161
Akron (G-201)		
Kleen Polymers Inc	F	
Wadsworth (G-15040)		
Macdivitt Rubber Company LLC	E	440 259-5937
Perry (G-12354)		
Mantaline Corporation	G	330 569-3147
Hiram (G-8486)		
Mantaline Corporation	G	330 274-2264
Mantua (G-9739)		
Mantaline Corporation	C	330 274-2264
Mantua (G-9740)		
Martin Industries Inc	F	419 862-2694
Elmore (G-7102)		
Meridian Industries Inc	D	330 673-1011
Kent (G-8834)		
Namoh Ohio Holdings Inc	E	
Norwood (G-11996)		
Performance Elastomers Corporation	D	330 297-2255
Ravenna (G-12727)		
Plabell Rubber Products Corp	E	419 691-5878
Toledo (G-14440)		
Q Holding Company	B	440 903-1827
Twinsburg (G-14720)		
Qualiform Inc	E	330 336-6777
Wadsworth (G-15057)		
Quanex Ig Systems Inc	E	740 439-2338
Cambridge (G-1950)		
Quanex Ig Systems Inc	D	216 910-1500
Akron (G-291)		
Robin Industries Inc	F	330 893-3501
Berlin (G-1308)		
Robin Industries Inc	E	330 695-9300
Fredericksburg (G-7732)		
Robin Industries Inc	E	330 359-5418
Winesburg (G-16082)		
Robin Industries Inc	F	216 631-7000
Independence (G-8684)		
Rubber-Tech Inc	E	937 274-1114
Dayton (G-6554)		
Shreiner Sole Company Inc	F	330 276-6135
Killbuck (G-8922)		
Soffseal Inc	E	513 934-0815
Cincinnati (G-3400)		
Sperry & Rice LLC	F	330 276-2801
Killbuck (G-8923)		
Sperry & Rice LLC	G	765 647-4141
Killbuck (G-8924)		
TAC Materials Inc	C	330 425-8472
Twinsburg (G-14740)		
The D S Brown Company	C	419 257-3561
North Baltimore (G-11701)		
Tigerpoly Manufacturing Inc	B	614 871-0045
Grove City (G-8122)		
Universal Urethane Pdts Inc	D	419 693-7400
Toledo (G-14514)		

Employee Codes: A=Over 500 employees, B=251-500, C=101-250, D=51-100, E=20-50, F=10-19, G=1-9

INDL SPLYS, WHOLESALE: Rubber Goods, Mechanical

Vertex Inc .... E 330 628-6210
  Mogadore (G-11090)
Woodlawn Rubber Co .... F 513 489-1718
  Blue Ash (G-1494)
Yokohama Tire Corporation .... D 440 352-3321
  Painesville (G-12281)
Yokohama Tws North America Inc .... E 866 633-8473
  Akron (G-379)

INDL SPLYS, WHOLESALE: Seals

Datwyler Sling Sltions USA Inc .... D 937 387-2800
  Vandalia (G-14937)
McNeil Industries Inc .... E 440 951-7756
  Painesville (G-12251)

INDL SPLYS, WHOLESALE: Tools

B W Grinding Co .... E 419 923-1376
  Lyons (G-9531)
H & D Steel Service Inc .... E 800 666-3390
  North Royalton (G-11878)
High Quality Tools Inc .... F 440 975-9684
  Eastlake (G-7036)
Ohio Drill & Tool Co .... E 330 525-7717
  Homeworth (G-8555)
Save Edge Inc .... E 937 376-8268
  Xenia (G-16272)
TCH Industries Incorporated .... F 330 487-5155
  Twinsburg (G-14741)
Tenney Tool & Supply Co .... G 330 666-2807
  Barberton (G-899)

INDL SPLYS, WHOLESALE: Valves & Fittings

Crane Pumps & Systems Inc .... C 937 773-2442
  Piqua (G-12508)
Pipe Products Inc .... C 513 587-7532
  West Chester (G-15480)
Quad Fluid Dynamics Inc .... F 330 220-3005
  Brunswick (G-1785)
Shaq Inc .... D 770 427-0402
  Beachwood (G-1023)
Victory White Metal Company .... D 216 271-1400
  Cleveland (G-4874)

INDUSTRIAL & COMMERCIAL EQPT INSPECTION SVCS

Quintus Technologies LLC .... E 614 891-2732
  Lewis Center (G-9176)

INFORMATION RETRIEVAL SERVICES

Advant-E Corporation .... F 937 429-4288
  Beavercreek (G-1039)
AGS Custom Graphics Inc .... D 330 963-7770
  Macedonia (G-9534)
Hkm Drect Mkt Cmmnications Inc .... C 800 860-4456
  Cleveland (G-4193)
Promatch Solutions LLC .... F 877 299-0185
  Moraine (G-11205)
Repro Acquisition Company LLC .... F 216 738-3800
  Cleveland (G-4626)
Welch Publishing Co .... E 419 874-2528
  Perrysburg (G-12444)

INFRARED OBJECT DETECTION EQPT

IEC Infrared Systems Inc .... E 440 234-8000
  Middleburg Heights (G-10719)

INGOT, EXTRUSION: Extrusion ingot, aluminum: rolling mills

Aluminum Extrusion Tech LLC .... G 330 533-3994
  Canfield (G-1999)

Powermount Systems Inc .... G 740 499-4330
  La Rue (G-8945)

INGOT: Aluminum

Homan Metals LLC .... G 513 721-5010
  Cincinnati (G-3004)

INK OR WRITING FLUIDS

Color Resolutions International LLC .... C 513 552-7200
  Fairfield (G-7349)
Sun Chemical Corporation .... E 513 671-0407
  Cincinnati (G-3427)

INK: Gravure

Superior Printing Ink Co Inc .... G 216 328-1720
  Cleveland (G-4750)

INK: Printing

American Inks and Coatings Co .... G 513 552-7200
  Fairfield (G-7334)
Chef Ink LLC .... G 937 474-2032
  Dayton (G-6252)
Eckart America Corporation .... D 440 954-7600
  Painesville (G-12231)
Flint CPS Inks North Amer LLC .... E 513 619-2089
  Cincinnati (G-2909)
Glass Coatings & Concepts LLC .... E 513 539-5300
  Monroe (G-11108)
Ink Technology Corporation .... E 216 486-6720
  Cleveland (G-4226)
INX International Ink Co .... F 707 693-2990
  Lebanon (G-9089)
Joules Angstrom Uv Prtg Inks C .... E 740 964-9113
  Pataskala (G-12299)
Kennedy Ink Company Inc .... F 513 871-2515
  Cincinnati (G-3074)
Kohl & Madden Inc .... F 513 326-6900
  Cincinnati (G-3086)
Magnum Magnetics Corporation .... E 740 516-6237
  Caldwell (G-1910)
Magnum Magnetics Corporation .... E 513 360-0790
  Middletown (G-10840)
Phoenix Inkjet Clour Sltons LL .... G 937 602-8486
  Dayton (G-6504)
Premier Ink Systems Inc .... F 513 367-2300
  Harrison (G-8286)
Printink Inc .... G 513 943-0599
  Amelia (G-461)
Red Tie Group Inc .... E
  Cleveland (G-4621)
Retail Project Management Inc .... G 614 299-9880
  Columbus (G-5721)
Sun Chemical Corporation .... D 513 753-9550
  Amelia (G-467)
Sun Chemical Corporation .... E 513 671-0407
  Cincinnati (G-3427)
Sun Chemical Corporation .... E 513 681-5950
  Cincinnati (G-3428)
Sun Chemical Corporation .... E 513 681-5950
  Cincinnati (G-3429)
Sun Chemical Corporation .... E 513 830-8667
  Cincinnati (G-3430)
Sun Chemical Corporation .... D 419 891-3514
  Maumee (G-10237)
Vibrantz Corporation .... C 216 875-6213
  Cleveland (G-4868)
Wikoff Color Corporation .... G 513 423-0727
  Middletown (G-10873)
Zeres Inc .... E 419 354-5555
  Bowling Green (G-1598)

INSECTICIDES

Abbott Laboratories .... D 847 937-6100
  Columbus (G-5787)

INSECTICIDES & PESTICIDES

A Best Trmt & Pest Ctrl Sups .... G 330 434-5555
  Akron (G-10)
Advanced Biological Mktg Inc .... E 419 232-2461
  Van Wert (G-14704)
Scotts Miracle-Gro Company .... B 937 644-0011
  Marysville (G-9535)

INSPECTION & TESTING SVCS

Brown Company of Findlay Ltd .... E 419 425-3002
  Findlay (G-7488)
Leak Finder Inc .... G 440 735-0130
  Hudson (G-8603)
National Wldg Tanker Repr LLC .... G 614 875-3399
  Grove City (G-5710)
Pioneer Solutions LLC .... E 216 383-3400
  Euclid (G-7292)
Supplier Inspection Svcs Inc .... F 877 263-7097
  Dayton (G-6600)

INSTRUMENTS & METERS: Measuring, Electric

Lake Shore Cryotonics Inc .... D 614 891-2243
  Westerville (G-1662)

INSTRUMENTS, LABORATORY: Analyzers, Automatic Chemical

Prospira America Corporation .... F 419 423-9552
  Findlay (G-7553)
Targeted Cmpund Monitoring LLC .... G 937 825-0842
  Dayton (G-6608)

INSTRUMENTS, LABORATORY: Spectrometers

Teledyne Instruments Inc .... D 603 886-8400
  Mason (G-10062)

INSTRUMENTS, MEASURING & CNTRL: Geophysical & Meteorological

Electric Speed Indicator Co .... F 216 251-2540
  Aurora (G-713)

INSTRUMENTS, MEASURING & CNTRL: Radiation & Testing, Nuclear

Fluke Biomedical LLC .... C 440 248-9300
  Solon (G-13351)
Nucon International Inc .... F 614 846-5710
  Columbus (G-5607)
Reuter-Stokes LLC .... B 330 425-3755
  Twinsburg (G-14724)

INSTRUMENTS, MEASURING & CNTRLG: Aircraft & Motor Vehicle

Nidec Avtron Automation Corporation .... C 216 642-1230
  Independence (G-3677)
Nidec Motor Corporation .... E 216 642-1230
  Cleveland (G-4453)

INSTRUMENTS, MEASURING & CNTRLNG: Nuclear Instrument Modules

Babcock & Wilcox Entps Inc .... C 330 753-4511
  Akron (G-74)

PRODUCT SECTION — INSTRUMENTS: Measuring, Electrical Energy

Overhoff Technology Corp............... F 513 248-2400
Milford *(G-10916)*

INSTRUMENTS, MEASURING & CONTROLLING: Cable Testing

Multilink Inc.. C 440 366-6966
Elyria *(G-7183)*

INSTRUMENTS, MEASURING & CONTROLLING: Magnetometers

Ceia Usa Ltd.. D 330 310-4741
Hudson *(G-8588)*

INSTRUMENTS, MEASURING & CONTROLLING: Ultrasonic Testing

Waygate Technologies Usa LP............ D 866 243-2638
Cincinnati *(G-3508)*

INSTRUMENTS, OPTICAL: Mirrors

Bruening Glass Works Inc.................... G 440 333-4768
Cleveland *(G-3765)*
Dale Kestler... G 513 871-9000
Cincinnati *(G-2817)*

INSTRUMENTS, OPTICAL: Test & Inspection

Lear Engineering Corp............................ G 937 429-0534
Beavercreek *(G-1054)*
Ncrx Optical Solutions Inc.................... G 330 239-5353
Hudson *(G-8607)*

INSTRUMENTS, SURGICAL & MED: Needles & Syringes, Hypodermic

Hgi Holdings Inc.................................. A 330 963-6996
Twinsburg *(G-14672)*

INSTRUMENTS, SURGICAL & MEDICAL: Blood & Bone Work

Findlay Amrcn Prsthtic Orthtic............. G 419 424-1622
Findlay *(G-7505)*
Innerdyne Holdings Inc........................ D 614 757-5000
Dublin *(G-6898)*
Mediview Xr Inc.................................... F 419 270-2774
Cleveland *(G-4388)*
Nervive Inc... F 847 274-1790
Cleveland *(G-4447)*
Resonetics LLC.................................... E 937 865-4070
Kettering *(G-8909)*
Troy Innovative Instrs Inc..................... E 440 834-9567
Middlefield *(G-10792)*

INSTRUMENTS, SURGICAL & MEDICAL: Inhalation Therapy

Invacare Holdings Corporation............ C 440 329-6000
Elyria *(G-7169)*
Pediavascular Inc.................................. G 216 236-5533
Chagrin Falls *(G-2414)*
Rhinosystems Inc................................. F 216 351-6262
Brooklyn *(G-1681)*

INSTRUMENTS, SURGICAL & MEDICAL: IV Transfusion

Smiths Medical Asd Inc....................... C 614 889-2220
Dublin *(G-6938)*

INSTRUMENTS, SURGICAL & MEDICAL: Operating Tables

Midmark Corporation............................ G 937 526-3662
Versailles *(G-14986)*

Midmark Corporation............................ A 937 528-7500
Miamisburg *(G-10661)*

INSTRUMENTS, SURGICAL/MED: Microsurgical, Exc Electromedical

Norman Noble Inc............................... E 216 851-4007
Euclid *(G-7289)*
Norman Noble Inc............................... B 216 761-5387
Highland Heights *(G-8389)*

INSTRUMENTS: Analytical

Affymetrix Inc....................................... E 800 321-9322
Cleveland *(G-3614)*
Affymetrix Inc....................................... E 419 887-1233
Maumee *(G-10160)*
American Scientific LLC....................... E 614 764-9002
Columbus *(G-5130)*
Bionix Safety Technologies Ltd............ E 419 727-0552
Maumee *(G-10172)*
Bridge Analyzers Inc............................ F 216 332-0592
Bedford Heights *(G-1165)*
Columbus Instruments LLC.................. E 614 276-0861
Columbus *(G-5267)*
Columbus Instruments Intl Corp........... E 614 276-0593
Columbus *(G-5268)*
Consoldted Anlytcal Systems In............ F 513 542-1200
Cincinnati *(G-2787)*
Dentronix Inc.. D 330 916-7300
Cuyahoga Falls *(G-6080)*
Environmental Sample Technology Inc. E 513 642-0100
West Chester *(G-15425)*
Laserlinc Inc... E 937 318-2440
Fairborn *(G-7318)*
Metron Instruments Inc........................ F 216 332-0592
Bedford Heights *(G-1176)*
Mettler-Toledo Intl Inc.......................... A 614 438-4511
Columbus *(G-5066)*
Mettlr-Tledo Globl Hldings LLC............ D 614 438-4511
Columbus *(G-5068)*
Nanotronics Imaging Inc...................... G 330 926-9809
Cuyahoga Falls *(G-6106)*
NDC Technologies Inc......................... C 937 233-9935
Dayton *(G-6468)*
Omnitech Electronics Inc..................... F 800 822-1344
Columbus *(G-5638)*
Orton Edward Jr Crmic Fndation.......... E 614 895-2663
Westerville *(G-15672)*
PMC Gage Inc...................................... E 440 953-1672
Willoughby *(G-15973)*
Precision Anlytical Instrs Inc................. G 513 984-1600
Blue Ash *(G-1455)*
Pts Prfssnal Technical Svc Inc............. E 513 642-0111
West Chester *(G-15488)*
Q-Lab Corporation.............................. D 440 835-8700
Westlake *(G-15776)*
Teledyne Instruments Inc..................... E 513 229-7000
Mason *(G-10063)*
Teledyne Tekmar Company.................. E 513 229-7000
Mason *(G-10064)*
Test-Fuchs Corporation........................ G 440 708-3505
Brecksville *(G-1635)*
Thermo Fisher Scientific Inc................. G 800 955-6288
Cincinnati *(G-3451)*
Thermo Fsher Scntfc Ashvlle L............. A 740 373-4763
Marietta *(G-9836)*
Trek Diagnostics Inc............................. F 440 808-0000
Brooklyn Heights *(G-1702)*
Viavi Solutions Inc................................ G 316 522-4981
Columbus *(G-5073)*
Weidmann Electrical Tech Inc............... G 937 508-2112
Cleveland *(G-4900)*

Xorb Corporation.................................. G 419 354-6021
Bowling Green *(G-1597)*
Ysi Environmental Inc.......................... D 937 767-7241
Yellow Springs *(G-16291)*

INSTRUMENTS: Combustion Control, Indl

Catacel Corp.. F
Ravenna *(G-12709)*
Cleveland Controls Inc........................ F 216 398-0330
Cleveland *(G-3837)*
Unison UCI Inc..................................... G
Cleveland *(G-4845)*

INSTRUMENTS: Electrocardiographs

Cardioinsight Technologies Inc............ G 216 274-2221
Independence *(G-8655)*
Synsei Medical...................................... G 609 759-1101
Dublin *(G-6950)*

INSTRUMENTS: Endoscopic Eqpt, Electromedical

Steris Corporation................................ A 440 354-2600
Mentor *(G-10563)*

INSTRUMENTS: Flow, Indl Process

Ernst Flow Industries LLC.................... F 732 938-5641
Strongsville *(G-13833)*
L J Star Incorporated........................... E 330 405-3040
Twinsburg *(G-14684)*

INSTRUMENTS: Indl Process Control

Aqua Technology Group LLC............... G 513 298-1183
West Chester *(G-15367)*
Clark-Reliance LLC.............................. C 440 572-1500
Strongsville *(G-13821)*
Facts Inc.. E 330 928-2332
Cuyahoga Falls *(G-6082)*
Journey Electronics Corp..................... G 513 539-9836
Monroe *(G-11112)*
Production Control Units Inc................ D 937 299-5594
Moraine *(G-11204)*

INSTRUMENTS: Infrared, Indl Process

L3harris Cincinnati Elec Corp............... A 513 573-6100
Mason *(G-10019)*

INSTRUMENTS: Laser, Scientific & Engineering

Tech4imaging LLC............................... F 614 214-2655
Columbus *(G-5817)*

INSTRUMENTS: Liquid Level, Indl Process

Dixon Bayco USA................................ G 513 874-8499
Fairfield *(G-7354)*

INSTRUMENTS: Measurement, Indl Process

Beaumont Machine LLC....................... F 513 701-0421
Mason *(G-9958)*
Command Alkon Incorporated............. E 614 799-0600
Dublin *(G-6876)*
Crawford United Corporation............... D 216 541-8060
Cleveland *(G-3916)*
Meech Sttic Elminators USA Inc........... F 330 564-2000
Copley *(G-5950)*
Nextech Materials Ltd.......................... D 614 842-6606
Lewis Center *(G-9174)*
Rickly Hydrological Co......................... E 614 297-9877
Columbus *(G-5722)*
Slone Gear International Inc................. G 507 401-4327
Tipp City *(G-14156)*

Employee Codes: A=Over 500 employees, B=251-500
C=101-250, D=51-100, E=20-50, F=10-19, G=1-9

INSTRUMENTS: Measuring, Electrical Energy

PRODUCT SECTION

INSTRUMENTS: Measuring, Electrical Energy

Company		Phone
Drs Signal Technologies Inc ..... E		937 429-7470
Beavercreek *(G-1048)*		
Tacoma Energy LLC ..... E		614 410-9000
Westerville *(G-15721)*		
Westerman Inc C		800 338-8265
Bremen *(G-1640)*		

INSTRUMENTS: Measuring, Electrical Power

F Squared Inc ..... G		419 752-7273
Greenwich *(G-8066)*		

INSTRUMENTS: Medical & Surgical

- Abbott Laboratories ..... D 847 937-6100
  Columbus *(G-5087)*
- Advanced Nanotherapies Inc ..... F 415 517-0867
  Cleveland *(G-3607)*
- Applied Medical Technology Inc ..... E 440 717-4000
  Brecksville *(G-1606)*
- Atc Group Inc ..... D 440 293-4064
  Andover *(G-484)*
- Avalign - Integrated LLC ..... F 440 269-6984
  Mentor *(G-10424)*
- Avalign Technologies Inc ..... C 419 542-7743
  Hicksville *(G-8372)*
- Aws Industries Inc ..... E 513 932-7941
  Lebanon *(G-9063)*
- Axon Medical Llc ..... E 216 276-0262
  Medina *(G-10299)*
- Beam Technologies Inc ..... B 800 648-1179
  Columbus *(G-5177)*
- Becton Dickinson and Company ..... G 858 617-4272
  Groveport *(G-8131)*
- Bexley Imaging ..... G 614 533-6560
  Columbus *(G-5185)*
- Boston Scntfic Nrmdlation Corp ..... F 513 377-6160
  Mason *(G-9966)*
- Boston Scntfic Nrmdlation Corp ..... G 330 372-2652
  Warren *(G-15147)*
- Bowden Manufacturing Corp ..... E 440 946-1770
  Willoughby *(G-15891)*
- Buckeye Medical Tech LLC ..... G 330 719-9868
  Warren *(G-15149)*
- Butler Cnty Surgical Prpts LLC ..... G 513 844-2200
  Hamilton *(G-8189)*
- Care Fusion ..... F 216 521-1220
  Lakewood *(G-8969)*
- Casco Mfg Solutions Inc ..... D 513 681-0003
  Cincinnati *(G-2706)*
- Cmd Medtech LLC ..... F 614 364-4243
  Columbus *(G-5257)*
- Codonics Inc ..... C 800 444-1198
  Cleveland *(G-3881)*
- Covidien Holding Inc ..... C 513 948-7219
  Cincinnati *(G-2799)*
- Cqt Kennedy LLC ..... D 419 238-2442
  Van Wert *(G-14912)*
- Dentronix Inc ..... D 330 916-7300
  Cuyahoga Falls *(G-6080)*
- Devicor Med Pdts Holdings Inc ..... A 513 864-9000
  Cincinnati *(G-2827)*
- Elite Biomedical Solutions LLC ..... F 513 207-0602
  Cincinnati *(G-2558)*
- Encore Industries Inc ..... C 419 626-8000
  Sandusky *(G-13053)*
- Frantz Medical Development Ltd ..... G 440 255-1155
  Mentor *(G-10457)*
- General Data Company Inc ..... B 513 752-7978
  Cincinnati *(G-2561)*
- Gentherm Medical LLC ..... C 513 772-8810
  Cincinnati *(G-2948)*
- Gyrus Acmi LP ..... C 419 668-8201
  Norwalk *(G-11971)*
- Haag-Streit Usa Inc ..... D 513 398-3937
  Mason *(G-10000)*
- Hammill Manufacturing Co ..... E 419 476-9125
  Toledo *(G-14311)*
- Howmedica Osteonics Corp ..... D 937 291-3900
  Dayton *(G-6374)*
- Icad Inc ..... F 866 280-2239
  Dayton *(G-6163)*
- Innovative Stoneworks Inc ..... G 440 352-2231
  Concord Township *(G-5907)*
- Inspyre Health Systems LLC ..... G 440 412-7916
  Grafton *(G-8002)*
- Kinetic Concepts Inc ..... F 440 234-8590
  Middleburg Heights *(G-10722)*
- Klarity Medical Products LLC ..... F 740 788-8107
  Heath *(G-8324)*
- KMC Holdings LLC ..... C 419 238-2442
  Van Wert *(G-14920)*
- Leica Biosystems - TAS ..... E 513 864-9671
  Cincinnati *(G-3101)*
- Life Sciences - Vandalia LLC ..... C 937 387-0880
  Dayton *(G-6407)*
- M&H Medical Holdings Inc ..... E 419 727-8421
  Maumee *(G-10215)*
- Markethtch Inc D/B/A Mh Eye CA ..... F 330 376-6363
  Akron *(G-236)*
- Medical Quant USA Inc ..... F 440 542-0761
  Solon *(G-13384)*
- Medtronic Inc ..... F 216 642-1977
  Cleveland *(G-4389)*
- Medtronic Inc ..... G 763 526-2566
  Independence *(G-8672)*
- Meridian LLC ..... G 330 995-0371
  Aurora *(G-724)*
- Micromd ..... G 850 217-7412
  Youngstown *(G-16399)*
- Minimally Invasive Devices Inc ..... G 614 484-5036
  Columbus *(G-5572)*
- Morris Technologies Inc ..... E 513 733-1611
  Cincinnati *(G-3174)*
- Morrison Medical Ltd ..... G 800 438-6677
  Columbus *(G-5581)*
- National Biological Corp ..... E 216 831-0600
  Beachwood *(G-1001)*
- Navigate Crdiac Structures Inc ..... G 949 482-5858
  Cleveland *(G-4441)*
- Norwood Medical LLC ..... D 937 228-4101
  Dayton *(G-6477)*
- Nuevue Solutions Inc ..... G 440 836-4772
  Rootstown *(G-12856)*
- OMI Surgical Products ..... F 513 561-2241
  Cincinnati *(G-3221)*
- Optoquest Corporation ..... F 216 445-3637
  Cleveland *(G-4507)*
- Patriot Products Inc ..... F 419 865-9712
  Holland *(G-8522)*
- Pemco Inc ..... E 216 524-2990
  Cleveland *(G-4539)*
- Percuvision LLC ..... F 614 891-4800
  Columbus *(G-5669)*
- Peritec Biosciences Ltd ..... F 216 445-3756
  Cleveland *(G-4541)*
- Phoenix Quality Mfg LLC ..... E 705 279-0538
  Jackson *(G-8722)*
- Pt Solutions LLC ..... G 844 786-6300
  Brunswick *(G-1784)*
- Pulse Worldwide Ltd ..... G 513 234-7829
  Mason *(G-10044)*
- Quality Electrodynamics LLC ..... C 440 638-5106
  Mayfield Village *(G-10261)*
- Realized Mfg LLC ..... F 330 535-3887
  Medina *(G-10309)*
- Respironics Novametrix LLC ..... A 800 345-6443
  Columbus *(G-5519)*
- Rultract Inc ..... G 330 856-9808
  Warren *(G-15204)*
- Smiths Medical Asd Inc ..... G 800 796-8701
  Dublin *(G-6937)*
- Smiths Medical North America ..... G 614 210-7300
  Dublin *(G-6939)*
- Southeastern Emergency Eqp Co ..... F 919 556-1890
  Dublin *(G-6942)*
- Spartronics Strongsville Inc ..... D 440 878-4630
  Strongsville *(G-3883)*
- Spring Hlthcare Dagnostics LLC ..... G 866 201-9503
  Jackson *(G-8727)*
- SRI Healthcare LLC ..... G 513 398-6406
  Mason *(G-10060)*
- Standard Bariatrics Inc ..... E 513 620-7751
  Blue Ash *(G-1409)*
- Steris Corporation ..... D 440 354-2600
  Mentor *(G-10567)*
- Steris Instrument MGT Svcs Inc ..... C 800 783-9251
  Stow *(G-13728)*
- Summit Online Products LLC ..... G 800 326-1972
  Powell *(G-1268)*
- Surgrx Inc ..... E 650 482-2400
  Blue Ash *(G-1475)*
- Theken Companies LLC ..... F 330 733-7600
  Akron *(G-353)*
- Thermo Fisher Scientific Inc ..... E 800 871-8909
  Oakwood Village *(G-12044)*
- Torbot Group Inc ..... F 419 724-1475
  Northwood *(G-1930)*
- United Medical Supply Company ..... F 866 678-8633
  Brunswick *(G-1727)*
- United Sttes Endoscopy Group In ..... C 440 639-4494
  Mentor *(G-10581)*
- Valensil Technologies LLC ..... E 440 937-8181
  Avon *(G-790)*
- Vesco Medical LLC ..... G 614 914-5991
  Westerville *(G-15723)*
- Ward Engineering Inc ..... G 614 442-8063
  Columbus *(G-5853)*

INSTRUMENTS: Particle Size Analyzers

- Rotex Global LLC ..... C 513 541-1236
  Cincinnati *(G-3351)*

INSTRUMENTS: Pressure Measurement, Indl

- Avure Autoclave Systems Inc ..... F 614 891-2732
  Columbus *(G-5157)*
- Cincinnati Test Systems Inc ..... D 513 202-5100
  Harrison *(G-8270)*
- Koester Corporation ..... E 419 599-0291
  Napoleon *(G-11522)*
- Solon Manufacturing Company ..... E 440 286-7149
  Chardon *(G-2468)*

INSTRUMENTS: Radio Frequency Measuring

- Dss Installations Ltd ..... F 513 761-7000
  Cincinnati *(G-2842)*
- Resonant Sciences LLC ..... E 937 431-8180
  Beavercreek *(G-1080)*

INSTRUMENTS: Signal Generators & Averagers

- Adams Elevator Equipment Co ..... D 847 581-2900
  Holland *(G-8492)*

INSTRUMENTS: Temperature Measurement, Indl

T E Brown LLC..................................F 937 223-2241
  Dayton *(G-6607)*
Thermo King Corporation....................G 567 280-9243
  Fremont *(G-7814)*

INSTRUMENTS: Test, Electrical, Engine

Nu-Di Products Co Inc........................D 216 251-9070
  Cleveland *(G-4487)*

INSTRUMENTS: Test, Electronic & Electric Measurement

Advanced Integration LLC..................E 614 863-2433
  Reynoldsburg *(G-12748)*
Advanced Kiffer Systems Inc...............E 216 267-8181
  Cleveland *(G-3606)*
Bionix Safety Technologies Ltd.............E 419 727-0552
  Maumee *(G-10172)*
Bird Electronic Corporation..................C 440 248-1200
  Solon *(G-13318)*
Bird Technologies Group Inc...............G 440 248-1200
  Solon *(G-13319)*
Field Apparatus Service & Tstg...........G 513 353-9399
  Cincinnati *(G-2902)*
Keithley Instruments LLC...................C 440 248-0400
  Solon *(G-13377)*
Mueller Electric Company Inc.............F 614 888-8855
  New Albany *(G-11384)*
Paneltech LLC..................................F 440 516-1300
  Chagrin Falls *(G-2413)*
Vmetro Inc..D 281 584-0728
  Fairborn *(G-7326)*

INSULATION & ROOFING MATERIALS: Wood, Reconstituted

Bmca Insulation Products Inc.............F 330 335-2501
  Wadsworth *(G-15020)*

INSULATION MATERIALS WHOLESALERS

Denizen Inc......................................F 937 615-9561
  Piqua *(G-12513)*
Tlg Cochran Inc.................................E 440 914-1122
  Twinsburg *(G-14744)*

INSULATION: Fiberglass

American Insulation Tech LLC............F 513 733-4248
  Milford *(G-10892)*
Blackthorn LLC.................................F 937 836-9296
  Clayton *(G-3564)*
Cpic Automotive Inc..........................G 740 587-3262
  Granville *(G-8015)*
Johns Manville Corporation................D 419 784-7000
  Defiance *(G-6685)*
Johns Manville Corporation................E 419 784-7000
  Defiance *(G-6686)*
Johns Manville Corporation................F 419 878-8111
  Defiance *(G-6687)*
Johns Manville Corporation................G 419 467-8189
  Maumee *(G-10209)*
Johns Manville Corporation................D 419 878-8111
  Waterville *(G-15246)*
Johns Manville Corporation................D 419 878-8112
  Waterville *(G-15247)*
Metal Building Intr Pdts Co.................F 440 322-6500
  Elyria *(G-7180)*
Owens Corning.................................F 614 754-4098
  Columbus *(G-5648)*

Owens Corning.................................G 419 248-8000
  Navarre *(G-11348)*
Owens Corning Roofg & Asp LLC.......E 877 858-3855
  Toledo *(G-14423)*
Owens Corning Sales LLC.................F 614 539-0830
  Grove City *(G-8114)*
Owens Corning Sales LLC.................E 740 928-6620
  Hebron *(G-8354)*
Owens Corning Sales LLC.................G 419 248-5751
  Swanton *(G-13979)*
Owens Corning Sales LLC.................A 419 248-8000
  Toledo *(G-14424)*
Owens Crning Inslting Systm.............A 740 328-2300
  Newark *(G-11600)*
Thermafiber Inc.................................D 260 563-2111
  Toledo *(G-14485)*

INSULATORS & INSULATION MATERIALS: Electrical

Bourbon Plastics Inc.........................E 574 342-0893
  Cuyahoga Falls *(G-6073)*
Koebbe Products Inc........................D 513 753-4200
  Amelia *(G-458)*
Monti Incorporated...........................D 513 761-7775
  Cincinnati *(G-3172)*
Mueller Electric Company Inc...........E 216 771-5225
  Akron *(G-256)*
Red Seal Electric Company...............E 216 941-3900
  Cleveland *(G-4620)*
Tlg Laporte Inc..................................G 440 914-1122
  Twinsburg *(G-14745)*
Von Roll Usa Inc...............................D 216 433-7474
  Cleveland *(G-4883)*

INSULATORS, PORCELAIN: Electrical

Ethima Inc...D 419 626-4912
  Sandusky *(G-13057)*
Newell - Psn LLC..............................G 304 387-2700
  Columbiana *(G-5046)*

INSURANCE BROKERS, NEC

Forge Industries Inc..........................A 330 960-2468
  Youngstown *(G-16359)*

INSURANCE CARRIERS: Life

Western & Southern Lf Insur Co........A 513 629-1800
  Cincinnati *(G-3517)*

INSURANCE CLAIM PROCESSING, EXC MEDICAL

Safelite Group Inc.............................A 614 210-9000
  Columbus *(G-5740)*

INSURANCE: Agents, Brokers & Service

Beam Technologies Inc.....................B 800 648-1179
  Columbus *(G-5177)*
Move Ez Inc.....................................D 844 466-8339
  Columbus *(G-5583)*

INTEGRATED CIRCUITS, SEMICONDUCTOR NETWORKS, ETC

A M D...G 440 918-8930
  Willoughby *(G-15872)*
Leidos Inc..D 937 656-6433
  Beavercreek *(G-1055)*

INTERIOR DESIGN SVCS, NEC

Nordic Light America Inc...................F 614 981-9497
  Canal Winchester *(G-1991)*

INTRAVENOUS SOLUTIONS

Clinical Specialties Inc......................D 888 873-7888
  Hudson *(G-8591)*
Molorokalin Inc.................................E 330 629-1332
  Canfield *(G-2012)*

INVERTERS: Nonrotating Electrical

Myers Controlled Power LLC............E 909 923-1800
  Canton *(G-2170)*
Vanner Holdings Inc.........................D 614 771-2718
  Hilliard *(G-8451)*

INVESTMENT ADVISORY SVCS

Linsalata Cpitl Prtners Fund I.............G 440 684-1400
  Cleveland *(G-4330)*

INVESTMENT FIRM: General Brokerage

Western & Southern Lf Insur Co........A 513 629-1800
  Cincinnati *(G-3517)*

INVESTORS, NEC

Alpha Zeta Holdings Inc....................G 216 271-1601
  Cleveland *(G-3640)*
Brantley Partners IV LP.....................G 216 464-8400
  Cleveland *(G-3754)*
Edgewater Capital Partners LP..........G 216 292-3838
  Independence *(G-8666)*
Kinetico Incorporated........................B 440 564-9111
  Newbury *(G-11628)*
Resilience Fund III LP.......................E 216 292-0200
  Cleveland *(G-4629)*

IRON & STEEL PRDTS: Hot-Rolled

Nucor Steel Marion Inc......................B 740 383-4011
  Marion *(G-9868)*

IRON ORE MINING

Cleveland-Cliffs Inc...........................E 419 243-8198
  Toledo *(G-14242)*
Cliffs Natural Resources Explo..........C 216 694-5700
  Cleveland *(G-3875)*
The Cleveland-Cliffs Iron Co..............C 216 694-5700
  Cleveland *(G-4781)*
Tilden Mining Company LC...............A 216 694-5700
  Cleveland *(G-4796)*
Wabush Mnes Clffs Min Mnging A....B 216 694-5700
  Cleveland *(G-4888)*

IRON ORES

Cleveland-Cliffs Intl Holdg Co............D 216 694-5700
  Cleveland *(G-3863)*
Cliffs & Associates Ltd......................G 216 694-5700
  Cleveland *(G-3869)*
Cliffs Empire Inc...............................G 216 694-5700
  Cleveland *(G-3870)*
Cliffs Mining Company......................F 216 694-5700
  Cleveland *(G-3872)*
Cliffs Mining Services Company........C 218 262-5913
  Cleveland *(G-3874)*

JACKS: Hydraulic

Joyce/Dayton Corp...........................E 937 294-6261
  Dayton *(G-6390)*

JEWELERS' FINDINGS & MATERIALS

Zero-D Products Inc.........................G 440 942-5005
  Willoughby *(G-16020)*

JEWELRY & PRECIOUS STONES WHOLESALERS

Employee Codes: A=Over 500 employees, B=251-500
C=101-250, D=51-100, E=20-50, F=10-19, G=1-9

JEWELRY REPAIR SVCS

Renoir Visions LLC .... G 419 586-5679
  Celina *(G-2345)*

JEWELRY REPAIR SVCS

Bensan Jewelers Inc .... G 216 221-1434
  Lakewood *(G-8967)*

Gustave Julian Jewelers Inc .... G 440 888-1100
  Cleveland *(G-4157)*

H P Nielsen Inc .... G 440 244-4255
  Lorain *(G-9413)*

Koop Diamond Cutters Inc .... F 513 621-2838
  Cincinnati *(G-3087)*

Michael W Hyes Desgr Goldsmith ...... G 440 519-0889
  Solon *(G-13389)*

Pughs Designer Jewelers Inc .... G 740 344-9259
  Newark *(G-11603)*

JEWELRY STORES

Farah Jewelers Inc .... F 614 438-6140
  Westerville *(G-15656)*

Markus Jewelers LLC .... G 513 474-4950
  Cincinnati *(G-3132)*

Michael W Hyes Desgr Goldsmith ...... G 440 519-0889
  Solon *(G-13389)*

Rosenfeld Jewelry Inc .... G 440 446-0099
  Cleveland *(G-4650)*

JEWELRY STORES: Precious Stones & Precious Metals

Bensan Jewelers Inc .... G 216 221-1434
  Lakewood *(G-8967)*

Em Es Be Company LLC .... G 216 761-9500
  Cleveland *(G-4008)*

Goyal Enterprises Inc .... F 513 874-9303
  West Chester *(G-15557)*

H P Nielsen Inc .... G 440 244-4255
  Lorain *(G-9413)*

Handcrafted Jewelry Inc .... G 330 650-9011
  Hudson *(G-8595)*

James C Free Inc .... G 513 793-0133
  Cincinnati *(G-3035)*

James C Free Inc .... E 937 298-0171
  Dayton *(G-6387)*

M B Saxon Co Inc .... G 440 229-5006
  Cleveland *(G-4345)*

Pughs Designer Jewelers Inc .... G 740 344-9259
  Newark *(G-11603)*

Robert W Johnson Inc .... D 614 336-4545
  Dublin *(G-6931)*

Sheiban Jewelry Inc .... F 440 238-0616
  Strongsville *(G-13879)*

White Jewelers Inc .... G 330 264-3324
  Wooster *(G-16182)*

JEWELRY STORES: Silverware

Gustave Julian Jewelers Inc .... G 440 888-1100
  Cleveland *(G-4157)*

JEWELRY, PRECIOUS METAL: Settings & Mountings

Prince & Izant LLC .... E 216 362-7000
  Cleveland *(G-4587)*

JEWELRY, WHOLESALE

Goyal Enterprises Inc .... F 513 874-9303
  West Chester *(G-15557)*

M B Saxon Co Inc .... G 440 229-5006
  Cleveland *(G-4345)*

Marfo Company .... D 614 276-3352
  Columbus *(G-5541)*

Scholz & Ey Engravers Inc .... F 614 444-8052
  Columbus *(G-5752)*

Sheiban Jewelry Inc .... F 440 238-0616
  Strongsville *(G-13879)*

Vy Inc .... F 513 421-8100
  Cincinnati *(G-3505)*

JEWELRY: Precious Metal

Associated Premium Corporation .... E 513 679-4444
  Cincinnati *(G-2637)*

Diamond Designs Inc .... G 330 434-6776
  Akron *(G-127)*

Don Basch Jewelers Inc .... E 330 467-2116
  Macedonia *(G-9547)*

Em Es Be Company LLC .... G 216 761-9500
  Cleveland *(G-4008)*

Ginos Awards Inc .... E 216 831-6565
  Warrensville Heights *(G-15229)*

Gustave Julian Jewelers Inc .... G 440 888-1100
  Cleveland *(G-4157)*

H P Nielsen Inc .... G 440 244-4255
  Lorain *(G-9413)*

Im Greenberg Inc .... G 440 461-4464
  Cleveland *(G-4214)*

James C Free Inc .... G 513 793-0133
  Cincinnati *(G-3035)*

James C Free Inc .... E 937 298-0171
  Dayton *(G-6387)*

Koop Diamond Cutters Inc .... F 513 621-2838
  Cincinnati *(G-3087)*

M B Saxon Co Inc .... G 440 229-5006
  Cleveland *(G-4345)*

Markus Jewelers LLC .... G 513 474-4950
  Cincinnati *(G-3132)*

Michael W Hyes Desgr Goldsmith ...... G 440 519-0889
  Solon *(G-13389)*

Robert W Johnson Inc .... D 614 336-4545
  Dublin *(G-6931)*

Rosenfeld Jewelry Inc .... G 440 446-0099
  Cleveland *(G-4650)*

Sheiban Jewelry Inc .... F 440 238-0616
  Strongsville *(G-13879)*

Signet Group Inc .... B 330 668-5000
  Fairlawn *(G-7450)*

Signet Group Services US Inc .... G 330 668-5000
  Fairlawn *(G-7451)*

Val Casting Inc .... F 419 562-2499
  Bucyrus *(G-1871)*

White Jewelers Inc .... G 330 264-3324
  Wooster *(G-16182)*

Whitehouse Bros Inc .... G 513 621-2259
  Blue Ash *(G-1491)*

JIGS & FIXTURES

Cmt Machining & Fabg LLC .... F 937 652-3740
  Urbana *(G-14827)*

Delta Tool & Die Stl Block Inc .... E 419 822-5939
  Delta *(G-6781)*

First Tool Corp .... E 937 254-6197
  Dayton *(G-6333)*

Homeworth Fabrication Mch Inc .... F 330 525-5459
  Homeworth *(G-8554)*

Jergens Inc .... C 216 486-5540
  Cleveland *(G-4253)*

Kilroy Company .... D 440 951-8700
  Cleveland *(G-4289)*

Krisdale Inc .... G 330 225-2392
  Valley City *(G-14875)*

Nation Tool & Die Ltd .... E 419 822-5939
  Delta *(G-6789)*

Northwestern Tools Inc .... F 937 298-9994
  Dayton *(G-6475)*

P O McIntire Company .... E 440 269-1848
  Wickliffe *(G-15844)*

JOB PRINTING & NEWSPAPER PUBLISHING COMBINED

County Classifieds .... G 937 592-8847
  Bellefontaine *(G-1203)*

Douthit Communications Inc .... D 419 855-7465
  Millbury *(G-10950)*

Douthit Communications Inc .... D 419 625-5825
  Sandusky *(G-1951)*

Hardin County Publishing Co .... E 419 674-4066
  Kenton *(G-8885)*

Ogden Newspapers Ohio Inc .... E 330 424-9541
  Lisbon *(G-9322)*

Springfield Newspapers Inc .... E 937 323-5533
  Springfield *(G-1635)*

Welch Publishing Co .... E 419 874-2528
  Perrysburg *(G-2444)*

Yellow Springs News Inc .... F 937 767-7373
  Yellow Springs *(G-16288)*

JOINTS: Expansion, Pipe

Bosch Rexroth Corporation .... C 330 263-3300
  Wooster *(G-16116)*

JOINTS: Swivel & Universal, Exc Aircraft & Auto

Excel Loading Systems LLC .... G 513 504-1069
  Hamilton *(G-8207)*

JOISTS: Long-Span Series, Open Web Steel

Socar of Ohio Inc .... D 419 596-3100
  Continental *(G-538)*

KILNS & FURNACES: Ceramic

Harrop Industries Inc .... E 614 231-3621
  Columbus *(G-542)*

I Cerco Inc .... C 330 567-2145
  Shreve *(G-1321)*

Star-Tjcm Inc .... E 740 342-3514
  New Lexington *(G-11458)*

KITCHEN CABINETS WHOLESALERS

Bison Builders LLC .... F 614 636-0365
  Columbus *(G-511)*

Custom Design Cabinets & Tops .... G 440 639-9900
  Painesville *(G-1225)*

Kitchen Designs R us Inc .... E 419 536-6605
  Toledo *(G-14348)*

Modern Builders Supply Inc .... E 419 526-0002
  Mansfield *(G-9690)*

Sims-Lohman Inc .... E 513 651-3510
  Cincinnati *(G-3395)*

KITCHEN UTENSILS: Food Handling & Processing Prdts, Wood

Alfrebro LLC .... F 513 539-7373
  Monroe *(G-11093)*

Katch Kitchen LLC .... E 513 537-8056
  Cincinnati *(G-3060)*

Mt Perry Foods Inc .... D 740 743-3890
  Mount Perry *(G-1251)*

Tok Dawgs Chicken LLC .... G 614 813-2698
  Columbus *(G-5820)*

KITCHENWARE STORES

Nacco Industries Inc .... E 440 229-5151
  Cleveland *(G-4434)*

PRODUCT SECTION — LABORATORY APPARATUS & FURNITURE

The Kitchen Collection LLC.................... A 740 773-9150
  Chillicothe (G-2538)
Wasserstrom Company............................ B 614 228-6525
  Columbus (G-5865)

KITCHENWARE: Plastic

HI Lite Plastic Products............................ G 614 235-9050
  Columbus (G-5432)

KITS: Plastic

RPM Consumer Holding Company............ E 330 273-5090
  Medina (G-10371)

KNIVES: Agricultural Or Indl

Advetech Inc... E 330 533-2227
  Canfield (G-1996)
Advetech Inc... E 330 533-2227
  Canfield (G-1995)
C B Mfg & Sls Co Inc............................... D 937 866-5986
  Miamisburg (G-10624)
Hamilton Industrial Grinding Inc.............. E 513 863-1221
  Hamilton (G-8218)
Handy Twine Knife Co............................. G 419 294-3424
  Upper Sandusky (G-14810)
Randolph Tool Company Inc................... F 330 877-4923
  Hartville (G-8304)
Superion Inc... E 937 374-0033
  Xenia (G-16274)

LABELS: Paper, Made From Purchased Materials

CCL Label Inc.. D 216 676-2703
  Cleveland (G-3801)
General Data Company Inc..................... B 513 752-7978
  Cincinnati (G-2561)
Label Aid Inc... E 419 433-2888
  Huron (G-8635)
Label Technique Southeast LLC............... E 440 951-7660
  Willoughby (G-15941)
Multi-Color Corporation........................... G 513 459-3283
  Mason (G-10032)
Multi-Color Corporation........................... F 513 381-1480
  Batavia (G-939)
Shore To Shore Inc................................. D 937 866-1908
  Dayton (G-6570)
T&T Graphics Inc.................................... D 937 847-6000
  Miamisburg (G-10688)
Tri State Media LLC................................ F 513 933-0101
  Wilmington (G-16061)
Verstrete In Mold Lbels USA In................ F 513 943-0080
  Batavia (G-959)

LABELS: Woven

Crane Consumables Inc........................... E 513 539-9980
  Middletown (G-10814)
Shore To Shore Inc................................. D 937 866-1908
  Dayton (G-6570)

LABORATORIES, TESTING: Food

Agrana Fruit Us Inc................................. C 937 693-3821
  Anna (G-488)

LABORATORIES, TESTING: Metallurgical

Metcut Research Associates Inc.............. D 513 271-5100
  Cincinnati (G-3156)
Mrl Materials Resources LLC................... E 937 531-6657
  Xenia (G-16269)
Phymet Inc... F 937 743-8061
  Springboro (G-13515)

LABORATORIES, TESTING: Pollution

Nucon International Inc.......................... F 614 846-5710
  Columbus (G-5607)

LABORATORIES, TESTING: Product Testing

Wallover Enterprises Inc......................... E 440 238-9250
  Strongsville (G-13893)

LABORATORIES, TESTING: Product Testing, Safety/Performance

Chemsultants International Inc................ G 440 974-3080
  Mentor (G-10437)
Global Manufacturing Solutions............... F 937 236-8315
  Dayton (G-6355)
Smithers Group Inc................................ D 330 833-8548
  Massillon (G-10145)

LABORATORIES: Biological Research

Mp Biomedicals LLC................................ C 440 337-1200
  Solon (G-13393)

LABORATORIES: Biotechnology

EMD Millipore Corporation...................... C 513 631-0445
  Norwood (G-11995)

LABORATORIES: Commercial Nonphysical Research

Intek Inc.. F 614 895-0301
  Westerville (G-15660)

LABORATORIES: Dental, Crown & Bridge Production

Dental Ceramics Inc............................... E 330 523-5240
  Richfield (G-12785)
Doling & Assoc Dntl Lab Inc................... F 937 254-0075
  Dayton (G-6300)
Sentage Corporation............................... G 419 842-6730
  Sylvania (G-14013)

LABORATORIES: Electronic Research

Barco Inc... E 937 372-7579
  Xenia (G-16250)
Electronic Concepts Engrg Inc................ F 419 861-9000
  Holland (G-8509)
Sierra Nevada Corporation...................... C 937 431-2800
  Beavercreek (G-1062)
Steiner Eoptics Inc................................. D 937 426-2341
  Miamisburg (G-10686)

LABORATORIES: Medical

Cellular Technology Limited.................... E 216 791-5084
  Shaker Heights (G-13152)
Mp Biomedicals LLC................................ C 440 337-1200
  Solon (G-13393)
Smithers Group Inc................................ D 330 833-8548
  Massillon (G-10145)

LABORATORIES: Noncommercial Research

Sdg Inc.. F 440 893-0771
  Cleveland (G-4682)
Tangent Company LLC............................ G 440 543-2775
  Chagrin Falls (G-2427)

LABORATORIES: Physical Research, Commercial

BASF Catalysts LLC................................ C 216 360-5005
  Cleveland (G-3723)
Borchers Americas Inc........................... D 440 899-2950
  Westlake (G-15741)
Circle Prime Manufacturing..................... E 330 923-0019
  Cuyahoga Falls (G-6074)
Copernicus Therapeutics Inc................... F 216 231-0227
  Cleveland (G-3904)
Curtiss-Wright Controls.......................... E 937 252-5601
  Fairborn (G-7312)
Defense Research Assoc Inc................... E 937 431-1644
  Dayton (G-6158)
Flexsys America LP................................ D 330 666-4111
  Akron (G-155)
KS Technologies & Cstm Mfg LLC............ G 419 426-0172
  Attica (G-701)
Lyondell Chemical Company................... C 513 530-4000
  Cincinnati (G-3118)
Medpace Holdings Inc............................ C 513 579-9911
  Cincinnati (G-3142)
Microweld Engineering Inc..................... G 614 847-9410
  Worthington (G-16204)
Northcoast Environmental Labs............... G 330 342-3377
  Streetsboro (G-13782)
Nsa Technologies LLC............................. G 330 576-4600
  Akron (G-269)
Open Additive LLC.................................. F 937 306-6140
  Dayton (G-6492)
Owens Corning Sales LLC....................... F 330 633-6735
  Tallmadge (G-14042)
Range Impact Inc................................... G 216 304-6556
  Cleveland (G-4615)
Sunpower Inc... D 740 594-2221
  Athens (G-699)
Trico Products Corporation..................... C 248 371-1700
  Cleveland (G-4829)
Vehicle Systems Inc............................... G 330 854-0535
  Massillon (G-10153)
Wiley Companies.................................... C 740 622-0755
  Coshocton (G-6000)

LABORATORIES: Testing

Personnel Selection Services................... F 440 835-3255
  Cleveland (G-4542)
Quest Diagnostics Incorporated.............. G 513 229-5500
  Mason (G-10045)
Balancing Company Inc.......................... E 937 898-9111
  Vandalia (G-14933)
Barr Engineering Incorporated................ E 614 714-0299
  Columbus (G-5175)
Curtiss-Wright Flow Ctrl Corp................. D 513 528-7900
  Cincinnati (G-2556)
Godfrey & Wing Inc................................ E 330 562-1440
  Aurora (G-716)
Jci Jones Chemicals Inc.......................... F 330 825-2531
  New Franklin (G-11438)
National Polymer Inc.............................. F 440 708-1245
  Chagrin Falls (G-2409)
Nelson Labs Fairfield Inc........................ E 973 227-6882
  Broadview Heights (G-1663)
Sample Machining Inc............................ E 937 258-3338
  Dayton (G-6558)
Tangent Company LLC............................ G 440 543-2775
  Chagrin Falls (G-2427)
Trico Products Corporation..................... C 248 371-1700
  Cleveland (G-4829)
Welding Consultants Inc......................... G 614 258-7018
  Columbus (G-5870)
Yoder Industries Inc............................... C 937 278-5769
  Dayton (G-6662)

LABORATORY APPARATUS & FURNITURE

Chemsultants International Inc................ G 513 860-1598
  West Chester (G-15392)
Chemsultants International Inc................ G 440 974-3080
  Mentor (G-10437)
Cortest Inc... F 440 942-1235
  Willoughby (G-15903)

Employee Codes: A=Over 500 employees, B=251-500
C=101-250, D=51-100, E=20-50, F=10-19, G=1-9

LABORATORY APPARATUS & FURNITURE

Dentronix Inc.................................. D 330 916-7300
Cuyahoga Falls *(G-6080)*

Gilson Company Inc........................ E 740 548-7298
Lewis Center *(G-9161)*

Ies Systems Inc.............................. E 330 533-6683
Canfield *(G-2008)*

Philips Med Systems Clvland In..... B 440 483-3000
Cleveland *(G-4547)*

Tech Pro Inc................................... G 330 923-3546
Akron *(G-350)*

Teledyne Instruments Inc.............. E 513 229-7000
Mason *(G-10063)*

Teledyne Tekmar Company........... E 513 229-7000
Mason *(G-10064)*

Waller Brothers Stone Company... E 740 858-1948
Mc Dermott *(G-10275)*

LABORATORY APPARATUS, EXC HEATING & MEASURING

Accuscan Instruments Inc.............. F 614 878-6644
Columbus *(G-5097)*

Caron Products and Svcs Inc........ E 740 373-6809
Marietta *(G-9781)*

LABORATORY APPARATUS: Freezers

Global Cooling Inc......................... C 740 274-7900
Athens *(G-685)*

LABORATORY APPARATUS: Pipettes, Hemocytometer

Mettler-Toledo Intl Fin Inc............. F 614 438-4511
Columbus *(G-5065)*

Mettler-Toledo LLC....................... A 614 438-4511
Columbus *(G-5067)*

LABORATORY CHEMICALS: Organic

Nationwide Chemical Products...... G 419 714-7075
Perrysburg *(G-12401)*

Polymer Diagnostics Inc................ F 440 930-1361
Avon Lake *(G-821)*

Rezkem Chemicals LLC................ F 330 653-9104
Hudson *(G-8610)*

LABORATORY EQPT, EXC MEDICAL: Wholesalers

Revvity Health Sciences Inc.......... E 330 825-4525
Akron *(G-303)*

Teledyne Instruments Inc.............. E 513 229-7000
Mason *(G-10063)*

Teledyne Tekmar Company........... E 513 229-7000
Mason *(G-10064)*

Test Mark Industries Inc................ F 330 426-2200
East Palestine *(G-7010)*

LABORATORY EQPT: Chemical

Cheminstruments Inc..................... G 513 860-1598
West Chester *(G-15390)*

Continntal Hydrdyne Systems In... E 330 494-2740
Canton *(G-2080)*

P212121 LLC.................................. G 253 229-9327
Toledo *(G-14427)*

LABORATORY EQPT: Clinical Instruments Exc Medical

Cellular Technology Limited.......... E 216 791-5084
Shaker Heights *(G-13152)*

Center For Excptonal Practices..... G 330 523-5240
Richfield *(G-12782)*

Strategic Technology Entp............ F 440 354-2600
Mentor *(G-10567)*

LABORATORY EQPT: Incubators

Health Aid of Ohio Inc................... E 216 252-3900
Cleveland *(G-4174)*

Malta Dynamics LLC..................... F 740 749-3512
Waterford *(G-15238)*

LABORATORY EQPT: Measuring

Mettler-Toledo Intl Inc................... A 614 438-4511
Columbus *(G-5066)*

LABORATORY EQPT: Sterilizers

American Sterilizer Company........ E 440 392-8328
Mentor *(G-10415)*

LABORATORY INSTRUMENT REPAIR SVCS

Tech Pro Inc................................... G 330 923-3546
Akron *(G-350)*

Tektronix Inc.................................. F 248 305-5200
West Chester *(G-15594)*

LADDERS: Metal

Bauer Corporation......................... E 800 321-4760
Wooster *(G-16102)*

Bc Investment Corporation........... G 330 262-3070
Wooster *(G-16103)*

LADLES: Metal Plate

Lincoln Electric Automtn Inc......... E 614 471-5926
Columbus *(G-5527)*

Rimrock Corporation..................... E 614 471-5926
Columbus *(G-5723)*

Rimrock Holdings Corporation..... C 614 471-5926
Columbus *(G-5724)*

Rose Metal Industries LLC............ F 216 881-3355
Cleveland *(G-4648)*

LAMINATED PLASTICS: Plate, Sheet, Rod & Tubes

Advanced Drainage Systems Inc... E 419 424-8324
Findlay *(G-7474)*

Advanced Drainage Systems Inc... E 419 599-9565
Napoleon *(G-11308)*

Advanced Drainage Systems Inc... E 330 264-4949
Wooster *(G-16095)*

Applied Medical Technology Inc... E 440 717-4000
Brecksville *(G-1606)*

Arthur Corporation........................ D 419 433-7202
Huron *(G-8627)*

Biothane Coated Webbing Corp.... E 440 327-0485
North Ridgeville *(G-11832)*

Cool Seal Usa LLC........................ F 419 666-1111
Perrysburg *(G-12371)*

Duracote Corporation................... E 330 296-9600
Ravenna *(G-12712)*

Durivage Pattern and Mfg Inc....... E 419 836-8655
Williston *(G-15870)*

Elster Perfection Corporation....... D 440 428-1171
Geneva *(G-7935)*

Flex Technologies Inc................... F 740 922-5992
Midvale *(G-10878)*

Fowler Products Inc...................... F 419 683-4057
Crestline *(G-6033)*

Hancor Inc...................................... B 614 658-0050
Hilliard *(G-8413)*

Iko Production Inc......................... E 937 746-4561
Franklin *(G-7682)*

Interntnal Cnvrter Cldwell Inc....... C 740 732-5665
Caldwell *(G-1909)*

Laminate Shop............................... F 740 749-3536
Waterford *(G-15237)*

Meridian Industries Inc.................. D 330 673-1011
Kent *(G-8834)*

Meridienne International Inc......... G 330 274-8317
Aurora *(G-725)*

Monarch Engraving Inc................. F 440 638-1500
Strongsville *(G-13857)*

Organized Living Inc..................... E 513 489-9300
Cincinnati *(G-3230)*

Overhead Door Corporation......... F 440 593-5226
Conneaut *(G-5929)*

Plaskolite LLC................................ E 614 294-3281
Columbus *(G-5677)*

Production Tube Cutting Inc........ F 937 254-6138
Dayton *(G-6530)*

Recto Molded Products Inc.......... D 513 871-5544
Cincinnati *(G-3328)*

Resinoid Engineering Corp.......... D 740 928-6115
Hebron *(G-8359)*

Rowmark LLC................................ D 419 425-8974
Findlay *(G-7557)*

Saint-Gobain Prfmce Plas Corp... C 330 798-6981
Akron *(G-324)*

Snyder Manufacturing Inc............. D 330 343-4456
Dover *(G-6844)*

Spartech LLC.................................. D 419 399-4050
Paulding *(G-12320)*

TS Trim Industries Inc................... B 614 837-4114
Canal Winchester *(G-1993)*

Wurms Woodworking Company... E 419 492-2184
New Washington *(G-11552)*

LAMINATING SVCS

Conversion Tech Intl Inc............... E 419 924-5566
West Unity *(G-15638)*

Kent Adhesive Products Co......... D 330 678-1626
Kent *(G-8821)*

Ohio Laminating & Binding Inc.... F 614 771-4868
Hilliard *(G-8426)*

Urban Industries of Ohio Inc........ E 419 468-3578
Galion *(G-7886)*

LAMP & LIGHT BULBS & TUBES

Carlisle and Finch Company......... E 513 681-6080
Cincinnati *(G-2703)*

Current Elec & Enrgy Solutions.... G 513 575-4600
Loveland *(G-9479)*

Current Lighting Solutions LLC... B 216 462-4700
Beachwood *(G-982)*

General Electric Company............ E 440 593-1156
Mc Donald *(G-10277)*

Kichler Lighting LLC..................... B 216 573-1000
Solon *(G-13379)*

Lumitex Inc..................................... D 440 243-8401
Strongsville *(G-13852)*

Osram Sylvania Inc....................... D 800 463-9275
Independence *(G-8678)*

Savant Technologies LLC............. A 800 435-4448
East Cleveland *(G-6983)*

LAMP BULBS & TUBES/PARTS, ELECTRIC: Generalized Applications

Advanced Lighting Tech LLC....... D 888 440-2358
Solon *(G-13306)*

LAMP SHADES: Glass

A Service Glass Inc....................... E 937 426-4920
Beavercreek *(G-1038)*

All State GL Block Fctry Inc.......... G 440 205-8410
Mentor *(G-10411)*

Blockamerica Corporation............ G 614 274-0700
Columbus *(G-5201)*

PRODUCT SECTION LEATHER & CUT STOCK WHOLESALERS

Dale Kestler... G 513 871-9000
  Cincinnati *(G-2817)*
Helios Quartz America Inc...................... G 419 882-3377
  Sylvania *(G-13999)*
Niles Mirror & Glass Inc........................... E 330 652-6277
  Niles *(G-11679)*
Oldcastle Buildingenvelope Inc............... D 800 537-4064
  Perrysburg *(G-12411)*

LAMPS: Fluorescent

Energy Focus Inc...................................... F 440 715-1300
  Solon *(G-13343)*
General Electric Company........................ B 419 563-1200
  Bucyrus *(G-1861)*

LAMPS: Table, Residential

J Schrader Company................................. F 216 961-2890
  Cleveland *(G-4246)*

LAND SUBDIVISION & DEVELOPMENT

Phillips Companies.................................... E 937 426-5461
  Beavercreek Township *(G-1089)*
Stonyridge Inc... F 937 845-9482
  New Carlisle *(G-11426)*

LASER SYSTEMS & EQPT

Eagle Welding & Fabg Inc........................ E 440 946-0692
  Willoughby *(G-15914)*
Fortec Medical Lithotripsy LLC................ F 330 656-4301
  Streetsboro *(G-13771)*
H W Fairway International Inc.................. F 330 678-2540
  Canton *(G-2119)*
Resonetics LLC... E 937 865-4070
  Kettering *(G-8909)*

LASERS: Welding, Drilling & Cutting Eqpt

Great Lakes Power Service Co................ G 440 259-0025
  Perry *(G-12351)*
Innovar Systems Limited.......................... E 330 538-3942
  North Jackson *(G-11784)*
Laser Automation Inc............................... F 440 543-9291
  Chagrin Falls *(G-2405)*
Lucky Thirteen Inc.................................... G 216 631-0013
  Cleveland *(G-4340)*
Peerless Laser Processors Inc................ F 614 836-5790
  Groveport *(G-8156)*
Pt Metals LLC.. E 330 767-3003
  Navarre *(G-11351)*

LATEX: Foamed

Firestone Polymers LLC........................... D 330 379-7000
  Akron *(G-153)*
Trexler Rubber Co Inc.............................. E 330 296-9677
  Ravenna *(G-12739)*

LATH: Expanded Metal

Nmc Metals Inc.. E 330 652-2501
  Niles *(G-11681)*

LAUNDRY EQPT: Commercial

Ha-International LLC................................ E 419 537-0096
  Toledo *(G-14308)*
Process Development Corp..................... E 937 890-3388
  Dayton *(G-6527)*
Whirlpool Corporation.............................. C 419 547-7711
  Clyde *(G-4979)*

LAUNDRY EQPT: Household

Kitchenaid Inc.. G 937 316-4782
  Greenville *(G-8049)*
Staber Industries Inc................................ E 614 836-5995
  Groveport *(G-8160)*

Whirlpool Corporation.............................. G 419 547-2610
  Clyde *(G-4980)*

LAWN & GARDEN EQPT

Cannon Salt & Supply Inc........................ G 440 232-1700
  Bedford *(G-1108)*
Commercial Turf Products Ltd................. D 330 995-7000
  Streetsboro *(G-13763)*
Elan Designs Inc....................................... G 614 985-5600
  Westerville *(G-15704)*
Erosion Control Products Corp................ F 302 815-6500
  West Chester *(G-15426)*
Extrudex Limited Partnership.................. E 440 352-7101
  Painesville *(G-12235)*
Finn Corporation....................................... E 513 874-2818
  West Chester *(G-15429)*
Franklin Equipment LLC........................... D 614 228-2014
  Groveport *(G-8143)*
Gardner Inc.. C 614 456-4000
  Columbus *(G-5395)*
Karl Kuemmerling Inc............................... F
  Massillon *(G-10114)*
Koenig Equipment Inc.............................. F 937 653-5281
  Urbana *(G-14842)*
Mtd Holdings Inc.. B 330 225-2600
  Valley City *(G-14882)*
Mtd International Operations................... C 330 225-2600
  Valley City *(G-14883)*
Mtd Products Inc....................................... C 419 342-6455
  Shelby *(G-13196)*
Mtd Products Inc....................................... B 330 225-1940
  Valley City *(G-14885)*
Mtd Products Inc....................................... C 419 951-9779
  Willard *(G-15861)*
Mtd Products Inc....................................... B 330 225-2600
  Valley City *(G-14884)*
Oase North America Inc.......................... G 800 365-3880
  Aurora *(G-728)*
Power Distributors LLC............................ D 614 876-3533
  Columbus *(G-5684)*
Scotts Company LLC................................ C 937 644-0011
  Marysville *(G-9934)*
Scotts Temecula Operations LLC........... E 800 221-1760
  Marysville *(G-9937)*
Smg Growing Media Inc.......................... F 937 644-0011
  Marysville *(G-9938)*
Tierra-Derco International LLC................ G 419 929-2240
  New London *(G-11471)*

LAWN & GARDEN EQPT: Grass Catchers, Lawn Mower

Cub Cadet Corporation Sales................. D 330 273-4550
  Valley City *(G-14867)*

LAWN & GARDEN EQPT: Lawnmowers, Residential, Hand Or Power

Johnson & Johnson Services LLC.......... F 513 289-4514
  Cincinnati *(G-3047)*
Mtd Products Inc....................................... C 330 225-9127
  Valley City *(G-14886)*

LAWN & GARDEN EQPT: Rototillers

Rotoline USA LLC..................................... G 330 677-3223
  Kent *(G-8856)*

LAWN & GARDEN EQPT: Tractors & Eqpt

Hawthorne Gardening Company............. E 360 883-8846
  Marysville *(G-9913)*
Mo-Trim Inc.. G 740 439-2725
  Cambridge *(G-1943)*

Mtd Consumer Group Inc......................... C 330 225-2600
  Valley City *(G-14881)*
Park-Ohio Holdings Corp.......................... F 440 947-2000
  Cleveland *(G-4524)*
Park-Ohio Industries Inc........................... C 440 947-2000
  Cleveland *(G-4525)*
Venture Products Inc................................ D 330 683-0075
  Orrville *(G-12160)*

LEAD & ZINC ORES

Abatement Lead Tstg Risk Assss............ G 330 785-6420
  Akron *(G-13)*

LEAD PENCILS & ART GOODS

North Shore Strapping Company............ E 216 661-5200
  Brooklyn Heights *(G-1696)*
Pulsar Ecoproducts LLC........................... F 216 861-8800
  Cleveland *(G-4600)*

LEASING & RENTAL SVCS: Cranes & Aerial Lift Eqpt

Rnm Holdings Inc...................................... F 614 444-5556
  Columbus *(G-5726)*

LEASING & RENTAL SVCS: Oil Field Eqpt

Eleet Cryogenics Inc................................ E 330 874-4009
  Bolivar *(G-1524)*

LEASING & RENTAL SVCS: Oil Well Drilling

Dover Fabrication and Burn Inc.............. G 330 339-1057
  Dover *(G-6819)*

LEASING & RENTAL: Construction & Mining Eqpt

Brewpro Inc.. G 513 577-7200
  Cincinnati *(G-2682)*
Efco Corp... G 614 876-1226
  Columbus *(G-5347)*
F & M Mafco Inc.. C 513 367-2151
  Harrison *(G-8273)*
Ioppolo Concrete Corporation................. E 440 439-6606
  Bedford *(G-1130)*
Lefeld Welding & Stl Sups Inc................. E 419 678-2397
  Coldwater *(G-4995)*
Ohio Machinery Co................................... C 440 526-6200
  Broadview Heights *(G-1665)*
Phillips Ready Mix Co............................... E 937 426-5151
  Beavercreek Township *(G-1090)*
Pollock Research & Design Inc............... E 330 332-3300
  Salem *(G-13023)*
The Wagner-Smith Company.................. B 866 338-0398
  Moraine *(G-11214)*

LEASING & RENTAL: Medical Machinery & Eqpt

Columbus Prescr Rehabilitation............... G 614 294-1600
  Westerville *(G-15696)*
Health Aid of Ohio Inc.............................. E 216 252-3900
  Cleveland *(G-4174)*
Kempf Surgical Appliances Inc................ F 513 984-5758
  Montgomery *(G-11130)*

LEASING & RENTAL: Trucks, Indl

Hull Ready Mix Concrete Inc................... F 419 625-8070
  Sandusky *(G-13064)*

LEASING & RENTAL: Trucks, Without Drivers

Knippen Chrysler Ddge Jeep Inc............ E 419 695-4976
  Delphos *(G-6767)*

LEATHER & CUT STOCK WHOLESALERS

PRODUCT SECTION

LEATHER & CUT STOCK WHOLESALERS

Weaver Leather LLC.................... D 330 674-7548
  Millersburg (G-11007)

LEATHER GOODS, EXC FOOTWEAR, GLOVES, LUGGAGE/ BELTING, WHOL

B D G Wrap-Tite Inc..................... E 440 349-5400
  Solon (G-13315)

LEATHER GOODS: Garments

LLC Bowman Leather..................... G 330 893-1954
  Millersburg (G-10976)

LEATHER GOODS: Holsters

Diy Holster LLC.......................... G 419 921-2168
  Elyria (G-7132)

LEATHER GOODS: Personal

Bison Leather Co......................... G 419 517-1737
  Toledo (G-14213)
Down Home............................... G 740 393-1186
  Mount Vernon (G-11271)
Ravenworks Deer Skin.................. G 937 354-5151
  Mount Victory (G-11302)
Total Education Solutions Inc......... D 330 668-4041
  Fairlawn (G-7453)
Weaver Leather LLC..................... D 330 674-7548
  Millersburg (G-11007)
Williams Leather Products Inc......... G 740 223-1604
  Marion (G-9890)

LEATHER GOODS: Wallets

Hugo Bosca Company Inc................ F 937 323-5523
  Springfield (G-13581)

LEATHER TANNING & FINISHING

Premier Tanning & Nutrition........... G 419 342-6259
  Shelby (G-13198)

LEGAL OFFICES & SVCS

Akron Legal News Inc................... F 330 296-7578
  Akron (G-35)
General Bar Inc............................ F 440 835-2000
  Westlake (G-15753)
Gongwer News Service Inc............. F 614 221-1992
  Columbus (G-5407)
Perfect Probate............................ G 513 791-4100
  Cincinnati (G-3246)

LEGAL SVCS: General Practice Attorney or Lawyer

Petro Quest Inc........................... G 740 593-3800
  Athens (G-690)

LICENSE TAGS: Automobile, Stamped Metal

Barbara A Lieurance...................... G 937 382-2864
  Wilmington (G-16041)
Clemens License Agency................ G 614 288-8007
  Pickerington (G-12459)
D J Klingler Inc........................... G 513 891-2284
  Montgomery (G-11129)
Middletown License Agency Inc....... G 513 422-7225
  Middletown (G-10844)
Ohio Department Public Safety........ G 440 943-5545
  Willowick (G-16033)
Parma Heights License Bureau......... G 440 888-0388
  Cleveland (G-4535)
Suburbanite Inc........................... G 419 756-4390
  Mansfield (G-9723)

LIGHTING EQPT: Area & Sports Luminaries

Jasper Paula............................... G 740 559-3983
  Pennsville (G-12348)

LIGHTING EQPT: Flashlights

Fulton Industries Inc.................... D 419 335-3015
  Wauseon (G-15261)

LIGHTING EQPT: Motor Vehicle

Atc Lighting & Plastics Inc............. C 440 466-7670
  Andover (G-485)
Lighting Products Inc.................... G 440 293-4064
  Andover (G-487)

LIGHTING EQPT: Motor Vehicle, Headlights

K-D Lamp Company....................... E 440 293-4064
  Andover (G-486)

LIGHTING EQPT: Motor Vehicle, NEC

Rvtronix Corporation.................... E 440 359-7200
  Eastlake (G-7048)
Stanley Electric US Co Inc.............. D 740 852-5200
  London (G-9394)
Washington Products Inc............... F 330 837-5101
  Massillon (G-10154)

LIGHTING EQPT: Outdoor

Holophane Corporation.................. C 866 759-1577
  Granville (G-8018)

LIGHTING FIXTURES WHOLESALERS

American De Rosa Lamparts LLC...... D
  Cuyahoga Falls (G-6063)
Architectural Busstrut Corp............ F 614 933-8695
  New Albany (G-11367)
B2d Solutions Inc......................... G 855 484-1145
  Cleveland (G-3718)
Cleanlife Energy LLC..................... F 800 316-2532
  Cleveland (G-3827)
Gt Industrial Supply Inc................ F 513 771-7000
  Cincinnati (G-2976)
LSI Industries Inc........................ C 913 281-1100
  Blue Ash (G-1425)

LIGHTING FIXTURES, NEC

Aat USA LLC................................ E 614 388-8866
  Columbus (G-5083)
Acuity Brands Lighting Inc............. D 740 349-4343
  Newark (G-11560)
Advanced Lighting Tech LLC........... D 888 440-2358
  Solon (G-13306)
Akron Brass Company................... E 614 529-7230
  Columbus (G-5109)
Atc Lighting & Plastics Inc............. C 440 466-7670
  Andover (G-485)
Beelighting Inc............................ G 937 296-4460
  Dayton (G-6224)
Brightguy Inc.............................. G 440 942-8318
  Willoughby (G-15893)
Cooper Lighting LLC..................... F 800 334-6871
  Columbus (G-5294)
Delta Power Supply Inc................. F 513 771-3835
  Cincinnati (G-2824)
Energy Focus Inc......................... F 440 715-1300
  Solon (G-13343)
Ericson Manufacturing Co.............. D 440 951-8000
  Willoughby (G-15917)
General Electric Company.............. E 330 373-1400
  Warren (G-15172)
Genesis Lamp Corp....................... F 440 354-0095
  Painesville (G-12239)
Global Lighting Tech Inc................ E 440 922-4584
  Brecksville (G-618)
Hughey & Phillips LLC................... E 937 652-3500
  Urbana (G-14806)
Kichler Lighting LLC..................... B 216 573-1000
  Solon (G-13379)
LSI Industries Inc........................ B 513 793-3200
  Cincinnati (G-3015)
Lumitex Inc................................ D 440 243-8401
  Strongsville (G-3852)
Midmark Corporation.................... G 937 526-3662
  Versailles (G-1986)
Midmark Corporation.................... E 937 526-8387
  Versailles (G-1987)
Midmark Corporation.................... A 937 528-7500
  Miamisburg (G-0661)
Pro Lighting LLC.......................... G 614 561-0089
  Hilliard (G-8433)
Smashray Ltd.............................. E 989 620-7507
  Maumee (G-1032)
Starbright Lighting USA LLC........... G 330 650-2000
  Hudson (G-8613)
Vanner Holdings Inc..................... D 614 771-2718
  Hilliard (G-8451)
Will-Burt Company....................... C 330 682-7015
  Orrville (G-1216)

LIGHTING FIXTURES: Decorative Area

B2d Solutions Inc......................... G 855 484-1145
  Cleveland (G-3718)

LIGHTING FIXTURES: Fluorescent, Commercial

Damak 1 LLC.............................. E 513 858-6004
  Fairfield (G-7350)
Magnum Asset Acquisition LLC........ E 330 915-2382
  Hudson (G-8603)

LIGHTING FIXTURES: Indl & Commercial

Acuity Brands Lighting Inc............. C 800 754-0463
  Granville (G-8014)
Acuity Brands Lighting Inc............. D 740 349-4343
  Newark (G-11560)
Acuity Brands Lighting Inc............. C 740 892-2011
  Utica (G-14856)
Advanced Lighting Tech LLC........... D 888 440-2358
  Solon (G-13306)
Besa Lighting Co Inc..................... E 614 475-7046
  Blacklick (G-1331)
Best Lighting Products Inc............. D 740 964-1198
  Etna (G-7254)
Current Lighting Solutions LLC........ B 216 266-4416
  Cleveland (G-3927)
Current Lighting Solutions LLC........ B 216 462-4700
  Beachwood (G-912)
Daycoa Inc................................. F 937 849-1315
  Medway (G-1039)
Evp International LLC................... G 513 761-7614
  Cincinnati (G-2890)
GE Lighting Inc........................... D 216 266-2121
  Cleveland (G-4102)
General Electric Company.............. E 330 458-3200
  Canton (G-2111)
Genesis Lamp Corp....................... F 440 354-0095
  Painesville (G-12239)
Grimes Aerospace Company............ A 937 484-2000
  Urbana (G-14830)
Hinkley Lighting Inc..................... E 440 653-5500
  Avon Lake (G-812)
Holophane Corporation.................. A 330 823-5535
  Alliance (G-406)

Holophane Corporation............................ F 740 349-4194
  Newark (G-11579)
Holophane Corporation............................ C 866 759-1577
  Granville (G-8018)
Importers Direct LLC............................... F 330 436-3260
  Akron (G-189)
J Schrader Company................................ F 216 961-2890
  Cleveland (G-4246)
JB Machining Concepts LLC...................... G 419 523-0096
  Ottawa (G-12182)
Led Lighting Center Inc............................ G 714 271-2633
  Toledo (G-14360)
Led Lighting Center LLC........................... F 888 988-6533
  Toledo (G-14361)
Light Craft Manufacturing Inc.................... F 419 332-0536
  Fremont (G-7795)
LSI Industries Inc.................................... C 913 281-1100
  Blue Ash (G-1425)
LSI Lightron Inc..................................... A 845 562-5500
  Blue Ash (G-1426)
Lumenforce Led LLC................................ E 330 330-8962
  Youngstown (G-16390)
Lumitex Inc... D 440 243-8401
  Strongsville (G-13852)
Mega Bright LLC................................... G 216 712-4689
  Cleveland (G-4390)
Mega Bright LLC................................... F 330 577-8859
  Cuyahoga Falls (G-6104)
Megalight Inc.. E 800 957-1797
  Hudson (G-8604)
NRG Industrial Lighting Mfg Co.................. G 419 354-8207
  Bowling Green (G-1578)
SMS Technologies Inc............................. F 419 465-4175
  Monroeville (G-11126)
Stress-Crete Company............................. E 440 576-9073
  Jefferson (G-8759)
Treemen Industries Inc............................ E 330 965-3777
  Boardman (G-1519)

LIGHTING FIXTURES: Motor Vehicle

Advanced Technology Corp........................ F 440 293-4064
  Andover (G-483)
Akron Brass Company.............................. E 614 529-7230
  Columbus (G-5109)
Akron Brass Company.............................. E 800 228-1161
  Wooster (G-16096)
Akron Brass Company.............................. B 330 264-5678
  Wooster (G-16097)
Akron Brass Holding Corp......................... E 330 264-5678
  Wooster (G-16098)
Atc Group Inc....................................... F 440 293-4064
  Andover (G-484)
Grimes Aerospace Company....................... D 937 484-2001
  Urbana (G-14832)
Grimes Aerospace Company....................... A 937 484-2000
  Urbana (G-14830)
Treemen Industries Inc............................ E 330 965-3777
  Boardman (G-1519)

LIGHTING FIXTURES: Ornamental, Commercial

King Luminaire Company Inc..................... E 440 576-9073
  Jefferson (G-8750)

LIGHTING FIXTURES: Public

Union Metal Corporation........................... B 330 456-7653
  Canton (G-2250)

LIGHTING FIXTURES: Residential, Electric

Architectural Busstrut Corp....................... F 614 933-8695
  New Albany (G-11367)

LIGHTING FIXTURES: Street

Miami Valley Lighting LLC........................ G 937 224-6000
  Dayton (G-6170)

LIME

Ayers Limestone Quarry Inc...................... F 740 633-2958
  Martins Ferry (G-9896)
Bluffton Stone Co................................... E 419 358-6941
  Bluffton (G-1501)
Graymont Dolime (oh) Inc......................... D 419 855-8682
  Genoa (G-7947)
Mineral Processing Company...................... G 419 396-3501
  Carey (G-2280)
National Lime and Stone Co....................... E 419 396-7671
  Carey (G-2281)
Piqua Materials Inc................................. F 937 773-4824
  Piqua (G-12547)
Shelly Materials Inc................................ E 740 666-5841
  Ostrander (G-12176)
Sugarcreek Lime Service........................... G 330 364-4460
  Dover (G-6845)

LIME ROCK: Ground

National Lime and Stone Co....................... E 419 396-7671
  Carey (G-2281)

LIMESTONE: Crushed & Broken

Allgeier & Son Inc.................................. F 513 574-3735
  Cincinnati (G-2611)
Beazer East Inc..................................... E 937 364-2311
  Hillsboro (G-8455)
Bluffton Stone Co................................... E 419 358-6941
  Bluffton (G-1501)
Carmeuse Lime Inc................................. E 419 986-5200
  Bettsville (G-1319)
Carmeuse Lime Inc................................. E 419 638-2511
  Millersville (G-11016)
Crushed Stone Sandusky.......................... G 419 483-4390
  Castalia (G-2321)
Cumberland Limestone LLC....................... E 740 638-3942
  Cumberland (G-6054)
Custar Stone Co..................................... E 419 669-4327
  Napoleon (G-11311)
Duff Quarry Inc...................................... F 419 273-2518
  Forest (G-7591)
Duff Quarry Inc...................................... F 937 686-2811
  Huntsville (G-8622)
Heidelberg Mtls Mdwest Agg Inc................. F 419 882-0123
  Sylvania (G-13997)
Kellstone Inc... E 419 746-2396
  Kelleys Island (G-8789)
King Limestone Inc................................. F 740 638-3942
  Cumberland (G-6055)
Lang Stone Company Inc.......................... E 614 235-4099
  Columbus (G-5520)
Marietta Martin Materials Inc..................... E 740 247-2211
  Racine (G-12694)
Marietta Martin Materials Inc..................... G 937 335-8313
  Troy (G-14596)
Martin Marietta Materials Inc..................... F 513 701-1120
  Mason (G-10025)
Martin Marietta Materials Inc..................... G 513 701-1140
  West Chester (G-15461)
Maysville Materials LLC........................... G 740 849-0474
  Mount Perry (G-11250)
National Lime and Stone Co....................... E 419 562-0771
  Bucyrus (G-1863)
National Lime and Stone Co....................... E 740 548-4206
  Delaware (G-6740)
National Lime and Stone Co....................... F 419 423-3400
  Findlay (G-7541)
National Lime and Stone Co....................... E 419 228-3434
  Lima (G-9273)
National Lime and Stone Co....................... G 330 966-4836
  North Canton (G-11748)
National Lime and Stone Co....................... G 419 657-6745
  Wapakoneta (G-15128)
Oglebay Norton Mar Svcs Co LLC................ A 216 861-3300
  Cleveland (G-4492)
Omya Industries Inc................................ D 513 387-4600
  Mason (G-10036)
Onco Wva Inc....................................... G 216 861-3300
  Cleveland (G-4505)
Ontex Inc... F 216 861-3300
  Cleveland (G-4506)
Oster Sand and Gravel Inc........................ G 330 833-2649
  Massillon (G-10133)
Ridge Township Stone Quarry..................... G 419 968-2222
  Van Wert (G-14925)
Sergeant Stone Inc................................. G 740 452-7434
  Corning (G-5959)
Shelly Company..................................... G 216 688-0684
  Cleveland (G-4691)
Shelly Materials Inc................................ E 740 666-5841
  Ostrander (G-12176)
Shelly Materials Inc................................ E 740 246-6315
  Toledo (G-14471)
Shelly Materials Inc................................ D 740 246-6315
  Thornville (G-14072)
Stoneco Inc.. E 419 893-7645
  Maumee (G-10236)
Stoneco Inc.. E 419 393-2555
  Oakwood (G-12033)
Stoneco Inc.. G 419 686-3311
  Portage (G-12637)
The National Lime and Stone Company. E 419 422-4341
  Findlay (G-7575)
Uniontown Stone.................................... G 740 968-4313
  Flushing (G-7588)
Wyandot Dolomite Inc............................. E 419 396-7641
  Carey (G-2286)

LIMESTONE: Cut & Shaped

Maple Grove Materials Inc........................ G 419 992-4235
  Tiffin (G-14093)
National Lime and Stone Co....................... G 419 657-6745
  Wapakoneta (G-15128)

LIMESTONE: Dimension

Gregory Stone Co Inc.............................. G 937 275-7455
  Dayton (G-6363)
National Lime and Stone Co....................... E 419 562-0771
  Bucyrus (G-1863)
S E Johnson Companies Inc....................... E 419 893-8731
  Maumee (G-10228)
Stoneco Inc.. E 419 422-8854
  Findlay (G-7569)
Waterloo Coal Company Inc....................... D 740 286-0004
  Jackson (G-8727)
Wyandot Dolomite Inc............................. E 419 396-7641
  Carey (G-2286)

LIMESTONE: Ground

Conag Inc.. F 419 394-8870
  Saint Marys (G-12950)
Heidelberg Mtls Mdwest Agg Inc................. G 419 983-2211
  Bloomville (G-1355)
Latham Limestone LLC............................ G 740 493-2677
  Latham (G-9051)
National Lime and Stone Co....................... E 740 387-3485
  Marion (G-9865)
Ohio Asphaltic Limestone Corp................... F 937 364-2191
  Hillsboro (G-8462)

LIMESTONE: Ground

Piqua Materials Inc..................D 937 773-4824
  Piqua (G-12547)
Piqua Materials Inc..................E 513 771-0820
  Cincinnati (G-3258)
Sharon Stone Inc....................G 740 732-7100
  Caldwell (G-1913)
Wagner Quarries Company.............E 419 625-8141
  Sandusky (G-13104)

LINENS & TOWELS WHOLESALERS

Standard Textile Co Inc..............B 513 761-9255
  Cincinnati (G-3415)

LINERS & COVERS: Fabric

Custom Canvas & Boat Repr Inc........G 419 732-3514
  Lakeside (G-8959)
Sailors Tailor Inc...................F 937 862-7781
  Spring Valley (G-13491)

LINERS & LINING

Flow-Liner Systems Ltd...............E 800 348-0020
  Zanesville (G-16531)
Ridge Corporation....................D 614 421-7434
  Etna (G-7256)

LININGS: Fabric, Apparel & Other, Exc Millinery

Fortner Upholstering Inc.............F 614 475-8282
  Columbus (G-5384)
Promospark Inc.......................F 513 844-2211
  Fairfield (G-7399)

LIQUEFIED PETROLEUM GAS DEALERS

Legacy Farmers Cooperative...........F 419 423-2611
  Findlay (G-7528)

LIQUEFIED PETROLEUM GAS WHOLESALERS

Centerra Co-Op.......................E 419 281-2153
  Ashland (G-562)

LIQUID CRYSTAL DISPLAYS

Cks Solution Incorporated............E 513 947-1277
  Fairfield (G-7348)
Cleanlife Energy LLC.................F 800 316-2532
  Cleveland (G-3827)
Kent Displays Inc....................D 330 673-8784
  Kent (G-8822)
S-Tek Inc............................G 440 439-8232
  Twinsburg (G-14732)

LITHOGRAPHIC PLATES

Gli Holdings Inc.....................D 440 892-7760
  Stow (G-13700)
Gli Holdings Inc.....................D 216 651-1500
  Stow (G-13701)
Kehl-Kolor Inc.......................E 419 281-3107
  Ashland (G-585)
R E May Inc..........................E 216 771-6332
  Cleveland (G-4612)

LIVESTOCK WHOLESALERS, NEC

Werling and Sons Inc.................F 937 338-3281
  Burkettsville (G-1879)

LOADS: Electronic

Omega Engineering Inc................E 740 965-9340
  Sunbury (G-13962)
Omegadyne Inc........................D 740 965-9340
  Sunbury (G-13963)

TL Industries Inc....................C 419 666-8144
  Perrysburg (G-12436)

LOCKERS

Industrial Mfg Co Intl LLC...........E 440 838-4555
  Upper Arlington (G-14801)
Industrial Mfg Co LLC................F 440 838-4700
  Brecksville (G-1621)
Republic Storage Systems LLC.........B 330 438-5800
  Canton (G-2215)
Tiffin Metal Products Co.............C 419 447-8414
  Tiffin (G-14110)

LOCKSMITHS

Deadbolts Plus.......................G 614 405-2117
  Columbus (G-5320)
Esmet Inc............................E 330 452-9132
  Canton (G-2098)
Kirk Key Interlock Company LLC.......E 330 833-8223
  North Canton (G-11740)
Medallion............................G 513 936-0597
  Blue Ash (G-1433)
Restricted Key.......................G 614 405-2109
  Columbus (G-5720)

LOCOMOTIVES & PARTS

B&C Machine Co LLC...................E 330 745-4013
  Barberton (G-859)

LOGGING

A and R Logging LLC..................G 740 352-6182
  Mc Dermott (G-10273)
Anthony W Hilderbrant................G 740 682-1035
  Oak Hill (G-12016)
Bailee Logging LLC...................G 330 881-4688
  Salineville (G-13038)
C & L Erectors & Riggers Inc.........F 740 332-7185
  Laurelville (G-9054)
Dale R Adkins........................G 740 682-7312
  Oak Hill (G-12017)
Geauga Counting Logging LLC..........G 440 478-7896
  Garrettsville (G-7915)
Gerald D Damron......................G 740 894-3680
  Chesapeake (G-2474)
Ghost Logging LLC....................G 740 504-1819
  Gambier (G-7906)
Giles Logging LLC....................G 406 855-5284
  Spencer (G-13481)
Haessly Lumber Sales Co..............D 740 373-6681
  Marietta (G-9798)
Jason C Gibson.......................F 740 663-4520
  Chillicothe (G-2514)
Kcox Enterprises LLC.................F 574 952-5084
  West Chester (G-15453)
Miller Logging Inc...................F 330 279-4721
  Holmesville (G-8550)
Morehouse Logging LLC................G 740 501-0256
  Thornville (G-14067)
Northeast Logging & Lumber LLC.......G 440 272-5100
  Middlefield (G-10778)
Powell Logging.......................G 740 372-6131
  Otway (G-12207)
Ray H Miller Logging Lumb............G 330 683-2055
  Apple Creek (G-509)
Raymond Robinson.....................G 937 890-1886
  Dayton (G-6542)
Select Logging.......................G 419 564-0361
  Marengo (G-9770)
Stark Truss Company Inc..............D 419 298-3777
  Edgerton (G-7082)
Sy Logging Llc.......................G 440 437-5744
  Orwell (G-12170)

Terry G Sickles......................G 740 286-8880
  Ray (G-12744)
Travis Cochran.......................G 740 294-2368
  Frazeysburg (G-7716)

LOGGING CAMPS & CONTRACTORS

Alfman Logging LLC...................F 740 982-6227
  Crooksville (G-4043)
Beachs Trees Sltive Hrvstg LL.......G 513 289-5976
  Cincinnati (G-253)
Biedenbach Logging...................G 740 732-6477
  Sarahsville (G-3105)
Blair Logging........................G 740 934-2730
  Lower Salem (G-9519)
Blankenship Logging LLC..............G 740 372-3833
  Otway (G-1220)
Border Lumber & Logging Ltd..........G 330 897-0177
  Fresno (G-7821)
Craig Saylor.........................G 740 352-8363
  Portland (G-1268)
Custom Material Hdlg Eqp LLC.........E 513 235-5336
  Cincinnati (G-258)
David Adkins Logging.................G 740 533-0297
  Kitts Hill (G-894)
Denver Adkins........................G 740 682-3123
  Oak Hill (G-1205)
HK Logging & Lumber Ltd..............G 440 632-1997
  Middlefield (G-1757)
Jefferson Logging Company LLC........G 304 634-9203
  Crown City (G-653)
JM Logging Inc.......................G 740 441-0941
  Gallipolis (G-785)
Joey Elliott Logging LLC.............G 740 626-0061
  South Salem (G-3475)
Miller Logging.......................G 440 693-4001
  Middlefield (G-169)
R & D Logging LLC....................G 740 259-6127
  Lucasville (G-955)
Randy Carter Logging Inc.............G 740 634-2604
  Bainbridge (G-83)
Rocky Mountain Logging Co LLC........G 440 313-8574
  Hiram (G-8488)
Sean Ison Logging LLC................G 740 835-7222
  Sardinia (G-1310)
Whites Logging & Land Clearin.......G 419 921-9878
  Fredericktown (G-7760)
Y&B Logging..........................G 440 437-1053
  Orwell (G-12172)

LOGGING: Timber, Cut At Logging Camp

Oakbridge Timber Framing.............G 419 994-1052
  Loudonville (G-950)
Superior Hardwoods of Ohio...........E 740 384-6862
  Jackson (G-8726)

LOGGING: Wooden Logs

Lee Saylor Logging LLC...............G 740 682-0479
  Oak Hill (G-12021)

LOGS: Gas, Fireplace

Specialty Ceramics Inc...............D 330 482-0800
  Columbiana (G-551)

LOTIONS OR CREAMS: Face

Beautyavenues LLC....................C 614 856-6000
  Reynoldsburg (G-2754)
Beiersdorf Inc.......................C 513 682-7300
  West Chester (G-541)
Bright Holdco LLC....................E 614 741-7458
  New Albany (G-11171)
Redex Industries Inc.................F 800 345-7339
  Salem (G-13026)

LUBRICANTS: Corrosion Preventive

Apex Advanced Technologies LLC........ G 216 898-1595
Cleveland *(G-3670)*

Dinol US Inc... E 740 548-1656
Lewis Center *(G-9157)*

Stellar Group Inc..................................... F 330 769-8484
Seville *(G-13145)*

LUBRICATING EQPT: Indl

Motionsource International LLC............. F 440 287-7037
Solon *(G-13392)*

R Holdings 2500 Co................................ E 800 883-7876
Columbus *(G-5707)*

LUBRICATING OIL & GREASE WHOLESALERS

American Ultra Specialties Inc................ F 330 656-5000
Hudson *(G-8584)*

Digilube Systems Inc............................... F 937 748-2209
Springboro *(G-13499)*

Functional Products Inc........................... F 330 963-3060
Macedonia *(G-9552)*

Lubriplate Lubricants Company............. G 419 691-2491
Toledo *(G-14372)*

LUBRICATION SYSTEMS & EQPT

Cleveland Gear Company Inc................. D 216 641-9000
Cleveland *(G-3840)*

Digilube Systems Inc............................... F 937 748-2209
Springboro *(G-13499)*

Groeneveld Atlantic South...................... G 330 225-4949
Brunswick *(G-1768)*

Koester Corporation................................ E 419 599-0291
Napoleon *(G-11322)*

Pax Products Inc..................................... F 419 586-2337
Celina *(G-2343)*

LUGGAGE & BRIEFCASES

Cleveland Canvas Goods Mfg Co........... E 216 361-4567
Cleveland *(G-3835)*

Kam Manufacturing Inc........................... C 419 238-6037
Van Wert *(G-14919)*

Plastic Forming Company Inc................. E 330 830-5167
Massillon *(G-10134)*

Weaver Leather LLC............................... D 330 674-7548
Millersburg *(G-11007)*

LUGGAGE & LEATHER GOODS STORES

Baggallini Inc... F 800 448-8753
Pickerington *(G-12456)*

LUGGAGE: Traveling Bags

Eagle Creek Inc....................................... D 513 385-4442
Cincinnati *(G-2852)*

LUMBER & BLDG MATLS DEALER, RET: Garage Doors, Sell/Install

A L Callahan Door Sales........................ G 419 884-3667
Mansfield *(G-9620)*

Jerry Harolds Doors Unlimited................ G 740 635-4949
Bridgeport *(G-1647)*

Nofziger Door Sales Inc.......................... F 419 445-2961
Archbold *(G-539)*

Overhead Inc... G 419 476-0300
Toledo *(G-14420)*

LUMBER & BLDG MATRLS DEALERS, RET: Bath Fixtures, Eqpt/Sply

Agean Marble Manufacturing.................. F 513 874-1475
West Chester *(G-15533)*

Marble Arch Products Inc....................... G 937 746-8388
Franklin *(G-7685)*

LUMBER & BLDG MATRLS DEALERS, RETAIL: Doors, Wood/Metal

American Quality Door Co...................... G 330 296-0393
Ravenna *(G-12705)*

Nofziger Door Sales Inc.......................... C 419 337-9900
Wauseon *(G-15271)*

LUMBER & BLDG MTRLS DEALERS, RET: Planing Mill Prdts/Lumber

Cox Wood Product Inc............................ F 740 372-4735
Otway *(G-12206)*

Marsh Industries Inc............................... E 330 308-8667
New Philadelphia *(G-11515)*

Yoder Lumber Co Inc.............................. D 330 893-3131
Sugarcreek *(G-13949)*

LUMBER & BUILDING MATERIALS DEALER, RET: Door & Window Prdts

Dale Kestler.. G 513 871-9000
Cincinnati *(G-2817)*

P & T Millwork Inc................................... F 440 543-2151
Chagrin Falls *(G-2412)*

Rockwood Products Ltd......................... E 330 893-2392
Millersburg *(G-10991)*

Seemray LLC... E 440 536-8705
Cleveland *(G-4685)*

Waxco International Inc.......................... F 937 746-4845
Miamisburg *(G-10701)*

LUMBER & BUILDING MATERIALS DEALER, RET: Masonry Matls/Splys

Associated Associates Inc...................... E 330 626-3300
Mantua *(G-9734)*

Feather Lite Innovations Inc................... E 937 743-9008
Springboro *(G-13501)*

Grafton Ready Mix Concret Inc.............. C 440 926-2911
Grafton *(G-8001)*

Gregory Stone Co Inc............................. G 937 275-7455
Dayton *(G-6363)*

Hazelbaker Industries Ltd...................... F
Columbus *(G-5424)*

Koltcz Concrete Block Co....................... E 440 232-3630
Bedford *(G-1132)*

Mack Industries....................................... E 419 353-7081
Bowling Green *(G-1572)*

Pleasant Valley Ready Mix Inc............... F 330 852-2613
Sugarcreek *(G-13934)*

Quikrete Companies LLC....................... E 330 296-6080
Ravenna *(G-12729)*

St Henry Tile Co Inc............................... G 937 548-1101
Greenville *(G-8061)*

St Henry Tile Co Inc............................... E 419 678-4841
Saint Henry *(G-12938)*

Stocker Concrete Company.................... F 740 254-4626
Gnadenhutten *(G-7989)*

Westview Concrete Corp........................ F 440 458-5800
Elyria *(G-7218)*

Westview Concrete Corp........................ E 440 235-1800
Olmsted Falls *(G-12084)*

LUMBER & BUILDING MATERIALS DEALERS, RET: Solar Heating Eqpt

Gopowerx Inc.. F 440 707-6029
Richfield *(G-12789)*

LUMBER & BUILDING MATERIALS DEALERS, RETAIL: Brick

American Concrete Products Inc............ F 937 224-1433
Dayton *(G-6200)*

Glen-Gery Corporation........................... D 419 845-3321
Caledonia *(G-1915)*

Huth Ready Mix & Supply Co................. E 330 833-4191
Massillon *(G-10108)*

Medina Supply Company........................ E 330 723-3681
Medina *(G-10352)*

The Ideal Builders Supply & Fuel Co Inc F 216 741-1600
Cleveland *(G-4787)*

LUMBER & BUILDING MATERIALS DEALERS, RETAIL: Cement

Ernst Enterprises Inc............................. E 614 443-9456
Columbus *(G-5358)*

Scioto Ready Mix LLC............................ D 740 924-9273
Pataskala *(G-12308)*

Smyrna Ready Mix Concrete LLC.......... E 937 855-0410
Germantown *(G-7952)*

LUMBER & BUILDING MATERIALS DEALERS, RETAIL: Modular Homes

Everything In America............................ G 347 871-6872
Cleveland *(G-4039)*

LUMBER & BUILDING MATERIALS DEALERS, RETAIL: Tile, Ceramic

Ohio Tile & Marble Co............................ E 513 541-4211
Cincinnati *(G-3217)*

Saint-Gobain Norpro Corp...................... C 330 673-5860
Stow *(G-13722)*

LUMBER & BUILDING MATERIALS RET DEALERS: Millwork & Lumber

Laborie Enterprises LLC........................ G 419 686-6245
Portage *(G-12634)*

Mohler Lumber Company....................... E 330 499-5461
North Canton *(G-11744)*

The Galehouse Companies Inc.............. E 330 658-2023
Doylestown *(G-6854)*

Walnut Creek Planing Ltd...................... D 330 893-3244
Millersburg *(G-11005)*

LUMBER & BUILDING MATLS DEALERS, RET: Concrete/Cinder Block

Encore Precast LLC............................... E 513 726-5678
Seven Mile *(G-13132)*

Ernst Enterprises Inc............................. E 419 222-2015
Lima *(G-9241)*

OK Brugmann Jr & Sons Inc................... F 330 274-2106
Mantua *(G-9741)*

Prairie Builders Supply Inc..................... G 419 332-7546
Fremont *(G-7802)*

LUMBER: Dimension, Hardwood

Halliday Holdings Inc.............................. E 740 335-1430
Wshngtn Ct Hs *(G-16233)*

J McCoy Lumber Co Ltd......................... F 937 587-3423
Peebles *(G-12328)*

Stephen M Trudick................................. E 440 834-1891
Burton *(G-1886)*

Woodcraft Industries Inc........................ D 440 632-9655
Middlefield *(G-10798)*

Woodcraft Industries Inc........................ C 440 437-7811
Orwell *(G-12171)*

LUMBER: Fiberboard

Frankes Wood Products LLC .... E 937 642-0706
  Marysville (G-9910)
Tectum Inc .... C 740 345-9691
  Newark (G-11608)

LUMBER: Flooring, Dressed, Softwood

Conover Lumber Company Inc .... F 937 368-3010
  Conover (G-5936)

LUMBER: Hardwood Dimension

Canfield Manufacturing Co Inc .... G 330 533-3333
  North Jackson (G-11780)
Cardinal Building Supply LLC .... E 614 706-4499
  Columbus (G-5237)
Itl LLC .... E 216 831-3140
  Beachwood (G-992)
McKay-Gross Division .... F 330 683-2055
  Apple Creek (G-504)
Ohio Valley Veneer Inc .... E 740 493-2901
  Piketon (G-12480)

LUMBER: Hardwood Dimension & Flooring Mills

Armstrong Custom Moulding Inc .... G 740 922-5931
  Uhrichsville (G-14761)
Baillie Lumber Co LP .... E 419 462-2000
  Galion (G-7861)
Beaver Wood Products .... F 740 226-6211
  Beaver (G-1035)
Carter-Jones Lumber Company .... F 330 674-9060
  Millersburg (G-10950)
Cherokee Hardwoods Inc .... G 440 632-0322
  Middlefield (G-10741)
Crownover Lumber Company Inc .... D 740 596-5229
  Mc Arthur (G-10263)
Denoon Lumber Company LLC .... D 740 768-2220
  Bergholz (G-1300)
Dutch Heritage Woodcraft .... F 330 893-2211
  Berlin (G-1306)
Gross Lumber Inc .... F 330 683-2055
  Apple Creek (G-501)
Haessly Lumber Sales Co .... D 740 373-6681
  Marietta (G-9798)
Hartzell Hardwoods Inc .... D 937 773-7054
  Piqua (G-12521)
Hochstetler Wood .... F 330 893-2384
  Millersburg (G-10961)
Holmes Lumber & Bldg Ctr Inc .... E 330 479-8314
  Canton (G-2125)
Holmes Lumber & Bldg Ctr Inc .... C 330 674-9060
  Millersburg (G-10967)
Itl Corp .... E 216 831-3140
  Cleveland (G-4240)
Knisley Lumber .... F 740 634-2935
  Bainbridge (G-831)
Mid Ohio Wood Products Inc .... E 740 323-0427
  Newark (G-11591)
Mohler Lumber Company .... E 330 499-5461
  North Canton (G-11744)
Roppe Holding Company .... B 419 435-8546
  Fostoria (G-7653)
Stony Point Hardwoods LLC .... G 330 852-4512
  Sugarcreek (G-13939)
Superior Hardwoods of Ohio .... F 740 596-2561
  Mc Arthur (G-10264)
Superior Hardwoods Ohio Inc .... E 740 439-2727
  Cambridge (G-1956)
Superior Hardwoods Ohio Inc .... D 740 384-4677
  Wellston (G-15332)

T & D Thompson Inc .... E 740 332-8515
  Laurelville (G-9056)
Trumbull County Hardwoods .... E 440 632-0555
  Middlefield (G-10794)
Wagner Farms Sawmill Ltd Lblty .... F 419 653-4126
  Leipsic (G-9141)
Walnut Creek Planing Ltd .... D 330 893-3244
  Millersburg (G-11005)
Wappoo Wood Products Inc .... E 937 492-1166
  Sidney (G-13294)
Wooden Horse .... G 740 503-5243
  Baltimore (G-849)
Yoder Lumber Co Inc .... D 330 893-3131
  Sugarcreek (G-13949)
Yoder Lumber Co Inc .... D 330 893-3121
  Millersburg (G-11008)

LUMBER: Kiln Dried

Blaney Hardwoods Ohio Inc .... D 740 678-8288
  Vincent (G-15006)
Itl Corp .... E 216 831-3140
  Cleveland (G-4240)
Miller Lumber Co Inc .... E 330 674-0273
  Millersburg (G-10981)

LUMBER: Plywood, Hardwood

Automated Bldg Components Inc .... E 419 257-2152
  North Baltimore (G-11694)
Beaver Wood Products .... F 740 226-6211
  Beaver (G-1035)
Bruewer Woodwork Mfg Co .... D 513 353-3505
  Cleves (G-4946)
Dimension Hardwood Veneers Inc .... E 419 272-2245
  Edon (G-7086)
Exhibit Concepts Inc .... D 937 890-7000
  Vandalia (G-14939)
Fifth Avenue Lumber Co .... E 614 833-6655
  Canal Winchester (G-1986)
Fryburg Door Inc .... D 330 674-5252
  Millersburg (G-10955)
Haessly Lumber Sales Co .... D 740 373-6681
  Marietta (G-9798)
Knisley Lumber .... F 740 634-2935
  Bainbridge (G-831)
Mac Lean J S Co .... E 614 878-5454
  Columbus (G-5538)
Miller Manufacturing Inc .... E 330 852-0689
  Sugarcreek (G-13931)
Mohler Lumber Company .... E 330 499-5461
  North Canton (G-11744)
Ohio Valley Veneer Inc .... E 740 493-2901
  Piketon (G-12480)
S & G Manufacturing Group LLC .... C 614 529-0100
  Hilliard (G-8437)
Sims-Lohman Inc .... E 513 651-3510
  Cincinnati (G-3395)
Stony Point Hardwoods LLC .... G 330 852-4512
  Sugarcreek (G-13939)
Universal Veneer Mill Corp .... C 740 522-1147
  Newark (G-11611)
Wappoo Wood Products Inc .... E 937 492-1166
  Sidney (G-13294)
Yoder Lumber Co Inc .... D 330 893-3131
  Sugarcreek (G-13949)

LUMBER: Plywood, Prefinished, Hardwood

Miller Crist .... G 330 359-7877
  Fredericksburg (G-7726)
Starecasing Systems Inc .... G 312 203-5632
  Columbus (G-5790)

LUMBER: Plywood, Softwood

Clopay Building Pdts Co Inc .... E 513 770-4800
  Mason (G-9978)

LUMBER: Treated

ISK Americas Incorporated .... F 440 357-4600
  Concord Township (G-5908)
The F A Requarth Company .... E 937 224-1141
  Dayton (G-6618)

LUMBER: Veneer, Softwood

American Veneer Edgebanding Co .... G 740 928-2700
  Heath (G-8316)

MACHINE PARTS: Stamped Or Pressed Metal

Abbott Tool Inc .... E 419 476-6742
  Toledo (G-1417)
Adh Industries Inc .... G 330 283-5822
  Akron (G-21)
Artisan Equipment Inc .... F 740 756-9135
  Carroll (G-2294)
Coreworth Holdings LLC .... G 419 468-7100
  Iberia (G-8647)
Diamond America Corporation .... E 330 762-9269
  Akron (G-126)
Gb Manufacturing Company .... D 419 822-5323
  Delta (G-6784)
Hidaka Usa Inc .... E 614 889-8611
  Dublin (G-6893)
Independent Power Cons Inc .... G 419 476-8383
  Toledo (G-14325)
Modern Engineering Inc .... E 440 593-5414
  Conneaut (G-5923)
MSC Industries Inc .... G 440 474-8788
  Rome (G-12849)
Northwood Industries Inc .... E 419 666-2100
  Perrysburg (G-12304)
P M Motor Company .... F 440 327-9999
  North Ridgeville (G-11852)
PE Usa LLC .... F 513 771-7374
  Cincinnati (G-324)
Perry Welding Service Inc .... F 330 425-2211
  Twinsburg (G-14714)
Plating Technology Inc .... D 937 268-6882
  Dayton (G-6507)
Saco Lowell Parts LLC .... E 330 794-1535
  Akron (G-322)
Spectrum Machine Inc .... F 330 626-3666
  Streetsboro (G-13793)
TEC Design & Manufacturing Inc .... F 937 435-2147
  Dayton (G-6611)
Tech-Med Inc .... F 216 486-0900
  Euclid (G-7301)
Tenacity Manufacturing Company .... F 513 821-0201
  West Chester (G-5514)
Thk Manufacturing America Inc .... C 740 928-1415
  Hebron (G-8365)
Voss Industries LLC .... C 216 771-7655
  Cleveland (G-4884)
Ysk Corporation .... B 740 774-7315
  Chillicothe (G-2541)

MACHINE TOOL ACCESS: Drill Bushings, Drilling Jig

Jergens Inc .... C 216 486-5540
  Cleveland (G-4253)

MACHINE TOOL ACCESS: Drills

H Machining Inc .... F 419 636-6890
  Bryan (G-1820)

PRODUCT SECTION

MACHINE TOOLS, METAL CUTTING: Tool Replacement & Rpr Parts

Sp3 Winco LLC.. E 937 667-4476
 Tipp City (G-14157)

MACHINE TOOL ACCESS: Tools & Access

Cowles Industrial Tool Co LLC.................. E 330 799-9100
 Austintown (G-751)
Furukawa Rock Drill USA Co Ltd............... F 330 673-5826
 Kent (G-8816)
H & S Tool Inc... F 330 335-1536
 Wadsworth (G-15034)
HI Carb Corp.. E 216 486-5000
 Eastlake (G-7035)
High Quality Tools Inc.............................. F 440 975-9684
 Eastlake (G-7036)
Imco Carbide Tool Inc.............................. D 419 661-6313
 Perrysburg (G-12390)
MSC Industries Inc.................................. G 440 474-8788
 Rome (G-12849)
Oakley Die & Mold Co.............................. E 513 754-8500
 Mason (G-10034)
Red Head Brass Inc................................. F 330 567-2903
 Shreve (G-13213)
Tomco Tool Inc....................................... G 937 322-5768
 Springfield (G-13649)

MACHINE TOOL ATTACHMENTS & ACCESS

Allied Machine & Engrg Corp..................... C 330 343-4283
 Dover (G-6807)
Carbide Probes Inc.................................. E 937 429-9123
 Beavercreek (G-1042)
D C Morrison Company Inc........................ E 859 581-7511
 Cincinnati (G-2812)
Frecon Technologies Inc........................... F 513 874-8981
 West Chester (G-15432)
Positrol Inc... E 513 272-0500
 Cincinnati (G-3267)
Retention Knob Supply & Mfg Co................ F 937 686-6405
 Huntsville (G-8624)
Riten Industries Incorporated..................... E 740 335-5353
 Wshngtn Ct Hs (G-16240)
Te-Co Inc... F 937 836-0961
 Union (G-14775)
Te-Co Manufacturing LLC.......................... D 937 836-0961
 Englewood (G-7244)

MACHINE TOOLS & ACCESS

Akron Gear & Engineering Inc.................... E 330 773-6608
 Akron (G-34)
Antwerp Tool & Die Inc............................. F 419 258-5271
 Antwerp (G-491)
Apollo Products Inc.................................. F 440 269-8551
 Willoughby (G-15880)
B & R Machine Co.................................... F 216 961-7370
 Cleveland (G-3715)
Bender Engineering Company.................... G 330 938-2355
 Beloit (G-1250)
Big Chief Manufacturing Ltd...................... E 513 934-3888
 Lebanon (G-9064)
Capital Tool Company............................... E 216 661-5750
 Cleveland (G-3787)
Coldwater Machine Company LLC............... C 419 678-4877
 Coldwater (G-4985)
Contour Tool Inc...................................... E 440 365-7333
 North Ridgeville (G-11836)
Covert Manufacturing Inc.......................... B 419 468-1761
 Galion (G-7868)
Dayton Progress Corporation..................... A 937 859-5111
 Dayton (G-6288)
Diamond Products Limited........................ G 440 323-4616
 Elyria (G-7129)
Diamond Products Limited........................ B 440 323-4616
 Elyria (G-7130)
Drt Mfg Co LLC....................................... D 937 297-2670
 Dayton (G-6307)
E & J Demark Inc..................................... E 419 337-5866
 Wauseon (G-15260)
Fischer Special Tooling Corp...................... E 440 951-8411
 Mentor (G-10455)
Gleason Metrology Systems Corp................ E 937 384-8901
 Dayton (G-6353)
Hudson Supply Company Inc..................... E 216 518-3000
 Cleveland (G-4207)
Hyper Tool Company................................ E 440 543-5151
 Chagrin Falls (G-2401)
Johnson Bros Rubber Co Inc...................... E 419 752-4814
 Greenwich (G-8067)
Kalt Manufacturing Company..................... D 440 327-2102
 North Ridgeville (G-11848)
Kiffer Industries Inc.................................. E 216 267-1818
 Cleveland (G-4288)
Kilroy Company...................................... D 440 951-8700
 Cleveland (G-4289)
Kongsberg Prcsion Cntng Systems.............. E 937 800-2169
 Miamisburg (G-10652)
Lincoln Electric Automtn Inc...................... C 419 678-4877
 Coldwater (G-4996)
Lord Corporation..................................... C 937 278-9431
 Dayton (G-6415)
Luther Machine Inc.................................. G 440 259-5014
 Perry (G-12353)
M & J Tooling Ltd..................................... F 937 951-3527
 Dayton (G-6417)
Matrix Tool & Machine Inc......................... F 440 255-0300
 Mentor (G-10500)
Mdf Tool Corporation............................... F 440 237-2277
 North Royalton (G-11887)
Medway Tool Corp................................... F 937 335-7717
 Troy (G-14597)
Metalex Manufacturing Inc........................ C 513 489-0507
 Blue Ash (G-1437)
Midwest Tool & Engineering Co.................. E
 Dayton (G-6445)
Obars Machine and Tool Company.............. E 419 535-6307
 Toledo (G-14403)
Ohio Broach & Machine Company............... E 440 946-1040
 Willoughby (G-15963)
Ohio Drill & Tool Co................................. E 330 525-7717
 Homeworth (G-8555)
Omwp Company...................................... E 330 453-8438
 Canton (G-2188)
Pemco Inc.. E 216 524-2990
 Cleveland (G-4539)
R T & T Machining Co Inc......................... F 440 974-8479
 Mentor (G-10543)
Rex International USA Inc......................... E 800 321-7950
 Ashtabula (G-659)
Rhgs Company.. G 513 721-6299
 Cincinnati (G-3334)
Ridge Tool Manufacturing Co..................... E 440 323-5581
 Elyria (G-7203)
Rol - Tech Inc... F 214 905-8050
 Fort Loramie (G-7606)
Setco Industries Inc................................. E 513 941-5110
 Cincinnati (G-3385)
Shl Liquidation Medina Inc........................ C
 Valley City (G-14895)
Skidmore-Wilhelm Mfg Company................ F 216 481-4774
 Solon (G-13422)
SL Endmills Inc....................................... F 513 851-6363
 West Chester (G-15586)
Sorbothane Inc.. E 330 678-9444
 Kent (G-8866)
Spectrum Machine Inc.............................. F 330 626-3666
 Streetsboro (G-13793)
Stanley Bittinger..................................... G 740 942-4302
 Cadiz (G-1904)
Starrett Communications Inc..................... G 614 798-0606
 Dublin (G-6946)
STC International Co Ltd........................... G 561 308-6002
 Lebanon (G-9112)
Sumitomo Elc Carbide Mfg Inc................... F 440 354-0600
 Grand River (G-8013)
Superion Inc... E 937 374-0033
 Xenia (G-16274)
Supplier Inspection Svcs Inc...................... F 877 263-7097
 Dayton (G-6600)
Technidrill Systems Inc............................. E 330 678-9980
 Kent (G-8872)
Troyke Manufacturing Company.................. F 513 769-4242
 Cincinnati (G-3467)
Wise Edge LLC.. G 330 208-0889
 Akron (G-376)
X-Press Tool Inc...................................... F 330 225-8748
 Brunswick (G-1802)

MACHINE TOOLS, METAL CUTTING: Drilling

Cincinnati Gilbert Mch Tl LLC.................... F 513 541-4815
 Cincinnati (G-2752)

MACHINE TOOLS, METAL CUTTING: Drilling & Boring

Barbco Inc... E 330 488-9400
 East Canton (G-6978)
Bor-It Mfg Co Inc..................................... E 419 289-6639
 Ashland (G-558)
Leland-Gifford Inc.................................... G 330 785-9730
 Akron (G-219)
Technidrill Systems Inc............................. E 330 678-9980
 Kent (G-8872)

MACHINE TOOLS, METAL CUTTING: Exotic, Including Explosive

C M M S - Re LLC.................................... F 513 489-5111
 Blue Ash (G-1375)
Fischer Special Tooling Corp...................... E 440 951-8411
 Mentor (G-10455)
National Machine Tool Company................. G 513 541-6682
 Cincinnati (G-3180)

MACHINE TOOLS, METAL CUTTING: Home Workshop

H & D Steel Service Inc............................ E 800 666-3390
 North Royalton (G-11878)

MACHINE TOOLS, METAL CUTTING: Numerically Controlled

Masters Prcision Machining Inc.................. F 330 419-1933
 Kent (G-8833)

MACHINE TOOLS, METAL CUTTING: Pipe Cutting & Threading

Rex International USA Inc......................... E 800 321-7950
 Ashtabula (G-659)
Ridge Tool Company................................ A 440 323-5581
 Elyria (G-7202)

MACHINE TOOLS, METAL CUTTING: Plasma Process

Cutting Systems Inc................................. F 216 928-0500
 Cleveland (G-3929)
Dbcr Inc.. E 330 920-1900
 Cuyahoga Falls (G-6078)

MACHINE TOOLS, METAL CUTTING: Tool Replacement & Rpr Parts

MACHINE TOOLS, METAL CUTTING: Tool Replacement & Rpr Parts

Cardinal Builders Inc .... E 614 237-1000
  Columbus (G-5236)
Drake Manufacturing Services Co .... D 330 847-7291
  Warren (G-15164)
Eagle Machinery & Supply Inc .... E 330 852-1300
  Sugarcreek (G-13924)
J-C-R Tech Inc .... F 937 783-2296
  Blanchester (G-1351)
Jrp Solutions Llc .... G 330 825-5989
  Norton (G-11946)
More Manufacturing LLC .... F 937 233-3898
  Tipp City (G-14142)
Ravana Industries Inc .... G 330 536-4015
  Lowellville (G-9518)

MACHINE TOOLS, METAL CUTTING: Vertical Turning & Boring

Axxess LLC .... G 330 861-0911
  Barberton (G-856)

MACHINE TOOLS, METAL FORMING: Bending

Addition Manufacturing Tech .... C 513 228-7000
  Lebanon (G-9059)
American Fluid Power Inc .... G 877 223-8742
  Elyria (G-7107)
Bendco Machine & Tool Inc .... F 419 628-3802
  Minster (G-11048)
K & L Tool Inc .... E 419 258-2086
  Antwerp (G-493)
Pines Manufacturing Inc .... E 440 835-5553
  Westlake (G-15775)
Ready Technology Inc .... F 937 866-7200
  Dayton (G-6544)

MACHINE TOOLS, METAL FORMING: Die Casting & Extruding

Tfi Manufacturing LLC .... G 440 290-9411
  Mentor (G-10575)

MACHINE TOOLS, METAL FORMING: Magnetic Forming

Green Corp Magnetic Inc .... F 614 801-4000
  Grove City (G-8096)

MACHINE TOOLS, METAL FORMING: Marking

Monode Marking Products Inc .... F 419 929-0346
  New London (G-11464)
Monode Marking Products Inc .... E 440 975-8802
  Mentor (G-10506)
Monode Steel Stamp Inc .... F 440 975-8802
  Mentor (G-10507)

MACHINE TOOLS, METAL FORMING: Mechanical, Pneumatic Or Hyd

Apeks LLC .... E 740 809-1174
  Johnstown (G-8769)
Compass Systems & Sales LLC .... D 330 733-2111
  Norton (G-11940)
Recycling Eqp Solutions Corp .... G 330 920-1500
  Cuyahoga Falls (G-6113)

MACHINE TOOLS, METAL FORMING: Pressing

Technical Machine Products Inc .... F
  Cleveland (G-4773)

MACHINE TOOLS, METAL FORMING: Rebuilt

Advanced Tech Utilization Co .... F 440 238-3770
  Strongsville (G-13802)

MACHINE TOOLS: Metal Cutting

Acro Tool & Die Company .... E 330 773-5173
  Akron (G-17)
Advanced Innovative Mfg Inc .... D 330 562-2468
  Aurora (G-705)
Advetech Inc .... E 330 533-2227
  Canfield (G-1995)
Alcon Tool Co Ltd .... G 330 773-9171
  Akron (G-50)
Alcon Tool Company .... E 330 773-9171
  Akron (G-51)
Arch Cutting Tls - Mentor LLC .... G 440 350-9393
  Mentor (G-10422)
Barth Industries Co LLC .... E 216 267-1950
  Cleveland (G-3722)
Beverly Dove Inc .... G 740 495-5200
  New Holland (G-11446)
Butech Inc .... C 330 337-0000
  Salem (G-12978)
Butech Inc .... D 330 337-0000
  Salem (G-12979)
Callahan Cutting Tools Inc .... G 614 294-1649
  Columbus (G-5227)
Carter Manufacturing Co Inc .... E 513 398-7303
  Mason (G-9968)
Channel Products Inc .... D 440 423-0113
  Solon (G-13328)
Chart-Tech Tool Inc .... E 937 667-3543
  Tipp City (G-14129)
Cincinnati Mine Machinery Co .... D 513 522-7777
  Cincinnati (G-2755)
Cincinnati Radiator Inc .... F 513 874-5555
  Hamilton (G-8193)
Commercial Grinding Svcs Inc .... E 330 273-5040
  Medina (G-10311)
Competetive Carbide Inc .... E 440 350-9393
  Madison (G-9590)
Criterion Tool & Die Inc .... E 216 267-1733
  Brookpark (G-1708)
Dayton Machine Tool Company .... E 937 222-6444
  Dayton (G-6282)
Desmond-Stephan Mfgcompany .... E 937 653-7181
  Urbana (G-14829)
Dixie Machinery Inc .... F 513 360-0091
  Monroe (G-11103)
Dmg Mori .... G 513 808-4842
  Cincinnati (G-2835)
Dmg Mori Usa Inc .... F 440 546-7088
  West Chester (G-15414)
Elliott Tool Technologies Ltd .... D 937 253-6133
  Dayton (G-6318)
Esi-Extrusion Services Inc .... E 330 374-3388
  Akron (G-143)
Falcon Industries Inc .... E 330 723-0099
  Medina (G-10322)
Falcon Tool & Machine Inc .... G 937 534-9999
  Dayton (G-6328)
Frazier Machine and Prod Inc .... E 419 874-7321
  Perrysburg (G-12383)
General Electric Company .... C 513 341-0214
  West Chester (G-15439)
Genex Tool and Die Inc .... F 330 788-2466
  Youngstown (G-16367)
George A Mitchell Company .... E 330 758-5777
  Youngstown (G-16368)
Glassline Corporation .... E 419 666-9712
  Perrysburg (G-2385)
Global TBM Company .... C 440 248-3303
  Solon (G-1335)
Glt Inc .... F 937 237-0055
  Dayton (G-635)
Hammer Jammer LLC .... G 937 549-4062
  Manchester (G-617)
Herco Inc .... F 740 498-5181
  Newcomerstown (G-11645)
Houston Machine Products Inc .... E 937 322-8022
  Springfield (G-1580)
Hyper Tool Company .... E 440 543-5151
  Chagrin Falls (G-2401)
Industrial Paper Shredders Inc .... F 888 637-4733
  North Lima (G-1806)
Interstate Tool Corporation .... E 216 671-1077
  Cleveland (G-434)
J & S Tool Corporation .... F 216 676-8330
  Cleveland (G-433)
K L M Manufacturing Company .... G 740 666-5171
  Ostrander (G-1274)
Ken Emerick Machine Products .... E 440 834-4501
  Burton (G-1883)
Kilroy Company .... D 440 951-8700
  Cleveland (G-429)
Lahm-Trosper Inc .... E 937 252-8791
  Dayton (G-6401)
Levan Enterprises Inc .... E 330 923-9797
  Stow (G-13706)
Lincoln Electric Automtn Inc .... E 614 471-5926
  Columbus (G-557)
Lower Investments LLC .... G 765 825-4151
  Mason (G-10022)
Makino .... B 513 573-7200
  Mason (G-10024)
Martindale Electric Company .... E 216 521-8567
  Cleveland (G-436)
Max - Pro Tools Inc .... F 800 456-0931
  Cleveland (G-435)
Melin Tool Company Inc .... D 216 362-4200
  Cleveland (G-432)
Michael Byrne Manufacturing Co Inc ...... E 419 525-1214
  Mansfield (G-969)
Midwest Knife Grinding Inc .... F 330 854-1030
  Canal Fulton (G-273)
Milacron Marketing Company LLC .... D 513 536-2000
  Batavia (G-936)
Monaghan & Associates Inc .... F 937 253-7706
  Dayton (G-6456)
Mrd Solutions LLC .... F 440 942-6969
  Eastlake (G-7043)
Nesco Inc .... F 440 461-6000
  Cleveland (G-444)
Northwood Industries Inc .... F 419 666-2100
  Perrysburg (G-1204)
Obars Machine and Tool Company .... E 419 535-6307
  Toledo (G-14403)
Page Slotting Saw Co Inc .... F 419 476-7475
  Toledo (G-14428)
Peerless Saw Company .... E 614 836-5790
  Groveport (G-815)
Phillips Manufacturing Co .... D 330 652-4335
  Niles (G-11682)
Portage Machine Concepts Inc .... F 330 628-2343
  Akron (G-282)
Rafter Equipment Corporation .... E 440 572-3700
  Strongsville (G-1371)

PRODUCT SECTION

MACHINERY & EQPT, INDL, WHOLESALE: Heat Exchange

Raymath Company..................................C 937 335-1860
  Troy *(G-14604)*

Reliable Products Co...........................G 419 394-5854
  Saint Marys *(G-12966)*

Ridge Tool Company............................D 740 432-8782
  Cambridge *(G-1951)*

Ridge Tool Company............................D 440 329-4737
  Elyria *(G-7201)*

Ridge Tool Manufacturing Co..............E 440 323-5581
  Elyria *(G-7203)*

Rimrock Corporation............................E 614 471-5926
  Columbus *(G-5723)*

Rimrock Holdings Corporation.............C 614 471-5926
  Columbus *(G-5724)*

Roto Tech Inc..F 937 859-8503
  Moraine *(G-11209)*

Sinico Mtm US Inc................................G 216 264-8344
  Middleburg Heights *(G-10727)*

Specialty Metals Proc Inc....................E 330 656-2767
  Hudson *(G-8614)*

Stadco Inc...E 937 878-0911
  Fairborn *(G-7322)*

STC International Co Ltd.....................G 561 308-6002
  Lebanon *(G-9112)*

Sumitomo Elc Carbide Mfg Inc...........F 440 354-0600
  Grand River *(G-8013)*

Superion Inc...E 937 374-0033
  Xenia *(G-16274)*

The Vulcan Tool Company..................G 937 253-6194
  Dayton *(G-6620)*

Tooling Connection Inc........................G 419 594-3339
  Oakwood *(G-12034)*

Tykma Inc..D 877 318-9562
  Chillicothe *(G-2540)*

U S Alloy Die Corp................................F 216 749-9700
  Cleveland *(G-4842)*

Updike Supply Company......................E 937 482-4000
  Huber Heights *(G-8580)*

Uvonics Co..F 614 458-1163
  Columbus *(G-5852)*

Walter Grinders Inc..............................F 937 859-1975
  Miamisburg *(G-10700)*

West Ohio Tool Co................................F 937 842-6688
  Russells Point *(G-12879)*

Willow Tool & Machining Ltd..............F 440 572-2288
  Strongsville *(G-13896)*

Wise Edge LLC.....................................G 330 208-0889
  Akron *(G-376)*

Wonder Machine Services Inc............E 440 937-7500
  Avon *(G-792)*

Zagar Inc...E 216 731-0500
  Cleveland *(G-4931)*

MACHINE TOOLS: Metal Forming

Anderson & Vreeland Inc....................D 419 636-5002
  Bryan *(G-1807)*

Barth Industries Co LLC.....................E 216 267-1950
  Cleveland *(G-3722)*

Brilex Industries Inc............................D 330 744-1114
  Youngstown *(G-16327)*

Brilex Industries Inc............................D 330 744-1114
  Youngstown *(G-16328)*

Carnaudmetalbox Machinery USA.....G 740 681-6788
  Lancaster *(G-8999)*

Columbus Water Section Permit........G 614 645-8039
  Columbus *(G-5281)*

D C Morrison Company Inc................E 859 581-7511
  Cincinnati *(G-2812)*

Decked LLC..F 208 806-0251
  Defiance *(G-6675)*

Elliott Tool Technologies Ltd...............D 937 253-6133
  Dayton *(G-6318)*

Exito Manufacturing LLC....................G 937 291-9871
  Beavercreek *(G-1073)*

F & G Tool and Die Co........................G 937 746-3658
  Franklin *(G-7673)*

First Tool Corp.....................................E 937 254-6197
  Dayton *(G-6333)*

Gem City Metal Tech LLC...................E 937 252-8998
  Dayton *(G-6349)*

H&G Legacy Co....................................F 513 921-1075
  Cincinnati *(G-2982)*

High Production Technology LLC.......G 419 599-1511
  Napoleon *(G-11317)*

J & S Tool Corporation.........................F 216 676-8330
  Cleveland *(G-4243)*

Kiraly Tool and Die Inc........................F 330 744-5773
  Youngstown *(G-16386)*

Levan Enterprises Inc.........................E 330 923-9797
  Stow *(G-13706)*

Madison Property Holdings Inc..........E 800 215-3210
  Cincinnati *(G-3124)*

McNeil & Nrm Inc.................................D 330 761-1855
  Akron *(G-240)*

Metal & Wire Products Company........E 330 332-9448
  Salem *(G-13016)*

Rafter Equipment Corporation............E 440 572-3700
  Strongsville *(G-13871)*

Risk Industries LLC.............................D 440 835-5553
  Westlake *(G-15779)*

Ritime Incorporated.............................G 330 273-3443
  Cleveland *(G-4636)*

Semtorq Inc..F 330 487-0600
  Twinsburg *(G-14734)*

Spencer Manufacturing Company Inc..D 330 648-2461
  Spencer *(G-13484)*

Starkey Machinery Inc........................E 419 468-2560
  Galion *(G-7885)*

Stolle Machinery Company LLC.........C 937 497-5400
  Sidney *(G-13291)*

Stover International LLC.....................E 740 363-5251
  Delaware *(G-6753)*

Taylor - Winfield Corporation..............C 330 259-8500
  Hubbard *(G-8571)*

TEC Design & Manufacturing Inc.......F 937 435-2147
  Dayton *(G-6611)*

Terminal Equipment Inds Inc.............G 330 468-0322
  Northfield *(G-11912)*

The Vulcan Tool Company..................G 937 253-6194
  Dayton *(G-6620)*

Trucut Incorporated.............................D 330 938-9806
  Sebring *(G-13127)*

Turner Machine Co..............................F 330 332-5821
  Salem *(G-13035)*

Twist Inc...G 937 675-9581
  Jamestown *(G-8743)*

Twist Inc...C 937 675-9581
  Jamestown *(G-8742)*

Uhrichsville Carbide Inc......................F 740 922-9197
  Uhrichsville *(G-14772)*

Valley Tool & Die Inc...........................D 440 237-0160
  North Royalton *(G-11900)*

MACHINERY & EQPT FINANCE LEASING

Ohio Machinery Co..............................C 440 526-6200
  Broadview Heights *(G-1665)*

MACHINERY & EQPT, AGRICULTURAL, WHOLESALE: Lawn & Garden

Arnold Corporation...............................C 330 225-2600
  Valley City *(G-14861)*

Hawthorne Gardening Company........E 360 883-8846
  Marysville *(G-9913)*

Karl Kuemmerling Inc..........................F
  Massillon *(G-10114)*

MACHINERY & EQPT, INDL, WHOLESALE: Chemical Process

Aldrich Chemical..................................D 937 859-1808
  Miamisburg *(G-10608)*

MACHINERY & EQPT, INDL, WHOLESALE: Conveyor Systems

Alba Manufacturing Inc.......................D 513 874-0551
  Fairfield *(G-7332)*

Digilube Systems Inc..........................F 937 748-2209
  Springboro *(G-13499)*

Logitech Inc...E 614 871-2822
  Grove City *(G-8102)*

Midwest Conveyor Products Inc.........E 419 281-1235
  Ashland *(G-592)*

Pomacon Inc..F 330 273-1576
  Brunswick *(G-1781)*

MACHINERY & EQPT, INDL, WHOLESALE: Cranes

Expert Crane Inc..................................E 216 451-9900
  Wellington *(G-15307)*

Hiab USA Inc..D 419 482-6000
  Perrysburg *(G-12388)*

Rnm Holdings Inc................................F 614 444-5556
  Columbus *(G-5726)*

Rnm Holdings Inc................................F 419 867-8712
  Holland *(G-8528)*

Venco Venturo Industries LLC............E 513 772-8448
  Cincinnati *(G-3490)*

MACHINERY & EQPT, INDL, WHOLESALE: Engines & Parts, Diesel

Industrial Parts Depot LLC.................G 440 237-9164
  North Royalton *(G-11880)*

Martin Diesel Inc..................................E 419 782-9911
  Defiance *(G-6691)*

Western Branch Diesel LLC................F 330 454-8800
  Canton *(G-2267)*

MACHINERY & EQPT, INDL, WHOLESALE: Engs & Parts, Air-Cooled

Power Distributors LLC.......................D 614 876-3533
  Columbus *(G-5684)*

MACHINERY & EQPT, INDL, WHOLESALE: Engs/Transportation Eqpt

Bulk Carriers Service Inc....................F 330 339-3333
  New Philadelphia *(G-11490)*

MACHINERY & EQPT, INDL, WHOLESALE: Fans

National Tool & Equipment Inc...........F 330 629-8665
  Youngstown *(G-16403)*

MACHINERY & EQPT, INDL, WHOLESALE: Food Product Manufacturng

Chemineer Inc......................................C 937 454-3200
  Dayton *(G-6254)*

Marengo Fabricated Steel Ltd............F 800 919-2652
  Cardington *(G-2276)*

MACHINERY & EQPT, INDL, WHOLESALE: Heat Exchange

MACHINERY & EQPT, INDL, WHOLESALE: Heat Exchange

PRODUCT SECTION

Gerow Equipment Company Inc............ G 216 383-8900
 Cleveland (G-4122)

Rayhaven Group Inc........................... G 330 659-3183
 Richfield (G-12795)

MACHINERY & EQPT, INDL, WHOLESALE: Hydraulic Systems

Breaker Technology Inc...................... F 440 248-7168
 Solon (G-13324)

Control Line Equipment Inc................ F 216 433-7766
 Cleveland (G-3903)

Depot Direct Inc................................. E 419 661-1233
 Perrysburg (G-12375)

Eaton Corporation............................... F 216 523-5000
 Willoughby (G-15916)

Fluid Power Solutions LLC................. G 614 777-8954
 Hilliard (G-8412)

Hydraulic Manifolds USA LLC............ E 973 728-1214
 Stow (G-13702)

Hydraulic Parts Store Inc.................... E 330 364-6667
 New Philadelphia (G-11505)

Hydro Supply Co................................. F 740 454-3842
 Zanesville (G-16537)

Ic-Fluid Power Inc............................... F 419 661-8811
 Rossford (G-12866)

Jay Dee Service Corporation.............. G 330 425-1546
 Macedonia (G-9558)

Lubrisource Inc.................................... F 937 432-9292
 Middletown (G-10836)

Mid-State Sales Inc............................. D 614 864-1811
 Columbus (G-5564)

Ohio Hydraulics Inc............................ E 513 771-2590
 Cincinnati (G-3215)

Parker-Hannifin Corporation............... G 216 433-1795
 Cleveland (G-4531)

R & M Fluid Power Inc........................ E 330 758-2766
 Youngstown (G-16425)

Robeck Fluid Power Co...................... D 330 562-1140
 Aurora (G-734)

Rumpke Transportation Co LLC......... F 513 851-0122
 Cincinnati (G-3355)

System Seals Inc................................. E 216 220-1800
 Brecksville (G-1632)

System Seals Inc................................. E 440 735-0200
 Cleveland (G-4763)

Taiyo America Inc............................... F 419 300-8811
 Saint Marys (G-12968)

MACHINERY & EQPT, INDL, WHOLESALE: Indl Machine Parts

Transducers Direct Llc....................... F 513 247-0601
 Cincinnati (G-3462)

MACHINERY & EQPT, INDL, WHOLESALE: Instruments & Cntrl Eqpt

Fcx Performance Inc........................... E 614 253-1996
 Columbus (G-5373)

Instrumentors Inc................................. G 440 238-3430
 Strongsville (G-13846)

South Shore Controls Inc.................... E 440 259-2500
 Mentor (G-10557)

MACHINERY & EQPT, INDL, WHOLESALE: Lift Trucks & Parts

Fastener Industries Inc........................ E 440 891-2031
 Berea (G-1279)

Fastener Industries Inc........................ G 440 243-0034
 Berea (G-1280)

Joseph Industries Inc........................... D 330 528-0091
 Streetsboro (G-13776)

Suspension Technology Inc................ F 330 458-3058
 Canton (G-2240)

MACHINERY & EQPT, INDL, WHOLESALE: Machine Tools & Access

Anthe Machine Works Inc................... G 859 431-1035
 Cincinnati (G-2552)

Imco Carbide Tool Inc......................... D 419 661-6313
 Perrysburg (G-12390)

Interstate Tool Corporation................. E 216 671-1077
 Cleveland (G-4234)

J & S Tool Corporation........................ F 216 676-8330
 Cleveland (G-4243)

Jergens Inc... C 216 486-5540
 Cleveland (G-4253)

Jis Distribution LLC............................ F 216 706-6552
 Cleveland (G-4256)

Neff Machinery and Supplies.............. F 740 454-0128
 Zanesville (G-16547)

Tool Systems Incorporated................. F 440 461-6363
 Cleveland (G-4801)

Wolf Machine Company...................... E 513 791-5194
 Blue Ash (G-1493)

MACHINERY & EQPT, INDL, WHOLESALE: Packaging

Alfons Haar Inc.................................... E 937 560-2031
 Springboro (G-13495)

Bollin & Sons Inc................................. E 419 693-6573
 Toledo (G-14216)

Millwood Inc.. E 513 860-4567
 West Chester (G-15464)

PE Usa LLC... F 513 771-7374
 Cincinnati (G-3244)

Toga-Pak Inc.. E 937 294-7311
 Dayton (G-6626)

MACHINERY & EQPT, INDL, WHOLESALE: Paint Spray

Kecamm LLC....................................... G 330 527-2918
 Garrettsville (G-7918)

MACHINERY & EQPT, INDL, WHOLESALE: Paper Manufacturing

Oak View Enterprises Inc.................... E 513 860-4446
 Bucyrus (G-1864)

MACHINERY & EQPT, INDL, WHOLESALE: Petroleum Industry

Stanwade Metal Products Inc............. E 330 772-2421
 Hartford (G-8298)

MACHINERY & EQPT, INDL, WHOLESALE: Processing & Packaging

Ampac Packaging LLC........................ C 513 671-1777
 Cincinnati (G-2623)

Kingsly Compression Inc.................... G 740 439-0772
 Cambridge (G-1939)

Proampac Orlando Inc......................... F 513 671-1777
 Cincinnati (G-3279)

MACHINERY & EQPT, INDL, WHOLESALE: Pulp Manufacturing, Wood

Advanced Green Tech Inc................... G 614 397-8130
 Plain City (G-12560)

MACHINERY & EQPT, INDL, WHOLESALE: Recycling

Axion International Inc........................ G 740 452-2500
 Zanesville (G-16502)

MACHINERY & EQPT, INDL, WHOLESALE: Safety Eqpt

A & A Safety Inc.................................. F 937 567-9781
 Beavercreek (G-1068)

A & A Safety Inc.................................. E 513 943-6100
 Amelia (G-447)

American Rescue Technology Inc...... F 937 293-6240
 Dayton (G-6203)

Cintas Corporation.............................. D 513 631-5750
 Cincinnati (G-2770)

Cintas Corporation.............................. A 513 459-1200
 Cincinnati (G-2769)

Cintas Corporation No 2..................... D 330 966-7800
 Canton (G-2074)

Impact Products LLC.......................... D 419 841-2891
 Toledo (G-14328)

Paul Peterson Company...................... F 614 486-4375
 Columbus (G-5660)

MACHINERY & EQPT, INDL, WHOLESALE: Trailers, Indl

Martin Allen Trailer LLC..................... F 330 942-0217
 Akron (G-238)

MACHINERY & EQPT, INDL, WHOLESALE: Water Pumps

Hawthorne Hydroponics LLC.............. F 888 478-6544
 Marysville (G-9914)

MACHINERY & EQPT, WHOLESALE: Construction, General

F & M Mafco Inc.................................. C 513 367-2151
 Harrison (G-8273)

Npk Construction Equipment Inc....... D 440 232-7900
 Bedford (G-1145)

Ohio Machinery Co............................. C 440 526-6200
 Broadview Heights (G-1665)

Thirion Brothers Eqp Co LLC............. G 440 357-8004
 Painesville (G-12271)

West Equipment Company Inc.......... G 419 698-1601
 Toledo (G-14522)

MACHINERY & EQPT, WHOLESALE: Oil Field Eqpt

Global Energy Partners LLC............... E 419 756-8027
 Mansfield (G-9660)

Petrox Inc... F 330 653-5526
 Streetsboro (G-13784)

MACHINERY & EQPT, WHOLESALE: Road Construction & Maintenance

Terry Asphalt Materials Inc................. E 513 874-6192
 Hamilton (G-8247)

MACHINERY & EQPT: Electroplating

Corrotec Inc... E 937 325-3585
 Springfield (G-13547)

Liquid Development Company........... G 216 641-9366
 Independence (G-8671)

Universal Rack & Eqp Co Inc............. D 330 963-6776
 Twinsburg (G-14751)

MACHINERY & EQPT: Farm

American Baler Co .... D 419 483-5790
  Bellevue *(G-1222)*
Buckeye Tractor Corporation .... G 419 659-2162
  Columbus Grove *(G-5896)*
Cailin Development LLC .... F 216 408-6261
  Cleveland *(G-3781)*
Country Manufacturing Inc .... F 740 694-9926
  Fredericktown *(G-7741)*
Creamer Metal Products Inc .... F 740 852-1752
  London *(G-9385)*
Empire Plow Company Inc .... E 216 641-2290
  Berea *(G-1276)*
Fecon LLC .... E 513 696-4430
  Lebanon *(G-9075)*
Fecon LLC .... D 513 696-4430
  Lebanon *(G-9076)*
Field Gymmy Inc .... G 419 538-6511
  Glandorf *(G-7978)*
Finn Corporation .... E 513 874-2818
  West Chester *(G-15429)*
Fremont Plastic Products Inc .... C 419 332-6407
  Fremont *(G-7783)*
H & S Company Inc .... E 419 394-4444
  Celina *(G-2335)*
Hog Slat Incorporated .... E 937 968-3890
  Union City *(G-14779)*
Hord Elevator LLC .... C 419 562-1198
  Edison *(G-7084)*
Intertec Corporation .... F 419 537-9711
  Toledo *(G-14335)*
J & M Manufacturing Co Inc .... C 419 375-2376
  Fort Recovery *(G-7620)*
Kts Equipment Inc .... E 440 647-2015
  Wellington *(G-15316)*
Ley Industries Inc .... G 419 238-6742
  Van Wert *(G-14922)*
M & S AG Solutions LLC .... F 419 598-8675
  Napoleon *(G-11323)*
Norden Mfg LLC .... E 440 693-4630
  North Bloomfield *(G-11712)*
Ntech Industries Inc .... E 707 467-3747
  Dayton *(G-6481)*
Ohio Machinery Co .... C 440 526-6200
  Broadview Heights *(G-1665)*
Pax Steel Products Inc .... G 419 678-1481
  Coldwater *(G-4999)*
Precision Assemblies Inc .... F 330 549-2630
  North Lima *(G-11809)*
Puehler Agco Inc .... G 419 388-6614
  Wauseon *(G-15273)*
Randall Brothers LLC .... G 419 395-1764
  Holgate *(G-8491)*
Reinke Company Inc .... G 614 570-2578
  Columbus *(G-5717)*
Safe-Grain Inc .... G 513 398-2500
  Dayton *(G-6557)*
Stephens Pipe & Steel LLC .... C 740 869-2257
  Mount Sterling *(G-11257)*
Tractor Supply Company .... G 740 963-8023
  Pataskala *(G-12310)*
Unverferth Mfg Co Inc .... C 419 532-3121
  Kalida *(G-8787)*

MACHINERY & EQPT: Liquid Automation

Dosmatic USA Inc .... F 972 245-9765
  Cincinnati *(G-2837)*
Fluid Automation Inc .... E 248 912-1970
  North Canton *(G-11728)*
Nov Inc .... D 937 454-3200
  Dayton *(G-6479)*

Nutro Corporation .... D 440 572-3800
  Strongsville *(G-13860)*

MACHINERY, CALCULATING: Calculators & Adding

Ganymede Technologies Corp .... G 419 562-5522
  Bucyrus *(G-1860)*

MACHINERY, EQPT & SUPPLIES: Parking Facility

Amano Cincinnati Incorporated .... F 513 697-9000
  Loveland *(G-9474)*
City of Cleveland .... B 216 664-2711
  Cleveland *(G-3823)*
Innoplast Inc .... F 440 543-8660
  Cleveland *(G-4227)*
Integrity Parking LLC .... F 440 543-4123
  Aurora *(G-720)*
Tiba LLC .... E 614 328-2040
  Columbus *(G-5826)*

MACHINERY, FOOD PRDTS: Beverage

Drink Modern Technologies LLC .... G 216 577-1536
  Cleveland *(G-3973)*
Mojonnier Usa LLC .... F 844 665-6664
  Streetsboro *(G-13780)*

MACHINERY, FOOD PRDTS: Cutting, Chopping, Grinding, Mixing

Lem Products Holding LLC .... E 513 202-1188
  West Chester *(G-15457)*

MACHINERY, FOOD PRDTS: Food Processing, Smokers

Frost Engineering Inc .... E 513 541-6330
  Cincinnati *(G-2923)*
Npk LLC .... G 740 927-2801
  New Albany *(G-11385)*

MACHINERY, FOOD PRDTS: Oilseed Crushing & Extracting

Simmons Feed & Supply LLC .... E 800 754-1228
  Salem *(G-13031)*

MACHINERY, FOOD PRDTS: Ovens, Bakery

Garland Commercial Industries LLC ...... E 800 338-2204
  Cleveland *(G-4103)*
Lincoln Foodservice Products LLC .... B 260 459-8200
  Cleveland *(G-4326)*
Total Baking Solutions LLC .... E
  Wilmington *(G-16060)*

MACHINERY, FOOD PRDTS: Processing, Poultry

Prime Equipment Group LLC .... D 614 253-8590
  Columbus *(G-5690)*

MACHINERY, METALWORKING: Coiling

Formtek Inc .... D 216 292-4460
  Cleveland *(G-4084)*
Kent Corporation .... E 440 582-3400
  North Royalton *(G-11881)*
Perfecto Industries Inc .... E 937 778-1900
  Piqua *(G-12542)*

MACHINERY, OFFICE: Paper Handling

Ricoh Usa Inc .... F 412 281-6700
  Cleveland *(G-4634)*

Symatic Inc .... F 330 225-1510
  Medina *(G-10381)*

MACHINERY, PACKAGING: Canning, Food

Scanacon Incorporated .... G 330 877-7600
  Hartville *(G-8306)*

MACHINERY, PACKAGING: Packing & Wrapping

Audion Automation Ltd .... F 216 267-1911
  Berea *(G-1266)*

MACHINERY, PACKAGING: Vacuum

Precision Replacement LLC .... G 330 908-0410
  Macedonia *(G-9569)*

MACHINERY, PAPER INDUSTRY: Converting, Die Cutting & Stampng

Jen-Coat Inc .... C 513 671-1777
  Cincinnati *(G-3040)*
Nilpeter Usa Inc .... C 513 489-4400
  Cincinnati *(G-3198)*
Spectex LLC .... F 603 330-3334
  Cincinnati *(G-3406)*

MACHINERY, PAPER INDUSTRY: Paper Mill, Plating, Etc

Miami Machine Corporation .... F 513 863-6707
  Overpeck *(G-12209)*
Press Technology & Mfg Inc .... G 937 327-0755
  Springfield *(G-13622)*

MACHINERY, PAPER INDUSTRY: Pulp Mill

Andritz Inc .... D 513 677-5620
  Loveland *(G-9476)*
Fq Sale Inc .... E
  Springfield *(G-13568)*
French Oil Mill Machinery Co .... D 937 773-3420
  Piqua *(G-12517)*

MACHINERY, PRINTING TRADES: Plates

Dynamic Dies Inc .... E 419 865-0249
  Holland *(G-8507)*
E C Shaw Company of Ohio .... E 513 721-6334
  Cincinnati *(G-2848)*
Flexoplate Inc .... F 513 489-0433
  Blue Ash *(G-1395)*
Flexotech Graphics Inc .... F 330 929-4743
  Stow *(G-13699)*

MACHINERY, SEWING: Sewing & Hat & Zipper Making

Production Design Services Inc .... D 937 866-3377
  Dayton *(G-6529)*
Ray Muro Inc .... G 440 984-8845
  Oberlin *(G-12056)*
Velocys Inc .... D 614 733-3300
  Plain City *(G-12599)*

MACHINERY, TEXTILE: Printing

Alley Cat Designs Inc .... G 937 291-8803
  Dayton *(G-6193)*

MACHINERY: Ammunition & Explosives Loading

Omco Usa LLC .... F 740 588-1722
  Zanesville *(G-16550)*
Roberts Machine Products LLC .... F 937 682-4015
  Rushsylvania *(G-12875)*

MACHINERY: Automotive Related

MACHINERY: Automotive Related

Company		Phone
Autotool Inc	E	614 733-0222
Plain City (G-12563)		
Cornerstone Wauseon Inc	C	419 337-0940
Wauseon (G-15259)		
Dengensha America Corporation	F	440 439-8081
Bedford (G-1115)		
Designetics Inc	D	419 866-0700
Holland (G-8504)		
Ganzcorp Investments Inc	D	330 963-5400
Twinsburg (G-14664)		
M W Solutions LLC	F	419 782-1611
Defiance (G-6689)		
Manufctring Bus Dev Sltons LLC	D	419 294-1313
Findlay (G-7530)		
Modular Assmbly Innvations LLC	E	614 389-4860
Dublin (G-6912)		
Process Development Corp	E	937 890-3388
Dayton (G-6527)		
Steelastic Company LLC	E	330 633-0505
Cuyahoga Falls (G-6119)		
Toney Tool Manufacturing Inc		937 890-8535
Dayton (G-6627)		

MACHINERY: Concrete Prdts

Company		Phone
Ernest Industries Inc	E	937 325-9851
Lowellville (G-9513)		

MACHINERY: Construction

Company		Phone
1062 Technologies Inc	G	303 453-9251
Youngstown (G-16295)		
Allied Consolidated Inds Inc	C	330 744-0808
Youngstown (G-16307)		
Altec Industries	G	419 289-6066
Ashland (G-550)		
Altec Industries Inc	G	614 295-4895
Columbus (G-5117)		
American Alloy Corporation	E	216 642-9638
Cleveland (G-3649)		
Ballinger Industries Inc	F	419 422-4533
Findlay (G-7482)		
Basetek LLC		877 712-2273
Middlefield (G-10733)		
Caterpillar Industrial Inc	E	440 247-8484
Chagrin Falls (G-2369)		
Chemineer Inc	C	937 454-3200
Dayton (G-6254)		
Cityscapes International Inc	E	614 850-2540
Hilliard (G-8406)		
Crane Pro Services	G	937 525-5555
Springfield (G-13549)		
Curtis Industires	G	216 430-5759
Cleveland (G-3921)		
CW Machine Worx Ltd	F	740 654-5304
Carroll (G-2295)		
DA Precision Products Inc	F	513 459-1113
West Chester (G-15411)		
Desco Corporation	G	614 888-8855
New Albany (G-11378)		
Dragon Products LLC	E	330 345-3968
Wooster (G-16214)		
Dynamic Plastics Inc	G	937 437-7261
New Paris (G-11481)		
E R Advanced Ceramics Inc	E	330 426-9433
East Palestine (G-7004)		
E Z Grout Corporation		740 749-3512
Malta (G-9606)		
Eagle Crusher Co Inc	D	419 562-1183
Bucyrus (G-1858)		
Eagle Crusher Co Inc	D	419 468-2288
Galion (G-7872)		
Enviri Corporation	F	740 387-1150
Marion (G-9851)		
Fecon LLC	D	513 696-4430
Lebanon (G-9076)		
Field Gymmy Inc	G	419 538-6511
Glandorf (G-7978)		
Fives St Corp	E	234 217-9070
Wadsworth (G-15029)		
Gradall Industries Inc	G	540 819-6638
Uhrichsville (G-14766)		
Gradall Industries LLC	C	330 339-2211
New Philadelphia (G-11504)		
Grand Harbor Yacht Sales & Svc	G	440 442-2919
Cleveland (G-4139)		
Hickmans Construction Co LLC	F	866 271-2565
Euclid (G-7273)		
Jlg Industries Inc	E	330 684-0132
Orrville (G-12130)		
Jlg Industries Inc	D	330 684-0200
Orrville (G-12131)		
Jordankelly LLC	F	216 855-8550
Akron (G-197)		
Kaffenbarger Truck Eqp Co	E	513 772-6800
Cincinnati (G-3056)		
Kubota Tractor Corporation	E	614 835-3800
Groveport (G-8150)		
Kundel Industries Inc	E	330 469-6147
Vienna (G-14996)		
Meyer Products LLC	E	216 486-1313
Cleveland (G-4397)		
Msk Trencher Mfg Inc	F	419 394-4444
Celina (G-2341)		
Murphy Tractor & Eqp Co Inc	G	330 220-4999
Brunswick (G-1774)		
Murphy Tractor & Eqp Co Inc	G	330 477-9304
Canton (G-2169)		
Murphy Tractor & Eqp Co Inc	G	614 876-1141
Columbus (G-5585)		
Murphy Tractor & Eqp Co Inc	G	419 221-3666
Lima (G-9272)		
Murphy Tractor & Eqp Co Inc	G	937 898-4198
Vandalia (G-14954)		
Norris Manufacturing LLC	F	330 602-5005
Dover (G-6838)		
Nov Inc	D	937 454-3200
Dayton (G-6479)		
Npk Construction Equipment Inc	D	440 232-7900
Bedford (G-1145)		
Otc Industrial Technologies	F	800 837-6827
Columbus (G-5646)		
Pace Consolidated Inc	D	440 942-1234
Willoughby (G-15967)		
Pace Engineering Inc	C	440 942-1234
Willoughby (G-15968)		
Paus North America Inc	G	775 778-5980
Solon (G-13402)		
Pubco Corporation	D	216 881-5300
Cleveland (G-4597)		
Roadsafe Traffic Systems Inc	G	614 274-9782
Columbus (G-5728)		
Sandvik Rock Proc Sltons N AME	F	216 431-2600
Cleveland (G-4671)		
Scott Port-A-Fold Inc	F	419 748-8880
Napoleon (G-11334)		
Terex Utilities Inc	F	419 470-8408
Perrysburg (G-12434)		
The Wagner-Smith Company	B	866 338-0398
Moraine (G-11214)		
Thorworks Industries Inc	C	419 626-4375
Sandusky (G-13096)		
Uhrden Inc	E	330 456-0031
Canton (G-2249)		
Werk Brau	G	419 421-4703
Findlay (G-758_)		

MACHINERY: Cryogenic, Industrial

Company		Phone
Chart International Inc	D	440 753-1490
Cleveland (G-3_12)		
Eden Cryogenic LLC	E	614 873-3949
Columbus (G-5_45)		
JC Carter LLC	G	440 569-1818
Richmond Heights (G-12808)		

MACHINERY: Custom

Company		Phone
A & R Machine Co Inc	G	330 832-4631
Massillon (G-10_73)		
Alfons Haar Inc	E	937 560-2031
Springboro (G-_3495)		
Alliance Automation LLC	D	419 238-2520
Van Wert (G-14_06)		
Artisan Equipment Inc	F	740 756-9135
Carroll (G-2294)		
Astro Technical Services Inc	E	
Warren (G-1514_)		
Autotec Corporation	E	419 885-2529
Toledo (G-1420_)		
Berran Industrial Group Inc	E	330 253-5800
Akron (G-83)		
Bonnot Company	E	330 896-6544
Akron (G-91)		
Boss Industries Inc	F	330 273-2266
Valley City (G-1_364)		
Bowdil Company	F	800 356-8663
Canton (G-2051)		
Cleveland Jsm Inc	E	440 876-3050
Strongsville (G-1_822)		
East End Welding LLC	C	330 677-6000
Kent (G-8811)		
Enprotech Industrial Tech LLC	E	216 883-3220
Cleveland (G-40_9)		
F & G Tool and Die Co	E	937 294-1405
Moraine (G-1118_)		
Farr Automation Inc	F	419 289-1883
Ashland (G-571)		
Ferry Industries Inc	D	330 920-9200
Stow (G-13698)		
Fluid Quip Custom MA	E	937 324-0662
Springfield (G-13_66)		
Fostoria MT&f Corp	F	419 435-7676
Fostoria (G-7636)		
Fredon Corporation	D	440 951-5200
Mentor (G-10458)		
Gasdorf Tool and Mch Co Inc	E	419 227-0103
Lima (G-9244)		
Global Srcing Support Svcs LLC	G	800 645-2986
Cincinnati (G-295_)		
Hahn Automation Group Us Inc	D	937 886-3232
Miamisburg (G-10_41)		
Heisler Tool Company	F	440 951-2424
Willoughby (G-15_27)		
Herd Manufacturing Inc	E	216 651-4221
Cleveland (G-418_)		
Htec Systems Inc	F	937 438-3010
Dayton (G-6376)		
Inovent Engineering Inc	G	330 468-0019
Macedonia (G-955_)		
Interscope Manufacturing Inc	E	513 423-8866
Middletown (G-10_32)		
Keban Industries Inc	G	216 446-0159
Broadview Heights (G-1659)		
Kiffer Industries Inc	E	216 267-1818
Cleveland (G-428_)		
Kimble Machines Inc	F	419 485-8449
Montpelier (G-111_)		

PRODUCT SECTION
MACHINERY: Pack-Up Assemblies, Wheel Overhaul

Last Arrow Manufacturing LLC............ D 330 683-7777
 Orrville *(G-12134)*
Latanick Equipment Inc........................ E 419 433-2200
 Huron *(G-8638)*
Lightning Mold & Machine Inc............. F 440 593-6460
 Conneaut *(G-5924)*
Logan Machine Company..................... D 330 633-6163
 Akron *(G-223)*
Markwith Tool Company Inc................. F 937 548-6808
 Greenville *(G-8051)*
Massillon Machine & Die Inc............... G 330 833-8913
 Massillon *(G-10122)*
Matrix Tool & Machine Inc.................... E 440 255-0300
 Mentor *(G-10500)*
McNeil & Nrm Inc................................... D 330 761-1855
 Akron *(G-240)*
McNeil & Nrm Intl Inc............................ D 330 253-2525
 Akron *(G-241)*
Metalex Manufacturing Inc.................... C 513 489-0507
 Blue Ash *(G-1437)*
Metro Design Inc................................... E 440 458-4200
 Elyria *(G-7181)*
Michael Byrne Manufacturing Co Inc... E 419 525-1214
 Mansfield *(G-9691)*
Midwest Laser Systems Inc.................. E 419 424-0062
 Alvada *(G-443)*
Modern Machine Development.............. F 937 253-4576
 Dayton *(G-6454)*
Narrow Way Custom Tech Inc............... E 937 743-1611
 Carlisle *(G-2290)*
Neil R Scholl Inc.................................... F 740 653-6593
 Lancaster *(G-9027)*
Odawara Automation Inc....................... E 937 667-8433
 Tipp City *(G-14145)*
Odyssey Machine Company Ltd........... G 419 455-6621
 Perrysburg *(G-12406)*
Path Robotics Inc.................................. D 614 816-1991
 Columbus *(G-5659)*
Path Robotics Inc.................................. D 330 808-2788
 Columbus *(G-5658)*
Perfecto Industries Inc.......................... E 937 778-1900
 Piqua *(G-12542)*
Perry Welding Service Inc..................... F 330 425-2211
 Twinsburg *(G-14714)*
Production Design Services Inc............ D 937 866-3377
 Dayton *(G-6529)*
Projects Designed & Built...................... E 419 726-7400
 Toledo *(G-14443)*
Quality Specialists Inc.......................... G 440 946-9129
 Willoughby *(G-15979)*
R J K Enterprises Inc............................ F 440 257-6018
 Mentor *(G-10542)*
Richmond Machine Co........................... E 419 485-5740
 Montpelier *(G-11142)*
Royalton Industries Inc........................ F 440 748-9900
 Columbia Station *(G-5020)*
RTZ Manufacturing Co........................... G 614 848-8366
 Heath *(G-8330)*
S-P Company Inc................................... D 330 782-5651
 Columbiana *(G-5050)*
Sample Machining Inc........................... E 937 258-3338
 Dayton *(G-6558)*
Sequa Can Machinery Inc..................... E 330 493-0444
 Canton *(G-2221)*
Siebtechnik Tema Inc............................ E 513 489-7811
 Cincinnati *(G-3390)*
Steel Eqp Specialists Inc...................... D 330 823-8260
 Alliance *(G-427)*
Systech Handling Inc............................ F 419 445-8226
 Archbold *(G-547)*
Terydon Inc.. E 330 879-2448
 Navarre *(G-11353)*

Ti Inc.. E 419 332-8484
 Fremont *(G-7815)*
Tru-Bore Machine Co Inc...................... G 330 928-6215
 Cuyahoga Falls *(G-6124)*
Tru-Fab Technology Inc........................ F 440 954-9760
 Willoughby *(G-16009)*

MACHINERY: Electronic Component Making

Azsr Technologies Distr LLC................ G 216 315-8285
 Brookpark *(G-1705)*
Inpower LLC... F 740 548-0965
 Lewis Center *(G-9164)*
Storetek Engineering Inc...................... D 330 294-0678
 Tallmadge *(G-14050)*
Summit Design and Tech Inc................ F 330 733-6662
 Akron *(G-339)*

MACHINERY: Gas Separators

Avc Inc... F 513 458-2600
 Cincinnati *(G-2647)*
H P E International............................... D 330 833-3161
 Massillon *(G-10104)*

MACHINERY: Ice Cream

Heavenly Creamery Inc......................... G 440 593-6080
 Conneaut *(G-5920)*
Norse Dairy Systems LP....................... B 614 294-4931
 Columbus *(G-5601)*

MACHINERY: Metalworking

Addition Manufacturing Tech................ C 513 228-7000
 Lebanon *(G-9059)*
ADS Machinery Corp.............................. D 330 399-3601
 Warren *(G-15134)*
Advance Manufacturing Corp................ E 216 333-1684
 Cleveland *(G-3603)*
Bardons & Oliver Inc............................. C 440 498-5800
 Solon *(G-13316)*
Barth Industries Co LLC........................ E 216 267-1950
 Cleveland *(G-3722)*
Berran Industrial Group Inc.................. E 330 253-5800
 Akron *(G-83)*
Brilex Industries Inc.............................. D 330 744-1114
 Youngstown *(G-16327)*
Brilex Industries Inc.............................. D 330 744-1114
 Youngstown *(G-16328)*
C A Litzler Co Inc................................... E 216 267-8020
 Cleveland *(G-3778)*
Cincinnati Incorporated......................... C 513 367-7100
 Harrison *(G-8269)*
Cline Machine and Automtn Inc............ E 740 474-4237
 Circleville *(G-3545)*
Ctm Integration Incorporated................ E 330 332-1800
 Salem *(G-12988)*
Dayton Machine Tool Company............ E 937 222-6444
 Dayton *(G-6282)*
Esi-Extrusion Services Inc.................... E 330 374-3388
 Akron *(G-143)*
Forrest Machine Pdts Co Ltd................ E 419 589-3774
 Mansfield *(G-9658)*
Gem City Engineering Co...................... C 937 223-5544
 Dayton *(G-6348)*
Gilson Machine & Tool Co Inc............... E 419 592-2911
 Napoleon *(G-11316)*
Glunt Industries Inc.............................. C 330 399-7585
 Warren *(G-15175)*
Hahn Manufacturing Company.............. E 216 391-9300
 Cleveland *(G-4163)*
Heisler Tool Company............................ F 440 951-2424
 Willoughby *(G-15927)*
Holdren Brothers Inc............................. F 937 465-7050
 West Liberty *(G-15622)*

J Horst Manufacturing Co..................... D 330 828-2216
 Dalton *(G-6133)*
Kalt Manufacturing Company................ D 440 327-2102
 North Ridgeville *(G-11848)*
Kilroy Company...................................... D 440 951-8700
 Cleveland *(G-4289)*
Master Marking Company Inc................ F 330 688-6797
 Cuyahoga Falls *(G-6102)*
Midwest Laser Systems Inc.................. E 419 424-0062
 Alvada *(G-443)*
Milacron LLC.. E 513 487-5000
 Blue Ash *(G-1439)*
Pines Manufacturing Inc....................... E 440 835-5553
 Westlake *(G-15775)*
Rafter Equipment Corporation.............. E 440 572-3700
 Strongsville *(G-13871)*
Riverside Mch & Automtn Inc................ D 419 855-8308
 Genoa *(G-7949)*
South Shore Controls Inc..................... E 440 259-2500
 Mentor *(G-10557)*
Stainless Automation............................ G 216 961-4550
 Cleveland *(G-4726)*
Stein LLC... D 216 883-7444
 Cleveland *(G-4734)*
Sticker Corporation............................... F 440 946-2100
 Willoughby *(G-15998)*
Todd Industries Inc............................... E 440 439-2900
 Cleveland *(G-4799)*
Tri-Mac Mfg & Svcs Co........................... F 513 896-4445
 Hamilton *(G-8251)*

MACHINERY: Mining

Bowdil Company..................................... F 800 356-8663
 Canton *(G-2051)*
Breaker Technology Inc........................ F 440 248-7168
 Solon *(G-13324)*
Cailin Development LLC........................ F 216 408-6261
 Cleveland *(G-3781)*
Carr Tool Company................................ E 513 825-2900
 Fairfield *(G-7343)*
Cleveland Vibrator Company................. F 800 221-3298
 Cleveland *(G-3859)*
Cool Machines Inc................................. F 419 232-4871
 Van Wert *(G-14909)*
Engines Inc of Ohio............................... E 740 377-9874
 South Point *(G-13466)*
Joy Global Underground Min LLC......... C 440 248-7970
 Solon *(G-13371)*
Kaffenbarger Truck Eqp Co................... E 513 772-6800
 Cincinnati *(G-3056)*
Kennametal Inc...................................... C 440 349-5151
 Solon *(G-13378)*
Komatsu Mining Corp............................. D 216 503-5029
 Independence *(G-8670)*
Nolan Company..................................... G 740 269-1512
 Bowerston *(G-1545)*
Nolan Company..................................... E 330 453-7922
 Canton *(G-2173)*
Npk Construction Equipment Inc......... D 440 232-7900
 Bedford *(G-1145)*
Penn Machine Company LLC................. D 814 288-1547
 Twinsburg *(G-14708)*
Strata Mine Services Inc....................... F 740 695-6880
 Saint Clairsville *(G-12926)*
Uhrden Inc... E 330 456-0031
 Canton *(G-2249)*
Warren Fabricating Corporation............ D 330 534-5017
 Hubbard *(G-8572)*
Zen Industries Inc................................. E 216 432-3240
 Cleveland *(G-4932)*

Employee Codes: A=Over 500 employees, B=251-500
C=101-250, D=51-100, E=20-50, F=10-19, G=1-9

MACHINERY: Pack-Up Assemblies, Wheel Overhaul

Aot Inc .... D 937 323-9669
  Springfield (G-13533)
Haeco Inc .... G 513 722-1030
  Loveland (G-9484)

MACHINERY: Packaging

Advanced Poly-Packaging Inc .... C 330 785-4000
  Akron (G-23)
Atmos360 Inc .... E 513 772-4777
  West Chester (G-15539)
Audion Automation Ltd .... E 216 267-1911
  Berea (G-1265)
Automated Packaging Systems LLC ... C 330 528-2000
  Streetsboro (G-13759)
Automated Packg Systems Inc .... E 330 342-2000
  Bedford (G-1103)
Automated Packg Systems Inc .... E 330 626-2313
  Streetsboro (G-13760)
Barry-Wehmiller Companies Inc .... F 330 923-0491
  Cuyahoga Falls (G-6072)
Combi Packaging Systems Llc .... D 330 456-9333
  Canton (G-2078)
Crown Closures Machinery .... E 740 681-6593
  Lancaster (G-9005)
Ctm Integration Incorporated .... E 330 332-1800
  Salem (G-12988)
Ctm Labeling Systems .... E 330 332-1800
  Salem (G-12989)
Darifill Inc .... F 614 890-3274
  Westerville (G-15698)
Exact Equipment Corporation .... E 215 295-2000
  Columbus (G-5062)
Expo Packaging Inc .... G 216 267-9700
  Cleveland (G-4043)
Food Equipment Mfg Corp .... E 216 672-5859
  Bedford Heights (G-1172)
G and J Automatic Systems Inc .... E 216 741-6070
  Cleveland (G-4097)
GL Industries Inc .... E 513 874-1233
  Hamilton (G-8212)
Gunnison Associates Llc .... G 330 562-5230
  Aurora (G-717)
H & G Equipment Inc .... E 513 761-2060
  Blue Ash (G-1401)
H&G Legacy Co .... F 513 921-1075
  Cincinnati (G-2982)
Kaufman Engineered Systems Inc ...... D 419 878-9727
  Waterville (G-15248)
Kennedy Group Incorporated .... D 440 951-7660
  Willoughby (G-15939)
Kolinahr Systems Inc .... F 513 745-9401
  Blue Ash (G-1417)
Millwood Inc .... E 513 860-4567
  West Chester (G-15464)
Millwood Natural Inc .... E 330 393-4400
  Vienna (G-15002)
Nilpeter Usa Inc .... E 513 489-4400
  Cincinnati (G-3198)
Norse Dairy Systems Inc .... C 614 294-4931
  Columbus (G-5600)
Ossid Inc .... G 724 463-3232
  Dublin (G-6919)
Pack Line Corp .... E 212 564-0664
  Cleveland (G-4519)
Pak Master LLC .... E 330 523-5319
  Richfield (G-12792)
PE Usa LLC .... F 513 771-7474
  Cincinnati (G-3244)

Reactive Resin Products Co .... E 419 666-6119
  Perrysburg (G-12423)
Recon Systems LLC .... G 330 488-0368
  East Canton (G-6980)
Rpmi Packaging Inc .... F 513 398-4040
  Lebanon (G-9109)
Switchback Group Inc .... E 216 290-6040
  Cleveland (G-4762)
System Packaging of Glassline .... D 419 666-9712
  Perrysburg (G-12427)
Titans Packaging LLC .... F 513 449-0014
  West Chester (G-15597)
Unity Enterprises Inc .... G 614 231-1370
  Columbus (G-5844)
Vistech Mfg Solutions LLC .... F 513 933-9300
  Lebanon (G-9120)
Vmi Americas Inc .... E 330 929-6800
  Stow (G-13738)

MACHINERY: Paint Making

Bethel Engineering and Eqp Inc .... E 419 568-1100
  New Hampshire (G-11445)
Cohesant Inc .... E 216 910-1700
  Beachwood (G-978)
Fawcett Co Inc .... G 330 659-4187
  Richfield (G-12787)
General Fabrications Corp .... E 419 625-6055
  Sandusky (G-13061)
Nutro Corporation .... D 440 572-3800
  Strongsville (G-13860)
Nutro Inc .... E 440 572-3800
  Strongsville (G-13861)
Woodman Agitator Inc .... F 440 937-9865
  Avon (G-793)

MACHINERY: Plastic Working

Alstart Enterprises LLC .... F 330 533-3222
  Canfield (G-1998)
American Plastic Tech Inc .... C 440 632-5203
  Middlefield (G-10731)
Budget Molders Supply Inc .... F 216 367-7050
  Macedonia (G-9540)
Encore Industries Inc .... C 419 626-8000
  Sandusky (G-13053)
Esi-Extrusion Services Inc .... E 330 374-3388
  Akron (G-143)
J McCaman Enterprises Inc .... G 330 825-2401
  New Franklin (G-11437)
Jaco Manufacturing Company .... E 440 234-4000
  Berea (G-1284)
Linden-Two Inc .... E 330 928-4064
  Cuyahoga Falls (G-6100)
Plastic Process Equipment Inc .... E 216 367-7000
  Macedonia (G-9566)
Tooltex Inc .... F 614 539-3222
  Grove City (G-8123)
Vulcan Machinery Corporation .... E 330 376-6025
  Akron (G-371)
Wentworth Mold Inc Electra .... D 937 898-8460
  Vandalia (G-14967)
Wesco Machine Inc .... F 330 688-6973
  Ravenna (G-12742)
Youngstown Plastic Tooling .... F 330 782-7222
  Youngstown (G-16485)
Zed Industries Inc .... D 937 667-8407
  Vandalia (G-14968)

MACHINERY: Printing Presses

Desco Equipment Corp .... E 330 405-1581
  Twinsburg (G-14648)
Graphic Systems Services Inc .... E 937 746-0708
  Springboro (G-13503)

Incorprted Trstees of The Gspl .... F 216 749-1428
  Cleveland (G-422)

MACHINERY: Recycling

Agmet Metals Inc .... E 440 439-7400
  Oakwood Village (G-12035)
ARS Recycling Systems LLC .... F 330 536-8210
  Lowellville (G-911)
Glenn Hunter & Associates Inc .... D 419 533-0925
  Delta (G-6785)
Prodeva Inc .... F 937 596-6713
  Jackson Center (G-8738)
RSI Company .... F 216 360-9800
  Beachwood (G-020)
SDS National LLC .... G 330 759-8066
  Youngstown (G-6436)

MACHINERY: Road Construction & Maintenance

2e Associates In .... E 440 975-9955
  Willoughby (G-12871)
American Highway Products LLC .... G 330 874-3270
  Bolivar (G-1522)
Concord Road Equipment Mfg Inc ...... E 440 357-5344
  Painesville (G-1223)
Concord Road Equipment Mfg LLC .... E 440 357-5344
  Mentor (G-10442)
Forge Industries Inc .... A 330 960-2468
  Youngstown (G-5359)
Gledhill Road Machinery Co .... E 419 468-4400
  Galion (G-7878)
Gradeworks .... G 440 487-4201
  Kirtland (G-8940)
Lake Township Trustees .... E 419 836-1143
  Millbury (G-1093)
Liverpool Township .... G 330 483-4747
  Valley City (G-1476)
Richland Township Bd Trustees .... F 419 358-4897
  Bluffton (G-1506)

MACHINERY: Robots, Molding & Forming Plastics

CAM-Lem Inc .... G 216 391-7750
  Cleveland (G-3758)
Force Robots LLC .... G 216 881-8360
  Cleveland (G-4089)
Lifeformations Inc .... E 419 352-2101
  Bowling Green (G-1571)
Sea Air Space Mchning Mlding L .... F 440 248-3025
  Streetsboro (G-13791)

MACHINERY: Rubber Working

Anderson International Corp .... D 216 641-1112
  Stow (G-13684)
Conviber Inc .... F 330 723-6006
  Medina (G-10313)
French Oil Mill Machinery Co .... F 937 773-3420
  Piqua (G-12517)
Kobelco Stewart Bolling Inc .... D 330 655-3111
  Hudson (G-8601)
McNeil & Nrm Inc .... D 330 761-1855
  Akron (G-240)
McNeil & Nrm Intl Inc .... D 330 253-2525
  Akron (G-241)
Rjs Corporation .... E 330 896-2387
  Akron (G-306)
RMS Equipment LLC .... A 330 564-1360
  Cuyahoga Falls (G-6115)
Rubber City Machinery Corp .... E 330 434-3500
  Akron (G-312)

Technical Machine Products Inc............ F
  Cleveland (G-4773)

MACHINERY: Screening Eqpt, Electric

Midwestern Industries Inc................ D 330 837-4203
  Massillon (G-10127)
Mjcj Holdings Inc............................. G 937 885-0800
  Miamisburg (G-10663)
Mm Industries Inc............................ E 330 332-5947
  Salem (G-13019)

MACHINERY: Semiconductor Manufacturing

Eaton Corporation............................ B 440 523-5000
  Cleveland (G-3994)
Rite Track Equipment Services LLC........ D 513 881-7820
  West Chester (G-15500)

MACHINERY: Separation Eqpt, Magnetic

Decision Systems Inc....................... F 330 456-7600
  Canton (G-2090)
Ohio Magnetics Inc........................... E 216 662-8484
  Maple Heights (G-9756)

MACHINERY: Sifting & Screening

Rotex Global LLC............................. C 513 541-1236
  Cincinnati (G-3351)

MACHINERY: Textile

C A Litzler Co Inc............................. E 216 267-8020
  Cleveland (G-3778)
Open Additive LLC........................... F 937 306-6140
  Dayton (G-6492)
Randy Gray..................................... G 513 533-3200
  Cincinnati (G-3324)
Slater Road Mills Inc......................... E 330 332-9951
  Salem (G-13032)
Wise Edge LLC................................. G 330 208-0889
  Akron (G-376)
Wolf Machine Company..................... E 513 791-5194
  Blue Ash (G-1493)

MACHINERY: Tire Retreading

American Manufacturing & Eqp............ G 513 829-2248
  Fairfield (G-7335)

MACHINERY: Wire Drawing

Carbide Specialist Inc....................... F 440 951-4027
  Willoughby (G-15896)
Lanko Industries Inc......................... G 440 269-1641
  Mentor (G-10491)

MACHINERY: Woodworking

Axiom Tool Group Inc....................... G 844 642-4902
  Westerville (G-15693)
Bent Wood Solutions LLC.................. G 330 674-1454
  Millersburg (G-10943)
Diamond Machinery LLC.................... G 216 312-1235
  Cleveland (G-3956)
General Intl Pwr Pdts LLC................... E 419 877-5234
  Whitehouse (G-15818)
Polychem Oms Systems LLC.............. F 330 427-1230
  North Canton (G-11750)
Trico Enterprises LLC........................ G 216 970-9984
  Lakewood (G-8983)

MACHINISTS' TOOLS & MACHINES: Measuring, Metalworking Type

Karma Metal Products Inc.................. F 419 524-4371
  Mansfield (G-9676)
PMC Gage Inc.................................. E 440 953-1672
  Willoughby (G-15973)

MACHINISTS' TOOLS: Measuring, Precision

Thaler Machine Company LLC............. C 937 550-2400
  Springboro (G-13521)
Thaler Machine Holdings LLC............. E 937 550-2400
  Springboro (G-13522)

MACHINISTS' TOOLS: Precision

Angstrom Precision Metals LLC........... F 440 255-6700
  Mentor (G-10417)
Chippewa Tool and Mfg Co................. F 419 849-2790
  Woodville (G-16091)
DA Precision Products Inc.................. F 513 459-1113
  West Chester (G-15411)
Kaeper Machine Inc........................... E 440 974-1010
  Mentor (G-10486)
Keb Industries Inc............................. G 440 953-4623
  Willoughby (G-15937)
Levan Enterprises Inc........................ E 330 923-9797
  Stow (G-13706)
M A Harrison Mfg Co Inc.................... E 440 965-4306
  Wakeman (G-15076)
Machining Technologies Inc................ E 419 862-3110
  Elmore (G-7101)
Sjk Machine LLC............................... F 330 868-3072
  North Lawrence (G-11799)
Tessa Precision Product Inc................ E 440 392-3470
  Painesville (G-12269)

MACHINISTS' TOOLS: Scales, Measuring, Precision

Cyber Shed Inc................................. G 419 724-5855
  Toledo (G-14256)

MAGNESIUM

Magnesium Refining Technologies Inc... D 419 483-9199
  Cleveland (G-4350)
Air Craft Wheels LLC......................... G 440 937-7903
  Ravenna (G-12701)
Lite Metals Company......................... E 330 296-6110
  Ravenna (G-12724)
Th Magnesium Inc............................. G 513 285-7568
  Cincinnati (G-3447)

MAGNETIC INK & OPTICAL SCANNING EQPT

Applied Vision Corporation.................. D 330 926-2222
  Cuyahoga Falls (G-6067)

MAGNETS: Permanent

Dura Magnetics Inc........................... F 419 882-0591
  Sylvania (G-13995)
Flexmag Industries Inc....................... D 740 373-3492
  Marietta (G-9793)
Magnet Engineering Inc...................... G 513 248-4578
  Batavia (G-930)
Magnum Magnetics Corporation........... D 740 373-7770
  Marietta (G-9805)
Ohio Magnetics Inc............................ E 216 662-8484
  Maple Heights (G-9756)
Sulo Enterprises Inc........................... F 440 926-3322
  Grafton (G-8005)
Walker National Inc........................... E 614 492-1614
  Columbus (G-5862)
Winkle Industries Inc.......................... D 330 823-9730
  Alliance (G-438)

MAIL-ORDER HOUSE, NEC

American Frame Corporation............... D 419 893-5595
  Maumee (G-10163)

Communication Concepts Inc.............. G 937 426-8600
  Beavercreek (G-1043)
Pardson Inc..................................... F 740 373-5285
  Marietta (G-9814)

MAIL-ORDER HOUSES: Educational Splys & Eqpt

Bendon Inc...................................... D 419 207-3600
  Ashland (G-556)
E-Z Grader Company......................... G 440 247-7511
  Chagrin Falls (G-2375)
Twin Sisters Productions LLC.............. E 330 631-0361
  Stow (G-13735)

MAILING & MESSENGER SVCS

Richardson Printing Corp.................... D 800 848-9752
  Marietta (G-9820)

MAILING LIST: Compilers

Brothers Publishing Co LLC................ E 937 548-3330
  Greenville (G-8040)
Cpmm Services Group Inc................... E 614 447-0165
  Columbus (G-5304)

MAILING SVCS, NEC

Aero Fulfillment Services Corp............. D 800 225-7145
  Mason (G-9945)
American Paper Group Inc.................. B 330 758-4545
  Youngstown (G-16309)
Bindery & Spc Pressworks Inc............. D 614 873-4623
  Plain City (G-12566)
Buckeye Business Forms Inc............... G 614 882-1890
  Westerville (G-15649)
Directconnectgroup Ltd....................... F 216 281-2866
  Cleveland (G-3960)
Eg Enterprise Services Inc.................. F 216 431-3300
  Cleveland (G-4001)
Fine Line Graphics Corp..................... C 614 486-0276
  Columbus (G-5375)
Hkm Drect Mkt Cmmnications Inc......... C 800 860-4456
  Cleveland (G-4193)
Macke Brothers Inc............................ E 513 771-7500
  Cincinnati (G-3123)
Master Printing Group Inc................... F 216 351-2246
  Berea (G-1287)
Northcoast Pmm LLC......................... F 419 540-8667
  Toledo (G-14399)
Porath Business Services Inc............... F 216 626-0060
  Cleveland (G-4564)
Victory Direct LLC............................. G 614 626-0000
  Gahanna (G-7852)
Youngstown Letter Shop Inc................ G 330 793-4935
  Youngstown (G-16484)

MANAGEMENT CONSULTING SVCS: Automation & Robotics

Projects Designed & Built................... E 419 726-7400
  Toledo (G-14443)
Recognition Robotics Inc..................... F 440 590-0499
  Elyria (G-7200)

MANAGEMENT CONSULTING SVCS: Business

5me LLC.. E 513 719-1600
  Cincinnati (G-2544)
Crimson Gate Consulting Co................ G 614 805-0897
  Dublin (G-6878)
Salient Systems Inc........................... E 614 792-5800
  Dublin (G-6934)

MANAGEMENT CONSULTING SVCS: Business

Sightgain Inc..................................F 202 494-9317
   Mason *(G-10056)*
Tha Presidential Suite LLC.............G 216 338-7287
   Dublin *(G-6952)*

MANAGEMENT CONSULTING SVCS: Business Planning & Organizing

Mag Resources LLC........................F 330 294-0494
   Barberton *(G-878)*

MANAGEMENT CONSULTING SVCS: Construction Project

Elite Property Group LLC..............F 216 356-7469
   Elyria *(G-7139)*

MANAGEMENT CONSULTING SVCS: Corporation Organizing

Comex North America Inc.............D 303 307-2100
   Cleveland *(G-3888)*
Pwi Inc..G 732 212-8110
   New Albany *(G-11389)*

MANAGEMENT CONSULTING SVCS: Distribution Channels

Tramonte & Sons LLC.....................F 513 770-5501
   Lebanon *(G-9114)*

MANAGEMENT CONSULTING SVCS: General

Quarrymasters Inc..........................G 330 612-0474
   Akron *(G-292)*

MANAGEMENT CONSULTING SVCS: Hospital & Health

Health Sense Inc............................G 440 354-8057
   Painesville *(G-12244)*

MANAGEMENT CONSULTING SVCS: Industrial

Alloy Extrusion Company...............E 330 677-4946
   Kent *(G-8798)*

MANAGEMENT CONSULTING SVCS: Industry Specialist

Applied Specialties Inc..................E 440 933-9442
   Avon Lake *(G-796)*
Chemsultants International Inc......G 440 974-3080
   Mentor *(G-10437)*
Ketman Corporation.......................G 330 262-1688
   Wooster *(G-16142)*
Telex Communications Inc............G 419 865-0972
   Toledo *(G-14482)*

MANAGEMENT CONSULTING SVCS: Information Systems

Millers Aplus Cmpt Svcs LLC........F 330 620-5288
   Akron *(G-250)*
Neurologix Technologies Inc.........F 512 914-7941
   Cleveland *(G-4451)*

MANAGEMENT CONSULTING SVCS: Training & Development

Honda Dev & Mfg Amer LLC...........C 937 644-0724
   Marysville *(G-9915)*
Leidos Inc.......................................D 937 656-8433
   Beavercreek *(G-1055)*

MANAGEMENT CONSULTING SVCS: Transportation

Integrity Parking LLC.....................F 440 543-4123
   Aurora *(G-720)*

MANAGEMENT SERVICES

Babcock & Wilcox Company..........A 330 753-4511
   Akron *(G-73)*
Cardinal Health Inc........................E 614 553-3830
   Dublin *(G-6871)*
Cardinal Health Inc........................G 614 757-2863
   Lewis Center *(G-9155)*
Cardinal Health Inc........................A 614 757-5000
   Dublin *(G-6872)*
Central Coca-Cola Btlg Co Inc........E 330 875-1487
   Akron *(G-105)*
Central Coca-Cola Btlg Co Inc........E 740 474-2180
   Circleville *(G-3543)*
CFM Religion Pubg Group LLC......D 513 931-4050
   Cincinnati *(G-2723)*
Coal Services Inc...........................B 740 795-5220
   Powhatan Point *(G-12684)*
Eleet Cryogenics Inc......................E 330 874-4009
   Bolivar *(G-1524)*
Instantwhip-Columbus Inc............E 614 871-9447
   Grove City *(G-8098)*
Integrated Resources Inc..............E 419 885-7122
   Sylvania *(G-14002)*
Kenyetta Bagby Enterprise LLC....F 614 584-3426
   Reynoldsburg *(G-12768)*
Kurtz Bros Compost Services........F 330 864-2621
   Akron *(G-213)*
Leadec Corp....................................E 513 731-3590
   Blue Ash *(G-1420)*
Momentum Fleet MGT Group Inc..D 440 759-2219
   Westlake *(G-15765)*
Ohio Designer Craftsmen Entps....F 614 486-7119
   Columbus *(G-5615)*
Pf Management Inc........................G 513 874-8741
   West Chester *(G-15575)*
RB Sigma LLC................................D 440 290-0577
   Mentor *(G-10545)*
Revolution Group Inc....................D 614 212-1111
   Westerville *(G-15675)*
Sand PROperties&landscaping......G 440 360-7386
   Westlake *(G-15781)*
TAC Industries Inc.........................B 937 328-5200
   Springfield *(G-13642)*

MANAGEMENT SVCS: Administrative

Instantwhip Foods Inc...................F 614 488-2536
   Columbus *(G-5464)*

MANAGEMENT SVCS: Business

Ironhawk Industrial Dist LLC.........G 216 502-3700
   Euclid *(G-7276)*
Ohio Clbrtive Lrng Sltons Inc.........E 216 595-5289
   Strongsville *(G-13862)*
Steward Edge Bus Solutions..........F 614 826-5305
   Columbus *(G-5795)*

MANAGEMENT SVCS: Construction

Elite Property Group LLC..............F 216 356-7469
   Elyria *(G-7139)*
Eric Allshouse LLC.........................G 330 533-4258
   Canfield *(G-2005)*
Ingle-Barr Inc.................................D 740 702-6117
   Chillicothe *(G-2513)*
Mel Heitkamp Builders Ltd............G 419 375-0405
   Fort Recovery *(G-7623)*

Protective Industrial Polymers......F 440 327-0015
   North Ridgeville *(G-11854)*

MANPOWER POOLS

Channel Products Inc....................D 440 423-0113
   Solon *(G-1332)*

MANUFACTURING INDUSTRIES, NEC

4S Company....................................F 330 792-5518
   Youngstown *(G-16296)*
Absolute Zero Mch & Design LLC..G 440 370-4172
   Lorain *(G-9400)*
Ace Assembly & Packaging Inc.....G 330 866-9117
   Waynesburg *(G-15292)*
Acoustech Systems LLC................G 270 796-5853
   Columbus *(G-5099)*
Actual Industries LLC....................G 614 379-2739
   Columbus *(G-5001)*
Agile Manufacturing Tech LLC......F 937 258-3338
   Dayton *(G-6191)*
AMG Industries Inc.......................G 740 397-4044
   Mount Vernon *(G-11260)*
Amy Industries Inc........................G 440 942-3478
   Mentor *(G-1041)*
ARS Recycling Systems 2019 LLC.E 330 536-8210
   Lowellville *(G-9512)*
B&M Underground LLC.................G 740 505-3096
   Wilmington *(G-1040)*
Bevcorp Industries LLC.................G 513 673-8520
   Blue Ash *(G-1369)*
Blackstar International Inc............G 917 510-5482
   Columbus *(G-5119)*
Brookville Glove Manufacturing....G 812 673-4893
   Uhrichsville *(G-1762)*
Byron Products Inc........................G 513 870-9111
   Fairfield *(G-7341)*
Cairns Industries LLC....................G 440 255-1190
   Mentor *(G-10436)*
CNB Machining and Mfg LLC........F 330 877-2786
   Hartville *(G-8299)*
Connelly Industries LLC................G 330 468-0675
   Macedonia *(G-9512)*
Csi America Inc..............................G 330 305-1403
   Canton *(G-2084)*
D Industries Inc..............................G 216 535-4900
   Cleveland *(G-3935)*
D Jacob Industries LLC..................F 440 292-7277
   Cleveland *(G-3935)*
Dalamer Industries LLC.................G 440 855-1368
   Cleveland *(G-3937)*
Datco Manufacturing LLC.............G 330 755-1414
   Struthers *(G-13903)*
Desco Machine Company LLC.......F 330 405-5181
   Twinsburg *(G-14649)*
DLAC Industries Inc......................G 330 519-4789
   Canfield *(G-2004)*
Donlon Manufacturing LLC...........G 847 437-7360
   Brecksville *(G-1671)*
DP Assembly LLC..........................G 740 225-4591
   Richwood *(G-12804)*
E-Z Shade LLC...............................G 419 340-2185
   Toledo *(G-14270)*
Eagle Industries.............................G 440 376-3885
   Cleveland *(G-3985)*
Elaire Corporation..........................G 419 843-2192
   Toledo *(G-14271)*
Endurance Industries LLC.............G 513 285-8503
   Cincinnati *(G-2870)*
Essentialware.................................G 888 975-0405
   Kirtland *(G-8939)*
FB Acquisition LLC........................E 513 459-7782
   Lebanon *(G-9074)*

PRODUCT SECTION

MARINE HARDWARE

Fbr Industries Inc .... G 330 701-7425
  Mineral Ridge *(G-11019)*
Five Star Fabrication LLC .... F 440 666-0427
  Wellington *(G-15308)*
Form Mfg .... G 419 763-1030
  Coldwater *(G-4989)*
Fortress Industries LLC .... G 614 402-3045
  Johnstown *(G-8773)*
Front Pocket Innovations LLC .... G 330 441-2365
  Wadsworth *(G-15031)*
Gateways Industries Inc .... G 330 505-0479
  Niles *(G-11669)*
Genergy .... G 937 477-3628
  Lebanon *(G-9078)*
Genesis One Industries LLC .... G 330 842-9428
  Silver Lake *(G-13297)*
Global Manufacturing Assoc Inc .... G 216 938-9056
  Cleveland *(G-4128)*
Gmx .... G 216 641-7502
  Cleveland *(G-4131)*
Groff Industries .... F 216 634-9100
  Cleveland *(G-4151)*
Honda Transmission Manufacturi ...... F 937 843-5555
  Marysville *(G-9919)*
Housing & Emrgncy Lgstcs Plnnr ...... E 209 201-7511
  Lisbon *(G-9315)*
Interarms Manufacturing Ltd .... G 440 201-9850
  Bedford *(G-1128)*
Item NA .... G 216 271-7241
  Akron *(G-194)*
Jameson Industries LLC .... G 330 533-5579
  Boardman *(G-1515)*
Jbs Industries Ltd .... G 513 314-5599
  Columbus *(G-5490)*
Jones Industries LLC .... F 440 810-1251
  Olmsted Twp *(G-12088)*
Juba Industries Inc .... G 440 655-9960
  Jefferson *(G-8747)*
Julius Patrick Industries LLC .... G 440 600-7369
  Solon *(G-13373)*
JW Manufacturing LLC .... G 419 375-5536
  Fort Recovery *(G-7622)*
Kanya Industries LLC .... G 330 722-5432
  Medina *(G-10340)*
Kayden Industries .... G 740 336-7801
  Marietta *(G-9804)*
King Industries LLC .... G 330 733-9106
  Akron *(G-209)*
Kitto Katsu Inc .... G 818 256-6997
  Clayton *(G-3567)*
KS Technologies & Cstm Mfg LLC .... G 419 426-0172
  Attica *(G-701)*
Kth Industries .... G 614 733-2020
  Plain City *(G-12585)*
LEPD Industries Ltd .... G 614 985-1470
  Powell *(G-12676)*
Lucys Barkery LLC .... G 419 886-3779
  Bellville *(G-1244)*
Lyle Industries Inc .... G 513 233-2803
  Cincinnati *(G-3117)*
M N M Mfg Inc .... F 330 256-5572
  Kent *(G-8829)*
Mako Finished Products Inc .... E 740 357-0839
  Lucasville *(G-9523)*
Mansfield Industries .... G 419 785-4510
  Defiance *(G-6690)*
Manufctred Assemblies Corp LLC ..... E 937 454-0722
  Vandalia *(G-14950)*
MCS Mfg LLC .... F 419 923-0169
  Lyons *(G-9532)*
Midwest Stamping & Mfg Co .... G 419 298-2394
  Edgerton *(G-7078)*

MODE Industries Inc .... G 614 504-8008
  Columbus *(G-5576)*
Morgan Site Services Inc .... E 330 823-6120
  Alliance *(G-416)*
Multi-Valve Technology Inc .... G 330 608-4096
  Akron *(G-257)*
My Splash Pad .... G 330 705-1802
  Louisville *(G-9465)*
Myriad Industries Inc .... G 619 232-6700
  Ostrander *(G-12175)*
New Republic Industries LLC .... G 614 580-9927
  Marysville *(G-9929)*
Nfi Industries Inc .... F 740 928-9522
  Hebron *(G-8352)*
Nhmf LLC .... G 614 444-2184
  Columbus *(G-5598)*
Nicholson Manufacturing Co LLC ...... G 978 776-2000
  Lebanon *(G-9101)*
Njf Manufacturing LLC .... G 419 294-0400
  Upper Sandusky *(G-14818)*
Norkaam Industries LLC .... G 330 873-9793
  Akron *(G-265)*
Norris North Manufacturing .... F 330 691-0449
  Canton *(G-2175)*
Noxgear LLC .... G 937 317-0199
  Worthington *(G-16206)*
P & R Mfg .... G 330 674-1431
  Millersburg *(G-10988)*
Padco Industries LLC .... F 440 564-7160
  Newbury *(G-11634)*
Palmer Donavin Manufacturing .... F 740 527-1111
  Hebron *(G-8355)*
Pavletich Manufacturing .... G 440 382-0997
  Brunswick *(G-1779)*
Perma Edge Industries LLC .... G 937 623-7819
  Vandalia *(G-14957)*
Platinum Industries LLC .... G 740 285-2641
  Ironton *(G-8699)*
Pragmatic Mfg LLC .... F 330 222-6051
  Brunswick *(G-1782)*
Proto Prcsion Mfg Slutions LLC .... F 614 771-0080
  Hilliard *(G-8434)*
Pyramid Industries LLC .... G 614 783-1543
  Columbus *(G-5699)*
R & D Industries LLC .... G 937 397-5836
  Medway *(G-10398)*
Rable Machine Inc .... E 740 689-9009
  Lancaster *(G-9036)*
Ransome AC LLC .... G 234 205-6907
  Akron *(G-297)*
RLM & Sqg Industries Inc .... G 513 527-4057
  Cincinnati *(G-3345)*
Ronfeldt Manufacturing .... F 419 382-5641
  Sylvania *(G-14012)*
RS&b Industries LLC .... F 330 255-6000
  Wooster *(G-16165)*
Rubber City Industries Inc .... G 330 990-9641
  Wadsworth *(G-15064)*
S & H Industries Inc .... G 216 831-0550
  Cleveland *(G-4665)*
Sdi Industries .... G 513 561-4032
  Cincinnati *(G-3372)*
Shafts Mfg .... G 440 942-6012
  Willoughby *(G-15989)*
Southpaw Industries LLC .... G 714 215-8592
  Westlake *(G-15789)*
Specialty Mfg & Service .... G 330 821-4675
  Alliance *(G-426)*
Spectre Industries LLC .... G 440 665-2600
  Chagrin Falls *(G-2423)*
Stevens Industries LLC .... G 937 266-8240
  Dayton *(G-6595)*

Tasyd Industries LLC .... G 440 352-8019
  Painesville *(G-12266)*
Teamfg LLC .... G 513 313-8855
  Fairfield *(G-7414)*
Teledoor Manufacturing LLC .... G 419 227-3000
  Lima *(G-9296)*
Terracotta Industries LLC .... G 513 313-6215
  Cincinnati *(G-3444)*
Texstone Industries .... G 419 722-4664
  Findlay *(G-7573)*
Tiger Inds Oil & Gas Lsg LLC .... G 330 533-1776
  Canfield *(G-2021)*
Travis Products Mfg Inc .... G 234 759-3741
  North Lima *(G-11815)*
Troyridge Mfg .... G 330 893-7516
  Millersburg *(G-11001)*
Ttr Manufacturing LLC .... G 440 366-5005
  Elyria *(G-7213)*
Tuffy Manufacturing .... F 330 940-2356
  Cuyahoga Falls *(G-6125)*
Turfware Manufacturing Inc .... G 330 688-8500
  Stow *(G-13734)*
Tyler Industries Inc .... G 440 578-1104
  Mentor *(G-10586)*
Universal Manufacturing .... G 816 396-0101
  Cleveland *(G-4850)*
Vic Maroscher .... F 330 332-4958
  Salem *(G-13036)*
Voo Doo Industries LLC .... G 440 653-5333
  Avon Lake *(G-826)*
VT Industries LLC .... G 614 804-6900
  Hilliard *(G-8453)*
Waterloo Industries Inc .... G 800 833-8851
  Cleveland *(G-4895)*
Weaver Industries Propak .... G 330 475-8160
  Akron *(G-373)*
Weaver Propack - Marc Drive .... G 330 379-3660
  Cuyahoga Falls *(G-6128)*
Wrayco Manufacturing In .... F 330 688-5617
  Stow *(G-13741)*
Yellow Creek Industries .... G 330 757-1065
  Youngstown *(G-16475)*
Yes Mfg LLC .... G 614 296-3553
  Lewis Center *(G-9184)*
Yoder Manufacturing .... G 740 504-5028
  Howard *(G-8560)*

MARBLE, BUILDING: Cut & Shaped

Accent Manufacturing Inc .... F 330 724-7704
  Akron *(G-15)*
Al-Co Products Inc .... G 419 399-3867
  Latty *(G-9053)*
Engineered Marble Inc .... G 614 308-0041
  Columbus *(G-5354)*
Heritage Marble of Ohio Inc .... F 614 436-1464
  Columbus *(G-5427)*
Ohio Tile & Marble Co .... E 513 541-4211
  Cincinnati *(G-3217)*
Pietra Naturale Inc .... F 937 438-8882
  Dayton *(G-6506)*
Piqua Granite & Marble Co Inc .... G 937 773-2000
  Piqua *(G-12546)*

MARINE CARGO HANDLING SVCS

McGinnis Inc .... C 740 377-4391
  South Point *(G-13470)*
McNational Inc .... D 740 377-4391
  South Point *(G-13471)*
Rayle Coal Co .... F 740 695-2197
  Saint Clairsville *(G-12920)*

MARINE HARDWARE PRODUCT SECTION

MARINE HARDWARE
Hydromotive Engineering Co .... G 330 425-4266
 Twinsburg *(G-14673)*
Racelite Southcoast Inc .... F 216 581-4600
 Maple Heights *(G-9759)*
Worthington Products Inc .... G 330 452-7400
 East Canton *(G-6982)*

MARINE SPLYS WHOLESALERS
Hydromotive Engineering Co .... G 330 425-4266
 Twinsburg *(G-14673)*
Werner G Smith Inc .... F 216 861-3676
 Cleveland *(G-4904)*

MARKETS: Meat & fish
D & H Meats Inc .... G 419 387-7767
 Vanlue *(G-14969)*
Riesbeck Food Markets Inc .... C 740 695-3401
 Saint Clairsville *(G-12921)*

MARKING DEVICES
Akron Paint & Varnish Inc .... D 330 773-8911
 Akron *(G-38)*
Bishop Machine Tool & Die .... F 740 453-8818
 Zanesville *(G-16510)*
Dayton Stencil Works Company .... F 937 223-3233
 Dayton *(G-6290)*
E C Shaw Company of Ohio .... E 513 721-6334
 Cincinnati *(G-2848)*
Hathaway Stamp Idntfction Cncn .... G 513 621-1052
 Cincinnati *(G-2990)*
Master Marking Company Inc .... F 330 688-6797
 Cuyahoga Falls *(G-6102)*
Metal Marker Manufacturing Co .... F 440 327-2300
 North Ridgeville *(G-11850)*
Microcom Corporation .... E 740 548-6262
 Lewis Center *(G-9171)*
Monode Marking Products Inc .... F 419 929-0346
 New London *(G-11464)*
Quick As A Wink Printing Co .... G 419 224-9786
 Lima *(G-9281)*
REA Elektronik Inc .... F 440 232-0555
 Bedford *(G-1151)*
Visual Marking Systems Inc .... D 330 425-7100
 Twinsburg *(G-14753)*
Volk Corporation .... G 513 621-1052
 Cincinnati *(G-3501)*

MARKING DEVICES: Canceling Stamps, Hand, Rubber Or Metal
Telesis Technologies Inc .... C 740 477-5000
 Circleville *(G-3558)*

MARKING DEVICES: Embossing Seals & Hand Stamps
Ace Rubber Stamp & Off Sup Co .... F 216 771-8483
 Cleveland *(G-3590)*
Hathaway Stamp Co .... E 513 621-1052
 Cincinnati *(G-2989)*
Marking Devices Inc .... G 216 861-4498
 Cleveland *(G-4359)*
Royal Acme Corporation .... E 216 241-1477
 Cleveland *(G-4654)*
System Seals Inc .... E 216 220-1800
 Brecksville *(G-1632)*
System Seals Inc .... E 440 735-0200
 Cleveland *(G-4763)*

MARKING DEVICES: Embossing Seals, Corporate & Official
Williams Steel Rule Die Co .... F 216 431-3232
 Cleveland *(G-4910)*

MATS OR MATTING, NEC: Rubber
DTR Equipment Inc .... F 419 692-3000
 Delphos *(G-6764)*
Durable Corporation .... D 800 537-1603
 Norwalk *(G-11962)*
Garro Tread Corporation .... G 330 376-3125
 Akron *(G-162)*
Ludlow Composites Corporation .... C 419 332-5531
 Fremont *(G-7796)*
R C Musson Rubber Co .... E 330 773-7651
 Akron *(G-294)*
Rubber Grinding Inc .... D 419 692-3000
 Delphos *(G-6771)*
Space-Links Inc .... E 330 788-2401
 Youngstown *(G-16442)*
Ultimate Rb Inc .... F 419 692-3000
 Delphos *(G-6774)*
Westlake Dimex LLC .... C 740 374-3100
 Marietta *(G-9844)*

MATS, MATTING & PADS: Nonwoven
Durable Corporation .... D 800 537-1603
 Norwalk *(G-11962)*
Spacelinks Enterprises Inc .... E 330 788-2401
 Youngstown *(G-16443)*
Tranzonic Companies .... C 440 446-0643
 Cleveland *(G-4818)*

MEAT MARKETS
Caven and Sons Meat Packing Co .... F 937 368-3841
 Conover *(G-5935)*
Dee-Jays Cstm Btchring Proc LL .... F 740 694-7492
 Fredericktown *(G-7743)*
Hoffman Meat Processing .... G 419 864-3994
 Cardington *(G-2275)*
Honeybaked Ham Company .... E 513 583-9700
 Cincinnati *(G-3006)*
John Krusinski .... F 216 441-0100
 Cleveland *(G-4258)*
John Stehlin & Sons Co .... F 513 385-6164
 Cincinnati *(G-3045)*
Lee Williams Meats Inc .... E 419 729-3893
 Toledo *(G-14362)*
Marshallville Packing Co Inc .... F 330 855-2871
 Marshallville *(G-9893)*
Mc Connells Market .... G 740 765-4300
 Richmond *(G-12802)*
North Country Charcuterie LLC .... F 614 670-5726
 Columbus *(G-5602)*
Pettisville Meats Incorporated .... F 419 445-0921
 Pettisville *(G-12453)*
Winesburg Meats Inc .... G 330 359-5092
 Winesburg *(G-16083)*

MEAT PRDTS: Bacon, Side & Sliced, From Purchased Meat
Honeybaked Foods Inc .... A 567 703-0002
 Holland *(G-8512)*
North Country Charcuterie LLC .... F 614 670-5726
 Columbus *(G-5602)*
Sugar Creek Packing Co .... G 937 268-6601
 Dayton *(G-6597)*
Sugar Creek Packing Co .... B 740 335-3586
 Blue Ash *(G-1472)*

MEAT PRDTS: Boxed Beef, From Slaughtered Meat
National Beef Ohio LLC .... D 800 449-2333
 North Baltimore *(G-11697)*

MEAT PRDTS: Cooked Meats, From Purchased Meat
King Kold Inc .... E 937 836-2731
 Englewood *(G-235)*

MEAT PRDTS: Frozen
A To Z Portion Ctrl Meats Inc .... E 419 358-2926
 Bluffton *(G-1498)*
Dee-Jays Cstm Btchring Proc LL .... F 740 694-7492
 Fredericktown *(G-7743)*
Frank Brunckhorst Company LLC .... G 614 662-5300
 Groveport *(G-8142)*
The Ellenbee-Leggett Company Inc .... C 513 874-3200
 Fairfield *(G-7412)*
White Castle System Inc .... B 614 228-5781
 Columbus *(G-5876)*

MEAT PRDTS: Luncheon Meat, From Purchased Meat
Fink Meat Company Inc .... G 937 390-2750
 Springfield *(G-13564)*

MEAT PRDTS: Prepared Beef Prdts From Purchased Beef
Advancepierre Foods Inc .... B 513 874-8741
 West Chester *(G-15531)*
Brinkman Turkey Farms Inc .... F 419 365-5127
 Findlay *(G-7487)*
Fresh Mark Inc .... B 330 832-7491
 Massillon *(G-10007)*
Pierre Holding Corp .... G 513 874-8741
 West Chester *(G-15576)*

MEAT PRDTS: Sausages & Related Prdts, From Purchased Meat
Owens Foods Inc .... B
 New Albany *(G-11388)*

MEAT PRDTS: Sausages, From Purchased Meat
Lous Sausage Ltd .... E 216 752-5060
 Cleveland *(G-4335)*
Rays Sausage Inc .... G 216 921-8782
 Cleveland *(G-4617)*

MEAT PRDTS: Snack Sticks, Incl Jerky, From Purchased Meat
Charqui Jerky Co .... G 614 286-2938
 Powell *(G-12668)*
Raneys Beef Jerky LLC .... G 606 694-1054
 Ironton *(G-8702)*
Simply Unique Snacks LLC .... G 513 223-7736
 Cincinnati *(G-3394)*

MEDIA: Magnetic & Optical Recording
CD Solutions Inc .... G 937 676-2376
 Pleasant Hill *(G-12506)*

MEDICAL & HOSPITAL EQPT WHOLESALERS
Boxout LLC .... C 833 462-7746
 Hudson *(G-8587)*

Homecare Mattress Inc .... F 937 746-2556
  Franklin (G-7680)
Optum Infusion Svcs 550 LLC .... D 866 442-4679
  Cincinnati (G-3227)
Smiths Medical North America .... G 614 210-7300
  Dublin (G-6939)
True Vision .... G 740 277-7550
  Lancaster (G-9048)

MEDICAL & SURGICAL SPLYS: Bandages & Dressings

Beiersdorf Inc .... C 513 682-7300
  West Chester (G-15541)
Jobskin Div of Torbot Group .... F 419 724-1475
  Northwood (G-11921)

MEDICAL & SURGICAL SPLYS: Braces, Elastic

Motion Mobility & Design Inc .... F 330 244-9723
  North Canton (G-11745)
Myfootshopcom LLC .... G 740 522-5681
  Newark (G-11595)

MEDICAL & SURGICAL SPLYS: Braces, Orthopedic

ABI Orthtc/Prosthetic Labs Ltd .... E 330 758-1143
  Youngstown (G-16299)
Akron Orthotic Solutions Inc .... G 330 253-3002
  Akron (G-37)
Anatomical Concepts Inc .... F 330 757-3569
  Youngstown (G-16312)
Bracemart LLC .... G 440 353-2830
  North Ridgeville (G-11833)
Cole Orthotics Prosthetic Ctr .... G 419 476-4248
  Toledo (G-14247)
Faretec Inc .... F 440 350-9510
  Painesville (G-12236)
Findlay Amrcn Prsthtic Orthtc .... G 419 424-1622
  Findlay (G-7505)
Opc Inc .... G 419 531-2222
  Toledo (G-14416)
Orthotics Prsthtics Rhblttion .... F 330 856-2553
  Warren (G-15197)

MEDICAL & SURGICAL SPLYS: Clothing, Fire Resistant & Protect

Barton-Carey Medical Pdts Inc .... E 419 887-1285
  Maumee (G-10169)
Lion First Responder Ppe Inc .... D 937 898-1949
  Dayton (G-6410)
Wcm Holdings Inc .... C 513 705-2100
  Cincinnati (G-3509)
West Chester Holdings LLC .... C 513 705-2100
  Cincinnati (G-3516)

MEDICAL & SURGICAL SPLYS: Foot Appliances, Orthopedic

Stable Step LLC .... C 800 491-1571
  Wadsworth (G-15068)

MEDICAL & SURGICAL SPLYS: Grafts, Artificial

Osteonovus Inc .... G 419 530-5940
  Toledo (G-14418)
Osteonovus Inc .... G 419 530-5940
  Toledo (G-14419)

MEDICAL & SURGICAL SPLYS: Limbs, Artificial

Capital Prsthtic Orthtic Ctr I .... F 614 451-0446
  Columbus (G-5232)
Fidelity Orthopedic Inc .... G 937 228-0682
  Dayton (G-6332)
Lower Limb Centers LLC .... G 440 365-2502
  Elyria (G-7175)
Luminaud Inc .... G 440 255-9082
  Mentor (G-10497)
Willowwood Global LLC .... C 740 869-3377
  Mount Sterling (G-11259)
Yanke Bionics Inc .... E 330 762-6411
  Akron (G-378)

MEDICAL & SURGICAL SPLYS: Orthopedic Appliances

Acor Orthopaedic Inc .... F 440 532-0117
  Cleveland (G-3593)
Gottfried Medical Inc .... F 419 474-2973
  Toledo (G-14301)
Matplus Ltd .... G 440 352-7201
  Painesville (G-12250)
Medical Device Bus Svcs Inc .... E 937 274-5850
  Dayton (G-6434)
Orthotic & Prosthetic Spc Inc .... E 216 531-2773
  Euclid (G-7291)
Sroufe Healthcare Products LLC .... E 260 894-4171
  Wadsworth (G-15067)
Zimmer Surgical Inc .... B 800 321-5533
  Dover (G-6851)

MEDICAL & SURGICAL SPLYS: Personal Safety Eqpt

Beeline Purchasing LLC .... G 513 703-3733
  Mason (G-9959)
Benchmark Shield LLC .... G 614 695-6500
  Gahanna (G-7831)

MEDICAL & SURGICAL SPLYS: Prosthetic Appliances

Acor Orthopaedic LLC .... E 216 662-4500
  Cleveland (G-3594)
American Orthopedics Inc .... F 614 291-6454
  Columbus (G-5128)
Form5 Prosthetics Inc .... F 614 226-1141
  New Albany (G-11379)
Presque Isle Orthtics Prsthtic .... G 216 371-0660
  Cleveland (G-4583)
Touch Bionics Inc .... G 800 233-6263
  Dublin (G-6953)

MEDICAL & SURGICAL SPLYS: Splints, Pneumatic & Wood

Avalign Technologies Inc .... C 419 542-7743
  Hicksville (G-8372)
Ferno-Washington Inc .... C 877 733-0911
  Wilmington (G-16050)

MEDICAL & SURGICAL SPLYS: Stretchers

Midmark Corporation .... G 937 526-3662
  Versailles (G-14986)
Midmark Corporation .... A 937 528-7500
  Miamisburg (G-10661)

MEDICAL EQPT REPAIR SVCS, NON-ELECTRIC

Elite Biomedical Solutions LLC .... F 513 207-0602
  Cincinnati (G-2558)

MEDICAL EQPT: Diagnostic

Bio Elctrctcal Scence Tech Inc .... G 888 614-1227
  Upper Arlington (G-14799)
Quidel Dhi .... F 740 589-3300
  Athens (G-696)

MEDICAL EQPT: Electromedical Apparatus

Cleveland Medical Devices Inc .... E 216 619-5928
  Cleveland (G-3846)
Great Lkes Nrotechnologies Inc .... E 855 456-3876
  Cleveland (G-4147)
Imalux Corporation .... F 216 502-0755
  Cleveland (G-4216)
Norwood Medical LLC .... D 937 228-4101
  Dayton (G-6477)
Relevium Labs Inc .... G 614 568-7000
  Oxford (G-12212)
Torax Medical Inc .... F 651 361-8900
  Blue Ash (G-1482)

MEDICAL EQPT: Sterilizers

Steris Corporation .... C 330 696-9946
  Mentor (G-10564)
Steris Corporation .... A 440 354-2600
  Mentor (G-10563)

MEDICAL EQPT: Ultrasonic Scanning Devices

Canary Health Technologies Inc .... F 617 784-4021
  Cleveland (G-3784)
Neurowave Systems Inc .... G 216 361-1591
  Beachwood (G-1002)

MEDICAL EQPT: X-Ray Apparatus & Tubes, Radiographic

General Electric Company .... E 216 663-2110
  Cleveland (G-4113)
Waygate Technologies Usa LP .... D 866 243-2638
  Cincinnati (G-3508)

MEDICAL INSURANCE CLAIM PROCESSING: Contract Or Fee Basis

Acu-Serve Corp .... C 330 923-5258
  Akron (G-18)
Mxr Imaging Inc .... G 614 219-2011
  Hilliard (G-8423)

MEDICAL SUNDRIES: Rubber

Philpott Rubber LLC .... G 330 225-3344
  Aurora (G-732)
Philpott Rubber LLC .... E 330 225-3344
  Brunswick (G-1780)

MEDICAL, DENTAL & HOSP EQPT, WHOLESALE: X-ray Film & Splys

Philips Med Systems Clvland In .... B 440 483-3000
  Cleveland (G-4547)

MEDICAL, DENTAL & HOSPITAL EQPT, WHOL: Hospital Eqpt & Splys

Kempf Surgical Appliances Inc .... F 513 984-5758
  Montgomery (G-11130)

MEDICAL, DENTAL & HOSPITAL EQPT, WHOL: Surgical Eqpt & Splys

MEDICAL, DENTAL & HOSPITAL EQPT, WHOL: Surgical Eqpt & Splys

PRODUCT SECTION

Cardinal Health Inc............................. E 614 553-3830
 Dublin (G-6871)
Cardinal Health Inc............................. G 614 757-2863
 Lewis Center (G-9155)
Cardinal Health Inc............................. A 614 757-5000
 Dublin (G-6872)

MELAMINE RESINS: Melamine-Formaldehyde

Bakelite Chemicals LLC......................... D 404 652-4000
 Columbus (G-5172)
Next Specialty Resins Inc...................... E 419 843-4600
 Sylvania (G-14009)

MEMBERSHIP ORGANIZATIONS, NEC: Personal Interest

American Gild of English Hndbe............. G 937 438-0085
 Cincinnati (G-2618)

MEN'S & BOYS' CLOTHING ACCESS STORES

Rnp Inc.. G
 Dellroy (G-6758)

MEN'S & BOYS' CLOTHING STORES

Benchmark Prints.................................. F 419 332-7640
 Fremont (G-7766)
City Apparel Inc.................................. F 419 434-1155
 Findlay (G-7493)
S F Mock & Associates LLC.................... F 937 438-0196
 Dayton (G-6556)

MEN'S & BOYS' CLOTHING WHOLESALERS, NEC

McCc Sportswear Inc............................ G 513 583-9210
 West Chester (G-15569)
West Chester Holdings LLC.................... C 513 705-2100
 Cincinnati (G-3516)

METAL & STEEL PRDTS: Abrasive

Cleveland Granite & Marble LLC............ E 216 291-7637
 Cleveland (G-3841)
Hoover Fabrication Ltd........................ G 330 575-1118
 Salem (G-13001)
Libra Guaymas LLC............................. C 440 974-7770
 Mentor (G-10492)
Steel Dynamics LLC............................. E
 Marietta (G-9830)
Tomson Steel Company....................... E 513 420-8600
 Middletown (G-10866)

METAL COMPONENTS: Prefabricated

Iron Works Inc.................................... F 937 420-2100
 Fort Loramie (G-7601)
Metal Mnkey Wldg Fbrcation LLC......... G 330 231-1490
 Sugarcreek (G-13929)
Pioneer Cldding Glzing Systems............ E 216 816-4242
 Cleveland (G-4554)

METAL DETECTORS

Ceia Usa Ltd...................................... D 330 310-4741
 Hudson (G-8588)
Ohio Magnetics Inc............................. E 216 662-8484
 Maple Heights (G-9756)

METAL FABRICATORS: Plate

Krendl Rack Co Inc.............................. G 419 667-4800
 Venedocia (G-14970)
Loveman Steel Corporation.................. D 440 232-6200
 Bedford (G-1135)

METAL FINISHING SVCS

Broco Products Inc.............................. G 216 531-0880
 Cleveland (G-3761)
Conforming Matrix Corporation............. E 419 729-3777
 Toledo (G-14249)
Luke Engineering & Mfg Corp............... E 330 335-1501
 Wadsworth (G-15043)
Taikisha Usa Inc................................. D 614 444-5602
 Columbus (G-5806)
Tom Richards Inc................................ C 440 974-1300
 Willoughby (G-16007)

METAL MINING SVCS

Cliffs UTAC Holding LLC...................... D 216 694-5700
 Cleveland (G-3877)
Mining and Reclamation Inc................ G 740 327-5555
 Dresden (G-6855)
Western Kentucky Coal Co LLC............. E 740 338-3334
 Saint Clairsville (G-12929)

METAL SERVICE CENTERS & OFFICES

American Tank & Fabricating Co........... D 216 252-1500
 Cleveland (G-3656)
Atlas Bolt & Screw Company LLC......... C 419 289-6171
 Ashland (G-554)
Canfield Coating LLC.......................... E 330 533-3311
 Canfield (G-2002)
Canfield Metal Coating Corp................ D 330 702-3876
 Canfield (G-2003)
EPI of Cleveland Inc........................... G 330 468-2872
 Twinsburg (G-14656)
Graber Metal Works Inc...................... F 440 237-8422
 North Royalton (G-11877)
Kirtland Capital Partners LP................. E 216 593-0100
 Beachwood (G-993)
Lake Building Products Inc.................. E 216 486-1500
 Cleveland (G-4306)
Merit Brass Co................................... C 216 261-9800
 Cleveland (G-4394)
Modern Welding Co Ohio Inc............... E 740 344-9425
 Newark (G-11593)
Nucor Steel Marion Inc....................... E 740 383-6068
 Marion (G-9867)
Ohio Steel Sheet and Plate Inc............. E 800 827-2401
 Hubbard (G-8569)
Oliver Steel Plate Co.......................... D 330 425-7000
 Twinsburg (G-14704)
Omega 1 Inc..................................... F 216 663-8424
 Willoughby (G-15965)
Panacea Products Corporation.............. E 614 850-7000
 Columbus (G-5652)
The Mansfield Strl & Erct Co............... F 419 522-5911
 Mansfield (G-9726)
Tricor Industrial Inc........................... D 330 264-3299
 Wooster (G-16178)
Tsk America Co Ltd............................ F 513 942-4002
 West Chester (G-15600)
Watteredge LLC................................. D 440 933-6110
 Avon Lake (G-828)
Wieland Metal Svcs Foils LLC.............. D 330 823-1700
 Alliance (G-437)
Worthington Enterprises Inc................ D 513 539-9291
 Monroe (G-11121)
Worthington Smuel Coil Proc LLC......... E 330 963-3777
 Twinsburg (G-14758)
Worthngton Stelpac Systems LLC......... C 614 438-3205
 Columbus (G-5886)

METAL STAMPING, FOR THE TRADE

AAA Stamping Inc.............................. E 216 749-4494
 Cleveland (G-3583)
Abl Products Inc................................. F 216 281-2400
 Cleveland (G-3588)
Acro Tool & Die Company.................... E 330 773-5173
 Akron (G-17)
Agb LLC.. G 419 924-5216
 West Unity (G-15636)
AJD Holding Co.................................. D 330 405-4477
 Twinsburg (G-1626)
Allied Tool & Die Inc.......................... F 216 941-6196
 Cleveland (G-337)
Amaroq Inc....................................... G 419 747-2110
 Mansfield (G-9023)
Amclo Group Inc................................ E 216 791-8400
 North Royalton (G-11867)
American Tool & Mfg Co...................... E 419 522-2452
 Mansfield (G-9025)
American Tool and Die Inc.................. F 419 726-5394
 Toledo (G-14190)
Ampex Metal Products Company.......... D 216 267-9242
 Brookpark (G-1704)
Andre Corporation.............................. E 574 293-0207
 Mason (G-9950)
Arbor Industries Inc............................ D 440 255-4720
 Mentor (G-10421)
ARC Metal Stamping LLC.................... D 517 448-8954
 Wauseon (G-15256)
Art Technologies LLC.......................... D 513 942-8800
 Hamilton (G-8150)
Artistic Metal Spinning Inc.................. G 216 961-3336
 Cleveland (G-3682)
Atlantic Tool & Die Company............... C 440 238-6931
 Strongsville (G-810)
Atra Metal Spinning Inc...................... F 440 354-9525
 Painesville (G-12216)
Automatic Stamp Products Inc............. F 216 781-7933
 Cleveland (G-3704)
Banner Metals Group Inc..................... E 614 291-3105
 Columbus (G-514)
Bayloff Stmped Prts Knsman Inc.......... D 330 876-4511
 Kinsman (G-8935)
Bennett Machine & Stamping Co.......... E 440 415-0401
 Geneva (G-7932)
Boehm Pressed Steel Company............. E 330 220-8000
 Valley City (G-14163)
Brainerd Industries Inc........................ F 937 228-0488
 Miamisburg (G-1522)
Buckley Manufacturing Company.......... F 513 821-4444
 Cincinnati (G-2650)
Carolina Stamping Company................ F 216 271-5100
 Highland Heights (G-8384)
Central Ohio Met Stmping Fbrct........... E 614 861-3332
 New Albany (G-11373)
Cleveland Die & Mfg Co...................... C 440 243-3404
 Middleburg Heights (G-10716)
Cleveland Metal Stamping Co............... F 440 234-0010
 Berea (G-1270)
Com-Corp Industries Inc..................... D 216 431-6266
 Cleveland (G-3882)
Continental Business Entps Inc............ F 440 439-4400
 Bedford (G-1113)
Dayton Rogers of Ohio Inc................... D 614 491-1477
 Obetz (G-12059)
Deerfield Manufacturing Inc................ E 513 398-2010
 Mason (G-9983)
Defiance Stamping Co......................... D 419 782-5781
 Napoleon (G-11317)
Dependable Stamping Company............ E 216 486-5522
 Cleveland (G-3952)
Die Co Inc... E 440 942-8856
 Eastlake (G-7025)
Die-Matic Corporation......................... D 216 749-4656
 Brooklyn Heights (G-1689)

PRODUCT SECTION — METAL STAMPING, FOR THE TRADE

Dove Die and Stamping Company .... E 216 267-3720
Cleveland *(G-3970)*

Dyco Manufacturing Inc .... F 419 485-5525
Montpelier *(G-11137)*

Eagle Precision Products LLC .... G 440 582-9393
North Royalton *(G-11873)*

Eisenhauer Mfg Co LLC .... D 419 238-0081
Van Wert *(G-14915)*

Elyria Spring Spclty Holdg Inc .... F 440 323-5502
Elyria *(G-7147)*

Englewood Precision Inc .... G 937 836-1910
Englewood *(G-7231)*

Ernst America Inc .... F 937 434-3133
Moraine *(G-11176)*

Ernst Metal Technologies LLC .... D 937 434-3133
Moraine *(G-11177)*

Ernst Metal Technologies LLC .... E 937 434-3133
Moraine *(G-11178)*

F C Brengman and Assoc LLC .... E 740 756-4308
Carroll *(G-2297)*

Fairfield Manufacturing Inc .... B 513 642-0081
Fairfield *(G-7358)*

Falls Stamping & Welding Co .... C 330 928-1191
Cuyahoga Falls *(G-6083)*

Falls Tool and Die Inc .... G 330 633-4884
Akron *(G-149)*

Famous Industries Inc .... F 740 685-2592
Byesville *(G-1896)*

Faull & Son LLC .... F 330 652-4341
Niles *(G-11668)*

Five Handicap Inc .... F 419 525-2511
Mansfield *(G-9656)*

Frepeg Industries Inc .... F 440 255-8595
Mentor *(G-10459)*

Fulton Industries Inc .... D 419 335-3015
Wauseon *(G-15261)*

Gentzler Tool & Die Corp .... E 330 896-1941
Akron *(G-168)*

Grenada Stamping Assembly Inc .... E 419 842-3600
Sylvania *(G-13996)*

Guarantee Specialties Inc .... D 216 451-9744
Strongsville *(G-13838)*

H&M Mtal Stamping Assembly Inc ..... F 216 898-9030
Brookpark *(G-1717)*

Hamlin Newco LLC .... D 330 753-7791
Akron *(G-178)*

Hamlin Steel Products LLC .... E 330 753-7791
Akron *(G-179)*

Hashier & Hashier Mfg .... G 440 933-4883
Avon Lake *(G-810)*

Herd Manufacturing Inc .... E 216 651-4221
Cleveland *(G-4184)*

Hill Manufacturing Inc .... E 419 335-5006
Wauseon *(G-15263)*

Ice Industries Inc .... E 513 398-2010
Mason *(G-10005)*

Ice Industries Inc .... E 419 842-3600
Sylvania *(G-14000)*

Impact Industries Inc .... E 440 327-2360
North Ridgeville *(G-11845)*

Imperial Die & Mfg Co .... F 440 268-9080
Strongsville *(G-13844)*

Imperial Metal Spinning Co .... G 216 524-5020
Cleveland *(G-4220)*

Independent Stamping Inc .... E 216 251-3500
Cleveland *(G-4223)*

Interlake Stamping Ohio Inc .... E 440 942-0800
Willoughby *(G-15934)*

J B Stamping Inc .... E 216 631-0013
Cleveland *(G-4244)*

K & H Industries LLC .... F 513 921-6770
Cincinnati *(G-3054)*

Kg63 LLC .... F 216 941-7766
Cleveland *(G-4287)*

Knowlton Manufacturing Co Inc .... F 513 631-7353
Cincinnati *(G-3085)*

Kreider Corp .... D 937 325-8787
Springfield *(G-13593)*

L & W Inc .... E 734 397-6300
Avon *(G-778)*

La Ganke & Sons Stamping Co .... F 216 451-0278
Columbia Station *(G-5013)*

Lakepark Industries Inc .... C 419 752-4471
Greenwich *(G-8068)*

Lextech Industries Ltd .... E 216 883-7900
Cleveland *(G-4322)*

Mahoning Valley Manufacturing .... E 330 537-4492
Beloit *(G-1251)*

Mansfield Industries Inc .... F 419 524-1300
Mansfield *(G-9686)*

Master Products Company .... D 216 341-1740
Cleveland *(G-4368)*

Maumee Assembly & Stamping LLC ... B 419 304-2887
Maumee *(G-10217)*

May Industries of Ohio Inc .... E 440 237-8012
North Royalton *(G-11886)*

McGlennon Metal Products Inc .... E 614 252-7114
Columbus *(G-5552)*

McGregor Mtal Innsfllen Wrks L .... C 937 322-3880
Springfield *(G-13602)*

McGregor Mtal Yllow Sprng Wrks ..... D 937 325-5561
Springfield *(G-13604)*

Metal & Wire Products Company .... F 330 332-1015
Salem *(G-13015)*

Metal & Wire Products Company .... E 330 332-9448
Salem *(G-13016)*

Metal Fabricating Corporation .... D 216 631-8121
Cleveland *(G-4396)*

Metal Products Company .... E 330 652-2558
Powell *(G-12677)*

Metal Stampings Unlimited Inc .... F 937 328-0206
Springfield *(G-13605)*

Mohawk Manufacturing Inc .... G 860 632-2345
Mount Vernon *(G-11279)*

Nasg Auto-Seat Tec LLC .... E 419 359-5954
Ridgeville Corners *(G-12815)*

Nasg Ohio Inc .... F 419 634-3125
Ada *(G-4)*

Nasg Seating Bryan LLC .... D 419 633-0662
Bryan *(G-1829)*

Nebraska Industries Corp .... F 419 335-6010
Wauseon *(G-15270)*

Neway Stamping & Mfg Inc .... D 440 951-8500
Willoughby *(G-15958)*

Niles Manufacturing & Finshg .... C 330 544-0402
Niles *(G-11678)*

Ohio Gasket and Shim Co Inc .... E 330 630-0626
Akron *(G-270)*

Ohio Valley Manufacturing Inc .... D 419 522-5818
Mansfield *(G-9707)*

Omni Manufacturing Inc .... F 419 394-7424
Saint Marys *(G-12963)*

Omni Manufacturing Inc .... D 419 394-7424
Saint Marys *(G-12962)*

Orick Stamping Inc .... D 419 331-0600
Elida *(G-7095)*

Pax Machine Works Inc .... D 419 586-2337
Celina *(G-2342)*

Peerless Metal Products Inc .... F 216 431-6905
Cleveland *(G-4538)*

Pennant Moldings Inc .... C 937 584-5411
Sabina *(G-12890)*

Pentaflex Inc .... C 937 325-5551
Springfield *(G-13617)*

Phillips Mch & Stamping Corp .... G 330 882-6714
New Franklin *(G-11441)*

Precision Metal Products Inc .... E 216 447-1900
Cleveland *(G-4575)*

Precision Metal Products Inc .... F 216 447-1900
Cleveland *(G-4576)*

Precision Pressed Powdered Met ...... F 937 433-6802
Dayton *(G-6517)*

Qfm Stamping Inc .... F 330 337-3311
Columbiana *(G-5048)*

Quality Fabricated Metals Inc .... E 330 332-7008
Salem *(G-13025)*

Quality Stamping Products Co .... E 216 441-2700
Cleveland *(G-4609)*

Quality Tool Company .... E 419 476-8228
Toledo *(G-14444)*

R K Metals Ltd .... E 513 874-6055
Fairfield *(G-7402)*

R L Rush Tool & Pattern Inc .... G 419 562-9849
Bucyrus *(G-1866)*

Ratliff Metal Spinning Company .... E 937 836-3900
Englewood *(G-7240)*

RB&w Manufacturing LLC .... G 234 380-8540
Streetsboro *(G-13787)*

Rjm Stamping Co .... F 614 443-1191
Columbus *(G-5725)*

Ronfeldt Associates Inc .... D 419 382-5641
Toledo *(G-14459)*

Ronfeldt Manufacturing LLC .... E 419 382-5641
Toledo *(G-14460)*

Ronlen Industries Inc .... E 330 273-6468
Brunswick *(G-1789)*

Schott Metal Products Company .... E 330 773-7873
Akron *(G-326)*

Service Stampings Inc .... E 440 946-2330
Willoughby *(G-15987)*

Seven Ranges Mfg Corp .... E 330 627-7155
Carrollton *(G-2315)*

Shl Liquidation Industries Inc .... D 440 647-2100
Wellington *(G-15322)*

Smithville Mfg Co .... F 330 345-5818
Wooster *(G-16173)*

Spirol Shim Corporation .... D 330 920-3655
Stow *(G-13726)*

Stamped Steel Products Inc .... F 330 538-3951
North Jackson *(G-11791)*

Stolle Machinery Company LLC .... C 937 497-5400
Sidney *(G-13291)*

Stripmatic Products Inc .... E 216 241-7143
Cleveland *(G-4740)*

Sunfield Inc .... D 740 928-0405
Hebron *(G-8364)*

Supply Technologies LLC .... G 937 898-5795
Dayton *(G-6601)*

Supply Technologies LLC .... C 440 947-2100
Cleveland *(G-4755)*

T and W Stamping Acquisition .... G 330 821-5777
Alliance *(G-432)*

T&W Stamping Inc .... G 330 270-0891
Austintown *(G-755)*

Takumi Stamping Inc .... C 513 642-0081
Fairfield *(G-7413)*

Talan Products Inc .... D 216 458-0170
Cleveland *(G-4766)*

Taylor Metal Products Co .... C 419 522-3471
Mansfield *(G-9724)*

The Kordenbrock Tool and Die Co .... F 513 326-4390
Cincinnati *(G-3449)*

The Reliable Spring Wire Frms .... E 440 365-7400
Elyria *(G-7211)*

Toledo Tool and Die Co Inc .... F 419 266-8458
Toledo *(G-14508)*

Employee Codes: A=Over 500 employees, B=251-500
C=101-250, D=51-100, E=20-50, F=10-19, G=1-9

2024 Harris Ohio Industrial Directory

METAL STAMPING, FOR THE TRADE

Toledo Tool and Die Co Inc..................B 419 476-4422
Toledo (G-14507)

Torrmetal LLC..................................E 216 671-1616
Cleveland (G-4807)

Torrmetal Corporation........................E 216 671-1616
Cleveland (G-4808)

Transue & Williams Stampg Corp..........E 330 821-5777
Austintown (G-756)

Triad Metal Products Company.............E 216 676-6505
Chagrin Falls (G-2430)

United Die & Mfg Sales Co..................E 330 938-6141
Sebring (G-13128)

Universal Metal Products Inc...............E 419 287-3223
Pemberville (G-12336)

Universal Metal Products Inc...............C 440 943-3040
Wickliffe (G-15857)

V K C Inc..F 440 951-9634
Mentor (G-10590)

Varbros LLC.....................................D 216 267-5200
Cleveland (G-4860)

Wedge Products Inc..........................B 330 405-4477
Twinsburg (G-14755)

Westlake Tool & Die Mfg Co................D 440 934-5305
Avon (G-791)

Willow Hill Industries LLC..................G 440 942-3003
Willoughby (G-16018)

WLS Stamping Co.............................D 216 271-5100
Cleveland (G-4914)

Wtd Real Estate Inc..........................D 440 934-5305
Avon (G-794)

METAL STAMPINGS: Perforated

A J Rose Mfg Co................................C 216 631-4645
Avon (G-758)

METAL TREATING COMPOUNDS

Broco Products Inc............................G 216 531-0880
Cleveland (G-3761)

Ferrum Industries Inc.........................G 440 519-1768
Twinsburg (G-14660)

Northern Chem Blnding Corp Inc..........G 216 781-7799
Cleveland (G-4476)

METAL, TITANIUM: Sponge & Granules

Advance Materials Products Inc............G 330 650-4000
Hudson (G-8582)

METAL: Battery

Cleanlife Energy LLC..........................F 800 316-2532
Cleveland (G-3827)

METALS SVC CENTERS & WHOLESALERS: Cable, Wire

Nimers & Woody II Inc........................C 937 454-0722
Vandalia (G-14955)

Radix Wire Co...................................D 216 731-9191
Solon (G-13411)

METALS SVC CENTERS & WHOLESALERS: Ferrous Metals

Curtis Steel & Supply Inc....................F 330 376-7141
Akron (G-119)

METALS SVC CENTERS & WHOLESALERS: Flat Prdts, Iron Or Steel

H & D Steel Service Inc.......................E 800 666-3390
North Royalton (G-11878)

Major Metals Company........................E 419 886-4600
Mansfield (G-9681)

METALS SVC CENTERS & WHOLESALERS: Pipe & Tubing, Steel

McWane Inc......................................B 740 622-6651
Coshocton (G-5983)

Pipe Products Inc...............................C 513 587-7532
West Chester (G-15480)

Shaq Inc..D 770 427-0402
Beachwood (G-1023)

METALS SVC CENTERS & WHOLESALERS: Sheets, Metal

Rockwell Metals Company LLC............F 440 242-2420
Lorain (G-9436)

METALS SVC CENTERS & WHOLESALERS: Steel

Alro Steel Corporation........................E 614 878-7271
Columbus (G-5116)

Alro Steel Corporation........................E 937 253-6121
Dayton (G-6196)

Alro Steel Corporation........................D 419 720-5300
Toledo (G-14184)

Aluminum Line Products Company........D 440 835-8880
Westlake (G-15729)

AM Castle & Co.................................F 330 425-7000
Bedford (G-1100)

American Ir Met Cleveland LLC............E 216 266-0509
Cleveland (G-3653)

American Posts LLC............................E 419 720-0652
Toledo (G-14191)

B&A Ison Steel Inc.............................F 216 663-4300
Cleveland (G-3716)

Berkshire Road Holdings Inc................F 216 883-4200
Cleveland (G-3731)

Bico Akron Inc..................................D 330 794-1716
Mogadore (G-11067)

Clifton Steel Company........................D 216 662-6111
Maple Heights (G-9749)

Conley Group Inc...............................E 330 372-2030
Warren (G-15158)

Contractors Steel Company.................D 330 425-3050
Twinsburg (G-14645)

Coventry Steel Services Inc.................F 216 883-4477
Cleveland (G-3909)

Efco Corp..G 614 876-1226
Columbus (G-5347)

General Steel Corporation....................F 216 883-4200
Cleveland (G-4118)

Grenga Machine & Welding..................F 330 743-1113
Youngstown (G-16374)

Hickman Williams & Company..............F 513 621-1946
Cincinnati (G-2998)

JSW Steel USA Ohio Inc.....................B 740 535-8172
Mingo Junction (G-11046)

Lapham-Hickey Steel Corp..................E 614 443-4881
Columbus (G-5521)

Latrobe Spcialty Mtls Dist Inc..............D 330 609-5137
Vienna (G-14997)

Louis Arthur Steel Company.................G 440 997-5545
Geneva (G-7941)

Master-Halco Inc...............................F 513 869-7600
Fairfield (G-7379)

McOn Inds Inc...................................E 937 294-2681
Moraine (G-11192)

Mid-America Steel Corp......................E 800 282-3466
Cleveland (G-4407)

Monarch Steel Company Inc................E 216 587-8000
Cleveland (G-4420)

Remington Steel Inc...........................D 937 322-2414
Springfield (G-13628)

Rex Welding Inc................................F 740 387-1650
Marion (G-9875)

Samuel Son & Co (usa) Inc..................D 740 522-2500
Heath (G-8331)

Sausser Steel Company Inc.................F 419 422-9632
Findlay (G-7559)

Scot Industries Inc.............................D 330 262-7585
Wooster (G-16159)

St Lawrence Holdings LLC..................E 330 562-9000
Maple Heights (G-9761)

St Lawrence Steel Corporation.............E 330 562-9000
Maple Heights (G-9762)

Thyssenkrupp Materials NA Inc............D 216 883-8100
Independence (G-8687)

Tomson Steel Company......................E 513 420-8600
Middletown (G-10866)

Universal Steel Company....................D 216 883-4972
Cleveland (G-4852)

Westfield Steel Inc............................D 937 322-2414
Springfield (G-13654)

Youngstown Specialty Mtls Inc............G 330 259-1110
Youngstown (G-6488)

METALS SVC CENTERS & WHOLESALERS: Tubing, Metal

Swagelok Company............................D 440 349-5934
Solon (G-13431)

Tubular Techniques Inc.......................G 614 529-4130
Hilliard (G-8450)

METALS: Precious NEC

Metallic Resources Inc........................E 330 425-3155
Twinsburg (G-14496)

METALS: Precious, Secondary

Auris Noble LLC................................E 330 321-6649
Akron (G-68)

Elemetal Refining LLC........................C 740 286-6457
Jackson (G-8714)

Materion Brush Inc.............................D 216 486-4200
Mayfield Heights (G-10250)

Materion Corporation..........................C 216 486-4200
Mayfield Heights (G-10251)

Mek Van Wert Inc..............................G 419 203-4902
Van Wert (G-14923)

Ohio Metal Processing LLC..................G 740 912-2057
Jackson (G-8719)

METALS: Primary Nonferrous, NEC

Aci Industries Ltd..............................E 740 368-4160
Delaware (G-6699)

American Spring Wire Corp..................C 216 292-4620
Bedford Heights (G-1163)

AMG Aluminum North America LLC......F 659 348-3620
Cambridge (G-1922)

Cleveland-Cliffs Inc............................E 216 694-5700
Toledo (G-14243)

Elemetal Refining LLC........................C 740 286-6457
Jackson (G-8714)

Elmet Euclid LLC...............................D 216 692-3990
Euclid (G-7267)

Elmet Technologies Inc......................D 216 692-3990
Cleveland (G-4007)

Galt Alloys Inc Main Ofc.....................G 330 453-4678
Canton (G-2109)

Rhenium Alloys Inc............................E 440 365-7388
North Ridgeville (G-11858)

Swift Manufacturing Co Inc.................G 740 237-4405
Ironton (G-8704)

METALWORK: Miscellaneous

Company	Code	Phone
Active Metal and Molds Inc — Ashland (G-549)	F	419 281-9623
Advance Industrial Mfg Inc — Grove City (G-8073)	E	614 871-3333
Arrow Tru-Line Inc — Bryan (G-1808)	G	419 636-7013
Burghardt Metal Fabg Inc — Akron (G-96)	F	330 794-1830
Fc Industries Inc — Dayton (G-6330)	E	937 275-8700
Fortin Welding & Mfg Inc — Columbus (G-5383)	E	614 291-4342
Kenton Strl & Orn Ir Works — Kenton (G-8887)	D	419 674-4025
Matteo Aluminum Inc — Wickliffe (G-15839)	E	440 585-5213
Metal Sales Manufacturing Corp — Jefferson (G-8753)	F	440 319-3779
Metalfab Group — Streetsboro (G-13778)	G	440 543-6234
Ohio Moulding Corporation — Wickliffe (G-15842)	E	440 944-2100
Omco Holdings Inc — Wickliffe (G-15843)	E	440 944-2100
Precision Impacts LLC — Miamisburg (G-10671)	D	937 530-8254
Simcote Inc — Marion (G-9882)	F	740 382-5000
T J F Inc — Waterville (G-15253)	F	419 878-4400
Ventari Corporation — Miamisburg (G-10697)	F	937 278-4269
Ver-Mac Industries Inc — Mount Vernon (G-11299)	E	740 397-6511
Watteredge LLC — Avon Lake (G-828)	D	440 933-6110
Will-Burt Company — Orrville (G-12162)	F	330 682-7015
Will-Burt Company — Orrville (G-12163)	C	330 682-7015

METALWORK: Ornamental

Company	Code	Phone
Cozmyk Enterprises Inc — Columbus (G-5303)	F	614 231-1370
Finelli Ornamental Iron Co — Cleveland (G-4061)	E	440 248-0050
Fortin Welding & Mfg Inc — Columbus (G-5383)	E	614 291-4342
Jason Incorporated — Hamilton (G-8224)	C	513 860-3400
L & L Ornamental Iron Co — Cleves (G-4958)	E	513 353-1930
Newman Brothers Inc — Cincinnati (G-3191)	E	
Okolona Iron & Metal LLC — Napoleon (G-11328)	F	419 758-3701
P & L Metalcrafts LLC — Youngstown (G-16409)	F	330 793-2178
Tarrier Steel Company Inc — Columbus (G-5811)	E	614 444-4000

METALWORKING MACHINERY WHOLESALERS

Company	Code	Phone
Advanced Tech Utilization Co — Strongsville (G-13802)	F	440 238-7770

METERING DEVICES: Flow Meters, Impeller & Counter Driven

Company	Code	Phone
Bif Co LLC — Akron (G-86)	F	330 564-0941

METERING DEVICES: Water Quality Monitoring & Control Systems

Company	Code	Phone
American Water Services Inc — Strongsville (G-13806)	G	440 243-9840
C H Washington Water Plan — Wshngtn Ct Hs (G-16227)	G	740 636-2382

METERS: Pyrometers, Indl Process

Company	Code	Phone
Marlin Manufacturing Corp — Cleveland (G-4360)	D	216 676-1340

MICROPHONES

Company	Code	Phone
C T I Audio Inc — Brooklyn Heights (G-1686)	G	440 593-1111
Cochran 6573 LLC — Solon (G-13333)	F	440 349-4900

MICROPROCESSORS

Company	Code	Phone
AT&T Corp — Cincinnati (G-2639)	G	513 792-9300
Salient Systems Inc — Dublin (G-6934)	E	614 792-5800

MICROWAVE COMPONENTS

Company	Code	Phone
Berry Investments Inc — Moraine (G-11162)	G	937 293-0398

MILITARY INSIGNIA

Company	Code	Phone
Gayston Corporation — Miamisburg (G-10640)	C	937 743-6050
Staco Energy Products Co — Miamisburg (G-10685)	G	937 253-1191

MILL PRDTS: Structural & Rail

Company	Code	Phone
Bd Laplace LLC — Cleveland (G-3725)	B	985 652-4900

MILLWORK

Company	Code	Phone
A & J Woodworking Inc — Delphos (G-6759)	G	419 695-5655
Aca Millworks Inc — Waynesfield (G-15295)	F	419 339-7600
Ace Lumber Company — Youngstown (G-16301)	F	330 744-3167
Advantage Tent Fittings Inc — Chillicothe (G-2491)	F	740 773-3015
Ailes Millwork Inc — Kent (G-8796)	E	330 678-4300
Anthony Flottemesch & Son Inc — Cincinnati (G-2628)	F	513 561-1212
Art Woodworking & Mfg Co — Cincinnati (G-2635)	E	513 681-2986
Automated Bldg Components Inc — North Baltimore (G-11694)	E	419 257-2152
Bench Made Woodworking LLC — Cincinnati (G-2664)	G	513 702-2698
Berlin Woodworking LLC — Millersburg (G-10945)	G	330 893-3234
Bruewer Woodwork Mfg Co — Cleves (G-4946)	D	513 353-3505
Buckeye Woodworking — Apple Creek (G-495)	G	330 698-1070
Burkholder Woodworking Llc — Middlefield (G-10735)	G	440 313-8203
C & W Custom Wdwkg Co Inc — Cincinnati (G-2697)	G	513 891-6340
C J Woodworking Inc — Wadsworth (G-15021)	G	330 607-4221
C L Woodworking LLC — Middlefield (G-10736)	G	440 487-7940
Carter-Jones Lumber Company — Millersburg (G-10950)	F	330 674-9060
Cassady Woodworks Inc — Dayton (G-6155)	E	937 256-7948
Cincinnati Stair & Handrail — Cincinnati (G-2761)	F	513 722-3947
Cindoco Wood Products Co — Mount Orab (G-11240)	F	937 444-2504
Country Comfort Wdwkg LLC — Fredericksburg (G-7720)	G	330 695-4408
Country Mile Woodworking — Walhonding (G-15091)	G	740 668-2452
Cox Interior Inc — Columbus (G-5302)	G	614 473-9169
Curves and More Woodworking — Columbus (G-5310)	G	614 239-7837
Custom Kerf Woodworking LLC — Barberton (G-865)	G	330 745-7651
Decker Custom Wood Llc — Fremont (G-7775)	G	419 332-3464
Dendratec Ltd — Dalton (G-6130)	G	330 473-4878
Dennelli Custom Wdwkg Inc — Pataskala (G-12296)	G	740 927-1900
Denoon Lumber Company LLC — Bergholz (G-1300)	D	740 768-2220
Display Dynamics Inc — Englewood (G-7229)	E	937 832-2830
Dlg Woodworks & Finishing Inc — Franklin (G-7670)	G	513 649-1245
Door Fabrication Services Inc — Vandalia (G-14938)	F	937 454-9207
Dublin Millwork Co Inc — Dublin (G-6882)	G	614 889-7776
Dutch Heritage Woodcraft — Berlin (G-1306)	F	330 893-2211
Duvall Woodworking Inc — Waterville (G-15242)	G	419 878-9581
Encompass Woodworking LLC — Cincinnati (G-2869)	G	513 569-2841
Fdi Cabinetry LLC — Cleves (G-4952)	G	513 353-4500
Fifth Avenue Lumber Co — Canal Winchester (G-1986)	E	614 833-6655
Fixture Dimensions Inc — Liberty Twp (G-9216)	E	513 360-7512
Forum III Inc — Cincinnati (G-2917)	G	513 961-5123
Forum Works LLC — Milford Center (G-10928)	E	937 349-8685
Freds Woodworking & Remodelin — Barberton (G-868)	G	330 802-8646
Gdw Woodworking LLC — South Lebanon (G-13461)	G	513 494-3041
Gerstenslager Construction — Massillon (G-10100)	G	330 832-3604
Gracie International Corp — Dublin (G-6887)	G	717 725-9138
Greenhart Rstoration Mllwk LLC — Boardman (G-1514)	G	330 502-6050
Gross & Sons Custom Millwork — Lima (G-9246)	G	419 227-0214
Heartland Stairways Inc — Holmesville (G-8543)	G	330 279-2554
Heirloom Woodworks LLC — Tipp City (G-14136)	G	937 430-0394
Hj Systems Inc — Columbus (G-5443)	F	614 351-9777
Hobby Hill Wood Working — Millersburg (G-10960)	G	330 893-4518

MILLWORK

PRODUCT SECTION

Holes Custom Woodworking .... G 419 586-8171
Celina *(G-2337)*

Holmes Custom Moulding Ltd .... E 330 893-3598
Millersburg *(G-10966)*

Holmes Lumber & Bldg Ctr Inc .... E 330 479-8314
Canton *(G-2125)*

Holmes Lumber & Bldg Ctr Inc .... C 330 674-9060
Millersburg *(G-10967)*

Hyde Park Lumber Company .... E 513 271-1500
Cincinnati *(G-3013)*

Icecap LLC .... G 216 548-4145
Wadsworth *(G-15036)*

Idx Corporation .... C 937 401-3225
Dayton *(G-6378)*

Jeffrey D Layton .... G 513 706-4352
Cincinnati *(G-3039)*

Jh Woodworking LLC .... G 330 276-7600
Killbuck *(G-8920)*

Judy Mills Company Inc .... E 513 271-4241
Cincinnati *(G-3053)*

L and J Woodworking .... F 330 359-3216
Dundee *(G-6966)*

Liechty Specialties Inc .... G 419 445-6696
Archbold *(G-534)*

Lima Millwork Inc .... F 419 331-3303
Elida *(G-7094)*

M H Woodworking LLC .... G 330 893-3929
Millersburg *(G-10977)*

Mac Lean J S Co .... E 614 878-5454
Columbus *(G-5538)*

Maple Hill Woodworking LLC .... G 330 674-2500
Millersburg *(G-10979)*

Marsh Industries Inc .... E 330 308-8667
New Philadelphia *(G-11515)*

MB Woodworking Llc .... G 330 808-5122
West Farmington *(G-15605)*

Mc Alister Woodworking .... G 614 989-6264
Columbus *(G-5549)*

McCoy Group Inc .... G 330 753-1041
Barberton *(G-881)*

Menard Inc .... F 513 250-4566
Cincinnati *(G-3148)*

Menard Inc .... C 419 998-4348
Lima *(G-9267)*

Menard Inc .... C 513 583-1444
Loveland *(G-9496)*

Midwest Commercial Mllwk Inc .... F 419 224-5001
Lima *(G-9271)*

Midwest Woodworking Co Inc .... F 513 631-6684
Cincinnati *(G-3164)*

Miller and Slay Wdwkg LLC .... G 513 265-3816
Morrow *(G-11224)*

Miller Manufacturing Inc .... E 330 852-0689
Sugarcreek *(G-13931)*

Mills Customs Woodworks .... G 216 407-3600
Cleveland *(G-4415)*

Millwood Wholesale Inc .... F 330 359-6109
Dundee *(G-6968)*

Millwork Elements LLC .... G 614 905-8163
Columbus *(G-5571)*

Millwork Enterprises LLC .... G 216 644-1481
Olmsted Falls *(G-12081)*

Moonlight Woodworks LLC .... G 440 836-3738
Bedford *(G-1139)*

Morningstar Cstm Woodworks LLC .... G 740 508-7178
Portland *(G-12639)*

Mount Hope Planing .... G 330 359-0538
Millersburg *(G-10984)*

National Door and Trim Inc .... E 419 238-9345
Van Wert *(G-14924)*

New Burlington Woodworks .... G 937 488-3503
Wilmington *(G-16056)*

Oak Pointe LLC .... E 740 498-9820
Newcomerstown *(G-11648)*

Ogonek Custom Hardwood Inc .... G 833 718-2531
Barberton *(G-885)*

Ohio Wood Connection LLC .... G 513 581-0361
Cincinnati *(G-3218)*

Ohio Woodworking Co Inc .... G 513 631-0870
Cincinnati *(G-3219)*

P & T Millwork Inc .... F 440 543-2151
Chagrin Falls *(G-2412)*

Ply-Trim Inc .... E 330 799-7876
Youngstown *(G-16419)*

Precise Custom Millwork Inc .... G 614 539-7855
Grove City *(G-8115)*

Prigge Woodworking .... G 419 274-1005
Hamler *(G-8260)*

Profac Inc .... D 440 942-0205
Mentor *(G-10533)*

Profac Inc .... C 440 942-0205
Mentor *(G-10532)*

Ramsey Stairs & Wdwkg LLC .... G 614 694-2101
Columbus *(G-5710)*

Raymond J Detweiler .... G 440 632-1255
Middlefield *(G-10783)*

Rebsco Inc .... F 937 548-2246
Greenville *(G-8057)*

Renewal By Andersen LLC .... G 614 781-9600
Columbus *(G-5070)*

Rick Alan Custom Woodworks Inc .... G 513 394-6957
Mason *(G-10050)*

Rinos Woodworking Shop Inc .... F 440 946-1718
Willoughby *(G-15984)*

Ripper Woodwork Inc .... G 513 922-1944
Cincinnati *(G-3342)*

Riverside Cnstr Svcs Inc .... E 513 723-0900
Cincinnati *(G-3344)*

Robertson Cabinets Inc .... F 937 698-3755
West Milton *(G-15631)*

Roettger Hardwood Inc .... F 937 693-6811
Kettlersville *(G-8912)*

Rush Fixture & Millwork Co .... F 216 241-9100
Cleveland *(G-4663)*

Rush Woodworks .... G 419 569-2370
Mansfield *(G-9715)*

S Holley Lumber LLC .... G 440 272-5315
Windsor *(G-16076)*

Salem Mill & Cabinet Co .... G 330 337-9568
Salem *(G-13028)*

Sheridan Woodworks Inc .... F 216 663-9333
Cleveland *(G-4692)*

Solid Surface Concepts Inc .... E 513 948-8677
Cincinnati *(G-3401)*

Stein Inc .... G 419 747-2611
Mansfield *(G-9721)*

Stephen M Trudick .... E 440 834-1891
Burton *(G-1886)*

Stony Point Hardwoods LLC .... G 330 852-4512
Sugarcreek *(G-13939)*

Stratton Creek Wood Works LLC .... F 330 876-0005
Kinsman *(G-8938)*

Summit Millwork LLC .... G 330 920-4000
Cuyahoga Falls *(G-6120)*

T & D Thompson Inc .... E 740 332-8515
Laurelville *(G-9056)*

Ted Bolle Millwork Inc .... F 937 325-8779
Springfield *(G-13645)*

The F A Requarth Company .... E 937 224-1141
Dayton *(G-6618)*

The Galehouse Companies Inc .... E 330 658-2023
Doylestown *(G-6854)*

Todco .... F 740 223-2542
Marion *(G-9886)*

Todd Peak Woodwork LLC .... G 513 560-6760
Maineville *(G-9702)*

Trimco .... G 614 679-3931
Westerville *(G-5684)*

Tuscarora Wood Midwest LLC .... G 937 603-8882
Covington *(G-6732)*

Village Woodworking .... G 740 326-4461
Fredericktown *(G-7758)*

Volpe Millwork Inc .... G 216 581-0200
Cleveland *(G-4782)*

Watson Wood Works .... G 513 233-5321
Somerville *(G-1453)*

Wengerd Wood Inc .... F 330 359-4300
Dundee *(G-6970)*

Whitmer Woodworks Inc .... G 614 873-1196
Plain City *(G-12702)*

Wilson Custom Woodworking Inc .... G 513 233-5613
Kings Mills *(G-8730)*

Windy Hills Woodworking .... G 419 892-3389
Lucas *(G-9520)*

Windy Knoll Woodworking LLC .... G 440 636-5092
Huntsburg *(G-8021)*

Wittrock Wdwkg & Mfg Co Inc .... D 513 891-5800
Blue Ash *(G-1452)*

Woodcraft Industries Inc .... D 440 632-9655
Middlefield *(G-10798)*

Woodcraft Industries Inc .... C 440 437-7811
Orwell *(G-12171)*

Woodgrain Enterprises LLC .... G 216 854-8151
Cleveland *(G-4919)*

Woodworks Design .... G 440 693-4414
Middlefield *(G-10799)*

Woodworks Unlimited .... G 740 574-0500
Franklin Furnace *(G-7713)*

Woodworks Zanesville .... G 740 624-3396
Mount Gilead *(G-11236)*

Wyman Woodworking .... G 614 338-0615
Columbus *(G-5858)*

Yoder Lumber Co Inc .... D 330 893-3121
Millersburg *(G-11908)*

Yoder Woodworking .... G 740 399-9400
Butler *(G-1892)*

Youngstown Shade & Alum LLC .... G 330 782-2373
Youngstown *(G-17487)*

Yutzy Woodworking Ltd .... E 330 359-6166
Dundee *(G-6975)*

MINE & QUARRY SVCS: Nonmetallic Minerals

M G Q Inc .... E 419 992-4236
Tiffin *(G-14092)*

Stoepfel Drilling Co .... G 419 532-3307
Ottawa *(G-12194)*

MINE DEVELOPMENT SVCS: Nonmetallic Minerals

Robin Industries Inc .... F 330 893-3501
Berlin *(G-1308)*

MINE PREPARATION SVCS

Strata Mine Services LLC .... F 740 695-0488
Saint Clairsville *(G-12927)*

MINERAL WOOL

Autoneum North America Inc .... B 419 693-0511
Oregon *(G-12103)*

Brendons Fiber Works .... G 614 353-6599
Columbus *(G-5205)*

ICP Adhesives and Sealants Inc .... E 330 753-4585
Norton *(G-11944)*

PRODUCT SECTION MOLDED RUBBER PRDTS

Johns Manville Corporation................... E 419 782-0180
  Defiance *(G-6684)*

Kinetics Noise Control Inc...................... C 614 889-0480
  Dublin *(G-6905)*

Midwest Acoust-A-Fiber Inc.................. F 740 369-3624
  Delaware *(G-6737)*

Owens Corning Roofg & Asp LLC......... E 330 764-7800
  Medina *(G-10360)*

Owens Corning Sales LLC..................... F 614 399-3915
  Mount Vernon *(G-11284)*

Premier Manufacturing Corp................... C 216 941-9700
  Cleveland *(G-4581)*

Refractory Specialties Inc........................ E 330 938-2101
  Sebring *(G-13125)*

Sorbothane Inc... E 330 678-9444
  Kent *(G-8866)*

Tectum Inc... C 740 345-9691
  Newark *(G-11608)*

MINERAL WOOL INSULATION PRDTS

Fibreboard Corporation........................... C 419 248-8000
  Toledo *(G-14287)*

MINERALS: Ground Or Otherwise Treated

Cimbar Performance Mnrl WV LLC......... E 330 532-2034
  Wellsville *(G-15334)*

Kish Company Inc................................... F 440 205-9970
  Mentor *(G-10487)*

MINERALS: Ground or Treated

Aquablok Ltd... G 419 825-1325
  Swanton *(G-13969)*

Continental Mineral Process.................... E 513 771-7190
  Cincinnati *(G-2790)*

Edw C Levy Co.. G 330 484-6328
  Canton *(G-2094)*

EMD Millipore Corporation...................... C 513 631-0445
  Norwood *(G-11995)*

Ethima Inc.. D 419 626-4912
  Sandusky *(G-13057)*

GRB Holdings Inc.................................... D 937 236-3250
  Dayton *(G-6360)*

Howard Industries Inc.............................. F 614 444-9900
  Columbus *(G-5447)*

Industrial Quartz Corporation................... E 440 942-0909
  Mentor *(G-10471)*

Seaforth Mineral & Ore Co Inc................ F 216 292-5820
  Beachwood *(G-1022)*

MINIATURES

Country Lane Custom Buildings............. G 740 485-8481
  Danville *(G-6148)*

On The Mantle LLC................................ G 740 702-1803
  Chillicothe *(G-2521)*

MINING EXPLORATION & DEVELOPMENT SVCS

Galt Alloys Enterprise.............................. F 330 309-8194
  Canton *(G-2108)*

Omega Cementing Co............................ G 330 695-7147
  Apple Creek *(G-508)*

MINING MACHINERY & EQPT WHOLESALERS

Unified Scrning Crshing - OH I................ G 937 836-3201
  Englewood *(G-7246)*

MIXTURES & BLOCKS: Asphalt Paving

Advanced Fiber LLC............................... E 419 562-1537
  Bucyrus *(G-1849)*

All Coatings Co Inc.................................. G 330 821-3806
  Alliance *(G-389)*

Aluminum Coating Manufacturers........... F 216 341-2000
  Cleveland *(G-3644)*

Asphalt Fabrics & Specialties.................. E 440 786-1077
  Solon *(G-13314)*

Atlas Roofing Corporation....................... C 937 746-9941
  Franklin *(G-7663)*

Bluffton Stone Co.................................... E 419 358-6941
  Bluffton *(G-1501)*

Bowerston Shale Company..................... E 740 269-2921
  Bowerston *(G-1544)*

Brewer Company..................................... G 800 394-0017
  Milford *(G-10896)*

Browns Handyman Remodeling.............. G 330 766-0925
  Warren *(G-15148)*

Crafco Inc.. F 330 270-3034
  Youngstown *(G-16342)*

Extendit Company................................... G 330 743-4343
  New Springfield *(G-11541)*

Gbr Property Maintenance LLC.............. F 937 879-0200
  Fairborn *(G-7316)*

Heidelberg Mtls Mdwest Agg Inc............ G 419 983-2211
  Bloomville *(G-1355)*

Holmes Supply Corp............................... G 330 279-2634
  Holmesville *(G-8547)*

Hy-Grade Corporation............................. E 216 341-7711
  Cleveland *(G-4210)*

Image Pavement Maintenance................ F 937 833-9200
  Brookville *(G-1739)*

Mae Materials LLC................................. F 740 778-2242
  South Webster *(G-13476)*

Mar-Zane Inc... F 740 453-0721
  Zanesville *(G-16543)*

Marathon Petroleum Company LP.......... F 419 422-2121
  Findlay *(G-7532)*

Miller Bros Paving Inc............................. F 419 445-1015
  Archbold *(G-536)*

Mplx Terminals LLC................................ D 330 479-5539
  Canton *(G-2167)*

Perma Edge Paver Edging..................... G 844 334-4464
  Dayton *(G-6502)*

Reading Rock Incorporated.................... C 513 874-2345
  West Chester *(G-15580)*

Rutland Township.................................... G 740 742-2805
  Bidwell *(G-1326)*

Seal Master Corporation......................... E 330 673-8410
  Kent *(G-8860)*

Seal Masters LLC................................... G 216 860-7710
  Parma *(G-12295)*

Shelly and Sands Inc.............................. G 740 859-2104
  Rayland *(G-12745)*

Shelly Materials Inc................................. F 419 622-2101
  Convoy *(G-5940)*

Shelly Materials Inc................................. E 740 246-5009
  Thornville *(G-14071)*

Shelly Materials Inc................................. G 419 273-2510
  Forest *(G-7592)*

Skyridge Roofing & Masnry LLC............ G 440 628-1983
  Willowick *(G-16034)*

Smalls Asphalt Paving Inc...................... F 740 427-4096
  Gambier *(G-7908)*

Smith & Thompson Entps LLC................ F 330 386-9345
  East Liverpool *(G-7000)*

Stark Materials Inc.................................. F 330 497-1648
  Canton *(G-2232)*

Stoneco Inc... E 419 393-2555
  Oakwood *(G-12033)*

Thorworks Industries Inc......................... C 419 626-4375
  Sandusky *(G-13096)*

Valley Asphalt Corporation...................... G 513 381-0652
  Morrow *(G-11226)*

MOBILE COMMUNICATIONS EQPT

Eei Acquisition Corp................................ E 440 564-5484
  Middlefield *(G-10749)*

Engineered Endeavors Inc...................... E 440 564-5484
  Newbury *(G-11623)*

Estone Group LLC.................................. E 888 653-2246
  Toledo *(G-14280)*

Sagequest LLC....................................... D 216 896-7243
  Solon *(G-13417)*

Wireless Retail LLC................................. F 614 657-5182
  Blacklick *(G-1345)*

MOBILE HOMES

Clayton Homes.. F 937 592-3039
  Bellefontaine *(G-1202)*

Freedom Homes...................................... G 740 446-3093
  Gallipolis *(G-7892)*

Mobile Conversions Inc........................... F 513 797-1991
  Amelia *(G-460)*

Skyline Corporation................................. C 330 852-2483
  Sugarcreek *(G-13938)*

MOBILE HOMES, EXC RECREATIONAL

Manufactured Housing Entps Inc............ E 419 636-4511
  Bryan *(G-1827)*

MOBILE HOMES: Personal Or Private Use

Palm Harbor Homes Inc.......................... G 937 725-9465
  New Vienna *(G-11543)*

MODELS: General, Exc Toy

3-D Technical Services Company........... E 937 746-2901
  Franklin *(G-7659)*

Anza Inc.. G 513 542-7337
  Cincinnati *(G-2629)*

King Model Company.............................. E 330 633-0491
  Akron *(G-210)*

MODULES: Computer Logic

Ezurio LLC... D 330 434-7929
  Akron *(G-146)*

MOLDED RUBBER PRDTS

Action Rubber Co Inc.............................. F 937 866-5975
  Dayton *(G-6182)*

American Pro-Mold Inc............................ F 330 336-4111
  Wadsworth *(G-15019)*

American Rubber Pdts Co Inc................. G 440 461-0900
  Solon *(G-13313)*

ARC Rubber Inc...................................... F 440 466-4555
  Geneva *(G-7931)*

Cardinal Rubber Company...................... E 330 745-2191
  Barberton *(G-864)*

Chardon Custom Polymers LLC............. F 440 285-2161
  Chardon *(G-2442)*

Clark Rubber & Plastic Company............ C 440 255-9793
  Mentor *(G-10439)*

Contitech Usa Inc.................................... F 330 664-7000
  Fairlawn *(G-7436)*

Custom Rubber Corporation................... D 216 391-2928
  Cleveland *(G-3926)*

Datwyler Sling Sltions USA Inc............... D 937 387-2800
  Vandalia *(G-14937)*

Eaton Aeroquip LLC................................ C 440 523-5000
  Cleveland *(G-3991)*

Enduro Rubber Company........................ G 330 296-9603
  Ravenna *(G-12713)*

Hytech Silicone Products Inc.................. G 330 297-1888
  Ravenna *(G-12720)*

Ier Fujikura Inc... C 330 425-7121
  Macedonia *(G-9556)*

MOLDED RUBBER PRDTS

James K Green Enterprises Inc............... G 614 878-6041
  Columbus (G-5487)
Jet Rubber Company............................... E 330 325-1821
  Rootstown (G-12853)
Karman Rubber Company........................ D 330 864-2161
  Akron (G-201)
Lauren International Ltd.......................... C 234 303-2400
  New Philadelphia (G-11510)
Macdivitt Rubber Company LLC................ E 440 259-5937
  Perry (G-12354)
Maine Rubber Preforms LLC................... G 216 387-1268
  Burton (G-1884)
May Lin Silicone Products Inc.................. G 330 825-9019
  Barberton (G-880)
Mullins Rubber Products Inc.................... G 937 233-4211
  Dayton (G-6461)
Neff-Perkins Company.............................. D 440 632-1658
  Middlefield (G-10776)
Newact Inc... F 513 321-5177
  Batavia (G-940)
Noster Rubber Company........................... G 419 299-3387
  Van Buren (G-14903)
Ottawa Rubber Company........................... F 419 865-1378
  Holland (G-8521)
Park-Ohio Holdings Corp........................... F 440 947-2000
  Cleveland (G-4524)
Park-Ohio Industries Inc........................... C 440 947-2000
  Cleveland (G-4525)
Park-Ohio Products Inc............................. D 216 961-7200
  Cleveland (G-4526)
Parkohio Worldwide LLC............................ E 440 947-2000
  Cleveland (G-4534)
Plabell Rubber Products Corp.................... E 419 691-5878
  Toledo (G-14440)
Profile Rubber Corporation........................ F 330 239-1703
  Wadsworth (G-15055)
Q Model Inc.. F 330 733-6545
  Akron (G-288)
Qualiform Inc... E 330 336-6777
  Wadsworth (G-15057)
Raydar Inc of Ohio.................................... G 330 334-6111
  Wadsworth (G-15061)
Robin Industries Inc.................................. F 330 893-3501
  Berlin (G-1308)
Robin Industries Inc.................................. E 330 695-9300
  Fredericksburg (G-7732)
Robin Industries Inc.................................. E 330 359-5418
  Winesburg (G-16082)
Robin Industries Inc.................................. F 216 631-7000
  Independence (G-8684)
Rubber Associates Inc............................... D 330 745-2186
  New Franklin (G-11443)
Rubber-Tech Inc.. E 937 274-1114
  Dayton (G-6554)
Shreiner Company..................................... G 800 722-9915
  Killbuck (G-8921)
Sorbothane Inc.. E 330 678-9444
  Kent (G-8866)
Sumiriko Ohio Inc..................................... E 419 358-2121
  Bluffton (G-1507)
Sur-Seal LLC... C 513 574-8500
  Cincinnati (G-3434)
The R C A Rubber Company....................... D 330 784-1291
  Akron (G-352)
Tmi Inc... E 330 270-9780
  Youngstown (G-16456)
Tristan Rubber Molding Inc........................ F 330 499-4055
  North Canton (G-11771)
Universal Polymer & Rubber Ltd................. F 330 633-1666
  Tallmadge (G-14055)
Universal Polymer & Rubber Ltd................. C 440 632-1691
  Middlefield (G-10795)
Universal Urethane Pdts Inc...................... D 419 693-7400
  Toledo (G-14514)
Vernay Manufacturing Inc......................... E 937 767-7261
  Yellow Springs (G-16286)
Woodlawn Rubber Co................................ F 513 489-1718
  Blue Ash (G-1494)
Yokohama Inds Amricas Ohio Inc............... D 440 352-3321
  Painesville (G-12280)

MOLDING COMPOUNDS

Ada Solutions Inc...................................... G 440 576-0423
  Jefferson (G-8744)
Clyde Tool & Die Inc................................. F 419 547-9574
  Clyde (G-4971)
Dentsply Sirona Inc................................... E 419 865-9497
  Maumee (G-10200)
Flex Technologies Inc................................ D 330 897-6311
  Baltic (G-836)
Hpc Holdings LLC..................................... A 440 224-7204
  North Kingsville (G-11796)
Hpc Holdings LLC..................................... D 330 666-3751
  Fairlawn (G-7442)
Incredible Solutions Inc............................. F 330 898-3878
  Warren (G-15177)
Industrial Thermoset Plas Inc.................... F 440 975-0411
  Mentor (G-10472)
Jain America Foods Inc............................. G 614 850-9400
  Columbus (G-5486)
JMS Industries Inc.................................... F 937 325-3502
  Springfield (G-13584)
Kirtley Mold Inc.. G 330 472-2427
  Akron (G-211)
Lyondllbsell Advnced Plymers I.................. C 330 773-2700
  Akron (G-226)
Lyondllbsell Advnced Plymers I.................. C 330 630-0308
  Akron (G-227)
Lyondllbsell Advnced Plymers I.................. D 330 630-3315
  Akron (G-228)
Meggitt (erlanger) LLC.............................. D 513 851-5550
  Cincinnati (G-3143)
Michael Day Enterprises LLC..................... E 330 335-5100
  Wadsworth (G-15044)
Ohio Rotational Molding LLC..................... F 419 608-5040
  Holgate (G-8490)
Polymer Stamping Tech LLC...................... G 616 371-4004
  Troy (G-14602)
Resinoid Engineering Corp......................... D 740 928-6115
  Hebron (G-8359)
Roechling Indus Cleveland LP.................... C 216 486-0100
  Cleveland (G-4645)
Uniloy Century LLC.................................. D 419 332-2693
  Fremont (G-7816)
Yoders Produce Inc.................................... E 330 695-5900
  Fredericksburg (G-7736)

MOLDINGS & TRIM: Metal, Exc Automobile

Aluminum Color Industries Inc.................. E 330 536-6295
  Lowellville (G-9510)

MOLDINGS & TRIM: Wood

Armstrong Custom Moulding Inc................ G 740 922-5931
  Uhrichsville (G-14761)
Dowel Yoder & Molding............................. G 330 231-2962
  Fredericksburg (G-7723)
Fairfield Wood Works Ltd.......................... G 740 689-1953
  Lancaster (G-9015)
Round Mate Systems................................ G 419 675-3334
  Kenton (G-8899)

MOLDINGS OR TRIM: Automobile, Stamped Metal

American Trim LLC................................... A 419 228-1145
  Sidney (G-132)
Florida Production Engrg Inc..................... D 937 996-4361
  New Madison (G-11474)
Kasai North America Inc........................... C 419 209-0399
  Upper Sandusky (G-14812)
Pennant Companies................................... E 614 451-1782
  Sabina (G-1285)
TS Trim Industries Inc.............................. B 614 837-4114
  Canal Winchester (G-1993)

MOLDS: Gra, Ingot, Cast Iron

Anchor Glass Container Corp..................... D 740 452-2743
  Zanesville (G-1500)
Ellwood Engineered Castings Co................ C 330 568-3000
  Hubbard (G-853)
Kenton Iron Products Inc.......................... E 419 674-4178
  Kenton (G-8886)

MOLDS: Indl

Aero Tech Tool & Mold Inc........................ G 440 942-3327
  Mentor (G-1040)
Akron Centl Engr Mold Mch Inc................. E 330 794-8704
  Akron (G-29)
American Cube Mold Inc............................ G 330 558-0044
  Brunswick (G-178)
Amerimold Inc... G 800 950-8020
  Mogadore (G-1166)
Apollo Plastics Inc.................................... F 440 951-7774
  Mentor (G-1042)
Caliber Mold and Machine Inc................... G 330 633-8171
  Akron (G-98)
CD Company LLC..................................... D 419 332-2693
  Fremont (G-777)
Deca Mfg Co... F 419 884-0071
  Mansfield (G-965)
Durivage Pattern and Mfg Inc.................... E 419 836-8655
  Williston (G-158)
Esterle Mold & Machine Co Inc.................. G 330 686-1685
  Stow (G-13695)
Ferriot Inc.. C 330 786-3000
  Akron (G-152)
H&M Machine & Tool LLC.......................... E 419 776-9220
  Toledo (G-14306)
Herbert Usa Inc.. D 330 929-4297
  Akron (G-181)
High-Tech Mold & Machine Inc.................. F 330 896-4466
  Uniontown (G-1435)
Home Asb & Mold Removal Inc................. G 216 661-6696
  Cleveland (G-419)
J M Mold Inc.. G 937 778-0077
  Piqua (G-12529)
Jamen Tool & Die Co................................ E 330 782-6731
  Youngstown (G-1382)
Kuhns Mold & Tool Co Inc......................... D 937 833-2178
  Brookville (G-174)
Lightning Mold & Machine Inc................... F 440 593-6460
  Conneaut (G-592)
Mallory Pattern Works Inc......................... G 419 726-8001
  Toledo (G-14377)
Mercury Machine Co................................. D 440 349-3222
  Solon (G-13386)
Midwest Mold & Texture Corp.................... E 513 732-1300
  Batavia (G-934)
Milacron Holdings Corp............................. C 513 487-5000
  Batavia (G-935)
Mold Surface Textures Inc......................... G 330 678-8590
  Kent (G-8838)
Monitor Mold & Machine Co...................... F 330 697-7800
  Rootstown (G-1285)
New Castings Inc...................................... C 330 645-6653
  Akron (G-262)

Nichols Mold Inc .... G 330 297-9719
  Ravenna (G-12726)
Numerics Unlimited Inc .... E 937 849-0100
  New Carlisle (G-11423)
Oakley Die & Mold Co .... E 513 754-8500
  Mason (G-10034)
Perfection Mold & Machine Co .... F 330 784-5435
  Twinsburg (G-14713)
Plastic Mold Technology Inc .... G 330 848-4921
  Barberton (G-890)
Precast Products LLC .... E 419 668-1639
  Norwalk (G-11986)
Reuther Mold & Mfg Co Inc .... D 330 923-5266
  Cuyahoga Falls (G-6114)
Ron-Al Mold & Machine Inc .... F 330 673-7919
  Kent (G-8855)
Saehwa IMC Na Inc .... D 330 645-6653
  Akron (G-323)
Seaway Pattern Mfg Inc .... E 419 865-5724
  Toledo (G-14465)
Stan-Kell LLC .... E 440 998-1116
  Ashtabula (G-661)
Superior Mold & Die Co .... F 330 688-8251
  Munroe Falls (G-11306)
Tempcraft Corporation .... A 216 391-3885
  Cleveland (G-4775)
Tom Smith Industries Inc .... D 937 832-1555
  Englewood (G-7245)
TW Manufacturing Co .... E 440 439-3243
  Cleveland (G-4838)
Twin Valley Mold & Tool LLC .... G 937 962-1403
  Lewisburg (G-9193)
Velocity Concept Dev Group LLC .... G 740 685-2637
  Byesville (G-1901)
XCEL Mold and Machine Inc .... E 330 499-8450
  Canton (G-2271)
Yugo Mold Inc .... F 330 606-0710
  Akron (G-380)

MOLYBDENUM SILICON, EXC MADE IN BLAST FURNACES

Newton Materion Inc .... B 216 692-3990
  Euclid (G-7287)

MOPS: Floor & Dust

Ekco Cleaning Inc .... C 513 733-8882
  Cincinnati (G-2860)
Ha-Ste Manufacturing Co Inc .... G 937 968-4858
  Union City (G-14778)
Impact Products LLC .... D 419 841-2891
  Toledo (G-14328)

MORTAR: High Temperature, Nonclay

Minteq International Inc .... F 419 636-4561
  Bryan (G-1828)

MOTOR & GENERATOR PARTS: Electric

Electrocraft Arkansas Inc .... D 501 268-4203
  Gallipolis (G-7890)
Parker-Hannifin Corporation .... E 330 336-3511
  Wadsworth (G-15051)
Swiger Coil Systems Ltd .... C 216 362-7500
  Cleveland (G-4760)
Wabtec Corporation .... F 216 362-7500
  Cleveland (G-4887)

MOTOR CONTROL CENTERS

Sdk Associates Inc .... G 330 745-3648
  Norton (G-11948)

MOTOR HOMES

Advanced Rv LLC .... E 440 283-0405
  Willoughby (G-15874)
Airstream Inc .... B 937 596-6111
  Jackson Center (G-8729)

MOTOR SCOOTERS & PARTS

Dco LLC .... E 419 931-9086
  Perrysburg (G-12373)

MOTOR VEHICLE ASSEMBLY, COMPLETE: Ambulances

Braun Industries Inc .... B 419 232-7020
  Van Wert (G-14907)
La Boit Specialty Vehicles .... D 614 231-7640
  Gahanna (G-7843)

MOTOR VEHICLE ASSEMBLY, COMPLETE: Buses, All Types

Eldorado National Kansas Inc .... C 937 596-6849
  Jackson Center (G-8732)
Thor Industries Inc .... F 937 596-6111
  Jackson Center (G-8739)

MOTOR VEHICLE ASSEMBLY, COMPLETE: Fire Department Vehicles

Copley Fire & Rescue Assn .... E 330 666-6464
  Copley (G-5947)
Sutphen Corporation .... C 800 726-7030
  Dublin (G-6949)

MOTOR VEHICLE ASSEMBLY, COMPLETE: Military Motor Vehicle

Warfighter Fcsed Logistics Inc .... E 740 513-4692
  West Chester (G-15526)

MOTOR VEHICLE ASSEMBLY, COMPLETE: Wreckers, Tow Truck

Horizon Global Corporation .... E 734 656-3000
  Cleveland (G-4200)

MOTOR VEHICLE DEALERS: Automobiles, New & Used

Doug Marine Motors Inc .... E 740 335-3700
  Wshngtn Ct Hs (G-16230)
Ford Motor Company .... C 440 933-1215
  Avon Lake (G-807)
Ford Motor Company .... A 419 226-7000
  Lima (G-9243)
General Motors LLC .... A 216 265-5000
  Cleveland (G-4116)
General Motors LLC .... C 330 824-5840
  Warren (G-15173)
Honda Dev & Mfg Amer LLC .... C 937 644-0724
  Marysville (G-9915)
Jmac Inc .... E 614 436-2418
  Columbus (G-5498)
Knippen Chrysler Ddge Jeep Inc .... E 419 695-4976
  Delphos (G-6767)
Mitsubishi Chemical Amer Inc .... D 419 483-2931
  Bellevue (G-1230)
Mitsubishi Elc Auto Amer Inc .... B 513 573-6614
  Mason (G-10030)
Subaru of A .... G 614 793-2358
  Dublin (G-6948)

MOTOR VEHICLE DEALERS: Vans, New & Used

Steves Vans ACC Unlimited LLC .... G 740 374-3154
  Marietta (G-9832)

MOTOR VEHICLE PARTS & ACCESS: Acceleration Eqpt

Oerlikon Friction Systems .... E 937 449-4000
  Dayton (G-6485)
Yachiyo of America Inc .... C 614 876-3220
  Columbus (G-5889)

MOTOR VEHICLE PARTS & ACCESS: Air Conditioner Parts

Aptiv Services Us LLC .... B 330 306-1000
  Warren (G-15142)
Ftd Investments LLC .... A 937 833-2161
  Brookville (G-1737)
Hanon Systems Usa LLC .... C 313 920-0583
  Carey (G-2279)
Mahle Behr Dayton LLC .... A 937 369-2900
  Dayton (G-6423)
Taiho Corporation of America .... C 419 443-1645
  Tiffin (G-14107)

MOTOR VEHICLE PARTS & ACCESS: Ball Joints

Torque 2020 CMA Acqisition LLC .... C 330 874-2900
  Bolivar (G-1539)

MOTOR VEHICLE PARTS & ACCESS: Bearings

Green Acquisition LLC .... F 440 930-7600
  Avon (G-776)
Kyklos Bearing International Llc .... A 419 627-7000
  Sandusky (G-13072)

MOTOR VEHICLE PARTS & ACCESS: Body Components & Frames

ARE Inc .... A 330 830-7800
  Massillon (G-10076)
Classic Reproductions .... G 937 548-9839
  Greenville (G-8042)
Frontier Tank Center Inc .... F 330 659-3888
  Richfield (G-12788)
Gerich Fiberglass Inc .... F 419 362-4591
  Mount Gilead (G-11233)
Green Tokai Co Ltd .... A 937 833-5444
  Brookville (G-1738)
Magna Modular Systems LLC .... D 419 324-3387
  Toledo (G-14376)
Oakley Inds Sub Assmbly Div In .... F 419 661-8888
  Northwood (G-11923)
TS Tech USA Corporation .... B 614 577-1088
  Reynoldsburg (G-12777)

MOTOR VEHICLE PARTS & ACCESS: Brakes, Air

Eaton Corporation .... C 216 281-2211
  Cleveland (G-3992)
Trulil Inc .... C 937 652-1242
  Urbana (G-14849)

MOTOR VEHICLE PARTS & ACCESS: Clutches

Luk Clutch Systems LLC .... E 330 264-4383
  Wooster (G-16147)
Pt Tech LLC .... D 330 239-4933
  Wadsworth (G-15056)

MOTOR VEHICLE PARTS & ACCESS: Clutches

Remington Steel Inc.................................. D 937 322-2414
 Springfield *(G-13628)*
Westfield Steel Inc.................................... D 937 322-2414
 Springfield *(G-13654)*

MOTOR VEHICLE PARTS & ACCESS: Connecting Rods

Usui International Corporation.............. C 513 448-0410
 Sharonville *(G-13174)*

MOTOR VEHICLE PARTS & ACCESS: Electrical Eqpt

Eaton Corporation...................................... B 440 523-5000
 Beachwood *(G-985)*
Maradyne Corporation............................... D 216 362-0755
 Cleveland *(G-4356)*
Mrs Electronic Inc...................................... F 937 660-6767
 Dayton *(G-6460)*
Stoneridge Inc.. A 419 884-1219
 Lexington *(G-9202)*
Weastec Incorporated............................... C 937 393-6800
 Hillsboro *(G-8469)*

MOTOR VEHICLE PARTS & ACCESS: Engines & Parts

Alegre Inc.. F 937 885-6786
 Miamisburg *(G-10609)*
Areway LLC... D 216 651-9022
 Brooklyn *(G-1676)*
Bucyrus Precision Tech Inc..................... C 419 563-9950
 Bucyrus *(G-1852)*
Detroit Toledo Fiber LLC........................... F 248 647-0400
 Toledo *(G-14265)*
Eaton Corporation...................................... B 440 523-5000
 Cleveland *(G-3994)*
Flaming River Industries Inc................... F 440 826-4488
 Berea *(G-1281)*
Ft Precision Inc.. A 740 694-1500
 Fredericktown *(G-7748)*
Gt Technologies Inc................................... D 419 782-8955
 Defiance *(G-6680)*
Gt Technologies Inc................................... D 419 324-7300
 Toledo *(G-14304)*
Hite Parts Exchange Inc........................... F 614 272-5115
 Columbus *(G-5442)*
L-H Battery Company Inc.......................... G 937 613-3769
 Jeffersonville *(G-8765)*
Linamar Strctures USA Mich Inc............. C 260 636-7030
 Edon *(G-7088)*
Linamar Strctures USA Mich Inc............. C 567 249-0838
 Edon *(G-7089)*
Lorain County Auto Systems Inc............ A 248 442-6800
 Lorain *(G-9421)*
Lorain County Auto Systems Inc............ E 440 960-7470
 Lorain *(G-9422)*
Mahle Behr Mt Sterling Inc...................... B 740 869-3333
 Mount Sterling *(G-11256)*
Neaton Auto Products Mfg Inc................ E 937 456-7103
 Eaton *(G-7066)*
Pullman Company....................................... C 419 592-2055
 Napoleon *(G-11331)*
Qualitor Inc... G 248 204-8600
 Cleveland *(G-4603)*
Rochling Automotive USA LLP................ D 330 400-5785
 Akron *(G-307)*
Schaeffler Transmission Llc.................... B 330 264-4383
 Wooster *(G-16168)*
Soundwich Inc.. E 216 249-4900
 Cleveland *(G-4715)*
Soundwich Inc.. D 216 486-2666
 Cleveland *(G-4716)*
ZF Active Safety US Inc............................ G 734 812-6979
 Findlay *(G-7584)*

MOTOR VEHICLE PARTS & ACCESS: Fuel Pumps

Bergstrom Company Ltd Partnr............... E 440 232-2282
 Cleveland *(G-3730)*

MOTOR VEHICLE PARTS & ACCESS: Fuel Systems & Parts

Interstate Diesel Service Inc................... C 216 881-0015
 Cleveland *(G-4233)*

MOTOR VEHICLE PARTS & ACCESS: Gas Tanks

Buckley Manufacturing Company............ F 513 821-4444
 Cincinnati *(G-2693)*

MOTOR VEHICLE PARTS & ACCESS: Gears

All Wright Enterprises LLC...................... G 440 259-5656
 Perry *(G-12349)*
Gear Company of America Inc................ D 216 671-5400
 Cleveland *(G-4107)*
Ig Watteeuw USA LLC................................ F 740 588-1722
 Zanesville *(G-16538)*
Scs Gearbox Inc... F 419 483-7278
 Bellevue *(G-1233)*

MOTOR VEHICLE PARTS & ACCESS: Heaters

Hdt Expeditionary Systems Inc............... F 216 438-6111
 Solon *(G-13360)*
Hdt Tactical Systems Inc......................... C 216 438-6111
 Solon *(G-13361)*
Jbar A/C Inc.. E 216 447-4294
 Cleveland *(G-4252)*
Lintern Corporation................................... E 440 255-9333
 Mentor *(G-10494)*

MOTOR VEHICLE PARTS & ACCESS: Instrument Board Assemblies

New Sabina Industries Inc....................... G 937 584-2433
 Grove City *(G-8111)*
New Sabina Industries Inc....................... E 937 584-2433
 Sabina *(G-12888)*

MOTOR VEHICLE PARTS & ACCESS: Lubrication Systems & Parts

Lubriquip Inc.. B 216 581-2000
 Cleveland *(G-4338)*

MOTOR VEHICLE PARTS & ACCESS: Mufflers, Exhaust

Allied Witan Company............................... F 440 237-9630
 North Royalton *(G-11866)*
Emssons Faurecia Ctrl Systems.............. C 812 341-2000
 Toledo *(G-14276)*
Midwest Muffler Pros & More.................. G 937 293-2450
 Moraine *(G-11195)*
Newman Technology Inc........................... A 419 525-1856
 Mansfield *(G-9704)*
Riker Products Inc.................................... D 419 729-1626
 Toledo *(G-14451)*
Supertrapp Industries Inc........................ D 216 265-8400
 Cleveland *(G-4754)*

MOTOR VEHICLE PARTS & ACCESS: Oil Strainers

Allied Separation Tech Inc....................... F 704 736-0420
 Twinsburg *(G-14629)*

MOTOR VEHICLE PARTS & ACCESS: Power Steering Eqpt

Maval Industries LLC................................ C 330 405-1600
 Twinsburg *(G-14692)*
Steer & Gear Inc.. F 614 231-4064
 Columbus *(G-5793)*

MOTOR VEHICLE PARTS & ACCESS: Propane Conversion Eqpt

Superior Energy Systems LLC................. F 440 236-6009
 Columbia Station *(G-5022)*

MOTOR VEHICLE PARTS & ACCESS: Pumps, Hydraulic Fluid Power

Eaton Corporation...................................... F 216 523-5000
 Willoughby *(G-15916)*

MOTOR VEHICLE PARTS & ACCESS: Rear Axel Housings

American Axle & Mfg Inc.......................... E 330 868-5761
 Minerva *(G-11026)*

MOTOR VEHICLE PARTS & ACCESS: Sanders, Safety

Doran Mfg LLC.. D 866 816-7233
 Blue Ash *(G-1385)*

MOTOR VEHICLE PARTS & ACCESS: Tire Valve Cores

31 Inc... D 740 498-8324
 Newcomerstown *(G-11640)*
Haltec Corporation.................................... C 330 222-1501
 Salem *(G-12999)*

MOTOR VEHICLE PARTS & ACCESS: Trailer Hitches

Horizon Global Corporation...................... E 734 656-3000
 Cleveland *(G-4200)*
Saf-Holland Inc.. G 513 874-7888
 Fairfield *(G-7404)*
White Mule Company................................. E 740 382-9008
 Ontario *(G-12097)*

MOTOR VEHICLE PARTS & ACCESS: Transmission Housings Or Parts

Oerlikon Friction Systems........................ E 937 449-4000
 Dayton *(G-6486)*
Torsion Control Products Inc.................. F 248 537-1900
 Wadsworth *(G-15070)*

MOTOR VEHICLE PARTS & ACCESS: Transmissions

Capco Automotive Products Corp........... A 216 523-5000
 Cleveland *(G-3786)*

MOTOR VEHICLE PARTS & ACCESS: Water Pumps

ASC Industries Inc.................................... D 800 253-6009
 North Canton *(G-11715)*

PRODUCT SECTION MOTORS: Generators

Hytec-Debartolo LLC...................................G..... 614 527-9370
 Columbus (G-5450)

MOTOR VEHICLE PARTS & ACCESS: Wiring Harness Sets

Connective Design Incorporated............F..... 937 746-8252
 Miamisburg (G-10628)
Designed Harness Systems Inc...............F..... 937 599-2485
 Bellefontaine (G-1206)
GSW Manufacturing Inc...........................B..... 419 423-7111
 Findlay (G-7516)
Sumitomo Elc Wirg Systems Inc..............E..... 937 642-7579
 Marysville (G-9941)

MOTOR VEHICLE SPLYS & PARTS WHOLESALERS: New

Anest Iwata Usa Inc....................................F..... 513 755-3100
 West Chester (G-15536)
ARE Inc..A..... 330 830-7800
 Massillon (G-10076)
Chemspec Usa Inc......................................D..... 330 669-8512
 Orrville (G-12121)
Doran Mfg LLC..D..... 866 816-7233
 Blue Ash (G-1385)
Emssons Faurecia Ctrl Systems................C..... 812 341-2000
 Toledo (G-14276)
Gear Star American Performance.............G..... 330 434-5216
 Akron (G-163)
Goodyear Tire & Rubber Company...........A..... 330 796-2121
 Akron (G-171)
Keystone Auto Glass Inc............................D..... 419 509-0497
 Maumee (G-10211)
Legacy Supplies Inc...................................F..... 330 405-4565
 Twinsburg (G-14685)
Mac Trailer Manufacturing Inc...................A..... 800 795-8454
 Alliance (G-411)
Neff Machinery and Supplies....................F..... 740 454-0128
 Zanesville (G-16547)
Qualitor Inc...G..... 248 204-8600
 Cleveland (G-4603)

MOTOR VEHICLE SPLYS & PARTS WHOLESALERS: Used

Lucas Sumitomo Brakes Inc......................E..... 513 934-0024
 Lebanon (G-9094)
Mac Trailer Manufacturing Inc...................A..... 800 795-8454
 Alliance (G-411)

MOTOR VEHICLE: Radiators

Albright Radiator Inc..................................G..... 330 264-8886
 Wooster (G-16100)
Thermal Solutions Mfg Inc.........................F..... 800 776-4225
 Brookpark (G-1726)

MOTOR VEHICLE: Shock Absorbers

Pullman Company......................................C..... 419 499-2541
 Milan (G-10885)
Thyssenkrupp Bilstein Amer Inc................C..... 513 881-7600
 Hamilton (G-8249)

MOTOR VEHICLE: Wheels

Accuride Corporation.................................E..... 812 962-5000
 Springfield (G-13527)
Forgeline Motorsports LLC........................E..... 800 886-0093
 Moraine (G-11181)
Goodrich Corporation.................................A..... 937 339-3811
 Troy (G-14574)
Honda Transmission Manufact..................A..... 937 843-5455
 Russells Point (G-12877)

Kosei St Marys Corporation......................A..... 419 394-7840
 Saint Marys (G-12955)
Oe Exchange LLC......................................G..... 440 266-1639
 Mentor (G-10514)

MOTOR VEHICLES & CAR BODIES

Airstream Inc..B..... 937 596-6111
 Jackson Center (G-8729)
Antique Auto Sheet Metal Inc....................F..... 937 833-4422
 Brookville (G-1729)
Autowax Inc..G..... 440 334-4417
 Strongsville (G-13813)
Bae Systems Survivability S......................A..... 513 881-9800
 West Chester (G-15372)
Bobbart Industries Inc...............................E..... 419 350-5477
 Sylvania (G-13991)
D&D Clssic Auto Rstoration Inc.................F..... 937 473-2229
 Covington (G-6021)
Ford Motor Company.................................C..... 440 933-1215
 Avon Lake (G-807)
FOXCONN EV SYSTEM LLC....................B..... 234 285-4001
 Warren (G-15171)
Galion-Godwin Truck Bdy Co LLC............F..... 330 359-5495
 Dundee (G-6965)
Halcore Group Inc......................................C..... 614 539-8181
 Grove City (G-8097)
Honda Dev & Mfg Amer LLC.....................C..... 937 644-0724
 Marysville (G-9915)
Honda Dev & Mfg Amer LLC.....................A..... 937 642-5000
 Marysville (G-9916)
Hyo Seong America Corporation...............F..... 513 682-6182
 Fairfield (G-7371)
Lordstown Ev Corporation.........................F..... 678 428-6558
 Warren (G-15185)
Subaru of A..G..... 614 793-2358
 Dublin (G-6948)
Toledo Pro Fiberglass Inc..........................F..... 419 241-9390
 Toledo (G-14503)
Tpam Inc...E..... 567 315-8694
 Toledo (G-14511)
Tremcar USA Inc.......................................D..... 330 878-7708
 Strasburg (G-13750)
Workhorse Technologies Inc.....................E..... 888 646-5205
 Sharonville (G-13176)

MOTOR VEHICLES, WHOLESALE: Fire Trucks

Fire Safety Services Inc............................F..... 937 686-2000
 Huntsville (G-8623)

MOTOR VEHICLES, WHOLESALE: Truck tractors

Kinstle Truck & Auto Svc Inc.....................F..... 419 738-7493
 Wapakoneta (G-15120)

MOTOR VEHICLES, WHOLESALE: Trucks, commercial

Youngstown-Kenworth Inc........................F..... 330 534-9761
 Hubbard (G-8574)

MOTORCYCLE ACCESS

B&D Truck Parts Sls & Svcs LLC.............G..... 419 701-7041
 Fostoria (G-7629)
Colony Machine & Tool Inc.......................G..... 330 225-3410
 Brunswick (G-1752)
Custom Cycle ACC Mfg Dstrg Inc............F..... 440 585-2200
 Wickliffe (G-15830)
Newman Technology Inc..........................A..... 419 525-1856
 Mansfield (G-9704)

Thomas D Epperson..................................G..... 937 855-3300
 Germantown (G-7954)

MOTORCYCLE PARTS: Wholesalers

L & R Racing Inc..E..... 330 220-3102
 Brunswick (G-1773)

MOTORCYCLES & RELATED PARTS

Cobra Motorcycles Mfg..............................F..... 330 207-3844
 North Lima (G-11802)
Sunstar Engrg Americas Inc.....................E..... 937 746-8575
 Springboro (G-13520)

MOTORS: Electric

Allied Motion At Dayton.............................F..... 937 228-3171
 Dayton (G-6194)
Ametek Tchnical Indus Pdts Inc................D..... 330 673-3451
 Kent (G-8799)
Dcm Manufacturing Inc..............................E..... 216 265-8006
 Cleveland (G-3948)
Dreison International Inc...........................C..... 216 362-0755
 Cleveland (G-3972)
Globe Motors Inc..C..... 334 983-3542
 Dayton (G-6356)
Hannon Company......................................D..... 330 456-4728
 Canton (G-2121)
Imperial Electric Company........................B..... 330 734-3600
 North Canton (G-11738)
Nidec Motor Corporation...........................C..... 575 434-0633
 Akron (G-264)
Ramco Electric Motors Inc........................D..... 937 548-2525
 Greenville (G-8056)
Regal Beloit America Inc...........................C..... 937 667-2431
 Tipp City (G-14151)
Siemens Industry Inc................................C..... 513 841-3100
 Norwood (G-12000)

MOTORS: Generators

Ares Inc..D..... 419 635-2175
 Port Clinton (G-12615)
Battle Motors Inc..C..... 888 328-5443
 New Philadelphia (G-11486)
Carter Carburetor LLC..............................A..... 216 314-2711
 Cleveland (G-3796)
Chemequip Sales Inc................................E..... 330 724-8300
 Coventry Township (G-6007)
City Machine Technologies Inc.................F..... 330 747-2639
 Youngstown (G-16336)
Crescent & Sprague..................................F..... 740 373-2331
 Marietta (G-9787)
Dayton-Phoenix Group Inc........................D..... 937 496-3900
 Dayton (G-6292)
Eagle Machining LLC................................C..... 419 237-1366
 Fayette (G-7462)
Energy Technologies Inc...........................D..... 419 522-4444
 Mansfield (G-9653)
GE Aviation Systems LLC.........................B..... 937 898-5881
 Vandalia (G-14941)
General Electric Company........................E..... 216 883-1000
 Cleveland (G-4115)
Gleason Metrology Systems Corp............E..... 937 384-8901
 Dayton (G-6353)
Grand-Rock Company Inc........................E..... 440 639-2000
 Painesville (G-12240)
HBD Industries Inc....................................E..... 614 526-7000
 Dublin (G-6891)
Hv Coil...F..... 330 260-4126
 Newcomerstown (G-11646)
Industrial and Mar Eng Svc Co.................F..... 740 694-0791
 Fredericktown (G-7749)
JD Power Systems LLC............................F..... 614 317-9394
 Hilliard (G-8416)

MOTORS: Generators

Linde Hydraulics Corporation............ E 330 533-6501
  Canfield *(G-2009)*

Lordstown Ev Corporation............. F 678 428-6558
  Warren *(G-15185)*

Ohio Magnetics Inc........................ E 216 662-8484
  Maple Heights *(G-9756)*

Ohio Semitronics Inc..................... D 614 777-1005
  Hilliard *(G-8427)*

Peerless-Winsmith Inc.................. B 330 399-3651
  Dublin *(G-6921)*

Regal Beloit America Inc............... E 608 364-8800
  Lima *(G-9284)*

Safran Usa Inc............................... C 513 247-7000
  Sharonville *(G-13173)*

Stateline Power Corp..................... F 937 547-1006
  Greenville *(G-8062)*

Tigerpoly Manufacturing Inc......... B 614 871-0045
  Grove City *(G-8122)*

Tremont Electric Incorporated...... G 888 214-3137
  Cleveland *(G-4820)*

Tridelta Industries Inc.................... E 440 255-1080
  Mentor *(G-10584)*

Vanner Holdings Inc...................... D 614 771-2718
  Hilliard *(G-8451)*

Waibel Electric Co Inc................... F 740 964-2956
  Etna *(G-7253)*

MOTORS: Pneumatic

Vickers International Inc................ E 419 867-2200
  Maumee *(G-10244)*

MOUTHWASHES

Oasis Consumer Healthcare LLC.......... G 216 394-0544
  Cleveland *(G-4489)*

MULTIPLEXERS: Telephone & Telegraph

7signal Inc..................................... E 216 777-2900
  Independence *(G-8650)*

AT&T Corp..................................... G 513 792-9300
  Cincinnati *(G-2639)*

Atx Networks.................................. G 440 427-9036
  Olmsted Twp *(G-12086)*

Cutting Edge Technologies Inc...... F 216 574-4759
  Cleveland *(G-3928)*

DTE Inc.. E 419 522-3428
  Mansfield *(G-9647)*

Dynalab Inc.................................... D 614 866-9999
  Reynoldsburg *(G-12764)*

Electrodata Inc.............................. F 216 663-3333
  Bedford Heights *(G-1170)*

Floyd Bell Inc................................. D 614 294-4000
  Columbus *(G-5381)*

Fremont Plastic Products Inc........ C 419 332-6407
  Fremont *(G-7783)*

Pro Oncall Technologies LLC........ F 614 761-1400
  Dublin *(G-6927)*

Vertiv Energy Systems Inc............ A 440 288-1122
  Lorain *(G-9443)*

Vertiv Group Corporation.............. G 440 460-3600
  Cleveland *(G-4864)*

Vertiv Group Corporation.............. G 440 288-1122
  Lorain *(G-9444)*

Wan Dynamics Inc......................... F 877 400-9490
  Medina *(G-10393)*

MUSICAL INSTRUMENTS & ACCESS: Carrying Cases

L M Engineering Inc....................... E 330 270-2400
  Austintown *(G-752)*

MUSICAL INSTRUMENTS & ACCESS: NEC

Bbb Music LLC............................... G 740 772-2262
  Chillicothe *(G-2494)*

Belco Works Inc............................. D 740 695-0500
  Saint Clairsville *(G-12897)*

D Picking & Co............................... G 419 562-6891
  Bucyrus *(G-1856)*

Grover Musical Products Inc......... E 216 391-1188
  Cleveland *(G-4153)*

Jatiga Inc....................................... D 859 817-7100
  Blue Ash *(G-1411)*

Loft Violin Shop.............................. F 614 267-7221
  Columbus *(G-5531)*

Muller Pipe Organ Co..................... F 740 893-1700
  Croton *(G-6051)*

The W L Jenkins Company............ F 330 477-3407
  Canton *(G-2244)*

Verdin Organ Division................... G 513 502-2333
  Cincinnati *(G-3495)*

MUSICAL INSTRUMENTS & PARTS: Percussion

Cardinal Percussion Inc................. G 330 707-4446
  Girard *(G-7964)*

MUSICAL INSTRUMENTS WHOLESALERS

Jatiga Inc....................................... D 859 817-7100
  Blue Ash *(G-1411)*

McHael D Goronok String Instrs......... G 216 421-4227
  Cleveland *(G-4380)*

MUSICAL INSTRUMENTS: Guitars & Parts, Electric & Acoustic

Conn-Selmer Inc............................ D 440 946-6100
  Willoughby *(G-15901)*

Dangelico Guitars.......................... G 513 218-3985
  Cincinnati *(G-2818)*

Earthquaker Devices LLC............. E 330 252-9220
  Akron *(G-136)*

S I T Strings Co Inc....................... E 330 434-8010
  Akron *(G-321)*

NAME PLATES: Engraved Or Etched

Etched Metal Company.................. E 440 248-0240
  Solon *(G-13347)*

Hathaway Stamp Idntfction Cncn........ G 513 621-1052
  Cincinnati *(G-2990)*

Industrial and Mar Eng Svc Co...... F 740 694-0791
  Fredericktown *(G-7749)*

Roemer Industries Inc................... D 330 448-2000
  Masury *(G-10158)*

Ryder Engraving Inc...................... G 740 927-7193
  Pataskala *(G-12307)*

Signature Partners Inc.................. D 419 678-1400
  Coldwater *(G-5001)*

Visionmark Nameplate Co LLC..... E 419 977-3131
  New Bremen *(G-11410)*

NATURAL GAS DISTRIBUTION TO CONSUMERS

City of Lancaster........................... E 740 687-6670
  Lancaster *(G-9002)*

National Gas & Oil Corporation..... E 740 344-2102
  Newark *(G-11596)*

NATURAL GAS LIQUIDS PRODUCTION

Condevco Inc................................. G 740 373-5302
  New Matamoras *(G-11476)*

H & S Operating Company Inc...... G 330 830-8178
  Winesburg *(G-16079)*

Markwest Utica Emg LLC.............. C 740 942-4810
  Jewett *(G-8767)*

NATURAL GAS PRODUCTION

Buckeye Franklin Co...................... F 330 859-2465
  Zoarville *(G-16575)*

D & L Energy Inc........................... E 330 270-1201
  Canton *(G-2087)*

Interstate Gas Supply LLC............ B 877 995-4447
  Dublin *(G-6900)*

RCM Engineering Company.......... G 330 666-0575
  Akron *(G-299)*

Temple Oil and Gas LLC................ F 740 452-7878
  Crooksville *(G-6050)*

Williams Partners LP..................... F 330 414-6201
  North Canton *(G-11775)*

NATURAL GAS TRANSMISSION

Knight Material Tech LLC.............. D 330 488-1651
  East Canton *(G-6979)*

National Gas & Oil Corporation..... E 740 344-2102
  Newark *(G-11596)*

NATURAL GAS TRANSMISSION & DISTRIBUTION

Ngo Development Corporation...... B 740 622-9560
  Coshocton *(G-5987)*

NATURAL GASOLINE PRODUCTION

Husky Marketing and Supply Co........... E 614 210-2300
  Dublin *(G-6894)*

RCM Engineering Company.......... G 330 666-0575
  Akron *(G-299)*

NATURAL PROPANE PRODUCTION

Consolidated Gas Coop Inc........... G 419 946-6600
  Mount Gilead *(G-11232)*

NAVIGATIONAL SYSTEMS & INSTRUMENTS

Cedar Elec Holdings Corp............. D 773 804-6288
  West Chester *(G-15388)*

Drs Advanced Isr LLC................... C 937 429-7408
  Beavercreek *(G-1046)*

L3 Technologies Inc...................... G 937 223-3285
  Dayton *(G-6400)*

Trimble Inc..................................... F 937 233-8921
  Dayton *(G-6634)*

Trimble Inc..................................... F 937 233-8921
  Tipp City *(G-14160)*

U S Army Corps of Engineers....... G 740 537-2571
  Toronto *(G-14536)*

NETS: Launderers & Dyers

TAC Industries Inc......................... B 937 328-5200
  Springfield *(G-13642)*

NEW & USED CAR DEALERS

Bwi North America Inc.................. E 937 253-1130
  Kettering *(G-8904)*

NEWS SYNDICATES

Ohio News Network....................... E 614 460-3700
  Columbus *(G-5622)*

NICKEL

Allied Mask and Tooling Inc.......... G 419 470-2555
  Toledo *(G-14183)*

Nickel Plate Railcar LLC................ G 440 382-6580
  Mentor *(G-10510)*

Nickels Marketing Group Inc........ G 440 835-1532
  Westlake *(G-15767)*

PRODUCT SECTION — OIL & GAS FIELD MACHINERY

NONCURRENT CARRYING WIRING DEVICES

- Arnco Corporation................................ D 800 847-7661
  Elyria *(G-7112)*
- Barracuda Technologies Inc................... G 216 469-1566
  Aurora *(G-708)*
- Danco Metal Products LLC..................... D 440 871-2300
  Avon Lake *(G-803)*
- Eaton Electric Holdings LLC.................... B 440 523-5000
  Cleveland *(G-3995)*
- Erico Products Inc................................. B 440 248-0100
  Cleveland *(G-4027)*
- Power Shelf LLC................................... G 419 775-6125
  Plymouth *(G-12609)*
- Regal Beloit America Inc....................... C 419 352-8441
  Bowling Green *(G-1588)*
- Roechling Indus Cleveland LP.................. C 216 486-0100
  Cleveland *(G-4645)*
- Standex International Corp.................... D 513 533-7171
  Fairfield *(G-7412)*
- Vertiv Energy Systems Inc...................... A 440 288-1122
  Lorain *(G-9443)*
- Vertiv Group Corporation...................... G 440 288-1122
  Lorain *(G-9444)*
- Zekelman Industries Inc........................ C 740 432-2146
  Cambridge *(G-1961)*

NONFERROUS: Rolling & Drawing, NEC

- BCi and V Investments Inc..................... F 330 538-0660
  North Jackson *(G-11778)*
- Bunting Bearings LLC............................ E 419 522-3323
  Mansfield *(G-9634)*
- Canton Drop Forge Inc.......................... B 330 477-4511
  Canton *(G-2061)*
- Consolidated Metal Pdts Inc.................. D 513 251-2624
  Cincinnati *(G-2788)*
- Contour Forming Inc............................. F 740 345-9777
  Newark *(G-11572)*
- Curtiss-Wright Flow Ctrl Corp................. D 216 267-3200
  Cleveland *(G-3922)*
- Economy Flame Hardening Inc............... F 216 431-9333
  Cleveland *(G-3999)*
- Elemetal Refining LLC........................... C 740 286-6457
  Jackson *(G-8714)*
- ESAB Group Incorporated..................... G 440 813-2506
  Ashtabula *(G-632)*
- G & S Titanium Inc............................... E 330 263-0564
  Wooster *(G-16122)*
- G A Avril Company............................... F 513 641-0566
  Cincinnati *(G-2925)*
- Gem City Metal Tech LLC...................... E 937 252-8998
  Dayton *(G-6349)*
- Kilroy Company................................... D 440 951-8700
  Cleveland *(G-4289)*
- Mestek Inc.. F 419 288-2703
  Bradner *(G-1603)*
- Metal Merchants Usa Inc...................... F 330 723-3228
  Medina *(G-10353)*
- Nova Machine Products Inc................... C 216 267-3200
  Middleburg Heights *(G-10724)*
- Patriot Special Metals Inc..................... D 330 580-9600
  Canton *(G-2194)*
- Titanium Metals Corporation................. A 740 537-1571
  Toronto *(G-14535)*

NOTEBOOKS, MADE FROM PURCHASED MATERIALS

- Avery Dennison Corporation.................. B 440 534-6000
  Mentor *(G-10426)*
- CCL Label Inc...................................... D 440 878-7000
  Strongsville *(G-13819)*

NOVELTIES

- Tiger Cat Furniture............................... G 330 220-7232
  Brunswick *(G-1794)*

NOVELTIES: Plastic

- Baker Plastics Inc................................. G 330 743-3142
  Youngstown *(G-16317)*
- CM Paula Company.............................. E 513 759-7473
  Mason *(G-9980)*
- Yachiyo of America Inc......................... C 614 876-3220
  Columbus *(G-5889)*

NOZZLES: Fire Fighting

- Premier Farnell Holding Inc................... E 330 523-4273
  Richfield *(G-12794)*
- Sensible Products Inc........................... G 330 659-4212
  Richfield *(G-12797)*

NOZZLES: Spray, Aerosol, Paint Or Insecticide

- Exair Corporation................................ E 513 671-3322
  Cincinnati *(G-2891)*
- J & J Performance Inc.......................... F 330 567-2455
  Shreve *(G-13211)*
- Vortec Corporation.............................. E
  Blue Ash *(G-1489)*

NUCLEAR SHIELDING: Metal Plate

- Laird Technologies Inc.......................... E 234 806-0105
  Warren *(G-15183)*

NURSERIES & LAWN & GARDEN SPLY STORES, RETAIL: Fertilizer

- Centerra Co-Op................................... E 419 281-2153
  Ashland *(G-562)*
- Insta-Gro Manufacturing Inc................. G 419 845-3046
  Caledonia *(G-1916)*
- K M B Inc.. E 330 889-3451
  Bristolville *(G-1652)*
- Keystone Cooperative Inc..................... G 937 884-5526
  Verona *(G-14975)*
- Mid-Wood Inc..................................... F 419 257-3331
  North Baltimore *(G-11696)*
- New Eezy-Gro Inc................................ F 419 927-6110
  Upper Sandusky *(G-14817)*
- Nutrien AG Solutions Inc...................... G 614 873-4253
  Milford Center *(G-10929)*
- Ohigro Inc... E 740 726-2429
  Waldo *(G-15090)*
- Premier Feeds LLC............................... G 937 584-2411
  Sabina *(G-12891)*

NURSING CARE FACILITIES: Skilled

- Ohio Home & Leisure Products I............ G 614 833-4144
  Pickerington *(G-12465)*
- Optum Infusion Svcs 550 LLC................ D 866 442-4679
  Cincinnati *(G-3227)*

NUTS: Metal

- Facil North America Inc........................ C 330 487-2500
  Twinsburg *(G-14659)*
- Industrial Nut Corp.............................. D 419 625-8543
  Sandusky *(G-13066)*
- Jerry Tools Inc..................................... F 513 242-3211
  Cincinnati *(G-3041)*
- Lear Mfg Co Inc................................... F 440 324-1111
  Elyria *(G-7173)*
- Ramco Specialties Inc.......................... D 330 653-5135
  Hudson *(G-8609)*

- Wheel Group Holdings LLC................... G 614 253-6247
  Columbus *(G-5875)*

NYLON FIBERS

- Cast Nylons Co Ltd............................... D 440 269-2300
  Willoughby *(G-15897)*
- Dowco LLC.. E 330 773-6654
  Akron *(G-133)*

OFFICE EQPT WHOLESALERS

- Friends Service Co Inc.......................... F 800 427-1704
  Dayton *(G-6339)*
- Friends Service Co Inc.......................... D 419 427-1704
  Findlay *(G-7512)*
- Mpc Inc.. E 440 835-1405
  Cleveland *(G-4424)*
- Symatic Inc... F 330 225-1510
  Medina *(G-10381)*

OFFICE EQPT, WHOLESALE: Photocopy Machines

- Ricoh Usa Inc...................................... F 412 281-6700
  Cleveland *(G-4634)*

OFFICE FURNITURE REPAIR & MAINTENANCE SVCS

- American Office Services Inc................. G 440 899-6888
  Westlake *(G-15731)*
- National Electro-Coatings Inc................ D 216 898-0080
  Cleveland *(G-4436)*
- Recycled Systems Furniture Inc............. E 614 880-9110
  Worthington *(G-16210)*

OFFICE SPLY & STATIONERY STORES: Office Forms & Splys

- Ace Rubber Stamp & Off Sup Co............ F 216 771-8483
  Cleveland *(G-3590)*
- Avon Lake Printing............................... G 440 933-2078
  Avon Lake *(G-799)*
- COS Blueprint Inc................................ E 330 376-0022
  Akron *(G-115)*
- Gordons Graphics Inc.......................... G 330 863-2322
  Malvern *(G-9613)*
- Hathaway Stamp Co............................ E 513 621-1052
  Cincinnati *(G-2989)*
- Hubbard Company............................... F 419 784-4455
  Defiance *(G-6682)*
- Murr Corporation................................ F 330 264-2223
  Wooster *(G-16154)*
- O Connor Office Pdts & Prtg................. G 740 852-2209
  London *(G-9392)*
- Quick Tech Graphics Inc....................... E 937 743-5952
  Springboro *(G-13518)*
- Warren Printing & Off Pdts Inc.............. F 419 523-3635
  Ottawa *(G-12196)*

OFFICE SPLYS, NEC, WHOLESALE

- Queen City Office Machine................... F 513 251-7200
  Cincinnati *(G-3317)*
- Wasserstrom Company......................... B 614 228-6525
  Columbus *(G-5865)*

OIL & GAS FIELD EQPT: Drill Rigs

- Buckeye Companies.............................. E 740 452-3641
  Zanesville *(G-16513)*

OIL & GAS FIELD MACHINERY

- Allied Machine Works Inc..................... G 740 454-2534
  Zanesville *(G-16499)*

Employee Codes: A=Over 500 employees, B=251-500
C=101-250, D=51-100, E=20-50, F=10-19, G=1-9

OIL & GAS FIELD MACHINERY

Black Gold Capital LLC .... E 614 348-7460
  Columbus *(G-5196)*

Cameron International Corp .... E 740 654-4260
  Lancaster *(G-8998)*

Electric Dsign For Indust Inc .... E 740 401-4000
  Belpre *(G-1252)*

H P E Inc .... G 330 833-3161
  Massillon *(G-10104)*

OSI Environmental LLC .... E 440 237-4600
  North Royalton *(G-11890)*

Pride of The Hills Manufacturing Inc ...... D 330 567-3108
  Big Prairie *(G-1329)*

Saint-Gobain Norpro Corp .... C 330 673-5860
  Stow *(G-13722)*

Timco Inc .... F 740 685-2594
  Byesville *(G-1900)*

OIL FIELD MACHINERY & EQPT

H & S Company Inc .... E 419 394-4444
  Celina *(G-2335)*

Multi Products Company .... G 330 674-5981
  Millersburg *(G-10986)*

OIL FIELD SVCS, NEC

Altier Brothers Inc .... F 740 347-4329
  Corning *(G-5957)*

Appalachian Oilfield Svcs LLC .... F 337 216-0066
  Sardis *(G-13110)*

Appalachian Well Surveys Inc .... G 740 255-7652
  Cambridge *(G-1922)*

B&L Services .... G 740 390-4272
  Fredericktown *(G-7738)*

Bhl International Inc .... G 216 458-8472
  Cleveland *(G-3734)*

Bijoe Development Inc .... E 330 674-5981
  Millersburg *(G-10946)*

Bishop Well Services Corp .... G 330 264-2023
  Wooster *(G-16104)*

Buckeye Pipe Inspection LLC .... G 440 476-8369
  Chardon *(G-2441)*

CDK Perforating LLC .... D 817 862-9834
  Marietta *(G-9783)*

Complete Energy Services Inc .... F 440 577-1070
  Pierpont *(G-12474)*

Crescent Services LLC .... G 405 603-1200
  Cambridge *(G-1930)*

Danos and Curole .... G 740 609-3599
  Martins Ferry *(G-9897)*

Darin Jordan .... G 740 819-3525
  Nashport *(G-11336)*

Everflow Eastern Partners LP .... G 330 537-3863
  Salem *(G-12993)*

Frantz Well Servicing Inc .... G 419 992-4564
  Tiffin *(G-14086)*

Full Circle Oil Field Svcs Inc .... F 740 371-5422
  Whipple *(G-15814)*

Genco .... G 419 207-7648
  Ashland *(G-576)*

Global Energy Partners LLC .... E 419 756-8027
  Mansfield *(G-9660)*

Hagen Well Service LLC .... G 330 264-7500
  Wooster *(G-16129)*

Halliburton Energy Svcs Inc .... F 740 617-2917
  Zanesville *(G-16535)*

Inland Tarp & Liner LLC .... E 419 436-6001
  Fostoria *(G-7638)*

JT Plus Well Service LLC .... F 740 347-0070
  Corning *(G-5958)*

Karlco Oilfield Services Inc .... F 440 576-3415
  Jefferson *(G-8748)*

Mac Oil Field Service Inc .... E 330 674-7371
  Millersburg *(G-10978)*

Nabors & Nabors Ltd .... G 440 846-0000
  Brunswick *(G-1775)*

Nine Downhole Technologies LLC .... G 817 862-9834
  Marietta *(G-9811)*

Northeastern Oilfield Svcs LLC .... G 330 581-3304
  Canton *(G-2178)*

Northfield Propane LLC .... G 330 854-4320
  Orrville *(G-12141)*

Panhandle Olfld Svc Cmpnies In .... E 330 340-9525
  Cambridge *(G-1947)*

Paragon Intgrted Svcs Group LL .... E 724 639-5126
  Newcomerstown *(G-11650)*

Petrox Inc .... F 330 653-5526
  Streetsboro *(G-13784)*

Pettigrew Pumping Inc .... F 330 297-7900
  Ravenna *(G-12728)*

Recon .... D 740 609-3050
  Bridgeport *(G-1648)*

Stallion Oilfield Cnstr LLC .... D 330 868-2083
  Paris *(G-12282)*

Stratagraph Ne Inc .... F 740 373-3091
  Marietta *(G-9834)*

Superior Energy Group Ltd .... E 216 282-4440
  Willoughby Hills *(G-16028)*

T A W Inc .... G 330 339-1212
  New Philadelphia *(G-11527)*

Tk Gas Services Inc .... E 740 826-0303
  New Concord *(G-11434)*

Tkn Oilfield Services LLC .... F 740 516-2583
  Marietta *(G-9837)*

Triple J Oilfield Services LLC .... G 740 609-3050
  Bridgeport *(G-1650)*

U S Weatherford L P .... C 330 746-2502
  Youngstown *(G-16463)*

United Chart Processors Inc .... G 740 373-5801
  Marietta *(G-9840)*

Universal Well Services Inc .... D 814 333-2656
  Millersburg *(G-11002)*

Vam Usa Llc .... E 330 742-3130
  Youngstown *(G-16467)*

W Pole Contracting Inc .... F 330 325-7177
  Ravenna *(G-12741)*

Well Service Group Inc .... G 330 308-0880
  New Philadelphia *(G-11532)*

Westerman Inc .... C 800 338-8265
  Bremen *(G-1640)*

Wyoming Casing Service Inc .... D 330 479-8785
  Canton *(G-2270)*

OIL TREATING COMPOUNDS

The Lubrizol Corporation .... A 440 943-4200
  Wickliffe *(G-15853)*

OILS & ESSENTIAL OILS

Lg Chem Ohio Petrochemical Inc .... G 470 792-5127
  Ravenna *(G-12723)*

Natural Essentials Inc .... C 330 562-8022
  Streetsboro *(G-13781)*

Peter Cremer North America LP .... D 513 471-7200
  Cincinnati *(G-3251)*

Unitrex Ltd .... D 216 831-1900
  Bedford Heights *(G-1180)*

OILS: Cutting

Dnd Emulsions Inc .... F 419 525-4988
  Mansfield *(G-9646)*

OILS: Lubricating

Functional Products Inc .... F 330 963-3060
  Macedonia *(G-9552)*

Oil Works LLC .... G 614 245-3090
  Columbus *(G-5635)*

OILS: Mineral, Natural

Gfl Environmental Svcs USA Inc .... E 614 441-4001
  Columbus *(G-5701)*

OLEFINS

Lyondell Chemical Company .... C 513 530-4000
  Cincinnati *(G-3718)*

OPERATOR TRAINING, COMPUTER

Computer Workshop Inc .... E 614 798-9505
  Dublin *(G-6877)*

Millers Aplus Cmpt Svcs LLC .... F 330 620-5288
  Akron *(G-250)*

OPHTHALMIC GOODS

Classic Optical Labs Inc .... C 330 759-8245
  Youngstown *(G-6339)*

Cleveland Hoya Corp .... E 440 234-5703
  Berea *(G-1269)*

DMV Corporation .... G 740 452-4787
  Zanesville *(G-1626)*

Luxottica of America Inc .... F 614 492-5610
  Lockbourne *(G-9339)*

Malta Dynamics LLC .... F 740 749-3512
  Waterford *(G-15738)*

Oakley Inc .... F 949 672-6560
  Dayton *(G-6483)*

Steiner Eoptics Inc .... D 937 426-2341
  Miamisburg *(G-7686)*

OPHTHALMIC GOODS WHOLESALERS

Haag-Streit Usa Inc .... D 513 398-3937
  Mason *(G-10000)*

OPHTHALMIC GOODS: Frames & Parts, Eyeglass & Spectacle

Luxottica North Amer Dist LLC .... G 614 492-5610
  Lockbourne *(G-9338)*

OPHTHALMIC GOODS: Frames, Lenses & Parts, Eyeglasses

Essilor of America Inc .... F 513 765-6000
  Mason *(G-9991)*

OPHTHALMIC GOODS: Lenses, Ophthalmic

Sticktite Lenses LLC .... F 571 276-9508
  New Albany *(G-1390)*

Volk Optical Inc .... D 440 942-6161
  Mentor *(G-10594)*

OPTICAL GOODS STORES

Central-1-Optical LLC .... D 330 783-9660
  Youngstown *(G-1334)*

Zenni USA LLC .... D 614 439-9850
  Obetz *(G-12065)*

OPTICAL INSTRUMENTS & APPARATUS

Greenlight Optics LLC .... E 513 247-9777
  Loveland *(G-9483)*

OPTICAL INSTRUMENTS & LENSES

Cincinnati Eye Inst Estgate .... F 513 984-5133
  Cincinnati *(G-2554)*

Cleveland Hoya Corp .... E 440 234-5703
  Berea *(G-1269)*

Genvac Aerospace Inc .... F 440 646-9986
  Highland Heights *(G-8386)*

Gooch & Housego (Ohio) LLC .... D 216 486-6100
  Highland Heights *(G-8387)*

Isomet LLC .... G 937 382-3867
  Wilmington *(G-16015)*

PRODUCT SECTION   PACKAGING MATERIALS: Paper

Krendl Machine Company.................... D 419 692-3060
  Delphos (G-6768)
Mercury Iron and Steel Co.................... F 440 349-1500
  Solon (G-13385)
Optics Incorporated............................... E 800 362-1337
  Brunswick (G-1777)
Punch Components Inc.......................... E 419 224-1242
  Lima (G-9280)
Seiler Enterprises LLC.......................... G 614 330-2220
  Hilliard (G-8439)
Sticktite Lenses LLC............................. F 571 276-9508
  New Albany (G-11390)
True Vision.. G 740 277-7550
  Lancaster (G-9048)
Volk Optical Inc..................................... D 440 942-6161
  Mentor (G-10594)
Vsp Lab Columbus................................ F 614 409-8900
  Lockbourne (G-9342)
Wilson Optical Labs Inc......................... E 440 357-7000
  Mentor (G-10595)

OPTICAL ISOLATORS

Viavi Solutions Inc................................. G 316 522-4981
  Columbus (G-5073)

ORGANIZATIONS: Medical Research

Mp Biomedicals LLC.............................. C 440 337-1200
  Solon (G-13393)
Valensil Technologies LLC.................... E 440 937-8181
  Avon (G-790)

ORGANIZATIONS: Physical Research, Noncommercial

Quasonix Inc.. E 513 942-1287
  West Chester (G-15491)
Sunpower Inc... D 740 594-2221
  Athens (G-699)

ORGANIZATIONS: Religious

Saint Ctherines Metalworks Inc............. G 216 409-0576
  Cleveland (G-4668)
Vista Community Church....................... F 614 718-2294
  Plain City (G-12600)

ORNAMENTS: Christmas Tree, Exc Electrical & Glass

Rhc Inc.. E 330 874-3750
  Bolivar (G-1536)

OVENS: Laboratory

Ignio Systems LLC................................ G 419 708-0503
  Toledo (G-14326)

PACKAGE DESIGN SVCS

Amatech Inc... E 614 252-2506
  Columbus (G-5119)

PACKAGING & LABELING SVCS

Ace Assembly & Packaging Inc............. G 330 866-9117
  Waynesburg (G-15292)
Advanced Specialty Products................ G 419 882-6528
  Bowling Green (G-1550)
Amros Industries Inc............................. E 216 433-0010
  Cleveland (G-3659)
Baumfolder Corporation......................... E 937 492-1281
  Sidney (G-13226)
BDS Packaging Inc................................ F 937 643-0530
  Moraine (G-11161)
Bernard Laboratories Inc....................... E 513 681-7373
  Cincinnati (G-2666)

Crane Consumables Inc......................... E 513 539-9980
  Middletown (G-10814)
Custom Products Corporation................ D 440 528-7100
  Solon (G-13334)
Domino Foods Inc................................. C 216 432-3222
  Cleveland (G-3968)
Expo Packaging Inc............................... E 216 267-9700
  Cleveland (G-4043)
First Choice Packaging Inc.................... C 419 333-4100
  Fremont (G-7778)
G and J Automatic Systems Inc............. E 216 741-6070
  Cleveland (G-4097)
G S K Inc... G 937 547-1611
  Greenville (G-8046)
GL Industries Inc................................... E 513 874-1233
  Hamilton (G-8212)
Groff Industries..................................... F 216 634-9100
  Cleveland (G-4151)
Howard Industries Inc............................ F 614 444-9900
  Columbus (G-5447)
Hunt Products Inc.................................. G 440 667-2457
  Newburgh Heights (G-11617)
Joseph T Snyder Industries Inc............. G 216 883-6900
  Cleveland (G-4260)
Magnaco Industries Inc......................... E 216 961-3636
  Lodi (G-9353)
Metzenbaum Sheltered Inds Inc............ D 440 729-1919
  Chesterland (G-2485)
Ohio Gasket and Shim Co Inc................ E 330 630-0626
  Akron (G-270)
Pactiv LLC.. D 614 771-5400
  Columbus (G-5650)
Pro-Pet LLC.. D 419 394-3374
  Saint Marys (G-12964)
Richland Newhope Inds Inc................... C 419 774-4400
  Mansfield (G-9712)
Safecor Health LLC............................... G 614 351-6117
  Columbus (G-5738)
Safecor Health LLC............................... F 781 933-8780
  Columbus (G-5739)
Systems Pack Inc.................................. E 330 467-5729
  Macedonia (G-9583)
Tekni-Plex Inc....................................... E 419 491-2399
  Holland (G-8532)
Teva Womens Health LLC..................... C 513 731-9900
  Cincinnati (G-3446)
Tko Mfg Services Inc............................. E 937 299-1637
  Moraine (G-11215)
Unique Packaging & Printing................. F 440 785-6730
  Mentor (G-10588)
Universal Packg Systems Inc................ C 513 732-2000
  Batavia (G-957)
Universal Packg Systems Inc................ C 513 735-4777
  Batavia (G-958)
Universal Packg Systems Inc................ C 513 674-9400
  Cincinnati (G-3483)
Welch Packaging Group Inc................... C 614 870-2000
  Columbus (G-5869)

PACKAGING MATERIALS, WHOLESALE

Advanced Poly-Packaging Inc................ C 330 785-4000
  Akron (G-23)
Allied Shipping and Packagi.................. F 937 222-7422
  Moraine (G-11155)
B B Bradley Company Inc..................... G 614 777-5600
  Columbus (G-5171)
BP 10 Inc... E 513 346-3900
  West Chester (G-15382)
Cambridge Packaging Inc..................... E 740 432-3351
  Cambridge (G-1925)
Custom Products Corporation................ D 440 528-7100
  Solon (G-13334)

Diversified Products & Svcs.................. F 740 393-6202
  Mount Vernon (G-11270)
Global-Pak Inc...................................... E 330 482-1993
  Lisbon (G-9312)
Gt Industrial Supply Inc......................... F 513 771-7000
  Cincinnati (G-2976)
Kopco Graphics Inc............................... E 513 874-7230
  West Chester (G-15456)
Protective Packg Solutions LLC............ E 513 769-5777
  Cincinnati (G-3306)
Putnam Plastics Inc.............................. G 937 866-6261
  Dayton (G-6535)
Samuel Son & Co (usa) Inc................... D 740 522-2500
  Heath (G-8331)
Skybox Packaging LLC.......................... C 419 525-7209
  Mansfield (G-9719)
Storopack Inc.. E 513 874-0314
  West Chester (G-15592)
Systems Pack Inc.................................. E 330 467-5729
  Macedonia (G-9583)
Toga-Pak Inc... E 937 294-7311
  Dayton (G-6626)
Tri-State Paper Inc................................ F 937 885-3365
  Dayton (G-6631)
Versa-Pak Ltd....................................... E 419 586-5466
  Celina (G-2355)

PACKAGING MATERIALS: Paper

American Corrugated Products Inc........ C 614 870-2000
  Columbus (G-5124)
Austin Tape and Label Inc..................... D 330 928-7999
  Stow (G-13686)
Bollin & Sons Inc.................................. E 419 693-6573
  Toledo (G-14216)
Colepak LLC... D 937 652-3910
  Urbana (G-14828)
Creative Packaging LLC........................ E 740 452-8497
  Zanesville (G-16524)
Custom Products Corporation................ D 440 528-7100
  Solon (G-13334)
Dubose Strapping Inc............................ E 419 221-0626
  Lima (G-9239)
E-Z Stop Service Center........................ G 330 448-2236
  Brookfield (G-1668)
Georgia-Pacific LLC.............................. C 740 477-3347
  Circleville (G-3553)
Gt Industrial Supply Inc......................... F 513 771-7000
  Cincinnati (G-2976)
Hunt Products Inc.................................. G 440 667-2457
  Newburgh Heights (G-11617)
Joseph T Snyder Industries Inc............. G 216 883-6900
  Cleveland (G-4260)
Kay Toledo Tag Inc................................ D 419 729-5479
  Toledo (G-14346)
Kroy LLC... C 216 426-5600
  Cleveland (G-4299)
Linneas Candy Supplies Inc.................. E 330 678-7112
  Kent (G-8828)
Liqui-Box Corporation............................ E 419 289-9696
  Ashland (G-589)
Loroco Industries Inc............................ D 513 891-9544
  Cincinnati (G-3113)
National Glass Svc Group LLC.............. F 614 652-3699
  Dublin (G-6914)
Nilpeter Usa Inc.................................... C 513 489-4400
  Cincinnati (G-3198)
Norse Dairy Systems Inc....................... C 614 294-4931
  Columbus (G-5600)
North American Plas Chem Inc.............. E 216 531-3400
  Euclid (G-7290)
Novacel Inc... C 937 335-5611
  Troy (G-14598)

PACKAGING MATERIALS: Paper

Orflex Inc.. B
   Cincinnati *(G-3228)*
Pioneer Labels Inc............................ C 618 546-5418
   West Chester *(G-15479)*
Plastic Works Inc.............................. F 440 331-5575
   Cleveland *(G-4560)*
Plastipak Packaging Inc................... B 937 596-6142
   Jackson Center *(G-8736)*
Prime Industries Inc........................... E
   Lorain *(G-9431)*
Safeway Packaging Inc.................... E 419 629-3200
   New Bremen *(G-11408)*
Schilling Graphics Inc....................... E 419 468-1037
   Galion *(G-7884)*
Schwarz Partners Packaging LLC........ F 317 290-1140
   Sidney *(G-13283)*
Signode Industrial Group LLC........... D 513 248-2990
   Loveland *(G-9505)*
Sonoco Products Company................ E 614 759-8470
   Columbus *(G-5778)*
Springdot Inc.................................... D 513 542-4000
   Cincinnati *(G-3411)*
Storopack Inc.................................... E 513 874-0314
   West Chester *(G-15592)*
Stretchtape Inc.................................. E 216 486-9400
   Cleveland *(G-4737)*
Sun America LLC.............................. E 330 821-6300
   Alliance *(G-429)*
Superior Label Systems Inc............... B 513 336-0825
   Mason *(G-10061)*
Tech/III Inc....................................... E 513 482-7500
   Fairfield *(G-7415)*
The Hooven - Dayton Corp................ C 937 233-4473
   Miamisburg *(G-10694)*
Thomas Products Co Inc................... E 513 756-9009
   Cincinnati *(G-3453)*
Visual Marking Systems Inc.............. D 330 425-7100
   Twinsburg *(G-14753)*
Zebco Industries Inc......................... F 740 654-4510
   Lancaster *(G-9049)*

PACKAGING MATERIALS: Paper, Coated Or Laminated

Ampac Plastics LLC......................... B 513 671-1777
   Cincinnati *(G-2624)*
Central Coated Products Inc............. D 330 821-9830
   Alliance *(G-398)*
Central Ohio Paper & Packg Inc........ F 419 621-9239
   Huron *(G-8629)*
Diversipak Inc.................................. E 513 321-7884
   Cincinnati *(G-2833)*
Octal Extrusion Corp........................ D 513 881-6100
   West Chester *(G-15574)*
Retterbush Graphics Packg Corp....... F 513 779-4466
   West Chester *(G-15498)*

PACKAGING MATERIALS: Plastic Film, Coated Or Laminated

Amatech Inc..................................... E 614 252-2506
   Columbus *(G-5119)*
Charter Next Generation Inc............. C 740 369-2770
   Delaware *(G-6709)*
Charter Next Generation Inc............. C 419 884-8150
   Lexington *(G-9195)*
Charter Next Generation Inc............. C 419 884-8150
   Lexington *(G-9196)*
Charter Next Generation Inc............. C 419 884-8150
   Lexington *(G-9197)*
Charter Next Generation Inc............. C 419 884-8150
   Lexington *(G-9198)*
Charter Next Generation Inc............. C 419 884-8150
   Lexington *(G-9199)*
Charter Next Generation Inc............. C 330 830-6030
   Massillon *(G-10084)*
Command Plastic Corporation............ F 800 321-8001
   Bedford *(G-1112)*
Cpg - Ohio LLC................................ D 513 825-4800
   Cincinnati *(G-2800)*
Crayex Corporation........................... D 937 773-7000
   Piqua *(G-12511)*
Engineered Films Division Inc........... D 419 884-8150
   Lexington *(G-9201)*
Future Polytech Inc.......................... E 614 942-1209
   Columbus *(G-5391)*
Polychem LLC.................................. C 440 357-1500
   Mentor *(G-10526)*
Universal Packg Systems Inc............. C 513 732-2000
   Batavia *(G-957)*
Universal Packg Systems Inc............. C 513 735-4777
   Batavia *(G-958)*
Universal Packg Systems Inc............. C 513 674-9400
   Cincinnati *(G-3483)*
Valgroup North America Inc.............. C 419 423-6500
   Findlay *(G-7577)*
Versa-Pak Ltd................................... E 419 586-5466
   Celina *(G-2355)*

PACKAGING: Blister Or Bubble Formed, Plastic

A Aabaco Plastics Inc....................... E 216 663-9494
   Cleveland *(G-3577)*
Alpha Inc.. G 419 996-7355
   Lima *(G-9303)*
Forrest Enterprises Inc..................... F 937 773-1714
   Piqua *(G-12516)*
Rohrer Corporation........................... C 330 335-1541
   Wadsworth *(G-15063)*
Sonoco Prtective Solutions Inc.......... E 419 420-0029
   Findlay *(G-7565)*
Truechoicepack Corp......................... F 937 630-3832
   West Chester *(G-15519)*

PACKING & CRATING SVC

Bates Metal Products Inc.................. D 740 498-8371
   Port Washington *(G-12631)*
Forrest Enterprises Inc..................... F 937 773-1714
   Piqua *(G-12516)*
Lalac One LLC................................. E 216 432-4422
   Cleveland *(G-4307)*

PADDING: Foamed Plastics

Aqua Lily Products LLC.................... G 951 322-0981
   Willoughby *(G-15884)*
J P Industrial Products Inc............... E 330 424-3388
   Lisbon *(G-9318)*
Team Wendy LLC.............................. D 216 738-2518
   Cleveland *(G-4770)*

PAINTS & ADDITIVES

Aexcel Corporation............................ E 440 974-3800
   Mentor *(G-10407)*
Akrochem Corporation....................... D 330 535-2100
   Akron *(G-26)*
Akron Paint & Varnish Inc................ D 330 773-8911
   Akron *(G-38)*
Akzo Nobel Paints LLC..................... A 440 297-8000
   Strongsville *(G-13803)*
All Coatings Co Inc.......................... G 330 821-3806
   Alliance *(G-389)*
Aluminum Coating Manufacturers...... F 216 341-2000
   Cleveland *(G-3644)*
Axalt Powde Coati Syste Usa I........ G 614 921-8000
   Hilliard *(G-8400)*
Axalt Powde Coati Syste Usa I........ G 614 600-4104
   Hilliard *(G-8401)*
Brinkman LLC................................... F 419 204-5934
   Lima *(G-9225)*
Certon Technologies Inc.................... F 440 786-7185
   Bedford *(G-1113)*
Chemspec Usa LLC........................... D 330 669-8512
   Orrville *(G-1212)*
Coloramics LLC................................ E 614 876-1171
   Hilliard *(G-8408)*
Comex North America Inc................ D 303 307-2100
   Cleveland *(G-3888)*
CPC Holding Inc............................... E 216 383-3932
   Cleveland *(G-3890)*
Dap Products Inc.............................. D 937 667-4461
   Tipp City *(G-14181)*
Kalcor Coatings Company.................. E 440 946-4700
   Willoughby *(G-15936)*
Karyall-Telday Inc............................. F 216 281-4063
   Cleveland *(G-4274)*
Nippon Paint Auto Americas Inc....... F 201 692-1111
   Cleveland *(G-4450)*
OPC Polymers LLC........................... C 614 253-8511
   Columbus *(G-5662)*
PPG Architectural Coatings LLC........ D 440 297-8000
   Strongsville *(G-13866)*
PPG Industries Inc............................ E 330 825-0831
   Barberton *(G-893)*
PPG Industries Ohio Inc.................... C 412 434-3888
   Cleveland *(G-4529)*
PPG Industries Ohio Inc.................... C 440 572-6777
   Strongsville *(G-13868)*
PPG Industries Ohio Inc.................... A 216 671-0050
   Cleveland *(G-4530)*
Sheffield Bronze Paint Corp.............. E 216 481-8330
   Cleveland *(G-4650)*
Sherwin-Williams Company................ C 330 830-6000
   Massillon *(G-10104)*

PAINTS & ALLIED PRODUCTS

Akzo Nobel Coatings Inc................... C 614 294-3361
   Columbus *(G-51?)*
Akzo Nobel Coatings Inc................... E 419 433-9143
   Huron *(G-8625)*
Americhem Inc................................... D 330 929-4213
   Cuyahoga Falls *(G-6064)*
Aps-Materials Inc.............................. D 937 278-6547
   Dayton *(G-6210)*
Avient Corporation............................. E 419 668-4844
   Norwalk *(G-11955)*
Basic Coatings LLC.......................... F 419 241-2156
   Bowling Green *(G-1553)*
Bollin & Sons Inc.............................. E 419 693-6573
   Toledo *(G-14216)*
Buckeye Fabric Finishers Inc............. F 740 622-3251
   Coshocton *(G-5977)*
Chemmasters Inc............................... E 440 428-2105
   Madison *(G-9589)*
Consolidated Coatings Corp............... A 216 514-7596
   Cleveland *(G-3898)*
CTS National Corporation................. E 216 566-2000
   Cleveland *(G-3918)*
Deco Plas Properties LLC................. F 419 485-0632
   Montpelier *(G-1113)*
Epsilon Management Corporation....... E 216 634-2500
   Cleveland *(G-4025)*
Fuchs Lubricants Co........................ F 330 963-0400
   Twinsburg *(G-14668)*
General Electric Company.................. E 216 268-3846
   Cleveland *(G-4114)*

Harrison Paint Company............................ E 330 455-5120
   Canton (G-2122)

Henkel US Operations Corp...................... C 216 475-3600
   Cleveland (G-4180)

Hexpol Compounding LLC......................... C 440 834-4644
   Burton (G-1880)

Hoover & Wells Inc................................... C 419 691-9220
   Toledo (G-14319)

Ineos Neal LLC... E 610 790-3333
   Dublin (G-6896)

Ineos Solvents Sales US Corp................... B 614 790-3333
   Dublin (G-6897)

Kardol Quality Products LLC..................... G 513 933-8206
   Blue Ash (G-1416)

Leonhardt Plating Company....................... F 513 242-1410
   Cincinnati (G-3102)

Mameco International Inc.......................... D 216 752-4400
   Cleveland (G-4354)

Matrix Sys Auto Finishes LLC.................... B 248 668-8135
   Massillon (G-10125)

McBmrdd... G 937 910-7301
   Dayton (G-6431)

McCann Color Inc....................................... E 330 498-4840
   Canton (G-2156)

Meggitt (erlanger) LLC............................... D 513 851-5550
   Cincinnati (G-3143)

Mid-America Chemical Corp...................... G 216 749-0100
   Cleveland (G-4406)

Npa Coatings Inc.. C 216 651-5900
   Cleveland (G-4486)

Parker Trutec Incorporated....................... D 937 653-8500
   Urbana (G-14846)

Perstorp Polyols Inc................................... C 419 729-5448
   Toledo (G-14434)

Plasti-Kote Co Inc...................................... C 330 725-4511
   Medina (G-10363)

Pmbp Legacy Co Inc.................................. E 330 253-8148
   Akron (G-278)

Polymerics Inc.. E 330 928-2210
   Cuyahoga Falls (G-6110)

Polynt Composites USA Inc...................... E 816 391-6000
   Sandusky (G-13088)

PPG Architectural Finishes Inc................. F 513 242-3050
   Cincinnati (G-3269)

PPG Architectural Finishes Inc................. F 513 563-0220
   Cincinnati (G-3270)

PPG Industries Inc..................................... E 740 774-8734
   Chillicothe (G-2526)

PPG Industries Inc..................................... E 740 774-7600
   Chillicothe (G-2527)

PPG Industries Inc..................................... E 740 774-7600
   Chillicothe (G-2528)

PPG Industries Inc..................................... C 740 474-3161
   Circleville (G-3554)

PPG Industries Inc..................................... E 216 671-7793
   Cleveland (G-4567)

PPG Industries Inc..................................... G 740 363-9610
   Delaware (G-6743)

PPG Industries Inc..................................... F 419 331-2011
   Lima (G-9277)

PPG Industries Inc..................................... D 440 572-2800
   Strongsville (G-13867)

PPG Industries Ohio Inc............................ B 740 363-9610
   Delaware (G-6744)

PPG Industries Ohio Inc............................ D 412 434-1542
   Euclid (G-7295)

Priest Services Inc..................................... G 440 333-1123
   Mayfield Heights (G-10254)

Republic Powdered Metals Inc................. D 330 225-3192
   Medina (G-10370)

Sherwin-Williams Company........................ G 216 566-2000
   Cleveland (G-4694)

Sherwin-Williams Company........................ G 330 528-0124
   Hudson (G-8611)

Sherwin-Williams Company........................ F 440 846-4328
   Strongsville (G-13880)

Sherwin-Williams Company........................ A 216 566-2000
   Cleveland (G-4693)

Sherwin-Williams Mfg Co........................... F 216 566-2000
   Cleveland (G-4695)

Sherwn-Wllams Auto Fnshes Corp........... E 216 332-8330
   Cleveland (G-4696)

Strong-Coat LLC.. G 440 299-2068
   Willoughby (G-16000)

Teknol Inc... D 937 264-0190
   Dayton (G-6613)

Tnemec Co Inc... G 614 850-8160
   Hilliard (G-8449)

Tremco Incorporated................................. B
   Beachwood (G-1031)

Universal Urethane Pdts Inc..................... D 419 693-7400
   Toledo (G-14514)

Urethane Polymers Intl............................. F 216 430-3655
   Cleveland (G-4855)

Vanguard Paints and Finishes Inc........... E 740 373-5261
   Marietta (G-9842)

Vibrantz Corporation................................. F 216 875-5600
   Mayfield Heights (G-10256)

Wooster Products Inc................................ D 330 264-2844
   Wooster (G-16186)

Zircoa Inc... C 440 248-0500
   Cleveland (G-4936)

PAINTS, VARNISHES & SPLYS WHOLESALERS

Autobody Supply Company Inc................. D 614 228-4328
   Columbus (G-5166)

Finishmaster Inc.. F 614 228-4328
   Groveport (G-8139)

Teknol Inc... D 937 264-0190
   Dayton (G-6613)

PAINTS, VARNISHES & SPLYS, WHOLESALE: Paints

Comex North America Inc......................... D 303 307-2100
   Cleveland (G-3888)

Jmac Inc... E 614 436-2418
   Columbus (G-5498)

Matrix Sys Auto Finishes LLC.................... B 248 668-8135
   Massillon (G-10125)

PAINTS: Oil Or Alkyd Vehicle Or Water Thinned

Akzo Nobel Coatings Inc........................... E 937 322-2671
   Springfield (G-13529)

Mansfield Paint Co Inc............................... G 330 725-2436
   Medina (G-10346)

Waterlox Coatings Corporation................ F 216 641-4877
   Cleveland (G-4896)

PALLET REPAIR SVCS

Able Pallet Mfg & Repr............................... G 614 444-2115
   Columbus (G-5091)

Mpi Logistics and Service Inc................... E 330 832-5309
   Massillon (G-10130)

PALLETIZERS & DEPALLETIZERS

Intelligrated Systems Ohio LLC................ A 513 701-7300
   Mason (G-10012)

PALLETS & SKIDS: Wood

Able Pallet Mfg & Repr............................... G 614 444-2115
   Columbus (G-5091)

Aero Pallets Inc... E 330 260-7107
   Carrollton (G-2303)

Arrowhead Pallet LLC................................ G 440 693-4241
   Middlefield (G-10732)

Belco Works Inc... D 740 695-0500
   Saint Clairsville (G-12897)

Boscowood Ventures Inc........................... F 440 429-5669
   Lorain (G-9404)

Clark Rm Inc... F 419 425-9889
   Findlay (G-7494)

D P Products Inc.. G 440 834-9663
   Middlefield (G-10747)

Haessly Lumber Sales Co.......................... D 740 373-6681
   Marietta (G-9798)

Hann Manufacturing Inc............................ E 740 962-3752
   Mcconnelsville (G-10281)

Makers Supply LLC.................................... G 937 203-8245
   Piqua (G-12534)

PRU Industries Inc..................................... F 937 746-8702
   Franklin (G-7694)

Quadco Rehabilitation Ctr Inc.................. E 419 445-1950
   Archbold (G-543)

Quadco Rehabilitation Ctr Inc.................. B 419 682-1011
   Stryker (G-13912)

Richland Newhope Inds Inc...................... C 419 774-4400
   Mansfield (G-9712)

Savvy Mtngs Special Events Ltd.............. G 916 774-3838
   Berea (G-1293)

Southwood Pallet LLC............................... D 330 682-3747
   Orrville (G-12158)

Troymill Manufacturing Inc....................... F 440 632-5580
   Middlefield (G-10793)

Tusco Hardwoods LLC............................... F 330 852-4281
   Sugarcreek (G-13946)

Wjf Enterprises LLC................................... G 513 871-7320
   Cincinnati (G-3523)

Yoder Lumber Co Inc................................ D 330 674-1435
   Millersburg (G-11009)

PALLETS: Plastic

Carbon Polymers Company....................... D 330 948-3007
   Lodi (G-9348)

Mye Automotive Inc................................... D 330 253-5592
   Akron (G-258)

Myers Industries Inc................................. E 330 253-5592
   Akron (G-260)

PALLETS: Wood & Metal Combination

Satco Inc... D 513 707-6150
   Loveland (G-9504)

PANEL & DISTRIBUTION BOARDS & OTHER RELATED APPARATUS

Acorn Technology Corporation................. E 216 663-1244
   Shaker Heights (G-13149)

Eaton Electric Holdings LLC...................... B 440 523-5000
   Cleveland (G-3995)

Jeff Bonham Electric Inc........................... E 937 233-7662
   Dayton (G-6388)

PANEL & DISTRIBUTION BOARDS: Electric

Assembly Works Inc.................................. G 419 433-5010
   Huron (G-8628)

Industrial Solutions Inc............................ E 614 431-8118
   Lewis Center (G-9163)

Osborne Coinage Company LLC.............. D 877 480-0456
   Blue Ash (G-1448)

Spectra-Tech Manufacturing Inc............. E 513 735-9300
   Batavia (G-949)

PANELS: Building, Plastic, NEC

Ad Industries Inc .... A 303 744-1911
Dayton (G-6183)

Fiberglass Technology Inds Inc .... E 740 335-9400
Wshngtn Ct Hs (G-16232)

Remram Recovery LLC .... F 740 667-0092
Tuppers Plains (G-14618)

PAPER & BOARD: Die-cut

Art Guild Binders Inc .... E 513 242-3000
Cincinnati (G-2634)

Buckeye Boxes Inc .... D 614 274-8484
Columbus (G-5219)

Chilcote Company .... C 216 781-6000
Cleveland (G-3819)

Foldedpak Inc .... G 740 527-1090
Hebron (G-8341)

Georgia-Pacific LLC .... C 740 477-3347
Circleville (G-3553)

Harris Paper Crafts Inc .... F 614 299-2141
Columbus (G-5421)

Honeymoon Paper Products Inc .... D 513 755-7200
Fairfield (G-7368)

Hunt Products Inc .... G 440 667-2457
Newburgh Heights (G-11617)

Kent Adhesive Products Co .... D 330 678-1626
Kent (G-8821)

Keyah International Trdg LLC .... E 937 399-3140
Springfield (G-13588)

Lam Pro Inc .... F 216 426-0661
Cleveland (G-4308)

Multi-Craft Litho Inc .... E 859 581-2754
Blue Ash (G-1442)

Nordec Inc .... D 330 940-3700
Stow (G-13715)

Printers Bindery Services Inc .... D 513 821-8039
Batavia (G-944)

Rohrer Corporation .... C 330 335-1541
Wadsworth (G-15063)

Southern Champion Tray LP .... D 513 755-7200
Fairfield (G-7410)

Springdot Inc .... D 513 542-4000
Cincinnati (G-3411)

Stuart Company .... E 513 621-9462
Cincinnati (G-3425)

Vya Inc .... E 513 772-5400
Cincinnati (G-3506)

PAPER & PAPER PRDTS: Crepe, Made From Purchased Materials

Cindus Corporation .... D 513 948-9951
Cincinnati (G-2766)

PAPER PRDTS: Infant & Baby Prdts

Sposie LLC .... F 888 977-2229
Maumee (G-10234)

PAPER PRDTS: Molded Pulp Prdts

Gr8 News Packaging LLC .... F 314 739-1202
Lockbourne (G-9235)

PAPER PRDTS: Napkins, Sanitary, Made From Purchased Material

Health Care Products Inc .... E 419 678-9620
Coldwater (G-4992)

Procter & Gamble Far East Inc .... C 513 983-1100
Cincinnati (G-3295)

Tranzonic Companies .... C 440 446-0643
Cleveland (G-4818)

Tranzonic Companies .... D 216 535-4300
Richmond Heights (G-12811)

Tz Acquisition Corp .... E 216 535-4300
Richmond Heights (G-12812)

PAPER PRDTS: Sanitary

Attends Healthcare Pdts Inc .... G 740 368-7880
Delaware (G-6703)

Eleeo Brands LLC .... G
Cincinnati (G-2863)

Eleeo Brands LLC .... G 513 572-8100
Cincinnati (G-2864)

Giant Industries Inc .... E 419 531-4600
Toledo (G-14300)

Linsalata Cpitl Prtners Fund I .... G 440 684-1400
Cleveland (G-4330)

Playtex Manufacturing Inc .... E 937 498-4710
Sidney (G-13271)

PAPER PRDTS: Tampons, Sanitary, Made From Purchased Material

Tambrands Sales Corp .... C 513 983-1100
Cincinnati (G-3441)

This Is L Inc .... G 415 630-5172
Cincinnati (G-3452)

PAPER, WHOLESALE: Printing

Millcraft Group LLC .... D 216 441-5500
Independence (G-8675)

PAPER: Adhesive

Acpo Ltd .... D 419 898-8273
Oak Harbor (G-12009)

Avery Dennison Corporation .... G 216 267-8700
Cleveland (G-3707)

Avery Dennison Corporation .... C 440 358-4691
Concord Township (G-5901)

Avery Dennison Corporation .... D 440 639-3900
Mentor (G-10427)

Avery Dennison Corporation .... F 937 865-2439
Miamisburg (G-10613)

Avery Dennison Corporation .... B 440 358-2564
Painesville (G-12218)

Avery Dennison Corporation .... B 440 878-7000
Strongsville (G-13814)

Avery Dennison Corporation .... B 440 534-6000
Mentor (G-10426)

Avery Dnnison G Holdings I LLC .... E 440 534-6000
Mentor (G-10429)

Bollin & Sons Inc .... E 419 693-6573
Toledo (G-14216)

CCL Label Inc .... D 216 676-2703
Cleveland (G-3801)

CCL Label Inc .... D 440 878-7000
Strongsville (G-13819)

GBS Corp .... C 330 863-1828
Malvern (G-9612)

Kent Adhesive Products Co .... D 330 678-1626
Kent (G-8821)

Linneas Candy Supplies Inc .... E 330 678-7112
Kent (G-8828)

Magnum Tapes Films .... G 877 460-8402
Caldwell (G-1911)

Miller Products Inc .... C 330 938-2134
Sebring (G-13122)

Miller Studio Inc .... E 330 339-1100
New Philadelphia (G-11519)

Morgan Adhesives Company LLC ...... B 330 688-1111
Stow (G-13709)

Stretchtape Inc .... E 216 486-9400
Cleveland (G-4737)

Technicote Inc .... E 800 358-4448
Miamisburg (G-10691)

Technicote Westfield Inc .... E 937 859-4448
Miamisburg (G-10692)

PAPER: Book

Glatfelter Corporation .... G 740 772-3893
Chillicothe (G-2706)

Glatfelter Corporation .... F 740 775-6119
Chillicothe (G-2707)

Glatfelter Corporation .... D 740 772-3111
Chillicothe (G-2708)

PAPER: Building, Insulating & Packaging

Avery Dennison Corporation .... C 440 358-4691
Concord Township (G-5901)

Avery Dennison Corporation .... D 440 639-3900
Mentor (G-10427)

PAPER: Cardboard

Valley Converting Co Inc .... E 740 537-2152
Toronto (G-14537)

PAPER: Cloth Lined, Made From Purchased Materials

Tekni-Plex Inc .... E 419 491-2399
Holland (G-8532)

PAPER: Coated & Laminated, NEC

3 Sigma LLC .... D 937 440-3400
Troy (G-14548)

Adcraft Decals Incorporated .... E 216 524-2934
Cleveland (G-3558)

Avery Dennison Corporation .... F 440 534-6527
Mentor (G-10425)

Avery Dennison Corporation .... F 419 898-8273
Oak Harbor (G-12010)

Avery Dennison Corporation .... C 440 358-3466
Painesville (G-12217)

BMC Growth Fund LLC .... C 937 291-4110
Miamisburg (G-10620)

Bucher Printing .... G 937 228-2022
Dayton (G-6238)

Central Coated Products Inc .... D 330 821-9830
Alliance (G-398)

Deco Tools Inc .... E 419 476-9321
Toledo (G-14262)

Dermamed Coatin .... F 330 474-3786
Kent (G-8809)

Gary I Teach Jr .... G 614 582-7483
London (G-9387)

Glatfelter Corporation .... G 419 333-6700
Fremont (G-7787)

Hall Company .... E 937 652-1376
Urbana (G-14833)

Kardol Quality Products LLC .... G 513 933-8206
Blue Ash (G-1416)

Label Technique Southeast LLC .... E 440 951-7660
Willoughby (G-15541)

Lam Pro Inc .... F 216 426-0661
Cleveland (G-4308)

Laminate Technologies Inc .... D 800 231-2523
Tiffin (G-14090)

Loroco Industries Inc .... G 513 891-9544
Cincinnati (G-3113)

Mr Label Inc .... E 513 681-2088
Cincinnati (G-3177)

Nilpeter Usa Inc .... C 513 489-4400
Cincinnati (G-3198)

Ohio Laminating & Binding Inc .... F 614 771-4868
Hilliard (G-8426)

PRODUCT SECTION PARTITIONS: Wood & Fixtures

Pioneer Labels Inc .... C 618 546-5418
  West Chester *(G-15479)*
R R Donnelley & Sons Company .... D 440 774-2101
  Oberlin *(G-12055)*
Roemer Industries Inc .... D 330 448-2000
  Masury *(G-10158)*
Sensical Inc .... D 216 641-1141
  Solon *(G-13420)*
Superior Label Systems Inc .... B 513 336-0825
  Mason *(G-10061)*
Thomas Products Co Inc .... E 513 756-9009
  Cincinnati *(G-3453)*
Waytek Corporation .... E 937 743-6142
  Franklin *(G-7711)*

PAPER: Coated, Exc Photographic, Carbon Or Abrasive

Domtar Corporation .... B 937 859-8261
  West Carrollton *(G-15353)*
Novacel Prfmce Coatings Inc .... D 937 552-4932
  Troy *(G-14599)*

PAPER: Fine

Billerud US Prod Holdg LLC .... B 877 855-7243
  Miamisburg *(G-10619)*
Blue Ridge Paper Products LLC .... D 440 235-7200
  Olmsted Falls *(G-12077)*

PAPER: Newsprint

B & B Paper Converters Inc .... F 216 941-8100
  Cleveland *(G-3713)*

PAPER: Packaging

Ampac Plastics LLC .... B 513 671-1777
  Cincinnati *(G-2624)*
Duracorp LLC .... D 740 549-3336
  Lewis Center *(G-9158)*
Graphic Paper Products Corp .... D 937 325-5503
  Springfield *(G-13570)*
Special Pack Inc .... E 330 458-3204
  Canton *(G-2229)*

PAPER: Specialty

Billerud Commercial LLC .... F 877 855-7243
  Miamisburg *(G-10617)*

PAPER: Specialty Or Chemically Treated

Gvs Industries Inc .... G 513 851-3606
  Hamilton *(G-8214)*
Novolyte Technologies Inc .... B 216 867-1040
  Cleveland *(G-4485)*
Pixelle Spcialty Solutions LLC .... A 740 772-3111
  Chillicothe *(G-2525)*
Pixelle Spcialty Solutions LLC .... C 419 333-6700
  Fremont *(G-7801)*

PAPER: Tissue

Novolex Holdings Inc .... B 937 746-1933
  Franklin *(G-7690)*

PAPER: Wrapping & Packaging

Corrchoice Cincinnati .... G 330 833-2884
  Massillon *(G-10086)*
Gvr Warehouse and Packg LLC .... G 440 272-1005
  Orwell *(G-12164)*
Polymer Packaging Inc .... D 330 832-2000
  North Canton *(G-11751)*
Specialty America Inc .... F 516 252-2438
  Columbus *(G-5781)*
Welch Packaging Group Inc .... C 614 870-2000
  Columbus *(G-5869)*

PAPERBOARD PRDTS: Folding Boxboard

Caraustar Industries Inc .... E 330 665-7700
  Copley *(G-5946)*
Graphic Packaging Intl LLC .... C 513 424-4200
  Middletown *(G-10828)*
Graphic Packaging Intl LLC .... C 440 248-4370
  Solon *(G-13357)*
Smith-Lustig Paper Box Mfg Co .... F 216 621-0453
  Bedford *(G-1155)*

PAPERBOARD PRDTS: Packaging Board

National Carton & Coating Company ..... D 937 347-1042
  Xenia *(G-16270)*
Saica Pack US LLC .... E 513 399-5602
  Hamilton *(G-8240)*
Thorwald Holdings Inc .... F 740 756-9271
  Lancaster *(G-9044)*

PARTICLEBOARD: Laminated, Plastic

Miller Manufacturing Inc .... E 330 852-0689
  Sugarcreek *(G-13931)*

PARTITIONS & FIXTURES: Except Wood

3-D Technical Services Company .... E 937 746-2901
  Franklin *(G-7659)*
Accel Group Inc .... D 330 336-0317
  Wadsworth *(G-15014)*
B-R-O-T Incorporated .... E 216 267-5335
  Cleveland *(G-3717)*
Benko Products Inc .... E 440 934-2180
  Sheffield Village *(G-13181)*
Cdc Corporation .... E 715 532-5548
  Maumee *(G-10173)*
Communication Exhibits Inc .... D 330 854-4040
  Canal Fulton *(G-1970)*
Component Systems Inc .... E 216 252-9292
  Cleveland *(G-3893)*
Control Electric Co .... E 216 671-8010
  Columbia Station *(G-5011)*
Crescent Metal Products Inc .... C 440 350-1100
  Mentor *(G-10445)*
Custom Millcraft Corp .... E 513 874-7080
  West Chester *(G-15410)*
Danco Metal Products LLC .... D 440 871-2300
  Avon Lake *(G-803)*
Display Dynamics Inc .... E 937 832-2830
  Englewood *(G-7229)*
Gwp Holdings Inc .... E 513 860-4050
  Fairfield *(G-7364)*
HP Manufacturing Company Inc .... D 216 361-6500
  Cleveland *(G-4204)*
Idx Dayton LLC .... C 937 401-3460
  Dayton *(G-6379)*
Integral Design Inc .... F 216 524-0555
  Cleveland *(G-4230)*
Kellogg Cabinets Inc .... G 614 833-9596
  Canal Winchester *(G-1988)*
Mac Lean J S Co .... E 614 878-5454
  Columbus *(G-5538)*
Marlite Inc .... C 330 343-6621
  Dover *(G-6833)*
Midmark Corporation .... E 937 526-3662
  Versailles *(G-14986)*
Midmark Corporation .... A 937 528-7500
  Miamisburg *(G-10661)*
Modern Retail Solutions LLC .... E 330 527-4308
  Garrettsville *(G-7923)*
Mro Built LLC .... D 330 526-0555
  North Canton *(G-11746)*
Myers Industries Inc .... D 330 336-6921
  Wadsworth *(G-15047)*
Ohio Displays Inc .... F 216 961-5600
  Elyria *(G-7189)*
Organized Living Inc .... E 513 489-9300
  Cincinnati *(G-3230)*
Panacea Products Corporation .... E 614 429-6320
  Columbus *(G-5653)*
Panacea Products Corporation .... E 614 850-7000
  Columbus *(G-5652)*
Pfi Displays Inc .... E 330 925-9015
  Rittman *(G-12826)*
Prestige Store Interiors Inc .... F 419 476-2106
  Maumee *(G-10224)*
Pucel Enterprises Inc .... D 216 881-4604
  Cleveland *(G-4598)*
Rack Processing Company Inc .... E 937 294-1911
  Moraine *(G-11206)*
Rogers Display Inc .... E 440 951-9200
  Mentor *(G-10547)*
Stanley Industrial & Auto LLC .... C 614 755-7089
  Dublin *(G-6943)*
Stein Holdings Inc .... D 440 526-9301
  Independence *(G-8686)*
Ternion Inc .... E 216 642-6180
  Cleveland *(G-4777)*
Tusco Limited Partnership .... C 740 254-4343
  Gnadenhutten *(G-7991)*
Valley Plastics Company Inc .... E 419 666-2349
  Toledo *(G-14518)*
W B Becherer Inc .... G 330 758-6616
  Youngstown *(G-16473)*
W J Egli Company Inc .... F 330 823-3666
  Alliance *(G-435)*

PARTITIONS: Solid Fiber, Made From Purchased Materials

Colepak LLC .... D 937 652-3910
  Urbana *(G-14828)*

PARTITIONS: Wood & Fixtures

A & J Woodworking Inc .... G 419 695-5655
  Delphos *(G-6759)*
Accent Manufacturing Inc .... F 330 724-7704
  Norton *(G-11936)*
Action Group Inc .... D 614 868-8868
  Blacklick *(G-1330)*
Amtekco Industries Inc .... E 614 228-6525
  Columbus *(G-5137)*
As America Inc .... E 419 522-4211
  Mansfield *(G-9626)*
Automated Bldg Components Inc .... E 419 257-2152
  North Baltimore *(G-11694)*
Creative Products Inc .... G 419 866-5501
  Holland *(G-8500)*
D Lewis Inc .... G 740 695-2615
  Saint Clairsville *(G-12901)*
Diversified Products & Svcs .... F 740 393-6202
  Mount Vernon *(G-11270)*
Forum III Inc .... G 513 961-5123
  Cincinnati *(G-2917)*
Geograph Industries Inc .... E 513 202-9200
  Harrison *(G-8276)*
Home Stor & Off Solutions Inc .... E 216 362-4660
  Cleveland *(G-4199)*
Kitchens By Rutenschroer Inc .... G 513 251-8333
  Cincinnati *(G-3080)*
L E Smith Company .... D 419 636-4555
  Bryan *(G-1825)*
Leiden Cabinet Company LLC .... G 330 425-8555
  Strasburg *(G-13748)*
Lemon Group LLC .... E 614 409-9850
  Obetz *(G-12060)*

Employee Codes: A=Over 500 employees, B=251-500
C=101-250, D=51-100, E=20-50, F=10-19, G=1-9

PARTITIONS: Wood & Fixtures

PRODUCT SECTION

Lima Millwork Inc .... F 419 331-3303
  Elida (G-7094)
Partitions Plus Incorporated .... E 419 422-2600
  Findlay (G-7550)
R & R Fabrications Inc .... E 419 678-4831
  Saint Henry (G-12937)
Reserve Millwork LLC .... E 216 531-6982
  Bedford (G-1153)
Riceland Cabinet Inc .... D 330 601-1071
  Wooster (G-16163)
Romline Express LLC .... G 234 855-1905
  Youngstown (G-16431)
Solid Surface Concepts Inc .... E 513 948-8677
  Cincinnati (G-3401)
Symatic Inc .... F 330 225-1510
  Medina (G-10381)
Thomas Cabinet Shop Inc .... F 937 847-8239
  Dayton (G-6621)
Tusco Limited Partnership .... C 740 254-4343
  Gnadenhutten (G-7991)
Wine Cellar Innovations LLC .... C 513 321-3733
  Cincinnati (G-3522)

PARTS: Metal

Allpass Corporation .... F 440 998-6300
  Madison (G-9587)
Cleveland Steel Specialty Co .... E 216 464-9400
  Bedford Heights (G-1168)
Clifton Steel Company .... D 216 662-6111
  Maple Heights (G-9749)
Diller Metals Inc .... G 419 943-3364
  Leipsic (G-9132)
Sharon Manufacturing Inc .... E 330 239-1561
  Sharon Center (G-13167)
Strohecker Incorporated .... E 330 426-9496
  East Palestine (G-7009)

PATIENT MONITORING EQPT WHOLESALERS

Neurowave Systems Inc .... G 216 361-1591
  Beachwood (G-1002)

PATTERNS: Indl

Advantic Building Group LLC .... F 513 290-4796
  Miamisburg (G-10606)
Air Power Dynamics LLC .... C 440 701-2100
  Mentor (G-10408)
Anchor Pattern Company .... G 614 443-2221
  Columbus (G-5142)
API Pattern Works Inc .... E 440 269-1766
  Willoughby (G-15879)
Cascade Pattern Company Inc .... E 440 323-4300
  Elyria (G-7122)
Clinton Foundry Ltd .... F 419 243-6885
  Toledo (G-14244)
Clinton Pattern Works Inc .... F 419 243-0855
  Toledo (G-14245)
Colonial Patterns Inc .... F 330 673-6475
  Kent (G-8805)
Dayton Pattern Inc .... G 937 277-0761
  Dayton (G-6286)
Design Pattern Works Inc .... G 937 252-0797
  Dayton (G-6297)
Elyria Pattern Co Inc .... G 440 323-1526
  Elyria (G-7144)
Feiner Pattern Works Inc .... F 513 851-9800
  Fairfield (G-7359)
Freeman Manufacturing & Sup Co .... E 440 934-1902
  Avon (G-775)
H&M Machine & Tool LLC .... E 419 776-9220
  Toledo (G-14306)
Industrial Pattern & Mfg Co .... F 614 252-0934
  Columbus (G-5457)
Industrial Technologies Inc .... G 330 434-2033
  Akron (G-190)
J-Lenco Inc .... E 740 499-2260
  Morral (G-11221)
Ketco Inc .... E 937 426-9331
  Beavercreek (G-1053)
Liberty Pattern and Mold Inc .... G 330 788-9463
  Youngstown (G-16389)
Lorain Modern Pattern Inc .... F 440 365-6780
  Elyria (G-7174)
Mold Masters Inc .... G 216 561-6653
  Shaker Heights (G-13157)
Past Patterns .... F 937 223-3722
  Dayton (G-6498)
R L Rush Tool & Pattern Inc .... G 419 562-9849
  Bucyrus (G-1866)
Reliable Castings Corporation .... D
  Cincinnati (G-3331)
Reliable Pattern Works Inc .... G 440 232-8820
  Cleveland (G-4623)
Ross Aluminum Castings LLC .... C 937 492-4134
  Sidney (G-13279)
Seaport Mold & Casting Company .... E 419 243-1422
  Toledo (G-14464)
Seaway Pattern Mfg Inc .... E 419 865-5724
  Toledo (G-14465)
Sherwood Rtm Corp .... G 330 875-7151
  Louisville (G-9471)
Spectracam Ltd .... G 937 223-3805
  Dayton (G-6582)
Tempcraft Corporation .... A 216 391-3885
  Cleveland (G-4775)
Th Manufacturing Inc .... G 330 893-3572
  Millersburg (G-10998)
Transducers Direct Llc .... F 513 247-0601
  Cincinnati (G-3462)
United States Drill Head Co .... E 513 941-0300
  Cincinnati (G-3482)

PAVERS

JB Pavers and Hardscapes LLC .... G 937 454-1145
  Vandalia (G-14946)

PAVING MIXTURES

Stoneco Inc .... G 419 693-3933
  Toledo (G-14475)

PAYROLL SVCS

Samb LLC Services .... G 937 660-0115
  Englewood (G-7241)

PENCILS & PENS WHOLESALERS

Identity Group LLC .... G 614 337-6167
  Westerville (G-15658)

PERFUME: Perfumes, Natural Or Synthetic

Aeroscena LLC .... F 800 671-1890
  Cleveland (G-3611)

PERFUMES

IMH LLC .... F 513 800-9830
  Columbus (G-5454)
IMH LLC .... G 614 436-0991
  Columbus (G-5455)

PERISCOPES

Miller-Holzwarth Inc .... D 330 342-7224
  Salem (G-13017)

PEST CONTROL IN STRUCTURES SVCS

A Best Trmt & Pest Ctrl Sups .... G 330 434-5555
  Akron (G-10)

PEST CONTROL SVCS

Hawthorne Gardening Company .... E 360 883-8846
  Marysville (G-9913)
Scotts Miracle-Gro Company .... B 937 644-0011
  Marysville (G-9935)

PESTICIDES

A Best Trmt & Pest Ctrl Sups .... G 330 434-5555
  Akron (G-10)

PET SPLYS

Aquatic Technology .... F 440 236-8330
  Columbia Station (G-5005)
Canine Creations Inc .... G 937 667-8576
  Tipp City (G-14125)
Crochet Kitty LLC .... G 440 340-5152
  Parma (G-12287)
Hartz Mountain Corporation .... D 513 877-2131
  Pleasant Plain (G-12607)
Heading4ward Investment Co .... G 937 293-9994
  Moraine (G-11185)

PETROLEUM & PETROLEUM PRDTS, WHOLESALE: Bulk Stations

Cincinnati - Vulcan Company .... D 513 242-5300
  Cincinnati (G-2736)
Universal Oil Inc .... E 216 771-4300
  Cleveland (G-4851)

PHARMACEUTICAL PREPARATIONS: Adrenal

Pharmaforce Inc C
  Columbus (G-5671)

PHARMACEUTICAL PREPARATIONS: Druggists' Preparations

Abbott Laboratories .... A 614 624-7677
  Columbus (G-5089)
CMC Pharmaceuticals Inc .... G 216 600-9430
  Solon (G-13331)
Flow Dry Technology Inc .... C 937 833-2161
  Brookville (G-1736)
Ftd Investments LLC .... A 937 833-2161
  Brookville (G-1737)
Hikma Labs Inc .... C 614 276-4000
  Columbus (G-5438)
Soleo Health Inc .... E 844 467-8200
  Dublin (G-6941)
West-Ward Columbus Inc .... A 614 276-4000
  Columbus (G-5873)

PHARMACEUTICAL PREPARATIONS: Pills

Sermonix Pharmaceuticals Inc .... F 614 864-4919
  Columbus (G-5760)

PHARMACEUTICAL PREPARATIONS: Proprietary Drug

Buderer Drug Company Inc .... E 419 627-2800
  Sandusky (G-13046)
Camargo Phrm Svcs LLC .... F 513 561-3329
  Cincinnati (G-2698)

PHARMACEUTICAL PREPARATIONS: Solutions

PRODUCT SECTION

Sara Wood Pharmaceuticals LLC .... G 513 833-5502
Mason *(G-10054)*

PHARMACEUTICALS

2 Retrievers LLC .... G 216 200-9040
Cleveland *(G-3571)*

Abbott .... F 608 931-1057
Columbus *(G-5084)*

Abbott Laboratories .... A 614 624-3191
Columbus *(G-5085)*

Abbott Laboratories .... F 614 624-3192
Columbus *(G-5086)*

Abbott Laboratories .... D 847 937-6100
Columbus *(G-5087)*

Abbott Laboratories .... C 800 551-5838
Columbus *(G-5088)*

Abbott Laboratories .... F 937 503-3405
Tipp City *(G-14119)*

Abeona Therapeutics Inc .... E 646 813-4701
Cleveland *(G-3586)*

Abitec Corporation .... E 614 429-6464
Columbus *(G-5090)*

Adare Pharmaceuticals Inc .... C 937 898-9669
Vandalia *(G-14931)*

Aerpio Therapeutics LLC .... E 513 985-1920
Blue Ash *(G-1360)*

Alkermes Inc .... E 937 382-5642
Wilmington *(G-16039)*

Allergan Sales LLC .... C 513 271-6800
Cincinnati *(G-2609)*

Allergan Sales LLC .... E 513 271-6800
Cincinnati *(G-2610)*

American Regent Inc .... D 614 436-2222
Columbus *(G-5129)*

American Regent Inc .... D 614 436-2222
Hilliard *(G-8397)*

American Regent Inc .... D 614 436-2222
New Albany *(G-11365)*

Amerix Ntra-Pharmaceutical Inc .... G 567 204-7756
Lima *(G-9222)*

Amylin Ohio .... E 512 592-8710
West Chester *(G-15364)*

Analiza Inc .... G 216 432-9050
Cleveland *(G-3660)*

Andelyn Biosciences Inc .... G 614 332-0554
Dublin *(G-6861)*

Andelyn Biosciences Inc .... C 844 228-2366
Columbus *(G-5143)*

Andrew M Farnham .... F 419 298-4300
Edgerton *(G-7071)*

Aprecia Pharmaceuticals LLC .... F 513 984-5000
Blue Ash *(G-1362)*

Astrazeneca Pharmaceuticals LP .... D 513 645-2600
West Chester *(G-15371)*

Barr Laboratories Inc .... A 513 731-9900
Cincinnati *(G-2657)*

BASF Corporation .... D 614 662-5682
Columbus *(G-5176)*

Baxters LLC .... G 234 678-5484
Akron *(G-79)*

Bayer .... E 513 336-6600
Fairfield *(G-7336)*

Ben Venue Laboratories Inc .... A 800 989-3320
Bedford *(G-1105)*

Biosortia Pharmaceuticals Inc .... F 614 636-4850
Dublin *(G-6867)*

Bld Pharmatech Co Limited .... G 330 333-6550
Blue Ash *(G-1371)*

Bnoat Oncology .... G 330 285-2537
Akron *(G-88)*

Boehrnger Inglheim Phrmcctcals .... E 440 286-5667
Chardon *(G-2440)*

Cardinal Health 414 LLC .... G 513 759-1900
West Chester *(G-15384)*

Cardinal Health 414 LLC .... C 614 757-5000
Dublin *(G-6873)*

Ceutix Pharma Inc .... G 614 388-8800
Columbus *(G-5245)*

Chester Labs Inc .... F 513 458-3871
Cincinnati *(G-2731)*

Clear Skies Ahead LLC .... G 440 632-3157
Middlefield *(G-10742)*

Diasome Pharmaceuticals Inc .... F 216 444-7110
Cleveland *(G-3957)*

Encapsulation Technologies LLC .... G 419 819-6319
Austinburg *(G-744)*

Galenas LLC .... F 330 208-9423
Akron *(G-161)*

Ganeden Biotech Inc .... E 440 229-5200
Mayfield Heights *(G-10249)*

Gebauer Company .... E 216 581-3030
Cleveland *(G-4108)*

Genoa Healthcare LLC .... G 513 727-0471
Middletown *(G-10826)*

Girindus America Inc .... E 513 679-3000
Cincinnati *(G-2952)*

Glaxosmithkline LLC .... G 330 608-2365
Copley *(G-5949)*

Hikma Labs Inc .... G 614 276-4000
Columbus *(G-5437)*

Hikma Pharmaceuticals USA Inc .... F 732 542-1191
Bedford *(G-1124)*

Hikma Pharmaceuticals USA Inc .... E 614 276-4000
Columbus *(G-5439)*

Hikma Pharmaceuticals USA Inc .... F 732 542-1191
Lockbourne *(G-9336)*

Hikma Specialty USA Inc .... E 856 489-2110
Columbus *(G-5440)*

Imcd Us LLC .... E 216 228-8900
Westlake *(G-15760)*

Invirsa Inc .... G 614 344-1765
Columbus *(G-5478)*

Isp Chemicals LLC .... D 614 876-3637
Columbus *(G-5481)*

Kurome Therapeutics Inc .... G 513 445-3852
Cincinnati *(G-3092)*

Lib Therapeutics Inc .... F 859 240-7764
Cincinnati *(G-3103)*

Lubrizol Global Management Inc .... F 216 447-5000
Cleveland *(G-4339)*

Masters Pharmaceutical Inc .... G 513 290-2969
Fairfield *(G-7380)*

Medpace Core Laboratories LLC .... F 513 579-9911
Cincinnati *(G-3141)*

Medpace Holdings Inc .... C 513 579-9911
Cincinnati *(G-3142)*

Meridian Bioscience Inc .... C 513 271-3700
Cincinnati *(G-3149)*

Mp Biomedicals LLC .... G 440 337-1200
Solon *(G-13393)*

Mvp Pharmacy .... G 614 449-8000
Columbus *(G-5586)*

Myers .... G 419 727-2010
Toledo *(G-14393)*

N-Molecular Inc .... F 440 439-5356
Oakwood Village *(G-12040)*

Navidea Biopharmaceuticals Inc .... G 614 793-7500
Dublin *(G-6915)*

Next Generation Hearing Case .... G 513 451-0360
Cincinnati *(G-3193)*

Nigerian Assn Pharmacists & PH .... G 513 861-2329
Cincinnati *(G-3197)*

Nnodum Pharmaceuticals Corp .... F 513 861-2329
Cincinnati *(G-3201)*

Novartis Corporation .... G 919 577-5000
Cincinnati *(G-3206)*

Oak Tree Intl Holdings Inc .... E 702 462-7295
Elyria *(G-7188)*

Oakwood Laboratories LLC .... E 440 359-0000
Oakwood Village *(G-12041)*

Omnicare Phrm of Midwest LLC .... D 513 719-2600
Cincinnati *(G-3222)*

Optum Infusion Svcs 550 LLC .... D 866 442-4679
Cincinnati *(G-3227)*

Organon Inc .... F 440 729-2290
Chesterland *(G-2487)*

Patheon Pharmaceuticals Inc .... A 513 948-9111
Blue Ash *(G-1450)*

Patheon Pharmaceuticals Inc .... A 513 948-9111
Cincinnati *(G-3235)*

Performanx Specialty Chem LLC .... G 614 300-7001
Waverly *(G-15290)*

Perrigo .... F 937 473-2050
Covington *(G-6030)*

Pharmacia Hepar LLC .... E 937 746-3603
Franklin *(G-7692)*

Prasco LLC .... E 513 204-1100
Mason *(G-10040)*

Principled Dynamics Inc .... F 419 351-6303
Holland *(G-8525)*

Pyros Pharmaceuticals Inc .... E 201 743-9468
Westerville *(G-15673)*

Quality Care Products LLC .... E 734 847-2704
Holland *(G-8526)*

Resilience Us Inc .... B 513 645-2600
West Chester *(G-15497)*

River City Pharma .... F 513 870-1680
Fairfield *(G-7403)*

Safecor Health LLC .... G 614 351-6117
Columbus *(G-5738)*

Safecor Health LLC .... F 781 933-8780
Columbus *(G-5739)*

Sarepta Therapeutics .... F 614 766-3296
Dublin *(G-6935)*

Sollis Therapeutics Inc .... E 614 701-9894
Columbus *(G-5776)*

Summit Research Group .... G 330 689-1778
Stow *(G-13730)*

Teva Womens Health LLC .... C 513 731-9900
Cincinnati *(G-3446)*

Tri-Tech Laboratories Inc .... C 740 927-2817
Johnstown *(G-8780)*

Tri-Tech Laboratories LLC .... C 434 845-7073
Johnstown *(G-8781)*

USB Corporation .... D 216 765-5000
Cleveland *(G-4857)*

Vincent Rx LLC .... G 740 678-2384
Vincent *(G-15010)*

Wedgewood Connect Ohio LLC .... G 800 331-8272
Albany *(G-382)*

WV CHS Pharmacy Services LLC .... G 844 595-4652
Blue Ash *(G-1496)*

PHOSPHATES

Scotts Company LLC .... C 937 644-0011
Marysville *(G-9934)*

PHOTOCOPY MACHINES

E-Waste Systems (ohio) Inc .... G 614 824-3057
Columbus *(G-5340)*

PHOTOCOPYING & DUPLICATING SVCS

A Grade Notes Inc .... G 614 299-9999
Dublin *(G-6856)*

A-A Blueprint Co Inc .... E 330 794-8803
Akron *(G-11)*

PHOTOCOPYING & DUPLICATING SVCS

Aztech Printing & Promotions .... G 937 339-0100
  Troy *(G-14551)*
Bethart Enterprises Inc .... F 513 863-6161
  Hamilton *(G-8185)*
Capitol Citicom Inc .... E 614 472-2679
  Columbus *(G-5234)*
Cincinnati Print Solutions LLC .... G 513 943-9500
  Milford *(G-10900)*
Colortech Graphics & Printing .... F 614 766-2400
  Columbus *(G-5260)*
Corporate Dcment Solutions Inc .... G 513 595-8200
  Cincinnati *(G-2797)*
Eg Enterprise Services Inc .... F 216 431-3300
  Cleveland *(G-4001)*
Geygan Enterprises Inc .... G 513 932-4222
  Lebanon *(G-9082)*
Hoster Graphics Company Inc .... F 614 299-9770
  Columbus *(G-5446)*
J & J Tire & Alignment .... G 330 424-5200
  Lisbon *(G-9316)*
Monks Copy Shop Inc .... F 614 461-6438
  Columbus *(G-5579)*
Morse Enterprises Inc .... G 513 229-3600
  Mason *(G-10031)*
Print-Digital Incorporated .... G 330 686-5945
  Stow *(G-13718)*
Printers Devil Inc .... E 330 650-1218
  Hudson *(G-8608)*
Rhoads Print Center Inc .... G 330 678-2042
  Tallmadge *(G-14045)*

PHOTOGRAPHIC EQPT & SPLYS

AGFA Corporation .... G 513 829-6292
  Fairfield *(G-7330)*
Dupont Specialty Pdts USA LLC .... E 740 474-0220
  Circleville *(G-3548)*
Eastman Kodak Company .... E 937 259-3000
  Kettering *(G-8906)*
Gary Dattilo .... G 513 671-2117
  Cincinnati *(G-2931)*
Kg63 LLC .... F 216 941-7766
  Cleveland *(G-4287)*
Miller-Holzwarth Inc .... D 330 342-7224
  Salem *(G-13017)*
Ohio Hd Video .... F 614 656-1162
  New Albany *(G-11387)*
Pulsar Ecoproducts LLC .... F 216 861-8800
  Cleveland *(G-4600)*

PHOTOGRAPHIC EQPT & SPLYS WHOLESALERS

Identiphoto Co Ltd .... F 440 306-9000
  Willoughby *(G-15930)*

PHOTOGRAPHIC EQPT & SPLYS: Film, Sensitized

Stretchtape Inc .... E 216 486-9400
  Cleveland *(G-4737)*

PHOTOGRAPHIC EQPT & SPLYS: Graphic Arts Plates, Sensitized

Plastigraphics Inc .... F 513 771-8848
  Cincinnati *(G-3261)*

PHOTOGRAPHIC EQPT & SPLYS: Printing Eqpt

Printer Components Inc .... G 585 924-5190
  Fairfield *(G-7397)*

PHOTOGRAPHY SVCS: Commercial

Queen City Reprographics .... C 513 326-2300
  Cincinnati *(G-3319)*
The Photo-Type Engraving Company ..... D 513 281-0999
  Cincinnati *(G-3450)*
Universal Ch Directories LLC .... G 419 522-5011
  Mansfield *(G-9729)*
Youngstown ARC Engraving Co .... G 330 793-2471
  Youngstown *(G-16476)*

PHYSICIANS' OFFICES & CLINICS: Medical doctors

Community Action Program Corp .... F 740 374-8501
  Marietta *(G-9786)*
Eye Surgery Center Ohio Inc .... E 614 228-3937
  Columbus *(G-5368)*
Francisco Jaume .... G 740 622-1200
  Coshocton *(G-5978)*
Lababidi Enterprises Inc .... G 330 733-2907
  Akron *(G-214)*
Nutritional Medicinals LLC .... F 937 433-4673
  West Chester *(G-15467)*
Orthotics Prsthtics Rhbltttion .... F 330 856-2553
  Warren *(G-15197)*
Volk Optical Inc .... D 440 942-6161
  Mentor *(G-10594)*

PICTURE FRAMES: Metal

Black Squirrel Holdings Inc .... E 513 577-7107
  Cincinnati *(G-2671)*
Frame Warehouse .... G 614 861-4582
  Reynoldsburg *(G-12765)*

PICTURE FRAMES: Wood

Bonfoey Co .... F 216 621-0178
  Cleveland *(G-3747)*
Cass Frames Inc .... G 419 468-2863
  Galion *(G-7863)*
Fenwick Gallery of Fine Arts .... G 419 475-1651
  Toledo *(G-14286)*
Frame Warehouse .... G 614 861-4582
  Reynoldsburg *(G-12765)*
Lazars Art Gllery Crtive Frmng .... G 330 477-8351
  Canton *(G-2144)*

PICTURE FRAMING SVCS, CUSTOM

American Frame Corporation .... D 419 893-5595
  Maumee *(G-10163)*

PIECE GOODS & NOTIONS WHOLESALERS

Sysco Guest Supply LLC .... E 440 960-2515
  Lorain *(G-9440)*

PIECE GOODS, NOTIONS/DRY GOODS, WHOL: Fabrics, Synthetic

Strata-Tac Inc .... F 630 879-9388
  Troy *(G-14613)*

PIGMENTS, INORGANIC: Metallic & Mineral, NEC

Enviri Corporation .... F 330 372-1781
  Warren *(G-15168)*
Obron Atlantic Corporation .... D 440 954-7600
  Painesville *(G-12252)*
Wogen Resources America LLC .... G 216 272-0062
  Valley City *(G-14901)*

PILOT SVCS: Aviation

Theiss Uav Solutions LLC .... G 330 584-2070
  North Benton *(G-11711)*

PINS

Altenloh Brinck & Co Inc .... C 419 636-6715
  Bryan *(G-1805)*
Express Trading Pins LLC .... G 419 394-2550
  Saint Marys *(G-12951)*
Lapel Pins Unlimited LLC .... G 614 562-3218
  Lewis Center *(G-9169)*
Paine Falls Centerpin LLC .... G 440 867-4954
  Thompson *(G-14061)*
Pin Oak Development LLC .... G 440 933-9862
  Avon Lake *(G-820)*

PINS: Dowel

Dayton Superior Corporation .... C 937 866-0711
  Miamisburg *(G-10633)*

PIPE & FITTINGS: Cast Iron

General Aluminum Mfg Company .... C 419 739-9300
  Wapakoneta *(G-15115)*
McWane Inc .... B 740 622-6651
  Coshocton *(G-5983)*
Tangent Air Inc .... E 740 474-1114
  Circleville *(G-3556)*

PIPE & TUBES: Seamless

Dom Tube Corp .... A 412 299-2616
  Alliance *(G-402)*
Reliacheck Manufacturing Inc .... E 440 933-6162
  Brookpark *(G-1724)*

PIPE FITTINGS: Plastic

Bay Corporation .... F 440 835-2212
  Westlake *(G-15735)*
Cantex Inc .... D 330 995-3665
  Aurora *(G-710)*
Elster Perfection Corporation .... D 440 428-1171
  Geneva *(G-7935)*
Indelco Custom Products Inc .... E 216 797-7300
  Euclid *(G-7274)*
Lenz Inc .... E 937 277-9364
  Dayton *(G-6405)*
Osburn Associates Inc .... F 740 385-5732
  Logan *(G-9372)*
Ppafco Inc .... E 614 488-7259
  Columbus *(G-5685)*

PIPE SECTIONS, FABRICATED FROM PURCHASED PIPE

Kottler Metal Products Co Inc .... E 440 946-7473
  Willoughby *(G-15940)*
Pioneer Pipe Inc .... A 740 376-2400
  Marietta *(G-9817)*
Scott Process Systems Inc .... C 330 877-2350
  Hartville *(G-8307)*

PIPE, CYLINDER: Concrete, Prestressed Or Pretensioned

Complete Cylinder Service Inc .... G 513 772-1500
  Cincinnati *(G-2784)*

PIPE, SEWER: Concrete

Ash Sewer & Drain Service .... G 330 376-9714
  Akron *(G-65)*

PIPE: Concrete

Haviland Culvert Company .... G 419 622-6951
  Haviland *(G-8311)*

PLASTICIZERS, ORGANIC: Cyclic & Acyclic

Northern Concrete Pipe Inc .... F 419 841-3361
  Sylvania *(G-14011)*

PIPE: Plastic

ADS .... G 419 422-6521
  Findlay *(G-7471)*

ADS International .... G 513 896-2094
  Hamilton *(G-8174)*

ADS International Inc .... E 614 658-0050
  Hilliard *(G-8392)*

ADS Ventures Inc .... G 614 658-0050
  Hilliard *(G-8393)*

Advanced Drainage of Ohio Inc .... D 614 658-0050
  Hilliard *(G-8395)*

Advanced Drainage Systems Inc ..... G 419 424-8222
  Findlay *(G-7473)*

Advanced Drainage Systems Inc ..... E 419 424-8324
  Findlay *(G-7474)*

Advanced Drainage Systems Inc ..... D 513 863-1384
  Hamilton *(G-8175)*

Advanced Drainage Systems Inc ..... C 740 852-2980
  London *(G-9379)*

Advanced Drainage Systems Inc ..... E 419 599-9565
  Napoleon *(G-11308)*

Advanced Drainage Systems Inc ..... E 330 264-4949
  Wooster *(G-16095)*

Advanced Drainage Systems Inc ..... D 614 658-0050
  Hilliard *(G-8396)*

Baughman Tile Company .... D 800 837-3160
  Paulding *(G-12311)*

Cantex Inc .... D 330 995-3665
  Aurora *(G-710)*

Contech Engnered Solutions Inc ..... E 513 645-7000
  West Chester *(G-15402)*

Contech Engnered Solutions LLC .... C 513 645-7000
  West Chester *(G-15403)*

Drainage Products Inc .... F 419 622-6951
  Haviland *(G-8310)*

Dura-Line Corporation .... D 440 322-1000
  Elyria *(G-7133)*

Dura-Line Services LLC .... D 440 322-1000
  Elyria *(G-7134)*

Elster Perfection Corporation .... D 440 428-1171
  Geneva *(G-7935)*

Flex Technologies Inc .... E 740 922-5992
  Midvale *(G-10878)*

Fowler Products Inc .... F 419 683-4057
  Crestline *(G-6033)*

Geon Performance Solutions LLC ... F 800 438-4366
  Westlake *(G-15754)*

Hancor Inc .... E 419 424-8222
  Findlay *(G-7520)*

Hancor Inc .... E 419 424-8225
  Findlay *(G-7521)*

Hancor Inc .... B 614 658-0050
  Hilliard *(G-8413)*

Harrison Mch & Plastic Corp .... E 330 527-5641
  Garrettsville *(G-7916)*

Heritage Plastics Liquidation Inc ...... D 330 627-8002
  Carrollton *(G-2309)*

Nupco Inc .... G 419 629-2259
  New Bremen *(G-11406)*

Plas-Tanks Industries Inc .... E 513 942-3800
  Hamilton *(G-8235)*

Ray Lewis Enterprises LLC .... G 330 424-9585
  Lisbon *(G-9325)*

Tolloti Pipe LLC .... F 330 364-6627
  New Philadelphia *(G-11529)*

Tolloti Plastic Pipe Inc .... F 330 364-6627
  New Philadelphia *(G-11530)*

PIPE: Sheet Metal

American Culvert & Fabg Co .... F 740 432-6334
  Cambridge *(G-1919)*

Shape Supply Inc .... G 513 863-6695
  Hamilton *(G-8242)*

PIPELINES: Natural Gas

Ngo Development Corporation .... E 740 344-3790
  Newark *(G-11598)*

PIPES & TUBES

George Manufacturing Inc .... F 513 932-1067
  Lebanon *(G-9079)*

Lokring Technology LLC .... D 440 942-0880
  Willoughby *(G-15946)*

Phillips Tube Group Inc .... E 205 338-4771
  Middletown *(G-10850)*

Prime Conduit Inc .... F 216 464-3400
  Beachwood *(G-1012)*

Sigma Tube Company .... G 419 729-9756
  Toledo *(G-14472)*

Trenchless Rsrces Globl Hldngs ..... F 419 419-6498
  Bowling Green *(G-1593)*

PIPES & TUBES: Steel

Alro Steel Corporation .... E 937 253-6121
  Dayton *(G-6196)*

Arcelrmttal Tblar Pdts Shlby L .... A 419 347-2424
  Shelby *(G-13191)*

Arcelrmttal Tblar Pdts USA LLC ...... A 419 347-2424
  Shelby *(G-13192)*

Busch & Thiem Inc .... E 419 625-7515
  Sandusky *(G-13047)*

Caparo Bull Moose Inc .... G 330 448-4878
  Masury *(G-10156)*

Cgi Group Benefits LLC .... E 440 246-6191
  Lorain *(G-9406)*

Chart International Inc .... D 440 753-1490
  Cleveland *(G-3812)*

Clevelnd-Clffs Tblar Cmpnnts L ..... C 419 661-4150
  Walbridge *(G-15080)*

Commercial Honing LLC .... D 330 343-8896
  Dover *(G-6813)*

Conduit Pipe Products Company ..... D 614 879-9114
  West Jefferson *(G-15609)*

Contech Engnered Solutions Inc ..... E 513 645-7000
  West Chester *(G-15402)*

Contech Engnered Solutions LLC ... C 513 645-7000
  West Chester *(G-15403)*

Crest Bending Inc .... E 419 492-2108
  New Washington *(G-11546)*

Dofasco Tubular Products .... G 419 342-1371
  Shelby *(G-13194)*

Fd Rolls Corp .... E 216 916-1922
  Solon *(G-13348)*

Grae-Con Process Piping LLC .... E 740 282-6830
  Marietta *(G-9796)*

H-P Products Inc .... C 330 875-5556
  Louisville *(G-9459)*

Jackson Tube Service Inc .... C 937 773-8550
  Piqua *(G-12530)*

James O Emert Jr .... E 330 650-6990
  Hudson *(G-8600)*

Kenco Products Co Inc .... E 216 351-7610
  Cleveland *(G-4282)*

Kirtland Capital Partners LP .... E 216 593-0100
  Beachwood *(G-993)*

Major Metals Company .... E 419 886-4600
  Mansfield *(G-9681)*

Mattr US Inc .... E 513 683-7800
  Loveland *(G-9495)*

Metallus Inc .... E 330 471-7000
  Canton *(G-2163)*

Phillips Mfg and Tower Co .... D 419 347-1720
  Shelby *(G-13197)*

PMC Industries Corp .... D 440 943-3300
  Wickliffe *(G-15848)*

Ptc Alliance LLC .... E 330 821-5700
  Alliance *(G-421)*

Shelar Inc .... C 419 729-9756
  Toledo *(G-14470)*

T & D Fabricating Inc .... E 440 951-5646
  Eastlake *(G-7051)*

TI Group Auto Systems LLC .... E 740 929-2049
  Hebron *(G-8366)*

Unison Industries LLC .... B 904 667-9904
  Dayton *(G-6175)*

Vallourec Star LP .... C 330 742-6227
  Girard *(G-7976)*

Wheatland Tube LLC .... C 724 342-6851
  Niles *(G-11692)*

Wheatland Tube LLC .... C 330 372-6611
  Warren *(G-15224)*

Woodsage LLC .... C 419 866-8000
  Holland *(G-8539)*

Zekelman Industries Inc .... E 216 910-3700
  Beachwood *(G-1033)*

PIPES & TUBES: Welded

Atlantic Welding LLC .... F 937 570-5094
  Piqua *(G-12505)*

Lock Joint Tube Ohio LLC .... C 210 278-3757
  Orwell *(G-12167)*

PIPES: Steel & Iron

Hickman Williams & Company .... F 513 621-1946
  Cincinnati *(G-2998)*

JSW Steel USA Ohio Inc .... B 740 535-8172
  Mingo Junction *(G-11046)*

Youngstown Bending Rolling Inc ..... F 330 898-3878
  Warren *(G-15225)*

Youngstown Tube Co .... E 330 743-7414
  Youngstown *(G-16490)*

PISTONS & PISTON RINGS

Ad Piston Ring LLC .... F 216 781-5200
  Cleveland *(G-3595)*

Celina Alum Precision Tech Inc ...... B 419 586-2278
  Celina *(G-2325)*

Race Winning Brands Inc .... B 440 951-6600
  Mentor *(G-10544)*

Seabiscuit Motorsports Inc .... B 440 951-6600
  Mentor *(G-10551)*

PLACER GOLD MINING

Ivi Mining Group Ltd .... G 740 418-7745
  Vinton *(G-15011)*

PLAQUES: Picture, Laminated

Gerber Wood Products Inc .... D 330 857-9007
  Kidron *(G-8914)*

Hafners Hrdwood Connection LLC . G 419 726-4828
  Toledo *(G-14309)*

Idx Corporation .... C 937 401-3225
  Dayton *(G-6378)*

Neff Motivation Inc .... C 937 548-3194
  Greenville *(G-8053)*

PLASTICIZERS, ORGANIC: Cyclic & Acyclic

Chemionics Corporation .... E 330 733-8834
  Tallmadge *(G-14024)*

OPC Polymers LLC .... C 614 253-8511
  Columbus *(G-5642)*

Employee Codes: A=Over 500 employees, B=251-500
C=101-250, D=51-100, E=20-50, F=10-19, G=1-9

PLASTICS FILM & SHEET

PLASTICS FILM & SHEET

Advanced Polymer Coatings Ltd............ E 440 937-6218
  Avon (G-761)
Berry Film Products Co Inc................ D 800 225-6729
  Mason (G-9960)
Berry Plastics Filmco Inc................. D 330 562-6111
  Aurora (G-709)
Clopay Corporation........................ C 800 282-2260
  Mason (G-9979)
Renegade Materials Corporation............ D 937 350-5274
  Miamisburg (G-10675)
Simona PMC LLC............................ D 419 429-0042
  Findlay (G-7561)
Specialty Films Inc....................... D 614 471-9100
  Columbus (G-5782)
Tsp Inc................................... E 513 732-8900
  Batavia (G-955)
Valgroup LLC.............................. E 419 423-6500
  Findlay (G-7576)

PLASTICS FILM & SHEET: Polyethylene

Blako Industries Inc...................... E 419 246-6172
  Dunbridge (G-6961)
General Films Inc......................... D 888 436-3456
  Covington (G-6023)
Magnum Tapes Films........................ G 877 460-8402
  Caldwell (G-1911)
New Tech Plastics Inc..................... D 937 473-3011
  Covington (G-6028)
Putnam Plastics Inc....................... G 937 866-6261
  Dayton (G-6535)

PLASTICS FILM & SHEET: Polypropylene

Crown Plastics Co LLC..................... D 513 367-0238
  Harrison (G-8272)

PLASTICS FILM & SHEET: Polyvinyl

Jain America Foods Inc.................... G 614 850-9400
  Columbus (G-5486)

PLASTICS FILM & SHEET: Vinyl

Clarkwestern Dietrich Building............ E 330 372-5564
  Warren (G-15154)
Clarkwstern Dtrich Bldg System............ C 513 870-1100
  West Chester (G-15396)
Ludlow Composites Corporation............. C 419 332-5531
  Fremont (G-7796)
Mikron Industries Inc..................... D 713 961-4600
  Akron (G-248)
Rotary Products Inc....................... F 740 747-2623
  Ashley (G-624)
Scherba Industries Inc.................... D 330 273-3200
  Brunswick (G-1790)
Walton Plastics Inc....................... E 440 786-7711
  Bedford (G-1160)
World Connections Corps................... F 419 363-2681
  Rockford (G-12835)

PLASTICS FINISHED PRDTS: Laminated

Bruewer Woodwork Mfg Co................... D 513 353-3505
  Cleves (G-4946)
Counter Concepts Inc...................... F 330 848-4848
  Doylestown (G-6853)
Designed Images Inc....................... G 440 708-2526
  Chagrin Falls (G-2392)
Designer Cntemporary Laminates............ G 440 946-8207
  Painesville (G-12228)
Fdi Cabinetry LLC......................... G 513 353-4500
  Cleves (G-4952)
Franklin Cabinet Company Inc.............. E 937 743-9606
  Franklin (G-7676)

General Electric Company.................. F 740 623-5379
  Coshocton (G-5979)
Idx Corporation........................... C 937 401-3225
  Dayton (G-6378)
Mkgs Corp................................. F 937 254-8181
  Dayton (G-6453)
Quality Rubber Stamp Inc.................. G 614 235-2700
  Lancaster (G-9034)
Southern Cabinetry Inc.................... E 740 245-5992
  Bidwell (G-1327)

PLASTICS MATERIAL & RESINS

A R E Logistics LLC....................... G 330 327-7315
  Massillon (G-10074)
A Westlake Axiall Co...................... G 614 754-3677
  Columbus (G-5081)
Accurate Plastics LLC..................... F 330 701-0019
  Kent (G-8793)
Al-Co Products Inc........................ G 419 399-3867
  Latty (G-9053)
Altera Polymers LLC....................... G 864 973-7000
  Jefferson (G-8745)
American Polymers Corporation............. G 330 666-6048
  Akron (G-61)
Americas Styrenics LLC.................... D 740 302-8667
  Ironton (G-8696)
Anchor Hocking Glass Company.............. G 740 681-6025
  Lancaster (G-8988)
Aptiv Services Us LLC..................... G 330 373-7614
  Warren (G-15141)
Arclin USA LLC............................ G 419 726-5013
  Toledo (G-14198)
Avient Corporation........................ F 440 930-3727
  Avon Lake (G-798)
Avient Corporation........................ F 800 727-4338
  Greenville (G-8037)
Avient Corporation........................ F 330 834-3812
  Massillon (G-10077)
Axiom International Inc................... G 330 396-5942
  Akron (G-71)
Bamberger Polymers Inc.................... F 614 718-9104
  Dublin (G-6866)
Benvic Trinity LLC........................ E 609 520-0000
  West Unity (G-15637)
Biobent Holdings LLC...................... G 513 658-5560
  Columbus (G-5190)
Biothane Coated Webbing Corp.............. G 440 327-0485
  North Olmsted (G-11819)
Biothane Coated Webbing Corp.............. E 440 327-0485
  North Ridgeville (G-11832)
Cameo Countertops Inc..................... E 419 865-6371
  Holland (G-8496)
Chem-Materials Inc........................ F 440 455-9465
  Westlake (G-15743)
Chemionics Corporation.................... E 330 733-8834
  Tallmadge (G-14024)
Chroma Color Corporation.................. E 740 363-6622
  Delaware (G-6710)
Concrete Sealants Inc..................... E 937 845-8776
  Tipp City (G-14130)
Covestro LLC.............................. C 740 929-2015
  Hebron (G-8337)
Crown Plastics Co LLC..................... D 513 367-0238
  Harrison (G-8272)
Cuyahoga Molded Plastics Co (inc)......... E 216 261-2744
  Euclid (G-7266)
Ddp Specialty Electronic MA............... C 937 839-4612
  West Alexandria (G-15341)
Diamant Polymers Inc...................... G 513 979-4011
  Cincinnati (G-2828)
Diamond Polymers Incorporated............. D 330 773-2700
  Akron (G-128)

Dupont Specialty Pdts USA LLC............. D 740 474-0635
  Circleville (G-3547)
Durez Corporation......................... E 567 295-6400
  Kenton (G-8882)
E C Shaw Company of Ohio.................. E 513 721-6334
  Cincinnati (G-2648)
E P S Specialists Ltd Inc................. E 513 489-3676
  Cincinnati (G-2650)
Eagle Elastomer Inc....................... E 330 923-7070
  Peninsula (G-1340)
Elyria Foundry Company LLC................ D 440 322-4657
  Elyria (G-7141)
Engineered Polymer Systems LLC............ G 216 255-2116
  Medina (G-10319)
Ep Bollinger LLC.......................... A 513 941-1101
  Cincinnati (G-2678)
Evans Adhesive Corporation Ltd............ E 614 451-2665
  Columbus (G-5353)
Fibre Glast Dvlpments Corp LLC............ F 937 833-5200
  Brookville (G-1715)
Flexsys America LP........................ D 330 666-4111
  Akron (G-155)
Franklin International Inc................ B 614 443-0241
  Columbus (G-5317)
Freeman Manufacturing & Sup Co............ E 440 934-1902
  Avon (G-775)
Freudenberg-Nok General Partnr............ E 937 335-3306
  Troy (G-14571)
Gabriel Phenoxies Inc..................... E 704 499-9801
  Akron (G-160)
Gayson Silicon Dispersions Inc............ G 330 848-8422
  Avon Lake (G-801)
Geo-Tech Polymers LLC..................... E 614 797-2300
  Waverly (G-15287)
Geon Performance Solutions LLC............ D 440 987-4553
  Elyria (G-7155)
Goldsmith & Eggleton Inc.................. F 330 336-6616
  Wadsworth (G-15032)
Goldsmith & Eggleton LLC.................. F 203 855-6000
  Wadsworth (G-15033)
Gsh Industries Inc........................ F 440 238-3009
  Strongsville (G-1337)
Hancor Inc................................ E 419 424-8225
  Findlay (G-7521)
Hexion US Finance Corp.................... E 614 225-4000
  Columbus (G-5437)
Hexpol Holding Inc........................ F 440 834-4644
  Burton (G-1882)
Hggc Citadel Plas Holdings Inc............ E 330 666-3751
  Fairlawn (G-7441)
Huntsman Advnce Mtls Amrcas L............. E 330 374-2424
  Akron (G-185)
Huntsman Advnce Mtls Amrcas L............. E 866 800-2436
  Akron (G-186)
Huntsman Corporation...................... D 330 374-2418
  Akron (G-187)
ICP Adhesives and Sealants Inc............ E 330 753-4585
  Norton (G-11944)
Ier Fujikura Inc.......................... C 330 425-7121
  Macedonia (G-955)
Ineos LLC................................. D 419 226-1200
  Lima (G-9255)
Ineos ABS (usa) LLC....................... C 513 467-2400
  Addyston (G-8)
Ineos Composites Us LLC................... D 614 790-9299
  Columbus (G-5455)
Ineos Neal LLC............................ E 610 790-3333
  Dublin (G-6896)
Ineos Nitriles USA LLC.................... F 281 535-6600
  Lima (G-9256)
Ineos Solvents Sales US Corp.............. B 614 790-3333
  Dublin (G-6897)

PRODUCT SECTION — PLASTICS PROCESSING

Integrated Chem Concepts Inc............ G 440 838-5666
  Brecksville *(G-1622)*
Interntnal Tchncal Plymr Syste............ E 330 505-1218
  Niles *(G-11672)*
Isochem Incorporated......................... G 614 775-9328
  New Albany *(G-11380)*
J P Industrial Products Inc................... F 330 627-1377
  Carrollton *(G-2310)*
J P Industrial Products Inc................... G 330 424-1110
  Lisbon *(G-9319)*
JB Polymers Inc.................................... G 216 941-7041
  Oberlin *(G-12053)*
Jeg Associates Inc............................... F 614 882-1295
  Westerville *(G-15711)*
Jerico Plastic Industries Inc................ E 330 868-4600
  Wadsworth *(G-15038)*
Kardol Quality Products LLC.............. G 513 933-8206
  Blue Ash *(G-1416)*
Kathom Manufacturing Co Inc............. E 513 868-8890
  Middletown *(G-10835)*
Kraton Corporation............................... D 740 423-7571
  Belpre *(G-1255)*
Kraton Polymers US LLC..................... B 740 423-7571
  Belpre *(G-1257)*
Lrbg Chemicals USA Inc...................... E 419 244-5856
  Toledo *(G-14371)*
Lubrizol Global Management Inc........ G 440 933-0400
  Avon Lake *(G-815)*
Lyondell Chemical Company............... C 440 352-9393
  Fairport Harbor *(G-7455)*
Lyondllbsell Advnced Plymers I........... E 330 498-4840
  Akron *(G-229)*
Lyondllbsell Advnced Plymers I........... E 440 224-7544
  Geneva *(G-7942)*
Lyondllbsell Advnced Plymers I........... D 419 872-1408
  Perrysburg *(G-12397)*
Lyondllbsell Advnced Plymers I........... E 419 682-3311
  Stryker *(G-13910)*
Material Processing & Hdlg Co........... F 419 436-9562
  Fostoria *(G-7643)*
Mitsubishi Chemical Amer Inc............. C 586 755-1660
  Bellevue *(G-1229)*
Modern Plastics Recovery Inc............ F 419 622-4611
  Haviland *(G-8314)*
Multi-Plastics Inc................................. D 740 548-4894
  Lewis Center *(G-9172)*
Multibase Inc.. D 330 666-0505
  Copley *(G-5952)*
National Polymer Dev Co Inc............... G 440 708-1245
  Chagrin Falls *(G-2408)*
Network Polymers Inc.......................... E 330 773-2700
  Akron *(G-261)*
Next Generation Plastics LLC............. F 330 668-1200
  Fairlawn *(G-7445)*
North American Composites................ G 440 930-0602
  Avon Lake *(G-819)*
Nu-Tech Polymers Co Inc................... G 513 942-6003
  Cincinnati *(G-3207)*
Occidental Chemical Corp................... E 513 242-2900
  Cincinnati *(G-3211)*
Ohio Foam Corporation........................ F 419 492-2151
  New Washington *(G-11550)*
Ohio Plastics & Belting Co LLC........... G 330 882-6764
  New Franklin *(G-11440)*
OK Industries Inc................................. E 419 435-2361
  Fostoria *(G-7649)*
OPC Polymers LLC............................... C 614 253-8511
  Columbus *(G-5642)*
OSI Global Sourcing LLC.................... F 614 471-4800
  Columbus *(G-5645)*
Ovation Plymr Tech Engnred Mtl......... E 330 723-5686
  Medina *(G-10359)*

Owens Corning Sales LLC.................. F 330 633-6735
  Tallmadge *(G-14042)*
Performnce Plymr Solutions Inc......... F 937 298-3713
  Moraine *(G-11196)*
Perstorp Polyols Inc............................. C 419 729-5448
  Toledo *(G-14434)*
Pilot Polymer Technologies................. G 412 735-4799
  West Chester *(G-15478)*
Plaskolite LLC...................................... C 614 294-3281
  Columbus *(G-5678)*
Plastic Compounders Inc................... E 740 432-7371
  Cambridge *(G-1948)*
Plastic Materials Inc............................ E 330 468-5706
  Macedonia *(G-9565)*
Plastic Suppliers Inc........................... E 614 471-9100
  Columbus *(G-5679)*
Polimeros Usa LLC.............................. G 216 591-0175
  Warrensville Heights *(G-15230)*
Polymer Packaging Inc........................ D 330 832-2000
  North Canton *(G-11751)*
Polymer Tech & Svcs Inc..................... F 740 929-5500
  Heath *(G-8327)*
Polymerics Inc..................................... E 330 677-1131
  Kent *(G-8845)*
Polymerics Inc..................................... E 330 928-2210
  Cuyahoga Falls *(G-6110)*
Polynew Inc... G 330 897-3202
  Baltic *(G-840)*
Polyone Corporation............................ D 330 467-8108
  Macedonia *(G-9568)*
Prime Industries Inc............................ E
  Lorain *(G-9431)*
Protech Pet LLC................................... F 419 552-4617
  Gibsonburg *(G-7955)*
Pyrograf Products Inc.......................... F 937 766-2020
  Cedarville *(G-2323)*
Rauh Polymers Inc............................... F 330 376-1120
  Akron *(G-298)*
Ravago Americas LLC.......................... E 330 825-2505
  Medina *(G-10368)*
Ravago Americas LLC.......................... D 419 924-9090
  West Unity *(G-15643)*
Ray Fogg Construction Inc.................. E 216 351-7976
  Cleveland *(G-4616)*
Renegade Materials Corp.................... G 513 469-9919
  Blue Ash *(G-1460)*
Return Polymers Inc............................ D 419 289-1998
  Ashland *(G-610)*
Rotopolymers....................................... F 216 645-0333
  Cleveland *(G-4653)*
Saco Aei Polymers Inc......................... F 330 995-1600
  Aurora *(G-735)*
Saint-Gobain Prfmce Plas Corp........... D 614 889-2220
  Dublin *(G-6933)*
Saint-Gobain Prfmce Plas Corp........... C 330 296-9948
  Ravenna *(G-12731)*
Scott Bader Inc..................................... G 330 920-4410
  Stow *(G-13723)*
Scott Molders Incorporated................ D 330 673-5777
  Kent *(G-8859)*
Sherwood Rtm Corp............................. G 330 875-7151
  Louisville *(G-9471)*
Soelter Corporation............................. F 800 838-8984
  Brookville *(G-1744)*
Solvay Spclty Polymers USA LLC........ F 740 373-9242
  Marietta *(G-9828)*
Sonoco Prtective Solutions Inc........... E 419 420-0029
  Findlay *(G-7565)*
Sorbothane Inc..................................... G 330 678-9444
  Kent *(G-8866)*
Spartech Mexico Holding Co Two....... E 440 930-3619
  Avon Lake *(G-824)*

Specialty Polymer Product.................. G 216 281-8300
  Rocky River *(G-12844)*
STC International Co Ltd..................... G 561 308-6002
  Lebanon *(G-9112)*
Tembec Btlsr Inc................................... E 419 244-5856
  Toledo *(G-14483)*
Thermocolor LLC.................................. E 419 626-5677
  Sandusky *(G-13095)*
Transdigm Inc...................................... F 330 676-7147
  Kent *(G-8878)*
Tribotech Composites Inc.................. G 216 901-1300
  Cleveland *(G-4826)*
Triple Arrow Industries Inc................ G 614 437-5588
  Marysville *(G-9943)*
Uniloy Milacron Inc.............................. D 513 487-5000
  Batavia *(G-956)*
Univar Solutions USA LLC................... F 800 531-7106
  Dublin *(G-6956)*
Urethane Polymers Intl........................ F 216 430-3655
  Cleveland *(G-4855)*
V & A Process Inc............................... F 440 288-8137
  Lorain *(G-9442)*
Vinyl Mng Llc DBA Vinylone................ E 440 261-5799
  Cleveland *(G-4876)*
Win Cd Inc... F 330 929-1999
  Cuyahoga Falls *(G-6129)*

PLASTICS MATERIALS, BASIC FORMS & SHAPES WHOLESALERS

Allied Shipping and Packagi................ F 937 222-7422
  Moraine *(G-11155)*
Ampacet Corporation........................... F 513 247-5400
  Cincinnati *(G-2625)*
Skybox Packaging LLC......................... C 419 525-7209
  Mansfield *(G-9719)*
United States Plastic Corp.................. D 419 228-2242
  Lima *(G-9299)*
Univar Solutions USA LLC................... F 800 531-7106
  Dublin *(G-6956)*

PLASTICS PROCESSING

American Plastics LLC......................... C 419 423-1213
  Findlay *(G-7476)*
AMS Global Ltd..................................... F 937 620-1036
  West Alexandria *(G-15339)*
Apogee Plastics Corp........................... F 937 864-1966
  Fairborn *(G-7310)*
Apollo Plastics Inc.............................. F 440 951-7774
  Mentor *(G-10420)*
Bc Investment Corporation................. G 330 262-3070
  Wooster *(G-16103)*
Bmf Devices Inc.................................. F 937 866-3451
  Miamisburg *(G-10621)*
C A Joseph Co...................................... G 330 385-6869
  East Liverpool *(G-6988)*
Dunstone Company Inc........................ F 704 841-1380
  Hiram *(G-8481)*
Fountain Specialists Inc..................... G 513 831-5717
  Milford *(G-10906)*
G I Plastek Inc...................................... G 440 230-1942
  Westlake *(G-15751)*
JPS Technologies Inc.......................... F 513 984-6400
  Blue Ash *(G-1415)*
JPS Technologies Inc.......................... F 513 984-6400
  Blue Ash *(G-1414)*
Liqui-Box Corporation.......................... E 419 289-9696
  Ashland *(G-589)*
Lotus Pipes & Rockdrills USA............. F 516 209-6995
  Cleveland *(G-4335)*
Mega Plastics Co................................. E 330 527-2211
  Garrettsville *(G-7922)*

Employee Codes: A=Over 500 employees, B=251-500
C=101-250, D=51-100, E=20-50, F=10-19, G=1-9

PLASTICS PROCESSING — PRODUCT SECTION

P T I Inc..E 419 445-2800
   Archbold *(G-540)*

Preferred Solutions Inc............................F 216 642-1200
   Independence *(G-8682)*

Radici Plastics Usa Inc...........................E 330 336-7611
   Wadsworth *(G-15059)*

Rexles Inc..G 419 732-8188
   Port Clinton *(G-12627)*

Samuel Son & Co (usa) Inc....................D 740 522-2500
   Heath *(G-8331)*

Starks Plastics LLC..................................F 513 541-4591
   Cincinnati *(G-3416)*

Steere Enterprises Inc............................D 330 633-4926
   Tallmadge *(G-14049)*

Tahoma Enterprises Inc.........................D 330 745-9016
   Barberton *(G-897)*

Tahoma Rubber & Plastics Inc..............D 330 745-9016
   Barberton *(G-898)*

Trinity Specialty Compounding Inc........F 419 924-9090
   West Unity *(G-15644)*

United Security Seals Inc.......................E 614 443-7633
   Columbus *(G-5843)*

United States Plastic Corp.....................D 419 228-2242
   Lima *(G-9299)*

Wyatt Industries LLC..............................G 330 954-1790
   Streetsboro *(G-13799)*

Y City Recycling LLC...............................F 740 452-2500
   Zanesville *(G-16572)*

PLASTICS SHEET: Packing Materials

Automated Packaging Systems LLC......C 330 528-2000
   Streetsboro *(G-13759)*

Automated Packg Systems Inc..............C 216 663-2000
   Cleveland *(G-3702)*

Automated Packg Systems Inc..............G 330 626-2313
   Streetsboro *(G-13760)*

Avery Dennison Corporation..................D 440 639-3900
   Mentor *(G-10427)*

Buckeye Packaging Co Inc....................D 330 935-0301
   Alliance *(G-396)*

Cool Seal Usa LLC..................................F 419 666-1111
   Perrysburg *(G-12371)*

MAI-Weave LLC.......................................D 937 322-1698
   Springfield *(G-13600)*

Ram Plastics Co.......................................G 330 549-3342
   Youngstown *(G-16427)*

Western Reserve Sleeve Inc..................F 440 238-8850
   Strongsville *(G-13895)*

PLASTICS: Blow Molded

Fremont Plastic Products Inc.................C 419 332-6407
   Fremont *(G-7783)*

Klw Plastics Inc.......................................G 513 539-2673
   Monroe *(G-11114)*

Paarlo Plastics Inc..................................D 330 494-3798
   North Canton *(G-11749)*

Plastic Forming Company Inc................E 330 830-5167
   Massillon *(G-10134)*

Thermoplastic Accessories Corp............F 614 771-4777
   Hilliard *(G-8448)*

Tigerpoly Manufacturing Inc..................B 614 871-0045
   Grove City *(G-8122)*

Tmd Wek North LLC................................C 440 576-6940
   Jefferson *(G-8761)*

PLASTICS: Extruded

Akron Polymer Products Inc..................D 330 628-5551
   Akron *(G-40)*

Axion Strl Innovations LLC.....................F 740 452-2500
   Zanesville *(G-16503)*

Cell-O-Core Co...E 330 239-4370
   Sharon Center *(G-13165)*

Clark Rubber & Plastic Company...........C 440 255-9793
   Mentor *(G-10439)*

Cleveland Specialty Pdts Inc..................E 216 281-8300
   Cleveland *(G-3855)*

Creative Extruded Products....................G 937 335-3336
   Troy *(G-14557)*

Custom Poly Bag LLC..............................D 330 935-2408
   Alliance *(G-399)*

D and D Plastics Inc................................F 330 376-0668
   Akron *(G-122)*

Extrudex Limited Partnership.................E 440 352-7101
   Painesville *(G-12235)*

Fowler Products Inc................................F 419 683-4057
   Crestline *(G-6033)*

HP Enterprise Inc....................................E 800 232-7950
   Streetsboro *(G-13773)*

Inventive Extrusions Corp.......................F 330 874-3000
   Bolivar *(G-1528)*

Malish Corporation..................................D 440 951-5356
   Mentor *(G-10499)*

Merryweather Foam Inc..........................E 330 753-0353
   Barberton *(G-882)*

Meteor Creative Inc................................E 800 273-1535
   Tipp City *(G-14141)*

Middlefield Plastics Inc...........................E 440 834-4638
   Middlefield *(G-10767)*

Mikron Industries Inc..............................D 713 961-4600
   Akron *(G-248)*

Montville Plastics & Rubber Inc..............E 440 548-3211
   Parkman *(G-12285)*

North Coast Seal Incorporated..............F 216 898-5000
   Brookpark *(G-1722)*

Overhead Door Corporation....................F 440 593-5226
   Conneaut *(G-5929)*

Plastic Extrusion Tech Ltd......................E 440 632-5611
   Middlefield *(G-10781)*

Profile Plastics Inc..................................E 330 452-7000
   Canton *(G-2204)*

Profusion Industries LLC........................G 800 938-2858
   Fairlawn *(G-7446)*

Roppe Holding Company........................G 419 435-6601
   Fostoria *(G-7652)*

Rowmark LLC...D 419 425-8974
   Findlay *(G-7557)*

Ryan Development Corporation.............F 937 587-2266
   Peebles *(G-12331)*

Spartech LLC..D 419 399-4050
   Paulding *(G-12320)*

The Crane Group Companies Limited....E 614 754-3000
   Columbus *(G-5821)*

Trellborg Sling Prfiles US Inc.................C 330 995-9725
   Aurora *(G-737)*

Universal Polymer & Rubber Ltd............C 440 632-1691
   Middlefield *(G-10795)*

Vts Co Ltd..G 419 273-4010
   Forest *(G-7594)*

PLASTICS: Finished Injection Molded

ABC Plastics Inc......................................E 330 948-3322
   Lodi *(G-9344)*

Akron Porcelain & Plastics Co................C 330 745-2159
   Akron *(G-41)*

Allied Moulded Products Inc..................C 419 636-4217
   Bryan *(G-1804)*

Atc Group Inc...D 440 293-4064
   Andover *(G-484)*

B & B Molded Products Inc....................E 419 592-8700
   Defiance *(G-6670)*

Bourbon Plastics Inc...............................E 574 342-0893
   Cuyahoga Falls *(G-6073)*

Caraustar Industries Inc.........................C 330 665-7700
   Copley *(G-5946)*

Design Molded Products LLC.................F 330 963-4400
   Macedonia *(G-5544)*

DJM Plastics Ltd.....................................F 419 424-5250
   Findlay *(G-7502)*

Edge Plastics Inc....................................C 419 522-6696
   Mansfield *(G-9651)*

Encore Industries....................................C 419 626-8000
   Sandusky *(G-12053)*

Global Plastic Tech Inc...........................E 330 963-6830
   Brecksville *(G-1519)*

Illinois Tool Works Inc.............................E 937 332-2839
   Troy *(G-14584)*

Interntnal Auto Cmpnnts Group.............A 419 433-5653
   Wauseon *(G-1565)*

Jaco Manufacturing Company................E 440 234-4000
   Berea *(G-1284)*

Jdh Holdings Inc......................................C 330 963-4400
   Macedonia *(G-5559)*

Kamco Industries Inc..............................B 419 924-5511
   West Unity *(G-15641)*

Kasai North America Inc........................E 614 356-1494
   Dublin *(G-6903)*

Kirtland Plastics Inc................................D 440 951-4466
   Kirtland *(G-8943)*

Kuhns Mold & Tool Co Inc......................D 937 833-2178
   Brookville *(G-1720)*

Marne Plastics LLC.................................G 614 732-4666
   Grove City *(G-8804)*

Mdi of Ohio Inc..E 937 866-2345
   Canton *(G-2155)*

Meese Inc...F 440 998-1202
   Ashtabula *(G-647)*

Moriroku Technology N Amer Inc..........A 937 548-3217
   Marysville *(G-9528)*

Myers Industries Inc...............................E 440 632-1006
   Middlefield *(G-1774)*

Novatex North America Inc....................D 419 282-4264
   Ashland *(G-595)*

Scientific Plastics Ltd.............................F 305 557-3737
   Ravenna *(G-12233)*

Sonoco Products Company....................E 614 759-8470
   Columbus *(G-5778)*

Stuchell Products LLC............................E 330 821-4299
   Alliance *(G-428)*

Tez Tool & Fabrication Inc.....................G 440 323-2300
   Elyria *(G-7210)*

Toledo Molding & Die LLC......................C 419 476-0581
   Toledo *(G-14500)*

Toledo Molding & Die LLC......................D 419 470-3950
   Toledo *(G-14499)*

Tom Smith Industries Inc.......................D 937 832-1555
   Englewood *(G-7745)*

Toth Mold & Die Inc................................F 440 232-8530
   Bedford *(G-1158)*

Tri-Craft Inc...E 440 826-1050
   Cleveland *(G-4822)*

Venture Packaging Inc...........................D 419 465-2534
   Monroeville *(G-7127)*

PLASTICS: Molded

Alpha Packaging Holdings Inc...............B 216 252-5595
   Cleveland *(G-3608)*

Astro Manufacturing & Design Inc........C 888 215-1746
   Eastlake *(G-7017)*

Beach Mfg Plastic Molding Div..............G 937 882-6400
   New Carlisle *(G-11411)*

Crg Plastics Inc.......................................F 937 298-2025
   Dayton *(G-6267)*

Cuyahoga Molded Plastics Co (inc).......E 216 261-2744
   Euclid *(G-7266)*

Don-Ell Corporation.................................E 419 841-7114
   Sylvania *(G-13913)*

PRODUCT SECTION

Flex Technologies Inc.............................. E 740 922-5992
  Midvale *(G-10878)*
Fortis Plastics LLC................................. F 937 382-0966
  Wilmington *(G-16051)*
G S K Inc.. G 937 547-1611
  Greenville *(G-8046)*
Industrial Farm Tank Inc....................... E 937 843-2972
  Lewistown *(G-9194)*
Liqui-Box Corporation........................... E 419 294-3884
  Upper Sandusky *(G-14814)*
Magic Molding Inc................................. G 937 778-0836
  Covington *(G-6027)*
Mar-Bal Inc.. D 440 543-7526
  Chagrin Falls *(G-2407)*
Meggitt (erlanger) LLC.......................... E 513 851-5550
  Cincinnati *(G-3143)*
Molded Fiber Glass Companies............. D 440 997-5851
  Ashtabula *(G-651)*
Molded Fiber Glass Companies............. A 440 997-5851
  Ashtabula *(G-650)*
Molders World Inc................................. F 513 469-6653
  Blue Ash *(G-1441)*
Myers Industries Inc............................. D 330 253-5592
  Akron *(G-259)*
North Coast Custom Molding Inc........... F 419 905-6447
  Dunkirk *(G-6976)*
Palpac Industries Inc............................ F 419 523-3230
  Ottawa *(G-12187)*
Plasticraft Usa LLC................................ G 513 761-2999
  Cincinnati *(G-3260)*
Podnar Plastics Inc............................... G 330 673-2255
  Kent *(G-8843)*
Priority Custom Molding Inc.................. F 937 431-8770
  Beavercreek *(G-1058)*
R and S Technologies Inc...................... F 419 483-3691
  Bellevue *(G-1232)*
RMC USA Incorporation......................... D 440 992-4906
  Jefferson *(G-8758)*
Step2 Company LLC.............................. B 419 938-6343
  Perrysville *(G-12449)*
Step2 Company LLC.............................. B 866 429-5200
  Streetsboro *(G-13794)*
Superior Plastics Inc............................. F 614 733-0307
  Plain City *(G-12593)*
Team Amity Mlds Plstic Injctio.............. G 937 667-7856
  Tipp City *(G-14158)*
U S Development Corp........................... D 330 673-6900
  Kent *(G-8879)*
Vnl Molding Ltd..................................... G 330 220-5951
  Brunswick *(G-1799)*
Wch Molding LLC................................... E 740 335-6320
  Wshngtn Ct Hs *(G-16244)*

PLASTICS: Polystyrene Foam

Acor Orthopaedic LLC........................... E 216 662-4500
  Cleveland *(G-3594)*
ADS Ventures Inc.................................. G 614 658-0050
  Hilliard *(G-8393)*
ADS Worldwide Inc................................ G 614 658-0050
  Hilliard *(G-8394)*
Advanced Drainage Systems Inc........... D 614 658-0050
  Hilliard *(G-8396)*
All Foam Products Co........................... G 330 849-3636
  Middlefield *(G-10730)*
Allied Shipping and Packagi.................. F 937 222-7422
  Moraine *(G-11155)*
Amatech Inc.. E 614 252-2506
  Columbus *(G-5119)*
American Corrugated Products Inc........ C 614 870-2000
  Columbus *(G-5124)*
Arkay Industries Inc.............................. E 513 360-0390
  Monroe *(G-11095)*

Armaly LLC.. E 740 852-3621
  London *(G-9381)*
Creative Foam Dayton Mold.................. F 937 279-9987
  Dayton *(G-6266)*
Ddp Specialty Electronic MA.................. C 937 839-4612
  West Alexandria *(G-15341)*
Deufol Worldwide Packaging LLC.......... E 440 232-1100
  Bedford *(G-1116)*
Extol of Ohio Inc.................................... F 419 668-2072
  Norwalk *(G-11964)*
Gdc Inc.. F 574 533-3128
  Wooster *(G-16123)*
Hedstrom Plastics LLC.......................... D 419 289-9310
  Ashland *(G-578)*
Hfi LLC... B 614 491-0700
  Canal Winchester *(G-1987)*
ICP Adhesives and Sealants Inc............ E 330 753-4585
  Norton *(G-11944)*
Interior Dnnage Spcialites Inc............... E 614 291-0900
  Columbus *(G-5473)*
ISO Technologies Inc............................ E 740 928-0084
  Heath *(G-8322)*
IVEX Protective Packaging LLC............. E 937 498-9298
  Sidney *(G-13256)*
Jain America Foods Inc........................ G 614 850-9400
  Columbus *(G-5486)*
M L B Molded Urethane Pdts LLC........... G 419 825-9140
  Swanton *(G-13976)*
Merryweather Foam Inc........................ E 330 753-0353
  Barberton *(G-882)*
Myers Industries Inc............................. E 330 253-5592
  Akron *(G-260)*
Ohio Decorative Products LLC.............. C 419 647-9033
  Spencerville *(G-13487)*
Ohio Foam Corporation......................... G 614 252-4877
  Columbus *(G-5619)*
Owens Corning Sales LLC..................... G 330 634-0460
  Tallmadge *(G-14041)*
Palpac Industries Inc............................ F 419 523-3230
  Ottawa *(G-12187)*
Plastic Forming Company Inc............... E 330 830-5167
  Massillon *(G-10134)*
Prime Industries Inc............................. E
  Lorain *(G-9431)*
S & A Industries Corporation................ E 330 733-6040
  Akron *(G-319)*
S & A Industries Corporation................ D 330 733-6040
  Akron *(G-320)*
Scott Port-A-Fold Inc............................ F 419 748-8880
  Napoleon *(G-11334)*
Smithers-Oasis Company..................... F 330 673-5831
  Kent *(G-8864)*
Sonoco Prtective Solutions Inc............. E 419 420-0029
  Findlay *(G-7565)*
Temprecision Intl Corp......................... G 855 891-7732
  Kent *(G-8873)*
Wellman Container Corporation............ E 513 860-3040
  Cincinnati *(G-3515)*

PLASTICS: Thermoformed

AMD Plastics Inc................................... F 216 289-4862
  Euclid *(G-7260)*
Arthur Corporation................................ D 419 433-7202
  Huron *(G-8627)*
Brittany Stamping LLC.......................... A 216 267-0850
  Cleveland *(G-3760)*
Comdess Company Inc......................... E 330 769-2094
  Seville *(G-13141)*
Corvac Composites LLC........................ D 248 807-0969
  Greenfield *(G-8028)*
Encore Industries Inc........................... C 419 626-8000
  Cambridge *(G-1935)*

PLATING & POLISHING SVC

First Choice Packaging Inc................... C 419 333-4100
  Fremont *(G-7778)*
I-Plus Inc.. G 216 432-9200
  Cleveland *(G-4213)*
Integral Design Inc............................... F 216 524-0555
  Cleveland *(G-4230)*
Kurz-Kasch Inc...................................... E 740 498-8343
  Newcomerstown *(G-11647)*
Maverick Corporation............................ F 513 469-9919
  Blue Ash *(G-1430)*
Neff-Perkins Company.......................... D 440 632-1658
  Middlefield *(G-10776)*
Plastikos Corporation........................... E 513 732-0961
  Batavia *(G-943)*
Progrssive Molding Bolivar Inc.............. E 330 874-3000
  Bolivar *(G-1534)*
Replex Mirror Company......................... E 740 397-5535
  Mount Vernon *(G-11291)*
Roechling Indus Cleveland LP............... C 216 486-0100
  Cleveland *(G-4645)*
Rubbermaid Home Products................ D 330 733-7771
  Mogadore *(G-11080)*
Saint-Gobain Prfmce Plas Corp............ D 440 836-6900
  Solon *(G-13418)*
Scott Molders Incorporated................... D 330 673-5777
  Kent *(G-8859)*
Tooling Tech Holdings LLC.................... F 937 295-3672
  Fort Loramie *(G-7612)*

PLATE WORK: Metalworking Trade

Alloy Engineering Company.................. D 440 243-6800
  Berea *(G-1264)*
Mercury Iron and Steel Co.................... F 440 349-1500
  Solon *(G-13385)*

PLATES: Steel

Churchill Steel Plate Ltd....................... E 330 425-9000
  Twinsburg *(G-14642)*
Evolve Solutions LLC............................. E 440 357-8964
  Painesville *(G-12233)*
Global Metal Services Ltd.................... G 440 591-1264
  Chagrin Falls *(G-2398)*

PLATING & POLISHING SVC

Ak-Isg Steel Coating Company.............. F 216 429-6901
  Cleveland *(G-3619)*
Allen Aircraft Products Inc.................... E 330 296-9621
  Ravenna *(G-12702)*
Aluminum Extruded Shapes Inc............ C 513 563-2205
  Cincinnati *(G-2613)*
Arem Co... F 440 974-6740
  Mentor *(G-10423)*
ATI Flat Rlled Pdts Hldngs LLC............. F 330 875-2244
  Louisville *(G-9455)*
Carlisle and Finch Company................. E 513 681-6080
  Cincinnati *(G-2703)*
Chemical Methods Incorporated........... E 216 476-8400
  Brunswick *(G-1751)*
Chromium Corporation.......................... E 216 271-4910
  Cleveland *(G-3821)*
Cincinnati Gearing Systems Inc............ D 513 527-8600
  Cincinnati *(G-2751)*
Cleveland-Cliffs Columbus LLC............. D 614 492-6800
  Richfield *(G-12784)*
Commercial Honing LLC........................ D 330 343-8896
  Dover *(G-6813)*
Conley Group Inc.................................. E 330 372-2030
  Warren *(G-15158)*
D-G Custom Chrome LLC....................... G 513 531-1881
  Cincinnati *(G-2815)*
Die Co Inc.. E 440 942-8856
  Eastlake *(G-7025)*

Employee Codes: A=Over 500 employees, B=251-500
C=101-250, D=51-100, E=20-50, F=10-19, G=1-9

2024 Harris Ohio Industrial Directory

PLATING & POLISHING SVC — PRODUCT SECTION

E L Stone Company .... E 330 825-4565
  Norton (G-11941)
Electro Prime Group LLC .... D 419 666-5000
  Rossford (G-12864)
Electro Prime Group LLC .... D 419 476-0100
  Toledo (G-14273)
Etched Metal Company .... E 440 248-0240
  Solon (G-13347)
GRB Holdings Inc .... D 937 236-3250
  Dayton (G-6360)
Hall Company .... E 937 652-1376
  Urbana (G-14833)
Hartzell Mfg Co LLC .... E 937 859-5955
  Miamisburg (G-10643)
Industrial Paint & Strip Inc .... E 419 568-2222
  Waynesfield (G-15296)
J Horst Manufacturing Co .... D 330 828-2216
  Dalton (G-6133)
Jason Incorporated .... C 513 860-3400
  Hamilton (G-8224)
JM Hamilton Group Inc .... E 419 229-4010
  Lima (G-9258)
Ledbetter Partners LLC .... G 937 253-5311
  Dayton (G-6402)
McGean-Rohco Inc .... F 216 441-4900
  Newburgh Heights (G-11618)
McGean-Rohco Inc .... D 216 441-4900
  Newburgh Heights (G-11619)
Metal Seal & Products Inc .... C 440 946-8500
  Mentor (G-10502)
Miba Bearings US LLC .... B 740 962-4242
  Mcconnelsville (G-10282)
Micro Lapping & Grinding Co .... F 216 267-6500
  Cleveland (G-4401)
Milestone Services Corp .... G 330 374-9988
  Akron (G-249)
Niles Manufacturing & Finshg .... C 330 544-0402
  Niles (G-11678)
Ohio Decorative Products LLC .... C 419 647-9033
  Spencerville (G-13487)
Ohio Metal Products Company .... E 937 228-6101
  Dayton (G-6489)
Ohio Roll Grinding Inc .... E 330 453-1884
  Louisville (G-9466)
P & L Heat Trting Grinding Inc .... E 330 746-1339
  Youngstown (G-16408)
Parker Rst-Proof Cleveland Inc .... E 216 481-6680
  Cleveland (G-4530)
Parker Trutec Incorporated .... D 937 653-8500
  Urbana (G-14846)
Polymet Recovery LLC .... G 330 630-9006
  Akron (G-281)
Rack Processing Company Inc .... E 937 294-1911
  Moraine (G-11206)
Reifel Industries Inc .... D 419 737-2138
  Pioneer (G-12498)
Sawyer Technical Materials LLC .... E 440 951-8770
  Willoughby (G-15985)
Scot Industries Inc .... D 330 262-7585
  Wooster (G-16169)
Springco Metal Coatings Inc .... C 216 941-0020
  Cleveland (G-4722)
Stuart-Dean Co Inc .... G 412 765-2752
  Cleveland (G-4742)
Thomas Steel Strip Corporation .... E 330 841-6429
  Warren (G-15210)
Tri-State Fabricators Inc .... E 513 752-5005
  Amelia (G-469)
Vectron Inc .... E 440 323-3369
  Elyria (G-7216)
Wieland Metal Svcs Foils LLC .... D 330 823-1700
  Alliance (G-437)

Worthington Enterprises Inc .... D 513 539-9291
  Monroe (G-11121)
Worthngton Smuel Coil Proc LLC .... E 330 963-3777
  Twinsburg (G-14758)
Yoder Industries Inc .... C 937 278-5769
  Dayton (G-6662)

PLATING COMPOUNDS

Coventya Inc .... F 315 768-6635
  Brooklyn Heights (G-1688)
Plating Process Systems Inc .... G
  Mentor (G-10525)

PLATING SVC: Chromium, Metals Or Formed Prdts

Archer Custom Chrome LLC .... G 216 441-2795
  Westlake (G-15734)
B & R Custom Chrome .... G 419 536-7215
  Toledo (G-14203)
Chrome Deposit Corporation .... E 330 773-7800
  Akron (G-109)
Chrome Deposit Corporation .... E 513 539-8486
  Monroe (G-11097)
Hale Performance Coatings Inc .... E 419 244-6451
  Toledo (G-14310)
Plate-All Metal Company Inc .... G 330 633-6166
  Akron (G-277)
Quality Plating Co .... G 216 361-0151
  Cleveland (G-4607)
R A Heller Company .... F 513 771-6100
  Cincinnati (G-3321)
Raf Acquisition Co .... E 440 572-5999
  Valley City (G-14888)
Youngstown Hard Chrome Pltg Gr .... E 330 758-9721
  Youngstown (G-16482)

PLAYGROUND EQPT

Funtown Playgrounds Inc .... F 513 871-8585
  Cincinnati (G-2559)
Meyer Design Inc .... E 330 434-9176
  Akron (G-247)
Ultrabuilt Play Systems Inc .... F 419 652-2294
  Nova (G-12005)

PLEATING & STITCHING FOR THE TRADE: Decorative & Novelty

Ideal Drapery Company Inc .... F 330 745-9873
  Barberton (G-874)

PLEATING & STITCHING SVC

Barbs Graffiti Inc .... E 216 881-5550
  Cleveland (G-3719)
Big Kahuna Graphics LLC .... G 330 455-2625
  Canton (G-2048)
Catania Medallic Specialty Inc .... E 440 933-9595
  Avon Lake (G-801)
Design Original Inc .... F 937 596-5121
  Jackson Center (G-8731)
Fineline Imprints Inc .... F 740 453-1083
  Zanesville (G-16530)
Finn Graphics Inc .... E 513 941-6161
  Cincinnati (G-2905)
Shamrock Companies Inc .... D 440 899-9510
  Westlake (G-15786)

PLUMBING FIXTURES

As America Inc .... F 330 332-9954
  Salem (G-12977)
Atlantic Co .... E 440 944-8988
  Willoughby Hills (G-16021)

Empire Brass Co .... G 216 431-6565
  Cleveland (G-4012)
Ferguson Enterprises LLC .... G 216 635-2493
  Parma (G-12287)
Field Stone Inc .... E 937 898-3236
  Tipp City (G-14135)
Fort Recovery Industries Inc .... D 419 375-3005
  Fort Recovery (G-7618)
Fort Recovery Industries Inc .... C 419 375-4121
  Fort Recovery (G-7617)
Krendl Machine Company .... D 419 692-3060
  Delphos (G-6763)
Lsq Manufacturing Inc .... F 330 725-4905
  Medina (G-10345)
Maass Midwest Mfg Inc .... G 419 894-6424
  Arcadia (G-516)
Mansfield Plumbing Pdts LLC .... A 419 938-5211
  Perrysville (G-12447)
Merit Brass Co .... C 216 261-9800
  Cleveland (G-4394)
Mssk Manufacturing Inc .... E 330 393-6624
  Warren (G-15197)
Next Gerenation Crimping .... G 440 237-6300
  North Royalton (G-11888)
W A S P Inc .... G 740 439-2398
  Cambridge (G-1560)
Waxman Industries Inc .... C 440 439-1830
  Bedford Heights (G-1181)
Wolff Bros Supply Inc .... F 440 327-1650
  North Ridgeville (G-11864)
Zekelman Industries Inc .... C 740 432-2146
  Cambridge (G-1551)

PLUMBING FIXTURES: Plastic

Add-A-Trap LLC .... G 330 750-0417
  Struthers (G-13808)
Bobbart Industries Inc .... E 419 350-5477
  Sylvania (G-13951)
Certified Walk In Tubs .... G 614 436-4848
  Columbus (G-524)
Cincinnati Machines Inc .... E 513 536-2432
  Batavia (G-915)
Cultured Marble Inc .... G 330 549-2282
  Poland (G-12610)
Dbhl Inc .... D 216 267-7100
  Cleveland (G-3945)
Hancor Inc .... B 614 658-0050
  Hilliard (G-8413)
Lubrizol Global Management Inc .... F 216 447-5000
  Cleveland (G-4337)
Mansfield Plumbing Pdts LLC .... A 419 938-5211
  Perrysville (G-12447)
Meese Inc .... F 440 998-1202
  Ashtabula (G-647)
Tower Industries Ltd .... E 330 837-2216
  Massillon (G-10159)

PLUMBING FIXTURES: Vitreous

Accent Manufacturing Inc .... F 330 724-7704
  Norton (G-11936)
As America Inc .... F 330 332-9954
  Salem (G-12977)
East Woodworking Company .... G 216 791-5950
  Cleveland (G-3990)
Mansfield Plumbing Pdts LLC .... A 419 938-5211
  Perrysville (G-12447)

PLUMBING FIXTURES: Vitreous China

As America Inc .... E 419 522-4211
  Mansfield (G-9626)
Watersource LLC .... G 419 747-9552
  Mansfield (G-9731)

POINT OF SALE DEVICES

NCR Technology Center............................ G 937 445-1936
 Dayton *(G-6466)*
Total Touch LLC.. E 800 726-2117
 Cleveland *(G-4811)*
Verifone Inc... C 800 837-4366
 Columbus *(G-5857)*

POLE LINE HARDWARE

Preformed Line Products Co.................... A 440 461-5200
 Mayfield Village *(G-10260)*

POLISHING SVC: Metals Or Formed Prdts

A & B Deburring Company....................... F 513 723-0444
 Cincinnati *(G-2582)*
Areway Acquisition Inc............................ D 216 651-9022
 Brooklyn *(G-1675)*
Bright-On Polishing & Mfg LLC................ G 937 489-3985
 Sidney *(G-13229)*
Charles J Meyers..................................... G 513 922-2866
 Cincinnati *(G-2726)*
Epsilon Management Corporation........... C 216 634-2500
 Cleveland *(G-4025)*
Gei of Columbiana Inc............................. E 330 783-0270
 Youngstown *(G-16364)*
General Extrusions Intl LLC..................... C 330 783-0270
 Youngstown *(G-16365)*
Hy-Blast Inc.. E 513 424-0704
 Middletown *(G-10829)*
Miami Valley Polishing LL....................... G 937 498-1634
 Sidney *(G-13265)*
Microtek Finishing LLC........................... E 513 766-5600
 West Chester *(G-15571)*
Shalmet Corporation................................ E 440 236-8840
 Elyria *(G-7204)*
Sun Polishing Corp.................................. G 440 237-5525
 Cleveland *(G-4746)*
Wall Polishing LLC.................................. G 937 698-1330
 Ludlow Falls *(G-9530)*

POLYESTERS

Dupont Specialty Pdts USA LLC............. E 740 474-0220
 Circleville *(G-3548)*
Illinois Tool Works Inc............................. C 513 489-7600
 Blue Ash *(G-1408)*
Maintenance Repair Supply Inc.............. F 740 922-3006
 Midvale *(G-10881)*
Mar-Bal Inc.. D 440 543-7526
 Chagrin Falls *(G-2407)*
Pet Processors LLc................................. D 440 354-4321
 Painesville *(G-12257)*
Polynt Composites USA Inc.................... E 816 391-6000
 Sandusky *(G-13088)*

POLYETHYLENE RESINS

Etna Products Incorporated.................... E 440 543-9845
 Chagrin Falls *(G-2395)*
Pitt Plastics Inc.. D 614 868-8660
 Columbus *(G-5675)*

POLYMETHYL METHACRYLATE RESINS: Plexiglas

Mexichem Specialty Resins Inc.............. E 440 930-1435
 Avon Lake *(G-817)*

POLYSTYRENE RESINS

Deltech Polymers LLC............................. G 937 339-3150
 Troy *(G-14561)*
Epsilyte Holdings LLC............................. D 937 778-9500
 Piqua *(G-12515)*

Evergreen Recycling LLC....................... E 419 547-1400
 Clyde *(G-4972)*
Progressive Foam Tech Inc..................... C 330 756-3200
 Beach City *(G-970)*

POLYTETRAFLUOROETHYLENE RESINS

Crg Plastics Inc....................................... F 937 298-2025
 Dayton *(G-6267)*

POLYURETHANE RESINS

Hfi LLC... B 614 491-0700
 Canal Winchester *(G-1987)*
Polymer Concepts Inc............................. G 440 953-9605
 Mentor *(G-10527)*

POLYVINYL CHLORIDE RESINS

Aurora Plastics LLC................................. E 330 422-0700
 Streetsboro *(G-13757)*
Carlisle Plastics Company...................... G 937 845-9411
 New Carlisle *(G-11412)*
Crane Blending Center............................ E 614 542-1199
 Columbus *(G-5305)*
Geon Company.. A 216 447-6000
 Cleveland *(G-4121)*
Prime Conduit Inc.................................... F 216 464-3400
 Beachwood *(G-1012)*
Win Plastic Extrusions LLC..................... E 330 929-1999
 Cincinnati *(G-3521)*

POULTRY & POULTRY PRDTS WHOLESALERS

Borden Dairy Co Cincinnati LLC............. E 513 948-8811
 Cleveland *(G-3748)*
Just Natural Provision Company............ G 216 431-7922
 Cleveland *(G-4267)*
Roots Poultry Inc..................................... F 419 332-0041
 Fremont *(G-7805)*

POULTRY & SMALL GAME SLAUGHTERING & PROCESSING

Cal-Maine Foods Inc............................... D 937 337-9576
 Rossburg *(G-12861)*
Case Farms.. G 330 452-0230
 Canton *(G-2070)*
Case Farms LLC...................................... E 330 832-0030
 Massillon *(G-10083)*
Cooper Foods... E 419 232-2440
 Van Wert *(G-14910)*
Daylay Egg Farm Inc............................... C 937 355-6531
 West Mansfield *(G-15625)*
Sid-Mar Foods Inc................................... G 330 743-0112
 Youngstown *(G-16437)*
The Ellenbee-Leggett Company Inc....... C 513 874-3200
 Fairfield *(G-7417)*
Weaver Bros Inc...................................... D 937 526-3907
 Versailles *(G-14992)*

POULTRY SLAUGHTERING & PROCESSING

Case Farms of Ohio Inc........................... D 330 878-7118
 Strasburg *(G-13745)*
Case Farms of Ohio Inc........................... C 330 359-7141
 Winesburg *(G-16078)*
Cooper Hatchery Inc................................ C 419 238-4869
 Van Wert *(G-14911)*
Just Natural Provision Company............ G 216 431-7922
 Cleveland *(G-4267)*

POWDER: Iron

Truck Fax Inc... G 216 921-8866
 Cleveland *(G-4835)*

POWDER: Metal

Additive Metal Alloys............................... G 419 215-5800
 Maumee *(G-10159)*
Additive Metal Alloys Ltd........................ G 800 687-6110
 Holland *(G-8493)*
Bogie Industries Inc Ltd.......................... E 330 745-3105
 Akron *(G-89)*
Duffee Finishing Inc................................ G 740 965-4848
 Sunbury *(G-13952)*
Eckart America Corporation................... D 440 954-7600
 Painesville *(G-12231)*
J & K Powder Coating............................. G 330 540-6145
 Mineral Ridge *(G-11020)*
Key Finishes LLC.................................... G 614 351-8393
 Columbus *(G-5510)*
Obron Atlantic Corporation..................... D 440 954-7600
 Painesville *(G-12252)*
Powdermet Inc... E 216 404-0053
 Euclid *(G-7293)*
Rmi Titanium Company LLC................... E 330 652-9952
 Niles *(G-11684)*

POWER GENERATORS

Babcock & Wilcox Entps Inc................... C 330 753-4511
 Akron *(G-74)*
Bwx Technologies Inc............................. D 740 687-4180
 Lancaster *(G-8996)*
Qaf Technologies Inc.............................. E 440 941-4348
 Columbus *(G-5701)*
Thermelectricity LLC............................... G 330 972-8054
 Akron *(G-355)*

POWER SPLY CONVERTERS: Static, Electronic Applications

Bennett & Bennett Inc............................. G 937 324-1100
 Yellow Springs *(G-16282)*

POWER SUPPLIES: All Types, Static

Dare Electronics Inc............................... E 937 335-0031
 Troy *(G-14559)*
Kontron America Incorporated.............. G 937 324-2420
 Springfield *(G-13591)*
Vertiv Group Corporation....................... A 614 888-0246
 Westerville *(G-15687)*
Vertiv JV Holdings LLC........................... A 614 888-0246
 Columbus *(G-5859)*

POWER SWITCHING EQPT

Layerzero Power Systems Inc................ E 440 399-9000
 Aurora *(G-721)*
Te Connectivity Corporation................... C 419 521-9500
 Mansfield *(G-9725)*
UCI Controls Inc...................................... E 216 398-0330
 Cleveland *(G-4843)*

PRECAST TERRAZZO OR CONCRETE PRDTS

Clark Grave Vault Company.................... C 614 294-3761
 Columbus *(G-5251)*

PRECIPITATORS: Electrostatic

Cleveland Roll Forming Envi................... F 440 899-3888
 Westlake *(G-15744)*
McGill Airclean LLC................................. D 614 829-1200
 Columbus *(G-5550)*
McGill Corporation................................... F 614 829-1200
 Groveport *(G-8153)*
Neundorfer Inc... E 440 942-8990
 Willoughby *(G-15957)*

PRESTRESSED CONCRETE PRDTS

United McGill Corporation..................... E 614 829-1200
  Groveport (G-8165)

PRESTRESSED CONCRETE PRDTS

Fabcon Companies LLC..................... D 614 875-8601
  Grove City (G-8093)

PRIMARY FINISHED OR SEMIFINISHED SHAPES

Dietrich Industries Inc..................... C 330 372-2868
  Warren (G-15162)

PRIMARY ROLLING MILL EQPT

Rki Inc..................... C 888 953-9400
  Mentor (G-10546)

PRINT CARTRIDGES: Laser & Other Computer Printers

All Write Ribbon Inc..................... F 513 753-8300
  Amelia (G-450)
Printer Components Inc..................... G 585 924-5190
  Fairfield (G-7397)
Wood County Ohio..................... G 419 353-1227
  Bowling Green (G-1596)

PRINTED CIRCUIT BOARDS

Accurate Electronics Inc..................... C 330 682-7015
  Orrville (G-12116)
Alektronics Inc..................... F 937 429-2118
  Beavercreek (G-1069)
Avcom Smt Inc..................... F 614 882-8176
  Westerville (G-15692)
Blue Creek Enterprises Inc..................... E 937 222-9969
  Dayton (G-6232)
C E Electronics Inc..................... D 419 636-6705
  Bryan (G-1813)
Cartessa Corp..................... F 513 738-4477
  Shandon (G-13159)
Circle Prime Manufacturing..................... E 330 923-0019
  Cuyahoga Falls (G-6074)
Circuit Center..................... G 513 435-2131
  Dayton (G-6256)
Cleveland Circuits Corp..................... E 216 267-9020
  Cleveland (G-3836)
Cleveland Coretec Inc..................... G 314 727-2087
  North Jackson (G-11781)
Co-Ax Technology Inc..................... C 440 914-9200
  Solon (G-13332)
Ddi North Jackson Corp..................... G 330 538-3900
  North Jackson (G-11782)
Deca Mfg Co..................... F 419 884-0071
  Mansfield (G-9645)
Dynalab Inc..................... D 614 866-9999
  Reynoldsburg (G-12764)
Flextronics Intl USA Inc..................... E 513 755-2500
  Liberty Township (G-9207)
Interactive Engineering Corp..................... E 330 239-6888
  Medina (G-10337)
Journey Electronics Corp..................... G 513 539-9836
  Monroe (G-11112)
L3 Technologies Inc..................... E 513 943-2000
  Cincinnati (G-2568)
Lad Technology Inc..................... F 561 543-9858
  Concord Township (G-5909)
Levison Enterprises LLC..................... E 419 838-7365
  Millbury (G-10935)
Libra Industries LLC..................... F 440 974-4770
  Mentor (G-10493)
Logisync Corporation..................... F 440 937-0388
  Avon (G-780)
McGregor & Associates Inc..................... C 937 833-6768
  Brookville (G-1741)
Metzenbaum Sheltered Inds Inc..................... D 440 729-1919
  Chesterland (G-2485)
Naprotek Holdings LLC..................... D 408 830-5000
  Independence (G-8676)
Npas Inc..................... F 614 595-6916
  Mansfield (G-9706)
Ohio Fire Suppression LLC..................... G 216 269-6032
  Aurora (G-729)
Philway Products Inc..................... C 419 281-7777
  Ashland (G-600)
Projects Unlimited Inc..................... C 937 918-2200
  Dayton (G-6534)
Qualtech Technologies Inc..................... E 440 946-8081
  Willoughby (G-15980)
Quarter Century Design LLC..................... G 937 434-5127
  Dayton (G-6536)
Sinbon Ohio LLC..................... C 937 415-2070
  Vandalia (G-14959)
Techtron Systems Inc..................... E 440 505-2990
  Solon (G-13436)
Tetrad Electronics Inc..................... D 440 946-6443
  Willoughby (G-16005)
Ttm Technologies Inc..................... C 330 538-3900
  North Jackson (G-11792)
Ttm Technologies North America LLC..... D 330 572-3400
  North Jackson (G-11793)
Uvonics Co..................... F 614 458-1163
  Columbus (G-5852)
Valtronic Technology Inc..................... D 440 349-1239
  Solon (G-13441)
Versitec Manufacturing Inc..................... E 440 354-4283
  Painesville (G-12274)
Vexos Inc..................... C 440 284-2500
  Lagrange (G-8957)
Vmetro Inc..................... D 281 584-0728
  Fairborn (G-7326)
Wurth Electronics Ics Inc..................... E 937 415-7700
  Miamisburg (G-10703)

PRINTERS & PLOTTERS

Gameday Vision..................... F 330 830-4550
  Massillon (G-10098)
Small Business Products..................... G 800 553-6485
  Cincinnati (G-3397)

PRINTERS' SVCS: Folding, Collating, Etc

Bookmasters Inc..................... C 419 281-1802
  Ashland (G-557)
Capitol Citicom Inc..................... E 614 472-2679
  Columbus (G-5234)
Printing Services..................... F 440 708-1999
  Chagrin Falls (G-2417)

PRINTERS: Computer

Microcom Corporation..................... E 740 548-6262
  Lewis Center (G-9171)

PRINTERS: Magnetic Ink, Bar Code

Hunkar Technologies Inc..................... C 513 272-1010
  Cincinnati (G-3012)
ID Images Inc..................... E 330 220-7300
  Brunswick (G-1769)

PRINTING & BINDING: Books

Bip Printing Solutions LLC..................... F 216 832-5673
  Beachwood (G-974)
Hf Group LLC..................... C 440 729-9411
  Chesterland (G-2481)
Star City Press LLC..................... G 740 500-0320
  Chillicothe (G-2535)

PRINTING & EMBOSSING: Plastic Fabric Articles

Plastic Card Inc..................... D 330 896-5555
  Uniontown (G-1790)
Solar Arts Graphic Designs..................... G 330 744-0535
  Youngstown (G-6441)

PRINTING & ENGRAVING: Card, Exc Greeting

1st Impressions Plus LLC..................... G 330 696-7605
  Akron (G-9)

PRINTING & ENGRAVING: Financial Notes & Certificates

Quick Tech Business Forms Inc..................... F 937 743-5952
  Springboro (G-1517)
Watson Haran & Company Inc..................... G 937 436-1414
  Dayton (G-6648)

PRINTING & STAMPING: Fabric Articles

City Apparel Inc..................... F 419 434-1155
  Findlay (G-7493)
Hollywood Imprints LLC..................... F 614 501-6040
  Gahanna (G-783)
Wholesale Imprints Inc..................... E 440 224-3527
  North Kingsville (G-11797)

PRINTING & WRITING PAPER WHOLESALERS

Gvs Industries Inc..................... G 513 851-3606
  Hamilton (G-821)
Microcom Corporation..................... E 740 548-6262
  Lewis Center (G-9171)

PRINTING MACHINERY

A/C Laser Technologies Inc..................... F 330 784-3355
  Akron (G-12)
Alchem Aluminum Europe Inc..................... G 216 910-3400
  Beachwood (G-92)
Anderson & Vreeland Inc..................... D 419 636-5002
  Bryan (G-1807)
Armor..................... G 614 459-1414
  Columbus (G-515)
Beehex Inc..................... G 512 633-5304
  Columbus (G-517)
Carco America LLC..................... G 216 928-5409
  Cleveland (G-379)
Commonwealth Aluminum Mtls LLC..... F 216 910-3400
  Beachwood (G-93)
Container Graphics Corp..................... F 937 746-5666
  Franklin (G-7667)
Finzer Roller Inc..................... F 937 746-4069
  Franklin (G-7675)
Gew Inc..................... G 440 237-4439
  Cleveland (G-412)
Hadronics Inc..................... D 513 321-9350
  Cincinnati (G-2983)
Imco Recycling of Indiana Inc..................... G 216 910-3400
  Beachwood (G-95)
Kase Equipment Corporation..................... D 216 642-9040
  Cleveland (G-4273)
Nilpeter Usa Inc..................... C 513 489-4400
  Cincinnati (G-3195)
R & D Equipment Inc..................... E 419 668-8439
  Norwalk (G-11987)
Roconex Corporation..................... F 937 339-2616
  Miamisburg (G-10178)
Schilling Graphics Inc..................... E 419 468-1037
  Galion (G-7884)

PRODUCT SECTION

PRINTING, COMMERCIAL: Screen

Suspension Feeder Corporation............ F 419 763-1377
  Fort Recovery *(G-7625)*
Wise Edge LLC... G 330 208-0889
  Akron *(G-376)*
Wood Graphics Inc................................. E 513 771-6300
  Cincinnati *(G-3525)*

PRINTING, COMMERCIAL: Bags, Plastic, NEC

Ray C Sprosty Bag Co Inc.................... F 330 669-0045
  Smithville *(G-13301)*
Trebnick Systems Inc............................. E 937 743-1550
  Springboro *(G-13524)*

PRINTING, COMMERCIAL: Business Forms, NEC

Carbonless Cut Sheet Forms Inc............ F 740 826-1700
  New Concord *(G-11431)*
PJ Bush Associates Inc.......................... E 216 362-6700
  Cleveland *(G-4556)*
R R Donnelley & Sons Company........... B 740 928-6110
  Hebron *(G-8358)*
S F Mock & Associates LLC................... F 937 438-0196
  Dayton *(G-6556)*
Smartbill Ltd... F 740 928-6909
  Hebron *(G-8362)*

PRINTING, COMMERCIAL: Calendars, NEC

Haman Enterprises Inc........................... F 614 888-7574
  Columbus *(G-5417)*
Proforma Systems Advantage................ G 419 224-8747
  Lima *(G-9279)*

PRINTING, COMMERCIAL: Decals, NEC

Boehm Inc... E 614 875-9010
  Grove City *(G-8080)*
Commercial Decal Ohio Inc.................... F 330 385-7178
  East Liverpool *(G-6991)*
T&T Graphics Inc.................................... D 937 847-6000
  Miamisburg *(G-10688)*

PRINTING, COMMERCIAL: Envelopes, NEC

Anthony Business Forms Inc.................. G 937 253-0072
  Dayton *(G-6153)*
McDaniel Envelope Company Inc........... G 330 868-5929
  Minerva *(G-11034)*
Ohio Envelope Manufacturing Co........... E 216 267-2920
  Cleveland *(G-4497)*

PRINTING, COMMERCIAL: Imprinting

Ableprint / Toucan Inc............................ F 419 522-9742
  Mansfield *(G-9621)*
Better Living Concepts Inc..................... F 330 494-2213
  Canton *(G-2047)*
Fair Publishing House Inc...................... E 419 668-3746
  Norwalk *(G-11967)*
Middaugh Enterprises Inc...................... G 330 852-2471
  Sugarcreek *(G-13930)*

PRINTING, COMMERCIAL: Labels & Seals, NEC

CCL Label Inc... D 856 273-0700
  New Albany *(G-11372)*
CCL Label Inc... B 440 878-7277
  Strongsville *(G-13820)*
Century Marketing Corporation.............. C 419 354-2591
  Bowling Green *(G-1558)*
CMC Group Inc....................................... D 419 354-2591
  Bowling Green *(G-1561)*
Collotype Labels Usa Inc....................... D 513 381-1480
  Batavia *(G-917)*
Contemprary Image Labeling Inc........... G 513 583-5699
  Lebanon *(G-9068)*
D&D Design Concepts Inc...................... F 513 752-2191
  Batavia *(G-919)*
Donprint Inc... E 847 573-7777
  Strongsville *(G-13828)*
Geygan Enterprises Inc.......................... F 513 932-4222
  Lebanon *(G-9082)*
Innovtive Lbling Solutions Inc............... D
  Hamilton *(G-8220)*
Jamac Inc... E 419 625-9790
  Sandusky *(G-13069)*
Label Aid Inc.. E 419 433-2888
  Huron *(G-8635)*
Label Technique Southeast LLC............. E 440 951-7660
  Willoughby *(G-15941)*
Labeltek Inc... D 330 335-3110
  Wadsworth *(G-15042)*
M PI Label Systems............................... G 330 938-2134
  Sebring *(G-13121)*
Markham Converting Limited................. F 419 353-2458
  Bowling Green *(G-1574)*
McC-Norway LLC................................... F 513 381-1480
  Batavia *(G-932)*
Miller Products Inc................................. F 330 335-3110
  Wadsworth *(G-15045)*
Miller Products Inc................................. D 330 335-3110
  Wadsworth *(G-15046)*
Model GRAphics& Media Inc.................. E 513 541-2355
  West Chester *(G-15465)*
Mpi Labels of Baltimore Inc................... G 330 938-2134
  Sebring *(G-13124)*
Multi-Color Corporation......................... G 513 459-3283
  Mason *(G-10032)*
Multi-Color Corporation......................... F 513 381-1480
  Batavia *(G-939)*
Ohio Label Inc....................................... F 614 777-0180
  Columbus *(G-5620)*
Performance Packaging Inc................... F 419 478-8805
  Toledo *(G-14433)*
Seneca Label Inc.................................... E 440 237-1600
  Brunswick *(G-1791)*
Storad Label Co..................................... F 740 382-6440
  Marion *(G-9885)*
Tech/III Inc... E 513 482-7500
  Fairfield *(G-7415)*
The Hooven - Dayton Corp..................... C 937 233-4473
  Miamisburg *(G-10694)*
The Label Team Inc................................ F 330 332-1067
  Salem *(G-13033)*
Verstrete In Mold Lbels USA In............... F 513 943-0080
  Batavia *(G-959)*
W/S Packaging Group Inc..................... D 513 459-8800
  Mason *(G-10069)*

PRINTING, COMMERCIAL: Letterpress & Screen

44stronger LLC...................................... G 440 371-6455
  Grafton *(G-7996)*
Club 513 LLC... G 800 530-2574
  Cincinnati *(G-2776)*

PRINTING, COMMERCIAL: Literature, Advertising, NEC

Bottomline Ink Corporation.................... E 419 897-8000
  Perrysburg *(G-12364)*
Multi-Color Australia LLC....................... D 513 381-1480
  Batavia *(G-938)*

PRINTING, COMMERCIAL: Magazines, NEC

Quebecor World Johnson Hardin............ E 614 326-0299
  Cincinnati *(G-3314)*

PRINTING, COMMERCIAL: Periodicals, NEC

1010 Magapp LLC.................................. G 210 701-1754
  Wooster *(G-16093)*
400 SW 7th Street Partners Ltd............. E 440 826-4700
  Cincinnati *(G-2580)*
AGS Custom Graphics Inc...................... D 330 963-7770
  Macedonia *(G-9534)*
Alcohol & Drug Addiction Svcs............... F 216 348-4830
  Cleveland *(G-3624)*
Center For Inquiry Inc............................ G 330 671-7192
  Peninsula *(G-12339)*
Clutch Mov... G 740 525-5510
  Marietta *(G-9784)*
Collective Arts Network.......................... G 216 235-3564
  Lakewood *(G-8971)*
Communication Resources Inc............... G 800 992-2144
  Canton *(G-2079)*
Crain Communications Inc..................... E 330 836-9180
  Cuyahoga Falls *(G-6077)*
Dominion Enterprises............................. G 216 472-1870
  Cleveland *(G-3967)*
Greater Cincinnati Bowl Assn................ E 513 761-7387
  Cincinnati *(G-2970)*
Kent Information Services Inc................ G 330 672-2110
  Kent *(G-8824)*
Liturgical Publications Inc..................... D 216 325-6825
  Cleveland *(G-4332)*
Matthew Bender & Company Inc............ C 518 487-3000
  Miamisburg *(G-10655)*
Pearson Education Inc............................ G 614 876-0371
  Columbus *(G-5663)*
Pearson Education Inc............................ E 614 841-3700
  Columbus *(G-5664)*
Relx Inc... G 937 865-6800
  Miamisburg *(G-10673)*
Rubber World Magazine Inc................... G 330 864-2122
  Akron *(G-313)*
Schaeffers Investment Research Inc....... D 513 589-3800
  Blue Ash *(G-1465)*
Sesh Communications............................ F 513 851-1693
  Cincinnati *(G-3384)*
Sterling Associates Inc.......................... G 330 630-3500
  Akron *(G-338)*
Telex Communications Inc..................... G 419 865-0972
  Toledo *(G-14482)*
University Sports Publications............... G 614 291-6416
  Columbus *(G-5847)*
Welch Publishing Co.............................. E 419 874-2528
  Perrysburg *(G-12444)*

PRINTING, COMMERCIAL: Promotional

Ad-Sensations Inc.................................. F 419 841-5395
  Sylvania *(G-13989)*
American Business Forms Inc................ E 513 312-2522
  West Chester *(G-15535)*
American Imprssions Sportswear........... G 614 848-6677
  Columbus *(G-5125)*
Dyenamo Distributing LLC..................... G 419 462-9474
  Galion *(G-7870)*
Everythings Image Inc............................ F 513 469-6727
  Blue Ash *(G-1392)*
Sensical Inc.. D 216 641-1141
  Solon *(G-13420)*
SRC Liquidation LLC............................... A 937 221-1000
  Dayton *(G-6586)*

Employee Codes: A=Over 500 employees, B=251-500
C=101-250, D=51-100, E=20-50, F=10-19, G=1-9

PRINTING, COMMERCIAL: Screen

PRINTING, COMMERCIAL: Screen

4d Screenprinting Ltd .... G 513 353-1070
  Cleves (G-4945)

Aardvark Screen Prtg & EMB LLC .... F 419 354-6686
  Bowling Green (G-1548)

Absolute Impressions Inc .... F 614 840-0599
  Lewis Center (G-9146)

Ace Transfer Company .... G 937 398-1103
  Springfield (G-13528)

Adcraft Decals Incorporated .... E 216 524-2934
  Cleveland (G-3598)

Advanced Incentives Inc .... G 419 471-9088
  Toledo (G-14178)

Airwaves LLC .... C 740 548-1200
  Lewis Center (G-9147)

Albany Screen Printing LLC .... F 614 585-3279
  Reynoldsburg (G-12750)

Alberts Screen Print Inc .... C 330 753-7559
  Norton (G-11938)

Allied Silk Screen Inc .... G 937 223-4921
  Dayton (G-6195)

Alvin L Roepke .... G 419 862-3891
  Elmore (G-7099)

Ares Sportswear Ltd .... D 614 767-1950
  Hilliard (G-8398)

Ashton LLC .... F 614 833-4165
  Pickerington (G-12455)

Assocted Vsual Cmmncations Inc .... E 330 452-4449
  Canton (G-2040)

Aztech Printing & Promotions .... G 937 339-0100
  Troy (G-14551)

Badlime Promo and Apparel LLC .... G 330 425-7100
  Twinsburg (G-14633)

Ball Jackets LLC .... E 937 572-1114
  Jamestown (G-8740)

Benchmark Prints .... F 419 332-7640
  Fremont (G-7766)

Big Kahuna Graphics LLC .... G 330 455-2625
  Canton (G-2048)

Campbell Signs & Apparel LLC .... F 330 386-4768
  East Liverpool (G-6989)

Casad Company Inc .... F 419 586-9457
  Coldwater (G-4984)

Clear Images LLC .... F 419 241-9347
  Toledo (G-14241)

Concept 9 Inc .... G 614 294-3743
  Columbus (G-5285)

Custom Deco LLC .... D 419 698-2900
  Toledo (G-14255)

Custom Sportswear Imprints LLC .... G 330 335-8326
  Wadsworth (G-15024)

Drycal Inc .... G 440 974-1999
  Mentor (G-10450)

Dynamic Design & Systems Inc .... G 440 708-1010
  Chagrin Falls (G-2393)

E & E Nameplates Inc .... G 419 468-3617
  Galion (G-7871)

First Impression Wear LLC .... G 937 456-3900
  Eaton (G-7059)

Foghorn Designs .... F 419 706-3861
  Norwalk (G-11968)

Fulton Sign & Decal Inc .... G 440 951-1515
  Mentor (G-10461)

Funky Ink Prints LLC .... G 330 241-7291
  Brunswick (G-1762)

Glavin Industries Inc .... E 440 349-0049
  Solon (G-13353)

Glen D Lala .... G 937 274-7770
  Dayton (G-6354)

Got Graphix Llc .... F 330 703-9047
  Fairlawn (G-7440)

Grady McCauley Inc .... D 330 494-9444
  Akron (G-172)

Graphix One Corporation .... G 513 870-0512
  West Chester (G-15558)

Green Leaf Printing and Design .... G 937 222-3634
  Dayton (G-6361)

Hartman Distributing LLC .... D 740 616-7764
  Heath (G-8321)

Homestretch Sportswear Inc .... G 419 678-4282
  Saint Henry (G-12936)

Industrial Screen Prcess Svc I .... F 419 255-4900
  Toledo (G-14330)

Ink Slingers LLC .... G 740 867-3528
  Chesapeake (G-2475)

Jupmode .... E 419 318-2029
  Toledo (G-14342)

Just Name It Inc .... G 614 626-8662
  Ashland (G-582)

Kaufman Container Company .... C 216 898-2000
  Cleveland (G-4276)

Kdm Signs Inc .... C 513 769-1932
  Cincinnati (G-3069)

Knight Line Signature AP Corp .... G 330 545-8108
  Girard (G-7970)

Lake Screen Printing Inc .... G 440 244-5707
  Lorain (G-9419)

Liberty Sportswear LLC .... G 513 755-8740
  Hamilton (G-8227)

License Ad Plate Company .... F 216 265-4200
  Cleveland (G-4323)

Lima Sporting Goods Inc .... E 419 222-1036
  Lima (G-9265)

M & H Screen Printing .... G 740 522-1957
  Newark (G-11587)

Markt LLC .... G 740 397-5900
  Mount Vernon (G-11278)

McC - Mason W&S .... C 513 459-1100
  Mason (G-10027)

Meder Special-Tees Ltd .... G 513 921-3800
  Cincinnati (G-3140)

Metro Flex Inc .... G 937 299-5360
  Moraine (G-11194)

Mid-Ohio Screen Print Inc .... G 614 875-1774
  Grove City (G-8106)

Moonshine Screen Printing Inc .... G 513 523-7775
  Oxford (G-12211)

Morrison Sign Company Inc .... E 614 276-1181
  Columbus (G-5582)

Mr O Fficials LLC .... G 216 240-2534
  Cleveland (G-4428)

Murphy Dog LLC .... E 614 755-4278
  Blacklick (G-1341)

Neff Motivation Inc .... C 937 548-3194
  Greenville (G-8053)

Nordec Inc .... D 330 940-3700
  Stow (G-13715)

Northeastern Plastics Inc .... G 330 453-5925
  Canton (G-2179)

Off Contact Inc .... F 419 255-5546
  Toledo (G-14406)

P S Graphics Inc .... G 440 356-9656
  Rocky River (G-12840)

Painted Hill Inv Group Inc .... F 937 339-1756
  Troy (G-14600)

Part 2 Screen Prtg Design Inc .... G 614 294-4429
  Columbus (G-5657)

Pops Printed Apparel LLC .... G 614 372-5651
  Columbus (G-5682)

Pounce Signs & Print Wear .... G 408 377-4680
  London (G-9393)

Precision Imprint .... G 740 592-5916
  Athens (G-692)

Primal Screen Inc .... F 330 677-1766
  Kent (G-8848)

Printeesweet .... G 888 410-2160
  Hopedale (G-857)

Prodigy Print Inc .... F
  Dayton (G-6528)

Promospark Inc .... G 513 844-2211
  Fairfield (G-7397)

Qualitee Design Sportswear Co .... F 740 333-8337
  Wshngtn Ct Hs (G-16237)

Queen City Spirit LLC .... G 513 533-2662
  Cincinnati (G-3320)

Schlabach Printers LLC .... E 330 852-4687
  Sugarcreek (G-3937)

Sit Inc .... E 330 758-8468
  Youngstown (G-6440)

Sk Screen Printing Inc .... E 330 475-0286
  Akron (G-332)

Spear Inc .... D 513 459-1100
  Mason (G-10052)

Specialty Printing and Proc .... F 614 322-9035
  Columbus (G-5763)

SRI Ohio Inc .... E 740 653-5800
  Lancaster (G-9061)

Standout Stickers Inc .... G 877 449-7703
  Brunswick (G-1772)

Steves Sports Inc .... G 440 735-0044
  Northfield (G-11511)

Studio Eleven Inc .... F 937 295-2225
  Fort Loramie (G-7611)

T & L Custom Screening Inc .... G 937 237-3121
  Dayton (G-6605)

T-Shirt Co .... E 513 821-7100
  Cincinnati (G-3439)

Tee Hee Co Inc .... G 614 515-5581
  Worthington (G-5215)

Transfer Express Inc .... D 440 918-1900
  Mentor (G-10581)

Traxler Tees LLC .... F 614 593-1270
  Columbus (G-5864)

Treefrogg Specialties Inc .... G 513 212-3581
  Batavia (G-954)

Underground Sports Shop Inc .... F 513 751-1662
  Cincinnati (G-3477)

Unisport Inc .... G 419 529-4727
  Ontario (G-12096)

United Sport Apparel .... F 330 722-0818
  Medina (G-10391)

Vandalia Sportswear LLC .... G 937 264-3204
  Vandalia (G-14960)

Vgu Industries Inc .... E 216 676-9093
  Cleveland (G-4860)

Viewpoint Graphic Design .... G 419 447-6073
  Tiffin (G-14114)

Water Drop Media Inc .... G 234 600-5817
  Vienna (G-15005)

Weaver Screen Print LLC .... G 440 725-0116
  Willoughby (G-16014)

PRINTING, COMMERCIAL: Stationery, NEC

Atelierkopii LLC .... G 216 559-0815
  Cleveland (G-3690)

CCL Label Inc .... D 216 676-2703
  Cleveland (G-3807)

Keeler Enterprises Inc .... G 330 336-7601
  Wadsworth (G-15039)

Westrock Mwv LLC .... D 937 495-6323
  Dayton (G-6651)

PRINTING, LITHOGRAPHIC: Calendars

Beach Company .... E 740 622-0905
  Coshocton (G-597)

PRODUCT SECTION

PRINTING: Commercial, NEC

Novelty Advertising Co Inc .... E 740 622-3113
 Coshocton *(G-5988)*

PRINTING, LITHOGRAPHIC: Circulars

Melnor Graphics LLC .... F 419 476-8808
 Toledo *(G-14382)*

PRINTING, LITHOGRAPHIC: Color

Fx Digital Media Inc .... F 216 241-4040
 Cleveland *(G-4095)*

PRINTING, LITHOGRAPHIC: Forms, Business

GBS Corp .... C 330 863-1828
 Malvern *(G-9612)*
Quick Tab II Inc .... D 419 448-6622
 Tiffin *(G-14101)*

PRINTING, LITHOGRAPHIC: Offset & photolithographic printing

Capitol Citicom Inc .... E 614 472-2679
 Columbus *(G-5234)*
Corporate Dcment Solutions Inc .... G 513 595-8200
 Cincinnati *(G-2797)*
Hecks Direct Mail & Prtg Svc .... E 419 661-6028
 Toledo *(G-14314)*
M Rosenthal Company .... F 513 563-0081
 Cincinnati *(G-3120)*
SMI Holdings Inc .... D 740 927-3464
 Pataskala *(G-12309)*

PRINTING, LITHOGRAPHIC: Posters

Frame Warehouse .... G 614 861-4582
 Reynoldsburg *(G-12765)*

PRINTING, LITHOGRAPHIC: Tags

Bainbridge419 Inc .... F 937 228-2181
 Toledo *(G-14204)*
Trebnick Systems Inc .... E 937 743-1550
 Springboro *(G-13524)*

PRINTING, LITHOGRAPHIC: Tickets

Premier Southern Ticket Co Inc .... E 513 489-6700
 Cincinnati *(G-3273)*

PRINTING: Books

1st Impressions Plus LLC .... G 330 696-7605
 Akron *(G-9)*
American Printing & Lithog Co .... F 513 867-0602
 Hamilton *(G-8177)*
Golf Marketing Group Inc .... G 330 963-5155
 Twinsburg *(G-14669)*
Hf Group LLC .... F 440 729-2445
 Aurora *(G-719)*
Hubbard Company .... E 419 784-4455
 Defiance *(G-6682)*
J & L Management Corporation .... G 440 205-1199
 Mentor *(G-10478)*
Multi-Craft Litho Inc .... E 859 581-2754
 Blue Ash *(G-1442)*
The Press of Ohio Inc .... B 330 678-5868
 Kent *(G-8875)*
Lsc Communications Inc .... A 419 935-0111
 Willard *(G-15860)*
Quebecor World Johnson Hardin ...... E 614 326-0299
 Cincinnati *(G-3314)*

PRINTING: Commercial, NEC

4 Over LLC .... E 937 610-0629
 Dayton *(G-6177)*

A E Wilson Holdings Inc .... G 330 405-0316
 Twinsburg *(G-14621)*
A To Z Paper Box Company .... G 330 325-8722
 Rootstown *(G-12850)*
Advanced Specialty Products .... G 419 882-6528
 Bowling Green *(G-1550)*
Advertising Joe LLC Mean .... G 440 247-8200
 Chagrin Falls *(G-2367)*
Aero Fulfillment Services Corp .... D 800 225-7145
 Mason *(G-9945)*
Agnone-Kelly Enterprises Inc .... G 800 634-6503
 Cincinnati *(G-2602)*
AGS Custom Graphics Inc .... D 330 963-7770
 Macedonia *(G-9534)*
American Printing & Lithog Co .... F 513 867-0602
 Hamilton *(G-8177)*
Anderson Graphics Inc .... E 330 745-2165
 Barberton *(G-855)*
Appleheart Inc .... G 937 384-0430
 Miamisburg *(G-10612)*
Austin Tape and Label Inc .... D 330 928-7999
 Stow *(G-13686)*
Bates Printing Inc .... F 330 833-5830
 Massillon *(G-10078)*
Bindery & Spc Pressworks Inc .... D 614 873-4623
 Plain City *(G-12566)*
Bizall Inc .... G 216 939-9580
 Cleveland *(G-3738)*
Bohlender Engraving Company .... G 513 621-4095
 Cincinnati *(G-2676)*
Bollin & Sons Inc .... E 419 693-6573
 Toledo *(G-14216)*
Brass Bull 1 LLC .... G 740 335-8030
 Wshngtn Ct Hs *(G-16226)*
Broadway Printing LLC .... G 513 621-3429
 Cincinnati *(G-2687)*
Brook & Whittle Limited .... E 513 860-2457
 Hamilton *(G-8187)*
Buckeye Packaging Co Inc .... D 330 935-0301
 Alliance *(G-396)*
C P S Enterprises Inc .... G 216 441-7969
 Cleveland *(G-3779)*
Carey Color Inc .... D 330 239-1835
 Sharon Center *(G-13164)*
Century Graphics Inc .... F 614 895-7698
 Westerville *(G-15651)*
Charles Huffman & Associates .... G 216 295-0850
 Warrensville Heights *(G-15228)*
Cincinnati Print Solutions LLC .... G 513 943-9500
 Milford *(G-10900)*
Coloring Book Solutions LLC .... G 419 281-9641
 Ashland *(G-566)*
Consolidated Graphics Group Inc ..... C 216 881-9191
 Cleveland *(G-3896)*
Corporate Dcment Solutions Inc .... G 513 595-8200
 Cincinnati *(G-2797)*
Culaine Inc .... G 419 345-4984
 Toledo *(G-14254)*
Custom Products Corporation .... D 440 528-7100
 Solon *(G-13334)*
Dayton Legal Blank Inc .... F 937 435-4405
 Dayton *(G-6281)*
Dbh Asscates - Ohio Ltd Partnr .... G 330 676-2006
 Kent *(G-8808)*
Delaware Data Products .... G 740 369-5449
 Delaware *(G-6713)*
Dietrich Von Hldbrand Lgacy PR .... G 703 496-7821
 Steubenville *(G-13666)*
Djsc Inc .... E 740 928-2697
 Hebron *(G-8340)*
Dlh Enterprises LLC .... G 330 253-6960
 Akron *(G-132)*

DSC Supply Company LLC .... G 614 891-1100
 Westerville *(G-15703)*
Dupli-Systems Inc .... C 440 234-9415
 Strongsville *(G-13830)*
Edge 247 Corp .... G 216 771-7000
 Cleveland *(G-4000)*
Electronic Imaging Svcs Inc .... F 740 549-2487
 Lewis Center *(G-9159)*
Engineered Imaging LLC .... F 419 255-1283
 Toledo *(G-14277)*
Equip Business Solutions Co .... G 614 854-9755
 Jackson *(G-8715)*
F J Designs Inc .... F 330 264-1377
 Wooster *(G-16117)*
Flexoparts Com .... G 513 932-2060
 Lebanon *(G-9077)*
Folks Creative Printers Inc .... F 740 383-6326
 Marion *(G-9852)*
Gb Liquidating Company Inc .... E 513 248-7600
 Milford *(G-10907)*
GBS Corp .... C 330 494-5330
 North Canton *(G-11729)*
General Data Company Inc .... B 513 752-7978
 Cincinnati *(G-2561)*
General Theming Contrs LLC .... C 614 252-6342
 Columbus *(G-5397)*
Gq Business Products Inc .... G 513 792-4750
 Loveland *(G-9482)*
Grafisk Maskinfabrik Amer LLC .... F 630 432-4370
 Lebanon *(G-9086)*
Graphic Stitch Inc .... G 937 642-6707
 Marysville *(G-9911)*
Grassroots Strategies LLC .... G 614 783-6515
 Columbus *(G-5411)*
Harper Engraving & Printing Co .... D 614 276-0700
 Columbus *(G-5420)*
Hecks Direct Mail Prtg Svc Inc .... F 419 697-3505
 Toledo *(G-14315)*
Hkm Drect Mkt Cmmnications Inc .... E 440 934-3060
 Sheffield Village *(G-13183)*
Hkm Drect Mkt Cmmnications Inc .... E 330 395-9538
 Warren *(G-15176)*
Hkm Drect Mkt Cmmnications Inc .... C 800 860-4456
 Cleveland *(G-4193)*
Horizon Ohio Publications Inc .... D 419 738-2128
 Wapakoneta *(G-15117)*
HP Industries Inc .... E 419 478-0695
 Toledo *(G-14322)*
Hr Graphics .... G 216 455-0534
 Cleveland *(G-4205)*
Humtown Pattern Company .... D 330 482-5555
 Columbiana *(G-5041)*
Imagine This Renovations .... G 330 833-6739
 Navarre *(G-11344)*
Innomark Communications LLC .... D 513 285-1040
 Fairfield *(G-7372)*
Jack Walker Printing Co .... F 440 352-4222
 Mentor *(G-10481)*
Kay Toledo Tag Inc .... D 419 729-5479
 Toledo *(G-14346)*
Kdm Signs Inc .... G 513 554-1393
 Cincinnati *(G-3068)*
Kenwel Printers Inc .... E 614 261-1011
 Columbus *(G-5508)*
Letterman Printing Inc .... G 513 523-1111
 Oxford *(G-12210)*
Lsc Communications Inc .... A 419 935-0111
 Willard *(G-15860)*
Marbee Inc .... G 419 422-9441
 Findlay *(G-7535)*
Marcus Uppe Inc .... E 216 263-4000
 Cleveland *(G-4357)*

Employee Codes: A=Over 500 employees, B=251-500
C=101-250, D=51-100, E=20-50, F=10-19, G=1-9

PRINTING: Commercial, NEC

Middleton Printing Co Inc .... G 614 294-7277
  Gahanna (G-7845)
ML Advertising & Design LLC .... G 419 447-6523
  Tiffin (G-14094)
Mmp Printing Inc .... E 513 381-0990
  Cincinnati (G-3168)
Multi-Craft Litho Inc .... E 859 581-2754
  Blue Ash (G-1442)
Mustang Printing .... F 419 592-2746
  Napoleon (G-11325)
Ncrformscom .... G 800 709-1938
  Hudson (G-8606)
Network Printing & Graphics .... F 614 230-2084
  Columbus (G-5593)
Nilpeter Usa Inc .... C 513 489-4400
  Cincinnati (G-3198)
OH Road LLC .... G 614 582-4765
  Columbus (G-5612)
Old Trail Printing Company .... C 614 443-4852
  Columbus (G-5636)
Onetouchpoint East Corp .... D 513 421-1600
  Cincinnati (G-3225)
Packaging Materials Inc .... E 740 432-6337
  Cambridge (G-1946)
Park PLC Prntg Cpyg & Dgtl IMG .... G 330 799-1739
  Youngstown (G-16414)
Penguin Enterprises Inc .... E 440 899-5112
  Westlake (G-15773)
Precision Business Solutions .... F 419 661-8700
  Perrysburg (G-12420)
Press of Ohio Inc .... E 330 678-5868
  Kent (G-8847)
Printing Dimensions Inc .... F 937 256-0044
  Dayton (G-6523)
Printing Unlimited Inc .... G 419 874-9828
  Perrysburg (G-12421)
Progressive Printers Inc .... D 937 222-1267
  Dayton (G-6533)
Quest Service Labs Inc .... F 330 405-0316
  Twinsburg (G-14721)
Quick As A Wink Printing Co .... G 419 224-9786
  Lima (G-9281)
R R Donnelley & Sons Company .... G 513 552-1512
  West Chester (G-15494)
R&D Marketing Group Inc .... G 216 398-9100
  Brooklyn Heights (G-1697)
Reece Brothers Inc .... G 419 212-9226
  Bryan (G-1837)
Repacorp Inc .... D 937 667-8496
  Tipp City (G-14152)
Reynolds and Reynolds Company ...... F 419 584-7000
  Celina (G-2346)
Schilling Graphics Inc .... E 419 468-1037
  Galion (G-7884)
Sekuworks LLC .... E 513 202-1210
  Harrison (G-8290)
Solution Ventures Inc .... G 330 858-1111
  Tallmadge (G-14047)
Springdot Inc .... D 513 542-4000
  Cincinnati (G-3411)
Standard Register Technologies .... G 937 443-1000
  Dayton (G-6590)
Stephen Andrews Inc .... G 330 725-2672
  Lodi (G-9357)
Stolle Machinery Company LLC .... C 937 497-5400
  Sidney (G-13291)
Suburban Press Incorporated .... E 216 961-0766
  Cleveland (G-4744)
Taylor Communications Inc .... E 419 678-6000
  Coldwater (G-5002)
Taylor Communications Inc .... E 937 221-1000
  Dayton (G-6609)

Taylor Communications Inc .... E 614 277-7500
  Urbancrest (G-14855)
The Cyril-Scott Company .... C 740 654-2112
  Lancaster (G-9043)
The D B Hess Company .... E 330 678-5868
  Kent (G-8874)
Tj Metzgers Inc .... D 419 861-8611
  Toledo (G-14487)
Toledo Ticket Company .... E 419 476-5424
  Toledo (G-14506)
Tpo Hess Holdings Inc .... E 815 334-6140
  Kent (G-8876)
Tree Free Resources LLC .... G 740 751-4844
  Marion (G-9887)
Universal North Inc .... F 440 230-1366
  North Royalton (G-11899)
Visual Marking Systems Inc .... D 330 425-7100
  Twinsburg (G-14753)
Vya Inc .... E 513 772-5400
  Cincinnati (G-3506)
Ward/Kraft Forms of Ohio Inc .... E 740 694-0015
  Fredericktown (G-7759)
West-Camp Press Inc .... D 614 882-2378
  Westerville (G-15725)
Western Ohio Graphics .... F 937 335-8769
  Troy (G-14616)
Western Roto Engravers Inc .... E 330 336-7636
  Wadsworth (G-15072)
Wfsr Holdings LLC .... A 877 735-4966
  Dayton (G-6654)
Williams Steel Rule Die Co .... F 216 431-3232
  Cleveland (G-4910)
Workflowone LLC .... A 877 735-4966
  Dayton (G-6661)
Yockey Group Inc .... F 513 860-9053
  West Chester (G-15529)
Youngstown ARC Engraving Co .... G 330 793-2471
  Youngstown (G-16476)

PRINTING: Flexographic

Custom Poly Bag LLC .... D 330 935-2408
  Alliance (G-399)
Ebel-Binder Printing Co Inc .... G 513 471-1067
  Cincinnati (G-2856)
Hawks & Associates Inc .... E 513 752-4311
  Cincinnati (G-2563)
HI Tech Printing Co Inc .... E 513 874-5325
  Fairfield (G-7366)
Kopco Graphics Inc .... E 513 874-7230
  West Chester (G-15456)
Mr Label Inc .... E 513 681-2088
  Cincinnati (G-3177)
Novavision LLC .... D 419 354-1427
  Bowling Green (G-1577)
Ohio Flexible Packaging Co .... F 513 494-1800
  South Lebanon (G-13462)
Omni Systems Inc .... D 216 377-5160
  Mayfield Village (G-10259)
Samuels Products Inc .... E 513 891-4456
  Blue Ash (G-1464)
Superior Label Systems Inc .... B 513 336-0825
  Mason (G-10061)
Thomas Products Co Inc .... E 513 756-9009
  Cincinnati (G-3453)
Warren Printing & Off Pdts Inc .... F 419 523-3635
  Ottawa (G-12196)
West Crrllton Prchment Cnvrtn .... E 513 594-3341
  West Carrollton (G-15358)

PRINTING: Gravure, Forms, Business

Dupli-Systems Inc .... C 440 234-9415
  Strongsville (G-13830)

Workflowone LLC .... A 877 735-4966
  Dayton (G-6663)

PRINTING: Gravure, Labels

Anthony Business Forms Inc .... G 937 253-0072
  Dayton (G-6153)
E-Z Stop Service Center .... G 330 448-2236
  Brookfield (G-1668)
M PI Label Systems .... G 330 938-2134
  Sebring (G-13121)
Mpi Labels of Baltimore Inc .... E 330 938-2134
  Sebring (G-13124)
Pioneer Labels Inc .... C 618 546-5418
  West Chester (G-15479)
Retterbush Graphics Packg Corp .... F 513 779-4466
  West Chester (G-15498)

PRINTING: Gravure, Rotogravure

Angstrom Graphics Inc .... C 216 271-5300
  Cleveland (G-358)
Brook & Whittle Limited .... E 513 860-2457
  Hamilton (G-817)
Lloyd F Helber .... G 740 756-9607
  Carroll (G-2299)
Multi-Color Australia LLC .... D 513 381-1480
  Batavia (G-938)
Ohio Gravure Technologies Inc .... F 937 439-1582
  Miamisburg (G-10668)
Sekuworks LLC .... E 513 202-1210
  Harrison (G-8290)
Shamrock Companies Inc .... D 440 899-9510
  Westlake (G-15776)
The Photo-Type Engraving Company ... D 513 281-0999
  Cincinnati (G-3430)
Wfsr Holdings LLC .... A 877 735-4966
  Dayton (G-6654)

PRINTING: Laser

Data Image .... G 740 763-7008
  Heath (G-8319)
Laser Printing Solutions Inc .... F 216 351-4444
  Cleveland (G-4315)
Microplex Printware Corp .... F 440 374-2424
  Solon (G-13390)
Queen City Office Machine .... F 513 251-7200
  Cincinnati (G-3317)
True Dinero Records & Tech LLC .... G 513 428-4610
  Cincinnati (G-3475)

PRINTING: Letterpress

A-A Blueprint Co Inc .... E 330 794-8803
  Akron (G-11)
Acme Printing Co Inc .... G 419 626-4426
  Sandusky (G-1301)
Akron Litho-Print Company Inc .... F 330 434-3145
  Akron (G-36)
All Points Printing Inc .... G 440 585-1125
  Wickliffe (G-15823)
Barnhart Printing Corp .... F 330 456-2279
  Canton (G-2044)
Berea Printing Company .... G 440 243-1080
  Berea (G-1268)
Bramkamp Printing Company Inc .... E 513 241-1865
  Blue Ash (G-1373)
Brothers Printing Co Inc .... F 216 621-6050
  Cleveland (G-3764)
Cox Printing Company .... G 937 382-2312
  Wilmington (G-16046)
Dee Printing Inc .... F 614 777-8700
  Columbus (G-5322)
Diocesan Publications Inc .... E 614 718-9500
  Dublin (G-6879)

PRINTING: Lithographic

E&O Fbn Inc .... F 513 241-5150
  Cincinnati (G-2851)

Eci Macola/Max LLC .... C 978 539-6186
  Dublin (G-6883)

Empire Printing Inc .... G 513 242-3900
  Fairfield (G-7356)

Foote Printing Company Inc .... F 216 431-1757
  Cleveland (G-4079)

Great Lakes Printing Inc .... F 440 993-8781
  Ashtabula (G-636)

Heskamp Printing Co Inc .... G 513 871-6770
  Cincinnati (G-2997)

Keystone Press Inc .... G 419 243-7326
  Toledo (G-14347)

KMS 2000 Inc .... F 330 454-9444
  Canton (G-2141)

Lee Corporation .... G 513 771-3602
  Cincinnati (G-3099)

Lilienthal/Southeastern Inc .... E 740 439-1640
  Cambridge (G-1940)

Lyle Printing & Publishing Co .... E 330 337-3419
  Salem (G-13013)

M Rosenthal Company .... F 513 563-0081
  Cincinnati (G-3120)

Mariotti Printing Co LLC .... G 440 245-4120
  Lorain (G-9424)

Odyssey Press Inc .... F 614 410-0356
  Huron (G-8642)

Post Printing Co .... D 859 254-7714
  Minster (G-11058)

Printex Incorporated .... F 740 773-0088
  Chillicothe (G-2529)

R R Donnelley & Sons Company .... D 440 774-2101
  Oberlin (G-12055)

Selby Service/Roxy Press Inc .... G 513 241-3445
  Cincinnati (G-3378)

Shreve Printing LLC .... F 330 567-2341
  Shreve (G-13215)

Slimans Printery Inc .... F 330 454-9141
  Canton (G-2226)

Snow Printing Co Inc .... F 419 229-7669
  Lima (G-9290)

Star Printing Company Inc .... E 330 376-0514
  Akron (G-336)

Starr Services Inc .... G 513 241-7708
  Cincinnati (G-3417)

Tope Printing Inc .... G 330 674-4993
  Millersburg (G-11000)

Traxium LLC .... E 330 572-8200
  Stow (G-13732)

William J Bergen & Co .... G 440 248-6132
  Solon (G-13448)

PRINTING: Lithographic

1one Stop Printing Inc .... F 614 216-1438
  Columbus (G-5074)

3d Printing .... G 501 248-0468
  Lewis Center (G-9143)

7 7 Print Solutions LLC .... F 513 600-4597
  Fairfield (G-7328)

Adcraft Decals Incorporated .... E 216 524-2934
  Cleveland (G-3598)

Akron Thermography Inc .... F 330 896-9712
  Akron (G-46)

Akron Thermography Inc .... F 330 896-9712
  Akron (G-47)

Alberts Screen Print Inc .... C 330 753-7559
  Norton (G-11938)

Alliance Publishing Co Inc .... C 330 453-1304
  Alliance (G-393)

AlphaGraphics .... G 513 204-6070
  Mason (G-9948)

AlphaGraphics 507 Inc .... G 440 878-9700
  Strongsville (G-13805)

Alvito Custom Imprints LLC .... G 614 207-1004
  Columbus (G-5118)

American Printing & Lithog Co .... F 513 867-0602
  Hamilton (G-8177)

Amsive OH LLC .... D 937 885-8000
  Miamisburg (G-10611)

Angstrom Graphics Inc .... C 216 271-5300
  Cleveland (G-3668)

Anthony Business Forms Inc .... G 937 253-0072
  Dayton (G-6153)

Artistic Photography Prtg Inc .... G 813 310-6965
  Bedford (G-1102)

Auld Corporation .... G 614 454-1010
  Columbus (G-5165)

Baesman Group Inc .... D 614 771-2300
  Hilliard (G-8402)

Banbury Investments Inc .... G 513 677-4500
  Cincinnati (G-2655)

BCT Alarm Services Inc .... G 440 669-8153
  Lorain (G-9402)

Best Graphics & Printing Inc .... G 513 535-3529
  Cincinnati (G-2668)

Black River Group Inc .... E 419 524-6699
  Mansfield (G-9628)

Bloch Printing Company .... G 330 576-6760
  Copley (G-5945)

Blooms Printing Inc .... F 740 922-1765
  Dennison (G-6793)

Blue Crescent Enterprises Inc .... G 440 878-9700
  Strongsville (G-13816)

Bohlender Engraving Company .... G 513 621-4095
  Cincinnati (G-2676)

Bookmasters Inc .... C 419 281-1802
  Ashland (G-557)

BP 10 Inc .... E 513 346-3900
  West Chester (G-15382)

Brandon Screen Printing .... F 419 229-9837
  Lima (G-9224)

Capehart Enterprises LLC .... F 614 769-7746
  Columbus (G-5230)

Cardpak Incorporated .... C 440 542-3100
  Solon (G-13326)

Cincinnati Convertors Inc .... F 513 731-6600
  Cincinnati (G-2744)

City of Cleveland .... E 216 664-3013
  Cleveland (G-3822)

Coachella Trotting & Prtg Ltd .... G 614 326-1009
  Columbus (G-5258)

County Classifieds .... G 937 592-8847
  Bellefontaine (G-1203)

Coyne Graphic Finishing Inc .... E 740 397-6232
  Mount Vernon (G-11269)

Culaine Inc .... G 419 345-4984
  Toledo (G-14254)

Custom Imprint .... F 440 238-4488
  Strongsville (G-13825)

Custom Needle-Print LLC .... G 330 432-5506
  New Philadelphia (G-11497)

Davis Printing Company .... E 330 745-3113
  Barberton (G-866)

Dayton Legal Blank Inc .... F 937 435-4405
  Dayton (G-6281)

DC Printing LLC .... G 937 640-1957
  Dayton (G-6294)

DC Reprographics Co .... F 614 297-1200
  Columbus (G-5319)

Denny Printing LLC .... G 417 825-4936
  Grove City (G-8088)

Digital Color Intl LLC .... F
  Akron (G-130)

Ditty Printing LLC .... G 614 893-7439
  Galena (G-7853)

Djsc Inc .... E 740 928-2697
  Hebron (G-8340)

Dla Document Services .... F 937 257-6014
  Dayton (G-6159)

Dupli-Systems Inc .... C 440 234-9415
  Strongsville (G-13830)

Electronic Printing Pdts Inc .... E 800 882-4050
  Stow (G-13694)

Enlarging Arts Inc .... G 330 434-3433
  Akron (G-142)

Ennis Inc .... E 800 537-8648
  Toledo (G-14278)

Enquirer Printing Company .... G 513 241-1956
  Cincinnati (G-2875)

Envoi Design Inc .... G 513 651-4229
  Cincinnati (G-2877)

Etched Metal Company .... E 440 248-0240
  Solon (G-13347)

Eugene Stewart .... G 937 898-1117
  Dayton (G-6325)

Fair Publishing House Inc .... E 419 668-3746
  Norwalk (G-11967)

Far Corner .... G 330 767-3734
  Navarre (G-11341)

Fleet Graphics Inc .... G 937 252-2552
  Dayton (G-6335)

Follow Print Club On Facebook .... G 216 707-2579
  Cleveland (G-4077)

Fremont Printing Inc .... F 480 272-3443
  Fremont (G-7784)

Friends Service Co Inc .... F 800 427-1704
  Dayton (G-6339)

Frisby Printing Company .... F 330 665-4565
  Fairlawn (G-7439)

Fully Involved Printing Co LLC .... G 440 635-6858
  Mentor (G-10460)

Gannett Stllite Info Ntwrk LLC .... E 419 334-1012
  Fremont (G-7785)

Geygan Enterprises Inc .... F 513 932-4222
  Lebanon (G-9082)

Gorilla Joe Printing Co LLC .... G 234 719-1861
  Youngstown (G-16372)

Graphic Paper Products Corp .... D 937 325-5503
  Springfield (G-13570)

Hawks & Associates Inc .... E 513 752-4311
  Cincinnati (G-2563)

Headlee Enterprises Ltd .... G 614 785-1476
  Columbus (G-5063)

Highland Computer Forms Inc .... D 937 393-4215
  Hillsboro (G-8459)

Hkm Drect Mkt Cmmnications Inc .... C 800 860-4456
  Cleveland (G-4193)

Horizon Ohio Publications Inc .... D 419 738-2128
  Wapakoneta (G-15117)

Howling Print and Promo Inc .... G 440 363-4999
  Chardon (G-2452)

Identity Group LLC .... G 614 337-6167
  Westerville (G-15658)

Imprint LLC .... G 216 233-0066
  Cleveland (G-4221)

Inkscape Print and Promos LLC .... F 330 893-0160
  Millersburg (G-10970)

Innovative Graphics Ltd .... F 877 406-3636
  Columbus (G-5461)

Instant Graphications Inc .... G 330 819-5267
  Akron (G-191)

Instant Replay Ltd .... G 937 592-0534
  Bellefontaine (G-1214)

Instant Surface Solutions Inc .... G 513 266-1667
  Cincinnati (G-2566)

PRINTING: Lithographic   PRODUCT SECTION

Company	Col	Phone
Isaac Foster Mack Co. Sandusky (G-13067)	C	419 625-5500
J Solutions LLC. Columbus (G-5484)	G	614 732-4857
Jay Tees LLC. Thornville (G-14066)	E	740 405-1579
Jk Digital Publishing LLC. Springboro (G-13506)	F	937 299-0185
Joe The Printer Guy LLC. Lakewood (G-8977)	G	216 651-3880
Kem Advertising and Prtg LLC. Barberton (G-876)	G	330 818-5061
Kinkos Inc. Cleveland (G-4291)	F	216 661-9950
Liturgical Publications Inc. Cleveland (G-4332)	D	216 325-6825
Loving Choice Adoption-Prntng. Canton (G-2146)	G	330 994-1451
Lsc Communications Inc. Willard (G-15860)	A	419 935-0111
Malik Media LLC. New Albany (G-11383)	F	614 933-0328
Master Printing Group Inc. Berea (G-1287)	F	216 351-2246
Minuteman Press. Dayton (G-6452)	G	937 701-7100
Minuteman Press. Hamilton (G-8229)	G	513 454-7318
Minuteman Press. Piqua (G-12537)	F	937 451-8222
Minuteman Press Inc. Cincinnati (G-3166)	F	513 741-9056
Mj Bornhorst Enterprises LLC. Fort Loramie (G-7604)	E	937 295-3469
Mmp Printing Inc. Cincinnati (G-3168)	E	513 381-0990
Monks Copy Shop Inc. Columbus (G-5579)	F	614 461-6438
Morse Enterprises Inc. Mason (G-10031)	G	513 229-3600
Multi-Color Australia LLC. Batavia (G-938)	D	513 381-1480
North Shore Printing LLC. Portsmouth (G-12651)	G	740 876-9066
Northcoast Pmm LLC. Toledo (G-14399)	F	419 540-8667
Northeast Blueprint and Sup Co. Cleveland (G-4475)	G	216 261-7500
Ohio Art Company. Bryan (G-1833)	D	419 636-3141
Onetouchpoint East Corp. Cincinnati (G-3225)	D	513 421-1600
Ovp Inc. Belpre (G-1259)	G	740 423-5171
Pamton 3d Printing LLC. Youngstown (G-16411)	G	330 792-5503
Precious Mmories Cstm Prtg Inc. Cleveland (G-4571)	G	216 721-3909
Premier Prtg Centl Ohio Ltd. Marysville (G-9932)	E	937 642-0988
Print Syndicate Inc. Columbus (G-5691)	E	617 290-9550
Print Syndicate LLC. Columbus (G-5692)	F	614 519-0341
Printers Edge Inc. Warren (G-15200)	F	330 372-2232
Printing Resources Inc. Cleveland (G-4588)	G	216 881-7660
Printing Services. Chagrin Falls (G-2417)	F	440 708-1999
Professional Screen Printing. Lancaster (G-9033)	G	740 687-0760
Proforma Prana. Wickliffe (G-15850)	G	440 345-6466
Promatch Solutions LLC. Moraine (G-11205)	F	877 299-0185
Quick Tech Graphics Inc. Springboro (G-13518)	E	937 743-5952
R R Donnelley & Sons Company. Oberlin (G-12055)	D	440 774-2101
R R Donnelley & Sons Company. Streetsboro (G-13786)	D	330 562-5250
R&D Marketing Group Inc. Brooklyn Heights (G-1697)	G	216 398-9100
Record Herald Publishing Co. Cincinnati (G-3327)	E	717 762-2151
Reliable Printing Solutions. Wilmington (G-16058)	G	937 486-5031
Reynolds and Reynolds Company. Celina (G-2346)	F	419 584-7000
RI Smith Graphics LLC. Youngstown (G-16428)	G	330 629-8616
Ron Toelke. Cincinnati (G-3350)	G	513 598-1881
Rotary Forms Press Inc. Hillsboro (G-8465)	E	937 393-3426
RS Imprints LLC. Newton Falls (G-11656)	G	330 872-5905
Schlabach Printers LLC. Sugarcreek (G-13937)	E	330 852-4687
Scott Francis Antique Prints. Cleveland (G-4679)	G	216 737-0873
Sdg News Group Inc. New London (G-11468)	F	419 929-3411
Sdo Sports Ltd. Cleveland (G-4683)	G	440 546-9998
Sekuworks LLC. Harrison (G-8290)	E	513 202-1210
Sensical Inc. Solon (G-13420)	D	216 641-1141
Shawnee Systems Inc. Cincinnati (G-3387)	D	513 561-9932
Shout Out Loud Prints. Columbus (G-5765)	G	614 432-8990
Soondook LLC. Columbus (G-5779)	E	614 389-5757
Start Printing Co LLC. Middletown (G-10859)	C	513 424-2121
Stephen Andrews Inc. Lodi (G-9357)	G	330 725-2672
Stepping Stone Enterprises Inc. Maumee (G-10235)	F	419 472-0505
Stevenson Color Inc. Cincinnati (G-3422)	C	513 321-7500
Swimmer Printing Inc. Cleveland (G-4761)	G	216 623-1005
Taylor Communications Inc. Columbus (G-5812)	F	614 351-6868
Taylor Communications Inc. Dayton (G-6609)	F	937 221-1000
Tiny Footprints Daycare LLC. Cleveland (G-4797)	G	216 938-7306
Tpl Holdings LLC. Mogadore (G-11088)	E	800 475-4030
Tribune Printing Inc. Hicksville (G-8382)	F	419 542-7764
United Trade Printers LLC. Dublin (G-6955)	E	614 326-4829
Vectra Inc. Columbus (G-5855)	C	614 351-6868
Vision Graphix Inc. Westlake (G-15800)	G	440 835-6540
Vya Inc. Cincinnati (G-3506)	E	513 772-5400
Welch Publishing Co. Perrysburg (G-2444)	E	419 874-2528
Westrock Commercial LLC. Toledo (G-14523)	D	419 476-9101
Wfsr Holdings LLC. Dayton (G-6654)	A	877 735-4966
Wicked Premiums LLC. Brecksville (G-1537)	G	216 364-0322
Woodrow Manufacturing Co. Springfield (G-1657)	E	937 399-9333
Workflowone LLC. Dayton (G-6661)	A	877 735-4966
Xenia Daily Gazette. Xenia (G-16281)	E	937 372-4444

PRINTING: Offset

Company	Col	Phone
A F Krainz Co. Cleveland (G-359)	G	216 431-4341
A Grade Notes Inc. Dublin (G-6856)	G	614 299-9999
A Z Printing Inc. Cincinnati (G-255)	G	513 733-3900
A-A Blueprint Co Inc. Akron (G-11)	G	330 794-8803
Academy Graphic Comm Inc. Cleveland (G-359)	E	216 661-2550
Acme Duplicating Co Inc. Westlake (G-1527)	G	216 241-1241
Acme Printing Co Inc. Sandusky (G-1341)	G	419 626-4426
Activities Press Inc. Mentor (G-10404)	E	440 953-1200
Ad Choice Inc. Oregon (G-12101)	G	419 697-8889
Admark Printing Inc. Brookville (G-173)	G	937 833-5111
Advantage Print Solutions LLC. Columbus (G-514)	G	614 519-2392
AGS Custom Graphics Inc. Macedonia (G-954)	D	330 963-7770
All Points Printing Inc. Wickliffe (G-1582)	G	440 585-1125
Allegra Print & Imaging. Findlay (G-7475)	G	419 427-8095
Allen Graphics Inc. Solon (G-13308)	G	440 349-4100
American Printing Inc. Akron (G-62)	F	330 630-1121
Anderson Graphics Inc. Barberton (G-855)	E	330 745-2165
Andrin Enterprises Inc. Moraine (G-11157)	F	937 276-7794
Angstrom Graphics Inc Midwest. Cleveland (G-3660)	C	216 271-5300
Arens Corporation. Covington (G-6010)	G	937 473-2028
Arens Corporation. Covington (G-6010)	F	937 473-2028
Artco LLC. Piketon (G-12475)	G	740 493-2901
Avon Lake Printing. Avon Lake (G-795)	G	440 933-2078
B & B Printing Graphics Inc. Maumee (G-10167)	F	419 893-7068
B R Printers Inc. Cincinnati (G-2652)	D	513 271-6035
Barnhart Printing Corp. Canton (G-2044)	F	330 456-2279
Bates Printing Inc. Massillon (G-1007)	F	330 833-5830
Bay Business Forms Inc. Springfield (G-1359)	E	937 322-3000

(G-0000) Company's Geographic Section entry number

PRODUCT SECTION — PRINTING: Offset

Beckman Xmo .... F 614 864-2232
  Columbus *(G-5178)*
Berea Printing Company .... G 440 243-1080
  Berea *(G-1268)*
Bethart Enterprises Inc .... F 513 863-6161
  Hamilton *(G-8185)*
Bindery & Spc Pressworks Inc .... D 614 873-4623
  Plain City *(G-12566)*
Bis Printing .... G 440 951-2606
  Willoughby *(G-15890)*
Bizzy Bee Printing Inc .... G 614 771-1222
  Columbus *(G-5192)*
Bodnar Printing Co Inc .... F 440 277-8295
  Lorain *(G-9403)*
Bolger .... G 440 979-9577
  Cleveland *(G-3745)*
Bornhorst Printing Company Inc .... G 419 738-5901
  Wapakoneta *(G-15107)*
Bramkamp Printing Company Inc .... E 513 241-1865
  Blue Ash *(G-1373)*
Brand Printer LLC .... G 614 404-2615
  Powell *(G-12664)*
Brass Bull 1 LLC .... G 740 335-8030
  Wshngtn Ct Hs *(G-16226)*
Brentwood Printing & Sty .... G 513 522-2679
  Cincinnati *(G-2680)*
Brothers Printing Co Inc .... F 216 621-6050
  Cleveland *(G-3764)*
Buckeye Business Forms Inc .... G 614 882-1890
  Westerville *(G-15649)*
Bucyrus Graphics Inc .... F 419 562-2906
  Bucyrus *(G-1851)*
Bush Inc .... F 216 362-6700
  Cleveland *(G-3775)*
C Massouh Printing Co Inc .... F 330 408-7330
  Canal Fulton *(G-1969)*
Capitol Square Printing Inc .... G 614 221-2850
  Columbus *(G-5235)*
Carbon Web Print LLC .... F 216 402-3504
  Willoughby Hills *(G-16022)*
Carbonless On Demandcom LLC .... F 330 837-8611
  Massillon *(G-10082)*
Cardinal Printing Inc .... G 330 773-7300
  Akron *(G-99)*
Castle Printing Inc .... G 740 439-2208
  Cambridge *(G-1926)*
Cbp Co Inc .... F 513 860-9053
  Cincinnati *(G-2710)*
Century Graphics Inc .... F 614 895-7698
  Westerville *(G-15651)*
Charger Press Inc .... G 513 542-3113
  Miamitown *(G-10707)*
Cincinnati Print Solutions LLC .... G 513 943-9500
  Milford *(G-10900)*
City Printing Co Inc .... E 330 747-5691
  Youngstown *(G-16337)*
Clancey Printing Inc .... G 740 275-4070
  Steubenville *(G-13665)*
Cleveland Letter Service Inc .... F 216 781-8300
  Chagrin Falls *(G-2371)*
Color Bar Printing Centers Inc .... G 216 595-3939
  Cleveland *(G-3883)*
Color Process Inc .... E 440 268-7100
  Strongsville *(G-13823)*
Coloramic Process Inc .... F 440 275-1199
  Austinburg *(G-743)*
Commercial Prtg Greenville Inc .... G 937 548-3835
  Greenville *(G-8043)*
Consolidated Graphics Group Inc .... C 216 881-9191
  Cleveland *(G-3896)*
Consolidated Graphics Inc .... C 740 654-2112
  Lancaster *(G-9003)*

Copley Ohio Newspapers Inc .... C 330 364-5577
  New Philadelphia *(G-11493)*
Copy King Inc .... E 216 861-3377
  Cleveland *(G-3905)*
COS Blueprint Inc .... E 330 376-0022
  Akron *(G-115)*
Cox Printing Company .... G 937 382-2312
  Wilmington *(G-16046)*
Cpmm Services Group Inc .... E 614 447-0165
  Columbus *(G-5304)*
Custom Graphics Inc .... C 330 963-7770
  Macedonia *(G-9543)*
Cwh Graphics LLC .... G 866 241-8515
  Bedford Heights *(G-1169)*
D & J Printing Inc .... B 330 678-5868
  Kent *(G-8806)*
Daubenmires Printing Co LLC .... G 513 425-7223
  Middletown *(G-10817)*
David A and Mary A Mathis .... G 330 837-8611
  Massillon *(G-10089)*
Deerfield Ventures Inc .... G 614 875-0688
  Grove City *(G-8087)*
Delphos Herald Inc .... D 419 695-0015
  Delphos *(G-6760)*
Direct Digital Graphics Inc .... G 330 405-3770
  Twinsburg *(G-14651)*
Directconnectgroup Ltd .... F 216 281-2866
  Cleveland *(G-3960)*
Distributor Graphics Inc .... G 440 260-0024
  Cleveland *(G-3963)*
Docmann Printing & Assoc Inc .... G 440 975-1775
  Solon *(G-13338)*
Document Concepts Inc .... E 330 575-5685
  North Canton *(G-11723)*
Doll Inc .... G 419 586-7880
  Celina *(G-2329)*
Dr JS Print Shop Ltd .... G 513 571-6553
  Monroe *(G-11105)*
Dsk Imaging LLC .... G 513 554-1797
  Blue Ash *(G-1386)*
Duke Graphics Inc .... E 440 946-0606
  Willoughby *(G-15911)*
Duncan Press Corporation .... F 330 477-4529
  North Canton *(G-11724)*
E Bee Printing Inc .... G 614 224-0416
  Columbus *(G-5338)*
E&O Fbn Inc .... G 513 241-5150
  Cincinnati *(G-2851)*
Eg Enterprise Services Inc .... F 216 431-3300
  Cleveland *(G-4001)*
Empire Printing Inc .... G 513 242-3900
  Fairfield *(G-7356)*
Engler Printing Co .... G 419 332-2181
  Fremont *(G-7777)*
Enquirer Printing Co Inc .... F 513 241-1956
  Cincinnati *(G-2874)*
Eurostampa North America Inc .... C 513 821-2275
  Cincinnati *(G-2885)*
Eveready Printing Inc .... E 216 587-2389
  Cleveland *(G-4038)*
Excelsior Printing Co .... G 740 927-2934
  Pataskala *(G-12297)*
Express Grphics Prtg Dsign Inc .... G 513 728-3344
  Cincinnati *(G-2892)*
Fgs-Wi LLC .... E 630 375-8597
  Newark *(G-11576)*
Fine Line Graphics Corp .... C 614 486-0276
  Columbus *(G-5375)*
Finn Graphics Inc .... E 513 941-6161
  Cincinnati *(G-2905)*
Folks Creative Printers Inc .... F 740 383-6926
  Marion *(G-9852)*

Foote Printing Company Inc .... F 216 431-1757
  Cleveland *(G-4079)*
Franklin Printing Company .... F 740 452-6375
  Zanesville *(G-16533)*
Freeport Press Inc .... C 330 308-3300
  New Philadelphia *(G-11503)*
Fx Digital Media Inc .... G 216 241-4040
  Cleveland *(G-4094)*
Galley Printing Inc .... E 330 220-5577
  Brunswick *(G-1763)*
Gaspar Services LLC .... G 330 467-8292
  Macedonia *(G-9554)*
Gergel-Kellem Company Inc .... D 216 398-2000
  Olmsted Falls *(G-12080)*
Gli Holdings Inc .... D 440 892-7760
  Stow *(G-13700)*
Gli Holdings Inc .... D 216 651-1500
  Stow *(G-13701)*
Globus Printing & Packg Co Inc .... D 419 628-2381
  Minster *(G-11053)*
Gordons Graphics Inc .... G 330 863-2322
  Malvern *(G-9613)*
Graphic Info Systems Inc .... F 513 948-1300
  Mason *(G-9999)*
Graphic Print Solutions Inc .... G 513 948-3344
  Cincinnati *(G-2969)*
Graphic Village LLC .... C 513 241-1865
  Blue Ash *(G-1399)*
Graphix Network .... G 740 941-3771
  Waverly *(G-15282)*
Graphtech Communications Inc .... F 216 676-1020
  Brunswick *(G-1766)*
Great Lakes Printing Inc .... F 440 993-8781
  Ashtabula *(G-636)*
Greenwood Prtg & Graphics Inc .... G 419 727-3275
  Toledo *(G-14303)*
Greg Blume .... G 740 574-2308
  Wheelersburg *(G-15809)*
Haman Enterprises Inc .... F 614 888-7574
  Columbus *(G-5417)*
Harper Engraving & Printing Co .... D 614 276-0700
  Columbus *(G-5420)*
Hartco Printing Company .... G 614 761-1292
  Dublin *(G-6890)*
Hartmann Inc .... G 513 276-7318
  Blue Ash *(G-1403)*
Hecks Direct Mail Prtg Svc Inc .... F 419 697-3505
  Toledo *(G-14315)*
Heeter Printing Company Inc .... E 440 946-0606
  Eastlake *(G-7034)*
Herald Inc .... E 419 492-2133
  New Washington *(G-11547)*
Heskamp Printing Co Inc .... G 513 871-6770
  Cincinnati *(G-2997)*
Hi-Point Graphics LLC .... G 937 407-6524
  Bellefontaine *(G-1211)*
Hilltop Printing .... G 419 782-9898
  Defiance *(G-6681)*
Holmes Printing Solutions LLC .... F 330 234-9699
  Fredericksburg *(G-7724)*
Holmes W & Sons Printing .... F 937 325-1509
  Springfield *(G-13577)*
Hoster Graphics Company Inc .... F 614 299-9770
  Columbus *(G-5446)*
HOT Graphic Services Inc .... E 419 242-7000
  Northwood *(G-11920)*
Howland Printing Inc .... G 330 637-8255
  Cortland *(G-5964)*
HP Acquisition II LLC .... F 216 241-4040
  Chagrin Falls *(G-2379)*
HP Industries Inc .... E 419 478-0695
  Toledo *(G-14322)*

Employee Codes: A=Over 500 employees, B=251-500
C=101-250, D=51-100, E=20-50, F=10-19, G=1-9

2024 Harris Ohio Industrial Directory

1453

PRINTING: Offset

Company	Location	Code	Phone
Hubbard Company	Defiance (G-6682)	E	419 784-4455
Hubbard Publishing Co	Bellefontaine (G-1212)	E	937 592-3060
Hyde Brothers Prtg & Mktg LLC	Marietta (G-9801)	G	740 373-2054
Image Concepts Inc	Cleveland (G-4215)	F	216 524-9000
Image Print Inc	Westerville (G-15709)	G	614 776-3985
Innomark Communications LLC	Miamisburg (G-10648)	C	937 454-5555
Inskeep Brothers Inc	Columbus (G-5462)	F	614 898-6620
Irwin Engraving & Printing Co	Cleveland (G-4238)	G	216 391-7300
J & J Bechke Inc	Strongsville (G-13847)	G	440 238-1441
J & L Management Corporation	Mentor (G-10478)	G	440 205-1199
Jack Walker Printing Co	Mentor (G-10481)	F	440 352-4222
Jakprints Inc	Cleveland (G-4249)	C	877 246-3132
Jakprints Inc	Willowick (G-16032)	G	216 246-3132
Jbnovember LLC	Cincinnati (G-3038)	G	513 272-7000
Jos Berning Printing Co	Cincinnati (G-3051)	F	513 721-0781
Jt Premier Printing Corp	Cleveland (G-4266)	F	216 831-8785
Kahny Printing Inc	Cincinnati (G-3057)	E	513 251-2911
Kay Toledo Tag Inc	Toledo (G-14346)	D	419 729-5479
Keener Printing Inc	Cleveland (G-4280)	F	216 531-7595
Kehl-Kolor Inc	Ashland (G-585)	G	419 281-3107
Kenwel Printers Inc	Columbus (G-5508)	E	614 261-1011
Kevin K Tidd	Sylvania (G-14003)	G	419 885-5603
Key Maneuvers Inc	Chardon (G-2454)	G	440 285-0774
Keystone Press Inc	Toledo (G-14347)	G	419 243-7326
Kimpton Printing & Spc Co	Macedonia (G-9561)	F	330 467-1640
Klingstedt Brothers Company	Canton (G-2140)	G	330 456-8319
KMS 2000 Inc	Canton (G-2141)	G	330 454-9444
Kramer Graphics Inc	Moraine (G-11188)	E	937 296-9600
Krehbiel Holdings Inc	Cincinnati (G-3089)	D	
Krieg Rev 2 Inc	Cincinnati (G-3090)	E	513 542-1522
L & T Collins Inc	Newark (G-11586)	G	740 345-4494
Lahlouh Inc	Monroe (G-11115)	G	650 692-6600
Lake Shore Graphic Inds Inc	Sandusky (G-13073)	F	419 626-8631
Larmax Inc	Blue Ash (G-1419)	G	513 984-0783
Laurenee Ltd	Cincinnati (G-3097)	G	513 662-2225
Lba Custom Printing	Toledo (G-14359)	F	419 535-3151
LBL Lithographers Inc	Painesville (G-12247)	G	440 350-0106
Lee Corporation	Cincinnati (G-3099)	G	513 771-3602
Legalcraft Inc	Canton (G-2145)	F	330 494-1261
Lesher Printers Inc	Fremont (G-7794)	F	419 332-8253
Letterman Printing Inc	Oxford (G-12210)	G	513 523-1111
Lilienthal/Southeastern Inc	Cambridge (G-1940)	G	740 439-1640
Litho-Print Ltd	Dayton (G-6413)	F	937 222-4351
Little Printing Company	Piqua (G-12532)	F	937 773-4595
LSc Service Corp	Cleveland (G-4337)	G	440 331-1359
Lyle Printing & Publishing Co	Salem (G-13013)	E	330 337-3419
Mansfield Journal Co	New Philadelphia (G-11513)	C	330 364-8641
Marbee Inc	Findlay (G-7535)	G	419 422-9441
Marco Printed Products Co	Dayton (G-6430)	F	937 433-7030
Mariotti Printing Co LLC	Lorain (G-9424)	G	440 245-4120
Mark Advertising Agency Inc	Sandusky (G-13079)	F	419 626-9000
Mathews Printing Company	Columbus (G-5546)	F	614 444-1010
Mbas Printing Inc	Blue Ash (G-1432)	G	513 489-3000
McNerney & Associates LLC	West Chester (G-15570)	E	513 241-9951
Mercer Color Corporation	Coldwater (G-4998)	G	419 678-8273
Messenger Publishing Company	Athens (G-688)	C	740 592-6612
Metzgers	Toledo (G-14383)	D	419 861-8611
Meyers Printing & Design Inc	Dayton (G-6437)	F	937 461-6000
Miami Valley Publishing LLC	Fairborn (G-7319)	C	937 879-5678
Middaugh Enterprises Inc	Sugarcreek (G-13930)	G	330 852-2471
Middleton Printing Co Inc	Gahanna (G-7845)	G	614 294-7277
Milford Printers	Milford (G-10914)	E	513 831-6630
Millennium Printing LLC	Blue Ash (G-1440)	G	513 489-3000
Mmp Toledo	Toledo (G-14388)	F	419 472-0505
Mound Printing Company Inc	Miamisburg (G-10664)	E	937 866-2872
Muir Graphics Inc	Sylvania (G-14007)	G	419 882-7993
Multi-Craft Litho Inc	Blue Ash (G-1442)	E	859 581-2754
Murr Corporation	Wooster (G-16154)	F	330 264-2223
Network Printing & Graphics	Columbus (G-5593)	F	614 230-2084
Newmast Mktg & Communications	Columbus (G-5597)	G	614 837-1200
News Gazette Printing Company	Lima (G-9274)	F	419 227-2527
North Coast Litho Inc	Cleveland (G-4470)	E	216 881-1952
North Toledo Graphics LLC	Toledo (G-14395)	D	419 476-8808
Nta Graphics Inc	Toledo (G-14407)	E	419 476-8808
O Connor Office Pdts & Prtg	London (G-9393)	G	740 852-2209
Odyssey Press Inc	Huron (G-8642)	F	614 410-0356
Ohio Esc Print Shop	Ontario (G-12092)	G	419 774-2512
Old Trail Printing Company	Columbus (G-5636)	C	614 443-4852
Oliver Printing & Packg Co LLC	Twinsburg (G-14703)	D	330 425-7890
Orange Blossom Press Inc	Willoughby (G-15966)	G	216 781-8655
Oregon Vlg Print Shoppe Inc	Dayton (G-6494)	F	937 222-9418
Orwell Printing	Chardon (G-2462)	G	440 285-2233
Page One Group	Mount Vernon (G-11286)	G	740 397-4240
Painesville Publishing Inc	Austinburg (G-728)	G	440 354-4142
Painted Hill Inv Group Inc	Troy (G-14600)	F	937 339-1756
Paragraphics Inc	Canton (G-2191)	G	330 493-1074
Park Press Direct	Sandusky (G-13086)	G	419 626-4426
Payday 124 Inc	Columbus (G-5662)	D	614 509-1080
PDQ Printing Service	Westlake (G-15772)	F	216 241-5443
Peerless Printing Company	Cincinnati (G-3245)	F	513 721-4657
Pen-Ann Corporation	Marietta (G-9816)	G	740 373-2054
Penguin Enterprises Inc	Westlake (G-15773)	E	440 899-5112
Perfection Printing	Fairfield (G-7394)	F	513 874-2173
Perrons Printing Company	Columbia Station (G-5016)	F	440 236-8870
Persistence of Vision Inc	Chagrin Falls (G-2415)	G	440 591-5443
Phil Vedda & Sons Inc	Cleveland (G-4547)	G	216 671-2222
Phoenix Grphics Communications	Munroe Falls (G-11304)	G	330 697-4171
Pinnacle Press Inc	Canton (G-2197)	F	330 453-7060
PIP Printing	Cincinnati (G-3257)	G	513 245-0590
PM Graphics Inc	Streetsboro (G-13785)	E	330 650-0861
Porath Business Services Inc	Cleveland (G-4564)	F	216 626-0060
Post Printing Co	Minster (G-11058)	D	859 254-7714
Preferred Printing	Sidney (G-13273)	F	937 492-6961
Preisser Inc	Columbus (G-5682)	E	614 345-0199
Premier Printing Corporation	Cleveland (G-4582)	F	216 478-9720
Prime Printing Inc	Dayton (G-6522)	E	937 438-3707
Print Centers of Ohio Inc	Mansfield (G-9711)	F	419 526-4139
Print Direct For Less 2 Inc	Columbia Station (G-5018)	F	440 236-8870

PRODUCT SECTION — PRINTING: Screen, Broadwoven Fabrics, Cotton

Print Factory PII .... G 330 549-9640
North Lima (G-11810)
Print Marketing Inc .... G 330 625-1500
Homerville (G-8553)
Print Shop of Canton Inc .... F 330 497-3212
Canton (G-2202)
Print-Digital Incorporated .... G 330 686-5945
Stow (G-13718)
Printers Devil Inc .... E 330 650-1218
Hudson (G-8608)
Printex Incorporated .... F 740 773-0088
Chillicothe (G-2529)
Printing Arts Press Inc .... G 740 397-6106
Mount Vernon (G-11289)
Printing Connection Inc .... G 216 898-4878
Brookpark (G-1723)
Printing Dimensions Inc .... F 937 256-0044
Dayton (G-6523)
Printing Express .... G 937 276-7794
Moraine (G-11203)
Printing Express Inc .... G 740 533-9217
Ironton (G-8701)
Printing Service Company .... D 937 425-6100
Miamisburg (G-10672)
Printing System Inc .... F 330 375-9128
Twinsburg (G-14718)
Printpoint Inc .... G 937 223-9041
Dayton (G-6524)
Program Managers Inc .... G 937 431-1982
Beavercreek (G-1078)
Progressive Printers Inc .... D 937 222-1267
Dayton (G-6533)
Progrssive Communications Corp .... D 740 397-5333
Mount Vernon (G-11290)
Quebecor World Johnson Hardin .... E 614 326-0299
Cincinnati (G-3314)
Quez Media Marketing Inc .... F 216 910-0202
Independence (G-8683)
Quick As A Wink Printing Co .... G 419 224-9786
Lima (G-9281)
R & J Bardon Inc .... G 614 457-5500
Columbus (G-5705)
R & J Printing Enterprises Inc .... F 330 343-1242
Stow (G-13719)
Randd Assoc Prtg & Promotions .... G 937 294-1874
Dayton (G-6541)
Rba Inc .... G 330 336-6700
Wadsworth (G-15062)
Repro Acquisition Company LLC .... F 216 738-3800
Cleveland (G-4626)
Resilient Holdings Inc .... F 614 847-5600
Columbus (G-5718)
Rhoads Print Center Inc .... G 330 678-2042
Tallmadge (G-14045)
Richardson Printing Corp .... D 800 848-9752
Marietta (G-9820)
Robert Becker Impressions Inc .... F 419 385-5303
Toledo (G-14456)
Robin Enterprises Company .... C 614 891-0250
Westerville (G-15719)
RPI Color Service Inc .... D 513 471-4040
Cincinnati (G-3353)
S Beckman Print Grphic Sltons .... E 614 864-2232
Columbus (G-5736)
Schuerholz Inc .... G 937 294-5218
Dayton (G-6561)
Scorecards Unlimited LLC .... G 614 885-0796
Columbus (G-5755)
Scratch Off Works LLC .... G 440 333-4302
Rocky River (G-12843)
Seemless Printing LLC .... G 513 871-2366
Cincinnati (G-3375)

Selby Service/Roxy Press Inc .... G 513 241-3445
Cincinnati (G-3378)
Sfc Graphics Cleveland Ltd .... E 419 255-1283
Toledo (G-14469)
Shamrock Printing LLC .... G 740 349-2244
Newark (G-11605)
Sharp Enterprises Inc .... F 937 295-2965
Fort Loramie (G-7609)
Shelby Printing Partners LLC .... F 419 342-3171
Shelby (G-13201)
Shreve Printing LLC .... G 330 567-2341
Shreve (G-13215)
Skladany Enterprises Inc .... G 614 823-6882
Westerville (G-15679)
Slimans Printery Inc .... F 330 454-9141
Canton (G-2226)
Snow Printing Co Inc .... F 419 229-7669
Lima (G-9290)
Source3media Inc .... E 330 467-9003
Macedonia (G-9575)
Southern Ohio Printing .... G 513 241-5150
Cincinnati (G-3404)
SP Mount Printing Company .... E 216 881-3316
Cleveland (G-4718)
SPAOS Inc .... G 937 890-0783
Dayton (G-6580)
Specialty Lithographing Co .... F 513 621-0222
Cincinnati (G-3405)
Springdot Inc .... D 513 542-4000
Cincinnati (G-3411)
Sprint Print Inc .... G 740 622-4429
Coshocton (G-5997)
Standard Printing Co of Canton .... D 330 453-8247
Canton (G-2230)
Star Printing Company Inc .... E 330 376-0514
Akron (G-336)
Starr Services Inc .... F 513 241-7708
Cincinnati (G-3417)
Stein-Palmer Printing Co .... G 740 633-3894
Saint Clairsville (G-12925)
Suburban Press Incorporated .... E 216 961-0766
Cleveland (G-4744)
Superior Impressions Inc .... G 419 244-8676
Toledo (G-14477)
T D Dynamics Inc .... F 216 881-0800
Cleveland (G-4765)
Taylor Quick Print .... G 740 439-2208
Cambridge (G-1957)
The Gazette Printing Co Inc .... G 440 593-6030
Conneaut (G-5934)
Theb Inc .... G 216 391-4800
Cleveland (G-4790)
Tj Metzgers Inc .... D 419 861-8611
Toledo (G-14487)
Tkm Print Solutions Inc .... F 330 237-4029
Uniontown (G-14795)
Tomahawk Printing Inc .... F 419 335-3161
Wauseon (G-15274)
Tope Printing Inc .... G 330 674-4993
Millersburg (G-11000)
Tradewinds Prin Twear .... G 740 214-5005
Roseville (G-12860)
Traxium LLC .... E 330 572-8200
Stow (G-13732)
Traxler Printing .... G 614 593-1270
Columbus (G-5833)
Tri-State Publishing Company .... E 740 283-3686
Steubenville (G-13679)
Truax Printing Inc .... E 419 994-4166
Loudonville (G-9452)
True Dinero Records & Tech LLC .... G 513 428-4610
Cincinnati (G-3470)

Tucker Printers Inc .... D 585 359-3030
West Chester (G-15520)
Ultimate Printing Co Inc .... G 330 847-2941
Warren (G-15213)
USA Quickprint Inc .... F 330 455-5119
Canton (G-2259)
V & C Enterprises Co .... G 614 221-1412
Columbus (G-5853)
Vision Press Inc .... G 440 357-6362
Painesville (G-12275)
Visual Art Graphic Services .... G 330 274-2775
Mantua (G-9745)
Vpp Industries Inc .... F 937 526-3775
Versailles (G-14991)
Warren Printing & Off Pdts Inc .... F 419 523-3635
Ottawa (G-12196)
Watkins Printing Company .... E 614 297-8270
Columbus (G-5867)
Wernet Inc .... G 330 452-2200
Canton (G-2266)
West Bend Printing & Pubg Inc .... G 419 258-2000
Antwerp (G-494)
West-Camp Press Inc .... D 614 882-2378
Westerville (G-15725)
Western Ohio Graphics .... F 937 335-8769
Troy (G-14616)
White Tiger Inc .... F 740 852-4873
London (G-9397)
William J Bergen & Co .... G 440 248-6132
Solon (G-13448)
Willoughby Printing Co Inc .... G 440 946-0800
Willoughby (G-16017)
Wis 1985 Inc .... F 423 581-4916
Dayton (G-6657)
Wooster Printing & Litho Inc .... E
Wooster (G-16185)
Yespress Graphics LLC .... G 614 899-1403
Westerville (G-15726)
Youngstown ARC Engraving Co .... G 330 793-2471
Youngstown (G-16476)
Youngstown Letter Shop Inc .... G 330 793-4935
Youngstown (G-16484)
Zip Publishing .... G 614 485-0721
Columbus (G-5893)
Zippitycom Print LLC .... F 216 438-0001
Cleveland (G-4935)

PRINTING: Photo-Offset

Deshea Printing Company .... G 330 336-7601
Wadsworth (G-15026)
Gerald L Herrmann Company Inc .... F 513 661-1818
Cincinnati (G-2949)

PRINTING: Photolithographic

Friends Service Co Inc .... D 419 427-1704
Findlay (G-7512)

PRINTING: Rotogravure

Western Roto Engravers Inc .... E 330 336-7636
Wadsworth (G-15072)

PRINTING: Screen, Broadwoven Fabrics, Cotton

Atlantis Sportswear Inc .... E 937 773-0680
Piqua (G-12506)
Image Group Inc .... E 419 866-3300
Holland (G-8514)
Phantasm Dsgns Sprtsn More Ltd ...... G 419 538-6737
Ottawa (G-12188)
Precision Imprint .... G 740 592-5916
Athens (G-692)

PRINTING: Screen, Fabric

West-Camp Press Inc .... D 216 426-2660
  Cleveland *(G-4905)*

PRINTING: Screen, Fabric

American Imprssions Sportswear .... G 614 848-6677
  Columbus *(G-5125)*
Bdp Services Inc .... G 740 828-9685
  Nashport *(G-11335)*
Brandon Screen Printing .... F 419 229-9837
  Lima *(G-9224)*
Cal Sales Embroidery .... G 440 236-3820
  Columbia Station *(G-5007)*
Charizma Corp .... G 216 621-2220
  Cleveland *(G-3807)*
Charles Wisvari .... G 740 671-9960
  Bellaire *(G-1184)*
Fineline Imprints Inc .... F 740 453-1083
  Zanesville *(G-16530)*
Greenfield Research Inc .... C 937 981-7763
  Greenfield *(G-8032)*
Kiwi Promotional AP & Prtg Co .... E 330 487-5115
  Twinsburg *(G-14681)*
Michigan Silkscreen Inc .... G 419 885-1163
  Sylvania *(G-14004)*
Mr Emblem Inc .... G 419 697-1888
  Oregon *(G-12108)*
Ohio State Institute Fin Inc .... G 614 861-8511
  Reynoldsburg *(G-12770)*
Painted Hill Inv Group Inc .... F 937 339-1756
  Troy *(G-14600)*
Peska Inc .... F 440 998-4664
  Ashtabula *(G-654)*
Quality Rubber Stamp Inc .... G 614 235-2700
  Lancaster *(G-9034)*
R & A Sports Inc .... E 216 289-2254
  Euclid *(G-7297)*
Roach Studios LLC .... F 614 725-1405
  Columbus *(G-5727)*
Sroufe Healthcare Products LLC .... E 260 894-4171
  Wadsworth *(G-15067)*
Stakes Manufacturing LLC .... D 216 245-4752
  Willowick *(G-16035)*
Tee Creations .... G 937 878-2822
  Fairborn *(G-7325)*
Tim L Humbert .... G 330 497-4944
  Canton *(G-2245)*
Triage Ortho Group .... G 937 653-6431
  Urbana *(G-14848)*
Vandava Inc .... G 614 277-8003
  Grove City *(G-8128)*
Vector International Corp .... G 440 942-2002
  Mentor *(G-10591)*
Zide Sport Shop of Ohio Inc .... F 740 373-8199
  Marietta *(G-9846)*

PRINTING: Screen, Manmade Fiber & Silk, Broadwoven Fabric

717 Inc .... G 440 925-0402
  Lakewood *(G-8965)*
B Richardson Inc .... G 330 724-2122
  Akron *(G-72)*
Flashions Sportswear Ltd .... G 937 323-5885
  Springfield *(G-13565)*
Kaylo Enterprises LLC .... G 330 535-1860
  Akron *(G-202)*
Phantasm Dsgns Sprtsn More Ltd .... G 419 538-6737
  Ottawa *(G-12188)*
Sportsco Imprinting .... G 513 641-5111
  Cincinnati *(G-3409)*

PRINTING: Thermography

A C Hadley - Printing Inc .... G 937 426-0952
  Beavercreek *(G-1037)*

PROFESSIONAL EQPT & SPLYS, WHOLESALE: Analytical Instruments

Consoldted Anlytcal Systems In .... F 513 542-1200
  Cincinnati *(G-2787)*
Gilson Company Inc .... E 740 548-7298
  Lewis Center *(G-9161)*
Mettler-Toledo Intl Fin Inc .... F 614 438-4511
  Columbus *(G-5065)*
Mettler-Toledo LLC .... A 614 438-4511
  Columbus *(G-5067)*

PROFESSIONAL EQPT & SPLYS, WHOLESALE: Engineers', NEC

S&V Industries Inc .... E 330 666-1986
  Medina *(G-10373)*
US Tsubaki Power Transm LLC .... C 419 626-4560
  Sandusky *(G-13102)*

PROFESSIONAL EQPT & SPLYS, WHOLESALE: Optical Goods

Diversified Ophthalmics Inc .... E 803 783-3454
  Cincinnati *(G-2832)*
Essilor Laboratories Amer Inc .... E 614 274-0840
  Columbus *(G-5361)*

PROFESSIONAL INSTRUMENT REPAIR SVCS

Certon Technologies Inc .... F 440 786-7185
  Bedford *(G-1111)*
Cleveland Electric Labs Co .... E 800 447-2207
  Twinsburg *(G-14643)*
Mettler-Toledo Intl Fin Inc .... F 614 438-4511
  Columbus *(G-5065)*
Mettler-Toledo LLC .... A 614 438-4511
  Columbus *(G-5067)*
UPA Technology Inc .... F 513 755-1380
  West Chester *(G-15522)*

PROFILE SHAPES: Unsupported Plastics

Advanced Composites Inc .... C 937 575-9800
  Sidney *(G-13218)*
Alkon Corporation .... E 614 799-6650
  Dublin *(G-6858)*
Bobbart Industries Inc .... E 419 350-5477
  Sylvania *(G-13991)*
Cosmo Plastics Company .... C 440 498-7500
  Cleveland *(G-3907)*
Dayton Technologies .... F 513 539-5474
  Monroe *(G-11100)*
Deceuninck North America LLC .... E 513 539-4444
  Monroe *(G-11101)*
Duracote Corporation .... E 330 296-9600
  Ravenna *(G-12712)*
Global Manufacturing Solutions .... F 937 236-8315
  Dayton *(G-6355)*
HP Manufacturing Company Inc .... D 216 361-6500
  Cleveland *(G-4204)*
Inventive Extrusions Corp .... F 330 874-3000
  Bolivar *(G-1528)*
Machining Technologies Inc .... E 419 862-3110
  Elmore *(G-7101)*
Meridian Industries Inc .... D 330 673-1011
  Kent *(G-8834)*
Roach Wood Products & Plas Inc .... G 740 532-4855
  Ironton *(G-8703)*
Wurms Woodworking Company .... E 419 492-2184
  New Washington *(G-11552)*

PROTECTION EQPT: Lightning

Amidac Wind Corporation .... G 213 973-4000
  Elyria *(G-7110)*
Innovest Energy Group LLC .... G 440 644-1027
  Chesterland *(G-2483)*

PROTECTIVE FOOTWEAR: Rubber Or Plastic

Advantage Products Corporation .... G 513 489-2283
  Blue Ash *(G-1319)*
Calzurocom .... G 800 257-9472
  Plain City *(G-1269)*

PUBLIC RELATIONS & PUBLICITY SVCS

Marketing Essentials LLC .... E 419 629-0080
  New Bremen *(G-11404)*

PUBLISHERS: Music Book & Sheet Music

Road Apple Music .... G 513 217-4444
  Middletown *(G-12856)*

PUBLISHERS: Music, Sheet

American Gild of English Hndbe .... G 937 438-0085
  Cincinnati *(G-268)*
Lorenz Corporation .... D 937 228-6118
  Dayton *(G-6416)*

PUBLISHERS: Sheet Music

Willis Music Company .... F 513 671-3288
  Cincinnati *(G-3520)*

PUBLISHERS: Telephone & Other Directory

ITM Marketing Inc .... C 740 295-3575
  Coshocton *(G-5591)*
Propress Inc .... F 216 631-8200
  Cleveland *(G-4553)*

PUBLISHING & BROADCASTING: Internet Only

Ahalogy .... E 314 974-5599
  Cincinnati *(G-268)*
Cerkl Incorporated .... D 513 813-8425
  Blue Ash *(G-1378)*
Chatterbox Sports LLC .... F 513 545-4754
  Hamilton *(G-8190)*
Clark Optimization LLC .... E 330 417-2164
  Canton *(G-2076)*
Deemsys Inc .... D 614 322-9928
  Gahanna *(G-7833)*
Dotcentral LLC .... F 330 809-0112
  Massillon *(G-10050)*
Evans Creative Group LLC .... G 614 657-9439
  Columbus *(G-5360)*
Intelacomm Inc .... G 888 610-9250
  Newbury *(G-11620)*
IPA Ltd .... F 614 523-3974
  Columbus *(G-5470)*
Legatum Project Inc .... G 216 533-8843
  Shaker Heights *(G-13155)*
Marketing Essentials LLC .... E 419 629-0080
  New Bremen *(G-11404)*
Organized Lightning LLC .... G 407 965-2730
  Blue Ash *(G-1447)*
Quadriga Americas LLC .... G 614 890-6090
  Westerville *(G-15674)*

PUBLISHING & PRINTING: Art Copy

Publishing Group Ltd .... F 614 572-1240
  Columbus *(G-5697)*

PUBLISHING & PRINTING: Book Music

PRODUCT SECTION
PUBLISHING & PRINTING: Newspapers

Swagg Productions2015llc.................... F 614 601-7414
  Worthington *(G-16213)*

PUBLISHING & PRINTING: Books

Bearing Precious Seed Intl Inc................. G 513 575-1706
  Milford *(G-10894)*
Gardner Business Media Inc................. F 513 527-8800
  Cincinnati *(G-2929)*
Kendall/Hunt Publishing Co.................... C 877 275-4725
  Cincinnati *(G-3073)*
Marysville Newspaper Inc........................ E 937 644-9111
  Marysville *(G-9926)*
McGraw-Hill Schl Edcatn Hldngs............. A 419 207-7400
  Ashland *(G-591)*
World Harvest Church Inc....................... C 614 837-1990
  Canal Winchester *(G-1994)*

PUBLISHING & PRINTING: Directories, NEC

Haines Publishing Inc............................. E 330 494-9111
  Canton *(G-2120)*
Lsc Communications Inc......................... A 419 935-0111
  Willard *(G-15860)*

PUBLISHING & PRINTING: Directories, Telephone

Berry Company.. G 513 768-7800
  Cincinnati *(G-2667)*
User Friendly Phone Book LLC................ E 216 674-6500
  Independence *(G-8689)*

PUBLISHING & PRINTING: Guides

Beaver Productions................................. G 330 352-4603
  Akron *(G-81)*
Trogdon Publishing Inc........................... E 330 721-7678
  Medina *(G-10389)*

PUBLISHING & PRINTING: Magazines: publishing & printing

614 Media Group LLC.............................. E 614 488-4400
  Columbus *(G-5079)*
Angstrom Graphics Inc........................... C 216 271-5300
  Cleveland *(G-3668)*
Breakwall Publishing LLC........................ G 813 575-2570
  Medina *(G-10306)*
Carmel Publishing Inc............................. F 330 478-9200
  Canton *(G-2069)*
Cars and Parts Magazine........................ D 937 498-0803
  Sidney *(G-13232)*
Cincinnati Media LLC.............................. E 513 562-2755
  Cincinnati *(G-2754)*
Cruisin Times Holdings LLC.................... G 234 646-2095
  Ashtabula *(G-629)*
Cruisin Times Magazine.......................... G 440 331-4615
  Rocky River *(G-12837)*
Family Motor Coach Assn Inc................. E 513 474-3622
  Cincinnati *(G-2894)*
Highlights For Children Inc..................... C 614 486-0631
  Columbus *(G-5436)*
Insights Sccess Media Tech LLC............. E 614 602-1754
  Dublin *(G-6899)*
North Coast Minority Media LLC............. G 216 407-4327
  Cleveland *(G-4472)*
Peninsula Publishing LLC........................ G 330 524-3359
  Independence *(G-8679)*
Publishing Group Ltd............................... F 614 572-1240
  Columbus *(G-5697)*
Venue Lifestyle & Event Guide................ F 513 405-6822
  Cincinnati *(G-3493)*
Youngs Publishing Inc............................. G 937 259-6575
  Dayton *(G-6176)*

PUBLISHING & PRINTING: Newsletters, Business Svc

Omnipresence Cleaning LLC.................... F 937 250-4749
  Dayton *(G-6491)*
Quality Solutions Inc............................... E 440 933-9946
  Cleveland *(G-4608)*
Questline Inc... E 614 255-3166
  Dublin *(G-6930)*

PUBLISHING & PRINTING: Newspapers

A Gatehouse Media Company.................. F 330 580-8579
  Canton *(G-2024)*
Active Daily Living LLC.......................... G 513 607-6769
  Cincinnati *(G-2596)*
Adams Publishing Group LLC.................. E 740 592-6612
  Athens *(G-673)*
Aim Media Midwest Oper LLC................. G 740 354-6621
  Portsmouth *(G-12640)*
Alderwoods (oklahoma) Inc..................... G 903 597-6611
  Cincinnati *(G-2606)*
Alliance Publishing Co Inc....................... C 330 453-1304
  Alliance *(G-393)*
American Community Newspapers.......... G 614 888-4567
  Columbus *(G-5123)*
Amos Media Company............................ C 937 638-0967
  Sidney *(G-13221)*
Ashland Publishing Co............................ B 419 281-0581
  Ashland *(G-552)*
At Your Service....................................... G 513 498-9392
  Hamilton *(G-8181)*
Atrium At Anna Maria Inc....................... F 330 562-7777
  Aurora *(G-706)*
Block Communications Inc..................... F 419 724-6212
  Toledo *(G-14214)*
Boardman News....................................... G 330 758-6397
  Boardman *(G-1510)*
Brecksvll-Brdview Hts Gztte In................ G 440 526-7977
  Brecksville *(G-1610)*
Brekkie Shack Grandview LLC................ G 614 306-5618
  Columbus *(G-5208)*
Bryan Publishing Company..................... D 419 636-1111
  Bryan *(G-1811)*
Bryan West Main Stop............................ G 419 636-1616
  Bryan *(G-1812)*
Business Journal.................................... E 330 744-5023
  Youngstown *(G-16330)*
Chagrin Valley Publishing Co.................. E 440 247-5335
  Chagrin Falls *(G-2370)*
Chesterland News Inc............................. G 440 729-7667
  Chesterland *(G-2480)*
Chronicle Telegram................................. G 330 725-4166
  Medina *(G-10309)*
Cincinnati Enquirer................................. D 513 721-2700
  Cincinnati *(G-2748)*
Cincinnati Ftn Sq News Inc..................... F 513 421-4049
  Mason *(G-9975)*
Cincinnati Site Solutions LLC................. G 513 373-5001
  Cincinnati *(G-2760)*
Cleveland Activist.................................... G 888 817-3777
  Cleveland *(G-3830)*
Cleveland Jewish Publ Co....................... E 216 454-8300
  Cleveland *(G-3844)*
Cleveland Jewish Publ Co Fdn................ F 216 454-8300
  Beachwood *(G-977)*
Coffee News... G 614 679-2967
  Hilliard *(G-8407)*
Columbus Jewish News........................... G 216 342-5184
  Beachwood *(G-979)*
Columbus Messenger Company.............. E 614 272-5422
  Columbus *(G-5272)*

Columbus Podcast Company LLC........... G 614 405-8298
  Columbus *(G-5274)*
Columbus-Sports Publications................ F 614 486-2202
  Columbus *(G-5282)*
Communicator Needs.............................. G 614 781-1160
  Columbus *(G-5283)*
Cox Newspapers LLC.............................. F 937 866-3331
  Miamisburg *(G-10629)*
Daily Fantasy Circuit Inc........................ G 614 989-8689
  Columbus *(G-5314)*
Daily Growler Inc.................................... G 614 656-2337
  Upper Arlington *(G-14800)*
Daily Needs Assistance Inc.................... G 614 824-8340
  Plain City *(G-12572)*
Daily Reporter.. E 614 224-4835
  Columbus *(G-5315)*
Dayton City Paper Group Llc.................. F 937 222-8855
  Dayton *(G-6275)*
Delphos Herald Inc................................. G 419 399-4015
  Paulding *(G-12312)*
Delphos Herald Inc................................. D 419 695-0015
  Delphos *(G-6760)*
Dispatch Consumer Services.................. C 740 687-1893
  Lancaster *(G-9013)*
Dispatch Printing Company..................... A
  Columbus *(G-5329)*
Dow Jones & Company Inc.................... E 419 352-4696
  Bowling Green *(G-1563)*
Eastern Ohio Newspapers Inc................. G 740 633-1131
  Martins Ferry *(G-9898)*
Euclid Media Group LLC.......................... F 216 241-7550
  Cleveland *(G-4035)*
Fire & Iron... G 937 470-8536
  W Carrollton *(G-15013)*
Funny Times Inc..................................... G 216 371-8600
  Cleveland *(G-4092)*
Gannett Stllite Info Ntwrk LLC............... E 419 334-1012
  Fremont *(G-7785)*
Gannett Stllite Info Ntwrk LLC............... E 304 485-1891
  Marietta *(G-9794)*
Gate West Coast Ventures LLC.............. F 513 891-1000
  Blue Ash *(G-1397)*
Graphic Publications Inc........................ G 330 343-4377
  Dover *(G-6825)*
Greater Cleveland FCC............................ G 440 333-5984
  Cleveland *(G-4149)*
Greenworld Enterprises Inc..................... G 800 525-6999
  West Chester *(G-15559)*
Harrison News Herald Inc....................... G 740 942-2118
  Cadiz *(G-1903)*
Hearth and Home At Urbana................... G 937 653-5263
  Urbana *(G-14834)*
Heartland Education Cmnty Inc.............. G 330 684-3034
  Orrville *(G-12127)*
Hirt Publishing Co Inc............................ E 419 946-3010
  Mount Gilead *(G-11234)*
Holmes County Hub Inc.......................... G 330 674-1811
  Millersburg *(G-10965)*
Journal News... G 513 829-7900
  Fairfield *(G-7376)*
Journal Register Company...................... D 440 245-6901
  Lorain *(G-9416)*
Journal Register Company...................... C 440 951-0000
  Willoughby *(G-15935)*
Keith O King.. G 419 339-5028
  Lima *(G-9259)*
Lake Community News............................ G 440 946-2577
  Willoughby *(G-15942)*
Lakewood Observer Inc.......................... G 216 712-7070
  Lakewood *(G-8978)*
Mansfield Journal Co.............................. C 330 364-8641
  New Philadelphia *(G-11513)*

Employee Codes: A=Over 500 employees, B=251-500
C=101-250, D=51-100, E=20-50, F=10-19, G=1-9

PUBLISHING & PRINTING: Newspapers

Marion Star .... G 740 328-8542
  Newark (G-11589)
Marysville Newspaper Inc .... E 937 644-9111
  Marysville (G-9926)
Medina Hntngton RE Group II LL .... E 330 591-2777
  Medina (G-10348)
Messenger Publishing Company ..... C 740 592-6612
  Athens (G-688)
Morgan County Publishing Co .... G 740 962-3377
  Mcconnelsville (G-10284)
Napoleon Inc .... F 419 592-5055
  Napoleon (G-11326)
News Watchman & Paper .... F 740 947-2149
  Waverly (G-15288)
Newspaper Network Central OH ..... G 419 524-3545
  Mansfield (G-9705)
Ogden Newspapers Ohio Inc .... F 419 448-3200
  Tiffin (G-14097)
Ohio Irish American News .... G 216 647-1144
  Cleveland (G-4498)
Ohio Newspaper Services Inc .... G 614 486-6677
  Columbus (G-5623)
Ohio Newspapers Foundation .... G 614 486-6677
  Columbus (G-5624)
Ohio Rights Group .... G 614 300-0529
  Columbus (G-5626)
Pataskala Post .... F 740 964-6226
  Pataskala (G-12303)
Perry County Tribune .... F 740 342-4121
  New Lexington (G-11455)
Plain Dealer Publishing Co .... G 216 999-5000
  Cleveland (G-4557)
PMG Cincinnati Inc .... F 513 421-7275
  Columbus (G-5681)
Premier Prtg Centl Ohio Ltd .... E 937 642-0988
  Marysville (G-9932)
Primrose School of Marysville .... G 937 642-2125
  Marysville (G-9933)
Pulse Journal .... G 513 829-7900
  Liberty Township (G-9209)
Ringer LLC .... G 216 228-1442
  Lakewood (G-8982)
Rockbrook Business Svcs LLC .... E 234 817-8107
  Youngstown (G-16430)
Sesh Communications .... F 513 851-1693
  Cincinnati (G-3384)
Shelby Daily Globe Inc .... F 419 342-4276
  Shelby (G-13200)
Sojourners Truth Inc .... F 419 243-0007
  Toledo (G-14474)
Spectrum News Ohio .... G 614 384-2640
  Columbus (G-5785)
Spectrum Publications .... G 740 439-3531
  Cambridge (G-1954)
Stark Cnty Fdrtion Cnsrvtion C .... E 330 268-1652
  Canton (G-2231)
Streamline Media & Pubg LLC .... G 614 822-1817
  Reynoldsburg (G-12774)
Summit Street News Inc .... G 330 609-5600
  Warren (G-15207)
Syracuse China LLC .... C 419 325-2100
  Toledo (G-14480)
The Cleveland Jewish Publ Co .... E 216 454-8300
  Beachwood (G-1027)
The Gazette Printing Co Inc .... D 440 576-9125
  Jefferson (G-8760)
The Vindicator Printing Company ... B 330 747-1471
  Youngstown (G-16454)
Trading Post .... G 740 922-1199
  Uhrichsville (G-14771)
Upper Arlington Crew Inc .... F 614 485-0089
  Columbus (G-5848)

Village Reporter .... G 419 485-4851
  Montpelier (G-11144)
Vindicator .... E 330 841-1600
  Warren (G-15216)
World Journal .... G 216 458-0988
  Cleveland (G-4922)
Xenia Daily Gazette .... E 937 372-4444
  Xenia (G-16281)
Ylt Red Cleveland LLC .... G 216 664-0941
  Cleveland (G-4928)

PUBLISHING & PRINTING: Pamphlets

Communication Resources Inc ...... G 800 992-2144
  Canton (G-2079)
Equipping Ministries Intl Inc .... G 513 742-1100
  Cincinnati (G-2882)
J S C Publishing .... G 614 424-6911
  Columbus (G-5483)
Liturgical Publications Inc .... D 216 325-6825
  Cleveland (G-4332)

PUBLISHING & PRINTING: Textbooks

Cengage Learning Inc .... B 415 839-2300
  Mason (G-9972)
Cengage Lrng Holdings II Inc .... E 617 289-7700
  Mason (G-9973)

PUBLISHING & PRINTING: Trade Journals

Benjamin Media Inc .... E 330 467-7588
  Brecksville (G-1608)

PULLEYS: Metal

J L R Products Inc .... F 330 832-9557
  Massillon (G-10112)

PULLEYS: Power Transmission

J L R Products Inc .... F 330 832-9557
  Massillon (G-10112)

PULP MILLS

Billerud Americas Corporation .... D 901 369-4105
  West Chester (G-15379)
Caraustar Industries Inc .... D 740 862-4167
  Baltimore (G-843)
Caraustar Industries Inc .... F 216 961-5060
  Cleveland (G-3788)
Mondi Pakaging .... G 541 686-2665
  Lancaster (G-9025)
Polymer Tech & Svcs Inc .... F 740 929-5500
  Heath (G-8327)
Rumpke Transportation Co LLC .... B 513 242-4600
  Cincinnati (G-3356)
The Mead Corporation .... B 937 495-6323
  Dayton (G-6619)
Waste Parchment Inc .... F 330 674-6868
  Millersburg (G-11006)

PULP MILLS: Mechanical & Recycling Processing

Flegal Brothers Inc .... E 419 298-3539
  Edgerton (G-7075)
Riverview Productions Inc .... G 740 441-1150
  Gallipolis (G-7900)
World Wide Recyclers Inc .... G 614 554-3296
  Columbus (G-5881)

PUMPS & PARTS: Indl

A & F Machine Products Co .... E 440 826-0959
  Berea (G-1263)
Ayling and Reichert Co Consent .... E 419 898-2471
  Oak Harbor (G-12011)

Cima Inc .... G 513 382-8976
  Hamilton (G-8112)
Columbia Industrial Pdts Inc .... F 216 431-6633
  Cleveland (G-3384)
Crane Pumps & Systems Inc .... B 937 773-2442
  Piqua (G-12505)
E R Advanced Ceramics Inc .... E 330 426-9433
  East Palestine (G-7004)
Fischer Global Enterprises LLC ..... F 513 583-4900
  Loveland (G-9440)
Flowserve Corporation .... E 937 226-4000
  Dayton (G-6337)
Flowserve Corporation .... G 513 874-6990
  Loveland (G-9441)
Fluid Automation Inc .... E 248 912-1970
  North Canton (G-11728)
Gerow Equipment Company Inc ... G 216 383-8800
  Cleveland (G-4122)
Gorman-Rupp Company .... B 419 755-1011
  Mansfield (G-9661)
Gorman-Rupp Company .... C 419 755-1011
  Mansfield (G-9663)
Molten Mtal Eqp Innvations LLC ... E 440 632-9119
  Middlefield (G-10771)
Pckd Enterprises Inc .... F 440 632-9119
  Middlefield (G-10779)
Thieman Tailgates Inc .... D 419 586-7727
  Celina (G-2353)
Valco Cincinnati Inc .... C 513 874-6550
  West Chester (G-15603)
Warren Rupp Inc .... C 419 524-8388
  Mansfield (G-9730)

PUMPS & PUMPING EQPT REPAIR SVCS

Certified Labs & Service Inc .... G 419 289-7462
  Ashland (G-563)
Eaton Industrial Corporation .... C 216 692-5456
  Cleveland (G-3957)
Thirion Brothers Eqp Co LLC .... G 440 357-8004
  Painesville (G-12271)
Wm Plotz Machine and Forge Co .. E 216 861-0441
  Cleveland (G-4975)

PUMPS & PUMPING EQPT WHOLESALERS

Advanced Fuel Systems Inc .... G 614 252-8422
  Columbus (G-5102)
Ashland Water Group Inc .... G 877 326-3561
  Ashland (G-553)
Bergstrom Company Ltd Partnr .... E 440 232-2282
  Cleveland (G-3737)
Bowden Manufacturing Corp .... E 440 946-1770
  Willoughby (G-15231)
Chaos Entertainment .... G 937 520-5260
  Dayton (G-6251)
Dreison International Inc .... C 216 362-0755
  Cleveland (G-3972)
Eaton Aeroquip LLC .... A 419 891-7775
  Maumee (G-10201)
Fill-Rite Company .... E 419 755-1011
  Mansfield (G-9655)
Flow Control US Holding Corp ...... C 419 289-1144
  Ashland (G-572)
General Electric Company .... E 216 883-1000
  Cleveland (G-4115)
Giant Industries Inc .... E 419 531-4600
  Toledo (G-14300)
Gorman-Rupp Company .... G 419 755-1245
  Mansfield (G-9662)
Hydromatic Pumps Inc .... D 419 289-1144
  Ashland (G-580)
Idex Corporation .... G 419 526-7222
  Mansfield (G-9670)

Indelco Custom Products Inc................ E 216 797-7300
  Euclid *(G-7274)*
Interstate Pump Company Inc.................. G 330 222-1006
  Salem *(G-13005)*
Keen Pump Company Inc...................... E 419 207-9400
  Ashland *(G-584)*
Lubrisource Inc..................................... F 937 432-9292
  Middletown *(G-10836)*
M T Systems Inc................................... G 330 453-4646
  Canton *(G-2150)*
Maag Reduction Inc............................... F 704 716-9000
  Kent *(G-8831)*
Magnum Piering Inc............................... E 513 759-3448
  West Chester *(G-15568)*
Metaullics Systems LP............................ C 509 926-6212
  Solon *(G-13387)*
Pentair... E 440 248-0100
  Solon *(G-13404)*
Pentair Pump Group Inc.......................... F 419 281-9918
  Ashland *(G-598)*
Quikstir Inc.. E 419 732-2601
  Port Clinton *(G-12625)*
Rumpke Transportation Co LLC................ F 513 851-0122
  Cincinnati *(G-3355)*
Seepex Inc... C 937 864-7150
  Enon *(G-7252)*
Stahl Gear & Machine Co........................ E 216 431-2820
  Cleveland *(G-4725)*
Suburban Manufacturing Co..................... D 440 953-2024
  Eastlake *(G-7050)*
Systecon LLC....................................... D 513 777-7722
  West Chester *(G-15513)*
Tark Inc... E 937 434-6766
  Miamisburg *(G-10689)*
Teikoku USA Inc.................................... F 304 699-1156
  Marietta *(G-9835)*
TJ Clark International LLC....................... G 614 388-8869
  Delaware *(G-6755)*
Tolco Corporation.................................. D 419 241-1113
  Toledo *(G-14491)*
Trane Technologies Company LLC............ E 419 633-6800
  Bryan *(G-1842)*
Trane Technologies Company LLC............ E 419 636-4242
  Bryan *(G-1843)*
Trane Technologies Company LLC............ E 513 459-4580
  Cincinnati *(G-3459)*
Transdigm Inc....................................... F 216 291-6025
  Cleveland *(G-4815)*
Transdigm Inc....................................... E 440 352-6182
  Painesville *(G-12272)*
Uhrden Inc... E 330 456-0031
  Canton *(G-2249)*
Vertiflo Pump Company.......................... F 513 530-0888
  Cincinnati *(G-3496)*
Vickers International Inc.......................... E 419 867-2200
  Maumee *(G-10244)*
Waterpro.. G 330 372-3565
  Warren *(G-15222)*

PUMPS: Domestic, Water Or Sump

Certified Labs & Service Inc.................... G 419 289-7462
  Ashland *(G-563)*
City of Newark...................................... E 740 349-6765
  Newark *(G-11570)*
Crane Pumps & Systems Inc.................... C 937 778-8947
  Piqua *(G-12510)*
Lakecraft Inc.. G 419 734-2828
  Port Clinton *(G-12621)*
Wayne/Scott Fetzer Company................... C 800 237-0987
  Harrison *(G-8296)*

PUMPS: Fluid Power

Alkid Corporation.................................. E 216 896-3000
  Cleveland *(G-3629)*
Custom Cltch Jint Hydrlics Inc.................. F 216 431-1630
  Cleveland *(G-3923)*
Danfoss Power Solutions II LLC................ G 419 238-1190
  Van Wert *(G-14913)*
Oase North America Inc......................... G 800 365-3880
  Aurora *(G-728)*
Parker-Hannifin Corporation.................... E 440 266-2300
  Mentor *(G-10520)*
Parker-Hannifin Corporation.................... A 216 896-3000
  Cleveland *(G-4532)*
Suburban Manufacturing Co..................... D 440 953-2024
  Eastlake *(G-7050)*
Vertiflo Pump Company.......................... F 513 530-0888
  Cincinnati *(G-3496)*

PUMPS: Gasoline, Measuring Or Dispensing

Field Stone Inc..................................... E 937 898-3236
  Tipp City *(G-14135)*

PUMPS: Hydraulic Power Transfer

Bosch Rexroth Corporation..................... C 330 263-3300
  Wooster *(G-16106)*
Eaton Corporation................................. B 440 523-5000
  Cleveland *(G-3994)*
Linde Hydraulics Corporation.................. E 330 533-6801
  Canfield *(G-2009)*
Parker-Hannifin Corporation.................... F 937 644-3915
  Marysville *(G-9930)*

PUMPS: Measuring & Dispensing

Bergstrom Company Ltd Partnr................ E 440 232-2282
  Cleveland *(G-3730)*
Cohesant Inc.. E 216 910-1700
  Beachwood *(G-978)*
Gojo Industries Inc................................ C 330 255-6000
  Akron *(G-170)*
Graco Ohio Inc..................................... D 330 494-1313
  North Canton *(G-11733)*
Seepex Inc... C 937 864-7150
  Enon *(G-7252)*
Tolco Corporation.................................. D 419 241-1113
  Toledo *(G-14491)*
Tranzonic Companies............................. D 216 535-4300
  Richmond Heights *(G-12811)*
Valco Cincinnati Inc............................... C 513 874-6550
  West Chester *(G-15603)*
WD Pumpco LLC................................... G 740 454-2576
  Zanesville *(G-16569)*

PUMPS: Oil Well & Field

GE Vernova International LLC.................. G 330 963-2066
  Twinsburg *(G-14665)*

PUMPS: Oil, Measuring Or Dispensing

Energy Manufacturing Ltd...................... G 419 355-9304
  Fremont *(G-7776)*
Lubrisource Inc..................................... F 937 432-9292
  Middletown *(G-10836)*

PUNCHES: Forming & Stamping

Cleveland Steel Tool Company................. E 216 681-7400
  Cleveland *(G-3856)*
Dayton Progress Corporation.................. A 937 859-5111
  Dayton *(G-6288)*
Miami Valley Punch & Mfg...................... F 937 237-0533
  Dayton *(G-6440)*
Stolle Machinery Company LLC................ C 937 497-5400
  Dayton *(G-6596)*

PURIFICATION & DUST COLLECTION EQPT

Ceco Group Global Holdings LLC............. G 513 458-2600
  Cincinnati *(G-2714)*
Dreison International Inc........................ C 216 362-0755
  Cleveland *(G-3972)*
Effox-Flextor-Mader Inc.......................... F 513 874-8915
  West Chester *(G-15549)*
Seneca Environmental Products Inc.......... E 419 447-1282
  Tiffin *(G-14104)*

RACEWAYS

Dees Family Raceway LLC....................... G 740 772-5431
  Chillicothe *(G-2501)*
Indian Lake Raceway LLC....................... G 937 837-7533
  Clayton *(G-3566)*
Raceway Beverage LLC.......................... G 513 932-2214
  Lebanon *(G-9107)*
Raceway Petroleum Inc.......................... F 440 989-2660
  Lorain *(G-9432)*
State of Ohio Dayton Raceway................. E 937 237-7802
  Dayton *(G-6592)*
Tri-State Hobbies Raceway LLC................ G 513 889-3954
  Hamilton *(G-8252)*

RADAR SYSTEMS & EQPT

Decibel Research Inc............................. E 256 705-3341
  Beavercreek *(G-1045)*
Dedrone Defense Inc............................. F 614 948-2002
  Westerville *(G-15700)*
Dragoon Technologies Inc...................... G 937 439-9223
  Dayton *(G-6303)*
Escort Inc... C 513 870-8500
  West Chester *(G-15427)*
Oculii Corp... E 937 912-9261
  Beavercreek Township *(G-1088)*
Valentine Research Inc.......................... E 513 984-8900
  Blue Ash *(G-1487)*

RADIO & TELEVISION COMMUNICATIONS EQUIPMENT

Pole/Zero LLC....................................... C 513 870-9060
  West Chester *(G-15481)*

RADIO BROADCASTING & COMMUNICATIONS EQPT

Circle Prime Manufacturing..................... E 330 923-0019
  Cuyahoga Falls *(G-6074)*
Gatesair Inc.. D 513 459-3400
  Mason *(G-9995)*
Imagine Communications Corp................. G 513 459-3400
  Mason *(G-10006)*

RADIO BROADCASTING STATIONS

Franklin Communications Inc................... E 614 459-9769
  Columbus *(G-5386)*
Iheartcommunications Inc....................... G 419 223-2060
  Lima *(G-9254)*
Isaac Foster Mack Co............................. C 419 625-5500
  Sandusky *(G-13067)*

RADIO COMMUNICATIONS: Airborne Eqpt

Quasonix Inc.. E 513 942-1287
  West Chester *(G-15491)*

RADIO COMMUNICATIONS: Carrier Eqpt

L-3 Cmmncations Nova Engrg Inc............. C 877 282-1168
  Mason *(G-10018)*

RADIO, TV & CONSUMER ELEC STORES: High Fidelity Stereo Eqpt

RADIO, TV & CONSUMER ELEC STORES: High Fidelity Stereo Eqpt

ABC Appliance Inc .... E 419 693-4414
Oregon (G-12099)

Tune Town Car Audio .... G 419 627-1100
Sandusky (G-13098)

RADIO, TV/CONSUMER ELEC STORES: Antennas, Satellite Dish

Dish One Up Satellite Inc .... D 216 482-3875
Cleveland (G-3961)

Dss Installations Ltd .... F 513 761-7000
Cincinnati (G-2842)

RAILINGS: Prefabricated, Metal

AT&f Advanced Metals LLC .... F 330 684-1122
Orrville (G-12117)

AT&f Advanced Metals LLC .... F 330 684-1122
Cleveland (G-3695)

Beacon Metal Fabricators Inc .... F 216 391-7444
Cleveland (G-3727)

Glas Ornamental Metals Inc .... G 330 753-0215
Barberton (G-869)

Hayes Bros Ornamental Ir Works .... F 419 531-1491
Toledo (G-14312)

RAILINGS: Wood

L & L Ornamental Iron Co .... E 513 353-1930
Cleves (G-4958)

RAILROAD CAR REPAIR SVCS

Andersons Inc .... G 419 536-0460
Toledo (G-14194)

Andersons Inc .... C 419 893-5050
Maumee (G-10165)

Jk-Co LLC .... E 419 422-5240
Findlay (G-7526)

RAILROAD EQPT

A Stucki Company .... G 412 424-0560
North Canton (G-11713)

Aliquippa & Ohio River RR Co .... G 740 622-8092
Youngstown (G-16306)

Alliance Castings Company LLC .... E 330 829-5600
Alliance (G-391)

Amsted Industries Incorporated .... D 614 836-2323
Groveport (G-8129)

Buck Equipment Inc .... E 614 539-3039
Grove City (G-8081)

Dayton-Phoenix Group Inc .... D 937 496-3900
Dayton (G-6292)

Great Lake Port Corporation .... G 330 718-3727
Poland (G-12611)

Gunderson Rail Services LLC .... D 330 792-6521
Youngstown (G-16376)

Johnson Bros Rubber Co Inc .... E 419 752-4814
Greenwich (G-8067)

K & G Machine Company .... F 216 732-7115
Cleveland (G-4268)

L B Foster Company .... F 330 652-1461
Mineral Ridge (G-11022)

Midwest Rlwy Prsrvtion Soc Inc .... G 216 781-3629
Cleveland (G-4412)

Nolan Company .... G 740 269-1512
Bowerston (G-1545)

Nolan Company .... G 330 453-7922
Canton (G-2173)

Ohio Valley Trackwork Inc .... F 740 446-0181
Bidwell (G-1325)

Progress Rail Services Corp .... B 216 641-4000
Cleveland (G-4591)

Progress Rail Services Corp .... E 614 850-1730
Columbus (G-5695)

R H Little Co .... G 330 477-3455
Canton (G-2208)

Shems Inc .... G 614 279-2342
Columbus (G-5762)

Transco Railway Products Inc .... E 330 872-0934
Newton Falls (G-11659)

Youngstown Belt Railroad Co .... G 740 622-8092
Youngstown (G-16477)

RAILROAD EQPT & SPLYS WHOLESALERS

Amsted Industries Incorporated .... D 614 836-2323
Groveport (G-8129)

Buck Equipment Inc .... E 614 539-3039
Grove City (G-8081)

Ysd Industries Inc .... E 330 792-6521
Youngstown (G-16491)

RAILROAD EQPT: Brakes, Air & Vacuum

Westinghouse A Brake Tech Corp .... G 419 526-5323
Mansfield (G-9733)

RAILROAD MAINTENANCE & REPAIR SVCS

Simpson & Sons Inc .... F 513 367-0152
Harrison (G-8292)

Tmt Inc .... F 419 592-1041
Perrysburg (G-12437)

RAILROAD RELATED EQPT

Youngstown Bending Rolling .... G 330 799-2227
Youngstown (G-16478)

RAMPS: Prefabricated Metal

Homecare Mattress Inc .... F 937 746-2556
Franklin (G-7680)

Jh Industries Inc .... E 330 963-4105
Twinsburg (G-14677)

Overhead Door Corporation .... F 419 294-3874
Upper Sandusky (G-14820)

Wyse Industrial Carts Inc .... F 419 923-7353
Wauseon (G-15277)

RAZORS, RAZOR BLADES

Edgewell Personal Care Company .... F 740 374-1905
Marietta (G-9791)

Gillette Company LLC .... D 513 983-1100
Cincinnati (G-2950)

Procter & Gamble Company .... D 513 983-1100
Cincinnati (G-3281)

Procter & Gamble Company .... F 513 266-4375
Cincinnati (G-3282)

Procter & Gamble Company .... G 513 871-7557
Cincinnati (G-3283)

Procter & Gamble Company .... F 513 482-6789
Cincinnati (G-3286)

Procter & Gamble Company .... C 513 983-3000
Cincinnati (G-3288)

Procter & Gamble Company .... E 513 627-7115
Cincinnati (G-3289)

Procter & Gamble Company .... F 513 945-0340
Cincinnati (G-3292)

Procter & Gamble Company .... D 513 622-1000
Mason (G-10043)

Procter & Gamble Company .... C 513 634-9600
West Chester (G-15486)

Procter & Gamble Company .... C 513 634-9100
West Chester (G-15487)

Procter & Gamble Company .... A 513 983-1100
Cincinnati (G-3280)

Procter & Gamble Mexico Inc .... G 513 983-1100
Cincinnati (G-3297)

RAZORS: Electric

Procter & Gamble Company .... A 513 983-1100
Cincinnati (G-3280)

REAL ESTATE AGENCIES & BROKERS

Lenz Inc .... E 937 277-9364
Dayton (G-6405)

Stonyridge Inc .... F 937 845-9482
New Carlisle (G-11426)

Wedco LLC .... G 513 309-0781
Mount Orab (G-1247)

REAL ESTATE AGENTS & MANAGERS

Hitti Enterprises Inc .... F 440 243-4100
Cleveland (G-4191)

Kenyetta Bagby Enterprise LLC .... F 614 584-3426
Reynoldsburg (G-12768)

Rona Enterprises Inc .... G 740 927-9971
Pataskala (G-12706)

REAL ESTATE INVESTMENT TRUSTS

Infinitaire Industries LLC .... G 216 600-2051
Euclid (G-7275)

RECEIVERS: Radio Communications

CDI Industries Inc .... E 440 243-1100
Cleveland (G-3802)

RECORDS & TAPES: Prerecorded

Cabconnect Inc .... F 773 282-3565
Dayton (G-6245)

Cuttercroix LLC .... F 330 289-6185
Cleveland (G-3957)

Fluid Handling Dynamics Ltd .... F 419 633-0560
Bryan (G-1818)

RECOVERY SVC: Iron Ore, From Open Hearth Slag

Stein LLC .... D 216 883-7444
Cleveland (G-4731)

Stein LLC .... F 440 526-9301
Independence (G-3685)

Waterford Tank Fabrication Ltd .... D 740 984-4100
Beverly (G-1323)

RECREATIONAL VEHICLE PARTS & ACCESS STORES

Mitchs Welding & Hitches .... G 419 893-3117
Maumee (G-1022)

Steves Vans ACC Unlimited LLC .... G 740 374-3154
Marietta (G-9832)

REFINERS & SMELTERS: Copper

Sam Dong Ohio Inc .... D 740 363-1985
Delaware (G-6748)

REFINERS & SMELTERS: Silicon, Primary, Over 99% Pure

Ferroglobe USA Mtlurgical Inc .... C 740 984-2361
Waterford (G-1523)

Silicon Processors Inc .... G 740 373-2252
Marietta (G-9823)

REFINING: Petroleum

Aecom Energy & Cnstr Inc .... G 419 698-6277
Oregon (G-12101)

Blaster Corporation .... F 216 901-5800
Medina (G-10302)

PRODUCT SECTION

BP Products North America Inc............ E 419 537-9540
  Toledo (G-14217)
Crowley Blue Wtr Partners LLC............ F 419 422-2121
  Findlay (G-7499)
Cyberutility LLC................................... G ... 216 291-8723
  Cleveland (G-3934)
Eidp Inc.. F 440 934-6444
  Avon (G-772)
Gfl Environmental Svcs USA Inc........... E 281 486-4182
  Norwalk (G-11969)
Isp Lima LLC....................................... E 419 998-8700
  Lima (G-9257)
Knight Material Tech LLC.................... D 330 488-1651
  East Canton (G-6979)
Lima Refining Company....................... E 419 226-2300
  Lima (G-9263)
Marathon Oil Company........................ E 419 422-2121
  Findlay (G-7531)
Marathon Petroleum Corporation......... A 419 422-2121
  Findlay (G-7533)
Marathon Ptro Cnada Trdg Sup U........ F 419 422-2121
  Findlay (G-7534)
Mkfour Inc.. G 620 629-1120
  Granville (G-8021)
Mplx GP LLC.. F 419 422-2121
  Findlay (G-7540)
National Staffing Services LLC............ G 785 731-2540
  Toledo (G-14395)
Ohio Refining Company LLC............... A 614 210-2300
  Dublin (G-6917)
Petroleum Holdings LLC..................... G 443 676-0150
  Salem (G-13021)
PSC 272 TRC Pbf................................ E 419 466-7129
  Oregon (G-12109)
Seneca Petroleum Co Inc.................... F 419 691-3581
  Toledo (G-14468)
Shacks Stop N Go LLC....................... G 614 296-9292
  Pickerington (G-12470)
Troy Valley Petroleum......................... G 937 604-0012
  Dayton (G-6636)

REFRACTORIES: Brick

Minteq International Inc...................... E 330 343-8821
  Dover (G-6836)
Plibrico Company LLC........................ F 740 682-7755
  Oak Hill (G-12023)

REFRACTORIES: Cement

Castruction Company Inc.................... F 330 332-9622
  Salem (G-12982)

REFRACTORIES: Clay

Afc Company....................................... F 330 533-5581
  Canfield (G-1997)
Bowerston Shale Company.................. E 740 269-2921
  Bowerston (G-1544)
Ferro Corp... G 800 245-8225
  Crooksville (G-6046)
Glen-Gery Corporation........................ D 419 845-3321
  Caledonia (G-1915)
Glen-Gery Corporation........................ E 419 468-5002
  Iberia (G-8648)
I Cerco Inc... C 740 982-2050
  Crooksville (G-6047)
Industrial Ceramic Products Inc.......... D 937 642-3897
  Marysville (G-9921)
Lakeway Mfg Inc................................. E 419 433-1010
  Huron (G-8637)
Magneco/Metrel Inc............................ D 330 426-9468
  Negley (G-11354)
Minteq International Inc...................... E 330 343-8821
  Dover (G-6836)

Nock and Son Company...................... F 740 682-7741
  Oak Hill (G-12022)
Resco Products Inc............................. G 330 488-1226
  East Canton (G-6981)
Selas Heat Technology Co LLC........... E 800 523-6500
  Streetsboro (G-13792)
Specialty Ceramics Inc........................ D 330 482-0800
  Columbiana (G-5051)
Stebbins Engineering & Mfg Co........... F 740 922-3012
  Uhrichsville (G-14770)
Summitville Tiles Inc........................... E 330 868-6463
  Minerva (G-11040)
United Refractories Inc........................ E 330 372-3716
  Warren (G-15215)
Whitacre Greer Company..................... E 330 823-1610
  Alliance (G-436)

REFRACTORIES: Foundry, Clay

Ethima Inc... D 419 626-4912
  Sandusky (G-13057)

REFRACTORIES: Graphite, Carbon Or Ceramic Bond

E I Ceramics LLC................................ D 513 772-7001
  Cincinnati (G-2849)
Refractory Specialties Inc.................... E 330 938-2101
  Sebring (G-13125)

REFRACTORIES: Nonclay

A & M Refractories Inc........................ E 740 456-8020
  New Boston (G-11396)
Allied Mineral Products LLC................ B 614 876-0244
  Columbus (G-5114)
Ethima Inc... D 419 626-4912
  Sandusky (G-13057)
Ets Schaefer LLC................................. F 330 468-6600
  Macedonia (G-9549)
Ets Schaefer LLC................................. E 330 468-6600
  Beachwood (G-987)
I Cerco Inc... C 740 982-2050
  Crooksville (G-6047)
Impact Armor Technologies LLC......... F 216 706-2024
  Cleveland (G-4218)
Industrial Ceramic Products Inc.......... D 937 642-3897
  Marysville (G-9921)
Johns Manville Corporation................. D 419 878-8111
  Waterville (G-15246)
Magneco/Metrel Inc............................ D 330 426-9468
  Negley (G-11354)
Martin Marietta Materials Inc.............. G 513 701-1140
  West Chester (G-15461)
Momentive Prfmce Mtls Qrtz Inc.......... D 440 878-5700
  Strongsville (G-13855)
Ohio Vly Stmpng-Assemblies Inc......... E 419 522-0983
  Mansfield (G-9708)
Ormet Primary Aluminum Corp........... A 740 483-1381
  Hannibal (G-8262)
Pmbp Legacy Co Inc........................... E 330 253-8148
  Akron (G-278)
Pyromatics Corp.................................. F 440 352-3500
  Mentor (G-10538)
Resco Products Inc............................. G 740 682-7794
  Oak Hill (G-12024)
Saint-Gobain Ceramics Plas Inc.......... C 330 673-5860
  Stow (G-13721)
US Refractory Products LLC............... E 440 386-4580
  North Ridgeville (G-11863)
Vacuform Inc....................................... E 330 938-9674
  Sebring (G-13129)
Wahl Refractory Solutions LLC............ D 419 334-2658
  Fremont (G-7819)

Zircoa Inc... C 440 248-0500
  Cleveland (G-4936)

REFRACTORIES: Tile & Brick, Exc Plastic

Seven Lakeway Refractories LLC......... F 419 433-3030
  Huron (G-8645)

REFRIGERATION & HEATING EQUIPMENT

A A S Amels Sheet Meta L Inc............. F 330 793-9326
  Youngstown (G-16297)
Bard Manufacturing Company Inc....... D 419 636-1194
  Bryan (G-1809)
Beckett Air Incorporated..................... D 440 327-9999
  North Ridgeville (G-11829)
Bessamaire Sales Inc.......................... E 440 439-1200
  Twinsburg (G-14635)
Bodor Vents Inc................................... G 513 348-3853
  Cincinnati (G-2674)
Briskheat Corporation......................... C 614 294-3376
  Columbus (G-5218)
Bry Air Inc... G 614 839-0250
  Columbus (G-5060)
C Nelson Mfg Co.................................. E 419 898-3305
  Oak Harbor (G-12012)
Cryogenic Equipment & Svcs Inc......... F 513 761-4200
  Hamilton (G-8196)
Csafe LLC.. G 513 360-7189
  Monroe (G-11099)
Daikin Applied Americas Inc................ G 614 351-9862
  Westerville (G-15697)
Dyoung Enterprise Inc......................... C 440 918-0505
  Willoughby (G-15913)
Ellis & Watts Global Inds Inc............... E 513 752-9000
  Batavia (G-922)
Emerson Network Power...................... F 614 841-8054
  Ironton (G-8697)
Famous Industries Inc......................... F 740 685-2592
  Byesville (G-1896)
Fire From Ice Ventures LLC................. E 419 944-6705
  Solon (G-13350)
Jnp Group LLC.................................... F 800 735-9645
  Wooster (G-16137)
Lennox Industries Inc.......................... G 216 739-1909
  Cleveland (G-4320)
Mahle Behr Dayton LLC....................... A 937 369-2000
  Dayton (G-6425)
Mahle Behr USA Inc............................ F 937 369-2610
  Xenia (G-16268)
Maverick Innvtive Slutions LLC............ D 419 281-7944
  Ashland (G-590)
Professional Supply Inc....................... F 419 332-7373
  Fremont (G-7803)
Royal Metal Products LLC................... C 740 397-8842
  Mount Vernon (G-11293)
RSI Company....................................... F 216 360-9800
  Beachwood (G-1020)
Rtx Corporation................................... B 330 784-5477
  North Canton (G-11757)
T J F Inc.. F 419 878-4400
  Waterville (G-15253)
Taiho Corporation of America............. C 419 443-1645
  Tiffin (G-14107)
Tempest Inc... E 216 883-6500
  Cleveland (G-4776)
Ten Dogs Global Industries LLC........... G 513 752-9000
  Batavia (G-952)
Trane Inc.. E 440 946-7823
  Cleveland (G-4814)
Trane US Inc.. D 513 771-8884
  Cincinnati (G-3460)
Trane US Inc.. C 614 473-3131
  Columbus (G-5830)

REFRIGERATION & HEATING EQUIPMENT — PRODUCT SECTION

Trane US Inc .... G 614 473-8701
 Columbus *(G-5831)*

Trane US Inc .... G 614 497-6300
 Groveport *(G-8163)*

Vertiv Corporation .... G 614 491-9286
 Groveport *(G-8166)*

Vortec Corporation .... E
 Blue Ash *(G-1489)*

REFRIGERATION EQPT & SPLYS WHOLESALERS

Modern Ice Equipment & Sup Co .... E 513 367-2101
 Cincinnati *(G-3170)*

REFRIGERATION EQPT: Complete

Hobart LLC .... E 937 332-2797
 Piqua *(G-12525)*

Hobart LLC .... E 937 332-3000
 Troy *(G-14581)*

Hobart LLC .... D 937 332-3000
 Troy *(G-14582)*

Northeastern Rfrgn Corp .... E 440 942-7676
 Willoughby *(G-15960)*

Nrc Inc .... E 440 975-9449
 Willoughby *(G-15961)*

REFRIGERATION REPAIR SVCS

Northeastern Rfrgn Corp .... E 440 942-7676
 Willoughby *(G-15960)*

REFRIGERATION SVC & REPAIR

Bell Industrial Services LLC .... F 937 507-9193
 Sidney *(G-13227)*

REFUSE SYSTEMS

A & B Iron & Metal Co Inc .... G 937 228-1561
 Dayton *(G-6178)*

Capital City Oil Inc .... G 740 397-4483
 Mount Vernon *(G-11266)*

Metalico Akron Inc .... F 330 376-1400
 Akron *(G-246)*

Rumpke Transportation Co LLC .... F 513 851-0122
 Cincinnati *(G-3355)*

Unlimited Energy Services LLC .... F 304 517-7097
 Beverly *(G-1322)*

REGISTERS: Air, Metal

Hart & Cooley LLC .... E 937 832-7800
 Englewood *(G-7232)*

REGULATORS: Power

Vertiv Corporation .... G 614 888-0246
 Lockbourne *(G-9341)*

Vertiv Corporation .... A 614 888-0246
 Westerville *(G-15686)*

REHABILITATION SVCS

Clovernook Ctr For Blind Vslly .... C 513 522-3860
 Cincinnati *(G-2775)*

RELAYS & SWITCHES: Indl, Electric

Control Electric Co .... E 216 671-8010
 Columbia Station *(G-5011)*

Controllix Corporation .... F 440 232-8757
 Walton Hills *(G-15097)*

Rogers Industrial Products Inc .... E 330 535-3331
 Akron *(G-309)*

Tridelta Industries Inc .... G 440 255-1080
 Mentor *(G-10584)*

Utility Relay Co Ltd .... E 440 708-1000
 Chagrin Falls *(G-2431)*

RELAYS: Control Circuit, Ind

Industrial and Mar Eng Svc Co .... F 740 694-0791
 Fredericktown *(G-7749)*

RELIGIOUS SPLYS WHOLESALERS

Novak J F Manufacturing Co LLC .... G 216 741-5112
 Cleveland *(G-4484)*

REMOVERS & CLEANERS

Cahill Services Inc .... G 216 410-5595
 Lakewood *(G-8968)*

Grand Archt Etrnl Eye 314 LLC .... F 800 377-8147
 Cleveland *(G-4138)*

High Life .... G 330 978-4124
 Cortland *(G-5963)*

REMOVERS: Paint

ABRA Auto Body & Glass LP .... G 513 247-3400
 Cincinnati *(G-2592)*

ABRA Auto Body & Glass LP .... G 513 367-9200
 Harrison *(G-8263)*

ABRA Auto Body & Glass LP .... F 513 755-7709
 West Chester *(G-15359)*

Treved Exteriors .... G 513 771-3888
 Cincinnati *(G-3463)*

RENTAL SVCS: Costume

Akron Design & Costume LLC .... G 330 644-0425
 Coventry Township *(G-6004)*

Costume Specialists Inc .... E 614 464-2115
 Columbus *(G-5298)*

Deborah Meredith .... G 330 644-0425
 Coventry Township *(G-6008)*

RENTAL SVCS: Eqpt, Theatrical

Schenz Theatrical Supply Inc .... F 513 542-6100
 Cincinnati *(G-3369)*

RENTAL SVCS: Sign

ABC Signs Inc .... F 513 241-8884
 Cincinnati *(G-2590)*

RENTAL SVCS: Sound & Lighting Eqpt

Importers Direct LLC .... F 330 436-3260
 Akron *(G-189)*

RENTAL SVCS: Tent & Tarpaulin

Galion Canvas Products .... G 419 468-5333
 Galion *(G-7876)*

Rainbow Industries Inc .... G 937 323-6493
 Springfield *(G-13623)*

South Akron Awning Co .... F 330 848-7611
 Akron *(G-333)*

Tarpco Inc .... F 330 677-8277
 Kent *(G-8871)*

Wolf G T Awning & Tent Co .... F 937 548-4161
 Greenville *(G-8065)*

RENTAL SVCS: Vending Machine

Cuyahoga Vending Co Inc .... C 440 353-9595
 North Ridgeville *(G-11837)*

RENTAL SVCS: Work Zone Traffic Eqpt, Flags, Cones, Etc

A & A Safety Inc .... F 937 567-9781
 Beavercreek *(G-1068)*

A & A Safety Inc .... E 513 943-6100
 Amelia *(G-447)*

Paul Peterson Company .... F 614 486-4375
 Columbus *(G-5660)*

Paul Peterson Safety Div Inc .... E 614 486-4375
 Columbus *(G-5661)*

RENTAL: Portable Toilet

BJ Equipment Ltd .... E 614 497-1188
 Columbus *(G-5893)*

RENTAL: Video Tape & Disc

Ohio Hd Video .... F 614 656-1162
 New Albany *(G-1387)*

RESEARCH & DEVELOPMENT SVCS, COMMERCIAL: Engineering Lab

Iconic Labs LLC .... F 216 759-4040
 Westlake *(G-15158)*

Morris Technologies Inc .... E 513 733-1611
 Cincinnati *(G-3174)*

RESEARCH, DEVELOPMENT & TESTING SVCS, COMM: Agricultural

Lifestyle Nutraceuticals Ltd .... G 513 376-7218
 Cincinnati *(G-3175)*

RESEARCH, DEVELOPMENT & TESTING SVCS, COMMERCIAL: Energy

Tacoma Energy LLC .... E 614 410-9000
 Westerville *(G-1721)*

RESEARCH, DEVELOPMENT & TESTING SVCS, COMMERCIAL: Medical

Applied Medical Technology Inc .... E 440 717-4000
 Brecksville *(G-106)*

RESEARCH, DEVELOPMENT & TESTING SVCS, COMMERCIAL: Physical

Ftech R&D North America Inc .... E 937 339-2777
 Troy *(G-14572)*

Ion Vacuum Ivac Tech Corp .... F 216 662-5158
 Cleveland *(G-425)*

Leidos Inc .... D 937 656-8433
 Beavercreek *(G-1055)*

Velocys Inc .... D 614 733-3300
 Plain City *(G-12529)*

RESINS: Custom Compound Purchased

Accel Corporation .... D 440 934-7711
 Avon *(G-759)*

Advanced Composites Inc .... C 937 575-9800
 Sidney *(G-13218)*

Aurora Plastics LLC .... E 330 422-0700
 Streetsboro *(G-13757)*

Avient Corporation .... E 419 668-4844
 Norwalk *(G-11955)*

Avient Corporation .... D 440 930-1000
 Avon Lake *(G-797)*

Bay State Polymer Distribution Inc .... F 440 892-8500
 Westlake *(G-15737)*

Chemionics Corporation .... E 330 733-8834
 Tallmadge *(G-1404)*

Deltech Polymers LLC .... G 937 339-3150
 Troy *(G-14561)*

Deltech Polymers Co LLC .... G 225 358-3306
 Troy *(G-14562)*

Dyneon LLC .... B 859 334-4500
 Cincinnati *(G-2846)*

Flex Technologies Inc .... D 330 897-6311
 Baltic *(G-836)*

Flex Technologies Inc .... E 740 922-5992
 Midvale *(G-10878)*

Freeman Manufacturing & Sup Co......... E 440 934-1902
  Avon (G-775)
General Color Investments Inc............... D 330 868-4161
  Minerva (G-11031)
Hexpol Compounding LLC...................... C 440 834-4644
  Burton (G-1880)
Hexpol Compounding LLC...................... C 440 632-1962
  Middlefield (G-10756)
Hexpol Compounding LLC...................... E 440 834-4644
  Burton (G-1881)
Hexpol Holding Inc................................. F 440 834-4644
  Burton (G-1882)
Howard Industries Inc............................. F 614 444-9900
  Columbus (G-5447)
Jpi Coastal LLC..................................... G 330 424-1110
  Lisbon (G-9320)
Killian Latex Inc..................................... F 330 644-6746
  Akron (G-207)
Lancer Dispersions Inc............................ D
  Akron (G-216)
McCann Plastics LLC............................ D 330 499-1515
  Canton (G-2157)
Nanosperse LLC................................... G 937 296-5050
  Kettering (G-8908)
Polymera Inc... G 740 527-2069
  Hebron (G-8357)
Polyone Corporation............................. D 330 467-8108
  Macedonia (G-9568)
Radici Plastics Usa Inc.......................... E 330 336-7611
  Wadsworth (G-15059)
Sherwin-Williams Company..................... C 330 830-6000
  Massillon (G-10144)
Thermafab Alloy Inc............................. F 216 861-0540
  Olmsted Falls (G-12082)
Tymex Plastics Inc................................ E 216 429-8950
  Cleveland (G-4841)
Vibrantz Color Solutions Inc................... C 440 997-5137
  Ashtabula (G-664)

RESISTORS & RESISTOR UNITS

Asco Power Technologies LP................ C 216 573-7600
  Cleveland (G-3685)
Avtron Loadbank Inc.............................. C 216 573-7600
  Cleveland (G-3711)

RESPIRATORS

Morning Pride Mfg LLC.......................... A 937 264-1726
  Dayton (G-6458)
Morning Pride Mfg LLC.......................... A 937 264-2662
  Dayton (G-6457)

RESTAURANT EQPT: Carts

Cateringstone....................................... G 513 410-1064
  Cincinnati (G-2709)
Darpro Storage Solutions LLC................ E 567 233-3190
  Marengo (G-9766)
Modroto.. G 440 998-1202
  Ashtabula (G-649)

RESTAURANT EQPT: Sheet Metal

D B S Stinless Stl Fabricators................ G 513 856-9600
  Hamilton (G-8198)
Porcelain Steel Buildings Company........ D 614 228-5781
  Columbus (G-5683)

RESTAURANTS: Full Svc, American

Brewpub Restaurant Corporation........... E 614 228-2537
  Columbus (G-5211)
Great Lakes Brewing Co........................ C 216 771-4404
  Cleveland (G-4142)
Velvet Ice Cream Company.................... D 740 892-3921
  Utica (G-14859)

RETAIL BAKERY: Bread

Blf Enterprises Inc................................. F 937 642-6425
  Westerville (G-15694)
Brooks Pastries Inc................................ G 614 274-4880
  Plain City (G-12567)
Busken Bakery Inc................................ D 513 871-2114
  Cincinnati (G-2695)
Investors United Inc.............................. F 419 473-8942
  Toledo (G-14336)
Norcia Bakery....................................... F 330 454-1077
  Canton (G-2174)
Schwebel Baking Company.................... G 330 783-2860
  Hebron (G-8361)
Unger Kosher Bakery Inc...................... F 216 321-7176
  Cleveland Heights (G-4944)

RETAIL BAKERY: Cakes

I Dream of Cakes.................................. G 937 533-6024
  Eaton (G-7061)

RETAIL BAKERY: Cookies

Cookie Bouquets Inc.............................. G 614 888-2171
  Columbus (G-5293)
Great American Cookie Company........... F 419 474-9417
  Toledo (G-14302)

RETAIL BAKERY: Doughnuts

Crispie Creme Chillicothe Inc................. G 740 774-3770
  Chillicothe (G-2500)
Dandi Enterprises Inc............................ G 419 516-9070
  Solon (G-13336)
Evans Bakery Inc.................................. G 937 228-4151
  Dayton (G-6326)
Kennedys Bakery Inc............................. F 740 432-2301
  Cambridge (G-1938)
Krispy Kreme Doughnut Corp................ E 614 798-0812
  Columbus (G-5515)
Krispy Kreme Doughnut Corp................ D 614 876-0058
  Columbus (G-5516)
Mary Ann Donut Shoppe Inc.................. G 330 478-1655
  Canton (G-2152)
McHappys Donuts of Parkersburg......... D 740 593-8744
  Athens (G-687)
Schulers Bakery Inc.............................. E 937 323-4154
  Springfield (G-13630)
Wal-Bon of Ohio Inc............................. F 740 423-8178
  Belpre (G-1262)

RETAIL BAKERY: Pastries

Meeks Pastry Shop............................... G 419 782-4871
  Defiance (G-6692)

RETAIL BAKERY: Pretzels

Chestnut Land Company........................ G 330 652-1939
  Niles (G-11663)

RETAIL STORES: Alcoholic Beverage Making Eqpt & Splys

Cineen Inc.. G 440 236-3658
  Columbia Station (G-5009)
Pomacon Inc.. F 330 273-1576
  Brunswick (G-1781)

RETAIL STORES: Audio-Visual Eqpt & Splys

Educational Direction Inc....................... G 330 836-8439
  Fairlawn (G-7437)
Findaway World LLC............................. E 440 893-0808
  Solon (G-13349)

RETAIL STORES: Batteries, Non-Automotive

Battery Unlimited.................................. G 740 452-5030
  Zanesville (G-16506)
One Wish LLC....................................... F 800 505-6883
  Bedford (G-1147)

RETAIL STORES: Business Machines & Eqpt

A/C Laser Technologies Inc................... F 330 784-3355
  Akron (G-12)

RETAIL STORES: Cake Decorating Splys

Hartville Chocolates Inc......................... F 330 877-1999
  Hartville (G-8300)

RETAIL STORES: Christmas Lights & Decorations

Rhc Inc.. E 330 874-3750
  Bolivar (G-1536)

RETAIL STORES: Cleaning Eqpt & Splys

Akron Cotton Products Inc..................... G 330 434-7171
  Akron (G-32)

RETAIL STORES: Communication Eqpt

Communications Aid Inc......................... F 513 475-8453
  Cincinnati (G-2783)

RETAIL STORES: Concrete Prdts, Precast

Artistic Rock LLC.................................. G 216 291-8856
  Cleveland (G-3683)
Michaels Pre-Cast Con Pdts................. F 513 683-1292
  Loveland (G-9497)

RETAIL STORES: Cosmetics

Boxout LLC... C 833 462-7746
  Hudson (G-8587)
Primal Life Organics LLC....................... E 800 260-4946
  Copley (G-5954)
Studgionsgroup LLC.............................. E 216 804-1561
  Cleveland (G-4743)

RETAIL STORES: Educational Aids & Electronic Training Mat

Bendon Inc.. D 419 207-3600
  Ashland (G-556)
Health Nuts Media LLC......................... G 818 802-5222
  Cleveland (G-4175)

RETAIL STORES: Electronic Parts & Eqpt

Mixed Logic LLC.................................... G 440 826-1676
  Valley City (G-14879)
Precision Replacement LLC................... G 330 908-0410
  Macedonia (G-9569)

RETAIL STORES: Flags

Flag Lady Inc.. G 614 263-1776
  Columbus (G-5378)
Mel Wacker Signs Inc............................ G 330 832-1726
  Massillon (G-10126)

RETAIL STORES: Hair Care Prdts

Natural Beauty Products Inc.................. F 513 420-9400
  Middletown (G-10847)

RETAIL STORES: Ice

Haller Enterprises Inc............................ F 330 733-9693
  Akron (G-177)
Home City Ice Company......................... G 937 461-6028
  Dayton (G-6371)
Home City Ice Company......................... F 614 836-2877
  Groveport (G-8146)

RETAIL STORES: Medical Apparatus & Splys
Health Aid of Ohio Inc .... E 216 252-3900
  Cleveland (G-4174)
Relevium Labs Inc .... G 614 568-7000
  Oxford (G-12212)
Schaerer Medical Usa Inc .... F 513 561-2241
  Cincinnati (G-3368)

RETAIL STORES: Orthopedic & Prosthesis Applications
Akron Orthotic Solutions Inc .... G 330 253-3002
  Akron (G-37)
Leimkuehler Inc .... E 440 899-7842
  Cleveland (G-4319)
Presque Isle Orthtics Prsthtic .... G 216 371-0660
  Cleveland (G-4583)
Stable Step LLC .... C 800 491-1571
  Wadsworth (G-15068)

RETAIL STORES: Pet Splys
Heading4ward Investment Co .... D 937 293-9994
  Moraine (G-11185)

RETAIL STORES: Religious Goods
Incorprted Trstees of The Gspl .... D 216 749-2100
  Middleburg Heights (G-10721)
Strictly Stitchery Inc .... F 440 543-7128
  Cleveland (G-4739)

RETAIL STORES: Safety Splys & Eqpt
Paul Peterson Safety Div Inc .... E 614 486-4375
  Columbus (G-5661)
Pneumatic Specialties Inc .... G 440 729-4400
  Chesterland (G-2488)

RETAIL STORES: Swimming Pools, Above Ground
Litehouse Products LLC .... E 440 638-2350
  Strongsville (G-13851)

RETAIL STORES: Telephone & Communication Eqpt
Securcom Inc .... E 419 628-1049
  Minster (G-11060)

RETAIL STORES: Tents
Rainbow Industries Inc .... G 937 323-6493
  Springfield (G-13623)

RETAIL STORES: Water Purification Eqpt
Enting Water Conditioning Inc .... E 937 294-5100
  Moraine (G-11175)
US Water Company LLC .... G 740 453-0604
  Zanesville (G-16567)
William R Hague Inc .... D 614 836-2115
  Groveport (G-8168)

RETAIL STORES: Welding Splys
ARC Solutions Inc .... E 419 542-9272
  Hicksville (G-8371)
Linde Gas & Equipment Inc .... G 513 821-2192
  Cincinnati (G-3107)
Mt Vernon Machine & Tool Inc .... E 740 397-0311
  Mount Vernon (G-11282)
Welders Supply Inc .... E 216 267-4470
  Brookpark (G-1727)
Welders Supply Inc .... F 216 241-1696
  Cleveland (G-4903)

REUPHOLSTERY & FURNITURE REPAIR
Custom Craft Collection Inc .... F 440 998-3000
  Ashtabula (G-630)
Fortner Upholstering Inc .... F 614 475-8282
  Columbus (G-5384)
Robert Mayo Industries .... G 330 426-2587
  East Palestine (G-7008)

RIBBONS & BOWS
Sylvan Studios Inc .... G 419 882-3423
  Sylvania (G-14016)

RIVETS: Metal
North Coast Rivet Inc .... F 440 366-6829
  Elyria (G-7187)

ROAD CONSTRUCTION EQUIPMENT WHOLESALERS
Brewpro Inc .... G 513 577-7200
  Cincinnati (G-2682)
Winter Equipment Company In .... E 440 946-8377
  Willoughby (G-16019)

ROBOTS: Assembly Line
Advanced Design Industries Inc .... E 440 277-4141
  Sheffield Village (G-13180)
Air Technical Industries Inc .... E 440 951-5191
  Mentor (G-10409)
Ats Systems Oregon Inc .... C 541 738-0932
  Lewis Center (G-9152)
Computer Allied Technology Co .... G 614 457-2292
  Columbus (G-5284)
Hitachi Automation Ohio Inc .... F 937 753-1148
  Covington (G-6025)
Kc Robotics Inc .... E 513 860-4442
  West Chester (G-15452)
Lincoln Electric Automtn Inc .... E 614 471-5926
  Columbus (G-5527)
Programmable Control Svc Inc .... G 740 927-0744
  Pataskala (G-12304)
Ready Robotics Corporation .... E 833 732-3967
  Columbus (G-5714)
Recognition Robotics Inc .... F 440 590-0499
  Elyria (G-7200)
Rennco Automation Systems Inc .... E 419 861-2340
  Holland (G-8527)
Rimrock Corporation .... E 614 471-5926
  Columbus (G-5723)
Rimrock Holdings Corporation .... E 614 471-5926
  Columbus (G-5724)
Rixan Associates Inc .... E 937 438-3005
  Dayton (G-6550)
Sensory Robotics Inc .... E 513 545-9501
  Cincinnati (G-3382)
Sentient Studios Ltd .... E 330 204-8636
  Fairlawn (G-7449)
Versatile Automation Tech Corp .... G 330 220-2600
  Brunswick (G-1798)
Versatile Automation Tech Ltd .... G 440 589-6700
  Solon (G-13442)
Yaskawa America Inc .... C 937 440-2600
  Troy (G-14617)

ROBOTS: Indl Spraying, Painting, Etc
Ats Ohio Inc .... C 614 888-2344
  Lewis Center (G-9151)
Rubberset Company .... G 800 345-4939
  Cleveland (G-4661)
Wiwa LP .... G 419 757-0141
  Alger (G-385)

RODS: Rolled, Aluminum
Kaiser Aluminum Fab Pdts LLC .... C 740 522-1151
  Heath (G-8323)

RODS: Steel & Iron, Made In Steel Mills
American Posts LLC .... E 419 720-0652
  Toledo (G-1419)
Buschman Corporation .... F 216 431-6633
  Cleveland (G-374)
Charter Manufacturing Co Inc .... D 216 883-3800
  Cleveland (G-313)
L&H Threaded Rods Corp .... C 937 294-6666
  Moraine (G-1119)

ROLL FORMED SHAPES: Custom
American Roll Formed Pdts Corp .... C 440 352-0753
  Youngstown (G-6310)
Cdh Custom Roll Form LLC .... F 330 984-0555
  Warren (G-1515)
Ej Usa Inc .... F 330 782-3900
  Youngstown (G-6354)
Formasters Corporation .... F 440 639-9206
  Mentor (G-1045)
Hynes Holding Company .... F 330 799-3221
  Youngstown (G-6377)
Hynes Industries Inc .... E 800 321-9257
  Youngstown (G-6378)
Lion Industries LLC .... E 740 676-1100
  Bellaire (G-1188)
Welser Profile North Amer LLC .... F 330 225-2500
  Valley City (G-14300)

ROLLING MILL EQPT: Finishing
Bardons & Oliver Inc .... C 440 498-5800
  Solon (G-13316)
Fives Bronx Inc .... D 330 244-1960
  North Canton (G-1727)

ROLLING MILL MACHINERY
Addition Manufacturing Tech .... C 513 228-7000
  Lebanon (G-905)
ADS Machinery Corp .... D 330 399-3601
  Warren (G-15134)
Bendco Machine & Tool Inc .... F 419 628-3802
  Minster (G-11048)
Circle Machine Rolls Inc .... E 330 938-9010
  Sebring (G-13115)
Cornerstone Wauseon Inc .... C 419 337-0940
  Wauseon (G-1529)
E R Advanced Ceramics Inc .... E 330 426-9433
  East Palestine (G-7004)
Element Machinery LLC .... G 855 447-7648
  Toledo (G-14274)
Enprotech Industrial Tech LLC .... E 216 883-3220
  Cleveland (G-401)
Formtek Metal Forming Inc .... D 216 292-4460
  Cleveland (G-408)
George A Mitchell Company .... E 330 758-5777
  Youngstown (G-1368)
H P E Inc .... G 330 833-3161
  Massillon (G-1010)
Hydranamics Inc .... D 419 468-3530
  Galion (G-7880)
J Horst Manufacturing Co .... D 330 828-2216
  Dalton (G-6133)
Kottler Metal Products Co Inc .... E 440 946-7473
  Willoughby (G-1590)
Park Corporation .... B 216 267-4870
  Medina (G-10362)
Perfecto Industries Inc .... E 937 778-1900
  Piqua (G-12542)

PRODUCT SECTION — SAND & GRAVEL

Pines Manufacturing Inc.............................. E 440 835-5553
  Westlake (G-15775)
Rafter Equipment Corporation.................... E 440 572-3700
  Strongsville (G-13871)
Ridge Tool Company.................................... A 440 323-5581
  Elyria (G-7202)
Ridge Tool Manufacturing Co...................... E 440 323-5581
  Elyria (G-7203)
Steel Eqp Specialists Inc............................. D 330 823-8260
  Alliance (G-427)
Sticker Corporation....................................... F 440 946-2100
  Willoughby (G-15998)
Turner Machine Co.. F 330 332-5821
  Salem (G-13035)
United Rolls Inc... D 330 456-2761
  Canton (G-2255)
Warren Fabricating Corporation................. D 330 534-5017
  Hubbard (G-8572)
Xtek Inc.. B 513 733-7800
  Cincinnati (G-3534)

ROLLING MILL ROLLS: Cast Steel

United Engineering & Fndry Co.................. E 330 456-2761
  Canton (G-2253)

ROLLS: Rubber, Solid Or Covered

United Roller Co LLC.................................... F 440 564-9698
  Newbury (G-11638)

ROOFING MATERIALS: Asphalt

Modern Builders Supply Inc....................... E 419 526-0002
  Mansfield (G-9698)

ROOFING MEMBRANE: Rubber

Hyload Inc... G 330 336-6604
  Seville (G-13142)
Republic Powdered Metals Inc.................. D 330 225-3192
  Medina (G-10370)
RPM International Inc.................................. D 330 273-5090
  Medina (G-10372)
Soprema USA Inc... E 330 334-0066
  Wadsworth (G-15066)
Synthomer Inc... C 216 682-7000
  Beachwood (G-1025)
Topps Products Inc..................................... F 913 685-2500
  Cleveland (G-4806)

RUBBER BANDS

Keener Rubber Company............................. F 330 821-1880
  Alliance (G-407)

RUBBER PRDTS: Appliance, Mechanical

Canton OH Rubber Specity Prods............... G 330 454-3847
  Canton (G-2065)

RUBBER PRDTS: Automotive, Mechanical

Cardinal Rubber Company.......................... E 330 745-2191
  Barberton (G-864)
Koneta Inc... D 419 739-4200
  Wapakoneta (G-15122)
Mm Outsourcing LLC................................... F 937 661-4300
  Leesburg (G-9126)
Prospira America Corporation.................... D 419 294-6989
  Upper Sandusky (G-14821)

RUBBER PRDTS: Medical & Surgical Tubing, Extrudd & Lathe-Cut

Saint-Gobain Prfmce Plas Corp.................. F 330 798-6981
  Akron (G-324)

RUBBER PRDTS: Oil & Gas Field Machinery, Mechanical

United Feed Screws Ltd.............................. F 330 798-5532
  Akron (G-367)
V & M Star LP.. F 330 742-6300
  Youngstown (G-16465)

RUBBER PRDTS: Silicone

Blair Sales Inc... D 330 769-5586
  Seville (G-13138)
Brain Child Products LLC............................ F 419 698-4020
  Toledo (G-14220)
North Coast Seal Incorporated................... F 216 898-5000
  Brookpark (G-1722)
Novagard Solutions Inc.............................. C 216 881-8111
  Cleveland (G-4483)
S P E Inc... E 330 733-0101
  Mogadore (G-11082)
Shin-Etsu Silicones of America Inc........... C 330 630-9460
  Akron (G-328)
Shincor Silicones Inc................................... E 330 630-9460
  Akron (G-329)

RUBBER PRDTS: Sponge

Chalfant Sew Fabricators Inc..................... E 216 521-7922
  Cleveland (G-3805)
Merryweather Foam Inc............................... E 330 753-0353
  Barberton (G-882)
Miles Rubber & Packing Company............ E 330 425-3888
  Twinsburg (G-14697)
North Coast Seal Incorporated................... F 216 898-5000
  Brookpark (G-1722)

RUBBER STRUCTURES: Air-Supported

Truflex Rubber Products Co....................... C 740 967-9015
  Johnstown (G-8782)

SAFE DEPOSIT BOXES

Hamilton Safe Co... F 513 874-3733
  Milford (G-10909)
Hamilton Security Products Co................. E 513 874-3733
  Milford (G-10910)
Williamson Safe Inc..................................... F 937 393-9919
  Hillsboro (G-8470)

SAFES & VAULTS: Metal

Cincy Safe Company................................... F 513 900-9152
  Milford (G-10901)
Diebold Nixdorf Incorporated.................... C 740 928-1010
  Hebron (G-8339)
Diebold Nixdorf Incorporated.................... A 330 490-4000
  North Canton (G-11722)
Linsalata Cpitl Prtners Fund I.................... G 440 684-1400
  Cleveland (G-4330)
McIntosh Safe Corp..................................... F 937 222-7008
  Dayton (G-6432)

SAFETY EQPT & SPLYS WHOLESALERS

All-American Fire Eqp Inc.......................... F 800 972-6035
  Wshngtn Ct Hs (G-16225)
Netherland Rubber Company..................... F 513 733-0883
  Cincinnati (G-3187)
Wcm Holdings Inc.. C 513 705-2100
  Cincinnati (G-3509)
West Chester Holdings LLC........................ C 513 705-2100
  Cincinnati (G-3516)

SAFETY INSPECTION SVCS

Industrial Power Systems Inc.................... B 419 531-3121
  Rossford (G-12867)

SALT

CJ Salt World.. G 440 343-5661
  Wickliffe (G-15827)
Morton Salt Inc... G 513 941-1578
  Cincinnati (G-3176)
Morton Salt Inc... D 216 664-0728
  Cleveland (G-4423)

SAND & GRAVEL

Bonsal American Inc.................................... F 513 398-7300
  Cincinnati (G-2677)
Broadway Sand and Gravel LLC................. G 937 853-5555
  Dayton (G-6237)
C F Poeppelman Inc..................................... E 937 448-2191
  Bradford (G-1600)
Central Allied Enterprises Inc.................... E 330 477-6751
  Canton (G-2071)
Constrction Aggrgtes Corp Mich............... E 616 842-7900
  Independence (G-8659)
Covia Solutions Inc..................................... G 404 214-3200
  Independence (G-8661)
Enon Sand and Gravel LLC........................ G 513 771-0820
  Cincinnati (G-2873)
Fisher Sand & Gravel Inc........................... G 330 745-9239
  Norton (G-11943)
Foundry Sand Service LLC......................... F 330 823-6152
  Sebring (G-13120)
Gravel Doctor of Ohio................................. G 844 472-8353
  Millersport (G-11011)
Hanson Aggregates East............................. G 513 353-1100
  Cleves (G-4953)
Hilltop Basic Resources Inc....................... D 513 621-1500
  Cincinnati (G-3000)
Hilltop Basic Resources Inc....................... F 937 859-3616
  Miamisburg (G-10646)
Hilltop Basic Resources Inc....................... F 937 882-6357
  Springfield (G-13576)
Holmes Redimix Inc.................................... E 330 674-0865
  Holmesville (G-8545)
Holmes Supply Corp................................... G 330 279-2634
  Holmesville (G-8547)
James Bunnell Inc....................................... F 513 353-1100
  Cleves (G-4955)
Kenmore Construction Co Inc................... D 330 832-8888
  Massillon (G-10116)
Lake Erie Aggregates Inc........................... G 419 541-0130
  Huron (G-8636)
Martin Marietta Materials Inc..................... G 513 701-1140
  West Chester (G-15461)
McClelland Inc.. E 740 452-3036
  Zanesville (G-16544)
Medina Supply Company............................ E 330 723-3681
  Medina (G-10352)
National Lime and Stone Co....................... E 419 396-7671
  Carey (G-2281)
Ohio Valley Sand LLC.................................. G 740 661-4240
  New Philadelphia (G-11521)
Ohio Valley Sand LLC.................................. G 330 440-6495
  Newcomerstown (G-11649)
Oster Sand and Gravel Inc........................ G 330 874-3322
  Bolivar (G-1531)
Oster Sand and Gravel Inc........................ G 330 833-2649
  Massillon (G-10133)
Parry Co... G 740 884-4893
  Chillicothe (G-2523)
Phillips Ready Mix Co................................. E 937 426-5151
  Beavercreek Township (G-1090)
Phoenix Asphalt Company Inc.................. G 330 339-4935
  Magnolia (G-9597)
Portable Crushing LLC................................ F 330 618-5251
  New Franklin (G-11442)

SAND & GRAVEL

Prairie Lane Corporation .... G 330 262-3322
 Wooster (G-16159)
Putnam Aggregates Co .... G 419 523-6004
 Ottawa (G-12189)
R W Sidley Incorporated .... G 440 564-2221
 Newbury (G-11635)
Rjw Trucking Company Ltd .... E 740 363-5343
 Delaware (G-6746)
Sand Rock Enterprises Inc .... F 740 407-2735
 Glenford (G-7979)
Sharps Valet Parking Svc Inc .... G 574 223-5230
 Cincinnati (G-3386)
Shelly Materials Inc .... G 740 247-2311
 Racine (G-12695)
Shelly Materials Inc .... D 740 246-6315
 Thornville (G-14072)
Smith Concrete Co .... E 740 373-7441
 Dover (G-6843)
Stafford Gravel Inc .... F 419 298-2440
 Edgerton (G-7081)
Stocker Concrete Company .... F 740 254-4626
 Gnadenhutten (G-7989)
Streamside Materials Llc .... G 419 423-1290
 Findlay (G-7570)
The Olen Corporation .... D 614 491-1515
 Columbus (G-5823)
Tiger Sand & Gravel LLC .... F 330 833-6325
 Massillon (G-10150)
Tri County Concrete Inc .... F 330 425-4464
 Twinsburg (G-14747)
Tuffco Sand and Gravel Inc .... F 614 873-3977
 Plain City (G-12596)
W&W Rock Sand and Gravel .... G 513 266-3708
 Williamsburg (G-15867)
Wayne Concrete Company LLC .... F 937 545-9919
 Medway (G-10400)
Welch Sand & Gravel Inc .... F 513 353-3220
 Cincinnati (G-3513)
White Gravel Mines Productions .... G 740 776-0510
 Portsmouth (G-12660)
Youngs Sand & Gravel Co Inc .... F 419 994-3040
 Loudonville (G-9454)

SAND LIME PRDTS

Holmes Supply Corp .... G 330 279-2634
 Holmesville (G-8547)

SAND MINING

Alden Sand & Gravel Co Inc .... G 330 928-3249
 Cuyahoga Falls (G-6061)
Carl E Oeder Sons Sand & Grav .... F 513 494-1555
 Lebanon (G-9066)
Central Ready Mix LLC .... E 513 402-5001
 Cincinnati (G-2717)
D H Bowman & Sons Inc .... G 419 886-2711
 Bellville (G-1241)
John R Jurgensen Co .... B 513 771-0820
 Cincinnati (G-3044)
Massillon Materials Inc .... F 330 837-4767
 Dalton (G-6136)
Phillips Companies .... E 937 426-5461
 Beavercreek Township (G-1089)
S & S Aggregates Inc .... F 740 453-0721
 Zanesville (G-16561)
The National Lime and Stone Company . E 419 422-4341
 Findlay (G-7575)
Ward Construction Co .... F 419 943-2450
 Leipsic (G-9142)

SANDBLASTING EQPT

L N Brut Manufacturing Co .... G 330 833-9045
 Shreve (G-13212)

SANITARY SVC, NEC

Ash Sewer & Drain Service .... G 330 376-9714
 Akron (G-65)
N-Viro International Corp .... F 419 535-6374
 Toledo (G-14394)

SANITARY SVCS: Liquid Waste Collection & Disposal

Koski Construction Co .... G 440 997-5337
 Ashtabula (G-644)

SANITARY SVCS: Refuse Collection & Disposal Svcs

Montgomerys Pallet Service Inc .... G 330 297-6677
 Ravenna (G-12725)

SANITARY SVCS: Waste Materials, Recycling

Auris Noble LLC .... E 330 321-6649
 Akron (G-68)
Cirba Solutions Us Inc .... E 740 653-6290
 Lancaster (G-9000)
Fpt Cleveland LLC .... C 216 441-3800
 Cleveland (G-4088)
Garden Street Iron & Metal Inc .... E 513 721-4660
 Cincinnati (G-2928)
Green Vision Materials Inc .... F 440 564-5500
 Newbury (G-11625)
H Hafner & Sons Inc .... E 513 321-1895
 Cincinnati (G-2979)
Homan Metals LLC .... G 513 721-5010
 Cincinnati (G-3004)
Hope Timber Pallet Recycl LLC .... E 740 344-1788
 Newark (G-11582)
Innovation Plastics LLC .... E 513 818-1771
 Fostoria (G-7639)
Magnus International Group Inc ...... G 216 592-8355
 Painesville (G-12248)
Mondo Polymer Technologies Inc ... E 740 376-9396
 Marietta (G-9810)
Novelis Alr Recycling Ohio LLC .... C 740 922-2373
 Uhrichsville (G-14767)
Perma-Fix of Dayton Inc .... F 937 268-6501
 Dayton (G-6503)
Polychem LLC .... D 419 547-1400
 Clyde (G-4975)
Pratt Paper (oh) LLC .... E 567 320-3353
 Wapakoneta (G-15129)
Resource Recycling Inc .... F 419 222-2702
 Lima (G-9285)
Roe Transportation Entps Inc .... G 937 497-7161
 Sidney (G-13278)
Rumpke Transportation Co LLC ...... B 513 242-4600
 Cincinnati (G-3356)
Synagro Midwest Inc .... F 937 384-0669
 Miamisburg (G-10687)
Waste Parchment Inc .... F 330 674-6868
 Millersburg (G-11006)
Werlor Inc .... E 419 784-4285
 Defiance (G-6698)

SASHES: Door Or Window, Metal

Rsl LLC .... E 330 392-8900
 Warren (G-15203)
YKK AP America Inc .... E 513 942-7200
 West Chester (G-15528)

SATELLITES: Communications

Great Lakes Telcom Ltd .... E 330 629-8848
 Youngstown (G-16373)

SAW BLADES

Cammel Saw Company .... F 330 477-3764
 Canton (G-2058)
Uhrichsville Carbide Inc .... F 740 922-9197
 Uhrichsville (G-4772)

SAWDUST & SHAVINGS

Sugarcreek Shavings LLC .... G 330 763-4239
 Sugarcreek (G-3942)

SCAFFOLDS: Mobile Or Stationary, Metal

Bil-Jax Inc .... F 419 445-8915
 Archbold (G-525)
Hansen Scaffolding LLC .... F 513 574-9000
 West Chester (G-15561)
Haulotte North America Mfg Inc .... G 567 444-4159
 Archbold (G-530)
Sky Climber Winc Solutions LLC ...... E 740 203-3900
 Delaware (G-6731)
Waco Scaffolding & Equipment Inc ... A 216 749-8900
 Cleveland (G-4889)

SCALES & BALANCES, EXC LABORATORY

Etched Metal Company .... E 440 248-0240
 Solon (G-13347)
Interface Logic Systems Inc .... G 614 236-8388
 Columbus (G-5422)
K Davis Inc .... G 419 307-7051
 Fremont (G-7797)
Rainin Instrument LLC .... E 510 564-1600
 Columbus (G-5069)

SCALES: Indl

Exact Equipment Corporation .... F 215 295-2000
 Columbus (G-5062)
Holtgreven Scale Elec Corp .... F 419 422-4779
 Findlay (G-7524)
Mettler-Toledo LLC .... C 614 841-7300
 Columbus (G-5560)
Mettler-Toledo LLC .... E 614 438-4511
 Worthington (G-15202)
Mettler-Toledo LLC .... C 614 438-4390
 Worthington (G-15203)
Mettler-Toledo Intl Fin Inc .... E 614 438-4511
 Columbus (G-5065)
Mettler-Toledo Intl Inc .... A 614 438-4511
 Columbus (G-5066)
Mettler-Toledo LLC .... A 614 438-4511
 Columbus (G-5067)

SCIENTIFIC EQPT REPAIR SVCS

Instrumentors Inc .... G 440 238-3430
 Strongsville (G-13746)

SCIENTIFIC INSTRUMENTS WHOLESALERS

Science/Electronics Inc .... F 937 224-4444
 Dayton (G-6562)

SCRAP & WASTE MATERIALS, WHOLESALE: Ferrous Metal

Agmet LLC .... F 216 663-8200
 Cleveland (G-3615)
Cohen Brothers Inc .... F 513 217-5200
 Middletown (G-10812)
Cohen Brothers Inc .... E 513 422-3696
 Middletown (G-10811)
Fpt Cleveland LLC .... C 216 441-3800
 Cleveland (G-4088)
Franklin Iron & Metal Corp .... C 937 253-8184
 Dayton (G-6338)

PRODUCT SECTION — SCREW MACHINE PRDTS

Homan Metals LLC .... G 513 721-5010
  Cincinnati (G-3004)
Metalico Akron Inc .... F 330 376-1400
  Akron (G-246)
R L S Corporation .... F 740 773-1440
  Chillicothe (G-2530)
Rm Advisory Group Inc .... E 513 242-2100
  Cincinnati (G-3346)

SCRAP & WASTE MATERIALS, WHOLESALE: Metal

A & B Iron & Metal Co Inc .... G 937 228-1561
  Dayton (G-6178)
Fex LLC .... F 412 604-0400
  Mingo Junction (G-11045)
Nucor Steel Marion Inc .... E 740 383-6068
  Marion (G-9867)
Triple Arrow Industries Inc .... G 614 437-5588
  Marysville (G-9943)

SCRAP & WASTE MATERIALS, WHOLESALE: Nonferrous Metals Scrap

Auris Noble LLC .... E 330 321-6649
  Akron (G-68)
W R G Inc .... E 216 351-8494
  Avon Lake (G-827)

SCRAP & WASTE MATERIALS, WHOLESALE: Paper

Sims Bros Inc .... D 740 387-9041
  Marion (G-9883)

SCRAP STEEL CUTTING

Geneva Liberty Steel Ltd .... E 330 740-0103
  Youngstown (G-16366)
Precision Cut Fabricating Inc .... F 440 877-1260
  North Royalton (G-11891)

SCREENS: Projection

Stewart Filmscreen Corp .... E 513 753-0800
  Amelia (G-466)

SCREENS: Window, Metal

Dale Kestler .... G 513 871-9000
  Cincinnati (G-2817)
M-D Building Products Inc .... F 513 539-2255
  Middletown (G-10837)
Renewal By Andersen LLC .... G 614 781-9600
  Columbus (G-5070)

SCREENS: Woven Wire

Kimmatt Corp .... G 937 228-3811
  West Alexandria (G-15342)
Yankee Wire Cloth Products Inc .... F 740 545-9129
  West Lafayette (G-15621)

SCREW MACHINE PRDTS

Abco Bar & Tube Cutng Svc Inc .... E 513 697-9487
  Maineville (G-9598)
Abel Manufacturing Company .... F 513 681-5000
  Cincinnati (G-2591)
Acme Machine Automatics Inc .... E 419 453-0010
  Ottoville (G-12197)
Adams Automatic Inc .... F 440 235-4416
  Olmsted Falls (G-12074)
Alco Manufacturing Corp LLC .... E 440 458-5165
  Elyria (G-7105)
Amco Products Inc .... F 937 433-7982
  Dayton (G-6152)
Amerascrew Inc .... E 419 522-2232
  Mansfield (G-9624)
American Aero Components Llc .... G 937 367-5068
  Dayton (G-6197)
American Micro Products Inc .... C 513 732-2674
  Batavia (G-908)
Amt Machine Systems Limited .... F 740 965-2693
  Columbus (G-5134)
Ashley F Ward Inc .... C 513 398-1414
  Mason (G-9955)
Atlas Machine Products Co .... G 216 228-3688
  Oberlin (G-12048)
Ban Inc .... E 937 325-5539
  Springfield (G-13538)
Bront Machining Inc .... E 937 228-4551
  Moraine (G-11164)
Chardon Metal Products Co .... E 440 285-2147
  Chardon (G-2443)
Clear Creek Screw Machine Co .... G 740 969-2113
  Amanda (G-445)
Condo Incorporated .... D 330 609-6021
  Warren (G-15157)
Day-Hio Products Inc .... F 937 445-0782
  Dayton (G-6272)
Deloscrew Products .... F 740 363-1971
  Delaware (G-6716)
Dunham Products Inc .... F 440 232-0885
  Walton Hills (G-15098)
Eastlake Machine Products LLC .... F 440 953-1014
  Willoughby (G-15915)
Ecm Industries LLC .... E 513 533-6242
  Cincinnati (G-2857)
Elyria Manufacturing Corp .... D 440 365-4171
  Elyria (G-7142)
Engstrom Manufacturing Inc .... G 513 573-0010
  Mason (G-9990)
Eureka Screw Machine Pdts Co .... G 216 883-1715
  Cleveland (G-4036)
Fairfield Machined Pdts Inc .... F 740 756-4409
  Carroll (G-2298)
Fannin Machine Company LLC .... G 419 524-9525
  Mansfield (G-9654)
Forrest Machine Pdts Co Ltd .... E 419 589-3774
  Mansfield (G-9658)
Gent Machine Company .... E 216 481-2334
  Cleveland (G-4120)
Global Precision Parts Inc .... F 260 563-9030
  Van Wert (G-14916)
H & S Precision Screw Pdts Inc .... F 937 437-0316
  New Paris (G-11482)
H & W Screw Products Inc .... F 937 866-2577
  Franklin (G-7679)
Helix Operating Company LLC .... G 855 435-4958
  Beachwood (G-990)
Heller Machine Products Inc .... G 216 281-2951
  Cleveland (G-4179)
Houston Machine Products Inc .... E 937 322-8022
  Springfield (G-13580)
Hy-Production Inc .... C 330 273-2400
  Valley City (G-14873)
Hyland Machine Company .... E 937 233-8600
  Dayton (G-6377)
Ilsco LLC .... C 513 533-6200
  Cincinnati (G-3017)
Integrity Manufacturing Corp .... F 937 233-6792
  Dayton (G-6386)
JAD Machine Company Inc .... F 419 256-6332
  Malinta (G-9605)
Karma Metal Products Inc .... F 419 524-4371
  Mansfield (G-9676)
Kernells Autmtc Machining Inc .... E 419 588-2164
  Berlin Heights (G-1315)
Kerr Lakeside Inc .... D 216 261-2100
  Euclid (G-7280)
Krausher Machining Inc .... G 440 839-2828
  Wakeman (G-15075)
Kts Met-Bar Products Inc .... G 440 288-9308
  Lorain (G-9417)
Lehner Screw Machine LLC .... E 330 688-6616
  Akron (G-218)
Lenco Industries Inc .... F 937 277-9364
  Dayton (G-6404)
Machine Tek Systems Inc .... E 330 527-4450
  Garrettsville (G-7921)
Magnetic Screw Machine Pdts .... E 937 348-2807
  Marysville (G-9925)
Maumee Machine & Tool Corp .... E 419 385-2501
  Toledo (G-14379)
McDaniel Products Inc .... F 419 524-5841
  Mansfield (G-9689)
McDaniel Products Inc .... E 419 524-5841
  Mansfield (G-9688)
McGregor Metal National Works LLC ... E 937 882-6347
  Springfield (G-13601)
McGregor Mtal Yllow Sprng Wrks .... D 937 325-5561
  Springfield (G-13604)
Meistermatic Inc .... E 216 481-7773
  Chesterland (G-2484)
Metal Seal & Products Inc .... C 440 946-8500
  Mentor (G-10502)
Mettlr-Tledo Globl Hldings LLC .... D 614 438-4511
  Columbus (G-5068)
Midwest Precision LLC .... E 440 951-2333
  Eastlake (G-7041)
Mosher Machine & Tool Co Inc .... E 937 258-8070
  Beavercreek Township (G-1085)
Murray Machine and Tool Inc .... G 216 267-1126
  Cleveland (G-4431)
Nolte Precise Manufacturing Inc .... D 513 923-3100
  Cincinnati (G-3203)
Nook Industries LLC .... B 216 271-7900
  Cleveland (G-4463)
NSK Industries Inc .... D 330 923-4112
  Cuyahoga Falls (G-6107)
Obars Machine and Tool Company ...... E 419 535-6307
  Toledo (G-14403)
Ohio Metal Products Company .... E 937 228-6101
  Dayton (G-6489)
Ohio Screw Products Inc .... D 440 322-6341
  Elyria (G-7191)
Paramont Machine Company LLC .... F 330 339-3489
  New Philadelphia (G-11522)
Pfi Precision Inc .... E 937 845-3563
  New Carlisle (G-11425)
Pohlman Precision LLC .... E 636 537-1909
  Massillon (G-10135)
Port Clinton Manufacturing LLC .... E 419 734-2141
  Port Clinton (G-12623)
Precision Engneered Components .... F 614 436-0392
  Worthington (G-16207)
Precision Fittings LLC .... E 440 647-4143
  Wellington (G-15320)
Premier Farnell Corp .... D 330 659-0459
  Richfield (G-12793)
Profile Grinding Inc .... E 216 351-0600
  Cleveland (G-4590)
Qcsm LLC .... G 216 650-8731
  Cleveland (G-4602)
Qualitor Subsidiary H Inc .... C 419 562-7987
  Bucyrus (G-1865)
Quality Machining and Mfg Inc .... F 419 899-2543
  Sherwood (G-13202)
R T & T Machining Co Inc .... F 440 974-8479
  Mentor (G-10543)

Employee Codes: A=Over 500 employees, B=251-500
C=101-250, D=51-100, E=20-50, F=10-19, G=1-9

SCREW MACHINE PRDTS

R W Screw Products Inc................... C 330 837-9211
  Massillon (G-10137)

Raka Corporation................................ D 419 476-6572
  Toledo (G-14449)

Rely-On Manufacturing Inc................ G 937 254-0118
  Dayton (G-6545)

Richland Screw Mch Pdts Inc............ E 419 524-1272
  Mansfield (G-9713)

Rtsi LLC.. G 440 542-3066
  Solon (G-13416)

Semtorq Inc... F 330 487-0600
  Twinsburg (G-14734)

Shanafelt Manufacturing Co................... 330 455-0315
  Canton (G-2223)

Soemhejee Inc.................................... E 419 298-2306
  Edgerton (G-7080)

Stadco Inc... E 937 878-0911
  Fairborn (G-7322)

Superior Bar Products Inc................. E 419 784-2590
  Defiance (G-6696)

Supply Technologies LLC.................. F 740 363-1971
  Delaware (G-6754)

Swagelok Zalo..................................... F 216 524-8950
  Solon (G-13432)

Tri-K Enterprises Inc.......................... E 330 832-7380
  Canton (G-2248)

Triangle Machine Products Co........... E 216 524-5872
  Cleveland (G-4824)

Twin Valley Metalcraft Asm LLC........ G 937 787-4634
  West Alexandria (G-15345)

Usm Precision Products Inc.............. D 440 975-8600
  Wickliffe (G-15858)

Valley Tool & Die Inc.......................... D 440 237-0160
  North Royalton (G-11900)

Vanamatic Company........................... D 419 692-6085
  Delphos (G-6778)

Vulcan Products Co Inc..................... F 419 468-1039
  Galion (G-7887)

Warren Screw Machine Inc............... F 330 609-6020
  Warren (G-15219)

Watters Manufacturing Co Inc........... G 216 281-8600
  Cleveland (G-4897)

Whirlaway Corporation........................ D 440 647-4711
  Wellington (G-15323)

Whirlaway Corporation........................ D 440 647-4711
  Wellington (G-15324)

Whirlaway Corporation........................ C 440 647-4711
  Wellington (G-15325)

Whiteford Industries Inc.................... F 419 381-1155
  Toledo (G-14524)

Wood-Sebring Corporation................ G 216 267-3191
  Cleveland (G-4918)

SCREWS: Metal

Agrati - Medina LLC........................... C 330 725-8853
  Medina (G-10289)

Agrati - Tiffin LLC............................... D 419 447-2221
  Tiffin (G-14074)

Akko Fastener Inc.............................. F 513 489-8300
  Middletown (G-10804)

Altenloh Brinck & Co US Inc.............. E 419 737-2381
  Pioneer (G-12489)

Altenloh Brinck & Co US Inc.............. F 419 636-6715
  Bryan (G-1806)

Engstrom Manufacturing Inc............. G 513 573-0010
  Mason (G-9990)

Hexagon Industries Inc..................... E 216 249-0200
  Cleveland (G-4187)

Tinnerman Palnut Engineered PR...... F 330 220-5100
  Brunswick (G-1795)

SEALANTS

Aluminum Coating Manufacturers..... F 216 341-2000
  Cleveland (G-3644)

Besten Equipment Inc....................... E 216 581-1166
  Akron (G-85)

Century Industries Corporation.......... E 330 457-2367
  New Waterford (G-11556)

Chemmasters Inc................................ E 440 428-2105
  Madison (G-9589)

Concrete Sealants Inc....................... E 937 845-8776
  Tipp City (G-14130)

Egc Operating Company LLC........... D 440 285-5835
  Chardon (G-2449)

ICP Adhesives and Sealants Inc....... E 330 753-4585
  Norton (G-11944)

Jetcoat LLC.. E 800 394-0047
  Columbus (G-5496)

Mameco International Inc.................. D 216 752-4400
  Cleveland (G-4354)

P & T Products Inc............................. E 419 621-1966
  Sandusky (G-13085)

Royal Adhesives & Sealants LLC...... F 440 708-1212
  Chagrin Falls (G-2421)

Sika Mbcc US LLC............................. A 216 839-7500
  Beachwood (G-1024)

Teknol Inc... D 937 264-0190
  Dayton (G-6613)

Tremco Cpg Inc.................................. F 216 514-7783
  Beachwood (G-1030)

Tremco Incorporated.......................... B
  Beachwood (G-1031)

Truseal Technologies Inc................... E 216 910-1500
  Akron (G-364)

SEALING COMPOUNDS: Sealing, synthetic rubber or plastic

FedPro Inc.. E 216 464-6440
  Cleveland (G-4055)

Technical Rubber Company Inc........ C 740 967-9015
  Johnstown (G-8779)

SEALS: Hermetic

Aeroseal LLC...................................... E 937 428-9300
  Dayton (G-6187)

Aeroseal LLC...................................... E 937 428-9300
  Miamisburg (G-10607)

Reliable Hermetic Seals LLC........... F 888 747-3250
  Beavercreek (G-1060)

SEARCH & NAVIGATION SYSTEMS

Accurate Electronics Inc................... C 330 682-7015
  Orrville (G-12116)

ADB Safegate Americas LLC............ C 614 861-1304
  Gahanna (G-7828)

Aero-Instruments Co LLC.................. E 216 671-3133
  Cleveland (G-3610)

Atk Space Systems LLC.................... C 937 490-4121
  Beavercreek (G-1070)

Atk Systems.. G 937 429-8632
  Beavercreek (G-1071)

Boeing Company................................ E 740 788-4000
  Heath (G-8318)

Btc Inc... G 740 549-2722
  Lewis Center (G-9153)

Btc Technology Services Inc............. G 740 549-2722
  Lewis Center (G-9154)

Drs Leonardo Inc............................... E 937 429-7408
  Beavercreek (G-1047)

Drs Leonardo Inc............................... E 513 943-1111
  Cincinnati (G-2557)

Enjet Aero Dayton Inc........................ E 937 878-3800
  Huber Heights (G-8576)

Eti Tech LLC....................................... F 937 832-4200
  Kettering (G-8957)

Ferrotherm Corporation..................... C 216 883-9350
  Cleveland (G-4158)

General Dynmics Mssion Systems... F 513 253-4770
  Beavercreek (G-1051)

Grimes Aerospace Company............ D 937 484-2001
  Urbana (G-14832)

Heller Machine Products Inc............ G 216 281-2951
  Cleveland (G-4179)

Hunter Defense Tech Inc.................. F 513 943-7880
  Cincinnati (G-2555)

Lake Shore Cryotronics Inc.............. D 614 891-2243
  Westerville (G-1662)

Lockheed Mrtin Intgrted System...... C 330 796-2800
  Akron (G-222)

Northrop Grmman Innvtion Syste.... C 937 429-9261
  Beavercreek (G-1076)

Northrop Grmman Tchncal Svcs I... D 937 320-3100
  Beavercreek Township (G-1086)

Northrop Grumman Systems Corp.. C 937 490-4111
  Beavercreek (G-1077)

Northrop Grumman Systems Corp.. D 937 429-6450
  Beavercreek Township (G-1087)

Northrop Grumman Systems Corp.. B 513 881-3296
  West Chester (G-15573)

Parker Aerospace............................... G 216 225-2721
  Cleveland (G-4517)

PCC Airfoils LLC................................. C 216 692-7900
  Cleveland (G-4527)

Reuter-Stokes LLC............................. B 330 425-3755
  Twinsburg (G-14724)

S&L Fleet Services Inc...................... E 740 549-2722
  Westerville (G-1577)

Star Dynamics Corporation................ D 614 334-4510
  Hilliard (G-8442)

Sunset Industries Inc......................... E 440 306-8284
  Mentor (G-10570)

Te Connectivity Corporation.............. C 419 521-9500
  Mansfield (G-9725)

Wall Colmonoy Corporation................ D 513 842-4200
  Cincinnati (G-3507)

Watts Antenna Company.................... G 740 797-9380
  The Plains (G-14460)

Yost Labs Inc...................................... F 740 876-4936
  Portsmouth (G-12561)

SEATING: Stadium

American Office Services Inc............ G 440 899-6888
  Westlake (G-1573)

Bill Davis Stadium............................. F 614 292-2624
  Columbus (G-5180)

SECURITY CONTROL EQPT & SYSTEMS

Checkpoint Systems Inc.................... D 330 456-7776
  Canton (G-2072)

Diebold Nixdorf Incorporated............. A 330 490-4000
  North Canton (G-1722)

Emx Industries Inc............................. F 216 518-9888
  Cleveland (G-4013)

Enterpriseid Inc.................................. G 330 963-0064
  Twinsburg (G-14635)

FM Systems.. F 330 273-3000
  Brunswick (G-1753)

Global Security Tech Inc.................... G 614 890-6400
  Westerville (G-1576)

Honeywell International Inc............... A 937 484-2000
  Urbana (G-14835)

Midwest Security Services................ E 937 853-9000
  Dayton (G-6444)

Pentagon Protection Usa LLC.............. F 614 734-7240
  Dublin (G-6922)
R F I... G 740 654-4502
  Lancaster (G-9035)
Securcom Inc... E 419 628-1049
  Minster (G-11060)
Securtex International Inc........................ F 937 312-1414
  Dayton (G-6565)
Technlogy Install Partners LLC............... E 888 586-7040
  Cleveland (G-4774)

SECURITY DEVICES

Ever Secure SEC Systems Inc................ F 937 369-8294
  Dayton (G-6327)
Invue Security Products Inc.................... E 330 456-7776
  Canton (G-2133)
Lindsay Precast LLC................................ E 800 837-7788
  Canal Fulton (G-1972)
Mace Security Intl Inc.............................. D 440 424-5325
  Cleveland (G-4349)
Ohio Home & Leisure Products I............ G 614 833-4144
  Pickerington (G-12465)
Sage Integration Holdings LLC............... E 330 733-8183
  Kent (G-8857)
Say Security Group USA LLC................. F 419 634-0004
  Ada (G-5)
The W L Jenkins Company...................... F 330 477-3407
  Canton (G-2244)

SECURITY SYSTEMS SERVICES

Fellhauer Mechanical Systems................ E 419 734-3674
  Port Clinton (G-12617)
Johnson Controls Inc................................ F 513 671-6338
  Cincinnati (G-3049)
Sage Integration Holdings LLC............... E 330 733-8183
  Kent (G-8857)
Say Security Group USA LLC................. F 419 634-0004
  Ada (G-5)
Securcom Inc... E 419 628-1049
  Minster (G-11060)
Sound Communications Inc..................... E 614 875-8500
  Grove City (G-8120)

SEMICONDUCTOR CIRCUIT NETWORKS

Micro Industries Corporation................... D 740 548-7878
  Westerville (G-15716)

SEMICONDUCTORS & RELATED DEVICES

Communication Concepts Inc.................. G 937 426-8600
  Beavercreek (G-1043)
Darrah Electric Company.......................... F 216 631-0912
  Cleveland (G-3942)
Em4 Inc.. E 608 240-4800
  Cleveland (G-4009)
Gen Digital Inc... G 330 252-1171
  Akron (G-165)
Gopowerx Inc... F 440 707-6029
  Richfield (G-12789)
Greenfield Solar Corp............................... G 216 535-9200
  North Ridgeville (G-11842)
Heraeus Electro-Nite Co LLC.................. G 330 725-1419
  Medina (G-10333)
Honeywell International Inc..................... D 302 327-8920
  Columbus (G-5444)
Hyper Tech Research Inc......................... F 614 481-8050
  Columbus (G-5449)
Intel Interpeace... G 330 922-4450
  Akron (G-192)
Lam Research Corporation....................... G 937 472-3311
  Eaton (G-7064)
Linear Asics Inc... G 330 474-3920
  Twinsburg (G-14690)

Materion Brush Inc.................................... D 216 486-4200
  Mayfield Heights (G-10250)
Materion Corporation................................ C 216 486-4200
  Mayfield Heights (G-10251)
Niobium Microsystems Inc....................... C 937 203-8117
  Dayton (G-6471)
Ohio Semitronics Inc................................. D 614 777-1005
  Hilliard (G-8427)
Pepperl + Fuchs Inc.................................. C 330 425-3555
  Twinsburg (G-14709)
Pepperl + Fuchs Entps Inc...................... F 330 425-3555
  Twinsburg (G-14710)
Powertech Inc... G 901 850-9393
  Beachwood (G-1011)
Rexon Components Inc............................ E 216 292-7373
  Beachwood (G-1018)
Saint-Gobain Ceramics Plas Inc............. B 440 542-2712
  Newbury (G-11637)
SCI Engineered Materials Inc.................. E 614 486-0261
  Columbus (G-5754)
Signature Technologies Inc...................... E 937 859-6323
  Miamisburg (G-10683)
Silfex Inc... B 937 324-2487
  Springfield (G-13632)
Silfex Inc... D 937 472-3311
  Eaton (G-7070)
Spang & Company.................................... E 440 350-6108
  Mentor (G-10558)
Tosoh SMD Inc.. C 614 875-7912
  Grove City (G-8125)
Ustek Incorporated................................... F 614 538-8000
  Columbus (G-5851)
Uvonics Co... F 614 458-1163
  Columbus (G-5852)

SENSORS: Temperature, Exc Indl Process

Krumor Inc.. F 216 328-9802
  Cleveland (G-4300)
Lake Shore Cryotronics Inc...................... D 614 891-2243
  Westerville (G-15662)
Safe-Grain Inc.. G 513 398-2500
  Loveland (G-9503)

SEPARATORS: Metal Plate

Allgaier Process Technology.................... G 513 402-2566
  West Chester (G-15363)

SEPTIC TANKS: Concrete

Allen Enterprises Inc................................. E 740 532-5913
  Ironton (G-8694)
Bluffton Precast Concrete Co.................. E 419 358-6946
  Bluffton (G-1500)
E A Cox Inc... G 740 858-4400
  Lucasville (G-9522)
Encore Precast LLC................................. E 513 726-5678
  Seven Mile (G-13132)
J K Precast LLC.. G 740 335-2188
  Wshngtn Ct Hs (G-16234)
James Kimmey.. F 740 335-5746
  Wshngtn Ct Hs (G-16235)
Lindsay Precast LLC................................ E 800 837-7788
  Canal Fulton (G-1972)
Quaker City Concrete Pdts LLC.............. G 330 427-2239
  Leetonia (G-9130)
Septic Products Inc................................... G 419 282-5933
  Ashland (G-613)
Stiger Pre Cast Inc.................................... G 740 482-2313
  Nevada (G-11362)

SEPTIC TANKS: Plastic

Hancor Inc.. E 419 424-8225
  Findlay (G-7521)

Hancor Inc.. B 614 658-0050
  Hilliard (G-8413)
J K Precast LLC.. G 740 335-2188
  Wshngtn Ct Hs (G-16234)

SEWAGE & WATER TREATMENT EQPT

Aqua Ohio Inc.. F 740 867-8700
  Chesapeake (G-2472)
Artesian of Pioneer Inc............................. F 419 737-2352
  Pioneer (G-12490)
City of Chardon... E 440 286-2657
  Chardon (G-2446)
City of Troy.. F 937 339-4826
  Troy (G-14555)
De Nora Tech LLC.................................... D 440 710-5334
  Concord Township (G-5905)
Eagle Crusher Co Inc............................... D 419 468-2288
  Galion (G-7872)
Greene County.. G 937 429-0127
  Dayton (G-6162)
Pelton Environmental Pdts Inc................ G 440 838-1221
  Lewis Center (G-9175)
Smart Sonic Corporation.......................... G 818 610-7900
  Cleveland (G-4707)
Tangent Company LLC............................ G 440 543-2775
  Chagrin Falls (G-2427)

SEWER CLEANING EQPT: Power

Best Equipment Co Inc............................ E 440 237-3515
  North Royalton (G-11868)
Electric Eel Mfg Co Inc............................ E 937 323-4644
  Springfield (G-13558)

SHADES: Window

Cincinnati Window Shade Inc.................. F 513 631-7200
  Cincinnati (G-2763)

SHAPES & PILINGS, STRUCTURAL: Steel

A-1 Welding & Fabrication....................... F 440 233-8474
  Lorain (G-9399)
Brenmar Construction Inc........................ D 740 286-2151
  Jackson (G-8711)
Steve Vore Welding and Steel................. F 419 375-4087
  Fort Recovery (G-7624)

SHAPES: Extruded, Aluminum, NEC

Gei of Columbiana Inc.............................. E 330 783-0270
  Youngstown (G-16364)
General Extrusions Intl LLC..................... C 330 783-0270
  Youngstown (G-16365)
Novelis Alr Aluminum LLC....................... A 216 910-3400
  Beachwood (G-1004)
Patton Aluminum Products Inc............... F 937 845-9404
  New Carlisle (G-11424)
Systems Kit LLC MB................................ E 330 945-4500
  Akron (G-343)
Vari-Wall Tube Specialists Inc................. D 330 482-0000
  Columbiana (G-5053)

SHAVING PREPARATIONS

Edgewell Personal Care LLC.................. C 937 492-1057
  Sidney (G-13244)

SHEET METAL SPECIALTIES, EXC STAMPED

Ahner Fabricating & Shtmtl Inc............... E 419 626-6641
  Sandusky (G-13042)
All Metal Fabricators Inc.......................... F 216 267-0033
  Cleveland (G-3630)
Allen County Fabrication Inc................... E 419 227-7447
  Lima (G-9219)
Allied Fabricating & Wldg Co.................. E 614 751-6664
  Columbus (G-5113)

SHEET METAL SPECIALTIES, EXC STAMPED

Buckeye Metal Works Inc..................G.....614 239-8000
  Columbus (G-5220)
C & R Inc..................................E.....614 497-1130
  Groveport (G-8134)
Columbus Steelmasters Inc................F.....614 231-2141
  Columbus (G-5279)
Cramers Inc...............................E.....330 477-4571
  Canton (G-2083)
Crown Electric Engrg & Mfg LLC...........E.....513 539-7394
  Middletown (G-10816)
Flood Heliarc Inc.........................F.....614 835-3929
  Groveport (G-8140)
G T Metal Fabricators Inc................E.....440 237-8745
  Cleveland (G-4098)
Hartzell Mfg Co LLC......................E.....937 859-5955
  Miamisburg (G-10643)
I-M-A Enterprises Inc....................F.....330 948-3535
  Lodi (G-9351)
Kirk & Blum Manufacturing Co.............C.....513 458-2600
  Cincinnati (G-3078)
Kuhlman Engineering Co...................F.....419 243-2196
  Toledo (G-14352)
Kuhn Fabricating Inc.....................G.....440 277-4182
  Lorain (G-9418)
Lambert Sheet Metal Inc..................F.....614 237-0384
  Columbus (G-5518)
M3 Technologies Inc......................F.....216 898-9936
  Cleveland (G-4347)
Metal-Max Inc.............................G.....330 673-9926
  Kent (G-8835)
Metlweb Ltd...............................F.....513 563-8822
  Cincinnati (G-3157)
Midwest Fabrications Inc.................E.....330 633-0191
  Tallmadge (G-14038)
Midwest Metal Fabricators Ltd............F.....419 739-7077
  Wapakoneta (G-15126)
Modern Manufacturing Inc.................G.....513 251-3600
  Cincinnati (G-3171)
National Indus Concepts Inc..............C.....615 989-9101
  Chillicothe (G-2520)
Paul Wilke & Son Inc.....................F.....513 921-3163
  Cincinnati (G-3241)
S&B Metal Pdts Twinsburg LLC.............E.....330 487-5790
  Twinsburg (G-14731)
Selmco Metal Fabricators Inc.............F.....937 498-1331
  Sidney (G-13285)
Seneca Sheet Metal Company...............F.....419 447-8434
  Tiffin (G-14105)
SFM Corp..................................E.....440 951-5500
  Willoughby (G-15988)
Sheet Metal Products Co Inc..............E.....440 392-9000
  Mentor (G-10554)
Varmland Inc..............................F.....216 741-1510
  Cleveland (G-4861)
Vicart Prcsion Fabricators Inc...........E.....614 771-0080
  Hilliard (G-8452)
Waterville Sheet Metal Company...........G.....419 878-5050
  Waterville (G-15255)
Weybridge LLC.............................E.....440 951-5500
  Willoughby (G-16015)
Wolf Metals Inc...........................G.....614 461-6361
  Columbus (G-5880)

SHEETS: Hard Rubber

Novex Operating Company LLC..............F.....330 335-2371
  Wadsworth (G-15049)

SHELVING, MADE FROM PURCHASED WIRE

Interntnal Tchncal Catings Inc...........C.....800 567-4592
  Columbus (G-5476)
KEffs Inc.................................E.....614 443-0586
  Columbus (G-5505)

SHIMS: Metal

Die-Cut Products Co......................F.....216 771-6994
  Cleveland (G-3958)
Ohio Gasket and Shim Co Inc..............E.....330 630-0626
  Akron (G-270)
Shim Shack................................G.....877 557-3930
  Harrison (G-8291)

SHOE STORES: Boots, Men's

Cobblers Corner LLC......................F.....330 482-4005
  Columbiana (G-5032)

SHOE STORES: Men's

Rnp Inc...................................G
  Dellroy (G-6758)

SHOES: Men's

Acor Orthopaedic LLC.....................E.....216 662-4500
  Cleveland (G-3594)
Careismatic Brands LLC...................G.....561 843-8727
  Groveport (G-8135)
Georgia-Boot Inc..........................D.....740 753-1951
  Nelsonville (G-11356)
Rocky Brands Inc..........................B.....740 753-9100
  Nelsonville (G-11359)

SHOES: Men's, Work

Rbr Enterprises LLC......................F.....866 437-9327
  Brecksville (G-1630)

SHOES: Plastic Or Rubber

Cobblers Corner LLC......................F.....330 482-4005
  Columbiana (G-5032)
Georgia-Boot Inc..........................D.....740 753-1951
  Nelsonville (G-11356)
Mettler Footwear Inc.....................G.....330 703-0079
  Hudson (G-8605)
Mulhern Belting Inc......................E.....201 337-5700
  Fairfield (G-7386)
Totes Isotoner Holdings Corp.............C.....513 682-8200
  West Chester (G-15599)
US Footwear Holdings LLC.................C.....740 753-9100
  Nelsonville (G-11360)

SHOES: Women's

Acor Orthopaedic LLC.....................E.....216 662-4500
  Cleveland (G-3594)
Careismatic Brands LLC...................G.....561 843-8727
  Groveport (G-8135)
Georgia-Boot Inc..........................D.....740 753-1951
  Nelsonville (G-11356)
Rocky Brands Inc..........................B.....740 753-9100
  Nelsonville (G-11359)

SHOES: Women's, Dress

FP Holdco Inc.............................G.....614 729-7205
  Pickerington (G-12462)

SHOT PEENING SVC

Metal Improvement Company LLC............D.....513 489-6484
  Blue Ash (G-1436)
Metal Improvement Company LLC............E.....330 425-1490
  Twinsburg (G-14695)
National Peening.........................F.....216 342-9155
  Bedford Heights (G-1178)

SHOWCASES & DISPLAY FIXTURES: Office & Store

CSM Concepts LLC.........................F.....330 483-1320
  Valley City (G-14866)

E-B Display Company Inc..................C.....330 833-4101
  Massillon (G-1092)
Pete Gaietto & Associates Inc............D.....513 771-0903
  Cincinnati (G-3249)

SHOWER STALLS: Plastic & Fiberglass

Closets By Mike..........................G.....740 607-2212
  Zanesville (G-1522)
Crane Plumbing LLC.......................A.....419 522-4211
  Mansfield (G-9692)

SHREDDERS: Indl & Commercial

Accushred LLC............................F.....419 244-7473
  Toledo (G-14170)

SHUTTERS, DOOR & WINDOW: Metal

Cleveland Shutters Inc...................G.....440 234-7600
  Berea (G-1271)

SHUTTERS, DOOR & WINDOW: Plastic

Dinesol Building Products Ltd............E.....330 270-0212
  Youngstown (G-6350)

SIDING MATERIALS

American Orginal Bldg Pdts LLC...........G.....330 786-3000
  Akron (G-60)
C Green & Sons Incorporated..............F.....740 745-2998
  Saint Louisville (G-12942)

SIDING: Plastic

Alside Inc................................D.....419 865-0934
  Maumee (G-10101)
Exterior Portfolio LLC...................C.....614 754-3400
  Columbus (G-5357)
Fibreboard Corporation...................C.....419 248-8000
  Toledo (G-14287)
Gentek Building Products Inc.............F.....800 548-4542
  Cuyahoga Falls (G-6086)

SIDING: Precast Stone

Headwaters Incorporated..................F.....989 671-1500
  Manchester (G-9618)

SIDING: Sheet Metal

Gentek Building Products Inc.............F.....800 548-4542
  Cuyahoga Falls (G-6086)
Metal Sales Manufacturing Corp...........F.....440 319-3779
  Jefferson (G-8753)
Owens Corning Sales LLC..................F.....740 983-1300
  Ashville (G-671)

SIGN PAINTING & LETTERING SHOP

Freds Sign Service Inc...................G.....937 335-1901
  Troy (G-14570)
General Theming Cntrs LLC................C.....614 252-6342
  Columbus (G-5392)
Ohio Shelterall Inc......................F.....614 882-1110
  Westerville (G-15717)
Quick As A Wink Pnting Co................G.....419 224-9786
  Lima (G-9281)
Triangle Sign Co LLC.....................G.....513 266-1009
  Hamilton (G-8254)

SIGNALS: Traffic Control, Electric

Athens Technical Specialists.............F.....740 592-2874
  Athens (G-676)
City Elyria Communication................G.....440 322-3329
  Elyria (G-7127)
City of Canton............................D.....330 489-3370
  Canton (G-2075)
Intelligent Signal Tech Intl.............G.....614 530-4784
  Loveland (G-9487)

PRODUCT SECTION
SIGNS & ADVERTISING SPECIALTIES

Paul Peterson Company .... F 614 486-4375
   Columbus *(G-5660)*

Security Fence Group Inc .... E 513 681-3700
   Cincinnati *(G-3374)*

Union Metal Industries Corp .... E 330 456-7653
   Canton *(G-2251)*

SIGNS & ADVERTISING SPECIALTIES

A & A Safety Inc .... F 937 567-9781
   Beavercreek *(G-1068)*

A & A Safety Inc .... E 513 943-6100
   Amelia *(G-447)*

A&E Signs and Lighting LLC .... F 513 541-0024
   Cincinnati *(G-2586)*

Abbott Image Solutions LLC .... F 937 382-6677
   Wilmington *(G-16037)*

Accent Signage Systems Inc .... E 612 377-9156
   Findlay *(G-7470)*

Adcraft Decals Incorporated .... E 216 524-2934
   Cleveland *(G-3598)*

Affinity Disp Expositions Inc .... F 513 771-2339
   Cincinnati *(G-2599)*

Agile Sign & Ltg Maint Inc .... E 440 918-1311
   Eastlake *(G-7017)*

Alberts Screen Print Inc .... C 330 753-7559
   Norton *(G-11938)*

Allied Sign Co .... F 614 443-9656
   Columbus *(G-5115)*

Alvin L Roepke .... G 419 862-3891
   Elmore *(G-7099)*

American Awards Inc .... F 614 875-1850
   Grove City *(G-8077)*

Apex Signs Inc .... G 330 952-2626
   Medina *(G-10295)*

Archer Corporation .... E 330 455-9995
   Canton *(G-2038)*

Associated Premium Corporation .... E 513 679-4444
   Cincinnati *(G-2637)*

Atlantic Sign Company Inc .... E 513 383-1504
   Cincinnati *(G-2640)*

Auto Dealer Designs Inc .... E 330 374-7666
   Akron *(G-70)*

Avid Signs Plus LLC .... G 513 932-7446
   Lebanon *(G-9062)*

Baker Plastics Inc .... G 330 743-3142
   Youngstown *(G-16317)*

Barnes Advertising Corporation .... E 740 453-6836
   Zanesville *(G-16505)*

Bates Metal Products Inc .... D 740 498-8371
   Port Washington *(G-12631)*

Belco Works Inc .... D 740 695-0500
   Saint Clairsville *(G-12897)*

Best Graphics .... G 614 327-7929
   Columbus *(G-5183)*

Blang Acquisition LLC .... F 937 223-2155
   Dayton *(G-6231)*

Brandon Screen Printing .... F 419 229-9837
   Lima *(G-9224)*

Brown Cnty Bd Mntal Rtardation .... E 937 378-4891
   Georgetown *(G-7950)*

Buckeye Boxes Inc .... D 614 274-8484
   Columbus *(G-5219)*

Busch & Thiem Inc .... E 419 625-7515
   Sandusky *(G-13047)*

Business Idntfction Systems In .... G 614 841-1255
   Columbus *(G-5223)*

C JS Signs .... G 330 821-7446
   Alliance *(G-397)*

Call Sign Alpha LLC .... G 330 842-6200
   Salem *(G-12980)*

Casad Company Inc .... F 419 586-9457
   Coldwater *(G-4984)*

Cgs Imaging Inc .... F 419 897-3000
   Holland *(G-8497)*

Chad Abbott Signs LLC .... G 937 393-8864
   Hillsboro *(G-8456)*

Chase Sign & Lighting Svc Inc .... G 567 128-3444
   Toledo *(G-14234)*

Cincinnati Custom Signs Inc .... G 513 322-2559
   Cincinnati *(G-2747)*

Cleveland E Speedpro Imaging .... G 216 342-4954
   Cleveland *(G-3839)*

Columbus Graphics Inc .... F 614 577-9360
   Reynoldsburg *(G-12759)*

Communication Exhibits Inc .... D 330 854-4040
   Canal Fulton *(G-1970)*

CSP Group Inc .... E 513 984-9500
   Cincinnati *(G-2804)*

Custom Sign & Design LLC .... G 419 202-3633
   Norwalk *(G-11960)*

Custom Sign Center .... G 614 279-6035
   Columbus *(G-5311)*

Davis Printing Company .... E 330 745-3113
   Barberton *(G-866)*

Dayton Wire Products Inc .... E 937 236-8000
   Dayton *(G-6291)*

Dee Sign Usa LLC .... F 513 779-3333
   West Chester *(G-15413)*

Dern Trophies Corp .... F 614 895-3260
   Westerville *(G-15653)*

Devries & Associates Inc .... G 614 890-3821
   Westerville *(G-15701)*

DJ Signs MD LLC .... G 330 344-6643
   Akron *(G-131)*

Djmc Partners Inc .... F 614 890-3821
   Westerville *(G-15702)*

Doxie Inc .... G 937 427-3431
   Dayton *(G-6160)*

Dualite Inc .... C 513 724-7100
   Williamsburg *(G-15864)*

Eaglestone Products LLC .... G 440 463-8715
   Brecksville *(G-1615)*

Eighth Floor Promotions LLC .... C 419 586-6433
   Celina *(G-2330)*

Enlarging Arts Inc .... G 330 434-3433
   Akron *(G-142)*

Etched Metal Company .... E 440 248-0240
   Solon *(G-13347)*

F J Designs Inc .... F 330 264-1377
   Wooster *(G-16117)*

Fair Publishing House Inc .... E 419 668-3746
   Norwalk *(G-11967)*

Fast Signs .... G 614 710-1312
   Hilliard *(G-8411)*

Fastsigns .... G 513 489-8989
   Cincinnati *(G-2896)*

Fastsigns .... G 937 890-6770
   Dayton *(G-6329)*

Fastsigns .... G 513 226-6733
   Liberty Township *(G-9206)*

Fastsigns .... G 330 952-2626
   Medina *(G-10323)*

Fastsigns .... G 440 954-9191
   Mentor *(G-10454)*

Fastsigns .... F 419 843-1073
   Toledo *(G-14284)*

Fdi Cabinetry LLC .... G 513 353-4500
   Cleves *(G-4952)*

Fineline Imprints Inc .... F 740 453-1083
   Zanesville *(G-16530)*

Flawless Signs & Wraps LLC .... G 937 559-0672
   Troy *(G-14569)*

Folks Creative Printers Inc .... F 740 383-6326
   Marion *(G-9852)*

Forty Nine Degrees LLC .... F 419 678-0100
   Coldwater *(G-4990)*

Fourteen Ventures Group LLC .... G 937 866-2341
   West Carrollton *(G-15354)*

Frontier Signs & Displays Inc .... G 513 367-0813
   Harrison *(G-8275)*

Gary Lawrence Enterprises Inc .... G 330 833-7181
   Massillon *(G-10099)*

Geograph Industries Inc .... E 513 202-9200
   Harrison *(G-8276)*

Ginos Awards Inc .... E 216 831-6565
   Warrensville Heights *(G-15229)*

Glavin Industries Inc .... E 440 349-0049
   Solon *(G-13353)*

Global Lighting Tech Inc .... E 440 922-4584
   Brecksville *(G-1618)*

Golf Marketing Group Inc .... G 330 963-5155
   Twinsburg *(G-14669)*

Hall Company .... E 937 652-1376
   Urbana *(G-14833)*

Ham Signs LLC DBA Fastsigns .... F 937 890-6770
   Dayton *(G-6365)*

Harbor Wraps LLC .... G 614 725-0429
   Columbus *(G-5419)*

Hart Advertising Inc .... F 419 668-1194
   Norwalk *(G-11972)*

Highrise Creative LLC .... F 614 890-3821
   Westerville *(G-15708)*

HP Manufacturing Company Inc .... D 216 361-6500
   Cleveland *(G-4204)*

Hy-Ko Products Company LLC .... E 330 467-7446
   Northfield *(G-11907)*

Identitek Systems Inc .... D 330 832-9844
   Massillon *(G-10111)*

Ike Smart City .... E 614 294-4898
   Columbus *(G-5453)*

Industrial and Mar Eng Svc Co .... F 740 694-0791
   Fredericktown *(G-7749)*

Innomark Group LLC .... G 419 720-8102
   Toledo *(G-14332)*

Integral Design Inc .... F 216 524-0555
   Cleveland *(G-4230)*

J Best Inc .... G 513 943-7000
   Cincinnati *(G-2567)*

Johnny Hulsman Signs .... G 513 638-9788
   Cincinnati *(G-3046)*

Kdm Signs Inc .... C 513 769-1932
   Cincinnati *(G-3069)*

Kinly Signs Corporation .... F 740 451-7446
   South Point *(G-13468)*

Kinoly Signs .... G 740 451-7446
   South Point *(G-13469)*

Kmgrafx Inc .... G 513 248-4100
   Loveland *(G-9490)*

Laad Sign & Lighting Inc .... F 330 379-2297
   Ravenna *(G-12721)*

Lake Erie Graphics Inc .... E 216 575-1333
   Brookpark *(G-1721)*

Lehner Signs Inc .... G 614 258-0500
   Columbus *(G-5523)*

Lightning Signs and Decals LLC .... G 304 403-1290
   New Philadelphia *(G-11511)*

Long Sign Co .... G 614 294-1057
   Columbus *(G-5532)*

Macray Co LLC .... G 937 325-1726
   Springfield *(G-13598)*

Masterpiece Signs & Graphics .... F 419 358-0077
   Bluffton *(G-1505)*

Mayfair Granite Co Inc .... G 216 382-8150
   Cleveland *(G-4372)*

Mes Painting and Graphics .... G 614 496-1696
   Westerville *(G-15714)*

Employee Codes: A=Over 500 employees, B=251-500
C=101-250, D=51-100, E=20-50, F=10-19, G=1-9

SIGNS & ADVERTISING SPECIALTIES

Mes Painting and Graphics Ltd .... E 614 496-1696
  Westerville (G-15715)
Mitchell Plastics Inc .... E 330 825-2461
  Barberton (G-883)
National Sign Systems Inc .... D 614 850-2540
  Hilliard (G-8424)
Neon Workshop .... G 216 832-5236
  Bedford (G-1143)
Nevco Services Ltd .... G 937 603-1500
  Dayton (G-6470)
North Coast Theatrical Inc .... G 330 762-1768
  Akron (G-266)
Norton Outdoor Advertising .... E 513 631-4864
  Cincinnati (G-3205)
Nrka Corp .... F 440 817-0700
  Broadview Heights (G-1664)
Ohio Shelterall Inc .... F 614 882-1110
  Westerville (G-15717)
Omni Media Cleveland Inc .... G 216 687-0077
  Cleveland (G-4503)
On Site Signs Ohio Ltd .... G 614 496-9400
  Hilliard (G-8428)
Onestop Signs .... F 513 722-7867
  Goshen (G-7994)
Orange Barrel Media LLC .... D 614 294-4898
  Columbus (G-5643)
Painted Hill Inv Group Inc .... G 937 339-1756
  Troy (G-14600)
Precision Signs & Graphics LLC .... G 740 446-1774
  Gallipolis (G-7898)
Pro A V of Ohio 877 812-5350
  New Philadelphia (G-11523)
Pro Image Sign & Design Inc .... E 440 986-8888
  Amherst (G-482)
Pro-Decal Inc .... G 330 484-0089
  Canton (G-2203)
Quality Custom Signs LLC .... G 614 580-7233
  Worthington (G-16209)
Queen Exhibits LLC .... G 937 615-6051
  Piqua (G-12551)
Ray Meyer Sign Company Inc .... E 513 984-5446
  Loveland (G-9500)
Renoir Visions LLC .... G 419 586-5679
  Celina (G-2345)
Retain Loyalty LLC .... G 330 830-0839
  Massillon (G-10139)
Ripped Vinyl .... G 330 332-5004
  Salem (G-13027)
Roemer Industries Inc .... D 330 448-2000
  Masury (G-10158)
Royal Acme Corporation 216 241-1477
  Cleveland (G-4654)
S&S Sign Service .... G 614 279-9722
  Columbus (G-5737)
Sabco Industries Inc .... E 419 531-5347
  Toledo (G-14461)
Screen Works Inc .... E 937 264-9111
  Dayton (G-6564)
Sdmk LLC .... G 330 965-0970
  Youngstown (G-16435)
Select Signs .... E 937 262-7095
  Dayton (G-6173)
Sensical Inc .... D 216 641-1141
  Solon (G-13420)
Sideway Signs LLC .... G 501 400-4013
  Cincinnati (G-3388)
Sign America Incorporated .... F 740 765-5555
  Richmond (G-12803)
Sign Technologies LLC .... G 937 439-3970
  Dayton (G-6573)
Sign Write .... G 937 559-4388
  Beavercreek (G-1063)

Signarama .... G 330 468-0556
  Macedonia (G-9573)
Signs Ohio Inc .... G 419 228-7446
  Lima (G-9289)
Signs Unlmted The Grphic Advnt .... G 614 836-7446
  Logan (G-9376)
Signwire Worldwide Inc .... G 937 428-6189
  Dayton (G-6574)
Speedpro Imaging .... G 513 771-4776
  Cincinnati (G-3407)
Speedpro Imaging .... G 513 753-5600
  Milford (G-10924)
Stratus Unlimited LLC .... C 440 209-6200
  Mentor (G-10568)
Super Signs Inc .... G 480 968-2200
  North Bend (G-11707)
Superior Label Systems Inc .... B 513 336-0825
  Mason (G-10061)
TCS Schindler & Co LLC .... G 937 836-9473
  Englewood (G-7243)
Ternion Inc .... E 216 642-6180
  Cleveland (G-4777)
The Hartman Corp .... G 614 475-5035
  Columbus (G-5822)
The Massillon-Cleveland-Akr .... C 330 833-3165
  Massillon (G-10149)
Toledo Sign Company Inc .... E 419 244-4444
  Toledo (G-14504)
Traffic Cntrl Sgnls Signs & MA .... G 740 670-7763
  Newark (G-11609)
Traffic Detectors & Signs Inc .... G 330 707-9060
  Youngstown (G-14657)
Traxx North America Inc .... F 513 554-4700
  Blue Ash (G-1485)
Triumph Signs & Consulting Inc .... E 513 576-8090
  Milford (G-10926)
Vista Creations LLC .... G 440 954-9191
  Mentor (G-10593)
Visual Marking Systems Inc .... D 330 425-7100
  Twinsburg (G-14753)
West 6th Products Company .... D 330 467-7446
  Northfield (G-11915)
Wettle Corp .... G 419 865-6923
  Holland (G-8537)
Williams Steel Rule Die Co .... F 216 431-3232
  Cleveland (G-4910)
Yesco Sign & Lighting Service .... G 419 407-6581
  Toledo (G-14531)
Zilla .... G 614 763-5311
  Dublin (G-6960)

SIGNS & ADVERTISING SPECIALTIES: Artwork, Advertising

1157 Designconcepts LLC .... E 937 497-1157
  Sidney (G-13216)
T&T Graphics Inc .... D 937 847-6000
  Miamisburg (G-10688)
Vision Graphix Inc .... G 440 835-6540
  Westlake (G-15800)

SIGNS & ADVERTISING SPECIALTIES: Displays, Paint Process

Ohio Displays Inc .... F 216 961-5600
  Elyria (G-7189)

SIGNS & ADVERTISING SPECIALTIES: Letters For Signs, Metal

Engravers Gallery & Sign Co .... G 330 830-1271
  Massillon (G-10094)

Interstate Sign Products Inc .... G 419 683-1962
  Crestline (G-6004)

SIGNS & ADVERTISING SPECIALTIES: Novelties

E P Gerber & Sons Inc .... D 330 857-2021
  Kidron (G-8913)
Finn Graphics Inc .... E 513 941-6161
  Cincinnati (G-2905)
Gerber Wood Products Inc .... D 330 857-9007
  Kidron (G-8914)
License Ad Plate Company .... F 216 265-4200
  Cleveland (G-4523)
Quikey Manufacturing Co Inc .... C 330 633-8106
  Akron (G-293)
W C Bunting Co Inc .... F 330 385-2050
  East Liverpool (G-7002)

SIGNS & ADVERTISING SPECIALTIES: Scoreboards, Electric

Industrial Electronic Service .... F 937 746-9750
  Carlisle (G-2288)
National Scoreboards LLC .... G 513 791-5244
  Cincinnati (G-3111)
Obhc Inc .... G 440 236-5112
  Columbia Station (G-5015)

SIGNS, ELECTRICAL: Wholesalers

Sign America Incorporated .... F 740 765-5555
  Richmond (G-12803)

SIGNS, EXC ELECTRIC, WHOLESALE

K Ventures Inc .... F 419 678-2308
  Coldwater (G-4904)
Macray Co LLC .... G 937 325-1726
  Springfield (G-13798)
Water Drop Media Inc .... G 234 600-5817
  Vienna (G-15005)

SIGNS: Electrical

ABC Signs Inc .... F 513 241-8884
  Cincinnati (G-2559)
All Signs of Chillicothe Inc .... G 740 773-5016
  Chillicothe (G-2452)
Allen Industries Inc .... D 567 408-7538
  Toledo (G-14182)
American Led-Gible Inc .... F 614 851-1100
  Columbus (G-5127)
Architctral Identification Inc .... F 614 868-8400
  Gahanna (G-7830)
Behrco Inc .... G 419 394-1612
  Saint Marys (G-1245)
Boyer Signs & Graphics Inc .... E 216 383-7242
  Columbus (G-5200)
Brilliant Electric Sign Co Ltd .... D 216 741-3800
  Brooklyn Heights (G-1685)
Danite Holdings LLC .... E 614 444-3333
  Columbus (G-5310)
Ellet Neon Sales & Service Inc .... E 330 628-9907
  Akron (G-137)
Federal Heath Sign Company LLC .... D 740 369-0999
  Delaware (G-6721)
Gardner Signs Inc .... F 419 385-6669
  Toledo (G-14297)
Grady McCauley Inc .... D 330 494-9444
  Akron (G-172)
Gus Holthaus Signs Inc .... E 513 861-0060
  Cincinnati (G-2978)
Hendricks Vacuum Forming Inc .... F 330 837-2040
  Massillon (G-10108)

PRODUCT SECTION   SPECIALTY FOOD STORES: Coffee

Insignia Signs Inc.................................... G 937 866-2341
 Moraine (G-11186)
Lettergraphics Inc................................... G 330 683-3903
 Orrville (G-12135)
LSI Industries Inc.................................... B 513 793-3200
 Cincinnati (G-3115)
National Illmination Sign Corp............... G 419 866-1666
 Holland (G-8520)
Ohio Awning & Manufacturing Co........... E 216 861-2400
 Cleveland (G-4494)
Signs Limited LLC.................................. G 740 282-7715
 Steubenville (G-13677)
Terry & Jack Neon Sign Co..................... G 419 229-0674
 Lima (G-9297)
United - Maier Signs Inc...................... D 513 681-6600
 Cincinnati (G-3478)

SIGNS: Neon

Cicogna Electric and Sign Co................. D 440 998-2637
 Ashtabula (G-627)
Columbus Sign Company........................ E 614 252-3133
 Columbus (G-5277)
Kasper Enterprises Inc.......................... G 419 841-6656
 Toledo (G-14345)
Moonshine Screen Printing Inc............... G 513 523-7775
 Oxford (G-12211)
Ruff Neon & Lighting Maint Inc.............. F 440 350-6267
 Painesville (G-12263)
Signcom Incorporated............................ F 614 228-9999
 Columbus (G-5770)
Triangle Sign Co LLC.............................. G 513 266-1009
 Hamilton (G-8254)
Wholesale Channel Letters................... G 440 256-3200
 Kirtland (G-8942)

SILICA MINING

Covia Holdings LLC................................ D 800 255-7263
 Independence (G-8660)

SILICON WAFERS: Chemically Doped

Techneglas LLC...................................... F 419 873-2000
 Perrysburg (G-12432)

SILICON: Pure

Ohio Valley Specialty Company............. F 740 373-2276
 Marietta (G-9813)

SILICONE RESINS

Poly-Carb Inc... D 440 248-1223
 Macedonia (G-9567)

SILICONES

Canton OH Rubber Speclty Prods........... G 330 454-3847
 Canton (G-2065)
Hexion Topco LLC................................... D 614 225-4000
 Columbus (G-5430)
Momentive Performance Mtls Inc.......... A 614 986-2495
 Columbus (G-5578)
Momentive Performance Mtls Inc.......... A 740 928-7010
 Hebron (G-8349)
Momentive Performance Mtls Inc.......... C 440 878-5705
 Richmond Heights (G-12809)
Momentive Prfmce Mtls Qrtz Inc........... D 440 878-5700
 Strongsville (G-13855)
Novagard Solutions Inc......................... C 216 881-8111
 Cleveland (G-4483)
Silicone Solutions Inc.......................... F 330 920-3125
 Cuyahoga Falls (G-6117)
Wacker Chemical Corporation............... C 330 899-0847
 Canton (G-2264)

SILK SCREEN DESIGN SVCS

Alvin L Roepke....................................... G 419 862-3891
 Elmore (G-7099)
Eastgate Custom Graphics Ltd.............. G 513 528-7922
 Cincinnati (G-2854)
Hollywood Imprints LLC......................... F 614 501-6040
 Gahanna (G-7838)
Kent Stow Screen Printing Inc............... G 330 923-5118
 Akron (G-205)
Kimpton Printing & Spc Co..................... F 330 467-1640
 Macedonia (G-9561)
Newmast Mktg & Communications........ G 614 837-1200
 Columbus (G-5597)
Professional Screen Printing................. G 740 687-0760
 Lancaster (G-9033)
Qualitee Design Sportswear Co............. F 740 333-8337
 Wshngtn Ct Hs (G-16237)
Red Barn Screen Printing & EMB............. G 740 474-6657
 Circleville (G-3555)
Roban Inc... G 330 794-1059
 Lakemore (G-8958)
Screen Works Inc.................................. E 937 264-9111
 Dayton (G-6564)
Wis 1985 Inc.. F 423 581-4916
 Dayton (G-6657)
Woodrow Manufacturing Co.................... E 937 399-9333
 Springfield (G-13657)

SILVERWARE & PLATED WARE

Professional Award Service................... G 513 389-3600
 Cincinnati (G-3301)

SIMULATORS: Flight

Flightsafety International Inc............... C 614 324-3500
 Columbus (G-5380)

SINTER: Iron

GKN Sinter Metals LLC........................... C 740 441-3203
 Gallipolis (G-7894)
Miba Sinter USA LLC.............................. F 740 962-4242
 Mcconnelsville (G-10283)

SLAG: Crushed Or Ground

Enviri Corporation................................. G 740 367-7322
 Cheshire (G-2477)
Trans Ash Inc.. F 859 341-1528
 Cincinnati (G-3461)

SMOKE DETECTORS

Voice Products Inc................................ F 216 360-0433
 Cleveland (G-4881)

SOFT DRINKS WHOLESALERS

Pepsi-Cola Metro Btlg Co Inc................. F 440 323-5524
 Elyria (G-7193)

SOFTWARE PUBLISHERS: Home Entertainment

Cake LLC.. G 614 592-7681
 Dublin (G-6870)
Cerner Corporation................................ D 740 826-7678
 New Concord (G-11432)
Mirus Adapted Tech LLC....................... E 614 402-4585
 Dublin (G-6910)
Whatifsportscom Inc............................. G 513 333-0313
 Blue Ash (G-1490)

SOFTWARE PUBLISHERS: Operating Systems

Steward Edge Bus Solutions................. F 614 826-5305
 Columbus (G-5795)

SOLAR CELLS

First Solar Inc....................................... E 419 661-1478
 Perrysburg (G-12382)
Isofoton North America Inc................... F 419 591-4330
 Napoleon (G-11321)
Mok Industries LLC................................ F 614 934-1734
 Columbus (G-5577)
Redhawk Energy Systems LLC.............. G 740 927-8244
 Pataskala (G-12305)
Rv Mobile Power LLC............................. G 855 427-7978
 Columbus (G-5735)
Toledo Solar Inc.................................... F 567 202-4145
 Perrysburg (G-12439)

SOLAR HEATING EQPT

Iosil Energy Corporation....................... F
 Groveport (G-8147)
Xunlight Corporation............................. D 419 469-8600
 Toledo (G-14529)

SOLES, BOOT OR SHOE: Rubber, Composition Or Fiber

Shreiner Sole Company Inc................... F 330 276-6135
 Killbuck (G-8922)

SOLID CONTAINING UNITS: Concrete

K-Mar Structures LLC............................ F 231 924-5777
 Junction City (G-8783)

SOLVENTS

Appalachian Solvents LLC..................... G 740 680-3649
 Cambridge (G-1921)
Solvent Solutions LLC........................... G 937 648-4962
 Dayton (G-6579)

SOLVENTS: Organic

Mid-America Chemical Corp................... G 216 749-0100
 Cleveland (G-4406)
Tedia Company LLC................................ C 513 874-5340
 Fairfield (G-7416)

SONAR SYSTEMS & EQPT

Raytheon Company................................ F 937 429-5429
 Beavercreek (G-1059)

SOUND EFFECTS & MUSIC PRODUCTION: Motion Picture

Swagg Productions2015llc..................... F 614 601-7414
 Worthington (G-16213)

SOUND EQPT: Electric

Fernandes Enterprises LLC................... F 937 890-6444
 Dayton (G-6331)
Holland Assocts LLC DBA Archou.......... F 513 891-0006
 Cincinnati (G-3003)
Mixed Logic LLC..................................... G 440 826-1676
 Valley City (G-14879)

SPEAKER SYSTEMS

Althar LLC.. F 216 408-9860
 Cleveland (G-3642)
J & C Group Inc of Ohio........................ F 440 205-9658
 Mentor (G-10477)
Phantom Sound...................................... G 513 759-4477
 Mason (G-10038)

SPECIALTY FOOD STORES: Coffee

Employee Codes: A=Over 500 employees, B=251-500
C=101-250, D=51-100, E=20-50, F=10-19, G=1-9

SPECIALTY FOOD STORES: Coffee

Boston Stoker Inc....................................F..... 937 890-6401
  Vandalia (G-14934)
Iron Bean Inc..F..... 518 641-9917
  Perrysburg (G-12393)
Ohio Coffee Collaborative Ltd................F..... 614 564-9852
  Columbus (G-5613)

SPECIALTY FOOD STORES: Eggs & Poultry

Roots Poultry Inc..................................F..... 419 332-0041
  Fremont (G-7805)

SPECIALTY FOOD STORES: Health & Dietetic Food

Premier Tanning & Nutrition...................G..... 419 342-6259
  Shelby (G-13198)

SPORTING & ATHLETIC GOODS: Basketball Eqpt & Splys, NEC

Huffy Sports Washington Inc..................F..... 937 865-2800
  Miamisburg (G-10647)

SPORTING & ATHLETIC GOODS: Camping Eqpt & Splys

Leisure Time Pdts Design Corp...............G..... 440 934-1032
  Avon (G-779)

SPORTING & ATHLETIC GOODS: Cases, Gun & Rod

Raven Concealment Systems LLC...........E..... 440 508-9000
  North Ridgeville (G-11856)

SPORTING & ATHLETIC GOODS: Fishing Eqpt

Crownplace Brands Ltd.........................G..... 888 332-5534
  Apple Creek (G-497)

SPORTING & ATHLETIC GOODS: Hunting Eqpt

Ghostblind Industries Inc.......................G..... 740 374-6766
  Belpre (G-1253)
Lem Products Holding LLC.....................E..... 513 202-1188
  West Chester (G-15457)

SPORTING & ATHLETIC GOODS: Shafts, Golf Club

Board of Park Commissioners................F..... 216 635-3200
  Cleveland (G-3743)
Nova Golf Corp....................................G..... 419 652-3160
  Nova (G-12004)

SPORTING & ATHLETIC GOODS: Team Sports Eqpt

Backyard Scoreboards LLC...................G..... 513 702-6561
  Middletown (G-10805)
Shoot-A-Way Inc..................................F..... 419 294-4654
  Nevada (G-11361)

SPORTING & ATHLETIC GOODS: Water Sports Eqpt

Kent Water Sports LLC.........................D..... 419 929-7021
  New London (G-11463)
Litehouse Products LLC........................E..... 440 638-2350
  Strongsville (G-13851)
Rain Drop Products Llc........................E..... 419 207-1229
  Ashland (G-609)

SPORTING & RECREATIONAL GOODS, WHOLESALE: Athletic Goods

Garick LLC..E..... 216 581-0100
  Cleveland (G-4102)

SPORTING & RECREATIONAL GOODS, WHOLESALE: Boat Access & Part

Atwood Rope Manufacturing Inc.............E..... 614 920-0534
  Canal Winchester (G-1979)

SPORTING GOODS STORES: Firearms

Area 419 Firearms LLC.........................F..... 419 830-8353
  Delta (G-6779)
R & S Monitions Inc..............................G..... 614 846-0597
  Columbus (G-5706)
Sportsmans Haven Inc..........................G..... 740 432-7243
  Cambridge (G-1955)
TS Sales LLC.......................................F..... 727 804-8060
  Akron (G-365)

SPORTING GOODS STORES: Playground Eqpt

Hershberger Lawn Structures................F..... 330 674-3900
  Millersburg (G-10957)

SPORTS APPAREL STORES

Shoot-A-Way Inc..................................F..... 419 294-4654
  Nevada (G-11361)
Tee Creations.....................................G..... 937 878-2822
  Fairborn (G-7325)
Trophy Sports Center LLC....................F..... 937 376-2311
  Xenia (G-16279)
Unisport Inc...F..... 419 529-4727
  Ontario (G-12096)

SPRINGS: Clock, Precision

Allied Shipping and Packagi..................F..... 937 222-7422
  Moraine (G-11155)
Malabar..E..... 419 866-6301
  Swanton (G-13978)

SPRINGS: Coiled Flat

Golden Spring Company Inc..................F..... 937 848-2513
  Bellbrook (G-1193)

SPRINGS: Leaf, Automobile, Locomotive, Etc

Liteflex Disc LLC..................................D..... 937 836-7025
  Dayton (G-6412)

SPRINGS: Mechanical, Precision

Kern-Liebers Usa Inc............................D..... 419 865-2437
  Holland (G-8517)
Spring Works Incorporated...................E..... 614 351-9345
  Columbus (G-5788)
Stalder Spring Works Inc......................E..... 937 322-6120
  Springfield (G-13637)
The Reliable Spring Wire Frms..............E..... 440 365-7400
  Elyria (G-7211)
Twist Inc...G..... 937 675-9581
  Jamestown (G-8743)
Twist Inc...C..... 937 675-9581
  Jamestown (G-8742)
Wire Products Company Inc.................G..... 216 267-0777
  Cleveland (G-4912)
Yost Superior Co.................................E..... 937 323-7591
  Springfield (G-13658)

SPRINGS: Precision

B & P Spring Production Co...................E..... 216 486-4260
  Cleveland (G-3714)
Tadd Spring Co Inc..............................F..... 440 572-1313
  Strongsville (G-3889)

SPRINGS: Steel

Betts Co DBA Betts Hd........................G..... 330 533-0111
  Canfield (G-2007)
Dayton Progress Corporation................A..... 937 859-5111
  Dayton (G-6288)
Elyria Spring & Specialty Inc.................F..... 440 323-5502
  Elyria (G-7146)
Hendrickson International Corp.............D..... 740 929-5600
  Hebron (G-8343)
Jamestown Industries Inc.....................D..... 330 779-0670
  Youngstown (G-16383)
Kern-Liebers Usa Inc............................D..... 419 865-2437
  Holland (G-8517)
Matthew Warren Inc.............................E..... 614 418-0250
  Columbus (G-5547)
Peterson American Corporation.............E..... 419 867-8711
  Holland (G-8523)
Service Spring Corp.............................G..... 419 867-0212
  Maumee (G-10270)
Service Spring Corp.............................D..... 419 838-6081
  Maumee (G-10271)
Tadd Spring Co Inc..............................F..... 440 572-1313
  Strongsville (G-3889)
Zsi Manufacturing Inc...........................F..... 440 266-0701
  Concord Township (G-5915)

SPRINGS: Torsion Bar

Napoleon Spring Works Inc...................C..... 419 445-1010
  Archbold (G-537)

SPRINGS: Wire

Aswpengg LLC....................................E..... 216 292-4620
  Bedford Heights (G-1164)
Barnes Group Inc.................................G..... 440 526-5900
  Brecksville (G-1677)
Barnes Group Inc.................................C..... 419 891-9292
  Maumee (G-10163)
Bloomngburg Spring Wire Form I..........E..... 740 437-7614
  Bloomingburg (G-1353)
Dayton Progress Corporation................A..... 937 859-5111
  Dayton (G-6288)
Elyria Spring & Specialty Inc.................F..... 440 323-5502
  Elyria (G-7146)
Elyria Spring Spclty Holdg Inc...............F..... 440 323-5502
  Elyria (G-7147)
Euclid Spring Co..................................E..... 440 943-3213
  Wickliffe (G-1583)
Kern-Liebers Texas Inc........................F..... 419 865-2437
  Holland (G-8516)
Matthew Warren Inc.............................E..... 614 418-0250
  Columbus (G-5547)
Ohio Wire Form & Spring Co.................E..... 614 444-3676
  Columbus (G-5630)
Six C Fabrication Inc...........................B..... 330 296-5594
  Ravenna (G-1273)
Solon Manufacturing Company..............E..... 440 286-7149
  Chardon (G-2468)
Spring Team Inc..................................D..... 440 275-5981
  Austinburg (G-750)
Supro Spring & Wire Forms Inc.............E..... 330 722-5628
  Medina (G-10380)
Timac Manufacturing Company.............F..... 937 372-3305
  Xenia (G-16275)
Trupoint Products LLC.........................F..... 330 204-3302
  Sugarcreek (G-13545)

SPROCKETS: Power Transmission

Abl Products Inc................................ F 216 281-2400
 Cleveland (G-3588)
Akron Gear & Engineering Inc........... E 330 773-6608
 Akron (G-34)
Robertson Manufacturing Co............ F 216 531-8222
 Concord Township (G-5912)

STAINLESS STEEL

Acme Surface Dynamics Inc.............. F 330 821-3900
 Alliance (G-388)
Aco Inc.. E 440 639-7230
 Mentor (G-10403)
ATI Flat Rlled Pdts Hldngs LLC........... F 330 875-2244
 Louisville (G-9455)
ATI Solutions Properties LLC............. G 937 609-7681
 Dayton (G-6216)
Challenger Hardware Company......... G 216 591-1141
 Independence (G-8656)
Cleveland-Cliffs Steel Corp................ B 419 755-3011
 Mansfield (G-9639)
Cleveland-Cliffs Steel Corp................ B 513 425-3694
 Middletown (G-10810)
Fulton County Processing Ltd........... C 419 822-9266
 Delta (G-6783)
Great Lakes Mfg Group Ltd.............. G 440 391-8266
 Rocky River (G-12838)
Kda Manufacturing LLC.................... F 330 590-7431
 Norton (G-11947)
Latrobe Spcialty Mtls Dist Inc............ D 330 609-5137
 Vienna (G-14997)
McIntosh Manufacturing LLC............ D 513 424-5307
 Middletown (G-10843)
Qual-Fab Inc.................................... E 440 327-5000
 Avon (G-784)
Quality Bar Inc................................. E 330 755-0000
 Struthers (G-13906)
Shaq Inc.. D 770 427-0402
 Beachwood (G-1023)

STAIRCASES & STAIRS, WOOD

Amcan Stair & Rail LLC.................... F 937 781-3484
 Springfield (G-13532)
Carolina Stair Supply Inc.................. E 740 922-3333
 Uhrichsville (G-14763)
Great Lakes Stair & Mllwk Co........... G 330 225-2005
 Hinckley (G-8473)
Hinckley Wood Products Ltd............ F 330 220-9999
 Hinckley (G-8474)

STAMPINGS: Automotive

Anchor Tool & Die Co...................... B 216 362-1850
 Cleveland (G-3664)
Cleveland Metal Processing Inc........ C 440 243-3404
 Cleveland (G-3848)
Cole Tool & Die Company................ E 419 522-1272
 Ontario (G-12090)
Compco Quaker Mfg Inc.................. E 330 482-0200
 Salem (G-12986)
Elyria Spring & Specialty Inc............ F 440 323-5502
 Elyria (G-7146)
Exact-Tool & Die Inc........................ E 216 676-9140
 Cleveland (G-4040)
Falls Stamping & Welding Co........... F 216 771-9635
 Cleveland (G-4049)
Falls Stamping & Welding Co........... C 330 928-1191
 Cuyahoga Falls (G-6083)
Falls Tool and Die Inc...................... G 330 633-4884
 Akron (G-149)
Feintool Cincinnati Inc..................... C 513 247-0110
 Blue Ash (G-1394)

Feintool US Operations Inc............... C 513 247-0110
 Cincinnati (G-2900)
Findlay Products Corporation........... C 419 423-3324
 Findlay (G-7509)
Grouper Acquisition Co LLC............. B 330 558-2600
 Wellington (G-15313)
Gt Technologies Inc......................... D 419 324-7300
 Toledo (G-14304)
Guarantee Specialties Inc................. D 216 451-9744
 Strongsville (G-13838)
Hayford Technologies Inc................. D 419 524-7627
 Mansfield (G-9667)
Honda Dev & Mfg Amer LLC............ C 937 644-0724
 Marysville (G-9915)
Hydro Extrusion Usa LLC.................. C 888 935-5759
 Sidney (G-13255)
JA Acquisition Corp......................... F 419 287-3223
 Pemberville (G-12335)
Kirchhoff Auto Waverly Inc.............. F 740 947-7763
 Waverly (G-15284)
L & W Inc.. E 734 397-6300
 Avon (G-778)
Lakepark Industries Inc.................... C 419 752-4471
 Greenwich (G-8068)
Langenau Manufacturing Company... E 216 651-3400
 Cleveland (G-4310)
Milark Industries Inc........................ D 419 524-7627
 Mansfield (G-9693)
Milark Industries Inc........................ D 419 524-7627
 Mansfield (G-9694)
Muncy Corporation.......................... D 937 346-0800
 Springfield (G-13608)
Namoh Ohio Holdings Inc................ E
 Norwood (G-11996)
Nebraska Industries Corp................. F 419 335-6010
 Wauseon (G-15270)
Nn Metal Stampings LLC.................. E 419 737-2311
 Pioneer (G-12493)
Northern Stamping Co..................... F 216 883-8888
 Cleveland (G-4477)
Northern Stamping Co..................... F 216 642-8081
 Cleveland (G-4479)
Northern Stamping Co..................... F 216 883-8888
 Cleveland (G-4478)
Oerlikon Frction Systems US In........ E 937 233-9191
 Dayton (G-6484)
P & A Industries Inc......................... D 419 422-7070
 Findlay (G-7549)
Quaker Mfg Corp............................. C 330 332-4631
 Salem (G-13024)
R K Industries Inc............................ D 419 523-5001
 Ottawa (G-12190)
Regal Metal Products Co.................. E 330 868-6343
 Minerva (G-11039)
Shiloh Industries Inc........................ A 330 558-2000
 Valley City (G-14890)
Shl Liquidation Inc Dickson.............. E 615 446-7725
 Valley City (G-14892)
Shl Liquidation Industries Inc........... B 248 299-7500
 Valley City (G-14893)
Shl Liquidation Jefferson Inc............ D
 Valley City (G-14894)
Shl Liquidation Mfg LLC................... E 330 558-2600
 Valley City (G-14896)
Shl Liquidation Stamping Inc........... D 330 558-2600
 Valley City (G-14898)
SSP Industrial Group Inc................... G 330 665-2900
 Fairlawn (G-7452)
Stamco Industries Inc...................... E 216 731-9333
 Cleveland (G-4727)
Stripmatic Products Inc.................... E 216 241-7143
 Cleveland (G-4740)

T A Bacon Co................................... E 216 851-1404
 Chesterland (G-2489)
Taylor Metal Products Co................. C 419 522-3471
 Mansfield (G-9724)
Tfo Tech Co Ltd............................... C 740 426-6381
 Jeffersonville (G-8766)
Tower Atmtive Oprtons USA I LL...... B 419 358-8966
 Bluffton (G-1508)
Triton Duro Werks Inc...................... F 216 267-1117
 Cleveland (G-4833)
Trucut Incorporated......................... D 330 938-9806
 Sebring (G-13127)
Twb Company LLC........................... E 330 558-2026
 Valley City (G-14899)
Valley Tool & Die Inc....................... D 440 237-0160
 North Royalton (G-11900)
Winzeler Stamping Co..................... E 419 485-3147
 Montpelier (G-11147)
Yachiyo of America Inc.................... C 614 876-3220
 Columbus (G-5889)
Yanfeng US Auto Intr Systems I........ D 419 633-1873
 Bryan (G-1847)

STAMPINGS: Metal

Stamped Steel Products Inc............. F 330 538-3951
 North Jackson (G-11791)

STAPLES: Steel, Wire Or Cut

Maverick Nail & Staple Ltd.............. G 513 843-5270
 Batavia (G-931)

STATIONERY & OFFICE SPLYS WHOLESALERS

AW Faber-Castell Usa Inc................. D 216 643-4660
 Independence (G-8654)
Equip Business Solutions Co............. G 614 854-9755
 Jackson (G-8715)
Friends Service Co Inc..................... F 800 427-1704
 Dayton (G-6339)
Friends Service Co Inc..................... C 419 427-1704
 Findlay (G-7512)
Gvs Industries Inc............................ G 513 851-3606
 Hamilton (G-8214)
Pulsar Ecoproducts LLC.................... F 216 861-8800
 Cleveland (G-4600)
Quick Tab II Inc............................... D 419 448-6622
 Tiffin (G-14101)
Westrock Commercial LLC............... D 419 476-9101
 Toledo (G-14523)

STATIONERY: Made From Purchased Materials

American Greetings Corporation...... A 216 252-7300
 Cleveland (G-3652)
CM Paula Company......................... E 513 759-7473
 Mason (G-9980)

STATUARY & OTHER DECORATIVE PRDTS: Nonmetallic

Aquablok Ltd................................... G 419 402-4170
 Swanton (G-13968)
Aquablok Ltd................................... G 419 825-1325
 Swanton (G-13969)
Fireline Inc...................................... C 330 743-1164
 Youngstown (G-16356)
Valutex Reinforcements Inc............. E 800 251-2507
 Wshngtn Ct Hs (G-16243)

STEEL & ALLOYS: Tool & Die

STEEL & ALLOYS: Tool & Die

American Steel & Alloys LLC .... F 330 847-0487
   Warren (G-15138)
CPM Tool Co LLC .... G 937 258-1176
   Dayton (G-6156)
Ernst America Inc .... F 937 434-3133
   Moraine (G-11176)
Ernst Metal Technologies LLC .... F 937 434-3133
   Moraine (G-11178)
Mercer Tool Corporation .... E 419 394-7277
   Saint Marys (G-12957)
Rmi Titanium Company LLC .... C 330 453-2118
   Canton (G-2217)
Thrift Tool Inc .... G 937 275-3600
   Dayton (G-6623)
Unlimited Machine and Tool LLC .... F 419 269-1730
   Toledo (G-14516)

STEEL, COLD-ROLLED: Flat Bright, From Purchased HotRolled

Clark Grave Vault Company .... C 614 294-5761
   Columbus (G-5251)
Geneva Liberty Steel Ltd .... E 330 740-0103
   Youngstown (G-16366)

STEEL, COLD-ROLLED: Sheet Or Strip, From Own HotRolled

American Hvy Plate Sltions LLC .... C 740 331-4620
   Clarington (G-3562)
Nucor Steel Marion Inc .... E 740 383-6068
   Marion (G-9867)
Steel Technologies LLC .... E 419 523-5199
   Ottawa (G-12192)
Suburban Steel Supply Co Li .... D 614 737-5501
   Gahanna (G-7850)

STEEL, COLD-ROLLED: Strip NEC, From Purchased HotRolled

Heidtman Steel Products Inc .... E 419 691-4646
   Toledo (G-14317)
Sandvik Inc .... C 614 438-6579
   Columbus (G-5745)
Worthington Industries Inc .... F 614 438-3113
   Columbus (G-5885)
Worthington Military Cnstr Inc .... F 615 599-6446
   Worthington (G-16222)
Worthington Services LLC .... G 937 848-2164
   Spring Valley (G-13492)
Worthngton Stl Mexico SA De Cv .... G 800 944-2255
   Worthington (G-16224)

STEEL, COLD-ROLLED: Strip Or Wire

Bekaert Corporation .... E 330 683-5060
   Orrville (G-12119)
Worthington Steel Company .... B 800 944-2255
   Worthington (G-16223)

STEEL, HOT-ROLLED: Sheet Or Strip

Cleveland-Cliffs Steel Corp .... D 216 694-5700
   Cleveland (G-3864)
Clevelnd-Cliffs Stl Holdg Corp .... B 216 694-5700
   Cleveland (G-3868)
Heidtman Steel Products Inc .... E 419 691-4646
   Toledo (G-14317)
L T V Steel Company Inc .... A 216 622-5000
   Cleveland (G-4303)
Ohio Steel Sheet and Plate Inc .... E 800 827-2401
   Hubbard (G-8569)
Precision Cut Fabricating Inc .... F 440 877-1260
   North Royalton (G-11891)

Republic Technology Corp .... F 216 622-5000
   Cleveland (G-4627)

STOCK SHAPES: Plastic

Swapil Inc .... D
   Columbus (G-5804)

STONE: Dimension, NEC

Heritage Marble of Ohio Inc .... F 614 436-1464
   Columbus (G-5427)
North Hill Marble & Granite Co .... F 330 253-2179
   Akron (G-267)
Solid Surface Concepts Inc .... E 513 948-8677
   Cincinnati (G-3401)

STONE: Quarrying & Processing, Own Stone Prdts

Beazer East Inc .... E 937 364-2311
   Hillsboro (G-8455)
Briar Hill Stone Co Inc .... D 216 377-5100
   Glenmont (G-7980)
Briar Hill Stone Company .... F 330 377-5100
   Glenmont (G-7981)
Cardinal Aggregate Inc .... F 419 872-4380
   Perrysburg (G-12368)
Kipton Properties Inc .... F 440 315-3699
   Oberlin (G-12054)
Terra Surfaces LLC .... G 937 836-1900
   Dayton (G-6614)
Waller Brothers Stone Company .... E 740 858-1948
   Mc Dermott (G-10275)

STONEWARE PRDTS: Pottery

Beaumont Bros Stoneware Inc .... E 740 982-0055
   Crooksville (G-6044)
Brittany Stamping LLC .... A 216 267-0850
   Cleveland (G-3760)
Clay Burley Products Co .... E 740 452-3633
   Roseville (G-12859)

STORE FIXTURES: Exc Wood

Cap & Associates Inc .... C 614 863-3363
   Columbus (G-5229)

STORE FIXTURES: Wood

Artistic Finishes Inc .... F 440 951-7850
   Willoughby (G-15886)
Baker Store Equipment Company .... F
   Shaker Heights (G-13150)
Cap & Associates Inc .... C 614 863-3363
   Columbus (G-5229)
CIP International Inc .... D 513 874-9925
   West Chester (G-15394)
Custom Surroundings Inc .... F 913 839-0100
   Valley City (G-14868)
Display Dynamics Inc .... E 937 832-2830
   Englewood (G-7229)
Leiden Cabinet Company LLC .... D 330 425-8555
   Twinsburg (G-14687)
Mac Lean J S Co .... E 614 878-5454
   Columbus (G-5538)
Norton Industries Inc .... E 888 357-2345
   Lakewood (G-8980)

STORES: Auto & Home Supply

Allen Aircraft Products Inc .... D 330 296-9621
   Ravenna (G-12704)
Doug Marine Motors Inc .... E 740 335-3700
   Wshngtn Ct Hs (G-16230)
Finale Products Inc .... G 419 874-2662
   Perrysburg (G-12381)

Keystone Auto Glass Inc .... D 419 509-0497
   Maumee (G-10211)
Knippen Chrysler Ddge Jeep Inc .... E 419 695-4976
   Delphos (G-6767)
Pattons Trck & Hvy Eqp Svc Inc .... E 740 385-4067
   Logan (G-9373)
Support Svc LLC .... G 419 617-0660
   Lexington (G-9203)
Vintage Automotive Elc Inc .... F 419 472-9349
   Toledo (G-14520)

STRAINERS: Line, Piping Systems

16363 Sca Inc .... G 330 448-0000
   Masury (G-1015)
Insulpro Inc .... F 614 262-3768
   Columbus (G-5459)

STRAWS: Drinking, Made From Purchased Materials

Solas Ltd .... E 650 501-0889
   Avon (G-788)

STRUCTURAL SUPPORT & BUILDING MATERIAL: Concrete

High Concrete Group LLC .... B 937 748-2412
   Springboro (G-1504)
Jet Stream International Inc .... D 330 505-9988
   Hubbard (G-8560)

STUDS & JOISTS: Sheet Metal

Clarkwestern Dietrich Building .... E 330 372-5564
   Warren (G-15154)
Clarkwstern Dtrich Bldg System .... C 513 870-1100
   West Chester (G-15396)

SUNDRIES & RELATED PRDTS: Medical & Laboratory, Rubber

Duramax Marine LLC .... D 440 834-5400
   Hiram (G-8483)
Elastostar Rubber Corp .... E 614 841-4400
   Plain City (G-12558)
Elbex Corporation .... D 330 673-3233
   Kent (G-8812)
Express Pharmacy & Dme LLC .... G 210 981-9690
   Columbus (G-5366)
Gdc Inc .... F 574 533-3128
   Wooster (G-16123)
Guardian Manufacturing Co LLC .... E 419 933-2711
   Willard (G-15859)
Hexpol Compounding LLC .... C 440 682-4038
   Akron (G-183)
Hygenic Company LLC .... B 330 633-8460
   Akron (G-188)
Kent Elastomer Products Inc .... C 330 673-1011
   Kent (G-8823)
Newell Brands Inc .... F 330 733-1184
   Kent (G-8839)
Plymouth Foam LLC .... D 740 254-1188
   Gnadenhutten (G-7987)
Rainbow Master Mixing Inc .... F 330 374-1810
   Akron (G-295)
Roller Source Inc .... F 440 748-4033
   Columbia Station (G-5019)
Vulcan International Corp .... G 513 621-2850
   Cincinnati (G-3503)

SURFACE ACTIVE AGENTS

BASF Corporation .... D 614 662-5682
   Columbus (G-5176)

Chemron Corp.................................. G 419 352-5565
  Bowling Green (G-1559)
Peter Cremer N Amer Enrgy Inc............. E 513 557-3943
  Cincinnati (G-3250)
Pilot Chemical Corp........................... C 513 326-0600
  West Chester (G-15477)

SURGICAL APPLIANCES & SPLYS

American Power LLC.......................... F 937 235-0418
  Dayton (G-6202)
Axon Medical Llc.............................. E 216 276-0262
  Medina (G-10299)
Cardinal Health Inc........................... E 614 553-3830
  Dublin (G-6871)
Cardinal Health Inc........................... G 614 757-2863
  Lewis Center (G-9155)
Cardinal Health Inc........................... A 614 757-5000
  Dublin (G-6872)
Cleveland Medical Devices Inc............... E 216 619-5928
  Cleveland (G-3846)
Deco Tools Inc................................. E 419 476-9321
  Toledo (G-14262)
Dentronix Inc................................... D 330 916-7300
  Cuyahoga Falls (G-6080)
Doling & Assoc Dntl Lab Inc................. F 937 254-0075
  Dayton (G-6300)
Ethicon Inc..................................... C 513 786-7000
  Blue Ash (G-1390)
Florida Invacare Holdings LLC............... E 800 333-6900
  Elyria (G-7152)
Francisco Jaume................................ G 740 622-1200
  Coshocton (G-5978)
Frohock-Stewart Inc........................... E 440 329-6000
  North Ridgeville (G-11840)
Gelok International Corp...................... E 419 352-1482
  Bowling Green (G-1566)
Gendron Inc.................................... E 419 636-0848
  Bryan (G-1819)
Guardian Manufacturing Co LLC............. E 419 933-2711
  Willard (G-15859)
Hdwt Holdings Inc............................. D 440 269-4984
  Mentor (G-10467)
Invacare Canadian Holdings Inc.............. E 440 329-6000
  Elyria (G-7161)
Invacare Canadian Holdings LLC............. E 440 329-6000
  Elyria (G-7162)
Invacare Continuing Care Inc................. G 800 668-2337
  Elyria (G-7163)
Invacare Corporation.......................... F 440 329-6000
  North Ridgeville (G-11846)
Invacare Corporation.......................... A 440 329-6000
  Elyria (G-7164)
Invacare Hcs LLC.............................. E 330 634-9925
  Elyria (G-7167)
Invacare Holdings LLC........................ E 440 329-6000
  Elyria (G-7168)
Jones Metal Products Co LLC................ E 740 545-6381
  West Lafayette (G-15618)
Jones Metal Products Company.............. E 740 545-6341
  West Lafayette (G-15619)
Kempf Surgical Appliances Inc............... F 513 984-5758
  Montgomery (G-11130)
Leimkuehler Inc................................ E 440 899-7842
  Cleveland (G-4319)
Medline Industries LP......................... E 614 879-9728
  West Jefferson (G-15612)
Meridian Industries Inc........................ D 330 673-1011
  Kent (G-8834)
Philips Med Systems Clvland In.............. B 440 483-3000
  Cleveland (G-4547)
Schaerer Medical Usa Inc..................... F 513 561-2241
  Cincinnati (G-3368)

Steris-IMS...................................... F 330 686-4557
  Stow (G-13729)
Thomas Products Co Inc...................... E 513 756-9009
  Cincinnati (G-3453)
Tilt 15 Inc...................................... D 330 239-4192
  Sharon Center (G-13169)
Tranzonic Companies.......................... D 216 535-4300
  Richmond Heights (G-12811)
Dan Allen Surgical LLC........................ F 800 261-9953
  Newbury (G-11622)
Marlen Manufacturing & Dev Co.............. G 216 292-7060
  Bedford (G-1137)
Steris Corporation............................. C 440 392-8079
  Mentor (G-10565)
Steris Corporation............................. C 440 354-2600
  Mentor (G-10566)
Surgical Appliance Inds Inc................... C 513 271-4594
  Cincinnati (G-3436)

SURGICAL IMPLANTS

Bahler Medical Inc............................. F 614 873-7600
  Plain City (G-12564)
Hammill Manufacturing Co.................... D 419 476-0789
  Maumee (G-10204)
Osteosymbionics LLC......................... E 216 881-8500
  Cleveland (G-4511)
Spinal Balance Inc............................. G 419 530-5935
  Swanton (G-13983)
Theken Spine LLC............................. F 330 773-7677
  Medina (G-10385)

SURGICAL INSTRUMENT REPAIR SVCS

Optimum Surgical.............................. F 216 870-8526
  Medina (G-10358)

SURVEYING INSTRUMENTS WHOLESALERS

Zaenkert Surveying Essentials................ G 513 738-2917
  Okeana (G-12070)

SUSPENSION SYSTEMS: Acoustical, Metal

Kinetics Noise Control Inc.................... C 614 889-0480
  Dublin (G-6905)
One Wish LLC.................................. F 800 505-6883
  Bedford (G-1147)
Wall Technology Inc........................... F 715 532-5548
  Toledo (G-14521)

SVC ESTABLISHMENT EQPT, WHOLESALE: Firefighting Eqpt

A-1 Sprinkler Company Inc................... D 937 859-6198
  Miamisburg (G-10604)
Action Coupling & Eqp Inc.................... D 330 279-4242
  Holmesville (G-8541)
Fire Safety Services Inc....................... F 937 686-2000
  Huntsville (G-8623)
Johnsons Fire Equipment Co................. F 740 357-4916
  Wellston (G-15330)
Sutphen Corporation........................... C 800 726-7030
  Dublin (G-6949)

SVC ESTABLISHMENT EQPT, WHOLESALE: Laundry Eqpt & Splys

Pneumatic Specialties Inc..................... G 440 729-4400
  Chesterland (G-2488)

SVC ESTABLISHMENT EQPT, WHOLESALE: Restaurant Splys

Martin-Brower Company LLC................. C 513 773-2301
  West Chester (G-15462)

Wasserstrom Company....................... B 614 228-6525
  Columbus (G-5865)

SWEEPING COMPOUNDS

B&D Water Inc................................. F 330 771-3318
  Quaker City (G-12691)
Nwp Manufacturing Inc........................ F 419 894-6871
  Waldo (G-15089)

SWIMMING POOL EQPT: Filters & Water Conditioning Systems

Aquapro Systems LLC........................ F 877 278-2797
  Oakwood (G-12026)
Hammersmith Bros Invstmnts Inc........... E 513 353-3000
  North Bend (G-11704)
Onesource Water LLC........................ F 866 917-7873
  Toledo (G-14414)

SWIMMING POOLS, EQPT & SPLYS: Wholesalers

Bradley Enterprises Inc....................... G 330 875-1444
  Louisville (G-9456)
Hammersmith Bros Invstmnts Inc........... E 513 353-3000
  North Bend (G-11704)
Litehouse Products LLC....................... E 440 638-2350
  Strongsville (G-13851)
Mc Alarney Pool Spas and Billd.............. F 740 373-6698
  Marietta (G-9808)

SWITCHBOARDS & PARTS: Power

Vacuum Electric Switch Co Inc.............. F 330 374-5156
  Mogadore (G-11089)

SWITCHES: Electric Power

Temple Israel................................... G 330 762-8617
  Akron (G-351)
Wes-Garde Components Group Inc......... G 614 885-0319
  Westerville (G-15724)

SWITCHES: Electronic

Black Box Corporation........................ G 855 324-9909
  Westlake (G-15738)
Don-Ell Corporation........................... E 419 841-7114
  Sylvania (G-13993)
Hall Company................................... E 937 652-1376
  Urbana (G-14833)
Quality Switch Inc............................. E 330 872-5707
  Newton Falls (G-11655)
Specialty Switch Company LLC.............. F 330 427-3000
  Youngstown (G-16444)

SWITCHES: Electronic Applications

Contact Industries Inc......................... E 419 884-9788
  Lexington (G-9200)
Twinsource LLC................................ F 440 248-6800
  Solon (G-13440)

SWITCHES: Time, Electrical Switchgear Apparatus

All Pack Services LLC......................... G 614 935-0964
  Grove City (G-8076)

SWITCHGEAR & SWITCHBOARD APPARATUS

ABB Inc.. F 614 818-6300
  Westerville (G-15646)
Asco Power Technologies LP................. C 216 573-7600
  Cleveland (G-3685)
Avtron Loadbank Inc.......................... C 216 573-7600
  Cleveland (G-3711)

Employee Codes: A=Over 500 employees, B=251-500
C=101-250, D=51-100, E=20-50, F=10-19, G=1-9

SWITCHGEAR & SWITCHBOARD APPARATUS

CDI Industries Inc .... E 440 243-1100
  Cleveland (G-3802)
Delta Systems Inc .... B 330 626-2811
  Streetsboro (G-13765)
Emerson Network Power .... F 614 841-8054
  Ironton (G-8697)
Flood Heliarc Inc .... F 614 835-3929
  Groveport (G-8140)
General Electric Company .... E 216 883-1000
  Cleveland (G-4115)
Joslyn Hi-Voltage Company LLC .... C 216 271-6600
  Cleveland (G-4261)
Mercury Iron and Steel Co .... F 440 349-1500
  Solon (G-13385)
Myers Power Products Inc .... C 330 834-3200
  North Canton (G-11747)
Npas Inc .... F 614 595-6916
  Mansfield (G-9706)
Roemer Industries Inc .... D 330 448-2000
  Masury (G-10158)
Schneider Automation Inc .... C 612 426-0709
  Fairfield (G-7405)
Schneider Electric Usa Inc .... D 513 777-4445
  West Chester (G-15506)
Siemens Industry Inc .... E 937 593-6010
  Bellefontaine (G-1219)
Toledo Transducers Inc .... E 419 724-4170
  Maumee (G-10242)
Westbrook Mfg Inc .... B 937 254-2004
  Dayton (G-6650)

SWITCHGEAR & SWITCHGEAR ACCESS, NEC

Ideal Electric Power Co .... E 419 522-3611
  Mansfield (G-9669)
Pacs Industries Inc .... D 740 397-5021
  Mount Vernon (G-11285)

SYNTHETIC RESIN FINISHED PRDTS, NEC

Orbis Corporation .... B 937 652-1361
  Urbana (G-14845)
Reactive Resin Products Co .... C 419 666-6119
  Perrysburg (G-12423)

SYRUPS, DRINK

Central Coca-Cola Btlg Co Inc .... C 419 476-6622
  Toledo (G-14230)
Dominion Liquid Tech LLC .... E 513 272-2824
  Cincinnati (G-2836)
Innovtive Cnfction Sltions LLC .... F 440 835-8001
  Westlake (G-15761)
Slush Puppie .... F 513 771-0940
  West Chester (G-15587)

SYSTEMS ENGINEERING: Computer Related

Freedom Usa Inc .... E 216 503-6374
  Twinsburg (G-14662)
Leidos Inc .... D 937 656-8433
  Beavercreek (G-1055)

SYSTEMS INTEGRATION SVCS

Advanced Prgrm Resources Inc .... E 614 761-9994
  Dublin (G-6857)
Creative Microsystems Inc .... D 937 836-4499
  Englewood (G-7227)
Data Processing Sciences Corporation . D 513 791-7100
  Cincinnati (G-2820)
Generic Systems Inc .... F 419 841-8460
  Holland (G-8510)
Kc Robotics Inc .... E 513 860-4442
  West Chester (G-15452)

Smartronix Inc .... F 216 378-3300
  Northfield (G-11910)
Systemax Manufacturing Inc .... D 937 368-2300
  Dayton (G-6604)

SYSTEMS INTEGRATION SVCS: Local Area Network

Town Cntry Technical Svcs Inc .... F 614 866-7700
  Reynoldsburg (G-12775)

SYSTEMS SOFTWARE DEVELOPMENT SVCS

CHI Corporation .... G 440 498-2300
  Cleveland (G-3818)
Cincinnati Ctrl Dynamics Inc .... G 513 242-7300
  Cincinnati (G-2746)
Deemsys Inc .... D 614 322-9928
  Gahanna (G-7833)
Dewesoft LLC .... D 855 339-3669
  Whitehouse (G-15817)
Drb Holdings LLC .... B 330 645-3299
  Akron (G-134)
Drb Systems LLC .... B 330 645-3299
  Akron (G-135)
Online Mega Sellers Corp .... G 888 384-6468
  Toledo (G-14415)
Pinnacle Data Systems Inc .... C 614 748-1150
  Groveport (G-8158)

TABLE OR COUNTERTOPS, PLASTIC LAMINATED

Archer Counter Design Inc .... G 513 396-7526
  Cincinnati (G-2631)
Customworks Inc .... G 614 262-1002
  Columbus (G-5312)
E J Skok Industries .... E 216 292-7533
  Bedford (G-1119)
Helmart Company Inc .... G 513 941-3095
  Cincinnati (G-2992)
Laminated Concepts Inc .... F 216 475-4141
  Maple Heights (G-9753)
Rusco Products Inc .... G 330 758-0378
  Youngstown (G-16432)
Scio Laminated Products Inc .... F 740 945-1321
  Scio (G-13112)
Shur-Fit Distributors Inc .... F 937 746-0567
  Franklin (G-7702)
Wdi Group Inc .... D 216 251-5509
  Cleveland (G-4898)
Youngstown Curve Form Inc .... F 330 744-3028
  Youngstown (G-16480)

TABLEWARE: Vitreous China

Libbey Inc .... C 419 325-2100
  Toledo (G-14366)

TAGS & LABELS: Paper

Kay Toledo Tag Inc .... D 419 729-5479
  Toledo (G-14346)
Kennedy Group Incorporated .... D 440 951-7660
  Willoughby (G-15939)
Markham Converting Limited .... F 419 353-2458
  Bowling Green (G-1574)
Orbytel Print and Packg Inc .... G 216 267-8734
  Cleveland (G-4508)
The Hooven - Dayton Corp .... C 937 233-4473
  Miamisburg (G-10694)
Warren Printing & Off Pdts Inc .... F 419 523-3635
  Ottawa (G-12196)

TANK REPAIR & CLEANING SVCS

Amko Service Company .... E 330 364-8857
  Midvale (G-10875)
Kars Ohio LLC .... G 614 655-1099
  Pataskala (G-12300)
National Wldg Tanker Repr LLC .... G 614 875-3399
  Grove City (G-8510)
Ohio Hydraulics Inc .... E 513 771-2590
  Cincinnati (G-3215)
Sabco Industries Inc .... E 419 531-5347
  Toledo (G-14460)

TANK REPAIR SVCS

Corrotec Inc .... E 937 325-3585
  Springfield (G-1547)
Frontier Tank Center Inc .... F 330 659-3888
  Richfield (G-12758)
Schaeffer Metal Products Inc .... G 330 296-6226
  Ravenna (G-12732)

TANK TOWERS: Metal Plate

Complete Mechanical Svcs LLC .... D 513 489-3080
  Blue Ash (G-1362)

TANKS & OTHER TRACKED VEHICLE CMPNTS

CSC .... G 419 221-7037
  Lima (G-9231)
Integris Composites Inc .... D 740 928-0326
  Hebron (G-8345)
Performance Tank Sales Inc .... G
  Dover (G-6839)
Tessec Manufacturing Svcs LLC .... E 937 985-3552
  Dayton (G-6616)
US Yachiyo Inc .... C 740 375-4687
  Marion (G-9888)
Weldon Pump LLC .... E 440 232-2282
  Oakwood Village (G-12047)

TANKS: Concrete

Star Manufacturing LLC .... C 330 740-8300
  Youngstown (G-1447)

TANKS: Cryogenic, Metal

Amko Service Company .... E 330 364-8857
  Midvale (G-10875)
Eleet Cryogenics Inc .... E 330 874-4009
  Bolivar (G-1524)
Fiba Technologies Inc .... F 330 602-7300
  Midvale (G-10877)

TANKS: For Tank Trucks, Metal Plate

Elliott Machine Works Inc .... E 419 468-4709
  Galion (G-7874)
Liquid Luggers LLC .... E 330 426-2538
  East Palestine (G-7006)

TANKS: Fuel, Including Oil & Gas, Metal Plate

Convault of Ohio Inc .... G 614 252-8422
  Columbus (G-5293)
Fabstar Tanks Inc .... G 419 587-3639
  Grover Hill (G-8162)
Stanwade Metal Products Inc .... E 330 772-2421
  Hartford (G-8298)

TANKS: Lined, Metal

Hamilton Tanks LLC .... F 614 445-8446
  Columbus (G-5418)

PRODUCT SECTION TEXTILE FINISHING: Napping, Manmade Fiber & Silk, Broadwoven

Modern Welding Co Ohio Inc............... E 740 344-9425
   Newark (G-11593)

TANKS: Military, Including Factory Rebuilding

General Dynmics Land Systems I........... B 419 221-7000
   Lima (G-9245)

TANKS: Plastic & Fiberglass

Aco Inc... E 440 639-7230
   Mentor (G-10403)
Alliance Equipment Company Inc.......... F 330 821-2291
   Alliance (G-392)
Industrial Container Svcs LLC................ E 513 921-2056
   Cincinnati (G-3020)
Kar-Del Plastics Inc................................ G 419 289-9739
   Ashland (G-583)
Norwesco Inc... F 740 654-6402
   Lancaster (G-9031)
R L Industries Inc................................... D 513 874-2800
   West Chester (G-15493)
Wasca LLC... E 937 723-9031
   Dayton (G-6647)

TANKS: Standard Or Custom Fabricated, Metal Plate

Buckeye Fabricating Company............... E 937 746-9822
   Springboro (G-13497)
Compco Columbiana Company............... D 330 482-0200
   Columbiana (G-5035)
Compco Youngstown Company............... D 330 482-6488
   Columbiana (G-5036)
Dabar Industries LLC............................. F 614 873-3949
   Columbus (G-5313)
Enerfab LLC... B 513 641-0500
   Cincinnati (G-2872)
Gaspar Inc.. D 330 477-2222
   Canton (G-2110)
Hason USA Corp..................................... F 513 248-0287
   Cincinnati (G-2988)
M & H Fabricating Co Inc....................... G 937 325-8708
   Springfield (G-13596)
Odom Industries Inc.............................. E 513 248-0287
   Milford (G-10915)
Rebsco Inc.. F 937 548-2246
   Greenville (G-8057)
S-P Company Inc.................................... D 330 782-5651
   Columbiana (G-5050)
Seneca Environmental Products Inc...... E 419 447-1282
   Tiffin (G-14104)

TANKS: Storage, Farm, Metal Plate

Industrial Farm Tank Inc....................... E 937 843-2972
   Lewistown (G-9194)
Rcr Partnership...................................... G 419 340-1202
   Genoa (G-7948)

TAPE DRIVES

CHI Corporation..................................... G 440 498-2300
   Cleveland (G-3818)

TAPES: Coated Fiberglass, Pipe Sealing Or Insulating

Richard Klinger Inc................................ G 937 498-2222
   Sidney (G-13276)

TAPES: Pressure Sensitive

Strata-Tac Inc.. F 630 879-9388
   Troy (G-14613)

TAPES: Pressure Sensitive, Rubber

3M Company... E 330 725-1444
   Medina (G-10288)
Austin Tape and Label Inc..................... D 330 928-7999
   Stow (G-13686)
Beiersdorf Inc... C 513 682-7300
   West Chester (G-15541)
Cortape Inc... F 330 929-6700
   Cuyahoga Falls (G-6076)
Lockfast LLC... G 800 543-7157
   Loveland (G-9491)
Progressive Supply LLC......................... F 570 688-9636
   Willoughby (G-15977)
The Hooven - Dayton Corp..................... C 937 233-4473
   Miamisburg (G-10694)

TARGET DRONES

Drone Express Inc................................. F 513 577-5152
   Dayton (G-6304)

TARPAULINS

Custom Tarpaulin Products Inc.............. F 330 758-1801
   Youngstown (G-16345)
Lesch Boat Cover Canvas Co LLC........... G 419 668-6374
   Norwalk (G-11977)
Rainbow Industries Inc.......................... G 937 323-6493
   Springfield (G-13623)
Tarpco Inc... F 330 677-8277
   Kent (G-8871)
Toledo Tarp Service Inc.......................... F 419 837-5098
   Perrysburg (G-12440)
Tri County Tarp LLC.............................. E 419 288-3350
   Gibsonburg (G-7956)

TARPAULINS, WHOLESALE

Berlin Truck Caps & Tarps Ltd............... F 330 893-2811
   Millersburg (G-10944)

TECHNICAL MANUAL PREPARATION SVCS

ONeil & Associates Inc.......................... C 937 865-0800
   Miamisburg (G-10669)

TELECOMMUNICATION EQPT REPAIR SVCS, EXC TELEPHONES

Cbst Acquisition LLC.............................. D 513 361-9600
   Cincinnati (G-2711)
Town Cntry Technical Svcs Inc............... F 614 866-7700
   Reynoldsburg (G-12775)
Vertiv Energy Systems Inc..................... A 440 288-1122
   Lorain (G-9443)
Vertiv Group Corporation....................... G 440 288-1122
   Lorain (G-9444)

TELEMETERING EQPT

L3 Technologies Inc............................... G 937 257-8501
   Dayton (G-6165)

TELEPHONE BOOTHS, EXC WOOD

Ray Communications Inc....................... G 330 686-0226
   Stow (G-13720)

TELEPHONE EQPT: Modems

Black Box Corporation............................ G 855 324-9909
   Westlake (G-15738)
C Dcap Modem Line............................... G 419 748-7409
   Mc Clure (G-10265)

TELEPHONE EQPT: NEC

Arnco Corporation.................................. D 800 847-7661
   Elyria (G-7112)

Commercial Electric Pdts Corp............... E 216 241-2886
   Cleveland (G-3889)
Siemens AG.. E 513 576-2451
   Mason (G-10055)
Siemens Energy Inc............................... E 740 393-8200
   Mount Vernon (G-11294)

TELEPHONE STATION EQPT & PARTS: Wire

Christopher Sweeney............................. G 513 276-4350
   Troy (G-14554)

TELEPHONE SVCS

Total Call Center Solutions.................... F 330 869-9844
   Akron (G-361)

TELEVISION BROADCASTING & COMMUNICATIONS EQPT

Nissin Precision N Amer Inc.................. D 937 836-1910
   Englewood (G-7238)
Punch Components Inc.......................... E 419 224-1242
   Lima (G-9280)

TELEVISION BROADCASTING STATIONS

Block Communications Inc.................... F 419 724-6212
   Toledo (G-14214)

TELEVISION: Closed Circuit Eqpt

Diamond Electronics Inc........................ D 740 652-9222
   Lancaster (G-9010)

TELEVISION: Monitors

Edl Displays Inc..................................... E 937 429-7423
   Beavercreek (G-1050)

TEMPORARY HELP SVCS

Cima Inc... G 513 382-8976
   Hamilton (G-8192)
Upshift Work LLC................................... C 513 813-5695
   Cincinnati (G-3485)

TERMINAL BOARDS

Osborne Coinage Company LLC............. D 877 480-0456
   Blue Ash (G-1448)

TESTERS: Battery

Battery Unlimited.................................. G 740 452-5030
   Zanesville (G-16506)
Zts Inc... F 513 271-2557
   Cincinnati (G-3538)

TESTERS: Physical Property

Kw Acquisition Inc................................. G 740 548-7298
   Lewis Center (G-9168)
Pressco Technology Inc.......................... D 440 498-2600
   Cleveland (G-4585)
Test Mark Industries Inc........................ F 330 426-2200
   East Palestine (G-7010)

TESTING SVCS

Alpha Technologies Svcs LLC................. D 330 745-1641
   Hudson (G-8583)
Orton Edward Jr Crmic Fndation............ E 614 895-2663
   Westerville (G-15672)

TEXTILE DESIGNERS

Standard Textile Co Inc......................... B 513 761-9255
   Cincinnati (G-3415)

TEXTILE FINISHING: Napping, Manmade Fiber & Silk, Broadwoven

TEXTILE FINISHING: Napping, Manmade Fiber & Silk, Broadwoven — PRODUCT SECTION

Tranzonic Companies............................ C 440 446-0643
　Cleveland (G-4818)
Tz Acquisition Corp.............................. E 216 535-4300
　Richmond Heights (G-12812)

TEXTILES: Linen Fabrics

Standard Textile Co Inc........................ B 513 761-9255
　Cincinnati (G-3415)

THEATRICAL PRODUCTION SVCS

North Coast Theatrical Inc.................... G 330 762-1768
　Akron (G-266)

THEATRICAL SCENERY

Erie Street Thea Svcs Inc..................... G 216 426-0050
　Cleveland (G-4028)
Scarefactory Inc.................................. F 614 565-3590
　Columbus (G-5750)
Schell Scenic Studio Inc...................... G 614 444-9550
　Millersport (G-11013)

THERMISTORS, EXC TEMPERATURE SENSORS

Measurement Specialties Inc................ E 937 427-1231
　Dayton (G-6433)

THERMOCOUPLES

Blaze Technical Services Inc................ E 330 923-0409
　Stow (G-13688)
Heraeus Electro-Nite Co LLC............... G 330 725-1419
　Medina (G-10333)

THERMOPLASTIC MATERIALS

Amros Industries Inc........................... E 216 433-0010
　Cleveland (G-3659)
Avient Corporation.............................. D 440 930-1000
　Avon Lake (G-797)
Genius Solutions Engrg Co................... E 419 794-9914
　Maumee (G-10202)
Geon Performance Solutions LLC......... E 440 930-1000
　Avon Lake (G-809)
Hexpol Compounding LLC.................... E 440 834-4644
　Burton (G-1881)
Integra Enclosures Limited.................. D 440 269-4966
　Mentor (G-10474)
Polyone Funding Corporation............... E 440 930-1000
　Avon Lake (G-822)
Polyone LLC.. E 440 930-1000
　Avon Lake (G-823)
Ppl Holding Company........................... E 216 514-1840
　Cleveland (G-4570)

THERMOSETTING MATERIALS

Current Inc... G 330 392-5151
　Warren (G-15159)
Hexion LLC... D 614 225-4000
　Columbus (G-5429)
Hexion Topco LLC................................ D 614 225-4000
　Columbus (G-5430)

TILE: Brick & Structural, Clay

Armstrong World Industries Inc............ E 614 771-9307
　Hilliard (G-8399)
Glen-Gery Corporation......................... F 419 468-4890
　Galion (G-7879)
Kepcor Inc.. F 330 868-6434
　Minerva (G-11032)
LBC Clay Co LLC................................. G 330 674-0674
　Millersburg (G-10972)
Minteq International Inc...................... E 330 343-3821
　Dover (G-6836)

Resco Products Inc.............................. G 740 682-7794
　Oak Hill (G-12024)
Stebbins Engineering & Mfg Co............ F 740 922-3012
　Uhrichsville (G-14770)

TILE: Clay, Drain & Structural

Haviland Drainage Products Co............. F 800 860-6294
　Haviland (G-8312)

TILE: Wall & Floor, Ceramic

Wccv Floor Coverings LLC................... F 330 688-0114
　Peninsula (G-12344)

TIN

Tin Wizard Heating & Coolg Inc............ G 330 467-9826
　Macedonia (G-9584)

TIRE & INNER TUBE MATERIALS & RELATED PRDTS

American Airless Inc............................ F 614 552-0146
　Reynoldsburg (G-12751)
Grove Engineered Products.................. G 419 659-5939
　Columbus Grove (G-5898)
Troy Engnred Cmpnnts Assmblies........ G 937 335-8070
　Dayton (G-6635)
Truflex Rubber Products Co................. C 740 967-9015
　Johnstown (G-8782)

TIRE & TUBE REPAIR MATERIALS, WHOLESALE

Mark Knupp Muffler & Tire Inc............. E 937 773-1334
　Piqua (G-12535)
Myers Industries Inc............................ E 330 253-5592
　Akron (G-260)
Technical Rubber Company Inc............ C 740 967-9015
　Johnstown (G-8779)

TIRE CORD & FABRIC

Cleveland Canvas Goods Mfg Co........... E 216 361-4567
　Cleveland (G-3835)
Mfh Partners Inc................................. B 440 461-4100
　Cleveland (G-4398)

TIRE SUNDRIES OR REPAIR MATERIALS: Rubber

31 Inc... D 740 498-8324
　Newcomerstown (G-11640)
Swiss Valley Tire LLC.......................... G 330 231-6187
　Wilmot (G-16069)
Technical Rubber Company Inc............ C 740 967-9015
　Johnstown (G-8779)

TIRES & INNER TUBES

B & S Transport Inc............................. G 330 767-4319
　Navarre (G-11340)
BF & CD Roberts RE Imprv.................. G 937 277-2632
　Dayton (G-6228)
Bkt USA Inc.. F 330 836-1090
　Copley (G-5944)
Bridgestone Amrcas Tire Oprtons........ D 330 379-3714
　Akron (G-92)
Empire Tire Inc.................................... G 330 983-4176
　Tallmadge (G-14030)
Jamies Tire & Service.......................... G 937 372-9254
　Xenia (G-16266)
North American Assemblies LLC.......... E 843 420-5354
　Dublin (G-6916)
Oliver Rubber Co................................. G 419 420-6235
　Findlay (G-7546)

Titan Tire Corporation......................... B 419 633-4221
　Bryan (G-1840)
Titan Tire Corporation Bryan................ E 419 633-4224
　Bryan (G-1841)
Umd Contractors Inc........................... F 740 694-8614
　Fredericktown (G-7757)

TIRES & TUBES WHOLESALERS

B & S Transport Inc............................. G 330 767-4319
　Navarre (G-11340)
Best One Tire & Svc Lima Inc.............. G 419 425-3322
　Findlay (G-7484)
Bob Sumerel Tire Co Inc...................... F 614 527-9700
　Columbus (G-5234)
Bob Sumerel Tire Co Inc...................... F 740 432-5200
　Lore City (G-945)
Bob Sumerel Tire Company Inc............ G 740 927-2811
　Reynoldsburg (G-12755)
Forklift Tire East Mich Inc................... F 586 771-1330
　Toledo (G-14292)
Gt Tire Service Inc............................... G 740 927-7226
　Pataskala (G-12298)

TIRES & TUBES, WHOLESALE: Automotive

AB Tire & Repair................................. G 440 543-2929
　Chagrin Falls (G-2386)
Associates Tire and Svc Inc................. F 937 436-4692
　Centerville (G-2359)
Bell Tire Co.. F 440 234-8022
　Olmsted Falls (G-12076)
Best One Tire & Svc Lima Inc.............. G 419 425-3322
　Findlay (G-7484)
Best One Tire & Svc Lima Inc.............. G 419 229-2380
　Lima (G-9223)
Bkt USA Inc.. F 330 836-1090
　Copley (G-5944)
Bob Sumerel Tire Co Inc...................... F 937 235-0062
　Dayton (G-6233)
Bob Sumerel Tire Co Inc...................... G 740 432-5200
　Lore City (G-9440)
Bob Sumerel Tire Co Inc...................... G 330 769-9092
　Seville (G-13140)
Bob Sumerel Tire Co Inc...................... G 740 454-9728
　Zanesville (G-16502)
Bob Sumerel Tire Company.................. G 330 262-1220
　Wooster (G-16100)
Bob Sumerel Tire Company Inc............ G 740 927-2811
　Reynoldsburg (G-12755)
Boy RAD Inc....................................... F 614 766-1228
　Dublin (G-6869)
Bridgestone Ret Operations LLC.......... G 740 592-3075
　Athens (G-677)
Bridgestone Ret Operations LLC.......... G 614 834-3672
　Canal Winchester (G-1982)
Bridgestone Ret Operations LLC.......... G 330 454-9478
　Canton (G-2053)
Bridgestone Ret Operations LLC.......... G 513 681-7682
　Cincinnati (G-2683)
Bridgestone Ret Operations LLC.......... G 513 793-4550
　Cincinnati (G-2684)
Bridgestone Ret Operations LLC.......... G 513 677-5200
　Cincinnati (G-2685)
Bridgestone Ret Operations LLC.......... G 440 842-3200
　Cleveland (G-3756)
Bridgestone Ret Operations LLC.......... G 440 461-4747
　Cleveland (G-3757)
Bridgestone Ret Operations LLC.......... G 216 229-2550
　Cleveland (G-3758)
Bridgestone Ret Operations LLC.......... G 216 382-8970
　Cleveland (G-3759)
Bridgestone Ret Operations LLC.......... F 614 864-3350
　Columbus (G-5214)

PRODUCT SECTION

TRAILERS & PARTS: Boat

Bridgestone Ret Operations LLC............ F 614 491-8062
Columbus (G-5215)

Bridgestone Ret Operations LLC............ G 614 224-4221
Columbus (G-5216)

Bridgestone Ret Operations LLC............ G 440 324-3327
Elyria (G-7117)

Bridgestone Ret Operations LLC............ G 440 365-8308
Elyria (G-7118)

Bridgestone Ret Operations LLC............ G 937 548-1197
Greenville (G-8039)

Bridgestone Ret Operations LLC............ G 513 868-7399
Hamilton (G-8186)

Bridgestone Ret Operations LLC............ G 330 673-1700
Kent (G-8803)

Bridgestone Ret Operations LLC............ F 440 299-6126
Mentor (G-10431)

Bridgestone Ret Operations LLC............ F 740 397-5601
Mount Vernon (G-11265)

Bridgestone Ret Operations LLC............ G 614 861-7994
Reynoldsburg (G-12756)

Bridgestone Ret Operations LLC............ G 419 625-6571
Sandusky (G-13045)

Bridgestone Ret Operations LLC............ G 937 325-4638
Springfield (G-13540)

Bridgestone Ret Operations LLC............ G 330 758-0921
Youngstown (G-16325)

Bridgestone Ret Operations LLC............ G 330 759-3697
Youngstown (G-16326)

Canton Bandag Co............ F 330 454-3025
Canton (G-2060)

Capital Tire Inc............ E 330 364-4731
Toledo (G-14227)

Colyer C & Sons Truck Service............ G 513 563-0663
Cincinnati (G-2781)

Custom Recapping Inc............ G 937 324-4331
Springfield (G-13550)

Exit 11 Truck Tire Service............ G 330 659-6372
Richfield (G-12786)

Garro Tread Corporation............ G 330 376-3125
Akron (G-162)

Goodyear Tire & Rubber Company............ F 419 643-8273
Beaverdam (G-1096)

Goodyear Tire & Rubber Company............ G 330 966-1274
Canton (G-2116)

Goodyear Tire & Rubber Company............ G 330 759-9343
Youngstown (G-16371)

Goodyear Tire & Rubber Company............ A 330 796-2121
Akron (G-171)

Grismer Tire Company............ E 937 643-2526
Centerville (G-2363)

JTL Enterprises LLC............ G 937 890-8189
Dayton (G-6392)

L & O Tire Service Inc............ G 937 394-8462
Anna (G-490)

Mid America Tire of Hillsboro Inc............ E 937 393-3520
Hillsboro (G-8461)

Mid-Wood Inc............ F 419 257-3331
North Baltimore (G-11696)

Mitchell Bros Tire Rtread Svc............ G 740 353-1551
Portsmouth (G-12649)

Ntb National Tire and Battery............ G 614 870-8945
Columbus (G-5606)

Paul Shovlin............ G 330 757-0032
Youngstown (G-16416)

Q T Columbus LLC............ G 800 758-2410
Columbus (G-5700)

QT Equipment Company............ E 330 724-3055
Akron (G-289)

Shrader Tire & Oil Inc............ G 419 420-4350
Perrysburg (G-12426)

Skinner Firestone Inc............ F 740 984-4247
Beverly (G-1321)

Snider Tire Inc............ E 740 439-2741
Cambridge (G-1953)

Tbc Retail Group Inc............ E 216 267-8040
Cleveland (G-4768)

Wayne A Whaley............ G 330 525-7779
Homeworth (G-8556)

Ziegler Tire and Supply Co............ G 330 434-7126
Akron (G-381)

Ziegler Tire and Supply Co............ G 330 477-3463
Canton (G-2273)

Ziegler Tire and Supply Co............ E 330 343-7739
Dover (G-6850)

TOBACCO & TOBACCO PRDTS WHOLESALERS

Scandinavian Tob Group Ln Ltd............ C 770 934-4594
Akron (G-325)

TOBACCO: Chewing & Snuff

Smoke Rings Inc............ G 419 420-9966
Findlay (G-7564)

TOBACCO: Cigarettes

Discount Smokes & Gifts Xenia............ G 937 372-0259
Xenia (G-16260)

Memphis Smokehouse Inc............ G 216 351-5321
Cleveland (G-4393)

TOBACCO: Smoking

Scandinavian Tob Group Ln Ltd............ C 770 934-4594
Akron (G-325)

TOILET PREPARATIONS

Barbasol LLC............ E 419 903-0738
Ashland (G-555)

Bocchi Laboratories Ohio LLC............ B 614 741-7458
New Albany (G-11370)

Noi Enhancements LLC............ G 216 218-4136
University Heights (G-14798)

Procter & Gamble Distrg Co............ G 513 983-1100
Cincinnati (G-3294)

Procter & Gamble Far East Inc............ C 513 983-1100
Cincinnati (G-3295)

Procter & Gamble Mfg Co............ F 513 983-1100
Cincinnati (G-3298)

TOILETRIES, WHOLESALE: Hair Preparations

ICM Distributing Company Inc............ E 234 212-3030
Twinsburg (G-14675)

TOILETRIES, WHOLESALE: Perfumes

Beautyavenues LLC............ C 614 856-6000
Reynoldsburg (G-12754)

TOILETRIES, WHOLESALE: Toiletries

Nehemiah Manufacturing Co LLC............ D 513 351-5700
Cincinnati (G-3185)

Walter F Stephens Jr Inc............ E 937 746-0521
Franklin (G-7709)

TOILETS: Portable Chemical, Plastics

Slm LLC............ G 330 874-7131
Bolivar (G-1537)

TOOL & DIE STEEL

Askar Productive Resources LLC............ G 440 946-0393
Willoughby (G-15887)

B & G Tool Company............ G 614 451-2538
Columbus (G-5170)

Carter Scott-Browne............ G 513 398-3970
Mason (G-9969)

Latrobe Specialty Mtls Co LLC............ E 419 335-8010
Wauseon (G-15266)

New Age Design & Tool Inc............ F 440 355-5400
Lagrange (G-8953)

Nichidai America Corporation............ F 419 423-7511
Findlay (G-7542)

OReilly Precision Pdts Inc............ E 937 526-4677
Russia (G-12886)

Quality Tool Company............ E 419 476-8228
Toledo (G-14444)

R & D Machine Inc............ F 937 339-2545
Troy (G-14603)

Seilkop Industries Inc............ F 513 353-3090
Miamitown (G-10709)

TOOLS: Hand, Mechanics

S & H Industries Inc............ E 216 831-0550
Cleveland (G-4664)

S & H Industries Inc............ F 216 831-0550
Bedford (G-1154)

The Cornwell Quality Tools Company............ D 330 336-3506
Wadsworth (G-15069)

TOWELS: Fabric & Nonwoven, Made From Purchased Materials

Saturday Knight Ltd............ D 513 641-1400
Cincinnati (G-3363)

TOWELS: Paper

Aci Industries Converting Ltd............ F 740 368-4160
Delaware (G-6700)

TOWERS, SECTIONS: Transmission, Radio & Television

Amto Acquisition Corp............ F 419 347-1185
Shelby (G-13190)

Warmus and Associates Inc............ F 330 659-4440
Bath (G-962)

TOWING SVCS: Marine

Great Lakes Group............ C 216 621-4854
Cleveland (G-4145)

TOYS & HOBBY GOODS & SPLYS, WHOLESALE: Toys & Games

Party Animal Inc............ F 440 471-1030
Westlake (G-15771)

TOYS & HOBBY GOODS & SPLYS, WHOLESALE: Toys, NEC

Advance Novelty Incorporated............ G 419 424-0363
Findlay (G-7472)

ICM Distributing Company Inc............ E 234 212-3030
Twinsburg (G-14675)

TOYS: Rubber

Pioneer National Latex Inc............ D 419 289-3300
Ashland (G-601)

Pioneer National Latex Inc............ E 419 289-3300
Ashland (G-602)

TRADE SHOW ARRANGEMENT SVCS

Downing Enterprises Inc............ D 330 666-3888
Copley (G-5948)

Publishing Group Ltd............ F 614 572-1240
Columbus (G-5697)

TRAILERS & PARTS: Boat

Hitch-Hiker Mfg Inc................................F 330 542-3052
New Middletown *(G-11478)*

Loadmaster Trailer Company Ltd..........F 419 732-3434
Port Clinton *(G-12622)*

TRAILERS & TRAILER EQPT

Blue Ribbon Trailers Ltd.......................G 330 538-4114
North Jackson *(G-11779)*

Buckeye Trailer & Fab Co LLC..............G 330 501-9440
Damascus *(G-6147)*

Fitchville East Corp..............................G 419 929-1510
New London *(G-11462)*

Hawkline Nevada LLC...........................G 937 444-4295
Mount Orab *(G-11241)*

Interstate Truckway Inc.......................F 614 771-1220
Columbus *(G-5477)*

Malabar..E 419 866-6301
Swanton *(G-13978)*

Otterbacher Trailers LLC.....................F 419 462-1975
Galion *(G-7882)*

Performance Tank Sales Inc................G
Dover *(G-6839)*

Prostar LLC..F 419 225-8806
Lima *(G-9306)*

Rankin Mfg Inc....................................E 419 929-8338
New London *(G-11466)*

TRAILERS: Semitrailers, Missile Transportation

Pdi Ground Support Systems Inc..........D 216 271-7344
Solon *(G-13403)*

TRAILERS: Semitrailers, Truck Tractors

4w Services...F 614 554-5427
Hebron *(G-8334)*

Nelson Manufacturing Company..........D 419 523-5321
Ottawa *(G-12185)*

TRANSDUCERS: Electrical Properties

Dcm Soundex Inc.................................F 937 522-0371
Dayton *(G-6295)*

Guitammer Company............................G 614 898-9370
Columbus *(G-5413)*

Ohio Semitronics Inc...........................D 614 777-1005
Hilliard *(G-8427)*

TRANSDUCERS: Pressure

Honeywell International Inc................D 302 327-8920
Columbus *(G-5444)*

Omega Engineering Inc.......................E 740 965-9340
Sunbury *(G-13962)*

Omegadyne Inc...................................D 740 965-9340
Sunbury *(G-13963)*

Sensotec LLC......................................G 614 481-8616
Hilliard *(G-8440)*

TRANSFORMERS: Distribution

Darrah Electric Company.....................F 216 631-0912
Cleveland *(G-3942)*

TRANSFORMERS: Distribution, Electric

Clark Substations LLC.........................F 330 452-5200
Canton *(G-2077)*

Tesa Inc...G 614 847-8200
Lewis Center *(G-9181)*

TRANSFORMERS: Instrument

Staco Energy Products Co...................E 937 253-1191
Dayton *(G-6587)*

TRANSFORMERS: Specialty

LTI Power Systems Inc........................E 440 327-5050
Elyria *(G-7176)*

TRANSFORMERS: Voltage Regulating

Transformer Associates Limited..........G 330 430-0750
Canton *(G-2247)*

TRANSMISSIONS: Motor Vehicle

Ada Technologies Inc..........................C 419 634-7000
Ada *(G-2)*

Askar Productive Resources LLC........G 440 946-0393
Willoughby *(G-15887)*

Comprehensive Logistics Co Inc..........E 440 934-3517
Avon *(G-768)*

Custom Cltch Jint Hydrlics Inc............F 216 431-1630
Cleveland *(G-3923)*

FCA North America Holdings LLC........C 419 661-3500
Perrysburg *(G-12380)*

Gear Star American Performance........G 330 434-5216
Akron *(G-163)*

Modern Transmission Dev Co..............C
Valley City *(G-14880)*

RTC Converters Inc.............................F 937 743-2300
Franklin *(G-7700)*

TRANSPORTATION EQPT & SPLYS WHOLESALERS, NEC

American Power LLC...........................F 937 235-0418
Dayton *(G-6202)*

Dircksen and Associates Inc................G 614 238-0413
Columbus *(G-5327)*

TRANSPORTATION SVCS, AIR, NONSCHEDULED: Air Cargo Carriers

Grand Aire Inc.....................................E 419 861-6700
Swanton *(G-13974)*

TRAVEL TRAILERS & CAMPERS

Airstream Inc.......................................B 937 596-6111
Jackson Center *(G-8729)*

ARE Inc..A 330 830-7800
Massillon *(G-10076)*

Gerich Fiberglass Inc..........................F 419 362-4591
Mount Gilead *(G-11233)*

Xtreme Outdoors LLC..........................E 330 731-4137
Uniontown *(G-14797)*

TROPHIES, NEC

Ginos Awards Inc................................E 216 831-6565
Warrensville Heights *(G-15229)*

Tempo Manufacturing Company...........G 937 773-6613
Piqua *(G-12556)*

TROPHIES, WHOLESALE

Behrco Inc...G 419 394-1612
Saint Marys *(G-12945)*

Dern Trophies Corp.............................F 614 895-3260
Westerville *(G-15653)*

Sharonco Inc.......................................G 419 882-3443
Sylvania *(G-14014)*

TROPHIES: Metal, Exc Silver

Dern Trophies Corp.............................F 614 895-3260
Westerville *(G-15653)*

Hit Trophy Inc.....................................G 419 445-5356
Archbold *(G-532)*

PS Superior Inc..................................E 216 587-1000
Cleveland *(G-4596)*

TRUCK & BUS BODIES: Bus Bodies

Gerich Fiberglass Inc..........................F 419 362-4591
Mount Gilead *(G-11233)*

TRUCK & BUS BODIES: Car Carrier

Kilar Manufacturing Inc.......................F 330 534-8961
Hubbard *(G-857)*

TRUCK & BUS BODIES: Cement Mixer

Kimble Mixer Company........................D 330 308-6700
New Philadelphia *(G-11509)*

McNeilus Truck and Mfg Inc................E 513 874-2022
Fairfield *(G-738)*

McNeilus Truck and Mfg Inc................E 614 868-0760
Gahanna *(G-784)*

TRUCK & BUS BODIES: Motor Vehicle, Specialty

Bush Specialty Vehicles Inc................F 937 382-5502
Wilmington *(G-15042)*

Lifeline Mobile Inc...............................D 614 497-8300
Obetz *(G-12061)*

Willard Machine & Welding Inc............F 330 467-0642
Macedonia *(G-9386)*

TRUCK & BUS BODIES: Truck Beds

Zie Bart Rhino Linings Toledo..............G 419 841-2886
Toledo *(G-14533)*

TRUCK & BUS BODIES: Utility Truck

Custom Truck One Source LP..............E 330 409-7291
Canton *(G-2085)*

Q T Columbus LLC..............................G 800 758-2410
Columbus *(G-5730)*

QT Equipment Company......................E 330 724-3055
Akron *(G-289)*

TRUCK BODIES: Body Parts

ARE Inc..A 330 830-7800
Massillon *(G-10076)*

Brothers Body and Eqp LLC.................F 419 462-1975
Galion *(G-7862)*

Composite Panel Tech Co....................G 704 310-5838
Strongsville *(G-13824)*

Contech Manufacturing Inc.................G 440 946-3322
Willoughby *(G-15902)*

Cota International Inc.........................F 937 526-5520
Versailles *(G-14978)*

Crane Carrier Company LLC................C 918 286-2889
New Philadelphia *(G-11495)*

Crane Carrier Holdings LLC.................C 918 286-2889
New Philadelphia *(G-11496)*

Dan Patrick Enterprises Inc................G 740 477-1006
Circleville *(G-3547)*

H & H Truck Parts LLC.........................E 216 642-4540
Cleveland *(G-4160)*

Kaffenbarger Truck Eqp Co..................E 513 772-6800
Cincinnati *(G-3057)*

Kimble Custom Chassis Company........D 877 546-2537
New Philadelphia *(G-11508)*

Mancor Ohio Inc..................................C 937 228-6141
Dayton *(G-6428)*

Mancor Ohio Inc..................................E 937 228-6141
Dayton *(G-6427)*

Sutphen Towers Inc.............................D 614 876-1262
Hilliard *(G-8444)*

Wilson Seat Company..........................F 513 732-2460
Batavia *(G-961)*

TRUCK BODY SHOP

PRODUCT SECTION

TRUCKS: Indl

Q T Columbus LLC.. G 800 758-2410
 Columbus *(G-5700)*

QT Equipment Company............................. E 330 724-3055
 Akron *(G-289)*

TRUCK GENERAL REPAIR SVC

Colyer C & Sons Truck Service................. G 513 563-0663
 Cincinnati *(G-2781)*

Dan Patrick Enterprises Inc...................... G 740 477-1006
 Circleville *(G-3546)*

Knippen Chrysler Ddge Jeep Inc............. E 419 695-4976
 Delphos *(G-6767)*

L & O Tire Service Inc................................. G 937 394-8462
 Anna *(G-490)*

M & W Trailers Inc....................................... F 419 453-3331
 Ottoville *(G-12201)*

TRUCK PARTS & ACCESSORIES: Wholesalers

Adelmans Truck Parts Corp...................... E 330 456-0206
 Canton *(G-2028)*

Buyers Products Company........................ C 440 974-8888
 Mentor *(G-10435)*

Crane Carrier Company LLC.................... C 918 286-2889
 New Philadelphia *(G-11495)*

Crane Carrier Holdings LLC..................... C 918 286-2889
 New Philadelphia *(G-11496)*

Dan Patrick Enterprises Inc...................... G 740 477-1006
 Circleville *(G-3546)*

East Manufacturing Corporation............. B 330 325-9921
 Randolph *(G-12697)*

Kaffenbarger Truck Eqp Co....................... C 937 845-3804
 New Carlisle *(G-11418)*

Perkins Motor Service Ltd......................... F 440 277-1256
 Lorain *(G-9430)*

Youngstown-Kenworth Inc........................ F 330 534-9761
 Hubbard *(G-8574)*

TRUCKING & HAULING SVCS: Contract Basis

Kmj Leasing Ltd... F 614 871-3883
 Orient *(G-12115)*

TRUCKING & HAULING SVCS: Lumber & Log, Local

Dale R Adkins.. G 740 682-7312
 Oak Hill *(G-12017)*

TRUCKING & HAULING SVCS: Machinery, Heavy

B M Machine.. E 419 595-2898
 New Riegel *(G-11534)*

TRUCKING: Except Local

American Power LLC.................................. F 937 235-0418
 Dayton *(G-6202)*

Barrett Paving Materials Inc..................... E 973 533-1001
 Hamilton *(G-8183)*

Bc Investment Corporation....................... G 330 262-3070
 Wooster *(G-16103)*

Buckeye Energy Resources Inc................ G 740 452-9506
 Zanesville *(G-16514)*

Chagrin Vly Stl Erectors Inc..................... F 440 975-1556
 Willoughby Hills *(G-16023)*

Custom Built Crates Inc............................ E
 Milford *(G-10904)*

Euclid Chemical Company........................ E 800 321-7628
 Cleveland *(G-4032)*

Flegal Brothers Inc..................................... E 419 298-3539
 Edgerton *(G-7075)*

Mpi Logistics and Service Inc.................. E 330 832-5309
 Massillon *(G-10130)*

Parobek Trucking Co.................................. G 419 869-7500
 West Salem *(G-15635)*

Sandwisch Enterprises Inc....................... G 419 944-6446
 Toledo *(G-14462)*

Shawn Fleming Ind Trckg LLC................. G 937 707-8539
 Dayton *(G-6568)*

Tk Gas Services Inc.................................... E 740 826-0303
 New Concord *(G-11434)*

TRUCKING: Local, With Storage

M G Q Inc.. E 419 992-4236
 Tiffin *(G-14092)*

Resource Recycling Inc............................. F 419 222-2702
 Lima *(G-9285)*

TRUCKING: Local, Without Storage

Corbett R Caudill Chipping Inc............... G 740 596-5984
 Hamden *(G-8172)*

Demilta Sand and Gravel Inc.................... E 440 942-2015
 Willoughby *(G-15907)*

Hershberger Manufacturing..................... E 440 272-5555
 Windsor *(G-16075)*

M & R Redi Mix Inc..................................... E 419 445-7771
 Pettisville *(G-12451)*

Mm Outsourcing LLC.................................. F 937 661-4300
 Leesburg *(G-9126)*

Parobek Trucking Co.................................. G 419 869-7500
 West Salem *(G-15635)*

Rjw Trucking Company Ltd...................... E 740 363-5343
 Delaware *(G-6746)*

S&M Trucking LLC....................................... F 661 310-2585
 Mason *(G-10052)*

Shawn Fleming Ind Trckg LLC................. G 937 707-8539
 Dayton *(G-6568)*

Tk Gas Services Inc.................................... E 740 826-0303
 New Concord *(G-11434)*

Ward Construction Co................................ F 419 943-2450
 Leipsic *(G-9142)*

Wooster Abruzzi Company........................ E 330 345-3968
 Wooster *(G-16183)*

TRUCKS & TRACTORS: Industrial

Back In Black Co... E 419 425-5555
 Findlay *(G-7479)*

Canton Elevator Inc.................................... D 330 833-3600
 North Canton *(G-11719)*

City Machine Technologies Inc................ F 330 747-2639
 Youngstown *(G-16336)*

Crescent Metal Products Inc.................... C 440 350-1100
 Mentor *(G-10445)*

Crown Equipment Corporation................ A 419 629-2311
 New Bremen *(G-11400)*

Dragon Products LLC................................. E 330 345-3968
 Wooster *(G-16114)*

Eagle Industrial Truck Mfg LLC................ E 419 866-6301
 Swanton *(G-13973)*

Enviri Corporation...................................... F 740 387-1150
 Marion *(G-9851)*

Forte Industrial Equipment Systems Inc E 513 398-2800
 Mason *(G-9993)*

G & T Manufacturing Co............................ F 440 639-7777
 Mentor *(G-10462)*

General Electric Company........................ E 513 977-1500
 Cincinnati *(G-2943)*

Gradall Industries LLC............................... C 330 339-2211
 New Philadelphia *(G-11504)*

Grand Harbor Yacht Sales & Svc............. G 440 442-2919
 Cleveland *(G-4139)*

Hobart Brothers LLC.................................. A 937 332-5429
 Troy *(G-14579)*

Jh Industries Inc... E 330 963-4105
 Twinsburg *(G-14677)*

Lane Field Materials Inc........................... G 330 526-8082
 Canton *(G-2143)*

Macton Corporation................................... D 330 259-8555
 Youngstown *(G-16393)*

Miller Products Inc.................................... E 330 308-5934
 New Philadelphia *(G-11518)*

Miners Tractor Sales Inc........................... F 330 325-9914
 Rootstown *(G-12854)*

Mitchs Welding & Hitches......................... G 419 893-3117
 Maumee *(G-10223)*

Parobek Trucking Co.................................. G 419 869-7500
 West Salem *(G-15635)*

Perfecto Industries Inc.............................. E 937 778-1900
 Piqua *(G-12542)*

Pollock Research & Design Inc................ E 330 332-3300
 Salem *(G-13023)*

Pucel Enterprises Inc................................ D 216 881-4604
 Cleveland *(G-4598)*

Saf-Holland Inc... G 513 874-7888
 Fairfield *(G-7404)*

Stock Fairfield Corporation...................... C 440 543-6000
 Solon *(G-13425)*

Sweet Manufacturing Company............... E 937 325-1511
 Springfield *(G-13641)*

Tarpco Inc.. F 330 677-8277
 Kent *(G-8871)*

Trailer Component Mfg Inc....................... E 440 255-2888
 Mentor *(G-10580)*

Transco Railway Products......................... G 419 562-1031
 Bucyrus *(G-1869)*

Uhrden Inc.. E 330 456-0031
 Canton *(G-2249)*

Volens LLC... G 216 544-1200
 Macedonia *(G-9585)*

Waltco Lift Corp... C 330 633-9191
 Streetsboro *(G-13798)*

Youngstown-Kenworth Inc........................ F 330 534-9761
 Hubbard *(G-8574)*

TRUCKS: Forklift

Forklift Solutions LLC................................ G 419 717-9496
 Napoleon *(G-11313)*

Freedom Forklift Sales LLC...................... G 330 289-0879
 Akron *(G-158)*

Hyster-Yale Materials Hdlg Inc................ C 440 449-9600
 Cleveland *(G-4211)*

TRUCKS: Indl

ADSr Ent LLC... F 773 280-2129
 Columbus *(G-5102)*

All Around Primo Logistics LLC............... G 513 725-7888
 Cincinnati *(G-2607)*

Elliott Machine Works Inc........................ E 419 468-4709
 Galion *(G-7874)*

Express Ground Services Inc................... G 216 870-9374
 Cleveland *(G-4044)*

Flawless Logistics LLC.............................. G 330 201-7070
 Canton *(G-2101)*

Grand Aire Inc... E 419 861-6700
 Swanton *(G-13974)*

Ken Beaverson Inc..................................... G 330 264-0378
 Wooster *(G-16140)*

Load32 LLC... F 614 984-6648
 Columbus *(G-5530)*

Newsafe Transport Service Inc............... F 740 387-1679
 Marion *(G-9866)*

Ready Rigs LLC.. F 740 963-9203
 Reynoldsburg *(G-12773)*

S&M Trucking LLC....................................... F 661 310-2585
 Mason *(G-10052)*

TRUCKS: Indl

Sb Trans LLC .... F 407 477-2545
  Cincinnati (G-3365)
Surplus Freight Inc .... G 614 235-7660
  Gahanna (G-7851)
Tbt Hauling LLC .... G 904 635-7631
  Bowling Green (G-1590)
Triumphant Enterprises Inc .... F 513 617-1668
  Goshen (G-7995)

TRUSSES & FRAMING: Prefabricated Metal

C Green & Sons Incorporated .... F 740 745-2998
  Saint Louisville (G-12942)
Jentgen Steel Services LLC .... F 614 268-6340
  Columbus (G-5493)

TRUSSES: Wood, Floor

Khempco Bldg Sup Co Ltd Partnr .... D 740 549-0465
  Delaware (G-6733)

TUBES: Paper

Ohio Paper Tube Co .... E 330 478-5171
  Canton (G-2185)
Sonoco Products Company .... G 937 429-0040
  Beavercreek Township (G-1094)

TUBES: Steel & Iron

Crest Bending Inc .... E 419 492-2108
  New Washington (G-11546)
Kirtland Capital Partners LP .... E 216 593-0100
  Beachwood (G-993)
Nanogate North America LLC .... B 419 747-1096
  Mansfield (G-9702)
Phillips Mfg and Tower Co .... D 419 347-1720
  Shelby (G-13197)
Universal Metals Cutting Inc .... G 330 580-5192
  Canton (G-2257)

TUBES: Wrought, Welded Or Lock Joint

Lsp Tubes Inc .... D 216 378-2092
  Orwell (G-12168)
Tubetech Inc .... G 330 426-9476
  East Palestine (G-7011)
United Tube Corporation .... D 330 725-4196
  Medina (G-10392)

TUBING: Copper

Arem Co .... F 440 974-6740
  Mentor (G-10423)

TUBING: Flexible, Metallic

Lincoln Electric Automtn Inc .... B 937 295-2120
  Fort Loramie (G-7603)
Tubular Techniques Inc .... G 614 529-4130
  Hilliard (G-8450)

TUBING: Glass

Glasstech Inc .... C 419 661-9500
  Perrysburg (G-12386)
Techneglas Inc .... E 419 873-2000
  Perrysburg (G-12431)

TUBING: Rubber

Eagle Elastomer Inc .... E 330 923-7070
  Peninsula (G-12340)
First Brnds Group Holdings LLC .... E 216 589-0198
  Cleveland (G-4063)
First Brnds Group Intrmdate LL .... F 216 589-0198
  Cleveland (G-4064)
Meridian Industries Inc .... D 330 673-1011
  Kent (G-8834)
Meridian Industries Inc .... D 330 359-5447
  Winesburg (G-16081)

Meteor Sealing Systems LLC .... C 330 343-9595
  Dover (G-6835)
Trico Products Corporation .... C 248 371-1700
  Cleveland (G-4829)

TUGBOAT SVCS

Shelly Materials Inc .... F 740 247-2311
  Racine (G-12695)
Shelly Materials Inc .... D 740 246-6315
  Thornville (G-14072)
The Great Lakes Towing Company .... D 216 621-4854
  Cleveland (G-4784)

TURBINES & TURBINE GENERATOR SETS

Alin Machining Company Inc .... D 740 223-0200
  Marion (G-9847)
Babcock & Wilcox Company .... D 740 687-6500
  Lancaster (G-8991)
Babcock & Wilcox Entps Inc .... F 740 687-4370
  Lancaster (G-8992)
Babcock & Wilcox Holdings Inc .... A 704 625-4900
  Akron (G-75)
Canvus Inc .... E 216 340-7500
  Rocky River (G-12836)
Diamond Power Intl Inc .... D 740 687-6500
  Lancaster (G-9012)
Eaton Leasing Corporation .... B 216 382-2292
  Beachwood (G-986)
Fluidpower Assembly Inc .... G 419 394-7486
  Saint Marys (G-12952)
Mendenhall Technical Services Inc ...... E 513 860-1280
  Fairfield (G-7383)
Metalex Manufacturing Inc .... C 513 489-0507
  Blue Ash (G-1437)
Miba Bearings US LLC .... B 740 962-4242
  Mcconnelsville (G-10282)
Pfpc Enterprises Inc .... F 513 941-6200
  Cincinnati (G-3253)
Precision Castparts Corp .... F 440 350-6150
  Painesville (G-12258)
Rolls-Royce Energy Systems Inc .... A 703 834-1700
  Mount Vernon (G-11292)
Siemens Energy Inc .... E 740 393-8897
  Mount Vernon (G-11295)

TURBINES: Gas, Mechanical Drive

Onpower Inc .... E 513 228-2100
  Lebanon (G-9103)

TURBINES: Hydraulic, Complete

Fluid System Service Inc .... G 216 651-2450
  Cleveland (G-4072)

TURBINES: Steam

Siemens Energy Inc .... E 740 504-1947
  Mount Vernon (G-11296)
Steam Trbine Altrntive Rsrces .... E 740 387-5535
  Marion (G-9884)

TYPESETTING SVC

A-A Blueprint Co Inc .... E 330 794-8803
  Akron (G-11)
Activities Press Inc .... E 440 953-1200
  Mentor (G-10404)
AGS Custom Graphics Inc .... D 330 963-7770
  Macedonia (G-9534)
American Printing & Lithog Co .... F 513 867-0602
  Hamilton (G-8177)
Anderson Graphics Inc .... E 330 745-2165
  Barberton (G-855)
Andrin Enterprises Inc .... F 937 276-7794
  Moraine (G-11157)

Anthony Business Forms Inc .... G 937 253-0072
  Dayton (G-6153)
Asist Translation Services .... F 614 451-6744
  Columbus (G-558)
Baesman Group Inc .... D 614 771-2300
  Hilliard (G-8402)
Bindery & Spc Pressworks Inc .... G 614 873-4623
  Plain City (G-12566)
Black River Group Inc .... E 419 524-6699
  Mansfield (G-9628)
Bookmasters Inc .... C 419 281-1802
  Ashland (G-557)
Brass Bull 1 LLC .... G 740 335-8030
  Wshngtn Ct Hs (G-16226)
Brothers Publishing Co LLC .... E 937 548-3330
  Greenville (G-8040)
Carlisle Prtg Walnut Creek Ltd .... E 330 852-9922
  Sugarcreek (G-13922)
Characters Inc .... G 937 335-1976
  Troy (G-14553)
Colortech Graphics & Printing .... F 614 766-2400
  Columbus (G-5250)
Consolidated Graphics Group Inc .... C 216 881-9191
  Cleveland (G-3896)
Copley Ohio Newspapers Inc .... C 330 364-5577
  New Philadelphia (G-11493)
COS Blueprint Inc .... E 330 376-0022
  Akron (G-115)
Daubenmires Printing Co LLC .... G 513 425-7223
  Middletown (G-12817)
Davis Printing Company .... E 330 745-3113
  Barberton (G-860)
Dayton Legal Blank Inc .... F 937 435-4405
  Dayton (G-6281)
Eugene Stewart .... G 937 898-1117
  Dayton (G-6325)
Flexoplate Inc .... F 513 489-0433
  Blue Ash (G-1395)
Franklin Printing Company .... F 740 452-6375
  Zanesville (G-16133)
Geygan Enterprises Inc .... F 513 932-4222
  Lebanon (G-9082)
Greg Blume .... G 740 574-2308
  Wheelersburg (G-15809)
Harlan Graphic Arts Svcs Inc .... E 513 251-5700
  Cincinnati (G-2985)
Hecks Direct Mail Prtg Svc Inc .... F 419 697-3505
  Toledo (G-14315)
Hkm Drect Mkt Cmmnications Inc .... C 800 860-4456
  Cleveland (G-4193)
HP Industries Inc .... E 419 478-0695
  Toledo (G-14322)
Hubbard Publishing Co .... E 937 592-3060
  Bellefontaine (G-1212)
Imprints .... F 330 650-0467
  Hudson (G-8599)
Jack Walker Printing Co .... F 440 352-4222
  Mentor (G-10481)
Keener Printing Inc .... F 216 531-7595
  Cleveland (G-4280)
Kehl-Kolor Inc .... E 419 281-3107
  Ashland (G-585)
Kevin K Tidd .... F 419 885-5603
  Sylvania (G-14003)
Keystone Press Inc .... G 419 243-7326
  Toledo (G-14347)
Laurenee Ltd .... G 513 662-2225
  Cincinnati (G-3097)
Lee Corporation .... G 513 771-3602
  Cincinnati (G-3099)
Middleton Printing Co Inc .... G 614 294-7277
  Gahanna (G-7845)

PRODUCT SECTION

Mmp Printing Inc............................... E 513 381-0990
  Cincinnati *(G-3168)*
Multi-Craft Litho Inc........................... E 859 581-2754
  Blue Ash *(G-1442)*
Network Printing & Graphics.............. F 614 230-2084
  Columbus *(G-5593)*
Old Trail Printing Company................ C 614 443-4852
  Columbus *(G-5636)*
Onetouchpoint East Corp.................... D 513 421-1600
  Cincinnati *(G-3225)*
Orange Blossom Press Inc................... G 216 781-8655
  Willoughby *(G-15966)*
Painesville Publishing Inc.................... D 440 354-4142
  Austinburg *(G-748)*
Penguin Enterprises Inc....................... E 440 899-5112
  Westlake *(G-15773)*
Preisser Inc....................................... E 614 345-0199
  Columbus *(G-5688)*
Prime Printing Inc............................... E 937 438-3707
  Dayton *(G-6522)*
Printing Arts Press Inc......................... F 740 397-6106
  Mount Vernon *(G-11289)*
Progrssive Communications Corp........ D 740 397-5333
  Mount Vernon *(G-11290)*
Quick As A Wink Printing Co................ G 419 224-9786
  Lima *(G-9281)*
Quick Tab II Inc.................................. D 419 448-6622
  Tiffin *(G-14101)*
Quick Tech Graphics Inc....................... E 937 743-5952
  Springboro *(G-13518)*
Robin Enterprises Company................. C 614 891-0250
  Westerville *(G-15719)*
Royal Acme Corporation..................... E 216 241-1477
  Cleveland *(G-4654)*
RR Donnelley & Sons Company........... G 614 221-8385
  Columbus *(G-5733)*
St Media Group Intl Inc........................ D 513 421-2050
  Blue Ash *(G-1467)*
Standard Printing Co of Canton............ D 330 453-8247
  Canton *(G-2230)*
Suburban Press Incorporated............... E 216 961-0766
  Cleveland *(G-4744)*
The Photo-Type Engraving Company.... D 513 281-0999
  Cincinnati *(G-3450)*
Tim L Humbert.................................... G 330 497-4944
  Canton *(G-2245)*
Watkins Printing Company................... E 614 297-8270
  Columbus *(G-5867)*
West-Camp Press Inc........................... D 614 882-2378
  Westerville *(G-15725)*
Western Roto Engravers Inc................. E 330 336-7636
  Wadsworth *(G-15072)*
Wfsr Holdings LLC............................. A 877 735-4966
  Dayton *(G-6654)*
Winkler Co Inc.................................... G 937 294-2662
  Dayton *(G-6655)*
Workflowone LLC............................... A 877 735-4966
  Dayton *(G-6661)*
Xenia Daily Gazette............................. E 937 372-4444
  Xenia *(G-16281)*
Youngstown ARC Engraving Co............ G 330 793-2471
  Youngstown *(G-16476)*

TYPESETTING SVC: Computer

Wolters Kluwer Clinical Dru................ D 330 650-6506
  Hudson *(G-8619)*

UNDERGROUND GOLD MINING

Fantasia Enterprises LLC..................... F 330 400-8741
  Massillon *(G-10095)*

UNIFORM SPLY SVCS: Indl

Cintas Corporation............................. D 513 631-5750
  Cincinnati *(G-2770)*
Cintas Corporation............................. A 513 459-1200
  Cincinnati *(G-2769)*
Cintas Sales Corporation..................... B 513 459-1200
  Cincinnati *(G-2771)*

UNIFORM STORES

K Ventures Inc.................................... F 419 678-2308
  Coldwater *(G-4994)*
Kip-Craft Incorporated........................ D 216 898-5500
  Cleveland *(G-4293)*
The Fechheimer Brothers Co................ C 513 793-5400
  Blue Ash *(G-1480)*

UNSUPPORTED PLASTICS: Floor Or Wall Covering

Rjf International Corporation.............. A 330 668-2069
  Fairlawn *(G-7447)*

UPHOLSTERY WORK SVCS

Casco Mfg Solutions Inc...................... D 513 681-0003
  Cincinnati *(G-2706)*

USED CAR DEALERS

Cars and Parts Magazine..................... D 937 498-0803
  Sidney *(G-13232)*
Dawn Enterprises Inc.......................... E 216 642-5506
  Cleveland *(G-3943)*
Knippen Chrysler Ddge Jeep Inc........... E 419 695-4976
  Delphos *(G-6767)*
Suburbanite Inc.................................. G 419 756-4390
  Mansfield *(G-9723)*
United Ignition Wire Corp.................... G 216 898-1112
  Cleveland *(G-4847)*

UTENSILS: Cast Aluminum, Cooking Or Kitchen

Range Kleen Mfg Inc........................... B 419 331-8000
  Elida *(G-7098)*

UTILITY TRAILER DEALERS

Custom Way Welding Inc..................... F 937 845-9469
  New Carlisle *(G-11414)*
M R Trailer Sales Inc........................... G 330 339-7701
  New Philadelphia *(G-11512)*
OReilly Equipment LLC....................... G 440 564-1234
  Newbury *(G-11633)*

VACUUM CLEANERS: Indl Type

Hi-Vac Corporation............................. C 740 374-2306
  Marietta *(G-9799)*

VALUE-ADDED RESELLERS: Computer Systems

Sutter Llc.. F 513 891-2261
  Blue Ash *(G-1476)*

VALVES

Aswpengg LLC.................................... E 216 292-4620
  Bedford Heights *(G-1164)*
Brooks Manufacturing......................... G 419 244-1777
  Toledo *(G-14221)*
Buckeye BOP LLC............................... G 740 498-9898
  Newcomerstown *(G-11643)*
Valv-Trol LLC..................................... F 330 686-2800
  Stow *(G-13736)*

VALVES & PARTS: Gas, Indl

Honeywell International Inc................. A 937 484-2000
  Urbana *(G-14835)*

VALVES & PIPE FITTINGS

Alloy Precision Tech Inc...................... D 440 266-7700
  Mentor *(G-10412)*
Anchor Flange Company...................... D 513 527-3512
  Cincinnati *(G-2626)*
Bay Corporation.................................. E 440 835-2212
  Westlake *(G-15735)*
Blackmer Pump................................... F 616 248-9239
  West Chester *(G-15380)*
Bowden Manufacturing Corp................ E 440 946-1770
  Willoughby *(G-15891)*
Bowes Manufacturing Inc.................... E 216 378-2110
  Solon *(G-13321)*
Calvin J Magsig.................................. G 419 862-3311
  Elmore *(G-7100)*
Crane Pumps & Systems Inc................ C 937 773-2442
  Piqua *(G-12508)*
Cylinders and Valves Inc..................... G 440 238-7343
  Strongsville *(G-13826)*
Eaton Corporation.............................. E 330 274-0743
  Aurora *(G-712)*
Edward W Daniel LLC......................... E 440 647-1960
  Wellington *(G-15306)*
Fcx Performance Inc............................ E 614 253-1996
  Columbus *(G-5373)*
General Aluminum Mfg Company......... C 419 739-9300
  Wapakoneta *(G-15115)*
H P E Inc.. G 330 833-3161
  Massillon *(G-10104)*
H-P Products Inc................................. C 330 875-5556
  Louisville *(G-9459)*
Impaction Co...................................... G 440 349-5652
  Solon *(G-13367)*
Kirtland Capital Partners LP................ E 216 593-0100
  Beachwood *(G-993)*
Knappco Corporation.......................... C 513 870-3100
  West Chester *(G-15455)*
Lsq Manufacturing Inc......................... F 330 725-4905
  Medina *(G-10345)*
Mack Iron Works Company.................. E 419 626-3712
  Sandusky *(G-13078)*
Northcoast Valve and Gate Inc............ G 440 392-9910
  Mentor *(G-10512)*
Nupro Company.................................. D 440 951-9729
  Willoughby *(G-15962)*
Opw Engineered Systems Inc.............. E 888 771-9438
  West Chester *(G-15471)*
Piersante and Associates Inc............... G 330 533-9904
  Canfield *(G-2014)*
Pima Valve LLC.................................. D 330 337-9535
  Salem *(G-13022)*
Precision McHning Cnnction LLC......... F 440 943-3300
  Wickliffe *(G-15849)*
Pressure Connections Corp.................. D 614 863-6930
  Columbus *(G-5689)*
Robeck Fluid Power Co........................ D 330 562-1140
  Aurora *(G-734)*
Spirex Corporation.............................. C 330 726-1166
  Youngstown *(G-16446)*
Stelter and Brinck Inc......................... E 513 367-9300
  Harrison *(G-8293)*
Stephens Pipe & Steel LLC.................. C 740 869-2257
  Mount Sterling *(G-11257)*
Superior Holding LLC......................... E 216 651-9400
  Cleveland *(G-4748)*
Superior Products LLC........................ D 216 651-9400
  Cleveland *(G-4751)*

VALVES & PIPE FITTINGS

Swagelok Company................... F 440 442-6611
  Cleveland (G-4757)
Swagelok Company................... D 440 349-5934
  Solon (G-13431)
The Sheffer Corporation............ D 513 489-9770
  Blue Ash (G-1481)
Thogus Products Company............ D 440 933-8850
  Avon Lake (G-825)
Tylok International Inc............ D 216 261-7310
  Cleveland (G-4840)
Victaulic.......................... G 513 479-1764
  Loveland (G-9508)
Waxman Industries Inc.............. C 440 439-1830
  Bedford Heights (G-1181)
William Powell Company............. D 513 852-2000
  Cincinnati (G-3519)
Xomox Pft Corp..................... B 936 271-6500
  Cincinnati (G-3532)

VALVES & REGULATORS: Pressure, Indl

Rogers Industrial Products Inc..... E 330 535-3331
  Akron (G-309)
Swagelok Company................... F 440 248-4600
  Solon (G-13427)
Swagelok Company................... F 440 349-5652
  Solon (G-13429)
Swagelok Company................... F 440 349-5836
  Solon (G-13430)
Swagelok Company................... D 440 248-4600
  Willoughby Hills (G-16029)
Swagelok Company................... A 440 248-4600
  Solon (G-13428)
Tylok International Inc............ D 216 261-7310
  Cleveland (G-4840)
William Powell Company............. D 513 852-2000
  Cincinnati (G-3519)

VALVES: Aerosol, Metal

Accurate Mechanical Inc............ D 740 681-1332
  Lancaster (G-8985)
B M Machine........................ E 419 595-2898
  New Riegel (G-11534)
Jfdb Ltd........................... C 513 870-0601
  Cincinnati (G-3042)

VALVES: Aircraft, Control, Hydraulic & Pneumatic

Eaton Corporation.................. B 440 523-5000
  Cleveland (G-3994)
Poc Hydraulic Technologies LLC..... G 614 761-8555
  Dublin (G-6924)

VALVES: Aircraft, Fluid Power

Malabar............................ E 419 866-6301
  Swanton (G-13978)
Taiyo America Inc.................. F 419 300-8811
  Saint Marys (G-12968)

VALVES: Aircraft, Hydraulic

Aerocontrolex Group Inc............ D 216 291-6025
  South Euclid (G-13457)
Hydraulic Manifolds USA LLC........ E 973 728-1214
  Stow (G-13702)
Parker-Hannifin Corporation........ F 419 542-6611
  Hicksville (G-8377)

VALVES: Control, Automatic

Flow Technology Inc................ E 513 745-6000
  Cincinnati (G-2910)
Superb Industries Inc.............. D 330 852-0500
  Sugarcreek (G-13943)

VALVES: Electrohydraulic Servo, Metal

Pioneer Solutions LLC.............. E 216 383-3400
  Euclid (G-7292)

VALVES: Fluid Power, Control, Hydraulic & pneumatic

Dana Limited....................... B 419 887-3000
  Maumee (G-10186)
DNC Hydraulics LLC................. F 419 963-2800
  Rawson (G-12743)
Hunt Valve Company Inc............. D 330 337-9535
  Salem (G-13004)
Hy-Production Inc.................. C 330 273-2400
  Valley City (G-14873)
Hydrotech Inc...................... D 888 651-5712
  West Chester (G-15563)
National Aviation Products Inc..... G 330 688-6494
  Stow (G-13713)
National Machine Company........... C 330 688-6494
  Stow (G-13714)
Parker-Hannifin Corporation........ A 216 896-3000
  Cleveland (G-4532)
SMC Corporation of America......... F 330 659-2006
  Richfield (G-12798)
The Sheffer Corporation............ D 513 489-9770
  Blue Ash (G-1481)
Valv-Trol LLC...................... F 330 686-2800
  Stow (G-13736)

VALVES: Gas Cylinder, Compressed

Kaplan Industries Inc.............. D 856 779-8181
  Harrison (G-8282)

VALVES: Indl

4matic Valve Automtn Ohio LLC...... F 614 806-1221
  Columbus (G-5077)
Alkon Corporation.................. E 614 799-6650
  Dublin (G-6858)
Bosch Rexroth Corporation.......... C 330 263-3300
  Wooster (G-16106)
Curtiss-Wright Flow Control........ E 440 838-7690
  Brecksville (G-1611)
Maass Midwest Mfg Inc.............. G 419 894-6424
  Arcadia (G-516)
Meador Supply Company Inc.......... F 330 405-4403
  Walton Hills (G-15101)
Nupro Company...................... D 440 951-9729
  Willoughby (G-15962)
Parker-Hannifin Corporation........ E 419 542-6611
  Hicksville (G-8377)
Parker-Hannifin Corporation........ F 937 644-3915
  Marysville (G-9930)
Pima Valve LLC..................... D 330 337-9535
  Salem (G-13022)
Richards Industrials Inc........... D 513 533-5600
  Cincinnati (G-3339)
S DH Flow Contro Ls LLC............ G 513 834-8432
  Amelia (G-463)
Seawin Inc......................... E 419 355-9111
  Fremont (G-7809)
Sherwood Valve LLC................. E 216 264-5023
  Cleveland (G-4697)
Valv-Trol LLC...................... F 330 686-2800
  Stow (G-13736)
Vickers International Inc.......... E 419 867-2200
  Maumee (G-10244)
Watts Water........................ F 614 491-5143
  Groveport (G-8167)
Waxman Industries Inc.............. C 440 439-1830
  Bedford Heights (G-1181)

VALVES: Plumbing & Heating

Xomox Corporation.................. E 936 271-6500
  Cincinnati (G-3531)

VALVES: Regulating & Control, Automatic

Elite Industrial Controls Inc...... G 440 477-6923
  Grafton (G-7999)

VALVES: Regulating, Process Control

Akron Steel Fabricators Co......... E 330 644-0616
  Akron (G-44)
Clark-Reliance LLC................. C 440 572-1500
  Strongsville (G-3821)
Hearth Products Controls Co........ F 937 436-9800
  Miamisburg (G-10644)
Xomox Corporation.................. G 513 745-6000
  Blue Ash (G-1497)
Xomox Pft Corp..................... B 936 271-6500
  Cincinnati (G-3532)

VAN CONVERSIONS

Mobile Conversions Inc............. F 513 797-1991
  Amelia (G-460)
National Fleet Svcs Ohio LLC....... F 440 930-5177
  Avon Lake (G-818)
Steves Vans ACC Unlimited LLC...... G 740 374-3154
  Marietta (G-9832)

VARNISHES, NEC

David E Easterday and Co Inc....... F 330 359-0700
  Wilmot (G-16067)
Superior Printing Ink Co Inc....... G 216 328-1720
  Cleveland (G-4730)

VAULTS & SAFES WHOLESALERS

McIntosh Safe Corp................. F 937 222-7008
  Dayton (G-6432)

VEHICLES: Recreational

Bulk Carriers Service Inc.......... F 330 339-3333
  New Philadelphia (G-11490)
L & R Racing Inc................... E 330 220-3102
  Brunswick (G-1733)
Rv Xpress Inc...................... G 937 418-0127
  Piqua (G-12553)
Thor Industries Inc................ F 937 596-6111
  Jackson Center (G-8739)

VENDING MACHINE REPAIR SVCS

Superior Soda Service LLC.......... G 937 657-9700
  Beavercreek (G-1981)

VENDING MACHINES & PARTS

Best Result Marketing Inc.......... G 234 212-1194
  Bedford (G-1106)
Five Star Healthy Vending LLC...... F 330 549-6011
  Akron (G-154)
Giant Industries Inc............... E 419 531-4600
  Toledo (G-14300)
Gold Medal Products Co............. B 513 769-7676
  Cincinnati (G-2962)
Innovative Vend Solutions LLC...... F 866 931-9413
  Dayton (G-6383)
Ring Snack LLC..................... G 216 334-4356
  Cleveland (G-4639)
Securastock LLC.................... F 330 957-5711
  Cleveland (G-4684)
Tranzonic Companies................ D 216 535-4300
  Richmond Heights (G-12811)
Ve Global Vending Inc.............. F 216 785-2611
  Cleveland (G-4862)

PRODUCT SECTION — WATER SUPPLY

VENTILATING EQPT: Metal
Famous Industries Inc.................... E 330 535-1811
  Akron (G-150)

VENTILATING EQPT: Sheet Metal
Burt Manufacturing Company Inc........... E 330 762-0061
  Akron (G-97)
Thermo Vent Manufacturing Inc............ F 330 239-0239
  Medina (G-10386)
Venti-Now............................... G 513 334-3375
  Montgomery (G-11132)

VENTURE CAPITAL COMPANIES
Brain Brew Ventures 30 Inc............... F 513 310-6374
  Newtown (G-11661)
Linsalata Cpitl Prtners Fund I........... G 440 684-1400
  Cleveland (G-4330)

VETERINARY PHARMACEUTICAL PREPARATIONS
Berlin Industries Inc.................... F 330 549-2100
  Youngstown (G-16319)

VIDEO TAPE PRODUCTION SVCS
Master Communications Inc................ G 208 821-3473
  Cincinnati (G-3133)
World Harvest Church Inc................. C 614 837-1990
  Canal Winchester (G-1994)

VIDEO TAPE WHOLESALERS, RECORDED
Allied Shipping and Packagi.............. F 937 222-7422
  Moraine (G-11155)

VIDEO TRIGGERS: Remote Control TV Devices
Universal Electronics Inc................ G 330 487-1110
  Twinsburg (G-14750)

VINYL RESINS, NEC
BCi and V Investments Inc................ F 330 538-0660
  North Jackson (G-11778)

VISUAL COMMUNICATIONS SYSTEMS
Findaway World LLC....................... E 440 893-0808
  Solon (G-13349)

VITAMINS: Natural Or Synthetic, Uncompounded, Bulk
Nomah Naturals Inc....................... G 330 212-8785
  Cleveland (G-4462)
Nufacturing Inc.......................... G 330 814-5259
  Brunswick (G-1776)

VOCATIONAL REHABILITATION AGENCY
Quadco Rehabilitation Ctr Inc............ E 419 445-1950
  Archbold (G-543)
Quadco Rehabilitation Ctr Inc............ B 419 682-1011
  Stryker (G-13912)

VOCATIONAL TRAINING AGENCY
Jeffco Sheltered Workshop................ F 740 264-4608
  Steubenville (G-13669)

WALL COVERINGS WHOLESALERS
The Blonder Company...................... C 216 431-3560
  Cleveland (G-4780)

WALL COVERINGS: Rubber
Rjf International Corporation............ A 330 668-2069
  Fairlawn (G-7447)

WALLPAPER & WALL COVERINGS
4wallscom LLC............................ F 216 432-1400
  Cleveland (G-3572)

WALLPAPER: Made From Purchased Paper
The Blonder Company...................... C 216 431-3560
  Cleveland (G-4780)

WALLS: Curtain, Metal
Midwest Curtainwalls Inc................. D 216 641-7900
  Cleveland (G-4410)
Wt Acquisition Company Ltd............... E 513 577-7980
  Cincinnati (G-3528)
YKK AP America Inc....................... E 513 942-7200
  West Chester (G-15528)

WAREHOUSING & STORAGE FACILITIES, NEC
Abbott Laboratories...................... D 847 937-6100
  Columbus (G-5087)
Ballreich Bros Inc....................... C 419 447-1814
  Tiffin (G-14078)
Kuhlman Corporation...................... E 419 897-6000
  Maumee (G-10213)
Lalac One LLC............................ E 216 432-4422
  Cleveland (G-4307)
Littlern Corporation..................... G 330 848-8847
  Fairlawn (G-7444)
SH Bell Company.......................... E 412 963-9910
  East Liverpool (G-6999)

WAREHOUSING & STORAGE, REFRIGERATED: Cold Storage Or Refrig
Youngs Locker Service Inc................ F 740 599-6833
  Danville (G-6150)

WAREHOUSING & STORAGE, REFRIGERATED: Frozen Or Refrig Goods
Pettisville Meats Incorporated........... F 419 445-0921
  Pettisville (G-12453)

WAREHOUSING & STORAGE: General
Cooper Tire Vhcl Test Ctr Inc............ F 419 423-1321
  Findlay (G-7498)
Dayton Bag & Burlap Co................... F 937 253-1722
  Dayton (G-6273)
Fuchs Lubricants Co...................... F 330 963-0400
  Twinsburg (G-14663)
Performance Packaging Inc................ F 419 478-8805
  Toledo (G-14433)
Precision Strip Inc...................... D 419 674-4186
  Kenton (G-8897)
Precision Strip Inc...................... D 937 667-6255
  Tipp City (G-14148)
SH Bell Company.......................... E 412 963-9910
  East Liverpool (G-6999)
Taylor Communications Inc................ F 614 351-6868
  Columbus (G-5812)
Trane Technologies Company LLC........... E 419 633-6800
  Bryan (G-1842)
Vectra Inc............................... C 614 351-6868
  Columbus (G-5855)
Victory White Metal Company.............. F 216 271-1400
  Cleveland (G-4875)
Workflowone LLC.......................... A 877 735-4966
  Dayton (G-6661)

WAREHOUSING & STORAGE: Refrigerated
Produce Packaging Inc.................... C 216 391-6129
  Willoughby Hills (G-16027)

WAREHOUSING & STORAGE: Self Storage
John D Oil and Gas Company............... G 440 255-6325
  Mentor (G-10484)
McCrary Metal Polishing Co Inc........... F 937 492-1979
  Port Jefferson (G-12630)

WARM AIR HEATING/AC EQPT/SPLYS, WHOL Warm Air Htg Eqpt/Splys
Air-Rite Inc............................. E 216 228-8200
  Cleveland (G-3617)
Shape Supply Inc......................... G 513 863-6695
  Hamilton (G-8242)

WASHERS
Die-Cut Products Co...................... F 216 771-6994
  Cleveland (G-3958)
Pressure Washer Mfrs Assn Inc............ G 216 241-7333
  Cleveland (G-4586)

WASHERS: Metal
Andre Corporation........................ E 574 293-0207
  Mason (G-9950)
Atlas Bolt & Screw Company LLC........... C 419 289-6171
  Ashland (G-554)
Master Products Company.................. D 216 341-1740
  Cleveland (G-4368)
Peterson American Corporation............ E 419 867-8711
  Holland (G-8523)

WATCH & CLOCK STORES
Quality Gold Inc......................... B 513 942-7659
  Fairfield (G-7400)

WATCH REPAIR SVCS
White Jewelers Inc....................... G 330 264-3324
  Wooster (G-16182)

WATER HEATERS
RAD Technologies Incorporated............ F 513 641-0523
  Cincinnati (G-3323)
Rv Mobile Power LLC...................... G 855 427-7978
  Columbus (G-5735)

WATER PURIFICATION EQPT: Household
De Nora Holdings Us Inc.................. B 440 710-5300
  Concord Township (G-5904)
Evoqua Water Technologies LLC............ G 614 491-5917
  Groveport (G-8138)
R D Baker Enterprises Inc................ G 937 461-5225
  Dayton (G-6537)
Wateropolis Corp......................... G 440 564-5061
  Newbury (G-11639)

WATER SOFTENING WHOLESALERS
R D Baker Enterprises Inc................ G 937 461-5225
  Dayton (G-6537)

WATER SUPPLY
American Water Services Inc.............. G 440 243-9840
  Strongsville (G-13806)
Aqua Pennsylvania Inc.................... G 440 257-6190
  Mentor On The Lake (G-10600)
City of Athens........................... E 740 592-3344
  Athens (G-679)
City of Middletown....................... D 513 425-7781
  Middletown (G-10807)
City of Troy............................. F 937 339-4826
  Troy (G-14555)

WATER SUPPLY

Greene County .... G 937 429-0127
  Dayton *(G-6162)*

Victory White Metal Company .... F 216 271-1400
  Cleveland *(G-4875)*

WATER TREATMENT EQPT: Indl

Advanced Green Tech Inc .... G 614 397-8130
  Plain City *(G-12560)*

Ameriwater LLC .... E 937 461-8833
  Dayton *(G-6205)*

Aqua Pennsylvania Inc .... G 440 257-6190
  Mentor On The Lake *(G-10600)*

Chemtreat .... F 937 644-2525
  East Liberty *(G-6985)*

Choice Ballast Solutions LLC .... G 440 973-9841
  Columbia Station *(G-5008)*

City of Athens .... E 740 592-3344
  Athens *(G-679)*

City of Middletown .... D 513 425-7781
  Middletown *(G-10807)*

City of Xenia .... E 937 376-7269
  Xenia *(G-16256)*

County of Lake .... F 440 428-1794
  Madison *(G-9591)*

Crown Solutions Co LLC .... C 937 890-4075
  Vandalia *(G-14936)*

De Nora North America Inc .... E 440 357-4000
  Painesville *(G-12226)*

De Nora Tech LLC .... G 440 285-0368
  Painesville *(G-12227)*

Imet Corporation .... G 440 799-3135
  Cleveland *(G-4217)*

Industrial Fluid MGT Inc .... F 419 748-7460
  Mc Clure *(G-10266)*

Kinetico Incorporated .... B 440 564-9111
  Newbury *(G-11628)*

McNish Corporation .... G 614 899-2282
  Westerville *(G-15667)*

Mt Vernon Cy Wastewater Trtmnt .... G 740 393-9502
  Mount Vernon *(G-11281)*

N-Viro International Corp .... F 419 535-6374
  Toledo *(G-14394)*

Norwalk Wastewater Eqp Co .... D 419 668-4471
  Norwalk *(G-11983)*

Or-Tec Inc .... G 216 475-5225
  Maple Heights *(G-9757)*

Tipton Environmental Intl Inc .... F 513 735-2777
  Batavia *(G-953)*

Total Water Solutions LLC .... G 234 567-5912
  Leetonia *(G-9131)*

Trinity Water Solutions LLC .... E 740 318-0585
  Caldwell *(G-1914)*

Trumbull Manufacturing Inc .... E 330 270-7888
  Youngstown *(G-16461)*

Under Pressure Systems Inc .... G 330 602-4466
  New Philadelphia *(G-11531)*

Veolia Wts Systems Usa Inc .... E 513 794-1010
  Cincinnati *(G-3494)*

Veolia Wts Systems Usa Inc .... F 330 929-1639
  Stow *(G-13737)*

Village of Ansonia .... E 937 337-5741
  Greenville *(G-8063)*

Water & Waste Water Eqp Co .... G 440 542-0972
  Solon *(G-13447)*

WATER: Distilled

Rambasek Realty Inc .... F 937 228-1189
  Dayton *(G-6540)*

WATER: Pasteurized, Canned & Bottled, Etc

On US LLC .... E 330 286-3436
  Kent *(G-8841)*

WATERPROOFING COMPOUNDS

Republic Powdered Metals Inc .... D 330 225-3192
  Medina *(G-10370)*

RP Hoskins Inc .... E 216 631-1000
  Cleveland *(G-4658)*

RPM International Inc .... D 330 273-5090
  Medina *(G-10372)*

Urethane Polymers Intl .... F 216 430-3655
  Cleveland *(G-4855)*

WAXES: Petroleum, Not Produced In Petroleum Refineries

The Kindt-Collins Company LLC .... D 216 252-4122
  Cleveland *(G-4788)*

WEATHER STRIP: Sponge Rubber

Canton OH Rubber Speclty Prods .... G 330 454-3847
  Canton *(G-2065)*

WEATHER STRIPS: Metal

M-D Building Products Inc .... C 513 539-2255
  Middletown *(G-10838)*

WEIGHING MACHINERY & APPARATUS

Hobart LLC .... E 937 332-2797
  Piqua *(G-12525)*

Hobart LLC .... E 937 332-3000
  Troy *(G-14581)*

Hobart LLC .... D 937 332-3000
  Troy *(G-14582)*

WELDING & CUTTING APPARATUS & ACCESS, NEC

Firelands Manufacturing LLC .... G 419 687-8237
  Plymouth *(G-12608)*

Kaliburn Inc .... E 843 695-4073
  Cleveland *(G-4273)*

Lincoln Electric Holdings Inc .... A 216 481-8100
  Cleveland *(G-4325)*

Luvata Ohio Inc .... D 740 363-1981
  Delaware *(G-6736)*

Miller Weldmaster Corporation .... D 330 833-6739
  Navarre *(G-11346)*

O E Meyer Co .... G 419 332-6931
  Fremont *(G-7798)*

Otto Konigslow Mfg Co .... F 216 851-7900
  Cleveland *(G-4513)*

Postle Industries Inc .... E 216 265-9000
  Cleveland *(G-4565)*

Quality Components Inc .... F 440 255-0606
  Mentor *(G-10540)*

Weld-Action Company Inc .... G 330 372-1063
  Warren *(G-15223)*

WELDING EQPT

Accurate Manufacturing Company ...... E 614 878-6510
  Columbus *(G-5096)*

Aerowave Inc .... G 440 731-8464
  Elyria *(G-7104)*

AK Fabrication Inc .... F 330 458-1037
  Canton *(G-2032)*

Ch Transition Company LLC .... C 800 543-6400
  Cincinnati *(G-2724)*

Harris Calorific Inc .... G 216 383-4107
  Cleveland *(G-4170)*

Hobart Brothers LLC .... G 937 332-5953
  Piqua *(G-12524)*

Hobart Brothers LLC .... A 937 332-5439
  Troy *(G-14579)*

Imax Industries Inc .... F 440 639-0242
  Painesville *(G-12246)*

Mansfield Welding Service LLC .... G 419 594-2738
  Oakwood *(G-12031)*

Nelson Stud Welding Inc .... D 440 329-0400
  Elyria *(G-7184)*

O E Meyer Co .... E 614 428-5656
  Columbus *(G-5209)*

Peco Holdings Corp .... D 937 667-5705
  Tipp City *(G-14247)*

Polymet Corporation .... E 513 874-3586
  West Chester *(G-15482)*

Process Development Corp .... E 937 890-3388
  Dayton *(G-6527)*

Romans Mobile Welding LLC .... E 513 603-0961
  Amelia *(G-462)*

Select-Arc Inc .... C 937 295-5215
  Fort Loramie *(G-7608)*

Semtorq Inc .... F 330 487-0600
  Twinsburg *(G-14734)*

Sherbrooke Corporation .... E 440 942-3520
  Willoughby *(G-15990)*

Sherbrooke Metals .... G 440 542-3066
  Willoughby *(G-15991)*

Smart Force LLC .... E 216 481-8100
  Cleveland *(G-4776)*

Spiegelberg Manufacturing Inc .... D 440 324-3042
  Strongsville *(G-15884)*

Stryver Mfg Inc .... E 937 854-3048
  Trotwood *(G-14516)*

Summit Machine Solutions LLC .... G 330 785-0781
  Akron *(G-340)*

Taylor - Winfield Corporation .... C 330 259-8500
  Hubbard *(G-8572)*

Taylor-Winfield Tech Inc .... E 330 259-8500
  Youngstown *(G-15451)*

Worker Automation Inc .... G 937 473-2111
  Dayton *(G-6660)*

WELDING EQPT & SPLYS WHOLESALERS

Addup Inc .... E 513 745-4510
  Blue Ash *(G-1357)*

Airgas Usa LLC .... G 937 222-8312
  Moraine *(G-1154)*

Airgas Usa LLC .... G 440 232-6397
  Twinsburg *(G-14625)*

ARC Solutions Inc .... E 419 542-9272
  Hicksville *(G-8373)*

Bickett Machine and Gas Supply .... G 740 353-5710
  Portsmouth *(G-12541)*

Delille Oxygen Company .... G 937 325-9595
  Springfield *(G-13853)*

Jerrys Welding Supply Inc .... G 937 364-1500
  Hillsboro *(G-8460)*

Lefeld Welding & Sl Sups Inc .... E 419 678-2397
  Coldwater *(G-4997)*

Linde Gas & Equipment Inc .... G 513 821-2192
  Cincinnati *(G-3107)*

Matheson Tri-Gas Inc .... E 419 865-8881
  Holland *(G-8518)*

Matheson Tri-Gas Inc .... E 513 727-9638
  Middletown *(G-10842)*

Modern Machine Development .... F 937 253-4576
  Dayton *(G-6454)*

Salem Welding & Supply Company ..... G 330 332-4517
  Salem *(G-13029)*

Sausser Steel Company Inc .... F 419 422-9632
  Findlay *(G-7559)*

T & D Fabricating Inc .... E 440 951-5646
  Eastlake *(G-7051)*

Weld-Action Company Inc .... G 330 372-1063
  Warren *(G-15223)*

Weldco Inc .... E 513 744-9353
  Cincinnati *(G-3514)*

PRODUCT SECTION — WELDING REPAIR SVC

Welders Supply Inc .... F 216 241-1696
  Cleveland *(G-4903)*
Wright Brothers Inc .... F 513 731-2222
  Cincinnati *(G-3527)*

WELDING EQPT & SPLYS: Gas

Rexarc International Inc .... E 937 839-4604
  West Alexandria *(G-15344)*

WELDING EQPT & SPLYS: Generators, Arc Welding, AC & DC

Lincoln Electric Company .... A 216 481-8100
  Cleveland *(G-4324)*

WELDING EQPT REPAIR SVCS

ARS Recycling Systems LLC .... F 330 536-8210
  Lowellville *(G-9511)*
Hannon Company .... F 330 343-7758
  Dover *(G-6826)*
Hannon Company .... F 740 453-0527
  Zanesville *(G-16536)*
Lyco Corporation .... E 412 973-9176
  Lowellville *(G-9517)*
Quality Components Inc .... F 440 255-0606
  Mentor *(G-10540)*
Unified Scrning Crshing - OH I .... G 937 836-3201
  Englewood *(G-7246)*

WELDING EQPT: Electric

Ivostud LLC .... G 440 925-4227
  Brookpark *(G-1719)*
Production Products Inc .... D 734 241-7242
  Columbus Grove *(G-5899)*
Tech-Sonic Inc .... F 614 792-3117
  Columbus *(G-5816)*

WELDING EQPT: Electrical

Pacific Highway Products LLC .... G 740 914-5217
  Marion *(G-9871)*

WELDING MACHINES & EQPT: Ultrasonic

Cecil C Peck Co .... F 330 785-0781
  Akron *(G-103)*

WELDING REPAIR SVC

3-B Welding Ltd .... G 740 819-4329
  New Concord *(G-11430)*
A & C Welding Inc .... E 330 762-4777
  Peninsula *(G-12337)*
A & G Manufacturing Co Inc .... F 419 468-7433
  Galion *(G-7858)*
A Tech Welding Products Inc .... G 614 296-1573
  Valley City *(G-14860)*
Abbott Tool Inc .... E 419 476-6742
  Toledo *(G-14174)*
Active Metal and Molds Inc .... F 419 281-9623
  Ashland *(G-549)*
Advanced Welding Inc .... E 937 746-6800
  Franklin *(G-7662)*
Advanced Wldg Fabrication Inc .... F 440 724-9165
  Sheffield Lake *(G-13178)*
Albright Radiator Inc .... G 330 264-8886
  Wooster *(G-16100)*
All - Do Weld & Fab LLC .... G 740 477-2133
  Circleville *(G-3540)*
All Ohio Welding Inc .... G 937 663-7116
  Saint Paris *(G-12970)*
All-Type Welding & Fabrication .... E 440 439-3990
  Cleveland *(G-3635)*
Allied Fabricating & Wldg Co .... E 614 751-6464
  Columbus *(G-5113)*

Almandrey Fabricating Tech .... G 937 408-0054
  Springfield *(G-13531)*
Amptech Machining & Welding .... G 419 652-3444
  Nova *(G-12002)*
Apollo Welding & Fabg Inc .... E 440 942-0227
  Willoughby *(G-15881)*
ARC Solutions Inc .... E 419 542-9272
  Hicksville *(G-8371)*
Arctech Fabricating Inc .... E 937 525-9353
  Springfield *(G-13535)*
Athens Mold and Machine Inc .... D 740 593-6613
  Athens *(G-675)*
B & R Fabricators & Maint Inc .... F 513 641-2222
  Cincinnati *(G-2650)*
Bamf Welding & Fabrication LLC .... G 440 862-8286
  Novelty *(G-12008)*
Baughman Machine & Weld Sp Inc .... G 330 866-9243
  Waynesburg *(G-15293)*
Bayloff Stmped Pdts Knsman Inc .... D 330 876-4511
  Kinsman *(G-8935)*
Bear Welding Services LLC .... F 740 630-7538
  Caldwell *(G-1907)*
Blackwood Sheet Metal Inc .... G 614 291-3115
  Columbus *(G-5200)*
Blevins Metal Fabrication Inc .... E 419 522-6082
  Mansfield *(G-9629)*
Bob Lanes Welding Inc .... F 740 373-3567
  Marietta *(G-9779)*
Brad Grizer On Spot Welding .... G 740 516-3436
  Whipple *(G-15813)*
Breitinger Company .... C 419 526-4255
  Mansfield *(G-9631)*
Buckeye State Wldg & Fabg Inc .... G 440 322-0344
  Elyria *(G-7119)*
Buckeye Welding .... G 330 674-0944
  Millersburg *(G-10948)*
Byron Products Inc .... D 513 870-9111
  Fairfield *(G-7340)*
C & R Inc .... E 614 497-1130
  Groveport *(G-8134)*
C-N-D Industries Inc .... E 330 478-8811
  Massillon *(G-10080)*
Camelot Manufacturing Inc .... E 419 678-2603
  Coldwater *(G-4983)*
Cardinal Welding Inc .... G 330 426-2404
  East Palestine *(G-7003)*
Carter Manufacturing Co Inc .... E 513 398-7303
  Mason *(G-9968)*
Case-Maul Manufacturing Co .... E 419 524-1061
  Mansfield *(G-9635)*
Ccr Fabrications LLC .... F 937 667-6632
  Tipp City *(G-14128)*
Ceramic Holdings Inc .... C 216 362-3900
  Brookpark *(G-1707)*
Certified Welding Co .... E 216 961-5410
  Cleveland *(G-3804)*
Chore Anden .... F 330 695-2300
  Fredericksburg *(G-7719)*
City Machine Technologies Inc .... F 330 747-2639
  Youngstown *(G-16336)*
Clemens Mobile Welding LLC .... E 419 782-4220
  Defiance *(G-6674)*
Cleveland Jsm Inc .... E 440 876-3050
  Strongsville *(G-13822)*
Clipsons Metal Working Inc .... G 513 772-6393
  Cincinnati *(G-2774)*
Cmt Machining & Fabg LLC .... F 937 652-3740
  Urbana *(G-14827)*
Columbus Mobile Welding LLC .... G 614 352-6052
  Centerburg *(G-2357)*
Columbus Pipe and Equipment Co .... F 614 444-7871
  Columbus *(G-5273)*

Combs Manufacturing Inc .... D 330 784-3151
  Akron *(G-114)*
Complete Metal Services .... G 740 694-0000
  Fredericktown *(G-7740)*
Complete Stud Welding Inc .... G 216 533-8482
  Chagrin Falls *(G-2372)*
Compton Metal Products Inc .... F 937 382-2403
  Wilmington *(G-16045)*
Comptons Precision Machine .... F 937 325-9139
  Springfield *(G-13546)*
Connaughton Wldg & Fence LLC .... G 513 867-0230
  Hamilton *(G-8195)*
Creative Fab & Welding LLC .... E 937 780-5000
  Leesburg *(G-9123)*
Creative Fabrication Ltd .... G 740 262-5789
  Richwood *(G-12813)*
Creative Mold and Machine Inc .... E 440 338-5146
  Newbury *(G-11621)*
Crest Bending Inc .... E 419 492-2108
  New Washington *(G-11546)*
Custom Machine Inc .... E 419 986-5122
  Tiffin *(G-14082)*
Custom Way Welding Inc .... F 937 845-9469
  New Carlisle *(G-11414)*
Custom Weld & Machine Corp .... F 330 452-3935
  Canton *(G-2086)*
Danny L Boyle .... G 330 206-1448
  Salem *(G-12990)*
Dayton Brick Company Inc .... F 937 293-4189
  Moraine *(G-11171)*
Dbcr Inc .... E 330 920-1900
  Cuyahoga Falls *(G-6078)*
Dover Fabrication and Burn Inc .... G 330 339-1057
  Dover *(G-6819)*
Dover Machine Co .... F 330 343-4123
  Dover *(G-6821)*
Drabik Manufacturing Inc .... F 216 267-1616
  Cleveland *(G-3971)*
Dragonfly Cstm Fabrication LLC .... G 614 522-9618
  Blacklick *(G-1336)*
Drj Welding Services LLC .... F 740 229-7428
  New Philadelphia *(G-11499)*
Ds Welding LLC .... G 330 893-4049
  Millersburg *(G-10953)*
Duco Tool & Die Inc .... F 419 628-2031
  Minster *(G-11050)*
Duray Machine Company Inc .... F 440 277-4119
  Amherst *(G-475)*
Dynamic Weld Corporation .... E 419 582-2900
  Osgood *(G-12173)*
E & M Liberty Welding Inc .... G 330 866-2338
  Waynesburg *(G-15294)*
E & R Welding Inc .... G 440 329-9387
  Berlin Heights *(G-1313)*
Eagle Welding & Fabg Inc .... E 440 946-0692
  Willoughby *(G-15914)*
East End Welding LLC .... C 330 677-6000
  Kent *(G-8811)*
Fabrication Shop Inc .... F 419 435-7934
  Fostoria *(G-7631)*
Falls Stamping & Welding Co .... C 330 928-1191
  Cuyahoga Falls *(G-6083)*
Finely Tuned Fabrications LLC .... E 216 513-6731
  Lagrange *(G-8947)*
Fleetpride Inc .... E 740 282-2711
  Steubenville *(G-13667)*
Fredrick Welding & Machining .... F 614 866-9650
  Reynoldsburg *(G-12766)*
Friess Welding Inc .... G 330 644-8160
  Coventry Township *(G-6009)*
G & R Welding Service LLC .... G 937 245-2341
  Middletown *(G-10825)*

Employee Codes: A=Over 500 employees, B=251-500, C=101-250, D=51-100, E=20-50, F=10-19, G=1-9

WELDING REPAIR SVC

G-Rod Welding & Fabg LLC .... G 740 588-0609
  Chandlersville *(G-2439)*
Gabel Welding Inc .... G 567 201-8217
  Port Clinton *(G-12619)*
Garland Welding Co Inc .... F 330 536-6506
  Lowellville *(G-9515)*
Gaspar Inc .... D 330 477-2222
  Canton *(G-2110)*
General Technologies Inc .... E 419 747-1800
  Mansfield *(G-9659)*
General Tool Company .... C 513 733-5500
  Cincinnati *(G-2946)*
George Steel Fabricating Inc .... E 513 932-2887
  Lebanon *(G-9080)*
Gilson Machine & Tool Co Inc .... E 419 592-2911
  Napoleon *(G-11316)*
Glenridge Machine Co .... E 440 975-1055
  Solon *(G-13354)*
Gmp Welding & Fabrication Inc .... E 513 825-7861
  Cincinnati *(G-2961)*
Gorski Welding LLC .... G 440 412-7910
  North Ridgeville *(G-11841)*
Greber Machine Tool Inc .... G 440 322-3685
  Elyria *(G-7156)*
Griffiths Mobile Welding .... G 937 750-3711
  New Carlisle *(G-11415)*
H & H Machine Shop Akron Inc .... E 330 773-3327
  Akron *(G-175)*
Habco Tool and Dev Co Inc .... E 440 946-5546
  Mentor *(G-10466)*
Harris Welding and Machine Co .... F 419 281-8351
  Ashland *(G-577)*
Harrison Welding Services LLC .... G 513 405-6581
  Amelia *(G-456)*
HI Tecmetal Group Inc .... E 216 881-8100
  Wickliffe *(G-15835)*
Hi-Tek Manufacturing Inc .... C 513 459-1094
  Mason *(G-10001)*
Highs Welding Inc .... G 937 464-3029
  Belle Center *(G-1197)*
Hobart Bros Stick Electrode .... F 937 332-5375
  Troy *(G-14578)*
Holdren Brothers Inc .... F 937 465-7050
  West Liberty *(G-15622)*
Holdsworth Industrial Fabg LLC .... G 330 874-3945
  Bolivar *(G-1527)*
Holmview Welding LLC .... F 330 359-5315
  Fredericksburg *(G-7725)*
Independent Machine & Wldg Inc .... G 937 339-7330
  Troy *(G-14586)*
J & S Industrial Mch Pdts Inc .... D 419 691-1380
  Toledo *(G-14341)*
J A B Welding Service Inc .... F 740 453-5868
  Zanesville *(G-16540)*
J&J Precision Fabricators Ltd .... F 330 482-4964
  Columbiana *(G-5043)*
Jerl Machine Inc .... D 419 873-0270
  Perrysburg *(G-12394)*
Jerrys Welding Supply Inc .... G 937 364-1500
  Hillsboro *(G-8460)*
JMw Welding and Mfg Inc .... E 330 484-2428
  Canton *(G-2136)*
Johns Welding & Towing Inc .... F 419 447-8937
  Tiffin *(G-14089)*
JP Suggins Mobile Wldg Inc .... F 216 566-7131
  Cleveland *(G-4265)*
Jrs MBL Wldg Fabrication LLC .... G 567 307-5460
  Ashland *(G-581)*
K & J Machine Inc .... F 740 425-3282
  Barnesville *(G-903)*
K-M-S Industries Inc .... F 440 243-6680
  Brookpark *(G-1720)*

Kda Manufacturing LLC .... F 330 590-7431
  Norton *(G-11947)*
Kellers Fine Line Welding LLC .... G 903 348-8304
  Tallmadge *(G-14035)*
Kellys Wldg & Fabrication Ltd .... G 440 593-6040
  Conneaut *(G-5922)*
Kendel Welding & Fabrication .... G 330 834-2429
  Massillon *(G-10115)*
Kings Welding and Fabg Inc .... F 330 738-3592
  Mechanicstown *(G-10287)*
Kinninger Prod Wldg Co Inc .... D 419 629-3491
  New Bremen *(G-11403)*
Kirbys Auto and Truck Repr Inc .... G 513 934-3999
  Lebanon *(G-9093)*
Kottler Metal Products Co Inc .... E 440 946-7473
  Willoughby *(G-15940)*
Kramer Power Equipment Co .... F 937 456-2232
  Eaton *(G-7063)*
KS Welding & Fabrication LLC .... G 937 420-2270
  Fort Loramie *(G-7602)*
Lakecraft Inc .... G 419 734-2828
  Port Clinton *(G-12621)*
Laserflex Corporation .... D 614 850-9600
  Hilliard *(G-8418)*
Lima Sheet Metal Machine & Mfg .... E 419 229-1161
  Lima *(G-9264)*
Lincoln Electric Automtn Inc .... B 937 295-2120
  Fort Loramie *(G-7603)*
Logan Welding Inc .... G 740 385-9651
  Logan *(G-9370)*
Long-Stanton Mfg Company .... E 513 874-8020
  West Chester *(G-15458)*
Lostcreek Tool & Machine Inc .... F 937 773-6022
  Piqua *(G-12533)*
Lunar Tool & Mold Inc .... E 440 237-2141
  North Royalton *(G-11884)*
M & M Certified Welding Inc .... F 330 467-1729
  Macedonia *(G-9562)*
M & M Concepts Inc .... G 937 355-1115
  West Mansfield *(G-15626)*
Majestic Tool and Machine Inc .... F 440 248-5058
  Solon *(G-13383)*
Marengo Fabricated Steel Ltd .... F 800 919-2652
  Cardington *(G-2276)*
Marsam Metalfab Inc .... E 330 405-1520
  Twinsburg *(G-14691)*
Martin Welding LLC .... F 937 687-3602
  New Lebanon *(G-11450)*
Matcor Metal Fabrication Inc .... G 419 298-2394
  Edgerton *(G-7076)*
Mc Elwain Industries Inc .... F 419 532-3126
  Ottawa *(G-12184)*
Mc Machine Llc .... E 216 398-3666
  Cleveland *(G-4378)*
Mdb Fabricating Inc .... G 216 799-7017
  Cleveland *(G-4385)*
Meta Manufacturing Corporation .... E 513 793-6382
  Blue Ash *(G-1435)*
Microweld Engineering Inc .... G 614 847-9410
  Worthington *(G-16204)*
Mike Loppe .... F 937 969-8102
  Tremont City *(G-14538)*
Millwrght Wldg Fbrication Svcs .... G 740 533-1510
  Kitts Hill *(G-8944)*
Mk Welding & Fabrication Inc .... G 937 603-4430
  Waynesville *(G-15299)*
Modern Machine Development .... F 937 253-4576
  Dayton *(G-6454)*
Montgomery & Montgomery LLC .... G 330 858-9533
  Akron *(G-252)*
Morrison Custom Welding Inc .... G 330 464-1637
  Fredericksburg *(G-7727)*

Ms Welding LLC .... G 419 925-4141
  Maria Stein *(G-1773)*
Mt Vernon Mold Works Inc .... E 618 242-6040
  Akron *(G-255)*
Nation Welding LLC .... G 419 466-2241
  Delta *(G-6790)*
National Wldg Tanker Repr LLC .... G 614 875-3399
  Grove City *(G-8810)*
Northwind Industries Inc .... E 216 433-0666
  Cleveland *(G-4381)*
Oaks Welding Inc .... G 330 482-4216
  Columbiana *(G-5047)*
Ohio Hydraulics Inc .... E 513 771-2590
  Cincinnati *(G-3275)*
Ohio Trailer Inc .... F 330 392-4444
  Warren *(G-15195)*
Ohio Trailer Supply Inc .... G 614 471-9121
  Columbus *(G-5629)*
Ottawa Defense Logistics LLC .... F 419 596-3202
  Ottawa *(G-12180)*
Patriot Stainless Welding .... F 740 297-6040
  Zanesville *(G-16653)*
Paul Wilke & Son Inc .... F 513 921-3163
  Cincinnati *(G-3271)*
Pentaflex Inc .... C 937 325-5551
  Springfield *(G-13517)*
Perry Welding Service Inc .... F 330 425-2211
  Twinsburg *(G-14714)*
Phillips Mfg and Tower Co .... D 419 347-1720
  Shelby *(G-13197)*
Phoenix Inds & Apparatus Inc .... F 513 722-1085
  Loveland *(G-9497)*
Piscione Welding .... G 440 653-3985
  Burbank *(G-1877)*
Pr-Weld & Manufacturing Ltd .... G 419 633-9204
  West Unity *(G-15542)*
Precision Assemblies Inc .... F 330 549-2630
  North Lima *(G-11809)*
Precision Mtal Fabrication Inc .... D 937 235-9261
  Dayton *(G-6516)*
Precision Reflex Inc .... F 419 629-2603
  New Bremen *(G-11407)*
Precision Weld Fab .... G 440 576-5800
  Jefferson *(G-8758)*
Precision Welding .... G 740 627-7320
  Howard *(G-8559)*
Precision Welding & Mfg Inc .... F 937 444-6925
  Mount Orab *(G-11245)*
Precision Welding Corporation .... E 216 524-6110
  Cleveland *(G-4577)*
Prout Boiler Htg & Wldg Inc .... E 330 744-0293
  Youngstown *(G-16423)*
Quality Welding Inc .... E 419 483-6067
  Bellevue *(G-1231)*
Quality Wldg & Fabrication LLC .... G 567 220-6639
  Tiffin *(G-14100)*
Quick Service Welding & Mch Co .... F 330 673-3818
  Kent *(G-8851)*
Rbm Environmental & Cnstr Inc .... F 419 693-5840
  Oregon *(G-12110)*
Rex Welding Inc .... F 740 387-1650
  Marion *(G-9875)*
RI Alto Mfg Inc .... F 740 914-4230
  Marion *(G-9876)*
Ridge Engineering Inc .... G 513 681-5500
  Cincinnati *(G-3340)*
Ridge Machine & Welding Co .... G 740 537-2821
  Toronto *(G-14534)*
Rodney Wells .... G 740 425-2266
  Barnesville *(G-904)*
Roetmans Welding LLC .... G 216 385-5938
  Akron *(G-308)*

PRODUCT SECTION — WINDOW & DOOR FRAMES

Romar Metal Fabricating Inc .... G 740 682-7731
Oak Hill (G-12025)

Rose Metal Industries LLC .... F 216 881-3355
Cleveland (G-4648)

Rsv Wlding Fbrction McHning In .... F 419 592-0993
Napoleon (G-11333)

Salem Welding & Supply Company ..... G 330 332-4517
Salem (G-13029)

Sauerwein Welding .... G 513 563-2979
Cincinnati (G-3364)

Schmidt Machine Company .... E 419 294-3814
Upper Sandusky (G-14823)

Semtorq .... F 330 487-0600
Twinsburg (G-14734)

Simpson & Sons Inc .... G 513 367-0152
Harrison (G-8292)

Sky Climber Fabricating LLC .... F 740 990-9430
Delaware (G-6750)

Smp Welding LLC .... F 440 205-9353
Mentor (G-10556)

Somerville Manufacturing Inc .... G 740 336-7847
Marietta (G-9829)

Spradlin Bros Welding Co .... F 800 219-2182
Springfield (G-13634)

Stan-Kell LLC .... E 440 998-1116
Ashtabula (G-661)

State Metal Hose Inc .... G 614 527-4700
Hilliard (G-8443)

Steve Vore Welding and Steel .... F 419 375-4087
Fort Recovery (G-7624)

Steven Crumbaker Jr .... G 740 995-0613
Zanesville (G-16566)

Stud Welding Associates .... F 216 392-7808
Elyria (G-7207)

Superior Weld and Fabg Co Inc .... G 216 249-5122
Cleveland (G-4753)

Systech Handling Inc .... F 419 445-8226
Archbold (G-547)

T & R Welding Systems Inc .... F 937 228-7517
Dayton (G-6606)

Tbone Sales LLC .... F 330 897-6131
Baltic (G-841)

Techniweld .... G 412 357-2176
Youngstown (G-16452)

Temperature Controls Co Inc .... F 330 773-6633
New Franklin (G-11444)

Terex Services .... G 440 262-3200
Brecksville (G-1634)

Toney Tool Manufacturing Inc .... E 937 890-8535
Dayton (G-6627)

Tonys Wldg & Fabrication LLC .... E 740 333-4000
Wshngtn Ct Hs (G-16242)

Tri-State Plating & Polishing .... G 304 529-2579
Proctorville (G-12688)

Tri-Weld Inc .... G 216 281-6009
Cleveland (G-4823)

Triangle Precision Industries .... D 937 299-6776
Dayton (G-6632)

Tru-Fab Technology Inc .... F 440 954-9760
Willoughby (G-16009)

United Abrasives & Welding LLC .... G 304 996-1490
Canton (G-2252)

US Welding Training LLC .... G 440 669-9380
Fairport Harbor (G-7459)

Valley Machine Tool Inc .... E 513 899-2737
Morrow (G-11227)

Viking Fabricators Inc .... E 740 374-5246
Marietta (G-9843)

Ways Cstm Wldg & Fabrication .... G 440 354-1350
Painesville (G-12276)

Webers Body & Frame Inc .... G 937 839-5946
West Alexandria (G-15346)

Welders Supply Inc .... E 216 267-4470
Brookpark (G-1727)

Welding Consultants Inc .... G 614 258-7018
Columbus (G-5870)

Welding Consultants LLC .... G 614 258-7018
Columbus (G-5871)

Weldments Inc .... F 937 235-9261
Dayton (G-6649)

Wengerds Welding & Repair LLC .... G 740 599-9071
Butler (G-1891)

Wenrick Machine and Tool Corp .... F 937 667-7307
Tipp City (G-14166)

Whitt Machine Inc .... F 513 423-7624
Middletown (G-10872)

Worthington Industries Inc .... E 614 438-3028
Columbus (G-5883)

Wpc Successor Inc .... G 937 233-6141
Tipp City (G-14167)

WELDING SPLYS, EXC GASES: Wholesalers

Airgas Usa LLC .... G 937 222-8312
Moraine (G-11154)

Airgas Usa LLC .... G 440 232-6397
Twinsburg (G-14625)

Delille Oxygen Company .... E 614 444-1177
Columbus (G-5324)

F & M Mafco Inc .... C 513 367-2151
Harrison (G-8273)

WELDING TIPS: Heat Resistant, Metal

Ohio Laser LLC .... E 614 873-7030
Plain City (G-12587)

WELDMENTS

A-1 Welding & Fabrication .... F 440 233-8474
Lorain (G-9399)

American Tank & Fabricating Co .... D 216 252-1500
Cleveland (G-3656)

Dj S Weld .... G 330 432-2206
Uhrichsville (G-14764)

Loveman Steel Corporation .... D 440 232-6200
Bedford (G-1135)

Northeast Fabricators LLC .... E 330 747-3484
Youngstown (G-16404)

Universal Design Fbrication LLC .... F 419 202-5269
Sandusky (G-13101)

WET CORN MILLING

Fluid Quip Ks LLC .... D 937 324-0352
Springfield (G-13567)

Primary Pdts Ingrdnts Amrcas L .... G 937 235-4074
Dayton (G-6521)

WHEELCHAIR LIFTS

Plumb Builders Inc .... F 937 293-1111
Dayton (G-6508)

Serving Veterans Mobility Inc .... G 937 746-4788
Franklin (G-7701)

Steves Vans ACC Unlimited LLC .... G 740 374-3154
Marietta (G-9832)

WHEELCHAIRS

Columbus Prescr Rehabilitation .... G 614 294-1600
Westerville (G-15696)

Healthwares Manufacturing .... F 513 353-3691
Cleves (G-4954)

Invacare Corporation .... F 440 329-6000
Elyria (G-7165)

Invacare Corporation .... G 800 333-6900
Elyria (G-7166)

Invacare Holdings Corporation .... C 440 329-6000
Elyria (G-7169)

Nmn Spinco Inc .... G 800 850-0335
Columbus (G-5599)

Reliable Wheelchair Trans .... G 216 390-3999
Beachwood (G-1017)

WHEELS & PARTS

Americana Development Inc .... D 330 633-3278
Tallmadge (G-14022)

Ernie Green Industries Inc .... F 614 219-1423
New Madison (G-11473)

Marion Industries LLC .... A 740 223-0075
Marion (G-9861)

Pacific Industries USA Inc .... E 513 860-3900
Fairfield (G-7389)

Piston Automotive LLC .... A 740 223-0075
Marion (G-9872)

Viper Acquisition I Inc .... D 216 589-0198
Cleveland (G-4877)

WHEELS, GRINDING: Artificial

Action Super Abrasive Pdts Inc .... E 330 673-7333
Kent (G-8795)

Carborundum Grinding Wheel .... E 740 385-2171
Logan (G-9360)

Performance Superabrasives LLC ...... G 440 946-7171
Mentor (G-10523)

WHEELS: Abrasive

Buckeye Abrasive Inc .... F 330 753-1041
Barberton (G-862)

Research Abrasive Products Inc .... E 440 944-3200
Wickliffe (G-15852)

WHEELS: Disc, Wheelbarrow, Stroller, Etc, Stamped Metal

IBI Brake Products Inc .... G 440 543-7962
Chagrin Falls (G-2402)

WHEELS: Iron & Steel, Locomotive & Car

Plymouth Locomotive Svc LLC .... G 419 896-2854
Shiloh (G-13205)

Xtek Inc .... B 513 733-7800
Cincinnati (G-3534)

WHEELS: Railroad Car, Cast Steel

Engines Inc of Ohio .... E 740 377-9874
South Point (G-13466)

WHITING MINING: Crushed & Broken

Ayers Limestone Quarry Inc .... F 740 633-2958
Martins Ferry (G-9896)

WINCHES

American Power Pull Corp .... G 419 335-7050
Archbold (G-520)

Drc Acquisition Inc .... E 330 656-1600
Streetsboro (G-13767)

Malta Dynamics LLC .... F 740 749-3512
Waterford (G-15238)

WINDINGS: Coil, Electronic

M2m Imaging Corporation .... G 440 684-9690
Cleveland (G-4346)

WINDMILLS: Electric Power Generation

Cleveland Wind Company LLC .... G 216 269-7667
Cleveland (G-3860)

Surenergy LLC .... G 419 626-8000
Oak Harbor (G-12015)

WINDOW & DOOR FRAMES

Employee Codes: A=Over 500 employees, B=251-500
C=101-250, D=51-100, E=20-50, F=10-19, G=1-9

WINDOW & DOOR FRAMES

Arch Angle Window and Door LLC .... F 800 548-0214
  Medina (G-10297)
Creative Millwork Ohio Inc .... D 440 992-3566
  Ashtabula (G-628)
Desco Corporation .... G 614 888-8855
  New Albany (G-11378)
Midwest Curtainwalls Inc .... D 216 641-7900
  Cleveland (G-4410)

WINDOW FRAMES & SASHES: Plastic

Champion Opco LLC .... B 513 327-7338
  Cincinnati (G-2725)
Creative Millwork Ohio Inc .... D 440 992-3566
  Ashtabula (G-628)
Vinylume Products Inc .... E 330 799-2000
  Youngstown (G-16472)

WINDOW FRAMES, MOLDING & TRIM: Vinyl

Builder Tech Wholesale LLC .... G 419 535-7606
  Toledo (G-14224)
Comfort Line Ltd .... D 419 729-8520
  Toledo (G-14248)
Duo-Corp .... F 330 549-2149
  North Lima (G-11804)
Great Lakes Window Inc .... A 419 666-5555
  Walbridge (G-15082)
Larmco Windows Inc .... E 216 502-2832
  Cleveland (G-4313)
Modern Builders Supply Inc .... C 419 241-3961
  Toledo (G-14389)
Owens Corning Sales LLC .... A 419 248-8000
  Toledo (G-14424)
Plastics Family Holdings Inc .... F 614 272-0777
  Columbus (G-5680)
Pvc Industries Inc .... E 518 877-8670
  Hamilton (G-8237)
Solutions In Polycarbonate LLC .... F 330 572-2860
  Medina (G-10378)
Stanek E F and Assoc Inc .... C 216 341-7700
  Macedonia (G-9580)
Tsp Inc .... E 513 732-8900
  Batavia (G-955)
Vinyl Design Corporation .... E 419 283-4009
  Holland (G-8536)

WINDOW SCREENING: Plastic

Gateway Industrial Pdts Inc .... E 440 324-4112
  Elyria (G-7154)

WINDOWS: Louver, Glass, Wood Framed

Logan Glass Technologies LLC .... G 740 385-2114
  Logan (G-9369)

WINDOWS: Wood

M21 Industries LLC .... E 937 781-1377
  Dayton (G-6419)
Yoder Window & Siding Ltd .... F 330 695-6960
  Fredericksburg (G-7735)

WINDSHIELD WIPER SYSTEMS

First Brands Group LLC .... F 248 371-1700
  Cleveland (G-4062)
Trico Products Corporation .... C 248 371-1700
  Cleveland (G-4829)

WINDSHIELDS: Plastic

Few Atmtive GL Applcations Inc .... D 234 249-1880
  Wooster (G-16118)

WIRE

Advance Industries Group LLC .... E 216 741-1800
  Cleveland (G-3602)

AJD Holding Co .... D 330 405-4477
  Twinsburg (G-14626)
Bekaert Corporation .... E 330 683-5060
  Orrville (G-12119)
Bekaert Corporation .... E 330 867-3325
  Fairlawn (G-7433)
D C Controls LLC .... G 513 225-0813
  West Chester (G-15548)
Hawthorne Wire Ltd .... F 216 712-4747
  Lakewood (G-8975)
Injection Alloys Incorporated .... F 513 422-8819
  Middletown (G-10830)
Madsen Wire Products Inc .... G 937 829-6561
  Dayton (G-6421)
Radix Wire & Cable LLC .... D 216 731-9191
  Solon (G-13410)
Reinforcement Systems of Ohio LLC .... G 330 469-6958
  Warren (G-15202)
Scovil Hanna LLC .... E 216 581-1500
  Cleveland (G-4681)

WIRE & CABLE: Aluminum

Mac Its LLC .... G 937 454-0722
  Vandalia (G-14947)

WIRE & CABLE: Nonferrous, Building

Ribbon Technology Corporation .... F 614 864-5444
  Gahanna (G-7848)

WIRE & WIRE PRDTS

Adcura Mfg .... G 937 222-3800
  Dayton (G-6184)
Advance Wire Forming Inc .... F 216 432-3250
  Cleveland (G-3605)
Alabama Sling Center Inc .... E 440 239-7000
  Cleveland (G-3620)
Alcan Corporation .... E 440 460-3307
  Cleveland (G-3622)
Amanda Bent Bolt Company .... C 740 385-6893
  Logan (G-9358)
Ametco Manufacturing Corp .... E 440 951-4300
  Willoughby (G-15876)
Bekaert Corporation .... F 330 683-5060
  Orrville (G-12118)
Bloomngburg Spring Wire Form I .... E 740 437-7614
  Bloomingburg (G-1353)
Brushes Inc .... F 216 267-8084
  Cleveland (G-3767)
Busch & Thiem Inc .... E 419 625-7515
  Sandusky (G-13047)
C & F Fabrications Inc .... E 937 666-3234
  East Liberty (G-6984)
C C M Wire Inc .... E 330 425-3421
  Twinsburg (G-14638)
Canron Manufacturing Inc .... F 330 497-1131
  Greentown (G-8034)
Conveyor Guard Corp .... G 614 337-1727
  Columbus (G-5292)
Dayton Wire Products Inc .... E 937 236-8000
  Dayton (G-6291)
Die Co Inc .... E 440 942-8856
  Eastlake (G-7025)
Dysinger Incorporated .... E 937 297-7761
  Dayton (G-6310)
Efco Corp .... G 614 876-1226
  Columbus (G-5347)
Elyria Spring & Specialty Inc .... F 440 323-5502
  Elyria (G-7146)
Engineered Wire Products Inc .... E 330 469-6958
  Warren (G-15167)
Engineered Wire Products Inc .... C 419 294-3817
  Upper Sandusky (G-14808)

Ever Roll Specialties Co .... E 937 964-1302
  Springfield (G-13561)
Fence One Inc .... F 216 441-2600
  Cleveland (G-4056)
G & S Titanium Inc .... E 330 263-0564
  Wooster (G-16122)
Gateway Con Forming Svcs Inc .... D 513 353-2000
  Miamitown (G-10708)
General Chain & Mfg Corp .... E 513 541-6005
  Cincinnati (G-2940)
Helical Line Products Co .... E 440 933-9263
  Avon Lake (G-811)
Illinois Tool Works Inc .... E 216 292-7161
  Bedford (G-1127)
Malin Wire Co .... E 216 267-9080
  Cleveland (G-4352)
Marik Spring Inc .... E 330 564-0617
  Tallmadge (G-14037)
Mazzella Jhh Company Inc .... D 440 239-7000
  Cleveland (G-4374)
Mazzella Lifting Tech Inc .... D 440 239-7000
  Cleveland (G-4375)
McM Ind Co Inc .... F 216 641-6300
  Cleveland (G-4383)
McM Ind Co Inc .... F 216 292-4506
  Cleveland (G-4382)
Meese Inc .... F 440 998-1202
  Ashtabula (G-647)
Merchants Metals LLC .... E 513 942-0268
  West Chester (G-15463)
Mid-West Fabricating Co .... C 740 969-4411
  Amanda (G-446)
Mueller Electric Company Inc .... E 216 771-5225
  Akron (G-256)
Ohio Wire Form & Spring Co .... E 614 444-3676
  Columbus (G-5630)
Options Plus Incorporated .... F 740 694-9811
  Fredericktown (G-7752)
Panacea Products Corporation .... E 614 429-6320
  Columbus (G-5653)
Panacea Products Corporation .... E 614 850-7000
  Columbus (G-5652)
Peterson American Corporation .... E 419 867-8711
  Holland (G-8523)
Polymet Corporation .... E 513 874-3586
  West Chester (G-15482)
Premier Manufacturing Corp .... C 216 941-9700
  Cleveland (G-4581)
Pwp Inc .... E 216 251-2181
  Ashland (G-607)
Qualtek Electronics Corp .... E 440 951-3300
  Mentor (G-10541)
R G Smith Company .... D 330 456-3415
  Canton (G-2207)
Rjs Corporation .... E 330 896-2387
  Akron (G-306)
Saxon Products Inc .... E 419 241-6771
  Toledo (G-14463)
Schweizer Dipple Inc .... D 440 786-8090
  Cleveland (G-4676)
Spring Team Inc .... D 440 275-5981
  Austinburg (G-750)
Starr Fabricating Inc .... D 330 394-9891
  Vienna (G-15004)
Stephens Pipe & Steel LLC .... C 740 869-2257
  Mount Sterling (G-11257)
Stolle Machinery Company LLC .... C 937 497-5400
  Dayton (G-6596)
T & R Welding Systems Inc .... F 937 228-7517
  Dayton (G-6606)
Therm-O-Link Inc .... D 330 527-2124
  Garrettsville (G-7926)

PRODUCT SECTION — WOMEN'S & GIRLS' SPORTSWEAR WHOLESALERS

Top Knotch Products Inc .... G 419 543-2266
 Cleveland *(G-4804)*

Tyler Haver Inc .... E 440 974-1047
 Mentor *(G-10585)*

Ver-Mac Industries Inc .... E 740 397-6511
 Mount Vernon *(G-11299)*

W J Egli Company Inc .... F 330 823-3666
 Alliance *(G-435)*

Willison Wred Den Incorporate .... G 440 236-9693
 Columbia Station *(G-5024)*

Wire Products Company LLC .... C 216 267-0777
 Cleveland *(G-4913)*

Wrwp LLC .... F 330 425-3421
 Twinsburg *(G-14759)*

WS Tyler Screening Inc .... E 440 974-1047
 Mentor *(G-10598)*

Yost Superior Co .... E 937 323-7591
 Springfield *(G-13658)*

WIRE CLOTH & WOVEN WIRE PRDTS, MADE FROM PURCHASED

Ofco Inc .... D 740 622-5922
 Coshocton *(G-5989)*

Unified Scrning Crshing - OH I .... G 937 836-3201
 Englewood *(G-7246)*

WIRE FABRIC: Welded Steel

S & S Wldg Fabg Machining Inc .... F 330 392-7878
 Newton Falls *(G-11657)*

WIRE MATERIALS: Aluminum

Alcan Corporation .... E 440 460-3307
 Cleveland *(G-3622)*

WIRE MATERIALS: Copper

Alcan Corporation .... E 440 460-3307
 Cleveland *(G-3622)*

American Wire & Cable Company .... E 440 235-1140
 Olmsted Twp *(G-12085)*

Commconnect .... F 937 414-0505
 Dayton *(G-6259)*

Core Optix Inc .... F 855 267-3678
 Cincinnati *(G-2796)*

Republic Wire Inc .... D 513 860-1800
 West Chester *(G-15496)*

WIRE MATERIALS: Steel

American Wire & Cable Company .... E 440 235-1140
 Olmsted Twp *(G-12085)*

Armco Inc .... G 740 829-3000
 Coshocton *(G-5971)*

Bayloff Stmped Pdts Knsman Inc .... D 330 876-4511
 Kinsman *(G-8935)*

Contour Forming Inc .... F 740 345-9777
 Newark *(G-11572)*

Custom Cltch Jint Hydrlics Inc .... F 216 431-1630
 Cleveland *(G-3923)*

D M L Steel Tech .... G 513 737-9911
 Liberty Twp *(G-9213)*

Dayton Superior Corporation .... C 937 866-0711
 Miamisburg *(G-10633)*

Engineered Wire Products Inc .... C 419 294-3817
 Upper Sandusky *(G-14808)*

JR Manufacturing Inc .... C 419 375-8021
 Fort Recovery *(G-7621)*

Midwestern Industries Inc .... D 330 837-4203
 Massillon *(G-10127)*

Pioneer Corp .... D 330 857-0267
 Dalton *(G-6140)*

Polymet Corporation .... E 513 874-3586
 West Chester *(G-15482)*

Regency Steel Supply Inc LLC .... G 440 306-0269
 Eastlake *(G-7046)*

Republic Steel Wire Proc LLC .... E 440 996-0740
 Solon *(G-13414)*

Republic Wire Inc .... D 513 860-1800
 West Chester *(G-15496)*

Save Edge Inc .... E 937 376-8268
 Xenia *(G-16272)*

Summit Engineered Products Inc .... F 330 854-5388
 Canal Fulton *(G-1975)*

Tru-Form Steel & Wire Inc .... F 765 348-5001
 Toledo *(G-14512)*

Unison Industries LLC .... F 937 426-0621
 Alpha *(G-439)*

WIRE PRDTS: Ferrous Or Iron, Made In Wiredrawing Plants

American Spring Wire Corp .... C 216 292-4620
 Bedford Heights *(G-1163)*

Fenix LLC .... F 419 739-3400
 Wapakoneta *(G-15110)*

Seneca Wire & Manufacturing Co Inc ...... F 419 435-9261
 Fostoria *(G-7655)*

WIRE PRDTS: Steel & Iron

North Shore Strapping Company .... E 216 661-5200
 Brooklyn Heights *(G-1696)*

Radix Wire & Cable LLC .... D 216 731-9191
 Solon *(G-13410)*

Trupoint Products LLC .... F 330 204-3302
 Sugarcreek *(G-13945)*

WIRE WINDING OF PURCHASED WIRE

Providence REES Inc .... F 614 833-6231
 Columbus *(G-5696)*

WIRE, FLAT: Strip, Cold-Rolled, Exc From Hot-Rolled Mills

American Spring Wire Corp .... C 216 292-4620
 Bedford Heights *(G-1163)*

Hynes Industries Inc .... C 800 321-9257
 Youngstown *(G-16378)*

WIRE: Communication

Astro Industries Inc .... E 937 429-5900
 Beavercreek *(G-1041)*

AT&T Corp .... G 513 792-9300
 Cincinnati *(G-2639)*

Ohio Associated Entps LLC .... F 440 354-3148
 Painesville *(G-12253)*

Xponet Inc .... E 440 354-6617
 Painesville *(G-12279)*

WIRE: Magnet

Sam Dong America Inc .... F 740 363-1985
 Delaware *(G-6747)*

WIRE: Mesh

Midwestern Industries Inc .... D 330 837-4203
 Massillon *(G-10127)*

WIRE: Nonferrous

Alcan Corporation .... E 440 460-3307
 Cleveland *(G-3622)*

American Wire & Cable Company .... E 440 235-1140
 Olmsted Twp *(G-12085)*

Arnco Corporation .... D 800 847-7661
 Elyria *(G-7112)*

Calvert Wire & Cable Corp .... E 330 494-3248
 North Canton *(G-11718)*

Connectors Unlimited Inc .... E 440 357-1161
 Painesville *(G-12224)*

Electrovations Inc .... G 330 274-3558
 Solon *(G-13341)*

Flex Technologies Inc .... E 740 922-5992
 Midvale *(G-10878)*

Legrand North America LLC .... B 937 224-0639
 Dayton *(G-6403)*

Mueller Electric Company Inc .... E 216 771-5225
 Akron *(G-256)*

Projects Unlimited Inc .... C 937 918-2200
 Dayton *(G-6534)*

Radix Wire Co .... F 330 995-3677
 Aurora *(G-733)*

Radix Wire Co .... F 216 731-9191
 Solon *(G-13412)*

Radix Wire Co .... D 216 731-9191
 Solon *(G-13411)*

Rah Investment Holding Inc .... D 330 832-8124
 Massillon *(G-10138)*

Schneider Electric Usa Inc .... B 513 523-4171
 Oxford *(G-12213)*

Scott Fetzer Company .... C 216 267-9000
 Cleveland *(G-4678)*

Therm-O-Link Inc .... E 330 393-7600
 Warren *(G-15209)*

Therm-O-Link Inc .... D 330 527-2124
 Garrettsville *(G-7926)*

Vulkor Incorporated .... E 330 393-7600
 Warren *(G-15217)*

Wiremax Ltd .... G 419 531-9500
 Toledo *(G-14525)*

WIRE: Steel, Insulated Or Armored

Euclid Steel & Wire Inc .... E 216 731-6744
 Lakewood *(G-8974)*

Marlin Thermocouple Wire Inc .... E 440 835-1950
 Westlake *(G-15764)*

Ram Sensors Inc .... E 440 835-3540
 Cleveland *(G-4613)*

WIRE: Wire, Ferrous Or Iron

Solon Specialty Wire Co .... E 440 248-7600
 Solon *(G-13424)*

WIRING DEVICES WHOLESALERS

Astro Industries Inc .... E 937 429-5900
 Beavercreek *(G-1041)*

WOMEN'S & CHILDREN'S CLOTHING WHOLESALERS, NEC

Fluff Boutique .... G 513 227-6614
 Cincinnati *(G-2911)*

McCc Sportswear Inc .... G 513 583-9210
 West Chester *(G-15569)*

West Chester Holdings LLC .... C 513 705-2100
 Cincinnati *(G-3516)*

Zimmer Enterprises Inc .... E 937 428-1057
 Dayton *(G-6663)*

WOMEN'S & GIRLS' SPORTSWEAR WHOLESALERS

Barbs Graffiti Inc .... E 216 881-5550
 Cleveland *(G-3719)*

Design Original Inc .... F 937 596-5121
 Jackson Center *(G-8731)*

Precision Imprint .... G 740 592-5916
 Athens *(G-692)*

R & A Sports Inc .... E 216 289-2254
 Euclid *(G-7297)*

Unisport Inc.. F 419 529-4727
  Ontario (G-12096)

WOMEN'S CLOTHING STORES

City Apparel Inc.. F 419 434-1155
  Findlay (G-7493)
Fancy ME Boutique LLC................................ G 419 357-8927
  Sandusky (G-13058)
Fluff Boutique.. G 513 227-6614
  Cincinnati (G-2911)

WOOD & WOOD BY-PRDTS, WHOLESALE

77 Coach Supply Ltd..................................... G 330 674-1454
  Millersburg (G-10937)
Cindoco Wood Products Co.......................... F 937 444-2504
  Mount Orab (G-11240)
Gross Lumber Inc... F 330 683-2055
  Apple Creek (G-501)

WOOD CHIPS, PRODUCED AT THE MILL

Calvin W Lafferty... G 740 498-6566
  Kimbolton (G-8927)
Miller Logging Inc.. F 330 279-4721
  Holmesville (G-8550)

WOOD FENCING WHOLESALERS

Df Supply Inc.. E 330 650-9226
  Twinsburg (G-14650)
Double D D Mtls Instlltion Inc...................... G 937 898-2534
  Dayton (G-6302)

WOOD PRDTS: Laundry

Adroit Thinking Inc....................................... F 419 542-9363
  Hicksville (G-8370)
P Graham Dunn Inc...................................... B 330 828-2105
  Dalton (G-6138)
Rcs Cross Woods Maple LLC....................... E 614 825-0670
  Columbus (G-5713)

WOOD PRDTS: Moldings, Unfinished & Prefinished

Cox Interior Inc... F 270 789-3129
  Norwood (G-11994)
Custom Carving Source LLC........................ G 513 407-1008
  Cincinnati (G-2807)
J McCoy Lumber Co Ltd............................... F 937 587-3423
  Peebles (G-12328)
Laborie Enterprises LLC.............................. G 419 686-6245
  Portage (G-12634)
Midwest Wood Trim Inc............................... E 419 592-3389
  Napoleon (G-11324)
Quality Woodproducts LLC.......................... G 330 279-2217
  Fredericksburg (G-7731)
Seneca Millwork Inc..................................... E 419 435-6671
  Fostoria (G-7654)

WOOD PRDTS: Mulch Or Sawdust

American Wood Fibers Inc........................... E 740 420-3233
  Circleville (G-3541)
Garick LLC.. E 216 581-0100
  Cleveland (G-4102)
Hope Timber & Marketing Group.................. F 740 344-1788
  Newark (G-11580)
Hope Timber Mulch LLC.............................. G 740 344-1788
  Newark (G-11581)

Roe Transportation Entps Inc....................... G 937 497-7161
  Sidney (G-13278)

WOOD PRDTS: Mulch, Wood & Bark

Gayston Corporation..................................... C 937 743-6050
  Miamisburg (G-10640)
H Hafner & Sons Inc.................................... E 513 321-1895
  Cincinnati (G-2979)
Hauser Services Llc..................................... E 440 632-5126
  Middlefield (G-10755)
Irvine Wood Recovery Inc............................ E 513 831-0060
  Miamiville (G-10711)
Latham Lumber & Pallet Co......................... G 740 493-2707
  Latham (G-9052)
Mulch Manufacturing Inc.............................. E 614 864-4004
  Reynoldsburg (G-12769)
Scotts Company LLC................................... C 937 644-0011
  Marysville (G-9934)
Yoder Lumber Co Inc................................... D 330 893-3121
  Millersburg (G-11008)

WOOD PRDTS: Novelties, Fiber

F J Designs Inc... F 330 264-1377
  Wooster (G-16117)

WOOD PRDTS: Outdoor, Structural

Luxcraft LLC... G 330 852-1036
  Sugarcreek (G-13928)

WOOD PRDTS: Plugs

Sealco Inc.. G 740 922-4122
  Uhrichsville (G-14768)

WOOD PRDTS: Signboards

Blang Acquisition LLC.................................. F 937 223-2155
  Dayton (G-6231)
Signature Sign Co Inc.................................. F 216 426-1234
  Cleveland (G-4702)

WOOD PRDTS: Trophy Bases

Akron Centl Engrv Mold Mch Inc.................. G 330 475-1388
  Akron (G-28)
Engraved In Usa LLC................................... G 513 301-7760
  Fairfield (G-7357)
Hit Trophy Inc... G 419 445-5356
  Archbold (G-532)
J & D Wood Ltd.. G 937 778-9663
  Piqua (G-12528)

WOOD TREATING: Millwork

Couch Business Development Inc................ F 937 253-1099
  Dayton (G-6264)
Joseph Sabatino... G 330 332-5879
  Salem (G-13007)

WOOD TREATING: Structural Lumber & Timber

Clark Rm Inc... F 419 425-9889
  Findlay (G-7494)
Flagship Trading Corporation....................... E
  Cleveland (G-4066)
Luxus Products LLC..................................... G 937 444-6500
  Mount Orab (G-11242)
Urbn Timber LLC.. G 614 981-3043
  Columbus (G-5850)

WOOD TREATING: Wood Prdts, Creosoted

Wood Duck Enterprises Ltd......................... G 937 776-0606
  Beavercreek (G-1067)

WOODWORK & TRIM: Exterior & Ornamental

Robura Inc.. G 330 857-7404
  Orrville (G-12148)

WOODWORK & TRIM: Interior & Ornamental

L E Smith Company..................................... D 419 636-4555
  Bryan (G-1825)
Richardson Woodworking............................. G 614 893-8850
  Blacklick (G-1343)
Turnwood Industry Inc.................................. G 330 278-2421
  Hinckley (G-8478)

WOODWORK: Interior & Ornamental, NEC

Saw Dust Ltd.. G 740 862-0612
  Baltimore (G-847)
Stull Woodworks Inc.................................... G 937 698-8181
  Troy (G-14614)

WORK EXPERIENCE CENTER

TAC Industries Inc.. B 937 328-5200
  Springfield (G-13642)

WOVEN WIRE PRDTS, NEC

Roy I Kaufman Inc.. G 740 382-0643
  Marion (G-9877)
Utility Wire Products Inc.............................. F 216 441-2180
  Cleveland (G-4858)

WRENCHES

Norbar Torque Tools Inc............................... F 440 953-1175
  Willoughby (G-15959)
Wright Tool Company................................... C 330 848-0600
  Barberton (G-901)

X-RAY EQPT & TUBES

Control-X Inc... G 614 777-9729
  Columbus (G-5290)
Dentsply Sirona Inc...................................... E 419 865-9497
  Maumee (G-10200)
Leisure Time Pdts Design Corp................... G 440 934-1032
  Avon (G-779)
Metro Design Inc.. E 440 458-4200
  Elyria (G-7181)
North Coast Medical Eqp Inc....................... F 440 243-6189
  Berea (G-1289)
Philips Med Systems Clvland In................... D 617 245-5510
  Beachwood (G-1010)
Philips Med Systems Clvland In................... B 440 483-3000
  Cleveland (G-4547)

X-RAY EQPT REPAIR SVCS

Metro Design Inc.. E 440 458-4200
  Elyria (G-7181)

YARN & YARN SPINNING

Unifi LLC... G 614 288-9217
  Reynoldsburg (G-12779)